LIFE APPLICATION® BIBLE

NEW INTERNATIONAL VERSION

LIFE APPLICATION® BIBLE

NEW INTERNATIONAL VERSION

KINGSWAY PUBLICATIONS

EASTBOURNE

ISBN 0 85476 312 0 (standard edition)
ISBN 0 85476 622 7 (limp edition)
ISBN 0 85476 339 0 (bonded leather-black)
ISBN 0 85476 340 6 (bonded leather-burgundy)

The publishers gratefully acknowledge the role of Youth for Christ (USA) in preparing the Life Application Notes and Bible Helps.

This edition 1992.
Reprinted 1993, 1995, 1998, 1999.

Published by
KINGSWAY PUBLICATIONS
Lottbridge Drove, Eastbourne, BN23 6NT, England
E-mail: books@kingsway.co.uk

Produced for the publishers by
Bookprint Creative Services, P.O. Box 827, BN21 3YJ, England.
Printed in Great Britain.

YOUR WORD IS A LAMP TO MY FEET AND
A LIGHT FOR MY PATH. PS 119:105

PRESENTED

TO

Isabel Mitchell

BY

The Mustard Seed
Fellowship.

ON

Easter Sunday, April 15th
2001

May the Lord be a lamp
in your life.

LOVE IS PATIENT, LOVE IS KIND ...
LOVE NEVER FAILS. 1 COR 13:4,8

MARRIAGE & FAMILY TREE

NAME

BIRTHPLACE DATE

NAME

BIRTHPLACE DATE

were united in
HOLY MATRIMONY
on ______________________
at ______________________
____

PARENTS

FATHER

NAME

BIRTHPLACE DATE

MOTHER

NAME

BIRTHPLACE DATE

FATHER

NAME

BIRTHPLACE DATE

MOTHER

NAME

BIRTHPLACE DATE

GRANDPARENTS

PATERNAL

GRANDFATHER

BIRTHPLACE DATE

GRANDMOTHER

BIRTHPLACE DATE

MATERNAL

GRANDFATHER

BIRTHPLACE DATE

GRANDMOTHER

BIRTHPLACE DATE

PATERNAL

GRANDFATHER

BIRTHPLACE DATE

GRANDMOTHER

BIRTHPLACE DATE

MATERNAL

GRANDFATHER

BIRTHPLACE DATE

GRANDMOTHER

BIRTHPLACE DATE

CONTENTS

LIST OF THE BOOKS OF THE BIBLE

THE NIV CROSS-REFERENCE SYSTEM

The New International Version has one of the most accurate and best-organised cross-reference systems available. The system used in this Bible contains more than 53,000 references.

The cross-references link words or phrases in the NIV text with counterpart biblical references listed in a side column on every page. The raised letters containing these cross-references are set in light italic typeface to distinguish them from the NIV text note letters, which use a bold typeface.

The lists of references are in biblical order with one exception: If reference is made to a verse within the same chapter, that verse (indicated by "ver") is listed first.

In the Old Testament, some references are marked with an asterisk (*), which means that the Old Testament verse or phrase is quoted in the New Testament (see, for example, Genesis 1:3). The corresponding information is provided in the New Testament by the NIV text note (see 2 Corinthians 4:6).

Following is a list of abbreviations used in the cross-references:

ABBREVIATIONS FOR THE BOOKS OF THE BIBLE

Genesis	Ge	Isaiah	Isa	Romans	Ro
Exodus	Ex	Jeremiah	Jer	1 Corinthians	1Co
Leviticus	Lev	Lamentations	La	2 Corinthians	2Co
Numbers	Nu	Ezekiel	Eze	Galatians	Gal
Deuteronomy	Dt	Daniel	Da	Ephesians	Eph
Joshua	Jos	Hosea	Hos	Philippians	Php
Judges	Jdg	Joel	Joel	Colossians	Col
Ruth	Ru	Amos	Am	1 Thessalonians	1Th
1 Samuel	1Sa	Obadiah	Ob	2 Thessalonians	2Th
2 Samuel	2Sa	Jonah	Jnh	1 Timothy	1Ti
1 Kings	1Ki	Micah	Mic	2 Timothy	2Ti
2 Kings	2Ki	Nahum	Na	Titus	Tit
1 Chronicles	1Ch	Habakkuk	Hab	Philemon	Phm
2 Chronicles	2Ch	Zephaniah	Zep	Hebrews	Heb
Ezra	Ezr	Haggai	Hag	James	Jas
Nehemiah	Ne	Zechariah	Zec	1 Peter	1Pe
Esther	Est	Malachi	Mal	2 Peter	2Pe
Job	Job	Matthew	Mt	1 John	1Jn
Psalms	Ps	Mark	Mk	2 John	2Jn
Proverbs	Pr	Luke	Lk	3 John	3Jn
Ecclesiastes	Ecc	John	Jn	Jude	Jude
Song of Songs	SS	Acts	Ac	Revelation	Rev

TRANSLATORS' PREFACE

The New International Version is a completely new translation of the Holy Bible made by over a hundred scholars working directly from the best available Hebrew, Aramaic and Greek texts. It had its beginning in 1965 when, after several years of exploratory study by committees from the Christian Reformed Church and the National Association of Evangelicals, a group of scholars met at Palos Heights, Illinois, and concurred in the need for a new translation of the Bible in contemporary English. This group, though not made up of official church representatives, was transdenominational. Its conclusion was endorsed by a large number of leaders from many denominations who met in Chicago in 1966.

Responsibility for the new version was delegated by the Palos Heights group to a self-governing body of fifteen, the Committee on Bible Translation, composed for the most part of biblical scholars from colleges, universities and seminaries. In 1967 the New York Bible Society (now the International Bible Society) generously undertook the financial sponsorship of the project—a sponsorship that made it possible to enlist the help of many distinguished scholars. The fact that participants from the United States, Great Britain, Canada, Australia and New Zealand worked together gave the project its international scope. That they were from many denominations—including Anglican, Assemblies of God, Baptist, Brethren, Christian Reformed, Church of Christ, Evangelical Free, Lutheran, Mennonite, Methodist, Nazarene, Presbyterian, Wesleyan and other churches—helped to safeguard the translation from sectarian bias.

How it was made helps to give the New International Version its distinctiveness. The translation of each book was assigned to a team of scholars. Next, one of the Intermediate Editorial Committees revised the initial translation, with constant reference to the Hebrew, Aramaic or Greek. Their work then went to one of the General Editorial Committees, which checked it in detail and made another thorough revision. This revision in turn was carefully reviewed by the Committee on Bible Translation, which made further changes and then released the final version for publication. In this way the entire Bible underwent three revisions, during each of which the translation was examined for its faithfulness to the original languages and for its English style.

All this involved many thousands of hours of research and discussion regarding the meaning of the texts and the precise way of putting them into English. It may well be that no other translation has been made by a more thorough process of review and revision from committee to committee than this one.

From the beginning of the project, the Committee on Bible Translation held to certain goals for the New International Version: that it would be an accurate translation and one that would have clarity and literary quality and so prove suitable for public and private reading, teaching, preaching, memorising and liturgical use. The Committee also sought to preserve some measure of continuity with the long tradition of translating the Scriptures into English.

In working towards these goals, the translators were united in their commitment to the authority and infallibility of the Bible as God's Word in written form. They believe that it contains the divine answer to the deepest needs of humanity, that it sheds unique light on our path in a dark world, and that it sets forth the way to our eternal well-being.

The first concern of the translators has been the accuracy of the translation and its fidelity to the thought of the biblical writers. They have weighed the significance of the lexical and grammatical details of the Hebrew, Aramaic and Greek texts. At the same time, they have striven for more than a word-for-word translation. Because thought patterns and syntax differ from language to language, faithful communication of the meaning of the writers of the Bible demands frequent modifications in sentence structure and constant regard for the contextual meanings of words.

A sensitive feeling for style does not always accompany scholarship. Accordingly the Committee on Bible Translation submitted the developing version to a number of stylistic consultants. Two of them read every book of both Old and New Testaments twice—once before and once after the last major revision—and made invaluable suggestions. Samples of the translation were tested for clarity and ease of reading by various kinds of people—young and old, highly educated and less well educated, ministers and laymen.

Concern for clear and natural English—that the New International Version should be idiomatic but not idiosyncratic, contemporary but not dated—motivated the translators and consultants. At the same time, they tried to reflect the differing styles of the biblical writers. In view of the international use of English, the translators sought to avoid obvious Americanisms on the one hand and obvious Anglicisms on the other. A British edition reflects the comparatively few differences of significant idiom and of spelling.

As for the traditional pronouns "thou", "thee" and "thine" in reference to the Deity, the translators judged that to use these archaisms (along with old verb forms such as "doest," "wouldest" and "hadst") would violate accuracy in translation. Neither Hebrew, Aramaic nor Greek uses special pronouns for the persons of the Godhead. A present-day translation is not enhanced by forms that in the time of the King James Version were used in everyday speech, whether referring to God or man.

For the Old Testament the standard Hebrew text, the Masoretic Text as published in the latest editions of *Biblia Hebraica*, was used throughout. The Dead Sea Scrolls contain material bearing on an earlier stage of the Hebrew text. They were consulted, as were the Samaritan Pentateuch and the ancient scribal traditions relating to textual changes. Sometimes a variant Hebrew reading in the margin of the Masoretic Text was followed instead of the text itself. Such instances, being variants within the Masoretic tradition, are not specified by footnotes. In rare cases, words in the consonantal text were divided differently from the way they appear in the Masoretic Text. Footnotes indicate this. The translators also consulted the more important early versions—the Septuagint; Aquila, Symmachus and Theodotion; the Vulgate; the Syriac Peshitta; the Targums; and for the Psalms the *Juxta Hebraica* of Jerome. Readings from these versions were occasionally followed where the Masoretic Text seemed doubtful and where accepted principles of textual criticism showed that one or more of these textual witnesses appeared to provide the correct reading. Such instances are footnoted. Sometimes vowel letters and vowel signs did not, in the judgment of the translators, represent the correct vowels for the original consonantal text. Accordingly some words were read with a different set of vowels. These instances are usually not indicated by footnotes.

The Greek text used in translating the New Testament was an eclectic one. No other piece of ancient literature has such an abundance of manuscript witnesses as does the New Testament. Where existing manuscripts differ, the translators made their choice of readings according to accepted principles of New Testament textual criticism. Footnotes call attention to places where there was uncertainty about what the original text was. The best current printed texts of the Greek New Testament were used.

There is a sense in which the work of translation is never wholly finished. This applies to all great literature and uniquely so to the Bible. In 1973 the New Testament in the New International Version was published. Since then, suggestions for corrections and revisions have been received from various sources. The Committee on Bible Translation carefully considered the suggestions and adopted a number of them. These were incorporated in the first printing of the entire Bible in 1978. Additional revisions were made by the Committee on Bible Translation in 1983 and appear in printings after that date.

As in other ancient documents, the precise meaning of the biblical texts is sometimes uncertain. This is more often the case with the Hebrew and Aramaic texts than with the Greek text. Although archaeological and linguistic discoveries in this century aid in understanding difficult passages, some uncertainties remain. The more significant of these have been called to the reader's attention in the footnotes.

In regard to the divine name *YHWH,* commonly referred to as the *Tetragrammaton,* the translators adopted the device used in most English versions of rendering that name as "LORD" in capital letters to distinguish it from *Adonai,* another Hebrew word rendered "Lord", for which small letters are used. Wherever the two names stand together in the Old Testament as a compound name of God, they are rendered "Sovereign LORD".

Because for most readers today the phrases "the LORD of hosts" and "God of hosts" have little meaning, this version renders them "the LORD Almighty" and "God Almighty". These renderings convey the sense of the Hebrew, namely, "he who is sovereign over all the 'hosts' (powers) in heaven and on earth, especially over the 'hosts' (armies) of Israel." For readers unacquainted with Hebrew this does not make clear the distinction between *Sabaoth* ("hosts" or "Almighty") and *Shaddai* (which can also be translated "Almighty"), but the latter occurs infrequently and is always footnoted. When *Adonai* and *YHWH Sabaoth* occur together, they are rendered "the Lord, the LORD Almighty".

As for other proper nouns, the familiar spellings of the Authorised Version are generally retained. Names traditionally spelled with "ch", except where it is final, are usually spelled in this translation with "k" or "c", since the biblical languages do not have the sound that "ch" frequently indicates in English—for example, in *chant*. For well-known names such as Zechariah, however, the traditional spelling has been retained. Variation in the spelling of names in the original languages has usually not been indicated. Where a person or place has two or more different names in the Hebrew, Aramaic or Greek texts, the more familiar one has generally been used, with footnotes where needed.

To achieve clarity the translators sometimes supplied words not in the original texts but required by the context. If there was uncertainty about such material, it is enclosed in brackets. Also for the sake of clarity or style, nouns, including some proper nouns, are sometimes substituted for pronouns, and vice versa. And though the Hebrew writers often shifted back and forth between first, second and third personal pronouns without change of antecedent, this translation often makes them uniform, in accordance with English style and without the use of footnotes.

Poetical passages are printed as poetry, that is, with indentation of lines and with separate stanzas. These are generally designed to reflect the structure of Hebrew poetry. This poetry is normally characterised by parallelism in balanced lines. Most of the poetry in the Bible is in the Old Testament, and scholars differ regarding the scansion of Hebrew lines. The translators determined the stanza divisions for the most part by analysis of the subject matter. The stanzas therefore serve as poetic paragraphs.

As an aid to the reader, italicised sectional headings are inserted in most of the books. They are not to be regarded as part of the NIV text, are not for oral reading, and are not intended to dictate the interpretation of the sections they head.

The footnotes in this version are of several kinds, most of which need no explanation. Those giving alternative translations begin with "Or" and generally introduce the alternative with the last word preceding it in the text, except when it is a single-word alternative; in poetry quoted in a footnote a slant mark indicates a line division. Footnotes introduced by "Or" do not have uniform significance. In some cases two possible translations were considered to have about equal validity. In other cases, though the translators were convinced that the translation in the text was correct, they judged that another interpretation was possible and of sufficient importance to be represented in a footnote.

In the New Testament, footnotes that refer to uncertainty regarding the original text are introduced by "Some manuscripts" or similar expressions. In the Old Testament, evidence for the reading chosen is given first and evidence for the alternative is added after a semicolon (for example: Septuagint; Hebrew *father*). In such notes the term "Hebrew" refers to the Masoretic Text.

It should be noted that minerals, flora and fauna, architectural details, articles of clothing and jewellery, musical instruments and other articles cannot always be identified with precision. Also measures of capacity in the biblical period are particularly uncertain (see the table of weights and measures following the text).

Like all translations of the Bible, made as they are by imperfect man, this one undoubtedly falls short of its goals. Yet we are grateful to God for the extent to which he has enabled us to realise these goals and for the strength he has given us and our colleagues to complete our task. We offer this version of the Bible to him in whose name and for whose glory it has been made. We pray that it will lead many into a better understanding of the Holy Scriptures and a fuller knowledge of Jesus Christ the incarnate Word, of whom the Scriptures so faithfully testify.

The Committee on Bible Translation
June 1978 (Revised August 1983)

Names of the translators and editors may be secured from the International Bible Society, P O Box 62970, Colorado Springs, CO 80962-2970 USA

CONTRIBUTORS

Senior Editorial Team
Dr. Bruce B. Barton
Ronald A. Beers
Dr. James C. Galvin
Linda Chaffee Taylor
David R. Veerman

General Editor
Dr. Bruce B. Barton

Zondervan Theological Editor
Dirk R. Buursma

Tyndale House Bible Editors
Dr. Philip W. Comfort
Mark Norton
Robert Brown

Book Introductions
David R. Veerman

Book Outlines, Blueprints, Harmony
Dr. James C. Galvin

Megathemes
Dr. Bruce B. Barton

Map Development & Computer Operation
Linda Chaffee Taylor

Charts & Diagrams
Neil S. Wilson
Ronald A. Beers
David R. Veerman
Pamela York

Personality Profiles
Neil S. Wilson

Design & Development Team
Dr. Bruce B. Barton
Ronald A. Beers
Dr. James C. Galvin
David R. Veerman

Tyndale House Production
Joan Major
Julee Schwarzburg
Jim Bolton
Linda Oswald

Zondervan Production
Caroline Blauwkamp
Randall VanderWel

Tyndale House Graphic Design
Timothy R. Botts

A Chronology of Bible Events and World Events
Dr. David Maas

Theological Reviewers

Dr. Kenneth S. Kantzer
General Theological Reviewer
Dean Emeritus and
Distinguished Professor of Bible and Systematic Theology
Trinity Evangelical Divinity School

Dr. V. Gilbert Beers
Senior Editor
Christianity Today, Inc.

Dr. Barry Beitzel
Associate Academic Dean
and Professor of Old Testament and Semitic Languages
Trinity Evangelical Divinity School

Dr. Edwin A. Blum
Associate Professor of Historical Theology
Dallas Theological Seminary

Dr. Geoffrey W. Bromiley
Professor
Fuller Theological Seminary

Dr. George K. Brushaber
President
Bethel College & Seminary

Dr. L. Russ Bush
Associate Professor
Philosophy & Religion
Southwestern Baptist Theological Seminary

C. Donald Cole
Pastor, Moody Radio Network

Mrs. Naomi E. Cole
Speaker & Seminar Leader

Dr. Walter A. Elwell
Dean
Wheaton College Graduate School

Dr. Gerald F. Hawthorne
Professor of Greek
Wheaton College

Dr. Howard G. Hendricks
Professor-at-Large
Chairman
Center for Christian Leadership
Dallas Theological Seminary

Dr. Grant R. Osborne
Professor of New Testament
Trinity Evangelical Divinity School

A special thanks to the nationwide staff of Youth for Christ/USA for their suggestions and field-testing, and to the following additional contributing writers: V. Gilbert Beers, Neil Wilson, John Crosby, Joan Young, Jack Crabtree, Philip Craven, Bob Black, Bur Schilling, Arthur Deyo, Annie Lafrentz, Danny Sartin, William Hanawalt, William Bonikowsky, Brian Rathbun, Pamela Barden, Thomas Stobie, Robert Arnold, Greg Monaco, Larry Dunn, Lynn Ziegenfuss, Mitzie Barton, Marijean Hamilton, Larry Kreider, Gary Dausey, William Roland, Kathy Howell, Philip Steffeck, James Coleman, Marty Grasley, O'Ann Steere, Julia Amstutz.

A special thanks also to the following people whose personal counsel, encouragement, and determination helped make this product a reality:

Dr. Kenneth N. Taylor
Translator of *The Living Bible*
Chairman of the Board
Tyndale House Publishers, Inc.

Mark D. Taylor
President
Tyndale House Publishers, Inc.

Dr. Wendell C. Hawley
Senior Vice President
Tyndale House Publishers, Inc.

Virginia Muir
Former Assistant Editor-In-Chief
Tyndale House Publishers, Inc.

Richard R. Wynn
President, Youth for Christ/USA

Dr. Jay L. Kesler
President, Taylor University

A CHRONOLOGY OF BIBLE EVENTS AND WORLD EVENTS

Creation
undated

Noah builds the ark
undated

Abraham born
2166

Abraham enters Canaan
2091

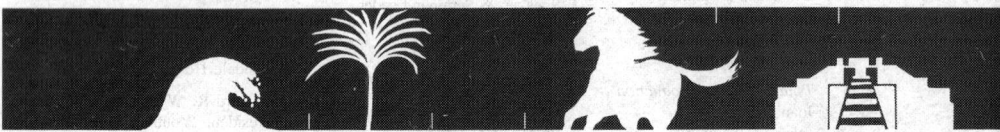

2500 B.C.
Egyptians discover papyrus and ink for writing and build the first libraries; iron objects manufactured in the ancient Near East

2400
Egyptians import gold from Africa

2331
Semitic chieftain, Sargon, conquers Sumer to become first "world conqueror"

2300
Horses domesticated in Egypt; chickens domesticated in Babylon; bows & arrows used in wars

2100
Glass made by the Mesopotamians; ziggurats (like the tower of Babel) built in Mesopotamia; earliest discovered drug, ethyl alcohol, used to alleviate pain

WHY THE LIFE APPLICATION BIBLE IS UNIQUE

Have you ever opened your Bible and asked the following:

- What does this passage really mean?
- How does it apply to my life?
- Why does some of the Bible seem irrelevant?
- What do these ancient cultures have to do with today?
- I love God; why can't I understand what he is saying to me through his word?
- What's going on in the lives of these Bible people?

Many Christians do not read the Bible regularly. Why? Because in the pressures of daily living they cannot find a connection between the timeless principles of Scripture and the ever-present problems of day-by-day living.

God urges us to apply his word (Isaiah 42:23; 1 Corinthians 10:11; 2 Thessalonians 3:4), but too often we stop at accumulating Bible knowledge. This is why the *Life Application Bible* was developed—to show how to put into practice what we have learned.

Applying God's word is a vital part of one's relationship with God; it is the evidence that we are obeying him. The difficulty in applying the Bible is not

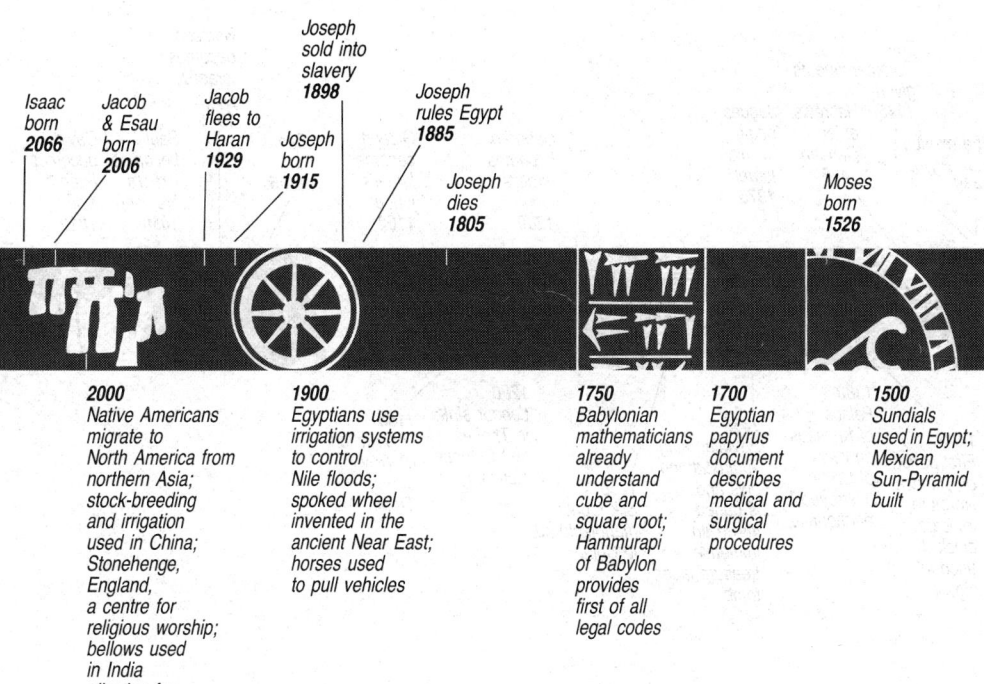

Isaac born ***2066***

Jacob & Esau born ***2006***

Jacob flees to Haran ***1929***

Joseph born ***1915***

Joseph sold into slavery ***1898***

Joseph rules Egypt ***1885***

Joseph dies ***1805***

Moses born ***1526***

2000 *Native Americans migrate to North America from northern Asia; stock-breeding and irrigation used in China; Stonehenge, England, a centre for religious worship; bellows used in India allowing for higher furnace temperatures*

1900 *Egyptians use irrigation systems to control Nile floods; spoked wheel invented in the ancient Near East; horses used to pull vehicles*

1750 *Babylonian mathematicians already understand cube and square root; Hammurapi of Babylon provides first of all legal codes*

1700 *Egyptian papyrus document describes medical and surgical procedures*

1500 *Sundials used in Egypt; Mexican Sun-Pyramid built*

with the Bible itself, but with the reader's inability to bridge the gap between the past and present, the conceptual and practical. When we don't or can't do this, spiritual dryness, shallowness, and indifference are the results.

The words of Scripture itself cry out to us, "Do not merely listen to the word, and so deceive yourselves. Do what it says" (James 1:22). The *Life Application Bible* does just that. Developed by an interdenominational team of pastors, scholars, family counselors, and a national organisation dedicated to promoting God's word and spreading the gospel, the *Life Application Bible* took many years to complete, and all the work was reviewed by several renowned theologians under the directorship of Dr. Kenneth Kantzer.

The *Life Application Bible* does what a good resource Bible should—it helps you understand the context of a passage, gives important background and historical information, explains difficult words and phrases, and helps you see the inter-relationships within Scripture. But it does much more. The *Life Application Bible* goes deeper into God's word, helping you discover the timeless truth being communicated, see the relevance for your life, and make a personal application. While some study Bibles attempt application, over 75% of this Bible is application-oriented. The notes answer the questions, "So what?" and "What does this passage mean to me, my family, my friends, my job, my neighbourhood, my church, my country?"

Imagine reading a familiar passage of Scripture and gaining fresh insight, as if it were the first time you had ever read it. How much richer your life would be if you left each Bible reading with a new perspective and a small change for the better. A small change every day adds up to a changed life—and that is the very purpose of Scripture.

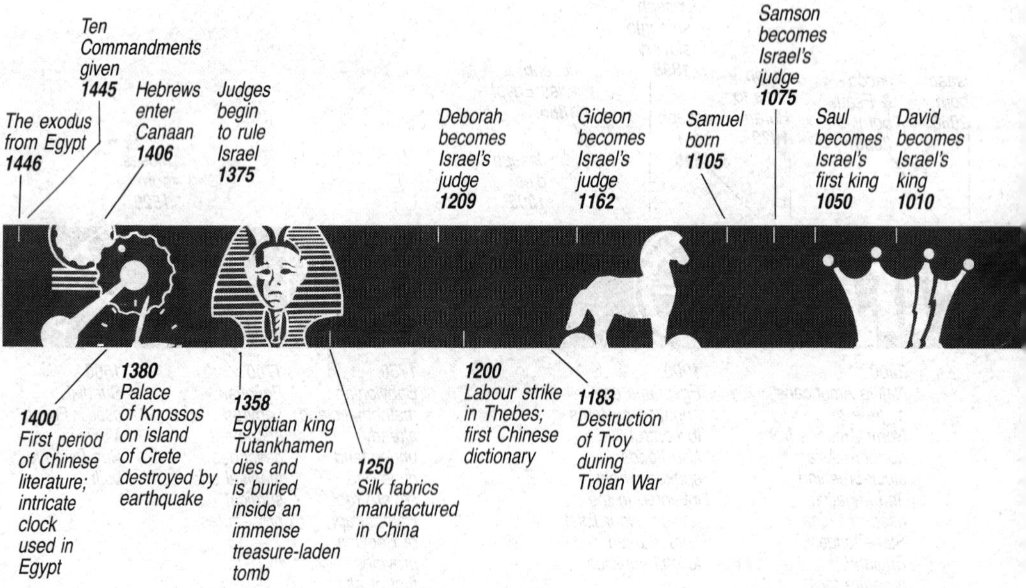
The exodus from Egypt 1446
Ten Commandments given 1445
Hebrews enter Canaan 1406
Judges begin to rule Israel 1375
Deborah becomes Israel's judge 1209
Gideon becomes Israel's judge 1162
Samuel born 1105
Samson becomes Israel's judge 1075
Saul becomes Israel's first king 1050
David becomes Israel's king 1010
1400 First period of Chinese literature; intricate clock used in Egypt
1380 Palace of Knossos on island of Crete destroyed by earthquake
1358 Egyptian king Tutankhamen dies and is buried inside an immense treasure-laden tomb
1250 Silk fabrics manufactured in China
1200 Labour strike in Thebes; first Chinese dictionary
1183 Destruction of Troy during Trojan War

The best way to define application is to first determine what it is *not*. Application is *not* just accumulating knowledge. This helps us discover and understand facts and concepts, but it stops there. History is filled with philosophers who knew what the Bible said, but failed to apply it to their lives, keeping them from believing and changing. Many think that understanding is the end goal of Bible study, but it is really only the beginning.

Application is *not* just illustration. Illustration only tells us how someone else handled a similar situation. While we may empathise with that person, we still have little direction for our personal situation.

Application is *not* just making a passage "relevant". Making the Bible relevant only helps us to see that the same lessons that were true in Bible times are true today; it does not show us how to apply them to the problems and pressures of our individual lives.

What, then, is application? Application begins by knowing and understanding God's word and its timeless truths. *But you cannot stop there*. If you do, God's word may not change your life, and it may become dull, difficult, tedious, and tiring. A good application focuses the truth of God's word, shows the reader what to do about what is being read, and motivates the reader to respond to what God is teaching. All three are essential to application.

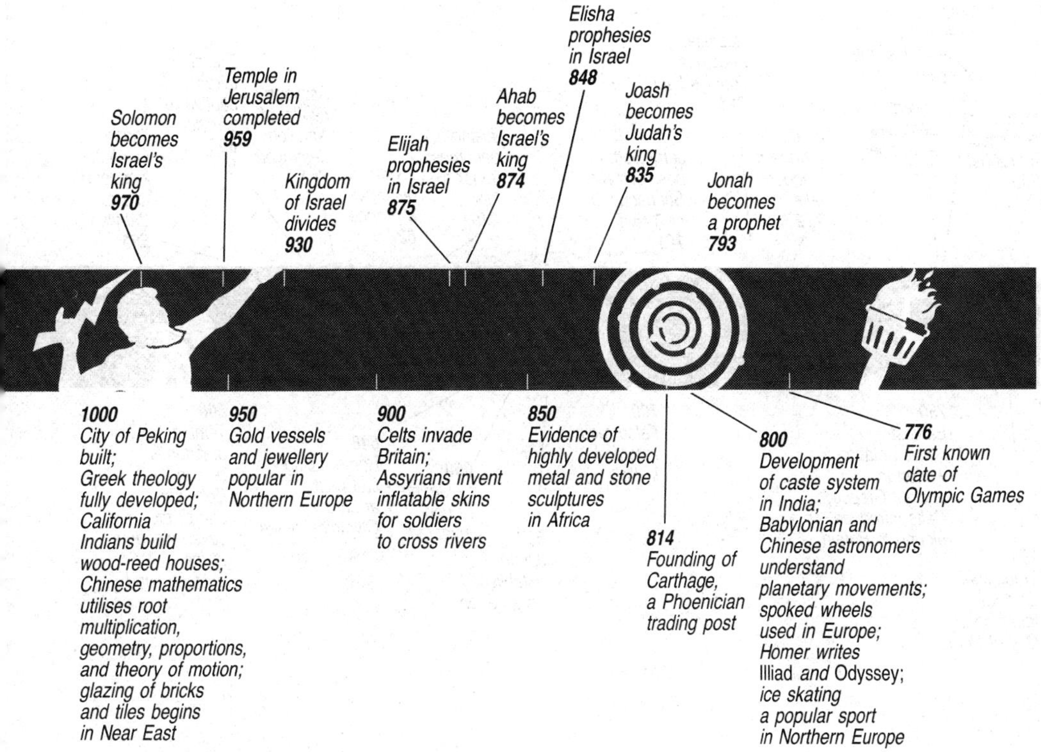
Solomon becomes Israel's king 970
Temple in Jerusalem completed 959
Kingdom of Israel divides 930
Elijah prophesies in Israel 875
Ahab becomes Israel's king 874
Elisha prophesies in Israel 848
Joash becomes Judah's king 835
Jonah becomes a prophet 793
1000 City of Peking built; Greek theology fully developed; California Indians build wood-reed houses; Chinese mathematics utilises root multiplication, geometry, proportions, and theory of motion; glazing of bricks and tiles begins in Near East
950 Gold vessels and jewellery popular in Northern Europe
900 Celts invade Britain; Assyrians invent inflatable skins for soldiers to cross rivers
850 Evidence of highly developed metal and stone sculptures in Africa
814 Founding of Carthage, a Phoenician trading post
800 Development of caste system in India; Babylonian and Chinese astronomers understand planetary movements; spoked wheels used in Europe; Homer writes Illiad and Odyssey; ice skating a popular sport in Northern Europe
776 First known date of Olympic Games

Application is putting into practice what we already know (see Mark 4:24 and Hebrews 5:14) and answering the question. "So what?" by confronting us with the right questions and motivating us to take action (see 1 John 2:5, 6 and James 2:17). Application is deeply personal—unique for each individual. It is making a relevant truth a personal truth, and involves developing a strategy and action plan to live your life in harmony with the Bible. It is the biblical "how to" of life.

You may ask, "How can your application notes be relevant to my life?" Each application note has three parts: (1) an *explanation* that ties the note directly to the Scripture passage and sets up the truth that is being taught, (2) the *bridge* that explains the timeless truth and makes it relevant for today, (3) the *application* that shows you how to take the timeless truth and apply it to your personal situation. No note, by itself, can apply Scripture directly to your life. It can only teach, direct, lead, guide, inspire, recommend, and urge. It can give you the resources and direction you need to apply the Bible; but only *you* can take these resources and put them into practice.

A good note, therefore, should not only give you knowledge and understanding, but point you to application. Before you buy any kind of resource Bible, you should evaluate the notes and ask the following questions: (1) Does the note contain enough information to help me understand the point of the Scripture passage? (2) Does the note assume I know too much? (3) Does the note avoid denominational bias? (4) Do the notes touch most of life's experiences? (5) Does the note help me *apply* God's word?

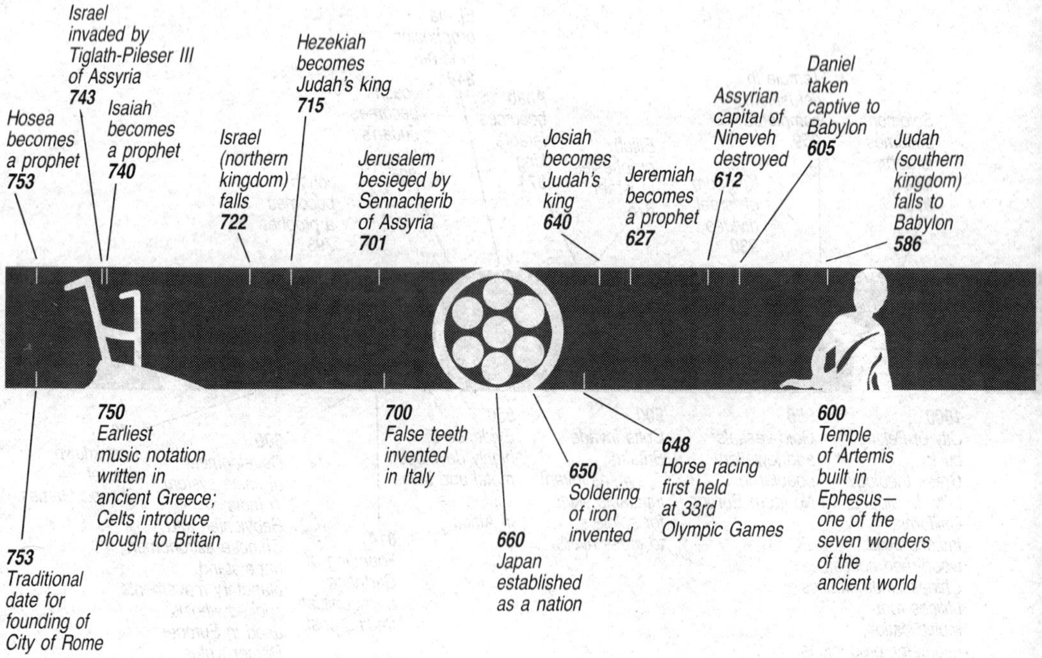

Israel invaded by Tiglath-Pileser III of Assyria 743
Hosea becomes a prophet 753
Isaiah becomes a prophet 740
Israel (northern kingdom) falls 722
Hezekiah becomes Judah's king 715
Jerusalem besieged by Sennacherib of Assyria 701
Josiah becomes Judah's king 640
Jeremiah becomes a prophet 627
Assyrian capital of Nineveh destroyed 612
Daniel taken captive to Babylon 605
Judah (southern kingdom) falls to Babylon 586
753 Traditional date for founding of City of Rome
750 Earliest music notation written in ancient Greece; Celts introduce plough to Britain
700 False teeth invented in Italy
660 Japan established as a nation
650 Soldering of iron invented
648 Horse racing first held at 33rd Olympic Games
600 Temple of Artemis built in Ephesus—one of the seven wonders of the ancient world

FEATURES OF THE LIFE APPLICATION BIBLE

NOTES

In addition to providing the reader with many application notes, the *Life Application Bible* offers several explanatory notes, which are notes that help the reader understand culture, history, context, difficult-to-understand passages, background, places, theological concepts, and the relationship of various passages in Scripture to other passages. Maps, charts, and diagrams are also found on the same page as the passages to which they relate. For an example of an application note, see Mark 15:47. For an example of an explanatory note, see Mark 11:1, 2.

BOOK INTRODUCTIONS

The Book Introductions are divided into several easy-to-find parts:

Timeline. This puts the Bible book into its historical setting. It lists the key events of each book and the date when they occurred.

Vital Statistics. This is a list of straight facts about the book—those pieces of information you need to know at a glance.

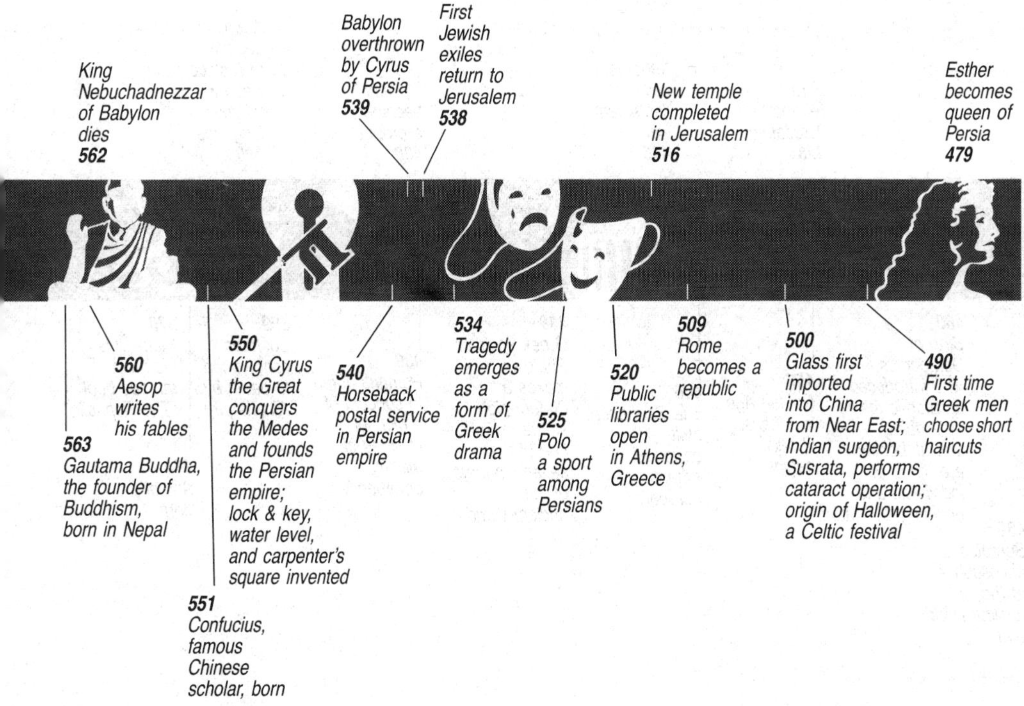
King Nebuchadnezzar of Babylon dies 562
Babylon overthrown by Cyrus of Persia 539
First Jewish exiles return to Jerusalem 538
New temple completed in Jerusalem 516
Esther becomes queen of Persia 479
563 Gautama Buddha, the founder of Buddhism, born in Nepal
560 Aesop writes his fables
551 Confucius, famous Chinese scholar, born
550 King Cyrus the Great conquers the Medes and founds the Persian empire; lock & key, water level, and carpenter's square invented
540 Horseback postal service in Persian empire
534 Tragedy emerges as a form of Greek drama
525 Polo a sport among Persians
520 Public libraries open in Athens, Greece
509 Rome becomes a republic
500 Glass first imported into China from Near East; Indian surgeon, Susrata, performs cataract operation; origin of Halloween, a Celtic festival
490 First time Greek men choose short haircuts

Overview. This is a summary of the book with general lessons and application that can be learned from the book as a whole.

Blueprint. This is the outline of the book. It is printed in easy-to-understand language and is designed for easy memorisation. To the right of each main heading is a key lesson that is taught in that particular section.

Megathemes. This section gives the main themes of the Bible book, explains their significance, and then tells why they are still important for us today.

Map. This shows the key places found in that book and retells the story of the book from a geographical point of view.

OUTLINE

The *Life Application Bible* has a new, custom-made outline that was designed specifically from an application point of view. Several unique features should be noted:

1. To avoid confusion and to aid memory work, each book outline has only three levels for headings. Main outline heads are marked with a capital letter. Subheads are marked by a number. Minor explanatory heads have no letter or number.

2. Each main outline head marked by a letter also has a brief paragraph below it summarising the Bible text and offering a general application.

3. Parallel passages are listed where they apply in the Gospels.

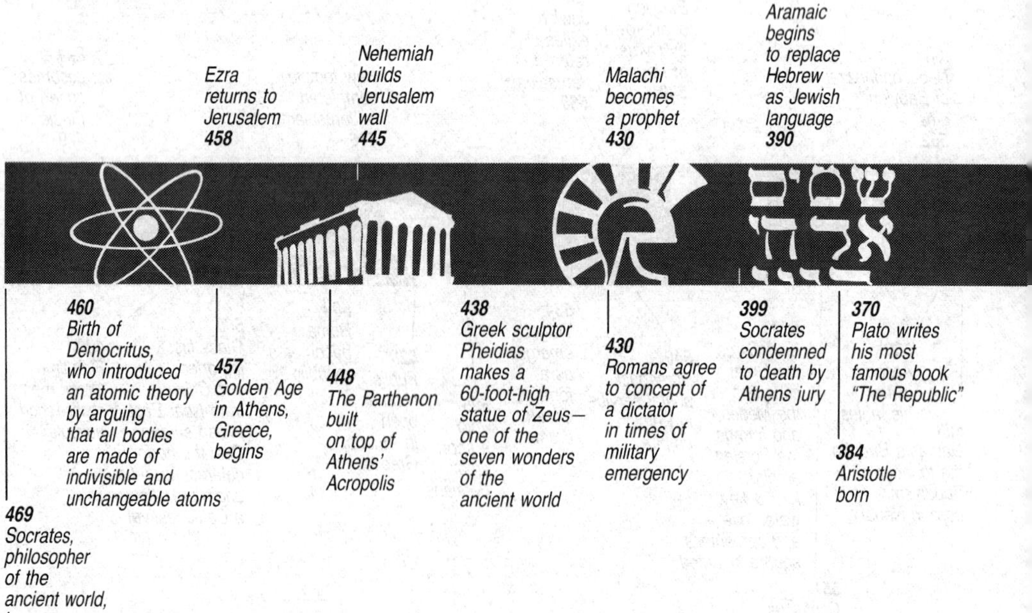

Ezra returns to Jerusalem 458
Nehemiah builds Jerusalem wall 445
Malachi becomes a prophet 430
Aramaic begins to replace Hebrew as Jewish language 390
469 Socrates, philosopher of the ancient world, born
460 Birth of Democritus, who introduced an atomic theory by arguing that all bodies are made of indivisible and unchangeable atoms
457 Golden Age in Athens, Greece, begins
448 The Parthenon built on top of Athens' Acropolis
438 Greek sculptor Pheidias makes a 60-foot-high statue of Zeus—one of the seven wonders of the ancient world
430 Romans agree to concept of a dictator in times of military emergency
399 Socrates condemned to death by Athens jury
370 Plato writes his most famous book "The Republic"
384 Aristotle born

HARMONY OF THE GOSPELS

A harmony of the Gospels was developed specifically for this Bible. It is the first harmony that has ever been incorporated into the Bible text. Through a unique and simple numbering system, you can read any Gospel account and see just where you are in relation to the entire life of Christ. The harmony is located after the Gospel of John and explained in detail there.

PROFILE NOTES

Another unique feature of this Bible is the profiles of many Bible people, including their strengths and weaknesses, greatest accomplishments and mistakes, and key lessons from their lives. The profiles of these people are found in the Bible books where their stories occur.

MAPS

The *Life Application Bible* has more maps than any other Bible. A thorough and comprehensive Bible atlas is built right into each Bible book. There are two kinds of maps: (1) A book introduction map, telling the story of that Bible book. (2) Thumb-nail maps in the notes, plotting most geographic movements in the Bible.

CHARTS AND DIAGRAMS

Hundreds of charts and diagrams are included to help the reader better visualise difficult concepts or relationships. Most charts not only present the needed information but show the significance of the information as well.

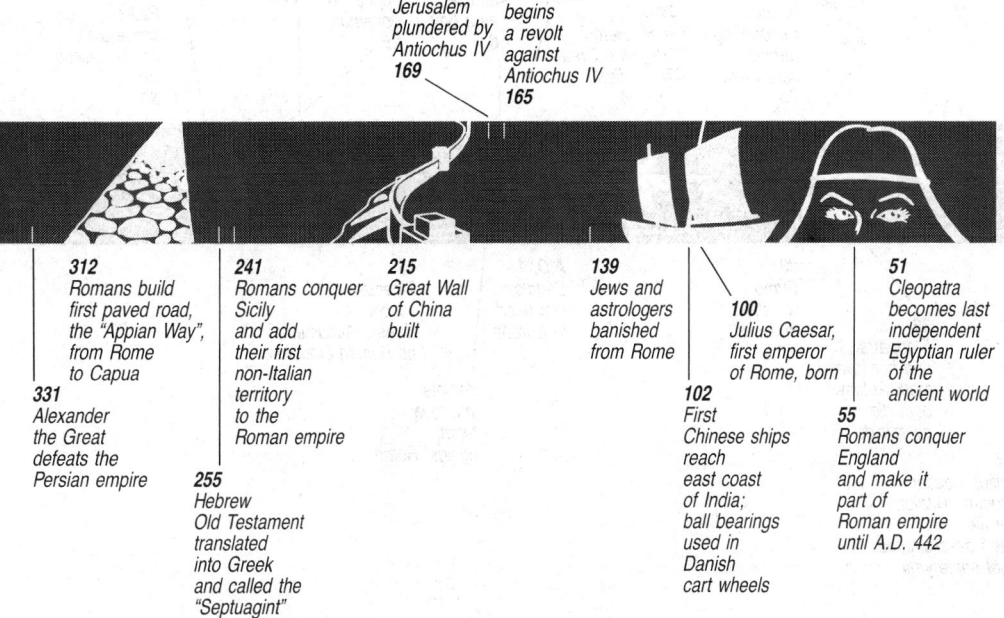

Temple of Jerusalem plundered by Antiochus IV
169

Judas Maccabeus begins a revolt against Antiochus IV
165

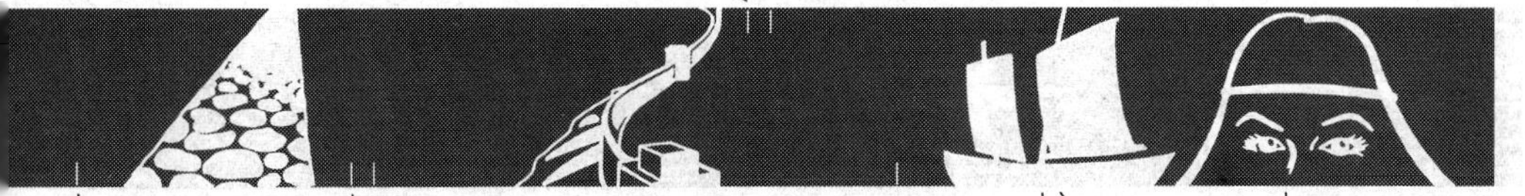

331
Alexander the Great defeats the Persian empire

312
Romans build first paved road, the "Appian Way", from Rome to Capua

255
Hebrew Old Testament translated into Greek and called the "Septuagint"

241
Romans conquer Sicily and add their first non-Italian territory to the Roman empire

215
Great Wall of China built

139
Jews and astrologers banished from Rome

102
First Chinese ships reach east coast of India; ball bearings used in Danish cart wheels

100
Julius Caesar, first emperor of Rome, born

55
Romans conquer England and make it part of Roman empire until A.D. 442

51
Cleopatra becomes last independent Egyptian ruler of the ancient world

CROSS-REFERENCES

A carefully organised cross-reference system in the margins of the Bible text helps the reader find related passages quickly. See page v for more information on the NIV Cross-Reference system.

TEXTUAL NOTES AND SECTIONAL HEADINGS

Directly related to the New International Version text, the textual notes examine such things as alternative translations, meaning of Hebrew and Greek terms, Old Testament quotations, and variant readings in ancient biblical manuscripts. The NIV text also contains sectional headings in order to help you more easily understand the subject and content of each section. NOTE: The standard New International Version section headings have been altered for this particular edition, particularly in the Gospels where they have been eliminated in favour of the "Harmony of the Gospels" feature.

INDEX

This book contains a complete index to all the notes, charts, maps, and personality profiles. With its emphasis on application, it is helpful for group Bible study, sermon preparation, teaching, or personal study.

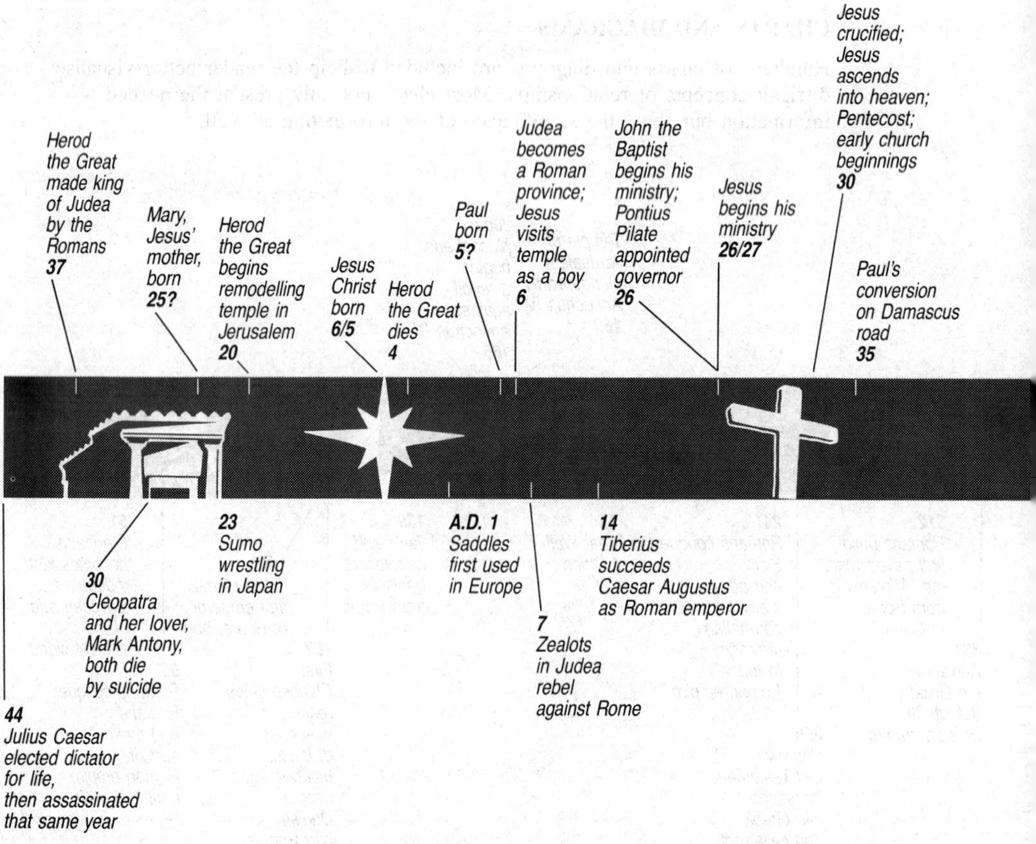
Herod the Great made king of Judea by the Romans 37
Mary, Jesus' mother, born 25?
Herod the Great begins remodelling temple in Jerusalem 20
Jesus Christ born 6/5
Herod the Great dies 4
Paul born 5?
Judea becomes a Roman province; Jesus visits temple as a boy 6
John the Baptist begins his ministry; Pontius Pilate appointed governor 26
Jesus begins his ministry 26/27
Jesus crucified; Jesus ascends into heaven; Pentecost; early church beginnings 30
Paul's conversion on Damascus road 35
44 Julius Caesar elected dictator for life, then assassinated that same year
30 Cleopatra and her lover, Mark Antony, both die by suicide
23 Sumo wrestling in Japan
A.D. 1 Saddles first used in Europe
7 Zealots in Judea rebel against Rome
14 Tiberius succeeds Caesar Augustus as Roman emperor

Herod Agrippa appointed king of Judea
40

43
London founded; first definite reference to diamonds

Paul begins first missionary journey
46

50
Romans begin using soap

54
Emperor Claudius poisoned by order of his wife; Nero becomes emperor

Paul writes Romans; Paul imprisoned in Caesarea
57

Paul's voyage to Rome
59

Paul writes "prison letters"
60

Paul released from prison
62

64
Fire burns much of Rome. Nero blames Christians for starting it

66
Painting on canvas

Paul martyred
67?

68
Romans destroy a Jewish religious commune of the Essene sect. Before the Essenes were captured they hid their library of Bible manuscripts in a cave in Qumran by the Dead Sea (discovered in 1948).

Romans destroy Jerusalem
70

960 Jews commit mass suicide at Masada while under Roman attack
73

74
China opens silk trade with the west

75
Rome begins construction of famous Colosseum

79
Mount Vesuvius in Italy erupts, killing 30,000 people and burying cities of Pompeii and Herculaneum

Apostle John writes Revelation
95

THE OLD TESTAMENT

GENESIS

Creation	Noah undated	Abram born 2166 B.C. (2000 B.C.)	Abram enters Canaan 2091 (1925)	Isaac born 2066 (1900)

VITAL STATISTICS

PURPOSE:
To record God's creation of the world and his desire to have a people set apart to worship him

AUTHOR:
Moses

TO WHOM WRITTEN:
The people of Israel

DATE WRITTEN:
1450–1410 B.C.

SETTING:
The region presently known as the Middle East

KEY VERSES:
"So God created man in his own image, in the image of God he created him; male and female he created them" (1:27). " 'I will make you into a great nation and I will bless you; I will make your name great, and you will be a blessing. I will bless those who bless you, and whoever curses you I will curse; and all peoples on earth will be blessed through you' " (12:2, 3).

KEY PEOPLE:
Adam, Eve, Noah, Abraham, Sarah, Isaac, Rebekah, Jacob, Joseph

BEGIN . . . start . . . commence . . . open. . . . There's something refreshing and optimistic about these words, whether they refer to the dawn of a new day, the birth of a child, the prelude of a symphony, or the first miles of a family holiday. Free of problems and full of promise, beginnings stir hope and imaginative visions of the future. Genesis means "beginnings" or "origin", and it unfolds the record of the beginning of the world, of human history, of family, of civilisation, of salvation. It is the story of God's purpose and plan for his creation. As the book of beginnings, Genesis sets the stage for the entire Bible. It reveals the person and nature of God (Creator, Sustainer, Judge, Redeemer); the value and dignity of human beings (made in God's image, saved by grace, used by God in the world); the tragedy and consequences of sin (the fall, separation from God, judgment); and the promise and assurance of salvation (covenant, forgiveness, promised Messiah).

God. That's where Genesis begins. All at once we see him creating the world in a majestic display of power and purpose, culminating with a man and woman made like himself (1:26, 27). But before long sin entered the world, and Satan was unmasked. Bathed in innocence, creation was shattered by the fall (the wilful disobedience of Adam and Eve). Fellowship with God was broken, and evil began weaving its destructive web. In rapid succession, we read how Adam and Eve were expelled from the beautiful garden, their first son turned murderer, and evil bred evil until God finally destroyed everyone on earth except a small family led by Noah, the only godly person left.

As we come to Abraham on the plains of Canaan, we discover the beginning of God's covenant people and the broad strokes of his salvation plan: salvation comes by faith, Abraham's descendants will be God's people, and the Saviour of the world will come through this chosen nation. The stories of Isaac, Jacob, and Joseph which follow are more than interesting biographies. They emphasise the promises of God and the proof that he is faithful. The people we meet in Genesis are simple, ordinary people, yet through them, God did great things. These are vivid pictures of how God can and does use all kinds of people to accomplish his good purposes . . . even people like you and me.

Read Genesis and be encouraged. There is hope! No matter how dark the world situation seems, God has a plan. No matter how insignificant or useless you feel, God loves you and wants to use you in his plan. No matter how sinful and separated from God you are, his salvation is available. Read Genesis . . . and hope!

Jacob & Esau born 2006 (1840)	*Jacob flees to Haran 1929 (1764)*	*Joseph born 1915 (1750)*	*Joseph sold into slavery 1898 (1733)*	*Joseph rules Egypt 1885 (1720)*	*Joseph dies 1805 (1640)*

THE BLUEPRINT

A. THE STORY OF CREATION (1:1—2:3)

God created the sky, seas, and land. He created the plants, animals, fish, and birds. But he created human beings in his own image. At times, others may treat us disrespectfully. But we can be certain of our dignity and worth because we have been created in the image of God.

B. THE STORY OF ADAM (2:4—5:32)
1. Adam and Eve
2. Cain and Abel
3. Adam's descendants

When Adam and Eve were created by God, they were without sin. But they became sinful when they disobeyed God and ate some fruit from the tree. Through Adam and Eve we learn about the destructive power of sin and its bitter consequences.

C. THE STORY OF NOAH (6:1—11:32)
1. The flood
2. Repopulating the earth
3. The tower of Babel

Noah was spared from the destruction of the flood because he obeyed God and built the ark. Just as God protected Noah and his family, he still protects those who are faithful to him today.

D. THE STORY OF ABRAHAM (12:1—25:18)
1. God promises a nation to Abram
2. Abram and Lot
3. God promises a son to Abram
4. Sodom and Gomorrah
5. Birth and near sacrifice of Isaac
6. Isaac and Rebekah
7. Abraham dies

Abraham was asked to leave his country, wander in Canaan, wait years for a son, and then sacrifice him as a burnt offering. Through these periods of sharp testing, Abraham remained faithful to God. His example teaches us what it means to live a life of faith.

E. THE STORY OF ISAAC (25:19—28:9)
1. Jacob and Esau
2. Isaac and Abimelech
3. Jacob gets Isaac's blessing

Isaac did not demand his own way. He did not resist when he was about to be sacrificed, and he gladly accepted a wife chosen for him by others. Like Isaac, we must learn to put God's will ahead of our own.

F. THE STORY OF JACOB (28:10—36:43)
1. Jacob starts a family
2. Jacob returns home

Jacob did not give up easily. He faithfully served Laban for over 14 years. Later, he wrestled with God. Although Jacob made many mistakes, his hard work teaches us about living a life of service for our Lord.

G. THE STORY OF JOSEPH (37:1—50:26)
1. Joseph is sold into slavery
2. Judah and Tamar
3. Joseph is thrown into prison
4. Joseph is placed in charge of Egypt
5. Joseph and his brothers meet in Egypt
6. Jacob's family moves to Egypt
7. Jacob and Joseph die in Egypt

Joseph was sold into slavery by his brothers and unjustly thrown into prison by his master. Through the life of Joseph, we learn that suffering, no matter how unfair, can develop strong character in us.

MEGATHEMES

THEME	EXPLANATION	IMPORTANCE
Beginnings	Genesis explains the beginning of many important realities: the universe, earth, people, sin, and God's plan of salvation.	Genesis teaches us that the earth is well made and good. Mankind is special to God and unique. God creates and sustains all life.
Disobedience	People are always facing great choices. Disobedience occurs when people choose not to follow God's plan of living.	Genesis explains why men are evil: they choose to do wrong. Even great Bible heroes failed God and disobeyed.
Sin	Sin ruins people's lives. It happens when we disobey God.	Living God's way makes life productive and fulfilling.

Promises	God makes promises to help and protect mankind. This kind of promise is called a "covenant".	God kept his promises then, and he keeps them now. He promises to love us, accept us, forgive us.
Obedience	The opposite of sin is obedience. Obeying God restores our relationship to him.	The only way to enjoy the benefits of God's promises is to obey him.
Prosperity	Prosperity is deeper than mere material wealth. True prosperity and fulfilment come as a result of obeying God.	When people obey God, they find peace with him, with others, and with themselves.
Israel	God started the nation of Israel in order to have a dedicated people who would (1) keep his ways alive in the world, (2) proclaim to the world what he is really like, and (3) prepare the world for the birth of Christ.	God is looking for people today to follow him. We are to proclaim God's truth and love to all nations, not just our own. We must be faithful to carry out the mission God has given us.

KEY PLACES IN GENESIS

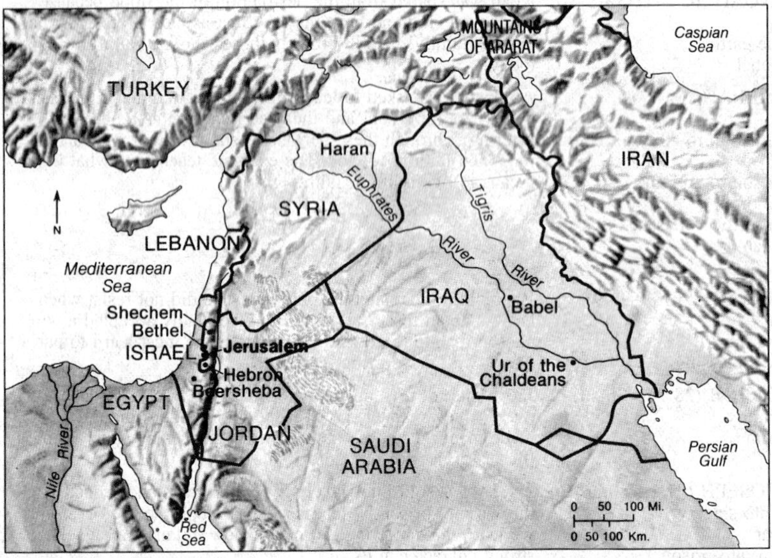

Modern names and boundaries are shown in grey.

God created the universe and the earth. Then he made man and woman, giving them a home in a beautiful garden. Unfortunately, Adam and Eve disobeyed God and were expelled from the garden (3:24).

1 **Mountains of Ararat** Adam and Eve's sin brought sin into the human race. Years later, sin had run rampant and God decided to destroy the earth with a great flood. But Noah, his family, and two of each animal were safe in the ark. When the floods receded, the ark rested on the mountains of Ararat (8:4).

2 **Babel** People never learn. Again sin abounded and the pride of the people led them to build a huge tower as a monument to their own greatness—obviously they had no thought of God. As punishment, God scattered the people by giving them different languages (11:8, 9).

3 **Ur of the Chaldeans** Abram, a descendant of Shem and father of the Hebrew nation, was born in this great city (11:28).

4 **Haran** Terah, Lot, Abram, and Sarai left Ur and, following the fertile crescent of the Euphrates River, headed towards the land of Canaan. Along the way, they settled in the city of Haran for a while (11:31).

5 **Shechem** God urged Abram to leave Haran and go to a place where he would become the father of a great nation (12:1, 2). So Abram, Lot, and Sarai travelled to the land of Canaan and settled near a city called Shechem (12:6).

6 **Hebron** Abraham moved on to Hebron where he put down his deepest roots (13:18). Abraham, Isaac, and Jacob all lived and were buried here.

7 **Beersheba** A well was dug here as a sign of an oath between Abraham and the army of King Abimelech (21:31). Years later, as Isaac was moving from place to place, God appeared to him here and passed on to him the covenant he had made with his father, Abraham (26:23–25).

8 **Bethel** After deceiving his brother, Jacob left Beersheba and fled to Haran. Along the way, God revealed himself to Jacob in a dream and passed on the covenant he had made with Abraham and Isaac (28:10–22). Jacob lived in Haran, worked for Laban, and married Leah and Rachel (29:15–28). After a tense meeting with his brother Esau, Jacob returned to Bethel (35:1).

9 **Egypt** Jacob had 12 sons, including Joseph, Jacob's favourite. Joseph's ten older brothers grew jealous, until one day the brothers sold him to Midianite merchants going to Egypt. Eventually, Joseph rose from Egyptian slave to Pharaoh's "right-hand man", saving Egypt from famine. His entire family moved from Canaan to Egypt and settled there (46:3, 4).

A. THE STORY OF CREATION (1:1 – 2:3)

We sometimes wonder how our world came to be. But here we find the answer. God created the earth and everything in it, and made man like himself. Although we may not understand the complexity of just how he did it, it is clear that God did create all life. This shows not only God's authority over humanity, but his deep love for all people.

The Beginning

1 In the beginning[a] God created the heavens and the earth.[b] 2 Now the earth
was[a] formless and empty,[c] darkness was over the surface of the deep, and the
Spirit of God[d] was hovering over the waters.
3 And God said,[e] "Let there be light," and there was light.[f] 4 God saw that the light
was good, and he separated the light from the darkness. 5 God called the light
"day", and the darkness he called "night".[g] And there was evening, and there
was morning — the first day.
6 And God said, "Let there be an expanse[h] between the waters to separate water from
water." 7 So God made the expanse and separated the water under the expanse
from the water above it.[i] And it was so. 8 God called the expanse "sky". And
there was evening, and there was morning — the second day.
9 And God said, "Let the water under the sky be gathered to one place,[j] and let dry
ground appear." And it was so. 10 God called the dry ground "land", and the
gathered waters he called "seas". And God saw that it was good.
11 Then God said, "Let the land produce vegetation:[k] seed-bearing plants and
trees on the land that bear fruit with seed in it, according to their various kinds."
And it was so. 12 The land produced vegetation: plants bearing seed according to
their kinds and trees bearing fruit with seed in it according to their kinds. And
God saw that it was good. 13 And there was evening, and there was morning — the third day.
14 And God said, "Let there be lights[l] in the expanse of the sky to separate the day

1:1 [a] Jn 1:1-2 [b] Job 38:4; Ps 90:2; Isa 42:5; 44:24; 45:12, 18; Ac 17:24; Heb 11:3; Rev 4:11
1:2 [c] Jer 4:23 [d] Ps 104:30
1:3 [e] Ps 33:6, 9; 148:5; Heb 11:3 [f] 2Co 4:6*
1:5 [g] Ps 74:16
1:6 [h] Jer 10:12
1:7 [i] Job 38:8-11, 16; Ps 148:4
1:9 [j] Job 38:8-11; Ps 104:6-9; Pr 8:29; Jer 5:22; 2Pe 3:5
1:11 [k] Ps 65:9-13; 104:14
1:14 [l] Ps 74:16

[a] *2* Or possibly *became*

1:1 The simple statement that God created the heavens and the earth is one of the most challenging concepts confronting the modern mind. The vast galaxy we live in is spinning at the incredible speed of 490,000 miles an hour. But even at this breakneck speed, our galaxy still needs 200 million years to make one rotation. And there are over one billion other galaxies just like ours in the universe.

Some scientists say that the number of stars in creation is equal to all the grains of all the sands on all the beaches of the world. Yet this complex sea of spinning stars functions with remarkable order and efficiency. To say that the universe "just happened" or "evolved" requires more faith than to believe that God is behind these amazing statistics. God truly did create a wonderful universe.

God did not *need* to create the universe; he *chose* to create it. Why? God is love, and love is best expressed towards something or someone else – so God created the world and people as an expression of his love. We should avoid reducing God's creation to merely scientific terms. Remember that God created the universe because he loves each of us.

1:1ff The creation story teaches us much about God and ourselves. First, we learn about God: (1) he is creative; (2) as the Creator he is distinct from his creation; (3) he is eternal and in control of the world. We also learn about ourselves: (1) since God chose to create us, we are valuable in his eyes; (2) we are more important than the animals. (See 1:28 for more on our role in the created order.)

1:1ff Just how did God create the earth? This is still a subject of great debate. Some say that there was a sudden explosion, and the universe appeared. Others say God started the process, and the universe evolved over billions of years. Almost every ancient religion has its own story to explain how the earth came to be. And almost every scientist has an opinion on the origin of the universe. But only the Bible shows one supreme God creating the earth out of his great love and giving all people a special place in it. We will never know all the answers to how God created the earth, but the Bible tells us that God did create it. That fact alone gives worth and dignity to all people.

1:2 The statement "the earth was formless and empty" provides the setting for the creation narrative that follows. During the second and third days of creation, God gave *form* to the universe; during the next three days, God *filled* the earth with living beings. The "darkness . . . over the surface of the deep" was dispelled on the first day, when God created light.

1:2 The image of the Spirit of God hovering over the waters is similar to a mother bird caring for and protecting her young (see Deuteronomy 32:11, 12; Isaiah 31:5). God's Spirit was actively involved in the creation of the world (see Job 33:4; Psalm 104:30). God's care and protection are still active.

1:3 – 2:7 How long did it take God to create the world? There are two basic views about the days of creation: (1) each day was a literal 24-hour period; (2) each day represents an indefinite period of time (even millions of years).

The Bible does not say how long these time periods were. The real question, however, is not how long God took, but how he did it. God created the earth in an orderly fashion (he did not make plants before light), and he created men and women as unique beings capable of communication with him. No other part of creation can claim that remarkable privilege. It is not important how long it took God to create the world, whether a few days or a few billion years, but that he created it just the way he wanted it.

1:6 The "expanse between the waters" was a separation between the sea and the mists of the skies.

from the night, and let them serve as signs[m] to mark seasons[n] and days and
years, 15 and let them be lights in the expanse of the sky to give light on the
earth." And it was so. 16 God made two great lights—the greater light to govern[o] the day and the lesser light to govern[p] the night. He also made the stars.[q]
17 God set them in the expanse of the sky to give light on the earth, 18 to govern
the day and the night,[r] and to separate light from darkness. And God saw that
it was good. 19 And there was evening, and there was morning—the fourth day.
20 And God said, "Let the water teem with living creatures, and let birds fly above the
earth across the expanse of the sky." 21 So God created the great creatures of the
sea and every living and moving thing with which the water teems,[s] according
to their kinds, and every winged bird according to its kind. And God saw that it
was good. 22 God blessed them and said, "Be fruitful and increase in number and
fill the water in the seas, and let the birds increase on the earth."[t] 23 And there
was evening, and there was morning—the fifth day.
24 And God said, "Let the land produce living creatures according to their kinds: livestock, creatures that move along the ground, and wild animals, each according
to its kind." And it was so. 25 God made the wild animals[u] according to their
kinds, the livestock according to their kinds, and all the creatures that move
along the ground according to their kinds. And God saw that it was good.
26 Then God said, "Let us[v] make man in our image,[w] in our likeness, and let
them rule[x] over the fish of the sea and the birds of the air, over the livestock,
over all the earth,[b] and over all the creatures that move along the ground."

[b] 26 Hebrew; Syriac *all the wild animals*

1:14 [m] Jer 10:2 [n] Ps 104:19
1:16 [o] Ps 136:8 [p] Ps 136:9 [q] Job 38:7, 31-32; Ps 8:3; Isa 40:26
1:18 [r] Jer 33:20, 25
1:21 [s] Ps 104:25-26
1:22 [t] ver 28; Ge 8:17
1:25 [u] Jer 27:5
1:26 [v] Ps 100:3 [w] Ge 9:6; Jas 3:9 [x] Ps 8:6-8

BEGINNINGS

The Bible does not discuss the subject of evolution. Rather, its worldview assumes God created the world. The biblical view of creation is not in conflict with science; rather, it is in conflict with any worldview that starts without a creator.

Equally committed and sincere Christians have struggled with the subject of beginnings and come to differing conclusions. This, of course, is to be expected because the evidence is very old and, due to the ravages of the ages, quite fragmented. Students of the Bible and of science should avoid polarisations and black/white thinking. Students of the Bible must be careful not to make the Bible say what it doesn't say, and students of science must not make science say what it doesn't say.

The most important aspect of the continuing discussion is not the *process* of creation, but the *origin* of creation. The world is not a product of blind chance and probability; God created it.

The Bible not only tells us that the world was created by God; more important, it tells us who this God is. It reveals God's personality, his character, and his plan for his creation. It also reveals God's deepest desire: to relate to and fellowship with the people he created. God took the ultimate step towards fellowship with us through his historic visit to this planet in the person of his Son, Jesus Christ. We can know this God who created the universe in a very personal way.

The heavens and the earth are here. We are here. God created all that we see and experience. The book of Genesis begins, "God created the heavens and the earth." Here we begin the most exciting and fulfilling journey imaginable.

1:25 God saw that his work was good. People sometimes feel guilty for having a good time or for feeling good about an accomplishment. This need not be so. Just as God felt good about his work, we can be pleased with ours. However, we should not feel good about our work if God would not be pleased with it. What are you doing that pleases both you and God?

1:26 Why does God use the plural form, "Let *us* make man in *our* image"? One view says this is a reference to the Trinity—God the Father, Jesus Christ his Son, and the Holy Spirit—all of whom are God. Another view is that the plural wording is used to denote majesty. Kings traditionally use the plural form in speaking of themselves. From Job 33:4 and Psalm 104:30, we do know that God's Spirit was present in the creation. From Colossians 1:16 we know that Christ, God's Son, was at work in the creation.

1:26 In what ways are we made in God's image? God obviously did not create us exactly like himself because God has no physical body. Instead, we are reflections of God's glory. Some feel that our reason, creativity, speech, or self-determination is the image of God. More likely, it is our entire self that reflects the image of God. We will never be totally like God because he is our supreme Creator. But we do have the ability to reflect his character in our love, patience, forgiveness, kindness, and faithfulness.

Knowing that we are made in God's image and thus share many of his characteristics provides a solid basis for self-worth. Human worth is not based on possessions, achievements, physical attractiveness, or public acclaim. Instead it is based on being made in God's image. Because we bear God's image, we can feel positive about ourselves. Criticising or downgrading ourselves is criticising what God has made and the abilities he has given us. Knowing that you are a person of worth helps you love God, know him personally, and make a valuable contribution to those around you.

27 So God created man in his own image,[y]
in the image of God he created him;
male and female[z] he created them.

28 God blessed them and said to them, "Be fruitful and increase in number; fill
the earth[a] and subdue it. Rule over the fish of the sea and the birds of the air and
over every living creature that moves on the ground."
29 Then God said, "I give you every seed-bearing plant on the face of the
whole earth and every tree that has fruit with seed in it. They will be yours for
food.[b] 30 And to all the beasts of the earth and all the birds of the air and all the
creatures that move on the ground—everything that has the breath of life in it—I
give every green plant for food.[c]" And it was so.
31 God saw all that he had made,[d] and it was very good.[e] And there was
evening, and there was morning—the sixth day.

2 Thus the heavens and the earth were completed in all their vast array.

2 By the seventh day God had finished the work he had been doing; so on the seventh
day he rested[a] from all his work.[a] 3 And God blessed the seventh day and made
it holy,[b] because on it he rested from all the work of creating that he had done.

B. THE STORY OF ADAM (2:4—5:32)

Learning about our ancestors often helps us understand ourselves. Adam and Eve, our first ancestors, were the highlight of God's creation—the very reason God made the world. But they didn't always live the way God intended. Through their mistakes, we can learn important lessons on how to live rightly. Adam and Eve teach us much about the nature of sin and its consequences.

1. Adam and Eve

4 This is the account of the heavens and the earth when they were created.

When the LORD God made the earth and the heavens—5 and no shrub of the field had

a 2 Or *ceased*; also in verse 3

1:27 [y] 1Co 11:7 [z] Ge 5:2; Mt 19:4*; Mk 10:6*
1:28 [a] Ge 9:1, 7; Lev 26:9
1:29 [b] Ps 104:14
1:30 [c] Ps 104:14, 27; 145:15
1:31 [d] Ps 104:24 [e] 1Ti 4:4
2:2 [a] Ex 20:11; 31:17; Heb 4:4*
2:3 [b] Lev 23:3; Isa 58:13

DAYS OF CREATION

First Day	Light (so there was light and darkness)
Second Day	Sky and water (waters separated)
Third Day	Land and seas (waters gathered); vegetation
Fourth Day	Sun, moon, and stars (to govern the day and the night and to mark seasons, days, and years)
Fifth Day	Fish and birds (to fill the waters and the sky)
Sixth Day	Animals (to fill the earth) Man and woman (to care for the earth and to commune with God)
Seventh Day	God rested and declared all he had made to be very good

1:27 God made both man and woman in his image. Neither man nor woman is made more in the image of God than the other. From the beginning the Bible places both man and woman at the pinnacle of God's creation. Neither sex is exalted, and neither is depreciated.

1:28 To "rule over" something is to have absolute authority and control over it. God has ultimate rule over the earth, and he exercises his authority with loving care. When God delegated some of his authority to the human race, he expected us to take responsibility for the environment and the other creatures that share our planet. We must not be careless and wasteful as we fulfil this charge. God was careful how he made this earth. We must not be careless about how we take care of it.

1:31 God saw that all he had created was very good. You are part of God's creation, and he is pleased with how he made you. If at times you feel worthless or of little value, remember that God made you for a good reason. You are valuable to him.

2:2, 3 We live in an action-oriented world! There always seems to be something to do and no time to rest. Yet God demonstrated that rest is appropriate and right. If God himself rested from his work, then it should not amaze us that we also need rest. Jesus demonstrated this principle when he and his disciples left in a boat to get away from the crowds (see Mark 6:31, 32). Our times of rest refresh us for times of service.

2:3 That God *blessed* the seventh day means that he set it apart for holy use. This act is picked up in the Ten Commandments (Exodus 20:1–17) where God commanded the observance of the Sabbath.

yet appeared on the earth[b] and no plant of the field had yet sprung up,[c] for the LORD
God had not sent rain on the earth[b][d] and there was no man to work the ground, 6 but
streams[c] came up from the earth and watered the whole surface of the ground—7 the
LORD God formed the man[d] from the dust[e] of the ground[f] and breathed into his
nostrils the breath[g] of life,[h] and the man became a living being.[i]
8 Now the LORD God had planted a garden in the east, in Eden;[j] and there he put the
man he had formed. 9 And the LORD God made all kinds of trees grow out of the
ground—trees that were pleasing to the eye and good for food. In the middle of the
garden were the tree of life[k] and the tree of the knowledge of good and evil.[l]
10 A river watering the garden flowed from Eden; from there it was separated into
four headwaters. 11 The name of the first is the Pishon; it winds through the entire land
of Havilah, where there is gold. 12 (The gold of that land is good; aromatic resin[e] and
onyx are also there.) 13 The name of the second river is the Gihon; it winds through the
entire land of Cush.[f] 14 The name of the third river is the Tigris;[m] it runs along the east
side of Asshur. And the fourth river is the Euphrates.
15 The LORD God took the man and put him in the Garden of Eden to work it and take
care of it. 16 And the LORD God commanded the man, "You are free to eat from any tree
in the garden; 17 but you must not eat from the tree of the knowledge of good and evil,
for when you eat of it you will surely die."[n]
18 The LORD God said, "It is not good for the man to be alone. I will make a helper
suitable for him."[o]
19 Now the LORD God had formed out of the ground all the beasts of the field[p] and
all the birds of the air. He brought them to the man to see what he would name them;
and whatever the man called each living creature,[q] that was its name. 20 So the man
gave names to all the livestock, the birds of the air and all the beasts of the field.
But for Adam[g] no suitable helper was found. 21 So the LORD God caused the man
to fall into a deep sleep; and while he was sleeping, he took one of the man's ribs[h] and
closed up the place with flesh. 22 Then the LORD God made a woman from the rib[i][r]
he had taken out of the man, and he brought her to the man.
23 The man said,

[b] *5* Or *land*; also in verse 6 [c] *6* Or *mist* [d] *7* The Hebrew for *man (adam)* sounds like and may be related to the Hebrew for *ground (adamah)*; it is also the name *Adam* (see Gen. 2:20). [e] *12* Or *good; pearls* [f] *13* Possibly south-east Mesopotamia [g] *20* Or *the man* [h] *21* Or *took part of the man's side* [i] *22* Or *part*

2:5 [c] Ge 1:11 [d] Ps 65:9-10
2:7 [e] Ge 3:19 [f] Ps 103:14 [g] Job 33:4 [h] Ac 17:25 [i] 1Co 15:45*
2:8 [j] Ge 3:23, 24; Isa 51:3
2:9 [k] Ge 3:22, 24; Rev 2:7; 22:2, 14, 19 [l] Eze 47:12
2:14 [m] Da 10:4
2:17 [n] Dt 30:15, 19; Ro 5:12; 6:23; Jas 1:15
2:18 [o] 1Co 11:9
2:19 [p] Ps 8:7 [q] Ge 1:24
2:22 [r] 1Co 11:8, 9, 12

2:7 "From the dust of the ground" implies that there is nothing fancy about the chemical elements making up our bodies. The body is a lifeless shell until God brings it alive with his "breath of life". When God removes his life-giving breath, our bodies once again return to dust. Therefore our life and worth come from God's Spirit. Many boast of their achievements and abilities as though they were the originator of their own strengths. Others feel worthless because their abilities do not stand out. In reality, our worth comes not from our achievements but from the God of the universe, who chooses to give us the mysterious and miraculous gift of life. Value life, as he does.

2:9 The name of the tree of the knowledge of good and evil implies that evil had already occurred, if not in the garden, then at the time of Satan's fall.

2:9, 16, 17 Were the tree of life and the tree of the knowledge of good and evil real trees? Two views are often expressed:

(1) *The trees were real, but symbolic.* Eternal life with God was pictured as eating from the tree of life.

(2) *The trees were real, possessing special properties.* By eating the fruit from the tree of life, Adam and Eve could have had eternal life, enjoying a permanent relationship as God's children.

In either case, Adam and Eve's sin separated them from the tree of life and thus kept them from obtaining eternal life. Interestingly, the tree of life again appears in a description in Revelation 22 of people enjoying eternal life with God.

2:15–17 God gave Adam responsibility for the garden and told him not to eat from the tree of the knowledge of good and evil. Rather than physically preventing him from eating, God gave Adam a choice, and thus the possibility of choosing wrongly. God still gives us choices, and we, too, often choose wrongly. These wrong choices may cause us pain, but they can help us learn and grow and make better choices in the future. Living with the consequences of our choices teaches us to think and choose more carefully.

2:16, 17 Why would God place a tree in the garden and then forbid Adam to eat from it? God wanted Adam to obey, but God gave Adam the freedom to choose. Without choice, Adam would have been like a prisoner, and his obedience would have been hollow. The two trees provided an exercise in choice, with rewards for choosing to obey and sad consequences for choosing to disobey. When you are faced with the choice, always choose to obey God.

2:18–24 God's creative work was not complete until he made woman. He could have made her from the dust of the ground, as he made man. God chose, however, to make her from the man's flesh and bone. In so doing, he illustrated for us that in marriage man and woman symbolically become one flesh. This is a mystical union of the couple's hearts and lives. Throughout the Bible, God treats this special partnership seriously. If you are married or planning to be married, are you willing to keep the commitment that makes the two of you one? The goal in marriage should be more than friendship; it should be oneness.

2:21–23 God forms and equips men and women for various tasks, but all these tasks lead to the same goal—honouring God. Man gives life to woman; woman gives life to the world. Each role carries exclusive privileges; there is no room for thinking that one sex is superior to the other.

2:23
[s]Ge 29:14;
Eph 5:28-30

2:24
[t]Mal 2:15
[u]Mt 19:5*;
Mk 10:7-8*;
1Co 6:16*;
Eph 5:31*

2:25
[v]Ge 3:7, 10-11

3:1
[a]2Co 11:3;
Rev 12:9; 20:2

"This is now bone of my bones
and flesh of my flesh;[s]
she shall be called 'woman',[j]
for she was taken out of man."

24For this reason a man will leave his father and mother and be united[t] to his wife, and
they will become one flesh.[u]
25The man and his wife were both naked,[v] and they felt no shame.

The Fall of Man

3 Now the serpent[a] was more crafty than any of the wild animals the LORD God had
made. He said to the woman, "Did God really say, 'You must not eat from any
tree in the garden'?"
2The woman said to the serpent, "We may eat fruit from the trees in the garden, 3but
God did say, 'You must not eat fruit from the tree that is in the middle of the garden,
and you must not touch it, or you will die.' "

[j] *23* The Hebrew for *woman* sounds like the Hebrew for *man.*

WHAT THE BIBLE SAYS ABOUT MARRIAGE

Genesis 2:18–24	Marriage is God's idea
Genesis 24:58–60	Commitment is essential to a successful marriage
Song of Songs 4:9, 10	Romance is important
Jeremiah 33:10, 11	Marriage holds times of great joy
Malachi 2:14, 15	Marriage creates the best environment for raising children
Matthew 5:32	Unfaithfulness breaks the bond of trust, the foundation of all relationships
Matthew 19:6	Marriage is permanent
Romans 7:2, 3	Ideally, only death should dissolve marriage
Ephesians 5:21–33	Marriage is based on the principled practice of love, not on feelings
Ephesians 5:23, 32	Marriage is a living symbol of Christ and the church
Hebrews 13:4	Marriage is good and honourable

2:24 God gave marriage as a gift to Adam and Eve. They were created perfect for each other. Marriage was not just for convenience, nor was it brought about by any culture. It was instituted by God and has three basic aspects: (1) the man leaves his parents and, in a public act, promises himself to his wife; (2) the man and woman are joined together by taking responsibility for each other's welfare and by loving the partner above all others; (3) the two become one flesh in the intimacy and commitment of sexual union that is reserved for marriage. Strong marriages include all three of these aspects.

2:25 Have you ever noticed how a little child can run naked through a room full of strangers without embarrassment? He is not aware of his nakedness, just as Adam and Eve were not embarrassed in their innocence. But after Adam and Eve sinned, shame and awkwardness followed, creating barriers between themselves and God. We often experience these same barriers in marriage. Ideally a husband and wife have no barriers, feeling no embarrassment in exposing themselves to each other or to God. But, like Adam and Eve (3:7), we put on fig leaves (barriers) because we have areas we don't want our spouse, or God, to know about. Then we hide, just as Adam and Eve hid from God. In marriage, lack of spiritual, emotional, and intellectual intimacy usually precedes a breakdown of physical intimacy. In the same way, when we fail to expose our secret thoughts to God, we break our lines of communication with him.

3:1 Disguised as a crafty serpent, Satan came to tempt Eve. Satan at one time was an angel who rebelled against God and was thrown out of heaven. As a created being, Satan has definite limitations. Although he is trying to tempt everyone away from God, he will not be the final victor. In 3:14, 15, God promises that Satan will be crushed by one of the woman's offspring, the Messiah.

3:1–6 Why does Satan tempt us? Temptation is Satan's invitation to give in to his kind of life and give up on God's kind of life. Satan tempted Eve and succeeded in getting her to sin. Ever since then, he's been busy getting people to sin. He even tempted Jesus (Matthew 4:11). But Jesus did not sin!

How could Eve have resisted temptation? By following the same guidelines we can follow. First, we must realise that *being tempted* is not a sin. We have not sinned until we *give in* to the temptation. Then, to resist temptation, we must (1) pray for strength to resist, (2) run, sometimes literally, and (3) say no when confronted with what we know is wrong. James 1:12 tells of the blessings and rewards for those who don't give in when tempted.

3:1–6 The serpent, Satan, tempted Eve by getting her to doubt God's goodness. He implied that God was strict, stingy, and selfish for not wanting Eve to share his knowledge of good and evil. Satan made Eve forget all that God had given her and, instead, focus on the one thing she couldn't have. We fall into trouble, too, when we dwell on the few things we don't have rather than on the countless things God has given us. The next time you are feeling sorry for yourself and what you don't have, consider all you *do* have and thank God. Then your doubts won't lead you into sin.

4"You will not surely die," the serpent said to the woman. [b] 5"For God knows that
when you eat of it your eyes will be opened, and you will be like God, [c] knowing good
and evil."
6When the woman saw that the fruit of the tree was good for food and pleasing to the
eye, and also desirable [d] for gaining wisdom, she took some and ate it. She also gave
some to her husband, who was with her, and he ate it. [e] 7Then the eyes of both of them
were opened, and they realised that they were naked; so they sewed fig leaves together
and made coverings for themselves.
8Then the man and his wife heard the sound of the LORD God as he was walking [f]
in the garden in the cool of the day, and they hid [g] from the LORD God among the trees
of the garden. 9But the LORD God called to the man, "Where are you?"
10He answered, "I heard you in the garden, and I was afraid because I was naked; so
I hid."
11And he said, "Who told you that you were naked? Have you eaten from the tree
from which I commanded you not to eat?"
12The man said, "The woman you put here with me—she gave me some fruit from
the tree, and I ate it."
13Then the LORD God said to the woman, "What is this you have done?"

3:4 [b] Jn 8:44; 2Co 11:3
3:5 [c] Isa 14:14; Eze 28:2
3:6 [d] Jas 1:14-15; 1Jn 2:16 [e] 1Ti 2:14
3:8 [f] Dt 23:14 [g] Job 31:33; Ps 139:7-12; Jer 23:24

3:5 Adam and Eve got what they wanted: an intimate knowledge of both good and evil. But they got it by doing evil, and the results were disastrous. Sometimes we have the illusion that freedom is doing anything we want. But God says that true freedom comes from obedience and knowing what *not* to do. The restrictions he gives us are for our good, helping us avoid evil. We have the freedom to walk in front of a speeding car, but we don't need to be hit to realise it would be foolish to do so. Don't listen to Satan's temptations. You don't have to do evil to gain more experience and learn more about life.

3:5 Satan used a sincere motive to tempt Eve—"you will be like God". It wasn't wrong of Eve to want to be like God. To become more like God is humanity's highest goal. It is what we are supposed to do. But Satan misled Eve concerning the right way to accomplish this goal. He told her that she could become more like God by defying God's authority, by taking God's place and deciding for herself what was best for her life. In effect, he told her to become her own god.

But to become like God is not the same as trying to become God. Rather, it is to reflect his characteristics and to recognise his authority over your life. Like Eve, we often have a worthy goal but try to achieve it in the wrong way. We act like a political candidate who makes empty promises in order to win votes. When he does this, serving the people is no longer his highest goal.

Self-exaltation leads to rebellion against God. As soon as we begin to leave God out of our plans, we are placing ourselves above him. This is exactly what Satan wants us to do.

3:6 Satan tried to make Eve think that sin is good, pleasant, and desirable. A knowledge of both good and evil seemed harmless to her. People usually choose wrong things because they have become convinced that those things are good, at least for themselves. Our sins do not always appear ugly to us, and the pleasant sins are the hardest to avoid. So prepare yourself for the attractive temptations that may come your way. We cannot always prevent temptation, but there is always a way of escape (1 Corinthians 10:13). Use God's word and God's people to help you stand against it.

3:6, 7 Notice what Eve did: She looked, she took, she ate, and she gave. The battle is often lost at the first look. Temptation often begins by simply seeing something you want. Are you struggling with temptation because you have not learned that looking is the first step towards sin? You would win over temptation more often if you followed Paul's advice to run from those things that produce evil thoughts (2 Timothy 2:22).

3:6, 7 One of the realities of sin is that its effects spread. After Eve sinned, she involved Adam in her wrongdoing. When we do something wrong, often we try to relieve our guilt by involving someone else. Like toxic waste spilled in a river, sin swiftly spreads. Recognise and confess your sin to God before you are tempted to pollute those around you.

3:7, 8 After sinning, Adam and Eve felt guilt and embarrassment over their nakedness. Their guilty feelings made them try to hide from God. A guilty conscience is a warning signal God placed inside you that goes off when you've done wrong. The worst step you could take is to eliminate the guilty feelings without eliminating the cause. That would be like using a pain killer but not treating the disease. Be glad those guilty feelings are there. They make you aware of your sin so you can ask God's forgiveness and then correct your wrongdoing.

3:8 The thought of two humans covered with fig leaves trying to hide from the all-seeing, all-knowing God is laughable. How could they be so silly as to think they could actually hide? Yet we do the same, acting as though God doesn't know what we're doing. Have the courage to share all you do and think with him. And don't try to hide—it can't be done. Honesty will strengthen your relationship with God.

3:8, 9 These verses show God's desire to have fellowship with us. They also show why we are afraid to have fellowship with him. Adam and Eve hid from God when they heard him approaching. God wanted to be with them, but because of their sin they were afraid to show themselves. Sin had broken their close relationship with God, just as it has broken ours. But Jesus Christ, God's Son, opens the way for us to renew our fellowship with him. God longs to be with us. He actively offers us his unconditional love. Our natural response is fear because we feel we can't live up to his standards. But understanding that he loves us, regardless of our faults, can help remove that dread.

3:11–13 Adam and Eve failed to heed God's warning recorded in 2:16, 17. They did not understand the reasons for his command, so they chose to act in another way that looked better to them. All of God's commands are for our own good, but we may not always understand the reasons behind them. People who trust God will obey because God asks them to, whether or not they understand why God commands it.

3:11–13 When God asked Adam about his sin, Adam blamed Eve. Then Eve blamed the serpent. How easy it is to excuse our sins by blaming someone else or circumstances. But God knows the truth, and he holds each of us responsible for what we do (see 3:14–19). Admit your wrong attitudes and actions and apologise to God. Don't try to get away with sin by blaming someone else.

3:13 [h]2Co 11:3; 1Ti 2:14
3:14 [i]Dt 28:15-20

The woman said, "The serpent deceived me,[h] and I ate."
14So the LORD God said to the serpent, "Because you have done this,

"Cursed[i] are you above all the livestock

ADAM

We can hardly imagine what it must have been like to be the first and only person on earth. It's one thing for us to be lonely; it was another for Adam, who had never known another human being. He missed much that makes us who we are—he had no childhood, no parents, no family or friends. He had to learn to be human on his own. Fortunately, God didn't let him struggle too long before presenting him with an ideal companion and mate, Eve. Theirs was a complete, innocent, and open oneness, without a hint of shame.

One of Adam's first conversations with his delightful new companion must have been about the rules of the garden. Before God made Eve he had already given Adam complete freedom in the garden, with the responsibility to tend and care for it. But one tree was off limits, the tree of the knowledge of good and evil. Adam would have told Eve all about this. She knew, when Satan approached her, that the tree's fruit was not to be eaten. However, she decided to eat the forbidden fruit. Then she offered some to Adam. At that moment, the fate of creation was on the line. Sadly, Adam didn't pause to consider the consequences. He went ahead and ate.

In that moment of small rebellion something large, beautiful, and free was shattered . . . God's perfect creation. Man was separated from God by his desire to act on his own. The effect on a plate glass window is the same whether a pebble or a boulder is hurled at it—the thousands of fragments can never be regathered.

In the case of man's sin, however, God already had a plan in motion to overcome the effects of the rebellion. The entire Bible is the story of how that plan unfolds, ultimately leading to God's own visit to earth through his Son, Jesus. His sinless life and death made it possible for God to offer forgiveness to all who want it. Our small and large acts of rebellion prove that we are descendants of Adam. Only by asking forgiveness of Jesus Christ can we become children of God.

Strengths and accomplishments:
- The first zoologist—namer of animals
- The first landscape architect, placed in the garden to care for it
- Father of the human race
- The first person made in the image of God, and the first human to share an intimate personal relationship with God

Weaknesses and mistakes:
- Avoided responsibility and blamed others; chose to hide rather than to confront; made excuses rather than admitting the truth
- Greatest mistake: teamed up with Eve to bring sin into the world

Lessons from his life:
- As Adam's descendants, we all reflect to some degree the image of God
- God wants people who, though free to do wrong, choose instead to love him
- We should not blame others for our faults
- We cannot hide from God

Vital statistics:
- Where: Garden of Eden
- Occupation: Caretaker, gardener, farmer
- Relatives: Wife: Eve. Sons: Cain, Abel, Seth. Numerous other children. The only man who never had an earthly mother or father

Key verses:
"The man said, 'The woman you put here with me—she gave me some fruit from the tree, and I ate it' " (Genesis 3:12).
"For as in Adam all die, so in Christ all will be made alive" (1 Corinthians 15:22).

Adam's story is told in Genesis 1:26—5:5. He is also mentioned in 1 Chronicles 1:1; Luke 3:38; Romans 5:14; 1 Corinthians 15:22, 45; 1 Timothy 2:13, 14.

3:14ff Adam and Eve chose their course of action (disobedience), and then God chose his. As a holy God, he could respond only in a way consistent with his perfect moral nature. He could not allow sin to go unchecked; he had to punish it. If the consequences of Adam and Eve's sin seem extreme, remember that their sin set in motion the world's tendency towards disobeying God. That is why we sin today: Every human being ever born, with the exception of Jesus, has inherited the sinful nature of Adam and Eve (Romans 5:12–21). Adam and Eve's punishment reflects how seriously God views sin of any kind.

3:14–19 Adam and Eve learned by painful experience that because God is holy and hates sin, he must punish sinners. The rest of the book of Genesis recounts painful stories of lives ruined as a result of the fall. Disobedience is sin, and it breaks our fellowship with God. But, fortunately, when we disobey, God is willing to forgive us and to restore our relationship with him.

and all the wild animals!
You will crawl on your belly
and you will eat dust[j]
all the days of your life.
15 And I will put enmity
between you and the woman,
and between your offspring[a][k] and hers;[l]
he will crush[b] your head,[m]
and you will strike his heel."

16 To the woman he said,

"I will greatly increase your pains in childbearing;
with pain you will give birth to children.
Your desire will be for your husband,
and he will rule over you.[n]"

17 To Adam he said, "Because you listened to your wife and ate from the tree about
which I commanded you, 'You must not eat of it,'

"Cursed[o] is the ground because of you;
through painful toil you will eat of it
all the days of your life.[p]
18 It will produce thorns and thistles for you,
and you will eat the plants of the field.[q]
19 By the sweat of your brow
you will eat your food[r]
until you return to the ground,
since from it you were taken;
for dust you are
and to dust you will return."[s]

20 Adam[c] named his wife Eve,[d] because she would become the mother of all the
living.
21 The LORD God made garments of skin for Adam and his wife and clothed them.
22 And the LORD God said, "The man has now become like one of us, knowing good
and evil. He must not be allowed to reach out his hand and take also from the tree of
life[t] and eat, and live for ever." 23 So the LORD God banished him from the Garden of
Eden[u] to work the ground[v] from which he had been taken. 24 After he drove the man
out, he placed on the east side[e] of the Garden of Eden cherubim[w] and a flaming
sword[x] flashing back and forth to guard the way to the tree of life.[y]

a 15 Or *seed* b 15 Or *strike* c 20 Or *The man* d 20 *Eve* probably means *living.* e 24 Or *placed in front*

3:14 [j] Isa 65:25; Mic 7:17
3:15 [k] Jn 8:44; Ac 13:10; 1Jn 3:8 [l] Isa 7:14; Mt 1:23; Rev 12:17 [m] Ro 16:20; Heb 2:14
3:16 [n] 1Co 11:3; Eph 5:22
3:17 [o] Ge 5:29; Ro 8:20-22 [p] Job 5:7; 14:1; Ecc 2:23
3:18 [q] Ps 104:14
3:19 [r] 2Th 3:10 [s] Ge 2:7; Ps 90:3; 104:29; Ecc 12:7
3:22 [t] Rev 22:14
3:23 [u] Ge 2:8 [v] Ge 4:2
3:24 [w] Ex 25:18-22 [x] Ps 104:4 [y] Ge 2:9

3:15 Satan is our enemy. He will do anything he can to get us to follow his evil, deadly path. The phrase "you will strike his heel" refers to Satan's repeated attempts to defeat Christ during his life on earth. "He will crush your head" foreshadows Satan's defeat when Christ rose from the dead. A strike on the heel is not deadly, but a crushing blow to the head is. Already God was revealing his plan to defeat Satan and offer salvation to the world through his Son, Jesus Christ.

3:17–19 Adam and Eve's disobedience and fall from God's gracious presence affected all creation, including the environment. Years ago people thought nothing of polluting streams with chemical wastes and garbage. This seemed so insignificant, so small. Now we know that just two or three parts per million of certain chemicals can damage human health. Sin in our lives is similar to pollution in streams. Even small amounts are deadly.

3:22–24 Life in the Garden of Eden was like living in heaven. Everything was perfect, and if Adam and Eve had obeyed God, they could have lived there for ever. But after disobeying, Adam and Eve no longer deserved paradise, and God told them to leave. If they had continued to live in the garden and eat from the tree of life, they would have lived for ever. But eternal life in a state of sin would mean for ever trying to hide from God. Like Adam and Eve, all of us have sinned and are separated from fellowship with God. We do not have to stay separated, however. God is preparing a new earth as an eternal paradise for his people (see Revelation 22).

3:24 The cherubim were mighty angels of the Lord.

3:24 This is how Adam and Eve broke their relationship with God: (1) they became convinced their way was better than God's; (2) they became self-conscious and hid; (3) they tried to excuse and defend themselves. To build a relationship with God we must reverse those steps: (1) we must drop our excuses and self-defences; (2) we must stop trying to hide from God; (3) we must become convinced that God's way is better than our way.

2. Cain and Abel

4 Adam[a] lay with his wife Eve, and she became pregnant and gave birth to Cain.[b]
She said, "With the help of the LORD I have brought forth[c] a man." 2 Later she
gave birth to his brother Abel.[a]
Now Abel kept flocks, and Cain worked the soil. 3 In the course of time Cain brought
some of the fruits of the soil as an offering to the LORD.[b] 4 But Abel brought fat portions[c] from some of the firstborn of his flock.[d] The LORD looked with favour on Abel
and his offering,[e] 5 but on Cain and his offering he did not look with favour. So Cain
was very angry, and his face was downcast.
6 Then the LORD said to Cain, "Why are you angry? Why is your face downcast? 7 If
you do what is right, will you not be accepted? But if you do not do what is right, sin
is crouching at your door;[f] it desires to have you, but you must master it.[g]"
8 Now Cain said to his brother Abel, "Let's go out to the field."[d] And while they
were in the field, Cain attacked his brother Abel and killed him.[h]
9 Then the LORD said to Cain, "Where is your brother Abel?"
"I don't know," he replied. "Am I my brother's keeper?"
10 The LORD said, "What have you done? Listen! Your brother's blood cries out to
me from the ground.[i] 11 Now you are under a curse and driven from the ground, which
opened its mouth to receive your brother's blood from your hand. 12 When you work
the ground, it will no longer yield its crops for you. You will be a restless wanderer on
the earth."

4:2 [a] Lk 11:51
4:3 [b] Nu 18:12
4:4 [c] Lev 3:16 [d] Ex 13:2, 12 [e] Heb 11:4
4:7 [f] Nu 32:23 [g] Ro 6:16
4:8 [h] Mt 23:35; 1Jn 3:12
4:10 [i] Ge 9:5; Nu 35:33; Heb 12:24; Rev 6:9-10

[a] *1* Or *The man* [b] *1* *Cain* sounds like the Hebrew for *brought forth* or *acquired.* [c] *1* Or *have acquired*
[d] *8* Samaritan Pentateuch, Septuagint, Vulgate and Syriac; Masoretic Text does not have *"Let's go out to the field."*

SATAN'S PLAN		
	Doubt	Makes you question God's word and his goodness
	Discouragement	Makes you look at your problems rather than at God
	Diversion	Makes the wrong things seem attractive so that you will want them more than the right things
	Defeat	Makes you feel like a failure so that you don't even try
	Delay	Makes you put off doing something so that it never gets done

4:1 The phrase *lay with* is literally *he knew* and means he "had sexual intercourse with". Sexual union means oneness and total knowledge of the other person. Sexual intercourse is the most intimate of acts, sealing a social, physical, and spiritual relationship. That is why God has reserved it for marriage alone.

4:2 No longer was everything provided for Adam and Eve as it was in the Garden of Eden, where their daily tasks were refreshing and delightful. Now they had to struggle against the elements in order to provide food, clothing, and shelter for themselves and their family. Cain became a farmer, while Abel was a shepherd. In parts of the Middle East today, these ancient occupations are still practised much as they were in Cain and Abel's time.

4:3–5 The Bible does not say why God rejected Cain's sacrifice. Perhaps Cain's attitude was improper, or perhaps his offering was not up to God's standards. Proverbs 21:27 says, "The sacrifice of the wicked is detestable – how much more so when brought with evil intent"! God evaluates both our motives and the quality of what we offer him. When we give to God and others, we should have a joyful heart because of what we are able to give. We should not worry about how much we are giving up, for all things are God's in the first place. Instead, we should joyfully give to God our best in time, money, possessions, and talents.

4:6, 7 How do you react when someone suggests you have done something wrong? Do you move to correct the mistake or deny that you need to correct it? After Cain's sacrifice was rejected, God gave him the chance to right his wrong and try again. God even encouraged him to do this! But Cain refused, and the rest of his life is a startling example of what happens to those who refuse to admit their mistakes. The next time someone suggests you are wrong, take an honest look at yourself and choose God's way instead of Cain's.

4:7 For Cain to master the sin lurking at the entrance to his desires, he would have to give up his jealous anger so that sin would not find a foothold in his life. Sin is still crouching at our doors today. Like Cain, we will be victims of sin if we do not master it. But we cannot master sin in our own strength. Instead, we must turn to God to receive faith for ourselves and faith and strength from other believers. The Holy Spirit will help us master sin. This will be a lifelong battle that will not be over until we are face to face with Christ.

4:8–10 This is the first murder – taking a life by shedding human blood. Blood represents life (Leviticus 17:10–14). If blood is removed from a living creature, it will die. Because God created life, only God should take life away.

4:8–10 Adam and Eve's disobedience brought sin into the human race. They may have thought their sin – eating a piece of fruit – wasn't very bad, but notice how quickly their sinful nature developed in their children. Simple disobedience quickly degenerated into outright murder. Adam and Eve acted only against God, but Cain acted against both God and man. A small sin has a way of growing out of control. Let God help you with your "little" sins before they turn into tragedies.

4:11–15 Cain was severely punished for this murder. God judges all sins and punishes appropriately, but not simply out of anger or vengeance. Rather, God's punishment is meant to correct us and restore our fellowship with him. When you're corrected, don't resent it. Instead, renew your fellowship with God.

13Cain said to the LORD, "My punishment is more than I can bear. 14Today you are
driving me from the land, and I will be hidden from your presence;[j] I will be a restless
wanderer on the earth, and whoever finds me will kill me."[k]
15But the LORD said to him, "Not so;[e] if anyone kills Cain[l], he will suffer vengeance seven times over.[m]" Then the LORD put a mark on Cain so that no-one who
found him would kill him. 16So Cain went out from the LORD's presence and lived in
the land of Nod,[f] east of Eden.[n]
17Cain lay with his wife, and she became pregnant and gave birth to Enoch. Cain
was then building a city, and he named it after his son[o] Enoch. 18To Enoch was born
Irad, and Irad was the father of Mehujael, and Mehujael was the father of Methushael,
and Methushael was the father of Lamech.
19Lamech married two women, one named Adah and the other Zillah. 20Adah gave
birth to Jabal; he was the father of those who live in tents and raise livestock. 21His
brother's name was Jubal; he was the father of all who play the harp and flute. 22Zillah
also had a son, Tubal-Cain, who forged all kinds of tools out of[g] bronze and iron.
Tubal-Cain's sister was Naamah.
23Lamech said to his wives,

"Adah and Zillah, listen to me;
wives of Lamech, hear my words.
I have killed[h][p] a man for wounding me,
a young man for injuring me.
24If Cain is avenged[q] seven times,[r]
then Lamech seventy-seven times."

25Adam lay with his wife again, and she gave birth to a son and named him Seth,[i][s]
saying, "God has granted me another child in place of Abel, since Cain killed him."[t]
26Seth also had a son, and he named him Enosh.
At that time men began to call on[j] the name of the LORD.[u]

3. Adam's descendants

From Adam to Noah

5 This is the written account of Adam's line.

When God created man, he made him in the likeness of God.[a] 2He created them
male and female[b] and blessed them. And when they were created, he called them
"man".[a]

e *15* Septuagint, Vulgate and Syriac; Hebrew *Very well* **f** *16* *Nod* means *wandering* (see verses 12 and 14).
g *22* Or *who instructed all who work in* **h** *23* Or *I will kill* **i** *25* *Seth* probably means *granted.* **j** *26* Or *to proclaim*
a *2* Hebrew *adam*

4:14
[j]2Ki 17:18; Ps 51:11; 139:7-12; Jer 7:15; 52:3
[k]Ge 9:6; Nu 35:19, 21, 27, 33

4:15
[l]Eze 9:4, 6
[m]ver 24; Ps 79:12

4:16
[n]Ge 2:8

4:17
[o]Ps 49:11

4:23
[p]Ex 20:13; Lev 19:18

4:24
[q]Dt 32:35
[r]ver 15

4:25
[s]Ge 5:3
[t]ver 8

4:26
[u]Ge 12:8; 1Ki 18:24; Ps 116:17; Joel 2:32; Zep 3:9; Ac 2:21; 1Co 1:2

5:1
[a]Ge 1:27; Eph 4:24; Col 3:10

5:2
[b]Ge 1:27; Mt 19:4; Mk 10:6; Gal 3:28

4:14 We have heard about only four people so far—Adam, Eve, Cain, and Abel. Two questions arise: Why was Cain worried about being killed by others, and where did he get his wife (see 4:17)?

Adam and Eve had numerous children; they had been told to "fill the earth" (1:28). Cain's guilt and fear over killing his brother were heavy, and he probably feared repercussions from his family. If he was capable of killing, so were they. The wife Cain chose may have been one of his sisters or a niece. The human race was still genetically pure, and there was no fear of side effects from marrying relatives.

4:15 The expression, "will suffer vengeance seven times over" means that the person's punishment would be complete, thorough, and much worse than that received by Cain for his sin.

4:19–26 Unfortunately, when left to themselves, people tend to get worse instead of better. This short summary of Lamech's family shows us the variety of talent and ability God gives humans. It also presents the continuous development of sin as time passes. Another killing occurred, presumably in self-defence. Violence is on the rise. Two distinct groups are appearing: (1) those who show indifference to sin and evil, and (2) those who call on the name of the Lord (the descendants of Seth, 4:26). Seth would take Abel's place as leader of a line of God's faithful people.

5:1ff The Bible contains several lists of ancestors, called *genealogies.* There are two basic views concerning these lists: (1) they are complete, recording the entire history of a family, tribe, or nation; or (2) they are not intended to be exhaustive and may include only famous people or the heads of families. "Became the father of" could also mean "was the ancestor of".

Why are genealogies included in the Bible? The Hebrews passed on their beliefs through oral tradition. For many years in many places, writing was primitive or non-existent. Stories were told to children who passed them on to their children. Genealogies gave a skeletal outline that helped people remember the stories. For centuries these genealogies were added to and passed down from family to family. Even more important than preserving family tradition, genealogies were included to confirm the Bible's promise that the coming Messiah, Jesus Christ, would be born into the line of Abraham.

Genealogies point out an interesting characteristic of God. People are important to him as individuals, not just as races or nations. Therefore God refers to people by name, mentioning their life span and descendants. The next time you feel overwhelmed in a vast

5:3 [c]Ge 1:26; 1Co 15:49
5:5 [d]Ge 3:19
5:18 [e]Jude 1:14

3 When Adam had lived 130 years, he had a son in his own likeness, in his own
image;[c] and he named him Seth. 4 After Seth was born, Adam lived 800 years and had
other sons and daughters. 5 Altogether, Adam lived 930 years, and then he died.[d]
6 When Seth had lived 105 years, he became the father[b] of Enosh. 7 And after he
became the father of Enosh, Seth lived 807 years and had other sons and daughters.
8 Altogether, Seth lived 912 years, and then he died.
9 When Enosh had lived 90 years, he became the father of Kenan. 10 And after he
became the father of Kenan, Enosh lived 815 years and had other sons and daughters.
11 Altogether, Enosh lived 905 years, and then he died.
12 When Kenan had lived 70 years, he became the father of Mahalalel. 13 And after
he became the father of Mahalalel, Kenan lived 840 years and had other sons and
daughters. 14 Altogether, Kenan lived 910 years, and then he died.
15 When Mahalalel had lived 65 years, he became the father of Jared. 16 And after he
became the father of Jared, Mahalalel lived 830 years and had other sons and daughters. 17 Altogether, Mahalalel lived 895 years, and then he died.
18 When Jared had lived 162 years, he became the father of Enoch.[e] 19 And after he

b 6 *Father* may mean *ancestor*; also in verses 7–26.

EVE

We know very little about Eve, the first woman in the world, yet she is the mother of us all. She was the final piece in the intricate and amazing puzzle of God's creation. Adam now had another human being with whom to fellowship—someone with an equal share in God's image. Here was someone alike enough for companionship, yet different enough for relationship. Together they were greater than either could have been alone.

Eve was approached by Satan in the Garden of Eden, where she and Adam lived. He questioned her contentment. How could she be happy when she was not allowed to eat from one of the fruit trees? Satan helped Eve shift her focus from all that God had done and given to the one thing he had withheld. And Eve was willing to accept Satan's viewpoint without checking with God.

Sound familiar? How often is our attention drawn from the much which is ours to the little that isn't? We get that "I've got to have it" feeling. Eve was typical of us all, and we consistently show we are her descendants by repeating her mistakes. Our desires, like Eve's, can be quite easily manipulated. They are not the best basis for actions. We need to keep God in our decision-making process always. His word, the Bible, is our guidebook in decision making.

Strengths and accomplishments:
- First wife and mother
- First female. As such she shared a special relationship with God, had co-responsibility with Adam over creation, and displayed certain characteristics of God

Weaknesses and mistakes:
- Allowed her contentment to be undermined by Satan
- Acted impulsively without talking either to God or to her partner
- Not only sinned, but shared her sin with Adam
- When confronted, blamed others

Lessons from her life:
- The female shares in the image of God
- The necessary ingredients for a strong marriage are commitment to each other, companionship with each other, complete oneness, absence of shame (2:24, 25)
- The basic human tendency to sin goes back to the beginning of the human race

Vital statistics:
- Where: Garden of Eden
- Occupation: Wife, helper, companion, co-manager of Eden
- Relatives: Husband: Adam. Sons: Cain, Abel, Seth. Numerous other children

Key verse:
"The LORD God said, 'It is not good for the man to be alone. I will make a helper suitable for him' " (Genesis 2:18).

Eve's story is told in Genesis 2:19—4:26. Her death is not mentioned in Scripture.

---

crowd, remember that the focus of God's attention and love is on the individual—and on you!

5:3–5 All human beings are related, going back to Adam and Eve. Mankind is a family that shares one flesh and blood. Remember this when prejudice enters your mind or hatred invades your feelings. Each person is a valuable and unique creation of God.

became the father of Enoch, Jared lived 800 years and had other sons and daughters.
20 Altogether, Jared lived 962 years, and then he died.
21 When Enoch had lived 65 years, he became the father of Methuselah. 22 And after
he became the father of Methuselah, Enoch walked with God[f] 300 years and had
other sons and daughters. 23 Altogether, Enoch lived 365 years. 24 Enoch walked with
God;[g] then he was no more, because God took him away.[h]
25 When Methuselah had lived 187 years, he became the father of Lamech. 26 And
after he became the father of Lamech, Methuselah lived 782 years and had other sons
and daughters. 27 Altogether, Methuselah lived 969 years, and then he died.
28 When Lamech had lived 182 years, he had a son. 29 He named him Noah[c] and
said, "He will comfort us in the labour and painful toil of our hands caused by the
ground the LORD has cursed.[i]" 30 After Noah was born, Lamech lived 595 years and
had other sons and daughters. 31 Altogether, Lamech lived 777 years, and then he died.
32 After Noah was 500 years old, he became the father of Shem, Ham and Japheth.

C. THE STORY OF NOAH (6:1—11:32)

Earth was no longer the perfect paradise that God had intended. It is frightening to see how quickly all of humanity forgot about God. Incredibly, in all the world, only one man and his family still worshipped God. That man was Noah. Because of his faithfulness and obedience, God saved him and his family from a vast flood that destroyed every other human being on earth. This section shows us how God hates sin and judges those who enjoy it.

1. The flood

6 When men began to increase in number on the earth[a] and daughters were born to
them, 2 the sons of God saw that the daughters of men were beautiful, and they
married any of them they chose. 3 Then the LORD said, "My Spirit will not contend
with[a] man for ever,[b] for he is mortal;[b][c] his days will be a hundred and twenty
years."
4 The Nephilim[d] were on the earth in those days—and also afterwards—when the
sons of God went to the daughters of men and had children by them. They were the
heroes of old, men of renown.
5 The LORD saw how great man's wickedness on the earth had become, and that
every inclination of the thoughts of his heart was only evil all the time.[e] 6 The LORD
was grieved[f] that he had made man on the earth, and his heart was filled with pain.
7 So the LORD said, "I will wipe mankind, whom I have created, from the face of the
earth—men and animals, and creatures that move along the ground, and birds of the

5:22 [f] ver 24; Ge 6:9; 17:1; 48:15; Mic 6:8; Mal 2:6

5:24 [g] ver 22 [h] 2Ki 2:1, 11; Heb 11:5

5:29 [i] Ge 3:17; Ro 8:20

6:1 [a] Ge 1:28

6:3 [b] Isa 57:16 [c] Ps 78:39

6:4 [d] Nu 13:33

6:5 [e] Ge 8:21; Ps 14:1-3

6:6 [f] 1Sa 15:11, 35; Isa 63:10

c 29 *Noah* sounds like the Hebrew for *comfort.* a 3 Or *My spirit will not remain in* b 3 Or *corrupt*

5:25–27 How did these people live so long? Some believe that the ages listed here were lengths of family dynasties rather than ages of individual men. Those who think these were actual ages offer three explanations: (1) the human race was more genetically pure in this early time period, so there was less disease to shorten life spans; (2) no rain had yet fallen on the earth, and the expanse of water "above" (1:7) kept out harmful cosmic rays and shielded people from environmental factors that hasten aging; (3) God gave people longer lives so they would have time to "fill the earth" (1:28).

6:1–4 Some people have thought that the "sons of God" were fallen angels. But the "sons of God" were probably not angels, because angels do not marry or reproduce (Matthew 22:30; Mark 12:25). Some scholars believe this phrase refers to the descendants of Seth who intermarried with Cain's evil descendants ("the daughters of men"). This would have weakened the good influence of the faithful and increased moral depravity in the world, resulting in an explosion of evil. *Nephilim* refers to a powerful race of giants.

6:3 "His days will be a hundred and twenty years" means that God was allowing the people of Noah's day 120 years to change their sinful ways. God shows his great patience with us as well. He is giving us time to stop living our way and begin living his way, the way he shows us in his word. While 120 years seems like a long time, eventually the time ran out and the floodwaters swept across the earth. Your time also may be running out. Turn to God to forgive your sins. You can't see the stopwatch of God's patience, and there is no bargaining for additional time.

6:4 The Nephilim were giants, people probably nine or ten feet tall. These may have been the same people mentioned in Numbers 13:33. Goliath, who was nine feet tall, appears in 1 Samuel 17. The Nephilim used their physical advantage to oppress the people around them.

6:6, 7 Does this mean that God regretted creating humanity? Was he admitting he made a mistake? No, God does not change his mind (1 Samuel 15:29). Instead, he was expressing sorrow for what the people had done to themselves, as a parent might express sorrow over a rebellious child. God was sorry that the people chose sin and death instead of a relationship with him.

6:6–8 The people's sin grieved God. Our sins break God's heart as much as sin did in Noah's day. Noah, however, pleased God, although he was far from perfect. We can follow Noah's example and find "favour in the eyes of the LORD" in spite of the sin that surrounds us.

6:8
[g]Ge 19:19; Ex 33:12, 13, 17; Lk 1:30; Ac 7:46
6:9
[h]Ge 7:1; Eze 14:14, 20; Heb 11:7; 2Pe 2:5
[i]Ge 5:22
6:10
[j]Ge 5:32
6:11
[k]Eze 7:23; 8:17
6:12
[l]Ps 14:1-3
6:13
[m]ver 17; Eze 7:2-3
6:14
[n]Heb 11:7; 1Pe 3:20
[o]Ex 2:3
6:17
[p]Ge 7:4, 21-23; 2Pe 2:5
6:18
[q]Ge 9:9-16
[r]Ge 7:1, 7, 13

air—for I am grieved that I have made them." 8But Noah found favour in the eyes of
the LORD.[g]

9This is the account of Noah.

Noah was a righteous man, blameless among the people of his time,[h] and he
walked with God.[i] 10Noah had three sons: Shem, Ham and Japheth.[j]
11Now the earth was corrupt in God's sight and was full of violence.[k] 12God saw
how corrupt the earth had become, for all the people on earth had corrupted their
ways.[l] 13So God said to Noah, "I am going to put an end to all people, for the earth
is filled with violence because of them. I am surely going to destroy both them and the
earth.[m] 14So make yourself an ark of cypress[c] wood;[n] make rooms in it and coat it
with pitch[o] inside and out. 15This is how you are to build it: The ark is to be 450 feet
long, 75 feet wide and 45 feet high.[d] 16Make a roof for it and finish[e] the ark to within
18 inches[f] of the top. Put a door in the side of the ark and make lower, middle and
upper decks. 17I am going to bring floodwaters on the earth to destroy all life under the
heavens, every creature that has the breath of life in it. Everything on earth will perish.[p] 18But I will establish my covenant with you,[q] and you will enter the ark[r]—you
and your sons and your wife and your sons' wives with you. 19You are to bring into the

c *14* The meaning of the Hebrew for this word is uncertain. d *15* Hebrew *300 cubits long, 50 cubits wide and 30 cubits high* (about 140 metres long, 23 metres wide and 13.5 metres high) e *16* Or *Make an opening for light by finishing* f *16* Hebrew *a cubit* (about 0.5 metre)

ABEL

Abel was the second child born into the world, but the first one to obey God. All we know about this man is that his parents were Adam and Eve, he was a shepherd, he presented pleasing sacrifices to God, and his short life was ended at the hands of his jealous older brother, Cain.

The Bible doesn't tell us why God liked Abel's gift and disliked Cain's, but both Cain and Abel knew what God expected. Only Abel obeyed. Throughout history, Abel is remembered for his obedience and faith (Hebrews 11:4), and he is called "righteous" (Matthew 23:35).

The Bible is filled with God's general guidelines and expectations for our lives. It is also filled with more specific directions. Like Abel, we must obey regardless of the cost and trust God to make things right.

Strengths and accomplishments:
- First member of the Hall of Faith in Hebrews 11
- First shepherd
- First martyr for truth (Matthew 23:35)

Lessons from his life:
- God hears those who come to him
- God recognises the innocent person and sooner or later punishes the guilty

Vital statistics:
- Where: Just outside of Eden
- Occupation: Shepherd
- Relatives: Parents: Adam and Eve. Brother: Cain

Key verse:
"By faith Abel offered God a better sacrifice than Cain did. By faith he was commended as a righteous man, when God spoke well of his offerings. And by faith he still speaks, even though he is dead" (Hebrews 11:4).

Abel's story is told in Genesis 4:1–8. He is also mentioned in Matthew 23:35; Luke 11:51; Hebrews 11:4 and 12:24.

6:9 To say that Noah was *righteous* and *blameless* does not mean that he never sinned (the Bible records one of his sins in 9:20ff). Rather it means that he wholeheartedly loved and obeyed God. For a lifetime he walked step by step in faith as a living example to his generation. Like Noah, we live in a world filled with evil. Are we influencing others or being influenced by them?

6:14 *Pitch* was a tarlike substance used to make the ark watertight.

6:15 The boat Noah built was no canoe! Picture yourself building a boat the length of one and a half football fields and as high as a four-storey building. The ark was exactly six times longer than it was wide—the same ratio used by modern shipbuilders. This huge boat was probably built miles from any body of water by only a few faithful men who believed God's promises and obeyed his commands.

6:18 A *covenant* is a promise. This is a familiar theme in Scripture—God making covenants with his people. How reassuring it is to know God's covenant is established with us. He is still our salvation and we are kept safe through our relationship with him. For more on the covenant see 9:8–17; 12:1–3; and 15:17–20.

ark two of all living creatures, male and female, to keep them alive with you. 20 Two[s]
of every kind of bird, of every kind of animal and of every kind of creature that moves
along the ground will come to you to be kept alive. 21 You are to take every kind of food
that is to be eaten and store it away as food for you and for them."
22 Noah did everything just as God commanded him.[t]
7 The LORD then said to Noah, "Go into the ark, you and your whole family,[a]
because I have found you righteous[b] in this generation. 2 Take with you seven[a]
of every kind of clean[c] animal, a male and its mate, and two of every kind of unclean
animal, a male and its mate, 3 and also seven of every kind of bird, male and female,
to keep their various kinds alive throughout the earth. 4 Seven days from now I will
send rain on the earth for forty days and forty nights, and I will wipe from the face of
the earth every living creature I have made."
5 And Noah did all that the LORD commanded him.[d]
6 Noah was six hundred years old when the floodwaters came on the earth. 7 And
Noah and his sons and his wife and his sons' wives entered the ark to escape the waters
of the flood. 8 Pairs of clean and unclean animals, of birds and of all creatures that
move along the ground, 9 male and female, came to Noah and entered the ark, as God
had commanded Noah. 10 And after the seven days the floodwaters came on the earth.
11 In the six hundredth year of Noah's life, on the seventeenth day of the second
month—on that day all the springs of the great deep[e] burst forth, and the floodgates
of the heavens[f] were opened. 12 And rain fell on the earth for forty days and forty
nights.[g]
13 On that very day Noah and his sons, Shem, Ham and Japheth, together with his
wife and the wives of his three sons, entered the ark. 14 They had with them every wild
animal according to its kind, all livestock according to their kinds, every creature that
moves along the ground according to its kind and every bird according to its kind,
everything with wings. 15 Pairs of all creatures that have the breath of life in them came
to Noah and entered the ark.[h] 16 The animals going in were male and female of every
living thing, as God had commanded Noah. Then the LORD shut him in.
17 For forty days[i] the flood kept coming on the earth, and as the waters increased
they lifted the ark high above the earth. 18 The waters rose and increased greatly on the
earth, and the ark floated on the surface of the water. 19 They rose greatly on the earth,
and all the high mountains under the entire heavens were covered.[j] 20 The waters rose
and covered the mountains to a depth of more than twenty feet.[b,c] 21 Every living
thing that moved on the earth perished—birds, livestock, wild animals, all the creatures that swarm over the earth, and all mankind.[k] 22 Everything on dry land that had
the breath of life[l] in its nostrils died. 23 Every living thing on the face of the earth was
wiped out; men and animals and the creatures that move along the ground and the birds
of the air were wiped from the earth.[m] Only Noah was left, and those with him in the
ark.[n]

a *2* Or *seven pairs*; also in verse 3 b *20* Hebrew *fifteen cubits* (about 6.9 metres) c *20* Or *rose more than twenty feet, and the mountains were covered*

6:20 s Ge 7:15
6:22 t Ge 7:5, 9, 16
7:1 a Mt 24:38; Heb 11:7; 1Pe 3:20; 2Pe 2:5 b Ge 6:9; Eze 14:14
7:2 c ver 8; Ge 8:20; Lev 10:10; 11:1-47
7:5 d Ge 6:22
7:11 e Eze 26:19 f Ge 8:2
7:12 g ver 4
7:15 h Ge 6:19
7:17 i ver 4
7:19 j Ps 104:6
7:21 k Ge 6:7, 13
7:22 l Ge 1:30
7:23 m Mt 24:39; Lk 17:27; 1Pe 3:20; 2Pe 2:5 n Heb 11:7

6:22 Noah got right to work when God told him to build the ark. Other people must have been warned about the coming disaster (1 Peter 3:20), but apparently they did not expect it to happen. Today things haven't changed much. Each day thousands of people are warned of God's inevitable judgment, yet most of them don't really believe it will happen. Don't expect people to welcome or accept your message of God's coming judgment on sin. Those who don't believe in God will deny his judgment and try to get you to deny God as well. But remember God's promise to Noah to keep him safe. This can inspire you to trust God for deliverance in the judgment that is sure to come.

7:1ff Pairs of every animal joined Noah in the ark; seven pairs were taken of those animals used for sacrifice—the "clean" animals. Scholars have estimated that almost 45,000 animals could have fit into the ark.

7:16 Many have wondered how this animal kingdom roundup happened. Did Noah and his sons spend years collecting all the animals? In reality the creation, along with Noah, was doing just as God had commanded. There seemed to be no problem gathering the animals—God took care of the details of that job while Noah was doing his part by building the ark. Often we do just the opposite of Noah. We worry about details over which we have no control, while neglecting specific areas (such as attitudes, relationships, responsibilities) that *are* under our control. Like Noah, concentrate on what God has given you to do, and leave the rest to God.

7:17-24 Was the flood a local event, or did it cover the entire earth? A universal flood was certainly possible. There is enough water on the earth to cover all dry land (the earth began that way; see 1:9, 10). Afterwards, God promised never again to destroy the earth with a flood. Thus this flood must have either covered the entire earth or destroyed all the inhabitants of the earth. Remember, God's reason for sending the flood was to destroy all the earth's wickedness. It would have taken a major flood to accomplish this.

7:24
[o]Ge 8:3

24 The waters flooded the earth for a hundred and fifty days.[o]
8 But God remembered[a] Noah and all the wild animals and the livestock that were
with him in the ark, and he sent a wind over the earth,[b] and the waters receded.
2 Now the springs of the deep and the floodgates of the heavens[c] had been closed, and
the rain had stopped falling from the sky. 3 The water receded steadily from the earth.
At the end of the hundred and fifty days the water had gone down, 4 and on the seventeenth day of the seventh month the ark came to rest on the mountains of Ararat. 5 The
waters continued to recede until the tenth month, and on the first day of the tenth month
the tops of the mountains became visible.
6 After forty days Noah opened the window he had made in the ark 7 and sent out a
raven, and it kept flying back and forth until the water had dried up from the earth.
8 Then he sent out a dove to see if the water had receded from the surface of the ground.
9 But the dove could find no place to set its feet because there was water over all the
surface of the earth; so it returned to Noah in the ark. He reached out his hand and took
the dove and brought it back to himself in the ark. 10 He waited seven more days and

8:1
[a]Ge 9:15; 19:29; Ex 2:24; 1Sa 1:11, 19
[b]Ex 14:21

8:2
[c]Ge 7:11

CAIN

In spite of parents' efforts and worries, conflicts between children in a family seem inevitable. Sibling relationships allow both competition and cooperation. In most cases, the mixture of loving and fighting eventually creates a strong bond between brothers and sisters. It isn't unusual, though, to hear parents say, "They fight so much I hope they don't kill each other before they grow up." In Cain's case, the troubling potential became a tragedy. And while we don't know many details of this first child's life, his story can still teach us.

Cain got angry. Furious. Both he and his brother Abel had made sacrifices to God, and his had been rejected. Cain's reaction gives us a clue that his attitude was probably wrong from the start. Cain had a choice to make. He could correct his attitude about his sacrifice to God, or he could take out his anger on his brother. His decision is a clear reminder of how often we are aware of opposite choices, yet choose the wrong just as Cain did. We may not be choosing to murder, but we are still intentionally choosing what we shouldn't.

The feelings motivating our behaviour can't always be changed by simple thought-power. But here we can begin to experience God's willingness to help. Asking for his help to do what is right can prevent us from setting into motion actions that we will later regret.

Strengths and accomplishments:
- First human child
- First to follow in father's profession, farming

Weaknesses and mistakes:
- When disappointed, reacted in anger
- Took the negative option even when a positive possibility was offered
- Was the first murderer

Lessons from his life:
- Anger is not necessarily a sin, but actions motivated by anger can be sinful. Anger should be the energy behind good action, not evil action
- What we offer to God must be from the heart—the best we are and have
- The consequences of sin may last a lifetime

Vital statistics:
- Where: Near Eden, which was probably located in present-day Iraq or Iran
- Occupation: Farmer, then wanderer
- Relatives: Parents: Adam and Eve. Brothers: Abel, Seth, and others not mentioned by name

Key verse:
"If you do what is right, will you not be accepted? But if you do not do what is right, sin is crouching at your door; it desires to have you, but you must master it" (Genesis 4:7).

Cain's story is told in Genesis 4:1–17. He is also mentioned in Hebrews 11:4; 1 John 3:12; Jude 11.

8:6–16 Occasionally Noah would send a bird out to test the earth and see if it was dry. But Noah didn't get out of the ark until God told him to. He was waiting for God's timing. God knew that even though the water was gone, the earth was not dry enough for Noah and his family to venture out. What patience Noah showed, especially after spending an entire year inside his boat! We, like Noah, must trust God to give us patience during those difficult times when we must wait.

again sent out the dove from the ark. 11When the dove returned to him in the evening,
there in its beak was a freshly plucked olive leaf! Then Noah knew that the water had
receded from the earth. 12He waited seven more days and sent the dove out again, but
this time it did not return to him.
13By the first day of the first month of Noah's six hundred and first year, the water
had dried up from the earth. Noah then removed the covering from the ark and saw that
the surface of the ground was dry. 14By the twenty-seventh day of the second month
the earth was completely dry.
15Then God said to Noah, 16"Come out of the ark, you and your wife and your sons
and their wives.[d] 17Bring out every kind of living creature that is with you — the birds,
the animals, and all the creatures that move along the ground — so they can multiply on
the earth and be fruitful and increase in number upon it."[e]
18So Noah came out, together with his sons and his wife and his sons' wives. 19All
the animals and all the creatures that move along the ground and all the
birds — everything that moves on the earth — came out of the ark, one kind after another.
20Then Noah built an altar to the LORD[f] and, taking some of all the clean animals
and clean[g] birds, he sacrificed burnt offerings[h] on it. 21The LORD smelled the pleasing aroma[i] and said in his heart: "Never again will I curse the ground[j] because of
man, even though[a] every inclination of his heart is evil from childhood.[k] And never
again will I destroy all living creatures,[l] as I have done.

22"As long as the earth endures,
seedtime and harvest,
cold and heat,
summer and winter,
day and night
will never cease."[m]

2. Repopulating the earth

God's Covenant With Noah

9 Then God blessed Noah and his sons, saying to them, "Be fruitful and increase in
number and fill the earth.[a] 2The fear and dread of you will fall upon all the beasts
of the earth and all the birds of the air, upon every creature that moves along the
ground, and upon all the fish of the sea; they are given into your hands. 3Everything
that lives and moves will be food for you.[b] Just as I gave you the green plants, I now
give you everything.
4"But you must not eat meat that has its lifeblood still in it.[c] 5And for your lifeblood

a 21 *Or man, for*

8:16 [d]Ge 7:13
8:17 [e]Ge 1:22
8:20 [f]Ge 12:7-8; 13:18; 22:9 [g]Ge 7:8; Lev 11:1-47 [h]Ge 22:2, 13; Ex 10:25
8:21 [i]Lev 1:9, 13; 2Co 2:15 [j]Ge 3:17 [k]Ge 6:5; Ps 51:5; Jer 17:9 [l]Ge 9:11, 15; Isa 54:9
8:22 [m]Ge 1:14; Jer 33:20, 25
9:1 [a]Ge 1:22
9:3 [b]Ge 1:29
9:4 [c]Lev 3:17; 17:10-14; Dt 12:16, 23-25; 1Sa 14:33

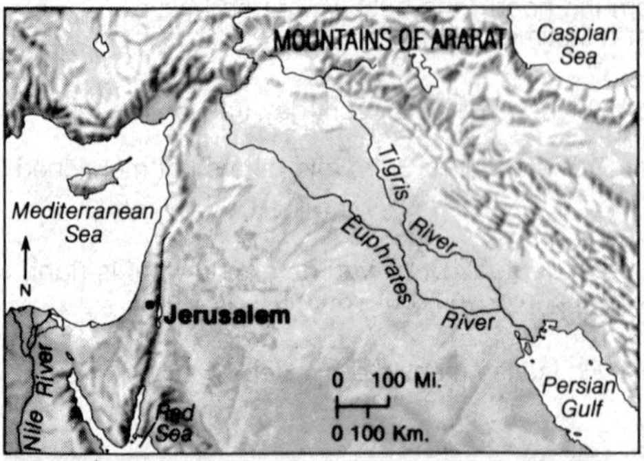

MOUNTAINS OF ARARAT The boat touched land in the mountains of Ararat, located in present-day Turkey near the USSR border. There it rested for almost eight months before Noah, his family, and the animals stepped onto dry land.

8:21, 22 Countless times throughout the Bible we see God showing his love and patience towards men and women in order to save them. Although he realises that their hearts are evil, he continues to try to reach them. When we sin or fall away from God, we surely deserve to be destroyed by his judgment. But God has promised never again to destroy everything on earth until the judgment day when Christ returns to destroy evil for ever. Now every change of season is a reminder of his promise.

9:5 To "demand an accounting" means that God will require each person to account for his or her actions. We cannot harm or kill another human being without answering to God. A penalty must be paid. Justice will be served.

9:5, 6 Here God explains why murder is so wrong: To kill a person is to kill one made in God's image. Because all human beings are made in God's image, all people possess the qualities that distinguish them from animals: morality, reason, creativity, and self-worth. When we interact with others, we are interacting with beings made by God, beings to whom God offers eternal life. God wants us to recognise his image in all people.

9:5 [d]Ex 21:28-32 [e]Ge 4:10
9:6 [f]Ge 4:14; Ex 21:12, 14; Lev 24:17; Mt 26:52 [g]Ge 1:26
9:7 [h]Ge 1:22
9:9 [i]Ge 6:18
9:11 [j]ver 16; Isa 24:5 [k]Ge 8:21; Isa 54:9
9:12 [l]ver 17; Ge 17:11
9:15 [m]Ex 2:24; Lev 26:42, 45; Dt 7:9; Eze 16:60

I will surely demand an accounting. I will demand an accounting from every animal.[d]
And from each man, too, I will demand an accounting for the life of his fellow man.[e]

6 "Whoever sheds the blood of man,
by man shall his blood be shed;[f]
for in the image of God[g]
has God made man.

7 As for you, be fruitful and increase in number; multiply on the earth and increase
upon it."[h]
8 Then God said to Noah and to his sons with him: 9 "I now establish my covenant
with you[i] and with your descendants after you 10 and with every living creature that
was with you—the birds, the livestock and all the wild animals, all those that came out
of the ark with you—every living creature on earth. 11 I establish my covenant[j] with
you: Never again will all life be cut off by the waters of a flood; never again will there
be a flood to destroy the earth.[k]"
12 And God said, "This is the sign of the covenant[l] I am making between me and
you and every living creature with you, a covenant for all generations to come: 13 I have
set my rainbow in the clouds, and it will be the sign of the covenant between me and
the earth. 14 Whenever I bring clouds over the earth and the rainbow appears in the
clouds, 15 I will remember my covenant[m] between me and you and all living creatures
of every kind. Never again will the waters become a flood to destroy all life. 16 When-

NOAH

The story of Noah's life involves not one, but two great and tragic floods. The world in Noah's day was flooded with evil. The number of those who remembered the God of creation, perfection, and love had dwindled to one. Of God's people, only Noah was left. God's response to the severe situation was a 120-year-long last chance, during which he had Noah build a graphic illustration of the message of his life. Nothing like a huge boat on dry land to make a point! For Noah, obedience meant a long-term commitment to a project.

Many of us have trouble sticking to any project, whether or not it is directed by God. It is interesting that the length of Noah's obedience was greater than the lifespan of people today. The only comparable long-term project is our very lives. But perhaps this is one great challenge Noah's life gives us—to live, in acceptance of God's grace, an entire lifetime of obedience and gratitude.

Strengths and accomplishments:
- Only follower of God left in his generation
- Second father of the human race
- Man of patience, consistency, and obedience
- First major shipbuilder

Weakness and mistake:
- Got drunk and embarrassed himself in front of his sons

Lessons from his life:
- God is faithful to those who obey him
- God does not always protect us from trouble, but cares for us in spite of trouble
- Obedience is a long-term commitment
- A man may be faithful, but his sinful nature always travels with him

Vital statistics:
- Where: We're not told how far from the Garden of Eden people had settled
- Occupation: Farmer, shipbuilder, preacher
- Relatives: Grandfather: Methuselah. Father: Lamech. Sons: Ham, Shem, and Japheth

Key verse:
"Noah did everything just as God commanded him" (Genesis 6:22).

Noah's story is told in Genesis 5:29—10:32. He is also mentioned in 1 Chronicles 1:3, 4; Isaiah 54:9; Ezekiel 14:14, 20; Matthew 24:37, 38; Luke 3:36; 17:26, 27; Hebrews 11:7; 1 Peter 3:20; 2 Peter 2:5.

9:8–17 Noah stepped out of the ark onto an earth devoid of human life. But God gave him a reassuring promise. This covenant had three parts: (1) never again will a flood cause such destruction; (2) as long as the earth remains, the seasons will always come as expected; (3) a rainbow will be visible when it rains as a sign to all that God will keep his promises. The earth's order and seasons are still preserved, and rainbows still remind us of God's faithfulness to his word.

ever the rainbow appears in the clouds, I will see it and remember the everlasting
covenant[n] between God and all living creatures of every kind on the earth."
17So God said to Noah, "This is the sign of the covenant[o] I have established between me and all life on the earth."

The Sons of Noah

18The sons of Noah who came out of the ark were Shem, Ham and Japheth. (Ham
was the father of Canaan.)[p] 19These were the three sons of Noah, and from them came
the people who were scattered over the earth.[q]
20Noah, a man of the soil, proceeded[a] to plant a vineyard. 21When he drank some
of its wine, he became drunk and lay uncovered inside his tent. 22Ham, the father of
Canaan, saw his father's nakedness and told his two brothers outside. 23But Shem and
Japheth took a garment and laid it across their shoulders; then they walked in backwards and covered their father's nakedness. Their faces were turned the other way so
that they would not see their father's nakedness.
24When Noah awoke from his wine and found out what his youngest son had done
to him, 25he said,

"Cursed be Canaan![r]
The lowest of slaves
will he be to his brothers.[s]"

26He also said,

"Blessed be the LORD, the God of Shem!
May Canaan be the slave of Shem.[b]
27May God extend the territory of Japheth;[c]
may Japheth live in the tents of Shem,
and may Canaan be his[d] slave."

28After the flood Noah lived 350 years. 29Altogether, Noah lived 950 years, and
then he died.

The Table of Nations

10 This is the account[a] of Shem, Ham and Japheth, Noah's sons, who themselves had sons after the flood.

The Japhethites

2The sons[a] of Japheth:
Gomer,[b] Magog,[c] Madai, Javan, Tubal,[d] Meshech and Tiras.
3The sons of Gomer:
Ashkenaz,[e] Riphath and Togarmah.[f]
4The sons of Javan:
Elishah, Tarshish,[g] the Kittim and the Rodanim.[b] 5(From these the maritime peoples spread out into their territories by their clans within their nations,
each with its own language.)

a *20* Or *soil, was the first* **b** *26* Or *be his slave* **c** *27* *Japheth* sounds like the Hebrew for *extend.* **d** *27* Or *their*
a *2* *Sons* may mean *descendants* or *successors* or *nations*; also in verses 3, 4, 6, 7, 20–23, 29 and 31.
b *4* Some manuscripts of the Masoretic Text and Samaritan Pentateuch (see also Septuagint and 1 Chron. 1:7); most manuscripts of the Masoretic Text *Dodanim*

9:16 [n]ver 11; Ge 17:7, 13, 19; 2Sa 7:13; 23:5
9:17 [o]ver 12; Ge 17:11
9:18 [p]ver 25-27; Ge 10:6, 15
9:19 [q]Ge 10:32
9:25 [r]ver 18 [s]Ge 25:23; Jos 9:23
10:1 [a]Ge 2:4
10:2 [b]Eze 38:6 [c]Eze 38:2; Rev 20:8 [d]Isa 66:19
10:3 [e]Jer 51:27 [f]Eze 27:14; 38:6
10:4 [g]Eze 27:12, 25; Jnh 1:3

9:20–27 Noah, the great hero of faith, got drunk—a poor example of godliness to his sons. Perhaps this story is included to show us that even godly people can sin and that their bad influence affects their families. Although the wicked people had all been killed, the possibility of evil still existed in the hearts of Noah and his family. Ham's mocking attitude revealed a severe lack of respect for his father and for God.

9:25 This verse has been wrongfully used to support racial prejudice and even slavery. Noah's curse, however, wasn't directed towards any particular race, but rather at the Canaanite nation—a nation God knew would become wicked. The curse was fulfilled when the Israelites entered the promised land and drove the Canaanites out (see the book of Joshua).

10:6 [h]ver 15; Ge 9:18
10:10 [i]Ge 11:9 [j]Ge 11:2
10:11 [k]Ps 83:8; Mic 5:6 [l]Jnh 1:2; 4:11; Na 1:1
10:14 [m]Ge 21:32, 34; 26:1, 8
10:15 [n]ver 6; Ge 9:18 [o]Eze 28:21 [p]Ge 23:3, 20
10:16 [q]1Ch 11:4
10:18 [r]Ge 12:6; Ex 13:11
10:19 [s]Ge 11:31; 13:12; 17:8 [t]ver 15
10:21 [u]ver 24; Nu 24:24
10:22 [v]Jer 49:34 [w]Lk 3:36
10:23 [x]Job 1:1
10:24 [y]ver 21

The Hamites

6 The sons of Ham:
Cush, Mizraim,[c] Put and Canaan.[h]
7 The sons of Cush:
Seba, Havilah, Sabtah, Raamah and Sabteca.
The sons of Raamah:
Sheba and Dedan.

8 Cush was the father[d] of Nimrod, who grew to be a mighty warrior on the earth.
9 He was a mighty hunter before the LORD; that is why it is said, "Like Nimrod, a
mighty hunter before the LORD." 10 The first centres of his kingdom were Babylon,[i]
Erech, Akkad and Calneh, in[e] Shinar.[f][j] 11 From that land he went to Assyria,[k]
where he built Nineveh,[l] Rehoboth Ir,[g] Calah 12 and Resen, which is between Nineveh and Calah; that is the great city.

13 Mizraim was the father of
the Ludites, Anamites, Lehabites, Naphtuhites, 14 Pathrusites, Casluhites
(from whom the Philistines[m] came) and Caphtorites.
15 Canaan[n] was the father of
Sidon[o] his firstborn,[h] and of the Hittites,[p] 16 Jebusites,[q] Amorites, Girgashites, 17 Hivites, Arkites, Sinites, 18 Arvadites, Zemarites and Hamathites.

Later the Canaanite[r] clans scattered 19 and the borders of Canaan[s] reached from
Sidon[t] towards Gerar as far as Gaza, and then towards Sodom, Gomorrah, Admah
and Zeboiim, as far as Lasha.
20 These are the sons of Ham by their clans and languages, in their territories and
nations.

The Semites

21 Sons were also born to Shem, whose older brother was[i] Japheth; Shem was the
ancestor of all the sons of Eber.[u]

22 The sons of Shem:
Elam,[v] Asshur, Arphaxad,[w] Lud and Aram.
23 The sons of Aram:
Uz,[x] Hul, Gether and Meshech.[j]
24 Arphaxad was the father of[k] Shelah,
and Shelah the father of Eber.[y]
25 Two sons were born to Eber:
One was named Peleg,[l] because in his time the earth was divided; his brother
was named Joktan.
26 Joktan was the father of
Almodad, Sheleph, Hazarmaveth, Jerah, 27 Hadoram, Uzal, Diklah, 28 Obal,
Abimael, Sheba, 29 Ophir, Havilah and Jobab. All these were sons of Joktan.

[c] *6* That is, Egypt; also in verse 13 [d] *8* *Father* may mean *ancestor* or *predecessor* or *founder*; also in verses 13, 15, 24 and 26. [e] *10* Or *Erech and Akkad—all of them in* [f] *10* That is, Babylonia [g] *11* Or *Nineveh with its city squares* [h] *15* Or *of the Sidonians, the foremost* [i] *21* Or *Shem, the older brother of* [j] *23* See Septuagint and 1 Chron. 1:17; Hebrew *Mash.* [k] *24* Hebrew; Septuagint *father of Cainan, and Cainan was the father of* [l] *25* *Peleg* means *division.*

BIBLE NATIONS DESCENDED FROM NOAH'S SONS

Shem	*Ham*	*Japheth*
Hebrews	Canaanites	Greeks
Chaldeans	Egyptians	Thracians
Assyrians	Philistines	Scythians
Persians	Hittites	
Syrians	Amorites	

Shem's descendants were called Semites. Abraham, David, and Jesus descended from Shem. Ham's descendants settled in Canaan, Egypt, and the rest of Africa. Japheth's descendants settled for the most part in Europe and Asia Minor.

10:8, 9 Who was Nimrod? Not much is known about him except that he was a mighty hunter. But people with great gifts can become proud, and that is probably what happened to Nimrod. Some consider him the founder of the great, godless Babylonian empire.

30 The region where they lived stretched from Mesha towards Sephar, in the eastern hill
country.
31 These are the sons of Shem by their clans and languages, in their territories and
nations.

32 These are the clans of Noah's sons,[z] according to their lines of descent, within
their nations. From these the nations spread out over the earth[a] after the flood.

3. The tower of Babel

11 Now the whole world had one language and a common speech. 2 As men moved
eastward,[a] they found a plain in Shinar[b][a] and settled there.
3 They said to each other, "Come, let's make bricks[b] and bake them thoroughly."
They used brick instead of stone, and bitumen[c] for mortar. 4 Then they said, "Come,
let us build ourselves a city, with a tower that reaches to the heavens,[d] so that we may
make a name[e] for ourselves and not be scattered over the face of the whole earth."[f]
5 But the LORD came down[g] to see the city and the tower that the men were building.
6 The LORD said, "If as one people speaking the same language they have begun to do
this, then nothing they plan to do will be impossible for them. 7 Come, let us[h] go down
and confuse their language so they will not understand each other."[i]
8 So the LORD scattered them from there over all the earth,[j] and they stopped building the city. 9 That is why it was called Babel[c][k]—because there the LORD confused
the language of the whole world. From there the LORD scattered them over the face of
the whole earth.

From Shem to Abram

10 This is the account of Shem.

Two years after the flood, when Shem was 100 years old, he became the father[d] of
Arphaxad. 11 And after he became the father of Arphaxad, Shem lived 500 years and
had other sons and daughters.
12 When Arphaxad had lived 35 years, he became the father of Shelah.[l] 13 And after
he became the father of Shelah, Arphaxad lived 403 years and had other sons and
daughters.[e]
14 When Shelah had lived 30 years, he became the father of Eber. 15 And after he

10:32 [z]ver 1 [a]Ge 9:19
11:2 [a]Ge 10:10
11:3 [b]Ex 1:14 [c]Ge 14:10
11:4 [d]Dt 1:28; 9:1 [e]Ge 6:4 [f]Dt 4:27
11:5 [g]ver 7; Ge 18:21; Ex 3:8; 19:11, 18, 20
11:7 [h]Ge 1:26 [i]Ge 42:23
11:8 [j]Ge 9:19; Lk 1:51
11:9 [k]Ge 10:10
11:12 [l]Lk 3:35

[a] 2 Or *from the east*; or *in the east* [b] 2 That is, Babylonia [c] 9 That is, Babylon; *Babel* sounds like the Hebrew for *confused*. [d] 10 *Father* may mean *ancestor*; also in verses 11–25. [e] 12,13 Hebrew; Septuagint (see also Luke 3:35, 36 and note at Gen. 10:24) *35 years, he became the father of Cainan. 13 And after he became the father of Cainan, Arphaxad lived 430 years and had other sons and daughters, and then he died. When Cainan had lived 130 years, he became the father of Shelah. And after he became the father of Shelah, Cainan lived 330 years and had other sons and daughters*

11:3 The brick used to build this tower was man-made and not as hard as stone.

11:3, 4 The tower of Babel was most likely a ziggurat, a common structure in Babylonia at this time. Most often built as temples, ziggurats looked like pyramids with steps or ramps leading up the sides. Ziggurats stood as high as 300 feet and were often just as wide; thus they were the focal point of the city. The people in this story built their tower as a monument to their own greatness, something for the whole world to see.

11:4 The tower of Babel was a great human achievement, a wonder of the world. But it was a monument to the people themselves rather than to God. We may build monuments to ourselves (expensive clothes, big house, fancy car, important job) to call attention to our achievements. These may not be wrong in themselves, but when we use them to give us identity and self-worth, they take God's place in our lives. We are free to develop in many areas, but we are not free to think we have replaced God. What "towers" have you built in your life?

11:10–27 In 9:24–27 we read Noah's curse on Canaan, Ham's son (10:6), ancestor of the evil Canaanites. Here and in 10:22–31 we have a list of Shem's descendants, who were blessed (9:26). From Shem's line came Abram and the entire Jewish nation, which would eventually conquer the land of Canaan in the days of Joshua.

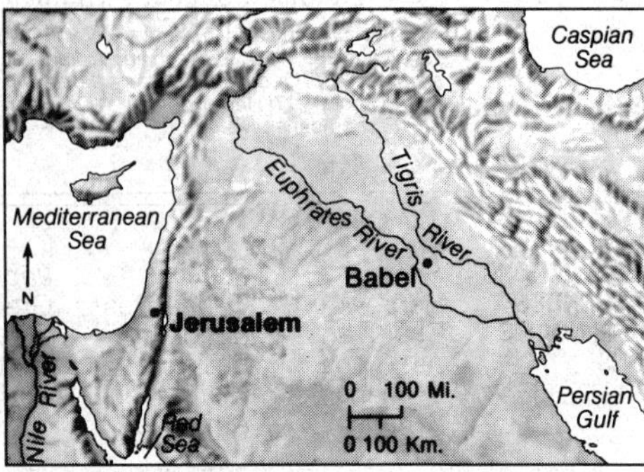

THE TOWER OF BABEL The plain between the Tigris and Euphrates rivers offered a perfect location for the city and tower "that reaches to the heavens".

11:20 [m]Lk 3:35

became the father of Eber, Shelah lived 403 years and had other sons and daughters.
16When Eber had lived 34 years, he became the father of Peleg. 17And after he
became the father of Peleg, Eber lived 430 years and had other sons and daughters.

11:24 [n]Lk 3:34

18When Peleg had lived 30 years, he became the father of Reu. 19And after he became the father of Reu, Peleg lived 209 years and had other sons and daughters.
20When Reu had lived 32 years, he became the father of Serug.[m] 21And after he
became the father of Serug, Reu lived 207 years and had other sons and daughters.

11:26 [o]Lk 3:34 [p]Jos 24:2

22When Serug had lived 30 years, he became the father of Nahor. 23And after he
became the father of Nahor, Serug lived 200 years and had other sons and daughters.
24When Nahor had lived 29 years, he became the father of Terah.[n] 25And after he
became the father of Terah, Nahor lived 119 years and had other sons and daughters.

11:27 [q]ver 31; Ge 12:4; 14:12; 19:1; 2Pe 2:7

26After Terah had lived 70 years, he became the father of Abram,[o] Nahor[p] and
Haran.

27This is the account of Terah.

11:28 [r]ver 31; Ge 15:7

Terah became the father of Abram, Nahor and Haran. And Haran became the father
of Lot.[q] 28While his father Terah was still alive, Haran died in Ur of the Chaldeans,[r]
in the land of his birth. 29Abram and Nahor both married. The name of Abram's wife
was Sarai,[s] and the name of Nahor's wife was Milcah;[t] she was the daughter of
Haran, the father of both Milcah and Iscah. 30Now Sarai was barren; she had no children.[u]

11:29 [s]Ge 17:15 [t]Ge 22:20

31Terah took his son Abram, his grandson Lot son of Haran, and his daughter-in-law
Sarai, the wife of his son Abram, and together they set out from Ur of the Chaldeans[v]
to go to Canaan.[w] But when they came to Haran, they settled there.
32Terah lived 205 years, and he died in Haran.

11:30 [u]Ge 16:1; 18:11

11:31 [v]Ge 15:7; Ne 9:7; Ac 7:4 [w]Ge 10:19

D. THE STORY OF ABRAHAM (12:1—25:18)

Despite God's swift judgment of sin, most people ignored him and continued to sin. But a handful of people genuinely tried to follow him. One of these was Abraham. God appeared to Abraham one day and promised to make his descendants into a great nation. Abraham's part of the agreement was to obey God. Through sharp testing and an incident that almost destroyed his family, Abraham remained faithful to God. Throughout this section we discover how to live a life of faith.

1. God promises a nation to Abram

The Call of Abram

12:1 [a]Ac 7:3*; Heb 11:8

12 The LORD had said to Abram, "Leave your country, your people and your
father's household and go to the land I will show you.[a]

12:2 [b]Ge 15:5; 17:2, 4; 18:18; 22:17; Dt 26:5 [c]Ge 24:1, 35

2"I will make you into a great nation[b]
and I will bless you;[c]
I will make your name great,
and you will be a blessing.

11:26–28 Abram grew up in Ur of the Chaldeans, an important city in the ancient world. Archaeologists have discovered evidence of a flourishing civilisation there in Abram's day. The city carried on an extensive trade with its neighbours and had a vast library. Growing up in Ur, Abram was probably well educated.

11:31 Terah left Ur to go to Canaan but settled in Haran instead. Why did he stop halfway? It may have been his health, the climate, or even fear. But this did not change Abram's calling ("the LORD had said to Abram", 12:1). He had respect for his father's leadership, but when Terah died Abram moved on to Canaan. God's will may come in stages. Just as the time in Haran was a transition period for Abram, so God may give us transition periods and times of waiting to help us depend on him and trust his timing. If we patiently do his will during the transition times, we will be better prepared to serve him as we should when he calls us.

12:1–3 When God called him, Abram moved out in faith from Ur to Haran and finally to Canaan. God then established a covenant with Abram, telling him that he would found a great nation. Not only would this nation be blessed, God said, but the other nations of the earth would be blessed through Abram's descendants. Israel, the nation that would come from Abram, was to follow God and influence those with whom it came in contact. Through Abram's family tree, Jesus Christ was born to save humanity. Through Christ, people can have a personal relationship with God and be blessed beyond measure.

12:2 God promised to bless Abram and make him great, but there was one condition. Abram had to do what God wanted him to do. This meant leaving his home and friends and travelling to a new land where God promised to build a great nation from Abram's family. Abram obeyed, walking away from his home for God's promise of even greater blessings in the future. God may be trying to lead you to a place of greater service and usefulness for him. Don't let the comfort and security of your present position make you miss God's plan for you.

3I will bless those who bless you,
and whoever curses you I will curse;[d]
and all peoples on earth
will be blessed through you.[e]"

4So Abram left, as the LORD had told him; and Lot went with him. Abram was
seventy-five years old when he set out from Haran.[f] 5He took his wife Sarai, his
nephew Lot, all the possessions they had accumulated and the people[g] they had acquired in Haran, and they set out for the land of Canaan, and they arrived there.
6Abram travelled through the land[h] as far as the site of the great tree of Moreh[i] at
Shechem. At that time the Canaanites[j] were in the land. 7The LORD appeared to
Abram[k] and said, "To your offspring[a] I will give this land."[l] So he built an altar
there to the LORD,[m] who had appeared to him.
8From there he went on towards the hills east of Bethel[n] and pitched his tent, with
Bethel on the west and Ai on the east. There he built an altar to the LORD and called on
the name of the LORD. 9Then Abram set out and continued towards the Negev.[o]

Abram in Egypt

10Now there was a famine in the land, and Abram went down to Egypt to live there
for a while because the famine was severe. 11As he was about to enter Egypt, he said

[a] 7 Or *seed*

12:3 [d]Ge 27:29; Ex 23:22; Nu 24:9 [e]Ge 18:18; 22:18; 26:4; Ac 3:25; Gal 3:8*
12:4 [f]Ge 11:31
12:5 [g]Ge 14:14; 17:23
12:6 [h]Heb 11:9 [i]Ge 35:4; Dt 11:30 [j]Ge 10:18
12:7 [k]Ge 17:1; 18:1; Ex 6:3 [l]Ge 13:15, 17; 15:18; 17:8; Ps 105:9-11 [m]Ge 13:4
12:8 [n]Ge 13:3
12:9 [o]Ge 13:1, 3

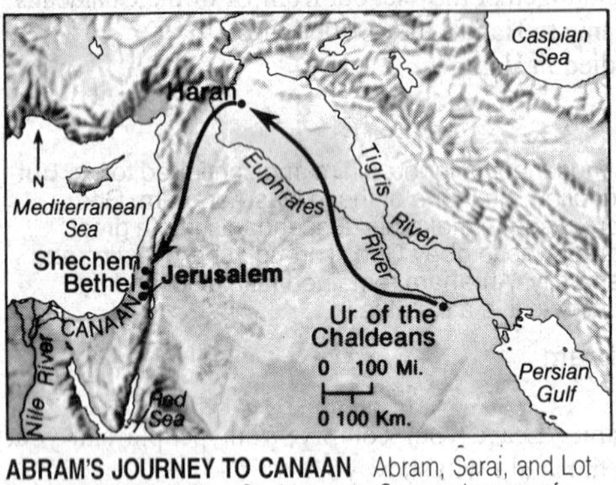

ABRAM'S JOURNEY TO CANAAN Abram, Sarai, and Lot travelled from Ur of the Chaldeans to Canaan by way of Haran. Though indirect, this route followed the rivers rather than attempting to cross the vast desert.

12:5 God planned to develop a nation of people he would call his own. He called Abram from the godless, self-centred city of Ur to a fertile region called Canaan, where a God-centred, moral nation could be established. Though small in dimension, the land of Canaan was the focal point for most of the history of Israel as well as for the rise of Christianity. This small land given to one man, Abram, has had a tremendous impact on world history.

12:7 Abram built an altar to the Lord. Altars were used in many religions, but for God's people, altars were more than places of sacrifice. For them, altars symbolised communion with God and commemorated notable encounters with him. Built of rough stones and earth, altars often remained in place for years as continual reminders of God's protection and promises.

Abram regularly built altars to God for two reasons: (1) for prayer and worship, and (2) as reminders of God's promise to bless him. Abram couldn't survive spiritually without regularly renewing his love and loyalty to God. Building altars helped Abram remember that God was at the centre of his life. Regular worship helps us remember what God desires and motivates us to obey him.

12:10 When famine struck, Abram went to Egypt where there was food. Why would there be a famine in the land where God had just called Abram? This was a test of Abram's faith, and Abram passed. He didn't question God's leading when facing this difficulty. Many believers find that when they determine to follow God, they immediately encounter great obstacles. The next time you face such a test, don't try to second-guess what God is doing. Use the intelligence God gave you, as Abram did when he temporarily moved to Egypt, and wait for new opportunities.

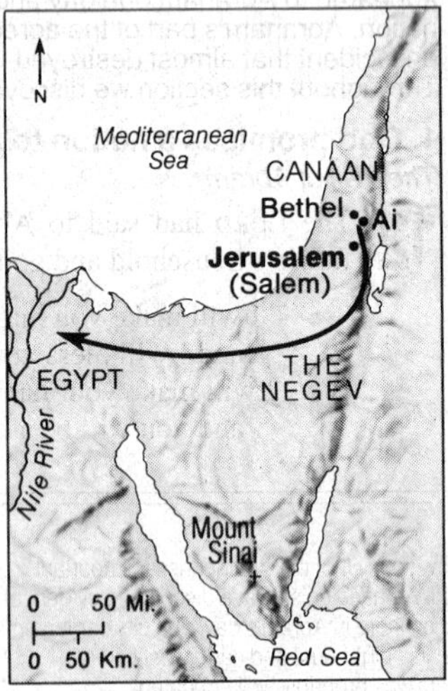

ABRAM'S JOURNEY TO EGYPT A famine could cause the loss of a shepherd's wealth. So Abram travelled through the Negev to Egypt, where there was plenty of food and good land for his flocks.

12:11–13 Abram, acting out of fear, asked Sarai to tell a half-truth by saying she was his sister. She *was* his half sister, but she was also his wife (see 20:12).

Abram's intent was to deceive the Egyptians. He feared that if they knew the truth, they would kill him to get Sarai. She would have been a desirable addition to Pharaoh's harem because of her wealth, beauty, and potential for political alliance. As Sarai's brother, Abram would have been given a place of honour. As her husband, however, his life would be in danger because Sarai could not enter Pharaoh's harem unless Abram was dead. So Abram lost faith in God's protection, even after all God had promised him, and told a half-truth. This shows how lying compounds

12:13 [p]Ge 20:2; 26:7
12:17 [q]1Ch 16:21
12:18 [r]Ge 20:9; 26:10
13:1 [a]Ge 12:9
13:3 [b]Ge 12:8
13:4 [c]Ge 12:7
13:6 [d]Ge 36:7
13:7 [e]Ge 26:20, 21 [f]Ge 12:6
13:8 [g]Pr 15:18; 20:3 [h]Ps 133:1
13:10 [i]Ge 2:8-10; Isa 51:3 [j]Ge 19:22, 30 [k]Ge 14:8; 19:17-29

to his wife Sarai, "I know what a beautiful woman you are. 12 When the Egyptians see
you, they will say, 'This is his wife.' Then they will kill me but will let you live. 13 Say
you are my sister,[p] so that I will be treated well for your sake and my life will be
spared because of you."
14 When Abram came to Egypt, the Egyptians saw that she was a very beautiful
woman. 15 And when Pharaoh's officials saw her, they praised her to Pharaoh, and she
was taken into his palace. 16 He treated Abram well for her sake, and Abram acquired
sheep and cattle, male and female donkeys, menservants and maidservants, and
camels.
17 But the LORD inflicted serious diseases on Pharaoh and his household[q] because of
Abram's wife Sarai. 18 So Pharaoh summoned Abram. "What have you done to me?"[r]
he said. "Why didn't you tell me she was your wife? 19 Why did you say, 'She is my
sister,' so that I took her to be my wife? Now then, here is your wife. Take her and go!"
20 Then Pharaoh gave orders about Abram to his men, and they sent him on his way,
with his wife and everything he had.

2. Abram and Lot

Abram and Lot Separate

13 So Abram went up from Egypt to the Negev,[a] with his wife and everything he
had, and Lot went with him. 2 Abram had become very wealthy in livestock and
in silver and gold.
3 From the Negev he went from place to place until he came to Bethel,[b] to the place
between Bethel and Ai where his tent had been earlier 4 and where he had first built an
altar.[c] There Abram called on the name of the LORD.
5 Now Lot, who was moving about with Abram, also had flocks and herds and tents.
6 But the land could not support them while they stayed together, for their possessions
were so great that they were not able to stay together.[d] 7 And quarrelling[e] arose between Abram's herdsmen and the herdsmen of Lot. The Canaanites and Perizzites
were also living in the land[f] at that time.
8 So Abram said to Lot, "Let's not have any quarrelling between you and me,[g] or
between your herdsmen and mine, for we are brothers.[h] 9 Is not the whole land before
you? Let's part company. If you go to the left, I'll go to the right; if you go to the right,
I'll go to the left."
10 Lot looked up and saw that the whole plain of the Jordan was well watered, like
the garden of the LORD,[i] like the land of Egypt, towards Zoar.[j] (This was before the
LORD destroyed Sodom and Gomorrah.)[k] 11 So Lot chose for himself the whole plain
of the Jordan and set out towards the east. The two men parted company: 12 Abram

---

the effects of sin. When he lied, Abram's problems multiplied.

13:1, 2 In Abram's day, sheep and cattle owners could acquire great wealth. Abram's wealth not only included silver and gold, but also livestock. These animals were a valuable commodity used for food, clothing, tent material, and sacrifices. They were often traded for other goods and services. Abram was able to watch his wealth grow and multiply daily.

13:5–9 Facing a potential conflict with his nephew Lot, Abram took the initiative in settling the dispute. He gave Lot first choice, even though Abram, being older, had the right to choose first. Abram also showed a willingness to risk being cheated. Abram's example shows us how to respond to difficult family situations: (1) take the initiative in resolving conflicts; (2) let others have first choice, even if that means not getting what we want; (3) put family peace above personal desires.

13:7, 8 Surrounded by hostile neighbours, the herdsmen of Abram and Lot should have pulled together. Instead, they let petty jealousy tear them apart. Similar situations exist today. Christians often bicker while Satan is at work all around them.

Rivalries, arguments, and disagreements among believers can be destructive in three ways. (1) They damage goodwill, trust, and peace – the foundations of good human relations. (2) They hamper progress towards important goals. (3) They make us self-centred rather than love-centred. Jesus understood how destructive arguments among brothers could be. In his final prayer before being betrayed and arrested, Jesus asked God that his followers be "one" (John 17:21).

13:10, 11 Lot's character is revealed by his choices. He took the best share of the land even though it meant living near Sodom, a city known for its sin. He was greedy, wanting the best for himself, without thinking about his uncle Abram's needs or what was fair.

Life is a series of choices. We too can choose the best while ignoring the needs and feelings of others. But this kind of choice, as Lot's life shows, leads to problems. When we stop making choices in God's direction, all that is left is to make choices in the wrong direction.

13:12 Good pasture and available water seemed like a wise choice to Lot at first. But he failed to recognise that wicked Sodom could provide temptations strong enough to destroy his family. Have you chosen to live or work in a "Sodom"? Even though you may be strong enough to resist the temptations, other members of your family may not. While God commands us to reach people in the "Sodom" near us, we must be careful not to become like the very people we are trying to reach.

lived in the land of Canaan, while Lot lived among the cities of the plain[l] and pitched
his tents near Sodom.[m] 13 Now the men of Sodom were wicked and were sinning
greatly against the LORD.[n]
14 The LORD said to Abram after Lot had parted from him, "Lift up your eyes from
where you are and look north and south, east and west.[o] 15 All the land that you see I
will give to you and your offspring[a] for ever.[p] 16 I will make your offspring like the
dust of the earth, so that if anyone could count the dust, then your offspring could be
counted. 17 Go, walk through the length and breadth of the land,[q] for I am giving it to
you."
18 So Abram moved his tents and went to live near the great trees of Mamre[r] at
Hebron,[s] where he built an altar to the LORD.[t]

Abram Rescues Lot

14 At this time Amraphel king of Shinar,[a][a] Arioch king of Ellasar, Kedorlaomer
king of Elam and Tidal king of Goiim 2 went to war against Bera king of Sodom,
Birsha king of Gomorrah, Shinab king of Admah, Shemeber king of Zeboiim,[b] and
the king of Bela (that is, Zoar).[c] 3 All these latter kings joined forces in the Valley of
Siddim (the Salt Sea[b][d]). 4 For twelve years they had been subject to Kedorlaomer, but
in the thirteenth year they rebelled.
5 In the fourteenth year, Kedorlaomer and the kings allied with him went out and
defeated the Rephaites[e] in Ashteroth Karnaim, the Zuzites in Ham, the Emites[f] in
Shaveh Kiriathaim 6 and the Horites[g] in the hill country of Seir,[h] as far as El Paran[i]
near the desert. 7 Then they turned back and went to En Mishpat (that is, Kadesh), and
they conquered the whole territory of the Amalekites, as well as the Amorites who
were living in Hazezon Tamar.[j]
8 Then the king of Sodom, the king of Gomorrah,[k] the king of Admah, the king of
Zeboiim[l] and the king of Bela (that is, Zoar) marched out and drew up their battle
lines in the Valley of Siddim 9 against Kedorlaomer king of Elam, Tidal king of Goiim,
Amraphel king of Shinar and Arioch king of Ellasar—four kings against five. 10 Now
the Valley of Siddim was full of tar pits, and when the kings of Sodom and Gomorrah
fled, some of the men fell into them and the rest fled to the hills.[m] 11 The four kings
seized all the goods of Sodom and Gomorrah and all their food; then they went away.
12 They also carried off Abram's nephew Lot and his possessions, since he was living
in Sodom.
13 One who had escaped came and reported this to Abram the Hebrew. Now Abram
was living near the great trees of Mamre[n] the Amorite, a brother[c] of Eshcol and
Aner, all of whom were allied with Abram. 14 When Abram heard that his relative had
been taken captive, he called out the 318 trained men born in his household[o] and went

13:12 [l]Ge 19:17, 25, 29 [m]Ge 14:12
13:13 [n]Ge 18:20; Eze 16:49-50; 2Pe 2:8
13:14 [o]Ge 28:14; Dt 3:27
13:15 [p]Ge 12:7; Gal 3:16*
13:17 [q]ver 15; Nu 13:17-25
13:18 [r]Ge 14:13, 24; 18:1 [s]Ge 35:27 [t]Ge 8:20
14:1 [a]Ge 10:10
14:2 [b]Ge 10:19 [c]Ge 13:10
14:3 [d]Nu 34:3, 12; Dt 3:17; Jos 3:16; 15:2, 5
14:5 [e]Ge 15:20; Dt 2:11, 20 [f]Dt 2:10
14:6 [g]Dt 2:12, 22 [h]Dt 2:1, 5, 22 [i]Ge 21:21; Nu 10:12
14:7 [j]2Ch 20:2
14:8 [k]Ge 13:10; 19:17-29 [l]Dt 29:23
14:10 [m]Ge 19:17, 30
14:13 [n]ver 24; Ge 13:18
14:14 [o]Ge 15:3

[a] *15* Or *seed*; also in verse 16 [a] *1* That is, Babylonia; also in verse 9 [b] *3* That is, the Dead Sea [c] *13* Or *a relative*; or *an ally*

14:4–16 Who was Kedorlaomer, and why was he important? In Abram's time, most cities had their own kings. Wars and rivalries among kings were common. A conquered city paid tribute to the victorious king. Nothing is known about Kedorlaomer except what we read in the Bible, but apparently he was quite powerful. Five cities including Sodom had paid tribute to him for 12 years. The five cities formed an alliance and rebelled by withholding tribute. Kedorlaomer reacted swiftly and reconquered them all. When he defeated Sodom, he captured Lot, his family, and his possessions. Abram, with only 318 men, chased Kedorlaomer's army and attacked him near Damascus. With God's help, he defeated them and recovered Lot, his family, and their possessions.

14:12 Lot's greedy desire for the best of everything led him into sinful surroundings. His burning desire for possessions and success cost him his freedom and enjoyment. As a captive to Kedorlaomer, he faced torture, slavery, or death. In much the same way, we can be enticed into doing things or going places we shouldn't. The prosperity we long for is captivating; it can both entice us and enslave us if our motives are not in line with God's desires.

14:14–16 These incidents portray two of Abram's characteristics:

14:14 *p* Dt 34:1; Jdg 18:29

in pursuit as far as Dan.[p] 15During the night Abram divided his men to attack them
and he routed them, pursuing them as far as Hobah, north of Damascus. 16He recov-

LOT

Some people simply drift through life. Their choices, when they can muster the will to choose, tend to follow the course of least resistance. Lot, Abram's nephew, was such a person.

While still young, Lot lost his father. Although this must have been hard on him, he was not left without strong role models in his grandfather Terah and his uncle Abram, who brought him up. Still, Lot did not develop their sense of purpose. Throughout his life he was so caught up in the present moment that he seemed incapable of seeing the consequences of his actions. It is hard to imagine what his life would have been like without Abram's careful attention and God's intervention.

By the time Lot drifted out of the picture, his life had taken an ugly turn. He had so blended into the sinful culture of his day that he did not want to leave it. Then his daughters committed incest with him. His drifting finally took him in a very specific direction—destruction.

Lot, however, is called "righteous" in the New Testament (2 Peter 2:7, 8). Ruth, a descendant of Moab, was an ancestor of Jesus, even though Moab was born as a result of Lot's incestuous relationship with one of his daughters. Lot's story gives hope to us that God forgives and often brings about positive circumstances from evil.

What is the direction of your life? Are you headed towards God or away from him? If you're a drifter, the choice for God may seem difficult, but it is the one choice that puts all other choices in a different light.

Strengths and accomplishments:
- He was a successful businessman
- Peter calls him a righteous man (2 Peter 2:7, 8)

Weaknesses and mistakes:
- When faced with decisions, he tended to put off deciding, then chose the easiest course of action
- When given a choice, his first reaction was to think of himself

Lesson from his life:
- God wants us to do more than drift through life; he wants us to be an influence for him

Vital statistics:
- Where: Lived first in Ur of the Chaldeans, then moved to Canaan with Abram. Eventually he moved to the wicked city of Sodom
- Occupation: Wealthy sheep and cattle farmer; also a city official
- Relatives: Father: Haran. Adopted by Abram when his father died. The name of his wife, who turned into a pillar of salt, is not mentioned

Key verse:
"When he hesitated, the men grasped his hand and the hands of his wife and of his two daughters and led them safely out of the city, for the LORD was merciful to them" (Genesis 19:16).

Lot's story is told in Genesis 11—14; 19. He is also mentioned in Deuteronomy 2:9; Luke 17:28–32; 2 Peter 2:7, 8.

---

(1) He had courage that came from God. Facing a powerful foe, he attacked. (2) He was prepared. He had taken time to train his men for a potential conflict. We never know when we will be called upon to complete difficult tasks. Like Abram, we should prepare for those times and take courage from God when they come.

14:14–16 When Abram learned that Lot was a prisoner, he immediately tried to rescue his nephew. It is easier and safer not to become involved. But with Lot in serious trouble, Abram acted at once. Sometimes we must get involved in a messy or painful situation in order to help others. We should be willing to act immediately when others need our help.

ered all the goods and brought back his relative Lot and his possessions, together with
the women and the other people.
17After Abram returned from defeating Kedorlaomer and the kings allied with him,
the king of Sodom came out to meet him in the Valley of Shaveh (that is, the King's
Valley).[q]
18Then Melchizedek[r] king of Salem[d][s] brought out bread and wine. He was priest
of God Most High, 19and he blessed Abram,[t] saying,

"Blessed be Abram by God Most High,
Creator[e] of heaven and earth.[u]
20And blessed be[f] God Most High,[v]
who delivered your enemies into your hand."

Then Abram gave him a tenth of everything.[w]
21The king of Sodom said to Abram, "Give me the people and keep the goods for
yourself."
22But Abram said to the king of Sodom, "I have raised my hand[x] to the LORD, God
Most High, Creator of heaven and earth,[y] and have taken an oath 23that I will accept
nothing belonging to you,[z] not even a thread or the thong of a sandal, so that you will
never be able to say, 'I made Abram rich.' 24I will accept nothing but what my men
have eaten and the share that belongs to the men who went with me—to Aner, Eshcol
and Mamre. Let them have their share."

3. God promises a son to Abram

God's Covenant With Abram

15 After this, the word of the LORD came to Abram[a] in a vision:

"Do not be afraid,[b] Abram.
I am your shield,[a][c]
your very great reward."[b]

2But Abram said, "O Sovereign LORD, what can you give me since I remain child-

[d] *18* That is, Jerusalem [e] *19* Or *Possessor*; also in verse 22 [f] *20* Or *And praise be to* [a] *1* Or *sovereign*
[b] *1* Or *shield; / your reward will be very great*

14:17 [q]2Sa 18:18
14:18 [r]Ps 110:4; Heb 5:6 [s]Ps 76:2; Heb 7:2
14:19 [t]Heb 7:6 [u]ver 22
14:20 [v]Ge 24:27 [w]Ge 28:22; Dt 26:12; Heb 7:4
14:22 [x]Ex 6:8; Da 12:7; Rev 10:5-6 [y]ver 19
14:23 [z]2Ki 5:16
15:1 [a]Da 10:1 [b]Ge 21:17; 26:24; 46:3; 2Ki 6:16; Ps 27:1; Isa 41:10, 13-14 [c]Dt 33:29; 2Sa 22:3, 31; Ps 3:3

LOT'S RESCUE
Having conquered Sodom, Kedorlaomer left for his home country, taking many captives with him. Abram learned what had happened and chased Kedorlaomer past Dan and beyond Damascus. There he defeated the king and rescued the captives, among them Lot.

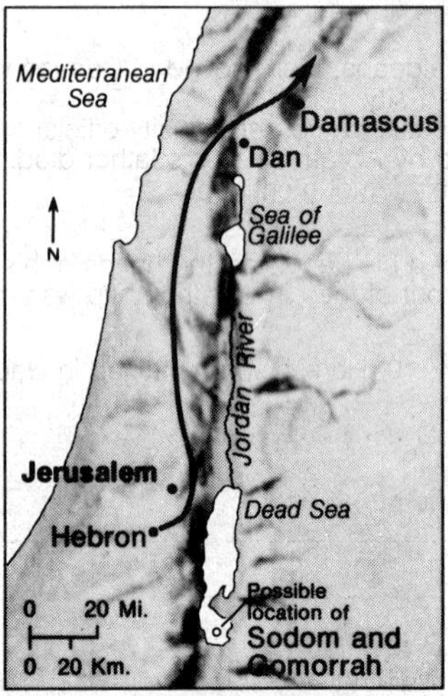

14:18 Who was Melchizedek? He was obviously a God-fearing man, for his name means "king of righteousness", and king of Salem means "king of peace". He was a "priest of God Most High" (Hebrews 7:1, 2). He recognised God as Creator of heaven and earth. What else is known about him? Four main theories have been suggested. (1) Melchizedek was a respected king of that region. Abram was simply showing him the respect he deserved. (2) The name Melchizedek may have been a standing title for all the kings of Salem. (3) Melchizedek was a type of Christ (Hebrews 7:3). A type is an Old Testament event or teaching that is so closely related to what Christ did that it illustrates a lesson about Christ. (4) Melchizedek was the appearance on earth of the preincarnate Christ in a temporary bodily form.

14:20 Abram gave one-tenth of the booty to Melchizedek. Even in some pagan religions, it was traditional to give a tenth of one's earnings to the gods. Abram followed accepted tradition; however, he refused to take any booty from the king of Sodom. Even though this huge amount would significantly increase what he could have given to God, he chose to reject it for more important reasons—he didn't want the ungodly king of Sodom to say, "I have made Abram rich." Instead, Abram wanted him to say, "God has made Abram rich." In this case, accepting the gifts would have focused everyone's attention on Abram or the king of Sodom rather than on God, the giver of victory. When people look at us, they need to see what God has accomplished in our lives.

15:1 Why would Abram be afraid? Perhaps he feared revenge from the kings he had just defeated (14:15). God gave him two good reasons for courage: (1) he promised to defend Abram ("I am your shield"), and (2) he promised to be Abram's "very great reward". When you fear what lies ahead, remember that God will stay with you through difficult times and that he has promised you great blessings.

15:2, 3 Eliezer was Abram's most trusted servant, acting as household administrator ("chief servant", see Genesis 24). Accord-

15:2 [d]Ac 7:5
15:3 [e]Ge 24:2, 34
15:4 [f]Gal 4:28
15:5 [g]Ps 147:4; Jer 33:22
[h]Ro 4:18*; Heb 11:12
15:6 [i]Ro 4:3*, 20-24*; Gal 3:6*; Jas 2:23*

less[d] and the one who will inherit[c] my estate is Eliezer of Damascus?" 3And Abram
said, "You have given me no children; so a servant[e] in my household will be my
heir."
4Then the word of the LORD came to him: "This man will not be your heir, but a son
coming from your own body will be your heir.[f]" 5He took him outside and said,
"Look up at the heavens and count the stars[g]—if indeed you can count them." Then
he said to him, "So shall your offspring be."[h]
6Abram believed the LORD, and he credited it to him as righteousness.[i]

[c] *2* The meaning of the Hebrew for this phrase is uncertain.

MELCHIZEDEK

Do you like a good mystery? History is full of them! They usually involve people. One of the most mysterious people in the Bible is the king of peace, Melchizedek. He appeared one day in the life of Abraham (then Abram) and was never heard from again. What happened that day, however, was to be remembered throughout history and eventually became a subject of a New Testament letter (Hebrews).

This meeting between Abram and Melchizedek was most unusual. Although the two men were strangers and foreigners to each other, they shared a most important characteristic: both worshipped and served the one God who made heaven and earth. This was a great moment of triumph for Abram. He had just defeated an army and regained the freedom of a large group of captives. If there was any doubt in his mind about whose victory it was, Melchizedek set the record straight by reminding Abram, "Blessed be God Most High, who delivered your enemies into your hand" (Genesis 14:20). Abram recognised that this man worshipped the same God he did.

Melchizedek was one of a small group of God-honouring people throughout the Old Testament who came in contact with the Jews (Israelites) but were not Jews themselves. This indicates that the requirement to be a follower of God is not genetic, but is based on faithfully obeying his teachings and recognising his greatness.

Do you let God speak to you through other people? In evaluating others, do you consider God's impact on their lives? Are you aware of the similarities between yourself and others who worship God, even if their form of worship is quite different from yours? Do you know the God of the Bible well enough to know if you truly worship him? Allow Melchizedek, Abraham, David, and Jesus, along with many other persons in the Bible, to show you this great God, Creator of heaven and earth. He wants you to know how much he loves you; he wants you to know him personally.

Strengths and accomplishments:
- The first priest/king of Scripture—a leader with a heart tuned to God
- Good at encouraging others to serve God wholeheartedly
- A man whose character reflected his love for God
- A person in the Old Testament who reminds us of Jesus and who some believe really was Jesus

Lesson from his life:
- Live for God and you're likely to be at the right place at the right time. Examine your heart: to whom or what is your greatest loyalty? If you can honestly answer *God,* you are living for him

Vital statistics:
- Where: Ruled in Salem, site of the future Jerusalem
- Occupation: King of Salem and priest of God Most High

Key verses:
"This Melchizedek was king of Salem and priest of God Most High. He met Abraham returning from the defeat of the kings and blessed him. . . . Just think how great he was: Even the patriarch Abraham gave him a tenth of the plunder!" (Hebrews 7:1, 4).

Melchizedek's story is told in Genesis 14:17–20. He is also mentioned in Psalm 110:4; Hebrews 5—7.

---

ing to custom, if Abram were to die without a son, his eldest servant would become his heir. Although Abram loved his servant, he wanted a son to carry on the family line.

15:5 Abram wasn't promised wealth or fame; he already had that. Instead God promised descendants like the stars in the sky or the grains of sand on the seashore (22:17), too numerous to count. To appreciate the vast number of stars scattered through the sky, you need to be, like Abram, away from any distractions. Or pick up a handful of sand and try to count the grains – it can't be done! Just when Abram was despairing of ever having an heir, God promised descendants too numerous to imagine. God's blessings are beyond our imaginations!

15:6 Although Abram had been demonstrating his faith through his actions, it was his belief in the Lord, not his actions, that made Abram right with God (Romans 4:1–5). We too can have a right relationship with God by trusting him. Our outward actions – church attendance, prayer, good deeds – will not by themselves make us right with God. A right relationship is based on faith – the heartfelt inner confidence that God is who he says he is and does what he says he will do. Right actions will follow naturally as by-products.

7He also said to him, "I am the LORD, who brought you out of Ur of the Chaldeans
to give you this land to take possession of it."
8But Abram said, "O Sovereign LORD, how can I know[j] that I shall gain possession
of it?"
9So the LORD said to him, "Bring me a heifer, a goat and a ram, each three years old,
along with a dove and a young pigeon."
10Abram brought all these to him, cut them in two and arranged the halves opposite
each other;[k] the birds, however, he did not cut in half.[l] 11Then birds of prey came
down on the carcasses, but Abram drove them away.
12As the sun was setting, Abram fell into a deep sleep,[m] and a thick and dreadful
darkness came over him. 13Then the LORD said to him, "Know for certain that your
descendants will be strangers in a country not their own, and they will be enslaved[n]
and ill-treated four hundred years.[o] 14But I will punish the nation they serve as slaves,
and afterwards they will come out[p] with great possessions.[q] 15You, however, will go
to your fathers in peace and be buried at a good old age.[r] 16In the fourth generation
your descendants will come back here, for the sin of the Amorites[s] has not yet reached
its full measure."
17When the sun had set and darkness had fallen, a smoking brazier with a blazing
torch appeared and passed between the pieces.[t] 18On that day the LORD made a covenant with Abram and said, "To your descendants I give this land,[u] from the river[d]
of Egypt[v] to the great river, the Euphrates—19the land of the Kenites, Kenizzites,
Kadmonites, 20Hittites, Perizzites, Rephaites, 21Amorites, Canaanites, Girgashites
and Jebusites."

Hagar and Ishmael

16 Now Sarai, Abram's wife, had borne him no children.[a] But she had an Egyptian maidservant[b] named Hagar; 2so she said to Abram, "The LORD has kept
me from having children. Go, sleep with my maidservant; perhaps I can build a family
through her."[c]
Abram agreed to what Sarai said. 3So after Abram had been living in Canaan[d] ten
years, Sarai his wife took her Egyptian maidservant Hagar and gave her to her husband
to be his wife. 4He slept with Hagar, and she conceived.
When she knew she was pregnant, she began to despise her mistress. 5Then Sarai
said to Abram, "You are responsible for the wrong I am suffering. I put my servant in

d *18 Or Wadi*

15:8 [j]Lk 1:18
15:10 [k]ver 17; Jer 34:18 [l]Lev 1:17
15:12 [m]Ge 2:21
15:13 [n]Ex 1:11 [o]ver 16; Ex 12:40; Ac 7:6, 17
15:14 [p]Ac 7:7* [q]Ex 12:32-38
15:15 [r]Ge 25:8
15:16 [s]1Ki 21:26
15:17 [t]ver 10
15:18 [u]Ge 12:7 [v]Nu 34:5
16:1 [a]Ge 11:30; Gal 4:24-25 [b]Ge 21:9
16:2 [c]Ge 30:3-4, 9-10
16:3 [d]Ge 12:5

15:8 Abram was looking for confirmation and assurance that he was doing God's will. We also want assurance when we ask for guidance. But we can know for sure that what we are doing is right if we do what the Bible says. Abram didn't have the Bible—we do.

15:13, 14 The book of Exodus tells the story of the enslavement and miraculous deliverance of Abram's descendants.

15:16 The Amorites were one of the nations living in Canaan, the land God promised Abram. God knew the people would grow more wicked and would someday need to be punished. Part of that punishment would involve taking away their land and giving it to Abram's descendants. God in his mercy was giving the Amorites plenty of time to repent, but he already knew they would not. At the right time, they would have to be punished. Everything God does is true to his character. He is merciful, knows all, and acts justly—and his timing is perfect.

15:17 Why did God send this strange vision to Abram? God's covenant with Abram was serious business. It represented an incredible promise from God and a huge responsibility for Abram. To confirm his promise, God gave Abram a sign—the smoking firepot and a blazing torch. The fire and smoke suggest God's holiness, his zeal for righteousness, and his judgment on all the nations. God took the initiative, gave the confirmation, and followed through on his promises. God's passing through the pieces was a visible assurance to Abram that the covenant God had made was real.

16:1–3 Sarai gave Hagar to Abram as a substitute wife, a common practice of that time. A married woman who could not have children was shamed by her peers and was often required to give a female servant to her husband in order to produce heirs. The children born to the servant woman were considered the children of the wife. Abram was acting in line with the custom of the day, but his action showed a lack of faith that God would fulfil his promise.

16:3 Sarai took matters into her own hands by giving Hagar to Abram. Like Abram she had trouble believing God's promise that was apparently directed specifically towards Abram and Sarai. Out of this lack of faith came a series of problems. This invariably happens when we take over for God, trying to make his promise come true through efforts that are not in line with his specific directions. In this case, time was the greatest test of Abram and Sarai's willingness to let God work in their lives. Sometimes we too must simply wait. When we ask God for something and have to wait, it is a temptation to take matters into our own hands and interfere with God's plans.

16:5 Although Sarai arranged for Hagar to have a child by Abram, she later blamed Abram for the results. It is often easier to strike out in frustration and accuse someone else than to admit an error and ask forgiveness. (Adam and Eve did the same thing in 3:12, 13.)

16:5 [e]Ge 31:53

your arms, and now that she knows she is pregnant, she despises me. May the LORD
judge between you and me."[e]
6"Your servant is in your hands," Abram said. "Do with her whatever you think
best." Then Sarai ill-treated Hagar; so she fled from her.
7The angel of the LORD[f] found Hagar near a spring in the desert; it was the spring
that is beside the road to Shur.[g] 8And he said, "Hagar, servant of Sarai, where have
you come from, and where are you going?"
"I'm running away from my mistress Sarai," she answered.
9Then the angel of the LORD told her, "Go back to your mistress and submit to her."

16:7 [f]Ge 21:17; 22:11, 15; 31:11 [g]Ge 20:1

ISHMAEL

Have you ever wondered if you were born into the wrong family? We don't know much about how Ishmael viewed life, but that question must have haunted him at times. His life, his name, and his position were bound up in a conflict between two jealous women. Sarah (Sarai), impatient with God's timetable, had taken matters into her own hands, deciding to have a child through another woman. Hagar, servant that she was, submitted to being used this way. But her pregnancy gave birth to strong feelings of superiority towards Sarah. Into this tense atmosphere, Ishmael was born.

For 13 years Abraham thought Ishmael's birth had fulfilled God's promise. He was surprised to hear God say that the promised child would be Abraham and Sarah's very own. Sarah's pregnancy and Isaac's birth must have had a devastating impact on Ishmael. Until then he had been treated as a son and heir, but this late arrival made his future uncertain. During Isaac's weaning celebration, Sarah caught Ishmael teasing his half brother. As a result, Hagar and Ishmael were permanently expelled from Abraham's family.

Much of what happened throughout his life cannot be blamed on Ishmael. He was caught in a process much bigger than himself. However, his own actions showed that he had chosen to become part of the problem and not part of the solution. He chose to live under his circumstances rather than above them.

The choice he made is one we must all make. There are circumstances over which we have no control (heredity, for instance), but there are others that we can control (decisions we make). At the heart of the matter is the sin-oriented nature we have all inherited. It can be partly controlled, although not overcome, by human effort. In the context of history, Ishmael's life represents the mess we make when we don't try to change the things we could change. The God of the Bible has offered a solution. His answer is not control, but a changed life. To have a changed life, turn to God, trust him to forgive your sinful past, and begin to change your attitude towards him and others.

Strengths and accomplishments:
- One of the first to experience the physical sign of God's covenant, circumcision
- Known for his ability as an archer and hunter
- Fathered 12 sons who became leaders of warrior tribes

Weakness and mistake:
- Failed to recognise the place of his half brother, Isaac, and mocked him

Lesson from his life:
- God's plans incorporate people's mistakes

Vital statistics:
- Where: Canaan and Egypt
- Occupation: Hunter, archer, warrior
- Relatives: Parents: Hagar and Abraham. Half brother: Isaac

Key verses:
"God heard the boy crying, and the angel of God called to Hagar from heaven and said to her, 'What is the matter, Hagar? Do not be afraid; God has heard the boy crying as he lies there. Lift the boy up and take him by the hand, for I will make him into a great nation' " (Genesis 21:17, 18).

Ishmael's story is told in Genesis 16—17; 25:12–18; 28:8, 9; 36:1–3. He is also mentioned in 1 Chronicles 1:28–31; Romans 9:7–9; Galatians 4:21–31.

16:6 Sarai took out her anger against Abram and herself on Hagar, and her treatment was harsh enough to cause Hagar to run away. Anger, especially when it arises from our own shortcomings, can be dangerous.

16:8 Hagar was running away from her mistress and her problem. The angel of the Lord gave her this advice: (1) to return and face Sarai, the cause of her problem, and (2) to submit to her. Hagar needed to work on her attitude towards Sarai, no matter how justified it may have been. Running away from our problems rarely solves them. It is wise to return to our problems, face them squarely, accept God's promise of help, correct our attitudes, and act as we should.

10The angel added, "I will so increase your descendants that they will be too numerous
to count."[h]
11The angel of the LORD also said to her:

> "You are now with child
> and you will have a son.
> You shall name him Ishmael,[a]
> for the LORD has heard of your misery.[i]
> 12He will be a wild donkey of a man;
> his hand will be against everyone
> and everyone's hand against him,
> and he will live in hostility
> towards[b] all his brothers.[j]"

13She gave this name to the LORD who spoke to her: "You are the God who sees
me," for she said, "I have now seen[c] the One who sees me."[k] 14That is why the well
was called Beer Lahai Roi;[d] it is still there, between Kadesh and Bered.
15So Hagar bore Abram a son,[l] and Abram gave the name Ishmael to the son she
had borne. 16Abram was eighty-six years old when Hagar bore him Ishmael.

The Covenant of Circumcision

17 When Abram was ninety-nine years old, the LORD appeared to him and said, "I
am God Almighty;[a][a] walk before me and be blameless.[b] 2I will confirm my
covenant between me and you[c] and will greatly increase your numbers."
3Abram fell face down, and God said to him, 4"As for me, this is my covenant with
you:[d] You will be the father of many nations.[e] 5No longer will you be called
Abram;[b] your name will be Abraham,[c][f] for I have made you a father of many nations.[g] 6I will make you very fruitful;[h] I will make nations of you, and kings will
come from you.[i] 7I will establish my covenant as an everlasting covenant between me
and you and your descendants after you for the generations to come, to be your God[j]
and the God of your descendants after you.[k] 8The whole land of Canaan,[l] where you
are now an alien,[m] I will give as an everlasting possession to you and your descendants
after you;[n] and I will be their God."
9Then God said to Abraham, "As for you, you must keep my covenant, you and
your descendants after you for the generations to come. 10This is my covenant with
you and your descendants after you, the covenant you are to keep: Every male among

[a] *11 Ishmael* means *God hears.* [b] *12* Or *live to the east of* [c] *13* Or *seen the back of* [d] *14 Beer Lahai Roi* means *well of the Living One who sees me.* [a] *1* Hebrew *El-Shaddai* [b] *5 Abram* means *exalted father.* [c] *5 Abraham* means *father of many.*

16:10 [h]Ge 13:16; 17:20
16:11 [i]Ex 2:24; 3:7, 9
16:12 [j]Ge 25:18
16:13 [k]Ge 32:30
16:15 [l]Gal 4:22
17:1 [a]Ge 28:3; Ex 6:3 [b]Dt 18:13
17:2 [c]Ge 15:18
17:4 [d]Ge 15:18 [e]ver 16; Ge 12:2; 35:11; 48:19
17:5 [f]ver 15; Ne 9:7 [g]Ro 4:17*
17:6 [h]Ge 35:11 [i]Mt 1:6
17:7 [j]Ex 29:45, 46 [k]Ro 9:8; Gal 3:16
17:8 [l]Ps 105:9, 11 [m]Ge 23:4; 28:4; Ex 6:4 [n]Ge 12:7

16:13 We have watched three people make serious mistakes: (1) Sarai, who took matters into her own hands and gave her maidservant to Abram; (2) Abram, who went along with the plan but, when circumstances began to go wrong, refused to help solve the problem; and (3) Hagar, who ran away from the problem. In spite of this messy situation, God demonstrated his ability to work in all things for good (Romans 8:28). Sarai and Abram still received the son they so desperately wanted, and God solved Hagar's problem despite Abram's refusal to get involved. No problem is too complicated for God if you are willing to let him help you.

17:1 The Lord told Abram, "I am God Almighty; walk before me and be blameless." God has the same message for us today. We are to obey the Lord in every respect because he is God – that is reason enough. If you don't think the benefits of obedience are worth it, consider who God is – the only one with the power and ability to meet your every need.

17:2–8 Why did God repeat his covenant to Abram? Twice before, he had mentioned this agreement (Genesis 12 and 15). Here, however, God was bringing it into focus and preparing to carry it out. He revealed to Abram several specific parts of his covenant: (1) God would give Abram many descendants; (2) many nations would descend from him; (3) God would maintain his covenant with Abram's descendants; (4) God would give Abram's descendants the land of Canaan.

17:5 God changed Abram's name to Abraham ("father of many") shortly before the promised son was conceived. From this point on, the Bible calls him Abraham.

17:5–14 God was making a covenant, or contract, between himself and Abraham. The terms were simple: Abraham would obey God and circumcise all the males in his household; God's part was to give Abraham heirs, property, power, and wealth. Most contracts are mutually beneficial: We give something and in turn receive something of equal value. But when we become part of God's covenant family, the blessings we receive far outweigh what we must give up.

17:9, 10 Why did God require circumcision? (1) As a sign of obedience to him in all matters. (2) As a sign of belonging to his covenant people. Once circumcised, there was no turning back. The man would be identified as a Jew for ever. (3) As a symbol of "cutting off" the old life of sin, purifying one's heart, and dedicating oneself to God. (4) Possibly as a health measure.

Circumcision more than any other practice separated God's people from their pagan neighbours. In Abraham's day, this was essential to develop the pure worship of the one true God.

17:10 [o]ver 23; Ge 21:4; Jn 7:22; Ac 7:8; Ro 4:11
17:11 [p]Ex 12:48; Dt 10:16 [q]Ro 4:11
17:12 [r]Lev 12:3; Lk 2:21
17:14 [s]Ex 4:24-26
17:16 [t]Ge 18:10 [u]Ge 35:11; Gal 4:31
17:17 [v]Ge 18:12; 21:6

you shall be circumcised.[o] 11 You are to undergo circumcision,[p] and it will be the
sign of the covenant[q] between me and you. 12 For the generations to come every male
among you who is eight days old must be circumcised,[r] including those born in your
household or bought with money from a foreigner—those who are not your offspring.
13 Whether born in your household or bought with your money, they must be circumcised. My covenant in your flesh is to be an everlasting covenant. 14 Any uncircumcised male, who has not been circumcised in the flesh, will be cut off from his people;[s] he has broken my covenant."
15 God also said to Abraham, "As for Sarai your wife, you are no longer to call her
Sarai; her name will be Sarah. 16 I will bless her and will surely give you a son by her.[t]
I will bless her so that she will be the mother of nations;[u] kings of peoples will come
from her."
17 Abraham fell face down; he laughed[v] and said to himself, "Will a son be born to

---

ABRAHAM

We all know that there are consequences to any action we take. What we do can set into motion a series of events that may continue long after we're gone. Unfortunately, when we are making a decision most of us think only of the immediate consequences. These are often misleading because they are short-lived.

Abraham had a choice to make. His decision was between setting out with his family and belongings for parts unknown or staying right where he was. He had to decide between the security of what he already had and the uncertainty of travelling under God's direction. All he had to go on was God's promise to guide and bless him. Abraham could hardly have been expected to visualise how much of the future was resting on his decision of whether to go or stay, but his obedience affected the history of the world. His decision to follow God set into motion the development of the nation that God would eventually use as his own when he visited earth himself. When Jesus Christ came to earth, God's promise was fulfilled; through Abraham the entire world was blessed.

You probably don't know the long-term effects of most decisions you make. But shouldn't the fact that there will be long-term results cause you to think carefully and seek God's guidance as you make choices and take action today?

Strengths and accomplishments:
- His faith pleased God
- Became the founder of the Jewish nation
- Was respected by others and was courageous in defending his family at any cost
- Was not only a caring father to his own family, but practised hospitality to others
- Was a successful and wealthy owner of livestock
- Usually avoided conflicts, but when they were unavoidable, he allowed his opponent to set the rules for settling the dispute

Weakness and mistake:
- Under direct pressure, he distorted the truth

Lessons from his life:
- God desires dependence, trust, and faith in him—not faith in our ability to please him
- God's plan from the beginning has been to make himself known to all people

Vital statistics:
- Where: Born in Ur of the Chaldeans; spent most of his life in the land of Canaan
- Occupation: Wealthy livestock owner
- Relatives: Brothers: Nahor and Haran. Father: Terah. Wife: Sarah. Nephew: Lot. Sons: Ishmael and Isaac
- Contemporaries: Abimelech, Melchizedek

Key verse:
"Abram believed the LORD, and he credited it to him as righteousness" (Genesis 15:6).

Abraham's story is told in Genesis 11—25. He is also mentioned in Exodus 2:24; Acts 7:2–8; Romans 4; Galatians 3; Hebrews 2, 6, 7, 11.

17:17–27 How could Abraham doubt God? It seemed incredible that he and Sarah in their advanced years could have a child. Abraham, the man God considered righteous because of his faith, had trouble believing God's promise to him. Despite his doubts, however, he followed God's commands (17:22–27). Even people of great faith may have doubts. When God seems to want the impossible and you begin to doubt his leading, be like Abraham. Focus on God's commitment to fulfil his promises to you, and then continue to obey.

a man a hundred years old? Will Sarah bear a child at the age of ninety?" 18 And Abraham said to God, "If only Ishmael might live under your blessing!"
19 Then God said, "Yes, but your wife Sarah will bear you a son,[w] and you will call
him Isaac.[d] I will establish my covenant with him[x] as an everlasting covenant for his
descendants after him. 20 And as for Ishmael, I have heard you: I will surely bless him;
I will make him fruitful and will greatly increase his numbers.[y] He will be the father
of twelve rulers,[z] and I will make him into a great nation.[a] 21 But my covenant I will
establish with Isaac, whom Sarah will bear to you by this time next year."[b] 22 When
he had finished speaking with Abraham, God went up from him.
23 On that very day Abraham took his son Ishmael and all those born in his household
or bought with his money, every male in his household, and circumcised them, as God
told him. 24 Abraham was ninety-nine years old when he was circumcised,[c] 25 and his
son Ishmael was thirteen; 26 Abraham and his son Ishmael were both circumcised on
that same day. 27 And every male in Abraham's household, including those born in his
household or bought from a foreigner, was circumcised with him.

4. Sodom and Gomorrah

The Three Visitors

18 The LORD appeared to Abraham near the great trees of Mamre[a] while he was
sitting at the entrance to his tent in the heat of the day. 2 Abraham looked up and
saw three men[b] standing nearby. When he saw them, he hurried from the entrance of
his tent to meet them and bowed low to the ground.
3 He said, "If I have found favour in your eyes, my lord,[a] do not pass your servant
by. 4 Let a little water be brought, and then you may all wash your feet[c] and rest under
this tree. 5 Let me get you something to eat,[d] so you can be refreshed and then go on
your way—now that you have come to your servant."
"Very well," they answered, "do as you say."
6 So Abraham hurried into the tent to Sarah. "Quick," he said, "get three seahs[b] of
fine flour and knead it and bake some bread."
7 Then he ran to the herd and selected a choice, tender calf and gave it to a servant,
who hurried to prepare it. 8 He then brought some curds and milk and the calf that had
been prepared, and set these before them.[e] While they ate, he stood near them under
a tree.
9 "Where is your wife Sarah?" they asked him.
"There, in the tent," he said.
10 Then the LORD[c] said, "I will surely return to you about this time next year, and
Sarah your wife will have a son."[f]
Now Sarah was listening at the entrance to the tent, which was behind him. 11 Abraham and Sarah were already old and well advanced in years,[g] and Sarah was past the
age of childbearing.[h] 12 So Sarah laughed[i] to herself as she thought, "After I am worn
out and my master[d][j] is old, will I now have this pleasure?"
13 Then the LORD said to Abraham, "Why did Sarah laugh and say, 'Will I really
have a child, now that I am old?' 14 Is anything too hard for the LORD?[k] I will return
to you at the appointed time next year and Sarah will have a son."

d 19 *Isaac* means *he laughs.* a 3 Or *O Lord* b 6 That is, probably about 39 pints (about 22 litres) c 10 Hebrew *Then he* d 12 Or *husband*

17:19 [w]Ge 18:14; 21:2 [x]Ge 26:3
17:20 [y]Ge 16:10 [z]Ge 25:12-16 [a]Ge 21:18
17:21 [b]Ge 21:2
17:24 [c]Ro 4:11
18:1 [a]Ge 13:18; 14:13
18:2 [b]ver 16, 22; Ge 32:24; Jos 5:13; Jdg 13:6-11; Heb 13:2
18:4 [c]Ge 19:2; 43:24
18:5 [d]Jdg 13:15
18:8 [e]Ge 19:3
18:10 [f]Ro 9:9*
18:11 [g]Ge 17:17 [h]Ro 4:19
18:12 [i]Ge 17:17; 21:6 [j]1Pe 3:6
18:14 [k]Jer 32:17, 27; Zec 8:6; Mt 19:26; Lk 1:37; Ro 4:21

17:20 God did not forget Ishmael. Although he was not to be Abraham's heir, he would also be the father of a great nation. Regardless of your circumstances, God has not forgotten you. Obey him and trust in his plan.

18:2–5 Abraham was eager to show hospitality to these three visitors, as was Lot (19:2). In Abraham's day, a person's reputation was largely connected to his hospitality—the sharing of home and food. Even strangers were to be treated as highly honoured guests. Meeting another's need for food or shelter was and still is one of the most immediate and practical ways to obey God. It is also a time-honoured relationship builder. Hebrews 13:2 suggests that we, like Abraham, might actually entertain angels. This thought should be on our minds the next time we have the opportunity to meet a stranger's needs.

18:14 "Is anything too hard for the LORD?" The obvious answer is, "Of course not!" This question reveals much about God. Make it a habit to insert your specific needs into the question. "Is this day in my life too hard for the Lord?" "Is this habit I'm trying to break too hard for him?" "Is the communication problem I'm having too hard for him?" Asking the question this way reminds you that God is personally involved in your life and nudges you to ask for his power to help you.

18:17
[l]Am 3:7
[m]Ge 19:24

18:18
[n]Gal 3:8*

18:19
[o]Dt 4:9-10; 6:7
[p]Jos 24:15; Eph 6:4

15 Sarah was afraid, so she lied and said, "I did not laugh."
But he said, "Yes, you did laugh."

Abraham Pleads for Sodom

16 When the men got up to leave, they looked down towards Sodom, and Abraham
walked along with them to see them on their way. 17 Then the LORD said, "Shall I hide
from Abraham[l] what I am about to do?[m] 18 Abraham will surely become a great and
powerful nation,[n] and all nations on earth will be blessed through him. 19 For I have
chosen him, so that he will direct his children[o] and his household after him to keep the
way of the LORD[p] by doing what is right and just, so that the LORD will bring about for
Abraham what he has promised him."

SARAH

There probably isn't anything harder to do than wait, whether we are expecting something good, something bad, or an unknown.

One way we often cope with a long wait (or even a short one) is to begin helping God to put his plan into action. Sarah tried this approach. She was too old to expect to have a child of her own, so she thought God must have something else in mind. From Sarah's limited point of view this could only be to give Abraham a son through another woman—a common practice in her day. The plan seemed harmless enough. Abraham would sleep with Sarah's maidservant, who would then give birth to a child. Sarah would take the child as her own. The plan worked beautifully—at first. But as you read about the events that followed, you will be struck by how often Sarah must have regretted the day she decided to push God's timetable ahead.

Another way we cope with a long wait is to gradually conclude that what we're waiting for is never going to happen. Sarah waited 90 years for a baby! When God told her she would finally have one of her own, she laughed, not so much from a lack of faith in what God could do, but from doubt about what he could do *through her.* When confronted about her laughter, she lied—as she had seen her husband do from time to time. She probably didn't want her true feelings to be known.

What parts of your life seem to be on hold right now? Do you understand that this may be part of God's plan for you? The Bible has more than enough clear direction to keep us busy while we're waiting for some particular part of life to move ahead.

Strengths and accomplishments:
- Was intensely loyal to her own child
- Became the mother of a nation and an ancestor of Jesus
- Was a woman of faith, the first woman listed in the Hall of Faith in Hebrews 11

Weaknesses and mistakes:
- Had trouble believing God's promises to her
- Attempted to work problems out on her own, without consulting God
- Tried to cover her faults by blaming others

Lessons from her life:
- God responds to faith even in the midst of failure
- God is not bound by what usually happens; he can stretch the limits and cause unheard-of events to occur

Vital statistics:
- Where: Married Abram in Ur of the Chaldeans, then moved with him to Canaan
- Occupation: Wife, mother, household manager
- Relatives: Father: Terah. Husband: Abraham. Half brothers: Nahor and Haran. Nephew: Lot. Son: Isaac

Key verse:
"By faith Abraham, even though he was past age—and Sarah herself was barren—was enabled to become a father because he considered him faithful who had made the promise" (Hebrews 11:11).

Sarah's story is told in Genesis 11—25. She is also mentioned in Isaiah 51:2; Romans 4:19; 9:9; Hebrews 11:11; 1 Peter 3:6.

18:15 Sarah lied because she was afraid of being discovered. Fear is the most common motive for lying. We are afraid that our inner thoughts and emotions will be exposed or our wrongdoings discovered. But lying causes greater complications than telling the truth and brings even more problems. If God can't be trusted with our innermost thoughts and fears, we are in greater trouble than we first imagined.

20Then the LORD said, "The outcry against Sodom and Gomorrah is so great and
their sin so grievous 21that I will go down[q] and see if what they have done is as bad
as the outcry that has reached me. If not, I will know."
22The men turned away and went towards Sodom,[r] but Abraham remained standing before the LORD.[e] 23Then Abraham approached him and said: "Will you sweep
away the righteous with the wicked?[s] 24What if there are fifty righteous people in the
city? Will you really sweep it away and not spare[f] the place for the sake of the fifty
righteous people in it?[t] 25Far be it from you to do such a thing—to kill the righteous
with the wicked, treating the righteous and the wicked alike. Far be it from you! Will
not the Judge[g] of all the earth do right?"[u]
26The LORD said, "If I find fifty righteous people in the city of Sodom, I will spare
the whole place for their sake.[v]"
27Then Abraham spoke up again: "Now that I have been so bold as to speak to the
Lord, though I am nothing but dust and ashes,[w] 28what if the number of the righteous
is five less than fifty? Will you destroy the whole city because of five people?"
"If I find forty-five there," he said, "I will not destroy it."
29Once again he spoke to him, "What if only forty are found there?"
He said, "For the sake of forty, I will not do it."
30Then he said, "May the Lord not be angry, but let me speak. What if only thirty
can be found there?"
He answered, "I will not do it if I find thirty there."
31Abraham said, "Now that I have been so bold as to speak to the Lord, what if only
twenty can be found there?"
He said, "For the sake of twenty, I will not destroy it."
32Then he said, "May the Lord not be angry, but let me speak just once more.[x]
What if only ten can be found there?"
He answered, "For the sake of ten,[y] I will not destroy it."
33When the LORD had finished speaking with Abraham, he left, and Abraham returned home.

Sodom and Gomorrah Destroyed

19 The two angels arrived at Sodom[a] in the evening, and Lot was sitting in the
gateway of the city.[b] When he saw them, he got up to meet them and bowed
down with his face to the ground. 2"My lords," he said, "please turn aside to your

18:21 [q]Ge 11:5
18:22 [r]Ge 19:1
18:23 [s]Nu 16:22
18:24 [t]Jer 5:1
18:25 [u]Job 8:3, 20; Ps 58:11; 94:2; Isa 3:10-11; Ro 3:6
18:26 [v]Jer 5:1
18:27 [w]Ge 2:7; 3:19; Job 30:19; 42:6
18:32 [x]Jdg 6:39 [y]Jer 5:1
19:1 [a]Ge 18:22 [b]Ge 18:1

[e] *22* Masoretic Text; an ancient Hebrew scribal tradition *but the LORD remained standing before Abraham*
[f] *24* Or *forgive*; also in verse 26 [g] *25* Or *Ruler*

18:20–33 Did Abraham change God's mind? Of course not. The more likely answer is that God changed Abraham's mind. Abraham knew that God is just and that he punishes sin, but he may have wondered about God's mercy. Abraham seemed to be probing God's mind to see how merciful he really was. He left his conversation with God convinced that God was both kind and fair. Our prayers won't change God's mind, but they may change ours just as Abraham's prayer changed his. Prayer helps us better understand the mind of God.

18:20–33 Why did God let Abraham question his justice and intercede for a wicked city? Abraham knew that God must punish sin, but he also knew from experience that God is merciful to sinners. God knew there were not ten righteous people in the city, but he was merciful enough to allow Abraham to intercede. He was also merciful enough to help Lot, Abraham's nephew, get out of Sodom before it was destroyed. God does not take pleasure in destroying the wicked, but he must punish sin. He is both just and merciful. We should be thankful that God's mercy extends to us.

18:21 God gave the men of Sodom a fair test. He was not ignorant of the city's wicked practices, but in his fairness and patience he gave the people of Sodom one last chance to repent. God is still waiting, giving people the opportunity to turn to him (2 Peter 3:9). Those who are wise will turn to him before his patience wears out.

18:25 Was God being unfair to the people of Sodom? Did he really plan to destroy the righteous with the wicked? On the contrary, God's fairness stood out. (1) He agreed to spare the entire city if only ten righteous people lived there. (2) He showed great mercy towards Lot, apparently the only man in the city who had any kind of relationship with him (and even that was questionable). (3) He showed great patience towards Lot, almost forcing him to leave Sodom before it was destroyed. Remember God's patience when you are tempted to think he is unfair. Even the most godly people deserve his justice. We should be glad God doesn't direct his justice towards us as he did towards Sodom.

18:33 God showed Abraham that asking for anything is allowed, with the understanding that God's answers come from God's perspective. They are not always in harmony with our expectations, for only he knows the whole story. Are you missing God's answer to a prayer because you haven't considered any possible answers other than the one you expect?

19:1 The gateway of the city was the meeting place for city officials and other men to discuss current events and transact business. It was a place of authority and status where a person could see and be seen. Evidently Lot held an important position in the government or associated with those who did because the angels found him at the city gate. Perhaps Lot's status in Sodom was one reason he was so reluctant to leave (19:16, 18–22).

servant's house. You can wash your feet[c] and spend the night and then go on your
way early in the morning."
"No," they answered, "we will spend the night in the square."
3 But he insisted so strongly that they did go with him and entered his house. He
prepared a meal for them, baking bread without yeast, and they ate.[d] 4 Before they had
gone to bed, all the men from every part of the city of Sodom—both young and
old—surrounded the house. 5 They called to Lot, "Where are the men who came to you
tonight? Bring them out to us so that we can have sex with them."[e]
6 Lot went outside to meet them[f] and shut the door behind him 7 and said, "No, my
friends. Don't do this wicked thing. 8 Look, I have two daughters who have never slept
with a man. Let me bring them out to you, and you can do what you like with them. But
don't do anything to these men, for they have come under the protection of my roof."[g]
9 "Get out of our way," they replied. And they said, "This fellow came here as an
alien, and now he wants to play the judge![h] We'll treat you worse than them." They
kept bringing pressure on Lot and moved forward to break down the door.
10 But the men inside reached out and pulled Lot back into the house and shut the
door. 11 Then they struck the men who were at the door of the house, young and old,
with blindness[i] so that they could not find the door.
12 The two men said to Lot, "Do you have anyone else here—sons-in-law, sons or
daughters, or anyone else in the city who belongs to you?[j] Get them out of here,
13 because we are going to destroy this place. The outcry to the LORD against its people
is so great that he has sent us to destroy it."[k]
14 So Lot went out and spoke to his sons-in-law, who were pledged to marry[a] his
daughters. He said, "Hurry and get out of this place, because the LORD is about to
destroy the city![l]" But his sons-in-law thought he was joking.[m]
15 With the coming of dawn, the angels urged Lot, saying, "Hurry! Take your wife
and your two daughters who are here, or you will be swept away[n] when the city is
punished.[o]"
16 When he hesitated, the men grasped his hand and the hands of his wife and of his
two daughters and led them safely out of the city, for the LORD was merciful to them.
17 As soon as they had brought them out, one of them said, "Flee for your lives![p] Don't
look back,[q] and don't stop anywhere in the plain! Flee to the mountains or you will be
swept away!"
18 But Lot said to them, "No, my lords,[b] please! 19 Your[c] servant has found favour
in your[c] eyes, and you[c] have shown great kindness to me in sparing my life. But I

a *14* Or *were married to* b *18* Or *No, Lord*; or *No, my lord* c *19* The Hebrew is singular.

19:2 [c]Ge 18:4; Lk 7:44
19:3 [d]Ge 18:6
19:5 [e]Jdg 19:22; Isa 3:9; Ro 1:24-27
19:6 [f]Jdg 19:23
19:8 [g]Jdg 19:24
19:9 [h]Ex 2:14; Ac 7:27
19:11 [i]Dt 28:28-29; 2Ki 6:18; Ac 13:11
19:12 [j]Ge 7:1
19:13 [k]1Ch 21:15
19:14 [l]Nu 16:21 [m]Ex 9:21; Lk 17:28
19:15 [n]Nu 16:26 [o]Rev 18:4
19:17 [p]Jer 48:6 [q]ver 26

19:8 How could any father give his daughters to be ravished by a mob of perverts, just to protect two strangers? Possibly Lot was scheming to save both the girls and the visitors, hoping the girls' fiancés would rescue them or that the homosexual men would be disinterested in the girls and simply go away. Although it was the custom of the day to protect guests at any cost, this terrible suggestion reveals how deeply sin had been absorbed into Lot's life. He had become hardened to evil acts in an evil city. Whatever Lot's motives were, we see here an illustration of Sodom's terrible wickedness—a wickedness so great that God had to destroy the entire city.

19:13 God promised to spare Sodom if only ten righteous people lived there (18:32). Obviously not even ten could be found, because the angels arrived to destroy the city. Archaeological evidence points to an advanced civilisation in this area during Abraham's day. Most researchers also confirm some kind of sudden and devastating destruction. It is now widely thought that the buried city lies beneath the waters of the southern end of the Dead Sea. The story of Sodom reveals that the people of Lot's day had to deal with the same kinds of repulsive sins the world faces today. We should follow Abraham's example of trusting God. His selfless faith contrasts with the self-gratifying people of Sodom.

19:14 Lot had lived so long and so contented among ungodly people that he was no longer a believable witness for God. He had allowed his environment to shape him, rather than he shaping his environment. Do those who know you see you as a witness for God, or are you just one of the crowd, blending in unnoticed? Lot had compromised to the point that he was almost useless to God. When he finally made a stand, nobody listened. Have you too become useless to God because you are too much like your environment? To make a difference, you must first decide to be different in your faith and your conduct.

19:16 Lot hesitated, so the angel grasped his hand and rushed him to safety. Lot did not want to abandon the wealth, position, and comfort he enjoyed in Sodom. It is easy to criticise Lot for being hypnotised by Sodom when the choice seems so clear to us. To be wiser than Lot, we must see that our hesitation to obey stems from the false attractions of our culture's pleasures.

19:16–29 Notice how God's mercy towards Abraham extended to Lot and his family. Because Abraham pleaded for Lot, God was merciful and saved Lot from the fiery destruction of Sodom. A righteous person can often affect others for good. James says that the prayers of a righteous person are powerful (see James 5:16). All Christians should follow Abraham's example and pray for others to be saved.

can't flee to the mountains; this disaster will overtake me, and I'll die. 20 Look, here is
a town near enough to run to, and it is small. Let me flee to it—it is very small, isn't
it? Then my life will be spared."
21 He said to him, "Very well, I will grant this request too; I will not overthrow the
town you speak of. 22 But flee there quickly, because I cannot do anything until you
reach it." (That is why the town was called Zoar.[d])
23 By the time Lot reached Zoar, the sun had risen over the land. 24 Then the LORD
rained down burning sulphur on Sodom and Gomorrah[r]—from the LORD out of the
heavens.[s] 25 Thus he overthrew those cities and the entire plain, including all those
living in the cities—and also the vegetation in the land.[t] 26 But Lot's wife looked
back,[u] and she became a pillar of salt.[v]
27 Early the next morning Abraham got up and returned to the place where he had
stood before the LORD.[w] 28 He looked down towards Sodom and Gomorrah, towards
all the land of the plain, and he saw dense smoke rising from the land, like smoke from
a furnace.[x]
29 So when God destroyed the cities of the plain, he remembered Abraham, and he
brought Lot out of the catastrophe[y] that overthrew the cities where Lot had lived.

Lot and His Daughters

30 Lot and his two daughters left Zoar and settled in the mountains,[z] for he was
afraid to stay in Zoar. He and his two daughters lived in a cave. 31 One day the older
daughter said to the younger, "Our father is old, and there is no man around here to lie
with us, as is the custom all over the earth. 32 Let's get our father to drink wine and then
lie with him and preserve our family line through our father."
33 That night they got their father to drink wine, and the older daughter went in and
lay with him. He was not aware of it when she lay down or when she got up.
34 The next day the older daughter said to the younger, "Last night I lay with my
father. Let's get him to drink wine again tonight, and you go in and lie with him so we
can preserve our family line through our father." 35 So they got their father to drink
wine that night also, and the younger daughter went and lay with him. Again he was
not aware of it when she lay down or when she got up.
36 So both of Lot's daughters became pregnant by their father. 37 The older daughter
had a son, and she named him Moab;[e] he is the father of the Moabites[a] of today.
38 The younger daughter also had a son, and she named him Ben-Ammi;[f] he is the
father of the Ammonites[b] of today.

[d] 22 *Zoar* means *small.* [e] 37 *Moab* sounds like the Hebrew for *from father.* [f] 38 *Ben-Ammi* means *son of my people.*

19:24 [r] Dt 29:23; Isa 1:9; 13:19 [s] Lk 17:29; 2Pe 2:6; Jude 7
19:25 [t] Ps 107:34; Eze 16:48
19:26 [u] ver 17 [v] Lk 17:32
19:27 [w] Ge 18:22
19:28 [x] Rev 9:2; 18:9
19:29 [y] 2Pe 2:7
19:30 [z] ver 19
19:37 [a] Dt 2:9
19:38 [b] Dt 2:19

19:24 In the story of Sodom and Gomorrah, we see two facets of God's character: his great patience (agreeing to spare a wicked city for ten good people) and his fierce anger (destroying both cities). As we grow spiritually, we should find ourselves developing a deeper respect for God because of his anger towards sin, and also a deeper love for God because of his patience when we sin.

19:26 Lot's wife turned back to look at the smouldering city of Sodom. Clinging to the past, she was unwilling to turn completely away. Are you looking back longingly at sin while trying to move forward with God? You can't make progress with God as long as you are holding on to pieces of your old life. Jesus said it this way in Matthew 6:24: "No-one can serve two masters."

19:30–38 In this pitiful sequel to the story of the destruction of Sodom, we see two women compelled to preserve their family line. They were driven not by lust, but by desperation—they feared they would never marry. Lot's tendency to compromise and refusal to act reached its peak. He should have found right partners for his daughters long before this; Abraham's family wasn't far away. Now the two daughters stooped to incest, showing their acceptance of the morals of Sodom. We are most likely to sin when we are desperate for what we feel we must have.

19:30–38 Why doesn't the Bible openly condemn these sisters for what they did? In many cases, the Bible does not judge people for their actions. It simply reports the events. However, incest is clearly condemned in other parts of Scripture (Leviticus 18:6–18; 20:11, 12, 17, 19–21; Deuteronomy 22:30; 27:20–23; Ezekiel 22:11; 1 Corinthians 5:1). Perhaps the consequence of their action—Moab and Ammon became enemies of Israel—was God's way of judging their sin.

19:37, 38 Moab and Ben-Ammi were the products of incest. They became the fathers of two of Israel's greatest enemies, the Moabites and the Ammonites. These nations settled east of the Jordan River, and Israel never conquered them. Because of the family connection, Moses was forbidden to attack them (Deuteronomy 2:9). Ruth, great-grandmother of David and an ancestor of Jesus, was from Moab.

Abraham and Abimelech

20 Now Abraham moved on from there[a] into the region of the Negev and lived
between Kadesh and Shur. For a while he stayed in Gerar,[b] 2and there Abraham said of his wife Sarah, "She is my sister.[c]" Then Abimelech king of Gerar sent
for Sarah and took her.[d]
3But God came to Abimelech in a dream[e] one night and said to him, "You are as
good as dead because of the woman you have taken; she is a married woman."[f]
4Now Abimelech had not gone near her, so he said, "Lord, will you destroy an
innocent nation?[g] 5Did he not say to me, 'She is my sister,' and didn't she also say,
'He is my brother'? I have done this with a clear conscience and clean hands."
6Then God said to him in the dream, "Yes, I know you did this with a clear conscience, and so I have kept[h] you from sinning against me. That is why I did not let you
touch her. 7Now return the man's wife, for he is a prophet, and he will pray for you[i]
and you will live. But if you do not return her, you may be sure that you and all yours
will die."
8Early the next morning Abimelech summoned all his officials, and when he told
them all that had happened, they were very much afraid. 9Then Abimelech called
Abraham in and said, "What have you done to us? How have I wronged you that you
have brought such great guilt upon me and my kingdom? You have done things to me
that should not be done.[j]" 10And Abimelech asked Abraham, "What was your reason
for doing this?"
11Abraham replied, "I said to myself, 'There is surely no fear of God[k] in this place,
and they will kill me because of my wife.'[l] 12Besides, she really is my sister, the
daughter of my father though not of my mother; and she became my wife. 13And when
God caused me to wander from my father's household, I said to her, 'This is how you
can show your love to me: Everywhere we go, say of me, "He is my brother." ' "
14Then Abimelech brought sheep and cattle and male and female slaves and gave
them to Abraham,[m] and he returned Sarah his wife to him. 15And Abimelech said,
"My land is before you; live wherever you like."[n]
16To Sarah he said, "I am giving your brother a thousand shekels[a] of silver. This is
to cover the offence against you before all who are with you; you are completely vindicated."
17Then Abraham prayed to God,[o] and God healed Abimelech, his wife and his
slave girls so they could have children again, 18for the LORD had closed up every
womb in Abimelech's household because of Abraham's wife Sarah.[p]

a *16* That is, about 25 pounds (about 11.5 kilograms)

20:1 [a]Ge 18:1 [b]Ge 26:1, 6, 17
20:2 [c]ver 12; Ge 12:13; 26:7 [d]Ge 12:15
20:3 [e]Job 33:15; Mt 27:19 [f]Ps 105:14
20:4 [g]Ge 18:25
20:6 [h]1Sa 25:26, 34
20:7 [i]ver 17; 1Sa 7:5; Job 42:8
20:9 [j]Ge 12:18; 26:10; 34:7
20:11 [k]Ge 42:18; Ps 36:1 [l]Ge 12:12; 26:7
20:14 [m]Ge 12:16
20:15 [n]Ge 13:9
20:17 [o]Job 42:9
20:18 [p]Ge 12:17

20:2 Abraham had used this same trick before to protect himself (12:11–13). Although Abraham is one of our heroes of faith, he did not learn his lesson well enough the first time. In fact, by giving in to the temptation again, he risked turning a sinful act into a sinful pattern of lying whenever he suspected his life was in danger.

No matter how much we love God, certain temptations are especially difficult to resist. These are the vulnerable spots in our spiritual armour. As we struggle with these weaknesses, we can be encouraged to know that God is watching out for us just as he did for Abraham.

20:6 Abimelech had unknowingly taken a married woman to be his wife and was about to commit adultery. But God somehow prevented him from touching Sarah and held him back from sinning. What mercy on God's part! How many times has God done the same for us, holding us back from sin in ways we can't even detect? We have no way of knowing – we just know from this story that he can. God works just as often in ways we can't see as in ways we can.

20:11–13 Because Abraham mistakenly assumed that Abimelech was a wicked man, he made a quick decision to tell a half-truth. Abraham thought it would be more effective to deceive Abimelech than to trust God to work in the king's life. Don't assume that God will not work in a situation that has potential problems. You may not completely understand the situation, and God may intervene when you least expect it.

20:17, 18 Why did God punish Abimelech when he had no idea Sarah was married? (1) Even though Abimelech's intentions were good, as long as Sarah was living in his harem he was in danger of sinning. A person who eats a poisonous toadstool, thinking it's a harmless mushroom, no doubt has perfectly good intentions – but will still suffer. Sin is a poison that damages us and those around us, whatever our intentions. (2) The punishment, closing up "every womb in Abimelech's household", lasted only as long as Abimelech was in danger of sleeping with Sarah. It was meant to change the situation, not to harm Abimelech. (3) The punishment clearly showed that Abraham was in league with Almighty God. This incident may have made Abimelech respect and fear Abraham's God.

5. Birth and near sacrifice of Isaac

The Birth of Isaac

21 Now the LORD was gracious to Sarah[a] as he had said, and the LORD did for
Sarah what he had promised.[b] 2Sarah became pregnant and bore a son[c] to
Abraham in his old age,[d] at the very time God had promised him. 3Abraham gave the
name Isaac[a][e] to the son Sarah bore him. 4When his son Isaac was eight days old,
Abraham circumcised him,[f] as God commanded him. 5Abraham was a hundred years
old when his son Isaac was born to him.
6Sarah said, "God has brought me laughter,[g] and everyone who hears about this
will laugh with me." 7And she added, "Who would have said to Abraham that Sarah
would nurse children? Yet I have borne him a son in his old age."

Hagar and Ishmael Sent Away

8The child grew and was weaned, and on the day Isaac was weaned Abraham held
a great feast. 9But Sarah saw that the son whom Hagar the Egyptian had borne to
Abraham[h] was mocking,[i] 10and she said to Abraham, "Get rid of that slave woman
and her son, for that slave woman's son will never share in the inheritance with my son
Isaac."[j]
11The matter distressed Abraham greatly because it concerned his son.[k] 12But God
said to him, "Do not be so distressed about the boy and your maidservant. Listen to
whatever Sarah tells you, because it is through Isaac that your offspring[b] will be reckoned.[l] 13I will make the son of the maidservant into a nation[m] also, because he is
your offspring."
14Early the next morning Abraham took some food and a skin of water and gave
them to Hagar. He set them on her shoulders and then sent her off with the boy. She
went on her way and wandered in the desert of Beersheba.[n]
15When the water in the skin was gone, she put the boy under one of the bushes.
16Then she went off and sat down nearby, about a bow-shot away, for she thought, "I
cannot watch the boy die." And as she sat there nearby, she[c] began to sob.
17God heard the boy crying,[o] and the angel of God called to Hagar from heaven and
said to her, "What is the matter, Hagar? Do not be afraid; God has heard the boy crying
as he lies there. 18Lift the boy up and take him by the hand, for I will make him into
a great nation.[p]"
19Then God opened her eyes[q] and she saw a well of water. So she went and filled
the skin with water and gave the boy a drink.
20God was with the boy[r] as he grew up. He lived in the desert and became an
archer. 21While he was living in the Desert of Paran, his mother got a wife for him[s]
from Egypt.

The Treaty at Beersheba

22At that time Abimelech and Phicol the commander of his forces said to Abraham,
"God is with you in everything you do. 23Now swear[t] to me here before God that you
will not deal falsely with me or my children or my descendants. Show to me and the
country where you are living as an alien the same kindness I have shown to you."
24Abraham said, "I swear it."
25Then Abraham complained to Abimelech about a well of water that Abimelech's

a 3 *Isaac* means *he laughs.* b 12 Or *seed* c 16 Hebrew; Septuagint *the child*

21:1 [a]1Sa 2:21 [b]Ge 8:1; 17:16, 21; Gal 4:23
21:2 [c]Ge 17:19 [d]Gal 4:22; Heb 11:11
21:3 [e]Ge 17:19
21:4 [f]Ge 17:10, 12; Ac 7:8
21:6 [g]Ge 17:17; Isa 54:1
21:9 [h]Ge 16:15 [i]Gal 4:29
21:10 [j]Gal 4:30*
21:11 [k]Ge 17:18
21:12 [l]Ro 9:7*; Heb 11:18*
21:13 [m]ver 18
21:14 [n]ver 31, 32
21:17 [o]Ex 3:7
21:18 [p]ver 13
21:19 [q]Nu 22:31
21:20 [r]Ge 26:3, 24; 28:15; 39:2, 21, 23
21:21 [s]Ge 24:4, 38
21:23 [t]ver 31; Jos 2:12

21:1–7 Who could believe that Abraham would have a son at 100 years of age—and live to raise him to adulthood? But doing the impossible is everyday business for God. Our big problems won't seem so impossible if we let God handle them.

21:7 After repeated promises, a visit by two angels, and the appearance of the Lord himself, Sarah finally cried out with surprise and joy at the birth of her son. Because of her doubt, worry, and fear, she had forfeited the peace she could have felt in God's wonderful promise to her. The way to bring peace to a troubled heart is to focus on God's promises. Trust him to do what he says.

21:18 What happened to Ishmael, and who are his descendants? Ishmael became ruler of a large tribe or nation. The Ishmaelites were nomads living in the Desert of Sinai and Paran, south of Israel. One of Ishmael's daughters married Esau, Ishmael's nephew (28:9). The Bible pictures the Ishmaelites as hostile to Israel and to God (Psalm 83:6).

servants had seized.[u] 26But Abimelech said, "I don't know who has done this. You
did not tell me, and I heard about it only today."
27So Abraham brought sheep and cattle and gave them to Abimelech, and the two
men made a treaty.[v] 28Abraham set apart seven ewe lambs from the flock, 29and
Abimelech asked Abraham, "What is the meaning of these seven ewe lambs you have
set apart by themselves?"
30He replied, "Accept these seven lambs from my hand as a witness[w] that I dug this
well."
31So that place was called Beersheba,[d][x] because the two men swore an oath there.
32After the treaty had been made at Beersheba, Abimelech and Phicol the commander of his forces returned to the land of the Philistines. 33Abraham planted a tamarisk tree in Beersheba, and there he called upon the name of the LORD,[y] the Eternal
God.[z] 34And Abraham stayed in the land of the Philistines for a long time.

Abraham Tested

22 Some time later God tested[a] Abraham. He said to him, "Abraham!"
"Here I am," he replied.
2Then God said, "Take your son[b], your only son, Isaac, whom you love, and go to
the region of Moriah.[c] Sacrifice him there as a burnt offering on one of the mountains
I will tell you about."
3Early the next morning Abraham got up and saddled his donkey. He took with him
two of his servants and his son Isaac. When he had cut enough wood for the burnt
offering, he set out for the place God had told him about. 4On the third day Abraham
looked up and saw the place in the distance. 5He said to his servants, "Stay here with
the donkey while I and the boy go over there. We will worship and then we will come
back to you."
6Abraham took the wood for the burnt offering and placed it on his son Isaac,[d] and
he himself carried the fire and the knife. As the two of them went on together, 7Isaac
spoke up and said to his father Abraham, "Father?"
"Yes, my son?" Abraham replied.

21:25 [u]Ge 26:15, 18, 20-22
21:27 [v]Ge 26:28, 31
21:30 [w]Ge 31:44, 47, 48, 50, 52
21:31 [x]Ge 26:33
21:33 [y]Ge 4:26 [z]Dt 33:27
22:1 [a]Dt 8:2, 16; Heb 11:17; Jas 1:12-13
22:2 [b]ver 12, 16; Jn 3:16; Heb 11:17; 1Jn 4:9 [c]2Ch 3:1
22:6 [d]Jn 19:17

d 31 *Beersheba* can mean *well of seven* or *well of the oath.*

21:31 Beersheba, the southernmost city of Israel, lay on the edge of a vast desert that stretched as far as Egypt to the southwest and Mount Sinai to the south. The phrase "from Dan to Beersheba" was often used to describe the traditional boundaries of the promised land (2 Samuel 17:11). Beersheba's southern location and the presence of several wells in the area may explain why Abraham settled there. Beersheba was also the home of Isaac, Abraham's son.

22:1 God tested Abraham, not to trip him and watch him fall, but to deepen his capacity to obey God and thus to develop his character. Just as fire refines ore to extract precious metals, God refines us through difficult circumstances. When we are tested we can complain, or we can try to see how God is stretching us to develop our character.

22:3 That morning Abraham began one of the greatest acts of obedience in recorded history. He travelled 50 miles to Mount Moriah near the site of Jerusalem. Over the years he had learned many tough lessons about the importance of obeying God. This time his obedience was prompt and complete. Obeying God is often a struggle because it may mean giving up something we truly want. We should not expect our obedience to God to be easy or to come naturally.

22:6 We don't know how Abraham carried the fire. Perhaps he carried a live coal or a flint to start a fire.

22:7, 8 Why did God ask Abraham to perform human sacrifice? Pagan nations practised human sacrifice, but God condemned this as a terrible sin (Leviticus 20:1–5). God did not want Isaac to die, but he wanted Abraham to sacrifice Isaac in his heart so it would be clear that Abraham loved God more than he loved his promised and long-awaited son. God was testing Abraham. The purpose of testing is to strengthen our character and deepen our commitment to God and his perfect timing. Through this difficult experience, Abraham strengthened his commitment to obey God. He also learned about God's ability to provide.

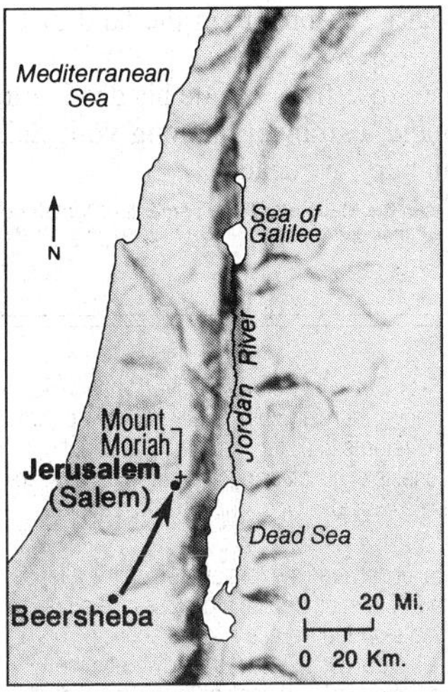

ABRAHAM'S TRIP TO MOUNT MORIAH
Abraham and Isaac travelled the 50 or 60 miles from Beersheba to Mount Moriah in about three days. This was a very difficult time for Abraham, who was on his way to sacrifice his beloved son, Isaac.

"The fire and wood are here," Isaac said, "but where is the lamb[e] for the burnt
offering?"
8Abraham answered, "God himself will provide the lamb for the burnt offering, my
son." And the two of them went on together.
9When they reached the place God had told him about, Abraham built an altar there
and arranged the wood on it. He bound his son Isaac and laid him on the altar,[f] on top
of the wood. 10Then he reached out his hand and took the knife to slay his son. 11But
the angel of the LORD called out to him from heaven, "Abraham! Abraham!"
"Here I am," he replied.
12"Do not lay a hand on the boy," he said. "Do not do anything to him. Now I know
that you fear God,[g] because you have not withheld from me your son, your only
son.[h]"
13Abraham looked up and there in a thicket he saw a ram[a] caught by its horns. He
went over and took the ram and sacrificed it as a burnt offering instead of his son.[i]
14So Abraham called that place The LORD Will Provide. And to this day it is said, "On
the mountain of the LORD it will be provided.[j]"
15The angel of the LORD called to Abraham from heaven a second time 16and said,
"I swear by myself,[k] declares the LORD, that because you have done this and have not
withheld your son, your only son, 17I will surely bless you and make your descendants[l] as numerous as the stars in the sky[m] and as the sand on the seashore.[n] Your
descendants will take possession of the cities of their enemies,[o] 18and through your
offspring[b] all nations on earth will be blessed,[p] because you have obeyed me."[q]
19Then Abraham returned to his servants, and they set off together for Beersheba.
And Abraham stayed in Beersheba.

Nahor's Sons

20Some time later Abraham was told, "Milcah is also a mother; she has borne sons
to your brother Nahor:[r] 21Uz the firstborn, Buz his brother, Kemuel (the father of
Aram), 22Kesed, Hazo, Pildash, Jidlaph and Bethuel." 23Bethuel became the father of
Rebekah.[s] Milcah bore these eight sons to Abraham's brother Nahor. 24His concubine, whose name was Reumah, also had sons: Tebah, Gaham, Tahash and Maacah.

The Death of Sarah

23 Sarah lived to be a hundred and twenty-seven years old. 2She died at Kiriath
Arba[a] (that is, Hebron)[b] in the land of Canaan, and Abraham went to mourn
for Sarah and to weep over her.
3Then Abraham rose from beside his dead wife and spoke to the Hittites.[a] He said,
4"I am an alien and a stranger[c] among you. Sell me some property for a burial site
here so that I can bury my dead."

a *13* Many manuscripts of the Masoretic Text, Samaritan Pentateuch, Septuagint and Syriac; most manuscripts of the Masoretic Text *a ram behind* ⌞*him*⌟ **b** *18* Or *seed* **a** *3* Or *the sons of Heth*; also in verses 5, 7, 10, 16, 18 and 20

22:7 [e]Lev 1:10
22:9 [f]Heb 11:17-19; Jas 2:21
22:12 [g]1Sa 15:22; Jas 2:21-22 [h]ver 2; Jn 3:16
22:13 [i]Ro 8:32
22:14 [j]ver 8
22:16 [k]Lk 1:73; Heb 6:13
22:17 [l]Heb 6:14* [m]Ge 15:5 [n]Ge 26:24; 32:12 [o]Ge 24:60
22:18 [p]Ge 12:2, 3; Ac 3:25*; Gal 3:8* [q]ver 10
22:20 [r]Ge 11:29
22:23 [s]Ge 24:15
23:2 [a]Jos 14:15 [b]ver 19; Ge 13:18
23:4 [c]Ge 17:8; 1Ch 29:15; Ps 105:12; Heb 11:9, 13

22:12 It is difficult to let go of what we deeply love. What could be more proper than to love your only child? Yet when we do give to God what he asks, he returns to us far more than we could dream. The spiritual benefits of his blessings far outweigh our sacrifices. Have you withheld your love, your children, or your time from him? Trust him to provide (22:8).

22:13 Notice the parallel between the ram offered on the altar as a substitute for Isaac and Christ offered on the cross as a substitute for us. Whereas God stopped Abraham from sacrificing his son, God did not spare his own Son, Jesus, from dying on the cross. If Jesus had lived, the rest of humankind would have died. God sent his only Son to die for us so that we can be spared from the eternal death we deserve and instead receive eternal life (John 3:16).

22:15–18 Abraham received abundant blessings because he did not hold back, but obeyed God. First, God gave Abraham's descendants the ability to conquer their enemies. Second, God promised Abraham children and grandchildren who would in turn bless the whole earth. People's lives would be changed as a result of knowing of the faith of Abraham and his descendants. Most often we think of blessings as gifts to be enjoyed. But when God blesses us, his blessings are intended to overflow to others.

23:1–4 In Abraham's day, death and burial were steeped in ritual and traditions. Failing to honour a dead person demonstrated the greatest possible lack of respect. An improper burial was the equivalent of a curse. Mourning was an essential part of the death ritual. Friends and relatives let out loud cries for the whole neighbourhood to hear. Because there were no funeral parlours or undertakers, these same friends and relatives helped prepare the body for burial, which usually took place on the same day because of the warm climate.

23:4–6 Abraham was in a foreign land looking for a place to bury his wife. Strangers offered to help him because he was "a mighty prince", and they respected him. Although Abraham had not es-

23:6 [d]Ge 14:14-16; 24:35

5 The Hittites replied to Abraham, 6 "Sir, listen to us. You are a mighty prince[d]
among us. Bury your dead in the choicest of our tombs. None of us will refuse you his
tomb for burying your dead."
7 Then Abraham rose and bowed down before the people of the land, the Hittites.
8 He said to them, "If you are willing to let me bury my dead, then listen to me and
intercede with Ephron son of Zohar[e] on my behalf 9 so that he will sell me the cave of
Machpelah, which belongs to him and is at the end of his field. Ask him to sell it to me
for the full price as a burial site among you."

23:8 [e]Ge 25:9

ISAAC

A name carries great authority. It sets you apart. It triggers memories. The sound of it calls you to attention anywhere.

Many Bible names accomplished even more. They were often descriptions of important facts about one's past and hopes for the future. The choice of the name *Isaac,* "he laughs", for Abraham and Sarah's son must have created a variety of feelings in them each time it was spoken. At times it must have recalled their shocked laughter at God's announcement that they would be parents in their old age. At other times, it must have brought back the joyful feelings of receiving their long-awaited answer to prayer for a child. Most important, it was a testimony to God's power in making his promise a reality.

In a family of forceful initiators, Isaac was the quiet, "mind-my-own-business" type unless he was specifically called on to take action. He was the protected only child from the time Sarah got rid of Ishmael until Abraham arranged his marriage to Rebekah.

In his own family, Isaac had the patriarchal position, but Rebekah had the power. Rather than stand his ground, Isaac found it easier to compromise or lie to avoid confrontations.

In spite of these shortcomings, Isaac was part of God's plan. The model his father gave him included a great gift of faith in the one true God. God's promise to create a great nation through which he would bless the world was passed on by Isaac to his twin sons.

It is usually not hard to identify with Isaac in his weaknesses. But consider for a moment that God works through people in spite of their shortcomings and, often, through them. As you pray, put into words your desire to be available to God. You will discover that his willingness to use you is even greater than your desire to be used.

Strengths and accomplishments:
- He was the miracle child born to Sarah and Abraham when she was 90 years old and he was 100
- He was the first descendant in fulfilment of God's promise to Abraham
- He seems to have been a caring and consistent husband, at least until his sons were born
- He demonstrated great patience

Weaknesses and mistakes:
- Under pressure he tended to lie
- In conflict he sought to avoid confrontation
- He played favourites between his sons and alienated his wife

Lessons from his life:
- Patience often brings rewards
- Both God's plans and his promises are larger than people
- God keeps his promises! He remains faithful though we are often faithless
- Playing favourites is sure to bring family conflict

Vital statistics:
- Where: The area called the Negev, in the southern part of Palestine, between Kadesh and Shur (Genesis 20:1)
- Occupation: Wealthy livestock owner
- Relatives: Parents: Abraham and Sarah. Half brother: Ishmael. Wife: Rebekah. Sons: Jacob and Esau

Key verse:
"Then God said, 'Yes, but your wife Sarah will bear you a son, and you will call him Isaac. I will establish my covenant with him as an everlasting covenant for his descendants after him' " (Genesis 17:19).

Isaac's story is told in Genesis 17:15—35:29. He is also mentioned in Romans 9:7, 8; Hebrews 11:17–20; James 2:21–24.

tablished roots in the area, his reputation was above reproach. Those who invest their time and money in serving God often earn a pleasant return on their investment—a good reputation and the respect of others.

10Ephron the Hittite was sitting among his people and he replied to Abraham in the
hearing of all the Hittites who had come to the gate[f] of his city. 11"No, my lord," he
said. "Listen to me; I give[b][g] you the field, and I give[b] you the cave that is in it. I
give[b] it to you in the presence of my people. Bury your dead."
12Again Abraham bowed down before the people of the land 13and he said to Ephron
in their hearing, "Listen to me, if you will. I will pay the price of the field. Accept it
from me so that I can bury my dead there."
14Ephron answered Abraham, 15"Listen to me, my lord; the land is worth four hundred shekels[c] of silver,[h] but what is that between me and you? Bury your dead."
16Abraham agreed to Ephron's terms and weighed out for him the price he had
named in the hearing of the Hittites: four hundred shekels of silver,[i] according to the
weight current among the merchants.
17So Ephron's field in Machpelah near Mamre[j]—both the field and the cave in it,
and all the trees within the borders of the field—was legally made over 18to Abraham
as his property in the presence of all the Hittites who had come to the gate of the city.
19Afterwards Abraham buried his wife Sarah in the cave in the field of Machpelah near
Mamre (which is at Hebron) in the land of Canaan. 20So the field and the cave in it
were legally made over[k] to Abraham by the Hittites as a burial site.

23:10 [f]Ge 34:20-24; Ru 4:4
23:11 [g]2Sa 24:23
23:15 [h]Eze 45:12
23:16 [i]Jer 32:9; Zec 11:12
23:17 [j]Ge 25:9; 49:30-32; 50:13; Ac 7:16
23:20 [k]Jer 32:10

6. Isaac and Rebekah

24 Abraham was now old and well advanced in years, and the LORD had blessed
him in every way.[a] 2He said to the chief[a] servant in his household, the one in
charge of all that he had,[b] "Put your hand under my thigh.[c] 3I want you to swear by
the LORD, the God of heaven and the God of earth,[d] that you will not get a wife for my
son[e] from the daughters of the Canaanites,[f] among whom I am living, 4but will go
to my country and my own relatives[g] and get a wife for my son Isaac."
5The servant asked him, "What if the woman is unwilling to come back with me to
this land? Shall I then take your son back to the country you came from?"
6"Make sure that you do not take my son back there," Abraham said. 7"The LORD,

24:1 [a]ver 35
24:2 [b]Ge 39:4-6 [c]ver 9; Ge 47:29
24:3 [d]Ge 14:19 [e]Ge 28:1; Dt 7:3 [f]Ge 10:15-19
24:4 [g]Ge 12:1; 28:2

[b] *11* Or *sell* [c] *15* That is, about 10 pounds (about 4.5 kilograms) [a] *2* Or *oldest*

CAVE OF MACHPELAH
Sarah died in Hebron. Abraham bought the cave of Machpelah, near Hebron, as her burial place. Abraham was also buried there, as were his son and grandson, Isaac and Jacob.

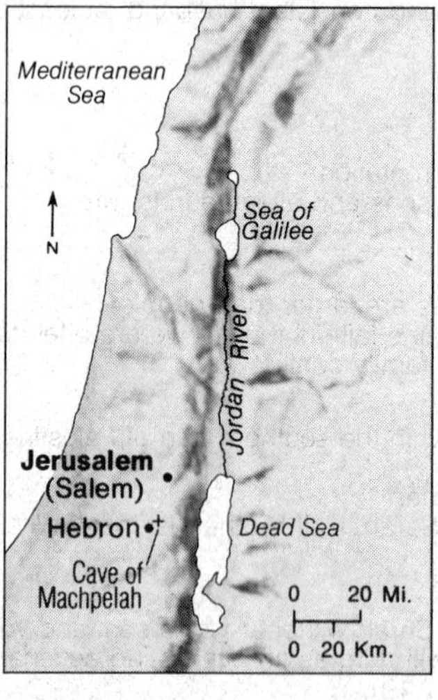

23:10–15 The polite interchange between Abraham and Ephron was typical of bargaining at that time. Ephron graciously offered to give his land to Abraham at no charge; Abraham insisted on paying for it; Ephron politely mentioned the price but said, in effect, that it wasn't important; Abraham paid the 400 shekels of silver. Both men knew what was going on as they went through the bargaining process. If Abraham had accepted the land as a gift when it was offered, he would have insulted Ephron, who then would have rescinded his offer. Many Middle Eastern shopkeepers still follow this ritual with their customers.

23:16 Four hundred shekels of silver was a high price for the piece of property Abraham bought. The Hittites weren't thrilled about foreigners buying their property, so Abraham had little bargaining leverage.

Ephron asked an outrageous price. The custom of the day was to ask double the fair market value of the land, fully expecting the buyer to offer half the stated price. Abraham, however, did not bargain. He simply paid the initial price. He was not trying to take anything he didn't deserve. Even though God had promised the land to Abraham, he did not just take it away from Ephron.

24:2, 9 In Abraham's culture, putting a hand under the thigh was how an agreement was sealed or a covenant ratified. To accomplish the same purpose, we shake hands, swear oaths, or sign documents in the presence of a witness.

24:4 Abraham wanted Isaac to marry within the family. This was a common and acceptable practice at this time that had the added advantage of avoiding intermarriage with pagan neighbours. A son's wife was usually chosen by the parents. It was common for a woman to be married in her early teens although Rebekah was probably older.

24:6 Abraham wanted Isaac to stay in Canaan, but he didn't want him to marry one of the local girls. This contrasts to the way Hagar selected a wife for Ishmael in 21:21. To have Isaac stay and marry, or send him back to marry a relative would have been easier. But Abraham wanted to obey God in the *who* as well as in the *where.* Make your obedience full and complete.

24:7
[h]Gal 3:16*
[i]Ge 12:7; 13:15
[j]Ex 23:20, 23

24:9
[k]ver 2

24:11
[l]Ex 2:15
[m]ver 13;
1Sa 9:11

24:12
[n]ver 27, 42, 48;
Ge 26:24;
Ex 3:6, 15, 16

the God of heaven, who brought me out of my father's household and my native land
and who spoke to me and promised me on oath, saying, 'To your offspring[b][h] I will
give this land'[i]—he will send his angel before you[j] so that you can get a wife for my
son from there. 8 If the woman is unwilling to come back with you, then you will be
released from this oath of mine. Only do not take my son back there." 9 So the servant
put his hand under the thigh[k] of his master Abraham and swore an oath to him concerning this matter.
10 Then the servant took ten of his master's camels and left, taking with him all kinds
of good things from his master. He set out for Aram Naharaim[c] and made his way to
the town of Nahor. 11 He made the camels kneel down near the well[l] outside the town;
it was towards evening, the time the women go out to draw water.[m]
12 Then he prayed, "O LORD, God of my master Abraham,[n] give me success today,
and show kindness to my master Abraham. 13 See, I am standing beside this spring, and

[b] 7 Or *seed* [c] 10 That is, North-west Mesopotamia

HAGAR

Escape of some kind is usually the most tempting solution to our problems. In fact, it can become a habit. Hagar was a person who used that approach. When the going got tough, she usually got going—in the other direction.

However, it is worthwhile to note that the biggest challenges Hagar faced were brought on by *other* people's choices. Sarah chose her to bear Abraham's child, and Hagar probably had little say in the matter.

It isn't hard to understand how Hagar's pregnancy caused her to look down on Sarah. But that brought on hard feelings, and Sarah consequently punished Hagar. This motivated her first escape. When she returned to the family and gave birth to Ishmael, Sarah's continued barrenness must have contributed to bitterness on both sides.

When Isaac was finally born, Sarah looked for any excuse to have Hagar and Ishmael sent away. She found it when she caught Ishmael teasing Isaac. In the desert, out of water and facing the death of her son, Hagar once again tried to escape. She walked away so she wouldn't have to watch her son die. Once again, God graciously intervened.

Have you noticed how patiently God operates to make our escape attempts fail? Have you begun to learn that escape is only a temporary solution? God's continual desire is for us to face our problems with his help. We experience his help most clearly in and through conflicts and difficulties, not away from them. Are there problems in your life for which you've been using the "Hagar solution"? Choose one of those problems, ask for God's help, and begin to face it today.

Strength and accomplishment:
- Mother of Abraham's first child, Ishmael, who became founder of the Arab nations

Weaknesses and mistakes:
- When faced with problems, she tended to run away
- Her pregnancy brought out strong feelings of pride and arrogance

Lessons from her life:
- God is faithful to his plan and promises, even when humans complicate the process
- God shows himself as one who knows us and wants to be known by us
- The New Testament uses Hagar as a symbol of those who would pursue favour with God by their own efforts, rather than by trusting in his mercy and forgiveness

Vital statistics:
- Where: Canaan and Egypt
- Occupation: Servant, mother
- Relatives: Son: Ishmael

Key verse:
"Then the angel of the LORD told her, 'Go back to your mistress and submit to her' " (Genesis 16:9).

Hagar's story is told in Genesis 16—21. She is also mentioned in Galatians 4:24, 25.

24:11 The well, the chief source of water for an entire village, was usually located outside town along the main road. Many people had to walk a mile or more for their water. They could use only what they could carry home. Farmers and shepherds would come from nearby fields to draw water for their animals. The well was a good place to meet new friends or to chat with old ones. Rebekah would have visited the well twice daily to draw water for her family.

24:12 Abraham's servant asked God for guidance in this very important task. Obviously Eliezer had learned much about faith and about God from his master. What are your family members, friends, and associates learning about God from watching you? Be like Abraham, setting an example of dependent faith. And be like Eliezer, asking God for guidance before any venture.

the daughters of the townspeople are coming out to draw water. 14May it be that when
I say to a girl, 'Please let down your jar that I may have a drink,' and she says, 'Drink,
and I'll water your camels too'—let her be the one you have chosen for your servant
Isaac. By this I will know[o] that you have shown kindness to my master."
15Before he had finished praying,[p] Rebekah[q] came out with her jar on her shoulder. She was the daughter of Bethuel son of Milcah,[r] who was the wife of Abraham's
brother Nahor.[s] 16The girl was very beautiful,[t] a virgin; no man had ever lain with
her. She went down to the spring, filled her jar and came up again.
17The servant hurried to meet her and said, "Please give me a little water from your
jar."
18"Drink,[u] my lord," she said, and quickly lowered the jar to her hands and gave
him a drink.
19After she had given him a drink, she said, "I'll draw water for your camels too,[v]
until they have finished drinking." 20So she quickly emptied her jar into the trough, ran
back to the well to draw more water, and drew enough for all his camels. 21Without
saying a word, the man watched her closely to learn whether or not the LORD had made
his journey successful.[w]
22When the camels had finished drinking, the man took out a gold nose ring[x]
weighing a beka[d] and two gold bracelets weighing ten shekels.[e] 23Then he asked,
"Whose daughter are you? Please tell me, is there room in your father's house for us
to spend the night?"
24She answered him, "I am the daughter of Bethuel, the son that Milcah bore to
Nahor.[y]" 25And she added, "We have plenty of straw and fodder, as well as room for
you to spend the night."
26Then the man bowed down and worshipped the LORD,[z] 27saying, "Praise be to
the LORD,[a] the God of my master Abraham, who has not abandoned his kindness and
faithfulness[b] to my master. As for me, the LORD has led me on the journey[c] to the
house of my master's relatives."[d]
28The girl ran and told her mother's household about these things. 29Now Rebekah
had a brother named Laban,[e] and he hurried out to the man at the spring. 30As soon
as he had seen the nose ring, and the bracelets on his sister's arms, and had heard
Rebekah tell what the man said to her, he went out to the man and found him standing
by the camels near the spring. 31"Come, you who are blessed by the LORD,"[f] he said.
"Why are you standing out here? I have prepared the house and a place for the camels."
32So the man went to the house, and the camels were unloaded. Straw and fodder
were brought for the camels, and water for him and his men to wash their feet.[g]
33Then food was set before him, but he said, "I will not eat until I have told you what
I have to say."
"Then tell us," ⌊Laban⌋ said.
34So he said, "I am Abraham's servant. 35The LORD has blessed my master abundantly,[h] and he has become wealthy. He has given him sheep and cattle, silver and
gold, menservants and maidservants, and camels and donkeys.[i] 36My master's wife

24:14 [o]Jdg 6:17, 37
24:15 [p]ver 45 [q]Ge 22:23 [r]Ge 22:20 [s]Ge 11:29
24:16 [t]Ge 26:7
24:18 [u]ver 14
24:19 [v]ver 14
24:21 [w]ver 12
24:22 [x]ver 47
24:24 [y]ver 15
24:26 [z]ver 48, 52; Ex 4:31
24:27 [a]Ex 18:10; Ru 4:14; 1Sa 25:32 [b]ver 49; Ge 32:10; Ps 98:3 [c]ver 21 [d]ver 12, 48
24:29 [e]ver 4; Ge 29:5, 12, 13
24:31 [f]Ge 26:29; Ru 3:10; Ps 115:15
24:32 [g]Ge 43:24; Jdg 19:21
24:35 [h]ver 1 [i]Ge 13:2

d *22* That is, about 1/5 ounce (about 6 grams) e *22* That is, about 4 ounces (about 115 grams)

24:14 Was it right for Abraham's servant to ask God for such a specific sign? The sign he requested was only slightly out of the ordinary. The hospitality of the day required women at the well to offer water to weary travellers, but not to their animals. Eliezer was simply asking God to show him a woman with an attitude of service—someone who would go beyond the expected. An offer to water his camels would indicate that kind of attitude. Eliezer did not ask for a woman with looks or wealth. He knew the importance of having the right heart, and he asked God to help him with his task.

24:15, 16 Rebekah had physical beauty, but the servant was looking for a sign of inner beauty. Appearance is important to us, and we spend time and money improving it. But how much effort do we put into developing our inner beauty? Patience, kindness, and joy are the beauty treatments that help us become truly lovely—on the inside.

24:18–21 Rebekah's servant spirit was clearly demonstrated as she willingly and quickly drew water for Eliezer and his camels. The pots used for carrying water were large and heavy. It took a lot of water to satisfy a thirsty camel—up to 25 gallons per camel after a week's travel. Seeing Rebekah go to work, Eliezer knew this was a woman with a heart for doing far more than the bare minimum. Do you have a servant spirit? When asked to help or when you see a need, go beyond the minimum.

24:26, 27 As soon as Abraham's servant knew that God had answered his prayer, he prayed and thanked God for his goodness and guidance. God will also use and lead us if we are available like Eliezer. And our first response should be praise and thanksgiving that God would choose to work in and through us.

24:36 [j]Ge 21:2, 10 [k]Ge 25:5
24:37 [l]ver 3
24:38 [m]ver 4
24:39 [n]ver 5
24:40 [o]ver 7
24:41 [p]ver 8
24:42 [q]ver 12
24:43 [r]ver 13

Sarah has borne him a son in her[f] old age,[j] and he has given him everything he
owns.[k] 37And my master made me swear an oath, and said, 'You must not get a wife
for my son from the daughters of the Canaanites, in whose land I live,[l] 38but go to my
father's family and to my own clan, and get a wife for my son.'[m]
39"Then I asked my master, 'What if the woman will not come back with me?'[n]
40"He replied, 'The LORD, before whom I have walked, will send his angel with
you[o] and make your journey a success, so that you can get a wife for my son from my
own clan and from my father's family. 41Then, when you go to my clan, you will be
released from my oath even if they refuse to give her to you—you will be released
from my oath.'[p]
42"When I came to the spring today, I said, 'O LORD, God of my master Abraham,
if you will, please grant success[q] to the journey on which I have come. 43See, I am
standing beside this spring;[r] if a maiden comes out to draw water and I say to her,

f 36 Or *his*

REBEKAH

Some people are initiators. They help get the ball rolling. Rebekah would easily stand out in this group. Her life was characterised by initiative. When she saw a need she took action, even though the action was not always right.

It was Rebekah's initiative that first caught the attention of Eliezer, the servant Abraham sent to find a wife for Isaac. It was common courtesy to give a drink to a stranger, but it took added character to fetch water for ten thirsty camels as well. Later, after hearing the details of Eliezer's mission, Rebekah was immediately willing to be Isaac's bride.

Several later events help us see how initiative can be misdirected. Rebekah was aware that God's plan would be channelled through Jacob, not Esau (Genesis 25:23). So not only did Jacob become her favourite; she actually planned ways to ensure that he would overshadow his older twin. Meanwhile, Isaac preferred Esau. This created a conflict between the couple. She felt justified in deceiving her husband when the time came to bless the sons, and her ingenious plan was carried out to perfection.

Most of the time we try to justify the things we choose to do. Often we attempt to add God's approval to our actions. While it is true that our actions will not spoil God's plan, it is also true that we are responsible for what we do and must always be cautious about our motives. When thinking about a course of action, are you simply seeking God's stamp of approval on something you've already decided to do? Or are you willing to set the plan aside if the principles and commands of God's word are against the action? Initiative and action are admirable and right when they are controlled by God's wisdom.

Strengths and accomplishments:
- When confronted with a need, she took immediate action
- She was accomplishment oriented

Weaknesses and mistakes:
- Her initiative was not always balanced by wisdom
- She favoured one of her sons
- She deceived her husband

Lessons from her life:
- Our actions must be guided by God's word
- God makes use even of our mistakes in his plan
- Parental favouritism hurts a family

Vital statistics:
- Where: Haran, Canaan
- Occupation: Wife, mother, household manager
- Relatives: Grandparents: Nahor and Milcah. Father: Bethuel. Husband: Isaac. Brother: Laban. Twin sons: Esau and Jacob

Key verses:
"Isaac brought her into the tent of his mother Sarah, and he married Rebekah. So she became his wife, and he loved her; and Isaac was comforted after his mother's death" (Genesis 24:67). "Isaac, who had a taste for wild game, loved Esau, but Rebekah loved Jacob" (Genesis 25:28).

Rebekah's story is told in Genesis 24—49. She is also mentioned in Romans 9:10.

24:42, 48 When Eliezer told his story to Laban, he spoke openly of God and his goodness. Often we do the opposite, afraid that we will be misunderstood or rejected or seen as too religious. Instead, we should share openly what God is doing for us.

"Please let me drink a little water from your jar,"[s] 44and if she says to me, "Drink, and
I'll draw water for your camels too," let her be the one the LORD has chosen for my
master's son.'
45"Before I finished praying in my heart,[t] Rebekah came out, with her jar on her
shoulder.[u] She went down to the spring and drew water, and I said to her, 'Please give
me a drink.'[v]
46"She quickly lowered her jar from her shoulder and said, 'Drink, and I'll water
your camels too.'[w] So I drank, and she watered the camels also.
47"I asked her, 'Whose daughter are you?'[x]
"She said, 'The daughter of Bethuel son of Nahor, whom Milcah bore to him.'[y]
"Then I put the ring in her nose and the bracelets on her arms,[z] 48and I bowed down
and worshipped the LORD.[a] I praised the LORD, the God of my master Abraham, who
had led me on the right road to get the granddaughter of my master's brother for his
son.[b] 49Now if you will show kindness and faithfulness[c] to my master, tell me; and
if not, tell me, so I may know which way to turn."
50Laban and Bethuel answered, "This is from the LORD;[d] we can say nothing to you
one way or the other.[e] 51Here is Rebekah; take her and go, and let her become the wife
of your master's son, as the LORD has directed."
52When Abraham's servant heard what they said, he bowed down to the ground
before the LORD.[f] 53Then the servant brought out gold and silver jewellery and articles of clothing and gave them to Rebekah; he also gave costly gifts[g] to her brother
and to her mother. 54Then he and the men who were with him ate and drank and spent
the night there.
When they got up the next morning, he said, "Send me on my way[h] to my master."
55But her brother and her mother replied, "Let the girl remain with us ten days or so;
then you[g] may go."
56But he said to them, "Do not detain me, now that the LORD has granted success to
my journey. Send me on my way so I may go to my master."
57Then they said, "Let's call the girl and ask her about it." 58So they called Rebekah
and asked her, "Will you go with this man?"
"I will go," she said.
59So they sent their sister Rebekah on her way, along with her nurse[i] and Abraham's servant and his men. 60And they blessed Rebekah and said to her,

"Our sister, may you increase
to thousands upon thousands;[j]
may your offspring possess
the gates of their enemies."[k]

61Then Rebekah and her maids got ready and mounted their camels and went back
with the man. So the servant took Rebekah and left.
62Now Isaac had come from Beer Lahai Roi,[l] for he was living in the Negev.[m]

[g] *55* Or *she*

24:43 [s]ver 14
24:45 [t]1Sa 1:13 [u]ver 15 [v]ver 17
24:46 [w]ver 18-19
24:47 [x]ver 23 [y]ver 24 [z]Eze 16:11-12
24:48 [a]ver 26 [b]ver 27
24:49 [c]Ge 47:29; Jos 2:14
24:50 [d]Ps 118:23 [e]Ge 31:7, 24, 29, 42
24:52 [f]ver 26
24:53 [g]ver 10, 22
24:54 [h]ver 56, 59
24:59 [i]Ge 35:8
24:60 [j]Ge 17:16 [k]Ge 22:17
24:62 [l]Ge 16:14; 25:11 [m]Ge 20:1

ELIEZER: PROFILE OF A TRUE SERVANT

Have you ever approached a responsibility with this kind of single-mindedness and careful planning, while ultimately depending on God?

24:3, 9	Accepted the challenge
24:5	Examined alternatives
24:9	Promised to follow instructions
24:12–14	Made a plan
24:12–14	Submitted the plan to God
24:12–14	Prayed for guidance
24:12–14	Devised a strategy with room for God to operate
24:21	Waited
24:21	Watched closely
24:26	Accepted the answer thankfully
24:34–49	Explained the situation to concerned parties
24:56	Refused unnecessary delay
24:66	Followed through with entire plan

24:60 "May your offspring possess the gates of their enemies" means "May you overcome all your enemies".

63He went out to the field one evening to meditate,[h][n] and as he looked up, he saw camels approaching. 64Rebekah also looked up and saw Isaac. She got down from her camel 65and asked the servant, "Who is that man in the field coming to meet us?"

"He is my master," the servant answered. So she took her veil and covered herself.

66Then the servant told Isaac all he had done. 67Isaac brought her into the tent of his mother Sarah, and he married Rebekah.[o] So she became his wife, and he loved her;[p] and Isaac was comforted after his mother's death.[q]

7. Abraham dies

The Death of Abraham

25 Abraham took[a] another wife, whose name was Keturah. 2She bore him Zimran, Jokshan, Medan, Midian, Ishbak and Shuah.[a] 3Jokshan was the father of Sheba and Dedan; the descendants of Dedan were the Asshurites, the Letushites and the Leummites. 4The sons of Midian were Ephah, Epher, Hanoch, Abida and Eldaah. All these were descendants of Keturah.

5Abraham left everything he owned to Isaac.[b] 6But while he was still living, he gave gifts to the sons of his concubines[c] and sent them away from his son Isaac[d] to the land of the east.

7Altogether, Abraham lived a hundred and seventy-five years. 8Then Abraham breathed his last and died at a good old age,[e] an old man and full of years; and he was gathered to his people.[f] 9His sons Isaac and Ishmael buried him[g] in the cave of Machpelah near Mamre, in the field of Ephron son of Zohar the Hittite,[h] 10the field Abraham had bought from the Hittites.[b][i] There Abraham was buried with his wife Sarah. 11After Abraham's death, God blessed his son Isaac, who then lived near Beer Lahai Roi.[j]

Ishmael's Sons

12This is the account of Abraham's son Ishmael, whom Sarah's maidservant, Hagar[k] the Egyptian, bore to Abraham.[l]

13These are the names of the sons of Ishmael, listed in the order of their birth: Nebaioth the firstborn of Ishmael, Kedar, Adbeel, Mibsam, 14Mishma, Dumah, Massa, 15Hadad, Tema, Jetur, Naphish and Kedemah. 16These were the sons of Ishmael, and these are the names of the twelve tribal rulers[m] according to their settlements and camps. 17Altogether, Ishmael lived a hundred and thirty-seven years. He breathed his last and died, and he was gathered to his people.[n] 18His descendants settled in the area from Havilah to Shur, near the border of Egypt, as you go towards Asshur. And they lived in hostility towards[c] all their brothers.[o]

E. THE STORY OF ISAAC (25:19–28:9)

Isaac inherited everything from his father, including God's promise to make his descendants into a great nation. As a boy, Isaac did not resist as his father prepared to sacrifice him, and as a man, he gladly accepted the wife that others chose for him. Through Isaac, we learn how to let God guide our life and place his will ahead of our own.

1. Jacob and Esau

19This is the account of Abraham's son Isaac.

Abraham became the father of Isaac, 20and Isaac was forty years old[p] when he married Rebekah[q] daughter of Bethuel the Aramean from Paddan Aram[d] and sister of Laban[r] the Aramean.

h *63* The meaning of the Hebrew for this word is uncertain. **a** *1* Or *had taken* **b** *10* Or *the sons of Heth* **c** *18* Or *lived to the east of* **d** *20* That is, North-west Mesopotamia

24:63 [n]Ps 1:2; 77:12; 119:15, 27, 48, 97, 148; 143:5; 145:5
24:67 [o]Ge 25:20 [p]Ge 29:18, 20 [q]Ge 23:1-2
25:2 [a]1Ch 1:32, 33
25:5 [b]Ge 24:36
25:6 [c]Ge 22:24 [d]Ge 21:10, 14
25:8 [e]Ge 15:15 [f]ver 17; Ge 35:29; 49:29, 33
25:9 [g]Ge 35:29 [h]Ge 50:13
25:10 [i]Ge 23:16
25:11 [j]Ge 16:14
25:12 [k]Ge 16:1 [l]Ge 16:15
25:16 [m]Ge 17:20
25:17 [n]ver 8
25:18 [o]Ge 16:12
25:20 [p]ver 26; Ge 26:34 [q]Ge 24:67 [r]Ge 24:29

24:64, 65 When Rebekah learned that the man coming to greet them was Isaac, her husband-to-be, she followed two oriental customs. She dismounted from her camel to show respect, and she placed a veil over her face as a bride.

25:1-6 Abraham took another wife, Keturah, after Sarah died. Although the sons and grandson of Abraham and Keturah received many gifts from Abraham, all his property and authority went to Isaac, his principal heir.

21 Isaac prayed to the LORD on behalf of his wife, because she was barren. The LORD
answered his prayer,[s] and his wife Rebekah became pregnant. 22 The babies jostled
each other within her, and she said, "Why is this happening to me?" So she went to
enquire of the LORD.[t]
23 The LORD said to her,

> "Two nations[u] are in your womb,
> and two peoples from within you will be separated;
> one people will be stronger than the other,
> and the older will serve the younger.[v]"

24 When the time came for her to give birth, there were twin boys in her womb.
25 The first to come out was red, and his whole body was like a hairy garment;[w] so they
named him Esau.[e] 26 After this, his brother came out, with his hand grasping Esau's
heel;[x] so he was named Jacob.[f][y] Isaac was sixty years old when Rebekah gave birth
to them.
27 The boys grew up, and Esau became a skilful hunter, a man of the open country,[z]
while Jacob was a quiet man, staying among the tents. 28 Isaac, who had a taste for wild
game,[a] loved Esau, but Rebekah loved Jacob.[b]
29 Once when Jacob was cooking some stew, Esau came in from the open country,
famished. 30 He said to Jacob, "Quick, let me have some of that red stew! I'm famished!" (That is why he was also called Edom.[g])
31 Jacob replied, "First sell me your birthright."
32 "Look, I am about to die," Esau said. "What good is the birthright to me?"
33 But Jacob said, "Swear to me first." So he swore an oath to him, selling his birthright[c] to Jacob.
34 Then Jacob gave Esau some bread and some lentil stew. He ate and drank, and
then got up and left.
So Esau despised his birthright.

2. Isaac and Abimelech

26 Now there was a famine in the land[a]—besides the earlier famine of Abraham's
time—and Isaac went to Abimelech king of the Philistines in Gerar.[b] 2 The
LORD appeared[c] to Isaac and said, "Do not go down to Egypt; live in the land where

e 25 *Esau* may mean *hairy*; he was also called Edom, which means *red*. f 26 *Jacob* means *he grasps the heel* (figuratively, *he deceives*). g 30 *Edom* means *red*.

25:21 s 1Ch 5:20; 2Ch 33:13; Ezr 8:23; Ps 127:3; Ro 9:10
25:22 t 1Sa 9:9; 10:22
25:23 u Ge 17:4 v Ge 27:29, 40; Mal 1:3; Ro 9:11-12*
25:25 w Ge 27:11
25:26 x Hos 12:3 y Ge 27:36
25:27 z Ge 27:3, 5
25:28 a Ge 27: 19 b Ge 27:6
25:33 c Ge 27:36; Heb 12:16
26:1 a Ge 12:10 b Ge 20:1
26:2 c Ge 12:7; 17:1; 18:1 d Ge 12:1

25:21 As Isaac pleaded with God for children, so the Bible encourages us to ask and even plead for our most personal and important requests. God wants to grant our requests, but he wants us to ask him. Even then, as Isaac learned, God may decide to withhold his answer for a while in order to (1) deepen our insight into what we really need, (2) broaden our appreciation of his answers, or (3) allow us to mature so we can use his gifts more wisely.

25:31 A birthright was a special honour given to the firstborn son. It included a double portion of the family inheritance along with the honour of one day becoming the family's leader. The oldest son could sell his birthright or give it away if he chose, but in so doing, he would lose both material goods and his leadership position. By trading his birthright, Esau showed complete disregard for the spiritual blessings that would have come his way if he had kept it. In effect, Esau "despised" his birthright (25:34).

25:32, 33 Esau traded the lasting benefits of his birthright for the immediate pleasure of food. He acted on impulse, satisfying his immediate desires without pausing to consider the long-term consequences of what he was about to do. We can fall into the same trap. When we see something we want, our first impulse is to get it. At first we feel intensely satisfied and sometimes even powerful because we have obtained what we set out to get. But immediate pleasure often loses sight of the future. We can avoid making Esau's mistake by comparing the short-term satisfaction with its long-term consequences before we act.

Esau exaggerated his hunger. "I am about to die," he said. This thought made his choice much easier because if he was starving, what good was an inheritance anyway? The pressure of the moment distorted his perspective and made his decision seem urgent. We often experience similar pressures. For example, when we feel sexual pressure, a marriage vow may seem unimportant. We might feel such great pressure in one area that nothing else seems to matter and we lose our perspective. Getting through that

26:3
[e] Ge 20:1; 28:15
[f] Ge 12:2; 22:16-18
[g] Ge 12:7; 13:15

I tell you to live.[d] 3 Stay in this land for a while,[e] and I will be with you and will bless
you.[f] For to you and your descendants I will give all these lands[g] and will confirm

---

ESAU

Common sense isn't all that common. In fact, the common thread in many decisions is that they don't make sense. Esau's life was filled with choices he must have regretted bitterly. He appears to have been a person who found it hard to consider consequences, reacting to the need of the moment without realising what he was giving up to meet that need. Trading his birthright for a bowl of stew was the clearest example of this weakness. He also chose wives in direct opposition to his parents' wishes. He learned the hard way.

What are you willing to trade for the things you want? Do you find yourself, at times, willing to negotiate *anything* for what you feel you need *now?* Do your family, spouse, integrity, body, or soul get included in these deals? Do you sometimes feel that the important parts of life escaped while you were grabbing for something else?

If so, your initial response, like Esau's, may be deep anger. In itself that isn't wrong, as long as you direct the energy of that anger towards a solution and not towards yourself or others as the cause of the problem. Your greatest need is to find a focal point other than "what I need now". The only worthy focal point is God. A relationship with him will not only give an ultimate purpose to your life; it will also be a daily guideline for living. Meet him in the pages of the Bible.

Strengths and accomplishments:
- Ancestor of the Edomites
- Known for his archery skill
- Able to forgive after explosive anger

Weaknesses and mistakes:
- When faced with important decisions, tended to choose according to the immediate need rather than the long-range effect
- Angered his parents by poor marriage choices

Lessons from his life:
- God allows certain events in our lives to accomplish his overall purposes, but we are still responsible for our actions
- Consequences are important to consider
- It is possible to have great anger and yet not sin

Vital statistics:
- Where: Canaan
- Occupation: Skilful hunter
- Relatives: Parents: Isaac and Rebekah. Brother: Jacob. Wives: Judith, Basemath, and Mahalath

Key verses:
"Make every effort to live in peace with all men and to be holy; without holiness no-one will see the Lord. See to it that no-one misses the grace of God and that no bitter root grows up to cause trouble and defile many. See that no-one is sexually immoral, or is godless like Esau, who for a single meal sold his inheritance rights as the oldest son. Afterwards, as you know, when he wanted to inherit this blessing, he was rejected. He could bring about no change of mind, though he sought the blessing with tears" (Hebrews 12:14–17).

Esau's story is told in Genesis 25—36. He is also mentioned in Malachi 1:2, 3; Romans 9:13; Hebrews 12:16, 17.

---

short, pressure-filled moment is often the most difficult part of overcoming a temptation.

26:1 The Philistine tribe would become one of Israel's fiercest enemies. The Philistines were one group of a number of migrating sea peoples from the Aegean Sea who settled in Palestine. They arrived by way of Crete and Cyprus and were used as mercenaries by Canaanite rulers. These people, living along the southwest coast, were few but ferocious in battle. Although friendly to Isaac, this small group was the forerunner of the nation that would plague Israel during the time of Joshua, the judges, and David. This King Abimelech was not the same Abimelech that Abraham encountered (chapter 22). *Abimelech* may have been a dynastic name of the Philistine rulers.

the oath I swore to your father Abraham. 4 I will make your descendants as numerous
as the stars in the sky[h] and will give them all these lands, and through your offspring[a]
all nations on earth will be blessed,[i] 5 because Abraham obeyed me[j] and kept my
requirements, my commands, my decrees and my laws." 6 So Isaac stayed in Gerar.
7 When the men of that place asked him about his wife, he said, "She is my sister,[k]"
because he was afraid to say, "She is my wife." He thought, "The men of this place
might kill me on account of Rebekah, because she is beautiful."
8 When Isaac had been there a long time, Abimelech king of the Philistines looked
down from a window and saw Isaac caressing his wife Rebekah. 9 So Abimelech summoned Isaac and said, "She is really your wife! Why did you say, 'She is my sister'?"
Isaac answered him, "Because I thought I might lose my life on account of her."
10 Then Abimelech said, "What is this you have done to us?[l] One of the men might
well have slept with your wife, and you would have brought guilt upon us."
11 So Abimelech gave orders to all the people: "Anyone who molests[m] this man or
his wife shall surely be put to death."
12 Isaac planted crops in that land and the same year reaped a hundredfold, because
the LORD blessed him.[n] 13 The man became rich, and his wealth continued to grow
until he became very wealthy.[o] 14 He had so many flocks and herds and servants[p] that
the Philistines envied him.[q] 15 So all the wells[r] that his father's servants had dug in
the time of his father Abraham, the Philistines stopped up,[s] filling them with earth.
16 Then Abimelech said to Isaac, "Move away from us; you have become too powerful for us.[t]"
17 So Isaac moved away from there and encamped in the Valley of Gerar and settled
there. 18 Isaac reopened the wells[u] that had been dug in the time of his father Abraham, which the Philistines had stopped up after Abraham died, and he gave them the
same names his father had given them.
19 Isaac's servants dug in the valley and discovered a well of fresh water there. 20 But
the herdsmen of Gerar quarrelled with Isaac's herdsmen and said, "The water is
ours!"[v] So he named the well Esek,[b] because they disputed with him. 21 Then they
dug another well, but they quarrelled over that one also; so he named it Sitnah.[c] 22 He

[a] 4 Or *seed* [b] 20 *Esek* means *dispute.* [c] 21 *Sitnah* means *opposition.*

26:4 [h] Ge 15:5; 22:17; Ex 32:13 [i] Ge 12:3; 22:18; Gal 3:8
26:5 [j] Ge 22:16
26:7 [k] Ge 12:13; 20:2, 12; Pr 29:25
26:10 [l] Ge 20:9
26:11 [m] Ps 105:15
26:12 [n] ver 3; Job 42:12
26:13 [o] Pr 10:22
26:14 [p] Ge 24:36 [q] Ge 37:11
26:15 [r] Ge 21:30 [s] Ge 21:25
26:16 [t] Ex 1:9
26:18 [u] Ge 21:30
26:20 [v] Ge 21:25

ISAAC'S MOVE TO GERAR
Isaac had settled near Beer Lahai Roi ("the well of the Living One who sees me"), where his sons, Jacob and Esau, were born. A famine drove him to Gerar. But when he became wealthy, his jealous neighbours asked him to leave. From Gerar he moved to Beersheba.

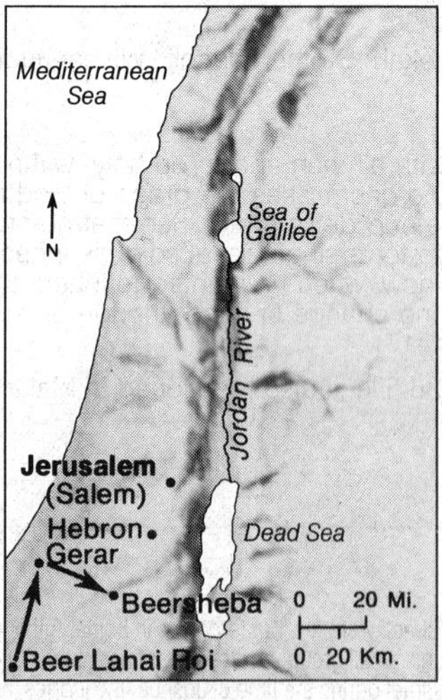

26:7–11 Isaac was afraid that the men in Gerar would kill him to get his beautiful wife, Rebekah. So he lied, claiming that Rebekah was his sister. Where did he learn that trick? He may have known about the actions of his father, Abraham (see 12:10–14 and 20:1–4). Parents help shape the world's future by the way they shape their children's values. The first step towards helping children live rightly is for the parents to live rightly. Your actions are often copied by those closest to you. What kind of example are you setting for your children?

26:12–16 God kept his promise to bless Isaac. The neighbouring Philistines grew jealous because everything Isaac did seemed to go right. So they plugged his wells and tried to get rid of him. Jealousy is a dividing force strong enough to tear apart the mightiest of nations or the closest of friends. It forces you to separate yourself from what you were longing for in the first place. When you find yourself becoming jealous of others, try thanking God for their good fortune. Before striking out in anger, consider what you could lose—a friend, a job, a spouse?

26:17, 18 The desolate Gerar area was located on the edge of a desert. Water was as precious as gold. If someone dug a well, he was staking a claim to the land. Some wells had locks to keep thieves from stealing the water. To "stop" or plug up someone's well was an act of war; it was one of the most serious crimes in the land. Isaac had every right to fight back when the Philistines ruined his wells, and yet he chose to keep the peace. In the end, the Philistines respected him for his patience.

26:17–22 Three times Isaac and his men dug new wells. When the first two disputes arose, Isaac moved on. Finally there was enough room for everyone. Rather than start a huge conflict, Isaac compromised for the sake of peace. Would you be willing to forsake an important position or valuable possession to keep peace? Ask God for the wisdom to know when to withdraw and when to stand and fight.

26:22 [w]Ge 17:6; Ex 1:7

moved on from there and dug another well, and no-one quarrelled over it. He named
it Rehoboth,[d] saying, "Now the LORD has given us room and we will flourish[w] in the
land."
23From there he went up to Beersheba. 24That night the LORD appeared to him and
said, "I am the God of your father Abraham.[x] Do not be afraid,[y] for I am with you;

26:24 [x]Ge 24:12; Ex 3:6 [y]Ge 15:1

[d] 22 *Rehoboth* means *room*.

JACOB

Abraham, Isaac, and Jacob are among the most significant people in the Old Testament. It is important to realise that this significance is not based upon their personal characters, but upon the character of God. They were all men who earned the grudging respect and even fear of their peers; they were wealthy and powerful, and yet each was capable of lying, deceit, and selfishness. They were not the perfect heroes we might have expected; instead, they were just like us, trying to please God, but often falling short.

Jacob was the third link in God's plan to start a nation from Abraham. The success of that plan was more often in spite of than because of Jacob's life. Before Jacob was born, God promised that his plan would be worked out through Jacob and not his twin brother, Esau. Although Jacob's methods were not always respectable, his skill, determination, and patience have to be admired. As we follow him from birth to death, we are able to see God's work.

Jacob's life had four stages, each marked by a personal encounter with God. In the first stage, Jacob lived up to his name, which means "he grasps the heel" (figuratively, "he deceives"). He grabbed Esau's heel at birth, and by the time he fled from home, he had also grabbed his brother's birthright and blessing. During his flight, God first appeared to him. Not only did God confirm to Jacob his blessing, but he awakened in Jacob a personal knowledge of himself. In the second stage, Jacob experienced life from the other side, being manipulated and deceived by Laban. But there is a curious change: the Jacob of stage one would simply have left Laban, whereas the Jacob of stage two, after deciding to leave, waited six years for God's permission. In the third stage, Jacob was in a new role as grabber. This time, by the Jordan River, he grabbed on to God and wouldn't let go. He realised his dependence on the God who had continued to bless him. His relationship to God became essential to his life, and his name was changed to Israel, "he struggles with God". Jacob's last stage of life was to *be* grabbed—God achieved a firm hold on him. In responding to Joseph's invitation to come to Egypt, Jacob was clearly unwilling to make a move without God's approval.

Can you think of times when God has made himself known to you? Do you allow yourself to meet him as you study his word? What difference have these experiences made in your life? Are you more like the young Jacob, forcing God to track you down in the desert of your own plans and mistakes? Or are you more like the Jacob who placed his desires and plans before God for his approval before taking any action?

Strengths and accomplishments:
- Father of the 12 tribes of Israel
- Third in the Abrahamic line of God's plan
- Determined, willing to work long and hard for what he wanted
- Good businessman

Weaknesses and mistakes:
- When faced with conflict, relied on his own resources rather than going to God for help
- Tended to accumulate wealth for its own sake

Lessons from his life:
- Security does not lie in the accumulation of goods
- All human intentions and actions—for good or evil—are woven by God into his ongoing plan

Vital statistics:
- Where: Canaan
- Occupation: Shepherd, livestock owner
- Relatives: Parents: Isaac and Rebekah. Brother: Esau. Father-in-law: Laban. Wives: Rachel and Leah. Twelve sons and one daughter are mentioned in the Bible

Key verse:
"I am with you and will watch over you wherever you go, and I will bring you back to this land. I will not leave you until I have done what I have promised you" (Genesis 28:15).

Jacob's story is told in Genesis 25—50. He is also mentioned in Hosea 12:2–5; Matthew 1:2; 22:32; Acts 3:13; 7:46; Romans 9:11–13; 11:26; Hebrews 11:9, 20, 21.

I will bless you and will increase the number of your descendants[z] for the sake of my
servant Abraham."[a]
25 Isaac built an altar[b] there and called on the name of the LORD. There he pitched
his tent, and there his servants dug a well.
26 Meanwhile, Abimelech had come to him from Gerar, with Ahuzzath his personal
adviser and Phicol the commander of his forces.[c] 27 Isaac asked them, "Why have you
come to me, since you were hostile to me and sent me away?[d]"
28 They answered, "We saw clearly that the LORD was with you;[e] so we said, 'There
ought to be a sworn agreement between us'—between us and you. Let us make a treaty
with you 29 that you will do us no harm, just as we did not molest you but always treated
you well and sent you away in peace. And now you are blessed by the LORD."[f]
30 Isaac then made a feast[g] for them, and they ate and drank. 31 Early the next morning the men swore an oath[h] to each other. Then Isaac sent them on their way, and they
left him in peace.
32 That day Isaac's servants came and told him about the well they had dug. They
said, "We've found water!" 33 He called it Shibah,[e] and to this day the name of the
town has been Beersheba.[f][i]
34 When Esau was forty years old,[j] he married Judith daughter of Beeri the Hittite,
and also Basemath daughter of Elon the Hittite.[k] 35 They were a source of grief to
Isaac and Rebekah.[l]

3. Jacob gets Isaac's blessing

27 When Isaac was old and his eyes were so weak that he could no longer see,[a] he
called for Esau his older son[b] and said to him, "My son."
"Here I am," he answered.
2 Isaac said, "I am now an old man and don't know the day of my death.[c] 3 Now
then, get your weapons—your quiver and bow—and go out to the open country[d] to
hunt some wild game for me. 4 Prepare me the kind of tasty food I like and bring it to
me to eat, so that I may give you my blessing[e] before I die."
5 Now Rebekah was listening as Isaac spoke to his son Esau. When Esau left for the
open country to hunt game and bring it back, 6 Rebekah said to her son Jacob,[f] "Look,
I overheard your father say to your brother Esau, 7 'Bring me some game and prepare
me some tasty food to eat, so that I may give you my blessing in the presence of the
LORD before I die.' 8 Now, my son, listen carefully and do what I tell you:[g] 9 Go out
to the flock and bring me two choice young goats, so that I can prepare some tasty food
for your father, just the way he likes it. 10 Then take it to your father to eat, so that he
may give you his blessing before he dies."
11 Jacob said to Rebekah his mother, "But my brother Esau is a hairy man,[h] and I'm

[e] 33 *Shibah* can mean *oath* or *seven*. [f] 33 *Beersheba* can mean *well of the oath* or *well of seven.*

26:24 [z]ver 4 [a]Ge 17:7
26:25 [b]Ge 12:7, 8; 13:4, 18; Ps 116:17
26:26 [c]Ge 21:22
26:27 [d]ver 16
26:28 [e]Ge 21:22
26:29 [f]Ge 24:31; Ps 115:15
26:30 [g]Ge 19:3
26:31 [h]Ge 21:31
26:33 [i]Ge 21:14
26:34 [j]Ge 25:20 [k]Ge 28:9; 36:2
26:35 [l]Ge 27:46
27:1 [a]Ge 48:10; 1Sa 3:2 [b]Ge 25:25
27:2 [c]Ge 47:29
27:3 [d]Ge 25:27
27:4 [e]ver 10, 25, 31; Ge 49:28; Dt 33:1; Heb 11:20
27:6 [f]Ge 25:28
27:8 [g]ver 13, 43
27:11 [h]Ge 25:25

26:26–31 With his enemies wanting to make a peace treaty, Isaac was quick to respond, turning the occasion into a celebration. We should be just as receptive to those who want to make peace with us. When God's influence in our lives attracts people—even enemies—we must take the opportunity to reach out to them with God's love.

26:34, 35 Esau married pagan women, and this upset his parents greatly. Most parents can be a source of good advice, because they have a lifetime of insight into their children's characters. You may not agree with everything your parents say, but at least talk with them and listen carefully. This will help avoid the hard feelings Esau experienced.

27:5–10 When Rebekah learned that Isaac was preparing to bless Esau, she quickly devised a plan to trick him into blessing Jacob instead. Although God had already told her that Jacob would become the family leader (25:23–26), Rebekah took matters into her own hands. She resorted to doing something wrong to try to bring about what God had already said would happen. For Rebekah, the end justified the means. No matter how good we think our goals are, we should not attempt to achieve them by doing what is wrong. Would God approve of the methods you are using to accomplish your goals?

27:11, 12 How we react to a moral dilemma often exposes our real motives. Frequently we are more worried about getting caught than about doing what is right. Jacob did not seem concerned about the deceitfulness of his mother's plan; instead he was afraid of getting into trouble while carrying it out. If you are worried about getting caught, you are probably in a position that is less than honest. Let your fear of getting caught be a warning to do right. Jacob paid a huge price for carrying out this dishonest plan.

27:11–13 Jacob hesitated when he heard Rebekah's deceitful plan. Although he questioned it for the wrong reason (fear of getting caught), he protested and thus gave her one last chance to reconsider. But Rebekah had become so wrapped up in her plan that she no longer saw clearly what she was doing. Sin had trapped her and was degrading her character. Correcting yourself in the middle of doing wrong may bring hurt and disappointment, but it will also bring freedom from sin's control.

a man with smooth skin. 12 What if my father touches me?[i] I would appear to be
tricking him and would bring down a curse on myself rather than a blessing."
13 His mother said to him, "My son, let the curse fall on me.[j] Just do what I say;[k]
go and get them for me."
14 So he went and got them and brought them to his mother, and she prepared some
tasty food, just the way his father liked it. 15 Then Rebekah took the best clothes[l] of
Esau her older son, which she had in the house, and put them on her younger son
Jacob. 16 She also covered his hands and the smooth part of his neck with the goatskins.
17 Then she handed to her son Jacob the tasty food and the bread she had made.
18 He went to his father and said, "My father."
"Yes, my son," he answered. "Who is it?"
19 Jacob said to his father, "I am Esau your firstborn. I have done as you told me.
Please sit up and eat some of my game so that you may give me your blessing."[m]
20 Isaac asked his son, "How did you find it so quickly, my son?"
"The LORD your God gave me success,[n]" he replied.
21 Then Isaac said to Jacob, "Come near so I can touch you,[o] my son, to know
whether you really are my son Esau or not."
22 Jacob went close to his father Isaac, who touched him and said, "The voice is the
voice of Jacob, but the hands are the hands of Esau." 23 He did not recognise him, for
his hands were hairy like those of his brother Esau;[p] so he blessed him. 24 "Are you
really my son Esau?" he asked.
"I am," he replied.
25 Then he said, "My son, bring me some of your game to eat, so that I may give you
my blessing."[q]
Jacob brought it to him and he ate; and he brought some wine and he drank. 26 Then
his father Isaac said to him, "Come here, my son, and kiss me."
27 So he went to him and kissed him[r]. When Isaac caught the smell of his clothes,[s]
he blessed him and said,

"Ah, the smell of my son
  is like the smell of a field
  that the LORD has blessed.[t]
28 May God give you of heaven's dew[u]
  and of earth's richness[v]—
  an abundance of grain and new wine.[w]
29 May nations serve you
  and peoples bow down to you.[x]
Be lord over your brothers,
  and may the sons of your mother bow down to you.[y]
May those who curse you be cursed
  and those who bless you be blessed.[z]"

30 After Isaac finished blessing him and Jacob had scarcely left his father's presence,
his brother Esau came in from hunting. 31 He too prepared some tasty food and brought
it to his father. Then he said to him, "My father, sit up and eat some of my game, so
that you may give me your blessing."[a]
32 His father Isaac asked him, "Who are you?"[b]
"I am your son," he answered, "your firstborn, Esau."

27:12 [i] ver 22
27:13 [j] Mt 27:25 [k] ver 8
27:15 [l] ver 27
27:19 [m] ver 4
27:20 [n] Ge 24:12
27:21 [o] ver 12
27:23 [p] ver 16
27:25 [q] ver 4
27:27 [r] Heb 11:20 [s] SS 4:11 [t] Ps 65:9-13
27:28 [u] Dt 33:13 [v] ver 39 [w] Ge 45:18; Nu 18:12; Dt 33:28
27:29 [x] Isa 45:14, 23; 49:7, 23 [y] Ge 9:25; 25:23; 37:7 [z] Ge 12:3; Nu 24:9; Zep 2:8
27:31 [a] ver 4
27:32 [b] ver 18

27:24 Although Jacob got the blessing he wanted, deceiving his father cost him dearly. These are some of the consequences of that deceit: (1) he never saw his mother again; (2) his brother wanted to kill him; (3) he was deceived by his uncle, Laban; (4) his family became torn by strife; (5) Esau became the founder of an enemy nation; (6) he was exiled from his family for years. Ironically, Jacob would have received the birthright and blessing anyway (25:23). Imagine how different his life would have been had he and his mother waited for God to work his way, in his time!

33 Isaac trembled violently and said, "Who was it, then, that hunted game and
brought it to me? I ate it just before you came and I blessed him—and indeed he will
be blessed![c]"
34 When Esau heard his father's words, he burst out with a loud and bitter cry[d] and
said to his father, "Bless me—me too, my father!"
35 But he said, "Your brother came deceitfully[e] and took your blessing."
36 Esau said, "Isn't he rightly named Jacob?[a][f] He has deceived me these two times:
He took my birthright,[g] and now he's taken my blessing!" Then he asked, "Haven't
you reserved any blessing for me?"
37 Isaac answered Esau, "I have made him lord over you and have made all his relatives his servants, and I have sustained him with grain and new wine.[h] So what can I
possibly do for you, my son?"
38 Esau said to his father, "Do you have only one blessing, my father? Bless me too,
my father!" Then Esau wept aloud.[i]
39 His father Isaac answered him,

"Your dwelling will be
away from the earth's richness,
away from the dew[j] of heaven above.
40 You will live by the sword
and you will serve[k] your brother.[l]
But when you grow restless,
you will throw his yoke
from off your neck.[m]"

Jacob Flees to Laban

41 Esau held a grudge[n] against Jacob[o] because of the blessing his father had given
him. He said to himself, "The days of mourning[p] for my father are near; then I will kill
my brother Jacob."[q]
42 When Rebekah was told what her older son Esau had said, she sent for her
younger son Jacob and said to him, "Your brother Esau is consoling himself with the
thought of killing you. 43 Now then, my son, do what I say:[r] Flee at once to my brother
Laban[s] in Haran.[t] 44 Stay with him for a while[u] until your brother's fury subsides.
45 When your brother is no longer angry with you and forgets what you did to him,[v]
I'll send word for you to come back from there. Why should I lose both of you in one
day?"
46 Then Rebekah said to Isaac, "I'm disgusted with living because of these Hittite
women. If Jacob takes a wife from among the women of this land, from Hittite women
like these, my life will not be worth living."[w]
28 So Isaac called for Jacob and blessed[a] him and commanded him: "Do not
marry a Canaanite woman.[a] 2 Go at once to Paddan Aram,[b] to the house of
your mother's father Bethuel.[b] Take a wife for yourself there, from among the daughters of Laban, your mother's brother. 3 May God Almighty[c][c] bless you and make you

27:33 [c] ver 29; Ge 28:3, 4; Ro 11:29
27:34 [d] Heb 12:17
27:35 [e] Jer 9:4; 12:6
27:36 [f] Ge 25:26 [g] Ge 25:33
27:37 [h] ver 28
27:38 [i] Heb 12:17
27:39 [j] ver 28
27:40 [k] 2Sa 8:14 [l] Ge 25:23 [m] 2Ki 8:20-22
27:41 [n] Ge 37:4 [o] Ge 32:11 [p] Ge 50:4, 10 [q] Ob 1:10
27:43 [r] ver 8 [s] Ge 24:29 [t] Ge 11:31
27:44 [u] Ge 31:38, 41
27:45 [v] ver 35
27:46 [w] Ge 26:35
28:1 [a] Ge 24:3
28:2 [b] Ge 25:20
28:3 [c] Ge 17:1

[a] *36 Jacob* means *he grasps the heel* (figuratively, *he deceives*). [a] *1* Or *greeted* [b] *2* That is, North-west Mesopotamia; also in verses 5, 6 and 7 [c] *3* Hebrew *El-Shaddai*

27:33 In ancient times, a person's word was binding (much like a written contract today), especially when it was a formal oath. This is why Isaac's blessing was irrevocable.

27:33–37 Before the father died, he performed a ceremony of blessing, in which he officially handed over the birthright to the rightful heir. Although the firstborn son was entitled to the birthright, it was not actually his until the blessing was pronounced. Before the blessing was given, the father could take the birthright away from the oldest son and give it to a more deserving son. But after the blessing was given, the birthright could no longer be taken away. This is why fathers usually waited until late in life to pronounce the blessing. Although Jacob had been given the birthright by his older brother years before, he still needed his father's blessing to make it binding.

27:41 Esau was so angry at Jacob that he failed to see his own wrong in giving away the birthright in the first place. Jealous anger blinds us to the benefits we have and makes us dwell on what we don't have.

27:41 When Esau lost the valuable family blessing, his future suddenly changed. Reacting in anger, he decided to kill Jacob. When you lose something of great value, or if others conspire against you and succeed, anger is the first and most natural reaction. But you can control your feelings by (1) recognising your reaction for what it is, (2) praying for strength, and (3) asking God for help to see the opportunities that even your bad situation may provide.

28:3 [d]Ge 17:6
28:4 [e]Ge 12:2, 3 [f]Ge 17:8
28:5 [g]Hos 12:12 [h]Ge 24:29
28:6 [i]ver 1
28:8 [j]Ge 24:3 [k]Ge 26:35
28:9 [l]Ge 25:13 [m]Ge 26:34
28:10 [n]Ge 11:31
28:12 [o]Ge 20:3 [p]Jn 1:51
28:13 [q]Ge 12:7; 35:7, 9; 48:3 [r]Ge 26:24 [s]Ge 13:15; 35:12
28:14 [t]Ge 26:4 [u]Ge 13:14 [v]Ge 12:3; 18:18; 22:18; Gal 3:8
28:15 [w]Ge 26:3; 48:21 [x]Nu 6:24; Ps 121:5, 7-8 [y]Dt 31:6, 8 [z]Nu 23:19
28:17 [a]Ex 3:5; Jos 5:15

fruitful[d] and increase your numbers until you become a community of peoples. 4 May
he give you and your descendants the blessing given to Abraham,[e] so that you may
take possession of the land where you now live as an alien,[f] the land God gave to
Abraham." 5 Then Isaac sent Jacob on his way, and he went to Paddan Aram,[g] to
Laban son of Bethuel the Aramean, the brother of Rebekah,[h] who was the mother of
Jacob and Esau.

6 Now Esau learned that Isaac had blessed Jacob and had sent him to Paddan Aram
to take a wife from there, and that when he blessed him he commanded him, "Do not
marry a Canaanite woman,"[i] 7 and that Jacob had obeyed his father and mother and
had gone to Paddan Aram. 8 Esau then realised how displeasing the Canaanite
women[j] were to his father Isaac;[k] 9 so he went to Ishmael and married Mahalath, the
sister of Nebaioth[l] and daughter of Ishmael son of Abraham, in addition to the wives
he already had.[m]

F. THE STORY OF JACOB (28:10–36:43)

Jacob did everything, both right and wrong, with great zeal. He deceived his own brother Esau and his father Isaac. He wrestled with an angel and worked fourteen years to marry the woman he loved. Through Jacob we learn how a strong leader can also be a servant. We also see how wrong actions will always come back to haunt us.

1. Jacob starts a family

Jacob's Dream at Bethel

10 Jacob left Beersheba and set out for Haran.[n] 11 When he reached a certain place,
he stopped for the night because the sun had set. Taking one of the stones there, he put
it under his head and lay down to sleep. 12 He had a dream[o] in which he saw a stairway**[d]** resting on the earth, with its top reaching to heaven, and the angels of God were
ascending and descending on it.[p] 13 There above it**[e]** stood the LORD,[q] and he said: "I
am the LORD, the God of your father Abraham and the God of Isaac.[r] I will give you
and your descendants the land[s] on which you are lying. 14 Your descendants will be
like the dust of the earth, and you[t] will spread out to the west and to the east, to the
north and to the south.[u] All peoples on earth will be blessed through you and your
offspring.[v] 15 I am with you[w] and will watch over you[x] wherever you go, and I will
bring you back to this land. I will not leave you[y] until I have done what I have promised you."[z]

16 When Jacob awoke from his sleep, he thought, "Surely the LORD is in this place,
and I was not aware of it." 17 He was afraid and said, "How awesome is this place![a]
This is none other than the house of God; this is the gate of heaven."

18 Early the next morning Jacob took the stone he had placed under his head and set

d *12* Or *ladder* **e** *13* Or *There beside him*

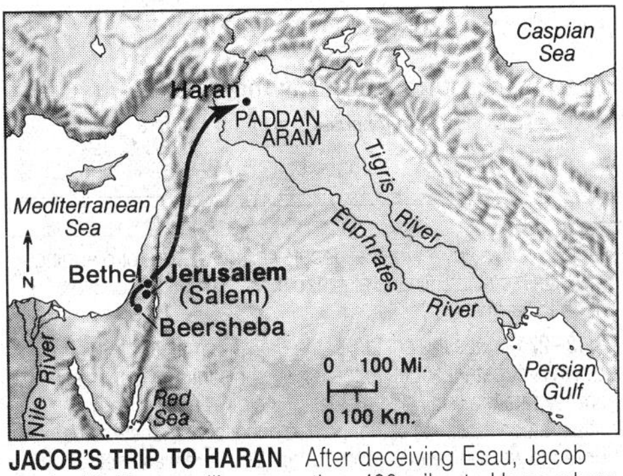

JACOB'S TRIP TO HARAN After deceiving Esau, Jacob ran for his life, travelling more than 400 miles to Haran where an uncle, Laban, lived. In Haran, Jacob married and started a family.

28:9 Ishmael was Isaac's half brother, the son of Abraham and Hagar, Sarah's maidservant (16:1–4, 15). After marrying two foreign girls (26:34), Esau hoped his marriage into Ishmael's family would please his parents, Isaac and Rebekah.

28:10–15 God's covenant promise to Abraham and Isaac was offered to Jacob as well. But it was not enough to be Abraham's grandson; Jacob had to establish his own personal relationship with God. God has no grandchildren; each of us must have a personal relationship with him. It is not enough to hear wonderful stories about Christians in your family. You need to become part of the story yourself (see Galatians 3:6, 7).

it up as a pillar[b] and poured oil on top of it.[c] 19 He called that place Bethel,[f] though
the city used to be called Luz.[d]
20 Then Jacob made a vow,[e] saying, "If God will be with me and will watch over
me[f] on this journey I am taking and will give me food to eat and clothes to wear 21 so
that I return safely[g] to my father's house, then the LORD[g] will be my God[h] 22 and[h]
this stone that I have set up as a pillar will be God's house,[i] and of all that you give
me I will give you a tenth.[j]"

Jacob Arrives in Paddan Aram

29 Then Jacob continued on his journey and came to the land of the eastern peoples.[a] 2 There he saw a well in the field, with three flocks of sheep lying near
it because the flocks were watered from that well. The stone over the mouth of the well
was large. 3 When all the flocks were gathered there, the shepherds would roll the stone
away from the well's mouth and water the sheep. Then they would return the stone to
its place over the mouth of the well.
4 Jacob asked the shepherds, "My brothers, where are you from?"
"We're from Haran,[b]" they replied.
5 He said to them, "Do you know Laban, Nahor's grandson?"
"Yes, we know him," they answered.
6 Then Jacob asked them, "Is he well?"
"Yes, he is," they said, "and here comes his daughter Rachel with the sheep."
7 "Look," he said, "the sun is still high; it is not time for the flocks to be gathered.
Water the sheep and take them back to pasture."
8 "We can't," they replied, "until all the flocks are gathered and the stone has been
rolled away from the mouth of the well. Then we will water the sheep."
9 While he was still talking with them, Rachel came with her father's sheep,[c] for
she was a shepherdess. 10 When Jacob saw Rachel daughter of Laban, his mother's
brother, and Laban's sheep, he went over and rolled the stone away from the mouth of
the well and watered his uncle's sheep.[d] 11 Then Jacob kissed Rachel and began to
weep aloud.[e] 12 He had told Rachel that he was a relative[f] of her father and a son of
Rebekah. So she ran and told her father.[g]
13 As soon as Laban[h] heard the news about Jacob, his sister's son, he hurried to
meet him. He embraced him and kissed him and brought him to his home, and there
Jacob told him all these things. 14 Then Laban said to him, "You are my own flesh and
blood."[i]

Jacob Marries Leah and Rachel

After Jacob had stayed with him for a whole month, 15 Laban said to him, "Just
because you are a relative of mine, should you work for me for nothing? Tell me what
your wages should be."
16 Now Laban had two daughters; the name of the older was Leah, and the name of
the younger was Rachel. 17 Leah had weak[a] eyes, but Rachel was lovely in form, and
beautiful. 18 Jacob was in love with Rachel and said, "I'll work for you seven years in
return for your younger daughter Rachel."[j]
19 Laban said, "It's better that I give her to you than to some other man. Stay here

28:18 [b]Ge 35:14 [c]Lev 8:11
28:19 [d]Jdg 1:23, 26
28:20 [e]Ge 31:13; Jdg 11:30; 2Sa 15:8 [f]ver 15
28:21 [g]Jdg 11:31 [h]Dt 26:17
28:22 [i]Ge 35:7, 14 [j]Ge 14:20; Lev 27:30
29:1 [a]Jdg 6:3, 33
29:4 [b]Ge 28:10
29:9 [c]Ex 2:16
29:10 [d]Ex 2:17
29:11 [e]Ge 33:4
29:12 [f]Ge 13:8; 14:14, 16 [g]Ge 24:28
29:13 [h]Ge 24:29
29:14 [i]Ge 2:23; Jdg 9:2; 2Sa 19:12-13
29:18 [j]Hos 12:12

[f] 19 Bethel means *house of God.* *[g] 20,21 Or Since God . . . father's house, the LORD* *[h] 21,22 Or house, and the LORD will be my God, 22 then* *[a] 17 Or delicate*

28:19 Bethel was about ten miles north of Jerusalem and 60 miles north of Beersheba, where Jacob left his family. This was where Abraham made one of his first sacrifices to God when he entered the land. At first, Bethel became an important centre for worship; later, it was a centre of idol worship. The prophet Hosea condemned its evil practices.

28:20–22 Was Jacob trying to bargain with God? It is possible that he, in his ignorance of how to worship and serve God, treated God like a servant who would perform a service for a tip. More likely, Jacob was not bargaining, but pledging his future to God. He may have been saying, in effect, "Because you have blessed me, I will follow you." Whether Jacob was bargaining or pledging, God blessed him. But God also had some difficult lessons for Jacob to learn.

29:18–27 It was the custom of the day for a man to present a dowry, or substantial gift, to the family of his future wife. This was to compensate the family for the loss of the girl. Jacob's dowry was not a material possession, for he had none to offer. Instead he agreed to work seven years for Laban. But there was another custom of the land that Laban did not tell Jacob. The older daughter had to be married first. By giving Jacob Leah and not Rachel, Laban tricked him into promising another seven years of hard work.

with me." 20 So Jacob served seven years to get Rachel, but they seemed like only a few
days to him because of his love for her.[k]
21 Then Jacob said to Laban, "Give me my wife. My time is completed, and I want
to lie with her.[l]"
22 So Laban brought together all the people of the place and gave a feast.[m] 23 But
when evening came, he took his daughter Leah and gave her to Jacob, and Jacob lay
with her. 24 And Laban gave his servant girl Zilpah to his daughter as her maidservant.
25 When morning came, there was Leah! So Jacob said to Laban, "What is this you
have done to me?[n] I served you for Rachel, didn't I? Why have you deceived me?[o]"
26 Laban replied, "It is not our custom here to give the younger daughter in marriage
before the older one. 27 Finish this daughter's bridal week;[p] then we will give you the
younger one also, in return for another seven years of work."
28 And Jacob did so. He finished the week with Leah, and then Laban gave him his
daughter Rachel to be his wife. 29 Laban gave his servant girl Bilhah[q] to his daughter
Rachel as her maidservant.[r] 30 Jacob lay with Rachel also, and he loved Rachel more
than Leah.[s] And he worked for Laban another seven years.[t]

Jacob's Children

31 When the LORD saw that Leah was not loved,[u] he opened her womb,[v] but Rachel
was barren. 32 Leah became pregnant and gave birth to a son. She named him Reuben,[b] for she said, "It is because the LORD has seen my misery.[w] Surely my husband
will love me now."
33 She conceived again, and when she gave birth to a son she said, "Because the
LORD heard that I am not loved, he gave me this one too." So she named him Simeon.[c][x]
34 Again she conceived, and when she gave birth to a son she said, "Now at last my
husband will become attached to me,[y] because I have borne him three sons." So he
was named Levi.[d][z]
35 She conceived again, and when she gave birth to a son she said, "This time I will
praise the LORD." So she named him Judah.[e][a] Then she stopped having children.

30 When Rachel saw that she was not bearing Jacob any children,[a] she became
jealous of her sister.[b] So she said to Jacob, "Give me children, or I'll die!"
2 Jacob became angry with her and said, "Am I in the place of God, who has kept you
from having children?"[c]

b *32 Reuben* sounds like the Hebrew for *he has seen my misery*; the name means *see, a son.* **c** *33 Simeon* probably means *one who hears.* **d** *34 Levi* sounds like and may be derived from the Hebrew for *attached.*
e *35 Judah* sounds like and may be derived from the Hebrew for *praise.*

29:20 [k]SS 8:7; Hos 12:12
29:21 [l]Jdg 15:1
29:22 [m]Jdg 14:10; Jn 2:1-2
29:25 [n]Ge 12:18 [o]Ge 27:36
29:27 [p]Jdg 14:12
29:29 [q]Ge 30:3 [r]Ge 16:1
29:30 [s]ver 16 [t]Ge 31:41
29:31 [u]Dt 21:15-17 [v]Ge 11:30; 30:1; Ps 127:3
29:32 [w]Ge 16:11; 31:42; Ex 4:31; Dt 26:7; Ps 25:18
29:33 [x]Ge 34:25; 49:5
29:34 [y]Ge 30:20; 1Sa 1:2-4 [z]Ge 49:5-7
29:35 [a]Ge 49:8; Mt 1:2-3
30:1 [a]Ge 29:31; 1Sa 1:5-6 [b]Lev 18:18
30:2 [c]Ge 16:2; 20:18; 29:31

29:20–28 People often wonder if working a long time for something they desire is worth it. Jacob worked seven years to marry Rachel. After being tricked, he agreed to work seven more years for her (although he did get to marry Rachel shortly after he married Leah)! The most important goals and desires are worth working and waiting for. Films and television have created the illusion that people have to wait only about an hour to solve their problems or get what they want. Don't be trapped into thinking the same is true in real life. Patience is hardest when we need it the most, but it is the key to achieving our goals.

29:23–25 Jacob was enraged when he learned that Laban had tricked him. The deceiver of Esau was now deceived himself. How natural it is for us to become upset at an injustice done to us while closing our eyes to the injustices we do to others. Sin has a way of coming back to haunt us.

29:28–30 Although Jacob was tricked by Laban, he kept his part of the bargain. There was more at stake than just Jacob's hurt. There was Rachel to think about, as well as God's plan for his life. When we are tricked by others, keeping our part of the bargain may still be wise. Nursing our wounds or plotting revenge makes us unable to see from God's perspective.

29:32 Today parents usually give their children names that sound good or have sentimental appeal. But the Old Testament portrays a more dynamic use of names. Parents often chose names that reflected the situation at the time of the birth. They sometimes hoped their children would fulfil the meaning of the names given them. Later the parents could look back and see if their grown children had lived up to their names. Sometimes a person's name was changed because his or her character and name did not match. This happened to Jacob ("he grasps the heel", figuratively, "he deceives"), whose name was changed to Israel ("he struggles with God"). Jacob's character had changed to the point that he was no longer seen as a deceiver, but as a God-honouring man.

3 Then she said, "Here is Bilhah, my maidservant. Sleep with her so that she can bear
children for me and that through her I too can build a family."[d]
4 So she gave him her servant Bilhah as a wife.[e] Jacob slept with her,[f] 5 and she
became pregnant and bore him a son. 6 Then Rachel said, "God has vindicated me;[g]
he has listened to my plea and given me a son." Because of this she named him
Dan.[a][h]
7 Rachel's servant Bilhah conceived again and bore Jacob a second son. 8 Then Rachel said, "I have had a great struggle with my sister, and I have won."[i] So she named
him Naphtali.[b][j]
9 When Leah saw that she had stopped having children, she took her maidservant
Zilpah and gave her to Jacob as a wife.[k] 10 Leah's servant Zilpah bore Jacob a son.
11 Then Leah said, "What good fortune!"[c] So she named him Gad.[d][l]
12 Leah's servant Zilpah bore Jacob a second son. 13 Then Leah said, "How happy I
am! The women will call me[m] happy."[n] So she named him Asher.[e][o]
14 During wheat harvest, Reuben went out into the fields and found some mandrake
plants,[p] which he brought to his mother Leah. Rachel said to Leah, "Please give me
some of your son's mandrakes."
15 But she said to her, "Wasn't it enough[q] that you took away my husband? Will you
take my son's mandrakes too?"
"Very well," Rachel said, "he can sleep with you tonight in return for your son's
mandrakes."
16 So when Jacob came in from the fields that evening, Leah went out to meet him.
"You must sleep with me," she said. "I have hired you with my son's mandrakes." So
he slept with her that night.
17 God listened to Leah,[r] and she became pregnant and bore Jacob a fifth son.
18 Then Leah said, "God has rewarded me for giving my maidservant to my husband."
So she named him Issachar.[f][s]
19 Leah conceived again and bore Jacob a sixth son. 20 Then Leah said, "God has
presented me with a precious gift. This time my husband will treat me with honour,
because I have borne him six sons." So she named him Zebulun.[g][t]
21 Some time later she gave birth to a daughter and named her Dinah.
22 Then God remembered Rachel;[u] he listened to her and opened her womb.[v]
23 She became pregnant and gave birth to a son[w] and said, "God has taken away my
disgrace."[x] 24 She named him Joseph,[h][y] and said, "May the LORD add to me another
son."[z]

Jacob's Flocks Increase

25 After Rachel gave birth to Joseph, Jacob said to Laban, "Send me on my way[a] so
that I can go back to my own homeland. 26 Give me my wives and children, for whom
I have served you,[b] and I will be on my way. You know how much work I've done for
you."
27 But Laban said to him, "If I have found favour in your eyes, please stay. I have

30:3 [d] Ge 16:2
30:4 [e] ver 9, 18 [f] Ge 16:3-4
30:6 [g] Ps 35:24; 43:1; La 3:59 [h] Ge 49:16-17
30:8 [i] Hos 12:3-4 [j] Ge 49:21
30:9 [k] ver 4
30:11 [l] Ge 49:19
30:13 [m] Ps 127:3 [n] Pr 31:28; Lk 1:48 [o] Ge 49:20
30:14 [p] SS 7:13
30:15 [q] Nu 16:9, 13
30:17 [r] Ge 25:21
30:18 [s] Ge 49:14
30:20 [t] Ge 35:23; 49:13; Mt 4:13
30:22 [u] Ge 8:1; 1Sa 1:19-20 [v] Ge 29:31
30:23 [w] ver 6 [x] Isa 4:1; Lk 1:25
30:24 [y] Ge 35:24; 37:2; 39:1; 49:22-26 [z] Ge 35:17
30:25 [a] Ge 24:54
30:26 [b] Ge 29:20, 30; Hos 12:12

a 6 *Dan* here means *he has vindicated.* b 8 *Naphtali* means *my struggle.* c 11 Or *"A troop is coming!"* d 11 *Gad* can mean *good fortune* or *a troop.* e 13 *Asher* means *happy.* f 18 *Issachar* sounds like the Hebrew for *reward.* g 20 *Zebulun* probably means *honour.* h 24 *Joseph* means *may he add.*

30:3 Each of the three great patriarchs (Abraham, Isaac, and Jacob) had wives who had difficulty conceiving children. It is interesting to note how each man reacted to his wife's predicament. Abraham had relations with Sarah's maidservant in order to have his own child, thus introducing bitterness and jealousy into his family. Isaac, by contrast, prayed to God when his wife was barren. God eventually answered his prayers, and Rebekah had twin sons. Jacob, however, followed his grandfather's example and had children by his wives' maidservants, leading to sad and sometimes bitter consequences.

30:4–13 Rachel and Leah were locked in a cruel contest. In their race to have more children, they both gave their maidservants to Jacob as concubines. Jacob would have been wise to refuse, even though this was an accepted custom of the day. The fact that a custom is socially acceptable does not mean it is wise or right. You will be spared much heartbreak if you look at the potential consequences, to you or others, of your actions. Are you doing anything now that might cause future problems?

30:22–24 Eventually God answered Rachel's prayers and gave her a child of her own. In the meantime, however, she had given her maidservant to Jacob. Trusting God when nothing seems to happen is difficult. But it is harder still to live with the consequences of taking matters into our own hands. Resist the temptation to think God has forgotten you. Have patience and courage to wait for God to act.

30:27 Laban claimed to have learned by divination that God had blessed him because of Jacob. In other words, he thought his idols had given him this insight.

learned by divination that[i] the LORD has blessed me because of you."[c] 28He added,
"Name your wages,[d] and I will pay them."
29Jacob said to him, "You know how I have worked for you[e] and how your livestock has fared under my care.[f] 30The little you had before I came has increased
greatly, and the LORD has blessed you wherever I have been. But now, when may I do
something for my own household?[g]"
31"What shall I give you?" he asked.
"Don't give me anything," Jacob replied. "But if you will do this one thing for me,
I will go on tending your flocks and watching over them: 32Let me go through all your
flocks today and remove from them every speckled or spotted sheep, every dark-
coloured lamb and every spotted or speckled goat.[h] They will be my wages. 33And
my honesty will testify for me in the future, whenever you check on the wages you

[i] 27 Or possibly *have become rich and*

30:27 [c]Ge 26:24; 39:3, 5
30:28 [d]Ge 29:15
30:29 [e]Ge 31:6 [f]Ge 31:38-40
30:30 [g]1Ti 5:8
30:32 [h]Ge 31:8, 12

RACHEL

History seems to repeat itself here. Twice a town well at Haran was the site of significant events in one family's story. It was here that Rebekah met Eliezer, Abraham's servant, who had come to find a wife for Isaac. Some 40 years later, Rebekah's son Jacob returned the favour by serving his cousin Rachel and her sheep from the same well. The relationship that developed between them not only reminds us that romance is not a modern invention, but also teaches us a few lessons about patience and love.

Jacob's love for Rachel was both patient and practical. Jacob had the patience to wait seven years for her, but he kept busy in the meantime. His commitment to Rachel kindled a strong loyalty within her. In fact, her loyalty to Jacob got out of hand and became self-destructive. She was frustrated by her barrenness and desperate to compete with her sister for Jacob's affection. She was trying to gain from Jacob what he had already given: devoted love.

Rachel's attempts to earn the unearnable are a picture of a much greater error we can make. Like her, we find ourselves trying somehow to earn love—God's love. But apart from his word, we end up with one of two false ideas. Either we think we've been good enough to deserve his love or we recognise we're not able to earn his love and assume that it cannot be ours. If the Bible makes no other point, it shouts this one: God loves us! His love had no beginning and is incredibly patient. All we need to do is respond, not try to earn what is freely offered. God has said in many ways, "I love you. I have demonstrated that love to you by all I've done for you. I have even sacrificed my Son, Jesus, to pay the price for what is unacceptable about you—your sin. Now, live because of my love. Respond to me; love me with your whole being; give yourself to me in thanksgiving, not as payment." Live life fully, in the freedom of knowing you are loved.

Strengths and accomplishments:
- She showed great loyalty to her family
- She mothered Joseph and Benjamin after being barren for many years

Weaknesses and mistakes:
- Her envy and competitiveness marred her relationship with her sister, Leah
- She was capable of dishonesty when she took her loyalty too far
- She failed to recognise that Jacob's devotion was not dependent on her ability to have children

Lessons from her life:
- Loyalty must be controlled by what is true and right
- Love is accepted, not earned

Vital statistics:
- Where: Haran
- Occupation: Shepherdess, housewife
- Relatives: Father: Laban. Aunt: Rebekah. Sister: Leah. Husband: Jacob. Sons: Joseph and Benjamin

Key verse:
"So Jacob served seven years to get Rachel, but they seemed like only a few days to him because of his love for her" (Genesis 29:20).

Rachel's story is told in Genesis 29—35:20. She is also mentioned in Ruth 4:11.

have paid me. Any goat in my possession that is not speckled or spotted, or any lamb 30:35 [i]Ge 31:1
that is not dark-coloured, will be considered stolen."
34"Agreed," said Laban. "Let it be as you have said." 35That same day he removed
all the male goats that were streaked or spotted, and all the speckled or spotted female
goats (all that had white on them) and all the dark-coloured lambs, and he placed them
in the care of his sons.[i] 36Then he put a three-day journey between himself and Jacob,
while Jacob continued to tend the rest of Laban's flocks.
37Jacob, however, took fresh-cut branches from poplar, almond and plane trees and
made white stripes on them by peeling the bark and exposing the white inner wood of
the branches. 38Then he placed the peeled branches in all the watering troughs, so that
they would be directly in front of the flocks when they came to drink. When the flocks
were in heat and came to drink, 39they mated in front of the branches. And they bore
young that were streaked or speckled or spotted. 40Jacob set apart the young of the
flock by themselves, but made the rest face the streaked and dark-coloured animals 30:43 [j]ver 30;
that belonged to Laban. Thus he made separate flocks for himself and did not put them Ge 12:16; 13:2;
with Laban's animals. 41Whenever the stronger females were in heat, Jacob would 24:35; 26:13-14
place the branches in the troughs in front of the animals so that they would mate near
the branches, 42but if the animals were weak, he would not place them there. So the
weak animals went to Laban and the strong ones to Jacob. 43In this way the man grew
exceedingly prosperous and came to own large flocks, and maidservants and menservants, and camels and donkeys.[j]

2. Jacob returns home

Jacob Flees From Laban

31 Jacob heard that Laban's sons were saying, "Jacob has taken everything our
father owned and has gained all this wealth from what belonged to our father."
2And Jacob noticed that Laban's attitude towards him was not what it had been.
3Then the LORD said to Jacob, "Go back[a] to the land of your fathers and to your 31:3 [a]ver 13;
relatives, and I will be with you."[b] Ge 32:9
4So Jacob sent word to Rachel and Leah to come out to the fields where his flocks [b]Ge 21:22; 26:3; 28:15

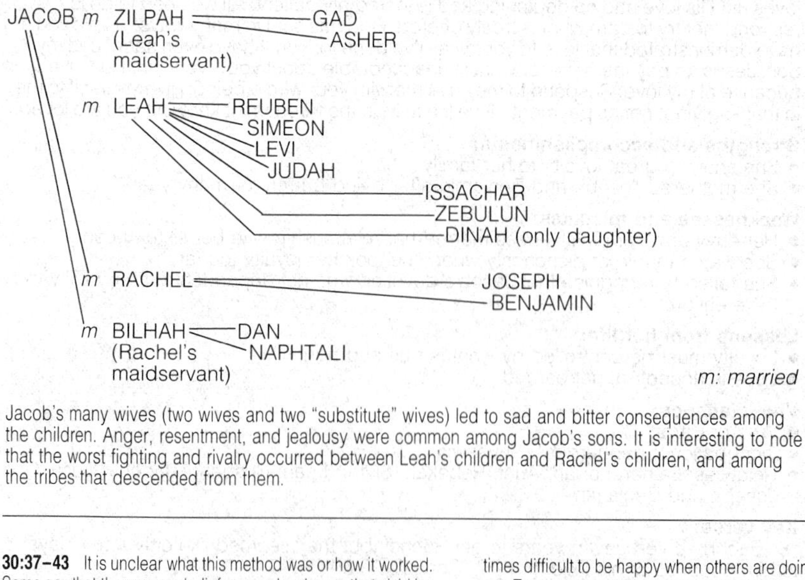

JACOB'S CHILDREN
This chart shows from left to right Jacob's children in the order in which they were born.

Jacob's many wives (two wives and two "substitute" wives) led to sad and bitter consequences among the children. Anger, resentment, and jealousy were common among Jacob's sons. It is interesting to note that the worst fighting and rivalry occurred between Leah's children and Rachel's children, and among the tribes that descended from them.

30:37–43 It is unclear what this method was or how it worked. Some say that there was a belief among herdsmen that vivid impressions at mating time influenced the offspring. Most likely, the selective breeding and God's promise of provision were the main reasons that Jacob's flocks increased.

31:1, 2 Jacob's wealth made Laban's sons jealous. It is sometimes difficult to be happy when others are doing better than we are. To compare our success with that of others is a dangerous way to judge the quality of our lives. By comparing ourselves to others, we may be giving jealousy a foothold. We can avoid jealousy by rejoicing in others' successes (see Romans 12:15).

31:4–13 Although Laban treated Jacob unfairly, God still in-

31:5 [c]Ge 21:22; 26:3
31:6 [d]Ge 30:29
31:7 [e]ver 41; Job 19:3 [f]ver 52; Ps 37:28; 105:14
31:8 [g]Ge 30:32
31:9 [h]ver 1, 16; Ge 30:42
31:11 [i]Ge 16:7; 48:16
31:12 [j]Ex 3:7
31:13 [k]Ge 28:10-22 [l]ver 3; Ge 32:9

were. 5He said to them, "I see that your father's attitude towards me is not what it was
before, but the God of my father has been with me.[c] 6You know that I've worked for
your father with all my strength,[d] 7yet your father has cheated me by changing my
wages ten times.[e] However, God has not allowed him to harm me.[f] 8If he said, 'The
speckled ones will be your wages,' then all the flocks gave birth to speckled young;
and if he said, 'The streaked ones will be your wages,'[g] then all the flocks bore
streaked young. 9So God has taken away your father's livestock and has given them to
me.[h]
10"In the breeding season I once had a dream in which I looked up and saw that the
male goats mating with the flock were streaked, speckled or spotted. 11The angel of
God[i] said to me in the dream, 'Jacob.' I answered, 'Here I am.' 12And he said, 'Look
up and see that all the male goats mating with the flock are streaked, speckled or spotted, for I have seen all that Laban has been doing to you.[j] 13I am the God of Bethel,[k]
where you anointed a pillar and where you made a vow to me. Now leave this land at
once and go back to your native land.[l]' "

LABAN

We're all selfish, but some of us seem to make a speciality out of the weakness. Laban's whole life was stamped by self-centredness. His chief goal was to look out for himself. The way he treated others was controlled by that goal. He made profitable arrangements for his sister Rebekah's marriage to Isaac and used his daughters' lives as bargaining chips. Jacob eventually outmanoeuvred Laban, but the older man was unwilling to admit defeat. His hold on Jacob was broken, but he still tried to maintain some kind of control by getting Jacob to promise to be gone for good. He realised that Jacob and Jacob's God were more than he could handle.

On the surface, we may find it difficult to identify with Laban. But his selfishness is one point we have in common. Like him, we often have a strong tendency to control people and events to our benefit. Our "good" reasons for treating others the way we do may simply be a thin cover on our self-centred motives. We may not even recognise our own selfishness. One way to discover it is to examine our willingness to admit we're wrong. Laban could not bring himself to do this. If you ever amaze yourself by what you say and do to avoid facing up to wrong actions, you are getting a glimpse of your selfishness in action. Recognising selfishness is painful, but it is the first step on the road back to God.

Strengths and accomplishments:
- Controlled two generations of marriages in the Abrahamic family (Rebekah, Rachel, Leah)
- Quick-witted

Weaknesses and mistakes:
- Manipulated others for his own benefit
- Unwilling to admit wrongdoing
- Benefited financially by using Jacob, but never fully benefited spiritually by knowing and worshipping Jacob's God

Lessons from his life:
- Those who set out to use people will eventually find themselves used
- God's plan cannot be blocked

Vital statistics:
- Where: Haran
- Occupation: Wealthy sheep breeder
- Relatives: Father: Bethuel. Sister: Rebekah. Brother-in-law: Isaac. Daughters: Rachel and Leah. Son-in-law: Jacob

Key verse:
"If the God of my father, the God of Abraham and the Fear of Isaac, had not been with me, you would surely have sent me away empty-handed. But God has seen my hardship and the toil of my hands, and last night he rebuked you" (Genesis 31:42).

Laban's story is told in Genesis 24:1—31:55.

creased Jacob's prosperity. God's power is not limited by lack of fair play. He has the ability to meet our needs and make us thrive even though others mistreat us. To give in and respond unfairly is to be no different from your enemies.

14 Then Rachel and Leah replied, "Do we still have any share in the inheritance of
our father's estate? 15 Does he not regard us as foreigners? Not only has he sold us, but
he has used up what was paid for us.[m] 16 Surely all the wealth that God took away from
our father belongs to us and our children. So do whatever God has told you."
17 Then Jacob put his children and his wives on camels, 18 and he drove all his livestock ahead of him, along with all the goods he had accumulated in Paddan Aram,[a] to
go to his father Isaac[n] in the land of Canaan.[o]
19 When Laban had gone to shear his sheep, Rachel stole her father's household
gods.[p] 20 Moreover, Jacob deceived[q] Laban the Aramean by not telling him he was
running away.[r] 21 So he fled with all he had, and crossing the River,[b] he headed for
the hill country of Gilead.[s]

Laban Pursues Jacob

22 On the third day Laban was told that Jacob had fled. 23 Taking his relatives with
him, he pursued Jacob for seven days and caught up with him in the hill country of
Gilead. 24 Then God came to Laban the Aramean in a dream at night and said to him,[t]
"Be careful not to say anything to Jacob, either good or bad."[u]
25 Jacob had pitched his tent in the hill country of Gilead when Laban overtook him,
and Laban and his relatives camped there too. 26 Then Laban said to Jacob, "What have
you done? You've deceived me,[v] and you've carried off my daughters like captives in
war.[w] 27 Why did you run off secretly and deceive me? Why didn't you tell me, so that
I could send you away with joy and singing to the music of tambourines[x] and harps?[y]
28 You didn't even let me kiss my grandchildren and my daughters good-bye.[z] You
have done a foolish thing. 29 I have the power to harm you;[a] but last night the God of
your father[b] said to me, 'Be careful not to say anything to Jacob, either good or bad.'
30 Now you have gone off because you longed to return to your father's house. But why
did you steal my gods?[c]"
31 Jacob answered Laban, "I was afraid, because I thought you would take your
daughters away from me by force. 32 But if you find anyone who has your gods, he
shall not live.[d] In the presence of our relatives, see for yourself whether there is anything of yours here with me; and if so, take it." Now Jacob did not know that Rachel
had stolen the gods.
33 So Laban went into Jacob's tent and into Leah's tent and into the tent of the two
maidservants, but he found nothing. After he came out of Leah's tent, he entered Rachel's tent. 34 Now Rachel had taken the household gods and put them inside her

a *18* That is, North-west Mesopotamia **b** *21* That is, the Euphrates

31:15 [m]Ge 29:20
31:18 [n]Ge 35:27 [o]Ge 10:19
31:19 [p]ver 30, 32, 34-35; Ge 35:2; Jdg 17:5; 1Sa 19:13; Hos 3:4
31:20 [q]Ge 27:36 [r]ver 27
31:21 [s]Ge 37:25
31:24 [t]Ge 20:3; Job 33:15 [u]Ge 24:50
31:26 [v]Ge 27:36 [w]1Sa 30:2-3
31:27 [x]Ex 15:20 [y]Ge 4:21
31:28 [z]ver 55
31:29 [a]ver 7 [b]ver 53
31:30 [c]ver 19; Jdg 18:24
31:32 [d]Ge 44:9

31:14, 15 Leaving home was not difficult for Rachel and Leah because their father had treated them as poorly as he had Jacob. According to custom, they were supposed to receive the benefits of the dowry Jacob paid for them, which was 14 years of hard work. When Laban did not give them what was rightfully theirs, they knew they would never inherit anything from their father. Thus they wholeheartedly approved of Jacob's plan to take the wealth he had gained and leave.

31:19 Many people kept small wooden or metal idols ("gods") in their homes. These idols were called *teraphim,* and they were thought to protect the home and offer advice in times of need. They had legal significance as well, for when they were passed on to an heir, the person who received them could rightfully claim the greatest part of the family inheritance. No wonder Laban was concerned when he realised his idols were missing (31:30). Most likely Rachel stole her father's idols because she was afraid Laban would consult them and learn where she and Jacob had gone, or perhaps she wanted to claim the family inheritance.

31:32 Do you remember feeling absolutely sure about something? Jacob was so sure that no-one had stolen Laban's idols that he vowed to kill the offender. Because Rachel took them, this statement put her safety in serious jeopardy. Even when you are absolutely sure about a matter, it is safer to avoid rash statements. Someone may hold you to them.

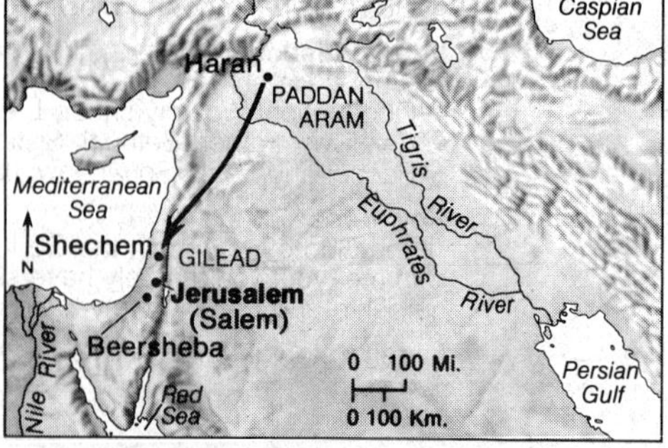

JACOB'S RETURN TO CANAAN God told Jacob to leave Haran and return to his homeland. Jacob took his family, crossed the Euphrates River, and headed first for the hill country of Gilead. Laban caught up with him there.

camel's saddle and was sitting on them. Laban searched[e] through everything in the
tent but found nothing.
35Rachel said to her father, "Don't be angry, my lord, that I cannot stand up in your
presence;[f] I'm having my period." So he searched but could not find the household
gods.
36Jacob was angry and took Laban to task. "What is my crime?" he asked Laban.
"What sin have I committed that you hunt me down? 37Now that you have searched
through all my goods, what have you found that belongs to your household? Put it here
in front of your relatives[g] and mine, and let them judge between the two of us.
38"I have been with you for twenty years now. Your sheep and goats have not mis-
carried, nor have I eaten rams from your flocks. 39I did not bring you animals torn by
wild beasts; I bore the loss myself. And you demanded payment from me for whatever
was stolen by day or night.[h] 40This was my situation: The heat consumed me in the
daytime and the cold at night, and sleep fled from my eyes. 41It was like this for the
twenty years I was in your household. I worked for you fourteen years for your two
daughters[i] and six years for your flocks, and you changed my wages ten times.[j] 42If
the God of my father,[k] the God of Abraham and the Fear of Isaac,[l] had not been with
me,[m] you would surely have sent me away empty-handed. But God has seen my hardship and the toil of my hands,[n] and last night he rebuked you."
43Laban answered Jacob, "The women are my daughters, the children are my children, and the flocks are my flocks. All you see is mine. Yet what can I do today about
these daughters of mine, or about the children they have borne? 44Come now, let's
make a covenant,[o] you and I, and let it serve as a witness between us."[p]
45So Jacob took a stone and set it up as a pillar.[q] 46He said to his relatives, "Gather
some stones." So they took stones and piled them in a heap, and they ate there by the
heap. 47Laban called it Jegar Sahadutha,[c] and Jacob called it Galeed.[d]
48Laban said, "This heap is a witness between you and me today." That is why it
was called Galeed. 49It was also called Mizpah,[e][r] because he said, "May the LORD
keep watch between you and me when we are away from each other. 50If you ill-treat
my daughters or if you take any wives besides my daughters, even though no-one is
with us, remember that God is a witness[s] between you and me."
51Laban also said to Jacob, "Here is this heap, and here is this pillar[t] I have set up
between you and me. 52This heap is a witness, and this pillar is a witness,[u] that I will
not go past this heap to your side to harm you and that you will not go past this heap
and pillar to my side to harm me.[v] 53May the God of Abraham[w] and the God of
Nahor, the God of their father, judge between us."[x]
So Jacob took an oath[y] in the name of the Fear of his father Isaac.[z] 54He offered
a sacrifice there in the hill country and invited his relatives to a meal. After they had
eaten, they spent the night there.
55Early the next morning Laban kissed his grandchildren and his daughters[a] and
blessed them. Then he left and returned home.[b]

Jacob Prepares to Meet Esau

32 Jacob also went on his way, and the angels of God[a] met him. 2When Jacob saw
them, he said, "This is the camp of God!"[b] So he named that place Mahanaim.[a][c]

31:34 [e]ver 37; Ge 44:12
31:35 [f]Ex 20:12; Lev 19:3, 32
31:37 [g]ver 23
31:39 [h]Ex 22:13
31:41 [i]Ge 29:30 [j]ver 7
31:42 [k]ver 5; Ex 3:15; 1Ch 12:17 [l]ver 53; Isa 8:13 [m]Ps 124:1-2 [n]Ge 29:32
31:44 [o]Ge 21:27; 26:28 [p]Jos 24:27
31:45 [q]Ge 28:18
31:49 [r]Jdg 11:29; 1Sa 7:5-6
31:50 [s]Jer 29:23; 42:5
31:51 [t]Ge 28:18
31:52 [u]Ge 21:30 [v]ver 7; Ge 26:29
31:53 [w]Ge 28:13 [x]Ge 16:5 [y]Ge 21:23, 27 [z]ver 42
31:55 [a]ver 28 [b]Ge 18:33; 30:25
32:1 [a]Ge 16:11; 2Ki 6:16-17; Ps 34:7; 91:11; Heb 1:14
32:2 [b]Ge 28:17 [c]2Sa 2:8, 29

c *47* The Aramaic *Jegar Sahadutha* means *witness heap.* **d** *47* The Hebrew *Galeed* means *witness heap.*
e *49 Mizpah* means *watchtower.* **a** *2 Mahanaim* means *two camps.*

31:38–42 Jacob made it a habit to do more than was expected of him. When his flocks were attacked, he took the losses rather than splitting them with Laban. He worked hard even after several pay cuts. His diligence eventually paid off; his flocks began to multiply. Making a habit of doing more than expected can pay off. It (1) pleases God, (2) earns recognition and advancement, (3) enhances your reputation, (4) builds others' confidence in you, (5) gives you more experience and knowledge, and (6) develops your spiritual maturity.

31:49 To be binding, an agreement had to be witnessed by a third party. In this case, Jacob and Laban used God as their witness that they would keep their word.

32:1 Why did angels of God meet Jacob? In the Bible, angels often intervened in human situations. Although angels often came in human form, these angels must have looked different, for Jacob recognised them at once. The reason these angels met Jacob is unclear; but because of their visit, Jacob knew God was with him.

3Jacob sent messengers ahead of him to his brother Esau[d] in the land of Seir, the
country of Edom.[e] 4He instructed them: "This is what you are to say to my master
Esau: 'Your servant Jacob says, I have been staying with Laban and have remained
there till now. 5I have cattle and donkeys, sheep and goats, menservants and maidservants.[f] Now I am sending this message to my lord, that I may find favour in your
eyes.[g]' "
6When the messengers returned to Jacob, they said, "We went to your brother Esau,
and now he is coming to meet you, and four hundred men are with him."[h]
7In great fear[i] and distress Jacob divided the people who were with him into two
groups,[b] and the flocks and herds and camels as well. 8He thought, "If Esau comes
and attacks one group,[c] the group[c] that is left may escape."
9Then Jacob prayed, "O God of my father Abraham, God of my father Isaac,[j]
O LORD, who said to me, 'Go back to your country and your relatives, and I will make
you prosper,'[k] 10I am unworthy of all the kindness and faithfulness[l] you have shown
your servant. I had only my staff when I crossed this Jordan, but now I have become
two groups. 11Save me, I pray, from the hand of my brother Esau, for I am afraid he
will come and attack me,[m] and also the mothers with their children.[n] 12But you have
said, 'I will surely make you prosper and will make your descendants like the sand[o]
of the sea, which cannot be counted.[p]' "
13He spent the night there, and from what he had with him he selected a gift[q] for his
brother Esau: 14two hundred female goats and twenty male goats, two hundred ewes
and twenty rams, 15thirty female camels with their young, forty cows and ten bulls,
and twenty female donkeys and ten male donkeys. 16He put them in the care of his
servants, each herd by itself, and said to his servants, "Go ahead of me, and keep some
space between the herds."
17He instructed the one in the lead: "When my brother Esau meets you and asks, 'To
whom do you belong, and where are you going, and who owns all these animals in
front of you?' 18then you are to say, 'They belong to your servant[r] Jacob. They are a
gift sent to my lord Esau, and he is coming behind us.' "
19He also instructed the second, the third and all the others who followed the herds:
"You are to say the same thing to Esau when you meet him. 20And be sure to say,
'Your servant Jacob is coming behind us.' " For he thought, "I will pacify him with
these gifts I am sending on ahead; later, when I see him, perhaps he will receive me."[s]
21So Jacob's gifts went on ahead of him, but he himself spent the night in the camp.

Jacob Wrestles With God

22That night Jacob got up and took his two wives, his two maidservants and his
eleven sons and crossed the ford of the Jabbok.[t] 23After he had sent them across the
stream, he sent over all his possessions. 24So Jacob was left alone, and a man[u] wrestled with him till daybreak. 25When the man saw that he could not overpower him, he
touched the socket of Jacob's hip[v] so that his hip was wrenched as he wrestled with
the man. 26Then the man said, "Let me go, for it is daybreak."
But Jacob replied, "I will not let you go unless you bless me."[w]
27The man asked him, "What is your name?"

[b] 7 *Or camps*; also in verse 10 [c] 8 *Or camp*

32:3 [d]Ge 27:41-42 [e]Ge 25:30; 36:8, 9
32:5 [f]Ge 12:16; 30:43 [g]Ge 33:8, 10, 15
32:6 [h]Ge 33:1
32:7 [i]ver 11
32:9 [j]Ge 28:13; 31:42 [k]Ge 31:13
32:10 [l]Ge 24:27
32:11 [m]Ps 59:2 [n]Ge 27:41
32:12 [o]Ge 22:17 [p]Ge 28:13-15; Hos 1:10; Ro 9:27
32:13 [q]Ge 43:11, 15, 25, 26; Pr 18:16
32:18 [r]Ge 18:3
32:20 [s]Ge 33:10; Pr 21:14
32:22 [t]Dt 2:37; 3:16; Jos 12:2
32:24 [u]Ge 18:2
32:25 [v]ver 32
32:26 [w]Hos 12:4

32:3 The last time Jacob had seen Esau, his brother was ready to kill him for stealing the family blessing (25:29–27:42). Esau was so angry he had vowed to kill Jacob as soon as their father, Isaac, died (27:41). Fearing their reunion, Jacob sent a messenger ahead with gifts. He hoped to buy Esau's favour.

32:9–12 How would you feel knowing you were about to meet the person you had cheated out of his most precious possession? Jacob had taken Esau's birthright (25:33) and his blessings (27:27–40). Now he was about to meet this brother for the first time in 20 years, and he was frantic with fear. He collected his thoughts, however, and decided to pray. When we face a difficult conflict, we can run about frantically or we can pause to pray. Which approach will be more effective?

32:26 Jacob continued this wrestling match all night just to be blessed. He was persistent. God encourages persistence in all areas of our lives, including the spiritual. Where in your spiritual life do you need more persistence? Strong character develops as you struggle through tough conditions.

32:27–29 God gave many Bible people new names (Abraham, Sarah, Peter). Their new names were symbols of how God had changed their lives. Here we see how Jacob's character had changed. Jacob, the ambitious deceiver, had now become Israel, the one who struggles with God and overcomes.

"Jacob," he answered.
28Then the man said, "Your name will no longer be Jacob, but Israel,[d][x] because
you have struggled with God and with men and have overcome."
29Jacob said, "Please tell me your name."[y]
But he replied, "Why do you ask my name?"[z] Then he blessed[a] him there.
30So Jacob called the place Peniel,[e] saying, "It is because I saw God face to face,[b]
and yet my life was spared."
31The sun rose above him as he passed Peniel,[f] and he was limping because of his
hip. 32Therefore to this day the Israelites do not eat the tendon attached to the socket
of the hip, because the socket of Jacob's hip was touched near the tendon.

Jacob Meets Esau

33 Jacob looked up and there was Esau, coming with his four hundred men;[a] so
he divided the children among Leah, Rachel and the two maidservants. 2He put
the maidservants and their children in front, Leah and her children next, and Rachel
and Joseph in the rear. 3He himself went on ahead and bowed down to the ground[b]
seven times as he approached his brother.
4But Esau ran to meet Jacob and embraced him; he threw his arms around his neck
and kissed him. And they wept.[c] 5Then Esau looked up and saw the women and
children. "Who are these with you?" he asked.
Jacob answered, "They are the children God has graciously given your servant.[d]"
6Then the maidservants and their children approached and bowed down. 7Next,
Leah and her children came and bowed down. Last of all came Joseph and Rachel, and
they too bowed down.
8Esau asked, "What do you mean by all these droves I met?"[e]
"To find favour in your eyes, my lord,"[f] he said.
9But Esau said, "I already have plenty, my brother. Keep what you have for yourself."
10"No, please!" said Jacob. "If I have found favour in your eyes, accept this gift
from me. For to see your face is like seeing the face of God,[g] now that you have
received me favourably.[h] 11Please accept the present[i] that was brought to you, for
God has been gracious to me[j] and I have all I need." And because Jacob insisted,
Esau accepted it.
12Then Esau said, "Let us be on our way; I'll accompany you."
13But Jacob said to him, "My lord knows that the children are tender and that I must
care for the ewes and cows that are nursing their young. If they are driven hard just one
day, all the animals will die. 14So let my lord go on ahead of his servant, while I move
along slowly at the pace of the droves before me and that of the children, until I come
to my lord in Seir.[k]"

d *28 Israel* means *he struggles with God.* **e** *30 Peniel* means *face of God.* **f** *31* Hebrew *Penuel,* a variant of *Peniel*

32:28 [x]Ge 17:5; 35:10; 1Ki 18:31
32:29 [y]Jdg 13:17 [z]Jdg 13:18 [a]Ge 35:9
32:30 [b]Ge 16:13; Ex 24:11; Nu 12:8; Jdg 6:22; 13:22
33:1 [a]Ge 32:6
33:3 [b]Ge 18:2; 42:6
33:4 [c]Ge 45:14-15
33:5 [d]Ge 48:9; Ps 127:3; Isa 8:18
33:8 [e]Ge 32:14-16 [f]Ge 24:9; 32:5
33:10 [g]Ge 16:13 [h]Ge 32:20
33:11 [i]1Sa 25:27 [j]Ge 30:43
33:14 [k]Ge 32:3

33:1–11 It is refreshing to see Esau's change of heart when the two brothers meet again. The bitterness over losing his birthright and blessing (25:29–34) seems gone. Instead Esau was content with what he had. Jacob even exclaimed how great it was to see his brother obviously pleased with him (33:10).

Life can bring us some bad situations. We can feel cheated, as Esau did, but we don't have to remain bitter. We can remove bitterness from our lives by honestly expressing our feelings to God, forgiving those who have wronged us, and being content with what we have.

33:3 Bowing to the ground seven times was the sign of respect given to a king. Jacob was taking every precaution as he met Esau, hoping to dispel any thoughts of revenge.

33:4 Esau greeted his brother, Jacob, with a great hug. Imagine how difficult this must have been for a man who once had actually plotted his brother's death (27:41). But time away from each other allowed the bitter wounds to heal. With the passing of time, each brother was able to see that their relationship was more important than their property.

33:11 Why did Jacob send gifts ahead for Esau? In Bible times, gifts were given for several reasons. (1) This may have been a bribe. Gifts are still given to win someone over or buy his or her support. Esau may first have refused Jacob's gifts (33:9) because he didn't want or need a bribe. He had already forgiven Jacob, and he had ample wealth of his own. (2) This may have been an expression of affection. (3) It may have been the customary way of greeting someone before an important meeting. Such gifts were often related to a person's occupation. This explains why Jacob sent Esau, who was a herdsman, sheep, goats, and cattle.

33:14–17 Why did Jacob imply that he was going to Seir but then stop at Succoth? We don't know the answer, but perhaps Jacob decided to stop there as they journeyed because Succoth is a beautiful site on the eastern side of the Jordan River. Whatever the reason, Jacob and Esau parted in peace. But they still lived fairly close to each other until after their father's death (36:6–8).

15 Esau said, "Then let me leave some of my men with you."
"But why do that?" Jacob asked. "Just let me find favour in the eyes of my lord."[l]
16 So that day Esau started on his way back to Seir. 17 Jacob, however, went to Succoth,[m] where he built a place for himself and made shelters for his livestock. That is
why the place is called Succoth.[a]
18 After Jacob came from Paddan Aram,[b][n] he arrived safely at the[c] city of Shechem[o] in Canaan and camped within sight of the city. 19 For a hundred pieces of silver,[d] he bought from the sons of Hamor, the father of Shechem,[p] the plot of ground[q]
where he pitched his tent. 20 There he set up an altar and called it El Elohe Israel.[e]

Dinah and the Shechemites

34 Now Dinah,[a] the daughter Leah had borne to Jacob, went out to visit the
women of the land. 2 When Shechem son of Hamor the Hivite, the ruler of that
area, saw her, he took her and raped her. 3 His heart was drawn to Dinah daughter of
Jacob, and he loved the girl and spoke tenderly to her. 4 And Shechem said to his father
Hamor, "Get me this girl as my wife."
5 When Jacob heard that his daughter Dinah had been defiled, his sons were in the
fields with his livestock; so he kept quiet about it until they came home.
6 Then Shechem's father Hamor went out to talk with Jacob.[b] 7 Now Jacob's sons
had come in from the fields as soon as they heard what had happened. They were filled
with grief and fury, because Shechem had done a disgraceful thing in[a] Israel[c] by
lying with Jacob's daughter—a thing that should not be done.[d]
8 But Hamor said to them, "My son Shechem has his heart set on your daughter.
Please give her to him as his wife. 9 Intermarry with us; give us your daughters and take
our daughters for yourselves. 10 You can settle among us;[e] the land is open to you.[f]
Live in it, trade[b] in it,[g] and acquire property in it."
11 Then Shechem said to Dinah's father and brothers, "Let me find favour in your
eyes, and I will give you whatever you ask. 12 Make the price for the bride[h] and the gift
I am to bring as great as you like, and I'll pay whatever you ask me. Only give me the
girl as my wife."
13 Because their sister Dinah had been defiled, Jacob's sons replied deceitfully as
they spoke to Shechem and his father Hamor. 14 They said to them, "We can't do such
a thing; we can't give our sister to a man who is not circumcised.[i] That would be a

[a] *17 Succoth* means *shelters.* [b] *18* That is, North-west Mesopotamia [c] *18* Or *arrived at Shalem, a*
[d] *19* Hebrew *hundred kesitahs*; a kesitah was a unit of money of unknown weight and value. [e] *20 El Elohe Israel* can mean *God, the God of Israel* or *mighty is the God of Israel.* [a] *7* Or *against* [b] *10* Or *move about freely*; also in verse 21

33:15 [l] Ge 34:11; 47:25; Ru 2:13
33:17 [m] Jos 13:27; Jdg 8:5, 6, 8, 14, 14-16, 15, 16; Ps 60:6
33:18 [n] Ge 25:20; 28:2 [o] Jos 24:1; Jdg 9:1
33:19 [p] Jos 24:32 [q] Jn 4:5
34:1 [a] Ge 30:21
34:6 [b] Jdg 14:2-5
34:7 [c] Dt 22:21; Jdg 20:6; 2Sa 13:12 [d] Jos 7:15
34:10 [e] Ge 47:6, 27 [f] Ge 13:9; 20:15 [g] Ge 42:34
34:12 [h] Ex 22:16; Dt 22:29; 1Sa 18:25
34:14 [i] Ge 17:14; Jdg 14:3

34:1–4 Shechem may have been a victim of "love at first sight", but his actions were impulsive and evil. Not only did he sin against Dinah; he sinned against the entire family (34:6, 7). The consequences of his deed were severe both for his family and for Jacob's (34:25–31). Even Shechem's declared love for Dinah could not excuse the evil he did by raping her. Don't allow sexual passion to boil over into evil actions. Passion must be controlled.

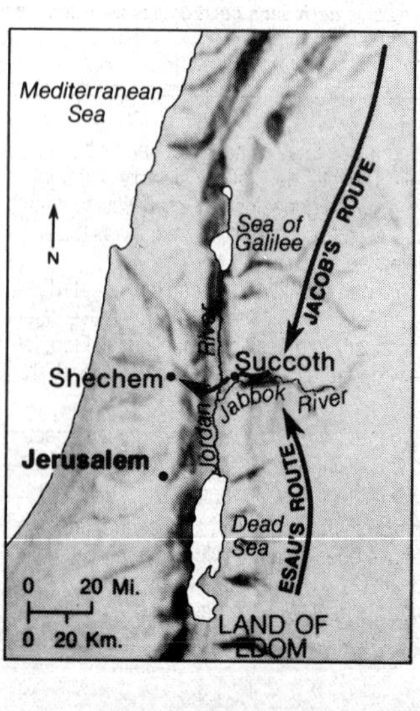

JACOB'S JOURNEY TO SHECHEM
After a joyful reunion with his brother Esau (who journeyed from Edom), Jacob set up camp in Succoth. Later he moved on to Shechem where his daughter, Dinah, was raped and two of his sons took revenge on the city.

34:15 [j]Ex 12:48
disgrace to us. 15We will give our consent to you on one condition only: that you
become like us by circumcising all your males.[j] 16Then we will give you our daughters and take your daughters for ourselves. We'll settle among you and become one
people with you. 17But if you will not agree to be circumcised, we'll take our sister[c]
and go."

34:19 [k]ver 3
18Their proposal seemed good to Hamor and his son Shechem. 19The young man,
who was the most honoured of all his father's household, lost no time in doing what
they said, because he was delighted with Jacob's daughter.[k] 20So Hamor and his son
Shechem went to the gate of their city[l] to speak to their fellow townsmen. 21"These
men are friendly towards us," they said. "Let them live in our land and trade in it; the
34:20 [l]Ru 4:1; 2Sa 15:2
land has plenty of room for them. We can marry their daughters and they can marry
ours. 22But the men will consent to live with us as one people only on the condition that
our males be circumcised, as they themselves are. 23Won't their livestock, their property and all their other animals become ours? So let us give our consent to them, and
they will settle among us."

34:24 [m]Ge 23:10
24All the men who went out of the city gate[m] agreed with Hamor and his son Shechem, and every male in the city was circumcised.

25Three days later, while all of them were still in pain, two of Jacob's sons, Simeon
and Levi, Dinah's brothers, took their swords[n] and attacked the unsuspecting city,
killing every male.[o] 26They put Hamor and his son Shechem to the sword and took
34:25 [n]Ge 49:5 [o]Ge 49:7
Dinah from Shechem's house and left. 27The sons of Jacob came upon the dead bodies
and looted the city where[d] their sister had been defiled. 28They seized their flocks and
herds and donkeys and everything else of theirs in the city and out in the fields. 29They
carried off all their wealth and all their women and children, taking as plunder everything in the houses.

30Then Jacob said to Simeon and Levi, "You have brought trouble on me by making
34:30 [p]Ex 5:21; 1Sa 13:4 [q]Ge 13:7 [r]Ge 46:27; 1Ch 16:19; Ps 105:12
me a stench[p] to the Canaanites and Perizzites, the people living in this land.[q] We are
few in number,[r] and if they join forces against me and attack me, I and my household
will be destroyed."

31But they replied, "Should he have treated our sister like a prostitute?"

Jacob Returns to Bethel

35 Then God said to Jacob, "Go up to Bethel[a] and settle there, and build an altar
there to God, who appeared to you when you were fleeing from your brother
35:1 [a]Ge 28:19 [b]Ge 27:43
Esau."[b]

[c] 17 Hebrew *daughter* [d] 27 Or *because*

JACOB'S JOURNEY BACK TO HEBRON
After Jacob's sons Simeon and Levi destroyed Shechem, God told Jacob to move to Bethel, where God reminded him that his name had been changed to Israel. He then travelled to Hebron, but along the way, his dear wife Rachel died in Ephrath (Bethlehem).

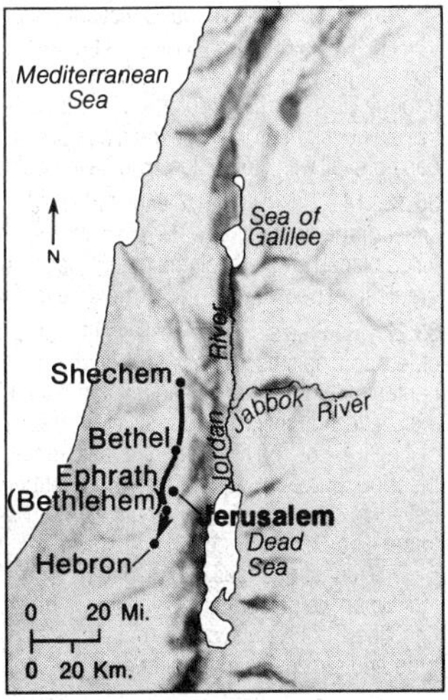

34:25–31 Why did Simeon and Levi take such harsh action against the city of Shechem? Jacob's family saw themselves as set apart from others. God wanted them to remain separate from their pagan neighbours. But the brothers wrongly thought that being set apart also meant being better. This arrogant attitude led to the terrible slaughter of innocent people.

34:27–29 When Shechem raped Dinah, the consequences were far greater than he could have imagined. Dinah's brothers were outraged and took revenge. Pain, deceit, and murder followed. Sexual sin is devastating because its consequences are so far reaching.

34:30, 31 In seeking revenge against Shechem, Simeon and Levi lied, stole, and murdered. Their desire for justice was right, but their ways of achieving it were wrong. Because of their sin, their father cursed them with his dying breath (49:5–7). Generations later, their descendants lost the part of the promised land allotted to them. When tempted to return evil for evil, leave revenge to God and spare yourself the dreadful consequences of sin.

2 So Jacob said to his household[c] and to all who were with him, "Get rid of the
foreign gods[d] you have with you, and purify yourselves and change your clothes.[e]
3 Then come, let us go up to Bethel, where I will build an altar to God, who answered
me in the day of my distress[f] and who has been with me wherever I have gone.[g]" 4 So
they gave Jacob all the foreign gods they had and the rings in their ears, and Jacob
buried them under the oak at Shechem.[h] 5 Then they set out, and the terror of God[i]
fell upon the towns all around them so that no-one pursued them.
6 Jacob and all the people with him came to Luz[j] (that is, Bethel) in the land of
Canaan. 7 There he built an altar, and he called the place El Bethel,[a] because it was
there that God revealed himself to him[k] when he was fleeing from his brother.
8 Now Deborah, Rebekah's nurse,[l] died and was buried under the oak below
Bethel. So it was named Allon Bacuth.[b]
9 After Jacob returned from Paddan Aram,[c] God appeared to him again and blessed
him.[m] 10 God said to him, "Your name is Jacob,[d] but you will no longer be called
Jacob; your name will be Israel."[e][n] So he named him Israel.
11 And God said to him, "I am God Almighty;[f][o] be fruitful and increase in number.
A nation[p] and a community of nations will come from you, and kings will come from
your body.[q] 12 The land I gave to Abraham and Isaac I also give to you, and I will give
this land to your descendants after you.[r]"[s] 13 Then God went up from him[t] at the
place where he had talked with him.
14 Jacob set up a stone pillar at the place where God had talked with him, and he
poured out a drink offering on it; he also poured oil on it.[u] 15 Jacob called the place
where God had talked with him Bethel.[g][v]

The Deaths of Rachel and Isaac

16 Then they moved on from Bethel. While they were still some distance from Ephrath, Rachel began to give birth and had great difficulty. 17 And as she was having great
difficulty in childbirth, the midwife said to her, "Don't be afraid, for you have another
son."[w] 18 As she breathed her last—for she was dying—she named her son Ben-
Oni.[h] But his father named him Benjamin.[i]
19 So Rachel died and was buried on the way to Ephrath (that is, Bethlehem[x]).
20 Over her tomb Jacob set up a pillar, and to this day that pillar marks Rachel's tomb.[y]
21 Israel moved on again and pitched his tent beyond Migdal Eder. 22 While Israel

[a] 7 *El Bethel* means *God of Bethel.* [b] 8 *Allon Bacuth* means *oak of weeping.* [c] 9 That is, North-west Mesopotamia; also in verse 26 [d] 10 *Jacob* means *he grasps the heel* (figuratively, *he deceives*). [e] 10 *Israel* means *he struggles with God.* [f] 11 Hebrew *El-Shaddai* [g] 15 *Bethel* means *house of God.* [h] 18 *Ben-Oni* means *son of my trouble.* [i] 18 *Benjamin* means *son of my right hand.*

35:2 [c] Ge 18:19; Jos 24:15 [d] Ge 31:19 [e] Ex 19:10, 14
35:3 [f] Ge 32:7 [g] Ge 28:15, 20-22; 31:3, 42
35:4 [h] Jos 24:25-26
35:5 [i] Ex 15:16; 23:27; Jos 2:9
35:6 [j] Ge 28:19; 48:3
35:7 [k] Ge 28:13
35:8 [l] Ge 24:59
35:9 [m] Ge 32:29
35:10 [n] Ge 17:5
35:11 [o] Ge 17:1; Ex 6:3 [p] Ge 28:3; 48:4 [q] Ge 17:6
35:12 [r] Ge 13:15; 28:13 [s] Ge 12:7; 26:3
35:13 [t] Ge 17:22
35:14 [u] Ge 28:18
35:15 [v] Ge 28:19
35:17 [w] Ge 30:24
35:19 [x] Ge 48:7; Ru 1:1, 19; Mic 5:2; Mt 2:16
35:20 [y] 1Sa 10:2

35:2 Why did the people have these idols ("foreign gods")? Idols were sometimes seen more as good luck charms than as gods. Some Israelites, even though they worshipped God, had idols in their homes, just as some Christians today own good luck trinkets. Jacob believed that idols should have no place in his household. He wanted nothing to divert his family's spiritual focus.

Jacob ordered his household to get rid of their gods. Unless we remove idols from our lives, they can ruin our faith. What idols do we have? An idol is anything we put before God. Idols don't have to be physical objects; they can be thoughts or desires. Like Jacob, we should get rid of anything that could stand between us and God.

35:4 Why did the people give Jacob their earrings? Jewelry in itself was not evil, but in Jacob's day earrings were often worn as good luck charms to ward off evil. The people in his family had to cleanse themselves of all pagan influences, including reminders of foreign gods.

35:10 God reminded Jacob of his new name, Israel, which meant "he struggles with God". Although Jacob's life was littered with difficulties and trials, his new name was a tribute to his desire to stay close to God despite life's disappointments.

Many people believe that Christianity should offer a problem-free life. Consequently, as life gets tough, they draw back disappointed. Instead, they should determine to prevail with God through life's storms. Problems and difficulties are painful but inevitable; you might as well see them as opportunities for growth. You can't prevail with God unless you have troubles to prevail over.

35:13, 14 This oil used to anoint the pillar was olive oil of the finest grade of purity. It was expensive, so using it showed the high value placed on the anointed object. Jacob was showing the greatest respect for the place where he met with God.

35:22 Reuben's sin was costly, although not right away. As the oldest son, he stood to receive a double portion of the family inheritance and a place of leadership among his people. Reuben may have thought he had got away with his sin. No more is mentioned of it until Jacob, on his deathbed, assembled his family for the final blessing. Suddenly Jacob took away Reuben's double portion and gave it to someone else. The reason? "You went up onto your father's bed, onto my couch and defiled it" (49:4).

Sin's consequences can plague us long after the sin is committed. When we do something wrong, we may think we can escape unnoticed, only to discover later that the sin has been quietly breeding serious consequences.

was living in that region, Reuben went in and slept with his father's concubine[z] Bilhah,[a] and Israel heard of it.

Jacob had twelve sons:
23 The sons of Leah:
Reuben the firstborn[b] of Jacob,
Simeon, Levi, Judah,[c] Issachar and Zebulun.[d]
24 The sons of Rachel:
Joseph[e] and Benjamin.[f]
25 The sons of Rachel's maidservant Bilhah:
Dan and Naphtali.[g]
26 The sons of Leah's maidservant Zilpah:
Gad[h] and Asher.[i]
These were the sons of Jacob, who were born to him in Paddan Aram.

27 Jacob came home to his father Isaac in Mamre,[j] near Kiriath Arba[k] (that is,
Hebron), where Abraham and Isaac had stayed. 28 Isaac lived a hundred and eighty
years.[l] 29 Then he breathed his last and died and was gathered to his people,[m] old and
full of years.[n] And his sons Esau and Jacob buried him.[o]

Esau's Descendants

36 This is the account of Esau (that is, Edom).[a]

2 Esau took his wives from the women of Canaan:[b] Adah daughter of Elon the
Hittite,[c] and Oholibamah daughter of Anah[d] and granddaughter of Zibeon the
Hivite — 3 also Basemath daughter of Ishmael and sister of Nebaioth.
4 Adah bore Eliphaz to Esau, Basemath bore Reuel,[e] 5 and Oholibamah bore
Jeush, Jalam and Korah. These were the sons of Esau, who were born to him in
Canaan.
6 Esau took his wives and sons and daughters and all the members of his household, as well as his livestock and all his other animals and all the goods he had
acquired in Canaan,[f] and moved to a land some distance from his brother Jacob.
7 Their possessions were too great for them to remain together; the land where
they were staying could not support them both because of their livestock.[g] 8 So
Esau[h] (that is, Edom) settled in the hill country of Seir.[i]

9 This is the account of Esau the father of the Edomites in the hill country of Seir.

10 These are the names of Esau's sons:
Eliphaz, the son of Esau's wife Adah, and Reuel, the son of Esau's wife Basemath.
11 The sons of Eliphaz:[j]
Teman,[k] Omar, Zepho, Gatam and Kenaz.
12 Esau's son Eliphaz also had a concubine named Timna, who bore him Amalek.[l] These were grandsons of Esau's wife Adah.[m]
13 The sons of Reuel:
Nahath, Zerah, Shammah and Mizzah. These were grandsons of Esau's wife
Basemath.
14 The sons of Esau's wife Oholibamah daughter of Anah and granddaughter of
Zibeon, whom she bore to Esau:
Jeush, Jalam and Korah.

15 These were the chiefs[n] among Esau's descendants:

35:22 [z]Ge 49:4; 1Ch 5:1 [a]Ge 29:29; Lev 18:8
35:23 [b]Ge 46:8 [c]Ge 29:35 [d]Ge 30:20
35:24 [e]Ge 30:24 [f]ver 18
35:25 [g]Ge 30:8
35:26 [h]Ge 30:11 [i]Ge 30:13
35:27 [j]Ge 13:18; 18:1 [k]Jos 14:15
35:28 [l]Ge 25:7, 20
35:29 [m]Ge 25:8; 49:33 [n]Ge 15:15 [o]Ge 25:9
36:1 [a]Ge 25:30
36:2 [b]Ge 28:8-9 [c]Ge 26:34 [d]ver 25
36:4 [e]1Ch 1:35
36:6 [f]Ge 12:5
36:7 [g]Ge 13:6; 17:8; 28:4
36:8 [h]Dt 2:4 [i]Ge 32:3
36:11 [j]ver 15-16; Job 2:11 [k]Am 1:12; Hab 3:3
36:12 [l]Ex 17:8, 16; Nu 24:20; 1Sa 15:2 [m]ver 16
36:15 [n]Ex 15:15

36:9 The Edomites were descendants of Esau who lived south and east of the Dead Sea. The country featured rugged mountains and desolate desert. Several major roads led through Edom because it was rich in natural resources. During the exodus, God told Israel to leave the Edomites alone (Deuteronomy 2:4, 5) because they were "brothers". But Edom refused to let them enter the land, and later they became bitter enemies of King David. The nations of Edom and Israel shared the same ancestor, Isaac, and the same border. Israel looked down on the Edomites because they intermarried with the Canaanites.

36:15ff The title "chief" is equivalent to "head of the clan".

The sons of Eliphaz the firstborn of Esau:
Chiefs Teman,[o] Omar, Zepho, Kenaz, 16Korah,[a] Gatam and Amalek.
These were the chiefs descended from Eliphaz in Edom; they were grandsons
of Adah.[p]
17The sons of Esau's son Reuel:[q]
Chiefs Nahath, Zerah, Shammah and Mizzah. These were the chiefs descended from Reuel in Edom; they were grandsons of Esau's wife Basemath.
18The sons of Esau's wife Oholibamah:
Chiefs Jeush, Jalam and Korah. These were the chiefs descended from Esau's wife Oholibamah daughter of Anah.
19These were the sons of Esau (that is, Edom),[r] and these were their chiefs.

20These were the sons of Seir the Horite,[s] who were living in the region:
Lotan, Shobal, Zibeon, Anah, 21Dishon, Ezer and Dishan. These sons of Seir
in Edom were Horite chiefs.
22The sons of Lotan:
Hori and Homam.[b] Timna was Lotan's sister.
23The sons of Shobal:
Alvan, Manahath, Ebal, Shepho and Onam.
24The sons of Zibeon:
Aiah and Anah. This is the Anah who discovered the hot springs[c] in the desert while he was grazing the donkeys of his father Zibeon.
25The children of Anah:
Dishon and Oholibamah daughter of Anah.
26The sons of Dishon:[d]
Hemdan, Eshban, Ithran and Keran.
27The sons of Ezer:
Bilhan, Zaavan and Akan.
28The sons of Dishan:
Uz and Aran.
29These were the Horite chiefs:
Lotan, Shobal, Zibeon, Anah, 30Dishon, Ezer and Dishan. These were the
Horite chiefs, according to their divisions, in the land of Seir.

The Rulers of Edom

31These were the kings who reigned in Edom before any Israelite king[t] reigned:[e]
32Bela son of Beor became king of Edom. His city was named Dinhabah.
33When Bela died, Jobab son of Zerah from Bozrah[u] succeeded him as king.
34When Jobab died, Husham from the land of the Temanites[v] succeeded him as king.
35When Husham died, Hadad son of Bedad, who defeated Midian in the country of Moab,[w] succeeded him as king. His city was named Avith.
36When Hadad died, Samlah from Masrekah succeeded him as king.
37When Samlah died, Shaul from Rehoboth on the river[f] succeeded him as king.
38When Shaul died, Baal-Hanan son of Acbor succeeded him as king.
39When Baal-Hanan son of Acbor died, Hadad[g] succeeded him as king. His city was named Pau, and his wife's name was Mehetabel daughter of Matred, the daughter of Me-Zahab.

40These were the chiefs descended from Esau, by name, according to their clans and regions:
Timna, Alvah, Jetheth, 41Oholibamah, Elah, Pinon, 42Kenaz, Teman, Mibzar, 43Magdiel and Iram. These were the chiefs of Edom, according to their settlements in the land they occupied.

This was Esau the father of the Edomites.

[a] *16* Masoretic Text; Samaritan Pentateuch (see also Gen. 36:11 and 1 Chron. 1:36) does not have *Korah.* [b] *22* Hebrew *Hemam,* a variant of *Homam* (see 1 Chron. 1:39) [c] *24* Vulgate; Syriac *discovered water*; the meaning of the Hebrew for this word is uncertain. [d] *26* Hebrew *Dishan,* a variant of *Dishon* [e] *31* Or *before an Israelite king reigned over them* [f] *37* Possibly the Euphrates [g] *39* Many manuscripts of the Masoretic Text, Samaritan Pentateuch and Syriac (see also 1 Chron. 1:50); most manuscripts of the Masoretic Text *Hadar*

36:15 [o] Job 2:11
36:16 [p] ver 12
36:17 [q] 1Ch 1:37
36:19 [r] Ge 25:30
36:20 [s] Ge 14:6; Dt 2:12, 22; 1Ch 1:38
36:31 [t] Ge 17:6; 1Ch 1:43
36:33 [u] Jer 49:13, 22
36:34 [v] Eze 25:13
36:35 [w] Ge 19:37; Nu 22:1; Dt 1:5; Ru 1:1, 6

37:1 [a]Ge 17:8 [b]Ge 10:19

G. THE STORY OF JOSEPH (37:1—50:26)

Joseph, one of Jacob's 12 sons, was obviously the favourite. Hated by his brothers for this, Joseph was sold to slave traders only to emerge as ruler of all Egypt. Through Joseph, we learn how suffering, no matter how unfair, develops strong character and deep wisdom.

1. Joseph is sold into slavery

37:2 [c]Ps 78:71 [d]Ge 35:25 [e]Ge 35:26 [f]1Sa 2:24

Joseph's Dreams

37 Jacob lived in the land where his father had stayed,[a] the land of Canaan.[b]
2This is the account of Jacob.

Joseph, a young man of seventeen, was tending the flocks[c] with his brothers, the
sons of Bilhah[d] and the sons of Zilpah,[e] his father's wives, and he brought their
father a bad report[f] about them.

37:3 [g]Ge 25:28

3Now Israel loved Joseph more than any of his other sons,[g] because he had been

---

JOSEPH

As a youngster, Joseph was overconfident. His natural self-assurance, increased by being Jacob's favourite son and by knowing of God's designs on his life, was unbearable to his ten older brothers, who eventually conspired against him. But this self-assurance, moulded by pain and combined with a personal knowledge of God, allowed him to survive and prosper where most would have failed. He added quiet wisdom to his confidence and won the hearts of everyone he met—Potiphar, the warden, other prisoners, the king, and after many years, even those ten brothers.

Perhaps you can identify with one or more of these hardships Joseph experienced: he was betrayed and deserted by his family, exposed to sexual temptation, and punished for doing the right thing; he endured a long imprisonment and was forgotten by those he helped. As you read his story, note what Joseph did in each case. His positive response transformed each setback into a step forward. He didn't spend much time asking "Why?" His approach was "What shall I do now?" Those who met Joseph were aware that wherever he went and whatever he did, God was with him. When you're facing a setback, the beginning of a Joseph-like attitude is to acknowledge that God is with you. There is nothing like his presence to shed new light on a dark situation.

Strengths and accomplishments:
- Rose in power from slave to ruler of Egypt
- Was known for his personal integrity
- Was a man of spiritual sensitivity
- Prepared a nation to survive a famine

Weakness and mistake:
- His youthful pride caused friction with his brothers

Lessons from his life:
- What matters is not so much the events or circumstances of life, but your response to them
- With God's help, any situation can be used for good, even when others intend it for evil

Vital statistics:
- Where: Canaan, Egypt
- Occupation: Shepherd, slave, convict, ruler
- Relatives: Parents: Jacob and Rachel. Eleven brothers and one sister named in the Bible. Wife: Asenath. Sons: Manasseh and Ephraim

Key verse:
"So Pharaoh asked them, 'Can we find anyone like this man, one in whom is the spirit of God?' " (Genesis 41:38).

Joseph's story is told in Genesis 30—50. He is also mentioned in Hebrews 11:22.

37:3 In Joseph's day, everyone had a robe or cloak. Robes were used to warm oneself, to bundle up belongings for a trip, to wrap babies, to sit on, or even to serve as security for a loan. Most robes were knee length, short sleeved, and plain. In contrast, Joseph's robe was probably of the kind worn by royalty—long sleeved, ankle length, and colourful. The robe became a symbol of Jacob's favouritism towards Joseph, and it aggravated the already strained relations between Joseph and his brothers. Favouritism in families may be unavoidable, but its divisive effects should be minimised. Parents may not be able to change their feelings towards a favourite child, but they can change their actions towards the others.

born to him in his old age;[h] and he made a richly ornamented[a] robe[i] for him. 4When
his brothers saw that their father loved him more than any of them, they hated him[j]
and could not speak a kind word to him.
5Joseph had a dream,[k] and when he told it to his brothers, they hated him all the
more. 6He said to them, "Listen to this dream I had: 7We were binding sheaves of corn
out in the field when suddenly my sheaf rose and stood upright, while your sheaves
gathered round mine and bowed down to it."[l]
8His brothers said to him, "Do you intend to reign over us? Will you actually rule
us?"[m] And they hated him all the more because of his dream and what he had said.
9Then he had another dream, and he told it to his brothers. "Listen," he said, "I had
another dream, and this time the sun and moon and eleven stars were bowing down to
me."
10When he told his father as well as his brothers,[n] his father rebuked him and said,
"What is this dream you had? Will your mother and I and your brothers actually come
and bow down to the ground before you?"[o] 11His brothers were jealous of him,[p] but
his father kept the matter in mind.[q]

Joseph Sold by His Brothers

12Now his brothers had gone to graze their father's flocks near Shechem, 13and
Israel said to Joseph, "As you know, your brothers are grazing the flocks near Shechem. Come, I am going to send you to them."
"Very well," he replied.
14So he said to him, "Go and see if all is well with your brothers and with the flocks,
and bring word back to me." Then he sent him off from the Valley of Hebron.[r]
When Joseph arrived at Shechem, 15a man found him wandering around in the fields
and asked him, "What are you looking for?"
16He replied, "I'm looking for my brothers. Can you tell me where they are grazing
their flocks?"
17"They have moved on from here," the man answered. "I heard them say, 'Let's go
to Dothan.[s]'"
So Joseph went after his brothers and found them near Dothan. 18But they saw him
in the distance, and before he reached them, they plotted to kill him.[t]
19"Here comes that dreamer!" they said to each other. 20"Come now, let's kill him
and throw him into one of these cisterns[u] and say that a ferocious animal devoured
him. Then we'll see what comes of his dreams."[v]

a 3 The meaning of the Hebrew for *richly ornamented* is uncertain; also in verses 23 and 32.

37:3 [h]Ge 44:20 [i]2Sa 13:18-19
37:4 [j]Ge 27:41; 49:22-23; Ac 7:9
37:5 [k]Ge 20:3; 28:12
37:7 [l]Ge 42:6, 9; 43:26, 28; 44:14; 50:18
37:8 [m]Ge 49:26
37:10 [n]ver 5 [o]ver 7; Ge 27:29
37:11 [p]Ac 7:9 [q]Lk 2:19, 51
37:14 [r]Ge 13:18; 35:27
37:17 [s]2Ki 6:13
37:18 [t]1Sa 19:1; Mk 14:1; Ac 23:12
37:20 [u]Jer 38:6, 9 [v]Ge 50:20

37:6-11 Joseph's brothers were already angry over the possibility of being ruled by their little brother. Joseph then fuelled the fire with his immature attitude and boastful manner. No-one enjoys a braggart. Joseph learned his lesson the hard way. His angry brothers sold him into slavery to get rid of him. After several years of hardship, Joseph learned an important lesson: Because our talents and knowledge come from God, it is more appropriate to thank him for them than to brag about them. Later, Joseph gives God the credit (41:16).

37:19, 20 Could jealousy ever make you feel like killing someone? Before saying, "Of course not," look at what happened in this story. Ten men were willing to kill their younger brother over a robe and a few reported dreams. Their deep jealousy had grown into ugly rage, completely blinding them to what was right. Jealousy can be difficult to recognise because our reasons for it seem to make sense. But left unchecked, jealousy grows quickly and leads to serious sins. The longer you cultivate jealous feelings, the harder it is to uproot them. The time to deal with jealousy is when you notice yourself keeping score of what others have.

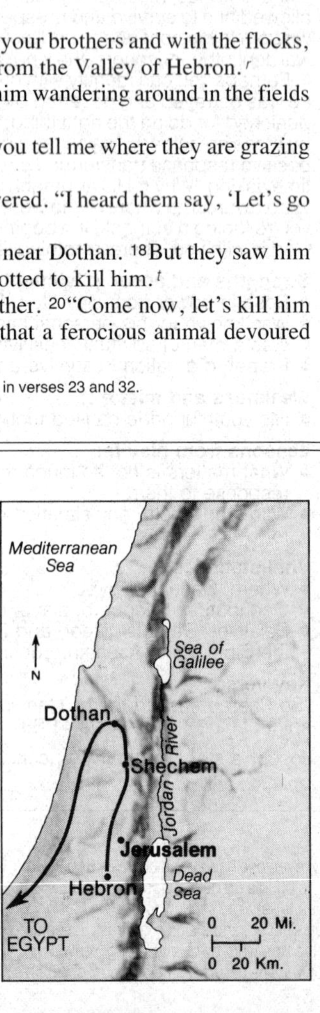

JOSEPH GOES TO MEET HIS BROTHERS
Jacob asked Joseph to go and find his brothers, who were grazing their flocks near Shechem. When Joseph arrived, he learned that his brothers had gone on to Dothan, which lay along a major trade route to Egypt. There the jealous brothers sold Joseph as a slave to a group of Midianite merchants on their way to Egypt.

37:21
[w]Ge 42:22

37:24
[x]Jer 41:7

37:25
[y]Ge 43:11
[z]ver 28

37:26
[a]ver 20;
Ge 4:10

37:27
[b]Ge 42:21

37:28
[c]Ge 25:2;
Jdg 6:1-3
[d]Ge 45:4-5;
Ps 105:17;
Ac 7:9

21 When Reuben heard this, he tried to rescue him from their hands. "Let's not take
his life," he said.[w] 22 "Don't shed any blood. Throw him into this cistern here in the
desert, but don't lay a hand on him." Reuben said this to rescue him from them and
take him back to his father.
23 So when Joseph came to his brothers, they stripped him of his robe—the richly
ornamented robe he was wearing—24 and they took him and threw him into the cistern.[x] Now the cistern was empty; there was no water in it.
25 As they sat down to eat their meal, they looked up and saw a caravan of Ishmaelites coming from Gilead. Their camels were loaded with spices, balm and myrrh,[y]
and they were on their way to take them down to Egypt.[z]
26 Judah said to his brothers, "What will we gain if we kill our brother and cover up
his blood?[a] 27 Come, let's sell him to the Ishmaelites and not lay our hands on him;
after all, he is our brother,[b] our own flesh and blood." His brothers agreed.
28 So when the Midianite[c] merchants came by, his brothers pulled Joseph up out of
the cistern and sold him for twenty shekels**b** of silver to the Ishmaelites, who took him
to Egypt.[d]

b *28* That is, about 8 ounces (about 0.2 kilogram)

REUBEN

Parents are usually the best judges of their children's character. Jacob summarised the personality of his son Reuben by comparing him to water. Except when frozen, water has no stable shape of its own. It always shapes itself to its container or environment. Reuben usually had good intentions, but he seemed unable to stand against a crowd. His instability made him hard to trust. He had both private and public values, but these contradicted each other. He went along with his brothers in their action against Joseph while hoping to counteract the evil in private. The plan failed. Compromise has a way of destroying convictions. Without convictions, lack of direction will destroy life. Reuben's sleeping with his father's concubine showed how little he had left of the integrity he had displayed earlier in life.

How consistent are your public and private lives? We may want to think they are separate, but we can't deny that they affect each other. What convictions are present in your life at all times? How closely does Jacob's description of his son—"turbulent as the waters"—describe your life?

Strengths and accomplishments:
- Saved Joseph's life by talking the other brothers out of murder
- Showed intense love for his father by offering his own sons as a guarantee that Benjamin's life would be safe

Weaknesses and mistakes:
- Gave in quickly to group pressure
- Did not directly protect Joseph from his brothers, although as oldest son he had the authority to do so
- Slept with his father's concubine

Lessons from his life:
- Public and private integrity must be the same, or one will destroy the other
- Punishment for sin may not be immediate, but it is certain

Vital statistics:
- Where: Canaan, Egypt
- Occupation: Shepherd
- Relatives: Parents: Jacob and Leah. Eleven brothers, one sister

Key verses:
"Reuben, you are my firstborn, my might, the first sign of my strength, excelling in honour, excelling in power. Turbulent as the waters, you will no longer excel, for you went up onto your father's bed, onto my couch and defiled it" (Genesis 49:3, 4).

Reuben's story is told in Genesis 29—50.

37:26, 27 The brothers were worried about bearing the guilt of Joseph's death. Judah suggested an option that was not right but would leave them guiltless of murder. Sometimes we jump at a solution because it is the lesser of two evils, but it is still not the right action to take. When someone proposes a seemingly workable solution, first ask, "Is it right?"

37:28 Although Joseph's brothers didn't kill him outright, they wouldn't expect him to survive for long as a slave. They were quite willing to let cruel slave traders do their dirty work for them. Joseph faced a 30-day journey through the desert, probably chained and on foot. He would be treated like baggage, and once in Egypt, would be sold as a piece of merchandise. His brothers thought they would never see him again. But God was in control of Joseph's life.

29When Reuben returned to the cistern and saw that Joseph was not there, he tore his
clothes.[e] 30He went back to his brothers and said, "The boy isn't there! Where can I
turn now?"[f]
31Then they got Joseph's robe,[g] slaughtered a goat and dipped the robe in the
blood. 32They took the ornamented robe back to their father and said, "We found this.
Examine it to see whether it is your son's robe."
33He recognised it and said, "It is my son's robe! Some ferocious animal[h] has devoured him. Joseph has surely been torn to pieces."[i]
34Then Jacob tore his clothes,[j] put on sackcloth[k] and mourned for his son many
days.[l] 35All his sons and daughters came to comfort him, but he refused to be comforted. "No," he said, "in mourning will I go down to the grave[c][m] to my son." So his
father wept for him.
36Meanwhile, the Midianites[d] sold Joseph in Egypt to Potiphar, one of Pharaoh's
officials, the captain of the guard.[n]

2. Judah and Tamar

38 At that time, Judah left his brothers and went down to stay with a man of Adullam named Hirah. 2There Judah met the daughter of a Canaanite man named
Shua.[a] He married her and lay with her; 3she became pregnant and gave birth to a son,
who was named Er.[b] 4She conceived again and gave birth to a son and named him
Onan. 5She gave birth to still another son and named him Shelah. It was at Kezib that
she gave birth to him.
6Judah got a wife for Er, his firstborn, and her name was Tamar. 7But Er, Judah's
firstborn, was wicked in the LORD's sight; so the LORD put him to death.[c]
8Then Judah said to Onan, "Lie with your brother's wife and fulfil your duty to her
as a brother-in-law to produce offspring for your brother."[d] 9But Onan knew that the
offspring would not be his; so whenever he lay with his brother's wife, he spilled his
semen on the ground to keep from producing offspring for his brother. 10What he did
was wicked in the LORD's sight; so he put him to death also.[e]
11Judah then said to his daughter-in-law Tamar, "Live as a widow in your father's
house until my son Shelah grows up."[f] For he thought, "He may die too, just like his
brothers." So Tamar went to live in her father's house.
12After a long time Judah's wife, the daughter of Shua, died. When Judah had recovered from his grief, he went up to Timnah,[g] to the men who were shearing his
sheep, and his friend Hirah the Adullamite went with him.
13When Tamar was told, "Your father-in-law is on his way to Timnah to shear his
sheep," 14she took off her widow's clothes, covered herself with a veil to disguise
herself, and then sat down at the entrance to Enaim, which is on the road to Timnah.

37:29 [e]ver 34; Ge 44:13; Job 1:20
37:30 [f]ver 22; Ge 42:13, 36
37:31 [g]ver 3, 23
37:33 [h]ver 20 [i]Ge 44:20, 28
37:34 [j]ver 29 [k]2Sa 3:31 [l]Ge 50:3, 10, 11
37:35 [m]Ge 42:38; 44:22, 29, 31
37:36 [n]Ge 39:1
38:2 [a]1Ch 2:3
38:3 [b]ver 6; Ge 46:12; Nu 26:19
38:7 [c]ver 10; Ge 46:12; 1Ch 2:3
38:8 [d]Dt 25:5-6; Mt 22:24-28
38:10 [e]Ge 46:12; Dt 25:7-10
38:11 [f]Ru 1:13
38:12 [g]ver 14; Jos 15:10, 57

c *35* Hebrew *Sheol* d *36* Samaritan Pentateuch, Septuagint, Vulgate and Syriac (see also verse 28); Masoretic Text *Medanites*

37:29, 30 Reuben returned to the pit to find Joseph, but his little brother was gone. His first response, in effect, was "What is going to happen to me?" rather than "What is going to happen to Joseph?" In a tough situation, are you usually concerned first about yourself? Consider the person most affected by the problem, and you will be more likely to find a solution for it.

37:31–35 To cover their evil action, Jacob's sons deceived their father into thinking Joseph was dead. Jacob himself had deceived others many times (including his own father; 27:35). Now, though blessed by God, he still had to face the consequences of his sins. God may not have punished Jacob immediately for his deceit, but the consequences came nevertheless and stayed with him for the rest of his life.

37:34 Tearing one's clothes and wearing sackcloth were signs of mourning, much like wearing black today.

37:36 Imagine the culture shock Joseph experienced upon arriving in Egypt. Joseph had lived as a nomad, travelling the countryside with his family, caring for sheep. Suddenly he was thrust into the world's most advanced civilisation with great pyramids, beautiful homes, sophisticated people, and a new language. While Joseph saw Egypt's skill and intelligence at their best, he also saw the Egyptians' spiritual blindness. They worshipped countless gods related to every aspect of life.

38:1ff This chapter vividly contrasts the immoral character of Judah with the moral character of Joseph. Judah's lack of integrity resulted in family strife and deception. In chapter 39, we see how Joseph's integrity and wise choices reflect his godly character. His faithfulness was rewarded with blessings greater than he could imagine, both for himself and for his family.

38:8–10 This law about marrying a widow in the family is explained in Deuteronomy 25:5–10. Its purpose was to ensure that a childless widow would have a son who would receive her late husband's inheritance and who, in turn, would care for her. Because Judah's son (Tamar's husband) had no children, there was no family line through which the inheritance and the blessing of the covenant could continue. God killed Onan because he refused to fulfil his obligation to his brother and to Tamar.

38:14 [h]ver 11
38:16 [i]Lev 18:15; 20:12
38:17 [j]Eze 16:33 [k]ver 20
38:18 [l]ver 25
38:19 [m]ver 14
38:21 [n]Lev 19:29; Hos 4:14
38:24 [o]Lev 21:9; Dt 22:21, 22
38:25 [p]ver 18
38:26 [q]1Sa 24:17 [r]ver 11
38:27 [s]Ge 25:24

For she saw that, though Shelah[h] had now grown up, she had not been given to him
as his wife.
15When Judah saw her, he thought she was a prostitute, for she had covered her
face. 16Not realising that she was his daughter-in-law,[i] he went over to her by the
roadside and said, "Come now, let me sleep with you."
"And what will you give me to sleep with you?" she asked.
17"I'll send you a young goat[j] from my flock," he said.
"Will you give me something as a pledge[k] until you send it?" she asked.
18He said, "What pledge should I give you?"
"Your seal[l] and its cord, and the staff in your hand," she answered. So he gave
them to her and slept with her, and she became pregnant by him. 19After she left, she
took off her veil and put on her widow's clothes[m] again.
20Meanwhile Judah sent the young goat by his friend the Adullamite in order to get
his pledge back from the woman, but he did not find her. 21He asked the men who lived
there, "Where is the shrine-prostitute[n] who was beside the road at Enaim?"
"There hasn't been any shrine-prostitute here," they said.
22So he went back to Judah and said, "I didn't find her. Besides, the men who lived
there said, 'There hasn't been any shrine-prostitute here.' "
23Then Judah said, "Let her keep what she has, or we will become a laughing-stock.
After all, I did send her this young goat, but you didn't find her."
24About three months later Judah was told, "Your daughter-in-law Tamar is guilty
of prostitution, and as a result she is now pregnant."
Judah said, "Bring her out and have her burned to death!"[o]
25As she was being brought out, she sent a message to her father-in-law. "I am
pregnant by the man who owns these," she said. And she added, "See if you recognise
whose seal and cord and staff these are."[p]
26Judah recognised them and said, "She is more righteous than I,[q] since I wouldn't
give her to my son Shelah.[r]" And he did not sleep with her again.
27When the time came for her to give birth, there were twin boys in her womb.[s]

WOMEN IN JESUS' FAMILY TREE

Tamar	Canaanite	Genesis 38:1–30
Rahab	Canaanite	Joshua 6:22–25
Ruth	Moabite	Ruth 4:13–22
Bathsheba	Israelite	2 Samuel 12:24, 25

38:15–23 Why does this story seem to take a light view of prostitution? Prostitutes were common in pagan cultures such as Canaan. Public prostitutes served Canaanite goddesses and were common elements of the religious cults. Fornication was encouraged to improve fertility in crops and flocks. They were more highly respected than private prostitutes who were sometimes punished when caught. Tamar was driven to seduce Judah because of her intense desire to have children and be the matriarch of Judah's oldest line; Judah was driven by his lust. Neither case was justified.

38:15–24 Why was Judah so open about his relations with a prostitute, yet ready to execute his daughter-in-law for being one? To understand this apparent contradiction, we must understand the place of women in Canaan. A woman's most important function was bearing children who would perpetuate the family line. To ensure that children belonged to the husband, the bride was expected to be a virgin and the wife was expected to have relations only with him. If a wife committed adultery, she could be executed. Some women, however, did not belong to families. They might be shrine prostitutes supported by offerings or common prostitutes supported by the men who used their services. Their children were nobody's heirs, and men who hired them adulterated nobody's bloodlines.

Judah saw no harm in hiring a prostitute for a night; after all, he was more than willing to pay. He was ready to execute Tamar, however, because if she was pregnant as a result of prostitution, his grandchild would not be part of his family line. Apparently the question of sexual morality never entered Judah's mind; his concern was for keeping his inheritance in the family. Ironically, it was Tamar, not Judah, who acted to provide him with legal heirs. By seducing him, she acted more in the spirit of the law than he did when he refused to send his third son to her.

This story in no way implies that God winks at prostitution. Throughout Scripture, prostitution is condemned as a serious sin. If the story has a moral, it is that faithfulness to family obligations is important. Incidentally, Judah and Tamar are direct ancestors of Jesus Christ (see Matthew 1:1–6).

38:18 A seal was a form of identification used to authenticate legal documents. Usually a unique design carved in stone and worn on a ring or necklace inseparable from its owner, the seal was used by the wealthy and powerful to mark clay or wax. Because Tamar had Judah's seal, she could prove beyond a doubt that he had been with her.

38:24–26 When Tamar revealed she was pregnant, Judah, who had unknowingly made her pregnant, moved to have her killed. Judah had concealed his own sin, yet he came down harshly on Tamar. Often the sins we try to cover up are the ones that anger us most when we see them in others. If you become indignant at the sins of others, you may have a similar tendency to sin that you don't wish to face. When we admit our sins and ask God to forgive us, forgiving others becomes easier.

28 As she was giving birth, one of them put out his hand; so the midwife took a scarlet
thread and tied it on his wrist and said, "This one came out first." 29 But when he drew
back his hand, his brother came out, and she said, "So this is how you have broken
out!" And he was named Perez.[a][t] 30 Then his brother, who had the scarlet thread on
his wrist, came out and he was given the name Zerah.[b][u]

3. Joseph is thrown into prison

Joseph and Potiphar's Wife

39 Now Joseph had been taken down to Egypt. Potiphar, an Egyptian who was one
of Pharaoh's officials, the captain of the guard,[a] bought him from the Ishmaelites who had taken him there.[b]
2 The LORD was with Joseph[c] and he prospered, and he lived in the house of his
Egyptian master. 3 When his master saw that the LORD was with him[d] and that the
LORD gave him success in everything he did,[e] 4 Joseph found favour in his eyes and
became his attendant. Potiphar put him in charge of his household, and he entrusted to
his care everything he owned.[f] 5 From the time he put him in charge of his household
and of all that he owned, the LORD blessed the household of the Egyptian because of
Joseph.[g] The blessing of the LORD was on everything Potiphar had, both in the house
and in the field. 6 So he left in Joseph's care everything he had; with Joseph in charge,
he did not concern himself with anything except the food he ate.
Now Joseph was well-built and handsome,[h] 7 and after a while his master's wife
took notice of Joseph and said, "Come to bed with me!"[i]
8 But he refused.[j] "With me in charge," he told her, "my master does not concern
himself with anything in the house; everything he owns he has entrusted to my care.
9 No-one is greater in this house than I am.[k] My master has withheld nothing from me
except you, because you are his wife. How then could I do such a wicked thing and sin
against God?"[l] 10 And though she spoke to Joseph day after day, he refused to go to
bed with her or even to be with her.
11 One day he went into the house to attend to his duties, and none of the household
servants was inside. 12 She caught him by his cloak[m] and said, "Come to bed with me!"
But he left his cloak in her hand and ran out of the house.
13 When she saw that he had left his cloak in her hand and had run out of the house,
14 she called her household servants. "Look," she said to them, "this Hebrew has been
brought to us to make sport of us! He came in here to sleep with me, but I screamed.[n]
15 When he heard me scream for help, he left his cloak beside me and ran out of the
house."
16 She kept his cloak beside her until his master came home. 17 Then she told him this
story:[o] "That Hebrew slave you brought us came to me to make sport of me. 18 But as
soon as I screamed for help, he left his cloak beside me and ran out of the house."

a 29 *Perez* means *breaking out.* b 30 *Zerah* can mean *scarlet* or *brightness.*

38:29 [t]Ge 46:12; Nu 26:20, 21; Ru 4:12, 18; 1Ch 2:4; Mt 1:3
38:30 [u]1Ch 2:4
39:1 [a]Ge 37:36 [b]Ge 37:25; Ps 105:17
39:2 [c]Ge 21:20, 22; Ac 7:9
39:3 [d]Ge 21:22; 26:28 [e]Ps 1:3
39:4 [f]ver 8, 22; Ge 24:2
39:5 [g]Ge 26:24; 30:27
39:6 [h]1Sa 16:12
39:7 [i]2Sa 13:11; Pr 7:15-18
39:8 [j]Pr 6:23-24
39:9 [k]Ge 41:33, 40 [l]Ge 20:6; 42:18; 2Sa 12:13
39:12 [m]Pr 7:13
39:14 [n]Dt 22:24, 27
39:17 [o]Ex 23:1, 7; Ps 101:5

39:1 The date of Joseph's arrival in Egypt is debatable. Many believe he arrived during the period of the Hyksos rulers, foreigners who came from the region of Canaan. They invaded Egypt and controlled the land for almost 150 years. If Joseph arrived during their rule, it is easy to see why he was rapidly promoted up the royal ladder. Because the Hyksos were foreigners themselves, they would not hold this brilliant young foreigner's ancestry against him.

39:1 *Pharaoh* was the general name for all the kings of Egypt. It was a title like "King" or "President" used to address the country's leader. The Pharaohs in Genesis and Exodus were different men.

39:1 Ancient Egypt was a land of great contrasts. People were either rich beyond measure or poverty stricken. There wasn't much middle ground. Joseph found himself serving Potiphar, an extremely rich officer in Pharaoh's service. Rich families like Potiphar's had elaborate homes two or three storeys high with beautiful gardens and balconies. They enjoyed live entertainment at home as they chose delicious fruit from expensive bowls. They surrounded themselves with alabaster vases, paintings, beautiful rugs, and hand-carved chairs. Dinner was served on golden tableware, and the rooms were lighted with gold lampstands. Servants, like Joseph, worked on the first floor, while the family occupied the upper storeys.

39:9 Potiphar's wife failed to seduce Joseph, who resisted this temptation by saying it would be a sin against God. Joseph didn't say, "I'd be hurting you," or "I'd be sinning against Potiphar," or "I'd be sinning against myself." Under pressure, such excuses are easily rationalised away. Remember that sexual sin is not just between two consenting adults. It is an act of disobedience against God.

39:10–15 Joseph avoided Potiphar's wife as much as possible. He refused her advances and finally *ran* from her. Sometimes merely trying to avoid temptation is not enough. We must turn and run, especially when the temptations seem very strong, as is often the case in sexual temptations.

39:20 Prisons were grim places with vile conditions. They were

19When his master heard the story his wife told him, saying, "This is how your slave
treated me," he burned with anger.[p] 20Joseph's master took him and put him in
prison,[q] the place where the king's prisoners were confined.
But while Joseph was there in the prison, 21the LORD was with him; he showed him
kindness and granted him favour in the eyes of the prison warder.[r] 22So the warder
put Joseph in charge of all those held in the prison, and he was made responsible for all
that was done there.[s] 23The warder paid no attention to anything under Joseph's care,
because the LORD was with Joseph and gave him success in whatever he did.[t]

The Cupbearer and the Baker

40 Some time later, the cupbearer[a] and the baker of the king of Egypt offended
their master, the king of Egypt. 2Pharaoh was angry[b] with his two officials, the
chief cupbearer and the chief baker, 3and put them in custody in the house of the captain of the guard,[c] in the same prison where Joseph was confined. 4The captain of the
guard assigned them to Joseph,[d] and he attended them.
After they had been in custody for some time, 5each of the two men—the cupbearer
and the baker of the king of Egypt, who were being held in prison—had a dream the
same night, and each dream had a meaning of its own.[e]
6When Joseph came to them the next morning, he saw that they were dejected. 7So
he asked Pharaoh's officials who were in custody with him in his master's house,
"Why are your faces so sad today?"[f]
8"We both had dreams," they answered, "but there is no-one to interpret them."[g]
Then Joseph said to them, "Do not interpretations belong to God?[h] Tell me your
dreams."
9So the chief cupbearer told Joseph his dream. He said to him, "In my dream I saw
a vine in front of me, 10and on the vine were three branches. As soon as it budded, it
blossomed, and its clusters ripened into grapes. 11Pharaoh's cup was in my hand, and
I took the grapes, squeezed them into Pharaoh's cup and put the cup in his hand."
12"This is what it means,[i]" Joseph said to him. "The three branches are three days.
13Within three days Pharaoh will lift up your head and restore you to your position, and
you will put Pharaoh's cup in his hand, just as you used to do when you were his
cupbearer. 14But when all goes well with you, remember me[j] and show me kindness;[k] mention me to Pharaoh and get me out of this prison. 15For I was forcibly
carried off from the land of the Hebrews,[l] and even here I have done nothing to deserve being put in a dungeon."
16When the chief baker saw that Joseph had given a favourable interpretation, he
said to Joseph, "I too had a dream: On my head were three baskets of bread.[a] 17In the
top basket were all kinds of baked goods for Pharaoh, but the birds were eating them
out of the basket on my head."
18"This is what it means," Joseph said. "The three baskets are three days.[m]
19Within three days Pharaoh will lift off your head[n] and hang you on a tree.[b] And the
birds will eat away your flesh."

a *16* Or *three wicker baskets* **b** *19* Or *and impale you on a pole*

39:19 [p]Pr 6:34
39:20 [q]Ge 40:3; Ps 105:18
39:21 [r]Ex 3:21
39:22 [s]ver 4
39:23 [t]ver 3
40:1 [a]Ne 1:11
40:2 [b]Pr 16:14, 15
40:3 [c]Ge 39:20
40:4 [d]Ge 39:4
40:5 [e]Ge 41:11
40:7 [f]Ne 2:2
40:8 [g]Ge 41:8, 15 [h]Ge 41:16; Da 2:22, 28, 47
40:12 [i]Ge 41:12, 15, 25; Da 2:36; 4:19
40:14 [j]Lk 23:42 [k]Jos 2:12; 1Sa 20:14, 42; 1Ki 2:7
40:15 [l]Ge 37:26-28
40:18 [m]ver 12
40:19 [n]ver 13

used to house forced labourers or, like Joseph, the accused who were awaiting trial. Prisoners were guilty until proved innocent, and there was no right to a speedy trial. Many prisoners never made it to court, because trials were held at the whim of the ruler. Joseph was in prison two years until he appeared before Pharaoh, and then he was called out to interpret a dream, not to stand trial.

39:21–23 As a prisoner and slave, Joseph could have seen his situation as hopeless. Instead, he did his best with each small task given him. His diligence and positive attitude were soon noticed by the warder, who promoted him to prison administrator. Are you facing a seemingly hopeless predicament? At work, at home, or at school, follow Joseph's example by taking each small task and doing your best. Remember how God turned Joseph's situation around. He will see your efforts and can reverse even overwhelming odds.

40:1–3 The cupbearer and the baker were two of the most trusted men in Pharaoh's kingdom. The baker was in charge of making the Pharaoh's food, and the cupbearer tasted all of his food and drink before giving it to him, in case any of it was contaminated or poisoned. These trusted men must have been suspected of a serious wrong, perhaps of conspiring against Pharaoh. Later the cupbearer was released and the baker executed.

40:8 When the subject of dreams came up, Joseph focused everyone's attention on God. Rather than using the situation to make himself look good, he turned it into a powerful witness for the Lord. One secret of effective witnessing is to recognise opportunities to relate God to the other person's experience. When the opportunity arises, we must have the courage to speak, as Joseph did.

20Now the third day was Pharaoh's birthday,[o] and he gave a feast for all his officials.[p] He lifted up the heads of the chief cupbearer and the chief baker in the presence
of his officials: 21He restored the chief cupbearer to his position, so that he once again
put the cup into Pharaoh's hand,[q] 22but he hanged[c] the chief baker,[r] just as Joseph
had said to them in his interpretation.[s]
23The chief cupbearer, however, did not remember Joseph; he forgot him.[t]

4. Joseph is placed in charge of Egypt

Pharaoh's Dreams

41 When two full years had passed, Pharaoh had a dream:[a] He was standing by the
Nile, 2when out of the river there came up seven cows, sleek and fat,[b] and they
grazed among the reeds.[c] 3After them, seven other cows, ugly and gaunt, came up out
of the Nile and stood beside those on the riverbank. 4And the cows that were ugly and
gaunt ate up the seven sleek, fat cows. Then Pharaoh woke up.
5He fell asleep again and had a second dream: Seven ears of corn, healthy and good,
were growing on a single stalk. 6After them, seven other ears of corn sprouted—thin
and scorched by the east wind. 7The thin ears of corn swallowed up the seven healthy,
full ears. Then Pharaoh woke up; it had been a dream.
8In the morning his mind was troubled,[d] so he sent for all the magicians[e] and wise
men of Egypt. Pharaoh told them his dreams, but no-one could interpret them for him.
9Then the chief cupbearer said to Pharaoh, "Today I am reminded of my shortcomings. 10Pharaoh was once angry with his servants,[f] and he imprisoned me and the
chief baker in the house of the captain of the guard.[g] 11Each of us had a dream the
same night, and each dream had a meaning of its own.[h] 12Now a young Hebrew was
there with us, a servant of the captain of the guard. We told him our dreams, and he
interpreted them for us, giving each man the interpretation of his dream.[i] 13And
things turned out exactly as he interpreted them to us: I was restored to my position,
and the other man was hanged."[a][j]
14So Pharaoh sent for Joseph, and he was quickly brought from the dungeon.[k]
When he had shaved and changed his clothes, he came before Pharaoh.
15Pharaoh said to Joseph, "I had a dream, and no-one can interpret it. But I have
heard it said of you that when you hear a dream you can interpret it."[l]
16"I cannot do it," Joseph replied to Pharaoh, "but God will give Pharaoh the answer
he desires."[m]
17Then Pharaoh said to Joseph, "In my dream I was standing on the bank of the Nile,
18when out of the river there came up seven cows, fat and sleek, and they grazed
among the reeds. 19After them, seven other cows came up—scrawny and very ugly
and lean. I had never seen such ugly cows in all the land of Egypt. 20The lean, ugly
cows ate up the seven fat cows that came up first. 21But even after they ate them,
no-one could tell that they had done so; they looked just as ugly as before. Then I woke
up.
22"In my dreams I also saw seven ears of corn, full and good, growing on a single

c *22 Or impaled* **a** *13 Or impaled*

40:20 [o]Mt 14:6-10 [p]Mk 6:21
40:21 [q]ver 13
40:22 [r]ver 19 [s]Ps 105:19
40:23 [t]Job 19:14; Ecc 9:15
41:1 [a]Ge 20:3
41:2 [b]ver 26 [c]Isa 19:6
41:8 [d]Da 2:1, 3; 4:5, 19 [e]Ex 7:11, 22; Da 1:20; 2:2, 27; 4:7
41:10 [f]Ge 40:2 [g]Ge 39:20
41:11 [h]Ge 40:5
41:12 [i]Ge 40:12
41:13 [j]Ge 40:22
41:14 [k]Ps 105:20; Da 2:25
41:15 [l]Da 5:16
41:16 [m]Ge 40:8; Da 2:30; Ac 3:12; 2Co 3:5

40:23 When Pharaoh's cupbearer was freed from prison, he forgot about Joseph, even though he had Joseph to thank for his freedom. It was two full years before Joseph had another opportunity to be freed (41:1). Yet Joseph's faith was deep, and he would be ready when the next chance came. When we feel passed by, overlooked, or forgotten, we shouldn't be surprised that people are often ungrateful. In similar situations, trust God as Joseph did. More opportunities may be waiting.

41:8 Magicians and wise men were common in the palaces of ancient rulers. Their job description included studying sacred arts and sciences, reading the stars, interpreting dreams, predicting the future, and performing magic. These men had power (see Exodus 7:11, 12), but their power was satanic. They were unable to interpret Pharaoh's dream, but God had revealed it to Joseph in prison.

41:14 Our most important opportunities may come when we least expect them. Joseph was brought hastily from the dungeon and pushed before Pharaoh. Did he have time to prepare? Yes and no. He had no warning that he would be suddenly pulled from prison and questioned by the king. Yet Joseph was ready for almost anything because of his right relationship with God. It was not Joseph's knowledge of dreams that helped him interpret their meaning. It was his knowledge of God. Be ready for opportunities by getting to know more about God. Then you will be ready to call on him when opportunities come your way.

41:16 Joseph made sure that he gave the credit to God. We should be careful to do the same. To take the honour for ourselves is a form of stealing God's honour. Don't be silent when you know you should be giving glory and credit to God.

41:24 [n]ver 8
41:25 [o]Da 2:45
41:26 [p]ver 2
41:27 [q]Ge 12:10; 2Ki 8:1
41:29 [r]ver 47
41:30 [s]ver 54; Ge 47:13 [t]ver 56
41:32 [u]Nu 23:19; Isa 46:10-11
41:33 [v]ver 39
41:34 [w]1Sa 8:15 [x]ver 48
41:35 [y]ver 48
41:36 [z]ver 56
41:37 [a]Ge 45:16
41:38 [b]Nu 27:18; Job 32:8; Da 4:8, 8-9, 18; 5:11, 14
41:40 [c]Ps 105:21-22; Ac 7:10
41:41 [d]Ge 42:6; Da 6:3
41:42 [e]Est 3:10 [f]Da 5:7, 16, 29
41:43 [g]Est 6:9
41:44 [h]Ps 105:22
41:45 [i]ver 50; Ge 46:20, 27

stalk. 23After them, seven other ears sprouted — withered and thin and scorched by the
east wind. 24The thin ears of corn swallowed up the seven good ears. I told this to the
magicians, but none could explain it to me.[n]"
25Then Joseph said to Pharaoh, "The dreams of Pharaoh are one and the same. God
has revealed to Pharaoh what he is about to do.[o] 26The seven good cows[p] are seven
years, and the seven good ears of corn are seven years; it is one and the same dream.
27The seven lean, ugly cows that came up afterwards are seven years, and so are the
seven worthless ears of corn scorched by the east wind: They are seven years of famine.[q]
28"It is just as I said to Pharaoh: God has shown Pharaoh what he is about to do.
29Seven years of great abundance[r] are coming throughout the land of Egypt, 30but
seven years of famine[s] will follow them. Then all the abundance in Egypt will be
forgotten, and the famine will ravage the land.[t] 31The abundance in the land will not
be remembered, because the famine that follows it will be so severe. 32The reason the
dream was given to Pharaoh in two forms is that the matter has been firmly decided[u]
by God, and God will do it soon.
33"And now let Pharaoh look for a discerning and wise man[v] and put him in charge
of the land of Egypt. 34Let Pharaoh appoint commissioners over the land to take a
fifth[w] of the harvest of Egypt during the seven years of abundance.[x] 35They should
collect all the food of these good years that are coming and store up the grain under the
authority of Pharaoh, to be kept in the cities for food.[y] 36This food should be held in
reserve for the country, to be used during the seven years of famine that will come
upon Egypt,[z] so that the country may not be ruined by the famine."
37The plan seemed good to Pharaoh and to all his officials.[a] 38So Pharaoh asked
them, "Can we find anyone like this man, one in whom is the spirit of God?"**[b]**[b]
39Then Pharaoh said to Joseph, "Since God has made all this known to you, there is
no-one so discerning and wise as you. 40You shall be in charge of my palace, and all
my people are to submit to your orders.[c] Only with respect to the throne will I be
greater than you."

Joseph in Charge of Egypt

41So Pharaoh said to Joseph, "I hereby put you in charge of the whole land of
Egypt."[d] 42Then Pharaoh took his signet ring[e] from his finger and put it on Joseph's
finger. He dressed him in robes of fine linen and put a gold chain around his neck.[f]
43He had him ride in a chariot as his second-in-command,**[c]** and men shouted before
him, "Make way!"**[d]**[g] Thus he put him in charge of the whole land of Egypt.
44Then Pharaoh said to Joseph, "I am Pharaoh, but without your word no-one will
lift hand or foot in all Egypt."[h] 45Pharaoh gave Joseph the name Zaphenath-Paneah
and gave him Asenath daughter of Potiphera, priest of On,**[e]** to be his wife.[i] And
Joseph went throughout the land of Egypt.

b *38* Or *of the gods* **c** *43* Or *in the chariot of his second-in-command*; or *in his second chariot* **d** *43* Or *Bow down* **e** *45* That is, Heliopolis; also in verse 50

41:28–36 After interpreting Pharaoh's dream, Joseph gave the king a survival plan for the next 14 years. The only way to prevent starvation was through careful planning; without a famine plan Egypt would have turned from prosperity to ruin. Many find detailed planning boring and unnecessary. But planning is a responsibility, not an option. Joseph was able to save a nation by translating God's plan for Egypt into practical actions (implementation). We must take time to translate God's plan for us into practical actions too.

41:38 Pharaoh recognised that Joseph was a man "in whom is the spirit of God". You probably won't get to interpret dreams for a king, but those who know you should be able to see God in you, through your kind words, merciful acts, and wise advice. Do your relatives, neighbours, and co-workers see you as a person in whom the Spirit of God lives?

41:39, 40 Joseph rose quickly to the top, from prison walls to Pharaoh's palace. His training for this important position involved being first a slave and then a prisoner. In each situation he learned the importance of serving God and others. Whatever your situation, no matter how undesirable, consider it part of your training programme for serving God.

41:45 Pharaoh may have been trying to make Joseph more acceptable by giving him an Egyptian name and wife. He probably wanted to (1) play down the fact that Joseph was a nomadic shepherd, an occupation disliked by the Egyptians, (2) make Joseph's name easier for Egyptians to pronounce and remember, and (3) show how highly he was honoured by giving him the daughter of a prominent Egyptian official.

46 Joseph was thirty years old[j] when he entered the service[k] of Pharaoh king of
Egypt. And Joseph went out from Pharaoh's presence and travelled throughout Egypt.
47 During the seven years of abundance the land produced plentifully. 48 Joseph collected all the food produced in those seven years of abundance in Egypt and stored it
in the cities. In each city he put the food grown in the fields surrounding it. 49 Joseph
stored up huge quantities of grain, like the sand of the sea; it was so much that he
stopped keeping records because it was beyond measure.

50 Before the years of famine came, two sons were born to Joseph by Asenath daughter of Potiphera, priest of On.[l] 51 Joseph named his firstborn[m] Manasseh[f] and said,
"It is because God has made me forget all my trouble and all my father's household."
52 The second son he named Ephraim[g][n] and said, "It is because God has made me
fruitful[o] in the land of my suffering."

53 The seven years of abundance in Egypt came to an end, 54 and the seven years of
famine began,[p] just as Joseph had said. There was famine in all the other lands, but
in the whole land of Egypt there was food. 55 When all Egypt began to feel the famine,[q] the people cried to Pharaoh for food. Then Pharaoh told all the Egyptians, "Go
to Joseph and do what he tells you."[r]

56 When the famine had spread over the whole country, Joseph opened the storehouses and sold grain to the Egyptians, for the famine[s] was severe throughout Egypt.
57 And all the countries came to Egypt to buy grain from Joseph,[t] because the famine
was severe in all the world.

5. Joseph and his brothers meet in Egypt

Joseph's Brothers Go to Egypt

42 When Jacob learned that there was grain in Egypt,[a] he said to his sons, "Why
do you just keep looking at each other?" 2 He continued, "I have heard that there
is grain in Egypt. Go down there and buy some for us, so that we may live and not
die."[b]

3 Then ten of Joseph's brothers went down to buy grain from Egypt. 4 But Jacob did
not send Benjamin, Joseph's brother, with the others, because he was afraid that harm
might come to him.[c] 5 So Israel's sons were among those who went to buy grain,[d] for
the famine was in the land of Canaan also.[e]

6 Now Joseph was the governor of the land,[f] the one who sold grain to all its people.
So when Joseph's brothers arrived, they bowed down to him with their faces to the
ground.[g] 7 As soon as Joseph saw his brothers, he recognised them, but he pretended
to be a stranger and spoke harshly to them.[h] "Where do you come from?" he asked.

"From the land of Canaan," they replied, "to buy food."

8 Although Joseph recognised his brothers, they did not recognise him.[i] 9 Then he

f 51 *Manasseh* sounds like and may be derived from the Hebrew for *forget.* g 52 *Ephraim* sounds like the Hebrew for *twice fruitful.*

41:46 [j]Ge 37:2 [k]1Sa 16:21; Da 1:19
41:50 [l]Ge 46:20; 48:5
41:51 [m]Ge 48:14, 18, 20
41:52 [n]Ge 48:1, 5; 50:23 [o]Ge 17:6;2 8:3; 49:22
41:54 [p]ver 30; Ps 105:11; Ac 7:11
41:55 [q]Dt 32:24 [r]ver 41
41:56 [s]Ge 12:10
41:57 [t]Ge 42:5; 47:15
42:1 [a]Ac 7:12
42:2 [b]Ge 43:8
42:4 [c]ver 38
42:5 [d]Ge 41:57 [e]Ge 12:10; Ac 7:11
42:6 [f]Ge 41:41 [g]Ge 37:7-10
42:7 [h]ver 30
42:8 [i]Ge 37:2

41:46 Joseph was 30 years old when he became governor of Egypt. He was 17 when he was sold into slavery by his brothers. Thus he must have spent 11 years as an Egyptian slave and two years in prison.

41:54 Famine was a catastrophe in ancient times, just as it still is in many parts of the world today. Almost perfect conditions were needed to produce good crops because there were no chemical fertilisers or pesticides. Any variances in rainfall or insect activity could cause crop failure and great hunger because the people relied almost exclusively on their own crops for food. Lack of storage, refrigeration, or transportation turned a moderate famine into a desperate situation. The famine Joseph prepared for was severe. Without God's intervention, the Egyptian nation would have crumbled.

42:1, 2 Why was grain so valuable in those days? As a food source it was universal and used in nearly everything eaten. It could be dried and stored much longer than any vegetables, milk products, or meat. It was so important that it was even used as money.

42:4 Jacob was especially fond of Benjamin because he was Joseph's only full brother and—as far as Jacob knew—the only surviving son of his beloved wife, Rachel. Benjamin was Jacob's youngest son and a child of his old age.

42:7 Joseph could have revealed his identity to his brothers at once. But Joseph's last memory of them was of staring in horror at their faces as slave traders carried him away. Were his brothers still evil and treacherous, or had they changed over the years? Joseph decided to put them through a few tests to find out.

42:8, 9 Joseph remembered his dreams about his brothers bowing down to him (37:6–9). Those dreams were coming true! As a young boy, Joseph was boastful about his dreams. As a man, he no longer flaunted his superior status. He did not feel the need to say "I told you so." It was not yet time to reveal his identity, so he kept quiet. Sometimes it is best for us to remain quiet, even when we would like to have the last word.

remembered his dreams[j] about them and said to them, "You are spies! You have
come to see where our land is unprotected."
10 "No, my lord," they answered. "Your servants have come to buy food. 11 We are
all the sons of one man. Your servants are honest men, not spies."
12 "No!" he said to them. "You have come to see where our land is unprotected."
13 But they replied, "Your servants were twelve brothers, the sons of one man, who
lives in the land of Canaan. The youngest is now with our father, and one is no
more."[k]
14 Joseph said to them, "It is just as I told you: You are spies! 15 And this is how you
will be tested: As surely as Pharaoh lives,[l] you will not leave this place unless your
youngest brother comes here. 16 Send one of your number to get your brother; the rest
of you will be kept in prison, so that your words may be tested to see if you are telling
the truth.[m] If you are not, then as surely as Pharaoh lives, you are spies!" 17 And he put
them all in custody[n] for three days.
18 On the third day, Joseph said to them, "Do this and you will live, for I fear God:[o]
19 If you are honest men, let one of your brothers stay here in prison, while the rest of
you go and take grain back for your starving households. 20 But you must bring your
youngest brother to me,[p] so that your words may be verified and that you may not
die." This they proceeded to do.
21 They said to one another, "Surely we are being punished because of our brother.[q]
We saw how distressed he was when he pleaded with us for his life, but we would not
listen; that's why this distress[r] has come upon us."
22 Reuben replied, "Didn't I tell you not to sin against the boy?[s] But you wouldn't
listen! Now we must give an accounting[t] for his blood."[u] 23 They did not realise that
Joseph could understand them, since he was using an interpreter.
24 He turned away from them and began to weep, but then turned back and spoke to
them again. He had Simeon taken from them and bound before their eyes.[v]
25 Joseph gave orders to fill their bags with grain,[w] to put each man's silver back in
his sack,[x] and to give them provisions for their journey.[y] After this was done for
them, 26 they loaded their grain on their donkeys and left.
27 At the place where they stopped for the night one of them opened his sack to get
feed for his donkey, and he saw his silver in the mouth of his sack.[z] 28 "My silver has
been returned," he said to his brothers. "Here it is in my sack."
Their hearts sank and they turned to each other trembling and said, "What is this that
God has done to us?"[a]
29 When they came to their father Jacob in the land of Canaan, they told him all that
had happened to them. They said, 30 "The man who is lord over the land spoke harshly
to us[b] and treated us as though we were spying on the land. 31 But we said to him, 'We
are honest men; we are not spies.[c] 32 We were twelve brothers, sons of one father. One
is no more, and the youngest is now with our father in Canaan.'
33 "Then the man who is lord over the land said to us, 'This is how I will know
whether you are honest men: Leave one of your brothers here with me, and take food
for your starving households and go.[d] 34 But bring your youngest brother to me so I
will know that you are not spies but honest men. Then I will give your brother back to
you, and you can trade[a] in the land.[e]' "
35 As they were emptying their sacks, there in each man's sack was his pouch of
silver! When they and their father saw the money pouches, they were frightened.[f]
36 Their father Jacob said to them, "You have deprived me of my children. Joseph is no
more and Simeon is no more, and now you want to take Benjamin.[g] Everything is
against me!"
37 Then Reuben said to his father, "You may put both of my sons to death if I do not
bring him back to you. Entrust him to my care, and I will bring him back."

a *34* Or *move about freely*

42:9 [j]Ge 37:7
42:13 [k]Ge 37:30, 33; 44:20
42:15 [l]1Sa 17:55
42:16 [m]ver 11
42:17 [n]Ge 40:4
42:18 [o]Ge 20:11; Lev 25:43
42:20 [p]ver 15, 34; Ge 43:5; 44:23
42:21 [q]Ge 37:26-28 [r]Hos 5:15
42:22 [s]Ge 37:21-22 [t]Ge 9:5 [u]1Ki 2:32; 2Ch 24:22; Ps 9:12
42:24 [v]ver 13; Ge 43:14, 23; 45:14-15
42:25 [w]Ge 43:2 [x]Ge 44:1, 8 [y]Ro 12:17, 20-21
42:27 [z]Ge 43:21-22
42:28 [a]Ge 43:23
42:30 [b]ver 7
42:31 [c]ver 11
42:33 [d]ver 19, 20
42:34 [e]Ge 34:10
42:35 [f]Ge 43:12, 15, 18
42:36 [g]Ge 43:14

42:15 Joseph was testing his brothers to make sure they had not been as cruel to Benjamin as they had been to him. Benjamin was his only full brother, and he wanted to see him face to face.

42:22 Reuben couldn't resist saying "I told you so". To "give an accounting for his blood" means that they thought they were being punished by God for what they had done to Joseph.

38 But Jacob said, "My son will not go down there with you; his brother is dead[h] and
he is the only one left. If harm comes to him[i] on the journey you are taking, you will
bring my grey head down to the grave[b][j] in sorrow.[k]"

The Second Journey to Egypt

43 Now the famine was still severe in the land.[a] 2 So when they had eaten all the
grain they had brought from Egypt, their father said to them, "Go back and buy
us a little more food."
3 But Judah said to him, "The man warned us solemnly, 'You will not see my face
again unless your brother is with you.'[b] 4 If you will send our brother along with us,
we will go down and buy food for you. 5 But if you will not send him, we will not go
down, because the man said to us, 'You will not see my face again unless your brother
is with you.[c]'"
6 Israel asked, "Why did you bring this trouble on me by telling the man you had
another brother?"
7 They replied, "The man questioned us closely about ourselves and our family. 'Is
your father still living?'[d] he asked us. 'Do you have another brother?'[e] We simply
answered his questions. How were we to know he would say, 'Bring your brother
down here'?"
8 Then Judah said to Israel his father, "Send the boy along with me and we will go
at once, so that we and you and our children may live and not die.[f] 9 I myself will
guarantee his safety; you can hold me personally responsible for him. If I do not bring
him back to you and set him here before you, I will bear the blame before you all my
life.[g] 10 As it is, if we had not delayed, we could have gone and returned twice."
11 Then their father Israel said to them, "If it must be, then do this: Put some of the
best products of the land in your bags and take them down to the man as a gift[h]—a
little balm[i] and a little honey, some spices[j] and myrrh, some pistachio nuts and
almonds. 12 Take double the amount of silver with you, for you must return the silver
that was put back into the mouths of your sacks.[k] Perhaps it was a mistake. 13 Take
your brother also and go back to the man at once. 14 And may God Almighty[a][l] grant
you mercy before the man so that he will let your other brother and Benjamin come
back with you.[m] As for me, if I am bereaved, I am bereaved."[n]
15 So the men took the gifts and double the amount of silver, and Benjamin also.
They hurried[o] down to Egypt and presented themselves[p] to Joseph. 16 When Joseph
saw Benjamin with them, he said to the steward of his house,[q] "Take these men to my
house, slaughter an animal and prepare dinner;[r] they are to eat with me at noon."
17 The man did as Joseph told him and took the men to Joseph's house. 18 Now the
men were frightened[s] when they were taken to his house. They thought, "We were
brought here because of the silver that was put back into our sacks the first time. He
wants to attack us and overpower us and seize us as slaves and take our donkeys."
19 So they went up to Joseph's steward and spoke to him at the entrance to the house.
20 "Please, sir," they said, "we came down here the first time to buy food.[t] 21 But at the
place where we stopped for the night we opened our sacks and each of us found his

[b] *38* Hebrew *Sheol* [a] *14* Hebrew *El-Shaddai*

42:38 [h] Ge 37:33 [i] ver 4 [j] Ge 37:35 [k] Ge 44:29, 34
43:1 [a] Ge 12:10; 41:56-57
43:3 [b] Ge 42:15; 44:23
43:5 [c] Ge 42:15; 2Sa 3:13
43:7 [d] ver 27 [e] Ge 42:13
43:8 [f] Ge 42:2; Ps 33:18-19
43:9 [g] Ge 42:37; 44:32; Phm 1:18-19
43:11 [h] Ge 32:20; Pr 18:16 [i] Ge 37:25; Jer 8:22 [j] 1Ki 10:2
43:12 [k] Ge 42:25
43:14 [l] Ge 17:1; 28:3; 35:11 [m] Ge 42:24 [n] Est 4:16
43:15 [o] Ge 45:9, 13 [p] Ge 47:2, 7
43:16 [q] Ge 44:1, 4, 12 [r] ver 31; Lk 15:23
43:18 [s] Ge 42:35
43:20 [t] Ge 42:3

43:1 Jacob and his sons had no relief from the famine. They could not see God's overall plan of sending them to Egypt to be re-united with Joseph and fed from Egypt's storehouses. If you are praying for relief from suffering or pressure and God is not bringing it as quickly as you would like, remember that God may be leading you to special treasures.

43:9 Judah accepted full responsibility for Benjamin's safety. He did not know what that might mean for him, but he was determined to do his duty. In the end it was Judah's stirring words that caused Joseph to break down with emotion and reveal himself to his brothers (44:18–34). Accepting responsibilities is difficult, but it builds character and confidence, earns others' respect, and motivates us to complete our work. When you have been given an assignment to complete or a responsibility to fulfil, commit yourself to seeing it through.

43:11 These gifts of balm, honey, spices, myrrh, pistachio nuts, and almonds were highly valuable specialities not common in Egypt. Because of the famine, they were even more rare.

43:12 Joseph's brothers arrived home from Egypt only to find in their grain sacks the money they had used to pay for the grain (42:35). Some months later, when it was time to return to Egypt for more food, Jacob instructed them to take extra money so they could pay for the previous purchase as well as for additional grain. Jacob did not try to get away with anything. He was a man of integrity who paid for what he bought, whether he had to or not. We should follow his example and guard our integrity. A reputation for honesty is worth far more than the money we might save by compromising it.

silver — the exact weight — in the mouth of his sack. So we have brought it back with
us.[u] 22We have also brought additional silver with us to buy food. We don't know
who put our silver in our sacks."
23"It's all right," he said. "Don't be afraid. Your God, the God of your father, has
given you treasure in your sacks;[v] I received your silver." Then he brought Simeon
out to them.[w]
24The steward took the men into Joseph's house,[x] gave them water to wash their
feet[y] and provided fodder for their donkeys. 25They prepared their gifts for Joseph's
arrival at noon, because they had heard that they were to eat there.
26When Joseph came home, they presented to him the gifts[z] they had brought into
the house, and they bowed down before him to the ground.[a] 27He asked them how
they were, and then he said, "How is your aged father you told me about? Is he still
living?"[b]
28They replied, "Your servant our father is still alive and well." And they bowed
low to pay him honour.[c]
29As he looked about and saw his brother Benjamin, his own mother's son, he
asked, "Is this your youngest brother, the one you told me about?"[d] And he said,
"God be gracious to you,[e] my son." 30Deeply moved[f] at the sight of his brother,
Joseph hurried out and looked for a place to weep. He went into his private room and
wept[g] there.
31After he had washed his face, he came out and, controlling himself,[h] said, "Serve
the food."
32They served him by himself, the brothers by themselves, and the Egyptians who
ate with him by themselves, because Egyptians could not eat with Hebrews,[i] for that
is detestable to Egyptians.[j] 33The men had been seated before him in the order of their
ages, from the firstborn to the youngest; and they looked at each other in astonishment.
34When portions were served to them from Joseph's table, Benjamin's portion was
five times as much as anyone else's.[k] So they feasted and drank freely with him.

A Silver Cup in a Sack

44 Now Joseph gave these instructions to the steward of his house: "Fill the men's
sacks with as much food as they can carry, and put each man's silver in the
mouth of his sack.[a] 2Then put my cup, the silver one, in the mouth of the youngest
one's sack, along with the silver for his grain." And he did as Joseph said.
3As morning dawned, the men were sent on their way with their donkeys. 4They had
not gone far from the city when Joseph said to his steward, "Go after those men at
once, and when you catch up with them, say to them, 'Why have you repaid good with
evil?[b] 5Isn't this the cup my master drinks from and also uses for divination?[c] This
is a wicked thing you have done.' "
6When he caught up with them, he repeated these words to them. 7But they said to
him, "Why does my lord say such things? Far be it from your servants to do anything
like that! 8We even brought back to you from the land of Canaan the silver we found
inside the mouths of our sacks.[d] So why would we steal silver or gold from your
master's house? 9If any of your servants is found to have it, he will die;[e] and the rest
of us will become my lord's slaves."
10"Very well, then," he said, "let it be as you say. Whoever is found to have it will
become my slave; the rest of you will be free from blame."
11Each of them quickly lowered his sack to the ground and opened it. 12Then the

43:21 [u]ver 15; Ge 42:27, 35
43:23 [v]Ge 42:28 [w]Ge 42:24
43:24 [x]ver 16 [y]Ge 18:4; 24:32
43:26 [z]Mt 2:11 [a]Ge 37:7, 10
43:27 [b]ver 7
43:28 [c]Ge 37:7
43:29 [d]Ge 42:13 [e]Nu 6:25; Ps 67:1
43:30 [f]Jn 11:33, 38 [g]Ge 42:24; 45:2, 14, 15; 46:29
43:31 [h]Ge 45:1
43:32 [i]Gal 2:12 [j]Ge 46:34; Ex 8:26
43:34 [k]Ge 37:3; 45:22
44:1 [a]Ge 42:25
44:4 [b]Ps 35:12
44:5 [c]Ge 30:27; Dt 18:10-14
44:8 [d]Ge 42:25; 43:21
44:9 [e]Ge 31:32

43:23 How did the money get into the sacks? Most likely, Joseph instructed his steward to replace the money and then explain it with this response. Note that the steward credited their God, not some Egyptian deity.

43:32 Why did Joseph eat by himself? He was following the laws of the Egyptians' caste system. Egyptians considered themselves highly intelligent and sophisticated. They looked upon shepherds and nomads as uncultured and even vulgar. As a Hebrew, Joseph could not eat with Egyptians even though he outranked them. As foreigners and shepherds, his brothers were lower in rank than any Egyptian citizens, so they had to eat separately too.

44:2 Joseph's silver cup was a symbol of his authority. It was thought to have supernatural powers, and to steal it was a serious crime. Such goblets were used for predicting the future. A person poured water into the cup and interpreted the reflections, ripples, and bubbles. Joseph wouldn't have needed his cup, since God told him everything he needed to know about the future.

steward proceeded to search, beginning with the oldest and ending with the youngest.
And the cup was found in Benjamin's sack.[f] 13 At this, they tore their clothes.[g] Then
they all loaded their donkeys and returned to the city.
14 Joseph was still in the house when Judah and his brothers came in, and they threw
themselves to the ground before him.[h] 15 Joseph said to them, "What is this you have
done? Don't you know that a man like me can find things out by divination?[i]"
16 "What can we say to my lord?" Judah replied. "What can we say? How can we
prove our innocence? God has uncovered your servants' guilt. We are now my lord's
slaves[j]—we ourselves and the one who was found to have the cup.[k]"
17 But Joseph said, "Far be it from me to do such a thing! Only the man who was
found to have the cup will become my slave. The rest of you, go back to your father in
peace."
18 Then Judah went up to him and said: "Please, my lord, let your servant speak a
word to my lord. Do not be angry[l] with your servant, though you are equal to Pharaoh
himself. 19 My lord asked his servants, 'Do you have a father or a brother?'[m] 20 And we
answered, 'We have an aged father, and there is a young son born to him in his old
age.[n] His brother is dead,[o] and he is the only one of his mother's sons left, and his
father loves him.'[p]
21 "Then you said to your servants, 'Bring him down to me so I can see him for
myself.'[q] 22 And we said to my lord, 'The boy cannot leave his father; if he leaves
him, his father will die.'[r] 23 But you told your servants, 'Unless your youngest brother
comes down with you, you will not see my face again.'[s] 24 When we went back to
your servant my father, we told him what my lord had said.
25 "Then our father said, 'Go back and buy a little more food.'[t] 26 But we said, 'We
cannot go down. Only if our youngest brother is with us will we go. We cannot see the
man's face unless our youngest brother is with us.'
27 "Your servant my father said to us, 'You know that my wife bore me two sons.[u]
28 One of them went away from me, and I said, "He has surely been torn to pieces."[v]
And I have not seen him since. 29 If you take this one from me too and harm comes to
him, you will bring my grey head down to the grave[a] in misery.'[w]
30 "So now, if the boy is not with us when I go back to your servant my father and
if my father, whose life is closely bound up with the boy's life,[x] 31 sees that the boy
isn't there, he will die. Your servants will bring the grey head of our father down to the
grave in sorrow. 32 Your servant guaranteed the boy's safety to my father. I said, 'If I
do not bring him back to you, I will bear the blame before you, my father, all my
life!'[y]
33 "Now then, please let your servant remain here as my lord's slave[z] in place of the

a *29* Hebrew *Sheol*; also in verse 31

44:12 [f] ver 2
44:13 [g] Ge 37:29; Nu 14:6; 2Sa 1:11
44:14 [h] Ge 37:7, 10
44:15 [i] ver 5; Ge 30:27
44:16 [j] ver 9; Ge 43:18 [k] ver 2
44:18 [l] Ge 18:30; Ex 32:22
44:19 [m] Ge 43:7
44:20 [n] Ge 37:3 [o] Ge 37:33 [p] Ge 42:13
44:21 [q] Ge 42:15
44:22 [r] Ge 37:35
44:23 [s] Ge 43:5
44:25 [t] Ge 43:2
44:27 [u] Ge 46:19
44:28 [v] Ge 37:33
44:29 [w] Ge 42:38
44:30 [x] 1Sa 18:1
44:32 [y] Ge 43:9
44:33 [z] Ge 43:18

44:13 Tearing clothes was an expression of deep sorrow, a customary manner of showing grief. The brothers were terrified that Benjamin might be harmed.

44:15 Did Joseph really practise divination? Probably not—he would have no desire or need to because of his relationship with God. This statement was probably part of the test to emphasise how important the cup was.

44:16–34 When Judah was younger, he showed no regard for his brother Joseph or his father, Jacob. First he convinced his brothers to sell Joseph as a slave (37:27); then he joined his brothers in lying to his father about Joseph's fate (37:32). But what a change had taken place in Judah! The man who sold one favoured little brother into slavery now offered to become a slave himself to save another favoured little brother. He was so concerned for his father and younger brother that he was willing to die for them. When you are ready to give up hope on yourself or others, remember that God can work a complete change in even the most selfish personality.

44:18–34 Judah finally could take no more and stepped forward to plead their case. This was risky because Joseph could have had him killed. But Judah courageously defended himself and his brothers and pleaded for mercy. And he offered to put himself in Benjamin's place. There are times when we should be silent, but there are also times when we should speak up, even if there could be serious repercussions. When faced with a situation that needs a strong voice and courageous action, remember Judah, and speak up.

44:32, 33 Judah had promised Jacob that he would guarantee young Benjamin's safety (43:9). Now Judah had a chance to keep that promise. Becoming a slave was a terrible fate, but Judah was determined to keep his word to his father. He showed great courage in carrying out his promise. Accepting a responsibility means carrying it out with determination and courage, regardless of the personal sacrifice.

44:33 Joseph wanted to see if his brothers' attitudes had changed for the better, so he tested the way they treated each other. Judah, the brother who had stepped forward with the plan to sell Joseph (37:27), now stepped forward to take Benjamin's punishment so that Benjamin could return to their father. This courageous act convinced Joseph that his brothers had dramatically changed for the better.

44:33 [a]Jn 15:13
44:34 [b]Est 8:6
45:1 [a]Ge 43:31
45:2 [b]Ge 29:11 [c]ver 16; Ge 46:29
45:3 [d]Ac 7:13 [e]ver 15
45:4 [f]Ge 37:28

boy,[a] and let the boy return with his brothers. 34How can I go back to my father if the
boy is not with me? No! Do not let me see the misery that would come upon my
father."[b]

Joseph Makes Himself Known

45 Then Joseph could no longer control himself[a] before all his attendants, and he
cried out, "Make everyone leave my presence!" So there was no-one with Joseph when he made himself known to his brothers. 2And he wept[b] so loudly that the
Egyptians heard him, and Pharaoh's household heard about it.[c]
3Joseph said to his brothers, "I am Joseph! Is my father still living?"[d] But his
brothers were not able to answer him,[e] because they were terrified at his presence.
4Then Joseph said to his brothers, "Come close to me." When they had done so, he
said, "I am your brother Joseph, the one you sold into Egypt![f] 5And now, do not be

JUDAH

People who are leaders stand out. They don't necessarily look or act a certain way until the need for their action is apparent. Among their skills are outspokenness, decisiveness, action, and control. These skills can be used for great good or great evil. Jacob's fourth son, Judah, was a natural leader. The events of his life provided many opportunities to exercise those skills. Unfortunately Judah's decisions were often shaped more by the pressures of the moment than by a conscious desire to cooperate with God's plan. But when he did recognise his mistakes, he was willing to admit them. His experience with Tamar and the final confrontation with Joseph are both examples of Judah's willingness to bear the blame when confronted. It was one of the qualities he passed on to his descendant David.

Whether or not we have Judah's natural leadership qualities, we share with him a tendency to be blind towards our own sin. Too often, however, we don't share his willingness to admit mistakes. From Judah we can learn that it is not wise to wait until our errors force us to admit to wrongdoing. It is far better to admit our mistakes openly, to shoulder the blame, and to seek forgiveness.

Strengths and accomplishments:
- Was a natural leader—outspoken and decisive
- Thought clearly and took action in high-pressure situations
- Was willing to stand by his word and put himself on the line when necessary
- Was the fourth son of 12, through whom God would eventually bring David and Jesus, the Messiah

Weaknesses and mistakes:
- Suggested to his brothers they sell Joseph into slavery
- Failed to keep his promise to his daughter-in-law, Tamar

Lessons from his life:
- God is in control, far beyond the immediate situation
- Procrastination often makes matters worse
- Judah's offer to substitute his life for Benjamin's is a picture of what his descendant Jesus would do for all people

Vital statistics:
- Where: Canaan and Egypt
- Occupation: Shepherd
- Relatives: Parents: Jacob and Leah. Wife: The daughter of Shua (1 Chronicles 2:3). Daughter-in-law: Tamar. Eleven brothers, at least one sister, and at least five sons

Key verses:
"Judah, your brothers will praise you; your hand will be on the neck of your enemies; your father's sons will bow down to you. You are a lion's cub, O Judah; you return from the prey, my son. Like a lion he crouches and lies down, like a lioness—who dares to rouse him? The scepter will not depart from Judah, nor the ruler's staff from between his feet, until he comes to whom it belongs and the obedience of the nations is his" (Genesis 49:8–10).

Judah's story is told in Genesis 29:35—50:26. He is also mentioned in 1 Chronicles 2—4.

45:4–8 Although Joseph's brothers had wanted to get rid of him, God used even their evil actions to fulfil his ultimate plan. He sent Joseph ahead to preserve their lives, save Egypt, and prepare the way for the beginning of the nation of Israel. God is sovereign. His plans are not dictated by human actions. When others intend evil towards you, remember that they are only God's tools. As Joseph said to his brothers, "You intended to harm me, but God intended it for good to accomplish what is now being done, the saving of many lives" (50:20).

distressed[g] and do not be angry with yourselves for selling me here,[h] because it was
to save lives that God sent me ahead of you.[i] 6For two years now there has been
famine in the land, and for the next five years there will not be ploughing and reaping.
7But God sent me ahead of you to preserve for you a remnant[j] on earth and to save
your lives by a great deliverance.[a][k]
8"So then, it was not you who sent me here, but God. He made me father[l] to Pharaoh, lord of his entire household and ruler of all Egypt.[m] 9Now hurry back to my father
and say to him, 'This is what your son Joseph says: God has made me lord of all Egypt.
Come down to me; don't delay.[n] 10You shall live in the region of Goshen[o] and be
near me—you, your children and grandchildren, your flocks and herds, and all you
have. 11I will provide for you there,[p] because five years of famine are still to come.
Otherwise you and your household and all who belong to you will become destitute.'
12"You can see for yourselves, and so can my brother Benjamin, that it is really I
who am speaking to you. 13Tell my father about all the honour accorded me in Egypt
and about everything you have seen. And bring my father down here quickly.[q]"
14Then he threw his arms around his brother Benjamin and wept, and Benjamin
embraced him, weeping. 15And he kissed[r] all his brothers and wept over them. Afterwards his brothers talked with him.[s]
16When the news reached Pharaoh's palace that Joseph's brothers had come,[t]
Pharaoh and all his officials were pleased. 17Pharaoh said to Joseph, "Tell your
brothers, 'Do this: Load your animals and return to the land of Canaan, 18and bring
your father and your families back to me. I will give you the best of the land of Egypt[u]
and you can enjoy the fat of the land.'[v]
19"You are also directed to tell them, 'Do this: Take some carts[w] from Egypt for
your children and your wives, and get your father and come. 20Never mind about your
belongings, because the best of all Egypt will be yours.' "
21So the sons of Israel did this. Joseph gave them carts, as Pharaoh had commanded,
and he also gave them provisions for their journey.[x] 22To each of them he gave new
clothing, but to Benjamin he gave three hundred shekels[b] of silver and five sets of
clothes.[y] 23And this is what he sent to his father: ten donkeys loaded with the best
things of Egypt, and ten female donkeys loaded with grain and bread and other provisions for his journey. 24Then he sent his brothers away, and as they were leaving he
said to them, "Don't quarrel on the way!"[z]
25So they went up out of Egypt and came to their father Jacob in the land of Canaan.
26They told him, "Joseph is still alive! In fact, he is ruler of all Egypt." Jacob was
stunned; he did not believe them.[a] 27But when they told him everything Joseph had
said to them, and when he saw the carts[b] Joseph had sent to carry him back, the spirit
of their father Jacob revived. 28And Israel said, "I'm convinced! My son Joseph is still
alive. I will go and see him before I die."

6. Jacob's family moves to Egypt

Jacob Goes to Egypt

46 So Israel set out with all that was his, and when he reached Beersheba,[a] he
offered sacrifices to the God of his father Isaac.[b]
2And God spoke to Israel in a vision at night[c] and said, "Jacob! Jacob!"
"Here I am,"[d] he replied.
3"I am God, the God of your father,"[e] he said. "Do not be afraid to go down to

a 7 Or *save you as a great band of survivors* b 22 That is, about 7½ pounds (about 3.5 kilograms)

45:5 [g]Ge 42:21 [h]Ge 42:22 [i]ver 7-8; Ge 50:20; Ps 105:17
45:7 [j]2Ki 19:4, 30, 31; Isa 10:20, 21; Mic 4:7; Zep 2:7 [k]Ex 15:2; Est 4:14; Isa 25:9
45:8 [l]Jdg 17:10 [m]Ge 41:41
45:9 [n]Ge 43:10
45:10 [o]Ge 46:28, 34; 47:1
45:11 [p]Ge 47:12
45:13 [q]Ac 7:14
45:15 [r]Lk 15:20 [s]ver 3
45:16 [t]Ac 7:13
45:18 [u]Ge 27:28; 46:34; 47:6, 11, 27; Nu 18:12, 29 [v]Ps 37:19
45:19 [w]Ge 46:5
45:21 [x]Ge 42:25
45:22 [y]Ge 37:3; 43:34
45:24 [z]Ge 42:21-22
45:26 [a]Ge 44:28
45:27 [b]ver 19
46:1 [a]Ge 21:14; 28:10 [b]Ge 26:24; 28:13; 31:42
46:2 [c]Ge 15:1; Job 33:14-15 [d]Ge 22:1; 31:11
46:3 [e]Ge 28:13

45:17–20 Joseph was rejected, kidnapped, enslaved, and imprisoned. Although his brothers had been unfaithful to him, he graciously forgave them and shared his prosperity. Joseph demonstrated how God forgives us and showers us with goodness even though we have sinned against him. The same forgiveness and blessings are ours if we ask for them.

45:26, 27 Jacob needed some evidence before he could believe the incredible news that Joseph was alive. Similarly, Thomas refused to believe that Jesus had risen from the dead until he could see and touch him (John 20:25). It is hard to change what you believe without all the facts—or sometimes even with the facts. Good news can be hard to believe. Don't ever give up hope that God has a wonderful future in store for you.

Egypt, for I will make you into a great nation[f] there.[g] 4I will go down to Egypt with
you, and I will surely bring you back again.[h] And Joseph's own hand will close your
eyes.[i]"
5Then Jacob left Beersheba, and Israel's sons took their father Jacob and their children and their wives in the carts[j] that Pharaoh had sent to transport him. 6They also
took with them their livestock and the possessions they had acquired in Canaan, and
Jacob and all his offspring went to Egypt.[k] 7He took with him to Egypt his sons and
grandsons and his daughters and granddaughters—all his offspring.[l]

8These are the names of the sons of Israel[m] (Jacob and his descendants) who went
to Egypt:

Reuben the firstborn of Jacob.
9The sons of Reuben:[n]
Hanoch, Pallu, Hezron and Carmi.
10The sons of Simeon:[o]
Jemuel,[p] Jamin, Ohad, Jakin, Zohar and Shaul the son of a Canaanite woman.
11The sons of Levi:[q]
Gershon, Kohath and Merari.
12The sons of Judah:[r]
Er, Onan, Shelah, Perez and Zerah (but Er and Onan had died in the land of Canaan).
The sons of Perez:[s]
Hezron and Hamul.
13The sons of Issachar:[t]
Tola, Puah,[a][u] Jashub[b] and Shimron.
14The sons of Zebulun:[v]
Sered, Elon and Jahleel.
15These were the sons Leah bore to Jacob in Paddan Aram,[c] besides his daughter
Dinah. These sons and daughters of his were thirty-three in all.

16The sons of Gad:[w]
Zephon,[d][x] Haggi, Shuni, Ezbon, Eri, Arodi and Areli.

a *13* Samaritan Pentateuch and Syriac (see also 1 Chron. 7:1); Masoretic Text *Puvah* b *13* Samaritan Pentateuch and some Septuagint manuscripts (see also Num. 26:24 and 1 Chron. 7:1); Masoretic Text *Job*
c *15* That is, North-west Mesopotamia d *16* Samaritan Pentateuch and Septuagint (see also Num. 26:15); Masoretic Text *Ziphion*

46:3 [f]Ge 12:2; Dt 26:5 [g]Ex 1:7
46:4 [h]Ge 28:15; 48:21; Ex 3:8 [i]Ge 50:1, 24
46:5 [j]Ge 45:19
46:6 [k]Dt 26:5; Jos 24:4; Ps 105:23; Isa 52:4; Ac 7:15
46:7 [l]Ge 45:10
46:8 [m]Ex 1:1; Nu 26:4
46:9 [n]1Ch 5:3
46:10 [o]Ge 29:33; Nu 26:14 [p]Ex 6:15
46:11 [q]Ge 29:34; Nu 3:17
46:12 [r]Ge 29:35 [s]1Ch 2:5; Mt 1:3
46:13 [t]Ge 30:18 [u]1Ch 7:1
46:14 [v]Ge 30:20
46:16 [w]Ge 30:11 [x]Nu 26:15

JACOB MOVES TO EGYPT
After hearing the joyful news that Joseph was alive, Jacob packed up and moved his family to Egypt. Stopping first in Beersheba, Jacob offered sacrifices and received assurance from God that Egypt was where he should go. Jacob and his family settled in the region of Goshen, in the north-eastern part of Egypt.

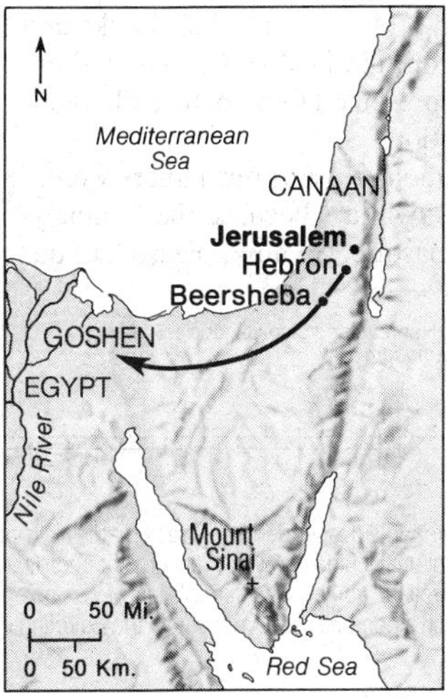

46:3, 4 The Israelites did become a great nation, and Jacob's descendants eventually returned to Canaan. The book of Exodus recounts the story of Israel's slavery in Egypt for 400 years (fulfilling God's words to Abraham in 15:13–16), and the book of Joshua gives an exciting account of the Israelites entering and conquering Canaan, the promised land.

46:3, 4 God told Jacob to leave his home and travel to a strange and faraway land. But God reassured him by promising to go with him and take care of him. When new situations or surroundings frighten you, recognise that experiencing fear is normal. To be paralysed by fear, however, is an indication that you question God's ability to take care of you.

46:4 Jacob never returned to Canaan. This was a promise to his descendants that they would return. "Joseph's own hand will close your eyes" refers to Joseph attending to Jacob as he faced death. It was God's promise to Jacob that he would never know the bitterness of being lonely again.

17The sons of Asher:[y]
Imnah, Ishvah, Ishvi and Beriah.
Their sister was Serah.
The sons of Beriah:
Heber and Malkiel.
18These were the children born to Jacob by Zilpah,[z] whom Laban had given to his
daughter Leah[a]—sixteen in all.

19The sons of Jacob's wife Rachel:
Joseph and Benjamin.[b] 20In Egypt, Manasseh[c] and Ephraim[d] were born to
Joseph by Asenath daughter of Potiphera, priest of On.[e]
21The sons of Benjamin:[e]
Bela, Beker, Ashbel, Gera, Naaman, Ehi, Rosh, Muppim, Huppim and Ard.
22These were the sons of Rachel who were born to Jacob—fourteen in all.

23The son of Dan:
Hushim.
24The sons of Naphtali:
Jahziel, Guni, Jezer and Shillem.
25These were the sons born to Jacob by Bilhah,[f] whom Laban had given to his
daughter Rachel[g]—seven in all.

26All those who went to Egypt with Jacob—those who were his direct descendants,
not counting his sons' wives—numbered sixty-six persons.[h] 27With the two sons[f]
who had been born to Joseph in Egypt, the members of Jacob's family, which went to
Egypt, were seventy[g] in all.[i]

28Now Jacob sent Judah ahead of him to Joseph to get directions to Goshen.[j] When
they arrived in the region of Goshen, 29Joseph had his chariot made ready and went to
Goshen to meet his father Israel. As soon as Joseph appeared before him, he threw his
arms around his father[h] and wept for a long time.[k]
30Israel said to Joseph, "Now I am ready to die, since I have seen for myself that you
are still alive."
31Then Joseph said to his brothers and to his father's household, "I will go up and
speak to Pharaoh and will say to him, 'My brothers and my father's household, who
were living in the land of Canaan, have come to me.[l] 32The men are shepherds; they
tend livestock, and they have brought along their flocks and herds and everything they
own.' 33When Pharaoh calls you in and asks, 'What is your occupation?'[m] 34you
should answer, 'Your servants have tended livestock from our boyhood on, just as our
fathers did.' Then you will be allowed to settle in the region of Goshen,[n] for all shepherds are detestable to the Egyptians.[o]"

47 Joseph went and told Pharaoh, "My father and brothers, with their flocks and
herds and everything they own, have come from the land of Canaan and are
now in Goshen."[a] 2He chose five of his brothers and presented them before Pharaoh.
3Pharaoh asked the brothers, "What is your occupation?"[b]
"Your servants are shepherds," they replied to Pharaoh, "just as our fathers were."
4They also said to him, "We have come to live here awhile,[c] because the famine is
severe in Canaan[d] and your servants' flocks have no pasture. So now, please let your
servants settle in Goshen."[e]

e *20* That is, Heliopolis **f** *27* Hebrew; Septuagint *the nine children* **g** *27* Hebrew (see also Exodus 1:5 and footnote); Septuagint (see also Acts 7:14) *seventy-five* **h** *29* Hebrew *around him*

46:17 [y]Ge 30:13; 1Ch 7:30-31
46:18 [z]Ge 30:10 [a]Ge 29:24
46:19 [b]Ge 44:27
46:20 [c]Ge 41:51 [d]Ge 41:52
46:21 [e]Nu 26:38-41; 1Ch 7:6-12; 8:1
46:25 [f]Ge 30:8 [g]Ge 29:29
46:26 [h]ver 5-7; Ex 1:5; Dt 10:22
46:27 [i]Ac 7:14
46:28 [j]Ge 45:10
46:29 [k]Ge 45:14-15; Lk 15:20
46:31 [l]Ge 47:1
46:33 [m]Ge 47:3
46:34 [n]Ge 45:10 [o]Ge 43:32; Ex 8:26
47:1 [a]Ge 46:31
47:3 [b]Ge 46:33
47:4 [c]Ge 15:13; Dt 26:5 [d]Ge 43:1 [e]Ge 46:34

46:31–34 Jacob moved his whole family to Egypt, but they wanted to live apart from the Egyptians. To ensure this, Joseph told them to let Pharaoh know they were shepherds. Although Pharaoh may have been sympathetic to shepherds (for he was probably descended from the nomadic Hyksos line), the Egyptian culture would not willingly accept shepherds among them. The strategy worked, and Jacob's family was able to benefit from Pharaoh's generosity as well as from the Egyptians' prejudice.

5Pharaoh said to Joseph, "Your father and your brothers have come to you, 6and the
land of Egypt is before you; settle your father and your brothers in the best part of the
land.[f] Let them live in Goshen. And if you know of any among them with special
ability,[g] put them in charge of my own livestock."
7Then Joseph brought his father Jacob in and presented him before Pharaoh. After
Jacob blessed[a] Pharaoh,[h] 8Pharaoh asked him, "How old are you?"
9And Jacob said to Pharaoh, "The years of my pilgrimage are a hundred and
thirty.[i] My years have been few and difficult,[j] and they do not equal the years of the
pilgrimage of my fathers.[k]" 10Then Jacob blessed[b] Pharaoh[l] and went out from his
presence.
11So Joseph settled his father and his brothers in Egypt and gave them property in
the best part of the land, the district of Rameses,[m] as Pharaoh directed. 12Joseph also
provided his father and his brothers and all his father's household with food, according
to the number of their children.[n]

Joseph and the Famine

13There was no food, however, in the whole region because the famine was severe;
both Egypt and Canaan wasted away because of the famine.[o] 14Joseph collected all
the money that was to be found in Egypt and Canaan in payment for the grain they were
buying, and he brought it to Pharaoh's palace.[p] 15When the money of the people of
Egypt and Canaan was gone, all Egypt came to Joseph and said, "Give us food. Why
should we die before your eyes?[q] Our money is used up."
16"Then bring your livestock," said Joseph. "I will sell you food in exchange for
your livestock, since your money is gone." 17So they brought their livestock to Joseph,
and he gave them food in exchange for their horses,[r] their sheep and goats, their cattle
and donkeys. And he brought them through that year with food in exchange for all their
livestock.
18When that year was over, they came to him the following year and said, "We
cannot hide from our lord the fact that since our money is gone and our livestock belongs to you, there is nothing left for our lord except our bodies and our land. 19Why
should we perish before your eyes—we and our land as well? Buy us and our land in
exchange for food, and we with our land will be in bondage to Pharaoh. Give us seed
so that we may live and not die, and that the land may not become desolate."
20So Joseph bought all the land in Egypt for Pharaoh. The Egyptians, one and all,
sold their fields, because the famine was too severe for them. The land became Pharaoh's, 21and Joseph reduced the people to servitude,[c] from one end of Egypt to the
other. 22However, he did not buy the land of the priests, because they received a regular allotment from Pharaoh and had food enough from the allotment[s] Pharaoh gave
them. That is why they did not sell their land.
23Joseph said to the people, "Now that I have bought you and your land today for
Pharaoh, here is seed for you so you can plant the ground. 24But when the crop comes
in, give a fifth[t] of it to Pharaoh. The other four-fifths you may keep as seed for the
fields and as food for yourselves and your households and your children."
25"You have saved our lives," they said. "May we find favour in the eyes of our
lord;[u] we will be in bondage to Pharaoh."
26So Joseph established it as a law concerning land in Egypt—still in force today—that a fifth of the produce belongs to Pharaoh. It was only the land of the priests
that did not become Pharaoh's.[v]
27Now the Israelites settled in Egypt in the region of Goshen. They acquired property there and were fruitful and increased greatly in number.[w]

a *7* Or *greeted* **b** *10* Or *said farewell to* **c** *21* Samaritan Pentateuch and Septuagint (see also Vulgate); Masoretic Text *and he moved the people into the cities*

47:6 [f]Ge 45:18 [g]Ex 18:21, 25
47:7 [h]ver 10; 2Sa 14:22
47:9 [i]Ge 25:7 [j]Heb 11:9, 13 [k]Ge 35:28
47:10 [l]ver 7
47:11 [m]Ex 1:11; 12:37
47:12 [n]Ge 45:11
47:13 [o]Ge 41:30; Ac 7:11
47:14 [p]Ge 41:56
47:15 [q]ver 19; Ex 16:3
47:17 [r]Ex 14:9
47:22 [s]Dt 14:28-29; Ezr 7:24
47:24 [t]Ge 41:34
47:25 [u]Ge 32:5
47:26 [v]ver 22
47:27 [w]Ge 17:6; 46:3; Ex 1:7

47:1-6 The faithfulness of Joseph affected his entire family. When he was in the pit and in prison, Joseph must have wondered about his future. Instead of despairing, he faithfully obeyed God and did what was right. Here we see one of the exciting results. We may not always see the effects of our faith, but we can be sure that God will honour faithfulness.

7. Jacob and Joseph die in Egypt

28Jacob lived in Egypt[x] seventeen years, and the years of his life were a hundred
and forty-seven. 29When the time drew near for Israel to die,[y] he called for his son
Joseph and said to him, "If I have found favour in your eyes, put your hand under my
thigh[z] and promise that you will show me kindness and faithfulness.[a] Do not bury
me in Egypt, 30but when I rest with my fathers, carry me out of Egypt and bury me
where they are buried."[b]
"I will do as you say," he said.
31"Swear to me,"[c] he said. Then Joseph swore to him,[d] and Israel worshipped as
he leaned on the top of his staff.[d][e]

Manasseh and Ephraim

48 Some time later Joseph was told, "Your father is ill." So he took his two sons
Manasseh and Ephraim[a] along with him. 2When Jacob was told, "Your son
Joseph has come to you," Israel rallied his strength and sat up on the bed.
3Jacob said to Joseph, "God Almighty[a] appeared to me at Luz[b] in the land of
Canaan, and there he blessed me[c] 4and said to me, 'I am going to make you fruitful
and will increase your numbers.[d] I will make you a community of peoples, and I will
give this land as an everlasting possession to your descendants after you.'
5"Now then, your two sons born to you in Egypt[e] before I came to you here will be
reckoned as mine; Ephraim and Manasseh will be mine,[f] just as Reuben and Simeon
are mine. 6Any children born to you after them will be yours; in the territory they
inherit they will be reckoned under the names of their brothers. 7As I was returning
from Paddan,[b] to my sorrow Rachel died in the land of Canaan while we were still on
the way, a little distance from Ephrath. So I buried her there beside the road to Ephrath" (that is, Bethlehem).[g]
8When Israel saw the sons of Joseph, he asked, "Who are these?"
9"They are the sons God has given me here,"[h] Joseph said to his father.
Then Israel said, "Bring them to me so that I may bless[i] them."
10Now Israel's eyes were failing because of old age, and he could hardly see.[j] So
Joseph brought his sons close to him, and his father kissed them[k] and embraced them.
11Israel said to Joseph, "I never expected to see your face again, and now God has
allowed me to see your children too."[l]
12Then Joseph removed them from Israel's knees and bowed down with his face to
the ground. 13And Joseph took both of them, Ephraim on his right towards Israel's left
hand and Manasseh on his left towards Israel's right hand,[m] and brought them close to
him. 14But Israel reached out his right hand and put it on Ephraim's head, though he
was the younger, and crossing his arms, he put his left hand on Manasseh's head, even
though Manasseh was the firstborn.[n]
15Then he blessed[o] Joseph and said,

> "May the God before whom my fathers

47:28 [x]Ps 105:23
47:29 [y]Dt 31:14 [z]Ge 24:2 [a]Ge 24:49
47:30 [b]Ge 49:29-32; 50:5, 13; Ac 7:15-16
47:31 [c]Ge 21:23 [d]Ge 24:3 [e]Heb 11:21 *fn* 1Ki 1:47
48:1 [a]Ge 41:52
48:3 [b]Ge 28:19 [c]Ge 28:13; 35:9-12
48:4 [d]Ge 17:6
48:5 [e]Ge 41:50-52; 46:20 [f]1Ch 5:1; Jos 14:4
48:7 [g]Ge 35:19
48:9 [h]Ge 33:5 [i]Ge 27:4
48:10 [j]Ge 27:1 [k]Ge 27:27
48:11 [l]Ge 50:23; Ps 128:6
48:13 [m]Ps 110:1
48:14 [n]Ge 41:51
48:15 [o]Ge 17:1

d *31* Or *Israel bowed down at the head of his bed* **a** *3* Hebrew *El-Shaddai* **b** *7* That is, North-west Mesopotamia

---

47:29–31 Putting a hand under the thigh was a sign of making a promise, much like shaking hands today. Jacob had Joseph promise to bury him in his homeland. Few things were written in this culture, so a person's word then carried as much force as a written contract today. People today seem to find it easy to say, "I didn't mean that." God's people, however, are to speak the truth and live the truth. Let your words be as binding as a written contract.

48:8–20 Jacob gave Ephraim, instead of his older brother Manasseh, the greater blessing. When Joseph objected, Jacob refused to listen because God had told him that Ephraim would become greater. God often works in unexpected ways. When he chooses people to fulfil his plans, he always goes deeper than appearance, tradition, or position. He sometimes surprises us by choosing the less obvious person, at least by human reasoning. God can use you to carry out his plans, even if you don't think you have all the qualifications.

48:11 When Joseph became a slave, Jacob thought he was dead and wept in despair (37:30). But eventually God's plan allowed Jacob to regain not only his son, but his grandchildren as well. Circumstances are never so bad that they are beyond God's help. Jacob regained his son. Job got a new family (Job 42:10–17). Mary regained her brother Lazarus (John 11:1–44). We need never despair because we belong to a loving God. We never know what good he will bring out of a seemingly hopeless situation.

48:15 Jacob spoke of God as his shepherd throughout his life. In his old age, he could clearly see his dependence upon God. This marks a total attitude change from that of his scheming and dishonest youth. To develop an attitude like Jacob's, let God shepherd you as you trust in his provision and care. When you realise that every good thing comes from God, you can cease trying to grab them for yourself.

Abraham and Isaac walked,
the God who has been my shepherd[p]
all my life to this day,
16the Angel who has delivered me from all harm
—may he bless these boys.[q]
May they be called by my name
and the names of my fathers Abraham and Isaac,[r]
and may they increase greatly
upon the earth."

17When Joseph saw his father placing his right hand on Ephraim's head[s] he was
displeased; so he took hold of his father's hand to move it from Ephraim's head to
Manasseh's head. 18Joseph said to him, "No, my father, this one is the firstborn; put
your right hand on his head."
19But his father refused and said, "I know, my son, I know. He too will become a
people, and he too will become great.[t] Nevertheless, his younger brother will be
greater than he,[u] and his descendants will become a group of nations." 20He blessed
them that day and said,

"In your**[c]** name will Israel pronounce this blessing:
'May God make you like Ephraim[v] and Manasseh.[w]' "

So he put Ephraim ahead of Manasseh.
21Then Israel said to Joseph, "I am about to die, but God will be with you**[d]**[x] and
take you**[d]** back to the land of your**[d]** fathers.[y] 22And to you, as one who is over your
brothers,[z] I give the ridge of land**[e]**[a] I took from the Amorites with my sword and my
bow."

Jacob Blesses His Sons

49 Then Jacob called for his sons and said: "Gather round so that I can tell you
what will happen to you in days to come.[a]

2"Assemble and listen, sons of Jacob;
listen to your father Israel.[b]

3"Reuben, you are my firstborn,[c]
my might, the first sign of my strength,[d]
excelling in honour, excelling in power.
4Turbulent as the waters,[e] you will no longer excel,
for you went up onto your father's bed,
onto my couch and defiled it.[f]

5"Simeon and Levi are brothers—
their swords**[a]** are weapons of violence.[g]
6Let me not enter their council,
let me not join their assembly,[h]
for they have killed men in their anger[i]
and hamstrung oxen as they pleased.
7Cursed be their anger, so fierce,
and their fury, so cruel!

48:15 [p]Ge 49:24
48:16 [q]Heb 11:21 [r]Ge 28:13
48:17 [s]ver 14
48:19 [t]Ge 17:20 [u]Ge 25:23
48:20 [v]Nu 2:18 [w]Nu 2:20; Ru 4:11
48:21 [x]Ge 26:3; 46:4 [y]Ge 28:13; 50:24
48:22 [z]Ge 37:8 [a]Jos 24:32; Jn 4:5
49:1 [a]Nu 24:14; Jer 23:20
49:2 [b]Ps 34:11
49:3 [c]Ge 29:32 [d]Dt 21:17; Ps 78:51
49:4 [e]Isa 57:20 [f]Ge 35:22; Dt 27:20
49:5 [g]Ge 34:25; Pr 4:17
49:6 [h]Pr 1:15; Eph 5:11 [i]Ge 34:26

c *20* The Hebrew is singular. **d** *21* The Hebrew is plural. **e** *22* Or *And to you I give one portion more than to your brothers—the portion* **a** *5* The meaning of the Hebrew for this word is uncertain.

48:20–22 Jacob was giving these young boys land occupied by the Philistines and Canaanites. His gift became reality when the tribes of Ephraim and Manasseh occupied the east and west sides of the Jordan River (Joshua 16).

49:3–28 Jacob blessed each of his sons and then made a prediction about each one's future. The way the men had lived played an important part in Jacob's blessing and prophecy. Our past also affects our present and future. By sunrise tomorrow, our actions of today will have become part of the past. Yet they will already have begun to shape the future. What actions can you choose or avoid that will positively shape your future?

49:4 The oldest son was supposed to receive a double inheritance, but Reuben lost his special honour. Unstable and untrustworthy, especially in his younger days, he had gone so far as to sleep with one of his father's concubines. Jacob could not give the birthright blessing to such a dishonourable son.

I will scatter them in Jacob
and disperse them in Israel.[j]

8"Judah,[b] your brothers will praise you;
your hand will be on the neck of your enemies;
your father's sons will bow down to you.[k]
9You are a lion[l]'s cub, O Judah;[m]
you return from the prey, my son.
Like a lion he crouches and lies down,
like a lioness — who dares to rouse him?
10The sceptre will not depart from Judah,[n]
nor the ruler's staff from between his feet,
until he comes to whom it belongs[c]
and the obedience of the nations is his.[o]
11He will tether his donkey to a vine,
his colt to the choicest branch;
he will wash his garments in wine,
his robes in the blood of grapes.
12His eyes will be darker than wine,
his teeth whiter than milk.[d]

13"Zebulun[p] will live by the seashore
and become a haven for ships;
his border will extend towards Sidon.

14"Issachar[q] is a scrawny[e] donkey
lying down between two saddlebags.[f]
15When he sees how good is his resting place
and how pleasant is his land,
he will bend his shoulder to the burden
and submit to forced labour.

16"Dan[g][r] will provide justice for his people
as one of the tribes of Israel.
17Dan[s] will be a serpent by the roadside,
a viper along the path,
that bites the horse's heels
so that its rider tumbles backwards.

18"I look for your deliverance, O LORD.[t]

19"Gad[h][u] will be attacked by a band of raiders,
but he will attack them at their heels.

20"Asher's[v] food will be rich;
he will provide delicacies fit for a king.

b 8 *Judah* sounds like and may be derived from the Hebrew for *praise.* c 10 Or *until Shiloh comes*; or *until he comes to whom tribute belongs* d 12 Or *will be dull from wine, / his teeth white from milk* e 14 Or *strong* f 14 Or *campfires* g 16 *Dan* here means *he provides justice.* h 19 *Gad* can mean *attack* and *band of raiders.*

49:7 j Jos 19:1, 9; 21:1-42
49:8 k Dt 33:7; 1Ch 5:2
49:9 l Nu 24:9; Eze 19:5; Mic 5:8 m Rev 5:5
49:10 n Nu 24:17, 19; Ps 60:7 o Ps 2:9; Isa 42:1, 4
49:13 p Ge 30:20; Dt 33:18-19; Jos 19:10-11
49:14 q Ge 30:18
49:16 r Ge 30:6; Dt 33:22; Jdg 18:26-27
49:17 s Jdg 18:27
49:18 t Ps 119:166, 174
49:19 u Ge 30:11; Dt 33:20; 1Ch 5:18
49:20 v Ge 30:13; Dt 33:24

49:8–12 Why was Judah – known for selling Joseph into slavery and trying to defraud his daughter-in-law – so greatly blessed? God had chosen Judah to be the ancestor of Israel's line of kings (that is the meaning of "the sceptre will not depart from Judah"). This may have been due to Judah's dramatic change of character (44:33, 34). Judah's line would produce the promised Messiah, Jesus.

49:10 "Until he comes to whom it belongs" may also be translated, "until Shiloh comes". What is *Shiloh?* The meaning of this difficult passage is disputed. Shiloh may be another name for the Messiah, because its literal meaning is "sent". Shiloh might also refer to the Tent of Meeting set up at the city of Shiloh (Joshua 18:1).

49:18 In the middle of his prophecy to Dan, Jacob exclaimed, "I look for your deliverance, O LORD." He was emphasising to Dan that he would be a strong leader only if his trust was in God, not in his natural strength or ability. Those who are strong, attractive, or talented often find it easier to trust in themselves than in God who gave them their gifts. Remember to thank God for what you are and have so your trust does not become misplaced.

49:21 [w]Ge 30:8; Dt 33:23
49:22 [x]Ge 30:24; Dt 33:13-17
49:23 [y]Ge 37:24
49:24 [z]Ps 18:34 [a]Ps 132:2, 5; Isa 1:24; 41:10 [b]Isa 28:16
49:25 [c]Ge 28:13 [d]Ge 27:28
49:26 [e]Dt 33:15-16
49:27 [f]Ge 35:18; Jdg 20:12-13

21 "Naphtali[w] is a doe set free
that bears beautiful fawns.[i]

22 "Joseph[x] is a fruitful vine,
a fruitful vine near a spring,
whose branches climb over a wall.[j]
23 With bitterness archers attacked him;
they shot at him with hostility.[y]
24 But his bow remained steady,
his strong arms[z] stayed[k] supple,
because of the hand of the Mighty One of Jacob,[a]
because of the Shepherd, the Rock of Israel,[b]
25 because of your father's God,[c] who helps you,
because of the Almighty,[l] who blesses you
with blessings of the heavens above,
blessings of the deep that lies below,[d]
blessings of the breast and womb.
26 Your father's blessings are greater
than the blessings of the ancient mountains,
than[m] the bounty of the age-old hills.
Let all these rest on the head of Joseph,
on the brow of the prince among[n] his brothers.[e]

27 "Benjamin[f] is a ravenous wolf;
in the morning he devours the prey,
in the evening he divides the plunder."

[i] *21* Or *free; / he utters beautiful words* [j] *22* Or *Joseph is a wild colt, / a wild colt near a spring, / a wild donkey on a terraced hill* [k] *23,24* Or *archers will attack . . . will shoot . . . will remain . . . will stay* [l] *25* Hebrew *Shaddai* [m] *26* Or *of my progenitors, / as great as* [n] *26* Or *the one separated from*

PARALLELS BETWEEN JOSEPH AND JESUS
Genesis 37–50

Joseph	*Parallels*	*Jesus*
37:3	Their fathers loved them dearly	Matthew 3:17
37:2	Shepherds of their fathers' sheep	John 10:11, 27
37:13, 14	Sent by father to brothers	Hebrews 2:11
37:4	Hated by brothers	John 7:5
37:20	Others plotted to harm them	John 11:53
39:7	Tempted	Matthew 4:1
37:25	Taken to Egypt	Matthew 2:14, 15
37:23	Robes taken from them	John 19:23
37:28	Sold for the price of a slave	Matthew 26:15
39:20	Bound in chains	Matthew 27:2
39:16–18	Falsely accused	Matthew 26:59, 60
40:2, 3	Placed with two other prisoners, one who was saved and the other lost	Luke 23:32
41:46	Both 30 years old at the beginning of public recognition	Luke 3:23
41:41	Exalted after suffering	Philippians 2:9–11
45:1–15	Forgave those who wronged them	Luke 23:34
45:7	Saved their nation	Matthew 1:21
50:20	What men did to hurt them God turned to good	1 Corinthians 2:7, 8

49:22 Joseph was indeed fruitful, with some heroic descendants. Among them were Joshua, who would lead the Israelites into the promised land (Joshua 1:10, 11); Deborah, Gideon, and Jephthah, judges of Israel (Judges 4:4; 6:11, 12; 11:11); and Samuel, a great prophet (1 Samuel 3:19).

49:23, 24 These verses celebrate the times God rescued Joseph when his enemies attacked him. So often we struggle by ourselves, forgetting that God is able to help us fight our battles, whether they are against men with weapons or against spiritual forces. Joseph was able to draw closer to God as adversity mounted. To trust God to rescue you shows great faith. Can you trust him when injury or persecution is directed at you? Such spiritual battles require teamwork between courageous, faithful people and a mighty God.

28 All these are the twelve tribes of Israel, and this is what their father said to them
when he blessed them, giving each the blessing appropriate to him.

The Death of Jacob

29 Then he gave them these instructions:[g] "I am about to be gathered to my people.[h] Bury me with my fathers[i] in the cave in the field of Ephron the Hittite, 30 the
cave in the field of Machpelah,[j] near Mamre in Canaan, which Abraham bought as a
burial place from Ephron the Hittite, along with the field.[k] 31 There Abraham[l] and
his wife Sarah[m] were buried, there Isaac and his wife Rebekah[n] were buried, and
there I buried Leah. 32 The field and the cave in it were bought from the Hittites."[o]
33 When Jacob had finished giving instructions to his sons, he drew his feet up into
the bed, breathed his last and was gathered to his people.[o]

50 Joseph threw himself upon his father and wept over him and kissed him.[a]
2 Then Joseph directed the physicians in his service to embalm his father Israel.
So the physicians embalmed him,[b] 3 taking a full forty days, for that was the time
required for embalming. And the Egyptians mourned for him seventy days.[c]
4 When the days of mourning had passed, Joseph said to Pharaoh's court, "If I have
found favour in your eyes, speak to Pharaoh for me. Tell him, 5 'My father made me
swear an oath[d] and said, "I am about to die; bury me in the tomb I dug for myself[e]
in the land of Canaan."[f] Now let me go up and bury my father; then I will return.' "
6 Pharaoh said, "Go up and bury your father, as he made you swear to do."
7 So Joseph went up to bury his father. All Pharaoh's officials accompanied
him—the dignitaries of his court and all the dignitaries of Egypt—8 besides all the
members of Joseph's household and his brothers and those belonging to his father's
household. Only their children and their flocks and herds were left in Goshen. 9 Chariots and horsemen[a] also went up with him. It was a very large company.
10 When they reached the threshing-floor of Atad, near the Jordan, they lamented
loudly and bitterly;[g] and there Joseph observed a seven-day period[h] of mourning for
his father. 11 When the Canaanites who lived there saw the mourning at the threshing-
floor of Atad, they said, "The Egyptians are holding a solemn ceremony of mourning."
That is why that place near the Jordan is called Abel Mizraim.[b]
12 So Jacob's sons did as he had commanded them: 13 They carried him to the land of

[o] *32* Or *the sons of Heth* [a] *9* Or *charioteers* [b] *11* *Abel Mizraim* means *mourning of the Egyptians.*

49:29 [g]Ge 50:16 [h]Ge 25:8 [i]Ge 15:15; 47:30; 50:13
49:30 [j]Ge 23:9 [k]Ge 23:20
49:31 [l]Ge 25:9 [m]Ge 23:19 [n]Ge 35:29
49:33 [o]ver 29; Ge 25:8; Ac 7:15
50:1 [a]Ge 46:4
50:2 [b]ver 26; 2Ch 16:14
50:3 [c]Ge 37:34; Nu 20:29; Dt 34:8
50:5 [d]Ge 47:31 [e]2Ch 16:14; Isa 22:16 [f]Ge 47:31
50:10 [g]2Sa 1:17; Ac 8:2 [h]1Sa 31:13; Job 2:13

JACOB'S SONS AND THEIR NOTABLE DESCENDANTS
Jacob's 12 sons were the ancestors of the 12 tribes of Israel. The entire nation of Israel came from these men.

REUBEN	none
SIMEON	none
LEVI	Aaron, Moses, Eli, John the Baptist
JUDAH	David, Jesus
DAN	Samson
NAPHTALI	Barak, Elijah (?)
GAD	Jephthah (?)
ASHER	none
ISSACHAR	none
ZEBULUN	none
JOSEPH	Joshua, Gideon, Samuel
BENJAMIN	Saul, Esther, Paul

50:1–11 When Jacob died at the age of 147, Joseph wept and mourned for months. When someone close to us dies, we need a long period of time to work through our grief. Crying and sharing our feelings with others helps us recover and go on with life. Allow yourself and others the freedom to grieve over the loss of a loved one, and give yourself time enough to complete your grieving process.

50:2, 3 Embalming was typical for Egyptians but unusual for nomadic shepherds. Believing that the dead went to the next world in their physical bodies, the Egyptians embalmed bodies to preserve them so they could function in the world to come. Jacob's family allowed him to be embalmed as a sign of courtesy and respect to the Egyptians.

50:5 Joseph had proved himself trustworthy as Pharaoh's adviser. Because of his good record, Pharaoh had little doubt that he would return to Egypt as promised after burying his father in Canaan. Privileges and freedom often result when we have demonstrated our trustworthiness. Since trust must be built gradually over time, take every opportunity to prove your reliability even in minor matters.

50:12, 13 Abraham had purchased the cave in the field of Machpelah as a burial place for his wife, Sarah (23:1–9). It was to be a burial place for his entire family. Jacob was Abraham's grandson,

Canaan and buried him in the cave in the field of Machpelah, near Mamre, which
Abraham had bought as a burial place from Ephron the Hittite, along with the field.[i]
14 After burying his father, Joseph returned to Egypt, together with his brothers and all
the others who had gone with him to bury his father.

Joseph Reassures His Brothers

15 When Joseph's brothers saw that their father was dead, they said, "What if Joseph
holds a grudge against us and pays us back for all the wrongs we did to him?"[j] 16 So
they sent word to Joseph, saying, "Your father left these instructions before he died:
17 'This is what you are to say to Joseph: I ask you to forgive your brothers the sins and
the wrongs they committed in treating you so badly.' Now please forgive the sins of the
servants of the God of your father." When their message came to him, Joseph wept.
18 His brothers then came and threw themselves down before him.[k] "We are your
slaves,"[l] they said.
19 But Joseph said to them, "Don't be afraid. Am I in the place of God?[m] 20 You
intended to harm me,[n] but God intended[o] it for good[p] to accomplish what is now
being done, the saving of many lives.[q] 21 So then, don't be afraid. I will provide for
you and your children.[r]" And he reassured them and spoke kindly to them.

The Death of Joseph

22 Joseph stayed in Egypt, along with all his father's family. He lived a hundred and
ten years[s] 23 and saw the third generation[t] of Ephraim's children. Also the children
of Makir[u] son of Manasseh were placed at birth on Joseph's knees.[c]
24 Then Joseph said to his brothers, "I am about to die.[v] But God will surely come
to your aid[w] and take you up out of this land to the land[x] he promised on oath to
Abraham, Isaac and Jacob."[y] 25 And Joseph made the sons of Israel swear an oath and
said, "God will surely come to your aid, and then you must carry my bones up from
this place."[z]
26 So Joseph died at the age of a hundred and ten. And after they embalmed him,[a]
he was placed in a coffin in Egypt.

c *23* That is, were counted as his

50:13 [i] Ge 23:20; Ac 7:16
50:15 [j] Ge 37:28; 42:21-22
50:18 [k] Ge 37:7 [l] Ge 43:18
50:19 [m] Ro 12:19; Heb 10:30
50:20 [n] Ge 37:20 [o] Mic 4:11-12 [p] Ro 8:28 [q] Ge 45:5
50:21 [r] Ge 45:11; 47:12
50:22 [s] Ge 25:7; Jos 24:29
50:23 [t] Job 42:16 [u] Nu 32:39, 40
50:24 [v] Ge 48:21 [w] Ex 3:16-17 [x] Ge 15:14 [y] Ge 12:7; 26:3; 28:13; 35:12
50:25 [z] Ge 47:29-30; Ex 13:19; Jos 24:32; Heb 11:22
50:26 [a] ver 2

---

and Jacob's sons returned to Canaan to bury him in this cave along with Abraham and Isaac. Their desire to be buried in this cave expressed their faith in God's promise to give their descendants the land of Canaan.

50:15–21 Now that Jacob (or Israel) was dead, the brothers feared revenge from Joseph. Could he really have forgiven them for selling him into slavery? But to their surprise, Joseph not only forgave them but reassured them, offering to care for them and their families. Joseph's forgiveness was complete. He demonstrated how God graciously accepts us even though we don't deserve it. Because God forgives us even when we have ignored or rejected him, we should graciously forgive others.

50:20 God brought good from the brothers' evil deed, Potiphar's wife's false accusation, the cupbearer's neglect, and seven years of famine. The experiences in Joseph's life taught him that God brings good from evil for those who trust him. Do you trust God enough to wait patiently for him to bring good out of bad situations? You can trust him because, as Joseph learned, God can overrule people's evil intentions to bring about his intended results.

50:24 Joseph was ready to die. He had no doubts that God would keep his promise and one day bring the Israelites back to their homeland. What a tremendous example! The secret of that kind of faith is a lifetime of trusting God. Your faith is like a muscle – it grows with exercise, gaining strength over time. After a lifetime of exercising trust, your faith can be as strong as Joseph's. Then at your death, you can be confident that God will fulfil all his promises to you and to all those faithful to him who may live after you.

50:24 This verse sets the stage for what would begin to happen in Exodus and come to completion in Joshua. God was going to make Jacob's family into a great nation, lead them out of Egypt, and bring them into the land he had promised them. The nation would rely heavily on this promise, and Joseph emphasised his belief that God would do what he had promised.

50:26 The book of Genesis gives us rich descriptions of the lives of many great men and women who walked with God. They sometimes succeeded and often failed. Yet we learn much by reading the biographies of these people. Where did they get their motivation and courage? They got it by realising God was with them despite their inadequacies. Knowing this should encourage us to be faithful to God, to rely on him for guidance, and to utilise the potential he has given us.

EXODUS

Joseph dies 1805 B.C. (1640 B.C.)

VITAL STATISTICS

PURPOSE:
To record the events of Israel's deliverance from Egypt and development as a nation

AUTHOR:
Moses

DATE WRITTEN:
1450–1410 B.C., approximately the same as Genesis

WHERE WRITTEN:
In the desert during Israel's wanderings, somewhere in the Sinai peninsula

SETTING:
Egypt. God's people, once highly favoured in the land, are now slaves. God is about to set them free.

KEY VERSES:
"The LORD said, 'I have indeed seen the misery of my people in Egypt. I have heard them crying out because of their slave drivers, and I am concerned about their suffering. . . . So now, go. I am sending you to Pharaoh to bring my people the Israelites out of Egypt' " (3:7, 10).

KEY PEOPLE:
Moses, Miriam, Pharaoh, Pharaoh's daughter, Jethro, Aaron, Joshua, Bezalel

KEY PLACES:
Egypt, Goshen, Nile River, Midian, Red Sea, Sinai peninsula, Mount Sinai

SPECIAL FEATURES:
Exodus relates more miracles than any other Old Testament book and is noted for containing the Ten Commandments

GET UP . . . leave . . . take off—these words are good ones for those trapped or enslaved. Some resist their marching orders, however, preferring present surroundings to a new, unknown environment. It's not easy to trade the comfortable security of the known for an uncertain future. But what if God gives the order to move? Will we follow his lead? Exodus describes a series of God's calls and the responses of his people.

Four hundred years had passed since Joseph moved his family to Egypt. These descendants of Abraham had now grown to over two million strong. To Egypt's new Pharaoh, these Hebrews were foreigners, and their numbers were frightening. Pharaoh decided to make them slaves so they wouldn't upset his balance of power. As it turned out, that was his biggest mistake, for God then came to the rescue of his people.

Through a series of strange events, a Hebrew boy named Moses became a prince in Pharaoh's palace and then an outcast in a desert land. God visited Moses in the mysterious flames of a burning bush, and, after some discussion, Moses agreed to return to Egypt to lead God's people out of slavery. Pharaoh was confronted, and, through a cycle of plagues and promises made and broken, Israel was torn from his grasp.

It was no easy task to mobilise this mass of humanity, but they marched out of Egypt, through the Red Sea, and into the desert behind Moses and the pillars of cloud and fire. Despite continual evidence of God's love and power, the people complained and began to yearn for their days in Egypt. God provided for their physical and spiritual needs with food and a place to worship, but he also judged their disobedience and unbelief. Then in the dramatic Sinai meeting with Moses, God gave his laws for right living.

God led Moses and the nation of Israel, and he wants to lead us as well. Is he preparing you, like Moses, for a specific task? He will be with you; obey and follow. Is he delivering you from an enemy or a temptation? Trust him, and do what he says. Have you heard his clear moral directions? Read, study, and obey his word. Is he calling you to true worship? Discover God's presence in your life, in your home, and in the body of assembled believers. Exodus is the exciting story of God's guidance. Read with the determination to follow God wherever he leads.

Moses born 1526 (1350)	*Exodus from Egypt 1446 (1280)*	*Ten Commandments given 1445 (1279)*	*Israel enters Canaan 1406 (1240)*	*Judges begin to rule 1375 (1220)*

THE BLUEPRINT

A. ISRAEL IN EGYPT (1:1—12:30) 1. Slavery in Egypt 2. God chooses Moses 3. God sends Moses to Pharaoh 4. Plagues strike Egypt 5. The Passover	When the Israelites were enslaved in Egypt, God heard their cries and rescued them. We can be confident that God still hears the cries of his people. Just as he delivered the Israelites from their captors, he delivers us from sin, death, and evil.
B. ISRAEL IN THE DESERT (12:31—18:27) 1. The exodus 2. Crossing the sea 3. Complaining in the desert	After crossing the Red Sea, the Israelites became quarrelsome and discontent. Like the Israelites, we find it easy to complain and be dissatisfied. Christians still have struggles, but we should never allow difficulties and unpleasant circumstances to turn us away from trusting God.
C. ISRAEL AT SINAI (19:1—40:38) 1. Giving the law 2. Tabernacle instructions 3. Breaking the law 4. Tabernacle construction	God revealed his law to the Israelites at Sinai. Through the law, they learned more about what God is like and how he expected his people to live. The law is still instructional for us, for it exposes our sin and shows us God's standard for living.

MEGATHEMES

THEME	EXPLANATION	IMPORTANCE
Slavery	The Israelites were slaves for 400 years. Pharaoh, the king of Egypt, oppressed them cruelly. They prayed to God for deliverance from this system.	Like the Israelites, we need both human and divine leadership to escape from the slavery of sin. After their escape, the memory of slavery helped the Israelites learn to treat others generously. We need to stand against those who oppress others.
Rescue/ Redemption	God rescued Israel through the leader Moses and through mighty miracles. The Passover celebration was an annual reminder of their escape from slavery.	God delivers us from the slavery of sin. Jesus Christ celebrated the Passover with his disciples at the Last Supper and then went on to rescue us from sin by dying in our place.
Guidance	God guided Israel out of Egypt by using the plagues, Moses' heroic courage, the miracle of the Red Sea, and the Ten Commandments. God is a trustworthy guide.	Although God is all-powerful and can do miracles, he normally leads us by wise leadership and team effort. His words give us the wisdom to make daily decisions and govern our lives.
Ten Commandments	God's law system had three parts. The Ten Commandments were the first part, containing the absolutes of spiritual and moral life. The civil law was the second part, giving the people rules to manage their lives. The ceremonial law was the third part, showing them patterns for building the tabernacle and regular worship.	God was teaching Israel the importance of choice and responsibility. When they obeyed the conditions of the law, he blessed them; if they forgot or disobeyed, he punished them or allowed calamities to come. Many great countries of the world base their laws on the moral system set up in the book of Exodus. God's moral law is valid today.
The Nation	God founded the nation of Israel to be the source of truth and salvation to all the world. His relationship to his people was loving yet firm. The Israelites had no army, schools, governors, mayors, or police when they left Egypt. God had to instruct them in their constitutional laws and daily practices. He showed them how to worship and how to have national holidays.	Israel's newly formed nation had all the behavioural characteristics of Christians today. We are often disorganised, sometimes rebellious, and sometimes victorious. God's Person and word are still our only guide. If our churches reflect his leadership, they will be effective in serving him.

KEY PLACES IN EXODUS

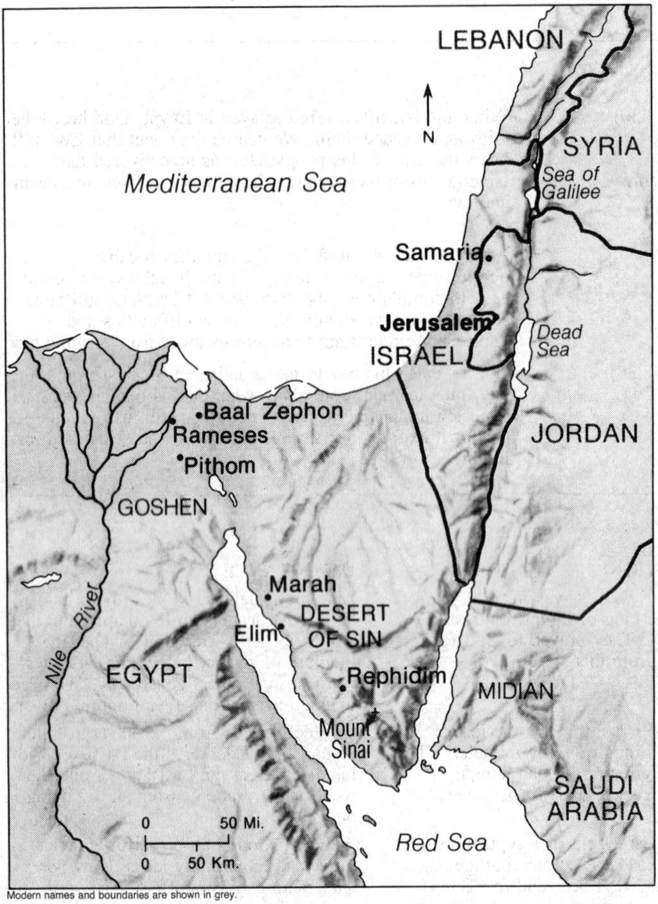

Modern names and boundaries are shown in grey.

1 Goshen This area was given to Jacob and his family when they moved to Egypt (Genesis 47:5, 6). It became the Hebrews' homeland for 400 years and remained separate from the main Egyptian centres, for Egyptian culture looked down upon shepherds and nomads. As the years passed, Jacob's family grew into a large nation (1:7).

2, 3 Pithom and Rameses After 400 years, a Pharaoh came to the throne who had no respect for these descendants of Joseph and feared their large numbers. He forced them into slavery in order to oppress and subdue them. Out of their slave labour, the supply cities of Pithom and Rameses were built (1:11).

4 Midian Moses, an Egyptian prince who was born a Hebrew, killed an Egyptian and fled for his life to Midian. Here he became a shepherd and married a woman named Zipporah. It was while he was here that God commissioned him for the job of leading the Hebrew people out of Egypt (2:15–4:31).

5 Baal Zephon Slavery was not to last because God planned to deliver his people. After choosing Moses and Aaron to be his spokesmen to Pharaoh, God worked a series of dramatic miracles in the land of Egypt to convince Pharaoh to let the Hebrews go (5:1–12:33). When finally freed, the entire nation set out with the riches of Egypt (12:34–36). One of their first stops was at Baal Zephon (14:1), where Pharaoh, who had changed his mind, chased the Hebrews and trapped them against the Red Sea. But God parted the waters and led the people through the sea on dry land. When Pharaoh's army tried to pursue, the waters collapsed around them, and they were drowned (14:5–31).

6 Marah Moses now led the people southwards. The long trek across the desert brought hot tempers and parched throats for this mass of people. At Marah, the water they found was bitter, but God sweetened it (15:22–25).

7 Elim As they continued their journey, the Hebrews (now called Israelites) came to Elim, an oasis with 12 springs (15:27).

8 Desert of Sin Leaving Elim, the people headed into the Desert of Sin. Here the people became hungry, so God provided them with manna that came from heaven and covered the ground each morning (16:1, 13–15). The people ate this manna until they entered the promised land.

9 Rephidim Moses led the people to Rephidim where they found no water. But God miraculously provided water from a rock (17:1, 5, 6). Here the Israelites encountered their first test in battle: the Amalekites attacked and were defeated (17:9–13). Moses' father-in-law, Jethro, then arrived on the scene with some sound advice on delegating responsibilities (18).

10 Mount Sinai God had previously appeared to Moses on this mountain and commissioned him to lead Israel (3:1, 2). Now Moses returned with the people God had asked him to lead. For almost a year the people camped at the foot of Mount Sinai. During this time God gave them his Ten Commandments as well as other laws for right living. He also provided the blueprint for building the tabernacle (19–40).

God was forging a holy nation, prepared to live for and serve him alone.

1:1 [a]Ge 46:8
1:5 [b]Ge 46:26
1:6 [c]Ge 50:26
1:7 [d]Ge 46:3; Dt 26:5; Ac 7:17
1:9 [e]Ps 105:24-25
1:10 [f]Ps 83:3 [g]Ac 7:17-19
1:11 [h]Ex 3:7 [i]Ge 15:13; Ex 2:11; 5:4; 6:6-7 [j]Ge 47:11 [k]1Ki 9:19; 2Ch 8:4
1:13 [l]Dt 4:20
1:14 [m]Ex 2:23; 6:9; Nu 20:15; Ps 81:6; Ac 7:19

A. ISRAEL IN EGYPT (1:1 – 12:30)

Joseph brought his family to Egypt and protected them there. But after Joseph's death, as they multiplied into a nation, they were forced into slavery. God then prepared Moses to free his people from slavery and lead them out of Egypt. To help Moses, God unleashed ten plagues upon the land. After the tenth plague, Pharaoh let the people go. On the night before the great exodus, God's new nation celebrated the Passover. Just as God delivered Israel from Egypt, he delivers us from sin, death, and evil.

1. Slavery in Egypt

The Israelites Oppressed

1 These are the names of the sons of Israel[a] who went to Egypt with Jacob, each
with his family: 2Reuben, Simeon, Levi and Judah; 3Issachar, Zebulun and
Benjamin; 4Dan and Naphtali; Gad and Asher. 5The descendants of Jacob numbered
seventy**[a]** in all;[b] Joseph was already in Egypt.
6Now Joseph and all his brothers and all that generation died,[c] 7but the Israelites
were fruitful and multiplied greatly and became exceedingly numerous,[d] so that the
land was filled with them.
8Then a new king, who did not know about Joseph, came to power in Egypt.
9"Look," he said to his people, "the Israelites have become much too numerous[e] for
us. 10Come, we must deal shrewdly[f] with them or they will become even more
numerous and, if war breaks out, will join our enemies, fight against us and leave the
country."[g]
11So they put slave masters[h] over them to oppress them with forced labour,[i] and
they built Pithom and Rameses[j] as store cities[k] for Pharaoh. 12But the more they
were oppressed, the more they multiplied and spread; so the Egyptians came to dread
the Israelites 13and worked them ruthlessly.[l] 14They made their lives bitter with hard
labour in brick and mortar and with all kinds of work in the fields; in all their hard
labour the Egyptians used them ruthlessly.[m]
15The king of Egypt said to the Hebrew midwives, whose names were Shiphrah
and Puah, 16"When you help the Hebrew women in childbirth and observe them on

a *5* Masoretic Text (see also Gen. 46:27); Dead Sea Scrolls and Septuagint (see also Acts 7:14 and note at Gen. 46:27) *seventy-five*

1:1 The children of Israel, or Israelites, were the descendants of Jacob, whose name was changed to Israel after he wrestled with the angel (see Genesis 32:24–30). Jacob's family had moved to Egypt at the invitation of Joseph, one of Jacob's sons who had become a great ruler under Pharaoh. Jacob's family grew into a large nation. But, as foreigners and newcomers, their lives were quite different from the Egyptians. The Hebrews worshipped one God; the Egyptians worshipped many gods. The Hebrews were wanderers; the Egyptians had a deeply rooted culture. The Hebrews were shepherds; the Egyptians were builders. The Hebrews were also physically separated from the rest of the Egyptians: They lived in Goshen, north of the great Egyptian cultural centres.

1:9, 10 Pharaoh was afraid the Israelites were becoming so numerous that they would organise and threaten his kingdom, so he made them slaves and oppressed them to kill their spirit and stop their growth. Slavery was an ancient practice used by almost all nations to employ conquered people and other captives. Most likely, the great pyramids of Egypt were built with slave labour. Although Israel was not a conquered nation, the people were foreigners and thus lacked the rights of native Egyptians.

1:11 There were levels of slavery in Egypt. Some slaves worked long hours in mud pits while others were skilled carpenters, jewellers, and craftsmen. Regardless of their skill or level, all slaves were watched closely by ruthless slave masters, supervisors whose assignment was to keep the slaves working as fast as possible. They were specialists at making a slave's life miserable.

1:11 Ancient records indicate that these cities were built in 1290 B.C., which is why some scholars believe the exodus occurred early in the 13th century. Looking at other evidence, however, other scholars believe the Hebrews left Egypt in 1446 B.C. How could they build two cities 150 years after they left? These scholars suggest that Rameses II, the pharaoh in 1290 B.C., did not build the cities of Pithom and Rameses. Instead, he renamed two cities that actually had been built 150 years previously. It was a common practice for an Egyptian ruler to make improvements to a city and then take credit for building it, thus wiping out all records of previous founders. Also see the second note on 13:17, 18.

1:12 The Egyptians tried to wear down the Hebrew people by forcing them into slavery and mistreating them. Instead, the Hebrews multiplied and grew stronger. When we are burdened or mistreated, we may feel defeated. But our burdens can make us stronger and develop qualities in us that will prepare us for the future. We cannot be overcomers without troubles to overcome. Be true to God in the hard times because even the worst situations can make us better people.

1:15–17 Shiphrah and Puah may have been supervisors over the midwives, or else these two were given special mention. Hebrew midwives helped women give birth and cared for the baby until the mother was stronger. When Pharaoh ordered the midwives to kill the Hebrew baby boys, he was asking the wrong group of people. Midwives were committed to helping babies be born, not to killing them. These women showed great courage and love for God by risking their lives to disobey Pharaoh's command. Note: A delivery stool was the stool upon which a woman crouched when delivering her baby.

the delivery stool, if it is a boy, kill him; but if it is a girl, let her live." 17The midwives,
however, feared[n] God and did not do what the king of Egypt had told them to do;[o]
they let the boys live. 18Then the king of Egypt summoned the midwives and asked
them, "Why have you done this? Why have you let the boys live?"
19The midwives answered Pharaoh, "Hebrew women are not like Egyptian women;
they are vigorous and give birth before the midwives arrive."[p]
20So God was kind to the midwives[q] and the people increased and became even
more numerous. 21And because the midwives feared God, he gave them families[r]
of their own.
22Then Pharaoh gave this order to all his people: "Every boy that is born[b] you must
throw into the Nile, but let every girl live."[s]

2. God chooses Moses

The Birth of Moses

2 Now a man of the house of Levi married a Levite woman,[a] 2and she became
pregnant and gave birth to a son. When she saw that he was a fine child, she hid
him for three months.[b] 3But when she could hide him no longer, she got a papyrus
basket for him and coated it with tar and pitch. Then she placed the child in it and
put it among the reeds along the bank of the Nile. 4His sister[c] stood at a distance
to see what would happen to him.
5Then Pharaoh's daughter went down to the Nile to bathe, and her attendants were
walking along the river bank.[d] She saw the basket among the reeds and sent her slave
girl to get it. 6She opened it and saw the baby. He was crying, and she felt sorry for
him. "This is one of the Hebrew babies," she said.
7Then his sister asked Pharaoh's daughter, "Shall I go and get one of the Hebrew
women to nurse the baby for you?"
8"Yes, go," she answered. And the girl went and got the baby's mother. 9Pharaoh's

1:17 [n]ver 21; Pr 16:6 [o]Da 3:16-18; Ac 4:18-20; 5:29
1:19 [p]Jos 2:4-6; 2Sa 17:20
1:20 [q]ver 12; Pr 11:18; Isa 3:10
1:21 [r]1Sa 2:35; 2Sa 7:11, 27-29; 1Ki 11:38
1:22 [s]Ac 7:19
2:1 [a]Ex 6:20; Nu 26:59
2:2 [b]Ac 7:20; Heb 11:23
2:4 [c]Ex 15:20; Nu 26:59
2:5 [d]Ex 7:15; 8:20

[b] *22* Masoretic Text; Samaritan Pentateuch, Septuagint and Targums *born to the Hebrews*

1:17–21 Against Pharaoh's orders, the midwives spared the Hebrew babies. Their faith in God gave them the courage to take a stand for what they knew was right. In this situation, disobeying the authority was proper. God does not expect us to obey those in authority when they ask us to disobey him or his word. The Bible is filled with examples of those who were willing to sacrifice their very lives in order to obey God or save others. Esther and Mordecai (Esther 3:2; 4:13–16) and Shadrach, Meshach, and Abednego (Daniel 3:16–18) are some of the people who took a bold stand for what was right. Whole nations can be caught up in immorality (racial hatred, slavery, prison cruelty); thus following the majority or the authority is not always right. Whenever we are ordered to disobey God's word, we must "obey God rather than men" (Acts 5:29).

1:19–21 Did God bless the Hebrew midwives for lying to Pharaoh? God blessed them not because they lied, but because they saved the lives of innocent children. This doesn't mean that a lie was necessarily the best way to answer Pharaoh. The midwives were blessed, however, for not violating the higher law of God that forbids the senseless slaughter of innocent lives.

2:1, 2 Although a name is not mentioned yet, the baby in this story was Moses. Moses' mother and father were named Jochebed and Amram. His brother was Aaron and his sister, Miriam.

2:3 This tiny boat made of papyrus reeds was fashioned by a woman who knew what she was doing. Egyptian river boats were made with these same reeds and waterproofed with tar. The reeds, which grew as tall as sixteen feet, could be gathered in swampy areas along the Nile. Thus a small basket hidden among the reeds would be well insulated from the weather and difficult to see.

2:3ff Moses' mother knew how wrong it would be to destroy her child. But there was little she could do to change Pharaoh's new law. Her only alternative was to hide the child and later place him in a tiny papyrus basket on the river. God used her courageous act to place her son, the Hebrew of his choice, in the house of Pharaoh. Do you sometimes feel surrounded by evil and frustrated by how little you can do about it? When faced with evil, look for ways to act against it. Then trust God to use your effort, however small it seems, in his war against evil.

2:5 Who was Pharaoh's daughter? There are two popular explanations. (1) Some think that Hatshepsut was the woman who pulled Moses from the river. Her husband was Pharaoh Thutmose II. (This would match the earlier exodus date.) Apparently Hatshepsut could not have children, so Thutmose had a son by another woman, and this son became heir to the throne. Hatshepsut would have considered Moses a gift from the gods because now she had her own son who would be the legal heir to the throne. (2) Some think the princess who rescued baby Moses was the daughter of Rameses II, an especially cruel Pharaoh who would have made life miserable for the Hebrew slaves. (This would match the later exodus date.)

2:7, 8 Miriam, the baby's sister, saw that Pharaoh's daughter had discovered Moses. Quickly she took the initiative to suggest a nurse (her mother) who might care for the baby. The Bible doesn't say if Miriam was afraid to approach the Egyptian princess, or if the princess was suspicious of the Hebrew girl. But Miriam did approach her, and the princess bought the services of Miriam and her mother. Their family was reunited. Special opportunities may come our way unexpectedly. Don't let the fear of what might happen cause you to miss an opportunity. Be alert for the opportunities God gives you, and take full advantage of them.

2:9 Moses' mother was reunited with her baby! God used her courageous act of saving and hiding her baby to begin his plan to rescue his people from Egypt. God doesn't need much from us to accomplish his plan for our lives. Focusing on our human predicament may paralyse us because the situation may appear humanly impossible. But concentrating on God and his power will help us

2:11 [e]Ac 7:23; Heb 11:24-26
2:13 [f]Ac 7:26
2:14 [g]Ac 7:27*
2:15 [h]Ac 7:29; Heb 11:27
2:16 [i]Ex 3:1 [j]Ge 24:11
2:17 [k]Ge 29:10
2:18 [l]Nu 10:29
2:20 [m]Ge 31:54
2:21 [n]Ex 18:2
2:22 [o]Ex 18:3-4; Heb 11:13
2:23 [p]Ac 7:30 [q]Ex 3:7, 9; Dt 26:7; Jas 5:4
2:24 [r]Ex 6:5; Ps 105:10, 42

daughter said to her, "Take this baby and nurse him for me, and I will pay you." So
the woman took the baby and nursed him. 10When the child grew older, she took him
to Pharaoh's daughter and he became her son. She named him Moses,[a] saying, "I
drew him out of the water."

Moses Flees to Midian

11One day, after Moses had grown up, he went out to where his own people[e] were
and watched them at their hard labour. He saw an Egyptian beating a Hebrew, one
of his own people. 12Glancing this way and that and seeing no-one, he killed the
Egyptian and hid him in the sand. 13The next day he went out and saw two Hebrews
fighting. He asked the one in the wrong, "Why are you hitting your fellow Hebrew?"[f]
14The man said, "Who made you ruler and judge over us?[g] Are you thinking of
killing me as you killed the Egyptian?" Then Moses was afraid and thought, "What
I did must have become known."
15When Pharaoh heard of this, he tried to kill Moses, but Moses fled from Pharaoh
and went to live in Midian,[h] where he sat down by a well. 16Now a priest of Midian[i]
had seven daughters, and they came to draw water[j] and fill the troughs to water their
father's flock. 17Some shepherds came along and drove them away, but Moses got
up and came to their rescue and watered their flock.[k]
18When the girls returned to Reuel[l] their father, he asked them, "Why have you
returned so early today?"
19They answered, "An Egyptian rescued us from the shepherds. He even drew water
for us and watered the flock."
20"And where is he?" he asked his daughters. "Why did you leave him? Invite him
to have something to eat."[m]
21Moses agreed to stay with the man, who gave his daughter Zipporah[n] to Moses
in marriage. 22Zipporah gave birth to a son, and Moses named him Gershom,[b]
saying, "I have become an alien[o] in a foreign land."
23During that long period,[p] the king of Egypt died. The Israelites groaned in their
slavery and cried out, and their cry[q] for help because of their slavery went up to God.
24God heard their groaning and he remembered his covenant[r] with Abraham, with

[a] *10 Moses* sounds like the Hebrew for *draw out.* [b] *22 Gershom* sounds like the Hebrew for *an alien there.*

---

see the way out. Right now you may feel unable to see through your troubles. Focus instead on God, and trust him for the way out. That is all he needs to begin his work in you.

2:12–14 Moses tried to make sure no-one was watching before he killed the Egyptian. But as it turned out, someone did see, and Moses had to flee the country. Sometimes we mistakenly think we can get away with doing wrong if no-one sees or catches us. Sooner or later, however, doing wrong will catch up with us as it did with Moses. Even if we are not caught in this life, we will still have to face God and his evaluation of our actions.

2:15 To escape punishment for killing the Egyptian, Moses ran away to Midian. He became a stranger in a strange land, separated from his home and family. It took many years after this incident for Moses to be ready to serve God. But he trusted God instead of fearing the king (Hebrews 11:27). We may feel abandoned or isolated because of something we have done. But though we feel afraid and separated, we should not give up. Moses didn't. He trusted God to deliver him, no matter how dark his past or bleak his future.

2:17 How did Moses handle these shepherds so easily? As an Egyptian prince, Moses would have been well trained in the Egyptian military, the most advanced army in the world. Even a large group of shepherds would have been no match for the sophisticated fighting techniques of this trained warrior.

2:18 Reuel is also called Jethro in 3:1.

2:23–25 God's rescue doesn't always come the moment we want it. God had promised to bring the Hebrew slaves out of Egypt (Genesis 15:16; 46:3, 4). The people had waited a long time for that promise to be kept, but God rescued them when he knew the right time had come. God knows the best time to act. When you feel that God has forgotten you in your troubles, remember that God has a time schedule we can't see.

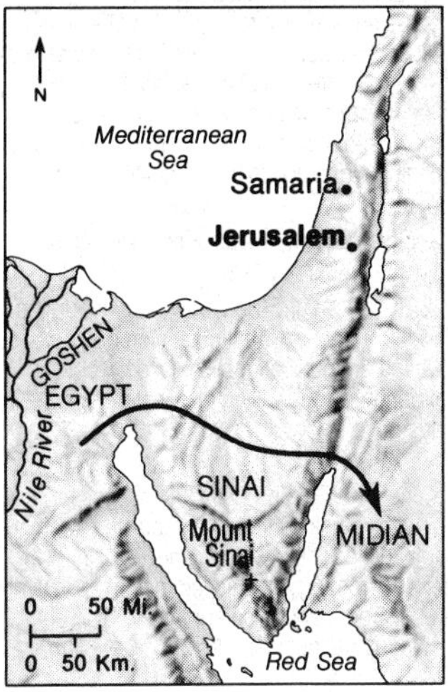

MOSES FLEES TO MIDIAN
After murdering an Egyptian, Moses escaped into Midian. There he married Zipporah and became a shepherd.

Isaac and with Jacob. 25So God looked on the Israelites and was concerned[s] about
them.

Moses and the Burning Bush

3 Now Moses was tending the flock of Jethro[a] his father-in-law, the priest of
Midian, and he led the flock to the far side of the desert and came to Horeb,[b]
the mountain[c] of God. 2There the angel of the LORD[d] appeared to him in flames of
fire from within a bush.[e] Moses saw that though the bush was on fire it did not burn
up. 3So Moses thought, "I will go over and see this strange sight—why the bush does
not burn up."
4When the LORD saw that he had gone over to look, God called to him from within
the bush, "Moses! Moses!"
And Moses said, "Here I am."
5"Do not come any closer," God said. "Take off your sandals, for the place where
you are standing is holy ground."[f] 6Then he said, "I am the God of your father, the
God of Abraham, the God of Isaac and the God of Jacob."[g] At this, Moses hid his
face, because he was afraid to look at God.
7The LORD said, "I have indeed seen the misery of my people in Egypt. I have heard
them crying out because of their slave drivers, and I am concerned[h] about their
suffering. 8So I have come down[i] to rescue them from the hand of the Egyptians
and to bring them up out of that land into a good and spacious land, a land flowing
with milk and honey[j]—the home of the Canaanites, Hittites, Amorites, Perizzites,
Hivites and Jebusites.[k] 9And now the cry of the Israelites has reached me, and I have
seen the way the Egyptians are oppressing[l] them. 10So now, go. I am sending you
to Pharaoh to bring my people the Israelites out of Egypt."[m]
11But Moses said to God, "Who am I,[n] that I should go to Pharaoh and bring the
Israelites out of Egypt?"
12And God said, "I will be with you.[o] And this will be the sign to you that it is
I who have sent you: When you have brought the people out of Egypt, you[a] will
worship God on this mountain."
13Moses said to God, "Suppose I go to the Israelites and say to them, 'The God

a 12 The Hebrew is plural.

2:25 [s]Ex 3:7; 4:31
3:1 [a]Ex 2:18 [b]1Ki 19:8 [c]Ex 18:5
3:2 [d]Ge 16:7 [e]Dt 33:16; Mk 12:26; Ac 7:30
3:5 [f]Ge 28:17; Jos 5:15; Ac 7:33*
3:6 [g]Ex 4:5; Mt 22:32*; Mk 12:26*; Lk 20:37*; Ac 7:32*
3:7 [h]Ex 2:25
3:8 [i]Ge 50:24 [j]ver 17; Ex 13:5; Dt 1:25 [k]Ge 15:18-21
3:9 [l]Ex 1:14; 2:23
3:10 [m]Mic 6:4
3:11 [n]Ex 6:12, 30; 1Sa 18:18
3:12 [o]Ge 31:3; Jos 1:5; Ro 8:31

3:1 What a contrast between Moses' life as an Egyptian prince and his life as a Midianite shepherd! As a prince he had everything done for him; he was the famous son of an Egyptian princess. As a shepherd he had to do everything for himself; he was holding the very job he had been taught to despise (Genesis 43:32; 46:32–34), and he lived as an unknown foreigner. What a humbling experience this must have been for Moses! But God was preparing him for leadership. Living the life of a shepherd and nomad, Moses learned about the ways of the people he would be leading and also about life in the desert. Moses couldn't appreciate this lesson, but God was getting him ready to free Israel from Pharaoh's grasp.

3:1 Mount Horeb is another name for Mount Sinai, where God would give the people his revealed law (3:12).

3:2 God spoke to Moses from an unexpected source: a burning bush. When Moses saw it, he went to investigate. God may use unexpected sources when communicating with us too, whether people, thoughts, or experiences. Be willing to investigate, and be open to God's surprises.

3:2–4 Moses saw a burning bush and spoke with God. Many people in the Bible experienced God in visible (not necessarily human) form. Abraham saw the smoking firepot and blazing torch (Genesis 15:17); Jacob wrestled with a man (Genesis 32:24–29). When the slaves were freed from Egypt, God led them by pillars of cloud and fire (13:17–22). God made such appearances to encourage his new nation, to guide them, and to prove the reliability of his verbal message.

3:5, 6 At God's command, Moses removed his sandals and covered his face. Taking off his shoes was an act of reverence, conveying his own unworthiness before God. God is our friend, but he is also our sovereign Lord. To approach him frivolously shows a lack of respect and sincerity. When you come to God in worship, do you approach him casually, or do you come as though you were an invited guest before a king? If necessary, adjust your attitude so it is suitable for approaching a holy God.

3:8 "The home of the Canaanites" is the land of Israel and Jordan today. *Canaanites* was a term for all the various tribes living in that land.

3:10ff Moses made excuses because he felt inadequate for the job God asked him to do. It was natural for him to feel that way. He *was* inadequate all by himself. But God wasn't asking Moses to work alone. He offered other resources to help (God himself, Aaron, and the ability to do miracles). God often calls us to tasks that seem too difficult, but he doesn't ask us to do them alone. God offers us his resources, just as he did to Moses. We should not hide behind our inadequacies, as Moses did, but look beyond ourselves to the great resources available. Then we can allow God to use our unique contributions.

3:13–15 The Egyptians had many gods by many different names. Moses wanted to know God's name so the Hebrew people would know exactly who had sent him to them. God called himself *I AM,* a name describing his eternal power and unchangeable character. In a world where values, morals, and laws change constantly, we can find stability and security in our unchanging God. The God who appeared to Moses is the same God who can live in us today. Hebrews 13:8 says God is the same "yesterday and to-

of your fathers has sent me to you,' and they ask me, 'What is his name?' Then what
shall I tell them?"
14God said to Moses, "I AM WHO I AM.[b] This is what you are to say to the Israelites:
'I AM[p] has sent me to you.' "
15God also said to Moses, "Say to the Israelites, 'The LORD,[c] the God of your
fathers — the God of Abraham, the God of Isaac and the God of Jacob — has sent me
to you.' This is my name[q] for ever, the name by which I am to be remembered from
generation to generation.
16"Go, assemble the elders[r] of Israel and say to them, 'The LORD, the God of your
fathers — the God of Abraham, Isaac and Jacob — appeared to me and said: I have
watched over you and have seen what has been done to you in Egypt. 17And I have
promised to bring you up out of your misery in Egypt[s] into the land of the Canaanites,
Hittites, Amorites, Perizzites, Hivites and Jebusites — a land flowing with milk and
honey.'
18"The elders of Israel will listen[t] to you. Then you and the elders are to go to
the king of Egypt and say to him, 'The LORD, the God of the Hebrews, has met with
us. Let us take a three-day journey into the desert to offer sacrifices[u] to the LORD
our God.' 19But I know that the king of Egypt will not let you go unless a mighty
hand[v] compels him. 20So I will stretch out my hand[w] and strike the Egyptians with
all the wonders[x] that I will perform among them. After that, he will let you go.[y]
21"And I will make the Egyptians favourably disposed[z] towards this people, so that
when you leave you will not go empty-handed.[a] 22Every woman is to ask her
neighbour and any woman living in her house for articles of silver and gold[b] and for
clothing, which you will put on your sons and daughters. And so you will plunder[c]
the Egyptians."

Signs for Moses

4 Moses answered, "What if they do not believe me or listen[a] to me and say, 'The
LORD did not appear to you'?"
2Then the LORD said to him, "What is that in your hand?"
"A staff,"[b] he replied.
3The LORD said, "Throw it on the ground."
Moses threw it on the ground and it became a snake, and he ran from it. 4Then the
LORD said to him, "Reach out your hand and take it by the tail." So Moses reached

b *14* Or *I WILL BE WHAT I WILL BE* **c** *15* The Hebrew for *LORD* sounds like and may be derived from the Hebrew for *I AM* in verse 14.

3:14 [p]Ex 6:2-3; Jn 8:58; Heb 13:8
3:15 [q]Ps 135:13; Hos 12:5
3:16 [r]Ex 4:29
3:17 [s]Ge 15:16; Jos 24:11
3:18 [t]Ex 4:1, 8, 31 [u]Ex 5:1, 3
3:19 [v]Ex 4:21; 5:2
3:20 [w]Ex 6:1, 6; 9:15 [x]Dt 6:22; Ne 9:10; Ac 7:36 [y]Ex 12:31-33
3:21 [z]Ex 12:36 [a]Ps 105:37
3:22 [b]Ex 11:2 [c]Eze 39:10
4:1 [a]Ex 3:18; 6:30
4:2 [b]ver 17, 20

---

day and for ever". Because God's nature is stable and trustworthy, we are free to follow and enjoy him rather than spend our time trying to figure him out.

3:14, 15 *Yahweh* is derived from the Hebrew word for "I AM". God reminded Moses of his covenant promises to Abraham (Genesis 12:1–3; 15; 17), Isaac (Genesis 26:2–5), and Jacob (Genesis 28:13–15), and used the name *I AM* to show his unchanging nature. What God promised to the great patriarchs hundreds of years earlier he would fulfil through Moses.

3:16, 17 God told Moses to tell the people what he saw and heard at the burning bush. Our God is a God who acts and speaks. One of the most convincing ways to tell others about him is to describe what he has done and how he has spoken to his people. If you are trying to explain God to others, talk about what he has done for you, for people you know, or for people whose stories are told in the Bible.

3:17 "A land flowing with milk and honey" is a poetic word picture expressing the beauty and productivity of the promised land.

3:18–20 The leaders of Israel would accept God's message, and the leaders of Egypt would reject it. God knew what both reactions would be before they happened. This is more than good psychology — God knows the future. Any believer can trust his or her future to God because God already knows what is going to happen.

3:22 The jewels and clothing were not merely borrowed — they were asked for and easily received. The Egyptians were so glad to see the Israelites go that they sent them out with gifts. These items were used later in building the tabernacle (35:5, 22). The promise of being able to plunder the Egyptians seemed impossible to Moses at this time.

4:1 Moses' reluctance and fear were caused by overanticipation. He was worried about how the people might respond to him. We often build up events in our minds and then panic over what might go wrong. God does not ask us to go where he has not provided the means to help. Go where he leads, trusting him to supply courage, confidence, and resources at the right moment.

4:2–4 A shepherd's staff was commonly a three- to six-foot wooden rod with a curved hook at the top. The shepherd used it for walking, guiding his sheep, killing snakes, and many other tasks. Still, it was just a stick. But God used the simple shepherd's staff Moses carried as a sign to teach him an important lesson. God sometimes takes joy in using ordinary things for extraordinary purposes. What are the ordinary things in your life — your voice, a pen, a hammer, a broom, a musical instrument? While it is easy to assume God can use only special skills, you must not hinder his use of the everyday contributions you can make. Little did Moses imagine the power his simple staff would wield when it became the staff of God.

out and took hold of the snake and it turned back into a staff in his hand. 5"This,"
said the LORD, "is so that they may believe[c] that the LORD, the God of their
fathers—the God of Abraham, the God of Isaac and the God of Jacob—has appeared
to you."
6Then the LORD said, "Put your hand inside your cloak." So Moses put his hand
into his cloak, and when he took it out, it was leprous,[a] like snow.[d]
7"Now put it back into your cloak," he said. So Moses put his hand back into his
cloak, and when he took it out, it was restored,[e] like the rest of his flesh.
8Then the LORD said, "If they do not believe you or pay attention to the first
miraculous sign, they may believe the second. 9But if they do not believe these two
signs or listen to you, take some water from the Nile and pour it on the dry ground.
The water you take from the river will become blood[f] on the ground."
10Moses said to the LORD, "O Lord, I have never been eloquent, neither in the past
nor since you have spoken to your servant. I am slow of speech and tongue."[g]
11The LORD said to him, "Who gave man his mouth? Who makes him deaf or mute?
Who gives him sight or makes him blind?[h] Is it not I, the LORD? 12Now go; I will
help you speak and will teach you what to say."[i]
13But Moses said, "O Lord, please send someone else to do it."
14Then the LORD's anger burned against Moses and he said, "What about your
brother, Aaron the Levite? I know he can speak well. He is already on his way to
meet[j] you, and his heart will be glad when he sees you. 15You shall speak to him
and put words in his mouth;[k] I will help both of you speak and will teach you what
to do. 16He will speak to the people for you, and it will be as if he were your mouth[l]
and as if you were God to him. 17But take this staff[m] in your hand so that you can
perform miraculous signs[n] with it."

Moses Returns to Egypt

18Then Moses went back to Jethro his father-in-law and said to him, "Let me go
back to my own people in Egypt to see if any of them are still alive."
Jethro said, "Go, and I wish you well."
19Now the LORD had said to Moses in Midian, "Go back to Egypt, for all the men
who wanted to kill[o] you are dead."[p] 20So Moses took his wife and sons, put them
on a donkey and started back to Egypt. And he took the staff[q] of God in his hand.
21The LORD said to Moses, "When you return to Egypt, see that you perform before
Pharaoh all the wonders[r] I have given you the power to do. But I will harden his
heart[s] so that he will not let the people go. 22Then say to Pharaoh, 'This is what the
LORD says: Israel is my firstborn son,[t] 23and I told you, "Let my son go,[u] so that
he may worship me." But you refused to let him go; so I will kill your firstborn
son.' "[v]
24At a lodging place on the way, the LORD met ⌞Moses⌟[b] and was about to kill[w]

[a] *6* The Hebrew word was used for various diseases affecting the skin—not necessarily leprosy. [b] *24* Or ⌞*Moses' son*⌟; Hebrew *him*

4:5 [c]Ex 19:9
4:6 [d]Nu 12:10; 2Ki 5:1, 27
4:7 [e]Nu 12:13-15; Dt 32:39; 2Ki 5:14; Mt 8:3
4:9 [f]Ex 7:17-21
4:10 [g]Ex 6:12; Jer 1:6
4:11 [h]Ps 94:9; Mt 11:5
4:12 [i]Isa 50:4; Jer 1:9; Mt 10:19-20; Mk 13:11; Lk 12:12; 21:14-15
4:14 [j]ver 27
4:15 [k]Nu 23:5, 12, 16
4:16 [l]Ex 7:1-2
4:17 [m]ver 2 [n]Ex 7:9-21
4:19 [o]Ex 2:15 [p]Ex 2:23
4:20 [q]Ex 17:9; Nu 20:8-9, 11
4:21 [r]Ex 3:19, 20 [s]Ex 7:3, 13; 9:12, 35; 14:4, 8; Dt 2:30; Isa 63:17; Jn 12:40; Ro 9:18
4:22 [t]Isa 63:16; 64:8; Jer 31:9; Hos 11:1; Ro 9:4
4:23 [u]Ex 5:1; 7:16 [v]Ex 11:5; 12:12, 29
4:24 [w]Nu 22:22

4:6, 7 Leprosy was one of the most feared diseases of this time. There was no cure, and a great deal of suffering preceded eventual death. Through this experience, Moses learned that God could cause or cure any kind of problem. He saw that God indeed had all power and was commissioning him to exercise that power to lead the Hebrews out of Egypt.

4:10–13 Moses pleaded with God to let him out of his mission. After all, he was not a good speaker and would probably embarrass himself and God. But God looked at Moses' problem quite differently. All Moses needed was some help, and who better than God could help him say and do the right things? God made his mouth and would give him the words to say. It is easy for us to focus on our weaknesses, but if God asks us to do something, then he will help us get the job done. If the job involves some of our weak areas, then we can trust that he will provide words, strength, courage, and ability where needed.

4:14 God finally agreed to let Aaron speak for Moses. Moses' feelings of inadequacy were so strong that he could not trust even God's ability to help him. Moses had to deal with his deep sense of inadequacy many times. When we face difficult or frightening situations, we must be willing to let God help us.

4:16 The phrase, "as if you were God to him", means that Moses would tell Aaron what to say as God was telling him.

4:17–20 Moses clung tightly to the shepherd's staff as he left for Egypt to face the greatest challenge of his life. The staff was his assurance of God's presence and power. When feeling uncertain, some people need something to stabilise and reassure them. For assurance when facing great trials, God has given promises from his word and examples from great heroes of faith. Any Christian may cling tightly to these.

4:24–26 God was about to kill Moses because Moses had not circumcised his son. Why hadn't Moses done this? Remember that

him. 25But Zipporah took a flint knife, cut off her son's foreskin[x] and touched
⌞Moses'⌟ feet with it.[c] "Surely you are a bridegroom of blood to me," she said. 26So
the LORD let him alone. (At that time she said "bridegroom of blood", referring to
circumcision.)
27The LORD said to Aaron, "Go into the desert to meet Moses." So he met Moses
at the mountain[y] of God and kissed[z] him. 28Then Moses told Aaron everything the
LORD had sent him to say,[a] and also about all the miraculous signs he had commanded
him to perform.
29Moses and Aaron brought together all the elders[b] of the Israelites, 30and Aaron
told them everything the LORD had said to Moses. He also performed the signs before
the people, 31and they believed.[c] And when they heard that the LORD was concerned[d] about them and had seen their misery, they bowed down and worshipped.

3. God sends Moses to Pharaoh

Bricks Without Straw

5 Afterwards Moses and Aaron went to Pharaoh and said, "This is what the LORD,
the God of Israel, says: 'Let my people go, so that they may hold a festival[a] to
me in the desert.' "
2Pharaoh said, "Who is the LORD,[b] that I should obey him and let Israel go? I do
not know the LORD and I will not let Israel go."[c]
3Then they said, "The God of the Hebrews has met with us. Now let us take a
three-day journey into the desert to offer sacrifices to the LORD our God, or he may
strike us with plagues[d] or with the sword."
4But the king of Egypt said, "Moses and Aaron, why are you taking the people away
from their labour?[e] Get back to your work!" 5Then Pharaoh said, "Look, the people
of the land are now numerous,[f] and you are stopping them from working."
6That same day Pharaoh gave this order to the slave drivers and foremen in charge

c 25 Or *and drew near ⌞Moses'⌟ feet*

4:25 [x]Ge 17:14; Jos 5:2, 3
4:27 [y]Ex 3:1 [z]ver 14
4:28 [a]ver 8-9, 16
4:29 [b]Ex 3:16
4:31 [c]ver 8; Ex 3:18 [d]Ex 2:25
5:1 [a]Ex 3:18
5:2 [b]2Ki 18:35; Job 21:15 [c]Ex 3:19
5:3 [d]Ex 3:18
5:4 [e]Ex 1:11
5:5 [f]Ex 1:7, 9

Moses had spent half his life in Pharaoh's palace and half his life in the Midianite desert. He might not have been too familiar with God's laws, especially since all the requirements of God's covenant with Israel (Genesis 17) had not been actively carried out for over 400 years. In addition, Moses' wife, due to her Midianite background, may have opposed circumcision. But Moses could not effectively serve as deliverer of God's people until he had fulfilled the conditions of God's covenant, and one of those conditions was circumcision. Before they could go any further, Moses and his family had to follow God's commands completely. Under Old Testament law, failing to circumcise your son was to remove yourself and your family from God's blessings. Moses learned that disobeying God was even more dangerous than tangling with an Egyptian pharaoh.

4:25, 26 Why did Zipporah perform the circumcision? It may have been Zipporah who, as a Midianite unfamiliar with the circumcision requirement, had persuaded Moses not to circumcise their son. If she prevented the action, now she would have to perform it. It is also possible that Moses became ill as a result of permitting disobedience, and so Zipporah had to perform the circumcision herself to save both her husband and son. This would not have made her happy—hence, her unflattering comment to Moses.

5:1, 2 Pharaoh was familiar with many gods (Egypt was filled with them), but he had never heard of the God of Israel. Pharaoh assumed that the God of the Hebrew slaves couldn't be very powerful. At first, Pharaoh was not at all worried about Moses' message, for he had not yet seen any evidence of the Lord's power.

5:3 Pharaoh would not listen to Moses and Aaron because he did not know or respect God. People who do not know God may not listen to his word or his messengers. Like Moses and Aaron, we need to persist. When others reject you or your faith, don't be surprised or discouraged. Continue to tell them about God, trusting him to open minds and soften stubborn hearts.

5:4–9 Moses and Aaron took their message to Pharaoh just as God directed. The unhappy result was harder work and more oppression for the Hebrews. Sometimes hardship comes as a result of obeying God. Are you following God but still suffering—or suffering even worse than before? If your life is miserable, don't assume you have fallen out of God's favour. You may be suffering for doing good in an evil world.

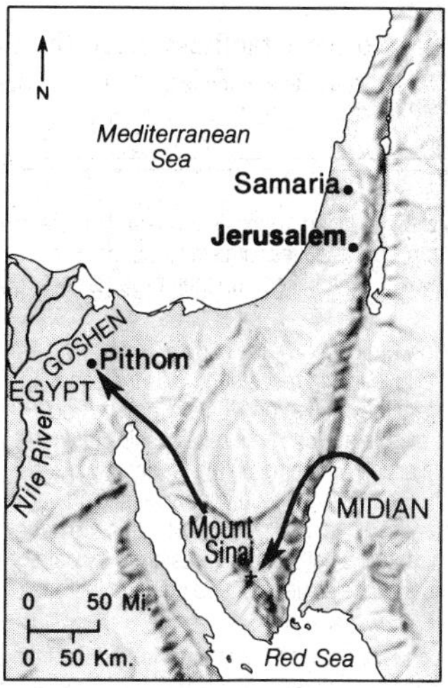

MOSES RETURNS TO EGYPT
God appeared to Moses in a mysterious burning bush on Mount Sinai (also called Mount Horeb). Later Aaron met Moses at the mountain and together they returned to Egypt, a 200-mile trip.

of the people: 7"You are no longer to supply the people with straw for making bricks;
let them go and gather their own straw. 8But require them to make the same number
of bricks as before; don't reduce the quota. They are lazy; that is why they are crying
out, 'Let us go and sacrifice to our God.' 9Make the work harder for the men so that
they keep working and pay no attention to lies."
10Then the slave drivers and the foremen went out and said to the people, "This
is what Pharaoh says: 'I will not give you any more straw. 11Go and get your own
straw wherever you can find it, but your work will not be reduced at all.'" 12So the
people scattered all over Egypt to gather stubble to use for straw. 13The slave drivers
kept pressing them, saying, "Complete the work required of you for each day, just
as when you had straw." 14The Israelite foremen appointed by Pharaoh's slave drivers
were beaten[g] and were asked, "Why didn't you meet your quota of bricks yesterday
or today, as before?"
15Then the Israelite foremen went and appealed to Pharaoh: "Why have you treated
your servants this way? 16Your servants are given no straw, yet we are told, 'Make
bricks!' Your servants are being beaten, but the fault is with your own people."
17Pharaoh said, "Lazy, that's what you are—lazy![h] That is why you keep saying,
'Let us go and sacrifice to the LORD.' 18Now get to work. You will not be given any
straw, yet you must produce your full quota of bricks."
19The Israelite foremen realised they were in trouble when they were told, "You
are not to reduce the number of bricks required of you for each day." 20When they
left Pharaoh, they found Moses and Aaron waiting to meet them, 21and they said,
"May the LORD look upon you and judge you! You have made us a stench[i] to Pharaoh
and his officials and have put a sword in their hand to kill us."[j]

God Promises Deliverance

22Moses returned to the LORD and said, "O Lord, why have you brought trouble
upon this people?[k] Is this why you sent me? 23Ever since I went to Pharaoh to speak
in your name, he has brought trouble upon this people, and you have not rescued[l]
your people at all."

6 Then the LORD said to Moses, "Now you will see what I will do to Pharaoh:
Because of my mighty hand[a] he will let them go;[b] because of my mighty hand
he will drive them out of his country."[c]
2God also said to Moses, "I am the LORD. 3I appeared to Abraham, to Isaac and
to Jacob as God Almighty,[a][d] but by my name[e] the LORD[b][f] I did not make myself
known to them.[c] 4I also established my covenant[g] with them to give them the land
of Canaan, where they lived as aliens.[h] 5Moreover, I have heard the groaning[i] of
the Israelites, whom the Egyptians are enslaving, and I have remembered my covenant.
6"Therefore, say to the Israelites: 'I am the LORD, and I will bring you out from

5:14 [g]Isa 10:24
5:17 [h]ver 8
5:21 [i]Ge 34:30 [j]Ex 14:11
5:22 [k]Nu 11:11
5:23 [l]Jer 4:10
6:1 [a]Ex 3:19 [b]Ex 3:20 [c]Ex 12:31, 33, 39
6:3 [d]Ge 17:1 [e]Ps 68:4; 83:18; Isa 52:6 [f]Ex 3:14
6:4 [g]Ge 15:18 [h]Ge 28:4, 13
6:5 [i]Ex 2:23

a 3 Hebrew *El-Shaddai* **b** 3 See note at Exodus 3:15. **c** 3 Or *Almighty, and by my name the LORD did I not let myself be known to them?*

5:7, 8 Mixing straw with mud made bricks stronger and more durable. Pharaoh had supplied the slaves with straw, but now he made them find their own straw and keep up their production quota as well.

5:15–21 The foremen were caught in the middle. First they tried to get the people to produce the same amount, then they complained to Pharaoh, finally they turned on Moses. Perhaps you have felt caught in the middle at work, or in relationships in your family or church. Complaining or turning on the leadership does not solve the problem. In the case of these supervisors, God had a larger purpose in mind, just as he might in your situation. So rather than turning on the leadership when you feel pressured by both sides, turn to God to see what else he might be doing in this situation.

5:22, 23 Pharaoh had just increased the Hebrews' workload, and Moses protested that God had not rescued his people. Moses expected faster results and fewer problems. When God is at work, suffering, setbacks, and hardship may still occur. In James 1:2–4, we are encouraged to be happy when difficulties come our way. Problems develop our patience and character by teaching us to (1) trust God to do what is best for us, (2) look for ways to honour God in our present situation, (3) remember that God will not abandon us, and (4) watch for God's plan for us.

6:6 Small problems need only small answers. But when we face great problems, God has an opportunity to exercise his great power. As the Hebrews' troubles grew steadily worse, God planned to intervene with his mighty power and perform great miracles to deliver them. How big are your problems? Big problems put you in a perfect position to watch God give big answers.

6:6–8 God's promises in these verses were fulfilled to the letter when the Hebrews left Egypt. He freed them from slavery, became their God, and accepted them as his people. Then he led them towards the land he had promised. When the Hebrews were rescued from slavery, they portrayed the drama of salvation for all of us.

under the yoke of the Egyptians. I will free you from being slaves to them, and I will
redeem[j] you with an outstretched arm[k] and with mighty acts of judgment. 7 I will
take you as my own people, and I will be your God.[l] Then you will know[m] that I
am the LORD your God, who brought you out from under the yoke of the Egyptians.
8 And I will bring you to the land[n] I swore with uplifted hand[o] to give to Abraham,
to Isaac and to Jacob.[p] I will give it to you as a possession. I am the LORD.' "
9 Moses reported this to the Israelites, but they did not listen to him because of their
discouragement and cruel bondage.
10 Then the LORD said to Moses, 11 "Go, tell Pharaoh king of Egypt to let the
Israelites go out of his country."
12 But Moses said to the LORD, "If the Israelites will not listen to me, why would
Pharaoh listen to me, since I speak with faltering lips?"[d][q]

Family Record of Moses and Aaron

13 Now the LORD spoke to Moses and Aaron about the Israelites and Pharaoh king
of Egypt, and he commanded them to bring the Israelites out of Egypt.

14 These were the heads of their families:[e][r]

The sons of Reuben the firstborn son of Israel were Hanoch and Pallu, Hezron
and Carmi. These were the clans of Reuben.
15 The sons of Simeon[s] were Jemuel, Jamin, Ohad, Jakin, Zohar and Shaul
the son of a Canaanite woman. These were the clans of Simeon.
16 These were the names of the sons of Levi according to their records: Gershon,[t] Kohath and Merari.[u] Levi lived 137 years.
17 The sons of Gershon, by clans, were Libni and Shimei.[v]
18 The sons of Kohath were Amram, Izhar, Hebron and Uzziel.[w] Kohath lived
133 years.
19 The sons of Merari were Mahli and Mushi.[x]
These were the clans of Levi according to their records.
20 Amram married his father's sister Jochebed, who bore him Aaron and
Moses.[y] Amram lived 137 years.
21 The sons of Izhar[z] were Korah, Nepheg and Zicri.
22 The sons of Uzziel were Mishael, Elzaphan[a] and Sithri.
23 Aaron married Elisheba, daughter of Amminadab[b] and sister of Nahshon,
and she bore him Nadab and Abihu,[c] Eleazar[d] and Ithamar.[e]
24 The sons of Korah[f] were Assir, Elkanah and Abiasaph. These were the
Korahite clans.
25 Eleazar son of Aaron married one of the daughters of Putiel, and she bore
him Phinehas.[g]

These were the heads of the Levite families, clan by clan.

26 It was this same Aaron and Moses to whom the LORD said, "Bring the Israelites

d *12* Hebrew *I am uncircumcised of lips;* also in verse 30 **e** *14* The Hebrew for *families* here and in verse 25 refers to units larger than clans.

6:6 j Dt 7:8; 1Ch 17:21 k Dt 26:8
6:7 l Dt 4:20; 2Sa 7:24 m Ex 16:12; Isa 41:20
6:8 n Ge 15:18; 26:3 o Ge 14:22 p Ps 136:21-22
6:12 q ver 30; Ex 4:10; Jer 1:6
6:14 r Ge 46:9
6:15 s Ge 46:10; 1Ch 4:24
6:16 t Ge 46:11 u Nu 3:17
6:17 v 1Ch 6:17
6:18 w 1Ch 6:2, 18
6:19 x 1Ch 6:19; 23:21
6:20 y Ex 2:1-2; Nu 26:59
6:21 z 1Ch 6:38
6:22 a Lev 10:4; Nu 3:30
6:23 b Ru 4:19, 20 c Lev 10:1 d Nu 3:2, 32 e Nu 26:60
6:24 f Nu 26:11
6:25 g Nu 25:7, 11; Jos 24:33; Ps 106:30

When God redeems us from sin he delivers us, accepts us, and becomes our God. Then he leads us to a new life as we follow him.

6:9–12 When Moses gave God's message to the people, they were too discouraged to listen. The Hebrews didn't want to hear any more about God and his promises because the last time they listened to Moses, all they got was more work and greater suffering. Sometimes a clear message from God is followed by a period when no change in the situation is apparent. During that time, seeming setbacks may turn people away from wanting to hear more about God. If you are a leader, don't give up. Keep bringing people God's message as Moses did. By focusing on God who must be obeyed rather than on the results to be achieved, good leaders see beyond temporary setbacks and reversals.

6:10–12 Think how hard it must have been for Moses to bring God's message to Pharaoh when his own people had trouble believing it. Eventually the Hebrews believed that God had sent Moses, but for a time he must have felt very alone. Moses obeyed God, however, and what a difference it made! When the chances for success appear slim, remember that anyone can obey God when the task is easy and everyone is behind it. Only those with persistent faith can obey when the task seems impossible.

6:14–25 This genealogy or family tree was placed here to identify Moses and Aaron more firmly. Genealogies were used to establish credentials and authority as well as outlining the history of a family.

6:26 To bring the Israelites out of Egypt by their divisions means that they would be brought out in tribes, clans, or family groups.

out of Egypt by their divisions."[h] 27They were the ones who spoke to Pharaoh king
of Egypt about bringing the Israelites out of Egypt. It was the same Moses and Aaron.

Aaron to Speak for Moses

28Now when the LORD spoke to Moses in Egypt, 29he said to him, "I am the LORD.[i]
Tell Pharaoh king of Egypt everything I tell you."
30But Moses said to the LORD, "Since I speak with faltering lips,[j] why would
Pharaoh listen to me?"
7 Then the LORD said to Moses, "See, I have made you like God[a] to Pharaoh, and
your brother Aaron will be your prophet. 2You are to say everything I command
you, and your brother Aaron is to tell Pharaoh to let the Israelites go out of his country.
3But I will harden Pharaoh's heart,[b] and though I multiply my miraculous signs and
wonders in Egypt, 4he will not listen[c] to you. Then I will lay my hand on Egypt and
with mighty acts of judgment[d] I will bring out my divisions, my people the Israelites.
5And the Egyptians will know that I am the LORD[e] when I stretch out my hand[f]
against Egypt and bring the Israelites out of it."
6Moses and Aaron did just as the LORD commanded[g] them. 7Moses was eighty
years old[h] and Aaron eighty-three when they spoke to Pharaoh.

Aaron's Staff Becomes a Snake

8The LORD said to Moses and Aaron, 9"When Pharaoh says to you, 'Perform a
miracle,'[i] then say to Aaron, 'Take your staff and throw it down before Pharaoh,'
and it will become a snake."[j]
10So Moses and Aaron went to Pharaoh and did just as the LORD commanded. Aaron
threw his staff down in front of Pharaoh and his officials, and it became a snake.
11Pharaoh then summoned the wise men and sorcerers, and the Egyptian magicians[k]
also did the same things by their secret arts:[l] 12Each one threw down his staff and
it became a snake. But Aaron's staff swallowed up their staffs. 13Yet Pharaoh's heart[m]
became hard and he would not listen to them, just as the LORD had said.

4. Plagues strike Egypt

The Plague of Blood

14Then the LORD said to Moses, "Pharaoh's heart is unyielding;[n] he refuses to let
the people go. 15Go to Pharaoh in the morning as he goes out to the water. Wait on
the bank of the Nile to meet him, and take in your hand the staff that was changed
into a snake. 16Then say to him, 'The LORD, the God of the Hebrews, has sent me
to say to you: Let my people go, so that they may worship[o] me in the desert. But
until now you have not listened. 17This is what the LORD says: By this you will know
that I am the LORD:[p] With the staff that is in my hand I will strike the water of the
Nile, and it will be changed into blood.[q] 18The fish in the Nile will die, and the river
will stink; the Egyptians will not be able to drink its water.' "[r]
19The LORD said to Moses, "Tell Aaron, 'Take your staff and stretch out your
hand[s] over the waters of Egypt—over the streams and canals, over the ponds and

6:26 [h]Ex 7:4; 12:17, 41, 51
6:29 [i]ver 11; Ex 7:2
6:30 [j]ver 12; Ex 4:10
7:1 [a]Ex 4:16
7:3 [b]Ex 4:21; 11:9
7:4 [c]Ex 11:9 [d]Ex 3:20; 6:6
7:5 [e]ver 17; Ex 8:19, 22 [f]Ex 3:20
7:6 [g]ver 2
7:7 [h]Dt 31:2; 34:7; Ac 7:23, 30
7:9 [i]Isa 7:11; Jn 2:18 [j]Ex 4:2-5
7:11 [k]Ge 41:8; 2Ti 3:8 [l]ver 22; Ex 8:7, 18
7:13 [m]Ex 4:21
7:14 [n]Ex 8:15, 32; 10:1, 20, 27
7:16 [o]Ex 3:18; 5:1, 3
7:17 [p]Ex 5:2 [q]Ex 4:9; Rev 11:6; 16:4
7:18 [r]ver 21, 24
7:19 [s]Ex 8:5-6, 16; 9:22; 10:12, 21; 14:21

7:1 God made Moses "like God to Pharaoh"—in other words, a powerful person who deserved to be listened to. Pharaoh himself was considered a god, so he recognised Moses as one of his peers. His refusal to give in to Moses shows, however, that he did not feel inferior to Moses.

7:11 How were these sorcerers and magicians able to duplicate Moses' miracles? Some of their feats involved trickery or illusion, and some may have used satanic power since worshipping gods of the underworld was part of their religion. Ironically, whenever the sorcerers duplicated one of Moses' plagues, it only made matters worse. If the magicians had been as powerful as God, they would have reversed the plagues, not added to them.

7:12 God performed a miracle by turning Aaron's staff into a snake, and Pharaoh's magicians did the same through trickery or sorcery. Although miracles can help us believe, it is dangerous to rely on them alone. Satan can imitate some parts of God's work and lead people astray. Pharaoh focused on the miracle rather than the message. We can avoid this error by letting the word of God be the basis of our faith. No miracle from God would endorse any message that is contrary to the teachings of his word.

7:17 God dramatically turned the waters of the Nile into blood to show Pharaoh who he was. Do you sometimes wish for miraculous signs so you can be sure about God? God has given you the miracle of eternal life through your faith in him, something Pharaoh never obtained. This is a quiet miracle and, though less evident right now, just as extraordinary as water turned to blood. The desire for spectacular signs may cause us to ignore the more subtle miracles God is working every day.

all the reservoirs’ — and they will turn to blood. Blood will be everywhere in Egypt,
even in the wooden buckets and stone jars.”
20 Moses and Aaron did just as the LORD had commanded. He raised his staff in the
presence of Pharaoh and his officials and struck the water of the Nile,[t] and all the
water was changed into blood.[u] 21 The fish in the Nile died, and the river smelled
so bad that the Egyptians could not drink its water. Blood was everywhere in Egypt.
22 But the Egyptian magicians did the same things by their secret arts,[v] and
Pharaoh’s heart became hard; he would not listen to Moses and Aaron, just as the LORD
had said. 23 Instead, he turned and went into his palace, and did not take even this to
heart. 24 And all the Egyptians dug along the Nile to get drinking water, because they
could not drink the water of the river.

The Plague of Frogs

8 25 Seven days passed after the LORD struck the Nile. 1 Then the LORD said to
Moses, “Go to Pharaoh and say to him, ‘This is what the LORD says: Let my
people go, so that they may worship[a] me. 2 If you refuse to let them go, I will plague
your whole country with frogs. 3 The Nile will teem with frogs. They will come up
into your palace and your bedroom and onto your bed, into the houses of your officials
and on your people,[b] and into your ovens and kneading troughs. 4 The frogs will go
up on you and your people and all your officials.’ ”
5 Then the LORD said to Moses, “Tell Aaron, ‘Stretch out your hand with your staff[c]
over the streams and canals and ponds, and make frogs come up on the land of
Egypt.’ ”
6 So Aaron stretched out his hand over the waters of Egypt, and the frogs[d] came
up and covered the land. 7 But the magicians did the same things by their secret arts;[e]
they also made frogs come up on the land of Egypt.
8 Pharaoh summoned Moses and Aaron and said, “Pray[f] to the LORD to take the
frogs away from me and my people, and I will let your people go to offer sacrifices[g]
to the LORD.”
9 Moses said to Pharaoh, “I leave to you the honour of setting the time for me to
pray for you and your officials and your people that you and your houses may be rid
of the frogs, except for those that remain in the Nile.”
10 “Tomorrow,” Pharaoh said.
Moses replied, “It will be as you say, so that you may know there is no-one like
the LORD our God.[h] 11 The frogs will leave you and your houses, your officials and
your people; they will remain only in the Nile.”
12 After Moses and Aaron left Pharaoh, Moses cried out to the LORD about the frogs
he had brought on Pharaoh. 13 And the LORD did what Moses asked. The frogs died
in the houses, in the courtyards and in the fields. 14 They were piled into heaps, and
the land reeked of them. 15 But when Pharaoh saw that there was relief, he hardened
his heart[i] and would not listen to Moses and Aaron, just as the LORD had said.

The Plague of Gnats

16 Then the LORD said to Moses, “Tell Aaron, ‘Stretch out your staff and strike the
dust of the ground,’ and throughout the land of Egypt the dust will become gnats.”

7:20 [t]Ex 17:5 [u]Ps 78:44; 105:29
7:22 [v]ver 11
8:1 [a]Ex 3:12, 18; 4:23
8:3 [b]Ex 10:6
8:5 [c]Ex 7:19
8:6 [d]Ps 78:45; 105:30
8:7 [e]Ex 7:11
8:8 [f]ver 28; Ex 9:28; 10:17 [g]ver 25
8:10 [h]Ex 9:14; Dt 4:35; 33:26; 2Sa 7:22; 1Ch 17:20; Ps 86:8; Isa 46:9; Jer 10:6
8:15 [i]Ex 7:14

7:20 Egypt was a large country, but most of the population lived along the banks of the Nile River. This 3,000-mile waterway was truly a river of life for the Egyptians. It made life possible in a land that was mostly desert by providing water for drinking, farming, bathing, and fishing. Egyptian society was a ribbon of civilisation lining the banks of this life source, rarely reaching very far into the surrounding desert. Without the Nile’s water, Egypt could not have existed. Imagine Pharaoh’s dismay when Moses turned this sacred river to blood!

8:3ff Moses predicted that every house in Egypt would be infested with frogs. The poor of Egypt lived in small, mud-brick houses of one or two rooms with palm-trunk roofs. The homes of the rich, however, were often two or three storeys high, surrounded by landscaped gardens and enclosed by a high wall. Servants lived and worked on the first floor while the family occupied the upper floors. Thus if the frogs got into the royal bedrooms, they had infiltrated even the upper floors. No place in Egypt would be safe from them.

8:15 After repeated warnings, Pharaoh still refused to obey God. He hardened his heart every time there was a break in the plagues. His stubborn disobedience brought suffering upon himself and his entire country. While persistence is good, stubbornness is usually self-centred. Stubbornness towards God is always disobedience. Avoid disobedience because the consequences may spill onto others.

17They did this, and when Aaron stretched out his hand with the staff and struck the
dust of the ground, gnats[j] came upon men and animals. All the dust throughout the
land of Egypt became gnats. 18But when the magicians[k] tried to produce gnats by
their secret arts,[l] they could not. And the gnats were on men and animals.
19The magicians said to Pharaoh, "This is the finger[m] of God." But Pharaoh's heart
was hard and he would not listen, just as the LORD had said.

The Plague of Flies

20Then the LORD said to Moses, "Get up early in the morning[n] and confront
Pharaoh as he goes to the water and say to him, 'This is what the LORD says: Let my
people go, so that they may worship[o] me. 21If you do not let my people go, I will
send swarms of flies on you and your officials, on your people and into your houses.
The houses of the Egyptians will be full of flies, and even the ground where they are.
22" 'But on that day I will deal differently with the land of Goshen, where my people
live;[p] no swarms of flies will be there, so that you will know[q] that I, the LORD, am
in this land. 23I will make a distinction[a] between my people and your people. This
miraculous sign will occur tomorrow.' "
24And the LORD did this. Dense swarms of flies poured into Pharaoh's palace and
into the houses of his officials, and throughout Egypt the land was ruined by the flies.[r]
25Then Pharaoh summoned[s] Moses and Aaron and said, "Go, sacrifice to your God
here in the land."
26But Moses said, "That would not be right. The sacrifices we offer the LORD our
God would be detestable to the Egyptians.[t] And if we offer sacrifices that are
detestable in their eyes, will they not stone us? 27We must take a three-day journey
into the desert to offer sacrifices[u] to the LORD our God, as he commands us."
28Pharaoh said, "I will let you go to offer sacrifices to the LORD your God in the
desert, but you must not go very far. Now pray[v] for me."
29Moses answered, "As soon as I leave you, I will pray to the LORD, and tomorrow
the flies will leave Pharaoh and his officials and his people. Only be sure that Pharaoh
does not act deceitfully[w] again by not letting the people go to offer sacrifices to the
LORD."
30Then Moses left Pharaoh and prayed to the LORD,[x] 31and the LORD did what
Moses asked: The flies left Pharaoh and his officials and his people; not a fly remained.
32But this time also Pharaoh hardened his heart[y] and would not let the people go.

The Plague on Livestock

9 Then the LORD said to Moses, "Go to Pharaoh and say to him, 'This is what the
LORD, the God of the Hebrews, says: "Let my people go, so that they may
worship[a] me." 2If you refuse to let them go and continue to hold them back, 3the
hand[b] of the LORD will bring a terrible plague on your livestock in the field—on your
horses and donkeys and camels and on your cattle and sheep and goats. 4But the LORD
will make a distinction between the livestock of Israel and that of Egypt,[c] so that no
animal belonging to the Israelites will die.' "
5The LORD set a time and said, "Tomorrow the LORD will do this in the land." 6And

a *23* Septuagint and Vulgate; Hebrew *will put a deliverance*

8:17 [j]Ps 105:31
8:18 [k]Ex 9:11; Da 5:8 [l]Ex 7:11
8:19 [m]Ex 7:5; 10:7; Ps 8:3; Lk 11:20
8:20 [n]Ex 7:15; 9:13 [o]ver 1; Ex 3:18
8:22 [p]Ex 9:4, 6, 26; 10:23; 11:7 [q]Ex 7:5; 9:29
8:24 [r]Ps 78:45; 105:31
8:25 [s]ver 8; Ex 9:27
8:26 [t]Ge 43:32; 46:34
8:27 [u]Ex 3:18
8:28 [v]ver 8; Ex 9:28; 1Ki 13:6
8:29 [w]ver 15
8:30 [x]ver 12
8:32 [y]ver 8, 15; Ex 4:21
9:1 [a]Ex 8:1
9:3 [b]Ex 7:4
9:4 [c]ver 26; Ex 8:22

8:19 Some people think, "If only I could see a miracle, I could believe in God." God gave Pharaoh just such an opportunity. When gnats infested Egypt, even the magicians agreed that this was God's work ("the finger of God")—but still Pharaoh refused to believe. He was stubborn, and stubbornness can blind a person to the truth. When you rid yourself of stubbornness, you may be surprised by abundant evidence of God's work in your life.

8:25–29 Pharaoh wanted a compromise. He would allow the Hebrews to sacrifice, but only if they would do it nearby. God's requirement, however, was firm: The Hebrews had to leave Egypt. Sometimes people urge believers to compromise and give only partial obedience to God's commands. But commitment and obedience to God cannot be negotiated. When it comes to obeying God, half measures won't do.

8:26 The Israelites would be sacrificing animals that the Egyptians regarded as sacred, and this would be offensive to them. Moses was concerned about a violent reaction to sacrificing these animals near the Egyptians.

9:1 This was the fifth time God sent Moses back to Pharaoh with the demand, "Let my people go!" By this time, Moses may have been tired and discouraged, but he continued to obey. Is there a difficult conflict you must face again and again? Don't give up when you know what is the right thing to do. As Moses discovered, persistence is rewarded.

9:6 [d] ver 19-21; Ex 11:5 [e] Ps 78:48-50
9:7 [f] Ex 7:14; 8:32
9:9 [g] Dt 28:27, 35; Rev 16:2
9:11 [h] Ex 8:18

the next day the LORD did it: All the livestock[d] of the Egyptians died,[e] but not one
animal belonging to the Israelites died. 7Pharaoh sent men to investigate and found
that not even one of the animals of the Israelites had died. Yet his heart was unyielding
and he would not let the people go.[f]

The Plague of Boils

8Then the LORD said to Moses and Aaron, "Take handfuls of soot from a furnace
and have Moses toss it into the air in the presence of Pharaoh. 9It will become fine
dust over the whole land of Egypt, and festering boils[g] will break out on men and
animals throughout the land."

10So they took soot from a furnace and stood before Pharaoh. Moses tossed it into
the air, and festering boils broke out on men and animals. 11The magicians[h] could
not stand before Moses because of the boils that were on them and on all the Egyptians.

THE PLAGUES

Reference	*Plague*	*What Happened*	*Result*
7:14–24	Blood	Fish die, the river smells, the people are without water	Pharaoh's magicians duplicate the miracle by "secret arts" and Pharaoh is unmoved
8:1–15	Frogs	Frogs come up from the water and completely cover the land	Again Pharaoh's magicians duplicate the miracle by sorcery and Pharaoh is unmoved
8:16–19	Gnats	All the dust of Egypt becomes a massive swarm of gnats	Magicians are unable to duplicate this; they say it is the "finger of God", but Pharaoh's heart remains hard
8:20–32	Flies	Swarms of flies cover the land	Pharaoh promises to let the Hebrews go, but then hardens his heart and refuses
9:1–7	Livestock	All the Egyptian livestock dies—but none of Israel's is even sick	Pharaoh still refuses to let the people go
9:8–12	Boils	Horrible boils break out on everyone in Egypt	Magicians cannot respond because they are struck down with boils as well—Pharaoh refuses to listen
9:13–35	Hail	Hailstorms kill all the slaves and animals left out or unprotected and strip or destroy almost every plant	Pharaoh admits his sin, but then changes his mind and refuses to let Israel go
10:1–20	Locusts	Locusts cover Egypt and eat everything left after the hail	Everyone advises Pharaoh to let the Hebrews go, but God hardens Pharaoh's heart and he refuses
10:21–29	Darkness	Total darkness covers Egypt for three days so no one can even move—except the Hebrews, who have light as usual	Pharaoh again promises to let Israel go, but again changes his mind
11:1—12:33	Death of Firstborn	The firstborn of all the people and cattle of Egypt die—but Israel is spared	Pharaoh and the Egyptians urge Israel to leave quickly; after they are gone, Pharaoh again changes his mind and chases after them

12 But the LORD hardened Pharaoh's heart[i] and he would not listen to Moses and
Aaron, just as the LORD had said to Moses.

The Plague of Hail

13 Then the LORD said to Moses, "Get up early in the morning, confront Pharaoh
and say to him, 'This is what the LORD, the God of the Hebrews, says: Let my people
go, so that they may worship[j] me, 14 or this time I will send the full force of my
plagues against you and against your officials and your people, so you may know[k]
that there is no-one like[l] me in all the earth. 15 For by now I could have stretched
out my hand and struck you and your people[m] with a plague that would have wiped
you off the earth. 16 But I have raised you up[a] for this very purpose,[n] that I might
show you my power[o] and that my name might be proclaimed in all the earth. 17 You
still set yourself against my people and will not let them go. 18 Therefore, at this time
tomorrow I will send the worst hailstorm[p] that has ever fallen on Egypt, from the
day it was founded till now.[q] 19 Give an order now to bring your livestock and
everything you have in the field to a place of shelter, because the hail will fall on every
man and animal that has not been brought in and is still out in the field, and they will
die.' "

20 Those officials of Pharaoh who feared[r] the word of the LORD hurried to bring
their slaves and their livestock inside. 21 But those who ignored the word of the LORD
left their slaves and livestock in the field.

22 Then the LORD said to Moses, "Stretch out your hand towards the sky so that hail
will fall all over Egypt—on men and animals and on everything growing in the fields
of Egypt." 23 When Moses stretched out his staff towards the sky, the LORD sent
thunder[s] and hail,[t] and lightning flashed down to the ground. So the LORD rained
hail on the land of Egypt; 24 hail fell and lightning flashed back and forth. It was the
worst storm in all the land of Egypt since it had become a nation. 25 Throughout Egypt
hail struck everything in the fields—both men and animals; it beat down everything
growing in the fields and stripped every tree.[u] 26 The only place it did not hail was
the land of Goshen,[v] where the Israelites were.[w]

27 Then Pharaoh summoned Moses and Aaron. "This time I have sinned,"[x] he said
to them. "The LORD is in the right,[y] and I and my people are in the wrong. 28 Pray[z]
to the LORD, for we have had enough thunder and hail. I will let you go;[a] you don't
have to stay any longer."

29 Moses replied, "When I have gone out of the city, I will spread out my hands[b]
in prayer to the LORD. The thunder will stop and there will be no more hail, so you
may know that the earth[c] is the LORD's. 30 But I know that you and your officials
still do not fear the LORD God."

31 (The flax and barley[d] were destroyed, since the barley was in the ear and the
flax was in bloom. 32 The wheat and spelt, however, were not destroyed, because they
ripen later.)

33 Then Moses left Pharaoh and went out of the city. He spread out his hands towards
the LORD; the thunder and hail stopped, and the rain no longer poured down on the
land. 34 When Pharaoh saw that the rain and hail and thunder had stopped, he sinned
again: He and his officials hardened their hearts. 35 So Pharaoh's heart[e] was hard and
he would not let the Israelites go, just as the LORD had said through Moses.

[a] 16 Or *have spared you*

9:12 [i]Ex 4:21
9:13 [j]Ex 8:20
9:14 [k]Ex 8:10 [l]2Sa 7:22; 1Ch 17:20; Ps 86:8; Isa 46:9; Jer 10:6
9:15 [m]Ex 3:20
9:16 [n]Pr 16:4 [o]Ro 9:17*
9:18 [p]ver 23 [q]ver 24
9:20 [r]Pr 13:13
9:23 [s]Ps 18:13 [t]Jos 10:11; Ps 78:47; 105:32; Isa 30:30; Eze 38:22; Rev 8:7; 16:21
9:25 [u]Ps 105:32-33
9:26 [v]ver 4 [w]Ex 8:22; 10:23; 11:7; 12:13
9:27 [x]Ex 10:16 [y]2Ch 12:6; Ps 129:4; La 1:18
9:28 [z]Ex 10:17 [a]Ex 8:8
9:29 [b]1Ki 8:22, 38; Ps 143:6; Isa 1:15 [c]Ex 19:5; Ps 24:1; 1Co 10:26
9:31 [d]Ru 1:22; 2:23
9:35 [e]Ex 4:21

9:12 God gave Pharaoh many opportunities to heed Moses' warnings. But finally God seemed to say, "All right, Pharaoh, have it your way," and Pharaoh's heart became permanently hardened. Did God intentionally harden Pharaoh's heart and overrule his free will? No, he simply confirmed that Pharaoh freely chose a life of resisting God. Similarly, after a lifetime of resisting God, you may find it impossible to turn to him. Don't wait until just the *right* time before turning to God. Do it now while you still have the chance. If you continually ignore God's voice, eventually you will be unable to hear it at all.

9:20, 21 If all the Egyptian livestock were killed in the earlier plague (9:6), how could the slaves of Pharaoh put their cattle inside? The answer is probably that the earlier plague killed all the animals in the fields (9:3), but not those in the shelters.

The Plague of Locusts

10 Then the LORD said to Moses, "Go to Pharaoh, for I have hardened his heart[a]
and the hearts of his officials so that I may perform these miraculous signs[b]
of mine among them 2 that you may tell your children[c] and grandchildren how I dealt
harshly with the Egyptians and how I performed my signs among them, and that you
may know that I am the LORD."
3 So Moses and Aaron went to Pharaoh and said to him, "This is what the LORD,
the God of the Hebrews, says: 'How long will you refuse to humble[d] yourself before
me? Let my people go, so that they may worship me. 4 If you refuse to let them go,
I will bring locusts[e] into your country tomorrow. 5 They will cover the face of the
ground so that it cannot be seen. They will devour what little you have left[f] after
the hail, including every tree that is growing in your fields. 6 They will fill your houses
and those of all your officials and all the Egyptians — something neither your fathers
nor your forefathers have ever seen from the day they settled in this land till now.' "
Then Moses turned and left Pharaoh.
7 Pharaoh's officials said to him, "How long will this man be a snare[g] to us? Let
the people go, so that they may worship the LORD their God. Do you not yet realise
that Egypt is ruined?"[h]
8 Then Moses and Aaron were brought back to Pharaoh. "Go, worship[i] the LORD
your God," he said. "But just who will be going?"
9 Moses answered, "We will go with our young and old, with our sons and daughters, and with our flocks and herds, because we are to celebrate a festival to the LORD."
10 Pharaoh said, "The LORD be with you — if I let you go, along with your women
and children! Clearly you are bent on evil.[a] 11 No! Let only the men go; and worship
the LORD, since that's what you have been asking for." Then Moses and Aaron were
driven out of Pharaoh's presence.
12 And the LORD said to Moses, "Stretch out your hand[j] over Egypt so that locusts
will swarm over the land and devour everything growing in the fields, everything left
by the hail."
13 So Moses stretched out his staff over Egypt, and the LORD made an east wind
blow across the land all that day and all that night. By morning the wind had brought
the locusts;[k] 14 they invaded all Egypt and settled down in every area of the country
in great numbers. Never before had there been such a plague of locusts,[l] nor will
there ever be again. 15 They covered all the ground until it was black. They devoured[m]
all that was left after the hail — everything growing in the fields and the fruit on the
trees. Nothing green remained on tree or plant in all the land of Egypt.
16 Pharaoh quickly summoned Moses and Aaron and said, "I have sinned[n] against
the LORD your God and against you. 17 Now forgive my sin once more and pray[o] to
the LORD your God to take this deadly plague away from me."
18 Moses then left Pharaoh and prayed to the LORD.[p] 19 And the LORD changed the
wind to a very strong west wind, which caught up the locusts and carried them into
the Red Sea.[b] Not a locust was left anywhere in Egypt. 20 But the LORD hardened
Pharaoh's heart,[q] and he would not let the Israelites go.

a *10* Or *Be careful, trouble is in store for you!* b *19* Hebrew *Yam Suph*; that is, Sea of Reeds

10:1 [a]Ex 4:21 [b]Ex 7:3
10:2 [c]Ex 12:26-27; 13:8, 14; Dt 4:9; Ps 44:1; 78:4, 5; Joel 1:3
10:3 [d]1Ki 21:29; Jas 4:10; 1Pe 5:6
10:4 [e]Rev 9:3
10:5 [f]Ex 9:32; Joel 1:4
10:7 [g]Ex 23:33; Jos 23:7-13; 1Sa 18:21; Ecc 7:26 [h]Ex 8:19
10:8 [i]Ex 8:8
10:12 [j]Ex 7:19
10:13 [k]Ps 105:34
10:14 [l]Ps 78:46; Joel 2:1-11, 25
10:15 [m]ver 5; Ps 105:34-35
10:16 [n]Ex 9:27
10:17 [o]Ex 8:8
10:18 [p]Ex 8:30
10:20 [q]Ex 4:21; 11:10

9:27-34 After promising to let the Hebrews go, Pharaoh immediately broke his promise and brought even more trouble upon the land. His actions reveal that his repentance was not real. We do damage to ourselves and to others if we pretend to change but don't mean it.

10:2 God told Moses that his miraculous experiences with Pharaoh should be retold to his descendants. What stories Moses had to tell! Living out one of the greatest dramas in biblical history, he witnessed events few people would ever see. It is important to tell our children about God's work in our past and to help them see what he is doing right now. What are the turning points in your life where God intervened? What is God doing for you now? Your stories will form the foundations of your children's belief in God.

The Plague of Darkness

21Then the LORD said to Moses, "Stretch out your hand towards the sky so that
darkness[r] will spread over Egypt – darkness that can be felt." 22So Moses stretched
out his hand towards the sky, and total darkness[s] covered all Egypt for three days.
23No-one could see anyone else or leave his place for three days. Yet all the Israelites
had light in the places where they lived.[t]
24Then Pharaoh summoned Moses and said, "Go, worship the LORD. Even your
women and children[u] may go with you; only leave your flocks and herds behind."
25But Moses said, "You must allow us to have sacrifices and burnt offerings to
present to the LORD our God. 26Our livestock too must go with us; not a hoof is to
be left behind. We have to use some of them in worshipping the LORD our God, and
until we get there we will not know what we are to use to worship the LORD."
27But the LORD hardened Pharaoh's heart,[v] and he was not willing to let them go.
28Pharaoh said to Moses, "Get out of my sight! Make sure you do not appear before
me again! The day you see my face you will die."
29"Just as you say," Moses replied, "I will never appear[w] before you again."

The Plague on the Firstborn

11 Now the LORD said to Moses, "I will bring one more plague on Pharaoh and
on Egypt. After that, he will let you go from here, and when he does, he will
drive you out completely. 2Tell the people that men and women alike are to ask their
neighbours for articles of silver and gold."[a] 3(The LORD made the Egyptians favourably disposed towards the people, and Moses himself was highly regarded[b] in Egypt
by Pharaoh's officials and by the people.)
4So Moses said, "This is what the LORD says: 'About midnight[c] I will go throughout Egypt. 5Every firstborn[d] son in Egypt will die, from the firstborn son of Pharaoh,
who sits on the throne, to the firstborn son of the slave girl, who is at her hand mill,
and all the firstborn of the cattle as well. 6There will be loud wailing[e] throughout
Egypt – worse than there has ever been or ever will be again. 7But among the Israelites
not a dog will bark at any man or animal.' Then you will know that the LORD makes
a distinction[f] between Egypt and Israel. 8All these officials of yours will come to
me, bowing down before me and saying, 'Go,[g] you and all the people who follow
you!' After that I will leave." Then Moses, hot with anger, left Pharaoh.
9The LORD had said to Moses, "Pharaoh will refuse to listen[h] to you – so that my
wonders may be multiplied in Egypt." 10Moses and Aaron performed all these won-

10:21 [r]Dt 28:29
10:22 [s]Ps 105:28; Rev 16:10
10:23 [t]Ex 8:22
10:24 [u]ver 8-10
10:27 [v]ver 20; Ex 4:21
10:29 [w]Heb 11:27
11:2 [a]Ex 3:21, 22
11:3 [b]Dt 34:11
11:4 [c]Ex 12:29
11:5 [d]Ex 4:23; Ps 78:51
11:6 [e]Ex 12:30
11:7 [f]Ex 8:22
11:8 [g]Ex 12:31-33
11:9 [h]Ex 7:4

10:22 As each gloomy plague descended upon the land, the Egyptian people realised how powerless their own gods were to stop it. Hapi, the god of the Nile River, could not prevent the waters from turning to blood (7:20). Hathor, the crafty cow-goddess, was helpless as Egyptian livestock died in droves (9:6). Amon-Re, the sun-god and chief of the Egyptian gods, could not stop an eerie darkness from covering the land for three full days (10:21, 22). The Egyptian gods were (1) non-personal, centring around images like the sun or the river; (2) numerous; (3) non-exclusive. By contrast, the God of the Hebrews was (1) a living personal Being, (2) the only true God, and (3) the only God who should be worshipped. God was proving to both the Hebrews and the Egyptians that he alone is the living and all-powerful God.

10:27, 28 Why was Pharaoh so reluctant to let the people go? The Hebrews were Egypt's free labour – the builders of their great cities. As Egypt's leader, Pharaoh would not easily let such a great resource go.

11:7 Moses told Pharaoh that God made a distinction between Egypt and Israel. At this time the distinction was very clear in God's mind: He knew the Hebrews would become his chosen people. The distinction was taking shape in Moses' mind also. But the Hebrews still saw the distinction only in terms of slave and free. Later, when they were in the desert, God would teach them the laws, principles, and values that would make them distinct as his people. Remember that God sees us in terms of what we will become and not just what we are right now.

11:9, 10 You may wonder how Pharaoh could be so foolish as to see God's miraculous power and still not listen to Moses. But Pharaoh had his mind made up long before the plagues began. He couldn't believe that someone was greater than he. This stubborn unbelief led to a heart so hard that even a major catastrophe couldn't soften him. Finally, it took the greatest of all calamities, the loss of his son, to force him to recognise God's authority. But even then he wanted God to leave, not to rule his country. We must not wait for great calamities to drive us to God, but must open our hearts and minds to his direction now.

11:10 Did God really harden Pharaoh's heart and force him to do wrong? Before the ten plagues began, Moses and Aaron announced what God would do if Pharaoh didn't let the people go. But their message only made Pharaoh stubborn – he was hardening his own heart. In so doing, he defied both God and his messengers. Through the first six plagues, Pharaoh's heart grew even more stubborn. After the sixth plague, God passed judgment. Sooner or later, evil people will be punished for their sins. When it became evident that Pharaoh wouldn't change, God confirmed Pharaoh's proud decision and set the painful consequences of his actions in motion. God didn't force Pharaoh to reject him; rather, he gave him every opportunity to change his mind. In Ezekiel 33:11, God says, "I take no pleasure in the death of the wicked."

11:10 [i]Ex 4:21; 10:20, 27

ders before Pharaoh, but the LORD hardened Pharaoh's heart,[i] and he would not let
the Israelites go out of his country.

5. The Passover

12 The LORD said to Moses and Aaron in Egypt, 2"This month is to be for you
the first month,[a] the first month of your year. 3Tell the whole community of
Israel that on the tenth day of this month each man is to take a lamb[a] for his family,
one for each household. 4If any household is too small for a whole lamb, they must
share one with their nearest neighbour, having taken into account the number of people
there are. You are to determine the amount of lamb needed in accordance with what
each person will eat. 5The animals you choose must be year-old males without

12:2 [a]Ex 13:4; Dt 16:1

[a] 3 The Hebrew word can mean *lamb* or *kid*; also in verse 4.

THE HEBREW CALENDAR
A Hebrew month began in the middle of a month on our calendar today. Crops are planted in November and December and harvested in March and April.

	Month	*Today's Calendar*	*Bible Reference*	*Israel's Holidays*
1	Nisan (Abib)	March–April	Exodus 13:4; 23:15; 34:18; Deuteronomy 16:1	Passover (Leviticus 23:5) Unleavened Bread (Leviticus 23:6) Firstfruits (Leviticus 23:10)
2	Iyyar (Ziv)	April–May	1 Kings 6:1, 37	Second Passover (Numbers 9:10,11)
3	Sivan	May–June	Esther 8:9	Pentecost (Weeks) (Leviticus 23:16)
4	Tammuz	June–July		
5	Ab	July–August		
6	Elul	August–September	Nehemiah 6:15	
7	Tishri (Ethanim)	September–October	1 Kings 8:2	Trumpets (Numbers 29:1; Leviticus 23:24) Day of Atonement (Leviticus 23:27) Tabernacles (Booths) (Leviticus 23:34)
8	Marcheshvan (Bul)	October–November	1 Kings 6:38	
9	Kislev	November–December	Nehemiah 1:1	Dedication (John 10:22)
10	Tebeth	December–January	Esther 2:16	
11	Shebat	January–February	Zechariah 1:7	
12	Adar	February–March	Esther 3:7	Purim (Esther 9:24-32)

12:1–3 Certain holidays were instituted by God himself. Passover was a holiday designed to celebrate Israel's deliverance from Egypt and to remind the people of what God had done. Holidays can be important today, too, as annual reminders of what God has done for us. Develop traditions in your family to highlight the religious significance of certain holidays. These serve as reminders to the older people and learning experiences for the younger ones.

12:3ff For the Israelites to be spared from the plague of death, a lamb with no defects had to be killed and its blood placed on the door-frames of each home. What was the significance of the lamb? In killing the lamb, the Israelites shed innocent blood. The lamb was a sacrifice, a substitute for the person who would have died in the plague. From this point on, the Hebrew people would clearly understand that for them to be spared from death, an innocent life had to be sacrificed in their place.

defect,[b] and you may take them from the sheep or the goats. 6Take care of them until
the fourteenth day of the month,[c] when all the people of the community of Israel must
slaughter them at twilight.[d] 7Then they are to take some of the blood and put it on
the sides and tops of the door-frames of the houses where they eat the lambs. 8That
same night[e] they are to eat the meat roasted[f] over the fire, along with bitter herbs,[g]
and bread made without yeast.[h] 9Do not eat the meat raw or cooked in water, but
roast it over the fire—head, legs and inner parts. 10Do not leave any of it till
morning;[i] if some is left till morning, you must burn it. 11This is how you are to
eat it: with your cloak tucked into your belt, your sandals on your feet and your staff
in your hand. Eat it in haste;[j] it is the LORD's Passover.[k]
12"On that same night I will pass through[l] Egypt and strike down every firstborn—both men and animals—and I will bring judgment on all the gods[m] of Egypt.
I am the LORD.[n] 13The blood will be a sign for you on the houses where you are;
and when I see the blood, I will pass over you. No destructive plague will touch you
when I strike Egypt.
14"This is a day you are to commemorate;[o] for the generations to come you shall
celebrate it as a festival to the LORD—a lasting ordinance.[p] 15For seven days you
are to eat bread made without yeast.[q] On the first day remove the yeast from your
houses, for whoever eats anything with yeast in it from the first day until the seventh
must be cut off[r] from Israel. 16On the first day hold a sacred assembly, and another
one on the seventh day. Do no work at all on these days, except to prepare food for
everyone to eat—that is all you may do.
17"Celebrate the Feast of Unleavened Bread, because it was on this very day that
I brought your divisions out of Egypt.[s] Celebrate this day as a lasting ordinance for
the generations to come. 18In the first month[t] you are to eat bread made without yeast,
from the evening of the fourteenth day until the evening of the twenty-first day. 19For
seven days no yeast is to be found in your houses. And whoever eats anything with
yeast in it must be cut off from the community of Israel, whether he is an alien or
native-born. 20Eat nothing made with yeast. Wherever you live, you must eat unleavened bread."
21Then Moses summoned all the elders of Israel and said to them, "Go at once and
select the animals for your families and slaughter the Passover[u] lamb. 22Take a bunch
of hyssop, dip it into the blood in the basin and put some of the blood[v] on the top
and on both sides of the door-frame. Not one of you shall go out of the door of his
house until morning. 23When the LORD goes through the land to strike down the
Egyptians, he will see the blood[w] on the top and sides of the door-frame and will pass
over[x] that doorway, and he will not permit the destroyer[y] to enter your houses and
strike you down.
24"Obey these instructions as a lasting ordinance for you and your descendants.
25When you enter the land that the LORD will give you as he promised, observe this
ceremony. 26And when your children[z] ask you, 'What does this ceremony mean to
you?' 27then tell them, 'It is the Passover[a] sacrifice to the LORD, who passed over
the houses of the Israelites in Egypt and spared our homes when he struck down the

12:5 [b]Lev 22:18-21; Heb 9:14
12:6 [c]Lev 23:5; Nu 9:1-3, 5, 11 [d]Ex 16:12; Dt 16:4, 6
12:8 [e]Ex 34:25; Nu 9:12 [f]Dt 16:7 [g]Nu 9:11 [h]Dt 16:3-4; 1Co 5:8
12:10 [i]Ex 23:18; 34:25
12:11 [j]Dt 16:3 [k]ver 13, 21, 27, 43; Dt 16:1
12:12 [l]Ex 11:4; Am 5:17 [m]Nu 33:4 [n]Ex 6:2
12:14 [o]Ex 13:9 [p]ver 17, 24; Ex 13:5, 10; 2Ki 23:21
12:15 [q]Ex 13:6-7; 23:15; 34:18; Lev 23:6; Dt 16:3 [r]Ge 17:14; Nu 9:13
12:17 [s]ver 41; Ex 13:3
12:18 [t]ver 2; Lev 23:5-8; Nu 28:16-25
12:21 [u]ver 11; Mk 14:12-16
12:22 [v]ver 7; Heb 11:28
12:23 [w]Rev 7:3 [x]ver 13 [y]1Co 10:10; Heb 11:28
12:26 [z]Ex 10:2; 13:8, 14-15; Jos 4:6
12:27 [a]ver 11

12:6–11 The Feast of the Passover was to be an annual holiday in honour of the night when the Lord "passed over" the homes of the Israelites. The Hebrews followed God's instructions by placing the blood of a lamb on the door-frames of their homes. That night the firstborn son of every family who did not have blood on the door-frames was killed. The lamb had to be killed in order to get the blood that would protect them. (This foreshadowed the blood of Christ, the Lamb of God, who gave his blood for the sins of all people.) Inside their homes, the Israelites ate a meal of roast lamb, bitter herbs, and bread made without yeast. Unleavened bread could be made quickly because the dough did not have to rise. Thus they could leave at any time. Bitter herbs signified the bitterness of slavery.

12:11 Eating the Passover feast while dressed for travel was a sign of the Hebrews' faith. Although they were not yet free, they were to prepare themselves, for God had said he would lead them out of Egypt. Their preparation was an act of faith. Preparing ourselves for the fulfilment of God's promises, however unlikely they may seem, demonstrates our faith.

12:17, 23 Passover became an annual remembrance of how God delivered the Hebrews from Egypt. Each year the people would pause to remember the day when the destroyer (God's angel of death) passed over their homes. They gave thanks to God for saving them from death and bringing them out of a land of slavery and sin. Believers today have experienced a day of deliverance as well—the day we were delivered from spiritual death and slavery to sin. The Lord's Supper is our Passover remembrance of our new life and freedom from sin. The next time struggles and trials come, remember how God has delivered you in the past and focus on his promise of new life with him.

Egyptians.' " Then the people bowed down and worshipped.[b] 28 The Israelites did just
what the LORD commanded Moses and Aaron.
29 At midnight[c] the LORD struck down all the firstborn[d] in Egypt, from the
firstborn of Pharaoh, who sat on the throne, to the firstborn of the prisoner, who was
in the dungeon, and the firstborn of all the livestock[e] as well. 30 Pharaoh and all his
officials and all the Egyptians got up during the night, and there was loud wailing[f]
in Egypt, for there was not a house without someone dead.

B. ISRAEL IN THE DESERT (12:31 – 18:27)

As Egypt buried its dead, the Hebrew slaves left the country, a free people at last. Pharaoh made one last attempt to bring them back, but the people escaped when God miraculously parted the waters of the Red Sea. But on the other side, the people soon became dissatisfied and complained bitterly to Moses and Aaron about their trek through the desert. Through these experiences of the Hebrews, we learn that the Christian life is not always trouble-free. We still have struggles and often complain bitterly to God about conditions in our lives.

1. The exodus

31 During the night Pharaoh summoned Moses and Aaron and said, "Up! Leave my
people, you and the Israelites! Go, worship[g] the LORD as you have requested. 32 Take
your flocks and herds,[h] as you have said, and go. And also bless me."
33 The Egyptians urged the people to hurry and leave[i] the country. "For otherwise,"
they said, "we will all die!" 34 So the people took their dough before the yeast was
added, and carried it on their shoulders in kneading troughs wrapped in clothing. 35 The
Israelites did as Moses instructed and asked the Egyptians for articles of silver and
gold[j] and for clothing. 36 The LORD had made the Egyptians favourably disposed
towards the people, and they gave them what they asked for; so they plundered[k] the
Egyptians.
37 The Israelites journeyed from Rameses to Succoth.[l] There were about six
hundred thousand men[m] on foot, besides women and children. 38 Many other people[n]
went up with them, as well as large droves of livestock, both flocks and herds. 39 With
the dough they had brought from Egypt, they baked cakes of unleavened bread. The
dough was without yeast because they had been driven out[o] of Egypt and did not have
time to prepare food for themselves.
40 Now the length of time the Israelite people lived in Egypt**b** was 430 years.[p] 41 At
the end of the 430 years, to the very day, all the LORD's divisions[q] left Egypt.[r]
42 Because the LORD kept vigil that night to bring them out of Egypt, on this night all
the Israelites are to keep vigil to honour the LORD for the generations to come.[s]

Passover Restrictions

43 The LORD said to Moses and Aaron, "These are the regulations for the Passover:[t]
"No foreigner[u] is to eat of it. 44 Any slave you have bought may eat of it after you

12:27 [b]Ex 4:31
12:29 [c]Ex 11:4 [d]Ex 4:23; Ps 78:51 [e]Ex 9:6
12:30 [f]Ex 11:6
12:31 [g]Ex 8:8
12:32 [h]Ex 10:9, 26
12:33 [i]Ps 105:38
12:35 [j]Ex 3:22
12:36 [k]Ex 3:22
12:37 [l]Nu 33:3-5 [m]Ex 38:26; Nu 1:46; 11:13, 21
12:38 [n]Nu 11:4
12:39 [o]ver 31-33; Ex 6:1; 11:1
12:40 [p]Ge 15:13; Ac 7:6; Gal 3:17
12:41 [q]ver 17; Ex 6:26 [r]Ex 3:10
12:42 [s]Ex 13:10; Dt 16:1, 6
12:43 [t]ver 11 [u]ver 48; Nu 9:14

b *40* Masoretic Text; Samaritan Pentateuch and Septuagint *Egypt and Canaan*

12:29, 30 Every firstborn child of the Egyptians died, but the Israelite children were spared because the blood of the lamb had been placed on their door-frames. So begins the story of redemption, the central theme of the Bible.

Redemption means "to buy back" or "to save from captivity by paying a ransom". One way to buy back a slave was to offer an equivalent or superior slave in exchange. That is the way God chose to buy us back – he offered his Son in exchange for us.

In Old Testament times, God accepted symbolic offerings. Jesus had not yet been sacrificed, so God accepted the life of an animal in place of the life of the sinner. When Jesus came, he substituted his perfect life for our sinful lives, taking the penalty for sin that we deserve. Thus he redeemed us from the power of sin and restored us to God. Jesus' sacrifice made animal sacrifice no longer necessary.

We must recognise that if we want to be freed from the deadly consequences of our sins, a tremendous price must be paid. But we don't have to pay it. Jesus Christ, our substitute, has already redeemed us by his death on the cross. Our part is to trust him and accept his gift of eternal life. Our sins have been paid for, and the way has been cleared for us to begin a relationship with God (Titus 2:14; Hebrews 9:13–15, 23–26).

12:34 A kneading trough was a large bowl made of wood, bronze, or pottery and used for kneading dough. Bread was made by mixing water and flour in the trough with a small piece of leavened dough saved from the previous day's batch. Bread was the primary food in the Hebrews' diet, and thus it was vital to bring the trough along. It could be easily carried on the shoulder.

12:37, 38 The total number of people leaving Egypt is estimated to have been about two million. The "many other people" may have been Egyptians and others who were drawn to the Hebrews by God's mighty works and who decided to leave Egypt with them.

have circumcised[v] him, 45 but a temporary resident and a hired worker[w] may not eat
of it.
46 "It must be eaten inside one house; take none of the meat outside the house. Do
not break any of the bones.[x] 47 The whole community of Israel must celebrate it.
48 "An alien living among you who wants to celebrate the LORD's Passover must
have all the males in his household circumcised; then he may take part like one born
in the land.[y] No uncircumcised male may eat of it. 49 The same law applies to the
native-born and to the alien[z] living among you."

50 All the Israelites did just what the LORD had commanded Moses and Aaron. 51 And
on that very day the LORD brought the Israelites out of Egypt by their divisions.[a]

Consecration of the Firstborn

13 The LORD said to Moses, 2 "Consecrate to me every firstborn male.[a] The first
offspring of every womb among the Israelites belongs to me, whether man or
animal."
3 Then Moses said to the people, "Commemorate this day, the day you came out
of Egypt, out of the land of slavery, because the LORD brought you out of it with a
mighty hand.[b] Eat nothing containing yeast.[c] 4 Today, in the month of Abib,[d] you
are leaving. 5 When the LORD brings you into the land of the Canaanites, Hittites,
Amorites, Hivites and Jebusites[e]—the land he swore to your forefathers to give you,
a land flowing with milk and honey—you are to observe this ceremony[f] in this
month: 6 For seven days eat bread made without yeast and on the seventh day hold
a festival[g] to the LORD. 7 Eat unleavened bread during those seven days; nothing with
yeast in it is to be seen among you, nor shall any yeast be seen anywhere within your
borders. 8 On that day tell your son,[h] 'I do this because of what the LORD did for me
when I came out of Egypt.' 9 This observance will be for you like a sign on your hand
and a reminder on your forehead[i] that the law of the LORD is to be on your lips. For
the LORD brought you out of Egypt with his mighty hand. 10 You must keep this
ordinance[j] at the appointed time year after year.
11 "After the LORD brings you into the land of the Canaanites and gives it to you,
as he promised on oath to you and your forefathers, 12 you are to give over to the LORD
the first offspring of every womb. All the firstborn males of your livestock belong
to the LORD.[k] 13 Redeem with a lamb every firstborn donkey, but if you do not redeem
it, break its neck.[l] Redeem every firstborn among your sons.[m]
14 "In days to come when your son[n] asks you, 'What does this mean?' say to him,
'With a mighty hand the LORD brought us out of Egypt, out of the land of slavery.[o]
15 When Pharaoh stubbornly refused to let us go, the LORD killed every firstborn in
Egypt, both man and animal. This is why I sacrifice to the LORD the first male
offspring of every womb and redeem each of my firstborn sons.'[p] 16 And it will be
like a sign on your hand and a symbol on your forehead[q] that the LORD brought us
out of Egypt with his mighty hand."

2. Crossing the sea

17 When Pharaoh let the people go, God did not lead them on the road through the
Philistine country, though that was shorter. For God said, "If they face war, they might

12:44 [v]Ge 17:12-13
12:45 [w]Lev 22:10
12:46 [x]Nu 9:12; Jn 19:36*
12:48 [y]Nu 9:14
12:49 [z]Nu 15:15-16, 29; Gal 3:28
12:51 [a]ver 41; Ex 6:26
13:2 [a]ver 12, 13, 15; Ex 22:29; Nu 3:13; Dt 15:19; Lk 2:23*
13:3 [b]Ex 3:20; 6:1 [c]Ex 12:19
13:4 [d]Ex 12:2
13:5 [e]Ex 3:8 [f]Ex 12:25-26
13:6 [g]Ex 12:15-20
13:8 [h]ver 14; Ex 10:2; Ps 78:5-6
13:9 [i]ver 16; Dt 6:8; 11:18
13:10 [j]Ex 12:24-25
13:12 [k]Lev 27:26; Lk 2:23*
13:13 [l]Ex 34:20 [m]Nu 18:15
13:14 [n]Ex 10:2; 12:26-27; Dt 6:20 [o]ver 3, 9
13:15 [p]Ex 12:29
13:16 [q]ver 9

13:2 *Consecrate* means to sacrifice or to consider something as belonging to God. This dedication practice described in 13:11–16 was to remind the people of their deliverance through God.

13:4 "In the month of Abib" corresponds to late March and early April on our calendar.

13:6–9 The Feast of Unleavened Bread marked the Hebrews as a unique people—as though they were branded on their hands and foreheads. What do you do that marks you as a follower of God? The way you raise your children, demonstrate love for others, show concern for the poor, and live in devotion to God—these actions will leave visible marks for all to see. While national groups are marked by customs and traditions, Christians are marked by loving one another (John 13:34, 35).

13:12–14 What did it mean to "redeem every firstborn among your sons"? During the night the Israelites escaped from Egypt, God spared the oldest son of every house marked with blood on the door-frames. Because God saved the lives of the firstborn, he had a rightful claim to them. But God commanded the Israelites to buy their sons back from him. This ritual served three main purposes: (1) it was a reminder to the people of how God had spared their sons from death and freed them all from slavery; (2) it showed God's high respect for human life in contrast to the pagan gods who, their worshippers believed, demanded human sacrifice; (3) it looked forward to the day when Jesus Christ would buy us back by paying the price for our sin once and for all.

change their minds and return to Egypt."[r] 18So God led[s] the people around by the
desert road towards the Red Sea.[a] The Israelites went up out of Egypt armed for
battle.[t]
19Moses took the bones of Joseph[u] with him because Joseph had made the sons
of Israel swear an oath. He had said, "God will surely come to your aid, and then
you must carry my bones up with you from this place."[b][v]
20After leaving Succoth they camped at Etham on the edge of the desert.[w] 21By
day the LORD went ahead of them in a pillar of cloud[x] to guide them on their way
and by night in a pillar of fire to give them light, so that they could travel by day or
night. 22Neither the pillar of cloud by day nor the pillar of fire by night left its place
in front of the people.

14 Then the LORD said to Moses, 2"Tell the Israelites to turn back and camp near
Pi Hahiroth, between Migdol[a] and the sea. They are to camp by the sea,
directly opposite Baal Zephon. 3Pharaoh will think, 'The Israelites are wandering
around the land in confusion, hemmed in by the desert.' 4And I will harden Pharaoh's
heart,[b] and he will pursue them. But I will gain glory[c] for myself through Pharaoh
and all his army, and the Egyptians will know that I am the LORD."[d] So the Israelites
did this.
5When the king of Egypt was told that the people had fled, Pharaoh and his officials
changed their minds about them and said, "What have we done? We have let the
Israelites go and have lost their services!" 6So he had his chariot made ready and took
his army with him. 7He took six hundred of the best chariots, along with all the other
chariots of Egypt, with officers over all of them. 8The LORD hardened the heart[e] of
Pharaoh king of Egypt, so that he pursued the Israelites, who were marching out
boldly.[f] 9The Egyptians—all Pharaoh's horses and chariots, horsemen[a] and

a *18* Hebrew *Yam Suph*; that is, Sea of Reeds b *19* See Gen. 50:25. a *9* Or *charioteers*; also in verses 17, 18, 23, 26 and 28

13:17 [r]Ex 14:11; Nu 14:1-4; Dt 17:16
13:18 [s]Ps 136:16 [t]Jos 1:14
13:19 [u]Jos 24:32; Ac 7:16 [v]Ge 50:24-25
13:20 [w]Nu 33:6
13:21 [x]Ex 14:19, 24; 33:9-10; Nu 9:16; Dt 1:33; Ne 9:12, 19; Ps 78:14; 99:7; 105:39; Isa 4:5; 1Co 10:1
14:2 [a]Nu 33:7; Jer 44:1
14:4 [b]Ex 4:21 [c]Ro 9:17, 22-23 [d]Ex 7:5
14:8 [e]ver 4; Ex 11:10 [f]Nu 33:3; Ac 13:17

THE EXODUS
The Israelites left Succoth and camped first at Etham before going towards Baal Zephon to camp by the sea (14:2). God miraculously brought them across the sea, into the desert of Shur (15:22). After stopping at the oasis of Elim, the people moved into the Desert of Sin (16:1).

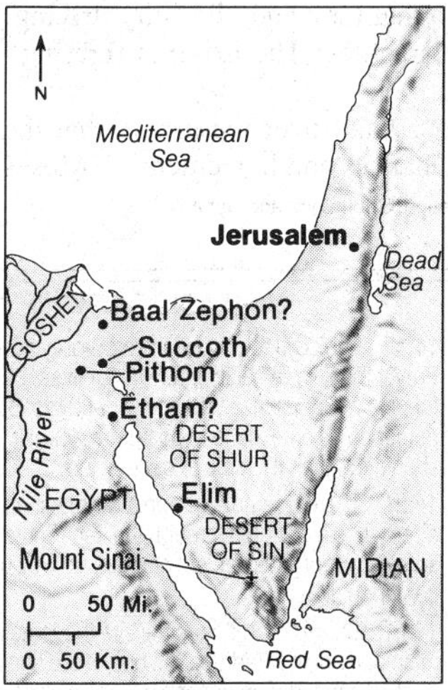

13:17, 18 God doesn't always work in the way that seems best to us. Instead of guiding the Israelites along the direct route from Egypt to the promised land, he took them by a longer route to avoid fighting with the Philistines. If God does not lead you along the shortest path to your goal, don't complain or resist. Follow him willingly and trust him to lead you safely around unseen obstacles. He can see the end of your journey from the beginning, and he knows the safest and best route.

13:17, 18 When did the Hebrews leave Egypt? There are two theories. The *early* theory says the exodus occurred around 1446–1445 B.C. The *late* theory suggests the exodus happened between 1300 and 1200 B.C. Those who hold to the earlier date point to 1 Kings 6:1, where the Bible clearly states that Solomon began building the temple 480 years after the Hebrews left Egypt. Since almost all scholars agree that Solomon began building the temple in 966, this puts the exodus in the year 1446. But those who hold to the later date suggest that the 480 years cannot be taken literally. They point to Exodus 1:11, which says that the Hebrews built the store cities of Pithom and Rameses, named after Pharaoh Rameses II, who reigned around 1290 B.C. Regardless of which date is correct, the fact is that God led the Hebrews out of Egypt, just as he had promised. This showed his great power and his great love for his people.

13:21, 22 God gave the Hebrews a pillar of cloud and a pillar of fire so they would know day and night that God was with them on their journey to the promised land. What has God given us so that we can have the same assurance? The Bible—something the Israelites did not have. Look to God's word for reassurance of his presence. As the Hebrews looked to the pillars of cloud and fire, we can look to God's word day and night to know he is with us, helping us on our journey.

13:21, 22 The pillars of fire and cloud were examples of *theophany*—God appearing in a physical form. In this form, God lighted Israel's path, protected them from their enemies, provided reassurance, controlled their movements, and inspired the burning zeal that Israel should have for their God.

14:6-9 Six hundred Egyptian war chariots were bearing down on the helpless Israelites, who were trapped between the mountains and the sea. The war chariots each carried two people—one to drive and one to fight. These chariots were made of a wood or leather cab placed over two wheels, and they were pulled by horses. These were the armoured tanks of Bible times. But even their power was no match for God, who destroyed both the chariots and their soldiers.

troops — pursued the Israelites and overtook[g] them as they camped by the sea near
Pi Hahiroth, opposite Baal Zephon.
10 As Pharaoh approached, the Israelites looked up, and there were the Egyptians,
marching after them. They were terrified and cried[h] out to the LORD. 11 They said
to Moses, "Was it because there were no graves in Egypt that you brought us to the
desert to die?[i] What have you done to us by bringing us out of Egypt? 12 Didn't we
say to you in Egypt, 'Leave us alone; let us serve the Egyptians'? It would have been
better for us to serve the Egyptians than to die in the desert!"
13 Moses answered the people, "Do not be afraid.[j] Stand firm and you will see[k]
the deliverance the LORD will bring you today. The Egyptians you see today you will
never see[l] again. 14 The LORD will fight[m] for you; you need only to be still."[n]
15 Then the LORD said to Moses, "Why are you crying out to me? Tell the Israelites
to move on. 16 Raise your staff[o] and stretch out your hand over the sea to divide the
water[p] so that the Israelites can go through the sea on dry ground. 17 I will harden
the hearts of the Egyptians so that they will go in after them.[q] And I will gain glory
through Pharaoh and all his army, through his chariots and his horsemen. 18 The
Egyptians will know that I am the LORD when I gain glory through Pharaoh, his
chariots and his horsemen."
19 Then the angel of God, who had been travelling in front of Israel's army,
withdrew and went behind them. The pillar of cloud[r] also moved from in front and
stood behind them, 20 coming between the armies of Egypt and Israel. Throughout the
night the cloud brought darkness to the one side and light to the other; so neither went
near the other all night long.
21 Then Moses stretched out his hand over the sea, and all that night the LORD drove
the sea back with a strong east wind[s] and turned it into dry land. The waters were
divided,[t] 22 and the Israelites went through the sea on dry ground,[u] with a wall of
water on their right and on their left.
23 The Egyptians pursued them, and all Pharaoh's horses and chariots and horsemen
followed them into the sea. 24 During the last watch of the night the LORD looked down
from the pillar of fire and cloud[v] at the Egyptian army and threw it into confusion.
25 He made the wheels of their chariots come off[b] so that they had difficulty driving.
And the Egyptians said, "Let's get away from the Israelites! The LORD is fighting[w]
for them against Egypt."
26 Then the LORD said to Moses, "Stretch out your hand over the sea so that the
waters may flow back over the Egyptians and their chariots and horsemen." 27 Moses

14:9 [g] Ex 15:9
14:10 [h] Jos 24:7; Ne 9:9; Ps 34:17
14:11 [i] Ps 106:7-8
14:13 [j] Ge 15:1 [k] 2Ch 20:17; Isa 41:10, 13-14 [l] ver 30
14:14 [m] ver 25; Ex 15:3; Dt 1:30; 3:22; 2Ch 20:29 [n] Ps 37:7; 46:10; Isa 30:15
14:16 [o] Ex 4:17; Nu 20:8-9, 11 [p] Isa 10:26
14:17 [q] ver 4
14:19 [r] Ex 13:21
14:21 [s] Ex 15:8 [t] Ps 74:13; 114:5; Isa 63:12
14:22 [u] Ex 15:19; Ne 9:11; Ps 66:6; Heb 11:29
14:24 [v] Ex 13:21
14:25 [w] ver 14

b 25 Or *He jammed the wheels of their chariots* (see Samaritan Pentateuch, Septuagint and Syriac)

14:10, 11 Trapped against the sea, the Israelites faced the Egyptian army sweeping in for the kill. The Israelites thought they were doomed. After watching God's powerful hand deliver them from Egypt, their only response was fear, whining, and despair. Where was their trust in God? Israel had to learn from repeated experience that God was able to provide for them. God has preserved these examples in the Bible so that we can learn to trust him the first time. By focusing on God's faithfulness in the past we can face crises with confidence rather than with fear and complaining.

14:11, 12 This is the first instance of grumbling and complaining by the Israelites. Their lack of faith in God is startling. Yet how often do we find ourselves doing the same thing — complaining over inconveniences or discomforts? The Israelites were about to learn some tough lessons. Had they trusted God, they would have been spared much grief.

14:13, 14 The people were hostile and despairing, but Moses encouraged them to watch the wonderful way God would rescue them. Moses had a positive attitude! When it looked as if they were trapped, Moses called upon God to intervene. We may not be chased by an army, but we may still feel trapped. Instead of giving in to despair, we should adopt Moses' attitude to "stand firm and . . . see the deliverance the Lord will bring".

14:15 The Lord told Moses to stop praying and get moving! Prayer must have a vital place in our lives, but there is also a place for action. Sometimes we know what to do, but we pray for more guidance as an excuse to postpone doing it. If we know what we should do, then it is time to get moving.

14:21 There was no apparent way of escape, but the Lord opened up a dry path through the sea. Sometimes we find ourselves caught in a problem and see no way out. Don't panic; God can open up a way.

14:21, 22 Some scholars believe the Israelites did not cross the main body of the Red Sea but one of the shallow lakes or marshes north of it that dry up at certain times of the year, or perhaps a smaller branch of the Red Sea where the water would have been shallow enough to wade across. But the Bible clearly states that the Lord "drove the sea back with a strong east wind and turned it into dry land" (14:21; see also Joshua 3:15, 16; and 2 Kings 2:13, 14). Also, the water was deep enough to cover the chariots (14:28). The God who created the earth and water performed a mighty miracle at exactly the right time to demonstrate his great power and love for his people.

14:27, 28 No evidence of this great exodus has been discovered in Egyptian historical records. This was because it was a common practice for Egyptian pharaohs not to record their defeats. They

14:27
[x]Jos 4:18
[y]Ex 15:1, 21; Ps 78:53; 106:11

14:29
[z]ver 22

stretched out his hand over the sea, and at daybreak the sea went back to its place.[x]
The Egyptians were fleeing towards[c] it, and the LORD swept them into the sea.[y]
28The water flowed back and covered the chariots and horsemen—the entire army of
Pharaoh that had followed the Israelites into the sea. Not one of them survived.
29But the Israelites went through the sea on dry ground,[z] with a wall of water on

[c] *27 Or from*

MOSES

Some people can't stay out of trouble. When conflict breaks out, they always manage to be nearby. Reaction is their favourite action. This was Moses. He seemed drawn to what needed to be righted. Throughout his life, he was at his finest and his worst responding to the conflicts around him. Even the burning bush experience was an illustration of his character. Having spotted the fire and seen that the bush did not burn, he had to investigate. Whether jumping into a fight to defend a Hebrew slave or trying to referee a struggle between two kinsmen, when Moses saw conflict, he reacted.

Over the years, however, an amazing thing happened to Moses' character. He didn't stop reacting, but rather learned to react correctly. The kaleidoscopic action of each day of leading two million people in the desert was more than enough challenge for Moses' reacting ability. Much of the time he served as a buffer between God and the people. At one moment he had to respond to God's anger at the people's stubbornness and forgetfulness. At another moment he had to react to the people's bickering and complaining. At still another moment he had to react to their unjustified attacks on his character.

Leadership often involves reaction. If we want to react with instincts consistent with God's will, we must develop habits of obedience to God. Consistent obedience to God is best developed in times of less stress. Then when stress comes, our natural reaction will be to obey God.

In our age of lowering moral standards, we find it almost impossible to believe that God would punish Moses for the one time he disobeyed outright. What we fail to see, however, is that God did not reject Moses; Moses simply disqualified himself from entering the promised land. Personal greatness does not make a person immune to error or its consequences.

In Moses we see an outstanding personality shaped by God. But we must not misunderstand what God did. He did not change who or what Moses was; he did not give Moses new abilities and strengths. Instead, he took Moses' characteristics and moulded them until they were suited to his purposes. Does knowing this make a difference in your understanding of God's purpose in your life? He is trying to take what he created in the first place and use it for its intended purposes. The next time you talk with God, don't ask, "What should I change into?" but "How should I use my own abilities and strengths to do your will?"

Strengths and accomplishments:
- Egyptian education; desert training
- Greatest Jewish leader; set the exodus in motion
- Prophet and law-giver; recorder of the Ten Commandments
- Author of the Pentateuch

Weaknesses and mistakes:
- Failed to enter the promised land because of disobedience to God
- Did not always recognise and use the talents of others

Lessons from his life:
- God prepares, then uses. His timetable is life-sized
- God does his greatest work through frail people

Vital statistics:
- Where: Egypt, Midian, Desert of Sinai
- Occupations: Prince, shepherd, leader of the Israelites
- Relatives: Sister: Miriam. Brother: Aaron. Wife: Zipporah. Sons: Gershom and Eliezer.

Key verses:
"By faith Moses, when he had grown up, refused to be known as the son of Pharaoh's daughter. He chose to be mistreated along with the people of God rather than to enjoy the pleasures of sin for a short time" (Hebrews 11:24, 25).

Moses' story is told in the books of Exodus to Deuteronomy. He is also mentioned in Acts 7:20–44; Hebrews 11:23–29.

---

even went so far as to take existing records and delete the names of traitors and political adversaries. Pharaoh would have been especially anxious not to record that his great army was destroyed chasing a band of runaway slaves. Since either the Egyptians failed to record the exodus or the record has not yet been found, it is impossible to place a precise date on the event.

their right and on their left. 30 That day the LORD saved[a] Israel from the hands of the
Egyptians, and Israel saw the Egyptians lying dead on the shore. 31 And when the
Israelites saw the great power the LORD displayed against the Egyptians, the people
feared the LORD and put their trust[b] in him and in Moses his servant.

The Song of Moses and Miriam

15 Then Moses and the Israelites sang this song[a] to the LORD:

"I will sing[b] to the LORD,
for he is highly exalted.
The horse and its rider
he has hurled into the sea.
2 The LORD is my strength[c] and my song;
he has become my salvation.[d]
He is my God,[e] and I will praise him,
my father's God, and I will exalt[f] him.
3 The LORD is a warrior;[g]
the LORD is his name.[h]
4 Pharaoh's chariots and his army[i]
he has hurled into the sea.
The best of Pharaoh's officers
are drowned in the Red Sea.[a]
5 The deep waters have covered them;
they sank to the depths like a stone.[j]

6 "Your right hand,[k] O LORD,
was majestic in power.
Your right hand, O LORD,
shattered the enemy.
7 In the greatness of your majesty
you threw down those who opposed you.
You unleashed your burning anger;[l]
it consumed them like stubble.
8 By the blast of your nostrils[m]
the waters piled up.[n]
The surging waters stood firm like a wall;[o]
the deep waters congealed in the heart of the sea.

9 "The enemy boasted,
'I will pursue,[p] I will overtake them.
I will divide the spoils;[q]
I will gorge myself on them.
I will draw my sword
and my hand will destroy them.'
10 But you blew with your breath,
and the sea covered them.
They sank like lead
in the mighty waters.[r]

11 "Who among the gods is like you,[s] O LORD?
Who is like you—

a 4 Hebrew *Yam Suph*; that is, Sea of Reeds; also in verse 22

14:30 [a]Ps 106:8, 10, 21
14:31 [b]Ps 106:12; Jn 2:11
15:1 [a]Rev 15:3 [b]Ps 106:12
15:2 [c]Ps 59:17 [d]Ps 18:2, 46; Isa 12:2; Hab 3:18 [e]Ge 28:21 [f]Ex 3:6, 15-16; Isa 25:1
15:3 [g]Ex 14:14; Ps 24:8; Rev 19:11 [h]Ex 6:2-3, 7-8; Ps 83:18
15:4 [i]Ex 14:6-7
15:5 [j]ver 10; Ne 9:11
15:6 [k]Ps 118:15
15:7 [l]Ps 78:49-50
15:8 [m]Ex 14:21 [n]Ps 78:13 [o]Ex 14:22
15:9 [p]Ex 14:5-9 [q]Jdg 5:30; Isa 53:12
15:10 [r]ver 5; Ex 14:27-28
15:11 [s]Ex 8:10; Dt 3:24; Ps 77:13

15:1ff Music played an important part in Israel's worship and celebration. Singing was an expression of love and thanks, and it was a creative way to pass down oral traditions. Some say this song of Moses is the oldest recorded song in the world. It was a festive epic poem celebrating God's victory, lifting the hearts and voices of the people outwards and upwards. After having been delivered from great danger, they sang with joy! Psalms and hymns can be great ways to express relief, praise, and thanks when you have been through trouble.

15:8 The phrase, "the deep waters congealed in the heart of the sea" means that the waters became like hard walls for them to walk between.

majestic in holiness,[t]
awesome in glory,[u]
working wonders?
12 You stretched out your right hand
and the earth swallowed them.

13 "In your unfailing love you will lead[v]
the people you have redeemed.
In your strength you will guide them
to your holy dwelling.[w]
14 The nations will hear and tremble;[x]
anguish will grip the people of Philistia.
15 The chiefs[y] of Edom will be terrified,
the leaders of Moab will be seized with trembling,[z]
the people[b] of Canaan will melt[a] away;
16 terror[b] and dread will fall upon them.
By the power of your arm
they will be as still as a stone[c]—
until your people pass by, O LORD,
until the people you bought[c][d] pass by.
17 You will bring them in and plant[e] them
on the mountain[f] of your inheritance—
the place, O LORD, you made for your dwelling,
the sanctuary, O Lord, your hands established.
18 The LORD will reign
for ever and ever."

19 When Pharaoh's horses, chariots and horsemen[d] went into the sea,[g] the LORD
brought the waters of the sea back over them, but the Israelites walked through the

[b] 15 Or *rulers* [c] 16 Or *created* [d] 19 Or *charioteers*

15:11 [t] Isa 6:3; Rev 4:8 [u] Ps 8:1
15:13 [v] Ne 9:12; Ps 77:20 [w] Ps 78:54
15:14 [x] Dt 2:25
15:15 [y] Ge 36:15 [z] Nu 22:3 [a] Jos 5:1
15:16 [b] Ex 23:27; Jos 2:9 [c] 1Sa 25:37 [d] Ps 74:2
15:17 [e] Ps 44:2 [f] Ps 78:54, 68
15:19 [g] Ex 14:28

FAMOUS SONGS IN THE BIBLE

Where	*Purpose of Song*
Exodus 15:1–21	Moses' song of victory and praise after God led Israel out of Egypt and saved them by parting the Red Sea; Miriam joined in the singing too
Numbers 21:17	Israel's song of praise to God for giving them water in the desert
Deuteronomy 32:1–43	Moses' song of Israel's history with thanksgiving and praise as the Hebrews were about to enter the promised land
Judges 5:2–31	Deborah and Barak's song of praise thanking God for Israel's victory over King Jabin's army at Mount Tabor
2 Samuel 22:2–51	David's song of thanks and praise to God for rescuing him from Saul and his other enemies
Song of Songs	Solomon's song of love celebrating the union of husband and wife
Isaiah 26:1	Isaiah's prophetic song about how the redeemed will sing in the new Jerusalem
Ezra 3:11	Israel's song of praise at the completion of the temple's foundation
Luke 1:46–55	Mary's song of praise to God for the conception of Jesus
Luke 1:68–79	Zechariah's song of praise for the promise of a son
Acts 16:25	Paul and Silas sang hymns in prison
Revelation 5:9, 10	The "new song" of the 24 elders acclaiming Christ as worthy to break the seven seals of God's scroll
Revelation 14:3	The song of the 144,000 redeemed from the earth
Revelation 15:3, 4	The song of all the redeemed in praise of the Lamb who redeemed them

sea on dry ground.[h] 20 Then Miriam[i] the prophetess,[j] Aaron's sister, took a tambourine in her hand, and all the women followed her, with tambourines and dancing.[k]
21 Miriam sang to them:

"Sing to the LORD,
for he is highly exalted.
The horse and its rider
he has hurled into the sea."[l]

3. Complaining in the desert

The Waters of Marah and Elim

22 Then Moses led Israel from the Red Sea and they went into the Desert of Shur.
For three days they travelled in the desert without finding water. 23 When they came
to Marah, they could not drink its water because it was bitter. (That is why the place
is called Marah.[e][m]) 24 So the people grumbled[n] against Moses, saying, "What are
we to drink?"
25 Then Moses cried out[o] to the LORD, and the LORD showed him a piece of wood.
He threw it into the water, and the water became sweet.
There the LORD made a decree and a law for them, and there he tested[p] them. 26 He
said, "If you listen carefully to the voice of the LORD your God and do what is right
in his eyes, if you pay attention to his commands and keep all his decrees,[q] I will
not bring on you any of the diseases[r] I brought on the Egyptians, for I am the LORD,
who heals[s] you."
27 Then they came to Elim, where there were twelve springs and seventy palm trees,
and they camped[t] there near the water.

Manna and Quail

16 The whole Israelite community set out from Elim and came to the Desert of
Sin,[a] which is between Elim and Sinai, on the fifteenth day of the second
month after they had come out of Egypt. 2 In the desert the whole community grumbled[b] against Moses and Aaron. 3 The Israelites said to them, "If only we had died
by the LORD's hand in Egypt![c] There we sat round pots of meat and ate all the food[d]
we wanted, but you have brought us out into this desert to starve this entire assembly
to death."
4 Then the LORD said to Moses, "I will rain down bread from heaven[e] for you. The
people are to go out each day and gather enough for that day. In this way I will test
them and see whether they will follow my instructions. 5 On the sixth day they are

[e] 23 *Marah* means *bitter.*

15:19 [h]Ex 14:22
15:20 [i]Nu 26:59 [j]Jdg 4:4 [k]Jdg 11:34; 1Sa 18:6; Ps 30:11; 150:4
15:21 [l]ver 1; Ex 14:27
15:23 [m]Nu 33:8
15:24 [n]Ex 14:12; 16:2
15:25 [o]Ex 14:10 [p]Jdg 3:4
15:26 [q]Dt 7:12 [r]Dt 28:27, 58-60 [s]Ex 23:25-26
15:27 [t]Nu 33:9
16:1 [a]Nu 33:11, 12
16:2 [b]Ex 14:11; 15:24; 1Co 10:10
16:3 [c]Ex 17:3 [d]Nu 11:4, 34
16:4 [e]Dt 8:3; Jn 6:31*

15:20 Miriam was called a prophetess not only because she received revelations from God (Numbers 12:1, 2; Micah 6:4) but also for her musical skill. Prophecy and music were often closely related in the Bible (1 Samuel 10:5; 1 Chronicles 25:1).

15:23, 27 The waters of Marah are contrasted with the springs of Elim. Marah stood for the unbelieving, grumbling attitude of the people who would not trust God. Elim stands for God's bountiful provision. How easy it is to grumble and complain too quickly, only to be embarrassed by God's help!

15:26 God promised that if the people obeyed him they would be free from the diseases that plagued the Egyptians. Little did they know that many of the moral laws he later gave them were designed to keep them free from sickness. For example, following God's law against prostitution would keep them free of venereal disease. God's laws for us are often designed to keep us from harm. Men and women are complex beings. Our physical, emotional, and spiritual lives are intertwined. Modern medicine is now acknowledging what these laws assumed. If we want God to care for us, we need to submit to his directions for living.

16:1 The Desert of Sin was a vast and hostile environment of sand and stone. Its barren surroundings provided the perfect place for God to test and shape the character of his people.

16:2 It happened again. As the Israelites encountered danger, shortages, and inconvenience, they complained bitterly and longed to be back in Egypt. But as always, God provided for their needs. Difficult circumstances often lead to stress, and complaining is a natural response. The Israelites didn't really want to be back in Egypt; they just wanted life to get a little easier. In the pressure of the moment, they could not focus on the cause of their stress (in this case, lack of trust in God); they could only think about the quickest way of escape. When pressure comes your way, resist the temptation to make a quick escape. Instead, focus on God's power and wisdom to help you deal with the cause of your stress.

16:4, 5 God promised to meet the Hebrews' need for food in the desert, but he decided to test their obedience. God wanted to see if they would obey his detailed instructions. We can learn to trust him as our Lord only by following. We can learn to obey by taking small steps of obedience.

to prepare what they bring in, and that is to be twice[f] as much as they gather on the
other days."
6So Moses and Aaron said to all the Israelites, "In the evening you will know that
it was the LORD who brought you out of Egypt,[g] 7and in the morning you will see
the glory[h] of the LORD, because he has heard your grumbling[i] against him. Who
are we, that you should grumble against us?"[j] 8Moses also said, "You will know that
it was the LORD when he gives you meat to eat in the evening and all the bread you
want in the morning, because he has heard your grumbling against him. Who are we?
You are not grumbling against us, but against the LORD."[k]
9Then Moses told Aaron, "Say to the entire Israelite community, 'Come before the
LORD, for he has heard your grumbling.' "
10While Aaron was speaking to the whole Israelite community, they looked towards
the desert, and there was the glory[l] of the LORD appearing in the cloud.[m]
11The LORD said to Moses, 12"I have heard the grumbling[n] of the Israelites. Tell
them, 'At twilight you will eat meat, and in the morning you will be filled with bread.
Then you will know that I am the LORD your God.' "
13That evening quail[o] came and covered the camp, and in the morning there was
a layer of dew[p] around the camp. 14When the dew was gone, thin flakes like frost[q]
on the ground appeared on the desert floor. 15When the Israelites saw it, they said
to each other, "What is it?" For they did not know what it was.
Moses said to them, "It is the bread[r] the LORD has given you to eat. 16This is what
the LORD has commanded: 'Each one is to gather as much as he needs. Take an
omer[a][s] for each person you have in your tent.' "
17The Israelites did as they were told; some gathered much, some little. 18And when
they measured it by the omer, he who gathered much did not have too much, and he
who gathered little did not have too little.[t] Each one gathered as much as he needed.
19Then Moses said to them, "No-one is to keep any of it until morning."[u]
20However, some of them paid no attention to Moses; they kept part of it until
morning, but it was full of maggots and began to smell. So Moses was angry with
them.
21Each morning everyone gathered as much as he needed, and when the sun grew
hot, it melted away. 22On the sixth day, they gathered twice[v] as much—two omers[b]
for each person—and the leaders of the community[w] came and reported this to Moses.
23He said to them, "This is what the LORD commanded: 'Tomorrow is to be a day
of rest, a holy Sabbath[x] to the LORD. So bake what you want to bake and boil what
you want to boil. Save whatever is left and keep it until morning.' "
24So they saved it until morning, as Moses commanded, and it did not stink or get
maggots in it. 25"Eat it today," Moses said, "because today is a Sabbath to the LORD.
You will not find any of it on the ground today. 26Six days you are to gather it, but
on the seventh day, the Sabbath,[y] there will not be any."
27Nevertheless, some of the people went out on the seventh day to gather it, but
they found none. 28Then the LORD said to Moses, "How long will you[c] refuse to keep
my commands[z] and my instructions? 29Bear in mind that the LORD has given you
the Sabbath; that is why on the sixth day he gives you bread for two days. Everyone
is to stay where he is on the seventh day; no-one is to go out." 30So the people rested
on the seventh day.
31The people of Israel called the bread manna.[d][a] It was white like coriander seed

16:5 [f]ver 22
16:6 [g]Ex 6:6
16:7 [h]ver 10; Isa 35:2; 40:5 [i]ver 12; Nu 14:2, 27, 28 [j]Nu 16:11
16:8 [k]1Sa 8:7; Ro 13:2
16:10 [l]ver 7; Nu 16:19 [m]Ex 13:21; 1Ki 8:10
16:12 [n]ver 7
16:13 [o]Nu 11:31; Ps 78:27-28; 105:40 [p]Nu 11:9
16:14 [q]ver 31; Nu 11:7-9; Ps 105:40
16:15 [r]ver 4; Jn 6:31
16:16 [s]ver 32, 36
16:18 [t]2Co 8:15*
16:19 [u]ver 23; Ex 12:10; 23:18
16:22 [v]ver 5 [w]Ex 34:31
16:23 [x]Ge 2:3; Ex 20:8; 23:12; Lev 23:3
16:26 [y]Ex 20:9-10
16:28 [z]2Ki 17:14; Ps 78:10; 106:13
16:31 [a]Nu 11:7-9

a *16* That is, probably about 4 pints (about 2 litres); also in verses 18, 32, 33 and 36 **b** *22* That is, probably about 7½ pints (about 4.5 litres) **c** *28* The Hebrew is plural. **d** *31* *Manna* means *What is it?* (see verse 15).

16:14–16 Manna (16:31) appeared on the ground each day as thin flakes like frost. The people gathered it, ground it like grain, and made it into honey-tasting pancakes. For the Israelites the manna was a gift—it came every day and was just what they needed. It satisfied their temporary physical need. In John 6:48–51 Jesus compares himself to manna. Christ is our daily bread who satisfies our eternal, spiritual need.

16:23 The Israelites were not to work on the Sabbath—not even to cook food. Why? God knew that the busy routine of daily living could distract people from worshipping him. It is so easy to let work, family responsibilities, and recreation crowd our schedules so tightly that we don't take time to worship. Carefully guard your time with God.

and tasted like wafers made with honey. 32Moses said, "This is what the LORD has
commanded: 'Take an omer of manna and keep it for the generations to come, so they
can see the bread I gave you to eat in the desert when I brought you out of Egypt.' "
33So Moses said to Aaron, "Take a jar and put an omer of manna[b] in it. Then place
it before the LORD to be kept for the generations to come."
34As the LORD commanded Moses, Aaron put the manna in front of the Testimony,[c] that it might be kept. 35The Israelites ate manna[d] for forty years,[e] until they
came to a land that was settled; they ate manna until they reached the border of
Canaan.[f]
36(An omer is one tenth of an ephah.)

Water From the Rock

17 The whole Israelite community set out from the Desert of Sin,[a] travelling from
place to place as the LORD commanded. They camped at Rephidim, but there
was no water[b] for the people to drink. 2So they quarrelled with Moses and said, "Give
us water[c] to drink."
Moses replied, "Why do you quarrel with me? Why do you put the LORD to the
test?"[d]
3But the people were thirsty for water there, and they grumbled[e] against Moses.
They said, "Why did you bring us up out of Egypt to make us and our children and
livestock die of thirst?"
4Then Moses cried out to the LORD, "What am I to do with these people? They are
almost ready to stone[f] me."
5The LORD answered Moses, "Walk on ahead of the people. Take with you some
of the elders of Israel and take in your hand the staff with which you struck the Nile,[g]
and go. 6I will stand there before you by the rock at Horeb. Strike the rock, and water[h]
will come out of it for the people to drink." So Moses did this in the sight of the elders
of Israel. 7And he called the place Massah[a] and Meribah[b][i] because the Israelites
quarrelled and because they tested the LORD saying, "Is the LORD among us or not?"

The Amalekites Defeated

8The Amalekites[j] came and attacked the Israelites at Rephidim. 9Moses said to
Joshua, "Choose some of our men and go out to fight the Amalekites. Tomorrow I
will stand on top of the hill with the staff[k] of God in my hands."

a 7 *Massah* means *testing*. b 7 *Meribah* means *quarrelling*.

16:33 [b]Heb 9:4
16:34 [c]Ex 25:16, 21, 22; 40:20; Nu 17:4, 10
16:35 [d]Jn 6:31, 49 [e]Ne 9:21 [f]Jos 5:12
17:1 [a]Ex 16:1 [b]Nu 33:14
17:2 [c]Nu 20:2 [d]Dt 6:16; Ps 78:18, 41; 1Co 10:9
17:3 [e]Ex 15:24; 16:2-3
17:4 [f]Nu 14:10; 1Sa 30:6
17:5 [g]Ex 7:20
17:6 [h]Nu 20:11; Ps 114:8; 1Co 10:4
17:7 [i]Nu 20:13, 24; Ps 81:7
17:8 [j]Ge 36:12; Dt 25:17-19
17:9 [k]Ex 4:17

16:32 The Hebrews put some manna in a special jar as a reminder of the way God provided for them in the desert. Symbols have always been an important part of Christian worship also. We use special objects as symbols to remind us of God's work. Such symbols can be valuable aids to our worship as long as we are careful to keep them from becoming objects of worship.

16:36 "An omer is one tenth of an ephah"—this is about two quarts or one tenth of a bushel.

17:2 Again the people complained about their problem instead of praying. Some problems can be solved by careful thought or by rearranging our priorities. Some can be solved by discussion and good counsel. But some problems can be solved only by prayer. We should make a determined effort to pray when we feel like complaining, because complaining only raises our level of stress. Prayer quiets our thoughts and emotions and prepares us to listen.

17:8 The Amalekites were descendants of Amalek, a grandson of Esau. They were a fierce nomadic tribe that lived in the desert region of the Dead Sea. They made part of their livelihood by conducting frequent raids on other settlements and carrying off booty. They killed for pleasure. One of the greatest insults in Israelite culture was to call someone "a friend of Amalek". When the Israelites entered the region, the Amalekites saw this as a perfect opportunity for both pleasure and profit. But this hostile tribe was moving in on the wrong group—a people led by God. For the Israelite slaves to defeat such a warlike nation was more than enough proof that God was with them as he had promised to be.

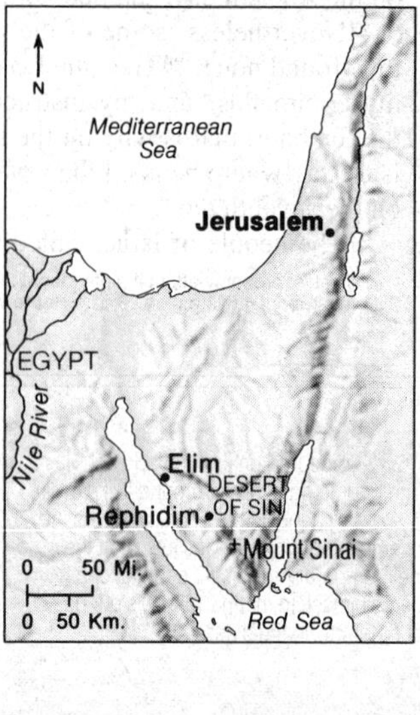

JOURNEY TO MOUNT SINAI
God miraculously supplied food and water in the desert for the Israelites. In the Desert of Sin, he provided manna (16). At Rephidim, he provided water from a rock (17:1–7). Finally God brought them to the foot of Mount Sinai, where he gave them his holy laws.

17:10 [l]Ex 24:14
17:11 [m]Jas 5:16
17:14 [n]Ex 24:4; 34:27; Nu 33:2 [o]1Sa 15:3; 30:17-18
18:1 [a]Ex 2:16; 3:1
18:2 [b]Ex 2:21; 4:25
18:3 [c]Ex 4:20; Ac 7:29 [d]Ex 2:22
18:4 [e]1Ch 23:15
18:5 [f]Ex 3:1
18:7 [g]Ge 43:28 [h]Ge 29:13
18:8 [i]Ex 15:6, 16; Ps 81:7
18:10 [j]Ge 14:20; Ps 68:19-20
18:11 [k]Ex 12:12; 15:11; 2Ch 2:5 [l]Lk 1:51
18:12 [m]Dt 12:7

10 So Joshua fought the Amalekites as Moses had ordered, and Moses, Aaron and
Hur[l] went to the top of the hill. 11 As long as Moses held up his hands, the Israelites
were winning,[m] but whenever he lowered his hands, the Amalekites were winning.
12 When Moses' hands grew tired, they took a stone and put it under him and he sat
on it. Aaron and Hur held his hands up—one on one side, one on the other—so that
his hands remained steady till sunset. 13 So Joshua overcame the Amalekite army with
the sword.
14 Then the LORD said to Moses, "Write[n] this on a scroll as something to be
remembered and make sure that Joshua hears it, because I will completely blot out
the memory of Amalek[o] from under heaven."
15 Moses built an altar and called it The LORD is my Banner. 16 He said, "For hands
were lifted up to the throne of the LORD. The[c] LORD will be at war against the
Amalekites from generation to generation."

Jethro Visits Moses

18 Now Jethro, the priest of Midian[a] and father-in-law of Moses, heard of
everything God had done for Moses and for his people Israel, and how the LORD
had brought Israel out of Egypt.
2 After Moses had sent away his wife Zipporah,[b] his father-in-law Jethro received
her 3 and her two sons.[c] One son was named Gershom,[a] for Moses said, "I have
become an alien in a foreign land";[d] 4 and the other was named Eliezer,[b][e] for he
said, "My father's God was my helper; he saved me from the sword of Pharaoh."
5 Jethro, Moses' father-in-law, together with Moses' sons and wife, came to him
in the desert, where he was camped near the mountain[f] of God. 6 Jethro had sent word
to him, "I, your father-in-law Jethro, am coming to you with your wife and her two
sons."
7 So Moses went out to meet his father-in-law and bowed down[g] and kissed[h] him.
They greeted each other and then went into the tent. 8 Moses told his father-in-law
about everything the LORD had done to Pharaoh and the Egyptians for Israel's sake
and about all the hardships they had met along the way and how the LORD had saved[i]
them.
9 Jethro was delighted to hear about all the good things the LORD had done for Israel
in rescuing them from the hand of the Egyptians. 10 He said, "Praise be to the LORD,[j]
who rescued you from the hand of the Egyptians and of Pharaoh, and who rescued
the people from the hand of the Egyptians. 11 Now I know that the LORD is greater
than all other gods,[k] for he did this to those who had treated Israel arrogantly."[l]
12 Then Jethro, Moses' father-in-law, brought a burnt offering and other sacrifices to
God, and Aaron came with all the elders of Israel to eat bread with Moses' father-in-
law in the presence[m] of God.

[c] *16* Or *"Because a hand was against the throne of the LORD, the* [a] *3* *Gershom* sounds like the Hebrew for *an alien there.* [b] *4* *Eliezer* means *my God is helper.*

17:9 Here we meet Joshua for the first time. Later he would become the great leader who brought God's people into the promised land. As a general of the Israelite army, he was gaining valuable experience for the greater battles to come.

17:10–13 Aaron and Hur stood by Moses' side and held up his arms to ensure victory against Amalek. We need to "lift up the hands" of our spiritual leaders as well. Shouldering some responsibility, lending a word of encouragement, or offering a prayer are ways of refreshing spiritual leaders in their work.

18:7 Jethro entered Moses' tent where the two talked. Tents were the homes of shepherds. In shape and design, they resembled the tents of today, but they were very large and made of a thick cloth woven from goat or camel hair. This fabric breathed in warm weather and contracted in stormy weather to offer protection from the winter winds and rains. The floor was often covered with animal-skin rugs, while curtains divided the inside space into rooms.

18:8–11 Moses told his father-in-law all that God had done, convincing him that the Lord was greater than any other god. Our relatives are often the hardest people to tell about God. Yet we should look for opportunities to tell them what God is doing in our lives because we can have an important influence on them.

18:12 This reunion turned into a large celebration. The Israelites frequently shared a sacrificial meal among themselves. A burnt offering was sacrificed to God, and then the meal taken from the sacrifice was dedicated to God and eaten ceremonially as a fellowship dinner.

13 The next day Moses took his seat to serve as judge for the people, and they stood
round him from morning till evening. 14 When his father-in-law saw all that Moses
was doing for the people, he said, "What is this you are doing for the people? Why
do you alone sit as judge, while all these people stand round you from morning till
evening?"
15 Moses answered him, "Because the people come to me to seek God's will.[n]
16 Whenever they have a dispute, it is brought to me, and I decide between the parties
and inform them of God's decrees and laws."[o]
17 Moses' father-in-law replied, "What you are doing is not good. 18 You and these
people who come to you will only wear yourselves out. The work is too heavy for
you; you cannot handle it alone.[p] 19 Listen now to me and I will give you some advice,
and may God be with you.[q] You must be the people's representative before God and
bring their disputes[r] to him. 20 Teach them the decrees and laws,[s] and show them
the way to live[t] and the duties they are to perform.[u] 21 But select capable men[v] from
all the people—men who fear God, trustworthy men who hate dishonest gain[w]—and
appoint them as officials[x] over thousands, hundreds, fifties and tens. 22 Have them
serve as judges for the people at all times, but have them bring every difficult case[y]
to you; the simple cases they can decide themselves. That will make your load lighter,
because they will share[z] it with you. 23 If you do this and God so commands, you
will be able to stand the strain, and all these people will go home satisfied."
24 Moses listened to his father-in-law and did everything he said. 25 He chose capable
men from all Israel and made them leaders of the people, officials over thousands,
hundreds, fifties and tens.[a] 26 They served as judges for the people at all times. The
difficult cases they brought to Moses, but the simple ones they decided themselves.[b]
27 Then Moses sent his father-in-law on his way, and Jethro returned to his own
country.[c]

C. ISRAEL AT SINAI (19:1—40:38)

After escaping through the Red Sea, the Hebrews travelled through the desert and arrived at Sinai, God's holy mountain. There they received the Ten Commandments, as well as instructions for building a tabernacle as a centre of worship. Through Israel's experiences at Mount Sinai, we learn about the importance of obedience in our relationship with God. His laws help expose sin, and they give standards for righteous living.

1. Giving the law

19 In the third month after the Israelites left Egypt—on the very day—they came
to the Desert of Sinai. 2 After they set out from Rephidim,[a] they entered the
Desert of Sinai, and Israel camped there in the desert in front of the mountain.[b]
3 Then Moses went up to God, and the LORD called[c] to him from the mountain and
said, "This is what you are to say to the house of Jacob and what you are to tell the
people of Israel: 4 'You yourselves have seen what I did to Egypt,[d] and how I carried
you on eagles' wings[e] and brought you to myself. 5 Now if you obey me fully[f] and

18:15 [n]Nu 9:6, 8; Dt 17:8-13
18:16 [o]Lev 24:12
18:18 [p]Nu 11:11, 14, 17
18:19 [q]Ex 3:12 [r]Nu 27:5
18:20 [s]Dt 5:1 [t]Ps 143:8 [u]Dt 1:18
18:21 [v]Ac 6:3 [w]Dt 16:19; Ps 15:5; Eze 18:8 [x]Dt 1:13, 15; 2Ch 19:5-10
18:22 [y]Dt 1:17-18 [z]Nu 11:17
18:25 [a]Dt 1:13-15
18:26 [b]ver 22
18:27 [c]Nu 10:29-30
19:2 [a]Ex 17:1 [b]Ex 3:1
19:3 [c]Ex 3:4; Ac 7:38
19:4 [d]Dt 29:2 [e]Isa 63:9
19:5 [f]Ex 15:26

18:13–26 Moses was spending so much time and energy hearing the Hebrews' complaints that he could not get to other important work. Jethro suggested that Moses delegate most of this work to others and focus his efforts on jobs only he could do. People in positions of responsibility sometimes feel they are the only ones who can do necessary tasks; but others are capable of handling part of the load. Delegation relieved Moses' stress and improved the quality of the government. It helped prepare them for the system of government set up in Canaan. Proper delegation can multiply your effectiveness while giving others a chance to grow.

18:16 Moses not only decided these cases, he also taught the people God's laws. Whenever we help others settle disputes or resolve conflicts, we should also look for opportunities to teach about God.

19:2, 3 Mount Sinai (also called Mount Horeb) is one of the most sacred locations in Israel's history. Located in the south-central Sinai peninsula, this mountain is where Moses met God in a burning bush, God made his covenant with Israel, and Elijah heard God in the gentle whisper. Here God gave his people the laws and guidelines for right living. They learned the potential blessings of obedience (34:4–28) and the tragic consequences of disobedience (34:32).

19:4–6 God had a reason for rescuing the Israelites from slavery. Now he was ready to tell them what it was: Israel was to become a kingdom of priests and a holy nation where anyone could approach God freely. It didn't take long, however, for the people to corrupt God's plan. God then established Aaron's descendants from the tribe of Levi as priests, representing what the entire nation should have been (Leviticus 8, 9). But with the coming of Jesus Christ, God has once again extended his plan to all believers. We are to become holy, a "royal priesthood" (1 Peter 2:9). The death and resurrection of Christ has allowed each of us to approach God freely.

19:5 Why did God choose Israel as his nation? God knew that no

19:5 [g]Dt 5:2 [h]Dt 14:2; Ps 135:4 [i]Ex 9:29; Dt 10:14 **19:6** [j]1Pe 2:5 [k]Dt 7:6; 26:19 **19:8** [l]Ex 24:3, 7; Dt 5:27 **19:9** [m]ver 16; Ex 24:15-16

keep my covenant,[g] then out of all nations you will be my treasured possession.[h]
Although the whole earth[i] is mine, 6you[a] will be for me a kingdom of priests[j] and
a holy nation.'[k] These are the words you are to speak to the Israelites."
7So Moses went back and summoned the elders of the people and set before them
all the words the LORD had commanded him to speak. 8The people all responded
together, "We will do everything the LORD has said."[l] So Moses brought their answer
back to the LORD.
9The LORD said to Moses, "I am going to come to you in a dense cloud,[m] so that

a 5,6 Or *possession, for the whole earth is mine.* 6 *You*

JETHRO

People such as Jethro and Melchizedek—not Israelites, but nevertheless worshippers of the true God—play an important role in the Old Testament. They remind us of God's commitment to the world. God chose one nation through which to work, but his love and concern are for all nations!

Jethro's religious background prepared him for, rather than prevented him from, responding in faith to God. When he saw and heard what God had done for the Israelites, he worshipped God wholeheartedly. We can guess that for 40 years as Moses' father-in-law, Jethro had been watching God at work, moulding a leader. Moses' and Jethro's relationship must have been close, for Moses readily accepted his father-in-law's advice. Each benefited from knowing the other. Jethro met God through Moses, and Moses received hospitality, his wife, and wisdom from Jethro.

The greatest gift one person can give another is an introduction to God. But that gift is hindered if the believer's attitude is, "I have the greatest gift to pass on to you, while you have nothing to give me in return." Real friends give to and receive from each other. The importance of introducing a friend to God does not make the friend's gifts to us insignificant. Rather, the believer is doubly blessed—first by receiving the gifts the friend wishes to give; then by growing in knowledge of the Lord. For we discover that in introducing another person to God, we increase our own awareness of God. As we give God away, he gives himself even more to us.

Is all you know about God a miscellaneous collection of trivia, or do you have a living relationship with him? Only with a vital relationship can you pass on to others the excitement of allowing God to guide your life. Have you reached the point of saying, with Jethro, "I know that the LORD is greater than all other gods" (Exodus 18:11)?

Strengths and accomplishments:
- As father-in-law to Moses, he came to recognise the one true God
- He was a practical troubleshooter and organiser

Lessons from his life:
- Supervision and administration are team efforts
- God's plan includes all nations

Vital statistics:
- Where: The land of Midian and the Desert of Sinai
- Occupations: Shepherd, priest
- Relatives: Daughter: Zipporah. Son-in-law: Moses. Son: Hobab

Key verse:
"Jethro was delighted to hear about all the good things the LORD had done for Israel in rescuing them from the hand of the Egyptians" (Exodus 18:9).

Jethro's story is told in Exodus 2:15—3:1; 18:1–27. He is also mentioned in Judges 1:16.

nation on earth was good enough to deserve to be called his people, his "treasured possession". He chose Israel, not because of anything they had done, but in his love and mercy he chose Israel in spite of the wrong the nation had done and would do. Why did he want to have a special nation on earth? To represent his way of life, to teach his word, and to be an agent of salvation to the world. "All nations on earth" would be blessed through Abraham's descendants (Genesis 18:18). Gentiles and kings would come to the Lord through Israel, predicted Isaiah (Isaiah 60:3). Through the nation of Israel, the Messiah, God's chosen Son, would be born. God chose one nation and put it through a rigorous training programme, so that one day it could be a channel for his blessings to the whole world.

19:5–8 In Genesis 15 and 17, God made a covenant with Abraham, promising to make his descendants into a great nation. Now that promise was being realised as God restated his agreement with the Israelite nation, the descendants of Abraham. God promised to bless and care for them. The people promised to obey him. The covenant was thus sealed. But the good intentions of the people quickly wore off. Have you made a commitment to God? How are you holding up your end of the bargain?

19:9–11 Moses was told to consecrate the people. This meant getting them physically and spiritually ready to meet God. The people were to set themselves apart from sin and even ordinary daily routine in order to dedicate themselves to God. The act of washing and preparing served to get their minds and hearts ready. When we meet God for worship, we should set aside the cares and preoccupations of everyday life. Use your time of physical preparation to get your mind ready to meet God.

the people will hear me speaking[n] with you and will always put their trust in you."
Then Moses told the LORD what the people had said.
10And the LORD said to Moses, "Go to the people and consecrate[o] them today and
tomorrow. Make them wash their clothes[p] 11and be ready by the third day,[q] because
on that day the LORD will come down on Mount Sinai in the sight of all the people.
12Put limits for the people around the mountain and tell them, 'Be careful that you
do not go up the mountain or touch the foot of it. Whoever touches the mountain shall
surely be put to death. 13He shall surely be stoned[r] or shot with arrows; not a hand
is to be laid on him. Whether man or animal, he shall not be permitted to live.' Only
when the ram's horn sounds a long blast may they go up to the mountain."
14After Moses had gone down the mountain to the people, he consecrated them,
and they washed their clothes. 15Then he said to the people, "Prepare yourselves for
the third day. Abstain from sexual relations."
16On the morning of the third day there was thunder and lightning, with a thick
cloud over the mountain, and a very loud trumpet blast.[s] Everyone in the camp
trembled.[t] 17Then Moses led the people out of the camp to meet with God, and they
stood at the foot of the mountain. 18Mount Sinai was covered with smoke,[u] because
the LORD descended on it in fire.[v] The smoke billowed up from it like smoke from
a furnace,[w] the whole mountain[b] trembled[x] violently, 19and the sound of the
trumpet grew louder and louder. Then Moses spoke and the voice[y] of God answered[z]
him.[c]
20The LORD descended to the top of Mount Sinai and called Moses to the top of
the mountain. So Moses went up 21and the LORD said to him, "Go down and warn
the people so they do not force their way through to see[a] the LORD and many of them
perish. 22Even the priests, who approach[b] the LORD, must consecrate themselves, or
the LORD will break out against them."[c]
23Moses said to the LORD, "The people cannot come up Mount Sinai, because you
yourself warned us, 'Put limits[d] around the mountain and set it apart as holy.'"
24The LORD replied, "Go down and bring Aaron[e] up with you. But the priests and
the people must not force their way through to come up to the LORD, or he will break
out against them."
25So Moses went down to the people and told them.

The Ten Commandments

20 And God spoke all these words:

2"I am the LORD your God, who brought you out of Egypt, out of the land
of slavery.[a]
3"You shall have no other gods before[a] me.[b]

b *18* Most Hebrew manuscripts; a few Hebrew manuscripts and Septuagint *all the people* **c** *19* Or *and God answered him with thunder* **a** *3* Or *besides*

19:9 [n]Dt 4:12, 36
19:10 [o]Lev 11:44; Heb 10:22 [p]Ge 35:2
19:11 [q]ver 16
19:13 [r]Heb 12:20*
19:16 [s]Heb 12:18-19; Rev 4:1 [t]Heb 12:21
19:18 [u]Ps 104:32 [v]Ex 3:2; 24:17; Dt 4:11; 2Ch 7:1; Ps 18:8; Heb 12:18 [w]Ge 19:28 [x]Jdg 5:5; Ps 68:8; Jer 4:24
19:19 [y]Ne 9:13 [z]Ps 81:7
19:21 [a]Ex 3:5; 1Sa 6:19
19:22 [b]Lev 10:3 [c]2Sa 6:7
19:23 [d]ver 12
19:24 [e]Ex 24:1, 9
20:2 [a]Ex 13:3
20:3 [b]Dt 6:14; Jer 35:15

19:22 By stating that he "will break out against them", the Lord was saying that he would destroy anyone who was not fully consecrated and ready to meet him.

20:1ff Why were the Ten Commandments necessary for God's new nation? At the foot of Mount Sinai, God showed his people the true function and beauty of his laws. The commandments were designed to lead Israel to a life of practical holiness. In them, people could see the nature of God and his plan for how they should live. The commands and guidelines were intended to direct the community to meet the needs of each individual in a loving and responsible manner. By Jesus' time, however, most people looked at the law the wrong way. They saw it as a means to prosperity in both this world and the next. And they thought that to obey every law was the way to earn God's protection from foreign invasion and natural disaster. Lawkeeping became an end in itself, not the means to fulfil God's ultimate law of love.

20:1–6 The Israelites had just come from Egypt, a land of many idols and many gods. Because each god represented a different aspect of life, it was common to worship many gods in order to get the maximum number of blessings. When God told his people to worship and believe in him, that wasn't so hard for them – he was just one more god to add to the list. But when he said, "You shall have no other gods before me," that was difficult for the people to accept. But if they didn't learn that the God who led them out of Egypt was the only true God, they could not be his people – no matter how faithfully they kept the other nine commandments. Thus, God made this his first commandment and emphasised it more than the others. Today we can allow many things to become gods to us. Money, fame, work, or pleasure can become gods when we concentrate too much on them for personal identity, meaning, and security. No-one sets out with the intention of worshipping these things. But by the amount of time we devote to them, they can grow into gods that ultimately control our thoughts and energies. Letting God hold the central place in our lives keeps these things from turning into gods.

20:4 [c]Lev 26:1; Dt 4:15-19, 23; 27:15
20:5 [d]Isa 44:15, 17, 19 [e]Ex 34:14; Dt 4:24 [f]Nu 14:18; Jer 32:18
20:6 [g]Dt 7:9
20:7 [h]Lev 19:12; Mt 5:33
20:8 [i]Ex 31:13-16; Lev 26:2
20:9 [j]Ex 34:21; Lk 13:14
20:11 [k]Ge 2:2

4“You shall not make for yourself an idol[c] in the form of anything in heaven
above or on the earth beneath or in the waters below. 5You shall not bow
down to them or worship[d] them; for I, the LORD your God, am a jealous
God,[e] punishing the children for the sin of the fathers to the third and
fourth generation[f] of those who hate me, 6but showing love to a thousand[g] ⌞generations⌟ of those who love me and keep my commandments.
7“You shall not misuse the name of the LORD your God, for the LORD will not
hold anyone guiltless who misuses his name.[h]
8“Remember the Sabbath[i] day by keeping it holy. 9Six days you shall labour
and do all your work,[j] 10but the seventh day is a Sabbath to the LORD your
God. On it you shall not do any work, neither you, nor your son or
daughter, nor your manservant or maidservant, nor your animals, nor the
alien within your gates. 11For in six days the LORD made the heavens and
the earth, the sea, and all that is in them, but he rested[k] on the seventh
day. Therefore the LORD blessed the Sabbath day and made it holy.

JESUS AND THE TEN COMMANDMENTS

The Ten Commandments said . . .	*Jesus said . . .*
Exodus 20:3 “You shall have no other gods before me”	Matthew 4:10 “Worship the Lord your God, and serve him only”
Exodus 20:4 “You shall not make for yourself an idol”	Luke 16:13 “No servant can serve two masters”
Exodus 20:7 “You shall not misuse the name of the LORD your God”	Matthew 5:34 “Do not swear at all: either by heaven, for it is God’s throne . . .”
Exodus 20:8 “Remember the Sabbath day by keeping it holy”	Mark 2:27, 28 “The Sabbath was made for man, not man for the Sabbath. So the Son of Man is Lord even of the Sabbath”
Exodus 20:12 “Honour your father and your mother”	Matthew 10:37 “Anyone who loves his father or mother more than me is not worthy of me”
Exodus 20:13 “You shall not murder”	Matthew 5:22 “Anyone who is angry with his brother will be subject to judgment”
Exodus 20:14 “You shall not commit adultery”	Matthew 5:28 “Anyone who looks at a woman lustfully has already committed adultery with her in his heart”
Exodus 20:15 “You shall not steal”	Matthew 5:40 “If someone wants to sue you and take your tunic, let him have your cloak as well”
Exodus 20:16 “You shall not give false testimony”	Matthew 12:36 “Men will have to give account on the day of judgment for every careless word they have spoken”
Exodus 20:17 “You shall not covet”	Luke 12:15 “Be on your guard against all kinds of greed”

20:7 God’s name is special because it carries his personal identity. Using it frivolously or in a curse is so common today that we may fail to realise how serious it is. The way we use God’s name conveys how we really feel about him. We should respect his name and use it appropriately, speaking it in praise or worship rather than in curse or jest. We should not take lightly the abuse or dishonour of his name.

20:8–11 The Sabbath was a day set aside for rest and worship. God commanded a Sabbath because human beings need to spend unhurried time in worship and rest each week. A God who is concerned enough to provide a day each week for us to rest is indeed wonderful. To observe a regular time of rest and worship in our fast-paced world demonstrates how important God is to us, and it gives us the extra benefit of refreshing our spirits. Don’t neglect God’s provision.

12"Honour your father and your mother,[l] so that you may live long in the land
the LORD your God is giving you.
13"You shall not murder.[m]
14"You shall not commit adultery.[n]
15"You shall not steal.[o]
16"You shall not give false testimony against your neighbour.[p]
17"You shall not covet[q] your neighbour's house. You shall not covet your
neighbour's wife, or his manservant or maidservant, his ox or donkey, or
anything that belongs to your neighbour."

18When the people saw the thunder and lightning and heard the trumpet[r] and saw
the mountain in smoke, they trembled with fear. They stayed at a distance 19and said
to Moses, "Speak to us yourself and we will listen. But do not have God speak to
us or we will die."[s]
20Moses said to the people, "Do not be afraid. God has come to test you, so that
the fear[t] of God will be with you to keep you from sinning."[u]
21The people remained at a distance, while Moses approached the thick darkness[v]
where God was.

Idols and Altars

22Then the LORD said to Moses, "Tell the Israelites this: 'You have seen for
yourselves that I have spoken to you from heaven:[w] 23Do not make any gods to be
alongside me;[x] do not make for yourselves gods of silver or gods of gold.[y]
24" 'Make an altar of earth for me and sacrifice on it your burnt offerings and
fellowship offerings,[b] your sheep and goats and your cattle. Wherever I cause my
name[z] to be honoured, I will come to you and bless[a] you. 25If you make an altar
of stones for me, do not build it with dressed stones, for you will defile it if you use
a tool[b] on it. 26And do not go up to my altar on steps, lest your nakedness be exposed
on it.'

[b] *24* Traditionally *peace offerings*

20:12 [l]Mt 15:4*; Mk 7:10*; Eph 6:2
20:13 [m]Mt 5:21*; Ro 13:9*
20:14 [n]Mt 19:18*
20:15 [o]Lev 19:11, 13; Mt 19:18*
20:16 [p]Ex 23:1, 7; Mt 19:18*
20:17 [q]Ro 7:7*; 13:9*; Eph 5:3
20:18 [r]Ex 19:16-19; Heb 12:18-19
20:19 [s]Dt 5:5, 23-27; Gal 3:19
20:20 [t]Dt 4:10; Isa 8:13 [u]Pr 16:6
20:21 [v]Dt 5:22
20:22 [w]Ne 9:13
20:23 [x]ver 3 [y]Ex 32:4, 8, 31
20:24 [z]Dt 12:5; 16:6, 11; 2Ch 6:6 [a]Ge 12:2
20:25 [b]Dt 27:5-6

20:12 This is the first commandment with a promise attached. To live in peace for generations in the promised land, the Israelites would need to respect authority and build strong families. But what does it mean to "honour" parents? Partly, it means speaking well of them and politely to them. It also means acting in a way that shows them courtesy and respect (but not to obey them if this means disobedience to God). It means following their teaching and example of putting God first. Parents have a special place in God's sight. Even those who find it difficult to get on with their parents are still commanded to honour them.

20:16 Giving false testimony means lying in court. God knew that Israel could not survive unless its system of justice was incorruptible. We should be honest in our private dealings as well as in our public statements. In either situation, we "give false testimony" by leaving something out of a story, telling a half-truth, twisting the facts, or inventing a falsehood. God warns us against deception. Even though deception is a way of life for many people, God's people must not give in to it!

20:17 To covet is to wish to have the possessions of others. It goes beyond simply admiring someone else's possessions or thinking, "I'd like to have one of those." Coveting includes envy – resenting the fact that others have what you don't. God knows, however, that possessions never make anyone happy for long. Since only God can supply all our needs, true contentment is found only in him. When you begin to covet, try to determine if a more basic need is leading you to envy. For example, you may covet someone's success, not because you want to take it away from him, but because you would like to feel as appreciated by others as he is. If this is the case, pray that God will help you deal with your resentment and meet your basic needs.

20:18 Sometimes God speaks to his people with a majestic display of power; at other times he speaks quietly. Why the difference? God speaks in the way that best accomplishes his purposes. At Sinai, the awesome display of light and sound was necessary to show Israel God's great power and authority. Only then would they listen to Moses and Aaron.

20:20 Throughout the Bible we find this phrase, "Do not be afraid." God wasn't trying to scare the people. He was showing his mighty power so the Israelites would know he was the true God and would therefore obey him. If they would do this, he would make his power available to them. God wants us to follow him out of love rather than fear. To overcome fear, we must think more about his love. 1 John 4:18 says, "Perfect love drives out fear."

20:24–26 Why were specific directions given for building altars? God's people had no Bible and few religious traditions to learn from. God had to start from scratch and teach them how to worship him. God gave specific instructions about building altars because he wanted to control the way sacrifices were offered. To prevent idolatry from creeping into worship, God did not allow the altar stones to be cut or shaped into any form. Nor did God let the people build an altar just anywhere. This was designed to prevent them from starting their own religions or making changes in the way God wanted things done. God is not against creativity, but he is against us creating our own religion.

21:1ff These laws were given because everything we do has consequences. It is vital to think before acting, to consider the effects of our choices. Think of your plans for today and consider

21 “These are the laws[a] you are to set before them:

Hebrew Servants

2“If you buy a Hebrew servant, he is to serve you for six years. But in the seventh
year, he shall go free,[b] without paying anything. 3If he comes alone, he is to go free
alone; but if he has a wife when he comes, she is to go with him. 4If his master gives
him a wife and she bears him sons or daughters, the woman and her children shall
belong to her master, and only the man shall go free.
5“But if the servant declares, ‘I love my master and my wife and children and do
not want to go free,’[c] 6then his master must take him before the judges.[a][d] He shall
take him to the door or the door-post and pierce his ear with an awl. Then he will
be his servant for life.[e]
7“If a man sells his daughter as a servant, she is not to go free as menservants do.
8If she does not please the master who has selected her for himself,[b] he must let her
be redeemed. He has no right to sell her to foreigners, because he has broken faith
with her. 9If he selects her for his son, he must grant her the rights of a daughter.
10If he marries another woman, he must not deprive the first one of her food, clothing
and marital rights.[f] 11If he does not provide her with these three things, she is to go
free, without any payment of money.

Personal Injuries

12“Anyone who strikes a man and kills him shall surely be put to death.[g] 13How-
ever, if he does not do it intentionally, but God lets it happen, he is to flee to a place[h]
I will designate. 14But if a man schemes and kills another man deliberately,[i] take
him away from my altar and put him to death.[j]
15“Anyone who attacks[c] his father or his mother must be put to death.
16“Anyone who kidnaps another and either sells[k] him or still has him when he is
caught must be put to death.[l]
17“Anyone who curses his father or mother must be put to death.[m]
18“If men quarrel and one hits the other with a stone or with his fist[d] and he does
not die but is confined to bed, 19the one who struck the blow will not be held
responsible if the other gets up and walks around outside with his staff; however, he
must pay the injured man for the loss of his time and see that he is completely healed.
20“If a man beats his male or female slave with a rod and the slave dies as a direct
result, he must be punished, 21but he is not to be punished if the slave gets up after
a day or two, since the slave is his property.[n]
22“If men who are fighting hit a pregnant woman and she gives birth prematurely[e]
but there is no serious injury, the offender must be fined whatever the woman’s
husband demands[o] and the court allows. 23But if there is serious injury, you are to
take life for life,[p] 24eye for eye, tooth for tooth,[q] hand for hand, foot for foot, 25burn
for burn, wound for wound, bruise for bruise.
26“If a man hits a manservant or maidservant in the eye and destroys it, he must
let the servant go free to compensate for the eye. 27And if he knocks out the tooth
of a manservant or maidservant, he must let the servant go free to compensate for the
tooth.

21:1 [a]Dt 4:14
21:2 [b]Jer 34:8, 14
21:5 [c]Dt 15:16
21:6 [d]Ex 22:8-9 [e]Ne 5:5
21:10 [f]1Co 7:3-5
21:12 [g]Ge 9:6; Mt 26:52
21:13 [h]Nu 35:10-34; Dt 19:2-13; Jos 20:9; 1Sa 24:4, 10, 18
21:14 [i]Heb 10:26 [j]Dt 19:11-12; 1Ki 2:28-34
21:16 [k]Ge 37:28 [l]Ex 22:4; Dt 24:7
21:17 [m]Lev 20:9-10; Mt 15:4*; Mk 7:10*
21:21 [n]Lev 25:44-46
21:22 [o]ver 30; Dt 22:18-19
21:23 [p]Lev 24:19; Dt 19:21
21:24 [q]Mt 5:38*

[a] 6 Or *before God* [b] 8 Or *master so that he does not choose her* [c] 15 Or *kills* [d] 18 Or *with a tool* [e] 22 Or *she has a miscarriage*

---

what their long-term results will be. As we deal with others, we should keep the principles of these laws in mind. We should act responsibly and justly with all people – friends and enemies alike.

21:2 The Hebrews, though freed from slavery, had slaves (or servants) themselves. A person could become a slave because of poverty, debt, or even crime. But Hebrew slaves were treated as humans, not property, and were allowed to work their way to freedom. The Bible acknowledges the existence of slavery but never encourages it.

21:24, 25 The “eye for eye” rule was instituted as a guide for judges, not as a rule for personal relationships or to justify revenge. This rule made the punishment fit the crime, thereby preventing the cruel and barbaric punishments that characterised many ancient countries. Jesus used this principle to teach us not to retaliate (Matthew 5:38–48). Judges, parents, teachers, and others who work with people must make wise decisions in order for discipline to be effective. A punishment too harsh is unfair, and one too lenient is powerless to teach. Ask God for wisdom before you judge.

28"If a bull gores a man or a woman to death, the bull must be stoned to death,[r]
and its meat must not be eaten. But the owner of the bull will not be held responsible.
29If, however, the bull has had the habit of goring and the owner has been warned
but has not kept it penned up and it kills a man or woman, the bull must be stoned
and the owner also must be put to death. 30However, if payment is demanded of him,
he may redeem his life by paying whatever is demanded.[s] 31This law also applies
if the bull gores a son or a daughter. 32If the bull gores a male or female slave, the
owner must pay thirty shekels[f][t] of silver to the master of the slave, and the bull must
be stoned.
33"If a man uncovers a pit or digs one and fails to cover it and an ox or a donkey
falls into it, 34the owner of the pit must pay for the loss; he must pay its owner, and
the dead animal will be his.
35"If a man's bull injures the bull of another and it dies, they are to sell the live
one and divide both the money and the dead animal equally. 36However, if it was
known that the bull had the habit of goring, yet the owner did not keep it penned up,
the owner must pay, animal for animal, and the dead animal will be his.

Protection of Property

22 "If a man steals an ox or a sheep and slaughters it or sells it, he must pay back[a]
five head of cattle for the ox and four sheep for the sheep.
2"If a thief is caught breaking in[b] and is struck so that he dies, the defender is not
guilty of bloodshed;[c] 3but if it happens[a] after sunrise, he is guilty of bloodshed.
"A thief must certainly make restitution, but if he has nothing, he must be sold[d]
to pay for his theft.
4"If the stolen animal is found alive in his possession—whether ox or donkey or
sheep—he must pay back double.[e]
5"If a man grazes his livestock in a field or vineyard and lets them stray and they
graze in another man's field, he must make restitution from the best of his own field
or vineyard.
6"If a fire breaks out and spreads into thornbushes so that it burns shocks of grain
or standing corn or the whole field, the one who started the fire must make restitution.
7"If a man gives his neighbour silver or goods for safekeeping and they are stolen
from the neighbour's house, the thief, if he is caught, must pay back double.[f] 8But
if the thief is not found, the owner of the house must appear before the judges[b][g] to
determine whether he has laid his hands on the other man's property. 9In all cases
of illegal possession of an ox, a donkey, a sheep, a garment, or any other lost property
about which somebody says, 'This is mine,' both parties are to bring their cases before
the judges.[h] The one whom the judges declare[c] guilty must pay back double to his
neighbour.
10"If a man gives a donkey, an ox, a sheep or any other animal to his neighbour
for safekeeping and it dies or is injured or is taken away while no-one is looking, 11the
issue between them will be settled by the taking of an oath[i] before the LORD that the
neighbour did not lay hands on the other person's property. The owner is to accept
this, and no restitution is required. 12But if the animal was stolen from the neighbour,
he must make restitution to the owner. 13If it was torn to pieces by a wild animal,
he shall bring in the remains as evidence and he will not be required to pay for the
torn animal.[j]

21:28 [r]ver 32; Ge 9:5
21:30 [s]ver 22; Nu 35:31
21:32 [t]Zec 11:12-13; Mt 26:15; 27:3, 9
22:1 [a]2Sa 12:6; Pr 6:31; Lk 19:8
22:2 [b]Mt 6:19-20; 24:43 [c]Nu 35:27
22:3 [d]Ex 21:2; Mt 18:25
22:4 [e]Ge 43:12
22:7 [f]ver 4
22:8 [g]Ex 21:6; Dt 17:8-9; 19:17
22:9 [h]ver 28; Dt 25:1
22:11 [i]Heb 6:16
22:13 [j]Ge 31:39

f *32* That is, about 12 ounces (about 0.3 kilogram) a *3* Or *if he strikes him* b *8* Or *before God*; also in verse 9
c *9* Or *whom God declares*

22:1ff These are not a collection of picky laws but are case studies of God's principles in action. God was taking potential situations and showing how his laws would work in the Israelites' everyday lives. These case studies had several objectives: (1) to protect the nation, (2) to organise the nation, and (3) to focus the nation's attention on God. The laws listed here do not cover every possible situation but give practical examples that make it easier to decide what God wants.

22:3ff Throughout chapter 22 we find examples of the principle of restitution—making wrongs right. For example, if a man stole an animal, he had to repay double the beast's market value. If you have done someone wrong, perhaps you should go beyond what is expected to make things right. This will (1) help ease any pain you've caused, (2) help the other person be more forgiving, and

14“If a man borrows an animal from his neighbour and it is injured or dies while
the owner is not present, he must make restitution. 15But if the owner is with the
animal, the borrower will not have to pay. If the animal was hired, the money paid
for the hire covers the loss.

Social Responsibility

16“If a man seduces a virgin[k] who is not pledged to be married and sleeps with
her, he must pay the bride-price, and she shall be his wife. 17If her father absolutely
refuses to give her to him, he must still pay the bride-price for virgins.
18“Do not allow a sorceress[l] to live.
19“Anyone who has sexual relations with an animal[m] must be put to death.
20“Whoever sacrifices to any god other than the LORD must be destroyed.[d][n]
21“Do not ill-treat an alien[o] or oppress him, for you were aliens[p] in Egypt.
22“Do not take advantage of a widow or an orphan.[q] 23If you do and they cry out[r]
to me, I will certainly hear their cry.[s] 24My anger will be aroused, and I will kill
you with the sword; your wives will become widows and your children fatherless.[t]
25“If you lend money to one of my people among you who is needy, do not be like
a money-lender; charge him no interest.[e][u] 26If you take your neighbour’s cloak as
a pledge,[v] return it to him by sunset, 27because his cloak is the only covering he has
for his body. What else will he sleep in? When he cries out to me, I will hear, for
I am compassionate.[w]
28“Do not blaspheme God[f][x] or curse the ruler of your people.[y]
29“Do not hold back offerings[z] from your granaries or your vats.[g]
“You must give me the firstborn of your sons.[a] 30Do the same with your cattle
and your sheep.[b] Let them stay with their mothers for seven days, but give them to
me on the eighth day.[c]
31“You are to be my holy people.[d] So do not eat the meat of an animal torn by
wild beasts;[e] throw it to the dogs.

Laws of Justice and Mercy

23 “Do not spread false reports.[a] Do not help a wicked man by being a malicious
witness.[b]
2“Do not follow the crowd in doing wrong. When you give testimony in a lawsuit,
do not pervert justice[c] by siding with the crowd, 3and do not show favouritism to
a poor man in his lawsuit.

d *20* The Hebrew term refers to the irrevocable giving over of things or persons to the LORD, often by totally destroying them. e *25* Or *excessive interest* f *28* Or *Do not revile the judges* g *29* The meaning of the Hebrew for this phrase is uncertain.

22:16 [k]Dt 22:28
22:18 [l]Lev 20:27; Dt 18:11; 1Sa 28:3
22:19 [m]Lev 18:23; Dt 27:21
22:20 [n]Dt 17:2-5
22:21 [o]Lev 19:33 [p]Dt 10:19
22:22 [q]Dt 24:6, 10, 12, 17
22:23 [r]Lk 18:7 [s]Dt 15:9; Ps 18:6
22:24 [t]Ps 69:24; 109:9
22:25 [u]Lev 25:35-37; Dt 23:20; Ps 15:5
22:26 [v]Dt 24:6
22:27 [w]Ex 34:6
22:28 [x]Lev 24:11, 16 [y]Ecc 10:20; Ac 23:5*
22:29 [z]Ex 23:15, 16, 19 [a]Ex 13:2
22:30 [b]Ex 13:12; Dt 15:19 [c]Lev 22:27
22:31 [d]Lev 19:2 [e]Eze 4:14
23:1 [a]Ex 20:16; Ps 101:5 [b]Ps 35:11; Ac 6:11
23:2 [c]Dt 16:19

---

(3) make you more likely to think before you do it again.

22:18 Why did God’s laws speak so strongly against sorcery (Leviticus 19:31; 20:6, 27; Deuteronomy 18:10–12)? Sorcery was punishable by death because it was a crime against God himself. To invoke evil powers violated the first commandment to “have no other gods”. Sorcery was rebellion against God and his authority. In essence, it was teaming up with Satan instead of with God.

22:21 God warned the Israelites not to treat aliens unfairly because they themselves were once strangers in Egypt. It is not easy coming into a new environment where you feel alone and out of place. Are there strangers in your corner of the world? Refugees? New arrivals at school? Immigrants from another country? Be sensitive to their struggles, and express God’s love by your kindness and generosity.

22:22–27 The Hebrew law code is noted for its fairness and social responsibility towards the poor. God insisted that the poor and powerless be well treated and given the chance to restore their fortunes. We should reflect God’s concern for the poor by helping those less fortunate than ourselves.

22:26 Why did the law insist on returning a person’s cloak by evening? The cloak was one of an Israelite’s most valuable possessions. Making clothing was difficult and time-consuming. As a result, cloaks were expensive, and most people owned only one. The cloak was used as a blanket, a sack to carry things in, a place to sit, a pledge for a debt, and, of course, clothing.

22:29 The Israelites were to be prompt in giving God their offerings. The first of the harvest was to be dedicated to him. Since God doesn’t send reminders, it is easy to take care of other financial responsibilities while letting our gifts to him slide. Giving to God first out of what he has allowed you to have demonstrates that he has first priority in your life.

23:1 Making up or spreading false reports was strictly forbidden by God. Gossip, slander, and false witnessing undermined families, strained neighbourhood co-operation, and made chaos of the justice system. Destructive gossip still causes problems. Even if you do not initiate a lie, you become responsible if you pass it on. Don’t circulate rumours; quench them.

23:2, 3 Justice is often perverted in favour of the rich. Here the people are warned against twisting justice in favour of the poor. Justice should be impartial, treating rich and poor alike. Giving special privileges to either rich or poor only makes justice for everyone more unlikely. Withstand the pressure of the crowd to sway your decision about a person. Let the fairness God shows to each of us guide your judgment.

4 "If you come across your enemy's ox or donkey wandering off, be sure to take
it back to him.[d] 5 If you see the donkey[e] of someone who hates you fallen down under
its load, do not leave it there; be sure you help him with it.
6 "Do not deny justice[f] to your poor people in their lawsuits. 7 Have nothing to do
with a false charge[g] and do not put an innocent or honest person to death, for I will
not acquit the guilty.
8 "Do not accept a bribe,[h] for a bribe blinds those who see and twists the words
of the righteous.
9 "Do not oppress an alien;[i] you yourselves know how it feels to be aliens, because
you were aliens in Egypt.

Sabbath Laws

10 "For six years you are to sow your fields and harvest the crops, 11 but during the
seventh year let the land lie unploughed and unused. Then the poor among your people
may get food from it, and the wild animals may eat what they leave. Do the same
with your vineyard and your olive grove.
12 "Six days do your work,[j] but on the seventh day do not work, so that your ox
and your donkey may rest and the slave born in your household, and the alien as well,
may be refreshed.
13 "Be careful[k] to do everything I have said to you. Do not invoke the names of
other gods; do not let them be heard on your lips.

The Three Annual Festivals

14 "Three times[l] a year you are to celebrate a festival to me.
15 "Celebrate the Feast of Unleavened Bread;[m] for seven days eat bread made
without yeast, as I commanded you. Do this at the appointed time in the month of
Abib, for in that month you came out of Egypt.
"No-one is to appear before me empty-handed.[n]
16 "Celebrate the Feast of Harvest with the firstfruits[o] of the crops you sow in your
field.
"Celebrate the Feast of Ingathering at the end of the year, when you gather in your
crops from the field.[p]
17 "Three times[q] a year all the men are to appear before the Sovereign LORD.
18 "Do not offer the blood of a sacrifice to me along with anything containing
yeast.[r]
"The fat of my festival offerings must not be kept until morning.[s]
19 "Bring the best of the firstfruits[t] of your soil to the house of the LORD your God.
"Do not cook a young goat in its mother's milk.[u]

God's Angel to Prepare the Way

20 "See, I am sending an angel[v] ahead of you to guard you along the way and to
bring you to the place I have prepared.[w] 21 Pay attention to him and listen[x] to what
he says. Do not rebel against him; he will not forgive your rebellion,[y] since my Name
is in him. 22 If you listen carefully to what he says and do all that I say, I will be an
enemy[z] to your enemies and will oppose those who oppose you. 23 My angel will go
ahead of you and bring you into the land of the Amorites, Hittites, Perizzites,
Canaanites, Hivites and Jebusites,[a] and I will wipe them out. 24 Do not bow down

23:4 [d] Dt 22:1-3
23:5 [e] Dt 22:4
23:6 [f] ver 2
23:7 [g] Eph 4:25
23:8 [h] Dt 10:17; 16:19; Pr 15:27
23:9 [i] Ex 22:21
23:12 [j] Ex 20:9
23:13 [k] 1Ti 4:16
23:14 [l] Ex 34:23, 24
23:15 [m] Ex 12:17 [n] Ex 34:20
23:16 [o] Ex 34:22 [p] Dt 16:13
23:17 [q] Dt 16:16
23:18 [r] Ex 34:25 [s] Dt 16:4
23:19 [t] Ex 22:29; Dt 26:2, 10 [u] Dt 14:21
23:20 [v] Ex 14:19; 32:34 [w] Ex 15:17
23:21 [x] Nu 14:11; Dt 18:19 [y] Ps 78:8, 40, 56
23:22 [z] Ge 12:3; Dt 30:7
23:23 [a] ver 20; Jos 24:8, 11

23:4, 5 The thought of being kind to enemies was new and startling in a world where revenge was the common form of justice. God not only introduced this idea to the Israelites, he made it law! If a man found a lost animal owned by his enemy, he was to return it at once, even if his enemy might use it to harm him. Jesus clearly taught in Luke 10:30–37 to reach out to all people in need, even our enemies. Following the laws of right living is hard enough with friends. When we apply God's laws of fairness and kindness to our enemies, we show how different we are from the world.

23:20, 21 Who was this angel that went with the Israelites? Most likely the angel was a manifestation of God. God was in the angel in the same way he was present in the pillars of cloud and fire (13:21, 22). "My Name is in him" means the essential nature and power of God were made known in this angel.

23:24, 25 If you're in the furnace, it's easy to catch fire. God warned the Israelites about their neighbours whose beliefs and actions could turn them away from him. We also live with neighbours whose values may be completely different from ours. We are called to maintain a life-style that shows our faith. This can be a struggle, especially if our Christian life-style differs from the norm. Our lives

before their gods or worship[b] them or follow their practices.[c] You must demolish[d]
them and break their sacred stones to pieces. 25 Worship the LORD your God,[e] and
his blessing[f] will be on your food and water. I will take away sickness[g] from among
you, 26 and none will miscarry or be barren[h] in your land. I will give you a full life
span.[i]

27 "I will send my terror[j] ahead of you and throw into confusion[k] every nation
you encounter. I will make all your enemies turn their backs and run. 28 I will send
the hornet[l] ahead of you to drive the Hivites, Canaanites and Hittites out of your way.
29 But I will not drive them out in a single year, because the land would become
desolate and the wild animals[m] too numerous for you. 30 Little by little I will drive
them out before you, until you have increased enough to take possession of the land.

31 "I will establish your borders from the Red Sea[a] to the Sea of the Philistines,[b]
and from the desert to the River.[c][n] I will hand over to you the people who live in
the land and you will drive them out[o] before you. 32 Do not make a covenant[p] with
them or with their gods. 33 Do not let them live in your land, or they will cause you
to sin against me, because the worship of their gods will certainly be a snare[q] to you."

The Covenant Confirmed

24 Then he said to Moses, "Come up to the LORD, you and Aaron, Nadab and
Abihu,[a] and seventy of the elders[b] of Israel. You are to worship at a distance,
2 but Moses alone is to approach the LORD; the others must not come near. And the
people may not come up with him."

3 When Moses went and told the people all the LORD's words and laws, they
responded with one voice, "Everything the LORD has said we will do."[c] 4 Moses then
wrote[d] down everything the LORD had said.

He got up early the next morning and built an altar at the foot of the mountain and
set up twelve stone pillars[e] representing the twelve tribes of Israel. 5 Then he sent
young Israelite men, and they offered burnt offerings and sacrificed young bulls as
fellowship offerings[a] to the LORD. 6 Moses took half of the blood[f] and put it in bowls,
and the other half he sprinkled on the altar. 7 Then he took the Book of the Covenant[g]
and read it to the people. They responded, "We will do everything the LORD has said;
we will obey."

8 Moses then took the blood, sprinkled it on the people and said, "This is the blood
of the covenant[h] that the LORD has made with you in accordance with all these
words."

9 Moses and Aaron, Nadab and Abihu, and the seventy elders[i] of Israel went up
10 and saw[j] the God of Israel. Under his feet was something like a pavement made
of sapphire,[b][k] clear as the sky[l] itself. 11 But God did not raise his hand against these
leaders of the Israelites; they saw[m] God, and they ate and drank.

a *31* Hebrew *Yam Suph*; that is, Sea of Reeds b *31* That is, the Mediterranean c *31* That is, the Euphrates
a *5* Traditionally *peace offerings* b *10* Or *lapis lazuli*

23:24 [b]Ex 20:5 [c]Dt 12:30-31 [d]Ex 34:13; Nu 33:52
23:25 [e]Dt 6:13; Mt 4:10 [f]Dt 7:12-15; 28:1-14 [g]Ex 15:26
23:26 [h]Dt 7:14; Mal 3:11 [i]Job 5:26
23:27 [j]Ex 15:14; Dt 2:25 [k]Dt 7:23
23:28 [l]Dt 7:20; Jos 24:12
23:29 [m]Dt 7:22
23:31 [n]Ge 15:18 [o]Jos 21:44; 24:12, 18
23:32 [p]Ex 34:12; Dt 7:2
23:33 [q]Dt 7:16; Ps 106:36
24:1 [a]Ex 6:23; Lev 10:1-2 [b]Nu 11:16
24:3 [c]Ex 19:8; Dt 5:27
24:4 [d]Dt 31:9 [e]Ge 28:18
24:6 [f]Heb 9:18
24:7 [g]Heb 9:19
24:8 [h]Heb 9:20*; 1Pe 1:2
24:9 [i]ver 1
24:10 [j]Mt 17:2; Jn 1:18; 6:46 [k]Eze 1:26 [l]Rev 4:3
24:11 [m]Ge 32:30; Ex 19:21

should show that we put obeying God before doing what is praised and accepted by society.

23:29 Not all of God's solutions are instantaneous. Nor does delay justify inaction. In this case, God's cause would require constant co-operation, persistence, and effort by the Israelites. Success would come step by step.

23:32, 33 God continually warned the people to avoid false religions and false gods. In Egypt they had been surrounded by idols and sorcerers, but leaving that land did not mean they were free from pagan religious influences. The land of Canaan was just as infested with idol worship. God knew his people needed extra strength, so he continually emphasised guarding against the influence of pagan religions.

24:6–8 To understand this unusual covenant ratification ceremony, we need to understand the Bible's view of sin and forgiveness. God is the sovereign judge of the universe. He is also absolutely holy. As the holy judge of all, he condemns sin and judges it worthy of death. In the Old Testament God accepted the death of an animal as a substitute for the sinner. The animal's shed blood was proof that one life had been given for another. So on the one hand, blood symbolised the death of the animal, but it also symbolised the life that was spared as a result. Of course the death of the animal that brought forgiveness in the Old Testament was only a temporary provision, looking forward to the death of Jesus Christ (Hebrews 9:9 – 10:24).

In this ceremony described here, Moses sprinkled half the blood from the sacrificed animals on the altar to show that the sinner could once again approach God because something had died in his place. He sprinkled the other half of the blood on the people to show that the penalty for their sin had been paid and they could be reunited with God. Through this symbolic act God's promises to Israel were reaffirmed and lessons are taught to us about the future sacrificial death (or atonement) of Jesus Christ.

12 The LORD said to Moses, "Come up to me on the mountain and stay here, and
I will give you the tablets of stone,[n] with the law and commands I have written for
their instruction."
13 Then Moses set out with Joshua[o] his assistant, and Moses went up on the
mountain[p] of God. 14 He said to the elders, "Wait here for us until we come back
to you. Aaron and Hur are with you, and anyone involved in a dispute can go to them."
15 When Moses went up on the mountain, the cloud[q] covered it, 16 and the glory[r]
of the LORD settled on Mount Sinai. For six days the cloud covered the mountain, and
on the seventh day the LORD called to Moses from within the cloud.[s] 17 To the
Israelites the glory of the LORD looked like a consuming fire[t] on top of the mountain.
18 Then Moses entered the cloud as he went on up the mountain. And he stayed on
the mountain forty[u] days and forty nights.[v]

2. Tabernacle instructions

Offerings for the Tabernacle

25 The LORD said to Moses, 2 "Tell the Israelites to bring me an offering. You are
to receive the offering for me from each man whose heart prompts[a] him to
give. 3 These are the offerings you are to receive from them: gold, silver and bronze;
4 blue, purple and scarlet yarn and fine linen; goat hair; 5 ram skins dyed red and hides
of sea cows;**[a]** acacia wood; 6 olive oil[b] for the light; spices for the anointing oil and
for the fragrant incense; 7 and onyx stones and other gems to be mounted on the
ephod[c] and breastpiece.[d]
8 "Then have them make a sanctuary[e] for me, and I will dwell[f] among them.
9 Make this tabernacle and all its furnishings exactly like the pattern[g] I will show you.

The Ark

10 "Have them make a chest[h] of acacia wood—two and a half cubits long, a cubit
and a half wide, and a cubit and a half high.**[b]** 11 Overlay it with pure gold, both inside
and out, and make a gold moulding around it. 12 Cast four gold rings for it and fasten
them to its four feet, with two rings on one side and two rings on the other. 13 Then
make poles of acacia wood and overlay them with gold. 14 Insert the poles into the
rings on the sides of the chest to carry it. 15 The poles are to remain in the rings of
this ark; they are not to be removed.[i] 16 Then put in the ark the Testimony,[j] which
I will give you.
17 "Make an atonement cover**[c]**[k] of pure gold—two and a half cubits long and a
cubit and a half wide.**[d]** 18 And make two cherubim out of hammered gold at the ends
of the cover. 19 Make one cherub on one end and the second cherub on the other; make
the cherubim of one piece with the cover, at the two ends. 20 The cherubim are to have
their wings spread upwards, overshadowing[l] the cover with them. The cherubim are
to face each other, looking towards the cover. 21 Place the cover on top of the ark[m]
and put in the ark the Testimony,[n] which I will give you. 22 There, above the cover
between the two cherubim[o] that are over the ark of the Testimony, I will meet[p] with
you and give you all my commands for the Israelites.

a *5* That is, large aquatic mammals **b** *10* That is, about 3¾ feet (about 1.1 metres) long and 2¼ feet (about 0.7 metre) wide and high **c** *17* Traditionally *a mercy seat* **d** *17* That is, about 3¾ feet (about 1.1 metres) long and 2¼ feet (about 0.7 metre) wide

24:12 [n]Ex 32:15-16
24:13 [o]Ex 17:9 [p]Ex 3:1
24:15 [q]Ex 19:9
24:16 [r]Ex 16:10 [s]Ps 99:7
24:17 [t]Ex 3:2; Dt 4:36; Heb 12:18, 29
24:18 [u]Dt 9:9 [v]Ex 34:28
25:2 [a]Ex 35:21; 1Ch 29:5, 7, 9; Ezr 2:68; 2Co 8:11-12; 9:7
25:6 [b]Ex 27:20; 30:22-32
25:7 [c]Ex 28:4, 6-14 [d]Ex 28:15-30
25:8 [e]Ex 36:1-5; Heb 9:1-2 [f]Ex 29:45; 1Ki 6:13; 2Co 6:16; Rev 21:3
25:9 [g]ver 40; Ac 7:44; Heb 8:5
25:10 [h]Dt 10:1-5; Heb 9:4
25:15 [i]1Ki 8:8
25:16 [j]Dt 31:26; Heb 9:4
25:17 [k]Ro 3:25
25:20 [l]1Ki 8:7; 1Ch 28:18; Heb 9:5
25:21 [m]Ex 26:34 [n]ver 16
25:22 [o]Nu 7:89; 1Sa 4:4; 2Sa 6:2; 2Ki 19:15; Ps 80:1; Isa 37:16 [p]Ex 29:42-43

25:1ff Chapters 25-31 record God's directions for building the tabernacle. Chapters 35-39 tell how these instructions were carried out. But what can all these ancient, complicated construction details show us today? First, the high quality of the precious materials making up the tabernacle shows God's greatness and transcendence. Second, the curtain surrounding the Most Holy Place shows God's moral perfection as symbolised by his separation from the common and unclean. Third, the portable nature of the tabernacle shows God's desire to be with his people as they travelled.

25:10 Much of the tabernacle and its furniture was made of acacia wood. Acacia trees flourished in barren regions and were fairly common in Old Testament times. The wood was brownish-orange and very hard, making it an excellent material for furniture. Acacia wood is still used in furniture-making today. A cubit is about 1½ feet or 0.43 metres.

25:17 The cover of the ark of the Testimony was called the atonement cover. This is where, between the two golden cherubim (mighty angels), the presence of God would dwell in a cloud above their outstretched wings. The atonement cover was where the highest and most perfect act of atonement would be made when the high priest would enter the Most Holy Place on the Day of Atonement to atone for the sins of all the people (30:10).

25:23
[q]Heb 9:2

The Table

23"Make a table[q] of acacia wood—two cubits long, a cubit wide and a cubit and
a half high.[e] 24Overlay it with pure gold and make a gold moulding around it. 25Also
make around it a rim a handbreadth[f] wide and put a gold moulding on the rim. 26Make
four gold rings for the table and fasten them to the four corners, where the four legs
are. 27The rings are to be close to the rim to hold the poles used in carrying the table.
28Make the poles of acacia wood, overlay them with gold and carry the table with
them. 29And make its plates and dishes of pure gold, as well as its pitchers and bowls
for the pouring out of offerings.[r] 30Put the bread of the Presence[s] on this table to
be before me at all times.

25:29
[r]Nu 4:7

The Lampstand

31"Make a lampstand[t] of pure gold and hammer it out, base and shaft; its flowerlike
cups, buds and blossoms shall be of one piece with it. 32Six branches are to extend
from the sides of the lampstand—three on one side and three on the other. 33Three
cups shaped like almond flowers with buds and blossoms are to be on one branch,
three on the next branch, and the same for all six branches extending from the
lampstand. 34And on the lampstand there are to be four cups shaped like almond
flowers with buds and blossoms. 35One bud shall be under the first pair of branches
extending from the lampstand, a second bud under the second pair, and a third bud
under the third pair—six branches in all. 36The buds and branches shall all be of one
piece with the lampstand, hammered out of pure gold.
37"Then make its seven lamps[u] and set them up on it so that they light the space
in front of it. 38Its wick trimmers and trays are to be of pure gold. 39A talent[g] of pure
gold is to be used for the lampstand and all these accessories. 40See that you make
them according to the pattern[v] shown you on the mountain.

25:30
[s]Lev 24:5-9

25:31
[t]1Ki 7:49; Zec 4:2; Heb 9:2; Rev 1:12

The Tabernacle

26 "Make the tabernacle with ten curtains of finely twisted linen and blue, purple
and scarlet yarn, with cherubim worked into them by a skilled craftsman. 2All
the curtains are to be the same size—twenty-eight cubits long and four cubits wide.[a]
3Join five of the curtains together, and do the same with the other five. 4Make loops
of blue material along the edge of the end curtain in one set, and do the same with
the end curtain in the other set. 5Make fifty loops on one curtain and fifty loops on
the end curtain of the other set, with the loops opposite each other. 6Then make fifty
gold clasps and use them to fasten the curtains together so that the tabernacle is a unit.
7"Make curtains of goat hair for the tent over the tabernacle—eleven altogether.
8All eleven curtains are to be the same size—thirty cubits long and four cubits wide.[b]
9Join five of the curtains together into one set and the other six into another set. Fold
the sixth curtain double at the front of the tent. 10Make fifty loops along the edge of

25:37
[u]Ex 27:21; Lev 24:3-4; Nu 8:2

25:40
[v]Ex 26:30; Nu 8:4; Ac 7:44; Heb 8:5*

[e] *23* That is, about 3 feet (about 0.9 metre) long and 1½ feet (about 0.5 metre) wide and 2¼ feet (about 0.7 metre) high [f] *25* That is, about 3 inches (about 8 centimetres) [g] *39* That is, about 75 pounds (about 34 kilograms) [a] *2* That is, about 42 feet (about 13 metres) long and 6 feet (about 1.8 metres) wide [b] *8* That is, about 45 feet (about 13.5 metres) long and 6 feet (about 1.8 metres) wide

THEOPHANIES IN THE SCRIPTURE

At the foot of Mount Sinai, God appeared to the people of Israel in a physical form. This is called a *theophany.* Here are some of the other times God appeared to Bible people.

Verse	*Theophany*
Genesis 16:7	The angel of the Lord appeared to Sarah's maidservant, Hagar, announcing the birth of Abraham's son, Ishmael
Genesis 18:1–11	The Lord appeared to Abraham, foretelling Isaac's birth
Genesis 22:11, 12	The angel of the Lord stopped Abraham from sacrificing Isaac
Exodus 3:2	The angel of the Lord appeared to Moses in flames in a bush
Exodus 14:19	God appeared to Israel in pillars of cloud and fire to guide them through the desert
Exodus 33:11	The Lord spoke to Moses face to face
Daniel 3:25	One "like a son of the gods" appeared as the fourth man with Shadrach, Meshach, and Abednego in the fiery furnace

("Angel of the Lord" is a reverential way to refer to God in these passages.)

the end curtain in one set and also along the edge of the end curtain in the other set.
11Then make fifty bronze clasps and put them in the loops to fasten the tent together
as a unit. 12As for the additional length of the tent curtains, the half curtain that is
left over is to hang down at the rear of the tabernacle. 13The tent curtains will be a
cubit[c] longer on both sides; what is left will hang over the sides of the tabernacle
so as to cover it. 14Make for the tent a covering of ram skins dyed red, and over that
a covering of hides of sea cows.[d][a]
15"Make upright frames of acacia wood for the tabernacle. 16Each frame is to be
ten cubits long and a cubit and a half wide,[e] 17with two projections set parallel to
each other. Make all the frames of the tabernacle in this way. 18Make twenty frames
for the south side of the tabernacle 19and make forty silver bases to go under
them — two bases for each frame, one under each projection. 20For the other side, the
north side of the tabernacle, make twenty frames 21and forty silver bases — two under
each frame. 22Make six frames for the far end, that is, the west end of the tabernacle,
23and make two frames for the corners at the far end. 24At these two corners they must
be double from the bottom all the way to the top, and fitted into a single ring; both
shall be like that. 25So there will be eight frames and sixteen silver bases — two under
each frame.
26"Also make crossbars of acacia wood: five for the frames on one side of the
tabernacle, 27five for those on the other side, and five for the frames on the west, at
the far end of the tabernacle. 28The centre crossbar is to extend from end to end at
the middle of the frames. 29Overlay the frames with gold and make gold rings to hold
the crossbars. Also overlay the crossbars with gold.
30"Set up the tabernacle according to the plan[b] shown you on the mountain.
31"Make a curtain[c] of blue, purple and scarlet yarn and finely twisted linen, with
cherubim[d] worked into it by a skilled craftsman. 32Hang it with gold hooks on four
posts of acacia wood overlaid with gold and standing on four silver bases. 33Hang the
curtain from the clasps and place the ark of the Testimony behind the curtain.[e] The
curtain will separate the Holy Place from the Most Holy Place.[f] 34Put the atonement
cover[g] on the ark of the Testimony in the Most Holy Place. 35Place the table[h] outside
the curtain on the north side of the tabernacle and put the lampstand[i] opposite it on
the south side.
36"For the entrance to the tent make a curtain of blue, purple and scarlet yarn and
finely twisted linen — the work of an embroiderer. 37Make gold hooks for this curtain
and five posts of acacia wood overlaid with gold. And cast five bronze bases for them.

The Altar of Burnt Offering

27 "Build an altar[a] of acacia wood, three cubits[a] high; it is to be square, five
cubits long and five cubits wide.[b] 2Make a horn[b] at each of the four corners,
so that the horns and the altar are of one piece, and overlay the altar with bronze.
3Make all its utensils of bronze — its pots to remove the ashes, and its shovels,
sprinkling bowls, meat forks and firepans. 4Make a grating for it, a bronze network,
and make a bronze ring at each of the four corners of the network. 5Put it under the
ledge of the altar so that it is halfway up the altar. 6Make poles of acacia wood for

c *13* That is, about 1½ feet (about 0.5 metre) d *14* That is, large aquatic mammals e *16* That is, about 15 feet (about 4.5 metres) long and 2¼ feet (about 0.7 metre) wide a *1* That is, about 4½ feet (about 1.4 metres) b *1* That is, about 7½ feet (about 2.3 metres) long and wide

26:14 [a]Ex 36:19; Nu 4:25
26:30 [b]Ex 25:9, 40; Ac 7:44; Heb 8:5
26:31 [c]2Ch 3:14; Mt 27:51; Heb 9:3 [d]Ex 36:35
26:33 [e]Ex 40:3, 21; Lev 16:2 [f]Heb 9:2-3
26:34 [g]Ex 25:21; 40:20; Heb 9:5
26:35 [h]Heb 9:2 [i]Ex 40:22, 24
27:1 [a]Eze 43:13
27:2 [b]Ps 118:27

26:31-33 This curtain separated the two sacred rooms in the tabernacle – the Holy Place and the Most Holy Place. The priest entered the Holy Place each day to commune with God and to tend to the altar of incense, the lampstand, and the table with the bread of the Presence. The Most Holy Place was where God himself dwelt, his presence resting on the atonement cover, which covered the ark of the Testimony. Only the high priest could enter the Most Holy Place. Even he could do so only once a year (on the Day of Atonement) to make atonement for the sins of the nation as a whole. When Jesus Christ died on the cross, the curtain in the temple (which had replaced the tabernacle) tore from top to bottom (Mark 15:38), symbolising our free access to God because of Jesus' death. No longer did people have to approach God through priests and sacrifices.

27:1 The altar of burnt offering was the first thing the Israelites saw as they entered the tabernacle courtyard. Here sacrifices were constantly made. Its vivid presence constantly reminded the people that they could only come to God by means of the sacrifice. It was the only way their sins could be forgiven and taken away. In Hebrews 10:1-18, Jesus Christ is portrayed as the ultimate sacrifice.

the altar and overlay them with bronze. 7The poles are to be inserted into the rings
so they will be on two sides of the altar when it is carried. 8Make the altar hollow,
out of boards. It is to be made just as you were shown[c] on the mountain.

The Courtyard

9"Make a courtyard for the tabernacle. The south side shall be a hundred cubits[c]
long and is to have curtains of finely twisted linen, 10with twenty posts and twenty
bronze bases and with silver hooks and bands on the posts. 11The north side shall also
be a hundred cubits long and is to have curtains, with twenty posts and twenty bronze
bases and with silver hooks and bands on the posts.
12"The west end of the courtyard shall be fifty cubits[d] wide and have curtains, with
ten posts and ten bases. 13On the east end, towards the sunrise, the courtyard shall
also be fifty cubits wide. 14Curtains fifteen cubits[e] long are to be on one side of the
entrance, with three posts and three bases, 15and curtains fifteen cubits long are to
be on the other side, with three posts and three bases.
16"For the entrance to the courtyard, provide a curtain twenty cubits[f] long, of blue,
purple and scarlet yarn and finely twisted linen—the work of an embroiderer—with
four posts and four bases. 17All the posts around the courtyard are to have silver bands
and hooks, and bronze bases. 18The courtyard shall be a hundred cubits long and fifty
cubits wide,[g] with curtains of finely twisted linen five cubits[h] high, and with bronze
bases. 19All the other articles used in the service of the tabernacle, whatever their
function, including all the tent pegs for it and those for the courtyard, are to be of
bronze.

Oil for the Lampstand

20"Command the Israelites to bring you clear oil of pressed olives for the light so
that the lamps may be kept burning. 21In the Tent of Meeting,[d] outside the curtain
that is in front of the Testimony,[e] Aaron and his sons are to keep the lamps[f] burning
before the LORD from evening till morning. This is to be a lasting ordinance[g] among
the Israelites for the generations to come.

The Priestly Garments

28 "Have Aaron[a] your brother brought to you from among the Israelites, with
his sons Nadab and Abihu, Eleazar and Ithamar, so that they may serve me
as priests.[b] 2Make sacred garments[c] for your brother Aaron, to give him dignity and
honour. 3Tell all the skilled men[d] to whom I have given wisdom[e] in such matters
that they are to make garments for Aaron, for his consecration, so that he may serve
me as priest. 4These are the garments they are to make: a breastpiece,[f] an ephod,
a robe,[g] a woven tunic,[h] a turban and a sash. They are to make these sacred garments
for your brother Aaron and his sons, so that they may serve me as priests. 5Make them
use gold, and blue, purple and scarlet yarn, and fine linen.

27:8 [c]Ex 25:9, 40

27:21 [d]Ex 28:43 [e]Ex 26:31, 33 [f]Ex 25:37; 30:8; 1Sa 3:3; 2Ch 13:11 [g]Ex 29:9; Lev 3:17; 16:34; Nu 18:23; 19:21

28:1 [a]Heb 5:4 [b]Nu 18:1-7; Heb 5:1

28:2 [c]Ex 29:5, 29; 31:10; 39:1; Lev 8:7-9, 30

28:3 [d]Ex 31:6; 36:1 [e]Ex 31:3

28:4 [f]ver 15-30 [g]ver 31-35 [h]ver 39

c *9* That is, about 150 feet (about 46 metres); also in verse 11 d *12* That is, about 75 feet (about 23 metres); also in verse 13 e *14* That is, about 22½ feet (about 6.9 metres); also in verse 15 f *16* That is, about 30 feet (about 9 metres) g *18* That is, about 150 feet (about 46 metres) long and 75 feet (about 23 metres) wide h *18* That is, about 7½ feet (about 2.3 metres)

28:1ff God was teaching his people how to worship him. To do so, he needed ministers to oversee the operations of the tabernacle and to help the people maintain their relationship with God. These men were called priests and Levites, and they could only be members of the tribe of Levi. Chapters 28 and 29 give some details about priests. Not only was a priest from the tribe of Levi, but he was also a descendant of Aaron, Israel's first high priest. Priests had more responsibilities than Levites. As high priest, Aaron was in charge of all the priests and Levites. The priests performed the daily sacrifices, maintained the tabernacle, and counselled the people on how to follow God. They were the people's representatives before God and thus were required to live worthy of their office. Jesus is now our high priest (Hebrews 8). Daily sacrifices are no longer required because he sacrificed himself on the cross for our sins. Today ministers no longer sacrifice animals. Instead they lead us in prayer and teach us about both the benefits and the commandments that characterise our new life as Christians.

28:3 The tailors who made Aaron's garments were given wisdom by God in order to do their task. All of us have special skills. God wants to fill us with his Spirit so we will use them for his glory. Think about your special talents and abilities and the ways you could use them for God's work in the world. A talent must be used or it will diminish.

The Ephod

6“Make the ephod of gold, and of blue, purple and scarlet yarn, and of finely twisted
linen—the work of a skilled craftsman. 7It is to have two shoulder pieces attached
to two of its corners, so that it can be fastened. 8Its skilfully woven waistband is to
be like it—of one piece with the ephod and made with gold, and with blue, purple
and scarlet yarn, and with finely twisted linen.
9“Take two onyx stones and engrave on them the names of the sons of Israel 10in
the order of their birth—six names on one stone and the remaining six on the other.
11Engrave the names of the sons of Israel on the two stones the way a gem cutter
engraves a seal. Then mount the stones in gold filigree settings 12and fasten them on
the shoulder pieces of the ephod as memorial stones for the sons of Israel. Aaron is
to bear the names on his shoulders as a memorial before the LORD. 13Make gold
filigree settings 14and two braided chains of pure gold, like a rope, and attach the
chains to the settings.

The Breastpiece

15“Fashion a breastpiece for making decisions—the work of a skilled craftsman.
Make it like the ephod: of gold, and of blue, purple and scarlet yarn, and of finely
twisted linen. 16It is to be square—a span[a] long and a span wide—and folded double.
17Then mount four rows of precious stones on it. In the first row there shall be a ruby,
a topaz and a beryl; 18in the second row a turquoise, a sapphire[b] and an emerald;
19in the third row a jacinth, an agate and an amethyst; 20in the fourth row a chrysolite,
an onyx and a jasper.[c] Mount them in gold filigree settings. 21There are to be twelve
stones, one for each of the names of the sons of Israel, each engraved like a seal with
the name of one of the twelve tribes.
22“For the breastpiece make braided chains of pure gold, like a rope. 23Make two
gold rings for it and fasten them to two corners of the breastpiece. 24Fasten the two
gold chains to the rings at the corners of the breastpiece, 25and the other ends of the
chains to the two settings, attaching them to the shoulder pieces of the ephod at the
front. 26Make two gold rings and attach them to the other two corners of the breastpiece on the inside edge next to the ephod. 27Make two more gold rings and attach
them to the bottom of the shoulder pieces on the front of the ephod, close to the seam
just above the waistband of the ephod. 28The rings of the breastpiece are to be tied
to the rings of the ephod with blue cord, connecting it to the waistband, so that the
breastpiece will not swing out from the ephod.
29“Whenever Aaron enters the Holy Place,[i] he will bear the names of the sons of
Israel over his heart on the breastpiece of decision as a continuing memorial before
the LORD. 30Also put the Urim and the Thummim[j] in the breastpiece, so they may
be over Aaron's heart whenever he enters the presence of the LORD. Thus Aaron will
always bear the means of making decisions for the Israelites over his heart before the
LORD.

Other Priestly Garments

31“Make the robe of the ephod entirely of blue cloth, 32with an opening for the head
in its centre. There shall be a woven edge like a collar[d] around this opening, so that
it will not tear. 33Make pomegranates of blue, purple and scarlet yarn around the hem
of the robe, with gold bells between them. 34The gold bells and the pomegranates are
to alternate around the hem of the robe. 35Aaron must wear it when he ministers. The

a *16* That is, about 9 inches (about 23 centimetres) b *18* Or *lapis lazuli* c *20* The precise identification of some of these precious stones is uncertain. d *32* The meaning of the Hebrew for this word is uncertain.

28:29 [i]ver 12

28:30 [j]Lev 8:8; Nu 27:21; Dt 33:8; Ezr 2:63; Ne 7:65

28:6–13 The ephod was a kind of apron elaborately embroidered with two pieces, back and front, joined at the shoulder with a band at the waist. On each shoulder strap was a stone with six of the 12 tribes of Israel engraved on it. The priest symbolically carried the burden of the whole nation on his shoulders as he represented them before God.

28:30 The Urim and the Thummim were used by the priest to make decisions. These names mean “Curses” and “Perfections” and refer to the nature of God whose will they revealed. They were kept in a pouch and taken out or shaken out to get either a yes or no decision.

29:1ff Why did God set up the priesthood? God had originally in-

sound of the bells will be heard when he enters the Holy Place before the LORD and
when he comes out, so that he will not die.
36“Make a plate of pure gold and engrave on it as on a seal: HOLY TO THE LORD.[k]
37Fasten a blue cord to it to attach it to the turban; it is to be on the front of the turban.
38It will be on Aaron's forehead, and he will bear the guilt[l] involved in the sacred
gifts the Israelites consecrate, whatever their gifts may be. It will be on Aaron's
forehead continually so that they will be acceptable to the LORD.
39“Weave the tunic of fine linen and make the turban of fine linen. The sash is to
be the work of an embroiderer. 40Make tunics, sashes and headbands for Aaron's
sons,[m] to give them dignity and honour. 41After you put these clothes on your brother
Aaron and his sons, anoint[n] and ordain them. Consecrate them so they may serve
me as priests.[o]
42“Make linen undergarments[p] as a covering for the body, reaching from the waist
to the thigh. 43Aaron and his sons must wear them whenever they enter the Tent of
Meeting[q] or approach the altar to minister in the Holy Place, so that they will not
incur guilt and die.[r]
“This is to be a lasting ordinance[s] for Aaron and his descendants.

Consecration of the Priests

29 “This is what you are to do to consecrate them, so that they may serve me as
priests: Take a young bull and two rams without defect. 2And from fine wheat
flour, without yeast, make bread, and cakes mixed with oil, and wafers spread with
oil.[a] 3Put them in a basket and present them in it—along with the bull and the two
rams. 4Then bring Aaron and his sons to the entrance to the Tent of Meeting and wash
them with water.[b] 5Take the garments[c] and dress Aaron with the tunic, the robe of
the ephod, the ephod itself and the breastpiece. Fasten the ephod on him by its skilfully
woven waistband.[d] 6Put the turban on his head and attach the sacred diadem[e] to the
turban. 7Take the anointing oil[f] and anoint him by pouring it on his head. 8Bring
his sons and dress them in tunics 9and put headbands on them. Then tie sashes on
Aaron and his sons.[a][g] The priesthood is theirs by a lasting ordinance.[h] In this way
you shall ordain Aaron and his sons.
10“Bring the bull to the front of the Tent of Meeting, and Aaron and his sons shall
lay their hands on its head.[i] 11Slaughter it in the LORD's presence at the entrance to
the Tent of Meeting. 12Take some of the bull's blood and put it on the horns[j] of the
altar with your finger, and pour out the rest of it at the base of the altar. 13Then take
all the fat[k] around the inner parts, the covering of the liver, and both kidneys with
the fat on them, and burn them on the altar. 14But burn the bull's flesh and its hide
and its offal outside the camp.[l] It is a sin offering.
15“Take one of the rams, and Aaron and his sons shall lay their hands on its head.
16Slaughter it and take the blood and sprinkle it against the altar on all sides. 17Cut
the ram into pieces and wash the inner parts and the legs, putting them with the head
and the other pieces. 18Then burn the entire ram on the altar. It is a burnt offering
to the LORD, a pleasing aroma,[m] an offering made to the LORD by fire.
19“Take the other ram,[n] and Aaron and his sons shall lay their hands on its head.

[a] *9* Hebrew; Septuagint *on them*

28:36 [k]Zec 14:20
28:38 [l]Lev 10:17; 22:9, 16; Nu 18:1; Heb 9:28; 1Pe 2:24
28:40 [m]ver 4; Ex 39:41
28:41 [n]Ex 29:7; Lev 10:7 [o]Ex 29:7-9; 30:30; 40:15; Lev 8:1-36; Heb 7:28
28:42 [p]Lev 6:10; 16:4, 23; Eze 44:18
28:43 [q]Ex 27:21 [r]Ex 20:26 [s]Lev 17:7
29:2 [a]Lev 2:1, 4; 6:19-23
29:4 [b]Ex 40:12; Heb 10:22
29:5 [c]Ex 28:2; Lev 8:7 [d]Ex 28:8
29:6 [e]Lev 8:9
29:7 [f]Ex 30:25, 30, 31; Lev 8:12; 21:10; Nu 35:25; Ps 133:2
29:9 [g]Ex 28:40 [h]Ex 40:15; Nu 3:10; 18:7; 25:13; Dt 18:5
29:10 [i]Lev 1:4
29:12 [j]Ex 27:2
29:13 [k]Lev 3:3, 5, 9
29:14 [l]Lev 4:11-12, 21; Heb 13:11
29:18 [m]Ge 8:21
29:19 [n]ver 3

tended that his chosen people be a “kingdom of priests” with both the nation as a whole and each individual dealing directly with God. But the people's sin prevented this from happening because a sinful person is not worthy to approach a perfect God. God then appointed priests from the tribe of Levi and set up the system of sacrifices to help the people approach him. He promised to forgive the people's sins if they would offer certain sacrifices administered by the priests on behalf of the people. Through these priests and their work, God wished to prepare all people for the coming of Jesus Christ, who would once again offer a direct relationship with God for anyone who would come to him. But until Christ came, the priests were the people's representatives before God. Through this Old Testament system, we can better understand the significance of what Christ did for us (see Hebrews 10:1–14).

29:10–41 Why were there such detailed rituals in connection with these sacrifices? Partly, it was for quality control. A centralised, standardised form of worship prevented problems of belief which could arise from individuals creating their own worship. Also, it differentiated the Hebrews from the pagan Canaanites they would meet in the promised land. By closely following God's instructions, the Hebrews could not possibly join the Canaanites in their immoral religious practices. Finally, it showed Israel that God was serious about his relationship with them.

20Slaughter it, take some of its blood and put it on the lobes of the right ears of Aaron
and his sons, on the thumbs of their right hands, and on the big toes of their right feet.
Then sprinkle blood against the altar on all sides. 21And take some of the blood[o] on
the altar and some of the anointing oil[p] and sprinkle it on Aaron and his garments
and on his sons and their garments. Then he and his sons and their garments will be
consecrated.[q]
22"Take from this ram the fat, the fat tail, the fat around the inner parts, the covering
of the liver, both kidneys with the fat on them, and the right thigh. (This is the ram
for the ordination.) 23From the basket of bread made without yeast, which is before
the LORD, take a loaf, and a cake made with oil, and a wafer. 24Put all these in the
hands of Aaron and his sons and wave them before the LORD as a wave offering.[r]
25Then take them from their hands and burn them on the altar along with the burnt
offering for a pleasing aroma to the LORD, an offering made to the LORD by fire.
26After you take the breast of the ram for Aaron's ordination, wave it before the LORD
as a wave offering, and it will be your share.[s]
27"Consecrate those parts of the ordination ram that belong to Aaron and his sons:[t]
the breast that was waved and the thigh that was presented. 28This is always to be
the regular share from the Israelites for Aaron and his sons. It is the contribution the
Israelites are to make to the LORD from their fellowship offerings.[b][u]
29"Aaron's sacred garments will belong to his descendants so that they can be
anointed and ordained in them.[v] 30The son[w] who succeeds him as priest and comes
to the Tent of Meeting to minister in the Holy Place is to wear them seven days.
31"Take the ram for the ordination and cook the meat in a sacred place. 32At the
entrance to the Tent of Meeting, Aaron and his sons are to eat the meat of the ram
and the bread[x] that is in the basket. 33They are to eat these offerings by which
atonement was made for their ordination and consecration. But no-one else may eat[y]
them, because they are sacred. 34And if any of the meat of the ordination ram or any
bread is left over till morning,[z] burn it up. It must not be eaten, because it is sacred.
35"Do for Aaron and his sons everything I have commanded you, taking seven days
to ordain them. 36Sacrifice a bull each day[a] as a sin offering to make atonement.
Purify the altar by making atonement for it, and anoint it to consecrate[b] it. 37For seven
days make atonement for the altar and consecrate it. Then the altar will be most holy,
and whatever touches it will be holy.[c]
38"This is what you are to offer on the altar regularly each day:[d] two lambs a year
old. 39Offer one in the morning and the other at twilight.[e] 40With the first lamb offer
a tenth of an ephah[c] of fine flour mixed with a quarter of a hin[d] of oil from pressed
olives, and a quarter of a hin of wine as a drink offering. 41Sacrifice the other lamb
at twilight with the same grain offering and its drink offering as in the morning—a
pleasing aroma, an offering made to the LORD by fire.
42"For the generations to come[f] this burnt offering is to be made regularly at the
entrance to the Tent of Meeting before the LORD. There I will meet you and speak
to you;[g] 43there also I will meet with the Israelites, and the place will be consecrated
by my glory.[h]
44"So I will consecrate the Tent of Meeting and the altar and will consecrate Aaron
and his sons to serve me as priests.[i] 45Then I will dwell[j] among the Israelites and
be their God.[k] 46They will know that I am the LORD their God, who brought them
out of Egypt so that I might dwell among them. I am the LORD their God.[l]

b *28* Traditionally *peace offerings* **c** *40* That is, probably about 4 pints (about 2 litres) **d** *40* That is, probably about 1½ pints (about 1 litre)

29:21 [o]Heb 9:22 [p]Ex 30:25, 31 [q]ver 1
29:24 [r]Lev 7:30
29:26 [s]Lev 7:31-34
29:27 [t]Lev 7:31, 34; Dt 18:3
29:28 [u]Lev 10:15
29:29 [v]Nu 20:26, 28
29:30 [w]Nu 20:28
29:32 [x]Mt 12:4
29:33 [y]Lev 10:14; 22:10, 13
29:34 [z]Ex 12:10
29:36 [a]Heb 10:11 [b]Ex 40:10
29:37 [c]Ex 30:28-29; 40:10; Mt 23:19
29:38 [d]Nu 28:3-8; 1Ch 16:40; Da 12:11
29:39 [e]Eze 46:13-15
29:42 [f]Ex 30:8 [g]Ex 25:22
29:43 [h]1Ki 8:11
29:44 [i]Lev 21:15
29:45 [j]Ex 25:8; Lev 26:12; Zec 2:10; Jn 14:17 [k]2Co 6:16; Rev 21:3
29:46 [l]Ex 20:2

29:37 Notice the overwhelming emphasis on the holiness of God. The priests, the clothes, the tabernacle, and the sacrifice had to be clean and consecrated, prepared to meet God. In contrast, today we tend to take God for granted, rushing into worship and treating him with almost casual disregard. But we worship the almighty Creator and Sustainer of the universe. Remember that profound truth when you pray or worship, and come before him with reverence and repentance.

29:45, 46 God's action in bringing the Israelites out of Egypt showed his great desire to be with them and protect them. Throughout the Bible, God shows that he is not an absentee landlord. He wants to live among us, even in our hearts. Don't exclude God from your life. Allow him to be your God as you obey his word and communicate with him in prayer. Let him be your resident landlord.

The Altar of Incense

30 "Make an altar[a] of acacia wood for burning incense.[b] 2It is to be square, a
cubit long and a cubit wide, and two cubits high**[a]**—its horns[c] of one piece
with it. 3Overlay the top and all the sides and the horns with pure gold, and make
a gold moulding around it. 4Make two gold rings for the altar below the moulding—two on opposite sides—to hold the poles used to carry it. 5Make the poles of
acacia wood and overlay them with gold. 6Put the altar in front of the curtain that is
before the ark of the Testimony—before the atonement cover[d] that is over the
Testimony—where I will meet with you.
7"Aaron must burn fragrant incense[e] on the altar every morning when he tends the
lamps. 8He must burn incense again when he lights the lamps at twilight so that incense
will burn regularly before the LORD for the generations to come. 9Do not offer on this
altar any other incense[f] or any burnt offering or grain offering, and do not pour a
drink offering on it. 10Once a year Aaron shall make atonement[g] on its horns. This
annual atonement must be made with the blood of the atoning sin offering for the
generations to come. It is most holy to the LORD."

Atonement Money

11Then the LORD said to Moses, 12"When you take a census[h] of the Israelites to
count them, each one must pay the LORD a ransom[i] for his life at the time he is
counted. Then no plague[j] will come on them when you number them. 13Each one
who crosses over to those already counted is to give a half shekel,**[b]** according to the
sanctuary shekel,[k] which weighs twenty gerahs. This half shekel is an offering to the
LORD. 14All who cross over, those twenty years old or more, are to give an offering
to the LORD. 15The rich are not to give more than a half shekel and the poor are not
to give less[l] when you make the offering to the LORD to atone for your lives.
16Receive the atonement money from the Israelites and use it for the service of the
Tent of Meeting.[m] It will be a memorial for the Israelites before the LORD, making
atonement for your lives."

Basin for Washing

17Then the LORD said to Moses, 18"Make a bronze basin,[n] with its bronze stand,
for washing. Place it between the Tent of Meeting and the altar, and put water in it.
19Aaron and his sons are to wash their hands and feet[o] with water[p] from it.
20Whenever they enter the Tent of Meeting, they shall wash with water so that they
will not die. Also, when they approach the altar to minister by presenting an offering
made to the LORD by fire, 21they shall wash their hands and feet so that they will not
die. This is to be a lasting ordinance[q] for Aaron and his descendants for the generations to come."

Anointing Oil

22Then the LORD said to Moses, 23"Take the following fine spices: 500 shekels**[c]**
of liquid myrrh,[r] half as much (that is, 250 shekels) of fragrant cinnamon, 250
shekels of fragrant cane, 24500 shekels of cassia[s]—all according to the sanctuary
shekel—and a hin**[d]** of olive oil. 25Make these into a sacred anointing oil, a fragrant
blend, the work of a perfumer.[t] It will be the sacred anointing oil.[u] 26Then use it

a *2* That is, about 1½ feet (about 0.5 metre) long and wide and about 3 feet (about 0.9 metre) high **b** *13* That is, about 1/5 ounce (about 6 grams); also in verse 15 **c** *23* That is, about 12½ pounds (about 6 kilograms)
d *24* That is, probably about 6½ pints (about 4 litres)

30:1 [a]Ex 37:25 [b]Rev 8:3
30:2 [c]Ex 27:2
30:6 [d]Ex 25:22; 26:34
30:7 [e]ver 34-35; Ex 27:21; 1Sa 2:28
30:9 [f]Lev 10:1
30:10 [g]Lev 16:18-19, 30
30:12 [h]Ex 38:25; Nu 1:2, 49; 2Sa 24:1 [i]Nu 31:50; Mt 20:28 [j]2Sa 24:13
30:13 [k]Nu 3:47; Mt 17:24
30:15 [l]Pr 22:2; Eph 6:9
30:16 [m]Ex 38:25-28
30:18 [n]Ex 38:8; 40:7, 30
30:19 [o]Ex 40:31-32; Isa 52:11 [p]Ps 26:6
30:21 [q]Ex 27:21; 28:43
30:23 [r]Ge 37:25
30:24 [s]Ps 45:8
30:25 [t]Ex 37:29 [u]Ex 40:9

30:10 This once-a-year ceremony was called the Day of Atonement. On this day a sacrifice was made for the sins of the entire Israelite nation. This was the only day the high priest could enter the Most Holy Place, the innermost room of the tabernacle. Here he asked God to forgive the people. The Day of Atonement served as a reminder that the daily, weekly, and monthly sacrifices could cover sins only temporarily. It pointed towards Jesus Christ, the perfect atonement, who could remove sins for ever.

30:11–16 The atonement money was like a census tax. It continued the principle that all the people belonged to God and therefore needed to be redeemed by a sacrifice. Whenever a census took place, everyone, both rich and poor, was required to pay a ransom. God does not discriminate between people (see Acts 10:34; Galatians 3:28). All of us need mercy and forgiveness because of our sinful thoughts and actions. There is no way the rich person can buy off God, and no way the poor can avoid paying. God's demand is that all of us come humbly before him to be forgiven and brought into his family.

to anoint[v] the Tent of Meeting, the ark of the Testimony, 27the table and all its
articles, the lampstand and its accessories, the altar of incense, 28the altar of burnt
offering and all its utensils, and the basin with its stand. 29You shall consecrate them
so they will be most holy, and whatever touches them will be holy.[w]
30"Anoint Aaron and his sons and consecrate[x] them so they may serve me as
priests. 31Say to the Israelites, 'This is to be my sacred anointing oil for the generations
to come. 32Do not pour it on men's bodies and do not make any oil with the same
formula. It is sacred, and you are to consider it sacred.[y] 33Whoever makes perfume
like it and whoever puts it on anyone other than a priest must be cut off[z] from his
people.' "

Incense

34Then the LORD said to Moses, "Take fragrant spices—gum resin, onycha and
galbanum—and pure frankincense, all in equal amounts, 35and make a fragrant blend
of incense, the work of a perfumer.[a] It is to be salted and pure and sacred. 36Grind
some of it to powder and place it in front of the Testimony in the Tent of Meeting,
where I will meet with you. It shall be most holy[b] to you. 37Do not make any incense
with this formula for yourselves; consider it holy[c] to the LORD. 38Whoever makes
any like it to enjoy its fragrance must be cut off[d] from his people."

Bezalel and Oholiab

31 Then the LORD said to Moses, 2"See I have chosen Bezalel[a] son of Uri, the
son of Hur, of the tribe of Judah, 3and I have filled him with the Spirit of God,
with skill, ability and knowledge in all kinds of crafts[b]—4to make artistic designs
for work in gold, silver and bronze, 5to cut and set stones, to work in wood, and to
engage in all kinds of craftsmanship. 6Moreover, I have appointed Oholiab son of
Ahisamach, of the tribe of Dan, to help him. Also I have given skill to all the craftsmen
to make everything I have commanded you: 7the Tent of Meeting,[c] the ark of the
Testimony[d] with the atonement cover[e] on it, and all the other furnishings of the
tent—8the table[f] and its articles, the pure gold lampstand[g] and all its accessories,
the altar of incense, 9the altar of burnt offering and all its utensils, the basin with its
stand—10and also the woven garments[h], both the sacred garments for Aaron the
priest and the garments for his sons when they serve as priests, 11and the anointing
oil[i] and fragrant incense for the Holy Place. They are to make them just as I
commanded you."

The Sabbath

12Then the LORD said to Moses, 13"Say to the Israelites, 'You must observe my
Sabbaths.[j] This will be a sign[k] between me and you for the generations to come,
so that you may know that I am the LORD, who makes you holy.[a][l]
14" 'Observe the Sabbath, because it is holy to you. Anyone who desecrates it must
be put to death;[m] whoever does any work on that day must be cut off from his people.
15For six days, work[n] is to be done, but the seventh day is a Sabbath of rest,[o] holy
to the LORD. Whoever does any work on the Sabbath day must be put to death. 16The
Israelites are to observe the Sabbath, celebrating it for the generations to come as a

a *13 Or who sanctifies you*; or *who sets you apart as holy*

30:26 [v]Ex 40:9; Lev 8:10; Nu 7:1
30:29 [w]Ex 29:37
30:30 [x]Ex 29:7; Lev 8:2, 12, 30
30:32 [y]ver 25, 37
30:33 [z]ver 38; Ge 17:14
30:35 [a]ver 25
30:36 [b]ver 32; Ex 29:37; Lev 2:3
30:37 [c]ver 32
30:38 [d]ver 33
31:2 [a]Ex 36:1, 2; 1Ch 2:20
31:3 [b]1Ki 7:14
31:7 [c]Ex 36:8-38 [d]Ex 37:1-5 [e]Ex 37:6
31:8 [f]Ex 37:10-16 [g]Ex 37:17-24
31:10 [h]Ex 28:2; 39:1, 41
31:11 [i]Ex 30:22-32
31:13 [j]Ex 20:8; Lev 19:3, 30 [k]Eze 20:12, 20 [l]Lev 11:44
31:14 [m]Nu 15:32-36
31:15 [n]Ex 20:8-11 [o]Ge 2:3; Ex 16:23

30:34–38 The Israelites often burned incense, but this holy incense could be burned only in the tabernacle. Here God gave the recipe for this special incense. The sweet-smelling incense was burned in shallow dishes called censers and was used to show honour and reverence to God. It was like prayer lifting up to God. It was also a vital part of the sacred ceremony on the Day of Atonement, when the high priest carried his smoking censer into the Most Holy Place. This incense, like the sacred anointing oil, was so holy that the people were strictly forbidden to copy it for personal use.

31:1–11 God regards all the skills of his people, not merely those with theological or ministerial abilities. Our tendency is to regard only those who are up front and in leadership roles. God gave Bezalel and Oholiab Spirit-filled abilities in artistic craftsmanship. Take notice of all the abilities God gives his people. Don't diminish your skills if they are not like Moses' and Aaron's.

31:12–17 The Sabbath had two purposes: It was a time *to rest* and a time *to remember* what God had done. We need rest. Without time out from the bustle, life loses its meaning. In our day, as in Moses' day, taking time out is not easy. But God reminds us that without Sabbaths we will forget the purpose for all of our activity and lose the balance crucial to a faithful life. Make sure your Sabbath provides a time of both refreshment and remembrance of God.

31:17 [p]ver 13 [q]Ge 2:2-3
31:18 [r]Ex 24:12 [s]Ex 32:15-16; 34:1, 28; Dt 4:13; 5:22

lasting covenant. 17It will be a sign[p] between me and the Israelites for ever, for in
six days the LORD made the heavens and the earth, and on the seventh day he abstained
from work and rested.[q]' "
18When the LORD finished speaking to Moses on Mount Sinai, he gave him the two
tablets of the Testimony, the tablets of stone[r] inscribed by the finger of God.[s]

3. Breaking the law

The Golden Calf

32:1 [a]Ex 24:18; Dt 9:9-12 [b]Ac 7:40*
32:2 [c]Ex 35:22

32 When the people saw that Moses was so long in coming down from the
mountain,[a] they gathered round Aaron and said, "Come, make us gods[a] who
will go before us. As for this fellow Moses who brought us up out of Egypt, we don't
know what has happened to him."[b]
2Aaron answered them, "Take off the gold ear-rings[c] that your wives, your sons

a *1* Or *a god*; also in verses 23 and 31

AARON

Effective teamwork happens when each team member uses his or her special skills. Ideally, each member's strengths will contribute something important to the team effort. In this way, members make up for one another's weaknesses. Aaron made a good team with Moses. He provided Moses with one skill Moses lacked—effective public speaking. But while Aaron was necessary to Moses, he needed Moses as well. Without a guide, Aaron had little direction of his own. There was never any doubt as to who God's chosen and trained leader was. The pliability that made Aaron a good follower made him a weak leader. His major failures were caused by his inability to stand alone. His yielding to public pressure and making an idol was a good example of this weakness.

Most of us have more of the follower than the leader in us. We may even be good followers, following a good leader. But no leader is perfect, and no human deserves our complete allegiance. Only God deserves our complete loyalty and obedience. We need to be effective team members in using the skills and abilities God has given us. But if the team or the leader goes against God's word, we must be willing to stand alone.

Strengths and accomplishments:
- First high priest of God in Israel
- Effective communicator; Moses' mouthpiece

Weaknesses and mistakes:
- Pliable personality; gave in to people's demands for a golden calf
- Joined with Moses in disobeying God's orders about the water-giving rock
- Joined sister Miriam in complaining against Moses

Lessons from his life:
- God gives individuals special abilities, which he weaves together for his use
- The very skills that make a good team player sometimes also make a poor leader

Vital statistics:
- Where: Egypt, Desert of Sinai
- Occupations: Priest; Moses' second in command
- Relatives: Brother: Moses. Sister: Miriam. Sons: Nadab, Abihu, Eleazar, and Ithamar

Key verses:
"Then the LORD's anger burned against Moses and he said, 'What about your brother, Aaron the Levite? I know he can speak well. He is already on his way to meet you, and his heart will be glad when he sees you. . . . He will speak to the people for you, and it will be as if he were your mouth and as if you were God to him' " (Exodus 4:14, 16).

Aaron's story is told in Exodus to Deuteronomy 10:6. He is also mentioned in Hebrews 7:11.

31:18 The two tablets of the Testimony contained the Ten Commandments. These were not the only code of laws in the ancient world. Other law codes had come into existence when cities or nations decided that there must be standards of judgment, ways to correct specific wrongs. But God's laws for Israel were unique in that: (1) they alleviated the harsh judgments typical of the day; (2) they were egalitarian – the poor and the powerful received the same punishment; (3) they did not separate religious and social law. All law rested on God's authority.

32:1–10 Idols again! Even though Israel had seen the invisible God in action, they still wanted the familiar gods they could see and shape into whatever image they desired. How much like them we are! Our great temptation is still to shape God to our liking, to make him convenient to obey or ignore. God responds in great anger when his mercy is trampled on. The gods we create blind us to the love our loving God wants to shower on us. God cannot work in us when we elevate anyone or anything above him. What false gods in your life are preventing the true God from living in you?

and your daughters are wearing, and bring them to me." 3So all the people took off
their ear-rings and brought them to Aaron. 4He took what they handed him and made
it into an idol cast in the shape of a calf,[d] fashioning it with a tool. Then they said,
"These are your gods,[b] O Israel, who brought you up out of Egypt."
5When Aaron saw this, he built an altar in front of the calf and announced,
"Tomorrow there will be a festival[e] to the LORD." 6So the next day the people rose
early and sacrificed burnt offerings and presented fellowship offerings.[c][f] Afterwards
they sat down to eat and drink and got up to indulge in revelry.[g]
7Then the LORD said to Moses, "Go down, because your people, whom you brought
up out of Egypt,[h] have become corrupt.[i] 8They have been quick to turn away from
what I commanded them and have made themselves an idol[j] cast in the shape of a
calf. They have bowed down to it and sacrificed[k] to it and have said, 'These are your
gods, O Israel, who brought you up out of Egypt.'[l]
9"I have seen these people," the LORD said to Moses, "and they are a stiff-necked[m]
people. 10Now leave me alone so that my anger may burn against them and that I may
destroy them. Then I will make you into a great nation."[n]
11But Moses sought the favour[o] of the LORD his God. "O LORD," he said, "why
should your anger burn against your people, whom you brought out of Egypt with great
power and a mighty hand?[p] 12Why should the Egyptians say, 'It was with evil intent
that he brought them out, to kill them in the mountains and to wipe them off the face
of the earth'?[q] Turn from your fierce anger; relent and do not bring disaster on your
people. 13Remember[r] your servants Abraham, Isaac and Israel, to whom you swore
by your own self:[s] 'I will make your descendants as numerous as the stars[t] in the
sky and I will give your descendants all this land[u] I promised them, and it will be
their inheritance for ever.'" 14Then the LORD relented[v] and did not bring on his
people the disaster he had threatened.
15Moses turned and went down the mountain with the two tablets of the Testimony[w]
in his hands.[x] They were inscribed on both sides, front and back. 16The tablets were
the work of God; the writing was the writing of God, engraved on the tablets.[y]
17When Joshua heard the noise of the people shouting, he said to Moses, "There
is the sound of war in the camp."
18Moses replied:

> "It is not the sound of victory,
> it is not the sound of defeat;
> it is the sound of singing that I hear."

19When Moses approached the camp and saw the calf[z] and the dancing, his anger

b 4 Or *This is your god*; also in verse 8 c 6 Traditionally *peace offerings*

32:4 [d]Dt 9:16; Ne 9:18; Ps 106:19; Ac 7:41
32:5 [e]Lev 23:2, 37; 2Ki 10:20
32:6 [f]Nu 25:2; Ac 7:41 [g]ver 17-19; 1Co 10:7*
32:7 [h]ver 4, 11 [i]Ge 6:11-12; Dt 9:12
32:8 [j]Ex 20:4 [k]Ex 22:20 [l]1Ki 12:28
32:9 [m]Ex 33:3, 5; 34:9; Isa 48:4; Ac 7:51
32:10 [n]Nu 14:12; Dt 9:14
32:11 [o]Dt 9:18 [p]Dt 9:26
32:12 [q]Nu 14:13-16; Dt 9:28
32:13 [r]Ex 2:24 [s]Ge 22:16; Heb 6:13 [t]Ge 15:5; 26:4 [u]Ge 12:7
32:14 [v]2Sa 24:16; Ps 106:45
32:15 [w]Ex 31:18 [x]Dt 9:15
32:16 [y]Ex 31:18
32:19 [z]Dt 9:16

32:4, 5 Two popular Egyptian gods, Hapi (Apis) and Hathor, were thought of as a bull and a heifer. The Canaanites around them worshipped Baal, thought of as a bull. Baal was their sacred symbol of power and fertility and was closely connected to immoral sexual practices. No doubt the Israelites, fresh from Egypt, found it quite natural to make a golden calf to represent the God that had just delivered them from their oppressors. They were weary of a god without a face. But in doing so, they were ignoring the command he had just given them: "You shall not make for yourself an idol in the form of anything in heaven above or on the earth beneath or in the waters below" (20:4). They may even have thought they were worshipping God. Their apparent sincerity was no substitute for obedience or excuse for disobedience.

Even if we do not make idols, we are often guilty of trying to make God in our image, moulding him to fit our expectations, desires, and circumstances. When we do this, we end up worshipping ourselves rather than the God who created us – and self-worship, today as in the Israelites' time, leads to all kinds of immorality. What is your favourite image of God? Is it biblical? Is it adequate? Do you need to destroy it in order to worship the immeasurably powerful God who delivered you from bondage to sin?

32:9–14 God was ready to destroy the whole nation because of their sin. But Moses pleaded for mercy, and God spared them. This is one of the countless examples in the Bible of God's mercy. Although we deserve his anger, he is willing to forgive and restore us to himself. We can receive God's forgiveness from sin by asking him. Like Moses, we can pray that he will forgive others and use us to bring them the message of his mercy.

32:14 How could God relent? God did not change his mind in the same way that a parent decides not to discipline a child. Instead, God changed his behaviour to remain consistent with his nature. When God first wanted to destroy the people, he was acting consistently with his justice. When Moses interceded for the people, God relented in order to act consistently with his mercy. God had often told the people that if they changed their ways, he would not condemn them. They changed, and God did as he promised.

32:19, 20 Overwhelmed by the actual sight of the blatant idolatry and revelry, Moses broke the tablets containing the commandments which had already been broken in the hearts and actions of the people. There is a place for righteous anger. However angry Moses might have been, God was angrier still – he wanted to kill all the people. Anger at sin is a sign of spiritual vitality. Don't

32:19 [a]Dt 9:17
32:20 [b]Dt 9:21
32:22 [c]Dt 9:24
32:23 [d]ver 1
32:24 [e]ver 4
32:27 [f]Nu 25:3, 5; Dt 33:9
32:30 [g]1Sa 12:20 [h]Lev 1:4; Nu 25:13
32:31 [i]Dt 9:18 [j]Ex 20:23
32:32 [k]Ro 9:3 [l]Ps 69:28; Da 12:1; Php 4:3; Rev 3:5; 21:27
32:33 [m]Dt 29:20; Ps 9:5
32:34 [n]Ex 3:17 [o]Ex 23:20 [p]Dt 32:35; Ps 99:8; Ro 2:5-6
32:35 [q]ver 4
33:1 [a]Ge 12:7
33:2 [b]Ex 32:34 [c]Ex 23:27-31; Jos 24:11
33:3 [d]Ex 3:8 [e]Ex 32:9 [f]Ex 32:10
33:4 [g]Nu 14:39
33:7 [h]Ex 29:42-43
33:8 [i]Nu 16:27
33:9 [j]Ex 13:21 [k]Ex 31:18; Ps 99:7

burned and he threw the tablets out of his hands, breaking them to pieces[a] at the foot of the mountain. 20And he took the calf they had made and burned it in the fire; then he ground it to powder, scattered it on the water[b] and made the Israelites drink it.

21He said to Aaron, "What did these people do to you, that you led them into such great sin?"

22"Do not be angry, my lord," Aaron answered. "You know how prone these people are to evil.[c] 23They said to me, 'Make us gods who will go before us. As for this fellow Moses who brought us up out of Egypt, we don't know what has happened to him.'[d] 24So I told them, 'Whoever has any gold jewellery, take it off.' Then they gave me the gold, and I threw it into the fire, and out came this calf!"[e]

25Moses saw that the people were running wild and that Aaron had let them get out of control and so become a laughing-stock to their enemies. 26So he stood at the entrance to the camp and said, "Whoever is for the LORD, come to me." And all the Levites rallied to him.

27Then he said to them, "This is what the LORD, the God of Israel, says: 'Each man strap a sword to his side. Go back and forth through the camp from one end to the other, each killing his brother and friend and neighbour.' "[f] 28The Levites did as Moses commanded, and that day about three thousand of the people died. 29Then Moses said, "You have been set apart to the LORD today, for you were against your own sons and brothers, and he has blessed you this day."

30The next day Moses said to the people, "You have committed a great sin.[g] But now I will go up to the LORD; perhaps I can make atonement[h] for your sin."

31So Moses went back to the LORD and said, "Oh, what a great sin these people have committed![i] They have made themselves gods of gold.[j] 32But now, please forgive their sin—but if not, then blot me[k] out of the book[l] you have written."

33The LORD replied to Moses, "Whoever has sinned against me I will blot out[m] of my book. 34Now go, lead the people to the place[n] I spoke of, and my angel[o] will go before you. However, when the time comes for me to punish,[p] I will punish them for their sin."

35And the LORD struck the people with a plague because of what they did with the calf[q] Aaron had made.

33 Then the LORD said to Moses, "Leave this place, you and the people you brought up out of Egypt, and go up to the land I promised on oath to Abraham, Isaac and Jacob, saying, 'I will give it to your descendants.'[a] 2I will send an angel[b] before you and drive out the Canaanites, Amorites, Hittites, Perizzites, Hivites and Jebusites.[c] 3Go up to the land flowing with milk and honey.[d] But I will not go with you, because you are a stiff-necked[e] people and I might destroy[f] you on the way."

4When the people heard these distressing words, they began to mourn[g] and no-one put on any ornaments. 5For the LORD had said to Moses, "Tell the Israelites, 'You are a stiff-necked people. If I were to go with you even for a moment, I might destroy you. Now take off your ornaments and I will decide what to do with you.' " 6So the Israelites stripped off their ornaments at Mount Horeb.

The Tent of Meeting

7Now Moses used to take a tent and pitch it outside the camp some distance away, calling it the "tent of meeting".[h] Anyone enquiring of the LORD would go to the tent of meeting outside the camp. 8And whenever Moses went out to the tent, all the people rose and stood at the entrances to their tents,[i] watching Moses until he entered the tent. 9As Moses went into the tent, the pillar of cloud[j] would come down and stay at the entrance, while the LORD spoke[k] with Moses. 10Whenever the people saw the

---

stifle this kind of anger. But when you are justifiably angry at sin, be careful not to do anything that you will regret later.

32:21–24 Aaron's decision nearly cost him his life. His absurd excuse shows the spiritual decline in his leadership and in the people. Those who function as spokespersons and assistants need to be doubly sure their theology and morality are in tune with God so they will not be influenced by pressure from people. For more information on Aaron, see his Profile in chapter 32.

33:5, 6 This ban on ornaments was not a permanent ban on all jewellery. It was a temporary sign of repentance and mourning. In 35:22 we read that the people had jewellery.

pillar of cloud standing at the entrance to the tent, they all stood and worshipped, each
at the entrance to his tent. 11The LORD would speak to Moses face to face,[l] as a man
speaks with his friend. Then Moses would return to the camp, but his young assistant
Joshua son of Nun did not leave the tent.

Moses and the Glory of the LORD

12Moses said to the LORD, "You have been telling me, 'Lead these people,'[m] but
you have not let me know whom you will send with me. You have said, 'I know you
by name[n] and you have found favour with me.' 13If you are pleased with me, teach
me your ways[o] so I may know you and continue to find favour with you. Remember
that this nation is your people."[p]
14The LORD replied, "My Presence[q] will go with you, and I will give you rest."[r]
15Then Moses said to him, "If your Presence does not go with us, do not send us
up from here. 16How will anyone know that you are pleased with me and with your
people unless you go with us?[s] What else will distinguish me and your people from
all the other people on the face of the earth?"[t]
17And the LORD said to Moses, "I will do the very thing you have asked, because
I am pleased with you and I know you by name."
18Then Moses said, "Now show me your glory."
19And the LORD said, "I will cause all my goodness to pass in front of you, and
I will proclaim my name, the LORD, in your presence. I will have mercy on whom
I will have mercy, and I will have compassion on whom I will have compassion.[u]
20But," he said, "you cannot see my face, for no-one may see[v] me and live."
21Then the LORD said, "There is a place near me where you may stand on a rock.
22When my glory passes by, I will put you in a cleft in the rock and cover you with
my hand[w] until I have passed by. 23Then I will remove my hand and you will see
my back; but my face must not be seen."

The New Stone Tablets

34 The LORD said to Moses, "Chisel out two stone tablets like the first ones, and
I will write on them the words that were on the first tablets,[a] which you
broke.[b] 2Be ready in the morning, and then come up on Mount Sinai.[c] Present
yourself to me there on top of the mountain. 3No-one is to come with you or be seen
anywhere on the mountain;[d] not even the flocks and herds may graze in front of the
mountain."
4So Moses chiselled out two stone tablets like the first ones and went up Mount
Sinai early in the morning, as the LORD had commanded him; and he carried the two
stone tablets in his hands. 5Then the LORD came down in the cloud and stood there
with him and proclaimed his name, the LORD.[e] 6And he passed in front of Moses,
proclaiming, "The LORD, the LORD, the compassionate[f] and gracious God, slow to
anger,[g] abounding in love[h] and faithfulness,[i] 7maintaining love to thousands,[j] and

33:11 [l]Nu 12:8; Dt 34:10
33:12 [m]Ex 3:10 [n]ver 17; Jn 10:14-15; 2Ti 2:19
33:13 [o]Ps 25:4; 86:11; 119:33 [p]Ex 34:9; Dt 9:26, 29
33:14 [q]Isa 63:9 [r]Jos 21:44; 22:4
33:16 [s]Nu 14:14 [t]Ex 34:10
33:19 [u]Ro 9:15*
33:20 [v]Ge 32:30; Isa 6:5
33:22 [w]Ps 91:4
34:1 [a]Dt 10:2, 4 [b]Ex 32:19
34:2 [c]Ex 19:11
34:3 [d]Ex 19:12-13, 21
34:5 [e]Ex 33:19
34:6 [f]Ps 86:15 [g]Nu 14:18; Ro 2:4 [h]Ne 9:17; Ps 103:8; Joel 2:13 [i]Ps 108:4
34:7 [j]Ex 20:6

33:11 God and Moses talked face to face in the Tent of Meeting, just as friends do. Why did Moses find such favour with God? It certainly was not because he was perfect, gifted, or powerful. Rather, it was because God chose Moses, and Moses in turn relied wholeheartedly on God's wisdom and direction. Friendship with God was a true privilege for Moses, out of reach for the other Hebrews. But it is not out of reach for us today. Jesus called his disciples – and, by extension, all of his followers – his friends (John 15:15). He has called you to be his friend. Will you trust him as Moses did?

33:11 Joshua, Moses' aide, did not leave the tent, probably because he was guarding it. No doubt there were curious people who would have dared to go inside.

33:18–23 Moses' prayer was to see the manifest glory of God. He wanted assurance of God's presence with him, Aaron, and Joshua, and also he desired to know that presence experientially. Because we are finite and morally imperfect, we cannot exist and see God as he is. To see God's back means we can only see where God has passed by. We can only know him by what he does and how he acts. We cannot comprehend God as he really is apart from Jesus Christ (John 14:9). Jesus promised to show himself to those who believe (John 14:21).

34:6, 7 Moses had asked to see God's glory (33:18), and this was God's response. What is God's glory? It is his character, his nature, his way of relating to his creatures. Notice that God did not give Moses a vision of his power and majesty, but rather of his love. God's glory is revealed in his mercy, grace, compassion, faithfulness, forgiveness, and justice. God's love and mercy are truly wonderful, and we benefit from them. We can respond and give glory to God when our characters resemble his.

34:7 Why would sins affect grandchildren and great-grandchildren? This is no arbitrary punishment. Children still suffer for the sins of their parents. Consider child abuse or alcoholism, for example. While these sins are obvious, sins like selfishness and

forgiving wickedness, rebellion and sin.[k] Yet he does not leave the guilty unpunished;[l] he punishes the children and their children for the sin of the fathers to the third and fourth generation."

8 Moses bowed to the ground at once and worshipped. 9 "O Lord, if I have found favour in your eyes," he said, "then let the Lord go with us.[m] Although this is a stiff-necked people, forgive our wickedness and our sin, and take us as your inheritance."[n]

10 Then the LORD said: "I am making a covenant[o] with you. Before all your people I will do wonders never before done in any nation in all the world.[p] The people you live among will see how awesome is the work that I, the LORD, will do for you. 11 Obey what I command you today. I will drive out before you the Amorites, Canaanites, Hittites, Perizzites, Hivites and Jebusites.[q] 12 Be careful not to make a treaty with those who live in the land where you are going, or they will be a snare[r] among you. 13 Break down their altars, smash their sacred stones and cut down their Asherah poles.[a][s] 14 Do not worship any other god,[t] for the LORD, whose name is Jealous, is a jealous God.[u]

15 "Be careful not to make a treaty with those who live in the land; for when they prostitute[v] themselves to their gods and sacrifice to them, they will invite you and you will eat their sacrifices.[w] 16 And when you choose some of their daughters as wives[x] for your sons and those daughters prostitute themselves to their gods,[y] they will lead your sons to do the same.

17 "Do not make cast idols.[z]

18 "Celebrate the Feast of Unleavened Bread.[a] For seven days eat bread made without yeast,[b] as I commanded you. Do this at the appointed time in the month of Abib,[c] for in that month you came out of Egypt.

19 "The first offspring[d] of every womb belongs to me, including all the firstborn males of your livestock, whether from herd or flock. 20 Redeem the firstborn donkey with a lamb, but if you do not redeem it, break its neck.[e] Redeem all your firstborn sons.

"No-one is to appear before me empty-handed.[f]

21 "Six days you shall labour, but on the seventh day you shall rest;[g] even during the ploughing season and harvest you must rest.

22 "Celebrate the Feast of Weeks with the firstfruits of the wheat harvest, and the Feast of Ingathering[h] at the turn of the year.[b] 23 Three times[i] a year all your men are to appear before the Sovereign LORD, the God of Israel. 24 I will drive out nations[j] before you and enlarge your territory, and no-one will covet your land when you go up three times each year to appear before the LORD your God.

25 "Do not offer the blood of a sacrifice to me along with anything containing yeast,[k] and do not let any of the sacrifice from the Passover Feast remain until morning.[l]

26 "Bring the best of the firstfruits of your soil to the house of the LORD your God.

"Do not cook a young goat in its mother's milk."[m]

27 Then the LORD said to Moses, "Write[n] down these words, for in accordance with

a *13* That is, symbols of the goddess Asherah b *22* That is, in the autumn

34:7 [k]Ps 103:3; 130:4, 8; Da 9:9; 1Jn 1:9 [l]Job 10:14; Na 1:3
34:9 [m]Ex 33:15 [n]Ps 33:12
34:10 [o]Dt 5:2-3 [p]Ex 33:16; Dt 4:32
34:11 [q]Ex 33:2
34:12 [r]Ex 23:32-33
34:13 [s]Ex 23:24; Dt 12:3; 2Ki 18:4
34:14 [t]Ex 20:3 [u]Ex 20:5; Dt 4:24
34:15 [v]Jdg 2:17 [w]Nu 25:2; 1Co 8:4
34:16 [x]Dt 7:3 [y]1Ki 11:4
34:17 [z]Ex 32:8
34:18 [a]Ex 12:17 [b]Ex 12:15 [c]Ex 12:2
34:19 [d]Ex 13:2
34:20 [e]Ex 13:13, 15 [f]Ex 23:15; Dt 16:16
34:21 [g]Ex 20:9; Lk 13:14
34:22 [h]Ex 23:16
34:23 [i]Ex 23:14
34:24 [j]Ex 23:28; 33:2; Ps 78:55
34:25 [k]Ex 23:18 [l]Ex 12:8, 10
34:26 [m]Ex 23:19
34:27 [n]Ex 17:14; 24:4

---

greed can be passed on as well. The dire consequences of sin are not limited to the individual family member. Be careful not to treat sin casually, but repent and turn from it. The sin may cause you little pain now, but it could sting in a most tender area of your life later—your children and grandchildren.

34:12–14 God told the Israelites not to join in religious rites with the sinful people around them, but to give their absolute loyalty and exclusive devotion to him. Pagan worship simply cannot be mixed with the worship of the holy God. As Jesus pointed out, "No servant can serve two masters. . . . You cannot serve both God and Money" (Luke 16:13). Love of money is the god of this age, and many Christians attempt to make a treaty with this enslaving god. Are you trying to worship two gods at once? Where is your first allegiance?

34:13 Asherah poles were wooden poles that stood by Baal's altar (see Judges 6:25). Asherah was the goddess who was the consort (wife) of Baal. She represented good luck in agriculture and fertility.

34:18 The month of Abib corresponds to the end of March and the beginning of April.

these words I have made a covenant with you and with Israel." 28 Moses was there
with the LORD forty days and forty nights[o] without eating bread or drinking water.
And he wrote on the tablets[p] the words of the covenant—the Ten Commandments.[q]

The Radiant Face of Moses

29 When Moses came down from Mount Sinai with the two tablets of the Testimony
in his hands,[r] he was not aware that his face was radiant[s] because he had spoken
with the LORD. 30 When Aaron and all the Israelites saw Moses, his face was radiant,
and they were afraid to come near him. 31 But Moses called to them; so Aaron and
all the leaders of the community came back to him, and he spoke to them. 32 Afterwards all the Israelites came near him, and he gave them all the commands[t] the LORD
had given him on Mount Sinai.
33 When Moses finished speaking to them, he put a veil[u] over his face. 34 But
whenever he entered the LORD's presence to speak with him, he removed the veil until
he came out. And when he came out and told the Israelites what he had been
commanded, 35 they saw that his face was radiant. Then Moses would put the veil back
over his face until he went in to speak with the LORD.

4. Tabernacle construction

Sabbath Regulations

35 Moses assembled the whole Israelite community and said to them, "These are
the things the LORD has commanded[a] you to do: 2 For six days, work is to be
done, but the seventh day shall be your holy day, a Sabbath[b] of rest to the LORD.
Whoever does any work on it must be put to death. 3 Do not light a fire in any of your
dwellings on the Sabbath day."[c]

Materials for the Tabernacle

4 Moses said to the whole Israelite community, "This is what the LORD has commanded: 5 From what you have, take an offering for the LORD. Everyone who is willing
is to bring to the LORD an offering of gold, silver and bronze; 6 blue, purple and scarlet
yarn and fine linen; goat hair; 7 ram skins dyed red and hides of sea cows;**a** acacia
wood; 8 olive oil for the light; spices for the anointing oil and for the fragrant incense;
9 and onyx stones and other gems to be mounted on the ephod and breastpiece.
10 "All who are skilled among you are to come and make everything the LORD has
commanded:[d] 11 the tabernacle[e] with its tent and its covering, clasps, frames, crossbars, posts and bases; 12 the ark[f] with its poles and the atonement cover and the curtain
that shields it; 13 the table[g] with its poles and all its articles and the bread of the
Presence; 14 the lampstand[h] that is for light with its accessories, lamps and oil for the
light; 15 the altar[i] of incense with its poles, the anointing oil[j] and the fragrant
incense;[k] the curtain for the doorway at the entrance to the tabernacle; 16 the altar[l]
of burnt offering with its bronze grating, its poles and all its utensils; the bronze basin
with its stand; 17 the curtains of the courtyard with its posts and bases, and the curtain
for the entrance to the courtyard;[m] 18 the tent pegs for the tabernacle and for the
courtyard, and their ropes; 19 the woven garments worn for ministering in the sanctuary—both the sacred garments[n] for Aaron the priest and the garments for his sons
when they serve as priests."
20 Then the whole Israelite community withdrew from Moses' presence, 21 and

a *7* That is, large aquatic mammals; also in verse 23

34:28 [o]Ge 7:4; Ex 24:18; Mt 4:2 [p]ver 1; Ex 31:18 [q]Dt 4:13; 10:4
34:29 [r]Ex 32:15 [s]Ps 34:5; Mt 17:2; 2Co 3:7, 13
34:32 [t]Ex 24:3
34:33 [u]2Co 3:13
35:1 [a]Ex 34:32
35:2 [b]Ex 20:9-10; 34:21; Lev 23:3
35:3 [c]Ex 16:23
35:10 [d]Ex 31:6
35:11 [e]Ex 26:1-37
35:12 [f]Ex 25:10-22
35:13 [g]Ex 25:23-30; Lev 24:5-6
35:14 [h]Ex 25:31
35:15 [i]Ex 30:1-6 [j]Ex 30:25 [k]Ex 30:34-38
35:16 [l]Ex 27:1-8
35:17 [m]Ex 27:9
35:19 [n]Ex 28:2; 31:10; 39:1

34:28–35 Moses' face was radiant after he spent time with God. The people could clearly see God's presence in him. How often do you spend time alone with God? Although your face may not light up a room, time spent in prayer, reading the Bible, and meditating should have such an effect on your life that people will know you have been with God.

35:5–21 God did not require these special offerings, but he appealed to people with generous hearts. Only those who were willing to give were invited to participate. God loves cheerful givers (2 Corinthians 9:7). Our giving should be from love and generosity, not from a guilty conscience.

35:10–19 Moses asked people with various abilities to help with the tabernacle. Every one of God's people has been given special abilities. We are responsible to develop these abilities—even the ones not considered religious—and to use them for God's glory. We can become skilled through study, by watching others, and through practice. Work on your skills or abilities that could help your church or community.

35:23 [o]1Ch 29:8
35:25 [p]Ex 28:3
35:27 [q]1Ch 29:6; Ezr 2:68

everyone who was willing and whose heart moved him came and brought an offering
to the LORD for the work on the Tent of Meeting, for all its service, and for the sacred
garments. 22All who were willing, men and women alike, came and brought gold
jewellery of all kinds: brooches, ear-rings, rings and ornaments. They all presented
their gold as a wave offering to the LORD. 23Everyone who had blue, purple or scarlet
yarn[o] or fine linen, or goat hair, ram skins dyed red or hides of sea cows brought
them. 24Those presenting an offering of silver or bronze brought it as an offering to
the LORD, and everyone who had acacia wood for any part of the work brought it.
25Every skilled woman[p] spun with her hands and brought what she had spun—blue,
purple or scarlet yarn or fine linen. 26And all the women who were willing and had
the skill spun the goat hair. 27The leaders[q] brought onyx stones and other gems to

KEY TABERNACLE PIECES

Name	*Function and Significance*
Ark of the Covenant	• A golden rectangular box that contained the Ten Commandments • Symbolised God's covenant with Israel's people • Located in the Most Holy Place
Atonement Cover	• The lid to the ark of the covenant • Symbolised the presence of God among his people
Curtain	• The curtain that divided the two sacred rooms of the tabernacle—the Holy Place and the Most Holy Place • Symbolised how the people were separated from God because of sin
Table	• A wooden table located in the Holy Place of the tabernacle. The bread of the Presence and various utensils were kept on this table
Bread of the Presence	• Twelve loaves of baked bread, one for each tribe of Israel • Symbolised the spiritual nourishment God offers his people
Lampstands and Lamps	• A golden lampstand located in the Holy Place, which held seven burning oil lamps • The lampstand lighted the Holy Place for the priests
Altar of Incense	• An altar in the Holy Place in front of the curtain • Used for burning God's special incense and symbolic of acceptable prayer
Anointing Oil	• A special oil used to anoint the priests and all the pieces in the tabernacle • A sign of being set apart for God
Altar of Burnt Offering	• The bronze altar outside the tabernacle used for the sacrifices • Symbolised how sacrifice restored one's relationship with God
Basin	• A large wash basin outside the tabernacle used by the priests to cleanse themselves before performing their duties • Symbolised the need for spiritual cleansing

35:20–24 Where did the Israelites, who were once Egyptian slaves, get all this gold and jewellery? When the Hebrews left Egypt, they took with them the spoils from the land—all the booty they could carry (12:35, 36). This included gold, silver, jewels, linen, skins, and other valuables.

35:21 Those whose hearts were stirred gave cheerfully to the Tent of Meeting (also called the tabernacle). With great enthusiasm they gave because they knew how important their giving was to the completion of God's house. Airline pilots and computer operators can push test buttons to see if their equipment is functioning properly. God has a quick test button he can push to see the level of our commitment—our wallets. Generous people aren't necessarily faithful to God. But faithful people are always generous.

35:26 Those who spun cloth made a beautiful contribution to the tabernacle. Good workers take pride in the quality and beauty of their work. God is concerned with the quality and beauty of what you do. Whether you are a business executive or a shop cashier, your work should reflect the creative abilities God has given you.

be mounted on the ephod and breastpiece. 28 They also brought spices and olive oil
for the light and for the anointing oil and for the fragrant incense.[r] 29 All the Israelite
men and women who were willing[s] brought to the LORD freewill offerings[t] for all
the work the LORD through Moses had commanded them to do.

Bezalel and Oholiab

30 Then Moses said to the Israelites, "See, the LORD has chosen Bezalel son of Uri,
the son of Hur, of the tribe of Judah, 31 and he has filled him with the Spirit of God,
with skill, ability and knowledge in all kinds of crafts[u]— 32 to make artistic designs
for work in gold, silver and bronze, 33 to cut and set stones, to work in wood and to
engage in all kinds of artistic craftsmanship. 34 And he has given both him and
Oholiab[v] son of Ahisamach, of the tribe of Dan, the ability to teach[w] others. 35 He
has filled them with skill to do all kinds of work[x] as craftsmen, designers, embroider-
ers in blue, purple and scarlet yarn and fine linen, and weavers—all of them master
36 craftsmen and designers. 1 So Bezalel, Oholiab and every skilled person[a] to
whom the LORD has given skill and ability to know how to carry out all the
work of constructing the sanctuary[b] are to do the work just as the LORD has commanded."
2 Then Moses summoned Bezalel[c] and Oholiab[d] and every skilled person to whom
the LORD had given ability and who was willing[e] to come and do the work. 3 They
received from Moses all the offerings[f] the Israelites had brought to carry out the work
of constructing the sanctuary. And the people continued to bring freewill offerings
morning after morning. 4 So all the skilled craftsmen who were doing all the work on
the sanctuary left their work 5 and said to Moses, "The people are bringing more than
enough[g] for doing the work the LORD commanded to be done."
6 Then Moses gave an order and they sent this word throughout the camp: "No man
or woman is to make anything else as an offering for the sanctuary." And so the people
were restrained from bringing more, 7 because what they already had was more[h] than
enough to do all the work.

The Tabernacle

8 All the skilled men among the workmen made the tabernacle with ten curtains of
finely twisted linen and blue, purple and scarlet yarn, with cherubim worked into them
by a skilled craftsman. 9 All the curtains were the same size—twenty-eight cubits long
and four cubits wide.**a** 10 They joined five of the curtains together and did the same
with the other five. 11 Then they made loops of blue material along the edge of the
end curtain in one set, and the same was done with the end curtain in the other set.
12 They also made fifty loops on one curtain and fifty loops on the end curtain of the
other set, with the loops opposite each other. 13 Then they made fifty gold clasps and
used them to fasten the two sets of curtains together so that the tabernacle was a unit.[i]
14 They made curtains of goat hair for the tent over the tabernacle—eleven altogether. 15 All eleven curtains were the same size—thirty cubits long and four cubits
wide.**b** 16 They joined five of the curtains into one set and the other six into another
set. 17 Then they made fifty loops along the edge of the end curtain in one set and also
along the edge of the end curtain in the other set. 18 They made fifty bronze clasps
to fasten the tent together as a unit.[j] 19 Then they made for the tent a covering of ram
skins dyed red, and over that a covering of hides of sea cows.**c**
20 They made upright frames of acacia wood for the tabernacle. 21 Each frame was
ten cubits long and a cubit and a half wide,**d** 22 with two projections set parallel to
each other. They made all the frames of the tabernacle in this way. 23 They made

a *9* That is, about 42 feet (about 13 metres) long and 6 feet (about 1.8 metres) wide **b** *15* That is, about 45 feet (about 13.5 metres) long and 6 feet (about 1.8 metres) wide **c** *19* That is, large aquatic mammals **d** *21* That is, about 15 feet (about 4.5 metres) long and 2¼ feet (about 0.7 metre) wide

35:28 [r] Ex 25:6
35:29 [s] ver 21; 1Ch 29:9 [t] ver 4-9; Ex 25:1-7; 36:3; 2Ki 12:4
35:31 [u] ver 35; 2Ch 2:7, 14
35:34 [v] Ex 31:6 [w] 2Ch 2:14
35:35 [x] ver 31; Ex 31:3, 6; 1Ki 7:14
36:1 [a] Ex 28:3 [b] Ex 25:8
36:2 [c] Ex 31:2 [d] Ex 31:6 [e] Ex 25:2; 35:21, 26; 1Ch 29:5
36:3 [f] Ex 35:29
36:5 [g] 2Ch 24:14; 31:10; 2Co 8:2-3
36:7 [h] 1Ki 7:47
36:13 [i] ver 18
36:18 [j] ver 13

36:8, 9 Making cloth (spinning and weaving) took a great deal of time in Moses' day. To own more than two or three changes of clothes was a sign of wealth. The effort involved in making enough cloth for the tabernacle was staggering. The tabernacle would never have been built without tremendous community involvement. Today, churches and neighbourhoods often require this same kind of pulling together. Without it, many essential services wouldn't get done.

twenty frames for the south side of the tabernacle 24and made forty silver bases to go under them—two bases for each frame, one under each projection. 25For the other side, the north side of the tabernacle, they made twenty frames 26and forty silver bases—two under each frame. 27They made six frames for the far end, that is, the west end of the tabernacle, 28and two frames were made for the corners of the tabernacle at the far end. 29At these two corners the frames were double from the bottom all the way to the top and fitted into a single ring; both were made alike. 30So there were eight frames and sixteen silver bases—two under each frame.

31They also made crossbars of acacia wood: five for the frames on one side of the tabernacle, 32five for those on the other side, and five for the frames on the west, at the far end of the tabernacle. 33They made the centre crossbar so that it extended from end to end at the middle of the frames. 34They overlaid the frames with gold and made gold rings to hold the crossbars. They also overlaid the crossbars with gold.

35They made the curtain[k] of blue, purple and scarlet yarn and finely twisted linen, with cherubim worked into it by a skilled craftsman. 36They made four posts of acacia wood for it and overlaid them with gold. They made gold hooks for them and cast their four silver bases. 37For the entrance to the tent they made a curtain of blue, purple and scarlet yarn and finely twisted linen—the work of an embroiderer;[l] 38and they made five posts with hooks for them. They overlaid the tops of the posts and their bands with gold and made their five bases of bronze.

The Ark

37 Bezalel[a] made the ark[b] of acacia wood—two and a half cubits long, a cubit and a half wide, and a cubit and a half high.**[a]** 2He overlaid it with pure gold,[c] both inside and out, and made a gold moulding around it. 3He cast four gold rings for it and fastened them to its four feet, with two rings on one side and two rings on the other. 4Then he made poles of acacia wood and overlaid them with gold. 5And he inserted the poles into the rings on the sides of the ark to carry it.

6He made the atonement cover[d] of pure gold—two and a half cubits long and a cubit and a half wide.**[b]** 7Then he made two cherubim[e] out of hammered gold at the ends of the cover. 8He made one cherub on one end and the second cherub on the other; at the two ends he made them of one piece with the cover. 9The cherubim had their wings spread upwards, overshadowing[f] the cover with them. The cherubim faced each other, looking towards the cover.[g]

The Table

10They**[c]** made the table[h] of acacia wood—two cubits long, a cubit wide, and a cubit and a half high.**[d]** 11Then they overlaid it with pure gold[i] and made a gold moulding around it. 12They also made around it a rim a handbreadth**[e]** wide and put a gold moulding on the rim. 13They cast four gold rings for the table and fastened them to the four corners, where the four legs were. 14The rings[j] were put close to the rim to hold the poles used in carrying the table. 15The poles for carrying the table were made of acacia wood and were overlaid with gold. 16And they made from pure gold the articles for the table—its plates and dishes and bowls and its pitchers for the pouring out of drink offerings.

a *1* That is, about 3¾ feet (about 1.1 metres) long and 2¼ feet (about 0.7 metre) wide and high **b** *6* That is, about 3¾ feet (about 1.1 metres) long and 2¼ feet (about 0.7 metre) wide **c** *10* Or *He*; also in verses 11–29 **d** *10* That is, about 3 feet (about 0.9 metre) long, 1½ feet (about 0.5 metre) wide, and 2¼ feet (about 0.7 metre) high **e** *12* That is, about 3 inches (about 8 centimetres)

36:35 [k]Ex 39:38; Mt 27:51; Lk 23:45; Heb 9:3
36:37 [l]Ex 27:16
37:1 [a]Ex 31:2 [b]Ex 30:6; 39:35; Dt 10:3
37:2 [c]ver 11, 26
37:6 [d]Ex 26:34; 31:7; Heb 9:5
37:7 [e]Eze 41:18
37:9 [f]Heb 9:5 [g]Dt 10:3
37:10 [h]Heb 9:2
37:11 [i]ver 2
37:14 [j]ver 27

36:35 Cherubim are mighty angels.

37:1 The ark (also called the ark of the Testimony or ark of the covenant) was built to hold the Ten Commandments. It symbolised God's covenant with his people. Two gold angels called cherubim were placed on its top. The ark was Israel's most sacred object and was kept in the Most Holy Place in the tabernacle. Only once each year, the high priest entered the Most Holy Place to sprinkle blood on the top of the ark (called the atonement cover) to atone for the sins of the entire nation.

The Lampstand

17 They made the lampstand[k] of pure gold and hammered it out, base and shaft;
its flowerlike cups, buds and blossoms were of one piece with it. 18 Six branches
extended from the sides of the lampstand — three on one side and three on the other.
19 Three cups shaped like almond flowers with buds and blossoms were on one branch,
three on the next branch and the same for all six branches extending from the
lampstand. 20 And on the lampstand were four cups shaped like almond flowers with
buds and blossoms. 21 One bud was under the first pair of branches extending from
the lampstand, a second bud under the second pair, and a third bud under the third
pair — six branches in all. 22 The buds and the branches were all of one piece with the
lampstand, hammered out of pure gold.[l]
23 They made its seven lamps,[m] as well as its wick trimmers and trays, of pure gold.
24 They made the lampstand and all its accessories from one talent[f] of pure gold.

The Altar of Incense

25 They made the altar of incense[n] out of acacia wood. It was square, a cubit long
and a cubit wide, and two cubits high[g] — its horns[o] of one piece with it. 26 They
overlaid the top and all the sides and the horns with pure gold, and made a gold
moulding around it. 27 They made two gold rings[p] below the moulding — two on
opposite sides — to hold the poles used to carry it. 28 They made the poles of acacia
wood and overlaid them with gold.[q]
29 They also made the sacred anointing oil[r] and the pure, fragrant incense[s] — the
work of a perfumer.

The Altar of Burnt Offering

38 They[a] built the altar of burnt offering of acacia wood, three cubits[b] high; it
was square, five cubits long and five cubits wide.[c] 2 They made a horn at each
of the four corners, so that the horns and the altar were of one piece, and they overlaid
the altar with bronze.[a] 3 They made all its utensils[b] of bronze — its pots, shovels,
sprinkling bowls, meat forks and firepans. 4 They made a grating for the altar, a bronze
network, to be under its ledge, halfway up the altar. 5 They cast bronze rings to hold
the poles for the four corners of the bronze grating. 6 They made the poles of acacia
wood and overlaid them with bronze. 7 They inserted the poles into the rings so they
would be on the sides of the altar for carrying it. They made it hollow, out of boards.

Basin for Washing

8 They made the bronze basin[c] and its bronze stand from the mirrors of the women[d]
who served at the entrance to the Tent of Meeting.

The Courtyard

9 Next they made the courtyard. The south side was a hundred cubits[d] long and had
curtains of finely twisted linen, 10 with twenty posts and twenty bronze bases, and with
silver hooks and bands on the posts. 11 The north side was also a hundred cubits long
and had twenty posts and twenty bronze bases, with silver hooks and bands on the
posts.
12 The west end was fifty cubits[e] wide and had curtains, with ten posts and ten
bases, with silver hooks and bands on the posts. 13 The east end, towards the sunrise,
was also fifty cubits wide. 14 Curtains fifteen cubits[f] long were on one side of the
entrance, with three posts and three bases, 15 and curtains fifteen cubits long were on
the other side of the entrance to the courtyard, with three posts and three bases. 16 All
the curtains around the courtyard were of finely twisted linen. 17 The bases for the posts
were bronze. The hooks and bands on the posts were silver, and their tops were
overlaid with silver; so all the posts of the courtyard had silver bands.
18 The curtain for the entrance to the courtyard was of blue, purple and scarlet yarn

f *24* That is, about 75 pounds (about 34 kilograms) g *25* That is, about 1½ feet (about 0.5 metre) long and wide, and about 3 feet (about 0.9 metre) high a *1* Or *He*; also in verses 2–9 b *1* That is, about 4½ feet (about 1.4 metres) c *1* That is, about 7½ feet (about 2.3 metres) long and wide d *9* That is, about 150 feet (about 46 metres) e *12* That is, about 75 feet (about 23 metres) f *14* That is, about 22½ feet (about 6.9 metres)

37:17 [k]Heb 9:2; Rev 1:12
37:22 [l]ver 17; Nu 8:4
37:23 [m]Ex 40:4, 25
37:25 [n]Ex 30:34-36; Lk 1:11; Heb 9:4; Rev 8:3 [o]Ex 27:2; Rev 9:13
37:27 [p]ver 14
37:28 [q]Ex 25:13
37:29 [r]Ex 31:11 [s]Ex 30:1, 25; 39:38
38:2 [a]2Ch 1:5
38:3 [b]Ex 31:9
38:8 [c]Ex 30:18; 40:7 [d]Dt 23:17; 1Sa 2:22; 1Ki 14:24

38:20
[e]Ex 35:18

and finely twisted linen—the work of an embroiderer. It was twenty cubits[g] long and,
like the curtains of the courtyard, five cubits[h] high, 19 with four posts and four bronze
bases. Their hooks and bands were silver, and their tops were overlaid with silver.
20 All the tent pegs[e] of the tabernacle and of the surrounding courtyard were bronze.

38:21
[f]Nu 1:50, 53; 8:24; 9:15; 10:11; 17:7; 1Ch 23:32; 2Ch 24:6; Ac 7:44; Rev 15:5
[g]Nu 4:28, 33

38:22
[h]Ex 31:2

38:23
[i]Ex 31:6

38:24
[j]Ex 30:16
[k]Ex 30:13; Lev 27:25; Nu 3:47; 18:16

38:25
[l]Ex 30:12

38:26
[m]Ex 30:12
[n]Ex 30:13
[o]Ex 30:14
[p]Ex 12:37; Nu 1:46

38:27
[q]Ex 26:19

39:1
[a]Ex 35:23
[b]Ex 35:19
[c]ver 41; Ex 28:2

The Materials Used

21 These are the amounts of the materials used for the tabernacle, the tabernacle of
the Testimony,[f] which were recorded at Moses' command by the Levites under the
direction of Ithamar[g] son of Aaron, the priest. 22 (Bezalel[h] son of Uri, the son of
Hur, of the tribe of Judah, made everything the LORD commanded Moses; 23 with him
was Oholiab[i] son of Ahisamach, of the tribe of Dan—a craftsman and designer, and
an embroiderer in blue, purple and scarlet yarn and fine linen.) 24 The total amount
of the gold from the wave offering used for all the work on the sanctuary[j] was 29
talents and 730 shekels,[i] according to the sanctuary shekel.[k]
25 The silver obtained from those of the community who were counted in the
census[l] was 100 talents and 1,775 shekels,[j] according to the sanctuary
shekel—26 one beka per person,[m] that is, half a shekel,[k] according to the sanctuary
shekel,[n] from everyone who had crossed over to those counted, twenty years old or
more,[o] a total of 603,550 men.[p] 27 The 100 talents[l] of silver were used to cast the
bases[q] for the sanctuary and for the curtain—100 bases from the 100 talents, one
talent for each base. 28 They used the 1,775 shekels[m] to make the hooks for the posts,
to overlay the tops of the posts, and to make their bands.
29 The bronze from the wave offering was 70 talents and 2,400 shekels.[n] 30 They
used it to make the bases for the entrance to the Tent of Meeting, the bronze altar with
its bronze grating and all its utensils, 31 the bases for the surrounding courtyard and
those for its entrance and all the tent pegs for the tabernacle and those for the
surrounding courtyard.

The Priestly Garments

39 From the blue, purple and scarlet yarn[a] they made woven garments for
ministering in the sanctuary.[b] They also made sacred garments[c] for Aaron,
as the LORD commanded Moses.

The Ephod

2 They[a] made the ephod of gold, and of blue, purple and scarlet yarn, and of finely
twisted linen. 3 They hammered out thin sheets of gold and cut strands to be worked
into the blue, purple and scarlet yarn and fine linen—the work of a skilled craftsman.
4 They made shoulder pieces for the ephod, which were attached to two of its corners,
so that it could be fastened. 5 Its skilfully woven waistband was like it—of one piece
with the ephod and made with gold, and with blue, purple and scarlet yarn, and with
finely twisted linen, as the LORD commanded Moses.
6 They mounted the onyx stones in gold filigree settings and engraved them like a
seal with the names of the sons of Israel. 7 Then they fastened them on the shoulder

[g] *18* That is, about 30 feet (about 9 meters) [h] *18* That is, about 7½ feet (about 2.3 metres) [i] *24* The weight of the gold was about one ton (about 1 metric ton). [j] *25* The weight of the silver was about 3⅓ tons (about 3.4 metric tons). [k] *26* That is, about ⅕ ounce (about 6 grams) [l] *27* That is, about 3⅓ tons (about 3.4 metric tons) [m] *28* That is, about 45 pounds (about 20 kilograms) [n] *29* The weight of the bronze was about 2⅓ tons (about 2.4 metric tons). [a] *2* Or *He*; also in verses 7, 8 and 22

38:21 In building the tabernacle, Moses laid out the steps, but Ithamar supervised the project. We all have different talents and abilities. God didn't ask Moses to build the tabernacle but to motivate the experts to do it. Look for the areas where God has gifted you and then seek opportunities to allow God to use your gifts.

39:1–21 The priests wore a uniform to the tabernacle each day. Some of the pieces of their uniform were not only beautiful but also significant. Two parts of the high priest's uniform were the ephod and breastpiece. The ephod looked like a vest and was worn over the outer clothing. The breastpiece was fitted to the ephod (and sometimes was called the ephod). The breastpiece was made of coloured linens about nine inches square. On its front were attached 12 precious stones, each inscribed with the name of a tribe of Israel. This symbolised how the high priest represented all the people before God. The breastpiece also contained pockets that held two stones or plates called the Urim and Thummim. The high priest could determine God's will for the nation by consulting the Urim and Thummim. (See the note on 28:30.)

pieces of the ephod as memorial[d] stones for the sons of Israel, as the LORD commanded Moses.

The Breastpiece

8They fashioned the breastpiece[e]—the work of a skilled craftsman. They made it
like the ephod: of gold, and of blue, purple and scarlet yarn, and of finely twisted
linen. 9It was square—a span[b] long and a span wide—and folded double. 10Then
they mounted four rows of precious stones on it. In the first row there was a ruby,
a topaz and a beryl; 11in the second row a turquoise, a sapphire[c] and an emerald;
12in the third row a jacinth, an agate and an amethyst; 13in the fourth row a chrysolite,
an onyx and a jasper.[d] They were mounted in gold filigree settings. 14There were
twelve stones, one for each of the names of the sons of Israel, each engraved like a
seal with the name of one of the twelve tribes.[f]
15For the breastpiece they made braided chains of pure gold, like a rope. 16They
made two gold filigree settings and two gold rings, and fastened the rings to two of
the corners of the breastpiece. 17They fastened the two gold chains to the rings at the
corners of the breastpiece, 18and the other ends of the chains to the two settings,
attaching them to the shoulder pieces of the ephod at the front. 19They made two gold
rings and attached them to the other two corners of the breastpiece on the inside edge
next to the ephod. 20Then they made two more gold rings and attached them to the
bottom of the shoulder pieces on the front of the ephod, close to the seam just above
the waistband of the ephod. 21They tied the rings of the breastpiece to the rings of
the ephod with blue cord, connecting it to the waistband so that the breastpiece would
not swing out from the ephod—as the LORD commanded Moses.

Other Priestly Garments

22They made the robe of the ephod entirely of blue cloth—the work of a
weaver—23with an opening in the centre of the robe like the opening of a collar,[e]
and a band around this opening, so that it would not tear. 24They made pomegranates
of blue, purple and scarlet yarn and finely twisted linen around the hem of the robe.
25And they made bells of pure gold and attached them around the hem between the
pomegranates. 26The bells and pomegranates alternated around the hem of the robe
to be worn for ministering, as the LORD commanded Moses.
27For Aaron and his sons, they made tunics of fine linen[g]—the work of a
weaver—28and the turban[h] of fine linen, the linen headbands and the undergarments
of finely twisted linen. 29The sash was of finely twisted linen and blue, purple and
scarlet yarn—the work of an embroiderer—as the LORD commanded Moses.
30They made the plate, the sacred diadem, out of pure gold and engraved on it, like
an inscription on a seal: HOLY TO THE LORD. 31Then they fastened a blue cord to it
to attach it to the turban, as the LORD commanded Moses.

Moses Inspects the Tabernacle

32So all the work on the tabernacle, the Tent of Meeting, was completed. The
Israelites did everything just as the LORD commanded Moses.[i] 33Then they brought
the tabernacle to Moses: the tent and all its furnishings, its clasps, frames, crossbars,
posts and bases; 34the covering of ram skins dyed red, the covering of hides of sea
cows[f] and the shielding curtain; 35the ark of the Testimony[j] with its poles and the
atonement cover; 36the table with all its articles and the bread of the Presence; 37the
pure gold lampstand[k] with its row of lamps and all its accessories, and the oil for
the light; 38the gold altar,[l] the anointing oil, the fragrant incense, and the curtain[m]

[b] *9* That is, about 9 inches (about 23 centimetres) [c] *11* Or *lapis lazuli* [d] *13* The precise identification of some of these precious stones is uncertain. [e] *23* The meaning of the Hebrew for this word is uncertain. [f] *34* That is, large aquatic mammals

39:7 [d]Lev 24:7; Jos 4:7
39:8 [e]Lev 8:8
39:14 [f]Rev 21:12
39:27 [g]Lev 6:10
39:28 [h]Ex 28:4
39:32 [i]ver 42-43; Ex 25:9
39:35 [j]Ex 30:6
39:37 [k]Ex 25:31
39:38 [l]Ex 30:1-10 [m]Ex 36:35

39:32 The tabernacle was finally complete to the last detail. God was keenly interested in every minute part. The Creator of the universe was concerned about even the little things. Matthew 10:30 says that God knows the number of hairs on our heads. This shows that God is greatly interested in you. Don't be afraid to talk to him about any of your concerns—no matter how small or unimportant they might seem.

39:40 [n]Ex 27:9-19
39:42 [o]Ex 25:9
39:43 [p]Lev 9:22, 23; Nu 6:23-27; 2Sa 6:18; 1Ki 8:14, 55; 2Ch 30:27
40:2 [a]Nu 1:1 [b]ver 17; Ex 12:2
40:3 [c]ver 21; Nu 4:5; Ex 26:33
40:4 [d]Ex 25:30 [e]ver 22-25; Ex 26:35
40:5 [f]ver 26; Ex 30:1
40:7 [g]ver 30; Ex 30:18
40:9 [h]Ex 30:26; Lev 8:10
40:10 [i]Ex 29:36
40:12 [j]Lev 8:1-13
40:13 [k]Ex 28:41 [l]Lev 8:12
40:15 [m]Ex 29:9; Nu 25:13
40:17 [n]Nu 7:1 [o]ver 2
40:20 [p]Ex 16:34; 25:16; Dt 10:5; 1Ki 8:9; Heb 9:4
40:21 [q]Ex 26:33
40:22 [r]Ex 26:35
40:23 [s]ver 4
40:24 [t]Ex 26:35

for the entrance to the tent; 39the bronze altar with its bronze grating, its poles and
all its utensils; the basin with its stand; 40the curtains of the courtyard with its posts
and bases, and the curtain for the entrance to the courtyard;[n] the ropes and tent pegs
for the courtyard; all the furnishings for the tabernacle, the Tent of Meeting; 41and
the woven garments worn for ministering in the sanctuary, both the sacred garments
for Aaron the priest and the garments for his sons when serving as priests.
42The Israelites had done all the work just as the LORD had commanded Moses.[o]
43Moses inspected the work and saw that they had done it just as the LORD had
commanded. So Moses blessed[p] them.

Setting Up the Tabernacle

40 Then the LORD said to Moses: 2"Set up the tabernacle, the Tent of Meeting,[a]
on the first day of the first month.[b] 3Place the ark[c] of the Testimony in it
and shield the ark with the curtain. 4Bring in the table and set out what belongs on
it.[d] Then bring in the lampstand[e] and set up its lamps. 5Place the gold altar[f] of
incense in front of the ark of the Testimony and put the curtain at the entrance to the
tabernacle.
6"Place the altar of burnt offering in front of the entrance to the tabernacle, the Tent
of Meeting; 7place the basin[g] between the Tent of Meeting and the altar and put water
in it. 8Set up the courtyard around it and put the curtain at the entrance to the courtyard.
9"Take the anointing oil and anoint[h] the tabernacle and everything in it; consecrate
it and all its furnishings, and it will be holy. 10Then anoint the altar of burnt offering
and all its utensils; consecrate[i] the altar, and it will be most holy. 11Anoint the basin
and its stand and consecrate them.
12"Bring Aaron and his sons to the entrance to the Tent of Meeting and wash them
with water.[j] 13Then dress Aaron in the sacred garments,[k] anoint him and consecrate[l] him so that he may serve me as priest. 14Bring his sons and dress them in tunics.
15Anoint them just as you anointed their father, so that they may serve me as priests.
Their anointing will be to a priesthood that will continue for all generations to
come.[m]" 16Moses did everything just as the LORD commanded him.
17So the tabernacle[n] was set up on the first day of the first month[o] in the second
year. 18When Moses set up the tabernacle, he put the bases in place, erected the
frames, inserted the crossbars and set up the posts. 19Then he spread the tent over the
tabernacle and put the covering over the tent, as the LORD commanded him.
20He took the Testimony[p] and placed it in the ark, attached the poles to the ark
and put the atonement cover over it. 21Then he brought the ark into the tabernacle and
hung the shielding curtain[q] and shielded the ark of the Testimony, as the LORD
commanded him.
22Moses placed the table[r] in the Tent of Meeting on the north side of the tabernacle
outside the curtain 23and set out the bread[s] on it before the LORD, as the LORD
commanded him.
24He placed the lampstand[t] in the Tent of Meeting opposite the table on the south

---

39:42 Moses had learned his management lesson well. He gave important responsibilities to others and then trusted them to do the job. Great leaders, like Moses, give plans and direction while letting others participate on the team. If you are a leader, trust your assistants with key responsibilities.

39:43 Moses inspected the finished work, saw that it was done the way God wanted, and then blessed the people. A good leader follows up on assigned tasks and gives rewards for good work. In whatever responsible position you find yourself, follow up to make sure that tasks are completed as intended, and show your appreciation to the people who have helped.

40:1ff Moses was careful to obey God's instructions in the smallest detail. Notice that he didn't make a reasonable facsimile of God's description, but an exact copy. We should follow Moses' example and be fastidious about our obedience. If God has told you to do something, do it, do it right, and do it completely.

40:16 God told Moses how to build the tabernacle, and Moses delegated jobs in order to do it. God allows people to participate with him in carrying out his will. Your task is not just to sit and watch God work, but to give your best effort when work needs to be done.

40:17–33 The physical care of the tabernacle required a long list of tasks, and each was important to the work of God's house. This principle is important to remember today when God's house is the church. There are many seemingly unimportant tasks that must be done to keep your church building maintained. Washing dishes, painting walls, or shovelling snow may not seem very spiritual. But they are vital to the ministry of the church and have an important role in our worship of God.

side of the tabernacle 25and set up the lamps[u] before the LORD, as the LORD commanded him.
26Moses placed the gold altar[v] in the Tent of Meeting in front of the curtain 27and
burned fragrant incense on it, as the LORD commanded[w] him. 28Then he put up the
curtain[x] at the entrance to the tabernacle.
29He set the altar of burnt offering near the entrance to the tabernacle, the Tent of
Meeting, and offered on it burnt offerings and grain offerings,[y] as the LORD commanded him.
30He placed the basin[z] between the Tent of Meeting and the altar and put water
in it for washing, 31and Moses and Aaron and his sons used it to wash their hands
and feet. 32They washed whenever they entered the Tent of Meeting or approached
the altar,[a] as the LORD commanded Moses.
33Then Moses set up the courtyard[b] around the tabernacle and altar and put up the
curtain[c] at the entrance to the courtyard. And so Moses finished the work.

The Glory of the LORD

34Then the cloud[d] covered the Tent of Meeting, and the glory of the LORD filled
the tabernacle. 35Moses could not enter the Tent of Meeting because the cloud had
settled upon it, and the glory of the LORD filled the tabernacle.[e]
36In all the travels of the Israelites, whenever the cloud lifted from above the
tabernacle, they would set out;[f] 37but if the cloud did not lift, they did not set
out—until the day it lifted. 38So the cloud[g] of the LORD was over the tabernacle by
day, and fire was in the cloud by night, in the sight of all the house of Israel during
all their travels.

40:25 [u]ver 4; Ex 25:37
40:26 [v]ver 5; Ex 30:6
40:27 [w]Ex 30:7
40:28 [x]Ex 26:36
40:29 [y]ver 6; Ex 29:38-42
40:30 [z]ver 7
40:32 [a]Ex 30:20
40:33 [b]Ex 27:9 [c]ver 8
40:34 [d]Nu 9:15-23; 1Ki 8:12
40:35 [e]1Ki 8:11; 2Ch 5:13-14
40:36 [f]Nu 9:17-23; 10:13; Ne 9:19
40:38 [g]Ex 13:21; Nu 9:15; 1Co 10:1

40:34 The tabernacle was God's home on earth. He filled it with his glory—the overpowering sense of his presence. Almost 500 years later, Solomon built the temple, which replaced the tabernacle as the central place of worship. God also filled the temple with his glory (2 Chronicles 5:13, 14). But when Israel turned from God, his glory and presence departed from the temple and it was destroyed by invading armies (2 Kings 25). The temple was rebuilt in 516 B.C. God's glory returned in even greater splendour nearly five centuries later when Jesus Christ, God's Son, entered it and taught. When Jesus was crucified, God's glory again left the temple. However, God no longer needed a physical building after Jesus rose from the dead. God's temple now is his church, the body of believers.

40:38 The Israelites were once Egyptian slaves making bricks without straw. Here they were following the pillar of cloud and the pillar of fire, carrying the tabernacle they had built for God. Exodus begins in gloom and ends in glory. This parallels our progress through the Christian life. We begin as slaves to sin, are redeemed by God, and end our pilgrimage living with God for ever. The lessons the Israelites learned along the way we also need to learn.

LEVITICUS

Joseph dies 1805 B.C. (1640 B.C.)	*SLAVERY IN EGYPT*	*Exodus from Egypt 1446 (1280)*	*Ten Command-ments given 1445 (1279)*	*Israel camps at Mount Sinai 1444 (1278)*	*Moses dies, Canaan entered 1406 (1240)*	*Judges begin to rule 1375 (1220)*	*United kingdom under Saul 1050 (1045)*

"GOD seems so far away . . . if only I could see or hear him." Have you ever felt this way—struggling with loneliness, burdened by despair, riddled with sin, overwhelmed by problems? Made in God's image, we were created to have a close relationship with him; and when fellowship is broken, we are incomplete and need restoration. Communion with the living God is the essence of worship. It is vital, touching the very core of our lives. Perhaps this is why a whole book of the Bible is dedicated to worship. After Israel's dramatic exit from Egypt, the nation was camped at the foot of Mount Sinai for two years to listen to God (Exodus 19 to Numbers 10). It was a time of resting, teaching, building, and meeting with him face to face. Redemption in Exodus is the foundation for cleansing, worship, and service in Leviticus.

The overwhelming message of Leviticus is the holiness of God—"Be holy because I, the LORD your God, am holy" (19:2). But how can unholy people approach a holy God? The answer—first sin must be dealt with. Thus the opening chapters of Leviticus give detailed instructions for offering sacrifices, which were the active symbols of repentance and obedience. Whether bulls, grain, goats, or sheep, the sacrificial offerings had to be perfect, with no defects or bruises—pictures of the ultimate sacrifice to come, Jesus, the Lamb of God. Jesus has come and opened the way to God by giving up his life as the final sacrifice in our place. True worship and oneness with God begin as we confess our sin and accept Christ as the only one who can redeem us from sin and help us approach God.

In Leviticus, sacrifices, priests, and the sacred Day of Atonement opened the way for the Israelites to come to God. God's people were also to worship him with their lives. Thus we read of purity laws (11—15) and rules for daily living concerning family responsibilities, sexual conduct, relationships, worldliness (18—20), and vows (27). These instructions involve one's holy walk with God, and the patterns of spiritual living still apply today. Worship, therefore, has a horizontal aspect—that is, God is honoured by our lives as we relate to others.

The final emphasis in Leviticus is celebration. The book gives instructions for the feasts. These were special, regular, and corporate occasions for remembering what God had done, giving thanks to him, and rededicating lives to his service (23). Our Christian traditions and holidays are different, but they are necessary ingredients of worship. We too need special days of worship and celebration with our brothers and sisters to remember God's goodness in our lives.

As you read Leviticus, rededicate yourself to holiness, worshipping God in private confession, public service, and group celebration.

VITAL STATISTICS

PURPOSE:
A handbook for the priests and Levites outlining their duties in worship, and a guidebook of holy living for the Hebrews

AUTHOR:
Moses

DATE OF EVENTS:
1445–1444 B.C.

SETTING:
At the foot of Mount Sinai. God is teaching the Israelites how to live as holy people.

KEY VERSE:
"Be holy because I, the LORD your God, am holy" (19:2).

KEY PEOPLE:
Moses, Aaron, Nadab, Abihu, Eleazar, Ithamar

KEY PLACE:
Mount Sinai

SPECIAL FEATURE:
Holiness is mentioned more times (152) than in any other book of the Bible.

THE BLUEPRINT

A. WORSHIPPING A HOLY GOD (1:1—17:16) 1. Instructions for the offerings 2. Instructions for the priests 3. Instructions for the people 4. Instructions for the altar	God provided specific directions for the kind of worship that would be pleasing to him. These instructions teach us about the nature of God and can help us develop a right attitude towards worship. Through the offerings we learn of the seriousness of sin and the importance of bringing our sins to God for forgiveness.
B. LIVING A HOLY LIFE (18:1—27:34) 1. Standards for the people 2. Rules for priests 3. Seasons and festivals 4. Receiving God's blessing	God gave clear standards for living a holy life to the Israelites. They were to be separate and distinct from the pagan nations around them. In the same way, all believers should be separated from sin and dedicated to God. God still wants to remove sin from the lives of his people.

MEGATHEMES

THEME	EXPLANATION	IMPORTANCE
Sacrifice/Offering	There are five kinds of offerings that fulfil two main purposes: one to show praise, thankfulness, and devotion; the other for atonement, the covering and removal of guilt and sin. Animal offerings demonstrated that the person was giving his or her life to God by means of the life of the animal.	The sacrifices (offerings) were for worship and forgiveness of sin. Through them we learn about the cost of sin, for we see that we cannot forgive ourselves. God's system says that a life must be given for a life. In the Old Testament, an animal's life was given to save the life of a person. But this was only a temporary measure until Jesus' death paid the penalty of sin for all people for ever.
Worship	Seven feasts were designated religious and national holidays. They were often celebrated in family settings. These events teach us much about worshipping God in both celebration and quiet dedication.	God's rules about worship set up an orderly, regular pattern of fellowship with him. They allowed times for celebration and thanksgiving as well as for reverence and rededication. Our worship should demonstrate our deep devotion.
Health	Civil rules for handling food, disease, and sex were taught. In these physical principles, many spiritual principles were suggested. Israel was to be different from the surrounding nations. God was preserving Israel from disease and community health problems.	We are to be different morally and spiritually from the unbelievers around us. Principles for healthy living are as important today as in Moses' time. A healthy environment and a healthy body make our service to God more effective.
Holiness	Holy means "separated" or "devoted". God removed his people from Egypt; now he was removing Egypt from the people. He was showing them how to exchange Egyptian ways of living and thinking for his ways.	We must devote every area of life to God. God desires absolute obedience in motives as well as practices. Though we do not observe all the worship practices of Israel, we are to have the same spirit of preparation and devotion.
Levites	The Levites and priests instructed the people in their worship. They were the ministers of their day. They also regulated the moral, civil, and ceremonial laws and supervised the health, justice, and welfare of the nation.	The Levites were servants who showed Israel the way to God. They provide the historical backdrop for Christ, who is our High Priest and yet our servant. God's true servants care for all the needs of their people.

1:1
[a]Ex 19:3; 25:22
[b]Nu 7:89

A. WORSHIPPING A HOLY GOD (1:1 – 17:16)

The Israelites have arrived safely at the foot of Mount Sinai, and the tabernacle has been completed. The people will spend a great deal of time here as God shows them a new way of life with clear instructions on how sinful people can relate to a holy God. These instructions help us avoid taking our relationship with the same holy God too lightly. We learn about the holiness and majesty of the God with whom we are allowed to have a personal relationship.

1. Instructions for the offerings

The Burnt Offering

1 The LORD called to Moses[a] and spoke to him from the Tent of Meeting.[b] He
said, 2"Speak to the Israelites and say to them: 'When any of you brings an
offering to the LORD, bring as your offering an animal from either the herd or the
flock.[c]

1:2
[c]Lev 22:18-19

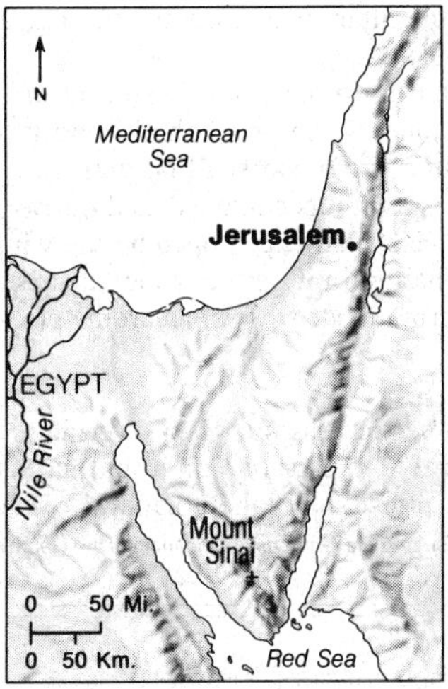

THE ISRAELITES AT MOUNT SINAI Throughout the book of Leviticus, the Israelites were camped at the foot of Mount Sinai. It was time to regroup as a nation and learn the importance of following God as they prepared to march towards the promised land.

1:1 The book of Leviticus begins where the book of Exodus ends – at the foot of Mount Sinai. The tabernacle was just completed (Exodus 35 – 40), and God was ready to teach the people how to worship there.

1:1 The Tent of Meeting was the smaller structure inside the larger tabernacle. The Tent of Meeting contained the sanctuary in one part and the Most Holy Place with the ark in another part. These two sections were separated by a curtain. God revealed himself to Moses in the Most Holy Place. Exodus 33:7 mentions a "tent of meeting" where Moses met God before the tabernacle was constructed. Many believe it served the same function as the one described here.

1:1ff We may be tempted to dismiss Leviticus as a record of bizarre rituals of a different age. But its practices made sense to the people of the day and offer important insights for us into God's nature and character. Animal sacrifice seems obsolete and repulsive to many people today, but animal sacrifices were practised in many cultures in the Middle East. God used the form of sacrifice to teach his people about faith. Sin needed to be taken seriously. When people saw the sacrificial animals being killed, they were made aware of the importance of their sin and guilt. Our culture's casual attitude towards sin ignores the cost of sin and need for repentance and restoration. Although many of the rituals of Leviticus were designed for the culture of the day, their purpose was to reveal a high and holy God who should be loved, obeyed, and worshipped. God's laws and sacrifices were intended to bring out true devotion of the heart. The ceremonies and rituals were the best way for the Israelites to focus their lives on God.

1:2 Was there any difference between a sacrifice and an offering? In Leviticus the words are interchanged. Usually a specific sacrifice is called an offering (burnt offering, grain offering, fellowship offering). Offerings in general are called sacrifices. The point is that each person *offered* a gift to God by *sacrificing* it on the altar. In the Old Testament, the sacrifice was the only way to approach God and restore a relationship with him. There was more than one kind of offering or sacrifice. The variety of sacrifices made them more meaningful because each one related to a specific life situation. Sacrifices were given in praise, worship, and thanksgiving, as well as for forgiveness and fellowship. The first seven chapters of Leviticus describe the variety of offerings and how they were to be used.

1:2 When God taught his people to worship him, he placed great emphasis on sacrifices. Why? Sacrifices were God's Old Testament way for people to ask forgiveness for their sins. Since creation, God has made it clear that sin separates people from him, and that those who sin deserve to die. Because "all have sinned" (Romans 3:23), God designed sacrifice as a way to seek forgiveness and restore a relationship with him. Because he is a God of love and mercy, God decided from the very first that he would come into our world and die to pay the penalty for all humans. This he did in his Son who, while still God, became a human being. In the meantime, before God made this ultimate sacrifice of his Son, he instructed people to kill animals as sacrifices for sin.

Animal sacrifice accomplished two purposes: (1) the animal symbolically took the sinner's place and paid the penalty for sin, and (2) the animal's death represented one life given so that another life could be saved. This method of sacrifice continued throughout Old Testament times. It was effective in teaching and guiding the people and bringing them back to God. But in New Testament times, Christ's death became the last sacrifice needed. He took our punishment once and for all. Animal sacrifice is no longer required. Now, all people can be freed from the penalty of sin by simply believing in Jesus and accepting the forgiveness he offers.

3“ ‘If the offering is a burnt offering from the herd, he is to offer a male without
defect.[d] He must present it at the entrance to the Tent[e] of Meeting so that it[a] will
be acceptable to the LORD. 4He is to lay his hand on the head[f] of the burnt offering,
and it will be accepted on his behalf to make atonement[g] for him. 5He is to slaughter[h]
the young bull before the LORD, and then Aaron’s sons the priests shall bring the blood
and sprinkle it against the altar on all sides[i] at the entrance to the Tent of Meeting.
6He is to skin[j] the burnt offering and cut it into pieces. 7The sons of Aaron the priest
are to put fire on the altar and arrange wood[k] on the fire. 8Then Aaron’s sons the
priests shall arrange the pieces, including the head and the fat,[l] on the burning wood
that is on the altar. 9He is to wash the inner parts and the legs with water, and the
priest is to burn all of it on the altar.[m] It is a burnt offering, an offering made by fire,
an aroma pleasing to the LORD.[n]
10“ ‘If the offering is a burnt offering from the flock, from either the sheep or the
goats,[o] he is to offer a male without defect. 11He is to slaughter it at the north side
of the altar before the LORD, and Aaron’s sons the priests shall sprinkle its blood
against the altar on all sides.[p] 12He is to cut it into pieces, and the priest shall arrange
them, including the head and the fat, on the burning wood that is on the altar. 13He
is to wash the inner parts and the legs with water, and the priest is to bring all of it
and burn it on the altar. It is a burnt offering, an offering made by fire, an aroma
pleasing to the LORD.
14“ ‘If the offering to the LORD is a burnt offering of birds, he is to offer a dove
or a young pigeon.[q] 15The priest shall bring it to the altar, wring off the head and
burn it on the altar; its blood shall be drained out on the side of the altar.[r] 16He is
to remove the crop with its contents[b] and throw it to the east side of the altar, where
the ashes[s] are. 17He shall tear it open by the wings, not severing it completely,[t] and
then the priest shall burn it on the wood[u] that is on the fire on the altar. It is a burnt
offering, an offering made by fire, an aroma pleasing to the LORD.

The Grain Offering

2 “ ‘When someone brings a grain offering[a] to the LORD, his offering is to be of
fine flour. He is to pour oil[b] on it, put incense on it 2and take it to Aaron’s sons
the priests. The priest shall take a handful of the fine flour[c] and oil, together with

[a] *3* Or *he* [b] *16* Or *crop and the feathers*; the meaning of the Hebrew for this word is uncertain.

1:3 [d]Ex 12:5; Dt 15:21; Heb 9:14; 1Pe 1:19 [e]Lev 17:9
1:4 [f]Ex 29:10, 15; Lev 3:2 [g]2Ch 29:23-24
1:5 [h]Lev 3:2, 8 [i]Heb 12:24; 1Pe 1:2
1:6 [j]Lev 7:8
1:7 [k]Lev 6:12
1:8 [l]ver 12
1:9 [m]Ex 29:18 [n]ver 13; Ge 8:21; Nu 15:8-10; Eph 5:2
1:10 [o]ver 3; Ex 12:5
1:11 [p]ver 5
1:14 [q]Ge 15:9; Lev 5:7; Lk 2:24
1:15 [r]Lev 5:9
1:16 [s]Lev 6:10
1:17 [t]Ge 15:10 [u]Lev 5:8
2:1 [a]Lev 6:14-18 [b]Nu 15:4
2:2 [c]Lev 5:11

1:3, 4 The first offering God describes is the burnt offering. A person who had sinned brought an animal with no defects to a priest. The unblemished animal symbolised the moral perfection demanded by a holy God and the perfect nature of the real sacrifice to come – Jesus Christ. The person then laid his hand on the head of the animal to symbolise the person’s complete identification with the animal as his substitute. Then he killed the animal and the priest sprinkled the blood. He symbolically transferred his sins to the animal, and thus his sins were taken away (atonement). Finally the animal (except for the blood and skin) was burned on the altar, signifying the person’s complete dedication to God. God required more than a sacrifice, of course. He also asked the sinner to have an attitude of repentance. The outward symbol (the sacrifice) and the inner change (repentance) were to work together. But it is important to remember that neither sacrifice nor repentance actually caused the sin to be taken away. God alone forgives sin. Fortunately for us, forgiveness is part of God’s loving nature. Have you come to him to receive forgiveness?

1:3ff What did sacrifices teach the people? (1) By requiring perfect animals and holy priests, they taught reverence for a holy God. (2) By demanding exact obedience, they taught total submission to God’s laws. (3) By requiring an animal of great value, they showed the high cost of sin and demonstrated the sincerity of their commitment to God.

1:3–13 Why are there such detailed regulations for each offering? God had a purpose in giving these commands. Starting from scratch, he was teaching his people a whole new way of life, cleansing them from the many pagan practices they had learned in Egypt, and restoring true worship of himself. The strict details kept Israel from slipping back into their old life-style. In addition, each law paints a graphic picture of the seriousness of sin and of God’s great mercy in forgiving sinners.

1:4ff Israel was not the only nation to sacrifice animals. Many other religions did it as well to try to please their gods. Some cultures even included human sacrifice, which was strictly forbidden by God. However, the meaning of Israel’s animal sacrifices was clearly different from that of their pagan neighbours. Israelites sacrificed animals, not just to appease God’s wrath, but as a substitute for the punishment they deserved for their sins. A sacrifice showed faith in God and commitment to his laws. Most important, this system foreshadowed the day when the Lamb of God (Jesus Christ) would die and conquer sin once and for all.

1:13 The “aroma pleasing to the LORD” is a way of saying that God accepted the sacrifice because of the people’s attitude.

2:1ff The grain offering accompanied all burnt offerings and was a gift of thanks to God. It reminded the people that their food came from God and that therefore they owed their lives to him. Three kinds of grain offerings are listed: (1) fine flour with oil and incense, (2) baked cakes or wafers of fine flour and oil, and (3) roasted kernels of grain (corn) with oil and incense. The absence of yeast symbolised the absence of sin, and the oil symbolised God’s presence. Part of the grain offering was burned on the altar as a gift to God, and the rest was eaten by the priests. The offerings helped support them in their work.

2:2 [d]Lev 6:15; Isa 66:3 [e]ver 9, 16; Lev 5:12; 6:15; 24:7; Ac 10:4
2:3 [f]ver 10; Lev 6:16; 10:12, 13
2:4 [g]Ex 29:2
2:7 [h]Lev 7:9
2:9 [i]ver 2 [j]Ex 29:18; Lev 6:15
2:10 [k]ver 3
2:11 [l]Ex 23:18; 34:25; Lev 6:16
2:12 [m]Lev 7:13; 23:10
2:13 [n]Nu 18:19; Eze 43:24
2:14 [o]Lev 23:10

all the incense,[d] and burn this as a memorial portion[e] on the altar, an offering made
by fire, an aroma pleasing to the LORD. 3The rest of the grain offering belongs to Aaron
and his sons;[f] it is a most holy part of the offerings made to the LORD by fire.
4" 'If you bring a grain offering baked in an oven, it is to consist of fine flour: cakes
made without yeast and mixed with oil, or[a] wafers made without yeast and spread
with oil.[g] 5If your grain offering is prepared on a griddle, it is to be made of fine
flour mixed with oil, and without yeast. 6Crumble it and pour oil on it; it is a grain
offering. 7If your grain offering is cooked in a pan,[h] it is to be made of fine flour
and oil. 8Bring the grain offering made of these things to the LORD; present it to the
priest, who shall take it to the altar. 9He shall take out the memorial portion[i] from
the grain offering and burn it on the altar as an offering made by fire, an aroma pleasing
to the LORD.[j] 10The rest of the grain offering belongs to Aaron and his sons;[k] it is
a most holy part of the offerings made to the LORD by fire.
11" 'Every grain offering you bring to the LORD must be made without yeast,[l] for
you are not to burn any yeast or honey in an offering made to the LORD by fire. 12You
may bring them to the LORD as an offering of the firstfruits,[m] but they are not to be
offered on the altar as a pleasing aroma. 13Season all your grain offerings with salt.
Do not leave the salt of the covenant[n] of your God out of your grain offerings; add
salt to all your offerings.
14" 'If you bring a grain offering of firstfruits[o] to the LORD, offer crushed heads

[a] 4 Or *and*

THE OFFERINGS
Listed here are the five key offerings the Israelites made to God. The Jews made these offerings in order to have their sins forgiven and to restore their fellowship with God. The death of Jesus Christ made these sacrifices unnecessary. Because of his death our sins were completely forgiven and fellowship with God has been restored.

Offering	*Purpose*	*Significance*	*Christ, the Perfect Offering*
Burnt Offering (Lev 1—voluntary)	To make payment for sins in general	Showed a person's devotion to God	Christ's death was the perfect offering
Grain Offering (Lev 2—voluntary)	To show honour and respect to God in worship	Acknowledged that all we have belongs to God	Christ was the perfect man, who gave all of himself to God and others
Fellowship Offering (Lev 3—voluntary)	To express gratitude to God	Symbolised peace and fellowship with God	Christ is the only way to fellowship with God
Sin Offering (Lev 4—required)	To make payment for unintentional sins of uncleanness, neglect, or thoughtlessness	Restored the sinner to fellowship with God; showed seriousness of sin	Christ's death restores our fellowship with God
Guilt Offering (Lev 5—required)	To make payment for sins against God and others. A sacrifice was made to God and the injured person was repaid or compensated	Provided compensation for injured parties	Christ's death takes away the deadly consequences of sin

2:11 Why was no yeast allowed in the grain offerings? Yeast is a bacterial fungus or mould and is, therefore, an appropriate symbol for sin. It grows in bread dough just as sin grows in a life. A little yeast will affect the whole loaf, just as a little sin can ruin a whole life. Jesus continued this analogy by warning about the "yeast of the Pharisees and Sadducees" (Matthew 16:6; Mark 8:15).

2:13 The offerings were seasoned with salt as a reminder of the people's covenant (contract) with God. Salt is a good symbol of God's activity in a person's life, because it penetrates, preserves, and aids in healing. God wants to be active in your life. Let him become part of you, penetrating every aspect of your life, preserving you from the evil all around, and healing you of your sins and shortcomings.

2:13 In Arab countries, an agreement was sealed with a gift of salt to show the strength and permanence of the contract. In Matthew 5:13 believers are called "the salt of the earth". Let the salt you use each day remind you that you are now one of God's covenant people who actively help preserve and purify the world.

2:14, 15 Crushed heads of new grain mixed with oil and baked was typical food for the average person. This offering was a token presentation of a person's daily food. In this way, people acknowledged God as provider of their food. Even a poor person could fulfil this offering. God was pleased by the motivation and the dedication of the persons making it.

of new grain roasted in the fire. 15 Put oil and incense on it; it is a grain offering. 16 The
priest shall burn the memorial portion[p] of the crushed grain and the oil, together with
all the incense, as an offering made to the LORD by fire.

The Fellowship Offering

3 " 'If someone's offering is a fellowship offering,[a][a] and he offers an animal from
the herd, whether male or female, he is to present before the LORD an animal
without defect.[b] 2 He is to lay his hand on the head[c] of his offering and slaughter
it[d] at the entrance to the Tent of Meeting. Then Aaron's sons the priests shall sprinkle
the blood against the altar on all sides. 3 From the fellowship offering he is to bring
a sacrifice made to the LORD by fire: all the fat[e] that covers the inner parts or is
connected to them, 4 both kidneys with the fat on them near the loins, and the covering
of the liver, which he will remove with the kidneys. 5 Then Aaron's sons[f] are to burn
it on the altar on top of the burnt offering[g] that is on the burning wood, as an offering
made by fire, an aroma pleasing to the LORD.
6 " 'If he offers an animal from the flock as a fellowship offering[h] to the LORD,
he is to offer a male or female without defect. 7 If he offers a lamb, he is to present
it before the LORD.[i] 8 He is to lay his hand on the head of his offering and slaughter
it[j] in front of the Tent of Meeting. Then Aaron's sons shall sprinkle its blood against
the altar on all sides. 9 From the fellowship offering he is to bring a sacrifice made
to the LORD by fire: its fat, the entire fat tail cut off close to the backbone, all the fat
that covers the inner parts or is connected to them, 10 both kidneys with the fat on them
near the loins, and the covering of the liver, which he will remove with the kidneys.
11 The priest shall burn them on the altar[k] as food,[l] an offering made to the LORD
by fire.
12 " 'If his offering is a goat, he is to present it before the LORD. 13 He is to lay his
hand on its head and slaughter it in front of the Tent of Meeting. Then Aaron's sons
shall sprinkle[m] its blood against the altar on all sides. 14 From what he offers he is
to make this offering to the LORD by fire: all the fat that covers the inner parts or is
connected to them, 15 both kidneys with the fat on them near the loins, and the covering
of the liver, which he will remove with the kidneys. 16 The priest shall burn them on
the altar as food, an offering made by fire, a pleasing aroma. All the fat is the
LORD's.[n]
17 " 'This is a lasting ordinance for the generations to come,[o] wherever you live:
You must not eat any fat or any blood.[p] ' "

The Sin Offering

4 The LORD said to Moses, 2 "Say to the Israelites: 'When anyone sins unintentionally[a] and does what is forbidden in any of the LORD's commands—
3 " 'If the anointed priest sins, bringing guilt on the people, he must bring to the
LORD a young bull[b] without defect as a sin offering[c] for the sin he has committed.
4 He is to present the bull at the entrance to the Tent of Meeting before the LORD.[d]
He is to lay his hand on its head and slaughter it before the LORD. 5 Then the anointed
priest shall take some of the bull's blood[e] and carry it into the Tent of Meeting. 6 He
is to dip his finger into the blood and sprinkle some of it seven times before the LORD,

a *1* Traditionally *peace offering*; also in verses 3, 6 and 9

2:16 [p]ver 2
3:1 [a]Lev 7:11-34 [b]Lev 1:3; 22:21
3:2 [c]Ex 29:10, 15 [d]Lev 1:5
3:3 [e]Ex 29:13
3:5 [f]Lev 7:29-34 [g]Ex 29:13, 38-42
3:6 [h]ver 1
3:7 [i]Lev 17:8-9
3:8 [j]ver 2; Lev 1:5
3:11 [k]ver 5 [l]ver 16; Lev 21:6, 17
3:13 [m]Ex 24:6
3:16 [n]1Sa 2:16
3:17 [o]Lev 6:18; 17:7 [p]Ge 9:4; Lev 7:25-26; 17:10-16; Dt 12:16; Ac 15:20
4:2 [a]Lev 5:15-18; Ps 19:12; Heb 9:7
4:3 [b]ver 14; Ps 66:15 [c]Lev 9:2-22; Heb 9:13-14
4:4 [d]Lev 1:3
4:5 [e]Lev 16:14

3:1ff A person gave a fellowship (or peace) offering as an expression of gratitude and a means of establishing fellowship between himself and God. Because it symbolised peace with God, part of the offering could be eaten by the person presenting it.

3:2 The altar was inside the walls of the tabernacle gate but outside the Tent of Meeting.

4:1ff Have you ever done something wrong without realising it until later? Although your sin was unintentional, it was still sin. One of the purposes of God's commands was to make the Israelites aware of their unintentional sins so they would not repeat them and so they could be forgiven for them. Leviticus 4 and 5 mention some of these unintentional sins and the way the Israelites could be forgiven for them. As you read more of God's laws, keep in mind that they were meant to teach and guide the people. Let them help you become more aware of sin in your life.

4:3 The sin offering was for those who (1) committed a sin without realising it or (2) committed a sin out of weakness or negligence as opposed to outright rebellion against God. Different animals were sacrificed for the different kinds of sin. The death of Jesus Christ was the final sin offering in the Bible (Hebrews 9:25–28 tells why).

in front of the curtain of the sanctuary. 7The priest shall then put some of the blood
on the horns of the altar of fragrant incense that is before the LORD in the Tent of
Meeting. The rest of the bull's blood he shall pour out at the base of the altar[f] of
burnt offering[g] at the entrance to the Tent of Meeting. 8He shall remove all the fat[h]
from the bull of the sin offering—the fat that covers the inner parts or is connected
to them, 9both kidneys with the fat on them near the loins, and the covering of the
liver, which he will remove with the kidneys[i]—10just as the fat is removed from the
ox[a] sacrificed as a fellowship offering.[b] Then the priest shall burn them on the altar
of burnt offering. 11But the hide of the bull and all its flesh, as well as the head and
legs, the inner parts and offal[j]—12that is, all the rest of the bull—he must take
outside the camp[k] to a place ceremonially clean,[l] where the ashes are thrown, and
burn it in a wood fire on the ash heap.

13" 'If the whole Israelite community sins unintentionally[m] and does what is forbidden in any of the LORD's commands, even though the community is unaware of the
matter, they are guilty. 14When they become aware of the sin they committed, the
assembly must bring a young bull[n] as a sin offering[o] and present it before the Tent
of Meeting. 15The elders of the community are to lay their hands on the bull's head[p]
before the LORD, and the bull shall be slaughtered before the LORD. 16Then the
anointed priest is to take some of the bull's blood[q] into the Tent of Meeting. 17He
shall dip his finger into the blood and sprinkle it before the LORD[r] seven times in
front of the curtain. 18He is to put some of the blood on the horns of the altar that
is before the LORD[s] in the Tent of Meeting. The rest of the blood he shall pour out
at the base of the altar of burnt offering at the entrance to the Tent of Meeting. 19He
shall remove all the fat[t] from it and burn it on the altar, 20and do with this bull just
as he did with the bull for the sin offering. In this way the priest will make atonement[u]
for them, and they will be forgiven.[v] 21Then he shall take the bull outside the camp
and burn it as he burned the first bull. This is the sin offering for the community.[w]

22" 'When a leader[x] sins unintentionally[y] and does what is forbidden in any of
the commands of the LORD his God, he is guilty. 23When he is made aware of the
sin he committed, he must bring as his offering a male goat without defect. 24He is
to lay his hand on the goat's head and slaughter it at the place where the burnt offering
is slaughtered before the LORD. It is a sin offering. 25Then the priest shall take some
of the blood of the sin offering with his finger and put it on the horns of the altar of
burnt offering and pour out the rest of the blood at the base of the altar.[z] 26He shall
burn all the fat on the altar as he burned the fat of the fellowship offering. In this way
the priest will make atonement for the man's sin, and he will be forgiven.[a]

27" 'If a member of the community sins unintentionally[b] and does what is forbidden
in any of the LORD's commands, he is guilty. 28When he is made aware of the sin
he committed, he must bring as his offering[c] for the sin he committed a female goat[d]
without defect. 29He is to lay his hand on the head[e] of the sin offering[f] and slaughter
it at the place of the burnt offering. 30Then the priest is to take some of the blood with
his finger and put it on the horns of the altar of burnt offering[g] and pour out the rest
of the blood at the base of the altar. 31He shall remove all the fat, just as the fat is
removed from the fellowship offering, and the priest shall burn it on the altar as an
aroma pleasing to the LORD.[h] In this way the priest will make atonement for him,
and he will be forgiven.
32" 'If he brings a lamb as his sin offering, he is to bring a female without defect.[i]
33He is to lay his hand on its head and slaughter it for a sin offering at the place where
the burnt offering is slaughtered.[j] 34Then the priest shall take some of the blood of
the sin offering with his finger and put it on the horns of the altar of burnt offering
and pour out the rest of the blood at the base of the altar.[k] 35He shall remove all the
fat, just as the fat is removed from the lamb of the fellowship offering, and the priest
shall burn it on the altar[l] on top of the offerings made to the LORD by fire. In this

a *10* The Hebrew word can include both male and female. b *10* Traditionally *peace offering;* also in verses 26, 31 and 35

4:7 f ver 34; Lev 8:15 g ver 18, 30; Lev 5:9; 9:9; 16:18
4:8 h Lev 3:3-5
4:9 i Lev 3:4
4:11 j Ex 29:14; Lev 9:11; Nu 19:5
4:12 k Heb 13:11 l Lev 6:11
4:13 m ver 2; Lev 5:2-4, 17; Nu 15:24-26
4:14 n ver 3 o ver 23, 28
4:15 p Lev 1:4; 8:14, 22; Nu 8:10
4:16 q ver 5
4:17 r ver 6
4:18 s ver 7
4:19 t ver 8
4:20 u Heb 10:10-12 v Nu 15:25
4:21 w Lev 16:5, 15
4:22 x Nu 31:13 y ver 2
4:25 z ver 7, 18, 30, 34; Lev 9:9
4:26 a Lev 5:10
4:27 b ver 2; Nu 15:27
4:28 c ver 23 d ver 3
4:29 e ver 4, 24 f Lev 1:4
4:30 g ver 7
4:31 h Ge 8:21
4:32 i ver 28
4:33 j ver 29
4:34 k ver 7
4:35 l ver 26, 31

way the priest will make atonement for him for the sin he has committed, and he will
be forgiven.

5 "'If a person sins because he does not speak up when he hears a public charge
to testify[a] regarding something he has seen or learned about, he will be held
responsible.[b]
2"'Or if a person touches anything ceremonially unclean—whether the carcasses
of unclean wild animals or of unclean livestock or of unclean creatures that move along
the ground[c]—even though he is unaware of it, he has become unclean and is guilty.
3"'Or if he touches human uncleanness[d]—anything that would make him unclean—even though he is unaware of it, when he learns of it he will be guilty.
4"'Or if a person thoughtlessly takes an oath[e] to do anything, whether good or
evil—in any matter one might carelessly swear about—even though he is unaware
of it, in any case when he learns of it he will be guilty.
5"'When anyone is guilty in any of these ways, he must confess[f] in what way he
has sinned 6and, as a penalty for the sin he has committed, he must bring to the LORD
a female lamb or goat from the flock as a sin offering;[g] and the priest shall make
atonement for him for his sin.
7"'If he cannot afford[h] a lamb, he is to bring two doves or two young pigeons
to the LORD as a penalty for his sin—one for a sin offering and the other for a burnt
offering. 8He is to bring them to the priest, who shall first offer the one for the sin
offering. He is to wring its head from its neck,[i] not severing it completely,[j] 9and
is to sprinkle some of the blood of the sin offering against the side of the altar; the
rest of the blood must be drained out at the base of the altar.[k] It is a sin offering.
10The priest shall then offer the other as a burnt offering in the prescribed way[l] and
make atonement for him for the sin he has committed, and he will be forgiven.[m]
11"'If, however, he cannot afford two doves or two young pigeons, he is to bring
as an offering for his sin a tenth of an ephah**[a]** of fine flour[n] for a sin offering. He
must not put oil or incense on it, because it is a sin offering. 12He is to bring it to
the priest, who shall take a handful of it as a memorial portion and burn it on the altar
on top of the offerings made to the LORD by fire. It is a sin offering. 13In this way
the priest will make atonement[o] for him for any of these sins he has committed, and
he will be forgiven. The rest of the offering will belong to the priest,[p] as in the case
of the grain offering.'"

The Guilt Offering

14The LORD said to Moses: 15"When a person commits a violation and sins unintentionally in regard to any of the LORD's holy things, he is to bring to the LORD as a
penalty[q] a ram[r] from the flock, one without defect and of the proper value in silver,
according to the sanctuary shekel.**[b]**[s] It is a guilt offering. 16He must make restitution[t] for what he has failed to do in regard to the holy things, add a fifth of the value[u]

a *11* That is, probably about 4 pints (about 2 litres) **b** *15* That is, about ⅖ ounce (about 11.5 grams)

5:1 [a]Pr 29:24 [b]ver 17
5:2 [c]Lev 11:11, 24-40; Dt 14:8
5:3 [d]Nu 19:11-16
5:4 [e]Nu 30:6, 8
5:5 [f]Lev 16:21; 26:40; Nu 5:7; Pr 28:13
5:6 [g]Lev 4:28
5:7 [h]Lev 12:8; 14:21
5:8 [i]Lev 1:15 [j]Lev 1:17
5:9 [k]Lev 4:7, 18
5:10 [l]Lev 1:14-17 [m]Lev 4:26
5:11 [n]Lev 2:1
5:13 [o]Lev 4:26 [p]Lev 2:3
5:15 [q]Lev 22:14 [r]Nu 5:8 [s]Ex 30:13
5:16 [t]Lev 6:4 [u]Lev 22:14; Nu 5:7

5:4 Have you ever sworn to do or not do something and then realised how foolish your promise was? God's people are called to keep their word, even if they make promises that are tough to keep. Jesus was warning against swearing (in the sense of making vows or oaths) when he said, "Simply let your 'Yes' be 'Yes', and your 'No,' 'No;' anything beyond this comes from the evil one" (Matthew 5:37). Our word should be enough. If we feel we have to strengthen it with an oath, something is wrong with our sincerity. The only promises we ought not to keep are promises that lead to sin. A wise and self-controlled person avoids making rash promises.

5:5 The entire system of sacrifices could not help a sinner unless he brought his offering with an attitude of repentance and a willingness to confess sin. Today, because of Christ's death on the cross, we do not have to sacrifice animals. But it is still vital to confess sin, because confession shows realisation of sin, awareness of God's holiness, humility before God, and willingness to turn from this sin (Psalm 51:16, 17). Even Jesus' death will be of little value to us if we do not repent and follow him. It is like a vaccine for a dangerous disease—it won't help unless it enters the bloodstream.

5:14–19 The guilt offering was a way of taking care of sin committed unintentionally. It was for those who sinned in some way against "holy things"—the tabernacle or the priesthood—as well as for those who unintentionally sinned against someone. In either case, a ram with no defects had to be sacrificed, plus those harmed by the sin had to be compensated for their loss, plus a 20 per cent penalty. Even though Christ's death has made guilt offerings unnecessary for us today, we still need to make things right with those we hurt.

to that and give it all to the priest, who will make atonement for him with the ram
as a guilt offering, and he will be forgiven.
17“If a person sins and does what is forbidden in any of the LORD’s commands, even
though he does not know it,[v] he is guilty and will be held responsible. 18He is to
bring to the priest as a guilt offering a ram from the flock, one without defect and
of the proper value. In this way the priest will make atonement for him for the wrong
he has committed unintentionally, and he will be forgiven.[w] 19It is a guilt offering;
he has been guilty of[c] wrongdoing against the LORD.”

6 The LORD said to Moses: 2“If anyone sins and is unfaithful to the LORD[a] by
deceiving his neighbour[b] about something entrusted to him or left in his care[c]
or stolen, or if he cheats him, 3or if he finds lost property and lies about it,[d] or if
he swears falsely, or if he commits any such sin that people may do—4when he thus
sins and becomes guilty, he must return[e] what he has stolen or taken by extortion,
or what was entrusted to him, or the lost property he found, 5or whatever it was he
swore falsely about. He must make restitution[f] in full, add a fifth of the value to it
and give it all to the owner on the day he presents his guilt offering.[g] 6And as a penalty
he must bring to the priest, that is, to the LORD, his guilt offering,[h] a ram from the
flock, one without defect and of the proper value. 7In this way the priest will make
atonement[i] for him before the LORD, and he will be forgiven for any of these things
he did that made him guilty.”

The Burnt Offering

8The LORD said to Moses: 9“Give Aaron and his sons this command: ‘These are
the regulations for the burnt offering: The burnt offering is to remain on the altar hearth
throughout the night, till morning, and the fire must be kept burning on the altar. 10The
priest shall then put on his linen clothes, with linen undergarments next to his body,[j]
and shall remove the ashes of the burnt offering that the fire has consumed on the altar
and place them beside the altar. 11Then he is to take off these clothes and put on others,
and carry the ashes outside the camp to a place that is ceremonially clean.[k] 12The
fire on the altar must be kept burning; it must not go out. Every morning the priest
is to add firewood and arrange the burnt offering on the fire and burn the fat of the
fellowship offerings[a] on it. 13The fire must be kept burning on the altar continuously;
it must not go out.

The Grain Offering

14“ ‘These are the regulations for the grain offering:[l] Aaron’s sons are to bring it
before the LORD, in front of the altar. 15The priest is to take a handful of fine flour
and oil, together with all the incense on the grain offering,[m] and burn the memorial
portion[n] on the altar as an aroma pleasing to the LORD. 16Aaron and his sons[o] shall
eat the rest[p] of it, but it is to be eaten without yeast[q] in a holy place;[r] they are to
eat it in the courtyard of the Tent of Meeting. 17It must not be baked with yeast; I
have given it as their share of the offerings made to me by fire. Like the sin offering
and the guilt offering, it is most holy.[s] 18Any male descendant of Aaron may eat it.[t]
It is his regular share of the offerings made to the LORD by fire for the generations
to come. Whatever touches it will become holy.’ ”[b][u]

c *19* Or *has made full expiation for his* a *12* Traditionally *peace offerings* b *18* Or *Whoever touches them must be holy*; similarly in verse 27

5:17 [v]ver 15; Lev 4:2
5:18 [w]ver 15
6:2 [a]Nu 5:6; Ac 5:4; Col 3:9 [b]Pr 24:28 [c]Ex 22:7
6:3 [d]Dt 22:1-3
6:4 [e]Lk 19:8
6:5 [f]Nu 5:7 [g]Lev 5:15
6:6 [h]Lev 5:15
6:7 [i]Lev 4:26
6:10 [j]Ex 28:39-42, 43; 39:28
6:11 [k]Lev 4:12
6:14 [l]Lev 2:1; 15:4
6:15 [m]Lev 2:9 [n]Lev 2:2
6:16 [o]Lev 2:3 [p]Eze 44:29 [q]Lev 2:11 [r]Lev 10:13
6:17 [s]ver 29; Ex 40:10; Nu 18:9, 10
6:18 [t]ver 29; Nu 18:9-10 [u]ver 27

6:1–7 Here we discover that stealing involves more than just taking from someone. Finding something and not returning it or refusing to return something borrowed are other forms of stealing. These are sins against God and not just your neighbour, a stranger, or a large business. If you have obtained something deceitfully, then confess your sin to God, apologise to the owner, and return the stolen items—with interest.

6:12, 13 While the previous offerings and sacrifices were ones that the people did, the section from 6:8—7:38 deals with priestly procedure. The burnt offering was presented in the morning and evening for the whole nation (see Exodus 29:38–43). The holy fire on the altar had to keep burning because God had started it. This represented God’s eternal presence in the sacrificial system. It showed the people that only by God’s gracious favour could their sacrifices be acceptable. God’s fire is present in each believer’s life today. He lights the fire when the Holy Spirit comes to live in us, and he tends it so that we will grow in grace as we walk with him. When we are aware that God lives in us, we have confidence to come to him for forgiveness and restoration. We can carry out our work with strength and enthusiasm.

19The LORD also said to Moses, 20"This is the offering Aaron and his sons are to
bring to the LORD on the day he[c] is anointed: a tenth of an ephah[d][v] of fine flour
as a regular grain offering,[w] half of it in the morning and half in the evening. 21Prepare
it with oil on a griddle;[x] bring it well-mixed and present the grain offering broken[e]
in pieces as an aroma pleasing to the LORD. 22The son who is to succeed him as
anointed priest shall prepare it. It is the LORD's regular share and is to be burned
completely. 23Every grain offering of a priest shall be burned completely; it must not
be eaten."

The Sin Offering

24The LORD said to Moses, 25"Say to Aaron and his sons: 'These are the regulations
for the sin offering: The sin offering is to be slaughtered before the LORD[y] in the
place[z] where the burnt offering is slaughtered; it is most holy. 26The priest who offers
it shall eat it; it is to be eaten in a holy place,[a] in the courtyard[b] of the Tent of
Meeting. 27Whatever touches any of the flesh will become holy,[c] and if any of the
blood is spattered on a garment, you must wash it in a holy place. 28The clay pot[d]
that the meat is cooked in must be broken; but if it is cooked in a bronze pot, the pot
is to be scoured and rinsed with water. 29Any male in a priest's family may eat it;[e]
it is most holy.[f] 30But any sin offering whose blood is brought into the Tent of
Meeting to make atonement in the Holy Place[g] must not be eaten; it must be burned.[h]

The Guilt Offering

7 " 'These are the regulations for the guilt offering,[a] which is most holy: 2The guilt
offering is to be slaughtered in the place where the burnt offering is slaughtered,
and its blood is to be sprinkled against the altar on all sides. 3All its fat[b] shall be
offered: the fat tail and the fat that covers the inner parts, 4both kidneys with the fat
on them near the loins, and the covering of the liver, which is to be removed with
the kidneys. 5The priest shall burn them on the altar as an offering made to the LORD
by fire. It is a guilt offering. 6Any male in a priest's family may eat it,[c] but it must
be eaten in a holy place; it is most holy.[d]
7" 'The same law applies to both the sin offering and the guilt offering: They belong
to the priest[e] who makes atonement with them. 8The priest who offers a burnt offering
for anyone may keep its hide for himself. 9Every grain offering baked in an oven or
cooked in a pan or on a griddle[f] belongs to the priest who offers it, 10and every grain
offering, whether mixed with oil or dry, belongs equally to all the sons of Aaron.

The Fellowship Offering

11" 'These are the regulations for the fellowship offering[a] a person may present
to the LORD:
12" 'If he offers it as an expression of thankfulness, then along with this thank-
offering[g] he is to offer cakes of bread made without yeast and mixed with oil, wafers[h]
made without yeast and spread with oil, and cakes of fine flour well-kneaded and
mixed with oil. 13Along with his fellowship offering of thanksgiving he is to present
an offering with cakes of bread made with yeast.[i] 14He is to bring one of each kind
as an offering, a contribution to the LORD; it belongs to the priest who sprinkles the
blood of the fellowship offerings. 15The meat of his fellowship offering of thanksgiving must be eaten on the day it is offered; he must leave none of it till morning.[j]
16" 'If, however, his offering is the result of a vow or is a freewill offering, the
sacrifice shall be eaten on the day he offers it, but anything left over may be eaten
on the next day.[k] 17Any meat of the sacrifice left over till the third day must be burned

[c] 20 Or *each* [d] 20 That is, probably about 4 pints (about 2 litres) [e] 21 The meaning of the Hebrew for this word is uncertain. [a] 11 Traditionally *peace offering*; also in verses 13–37

6:20 [v]Ex 16:36 [w]Ex 29:2
6:21 [x]Lev 2:5
6:25 [y]Lev 1:3 [z]Lev 1:5, 11
6:26 [a]ver 16 [b]Lev 10:17-18
6:27 [c]Ex 29:37
6:28 [d]Lev 11:33; 15:12
6:29 [e]ver 18 [f]ver 17
6:30 [g]Lev 4:18 [h]Lev 4:12
7:1 [a]Lev 5:14-6:7
7:3 [b]Ex 29:13; Lev 3:4, 9
7:6 [c]Lev 6:18; Nu 18:9-10 [d]Lev 2:3
7:7 [e]Lev 6:17, 26; 1Co 9:13
7:9 [f]Lev 2:5
7:12 [g]ver 13, 15 [h]Lev 2:4; Nu 6:15
7:13 [i]Lev 23:17; Am 4:5
7:15 [j]Lev 22:30
7:16 [k]Lev 19:5-8

7:11–18 The fellowship offering was divided into three kinds according to purpose: thanksgiving offering, vow offering, and freewill offering. A thanksgiving offering was appropriate whenever one wished to show thanks to God, as when recovering from a serious illness, or surviving a dangerous calamity (Psalm 107). A vow offering was given in fulfilment of a vow (2 Samuel 15:7, 8). The freewill offering, however, needed no special occasion or reason.

up. 18 If any meat of the fellowship offering is eaten on the third day, it will not be
accepted.[l] It will not be credited[m] to the one who offered it, for it is impure; the
person who eats any of it will be held responsible.
19 " 'Meat that touches anything ceremonially unclean must not be eaten; it must be
burned up. As for other meat, anyone ceremonially clean may eat it. 20 But if anyone
who is unclean eats any meat of the fellowship offering belonging to the LORD, that
person must be cut off from his people.[n] 21 If anyone touches something unclean[o]—whether human uncleanness or an unclean animal or any unclean, detestable
thing—and then eats any of the meat of the fellowship offering belonging to the LORD,
that person must be cut off from his people.' "

Eating Fat and Blood Forbidden

22 The LORD said to Moses, 23 "Say to the Israelites: 'Do not eat any of the fat of
cattle, sheep or goats.[p] 24 The fat of an animal found dead or torn by wild animals[q]
may be used for any other purpose, but you must not eat it. 25 Anyone who eats the
fat of an animal from which an offering by fire may be[b] made to the LORD must be
cut off from his people. 26 And wherever you live, you must not eat the blood[r] of
any bird or animal. 27 If anyone eats blood,[s] that person must be cut off from his
people.' "

The Priests' Share

28 The LORD said to Moses, 29 "Say to the Israelites: 'Anyone who brings a fellowship offering to the LORD is to bring part of it as his sacrifice to the LORD. 30 With
his own hands he is to bring the offering made to the LORD by fire; he is to bring the
fat, together with the breast, and wave the breast before the LORD as a wave offering.[t]
31 The priest shall burn the fat on the altar, but the breast belongs to Aaron and his
sons.[u] 32 You are to give the right thigh of your fellowship offerings to the priest as
a contribution.[v] 33 The son of Aaron who offers the blood and the fat of the fellowship
offering shall have the right thigh as his share. 34 From the fellowship offerings of the
Israelites, I have taken the breast that is waved and the thigh[w] that is presented and
have given them to Aaron the priest and his sons[x] as their regular share from the
Israelites.' "
35 This is the portion of the offerings made to the LORD by fire that were allotted
to Aaron and his sons on the day they were presented to serve the LORD as priests.
36 On the day they were anointed,[y] the LORD commanded that the Israelites give this
to them as their regular share for the generations to come.

37 These, then, are the regulations for the burnt offering,[z] the grain offering,[a] the
sin offering, the guilt offering, the ordination offering[b] and the fellowship offering,
38 which the LORD gave Moses on Mount Sinai on the day he commanded the Israelites
to bring their offerings to the LORD,[c] in the Desert of Sinai.

[b] 25 Or *fire is*

7:18 [l] Lev 19:7 [m] Nu 18:27
7:20 [n] Lev 22:3-7
7:21 [o] Lev 5:2; 11:24, 28
7:23 [p] Lev 3:17; 17:13-14
7:24 [q] Ex 22:31
7:26 [r] Ge 9:4
7:27 [s] Lev 17:10-24; Ac 15:20, 29
7:30 [t] Ex 29:24; Nu 6:20
7:31 [u] ver 34
7:32 [v] ver 34; Lev 9:21; Nu 6:20
7:34 [w] Lev 10:15 [x] Ex 29:27; Nu 18:18-19
7:36 [y] Ex 40:13, 15; Lev 8:12, 30
7:37 [z] Lev 6:9 [a] Lev 6:14 [b] ver 1, 11
7:38 [c] Lev 1:2

7:22–27 The fat portions were regarded as the best portions; therefore, it was appropriate to dedicate them only to God. Because blood was the river of life, and life was God's gift and his alone, blood had to be returned to God and not used by people.

7:28–30 God told the people of Israel to bring their fellowship offerings personally, with their own hands. They were to take time and effort to express thanks to God. You are the only person who can express your thankfulness to God and to others. Do you leave it to others to express thanks for what people have done? Do you rely on the one leading the prayer to thank God for you? Take time yourself to express thanks both to God and to others who have helped and blessed you.

7:31–36 The offering that was waved before the altar was called the wave offering. The part of the offering the priests waved was theirs to keep. The waving motion towards and away from the altar symbolised the offering of the sacrifice to God and his returning it to the priests. These offerings helped to care for the priests, who cared for God's house. The New Testament teaches that ministers should be paid by the people they serve (1 Corinthians 9:10). We should give generously to those who minister to us.

7:37 The ordination offering refers to the offering given at the ceremony when priests were inducted into office (8:22).

7:38 God gave his people many rituals and instructions to follow. All the rituals in Leviticus were meant to teach the people valuable lessons. But over time, the people became indifferent to the meanings of these rituals and they began to lose touch with God. When your church appears to be conducting dry, meaningless rituals, try rediscovering the original meaning and purpose behind each. Your worship will be revitalised.

2. Instructions for the priests

The Ordination of Aaron and His Sons

8 The LORD said to Moses, 2"Bring Aaron and his sons, their garments, the
anointing oil,[a] the bull for the sin offering, the two rams and the basket containing bread made without yeast,[b] 3and gather the entire assembly[c] at the entrance to
the Tent of Meeting." 4Moses did as the LORD commanded him, and the assembly
gathered at the entrance to the Tent of Meeting.
5Moses said to the assembly, "This is what the LORD has commanded to be done."
6Then Moses brought Aaron and his sons forward and washed them with water.[d] 7He
put the tunic on Aaron, tied the sash around him, clothed him with the robe and put
the ephod on him. He also tied the ephod to him by its skilfully woven waistband;
so it was fastened on him.[e] 8He placed the breastpiece on him and put the Urim and
Thummim[f] in the breastpiece. 9Then he placed the turban on Aaron's head and set
the gold plate, the sacred diadem,[g] on the front of it, as the LORD commanded Moses.
10Then Moses took the anointing oil[h] and anointed[i] the tabernacle and everything
in it, and so consecrated them. 11He sprinkled some of the oil on the altar seven times,
anointing the altar and all its utensils and the basin with its stand, to consecrate them.[j]
12He poured some of the anointing oil on Aaron's head and anointed[k] him to
consecrate him.[l] 13Then he brought Aaron's sons forward, put tunics on them, tied
sashes around them and put headbands on them, as the LORD commanded Moses.
14He then presented the bull[m] for the sin offering,[n] and Aaron and his sons laid
their hands on its head. 15Moses slaughtered the bull and took some of the blood, and
with his finger he put it on all the horns of the altar[o] to purify the altar.[p] He poured
out the rest of the blood at the base of the altar. So he consecrated it to make atonement
for it.[q] 16Moses also took all the fat around the inner parts, the covering of the liver,
and both kidneys and their fat, and burned it on the altar. 17But the bull with its hide
and its flesh and its offal[r] he burned up outside the camp,[s] as the LORD commanded
Moses.
18He then presented the ram[t] for the burnt offering, and Aaron and his sons laid
their hands on its head. 19Then Moses slaughtered the ram and sprinkled the blood
against the altar on all sides. 20He cut the ram into pieces and burned the head, the
pieces and the fat. 21He washed the inner parts and the legs with water and burned
the whole ram on the altar as a burnt offering, a pleasing aroma, an offering made
to the LORD by fire, as the LORD commanded Moses.

8:2 [a]Ex 30:23-25, 30 [b]Ex 29:2-3
8:3 [c]Nu 8:9
8:6 [d]Ex 29:4; 30:19; Ps 26:6; Ac 22:16; 1Co 6:11; Eph 5:26
8:7 [e]Ex 28:4
8:8 [f]Ex 28:30
8:9 [g]Ex 28:36
8:10 [h]ver 2 [i]Ex 30:26
8:11 [j]Ex 30:29
8:12 [k]Lev 21:10, 12 [l]Ex 30:30
8:14 [m]Lev 4:3 [n]Ps 66:15; Eze 43:19
8:15 [o]Lev 4:7 [p]Heb 9:22 [q]Eze 43:20
8:17 [r]Lev 4:11 [s]Lev 4:12
8:18 [t]ver 2

8:1ff Why did Aaron and his sons need to be cleansed and set apart? Although all the men from the tribe of Levi were dedicated for service to God, only Aaron's descendants could be priests. They alone had the honour and responsibility of performing the sacrifices. These priests had to cleanse and dedicate themselves before they could help the people do the same.

The ceremony described in Leviticus 8 and 9 was their ordination ceremony. Aaron and his sons were washed with water (8:6), clothed with special garments (8:7–9), and anointed with oil (8:12). They placed their hands on a young bull as it was killed (8:14), and on two rams as they were killed (8:18, 19, 22). This showed that holiness came from God alone, not from the priestly role. Similarly, we are not spiritually cleansed because we have a religious position. Spiritual cleansing comes only from God. No matter how high our position or how long we have held it, we must depend on God for spiritual vitality.

8:2, 3 Why were priests needed in Israel? In Exodus 19:6, the Israelites were instructed to be a kingdom of priests; ideally they would all be holy and relate to God. But from the time of Adam's fall, sin has separated man and God, and people have needed mediators to help them find forgiveness. At first, the patriarchs – heads of households like Abraham and Job – were priests of the house or clan and made sacrifices for the family. When the Israelites left Egypt, the descendants of Aaron were chosen to serve as priests for the nation. The priests stood in the gap between God and man. They were the full-time spiritual leaders and overseers of offerings. The priestly system was a concession to people's inability, because of sin, to confront and relate to God individually and corporately. In Christ, this imperfect system was transformed. Jesus Christ himself is our High Priest. Now all believers can approach God through him.

8:8 What were the Urim and Thummim? Little is known about them, but they were probably precious stones or flat objects that God used to give guidance to his people. The high priest kept them in a pouch attached to his breastpiece. Some scholars think the Urim may have been the *no* answer and the Thummim the *yes* answer. After a time of prayer for guidance, the priest would shake one of the stones out of the pouch, and God would cause the appropriate one to fall out. Another view is that the Urim and Thummim were small flat objects, each with a *yes* side and a *no* side. The priest spilled both from his pouch. If both landed on their *yes* sides, God's answer was positive. Two *no* sides were negative. A *yes* and a *no* meant no reply. God had a specific purpose for using this method of guidance – he was teaching a nation the principles of following him. Our situation is not the same, however, so we must not invent ways like this for God to guide us.

8:12 What was the significance of anointing Aaron as high priest? The high priest had special duties that no other priest had. He alone could enter the Most Holy Place in the tabernacle on the yearly Day of Atonement to atone for the sins of the nation. Therefore he was in charge of all the other priests. The high priest was a picture of Jesus Christ, who is our High Priest (Hebrews 7:26–28).

[22]He then presented the other ram, the ram for the ordination,[u] and Aaron and his sons laid their hands on its head. [23]Moses slaughtered the ram and took some of its blood and put it on the lobe of Aaron's right ear, on the thumb of his right hand and on the big toe of his right foot. [24]Moses also brought Aaron's sons forward and put some of the blood on the lobes of their right ears, on the thumbs of their right hands and on the big toes of their right feet. Then he sprinkled blood against the altar on all sides.[v] [25]He took the fat, the fat tail, all the fat around the inner parts, the covering of the liver, both kidneys and their fat and the right thigh. [26]Then from the basket of bread made without yeast, which was before the LORD, he took a cake of bread, and one made with oil, and a wafer; he put these on the fat portions and on the right thigh. [27]He put all these in the hands of Aaron and his sons and waved them before the LORD as a wave offering. [28]Then Moses took them from their hands and burned them on the altar on top of the burnt offering as an ordination offering, a pleasing aroma, an offering made to the LORD by fire. [29]He also took the breast—Moses' share of the ordination ram[w]—and waved it before the LORD as a wave offering, as the LORD commanded Moses.

[30]Then Moses took some of the anointing oil and some of the blood from the altar and sprinkled them on Aaron and his garments[x] and on his sons and their garments. So he consecrated[y] Aaron and his garments and his sons and their garments.

[31]Moses then said to Aaron and his sons, "Cook the meat at the entrance to the Tent of Meeting and eat it there with the bread from the basket of ordination offerings, as I commanded, saying,**[a]** 'Aaron and his sons are to eat it.' [32]Then burn up the rest of the meat and the bread. [33]Do not leave the entrance to the Tent of Meeting for seven days, until the days of your ordination are completed, for your ordination will last seven days. [34]What has been done today was commanded by the LORD[z] to make atonement for you. [35]You must stay at the entrance to the Tent of Meeting day and night for seven days and do what the LORD requires,[a] so that you will not die; for that is what I have been commanded." [36]So Aaron and his sons did everything the LORD commanded through Moses.

The Priests Begin Their Ministry

9 On the eighth day[a] Moses summoned Aaron and his sons and the elders of Israel. [2]He said to Aaron, "Take a bull calf for your sin offering and a ram for your burnt offering, both without defect, and present them before the LORD. [3]Then say to the Israelites: 'Take a male goat for a sin offering, a calf and a lamb—both a year old and without defect—for a burnt offering, [4]and an ox**[a]** and a ram for a fellowship offering**[b]** to sacrifice before the LORD, together with a grain offering mixed with oil. For today the LORD will appear to you.[b]' "

[5]They took the things Moses commanded to the front of the Tent of Meeting, and the entire assembly came near and stood before the LORD. [6]Then Moses said, "This is what the LORD has commanded you to do, so that the glory of the LORD[c] may appear to you."

[7]Moses said to Aaron, "Come to the altar and sacrifice your sin offering and your burnt offering and make atonement for yourself and the people; sacrifice the offering that is for the people and make atonement for them, as the LORD has commanded.[d]"

[8]So Aaron came to the altar and slaughtered the calf as a sin offering[e] for himself. [9]His sons brought the blood to him,[f] and he dipped his finger into the blood and put it on the horns of the altar; the rest of the blood he poured out at the base of the altar.[g] [10]On the altar he burned the fat, the kidneys and the covering of the liver from the

a *31* Or *I was commanded:* **a** *4* The Hebrew word can include both male and female; also in verses 18 and 19.
b *4* Traditionally *peace offering*; also in verses 18 and 22

8:22 [u]ver 2
8:24 [v]Heb 9:18-22
8:29 [w]Lev 7:31-34
8:30 [x]Ex 28:2 [y]Nu 3:3
8:34 [z]Heb 7:16
8:35 [a]Nu 3:7; 9:19; Dt 11:1; 1Ki 2:3; Eze 48:11
9:1 [a]Eze 43:27
9:4 [b]Ex 29:43
9:6 [c]ver 23; Ex 24:16
9:7 [d]Heb 5:1, 3; 7:27
9:8 [e]Lev 4:1-12
9:9 [f]ver 12, 18 [g]Lev 4:7

8:36 Aaron and his sons did "everything the LORD commanded". Considering the many detailed lists of Leviticus, that was a remarkable feat. They knew what God wanted, how he wanted it done, and with what attitude it was to be carried out. This can serve as a model for how carefully we ought to obey God. God wants us to be thoroughly holy people, not a rough approximation of the way his followers should be.

sin offering, as the LORD commanded Moses; 11 the flesh and the hide[h] he burned up
outside the camp.[i]
12 Then he slaughtered the burnt offering. His sons handed him the blood, and he
sprinkled it against the altar on all sides. 13 They handed him the burnt offering piece
by piece, including the head, and he burned them on the altar.[j] 14 He washed the inner
parts and the legs and burned them on top of the burnt offering on the altar.
15 Aaron then brought the offering that was for the people.[k] He took the goat for
the people's sin offering and slaughtered it and offered it for a sin offering as he did
with the first one.
16 He brought the burnt offering and offered it in the prescribed way.[l] 17 He also
brought the grain offering, took a handful of it and burned it on the altar in addition
to the morning's burnt offering.[m]
18 He slaughtered the ox and the ram as the fellowship offering for the people.[n]
His sons handed him the blood, and he sprinkled it against the altar on all sides. 19 But
the fat portions of the ox and the ram—the fat tail, the layer of fat, the kidneys and
the covering of the liver—20 these they laid on the breasts, and then Aaron burned the
fat on the altar. 21 Aaron waved the breasts and the right thigh before the LORD as a
wave offering,[o] as Moses commanded.
22 Then Aaron lifted his hands towards the people and blessed them.[p] And having
sacrificed the sin offering, the burnt offering and the fellowship offering, he stepped
down.
23 Moses and Aaron then went into the Tent of Meeting. When they came out, they
blessed the people; and the glory of the LORD[q] appeared to all the people. 24 Fire[r]
came out from the presence of the LORD and consumed the burnt offering and the fat
portions on the altar. And when all the people saw it, they shouted for joy and fell
face down.[s]

The Death of Nadab and Abihu

10 Aaron's sons Nadab and Abihu[a] took their censers, put fire in them[b] and
added incense; and they offered unauthorised fire before the LORD, contrary to
his command.[c] 2 So fire came out from the presence of the LORD and consumed
them,[d] and they died before the LORD. 3 Moses then said to Aaron, "This is what the
LORD spoke of when he said:

" 'Among those who approach me[e]
I will show myself holy;[f]
in the sight of all the people
I will be honoured.[g]' "

Aaron remained silent.

9:11 [h] Lev 4:11 [i] Lev 4:12; 8:17
9:13 [j] Lev 1:8
9:15 [k] Lev 4:27-31
9:16 [l] Lev 1:1-13
9:17 [m] Lev 2:1-2; 3:5
9:18 [n] Lev 3:1-11
9:21 [o] Ex 29:24, 26; Lev 7:30-34
9:22 [p] Nu 6:23; Dt 21:5; Lk 24:50
9:23 [q] ver 6
9:24 [r] Jdg 6:21; 2Ch 7:1 [s] 1Ki 18:39
10:1 [a] Ex 24:1; Nu 3:2-4; 26:61 [b] Lev 16:12 [c] Ex 30:9
10:2 [d] Nu 3:4; 16:35; 26:61
10:3 [e] Ex 19:22 [f] Ex 30:29; Lev 21:6; Eze 28:22 [g] Ex Isa 49:3

9:22, 23 In 9:6 Moses said to the people, "This is what the LORD has commanded you to do, so that the glory of the LORD may appear to you." Moses, Aaron, and the people then got to work and followed God's instructions. Soon after, the glory of the Lord appeared. Often we look for God's glorious acts without concern for following his instructions. Do you serve God in the daily routines of life, or do you wait for him to do a mighty act? If you depend on his glorious acts, you may find yourself sidestepping your everyday duty to obey.

9:24 As a display of his mighty power, God sent fire from the sky to consume Aaron's offering. The people fell to the ground in awe. Some people wonder if God really exists because they don't see his activity in the world. But God is at work in today's world just as he was in Moses' world. Where a large body of believers is active for him, God tends not to display his power in the form of mighty physical acts. Instead he works to change the world through the work of these believers. When you realise that, you will begin to see acts of love and faith that are just as supernatural.

10:1 What was the unauthorised fire that Nadab and Abihu offered before the Lord? The fire on the altar of burnt offering was never to go out (6:12, 13), implying that it was holy. It is possible that Nadab and Abihu brought coals of fire to the altar from another source, making the sacrifice unholy. It has also been suggested that the two priests gave an offering at an unprescribed time. Whatever explanation is correct, the point is that Nadab and Abihu abused their office as priests in a flagrant act of disrespect to God, who had just reviewed with them precisely how they were to conduct worship. As leaders, they had special responsibility to obey God. In their position, they could easily lead many people astray. If God has commissioned you to lead or teach others, be sure to stay close to him and follow his advice.

10:2 Aaron's sons were careless about following the laws for sacrifices. In response, God destroyed them with a blast of fire. Performing the sacrifices was an act of obedience. Doing them correctly showed respect for God. It is easy for us to grow careless about obeying God, to live our way instead of God's. But if one way were just as good as another, God would not have commanded us to live his way. He always has good reasons for his commands, and we always place ourselves in danger when we consciously or carelessly disobey them.

10:4 [h]Ex 6:22 [i]Ex 6:18 [j]Ac 5:6, 9, 10
10:5 [k]Lev 8:13
10:6 [l]Lev 21:10 [m]Nu 1:53; 16:22; Jos 7:1; 22:18;
10:7 [n]Ex 28:41; Lev 21:12
10:9 [o]Hos 4:11 [p]Eze 44:21; Lk 1:15; Eph 5:18; 1Ti 3:3; Tit 1:7
10:10 [q]Lev 11:47; 20:25; Eze 22:26
10:11 [r]Mal 2:7 [s]Dt 24:8

4Moses summoned Mishael and Elzaphan,[h] sons of Aaron's uncle Uzziel,[i] and
said to them, "Come here; carry your cousins outside the camp,[j] away from the front
of the sanctuary." 5So they came and carried them, still in their tunics,[k] outside the
camp, as Moses ordered.
6Then Moses said to Aaron and his sons Eleazar and Ithamar, "Do not let your hair
become unkempt,[a][l] and do not tear your clothes, or you will die and the LORD will
be angry with the whole community.[m] But your relatives, all the house of Israel, may
mourn for those the LORD has destroyed by fire. 7Do not leave the entrance to the Tent
of Meeting or you will die, because the LORD's anointing oil[n] is on you." So they
did as Moses said.
8Then the LORD said to Aaron, 9"You and your sons are not to drink wine[o] or other
fermented drink[p] whenever you go into the Tent of Meeting, or you will die. This
is a lasting ordinance for the generations to come. 10You must distinguish between
the holy and the common, between the unclean and the clean,[q] 11and you must teach[r]
the Israelites all the decrees the LORD has given them through Moses.[s]"

[a] 6 Or *Do not uncover your heads*

NADAB/ABIHU

Some brothers, like Cain and Abel or Jacob and Esau, get each other into trouble. Nadab and Abihu got into trouble together.

Although little is known of their early years, the Bible gives us an abundance of information about the environment in which they grew up. Born in Egypt, they were eye-witnesses of God's mighty acts of the exodus. They saw their father, Aaron, their uncle, Moses, and their aunt, Miriam, in action many times. They had first-hand knowledge of God's holiness as few men have ever had, and for a while at least, they followed God wholeheartedly (Leviticus 8:36). But at a crucial moment they chose to treat with indifference the clear instructions from God. The consequence of their sin was fiery, instant, and shocking to all.

We are in danger of making the same mistake as these brothers when we treat lightly the justice and holiness of God. We must draw near to God while realising that there is a proper fear of God. Don't forget that the opportunity to know God personally is based on his gracious invitation to an always unworthy people, not a gift to be taken for granted. Do your thoughts about God include a humble recognition of his great holiness?

Strengths and accomplishments:
- Oldest sons of Aaron
- Primary candidates to become high priest after their father
- Involved with the original consecration of the tabernacle
- Commended for doing "everything the LORD commanded" (Leviticus 8:36)

Weakness and mistake:
- Treated lightly God's direct commands

Lesson from their lives:
- Sin has deadly consequences

Vital statistics:
- Where: The Sinai peninsula
- Occupation: Priests-in-training
- Relatives: Father: Aaron. Uncle and Aunt: Moses and Miriam. Brothers: Eleazar and Ithamar

Key verses:
"Aaron's sons Nadab and Abihu took their censers, put fire in them and added incense; and they offered unauthorised fire before the LORD, contrary to his command. So fire came out from the presence of the LORD and consumed them, and they died before the LORD" (Leviticus 10:1, 2).

The story of Nadab and Abihu is told in Leviticus 8—10. They are also mentioned in Exodus 24:1, 9; 28:1; Numbers 3:2–4; 26:60, 61.

10:8–11 The priests were not to drink wine or other alcoholic beverages before going into the tabernacle. If their senses were dulled by alcohol, they might repeat Nadab and Abihu's sin and bring something unholy into the worship ceremony. In addition, drinking would disqualify them to teach the people God's requirements of self-discipline. Drunkenness was associated with pagan practices and the Jewish priests were supposed to be distinctively different.

10:10, 11 This passage (along with 19:1, 2) shows the focus of Leviticus. The Ten Commandments recorded in Exodus 20 were God's fundamental laws. Leviticus explained and supplemented those laws with many other guidelines and principles that helped the Israelites put them into practice. The purpose of God's laws was to teach people how to distinguish right from wrong, the holy from the common. The nation who lived by God's laws would obviously be set apart, dedicated to his service.

12Moses said to Aaron and his remaining sons, Eleazar and Ithamar, "Take the grain
offering left over from the offerings made to the LORD by fire and eat it prepared
without yeast beside the altar,[t] for it is most holy. 13Eat it in a holy place, because
it is your share and your sons' share of the offerings made to the LORD by fire; for
so I have been commanded. 14But you and your sons and your daughters may eat the
breast that was waved and the thigh that was presented. Eat them in a ceremonially
clean place;[u] they have been given to you and your children as your share of the
Israelites' fellowship offerings.[b] 15The thigh[v] that was presented and the breast that
was waved must be brought with the fat portions of the offerings made by fire, to be
waved before the LORD as a wave offering. This will be the regular share for you and
your children, as the LORD has commanded."
16When Moses enquired about the goat of the sin offering[w] and found that it had
been burned up, he was angry with Eleazar and Ithamar, Aaron's remaining sons, and
asked, 17"Why didn't you eat the sin offering[x] in the sanctuary area? It is most holy;
it was given to you to take away the guilt of the community by making atonement
for them before the LORD. 18Since its blood was not taken into the Holy Place,[y] you
should have eaten the goat in the sanctuary area, as I commanded."
19Aaron replied to Moses, "Today they sacrificed their sin offering and their burnt
offering[z] before the LORD, but such things as this have happened to me. Would the
LORD have been pleased if I had eaten the sin offering today?" 20When Moses heard
this, he was satisfied.

3. Instructions for the people

Clean and Unclean Food

11 The LORD said to Moses and Aaron, 2"Say to the Israelites: 'Of all the animals
that live on land, these are the ones you may eat:[a] 3You may eat any animal
that has a split hoof completely divided and that chews the cud.
4" 'There are some that only chew the cud or only have a split hoof, but you must
not eat them. The camel, though it chews the cud, does not have a split hoof; it is
ceremonially unclean for you. 5The coney,[a] though it chews the cud, does not have
a split hoof; it is unclean for you. 6The rabbit, though it chews the cud, does not have
a split hoof; it is unclean for you. 7And the pig,[b] though it has a split hoof completely
divided, does not chew the cud; it is unclean for you. 8You must not eat their meat
or touch their carcasses; they are unclean for you.[c]
9" 'Of all the creatures living in the water of the seas and the streams, you may eat
any that have fins and scales. 10But all creatures in the seas or streams that do not
have fins and scales—whether among all the swarming things or among all the other
living creatures in the water—you are to detest.[d] 11And since you are to detest them,
you must not eat their meat and you must detest their carcasses. 12Anything living
in the water that does not have fins and scales is to be detestable to you.
13" 'These are the birds you are to detest and not eat because they are detestable:
the eagle, the vulture, the black vulture, 14the red kite, any kind of black kite, 15any
kind of raven, 16the horned owl, the screech owl, the gull, any kind of hawk, 17the
little owl, the cormorant, the great owl, 18the white owl, the desert owl, the osprey,
19the stork, any kind of heron, the hoopoe and the bat.[b]
20" 'All flying insects that walk on all fours are to be detestable to you.[e] 21There
are, however, some winged creatures that walk on all fours that you may eat: those

b *14* Traditionally *peace offerings* **a** *5* That is, the hyrax or rock badger **b** *19* The precise identification of some of the birds, insects and animals in this chapter is uncertain.

10:12 [t]Lev 6:14-18; 21:22
10:14 [u]Ex 29:24, 26-27; Lev 7:31, 34; Nu 18:11
10:15 [v]Lev 7:34
10:16 [w]Lev 9:3
10:17 [x]Lev 6:24-30
10:18 [y]Lev 6:26, 30
10:19 [z]Lev 9:12
11:2 [a]Ac 10:12-14
11:7 [b]Isa 65:4; 66:3, 17
11:8 [c]Isa 52:11; Heb 9:10
11:10 [d]Lev 7:18
11:20 [e]Ac 10:14

10:16–20 The priest who offered the sin offering was supposed to eat a portion of the animal and then burn the rest (6:24–30). Moses was angry because Eleazar and Ithamar burned the sin offering, but did not eat any of it. Aaron explained to Moses that his two sons did not feel it appropriate to eat the sacrifice after their two brothers, Nadab and Abihu, had just been killed for sacrificing wrongly. Moses then understood that Eleazar and Ithamar were not trying to disobey God. They were simply afraid and upset over what had just happened to their brothers.

11:8 God had strictly forbidden eating the meat of certain "unclean" animals; to make sure, he forbade even touching them. He wanted the people to be totally separated from those things he had forbidden. So often we flirt with temptation, rationalising that at least we are technically keeping the commandment not to commit the sin. But God wants us to separate ourselves completely from all sin and tempting situations.

that have jointed legs for hopping on the ground. 22Of these you may eat any kind
of locust,[f] katydid, cricket or grasshopper. 23But all other winged creatures that have
four legs you are to detest.
24" 'You will make yourselves unclean by these; whoever touches their carcasses
will be unclean till evening. 25Whoever picks up one of their carcasses must wash his
clothes,[g] and he will be unclean till evening.[h]
26" 'Every animal that has a split hoof not completely divided or that does not chew
the cud is unclean for you; whoever touches ⌊the carcass of⌋ any of them will be
unclean. 27Of all the animals that walk on all fours, those that walk on their paws are
unclean for you; whoever touches their carcasses will be unclean till evening. 28Any-
one who picks up their carcasses must wash his clothes, and he will be unclean till
evening. They are unclean for you.
29" 'Of the animals that move about on the ground, these are unclean for you: the
weasel, the rat,[i] any kind of great lizard, 30the gecko, the monitor lizard, the wall
lizard, the skink and the chameleon. 31Of all those that move along the ground, these
are unclean for you. Whoever touches them when they are dead will be unclean till
evening. 32When one of them dies and falls on something, that article, whatever its
use, will be unclean, whether it is made of wood, cloth, hide or sackcloth.[j] Put it
in water; it will be unclean till evening, and then it will be clean. 33If one of them
falls into a clay pot, everything in it will be unclean, and you must break the pot.[k]
34Any food that could be eaten but has water on it from such a pot is unclean, and
any liquid that could be drunk from it is unclean. 35Anything that one of their carcasses
falls on becomes unclean; an oven or cooking pot must be broken up. They are
unclean, and you are to regard them as unclean. 36A spring, however, or a cistern for
collecting water remains clean, but anyone who touches one of these carcasses is
unclean. 37If a carcass falls on any seeds that are to be planted, they remain clean.
38But if water has been put on the seed and a carcass falls on it, it is unclean for you.
39" 'If an animal that you are allowed to eat dies, anyone who touches the carcass
will be unclean till evening. 40Anyone who eats some of the carcass must wash his
clothes, and he will be unclean till evening.[l] Anyone who picks up the carcass must
wash his clothes, and he will be unclean till evening.
41" 'Every creature that moves about on the ground is detestable; it is not to be eaten.
42You are not to eat any creature that moves about on the ground, whether it moves
on its belly or walks on all fours or on many feet; it is detestable. 43Do not defile
yourselves by any of these creatures.[m] Do not make yourselves unclean by means of
them or be made unclean by them. 44I am the LORD your God;[n] consecrate yourselves[o] and be holy,[p] because I am holy.[q] Do not make yourselves unclean by any
creature that moves about on the ground. 45I am the LORD who brought you up out
of Egypt[r] to be your God;[s] therefore be holy, because I am holy.[t]
46" 'These are the regulations concerning animals, birds, every living thing that

11:22 [f]Mt 3:4; Mk 1:6

11:25 [g]Lev 14:8, 47; 15:5 [h]ver 40; Nu 31:24

11:29 [i]Isa 66:17

11:32 [j]Lev 15:12

11:33 [k]Lev 6:28; 15:12

11:40 [l]Lev 17:15; 22:8; Eze 44:31

11:43 [m]Lev 20:25

11:44 [n]Ex 6:2, 7; Isa 43:3; 51:15 [o]Lev 20:7 [p]Ex 19:6 [q]Lev 19:2; Ps 99:3; Eph 1:4; 1Th 4:7; 1Pe 1:15, 16*

11:45 [r]Lev 25:38, 55; Ex 6:7; 20:2 [s]Ge 17:7 [t]Ex 19:6; 1Pe 1:16*

11:25 In order to worship, people need to be prepared. There were some acts of disobedience, some natural acts (such as childbirth, menstruation, or sex), or some accidents (such as touching a dead or diseased body) that would make a person ceremonially unclean and thus forbidden to participate in worship. This did not imply that they had sinned or were rejected by God, but it ensured that all worship was done decently and in order. This chapter describes many of the intentional or accidental occurrences that would disqualify a person from worship until they were "cleansed" or straightened out. A person had to be *prepared* for worship. Similarly, we cannot live any way we want during the week and then rush into God's presence on Sunday. We should prepare ourselves through repentance and cleansing.

11:44, 45 There is more to this chapter than eating right. These verses provide a key to understanding all the laws and regulations in Leviticus. God wanted his people to be *holy* (set apart, different, unique), just as he is holy. He knew they had only two options: to be separate and holy, or to compromise with their pagan neighbours and become corrupt. That is why he called them out of idolatrous Egypt and set them apart as a unique nation, dedicated to worshipping him alone and leading moral lives. That is also why he designed laws and restrictions to help them remain separate—both socially and spiritually—from the wicked pagan nations they would encounter in Canaan. Christians also are called to be holy (1 Peter 1:15). Like the Israelites, we should remain spiritually separate from the world's wickedness, even though unlike them, we rub shoulders with unbelievers every day. It is no easy task to be holy in an unholy world, but God doesn't ask you to accomplish this on your own. Through the death of his Son, he will "present you holy in his sight, without blemish and free from accusation" (Colossians 1:22).

moves in the water and every creature that moves about on the ground. 47You must
distinguish between the unclean and the clean, between living creatures that may be
eaten and those that may not be eaten.[u]' "

Purification After Childbirth

12 The LORD said to Moses, 2"Say to the Israelites: 'A woman who becomes
pregnant and gives birth to a son will be ceremonially unclean for seven days,
just as she is unclean during her monthly period.[a] 3On the eighth day the boy is to
be circumcised.[b] 4Then the woman must wait thirty-three days to be purified from
her bleeding. She must not touch anything sacred or go to the sanctuary until the days
of her purification are over. 5If she gives birth to a daughter, for two weeks the woman
will be unclean, as during her period. Then she must wait sixty-six days to be purified
from her bleeding.
6" 'When the days of her purification for a son or daughter are over,[c] she is to bring
to the priest at the entrance to the Tent of Meeting a year-old lamb[d] for a burnt offering
and a young pigeon or a dove for a sin offering.[e] 7He shall offer them before the
LORD to make atonement for her, and then she will be ceremonially clean from her
flow of blood.
" 'These are the regulations for the woman who gives birth to a boy or a girl. 8If
she cannot afford a lamb, she is to bring two doves or two young pigeons,[f] one for
a burnt offering and the other for a sin offering.[g] In this way the priest will make
atonement for her, and she will be clean.[h]' "

Regulations About Infectious Skin Diseases

13 The LORD said to Moses and Aaron, 2"When anyone has a swelling[a] or a rash
or a bright spot[b] on his skin that may become an infectious skin disease,**[a]**[c]
he must be brought to Aaron the priest[d] or to one of his sons**[b]** who is a priest. 3The
priest is to examine the sore on his skin, and if the hair in the sore has turned white
and the sore appears to be more than skin deep,**[c]** it is an infectious skin disease. When
the priest examines him, he shall pronounce him ceremonially unclean.[e] 4If the spot[f]
on his skin is white but does not appear to be more than skin deep and the hair in it
has not turned white, the priest is to put the infected person in isolation for seven
days.[g] 5On the seventh day[h] the priest is to examine him,[i] and if he sees that the
sore is unchanged and has not spread in the skin, he is to keep him in isolation another
seven days. 6On the seventh day the priest is to examine him again, and if the sore
has faded and has not spread in the skin, the priest shall pronounce him clean;[j] it
is only a rash. The man must wash his clothes,[k] and he will be clean.[l] 7But if the

11:47 [u]Lev 10:10
12:2 [a]Lev 15:19; 18:19
12:3 [b]Ge 17:12; Lk 1:59; 2:21
12:6 [c]Lk 2:22 [d]Ex 29:38; Lev 23:12; Nu 6:12, 14; 7:15 [e]Lev 5:7
12:8 [f]Ge 15:9; Lev 14:22 [g]Lev 5:7; Lk 2:22-24* [h]Lev 4:26
13:2 [a]ver 10, 19, 28, 43 [b]ver 4, 38, 39; Lev 14:56 [c]ver 3, 9, 15; Ex 4:6; Lev 14:3, 32; Nu 5:2; Dt 24:8 [d]Dt 24:8
13:3 [e]ver 8, 11, 20, 30; Lev 21:1; Nu 9:6
13:4 [f]ver 2 [g]ver 5, 21, 26, 33, 46; Lev 14:38; Nu 12:14, 15; Dt 24:9
13:5 [h]Lev 14:9 [i]ver 27, 32, 34, 51
13:6 [j]ver 13, 17, 23, 28, 34; Mt 8:3; Lk 5:12-14 [k]Lev 11:25 [l]Lev 11:25; 14:8, 9, 20, 48; 15:8; Nu 8:7

a *2* Traditionally *leprosy*; the Hebrew word was used for various diseases affecting the skin—not necessarily leprosy; also elsewhere in this chapter. **b** *2* Or *descendants* **c** *3* Or *be lower than the rest of the skin*; also elsewhere in this chapter

11:47 The designations *clean* and *unclean* were used to define the kind of animals the Israelites could and could not eat. There were several reasons for this restricted diet: (1) To ensure the health of the nation. The forbidden foods were usually scavenging animals that fed on dead animals; thus disease could be transmitted through them. (2) To visibly distinguish Israel from other nations. The pig, for example, was a common sacrifice of pagan religions. (3) To avoid objectionable associations. The creatures that move about on the ground, for example, were reminiscent of serpents, which often symbolised sin.

12:1–4 Why was a woman considered "ceremonially unclean" after the wonderful miracle of birth? It was due to the bodily emissions and secretions occurring during and after childbirth. These were considered unclean and made the woman unprepared to enter the pure surroundings of the tabernacle.

12:1–4 *Unclean* did not mean sinful or dirty. God created us male and female, and he ordered us to be fruitful and multiply (Genesis 1:27, 28). He did not change his mind and say that sex and procreation were now somehow unclean. Instead, he made a distinction between his worship and the popular worship of fertility gods and goddesses. Canaanite religions incorporated prostitution and immoral rites as the people begged their gods to make their crops, herds, and families increase. By contrast, Israel's religion avoided all sexual connotations. By keeping worship and sex entirely separate, God helped the Israelites avoid confusion with pagan rites. The Israelites worshipped God as their loving Creator and Provider, and they thanked him for bountiful crops and safe childbirth.

13:1ff Leprosy (here called "infectious skin disease") is a name applied to several different diseases, and was greatly feared in Bible times. Some of these diseases, unlike the disease we call leprosy or Hansen's disease today, were highly contagious. The worst of them slowly ruined the body and, in most cases, were fatal. Lepers were separated from family and friends and confined outside the camp. Since priests were responsible for the health of the camp, it was their duty to expel and readmit lepers. If someone's leprosy appeared to go away, only the priest could decide if that person was truly cured. Leprosy is often used in the Bible as an illustration of sin because sin is contagious and destructive and leads to separation.

rash does spread in his skin after he has shown himself to the priest to be pronounced
clean, he must appear before the priest again.[m] 8The priest is to examine him, and
if the rash has spread in the skin, he shall pronounce him unclean; it is an infectious
disease.
9"When anyone has an infectious skin disease, he must be brought to the priest.
10The priest is to examine him, and if there is a white swelling in the skin that has
turned the hair white and if there is raw flesh in the swelling, 11it is a chronic skin
disease[n] and the priest shall pronounce him unclean. He is not to put him in isolation,
because he is already unclean.
12"If the disease breaks out all over his skin and, so far as the priest can see, it covers
all the skin of the infected person from head to foot, 13the priest is to examine him,
and if the disease has covered his whole body, he shall pronounce that person clean.
Since it has all turned white, he is clean. 14But whenever raw flesh appears on him,
he will be unclean. 15When the priest sees the raw flesh, he shall pronounce him
unclean. The raw flesh is unclean; he has an infectious disease.[o] 16Should the raw
flesh change and turn white, he must go to the priest. 17The priest is to examine him,
and if the sores have turned white, the priest shall pronounce the infected person
clean;[p] then he will be clean.
18"When someone has a boil[q] on his skin and it heals, 19and in the place where
the boil was, a white swelling or reddish-white[r] spot[s] appears, he must present
himself to the priest. 20The priest is to examine it, and if it appears to be more than
skin deep and the hair in it has turned white, the priest shall pronounce him unclean.
It is an infectious skin disease[t] that has broken out where the boil was. 21But if, when
the priest examines it, there is no white hair in it and it is not more than skin deep
and has faded, then the priest is to put him in isolation for seven days. 22If it is
spreading in the skin, the priest shall pronounce him unclean; it is infectious. 23But
if the spot is unchanged and has not spread, it is only a scar from the boil, and the
priest shall pronounce him clean.[u]
24"When someone has a burn on his skin and a reddish-white or white spot appears
in the raw flesh of the burn, 25the priest is to examine the spot, and if the hair in it
has turned white, and it appears to be more than skin deep, it is an infectious disease
that has broken out in the burn. The priest shall pronounce him unclean; it is an
infectious skin disease.[v] 26But if the priest examines it and there is no white hair in
the spot and if it is not more than skin deep and has faded, then the priest is to put
him in isolation for seven days.[w] 27On the seventh day the priest is to examine him,[x]
and if it is spreading in the skin, the priest shall pronounce him unclean; it is an
infectious skin disease. 28If, however, the spot is unchanged and has not spread in
the skin but has faded, it is a swelling from the burn, and the priest shall pronounce
him clean; it is only a scar from the burn.[y]
29"If a man or woman has a sore on the head[z] or on the chin, 30the priest is to
examine the sore, and if it appears to be more than skin deep and the hair in it is yellow
and thin, the priest shall pronounce that person unclean; it is an itch, an infectious
disease of the head or chin. 31But if, when the priest examines this kind of sore, it
does not seem to be more than skin deep and there is no black hair in it, then the priest
is to put the infected person in isolation for seven days.[a] 32On the seventh day the
priest is to examine the sore,[b] and if the itch has not spread and there is no yellow
hair in it and it does not appear to be more than skin deep, 33he must be shaved except
for the diseased area, and the priest is to keep him in isolation another seven days.
34On the seventh day the priest is to examine the itch,[c] and if it has not spread in
the skin and appears to be no more than skin deep, the priest shall pronounce him
clean. He must wash his clothes, and he will be clean.[d] 35But if the itch does spread
in the skin after he is pronounced clean, 36the priest is to examine him, and if the itch
has spread in the skin, the priest does not need to look for yellow hair; the person is
unclean.[e] 37If, however, in his judgment it is unchanged and black hair has grown
in it, the itch is healed. He is clean, and the priest shall pronounce him clean.
38"When a man or woman has white spots on the skin, 39the priest is to examine
them, and if the spots are dull white, it is a harmless rash that has broken out on the
skin; that person is clean.

13:7 [m] Lk 5:14
13:11 [n] Ex 4:6; Lev 14:8; Nu 12:10; Mt 8:2
13:15 [o] ver 2
13:17 [p] ver 6
13:18 [q] Ex 9:9
13:19 [r] ver 24, 42; Lev 14:37 [s] ver 2
13:20 [t] ver 2
13:23 [u] ver 6
13:25 [v] ver 11
13:26 [w] ver 4
13:27 [x] ver 5
13:28 [y] ver 2
13:29 [z] ver 43, 44
13:31 [a] ver 4
13:32 [b] ver 5
13:34 [c] ver 5 [d] Lev 11:25
13:36 [e] ver 30

40“When a man has lost his hair and is bald,[f] he is clean. 41If he has lost his hair
from the front of his scalp and has a bald forehead, he is clean. 42But if he has a
reddish-white sore on his bald head or forehead, it is an infectious disease breaking
out on his head or forehead. 43The priest is to examine him, and if the swollen sore
on his head or forehead is reddish-white like an infectious skin disease, 44the man is
diseased and is unclean. The priest shall pronounce him unclean because of the sore
on his head.

45“The person with such an infectious disease must wear torn clothes,[g] let his hair
be unkempt,[d] cover the lower part of his face[h] and cry out, ‘Unclean! Unclean!’[i]
46As long as he has the infection he remains unclean. He must live alone; he must
live outside the camp.[j]

Regulations About Mildew

47“If any clothing is contaminated with mildew—any woollen or linen clothing,
48any woven or knitted material of linen or wool, any leather or anything made of
leather—49and if the contamination in the clothing, or leather, or woven or knitted
material, or any leather article, is greenish or reddish, it is a spreading mildew and
must be shown to the priest.[k] 50The priest is to examine the mildew[l] and isolate the
affected article for seven days. 51On the seventh day he is to examine it,[m] and if the
mildew has spread in the clothing, or the woven or knitted material, or the leather,
whatever its use, it is a destructive mildew; the article is unclean.[n] 52He must burn
up the clothing, or the woven or knitted material of wool or linen, or any leather article
that has the contamination in it, because the mildew is destructive; the article must
be burned up.[o]

53“But if, when the priest examines it, the mildew has not spread in the clothing,
or the woven or knitted material, or the leather article, 54he shall order that the
contaminated article be washed. Then he is to isolate it for another seven days. 55After
the affected article has been washed, the priest is to examine it, and if the mildew has
not changed its appearance, even though it has not spread, it is unclean. Burn it with
fire, whether the mildew has affected one side or the other. 56If, when the priest
examines it, the mildew has faded after the article has been washed, he is to tear the
contaminated part out of the clothing, or the leather, or the woven or knitted material.
57But if it reappears in the clothing, or in the woven or knitted material, or in the
leather article, it is spreading, and whatever has the mildew must be burned with fire.
58The clothing, or the woven or knitted material, or any leather article that has been
washed and is rid of the mildew, must be washed again, and it will be clean.”

59These are the regulations concerning contamination by mildew in woollen or linen
clothing, woven or knitted material, or any leather article, for pronouncing them clean
or unclean.

Cleansing From Infectious Skin Diseases

14 The LORD said to Moses, 2“These are the regulations for the diseased person
at the time of his ceremonial cleansing, when he is brought to the priest:[a] 3The
priest is to go outside the camp and examine him.[b] If the person has been healed of
his infectious skin disease,[a] 4the priest shall order that two live clean birds and some
cedar wood, scarlet yarn and hyssop be brought for the one to be cleansed.[c] 5Then
the priest shall order that one of the birds be killed over fresh water in a clay pot. 6He
is then to take the live bird and dip it, together with the cedar wood, the scarlet yarn
and the hyssop, into the blood of the bird that was killed over the fresh water.[d] 7Seven

d *45* Or *clothes, uncover his head* **a** *3* Traditionally *leprosy*; the Hebrew word was used for various diseases affecting the skin—not necessarily leprosy; also elsewhere in this chapter.

13:40 f Lev 21:5; 2Ki 2:23; Isa 3:24; 15:2; 22:12; Eze 27:31; 29:18; Am 8:10; Mic 1:16
13:45 g Lev 10:6 h Eze 24:17, 22; Mic 3:7 i Lev 5:2; La 4:15; Lk 17:12
13:46 j Nu 5:1-4; 12:14; 2Ki 7:3; 15:5; Lk 17:12
13:49 k Mk 1:44
13:50 l Eze 44:23
13:51 m ver 5 n Lev 14:44
13:52 o ver 55, 57
14:2 a Mt 8:2-4; Mk 1:40-44; Lk 5:12-14; 17:14
14:3 b Lev 13:46
14:4 c ver 6, 49, 51, 52; Nu 19:6; Ps 51:7
14:6 d ver 4

13:45, 46 A person with an infectious skin disease had to perform this strange ritual to protect others from coming too near. Because the disease described in Leviticus was often contagious, it was important that people stay away from those who had it.

times he shall sprinkle[e] the one to be cleansed of the infectious disease and pronounce
him clean. Then he is to release the live bird in the open fields.
8"The person to be cleansed must wash his clothes,[f] shave off all his hair and bathe
with water;[g] then he will be ceremonially clean.[h] After this he may come into the
camp,[i] but he must stay outside his tent for seven days. 9On the seventh day he must
shave off all his hair; he must shave his head, his beard, his eyebrows and the rest
of his hair. He must wash his clothes and bathe himself with water, and he will be
clean.
10"On the eighth day[j] he must bring two male lambs and one ewe lamb a year old,
each without defect, along with three-tenths of an ephah**[b]** of fine flour mixed with
oil for a grain offering,[k] and one log**[c]** of oil.[l] 11The priest who pronounces him
clean shall present both the one to be cleansed and his offerings before the LORD at
the entrance to the Tent of Meeting.
12"Then the priest is to take one of the male lambs and offer it as a guilt offering,[m]
along with the log of oil; he shall wave them before the LORD as a wave offering.[n]
13He is to slaughter the lamb in the holy place[o] where the sin offering and the burnt
offering are slaughtered. Like the sin offering, the guilt offering belongs to the
priest;[p] it is most holy. 14The priest is to take some of the blood of the guilt offering
and put it on the lobe of the right ear of the one to be cleansed, on the thumb of his
right hand and on the big toe of his right foot.[q] 15The priest shall then take some of
the log of oil, pour it in the palm of his own left hand, 16dip his right forefinger into
the oil in his palm, and with his finger sprinkle some of it before the LORD seven times.
17The priest is to put some of the oil remaining in his palm on the lobe of the right
ear of the one to be cleansed, on the thumb of his right hand and on the big toe of
his right foot, on top of the blood of the guilt offering. 18The rest of the oil in his
palm the priest shall put on the head of the one to be cleansed and make atonement
for him before the LORD.
19"Then the priest is to sacrifice the sin offering and make atonement for the one
to be cleansed from his uncleanness. After that, the priest shall slaughter the burnt
offering 20and offer it on the altar, together with the grain offering, and make
atonement for him, and he will be clean.[r]
21"If, however, he is poor[s] and cannot afford these,[t] he must take one male lamb
as a guilt offering to be waved to make atonement for him, together with a tenth of
an ephah**[d]** of fine flour mixed with oil for a grain offering, a log of oil, 22and two
doves or two young pigeons,[u] which he can afford, one for a sin offering and the
other for a burnt offering.
23"On the eighth day he must bring them for his cleansing to the priest at the
entrance to the Tent of Meeting, before the LORD.[v] 24The priest is to take the lamb
for the guilt offering,[w] together with the log of oil,[x] and wave them before the LORD
as a wave offering.[y] 25He shall slaughter the lamb for the guilt offering and take some
of its blood and put it on the lobe of the right ear of the one to be cleansed, on the
thumb of his right hand and on the big toe of his right foot.[z] 26The priest is to pour
some of the oil into the palm of his own left hand,[a] 27and with his right forefinger
sprinkle some of the oil from his palm seven times before the LORD. 28Some of the
oil in his palm he is to put on the same places he put the blood of the guilt offering—on
the lobe of the right ear of the one to be cleansed, on the thumb of his right hand and
on the big toe of his right foot. 29The rest of the oil in his palm the priest shall put
on the head of the one to be cleansed, to make atonement for him before the LORD.[b]
30Then he shall sacrifice the doves or the young pigeons, which the person can
afford,[c] 31one**[e]** as a sin offering and the other as a burnt offering,[d] together with
the grain offering. In this way the priest will make atonement before the LORD on
behalf of the one to be cleansed.[e]"
32These are the regulations for anyone who has an infectious skin disease[f] and who
cannot afford the regular offerings[g] for his cleansing.

b *10* That is, probably about 11½ pints (about 6.5 litres) **c** *10* That is, probably about ½ pint (about 0.3 litre); also in verses 12, 15, 21 and 24 **d** *21* That is, probably about 4 pints (about 2 litres) **e** *31* Septuagint and Syriac; Hebrew *31 such as the person can afford, one*

14:7 [e]2Ki 5:10, 14; Isa 52:15; Eze 36:25
14:8 [f]Lev 11:25; 13:6 [g]ver 9 [h]ver 20 [i]Nu 5:2, 3; 12:14, 15; 2Ch 26:21
14:10 [j]Mt 8:4; Mk 1:44; Lk 5:14 [k]Lev 2:1 [l]ver 12, 15, 21, 24
14:12 [m]Lev 5:18; 6:6-7 [n]Ex 29:24
14:13 [o]Ex 29:11 [p]Lev 6:24-30; 7:7
14:14 [q]Ex 29:20; Lev 8:23
14:20 [r]ver 8
14:21 [s]Lev 5:7; 12:8 [t]ver 22, 32
14:22 [u]Lev 5:7
14:23 [v]ver 10, 11
14:24 [w]Nu 6:14 [x]ver 10 [y]ver 12
14:25 [z]ver 14; Ex 29:20
14:26 [a]ver 15
14:29 [b]ver 18
14:30 [c]Lev 5:7
14:31 [d]ver 22; Lev 5:7; 15:15, 30 [e]ver 18, 19
14:32 [f]Lev 13:2 [g]ver 21

Cleansing From Mildew

33 The LORD said to Moses and Aaron, 34 "When you enter the land of Canaan,[h]
which I am giving you as your possession,[i] and I put a spreading mildew in a house
in that land, 35 the owner of the house must go and tell the priest, 'I have seen
something that looks like mildew in my house.' 36 The priest is to order the house to
be emptied before he goes in to examine the mildew, so that nothing in the house will
be pronounced unclean. After this the priest is to go in and inspect the house. 37 He
is to examine the mildew on the walls, and if it has greenish or reddish[j] depressions
that appear to be deeper than the surface of the wall, 38 the priest shall go out of the
doorway of the house and close it up for seven days.[k] 39 On the seventh day[l] the
priest shall return to inspect the house. If the mildew has spread on the walls, 40 he
is to order that the contaminated stones be torn out and thrown into an unclean place
outside the town.[m] 41 He must have all the inside walls of the house scraped and the
material that is scraped off dumped into an unclean place outside the town. 42 Then
they are to take other stones to replace these and take new clay and plaster the house.
43 "If the mildew reappears in the house after the stones have been torn out and the
house scraped and plastered, 44 the priest is to go and examine it and, if the mildew
has spread in the house, it is a destructive mildew; the house is unclean.[n] 45 It must
be torn down—its stones, timbers and all the plaster—and taken out of the town to
an unclean place.
46 "Anyone who goes into the house while it is closed up will be unclean till
evening.[o] 47 Anyone who sleeps or eats in the house must wash his clothes.[p]
48 "But if the priest comes to examine it and the mildew has not spread after the
house has been plastered, he shall pronounce the house clean,[q] because the mildew
is gone. 49 To purify the house he is to take two birds and some cedar wood, scarlet
yarn and hyssop.[r] 50 He shall kill one of the birds over fresh water in a clay pot.[s]
51 Then he is to take the cedar wood, the hyssop,[t] the scarlet yarn and the live bird,
dip them into the blood of the dead bird and the fresh water, and sprinkle the house
seven times.[u] 52 He shall purify the house with the bird's blood, the fresh water, the
live bird, the cedar wood, the hyssop and the scarlet yarn. 53 Then he is to release the
live bird in the open fields[v] outside the town. In this way he will make atonement
for the house, and it will be clean.[w]"
54 These are the regulations for any infectious skin disease,[x] for an itch, 55 for
mildew[y] in clothing or in a house, 56 and for a swelling, a rash or a bright spot,[z]
57 to determine when something is clean or unclean.
These are the regulations for infectious skin diseases and mildew.[a]

Discharges Causing Uncleanness

15 The LORD said to Moses and Aaron, 2 "Speak to the Israelites and say to them:
'When any man has a bodily discharge,[a] the discharge is unclean. 3 Whether
it continues flowing from his body or is blocked, it will make him unclean. This is
how his discharge will bring about uncleanness:

14:34 [h] Ge 12:5; Ex 6:4; Nu 13:2 [i] Ge 17:8; 48:4; Nu 27:12; 32:22; Dt 3:27; 7:1; 32:49
14:37 [j] Lev 13:19
14:38 [k] Lev 13:4
14:39 [l] Lev 13:5
14:40 [m] ver 45
14:44 [n] Lev 13:51
14:46 [o] Lev 11:24
14:47 [p] Lev 11:25
14:48 [q] Lev 13:6
14:49 [r] ver 4; 1Ki 4:33
14:50 [s] ver 5
14:51 [t] ver 6; Ps 51:7 [u] ver 4, 7
14:53 [v] ver 7 [w] ver 20
14:54 [x] Lev 13:2, 30
14:55 [y] Lev 13:47-52
14:56 [z] Lev 13:2
14:57 [a] Lev 10:10
15:2 [a] ver 16, 32; Lev 22:4; Nu 5:2; 2Sa 3:29; Mt 9:20

14:34, 35 This mildew was dry rot or mineral crystals affecting stone walls. There were specific cleansing procedures designated for mildewed clothing and buildings. These were fully required by the law (vv. 44–57). This fungus could spread rapidly and promote disease. It was therefore important to check its spread as soon as possible. In extreme cases, if the fungus had done enough damage, the clothing was burned or the house destroyed. Why was mildew so dangerous?

14:54–57 God told the Israelites how to diagnose infectious skin diseases and mildew so they could avoid them or treat them. These laws were given for the people's health and protection. They helped the Israelites avoid diseases that were serious threats in that time and place. Although they wouldn't have understood the medical reasons for some of these laws, their obedience to them made them healthier. Many of God's laws must have seemed strange to the Israelites. His laws, however, helped them avoid not only physical contamination, but also moral and spiritual infection.

The word of God still provides a pattern for physically, spiritually, and morally healthy living. We may not always understand the wisdom of God's laws, but if we obey them, we will thrive. Does this mean we are to follow the Old Testament health and dietary restrictions? In general, the basic principles of health and cleanliness are still healthful practices, but it would be legalistic, if not wrong, to adhere to each specific restriction today. Some of these regulations were intended to mark the Israelites as different from the wicked people around them. Others were given to prevent God's people from becoming involved in pagan religious practices, one of the most serious problems of the day. Still others related to quarantines in a culture where exact medical diagnosis was impossible. Today, for example, physicians can diagnose the different forms of leprosy, and they know which ones are contagious. Treatment methods have greatly improved, and quarantine for leprosy is rarely necessary.

4" 'Any bed the man with a discharge lies on will be unclean, and anything he sits
on will be unclean. 5Anyone who touches his bed must wash his clothes[b] and bathe
with water,[c] and he will be unclean till evening.[d] 6Whoever sits on anything that
the man with a discharge sat on must wash his clothes and bathe with water, and he
will be unclean till evening.
7" 'Whoever touches the man[e] who has a discharge[f] must wash his clothes and
bathe with water, and he will be unclean till evening.
8" 'If the man with the discharge spits[g] on someone who is clean, that person must
wash his clothes and bathe with water, and he will be unclean till evening.
9" 'Everything the man sits on when riding will be unclean, 10and whoever touches
any of the things that were under him will be unclean till evening; whoever picks up
those things[h] must wash his clothes and bathe with water, and he will be unclean till
evening.
11" 'Anyone the man with a discharge touches without rinsing his hands with water
must wash his clothes and bathe with water, and he will be unclean till evening.
12" 'A clay pot[i] that the man touches must be broken, and any wooden article[j]
is to be rinsed with water.
13" 'When a man is cleansed from his discharge, he is to count off seven days[k]
for his ceremonial cleansing; he must wash his clothes and bathe himself with fresh
water, and he will be clean.[l] 14On the eighth day he must take two doves or two young
pigeons[m] and come before the LORD to the entrance to the Tent of Meeting and give
them to the priest. 15The priest is to sacrifice them, the one for a sin offering[n] and
the other for a burnt offering.[o] In this way he will make atonement before the LORD
for the man because of his discharge.[p]
16" 'When a man has an emission of semen,[q] he must bathe his whole body with
water, and he will be unclean till evening.[r] 17Any clothing or leather that has semen
on it must be washed with water, and it will be unclean till evening. 18When a man
lies with a woman and there is an emission of semen,[s] both must bathe with water,
and they will be unclean till evening.
19" 'When a woman has her regular flow of blood, the impurity of her monthly
period[t] will last seven days, and anyone who touches her will be unclean till evening.
20" 'Anything she lies on during her period will be unclean, and anything she sits
on will be unclean. 21Whoever touches her bed must wash his clothes and bathe with
water, and he will be unclean till evening.[u] 22Whoever touches anything she sits on
must wash his clothes and bathe with water, and he will be unclean till evening.
23Whether it is the bed or anything she was sitting on, when anyone touches it, he
will be unclean till evening.
24" 'If a man lies with her and her monthly flow[v] touches him, he will be unclean
for seven days; any bed he lies on will be unclean.
25" 'When a woman has a discharge of blood for many days at a time other than
her monthly period[w] or has a discharge that continues beyond her period, she will
be unclean as long as she has the discharge, just as in the days of her period. 26Any
bed she lies on while her discharge continues will be unclean, as is her bed during
her monthly period, and anything she sits on will be unclean, as during her period.
27Whoever touches them will be unclean; he must wash his clothes and bathe with
water, and he will be unclean till evening.
28" 'When she is cleansed from her discharge, she must count off seven days, and
after that she will be ceremonially clean. 29On the eighth day she must take two doves
or two young pigeons[x] and bring them to the priest at the entrance to the Tent of
Meeting. 30The priest is to sacrifice one for a sin offering and the other for a burnt
offering. In this way he will make atonement for her before the LORD for the uncleanness of her discharge.[y]

15:5 [b]Lev 11:25 [c]Lev 14:8 [d]Lev 11:24
15:7 [e]ver 19; Lev 22:5 [f]ver 16; Lev 22:4
15:8 [g]Nu 12:14
15:10 [h]Nu 19:10
15:12 [i]Lev 6:28 [j]Lev 11:32
15:13 [k]Lev 8:33 [l]ver 5
15:14 [m]Lev 14:22
15:15 [n]Lev 5:7 [o]Lev 14:31 [p]Lev 14:18, 19
15:16 [q]ver 2; Lev 22:4; Dt 23:10 [r]ver 5; Dt 23:11
15:18 [s]1Sa 21:4
15:19 [t]ver 24; Lev 12:2
15:21 [u]ver 27
15:24 [v]ver 19; Lev 12:2; 18:19; 20:18; Eze 18:6
15:25 [w]Mt 9:20; Mk 5:25; Lk 8:43
15:29 [x]Lev 14:22
15:30 [y]Lev 5:10; 14:20, 31; 18:19; 2Sa 11:4; Mk 5:25; Lk 8:43

15:18 This verse is not implying that sex is dirty or disgusting. God created sex for the enjoyment of married couples as well as for continuing the race and continuing the covenant. Everything must be seen and done with a view towards God's love and control. Sex is not separate from spirituality and God's care. God is concerned about our sexual habits. We tend to separate our physical and spiritual lives, but there is an inseparable intertwining. God must be Lord over our whole selves – including our private lives.

31 " 'You must keep the Israelites separate from things that make them unclean, so
they will not die in their uncleanness for defiling my dwelling-place,[a][z] which is
among them.' "
32 These are the regulations for a man with a discharge, for anyone made unclean
by an emission of semen,[a] 33 for a woman in her monthly period, for a man or a
woman with a discharge, and for a man who lies with a woman who is ceremonially
unclean.[b]

4. Instructions for the altar

The Day of Atonement

16 The LORD spoke to Moses after the death of the two sons of Aaron who died
when they approached the LORD.[a] 2 The LORD said to Moses: "Tell your brother
Aaron not to come whenever he chooses[b] into the Most Holy Place[c] behind the
curtain in front of the atonement cover on the ark, or else he will die, because I
appear[d] in the cloud[e] over the atonement cover.
3 "This is how Aaron is to enter the sanctuary area:[f] with a young bull for a sin
offering and a ram for a burnt offering. 4 He is to put on the sacred linen tunic, with
linen undergarments next to his body; he is to tie the linen sash around him and put
on the linen turban.[g] These are sacred garments;[h] so he must bathe himself with
water[i] before he puts them on. 5 From the Israelite community[j] he is to take two
male goats[k] for a sin offering and a ram for a burnt offering.
6 "Aaron is to offer the bull for his own sin offering to make atonement for himself
and his household.[l] 7 Then he is to take the two goats and present them before the
LORD at the entrance to the Tent of Meeting. 8 He is to cast lots for the two goats—one
lot for the LORD and the other for the scapegoat.[a] 9 Aaron shall bring the goat whose
lot falls to the LORD and sacrifice it for a sin offering. 10 But the goat chosen by lot
as the scapegoat shall be presented alive before the LORD to be used for making
atonement[m] by sending it into the desert as a scapegoat.
11 "Aaron shall bring the bull for his own sin offering to make atonement for himself
and his household,[n] and he is to slaughter the bull for his own sin offering. 12 He is
to take a censer full of burning coals[o] from the altar before the LORD and two handfuls
of finely ground fragrant incense[p] and take them behind the curtain. 13 He is to put
the incense on the fire before the LORD, and the smoke of the incense will conceal
the atonement cover above the Testimony, so that he will not die.[q] 14 He is to take
some of the bull's blood[r] and with his finger sprinkle it on the front of the atonement

[a] *31* Or *my tabernacle* [a] *8* That is, the goat of removal; Hebrew *azazel*; also in verses 10 and 26

15:31 [z]Lev 20:3; Nu 5:3; 19:13, 20; 2Sa 15:25; 2Ki 21:7; Ps 33:14; 74:7; 76:2; Eze 5:11; 23:38
15:32 [a]ver 2
15:33 [b]ver 19, 24, 25
16:1 [a]Lev 10:1
16:2 [b]Ex 30:10; Heb 9:7 [c]Heb 9:25; 10:19 [d]Ex 25:22 [e]Ex 40:34
16:3 [f]Heb 9:24, 25
16:4 [g]Ex 28:39 [h]Ex 28:42 [i]ver 24; Heb 10:22
16:5 [j]Lev 4:13-21 [k]2Ch 29:23
16:6 [l]Lev 9:7; Heb 5:3; 7:27; 9:7, 12
16:10 [m]Isa 53:4-10; Ro 3:25; 1Jn 2:2
16:11 [n]Heb 7:27; 9:7
16:12 [o]Lev 10:1 [p]Ex 30:34-38
16:13 [q]Ex 28:43; Lev 22:9
16:14 [r]Lev 4:5; Heb 9:7, 13, 25

15:32, 33 God is concerned about health, the dignity of the person, the dignity of the body, and the dignity of the sexual experience. His commands call the people to avoid unhealthy practices and promote healthy ones. To wash was the physical health response, to be purified or cleansed was the spiritual dignity response. This shows God's high regard for sex and sexuality. In our day, sex has been degraded by publicity; it has become public domain, not private celebration. We are called to have a high regard for sex, both in good health and purity.

16:1ff The Day of Atonement was the greatest day of the year for Israel. The Hebrew word for *atone* means "to cover". Old Testament sacrifices could not actually remove sins, only cover them. On this day, the people confessed their sins as a nation, and the high priest went into the Most Holy Place to make atonement for them. Sacrifices were made and blood was shed so that the people's sins could be "covered" until Christ's sacrifice on the cross would give people the opportunity to have their sin removed for ever.

16:1–25 Aaron had to spend hours preparing himself to meet God. But we can approach God anytime (Hebrews 4:16). What a privilege! We are offered easier access to God than the high priests of Old Testament times! Still, we must never forget that God is holy nor let this privilege cause us to approach God carelessly. The way to God has been opened to us by Christ. But easy access to God does not eliminate our need to prepare our hearts as we draw near in prayer.

16:5–28 This event with the two goats occurred on the Day of Atonement. The two goats represented the two ways God was dealing with the Israelites' sin: (1) he was forgiving their sin through the first goat, which was sacrificed, and (2) he was removing their guilt through the second goat, the scapegoat that was sent into the desert. The same ritual had to be repeated every year. Jesus Christ's death replaced this system once and for all. We can have our sins forgiven and guilt removed by placing our trust in Christ (Hebrews 10:1–18).

16:12 A censer was a dish or shallow bowl that hung by a chain or was carried with tongs. Inside the censer were placed incense (a combination of sweet-smelling spices) and burning coals from the altar. On the Day of Atonement, the high priest entered the Most Holy Place carrying a smoking censer. The smoke shielded him from the ark of the covenant and the presence of God—otherwise he would die. Incense may also have had a very practical purpose. The sweet smell drew the people's attention to the morning and evening sacrifices and helped cover the sometimes foul smell.

cover; then he shall sprinkle some of it with his finger seven times before the
atonement cover.[s]
15“He shall then slaughter the goat for the sin offering for the people[t] and take
its blood behind the curtain[u] and do with it as he did with the bull’s blood: He shall
sprinkle it on the atonement cover and in front of it. 16In this way he will make
atonement[v] for the Most Holy Place because of the uncleanness and rebellion of the
Israelites, whatever their sins have been. He is to do the same for the Tent of Meeting,
which is among them in the midst of their uncleanness. 17No-one is to be in the Tent
of Meeting from the time Aaron goes in to make atonement in the Most Holy Place
until he comes out, having made atonement for himself, his household and the whole
community of Israel.
18“Then he shall come out to the altar[w] that is before the LORD and make atonement
for it. He shall take some of the bull’s blood and some of the goat’s blood and put
it on all the horns of the altar.[x] 19He shall sprinkle some of the blood on it with his
finger seven times to cleanse it and consecrate it from the uncleanness of the Israelites.[y]
20“When Aaron has finished making atonement for the Most Holy Place, the Tent
of Meeting and the altar, he shall bring forward the live goat. 21He is to lay both hands
on the head of the live goat and confess[z] over it all the wickedness and rebellion of
the Israelites — all their sins — and put them on the goat’s head. He shall send the goat
away into the desert in the care of a man appointed for the task. 22The goat will carry
on itself all their sins[a] to a solitary place; and the man shall release it in the desert.
23“Then Aaron is to go into the Tent of Meeting and take off the linen garments
he put on before he entered the Most Holy Place, and he is to leave them there.[b] 24He
shall bathe himself with water in a holy place and put on his regular garments.[c] Then
he shall come out and sacrifice the burnt offering for himself and the burnt offering
for the people, to make atonement for himself and for the people. 25He shall also burn
the fat of the sin offering on the altar.
26“The man who releases the goat as a scapegoat must wash his clothes[d] and bathe
himself with water; afterwards he may come into the camp. 27The bull and the goat
for the sin offerings, whose blood was brought into the Most Holy Place to make
atonement, must be taken outside the camp;[e] their hides, flesh and offal are to be
burned up. 28The man who burns them must wash his clothes and bathe himself with
water; afterwards he may come into the camp.
29“This is to be a lasting ordinance for you: On the tenth day of the seventh month

16:14 [s]Lev 4:6
16:15 [t]Heb 9:7, 12 [u]Heb 9:3
16:16 [v]Ex 29:36
16:18 [w]Lev 4:7 [x]Lev 4:25
16:19 [y]Eze 43:20
16:21 [z]Lev 5:5
16:22 [a]Isa 53:12
16:23 [b]Eze 42:14; 44:19
16:24 [c]ver 3-5
16:26 [d]Lev 11:25
16:27 [e]Lev 4:12, 21; Heb 13:11

OLD/NEW SYSTEMS OF SACRIFICE

Old System of Sacrifice	*New System of Sacrifice*
Was temporary (Hebrews 8:13)	Is permanent (Hebrews 7:21)
Aaron first high priest (Leviticus 16:32)	Jesus only High Priest (Hebrews 4:14)
From tribe of Levi (Hebrews 7:5)	From tribe of Judah (Hebrews 7:14)
Ministered on earth (Hebrews 8:4)	Ministers in heaven (Hebrews 8:1,2)
Used blood of animals (Leviticus 16:15)	Uses blood of Christ (Hebrews 10:5)
Required many sacrifices (Leviticus 22:19)	Requires one sacrifice (Hebrews 9:28)
Needed perfect animals (Leviticus 22:19)	Needs a perfect life (Hebrews 5:9)
Required careful approach to tabernacle (Leviticus 16:2)	Encourages confident approach to throne (Hebrews 4:16)
Looked forward to new system (Hebrews 10:1)	Sets aside old system (Hebrews 10:9)

you must deny yourselves[b][f] and not do any work—whether native-born or an alien
living among you—30because on this day atonement will be made for you, to cleanse
you. Then, before the LORD, you will be clean from all your sins.[g] 31It is a sabbath
of rest, and you must deny yourselves;[h] it is a lasting ordinance. 32The priest who
is anointed and ordained to succeed his father as high priest is to make atonement.
He is to put on the sacred linen garments[i] 33and make atonement for the Most Holy
Place, for the Tent of Meeting and the altar, and for the priests and all the people of
the community.[j]
34"This is to be a lasting ordinance for you: Atonement is to be made once a year[k]
for all the sins of the Israelites."
And it was done, as the LORD commanded Moses.

Eating Blood Forbidden

17 The LORD said to Moses, 2"Speak to Aaron and his sons and to all the Israelites
and say to them: 'This is what the LORD has commanded: 3Any Israelite who
sacrifices an ox,[a] a lamb or a goat in the camp or outside of it 4instead of bringing
it to the entrance to the Tent of Meeting to present it as an offering to the LORD in
front of the tabernacle of the LORD[a]—that man shall be considered guilty of bloodshed; he has shed blood and must be cut off from his people.[b] 5This is so that the
Israelites will bring to the LORD the sacrifices they are now making in the open fields.
They must bring them to the priest, that is, to the LORD, at the entrance to the Tent
of Meeting and sacrifice them as fellowship offerings.[b] 6The priest is to sprinkle the
blood against the altar of the LORD[c] at the entrance to the Tent of Meeting and burn
the fat as an aroma pleasing to the LORD.[d] 7They must no longer offer any of their
sacrifices to the goat idols[c][e] to whom they prostitute themselves.[f] This is to be a
lasting ordinance for them and for the generations to come.'
8"Say to them: 'Any Israelite or any alien living among them who offers a burnt
offering or sacrifice 9and does not bring it to the entrance to the Tent of Meeting[g]
to sacrifice it to the LORD—that man must be cut off from his people.
10" 'Any Israelite or any alien living among them who eats any blood—I will set
my face against that person who eats blood[h] and will cut him off from his people.
11For the life of a creature is in the blood,[i] and I have given it to you to make
atonement for yourselves on the altar; it is the blood that makes atonement for one's
life.[j] 12Therefore I say to the Israelites, "None of you may eat blood, nor may an
alien living among you eat blood."
13" 'Any Israelite or any alien living among you who hunts any animal or bird that
may be eaten must drain out the blood and cover it with earth,[k] 14because the life

16:29 [f]Lev 23:27, 32; Nu 29:7; Isa 58:3
16:30 [g]Jer 33:8; Eph 5:26
16:31 [h]Isa 58:3, 5
16:32 [i]ver 4; Nu 20:26, 28
16:33 [j]ver 11, 16-18
16:34 [k]Heb 9:7, 25
17:4 [a]Dt 12:5-21 [b]Ge 17:14
17:6 [c]Lev 3:2 [d]Nu 18:17
17:7 [e]Ex 22:20; 2Ch 11:15 [f]Ex 32:8; 34:15; Dt 32:17; 1Co 10:20
17:9 [g]ver 4
17:10 [h]Ge 9:4; Lev 3:17; Dt 12:16, 23; 1Sa 14:33
17:11 [i]ver 14; Ge 9:4 [j]Heb 9:22
17:13 [k]Lev 7:26; Dt 12:16

[b] 29 Or *must fast*; also in verse 31 [a] 3 The Hebrew word can include both male and female. [b] 5 Traditionally *peace offerings* [c] 7 Or *demons*

17:1ff Chapters 17–26 are sometimes called the "holiness code" because they focus on what it means to live a holy life. The central verse is 19:2, "Be holy because I, the LORD your God, am holy."

17:3–9 Why were the Israelites prohibited from sacrificing outside the tabernacle area? God had established specific times and places for sacrifices, and each occasion was permeated with symbolism. If people sacrificed on their own, they might easily add to or subtract from God's laws to fit their own life-styles. Many pagan religions allowed every individual priest to set his own rules; God's command helped the Israelites resist the temptation to follow the pagan pattern. When the Israelites slipped into idolatry, it was because "everyone did as he saw fit" (Judges 17:6).

17:7 The goat idols (also called demons) were objects of worship and sacrifice in ancient times, particularly in Egypt from which they had recently escaped. God did not want the people to make this kind of sacrifice in the desert or in the promised land where they were heading.

17:11–14 How does blood make atonement for sin? When offered with the right attitude, the sacrifice and the blood shed from it made forgiveness of sin possible. On the one hand, blood represented the sinner's life, infected by his sin and headed for death. On the other hand, the blood represented the innocent life of the animal that was sacrificed in place of the guilty person making the offering. The death of the animal (of which the blood was proof) fulfilled the penalty of death. God therefore granted forgiveness to the sinner. It is God who forgives based on the faith of the person doing the sacrificing.

17:14 Why was eating or drinking blood prohibited? The prohibition against eating blood can be traced all the way back to Noah (Genesis 9:4). God prohibited eating or drinking blood for several reasons. (1) To discourage pagan practices. Israel was to be separate and distinct from the foreign nations around them. Eating blood was a common pagan practice. It was often done in hopes of gaining the characteristics of the slain animal (strength, speed, etc.). God's people were to rely on him, not on ingested blood, for their strength. (2) To preserve the symbolism of the sacrifice. Blood symbolised the life of the animal that was sacrificed in the sinner's place. To drink it would change the symbolism of the sacrificial penalty and destroy the evidence of the sacrifice. (3) To protect the people from infection because many deadly diseases are

of every creature is its blood. That is why I have said to the Israelites, "You must not eat the blood of any creature, because the life of every creature is its blood; anyone who eats it must be cut off."[l]

15" 'Anyone, whether native-born or alien, who eats anything found dead or torn by wild animals[m] must wash his clothes and bathe with water, and he will be ceremonially unclean till evening; then he will be clean. 16But if he does not wash his clothes and bathe himself, he will be held responsible.' "

B. LIVING A HOLY LIFE (18:1 – 27:34)

After the sacrificial system for forgiving sins was in place, the people were instructed on how to live as forgiven people. Applying these standards to our lives helps us grow in obedience and live a life pleasing to God.

1. Standards for the people

Unlawful Sexual Relations

18 The LORD said to Moses, 2"Speak to the Israelites and say to them: 'I am the LORD your God.[a] 3You must not do as they do in Egypt, where you used to live, and you must not do as they do in the land of Canaan, where I am bringing you. Do not follow their practices.[b] 4You must obey my laws and be careful to follow my decrees. I am the LORD your God.[c] 5Keep my decrees and laws, for the man who obeys them will live by them.[d] I am the LORD.

6" 'No-one is to approach any close relative to have sexual relations. I am the LORD.

7" 'Do not dishonour your father[e] by having sexual relations with your mother.[f] She is your mother; do not have relations with her.

8" 'Do not have sexual relations with your father's wife;[g] that would dishonour your father.[h]

9" 'Do not have sexual relations with your sister,[i] either your father's daughter or your mother's daughter, whether she was born in the same home or elsewhere.

10" 'Do not have sexual relations with your son's daughter or your daughter's daughter; that would dishonour you.

11" 'Do not have sexual relations with the daughter of your father's wife, born to your father; she is your sister.

12" 'Do not have sexual relations with your father's sister;[j] she is your father's close relative.

13" 'Do not have sexual relations with your mother's sister, because she is your mother's close relative.

14" 'Do not dishonour your father's brother by approaching his wife to have sexual relations; she is your aunt.[k]

15" 'Do not have sexual relations with your daughter-in-law.[l] She is your son's wife; do not have relations with her.

17:14 [l]ver 11; Ge 9:4
17:15 [m]Ex 22:31; Dt 14:21
18:2 [a]Ex 6:7; Lev 11:44; Eze 20:5
18:3 [b]ver 24-30; Ex 23:24; Lev 20:23
18:4 [c]ver 2
18:5 [d]Eze 20:11; Ro 10:5*; Gal 3:12*
18:7 [e]Lev 20:11 [f]Eze 22:10
18:8 [g]1Co 5:1 [h]Lev 20:11
18:9 [i]Lev 20:17
18:12 [j]Lev 20:19
18:14 [k]Lev 20:20
18:15 [l]Lev 20:12

---

transmitted through the blood. The Jews took this prohibition seriously, and that is why Jesus' hearers were so upset when Jesus told them to drink his blood (John 6:53–56). However, Jesus, as God himself and the last sacrifice ever needed for sins, was asking believers to identify with him completely. He wants us to take his life into us, and he wants to participate in our lives as well.

18:3 The Israelites moved from one idol-infested country to another. As God helped them form a new culture, he warned them to leave all aspects of their pagan background behind. He also warned them how easy it would be to slip into the pagan culture of Canaan, where they were going. Canaan's society and religions appealed to worldly desires, especially sexual immorality and drunkenness. The Israelites were to keep themselves pure and set apart for God. God did not want his people absorbed into the surrounding culture and environment. Society may pressure us to conform to its way of life and thought, but yielding to that pressure will (1) create confusion as to which side we should be on and (2) eliminate our effectiveness in serving God. Follow God, and don't let the culture around you mould your thoughts and actions.

18:6–18 Marrying relatives was prohibited by God for physical, social, and moral reasons. Children born to near relatives may experience serious health problems. Without these specific laws, sexual promiscuity would have been more likely, first in families, then outside. Improper sexual relations destroy family life.

18:6–27 Several abominations, or wicked actions, are listed here: (1) having sexual relations with close relatives, (2) committing adultery, (3) offering children as sacrifices, (4) having homosexual relations, and (5) having sexual relations with animals. These practices were common in pagan religions and cultures, and it is easy to see why God dealt harshly with those who began to follow them. Such practices lead to disease, deformity, and death. They disrupt family life and society and reveal a low regard for the value of oneself and of others. Society today takes some of these practices lightly, even trying to make them acceptable. But they are still sins in God's eyes. If you consider them acceptable, you are not judging by God's standards.

16" 'Do not have sexual relations with your brother's wife;[m] that would dishonour
your brother.
17" 'Do not have sexual relations with both a woman and her daughter.[n] Do not
have sexual relations with either her son's daughter or her daughter's daughter; they
are her close relatives. That is wickedness.
18" 'Do not take your wife's sister as a rival wife and have sexual relations with
her while your wife is living.
19" 'Do not approach a woman to have sexual relations during the uncleanness of
her monthly period.[o]
20" 'Do not have sexual relations with your neighbour's wife[p] and defile yourself
with her.
21" 'Do not give any of your children[q] to be sacrificed[a] to Molech,[r] for you must
not profane the name of your God.[s] I am the LORD.
22" 'Do not lie with a man as one lies with a woman;[t] that is detestable.
23" 'Do not have sexual relations with an animal and defile yourself with it. A
woman must not present herself to an animal to have sexual relations with it; that is
a perversion.[u]
24" 'Do not defile yourselves in any of these ways, because this is how the nations
that I am going to drive out before you[v] became defiled.[w] 25Even the land was
defiled; so I punished it for its sin,[x] and the land vomited out its inhabitants.[y] 26But
you must keep my decrees and my laws. The native-born and the aliens living among
you must not do any of these detestable things, 27for all these things were done by
the people who lived in the land before you, and the land became defiled. 28And if
you defile the land, it will vomit you out as it vomited out the nations that were before
you.
29" 'Everyone who does any of these detestable things—such persons must be cut
off from their people. 30Keep my requirements[z] and do not follow any of the
detestable customs that were practised before you came and do not defile yourselves
with them. I am the LORD your God.[a]' "

Various Laws

19 The LORD said to Moses, 2"Speak to the entire assembly of Israel and say to
them: 'Be holy because I, the LORD your God, am holy.[a]
3" 'Each of you must respect his mother and father,[b] and you must observe my
Sabbaths. I am the LORD your God.[c]
4" 'Do not turn to idols or make gods of cast metal for yourselves.[d] I am the LORD
your God.
5" 'When you sacrifice a fellowship offering[a] to the LORD, sacrifice it in such a
way that it will be accepted on your behalf. 6It shall be eaten on the day you sacrifice
it or on the next day; anything left over until the third day must be burned up. 7If any
of it is eaten on the third day, it is impure and will not be accepted. 8Whoever eats
it will be held responsible because he has desecrated what is holy to the LORD; that
person must be cut off from his people.
9" 'When you reap the harvest of your land, do not reap to the very edges of your
field or gather the gleanings of your harvest.[e] 10Do not go over your vineyard a
second time or pick up the grapes that have fallen. Leave them for the poor and the
alien. I am the LORD your God.

a *21* Or *to be passed through* ⌞*the fire*⌟ a *5* Traditionally *peace offering*

18:16 [m]Lev 20:21
18:17 [n]Lev 20:14
18:19 [o]Lev 15:24; 20:18
18:20 [p]Ex 20:14; Lev 20:10; Mt 5:27, 28; 1Co 6:9; Heb 13:4
18:21 [q]Dt 12:31 [r]Lev 20:2-5 [s]Lev 19:12; 21:6; Eze 36:20
18:22 [t]Lev 20:13; Dt 23:18; Ro 1:27
18:23 [u]Ex 22:19; Lev 20:15; Dt 27:21
18:24 [v]ver 3, 27, 30 [w]Dt 18:12
18:25 [x]Lev 20:23; Dt 9:5; 18:12 [y]ver 28; Lev 20:22
18:30 [z]Dt 11:1 [a]ver 2
19:2 [a]1Pe 1:16*; Lev 11:44
19:3 [b]Ex 20:12 [c]Lev 11:44
19:4 [d]Ex 20:4, 23; 34:17; Lev 26:1; Ps 96:5; 115:4-7
19:9 [e]Lev 23:10, 22; Dt 24:19-22

19:9, 10 This law was a protection for the poor and the alien (foreigner) and a reminder that God owned the land; the people were only caretakers. Laws such as this showed God's generosity and liberality. As people of God, the Israelites were to reflect his nature and characteristics in their attitudes and actions. Ruth and Naomi were two people who benefited from this merciful law (Ruth 2:2).

19:9, 10 God instructed the Hebrews to provide for those in need. He required that the people leave the edges of their fields unharvested, providing food for travellers and the poor. It is easy to ignore the poor or forget about those who have less than we do. But God desires generosity. In what ways can you leave the "edges of your field" for those in need?

19:10–35 "Do not . . ." Some people think the Bible is nothing but a book of don'ts. But Jesus neatly summarised all these rules when he said to love God with all your heart, and your neighbour as yourself. He called these the greatest commandments (or rules) of all (Matthew 22:34–40). By carrying out Jesus' simple commands, we find ourselves following all of God's other laws as well.

11“ ‘Do not steal.[f]
“ ‘Do not lie.[g]
“ ‘Do not deceive one another.
12“ ‘Do not swear falsely by my name[h] and so profane the name of your God. I
am the LORD.
13“ ‘Do not defraud your neighbour or rob him.[i]
“ ‘Do not hold back the wages of a hired man overnight.[j]
14“ ‘Do not curse the deaf or put a stumbling-block in front of the blind,[k] but fear
your God. I am the LORD.
15“ ‘Do not pervert justice;[l] do not show partiality[m] to the poor or favouritism to
the great, but judge your neighbour fairly.
16“ ‘Do not go about spreading slander[n] among your people.
“ ‘Do not do anything that endangers your neighbour's life.[o] I am the LORD.
17“ ‘Do not hate your brother in your heart.[p] Rebuke your neighbour frankly[q] so
that you will not share in his guilt.
18“ ‘Do not seek revenge[r] or bear a grudge[s] against one of your people, but love
your neighbour as yourself.[t] I am the LORD.
19“ ‘Keep my decrees.
“ ‘Do not mate different kinds of animals.
“ ‘Do not plant your field with two kinds of seed.[u]
“ ‘Do not wear clothing woven of two kinds of material.[v]
20“ ‘If a man sleeps with a woman who is a slave girl promised to another man but
who has not been ransomed or given her freedom, there must be due punishment. Yet
they are not to be put to death, because she had not been freed. 21The man, however,
must bring a ram to the entrance to the Tent of Meeting for a guilt offering to the
LORD.[w] 22With the ram of the guilt offering the priest is to make atonement for him
before the LORD for the sin he has committed, and his sin will be forgiven.
23“ ‘When you enter the land and plant any kind of fruit tree, regard its fruit as
forbidden.[b] For three years you are to consider it forbidden;[b] it must not be eaten.
24In the fourth year all its fruit will be holy,[x] an offering of praise to the LORD. 25But
in the fifth year you may eat its fruit. In this way your harvest will be increased. I
am the LORD your God.
26“ ‘Do not eat any meat with the blood still in it.[y]
“ ‘Do not practise divination or sorcery.[z]
27“ ‘Do not cut the hair at the sides of your head or clip off the edges of your beard.[a]
28“ ‘Do not cut your bodies for the dead or put tattoo marks on yourselves. I am
the LORD.
29“ ‘Do not degrade your daughter by making her a prostitute,[b] or the land will
turn to prostitution and be filled with wickedness.
30“ ‘Observe my Sabbaths and have reverence for my sanctuary. I am the LORD.[c]
31“ ‘Do not turn to mediums or seek out spiritists,[d] for you will be defiled by them.
I am the LORD your God.
32“ ‘Rise in the presence of the aged, show respect for the elderly[e] and revere your
God. I am the LORD.
33“ ‘When an alien lives with you in your land, do not ill-treat him. 34The alien
living with you must be treated as one of your native-born.[f] Love him as yourself,
for you were aliens in Egypt.[g] I am the LORD your God.
35“ ‘Do not use dishonest standards when measuring length, weight or quantity.

b 23 Hebrew *uncircumcised*

19:11 [f]Ex 20:15 [g]Eph 4:25
19:12 [h]Ex 20:7; Mt 5:33
19:13 [i]Ex 22:15, 25-27 [j]Dt 24:15; Jas 5:4
19:14 [k]Dt 27:18
19:15 [l]Ex 23:2, 6 [m]Dt 1:17
19:16 [n]Ps 15:3; Eze 22:9 [o]Ex 23:7
19:17 [p]1Jn 2:9; 3:15 [q]Mt 18:15; Lk 17:3
19:18 [r]Ro 12:19 [s]Ps 103:9 [t]Mt 5:43*; 19:16*; 22:39*; Mk 12:31*; Lk 10:27*; Jn 13:34; Ro 13:9*; Gal 5:14*; Jas 2:8*
19:19 [u]Dt 22:9 [v]Dt 22:11
19:21 [w]Lev 5:15
19:24 [x]Pr 3:9
19:26 [y]Lev 17:10 [z]Dt 18:10
19:27 [a]Lev 21:5
19:29 [b]Dt 23:18
19:30 [c]Lev 26:2
19:31 [d]Lev 20:6; Isa 8:19
19:32 [e]1Ti 5:1
19:34 [f]Ex 12:48 [g]Dt 10:19

19:32 People often find it easy to dismiss the opinions of the elderly and avoid taking time to visit them. But the fact that God commanded the Israelites to honour the elderly shows how seriously we should take the responsibility of respecting those older than we. Their wisdom gained from experience can save us from many pitfalls.

19:33, 34 How do you feel when you encounter foreigners (aliens), especially those who don't speak your language? Are you impatient? Do you think or act as if they should go back where they came from? Are you tempted to take advantage of them? God says to treat foreigners as you'd treat fellow countrymen, to love them as you love yourself. In reality, we are all foreigners in this world, because it is only our temporary home. View strangers, newcomers, and foreigners as opportunities to demonstrate God's love.

36 Use honest scales and honest weights, an honest ephah[c] and an honest hin.[d][h] I
am the LORD your God, who brought you out of Egypt.
37 " 'Keep all my decrees and all my laws and follow them. I am the LORD.' "

Punishments for Sin

20 The LORD said to Moses, 2 "Say to the Israelites: 'Any Israelite or any alien
living in Israel who gives[a] any of his children to Molech must be put to death.
The people of the community are to stone him. 3 I will set my face against that man
and I will cut him off from his people; for by giving his children to Molech, he has
defiled my sanctuary[a] and profaned my holy name.[b] 4 If the people of the community
close their eyes when that man gives one of his children to Molech and they fail to
put him to death,[c] 5 I will set my face against that man and his family and will cut
off from their people both him and all who follow him in prostituting themselves to
Molech.
6 " 'I will set my face against the person who turns to mediums and spiritists to
prostitute himself by following them, and I will cut him off from his people.[d]
7 " 'Consecrate yourselves and be holy,[e] because I am the LORD your God. 8 Keep
my decrees and follow them. I am the LORD, who makes you holy.[b][f]
9 " 'If anyone curses his father or mother,[g] he must be put to death.[h] He has cursed
his father or his mother, and his blood will be on his own head.[i]
10 " 'If a man commits adultery with another man's wife[j]—with the wife of his
neighbour—both the adulterer and the adulteress must be put to death.
11 " 'If a man sleeps with his father's wife, he has dishonoured his father.[k] Both
the man and the woman must be put to death; their blood will be on their own heads.
12 " 'If a man sleeps with his daughter-in-law,[l] both of them must be put to death.
What they have done is a perversion; their blood will be on their own heads.
13 " 'If a man lies with a man as one lies with a woman, both of them have done
what is detestable.[m] They must be put to death; their blood will be on their own heads.
14 " 'If a man marries both a woman and her mother,[n] it is wicked. Both he and
they must be burned in the fire, so that no wickedness will be among you.[o]
15 " 'If a man has sexual relations with an animal,[p] he must be put to death, and
you must kill the animal.
16 " 'If a woman approaches an animal to have sexual relations with it, kill both the
woman and the animal. They must be put to death; their blood will be on their own
heads.
17 " 'If a man marries his sister[q], the daughter of either his father or his mother,

c 36 An ephah was a dry measure. d 36 A hin was a liquid measure. a 2 Or *sacrifices*; also in verses 3 and 4
b 8 Or *who sanctifies you*; or *who sets you apart as holy*

19:36 [h]Dt 25:13-15
20:3 [a]Lev 15:31 [b]Lev 18:21
20:4 [c]Dt 17:2-5
20:6 [d]Lev 19:31
20:7 [e]Eph 1:4; 1Pe 1:16*
20:8 [f]Ex 31:13
20:9 [g]Dt 27:16 [h]Ex 21:17; Mt 15:4*; Mk 7:10* [i]ver 11; 2Sa 1:16
20:10 [j]Ex 20:14; Dt 5:18; 22:22
20:11 [k]Lev 18:7; Dt 27:23
20:12 [l]Lev 18:15
20:13 [m]Lev 18:22
20:14 [n]Lev 18:17 [o]Dt 27:23
20:15 [p]Lev 18:23
20:17 [q]Lev 18:9

20:1-3 Sacrificing children to the gods was a common practice in ancient religions. The Ammonites, Israel's neighbours, made child sacrifice to Molech (their national god) a vital part of their religion. They saw this as the greatest gift they could offer to ward off evil or appease angry gods. God made it clear that this practice was detestable and strictly forbidden. In Old Testament times as well as New, his character made human sacrifice unthinkable. (1) Unlike the pagan gods, he is a God of love, who does not need to be appeased (Exodus 34:6). (2) He is a God of life, who prohibits murder and encourages practices that lead to health and happiness (Deuteronomy 30:15, 16). (3) He is God of the helpless, who shows special concern for children (Psalm 72:4). (4) He is a God of unselfishness, who instead of demanding blood gives his life for others (Isaiah 53:4, 5).

20:6 Everyone is interested in what the future holds, and we often look to others for guidance. But God warned about looking to the occult for advice. Mediums and spiritists were outlawed because God was not the source of their information. At best, occult practitioners are fakes whose predictions cannot be trusted. At worst, they are in contact with evil spirits and are thus extremely dangerous. We don't need to look to the occult for information about the future. God has given us the Bible so that we may obtain all the information we need—and the Bible's teaching is trustworthy.

20:10-21 This list of commands against sexual sins includes extremely harsh punishments. Why? God had no tolerance for such acts for the following reasons: (1) they shatter the mutual commitment of married partners; (2) they destroy the sanctity of the family; (3) they twist people's mental well-being; and (4) they spread disease. Sexual sin has always been widespread, but the glorification of sex between people who are not married to each other often hides deep tragedy and hurt behind the scenes. When society portrays sexual sins as attractive, it is easy to forget the dark side. God had good reasons for prohibiting sexual sins: He loves us and wants the very best for us.

20:10-21 The detestable acts listed here were very common in the pagan nations of Canaan; their religions were rampant with sex goddesses, temple prostitution, and other gross sins. The Canaanites' immoral religious practices reflected a decadent culture that tended to corrupt whoever came in contact with it. By contrast, God was building a nation to make a positive influence on the world. He did not want the Israelites to adopt the Canaanites' practices and slide into debauchery. So he prepared the people for what they would face in the promised land by commanding them to steer clear of sexual sins.

and they have sexual relations, it is a disgrace. They must be cut off before the eyes
of their people. He has dishonoured his sister and will be held responsible.
18“ ‘If a man lies with a woman during her monthly period[r] and has sexual relations
with her, he has exposed the source of her flow, and she has also uncovered it. Both
of them must be cut off from their people.
19“ ‘Do not have sexual relations with the sister of either your mother or your
father,[s] for that would dishonour a close relative; both of you would be held responsible.
20“ ‘If a man sleeps with his aunt,[t] he has dishonoured his uncle. They will be
held responsible; they will die childless.
21“ ‘If a man marries his brother’s wife,[u] it is an act of impurity; he has dishonoured
his brother. They will be childless.
22“ ‘Keep all my decrees and laws and follow them, so that the land[v] where I am
bringing you to live may not vomit you out. 23You must not live according to the
customs of the nations[w] I am going to drive out before you.[x] Because they did all
these things, I abhorred them. 24But I said to you, “You will possess their land; I will
give it to you as an inheritance, a land flowing with milk and honey.”[y] I am the LORD
your God, who has set you apart from the nations.[z]
25“ ‘You must therefore make a distinction between clean and unclean animals and
between unclean and clean birds.[a] Do not defile yourselves by any animal or bird
or anything that moves along the ground—those which I have set apart as unclean
for you. 26You are to be holy to me[c] because I, the LORD, am holy,[b] and I have
set you apart from the nations to be my own.
27“ ‘A man or woman who is a medium or spiritist among you must be put to
death.[c] You are to stone them; their blood will be on their own heads.’ ”

2. Rules for priests

21 The LORD said to Moses, “Speak to the priests, the sons of Aaron, and say to
them: ‘A priest must not make himself ceremonially unclean for any of his
people who die,[a] 2except for a close relative, such as his mother or father, his son
or daughter, his brother, 3or an unmarried sister who is dependent on him since she
has no husband—for her he may make himself unclean. 4He must not make himself
unclean for people related to him by marriage,[a] and so defile himself.
5“ ‘Priests must not shave their heads or shave off the edges of their beards[b] or
cut their bodies.[c] 6They must be holy to their God and must not profane the name
of their God.[d] Because they present the offerings made to the LORD by fire,[e] the
food of their God, they are to be holy.
7“ ‘They must not marry women defiled by prostitution or divorced from their
husbands,[f] because priests are holy to their God.[g] 8Regard them as holy,[h] because
they offer up the food of your God. Consider them holy, because I the LORD am
holy—I who make you holy.[b]
9“ ‘If a priest’s daughter defiles herself by becoming a prostitute, she disgraces her
father; she must be burned in the fire.[i]
10“ ‘The high priest, the one among his brothers who has had the anointing oil
poured on his head and who has been ordained to wear the priestly garments,[j] must
not let his hair become unkempt[c] or tear his clothes.[k] 11He must not enter a place
where there is a dead body.[l] He must not make himself unclean,[m] even for his father
or mother, 12nor leave the sanctuary of his God or desecrate it, because he has been
dedicated by the anointing oil[n] of his God. I am the LORD.

c 26 Or *be my holy ones* a 4 Or *unclean as a leader among his people* b 8 Or *who sanctify you*; or *who set you apart as holy* c 10 Or *not uncover his head*

20:18 [r]Lev 15:24; 18:19
20:19 [s]Lev 18:12-13
20:20 [t]Lev 18:14
20:21 [u]Lev 18:16
20:22 [v]Lev 18:25-28
20:23 [w]Lev 18:3 [x]Lev 18:24, 27, 30
20:24 [y]Ex 3:8; 13:5; 33:3 [z]Ex 33:16
20:25 [a]Lev 11:1-47; Dt 14:3-21
20:26 [b]Lev 19:2
20:27 [c]Lev 19:31
21:1 [a]Eze 44:25
21:5 [b]Eze 44:20 [c]Lev 19:28; Dt 14:1
21:6 [d]Lev 18:21 [e]Lev 3:11
21:7 [f]ver 13, 14 [g]Eze 44:22
21:8 [h]ver 6
21:9 [i]Ge 38:24; Lev 19:29
21:10 [j]Lev 16:32 [k]Lev 10:6
21:11 [l]Nu 19:11, 13, 14 [m]Lev 19:28
21:12 [n]Ex 29:6-7; Lev 10:7

20:22, 23 God gave many rules to his people—but not without reason. He did not withhold good from them; he only prohibited those acts that would bring them to ruin. All of us understand God’s physical laws of nature. For example, jumping off a ten-storey building means death because of the law of gravity. But some of us don’t understand how God’s spiritual laws work. God forbids us to do certain things because he wants to keep us from self-destruction. Next time you are drawn to a forbidden physical or emotional pleasure, remind yourself that its consequences might be suffering and separation from the God who is trying to help you.

21:1, 2 To become ceremonially unclean for “any of his people who die” means touching a dead body.

13“ ‘The woman he marries must be a virgin.[o] 14He must not marry a widow, a
divorced woman, or a woman defiled by prostitution, but only a virgin from his own
people, 15so that he will not defile his offspring among his people. I am the LORD,
who makes him holy.’ ”[d]
16The LORD said to Moses, 17“Say to Aaron: ‘For the generations to come none of
your descendants who has a defect may come near to offer the food of his God.[p] 18No
man who has any defect[q] may come near: no man who is blind or lame, disfigured
or deformed; 19no man with a crippled foot or hand, 20or who is hunchbacked or
dwarfed, or who has any eye defect, or who has festering or running sores or damaged
testicles.[r] 21No descendant of Aaron the priest who has any defect is to come near
to present the offerings made to the LORD by fire. He has a defect; he must not come
near to offer the food of his God. 22He may eat the most holy food of his God,[s] as
well as the holy food; 23yet because of his defect, he must not go near the curtain or
approach the altar, and so desecrate my sanctuary. I am the LORD, who makes them
holy.’ ”[e]
24So Moses told this to Aaron and his sons and to all the Israelites.

22 The LORD said to Moses, 2“Tell Aaron and his sons to treat with respect the
sacred offerings the Israelites consecrate to me, so that they will not profane
my holy name. I am the LORD.
3“Say to them: ‘For the generations to come, if any of your descendants is ceremonially unclean and yet comes near the sacred offerings that the Israelites consecrate to
the LORD, that person must be cut off from my presence.[a] I am the LORD.
4“ ‘If a descendant of Aaron has an infectious skin disease[a] or a bodily discharge,[b]
he may not eat the sacred offerings until he is cleansed. He will also be unclean if
he touches something defiled by a corpse[c] or by anyone who has an emission of
semen, 5or if he touches any crawling thing[d] that makes him unclean, or any person[e]
who makes him unclean, whatever the uncleanness may be. 6The one who touches
any such thing will be unclean till evening. He must not eat any of the sacred offerings
unless he has bathed himself with water. 7When the sun goes down, he will be clean,
and after that he may eat the sacred offerings, for they are his food.[f] 8He must not
eat anything found dead[g] or torn by wild animals,[h] and so become unclean[i] through
it. I am the LORD.
9“ ‘The priests are to keep my requirements so that they do not become guilty and
die[j] for treating them with contempt. I am the LORD, who makes them holy.[b]
10“ ‘No-one outside a priest’s family may eat the sacred offering, nor may the guest
of a priest or his hired worker eat it. 11But if a priest buys a slave with money, or
if a slave is born in his household, that slave may eat his food.[k] 12If a priest’s daughter
marries anyone other than a priest, she may not eat any of the sacred contributions.
13But if a priest’s daughter becomes a widow or is divorced, yet has no children, and
she returns to live in her father’s house as in her youth, she may eat of her father’s
food. No unauthorised person, however, may eat any of it.
14“ ‘If anyone eats a sacred offering by mistake, he must make restitution to the
priest for the offering and add a fifth of the value[l] to it. 15The priests must not

d *15* Or *who sanctifies him*; or *who sets him apart as holy* **e** *23* Or *who sanctifies them*; or *who sets them apart as holy* **a** *4* Traditionally *leprosy*; the Hebrew word was used for various diseases affecting the skin—not necessarily leprosy. **b** *9* Or *who sanctifies them*; or *who sets them apart as holy*; also in verse 16

21:13 [o]Eze 44:22
21:17 [p]ver 6
21:18 [q]Lev 22:19-25
21:20 [r]Dt 23:1; Isa 56:3
21:22 [s]1Co 9:13
22:3 [a]Lev 7:20, 21; Nu 19:13
22:4 [b]Lev 14:1-32; 15:2-15 [c]Lev 11:24-28, 39
22:5 [d]Lev 11:24-28, 43 [e]Lev 15:7
22:7 [f]Nu 18:11
22:8 [g]Lev 11:39 [h]Ex 22:31; Lev 17:15 [i]Lev 11:40
22:9 [j]ver 16; Ex 28:43
22:11 [k]Ge 17:13; Ex 12:44
22:14 [l]Lev 5:15

21:16–23 Was God unfairly discriminating against handicapped people when he said they were unqualified to offer sacrifices? Just as God demanded that no imperfect animals be used for sacrifice, he required that no handicapped priests offer sacrifices. This was not meant as an insult; rather, it had to do with the fact that the priest must match as closely as possible the perfect God he served. Of course, such perfection was not fully realised until Jesus Christ came. As Levites, the handicapped priests were protected and supported with food from the sacrifices. They were not abandoned because they still performed many essential services within the tabernacle.

22:1–9 Why were there so many specific guidelines for the priests? The Israelites would have been quite familiar with priests from Egypt. Egyptian priests were mainly interested in politics. They viewed religion as a way to gain power. Thus the Israelites would have been suspicious of the establishment of a new priestly order. But God wanted his priests to serve him and the people. Their duties were religious—to help people draw near to God and worship him. They could not use their position to gain power because they were not allowed to own land or take money from anyone. All these guidelines reassured the people and helped the priests accomplish their purpose.

desecrate the sacred offerings the Israelites present to the LORD[m] 16by allowing them
to eat the sacred offerings and so bring upon them guilt requiring payment.[n] I am
the LORD, who makes them holy.' "

Unacceptable Sacrifices

17The LORD said to Moses, 18"Speak to Aaron and his sons and to all the Israelites
and say to them: 'If any of you—either an Israelite or an alien living in Israel—presents a gift[o] for a burnt offering to the LORD, either to fulfil a vow or as
a freewill offering, 19you must present a male without defect[p] from the cattle, sheep
or goats in order that it may be accepted on your behalf. 20Do not bring anything with
a defect,[q] because it will not be accepted on your behalf. 21When anyone brings from
the herd or flock a fellowship offering[c][r] to the LORD to fulfil a special vow or as
a freewill offering, it must be without defect or blemish to be acceptable. 22Do not
offer to the LORD the blind, the injured or the maimed, or anything with warts or
festering or running sores. Do not place any of these on the altar as an offering made
to the LORD by fire. 23You may, however, present as a freewill offering an ox[d] or
a sheep that is deformed or stunted, but it will not be accepted in fulfilment of a vow.
24You must not offer to the LORD an animal whose testicles are bruised, crushed, torn
or cut.[s] You must not do this in your own land, 25and you must not accept such
animals from the hand of a foreigner and offer them as the food of your God.[t] They
will not be accepted on your behalf, because they are deformed and have defects.' "

26The LORD said to Moses, 27"When a calf, a lamb or a goat is born, it is to remain
with its mother for seven days.[u] From the eighth day on, it will be acceptable as an
offering made to the LORD by fire. 28Do not slaughter a cow or a sheep and its young
on the same day.[v]

29"When you sacrifice a thank-offering[w] to the LORD, sacrifice it in such a way
that it will be accepted on your behalf. 30It must be eaten that same day; leave none
of it till morning.[x] I am the LORD.

31"Keep[y] my commands and follow them. I am the LORD. 32Do not profane my
holy name.[z] I must be acknowledged as holy by the Israelites.[a] I am the LORD, who
makes[e] you holy[f] 33and who brought you out of Egypt to be your God.[b] I am the
LORD."

3. Seasons and festivals

23 The LORD said to Moses, 2"Speak to the Israelites and say to them: 'These are
my appointed feasts,[a] the appointed feasts of the LORD, which you are to
proclaim as sacred assemblies.[b]

The Sabbath

3" 'There are six days when you may work,[c] but the seventh day is a Sabbath of
rest,[d] a day of sacred assembly. You are not to do any work; wherever you live, it
is a Sabbath to the LORD.

The Passover and Unleavened Bread

4" 'These are the LORD's appointed feasts, the sacred assemblies you are to proclaim
at their appointed times: 5The LORD's Passover begins at twilight on the fourteenth

c 21 Traditionally *peace offering* d 23 The Hebrew word can include both male and female. e 32 Or *made*
f 32 Or *who sanctifies you*; or *who sets you apart as holy*

22:15 [m]Nu 18:32
22:16 [n]ver 9
22:18 [o]Lev 1:2
22:19 [p]Lev 1:3
22:20 [q]Dt 15:21; 17:1; Mal 1:8, 14; Heb 9:14; 1Pe 1:19
22:21 [r]Lev 3:6; Nu 15:3, 8
22:24 [s]Lev 21:20
22:25 [t]Lev 21:6
22:27 [u]Ex 22:30
22:28 [v]Dt 22:6, 7
22:29 [w]Lev 7:12; Ps 107:22
22:30 [x]Lev 7:15
22:31 [y]Dt 4:2, 40; Ps 105:45
22:32 [z]Lev 18:21 [a]Lev 10:3
22:33 [b]Lev 11:45
23:2 [a]ver 4, 37, 44; Nu 29:39 [b]ver 21, 27
23:3 [c]Ex 20:9 [d]Ex 20:10; 31:13-17; Lev 19:3; Dt 5:13; Heb 4:9, 10

22:19–25 Animals with defects were not acceptable as sacrifices because they did not represent God's holy nature. Furthermore, the animal had to be without blemish in order to foreshadow the perfect, sinless life of Jesus Christ. When we give our best time, talent, and treasure to God rather than what is tarnished or common, we show the true meaning of worship and testify to God's supreme worth.

23:1ff Feasts played a major role in Israel's culture. Israel's feasts were different from those of any other nation because, being ordained by God, they were times of celebrating with him, not times of moral depravity. God wanted to set aside special days for the people to come together for rest, refreshment, and remembering with thanksgiving all he had done for them.

23:1–4 God established several national holidays each year for celebration, fellowship, and worship. Much can be learned about people by observing the holidays they celebrate and the way they celebrate them. Take note of your holiday traditions. What do they say about your values?

day of the first month.[e] 6On the fifteenth day of that month the LORD's Feast of
Unleavened Bread begins; for seven days you must eat bread made without yeast. 7On
the first day hold a sacred assembly[f] and do no regular work. 8For seven days present
an offering made to the LORD by fire. And on the seventh day hold a sacred assembly
and do no regular work.' "

Firstfruits

9The LORD said to Moses, 10"Speak to the Israelites and say to them: 'When you
enter the land I am going to give you and you reap its harvest, bring to the priest a
sheaf[g] of the first grain you harvest. 11He is to wave the sheaf before the LORD[h]
so it will be accepted on your behalf; the priest is to wave it on the day after the
Sabbath. 12On the day you wave the sheaf, you must sacrifice as a burnt offering to
the LORD a lamb a year old without defect, 13together with its grain offering[i] of
two-tenths of an ephah**a** of fine flour mixed with oil—an offering made to the LORD
by fire, a pleasing aroma—and its drink offering of a quarter of a hin**b** of wine. 14You
must not eat any bread, or roasted or new grain, until the very day you bring this
offering to your God.[j] This is to be a lasting ordinance for the generations to come,[k]
wherever you live.

Feast of Weeks

15" 'From the day after the Sabbath, the day you brought the sheaf of the wave
offering, count off seven full weeks. 16Count off fifty days up to the day after the
seventh Sabbath,[l] and then present an offering of new grain to the LORD. 17From
wherever you live, bring two loaves made of two-tenths of an ephah of fine flour,
baked with yeast, as a wave offering of firstfruits[m] to the LORD. 18Present with this
bread seven male lambs, each a year old and without defect, one young bull and two
rams. They will be a burnt offering to the LORD, together with their grain offerings
and drink offerings—an offering made by fire, an aroma pleasing to the LORD. 19Then
sacrifice one male goat for a sin offering and two lambs, each a year old, for a
fellowship offering.**c** 20The priest is to wave the two lambs before the LORD as a wave
offering, together with the bread of the firstfruits. They are a sacred offering to the
LORD for the priest. 21On that same day you are to proclaim a sacred assembly[n] and
do no regular work.[o] This is to be a lasting ordinance for the generations to come,
wherever you live.

22" 'When you reap the harvest[p] of your land, do not reap to the very edges of your
field or gather the gleanings of your harvest.[q] Leave them for the poor and the alien.
I am the LORD your God.' "

Feast of Trumpets

23The LORD said to Moses, 24"Say to the Israelites: 'On the first day of the seventh
month you are to have a day of rest, a sacred assembly commemorated with trumpet
blasts.[r] 25Do no regular work,[s] but present an offering made to the LORD by fire.' "

23:5 [e]Ex 12:18-19; Nu 28:16-17; Dt 16:1-8
23:7 [f]ver 3, 8
23:10 [g]Ex 23:16, 19; 34:26
23:11 [h]Ex 29:24
23:13 [i]Lev 2:14-16; 6:20
23:14 [j]Ex 34:26 [k]Nu 15:21
23:16 [l]Nu 28:26; Ac 2:1
23:17 [m]Ex 34:22; Lev 2:12
23:21 [n]ver 2 [o]ver 3
23:22 [p]Lev 19:9 [q]Lev 19:10; Dt 24:19-21; Ru 2:15
23:24 [r]Lev 25:9; Nu 10:9, 10; 29:1
23:25 [s]ver 21

a *13* That is, probably about 7½ pints (about 4.5 litres); also in verse 17 **b** *13* That is, probably about 1½ pints (about 1 litre) **c** *19* Traditionally *peace offering*

23:6 The Feast of Unleavened Bread reminded Israel of their escape from Egypt. For seven days they ate unleavened bread, just as they had eaten it back then (Exodus 12:14, 15). The symbolism of this bread made without yeast was important to the Israelites. First, because the bread was unique, it illustrated Israel's uniqueness as a nation. Second, because yeast was a symbol of sin, the bread represented Israel's moral purity. Third, the bread reminded them to obey quickly. Their ancestors left the yeast out of their dough so they could leave Egypt quickly without waiting for the dough to rise.

23:9–14 The Feast of Firstfruits required that the first crops harvested be offered to God. The Israelites could not eat the food from their harvest until they had made this offering. Today God still expects us to set aside his portion first, not last. Giving leftovers to God is no way to express thanks.

23:15–22 The Feast of Weeks was a festival praising God for a bountiful harvest.

23:23, 24 Most of the trumpets used were rams' horns, although some of the more special trumpets were made of beaten silver. Trumpets were blown to announce the beginning of each month as well as the start of festivals.

Day of Atonement

26 The LORD said to Moses, 27 "The tenth day of this seventh month[t] is the Day
of Atonement.[u] Hold a sacred assembly[v] and deny yourselves,[d] and present an
offering made to the LORD by fire. 28 Do no work on that day, because it is the Day
of Atonement, when atonement is made for you before the LORD your God. 29 Anyone
who does not deny himself on that day must be cut off from his people.[w] 30 I will
destroy from among his people[x] anyone who does any work on that day. 31 You shall
do no work at all. This is to be a lasting ordinance for the generations to come,
wherever you live. 32 It is a sabbath of rest for you, and you must deny yourselves.
From the evening of the ninth day of the month until the following evening you are
to observe your sabbath."

Feast of Tabernacles

33 The LORD said to Moses, 34 "Say to the Israelites: 'On the fifteenth day of the
seventh month the LORD's Feast of Tabernacles[y] begins, and it lasts for seven days.
35 The first day is a sacred assembly; do no regular work. 36 For seven days present
offerings made to the LORD by fire, and on the eighth day hold a sacred assembly[z]
and present an offering made to the LORD by fire. It is the closing assembly; do no
regular work.

37 (" 'These are the LORD's appointed feasts, which you are to proclaim as sacred
assemblies for bringing offerings made to the LORD by fire—the burnt offerings and
grain offerings, sacrifices and drink offerings[a] required for each day. 38 These offerings are in addition to those for the LORD's Sabbaths[b] and[e] in addition to your gifts
and whatever you have vowed and all the freewill offerings you give to the LORD.)

23:27 [t]Lev 16:29 [u]Ex 30:10 [v]Nu 29:7
23:29 [w]Ge 17:14; Nu 5:2
23:30 [x]Lev 20:3
23:34 [y]Ex 23:16; Dt 16:13; Ezr 3:4; Ne 8:14; Zec 14:16; Jn 7:2
23:36 [z]2Ch 7:9; Ne 8:18; Jn 7:37
23:37 [a]ver 2, 4
23:38 [b]Eze 45:17

[d] 27 Or *and fast*; also in verses 29 and 32 [e] 38 Or *These feasts are in addition to the LORD's Sabbaths, and these offerings are*

THE FEASTS Besides enjoying one Sabbath day of rest each week, the Israelites also enjoyed 19 days when national holidays were celebrated.

Feast	*What It Celebrated*	*Its Importance*
Passover One day (Leviticus 23:5)	When God spared the lives of Israel's firstborn children in Egypt and freed the Hebrews from slavery	Reminded the people of God's deliverance
Unleavened Bread Seven days (Leviticus 23:6–8)	The exodus from Egypt	Reminded the people they were leaving the old life behind and entering a new way of living
Firstfruits One day (Leviticus 23:9–14)	The first crops of the barley harvest	Reminded the people how God provided for them
Weeks One day (Leviticus 23:15–22)	The end of the barley harvest and beginning of the wheat harvest	Showed joy and thanksgiving over the bountiful harvest
Trumpets One day (Leviticus 23:23–25)	The beginning of the seventh month (civil new year)	Expressed joy and thanksgiving to God
Day of Atonement One day (Leviticus 23:26–32)	The removal of sin from the people and the nation	Restored fellowship with God
Tabernacles Seven days (Leviticus 23:33–43)	God's protection and guidance in the desert	Renewed Israel's commitment to God and trust in his guidance and protection

23:33–43 The Feast of Tabernacles, also called the Feast of Ingathering, was a special celebration involving the whole family (see 23:34; Exodus 23:16; Deuteronomy 16:13). Like Passover, this feast taught family members of all ages about God's nature and what he had done for them and was a time of renewed commitment to God. Our families also need rituals of celebration to renew our faith and to pass it on to our children. In addition to Christmas and Easter, we should select other special days to commemorate God's goodness.

39" 'So beginning with the fifteenth day of the seventh month, after you have
gathered the crops of the land, celebrate the festival to the LORD for seven days;[c] the
first day is a day of rest, and the eighth day also is a day of rest. 40On the first day
you are to take choice fruit from the trees, and palm fronds, leafy branches and
poplars,[d] and rejoice before the LORD your God for seven days. 41Celebrate this as
a festival to the LORD for seven days each year. This is to be a lasting ordinance for
the generations to come; celebrate it in the seventh month. 42Live in booths[e] for seven
days: All native-born Israelites are to live in booths 43so that your descendants will
know[f] that I made the Israelites live in booths when I brought them out of Egypt.
I am the LORD your God.' "
44So Moses announced to the Israelites the appointed feasts of the LORD.

Oil and Bread Set Before the LORD

24 The LORD said to Moses, 2"Command the Israelites to bring you clear oil of
pressed olives for the light so that the lamps may be kept burning continually.
3Outside the curtain of the Testimony in the Tent of Meeting, Aaron is to tend the
lamps before the LORD from evening till morning, continually. This is to be a lasting
ordinance for the generations to come. 4The lamps on the pure gold lampstand[a] before
the LORD must be tended continually.
5"Take fine flour and bake twelve loaves of bread,[b] using two-tenths of an ephah[a]
for each loaf. 6Set them in two rows, six in each row, on the table of pure gold[c] before
the LORD. 7Along each row put some pure incense as a memorial portion[d] to represent
the bread and to be an offering made to the LORD by fire. 8This bread is to be set out
before the LORD regularly,[e] Sabbath after Sabbath,[f] on behalf of the Israelites, as
a lasting covenant. 9It belongs to Aaron and his sons,[g] who are to eat it in a holy
place, because it is a most holy part of their regular share of the offerings made to
the LORD by fire."

A Blasphemer Stoned

10Now the son of an Israelite mother and an Egyptian father went out among the
Israelites, and a fight broke out in the camp between him and an Israelite. 11The son
of the Israelite woman blasphemed the Name[h] with a curse; so they brought him to
Moses. (His mother's name was Shelomith, the daughter of Dibri the Danite.) 12They
put him in custody until the will of the LORD should be made clear to them.[i]
13Then the LORD said to Moses: 14"Take the blasphemer outside the camp. All those
who heard him are to lay their hands on his head, and the entire assembly is to stone
him.[j] 15Say to the Israelites: 'If anyone curses his God,[k] he will be held responsible;
16anyone who blasphemes the name of the LORD must be put to death.[l] The entire
assembly must stone him. Whether an alien or native-born, when he blasphemes the
Name, he must be put to death.
17" 'If anyone takes the life of a human being, he must be put to death.[m] 18Anyone
who takes the life of someone's animal must make restitution[n]—life for life. 19If
anyone injures his neighbour, whatever he has done must be done to him: 20fracture
for fracture, eye for eye, tooth for tooth.[o] As he has injured the other, so he is to
be injured. 21Whoever kills an animal must make restitution, but whoever kills a man
must be put to death.[p] 22You are to have the same law for the alien[q] and the
native-born.[r] I am the LORD your God.' "

[a] 5 That is, probably about 7½ pints (about 4.5 litres)

23:39 [c]Ex 23:16; Dt 16:13
23:40 [d]Ne 8:14-17
23:42 [e]Ne 8:14-16
23:43 [f]Dt 31:13; Ps 78:5
24:4 [a]Ex 25:31; 31:8
24:5 [b]Ex 25:30
24:6 [c]Ex 25:23-30; 1Ki 7:48
24:7 [d]Lev 2:2
24:8 [e]Nu 4:7; 1Ch 9:32; 2Ch 2:4 [f]Mt 12:5
24:9 [g]Lev 8:31; Mt 12:4; Mk 2:26; Lk 6:4
24:11 [h]Ex 3:15
24:12 [i]Ex 18:16; Nu 15:34
24:14 [j]Lev 20:27; Dt 13:9; 17:5, 7; 21:21
24:15 [k]Ex 22:28
24:16 [l]1Ki 21:10, 13; Mt 26:66
24:17 [m]Ge 9:6; Ex 21:12; Nu 35:30-31; Dt 27:24
24:18 [n]ver 21
24:20 [o]Ex 21:24; Mt 5:38*
24:21 [p]ver 17
24:22 [q]Ex 12:49 [r]Nu 9:14; 15:16

23:44 Worship involves both celebration and confession. But in Israel's national holidays, the balance seems heavily tipped in favour of celebration—five joyous occasions to two solemn ones. The God of the Bible encourages joy! God does not intend for religion to be only meditation and introspection. He also wants us to celebrate. Serious reflection and immediate confession of sin is essential, of course. But this should be balanced by celebrating who God is and what he has done for his people.

24:13 This punishment for blasphemy (cursing God) seems extreme by modern standards. But it shows how seriously God expects us to take our relationship with him. Often we use his name in swearing, or we act as though he doesn't exist. We should be careful how we speak and act, treating God with reverence. Eventually, he will have the last word.

24:17–22 This was a code for judges, not an endorsement of personal vengeance. In effect, it was saying that the punishment should fit the crime, but it should not go beyond.

23 Then Moses spoke to the Israelites, and they took the blasphemer outside the camp and stoned him. The Israelites did as the LORD commanded Moses.

The Sabbath Year

25 The LORD said to Moses on Mount Sinai, 2 "Speak to the Israelites and say to them: 'When you enter the land I am going to give you, the land itself must observe a sabbath to the LORD. 3 For six years sow your fields, and for six years prune your vineyards and gather their crops.[a] 4 But in the seventh year the land is to have a sabbath of rest, a sabbath to the LORD. Do not sow your fields or prune your vineyards. 5 Do not reap what grows of itself or harvest the grapes of your untended vines. The land is to have a year of rest. 6 Whatever the land yields during the sabbath year[b] will be food for you—for yourself, your manservant and maidservant, and the hired worker and temporary resident who live among you, 7 as well as for your livestock and the wild animals in your land. Whatever the land produces may be eaten.

The Year of Jubilee

8 " 'Count off seven sabbaths of years—seven times seven years—so that the seven sabbaths of years amount to a period of forty-nine years. 9 Then have the trumpet[c] sounded everywhere on the tenth day of the seventh month; on the Day of Atonement sound the trumpet throughout your land. 10 Consecrate the fiftieth year and proclaim liberty[d] throughout the land to all its inhabitants. It shall be a jubilee[e] for you; each one of you is to return to his family property and each to his own clan. 11 The fiftieth year shall be a jubilee for you; do not sow and do not reap what grows of itself or harvest the untended vines. 12 For it is a jubilee and is to be holy for you; eat only what is taken directly from the fields.

13 " 'In this Year of Jubilee[f] everyone is to return to his own property.

14 " 'If you sell land to one of your countrymen or buy any from him, do not take advantage of each other.[g] 15 You are to buy from your countryman on the basis of the number of years[h] since the Jubilee. And he is to sell to you on the basis of the number of years left for harvesting crops. 16 When the years are many, you are to increase the price, and when the years are few, you are to decrease the price,[i] because what he is really selling you is the number of crops. 17 Do not take advantage of each other,[j] but fear your God.[k] I am the LORD your God.[l]

18 " 'Follow my decrees and be careful to obey my laws, and you will live safely in the land.[m] 19 Then the land will yield its fruit,[n] and you will eat your fill and live there in safety. 20 You may ask, "What will we eat in the seventh year[o] if we do not plant or harvest our crops?" 21 I will send you such a blessing[p] in the sixth year that the land will yield enough for three years. 22 While you plant during the eighth year, you will eat from the old crop and will continue to eat from it until the harvest of the ninth year comes in.[q]

23 " 'The land must not be sold permanently, because the land is mine[r] and you are but aliens[s] and my tenants. 24 Throughout the country that you hold as a possession, you must provide for the redemption[t] of the land.

25 " 'If one of your countrymen becomes poor and sells some of his property, his nearest relative[u] is to come and redeem[v] what his countryman has sold. 26 If, however, a man has no-one to redeem it for him but he himself prospers and acquires sufficient means to redeem it, 27 he is to determine the value for the years since he sold it and refund the balance to the man to whom he sold it; he can then go back

25:3 [a] Ex 23:10
25:6 [b] ver 20
25:9 [c] Lev 23:24
25:10 [d] Isa 61:1; Jer 34:8, 15, 17; Lk 4:19 [e] Nu 36:4
25:13 [f] ver 10
25:14 [g] Lev 19:13; 1Sa 12:3, 4
25:15 [h] Lev 27:18, 23
25:16 [i] ver 27, 51, 52
25:17 [j] Pr 22:22; Jer 7:5, 6; 1Th 4:6 [k] Lev 19:14 [l] Lev 19:32
25:18 [m] Lev 26:4, 5; Dt 12:10; Ps 4:8; Jer 23:6
25:19 [n] Lev 26:4
25:20 [o] ver 4
25:21 [p] Dt 28:8, 12; Hag 2:19; Mal 3:10
25:22 [q] Lev 26:10
25:23 [r] Ex 19:5 [s] Ge 23:4; 1Ch 29:15; Ps 39:12; Heb 11:13; 1Pe 2:11
25:24 [t] ver 29, 48; Ru 4:7
25:25 [u] Ru 2:20; Jer 32:7 [v] Lev 27:13, 19, 31; Ru 4:4

25:1–7 The sabbath year provided one year in seven for the fields to lay fallow (unploughed). This was good management of natural resources and reminded the people of God's control and provision for them.

25:8–17 The Year of Jubilee was meant to be celebrated every 50 years. It included cancelling all debts, freeing all slaves, and returning to its original owners all land that had been sold. There is no indication in the Bible that the Year of Jubilee was ever carried out. If Israel had followed this practice faithfully, they would have been a society without permanent poverty.

25:23 The people would one day possess land in Canaan, but in God's plan, only God's ownership was absolute. He wanted his people to avoid greed and materialism. If you have the attitude that you are taking care of the Lord's property, you will make what you have more available to others. This is difficult to do if you have an attitude of ownership. Think of yourself as a manager of all that is under your care, not as an owner.

to his own property. 28But if he does not acquire the means to repay him, what he
sold will remain in the possession of the buyer until the Year of Jubilee. It will be
returned in the Jubilee, and he can then go back to his property.[w]
29" 'If a man sells a house in a walled city, he retains the right of redemption a full
year after its sale. During that time he may redeem it. 30If it is not redeemed before
a full year has passed, the house in the walled city shall belong permanently to the
buyer and his descendants. It is not to be returned in the Jubilee. 31But houses in
villages without walls round them are to be considered as open country. They can be
redeemed, and they are to be returned in the Jubilee.
32" 'The Levites always have the right to redeem their houses in the Levitical
towns,[x] which they possess. 33So the property of the Levites is redeemable—that is,
a house sold in any town they hold—and is to be returned in the Jubilee, because the
houses in the towns of the Levites are their property among the Israelites. 34But the
pasture-land belonging to their towns must not be sold; it is their permanent possession.[y]
35" 'If one of your countrymen becomes poor[z] and is unable to support himself
among you, help him[a] as you would an alien or a temporary resident, so that he can
continue to live among you. 36Do not take interest[b] of any kind**a** from him, but fear
your God, so that your countryman may continue to live among you. 37You must not
lend him money at interest or sell him food at a profit. 38I am the LORD your God,
who brought you out of Egypt to give you the land of Canaan and to be your God.[c]
39" 'If one of your countrymen becomes poor among you and sells himself to you,
do not make him work as a slave.[d] 40He is to be treated as a hired worker or a
temporary resident among you; he is to work for you until the Year of Jubilee. 41Then
he and his children are to be released, and he will go back to his own clan and to the
property[e] of his forefathers. 42Because the Israelites are my servants, whom I brought
out of Egypt, they must not be sold as slaves. 43Do not rule over them ruthlessly,[f]
but fear your God.
44" 'Your male and female slaves are to come from the nations around you; from
them you may buy slaves. 45You may also buy some of the temporary residents living
among you and members of their clans born in your country, and they will become
your property. 46You can will them to your children as inherited property and can
make them slaves for life, but you must not rule over your fellow Israelites ruthlessly.
47" 'If an alien or a temporary resident among you becomes rich and one of your
countrymen becomes poor and sells himself to the alien living among you or to a
member of the alien's clan, 48he retains the right of redemption after he has sold
himself. One of his relatives[g] may redeem him: 49An uncle or a cousin or any
blood-relative in his clan may redeem him. Or if he prospers,[h] he may redeem
himself. 50He and his buyer are to count the time from the year he sold himself up
to the Year of Jubilee. The price for his release is to be based on the rate paid to a
hired man[i] for that number of years. 51If many years remain, he must pay for his
redemption a larger share of the price paid for him. 52If only a few years remain until
the Year of Jubilee, he is to compute that and pay for his redemption accordingly.

a *36* Or *take excessive interest*; similarly in verse 37

25:28 [w]ver 10
25:32 [x]Nu 35:1-8; Jos 21:2
25:34 [y]Nu 35:2-5
25:35 [z]Dt 24:14, 15 [a]Dt 15:8; Ps 37:21, 26; Lk 6:35
25:36 [b]Ex 22:25; Dt 23:19-20
25:38 [c]Ge 17:7; Lev 11:45
25:39 [d]Ex 21:2; Dt 15:12; 1Ki 9:22
25:41 [e]ver 28
25:43 [f]Ex 1:13; Eze 34:4; Col 4:1
25:48 [g]Ne 5:5
25:49 [h]ver 26
25:50 [i]Job 7:1; Isa 16:14; 21:16

25:35ff The Bible places great emphasis on assisting the poor and helpless, especially orphans, widows, and the handicapped. In Israelite society, no paid work was available to women; thus, a widow and her children had no livelihood. Neither was there work available for the seriously handicapped in this nation of farmers and shepherds. The poor were to be helped without charging any interest. Individual and family responsibility for the poor was crucial since there was no government aid.

25:35–37 God said that neglecting the poor was a sin. Permanent poverty was not allowed in Israel. Financially secure families were responsible to help and house those in need. Many times we do nothing, not because we lack compassion, but because we are overwhelmed by the size of the problem and don't know where to begin. God doesn't expect you to eliminate poverty, nor does he expect you to neglect your family while providing for others. He does, however, expect that when you see an individual in need, you will reach out with whatever help you can offer, including hospitality.

25:44 Why did God allow the Israelites to purchase slaves? Under Hebrew laws, slaves were treated differently from slaves in other nations. They were seen as human beings with dignity, and not as animals. Hebrew slaves, for example, took part in the religious festivals and rested on the Sabbath. Nowhere does the Bible condone slavery, but it recognises its existence. God's laws offered many guidelines for treating slaves properly.

53He is to be treated as a man hired from year to year; you must see to it that his owner
does not rule over him ruthlessly.
54" 'Even if he is not redeemed in any of these ways, he and his children are to be
released in the Year of Jubilee, 55for the Israelites belong to me as servants. They are
my servants, whom I brought out of Egypt. I am the LORD your God.

4. Receiving God's blessing

Reward for Obedience

26 " 'Do not make idols[a] or set up an image or a sacred stone[b] for yourselves,
and do not place a carved stone[c] in your land to bow down before it. I am
the LORD your God.
2" 'Observe my Sabbaths and have reverence for my sanctuary.[d] I am the LORD.
3" 'If you follow my decrees and are careful to obey[e] my commands, 4I will send
you rain[f] in its season, and the ground will yield its crops and the trees of the field
their fruit.[g] 5Your threshing will continue until grape harvest and the grape harvest
will continue until planting, and you will eat all the food you want[h] and live in safety
in your land.[i]
6" 'I will grant peace in the land,[j] and you will lie down[k] and no-one will make
you afraid.[l] I will remove savage beasts[m] from the land, and the sword will not pass
through your country. 7You will pursue your enemies, and they will fall by the sword
before you. 8Five of you will chase a hundred, and a hundred of you will chase ten
thousand, and your enemies will fall by the sword before you.[n]
9" 'I will look on you with favour and make you fruitful and increase your numbers,[o] and I will keep my covenant[p] with you. 10You will still be eating last year's
harvest when you will have to move it out to make room for the new.[q] 11I will put
my dwelling-place[a][r] among you, and I will not abhor you. 12I will walk[s] among
you and be your God, and you will be my people.[t] 13I am the LORD your God, who
brought you out of Egypt so that you would no longer be slaves to the Egyptians; I
broke the bars of your yoke[u] and enabled you to walk with heads held high.

Punishment for Disobedience

14" 'But if you will not listen to me and carry out all these commands,[v] 15and if
you reject my decrees and abhor my laws and fail to carry out all my commands and
so violate my covenant, 16then I will do this to you: I will bring upon you sudden
terror, wasting diseases and fever[w] that will destroy your sight and drain away your
life.[x] You will plant seed in vain, because your enemies will eat it.[y] 17I will set my
face[z] against you so that you will be defeated by your enemies; those who hate you
will rule over you,[a] and you will flee even when no-one is pursuing you.[b]
18" 'If after all this you will not listen to me, I will punish you for your sins seven
times over.[c] 19I will break down your stubborn pride[d] and make the sky above you
like iron and the ground beneath you like bronze.[e] 20Your strength will be spent in

26:1 [a]Ex 20:4; Lev 19:4; Dt 5:8 [b]Ex 23:24 [c]Nu 33:52
26:2 [d]Lev 19:30
26:3 [e]Dt 7:12; 11:13, 22; 28:1, 9
26:4 [f]Dt 11:14 [g]Ps 67:6
26:5 [h]Dt 11:15; Joel 2:19, 26; Am 9:13 [i]Lev 25:18
26:6 [j]Ps 29:11; 85:8; 147:14 [k]Ps 4:8 [l]Zep 3:13 [m]ver 22
26:8 [n]Dt 32:30; Jos 23:10
26:9 [o]Ge 17:6; Ne 9:23 [p]Ge 17:7
26:10 [q]Lev 25:22
26:11 [r]Ex 25:8; Ps 76:2; Eze 37:27
26:12 [s]Ge 3:8 [t]2Co 6:16*
26:13 [u]Eze 34:27
26:14 [v]Dt 28:15-68; Mal 2:2
26:16 [w]Dt 28:22, 35 [x]1Sa 2:33 [y]Job 31:8
26:17 [z]Lev 17:10 [a]Ps 106:41 [b]ver 36, 37; Dt 28:7, 25; Ps 53:5
26:18 [c]ver 21
26:19 [d]Isa 25:11 [e]Dt 28:23

a *11* Or *my tabernacle*

26:1ff This chapter presents the two paths of obedience and disobedience that God set before the people (see also Deuteronomy 28). The people of the Old Testament were warned over and over against worshipping idols. We wonder how they could deceive themselves with these objects of wood and stone. Yet God could well give us the same warning, for we are prone to put idols before him. Idolatry is making anything more important than God, and our lives are full of that temptation. Money, looks, success, reputation, security – these are today's idols. As you look at these false gods that promise everything you want but nothing you need, does idolatry seem so far removed from your experience?

26:13 Imagine the joy of a slave set free. God took the children of Israel out of bitter slavery and gave them freedom and dignity. We too are set free when we accept Christ's payment that redeems us from sin's slavery. We no longer need to be bogged down in shame over our past sins; we can walk with dignity because God has forgiven us and forgotten them. But just as the Israelites were still in danger of returning to a slave mentality, we need to beware of the temptation to return to our former sinful patterns.

26:18 If the Israelites obeyed, there would be peace in the land. If they disobeyed, disaster would follow. God used sin's consequences to draw them to repentance, not to get back at them. Today, sin's consequences are not always so apparent. When calamity strikes us we may not know the reason. It may be (1) the result of our own disobedience, (2) the result of someone else's sin, (3) the result of natural disaster. Because we don't know, we should search our hearts and be sure we are at peace with God. His Spirit, like a great searchlight, will reveal those areas we need to deal with. Because calamity is not always the result of wrongdoing, we must guard against assigning or accepting blame for every tragedy we encounter. Misplaced guilt is one of Satan's favourite weapons against believers.

vain,[f] because your soil will not yield its crops, nor will the trees of the land yield
their fruit.[g]
21“ ‘If you remain hostile towards me and refuse to listen to me, I will multiply your
afflictions seven times over,[h] as your sins deserve. 22I will send wild animals[i]
against you, and they will rob you of your children, destroy your cattle and make you
so few in number that your roads will be deserted.
23“ ‘If in spite of these things you do not accept my correction[j] but continue to
be hostile towards me, 24I myself will be hostile towards you and will afflict you for
your sins seven times over. 25And I will bring the sword upon you to avenge the
breaking of the covenant. When you withdraw into your cities, I will send a plague[k]
among you, and you will be given into enemy hands. 26When I cut off your supply
of bread,[l] ten women will be able to bake your bread in one oven, and they will dole
out the bread by weight. You will eat, but you will not be satisfied.
27“ ‘If in spite of this you still do not listen to me but continue to be hostile towards
me, 28then in my anger I will be hostile towards you, and I myself will punish you
for your sins seven times over. 29You will eat the flesh of your sons and the flesh of
your daughters.[m] 30I will destroy your high places,[n] cut down your incense altars[o]
and pile your dead bodies on the lifeless forms of your idols,[p] and I will abhor you.
31I will turn your cities into ruins and lay waste your sanctuaries,[q] and I will take
no delight in the pleasing aroma of your offerings. 32I will lay waste the land,[r] so
that your enemies who live there will be appalled. 33I will scatter you among the
nations[s] and will draw out my sword and pursue you. Your land will be laid waste,
and your cities will lie in ruins. 34Then the land will enjoy its sabbath years all the
time that it lies desolate and you are in the country of your enemies;[t] then the land
will rest and enjoy its sabbaths. 35All the time that it lies desolate, the land will have
the rest it did not have during the sabbaths you lived in it.
36“ ‘As for those of you who are left, I will make their hearts so fearful in the lands
of their enemies that the sound of a wind-blown leaf will put them to flight.[u] They
will run as though fleeing from the sword, and they will fall, even though no-one is
pursuing them. 37They will stumble over one another as though fleeing from the
sword, even though no-one is pursuing them. So you will not be able to stand before
your enemies.[v] 38You will perish among the nations; the land of your enemies will
devour you.[w] 39Those of you who are left will waste away in the lands of their enemies
because of their sins; also because of their fathers’ sins they will waste away.[x]
40“ ‘But if they will confess their sins and the sins of their fathers[y]—their treachery
against me and their hostility towards me, 41which made me hostile towards them so
that I sent them into the land of their enemies—then when their uncircumcised hearts[z]
are humbled and they pay for their sin, 42I will remember my covenant with Jacob[a]
and my covenant with Isaac[b] and my covenant with Abraham, and I will remember
the land. 43For the land will be deserted by them and will enjoy its sabbaths while
it lies desolate without them. They will pay for their sins because they rejected my
laws and abhorred my decrees. 44Yet in spite of this, when they are in the land of
their enemies, I will not reject them or abhor[c] them so as to destroy them completely,[d] breaking my covenant[e] with them. I am the LORD their God. 45But for their
sake I will remember[f] the covenant with their ancestors whom I brought out of
Egypt[g] in the sight of the nations to be their God. I am the LORD.’ ”

26:20 [f]Ps 127:1; Isa 17:11 [g]Dt 11:17
26:21 [h]ver 18
26:22 [i]Dt 32:24
26:23 [j]Jer 2:30; 5:3
26:25 [k]Nu 14:12; Eze 5:17
26:26 [l]Ps 105:16; Isa 3:1; Mic 6:14
26:29 [m]Dt 28:53
26:30 [n]2Ch 34:3; Eze 6:3 [o]Eze 6:6 [p]Eze 6:13
26:31 [q]Ps 74:3-7
26:32 [r]Jer 9:11
26:33 [s]Dt 4:27; Eze 12:15; 20:23; Zec 7:14
26:34 [t]ver 43; 2Ch 36:21
26:36 [u]Eze 21:7
26:37 [v]Jos 7:12
26:38 [w]Dt 4:26
26:39 [x]Eze 4:17
26:40 [y]Jer 3:12-15; Lk 15:18; 1Jn 1:9
26:41 [z]Eze 44:7, 9; Ac 7:51
26:42 [a]Ge 22:15-18; 28:15 [b]Ge 26:5
26:44 [c]Ro 11:2 [d]Dt 4:31; Jer 30:11 [e]Jer 33:26
26:45 [f]Ge 17:7 [g]Ex 6:8; Lev 25:38

26:33–35 In 2 Kings 17 and 25 the warning pronounced in these verses came true. The people persistently disobeyed, and eventually they were conquered and carried off to the lands of Assyria and Babylonia. The nation was held in captivity for 70 years, making up for all of the years that the Israelites did not observe the law of the sabbath year (2 Chronicles 36:21).

26:40–45 These verses show what God meant when he said he is slow to anger (Exodus 34:6). Even if the Israelites chose to disobey and were scattered among their enemies, God would still give them the opportunity to repent and return to him. His purpose was not to destroy them, but to help them grow. Our day-to-day experiences and hardships are sometimes overwhelming; unless we can see that God’s purpose is to bring about continual growth in us, we may despair. The hope we need is well expressed in Jeremiah 29:11, 12: “ ‘For I know the plans I have for you,’ declares the LORD, ‘plans to prosper you and not to harm you, plans to give you hope and a future. Then you will call upon me and come and pray to me, and I will listen to you.’ ” To retain hope while we suffer shows we understand God’s merciful ways of relating to his people.

46These are the decrees, the laws and the regulations that the LORD established on
Mount Sinai between himself and the Israelites through Moses.[h]

Redeeming What Is the LORD's

27 The LORD said to Moses, 2"Speak to the Israelites and say to them: 'If anyone
makes a special vow[a] to dedicate persons to the LORD by giving equivalent
values, 3set the value of a male between the ages of twenty and sixty at fifty shekels[a]
of silver, according to the sanctuary shekel;[b][b] 4and if it is a female, set her value
at thirty shekels.[c] 5If it is a person between the ages of five and twenty, set the value
of a male at twenty shekels[d] and of a female at ten shekels.[e] 6If it is a person between
one month and five years, set the value of a male at five shekels[f][c] of silver and that
of a female at three shekels[g] of silver. 7If it is a person sixty years old or more, set
the value of a male at fifteen shekels[h] and of a female at ten shekels. 8If anyone
making the vow is too poor to pay[d] the specified amount, he is to present the person
to the priest, who will set the value[e] for him according to what the man making the
vow can afford.

9" 'If what he vowed is an animal that is acceptable as an offering to the LORD, such
an animal given to the LORD becomes holy. 10He must not exchange it or substitute
a good one for a bad one, or a bad one for a good one;[f] if he should substitute one
animal for another, both it and the substitute become holy. 11If what he vowed is a
ceremonially unclean animal—one that is not acceptable as an offering to the
LORD—the animal must be presented to the priest, 12who will judge its quality as good
or bad. Whatever value the priest then sets, that is what it will be. 13If the owner wishes
to redeem[g] the animal, he must add a fifth to its value.

14" 'If a man dedicates his house as something holy to the LORD, the priest will judge
its quality as good or bad. Whatever value the priest then sets, so it will remain. 15If
the man who dedicates his house redeems it,[h] he must add a fifth to its value, and
the house will again become his.

16" 'If a man dedicates to the LORD part of his family land, its value is to be set
according to the amount of seed required for it—fifty shekels of silver to a homer[i]
of barley seed. 17If he dedicates his field during the Year of Jubilee, the value that
has been set remains. 18But if he dedicates his field after the Jubilee, the priest will
determine the value according to the number of years that remain[i] until the next Year
of Jubilee, and its set value will be reduced. 19If the man who dedicates the field
wishes to redeem it, he must add a fifth to its value, and the field will again become
his. 20If, however, he does not redeem the field, or if he has sold it to someone else,
it can never be redeemed. 21When the field is released in the Jubilee,[j] it will become
holy, like a field devoted to the LORD;[k] it will become the property of the priests.[j]

22" 'If a man dedicates to the LORD a field he has bought, which is not part of his
family land, 23the priest will determine its value up to the Year of Jubilee, and the
man must pay its value on that day as something holy to the LORD. 24In the Year of
Jubilee the field will revert to the person from whom he bought it,[l] the one whose

26:46 [h]Lev 7:38; 27:34
27:2 [a]Nu 6:2
27:3 [b]Ex 30:13; Nu 3:47; 18:16
27:6 [c]Nu 18:16
27:8 [d]Lev 5:11 [e]ver 12, 14
27:10 [f]ver 33
27:13 [g]ver 15, 19; Lev 25:25
27:15 [h]ver 13, 20
27:18 [i]Lev 25:15
27:21 [j]Lev 25:10 [k]ver 28; Nu 18:14; Eze 44:29
27:24 [l]Lev 25:28

a *3* That is, about 1¼ pounds (about 0.6 kilogram); also in verse 16 b *3* That is, about ⅖ ounce (about 11.5 grams); also in verse 25 c *4* That is, about 12 ounces (about 0.3 kilogram) d *5* That is, about 8 ounces (about 0.2 kilogram) e *5* That is, about 4 ounces (about 115 grams); also in verse 7 f *6* That is, about 2 ounces (about 55 grams) g *6* That is, about 1¼ ounces (about 35 grams) h *7* That is, about 6 ounces (about 170 grams) i *16* That is, probably about 6 bushels (about 220 litres) j *21* Or *priest*

27:1ff The Israelites were required to give or dedicate certain things to the Lord and to his service: the firstfruits of their harvests, firstborn animals, their firstborn sons, a tithe of their increase. Many wished to go beyond this and dedicate themselves or another family member, additional animals, a house, or a field to God. In these cases, it was possible to donate money instead of the actual person, animal, or property. Some people made rash or unrealistic vows. To urge them to think about it first, a 20 per cent penalty was put on those items purchased back by money. This chapter explains how valuations were to be made and what to do if a donor later wished to buy back what had been donated to God.

27:9, 10 God taught the Israelites that when they made a vow to him, they must not go back on their promise even if it turned out to cost more than expected. (This applied to animals; humans could be redeemed or purchased back.) God takes our promises seriously. If you vow to give 10 per cent of your income and suddenly some unexpected bills come along, your faithful stewardship will be costly. God, however, expects you to fulfil your vow even if it is difficult to do so.

27:14-25 Property could be given as a voluntary offering in much the same way that today people give property through a will or donate the proceeds from the sale of property to the church or Christian organisations.

land it was. 25 Every value is to be set according to the sanctuary shekel,[m] twenty
gerahs[n] to the shekel.
26 " 'No-one, however, may dedicate the firstborn of an animal, since the firstborn
already belongs to the LORD;[o] whether an ox[k] or a sheep, it is the LORD's. 27 If it
is one of the unclean animals,[p] he may buy it back at its set value, adding a fifth
of the value to it. If he does not redeem it, it is to be sold at its set value.
28 " 'But nothing that a man owns and devotes[l][q] to the LORD—whether man or
animal or family land—may be sold or redeemed; everything so devoted is most holy
to the LORD.
29 " 'No person devoted to destruction[m] may be ransomed; he must be put to death.
30 " 'A tithe[r] of everything from the land, whether grain from the soil or fruit from
the trees, belongs to the LORD; it is holy to the LORD. 31 If a man redeems any of his
tithe, he must add a fifth of the value to it. 32 The entire tithe of the herd and
flock—every tenth animal that passes under the shepherd's rod[s]—will be holy to the
LORD. 33 He must not pick out the good from the bad or make any substitution.[t] If
he does make a substitution, both the animal and its substitute become holy and cannot
be redeemed.' "

34 These are the commands the LORD gave Moses on Mount Sinai for the Israelites.[u]

[k] 26 The Hebrew word can include both male and female. [l] 28 The Hebrew term refers to the irrevocable giving over of things or persons to the LORD. [m] 29 The Hebrew term refers to the irrevocable giving over of things or persons to the LORD, often by totally destroying them.

27:25 [m] Ex 30:13; Nu 18:16 [n] Nu 3:47; Eze 45:12
27:26 [o] Ex 13:2, 12
27:27 [p] ver 11
27:28 [q] Nu 18:14; Jos 6:17-19
27:30 [r] Ge 28:22; 2Ch 31:6; Mal 3:8
27:32 [s] Jer 33:13; Eze 20:37
27:33 [t] ver 10
27:34 [u] Lev 26:46; Dt 4:5

27:29 Things devoted to destruction applies to personal property or persons placed under God's ban, such as captured booty from idol-worshippers or idols themselves. These were to be destroyed and could not be redeemed.

27:33 Many of the principles regarding sacrifices and tithes were intended to encourage inward attitudes as well as outward actions. If a person gives grudgingly, he shows that he has a stingy heart. God wants us to be cheerful givers (2 Corinthians 9:7) who give with gratitude to him.

27:34 The book of Leviticus is filled with the commands God gave his people at the foot of Mount Sinai. From these commands we can learn much about God's nature and character. At first glance, Leviticus seems irrelevant to our high-tech world. But digging a little deeper, we realise that the book still speaks to us today—God has not changed, and his principles are for all times. As people and society change, we need constantly to search for ways to apply the principles of God's law to our present circumstances. God was the same in Leviticus as he is today and will be for ever (Hebrews 13:8).

KEY PLACES IN NUMBERS

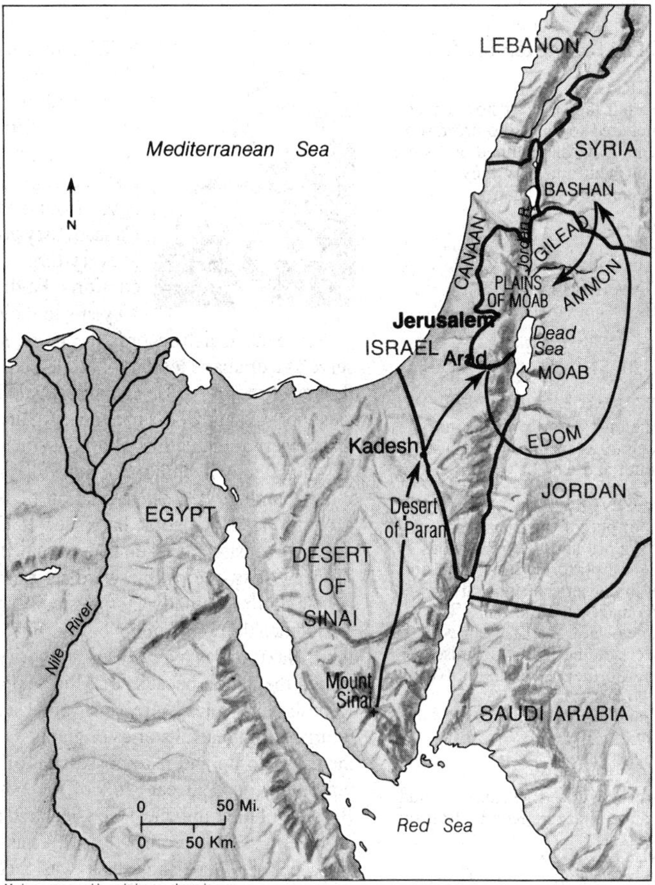

Modern names and boundaries are shown in grey.

1 Mount Sinai Numbers begins at Mount Sinai in the Desert of Sinai with Moses taking a census of the men eligible for battle. As the battle preparations began, the people also prepared for the spiritual warfare they would face. The promised land was full of wicked people who would try to entice the Israelites to sin. God, therefore, taught Moses and the Israelites how to live rightly (1:1–12:15).

2 Desert of Paran After a full year at Mount Sinai, the Israelites broke camp and began their march towards the promised land by moving into the Desert of Paran. From there, one leader from each tribe was sent to spy out the new land. After 40 days they returned, and all but Joshua and Caleb were too afraid to enter. Because of their lack of faith, the Israelites were made to wander in the desert for 40 years (12:16–19:22).

3 Kadesh With the years of wandering nearing an end, the Israelites set their sights once again on the promised land. Kadesh was the oasis where they spent most of their desert years. Miriam died here. And it was here that Moses angrily struck the rock, which kept him from entering the promised land (20).

4 Arad When the king there heard that Israel was on the move, he attacked, but he was soundly defeated. Moses then led the people southwards and eastwards around the Dead Sea (21:1–3).

5 Edom The Israelites wanted to travel through Edom, but the king of Edom refused them passage (20:14–22). So they travelled around Edom and became very discouraged. The people complained, and God sent venomous snakes to punish them. Only by looking at a bronze snake on a pole could those bitten be healed (21:4–9).

6 Ammon Next, King Sihon of the Amorites refused Israel passage. When he attacked, Israel defeated his army and conquered the territory as far as the border of Ammon (21:21–32).

7 Bashan Moses sent spies to Bashan. King Og attacked, but he was also defeated (21:33–35).

8 Plains of Moab The people camped on the plains of Moab, east of the Jordan River across from Jericho. They were on the verge of entering the promised land (22:1).

9 Moab King Balak of Moab, terrified of the Israelites, called upon Balaam, a famous sorcerer, to curse Israel from the mountains above where the Israelites camped. But the Lord caused Balaam to bless them instead (22:2–24:25).

10 Gilead The tribes of Reuben and Gad decided to settle in the fertile country of Gilead east of the Jordan River because it was a good land for their sheep. But first they promised to help the other tribes conquer the land west of the Jordan River (32).

NUMBERS

Joseph dies 1805 B.C. (1640 B.C.)	*SLAVERY IN EGYPT*	*Exodus from Egypt 1446 (1280)*	*Ten Command-ments given 1445 (1279)*	*First census 1444 (1278)*	*First spy mission 1443 (1277)*

VITAL STATISTICS

PURPOSE:
To tell the story of how Israel prepared to enter the promised land, how they sinned and were punished, and how they prepared to try again

AUTHOR:
Moses

TO WHOM WRITTEN:
The people of Israel

DATE WRITTEN:
1450–1410 B.C.

SETTING:
The vast desert of the Sinai region, as well as lands just south and east of Canaan

KEY VERSES:
"Not one of the men who saw my glory and the miraculous signs I performed in Egypt and in the desert but who disobeyed me and tested me ten times—not one of them will ever see the land I promised on oath to their forefathers. No-one who has treated me with contempt will ever see it" (14:22, 23).

KEY PEOPLE:
Moses, Aaron, Miriam, Joshua, Caleb, Eleazar, Korah, Balaam

KEY PLACES:
Mount Sinai, promised land (Canaan), Kadesh, Mount Hor, plains of Moab

EVERY parent knows the shrill whine of a young child—a slow, high-pitched complaint that grates on the eardrums and aggravates the soul. The tone of voice is difficult to bear, but the real irritation is the underlying cause—discontentment and disobedience. As the "children" of Israel journeyed from the foot of Mount Sinai to the land of Canaan, they grumbled, whined, and complained at every turn. They focused on their present discomforts. Faith had fled, and they added an extra 40 years to their trip.

Numbers, which records the tragic story of Israel's unbelief, should serve as a dramatic lesson for all of God's people. God loves us and wants the very best for us. He can and should be trusted. Numbers also gives a clear portrayal of God's patience. Again and again he withholds judgment and preserves the nation. But his patience must not be taken for granted. His judgment will come. We must obey.

As Numbers begins, the nation of Israel was camped at the foot of Mount Sinai. The people had received God's laws and were preparing to move. A census was taken to determine the number of men fit for military service. Next, the people were set apart for God. God was making the people, both spiritually and physically, ready to receive their inheritance.

But then the complaining began. First, the people complained about the food. Next, it was over Moses' authority. God punished some people but spared the nation because of Moses' prayers. The nation then arrived at Kadesh, and spies were sent into Canaan to assess its strength. Ten returned with fearful stories of giants. Only Caleb and Joshua encouraged them to "go up and take possession of the land" (13:28). The minority report fell on deaf ears full of the ominous message of the majority. Because of their unbelief, God declared that the present generation would not live to see the promised land. Thus the "wanderings" began. During these desert wanderings there was a continuous pattern of grumbling, defiance, discipline, and death. How much better it would have been to have trusted God and entered his land! Then the terrible waiting began—waiting for the old generation to die off and waiting to see if the new generation could faithfully obey God.

Numbers ends as it begins, with preparation. This new generation of Israelites were numbered and sanctified. After defeating numerous armies, they settle on the east side of the Jordan River. Then they faced their greatest test: to cross the river and possess the beautiful land God promised them.

The lesson is clear. God's people must trust him, moving ahead by *faith*, if they are to claim his promised land.

DESERT WANDERINGS	*Second census, Balaam prophesies 1407 (1241)*	*Joshua appointed, Canaan entered 1406 (1240)*	*Judges begin to rule 1375 (1220)*	*United kingdom under Saul 1050 (1045)*

THE BLUEPRINT

A. PREPARING FOR THE JOURNEY (1:1—10:10)
1. The first census of the nation
2. The role of the Levites
3. The purity of the camp
4. Receiving guidance for the journey

As part of their preparations, the Lord gave strict guidelines to the Israelites regarding purity in the camp. He wanted them to have a lifestyle distinct from the nations around them. He wanted them to be a holy people. Similarly, we should concern ourselves with purity in the church.

B. FIRST APPROACH TO THE PROMISED LAND (10:11—14:45)
1. The people complain
2. Miriam and Aaron oppose Moses
3. The spies incite rebellion

The Israelites were prevented from entering the promised land because of their unbelief. Throughout history, God's people have continued to struggle with lack of faith.We must prevent unbelief from gaining a foothold in our lives, for it will keep us from enjoying the blessings that God has promised.

C. WANDERING IN THE DESERT (15:1—21:35)
1. Additional regulations
2. Many leaders rebel against Moses
3. Duties of priests and Levites
4. The new generation

When the people complained against God and criticised Moses they were severely punished. Over 14,000 people died as a result of rebellion against Moses. As a result of Korah's rebellion, Korah, Dathan, and Abiram and their households died, along with 250 false priests. Dissatisfaction and discontent, if allowed to remain in our lives, can easily lead to disaster. We should refrain from complaining and criticising our leaders.

D. SECOND APPROACH TO THE PROMISED LAND (22:1—36:13)
1. The story of Balaam
2. The second census of the nation
3. Instructions concerning offerings
4. Vengeance on the Midianites
5. The Transjordan tribes
6. Camped on the plains of Moab

The Moabites and Midianites could not get Balaam to curse Israel, but they did get him to give advice on how to draw the Israelites to idol worship. Balaam knew what was right, but he gave in to the temptation of material rewards and sinned. Knowing what is right alone is never enough. We must also do what is right.

MEGATHEMES

THEME	EXPLANATION	IMPORTANCE
Census	Moses counted the Israelites twice. The first census organised the people into marching units to better defend themselves. The second prepared them to conquer the country east of the Jordan River.	People have to be organised, trained, and led to be effective in great movements. It is always wise to count the cost before setting out on some great undertaking. When we are aware of the obstacles before us we can more easily avoid them. In God's work, we must remove barriers in our relationships with others so that our effectiveness is not diminished.
Rebellion	At Kadesh, 12 spies were sent out into the land of Canaan to report on the fortifications of the enemies. When the spies returned, 10 said that they should give up and go back to Egypt. As a result, the people refused to enter the land. Faced with a choice, Israel rebelled against God. Rebellion did not start with an uprising, but with griping and murmuring against Moses and God.	Rebellion against God is always a serious matter. It is not something to take lightly, for God's punishment for sin is often very severe. Our rebellion does not usually begin with all-out warfare, but in subtle ways—with griping and criticising. Make sure your negative comments are not the product of a rebellious spirit.

Wandering	Because they rebelled, the Israelites wandered 40 years in the desert. This shows how severely God can punish sin. Forty years was enough time for all those who held on to Egypt's customs and values to die off. It gave time to train up a new generation in the ways of God.	God judges sin harshly because he is holy. The wanderings in the desert demonstrate how serious God considers flagrant disobedience of his commands. Purging our lives of sin is vital to God's purpose.
Canaan	Canaan is the promised land. It was the land God had promised to Abraham, Isaac, and Jacob—the land of the covenant. Canaan was to be the dwelling place of God's people, those set apart for true spiritual worship.	Although God's punishment for sin is often severe, he offers reconciliation and hope—his love is truly amazing. Just as God's love and law led Israel to the promised land, God desires to give purpose and destiny to our lives.

A. PREPARING FOR THE JOURNEY (1:1—10:10)

At Mount Sinai, the Israelites received specific directions for their lifestyle in the new land God would give to them. A census was taken and the second passover was celebrated, marking one year of freedom from slavery in Egypt. The people were now prepared to continue their journey to the promised land. Just as the Lord prepared the Israelites, he prepares us for our journey through life.

1. The first census of the nation

1 The LORD spoke to Moses in the Tent of Meeting[a] in the Desert of Sinai[b] on
the first day of the second month[c] of the second year after the Israelites came
out of Egypt. He said: 2“Take a census[d] of the whole Israelite community by their
clans and families, listing every man by name, one by one. 3You and Aaron are to
number by their divisions all the men in Israel twenty years old or more[e] who are
able to serve in the army. 4One man from each tribe, each the head of his family,[f]
is to help you.[g] 5These are the names of the men who are to assist you:

from Reuben,[h] Elizur son of Shedeur;
6from Simeon, Shelumiel son of Zurishaddai;
7from Judah,[i] Nahshon son of Amminadab;[j]
8from Issachar,[k] Nethanel son of Zuar;
9from Zebulun,[l] Eliab son of Helon;
10from the sons of Joseph:
from Ephraim,[m] Elishama son of Ammihud;
from Manasseh, Gamaliel son of Pedahzur;
11from Benjamin, Abidan son of Gideoni;
12from Dan,[n] Ahiezer son of Ammishaddai;
13from Asher,[o] Pagiel son of Ocran;
14from Gad, Eliasaph son of Deuel;[p]
15from Naphtali,[q] Ahira son of Enan.”

1:1 [a]Ex 40:2 [b]Ex 19:1 [c]Ex 40:17
1:2 [d]Ex 30:11-16; Nu 26:2
1:3 [e]Ex 30:14
1:4 [f]ver 16 [g]Ex 18:21; Dt 1:15
1:5 [h]Ge 29:32; Dt 33:6
1:7 [i]Ge 29:35; Ps 78:68 [j]Ru 4:20; Lk 3:32
1:8 [k]Ge 30:18
1:9 [l]ver 30
1:10 [m]ver 32
1:12 [n]ver 38
1:13 [o]ver 40
1:14 [p]Nu 2:14
1:15 [q]ver 42

1:1 As the book of Numbers opens, the Israelites had been camped near Mount Sinai for more than a year. There they had received all the laws and regulations recorded in the book of Leviticus. They had been transformed into a new nation and equipped for their task. At this time, they were ready to move out and receive their land. In preparation, Moses and Aaron were told to number all the men who were able to serve in the army. This book is named for this census, or numbering, of the people.

1:1 The Tent of Meeting was the smaller structure inside the larger tabernacle. The Tent of Meeting contained the sanctuary (or Holy Place) in one part, and the Most Holy Place with the ark in another part. These two parts were separated by a curtain. God revealed himself to Moses in the Most Holy Place. Sometimes the Tent of Meeting refers to the whole tabernacle (see 2:2).

Exodus 33:7 mentions the “tent of meeting” as the place where Moses met with God before the tabernacle was constructed. Many believe that the tent of meeting in Exodus served the same function as the one described here.

1:2–15 Taking a census was long and tedious, but it was an important task. The fighting men had to be counted to determine Israel's military strength before entering the promised land. In addition, the tribes had to be organised to determine the amount of land each would need, as well as to provide genealogical records. Without such a census, the task of conquering and organising the promised land would have been more difficult. Whenever we are at a crossroads, it is important to take stock of our resources. We will serve more effectively if, before plunging in, we set aside time to take a “census” of all we have—possessions, relationships, spiritual condition, time, goals.

16 These were the men appointed from the community, the leaders[r] of their ancestral tribes. They were the heads of the clans of Israel.[s]

17 Moses and Aaron took these men whose names had been given, 18 and they called the whole community together on the first day of the second month.[t] The people indicated their ancestry[u] by their clans and families, and the men twenty years old or more were listed by name, one by one, 19 as the LORD commanded Moses. And so he counted them in the Desert of Sinai:

20 From the descendants of Reuben[v] the firstborn son of Israel:

All the men twenty years old or more who were able to serve in the army were listed by name, one by one, according to the records of their clans and families. 21 The number from the tribe of Reuben was 46,500.

22 From the descendants of Simeon:[w]

All the men twenty years old or more who were able to serve in the army were counted and listed by name, one by one, according to the records of their clans and families. 23 The number from the tribe of Simeon was 59,300.

24 From the descendants of Gad:[x]

All the men twenty years old or more who were able to serve in the army were listed by name, according to the records of their clans and families. 25 The number from the tribe of Gad was 45,650.

26 From the descendants of Judah:[y]

All the men twenty years old or more who were able to serve in the army were listed by name, according to the records of their clans and families. 27 The number from the tribe of Judah was 74,600.

28 From the descendants of Issachar:[z]

All the men twenty years old or more who were able to serve in the army were listed by name, according to the records of their clans and families. 29 The number from the tribe of Issachar was 54,400.

30 From the descendants of Zebulun:[a]

All the men twenty years old or more who were able to serve in the army were listed by name, according to the records of their clans and families. 31 The number from the tribe of Zebulun was 57,400.

32 From the sons of Joseph:

From the descendants of Ephraim:[b]

All the men twenty years old or more who were able to serve in the army were listed by name, according to the records of their clans and families. 33 The number from the tribe of Ephraim was 40,500.

34 From the descendants of Manasseh:[c]

All the men twenty years old or more who were able to serve in the army were listed by name, according to the records of their clans and families. 35 The number from the tribe of Manasseh was 32,200.

36 From the descendants of Benjamin:[d]

All the men twenty years old or more who were able to serve in the army were listed by name, according to the records of their clans and families. 37 The number from the tribe of Benjamin was 35,400.

38 From the descendants of Dan:[e]

1:16 [r]Ex 18:25 [s]ver 4; Ex 18:21; Nu 7:2
1:18 [t]ver 1 [u]Ezr 2:59; Heb 7:3
1:20 [v]Nu 26:5-11; Rev 7:5
1:22 [w]Nu 26:12-14; Rev 7:7
1:24 [x]Ge 30:11; Nu 26:15-18; Rev 7:5
1:26 [y]Ge 29:35; Nu 26:19-22; Mt 1:2; Rev 7:5
1:28 [z]Nu 26:23-25; Rev 7:7
1:30 [a]Nu 26:26-27; Rev 7:8
1:32 [b]Nu 26:35-37
1:34 [c]Nu 26:28-34; Rev 7:6
1:36 [d]Nu 26:38-41; 2Ch 17:17; Rev 7:8
1:38 [e]Ge 30:6; Nu 26:42-43

1:20–46 If there were 603,550 men, not counting the Levites or women and children, the total population must have numbered more than two million Israelites. How could such a large population grow from Jacob's family of 70 who moved down to Egypt? The book of Exodus tells us that the Israelites who descended from Jacob's family "multiplied greatly" (Exodus 1:7). Because they remained in Egypt more than 400 years, they had plenty of time to grow into a large group of people. After leaving Egypt, they were able to survive in the desert because God miraculously provided the food and water they needed. The leaders of Moab were terrified because of the large number of Israelites (22:3).

All the men twenty years old or more who were able to serve in the army were
listed by name, according to the records of their clans and families. 39The
number from the tribe of Dan was 62,700.

40From the descendants of Asher:[f]
All the men twenty years old or more who were able to serve in the army were
listed by name, according to the records of their clans and families. 41The
number from the tribe of Asher was 41,500.

42From the descendants of Naphtali:[g]
All the men twenty years old or more who were able to serve in the army were
listed by name, according to the records of their clans and families. 43The
number from the tribe of Naphtali was 53,400.

44These were the men counted by Moses and Aaron[h] and the twelve leaders of
Israel, each one representing his family. 45All the Israelites twenty years old or more
who were able to serve in Israel's army were counted according to their families. 46The
total number was 603,550.[i]
47The families of the tribe of Levi,[j] however, were not counted[k] along with the
others. 48The LORD had said to Moses: 49"You must not count the tribe of Levi or
include them in the census of the other Israelites. 50Instead, appoint the Levites to be
in charge of the tabernacle of the Testimony[l]—over all its furnishings and everything
belonging to it. They are to carry the tabernacle and all its furnishings; they are to
take care of it and encamp round it. 51Whenever the tabernacle is to move, the Levites
are to take it down, and whenever the tabernacle is to be set up, the Levites shall do
it.[m] Anyone else who goes near it shall be put to death. 52The Israelites are to set
up their tents by divisions, each man in his own camp under his own standard.[n] 53The
Levites, however, are to set up their tents round the tabernacle of the Testimony so
that wrath will not fall[o] on the Israelite community. The Levites are to be responsible
for the care of the tabernacle of the Testimony.[p]"
54The Israelites did all this just as the LORD commanded Moses.

The Arrangement of the Tribal Camps

2 The LORD said to Moses and Aaron: 2"The Israelites are to camp round the Tent
of Meeting some distance from it, each man under his standard[a] with the banners
of his family."

3On the east, towards the sunrise, the divisions of the camp of Judah are to
encamp under their standard. The leader of the people of Judah is Nahshon son
of Amminadab.[b] 4His division numbers 74,600.
5The tribe of Issachar will camp next to them. The leader of the people of
Issachar is Nethanel son of Zuar.[c] 6His division numbers 54,400.
7The tribe of Zebulun will be next. The leader of the people of Zebulun is Eliab
son of Helon.[d] 8His division numbers 57,400.
9All the men assigned to the camp of Judah, according to their divisions,
number 186,400. They will set out first.[e]

10On the south will be the divisions of the camp of Reuben under their
standard. The leader of the people of Reuben is Elizur son of Shedeur.[f] 11His
division numbers 46,500.
12The tribe of Simeon will camp next to them. The leader of the people of
Simeon is Shelumiel son of Zurishaddai.[g] 13His division numbers 59,300.

1:40 [f]Nu 26:44-47; Rev 7:6
1:42 [g]Nu 26:48-50; Rev 7:6
1:44 [h]Nu 26:64
1:46 [i]Ex 12:37; 38:26; Nu 2:32; 26:51
1:47 [j]Nu 2:33; 26:57 [k]Nu 4:3, 49
1:50 [l]Ex 38:21; Ac 7:44
1:51 [m]Nu 3:38; 4:1-33
1:52 [n]Nu 2:2; Ps 20:5
1:53 [o]Lev 10:6; Nu 16:46; 18:5 [p]Nu 18:2-4
2:2 [a]Nu 1:52; Ps 74:4; Isa 31:9
2:3 [b]Nu 10:14; Ru 4:20; 1Ch 2:10
2:5 [c]Nu 1:8
2:7 [d]Nu 1:9
2:9 [e]Nu 10:14
2:10 [f]Nu 1:5
2:12 [g]Nu 1:6

2:2 The nation of Israel was organised according to tribes for several reasons. (1) It was an effective way to manage and govern a large group. (2) It made dividing the promised land easier. (3) It was part of their culture and heritage (people were not known by a last name, but by their family, clan, and tribe). (4) It made it easier to keep detailed genealogies, and genealogies were the only way to prove membership in God's chosen nation. (5) It made travel much more efficient. The people followed the tribe's standard (a kind of flag) and thus stayed together and kept from getting lost.

2:14 [h]Nu 1:14
2:16 [i]Nu 10:18
2:17 [j]Nu 1:53; 10:21
2:18 [k]Ge 48:20; Jer 31:18-20 [l]Nu 1:10
2:20 [m]Nu 1:10
2:22 [n]Nu 1:11; Ps 68:27
2:24 [o]Nu 10:22 [p]Ps 80:2
2:25 [q]Nu 1:12
2:27 [r]Nu 1:13
2:29 [s]Nu 1:15
2:31 [t]Nu 10:25
2:32 [u]Ex 38:26; Nu 1:46
2:33 [v]Nu 1:47; 26:57-62

14The tribe of Gad will be next. The leader of the people of Gad is Eliasaph
son of Deuel.[a][h] 15His division numbers 45,650.
16All the men assigned to the camp of Reuben,[i] according to their divisions,
number 151,450. They will set out second.

17Then the Tent of Meeting and the camp of the Levites[j] will set out in the
middle of the camps. They will set out in the same order as they encamp, each
in his own place under his standard.

18On the west will be the divisions of the camp of Ephraim[k] under their
standard. The leader of the people of Ephraim is Elishama son of Ammihud.[l]
19His division numbers 40,500.
20The tribe of Manasseh will be next to them. The leader of the people of
Manasseh is Gamaliel son of Pedahzur.[m] 21His division numbers 32,200.
22The tribe of Benjamin will be next. The leader of the people of Benjamin
is Abidan son of Gideoni.[n] 23His division numbers 35,400.
24All the men assigned to the camp of Ephraim,[o] according to their divisions,
number 108,100. They will set out third.[p]

25On the north will be the divisions of the camp of Dan, under their standard.
The leader of the people of Dan is Ahiezer son of Ammishaddai.[q] 26His division
numbers 62,700.
27The tribe of Asher will camp next to them. The leader of the people of Asher
is Pagiel son of Ocran.[r] 28His division numbers 41,500.
29The tribe of Naphtali will be next. The leader of the people of Naphtali is
Ahira son of Enan.[s] 30His division numbers 53,400.
31All the men assigned to the camp of Dan number 157,600. They will set out
last,[t] under their standards.

32These are the Israelites, counted according to their families. All those in the
camps, by their divisions, number 603,550.[u] 33The Levites, however, were not
counted[v] along with the other Israelites, as the LORD commanded Moses.

34So the Israelites did everything the LORD commanded Moses; that is the way they
encamped under their standards, and that is the way they set out, each with his clan
and family.

a *14* Many manuscripts of the Masoretic Text, Samaritan Pentateuch and Vulgate (see also Num. 1:14); most manuscripts of the Masoretic Text *Reuel*

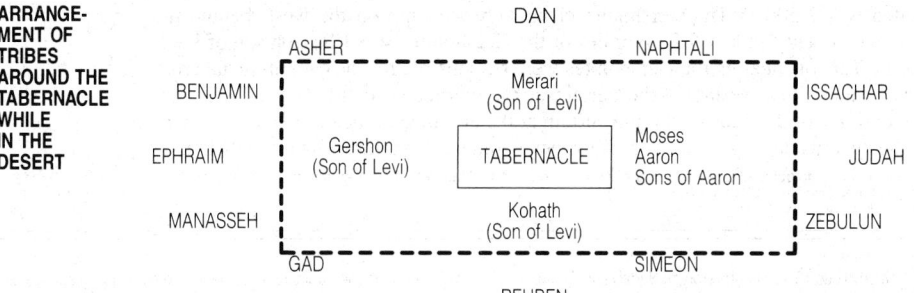

ARRANGEMENT OF TRIBES AROUND THE TABERNACLE WHILE IN THE DESERT

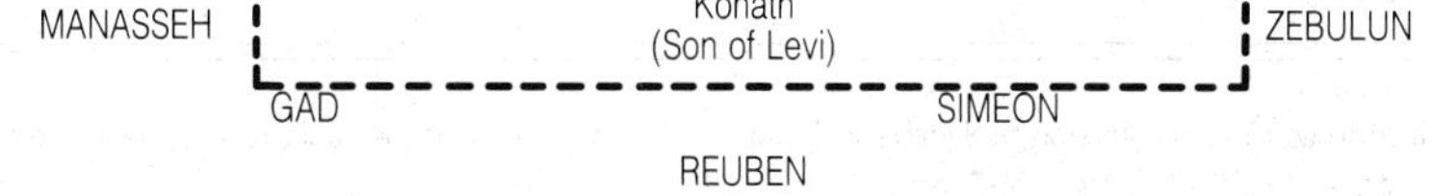

2:34 This must have been one of the biggest campsites the world has ever seen! It would have taken about 12 square miles to set up tents for just the 600,000 fighting men – not to mention the women and children. Moses must have had a difficult time managing such a group. In the early stages of the journey and at Mount Sinai, the people were generally obedient to both God and Moses. But when the people left Mount Sinai and travelled across the rugged desert, they began to complain, grumble, and disobey. Soon problems erupted, and Moses could no longer effectively manage the Israelites. The books of Exodus, Leviticus, and Numbers present a striking contrast between how much we can accomplish when we obey God and how little we can accomplish when we don't.

2. The role of the Levites

The Levites

3 This is the account of the family of Aaron and Moses[a] at the time the LORD talked
with Moses on Mount Sinai.
2The names of the sons of Aaron were Nadab the firstborn and Abihu, Eleazar and
Ithamar.[b] 3Those were the names of Aaron's sons, the anointed priests,[c] who were
ordained to serve as priests. 4Nadab and Abihu, however, fell dead before the LORD[d]
when they made an offering with unauthorised fire before him in the Desert of Sinai.[e]
They had no sons; so only Eleazar and Ithamar served as priests during the lifetime
of their father Aaron.[f]
5The LORD said to Moses, 6"Bring the tribe of Levi[g] and present them to Aaron
the priest to assist him.[h] 7They are to perform duties for him and for the whole
community at the Tent of Meeting by doing the work[i] of the tabernacle. 8They are
to take care of all the furnishings of the Tent of Meeting, fulfilling the obligations of
the Israelites by doing the work of the tabernacle. 9Give the Levites to Aaron and his
sons;[j] they are the Israelites who are to be given wholly to him.**a** 10Appoint Aaron
and his sons to serve as priests;[k] anyone else who approaches the sanctuary must be
put to death."[l]
11The LORD also said to Moses, 12"I have taken the Levites[m] from among the
Israelites in place of the first male offspring[n] of every Israelite woman. The Levites
are mine,[o] 13for all the firstborn are mine.[p] When I struck down all the firstborn
in Egypt, I set apart for myself every firstborn in Israel, whether man or animal. They
are to be mine. I am the LORD."
14The LORD said to Moses in the Desert of Sinai, 15"Count[q] the Levites by their
families and clans. Count every male a month old or more."[r] 16So Moses counted
them, as he was commanded by the word of the LORD.
17These were the names of the sons of Levi:[s]
Gershon, Kohath and Merari.[t]
18These were the names of the Gershonite clans:
Libni and Shimei.[u]
19The Kohathite clans:
Amram, Izhar, Hebron and Uzziel.[v]
20The Merarite clans:[w]
Mahli and Mushi.[x]
These were the Levite clans, according to their families.

21To Gershon belonged the clans of the Libnites and Shimeites;[y] these were the
Gershonite clans. 22The number of all the males a month old or more who were
counted was 7,500. 23The Gershonite clans were to camp on the west, behind the
tabernacle. 24The leader of the families of the Gershonites was Eliasaph son of Lael.
25At the Tent of Meeting the Gershonites were responsible for the care of the tabernacle[z] and tent, its coverings,[a] the curtain at the entrance[b] to the Tent of Meeting,
26the curtains of the courtyard[c], the curtain at the entrance to the courtyard surrounding the tabernacle and altar, and the ropes[d]—and everything related to their use.

a 9 Most manuscripts of the Masoretic Text; some manuscripts of the Masoretic Text, Samaritan Pentateuch and Septuagint (see also Num. 8:16) *to me*

3:1 [a]Ex 6:27
3:2 [b]Ex 6:23; Nu 26:60
3:3 [c]Ex 28:41
3:4 [d]Lev 10:2 [e]Lev 10:1 [f]1Ch 24:1
3:6 [g]Dt 10:8; 31:9; 1Ch 15:2 [h]Nu 8:6-22; 18:1-7; 2Ch 29:11
3:7 [i]Lev 8:35; Nu 1:50
3:9 [j]Nu 8:19; 18:6
3:10 [k]Ex 29:9 [l]Nu 1:51
3:12 [m]Mal 2:4 [n]ver 41; Nu 8:16, 18 [o]Ex 13:2
3:13 [p]Ex 13:12
3:15 [q]ver 39 [r]Nu 26:62
3:17 [s]Ge 46:11 [t]Ex 6:16
3:18 [u]Ex 6:17
3:19 [v]Ex 6:18
3:20 [w]Ge 46:11 [x]Ex 6:19
3:21 [y]Ex 6:17
3:25 [z]Ex 25:9 [a]Ex 26:14 [b]Ex 26:36; Nu 4:25
3:26 [c]Ex 27:9 [d]Ex 35:18

3:4 See Leviticus 10:1, 2 for the story of Nadab and Abihu.

3:5–13 At the time of the first Passover (Exodus 13:2), God instructed every Israelite family to dedicate its firstborn son to him (see 3:40–51 and 8:16). They were set apart to assist Moses and Aaron in ministering to the people. This was only a temporary measure, however. Here God chose all the men from the tribe of Levi to replace the firstborn sons from every Israelite tribe. These men, called Levites, were set apart to care for the tabernacle and minister to the people. All the priests had to belong to the tribe of Levi, but not all Levites were priests. The Levites were to be 25 years old before entering service. They probably received five years of on-the-job training before being admitted to full service at the age of 30.

3:10 Aaron and his descendants were appointed to the priesthood. There is a tremendous contrast between the priesthood of Aaron in the Old Testament and the priesthood of Christ in the New Testament. Aaron and his descendants were the only ones who could carry out the duties of the priests and approach God's dwelling place. Now that Christ is our High Priest – our intermediary with God – anyone who follows him is also called a priest (1 Peter 2:5, 9). Now all Christians may come into God's presence without fear because God's own Son encourages his followers to do so. We can put guilt behind us when we have a special relationship with

27To Kohath belonged the clans of the Amramites, Izharites, Hebronites and Uzzielites;[e] these were the Kohathite clans. 28The number of all the males a month old or more was 8,600.[b] The Kohathites were responsible for the care of the sanctuary. 29The Kohathite clans were to camp on the south side[f] of the tabernacle. 30The leader of the families of the Kohathite clans was Elizaphan son of Uzziel. 31They were responsible for the care of the ark,[g] the table,[h] the lampstand,[i] the altars,[j] the articles of the sanctuary used in ministering, the curtain,[k] and everything related to their use.[l] 32The chief leader of the Levites was Eleazar son of Aaron, the priest. He was appointed over those who were responsible for the care of the sanctuary.

33To Merari belonged the clans of the Mahlites and the Mushites;[m] these were the Merarite clans. 34The number of all the males a month old or more who were counted was 6,200. 35The leader of the families of the Merarite clans was Zuriel son of Abihail; they were to camp on the north side of the tabernacle.[n] 36The Merarites were appointed[o] to take care of the frames of the tabernacle, its crossbars, posts, bases, all its equipment, and everything related to their use, 37as well as the posts of the surrounding courtyard with their bases, tent pegs and ropes.

38Moses and Aaron and his sons were to camp to the east[p] of the tabernacle, towards the sunrise, in front of the Tent of Meeting.[q] They were responsible for the care of the sanctuary[r] on behalf of the Israelites. Anyone else who approached the sanctuary was to be put to death.[s]

39The total number of Levites counted at the LORD's command by Moses and Aaron according to their clans, including every male a month old or more, was 22,000.[t]

40The LORD said to Moses, "Count all the firstborn Israelite males who are a month old or more[u] and make a list of their names. 41Take the Levites for me in place of all the firstborn of the Israelites,[v] and the livestock of the Levites in place of all the firstborn of the livestock of the Israelites. I am the LORD."

42So Moses counted all the firstborn of the Israelites, as the LORD commanded him. 43The total number of firstborn males a month old or more, listed by name, was 22,273.[w]

44The LORD also said to Moses, 45"Take the Levites in place of all the firstborn of Israel, and the livestock of the Levites in place of their livestock. The Levites are to be mine. I am the LORD. 46To redeem[x] the 273 firstborn Israelites who exceed the number of the Levites, 47collect five shekels[c][y] for each one, according to the sanctuary shekel,[z] which weighs twenty gerahs.[a] 48Give the money for the redemption of the additional Israelites to Aaron and his sons."

49So Moses collected the redemption money from those who exceeded the number redeemed by the Levites. 50From the firstborn of the Israelites he collected silver weighing 1,365 shekels,[d][b] according to the sanctuary shekel. 51Moses gave the redemption money to Aaron and his sons, as he was commanded by the word of the LORD.

The Kohathites

4 The LORD said to Moses and Aaron: 2"Take a census[a] of the Kohathite branch of the Levites by their clans and families. 3Count all the men from thirty to fifty years of age[b] who come to serve in the work in the Tent of Meeting.

4"This is the work of the Kohathites in the Tent of Meeting: the care of the most

3:27 [e] 1Ch 26:23
3:29 [f] Nu 1:53
3:31 [g] Ex 25:10-22 [h] Ex 25:23 [i] Ex 25:31 [j] Ex 27:1; 30:1 [k] Ex 26:33 [l] Nu 4:15
3:33 [m] Ex 6:19
3:35 [n] Nu 1:53; 2:25
3:36 [o] Nu 4:32
3:38 [p] Nu 2:3 [q] Nu 1:53 [r] ver 7; Nu 18:5 [s] ver 10; Nu 1:51
3:39 [t] Nu 26:62
3:40 [u] ver 15
3:41 [v] ver 12
3:43 [w] ver 39
3:46 [x] Ex 13:13; Nu 18:15
3:47 [y] Lev 27:6 [z] Ex 30:13 [a] Lev 27:25
3:50 [b] ver 46-48
4:2 [a] Ex 30:12
4:3 [b] ver 23; Nu 8:25; 1Ch 23:3, 24, 27; Ezr 3:8

b *28* Hebrew; some Septuagint manuscripts *8,300* c *47* That is, about 2 ounces (about 55 grams) d *50* That is, about 35 pounds (about 15.5 kilograms)

God based on what Christ has done for us.

4:2ff The Kohathites, Gershonites (4:21), and Merarites (4:29) were families of Levites who were assigned special tasks in Israel's worship. For the jobs described in this chapter, a Levite had to be between 30 and 50 years old. They were expected to carry out their duties as described here in every detail. In fact, failure to do so would mean death (4:20). Worshipping our holy God must not be taken lightly.

holy things.[c] 5When the camp is to move, Aaron and his sons are to go in and take
down the shielding curtain[d] and cover the ark of the Testimony with it.[e] 6Then they
are to cover this with hides of sea cows,[a] spread a cloth of solid blue over that and
put the poles[f] in place.
7"Over the table of the Presence[g] they are to spread a blue cloth and put on it the
plates, dishes and bowls, and the jars for drink offerings; the bread that is continually
there[h] is to remain on it. 8Over these they are to spread a scarlet cloth, cover that
with hides of sea cows and put its poles in place.
9"They are to take a blue cloth and cover the lampstand that is for light, together
with its lamps, its wick trimmers and trays,[i] and all its jars for the oil used to supply
it. 10Then they are to wrap it and all its accessories in a covering of hides of sea cows
and put it on a carrying frame.
11"Over the gold altar[j] they are to spread a blue cloth and cover that with hides
of sea cows and put its poles in place.
12"They are to take all the articles used for ministering in the sanctuary, wrap them
in a blue cloth, cover that with hides of sea cows and put them on a carrying frame.
13"They are to remove the ashes from the bronze altar[k] and spread a purple cloth
over it. 14Then they are to place on it all the utensils used for ministering at the altar,
including the firepans, meat forks,[l] shovels and sprinkling bowls.[m] Over it they are
to spread a covering of hides of sea cows and put its poles[n] in place.
15"After Aaron and his sons have finished covering the holy furnishings and all the
holy articles, and when the camp is ready to move, the Kohathites are to come to do
the carrying.[o] But they must not touch the holy things or they will die.[p] The
Kohathites are to carry those things that are in the Tent of Meeting.
16"Eleazar[q] son of Aaron, the priest, is to have charge of the oil for the light,[r]
the fragrant incense, the regular grain offering[s] and the anointing oil. He is to be in
charge of the entire tabernacle and everything in it, including its holy furnishings and
articles."
17The LORD said to Moses and Aaron, 18"See that the Kohathite tribal clans are not
cut off from the Levites. 19So that they may live and not die when they come near
the most holy things,[t] do this for them: Aaron and his sons are to go into the sanctuary
and assign to each man his work and what he is to carry. 20But the Kohathites must
not go in to look[u] at the holy things, even for a moment, or they will die."

The Gershonites

21The LORD said to Moses, 22"Take a census also of the Gershonites by their
families and clans. 23Count all the men from thirty to fifty years of age[v] who come
to serve in the work at the Tent of Meeting.
24"This is the service of the Gershonite clans as they work and carry burdens:
25They are to carry the curtains of the tabernacle,[w] the Tent of Meeting,[x] its
covering[y] and the outer covering of hides of sea cows, the curtains for the entrance
to the Tent of Meeting, 26the curtains of the courtyard surrounding the tabernacle and
altar, the curtain for the entrance, the ropes and all the equipment used in its service.
The Gershonites are to do all that needs to be done with these things. 27All their
service, whether carrying or doing other work, is to be done under the direction of
Aaron and his sons. You shall assign to them as their responsibility all they are to
carry. 28This is the service of the Gershonite clans[z] at the Tent of Meeting. Their
duties are to be under the direction of Ithamar son of Aaron, the priest.

[a] *6* That is, large aquatic mammals; also elsewhere in this chapter

4:4 [c] ver 19
4:5 [d] Ex 26:31, 33 [e] Ex 25:10, 16
4:6 [f] Ex 25:13-15; 1Ki 8:7; 2Ch 5:8
4:7 [g] Ex 25:23, 29; Lev 24:6 [h] Ex 25:30
4:9 [i] Ex 25:31, 37, 38
4:11 [j] Ex 30:1
4:13 [k] Ex 27:1-8
4:14 [l] 2Ch 4:16 [m] Jer 52:18 [n] Ex 27:6
4:15 [o] Nu 7:9 [p] Nu 1:51; 2Sa 6:6, 7
4:16 [q] Lev 10:6 [r] Ex 25:6 [s] Ex 29:41; Lev 6:14-23
4:19 [t] ver 15
4:20 [u] Ex 19:21; 1Sa 6:19
4:23 [v] ver 3; 1Ch 23:3, 24, 27
4:25 [w] Ex 27:10-18; Nu 3:26 [x] Nu 3:25 [y] Ex 26:14
4:28 [z] Nu 7:7

4:27, 28 The Gershonites could receive directions from any of Aaron's sons, but they were directly responsible to Ithamar only. The lines of authority and accountability were clearly communicated to all. As you function with others in service to God, make sure the lines of authority between you and those you work with are clearly understood. Good communication builds good relationships.

The Merarites

29“Count the Merarites by their clans and families.[a] 30Count all the men from thirty
to fifty years of age who come to serve in the work at the Tent of Meeting. 31This
is their duty as they perform service at the Tent of Meeting: to carry the frames of
the tabernacle, its crossbars, posts and bases,[b] 32as well as the posts of the surrounding courtyard with their bases, tent pegs, ropes, all their equipment and everything
related to their use. Assign to each man the specific things he is to carry. 33This is
the service of the Merarite clans as they work at the Tent of Meeting under the direction
of Ithamar son of Aaron, the priest.”

The Numbering of the Levite Clans

34Moses, Aaron and the leaders of the community counted the Kohathites[c] by their
clans and families. 35All the men from thirty to fifty years of age who came to serve
in the work in the Tent of Meeting, 36counted by clans, were 2,750. 37This was the
total of all those in the Kohathite clans[d] who served in the Tent of Meeting. Moses
and Aaron counted them according to the LORD’s command through Moses.
38The Gershonites[e] were counted by their clans and families. 39All the men from
thirty to fifty years of age who came to serve in the work at the Tent of Meeting,
40counted by their clans and families, were 2,630. 41This was the total of those in
the Gershonite clans who served at the Tent of Meeting. Moses and Aaron counted
them according to the LORD’s command.
42The Merarites were counted by their clans and families. 43All the men from thirty
to fifty years of age who came to serve in the work at the Tent of Meeting, 44counted
by their clans, were 3,200. 45This was the total of those in the Merarite clans.[f] Moses
and Aaron counted them according to the LORD’s command through Moses.
46So Moses, Aaron and the leaders of Israel counted all the Levites by their clans
and families. 47All the men from thirty to fifty years of age[g] who came to do the work
of serving and carrying the Tent of Meeting 48numbered 8,580.[h] 49At the LORD’s
command through Moses, each was assigned his work and told what to carry.
Thus they were counted,[i] as the LORD commanded Moses.

3. The purity of the camp

5 The LORD said to Moses, 2“Command the Israelites to send away from the camp
anyone who has an infectious skin disease**a**[a] or a discharge[b] of any kind, or
who is ceremonially unclean[c] because of a dead body. 3Send away male and female
alike; send them outside the camp so that they will not defile their camp, where I dwell
among them.[d]” 4The Israelites did this; they sent them outside the camp. They did
just as the LORD had instructed Moses.

Restitution for Wrongs

5The LORD said to Moses, 6“Say to the Israelites: ‘When a man or woman wrongs
another in any way**b** and so is unfaithful[e] to the LORD, that person is guilty[f] 7and
must confess[g] the sin he has committed. He must make full restitution[h] for his
wrong, add one fifth to it and give it all to the person he has wronged. 8But if that
person has no close relative to whom restitution can be made for the wrong, the
restitution belongs to the LORD and must be given to the priest, along with the ram
with which atonement is made for him.[i] 9All the sacred contributions the Israelites
bring to a priest will belong to him.[j] 10Each man’s sacred gifts are his own, but what
he gives to the priest will belong to the priest.[k]’ ”

a *2* Traditionally *leprosy*; the Hebrew word was used for various diseases affecting the skin—not necessarily leprosy. **b** *6* Or *woman commits any wrong common to mankind*

4:29 [a]Ge 46:11
4:31 [b]Nu 3:36
4:34 [c]ver 2
4:37 [d]Nu 3:27
4:38 [e]Ge 46:11
4:45 [f]ver 29
4:47 [g]ver 3
4:48 [h]Nu 3:39
4:49 [i]Nu 1:47
5:2 [a]Lev 13:46 [b]Lev 15:2; Mt 9:20 [c]Lev 13:3; Nu 9:6-10
5:3 [d]Lev 26:12; Nu 35:34; 2Co 6:16
5:6 [e]Lev 6:2 [f]Lev 5:14-6:7
5:7 [g]Lev 5:5; 26:40; Jos 7:19; Lk 19:8 [h]Lev 6:5
5:8 [i]Lev 6:6, 7; 7:7
5:9 [j]Lev 6:17; 7:6-14
5:10 [k]Lev 10:13

5:5–8 God included restitution, a unique concept for that day, as part of his law for Israel. When someone was robbed, the guilty person was required to restore the loss to the victim and pay an additional interest penalty. When we have wronged others, we ought to do more than apologise. We should look for ways to set matters right and, if possible, leave the victim even better off than when we harmed him or her. When we have been wronged, we should still seek restoration rather than striking out in revenge.

The Test for an Unfaithful Wife

11 Then the LORD said to Moses, 12 "Speak to the Israelites and say to them: 'If a
man's wife goes astray[l] and is unfaithful to him 13 by sleeping with another man,[m]
and this is hidden from her husband and her impurity is undetected (since there is no
witness against her and she has not been caught in the act), 14 and if feelings of
jealousy[n] come over her husband and he suspects his wife and she is impure—or if
he is jealous and suspects her even though she is not impure— 15 then he is to take
his wife to the priest. He must also take an offering of a tenth of an ephah[c][o] of barley
flour[p] on her behalf. He must not pour oil on it or put incense on it, because it is
a grain offering for jealousy, a reminder[q] offering to draw attention to guilt.
16 " 'The priest shall bring her and make her stand before the LORD. 17 Then he shall
take some holy water in a clay jar and put some dust from the tabernacle floor into
the water. 18 After the priest has made the woman stand before the LORD, he shall
loosen her hair[r] and place in her hands the reminder offering, the grain offering for
jealousy, while he himself holds the bitter water that brings a curse. 19 Then the priest
shall put the woman under oath and say to her, "If no other man has slept with you
and you have not gone astray[s] and become impure while married to your husband,
may this bitter water that brings a curse not harm you. 20 But if you have gone astray[t]
while married to your husband and you have defiled yourself by sleeping with a man
other than your husband"— 21 here the priest is to put the woman under this curse of
the oath[u]—"may the LORD cause your people to curse and denounce you when he
causes your thigh to waste away and your abdomen to swell.[d] 22 May this water[v]
that brings a curse[w] enter your body so that your abdomen swells and your thigh
wastes away."[e]
" 'Then the woman is to say, "Amen. So be it.[x]"
23 " 'The priest is to write these curses on a scroll[y] and then wash them off into
the bitter water. 24 He shall make the woman drink the bitter water that brings a curse,
and this water will enter her and cause bitter suffering. 25 The priest is to take from
her hands the grain offering for jealousy, wave it before the LORD[z] and bring it to
the altar. 26 The priest is then to take a handful of the grain offering as a memorial
offering and burn it on the altar; after that, he is to make the woman drink the water.
27 If she has defiled herself and been unfaithful to her husband, then when she is made
to drink the water that brings a curse, it will go into her and cause bitter suffering;
her abdomen will swell and her thigh waste away,[f] and she will become accursed[a]
among her people. 28 If, however, the woman has not defiled herself and is free from
impurity, she will be cleared of guilt and will be able to have children.
29 " 'This, then, is the law of jealousy when a woman goes astray[b] and defiles
herself while married to her husband, 30 or when feelings of jealousy come over a man
because he suspects his wife. The priest is to make her stand before the LORD and is
to apply this entire law to her. 31 The husband will be innocent of any wrongdoing,
but the woman will bear the consequences[c] of her sin.' "

The Nazirite

6 The LORD said to Moses, 2 "Speak to the Israelites and say to them: 'If a man or
woman wants to make a special vow[a], a vow of separation to the LORD as a
Nazirite,[b] 3 he must abstain from wine[c] and other fermented drink and must not drink

[c] *15* That is, probably about 4 pints (about 2 litres) [d] *21* Or *causes you to have a miscarrying womb and barrenness* [e] *22* Or *body and cause you to be barren and have a miscarrying womb* [f] *27* Or *suffering; she will have barrenness and a miscarrying womb*

5:12 [l] Ex 20:14
5:13 [m] Lev 18:20; 20:10
5:14 [n] Pr 6:34; SS 8:6
5:15 [o] Ex 16:36 [p] Lev 6:20 [q] Eze 29:16
5:18 [r] Lev 10:6; 1Co 11:6
5:19 [s] ver 12, 29
5:20 [t] ver 12
5:21 [u] Jos 6:26; 1Sa 14:24; Ne 10:29
5:22 [v] Ps 109:18 [w] ver 18 [x] Dt 27:15
5:23 [y] Jer 45:1
5:25 [z] Lev 8:27
5:27 [a] Isa 43:28; 65:15; Jer 26:6; 29:18; 42:18; 44:12, 22; Zec 8:13
5:29 [b] ver 19
5:31 [c] Lev 5:1; 20:17
6:2 [a] Ge 28:20; Ac 21:23 [b] Jdg 13:5; 16:17; Am 2:11, 12
6:3 [c] Lk 1:15

5:11–31 This test for adultery served to remove a jealous husband's suspicion. Trust between husband and wife had to be completely eroded for a man to bring his wife to the priest for this type of test. Today priests and pastors help restore marriages by counselling couples who have lost faith in each other. Whether justified or not, suspicion must be removed for a marriage to survive and trust to be restored.

6:1, 2 In Moses' day, a personal vow was as binding as a written contract. It was one thing to say you would do something, but it was considered much more serious when you made a solemn vow to do it. God instituted the Nazirite vow for people who wanted to devote some time exclusively to serving him. This vow could be taken for as little as 30 days or as long as a lifetime. It was voluntary, with one exception—parents could take the vow for their young children, making them Nazirites for life. The vow included three distinct restrictions: (1) he must abstain from wine and fermented drink; (2) the hair could not be cut, and the beard could not be shaved; (3) touching a dead body was prohibited. The pur-

vinegar[d] made from wine or from other fermented drink. He must not drink grape
juice or eat grapes or raisins. 4As long as he is a Nazirite, he must not eat anything
that comes from the grapevine, not even the seeds or skins.
5" 'During the entire period of his vow of separation no razor[e] may be used on
his head.[f] He must be holy until the period of his separation to the LORD is over;
he must let the hair of his head grow long. 6Throughout the period of his separation
to the LORD he must not go near a dead body.[g] 7Even if his own father or mother
or brother or sister dies, he must not make himself ceremonially unclean[h] on account
of them, because the symbol of his separation to God is on his head. 8Throughout
the period of his separation he is consecrated to the LORD.
9" 'If someone dies suddenly in his presence, thus defiling the hair he has dedicated,[i] he must shave his head on the day of his cleansing[j]—the seventh day.
10Then on the eighth day he must bring two doves or two young pigeons[k] to the priest
at the entrance to the Tent of Meeting. 11The priest is to offer one as a sin offering
and the other as a burnt offering[l] to make atonement[m] for him because he sinned
by being in the presence of the dead body. That same day he is to consecrate his head.
12He must dedicate himself to the LORD for the period of his separation and must bring
a year-old male lamb as a guilt offering. The previous days do not count, because he
became defiled during his separation.
13" 'Now this is the law for the Nazirite when the period of his separation is over.[n]
He is to be brought to the entrance to the Tent of Meeting. 14There he is to present
his offerings to the LORD: a year-old male lamb without defect for a burnt offering,
a year-old ewe lamb without defect for a sin offering,[o] a ram without defect for a
fellowship offering,[a] 15together with their grain offerings and drink offerings,[p] and
a basket of bread made without yeast—cakes made of fine flour mixed with oil, and
wafers spread with oil.[q]
16" 'The priest is to present them before the LORD and make the sin offering and
the burnt offering. 17He is to present the basket of unleavened bread and is to sacrifice
the ram as a fellowship offering to the LORD, together with its grain offering and drink
offering.
18" 'Then at the entrance to the Tent of Meeting, the Nazirite must shave off the
hair that he dedicated.[r] He is to take the hair and put it in the fire that is under the
sacrifice of the fellowship offering.
19" 'After the Nazirite has shaved off the hair of his dedication, the priest is to place
in his hands a boiled shoulder of the ram, and a cake and a wafer from the basket,
both made without yeast. 20The priest shall then wave them before the LORD as a wave
offering; they are holy and belong to the priest, together with the breast that was waved
and the thigh that was presented. After that, the Nazirite may drink wine.[s]
21" 'This is the law of the Nazirite who vows his offering to the LORD in accordance
with his separation, in addition to whatever else he can afford. He must fulfil the vow
he has made, according to the law of the Nazirite.' "

The Priestly Blessing

22The LORD said to Moses, 23"Tell Aaron and his sons, 'This is how you are to
bless[t] the Israelites. Say to them:

24" ' "The LORD bless you[u]
and keep you;[v]
25the LORD make his face shine upon you[w]

a 14 Traditionally *peace offering*; also in verses 17 and 18

6:3 [d]Ru 2:14; Ps 69:21; Pr 10:26
6:5 [e]Ps 52:2; 57:4; 59:7; Isa 7:20; Eze 5:1 [f]1Sa 1:11
6:6 [g]Lev 21:1-3; Nu 19:11-22
6:7 [h]Nu 9:6
6:9 [i]ver 18 [j]Lev 14:9
6:10 [k]Lev 5:7; 14:22
6:11 [l]Ge 8:20 [m]Ex 29:36
6:13 [n]Ac 21:26
6:14 [o]Lev 14:10; Nu 15:27
6:15 [p]Nu 15:1-7 [q]Ex 29:2; Lev 2:4
6:18 [r]ver 9; Ac 21:24
6:20 [s]Ecc 9:7
6:23 [t]Dt 21:5; 1Ch 23:13
6:24 [u]Dt 28:3-6; Ps 28:9 [v]1Sa 2:9; Ps 17:8
6:25 [w]Job 29:24; Ps 31:16; 80:3; 119:135

---

pose of the Nazirite vow was to raise up a group of leaders devoted completely to God. Samson, Samuel, and John the Baptist were probably Nazirites for life.

6:24–26 A blessing was one way of asking for God's divine favour to rest upon others. The ancient blessing in these verses helps us understand what a blessing was supposed to do. Its five parts conveyed hope that God would (1) bless and keep them (favour and protect); (2) make his face shine upon them (be pleased); (3) be gracious (merciful and compassionate); (4) turn his face towards them (give his approval); (5) give peace. When you ask God to bless others or yourself, you are asking him to do these five things. The blessing you offer will not only help the one receiving it, it will also demonstrate love, encourage others, and provide a model of caring to others.

and be gracious to you;[x]
26the LORD turn his face[y] towards you
and give you peace.[z]" '

27"So they will put my name[a] on the Israelites, and I will bless them."

Offerings at the Dedication of the Tabernacle

7 When Moses finished setting up the tabernacle,[a] he anointed it and consecrated
it and all its furnishings.[b] He also anointed and consecrated the altar and all its
utensils.[c] 2Then the leaders of Israel,[d] the heads of families who were the tribal
leaders in charge of those who were counted, made offerings. 3They brought as their
gifts before the LORD six covered carts and twelve oxen—an ox from each leader and
a cart from every two. These they presented before the tabernacle.
4The LORD said to Moses, 5"Accept these from them, that they may be used in the
work at the Tent of Meeting. Give them to the Levites as each man's work requires."
6So Moses took the carts and oxen and gave them to the Levites. 7He gave two
carts and four oxen to the Gershonites,[e] as their work required, 8and he gave four
carts and eight oxen to the Merarites,[f] as their work required. They were all under
the direction of Ithamar son of Aaron, the priest. 9But Moses did not give any to the
Kohathites, because they were to carry on their shoulders[g] the holy things, for which
they were responsible.
10When the altar was anointed,[h] the leaders brought their offerings for its dedication[i] and presented them before the altar. 11For the LORD had said to Moses, "Each
day one leader is to bring his offering for the dedication of the altar."

12The one who brought his offering on the first day was Nahshon son of Amminadab
of the tribe of Judah.
13His offering was one silver plate weighing a hundred and thirty shekels,[a] and
one silver sprinkling bowl weighing seventy shekels,[b] both according to the
sanctuary shekel,[j] each filled with fine flour mixed with oil as a grain offering;[k]
14one gold dish weighing ten shekels,[c] filled with incense;[l] 15one young bull,[m]
one ram and one male lamb a year old, for a burnt offering;[n] 16one male goat
for a sin offering;[o] 17and two oxen, five rams, five male goats and five male
lambs a year old, to be sacrificed as a fellowship offering.[d][p] This was the
offering of Nahshon son of Amminadab.[q]

18On the second day Nethanel son of Zuar,[r] the leader of Issachar, brought his
offering.
19The offering he brought was one silver plate weighing a hundred and thirty
shekels, and one silver sprinkling bowl weighing seventy shekels, both according
to the sanctuary shekel, each filled with fine flour mixed with oil as a grain
offering; 20one gold dish[s] weighing ten shekels, filled with incense; 21one young
bull, one ram and one male lamb a year old, for a burnt offering; 22one male goat
for a sin offering; 23and two oxen, five rams, five male goats and five male lambs
a year old, to be sacrificed as a fellowship offering. This was the offering of
Nethanel son of Zuar.

24On the third day, Eliab son of Helon,[t] the leader of the people of Zebulun, brought
his offering.
25His offering was one silver plate weighing a hundred and thirty shekels, and
one silver sprinkling bowl weighing seventy shekels, both according to the
sanctuary shekel, each filled with fine flour mixed with oil as a grain offering;
26one gold dish weighing ten shekels, filled with incense; 27one young bull, one

a *13* That is, about 3¼ pounds (about 1.5 kilograms); also elsewhere in this chapter **b** *13* That is, about 1¾ pounds (about 0.8 kilogram); also elsewhere in this chapter **c** *14* That is, about 4 ounces (about 115 grams); also elsewhere in this chapter **d** *17* Traditionally *peace offering*; also elsewhere in this chapter

6:25 [x]Ge 43:29; Ps 25:16; 86:16
6:26 [y]Ps 4:6; 44:3 [z]Ps 29:11; 37:11, 37; Jn 14:27
6:27 [a]Dt 28:10; 2Sa 7:23; 2Ch 7:14; Ne 9:10; Jer 25:29
7:1 [a]Ex 40:17 [b]Ex 40:9 [c]ver 84, 88; Ex 40:10
7:2 [d]Nu 1:5-16
7:7 [e]Nu 4:24-26, 28
7:8 [f]Nu 4:31-33
7:9 [g]Nu 4:15
7:10 [h]ver 1 [i]2Ch 7:9
7:13 [j]Ex 30:13; Nu 3:47 [k]Lev 2:1
7:14 [l]Ex 30:34
7:15 [m]Ex 24:5; 29:3; Nu 28:11 [n]Lev 1:3
7:16 [o]Lev 4:3, 23
7:17 [p]Lev 3:1 [q]Nu 1:7
7:18 [r]Nu 1:8
7:20 [s]ver 14
7:24 [t]Nu 1:9

7:1ff After the tabernacle was set up, anointed, and consecrated, the leaders of the 12 tribes brought gifts and offerings for its use and maintenance. All of the people participated—it was everyone's tabernacle.

7:30 [u]Nu 1:5

ram and one male lamb a year old, for a burnt offering; 28 one male goat for a
sin offering; 29 and two oxen, five rams, five male goats and five male lambs a
year old, to be sacrificed as a fellowship offering. This was the offering of Eliab
son of Helon.

30 On the fourth day Elizur son of Shedeur,[u] the leader of the people of Reuben,
brought his offering.

31 His offering was one silver plate weighing a hundred and thirty shekels, and
one silver sprinkling bowl weighing seventy shekels, both according to the
sanctuary shekel, each filled with fine flour mixed with oil as a grain offering;
32 one gold dish weighing ten shekels, filled with incense; 33 one young bull, one
ram and one male lamb a year old, for a burnt offering; 34 one male goat for a
sin offering; 35 and two oxen, five rams, five male goats and five male lambs a
year old, to be sacrificed as a fellowship offering. This was the offering of Elizur
son of Shedeur.

7:36 [v]Nu 1:6

36 On the fifth day Shelumiel son of Zurishaddai,[v] the leader of the people of Simeon,
brought his offering.

37 His offering was one silver plate weighing a hundred and thirty shekels, and
one silver sprinkling bowl weighing seventy shekels, both according to the
sanctuary shekel, each filled with fine flour mixed with oil as a grain offering;
38 one gold dish weighing ten shekels, filled with incense; 39 one young bull, one
ram and one male lamb a year old, for a burnt offering; 40 one male goat for a
sin offering; 41 and two oxen, five rams, five male goats and five male lambs a
year old, to be sacrificed as a fellowship offering. This was the offering of
Shelumiel son of Zurishaddai.

7:42 [w]Nu 1:14

42 On the sixth day Eliasaph son of Deuel,[w] the leader of the people of Gad, brought
his offering.

43 His offering was one silver plate weighing a hundred and thirty shekels, and
one silver sprinkling bowl weighing seventy shekels, both according to the
sanctuary shekel, each filled with fine flour mixed with oil as a grain offering;
44 one gold dish weighing ten shekels, filled with incense; 45 one young bull, one
ram and one male lamb a year old, for a burnt offering; 46 one male goat for a
sin offering; 47 and two oxen, five rams, five male goats and five male lambs a
year old, to be sacrificed as a fellowship offering. This was the offering of
Eliasaph son of Deuel.

7:48 [x]Nu 1:10

48 On the seventh day Elishama son of Ammihud,[x] the leader of the people of
Ephraim, brought his offering.

49 His offering was one silver plate weighing a hundred and thirty shekels, and
one silver sprinkling bowl weighing seventy shekels, both according to the
sanctuary shekel, each filled with fine flour mixed with oil as a grain offering;
50 one gold dish weighing ten shekels, filled with incense; 51 one young bull, one
ram and one male lamb a year old, for a burnt offering; 52 one male goat for a
sin offering; 53 and two oxen, five rams, five male goats and five male lambs a
year old, to be sacrificed as a fellowship offering. This was the offering of
Elishama son of Ammihud.[y]

7:53 [y]Nu 1:10

7:54 [z]Nu 1:10; 2:20

54 On the eighth day Gamaliel son of Pedahzur,[z] the leader of the people of Manasseh,
brought his offering.

55 His offering was one silver plate weighing a hundred and thirty shekels, and
one silver sprinkling bowl weighing seventy shekels, both according to the
sanctuary shekel, each filled with fine flour mixed with oil as a grain offering;
56 one gold dish weighing ten shekels, filled with incense; 57 one young bull, one
ram and one male lamb a year old, for a burnt offering; 58 one male goat for a
sin offering; 59 and two oxen, five rams, five male goats and five male lambs a
year old, to be sacrificed as a fellowship offering. This was the offering of
Gamaliel son of Pedahzur.

60On the ninth day Abidan son of Gideoni,[a] the leader of the people of Benjamin, 7:60 [a]Nu 1:11
brought his offering.
61His offering was one silver plate weighing a hundred and thirty shekels, and
one silver sprinkling bowl weighing seventy shekels, both according to the
sanctuary shekel, each filled with fine flour mixed with oil as a grain offering;
62one gold dish weighing ten shekels, filled with incense; 63one young bull, one
ram and one male lamb a year old, for a burnt offering; 64one male goat for a
sin offering; 65and two oxen, five rams, five male goats and five male lambs a
year old, to be sacrificed as a fellowship offering. This was the offering of Abidan
son of Gideoni. 7:66 [b]Nu 1:12; 2:25

66On the tenth day Ahiezer son of Ammishaddai,[b] the leader of the people of Dan,
brought his offering.
67His offering was one silver plate weighing a hundred and thirty shekels, and
one silver sprinkling bowl weighing seventy shekels, both according to the
sanctuary shekel, each filled with fine flour mixed with oil as a grain offering;
68one gold dish weighing ten shekels, filled with incense; 69one young bull, one
ram and one male lamb a year old, for a burnt offering; 70one male goat for a
sin offering; 71and two oxen, five rams, five male goats and five male lambs a 7:72 [c]Nu 1:13
year old, to be sacrificed as a fellowship offering. This was the offering of
Ahiezer son of Ammishaddai.

72On the eleventh day Pagiel son of Ocran,[c] the leader of the people of Asher, brought
his offering.
73His offering was one silver plate weighing a hundred and thirty shekels, and
one silver sprinkling bowl weighing seventy shekels, both according to the
sanctuary shekel, each filled with fine flour mixed with oil as a grain offering;
74one gold dish weighing ten shekels, filled with incense; 75one young bull, one
ram and one male lamb a year old, for a burnt offering; 76one male goat for a 7:78 [d]Nu 1:15; 2:29
sin offering; 77and two oxen, five rams, five male goats and five male lambs a
year old, to be sacrificed as a fellowship offering. This was the offering of Pagiel
son of Ocran.

78On the twelfth day Ahira son of Enan,[d] the leader of the people of Naphtali, brought
his offering.
79His offering was one silver plate weighing a hundred and thirty shekels, and
one silver sprinkling bowl weighing seventy shekels, both according to the
sanctuary shekel, each filled with fine flour mixed with oil as a grain offering; 7:84 [e]ver 1, 10
80one gold dish weighing ten shekels, filled with incense; 81one young bull, one [f]Nu 4:14
ram and one male lamb a year old, for a burnt offering; 82one male goat for a [g]ver 14
sin offering; 83and two oxen, five rams, five male goats and five male lambs a
year old, to be sacrificed as a fellowship offering. This was the offering of Ahira
son of Enan.

84These were the offerings of the Israelite leaders for the dedication of the altar when
it was anointed:[e] twelve silver plates, twelve silver sprinkling bowls[f] and twelve
gold dishes.[g] 85Each silver plate weighed a hundred and thirty shekels, and each
sprinkling bowl seventy shekels. Altogether, the silver dishes weighed two thousand
four hundred shekels,[e] according to the sanctuary shekel. 86The twelve gold dishes 7:88 [h]ver 1, 10
filled with incense weighed ten shekels each, according to the sanctuary shekel.
Altogether, the gold dishes weighed a hundred and twenty shekels.[f] 87The total
number of animals for the burnt offering came to twelve young bulls, twelve rams
and twelve male lambs a year old, together with their grain offering. Twelve male
goats were used for the sin offering. 88The total number of animals for the sacrifice
of the fellowship offering came to twenty-four oxen, sixty rams, sixty male goats and
sixty male lambs a year old. These were the offerings for the dedication of the altar
after it was anointed.[h]
89When Moses entered the Tent of Meeting to speak with the LORD,[i] he heard the 7:89 [i]Ex 25:21, 22; 33:9, 11

[e] *85* That is, about 61 pounds (about 28 kilograms) [f] *86* That is, about 3 pounds (about 1.4 kilograms)

voice speaking to him from between the two cherubim above the atonement cover[j]
on the ark of the Testimony. And he spoke with him.

Setting Up the Lamps

8 The LORD said to Moses, 2 "Speak to Aaron and say to him, 'When you set up
the seven lamps, they are to light the area in front of the lampstand.[a]' "
3 Aaron did so; he set up the lamps so that they faced forward on the lampstand,
just as the LORD commanded Moses. 4 This is how the lampstand was made: It was
made of hammered gold[b]—from its base to its blossoms. The lampstand was made
exactly like the pattern[c] the LORD had shown Moses.

The Setting Apart of the Levites

5 The LORD said to Moses: 6 "Take the Levites from among the other Israelites and
make them ceremonially clean.[d] 7 To purify them, do this: Sprinkle the water of
cleansing[e] on them; then make them shave their whole bodies[f] and wash their
clothes,[g] and so purify themselves. 8 Make them take a young bull with its grain
offering of fine flour mixed with oil;[h] then you are to take a second young bull for
a sin offering. 9 Bring the Levites to the front of the Tent of Meeting[i] and assemble
the whole Israelite community.[j] 10 You are to bring the Levites before the LORD,
and the Israelites are to lay their hands on them.[k] 11 Aaron is to present the Levites
before the LORD as a wave offering[l] from the Israelites, so that they may be ready
to do the work of the LORD.
12 "After the Levites lay their hands on the heads of the bulls,[m] use the one for a
sin offering to the LORD and the other for a burnt offering, to make atonement[n] for
the Levites. 13 Make the Levites stand in front of Aaron and his sons and then present
them as a wave offering to the LORD. 14 In this way you are to set the Levites apart
from the other Israelites, and the Levites will be mine.[o]
15 "After you have purified the Levites and presented them as a wave offering,[p]
they are to come to do their work at the Tent of Meeting. 16 They are the Israelites
who are to be given wholly to me. I have taken them as my own in place of the
firstborn, the first male offspring[q] from every Israelite woman. 17 Every firstborn
male in Israel, whether man or animal,[r] is mine. When I struck down all the firstborn
in Egypt, I set them apart for myself.[s] 18 And I have taken the Levites in place of
all the firstborn sons in Israel.[t] 19 Of all the Israelites, I have given the Levites as
gifts to Aaron and his sons[u] to do the work at the Tent of Meeting on behalf of the
Israelites[v] and to make atonement for them[w] so that no plague will strike the Israelites
when they go near the sanctuary."
20 Moses, Aaron and the whole Israelite community did with the Levites just as the
LORD commanded Moses. 21 The Levites purified themselves and washed their
clothes.[x] Then Aaron presented them as a wave offering before the LORD and made
atonement for them to purify them.[y] 22 After that, the Levites came to do their work
at the Tent of Meeting under the supervision of Aaron and his sons. They did with
the Levites just as the LORD commanded Moses.
23 The LORD said to Moses, 24 "This applies to the Levites: Men twenty-five years
old or more[z] shall come to take part in the work at the Tent of Meeting,[a] 25 but at

7:89 [j] Ps 80:1; 99:1
8:2 [a] Ex 25:37; Lev 24:2, 4
8:4 [b] Ex 25:18, 36 [c] Ex 25:9
8:6 [d] Lev 22:2; Isa 1:16; 52:11
8:7 [e] Nu 19:9, 17 [f] Lev 14:9; Dt 21:12 [g] Lev 14:8
8:8 [h] Lev 2:1; Nu 15:8-10
8:9 [i] Ex 40:12 [j] Lev 8:3
8:10 [k] Ac 6:6
8:11 [l] Lev 7:30
8:12 [m] Ex 29:10 [n] Ex 29:36
8:14 [o] Nu 3:12
8:15 [p] Ex 29:24
8:16 [q] Nu 3:12
8:17 [r] Ex 4:23 [s] Ex 13:2; Lk 2:23
8:18 [t] Nu 3:12
8:19 [u] Nu 3:9 [v] Nu 1:53 [w] Nu 16:46
8:21 [x] ver 7 [y] ver 12
8:24 [z] 1Ch 23:3 [a] Ex 38:21; Nu 4:3

7:89 Imagine hearing the very voice of God! Moses must have trembled at the sound. Yet we have God's words recorded for us in the Bible, and we should have no less reverence and awe for them. God sometimes spoke directly to his people to tell them the proper way to live. The Bible records these conversations to give us insights into God's character. How tragic when we take these very words of God lightly. Like Moses, we have the privilege of talking to God, but God answers us differently—through his written word and the guidance of his Holy Spirit. To receive this guidance, we need to seek to know God as Moses did.

8:1–4 The lamps provided light for the priests as they carried out their duties. The light was also an expression of God's presence. Jesus said, "I am the light of the world" (John 8:12). The golden lampstand is still one of the major symbols of the Jewish faith.

8:25, 26 Why were the Levites supposed to retire at the age of 50? The reasons were probably more practical than theological. (1) Moving the tabernacle and its furniture through the desert required strength. The younger men were more suited for the work of lifting the heavy articles. (2) The Levites over 50 did not stop working altogether. They were allowed to assist with various light duties in the tabernacle. This helped the younger men assume more responsibilities, and it allowed the older men to be in a position to advise and counsel them.

the age of fifty, they must retire from their regular service and work no longer. 26They
may assist their brothers in performing their duties at the Tent of Meeting, but they
themselves must not do the work. This, then, is how you are to assign the responsibilities of the Levites."

The Passover

9 The LORD spoke to Moses in the Desert of Sinai in the first month[a] of the second
year after they came out of Egypt.[b] He said, 2"Make the Israelites celebrate the
Passover at the appointed time. 3Celebrate it at the appointed time, at twilight on the
fourteenth day of this month, in accordance with all its rules and regulations.[c]"
4So Moses told the Israelites to celebrate the Passover, 5and they did so in the Desert
of Sinai at twilight on the fourteenth day of the first month.[d] The Israelites did
everything just as the LORD commanded Moses.
6But some of them could not celebrate the Passover on that day because they were
ceremonially unclean[e] on account of a dead body. So they came to Moses and
Aaron[f] that same day 7and said to Moses, "We have become unclean because of a
dead body, but why should we be kept from presenting the LORD's offering with the
other Israelites at the appointed time?"
8Moses answered them, "Wait until I find out what the LORD commands concerning
you."[g]
9Then the LORD said to Moses, 10"Tell the Israelites: 'When any of you or your
descendants are unclean because of a dead body or are away on a journey, they may
still celebrate[h] the LORD's Passover. 11They are to celebrate it on the fourteenth day
of the second month at twilight. They are to eat the lamb, together with unleavened
bread and bitter herbs.[i] 12They must not leave any of it till morning[j] or break any
of its bones.[k] When they celebrate the Passover, they must follow all the regulations.
13But if a man who is ceremonially clean and not on a journey fails to celebrate the
Passover, that person must be cut off from his people[l] because he did not present
the LORD's offering at the appointed time. That man will bear the consequences of
his sin.
14" 'An alien[m] living among you who wants to celebrate the LORD's Passover must
do so in accordance with its rules and regulations. You must have the same regulations
for the alien and the native-born.' "

4. Receiving guidance for the journey

The Cloud Above the Tabernacle

15On the day the tabernacle, the Tent of the Testimony, was set up, the cloud[n]
covered it. From evening till morning the cloud above the tabernacle looked like fire.[o]
16That is how it continued to be; the cloud covered it, and at night it looked like fire.

9:1 [a]Ex 40:2 [b]Nu 1:1
9:3 [c]Ex 12:2-11, 43-49; Lev 23:5-8; Dt 16:1-8
9:5 [d]Ex 12:1-13; Jos 5:10
9:6 [e]Lev 5:3 [f]Ex 18:15; Nu 27:2
9:8 [g]Ex 18:15; Nu 27:5, 21; Ps 85:8
9:10 [h]2Ch 30:2
9:11 [i]Ex 12:8
9:12 [j]Ex 12:10, 43 [k]Ex 12:46; Jn 19:36*
9:13 [l]Ge 17:14; Ex 12:15
9:14 [m]Ex 12:48, 49
9:15 [n]Ex 40:34 [o]Ex 13:21

9:2 This is the second Passover. The first was instituted in Egypt and recorded in Exodus 12. Passover and the Feast of Unleavened Bread were an eight-day religious observance (Leviticus 23:5, 6) commemorating the Israelites' escape from slavery in Egypt by God's power.

9:6–12 Several men came to Moses because of the predicament they faced: They were "unclean" because of contact with a dead body (or entering the home of a person who had died), and this prevented them from participating in the Passover meal. Notice that God did not adjust the requirements of the Passover. The standards of holiness were maintained, and the men were not allowed to participate. But God did make an exception and allowed the men to celebrate the Passover at a later date. This upheld the sacred requirements while allowing the men to participate in the feast – a duty for all Israelite men. Sometimes we face predicaments where the most obvious solution might cause us to compromise God's standards. Like Moses, we should use wisdom and prayer to reach a workable solution.

9:14 Sometimes we are tempted to excuse non-Christians from following God's guidelines for living. Christmas and Easter, for example, often have other meanings for them. We would not expect them to understand Lent. Yet foreigners at this time were expected to follow the same laws and ordinances as the Israelites. God did not have a separate set of standards for unbelievers and he still does not today. The phrase "You must have the same regulations" emphasises that non-Israelites were also subject to God's commands and promises. God singled out Israel for a special purpose – to be an example of how one nation could, and should, follow him. His aim, however, was to have all people obey and worship him.

9:15–22 A pillar of cloud by day and a pillar of fire by night guided and protected the Israelites as they travelled across the desert. Some have said this pillar may have been a burning bowl of pitch whose smoke was visible during the day and whose fire could be seen at night. However, a bowl of pitch would not have lifted itself up and moved ahead of the people, and the Bible is clear that the cloud and fire moved in accordance with the will of God. The cloud and the fire were not merely natural phenomena; they were the vehicle of God's presence and the visible evidence of his moving and directing his people.

[17]Whenever the cloud lifted from above the Tent, the Israelites set out; wherever the
cloud settled, the Israelites encamped.[p] [18]At the LORD's command the Israelites set
out, and at his command they encamped. As long as the cloud stayed over the
tabernacle, they remained in camp. [19]When the cloud remained over the tabernacle
a long time, the Israelites obeyed the LORD's order and did not set out. [20]Sometimes
the cloud was over the tabernacle only a few days; at the LORD's command they would
encamp, and then at his command they would set out. [21]Sometimes the cloud stayed
only from evening till morning, and when it lifted in the morning, they set out.
Whether by day or by night, whenever the cloud lifted, they set out. [22]Whether the
cloud stayed over the tabernacle for two days or a month or a year, the Israelites would
remain in camp and not set out; but when it lifted, they would set out. [23]At the LORD's
command they encamped, and at the LORD's command they set out. They obeyed the
LORD's order, in accordance with his command through Moses.

The Silver Trumpets

10 The LORD said to Moses: [2]"Make two trumpets[a] of hammered silver, and use
them for calling the community[b] together and for having the camps set out.
[3]When both are sounded, the whole community is to assemble before you at the
entrance to the Tent of Meeting. [4]If only one is sounded, the leaders[c] — the heads
of the clans of Israel — are to assemble before you. [5]When a trumpet blast is sounded,
the tribes camping on the east are to set out.[d] [6]At the sounding of a second blast,
the camps on the south are to set out.[e] The blast will be the signal for setting out.
[7]To gather the assembly, blow the trumpets,[f] but not with the same signal.[g]

[8]"The sons of Aaron, the priests, are to blow the trumpets. This is to be a lasting
ordinance for you and the generations to come.[h] [9]When you go into battle in your
own land against an enemy who is oppressing you,[i] sound a blast on the trumpets.
Then you will be remembered[j] by the LORD your God and rescued from your
enemies.[k] [10]Also at your times of rejoicing — your appointed feasts and New Moon
festivals[l] — you are to sound the trumpets[m] over your burnt offerings and fellowship
offerings,[a] and they will be a memorial for you before your God. I am the LORD your
God."

B. FIRST APPROACH TO THE PROMISED LAND (10:11 — 14:45)

As the Israelites approached the promised land, Moses sent leaders to spy out the land and its people. But the spies returned with a discouraging report. " Although Joshua and Caleb disagreed, the Israelites had already made up their minds and began to complain. As punishment for their lack of faith, God condemned them to wander in the desert for 40 years. Our obedience must be complete and timely.

1. The people complain

The Israelites Leave Sinai

[11]On the twentieth day of the second month of the second year,[n] the cloud lifted[o]
from above the tabernacle of the Testimony. [12]Then the Israelites set out from the
Desert of Sinai and travelled from place to place until the cloud came to rest in the
Desert of Paran. [13]They set out, this first time, at the LORD's command through
Moses.[p]

[14]The divisions of the camp of Judah went first, under their standard.[q] Nahshon
son of Amminadab[r] was in command. [15]Nethanel son of Zuar was over the division
of the tribe of Issachar, [16]and Eliab son of Helon was over the division of the tribe

a *10* Traditionally *peace offerings*

9:17 p Ex 40:36-38; Nu 10:11, 12; 1Co 10:1
10:2 a Ne 12:35; Ps 47:5 b Jer 4:5, 19; 6:1; Hos 5:8; Joel 2:1, 15; Am 3:6
10:4 c Ex 18:21; Nu 1:16; 7:2
10:5 d ver 14
10:6 e ver 18
10:7 f Eze 33:3; Joel 2:1 g 1Co 14:8
10:8 h Nu 31:6
10:9 i Jdg 2:18; 6:9; 1Sa 10:18; Ps 106:42 j Ge 8:1 k Ps 106:4
10:10 l Ps 81:3 m Lev 23:24
10:11 n Ex 40:17 o Nu 9:17
10:13 p Dt 1:6
10:14 q Nu 2:3-9 r Nu 1:7

9:23 The Israelites travelled and camped as God guided. When you follow God's guidance, you know you are where God wants you, whether you're moving or staying in one place. You are physically somewhere right now. Instead of praying, "God, what do you want me to do next?" ask, "God, what do you want me to do while I'm right here?" Direction from God is not just for your next big move. He has a purpose in placing you where you are right now. Begin to understand God's purpose for your life by discovering what he wants you to do now!

10:1-10 The two silver trumpets were used to coordinate the tribes as they moved through the desert. To keep so many people in tight formations required clear communication and control. Trumpet blasts also reminded Israel of God's protection over them.

of Zebulun. 17 Then the tabernacle was taken down, and the Gershonites and Merarites, who carried it, set out.[s]
18 The divisions of the camp of Reuben went next, under their standard.[t] Elizur
son of Shedeur was in command. 19 Shelumiel son of Zurishaddai was over the division
of the tribe of Simeon, 20 and Eliasaph son of Deuel was over the division of the tribe
of Gad. 21 Then the Kohathites set out, carrying the holy things.[u] The tabernacle was
to be set up before they arrived.[v]
22 The divisions of the camp of Ephraim[w] went next, under their standard. Elishama
son of Ammihud was in command. 23 Gamaliel son of Pedahzur was over the division
of the tribe of Manasseh, 24 and Abidan son of Gideoni was over the division of the
tribe of Benjamin.
25 Finally, as the rear guard[x] for all the units, the divisions of the camp of Dan set
out, under their standard. Ahiezer son of Ammishaddai was in command. 26 Pagiel son
of Ocran was over the division of the tribe of Asher, 27 and Ahira son of Enan was
over the division of the tribe of Naphtali. 28 This was the order of march for the Israelite
divisions as they set out.
29 Now Moses said to Hobab[y] son of Reuel[z] the Midianite, Moses' father-in-
law,[a] "We are setting out for the place about which the LORD said, 'I will give it
to you.'[b] Come with us and we will treat you well, for the LORD has promised good
things to Israel."
30 He answered, "No, I will not go;[c] I am going back to my own land and my own
people."
31 But Moses said, "Please do not leave us. You know where we should camp in
the desert, and you can be our eyes.[d] 32 If you come with us, we will share with you[e]
whatever good things the LORD gives us.[f]"
33 So they set out[g] from the mountain of the LORD and travelled for three days. The
ark of the covenant of the LORD[h] went before them during those three days to find
them a place to rest. 34 The cloud of the LORD was over them by day when they set
out from the camp.[i]
35 Whenever the ark set out, Moses said,

"Rise up, O LORD!
May your enemies be scattered;[j]
may your foes flee before you.[k]"

36 Whenever it came to rest, he said,

"Return,[l] O LORD,
to the countless thousands of Israel.[m]"

10:17 [s]Nu 4:21-32
10:18 [t]Nu 2:10-16
10:21 [u]Nu 4:20 [v]ver 17
10:22 [w]Nu 2:24
10:25 [x]Nu 2:31; Jos 6:9
10:29 [y]Jdg 4:11 [z]Ex 2:18 [a]Ex 3:1 [b]Ge 12:7
10:30 [c]Mt 21:29
10:31 [d]Job 29:15
10:32 [e]Dt 10:18 [f]Ps 22:27-31; 67:5-7
10:33 [g]ver 12; Dt 1:33 [h]Jos 3:3
10:34 [i]Nu 9:15-23
10:35 [j]Ps 68:1 [k]Dt 7:10; 32:41; Ps 68:2; Isa 17:12-14
10:36 [l]Isa 63:17 [m]Dt 1:10

10:21 Those who travel, move, or face new challenges know what it is to be uprooted. Life is full of changes, and few things remain stable. The Israelites were constantly moving through the desert. They were able to handle change only because God's presence in the tabernacle was always with them. The portable tabernacle signified God and his people moving together. For us, stability does not mean lack of change, but moving with God in every circumstance.

10:29–32 By complimenting Hobab's desert skills, Moses let him know he was needed. People cannot know you appreciate them if you do not tell them they are important to you. Complimenting those who deserve it builds lasting relationships and helps people know they are valued. Think about those who have helped you this month. What can you do to let them know how much you need and appreciate them?

ISRAEL'S DEPARTURE FROM SINAI
It has been two years since Israel left Egypt. Having received God's travel instructions through Moses, Israel set out from Mount Sinai into the Desert of Paran on their way towards the promised land.

11:1
a Lev 10:2

11:2
b Nu 21:7

11:3
c Dt 9:22

11:4
d Ex 12:38
e Ps 78:18;
1Co 10:6

Fire From the LORD

11 Now the people complained about their hardships in the hearing of the LORD,
and when he heard them his anger was aroused. Then fire from the LORD burned
among them[a] and consumed some of the outskirts of the camp. 2When the people
cried out to Moses, he prayed to the LORD[b] and the fire died down. 3So that place
was called Taberah,[a][c] because fire from the LORD had burned among them.

Quail From the LORD

4The rabble with them began to crave other food,[d] and again the Israelites started
wailing[e] and said, "If only we had meat to eat! 5We remember the fish we ate in Egypt

a 3 *Taberah* means *burning.*

ISRAEL'S COMPLAINING

Reference	*Complaint*	*Sin*	*Result*
11:1	About their hardships	Complained about their problems instead of praying to God about them	Thousands of people were destroyed when God sent a plague of fire to punish them
11:4	About the lack of meat	Lusted after things they didn't have	God sent quail; but as the people began to eat, God struck them with a plague that killed many
14:1–4	About being stuck in the desert, facing the giants of the promised land, and wishing to return to Egypt	Openly rebelled against God's leaders and failed to trust in his promises	All who complained were not allowed to enter the promised land, being doomed to wander in the desert until they died
16:3	About Moses' and Aaron's authority and leadership	Were greedy for more power and authority	The families, friends, and possessions of Korah, Dathan, and Abiram were swallowed up by the earth. Fire then burned up the other 250 men who rebelled
16:41	That Moses and Aaron caused the deaths of Korah and his conspirators	Blamed others for their own troubles	God began to destroy Israel with a plague. Moses and Aaron made atonement for the people, but 14,700 of them were killed
20:2, 3	About the lack of water	Refused to believe that God would provide as he had promised	Moses sinned along with the people. For this he was barred from entering the promised land
21:5	That God and Moses brought them into the desert	Failed to recognise that their problems were brought on by their own disobedience	God sent venomous snakes that killed many people and seriously injured many others

11:1, 6–15 The Israelites complained, and then Moses complained. But God responded positively to Moses and negatively to the rest of the people. Why? The people complained *to one another,* and nothing was accomplished. Moses took his complaint *to God,* who could solve any problem. Many of us are good at complaining to each other. We need to learn to take our problems to the One who can do something about them.

11:4 The *rabble* refers to a mixed crowd of Egyptians and others who had followed Israel out of Egypt (Exodus 12:38).

11:4–6 Dissatisfaction comes when our attention shifts from what we have to what we don't have. The people of Israel didn't seem to notice what God was doing for them – setting them free, making them a nation, giving them a new land – because they were so wrapped up in what God wasn't doing for them. They could think of nothing but the delicious Egyptian food they had left behind. Somehow they forgot that the brutal whip of Egyptian slavery was the cost of eating that food. Before we judge the Israelites too harshly, it's helpful to think about what occupies our attention most of the time. Are we grateful for what God has given us, or are we always thinking about what we would like to have? We should not allow our unfulfilled desires to cause us to forget God's gifts of life, food, health, work, and friends.

11:4–9 Every morning the Israelites drew back their tent doors and witnessed a miracle. Covering the ground was white, fluffy manna – food from heaven. But soon that wasn't enough. Feeling it was their right to have more, they forgot what they already had. They didn't ask God to fill their need; instead they demanded meat, and they stopped trusting God to care for them. "If only we had meat to eat!" they complained to Moses as they reminisced about the good food they had in Egypt. God gave them what they asked for, but they paid dearly for it when a plague struck the camp (see 11:18–20, 31–34). When you ask God for something, he may grant your request. But if you approach him with a sinful attitude, getting what you want may prove costly.

at no cost—also the cucumbers, melons, leeks, onions and garlic.[f] 6But now we have
lost our appetite; we never see anything but this manna!"
7The manna was like coriander seed[g] and looked like resin.[h] 8The people went
around gathering it, and then ground it in a hand mill or crushed it in a mortar. They
cooked it in a pot or made it into cakes. And it tasted like something made with olive
oil. 9When the dew[i] settled on the camp at night, the manna also came down.
10Moses heard the people of every family wailing, each at the entrance to his tent.
The LORD became exceedingly angry, and Moses was troubled. 11He asked the LORD,
"Why have you brought this trouble on your servant? What have I done to displease
you that you put the burden of all these people on me?[j] 12Did I conceive all these
people? Did I give them birth? Why do you tell me to carry them in my arms, as a
nurse carries an infant,[k] to the land you promised on oath to their forefathers?[l]
13Where can I get meat for all these people?[m] They keep wailing to me, 'Give us meat
to eat!' 14I cannot carry all these people by myself; the burden is too heavy for me.[n]
15If this is how you are going to treat me, put me to death[o] right now[p]—if I have
found favour in your eyes—and do not let me face my own ruin."
16The LORD said to Moses: "Bring me seventy of Israel's elders who are known
to you as leaders and officials among the people. Make them come to the Tent of
Meeting, that they may stand there with you. 17I will come down and speak with you
there, and I will take of the Spirit that is on you and put the Spirit on them.[q] They
will help you carry the burden of the people so that you will not have to carry it alone.
18"Tell the people: 'Consecrate yourselves[r] in preparation for tomorrow, when you
will eat meat. The LORD heard you when you wailed,[s] "If only we had meat to eat!
We were better off in Egypt!"[t] Now the LORD will give you meat, and you will eat
it. 19You will not eat it for just one day, or two days, or five, ten or twenty days,
20but for a whole month—until it comes out of your nostrils and you loathe
it[u]—because you have rejected the LORD,[v] who is among you, and have wailed
before him, saying, "Why did we ever leave Egypt?" ' "
21But Moses said, "Here I am among six hundred thousand men[w] on foot, and you
say, 'I will give them meat to eat for a whole month!' 22Would they have enough if
flocks and herds were slaughtered for them? Would they have enough if all the fish
in the sea were caught for them?"[x]
23The LORD answered Moses, "Is the LORD's arm too short?[y] You will now see
whether or not what I say will come true for you."[z]
24So Moses went out and told the people what the LORD had said. He brought
together seventy of their elders and made them stand round the Tent. 25Then the LORD
came down in the cloud[a] and spoke with him,[b] and he took of the Spirit[c] that was
on him and put the Spirit on the seventy elders.[d] When the Spirit rested on them,
they prophesied,[e] but they did not do so again.[b]
26However, two men, whose names were Eldad and Medad, had remained in the
camp. They were listed among the elders, but did not go out to the Tent. Yet the Spirit
also rested on them, and they prophesied in the camp. 27A young man ran and told
Moses, "Eldad and Medad are prophesying in the camp."
28Joshua son of Nun, who had been Moses' assistant[f] since youth, spoke up and
said, "Moses, my lord, stop them!"[g]

[b] 25 Or *prophesied and continued to do so*

11:5 [f]Ex 16:3
11:7 [g]Ex 16:31 [h]Ge 2:12
11:9 [i]Ex 16:13
11:11 [j]Ex 5:22
11:12 [k]Isa 40:11; 49:23 [l]Ex 13:5
11:13 [m]Jn 6:5-9
11:14 [n]Ex 18:18
11:15 [o]Ex 32:32 [p]1Ki 19:4; Jnh 4:3
11:17 [q]ver 25, 29; 1Sa 10:6; 2Ki 2:9, 15; Joel 2:28
11:18 [r]Ex 19:10 [s]Ex 16:7 [t]ver 5; Ac 7:39
11:20 [u]Ps 78:29; 106:14, 15 [v]Jos 24:27; 1Sa 10:19
11:21 [w]Ex 12:37
11:22 [x]Mt 15:33
11:23 [y]Isa 50:2; 59:1 [z]Nu 23:19; Eze 12:25; 24:14
11:25 [a]Nu 12:5 [b]ver 17 [c]1Sa 10:6 [d]Ac 2:17 [e]1Sa 10:10
11:28 [f]Ex 33:11; Jos 1:1 [g]Mk 9:38-40

11:21, 22 Moses had witnessed God's power in spectacular miracles, yet at this time he questioned God's ability to feed the wandering Israelites. If Moses doubted God's power, how much easier it is for us to do the same. But completely depending upon God is essential, regardless of our level of spiritual maturity. When we begin to rely on our own understanding, we are in danger of ignoring God's assessment of the situation. By remembering his past works and his present power, we can be sure that we are not cutting off his potential help.

11:23 How strong is God? It is easy to trust God when we see his mighty acts (the Israelites saw many), but after a while, in the routine of daily life, his strength may appear to diminish. God doesn't change, but our view of him often does. The monotony of day-by-day living lulls us into forgetting how powerful God can be. As Moses learned, God's strength is always available.

11:26–29 This incident is similar to a story told in Mark 9:38–41. The disciples wanted Jesus to forbid others to drive out demons because they were not part of the disciples' group. But this type of narrow attitude was condemned by both Moses and Jesus. Beware of putting limits on God—he can work through whomever he chooses.

11:29 [h]1Co 14:5
11:31 [i]Ex 16:13; Ps 78:26-28
11:33 [j]Ps 78:30 [k]Ps 106:15
11:34 [l]Dt 9:22
11:35 [m]Nu 33:17
12:1 [a]Ex 2:21
12:2 [b]Nu 16:3 [c]Nu 11:1
12:3 [d]Mt 11:29
12:5 [e]Nu 11:25
12:6 [f]Ge 15:1; 46:2 [g]Ge 31:10; 1Ki 3:5; Heb 1:1
12:7 [h]Jos 1:1-2; Ps 105:26 [i]Heb 3:2, 5
12:8 [j]Dt 34:10 [k]Ex 20:4; Ps 17:15
12:9 [l]Ge 17:22
12:10 [m]Ex 4:6; Dt 24:9 [n]2Ki 5:1, 27

29 But Moses replied, "Are you jealous for my sake? I wish that all the LORD's people were prophets[h] and that the LORD would put his Spirit on them!" 30 Then Moses and the elders of Israel returned to the camp.

31 Now a wind went out from the LORD and drove quail[i] in from the sea. It brought them[c] down all around the camp to about three feet[d] above the ground, as far as a day's walk in any direction. 32 All that day and night and all the next day the people went out and gathered quail. No-one gathered less than ten homers.[e] Then they spread them out all around the camp. 33 But while the meat was still between their teeth[j] and before it could be consumed, the anger of the LORD burned against the people, and he struck them with a severe plague.[k] 34 Therefore the place was named Kibroth Hattaavah,[f][l] because there they buried the people who had craved other food.

35 From Kibroth Hattaavah the people travelled to Hazeroth[m] and stayed there.

2. Miriam and Aaron oppose Moses

12 Miriam and Aaron began to talk against Moses because of his Cushite wife,[a] for he had married a Cushite. 2 "Has the LORD spoken only through Moses?" they asked. "Hasn't he also spoken through us?"[b] And the LORD heard this.[c]

3 (Now Moses was a very humble man,[d] more humble than anyone else on the face of the earth.)

4 At once the LORD said to Moses, Aaron and Miriam, "Come out to the Tent of Meeting, all three of you." So the three of them came out. 5 Then the LORD came down in a pillar of cloud;[e] he stood at the entrance to the Tent and summoned Aaron and Miriam. When both of them stepped forward, 6 he said, "Listen to my words:

"When a prophet of the LORD is among you,
I reveal myself to him in visions,[f]
I speak to him in dreams.[g]
7 But this is not true of my servant Moses;[h]
he is faithful in all my house.[i]
8 With him I speak face to face,
clearly and not in riddles;[j]
he sees the form of the LORD.[k]
Why then were you not afraid
to speak against my servant Moses?"

9 The anger of the LORD burned against them, and he left them.[l]

10 When the cloud lifted from above the Tent, there stood Miriam—leprous,[a] like snow.[m] Aaron turned towards her and saw that she had leprosy;[n] 11 and he said to

c *31* Or *They flew* d *31* Hebrew *two cubits* (about 0.9 metre) e *32* That is, probably about 60 bushels (about 2.2 kilolitres) f *34* *Kibroth Hattaavah* means *graves of craving.* a *10* The Hebrew word was used for various diseases affecting the skin—not necessarily leprosy.

11:34 Craving or lusting is more than inappropriate sexual desire. It can be an unnatural or greedy desire for anything (sports, knowledge, possessions, influence over others). In this circumstance, God punished the Israelites for craving good food! Their desire was not wrong; the sin was in allowing that desire to turn into greed. They felt it was their right to have fine food, and they could think of nothing else. When you become preoccupied with something until it affects your perspective on everything else, you have moved from desire to lust.

12:1 Moses didn't have a Jewish wife because he lived with the Egyptians the first 40 years of his life, and he was in the desert the next 40 years. The woman is probably not Zipporah, his first wife, who was a Midianite (see Exodus 2:21). A Cushite was an Ethiopian. There is no explanation given for why Miriam objected to this woman.

12:1 People often argue over minor disagreements, leaving the real issue untouched. Such was the case when Miriam and Aaron came to Moses with a complaint. They represented the priests and the prophets, the two most powerful groups next to Moses. The real issue was their growing jealousy of Moses' position and influence. Since they could not find fault with the way Moses was leading the people, they chose to criticise his wife. Rather than face the problem squarely by dealing with their envy and pride, they chose to create a diversion from the real issue. When you are in a disagreement, stop and ask yourself if you are arguing over the real issue or if you have introduced a smoke screen by attacking someone's character. If you are unjustly criticised, remember that your critics may be afraid to face the real problem. Don't take this type of criticism personally. Ask God to help you identify the real issue and deal with it.

12:11 Aaron asked that the sin he and Miriam committed not be held against them. It is easy to look back at our mistakes and recognise their foolishness. It is much harder to recognise foolish plans while we are carrying them out because somehow then they seem appropriate. To get rid of foolish ideas before they turn into foolish actions requires eliminating our wrong thoughts and motives. Failing to do this caused Miriam and Aaron much grief.

Moses, "Please, my lord, do not hold against us the sin we have so foolishly committed.[o] 12Do not let her be like a stillborn infant coming from its mother's womb with
its flesh half eaten away."
13So Moses cried out to the LORD, "O God, please heal her![p]"
14The LORD replied to Moses, "If her father had spat in her face,[q] would she not
have been in disgrace for seven days? Confine her outside the camp[r] for seven days;
after that she can be brought back." 15So Miriam was confined outside the camp for
seven days, and the people did not move on till she was brought back.
16After that, the people left Hazeroth[s] and encamped in the Desert of Paran.

3. The spies incite rebellion

Exploring Canaan

13 The LORD said to Moses, 2"Send some men to explore[a] the land of Canaan,
which I am giving to the Israelites. From each ancestral tribe send one of its
leaders."
3So at the LORD's command Moses sent them out from the Desert of Paran. All
of them were leaders of the Israelites. 4These are their names:

from the tribe of Reuben, Shammua son of Zaccur;
5from the tribe of Simeon, Shaphat son of Hori;
6from the tribe of Judah, Caleb son of Jephunneh;[b]
7from the tribe of Issachar, Igal son of Joseph;
8from the tribe of Ephraim, Hoshea son of Nun;
9from the tribe of Benjamin, Palti son of Raphu;
10from the tribe of Zebulun, Gaddiel son of Sodi;
11from the tribe of Manasseh (a tribe of Joseph), Gaddi son of Susi;
12from the tribe of Dan, Ammiel son of Gemalli;
13from the tribe of Asher, Sethur son of Michael;
14from the tribe of Naphtali, Nahbi son of Vophsi;
15from the tribe of Gad, Geuel son of Maki.

16These are the names of the men Moses sent to explore the land. (Moses gave Hoshea
son of Nun[c] the name Joshua.)[d]
17When Moses sent them to explore Canaan, he said, "Go up through the Negev[e]
and on into the hill country.[f] 18See what the land is like and whether the people
who live there are strong or weak, few or many. 19What kind of land do they live
in? Is it good or bad? What kind of towns do they live in? Are they unwalled or fortified? 20How is the soil? Is it fertile or poor? Are there trees on it or not? Do your
best to bring back some of the fruit of the land.[g]" (It was the season for the first ripe
grapes.)
21So they went up and explored the land from the Desert of Zin[h] as far as Rehob,[i]
towards Lebo[a] Hamath.[j] 22They went up through the Negev and came to Hebron,
where Ahiman, Sheshai and Talmai,[k] the descendants of Anak,[l] lived. (Hebron had
been built seven years before Zoan in Egypt.)[m] 23When they reached the Valley of

a 21 *Or towards the entrance to*

12:11 [o] 2Sa 19:19; 24:10
12:13 [p] Isa 30:26; Jer 17:14
12:14 [q] Dt 25:9; Job 17:6; 30:9-10; Isa 50:6 [r] Lev 13:46; Nu 5:2-3
12:16 [s] Nu 11:35
13:2 [a] Dt 1:22
13:6 [b] ver 30; Nu 14:6, 24; 34:19; Jdg 1:12-15
13:16 [c] ver 8 [d] Dt 32:44
13:17 [e] Ge 12:9 [f] Jdg 1:9
13:20 [g] Dt 1:25
13:21 [h] Nu 20:1; 27:14; 33:36; Jos 15:1 [i] Jos 19:28 [j] Jos 13:5
13:22 [k] Jos 15:14 [l] Jos 15:13 [m] Ps 78:12, 43; Isa 19:11, 13

12:14 Spitting in someone's face was considered the ultimate insult and a sign of shame imposed on wrongdoers. The religious leaders spat in Jesus' face to insult him (Matthew 26:67). God punished Miriam for her smug attitude towards not only Moses' authority, but also God's. He struck her with leprosy, then ordered her out of the camp for a week. This punishment was actually quite lenient. A week was the length of time she would have been excluded if her father had spat in her face. How much more she deserved for wronging God! Once again, God was merciful while retaining an effective discipline.

13:17–20 Moses decided what information was needed before the people could enter the promised land, and he took careful steps to get that information. When you are making decisions or assuming new responsibilities, remember these two important steps. Ask yourself what you need to know about the opportunity, and then obtain that knowledge. Common sense is a valuable aid in accomplishing God's purposes.

Eshcol,[b] they cut off a branch bearing a single cluster of grapes. Two of them carried it on a pole between them, along with some pomegranates and figs. [24]That place was called the Valley of Eshcol because of the cluster of grapes the Israelites cut off there. [25]At the end of forty days they returned from exploring the land.

b 23 *Eshcol* means *cluster*; also in verse 24.

MIRIAM

Ask older brothers or sisters what their greatest trial in life is and they will often answer, "My younger brother (or sister)!" This is especially true when the younger sibling is more successful than the older. The bonds of family loyalty can be strained to the breaking point.

When we first meet Miriam she is involved in one of history's most unusual baby-sitting jobs. She is watching her infant brother float on the Nile River in a waterproof cradle. Miriam's quick thinking allowed Moses to be raised by his own mother. Her protective superiority, reinforced by that event, must have been hard to give up as she watched her little brother rise to greatness.

Eventually Moses' choice of a wife gave Miriam an opportunity to criticise. It was natural for her insecurity to break out over this issue. With Moses married, Miriam was clearly no longer the most important woman in his life. The real issue, however, was not the kind of woman Moses had married. It was the fact that he was now the most important man in Israel. "Has the LORD spoken only through Moses? . . . Hasn't he also spoken through us?" No mention is made of Moses' response, but God had a quick answer for Miriam and Aaron. Without denying their role in his plan, God clearly pointed out his special relationship with Moses. Miriam was stricken with leprosy, a deadly disease, as punishment for her insubordination. But Moses, true to his character, intervened for his sister so that God healed Miriam of her leprosy.

Before criticising someone else, we need to pause long enough to discover our own motives. Failing to do this can bring disastrous results. What is often labelled "constructive criticism" may actually be destructive jealousy, since the easiest way to raise our own status is to bring someone else down. Are you willing to question your motives before you offer criticism? Does the critical finger you point need to be pointed first towards yourself?

Strengths and accomplishments:
- Quick thinker under pressure
- Able leader
- Songwriter
- Prophetess

Weaknesses and mistakes:
- Was jealous of Moses' authority
- Openly criticised Moses' leadership

Lesson from her life:
- The motives behind criticism are often more important to deal with than the criticism itself

Vital statistics:
- Where: Egypt, Sinai peninsula
- Relatives: Brothers: Aaron and Moses

Key verses:
"Then Miriam the prophetess, Aaron's sister, took a tambourine in her hand, and all the women followed her, with tambourines and dancing. Miriam sang to them: 'Sing to the LORD, for he is highly exalted. The horse and its rider he has hurled into the sea'." (Exodus 15:20, 21).

Miriam's story is told in Exodus 2; 15 and Numbers 12; 20. She is also mentioned in Deuteronomy 24:9; 1 Chronicles 6:3; Micah 6:4.

13:25–29 God told the Israelites that the promised land was rich and fertile. Not only that, he promised that this bountiful land would be theirs. When the spies reported back to Moses, they gave plenty of good reasons for entering the land, but they couldn't stop focusing on their fear. Talk of giants (descendants of Anak) and fortified cities made it easy to forget about God's promise to help. When facing a tough decision, don't let the negatives cause you to lose sight of the positives. Weigh both sides carefully. Don't let potential difficulties blind you to God's power to help and his promise to guide.

Report on the Exploration

26They came back to Moses and Aaron and the whole Israelite community at Kadesh
in the Desert of Paran. There they reported to them[n] and to the whole assembly and
showed them the fruit of the land. 27They gave Moses this account: "We went into
the land to which you sent us, and it does flow with milk and honey![o] Here is its
fruit.[p] 28But the people who live there are powerful, and the cities are fortified and
very large.[q] We even saw descendants of Anak there. 29The Amalekites live in the
Negev; the Hittites, Jebusites and Amorites live in the hill country; and the Canaanites
live near the sea and along the Jordan."
30Then Caleb silenced the people before Moses and said, "We should go up and
take possession of the land, for we can certainly do it."
31But the men who had gone up with him said, "We can't attack those people; they
are stronger than we are."[r] 32And they spread among the Israelites a bad report[s]
about the land they had explored. They said, "The land we explored devours[t] those
living in it. All the people we saw there are of great size.[u] 33We saw the Nephilim[v]
there (the descendants of Anak[w] come from the Nephilim). We seemed like grasshoppers in our own eyes, and we looked the same to them."

The People Rebel

14 That night all the people of the community raised their voices and wept aloud.
2All the Israelites grumbled against Moses and Aaron, and the whole assembly
said to them, "If only we had died in Egypt! Or in this desert![a] 3Why is the LORD

13:26 [n]Nu 32:8
13:27 [o]Ex 3:8 [p]Dt 1:25
13:28 [q]Dt 1:28; 9:1, 2
13:31 [r]Dt 1:28; 9:1; Jos 14:8
13:32 [s]Nu 14:36, 37 [t]Eze 36:13, 14 [u]Am 2:9
13:33 [v]Ge 6:4 [w]Dt 1:28
14:2 [a]Nu 11:1

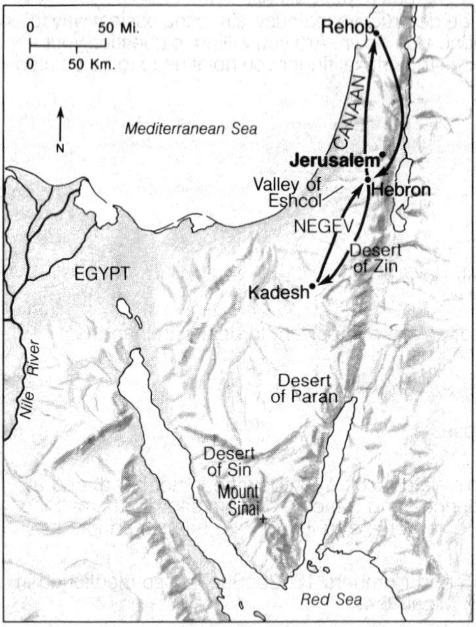

ROUTE OF THE SPIES The spies travelled from Kadesh at the southernmost edge of the Desert of Zin to Rehob at the northernmost edge and back, a round trip of about 500 miles.

13:26 Although Kadesh was only a desert oasis, it was a crossroads in Israel's history. When the spies returned to Kadesh from reconnoitring the new land, the people had to decide either to enter the land or to retreat. They chose to retreat and were condemned to wander 40 years in the desert. It was also at Kadesh that Moses disobeyed God (20:7–12). For this, he too was denied entrance into the promised land. Aaron and Miriam died there, for they could not enter the new land either. Kadesh was near Canaan's southern borders, but because of the Israelites' lack of faith, they needed more than a lifetime to go from Kadesh to the promised land.

13:27 The promised land, also called the land of Canaan, was indeed magnificent, as the 12 spies discovered. The Bible often calls it the land flowing with milk and honey. Although the land was relatively small — 150 miles long and 60 miles wide — its lush hillsides were covered with fig, date, and nut trees. It was the land God had promised to Abraham, Isaac, and Jacob.

13:28 The "descendants of Anak" were a race of abnormally large people. The family of Goliath may have been descended from these people (see 2 Samuel 21:16–22).

13:28, 29 The fortified cities the spies talked about were surrounded by high walls as much as 20 feet thick and 25 feet tall. Guards were often stationed on top, where there was a commanding view of the countryside. Some of the inhabitants, said the spies, were formidable men — from seven to nine feet tall — so that the Israelites felt like grasshoppers next to them (13:33). The fortified cities and the giants struck fear into the hearts of most of the spies.

13:30–32 Imagine standing before a crowd and loudly voicing an unpopular opinion! Caleb was willing to take the unpopular stand to do as God had commanded. To be effective when you go against the crowd, you must: (1) have the facts (Caleb had seen the land himself); (2) have the right attitude (Caleb trusted God's promise to give Israel the land); (3) state clearly what you believe (Caleb said, "We can certainly do it").

13:33 The Nephilim were giants who lived on the earth before the flood (Genesis 6:4).

13:33 – 14:4 The negative opinion of ten men caused a great rebellion among the people. Because it is human nature to accept opinion as fact, we must be especially careful when voicing our negative opinions. What we say may heavily influence the actions of those who trust us to give sound advice.

14:4 [b]Ne 9:17
14:5 [c]Nu 16:4, 22, 45
14:7 [d]Nu 13:27; Dt 1:25
14:8 [e]Dt 10:15 [f]Nu 13:27
14:9 [g]Dt 1:26; 9:7, 23, 24 [h]Dt 1:21; 7:18; 20:1
14:10 [i]Ex 17:4 [j]Lev 9:23
14:11 [k]Ps 78:22; 106:24
14:12 [l]Ex 32:10
14:13 [m]Ex 32:11-14; Ps 106:23
14:14 [n]Ex 15:14 [o]Ex 13:21
14:16 [p]Jos 7:7
14:18 [q]Ex 34:6; Ps 145:8; Jnh 4:2 [r]Ex 20:5
14:19 [s]Ex 34:9 [t]Ps 106:45 [u]Ps 78:38
14:20 [v]Ps 106:23; Mic 7:18-20

bringing us to this land only to let us fall by the sword? Our wives and children will be taken as plunder. Wouldn't it be better for us to go back to Egypt?" 4And they said to each other, "We should choose a leader and go back to Egypt.[b]"

5Then Moses and Aaron fell face down[c] in front of the whole Israelite assembly gathered there. 6Joshua son of Nun and Caleb son of Jephunneh, who were among those who had explored the land, tore their clothes 7and said to the entire Israelite assembly, "The land we passed through and explored is exceedingly good.[d] 8If the LORD is pleased with us,[e] he will lead us into that land, a land flowing with milk and honey,[f] and will give it to us. 9Only do not rebel[g] against the LORD. And do not be afraid of the people of the land,[h] because we will swallow them up. Their protection is gone, but the LORD is with us. Do not be afraid of them."

10But the whole assembly talked about stoning[i] them. Then the glory of the LORD[j] appeared at the Tent of Meeting to all the Israelites. 11The LORD said to Moses, "How long will these people treat me with contempt? How long will they refuse to believe in me,[k] in spite of all the miraculous signs I have performed among them? 12I will strike them down with a plague and destroy them, but I will make you into a nation[l] greater and stronger than they."

13Moses said to the LORD, "Then the Egyptians will hear about it! By your power you brought these people up from among them.[m] 14And they will tell the inhabitants of this land about it. They have already heard[n] that you, O LORD, are with these people and that you, O LORD, have been seen face to face, that your cloud stays over them, and that you go before them in a pillar of cloud by day and a pillar of fire by night.[o] 15If you put these people to death all at one time, the nations who have heard this report about you will say, 16'The LORD was not able to bring these people into the land he promised them on oath; so he slaughtered them in the desert.'[p]

17"Now may the Lord's strength be displayed, just as you have declared: 18'The LORD is slow to anger, abounding in love and forgiving sin and rebellion.[q] Yet he does not leave the guilty unpunished; he punishes the children for the sin of the fathers to the third and fourth generation.'[r] 19In accordance with your great love, forgive[s] the sin of these people,[t] just as you have pardoned them from the time they left Egypt until now."[u]

20The LORD replied, "I have forgiven them,[v] as you asked. 21Nevertheless, as

---

14:1–4 When the chorus of despair went up, everyone joined in. Their greatest fears were being realised. Losing their perspective, the people were caught up in the emotion of the moment, forgetting what they knew about God's character. What if the people had spent as much energy moving forward as they did moving back? They could have enjoyed their land – instead they never even entered it. When a cry of despair goes up around you, consider the larger perspective before you join in. You have better ways to use your energy than to complain.

14:5–9 With great miracles, God had led the Israelites out of slavery, through the desolate desert, and up to the very edge of the promised land. He had protected them, fed them, and fulfilled every promise. Yet when encouraged to take that last step of faith and enter the land, the people refused. After witnessing so many miracles, why did they stop trusting God? Why did they refuse to enter the promised land when that had been their goal since leaving Egypt? They were afraid. Often we do the same thing. We trust God to handle the smaller issues but doubt his ability to take care of the big problems, the tough decisions, the frightening situations. Don't stop trusting God just as you are ready to reach your goal. He brought you this far and won't let you down now. We can continue trusting God by remembering all he has done for us.

14:6 Tearing clothing was a customary way of showing deep sorrow, mourning, or despair. Joshua and Caleb were greatly distressed by the people's refusal to enter the land.

14:6–10 Two wise men, Joshua and Caleb, encouraged the people to act on God's promise and move ahead into the land. The people rejected their advice and even talked of killing them. Don't be too quick to reject advice you don't like. Evaluate it carefully, comparing it to the teaching in God's word. The advice may be God's message.

14:17–20 Moses pleaded with God, asking him to forgive his people. His plea reveals several characteristics of God: (1) God is immensely patient; (2) God's love is one promise we can always count on; (3) God forgives again and again; (4) God is merciful, listening to and answering our requests. God has not changed since Moses' day. Like Moses, we can rely on God's love, patience, forgiveness, and mercy.

14:20–23 The people of Israel had a clearer view of God than any people before them, for they had both his laws and his physical presence. Their refusal to follow God after witnessing his miraculous deeds and listening to his words made the judgment against them more severe. Increased opportunity brings increased responsibility. As Jesus said: "From everyone who has been given much, much will be demanded" (Luke 12:48). How much greater is our responsibility to obey and serve God – we have the whole Bible, and we know God's Son, Jesus Christ.

surely as I live[w] and as surely as the glory of the LORD fills the whole earth,[x] 22not
one of the men who saw my glory and the miraculous signs I performed in Egypt and
in the desert but who disobeyed me and tested me ten times[y]—23not one of them will
ever see the land I promised on oath[z] to their forefathers. No-one who has treated
me with contempt will ever see it.[a] 24But because my servant Caleb has a different
spirit and follows me wholeheartedly,[b] I will bring him into the land he went to, and
his descendants will inherit it.[c] 25Since the Amalekites and Canaanites are living in
the valleys, turn[d] back tomorrow and set out towards the desert along the route to
the Red Sea."[a]
26The LORD said to Moses and Aaron: 27"How long will this wicked community
grumble against me? I have heard the complaints of these grumbling Israelites.[e] 28So
tell them, 'As surely as I live,[f] declares the LORD, I will do to you the very things
I heard you say: 29In this desert your bodies will fall[g]—every one of you twenty years
old or more[h] who was counted in the census and who has grumbled against me. 30Not
one of you will enter the land I swore with uplifted hand to make your home, except
Caleb son of Jephunneh and Joshua son of Nun. 31As for your children that you said
would be taken as plunder, I will bring them in to enjoy the land you have rejected.[i]
32But you—your bodies will fall[j] in this desert. 33Your children will be shepherds
here for forty years, suffering for your unfaithfulness, until the last of your bodies lies
in the desert. 34For forty years—one year for each of the forty days you explored the
land[k]—you will suffer for your sins and know what it is like to have me against you.'
35I, the LORD, have spoken, and I will surely do these things[l] to this whole wicked
community, which has banded together against me. They will meet their end in this
desert; here they will die."
36So the men Moses had sent[m] to explore the land, who returned and made the
whole community grumble against him by spreading a bad report[n] about it—37these
men responsible for spreading the bad report[o] about the land were struck down and
died of a plague[p] before the LORD. 38Of the men who went to explore the land, only
Joshua son of Nun and Caleb son of Jephunneh survived.[q]
39When Moses reported this to all the Israelites, they mourned[r] bitterly. 40Early
the next morning they went up towards the high hill country. "We have sinned[s],"
they said. "We will go up to the place the LORD promised."
41But Moses said, "Why are you disobeying the LORD's command? This will not
succeed![t] 42Do not go up, because the LORD is not with you. You will be defeated
by your enemies,[u] 43for the Amalekites and Canaanites will face you there. Because
you have turned away from the LORD, he will not be with you and you will fall by
the sword."

a 25 Hebrew *Yam Suph*; that is, Sea of Reeds

14:21 [w]Dt 32:40; Isa 49:18 [x]Ps 72:19; Isa 6:3; Hab 2:14
14:22 [y]Ex 14:11; 32:1; 1Co 10:5
14:23 [z]Nu 32:11 [a]Heb 3:18
14:24 [b]ver 6-9; Jos 14:8, 14 [c]Nu 32:12
14:25 [d]Dt 1:40
14:27 [e]Ex 16:12
14:28 [f]ver 21
14:29 [g]Nu 26:65 [h]Nu 1:45
14:31 [i]Ps 106:24
14:32 [j]1Co 10:5
14:34 [k]Nu 13:25
14:35 [l]Nu 23:19
14:36 [m]Nu 13:4-16 [n]Nu 13:32
14:37 [o]1Co 10:10 [p]Nu 16:49
14:38 [q]Jos 14:6
14:39 [r]Ex 33:4
14:40 [s]Dt 1:41
14:41 [t]2Ch 24:20
14:42 [u]Dt 1:42

14:22 God wasn't exaggerating when he said that the Israelites had already failed ten times to trust and obey him. Here is a list of their ten failures: (1) lacking trust at the crossing of the Red Sea (Exodus 14:11, 12); (2) complaining over bitter water at Marah (Exodus 15:24); (3) complaining in the Desert of Sin (Exodus 16:3); (4) collecting more than the daily quota of manna (Exodus 16:20); (5) collecting manna on the Sabbath (Exodus 16:27–29); (6) complaining over lack of water at Rephidim (Exodus 17:2, 3); (7) engaging in idolatry with a golden calf (Exodus 32:7–10); (8) complaining at Taberah (Numbers 11:1, 2); (9) more complaining over the lack of delicious food (Numbers 11:4); (10) failing to trust God and enter the promised land (Numbers 14:1–4).

14:24 The fulfilment of this verse is recorded in Joshua 14:6–15 when Caleb received his inheritance in the promised land. Caleb followed God with all his heart and was rewarded for his obedience. Are you wholehearted in your commitment to obey God?

14:34 God's judgment came in the form the people feared most. The people were afraid of dying in the desert, so God punished them by making them wander in the desert until they died. Now they wished they had the problem of facing the giants and the fortified cities of the promised land. Failing to trust God often brings even greater problems than those we originally faced. When we run from God, we inevitably run into problems.

14:35 Was this judgment—wandering 40 years in the desert—too harsh? Not compared to the instant death that God first threatened (14:12). Instead, God allowed the people to live. God had brought his people to the edge of the promised land, just as he said he would. He was ready to give them the rich land, but the people didn't want it (14:1, 2). By this time, God had put up with a lot. At least ten times the people had refused to trust and obey him (14:22). The whole nation (except for Joshua, Caleb, Moses, and Aaron) showed contempt for and distrust of God. But God's punishment was not permanent. In 40 years, a new generation would have a chance to enter Canaan (Joshua 1–3).

14:40–44 When the Israelites realised their foolish mistake, they were suddenly ready to return to God. But God didn't confuse their admission of guilt with true repentance because he knew their hearts. Sure enough, they soon went their own way again. Sometimes right actions or good intentions come too late. We must not

14:44 [v]Dt 1:43 [w]Nu 31:6

14:45 [x]Nu 21:3; Dt 1:44; Jdg 1:17

15:2 [a]Lev 23:10

15:3 [b]Lev 1:2 [c]ver 24; Ge 8:21; Ex 29:18 [d]Nu 28:19, 27 [e]Lev 22:18, 21; Ezr 1:4 [f]Lev 23:1-44

15:4 [g]Lev 2:1; 6:14

44Nevertheless, in their presumption they went up[v] towards the high hill country,
though neither Moses nor the ark of the LORD's covenant moved from the camp.[w]
45Then the Amalekites and Canaanites who lived in that hill country came down and
attacked them and beat them down all the way to Hormah.[x]

C. WANDERING IN THE DESERT (15:1—21:35)

After their disobedience and unsuccessful attempt to enter the promised land, the Israelites are condemned to wander 40 years in the desert. Even in the midst of this punishment, the people continued to rebel and thus God continued to punish them. But the hearts of the people remained hard and rebellious. Hard hearts towards God may bring similar calamity to us.

1. Additional regulations

Supplementary Offerings

15 The LORD said to Moses, 2"Speak to the Israelites and say to them: 'After you
enter the land I am giving you[a] as a home 3and you present to the LORD
offerings made by fire, from the herd or the flock,[b] as an aroma pleasing to the
LORD[c]—whether burnt offerings[d] or sacrifices, for special vows or freewill offerings[e] or festival offerings[f]—4then the one who brings his offering shall present to
the LORD a grain offering[g] of a tenth of an ephah[a] of fine flour mixed with a quarter

a *4* That is, probably about 4 pints (about 2 litres)

CALEB

The voice of the minority is not often given a hearing. Nevertheless, truth cannot be measured by numbers. On the contrary, it often stands against majority opinion. Truth remains unchanged because it is guaranteed by the character of God. God is truth; what he says is the last word. At times, a person must even stand alone on the side of truth.

Caleb was not so much a man of great faith as a man of faith in a great God! His boldness rested on his understanding of God, not on his confidence in Israel's abilities to conquer the land. He could not agree with the majority, for that would be to disagree with God.

We, on the other hand, often base our decisions on what everyone else is doing. Few of us are first-order cowards like the ten spies. We are more like the people of Israel, getting our cowardice secondhand. Our search for right and wrong usually starts with questions such as "What do the experts say?" or "What do my friends say?" The question we most often avoid is "What does God say?" The principles we learn as we study the Bible provide a dependable road map for life. They draw us into a personal relationship with the God whose word is the Bible. The God who gave Caleb his boldness is the same God who offers us the gift of eternal life through his Son, Jesus. That's truth worth believing!

Strengths and accomplishments:
- One of the spies sent by Moses to survey the land of Canaan
- One of the only two adults who left Egypt and entered the promised land
- Voiced the minority opinion in favour of conquering the land
- Expressed faith in God's promises, in spite of apparent obstacles

Lessons from his life:
- Majority opinion is not an accurate measurement of right and wrong
- Boldness based on God's faithfulness is appropriate
- For courage and faith to be effective, they must combine words and actions

Vital statistics:
- Where: From Egypt to the Sinai peninsula to the promised land, specifically Hebron
- Occupations: Spy, soldier, shepherd

Key verse:
"But because my servant Caleb has a different spirit and follows me wholeheartedly, I will bring him into the land he went to, and his descendants will inherit it" (Numbers 14:24).

Caleb's story is told in Numbers 13; 14 and Joshua 14; 15. He is also mentioned in Judges 1 and 1 Chronicles 4:15.

---

only do what is right, but also do it at the right time. God wants complete and instant obedience.

15:3 "An aroma pleasing to the LORD" means that God would be pleased with their sacrifices.

of a hin[b] of oil. 5 With each lamb for the burnt offering or the sacrifice, prepare a
quarter of a hin of wine[h] as a drink offering.
6 " 'With a ram[i] prepare a grain offering[j] of two-tenths of an ephah[c] of fine flour
mixed with a third of a hin[d] of oil,[k] 7 and a third of a hin of wine as a drink offering.
Offer it as an aroma pleasing to the LORD.
8 " 'When you prepare a young bull as a burnt offering or sacrifice, for a special
vow or a fellowship offering[e][l] to the LORD, 9 bring with the bull a grain offering
of three-tenths of an ephah[f][m] of fine flour mixed with half a hin[g] of oil. 10 Also bring
half a hin of wine as a drink offering. It will be an offering made by fire, an aroma
pleasing to the LORD. 11 Each bull or ram, each lamb or young goat, is to be prepared
in this manner. 12 Do this for each one, for as many as you prepare.
13 " 'Everyone who is native-born[n] must do these things in this way when he brings
an offering made by fire as an aroma pleasing to the LORD. 14 For the generations to
come, whenever an alien or anyone else living among you presents an offering made
by fire as an aroma pleasing to the LORD, he must do exactly as you do. 15 The
community is to have the same rules for you and for the alien living among you; this
is a lasting ordinance for the generations to come.[o] You and the alien shall be the
same before the LORD: 16 The same laws and regulations will apply both to you and
to the alien living among you.[p]' "
17 The LORD said to Moses, 18 "Speak to the Israelites and say to them: 'When you
enter the land to which I am taking you 19 and you eat the food of the land,[q] present
a portion as an offering to the LORD. 20 Present a cake from the first of your ground
meal[r] and present it as an offering from the threshing-floor.[s] 21 Throughout the
generations to come you are to give this offering to the LORD from the first of your
ground meal.[t]

Offerings for Unintentional Sins

22 " 'Now if you unintentionally fail to keep any of these commands the LORD gave
Moses[u]—23 any of the LORD's commands to you through him, from the day the LORD
gave them and continuing through the generations to come—24 and if this is done
unintentionally without the community being aware of it,[v] then the whole community
is to offer a young bull for a burnt offering[w] as an aroma pleasing to the LORD, along
with its prescribed grain offering and drink offering, and a male goat for a sin
offering.[x] 25 The priest is to make atonement for the whole Israelite community, and
they will be forgiven,[y] for it was not intentional and they have brought to the LORD
for their wrong an offering made by fire and a sin offering. 26 The whole Israelite
community and the aliens living among them will be forgiven, because all the people
were involved in the unintentional wrong.[z]
27 " 'But if just one person sins unintentionally,[a] he must bring a year-old female
goat for a sin offering. 28 The priest is to make atonement before the LORD for the one
who erred by sinning unintentionally, and when atonement has been made for him,
he will be forgiven.[b] 29 One and the same law applies to everyone who sins unintentionally, whether he is a native-born Israelite or an alien.
30 " 'But anyone who sins defiantly,[c] whether native-born or alien,[d] blasphemes
the LORD, and that person must be cut off from his people. 31 Because he has despised
the LORD's word and broken his commands,[e] that person must surely be cut off; his
guilt remains on him.[f]' "

b *4* That is, probably about 1½ pints (about 1 litre); also in verse 5 c *6* That is, probably about 7½ pints (about 4.5 litres) d *6* That is, probably about 2¼ pints (about 1.2 litres); also in verse 7 e *8* Traditionally *peace offering* f *9* That is, probably about 11½ pints (about 6.5 litres) g *9* That is, probably about 3 pints (about 2 litres); also in verse 10

15:5 h Nu 28:7, 14
15:6 i Lev 5:15; j Nu 28:12; k Eze 46:14
15:8 l Lev 1:3; 3:1
15:9 m Lev 14:10
15:13 n Lev 16:29
15:15 o ver 29; Nu 9:14
15:16 p Nu 9:14
15:19 q Jos 5:11, 12
15:20 r Ex 34:26; Lev 23:14; Dt 26:2, 10; s Lev 2:14
15:21 t Ro 11:16
15:22 u Lev 4:2
15:24 v Lev 5:15; w Lev 4:14; x Lev 4:3
15:25 y Lev 4:20; Ro 3:25; Heb 2:17
15:26 z ver 24
15:27 a Lev 4:27
15:28 b Lev 4:35
15:30 c Nu 14:40-44; Dt 1:43; 17:13; Ps 19:13; d ver 14
15:31 e 2Sa 12:9; Ps 119:126; Pr 13:13; f Lev 5:1; Eze 18:20

15:30, 31 God was willing to forgive those who made unintentional errors if they realised their mistakes quickly and corrected them. However, those who defiantly and deliberately sinned received a harsher judgment. Intentional sin grows out of an improper attitude towards God. A child who knowingly disobeys his parents challenges their authority and dares them to respond. Both the act and the attitude have to be dealt with.

15:32
[g]Ex 31:14, 15; 35:2, 3
15:34
[h]Nu 9:8
15:35
[i]Ex 31:14, 15; Dt 21:21
[j]Lev 20:2; 24:14; Ac 7:58
15:38
[k]Dt 22:12; Mt 23:5
15:39
[l]Dt 4:23; 6:12; Ps 73:27
15:40
[m]Lev 11:44; Ro 12:1; Col 1:22; 1Pe 1:15
16:1
[a]Jude 1:11
[b]Nu 26:8; Dt 11:6
16:2
[c]Nu 1:16; 26:9
16:3
[d]ver 7; Ps 106:16
[e]Ex 19:6
[f]Nu 14:14
[g]Nu 12:2
16:4
[h]Nu 14:5
16:5
[i]Lev 10:3; 2Ti 2:19*
[j]Nu 17:5; Ps 65:4
16:9
[k]Nu 3:6; Dt 10:8
16:10
[l]Nu 3:10; 18:7
16:11
[m]1Co 10:10
[n]Ex 16:7

The Sabbath-Breaker Put to Death

32 While the Israelites were in the desert, a man was found gathering wood on the
Sabbath day.[g] 33 Those who found him gathering wood brought him to Moses and
Aaron and the whole assembly, 34 and they kept him in custody, because it was not
clear what should be done to him.[h] 35 Then the LORD said to Moses, "The man must
die.[i] The whole assembly must stone him outside the camp.[j]" 36 So the assembly
took him outside the camp and stoned him to death, as the LORD commanded Moses.

Tassels on Garments

37 The LORD said to Moses, 38 "Speak to the Israelites and say to them: 'Throughout
the generations to come you are to make tassels on the corners of your garments,[k]
with a blue cord on each tassel. 39 You will have these tassels to look at and so you
will remember[l] all the commands of the LORD, that you may obey them and not
prostitute yourselves by going after the lusts of your own hearts and eyes. 40 Then you
will remember to obey all my commands and will be consecrated to your God.[m] 41 I
am the LORD your God, who brought you out of Egypt to be your God. I am the LORD
your God.' "

2. Many leaders rebel against Moses

Korah, Dathan and Abiram

16 Korah[a] son of Izhar, the son of Kohath, the son of Levi, and certain Reubenites—Dathan and Abiram, sons of Eliab,[b] and On son of Peleth—became
insolent[a] 2 and rose up against Moses. With them were 250 Israelite men, well-known
community leaders who had been appointed members of the council.[c] 3 They came
as a group to oppose Moses and Aaron[d] and said to them, "You have gone too far!
The whole community is holy,[e] every one of them, and the LORD is with them.[f]
Why then do you set yourselves above the LORD's assembly?"[g]
4 When Moses heard this, he fell face down.[h] 5 Then he said to Korah and all his
followers: "In the morning the LORD will show who belongs to him and who is holy,[i]
and he will make that person come near him. The man he chooses[j] he will cause to
come near him. 6 You, Korah, and all your followers are to do this: Take censers 7 and
tomorrow put fire and incense in them before the LORD. The man the LORD chooses
will be the one who is holy. You Levites have gone too far!"
8 Moses also said to Korah, "Now listen, you Levites! 9 Isn't it enough for you that
the God of Israel has separated you from the rest of the Israelite community and
brought you near himself to do the work at the LORD's tabernacle and to stand before
the community and minister to them?[k] 10 He has brought you and all your fellow
Levites near himself, but now you are trying to get the priesthood too.[l] 11 It is against
the LORD that you and all your followers have banded together. Who is Aaron that
you should grumble[m] against him?[n]"
12 Then Moses summoned Dathan and Abiram, the sons of Eliab. But they said, "We

a *1* Or *Peleth—took* ˌ*men*ˌ

15:32–36 Stoning a man for gathering wood on the Sabbath seems like a severe punishment, and it was. This act was a deliberate sin, defying God's law against working on the Sabbath. Perhaps the man was trying to get ahead of everyone else, in addition to breaking the Sabbath.

15:39 The tassels were to remind people not to seek after their own lustful desires, but to seek the Lord. Idol worship is self-centred, focusing on what a person can get from serving an idol. Good luck, prosperity, long life, and success in battle were expected from the gods. So were power and prestige. The worship of God is the opposite. Believers are to be selfless rather than self-centred. Instead of expecting God to serve us, we are to serve him, expecting nothing in return. We serve God for who he is, not for what we get from him.

16:1–3 Korah and his associates had seen the advantages of the priesthood in Egypt. Egyptian priests had great wealth and political influence, something Korah wanted for himself. Korah may have assumed that Moses, Aaron, and his sons were trying to make the Israelite priesthood the same kind of political machine, and he wanted to be a part of it. He did not understand that Moses' main ambition was to serve God rather than to control others.

16:8–10 Moses saw through their charge to their true motivation—some of the Levites wanted the power of the priesthood. Like Korah, we often desire the special qualities God has given others. Korah had significant, worthwhile abilities and responsibilities of his own. In the end, however, his ambition for more caused him to lose everything. Inappropriate ambition is greed in disguise. Concentrate on finding the special purpose God has for you.

will not come! 13 Isn't it enough that you have brought us up out of a land flowing
with milk and honey to kill us in the desert?[o] And now you also want to lord it over
us?[p] 14 Moreover, you haven't brought us into a land flowing with milk and honey[q]
or given us an inheritance of fields and vineyards.[r] Will you gouge out the eyes of[b]
these men?[s] No, we will not come!"
15 Then Moses became very angry and said to the LORD, "Do not accept their
offering. I have not taken so much as a donkey[t] from them, nor have I wronged any
of them."
16 Moses said to Korah, "You and all your followers are to appear before the LORD
tomorrow—you and they and Aaron.[u] 17 Each man is to take his censer and put
incense in it—250 censers in all—and present it before the LORD. You and Aaron
are to present your censers also." 18 So each man took his censer, put fire and incense
in it, and stood with Moses and Aaron at the entrance to the Tent of Meeting. 19 When
Korah had gathered all his followers in opposition to them[v] at the entrance to the Tent
of Meeting, the glory of the LORD[w] appeared to the entire assembly. 20 The LORD said
to Moses and Aaron, 21 "Separate yourselves from this assembly so that I can put an
end to them at once."[x]
22 But Moses and Aaron fell face down[y] and cried out, "O God, God of the spirits
of all mankind,[z] will you be angry with the entire assembly when only one man
sins?"[a]
23 Then the LORD said to Moses, 24 "Say to the assembly, 'Move away from the tents
of Korah, Dathan and Abiram.' "
25 Moses got up and went to Dathan and Abiram, and the elders of Israel followed
him. 26 He warned the assembly, "Move back from the tents of these wicked men![b]
Do not touch anything belonging to them, or you will be swept away[c] because of
all their sins." 27 So they moved away from the tents of Korah, Dathan and Abiram.
Dathan and Abiram had come out and were standing with their wives, children and
little ones at the entrances to their tents.
28 Then Moses said, "This is how you will know that the LORD has sent me[d] to
do all these things and that it was not my idea: 29 If these men die a natural death and
experience only what usually happens to men, then the LORD has not sent me.[e] 30 But
if the LORD brings about something totally new, and the earth opens its mouth and
swallows them, with everything that belongs to them, and they go down alive into
the grave,[c][f] then you will know that these men have treated the LORD with contempt."
31 As soon as he finished saying all this, the ground under them split apart[g] 32 and
the earth opened its mouth and swallowed them,[h] with their households and all
Korah's men and all their possessions. 33 They went down alive into the grave, with
everything they owned; the earth closed over them, and they perished and were gone
from the community. 34 At their cries, all the Israelites around them fled, shouting,
"The earth is going to swallow us too!"
35 And fire came out from the LORD[i] and consumed[j] the 250 men who were
offering the incense.
36 The LORD said to Moses, 37 "Tell Eleazar son of Aaron, the priest, to take the

16:13 [o]Nu 14:2 [p]Ac 7:27, 35
16:14 [q]Lev 20:24 [r]Ex 22:5; 23:11; Nu 20:5 [s]Jdg 16:21; 1Sa 11:2
16:15 [t]1Sa 12:3
16:16 [u]ver 6
16:19 [v]ver 42 [w]Ex 16:7; Nu 14:10; 20:6
16:21 [x]Ex 32:10
16:22 [y]Nu 14:5 [z]Nu 27:16; Job 12:10; Heb 12:9 [a]Ge 18:23
16:26 [b]Isa 52:11 [c]Ge 19:15
16:28 [d]Ex 3:12; Jn 5:36; 6:38
16:29 [e]Ecc 3:19
16:30 [f]ver 33; Ps 55:15
16:31 [g]Mic 1:3-4
16:32 [h]Nu 26:11; Dt 11:6; Ps 106:17
16:35 [i]Nu 11:1-3; 26:10 [j]Lev 10:2

b *14* Or *you make slaves of*; or *you deceive* **c** *30* Hebrew *Sheol*; also in verse 33

16:13, 14 One of the easiest ways to fall away from following God is to look at our present problems and exaggerate them. Dathan and Abiram did just that when they began to long for better food and more pleasant surroundings. Egypt, the place they had longed to leave, was now looking better and better—not because of slavery and taskmasters, of course, but because of its mouth-watering food! These two men and their followers had completely lost their perspective. When we take our eyes off God and start looking at ourselves and our problems, we begin to lose our perspective as well. Overrating problems can hinder our relationship with God. Don't let difficulties make you lose sight of God's direction for your life.

16:26 The Israelites were told not even to touch the belongings of the wicked rebels. In this case, doing so would have shown sympathy to their cause and agreement with their principles. Korah, Dathan, and Abiram were directly challenging Moses and God. Moses clearly stated what God intended to do to the rebels (16:28–30). He did this so that everyone would have to choose between following Korah or following Moses, God's chosen leader. When God asks us to make a fundamental choice between siding

16:38
[k]Pr 20:2
[l]Nu 26:10;
Eze 14:8;
2Pe 2:6

16:40
[m]Ex 30:7-10;
Nu 1:51
[n]2Ch 26:18
[o]Nu 3:10

censers out of the smouldering remains and scatter the coals some distance away, for
the censers are holy—38the censers of the men who sinned at the cost of their lives.[k]
Hammer the censers into sheets to overlay the altar, for they were presented before
the LORD and have become holy. Let them be a sign[l] to the Israelites."
39So Eleazar the priest collected the bronze censers brought by those who had been
burned up, and he had them hammered out to overlay the altar, 40as the LORD directed
him through Moses. This was to remind the Israelites that no-one except a descendant
of Aaron should come to burn incense[m] before the LORD,[n] or he would become like
Korah and his followers.[o]

KORAH

Some notorious historical figures might have remained anonymous if they hadn't tried to grab on to more than they could hold. But by refusing to be content with what they had, and by trying to get more than they deserved, they ended up with nothing. Korah, one of the Israelite leaders, was such a person.

Korah was a Levite who assisted in the daily functions of the tabernacle. Shortly after Israel's great rebellion against God (Numbers 13; 14), Korah instigated his own mini-rebellion. He recruited a grievance committee and confronted Moses and Aaron. Their list of complaints boils down to three statements: (1) you are no better than anyone else; (2) everyone in Israel has been chosen of the Lord; (3) we don't need to obey you. It is amazing to see how Korah twisted the first two statements—both true—to reach the wrong conclusion.

Moses would have agreed that he was no better than anyone else. He would also have agreed that all Israelites were God's chosen people. But Korah's application of these truths was wrong. Not all Israelites were chosen to lead. Korah's hidden claim was this: "I have as much right to lead as Moses does." His error cost him not only his job—a position of service that he enjoyed—but also his life.

Korah's story gives us numerous warnings: (1) Don't let desire for what someone else has make you discontented with what you already have. (2) Don't try to raise your own self-esteem by attacking someone else's. (3) Don't use part of God's word to support what you want, rather than allowing its entirety to shape your wants. (4) Don't expect to find satisfaction in power and position; God may want to work through you in the position you are now in.

Strengths and accomplishments:
- Popular leader; influential figure during the exodus
- Mentioned among the chief men of Israel (Exodus 6)
- One of the first Levites appointed for special service in the tabernacle

Weaknesses and mistakes:
- Failed to recognise the significant position God had placed him in
- Forgot that his fight was against someone greater than Moses
- Allowed greed to blind his common sense

Lessons from his life:
- There is sometimes a fine line between goals and greed
- If we are discontented with what we have, we may lose it without gaining anything better

Vital statistics:
- Where: Egypt, Sinai peninsula
- Occupation: Levite (tabernacle assistant)

Key verses:
"Moses also said to Korah, 'Now listen, you Levites! Isn't it enough for you that the God of Israel has separated you from the rest of the Israelite community and brought you near himself to do the work at the LORD's tabernacle and to stand before the community and minister to them? He has brought you and all your fellow Levites near himself, but now you are trying to get the priesthood too' "(Numbers 16:8–10).

Korah's story is told in Numbers 16:1–40. He is also mentioned in Numbers 26:9; Jude 11.

with wicked people or siding with him, we should not hesitate but commit ourselves to be 100 per cent on the Lord's side.

16:27–35 Although the families of Dathan and Abiram were swallowed up, the sons of Korah were not wiped out (see 26:11).

41The next day the whole Israelite community grumbled against Moses and Aaron.
"You have killed the LORD's people," they said.
42But when the assembly gathered in opposition[p] to Moses and Aaron and turned
towards the Tent of Meeting, suddenly the cloud covered it and the glory of the LORD
appeared. 43Then Moses and Aaron went to the front of the Tent of Meeting, 44and
the LORD said to Moses, 45"Get away from this assembly so that I can put an end to
them at once." And they fell face down.
46Then Moses said to Aaron, "Take your censer and put incense in it, along with
fire from the altar, and hurry to the assembly[q] to make atonement[r] for them. Wrath
has come out from the LORD; the plague[s] has started." 47So Aaron did as Moses said,
and ran into the midst of the assembly. The plague had already started among the
people,[t] but Aaron offered the incense and made atonement for them. 48He stood
between the living and the dead, and the plague stopped.[u] 49But 14,700 people died
from the plague, in addition to those who had died because of Korah.[v] 50Then Aaron
returned to Moses at the entrance to the Tent of Meeting, for the plague had stopped.

The Budding of Aaron's Staff

17 The LORD said to Moses, 2"Speak to the Israelites and get twelve staffs from
them, one from the leader of each of their ancestral tribes. Write the name of
each man on his staff. 3On the staff of Levi write Aaron's name,[a] for there must be
one staff for the head of each ancestral tribe. 4Place them in the Tent of Meeting in
front of the Testimony,[b] where I meet with you.[c] 5The staff belonging to the man
I choose[d] will sprout, and I will rid myself of this constant grumbling against you
by the Israelites."
6So Moses spoke to the Israelites, and their leaders gave him twelve staffs, one for
the leader of each of their ancestral tribes, and Aaron's staff was among them. 7Moses
placed the staffs before the LORD in the Tent of the Testimony.[e]
8The next day Moses entered the Tent of the Testimony and saw that Aaron's staff,
which represented the house of Levi, had not only sprouted but had budded, blossomed and produced almonds.[f] 9Then Moses brought out all the staffs from the
LORD's presence to all the Israelites. They looked at them, and each man took his own
staff.
10The LORD said to Moses, "Put back Aaron's staff in front of the Testimony, to
be kept as a sign to the rebellious.[g] This will put an end to their grumbling against
me, so that they will not die." 11Moses did just as the LORD commanded him.
12The Israelites said to Moses, "We shall die! We are lost, we are all lost![h]
13Anyone who even comes near the tabernacle of the LORD will die.[i] Are we all going
to die?"

3. Duties of priests and Levites

18 The LORD said to Aaron, "You, your sons and your father's family are to bear
the responsibility for offences against the sanctuary,[a] and you and your sons
alone are to bear the responsibility for offences against the priesthood. 2Bring your
fellow Levites from your ancestral tribe to join you and assist you when you and your

16:42 [p]ver 19; Nu 20:6
16:46 [q]Lev 10:6 [r]Nu 18:5; 25:13; Dt 9:22 [s]Nu 8:19; Ps 106:29
16:47 [t]Nu 25:6-8
16:48 [u]Nu 25:8; Ps 106:30
16:49 [v]ver 32
17:3 [a]Nu 1:3
17:4 [b]ver 7 [c]Ex 25:22
17:5 [d]Nu 16:5
17:7 [e]Ex 38:21; Ac 7:44
17:8 [f]Eze 17:24; Heb 9:4
17:10 [g]Dt 9:24
17:12 [h]Isa 6:5
17:13 [i]Nu 1:51
18:1 [a]Ex 28:38

16:41 Just one day after Korah and his followers were executed for grumbling and complaining against God, the Israelites started again with more muttering and complaining. Their negative attitude only caused them to rebel even more and to bring about even greater trouble. It eroded their faith in God and encouraged thoughts of giving up and turning back. The path to open rebellion against God begins with dissatisfaction and scepticism, then moves to grumbling about both God and present circumstances. Next comes bitterness and resentment, followed finally by rebellion and open hostility. If you are often dissatisfied, sceptical, complaining, or bitter – beware! These attitudes lead to rebellion and separation from God. Any choice to side against God is a step in the direction of letting go of him completely and making your own way through life.

17:5, 10 After witnessing spectacular miracles, seeing the Egyptians punished by the plagues, and experiencing the actual presence of God, the Israelites still complained and rebelled. We wonder how they could be so blind and ignorant, and yet we often repeat this same pattern. We have centuries of evidence, the Bible in many translations, and the convincing results of archaeological and historical studies. But people today continue to disobey God and go their own way. Like the Israelites, we are more concerned about our physical condition than our spiritual condition. We can escape this pattern only by paying attention to all the signs of God's presence that we have been given. Has God guided and protected you? Has he answered your prayers? Do you know peo-

sons minister[b] before the Tent of the Testimony. 3They are to be responsible to you
and are to perform all the duties of the Tent,[c] but they must not go near the furnishings
of the sanctuary or the altar, or both they and you will die.[d] 4They are to join you
and be responsible for the care of the Tent of Meeting—all the work at the Tent—and
no-one else may come near where you are.
5"You are to be responsible for the care of the sanctuary and the altar,[e] so that
wrath will not fall on the Israelites again. 6I myself have selected your fellow Levites
from among the Israelites as a gift to you,[f] dedicated to the LORD to do the work
at the Tent of Meeting. 7But only you and your sons may serve as priests in connection
with everything at the altar and inside the curtain.[g] I am giving you the service of
the priesthood as a gift.[h] Anyone else who comes near the sanctuary must be put to
death.[i]"

Offerings for Priests and Levites

8Then the LORD said to Aaron, "I myself have put you in charge of the offerings
presented to me; all the holy offerings the Israelites give me I give to you and your
sons as your portion and regular share.[j] 9You are to have the part of the most holy
offerings that is kept from the fire. From all the gifts they bring me as most holy
offerings, whether grain[k] or sin[l] or guilt offerings,[m] that part belongs to you and
your sons. 10Eat it as something most holy; every male shall eat it.[n] You must regard
it as holy.
11"This also is yours: whatever is set aside from the gifts of all the wave offerings[o]
of the Israelites. I give this to you and your sons and daughters as your regular share.
Everyone in your household who is ceremonially clean[p] may eat it.
12"I give you all the finest olive oil and all the finest new wine and grain they give
to the LORD as the firstfruits of their harvest.[q] 13All the land's firstfruits that they
bring to the LORD will be yours.[r] Everyone in your household who is ceremonially
clean may eat it.
14"Everything in Israel that is devoted**[a]** to the LORD[s] is yours. 15The first offspring
of every womb, both man and animal, that is offered to the LORD is yours.[t] But you
must redeem[u] every firstborn son and every firstborn male of unclean animals.[v]
16When they are a month old, you must redeem them at the redemption price set at
five shekels**[b]**[w] of silver, according to the sanctuary shekel,[x] which weighs twenty
gerahs.
17"But you must not redeem the firstborn of an ox, a sheep or a goat; they are holy.[y]
Sprinkle their blood[z] on the altar and burn their fat as an offering made by fire, an
aroma pleasing to the LORD. 18Their meat is to be yours, just as the breast of the wave
offering[a] and the right thigh are yours. 19Whatever is set aside from the holy offerings
the Israelites present to the LORD I give to you and your sons and daughters as your
regular share. It is an everlasting covenant of salt[b] before the LORD for both you and
your offspring."
20The LORD said to Aaron, "You will have no inheritance in their land, nor will
you have any share among them;[c] I am your share and your inheritance[d] among the
Israelites.
21"I give to the Levites all the tithes[e] in Israel as their inheritance[f] in return for
the work they do while serving at the Tent of Meeting. 22From now on the Israelites
must not go near the Tent of Meeting, or they will bear the consequences of their sin
and will die.[g] 23It is the Levites who are to do the work at the Tent of Meeting and
bear the responsibility for offences against it. This is a lasting ordinance for the
generations to come. They will receive no inheritance[h] among the Israelites. 24In-
stead, I give to the Levites as their inheritance the tithes that the Israelites present as

18:2 [b]Nu 3:10
18:3 [c]Nu 1:51 [d]ver 7; Nu 4:15
18:5 [e]Nu 16:46
18:6 [f]Nu 3:9
18:7 [g]Heb 9:3, 6 [h]ver 20; Ex 29:9 [i]Nu 3:10
18:8 [j]Lev 6:16; 7:6, 31-34, 36
18:9 [k]Lev 2:1 [l]Lev 6:25 [m]Lev 5:15; 7:7
18:10 [n]Lev 6:16
18:11 [o]Ex 29:26 [p]Lev 22:1-16
18:12 [q]Ex 23:19; Ne 10:35
18:13 [r]Ex 22:29; 23:19
18:14 [s]Lev 27:28
18:15 [t]Ex 13:2 [u]Nu 3:46 [v]Ex 13:13
18:16 [w]Lev 27:6 [x]Ex 30:13
18:17 [y]Dt 15:19 [z]Lev 3:2
18:18 [a]Lev 7:30
18:19 [b]Lev 2:13; 2Ch 13:5
18:20 [c]Dt 12:12 [d]Dt 10:9; 14:27; 18:1-2; Jos 13:33; Eze 44:28
18:21 [e]Dt 14:22; Mal 3:8 [f]Lev 27:30-33; Heb 7:5
18:22 [g]Lev 22:9; Nu 1:51
18:23 [h]ver 20

a *14* The Hebrew term refers to the irrevocable giving over of things or persons to the LORD. **b** *16* That is, about 2 ounces (about 55 grams)

ple who have experienced remarkable blessings and healings? Do you know Bible stories about the way God has led his people? Focus your thoughts on what God has done, and rebellion will become unthinkable.

an offering to the LORD. That is why I said concerning them: 'They will have no
inheritance among the Israelites.' "
25The LORD said to Moses, 26"Speak to the Levites and say to them: 'When you
receive from the Israelites the tithe I give you[i] as your inheritance, you must present
a tenth of that tithe as the LORD's offering.[j] 27Your offering will be reckoned to you
as grain from the threshing-floor or juice from the winepress. 28In this way you also
will present an offering to the LORD from all the tithes[k] you receive from the Israelites.
From these tithes you must give the LORD's portion to Aaron the priest. 29You must
present as the LORD's portion the best and holiest part of everything given to you.'
30"Say to the Levites: 'When you present the best part, it will be reckoned to you
as the product of the threshing-floor or the winepress.[l] 31You and your households
may eat the rest of it anywhere, for it is your wages for your work at the Tent of
Meeting. 32By presenting the best part[m] of it you will not be guilty in this matter;
then you will not defile the holy offerings[n] of the Israelites, and you will not die.' "

The Water of Cleansing

19 The LORD said to Moses and Aaron: 2"This is a requirement of the law that the
LORD has commanded: Tell the Israelites to bring you a red heifer[a] without
defect or blemish[b] and that has never been under a yoke.[c] 3Give it to Eleazar[d] the
priest; it is to be taken outside the camp[e] and slaughtered in his presence. 4Then
Eleazar the priest is to take some of its blood on his finger and sprinkle[f] it seven times
towards the front of the Tent of Meeting. 5While he watches, the heifer is to be
burned—its hide, flesh, blood and offal.[g] 6The priest is to take some cedar wood,
hyssop[h] and scarlet wool[i] and throw them onto the burning heifer. 7After that, the
priest must wash his clothes and bathe himself with water.[j] He may then come into
the camp, but he will be ceremonially unclean till evening. 8The man who burns it
must also wash his clothes and bathe with water, and he too will be unclean till
evening.
9"A man who is clean shall gather up the ashes of the heifer[k] and put them in a
ceremonially clean place outside the camp. They shall be kept by the Israelite community for use in the water of cleansing;[l] it is for purification from sin. 10The man who
gathers up the ashes of the heifer must also wash his clothes, and he too will be unclean
till evening. This will be a lasting ordinance both for the Israelites and for the aliens
living among them.
11"Whoever touches the dead body[m] of anyone will be unclean for seven days.[n]
12He must purify himself with the water on the third day and on the seventh day;[o]
then he will be clean. But if he does not purify himself on the third and seventh days,
he will not be clean. 13Whoever touches the dead body[p] of anyone and fails to purify
himself defiles the LORD's tabernacle.[q] That person must be cut off from Israel.[r]
Because the water of cleansing has not been sprinkled on him, he is unclean;[s] his
uncleanness remains on him.
14"This is the law that applies when a person dies in a tent: Anyone who enters the
tent and anyone who is in it will be unclean for seven days, 15and every open container
without a lid fastened on it will be unclean.
16"Anyone out in the open who touches someone who has been killed with a sword
or someone who has died a natural death,[t] or anyone who touches a human bone or
a grave,[u] will be unclean for seven days.

18:26 [i]ver 21 [j]Ne 10:38
18:28 [k]Mal 3:8
18:30 [l]ver 27
18:32 [m]Lev 22:15 [n]Lev 19:8
19:2 [a]Ge 15:9; Heb 9:13 [b]Lev 22:19-25 [c]Dt 21:3; 1Sa 6:7
19:3 [d]Nu 3:4 [e]Lev 4:12, 21; Heb 13:11
19:4 [f]Lev 4:17
19:5 [g]Ex 29:14
19:6 [h]ver 18; Ps 51:7 [i]Lev 14:4
19:7 [j]Lev 11:25; 16:26, 28; 22:6
19:9 [k]Heb 9:13 [l]ver 13; Nu 8:7
19:11 [m]Lev 21:1; Nu 5:2 [n]Nu 31:19
19:12 [o]ver 19; Nu 31:19
19:13 [p]Lev 20:3 [q]Lev 15:31; 2Ch 36:14 [r]Lev 7:20; 22:3 [s]Hag 2:13
19:16 [t]Nu 31:19 [u]Mt 23:27

18:25, 26 Even the Levites, who were ministers, had to tithe to support the Lord's work. No-one was exempt from returning to God a portion of what was received. Though the Levites owned no land and operated no great enterprises, they were to treat their income the same as everyone else did by giving a portion to care for the needs of the other Levites and of the tabernacle. The tithing principle is still relevant. God expects all his followers to supply the material needs of those who devote themselves to meeting the spiritual needs of the community of faith.

19:9, 10 What is the significance of the red heifer's ashes? When a person touched a dead body, he was considered unclean (i.e., unable to approach God in worship). This ritual purified the unclean person so that once again he could offer sacrifices and worship God. Death was the strongest of defilements because it was the final result of sin. Thus a special sacrifice—a red heifer—was required. It had to be offered by someone who was not unclean. When it had been burned on the altar, its ashes were used to purify water for ceremonial cleansing—not so much literally as symbolically. The unclean person then washed himself, and often his clothes and belongings, with this purified water as an act of becoming clean again.

19:17 [v]ver 9
19:18 [w]ver 6
19:19 [x]Eze 36:25; Heb 10:22
19:22 [y]Lev 5:2; Hag 2:13, 14
20:1 [a]Nu 13:21 [b]Nu 33:36 [c]Ex 15:20
20:2 [d]Ex 17:1 [e]Nu 16:19
20:3 [f]Ex 17:2 [g]Nu 14:2; 16:31-35
20:4 [h]Ex 14:11; 17:3; Nu 14:3; 16:13
20:5 [i]Nu 16:14
20:6 [j]Nu 14:5 [k]Nu 16:19
20:8 [l]Ex 4:17, 20 [m]Ex 17:6; Isa 43:20
20:9 [n]Nu 17:10
20:10 [o]Ps 106:32, 33

17“For the unclean person, put some ashes[v] from the burned purification offering
into a jar and pour fresh water over them. 18Then a man who is ceremonially clean
is to take some hyssop,[w] dip it in the water and sprinkle the tent and all the furnishings
and the people who were there. He must also sprinkle anyone who has touched a
human bone or a grave or someone who has been killed or someone who has died a
natural death. 19The man who is clean is to sprinkle the unclean person on the third
and seventh days, and on the seventh day he is to purify him.[x] The person being
cleansed must wash his clothes and bathe with water, and that evening he will be clean.
20But if a person who is unclean does not purify himself, he must be cut off from the
community, because he has defiled the sanctuary of the LORD. The water of cleansing
has not been sprinkled on him, and he is unclean. 21This is a lasting ordinance for
them.

“The man who sprinkles the water of cleansing must also wash his clothes, and
anyone who touches the water of cleansing will be unclean till evening. 22Anything
that an unclean[y] person touches becomes unclean, and anyone who touches it becomes unclean till evening.”

4. The new generation

Water From the Rock

20 In the first month the whole Israelite community arrived at the Desert of Zin,[a]
and they stayed at Kadesh.[b] There Miriam[c] died and was buried.

2Now there was no water for the community,[d] and the people gathered in opposition[e] to Moses and Aaron. 3They quarrelled[f] with Moses and said, “If only we had
died when our brothers fell dead before the LORD![g] 4Why did you bring the LORD’s
community into this desert, that we and our livestock should die here?[h] 5Why did
you bring us up out of Egypt to this terrible place? It has no grain or figs, grapevines
or pomegranates.[i] And there is no water to drink!”

6Moses and Aaron went from the assembly to the entrance to the Tent of Meeting
and fell face down,[j] and the glory of the LORD[k] appeared to them. 7The LORD said
to Moses, 8“Take the staff,[l] and you and your brother Aaron gather the assembly
together. Speak to that rock before their eyes and it will pour out its water.[m] You will
bring water out of the rock for the community so that they and their livestock can
drink.”

9So Moses took the staff from the LORD’s presence,[n] just as he commanded him.
10He and Aaron gathered the assembly together in front of the rock and Moses said
to them, “Listen, you rebels, must we bring you water out of this rock?”[o] 11Then

EVENTS AT KADESH
After wandering in the desert for 40 years, Israel arrived at Kadesh, where Miriam died. There was not enough water and the people complained bitterly. Moses struck a rock, and it gave enough water for everyone. The king of Edom refused Israel passage through his land, forcing them to travel around his country.

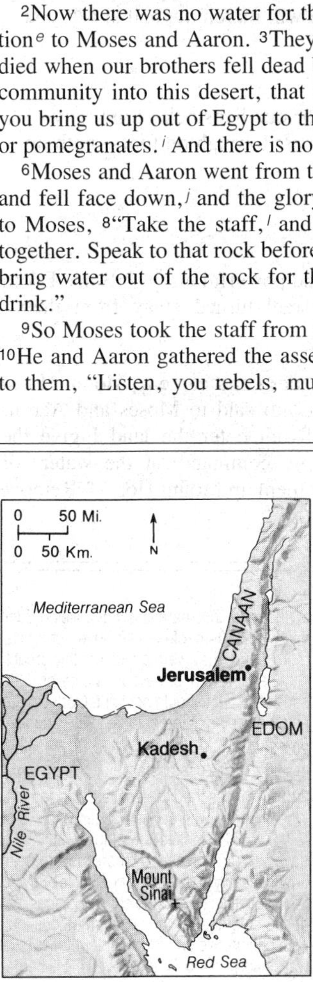

20:1 It had been 37 years since Israel’s first spy mission into the promised land (Numbers 13, 14) and 40 years since the exodus from Egypt. The Bible is virtually silent about those 37 years of aimless wandering. The generation of those who had lived in Egypt had almost died off, and the new generation would soon be ready to enter the land. Moses, Aaron, Joshua, and Caleb were among the few who remained from those who had left Egypt. Once again they camped at Kadesh, the site of the first spy mission that had ended in disaster. Moses hoped the people were ready for a fresh start.

20:3–5 After 37 years in the desert, the Israelites forgot that their wanderings were a result of their parents’ and their own sin. They could not accept the fact that they brought their problems upon themselves, so they blamed Moses for their condition. Often our troubles result from our own disobedience or lack of faith. We cannot blame God for our sins. Until we face this reality, we will have little peace and no spiritual growth.

Moses raised his arm and struck the rock twice with his staff. Water[p] gushed out,
and the community and their livestock drank.
12 But the LORD said to Moses and Aaron, "Because you did not trust in me enough
to honour me as holy[q] in the sight of the Israelites, you will not bring this community
into the land I give them."[r]
13 These were the waters of Meribah,[a][s] where the Israelites quarrelled[t] with the
LORD and where he showed himself holy among them.

Edom Denies Israel Passage

14 Moses sent messengers from Kadesh[u] to the king of Edom,[v] saying:

"This is what your brother Israel says: You know[w] about all the hardships that
have come upon us. 15 Our forefathers went down into Egypt,[x] and we lived there
many years.[y] The Egyptians ill-treated[z] us and our fathers, 16 but when we cried
out to the LORD, he heard our cry[a] and sent an angel[b] and brought us out of
Egypt.

"Now we are here at Kadesh, a town on the edge of your territory. 17 Please
let us pass through your country. We will not go through any field or vineyard,
or drink water from any well. We will travel along the king's highway and not
turn to the right or to the left until we have passed through your territory.[c]"
18 But Edom answered:

"You may not pass through here; if you try, we will march out and attack you
with the sword."

19 The Israelites replied:

"We will go along the main road, and if we or our livestock[d] drink any of
your water, we will pay for it.[e] We only want to pass through on foot—nothing
else."

20 Again they answered:

"You may not pass through."

Then Edom came out against them with a large and powerful army. 21 Since Edom
refused to let them go through their territory, Israel turned away from them.[f]

The Death of Aaron

22 The whole Israelite community set out from Kadesh and came to Mount Hor.[g]
23 At Mount Hor, near the border of Edom,[h] the LORD said to Moses and Aaron,
24 "Aaron will be gathered to his people.[i] He will not enter the land I give the
Israelites, because both of you rebelled against my command[j] at the waters of
Meribah. 25 Call Aaron and his son Eleazar and take them up Mount Hor.[k] 26 Remove

[a] 13 *Meribah* means *quarrelling.*

20:11 [p]Ex 17:6; Dt 8:15; Ps 78:16; Isa 48:2; 1Co 10:4
20:12 [q]Nu 27:14 [r]ver 24; Dt 1:37; 3:27
20:13 [s]Ex 17:7 [t]Dt 33:8; Ps 95:8; 106:32
20:14 [u]Jdg 11:16-17 [v]Dt 2:4 [w]Jos 2:11; 9:9
20:15 [x]Ge 46:6 [y]Ge 15:13; Ex 12:40 [z]Ex 1:11; Dt 26:6
20:16 [a]Ex 2:23; 3:7 [b]Ex 14:19
20:17 [c]Nu 21:22
20:19 [d]Ex 12:38 [e]Dt 2:6, 28
20:21 [f]Dt 2:8; Jdg 11:18
20:22 [g]Nu 33:37
20:23 [h]Nu 33:37
20:24 [i]Ge 25:8 [j]ver 10
20:25 [k]Nu 33:38

20:12 The Lord had told Moses to speak to the rock; however, Moses struck it, not once, but twice. God did the miracle; yet Moses was taking credit for it when he said, "We bring you water out of this rock." For this he was forbidden to enter the promised land. Was God's punishment of Moses too harsh? After all, the people had nagged him, slandered him, and rebelled against both him and God. Now they were at it again (20:5). But Moses was the leader and model for the entire nation. Because of this great responsibility to the people, he could not be let off lightly. By striking the rock, Moses disobeyed God's direct command and dishonoured God in the presence of his people.

20:14 Two brothers became the ancestors of two nations. The Edomites descended from Esau; the Israelites from Jacob. Thus the Edomites were "brothers" to the Israelites. Israel sent a brotherly message to Edom requesting passage through their land on the main road, a well-travelled trade route. Israel promised to stay on the road, thus harmlessly bypassing Edom's fields, vineyards, and wells. Edom refused, however, because they did not trust Israel's word. They were afraid that this great horde of people would either attack them or devour their crops (Deuteronomy 2:4, 5). Because brothers should not fight, God told the Israelites to turn back and travel by a different route to the promised land.

20:17 The king's highway was an old caravan route. Long before this time it was used as a major public road.

20:21 Moses tried to negotiate and reason with the Edomite king. When nothing worked, he was left with two choices—force a conflict or avoid it. Moses knew there would be enough barriers in the days and months ahead. There was no point in adding another one unnecessarily. Sometimes conflict is unavoidable. Sometimes, however, it isn't worth the consequences. Open warfare may seem heroic, courageous, and even righteous, but it is not always the best choice. We should consider Moses' example and find another way to solve our problems, even if it is harder for us to do.

Aaron's garments and put them on his son Eleazar, for Aaron will be gathered to his
people;[l] he will die there."
27 Moses did as the LORD commanded: They went up Mount Hor in the sight of the
whole community. 28 Moses removed Aaron's garments and put them on his son
Eleazar.[m] And Aaron died there[n] on top of the mountain. Then Moses and Eleazar
came down from the mountain, 29 and when the whole community learned that Aaron
had died, the entire house of Israel mourned for him[o] thirty days.

Arad Destroyed

21 When the Canaanite king of Arad,[a] who lived in the Negev,[b] heard that Israel
was coming along the road to Atharim, he attacked the Israelites and captured
some of them. 2 Then Israel made this vow to the LORD: "If you will deliver these
people into our hands, we will totally destroy[a] their cities." 3 The LORD listened to
Israel's plea and gave the Canaanites over to them. They completely destroyed them
and their towns; so the place was named Hormah.[b]

The Bronze Snake

4 They travelled from Mount Hor[c] along the route to the Red Sea,[c] to go round
Edom. But the people grew impatient on the way;[d] 5 they spoke against God[e] and

20:26 [l]ver 24
20:28 [m]Ex 29:29 [n]Nu 33:38; Dt 10:6; 32:50
20:29 [o]Dt 34:8
21:1 [a]Nu 33:40; Jos 12:14 [b]Jdg 1:9, 16
21:4 [c]Nu 20:22 [d]Dt 2:8; Jdg 11:18
21:5 [e]Ps 78:19

a 2 The Hebrew term refers to the irrevocable giving over of things or persons to the LORD, often by totally destroying them; also in verse 3. b 3 *Hormah* means *destruction.* c 4 Hebrew *Yam Suph*; that is, Sea of Reeds

ELEAZAR

An understudy must know the lead role completely and be willing to step into it at a moment's notice. Eleazar was an excellent understudy, well trained for his eventual leading role. However, his moments in the spotlight were painful. On one occasion, he watched his two older brothers burn to death for failing to take God's holiness seriously. Later, as his father was dying, he was made high priest, surely one of the most responsible—and therefore potentially most stressful—positions in Israel.

An understudy benefits from having both the script and a human model of the role. Ever since childhood, Eleazar had been able to observe Moses and Aaron. Now he could learn from watching Joshua. In addition, he had God's laws to guide him as he worked as priest and adviser to Joshua.

Strengths and accomplishments:
- Succeeded his father, Aaron, as high priest
- Completed his father's work by helping lead the people into the promised land
- Teamed up with Joshua
- Acted as God's spokesman to the people

Lessons from his life:
- Concentrating on our present challenges and responsibilities is the best way to prepare for what God has planned for our future
- God's desire is consistent obedience throughout our lives

Vital statistics:
- Where: Desert of Sinai, promised land
- Occupations: Priest and high priest
- Relatives: Father: Aaron. Brothers: Nadab and Abihu. Aunt and uncle: Miriam and Moses.
- Contemporaries: Joshua, Caleb

Key verses:
"At Mount Hor, near the border of Edom, the LORD said to Moses and Aaron . . . 'Call Aaron and his son Eleazar and take them up Mount Hor. Remove Aaron's garments and put them on his son Eleazar' " (Numbers 20:23–26).

Eleazar is mentioned in Exodus 6:23; Leviticus 10:16–20; Numbers 3:1–4; 4:16; 16:36–40; 20:25–29; 26:1–3, 63; 27:2, 15–23; 32:2; 34:17; Deuteronomy 10:6; Joshua 14:1; 17:4; 24:33.

20:28 Aaron died just before entering the promised land, probably as punishment for his sin of rebellion (Exodus 32; Numbers 12:1–9). This was the first time that a new high priest was appointed. The priestly clothing was removed from Aaron and placed on his son Eleazar, following the commands recorded in the book of Leviticus.

21:5 In Psalm 78, we learn the sources of Israel's complaining: (1) their spirits were not faithful to God (78:8); (2) they refused to obey God's law (78:10); (3) they forgot the miracles God had done for them (78:11). Our complaining often has its roots in one of these thoughtless actions and attitudes. If we can deal with the cause of our complaining, it will not take hold and grow in our lives.

against Moses, and said, "Why have you brought us up out of Egypt to die in the
desert?[f] There is no bread! There is no water! And we detest this miserable food!"[g]
6Then the LORD sent venomous snakes[h] among them; they bit the people and many
Israelites died.[i] 7The people came to Moses[j] and said, "We sinned when we spoke
against the LORD and against you. Pray that the LORD[k] will take the snakes away from
us." So Moses prayed[l] for the people.
8The LORD said to Moses, "Make a snake and put it up on a pole;[m] anyone who
is bitten can look at it and live." 9So Moses made a bronze snake[n] and put it up on
a pole. Then when anyone was bitten by a snake and looked at the bronze snake, he
lived.[o]

The Journey to Moab

10The Israelites moved on and camped at Oboth.[p] 11Then they set out from Oboth
and camped in Iye Abarim, in the desert that faces Moab[q] towards the sunrise. 12From
there they moved on and camped in the Zered Valley.[r] 13They set out from there and
camped alongside the Arnon[s], which is in the desert extending into Amorite territory.
The Arnon is the border of Moab, between Moab and the Amorites. 14That is why
the Book of the Wars of the LORD says:

"... Waheb in Suphah[d] and the ravines,
the Arnon 15and[e] the slopes of the ravines
that lead to the site of Ar[t]
and lie along the border of Moab."

16From there they continued on to Beer,[u] the well where the LORD said to Moses,
"Gather the people together and I will give them water."

d *14* The meaning of the Hebrew for this phrase is uncertain. e *14,15* Or *"I have been given from Suphah and the ravines / of the Arnon 15to*

21:5 [f]Nu 14:2, 3 [g]Nu 11:6
21:6 [h]Dt 8:15; Jer 8:17 [i]1Co 10:9
21:7 [j]Ps 78:34; Hos 5:15 [k]Ex 8:8; Ac 8:24 [l]Nu 11:2
21:8 [m]Jn 3:14
21:9 [n]2Ki 18:4 [o]Jn 3:14-15
21:10 [p]Nu 33:43
21:11 [q]Nu 33:44
21:12 [r]Dt 2:13, 14
21:13 [s]Nu 22:36; Jdg 11:13, 18
21:15 [t]ver 28; Dt 2:9, 18
21:16 [u]Jdg 9:21

21:6 God used venomous snakes to punish the people for their unbelief and complaining. The Desert of Sinai has a variety of snakes. Some hide in the sand and attack without warning. Both the Israelites and the Egyptians had a great fear of snakes. A bite by a poisonous snake often meant a slow death with intense suffering.

21:8, 9 When the bronze snake was hung on the pole, the Israelites didn't know the fuller meaning Jesus Christ would bring to this event (see John 3:14, 15). Jesus explained that just as the Israelites were healed of their sickness by looking at the snake on the pole, all believers today can be saved from the sickness of sin by looking to Jesus' death on the cross. It was not the snake that healed the people, but their belief that God could heal them. This belief was demonstrated by their obedience to God's instructions. In the same way, we should continue to look to Christ (see Hebrews 12:2).

21:14 There is no existing record of the Book of the Wars of the Lord. Most likely, it was a collection of victory songs or poems.

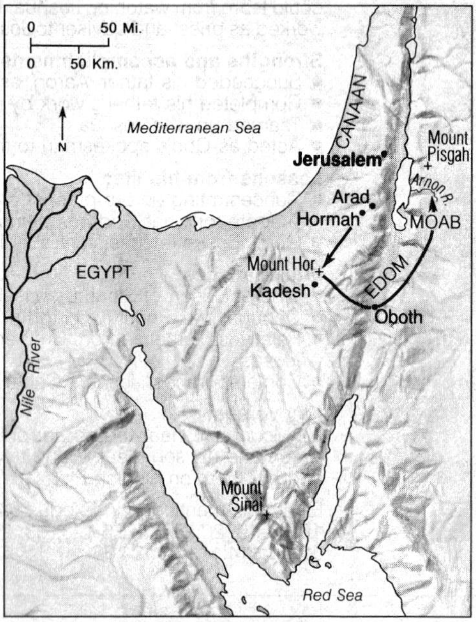

EVENTS IN THE DESERT Israel next met resistance from the king of Arad, but soundly defeated him. The next stop was Mount Hor (where Aaron had died); then they travelled south and east around Edom. After camping at Oboth, they moved towards the Arnon River and onto the plains of Moab near Mount Pisgah.

21:17 [v]Ex 15:1
21:21 [w]Dt 1:4; 2:26-27; Jdg 11:19-21
21:22 [x]Nu 20:17
21:23 [y]Nu 20:21 [z]Dt 2:32; Jdg 11:20
21:24 [a]Dt 2:33; Ps 135:10-11; Am 2:9 [b]Dt 2:37
21:25 [c]Nu 13:29; Jdg 10:11; Am 2:10
21:26 [d]Dt 29:7; Ps 135:11

17 Then Israel sang this song:[v]

"Spring up, O well!
  Sing about it,
18 about the well that the princes dug,
  that the nobles of the people sank—
  the nobles with sceptres and staffs."

Then they went from the desert to Mattanah, 19 from Mattanah to Nahaliel, from
Nahaliel to Bamoth, 20 and from Bamoth to the valley in Moab where the top of Pisgah
overlooks the wasteland.

Defeat of Sihon and Og

21 Israel sent messengers to say to Sihon[w] king of the Amorites:

22 "Let us pass through your country. We will not turn aside into any field or
vineyard, or drink water from any well. We will travel along the king's highway
until we have passed through your territory.[x]"

23 But Sihon would not let Israel pass through his territory.[y] He mustered his entire
army and marched out into the desert against Israel. When he reached Jahaz,[z] he
fought with Israel. 24 Israel, however, put him to the sword[a] and took over his land
from the Arnon to the Jabbok, but only as far as the Ammonites,[b] because their border
was fortified. 25 Israel captured all the cities of the Amorites[c] and occupied them,
including Heshbon and all its surrounding settlements. 26 Heshbon was the city of
Sihon[d] king of the Amorites, who had fought against the former king of Moab and
had taken from him all his land as far as the Arnon.
27 That is why the poets say:

"Come to Heshbon and let it be rebuilt;
  let Sihon's city be restored.

THE SNAKE IN THE DESERT
Compare the texts for yourself: Numbers 21:7–9 and John 3:14, 15.

Israelites	*Christians*
Bitten by snakes	Bitten by sin
Little initial pain, then intense suffering	Little initial pain, then intense suffering
Physical death from snakes' poison	Spiritual death from sin's poison
Bronze snake lifted up in the desert	Christ lifted up on the cross
Looking to the snake spared one's life	Looking to Christ saves from eternal death

BATTLES WITH SIHON AND OG
King Sihon refused passage to the Israelites through his land, and he attacked Israel at Jahaz. Israel defeated him, occupying the land between the Arnon and Jabbok rivers, including the capital city, Heshbon. As they moved north, they defeated King Og of Bashan at Edrei.

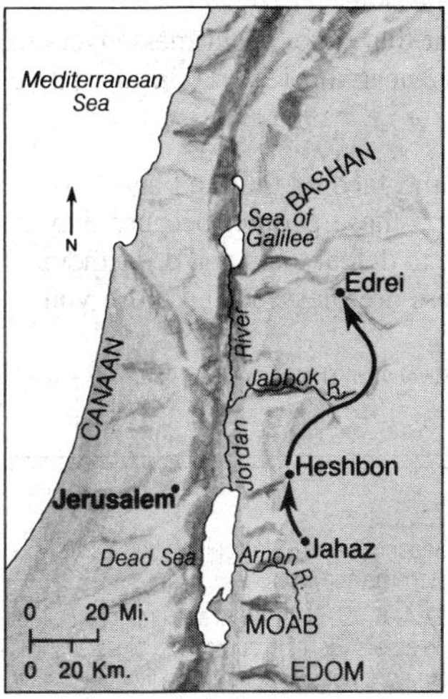

21:27–30 Chemosh, the national god of Moab, was worshipped as a god of war. This false god, however, was no help to this nation when it fought against Israel. Israel's God was stronger than any of Canaan's war gods.

28"Fire went out from Heshbon,
a blaze from the city of Sihon.[e]
It consumed Ar[f] of Moab,
the citizens of Arnon's heights.[g]
29Woe to you, O Moab![h]
You are destroyed, O people of Chemosh![i]
He has given up his sons as fugitives[j]
and his daughters as captives[k]
to Sihon king of the Amorites.

30"But we have overthrown them;
Heshbon is destroyed all the way to Dibon.[l]
We have demolished them as far as Nophah,
which extends to Medeba."

31So Israel settled in the land of the Amorites.
32After Moses had sent spies to Jazer,[m] the Israelites captured its surrounding
settlements and drove out the Amorites who were there. 33Then they turned and went
up along the road towards Bashan[n],[o] and Og king of Bashan and his whole army
marched out to meet them in battle at Edrei.[p]
34The LORD said to Moses, "Do not be afraid of him, for I have handed him over
to you, with his whole army and his land. Do to him what you did to Sihon king of
the Amorites, who reigned in Heshbon.[q]"
35So they struck him down, together with his sons and his whole army, leaving them
no survivors. And they took possession of his land.

D. SECOND APPROACH TO THE PROMISED LAND (22:1—36:13)

Now the old generation has died and a new generation stands poised at the border, ready to enter the promised land. Neighbouring nations, however, cause Israel to begin worshipping other gods. Without Moses' quick action, the nation may never have entered Canaan. We must never let down our guard in resisting sin.

1. The story of Balaam

Balak Summons Balaam

22 Then the Israelites travelled to the plains of Moab and camped along the Jordan
across from Jericho.[a][a]
2Now Balak son of Zippor[b] saw all that Israel had done to the Amorites, 3and Moab
was terrified because there were so many people. Indeed, Moab was filled with
dread[c] because of the Israelites.
4The Moabites said to the elders of Midian, "This horde is going to lick up
everything around us, as an ox licks up the grass of the field."
So Balak son of Zippor, who was king of Moab at that time, 5sent messengers to
summon Balaam son of Beor,[d] who was at Pethor, near the River,[b] in his native
land. Balak said:

"A people has come out of Egypt; they cover the face of the land and have
settled next to me. 6Now come and put a curse[e] on these people, because they
are too powerful for me. Perhaps then I will be able to defeat them and drive them
out of the country. For I know that those you bless are blessed, and those you
curse are cursed."

a *1* Hebrew *Jordan of Jericho*; possibly an ancient name for the Jordan River b *5* That is, the Euphrates

21:28 [e]Jer 48:45 [f]ver 15 [g]Nu 22:41; Isa 15:2
21:29 [h]Isa 25:10; Jer 48:46 [i]Jdg 11:24; 1Ki 11:7, 33; 2Ki 23:13; Jer 48:7, 46 [j]Isa 15:5 [k]Isa 16:2
21:30 [l]Nu 32:3; Isa 15:2; Jer 48:18, 22
21:32 [m]Nu 32:1, 3, 35; Jer 48:32
21:33 [n]Dt 3:3 [o]Dt 3:4 [p]Dt 1:4; 3:1, 10; Jos 13:12, 31
21:34 [q]Dt 3:2
22:1 [a]Nu 33:48
22:2 [b]Jdg 11:25
22:3 [c]Ex 15:15
22:5 [d]Dt 23:4; Jos 13:22; 24:9; Ne 13:2; Mic 6:5; 2Pe 2:15
22:6 [e]ver 12, 17; Nu 23:7, 11, 13

21:34 God assured Moses that Israel's enemy was conquered even before the battle began! God wants to give us victory over our enemies (which are usually problems related to sin rather than armed soldiers). But first we must believe that he can help us. Second, we must trust him to help us. Third, we must take the steps he shows us.

22:4–6 Balaam was a sorcerer, one called upon to place curses on others. Belief in curses and blessings was common in Old Testament times. Sorcerers were thought to have power with the gods.

22:7
[f] Nu 23:23; 24:1

7 The elders of Moab and Midian left, taking with them the fee for divination.[f]
When they came to Balaam, they told him what Balak had said.

BALAAM

Balaam was one of those noteworthy Old Testament characters who, though not one of God's chosen people, was willing to acknowledge that Yahweh (the Lord) was indeed a powerful God. But he did not believe in the Lord as the only true God. His story exposes the deception of maintaining an outward facade of spirituality over a corrupt inward life. Balaam was a man ready to obey God's command as long as he could profit from doing so. This mixture of motives—obedience and profit—eventually led to Balaam's death. Although he realised the awesome power of Israel's God, his heart was occupied with the wealth he could gain in Moab. There he returned to die when the armies of Israel invaded.

Eventually, each of us lives through the same process. Who and what we are will somehow come to the surface, destroying any masks we may have put on to cover up our real selves. Efforts spent on keeping up appearances would be much better spent on finding the answer to sin in our lives. We can avoid Balaam's mistake by facing ourselves and realising that God is willing to accept us, forgive us, and literally make us new from within. Don't miss this great discovery that eluded Balaam.

Strengths and accomplishments:
- Widely known for his effective curses and blessings
- Obeyed God and blessed Israel, in spite of Balak's bribe

Weaknesses and mistakes:
- Encouraged the Israelites to worship idols (Numbers 31:16)
- Returned to Moab and was killed in war

Lessons from his life:
- Motives are just as important as actions
- Your treasure is where your heart is

Vital statistics:
- Where: Lived near the Euphrates River, travelled to Moab
- Occupations: Sorcerer, prophet
- Relative: Father: Beor
- Contemporaries: Balak (king of Moab), Moses, Aaron

Key verses:
"They have left the straight way and wandered off to follow the way of Balaam son of Beor, who loved the wages of wickedness. But he was rebuked for his wrongdoing by a donkey—a beast without speech—who spoke with a man's voice and restrained the prophet's madness" (2 Peter 2:15, 16).

Balaam's story is told in Numbers 22:1—24:25. He is also mentioned in Numbers 31:7, 8, 16; Deuteronomy 23:4, 5; Joshua 24:9, 10; Nehemiah 13:2; Micah 6:5; 2 Peter 2:15, 16; Jude 11; Revelation 2:14.

THE STORY OF BALAAM
At King Balak's request Balaam travelled nearly 400 miles to curse Israel. Balak took Balaam to Bamoth Baal ("the high places of Baal"), then to Mount Pisgah, and finally to Mount Peor. Each place overlooked the plains of Moab where the Israelites were camped. But to the king's dismay, Balaam blessed, not cursed, Israel.

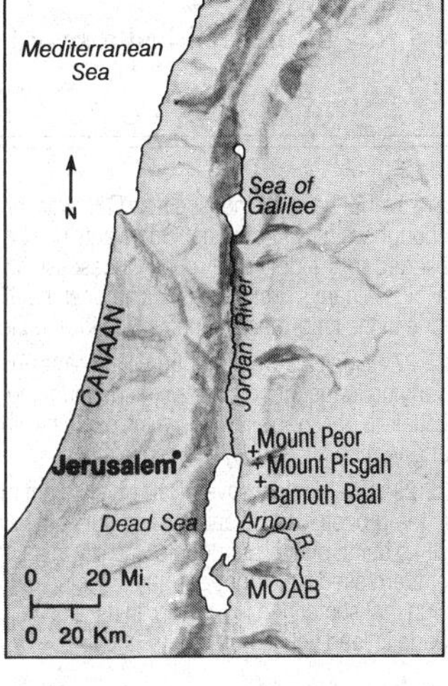

Thus the king of Moab wanted Balaam to use his powers with the God of Israel to place a curse on Israel—hoping that, by magic, God would turn against his people. Neither Balaam nor Balak had any idea whom they were dealing with!

8“Spend the night here,” Balaam said to them, “and I will bring you back the answer
the LORD gives me.[g]” So the Moabite princes stayed with him.
9God came to Balaam[h] and asked,[i] “Who are these men with you?”
10Balaam said to God, “Balak son of Zippor, king of Moab, sent me this message:
11‘A people that has come out of Egypt covers the face of the land. Now come and
put a curse on them for me. Perhaps then I will be able to fight them and drive them
away.’ ”
12But God said to Balaam, “Do not go with them. You must not put a curse on those
people, because they are blessed.[j]”
13The next morning Balaam got up and said to Balak’s princes, “Go back to your
own country, for the LORD has refused to let me go with you.”
14So the Moabite princes returned to Balak and said, “Balaam refused to come with
us.”
15Then Balak sent other princes, more numerous and more distinguished than the
first. 16They came to Balaam and said:

> “This is what Balak son of Zippor says: Do not let anything keep you from
> coming to me, 17because I will reward you handsomely[k] and do whatever you
> say. Come and put a curse[l] on these people for me.”

18But Balaam answered them, “Even if Balak gave me his palace filled with silver
and gold, I could not do anything great or small to go beyond the command of the
LORD my God.[m] 19Now stay here tonight as the others did, and I will find out what
else the LORD will tell me.[n]”
20That night God came to Balaam[o] and said, “Since these men have come to
summon you, go with them, but do only what I tell you.”[p]

Balaam’s Donkey

21Balaam got up in the morning, saddled his donkey and went with the princes of
Moab. 22But God was very angry[q] when he went, and the angel of the LORD[r] stood
in the road to oppose him. Balaam was riding on his donkey, and his two servants
were with him. 23When the donkey saw the angel of the LORD standing in the road
with a drawn sword[s] in his hand, she turned off the road into a field. Balaam beat
her[t] to get her back on the road.
24Then the angel of the LORD stood in a narrow path between two vineyards, with
walls on both sides. 25When the donkey saw the angel of the LORD, she pressed close
to the wall, crushing Balaam’s foot against it. So he beat her again.
26Then the angel of the LORD moved on ahead and stood in a narrow place where
there was no room to turn, either to the right or to the left. 27When the donkey saw
the angel of the LORD, she lay down under Balaam, and he was angry[u] and beat her
with his staff. 28Then the LORD opened the donkey’s mouth,[v] and she said to Balaam,
“What have I done to you to make you beat me these three times?[w]”
29Balaam answered the donkey, “You have made a fool of me! If I had a sword
in my hand, I would kill you right now.[x]”

22:8 [g]ver 19
22:9 [h]Ge 20:3 [i]ver 20
22:12 [j]Ge 12:2; 22:17; Nu 23:20
22:17 [k]ver 37; Nu 24:11 [l]ver 6
22:18 [m]ver 38; Nu 23:12, 26; 24:13; 1Ki 22:14; 2Ch 18:13; Jer 42:4
22:19 [n]ver 8
22:20 [o]Ge 20:3 [p]ver 35, 38; Nu 23:5, 12, 16, 26; 24:13; 2Ch 18:13
22:22 [q]Ex 4:14 [r]Ge 16:7; Ex 23:20; Jdg 13:3, 6, 13
22:23 [s]Jos 5:13 [t]ver 25, 27
22:27 [u]Nu 11:1; Jas 1:19
22:28 [v]2Pe 2:16 [w]ver 32
22:29 [x]Dt 25:4; Pr 12:10; 27:23-27; Mt 15:19

22:9 Why would God speak through a sorcerer like Balaam? God wanted to give a message to the Moabites, and they had already chosen to employ Balaam. So Balaam was available for God to use, much as he used the wicked pharaoh to accomplish his will in Egypt (Exodus 10:1). Balaam entered into his prophetic role seriously, but his heart was mixed. He had some knowledge of God, but not enough to forsake his magic and turn wholeheartedly to God. Although this story leads us to believe he turned completely to God, later passages in the Bible show that Balaam couldn’t resist the tempting pull of money and idolatry (31:16; 2 Peter 2:15; Jude 11).

22:20–23 God let Balaam go with Balak’s messengers, but he was angry about Balaam’s greedy attitude. Balaam claimed that he would not go against God just for money, but his resolve was beginning to slip. His greed for the wealth offered by the king blinded him so that he could not see how God was trying to stop him. Though we may know what God wants us to do, we can become blinded by the desire for money, possessions, or prestige. We can avoid Balaam’s mistake by looking past the allure of fame or fortune to the long-range benefits of following God.

22:27 Donkeys were all-purpose vehicles used for transportation, carrying loads, grinding grain, and ploughing fields. They were usually highly dependable, which explains why Balaam became so angry when his donkey refused to move.

22:29 The donkey saved Balaam’s life but made him look foolish in the process, so Balaam lashed out at the donkey. We sometimes strike out at blameless people who get in our way because we are embarrassed or our pride is hurt. Lashing out at others can be a sign that something is wrong with us. Don’t allow your own hurt pride to lead you to hurt others.

30The donkey said to Balaam, "Am I not your own donkey, which you have always
ridden, to this day? Have I been in the habit of doing this to you?"
"No," he said.
31Then the LORD opened Balaam's eyes,[y] and he saw the angel of the LORD
standing in the road with his sword drawn. So he bowed low and fell face down.
32The angel of the LORD asked him, "Why have you beaten your donkey these three
times? I have come here to oppose you because your path is a reckless one before me.[c]
33The donkey saw me and turned away from me these three times. If she had not turned
away, I would certainly have killed you by now,[z] but I would have spared her."
34Balaam said to the angel of the LORD, "I have sinned.[a] I did not realise you were
standing in the road to oppose me. Now if you are displeased, I will go back."
35The angel of the LORD said to Balaam, "Go with the men, but speak only what
I tell you." So Balaam went with the princes of Balak.
36When Balak heard that Balaam was coming, he went out to meet him at the
Moabite town on the Arnon[b] border, at the edge of his territory. 37Balak said to
Balaam, "Did I not send you an urgent summons? Why didn't you come to me? Am I
really not able to reward you?"
38"Well, I have come to you now," Balaam replied. "But can I say just anything?
I must speak only what God puts in my mouth."[c]
39Then Balaam went with Balak to Kiriath Huzoth. 40Balak sacrificed cattle and
sheep,[d] and gave some to Balaam and the princes who were with him. 41The next
morning Balak took Balaam up to Bamoth Baal,[e] and from there he saw part of the
people.[f]

Balaam's First Oracle

23 Balaam said, "Build me seven altars here, and prepare seven bulls and seven
rams[a] for me." 2Balak did as Balaam said, and the two of them offered a bull
and a ram on each altar.[b]
3Then Balaam said to Balak, "Stay here beside your offering while I go aside.
Perhaps the LORD will come to meet with me.[c] Whatever he reveals to me I will tell
you." Then he went off to a barren height.
4God met with him,[d] and Balaam said, "I have prepared seven altars, and on each
altar I have offered a bull and a ram."
5The LORD put a message in Balaam's mouth[e] and said, "Go back to Balak and
give him this message."[f]
6So he went back to him and found him standing beside his offering, with all the
princes of Moab.[g] 7Then Balaam[h] uttered his oracle:[i]

"Balak brought me from Aram,
 the king of Moab from the eastern mountains.
'Come,' he said, 'curse Jacob for me;
 come, denounce Israel.'[j]
8How can I curse
 those whom God has not cursed?[k]
How can I denounce
 those whom the LORD has not denounced?
9From the rocky peaks I see them,
 from the heights I view them.
I see people who live apart
 and do not consider themselves one of the nations.[l]
10Who can count the dust of Jacob[m]

c 32 The meaning of the Hebrew for this clause is uncertain.

22:41 Bamoth Baal means the high places of Baal near Heshbon and Dibon. It was the first stopping point on the way to the high plains of Moab. From this vantage point, they could see the entire Israelite camp.

23:1–3 The number seven was sacred among many of the nations and religions at this time. A "barren height" means a place at a higher elevation on the mountain, without foliage.

22:31 [y]Ge 21:19
22:33 [z]ver 29
22:34 [a]Ge 39:9; Nu 14:40; 1Sa 15:24, 30; 2Sa 12:13; 24:10; Job 33:27; Ps 51:4
22:36 [b]Nu 21:13
22:38 [c]Nu 23:5, 16, 26
22:40 [d]Nu 23:1, 14, 29; Eze 45:23
22:41 [e]Nu 21:28 [f]Nu 23:13
23:1 [a]Nu 22:40
23:2 [b]ver 14, 30
23:3 [c]ver 15
23:4 [d]ver 16
23:5 [e]Dt 18:18; Jer 1:9 [f]Nu 22:20
23:6 [g]ver 17
23:7 [h]Nu 22:5 [i]ver 18; Nu 24:3, 21 [j]Nu 22:6; Dt 23:4
23:8 [k]Nu 22:12
23:9 [l]Ex 33:16; Dt 32:8; 33:28
23:10 [m]Ge 13:16

or number the fourth part of Israel?
Let me die the death of the righteous,[n]
and may my end be like theirs![o]"

11Balak said to Balaam, "What have you done to me? I brought you to curse my
enemies, but you have done nothing but bless them!"[p]
12He answered, "Must I not speak what the LORD puts in my mouth?"[q]

Balaam's Second Oracle

13Then Balak said to him, "Come with me to another place where you can see them;
you will see only a part but not all of them. And from there, curse them for me." 14So
he took him to the field of Zophim on the top of Pisgah, and there he built seven altars
and offered a bull and a ram on each altar.[r]
15Balaam said to Balak, "Stay here beside your offering while I meet with him over
there."
16The LORD met with Balaam and put a message in his mouth[s] and said, "Go back
to Balak and give him this message."
17So he went to him and found him standing beside his offering, with the princes
of Moab. Balak asked him, "What did the LORD say?"
18Then he uttered his oracle:

"Arise, Balak, and listen;
hear me, son of Zippor.
19God is not a man,[t] that he should lie,
nor a son of man, that he should change his mind.[u]
Does he speak and then not act?
Does he promise and not fulfil?
20I have received a command to bless;
he has blessed,[v] and I cannot change it.[w]

21"No misfortune is seen in Jacob,[x]
no misery observed in Israel.[a][y]
The LORD their God is with them;[z]
the shout of the King[a] is among them.
22God brought them out of Egypt;[b]
they have the strength of a wild ox.[c]
23There is no sorcery against Jacob,
no divination[d] against Israel.
It will now be said of Jacob
and of Israel, 'See what God has done!'
24The people rise like a lioness;[e]
they rouse themselves like a lion[f]
that does not rest till he devours his prey
and drinks the blood of his victims."

25Then Balak said to Balaam, "Neither curse them at all nor bless them at all!"
26Balaam answered, "Did I not tell you I must do whatever the LORD says?"

Balaam's Third Oracle

27Then Balak said to Balaam, "Come, let me take you to another place.[g] Perhaps
it will please God to let you curse them for me from there." 28And Balak took Balaam
to the top of Peor,[h] overlooking the wasteland.

a 21 *Or He has not looked on Jacob's offences / or on the wrongs found in Israel.*

23:10 [n]Ps 116:15; Isa 57:1 [o]Ps 37:37
23:11 [p]Nu 24:10; Ne 13:2
23:12 [q]Nu 22:20, 38
23:14 [r]ver 2
23:16 [s]Nu 22:38
23:19 [t]Isa 55:9; Hos 11:9 [u]1Sa 15:29; Mal 3:6; Tit 1:2; Jas 1:17
23:20 [v]Ge 22:17; Nu 22:12 [w]Isa 43:13
23:21 [x]Ps 32:2, 5; Ro 4:7-8 [y]Isa 40:2; Jer 50:20 [z]Ex 29:45, 46; Ps 145:18 [a]Dt 33:5; Ps 89:15-18
23:22 [b]Nu 24:8 [c]Dt 33:17; Job 39:9
23:23 [d]Nu 24:1; Jos 13:22
23:24 [e]Na 2:11 [f]Ge 49:9
23:27 [g]ver 13
23:28 [h]Ps 106:28

23:27 Balak took Balaam to several places to try to entice him to curse the Israelites. He thought a change of scenery might help change Balaam's mind. But changing locations won't change God's will. We must learn to face the source of our problems. Moving to escape problems only makes solving them more difficult. Problems rooted in us are not solved by a change of scenery. A change in location or job may only distract us from the need for us to change our heart.

29 Balaam said, "Build me seven altars here, and prepare seven bulls and seven rams
for me." 30 Balak did as Balaam had said, and offered a bull and a ram on each
altar.

24 Now when Balaam saw that it pleased the LORD to bless Israel, he did not resort
to sorcery[a] as at other times, but turned his face towards the desert.[b] 2 When
Balaam looked out and saw Israel encamped tribe by tribe, the Spirit of God came
upon him[c] 3 and he uttered his oracle:

"The oracle of Balaam son of Beor,
the oracle of one whose eye sees clearly,
4 the oracle of one who hears the words of God,[d]
who sees a vision from the Almighty,[a][e]
who falls prostrate, and whose eyes are opened:

5 "How beautiful are your tents, O Jacob,
your dwelling-places, O Israel!

6 "Like valleys they spread out,
like gardens beside a river,
like aloes[f] planted by the LORD,
like cedars beside the waters.[g]
7 Water will flow from their buckets;
their seed will have abundant water.

"Their king will be greater than Agag;[h]
their kingdom will be exalted.[i]

8 "God brought them out of Egypt;
they have the strength of a wild ox.
They devour hostile nations
and break their bones in pieces;[j]
with their arrows they pierce them.[k]
9 Like a lion they crouch and lie down,
like a lioness[l]—who dares to rouse them?

"May those who bless you be blessed
and those who curse you be cursed!"[m]

10 Then Balak's anger burned against Balaam. He struck his hands together[n] and
said to him, "I summoned you to curse my enemies, but you have blessed them[o] these
three times.[p] 11 Now leave at once and go home! I said I would reward you hand-
somely,[q] but the LORD has kept you from being rewarded."

12 Balaam answered Balak, "Did I not tell the messengers you sent me,[r] 13 'Even
if Balak gave me his palace filled with silver and gold, I could not do anything
of my own accord, good or bad, to go beyond the command of the LORD[s]—and I
must say only what the LORD says'?[t] 14 Now I am going back to my people, but
come, let me warn you of what this people will do to your people in days to
come."[u]

[a] 4 Hebrew *Shaddai*; also in verse 16

24:1 [a]Nu 23:23 [b]Nu 23:28
24:2 [c]Nu 11:25, 26; 1Sa 10:10; 19:20; 2Ch 15:1
24:4 [d]Nu 22:20 [e]Ge 15:1
24:6 [f]Ps 45:8 [g]Ps 1:3; 104:16
24:7 [h]1Sa 15:8 [i]2Sa 5:12; 1Ch 14:2; Ps 145:11-13
24:8 [j]Ps 2:9; Jer 50:17 [k]Ps 45:5
24:9 [l]Ge 49:9; Nu 23:24 [m]Ge 12:3
24:10 [n]Eze 21:14 [o]Nu 23:11 [p]Ne 13:2
24:11 [q]Nu 22:17
24:12 [r]Nu 22:18
24:13 [s]Nu 22:18 [t]Nu 22:20
24:14 [u]Ge 49:1; Nu 31:8, 16; Da 2:28; Mic 6:5

24:1 Because Balaam was a sorcerer, he would look for omens or signs to help him tell the future. In this situation, however, it was clear that God himself was speaking, and so Balaam needed no other signs, real or imagined.

24:7 Who was Agag? *Agag* was the title for the king of the Amalekites, just as *Pharaoh* was the ruler of Egypt. Saul, the first king of Israel, defeated Agag (1 Samuel 15:8). Balaam has prophesied correctly the ruin of Israel's oldest enemy (Exodus 17:14–16).

24:11 Although Balaam's motives were not correct, in blessing Israel he acted with integrity. God's message had so filled him that Balaam spoke the truth. In so doing, he forfeited the reward that had lured him to speak in the first place. Staying true to God's word may cost us promotions and advantages in the short run, but those who choose God over money will one day acquire heavenly wealth beyond measure (Matthew 6:19–21).

Balaam's Fourth Oracle

15Then he uttered his oracle:

"The oracle of Balaam son of Beor,
the oracle of one whose eye sees clearly,
16the oracle of one who hears the words of God,
who has knowledge from the Most High,
who sees a vision from the Almighty,
who falls prostrate, and whose eyes are opened:

17"I see him, but not now;
I behold him, but not near.[v]
A star will come out of Jacob;[w]
a sceptre will rise out of Israel.[x]
He will crush the foreheads of Moab,[y]
the skulls[b] of[c] all the sons of Sheth.[d]
18Edom[z] will be conquered;
Seir, his enemy, will be conquered,
but Israel will grow strong.
19A ruler will come out of Jacob[a]
and destroy the survivors of the city."

Balaam's Final Oracles

20Then Balaam saw Amalek[b] and uttered his oracle:

"Amalek was first among the nations,
but he will come to ruin at last."

21Then he saw the Kenites[c] and uttered his oracle:

"Your dwelling-place is secure,
your nest is set in a rock;
22yet you Kenites will be destroyed
when Asshur[d] takes you captive."

23Then he uttered his oracle:

"Ah, who can live when God does this?[e]
24 Ships will come from the shores of Kittim;[e]
they will subdue Asshur and Eber,[f]
but they too will come to ruin.[g]"

25Then Balaam[h] got up and returned home and Balak went his own way.

Moab Seduces Israel

25 While Israel was staying in Shittim,[a] the men began to indulge in sexual
immorality[b] with Moabite women,[c] 2who invited them to the sacrifices[d] to
their gods.[e] The people ate and bowed down before these gods. 3So Israel joined in
worshipping the Baal of Peor.[f] And the LORD's anger burned against them.

b *17* Samaritan Pentateuch (see also Jer. 48:45); the meaning of the word in the Masoretic Text is uncertain.
c *17* Or possibly *Moab, / batter* **d** *17* Or *all the noisy boasters* **e** *23* Masoretic Text; with a different word division of the Hebrew *A people will gather from the north.*

24:17 [v]Rev 1:7 [w]Mt 2:2 [x]Ge 49:10 [y]Nu 21:29; Isa 15:1-16:14
24:18 [z]Am 9:12
24:19 [a]Ge 49:10; Mic 5:2
24:20 [b]Ex 17:14
24:21 [c]Ge 15:19
24:22 [d]Ge 10:22
24:24 [e]Ge 10:4 [f]Ge 10:21 [g]ver 20
24:25 [h]Nu 31:8
25:1 [a]Jos 2:1; Mic 6:5 [b]1Co 10:8; Rev 2:14 [c]Nu 31:16
25:2 [d]Ex 34:15 [e]Ex 20:5; Dt 32:38; 1Co 10:20
25:3 [f]Ps 106:28; Hos 9:10

24:15–19 The star out of Jacob is often thought to refer to the coming Messiah. It was probably this prophecy that convinced the Magi to travel to Israel to search for the baby Jesus (see Matthew 2:1, 2). It seems strange that God would use a sorcerer like Balaam to foretell the coming of the Messiah. But this teaches us that God can use anything or anyone to accomplish his plans. By using a sorcerer, God did not make sorcery acceptable; in fact, the Bible condemns it in several places (Exodus 22:18; 2 Chronicles 33:6; Revelation 18:23). Rather, God showed his ultimate sovereignty over good and evil.

25:1 This verse shows the great challenge Israel had to face. The most dangerous problem for Moses and Joshua was not Jericho's hostile army, but the ever-present temptation to compromise with the pagan Canaanite religions and cultures.

25:1, 2 The Bible doesn't say how the Israelite men got involved in sexual immorality. We do know that sacred prostitution was a common practice among Canaanite religions. At first, they didn't think about worshipping idols; they were just interested in sex. Before long they started attending local feasts and family celebrations that involved idol worship. Soon they were in over their heads, ab-

25:4 [g]Dt 4:3 [h]Dt 13:17
25:5 [i]Ex 32:27
25:8 [j]Nu 16:46-48; Ps 106:30
25:9 [k]Nu 14:37; 1Co 10:8 [l]Nu 31:16
25:11 [m]Ps 106:30 [n]Ex 20:5; Dt 32:16, 21; Ps 78:58
25:12 [o]Isa 54:10; Eze 34:25; Mal 2:4, 5
25:13 [p]Ex 29:9 [q]Nu 16:46
25:15 [r]ver 18 [s]Nu 31:8; Jos 13:21
25:17 [t]Nu 31:1-3
25:18 [u]Nu 31:16
26:2 [a]Ex 30:11-16; 38:25-26; Nu 1:2 [b]Nu 1:3
26:3 [c]Nu 33:48 [d]Nu 22:1
26:5 [e]Ge 46:9 [f]1Ch 5:3

4The LORD said to Moses, "Take all the leaders of these people, kill them and
expose them in broad daylight before the LORD,[g] so that the LORD's fierce anger[h]
may turn away from Israel."
5So Moses said to Israel's judges, "Each of you must put to death[i] those of your
men who have joined in worshipping the Baal of Peor."
6Then an Israelite man brought to his family a Midianite woman right before the
eyes of Moses and the whole assembly of Israel while they were weeping at the
entrance to the Tent of Meeting. 7When Phinehas son of Eleazar, the son of Aaron,
the priest, saw this, he left the assembly, took a spear in his hand 8and followed the
Israelite into the tent. He drove the spear through both of them — through the Israelite
and into the woman's body. Then the plague against the Israelites was stopped;[j] 9but
those who died in the plague[k] numbered 24,000.[l]
10The LORD said to Moses, 11"Phinehas son of Eleazar, the son of Aaron, the priest,
has turned my anger away from the Israelites;[m] for he was as zealous as I am for my
honour[n] among them, so that in my zeal I did not put an end to them. 12Therefore
tell him I am making my covenant of peace[o] with him. 13He and his descendants will
have a covenant of a lasting priesthood,[p] because he was zealous for the honour of
his God and made atonement[q] for the Israelites."
14The name of the Israelite who was killed with the Midianite woman was Zimri
son of Salu, the leader of a Simeonite family. 15And the name of the Midianite woman
who was put to death was Cozbi[r] daughter of Zur, a tribal chief of a Midianite
family.[s]
16The LORD said to Moses, 17"Treat the Midianites[t] as enemies and kill them,
18because they treated you as enemies when they deceived you in the affair of Peor[u]
and their sister Cozbi, the daughter of a Midianite leader, the woman who was killed
when the plague came as a result of Peor."

2. The second census of the nation

26 After the plague the LORD said to Moses and Eleazar son of Aaron, the priest,
2"Take a census[a] of the whole Israelite community by families — all those
twenty years old or more who are able to serve in the army[b] of Israel." 3So on the
plains of Moab[c] by the Jordan across from Jericho,[a][d] Moses and Eleazar the priest
spoke with them and said, 4"Take a census of men twenty years old or more, as the
LORD commanded Moses."

These were the Israelites who came out of Egypt:

5The descendants of Reuben, the firstborn son of Israel, were:
through Hanoch,[e] the Hanochite clan;
through Pallu,[f] the Palluite clan;

[a] 3 Hebrew *Jordan of Jericho*; possibly an ancient name for the Jordan River; also in verse 63

sorbed into the practices of the pagan culture. Their desire for fun and pleasure caused them to loosen their spiritual commitment. Have you relaxed your standards in order to justify your desires?

25:1–3 This combination of sexual sin and idolatry, it turns out, was Balaam's idea (see 31:16; Revelation 2:14), the same Balaam who had just blessed Israel and who appeared to be on their side. It is easy to see how the Israelites were misled, for Balaam seemed to say and do all the right things — at least for a while (22 – 24). Not until Balaam had inflicted great damage on them did the Israelites realise that he was greedy, used sorcery, and was deeply involved in pagan religious practices. We must be careful to weigh both the words and the deeds of those who claim to offer spiritual help.

25:3 Baal was the most popular god in Canaan, the land Israel was about to enter. Represented by a bull, symbol of strength and fertility, he was the god of the rains and harvest. The Israelites were continually attracted to Baal worship, in which prostitution played a large part, throughout their years in Canaan. Because Baal was so popular, his name was often used as a generic title for all the local gods.

25:6 The phrase "brought to his family" referred to the person's inner room of his tent. Clearly the woman was brought into his tent for sex. Zimri so disregarded the law of God that he brought that woman right into the camp.

25:10, 11 It is clear from Phinehas's story that some anger is proper and justified. Phinehas was angry because of his zeal for the Lord. But how can we know when our anger is appropriate and when it should be restrained? Ask these questions when you become angry: (1) Why am I angry? (2) Whose rights are being violated (mine or another's)? (3) Is the truth (a principle of God) being violated? If only your rights are at stake, it may be wiser to keep angry feelings under control. But if the truth is at stake, anger is often justified, although violence and retaliation are usually the wrong way to express it (Phinehas's case was unique). If we are becoming more and more like God, we should be angered by sin.

25:12, 13 Phinehas's act made atonement for the nation of Israel; in effect, what he did averted God's judgment. Because of this, his descendants would become the high priests of Israel. They continued so throughout the history of the tabernacle and the temple.

6 through Hezron, the Hezronite clan;
through Carmi, the Carmite clan.
7 These were the clans of Reuben; those numbered were 43,730.
8 The son of Pallu was Eliab, 9 and the sons of Eliab[g] were Nemuel, Dathan and
Abiram. The same Dathan and Abiram were the community[h] officials who rebelled
against Moses and Aaron and were among Korah's followers when they rebelled
against the LORD.[i] 10 The earth opened its mouth and swallowed them along with
Korah, whose followers died when the fire devoured the 250 men. And they served
as a warning sign.[j] 11 The line of Korah,[k] however, did not die out.[l]

12 The descendants of Simeon by their clans were:
through Nemuel, the Nemuelite clan;
through Jamin,[m] the Jaminite clan;
through Jakin, the Jakinite clan;
13 through Zerah,[n] the Zerahite clan;
through Shaul, the Shaulite clan.
14 These were the clans of Simeon; there were 22,200 men.[o]

15 The descendants of Gad by their clans were:
through Zephon,[p] the Zephonite clan;
through Haggi, the Haggite clan;
through Shuni, the Shunite clan;
16 through Ozni, the Oznite clan;
through Eri, the Erite clan;
17 through Arodi,**b** the Arodite clan;
through Areli, the Arelite clan.
18 These were the clans of Gad;[q] those numbered were 40,500.

19 Er and Onan were sons of Judah, but they died[r] in Canaan.
20 The descendants of Judah by their clans were:
through Shelah,[s] the Shelanite clan;
through Perez, the Perezite clan;
through Zerah, the Zerahite clan.[t]
21 The descendants of Perez were:
through Hezron,[u] the Hezronite clan;
through Hamul, the Hamulite clan.
22 These were the clans of Judah;[v] those numbered were 76,500.

23 The descendants of Issachar by their clans were:
through Tola,[w] the Tolaite clan;
through Puah, the Puite**c** clan;
24 through Jashub,[x] the Jashubite clan;
through Shimron, the Shimronite clan.
25 These were the clans of Issachar;[y] those numbered were 64,300.

26 The descendants of Zebulun by their clans were:
through Sered, the Seredite clan;
through Elon, the Elonite clan;
through Jahleel, the Jahleelite clan.
27 These were the clans of Zebulun;[z] those numbered were 60,500.

28 The descendants of Joseph by their clans through Manasseh and Ephraim were:

29 The descendants of Manasseh:
through Makir,[a] the Makirite clan (Makir was the father of Gilead[b]);
through Gilead, the Gileadite clan.
30 These were the descendants of Gilead:
through Iezer,[c] the Iezerite clan;
through Helek, the Helekite clan;

b *17* Samaritan Pentateuch and Syriac (see also Gen. 46:16); Masoretic Text *Arod* **c** *23* Samaritan Pentateuch, Septuagint, Vulgate and Syriac (see also 1 Chron. 7:1); Masoretic Text *through Puvah, the Punite*

26:9 [g]Nu 16:1 [h]Nu 1:16 [i]Nu 16:2
26:10 [j]Nu 16:35, 38
26:11 [k]Ex 6:24 [l]Nu 16:33; Dt 24:16
26:12 [m]1Ch 4:24
26:13 [n]Ge 46:10
26:14 [o]Nu 1:23
26:15 [p]Ge 46:16
26:18 [q]Nu 1:25; Jos 13:24-28
26:19 [r]Ge 38:2-10; 46:12
26:20 [s]1Ch 2:3 [t]Jos 7:17
26:21 [u]Ru 4:19; 1Ch 2:9
26:22 [v]Nu 1:27
26:23 [w]Ge 46:13; 1Ch 7:1
26:24 [x]Ge 46:13
26:25 [y]Nu 1:29
26:27 [z]Nu 1:31
26:29 [a]Jos 17:1 [b]Jdg 11:1
26:30 [c]Jos 17:2; Jdg 6:11

31 through Asriel, the Asrielite clan;
through Shechem, the Shechemite clan;
32 through Shemida, the Shemidaite clan;
through Hepher, the Hepherite clan.
33 (Zelophehad[d] son of Hepher had no sons; he had only daughters, whose names were Mahlah, Noah, Hoglah, Milcah and Tirzah.)[e]
34 These were the clans of Manasseh; those numbered were 52,700.[f]

35 These were the descendants of Ephraim by their clans:
through Shuthelah, the Shuthelahite clan;
through Beker, the Bekerite clan;
through Tahan, the Tahanite clan.
36 These were the descendants of Shuthelah:
through Eran, the Eranite clan.
37 These were the clans of Ephraim;[g] those numbered were 32,500.

These were the descendants of Joseph by their clans.

38 The descendants of Benjamin[h] by their clans were:
through Bela, the Belaite clan;
through Ashbel, the Ashbelite clan;
through Ahiram, the Ahiramite clan;
39 through Shupham,**d** the Shuphamite clan;
through Hupham, the Huphamite clan.
40 The descendants of Bela through Ard[i] and Naaman were:
through Ard,**e** the Ardite clan;
through Naaman, the Naamite clan.
41 These were the clans of Benjamin;[j] those numbered were 45,600.

42 These were the descendants of Dan by their clans:
through Shuham,[k] the Shuhamite clan.
These were the clans of Dan:
43 All of them were Shuhamite clans; and those numbered were 64,400.

44 The descendants of Asher by their clans were:
through Imnah, the Imnite clan;
through Ishvi, the Ishvite clan;
through Beriah, the Beriite clan;
45 and through the descendants of Beriah:
through Heber, the Heberite clan;
through Malkiel, the Malkielite clan.
46 (Asher had a daughter named Serah.)
47 These were the clans of Asher;[l] those numbered were 53,400.

48 The descendants of Naphtali[m] by their clans were:
through Jahzeel, the Jahzeelite clan;
through Guni, the Gunite clan;
49 through Jezer, the Jezerite clan;
through Shillem, the Shillemite clan.
50 These were the clans of Naphtali;[n] those numbered were 45,400.

51 The total number of the men of Israel was 601,730.[o]

52 The LORD said to Moses,
53 "The land is to be allotted to them as an inheritance based on the number of names.[p]
54 To a larger group give a larger inheritance, and to a smaller group a smaller one; each is to receive its inheritance according to the number[q] of those listed.
55 Be sure that the land is distributed by lot.[r] What each

26:33 [d] Nu 27:1 [e] Nu 36:11
26:34 [f] Nu 1:35
26:37 [g] Nu 1:33
26:38 [h] Ge 46:21; 1Ch 7:6
26:40 [i] Ge 46:21; 1Ch 8:3
26:41 [j] Nu 1:37
26:42 [k] Ge 46:23
26:47 [l] Nu 1:41
26:48 [m] Ge 46:24; 1Ch 7:13
26:50 [n] Nu 1:43
26:51 [o] Ex 12:37; 38:26; Nu 1:46; 11:21
26:53 [p] Jos 11:23; 14:1; Eze 45:8
26:54 [q] Nu 33:54
26:55 [r] Nu 34:14

d *39* A few manuscripts of the Masoretic Text, Samaritan Pentateuch, Vulgate and Syriac (see also Septuagint); most manuscripts of the Masoretic Text *Shephupham* **e** *40* Samaritan Pentateuch and Vulgate (see also Septuagint); Masoretic Text does not have *through Ard,*

group inherits will be according to the names for its ancestral tribe. 56 Each inheritance
is to be distributed by lot among the larger and smaller groups."

57 These were the Levites[s] who were counted by their clans:
through Gershon, the Gershonite clan;
through Kohath, the Kohathite clan;
through Merari, the Merarite clan.
58 These also were Levite clans:
the Libnite clan,
the Hebronite clan,
the Mahlite clan,
the Mushite clan,
the Korahite clan.
(Kohath was the forefather of Amram;[t] 59 the name of Amram's wife was
Jochebed,[u] a descendant of Levi, who was born to the Levites[f] in Egypt. To
Amram she bore Aaron, Moses[v] and their sister Miriam. 60 Aaron was the father
of Nadab and Abihu, Eleazar and Ithamar.[w] 61 But Nadab and Abihu[x] died when
they made an offering before the LORD with unauthorised fire.)[y]

62 All the male Levites a month old or more numbered 23,000.[z] They were not
counted[a] along with the other Israelites because they received no inheritance[b] among
them.[c]

63 These are the ones counted by Moses and Eleazar the priest when they counted
the Israelites on the plains of Moab[d] by the Jordan across from Jericho. 64 Not one
of them was among those counted[e] by Moses and Aaron the priest when they counted
the Israelites in the Desert of Sinai. 65 For the LORD had told those Israelites they would
surely die in the desert,[f] and not one of them was left except Caleb son of Jephunneh
and Joshua son of Nun.[g]

Zelophehad's Daughters

27 The daughters of Zelophehad[a] son of Hepher,[b] the son of Gilead, the son of
Makir,[c] the son of Manasseh, belonged to the clans of Manasseh son of
Joseph. The names of the daughters were Mahlah, Noah, Hoglah, Milcah and Tirzah.
They approached 2 the entrance to the Tent of Meeting and stood before Moses, Eleazar
the priest, the leaders and the whole assembly, and said, 3 "Our father died in the
desert.[d] He was not among Korah's followers, who banded together against the
LORD,[e] but he died for his own sin and left no sons.[f] 4 Why should our father's name
disappear from his clan because he had no son? Give us property among our father's
relatives."

5 So Moses brought their case[g] before the LORD[h] 6 and the LORD said to him,
7 "What Zelophehad's daughters are saying is right. You must certainly give them
property as an inheritance[i] among their father's relatives and give their father's
inheritance over to them.[j]

8 "Say to the Israelites, 'If a man dies and leaves no son, give his inheritance over
to his daughter. 9 If he has no daughter, give his inheritance to his brothers. 10 If he

f 59 *Or Jochebed, a daughter of Levi, who was born to Levi*

26:57 [s]Ge 46:11; Ex 6:16-19
26:58 [t]Ex 6:20
26:59 [u]Ex 2:1 [v]Ex 6:20
26:60 [w]Nu 3:2
26:61 [x]Lev 10:1-2 [y]Nu 3:4
26:62 [z]Nu 3:39 [a]Nu 1:47 [b]Nu 18:23 [c]Nu 2:33; Dt 10:9
26:63 [d]ver 3
26:64 [e]Nu 14:29; Dt 2:14-15; Heb 3:17
26:65 [f]Nu 14:28; 1Co 10:5 [g]Jos 14:6-10
27:1 [a]Nu 26:33 [b]Jos 17:2, 3 [c]Nu 36:1
27:3 [d]Nu 26:65 [e]Nu 16:2 [f]Nu 26:33
27:5 [g]Ex 18:19 [h]Nu 9:8
27:7 [i]Job 42:15 [j]Jos 17:4

26:64 A new census for a new generation. Thirty-eight years had elapsed since the first great census recorded in Numbers (see 1:1–2:33). During that time, every Israelite man and woman over 20 years of age – except Caleb, Joshua, and Moses – had died, and yet God's laws and the spiritual character of the nation were still intact. Numbers records some dramatic miracles. This is a quiet but powerful miracle often overlooked: A whole nation moved from one land to another, lost its entire adult population, yet managed to maintain its spiritual direction. Sometimes it may feel like God isn't working dramatic miracles in our lives. But God often works in quiet ways to bring about his long-range purposes.

27:3 "Died for his own sin" means that he died a natural death. His death fell under the judgment of the entire nation for believing the faithless spies.

27:3, 4 Up to this point, the Hebrew law gave sons alone the right to inherit. The daughters of Zelophehad, having no brothers, came to Moses to ask for their father's possessions. God told Moses that if a man died without sons, his inheritance would go to his daughters (27:8). But the daughters could keep it only if they married within their own tribe, probably so the territorial lines would remain intact (36:5–12).

27:11 [k]Nu 35:29
27:12 [l]Nu 33:47; Jer 22:20 [m]Dt 3:23-27; 32:48-52
27:13 [n]Nu 31:2 [o]Nu 20:28
27:14 [p]Nu 20:12 [q]Ex 17:7; Dt 32:51; Ps 106:32
27:16 [r]Nu 16:22
27:17 [s]Dt 31:2; 1Ki 22:17; Eze 34:5; Zec 10:2; Mt 9:36; Mk 6:34
27:18 [t]Ge 41:38; Nu 11:25-29 [u]ver 23; Dt 34:9
27:19 [v]Dt 3:28; 31:14, 23 [w]Dt 31:7
27:20 [x]Jos 1:16, 17
27:21 [y]Jos 9:14 [z]Ex 28:30
28:2 [a]Lev 3:11
28:3 [b]Ex 29:38
28:5 [c]Lev 2:1; Nu 15:4
28:6 [d]Ex 19:3
28:7 [e]Ex 29:41 [f]Lev 3:7
28:8 [g]Lev 1:9

has no brothers, give his inheritance to his father's brothers. 11If his father had no
brothers, give his inheritance to the nearest relative in his clan, that he may possess
it. This is to be a legal requirement[k] for the Israelites, as the LORD commanded
Moses.' "

Joshua to Succeed Moses

12Then the LORD said to Moses, "Go up this mountain in the Abarim Range[l] and
see the land[m] I have given the Israelites. 13After you have seen it, you too will be
gathered to your people,[n] as your brother Aaron[o] was, 14for when the community
rebelled at the waters in the Desert of Zin, both of you disobeyed my command to
honour me as holy[p] before their eyes." (These were the waters of Meribah[q] Kadesh,
in the Desert of Zin.)

15Moses said to the LORD, 16"May the LORD, the God of the spirits of all mankind,[r]
appoint a man over this community 17to go out and come in before them, one who
will lead them out and bring them in, so that the LORD's people will not be like sheep
without a shepherd."[s]

18So the LORD said to Moses, "Take Joshua son of Nun, a man in whom is the
spirit,[a][t] and lay your hand on him.[u] 19Make him stand before Eleazar the priest
and the entire assembly and commission him[v] in their presence.[w] 20Give him some
of your authority so that the whole Israelite community will obey him.[x] 21He is to
stand before Eleazar the priest, who will obtain decisions for him by enquiring[y] of
the Urim[z] before the LORD. At his command he and the entire community of the
Israelites will go out, and at his command they will come in."

22Moses did as the LORD commanded him. He took Joshua and made him stand
before Eleazar the priest and the whole assembly. 23Then he laid his hands on him
and commissioned him, as the LORD instructed through Moses.

3. Instructions concerning offerings

Daily Offerings

28 The LORD said to Moses, 2"Give this command to the Israelites and say to them:
'See that you present to me at the appointed time the food[a] for my offerings
made by fire, as an aroma pleasing to me.' 3Say to them: 'This is the offering made
by fire that you are to present to the LORD: two lambs a year old without defect, as
a regular burnt offering each day.[b] 4Prepare one lamb in the morning and the other
at twilight, 5together with a grain offering of a tenth of an ephah[a] of fine flour mixed
with a quarter of a hin[b] of oil[c] from pressed olives. 6This is the regular burnt offering
instituted at Mount Sinai[d] as a pleasing aroma, an offering made to the LORD by fire.
7The accompanying drink offering[e] is to be a quarter of a hin of fermented drink with
each lamb. Pour out the drink offering to the LORD at the sanctuary.[f] 8Prepare the
second lamb at twilight, along with the same kind of grain offering and drink offering
that you prepare in the morning. This is an offering made by fire, an aroma pleasing
to the LORD.[g]

a *18* Or *Spirit* a *5* That is, probably about 4 pints (about 2 litres); also in verses 13, 21 and 29 b *5* That is, probably about 1½ pints (about 1 litre); also in verses 7 and 14

27:15–17 Moses asked God to appoint a leader who was capable of directing both external and internal affairs – one who could lead them in battle, but who would also care for their needs. The Lord responded by appointing Joshua. Many people want to be known as leaders. Some are very capable of reaching their goals, while others care deeply for the people in their charge. The best leaders are both goal-oriented and people-oriented.

27:15–21 Moses did not want to leave his work without making sure a new leader was ready to replace him. First he asked God to help him find a replacement. Then, when Joshua was selected, Moses gave him a variety of tasks to ease the transition into his new position. Moses also clearly told the people that Joshua had the authority and the ability to lead the nation. His display of confidence in Joshua was good for both Joshua and the people. To minimise leadership gaps, anyone in a leadership position should train others to carry on the duties should he or she suddenly or eventually have to leave. While you have the opportunity, follow Moses' pattern: pray, select, develop, and commission.

28:1, 2 Offerings had to be brought regularly and presented according to prescribed rituals under the priests' supervision. Following these rituals took time, and this gave the people the opportunity to prepare their hearts for worship. Unless our hearts are ready, worship is meaningless. By contrast, God is delighted, and we get more from it, when our hearts are prepared to come before him in a spirit of thankfulness.

Sabbath Offerings

9" 'On the Sabbath[h] day, make an offering of two lambs a year old without defect,
together with its drink offering and a grain offering of two-tenths of an ephah[c][i] of
fine flour mixed with oil. 10This is the burnt offering for every Sabbath, in addition
to the regular burnt offering[j] and its drink offering.

Monthly Offerings

11" 'On the first of every month,[k] present to the LORD a burnt offering of two young
bulls, one ram and seven male lambs a year old, all without defect.[l] 12With each
bull there is to be a grain offering[m] of three-tenths of an ephah[d][n] of fine flour mixed
with oil; with the ram, a grain offering of two-tenths of an ephah of fine flour mixed
with oil; 13and with each lamb, a grain offering[o] of a tenth of an ephah of fine flour
mixed with oil. This is for a burnt offering, a pleasing aroma, an offering made to
the LORD by fire. 14With each bull there is to be a drink offering[p] of half a hin[e] of
wine; with the ram, a third of a hin;[f] and with each lamb, a quarter of a hin. This
is the monthly burnt offering to be made at each new moon[q] during the year.
15Besides the regular burnt offering[r] with its drink offering, one male goat is to be
presented to the LORD as a sin offering.[s]

The Passover

16" 'On the fourteenth day of the first month the LORD's Passover[t] is to be held.
17On the fifteenth day of this month there is to be a festival; for seven days[u] eat bread
made without yeast.[v] 18On the first day hold a sacred assembly and do no regular
work.[w] 19Present to the LORD an offering made by fire, a burnt offering of two young
bulls, one ram and seven male lambs a year old, all without defect. 20With each bull
prepare a grain offering of three-tenths of an ephah[x] of fine flour mixed with oil; with
the ram, two-tenths; 21and with each of the seven lambs, one-tenth. 22Include one male
goat as a sin offering[y] to make atonement for you.[z] 23Prepare these in addition to
the regular morning burnt offering. 24In this way prepare the food for the offering
made by fire every day for seven days as an aroma pleasing to the LORD; it is to be
prepared in addition to the regular burnt offering and its drink offering. 25On the
seventh day hold a sacred assembly and do no regular work.

Feast of Weeks

26" 'On the day of firstfruits,[a] when you present to the LORD an offering of new
grain during the Feast of Weeks,[b] hold a sacred assembly and do no regular work.[c]
27Present a burnt offering of two young bulls, one ram and seven male lambs a year
old as an aroma pleasing to the LORD. 28With each bull there is to be a grain offering
of three-tenths of an ephah of fine flour mixed with oil; with the ram, two-tenths; 29and
with each of the seven lambs, one-tenth.[d] 30Include one male goat to make atonement
for you. 31Prepare these together with their drink offerings, in addition to the regular
burnt offering[e] and its grain offering. Be sure the animals are without defect.

Feast of Trumpets

29 " 'On the first day of the seventh month hold a sacred assembly and do no
regular work.[a] It is a day for you to sound the trumpets. 2As an aroma pleasing
to the LORD,[b] prepare a burnt offering of one young bull, one ram and seven male

28:9 [h]Ex 20:10 [i]Lev 23:13
28:10 [j]ver 3
28:11 [k]Nu 10:10 [l]Lev 1:3
28:12 [m]Nu 15:6 [n]Nu 15:9
28:13 [o]Lev 6:14
28:14 [p]Nu 15:7 [q]Ezr 3:5
28:15 [r]ver 3, 23, 24 [s]Lev 4:3
28:16 [t]Ex 12:6, 18; Lev 23:5; Dt 16:1
28:17 [u]Ex 12:19 [v]Ex 23:15; 34:18; Lev 23:6; Dt 16:3-8
28:18 [w]Ex 12:16; Lev 23:7
28:20 [x]Lev 14:10
28:22 [y]Ro 8:3 [z]Nu 15:28
28:26 [a]Ex 34:22 [b]Ex 23:16 [c]ver 18; Dt 16:10
28:29 [d]ver 13
28:31 [e]ver 3, 19
29:1 [a]Lev 23:24
29:2 [b]Nu 28:2

c *9* That is, probably about 7½ pints (about 4.5 litres); also in verses 12, 20 and 28 **d** *12* That is, probably about 11½ pints (about 6.5 litres); also in verses 20 and 28 **e** *14* That is, probably about 3 pints (about 2 litres)
f *14* That is, probably about 2¼ pints (about 1.2 litres)

28:9, 10 Why were extra offerings made on the Sabbath day? The Sabbath was a special day of rest and worship commemorating both creation (Exodus 20:8–11) and the deliverance from Egypt (Deuteronomy 5:12–15). Because of the significance of this special day, it was only natural to offer extra sacrifices on it.

29:1ff God placed many holidays on Israel's calendar. The Feast of Trumpets was one of three great holidays celebrated in the seventh month (the Feast of Tabernacles and Day of Atonement were the other two). These holidays provided a time to refresh the mind and body and to renew one's commitment to God. If you feel tired or far from God, try taking a "spiritual holiday". Separate yourself from your daily routine and concentrate on renewing your commitment to God.

29:1, 2 The Feast of Trumpets demonstrated three important

lambs a year old, all without defect.[c] 3With the bull prepare a grain offering of
three-tenths of an ephah[a] of fine flour mixed with oil; with the ram, two-tenths;[b]
4and with each of the seven lambs, one-tenth.[c] 5Include one male goat[d] as a sin
offering to make atonement for you. 6These are in addition to the monthly[e] and daily
burnt offerings[f] with their grain offerings and drink offerings as specified. They are
offerings made to the LORD by fire — a pleasing aroma.

Day of Atonement

7" 'On the tenth day of this seventh month hold a sacred assembly. You must deny
yourselves[d][g] and do no work.[h] 8Present as an aroma pleasing to the LORD a burnt
offering of one young bull, one ram and seven male lambs a year old, all without
defect. 9With the bull prepare a grain offering[i] of three-tenths of an ephah of fine
flour mixed with oil; with the ram, two-tenths; 10and with each of the seven lambs,
one-tenth.[j] 11Include one male goat as a sin offering, in addition to the sin offering
for atonement and the regular burnt offering[k] with its grain offering, and their drink
offerings.

Feast of Tabernacles

12" 'On the fifteenth day of the seventh[l] month,[m] hold a sacred assembly and do
no regular work. Celebrate a festival to the LORD for seven days. 13Present an offering
made by fire as an aroma pleasing to the LORD, a burnt offering of thirteen young bulls,
two rams and fourteen male lambs a year old, all without defect. 14With each of the
thirteen bulls prepare a grain offering[n] of three-tenths of an ephah of fine flour mixed
with oil; with each of the two rams, two-tenths; 15and with each of the fourteen lambs,
one-tenth. 16Include one male goat as a sin offering, in addition to the regular burnt
offering with its grain offering and drink offering.[o]
17" 'On the second day[p] prepare twelve young bulls, two rams and fourteen male
lambs a year old, all without defect.[q] 18With the bulls, rams and lambs, prepare their
grain offerings[r] and drink offerings[s] according to the number specified.[t] 19Include
one male goat as a sin offering,[u] in addition to the regular burnt offering with its grain
offering, and their drink offerings.
20" 'On the third day prepare eleven bulls, two rams and fourteen male lambs a year
old, all without defect.[v] 21With the bulls, rams and lambs, prepare their grain
offerings and drink offerings according to the number specified.[w] 22Include one male
goat as a sin offering, in addition to the regular burnt offering with its grain offering
and drink offering.
23" 'On the fourth day prepare ten bulls, two rams and fourteen male lambs a year
old, all without defect. 24With the bulls, rams and lambs, prepare their grain offerings
and drink offerings according to the number specified. 25Include one male goat as a
sin offering, in addition to the regular burnt offering with its grain offering and drink
offering.
26" 'On the fifth day prepare nine bulls, two rams and fourteen male lambs a year
old, all without defect. 27With the bulls, rams and lambs, prepare their grain offerings
and drink offerings according to the number specified. 28Include one male goat as a
sin offering, in addition to the regular burnt offering with its grain offering and drink
offering.
29" 'On the sixth day prepare eight bulls, two rams and fourteen male lambs a year
old, all without defect. 30With the bulls, rams and lambs, prepare their grain offerings
and drink offerings according to the number specified. 31Include one male goat as a

29:2 [c]Nu 28:3
29:5 [d]Nu 28:15
29:6 [e]Nu 28:11 [f]Nu 28:3
29:7 [g]Ac 27:9 [h]Ex 31:15; Lev 16:29; 23:26-32
29:9 [i]ver 3, 18
29:10 [j]Nu 28:13
29:11 [k]Lev 16:3; Nu 28:3
29:12 [l]1Ki 8:2 [m]Lev 23:24
29:14 [n]ver 3
29:16 [o]ver 6
29:17 [p]Lev 23:36 [q]Nu 28:3
29:18 [r]ver 9 [s]Nu 28:7 [t]Nu 15:4-12
29:19 [u]Nu 28:15
29:20 [v]ver 17
29:21 [w]ver 18

a *3* That is, probably about 11½ pints (about 6.5 litres); also in verses 9 and 14 **b** *3* That is, probably about 7½ pints (about 4.5 litres); also in verses 9 and 14 **c** *4* That is, probably about 4 pints (about 2 litres); also in verses 10 and 15 **d** *7* Or *must fast*

principles that we should follow in our worship today: (1) The people gathered together to celebrate and worship. There is an extra benefit to be gained from worshipping with other believers. (2) The normal daily routine was suspended, and no hard work was done. It takes time to worship, and setting aside the time allows us to adjust our attitudes before and reflect afterwards. (3) The people sacrificed animals as burnt offerings to God. We show our commitment to God when we give something of value to him. The best gift, of course, is ourselves.

sin offering, in addition to the regular burnt offering with its grain offering and drink
offering.
32" 'On the seventh day prepare seven bulls, two rams and fourteen male lambs a
year old, all without defect. 33With the bulls, rams and lambs, prepare their grain
offerings and drink offerings according to the number specified. 34Include one male
goat as a sin offering, in addition to the regular burnt offering with its grain offering
and drink offering.
35" 'On the eighth day hold an assembly[x] and do no regular work. 36Present an
offering made by fire as an aroma pleasing to the LORD,[y] a burnt offering of one bull,
one ram and seven male lambs a year old,[z] all without defect. 37With the bull, the
ram and the lambs, prepare their grain offerings and drink offerings according to the
number specified. 38Include one male goat as a sin offering, in addition to the regular
burnt offering with its grain offering and drink offering.
39" 'In addition to what you vow[a] and your freewill offerings, prepare these for
the LORD at your appointed feasts:[b] your burnt offerings,[c] grain offerings, drink
offerings and fellowship offerings.' "[e]
40Moses told the Israelites all that the LORD commanded him.

Vows

30 Moses said to the heads of the tribes of Israel:[a] "This is what the LORD
commands: 2When a man makes a vow to the LORD or takes an oath to bind
himself by a pledge, he must not break his word but must do everything he said.[b]
3"When a young woman still living in her father's house makes a vow to the LORD
or binds herself by a pledge 4and her father hears about her vow or pledge but says
nothing to her, then all her vows and every pledge by which she bound herself will
stand.[c] 5But if her father forbids her when he hears about it, none of her vows or
the pledges by which she bound herself will stand; the LORD will release her because
her father has forbidden her.
6"If she marries after she makes a vow[d] or after her lips utter a rash promise by
which she binds herself 7and her husband hears about it but says nothing to her, then
her vows or the pledges by which she bound herself will stand. 8But if her husband[e]
forbids her when he hears about it, he nullifies the vow that binds her or the rash
promise by which she binds herself, and the LORD will release her.
9"Any vow or obligation taken by a widow or divorced woman will be binding on
her.
10"If a woman living with her husband makes a vow or binds herself by a pledge
under oath 11and her husband hears about it but says nothing to her and does not forbid
her, then all her vows or the pledges by which she bound herself will stand. 12But
if her husband nullifies them when he hears about them, then none of the vows or
pledges that came from her lips will stand.[f] Her husband has nullified them, and the
LORD will release her. 13Her husband may confirm or nullify any vow she makes or
any sworn pledge to deny herself. 14But if her husband says nothing to her about it
from day to day, then he confirms all her vows or the pledges binding on her. He
confirms them by saying nothing to her when he hears about them. 15If, however, he
nullifies them some time after he hears about them, then he is responsible for her
guilt."
16These are the regulations the LORD gave Moses concerning relationships between

e *39* Traditionally *peace offerings*

29:35 [x]Lev 23:36
29:36 [y]Lev 1:9 [z]ver 2
29:39 [a]Nu 6:2 [b]Lev 23:2 [c]Lev 1:3; 1Ch 23:31; 2Ch 31:3
30:1 [a]Nu 1:4
30:2 [b]Dt 23:21-23; Jdg 11:35; Job 22:27; Ps 22:25; 50:14; 116:14; Pr 20:25; Ecc 5:4, 5; Jnh 1:16
30:4 [c]ver 7
30:6 [d]Lev 5:4
30:8 [e]Ge 3:16
30:12 [f]Eph 5:22; Col 3:18

30:1, 2 Moses reminded the people that their promises to God and others must be kept. In ancient times, people did not sign written contracts. A person's word was as binding as a signature. To make a vow even more binding, an offering was given along with it. No-one was forced by law to make a vow; but once made, vows had to be fulfilled. Breaking a vow meant a broken trust and a broken relationship. Trust is still the basis of our relationships with God and others. A broken promise today is just as harmful as it was in Moses' day.

30:3–8 Under Israelite law, parents could overrule their children's vows. This helped young people avoid the consequences of making foolish promises or costly commitments. From this law comes an important principle for both parents and children. Young people still living at home should seek their parents' help when they make decisions. A parent's experience could save a child from a serious mistake. Parents, however, should exercise their authority with caution and grace. They should let children learn from their mistakes while protecting them from disaster.

a man and his wife, and between a father and his young daughter still living in his
house.

4. Vengance on the Midianites

31 The LORD said to Moses, 2"Take vengeance on the Midianites[a] for the Israelites. After that, you will be gathered to your people.[b]"
3So Moses said to the people, "Arm some of your men to go to war against the
Midianites and to carry out the LORD's vengeance[c] on them. 4Send into battle a
thousand men from each of the tribes of Israel." 5So twelve thousand men armed for
battle, a thousand from each tribe, were supplied from the clans of Israel. 6Moses sent
them into battle, a thousand from each tribe, along with Phinehas son of Eleazar, the
priest, who took with him articles from the sanctuary[d] and the trumpets[e] for signal-
ling.
7They fought against Midian, as the LORD commanded Moses, and killed every
man.[f] 8Among their victims were Evi, Rekem, Zur, Hur and Reba[g]—the five kings
of Midian.[h] They also killed Balaam son of Beor with the sword.[i] 9The Israelites
captured the Midianite women and children and took all the Midianite herds, flocks
and goods as plunder. 10They burned all the towns where the Midianites had settled,
as well as all their camps.[j] 11They took all the plunder and spoils, including the
people and animals,[k] 12and brought the captives, spoils and plunder to Moses and
Eleazar the priest and the Israelite assembly[l] at their camp on the plains of Moab,
by the Jordan across from Jericho.[a]
13Moses, Eleazar the priest and all the leaders of the community went to meet them
outside the camp. 14Moses was angry with the officers of the army[m]—the commanders of thousands and commanders of hundreds—who returned from the battle.
15"Have you allowed all the women to live?" he asked them. 16"They were the ones
who followed Balaam's advice[n] and were the means of turning the Israelites away
from the LORD in what happened at Peor,[o] so that a plague struck the LORD's people.
17Now kill all the boys. And kill every woman who has slept with a man,[p] 18but save
for yourselves every girl who has never slept with a man.
19"All of you who have killed anyone or touched anyone who was killed[q] must
stay outside the camp seven days. On the third and seventh days you must purify
yourselves[r] and your captives. 20Purify every garment[s] as well as everything made
of leather, goat hair or wood."
21Then Eleazar the priest said to the soldiers who had gone into battle, "This is the
requirement of the law that the LORD gave Moses: 22Gold, silver, bronze, iron,[t] tin,
lead 23and anything else that can withstand fire must be put through the fire,[u] and
then it will be clean. But it must also be purified with the water of cleansing.[v] And
whatever cannot withstand fire must be put through that water. 24On the seventh
day wash your clothes and you will be clean.[w] Then you may come into the
camp."

a *12* Hebrew *Jordan of Jericho*; possibly an ancient name for the Jordan River

31:2
[a]Ge 25:2
[b]Nu 20:26; 27:13

31:3
[c]Jdg 11:36; 1Sa 24:12; 2Sa 4:8; 22:48; Ps 94:1; 149:7

31:6
[d]Nu 14:44
[e]Nu 10:9

31:7
[f]Dt 20:13; Jdg 21:11; 1Ki 11:15, 16

31:8
[g]Jos 13:21
[h]Nu 25:15
[i]Jos 13:22

31:10
[j]Ge 25:16; 1Ch 6:54; Ps 69:25; Eze 25:4

31:11
[k]Dt 20:14

31:12
[l]Nu 27:2

31:14
[m]ver 48; Ex 18:21; Dt 1:15

31:16
[n]2Pe 2:15; Rev 2:14
[o]Nu 25:1-9

31:17
[p]Dt 7:2; 20:16-18; Jdg 21:11

31:19
[q]Nu 19:16
[r]Nu 19:12

31:20
[s]Nu 19:19

31:22
[t]Jos 6:19; 22:8

31:23
[u]1Co 3:13
[v]Nu 19:9, 17

31:24
[w]Lev 11:25

31:1ff The Midianites were a nomadic people who descended from Abraham and his second wife, Keturah. The land of Midian lay far to the south of Canaan, but large bands of Midianites roamed many miles from their homeland, searching for grazing areas for their flocks. Such a group was near the promised land when the Israelites arrived. When Moses fled from Egypt (Exodus 2), he took refuge in the land of Midian. His wife and father-in-law were Midianites. Despite this alliance, the Israelites and Midianites were always bitter enemies.

31:14–16 Because Midianites were responsible for enticing Israel into Baal worship, God commanded Israel to destroy them (25:16–18). But Israel took the women as captives, rather than killing them, probably because of the tempting enticements of the Midianites' sinful life-style. When we discover sin in our lives, we must deal with it completely. When the Israelites later entered the promised land, it was their indifferent attitude to sin that eventually ruined them. Moses dealt with the sin promptly and completely. When God points out sin, move quickly to remove it from your life.

31:16 Balaam's story (22:1–24:25), taken alone, would lead us to believe that Balaam was an honest and God-fearing man. But here is the first of much biblical evidence that Balaam was not the good man he might appear to be. For more on Balaam, see the notes on 22:9 and 25:1–3, and Balaam's Profile in chapter 22.

Dividing the Spoils

25The LORD said to Moses, 26"You and Eleazar the priest and the family heads of
the community are to count all the people[x] and animals that were captured. 27Divide[y]
the spoils between the soldiers who took part in the battle and the rest of the community. 28From the soldiers who fought in the battle, set apart as tribute for the LORD[z]
one out of every five hundred, whether persons, cattle, donkeys, sheep or goats.
29Take this tribute from their half share and give it to Eleazar the priest as the LORD's
part. 30From the Israelites' half, select one out of every fifty, whether persons, cattle,
donkeys, sheep, goats or other animals. Give them to the Levites, who are responsible
for the care of the LORD's tabernacle.[a]" 31So Moses and Eleazar the priest did as the
LORD commanded Moses.
32The plunder remaining from the spoils that the soldiers took was 675,000 sheep,
3372,000 cattle, 3461,000 donkeys 35and 32,000 women who had never slept with a
man.
36The half share of those who fought in the battle was:

337,500 sheep, 37of which the tribute for the LORD[b] was 675;
3836,000 cattle, of which the tribute for the LORD was 72;
3930,500 donkeys, of which the tribute for the LORD was 61;
4016,000 people, of which the tribute for the LORD was 32.

41Moses gave the tribute to Eleazar the priest as the LORD's part,[c] as the LORD
commanded Moses.
42The half belonging to the Israelites, which Moses set apart from that of the
fighting men—43the community's half—was 337,500 sheep, 4436,000 cattle,
4530,500 donkeys 46and 16,000 people. 47From the Israelites' half, Moses selected
one out of every fifty persons and animals, as the LORD commanded him, and gave
them to the Levites, who were responsible for the care of the LORD's tabernacle.
48Then the officers who were over the units of the army—the commanders of
thousands and commanders of hundreds—went to Moses 49and said to him, "Your
servants have counted the soldiers under our command, and not one is missing.[d] 50So
we have brought as an offering to the LORD the gold articles each of us acquired—armlets, bracelets, signet rings, ear-rings and necklaces—to make atonement
for ourselves[e] before the LORD."
51Moses and Eleazar the priest accepted from them the gold—all the handcrafted
articles. 52All the gold from the commanders of thousands and commanders of
hundreds that Moses and Eleazar presented as a gift to the LORD weighed 16,750
shekels.[b] 53Each soldier had taken plunder[f] for himself. 54Moses and Eleazar the
priest accepted the gold from the commanders of thousands and commanders of
hundreds and brought it into the Tent of Meeting as a memorial[g] for the Israelites
before the LORD.

5. The Transjordan tribes

32 The Reubenites and Gadites, who had very large herds and flocks, saw that
the lands of Jazer[a] and Gilead were suitable for livestock.[b] 2So they came
to Moses and Eleazar the priest and to the leaders of the community, and said,
3"Ataroth,[c] Dibon, Jazer, Nimrah,[d] Heshbon, Elealeh,[e] Sebam, Nebo and

b *52* That is, about 420 pounds (about 190 kilograms)

31:26 [x]Nu 1:19
31:27 [y]Jos 22:8; 1Sa 30:24
31:28 [z]Nu 18:21
31:30 [a]Nu 3:7; 18:3
31:37 [b]ver 38-41
31:41 [c]Nu 5:9; 18:8
31:49 [d]Jer 23:4
31:50 [e]Ex 30:16
31:53 [f]Dt 20:14
31:54 [g]Ex 28:12
32:1 [a]Nu 21:32 [b]Ex 12:38
32:3 [c]ver 34 [d]ver 36 [e]ver 37; Isa 15:4; 16:9; Jer 48:34

31:25–30 Moses told the Israelites to give a portion of the war spoils to God. Another portion was to go to the people who remained behind. Similarly, the money we earn is not ours alone. Everything we possess comes directly or indirectly from God and ultimately belongs to him. We should return a portion to him (a "tribute") and also share a portion with those in need.

31:48–50 After carefully accounting for all their men, the officers discovered that not one soldier had been lost in battle. At once they thanked God. After going through tough times, we should be quick to thank God for delivering us and protecting us from severe loss.

32:1ff Three tribes (Reuben, Gad, and the half-tribe of Manasseh) wanted to live east of the Jordan River (referred to as the Transjordan area) on land they had already conquered. Moses immediately assumed they had selfish motives and were trying to avoid helping the others fight for the land across the river. But Moses jumped to the wrong conclusion. In dealing with people, we

Beon[f]—4the land the LORD subdued[g] before the people of Israel—are suitable for
livestock,[h] and your servants have livestock. 5If we have found favour in your eyes,"
they said, "let this land be given to your servants as our possession. Do not make us
cross the Jordan."

6Moses said to the Gadites and Reubenites, "Shall your countrymen go to war while
you sit here? 7Why do you discourage the Israelites from going over into the land the
LORD has given them?[i] 8This is what your fathers did when I sent them from Kadesh
Barnea to look over the land.[j] 9After they went up to the Valley of Eshcol[k] and
viewed the land, they discouraged the Israelites from entering the land the LORD had
given them. 10The LORD's anger was aroused[l] that day and he swore this oath:
11'Because they have not followed me wholeheartedly, not one of the men twenty
years old or more[m] who came up out of Egypt will see the land I promised on oath[n]
to Abraham, Isaac and Jacob[o]—12not one except Caleb son of Jephunneh the Kenizzite and Joshua son of Nun, for they followed the LORD wholeheartedly.'[p] 13The
LORD's anger burned against Israel[q] and he made them wander in the desert for forty
years, until the whole generation of those who had done evil in his sight was gone.[r]

14"And here you are, a brood of sinners, standing in the place of your fathers and
making the LORD even more angry with Israel.[s] 15If you turn away from following
him, he will again leave all this people in the desert, and you will be the cause of their
destruction.[t]"

16Then they came up to him and said, "We would like to build pens here for our
livestock[u] and cities for our women and children. 17But we are ready to arm ourselves
and go ahead of the Israelites[v] until we have brought them to their place.[w] Meanwhile
our women and children will live in fortified cities, for protection from the inhabitants
of the land. 18We will not return to our homes until every Israelite has received his
inheritance.[x] 19We will not receive any inheritance with them on the other side of
the Jordan, because our inheritance has come to us on the east side of the Jordan."[y]

20Then Moses said to them, "If you will do this—if you will arm yourselves before
the LORD for battle,[z] 21and if all of you will go armed over the Jordan before the
LORD until he has driven his enemies out before him—22then when the land is subdued
before the LORD, you may return[a] and be free from your obligation to the LORD and
to Israel. And this land will be your possession before the LORD.[b]

23"But if you fail to do this, you will be sinning against the LORD; and you may
be sure that your sin will find you out.[c] 24Build cities for your women and children,
and pens for your flocks,[d] but do what you have promised.[e]"

25The Gadites and Reubenites said to Moses, "We your servants will do as our lord

32:3 [f]ver 38; Jos 13:17; Eze 25:9
32:4 [g]Nu 21:34 [h]Ex 12:38
32:7 [i]Nu 13:27-14:4
32:8 [j]Nu 13:3, 26; Dt 1:19-25
32:9 [k]Nu 13:23; Dt 1:24
32:10 [l]Nu 11:1
32:11 [m]Ex 30:14 [n]Nu 14:23 [o]Nu 14:28-30
32:12 [p]Nu 14:24, 30; Dt 1:36; Ps 63:8
32:13 [q]Ex 4:14 [r]Nu 14:28-35; 26:64, 65
32:14 [s]ver 10; Dt 1:34; Ps 78:59
32:15 [t]Dt 30:17-18; 2Ch 7:20
32:16 [u]Ex 12:38; Dt 3:19
32:17 [v]Jos 4:12, 13 [w]Nu 22:4; Dt 3:20
32:18 [x]Jos 22:1-4
32:19 [y]Jos 12:1
32:20 [z]Dt 3:18
32:22 [a]Jos 22:4 [b]Dt 3:18-20
32:23 [c]Ge 4:7; 44:16; Isa 59:12
32:24 [d]ver 1, 16 [e]Nu 30:2

PREPARING TO ENTER THE PROMISED LAND
The Israelites had been camped in the plains of Moab, across from Jericho. From this position, they were ready to enter the promised land.

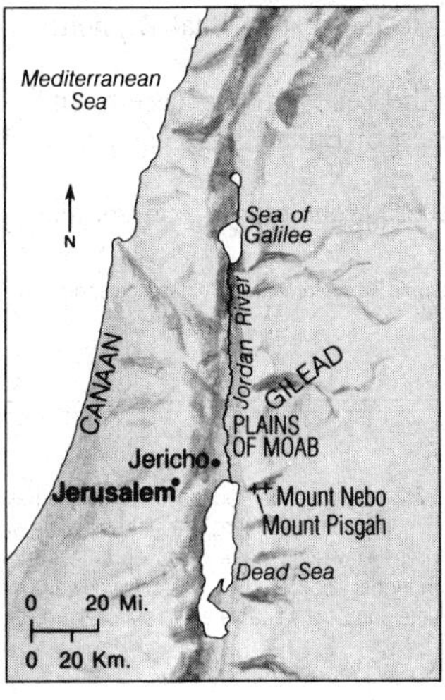

must find out all the facts before making up our minds. We shouldn't automatically assume that their motives are wrong, even if their plans sound suspicious.

32:16 A simple pen for livestock had four roughly built stone walls, high enough to keep wild animals out. Sometimes the top of the wall was lined with thorns to further discourage predators and thieves. The pen's single entrance made it easier for a shepherd to guard his flock. Often several shepherds used a single pen and took turns guarding the entrance. Mingling the animals was no problem since each flock responded readily to its own shepherd's voice. The three tribes who chose to remain east of the Jordan River wanted to build pens to protect their flocks and cities to protect their families before the men crossed the river to help the rest of the tribes conquer the promised land.

32:16–19 The land on the east side of the Jordan had been conquered. The hard work was done by all of the tribes together. But the tribes of Reuben and Gad and the half-tribe of Manasseh did not stop after their land was cleared. They promised to keep working with the others until everyone's land was conquered. After others have helped you, do you make excuses to escape helping them? Finish the whole job, even those parts that may not benefit you directly.

commands. 26Our children and wives, our flocks and herds will remain here in the
cities of Gilead.[f] 27But your servants, every man armed for battle, will cross over
to fight before the LORD, just as our lord says."
28Then Moses gave orders about them[g] to Eleazar the priest and Joshua son of Nun
and to the family heads of the Israelite tribes. 29He said to them, "If the Gadites and
Reubenites, every man armed for battle, cross over the Jordan with you before the
LORD, then when the land is subdued before you, give them the land of Gilead as their
possession. 30But if they do not cross over with you armed, they must accept their
possession with you in Canaan."
31The Gadites and Reubenites answered, "Your servants will do what the LORD has
said.[h] 32We will cross over before the LORD into Canaan armed, but the property we
inherit will be on this side of the Jordan."
33Then Moses gave to the Gadites,[i] the Reubenites and the half-tribe of Manasseh son of Joseph the kingdom of Sihon king of the Amorites[j] and the kingdom of Og king of Bashan—the whole land with its cities and the territory around
them.[k]
34The Gadites built up Dibon, Ataroth, Aroer,[l] 35Atroth Shophan, Jazer,[m] Jogbehah, 36Beth Nimrah[n] and Beth Haran as fortified cities, and built pens for their flocks.
37And the Reubenites rebuilt Heshbon, Elealeh and Kiriathaim, 38as well as Nebo[o]
and Baal Meon (these names were changed) and Sibmah. They gave names to the cities
they rebuilt.
39The descendants of Makir[p] son of Manasseh went to Gilead, captured it and
drove out the Amorites who were there. 40So Moses gave Gilead to the Makirites,[q]
the descendants of Manasseh, and they settled there. 41Jair, a descendant of Manasseh,
captured their settlements and called them Havvoth Jair.[a][r] 42And Nobah captured
Kenath and its surrounding settlements and called it Nobah after himself.[s]

6. Camped on the plains of Moab

Stages in Israel's Journey

33 Here are the stages in the journey of the Israelites when they came out of
Egypt[a] by divisions under the leadership of Moses and Aaron.[b] 2At the
LORD's command Moses recorded the stages in their journey. This is their journey by
stages:

3The Israelites set out from Rameses on the fifteenth day of the first month,
the day after the Passover.[c] They marched out boldly[d] in full view of all the
Egyptians, 4who were burying all their firstborn, whom the LORD had struck
down among them; for the LORD had brought judgment on their gods.[e]

5The Israelites left Rameses and camped at Succoth.[f]

6They left Succoth and camped at Etham, on the edge of the desert.[g]

7They left Etham, turned back to Pi Hahiroth, to the east of Baal Zephon,[h]
and camped near Migdol.[i]

8They left Pi Hahiroth[a] and passed through the sea[j] into the desert, and
when they had travelled for three days in the Desert of Etham, they camped at
Marah.[k]

9They left Marah and went to Elim, where there were twelve springs and
seventy palm trees, and they camped[l] there.

[a] *41* Or *them the settlements of Jair* [a] *8* Many manuscripts of the Masoretic Text, Samaritan Pentateuch and Vulgate; most manuscripts of the Masoretic Text *left from before Hahiroth*

32:26 [f]Jos 1:14
32:28 [g]Dt 3:18-20; Jos 1:13
32:31 [h]ver 29
32:33 [i]Jos 13:24-28; 1Sa 13:7 [j]Dt 2:26 [k]Nu 21:24; Jos 12:6
32:34 [l]Dt 2:36; Jdg 11:26
32:35 [m]ver 3
32:36 [n]ver 3
32:38 [o]ver 3; Isa 15:2; Jer 48:1, 22
32:39 [p]Ge 50:23
32:40 [q]Dt 3:15; Jos 17:1
32:41 [r]Dt 3:14; Jos 13:30; Jdg 10:4; 1Ch 2:23
32:42 [s]2Sa 18:18; Ps 49:11
33:1 [a]Mic 6:4 [b]Ps 77:20
33:3 [c]Ex 13:4 [d]Ex 14:8
33:4 [e]Ex 12:12
33:5 [f]Ex 12:37
33:6 [g]Ex 13:20
33:7 [h]Ex 14:9 [i]Ex 14:2
33:8 [j]Ex 14:22 [k]Ex 15:23
33:9 [l]Ex 15:27

33:1ff Look at the map in the introduction to the book of Numbers to see the travels of the Israelites.

33:2 Moses recorded the Israelites' journeys as God instructed him, providing a record of their spiritual as well as geographic progress. Have you made spiritual progress lately? Recording your thoughts about God and lessons you have learned over a period of time can be a valuable aid to spiritual growth. A record of your

33:11 [m]Ex 16:1
33:15 [n]Ex 17:1 [o]Ex 19:1
33:16 [p]Nu 11:34
33:17 [q]Nu 11:35
33:20 [r]Jos 10:29
33:30 [s]Dt 10:6
33:33 [t]Dt 10:7
33:35 [u]Dt 2:8; 1Ki 9:26; 22:48
33:36 [v]Nu 20:1
33:37 [w]Nu 20:22 [x]Nu 20:16; 21:4
33:38 [y]Dt 10:6 [z]Nu 20:25-28
33:40 [a]Nu 21:1
33:43 [b]Nu 21:10
33:44 [c]Nu 21:11
33:47 [d]Nu 27:12
33:48 [e]Nu 22:1
33:49 [f]Nu 25:1

10 They left Elim and camped by the Red Sea.[b]
11 They left the Red Sea and camped in the Desert of Sin.[m]
12 They left the Desert of Sin and camped at Dophkah.
13 They left Dophkah and camped at Alush.
14 They left Alush and camped at Rephidim, where there was no water for the
people to drink.
15 They left Rephidim[n] and camped in the Desert of Sinai.[o]
16 They left the Desert of Sinai and camped at Kibroth Hattaavah.[p]
17 They left Kibroth Hattaavah and camped at Hazeroth.[q]
18 They left Hazeroth and camped at Rithmah.
19 They left Rithmah and camped at Rimmon Perez.
20 They left Rimmon Perez and camped at Libnah.[r]
21 They left Libnah and camped at Rissah.
22 They left Rissah and camped at Kehelathah.
23 They left Kehelathah and camped at Mount Shepher.
24 They left Mount Shepher and camped at Haradah.
25 They left Haradah and camped at Makheloth.
26 They left Makheloth and camped at Tahath.
27 They left Tahath and camped at Terah.
28 They left Terah and camped at Mithcah.
29 They left Mithcah and camped at Hashmonah.
30 They left Hashmonah and camped at Moseroth.[s]
31 They left Moseroth and camped at Bene Jaakan.
32 They left Bene Jaakan and camped at Hor Haggidgad.
33 They left Hor Haggidgad and camped at Jotbathah.[t]
34 They left Jotbathah and camped at Abronah.
35 They left Abronah and camped at Ezion Geber.[u]
36 They left Ezion Geber and camped at Kadesh, in the Desert of Zin.[v]
37 They left Kadesh and camped at Mount Hor,[w] on the border of Edom.[x] 38 At
the LORD's command Aaron the priest went up Mount Hor, where he died[y] on
the first day of the fifth month of the fortieth year after the Israelites came out
of Egypt.[z] 39 Aaron was a hundred and twenty-three years old when he died on
Mount Hor.
40 The Canaanite king of Arad,[a] who lived in the Negev of Canaan, heard that
the Israelites were coming.
41 They left Mount Hor and camped at Zalmonah.
42 They left Zalmonah and camped at Punon.
43 They left Punon and camped at Oboth.[b]
44 They left Oboth and camped at Iye Abarim, on the border of Moab.[c]
45 They left Iyim[c] and camped at Dibon Gad.
46 They left Dibon Gad and camped at Almon Diblathaim.
47 They left Almon Diblathaim and camped in the mountains of Abarim,[d] near
Nebo.
48 They left the mountains of Abarim and camped on the plains of Moab by
the Jordan across from Jericho.[d][e] 49 There on the plains of Moab they camped
along the Jordan from Beth Jeshimoth to Abel Shittim.[f]

b *10* Hebrew *Yam Suph*; that is, Sea of Reeds; also in verse 11 **c** *45* That is, Iye Abarim **d** *48* Hebrew *Jordan of Jericho*; possibly an ancient name for the Jordan River; also in verse 50

spiritual pilgrimage will let you check up on your progress and avoid repeating past mistakes.

33:4 God "brought judgment on their gods" by sending the plagues. See the note on Exodus 10:22 for a further explanation.

50 On the plains of Moab by the Jordan across from Jericho the LORD said to Moses,
51 "Speak to the Israelites and say to them: 'When you cross the Jordan into Canaan,[g]
52 drive out all the inhabitants of the land before you. Destroy all their carved images
and their cast idols, and demolish all their high places.[h] 53 Take possession of the land
and settle in it, for I have given you the land to possess.[i] 54 Distribute the land by
lot, according to your clans.[j] To a larger group give a larger inheritance, and to a
smaller group a smaller one. Whatever falls to them by lot will be theirs. Distribute
it according to your ancestral tribes.
55 " 'But if you do not drive out the inhabitants of the land, those you allow to remain
will become barbs in your eyes and thorns[k] in your sides. They will give you trouble
in the land where you will live. 56 And then I will do to you what I plan to do to them.' "

Boundaries of Canaan

34 The LORD said to Moses, 2 "Command the Israelites and say to them: 'When
you enter Canaan, the land that will be allotted to you as an inheritance[a] will
have these boundaries:[b]
3 " 'Your southern side will include some of the Desert of Zin[c] along the border
of Edom. On the east, your southern boundary will start from the end of the Salt
Sea,[a][d] 4 cross south of Scorpion[b] Pass,[e] continue on to Zin and go south of Kadesh
Barnea.[f] Then it will go to Hazar Addar and over to Azmon, 5 where it will turn,
join the Wadi of Egypt[g] and end at the Sea.[c]
6 " 'Your western boundary will be the coast of the Great Sea. This will be your
boundary on the west.
7 " 'For your northern boundary,[h] run a line from the Great Sea to Mount Hor 8 and

a 3 That is, the Dead Sea; also in verse 12 b 4 Hebrew *Akrabbim* c 5 That is, the Mediterranean; also in verses 6 and 7

33:51 [g] Jos 3:17
33:52 [h] Ex 23:24; 34:13; Lev 26:1; Dt 7:2, 5; 12:3; Jos 11:12; Ps 106:34-36
33:53 [i] Dt 11:31; Jos 21:43
33:54 [j] Nu 26:54
33:55 [k] Jos 23:13; Jdg 2:3; Ps 106:36
34:2 [a] Ge 17:8; Dt 1:7-8; Ps 78:54-55 [b] Eze 47:15
34:3 [c] Jos 15:1-3 [d] Ge 14:3
34:4 [e] Jos 15:3 [f] Nu 32:8
34:5 [g] Ge 15:18; Jos 15:4
34:7 [h] Eze 47:15-17

33:50–53 God told Moses that before the Israelites settled in the promised land they should drive out the wicked inhabitants and destroy their idols. In Colossians 3, Paul encourages us to live as Christians in the same manner: throwing away our old way of living and moving ahead into our new life of obedience to God and faith in Jesus Christ. Like the Israelites moving into the promised land, we can destroy the wickedness in our lives or we can settle down and live with it. To move in and possess the new life, we must drive out the sinful thoughts and practices to make room for the new.

33:50–56 Why were the Israelites told to destroy the people living in Canaan? God had several compelling reasons for giving this command: (1) God was stamping out the wickedness of an extremely sinful nation. The Canaanites brought on their own punishment. Idol worship expressed their deepest evil desires. It ultimately led to the worship of Satan and the total rejection of God. (2) God was using Moses and Israel to judge Canaan for its sins in fulfilment of the prophecy in Genesis 9:25. (3) God wanted to remove all trace of pagan beliefs and practices from the land. He did not want his people to mix or compromise with idolatry in any way. The Israelites did not fully understand God's reasons, and they did not carry out his command. This eventually led them to compromise and corruption. In all areas of life, we should obey God's word without question because we know he is just, even if we cannot fully understand his overall purposes.

33:55 If you don't do the job right the first time, it often becomes much more difficult to accomplish. God warned that if the Israelites did not drive the wicked inhabitants out of the promised land, later these people would become a source of great irritation. That is exactly what happened. Just as the Israelites were hesitant to clear out all the wicked people, we are sometimes hesitant to clear out all the sin in our lives, either because we are afraid of it (as the Israelites feared the giants), or because it seems harmless and attractive (as sexual sin seemed). But Hebrews 12:1, 2 tells us to throw off "the sin that so easily entangles" us. We all have "idols" we don't want to let go of (a bad habit, an unhealthy relationship, a certain life-style). If we allow these idols to dominate us, they will cause serious problems later.

34:1ff The land was given by God as an inheritance; no tribe was to claim its own land. The boundaries declared by God are larger than the area actually occupied by the Hebrews. The boundaries correspond more to the land conquered by David and to the ideal territory portrayed by Ezekiel (Ezekiel 47, 48). The size of the land portrays God's generosity. He always gives us more than we could ask or think.

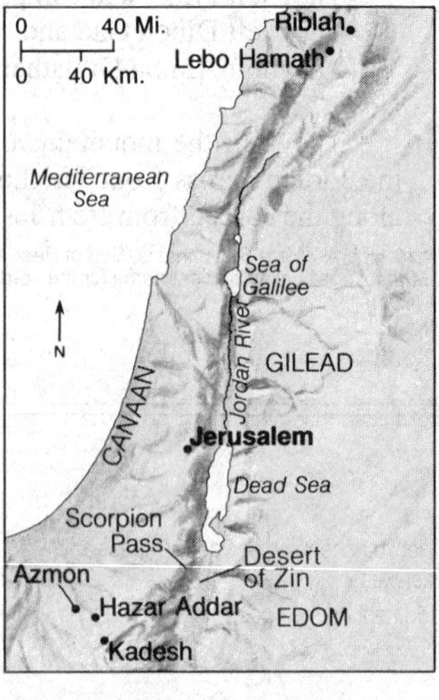

THE BORDERS OF THE PROMISED LAND
The borders of the promised land stretched from the Desert of Zin and Kadesh in the south to Lebo Hamath and Riblah in the north, and from the Mediterranean coast (the Great Sea) on the west to the Jordan River on the east. The land of Gilead was also included.

from Mount Hor to Lebo[d] Hamath.[i] Then the boundary will go to Zedad, 9continue
to Ziphron and end at Hazar Enan. This will be your boundary on the north.
10" 'For your eastern boundary, run a line from Hazar Enan to Shepham. 11The
boundary will go down from Shepham to Riblah[j] on the east side of Ain and continue
along the slopes east of the Sea of Kinnereth.[e][k] 12Then the boundary will go down
along the Jordan and end at the Salt Sea.

" 'This will be your land, with its boundaries on every side.' "

13Moses commanded the Israelites: "Assign this land by lot as an inheritance.[l] The
LORD has ordered that it be given to the nine and a half tribes, 14because the families
of the tribe of Reuben, the tribe of Gad and the half-tribe of Manasseh have received
their inheritance.[m] 15These two and a half tribes have received their inheritance on
the east side of the Jordan of Jericho,[f] towards the sunrise."

16The LORD said to Moses, 17"These are the names of the men who are to assign
the land for you as an inheritance: Eleazar the priest and Joshua[n] son of Nun. 18And
appoint one leader from each tribe to help[o] assign the land. 19These are their names:

Caleb[p] son of Jephunneh,
  from the tribe of Judah;[q]
20Shemuel son of Ammihud,
  from the tribe of Simeon;[r]
21Elidad son of Kislon,
  from the tribe of Benjamin;[s]
22Bukki son of Jogli,
  the leader from the tribe of Dan;
23Hanniel son of Ephod,
  the leader from the tribe of Manasseh son of Joseph;
24Kemuel son of Shiphtan,
  the leader from the tribe of Ephraim son of Joseph;
25Elizaphan son of Parnach,
  the leader from the tribe of Zebulun;
26Paltiel son of Azzan,
  the leader from the tribe of Issachar;
27Ahihud son of Shelomi,
  the leader from the tribe of Asher;[t]
28Pedahel son of Ammihud,
  the leader from the tribe of Naphtali."

29These are the men the LORD commanded to assign the inheritance to the Israelites
in the land of Canaan.

Towns for the Levites

35 On the plains of Moab by the Jordan across from Jericho,[a] the LORD said to
Moses, 2"Command the Israelites to give the Levites towns to live in[a] from
the inheritance the Israelites will possess. And give them pasture-lands around the
towns. 3Then they will have towns to live in and pasture-lands for their cattle, flocks
and all their other livestock.

4"The pasture-lands around the towns that you give the Levites will extend out
fifteen hundred feet[b] from the town wall. 5Outside the town, measure three thousand
feet[c] on the east side, three thousand on the south side, three thousand on the west

34:8 [i]Nu 13:21; Jos 13:5
34:11 [j]2Ki 23:33; Jer 39:5 [k]Dt 3:17; Jos 11:2; 13:27
34:13 [l]Jos 14:1-5
34:14 [m]Nu 32:33; Jos 14:3
34:17 [n]Jos 14:1
34:18 [o]Nu 1:4, 16
34:19 [p]Nu 26:65 [q]Ge 29:35; Dt 33:7
34:20 [r]Ge 49:5
34:21 [s]Ge 49:27; Ps 68:27
34:27 [t]Nu 1:40
35:2 [a]Lev 25:32-34; Jos 14:3, 4

[d] *8* Or *to the entrance to* [e] *11* That is, Galilee [f] *15* *Jordan of Jericho* was possibly an ancient name for the Jordan River. [a] *1* Hebrew *Jordan of Jericho*; possibly an ancient name for the Jordan River [b] *4* Hebrew *a thousand cubits* (about 450 metres) [c] *5* Hebrew *two thousand cubits* (about 900 metres)

34:16–29 In God's plan for settling the land, he (1) explained what to do, (2) communicated this clearly to Moses, and (3) assigned specific people to oversee the apportionment of the land. No plan is complete until each job is assigned and everyone understands his or her responsibilities. When you have a job to do, determine what must be done, give clear instructions, and put people in charge of each part.

35:2, 3 The Levites were ministers. They were supported by the tithes of the people who gave them homes, flocks, and pasture-lands. Likewise, we are responsible to provide for the needs of our ministers and missionaries so they can be free to do their God-ordained work.

and three thousand on the north, with the town in the centre. They will have this area
as pasture-land for the towns.

Cities of Refuge

6“Six of the towns you give the Levites will be cities of refuge, to which a person
who has killed someone may flee. [b] In addition, give them forty-two other towns. 7In
all you must give the Levites forty-eight towns, together with their pasture-lands. 8The
towns you give the Levites from the land the Israelites possess are to be given in
proportion to the inheritance of each tribe: Take many towns from a tribe that has
many, but few from one that has few.” [c]
9Then the LORD said to Moses: 10“Speak to the Israelites and say to them: ‘When
you cross the Jordan into Canaan, [d] 11select some towns to be your cities of refuge,
to which a person who has killed someone[e] accidentally[f] may flee. 12They will be
places of refuge from the avenger, [g] so that a person accused of murder may not die
before he stands trial before the assembly. 13These six towns you give will be your
cities of refuge. 14Give three on this side of the Jordan and three in Canaan as cities
of refuge. 15These six towns will be a place of refuge for Israelites, aliens and any
other people living among them, so that anyone who has killed another accidentally
can flee there.
16“ ‘If a man strikes someone with an iron object so that he dies, he is a murderer;
the murderer shall be put to death. [h] 17Or if anyone has a stone in his hand that could
kill, and he strikes someone so that he dies, he is a murderer; the murderer shall be
put to death. 18Or if anyone has a wooden object in his hand that could kill, and he
hits someone so that he dies, he is a murderer; the murderer shall be put to death. 19The
avenger of blood shall put the murderer to death; when he meets him, he shall put
him to death. [i] 20If anyone with malice aforethought pushes another or throws
something at him intentionally[j] so that he dies 21or if in hostility he hits him with
his fist so that he dies, that person shall be put to death; he is a murderer. The avenger
of blood shall put the murderer to death when he meets him.
22“ ‘But if without hostility someone suddenly pushes another or throws something
at him unintentionally[k] 23or, without seeing him, drops a stone on him that could kill
him, and he dies, then since he was not his enemy and he did not intend to harm him,
24the assembly[l] must judge between him and the avenger of blood according to these

35:6 [b]Jos 20:7-9; 21:3, 13
35:8 [c]Nu 26:54; 33:54; Jos 21:1-42
35:10 [d]Jos 20:2
35:11 [e]ver 22-25 [f]Ex 21:13; Dt 19:1-13
35:12 [g]Dt 19:6; Jos 20:3
35:16 [h]Ex 21:12; Lev 24:17
35:19 [i]ver 21
35:20 [j]Ge 4:8; Ex 21:14; Dt 19:11; 2Sa 3:27; 20:10
35:22 [k]ver 11; Ex 21:13
35:24 [l]ver 12; Jos 20:6

35:6 Of the 48 cities given to the Levites, six were cities of refuge. These six cities were probably put under the Levites' supervision because they would be the most impartial judges. Such cities were needed because the ancient customs of justice called for revenge in the event of the death of a relative or loved one (2 Samuel 14:7). The Levites would hold a preliminary hearing outside the gates while the accused person was kept in the city until the time of his trial. If the killing was judged accidental, the person would stay in the city until the death of the high priest. At that time, he would be allowed to go free, and he could start a new life without worrying about avengers. If it was not accidental, the person would be delivered to the slain person's avengers. This system of justice shows how God's law and his mercy go hand in hand.

35:11–28 If anyone died because of violence, murder was assumed, but the murder suspect was not automatically assumed guilty. The cities of refuge assured the accused that justice would be served. But if he or she left the city, then he or she would be assumed guilty and able to be killed by the avenging party. The people were to be intolerant of the sin, yet impartial to the accused so that he or she could have a fair trial. The cities of refuge represented God's concern for justice in a culture that did not always protect the innocent. It is unjust both to overlook wrongdoing and to jump to conclusions about guilt. When someone is accused of wrongdoing, stand up for justice, protect those not yet proven guilty, and listen carefully to all sides of the story.

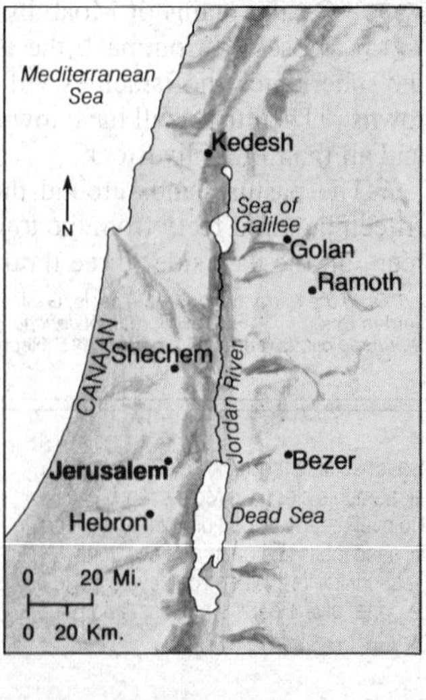

CITIES OF REFUGE
Six of the Levites' cities were designated as cities of refuge. They were spaced throughout the land and protected those who had accidentally committed a crime or who were awaiting trial.

35:25
[m]Ex 29:7

35:29
[n]Nu 27:11

35:30
[o]ver 16;
Dt 17:6; 19:15;
Mt 18:16;
Jn 7:51;
2Co 13:1;
Heb 10:28

35:33
[p]Ge 9:6;
Ps 106:38;
Mic 4:11

35:34
[q]Lev 18:24, 25
[r]Ex 29:45

regulations. 25 The assembly must protect the one accused of murder from the avenger
of blood and send him back to the city of refuge to which he fled. He must stay there
until the death of the high priest, who was anointed with holy oil.[m]
26 " 'But if the accused ever goes outside the limits of the city of refuge to which
he has fled 27 and the avenger of blood finds him outside the city, the avenger of blood
may kill the accused without being guilty of murder. 28 The accused must stay in his
city of refuge until the death of the high priest; only after the death of the high priest
may he return to his own property.
29 " 'These are to be legal requirements[n] for you throughout the generations to
come, wherever you live.
30 " 'Anyone who kills a person is to be put to death as a murderer only on the
testimony of witnesses. But no-one is to be put to death on the testimony of only one
witness.[o]
31 " 'Do not accept a ransom for the life of a murderer, who deserves to die. He must
surely be put to death.
32 " 'Do not accept a ransom for anyone who has fled to a city of refuge and so allow
him to go back and live on his own land before the death of the high priest.
33 " 'Do not pollute the land where you are. Bloodshed pollutes the land,[p] and
atonement cannot be made for the land on which blood has been shed, except by the
blood of the one who shed it. 34 Do not defile the land[q] where you live and where
I dwell,[r] for I, the LORD, dwell among the Israelites.' "

PRIESTS IN ISRAEL'S HISTORY
Numbers 35:25–28 mentions the death of a high priest. Each new high priest had to come from the lineage of Aaron. Listed here are the ones whose stories are told elsewhere in the Bible.

Priest	*Importance*	*Reference*
Aaron	Moses' brother and first priest	Exodus 28:1–3
Eleazar	Watched two of his brothers die in a fire from God because they did not follow God's instructions. He obeyed God and became chief leader of the tabernacle.	Leviticus 10 Numbers 3:32
Phinehas	Executed a young Israelite idol worshipper and his Midianite mistress to end a plague. He was then promised that his priestly line would never end.	Numbers 25:1–15
Ahitub	A priest during King Saul's reign	1 Samuel 14:3
Zadok	A faithful high priest under King David. He and Nathan anointed Solomon as the next king.	2 Samuel 8:17 1 Kings 1:38, 39
Ahimaaz	Carried the message of Absalom's death to King David, but was apparently afraid to tell about it.	2 Samuel 18:19–29
Azariah	High priest under King Solomon	1 Kings 4:2
Azariah	High priest under Uzziah. He rebuked the king for burning incense himself.	2 Chronicles 26:17–21
	When Hezekiah became king he reopened the temple. Azariah again served as high priest.	2 Chronicles 26:17–21
Amariah	King Jehoshaphat appointed him to judge religious disputes.	2 Chronicles 19:11
Hilkiah	Found the Book of the Law during Josiah's reign	2 Kings 22:3–13 2 Chronicles 34:14–21
Azariah	Probably one of the first to return to Israel from Babylon	1 Chronicles 9:10, 11
Seraiah	The father of Ezra	Ezra 7:1–5

Inheritance of Zelophehad's Daughters

36 The family heads of the clan of Gilead[a] son of Makir, the son of Manasseh,
who were from the clans of the descendants of Joseph, came and spoke before
Moses and the leaders,[b] the heads of the Israelite families. 2They said, "When the
LORD commanded my lord to give the land as an inheritance to the Israelites by lot,
he ordered you to give the inheritance of our brother Zelophehad[c] to his daughters.
3Now suppose they marry men from other Israelite tribes; then their inheritance will
be taken from our ancestral inheritance and added to that of the tribe they marry into.
And so part of the inheritance allotted to us will be taken away. 4When the Year of
Jubilee[d] for the Israelites comes, their inheritance will be added to that of the tribe
into which they marry, and their property will be taken from the tribal inheritance of
our forefathers."
5Then at the LORD's command Moses gave this order to the Israelites: "What the
tribe of the descendants of Joseph is saying is right. 6This is what the LORD commands
for Zelophehad's daughters: They may marry anyone they please as long as they marry
within the tribal clan of their father. 7No inheritance[e] in Israel is to pass from tribe
to tribe, for every Israelite shall keep the tribal land inherited from his forefathers.
8Every daughter who inherits land in any Israelite tribe must marry someone in her
father's tribal clan,[f] so that every Israelite will possess the inheritance of his fathers.
9No inheritance may pass from tribe to tribe, for each Israelite tribe is to keep the land
it inherits."
10So Zelophehad's daughters did as the LORD commanded Moses. 11Zelophehad's
daughters—Mahlah, Tirzah, Hoglah, Milcah and Noah[g]—married their cousins on
their father's side. 12They married within the clans of the descendants of Manasseh
son of Joseph, and their inheritance remained in their father's clan and tribe.
13These are the commands and regulations the LORD gave through Moses[h] to the
Israelites on the plains of Moab by the Jordan across from Jericho.[a][i]

a *13* Hebrew *Jordan of Jericho*; possibly an ancient name for the Jordan River

36:1 [a]Nu 26:29 [b]Nu 27:2
36:2 [c]Nu 26:33; 27:1, 7
36:4 [d]Lev 25:10
36:7 [e]1Ki 21:3
36:8 [f]1Ch 23:22
36:11 [g]Nu 26:33; 27:1
36:13 [h]Lev 26:46; 27:34 [i]Nu 22:1

36:1-9 Zelophehad had five daughters but no sons. After he died, his daughters appealed to Moses. Because the inheritance normally passed only through the male line, the family line of Zelophehad would have disappeared. God told Moses that if a man died without sons, then the inheritance would go to his daughters (27:8). But the question of marriage arose. If the daughters were to marry outside of their tribe, the land would belong to another tribe at the Year of Jubilee. So Moses commanded that in such cases the women should marry men in their own clan and tribe so that each tribe would retain its original inheritance. Later, when the tribes received their land under Joshua, the daughters of Zelophehad received their inheritance as God had instructed (Joshua 17:3–6).

We don't have to look far to find those who want to be considered "special cases" and "exceptions to the rule", but wise leaders will sort out those who have legitimate concerns and make sure that justice is done in these special situations.

36:13 The book of Numbers covers 39 years and closes with the Israelites poised near the banks of the Jordan River with the promised land in sight. The wanderings in the desert have come to an end, and the people are preparing for their next big move—the conquest of the land. The apostle Paul says that the events described in Numbers are examples that warn us and help us avoid the Israelites' mistakes (1 Corinthians 10:1–12). From their experiences we learn that unbelief is disastrous. We also learn not to long for the sinful pleasures of the past, to avoid complaining, and to stay away from all forms of compromise. If we choose to let God lead our lives, we should not ignore his message in the book of Numbers.

EIGHT WORDS FOR LAW

Hebrew law served as the personal and national guide for living under God's authority. It directed the moral, spiritual, and social life. Its purpose was to produce better understanding of God and greater commitment to him.

Word	*Meaning*	*Examples*	*Significance*
Torah	Direction, Guidance, Instruction	Exodus 24:12; Isaiah 12:23; 30:20	Need for law in general; a command from a higher person to a lower.
Mitswah	Commandment, Command	Genesis 25:5; Exodus 15:26; 20:2-17 Deuteronomy 5:6-21	God's specific instruction to be obeyed rather than a general law; used of the Ten Commandments.
Mishpat	Judgment, Ordinance	Genesis 18:19; Deuteronomy 34:2; 16:18; 17:9	Refers to the civil, social, and sanitation laws.
Eduth	Admonition, Testimony	Exodus 25:22	Refers to God's law as he deals with his people.
Huqqim	Statutes, Oracles	Leviticus 18:4; Deuteronomy 4:1	Dealt with the royal pronouncements; mainly connected to worship and feasts.
Piqqudim	Orders, Precepts	Psalms 19:8; 103:8	Used often in the psalms to describe God's orders and assignments.
Dabar	Word	Exodus 34:28; Deuteronomy 4:13	Used to indicate divine oracles or revelations of God.
Dath	Royal Edict Public law	Ezekiel 7:26; Daniel 2:3, 15; 6:8, 12	Refers to the divine law or Jewish religious traditions in general.

DEUTERONOMY

Joseph dies 1805 B.C. (1640 B.C.) — S L A V E R Y I N E G Y P T — Exodus from Egypt 1446 (1280) — Ten Commar ments given 1445 (1279)

DESERT WANDERI

VITAL STATISTICS

PURPOSE:
To remind the people of what God had done and encourage them to rededicate their lives to him

AUTHOR:
Moses (except for the final summary, which was probably written by Joshua after Moses' death)

TO WHOM WRITTEN:
Israel (the new generation entering the promised land)

DATE WRITTEN:
About 1407/6 B.C.

SETTING:
The east side of the Jordan River, in view of Canaan

KEY VERSE:
"Know therefore that the LORD your God is God; he is the faithful God, keeping his covenant of love to a thousand generations of those who love him and keep his commands" (7:9).

KEY PEOPLE:
Moses, Joshua

KEY PLACE:
The Arabah in Moab

SCHOOL reunions, scrapbooks and photo albums, familiar songs, and old neighbourhoods—like long-time friends they awaken our memories and stir our emotions. The past is a kaleidoscope of promises, failures, victories, and embarrassments. Sometimes we want to forget memories that are too painful. However, as the years pass, remembrances of unpleasant events usually fade into our subconscious. But there is a time to remember: mistakes should not be repeated; commitments made must be fulfilled; and the memory of special events can encourage us and move us to action.

The book of Deuteronomy is written in the form of a treaty between a king and his vassal state typical of the second millennium B.C. It calls Israel to remember who God is and what he has done. Lacking faith, the old generation had wandered for 40 years and died in the desert. They left Egypt behind, but never knew the promised land. Then on the east bank of the Jordan River, Moses prepared the sons and daughters of that faithless generation to possess the land. After a brief history lesson emphasising God's great acts on behalf of his people, Moses reviewed the law. Then he restated the covenant—God's contract with his people.

The lessons are clear. Because of what God has done, Israel should have hope and follow him; because of what he expects, they should listen and obey; because of who he is, they should love him completely. Learning these lessons will prepare them to possess the promised land.

As you hear the message of Deuteronomy, remember how God has expressed his kindness in your life, and then commit yourself anew to trust, love, and obey him.

THE BLUEPRINT

A. WHAT GOD HAS DONE FOR US: MOSES' FIRST ADDRESS (1:1—4:43)

Moses reviewed the mighty acts of God for the nation of Israel. Remembering God's special involvement in our lives gives us hope and encouragement for the future.

B. PRINCIPLES FOR GODLY LIVING: MOSES' SECOND ADDRESS (4:44—28:68)
1. The Ten Commandments
2. Love the Lord your God
3. Laws for proper worship
4. Laws for ruling the nation
5. Laws for human relationships
6. Consequences of obedience and disobedience

Obeying God's laws brought blessings to the Israelites and disobeying brought misfortune. This was part of the written agreement God made with his people. Although we are not part of this covenant, the principle holds true: obedience and disobedience carry inevitable consequences in this life and the next.

Moses' death; Israelites enter Canaan 1406 (1240)	*Judges begin to rule 1375 (1220)*	*United kingdom under Saul 1050 (1045)*

C. A CALL FOR COMMITMENT TO GOD: MOSES' THIRD ADDRESS (29:1—30:20)	Moses called the people to commitment. God still calls us to be committed to love him with all our heart, soul, mind, and strength.
D. THE CHANGE IN LEADERSHIP: MOSES' LAST DAYS (31:1—34:12)	Although Moses made some serious mistakes, he had lived uprightly and carried out God's commands. Moses died with integrity. We too may make some serious mistakes, but that should not stop us from living with integrity and godly commitment.

MEGATHEMES

THEME	EXPLANATION	IMPORTANCE
History	Moses reviewed the mighty acts of God whereby he liberated Israel from slavery in Egypt. He recounted how God had helped them and how the people had disobeyed.	By reviewing God's promises and mighty acts in history, we can learn about his character. We come to know God more intimately through understanding how he has acted in the past. We can also avoid mistakes in our own lives through learning from Israel's past failures.
Laws	God reviewed his laws for the people. The legal contract between God and his people had to be renewed by the new generation about to enter the promised land.	Commitment to God and his truth cannot be taken for granted. Each generation and each person must respond afresh to God's call for obedience.
Love	God's faithful and patient love is portrayed more often than his punishment. God shows his love by being faithful to his people and his promises. In response, God desires love from the heart, not merely legalistically keeping his law.	God's love forms the foundation for our trust in him. We trust him because he loves us. Because God loves us, we should maintain justice and respect.
Choices	God reminded his people that in order to ratify his agreement they must choose the path of obedience. A personal decision to obey would bring benefits to their lives; rebellion would bring severe calamity.	Our choices make a difference. Choosing to follow God benefits us and improves our relationships with others. Choosing to abandon God's ways brings harm to ourselves and others.
Teaching	God commanded the Israelites to teach their children his ways. They were to use ritual, instruction, and memorisation to make sure their children understood God's principles and passed them on to the next generation.	Quality teaching for our children must be a priority. It is important to pass on God's truth to future generations in our traditions. But God desires that his truth be in our hearts and minds and not merely in our traditions.

A. WHAT GOD HAS DONE FOR US: MOSES' FIRST ADDRESS (1:1—4:43)

God has led his people out of Egypt and across the great desert. Now they stand ready to enter the promised land. But before the Israelites go into the land, Moses has some important advice to give them. He delivers his advice in three parts. In the first part, Moses reviews the history of God's previous care for the people of Israel. Through God's actions in the past, we can learn about the God we serve today.

The Command to Leave Horeb

1 These are the words Moses spoke to all Israel in the desert east of the Jordan—that
is, in the Arabah—opposite Suph, between Paran and Tophel, Laban, Hazeroth
and Dizahab. 2(It takes eleven days to go from Horeb[a] to Kadesh Barnea[b] by the
Mount Seir road.)
3In the fortieth year,[c] on the first day of the eleventh month, Moses proclaimed[d]
to the Israelites all that the LORD had commanded him concerning them. 4This was
after he had defeated Sihon[e] king of the Amorites, who reigned in Heshbon,[f] and
at Edrei had defeated Og[g] king of Bashan, who reigned in Ashtaroth.
5East of the Jordan in the territory of Moab, Moses began to expound this law,
saying:

6The LORD our God said to us[h] at Horeb,[i] "You have stayed long enough at this
mountain. 7Break camp and advance into the hill country of the Amorites; go to all
the neighbouring peoples in the Arabah, in the mountains, in the western foothills,
in the Negev[j] and along the coast, to the land of the Canaanites and to Lebanon,[k]
as far as the great river, the Euphrates. 8See, I have given you this land. Go in and
take possession of the land that the LORD swore[l] he would give to your fathers—to
Abraham, Isaac and Jacob—and to their descendants after them."

The Appointment of Leaders

9At that time I said to you, "You are too heavy a burden for me to carry alone.[m]
10The LORD your God has increased your numbers so that today you are as many[n]

1:2 [a]Ex 3:1 [b]Nu 13:26; Dt 9:23
1:3 [c]Nu 33:38 [d]Dt 4:1-2
1:4 [e]Nu 21:21-26 [f]Nu 21:25 [g]Nu 21:33-35; Jos 13:12
1:6 [h]Nu 10:13 [i]Ex 3:1
1:7 [j]Jos 10:40 [k]Dt 11:24
1:8 [l]Ge 12:7; 15:18; 17:7-8; 26:4; 28:13
1:9 [m]Ex 18:18
1:10 [n]Ge 15:5

1:1, 2 The Israelites spent 40 years on a journey that should have lasted 11 days. It wasn't distance that stood between them and the promised land. It was the condition of their hearts. God's purpose went deeper than simply transporting a huge group of people to a new land. He was preparing them to live in obedience to him once they arrived. What good was the promised land if the Israelites were just as wicked as the nations already living there? The journey was a painful but necessary part of their preparation. Through it God taught the Israelites who he was: the living God, the Leader of their nation. He also taught them who they were: people who were fallen, sinful, prone to rebellion and doubt. He gave his rebellious people the law to help them understand how to relate to God and to other people. Your spiritual pilgrimage may be lengthy, and you may face pain, discouragement, and difficulties. But remember that God isn't just trying to keep you alive. He wants to prepare you to live in service and devotion to him.

1:1–5 The 40 years of desert wandering come to an end in this book. The events of Deuteronomy cover only a week or two of the 11th month of the 40th year (1:3). The 12th and last month was spent in mourning for Moses (34:8). Then the Israelites entered the promised land the first month of the 41st year after the exodus (Joshua 4:19).

1:6, 7 Notice that Moses' summary of Israel's 40-year journey begins at Mount Horeb (Sinai), not in Egypt. Why did Moses leave out the first part of the exodus? Moses was not giving an itinerary—he was summarising the nation's development. In Moses' mind the nation of Israel began at the base of Mount Sinai, not in Egypt, for it was at Mount Sinai that God gave his covenant to the people (Exodus 19, 20). Along with this covenant came knowledge and responsibility. After the people chose to follow God (and it was their choice), they had to know *how* to follow him. Therefore, God gave them a comprehensive set of laws and guidelines that stated how he wanted them to live (these are found in the books of Exodus, Leviticus, and Numbers). The people could no longer say they didn't know the difference between right and wrong. Now that the people had promised to follow God and knew how to follow him, they had a responsibility to do it. When God tells you to break camp and move out to face a challenge he gives you, will you be ready to obey?

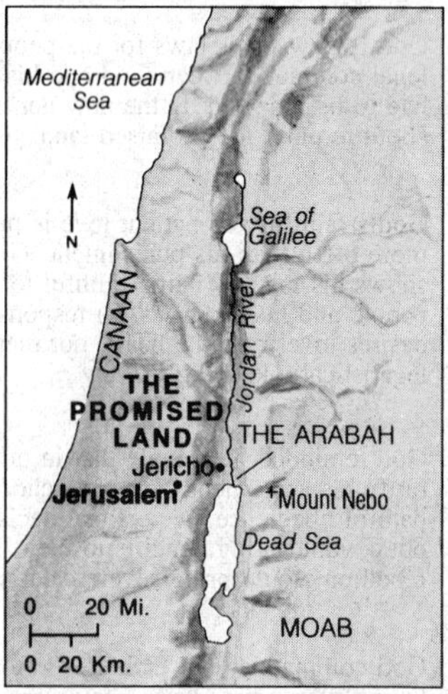

EVENTS IN DEUTERONOMY The book of Deuteronomy opens with Israel camped east of the Jordan River in the Arabah in the land of Moab. Just before the people crossed the river into the promised land, Moses delivered an inspirational speech indicating how they were to live.

1:9–13 It was a tremendous burden for Moses to lead the nation by himself. He could not accomplish the task single-handedly. Like nations, as organisations and churches grow, they become in-

as the stars in the sky.[o] 11May the LORD, the God of your fathers, increase you a
thousand times and bless you as he has promised![p] 12But how can I bear your
problems and your burdens and your disputes all by myself? 13Choose some wise,
understanding and respected men[q] from each of your tribes, and I will set them over
you."
14You answered me, "What you propose to do is good."
15So I took[r] the leading men of your tribes, wise and respected men, and appointed
them to have authority over you—as commanders of thousands, of hundreds, of fifties
and of tens and as tribal officials. 16And I charged your judges at that time: Hear the
disputes between your brothers and judge fairly,[s] whether the case is between brother
Israelites or between one of them and an alien.[t] 17Do not show partiality[u] in judging;
hear both small and great alike. Do not be afraid of any man,[v] for judgment belongs
to God. Bring me any case too hard for you, and I will hear it.[w] 18And at that time
I told you everything you were to do.

Spies Sent Out

19Then, as the LORD our God commanded us, we set out from Horeb and went
towards the hill country of the Amorites through all that vast and dreadful desert[x]
that you have seen, and so we reached Kadesh Barnea.[y] 20Then I said to you, "You
have reached the hill country of the Amorites, which the LORD our God is giving us.
21See, the LORD your God has given you the land. Go up and take possession of it
as the LORD, the God of your fathers, told you. Do not be afraid;[z] do not be
discouraged."
22Then all of you came to me and said, "Let us send men ahead to spy out the land
for us and bring back a report about the route we are to take and the towns we will
come to."
23The idea seemed good to me; so I selected[a] twelve of you, one man from each
tribe. 24They left and went up into the hill country, and came to the Valley of Eshcol[b]
and explored it. 25Taking with them some of the fruit of the land, they brought it down
to us and reported,[c] "It is a good land that the LORD our God is giving us."

Rebellion Against the LORD

26But you were unwilling to go up;[d] you rebelled against the command of the LORD
your God. 27You grumbled[e] in your tents and said, "The LORD hates us; so he brought
us out of Egypt to deliver us into the hands of the Amorites to destroy us. 28Where
can we go? Our brothers have made us lose heart. They say, 'The people are stronger
and taller[f] than we are; the cities are large, with walls up to the sky. We even saw
the Anakites[g] there.' "
29Then I said to you, "Do not be terrified; do not be afraid of them. 30The LORD

1:10 [o]Dt 10:22; 28:62
1:11 [p]Ge 22:17; Ex 32:13
1:13 [q]Ex 18:21
1:15 [r]Ex 18:25
1:16 [s]Dt 16:18; Jn 7:24 [t]Lev 24:22
1:17 [u]Lev 19:15; Dt 16:19; Pr 24:23; Jas 2:1 [v]2Ch 19:6 [w]Ex 18:26
1:19 [x]Dt 8:15; Jer 2:2, 6 [y]ver 2; Nu 13:26
1:21 [z]Jos 1:6, 9, 18
1:23 [a]Nu 13:1-3
1:24 [b]Nu 13:21-25
1:25 [c]Nu 13:27
1:26 [d]Nu 14:1-4
1:27 [e]Dt 9:28; Ps 106:25
1:28 [f]Nu 13:32 [g]Nu 13:33; Dt 9:1-3

---

creasingly complex. Conflicting needs and quarrels arise. No longer can one leader make all the decisions. Like Moses, you may have a natural tendency to try to do all the work alone. You may be afraid or embarrassed to ask for help. Moses made a wise decision to share the leadership with others. Rather than trying to handle larger responsibilities alone, look for ways of sharing the load so that others may exercise their God-given gifts and abilities.

1:13–18 Moses identified some of the inner qualities of good leaders: (1) wisdom, (2) understanding, and (3) respect. These characteristics differ markedly from the ones that often help elect leaders today: good looks, wealth, popularity, willingness to do anything to get to the top. The qualities Moses identified should be evident in us as we lead, and we should look for them in those we elect to positions of leadership.

1:22 The spies were sent into the land to determine not *whether* they should enter, but *where* they should enter. Upon returning, however, most of the spies concluded that the land was not worth the obstacles. God would give the Israelites the power to conquer the land, but they were afraid of the risk and decided not to enter. God gives us the power to overcome our obstacles, but like the Israelites filled with fear and scepticism, we often let difficulties control our lives. Following God regardless of the difficulties is the way to have courageous, overcoming faith.

1:23–40 Moses retold the story of the spy mission into the promised land (Numbers 13; 14). When the spies returned with reports of giants (Anakites) and walled cities, the people were afraid to move ahead and began to complain about their predicament. But the minority report of Joshua and Caleb pointed out that the land was fertile, the enemy was vulnerable, and God was on their side. We become fearful and immobile when we focus on the negative aspects of a situation. How much better it is to focus on the positive—God's direction and promises. When confronted with an important decision and you know what you should do, move out in faith. Focus on the positives while trusting God to overcome the negatives. Problems don't have to rob you of the victory.

1:28 Canaan was a land with giants and imposing fortresses. The "Anakites" may have been seven to nine feet tall. Many of the land's fortified cities had walls as high as 30 feet. The Israelites' fear was understandable, but not justified, for the all-powerful God had already promised them victory.

your God, who is going before you, will fight[h] for you, as he did for you in Egypt,
before your very eyes, 31and in the desert. There you saw how the LORD your God
carried[i] you, as a father carries his son, all the way you went until you reached this
place."
32In spite of this, you did not trust[j] in the LORD your God, 33who went ahead of
you on your journey, in fire by night and in a cloud by day,[k] to search[l] out places
for you to camp and to show you the way you should go.
34When the LORD heard what you said, he was angry and solemnly swore:[m] 35"Not
a man of this evil generation shall see the good land[n] I swore to give your forefathers,
36except Caleb son of Jephunneh. He will see it, and I will give him and his descendants the land he set his feet on, because he followed the LORD wholeheartedly.[o]"
37Because of you the LORD became angry[p] with me also and said, "You shall not
enter[q] it, either. 38But your assistant, Joshua[r] son of Nun, will enter it. Encourage[s]
him, because he will lead[t] Israel to inherit it. 39And the little ones that you said would
be taken captive,[u] your children who do not yet know[v] good from bad—they will
enter the land. I will give it to them and they will take possession of it. 40But as for
you, turn round and set out towards the desert along the route to the Red Sea."[a][w]
41Then you replied, "We have sinned against the LORD. We will go up and fight,
as the LORD our God commanded us." So every one of you put on his weapons,
thinking it easy to go up into the hill country.
42But the LORD said to me, "Tell them, 'Do not go up and fight, because I will not
be with you. You will be defeated by your enemies.' "[x]
43So I told you, but you would not listen. You rebelled against the LORD's command
and in your arrogance you marched up into the hill country. 44The Amorites who lived
in those hills came out against you; they chased you like a swarm of bees[y] and beat
you down from Seir all the way to Hormah. 45You came back and wept before the
LORD, but he paid no attention to your weeping and turned a deaf ear to you. 46And
so you stayed in Kadesh[z] many days—all the time you spent there.

Wanderings in the Desert

2 Then we turned back and set out towards the desert along the route to the Red
Sea,[a][a] as the LORD had directed me. For a long time we made our way around
the hill country of Seir.
2Then the LORD said to me, 3"You have made your way around this hill country
long enough; now turn north. 4Give the people these orders:[b] 'You are about to pass
through the territory of your brothers the descendants of Esau, who live in Seir. They
will be afraid of you, but be very careful. 5Do not provoke them to war, for I will
not give you any of their land, not even enough to put your foot on. I have given Esau
the hill country of Seir as his own.[c] 6You are to pay them in silver for the food you
eat and the water you drink.' "
7The LORD your God has blessed you in all the work of your hands. He has
watched[d] over your journey through this vast desert. These forty years the LORD your
God has been with you, and you have not lacked anything.
8So we went on past our brothers the descendants of Esau, who live in Seir. We
turned from the Arabah road, which comes up from Elath and Ezion Geber,[e] and
travelled along the desert road of Moab.[f]
9Then the LORD said to me, "Do not harass the Moabites or provoke them to war,
for I will not give you any part of their land. I have given Ar[g] to the descendants
of Lot[h] as a possession."
10(The Emites[i] used to live there—a people strong and numerous, and as tall as

1:30 [h]Ex 14:14; Dt 3:22; Ne 4:20
1:31 [i]Dt 32:10-12; Isa 46:3-4; 63:9; Hos 11:3; Ac 13:18
1:32 [j]Ps 106:24; Jude 1:5
1:33 [k]Ex 13:21; Ps 78:14 [l]Nu 10:33
1:34 [m]Nu 14:23, 28-30
1:35 [n]Ps 95:11
1:36 [o]Nu 14:24; Jos 14:9
1:37 [p]Dt 3:26; 4:21 [q]Nu 20:12
1:38 [r]Nu 14:30 [s]Dt 31:7 [t]Dt 3:28
1:39 [u]Nu 14:3 [v]Isa 7:15-16
1:40 [w]Nu 14:25
1:42 [x]Nu 14:41-43
1:44 [y]Ps 118:12
1:46 [z]Nu 20:1; Jdg 11:17
2:1 [a]Nu 21:4
2:4 [b]Nu 20:14-21
2:5 [c]Ge 36:8; Jos 24:4
2:7 [d]Dt 8:2-4
2:8 [e]1Ki 9:26 [f]Jdg 11:18
2:9 [g]Nu 21:15 [h]Ge 19:36-38
2:10 [i]Ge 14:5

[a] 40 Hebrew *Yam Suph*; that is, Sea of Reeds [a] 1 Hebrew *Yam Suph*; that is, Sea of Reeds

2:4–6 When the Israelites passed through Seir, God advised them to be careful. The Israelites were known as warriors, and the children of Esau—the Edomites—would be understandably nervous as the great crowd passed through their land. God warned the Israelites not to start a fight, to respect the Edomites' territory, and to pay for whatever they used. God wanted the Israelites to deal justly with these neighbours. We must also act justly in dealing with others. Recognise the rights of others, even your opponents. By behaving wisely and justly you may be able to establish or restore a relationship.

the Anakites.[j] 11Like the Anakites, they too were considered Rephaites, but the Moabites called them Emites. 12Horites used to live in Seir, but the descendants of Esau drove them out. They destroyed the Horites from before them and settled in their place, just as Israel did[k] in the land the LORD gave them as their possession.)

13And the LORD said, "Now get up and cross the Zered Valley." So we crossed the valley.

14Thirty-eight years passed from the time we left Kadesh Barnea[l] until we crossed the Zered Valley. By then, that entire generation[m] of fighting men had perished from the camp, as the LORD had sworn to them.[n] 15The LORD's hand was against them until he had completely eliminated[o] them from the camp.

16Now when the last of these fighting men among the people had died, 17the LORD said to me, 18"Today you are to pass by the region of Moab at Ar. 19When you come to the Ammonites,[p] do not harass them or provoke them to war, for I will not give you possession of any land belonging to the Ammonites. I have given it as a possession to the descendants of Lot.[q]"

20(That too was considered a land of the Rephaites, who used to live there; but the Ammonites called them Zamzummites. 21They were a people strong and numerous, and as tall as the Anakites.[r] The LORD destroyed them from before the Ammonites, who drove them out and settled in their place. 22The LORD had done the same for the descendants of Esau, who lived in Seir,[s] when he destroyed the Horites from before them. They drove them out and have lived in their place to this day. 23And as for the Avvites[t] who lived in villages as far as Gaza, the Caphtorites[u] coming out from Caphtor[b][v] destroyed them and settled in their place.)

Defeat of Sihon King of Heshbon

24"Set out now and cross the Arnon Gorge.[w] See, I have given into your hand Sihon the Amorite, king of Heshbon, and his country. Begin to take possession of it and engage him in battle. 25This very day I will begin to put the terror[x] and fear[y] of you on all the nations under heaven. They will hear reports of you and will tremble[z] and be in anguish because of you."

26From the desert of Kedemoth I sent messengers to Sihon king of Heshbon offering peace and saying, 27"Let us pass through your country. We will stay on the main road; we will not turn aside to the right or to the left.[a] 28Sell us food to eat and water to drink for their price in silver. Only let us pass through on foot[b]— 29as the descendants of Esau, who live in Seir, and the Moabites, who live in Ar, did for us—until we cross the Jordan into the land the LORD our God is giving us." 30But Sihon king of Heshbon refused to let us pass through. For the LORD[c] your God had made his spirit stubborn[d] and his heart obstinate in order to give him into your hands, as he has now done.

31The LORD said to me, "See, I have begun to deliver Sihon and his country over to you. Now begin to conquer and possess his land."[e]

32When Sihon and all his army came out to meet us in battle[f] at Jahaz, 33the LORD our God delivered him over to us and we struck him down,[g] together with his sons and his whole army. 34At that time we took all his towns and completely destroyed[c][h] them—men, women and children. We left no survivors. 35But the livestock and the

b *23* That is, Crete **c** *34* The Hebrew term refers to the irrevocable giving over of things or persons to the LORD, often by totally destroying them.

2:10 [j]Nu 13:22, 33
2:12 [k]ver 22
2:14 [l]Nu 13:26 [m]Nu 14:29-35 [n]Dt 1:34-35
2:15 [o]Ps 106:26
2:19 [p]Ge 19:38 [q]ver 9
2:21 [r]ver 10
2:22 [s]Ge 36:8
2:23 [t]Jos 13:3 [u]Ge 10:14 [v]Am 9:7
2:24 [w]Nu 21:13-14; Jdg 11:13, 18
2:25 [x]Dt 11:25 [y]Jos 2:9, 11 [z]Ex 15:14-16
2:27 [a]Nu 21:21-22
2:28 [b]Nu 20:19
2:30 [c]Jos 11:20 [d]Ex 4:21; Nu 21:23; Ro 9:18
2:31 [e]Dt 1:8
2:32 [f]Nu 21:23
2:33 [g]Dt 29:7
2:34 [h]Dt 3:6; 7:2

2:11 Both Moab and Ammon had removed a tall Anakim-like people usually known as the Rephaites, but called Emites by the Moabites and Zamzummites by the Ammonites (2:20). If our enemies seem overwhelming, we must remember that God can deliver us as he did the Israelites.

2:14, 15 Israel did not have to spend 40 years on the way to the promised land. God sentenced them to desert wanderings because they rejected his love, rebelled against his authority, ignored his commands for right living, and wilfully broke their end of the agreement made in Exodus 19:8 and 24:3–8. In short, they disobeyed God. We often make life's journey more difficult than necessary by disobedience. Accept God's love, read and follow his commands in the Bible, and make a promise to stick with God whatever your situation. You will find that your life will be less complicated and more rewarding.

2:25 God told Moses he would make the enemy nations afraid of Israel. By worldly standards, Israel's army was not intimidating, but Israel had God on its side. Moses no longer had to worry about his enemies because his enemies were worried about him. God often goes before us in our daily battles, preparing the way and overcoming barriers. We need to follow him wholeheartedly and be alert to his leading.

plunder from the towns we had captured we carried off for ourselves. 36 From Aroer[i]
on the rim of the Arnon Gorge, and from the town in the gorge, even as far as Gilead,
not one town was too strong for us. The LORD our God gave[j] us all of them. 37 But
in accordance with the command of the LORD our God,[k] you did not encroach on
any of the land of the Ammonites,[l] neither the land along the course of the Jabbok[m]
nor that around the towns in the hills.

Defeat of Og King of Bashan

3 Next we turned and went up along the road towards Bashan, and Og king of
Bashan with his whole army marched out to meet us in battle at Edrei.[a] 2 The
LORD said to me, "Do not be afraid[b] of him, for I have handed him over to you with
his whole army and his land. Do to him what you did to Sihon king of the Amorites,
who reigned in Heshbon."
3 So the LORD our God also gave into our hands Og king of Bashan and all his army.
We struck them down, leaving no survivors.[c] 4 At that time we took all his cities.
There was not one of the sixty cities that we did not take from them—the whole region
of Argob, Og's kingdom in Bashan.[d] 5 All these cities were fortified with high walls
and with gates and bars, and there were also a great many unwalled villages. 6 We
completely destroyed**[a]** them, as we had done with Sihon king of Heshbon, destroying**[a]**[e] every city—men, women and children. 7 But all the livestock and the plunder
from their cities we carried off for ourselves.
8 So at that time we took from these two kings of the Amorites the territory east of
the Jordan, from the Arnon Gorge as far as Mount Hermon. 9 (Hermon is called
Sirion[f] by the Sidonians; the Amorites call it Senir.)[g] 10 We took all the towns on
the plateau, and all Gilead, and all Bashan as far as Salecah[h] and Edrei, towns of
Og's kingdom in Bashan. 11 (Only Og king of Bashan was left of the remnant of the
Rephaites.[i] His bed**[b]** was made of iron and was more than thirteen feet long and
six feet wide.**[c]** It is still in Rabbah[j] of the Ammonites.)

Division of the Land

12 Of the land that we took over at that time, I gave the Reubenites and the Gadites
the territory north of Aroer[k] by the Arnon Gorge, including half the hill country of
Gilead, together with its towns. 13 The rest of Gilead and also all of Bashan, the
kingdom of Og, I gave to the half-tribe of Manasseh. (The whole region of Argob
in Bashan used to be known as a land of the Rephaites. 14 Jair,[l] a descendant of
Manasseh, took the whole region of Argob as far as the border of the Geshurites and
the Maacathites; it was named after him, so that to this day Bashan is called Havvoth
Jair.**[d]**) 15 And I gave Gilead to Makir.[m] 16 But to the Reubenites and the Gadites I
gave the territory extending from Gilead down to the Arnon Gorge (the middle of the
gorge being the border) and out to the Jabbok River,[n] which is the border of the
Ammonites. 17 Its western border was the Jordan in the Arabah, from Kinnereth[o] to
the Sea of the Arabah (the Salt Sea**[e]**[p]), below the slopes of Pisgah.
18 I commanded you at that time: "The LORD your God has given you this land to
take possession of it. But all your able-bodied men, armed for battle, must cross over
ahead of your brother Israelites.[q] 19 However, your wives, your children and your
livestock (I know you have much livestock) may stay in the towns I have given you,
20 until the LORD gives rest to your brothers as he has to you, and they too have taken
over the land that the LORD your God is giving them, across the Jordan. After that,
each of you may go back to the possession I have given you."

2:36 [i]Dt 3:12; 4:48; Jos 13:9 [j]Ps 44:3
2:37 [k]ver 18-19 [l]Nu 21:24 [m]Ge 32:22; Dt 3:16
3:1 [a]Nu 21:33
3:2 [b]Nu 21:34
3:3 [c]Nu 21:35
3:4 [d]1Ki 4:13
3:6 [e]Dt 2:24, 34
3:9 [f]Dt 4:48; Ps 29:6 [g]1Ch 5:23
3:10 [h]Jos 13:11
3:11 [i]Ge 14:5 [j]2Sa 12:26; Jer 49:2
3:12 [k]Nu 32:32-38; Dt 2:36; Jos 13:8-13
3:14 [l]Nu 32:41; 1Ch 2:22
3:15 [m]Nu 32:39-40
3:16 [n]Nu 21:24
3:17 [o]Nu 34:11; Jos 13:27 [p]Ge 14:3; Jos 12:3
3:18 [q]Nu 32:17

a *6* The Hebrew term refers to the irrevocable giving over of things or persons to the LORD, often by totally destroying them. **b** *11* Or *sarcophagus* **c** *11* Hebrew *nine cubits long and four cubits wide* (about 4 metres long and 1.8 metres wide) **d** *14* Or *called the settlements of Jair* **e** *17* That is, the Dead Sea

---

3:1–3 The Israelites faced a big problem—the well-trained army of Og, king of Bashan. The Israelites hardly stood a chance. But they won because God fought for them. God can help his people regardless of the problems they face. No matter how insurmountable the obstacles may seem, remember that God is sovereign, and he will keep his promises.

3:22
[r]Dt 1:29
[s]Ex 14:14; Dt 20:4

3:24
[t]Dt 11:2
[u]Ex 15:11; Ps 86:8
[v]Ps 71:16, 19
[w]2Sa 7:22

3:25
[x]Dt 4:22

3:26
[y]Dt 1:37; 31:2

3:27
[z]Nu 27:12

3:28
[a]Nu 27:18-23
[b]Dt 31:3, 23

3:29
[c]Dt 4:46; 34:6

4:1
[a]Dt 5:33; 8:1; 16:20; 30:15-20; Eze 20:11; Ro 10:5

4:2
[b]Dt 12:32; Jos 1:7; Rev 22:18-19

4:3
[c]Nu 25:1-9; Ps 106:28

4:6
[d]Dt 30:19-20; Ps 19:7; Pr 1:7
[e]Job 28:28

4:7
[f]2Sa 7:23
[g]Ps 46:1; Isa 55:6

Moses Forbidden to Cross the Jordan

21 At that time I commanded Joshua: "You have seen with your own eyes all that
the LORD your God has done to these two kings. The LORD will do the same to all
the kingdoms over there where you are going. 22 Do not be afraid[r] of them; the LORD
your God himself will fight[s] for you."
23 At that time I pleaded with the LORD: 24 "O Sovereign LORD, you have begun to
show to your servant your greatness[t] and your strong hand. For what god[u] is there
in heaven or on earth who can do the deeds and mighty works[v] you do?[w] 25 Let me
go over and see the good land[x] beyond the Jordan—that fine hill country and
Lebanon."
26 But because of you the LORD was angry[y] with me and would not listen to me.
"That is enough," the LORD said. "Do not speak to me any more about this matter.
27 Go up to the top of Pisgah and look west and north and south and east. Look at the
land with your own eyes, since you are not going to cross this Jordan.[z] 28 But
commission[a] Joshua, and encourage and strengthen him, for he will lead this people
across[b] and will cause them to inherit the land that you will see." 29 So we stayed
in the valley near Beth Peor.[c]

Obedience Commanded

4 Hear now, O Israel, the decrees and laws I am about to teach you. Follow them
so that you may live[a] and may go in and take possession of the land that the
LORD, the God of your fathers, is giving you. 2 Do not add[b] to what I command you
and do not subtract from it, but keep the commands of the LORD your God that I give
you.
3 You saw with your own eyes what the LORD did at Baal Peor.[c] The LORD your
God destroyed from among you everyone who followed the Baal of Peor, 4 but all of
you who held fast to the LORD your God are still alive today.
5 See, I have taught you decrees and laws as the LORD my God commanded me,
so that you may follow them in the land you are entering to take possession of it.
6 Observe them carefully, for this will show your wisdom[d] and understanding to the
nations, who will hear about all these decrees and say, "Surely this great nation is a
wise and understanding people."[e] 7 What other nation is so great[f] as to have their
gods near[g] them the way the LORD our God is near us whenever we pray to him?
8 And what other nation is so great as to have such righteous decrees and laws as this
body of laws I am setting before you today?

3:21, 22 What encouraging news for Joshua, who was to lead his men against the persistent forces of evil in the promised land! Since God promised to help him win every battle, he had nothing to fear. Our battles may not be against godless armies, but they are just as real as Joshua's. Whether we are resisting temptation or battling fear, God has promised to fight with and for us as we obey him.

3:26–28 God had made it clear that Moses would not enter the promised land (Numbers 20:12). So God told Moses to commission Joshua as the new leader and encourage him in this new role. This is a good example to churches and organisations who must eventually replace their leaders. Good leaders prepare their people to function without them by discovering those with leadership potential, providing the training they need, and looking for ways to encourage them.

4:2 What is meant by adding to or subtracting from God's commands? These laws were the word of God, and they were complete. How could any human being, with limited wisdom and knowledge, edit God's perfect laws? To add to the laws would make them a burden; to subtract from the laws would make them incomplete. Thus the laws were to remain unchanged. To presume to make changes in God's law is to assume a position of authority over God who gave the laws (Matthew 5:17–19; 15:3–9; Revelation 22:18, 19). The religious leaders at the time of Christ did exactly this; they elevated their own laws to the same level as God's. Jesus rebuked them for this (Matthew 23:1–4).

4:8 Do the laws God gave to the Israelites still apply to Christians today? God's laws are designed to guide all people towards life-styles that are healthy, upright, and devoted to God. Their purpose was to point out sin (or potential sin) and show the proper way to deal with that sin. The Ten Commandments, the heart of God's law, are just as applicable today as they were 3,000 years ago because they proclaim a life-style endorsed by God. They are the perfect expression of who God is and how he wants people to live.

But God gave other laws besides the Ten Commandments. Are these just as important? God never issued a law that didn't have a purpose. However, many of the laws we read in the Pentateuch were directed specifically to people of that time and culture. Although a specific law may not apply to us, the timeless truth or principle behind the law does.

For example, Christians do not practise animal sacrifice in worship. However, the principles behind the sacrifices—forgiveness for sin and thankfulness to God—still apply. The sacrifices pointed to the ultimate sacrifice made for us by Jesus Christ. The New Testament says that with the death and resurrection of Jesus Christ the Old Testament laws were fulfilled. This means that while the Old Testament laws help us recognise our sins and correct our wrongdoings, it is Jesus Christ who takes our sins away. Jesus is now our primary example to follow because he alone perfectly obeyed the law and modelled its true intent.

9Only be careful,[h] and watch yourselves closely so that you do not forget the things
your eyes have seen or let them slip from your heart as long as you live. Teach[i] them
to your children[j] and to their children after them. 10Remember the day you stood
before the LORD your God at Horeb,[k] when he said to me, "Assemble the people
before me to hear my words so that they may learn to revere me as long as they live
in the land and may teach them to their children." 11You came near and stood at the
foot of the mountain while it blazed with fire[l] to the very heavens, with black clouds
and deep darkness. 12Then the LORD spoke[m] to you out of the fire. You heard the
sound of words but saw no form; there was only a voice. 13He declared to you his
covenant,[n] the Ten Commandments,[o] which he commanded you to follow and then
wrote them on two stone tablets. 14And the LORD directed me at that time to teach
you the decrees and laws you are to follow in the land that you are crossing the Jordan
to possess.

Idolatry Forbidden

15You saw no form[p] of any kind the day the LORD spoke to you at Horeb out of
the fire. Therefore watch yourselves very carefully,[q] 16so that you do not become
corrupt and make for yourselves an idol,[r] an image of any shape, whether formed
like a man or a woman, 17or like any animal on earth or any bird that flies in the air,
18or like any creature that moves along the ground or any fish in the waters below.
19And when you look up to the sky and see the sun,[s] the moon and the stars—all
the heavenly array[t]—do not be enticed into bowing down to them and worshipping
things the LORD your God has apportioned to all the nations under heaven. 20But as
for you, the LORD took you and brought you out of the iron-smelting furnace,[u] out
of Egypt, to be the people of his inheritance,[v] as you now are.
21The LORD was angry with me[w] because of you, and he solemnly swore that I
would not cross the Jordan and enter the good land the LORD your God is giving you
as your inheritance. 22I will die in this land; I will not cross the Jordan; but you are
about to cross over and take possession of that good land.[x] 23Be careful not to forget
the covenant[y] of the LORD your God that he made with you; do not make for
yourselves an idol[z] in the form of anything the LORD your God has forbidden. 24For
the LORD your God is a consuming fire,[a] a jealous God.
25After you have had children and grandchildren and have lived in the land a long
time—if you then become corrupt and make any kind of idol, doing evil[b] in the eyes
of the LORD your God and provoking him to anger, 26I call heaven and earth as
witnesses against you[c] this day that you will quickly perish from the land that you
are crossing the Jordan to possess. You will not live there long but will certainly be

4:9 [h]Pr 4:23 [i]Ge 18:19; Eph 6:4 [j]Ps 78:5-6
4:10 [k]Ex 19:9, 16
4:11 [l]Ex 19:18; Heb 12:18-19
4:12 [m]Ex 20:22; Dt 5:4, 22
4:13 [n]Dt 9:9, 11 [o]Ex 24:12; 31:18; 34:28
4:15 [p]Isa 40:18 [q]Jos 23:11
4:16 [r]Ex 20:4-5; 32:7; Dt 5:8; Ro 1:23
4:19 [s]Dt 17:3; Job 31:26 [t]2Ki 17:16; 21:3; Ro 1:25
4:20 [u]1Ki 8:51; Jer 11:4 [v]Ex 19:5; Dt 9:29
4:21 [w]Nu 20:12; Dt 1:37
4:22 [x]Dt 3:25
4:23 [y]ver 9, 16 [z]Ex 20:4
4:24 [a]Ex 24:17; Dt 9:3; Heb 12:29
4:25 [b]2Ki 17:2, 17
4:26 [c]Dt 30:18-19; Isa 1:2; Mic 6:2

4:9 Moses wanted to make sure that the people did not forget all they had seen God do, so he urged parents to teach their children about God's great miracles. This helped parents remember God's faithfulness and provided the means for passing on from one generation to the next the stories recounting God's great acts. It is easy to forget the wonderful ways God has worked in the lives of his people. But you can remember God's great acts of faithfulness by telling your children, friends, or associates what you have seen him do.

4:19 God was not excusing the other nations for their idol worship. He was simply saying that while judgment might be delayed for those other nations, it would be swift and complete for Israel because Israel knew God's laws. We must remember that idol worship was not just keeping statues around the house—harmless lumps of clay, wood, or iron. It was the commitment to the other evil qualities, beliefs, and practices the idol represented (such as murder, prostitution, cruelty in war, self-centredness) or to strengths and attributes of mankind, the animal kingdom, or the orderliness of stars that were revered without reference to God who created them. Because God had so clearly revealed himself in Israel's history, the Israelites had no excuse for worshipping anyone but the true God.

4:24 God is a consuming fire. Because he is morally perfect, he hates sin and cannot accept those who practise it. Moses' sin kept him from entering the promised land, and no sacrifice could remove that judgment. Sin kept us from entering God's presence, but Jesus Christ paid the penalty for our sin and removed God's judgment for ever by his death. Trusting in Jesus Christ will save you from God's anger and will allow you to begin a personal relationship with him.

4:24 Jealousy is a demand for someone else's exclusive affection or loyalty. Some jealousy is bad. It is destructive for a man to get upset when his wife talks pleasantly with another man. But other jealousy is good. It is right for a man to demand that his wife treat him, and only him, as her husband. Usually we use the word *jealousy* only for the bad reaction. But God's kind of jealousy is appropriate and good. He is defending his word and his high honour. He makes a strong, exclusive demand on us: We must treat only the Lord—and no-one else in all the universe—as God.

destroyed. 27The LORD will scatter[d] you among the peoples, and only a few of you
will survive among the nations to which the LORD will drive you. 28There you will
worship man-made gods[e] of wood and stone, which cannot see or hear or eat or
smell.[f] 29But if from there you seek[g] the LORD your God, you will find him if you
look for him with all your heart[h] and with all your soul.[i] 30When you are in distress
and all these things have happened to you, then in later days[j] you will return to the
LORD your God and obey him. 31For the LORD your God is a merciful[k] God; he will
not abandon or destroy you or forget the covenant with your forefathers, which he
confirmed to them by oath.

The LORD Is God

32Ask[l] now about the former days, long before your time, from the day God
created man on the earth;[m] ask from one end of the heavens to the other.[n] Has
anything so great as this ever happened, or has anything like it ever been heard of?
33Has any other people heard the voice of God[a] speaking out of fire, as you have,
and lived?[o] 34Has any god ever tried to take for himself one nation out of another
nation,[p] by testings, by miraculous signs[q] and wonders,[r] by war, by a mighty hand
and an outstretched arm,[s] or by great and awesome deeds,[t] like all the things the
LORD your God did for you in Egypt before your very eyes?
35You were shown these things so that you might know that the LORD is God;
besides him there is no other.[u] 36From heaven he made you hear his voice[v] to
discipline you. On earth he showed you his great fire, and you heard his words from
out of the fire. 37Because he loved[w] your forefathers and chose their descendants after
them, he brought you out of Egypt by his Presence and his great strength,[x] 38to drive
out before you nations greater and stronger than you and to bring you into their land
to give it to you for your inheritance,[y] as it is today.
39Acknowledge and take to heart this day that the LORD is God in heaven above
and on the earth below. There is no other.[z] 40Keep[a] his decrees and commands,
which I am giving you today, so that it may go well[b] with you and your children
after you and that you may live long[c] in the land the LORD your God gives you for
all time.

Cities of Refuge

41Then Moses set aside three cities east of the Jordan, 42to which anyone who had
killed a person could flee if he had unintentionally killed his neighbour without malice
aforethought. He could flee into one of these cities and save his life. 43The cities were
these: Bezer in the desert plateau, for the Reubenites; Ramoth in Gilead, for the
Gadites; and Golan in Bashan, for the Manassites.

a 33 Or *of a god*

4:27 [d]Lev 26:33; Dt 28:36, 64; Ne 1:8
4:28 [e]Dt 28:36, 64; 1Sa 26:19; Jer 16:13 [f]Ps 115:4-8; 135:15-18
4:29 [g]2Ch 15:4; Isa 55:6 [h]Jer 29:13 [i]Dt 30:1-3, 10
4:30 [j]Dt 31:29; Jer 23:20; Hos 3:5
4:31 [k]2Ch 30:9; Ne 9:31; Ps 116:5; Jnh 4:2
4:32 [l]Dt 32:7; Job 8:8 [m]Ge 1:27 [n]Mt 24:31
4:33 [o]Ex 20:22; Dt 5:24-26
4:34 [p]Ex 6:6 [q]Ex 7:3 [r]Dt 7:19; 26:8 [s]Ex 13:3 [t]Dt 34:12
4:35 [u]Dt 32:39; 1Sa 2:2; Isa 45:5, 18
4:36 [v]Ex 19:9, 19
4:37 [w]Dt 10:15 [x]Ex 13:3, 9, 14
4:38 [y]Dt 7:1; 9:5
4:39 [z]ver 35; Jos 2:11
4:40 [a]Lev 22:31; Dt 5:33 [b]Dt 5:16 [c]Dt 6:3, 18; Eph 6:2-3

4:29 Do you want to know God? God promised the Israelites that they would find him when they searched with all their hearts and souls. God is knowable and wants to be known – but we have to want to know him. Acts of service and worship must be accompanied by sincere devotion of the heart. As Hebrews 11:6 says, "Anyone who comes to him must believe that he exists and that he rewards those who earnestly seek him." God will reward those who pursue a relationship with him.

4:32 How tempted we are to look everywhere else but to God for our guidance and leadership! We trust medical doctors, financial advisers, and news commentators, but do we trust God? Get God's advice first (4:39, 40), and recognise his authority over every dimension of life.

4:40 Was Israel guaranteed prosperity for obeying God's laws? Yes – but we have to look carefully at what that means. God's laws were designed to make his chosen nation healthy, just, and merciful. When the people followed those laws, they prospered. This does not mean, however, that no sickness, no sadness, and no misunderstandings existed among them. Rather, it means that as a nation they prospered and that individuals' problems were handled as fairly as possible. Today God's promise of prosperity – his constant presence, comfort, and the resources to live as we should – extends to all believers. We will face trials; Jesus assured us of that. But we will avoid the misery that directly results from intentional sin, and we will know that a great treasure awaits us in heaven.

B. PRINCIPLES FOR GODLY LIVING: MOSES' SECOND ADDRESS (4:44–29:1)

After reviewing the history of Israel's journey, Moses recounts the Ten Commandments and the other laws given to the Israelites at Mount Sinai. He urges them to obey the law and reminds them of the consequences of disobeying God's laws. The Ten Commandments and all of God's laws point out to us where we fall short and show us how we should act as God's people.

Introduction to the Law

44 This is the law Moses set before the Israelites. 45 These are the stipulations,
decrees and laws Moses gave them when they came out of Egypt 46 and were in the
valley near Beth Peor east of the Jordan, in the land of Sihon[d] king of the Amorites,
who reigned in Heshbon and was defeated by Moses and the Israelites as they came
out of Egypt. 47 They took possession of his land and the land of Og king of Bashan,
the two Amorite kings east of the Jordan. 48 This land extended from Aroer[e] on the
rim of the Arnon Gorge to Mount Siyon[b][f] (that is, Hermon), 49 and included all the
Arabah east of the Jordan, as far as the Sea of the Arabah,[c] below the slopes of
Pisgah.

1. The Ten Commandments

5 Moses summoned all Israel and said:
Hear, O Israel, the decrees and the laws I declare in your hearing today. Learn
them and be sure to follow them. 2 The LORD our God made a covenant[a] with us at
Horeb. 3 It was not with our fathers that the LORD made this covenant, but with us,
with all of us who are alive here today.[b] 4 The LORD spoke[c] to you face to face out
of the fire on the mountain. 5 (At that time I stood between[d] the LORD and you to
declare to you the word of the LORD, because you were afraid[e] of the fire and did
not go up the mountain.) And he said:

6 "I am the LORD your God, who brought you out of Egypt, out of the land
of slavery.
7 "You shall have no other gods before[a] me.
8 "You shall not make for yourself an idol in the form of anything in heaven above
or on the earth beneath or in the waters below. 9 You shall not bow down
to them or worship them; for I, the LORD your God, am a jealous God,
punishing the children for the sin of the fathers to the third and fourth
generation of those who hate me,[f] 10 but showing love to a thousand
⌞generations⌟ of those who love me and keep my commandments.[g]
11 "You shall not misuse the name of the LORD your God, for the LORD will not
hold anyone guiltless who misuses his name.[h]
12 "Observe the Sabbath day by keeping it holy,[i] as the LORD your God has

b 48 Hebrew; Syriac (see also Deut. 3:9) *Sirion* c 49 That is, the Dead Sea a 7 Or *besides*

4:46 d Nu 21:26; Dt 3:29
4:48 e Dt 2:36 f Dt 3:9
5:2 a Ex 19:5
5:3 b Heb 8:9
5:4 c Dt 4:12, 33, 36
5:5 d Gal 3:19 e Ex 20:18, 21
5:9 f Ex 34:7
5:10 g Jer 32:18
5:11 h Lev 19:12; Mt 5:33-37
5:12 i Ex 20:8

5:1 The people had entered into a covenant with God, and Moses commanded them to hear, learn, and follow his statutes. Christians also have entered into a covenant with God (through Jesus Christ) and should be responsive to what God expects. Moses' threefold command to the Israelites is excellent advice for all God's followers. *Hearing* is absorbing and accepting information about God. *Learning* is understanding its meaning and implications. *Following* is putting into action all we have learned and understood. All three parts are essential to a growing relationship with God.

5:7 A *god* is whatever people put first in their lives. Some people literally worship other gods by joining cults or strange religions. In a more subtle way, many of us worship other gods by building our lives around something other than the one true God. If your greatest desire is for popularity, power, or money, you are devoting yourself to something other than God. To put God first, (1) recognise what is taking his place in your life; (2) renounce this substitute god as unworthy of your devotion; (3) ask God for forgiveness; (4) restructure your priorities so that love for God is the motive for everything you do; (5) examine yourself daily to be sure you are giving God first place.

5:8, 9 How would you feel if someone took a picture of you, framed it, stared at it a lot, showed it to others, but completely ignored the real you? God does not want to be treated this way either. He wants a genuine relationship with us, not mere ritual. He wants us to know him. God knows that if we put anything other than him at the centre of our lives, we will not reach our potential and become all that he wants us to be.

5:11 We are familar with the sin to be avoided in this commandment, that we should not misuse the name of the Lord by saying it in an empty or worthless way. But there is also a good work that is commanded: to use God's name to praise him and ascribe to him glory. This is the opposite of misusing his name. While you might be able to keep yourself from swearing, how have you done at finding time to praise God and honour his name?

commanded you. 13Six days you shall labour and do all your work, 14but
the seventh day[j] is a Sabbath to the LORD your God. On it you shall not
do any work, neither you, nor your son or daughter, nor your manservant
or maidservant, nor your ox, your donkey or any of your animals, nor the
alien within your gates, so that your manservant and maidservant may rest,
as you do. 15Remember that you were slaves in Egypt and that the LORD
your God brought you out of there with a mighty hand and an outstretched
arm.[k] Therefore the LORD your God has commanded you to observe the
Sabbath day.

16"Honour your father and your mother,[l] as the LORD your God has commanded
you, so that you may live long[m] and that it may go well with you in the
land the LORD your God is giving you.

17"You shall not murder.[n]

18"You shall not commit adultery.[o]

19"You shall not steal.

20"You shall not give false testimony against your neighbour.

21"You shall not covet your neighbour's wife. You shall not set your desire on
your neighbour's house or land, his manservant or maidservant, his ox or
donkey, or anything that belongs to your neighbour."[p]

22These are the commandments the LORD proclaimed in a loud voice to your whole

5:14 [j]Ge 2:2; Heb 4:4
5:15 [k]Dt 4:34
5:16 [l]Ex 20:12; Lev 19:3; Dt 27:16; Eph 6:2-3*; Col 3:20 [m]Dt 4:40
5:17 [n]Mt 5:21-22*
5:18 [o]Mt 5:27-30; Lk 18:20*; Jas 2:11*
5:21 [p]Ro 7:7*; 13:9*

BROKEN COMMANDMENTS

The Ten Commandments were God's standards for right living. To obey them was to obey God. Yet throughout the Old Testament, we can see how each commandment was broken. As you read the stories, notice the tragic consequences that occurred as a result of violating God's law.

Ten Commandments	*Notable Violations*
"You shall have no other gods before me."	Solomon (1 Kings 11)
"You shall not make for yourself an idol . . . . You shall not bow down to them or worship them . . . ."	The golden calf-idol incident (Exodus 32); generations after Joshua (Judges 2:10–14; 2 Kings 21:1–15; Jeremiah 1:16)
"You shall not misuse the name of the LORD your God . . . ."	Zedekiah (Ezekiel 17:15–21)
"Observe the Sabbath day by keeping it holy."	Judah (2 Chronicles 36:21)
"Honour your father and your mother . . . ."	Eli's sons—Hophni and Phinehas (1 Samuel 2:12, 23–25)
"You shall not murder."	Hazael (2 Kings 8:15)
"You shall not commit adultery."	David (2 Samuel 11:2–5)
"You shall not steal."	Ahab (1 Kings 21:1–19)
"You shall not give false testimony against your neighbour."	Saul (1 Samuel 15:13–25)
"You shall not covet your neighbour's wife. You shall not set your desire on your neighbour's house, or land . . . or anything that belongs to your neighbour."	Achan (Joshua 7:19–26)

5:16 Obeying our parents is our main task when we are young, but honouring them should continue even beyond their death. One way to honour parents is to provide for them in times of financial need or when they are ill and unable to care for themselves. Perhaps the best way to honour them is to pass on their godly values to our children. Honouring involves all that sons and daughters do with their lives—the way they work and talk, the values they hold, and the morals they practise. What are you doing to show respect to your parents? Are you living in a way that brings honour to them?

5:17 "But I don't murder people," you may say. Good. That fulfils the letter of the law. But Jesus explained that hateful anger breaks this commandment (Matthew 5:21, 22). Have you ever been so angry with someone who mistreated you that for a moment you wished that person were dead? Have you ever fantasised that you could do someone in? Jesus' teaching concerning this law demonstrates that we are capable of murder in our hearts. Even if we are legally innocent, we are all morally guilty of murder and need to ask God's forgiveness. We need to commit ourselves to the opposite of hatred and anger—love and reconciliation.

5:21 To covet is to desire another person's prosperity. We are not to set our desires on anything that belongs to someone else. Not only can such desires make us miserable, they can also lead us to other sins such as adultery and stealing. Envying others is a useless exercise because God is able to provide everything we really need, even if he does not always give us everything we want. To stop coveting, we need to practise being content with what we have. The apostle Paul emphasises the significance of contentment in Philippians 4:11. It's a matter of perspective. Instead of thinking about what we don't have, we should thank God for what he has given and strive to be content. After all, our most important possession is free and available to everyone—eternal life through Christ.

assembly there on the mountain from out of the fire, the cloud and the deep darkness;
and he added nothing more. Then he wrote them on two stone tablets[q] and gave them
to me.
23When you heard the voice out of the darkness, while the mountain was ablaze
with fire, all the leading men of your tribes and your elders came to me. 24And you
said, "The LORD our God has shown us his glory and his majesty, and we have heard
his voice from the fire. Today we have seen that a man can live even if God speaks
with him.[r] 25But now, why should we die? This great fire will consume us, and we
will die if we hear the voice of the LORD our God any longer.[s] 26For what mortal
man has ever heard the voice of the living God speaking out of fire, as we have, and
survived?[t] 27Go near and listen to all that the LORD our God says. Then tell us
whatever the LORD our God tells you. We will listen and obey."
28The LORD heard you when you spoke to me and the LORD said to me, "I have
heard what this people said to you. Everything they said was good.[u] 29Oh, that their
hearts would be inclined to fear me[v] and keep all my commands[w] always, so that
it might go well with them and their children for ever![x]
30"Go, tell them to return to their tents. 31But you stay here[y] with me so that I
may give you all the commands, decrees and laws that you are to teach them to follow
in the land I am giving them to possess."
32So be careful to do what the LORD your God has commanded you; do not turn
aside to the right or to the left.[z] 33Walk in all the way that the LORD your God has
commanded you,[a] so that you may live and prosper and prolong your days[b] in the
land that you will possess.

2. Love the LORD your God

6 These are the commands, decrees and laws the LORD your God directed me to
teach you to observe in the land that you are crossing the Jordan to possess, 2so
that you, your children and their children after them may fear[a] the LORD your God
as long as you live by keeping all his decrees and commands that I give you, and so
that you may enjoy long life. 3Hear, O Israel, and be careful to obey so that it may
go well with you and that you may increase greatly[b] in a land flowing with milk and
honey,[c] just as the LORD, the God of your fathers, promised you.
4Hear, O Israel: The LORD our God, the LORD is one.[a][d] 5Love[e] the LORD your
God with all your heart and with all your soul and with all your strength.[f] 6These
commandments that I give you today are to be upon your hearts.[g] 7Impress them on

a 4 Or *The LORD our God is one LORD*; or *The LORD is our God, the LORD is one*; or *The LORD is our God, the LORD alone*

5:22 [q]Ex 24:12; 31:18; Dt 4:13
5:24 [r]Ex 19:19
5:25 [s]Dt 18:16
5:26 [t]Dt 4:33
5:28 [u]Dt 18:17
5:29 [v]Ps 81:8, 13 [w]Dt 11:1; Isa 48:18 [x]Dt 4:1, 40
5:31 [y]Ex 24:12
5:32 [z]Dt 17:11, 20; 28:14; Jos 1:7; 23:6; Pr 4:27
5:33 [a]Jer 7:23 [b]Dt 4:40
6:2 [a]Ex 20:20; Dt 10:12-13
6:3 [b]Dt 5:33 [c]Ex 3:8
6:4 [d]Mk 12:29*; 1Co 8:4
6:5 [e]Mt 22:37*; Mk 12:30*; Lk 10:27* [f]Dt 10:12
6:6 [g]Dt 11:18

5:29 God told Moses that he wanted the people to incline their hearts to fear him – to *want* to respect and obey him. There is a difference between doing something because it is required and doing something because we want to. God is not interested in forced religious exercises and rule-keeping. He wants our hearts and lives completely dedicated to him. If we love him, obedience will follow.

6:3 For a nation that had wandered 40 years in a parched desert, a land flowing with milk and honey sounded like paradise. It brought to mind rich crops, rushing streams, gentle rains, and lush fields filled with livestock. The Israelites could have had all that 40 years earlier. Numbers 13 and 14 explain how the people missed their chance. Now Moses was determined to help the people avoid the same mistake by whetting their appetite for the beautiful land and then clearly explaining the conditions for entering the land.

6:4 Monotheism – belief in only one God – was a distinctive feature of Hebrew religion. Many ancient religions believed in many gods. But the God of Abraham, Isaac, and Jacob is the God of the whole earth, the only true God. This was an important insight for the nation of Israel because they were about to enter a land filled with people who believed in many gods. Both then and today, there are people who prefer to place their trust in many different "gods". But the day is coming when God will be recognised as the only one. He will be the king over the whole earth (Zechariah 14:9).

6:4-9 This passage provides the central theme of Deuteronomy. It sets a pattern that helps us relate the word of God to our daily lives. We are to love God, think constantly about his commandments, teach his commandments to our children, and live each day by the guidelines in his word. God emphasised the importance of parents' teaching the Bible to their children. The church and Christian schools cannot be used to escape from this responsibility. The Bible provides so many opportunities for object lessons and practical teaching that it would be a shame to study it only one day a week. Eternal truths are most effectively learned in the loving environment of a God-fearing home.

6:5 Jesus said that loving God with all of ourselves is the first and greatest commandment (Matthew 22:37–39). This command, combined with the command to love your neighbour (Leviticus 19:18), encompasses all the other Old Testament laws.

6:7 The Hebrews were extremely successful at making religion an integral part of life. The reason for their success was that religious education was life-oriented, not information-oriented. They used the context of daily life to teach about God. The key to teaching your children to love God is stated simply and clearly in these verses. If you want your children to follow God, you must make God a part of your everyday experiences. You must teach your

your children. Talk about them when you sit at home and when you walk along the
road, when you lie down and when you get up.[h] 8Tie them as symbols on your hands
and bind them on your foreheads.[i] 9Write them on the door-frames of your houses
and on your gates.[j]
10When the LORD your God brings you into the land he swore to your fathers, to
Abraham, Isaac and Jacob, to give you—a land with large, flourishing cities you did
not build,[k] 11houses filled with all kinds of good things you did not provide, wells
you did not dig, and vineyards and olive groves you did not plant—then when you
eat and are satisfied,[l] 12be careful that you do not forget the LORD, who brought you
out of Egypt, out of the land of slavery.
13Fear the LORD[m] your God, serve him only[n] and take your oaths in his name.
14Do not follow other gods, the gods of the peoples around you; 15for the LORD your
God[o], who is among you, is a jealous God and his anger will burn against you, and
he will destroy you from the face of the land. 16Do not test the LORD your God[p] as
you did at Massah. 17Be sure to keep the commands of the LORD your God and the
stipulations and decrees he has given you.[q] 18Do what is right and good in the LORD's
sight, so that it may go well[r] with you and you may go in and take over the good
land that the LORD promised on oath to your forefathers, 19thrusting out all your
enemies before you, as the LORD said.
20In the future, when your son asks you,[s] "What is the meaning of the stipulations,
decrees and laws the LORD our God has commanded you?" 21tell him: "We were slaves
of Pharaoh in Egypt, but the LORD brought us out of Egypt with a mighty hand.
22Before our eyes the LORD sent miraculous signs and wonders—great and terrible—upon Egypt and Pharaoh and his whole household. 23But he brought us out from
there to bring us in and give us the land that he promised on oath to our forefathers.
24The LORD commanded us to obey all these decrees and to fear the LORD our God,[t]
so that we might always prosper and be kept alive, as is the case today.[u] 25And if

6:7 [h]Dt 4:9; 11:19; Eph 6:4
6:8 [i]Ex 13:9, 16; Dt 11:18
6:9 [j]Dt 11:20
6:10 [k]Jos 24:13
6:11 [l]Dt 8:10
6:13 [m]Dt 10:20 [n]Mt 4:10*; Lk 4:8
6:15 [o]Dt 4:24
6:16 [p]Ex 17:7; Mt 4:7*; Lk 4:12*
6:17 [q]Dt 11:22; Ps 119:4
6:18 [r]Dt 4:40
6:20 [s]Ex 13:14
6:24 [t]Dt 10:12; Jer 32:39 [u]Ps 41:2

DANGER IN PLENTY

"... when you eat and are satisfied, be careful that you do not forget the LORD ..." (Deuteronomy 6:11, 12). It is often most difficult to follow God when life is easy—we can fall prey to temptation and fall away from God. Here are some notable examples of this truth.

Person	*Reference*	*Comment*
Adam	Genesis 3	Adam lived in a perfect world and had a perfect relationship with God. His needs were met; he had everything. But he fell prey to Satan's deception.
Noah	Genesis 9	Noah and his family had survived the flood and the whole world was theirs. They were prosperous, and life was easy. Noah shamed himself by becoming drunk and cursed his son Ham.
The nation of Israel	Judges 2	God had given Israel the promised land—rest at last with no more wandering. But as soon as brave and faithful Joshua died, they fell into the idolatrous practices of the Canaanites.
David	2 Samuel 11	David ruled well, and Israel was a dominant nation, politically, economically, and militarily. In the midst of prosperity and success, he committed adultery with Bathsheba and had her husband Uriah murdered.
Solomon	1 Kings 11	Solomon truly had it all: power, wealth, fame, and wisdom. But his very abundance was the source of his downfall. He loved his pagan, idolatrous wives so much that he allowed himself and Israel to copy their detestable religious rites.

children diligently to see God in all aspects of life, not just those that are church related.

6:10–13 Moses warned the people not to forget God when they entered the promised land and became prosperous. Prosperity, more than poverty, can dull our spiritual vision because it tends to make us self-sufficient and eager to acquire still more of everything—except God. The same thing can happen in our church. Once we become successful in terms of numbers, programmes, and buildings, we can easily become self-sufficient and less sensitive to our need for God. This leads us to concentrate on self-preservation rather than thankfulness and service to God.

6:24 Does the phrase "so that we might always prosper" mean that we can expect only prosperity and no suffering when we obey God? What is promised here is a right relationship with God for all those who love him with all their heart. It speaks of a good relationship with God and the ultimate benefit of knowing him. It is not blanket protection against poverty, adversity, or suffering. We can have this right relationship with God by obeying his command to love him with all that we are.

we are careful to obey all this law before the LORD our God, as he has commanded
us, that will be our righteousness."[v]

Driving Out the Nations

7 When the LORD your God brings you into the land you are entering to possess
and drives out before you many nations[a]—the Hittites, Girgashites, Amorites,
Canaanites, Perizzites, Hivites and Jebusites, seven nations larger and stronger than
you—2and when the LORD your God has delivered them over to you and you have
defeated them, then you must destroy them totally.[a] Make no treaty[b] with them, and
show them no mercy.[c] 3Do not intermarry with them.[d] Do not give your daughters
to their sons or take their daughters for your sons, 4for they will turn your sons away
from following me to serve other gods, and the LORD's anger will burn against you
and will quickly destroy[e] you. 5This is what you are to do to them: Break down their
altars, smash their sacred stones, cut down their Asherah poles[b] and burn their idols
in the fire.[f] 6For you are a people holy[g] to the LORD your God.[h] The LORD your
God has chosen[i] you out of all the peoples on the face of the earth to be his people,
his treasured possession.
7The LORD did not set his affection on you and choose you because you were more
numerous than other peoples, for you were the fewest of all peoples.[j] 8But it was
because the LORD loved[k] you and kept the oath he swore[l] to your forefathers that
he brought you out with a mighty hand and redeemed you from the land of slavery,[m]
from the power of Pharaoh king of Egypt. 9Know therefore that the LORD your God
is God;[n] he is the faithful God,[o] keeping his covenant of love[p] to a thousand
generations of those who love him and keep his commands. 10But

those who hate him he will repay to their face by destruction;
he will not be slow to repay to their face those who hate him.

11Therefore, take care to follow the commands, decrees and laws I give you today.
12If you pay attention to these laws and are careful to follow them, then the LORD
your God will keep his covenant of love with you, as he swore to your forefathers.[q]
13He will love you and bless you[r] and increase your numbers. He will bless the fruit
of your womb, the crops of your land—your grain, new wine and oil—the calves of
your herds and the lambs of your flocks in the land that he swore to your forefathers
to give you.[s] 14You will be blessed more than any other people; none of your men
or women will be childless, nor any of your livestock without young.[t] 15The LORD
will keep you free from every disease.[u] He will not inflict on you the horrible diseases
you knew in Egypt, but he will inflict them on all who hate you. 16You must destroy
all the peoples the LORD your God gives over to you. Do not look on them with pity[v]
and do not serve their gods, for that will be a snare[w] to you.
17You may say to yourselves, "These nations are stronger than we are. How can
we drive them out?[x]" 18But do not be afraid[y] of them; remember well what the LORD
your God did to Pharaoh and to all Egypt.[z] 19You saw with your own eyes the great
trials, the miraculous signs and wonders, the mighty hand and outstretched arm, with

[a] *2* The Hebrew term refers to the irrevocable giving over of things or persons to the LORD, often by totally destroying them; also in verse 26. [b] *5* That is, symbols of the goddess Asherah; here and elsewhere in Deuteronomy

6:25 [v] Dt 24:13; Ro 10:3, 5
7:1 [a] Dt 31:3; Ac 13:19
7:2 [b] Ex 23:32 [c] Dt 13:8
7:3 [d] Ex 34:15-16; Ezr 9:2
7:4 [e] Dt 6:15
7:5 [f] Ex 23:24; Dt 12:2-3
7:6 [g] Ex 19:5-6; 1Pe 2:9 [h] Ps 50:5; Jer 2:3 [i] Dt 14:2
7:7 [j] Dt 10:22
7:8 [k] Dt 10:15 [l] Ex 32:13 [m] Ex 13:14
7:9 [n] Dt 4:35 [o] 1Co 1:9; 2Ti 2:13 [p] Ne 1:5; Da 9:4
7:12 [q] Lev 26:3-13; Dt 28:1-14; Ps 105:8-9
7:13 [r] Jn 14:21 [s] Dt 28:4
7:14 [t] Ex 23:26
7:15 [u] Ex 15:26
7:16 [v] ver 2; Ex 23:33 [w] Jdg 8:27
7:17 [x] Nu 33:53
7:18 [y] Dt 31:6 [z] Ps 105:5

7:2 God told the Israelites to destroy their enemies totally. How can a God of love and mercy wipe out everyone, even children? Although God is loving and merciful, he is also just. These enemy nations were as much a part of God's creation as Israel was, and God does not allow evil to continue unchecked. God had punished Israel by keeping out of the promised land all those who had disobeyed. The command to destroy these nations was both a judgment (9:4–6) and a safety measure. On one hand, the people living in the land were being judged for their sin, and Israel was God's instrument of judgment—just as God would one day use other nations to judge Israel for its sin (2 Chronicles 36:17; Isaiah 10:12). On the other hand, God's command was designed to protect the nation of Israel from being ruined by the idolatry and immorality of its enemies. To think that God is too "nice" to judge sin would be to underestimate him.

7:5 Asherah was a Canaanite mother goddess of the sea, associated with Baal.

7:6 How did Israel deserve to be chosen above all of the other nations at that time? It was not a matter of Israel's merit, but of God keeping his promise to their ancestors. Just as God chose the nation of Israel, he has chosen all believers today to be a part of his treasured possession. Similarly, it is not because of our merit that we have come to faith in Christ. Instead God chose us out of his goodness and grace.

7:19
[a]Dt 4:34
7:20
[b]Ex 23:28; Jos 24:12
7:21
[c]Jos 3:10
[d]Dt 10:17; Ne 9:32
7:22
[e]Ex 23:28-30
7:24
[f]Jos 23:9
7:25
[g]Ex 32:20; 1Ch 14:12
[h]Jos 7:21
[i]Jdg 8:27
[j]Dt 17:1
7:26
[k]Lev 27:28-29
8:1
[a]Dt 4:1
8:2
[b]Am 2:10
8:3
[c]Ex 16:12, 14, 35
[d]Ex 16:2-3; Mt 4:4*; Lk 4:4*
8:4
[e]Dt 29:5; Ne 9:21
8:5
[f]2Sa 7:14; Pr 3:11-12; Heb 12:5-11; Rev 3:19

which the LORD your God brought you out. The LORD your God will do the same to
all the peoples you now fear.[a] 20 Moreover, the LORD your God will send the hornet[b]
among them until even the survivors who hide from you have perished. 21 Do not be
terrified by them, for the LORD your God, who is among you,[c] is a great and awesome
God.[d] 22 The LORD your God will drive out those nations before you, little by little.[e]
You will not be allowed to eliminate them all at once, or the wild animals will multiply
around you. 23 But the LORD your God will deliver them over to you, throwing them
into great confusion until they are destroyed. 24 He will give their kings into your hand,
and you will wipe out their names from under heaven. No-one will be able to stand
up against you;[f] you will destroy them. 25 The images of their gods you are to burn[g]
in the fire. Do not covet[h] the silver and gold on them, and do not take it for yourselves,
or you will be ensnared[i] by it, for it is detestable[j] to the LORD your God. 26 Do not
bring a detestable thing into your house or you, like it, will be set apart for destruction.[k] Utterly abhor and detest it, for it is set apart for destruction.

Do Not Forget the LORD

8 Be careful to follow every command I am giving you today, so that you may live[a]
and increase and may enter and possess the land that the LORD promised on oath
to your forefathers. 2 Remember how the LORD your God led[b] you all the way in the
desert these forty years, to humble you and to test you in order to know what was
in your heart, whether or not you would keep his commands. 3 He humbled you,
causing you to hunger and then feeding you with manna,[c] which neither you nor your
fathers had known, to teach you that man does not live on bread alone but on every
word that comes from the mouth of the LORD.[d] 4 Your clothes did not wear out and
your feet did not swell during these forty years.[e] 5 Know then in your heart that as
a man disciplines his son, so the LORD your God disciplines you.[f]
6 Observe the commands of the LORD your God, walking in his ways and revering

OBEDIENCE
Deuteronomy 8:1 tells us to obey God's commandments. We do this by obeying God with . . .

OUR HEART	By loving him more than any relationship, activity, achievement, or possession.
OUR WILL	By committing ourselves completely to him.
OUR MIND	By seeking to know him and his word, so that his principles and values form the foundation of all we think and do.
OUR BODY	By recognising that our strengths, talents, and sexuality are given to us by God to be used for pleasure and fulfilment according to his rules, not ours.
OUR FINANCES	By deciding that all of the resources we have ultimately come from God, and that we are to be managers of them and not owners.
OUR FUTURE	By deciding to make service to God and man the main purpose of our life's work.

7:21–24 Moses told the Israelites that God would destroy Israel's enemies, but not all at once. God had the power to destroy those nations instantly, but he chose to do it in stages. In the same way and with the same power, God could miraculously and instantaneously change your life. Usually, however, he chooses to help you gradually, teaching you one lesson at a time. Rather than expecting instant spiritual maturity and solutions to all your problems, slow down and work one step at a time, trusting God to make up the difference between where you should be and where you are now. You'll soon look back and see that a miraculous transformation has occurred.

7:25, 26 Moses warned Israel against becoming ensnared by the idols of the defeated nations by coveting the silver or gold on them. We may think it's all right to be close to sin as long as we don't participate. "After all," we say, "I won't do anything wrong!" But being close can hurt us as we become attracted and finally give in. The only sure way to stay away from sin is to stay away!

8:3 Jesus quoted this verse when the devil tempted him to turn stones into bread (Matthew 4:4). Many people think that life is based on satisfying their appetites. If they can earn enough money to dress, eat, and play in high style, they think they are living "the good life". But such things do not satisfy our deepest longings. In the end they leave us empty and dissatisfied. Real life, according to Moses, comes from total commitment to God, the one who created life itself. It requires discipline, sacrifice, and hard work, and that's why most people never find it.

8:4 It's usually easy for us to take God's protection for granted. We seldom take notice or thank God when our car doesn't break down, our clothes don't rip, or our tools don't break. The people of Israel also failed to take notice, it seems, for they didn't even notice that in 40 years of wandering in the desert, their clothes didn't wear out and their feet didn't swell. Thus, they did not remember to give thanks to God for these blessings. What has been working well for you? What has been giving you good service? What has been lasting for a long time without breaking down or apart? Remember to thank God for these quiet blessings.

him.[g] 7For the LORD your God is bringing you into a good land—a land with streams
and pools of water, with springs flowing in the valleys and hills;[h] 8a land with wheat
and barley, vines and fig-trees, pomegranates, olive oil and honey; 9a land where
bread will not be scarce and you will lack nothing; a land where the rocks are iron
and you can dig copper out of the hills.
10When you have eaten and are satisfied,[i] praise the LORD your God for the good
land he has given you. 11Be careful that you do not forget the LORD your God, failing
to observe his commands, his laws and his decrees that I am giving you this day.
12Otherwise, when you eat and are satisfied, when you build fine houses and settle
down,[j] 13and when your herds and flocks grow large and your silver and gold
increase and all you have is multiplied, 14then your heart will become proud and you
will forget[k] the LORD your God, who brought you out of Egypt, out of the land of
slavery. 15He led you through the vast and dreadful desert,[l] that thirsty and waterless
land, with its venomous snakes[m] and scorpions. He brought you water out of hard
rock.[n] 16He gave you manna to eat in the desert, something your fathers had never
known,[o] to humble and to test you so that in the end it might go well with you. 17You
may say to yourself,[p] "My power and the strength of my hands have produced this
wealth for me." 18But remember the LORD your God, for it is he who gives you the
ability to produce wealth,[q] and so confirms his covenant, which he swore to your
forefathers, as it is today.
19If you ever forget the LORD your God and follow other gods and worship and bow
down to them, I testify against you today that you will surely be destroyed.[r] 20Like
the nations the LORD destroyed before you, so you will be destroyed for not obeying
the LORD your God.

Not Because of Israel's Righteousness

9 Hear, O Israel. You are now about to cross the Jordan to go in and dispossess
nations greater and stronger than you,[a] with large cities that have walls up to
the sky.[b] 2The people are strong and tall—Anakites! You know about them and have
heard it said: "Who can stand up against the Anakites?"[c] 3But be assured today that
the LORD your God is the one who goes across ahead of you[d] like a devouring fire.[e]
He will destroy them; he will subdue them before you. And you will drive them out
and annihilate them quickly,[f] as the LORD has promised you.
4After the LORD your God has driven them out before you, do not say to yourself,[g]
"The LORD has brought me here to take possession of this land because of my
righteousness." No, it is on account of the wickedness of these nations[h] that the LORD
is going to drive them out before you. 5It is not because of your righteousness or your
integrity[i] that you are going in to take possession of their land; but on account of
the wickedness of these nations, the LORD your God will drive them out before you,
to accomplish what he swore[j] to your fathers, to Abraham, Isaac and Jacob. 6Under-
stand, then, that it is not because of your righteousness that the LORD your God is
giving you this good land to possess, for you are a stiff-necked people.[k]

The Golden Calf

7Remember this and never forget how you provoked the LORD your God to anger
in the desert. From the day you left Egypt until you arrived here, you have been

8:6 [g]Dt 5:33
8:7 [h]Dt 11:9-12
8:10 [i]Dt 6:10-12
8:12 [j]Hos 13:6
8:14 [k]Ps 106:21
8:15 [l]Jer 2:6 [m]Nu 21:6 [n]Nu 20:11; Ps 78:15; 114:8
8:16 [o]Ex 16:15
8:17 [p]Dt 9:4, 7, 24
8:18 [q]Pr 10:22; Hos 2:8
8:19 [r]Dt 4:26; 30:18
9:1 [a]Dt 4:38; 11:23, 31 [b]Dt 1:28
9:2 [c]Nu 13:22, 28, 32-33
9:3 [d]Dt 31:3; Jos 3:11 [e]Dt 4:24; Heb 12:29 [f]Ex 23:31; Dt 7:23-24
9:4 [g]Dt 8:17 [h]Lev 18:21, 24-30; Dt 18:9-14
9:5 [i]Tit 3:5 [j]Ge 12:7; 13:15; 15:7; 17:8; 26:4
9:6 [k]ver 13; Ex 32:9; Dt 31:27

8:10 This verse is traditionally cited as the reason we say grace before or after meals. Its purpose, however, was to warn the Israelites not to forget God when their needs and wants were satisfied. Let your table prayers serve as a constant reminder of the Lord's goodness to you and your duty to those who are less fortunate.

8:11–20 In times of plenty, we often take credit for our prosperity and become proud that our own hard work and cleverness have made us rich. It is easy to get so busy collecting and managing wealth that we push God right out of our lives. But it is God who gives us everything we have, and it is God who asks us to manage it for him.

9:2, 3 The Anakites were enormous people, some seven to nine feet tall. Goliath, probably a descendant of this race, was over nine feet tall (1 Samuel 17:4–7). Unfortunately, these great men used their stature as a means of intimidation rather than for noble causes. Their appearance alone frightened the Israelite spies (Numbers 13:28), and their bad reputation may have been the deciding factor that kept the Israelites out of the land 40 years earlier (Numbers 13, 14). Moses used all his persuasive power to convince his people that God could handle these bullies. He used the illustration of God as a devouring fire, for not even a giant could stand up to that.

rebellious against the LORD. 8 At Horeb you aroused the LORD's wrath so that he was
angry enough to destroy you.[l] 9 When I went up on the mountain to receive the tablets
of stone, the tablets of the covenant that the LORD had made with you, I stayed on
the mountain forty days and forty nights; I ate no bread and drank no water.[m] 10 The
LORD gave me two stone tablets inscribed by the finger of God.[n] On them were all
the commandments the LORD proclaimed to you on the mountain out of the fire, on
the day of the assembly.

11 At the end of the forty days and forty nights, the LORD gave me the two stone
tablets, the tablets of the covenant. 12 Then the LORD told me, "Go down from here
at once, because your people whom you brought out of Egypt have become corrupt.[o]
They have turned away quickly[p] from what I commanded them and have made a cast
idol for themselves."

13 And the LORD said to me, "I have seen this people[q], and they are a stiff-necked
people indeed! 14 Let me alone,[r] so that I may destroy them and blot out[s] their name
from under heaven. And I will make you into a nation stronger and more numerous
than they."

15 So I turned and went down from the mountain while it was ablaze with fire. And
the two tablets of the covenant were in my hands.[a][t] 16 When I looked, I saw that
you had sinned against the LORD your God; you had made for yourselves an idol cast
in the shape of a calf.[u] You had turned aside quickly from the way that the LORD
had commanded you. 17 So I took the two tablets and threw them out of my hands,
breaking them to pieces before your eyes.

18 Then once again I fell[v] prostrate before the LORD for forty days and forty nights;
I ate no bread and drank no water, because of all the sin you had committed, doing
what was evil in the LORD's sight and so provoking him to anger. 19 I feared the anger
and wrath of the LORD, for he was angry enough with you to destroy you.[w] But again
the LORD listened to me.[x] 20 And the LORD was angry enough with Aaron to destroy
him, but at that time I prayed for Aaron too. 21 Also I took that sinful thing of yours,
the calf you had made, and burned it in the fire. Then I crushed it and ground it to
powder as fine as dust and threw the dust into a stream that flowed down the
mountain.[y]

22 You also made the LORD angry at Taberah,[z] at Massah[a] and at Kibroth Hattaavah.[b]

23 And when the LORD sent you out from Kadesh Barnea, he said, "Go up and take
possession of the land I have given you." But you rebelled against the command of
the LORD your God. You did not trust[c] him or obey him. 24 You have been rebellious
against the LORD ever since I have known you.[d]

25 I lay prostrate before the LORD those forty days and forty nights because the LORD
had said he would destroy you.[e] 26 I prayed to the LORD and said, "O Sovereign LORD,
do not destroy your people, your own inheritance that you redeemed by your great
power and brought out of Egypt with a mighty hand.[f] 27 Remember your servants
Abraham, Isaac and Jacob. Overlook the stubbornness of this people, their wickedness
and their sin. 28 Otherwise, the country from which you brought us will say, 'Because
the LORD was not able to take them into the land he had promised them, and because
he hated them, he brought them out to put them to death in the desert.'[g] 29 But they
are your people, your inheritance[h] that you brought out by your great power and your
outstretched arm.[i]"

a 15 Or *And I had the two tablets of the covenant with me, one in each hand*

9:8 [l]Ex 32:7-10; Ps 106:19
9:9 [m]Ex 24:12, 15, 18; 34:28
9:10 [n]Ex 31:18; Dt 4:13
9:12 [o]Ex 32:7-8; Dt 31:29 [p]Jdg 2:17
9:13 [q]ver 6; Ex 32:9; Dt 10:16
9:14 [r]Ex 32:10 [s]Nu 14:12; Dt 29:20
9:15 [t]Ex 19:18; 32:15
9:16 [u]Ex 32:19
9:18 [v]Ex 34:28
9:19 [w]Ex 32:10-11, 14 [x]Dt 10:10
9:21 [y]Ex 32:20
9:22 [z]Nu 11:3 [a]Ex 17:7 [b]Nu 11:34
9:23 [c]Ps 106:24
9:24 [d]ver 7; Dt 31:27
9:25 [e]ver 18
9:26 [f]Ex 32:11
9:28 [g]Ex 32:12; Nu 14:16
9:29 [h]Dt 4:20; 1Ki 8:51 [i]Dt 4:34; Ne 1:10

9:18 From the record of this event in Exodus 32, it seems as though Moses acted immediately, grinding the golden calf into powder, and forcing the people to drink water mixed with it. But evidently, Moses spent 40 days and nights interceding for the people.

9:23 Moses was reminding the people of the nation's unbelief 40 years earlier, when they were afraid to enter Canaan. The Israelites had not believed God would be able to help them in spite of all he had already done. They refused to follow because they looked only to their own limited resources instead of to God. Unbelief is the root of many sins and problems. When you feel lost, it may be because you're looking everywhere but to God for your help and guidance. (See Psalms 81:6–12; 95:8; 106:13–20; Hebrews 3.)

Tablets Like the First Ones

10 At that time the LORD said to me, "Chisel out two stone tablets[a] like the first
ones and come up to me on the mountain. Also make a wooden chest.[a] 2I will
write on the tablets the words that were on the first tablets, which you broke. Then
you are to put them in the chest."[b]
3So I made the ark out of acacia wood[c] and chiselled[d] out two stone tablets like
the first ones, and I went up on the mountain with the two tablets in my hands. 4The
LORD wrote on these tablets what he had written before, the Ten Commandments he
had proclaimed[e] to you on the mountain, out of the fire, on the day of the assembly.
And the LORD gave them to me. 5Then I came back down the mountain[f] and put the
tablets in the ark[g] I had made, as the LORD commanded me, and they are there now.[h]
6(The Israelites travelled from the wells of the Jaakanites to Moserah.[i] There
Aaron died and was buried, and Eleazar his son succeeded him as priest.[j] 7From there
they travelled to Gudgodah and on to Jotbathah, a land with streams of water.[k] 8At
that time the LORD set apart the tribe of Levi[l] to carry the ark of the covenant of the
LORD, to stand before the LORD to minister[m] and to pronounce blessings[n] in his name,
as they still do today. 9That is why the Levites have no share or inheritance among
their brothers; the LORD is their inheritance,[o] as the LORD your God told them.)
10Now I had stayed on the mountain forty days and nights, as I did the first time,
and the LORD listened to me at this time also. It was not his will to destroy you.[p]
11"Go," the LORD said to me, "and lead the people on their way, so that they may
enter and possess the land that I swore to their fathers to give them."

Fear the LORD

12And now, O Israel, what does the LORD your God ask of you[q] but to fear the
LORD your God, to walk in all his ways, to love him,[r] to serve the LORD your God
with all your heart[s] and with all your soul, 13and to observe the LORD's commands
and decrees that I am giving you today for your own good?
14To the LORD your God belong the heavens, even the highest heavens,[t] the earth
and everything in it.[u] 15Yet the LORD set his affection on your forefathers and loved[v]
them, and he chose you, their descendants, above all the nations, as it is today.
16Circumcise[w] your hearts, therefore, and do not be stiff-necked[x] any longer. 17For
the LORD your God is God of gods[y] and Lord of lords, the great God, mighty and
awesome, who shows no partiality[z] and accepts no bribes. 18He defends the cause
of the fatherless and the widow,[a] and loves the alien, giving him food and clothing.
19And you are to love those who are aliens, for you yourselves were aliens in Egypt.[b]
20Fear the LORD your God and serve him.[c] Hold fast[d] to him and take your oaths
in his name.[e] 21He is your praise;[f] he is your God, who performed for you those
great and awesome wonders[g] you saw with your own eyes. 22Your forefathers who

[a] 1 That is, an ark

10:1 [a]Ex 25:10; 34:1-2
10:2 [b]Ex 25:16, 21; Dt 4:13
10:3 [c]Ex 25:5, 10; 37:1-9 [d]Ex 34:4
10:4 [e]Ex 20:1
10:5 [f]Ex 34:29 [g]Ex 40:20 [h]1Ki 8:9
10:6 [i]Nu 33:30-31, 38 [j]Nu 20:25-28
10:7 [k]Nu 33:32-34
10:8 [l]Nu 3:6 [m]Dt 18:5 [n]Dt 21:5
10:9 [o]Nu 18:20; Dt 18:1-2; Eze 44:28
10:10 [p]Ex 33:17; 34:28; Dt 9:18-19, 25
10:12 [q]Mic 6:8 [r]Dt 5:33; 6:13; Mt 22:37 [s]Dt 6:5
10:14 [t]1Ki 8:27 [u]Ex 19:5
10:15 [v]Dt 4:37
10:16 [w]Jer 4:4 [x]Dt 9:6
10:17 [y]Jos 22:22; Da 2:47 [z]Ac 10:34; Ro 2:11; Eph 6:9
10:18 [a]Ps 68:5
10:19 [b]Lev 19:34
10:20 [c]Mt 4:10 [d]Dt 11:22 [e]Ps 63:11
10:21 [f]Ex 15:2; Jer 17:14 [g]Ps 106:21-22

10:5 The tablets of the law were still in the ark about 500 years later when Solomon put it in his newly built temple (1 Kings 8:9). The ark last appears in the Israelites' history during the reign of Josiah, about 300 years after Solomon (2 Chronicles 35:3).

10:12, 13 Often we ask, "What does God expect of me?" Here Moses gives a summary that is simple in form and easy to remember. Here are the essentials: (1) Fear God (have reverence for him). (2) Walk in all his ways. (3) Love him. (4) Serve him with all your heart and soul. (5) Observe his commands. How often we complicate faith with man-made rules, regulations, and requirements. Are you frustrated and burned out from trying hard to please God? Concentrate on his real requirements and find peace. Respect, follow, love, serve, and obey.

10:16–19 God required all male Israelites to be circumcised, but he wanted them to go beyond performing the surgery to understanding its meaning. They needed to submit to God inside, in their hearts, as well as outside, in their bodies. Then they could begin to imitate God's love and justice in their relationships with others. If our hearts are right with God, then our relationships with other people can be made right too. When your heart has been cleansed and you have been reconciled to God, you will begin to see a difference in the way you treat others.

10:17 In saying that the Lord is God of gods and Lord of lords, Moses was distinguishing the true God from all the local gods worshipped throughout the land. Then Moses went a step further, calling God "mighty and awesome". He has such awesome power and justice that people cannot stand before him without his mercy. Fortunately, his mercy towards his people is unlimited. When we begin to grasp the extent of God's mercy towards us, we see what true love is and how deeply God loves us. Although our sins deserve severe judgment, God has chosen to show love and mercy to all who seek him.

10:20 "Take your oaths in his name" means that God alone should have their allegiance.

went down into Egypt were seventy in all,[h] and now the LORD your God has made you as numerous as the stars in the sky.[i]

Love and Obey the LORD

11 Love[a] the LORD your God and keep his requirements, his decrees, his laws and his commands always.[b] 2Remember today that your children were not the ones who saw and experienced the discipline of the LORD your God:[c] his majesty, his mighty hand, his outstretched arm; 3the signs he performed and the things he did in the heart of Egypt, both to Pharaoh king of Egypt and to his whole country; 4what he did to the Egyptian army, to its horses and chariots, how he overwhelmed them with the waters of the Red Sea[a][d] as they were pursuing you, and how the LORD brought lasting ruin on them. 5It was not your children who saw what he did for you in the desert until you arrived at this place, 6and what he did[e] to Dathan and Abiram, sons of Eliab the Reubenite, when the earth opened its mouth right in the middle of all Israel and swallowed them up with their households, their tents and every living thing that belonged to them. 7But it was your own eyes that saw all these great things the LORD has done.

8Observe therefore all the commands I am giving you today, so that you may have the strength to go in and take over the land that you are crossing the Jordan to possess,[f] 9and so that you may live long[g] in the land that the LORD swore[h] to your forefathers to give to them and their descendants, a land flowing with milk and honey.[i] 10The land you are entering to take over is not like the land of Egypt, from which you have come, where you planted your seed and irrigated it by foot as in a vegetable garden. 11But the land you are crossing the Jordan to take possession of is a land of mountains and valleys that drinks rain from heaven.[j] 12It is a land the LORD your God cares for; the eyes[k] of the LORD your God are continually on it from the beginning of the year to its end.

13So if you faithfully obey[l] the commands I am giving you today—to love[m] the LORD your God and to serve him with all your heart and with all your soul—14then I will send rain[n] on your land in its season, both autumn and spring rains,[o] so that you may gather in your grain, new wine and oil. 15I will provide grass[p] in the fields for your cattle, and you will eat and be satisfied.[q]

16Be careful, or you will be enticed to turn away and worship other gods and bow down to them.[r] 17Then the LORD's anger[s] will burn against you, and he will shut[t] the heavens so that it will not rain and the ground will yield no produce, and you will soon perish[u] from the good land the LORD is giving you. 18Fix these words of mine in your hearts and minds; tie them as symbols on your hands and bind them on your foreheads.[v] 19Teach them to your children,[w] talking about them when you sit at home and when you walk along the road, when you lie down and when you get up.[x] 20Write them on the door-frames of your houses and on your gates,[y] 21so that your days and the days of your children may be many[z] in the land that the LORD swore to give your forefathers, as many as the days that the heavens are above the earth.[a]

22If you carefully observe[b] all these commands I am giving you to follow—to love the LORD your God, to walk in all his ways and to hold fast[c] to him—23then the LORD will drive out all these nations before you, and you will dispossess nations larger and stronger than you.[d] 24Every place where you set your foot will be yours:[e] Your territory will extend from the desert to Lebanon, and from the Euphrates River to the western sea.[b] 25No man will be able to stand against you. The LORD your God, as

a *4* Hebrew *Yam Suph*; that is, Sea of Reeds   b *24* That is, the Mediterranean

10:22 [h]Ge 46:26-27 [i]Ge 15:5; Dt 1:10
11:1 [a]Dt 10:12 [b]Zec 3:7
11:2 [c]Dt 5:24; 8:5
11:4 [d]Ex 14:27
11:6 [e]Nu 16:1-35
11:8 [f]Jos 1:7
11:9 [g]Dt 4:40; Pr 10:27 [h]Dt 9:5 [i]Ex 3:8
11:11 [j]Dt 8:7
11:12 [k]1Ki 9:3
11:13 [l]Dt 6:17 [m]Dt 10:12
11:14 [n]Lev 26:4; Dt 28:12 [o]Joel 2:23; Jas 5:7
11:15 [p]Ps 104:14 [q]Dt 6:11
11:16 [r]Dt 8:19; 29:18; Job 31:9, 27
11:17 [s]Dt 6:15 [t]1Ki 8:35; 2Ch 6:26 [u]Dt 4:26
11:18 [v]Dt 6:6-8
11:19 [w]Dt 6:7 [x]Dt 4:9-10
11:20 [y]Dt 6:9
11:21 [z]Pr 3:2; 4:10 [a]Ps 72:5
11:22 [b]Dt 6:17 [c]Dt 10:20
11:23 [d]Dt 4:38; 9:1
11:24 [e]Ge 15:18; Ex 23:31; Jos 1:3; 14:9

11:7 Israel had strong reasons to believe in God and obey his commands. They had witnessed a parade of mighty miracles that demonstrated God's love and care for them. Incredibly, they still had trouble remaining faithful. Because few of us have seen such dramatic miracles, it may seem even more difficult for us to obey God and remain faithful. But we have the Bible, the written record of God's acts throughout history. Reading God's word gives us a panoramic view of both the miracles Israel saw and others they didn't see. The lessons from the past, the instructions for the present, and the glimpses into the future give us many opportunities to strengthen our faith in God.

he promised you, will put the terror and fear of you on the whole land, wherever you
go.[f]
26See, I am setting before you today a blessing and a curse[g]—27the blessing[h] if
you obey the commands of the LORD your God that I am giving you today; 28the curse
if you disobey[i] the commands of the LORD your God and turn from the way that I
command you today by following other gods, which you have not known. 29When
the LORD your God has brought you into the land you are entering to possess, you
are to proclaim on Mount Gerizim the blessings, and on Mount Ebal the curses.[j] 30As
you know, these mountains are across the Jordan, west of the road,[c] towards the
setting sun, near the great trees of Moreh,[k] in the territory of those Canaanites living
in the Arabah in the vicinity of Gilgal.[l] 31You are about to cross the Jordan to enter
and take possession[m] of the land the LORD your God is giving you. When you have
taken it over and are living there, 32be sure that you obey all the decrees and laws
I am setting before you today.

3. Laws for proper worship

The One Place of Worship

12 These are the decrees and laws you must be careful to follow in the land that
the LORD, the God of your fathers, has given you to possess—as long as you
live in the land.[a] 2Destroy completely all the places on the high mountains and on
the hills and under every spreading tree[b] where the nations you are dispossessing
worship their gods. 3Break down their altars, smash[c] their sacred stones and burn
their Asherah poles in the fire; cut down the idols of their gods and wipe out their
names from those places.
4You must not worship the LORD your God in their way. 5But you are to seek the
place the LORD your God will choose from among all your tribes to put his Name there
for his dwelling.[d] To that place you must go; 6there bring your burnt offerings and
sacrifices, your tithes[e] and special gifts, what you have vowed to give and your
freewill offerings, and the firstborn of your herds and flocks. 7There, in the presence
of the LORD your God, you and your families shall eat and shall rejoice[f] in everything
you have put your hand to, because the LORD your God has blessed you.
8You are not to do as we do here today, everyone as he sees fit, 9since you have
not yet reached the resting place and the inheritance the LORD your God is giving you.
10But you will cross the Jordan and settle in the land the LORD your God is giving[g]
you as an inheritance, and he will give you rest from all your enemies around you
so that you will live in safety. 11Then to the place the LORD your God will choose
as a dwelling for his Name[h]—there you are to bring everything I command you: your
burnt offerings and sacrifices, your tithes and special gifts, and all the choice possessions you have vowed to the LORD. 12And there rejoice[i] before the LORD your God,

[c] 30 Or *Jordan, westward*

11:25 [f]Ex 23:27; Dt 7:24
11:26 [g]Dt 30:1, 15, 19
11:27 [h]Dt 28:1-14
11:28 [i]Dt 28:15
11:29 [j]Dt 27:12-13; Jos 8:33
11:30 [k]Ge 12:6 [l]Jos 4:19
11:31 [m]Dt 9:1; Jos 1:11
12:1 [a]Dt 4:9-10; 1Ki 8:40
12:2 [b]2Ki 16:4; 17:10
12:3 [c]Nu 33:52; Dt 7:5; Jdg 2:2
12:5 [d]ver 11, 13; 2Ch 7:12, 16
12:6 [e]Dt 14:22-23
12:7 [f]ver 12, 18; Lev 23:40; Dt 14:26
12:10 [g]Dt 11:31
12:11 [h]ver 5; Dt 15:20; 16:2
12:12 [i]ver 7

11:26 What is God's curse? It is not a magician's spell. To understand it, we must remember the conditions of the covenant between God and Israel. Both parties had agreed to the terms. The blessings would benefit Israel if they kept their part of the covenant: They would receive the land, live there for ever, have fruitful crops, and expel their enemies. The curse would fall on Israel only if they broke their agreement; then they would forfeit God's blessing and would be in danger of crop failure, invasion, and expulsion from their land. Joshua later reviewed these blessings and curses with the entire nation (Joshua 8:34).

11:26 It is amazing that God set before the Israelites a choice between blessings and curses. It is even more amazing that most of them, through their disobedience, chose the curses. We have the same fundamental choice today. We can live for ourselves or live in service to God. To choose our own way is to travel on a dead-end road, but to choose God's way is to receive eternal life (John 5:24).

12:2, 3 When taking over a nation, the Israelites were supposed to destroy every pagan altar and idol in the land. God knew it would be easy for them to change their beliefs if they started using those altars, so nothing was to remain that might tempt them to worship idols. We too should ruthlessly find and remove any centres of false worship in our lives. These may be activities, attitudes, possessions, relationships, places, or habits—anything that tempts us to turn our hearts from God and do wrong. We should never flatter ourselves by thinking we're too strong to be tempted. Israel learned that lesson.

12:12, 18 The Hebrews placed great emphasis on family worship. Whether offering a sacrifice or attending a great feast, the family was often together. This gave the children a healthy attitude towards worship, and it put extra meaning into it for the adults. Watching a family member confess his or her sin was just as important as celebrating a great holiday together. Although there are appropriate times to separate people by ages, some of the most meaningful worship can be experienced only when shared by old and young.

you, your sons and daughters, your menservants and maidservants, and the Levites
from your towns, who have no allotment or inheritance[j] of their own. 13 Be careful
not to sacrifice your burnt offerings anywhere you please. 14 Offer them only at the
place the LORD will choose[k] in one of your tribes, and there observe everything I
command you.
15 Nevertheless, you may slaughter your animals in any of your towns and eat as
much of the meat as you want, as if it were gazelle or deer,[l] according to the blessing
the LORD your God gives you. Both the ceremonially unclean and the clean may eat
it. 16 But you must not eat the blood;[m] pour it out on the ground like water.[n] 17 You
must not eat in your own towns the tithe of your grain and new wine and oil, or the
firstborn of your herds and flocks, or whatever you have vowed to give, or your
freewill offerings or special gifts. 18 Instead, you are to eat[o] them in the presence
of the LORD your God at the place the LORD your God will choose[p]—you, your
sons and daughters, your menservants and maidservants, and the Levites from
your towns—and you are to rejoice[q] before the LORD your God in everything you put
your hand to. 19 Be careful not to neglect the Levites[r] as long as you live in your
land.
20 When the LORD your God has enlarged your territory[s] as he promised[t] you, and
you crave meat and say, "I would like some meat," then you may eat as much of it
as you want. 21 If the place where the LORD your God chooses to put his Name is too
far away from you, you may slaughter animals from the herds and flocks the LORD
has given you, as I have commanded you, and in your own towns you may eat as much
of them as you want. 22 Eat them as you would gazelle or deer.[u] Both the ceremonially
unclean and the clean may eat. 23 But be sure you do not eat the blood,[v] because the
blood is the life, and you must not eat the life with the meat. 24 You must not eat the
blood; pour it out on the ground like water. 25 Do not eat it, so that it may go well[w]
with you and your children after you, because you will be doing what is right[x] in
the eyes of the LORD.
26 But take your consecrated things and whatever you have vowed to give,[y] and
go to the place the LORD will choose. 27 Present your burnt offerings[z] on the altar of
the LORD your God, both the meat and the blood. The blood of your sacrifices must
be poured beside the altar of the LORD your God, but you may eat the meat. 28 Be
careful to obey all these regulations I am giving you, so that it may always go well[a]
with you and your children after you, because you will be doing what is good and
right in the eyes of the LORD your God.
29 The LORD your God will cut off[b] before you the nations you are about to invade
and dispossess. But when you have driven them out and settled in their land, 30 and
after they have been destroyed before you, be careful not to be ensnared by enquiring
about their gods, saying, "How do these nations serve their gods? We will do the
same." 31 You must not worship the LORD your God in their way, because in worshipping their gods, they do all kinds of detestable things the LORD hates.[c] They even
burn their sons[d] and daughters in the fire as sacrifices to their gods.
32 See that you do all I command you; do not add[e] to it or take away from it.

12:12 [j] Dt 10:9; 14:29
12:14 [k] ver 11
12:15 [l] ver 20-23; Dt 14:5; 15:22
12:16 [m] Ge 9:4; Lev 7:26; 17:10-12 [n] Dt 15:23
12:18 [o] Dt 14:23 [p] ver 5 [q] ver 7, 12
12:19 [r] Dt 14:27
12:20 [s] Dt 19:8 [t] Ge 15:18; Dt 11:24
12:22 [u] ver 15
12:23 [v] ver 16; Ge 9:4; Lev 17:11, 14
12:25 [w] Dt 4:40; Isa 3:10 [x] Ex 15:26; Dt 13:18; 1Ki 11:38
12:26 [y] ver 17; Nu 5:9-10
12:27 [z] Lev 1:5, 9, 13
12:28 [a] ver 25; Dt 4:40
12:29 [b] Jos 23:4
12:31 [c] Dt 9:5 [d] Dt 18:10; Jer 32:35
12:32 [e] Dt 4:2; Jos 1:7; Rev 22:18-19

12:13, 14 While the pagans offered sacrifices to their gods, they offered them in many places. In contrast, the Israelites were only to offer sacrifices in the prescribed manner and in the prescribed places. This restriction was meant to ensure purity of worship for the nation of Israel. Later, they would neglect this injunction and offer sacrifices at the high places where pagan deities were worshipped. (See, for example, 2 Kings 23 where Josiah destroyed the other altars.) We should take steps to safeguard the purity of worship in our congregations. If we all individualised and customised worship to suit our own preferences, we would lose the benefit of worshipping as a body of believers.

12:16 Eating blood was forbidden for several reasons: (1) it was an integral part of the pagan practices of the land the Israelites were about to enter; (2) it represented life, which is sacred to God; (3) it was a symbol of the sacrifice that had to be made for sin. (For more on why eating blood was prohibited, see the note on Leviticus 17:14.)

12:30, 31 God did not want the Israelites even to ask about the pagan religions surrounding them. Idolatry completely permeated the land of Canaan. It was too easy to get drawn into the subtle temptations of seemingly harmless practices. Sometimes curiosity can cause us to stumble. Knowledge of evil is harmful if the evil becomes too tempting to resist. To resist curiosity about harmful practices shows discretion and obedience.

Worshipping Other Gods

13 If a prophet,[a] or one who foretells by dreams, appears among you and announces to you a miraculous sign or wonder, 2and if the sign or wonder of which
he has spoken takes place, and he says, "Let us follow other gods"[b] (gods you have
not known) "and let us worship them," 3you must not listen to the words of that prophet
or dreamer. The LORD your God is testing[c] you to find out whether you love him
with all your heart and with all your soul. 4It is the LORD your God you must follow,[d]
and him you must revere. Keep his commands and obey him; serve him and hold fast[e]
to him. 5That prophet or dreamer must be put to death, because he preached rebellion
against the LORD your God, who brought you out of Egypt and redeemed you from
the land of slavery; he has tried to turn you from the way the LORD your God
commanded you to follow. You must purge the evil[f] from among you.
6If your very own brother, or your son or daughter, or the wife you love, or your
closest friend secretly entices[g] you, saying, "Let us go and worship other gods" (gods
that neither you nor your fathers have known, 7gods of the peoples around you,
whether near or far, from one end of the land to the other), 8do not yield[h] to him
or listen to him. Show him no pity. Do not spare him or shield him. 9You must
certainly put him to death.[i] Your hand must be the first in putting him to death, and
then the hands of all the people. 10Stone him to death, because he tried to turn you
away from the LORD your God, who brought you out of Egypt, out of the land of
slavery. 11Then all Israel will hear and be afraid,[j] and no-one among you will do
such an evil thing again.
12If you hear it said about one of the towns the LORD your God is giving you to
live in 13that wicked men[k] have arisen among you and have led the people of their
town astray, saying, "Let us go and worship other gods" (gods you have not known),
14then you must enquire, probe and investigate it thoroughly. And if it is true and it
has been proved that this detestable thing has been done among you, 15you must
certainly put to the sword all who live in that town. Destroy it completely,**[a]** both its
people and its livestock. 16Gather all the plunder of the town into the middle of the
public square and completely burn the town and all its plunder as a whole burnt
offering to the LORD your God.[l] It is to remain a ruin[m] for ever, never to be rebuilt.
17None of those condemned things**[a]** shall be found in your hands, so that the LORD
will turn from his fierce anger;[n] he will show you mercy, have compassion[o] on you,
and increase your numbers,[p] as he promised[q] on oath to your forefathers, 18because
you obey the LORD your God, keeping all his commands that I am giving you today
and doing what is right[r] in his eyes.

a *15, 17* The Hebrew term refers to the irrevocable giving over of things or persons to the LORD, often by totally destroying them.

13:1 [a]Mt 24:24; Mk 13:22; 2Th 2:9
13:2 [b]ver 6, 13
13:3 [c]Dt 8:2, 16
13:4 [d]2Ki 23:3; 2Ch 34:31 [e]Dt 10:20
13:5 [f]Dt 17:7, 12; 1Co 5:13
13:6 [g]Dt 17:2-7; 29:18
13:8 [h]Pr 1:10
13:9 [i]Dt 17:5, 7
13:11 [j]Dt 19:20
13:13 [k]ver 2, 6; 1Jn 2:19
13:16 [l]Jos 6:24 [m]Jos 8:28; Jer 49:2
13:17 [n]Nu 25:4 [o]Dt 30:3 [p]Dt 7:13 [q]Ge 22:17; 26:4, 24; 28:14
13:18 [r]Dt 12:25, 28

13:1–3 Attractive leaders are not always led by God. Moses warned the Israelites against false prophets who encouraged worship of other gods. New ideas from inspiring people may sound good, but we must judge them by whether or not they are consistent with God's word. When people claim to speak for God today, check them in these areas: Are they telling the truth? Is their focus on God? Are their words consistent with what you already know to be true? Some people speak the truth while directing you towards God, but others speak persuasively while directing you towards themselves. It is even possible to say the right words but still lead people in the wrong direction. God is not against new ideas, but he is for discernment. When you hear a new, attractive idea, examine it carefully before getting too excited. False prophets are still around today. The wise person will carefully test ideas against the truth of God's word.

13:2–11 The Israelites were warned not to listen to false prophets or to anyone else who tried to get them to worship other gods—even if this person was a close friend or family member. The temptation to abandon God's commands often sneaks up on us. It may come not with a loud shout but in a whispering doubt. And whispers can be very persuasive, especially if they come from loved ones. But love for relatives should not take precedence over devotion to God. We can overcome whispered temptations by pouring out our hearts to God in prayer and by diligently studying his word.

13:12–16 A city that completely rejected God was to be destroyed so as not to lead the rest of the nation astray. But Israel was not to take action against a city until the rumour about its rejecting God was proved true. This guideline saved many lives when the leaders of Israel wrongly accused three tribes of falling away from their faith (Joshua 22). If we hear of friends who have wandered from the Lord or of entire congregations that have fallen away, we should check the facts and find the truth before doing or saying anything that could prove harmful. There are times, of course, when God wants us to take action—to rebuke a wayward friend, to discipline a child, to reject false teaching—but first we must be sure we have all the facts straight.

Clean and Unclean Food

14 You are the children[a] of the LORD your God. Do not cut yourselves or shave
the front of your heads for the dead, 2for you are a people holy to the LORD
your God.[b] Out of all the peoples on the face of the earth, the LORD has chosen you
to be his treasured possession.[c]
3Do not eat any detestable thing.[d] 4These are the animals you may eat:[e] the ox,
the sheep, the goat, 5the deer, the gazelle, the roe deer, the wild goat, the ibex, the
antelope and the mountain sheep.**a** 6You may eat any animal that has a split hoof
divided in two and that chews the cud. 7However, of those that chew the cud or that
have a split hoof completely divided you may not eat the camel, the rabbit or the
coney.**b** Although they chew the cud, they do not have a split hoof; they are
ceremonially unclean for you. 8The pig is also unclean; although it has a split hoof,
it does not chew the cud. You are not to eat their meat or touch their carcasses.[f]
9Of all the creatures living in the water, you may eat any that has fins and scales.
10But anything that does not have fins and scales you may not eat; for you it is unclean.
11You may eat any clean bird. 12But these you may not eat: the eagle, the vulture,
the black vulture, 13the red kite, the black kite, any kind of falcon, 14any kind of raven,
15the horned owl, the screech owl, the gull, any kind of hawk, 16the little owl, the
great owl, the white owl, 17the desert owl, the osprey, the cormorant, 18the stork, any
kind of heron, the hoopoe and the bat.
19All flying insects that swarm are unclean to you; do not eat them. 20But any
winged creature that is clean you may eat.
21Do not eat anything you find already dead.[g] You may give it to an alien living
in any of your towns, and he may eat it, or you may sell it to a foreigner. But you
are a people holy to the LORD your God.[h]
Do not cook a young goat in its mother's milk.[i]

Tithes

22Be sure to set aside a tenth[j] of all that your fields produce each year. 23Eat the
tithe of your grain, new wine and oil, and the firstborn of your herds and flocks in
the presence of the LORD your God at the place he will choose as a dwelling for his
Name,[k] so that you may learn[l] to revere the LORD your God always. 24But if that
place is too distant and you have been blessed by the LORD your God and cannot carry
your tithe (because the place where the LORD will choose to put his Name is so far
away), 25then exchange your tithe for silver, and take the silver with you and go to
the place the LORD your God will choose. 26Use the silver to buy whatever you like:
cattle, sheep, wine or other fermented drink, or anything you wish. Then you and your
household shall eat there in the presence of the LORD your God and rejoice.[m] 27And

14:1 [a]Lev 19:28; 21:5; Jer 16:6; 41:5; Ro 8:14; 9:8; Gal 3:26
14:2 [b]Lev 20:26 [c]Dt 7:6; 26:18-19
14:3 [d]Eze 4:14
14:4 [e]Lev 11:2-45; Ac 10:14
14:8 [f]Lev 11:26-27
14:21 [g]Lev 17:15; 22:8 [h]ver 2 [i]Ex 23:19; 34:26
14:22 [j]Lev 27:30; Dt 12:6, 17; Ne 10:37
14:23 [k]Dt 12:5 [l]Dt 4:10
14:26 [m]Dt 12:7-8

a *5* The precise identification of some of the birds and animals in this chapter is uncertain. **b** *7* That is, the hyrax or rock badger

---

14:1 The actions described here refer to a cult of the dead. Many other religions today have some kind of worship of or service to the dead. But Christianity and Judaism are very different from other religions because they focus on serving God in this life. Don't let concern or worry over the dead distract you from the tasks that God has for you while you are still alive.

14:3–21 Why was Israel forbidden to eat certain foods? There are several reasons: (1) Predatory animals ate the blood of other animals, and scavengers ate dead animals. Because the people could not eat blood or animals they found dead, they could not eat animals that did these things either. (2) Some forbidden animals had bad associations in the Israelite culture, as bats, snakes, and spiders do for some people today. Some may have been used in pagan religious practices (Isaiah 66:17). To the Israelites, the unclean animals represented sin or unhealthy habits. (3) Perhaps some restrictions were given to Israel just to remind them continually that they were a different and separate people committed to God. Although we no longer must follow these laws about food (Acts 10:9–16), we can still learn from them the lesson that holiness is to be carried into all parts of life. We can't restrict holiness only to the spiritual side; we must be holy in the everyday practical part of life as well. Health practices, finances, use of leisure – all provide opportunities to put holy living into daily living.

14:21 This prohibition against cooking a young goat in its mother's milk may reflect a Canaanite fertility rite. Or it may just mean that the Israelites were not to take what was intended to promote life and use it to kill or destroy life. This commandment is also given in Exodus 23:19.

14:22, 23 The Bible makes the purpose of tithing very clear – to put God first in our lives. We are to give God the first and best of what we earn. For example, what we do first with our money shows what we value most. Giving the first part of our pay cheque to God immediately focuses our attention on him. It also reminds us that all we have belongs to him. A habit of regular tithing can keep God at the top of our priority list and give us a proper perspective on everything else we have.

do not neglect the Levites[n] living in your towns, for they have no allotment or inheritance of their own.[o]

28At the end of every three years, bring all the tithes of that year's produce and store it in your towns,[p] 29so that the Levites (who have no allotment[q] or inheritance of their own) and the aliens,[r] the fatherless and the widows who live in your towns may come and eat and be satisfied, and so that the LORD your God may bless[s] you in all the work of your hands.

The Year for Cancelling Debts

15 At the end of every seven years you must cancel debts.[a] 2This is how it is to be done: Every creditor shall cancel the loan he has made to his fellow Israelite. He shall not require payment from his fellow Israelite or brother, because the LORD's time for cancelling debts has been proclaimed. 3You may require payment from a foreigner,[b] but you must cancel any debt your brother owes you. 4However, there should be no poor among you, for in the land the LORD your God is giving you to possess as your inheritance, he will richly bless[c] you, 5if only you fully obey the LORD your God and are careful to follow[d] all these commands I am giving you today. 6For the LORD your God will bless you as he has promised, and you will lend to many nations but will borrow from none. You will rule over many nations but none will rule over you.[e]

7If there is a poor man among your brothers in any of the towns of the land that the LORD your God is giving you, do not be hard-hearted or tight-fisted[f] towards your poor brother. 8Rather be open-handed[g] and freely lend him whatever he needs. 9Be careful not to harbour this wicked thought: "The seventh year, the year for cancelling debts,[h] is near," so that you do not show ill will[i] towards your needy brother and give him nothing. He may then appeal to the LORD against you, and you will be found guilty of sin.[j] 10Give generously to him and do so without a grudging heart;[k] then because of this the LORD your God will bless[l] you in all your work and in everything you put your hand to. 11There will always be poor people in the land. Therefore I command you to be open-handed towards your brothers and towards the poor and needy in your land.[m]

Freeing Servants

12If a fellow Hebrew, a man or woman, sells himself to you and serves you six years, in the seventh year you must let him go free.[n] 13And when you release him, do not send him away empty-handed. 14Supply him liberally from your flock, your threshing-floor and your winepress. Give to him as the LORD your God has blessed

14:27 [n]Dt 12:19 [o]Nu 18:20
14:28 [p]Dt 26:12
14:29 [q]ver 27 [r]Dt 26:12 [s]Dt 15:10; Mal 3:10
15:1 [a]Dt 31:10
15:3 [b]Dt 23:20
15:4 [c]Dt 28:8
15:5 [d]Dt 28:1
15:6 [e]Dt 28:12-13, 44
15:7 [f]1Jn 3:17
15:8 [g]Mt 5:42; Lk 6:34
15:9 [h]ver 1 [i]Mt 20:15 [j]Dt 24:15
15:10 [k]2Co 9:5 [l]Dt 14:29; 24:19
15:11 [m]Mt 26:11; Mk 14:7; Jn 12:8
15:12 [n]Ex 21:2; Lev 25:39; Jer 34:14

14:28, 29 The Bible supports an organised system of caring for the poor. God told his people to use their tithe every third year for those who were helpless, hungry, or poor. These regulations were designed to prevent the country from sinking under crushing poverty and oppression. It was everyone's responsibility to care for those less fortunate. Families were to help other family members, and towns were to help members of their community. National laws protected the rights of the poor, but helping the poor was also an active part of religious life. God counts on believers to provide for the needy, and we should use what God has given us to aid those less fortunate. Look beyond your regular giving and think of ways to help the needy. This will help you show your regard for God as Creator of all people, share God's goodness with others, and draw them to him. It is a practical and essential way to make faith work in everyday life.

15:7–11 God told the Israelites to help the poor among them when they arrived in the promised land. This was an important part of possessing the land. Many people conclude that people are poor through some fault of their own. This kind of reasoning makes it easy to close their hearts and hands to the needy. But we are not to invent reasons for ignoring the poor. We are to respond to their needs no matter who or what was responsible for their condition. Who are the poor in your community? How could your church help them? If your church does not have a programme to identify the poor and assist in fulfilling their needs, why not help start one? What can you do to help someone in need?

15:12–15 The Israelites were to release their servants after six years, sending them away with enough food so that they would be amply supplied until their needs could be met by some other means. This humanitarian act recognised that God created each person with dignity and worth. It also reminded the Israelites that they, too, had once been slaves in Egypt, and that their present freedom was a gift from God. We do not have servants such as these today, but God's instructions still apply to us: We must still be sure to treat our employees with respect and economic fairness.

you. 15 Remember that you were slaves[o] in Egypt and the LORD your God redeemed
you.[p] That is why I give you this command today.
16 But if your servant says to you, "I do not want to leave you," because he loves
you and your family and is well off with you, 17 then take an awl and push it through
his ear lobe into the door, and he will become your servant for life. Do the same for
your maidservant.
18 Do not consider it a hardship to set your servant free, because his service to you
these six years has been worth twice as much as that of a hired hand. And the LORD
your God will bless you in everything you do.

The Firstborn Animals

19 Set apart for the LORD your God every firstborn male[q] of your herds and flocks.
Do not put the firstborn of your oxen to work, and do not shear the firstborn of your
sheep. 20 Each year you and your family are to eat them in the presence of the LORD
your God at the place he will choose.[r] 21 If an animal has a defect, is lame or blind,
or has any serious flaw, you must not sacrifice it to the LORD your God.[s] 22 You are
to eat it in your own towns. Both the ceremonially unclean and the clean may eat it,
as if it were gazelle or deer.[t] 23 But you must not eat the blood; pour it out on the
ground like water.[u]

Passover

16 Observe the month of Abib[a] and celebrate the Passover of the LORD your God,
because in the month of Abib he brought you out of Egypt by night. 2 Sacrifice
as the Passover to the LORD your God an animal from your flock or herd at the place
the LORD will choose as a dwelling for his Name.[b] 3 Do not eat it with bread made
with yeast, but for seven days eat unleavened bread, the bread of affliction,[c] because
you left Egypt in haste[d]—so that all the days of your life you may remember the time
of your departure from Egypt.[e] 4 Let no yeast be found in your possession in all your
land for seven days. Do not let any of the meat you sacrifice on the evening of the
first day remain until morning.[f]
5 You must not sacrifice the Passover in any town the LORD your God gives you
6 except in the place he will choose as a dwelling for his Name. There you must
sacrifice the Passover in the evening, when the sun goes down, on the anniversary[a][g]
of your departure from Egypt. 7 Roast[h] it and eat it at the place the LORD your God
will choose. Then in the morning return to your tents. 8 For six days eat unleavened
bread and on the seventh day hold an assembly[i] to the LORD your God and do no
work.

Feast of Weeks

9 Count off seven weeks[j] from the time you begin to put the sickle to the standing
corn.[k] 10 Then celebrate the Feast of Weeks to the LORD your God by giving a freewill
offering in proportion to the blessings the LORD your God has given you. 11 And
rejoice[l] before the LORD your God at the place he will choose as a dwelling for his
Name—you, your sons and daughters, your menservants and maidservants, the
Levites[m] in your towns, and the aliens, the fatherless and the widows living among
you. 12 Remember that you were slaves in Egypt,[n] and follow carefully these decrees.

Feast of Tabernacles

13 Celebrate the Feast of Tabernacles for seven days after you have gathered the
produce of your threshing-floor[o] and your winepress.[p] 14 Be joyful[q] at your
Feast—you, your sons and daughters, your menservants and maidservants, and the
Levites, the aliens, the fatherless and the widows who live in your towns. 15 For seven
days celebrate the Feast to the LORD your God at the place the LORD will choose. For
the LORD your God will bless you in all your harvest and in all the work of your hands,
and your joy[r] will be complete.

[a] 6 Or *down, at the time of day*

15:15 [o] Dt 5:15 [p] Dt 16:12
15:19 [q] Ex 13:2
15:20 [r] Dt 12:5-7, 17, 18; 14:23
15:21 [s] Lev 22:19-25
15:22 [t] Dt 12:15, 22
15:23 [u] Dt 12:16
16:1 [a] Ex 12:2; 13:4
16:2 [b] Dt 12:5, 26
16:3 [c] Ex 12:8, 39; 34:18 [d] Ex 12:11, 15, 19 [e] Ex 13:3, 6-7
16:4 [f] Ex 12:10; 34:25
16:6 [g] Ex 12:6; Dt 12:5
16:7 [h] Ex 12:8; 2Ch 35:13
16:8 [i] Ex 12:16; 13:6; Lev 23:8
16:9 [j] Ex 34:22; Lev 23:15 [k] Ex 23:16; Nu 28:26
16:11 [l] Dt 12:7 [m] Dt 12:12
16:12 [n] Dt 15:15
16:13 [o] Lev 23:34 [p] Ex 23:16
16:14 [q] ver 11
16:15 [r] Lev 23:39

16 Three times a year all your men must appear before the LORD your God at the
place he will choose: at the Feast of Unleavened Bread, the Feast of Weeks and the
Feast of Tabernacles.[s] No man should appear before the LORD empty-handed:[t]
17 Each of you must bring a gift in proportion to the way the LORD your God has blessed
you.

4. Laws for ruling the nation

Judges

18 Appoint judges[u] and officials for each of your tribes in every town the LORD your
God is giving you, and they shall judge the people fairly. 19 Do not pervert justice[v]
or show partiality.[w] Do not accept a bribe,[x] for a bribe blinds the eyes of the wise
and twists the words of the righteous. 20 Follow justice and justice alone, so that you
may live and possess the land the LORD your God is giving you.

Worshipping Other Gods

21 Do not set up any wooden Asherah pole[b][y] beside the altar you build to the LORD
your God,[z] 22 and do not erect a sacred stone,[a] for these the LORD your God hates.
17 Do not sacrifice to the LORD your God an ox or a sheep that has any defect[a]
or flaw in it, for that would be detestable to him.[b]
2 If a man or woman living among you in one of the towns the LORD gives you is
found doing evil in the eyes of the LORD your God in violation of his covenant,[c] 3 and
contrary to my command[d] has worshipped other gods, bowing down to them or to
the sun[e] or the moon or the stars of the sky, 4 and this has been brought to your
attention, then you must investigate it thoroughly. If it is true and it has been proved
that this detestable thing has been done in Israel,[f] 5 take the man or woman who has
done this evil deed to your city gate and stone that person to death.[g] 6 On the testimony
of two or three witnesses a man shall be put to death, but no-one shall be put to death
on the testimony of only one witness.[h] 7 The hands of the witnesses must be the first
in putting him to death, and then the hands of all the people. You must purge the evil[i]
from among you.

Law Courts

8 If cases come before your courts that are too difficult for you to judge—whether
bloodshed, lawsuits or assaults[j]—take them to the place the LORD your God will
choose.[k] 9 Go to the priests, who are Levites, and to the judge who is in office at that
time. Enquire of them and they will give you the verdict.[l] 10 You must act according
to the decisions they give you at the place the LORD will choose. Be careful to do
everything they direct you to do. 11 Act according to the law they teach you and the

b *21* Or *Do not plant any tree dedicated to Asherah*

16:16 [s]Ex 23:14, 16 [t]Ex 34:20
16:18 [u]Dt 1:16
16:19 [v]Ex 23:2, 8 [w]Lev 19:15; Dt 1:17 [x]Ecc 7:7
16:21 [y]Dt 7:5 [z]Ex 34:13; 2Ki 17:16; 21:3; 2Ch 33:3
16:22 [a]Lev 26:1
17:1 [a]Mal 1:8, 13 [b]Dt 15:21
17:2 [c]Dt 13:6-11
17:3 [d]Jer 7:22-23 [e]Job 31:26
17:4 [f]Dt 13:12-14
17:5 [g]Lev 24:14
17:6 [h]Nu 35:30; Dt 19:15; Jos 7:25; Mt 18:16; Jn 8:17; 2Co 13:1; 1Ti 5:19; Heb 10:28
17:7 [i]Dt 13:5, 9
17:8 [j]2Ch 19:10 [k]Dt 12:5; Hag 2:11
17:9 [l]Dt 19:17; Eze 44:24

16:16, 17 Three times a year every male was to make a journey to the sanctuary in the city that would be designated as Israel's religious capital. At these festivals, each participant was encouraged to give what he could in proportion to what God had given him. God does not expect us to give more than we can, but we will be blessed when we give cheerfully. For some, 10 per cent may be a burden. For most of us, that would be far too little. Look at what you have and then give in proportion to what you have been given.

16:18–20 These verses anticipated a great problem the Israelites would face when they arrived in the promised land. Although they had Joshua as their national leader, they failed to complete the task and choose other spiritual leaders who would lead the tribes, districts, and cities with justice and God's wisdom. Because they did not appoint wise judges and faithful administrators, rebellion and injustice plagued their communities. It is a serious responsibility to appoint or elect wise and just officials. In your sphere of influence—home, church, school, job—are you ensuring that justice and godliness prevail? Failing to choose leaders who uphold justice can lead to much trouble, as Israel would discover.

17:1 The fact that this command was included probably indicates that some Israelites were sacrificing imperfect or deformed animals to God. Then, as now, it is difficult and expensive to offer God our best (i.e., the first part of what we earn). It is always tempting to shortchange God because we think we won't get caught. But our giving shows our real priorities. When we give God the leftovers, it is obvious that he is not at the centre of our lives. Give God the honour of having first claim on your money, time, and talents.

17:6, 7 A person was not put to death on the testimony of only one witness. On the witness of two or three, a person could be condemned and then sentenced to death by stoning. The condemned person was taken outside the city gates, and the witnesses were the first to throw heavy stones down on him or her. Bystanders would then pelt the dying person with stones. This system would "purge the evil" by putting the idolater to death. At the same time, it protected the rights of accused persons in two ways. First, by requiring several witnesses, it prevented any angry individual from giving "false testimony". Second, by requiring the accusers to throw the first stones, it made them think twice about accusing unjustly. They were responsible to finish what they had started.

decisions they give you. Do not turn aside from what they tell you, to the right or
to the left.[m] 12 The man who shows contempt[n] for the judge or for the priest who
stands ministering there to the LORD your God must be put to death. You must purge
the evil from Israel. 13 All the people will hear and be afraid, and will not be
contemptuous again.[o]

The King

14 When you enter the land the LORD your God is giving you and have taken
possession of it and settled in it, and you say, "Let us set a king over us like all the
nations around us,"[p] 15 be sure to appoint over you the king the LORD your God
chooses. He must be from among your own brothers.[q] Do not place a foreigner over
you, one who is not a brother Israelite. 16 The king, moreover, must not acquire great
numbers of horses for himself[r] or make the people return to Egypt[s] to get more of
them,[t] for the LORD has told you, "You are not to go back that way again."[u] 17 He
must not take many wives,[v] or his heart will be led astray. He must not accumulate
large amounts of silver and gold.

18 When he takes the throne of his kingdom, he is to write[w] for himself on a scroll
a copy of this law, taken from that of the priests, who are Levites. 19 It is to be with
him, and he is to read it all the days of his life[x] so that he may learn to revere the
LORD his God and follow carefully all the words of this law and these decrees 20 and
not consider himself better than his brothers and turn from the law[y] to the right or
to the left.[z] Then he and his descendants will reign a long time over his kingdom
in Israel.

Offerings for Priests and Levites

18 The priests, who are Levites—indeed the whole tribe of Levi—are to have no
allotment or inheritance with Israel. They shall live on the offerings made to
the LORD by fire, for that is their inheritance.[a] 2 They shall have no inheritance among
their brothers; the LORD is their inheritance, as he promised them.

3 This is the share due to the priests from the people who sacrifice a bull or a sheep:
the shoulder, the jowls and the inner parts.[b] 4 You are to give them the firstfruits of
your grain, new wine and oil, and the first wool from the shearing of your sheep,[c]
5 for the LORD your God has chosen them[d] and their descendants out of all your tribes
to stand and minister[e] in the LORD's name always.

6 If a Levite moves from one of your towns anywhere in Israel where he is living,
and comes in all earnestness to the place the LORD will choose,[f] 7 he may minister
in the name of the LORD his God like all his fellow Levites who serve there in the
presence of the LORD. 8 He is to share equally in their benefits even though he has
received money from the sale of family possessions.[g]

17:11 [m] Dt 25:1
17:12 [n] Nu 15:30
17:13 [o] Dt 13:11; 19:20
17:14 [p] Dt 11:31; 1Sa 8:5, 19-20
17:15 [q] Jer 30:21
17:16 [r] 1Ki 4:26; 10:26 [s] Isa 31:1; Hos 11:5 [t] 1Ki 10:28; Eze 17:15 [u] Ex 13:17
17:17 [v] 1Ki 11:3
17:18 [w] Dt 31:22, 24
17:19 [x] Jos 1:8
17:20 [y] 1Ki 15:5 [z] Dt 5:32
18:1 [a] Dt 10:9; 1Co 9:13
18:3 [b] Lev 7:28-34
18:4 [c] Ex 22:29; Nu 18:12
18:5 [d] Ex 28:1 [e] Dt 10:8
18:6 [f] Nu 35:2-3
18:8 [g] 2Ch 31:4; Ne 12:44, 47

17:14-20 God was not encouraging Israel to appoint a king to rule their nation. He was actually against the idea because he was their King, and the people were to obey and follow him. But God knew that the people would one day demand a king for selfish reasons—they would want to be like the nations around them (1 Samuel 8). If they insisted on having a king, he wanted to make sure they chose the right person. That is why he included these instructions both for the people's benefit as they chose their king and for the king himself as he sought to lead the nation according to God's laws.

17:16, 17 Israel's kings did not heed this warning, and their behaviour led to their downfall. Solomon had everything going for him, but when he became rich, built up a large army, and married many wives, his heart turned from God (1 Kings 11). Out of Solomon's sin came Israel's disobedience, division, and captivity.

17:18-20 The king was to be a man of God's word. He was to (1) have a copy of the law made for his personal use, (2) keep it with him all the time, (3) read from it every day, and (4) obey it completely. Through this process he would learn respect for God, keep himself from feeling more important than others, and avoid neglecting God in times of prosperity. We can't know what God wants except through his word, and his word won't affect our lives unless we read and think about it regularly. With the abundant availability of the Bible today, it is not difficult to gain access to the source of the king's wisdom. What is more of a challenge is following its directives.

18:1-8 The priests and Levites served much the same function as our ministers today. Their duties included (1) teaching the people about God, (2) setting an example of godly living, (3) caring for the sanctuary and its workers, and (4) distributing the offerings. Because priests could not own property or pursue outside business interests, God made special arrangements so that people would not take advantage of them. Often churches take advantage of the men and women God has brought to lead them. For example, ministers may not be paid in accordance with their skills or the time they put in. Or pastors may be expected to attend every evening meeting, even if this continual absence is harmful to their families. As you look at your own church in the light of God's word, what ways do you see to honour the leaders God has given you?

Detestable Practices

9When you enter the land the LORD your God is giving you, do not learn to imitate[h]
the detestable ways of the nations there. 10Let no-one be found among you who
sacrifices his son or daughter in[a] the fire, who practises divination[i] or sorcery,
interprets omens, engages in witchcraft,[j] 11or casts spells, or who is a medium or
spiritist or who consults the dead. 12Anyone who does these things is detestable to
the LORD, and because of these detestable practices the LORD your God will drive out
those nations before you.[k] 13You must be blameless before the LORD your God.

The Prophet

14The nations you will dispossess listen to those who practise sorcery or divination.
But as for you, the LORD your God has not permitted you to do so. 15The LORD your
God will raise up for you a prophet like me from among your own brothers.[l] You
must listen to him. 16For this is what you asked of the LORD your God at Horeb on
the day of the assembly when you said, "Let us not hear the voice of the LORD our
God nor see this great fire any more, or we will die."[m]
17The LORD said to me: "What they say is good. 18I will raise up for them a prophet
like you from among their brothers; I will put my words[n] in his mouth, and he will
tell them everything I command him.[o] 19If anyone does not listen to my words that
the prophet speaks in my name, I myself will call him to account.[p] 20But a prophet
who presumes to speak in my name anything I have not commanded him to say, or
a prophet who speaks in the name of other gods,[q] must be put to death."[r]
21You may say to yourselves, "How can we know when a message has not been
spoken by the LORD?" 22If what a prophet proclaims in the name of the LORD does
not take place or come true, that is a message the LORD has not spoken.[s] That prophet
has spoken presumptuously.[t] Do not be afraid of him.

Cities of Refuge

19 When the LORD your God has destroyed the nations whose land he is giving
you, and when you have driven them out and settled in their towns and
houses,[a] 2then set aside for yourselves three cities centrally located in the land the
LORD your God is giving you to possess. 3Build roads to them and divide into three

18:9 [h]Dt 12:29-31
18:10 [i]Dt 12:31 [j]Lev 19:31
18:12 [k]Lev 18:24; Dt 9:4
18:15 [l]Jn 1:21; Ac 3:22*; 7:37*
18:16 [m]Ex 20:19; Dt 5:23-27
18:18 [n]Isa 51:16; Jn 17:8 [o]Jn 4:25-26; 8:28; 12:49-50
18:19 [p]Ac 3:23*
18:20 [q]Jer 14:14 [r]Dt 13:1-5
18:22 [s]Jer 28:9 [t]ver 20
19:1 [a]Dt 12:29

a *10 Or who makes his son or daughter pass through*

18:10 Child sacrifice and occult practices were strictly forbidden by God. These practices were common among pagan religions. Israel's own neighbours actually sacrificed their children to the god Molech (Leviticus 20:2–5). Other neighbouring religions used supernatural means, such as contacting the spirit world, to foretell the future and gain guidance. Because of these wicked practices, God would drive out the pagan nations (18:12). The Israelites were to replace their evil practices with the worship of the one true God.

18:10–13 The Israelites were naturally curious about the occult practices of the Canaanite religions. But Satan is behind the occult, and God flatly forbade Israel to have anything to do with it. Today people are still fascinated by horoscopes, fortune-telling, witchcraft, and bizarre cults. Often their interest comes from a desire to know and control the future. But Satan is no less dangerous today than he was in Moses' time. In the Bible, God tells us all we need to know about what is going to happen. The information Satan offers is likely to be distorted or completely false. With the trustworthy guidance of the Holy Spirit through the Bible and the church, we don't need to turn to occult sources for faulty information.

18:15 Who is this prophet? Stephen used this verse to support his claim that Jesus Christ is God's Son, the Messiah (Acts 7:37). The coming of Jesus Christ to earth was not an afterthought, but part of God's original plan.

18:21, 22 As in the days of ancient Israel, some people today claim to have messages from God. God still speaks to his people, but we must be cautious before saying that someone is God's spokesman. How can we tell when people are speaking for the Lord? (1) We can see whether or not their prophecies come true – the ancient test for judging prophets. (2) We can check their words against the Bible. God never contradicts himself, so if someone says something contrary to the Bible, we can know that this is not God's word.

19:2, 3 The Israelites were told to build roads because these cities of refuge would have been ineffective if the roads that led to them were in disrepair. Many who came to the cities were literally running for their lives. A well-maintained road could have meant the difference between life and death. This involved continued maintenance, because these were dirt roads that could easily be washed away, covered by sand, or crisscrossed with deep ruts. It was important not only to initiate this system of justice, but to provide the necessary means of maintaining it.

19:2–7 Every society must deal with the problem of murder. But how should society treat those who have innocently or accidentally killed someone? God had an answer for the Israelites. Since revenge was common and swift in Moses' day, God had the Israelites set apart several "cities of refuge". Anyone who claimed to have accidentally killed someone could flee to one of these cities until he could have a fair trial. If he was found innocent of intentional murder, he could remain in that city and be safe from those seeking revenge. This is a beautiful example of how God blended his justice and mercy towards his people. (For more information on cities of refuge, see the note on Numbers 35:6.)

19:6 [b]Nu 35:12
19:9 [c]Jos 20:7-8
19:10 [d]Nu 35:33; Dt 21:1-9
19:11 [e]Nu 35:16
19:13 [f]Dt 7:2 [g]1Ki 2:31
19:14 [h]Dt 27:17; Pr 22:28; Hos 5:10
19:15 [i]Nu 35:30; Dt 17:6; Mt 18:16*; Jn 8:17; 2Co 13:1*; 1Ti 5:19; Heb 10:28
19:16 [j]Ex 23:1; Ps 27:12
19:17 [k]Dt 17:9
19:19 [l]Pr 19:5, 9
19:20 [m]Dt 17:13; 21:21
19:21 [n]ver 13 [o]Ex 21:24; Lev 24:20; Mt 5:38*
20:1 [a]Ps 20:7; Isa 31:1 [b]Dt 31:6, 8 [c]2Ch 32:7-8
20:3 [d]Jos 23:10

parts the land the LORD your God is giving you as an inheritance, so that anyone who
kills a man may flee there.
4This is the rule concerning the man who kills another and flees there to save his
life — one who kills his neighbour unintentionally, without malice aforethought. 5For
instance, a man may go into the forest with his neighbour to cut wood, and as he
swings his axe to fell a tree, the head may fly off and hit his neighbour and kill him.
That man may flee to one of these cities and save his life. 6Otherwise, the avenger
of blood[b] might pursue him in a rage, overtake him if the distance is too great, and
kill him even though he is not deserving of death, since he did it to his neighbour
without malice aforethought. 7This is why I command you to set aside for yourselves
three cities.
8If the LORD your God enlarges your territory, as he promised on oath to your
forefathers, and gives you the whole land he promised them, 9because you carefully
follow all these laws I command you today — to love the LORD your God and to walk
always in his ways[c] — then you are to set aside three more cities. 10Do this so that
innocent blood will not be shed in your land, which the LORD your God is giving you
as your inheritance, and so that you will not be guilty of bloodshed.[d]
11But if a man hates his neighbour and lies in wait for him, assaults and kills him,[e]
and then flees to one of these cities, 12the elders of his town shall send for him, bring
him back from the city, and hand him over to the avenger of blood to die. 13Show
him no pity.[f] You must purge from Israel the guilt of shedding innocent blood,[g]
so that it may go well with you.
14Do not move your neighbour's boundary stone set up by your predecessors in the
inheritance you receive in the land the LORD your God is giving you to possess.[h]

Witnesses

15One witness is not enough to convict a man accused of any crime or offence he
may have committed. A matter must be established by the testimony of two or three
witnesses.[i]
16If a malicious witness[j] takes the stand to accuse a man of a crime, 17the two
men involved in the dispute must stand in the presence of the LORD before the priests
and the judges[k] who are in office at the time. 18The judges must make a thorough
investigation, and if the witness proves to be a liar, giving false testimony against his
brother, 19then do to him as he intended to do to his brother.[l] You must purge the
evil from among you. 20The rest of the people will hear of this and be afraid,[m] and
never again will such an evil thing be done among you. 21Show no pity:[n] life for life,
eye for eye, tooth for tooth, hand for hand, foot for foot.[o]

Going to War

20 When you go to war against your enemies and see horses and chariots and an
army greater than yours,[a] do not be afraid[b] of them,[c] because the LORD your
God, who brought you up out of Egypt, will be with you. 2When you are about to
go into battle, the priest shall come forward and address the army. 3He shall say:
"Hear, O Israel, today you are going into battle against your enemies. Do not be
faint-hearted[d] or afraid; do not be terrified or give way to panic before them. 4For

19:12 The "avenger of blood" was the nearest male relative to the person killed. He acted as the family protector (see Numbers 35:19).

19:21 This principle was for the judges to use, not a plan for personal vengeance. This attitude towards punishment may seem primitive, but it was actually a breakthrough for justice and fairness in ancient times when most nations used arbitrary methods to punish criminals. This guideline reflects a concern for evenhandedness and justice — ensuring that those who violated the law were not punished more severely than their particular crime deserved. In the same spirit of justice, a false witness was to receive the same punishment the accused person would have suffered. The principle of making the punishment fit the crime should still be observed today.

20:1 Just like the Israelites, we sometimes face overwhelming opposition. Whether at school, at work, or even at home, we can feel outnumbered and helpless. God bolstered the Israelites' confidence by reminding them that he was always with them and that he had already saved them from the potential danger. We too can feel secure when we consider that God is able to overcome even the most difficult odds.

the LORD your God is the one who goes with you to fight[e] for you against your
enemies to give you victory."
5The officers shall say to the army: "Has anyone built a new house and not
dedicated[f] it? Let him go home, or he may die in battle and someone else may
dedicate it. 6Has anyone planted a vineyard and not begun to enjoy it? Let him go
home, or he may die in battle and someone else enjoy it. 7Has anyone become pledged
to a woman and not married her? Let him go home, or he may die in battle and someone
else marry her.[g]" 8Then the officers shall add, "Is any man afraid or faint-hearted?
Let him go home so that his brothers will not become disheartened too."[h] 9When the
officers have finished speaking to the army, they shall appoint commanders over it.
10When you march up to attack a city, make its people an offer of peace.[i] 11If
they accept and open their gates, all the people in it shall be subject to forced labour[j]
and shall work for you. 12If they refuse to make peace and they engage you in battle,
lay siege to that city. 13When the LORD your God delivers it into your hand, put to
the sword all the men in it.[k] 14As for the women, the children, the livestock[l] and
everything else in the city, you may take these as plunder for yourselves. And you
may use the plunder the LORD your God gives you from your enemies. 15This is how
you are to treat all the cities that are at a distance from you and do not belong to the
nations nearby.
16However, in the cities of the nations the LORD your God is giving you as an
inheritance, do not leave alive anything that breathes.[m] 17Completely destroy[a]
them—the Hittites, Amorites, Canaanites, Perizzites, Hivites and Jebusites—as the
LORD your God has commanded you. 18Otherwise, they will teach you to follow all
the detestable things they do in worshipping their gods,[n] and you will sin[o] against
the LORD your God.
19When you lay siege to a city for a long time, fighting against it to capture it, do
not destroy its trees by putting an axe to them, because you can eat their fruit. Do
not cut them down. Are the trees of the field people, that you should besiege them?[b]
20However, you may cut down trees that you know are not fruit trees and use them
to build siege works until the city at war with you falls.

5. Laws for human relationships

Atonement for an Unsolved Murder

21 If a man is found slain, lying in a field in the land the LORD your God is giving
you to possess, and it is not known who killed him, 2your elders and judges
shall go out and measure the distance from the body to the neighbouring towns. 3Then
the elders of the town nearest the body shall take a heifer that has never been worked
and has never worn a yoke 4and lead her down to a valley that has not been ploughed
or planted and where there is a flowing stream. There in the valley they are to break
the heifer's neck. 5The priests, the sons of Levi, shall step forward, for the LORD your
God has chosen them to minister and to pronounce blessings[a] in the name of the LORD
and to decide all cases of dispute and assault.[b] 6Then all the elders of the town nearest
the body shall wash their hands[c] over the heifer whose neck was broken in the valley,
7and they shall declare: "Our hands did not shed this blood, nor did our eyes see it
done. 8Accept this atonement for your people Israel, whom you have redeemed,

a *17* The Hebrew term refers to the irrevocable giving over of things or persons to the LORD, often by totally destroying them. b *19* Or *down to use in the siege, for the fruit trees are for the benefit of man.*

20:4 [e] Dt 1:30; 3:22; Jos 23:10
20:5 [f] Ne 12:27
20:7 [g] Dt 24:5
20:8 [h] Jdg 7:3
20:10 [i] Lk 14:31-32
20:11 [j] 1Ki 9:21
20:13 [k] Nu 31:7
20:14 [l] Jos 8:2; 22:8
20:16 [m] Ex 23:31-33; Nu 21:2-3; Dt 7:2; Jos 11:14
20:18 [n] Ex 34:16; Dt 7:4; 12:30-31 [o] Ex 23:33
21:5 [a] 1Ch 23:13 [b] Dt 17:8-11
21:6 [c] Mt 27:24

20:13–18 "Put to the sword" means to kill. How could a merciful and just God order the destruction of entire population centres? He did this to protect his people from idol worship, which was certain to bring ruin to Israel (20:18). In fact, because Israel did not completely destroy these evil people as God commanded, Israel was constantly oppressed by them and experienced greater bloodshed and destruction than if they had followed God's instructions in the first place.

20:20 Archaeologists have uncovered the remnants of many well-fortified cities in Canaan. Some had tall walls (up to 30 feet high), ramparts, moats, and towers. Accustomed to fighting on the open plains, the Israelites were going to have to learn new battle strategies to conquer these massive fortresses.

21:1–9 When a crime was committed and the criminal got away, the whole community was held responsible. In much the same way, if a city has a dangerous intersection and someone is killed there, the community may be held responsible for both damages and repairs. God was pointing to the need for the whole community to feel a keen sense of responsibility for what was going on around them and to move to correct any situations that were potentially harmful—physically, socially, or morally.

O LORD, and do not hold your people guilty of the blood of an innocent man." And
the bloodshed will be atoned for.[d] 9 So you will purge[e] from yourselves the guilt of
shedding innocent blood, since you have done what is right in the eyes of the LORD.

Marrying a Captive Woman

10 When you go to war against your enemies and the LORD your God delivers them
into your hands[f] and you take captives, 11 if you notice among the captives a beautiful
woman and are attracted to her, you may take her as your wife. 12 Bring her into your
home and make her shave her head,[g] trim her nails 13 and put aside the clothes she
was wearing when captured. After she has lived in your house and mourned her father
and mother for a full month,[h] then you may go to her and be her husband and she
shall be your wife. 14 If you are not pleased with her, let her go wherever she wishes.
You must not sell her or treat her as a slave, since you have dishonoured her.[i]

The Right of the Firstborn

15 If a man has two wives, and he loves one but not the other, and both bear him
sons but the firstborn is the son of the wife he does not love,[j] 16 when he wills his
property to his sons, he must not give the rights of the firstborn to the son of the wife
he loves in preference to his actual firstborn, the son of the wife he does not love.[k]
17 He must acknowledge the son of his unloved wife as the firstborn by giving him
a double share of all he has. That son is the first sign of his father's strength.[l] The
right of the firstborn belongs to him.[m]

A Rebellious Son

18 If a man has a stubborn and rebellious son who does not obey his father and
mother[n] and will not listen to them when they discipline him, 19 his father and mother
shall take hold of him and bring him to the elders at the gate of his town. 20 They shall
say to the elders, "This son of ours is stubborn and rebellious. He will not obey us.
He is a profligate and a drunkard." 21 Then all the men of his town shall stone him
to death. You must purge the evil[o] from among you. All Israel will hear of it and
be afraid.[p]

Various Laws

22 If a man guilty of a capital offence[q] is put to death and his body is hung on a
tree, 23 you must not leave his body on the tree overnight.[r] Be sure to bury him that
same day, because anyone who is hung on a tree is under God's curse.[s] You must
not desecrate[t] the land the LORD your God is giving you as an inheritance.

22 If you see your brother's ox or sheep straying, do not ignore it but be sure to
take it back to him.[a] 2 If the brother does not live near you or if you do not
know who he is, take it home with you and keep it until he comes looking for it. Then
give it back to him. 3 Do the same if you find your brother's donkey or his cloak or
anything he loses. Do not ignore it.

4 If you see your brother's donkey[b] or his ox fallen on the road, do not ignore it.
Help him to get it to its feet.

5 A woman must not wear men's clothing, nor a man wear women's clothing, for
the LORD your God detests anyone who does this.

6 If you come across a bird's nest beside the road, either in a tree or on the ground,
and the mother is sitting on the young or on the eggs, do not take the mother with

21:8 [d]Nu 35:33-34
21:9 [e]Dt 19:13
21:10 [f]Jos 21:44
21:12 [g]Lev 14:9; Nu 6:9
21:13 [h]Ps 45:10
21:14 [i]Ge 34:2
21:15 [j]Ge 29:33
21:16 [k]1Ch 26:10
21:17 [l]Ge 49:3 [m]Ge 25:31
21:18 [n]Pr 1:8; Isa 30:1; Eph 6:1-3
21:21 [o]Dt 19:19 [p]Dt 13:11
21:22 [q]Dt 22:26; Mk 14:64; Ac 23:29
21:23 [r]Jos 8:29; 10:27; Jn 19:31 [s]Gal 3:13* [t]Lev 18:25; Nu 35:34
22:1 [a]Ex 23:4-5
22:4 [b]Ex 23:5

21:18–21 Disobedient and rebellious children were to be brought before the elders of the city and stoned to death. There is no biblical or archaeological evidence that this punishment was ever carried out, but the point was that disobedience and rebellion were not to be tolerated in the home or allowed to continue unchecked.

22:1–4 The Hebrews were to care for and return lost animals or possessions to their rightful owners. The way of the world, by contrast, is "Finders keepers, losers weepers". To go beyond the finders-keepers rule by protecting and returning the property of others keeps us from being envious and greedy.

22:5 This verse commands men and women not to reverse their sexual roles. It is not a statement about clothing styles. Today role rejections are common – there are men who want to become women and women who want to become men. It's not the clothing style that offends God, but using the style to act out a different sex role. God had a purpose in making us uniquely male and female.

the young.[c] 7You may take the young, but be sure to let the mother go, so that it
may go well with you and you may have a long life.[d]
8When you build a new house, make a parapet around your roof so that you may
not bring the guilt of bloodshed on your house if someone falls from the roof.
9Do not plant two kinds of seed in your vineyard;[e] if you do, not only the crops
you plant but also the fruit of the vineyard will be defiled.[a]
10Do not plough with an ox and a donkey yoked together.[f]
11Do not wear clothes of wool and linen woven together.[g]
12Make tassels on the four corners of the cloak you wear.[h]

Marriage Violations

13If a man takes a wife and, after lying with her[i], dislikes her 14and slanders her
and gives her a bad name, saying, "I married this woman, but when I approached her,
I did not find proof of her virginity," 15then the girl's father and mother shall bring
proof that she was a virgin to the town elders at the gate. 16The girl's father will say
to the elders, "I gave my daughter in marriage to this man, but he dislikes her. 17Now
he has slandered her and said, 'I did not find your daughter to be a virgin.' But here
is the proof of my daughter's virginity." Then her parents shall display the cloth before
the elders of the town, 18and the elders[j] shall take the man and punish him. 19They
shall fine him a hundred shekels of silver[b] and give them to the girl's father, because
this man has given an Israelite virgin a bad name. She shall continue to be his wife;
he must not divorce her as long as he lives.
20If, however, the charge is true and no proof of the girl's virginity can be found,
21she shall be brought to the door of her father's house and there the men of her town
shall stone her to death. She has done a disgraceful thing[k] in Israel by being
promiscuous while still in her father's house. You must purge the evil from among
you.
22If a man is found sleeping with another man's wife, both the man who slept with
her and the woman must die.[l] You must purge the evil from Israel.
23If a man happens to meet in a town a virgin pledged to be married and he sleeps
with her, 24you shall take both of them to the gate of that town and stone them to
death—the girl because she was in a town and did not scream for help, and the man
because he violated another man's wife. You must purge the evil from among you.[m]
25But if out in the country a man happens to meet a girl pledged to be married and
rapes her, only the man who has done this shall die. 26Do nothing to the girl; she has
committed no sin deserving death. This case is like that of someone who attacks and
murders his neighbour, 27for the man found the girl out in the country, and though
the betrothed girl screamed, there was no-one to rescue her.
28If a man happens to meet a virgin who is not pledged to be married and rapes
her and they are discovered,[n] 29he shall pay the girl's father fifty shekels of silver.[c]
He must marry the girl, for he has violated her. He can never divorce her as long as
he lives.
30A man is not to marry his father's wife; he must not dishonour his father's bed.[o]

a 9 Or *be forfeited to the sanctuary* b 19 That is, about 2½ pounds (about 1 kilogram) c 29 That is, about 1¼ pounds (about 0.6 kilogram)

22:6 c Lev 22:28
22:7 d Dt 4:40
22:9 e Lev 19:19
22:10 f 2Co 6:14
22:11 g Lev 19:19
22:12 h Nu 15:37-41; Mt 23:5
22:13 i Dt 24:1
22:18 j Ex 18:21
22:21 k Ge 34:7; Dt 13:5; 23:17-18; Jdg 20:6; 2Sa 13:12
22:22 l Lev 20:10; Jn 8:5
22:24 m ver 21-22; 1Co 5:13*
22:28 n Ex 22:16
22:30 o Lev 18:8; 20:11; Dt 27:20; 1Co 5:1

22:8–11 These are practical laws, helpful for establishing good habits for everyday living. Verse 8: Since people used their flat roofs as balconies, a guardrail (parapet) was a wise safety precaution. Verse 9: If you plant two different crops side by side, one of them will not survive, since the stronger, taller one will block the sunlight and take most of the vital nutrients from the soil. Verse 10: A donkey and an ox, due to differences in strength and size, cannot pull a plough evenly. Verse 11: Two different kinds of thread wear unevenly and wash differently. Combining them reduces the life of the garment. Don't think of God's laws as arbitrary restrictions. Look for the reasons behind the laws. They are not made just to teach or restrict, but also to protect.

22:13–30 Why did God include all these laws about sexual sins? Instructions about sexual behaviour would have been vital for three million people on a 40-year camping trip. But they would be equally important when they entered the promised land and settled down as a nation. Paul, in Colossians 3:5–8, recognises the importance of strong rules about sex for believers because sexual sins have the power to disrupt and destroy the church. Sins involving sex are not innocent dabblings in forbidden pleasures, as is so often portrayed, but powerful destroyers of relationships. They confuse and tear down the climate of respect, trust, and credibility so essential for solid marriages and secure children.

Exclusion From the Assembly

23 No-one who has been emasculated by crushing or cutting may enter the assembly of the LORD.

2 No-one born of a forbidden marriage[a] nor any of his descendants may enter the assembly of the LORD, even down to the tenth generation.

3 No Ammonite or Moabite or any of his descendants may enter the assembly of the LORD, even down to the tenth generation.[a] 4 For they did not come to meet you with bread and water on your way when you came out of Egypt, and they hired Balaam[b] son of Beor from Pethor in Aram Naharaim[b] to pronounce a curse on you. 5 However, the LORD your God would not listen to Balaam but turned the curse[c] into a blessing for you, because the LORD your God loves you. 6 Do not seek a treaty of friendship with them as long as you live.[d]

7 Do not abhor an Edomite, for he is your brother.[e] Do not abhor an Egyptian, because you lived as an alien in his country.[f] 8 The third generation of children born to them may enter the assembly of the LORD.

Uncleanness in the Camp

9 When you are encamped against your enemies, keep away from everything impure. 10 If one of your men is unclean because of a nocturnal emission, he is to go outside the camp and stay there.[g] 11 But as evening approaches he is to wash himself, and at sunset he may return to the camp.

12 Designate a place outside the camp where you can go to relieve yourself. 13 As part of your equipment have something to dig with, and when you relieve yourself, dig a hole and cover up your excrement. 14 For the LORD your God moves[h] about in your camp to protect you and to deliver your enemies to you. Your camp must be holy,[i] so that he will not see among you anything indecent and turn away from you.

Miscellaneous Laws

15 If a slave has taken refuge with you, do not hand him over to his master.[j] 16 Let him live among you wherever he likes and in whatever town he chooses. Do not oppress[k] him.

17 No Israelite man[l] or woman is to become a shrine-prostitute.[m] 18 You must not bring the earnings of a female prostitute or of a male prostitute[c] into the house of the LORD your God to pay any vow, because the LORD your God detests them both.

19 Do not charge your brother interest, whether on money or food or anything else that may earn interest.[n] 20 You may charge a foreigner interest, but not a brother Israelite, so that the LORD your God may bless[o] you in everything you put your hand to in the land you are entering to possess.

21 If you make a vow to the LORD your God, do not be slow to pay it, for the LORD your God will certainly demand it of you and you will be guilty of sin.[p] 22 But if you refrain from making a vow, you will not be guilty. 23 Whatever your lips utter you must be sure to do, because you made your vow freely to the LORD your God with your own mouth.

24 If you enter your neighbour's vineyard, you may eat all the grapes you want, but do not put any in your basket. 25 If you enter your neighbour's cornfield, you may pick the ears with your hands, but you must not put a sickle to his standing corn.[q]

a 2 Or *one of illegitimate birth* b 4 That is, North-west Mesopotamia c 18 Hebrew *of a dog*

23:3 [a]Ne 13:2
23:4 [b]Nu 22:5-6; 23:7; 2Pe 2:15
23:5 [c]Pr 26:2
23:6 [d]Ezr 9:12
23:7 [e]Ge 25:26; Ob 1:10, 12 [f]Ex 22:21; 23:9; Lev 19:34; Dt 10:19
23:10 [g]Lev 15:16
23:14 [h]Lev 26:12 [i]Ex 3:5
23:15 [j]1Sa 30:15
23:16 [k]Ex 22:21
23:17 [l]Ge 19:25; 2Ki 23:7 [m]Lev 19:29; Dt 22:21
23:19 [n]Ex 22:25; Lev 25:35-37
23:20 [o]Dt 15:10; 28:12
23:21 [p]Nu 30:1-2; Ecc 5:4-5; Mt 5:33
23:25 [q]Mt 12:1; Mk 2:23; Lk 6:1

23:17, 18 Prostitution was not overlooked in God's law — it was strictly forbidden. To forbid this practice may seem obvious to us, but it may not have been so obvious to the Israelites. Almost every other religion known to them included prostitution as an integral part of its worship services. Prostitution makes a mockery of God's original idea for sex, treating sex as an isolated physical act rather than an act of commitment to another. Outside of marriage, sex destroys relationships. Within marriage, if approached with the right attitude, it can be a relationship builder. God frequently had to warn the people against the practice of extramarital sex. Today we still need to hear his warnings; young people need to be reminded about premarital sex, and adults need to be reminded about sexual fidelity.

23:24, 25 This commandment guarded against selfishly holding on to one's possessions. It also ensured that no-one had to go hungry. It was not, however, an excuse for taking advantage of one's neighbour. The Pharisees did not interpret this appropriately when they accused Jesus and the disciples of harvesting on the Sabbath (Matthew 12:1, 2).

24 If a man marries a woman who becomes displeasing to him[a] because he finds
something indecent about her, and he writes her a certificate of divorce,[b] gives
it to her and sends her from his house, 2and if after she leaves his house she becomes
the wife of another man, 3and her second husband dislikes her and writes her a
certificate of divorce, gives it to her and sends her from his house, or if he dies, 4then
her first husband, who divorced her, is not allowed to marry her again after she has
been defiled. That would be detestable in the eyes of the LORD. Do not bring sin upon
the land the LORD[c] your God is giving you as an inheritance.
5If a man has recently married, he must not be sent to war or have any other duty
laid on him. For one year he is to be free to stay at home and bring happiness to the
wife he has married.[d]
6Do not take a pair of millstones — not even the upper one — as security for a debt,
because that would be taking a man's livelihood as security.
7If a man is caught kidnapping one of his brother Israelites and treats him as a slave
or sells him, the kidnapper must die.[e] You must purge the evil from among you.
8In cases of leprous[a] diseases be very careful to do exactly as the priests, who are
Levites, instruct you. You must follow carefully what I have commanded them.[f]
9Remember what the LORD your God did to Miriam along the way after you came
out of Egypt.[g]
10When you make a loan of any kind to your neighbour, do not go into his house
to get what he is offering as a pledge. 11Stay outside and let the man to whom you
are making the loan bring the pledge out to you. 12If the man is poor, do not go to
sleep with his pledge in your possession. 13Return his cloak to him by sunset[h] so that
he may sleep in it. Then he will thank you, and it will be regarded as a righteous act
in the sight of the LORD your God.[i]
14Do not take advantage of a hired man who is poor and needy, whether he is a
brother Israelite or an alien living in one of your towns.[j] 15Pay him his wages each
day before sunset, because he is poor[k] and is counting on it.[l] Otherwise he may cry
to the LORD against you, and you will be guilty of sin.[m]
16Fathers shall not be put to death for their children, nor children put to death for
their fathers; each is to die for his own sin.[n]
17Do not deprive the alien or the fatherless of justice,[o] or take the cloak of the
widow as a pledge. 18Remember that you were slaves in Egypt and the LORD your
God redeemed you from there. That is why I command you to do this.
19When you are harvesting in your field and you overlook a sheaf, do not go back
to get it.[p] Leave it for the alien, the fatherless and the widow, so that the LORD your
God may bless[q] you in all the work of your hands. 20When you beat the olives from
your trees, do not go over the branches a second time.[r] Leave what remains for the
alien, the fatherless and the widow. 21When you harvest the grapes in your vineyard,

[a] 8 The Hebrew word was used for various diseases affecting the skin—not necessarily leprosy.

24:1 [a]Dt 22:13 [b]Mt 5:31*; 19:7-9; Mk 10:4-5
24:4 [c]Jer 3:1
24:5 [d]Dt 20:7
24:7 [e]Ex 21:16
24:8 [f]Lev 13:1-46; 14:2
24:9 [g]Nu 12:10
24:13 [h]Ex 22:26 [i]Dt 6:25; Da 4:27
24:14 [j]Lev 25:35-43; Dt 15:12-18
24:15 [k]Jer 22:13 [l]Lev 19:13 [m]Dt 15:9; Jas 5:4
24:16 [n]2Ki 14:6; 2Ch 25:4; Jer 31:29-30; Eze 18:20
24:17 [o]Dt 1:17; 10:17-18; 16:19
24:19 [p]Lev 19:9; 23:22 [q]Pr 19:17
24:20 [r]Lev 19:10

24:1-4 Some think this passage supports divorce, but that is not the case. It simply recognises a practice that already existed in Israel. All four verses must be read to understand the point of the passage; it certainly is not suggesting that a man divorce his wife on a whim. Divorce was a permanent and final act for the couple. Once divorced and remarried to others, they could never be remarried to each other (24:4). This restriction was to prevent casual remarriage after a frivolous separation. The intention was to make people think twice before divorcing.

24:5 Recently married couples were to remain together their first year. This was to avoid placing an excessive burden upon a new, unproven relationship and to give it a chance to mature and strengthen before confronting it with numerous responsibilities. A gardener starts a tiny seedling in a small pot and allows it to take root before planting it in the field. Let your marriage grow strong by protecting your relationship from too many outside pressures and distractions – especially in the beginning. And don't expect or demand so much from newlyweds that they have inadequate time or energy to establish their marriage.

24:10-22 Throughout the Old Testament God told his people to treat the poor with justice. The powerless and poverty-stricken are often looked upon as incompetent or lazy when, in fact, they may be victims of oppression and circumstance. God says we must do all we can to help these needy ones. His justice did not permit the Israelites to insist on profits or quick payment from those who were less fortunate. Instead, his laws gave the poor every opportunity to better their situation, while providing humane options for those who couldn't. None of us is completely isolated from the poor. God wants us to treat them fairly and do our part to see that their needs are met.

24:19-21 God's people were instructed to leave some of their harvest in the fields so travellers and the poor could gather it. This second gathering, called gleaning, was a way for them to provide food for themselves. Years later, Ruth obtained food for herself and Naomi by gleaning behind the reapers in Boaz's field, picking up the leftovers (Ruth 2:2). Because this law was being obeyed years after it was written, Ruth, a woman in Christ's lineage, was able to find food.

do not go over the vines again. Leave what remains for the alien, the fatherless and
the widow. 22 Remember that you were slaves in Egypt. That is why I command you
to do this.[s]

25 When men have a dispute, they are to take it to court and the judges will decide
the case,[a] acquitting the innocent and condemning the guilty.[b] 2 If the guilty
man deserves to be beaten,[c] the judge shall make him lie down and have him flogged
in his presence with the number of lashes his crime deserves, 3 but he must not give
him more than forty lashes.[d] If he is flogged more than that, your brother will be
degraded in your eyes.[e]

4 Do not muzzle an ox while it is treading out the grain.[f]

5 If brothers are living together and one of them dies without a son, his widow must
not marry outside the family. Her husband's brother shall take her and marry her and
fulfil the duty of a brother-in-law to her.[g] 6 The first son she bears shall carry on the
name of the dead brother so that his name will not be blotted out from Israel.[h]

7 However, if a man does not want to marry his brother's wife, she shall go to the
elders at the town gate and say, "My husband's brother refuses to carry on his brother's
name in Israel. He will not fulfil the duty of a brother-in-law to me."[i] 8 Then the elders
of his town shall summon him and talk to him. If he persists in saying, "I do not want
to marry her," 9 his brother's widow shall go up to him in the presence of the elders,
take off one of his sandals,[j] spit in his face and say, "This is what is done to the
man who will not build up his brother's family line." 10 That man's line shall be known
in Israel as The Family of the Unsandalled.

11 If two men are fighting and the wife of one of them comes to rescue her husband
from his assailant, and she reaches out and seizes him by his private parts, 12 you shall
cut off her hand. Show her no pity.[k]

13 Do not have two differing weights in your bag—one heavy, one light.[l] 14 Do
not have two differing measures in your house—one large, one small. 15 You must
have accurate and honest weights and measures, so that you may live long[m] in the
land the LORD your God is giving you. 16 For the LORD your God detests anyone who
does these things, anyone who deals dishonestly.[n]

17 Remember what the Amalekites[o] did to you along the way when you came out
of Egypt. 18 When you were weary and worn out, they met you on your journey and
cut off all who were lagging behind; they had no fear of God.[p] 19 When the LORD
your God gives you rest from all the enemies around you in the land he is giving you
to possess as an inheritance, you shall blot out the memory of Amalek[q] from under
heaven. Do not forget!

Firstfruits and Tithes

26 When you have entered the land that the LORD your God is giving you as an
inheritance and have taken possession of it and settled in it, 2 take some of the
firstfruits[a] of all that you produce from the soil of the land that the LORD your God
is giving you and put them in a basket. Then go to the place that the LORD your God
will choose as a dwelling for his Name[b] 3 and say to the priest in office at the time,

24:22 [s] ver 18
25:1 [a] Dt 19:17 [b] Dt 1:16-17
25:2 [c] Lk 12:47-48
25:3 [d] 2Co 11:24 [e] Job 18:3
25:4 [f] Pr 12:10; 1Co 9:9*; 1Ti 5:18*
25:5 [g] Mt 22:24; Mk 12:19; Lk 20:28
25:6 [h] Ge 38:9; Ru 4:5, 10
25:7 [i] Ru 4:1-2, 5-6
25:9 [j] Ru 4:7-8, 11
25:12 [k] Dt 19:13
25:13 [l] Lev 19:35-37; Pr 11:1; Eze 45:10; Mic 6:11
25:15 [m] Ex 20:12
25:16 [n] Pr 11:1
25:17 [o] Ex 17:8
25:18 [p] Ps 36:1; Ro 3:18
25:19 [q] 1Sa 15:2-3
26:2 [a] Ex 22:29; 23:16, 19; Nu 18:13; Pr 3:9 [b] Dt 12:5

25:1–3 At first glance these verses appear irrelevant today. But a closer look reveals some important principles about discipline. Are you responsible for the discipline of a child, a student, or an employee? Three important points will help you carry out your responsibility: (1) let the punishment follow quickly after the offence; (2) let the degree of punishment reflect the seriousness of the offence; and (3) don't overdo the punishment. Discipline that is swift, just, and restrained makes its point while preserving the dignity of the offender.

25:4 What is the point of this Old Testament regulation? Oxen were often used to tread out the grain on a threshing floor. The animal was attached by poles to a large millstone. As it walked around the millstone, its hooves trampled the grain, separating the kernels from the chaff. At the same time, the millstone ground the grain into flour. To muzzle the ox would prevent it from eating while it was working. Paul used this illustration in the New Testament to argue that people productive in Christian work should not be denied its benefits—they should receive financial support (2 Corinthians 9:10; 1 Timothy 5:17, 18). The fact that a person is in Christian ministry doesn't mean he or she should be unfairly paid. There is also a broader application: Don't be stingy with those who work for you.

25:5–10 This law describes a "levirate" marriage, the marriage of a widow to the brother of her dead husband. The purpose of such a marriage was to carry on the dead man's name and inheritance. Family ties were an important aspect of Israelite culture. The best way to be remembered was through your line of descendants. If a widow married someone outside the family, her first husband's line would come to an end. Tamar fought for this right in Genesis 38.

"I declare today to the LORD your God that I have come to the land that the LORD swore
to our forefathers to give us." 4The priest shall take the basket from your hands and
set it down in front of the altar of the LORD your God. 5Then you shall declare before
the LORD your God: "My father was a wandering Aramean,[c] and he went down into
Egypt with a few people[d] and lived there and became a great nation, powerful and
numerous. 6But the Egyptians ill-treated us and made us suffer,[e] putting us to hard
labour. 7Then we cried out to the LORD, the God of our fathers, and the LORD heard
our voice[f] and saw[g] our misery, toil and oppression. 8So the LORD brought us out
of Egypt with a mighty hand and an outstretched arm, with great terror and with
miraculous signs and wonders.[h] 9He brought us to this place and gave us this land,
a land flowing with milk and honey;[i] 10and now I bring the firstfruits of the soil that
you, O LORD, have given me." Place the basket before the LORD your God and bow
down before him. 11And you and the Levites[j] and the aliens among you shall
rejoice[k] in all the good things the LORD your God has given to you and your
household.
12When you have finished setting aside a tenth[l] of all your produce in the third
year, the year of the tithe,[m] you shall give it to the Levite, the alien, the fatherless
and the widow, so that they may eat in your towns and be satisfied. 13Then say to
the LORD your God: "I have removed from my house the sacred portion and have given
it to the Levite, the alien, the fatherless and the widow, according to all you commanded. I have not turned aside from your commands nor have I forgotten any of
them.[n] 14I have not eaten any of the sacred portion while I was in mourning, nor have
I removed any of it while I was unclean,[o] nor have I offered any of it to the dead.
I have obeyed the LORD my God; I have done everything you commanded me. 15Look
down from heaven,[p] your holy dwelling-place, and bless your people Israel and the
land you have given us as you promised on oath to our forefathers, a land flowing
with milk and honey."

Follow the LORD's Commands

16The LORD your God commands you this day to follow these decrees and laws;
carefully observe them with all your heart and with all your soul.[q] 17You have
declared this day that the LORD is your God and that you will walk in his ways, that
you will keep his decrees, commands and laws, and that you will obey him. 18And
the LORD has declared this day that you are his people, his treasured possession[r] as
he promised, and that you are to keep all his commands. 19He has declared that he
will set you in praise, fame and honour high above all the nations[s] he has made and
that you will be a people holy[t] to the LORD your God, as he promised.

6. Consequences of obedience and disobedience

The Altar on Mount Ebal

27 Moses and the elders of Israel commanded the people: "Keep all these commands that I give you today. 2When you have crossed the Jordan into the land
the LORD your God is giving you, set up some large stones and coat them with
plaster.[a] 3Write on them all the words of this law when you have crossed over to
enter the land the LORD your God is giving you, a land flowing with milk and honey,[b]
just as the LORD, the God of your fathers, promised you. 4And when you have crossed
the Jordan, set up these stones on Mount Ebal,[c] as I command you today, and coat
them with plaster. 5Build there an altar[d] to the LORD your God, an altar of stones.

26:5 [c]Hos 12:12 [d]Ge 43:1-2; 45:7, 11; 46:27; Dt 10:22
26:6 [e]Ex 1:11, 14
26:7 [f]Ex 2:23-25 [g]Ex 3:9
26:8 [h]Dt 4:34
26:9 [i]Ex 3:8
26:11 [j]Dt 12:7 [k]Dt 16:11
26:12 [l]Lev 27:30 [m]Nu 18:24; Dt 14:28-29; Heb 7:5, 9
26:13 [n]Ps 119:141, 153, 176
26:14 [o]Lev 7:20; Hos 9:4
26:15 [p]Isa 63:15; Zec 2:13
26:16 [q]Dt 4:29
26:18 [r]Ex 6:7; 19:5; Dt 7:6; 14:2; 28:9
26:19 [s]Dt 4:7-8; 28:1, 13, 44 [t]Ex 19:6; Dt 7:6; 1Pe 2:9
27:2 [a]Jos 8:31
27:3 [b]Dt 26:9
27:4 [c]Dt 11:29
27:5 [d]Jos 8:31

26:5–10 This recitation of God's dealings with his people helped the people remember what God had done for them. What is the history of your relationship with God? Can you put into clear and concise words what God has done for you? Find a friend with whom you can share your spiritual journey. Telling your stories to each other will help you clearly understand your personal spiritual history, as well as encouraging and inspiring you both. Note: *Wandering* can mean lost or dying. Also, Arameans were the people of northern Syria and among the ancestors of Abraham. This is also used as a reference to Jacob, who spent many years there (Genesis 29 – 31) and found his two wives in Aram.

26:18 Moses said that because the Israelites were now God's people, they needed to start obeying God's commands.

27:5, 6 The Lord had specified an altar made of uncut stones (field stones) so that the people would not begin worshipping the altars as idols. To use a chisel on a stone of the altar would be to profane it (Exodus 20:24–26). Additionally, because the Israelites did not have the capacity to work with iron at this time, using iron

Do not use any iron tool[e] upon them. [6]Build the altar of the LORD your God with
stones from the field and offer burnt offerings on it to the LORD your God. [7]Sacrifice
fellowship offerings[a] there, eating them and rejoicing in the presence of the LORD
your God. [8]And you shall write very clearly all the words of this law on these stones
you have set up."

Curses From Mount Ebal

[9]Then Moses and the priests, who are Levites, said to all Israel, "Be silent, O Israel,
and listen! You have now become the people of the LORD your God.[f] [10]Obey the
LORD your God and follow his commands and decrees that I give you today."
[11]On the same day Moses commanded the people:
[12]When you have crossed the Jordan, these tribes shall stand on Mount Gerizim[g]
to bless the people: Simeon, Levi, Judah, Issachar, Joseph and Benjamin.[h] [13]And
these tribes shall stand on Mount Ebal to pronounce curses: Reuben, Gad, Asher,
Zebulun, Dan and Naphtali.
[14]The Levites shall recite to all the people of Israel in a loud voice:

[15]"Cursed is the man who carves an image or casts an idol[i]—a thing detest-
able to the LORD, the work of the craftsman's hands—and sets it up in secret."
Then all the people shall say,
"Amen!"

[16]"Cursed is the man who dishonours his father or his mother."[j]
Then all the people shall say,
"Amen!"

[17]"Cursed is the man who moves his neighbour's boundary stone."[k]
Then all the people shall say,
"Amen!"

[18]"Cursed is the man who leads the blind astray on the road."[l]
Then all the people shall say,
"Amen!"

[19]"Cursed is the man who withholds justice from the alien,[m] the fatherless or
the widow."[n]
Then all the people shall say,
"Amen!"

[20]"Cursed is the man who sleeps with his father's wife, for he dishonours his
father's bed."[o]
Then all the people shall say,
"Amen!"

[21]"Cursed is the man who has sexual relations with any animal."[p]
Then all the people shall say,
"Amen!"

[22]"Cursed is the man who sleeps with his sister, the daughter of his father or
the daughter of his mother."[q]

a 7 Traditionally *peace offerings*

27:5 e Ex 20:25
27:9 f Dt 26:18
27:12 g Dt 11:29 h Jos 8:35
27:15 i Ex 20:4; 34:17; Lev 19:4; 26:1; Dt 4:16, 23; 5:8; Isa 44:9
27:16 j Ex 20:12; 21:17; Lev 19:3; 20:9
27:17 k Dt 19:14; Pr 22:28
27:18 l Lev 19:14
27:19 m Ex 22:21; Dt 24:19 n Dt 10:18
27:20 o Lev 18:7; Dt 22:30
27:21 p Lev 18:23
27:22 q Lev 18:9; 20:17

---

tools might mean using the cooperation and expertise of other nations.

27:9, 10 Moses was reviewing the law with the new generation of people. When we decide to believe in God, we must also decide to follow his ways. What we do shows what we really believe. Can people tell that you are a member of God's family?

27:15–26 These curses were a series of oaths, spoken by the priests and affirmed by the people, by which the people promised to stay away from wrong actions. By saying *Amen,* "So be it", the people took responsibility for their actions. Sometimes looking at a list of curses like this gives us the idea that God has a bad temper and is out to crush anyone who steps out of line. But we need to see these restrictions not as threats, but as loving warnings about the plain facts of life. Just as we warn children to stay away from hot stoves and busy streets, God warns us to stay away from dangerous actions. The natural law of his universe makes it clear that wrongdoing towards others or God has tragic consequences. God is merciful enough to tell us this truth plainly. Motivated by love and not anger, his strong words help us avoid the serious consequences that result from neglecting God or wronging others. But God does not leave us with only curses or consequences. Immediately following these curses, we discover the great blessings (positive consequences) that come from living for God (28:1–14). These give us extra incentive to obey God's laws. While all these blessings may not come in our lifetime on earth, those who obey God will experience the fullness of his blessing when he establishes the new heaven and the new earth.

Then all the people shall say,
"Amen!"
23"Cursed is the man who sleeps with his mother-in-law."[r]
Then all the people shall say,
"Amen!"
24"Cursed is the man who kills[s] his neighbour secretly."
Then all the people shall say,
"Amen!"
25"Cursed is the man who accepts a bribe to kill an innocent person."[t]
Then all the people shall say,
"Amen!"
26"Cursed is the man who does not uphold the words of this law by carrying
them out."[u]
Then all the people shall say,
"Amen!"

Blessings for Obedience

28 If you fully obey the LORD your God and carefully follow all his commands[a]
that I give you today, the LORD your God will set you high above all the nations
on earth.[b] 2All these blessings will come upon you[c] and accompany you if you obey
the LORD your God:

3You will be blessed[d] in the city and blessed in the country.[e]
4The fruit of your womb will be blessed, and the crops of your land and the
young of your livestock—the calves of your herds and the lambs of your flocks.[f]
5Your basket and your kneading trough will be blessed.
6You will be blessed when you come in and blessed when you go out.[g]

7The LORD will grant that the enemies who rise up against you will be defeated
before you. They will come at you from one direction but flee from you in seven.[h]
8The LORD will send a blessing on your barns and on everything you put your hand
to. The LORD your God will bless you in the land he is giving you.
9The LORD will establish you as his holy people,[i] as he promised you on oath,
if you keep the commands of the LORD your God and walk in his ways. 10Then all
the peoples on earth will see that you are called by the name[j] of the LORD, and they
will fear you. 11The LORD will grant you abundant prosperity—in the fruit of your
womb, the young of your livestock and the crops of your ground—in the land he swore
to your forefathers to give you.[k]
12The LORD will open the heavens, the storehouse of his bounty, to send rain[l] on
your land in season and to bless all the work of your hands. You will lend to many
nations but will borrow from none.[m] 13The LORD will make you the head, not the
tail. If you pay attention to the commands of the LORD your God that I give you this
day and carefully follow them, you will always be at the top, never at the bottom.
14Do not turn aside from any of the commands I give you today, to the right or to
the left,[n] following other gods and serving them.

Curses for Disobedience

15However, if you do not obey[o] the LORD your God and do not carefully follow
all his commands and decrees I am giving you today, all these curses will come upon
you and overtake you:[p]

16You will be cursed in the city and cursed in the country.
17Your basket and your kneading trough will be cursed.
18The fruit of your womb will be cursed, and the crops of your land, and the
calves of your herds and the lambs of your flocks.
19You will be cursed when you come in and cursed when you go out.

20The LORD will send on you curses,[q] confusion and rebuke[r] in everything you
put your hand to, until you are destroyed and come to sudden ruin[s] because of the

27:23 [r]Lev 20:14
27:24 [s]Lev 24:17; Nu 35:31
27:25 [t]Ex 23:7-8; Dt 10:17; Eze 22:12
27:26 [u]Jer 11:3; Gal 3:10*
28:1 [a]Ex 15:26; Lev 26:3; Dt 7:12-26 [b]Dt 26:19
28:2 [c]Zec 1:6
28:3 [d]Ps 128:1, 4 [e]Ge 39:5
28:4 [f]Ge 49:25; Pr 10:22
28:6 [g]Ps 121:8
28:7 [h]Lev 26:8, 17
28:9 [i]Ex 19:6; Dt 7:6
28:10 [j]2Ch 7:14
28:11 [k]Dt 30:9; Pr 10:22
28:12 [l]Lev 26:4 [m]Dt 15:3, 6
28:14 [n]Dt 5:32
28:15 [o]Lev 26:14 [p]Jos 23:15; Da 9:11; Mal 2:2
28:20 [q]Mal 2:2 [r]Isa 51:20; 66:15 [s]Dt 4:26

28:21 [t]Lev 26:25; Jer 24:10
28:22 [u]Lev 26:16 [v]Am 4:9
28:23 [w]Lev 26:19
28:25 [x]Isa 30:17 [y]Jer 15:4; 24:9; Eze 23:46
28:26 [z]Jer 7:33; 16:4; 34:20
28:27 [a]ver 60-61; 1Sa 5:6
28:29 [b]Job 5:14; Isa 59:10
28:30 [c]Job 31:10; Jer 8:10 [d]Am 5:11 [e]Jer 12:13
28:32 [f]ver 41
28:33 [g]Jer 5:15-17
28:35 [h]ver 27
28:36 [i]2Ki 17:4, 6; 24:12, 14; 25:7, 11 [j]Jer 16:13 [k]Dt 4:28
28:37 [l]Jer 24:9
28:38 [m]Mic 6:15; Hag 1:6, 9 [n]Joel 1:4
28:39 [o]Isa 5:10; 17:10-11
28:40 [p]Mic 6:15
28:41 [q]ver 32
28:43 [r]ver 13
28:44 [s]ver 12 [t]ver 13
28:45 [u]ver 15
28:46 [v]Isa 8:18; Eze 14:8
28:47 [w]Dt 32:15 [x]Ne 9:35
28:48 [y]Jer 28:13-14

evil you have done in forsaking him.[a] 21The LORD will plague you with diseases until
he has destroyed you from the land you are entering to possess.[t] 22The LORD will
strike you with wasting disease, with fever and inflammation, with scorching heat and
drought,[u] with blight and mildew, which will plague you until you perish.[v] 23The
sky over your head will be bronze, the ground beneath you iron.[w] 24The LORD will
turn the rain of your country into dust and powder; it will come down from the skies
until you are destroyed.

25The LORD will cause you to be defeated before your enemies. You will come at
them from one direction but flee from them in seven,[x] and you will become a thing
of horror to all the kingdoms on earth.[y] 26Your carcasses will be food for all the birds
of the air and the beasts of the earth, and there will be no-one to frighten them away.[z]
27The LORD will afflict you with the boils of Egypt[a] and with tumours, festering sores
and the itch, from which you cannot be cured. 28The LORD will afflict you with
madness, blindness and confusion of mind. 29At midday you will grope[b] about like
a blind man in the dark. You will be unsuccessful in everything you do; day after day
you will be oppressed and robbed, with no-one to rescue you.

30You will be pledged to be married to a woman, but another will take her and ravish
her.[c] You will build a house, but you will not live in it.[d] You will plant a vineyard,
but you will not even begin to enjoy its fruit.[e] 31Your ox will be slaughtered before
your eyes, but you will eat none of it. Your donkey will be forcibly taken from you
and will not be returned. Your sheep will be given to your enemies, and no-one will
rescue them. 32Your sons and daughters will be given to another nation,[f] and you
will wear out your eyes watching for them day after day, powerless to lift a hand. 33A
people that you do not know will eat what your land and labour produce, and you will
have nothing but cruel oppression all your days.[g] 34The sights you see will drive you
mad. 35The LORD will afflict your knees and legs with painful boils[h] that cannot be
cured, spreading from the soles of your feet to the top of your head.

36The LORD will drive you and the king[i] you set over you to a nation unknown
to you or your fathers.[j] There you will worship other gods, gods of wood and stone.[k]
37You will become a thing of horror and an object of scorn and ridicule to all the
nations where the LORD will drive you.[l]

38You will sow much seed in the field but you will harvest little,[m] because locusts
will devour[n] it. 39You will plant vineyards and cultivate them but you will not drink
the wine or gather the grapes, because worms will eat them.[o] 40You will have olive
trees throughout your country but you will not use the oil, because the olives will drop
off.[p] 41You will have sons and daughters but you will not keep them, because they
will go into captivity.[q] 42Swarms of locusts will take over all your trees and the crops
of your land.

43The alien who lives among you will rise above you higher and higher, but you
will sink lower and lower.[r] 44He will lend to you, but you will not lend to him.[s]
He will be the head, but you will be the tail.[t]

45All these curses will come upon you. They will pursue you and overtake you until
you are destroyed,[u] because you did not obey the LORD your God and observe the
commands and decrees he gave you. 46They will be a sign and a wonder to you and
your descendants for ever.[v] 47Because you did not serve[w] the LORD your God
joyfully and gladly[x] in the time of prosperity, 48therefore in hunger and thirst, in
nakedness and dire poverty, you will serve the enemies the LORD sends against you.
He will put an iron yoke[y] on your neck until he has destroyed you.

49The LORD will bring a nation against you from far away, from the ends of the

a *20* Hebrew *me*

28:23, 24 This curse is referring to a drought.

28:34 One of the curses for those who rejected God was that they would go mad from seeing all the tragedy around them. Do you ever feel that you will go crazy if you hear about one more rape, kidnapping, murder, or war? Much of the world's evil is a result of people's failure to acknowledge and serve God. When you hear bad news, don't groan helplessly as do unbelievers who have no hope for the future. Remind yourself that in spite of it all, God has ultimate control and will one day come back to make everything right.

28:36 This happened when Assyria and Babylonia took the Israelites captive to their lands (2 Kings 17:23; 25:11).

earth,[z] like an eagle[a] swooping down, a nation whose language you will not
understand, 50a fierce-looking nation without respect for the old[b] or pity for the
young. 51They will devour the young of your livestock and the crops of your land until
you are destroyed. They will leave you no grain, new wine or oil, nor any calves of
your herds or lambs of your flocks until you are ruined.[c] 52They will lay siege to
all the cities throughout your land until the high fortified walls in which you trust fall
down. They will besiege all the cities throughout the land the LORD your God is giving
you.[d]

53Because of the suffering that your enemy will inflict on you during the siege, you
will eat the fruit of the womb, the flesh of the sons and daughters the LORD your God
has given you.[e] 54Even the most gentle and sensitive man among you will have no
compassion on his own brother or the wife he loves or his surviving children, 55and
he will not give to one of them any of the flesh of his children that he is eating. It
will be all he has left because of the suffering that your enemy will inflict on you during
the siege of all your cities. 56The most gentle and sensitive[f] woman among you—so
sensitive and gentle that she would not venture to touch the ground with the sole of
her foot—will begrudge the husband she loves and her own son or daughter 57the
afterbirth from her womb and the children she bears. For she intends to eat them
secretly during the siege and in the distress that your enemy will inflict on you in your
cities.

58If you do not carefully follow all the words of this law, which are written in this
book, and do not revere[g] this glorious and awesome name[h]—the LORD your
God—59the LORD will send fearful plagues on you and your descendants, harsh and
prolonged disasters, and severe and lingering illnesses. 60He will bring upon you all
the diseases of Egypt[i] that you dreaded, and they will cling to you. 61The LORD will
also bring on you every kind of sickness and disaster not recorded in this Book of the
Law, until you are destroyed.[j] 62You who were as numerous as the stars in the sky[k]
will be left but few in number, because you did not obey the LORD your God. 63Just
as it pleased[l] the LORD to make you prosper and increase in number, so it will please[m]
him to ruin and destroy you. You will be uprooted[n] from the land you are entering
to possess.

64Then the LORD will scatter[o] you among all nations,[p] from one end of the earth
to the other. There you will worship other gods—gods of wood and stone, which
neither you nor your fathers have known. 65Among those nations you will find no
repose, no resting place for the sole of your foot. There the LORD will give you an
anxious mind, eyes weary with longing, and a despairing heart.[q] 66You will live in
constant suspense, filled with dread both night and day, never sure of your life. 67In
the morning you will say, "If only it were evening!" and in the evening, "If only it
were morning!"—because of the terror that will fill your hearts and the sights that your
eyes will see.[r] 68The LORD will send you back in ships to Egypt on a journey I said
you should never make again. There you will offer yourselves for sale to your enemies
as male and female slaves, but no-one will buy you.

C. A CALL FOR COMMITMENT TO GOD: MOSES' THIRD ADDRESS (29:1—30:20)

After reviewing God's laws, Moses calls for commitment, urging the people to honour the contract they had previously made with God. Knowing God's word is not enough; we must obey it.

Renewal of the Covenant

29 These are the terms of the covenant the LORD commanded Moses to make with
the Israelites in Moab, in addition to the covenant he had made with them at
Horeb.[a]

28:49 [z]Jer 5:15; 6:22 [a]La 4:19; Hos 8:1
28:50 [b]Isa 47:6
28:51 [c]ver 33
28:52 [d]Jer 10:18; Zep 1:14-16, 17
28:53 [e]Lev 26:29; 2Ki 6:28-29; Jer 19:9; La 2:20; 4:10
28:56 [f]ver 54
28:58 [g]Mal 1:14 [h]Ex 6:3
28:60 [i]ver 27
28:61 [j]Dt 4:25-26
28:62 [k]Dt 4:27; 10:22; Ne 9:23
28:63 [l]Jer 32:41 [m]Pr 1:26 [n]Jer 12:14; 45:4
28:64 [o]Lev 26:33; Dt 4:27 [p]Ne 1:8
28:65 [q]Lev 26:16, 36
28:67 [r]ver 34; Job 7:4
29:1 [a]Dt 5:2-3

28:64 This severe warning tragically came true when Israel was defeated and carried away into captivity by Assyria (722 B.C.), and Judah to Babylonia (586 B.C.). Later, in A.D. 70, Roman oppression forced many Jews to flee their homeland. Thus the people were dispersed throughout the various nations.

29:1ff At Mount Sinai, 40 years earlier, God and Israel had made a covenant (Exodus 19, 20). Although there were many parts to the covenant (read the books of Exodus, Leviticus, and Numbers), its purpose can be summed up in two sentences: God promised to bless the Israelites by making them the nation through whom the

2 Moses summoned all the Israelites and said to them:

Your eyes have seen all that the LORD did in Egypt to Pharaoh, to all his officials and to all his land.[b] 3 With your own eyes you saw those great trials, those miraculous signs and great wonders.[c] 4 But to this day the LORD has not given you a mind that understands or eyes that see or ears that hear.[d] 5 During the forty years that I led you through the desert, your clothes did not wear out, nor did the sandals on your feet.[e] 6 You ate no bread and drank no wine or other fermented drink. I did this so that you might know that I am the LORD your God.[f]

7 When you reached this place, Sihon[g] king of Heshbon and Og king of Bashan came out to fight against us, but we defeated them.[h] 8 We took their land and gave it as an inheritance to the Reubenites, the Gadites and the half-tribe of Manasseh.[i]

9 Carefully follow[j] the terms of this covenant, so that you may prosper in everything you do.[k] 10 All of you are standing today in the presence of the LORD your God — your leaders and chief men, your elders and officials, and all the other men of Israel, 11 together with your children and your wives, and the aliens living in your camps who chop your wood and carry your water.[l] 12 You are standing here in order to enter into a covenant with the LORD your God, a covenant the LORD is making with you this day and sealing with an oath, 13 to confirm you this day as his people,[m] that he may be your God[n] as he promised you and as he swore to your fathers, Abraham, Isaac and Jacob. 14 I am making this covenant,[o] with its oath, not only with you 15 who are standing here with us today in the presence of the LORD our God but also with those who are not here today.[p]

16 You yourselves know how we lived in Egypt and how we passed through the countries on the way here. 17 You saw among them their detestable images and idols of wood and stone, of silver and gold.[q] 18 Make sure there is no man or woman, clan or tribe among you today whose heart turns away from the LORD our God to go and worship the gods of those nations; make sure there is no root among you that produces such bitter poison.[r]

19 When such a person hears the words of this oath, he invokes a blessing on himself and therefore thinks, "I will be safe, even though I persist in going my own way." This will bring disaster on the watered land as well as the dry.[a] 20 The LORD will never be willing to forgive him; his wrath and zeal[s] will burn[t] against that man. All the curses written in this book will fall upon him, and the LORD will blot[u] out his name from under heaven. 21 The LORD will single him out from all the tribes of Israel for disaster, according to all the curses of the covenant written in this Book of the Law.

22 Your children who follow you in later generations and foreigners who come from distant lands will see the calamities that have fallen on the land and the diseases with which the LORD has afflicted it.[v] 23 The whole land will be a burning waste[w] of salt[x] and sulphur — nothing planted, nothing sprouting, no vegetation growing on it. It will be like the destruction of Sodom and Gomorrah,[y] Admah and Zeboiim, which the LORD overthrew in fierce anger. 24 All the nations will ask: "Why has the LORD done this to this land?[z] Why this fierce, burning anger?"

a *19 Or way, in order to add drunkenness to thirst."*

29:2 b Ex 19:4
29:3 c Dt 4:34; 7:19
29:4 d Isa 6:10; Ac 28:26-27; Ro 11:8*; Eph 4:18
29:5 e Dt 8:4
29:6 f Dt 8:3
29:7 g Dt 2:32; 3:1 h Nu 21:21-24, 33-35
29:8 i Nu 32:33; Dt 3:12-13
29:9 j Dt 4:6; Jos 1:7 k 1Ki 2:3
29:11 l Jos 9:21, 23, 27
29:13 m Dt 28:9 n Ge 17:7; Ex 6:7
29:14 o Jer 31:31
29:15 p Ac 2:39
29:17 q Dt 28:36
29:18 r Dt 11:16; Heb 12:15
29:20 s Eze 23:25 t Ps 74:1; 79:5 u Ex 32:33; Dt 9:14
29:22 v Jer 19:8
29:23 w Isa 34:9 x Jer 17:6 y Ge 19:24, 25; Zep 2:9
29:24 z 1Ki 9:8; Jer 22:8-9

rest of the world could know God. In return, the Israelites promised to love and obey God in order to receive physical and spiritual blessings. Here Moses reviewed this covenant. God was still keeping his part of the bargain (and he always would), but the Israelites were already neglecting their part. Moses restated the covenant to warn the people that if they did not keep their part of the agreement, they would experience severe discipline.

29:5 Just as the people of Israel did not notice God's care for them along their journey, we sometimes do not notice all of the ways that God takes care of us — that all of our daily needs have been supplied and we have been well fed and well clothed. Worse still, we mistakenly take the credit ourselves for being good providers instead of recognising God's hand in the process.

29:9 What is the best way to prosper in life? For the Israelites, their first step was to keep their part of the covenant. They were to love God with all of their heart, soul, and strength (6:4, 5). We, too, are to seek first the kingdom of God and his righteousness (Mathew 6:33); then true success in life will follow as a blessing from the hand of God.

29:18 Moses cautioned that the day the Hebrews chose to turn from God, a root would be planted that would produce bitter poison (see Hebrews 12:15). When we decide to do what we know is wrong, we plant an evil seed that begins to grow out of control, eventually yielding a crop of sorrow and pain. But we can prevent those seeds of sin from taking root. If you have done something wrong, confess it to God and others immediately. If the seed never finds fertile soil, its bitter fruit will never ripen.

25 And the answer will be: "It is because this people abandoned the covenant of the
LORD, the God of their fathers, the covenant he made with them when he brought them
out of Egypt. 26 They went off and worshipped other gods and bowed down to them,
gods they did not know, gods he had not given them. 27 Therefore the LORD's anger
burned against this land, so that he brought on it all the curses written in this book.[a]
28 In furious anger and in great wrath the LORD uprooted[b] them from their land and
thrust them into another land, as it is now."
29 The secret things belong to the LORD our God, but the things revealed belong to
us and to our children for ever, that we may follow all the words of this law.

Prosperity After Turning to the LORD

30 When all these blessings and curses[a] I have set before you come upon you
and you take them to heart wherever the LORD your God disperses you among
the nations,[b] 2 and when you and your children return[c] to the LORD your God and
obey him with all your heart and with all your soul according to everything I command
you today, 3 then the LORD your God will restore your fortunes[a][d] and have compassion on you and gather[e] you again from all the nations where he scattered you.[f]
4 Even if you have been banished to the most distant land under the heavens, from there
the LORD your God will gather you and bring you back.[g] 5 He will bring[h] you to the
land that belonged to your fathers, and you will take possession of it. He will make
you more prosperous and numerous than your fathers. 6 The LORD your God will
circumcise your hearts and the hearts of your descendants,[i] so that you may love him
with all your heart and with all your soul, and live. 7 The LORD your God will put all
these curses on your enemies who hate and persecute you.[j] 8 You will again obey
the LORD and follow all his commands I am giving you today. 9 Then the LORD your
God will make you most prosperous in all the work of your hands and in the fruit of
your womb, the young of your livestock and the crops of your land.[k] The LORD will
again delight in you and make you prosperous, just as he delighted in your fathers,
10 if you obey the LORD your God and keep his commands and decrees that are written
in this Book of the Law and turn to the LORD your God with all your heart and with
all your soul.[l]

The Offer of Life or Death

11 Now what I am commanding you today is not too difficult for you or beyond your
reach.[m] 12 It is not up in heaven, so that you have to ask, "Who will ascend into heaven
to get it and proclaim it to us so that we may obey it?"[n] 13 Nor is it beyond the sea,
so that you have to ask, "Who will cross the sea to get it and proclaim it to us so that
we may obey it?" 14 No, the word is very near you; it is in your mouth and in your
heart so that you may obey it.
15 See, I set before you today life and prosperity, death and destruction.[o] 16 For I

a 3 *Or will bring you back from captivity*

29:27 [a] Da 9:11, 13, 14
29:28 [b] 1Ki 14:15; 2Ch 7:20; Ps 52:5; Pr 2:22
30:1 [a] ver 15, 19; Dt 11:26 [b] Lev 26:40-45; Dt 28:64; 29:28; 1Ki 8:47
30:2 [c] Dt 4:30; Ne 1:9
30:3 [d] Ps 126:4 [e] Ps 147:2; Jer 32:37; Eze 34:13 [f] Jer 29:14
30:4 [g] Ne 1:8-9; Isa 43:6
30:5 [h] Jer 29:14
30:6 [i] Dt 10:16; Jer 32:39
30:7 [j] Dt 7:15
30:9 [k] Dt 28:11; Jer 31:28; 32:41
30:10 [l] Dt 4:29
30:11 [m] Isa 45:19, 23
30:12 [n] Ro 10:6*
30:15 [o] Dt 11:26

29:29 There are some secrets God has chosen not to reveal to us, possibly for the following reasons: (1) our finite minds cannot fully understand the infinite aspects of God's nature and the universe (Ecclesiastes 3:11); (2) some things are unnecessary for us to know until we are more mature; (3) God is infinite and all-knowing, and we do not have the capacity to know everything he does. This verse shows that although God has not told us everything there is to know about obeying him, he has told us enough. Thus disobedience comes from an act of the will, not a lack of knowledge. Through God's word we know enough about him to be saved by faith and to serve him. We must not use the limitation of our knowledge as an excuse to reject his claim on our life.

30:1–6 Moses told the Hebrews that when they were ready to return to God, he would be ready to receive them. God's mercy is unbelievable. It goes far beyond what we can imagine. Even if the Jews deliberately walked away from him and ruined their lives, God would still take them back. God would give them inward spiritual renewal (circumcise their hearts). God wants to forgive us and bring us back to himself too. Some people will not learn this until their world has crashed in around them. Then the sorrow and pain seem to open their eyes to what God has been saying all along. Are you separated from God by sin? No matter how far you have wandered, God promises a fresh beginning if only you will turn to him.

30:11–14 God has called us to keep his commands, while reminding us that his laws are not hidden from us or beyond our reach. Have you ever said you would obey God if you knew what he wanted? Have you ever complained that obedience is too difficult for a mere human? These are unacceptable excuses. God's laws are written in the Bible and are clearly evident in the world around us. Obeying them is reasonable, sensible, and beneficial. The most difficult part of obeying God's laws is simply deciding to start now. Paul refers to this passage in Romans 10:5–8.

command you today to love the LORD your God, to walk in his ways, and to keep
his commands, decrees and laws; then you will live and increase, and the LORD your
God will bless you in the land you are entering to possess.
[17]But if your heart turns away and you are not obedient, and if you are drawn away
to bow down to other gods and worship them, [18]I declare to you this day that you
will certainly be destroyed.[p] You will not live long in the land you are crossing the
Jordan to enter and possess.
[19]This day I call heaven and earth as witnesses against you[q] that I have set before
you life and death, blessings and curses.[r] Now choose life, so that you and your
children may live [20]and that you may love[s] the LORD your God, listen to his voice,
and hold fast to him. For the LORD is your life,[t] and he will give you many years
in the land he swore to give to your fathers, Abraham, Isaac and Jacob.

D. THE CHANGE IN LEADERSHIP: MOSES' LAST DAYS (31:1–34:12)

Realising that he is about to die, Moses commissions Joshua, records the laws in a permanent form, and teaches a special song to the Israelites. Thus Moses prepared the people for his departure. Similarly, we should not allow others to become dependent upon us for their spiritual growth, but help them to become dependent upon God.

Joshua to Succeed Moses

31 Then Moses went out and spoke these words to all Israel: [2]"I am now a hundred
and twenty years old[a] and I am no longer able to lead you.[b] The LORD has
said to me, 'You shall not cross the Jordan.'[c] [3]The LORD your God himself will
cross[d] over ahead of you.[e] He will destroy these nations before you, and you will
take possession of their land. Joshua also will cross[f] over ahead of you, as the LORD
said. [4]And the LORD will do to them what he did to Sihon and Og, the kings of the
Amorites, whom he destroyed along with their land. [5]The LORD will deliver[g] them
to you, and you must do to them all that I have commanded you. [6]Be strong and
courageous.[h] Do not be afraid or terrified[i] because of them, for the LORD your God
goes with you;[j] he will never leave you[k] nor forsake[l] you."
[7]Then Moses summoned Joshua and said[m] to him in the presence of all Israel, "Be
strong and courageous, for you must go with this people into the land that the LORD
swore to their forefathers to give them, and you must divide it among them as their
inheritance. [8]The LORD himself goes before you and will be with you;[n] he will never
leave you nor forsake you. Do not be afraid; do not be discouraged."

The Reading of the Law

[9]So Moses wrote down this law and gave it to the priests, the sons of Levi, who
carried[o] the ark of the covenant of the LORD, and to all the elders of Israel. [10]Then
Moses commanded them: "At the end of every seven years, in the year for cancelling
debts,[p] during the Feast of Tabernacles,[q] [11]when all Israel comes to appear[r] before
the LORD your God at the place he will choose, you shall read this law[s] before them
in their hearing. [12]Assemble the people—men, women and children, and the aliens
living in your towns—so that they can listen and learn[t] to fear the LORD your God
and follow carefully all the words of this law. [13]Their children,[u] who do not know
this law, must hear it and learn to fear the LORD your God as long as you live in the
land you are crossing the Jordan to possess."

30:18 [p]Dt 8:19
30:19 [q]Dt 4:26 [r]ver 1
30:20 [s]Dt 6:5; 10:20 [t]Ps 27:1; Jn 11:25
31:2 [a]Dt 34:7 [b]Nu 27:17; 1Ki 3:7 [c]Dt 3:23, 26
31:3 [d]Nu 27:18 [e]Dt 9:3 [f]Dt 3:28
31:5 [g]Dt 7:2
31:6 [h]Jos 10:25; 1Ch 22:13 [i]Dt 7:18 [j]Dt 1:29; 20:4 [k]Jos 1:5 [l]Heb 13:5*
31:7 [m]Dt 1:38; 3:28
31:8 [n]Ex 13:21; 33:14
31:9 [o]ver 25; Nu 4:15; Jos 3:3
31:10 [p]Dt 15:1 [q]Lev 23:34
31:11 [r]Dt 16:16 [s]Jos 8:34-35; 2Ki 23:2
31:12 [t]Dt 4:10
31:13 [u]Dt 11:2; Ps 78:6-7

30:19, 20 Moses challenged Israel to choose life, to obey God, and therefore continue to experience his blessings. God doesn't force his will on anyone. He lets us decide whether to follow him or reject him. This decision, however, is a life-or-death matter. God wants us to realise this, for he would like us all to choose life. Daily, in each new situation, we must affirm and reinforce this commitment.

31:10–13 The laws were to be read to the whole assembly so that everyone, including the children, could hear them. Every seven years the entire nation would gather together and listen as a priest read the law to them. There were no books, Bibles, or newspapers to spread God's word, so the people had to rely on word of mouth and an accurate memory. Memorisation was an important part of worship because if everyone knew the law, ignorance would be no excuse for breaking it. To fulfil God's purpose and will in our lives, we need the content and substance of his word in our hearts and minds. For the Hebrews, this process began in childhood. Teaching our children and new believers should be one of our top priorities. Our finest teachers, best resources, and most careful thought should be directed towards showing young believers how to follow God in all life's situations.

Israel's Rebellion Predicted

14The LORD said to Moses, "Now the day of your death[v] is near. Call Joshua and
present yourselves at the Tent of Meeting, where I will commission him." So Moses
and Joshua came and presented themselves at the Tent of Meeting.
15Then the LORD appeared at the Tent in a pillar of cloud, and the cloud stood over
the entrance to the Tent.[w] 16And the LORD said to Moses: "You are going to rest with
your fathers, and these people will soon prostitute[x] themselves to the foreign gods
of the land they are entering. They will forsake[y] me and break the covenant I made
with them. 17On that day I will become angry[z] with them and forsake[a] them; I will
hide[b] my face from them, and they will be destroyed. Many disasters and difficulties
will come upon them, and on that day they will ask, 'Have not these disasters come
upon us because our God is not with us?'[c] 18And I will certainly hide my face on
that day because of all their wickedness in turning to other gods.
19"Now write down for yourselves this song and teach it to the Israelites and make
them sing it, so that it may be a witness for me against them. 20When I have brought
them into the land flowing with milk and honey, the land I promised on oath to their
forefathers,[d] and when they eat their fill and thrive, they will turn to other gods[e]
and worship them, rejecting me and breaking my covenant.[f] 21And when many
disasters and difficulties come upon them,[g] this song will testify against them,
because it will not be forgotten by their descendants. I know what they are disposed
to do,[h] even before I bring them into the land I promised them on oath." 22So Moses
wrote[i] down this song that day and taught it to the Israelites.
23The LORD gave this command[j] to Joshua son of Nun: "Be strong and courageous,[k] for you will bring the Israelites into the land I promised them on oath, and
I myself will be with you."
24After Moses finished writing in a book the words of this law from beginning to
end, 25he gave this command to the Levites who carried the ark of the covenant of
the LORD: 26"Take this Book of the Law and place it beside the ark of the covenant
of the LORD your God. There it will remain as a witness against you.[l] 27For I know
how rebellious and stiff-necked[m] you are. If you have been rebellious against the
LORD while I am still alive and with you, how much more will you rebel after I die!
28Assemble before me all the elders of your tribes and all your officials, so that I can
speak these words in their hearing and call heaven and earth to testify against them.[n]
29For I know that after my death you are sure to become utterly corrupt[o] and to turn
from the way I have commanded you. In days to come, disaster[p] will fall upon you
because you will do evil in the sight of the LORD and provoke him to anger by what
your hands have made."

The Song of Moses

30And Moses recited the words of this song from beginning to end in the hearing
of the whole assembly of Israel:

31:14 [v] Nu 27:13; Dt 32:49-50
31:15 [w] Ex 33:9
31:16 [x] Jdg 2:12 [y] Jdg 10:6, 13
31:17 [z] Jdg 2:14, 20 [a] Jdg 6:13; 2Ch 15:2 [b] Dt 32:20; Isa 1:15; 8:17 [c] Nu 14:42
31:20 [d] Dt 6:10-12 [e] Dt 32:15-17 [f] ver 16
31:21 [g] ver 17 [h] Hos 5:3
31:22 [i] ver 19
31:23 [j] ver 7 [k] Jos 1:6
31:26 [l] ver 19
31:27 [m] Ex 32:9; Dt 9:6, 24
31:28 [n] Dt 4:26; 30:19; 32:1
31:29 [o] Dt 32:5; Jdg 2:19 [p] Dt 28:15

31:19–21 There is a place for music in Christian education, and for the building up of all believers. Some people memorise classic hymns of the church to help them think of what is true, right, and good. Others find tapes to play when they are in the car or at home. What creative ways can music be used to teach in your church? How might you maximise the benefit of music in your family?

31:23 Joshua had been appointed to take over the leadership of Israel and guide the people into the promised land (Moses could not enter the land due to his disobedience – Numbers 20:12). Joshua, first mentioned in Exodus 17:9, had been Moses' assistant for many years (Joshua 1:1). One of his key qualifications was his faith. As one of the 12 spies to first enter Canaan, only he and Caleb believed that God could help Israel conquer the land (Numbers 13:1 – 14:30). Moses told Joshua to be strong and courageous twice in this chapter (31:7, 23). Indeed, this was a frightening task with three million people to care for, settle disputes for, and lead into battle. Finding courage would be Joshua's greatest test. He was strong and courageous because he knew God was with him and because he had faith that God would do all he had promised Israel.

31:27–29 Moses knew that the Israelites, in spite of all they had seen of God's work, were rebellious at heart. They deserved God's punishment, although they often received his mercy instead. We too are stubborn and rebellious by nature. Throughout our lives we struggle with sin. Repentance once a month or once a week is not enough. We must constantly turn from our sins to God and let him, in his mercy, save us.

32:1 [a]Isa 1:2
32:2 [b]Isa 55:11 [c]Ps 72:6
32:3 [d]Ex 33:19 [e]Dt 3:24
32:4 [f]ver 15, 18, 30 [g]2Sa 22:31 [h]Dt 7:9
32:5 [i]Dt 31:29
32:6 [j]Ps 116:12 [k]Ps 74:2 [l]Dt 1:31; Isa 63:16 [m]ver 15
32:7 [n]Ex 13:14
32:8 [o]Ge 11:8; Ac 17:26
32:9 [p]Jer 10:16 [q]1Ki 8:51, 53
32:10 [r]Jer 2:6 [s]Ps 17:8; Zec 2:8
32:11 [t]Ex 19:4

32 Listen, O heavens,[a] and I will speak;
hear, O earth, the words of my mouth.
2 Let my teaching fall like rain
and my words descend like dew,[b]
like showers[c] on new grass,
like abundant rain on tender plants.

3 I will proclaim the name of the LORD.[d]
Oh, praise the greatness[e] of our God!
4 He is the Rock,[f] his works are perfect,[g]
and all his ways are just.
A faithful God[h] who does no wrong,
upright and just is he.

5 They have acted corruptly towards him;
to their shame they are no longer his children,
but a warped and crooked generation.[a][i]
6 Is this the way you repay[j] the LORD,
O foolish and unwise people?[k]
Is he not your Father,[l] your Creator,[b]
who made you and formed you?[m]

7 Remember the days of old;
consider the generations long past.
Ask your father and he will tell you,
your elders, and they will explain to you.[n]
8 When the Most High gave the nations their inheritance,
when he divided all mankind,[o]
he set up boundaries for the peoples
according to the number of the sons of Israel.[c]
9 For the LORD's portion[p] is his people,
Jacob his allotted inheritance.[q]

10 In a desert[r] land he found him,
in a barren and howling waste.
He shielded him and cared for him;
he guarded him as the apple of his eye,[s]
11 like an eagle that stirs up its nest
and hovers over its young,[t]

[a] *5* Or *Corrupt are they and not his children, / a generation warped and twisted to their shame* [b] *6* Or *Father, who bought you* [c] *8* Masoretic Text; Dead Sea Scrolls (see also Septuagint) *sons of God*

VARIETY IN WORSHIP

Israel's worship used all of the senses. They reinforced the meaning of the ceremony. Every sense can be used to worship God.

SIGHT	the beauty and symbolism of the tabernacle; every colour and hue had a meaning
HEARING	the use of music; there were instructions for the use of a variety of instruments, and the Bible records many songs
TOUCH	the head of the animal to be sacrificed was touched, symbolising the fact that it was taking their place
SMELL	the sacrifices were burned, emitting a familiar aroma
TASTE	the feasts were celebrations and memorials—much of the food was symbolic

32:1ff Moses was not only a great prophet but also a song leader. After three sermons, he changed the form of his message to singing. Sometimes reciting something in a different form makes it easier to remember. This song gives a brief history of Israel. It reminds the people of their mistakes, warns them to avoid repetition of those mistakes, and offers the hope that comes only in trusting God.

32:10 The Israelites had no excuse for abandoning God. He had shielded them like a kindly shepherd. He had guarded them like a person protects the pupil (apple) of his eye. He had been the encircling protector, like a mother eagle who protects her young. The Lord alone had led them. And he alone leads us. Let us remember to trust in him.

that spreads its wings to catch them
and carries them on its pinions.
12The LORD alone led him;
no foreign god was with him.[u]

13He made him ride on the heights[v] of the land
and fed him with the fruit of the fields.
He nourished him with honey from the rock,
and with oil[w] from the flinty crag,
14with curds and milk from herd and flock
and with fattened lambs and goats,
with choice rams of Bashan
and the finest grains of wheat.[x]
You drank the foaming blood of the grape.[y]

15Jeshurun[d] grew fat[z] and kicked;
filled with food, he became heavy and sleek.
He abandoned[a] the God who made him
and rejected the Rock[b] his Saviour.
16They made him jealous[c] with their foreign gods
and angered[d] him with their detestable idols.
17They sacrificed to demons, which are not God—
gods they had not known,[e]
gods that recently appeared,[f]
gods your fathers did not fear.
18You deserted the Rock, who fathered you;
you forgot[g] the God who gave you birth.

19The LORD saw this and rejected them[h]
because he was angered by his sons and daughters.[i]
20"I will hide my face[j] from them," he said,
"and see what their end will be;
for they are a perverse generation,[k]
children who are unfaithful.
21They made me jealous[l] by what is no god
and angered me with their worthless idols.[m]
I will make them envious by those who are not a people;
I will make them angry by a nation that has no
understanding.[n]
22For a fire has been kindled by my wrath,
one that burns to the realm of death[e] below.[o]
It will devour the earth and its harvests
and set on fire the foundations of the mountains.

23"I will heap calamities[p] upon them
and expend my arrows[q] against them.
24I will send wasting famine against them,
consuming pestilence[r] and deadly plague;[s]
I will send against them the fangs of wild beasts,[t]
the venom of vipers[u] that glide in the dust.
25In the street the sword will make them childless;
in their homes terror will reign.[v]
Young men and young women will perish,
infants and grey-haired men.[w]
26I said I would scatter[x] them
and blot out their memory from mankind,[y]
27but I dreaded the taunt of the enemy,
lest the adversary misunderstand

d *15 Jeshurun* means *the upright one,* that is, Israel. **e** *22* Hebrew *to Sheol*

32:12 [u]ver 39
32:13 [v]Isa 58:14 [w]Job 29:6
32:14 [x]Ps 81:16; 147:14 [y]Ge 49:11
32:15 [z]Dt 31:20 [a]ver 6; Isa 1:4, 28 [b]ver 4
32:16 [c]1Co 10:22 [d]Ps 78:58
32:17 [e]Dt 28:64 [f]Jdg 5:8
32:18 [g]Isa 17:10
32:19 [h]Jer 44:21-23 [i]Ps 106:40
32:20 [j]Dt 31:17, 29 [k]ver 5
32:21 [l]1Co 10:22 [m]1Ki 16:13, 26 [n]Ro 10:19*
32:22 [o]Ps 18:7-8; Jer 15:14; La 4:11
32:23 [p]Dt 29:21 [q]Ps 7:13; Eze 5:16
32:24 [r]Dt 28:22 [s]Ps 91:6 [t]Lev 26:22 [u]Am 5:18-19
32:25 [v]Eze 7:15 [w]2Ch 36:17; La 2:21
32:26 [x]Dt 4:27 [y]Ps 34:16

and say, 'Our hand has triumphed;
the LORD has not done all this.' "[z]

28They are a nation without sense,
there is no discernment in them.
29If only they were wise and would understand this[a]
and discern what their end will be!
30How could one man chase a thousand,
or two put ten thousand to flight,[b]
unless their Rock had sold them,
unless the LORD had given them up?[c]
31For their rock is not like our Rock,
as even our enemies concede.
32Their vine comes from the vine of Sodom
and from the fields of Gomorrah.
Their grapes are filled with poison,
and their clusters with bitterness.
33Their wine is the venom of serpents,
the deadly poison of cobras.[d]

34"Have I not kept this in reserve
and sealed it in my vaults?[e]
35It is mine to avenge; I will repay.[f]
In due time their foot will slip;[g]
their day of disaster is near
and their doom rushes upon them.[h]"

36The LORD will judge his people
and have compassion on his servants[i]
when he sees their strength is gone
and no-one is left, slave or free.
37He will say: "Now where are their gods,
the rock they took refuge in,[j]
38the gods who ate the fat of their sacrifices
and drank the wine of their drink offerings?
Let them rise up to help you!
Let them give you shelter!

39"See now that I myself am He![k]
There is no god besides me.[l]
I put to death and I bring to life,[m]
I have wounded and I will heal,[n]
and no-one can deliver out of my hand.[o]
40I lift my hand to heaven and declare:
As surely as I live for ever,
41when I sharpen my flashing sword[p]
and my hand grasps it in judgment,
I will take vengeance on my adversaries
and repay those who hate me.[q]
42I will make my arrows drunk with blood,[r]
while my sword devours flesh:[s]
the blood of the slain and the captives,
the heads of the enemy leaders."

43Rejoice,[t] O nations, with his people,[f,g]
for he will avenge the blood of his servants;[u]
he will take vengeance on his enemies
and make atonement for his land and people.[v]

32:27 [z] Isa 10:13
32:29 [a] Dt 5:29; Ps 81:13
32:30 [b] Lev 26:8 [c] Ps 44:12
32:33 [d] Ps 58:4
32:34 [e] Jer 2:22; Hos 13:12
32:35 [f] Ro 12:19*; Heb 10:30* [g] Jer 23:12 [h] Eze 7:8-9
32:36 [i] Dt 30:1-3; Ps 135:14; Joel 2:14
32:37 [j] Jdg 10:14; Jer 2:28
32:39 [k] Isa 41:4 [l] Isa 45:5 [m] 1Sa 2:6; Ps 68:20 [n] Hos 6:1 [o] Ps 50:22
32:41 [p] Isa 34:6; 66:16; Eze 21:9-10 [q] Jer 50:29
32:42 [r] ver 23 [s] Jer 46:10, 14
32:43 [t] Ro 15:10* [u] 2Ki 9:7 [v] Ps 65:3; 85:1; Rev 19:2

f *43* Or *Make his people rejoice, O nations* **g** *43* Masoretic Text; Dead Sea Scrolls (see also Septuagint) *people, / and let all the angels worship him /*

44Moses came with Joshua[h][w] son of Nun and spoke all the words of this song in
the hearing of the people. 45When Moses finished reciting all these words to all Israel,
46he said to them, "Take to heart all the words I have solemnly declared to you this
day,[x] so that you may command your children to obey carefully all the words of this
law. 47They are not just idle words for you—they are your life.[y] By them you will
live long in the land you are crossing the Jordan to possess."

Moses to Die on Mount Nebo

48On that same day the LORD told Moses, 49"Go up into the Abarim[z] Range to
Mount Nebo in Moab, across from Jericho, and view Canaan, the land I am giving
the Israelites as their own possession. 50There on the mountain that you have climbed
you will die[a] and be gathered to your people, just as your brother Aaron died on
Mount Hor and was gathered to his people. 51This is because both of you broke faith
with me in the presence of the Israelites at the waters of Meribah Kadesh in the Desert
of Zin[b] and because you did not uphold my holiness among the Israelites.[c] 52There-
fore, you will see the land only from a distance;[d] you will not enter[e] the land I am
giving to the people of Israel."

Moses Blesses the Tribes

33 This is the blessing that Moses the man of God[a] pronounced on the Israelites
before his death. 2He said:

"The LORD came from Sinai[b]
and dawned over them from Seir;[c]
he shone forth from Mount Paran.[d]
He came with[a] myriads of holy ones[e]
from the south, from his mountain slopes.[b]
3Surely it is you who love[f] the people;
all the holy ones are in your hand.[g]
At your feet they all bow down,[h]
and from you receive instruction,
4the law that Moses gave us,[i]
the possession of the assembly of Jacob.[j]
5He was king over Jeshurun[c]
when the leaders of the people assembled,
along with the tribes of Israel.

6"Let Reuben live and not die,
nor[d] his men be few."

7And this he said about Judah:[k]

"Hear, O LORD, the cry of Judah;
bring him to his people.
With his own hands he defends his cause.
Oh, be his help against his foes!"

8About Levi he said:

"Your Thummim and Urim[l] belong

h 44 Hebrew *Hoshea,* a variant of *Joshua* a 2 Or *from* b 2 The meaning of the Hebrew for this phrase is uncertain. c 5 *Jeshurun* means *the upright one,* that is, Israel; also in verse 26. d 6 Or *but let*

32:44 [w]Nu 13:8, 16
32:46 [x]Eze 40:4
32:47 [y]Dt 30:20
32:49 [z]Nu 27:12
32:50 [a]Ge 25:8
32:51 [b]Nu 20:11-13 [c]Nu 27:14
32:52 [d]Dt 34:1-3 [e]Dt 1:37
33:1 [a]Jos 14:6
33:2 [b]Ex 19:18; Ps 68:8 [c]Jdg 5:4 [d]Hab 3:3 [e]Da 7:10; Ac 7:53; Rev 5:11
33:3 [f]Hos 11:1 [g]Dt 14:2 [h]Lk 10:39
33:4 [i]Jn 1:17 [j]Ps 119:111
33:7 [k]Ge 49:10
33:8 [l]Ex 28:30

32:46, 47 Moses urged the people to think about God's word and teach it to their children. The Bible can sit on your bookshelf and gather dust, or you can make it a vital part of your life by regularly setting aside time to study it. When you discover the wisdom of God's message, you will want to apply it to your life and pass it on to your family and others. The Bible is not merely good reading—it's real help for real life.

33:6–25 Note the difference in blessings God gave each tribe. To one he gave the best land, to another strength, to another safety. Too often we see someone with a particular blessing and think that God must love that person more than others. Think rather that God draws out in all people their unique talents. All these gifts are needed to complete his plan. Don't be envious of the gifts others have. Instead, look for the gifts God has given you, and resolve to do the tasks he has uniquely qualified you to do.

33:8
[m]Ex 17:7

to the man you favoured.
You tested him at Massah;
you contended with him at the waters of Meribah.[m]
9He said of his father and mother,[n]
'I have no regard for them.'
He did not recognise his brothers
or acknowledge his own children,
but he watched over your word
and guarded your covenant.[o]
10He teaches your precepts to Jacob
and your law to Israel.[p]
He offers incense before you
and whole burnt offerings on your altar.[q]
11Bless all his skills, O LORD,
and be pleased with the work of his hands.[r]
Smite the loins of those who rise up against him;
strike his foes till they rise no more."

33:9
[n]Ex 32:26-29
[o]Mal 2:5

33:10
[p]Lev 10:11; Dt 31:9-13
[q]Ps 51:19

33:11
[r]2Sa 24:23

12About Benjamin he said:

"Let the beloved of the LORD rest secure in him,[s]
for he shields him all day long,
and the one the LORD loves rests between his shoulders.[t]"

33:12
[s]Dt 12:10
[t]Ex 28:12

13About Joseph[u] he said:

"May the LORD bless his land
with the precious dew from heaven above
and with the deep waters that lie below;[v]
14with the best the sun brings forth
and the finest the moon can yield;
15with the choicest gifts of the ancient mountains[w]
and the fruitfulness of the everlasting hills;
16with the best gifts of the earth and its fulness
and the favour of him who dwelt in the burning bush.[x]
Let all these rest on the head of Joseph,
on the brow of the prince among[e] his brothers.
17In majesty he is like a firstborn bull;
his horns are the horns of a wild ox.[y]
With them he will gore[z] the nations,
even those at the ends of the earth.
Such are the ten thousands of Ephraim;
such are the thousands of Manasseh."

33:13
[u]Ge 49:25
[v]Ge 27:28

33:15
[w]Hab 3:6

33:16
[x]Ex 3:2

33:17
[y]Nu 23:22
[z]1Ki 22:11; Ps 44:5

18About Zebulun[a] he said:

"Rejoice, Zebulun, in your going out,
and you, Issachar, in your tents.
19They will summon peoples to the mountain[b]
and there offer sacrifices of righteousness;[c]
they will feast on the abundance of the seas,[d]
on the treasures hidden in the sand."

33:18
[a]Ge 49:13-15

33:19
[b]Ex 15:17; Isa 2:3
[c]Ps 4:5
[d]Isa 60:5, 11

20About Gad[e] he said:

33:20
[e]Ge 49:19

e *16* Or *of the one separated from*

33:20, 21 The people of the tribe of Gad received the best of the new land because they obeyed God by punishing Israel's wicked enemies. Punishment is unpleasant for both the giver and the receiver, but it is a necessary part of growth. If you are in a position that sometimes requires you to correct others, don't hold back from fulfilling your task. Understand that realistic discipline is important to character development. Always strive to be both just and merciful, keeping in mind the best interests of the person who must receive the punishment.

"Blessed is he who enlarges Gad's domain!
Gad lives there like a lion,
tearing at arm or head.
21 He chose the best land for himself;[f]
the leader's portion was kept for him.
When the heads of the people assembled,
he carried out the LORD's righteous will,[g]
and his judgments concerning Israel."

22 About Dan[h] he said:

"Dan is a lion's cub,
springing out of Bashan."

23 About Naphtali he said:

"Naphtali is abounding with the favour of the LORD
and is full of his blessing;
he will inherit southward to the lake."

24 About Asher[i] he said:

"Most blessed of sons is Asher;
let him be favoured by his brothers,
and let him bathe his feet in oil.[j]
25 The bolts of your gates will be iron and bronze,
and your strength will equal your days.[k]
26 "There is no-one like the God of Jeshurun,[l]
who rides on the heavens to help you[m]
and on the clouds in his majesty.
27 The eternal God is your refuge,[n]
and underneath are the everlasting arms.
He will drive out your enemy before you,[o]
saying, 'Destroy him!'[p]
28 So Israel will live in safety alone;[q]
Jacob's spring is secure
in a land of grain and new wine,
where the heavens drop dew.[r]
29 Blessed are you, O Israel![s]
Who is like you,[t]
a people saved by the LORD?[u]
He is your shield and helper[v]
and your glorious sword.
Your enemies will cower before you,
and you will trample down their high places."[f][w]

The Death of Moses

34 Then Moses climbed Mount Nebo from the plains of Moab to the top of Pisgah,
across from Jericho.[a] There the LORD showed[b] him the whole land—from
Gilead to Dan, 2 all of Naphtali, the territory of Ephraim and Manasseh, all the land
of Judah as far as the western sea,[a][c] 3 the Negev and the whole region from the Valley
of Jericho, the City of Palms,[d] as far as Zoar. 4 Then the LORD said to him, "This

f 29 Or *will tread upon their bodies* a 2 That is, the Mediterranean

33:21 [f] Nu 32:1-5, 31-32 [g] Jos 4:12; 22:1-3
33:22 [h] Ge 49:16
33:24 [i] Ge 49:21 [j] Ge 49:20; Job 29:6
33:25 [k] Dt 4:40; 32:47
33:26 [l] Ex 15:11 [m] Ps 104:3
33:27 [n] Ps 90:1 [o] Jos 24:18 [p] Dt 7:2
33:28 [q] Nu 23:9; Jer 23:6 [r] Ge 27:28
33:29 [s] Ps 144:15 [t] Ps 18:44 [u] 2Sa 7:23 [v] Ps 115:9-11 [w] Dt 32:13
34:1 [a] Dt 32:49 [b] Dt 32:52
34:2 [c] Dt 11:24
34:3 [d] Jdg 1:16; 3:13; 2Ch 28:15

33:24 Bathing feet in oil was a sign of prosperity.

33:27 Moses' song declares that God is our refuge, our only true security. How often we entrust our lives to other things—perhaps money, career, a noble cause, or a lifelong dream. But our only true refuge is the eternal God, who always holds out his arms to catch us when the shaky supports that we trust collapse and we fall. No storm can destroy us when we take refuge in him. Those without God, however, must for ever be cautious. One mistake may wipe them out. Living for God in this world may look like a risky business. But it is the godless who are on shaky ground. Because God is our refuge, we can dare to be bold.

34:4
[e]Ge 28:13
[f]Ge 12:7
[g]Dt 3:27
34:5
[h]Nu 12:7
[i]Dt 32:50;
Jos 1:1-2
34:6
[j]Dt 3:29
[k]Jude 1:9
34:7
[l]Dt 31:2
[m]Ge 27:1
34:8
[n]Ge 50:3, 10;
2Sa 11:27
34:9
[o]Ge 41:38;
Isa 11:2;
Da 6:3
[p]Nu 27:18, 23
34:10
[q]Dt 18:15, 18
[r]Ex 33:11;
Nu 12:6, 8;
Dt 5:4
34:11
[s]Dt 4:34
[t]Dt 7:19

is the land I promised on oath[e] to Abraham, Isaac and Jacob when I said, 'I will give
it[f] to your descendants.' I have let you see it with your eyes, but you will not cross[g]
over into it."
5And Moses the servant of the LORD[h] died[i] there in Moab, as the LORD had said.
6He buried him[b] in Moab, in the valley opposite Beth Peor,[j] but to this day no-one
knows where his grave is.[k] 7Moses was a hundred and twenty years old[l] when he
died, yet his eyes were not weak[m] nor his strength gone. 8The Israelites grieved for
Moses in the plains of Moab thirty days, until the time of weeping and mourning[n]
was over.
9Now Joshua son of Nun was filled with the spirit[c] of wisdom[o] because Moses
had laid his hands on him.[p] So the Israelites listened to him and did what the LORD
had commanded Moses.
10Since then, no prophet has risen in Israel like Moses,[q] whom the LORD knew
face to face,[r] 11who did all those miraculous signs and wonders[s] the LORD sent him
to do in Egypt—to Pharaoh and to all his officials[t] and to his whole land. 12For
no-one has ever shown the mighty power or performed the awesome deeds that Moses
did in the sight of all Israel.

b *6 Or He was buried* **c** *9 Or Spirit*

34:4, 10 Moses was the only person who ever spoke with God face to face (Exodus 33:11; Numbers 12:8). He was called Israel's greatest prophet. Yet even this great man was not allowed to enter the promised land because he disobeyed God (Numbers 20:12). No matter how good we are, or how much we've done for God, we sometimes disobey him. The result of our disobedience is that we will be disciplined. God disciplined Moses severely, but still called him his friend. When you experience the sting of God's discipline, respond as Moses did. Don't turn away in anger, embarrassment, or resentment. Instead, turn towards God with love, openness, and a desire to do better.

34:10–12 Moses, the man who did not want to be sent to Egypt because he was "slow of speech" (Exodus 4:10), delivered the three addresses to Israel that make up the book of Deuteronomy. God gave him the power to develop from a stuttering shepherd into a national leader and powerful orator. His courage, humility, and wisdom moulded the Hebrew slaves into a nation. But Moses was one person who did not let success go to his head. In the end, God was still Moses' best friend. His love, respect, and awe for God had grown daily throughout his life. Moses knew that it was not any greatness in himself that made him successful; it was the greatness of the all-powerful God in whom he trusted. There were many great and powerful prophets during the time of the kings. But it would be more than a thousand years before one greater than Moses would appear—Jesus.

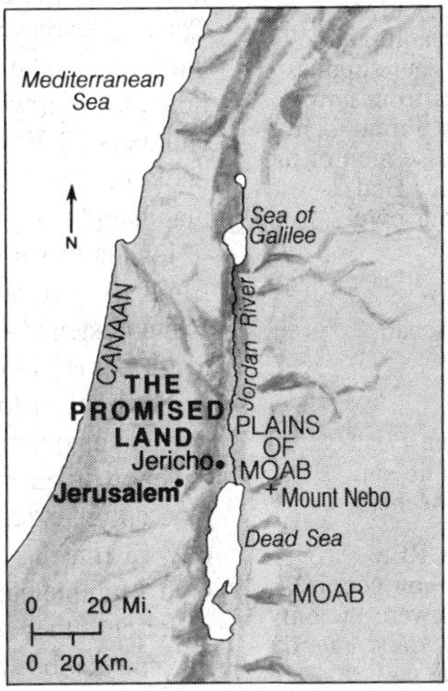

THE DEATH OF MOSES
Just before Moses died, he climbed Mount Nebo. Although he could not enter the promised land, God showed him its beauty from Mount Nebo's peak.

J O S H U A

Exodus from Egypt 1446 B.C. (1280 B.C.)	Israelites enter Canaan 1406 (1240)	Judges begin to rule 1375 (1220)	T H E D A Y S O

CONQUEST OF CANAAN

VITAL STATISTICS

PURPOSE:
To give the history of Israel's conquest of the promised land

AUTHOR:
Joshua, except for the ending which may have been written by the high priest Phinehas, an eyewitness to the events recounted there

SETTING:
Canaan, also called the promised land, which occupied the same general geographical territory as modern-day Israel

KEY VERSE:
"Go through the camp and tell the people, 'Get your supplies ready. Three days from now you will cross the Jordan here to go in and take possession of the land the LORD your God is giving you for your own' " (1:11).

KEY PEOPLE:
Joshua, Rahab, Achan, Phinehas, Eleazar

KEY PLACES:
Jericho, Ai, Mount Ebal, Mount Gerizim, Gibeon, Gilgal, Shiloh, Shechem

SPECIAL FEATURE:
Out of over a million people, Joshua and Caleb were the only two who left Egypt and entered the promised land.

REMEMBER the childhood game "follow my leader"? The idea was to mimic the antics of the person in front of you. Being a follower was all right, but being leader was the most fun, creating imaginative actions for everyone else to copy.

In real life, great leaders are rare. Often, men and women are elected or appointed to leadership positions, but then falter or fail to act. Others abuse their power to satisfy their egos, crushing their subjects and squandering resources. But without faithful, ethical, and effective leaders, people wander.

For 40 years, Israel had journeyed a circuitous route through the desert, but *not* because they were following their leader. Quite the opposite was true—with failing faith, they had refused to obey God and to conquer Canaan. So they wandered. Finally, the new generation was ready to cross the Jordan and possess the land. Having distinguished himself as a man of faith and courage (he and Caleb gave the minority spy report recorded in Numbers 13:30—14:9), Joshua was chosen to be Moses' successor. This book records Joshua's leadership of the people of God as they finish their march and conquer the promised land.

Joshua was a brilliant military leader and a strong spiritual influence. But the key to his success was his submission to God. When God spoke, Joshua listened and obeyed. Joshua's obedience served as a model. As a result, Israel remained faithful to God throughout Joshua's lifetime.

The book of Joshua is divided into two main parts. The first narrates the events surrounding the conquest of Canaan. After crossing the Jordan River on dry ground, the Israelites camped near the mighty city of Jericho. God commanded the people to conquer Jericho by marching around the city 13 times, blowing trumpets, and shouting. Because they followed God's unique battle strategy, they won (chapter 6). After the destruction of Jericho, they set out against the small town of Ai. Their first attack was driven back because one of the Israelites (Achan) had sinned (chapter 7). After the men of Israel stoned Achan and his family—purging the community of its sin—the Israelites succeeded in capturing Ai (chapter 8). In their next battle against the Amorites, God even made the sun stand still to aid them in their victory (chapter 10). Finally, after defeating other assorted Canaanites led by Jabin and his allies (chapter 11), they possessed most of the land.

Part two of the book of Joshua records the assignment and settlement of the captured territory (chapters 13—22). The book concludes with Joshua's farewell address and his death (chapters 23, 24).

Joshua was committed to obeying God, and this book is about obedience. Whether conquering enemies or settling in the land, God's people were required to do it God's way. In his final message to the people, Joshua underscored the importance of obeying God. "So be very careful to love the LORD your God" (23:11), and "choose for yourselves this day whom you will serve . . . . But as for me and my household, we will serve the LORD" (24:15). Read Joshua and make a fresh commitment to obey God today. Decide to follow your Lord wherever he leads and whatever it costs.

T H E J U D G E S

United kingdom under Saul 1050 (1045)

David becomes king 1010

THE BLUEPRINT

A. ENTERING THE PROMISED LAND (1:1–5:12) 1. Joshua leads the nation 2. Crossing the Jordan	Joshua demonstrated his faith in God as he took up the challenge to lead the nation. The Israelites reaffirmed their commitment to God by obediently setting out across the Jordan River to possess the land. As we live the Christian life, we need to cross over from the old life to the new, put off our selfish desires, and press on to possess all God has planned for us. Like Joshua and Israel, we need courageous faith to live the new life.
B. CONQUERING THE PROMISED LAND (5:13–12:24) 1. Joshua attacks the centre of the land 2. Joshua attacks the southern kings 3. Joshua attacks the northern kings 4. Summary of conquests	Joshua and his army moved from city to city, cleansing the land of its wickedness by destroying every trace of idol worship. Conflict with evil is inevitable, and we should be as merciless as Israel in destroying sin in our lives.
C. DIVIDING THE PROMISED LAND (13:1–24:33) 1. The tribes receive their land 2. Special cities are set aside 3. Eastern tribes return home 4. Joshua's farewell to the leaders	Joshua urged the Israelites to continue to follow the Lord and worship him alone. The people had seen God deliver them from many enemies and miraculously provide for all their needs, but they were prone to wandering from the Lord. Even though we may have experienced God at work in our lives, we too must continually renew our commitment to obey him above all other authority and to worship him alone.

MEGATHEMES

THEME	EXPLANATION	IMPORTANCE
Success	God gave success to the Israelites when they obeyed his master plan, not when they followed their own desires. Victory came when they trusted in him rather than in their military power, money, muscle, or mental capacity.	God's work done in God's way will bring his success. The standard for success, however, is not to be set by the society around us but by God's word. We must adjust our minds to God's way of thinking in order to see his standard for success.
Faith	The Israelites demonstrated their faith by trusting God daily to save and guide them. By noticing how God fulfilled his promises in the past, they developed strong confidence that he would be faithful in the future.	Our strength to do God's work comes from trusting him. His promises reassure us of his love and that he will be there to guide us in the decisions and struggles we face. Faith begins with believing he can be trusted.
Guidance	God gave instructions to Israel for every aspect of their lives. His law guided their daily living and his specific marching orders gave them victory in battle.	Guidance from God for daily living can be found in his word. By staying in touch with God, we will have the needed wisdom to meet the great challenges of life.
Leadership	Joshua was an example of an excellent leader. He was confident in God's strength, courageous in the face of opposition, and willing to seek God's advice.	To be a strong leader like Joshua we must be ready to listen and to move quickly when God instructs us. Once we have his instructions, we must be diligent in carrying them out. Strong leaders are led by God.
Conquest	God commanded his people to conquer the Canaanites and take all their land. Completing this mission would have fulfilled God's promise to Abraham and brought judgment on the evil people living there. Unfortunately, Israel never finished the job.	Israel was faithful in accomplishing their mission at first, but their commitment faltered. To love God means more than being enthusiastic about him. We must complete all the work he gives us and apply his instructions to every corner of our lives.

KEY PLACES IN JOSHUA

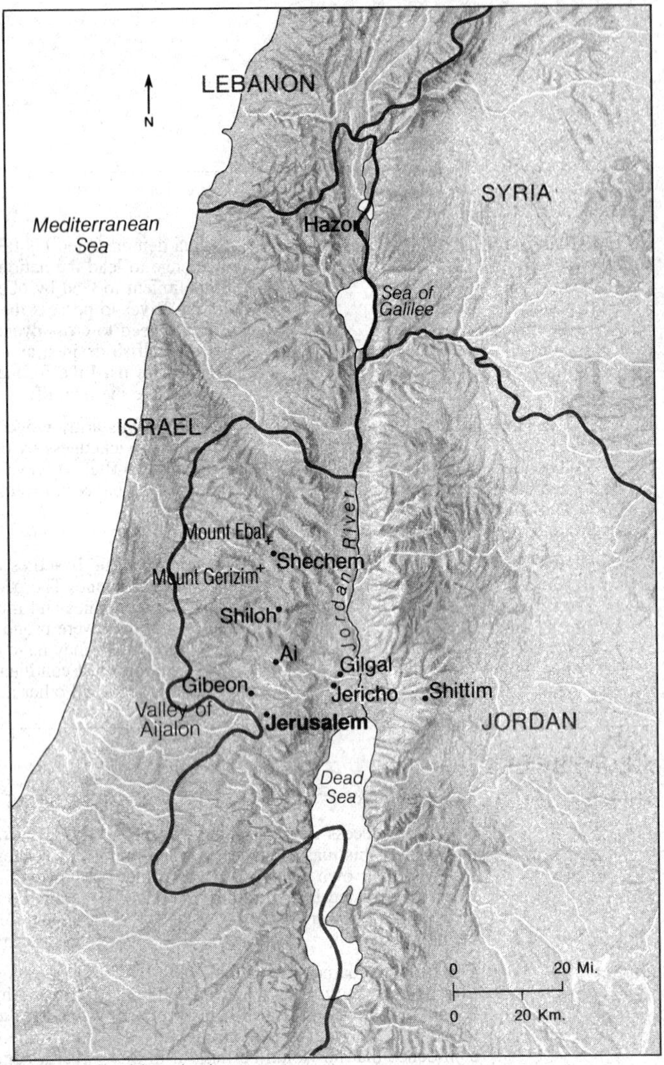

Modern names and boundaries are shown in grey.

1 Shittim The story of Joshua begins with the Israelites camping at Shittim. The Israelites under Joshua were ready to enter and conquer Canaan. But before the nation moved out, Joshua received instructions from God (1:1–18).

2 Jordan River The entire nation prepared to cross this river, which was swollen from spring rains. After the spies returned from Jericho with a positive report, Joshua prepared the priests and people for a miracle. As the priests carried the ark into the Jordan River, the water stopped flowing and the entire nation crossed on dry ground into the promised land (2:1–4:24).

3 Gilgal After crossing the Jordan River, the Israelites camped at Gilgal where they renewed their commitment to God and celebrated the Passover, the feast commemorating their deliverance from Egypt (see Exodus). As Joshua made plans for the attack on Jericho, an angel appeared to him (5:1–15).

4 Jericho The walled city of Jericho seemed a formidable enemy. But when Joshua followed God's plans, the great walls were no obstacle. The city was conquered with only the obedient marching of the people (6:1–27).

5 Ai Victory could not continue without obedience to God. That is why the disobedience of one man, Achan, brought defeat to the entire nation in the first battle against Ai. But once the sin was recognised and punished, God told Joshua to take heart and try Ai once again. This time the city was taken (7:1–8:29).

6 The Mountains of Ebal and Gerizim After the defeat of Ai, Joshua built an altar at Mount Ebal. Then the people divided themselves, half at the foot of Mount Ebal, half at the foot of Mount Gerizim. The priests stood between the mountains holding the ark of the covenant as Joshua read God's law to all the people (8:30–35).

7 Gibeon It was just after the Israelites reaffirmed their covenant with God that their leaders made a major mistake in judgment: they were tricked into making a peace treaty with the city of Gibeon. The Gibeonites pretended that they had travelled a long distance and asked the Israelites for a treaty. The leaders made the agreement without consulting God. The trick was soon discovered, but because the treaty had been made, Israel could not go back on its word. As a result, the Gibeonites saved their own lives, but they were forced to become Israel's slaves (9:1–27).

8 Valley of Aijalon The king of Jerusalem was very angry at Gibeon for making a peace treaty with the Israelites. He gathered armies from four other cities to attack the city. Gibeon summoned Joshua for help. Joshua took immediate action. Leaving Gilgal, he attacked the coalition by surprise. As the battle waged on and moved into the Valley of Aijalon, Joshua prayed for the sun to stand still until the enemy could be destroyed (10:1–43).

9 Hazor Up north in Hazor, King Jabin mobilised the kings of the surrounding cities to unite and crush Israel. But God gave Joshua and Israel victory (11:1–23).

10 Shiloh After the armies of Canaan were conquered, Israel gathered at Shiloh to set up the tabernacle. This movable building had been the nation's centre of worship during their years of wandering. The seven tribes who had not received their land were given their allotments (18:1–19:51).

11 Shechem Before Joshua died he called the entire nation together at Shechem to remind them that it was God who had given them their land and that only with God's help could they keep it. The people vowed to follow God. As long as Joshua was alive, the land was at rest from war and trouble (24:1–33).

1:1
[a]Nu 12:7; Dt 34:5
[b]Ex 24:13; Dt 1:38

1:2
[c]ver 11

1:3
[d]Dt 11:24

1:4
[e]Ge 15:18
[f]Nu 34:2-12

1:5
[g]Dt 7:24
[h]Jos 3:7; 6:27
[i]Dt 31:6-8

A. ENTERING THE PROMISED LAND (1:1–5:12)

After wandering for 40 years in the desert, a new generation is ready to enter Canaan. But first God prepares both Joshua and the nation by teaching them the importance of courageous and consistent faith. The nation then miraculously crosses the Jordan River to begin the long-awaited conquest of the promised land. Like Joshua, we too need faith to begin and continue living the Christian life.

1. Joshua leads the nation

The LORD Commands Joshua

1 After the death of Moses the servant of the LORD,[a] the LORD said to Joshua[b]
son of Nun, Moses' assistant: 2"Moses my servant is dead. Now then, you and
all these people, get ready to cross the Jordan River[c] into the land I am about to give
to them—to the Israelites. 3I will give you every place where you set your foot,[d]
as I promised Moses. 4Your territory will extend from the desert to Lebanon, and from
the great river, the Euphrates[e]—all the Hittite country—to the Great Sea[a] on the
west.[f] 5No-one will be able to stand up against you[g] all the days of your life. As
I was with[h] Moses, so I will be with you; I will never leave you nor forsake[i] you.

a 4 That is, the Mediterranean

TAKE THE LAND

God told Joshua to lead the Israelites into the promised land (also called Canaan) and conquer it. This was not an act of imperialism or aggression, but an act of judgment. Here are some of the earlier passages in the Bible where God promised to give this land to the Israelites and the reasons for doing so.

Genesis 12:1–3	God promised to bless Abraham and make his descendants into a great nation
Genesis 15:16	God would choose the right time for Israel to enter Canaan because the nations living there then would be wicked and ripe for judgment (their sin would reach full measure)
Genesis 17:7, 8	God promised to give all the land of Canaan to Abraham's descendants
Exodus 33:1–3	God promised to help the Israelites drive out all the evil nations from Canaan
Deuteronomy 4:5–8	The Israelites were to be an example of right living to the whole world; this would not work if they intermingled with the wicked Canaanites
Deuteronomy 7:1–5	The Israelites were to utterly wipe the Canaanites out because of their wickedness and because of Israel's call to purity
Deuteronomy 12:2	The Israelites were to destroy the Canaanite altars completely so that nothing would tempt them away from worshipping God alone

1:1 As the book of Joshua opens, the Israelites are camped along the east bank of the Jordan River at the very edge of the promised land and they are completing the mourning period for Moses, who has just died (Deuteronomy 34:7, 8). Thirty-nine years earlier (after spending a year at Mount Sinai receiving God's law), the Israelites had an opportunity to enter the promised land, but they failed to trust God to give them victory. As a result, God did not allow them to enter the land, but made them wander in the desert until the disobedient generation had all died.

During their desert wanderings, the Israelites obeyed God's laws. They also taught the new generation to obey God's laws so that they might enter the promised land (also called Canaan). As the children grew, they were often reminded that faith and obedience to God brought victory, while unbelief and disobedience brought tragedy. When the last of the older generation had died and the new generation had become adults, the Israelites prepared to make their long-awaited claim on the promised land.

1:1–5 Joshua succeeded Moses as Israel's leader. What qualifications did he have to become the leader of a nation? (1) God appointed him (Numbers 27:18–23). (2) He was one of only two living eyewitnesses to the Egyptian plagues and the exodus from Egypt. (3) He was Moses' personal aide for 40 years. (4) Of the 12 spies, only he and Caleb showed complete confidence that God would help them conquer the land.

1:2 Because Joshua had assisted Moses for many years, he was well prepared to take over the leadership of the nation. Changes in leadership are common in many organisations. At such times, a smooth transition is essential for the establishment of the new administration. This doesn't happen unless new leaders are trained. If you are currently in a leadership position, begin preparing someone to take your place. Then, when you leave or are promoted, operations can continue to run efficiently. If you want to be a leader, learn from others so that you will be prepared when the opportunity comes.

1:5 Joshua's new job consisted of leading more than two million people into a strange new land and conquering it. What a challenge—even for a man of Joshua's calibre! Every new job is a challenge. Without God it can be frightening. With God it can be a great adventure. Just as God was with Joshua, he is with us as we face our new challenges. We may not conquer nations, but every day we face tough situations, difficult people, and temptations. However, God promises that he will never abandon us or fail to help us. By asking God to direct us we can conquer many of life's challenges.

6 "Be strong and courageous, because you will lead these people to inherit the land
I swore to their forefathers[j] to give them. 7 Be strong and very courageous. Be careful
to obey all the law my servant Moses gave you; do not turn from it to the right or
to the left,[k] that you may be successful wherever you go.[l] 8 Do not let this Book
of the Law depart from your mouth; meditate on it day and night, so that you may
be careful to do everything written in it. Then you will be prosperous and successful.[m]
9 Have I not commanded you? Be strong and courageous. Do not be terrified;[n] do not
be discouraged, for the LORD your God will be with you wherever you go."[o]
10 So Joshua ordered the officers of the people: 11 "Go through the camp and tell the
people, 'Get your supplies ready. Three days from now you will cross the Jordan here
to go in and take possession[p] of the land the LORD your God is giving you for your
own.' "
12 But to the Reubenites, the Gadites and the half-tribe of Manasseh,[q] Joshua said,
13 "Remember the command that Moses the servant of the LORD gave you: 'The LORD
your God is giving you rest[r] and has granted you this land.' 14 Your wives, your
children and your livestock may stay in the land that Moses gave you east of the
Jordan, but all your fighting men, fully armed, must cross over ahead of your brothers.
You are to help your brothers 15 until the LORD gives them rest, as he has done for
you, and until they too have taken possession of the land that the LORD your God is
giving them. After that, you may go back and occupy your own land, which Moses
the servant of the LORD gave you east of the Jordan towards the sunrise."[s]
16 Then they answered Joshua, "Whatever you have commanded us we will do, and
wherever you send us we will go. 17 Just as we fully obeyed Moses, so we will obey
you.[t] Only may the LORD your God be with you as he was with Moses. 18 Whoever
rebels against your word and does not obey your words, whatever you may command
them, will be put to death. Only be strong and courageous!"

Rahab and the Spies

2 Then Joshua son of Nun secretly sent two spies[a] from Shittim.[b] "Go, look over
the land," he said, "especially Jericho." So they went and entered the house of
a prostitute[a] named Rahab[c] and stayed there.

a 1 Or possibly *an innkeeper*

1:6 [j] Dt 31:23
1:7 [k] Dt 5:32; 28:14 [l] Jos 11:15
1:8 [m] Dt 29:9; Ps 1:1-3
1:9 [n] Ps 27:1 [o] ver 7; Dt 31:7-8; Jer 1:8
1:11 [p] Joel 3:2
1:12 [q] Nu 32:20-22
1:13 [r] Dt 3:18-20
1:15 [s] Jos 22:1-4
1:17 [t] ver 5, 9
2:1 [a] Jas 2:25 [b] Nu 25:1; Jos 3:1 [c] Heb 11:31

1:6–8 Many people think that prosperity and success come from having power, influential personal contacts, and a relentless desire to get ahead. But the strategy for gaining prosperity that God taught Joshua goes against such criteria. He said that to succeed Joshua must (1) be strong and courageous because the task ahead would not be easy, (2) obey God's law, and (3) constantly read and study the Book of the Law – God's word. To be successful, follow God's words to Joshua. You may not succeed by the world's standards, but you will be a success in God's eyes – and his opinion lasts for ever.

1:12–15 During the previous year, the tribes of Reuben and Gad and the half-tribe of Manasseh had asked Moses if they could settle just east of the promised land. The area was excellent pastureland for their large flocks. Moses agreed to give them the land on one condition – that they help their fellow tribes enter and conquer the promised land. Only after the land was conquered could they return to their homes. Now it was time for these three tribes to live up to their agreement.

1:13 God was giving the people rest. This was wonderful news to these people who had been on the move for their entire lives. The people who had no land would be given a land of their own, and they would be able to settle and to "rest".

1:16 If everyone had tried to conquer the promised land his own way, chaos would have resulted. In order to complete the enormous task of conquering the land, everyone had to agree to the leader's plan and be willing to support and obey him. If we are going to complete the tasks God has given us, we must fully agree to his plan, pledge ourselves to obey it, and put his principles into action. Agreeing to God's plan means both knowing what the plan is (as found in the Bible) and carrying it out daily.

1:18 When God commissioned Joshua, he was told three times to be strong and courageous (see 1:6, 7, 9). Here, Joshua was given the same kind of encouragement from the people. Apparently, he took God's message to heart, and found the strength and courage he needed in his relationship with God. The next time you are afraid to do what you know is right, remember that strength and courage are readily available from God.

2:1 Why did Joshua send the spies secretly? As far as he knew, he would be attacking a heavily fortified city using conventional warfare tactics. He needed strategic information about the city for the forthcoming battle. But he also knew that this might draw criticism from the other leaders. After all, the last time spies were sent, the report they brought back caused disastrous problems (see Numbers 13:1 – 14:4). While he did not want to move ahead without information, he also did not want to cause the people to stumble and question his wisdom and ability to lead the nation.

2:1 Why would the spies stop at the house of Rahab, a prostitute? (1) It was a good place to gather information and have no questions asked in return. (2) Rahab's house was in an ideal location for a quick escape because it was built into the city wall (2:15).

2The king of Jericho was told, "Look! Some of the Israelites have come here tonight
to spy out the land." 3So the king of Jericho sent this message to Rahab: "Bring out
the men who came to you and entered your house, because they have come to spy
out the whole land."

JOSHUA

One of the greatest challenges facing leaders is to replace themselves, training others to become leaders. Many outstanding accomplishments have been started by someone with great ability whose life or career ended before the vision became reality. The fulfilment of that dream then became the responsibility of that person's successor. Death is the ultimate deadline for leadership. One of the best tests of our leadership is our willingness and ability to train another for our position.

Moses made an excellent decision when he chose Joshua as his assistant. That choice was later confirmed by God himself when he instructed Moses to commission Joshua as his successor (Numbers 27:15–23). Joshua had played a key role in the exodus from Egypt. Introduced as the field general of Israel's army, he was the only person allowed to accompany Moses part of the way up the mountain when Moses received the law. Joshua and Caleb were the only two among the 12 spies to bring back an encouraging report after being sent into the promised land the first time. Other references show him to have been Moses' constant shadow. His basic training was living with Moses—experiencing firsthand what it meant to lead God's people. This was modelling at its best!

Who is your Moses? Who is your Joshua? You are part of the chain of God's ongoing work in the world. You are modelling yourself on others, and others are patterning their lives after you. How important is God to those you want to be like? Do those who are watching you see God reflected in every area of your life? Ask God to lead you to a trustworthy Moses. Ask him to make you a good Joshua.

Strengths and accomplishments:
- Moses' assistant and successor
- One of only two adults who experienced Egyptian slavery and lived to enter the promised land
- Led the Israelites into their God-given homeland
- Brilliant military strategist
- Faithful to ask God's direction in the challenges he faced

Lessons from his life:
- Effective leadership is often the product of good preparation and encouragement
- The persons after whom we pattern ourselves will have a definite effect on us
- A person committed to God provides the best model for us

Vital statistics:
- Where: Egypt, the Desert of Sinai, and Canaan (the promised land)
- Occupations: Special assistant to Moses, warrior, leader
- Relative: Father: Nun
- Contemporaries: Moses, Caleb, Miriam, Aaron

Key verses:
"Moses did as the LORD commanded him. He took Joshua and made him stand before Eleazar the priest and the whole assembly. Then he laid his hands on him and commissioned him, as the LORD instructed through Moses" (Numbers 27:22, 23).

Joshua is also mentioned in Exodus 17:9–14; 24:13; 32:17; 33:11; Numbers 11:28; 13; 14; 26:65; 27:18–23; 32:11–12, 28; 34:17; Deuteronomy 1:38; 3:21, 28; 31:3, 7, 14, 23; 34:9; the book of Joshua; Judges 2:6–9; and 1 Kings 16:34.

(3) God directed the spies to Rahab's house because he knew her heart was open to him and that she would be instrumental in the Israelite victory over Jericho. God often uses people with simple faith to accomplish his great purposes, no matter what kind of past they have had or how insignificant they seem to be. Rahab didn't allow her past to keep her from the new role God had for her.

[4]But the woman had taken the two men and hidden them.[d] She said, "Yes, the
men came to me, but I did not know where they had come from. [5]At dusk, when it
was time to close the city gate, the men left. I don't know which way they went. Go
after them quickly. You may catch up with them." [6](But she had taken them up to
the roof and hidden them under the stalks of flax[e] she had laid out on the roof.)[f]
[7]So the men set out in pursuit of the spies on the road that leads to the fords of the
Jordan, and as soon as the pursuers had gone out, the gate was shut.
[8]Before the spies lay down for the night, she went up on the roof [9]and said to them,
"I know that the LORD has given this land to you and that a great fear[g] of you has
fallen on us, so that all who live in this country are melting in fear because of you.
[10]We have heard how the LORD dried up[h] the water of the Red Sea**[b]** for you when
you came out of Egypt,[i] and what you did to Sihon and Og,[j] the two kings of the
Amorites east of the Jordan, whom you completely destroyed.**[c]** [11]When we heard of
it, our hearts sank**[d]** and everyone's courage failed because of you,[k] for the LORD
your God is God in heaven above and on the earth[l] below. [12]Now then, please swear
to me by the LORD that you will show kindness to my family, because I have shown
kindness to you. Give me a sure sign[m] [13]that you will spare the lives of my father
and mother, my brothers and sisters, and all who belong to them, and that you will
save us from death."
[14]"Our lives for your lives!" the men assured her. "If you don't tell what we
are doing, we will treat you kindly and faithfully[n] when the LORD gives us the
land."
[15]So she let them down by a rope through the window,[o] for the house she lived

b *10* Hebrew *Yam Suph*; that is, Sea of Reeds **c** *10* The Hebrew term refers to the irrevocable giving over of things or persons to the LORD, often by totally destroying them. **d** *11* Hebrew *melted*

2:4 [d]2Sa 17:19-20
2:6 [e]Jas 2:25 [f]Ex 1:17, 19; 2Sa 17:19
2:9 [g]Ge 35:5; Ex 23:27; Dt 2:25
2:10 [h]Ex 14:21 [i]Nu 23:22 [j]Nu 21:21, 24, 34-35
2:11 [k]Ex 15:14; Jos 5:1; 7:5; Ps 22:14; Isa 13:7 [l]Dt 4:39
2:12 [m]ver 18
2:14 [n]Jdg 1:24; Mt 5:7
2:15 [o]Ac 9:25

SPY MISSION TO JERICHO
Two spies left the Israelite camp at Shittim, crossed the Jordan River, and slipped into Jericho. The city was built around an oasis in the midst of a hot and desolate valley 840 feet below sea level. Jericho was the first major city the Israelites set out to conquer.

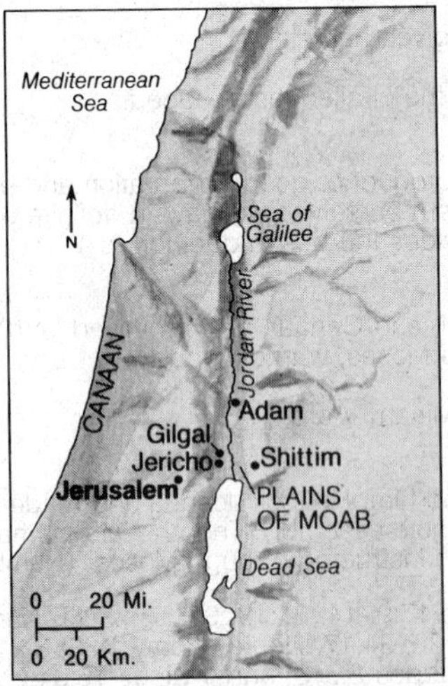

2:4, 5 Was Rahab justified in lying to save the lives of the spies? Although the Bible does not speak negatively about her lie, it is clear that lying is sin. In Hebrews 11:31, however, Rahab is commended for her faith in God. Her lie is not mentioned. Several explanations have been offered: (1) God forgave Rahab's lie because of her faith; (2) Rahab was simply deceiving the enemy, a normal and acceptable practice in wartime; (3) because Rahab was not a Jew, she could not be held responsible for keeping the moral standards set forth in God's law; (4) Rahab broke a lesser principle—telling the truth—to uphold a higher principle—protecting God's people.

There may have been another way to save the lives of the Israelite spies. But under the pressure of the moment, Rahab had to make a choice. Most of us will face dilemmas at one time or another. We may feel that there is no perfect solution to our problem. Fortunately, God does not demand that our judgment be perfect in all situations. He simply asks us to put our trust in him and to do the best we know how. Rahab did that and was commended for her faith.

2:6 Flax was harvested in the fields and piled high on the rooftops to dry. It was then made into yarn which was used to make linen cloth. Flax grows to a height of three or four feet. Stacked on the roof, it made an excellent hiding place for the spies.

2:8–13 Many would assume that Rahab—a pagan, a Canaanite, and a prostitute—would never be interested in God. Yet Rahab was willing to risk everything she had for a God she barely knew. We must not gauge a person's interest in God by his or her background, life-style, or appearance. We should let nothing get in the way of our telling people about God.

2:11 Rahab recognised something that many of the Israelites did not—the God of heaven is not an ordinary god! He is all-powerful. The people of Jericho were afraid because they had heard the news of God's extraordinary power in defeating the armies across the Jordan River. Today we can worship this same powerful, miracle-working God. He is powerful enough to destroy mighty, wicked armies, as he did in Jericho. He is also powerful enough to save us from certain death, as he did with Rahab.

2:15 In Joshua's day it was common to build houses on city walls. Many cities had two walls about 12 to 15 feet apart. Houses were built on wooden logs laid across the tops of the two walls. Rahab may have lived in such a house with a window that looked out over the outside wall.

in was part of the city wall. 16Now she had said to them, “Go to the hills so that the
pursuers will not find you. Hide yourselves there three days[p] until they return, and
then go on your way.”[q]
17The men said to her, “This oath[r] you made us swear will not be binding on us
18unless, when we enter the land, you have tied this scarlet cord in the window through
which you let us down, and unless you have brought your father and mother, your
brothers and all your family[s] into your house. 19If anyone goes outside your house
into the street, his blood will be on his own head;[t] we will not be responsible. As
for anyone who is in the house with you, his blood will be on our head[u] if a hand
is laid on him. 20But if you tell what we are doing, we will be released from the oath
you made us swear.”
21“Agreed,” she replied. “Let it be as you say.” So she sent them away and they
departed. And she tied the scarlet cord in the window.
22When they left, they went into the hills and stayed there three days, until the
pursuers had searched all along the road and returned without finding them. 23Then
the two men started back. They went down out of the hills, forded the river and came
to Joshua son of Nun and told him everything that had happened to them. 24They said
to Joshua, “The LORD has surely given the whole land into our hands;[v] all the people
are melting in fear because of us.”

2:16 [p] Jas 2:25 [q] Heb 11:31
2:17 [r] Ge 24:8
2:18 [s] ver 12; Jos 6:23
2:19 [t] Eze 33:4 [u] Mt 27:25
2:24 [v] ver 9; Jos 6:2

RAHAB

Rahab was a prostitute in the city of Jericho. As a prostitute, she lived on the edge of society, one stop short of rejection. Her house, built right into the city wall, provided both lodging and favours to travellers. It was a natural place for the Israelite spies to stay, as they would be mistaken for Rahab’s clients.

Stories about the Israelites had been circulating for some time, but now it was evident that the Israelites were about to invade. Living on the wall, Rahab felt especially vulnerable. Yet while she shared the general mood of fear with the rest of Jericho’s population, she alone turned to the Lord for her salvation. Her faith gave her the courage to hide the spies and lie to the authorities. Rahab knew her position was dangerous; she could have been killed if she were caught harbouring the Israelites. Rahab took the risk, however, because she sensed that the Israelites relied on a God worth trusting. And God rewarded Rahab by promising safety for her and her family.

God works through people—like Rahab—whom we are inclined to reject. God remembers her because of her faith, not her profession. If at times you feel like a failure, remember that Rahab rose above her situation through her trust in God. You can do the same!

Strengths and accomplishments:
- Relative of Boaz, and thus an ancestor of David and Jesus
- One of only two women listed in the Hall of Faith in Hebrews 11
- Resourceful, willing to help others at great cost to herself

Weakness and mistake:
- She was a prostitute

Lesson from her life:
- She did not let fear affect her faith in God’s ability to deliver

Vital statistics:
- Where: Jericho
- Occupations: Prostitute/innkeeper, later became a wife
- Relatives: Ancestor of David and Jesus (Matthew 1:5)
- Contemporary: Joshua

Key verse:
“By faith the prostitute Rahab, because she welcomed the spies, was not killed with those who were disobedient” (Hebrews 11:31).

Rahab’s story is told in Joshua 2 and 6:22, 23. She is also mentioned in Matthew 1:5; Hebrews 11:31; and James 2:25.

2. Crossing the Jordan

3 Early in the morning Joshua and all the Israelites set out from Shittim[a] and went
to the Jordan, where they camped before crossing over. 2After three days the
officers went throughout the camp,[b] 3giving orders to the people: "When you see the
ark of the covenant[c] of the LORD your God, and the priests,[d] who are Levites,
carrying it, you are to move out from your positions and follow it. 4Then you will
know which way to go, since you have never been this way before. But keep a distance
of about a thousand yards**a** between you and the ark; do not go near it."
5Joshua told the people, "Consecrate yourselves,[e] for tomorrow the LORD will do
amazing things among you."
6Joshua said to the priests, "Take up the ark of the covenant and pass on ahead of
the people." So they took it up and went ahead of them.
7And the LORD said to Joshua, "Today I will begin to exalt you[f] in the eyes of
all Israel, so that they may know that I am with you as I was with Moses.[g] 8Tell the
priests[h] who carry the ark of the covenant: 'When you reach the edge of the Jordan's
waters, go and stand in the river.' "
9Joshua said to the Israelites, "Come here and listen to the words of the LORD your
God. 10This is how you will know that the living God[i] is among you and that he
will certainly drive out before you the Canaanites, Hittites, Hivites, Perizzites, Girgashites, Amorites and Jebusites.[j] 11See, the ark of the covenant of the Lord of all the
earth[k] will go into the Jordan ahead of you. 12Now then, choose twelve men[l] from
the tribes of Israel, one from each tribe. 13And as soon as the priests who carry the
ark of the LORD—the Lord of all the earth[m]—set foot in the Jordan, its waters flowing
downstream[n] will be cut off and stand up in a heap.[o]"
14So when the people broke camp to cross the Jordan, the priests carrying the ark
of the covenant[p] went ahead[q] of them. 15Now the Jordan is in flood[r] all during

3:1 [a]Jos 2:1
3:2 [b]Jos 1:11
3:3 [c]Nu 10:33 [d]Dt 31:9
3:5 [e]Ex 19:10, 14; Lev 20:7; Jos 7:13; 1Sa 16:5; Joel 2:16
3:7 [f]Jos 4:14; 1Ch 29:25 [g]Jos 1:5
3:8 [h]ver 3
3:10 [i]Dt 5:26; 1Sa 17:26, 36; 2Ki 19:4, 16; Hos 1:10; Mt 16:16; 1Th 1:9 [j]Ex 33:2; Dt 7:1
3:11 [k]ver 13; Job 41:11; Zec 6:5
3:12 [l]Jos 4:2, 4
3:13 [m]ver 11 [n]ver 16 [o]Ex 15:8; Ps 78:13
3:14 [p]Ps 132:8 [q]Ac 7:44-45
3:15 [r]Jos 4:18; 1Ch 12:15

a 4 Hebrew *about two thousand cubits* (about 900 metres)

3:2–4 The ark of the covenant was Israel's most sacred treasure. It was a symbol of God's presence and power. The ark was a golden rectangular box with two cherubim (angels) facing each other on the lid. Inside the ark were the tablets of the Ten Commandments Moses received from God, a jar of manna (the bread God miraculously sent from heaven during the desert wanderings), and Aaron's staff (the symbol of the high priest's authority). According to God's law, only the Levites could carry the ark. The ark was constructed at the same time as the tabernacle (Exodus 37:1–9) and placed in the sanctuary's most sacred room.

3:5 Before entering the promised land, the Israelites were to perform a consecration (purification) ceremony. This was often done before making a sacrifice or, as in this case, before witnessing a great act of God. God's law stated that a person could become unclean for many reasons – eating certain foods (Leviticus 11), childbirth (Leviticus 12), disease (Leviticus 13, 14), touching a dead person (Numbers 19:11–22). God used these various outward signs of uncleanness to illustrate man's inward uncleanness that comes as a result of sin. The consecration ceremony pictured the importance of approaching God with a pure heart. Like the Israelites, we need God's forgiveness before we approach him.

3:9 Just before crossing over into the promised land, Joshua gathered the people to hear the words of the Lord. Their excitement was high. No doubt they wanted to rush on, but Joshua made them stop and listen. We live in a fast-paced age where everyone rushes just to keep up. It is easy to get caught up in our tasks, becoming too busy for what God says is most important – listening to his words. Before making your schedule, take time to focus on what God wants from all your activities. Knowing what God has said before you rush into your day may help you avoid foolish mistakes.

3:10 Why would God help the Israelites drive out these nations from their native land? God had punished Israel first for its disobedience. He then turned to the rest of the nations. Genesis 15:16 implies that the people of Canaan were wicked and deserved to be punished for their terrible sins. Israel was to be a vehicle for this punishment. More important was the fact that Israel, as a holy nation, could not live among such evil and idolatrous people. To do so would be to invite sin into their lives. The only way to prevent Israel from being infected by evil religions was to drive out those who practised them. Israel, however, failed to drive everyone out as God had told them to do. It wasn't long before Israel – the nation God chose to be his holy people – began following the evil practices of the Canaanites.

3:13, 14 The Israelites were eager to enter the promised land, conquer nations, and live peacefully. But first they had to cross the flood-level waters of the Jordan River. God gave them specific instructions: in order to cross, the priests had to step into the water. What if these priests had been afraid to take that first step? Often God provides no solution to our problems until we trust him and move ahead with what we know we should do. What are the rivers, or obstacles, in your life? In obedience to God, take that first step into the water.

3:13–17 God had parted the waters of the Red Sea to let the people out of Egypt (Exodus 14), and here he parted the Jordan River to let them enter Canaan. These miracles showed Israel that God keeps his promises. God's presence among his people and his faithfulness to them made the entire journey from Egypt to the promised land possible. He was with them at the end of their wanderings just as he was with them in the beginning.

3:15, 16 The Israelites crossed the Jordan River in the spring, when it was overflowing its banks. God chose the time when the river was at its highest to demonstrate his power – parting the waters so that the entire nation could cross on dry ground. Some say that God used a natural occurrence (such as a landslide) to stop the waters of the Jordan; others say he did it by a direct miracle. In either case, God showed his great power by working a miracle of timing and location to allow his people to cross the river on

3:16 [s]Ps 66:6; 74:15 [t]1Ki 4:12; 7:46 [u]ver 13 [v]Dt 1:1 [w]Ge 14:3
3:17 [x]Ex 14:22, 29
4:1 [a]Dt 27:2
4:2 [b]Jos 3:12
4:3 [c]ver 20 [d]ver 19
4:6 [e]ver 21; Ex 12:26; 13:14
4:7 [f]Jos 3:13 [g]Ex 12:14
4:8 [h]ver 20
4:9 [i]Ge 28:18; Jos 24:26; 1Sa 7:12
4:12 [j]Nu 32:27
4:14 [k]Jos 3:7
4:16 [l]Ex 25:22
4:18 [m]Jos 3:15
4:19 [n]Jos 5:9

harvest. Yet as soon as the priests who carried the ark reached the Jordan and their
feet touched the water's edge, 16the water from upstream stopped flowing.[s] It piled
up in a heap a great distance away, at a town called Adam in the vicinity of Zarethan,[t]
while the water flowing down[u] to the Sea of the Arabah[v] (the Salt Sea[b][w]) was
completely cut off. So the people crossed over opposite Jericho. 17The priests who
carried the ark of the covenant of the LORD stood firm on dry ground in the middle
of the Jordan, while all Israel passed by until the whole nation had completed the
crossing on dry ground.[x]

4 When the whole nation had finished crossing the Jordan,[a] the LORD said to
Joshua, 2"Choose twelve men[b] from among the people, one from each tribe,
3and tell them to take up twelve stones[c] from the middle of the Jordan from right
where the priests stood and to carry them over with you and put them down at the
place where you stay tonight.[d]"

4So Joshua called together the twelve men he had appointed from the Israelites, one
from each tribe, 5and said to them, "Go over before the ark of the LORD your God
into the middle of the Jordan. Each of you is to take up a stone on his shoulder,
according to the number of the tribes of the Israelites, 6to serve as a sign among you.
In the future, when your children ask you, 'What do these stones mean?'[e] 7tell them
that the flow of the Jordan was cut off[f] before the ark of the covenant of the LORD.
When it crossed the Jordan, the waters of the Jordan were cut off. These stones are
to be a memorial[g] to the people of Israel for ever."

8So the Israelites did as Joshua commanded them. They took twelve stones from
the middle of the Jordan, according to the number of the tribes of the Israelites, as
the LORD had told Joshua;[h] and they carried them over with them to their camp, where
they put them down. 9Joshua set up the twelve stones[i] that had been[a] in the middle
of the Jordan at the spot where the priests who carried the ark of the covenant had
stood. And they are there to this day.

10Now the priests who carried the ark remained standing in the middle of the Jordan
until everything the LORD had commanded Joshua was done by the people, just as
Moses had directed Joshua. The people hurried over, 11and as soon as all of them had
crossed, the ark of the LORD and the priests came to the other side while the people
watched. 12The men of Reuben, Gad and the half-tribe of Manasseh crossed over,
armed, in front of the Israelites,[j] as Moses had directed them. 13About forty thousand
armed for battle crossed over before the LORD to the plains of Jericho for war.

14That day the LORD exalted[k] Joshua in the sight of all Israel; and they revered
him all the days of his life, just as they had revered Moses.

15Then the LORD said to Joshua, 16"Command the priests carrying the ark of the
Testimony[l] to come up out of the Jordan."

17So Joshua commanded the priests, "Come up out of the Jordan."

18And the priests came up out of the river carrying the ark of the covenant of the
LORD. No sooner had they set their feet on the dry ground than the waters of the Jordan
returned to their place and ran in flood[m] as before.

19On the tenth day of the first month the people went up from the Jordan and camped
at Gilgal[n] on the eastern border of Jericho. 20And Joshua set up at Gilgal the twelve

b *16* That is, the Dead Sea **a** *9* Or *Joshua also set up twelve stones*

---

dry ground. This testimony of God's supernatural power served to build the Israelites' hope in God and to give them a great reputation with their enemies, who greatly outnumbered them.

4:1ff After the people safely crossed the river, what would be next? Conquering the land? Not yet. First, God directed them to build a memorial from 12 stones drawn from the river by 12 men, one from each tribe. This may seem like an insignificant step in their mission of conquering the land, but God did not want his people to plunge into their task unprepared. They were to focus on him and remember who was guiding them. As you are busy doing your God-given tasks, set aside quiet moments, times to build your own memorial to God's power. Too much activity may shift your focus away from God.

4:14 The Israelites revered Joshua for his role in leading them across the Jordan River. He, like Moses, would receive Israel's praises generation after generation. Although Israel was not a world power at that time, Joshua's reputation for handling his responsibilities God's way brought him greater glory than if he had been a hero in a "superpower" nation. Doing right is more important than doing well.

stones[o] they had taken out of the Jordan. 21 He said to the Israelites, "In the future
when your descendants ask their fathers, 'What do these stones mean?'[p] 22 tell them,
'Israel crossed the Jordan on dry ground.'[q] 23 For the LORD your God dried up the
Jordan before you until you had crossed over. The LORD your God did to the Jordan
just what he had done to the Red Sea[b] when he dried it up before us until we had
crossed over.[r] 24 He did this so that all the peoples of the earth might know[s] that
the hand of the LORD is powerful[t] and so that you might always fear the LORD your
God.[u]"

Circumcision at Gilgal

5 Now when all the Amorite kings west of the Jordan and all the Canaanite kings
along the coast[a] heard how the LORD had dried up the Jordan before the Israelites
until we had crossed over, their hearts sank[a][b] and they no longer had the courage
to face the Israelites.
2 At that time the LORD said to Joshua, "Make flint knives[c] and circumcise the
Israelites again." 3 So Joshua made flint knives and circumcised the Israelites at
Gibeath Haaraloth.[b]
4 Now this is why he did so: All those who came out of Egypt—all the men of
military age—died in the desert on the way after leaving Egypt.[d] 5 All the people that
came out had been circumcised, but all the people born in the desert during the journey
from Egypt had not. 6 The Israelites had moved about in the desert forty years[e] until
all the men who were of military age when they left Egypt had died, since they had
not obeyed the LORD. For the LORD had sworn to them that they would not see the
land that he had solemnly promised their fathers to give us,[f] a land flowing with milk
and honey.[g] 7 So he raised up their sons in their place, and these were the ones Joshua
circumcised. They were still uncircumcised because they had not been circumcised
on the way. 8 And after the whole nation had been circumcised, they remained where
they were in camp until they were healed.[h]
9 Then the LORD said to Joshua, "Today I have rolled away the reproach of Egypt
from you." So the place has been called Gilgal[c] to this day.
10 On the evening of the fourteenth day of the month,[i] while camped at Gilgal on

b 23 Hebrew *Yam Suph*; that is, Sea of Reeds a 1 Hebrew *melted* b 3 *Gibeath Haaraloth* means *hill of foreskins.* c 9 *Gilgal* sounds like the Hebrew for *roll.*

4:20 [o]ver 3, 8
4:21 [p]ver 6
4:22 [q]Jos 3:17
4:23 [r]Ex 14:21
4:24 [s]1Ki 8:42-43; 2Ki 19:19; Ps 106:8; Jer 10:7 [t]Ex 15:16; 1Ch 29:12; Ps 89:13 [u]Ex 14:31
5:1 [a]Nu 13:29 [b]Jos 2:9-11
5:2 [c]Ex 4:25
5:4 [d]Dt 2:14
5:6 [e]Dt 2:7 [f]Nu 14:23, 29-35; Dt 2:14 [g]Ex 3:8
5:8 [h]Ge 34:25
5:10 [i]Ex 12:6

4:21–24 The memorial of 12 stones was to be a constant reminder of the day the Israelites crossed the Jordan River on dry ground. Their children would see the stones, hear the story, and learn about God. Do you have traditions—special dates or special places—to help your children learn about God's work in your life? Do you take time to tell them what God has done for you—forgiving and saving you, answering your prayers, supplying your needs? Retelling your story will help keep memories of God's faithfulness alive in your family.

5:1 The Amorites and Canaanites were the two major groups living in Canaan at the time of Israel's invasion. The Canaanites worshipped a variety of gods, but Baal was their favourite. Canaanite culture was materialistic, and their religion, sensual. The Israelites continually turned to Baal after entering Canaan. The Amorite gods also infected Israel's worship and turned people away from worshipping the true God. Worshipping these false gods eventually brought about Israel's downfall.

5:1 The Israelites spent 39 years in the desert unnecessarily because they were terrified of the Canaanites. They underestimated God's ability. The Israelites' first attempt to enter the promised land had failed (Numbers 13, 14). Here Israel saw that the Canaanites were terrified of their army. The Canaanites had heard about Israel's great victories through God (2:9–11), and they hoped that the Jordan River would slow Israel down or discourage them from entering Canaan. But news that the Israelites had crossed the Jordan on dry land caused any courage the Canaanites still had to melt away.

Don't underestimate God. If we are faithful to God, he will cause great opposition to disappear. God can change the attitudes of those who oppose him.

5:2, 3 The rite of circumcision marked Israel's position as God's covenant people. When God made the original covenant with Abraham, he required that each male be circumcised as a sign of cutting off the old life and beginning a new life with God (Genesis 17:13). Other cultures at that time used circumcision as a sign of entry into adulthood, but only Israel used it as a sign of following God. A man would only be circumcised once. "Again" here refers to the fact that many of the young men were uncircumcised at this time (see 5:5).

5:8, 9 Located about two miles northeast of Jericho, Gilgal was Israel's base camp and their temporary centre of government and worship during their invasion of Canaan. Here the people renewed their commitment to God and covenant with him before attempting to conquer the new land. At Gilgal the angelic commander of the Lord's army appeared to Joshua with further instructions for battle and encouragement for the conquest (5:13–15). After the conquest, Gilgal continued to be an important place in Israel. It was here that Israel's first king, Saul, was crowned (1 Samuel 11:14, 15).

5:10 This joyous Passover was the first to be celebrated in the promised land and only the third celebrated by Israel since the exodus from Egypt. The last time was at the foot of Mount Sinai, 39 years earlier. This celebration reminded Israel of God's mighty miracles that brought them out of Egypt. There they had to eat in fear and haste; here they ate in celebration of God's blessings and promises. (See Exodus 12 for a description of the night the angel

5:11 [j]Nu 15:19 [k]Lev 23:14
5:12 [l]Ex 16:35
5:13 [m]Ge 18:2; 32:24 [n]Nu 22:23
5:14 [o]Ge 17:3
5:15 [p]Ex 3:5; Ac 7:33
6:1 [a]Jos 24:11
6:2 [b]Dt 7:24; Jos 2:9, 24; 8:1

the plains of Jericho, the Israelites celebrated the Passover. 11The day after the Passover, that very day, they ate some of the produce of the land:[j] unleavened bread and roasted grain.[k] 12The manna stopped the day after[d] they ate this food from the land; there was no longer any manna for the Israelites, but that year they ate of the produce of Canaan.[l]

B. CONQUERING THE PROMISED LAND (5:13 – 12:24)

After crossing the Jordan River, the Israelites begin to conquer Canaan. Jericho is the first to fall. Then Israel suffers its first defeat because of one man's disobedience. After the people remove the sin from their community, they strike again – this time with success. Soon great kings attack from the north and south, but they are defeated because God is with Israel. Evil could not be tolerated in the promised land, nor can it be tolerated in our lives. We, like Israel, must ruthlessly remove sin from our lives before it takes control of us.

1. Joshua attacks the centre of the land

The Fall of Jericho

13Now when Joshua was near Jericho, he looked up and saw a man[m] standing in front of him with a drawn sword[n] in his hand. Joshua went up to him and asked, "Are you for us or for our enemies?"

14"Neither," he replied, "but as commander of the army of the LORD I have now come." Then Joshua fell face down[o] to the ground in reverence, and asked him, "What message does my Lord[e] have for his servant?"

15The commander of the LORD's army replied, "Take off your sandals, for the place where you are standing is holy."[p] And Joshua did so.

6 Now Jericho[a] was tightly shut up because of the Israelites. No-one went out and no-one came in.

2Then the LORD said to Joshua, "See, I have delivered[b] Jericho into your hands, along with its king and its fighting men. 3March around the city once with all the armed men. Do this for six days. 4Make seven priests carry trumpets of rams' horns in front of the ark. On the seventh day, march around the city seven times, with the priests

[d] *12 Or the day* [e] *14 Or lord*

"passed over" the Israelites' homes.)

5:11, 12 God had miraculously supplied manna to the hungry Israelites during their 40 years in the desert (Exodus 16:14–31). In the bountiful promised land they no longer needed this daily food supply because the land was ready for planting and harvesting. God had miraculously provided food for the Israelites while they were in the desert; here he provided food from the land itself. Prayer is not an alternative to preparation, and faith is not a substitute for hard work. God can and does provide miraculously for his people as needed, but he also expects them to use their God-given talents and resources to provide for themselves. If your prayers have gone unanswered, perhaps what you need is within your reach. Pray instead for the wisdom to see it and the energy and motivation to do it.

5:14, 15 This was an angel of superior rank, the commander of the Lord's army. Some say he was an appearance of God in human form. As a sign of respect, Joshua took off his sandals. Although Joshua was Israel's leader, he was still subordinate to God, the absolute Leader. Awe and respect are the responses due to our holy God. How can we show respect for God? By our attitudes and actions. We should recognise God's power, authority, and deep love, and our actions must model our attitudes before others. Respect for God is just as important today as it was in Joshua's day, even though removing shoes is no longer our cultural way of showing it.

6:1 The city of Jericho, built thousands of years before Joshua was born, was one of the oldest cities in the world. In some places it had fortified walls up to 25 feet high and 20 feet thick. Soldiers standing guard on top of the walls could see for miles. Jericho was a symbol of military power and strength – the Canaanites considered it invincible. Israel would attack this city first, and its destruction would put the fear of Israel into the heart of every person in Canaan. The Canaanites saw Israel's God as a nature god because he parted the Jordan and as a war god because he defeated Sihon and Og. But the Canaanites did not consider him a fortress god – one who could prevail against a walled city. The defeat of Jericho showed not only that Israel's God was superior to the Canaanite gods, but also that he was invincible.

6:2–5 God told Joshua that Jericho was already delivered into his hands – the enemy was already defeated! What confidence Joshua must have had as he went into battle! Christians also fight against a defeated enemy. Our enemy, Satan, has been defeated by Christ (Romans 8:37–39; Hebrews 2:14, 15; 1 John 3:8). Although we still fight battles every day and sin runs rampant in the world, we have the assurance that the war has already been won. We do not have to be paralysed by the power of a defeated enemy; we can overcome him through Christ's power.

6:3–5 Why did God give Joshua all these complicated instructions for the battle? Several answers are possible: (1) God was making it undeniably clear that the battle would depend upon him, and not upon Israel's weapons and expertise. This is why priests carrying the ark, not soldiers, led the Israelites into battle. (2) God's method of taking the city accentuated the terror already felt in Jericho (2:9). (3) This strange military manoeuvre was a test of the Israelites' faith and their willingness to follow God completely. The blowing of the trumpets had a special significance. They had been instructed to blow the same trumpets used in the religious festivals in their battles to remind them that their victory would come from the Lord, not their own military might (Numbers 10:9).

blowing the trumpets.[c] 5When you hear them sound a long blast[d] on the trumpets,
make all the people give a loud shout;[e] then the wall of the city will collapse and
the people will go up, every man straight in."
6So Joshua son of Nun called the priests and said to them, "Take up the ark of the
covenant of the LORD and make seven priests carry trumpets in front of it." 7And he
ordered the people, "Advance[f]! March around the city, with the armed guard going
ahead of the ark of the LORD."
8When Joshua had spoken to the people, the seven priests carrying the seven
trumpets before the LORD went forward, blowing their trumpets, and the ark of the
LORD's covenant followed them. 9The armed guard marched ahead of the priests who
blew the trumpets, and the rear guard[g] followed the ark. All this time the trumpets
were sounding. 10But Joshua had commanded the people, "Do not give a war cry,
do not raise your voices, do not say a word until the day I tell you to shout. Then
shout![h]" 11So he had the ark of the LORD carried around the city, circling it once.
Then the people returned to camp and spent the night there.
12Joshua got up early the next morning and the priests took up the ark of the LORD.
13The seven priests carrying the seven trumpets went forward, marching before the
ark of the LORD and blowing the trumpets. The armed men went ahead of them and
the rear guard followed the ark of the LORD, while the trumpets kept sounding. 14So
on the second day they marched around the city once and returned to the camp. They
did this for six days.
15On the seventh day, they got up at daybreak and marched around the city seven
times in the same manner, except that on that day they circled the city seven times.[i]
16The seventh time around, when the priests sounded the trumpet blast, Joshua
commanded the people, "Shout! For the LORD has given you the city! 17The city and
all that is in it are to be devoted[a][j] to the LORD. Only Rahab the prostitute[b] and all
who are with her in her house shall be spared, because she hid[k] the spies we sent.
18But keep away from the devoted things,[l] so that you will not bring about your own
destruction by taking any of them. Otherwise you will make the camp of Israel liable
to destruction[m] and bring trouble[n] on it. 19All the silver and gold and the articles
of bronze and iron[o] are sacred to the LORD and must go into his treasury."
20When the trumpets sounded,[p] the people shouted, and at the sound of the
trumpet, when the people gave a loud shout,[q] the wall collapsed; so every man
charged straight in, and they took the city.[r] 21They devoted the city to the LORD and
destroyed[s] with the sword every living thing in it—men and women, young and old,
cattle, sheep and donkeys.
22Joshua said to the two men who had spied out the land, "Go into the prostitute's
house and bring her out and all who belong to her, in accordance with your oath to
her.[t]" 23So the young men who had done the spying went in and brought out Rahab,
her father and mother and brothers and all who belonged to her.[u] They brought out
her entire family and put them in a place outside the camp of Israel.
24Then they burned the whole city and everything in it, but they put the silver and
gold and the articles of bronze and iron[v] into the treasury of the LORD's house. 25But
Joshua spared Rahab the prostitute,[w] with her family and all who belonged to her,

a *17* The Hebrew term refers to the irrevocable giving over of things or persons to the LORD, often by totally destroying them; also in verses 18 and 21. b *17* Or possibly *innkeeper*; also in verses 22 and 25

6:4 [c]Lev 25:9; Nu 10:8
6:5 [d]Ex 19:13 [e]ver 20; 1Sa 4:5; Ps 42:4; Isa 42:13
6:7 [f]Ex 14:15
6:9 [g]ver 13; Isa 52:12
6:10 [h]ver 20
6:15 [i]1Ki 18:44
6:17 [j]Lev 27:28; Dt 20:17 [k]Jos 2:4
6:18 [l]Jos 7:1 [m]Jos 7:12 [n]Jos 7:25, 26
6:19 [o]ver 24; Nu 31:22
6:20 [p]Jdg 6:34; Jer 4:21; Am 2:2 [q]ver 5 [r]Heb 11:30
6:21 [s]Dt 20:16
6:22 [t]Jos 2:14; Heb 11:31
6:23 [u]Jos 2:13
6:24 [v]ver 19
6:25 [w]Heb 11:31

6:21 Why did God demand that the Israelites destroy almost everyone and everything in Jericho? He was carrying out severe judgment against the wickedness of the Canaanites. This judgment, or *ban*, usually required that everything be destroyed (Deuteronomy 12:2, 3; 13:12–18). Because of their evil practices and intense idolatry, the Canaanites were a stronghold of rebellion against God. This threat to the right kind of living that God required had to be removed. If not, it would affect all Israel like a cancerous growth (as it did in the sad story told in the book of Judges). A few people and some items in Jericho were not destroyed, but this was a special case. Rahab and her household were saved because she had faith in God and because she helped the Israelite spies. The silver and gold and articles of bronze and iron were kept, not to enrich the people, but to beautify the tabernacle and its services.

God's purpose in all this was to keep the people's faith and religion uncontaminated. He did not want the plunder to remind Israel of Canaanite practices.

God also wants us to be pure. He wants us to clean up our behaviour when we begin a new life with him. We must not let the desire for personal gain distract us from our spiritual purpose. We must also reject any objects that are reminders of a life of rebellion against God. (For more information on how Israel handled its plunder, see the note on Numbers 31:25–30.)

because she hid the men Joshua had sent as spies to Jericho[x]—and she lives among
the Israelites to this day.
26 At that time Joshua pronounced this solemn oath: "Cursed before the LORD is the
man who undertakes to rebuild this city, Jericho:

"At the cost of his firstborn son
  will he lay its foundations;
at the cost of his youngest
  will he set up its gates."[y]

27 So the LORD was with Joshua,[z] and his fame spread[a] throughout the land.

Achan's Sin

7 But the Israelites acted unfaithfully in regard to the devoted things;[a][a] Achan son
of Carmi, the son of Zimri,[b] the son of Zerah,[b] of the tribe of Judah, took some
of them. So the LORD's anger burned against Israel.
2 Now Joshua sent men from Jericho to Ai, which is near Beth Aven[c] to the east
of Bethel, and told them, "Go up and spy out the region." So the men went up and
spied out Ai.
3 When they returned to Joshua, they said, "Not all the people will have to go up
against Ai. Send two or three thousand men to take it and do not weary all the people,
for only a few men are there." 4 So about three thousand men went up; but they were
routed by the men of Ai,[d] 5 who killed about thirty-six of them. They chased the
Israelites from the city gate as far as the stone quarries[c] and struck them down on
the slopes. At this the hearts of the people melted[e] and became like water.
6 Then Joshua tore his clothes[f] and fell face down to the ground before the ark of
the LORD, remaining there till evening. The elders of Israel did the same, and sprinkled
dust[g] on their heads. 7 And Joshua said, "Ah, Sovereign LORD, why did you ever
bring this people across the Jordan to deliver us into the hands of the Amorites to
destroy us?[h] If only we had been content to stay on the other side of the Jordan! 8 O
Lord, what can I say, now that Israel has been routed by its enemies? 9 The Canaanites
and the other people of the country will hear about this and they will surround us and
wipe out our name from the earth.[i] What then will you do for your own great name?"

a *1* The Hebrew term refers to the irrevocable giving over of things or persons to the LORD, often by totally destroying them; also in verses 11, 12, 13 and 15. **b** *1* See Septuagint and 1 Chron. 2:6; Hebrew *Zabdi*; also in verses 17 and 18. **c** *5* Or *as far as Shebarim*

6:25 [x]Jos 2:6
6:26 [y]1Ki 16:34
6:27 [z]Ge 39:2; Jos 1:5 [a]Jos 9:1
7:1 [a]Jos 6:18 [b]Jos 22:20
7:2 [c]Jos 18:12; 1Sa 13:5; 14:23
7:4 [d]Lev 26:17; Dt 28:25
7:5 [e]Lev 26:36; Jos 2:9, 11; Eze 21:7; Na 2:10
7:6 [f]Ge 37:29 [g]1Sa 4:12; 2Sa 13:19; Ne 9:1; Job 2:12; La 2:10; Rev 18:19
7:7 [h]Ex 5:22
7:9 [i]Ex 32:12; Dt 9:28

6:26 This curse was fulfilled in 1 Kings 16:34 when a man, Hiel, rebuilt Jericho and consequently lost his oldest and youngest sons. It is very possible that Hiel sacrificed his sons and placed them in the foundation and gate masonry to ward off evil.

7:1 "The devoted things" refers to all the clothing, cattle, and other plunder that God said Israel should destroy when they conquered Jericho (see 6:17–19). It was not that they found a good use for something that was going to be thrown out anyway. This was a serious offence because it was in direct defiance to an explicit command of God (see Deuteronomy 20:16–18).

7:1ff Notice the results of Achan's sin: (1) many men died (7:5); (2) Israel's army melted in fear (7:5); (3) Joshua questioned God (7:7–9); (4) God threatened to withdraw his presence from the people (7:12); (5) Achan and his family had to be destroyed (7:24–26).

When Israel eliminated the sin from their community, these were the results: (1) encouragement from God (8:1); (2) God's presence in battle (8:1); (3) God's guidance and promise of victory (8:2); (4) God's permission to keep the plunder and livestock from the battle for themselves (8:2). Throughout Israel's history, blessings came when the people got rid of their sin. You will also experience victory when you turn from your sin and follow God's plan wholeheartedly.

7:6 Joshua and the elders tore their clothing and sprinkled dust on their heads as signs of deep mourning before God. They were confused by their defeat at the small city of Ai after the spectacular Jericho victory, so they went before God in deep humility and sorrow to receive his instructions. When our lives fall apart, we also should turn to God for direction and help. Like Joshua and the elders, we should humble ourselves so that we will be able to hear his words.

7:7 When Joshua first went against Ai (7:3), he did not consult God but relied on the strength of his army to defeat the small city. Only after Israel was defeated did they turn to God and ask what happened.

Too often we rely on our own skills and strength, especially when the task before us seems easy. We go to God only when the obstacles seem too great. However, only God knows what lies ahead. Consulting him, even when we are on a winning streak, may save us from grave mistakes or misjudgments. God may want us to learn lessons, remove pride, or consult others before he will work through us.

7:7–9 Imagine praying this way to God. This is not a formal church prayer; it is the prayer of a man who is afraid and confused by what is happening around him. Joshua poured out his real thoughts to God. Hiding your needs from God is ignoring the only one who can really help. God welcomes your honest prayers and wants you to express your true feelings to him. Any believer can become more honest in prayer by remembering that God is all-knowing and all-powerful and that his love is everlasting.

10The LORD said to Joshua, "Stand up! What are you doing down on your face?
11Israel has sinned; they have violated my covenant,[j] which I commanded them to
keep. They have taken some of the devoted things; they have stolen, they have lied,[k]
they have put them with their own possessions. 12That is why the Israelites cannot
stand against their enemies;[l] they turn their backs and run because they have been
made liable to destruction.[m] I will not be with you any more unless you destroy
whatever among you is devoted to destruction.
13"Go, consecrate the people. Tell them, 'Consecrate yourselves[n] in preparation
for tomorrow; for this is what the LORD, the God of Israel, says: That which is devoted
is among you, O Israel. You cannot stand against your enemies until you remove it.
14" 'In the morning, present yourselves tribe by tribe. The tribe that the LORD
takes[o] shall come forward clan by clan; the clan that the LORD takes shall come
forward family by family; and the family that the LORD takes shall come forward man
by man. 15He who is caught with the devoted things shall be destroyed by fire, along
with all that belongs to him.[p] He has violated the covenant[q] of the LORD and has
done a disgraceful thing in Israel!' "[r]
16Early the next morning Joshua had Israel come forward by tribes, and Judah was
taken. 17The clans of Judah came forward, and he took the Zerahites.[s] He had the
clan of the Zerahites come forward by families, and Zimri was taken. 18Joshua had
his family come forward man by man, and Achan son of Carmi, the son of Zimri,
the son of Zerah, of the tribe of Judah, was taken.
19Then Joshua said to Achan, "My son, give glory[t] to the LORD,[d] the God of
Israel, and give him the praise.[e] Tell[u] me what you have done; do not hide it from
me."
20Achan replied, "It is true! I have sinned against the LORD, the God of Israel. This
is what I have done: 21When I saw in the plunder a beautiful robe from Babylonia,[f]
two hundred shekels[g] of silver and a wedge of gold weighing fifty shekels,[h] I
coveted[v] them and took them. They are hidden in the ground inside my tent, with
the silver underneath."
22So Joshua sent messengers, and they ran to the tent, and there it was, hidden in
his tent, with the silver underneath. 23They took the things from the tent, brought them
to Joshua and all the Israelites and spread them out before the LORD.
24Then Joshua, together with all Israel, took Achan son of Zerah, the silver, the
robe, the gold wedge, his sons and daughters, his cattle, donkeys and sheep, his tent
and all that he had, to the Valley of Achor.[w] 25Joshua said, "Why have you brought
this trouble[x] on us? The LORD will bring trouble on you today."

d *19* A solemn charge to tell the truth e *19* Or *and confess to him* f *21* Hebrew *Shinar* g *21* That is, about 5 pounds (about 2.3 kilograms) h *21* That is, about 1¼ pounds (about 0.6 kilogram)

7:11 [j]Jos 6:17-19 [k]Ac 5:1-2
7:12 [l]Nu 14:45; Jdg 2:14 [m]Jos 6:18
7:13 [n]Jos 3:5; 6:18
7:14 [o]Pr 16:33
7:15 [p]1Sa 14:39 [q]ver 11 [r]Ge 34:7
7:17 [s]Nu 26:20
7:19 [t]1Sa 6:5; Jer 13:16; Jn 9:24* [u]1Sa 14:43
7:21 [v]Dt 7:25; Eph 5:5; 1Ti 6:10
7:24 [w]ver 26; Jos 15:7
7:25 [x]Jos 6:18

7:10–12 Why did Achan's sin bring judgment on the entire nation? Although it was one man's failure, God saw it as national disobedience to a national law. God needed the entire nation to be committed to the job they had agreed to do – conquer the land. Thus, when one person failed, everyone failed. If Achan's sin went unpunished, unlimited looting could break out. The nation as a whole had to take responsibility for preventing this undisciplined disobedience.

Achan's sin was not merely his keeping some of the plunder (God allowed it in some cases), but his disobeying God's explicit command to destroy everything connected with Jericho. His sin was indifference to the evil and idolatry of the city, not just a desire for money and clothes. God would not protect Israel's army again until the sin was removed and the army returned to obeying him without reservation. God is not content with our doing what is right some of the time. He wants us to do what is right all the time. We are under his orders to eliminate any thoughts, practices, or possessions that hinder our devotion to him.

7:13 "Consecrate yourselves" meant that the Israelites were to undergo purification rites like those mentioned in 3:5 when they were preparing to cross the Jordan River. Such rites prepared the people to approach God and constantly reminded them of their sinfulness and his holiness.

7:24, 25 Achan underestimated God and didn't take his commands seriously (6:18). It may have seemed a small thing to Achan, but the effects of his sin were felt by the entire nation, especially his family. Like Achan, our actions affect more people than just ourselves. Beware of the temptation to rationalise your sins by saying they are too small or too personal to hurt anyone but you.

7:24–26 Why did Achan's entire family pay for his sin? The biblical record does not tell us if they were accomplices to his crime, but in the ancient world, the family was treated as a whole. Achan, as the head of his family, was like a tribal chief. If he prospered, the family prospered with him. If he suffered, so did they. Many Israelites had already died in battle because of Achan's sin. Now he was to be completely cut off from Israel.

Achan's entire family was to be stoned along with him so that no trace of the sin would remain in Israel. In our permissive and individualistic culture we have a hard time understanding such a decree, but in ancient cultures it was a common punishment. The punishment fit the crime: Achan had disobeyed God's command to destroy everything in Jericho; thus everything that belonged to Achan had to be destroyed. Sin has drastic consequences, so we should take drastic measures to avoid it.

7:25 [y]Dt 17:5
7:26 [z]Nu 25:4; Dt 13:17 [a]ver 24; Isa 65:10; Hos 2:15
8:1 [a]Dt 31:6 [b]Dt 1:21; 7:18; Jos 1:9 [c]Jos 10:7 [d]Jos 6:2
8:2 [e]ver 27; Dt 20:14
8:7 [f]Jdg 7:7; 1Sa 23:4
8:8 [g]Jdg 20:29-38 [h]ver 19
8:9 [i]2Ch 13:13
8:10 [j]Ge 22:3 [k]Jos 7:6
8:14 [l]Dt 1:1

Then all Israel stoned him,[y] and after they had stoned the rest, they burned them.
26Over Achan they heaped up a large pile of rocks, which remains to this day. Then
the LORD turned from his fierce anger.[z] Therefore that place has been called the
Valley of Achor[i][a] ever since.

Ai Destroyed

8 Then the LORD said to Joshua, "Do not be afraid;[a] do not be discouraged.[b] Take
the whole army[c] with you, and go up and attack Ai. For I have delivered[d] into
your hands the king of Ai, his people, his city and his land. 2You shall do to Ai and
its king as you did to Jericho and its king, except that you may carry off their plunder
and livestock for yourselves.[e] Set an ambush behind the city."
3So Joshua and the whole army moved out to attack Ai. He chose thirty thousand
of his best fighting men and sent them out at night 4with these orders: "Listen
carefully. You are to set an ambush behind the city. Don't go very far from it. All
of you be on the alert. 5I and all those with me will advance on the city, and when
the men come out against us, as they did before, we will flee from them. 6They will
pursue us until we have lured them away from the city, for they will say, 'They are
running away from us as they did before.' So when we flee from them, 7you are to
rise up from ambush and take the city. The LORD your God will give it into your
hand.[f] 8When you have taken the city, set it on fire.[g] Do what the LORD has
commanded.[h] See to it; you have my orders."
9Then Joshua sent them off, and they went to the place of ambush[i] and lay in wait
between Bethel and Ai, to the west of Ai—but Joshua spent that night with the people.
10Early the next morning[j] Joshua mustered his men, and he and the leaders of
Israel[k] marched before them to Ai. 11The entire force that was with him marched up
and approached the city and arrived in front of it. They set up camp north of Ai, with
the valley between them and the city. 12Joshua had taken about five thousand men
and set them in ambush between Bethel and Ai, to the west of the city. 13They had
the soldiers take up their positions—all those in the camp to the north of the city and
the ambush to the west of it. That night Joshua went into the valley.
14When the king of Ai saw this, he and all the men of the city hurried out early
in the morning to meet Israel in battle at a certain place overlooking the Arabah.[l]

[i] 26 *Achor* means *trouble.*

8:1 After Israel had been cleansed from Achan's sin, Joshua prepared to attack Ai again—this time to win. Joshua had learned some lessons that we can follow: (1) confess your sins when God reveals them to you (7:19–21); (2) when you fail, refocus on God, deal with the problem, and move on (7:22–25; 8:1). God wants the cycle of sin, repentance, and forgiveness to strengthen us, not weaken us. The lessons we learn from our failures should make us better able to handle the same situation the second time around. Because God is eager to give us cleansing, forgiveness, and strength, the only way to lose is to give up. We can tell what kind of people we are by what we do on the second and third attempts.

8:2 Why did God allow the Israelites to keep the plunder and livestock this time? Israel's laws for handling the spoils of war covered two situations. (1) Cities like Jericho which were under God's *ban* (judgment for idolatry) could not be looted (see Deuteronomy 20:16–18). God's people were to be kept holy and separate from every influence of idolatry. (2) The distribution of plunder from cities not under the ban was a normal part of warfare. It provided the army and the nation with the necessary food, flocks, and weapons needed to sustain itself in wartime. Ai was not under the ban. The conquering army needed the food and equipment. Because soldiers were not paid, the loot was part of their incentive and reward for going to war.

8:3 The conquest of Ai was very important to the Israelites. Only 11 miles away from Jericho, Ai was a key stronghold for the Caananites and a buffer fortress for Bethel (8:12). If the Caananite kings got wind of an Israelite defeat at Ai, they could unite in a coordinated attack. They did not know that God had restored his power and protection to Joshua's troops. We must depend on God with absolute obedience to be sure of the victory he has promised.

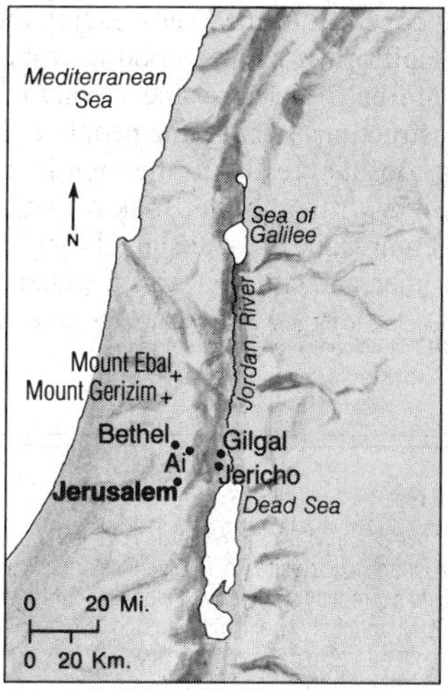

THE BATTLE FOR Ai
During the night, Joshua sent one detachment of soldiers to the west of Ai to lie in wait. The next morning he led a second group north of Ai. When the army of Ai attacked, the Israelites to the north pretended to scatter, only to turn on the enemy as the men lying in ambush moved in and burned the city.

But he did not know[m] that an ambush had been set against him behind the city.
15 Joshua and all Israel let themselves be driven back[n] before them, and they fled
towards the desert.[o] 16 All the men of Ai were called to pursue them, and they pursued
Joshua and were lured away[p] from the city. 17 Not a man remained in Ai or Bethel
who did not go after Israel. They left the city open and went in pursuit of Israel.
18 Then the LORD said to Joshua, "Hold out towards Ai the javelin[q] that is in your
hand,[r] for into your hand I will deliver the city." So Joshua held out his javelin[s]
towards Ai. 19 As soon as he did this, the men in the ambush rose quickly[t] from their
position and rushed forward. They entered the city and captured it and quickly set it
on fire.[u]
20 The men of Ai looked back and saw the smoke of the city rising against the sky,[v]
but they had no chance to escape in any direction, for the Israelites who had been
fleeing towards the desert had turned back against their pursuers. 21 For when Joshua
and all Israel saw that the ambush had taken the city and that smoke was going up
from the city, they turned round and attacked the men of Ai. 22 The men of the ambush
also came out of the city against them, so that they were caught in the middle, with
Israelites on both sides. Israel cut them down, leaving them neither survivors nor
fugitives.[w] 23 But they took the king of Ai alive[x] and brought him to Joshua.
24 When Israel had finished killing all the men of Ai in the fields and in the desert
where they had chased them, and when every one of them had been put to the sword,
all the Israelites returned to Ai and killed those who were in it. 25 Twelve thousand
men and women fell that day—all the people of Ai.[y] 26 For Joshua did not draw back
the hand that held out his javelin until he had destroyed[a][z] all who lived in Ai.[a] 27 But
Israel did carry off for themselves the livestock and plunder of this city, as the LORD
had instructed Joshua.[b]
28 So Joshua burned[c] Ai[d] and made it a permanent heap of ruins,[e] a desolate place
to this day.[f] 29 He hung the king of Ai on a tree and left him there until evening. At
sunset,[g] Joshua ordered them to take his body from the tree and throw it down at the
entrance of the city gate. And they raised a large pile of rocks[h] over it, which remains
to this day.

The Covenant Renewed at Mount Ebal

30 Then Joshua built on Mount Ebal[i] an altar[j] to the LORD, the God of Israel, 31 as
Moses the servant of the LORD had commanded the Israelites. He built it according
to what is written in the Book of the Law of Moses—an altar of uncut stones, on which
no iron tool[k] had been used. On it they offered to the LORD burnt offerings and
sacrificed fellowship offerings.[b][l] 32 There, in the presence of the Israelites, Joshua
copied on stones the law of Moses, which he had written.[m] 33 All Israel, aliens and
citizens[n] alike, with their elders, officials and judges, were standing on both sides
of the ark of the covenant of the LORD, facing those who carried it—the priests, who
were Levites.[o] Half of the people stood in front of Mount Gerizim and half of them
in front of Mount Ebal,[p] as Moses the servant of the LORD had formerly commanded
when he gave instructions to bless the people of Israel.
34 Afterwards, Joshua read all the words of the law—the blessings and the
curses—just as it is written in the Book of the Law.[q] 35 There was not a word of all
that Moses had commanded that Joshua did not read to the whole assembly of Israel,
including the women and children, and the aliens who lived among them.[r]

a *26* The Hebrew term refers to the irrevocable giving over of things or persons to the LORD, often by totally destroying them. b *31* Traditionally *peace offerings*

8:14 [m]Jdg 20:34
8:15 [n]Jdg 20:36 [o]Jos 15:61; 16:1; 18:12
8:16 [p]Jdg 20:31
8:18 [q]Job 41:26; Ps 35:3 [r]Ex 4:2; 14:16; 17:9-12 [s]ver 26
8:19 [t]Jdg 20:33 [u]ver 8
8:20 [v]Jdg 20:40
8:22 [w]Dt 7:2; Jos 10:1
8:23 [x]1Sa 15:8
8:25 [y]Dt 20:16-18
8:26 [z]Nu 21:2 [a]Ex 17:12
8:27 [b]ver 2
8:28 [c]Nu 31:10 [d]Jos 7:2; Jer 49:3 [e]Dt 13:16; Jos 10:1 [f]Ge 35:20
8:29 [g]Dt 21:23; Jn 19:31 [h]2Sa 18:17
8:30 [i]Dt 11:29 [j]Ex 20:24
8:31 [k]Ex 20:25 [l]Dt 27:6-7
8:32 [m]Dt 27:8
8:33 [n]Lev 16:29 [o]Dt 31:12 [p]Dt 11:29; 27:11-14
8:34 [q]Dt 28:61; 31:11; Jos 1:8
8:35 [r]Ex 12:38; Dt 31:12

8:18, 19 The Lord gave Joshua the city. Yesterday's defeat became today's victory. Once sin is dealt with, forgiveness and victory lie ahead. With God's direction we need not stay discouraged or burdened with guilt. No matter how difficult a setback sin may bring, we must renew our efforts to carry out God's will.

8:30, 31 The altar was to be built out of uncut stones so it would not be profaned (see Exodus 20:25). This would prevent the people from worshipping altars like idols, or worshipping the craftsmanship of the workers rather than the great works of God.

8:32 It was most likely the Ten Commandments (recorded in Exodus 20) that Joshua copied on stones. These were the heart of all God's laws, and they are still relevant today.

2. Joshua attacks the southern kings

The Gibeonite Deception

9 Now when all the kings west of the Jordan heard about these things—those in
the hill country, in the western foothills, and along the entire coast of the Great
Sea[a][a] as far as Lebanon (the kings of the Hittites, Amorites, Canaanites, Perizzites,
Hivites and Jebusites)[b]—2they came together to make war against Joshua and Israel.
3However, when the people of Gibeon[c] heard what Joshua had done to Jericho and
Ai, 4they resorted to a ruse: They went as a delegation whose donkeys were loaded[b]
with worn-out sacks and old wineskins, cracked and mended. 5The men put worn and
patched sandals on their feet and wore old clothes. All the bread of their food supply
was dry and mouldy. 6Then they went to Joshua in the camp at Gilgal[d] and said to
him and the men of Israel, "We have come from a distant country; make a treaty with
us."
7The men of Israel said to the Hivites,[e] "But perhaps you live near us. How then
can we make a treaty[f] with you?"
8"We are your servants,[g]" they said to Joshua.
But Joshua asked, "Who are you and where do you come from?"
9They answered: "Your servants have come from a very distant country[h] because
of the fame of the LORD your God. For we have heard reports[i] of him: all that he
did in Egypt, 10and all that he did to the two kings of the Amorites east of the
Jordan—Sihon king of Heshbon, and Og king of Bashan,[j] who reigned in Ashtaroth.[k] 11And our elders and all those living in our country said to us, 'Take provisions
for your journey; go and meet them and say to them, "We are your servants; make
a treaty with us." ' 12This bread of ours was warm when we packed it at home on the
day we left to come to you. But now see how dry and mouldy it is. 13And these
wineskins that we filled were new, but see how cracked they are. And our clothes and
sandals are worn out by the very long journey."
14The men of Israel sampled their provisions but did not enquire[l] of the LORD.
15Then Joshua made a treaty of peace[m] with them to let them live, and the leaders
of the assembly ratified it by oath.
16Three days after they made the treaty with the Gibeonites, the Israelites heard that
they were neighbours, living near them. 17So the Israelites set out and on the third
day came to their cities: Gibeon, Kephirah, Beeroth[n] and Kiriath Jearim.[o] 18But the
Israelites did not attack them, because the leaders of the assembly had sworn an oath[p]
to them by the LORD, the God of Israel.
The whole assembly grumbled[q] against the leaders, 19but all the leaders answered,
"We have given them our oath by the LORD, the God of Israel, and we cannot touch
them now. 20This is what we will do to them: We will let them live, so that wrath
will not fall on us for breaking the oath we swore to them." 21They continued, "Let
them live,[r] but let them be woodcutters and water-carriers[s] for the entire community." So the leaders' promise to them was kept.
22Then Joshua summoned the Gibeonites and said, "Why did you deceive us by

9:1 [a]Nu 34:6 [b]Ex 3:17; Jos 3:10
9:3 [c]ver 17; Jos 10:2; 2Sa 2:12; 2Ch 1:3; Isa 28:21
9:6 [d]Jos 5:10
9:7 [e]ver 1; Jos 11:19 [f]Ex 23:32; Dt 7:2
9:8 [g]Dt 20:11; 2Ki 10:5
9:9 [h]Dt 20:15 [i]ver 24; Jos 2:9
9:10 [j]Nu 21:33 [k]Nu 21:24, 35
9:14 [l]Nu 27:21
9:15 [m]Ex 23:32; Jos 11:19; 2Sa 21:2
9:17 [n]Jos 18:25 [o]1Sa 7:1-2
9:18 [p]Ps 15:4 [q]Ex 15:24
9:21 [r]ver 15 [s]Dt 29:11

a *1* That is, the Mediterranean **b** *4* Most Hebrew manuscripts; some Hebrew manuscripts, Vulgate and Syriac (see also Septuagint) *They prepared provisions and loaded their donkeys*

9:1–6 As the news about their victory became widespread, the Israelites experienced opposition in two forms: direct (kings in the area began to unite against them); and indirect (the Gibeonites resorted to deception). We can expect similar opposition as we obey God's commands. To guard against these pressures, we must rely on God and communicate daily with him. He will give us strength to endure the direct pressures and wisdom to see through the trickery.

9:14–17 When the leaders sampled these men's provisions, they saw that the bread was dry and mouldy, the wineskins were cracked, and the clothes and sandals worn out. But they did not see through the deception. After the promise had been made and the treaty ratified, the facts came out—Israel's leaders had been deceived. God had specifically instructed Israel to make no treaties with the inhabitants of Canaan (Exodus 23:32; 34:12; Numbers 33:55; Deuteronomy 7:2; 20:17, 18). As a strategist, Joshua knew enough to talk to God before leading his troops into battle. But the peace treaty seemed innocent enough, so Joshua and the leaders made this decision on their own. By failing to seek God's guidance and rushing ahead with their own plans, they had to deal with angry people and an awkward alliance.

9:19, 20 Joshua and his advisers had made a mistake. But because they had given an oath to protect the Gibeonites, they would keep their word. The oath was not nullified by the Gibeonites' trickery. God had commanded that oaths be kept (Leviticus 5:4; 27:1, 28), and breaking an oath was serious. This encourages us not to take our promises lightly.

saying, 'We live a long way[t] from you,' while actually you live near[u] us? 23 You
are now under a curse:[v] You will never cease to serve as woodcutters and water-
carriers for the house of my God."
24 They answered Joshua, "Your servants were clearly told[w] how the LORD your
God had commanded his servant Moses to give you the whole land and to wipe out
all its inhabitants from before you. So we feared for our lives because of you, and
that is why we did this. 25 We are now in your hands.[x] Do to us whatever seems good
and right to you."
26 So Joshua saved them from the Israelites, and they did not kill them. 27 That day
he made the Gibeonites woodcutters and water-carriers for the community and for the
altar of the LORD at the place the LORD would choose.[y] And that is what they are
to this day.

The Sun Stands Still

10 Now Adoni-Zedek king of Jerusalem[a] heard that Joshua had taken Ai[b] and
totally destroyed[a c] it, doing to Ai and its king as he had done to Jericho and
its king, and that the people of Gibeon had made a treaty of peace[d] with Israel and
were living near them. 2 He and his people were very much alarmed at this, because
Gibeon was an important city, like one of the royal cities; it was larger than Ai, and
all its men were good fighters. 3 So Adoni-Zedek king of Jerusalem appealed to Hoham
king of Hebron,[e] Piram king of Jarmuth, Japhia king of Lachish[f] and Debir king
of Eglon. 4 "Come up and help me attack Gibeon," he said, "because it has made
peace[g] with Joshua and the Israelites."
5 Then the five kings of the Amorites[h]—the kings of Jerusalem, Hebron, Jarmuth,
Lachish and Eglon—joined forces. They moved up with all their troops and took up
positions against Gibeon and attacked it.
6 The Gibeonites then sent word to Joshua in the camp at Gilgal: "Do not abandon
your servants. Come up to us quickly and save us! Help us, because all the Amorite
kings from the hill country have joined forces against us."
7 So Joshua marched up from Gilgal with his entire army,[i] including all the best
fighting men. 8 The LORD said to Joshua, "Do not be afraid[j] of them; I have given
them into your hand. Not one of them will be able to withstand you."
9 After an all-night march from Gilgal, Joshua took them by surprise. 10 The LORD
threw them into confusion before Israel,[k] who defeated them in a great victory at
Gibeon. Israel pursued them along the road going up to Beth Horon[l] and cut them
down all the way to Azekah[m] and Makkedah. 11 As they fled before Israel on the road

a 1 The Hebrew term refers to the irrevocable giving over of things or persons to the LORD, often by totally destroying them; also in verses 28, 35, 37, 39 and 40.

9:22 [t] ver 6 [u] ver 16
9:23 [v] Ge 9:25
9:24 [w] ver 9
9:25 [x] Ge 16:6
9:27 [y] Dt 12:5
10:1 [a] Jdg 1:7 [b] Jos 8:1 [c] Dt 20:16; Jos 8:22 [d] Jos 9:15
10:3 [e] Ge 13:18 [f] 2Ch 11:9; 25:27; Ne 11:30; Isa 36:2; 37:8; Jer 34:7; Mic 1:13
10:4 [g] Jos 9:15
10:5 [h] Nu 13:29
10:7 [i] Jos 8:1
10:8 [j] Dt 3:2; Jos 1:9
10:10 [k] Dt 7:23 [l] Jos 16:3, 5 [m] Jos 15:35

10:5-8 This alliance of enemy kings from the south actually helped Joshua and his army. Because the enemies had united to attack Gibeon, Joshua didn't have to spend the time and resources required to wage separate campaigns against each fortified city represented in the coalition. Joshua confidently confronted this coalition of armies and defeated them in a single battle because he trusted God to give Israel the victory.

10:6, 7 Joshua's response shows his integrity. After having been deceived by the Gibeonites, Joshua and the leaders could have been slow about their attempt to rescue them. Instead, they immediately responded to their call for help. How willing would you be to help someone who had deceived you, even though you had forgiven him or her? We should take our word just as seriously as Joshua did.

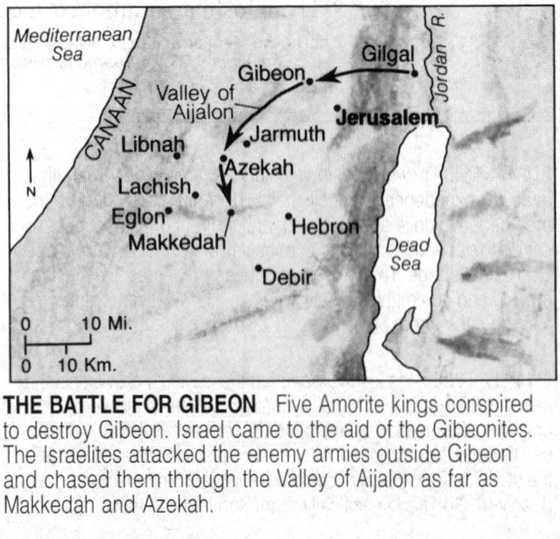

THE BATTLE FOR GIBEON Five Amorite kings conspired to destroy Gibeon. Israel came to the aid of the Gibeonites. The Israelites attacked the enemy armies outside Gibeon and chased them through the Valley of Aijalon as far as Makkedah and Azekah.

10:11 [n]Ps 18:12; Isa 28:2, 17

down from Beth Horon to Azekah, the LORD hurled large hailstones[n] down on them from the sky, and more of them died from the hailstones than were killed by the swords of the Israelites.
12On the day the LORD gave the Amorites[o] over to Israel, Joshua said to the LORD in the presence of Israel:

10:12 [o]Am 2:9 [p]Jdg 1:35; 12:12

"O sun, stand still over Gibeon,
O moon, over the Valley of Aijalon.[p]"
13So the sun stood still,[q]
and the moon stopped,
till the nation avenged itself on[b] its enemies,

10:13 [q]Hab 3:11 [r]2Sa 1:18 [s]Isa 38:8

as it is written in the Book of Jashar.[r]
The sun stopped[s] in the middle of the sky and delayed going down about a full day. 14There has never been a day like it before or since, a day when the LORD listened to a man. Surely the LORD was fighting[t] for Israel!
15Then Joshua returned with all Israel to the camp at Gilgal.[u]

10:14 [t]ver 42; Ex 14:14; Dt 1:30; Ps 106:43; 136:24

Five Amorite Kings Killed

16Now the five kings had fled and hidden in the cave at Makkedah. 17When Joshua was told that the five kings had been found hiding in the cave at Makkedah, 18he said, "Roll large rocks up to the mouth of the cave, and post some men there to guard it.
19But don't stop! Pursue your enemies, attack them from the rear and don't let them reach their cities, for the LORD your God has given them into your hand."
20So Joshua and the Israelites destroyed them completely[v]—almost to a man—but the few who were left reached their fortified cities. 21The whole army then returned safely to Joshua in the camp at Makkedah, and no-one uttered a word against the Israelites.
22Joshua said, "Open the mouth of the cave and bring those five kings out to me."
23So they brought the five kings out of the cave—the kings of Jerusalem, Hebron, Jarmuth, Lachish and Eglon. 24When they had brought these kings to Joshua, he summoned all the men of Israel and said to the army commanders who had come with him, "Come here and put your feet[w] on the necks of these kings." So they came forward and placed their feet[x] on their necks.
25Joshua said to them, "Do not be afraid; do not be discouraged. Be strong and courageous.[y] This is what the LORD will do to all the enemies you are going to fight."
26Then Joshua struck and killed the kings and hung them on five trees, and they were left hanging on the trees until evening.
27At sunset[z] Joshua gave the order and they took them down from the trees and threw them into the cave where they had been hiding. At the mouth of the cave they placed large rocks, which are there to this day.

10:15 [u]ver 43

10:20 [v]Dt 20:16

10:24 [w]Mal 4:3 [x]Ps 110:1

10:25 [y]Dt 31:6

10:27 [z]Dt 21:23; Jos 8:9, 29

b 13 *Or nation triumphed over*

10:12–14 How did the sun stand still? Of course, in relation to the earth the sun always stands still—it is the earth that travels around the sun. But the terminology used in Joshua should not cause us to doubt the miracle. After all, we are not confused when someone tells us the sun rises or sets. The point is that the day was prolonged, not that God used a particular method to prolong it.

Two explanations have been given for how this event occurred: (1) A slowing of the earth's normal rotation gave Joshua more time, as the original Hebrew language seems to indicate. (2) Some unusual refraction of the sun's rays gave additional hours of light. Regardless of God's chosen method, the Bible is clear that the day was prolonged by a miracle, and that God's intervention turned the tide of battle for his people.

10:13 The Book of Jashar (also mentioned in 2 Samuel 1:18) was probably a collection of historical events put to music. Many parts of the Bible contain quotations from previous books, songs, poems, or other spoken and written materials. Because God guided the writer of this book to select this material, his message comes with divine authority.

10:24 Placing a foot on the neck of a captive was a common military practice in the ancient Near East. It symbolised the victor's domination of his captives. These proud kings had boasted of their power. Now all Israel could see that God was superior to any earthly army.

10:25 With God's help, Israel won the battle against five Amorite armies. Such a triumph was part of God's daily business as he worked with his people for victory. Joshua told his men never to be afraid because God would give them similar victories over all their enemies. God has often protected us and won victories for us. The same God who empowered Joshua and who has led us in the past will help us with our present and future needs. Reminding ourselves of his help in the past will give us hope for the struggles that lie ahead.

28That day Joshua took Makkedah. He put the city and its king to the sword and
totally destroyed everyone in it. He left no survivors.[a] And he did to the king of
Makkedah as he had done to the king of Jericho.[b]

Southern Cities Conquered

29Then Joshua and all Israel with him moved on from Makkedah to Libnah and
attacked it. 30The LORD also gave that city and its king into Israel's hand. The city
and everyone in it Joshua put to the sword. He left no survivors there. And he did
to its king as he had done to the king of Jericho.
31Then Joshua and all Israel with him moved on from Libnah to Lachish; he took
up positions against it and attacked it. 32The LORD handed Lachish over to Israel, and
Joshua took it on the second day. The city and everyone in it he put to the sword,
just as he had done to Libnah. 33Meanwhile, Horam king of Gezer[c] had come up
to help Lachish, but Joshua defeated him and his army – until no survivors were left.
34Then Joshua and all Israel with him moved on from Lachish to Eglon; they took
up positions against it and attacked it. 35They captured it that same day and put it to
the sword and totally destroyed everyone in it, just as they had done to Lachish.
36Then Joshua and all Israel with him went up from Eglon to Hebron[d] and attacked
it. 37They took the city and put it to the sword, together with its king, its villages and
everyone in it. They left no survivors. Just as at Eglon, they totally destroyed it and
everyone in it.
38Then Joshua and all Israel with him turned round and attacked Debir.[e] 39They
took the city, its king and its villages, and put them to the sword. Everyone in it they
totally destroyed. They left no survivors. They did to Debir and its king as they had
done to Libnah and its king and to Hebron.
40So Joshua subdued the whole region, including the hill country, the Negev,[f] the
western foothills and the mountain slopes,[g] together with all their kings.[h] He left
no survivors. He totally destroyed all who breathed, just as the LORD, the God of
Israel, had commanded.[i] 41Joshua subdued them from Kadesh Barnea[j] to Gaza[k]
and from the whole region of Goshen[l] to Gibeon. 42All these kings and their lands
Joshua conquered in one campaign, because the LORD, the God of Israel, fought[m] for
Israel.
43Then Joshua returned with all Israel to the camp at Gilgal.[n]

3. Joshua attacks the northern kings

11 When Jabin[a] king of Hazor[b] heard of this, he sent word to Jobab king of
Madon, to the kings of Shimron[c] and Acshaph, 2and to the northern kings who
were in the mountains, in the Arabah[d] south of Kinnereth,[e] in the western foothills
and in Naphoth Dor[a][f] on the west; 3to the Canaanites in the east and west; to the
Amorites, Hittites, Perizzites and Jebusites in the hill country; and to the Hivites[g]
below Hermon in the region of Mizpah.[h] 4They came out with all their troops and
a large number of horses and chariots – a huge army, as numerous as the sand on the
seashore.[i] 5All these kings joined forces[j] and made camp together at the Waters
of Merom, to fight against Israel.
6The LORD said to Joshua, "Do not be afraid of them, because by this time tomorrow

[a] 2 *Or in the heights of Dor*

10:28 [a]Dt 20:16 [b]Jos 6:21
10:33 [c]Jos 16:3, 10; Jdg 1:29; 1Ki 9:15
10:36 [d]Jos 14:13; 15:13; Jdg 1:10
10:38 [e]Jos 15:15; Jdg 1:11
10:40 [f]Ge 12:9; Jos 12:8 [g]Dt 1:7 [h]Dt 7:24 [i]Dt 20:16-17
10:41 [j]Ge 14:7 [k]Ge 10:19 [l]Jos 11:16; 15:51
10:42 [m]ver 14
10:43 [n]ver 15; Jos 5:9
11:1 [a]Jdg 4:2, 7, 23 [b]ver 10; 1Sa 12:9 [c]Jos 19:15
11:2 [d]Jos 12:3 [e]Nu 34:11 [f]Jos 17:11; Jdg 1:27; 1Ki 4:11
11:3 [g]Dt 7:1; Jdg 3:3, 5; 1Ki 9:20 [h]Ge 31:49; Jos 15:38; 18:26
11:4 [i]Jdg 7:12; 1Sa 13:5
11:5 [j]Jdg 5:19

10:32 Notice that in every Israelite victory, the text gives the credit to the Lord. All of Israel's victories came from God. When we are successful, the temptation is to take all the credit and glory as though we did it by ourselves, in our own strength. In reality, *God* gives us the victories; and he alone delivers us from our enemies. We should give him the credit and praise him for his goodness.

10:40–43 God had commanded Joshua to take the leadership in ridding the land of sin so God's people could occupy it. Joshua did his part thoroughly – leading the united army to weaken the inhabitants. When God orders us to stop sinning, we must not pause to debate, consider the options, negotiate a compromise, or rationalise. Instead, like Joshua, our response must be swift and complete. We must be ruthless in avoiding relationships and activities that can lead us into sin.

11:1–5 There were two kings of Hazor named Jabin. The other, apparently a weak ruler, is mentioned in Judges 4:2, 3. The Jabin of this story was quite powerful because he was able to build an alliance with dozens of kings. By all appearances, Jabin had a clear advantage over Joshua and his outnumbered forces. But those who honour God can be victorious regardless of the odds.

11:6 [k]Jos 10:8 [l]2Sa 8:4
11:8 [m]Jos 13:6
11:11 [n]Dt 20:16-17
11:12 [o]Nu 33:50-52; Dt 7:2
11:14 [p]Nu 31:11-12
11:15 [q]Ex 34:11; Jos 1:7
11:16 [r]Jos 10:41
11:17 [s]Jos 12:7 [t]Dt 7:24
11:19 [u]Jos 9:3
11:20 [v]Ex 14:17; Ro 9:18 [w]Dt 7:16; Jdg 14:4
11:21 [x]Nu 13:22, 33; Dt 9:2

I will hand all of them over[k] to Israel, slain. You are to hamstring[l] their horses and
burn their chariots."
7So Joshua and his whole army came against them suddenly at the Waters of Merom
and attacked them, 8and the LORD gave them into the hand of Israel. They defeated
them and pursued them all the way to Greater Sidon, to Misrephoth Maim,[m] and to
the Valley of Mizpah on the east, until no survivors were left. 9Joshua did to them
as the LORD had directed: He hamstrung their horses and burned their chariots.
10At that time Joshua turned back and captured Hazor and put its king to the sword.
(Hazor had been the head of all these kingdoms.) 11Everyone in it they put to the
sword. They totally destroyed[b] them, not sparing anything that breathed,[n] and he
burned up Hazor itself.
12Joshua took all these royal cities and their kings and put them to the sword. He
totally destroyed them, as Moses the servant of the LORD had commanded.[o] 13Yet
Israel did not burn any of the cities built on their mounds—except Hazor, which
Joshua burned. 14The Israelites carried off for themselves all the plunder and livestock
of these cities, but all the people they put to the sword until they completely destroyed
them, not sparing anyone that breathed.[p] 15As the LORD commanded his servant
Moses, so Moses commanded Joshua, and Joshua did it; he left nothing undone of
all that the LORD commanded Moses.[q]

4. Summary of conquests

16So Joshua took this entire land: the hill country, all the Negev, the whole region
of Goshen, the western foothills,[r] the Arabah and the mountains of Israel with their
foothills, 17from Mount Halak, which rises towards Seir, to Baal Gad in the Valley
of Lebanon[s] below Mount Hermon. He captured all their kings and struck them
down, putting them to death.[t] 18Joshua waged war against all these kings for a long
time. 19Except for the Hivites living in Gibeon,[u] not one city made a treaty of peace
with the Israelites, who took them all in battle. 20For it was the LORD himself who
hardened their hearts[v] to wage war against Israel, so that he might destroy them
totally, exterminating them without mercy, as the LORD had commanded Moses.[w]
21At that time Joshua went and destroyed the Anakites[x] from the hill country: from

b *11* The Hebrew term refers to the irrevocable giving over of things or persons to the LORD, often by totally destroying them; also in verses 12, 20 and 21.

THE BATTLE FOR HAZOR
Kings from the north joined together to battle against the Israelites who controlled the southern half of Canaan. They gathered by the Waters of Merom, but Joshua attacked them by surprise—the enemies' chariots were useless in the dense forests. Hazor, the largest Canaanite centre in Galilee, was destroyed.

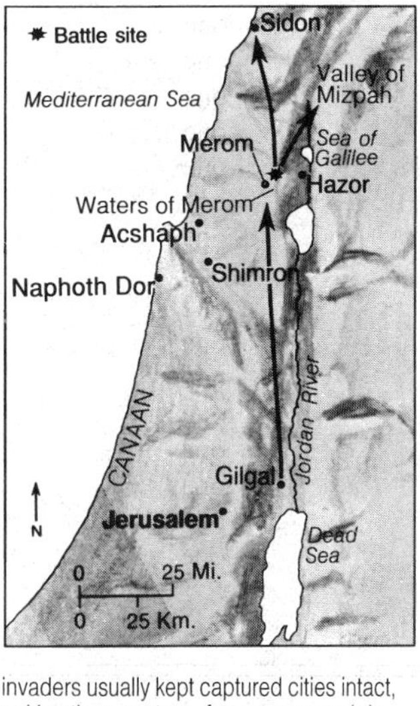

11:10–13 Victorious invaders usually kept captured cities intact, moving into them and making them centres of commerce and defence. For example, Moses predicted in Deuteronomy 6:10–12 that Israel would occupy cities they themselves had not built. Hazor, however, was burned. As a former capital of the land, it symbolised the wicked culture that Israel had come to destroy. In addition, its capture and destruction broke the backbone of the federation and weakened the will of the people to resist.

11:15 Joshua carefully obeyed all the instructions given by God. This theme of obedience is repeated frequently in the book of Joshua, partly because obedience is one aspect of life the individual believer can control. We can't always control our understanding because we may not have all the facts. We can't control what other people do or how they treat us. However, we can control our choice to obey God. Whatever new challenges we may face, the Bible contains relevant instructions that we can choose to ignore or choose to follow.

11:18 The conquest of much of the land of Canaan seems to have happened quickly (we can read about it in one sitting), but it actually took seven years. We often expect quick changes in our lives and quick victories over sin. But our journey with God is a lifelong process, and the changes and victories may take time. It is easy to grow impatient with God and feel like giving up hope because things are moving too slowly. When we are close to a situation, it is difficult to see progress. But when we look back we can see that God never stopped working.

11:21, 22 The Anakites were the tribes of giants the Israelite spies described when they gave their negative report on the promised land (Numbers 13, 14). This time the people did not let their fear of the giants prevent them from engaging in battle and claiming the land God had promised.

Hebron, Debir and Anab, from all the hill country of Judah, and from all the hill
country of Israel. Joshua totally destroyed them and their towns. 22 No Anakites were
left in Israelite territory; only in Gaza, Gath[y] and Ashdod[z] did any survive. 23 So
Joshua took the entire land,[a] just as the LORD had directed Moses, and he gave it
as an inheritance[b] to Israel according to their tribal divisions.[c]
Then the land had rest from war.[d]

List of Defeated Kings

12 These are the kings of the land whom the Israelites had defeated and whose
territory they took over east of the Jordan, from the Arnon Gorge to Mount
Hermon,[a] including all the eastern side of the Arabah:

2 Sihon king of the Amorites,
who reigned in Heshbon. He ruled from Aroer on the rim of the Arnon
Gorge — from the middle of the gorge — to the Jabbok River, which is the border
of the Ammonites. This included half of Gilead.[b] 3 He also ruled over the eastern
Arabah from the Sea of Kinnereth[a][c] to the Sea of the Arabah (the Salt Sea[b]),
to Beth Jeshimoth,[d] and then southward below the slopes of Pisgah.

4 And the territory of Og king of Bashan,[e]
one of the last of the Rephaites, who reigned in Ashtaroth[f] and Edrei. 5 He ruled
over Mount Hermon, Salecah,[g] all of Bashan to the border of the people of
Geshur[h] and Maacah,[i] and half of Gilead to the border of Sihon king of
Heshbon.

6 Moses, the servant of the LORD, and the Israelites conquered them. And Moses
the servant of the LORD gave their land to the Reubenites, the Gadites and the half-tribe
of Manasseh to be their possession.[j]
7 These are the kings of the land that Joshua and the Israelites conquered on the west
side of the Jordan, from Baal Gad in the Valley of Lebanon[k] to Mount Halak, which
rises towards Seir (their lands Joshua gave as an inheritance to the tribes of Israel
according to their tribal divisions — 8 the hill country, the western foothills, the Arabah, the mountain slopes, the desert and the Negev[l] — the lands of the Hittites,
Amorites, Canaanites, Perizzites, Hivites and Jebusites):

9 the king of Jericho[m]	one
the king of Ai[n] (near Bethel)	one
10 the king of Jerusalem[o]	one
the king of Hebron	one
11 the king of Jarmuth	one
the king of Lachish	one
12 the king of Eglon	one
the king of Gezer[p]	one
13 the king of Debir	one
the king of Geder	one
14 the king of Hormah	one
the king of Arad[q]	one
15 the king of Libnah	one
the king of Adullam	one
16 the king of Makkedah	one
the king of Bethel[r]	one
17 the king of Tappuah	one
the king of Hepher[s]	one
18 the king of Aphek[t]	one

a *3* That is, Galilee **b** *3* That is, the Dead Sea

11:22 [y] 1Sa 17:4; 1Ki 2:39; 1Ch 8:13 [z] 1Sa 5:1; Isa 20:1
11:23 [a] Jos 21:43-45 [b] Dt 1:38; 12:9-10; 25:19 [c] Nu 26:53 [d] Jos 14:15
12:1 [a] Dt 3:8
12:2 [b] Dt 2:36
12:3 [c] Jos 11:2 [d] Jos 13:20
12:4 [e] Nu 21:21, 33; Dt 3:11 [f] Dt 1:4
12:5 [g] Dt 3:10 [h] 1Sa 27:8 [i] Dt 3:14
12:6 [j] Nu 32:29, 33; Jos 13:8
12:7 [k] Jos 11:17
12:8 [l] Jos 11:16
12:9 [m] Jos 6:2 [n] Jos 8:29
12:10 [o] Jos 10:23
12:12 [p] Jos 10:33
12:14 [q] Nu 21:1
12:16 [r] Jos 7:2
12:17 [s] 1Ki 4:10
12:18 [t] Jos 13:4

12:1ff Chapter 12 is a summary of the first half of the book of Joshua. It lists the kings and nations conquered by Joshua to both the east and the west of the Jordan River. As long as the people trusted and obeyed God, one evil nation after another fell in defeat.

12:20 *u*Jos 11:1
12:22 *v*Jos 19:37; 20:7; 21:32 *w*1Sa 15:12
12:23 *x*Jos 11:2
12:24 *y*Ps 135:11; Dt 7:24

the king of Lasharon one
19 the king of Madon one
the king of Hazor one
20 the king of Shimron Meron one
the king of Acshaph[u] one
21 the king of Taanach one
the king of Megiddo one
22 the king of Kedesh[v] one
the king of Jokneam in Carmel[w] one
23 the king of Dor (in Naphoth Dor[c x]) one
the king of Goyim in Gilgal one
24 the king of Tirzah one
thirty-one kings in all.[y]

c 23 Or *in the heights of Dor*

THE CONQUERED LAND
Joshua displayed brilliant military strategy in the way he went about conquering the land of Canaan. He first captured the well-fortified Jericho to gain a foothold in Canaan and to demonstrate the awesome might of the God of Israel. Then he gained the hill country around Bethel and Gibeon. From there he subdued towns in the lowlands. Then his army conquered important cities in the north, such as Hazor. In all, Israel conquered land both east (12:1–6) and west (12:7–24) of the Jordan River; from Mount Hermon in the north to beyond the Negev to Mount Halak in the south. Thirty-one kings and their cities had been defeated. The Israelites had over-powered the Hittites, the Amorites, the Canaanites, the Perizzites, the Hivites, and the Jebusites. Other peoples living in Canaan were yet to be conquered.

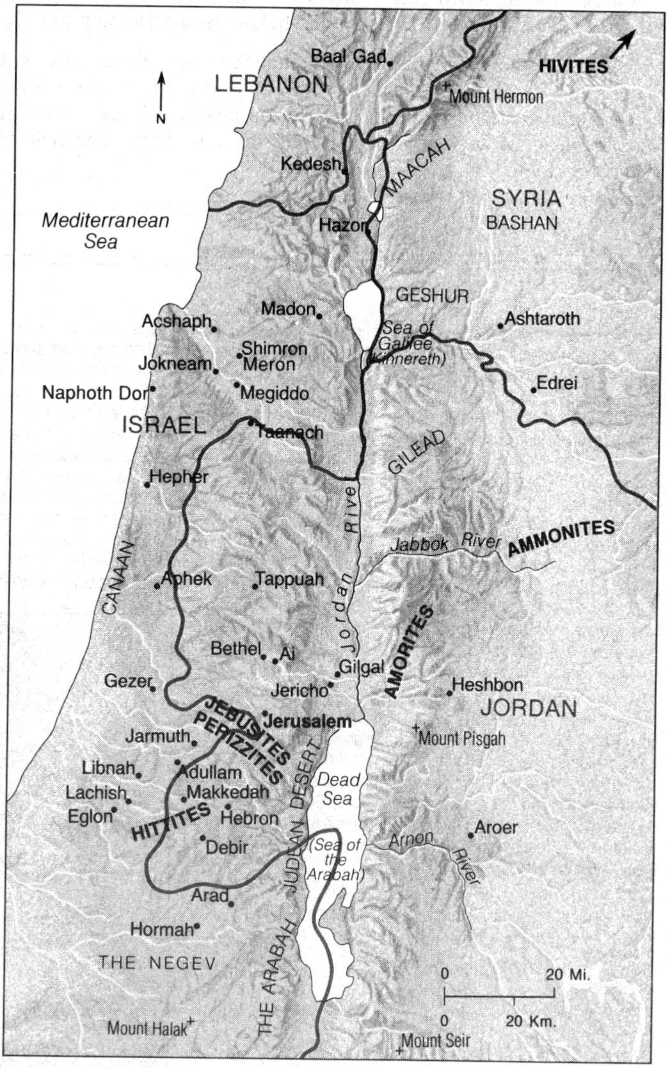

C. DIVIDING THE PROMISED LAND (13:1—24:33)

After seven years of battle, Israel gained control of the land, which was then divided and allotted to the tribes. Joshua dismisses the army, for it was now each tribe's responsibility to clear out the remaining enemies from their own areas. Joshua continues to encourage the people to remain faithful to God so they can remain in the land. The promised land was Israel's earthly inheritance. But Israel also had a spiritual inheritance in which we can share when we live a life of faithfulness to God.

1. The tribes receive their land

Land Still to Be Taken

13 When Joshua was old and well advanced in years,[a] the LORD said to him, "You
are very old, and there are still very large areas of land to be taken over.
2"This is the land that remains: all the regions of the Philistines and Geshurites:
3from the Shihor River[b] on the east of Egypt to the territory of Ekron[c] on the
north, all of it counted as Canaanite (the territory of the five Philistine rulers[d]
in Gaza, Ashdod, Ashkelon, Gath and Ekron—that of the Avvites);[e] 4from the
south, all the land of the Canaanites, from Arah of the Sidonians as far as
Aphek,[f] the region of the Amorites,[g] 5the area of the Gebalites;[a][h] and all
Lebanon[i] to the east, from Baal Gad below Mount Hermon to Lebo[b] Hamath.
6"As for all the inhabitants of the mountain regions from Lebanon to Misrephoth
Maim,[j] that is, all the Sidonians, I myself will drive them out before the Israelites.
Be sure to allocate this land to Israel for an inheritance, as I have instructed you,[k]
7and divide it as an inheritance[l] among the nine tribes and half of the tribe of
Manasseh."

a 5 That is, the area of Byblos b 5 *Or to the entrance to*

13:1 [a]Ge 24:1; Jos 14:10
13:3 [b]Jer 2:18 [c]Jdg 1:18 [d]Jdg 3:3 [e]Dt 2:23
13:4 [f]Jos 12:18; 19:30 [g]Am 2:10
13:5 [h]1Ki 5:18; Ps 83:7; Eze 27:9 [i]Jos 12:7
13:6 [j]Jos 11:8 [k]Nu 33:54
13:7 [l]Jos 11:23; Ps 78:55

13–19 The following chapters describe how the promised land was to be divided among the 12 tribes. First, the tribe of Levi was not to have any land because they were to spend all their energies serving the people, not their own interests (13:14; 21). Second, the tribes of Reuben and Gad and the half-tribe of Manasseh had already received land east of the Jordan River, which had been given to them by Moses (Numbers 32). Third, the tribes of Judah and Joseph (Ephraim and the other half-tribe of Manasseh) had received land that their ancestor Jacob had promised them 450 years earlier (Genesis 48:22; Joshua 15–17). The rest of the tribes divided up the remaining land by casting lots (chapter 18).

Through Jacob's original blessing of his sons (Genesis 49) and Moses' blessing of the 12 tribes (Deuteronomy 33), the type of land each tribe would receive was already known. The two blessings were prophetic, for although Joshua cast lots to determine the land to be given to each of the remaining tribes, the allotments came out just as Jacob and Moses had predicted.

13:1 Joshua was getting old—he was between 85 and 100 years of age at this time. God, however, still had work for him to do. Our culture often glorifies the young and strong and sets aside those who are older. Yet older people are filled with the wisdom that comes with experience. They are very capable of serving if given the chance and should be encouraged to do so. Believers are never allowed to retire from God's service. Those past retirement age should not assume that age alone disqualifies or excuses them from serving God.

13:7 Much of the land was unconquered at this point, but God's plan was to go ahead and include it in the divisions among the tribes. God's desire was that it would eventually be conquered by the Israelites. God knows the future, and as he leads you he already knows about the victories that lie ahead. But just as the Israelites still had to go to battle and fight, we must still face the trials and fight the battles of our unconquered land.

What are our unconquered lands? They may be overseas missionary territories, new languages in which to translate the Bible, new missionary areas in our neighbourhoods, interest groups or institutions that need redemptive work, unchallenged public problems or ethical issues, unconfessed sin in our lives, or underdeveloped talents and resources. What territory has God given you to conquer? This territory is your "promised land". Our inheritance will be a new heaven and a new earth (Revelation 21:1) if we fulfil the mission God has given us to do.

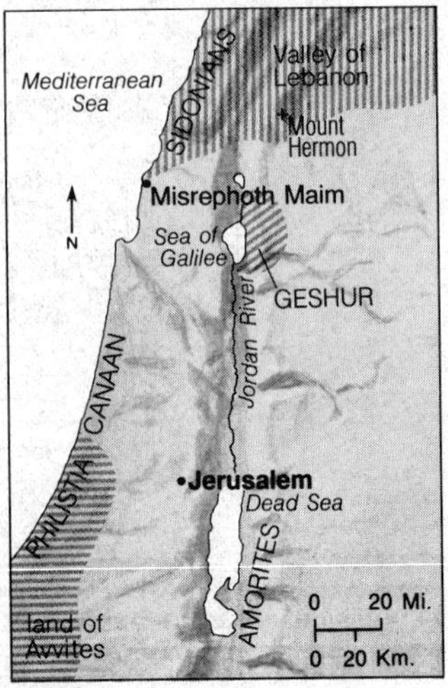

THE LAND YET TO BE CONQUERED
Canaan was now controlled by the Israelites, although much land and several cities still needed to be conquered. Joshua told the people to include both conquered and unconquered lands in the territorial allotments (13:7). He was certain the people would complete the conquest as God had commanded.

13:8 [m]Jos 12:6
13:9 [n]ver 16 [o]Jer 48:8, 21 [p]Nu 21:30
13:10 [q]Nu 21:24
13:11 [r]Jos 12:5
13:12 [s]Dt 3:11 [t]Jos 12:4 [u]Ge 14:5
13:13 [v]Jos 12:5 [w]Dt 3:14
13:14 [x]ver 33; Dt 18:1-2
13:16 [y]ver 9; Jos 12:2 [z]Nu 21:30
13:17 [a]Nu 32:3 [b]1Ch 5:8
13:18 [c]Nu 21:23 [d]Jer 48:21
13:19 [e]Nu 32:37
13:20 [f]Dt 3:29
13:21 [g]Nu 25:15 [h]Nu 31:8
13:22 [i]Nu 22:5; 31:8
13:25 [j]Nu 21:32; Jos 21:39
13:26 [k]Nu 21:25; Jer 49:3

Division of the Land East of the Jordan

8The other half of Manasseh,[c] the Reubenites and the Gadites had received the
inheritance that Moses had given them east of the Jordan, as he, the servant of the
LORD, had assigned[m] it to them.

9It extended from Aroer[n] on the rim of the Arnon Gorge, and from the town
in the middle of the gorge, and included the whole plateau[o] of Medeba as far
as Dibon,[p] 10and all the towns of Sihon king of the Amorites, who ruled in
Heshbon, out to the border of the Ammonites.[q] 11It also included Gilead, the
territory of the people of Geshur and Maacah, all of Mount Hermon and all
Bashan as far as Salecah[r]—12that is, the whole kingdom of Og in Bashan,[s]
who had reigned in Ashtaroth[t] and Edrei and had survived as one of the last
of the Rephaites.[u] Moses had defeated them and taken over their land. 13But
the Israelites did not drive out the people of Geshur[v] and Maacah,[w] so they
continue to live among the Israelites to this day.

14But to the tribe of Levi he gave no inheritance, since the offerings made by fire
to the LORD, the God of Israel, are their inheritance, as he promised them.[x]

15This is what Moses had given to the tribe of Reuben, clan by clan:

16The territory from Aroer[y] on the rim of the Arnon Gorge, and from the town
in the middle of the gorge, and the whole plateau past Medeba[z] 17to Heshbon
and all its towns on the plateau, including Dibon,[a] Bamoth Baal, Beth Baal
Meon,[b] 18Jahaz,[c] Kedemoth, Mephaath,[d] 19Kiriathaim,[e] Sibmah, Zereth
Shahar on the hill in the valley, 20Beth Peor,[f] the slopes of Pisgah, and Beth
Jeshimoth 21—all the towns on the plateau and the entire realm of Sihon king
of the Amorites, who ruled at Heshbon. Moses had defeated him and the Midianite chiefs,[g] Evi, Rekem, Zur, Hur and Reba[h]—princes allied with Sihon—who lived in that country. 22In addition to those slain in battle, the
Israelites had put to the sword Balaam son of Beor,[i] who practised divination.
23The boundary of the Reubenites was the bank of the Jordan. These towns and
their villages were the inheritance of the Reubenites, clan by clan.

24This is what Moses had given to the tribe of Gad, clan by clan:

25The territory of Jazer,[j] all the towns of Gilead and half the Ammonite country
as far as Aroer, near Rabbah; 26and from Heshbon[k] to Ramath Mizpah and

c 8 Hebrew *With it* (that is, with the other half of Manasseh)

THE TRIBES EAST OF THE JORDAN
Joshua assigned territory to the tribes of Reuben, Gad, and the half-tribe of Manasseh on the east side of the Jordan where they had chosen to remain because of the wonderful livestock country (Numbers 32:1–5).

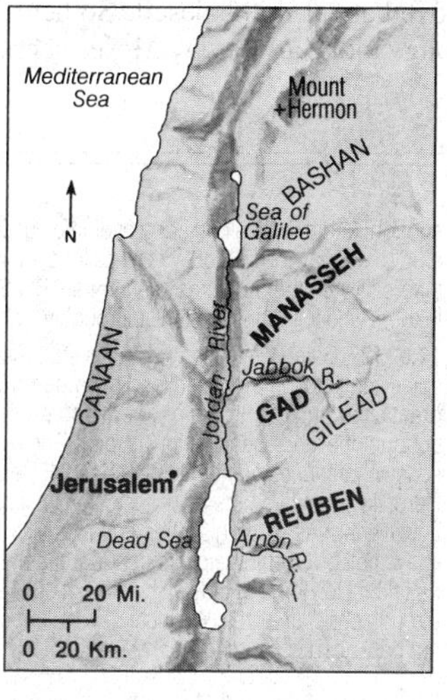

13:13 One reason the Israelites encountered so many problems as they settled the land was that they failed to conquer *fully* the land and drive out all its inhabitants. The cancer-like presence of the remaining pagan peoples of Canaan caused unending difficulties for the Israelites, as the book of Judges records. Just as they failed to remove completely the sin from the land, believers today often fail to remove completely the sin from their lives—with equally disastrous results. As a self-test, reread the Ten Commandments in Exodus 20:1–17. Ask yourself, Am I tolerating sinful practices or thoughts? Have I accepted half-measures as good enough? Do I condemn the faults of others but condone my own?

13:15–23 There is often an interesting connection between the land a tribe received and the character of the tribe's founder. For example, because of Joseph's godly character (Genesis 49:22–26), the tribes descended from him—Ephraim and Manasseh—were given the richest, most fertile land in all of Canaan. Judah, who offered himself in exchange for his brother Benjamin's safety (Genesis 44:18–34), received the largest portion of land, which eventually became the southern kingdom and the seat of David's dynasty. Reuben, who slept with one of his father's wives (Genesis 49:4), was given desert land, the region described here.

Betonim, and from Mahanaim to the territory of Debir;[l] 27and in the valley, Beth
Haram, Beth Nimrah, Succoth[m] and Zaphon with the rest of the realm of Sihon
king of Heshbon (the east side of the Jordan, the territory up to the end of the
Sea of Kinnereth[d][n]). 28These towns and their villages were the inheritance of
the Gadites,[o] clan by clan.

29This is what Moses had given to the half-tribe of Manasseh, that is, to half the family
of the descendants of Manasseh, clan by clan:

30The territory extending from Mahanaim[p] and including all of Bashan, the
entire realm of Og king of Bashan—all the settlements of Jair[q] in Bashan, sixty
towns, 31half of Gilead, and Ashtaroth and Edrei (the royal cities of Og in
Bashan). This was for the descendants of Makir[r] son of Manasseh—for half of
the sons of Makir, clan by clan.

32This is the inheritance Moses had given when he was in the plains of Moab across
the Jordan east of Jericho. 33But to the tribe of Levi, Moses had given no inheritance;
the LORD, the God of Israel, is their inheritance,[s] as he promised them.[t]

Division of the Land West of the Jordan

14 Now these are the areas the Israelites received as an inheritance in the land of
Canaan, which Eleazar the priest, Joshua son of Nun and the heads of the tribal
clans of Israel allotted to them.[a] 2Their inheritances were assigned by lot[b] to the
nine-and-a-half tribes, as the LORD had commanded through Moses. 3Moses had
granted the two-and-a-half tribes their inheritance east of the Jordan[c] but had not
granted the Levites an inheritance among the rest,[d] 4for the sons of Joseph had
become two tribes—Manasseh and Ephraim.[e] The Levites received no share of the
land but only towns to live in, with pasture-lands for their flocks and herds. 5So the
Israelites divided the land, just as the LORD had commanded Moses.[f]

Hebron Given to Caleb

6Now the men of Judah approached Joshua at Gilgal, and Caleb son of Jephunneh[g]
the Kenizzite said to him, "You know what the LORD said to Moses the man of God
at Kadesh Barnea[h] about you and me. 7I was forty years old when Moses the servant
of the LORD sent me from Kadesh Barnea to explore the land.[i] And I brought him
back a report according to my convictions,[j] 8but my brothers who went up with me
made the hearts of the people sink.[a][k] I, however, followed the LORD my God
wholeheartedly.[l] 9So on that day Moses swore to me, 'The land on which your feet
have walked will be your inheritance and that of your children[m] for ever, because you
have followed the LORD my God wholeheartedly.'[b]

10"Now then, just as the LORD promised,[n] he has kept me alive for forty-five years
since the time he said this to Moses, while Israel moved about in the desert. So here
I am today, eighty-five years old! 11I am still as strong[o] today as the day Moses sent

[d] *27* That is, Galilee [a] *8* Hebrew *melt* [b] *9* Deut. 1:36

13:26 [l] Jos 10:3
13:27 [m] Ge 33:17 [n] Nu 34:11
13:28 [o] Nu 32:33
13:30 [p] Ge 32:2 [q] Nu 32:41
13:31 [r] Ge 50:23
13:33 [s] Nu 18:20 [t] ver 14; Jos 18:7
14:1 [a] Nu 34:17-18
14:2 [b] Nu 26:55
14:3 [c] Nu 32:33 [d] Jos 13:14
14:4 [e] Ge 41:52; 48:5
14:5 [f] Nu 34:13; 35:2; Jos 21:2
14:6 [g] Nu 13:6; 14:30 [h] Nu 13:26
14:7 [i] Nu 13:17 [j] Nu 13:30; 14:6-9
14:8 [k] Nu 13:31 [l] Nu 14:24
14:9 [m] Nu 14:24; Dt 1:36
14:10 [n] Nu 14:30
14:11 [o] Dt 34:7

13:29 The tribe of Manasseh was divided into two half-tribes. This occurred when many people from the tribe wanted to settle east of the Jordan River in an area that was especially suited for their flocks (Numbers 32:33). The rest of the tribe preferred to settle west of the Jordan River in the land of Canaan.

13:33 The tribe of Levi was dedicated to serving God. The Levites needed more time and mobility than a landowner could possibly have. Giving them land would mean saddling them with responsibilities and loyalties that would hinder their service to God. Instead, God arranged for the other tribes to meet the Levites' needs through donations. (See Numbers 35:2–4 for how the Levites were to receive cities within each tribal territory.)

14:5 The land was divided exactly as God had instructed Moses years before. Joshua did not change a word. He followed God's commands precisely. Often we believe that *almost* is close enough, and this idea can carry over into our spiritual lives. For example, we may follow God's word as long as we agree with it, but ignore it when the demands seem harsh. But God is looking for leaders who follow instructions thoroughly.

14:6–12 Caleb was faithful from the start. As one of the original spies sent into the promised land (Numbers 13:30–33), he saw great cities and giants, yet he knew God would help the people conquer the land. Because of his faith, God promised him a personal inheritance of land (Numbers 14:24; Deuteronomy 1:34–36). Here, 45 years later, the land was given to him. His faith was still unwavering. Although his inherited land still had giants, Caleb knew the Lord would help him conquer them. Like Caleb, we must be faithful to God, not only at the start of our walk with him, but through our entire lives. We must never allow ourselves to rest on our past accomplishments or reputations.

me out; I'm just as vigorous to go out to battle now as I was then. 12Now give me
this hill country that the LORD promised me that day. You yourself heard then that
the Anakites[p] were there and their cities were large and fortified,[q] but, the LORD
helping me, I will drive them out just as he said."
13Then Joshua blessed[r] Caleb son of Jephunneh and gave him Hebron[s] as his
inheritance.[t] 14So Hebron has belonged to Caleb son of Jephunneh the Kenizzite ever
since, because he followed the LORD, the God of Israel, wholeheartedly. 15(Hebron
used to be called Kiriath Arba[u] after Arba,[v] who was the greatest man among the
Anakites.)

Then the land had rest[w] from war.

Allotment for Judah

15 The allotment for the tribe of Judah, clan by clan, extended down to the territory
of Edom,[a] to the Desert of Zin[b] in the extreme south.
2Their southern boundary started from the bay at the southern end of the Salt
Sea,[a] 3crossed south of Scorpion[b] Pass,[c] continued on to Zin and went over
to the south of Kadesh Barnea. Then it ran past Hezron up to Addar and curved
around to Karka. 4It then passed along to Azmon[d] and joined the Wadi of
Egypt,[e] ending at the sea. This is their[c] southern boundary.
5The eastern boundary[f] is the Salt Sea as far as the mouth of the Jordan.
The northern boundary[g] started from the bay of the sea at the mouth of the
Jordan, 6went up to Beth Hoglah[h] and continued north of Beth Arabah to the
Stone of Bohan[i] son of Reuben. 7The boundary then went up to Debir from the
Valley of Achor[j] and turned north to Gilgal, which faces the Pass of Adummim
south of the gorge. It continued along to the waters of En Shemesh and came
out at En Rogel.[k] 8Then it ran up the Valley of Ben Hinnom along the southern
slope of the Jebusite[l] city (that is, Jerusalem). From there it climbed to the top
of the hill west of the Hinnom Valley at the northern end of the Valley of
Rephaim. 9From the hilltop the boundary headed towards the spring of the waters
of Nephtoah,[m] came out at the towns of Mount Ephron and went down towards
Baalah[n] (that is, Kiriath Jearim). 10Then it curved westward from Baalah to
Mount Seir, ran along the northern slope of Mount Jearim (that is, Kesalon),
continued down to Beth Shemesh and crossed to Timnah.[o] 11It went to the
northern slope of Ekron, turned towards Shikkeron, passed along to Mount
Baalah and reached Jabneel.[p] The boundary ended at the sea.
12The western boundary is the coastline of the Great Sea.[d][q]

These are the boundaries around the people of Judah by their clans.

13In accordance with the LORD's command to him, Joshua gave to Caleb son of
Jephunneh a portion in Judah — Kiriath Arba, that is, Hebron. (Arba was the forefather
of Anak.)[r] 14From Hebron Caleb drove out the three Anakites[s] — Sheshai, Ahiman
and Talmai[t] — descendants of Anak.[u] 15From there he marched against the people
living in Debir (formerly called Kiriath Sepher). 16And Caleb said, "I will give my
daughter Acsah[v] in marriage to the man who attacks and captures Kiriath Sepher."
17Othniel[w] son of Kenaz, Caleb's brother, took it; so Caleb gave his daughter Acsah
to him in marriage.
18One day when she came to Othniel, she urged him[e] to ask her father for a field.
When she got off her donkey, Caleb asked her, "What can I do for you?"

a *2* That is, the Dead Sea; also in verse 5 b *3* Hebrew *Akrabbim* c *4* Hebrew *your* d *12* That is, the Mediterranean; also in verse 47 e *18* Hebrew and some Septuagint manuscripts; other Septuagint manuscripts (see also note at Judges 1:14) *Othniel, he urged her*

14:12 p Nu 13:33 q Nu 13:28
14:13 r Jos 22:6, 7 s Jos 10:36 t Jdg 1:20; 1Ch 6:56
14:15 u Ge 23:2 v Jos 15:13 w Jos 11:23
15:1 a Nu 34:3 b Nu 33:36
15:3 c Nu 34:4
15:4 d Nu 34:5 e Ge 15:18
15:5 f Nu 34:10 g Jos 18:15-19
15:6 h Jos 18:19, 21 i Jos 18:17
15:7 j Jos 7:24 k 2Sa 17:17; 1Ki 1:9
15:8 l ver 63; Jos 18:16, 28; Jdg 1:21; 19:10
15:9 m Jos 18:15 n 1Ch 13:6
15:10 o Ge 38:12; Jdg 14:1
15:11 p Jos 19:33
15:12 q Nu 34:6
15:13 r Jos 14:13-15
15:14 s Nu 13:33 t Nu 13:22 u Jdg 1:10, 20
15:16 v Jdg 1:12
15:17 w Jdg 3:9, 11

14:15 The Anakites were a race of giants who inhabited parts of the land before Joshua's conquest.

15:4 Notice that these boundaries and descriptions of the promised land are very specific. God was telling Israel exactly what to do, and he was giving them just what they needed. There was no excuse for disobedience.

15:16–19 Othniel became Israel's first judge after Joshua's death (Judges 1:13; 3:9–11). He played an important role in reforming Israel by chasing away an oppressive enemy army and bringing peace back to the land. Thus Caleb's legacy of faithfulness continued to the next generation.

19She replied, "Do me a special favour. Since you have given me land in the Negev,
give me also springs of water." So Caleb gave her the upper and lower springs.
20This is the inheritance of the tribe of Judah, clan by clan:

21The southernmost towns of the tribe of Judah in the Negev towards the boundary
of Edom were:
Kabzeel, Eder,[x] Jagur, 22Kinah, Dimonah, Adadah, 23Kedesh, Hazor, Ith-
nan, 24Ziph,[y] Telem, Bealoth, 25Hazor Hadattah, Kerioth Hezron (that is,
Hazor), 26Amam, Shema, Moladah,[z] 27Hazar Gaddah, Heshmon, Beth Pelet,
28Hazar Shual, Beersheba,[a] Biziothiah, 29Baalah,[b] Iim, Ezem, 30Eltolad,[c]
Kesil, Hormah, 31Ziklag,[d] Madmannah, Sansannah, 32Lebaoth, Shilhim, Ain
and Rimmon[e]—a total of twenty-nine towns and their villages.

33In the western foothills:
Eshtaol,[f] Zorah, Ashnah, 34Zanoah,[g] En Gannim, Tappuah, Enam, 35Jar-
muth,[h] Adullam,[i] Socoh, Azekah, 36Shaaraim, Adithaim and Gederah[j] (or
Gederothaim)**f**—fourteen towns and their villages.
37Zenan, Hadashah, Migdal Gad, 38Dilean, Mizpah, Joktheel,[k] 39Lachish,[l]
Bozkath,[m] Eglon, 40Cabbon, Lahmas, Kitlish, 41Gederoth, Beth Dagon, Naamah and Makkedah[n]—sixteen towns and their villages.
42Libnah, Ether, Ashan,[o] 43Iphtah, Ashnah, Nezib, 44Keilah, Aczib[p] and
Mareshah[q]—nine towns and their villages.
45Ekron, with its surrounding settlements and villages; 46west of Ekron, all
that were in the vicinity of Ashdod, together with their villages; 47Ashdod,[r] its
surrounding settlements and villages; and Gaza, its settlements and villages, as
far as the Wadi of Egypt[s] and the coastline of the Great Sea.[t]

48In the hill country:
Shamir, Jattir,[u] Socoh, 49Dannah, Kiriath Sannah (that is, Debir[v]), 50Anab,
Eshtemoh,[w] Anim, 51Goshen,[x] Holon and Giloh—eleven towns and their
villages.
52Arab, Dumah,[y] Eshan, 53Janim, Beth Tappuah, Aphekah, 54Humtah, Kiriath Arba (that is, Hebron) and Zior—nine towns and their villages.
55Maon, Carmel,[z] Ziph, Juttah, 56Jezreel,[a] Jokdeam, Zanoah, 57Kain, Gibeah[b] and Timnah—ten towns and their villages.
58Halhul, Beth Zur,[c] Gedor, 59Maarath, Beth Anoth and Eltekon—six towns
and their villages.
60Kiriath Baal (that is, Kiriath Jearim[d]) and Rabbah[e]—two towns and their
villages.

61In the desert:
Beth Arabah, Middin, Secacah, 62Nibshan, the City of Salt and En
Gedi[f]—six towns and their villages.
63Judah could not[g] dislodge the Jebusites[h], who were living in Jerusalem; to this
day the Jebusites live there with the people of Judah.

Allotment for Ephraim and Manasseh

16 The allotment for Joseph began at the Jordan of Jericho,**a** east of the
waters of Jericho, and went up from there through the desert[a] into the hill
country of Bethel. 2It went on from Bethel (that is, Luz[b]),**b** crossed over to the
territory of the Arkites in Ataroth, 3descended westward to the territory of the

f *36* Or *Gederah and Gederothaim* **a** *1* *Jordan of Jericho* was possibly an ancient name for the Jordan River.
b *2* Septuagint; Hebrew *Bethel to Luz*

15:21 [x]Ge 35:21
15:24 [y]1Sa 23:14
15:26 [z]1Ch 4:28
15:28 [a]Ge 21:31
15:29 [b]ver 9
15:30 [c]Jos 19:4
15:31 [d]1Sa 27:6
15:32 [e]Jdg 20:45
15:33 [f]Jdg 13:25; 16:31
15:34 [g]1Ch 4:18; Ne 3:13
15:35 [h]Jos 10:3 [i]1Sa 22:1
15:36 [j]1Ch 12:4
15:38 [k]2Ki 14:7
15:39 [l]Jos 10:3; 2Ki 14:19 [m]2Ki 22:1
15:41 [n]Jos 10:10
15:42 [o]1Sa 30:30
15:44 [p]Jdg 1:31 [q]Mic 1:15
15:47 [r]Jos 11:22 [s]ver 4 [t]Nu 34:6
15:48 [u]1Sa 30:27
15:49 [v]Jos 10:3
15:50 [w]Jos 21:14
15:51 [x]Jos 10:41; 11:16
15:52 [y]Ge 25:14
15:55 [z]Jos 12:22
15:56 [a]Jos 17:16
15:57 [b]Jos 18:28; Jdg 19:12
15:58 [c]1Ch 2:45
15:60 [d]Jos 18:14 [e]Dt 3:11
15:62 [f]1Sa 23:29
15:63 [g]Jdg 1:21 [h]2Sa 5:6
16:1 [a]Jos 8:15; 18:12
16:2 [b]Jos 18:13

15:19 Acsah asked Caleb for springs of water because her land was in the south and was very arid. Caleb probably granted her request as a wedding present (see 15:17).

16:1ff Although Joseph was one of Jacob's 12 sons, he did not have a tribe named after him. This was because Joseph, as the oldest son of Jacob's wife Rachel, received a double portion of the inheritance. This double portion was given to Joseph's two sons, Ephraim and Manasseh, whom Jacob considered as his own (Genesis 48:5). The largest territory and the greatest influence in the northern half of Israel belonged to their tribes.

Japhletites as far as the region of Lower Beth Horon[c] and on to Gezer,[d] ending
at the sea.
4 So Manasseh and Ephraim, the descendants of Joseph, received their inheritance.[e]

5 This was the territory of Ephraim, clan by clan:
The boundary of their inheritance went from Ataroth Addar[f] in the east to
Upper Beth Horon 6 and continued to the sea. From Micmethath[g] on the north
it curved eastward to Taanath Shiloh, passing by it to Janoah on the east. 7 Then
it went down from Janoah to Ataroth[h] and Naarah, touched Jericho and came
out at the Jordan. 8 From Tappuah the border went west to the Kanah Ravine[i]
and ended at the sea. This was the inheritance of the tribe of the Ephraimites,
clan by clan. 9 It also included all the towns and their villages that were set aside
for the Ephraimites within the inheritance of the Manassites.
10 They did not dislodge the Canaanites living in Gezer; to this day the Canaanites live
among the people of Ephraim but are required to do forced labour.[j]

17 This was the allotment for the tribe of Manasseh as Joseph's firstborn,[a] that
is, for Makir,[b] Manasseh's firstborn. Makir was the ancestor of the Gileadites,
who had received Gilead and Bashan because the Makirites were great soldiers. 2 So
this allotment was for the rest of the people of Manasseh—the clans of Abiezer,[c]
Helek, Asriel, Shechem, Hepher and Shemida. These are the other male descendants
of Manasseh son of Joseph by their clans.
3 Now Zelophehad son of Hepher,[d] the son of Gilead, the son of Makir, the son
of Manasseh, had no sons but only daughters,[e] whose names were Mahlah, Noah,
Hoglah, Milcah and Tirzah. 4 They went to Eleazar the priest, Joshua son of Nun, and
the leaders and said, "The LORD commanded Moses to give us an inheritance among
our brothers." So Joshua gave them an inheritance along with the brothers of their
father, according to the LORD's command.[f] 5 Manasseh's share consisted of ten tracts
of land besides Gilead and Bashan east of the Jordan, 6 because the daughters of the
tribe of Manasseh received an inheritance among the sons. The land of Gilead
belonged to the rest of the descendants of Manasseh.
7 The territory of Manasseh extended from Asher to Micmethath[g] east of
Shechem.[h] The boundary ran southward from there to include the people living
at En Tappuah. 8 (Manasseh had the land of Tappuah, but Tappuah[i] itself, on
the boundary of Manasseh, belonged to the Ephraimites.) 9 Then the boundary
continued south to the Kanah Ravine.[j] There were towns belonging to Ephraim
lying among the towns of Manasseh, but the boundary of Manasseh was the
northern side of the ravine and ended at the sea. 10 On the south the land belonged
to Ephraim, on the north to Manasseh. The territory of Manasseh reached the sea
and bordered Asher on the north and Issachar[k] on the east.
11 Within Issachar and Asher, Manasseh also had Beth Shan,[l] Ibleam and the
people of Dor,[m] Endor,[n] Taanach and Megiddo,[o] together with their surrounding settlements (the third in the list is Naphoth[a]).
12 Yet the Manassites were not able[p] to occupy these towns, for the Canaanites were
determined to live in that region. 13 However, when the Israelites grew stronger, they
subjected the Canaanites to forced labour but did not drive them out completely.[q]

a *11* That is, Naphoth Dor

16:3 c 2Ch 8:5 d Jos 10:33; 1Ki 9:15
16:4 e Jos 17:14
16:5 f Jos 18:13
16:6 g Jos 17:7
16:7 h 1Ch 7:28
16:8 i Jos 17:9
16:10 j Jos 17:13; Jdg 1:28-29; 1Ki 9:16
17:1 a Ge 41:51 b Ge 50:23
17:2 c Nu 26:30; 1Ch 7:18
17:3 d Nu 27:1 e Nu 26:33
17:4 f Nu 27:5-7
17:7 g Jos 16:6 h Ge 12:6; Jos 21:21
17:8 i Jos 16:8
17:9 j Jos 16:8
17:10 k Ge 30:18
17:11 l 1Sa 31:10; 1Ki 4:12; 1Ch 7:29 m Jos 11:2 n 1Sa 28:7; Ps 83:10 o 1Ki 9:15
17:12 p Jdg 1:27
17:13 q Jos 16:10

16:10 Occasionally this short phrase appears: "They did not dislodge" the people of the land (see also 15:63; 17:12). This was contrary to God's explicit desire and command (13:1–6). The failure to remove completely the pagan people and their gods from the land would cause many problems for the nation. The book of Judges records many of these struggles.

17:3, 4 Although women did not traditionally inherit property in Israelite society, Moses put justice ahead of tradition and gave these five women the land they deserved (see Numbers 27:1–11). In fact, God told Moses to add a law that would help other women in similar circumstances inherit property as well. Joshua was now carrying out this law. It is easy to refuse to honour a reasonable request because "things have never been done that way before". But, like Moses and Joshua, it is best to look carefully at the purpose of the law and the merits of each case before deciding.

14The people of Joseph said to Joshua, "Why have you given us only one allotment
and one portion for an inheritance? We are a numerous people and the LORD has
blessed us abundantly."[r]
15"If you are so numerous," Joshua answered, "and if the hill country of Ephraim
is too small for you, go up into the forest and clear land for yourselves there in the
land of the Perizzites and Rephaites.[s]"
16The people of Joseph replied, "The hill country is not enough for us, and all the
Canaanites who live in the plain have iron chariots,[t] both those in Beth Shan and
its settlements and those in the Valley of Jezreel."
17But Joshua said to the house of Joseph—to Ephraim and Manasseh—"You are
numerous and very powerful. You will have not only one allotment 18but the forested
hill country as well. Clear it, and its farthest limits will be yours; though the Canaanites
have iron chariots[u] and though they are strong, you can drive them out."

Division of the Rest of the Land

18 The whole assembly of the Israelites gathered at Shiloh[a] and set up the Tent
of Meeting[b] there. The country was brought under their control, 2but there
were still seven Israelite tribes who had not yet received their inheritance.
3So Joshua said to the Israelites: "How long will you wait before you begin to take
possession of the land that the LORD, the God of your fathers, has given you? 4Appoint
three men from each tribe. I will send them out to make a survey of the land and to
write a description of it, according to the inheritance of each.[c] Then they will return
to me. 5You are to divide the land into seven parts. Judah is to remain in its territory
on the south[d] and the house of Joseph in its territory on the north.[e] 6After you have
written descriptions of the seven parts of the land, bring them here to me and I will
cast lots[f] for you in the presence of the LORD our God. 7The Levites, however, do

17:14 [r]Nu 26:28-37
17:15 [s]Ge 14:5
17:16 [t]Jdg 1:19; 4:3, 13
17:18 [u]ver 16
18:1 [a]Jos 19:51; 21:2; Jdg 18:31; 21:12, 19; 1Sa 1:3; 4:3; Jer 7:12; 26:6 [b]Ex 27:21
18:4 [c]Mic 2:5
18:5 [d]Jos 15:1 [e]Jos 16:1-4
18:6 [f]Jos 14:2

17:14, 15 Notice the two contrasting attitudes towards settling the promised land: Caleb took what God gave him and moved ahead to fulfil God's plan for him (14:12). He was confident that God would help him drive out the wicked inhabitants and that he would soon fully occupy his land (15:14, 15). In contrast, the two tribes of Joseph were given rich land and lots of it, but they were afraid to drive out the inhabitants and take full possession of it. Instead they begged for more land. But Joshua asked them to prove their sincerity first by clearing the unclaimed forest areas. They agreed, but they failed to carry this through (Judges 1:27).

18:1, 2 With most of the conquest behind them, Israel moved their religious centre from Gilgal (see the note on 5:8, 9) to Shiloh. This was probably the first place where the tabernacle was set up permanently. The Tent of Meeting was part of the tabernacle and was where God lived among his people (Exodus 25:8). Its central location in the land made it easier for the people to attend the special worship services and yearly feasts.

The family of Samuel, a great priest and prophet, often travelled to Shiloh, and Samuel was taken there when he was a small boy (1 Samuel 1:3, 22). The tabernacle remained in Shiloh through the period of the judges (about 300 years). Apparently the city was destroyed by the Philistines when the ark of the covenant was captured (1 Samuel 4, 5). Shiloh never lived up to its reputation as Israel's religious centre, for later references in the Bible point to the wickedness and idolatry in the city (Psalm 78:56–60; Jeremiah 7:12–15).

18:2ff Seven of the tribes had not yet been assigned their land. They gathered at Shiloh, where Joshua cast lots to determine which areas would be given to them. Using the sacred lottery, God would make the choice, not Joshua or any other human leader.

By this time, the Canaanites were, in most places, so weakened that they were no longer a threat. Instead of fulfilling God's command to destroy the remaining Canaanites, however, these seven tribes would often take the path of least resistance. As nomadic people, they may have been reluctant to settle down, preferring to depend economically on the people they were supposed to eliminate. Others may have feared the high cost of continued warfare. It was easier and more profitable to trade for goods than to destroy the suppliers and have to provide for themselves.

18:3–6 Joshua asked why some of the tribes were putting off the job of possessing the land. Often we delay doing jobs that seem large, difficult, boring, or disagreeable. But to continue putting them off shows lack of discipline, poor stewardship of time, and, in some cases, disobedience to God. Jobs we don't enjoy require concentration, teamwork, twice as much time, lots of encouragement, and accountability. Remember this when you are tempted to procrastinate.

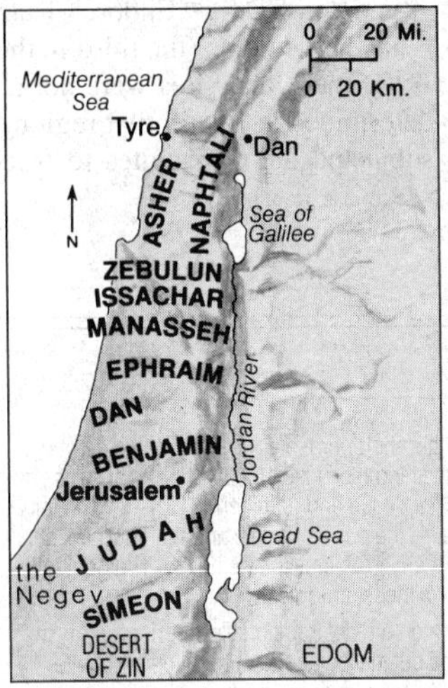

THE TRIBES WEST OF THE JORDAN
Judah, Ephraim, and the other half-tribe of Manasseh were the first tribes to receive land west of the Jordan because of their past acts of faith. The remaining seven tribes—Benjamin, Zebulun, Issachar, Asher, Naphtali, Simeon, and Dan—were slow to conquer and possess the land allotted to them.

not get a portion among you, because the priestly service of the LORD is their inheritance.[g] And Gad, Reuben and the half-tribe of Manasseh have already received their inheritance on the east side of the Jordan. Moses the servant of the LORD gave it to them.[h]"

8 As the men started on their way to map out the land, Joshua instructed them, "Go and make a survey of the land and write a description of it. Then return to me, and I will cast lots for you here at Shiloh[i] in the presence of the LORD." 9 So the men left and went through the land. They wrote its description on a scroll, town by town, in seven parts, and returned to Joshua in the camp at Shiloh. 10 Joshua then cast lots[j] for them in Shiloh in the presence[k] of the LORD, and there he distributed the land to the Israelites according to their tribal divisions.[l]

Allotment for Benjamin

11 The lot came up for the tribe of Benjamin, clan by clan. Their allotted territory lay between the tribes of Judah and Joseph:

12 On the north side their boundary began at the Jordan, passed the northern slope of Jericho and headed west into the hill country, coming out at the desert[m] of Beth Aven.[n] 13 From there it crossed to the south slope of Luz[o] (that is, Bethel[p]) and went down to Ataroth Addar[q] on the hill south of Lower Beth Horon.

14 From the hill facing Beth Horon[r] on the south the boundary turned south along the western side and came out at Kiriath Baal (that is, Kiriath Jearim), a town of the people of Judah. This was the western side.

15 The southern side began at the outskirts of Kiriath Jearim on the west, and the boundary came out at the spring of the waters of Nephtoah.[s] 16 The boundary went down to the foot of the hill facing the Valley of Ben Hinnom, north of the Valley of Rephaim. It continued down the Hinnom Valley[t] along the southern slope of the Jebusite city and so to En Rogel.[u] 17 It then curved north, went to En Shemesh, continued to Geliloth, which faces the Pass of Adummim, and ran down to the Stone of Bohan[v] son of Reuben. 18 It continued to the northern slope of Beth Arabah[a][w] and on down into the Arabah. 19 It then went to the northern slope of Beth Hoglah and came out at the northern bay of the Salt Sea,[b][x] at the mouth of the Jordan in the south. This was the southern boundary.

20 The Jordan formed the boundary on the eastern side.

These were the boundaries that marked out the inheritance of the clans of Benjamin on all sides.[y]

21 The tribe of Benjamin, clan by clan, had the following cities:

Jericho, Beth Hoglah, Emek Keziz, 22 Beth Arabah, Zemaraim, Bethel,[z] 23 Avvim, Parah, Ophrah, 24 Kephar Ammoni, Ophni and Geba[a]—twelve towns and their villages.

25 Gibeon,[b] Ramah,[c] Beeroth,[d] 26 Mizpah,[e] Kephirah, Mozah, 27 Rekem, Irpeel, Taralah, 28 Zelah,[f] Haeleph, the Jebusite city[g] (that is, Jerusalem[h]), Gibeah[i] and Kiriath—fourteen towns and their villages.

This was the inheritance of Benjamin for its clans.

a 18 Septuagint; Hebrew *slope facing the Arabah* b 19 That is, the Dead Sea

18:7 g Jos 13:33 h Jos 13:8
18:8 i ver 1
18:10 j Nu 34:13 k ver 1; Jer 7:12 l Nu 33:54; Jos 19:51
18:12 m Jos 16:1 n Jos 7:2
18:13 o Ge 28:19 p Jdg 1:23 q Jos 16:5
18:14 r Jos 10:10
18:15 s Jos 15:9
18:16 t Jos 15:8; 2Ki 23:10 u Jos 15:7
18:17 v Jos 15:6
18:18 w Jos 15:6
18:19 x Ge 14:3
18:20 y Jos 21:4, 17; 1Sa 9:1
18:22 z Jos 16:1
18:24 a Isa 10:29
18:25 b Jos 9:3 c Jdg 4:5 d Jos 9:17
18:26 e Jos 11:3
18:28 f 2Sa 21:14 g Jos 15:8 h Jos 10:1 i Jos 15:57

18:8 Making decisions by casting lots was a common practice among the Hebrews. Little is known about the actual method used in Joshua's day. Dice may have been used. Another possibility is that two urns were used: one containing tribal names; the other, the divisions of the land. Drawing one name from each urn matched a tribe to a region. The Urim and Thummim (explained in the note on Leviticus 8:8) may also have been used. No matter how it was done, the process removed human choice from the decision-making process and allowed God to match tribes and lands as he saw fit.

18:11 The tribe of Benjamin was given a narrow strip of land that served as a buffer zone between Judah and Ephraim, the two tribes that would later dominate the land.

18:16 The Valley of Ben Hinnom became associated with the worship of Molech (the Ammonite god) in Jeremiah's time. These terrible rites involved the sacrifice of children. Later the valley was used for burning garbage and the corpses of criminals and animals. Thus the name became a synonym for hell.

Allotment for Simeon

19 The second lot came out for the tribe of Simeon, clan by clan. Their inheritance
lay within the territory of Judah.[a] 2It included:
Beersheba[b] (or Sheba),[a] Moladah, 3Hazar Shual, Balah, Ezem, 4Eltolad,
Bethul, Hormah, 5Ziklag, Beth Marcaboth, Hazar Susah, 6Beth Lebaoth and
Sharuhen—thirteen towns and their villages;
7Ain, Rimmon, Ether and Ashan[c]—four towns and their villages—8and all
the villages around these towns as far as Baalath Beer (Ramah in the Negev).[d]
This was the inheritance of the tribe of the Simeonites, clan by clan. 9The inheritance
of the Simeonites was taken from the share of Judah,[e] because Judah's portion was
more than they needed. So the Simeonites received their inheritance within the
territory of Judah.[f]

Allotment for Zebulun

10The third lot came up for Zebulun,[g] clan by clan:
The boundary of their inheritance went as far as Sarid. 11Going west it ran to
Maralah, touched Dabbesheth, and extended to the ravine near Jokneam.[h] 12It
turned east from Sarid towards the sunrise to the territory of Kisloth Tabor and
went on to Daberath and up to Japhia. 13Then it continued eastward to Gath
Hepher and Eth Kazin; it came out at Rimmon[i] and turned towards Neah.
14There the boundary went round on the north to Hannathon and ended at the
Valley of Iphtah El. 15Included were Kattath, Nahalal, Shimron, Idalah and
Bethlehem.[j] There were twelve towns and their villages.
16These towns and their villages were the inheritance of Zebulun,[k] clan by clan.[l]

Allotment for Issachar

17The fourth lot came out for Issachar,[m] clan by clan. 18Their territory included:
Jezreel,[n] Kesulloth, Shunem,[o] 19Hapharaim, Shion, Anaharath, 20Rabbith,
Kishion, Ebez, 21Remeth, En Gannim, En Haddah and Beth Pazzez. 22The
boundary touched Tabor,[p] Shahazumah and Beth Shemesh,[q] and ended at the
Jordan. There were sixteen towns and their villages.
23These towns and their villages were the inheritance of the tribe of Issachar,[r] clan
by clan.[s]

Allotment for Asher

24The fifth lot came out for the tribe of Asher,[t] clan by clan. 25Their territory
included:
Helkath, Hali, Beten, Acshaph, 26Allammelech, Amad and Mishal. On the
west the boundary touched Carmel[u] and Shihor Libnath. 27It then turned east
towards Beth Dagon, touched Zebulun[v] and the Valley of Iphtah El, and went
north to Beth Emek and Neiel, passing Cabul[w] on the left. 28It went to Abdon,[b]
Rehob,[x] Hammon[y] and Kanah, as far as Greater Sidon.[z] 29The boundary then
turned back towards Ramah[a] and went to the fortified city of Tyre,[b] turned
towards Hosah and came out at the sea in the region of Aczib,[c] 30Ummah,
Aphek and Rehob. There were twenty-two towns and their villages.
31These towns and their villages were the inheritance of the tribe of Asher,[d] clan by
clan.

Allotment for Naphtali

32The sixth lot came out for Naphtali, clan by clan:
33Their boundary went from Heleph and the large tree in Zaanannim, passing
Adami Nekeb and Jabneel to Lakkum and ending at the Jordan. 34The boundary
ran west through Aznoth Tabor and came out at Hukkok. It touched Zebulun on
the south, Asher on the west and the Jordan[c] on the east. 35The fortified cities
were Ziddim, Zer, Hammath, Rakkath, Kinnereth,[e] 36Adamah, Ramah,[f] Ha-

[a] 2 Or *Beersheba, Sheba*; 1 Chron. 4:28 does not have *Sheba*. [b] 28 Some Hebrew manuscripts (see also Joshua 21:30); most Hebrew manuscripts *Ebron* [c] 34 Septuagint; Hebrew *west, and Judah, the Jordan,*

19:1 [a] ver 9; Ge 49:7
19:2 [b] Ge 21:14; 1Ki 19:3
19:7 [c] Jos 15:42
19:8 [d] Jos 10:40
19:9 [e] Ge 49:7 [f] Eze 48:24
19:10 [g] Jos 21:7, 34
19:11 [h] Jos 12:22
19:13 [i] Jos 15:32
19:15 [j] Ge 35:19
19:16 [k] ver 10; Jos 21:7 [l] Eze 48:26
19:17 [m] Ge 30:18
19:18 [n] Jos 15:56 [o] 1Sa 28:4; 2Ki 4:8
19:22 [p] Jdg 4:6, 12; Ps 89:12 [q] Jos 15:10
19:23 [r] Jos 17:10 [s] Ge 49:15; Eze 48:25
19:24 [t] Jos 17:7
19:26 [u] Jos 12:22
19:27 [v] ver 10 [w] 1Ki 9:13
19:28 [x] Jdg 1:31 [y] 1Ch 6:76 [z] Ge 10:19; Jos 11:8
19:29 [a] Jos 18:25 [b] 2Sa 5:11; 24:7; Isa 23:1; Jer 25:22; Eze 26:2 [c] Jdg 1:31
19:31 [d] Ge 30:13; Eze 48:2
19:35 [e] Jos 11:2
19:36 [f] Jos 18:25

zor,[g] 37Kedesh, Edrei,[h] En Hazor, 38Iron, Migdal El, Horem, Beth Anath and
Beth Shemesh. There were nineteen towns and their villages.
39These towns and their villages were the inheritance of the tribe of Naphtali, clan
by clan.[i]

Allotment for Dan

40The seventh lot came out for the tribe of Dan, clan by clan. 41The territory of their
inheritance included:
Zorah, Eshtaol, Ir Shemesh, 42Shaalabbin, Aijalon,[j] Ithlah, 43Elon, Timnah,[k] Ekron, 44Eltekeh, Gibbethon, Baalath, 45Jehud, Bene Berak, Gath Rimmon,[l] 46Me Jarkon and Rakkon, with the area facing Joppa.[m]
47(But the Danites had difficulty taking possession of their territory,[n] so they went
up and attacked Leshem[o], took it, put it to the sword and occupied it. They settled
in Leshem and named it Dan after their forefather.)[p]
48These towns and their villages were the inheritance of the tribe of Dan,[q] clan by
clan.

Allotment for Joshua

49When they had finished dividing the land into its allotted portions, the Israelites
gave Joshua son of Nun an inheritance among them, 50as the LORD had commanded.
They gave him the town he asked for—Timnath Serah[d][r] in the hill country of
Ephraim. And he built up the town and settled there.
51These are the territories that Eleazar the priest, Joshua son of Nun and the heads
of the tribal clans of Israel assigned by lot at Shiloh in the presence of the LORD at
the entrance to the Tent of Meeting. And so they finished dividing the land.[s]

2. Special cities are set aside

Cities of Refuge

20 Then the LORD said to Joshua: 2"Tell the Israelites to designate the cities of
refuge, as I instructed you through Moses, 3so that anyone who kills a person
accidentally and unintentionally[a] may flee there and find protection from the avenger
of blood.[b]
4"When he flees to one of these cities, he is to stand in the entrance of the city gate[c]
and state his case before the elders[d] of that city. Then they are to admit him into their
city and give him a place to live with them. 5If the avenger of blood pursues him,

d 50 Also known as *Timnath Heres* (see Judges 2:9)

19:36 g Jos 11:1
19:37 h Nu 21:33
19:39 i Dt 33:23; Eze 48:3
19:42 j Jdg 1:35
19:43 k Ge 38:12
19:45 l Jos 21:24; 1Ch 6:69
19:46 m 2Ch 2:16; Jnh 1:3
19:47 n Jdg 18:1 o Jdg 18:7, 14 p Jdg 18:27, 29
19:48 q Ge 30:6
19:50 r Jos 24:30
19:51 s Jos 14:1; 18:10; Ac 13:19
20:3 a Lev 4:2 b Nu 35:12
20:4 c Ru 4:1; Jer 38:7 d Jos 7:6

THE CITIES OF REFUGE
A city of refuge was just that—refuge for someone who committed an unintentional murder that would evoke revenge from the victim's friends and relatives. The six cities of refuge were spaced throughout the land so that a person was never too far from one.

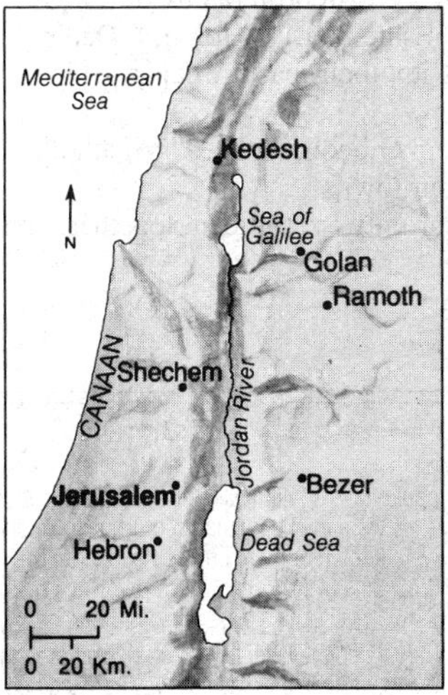

19:47, 48 The tribe of Dan found that some of their land was difficult to conquer, so they chose to migrate to Leshem where they knew victory would be easier. Anyone can trust God when the going is easy. It is when everything looks impossible that our faith and courage are put to the test. Have faith that God is great enough to tackle your most difficult situations.

19:49 There were several good reasons for establishing these well-set boundaries instead of turning the promised land into a single undivided nation. (1) The boundaries gave each tribe ownership of an area, promoting loyalty and unity that would strengthen each tribe. (2) The boundaries delineated areas of responsibility and privilege, which would help each tribe develop and mature. (3) The boundaries reduced conflicts that might have broken out if everyone had wanted to live in the choicest areas. (4) The boundaries fulfilled the promised inheritance to each tribe that began to be given as early as the days of Jacob (Genesis 48:21, 22).

they must not surrender the one accused, because he killed his neighbour unintentionally and without malice aforethought. 6He is to stay in that city until he has stood
trial before the assembly[e] and until the death of the high priest who is serving at that
time. Then he may go back to his own home in the town from which he fled."
7So they set apart Kedesh[f] in Galilee in the hill country of Naphtali, Shechem[g]
in the hill country of Ephraim, and Kiriath Arba (that is, Hebron[h]) in the hill country
of Judah.[i] 8On the east side of the Jordan of Jericho[a] they designated Bezer[j] in
the desert on the plateau in the tribe of Reuben, Ramoth in Gilead[k] in the tribe of
Gad, and Golan in Bashan in the tribe of Manasseh. 9Any of the Israelites or any alien
living among them who killed someone accidentally could flee to these designated
cities and not be killed by the avenger of blood prior to standing trial before the
assembly.[l]

Towns for the Levites

21 Now the family heads of the Levites approached Eleazar the priest, Joshua son
of Nun, and the heads of the other tribal families of Israel[a] 2at Shiloh[b] in
Canaan and said to them, "The LORD commanded through Moses that you give us
towns to live in, with pasture-lands for our livestock."[c] 3So, as the LORD had
commanded, the Israelites gave the Levites the following towns and pasture-lands out
of their own inheritance:
4The first lot came out for the Kohathites, clan by clan. The Levites who were
descendants of Aaron the priest were allotted thirteen towns from the tribes of Judah,
Simeon and Benjamin.[d] 5The rest of Kohath's descendants were allotted ten towns
from the clans of the tribes of Ephraim, Dan and half of Manasseh.[e]
6The descendants of Gershon were allotted thirteen towns from the clans of the
tribes of Issachar,[f] Asher, Naphtali and the half-tribe of Manasseh in Bashan.
7The descendants of Merari,[g] clan by clan, received twelve towns from the tribes
of Reuben, Gad and Zebulun.[h]
8So the Israelites allotted to the Levites these towns and their pasture-lands, as the
LORD had commanded through Moses.

9From the tribes of Judah and Simeon they allotted the following towns by name
10(these towns were assigned to the descendants of Aaron who were from the Kohathite clans of the Levites, because the first lot fell to them):

11They gave them Kiriath Arba (that is, Hebron[i]), with its surrounding
pasture-land, in the hill country of Judah. (Arba was the forefather of Anak.)
12But the fields and villages around the city they had given to Caleb son of
Jephunneh as his possession.

13So to the descendants of Aaron the priest they gave Hebron (a city of refuge
for one accused of murder), Libnah,[j] 14Jattir,[k] Eshtemoa,[l] 15Holon,[m] Debir,
16Ain, Juttah[n] and Beth Shemesh,[o] together with their pasture-lands—nine
towns from these two tribes.

17And from the tribe of Benjamin they gave them Gibeon, Geba,[p] 18Anathoth
and Almon, together with their pasture-lands—four towns.

19All the towns for the priests, the descendants of Aaron, were thirteen, together with
their pasture-lands.

a 8 *Jordan of Jericho* was possibly an ancient name for the Jordan River.

20:6 e Nu 35:12
20:7 f Jos 21:32; 1Ch 6:76 g Ge 12:6 h Jos 10:36; 21:11 i Lk 1:39
20:8 j Jos 21:36; 1Ch 6:78 k Jos 12:2
20:9 l Ex 21:13; Nu 35:15
21:1 a Jos 14:1
21:2 b Jos 18:1 c Nu 35:2-3
21:4 d ver 19
21:5 e ver 26
21:6 f Ge 30:18
21:7 g Ex 6:16 h Jos 19:10
21:11 i Jos 15:13; 1Ch 6:55
21:13 j Jos 15:42; 1Ch 6:57
21:14 k Jos 15:48 l Jos 15:50
21:15 m Jos 15:51
21:16 n Jos 15:55 o Jos 15:10
21:17 p Jos 18:24

20:6 A new nation in a new land needed a new government. Many years earlier God had told Moses how this government should function. One of the tasks God wanted the Israelites to do when they entered the promised land was to designate certain cities as "cities of refuge". These were to be scattered throughout the land. Their purpose was to prevent injustice, especially in cases of revenge. For example, if someone accidentally killed another person, he could flee to a city of refuge where he was safe until he could have a fair trial. The Levites were in charge of these cities. They were to ensure that God's principles of justice and fairness were kept. (For more on cities of refuge, see the notes on Numbers 35:6; 35:11–28.)

21:2 The Levites were to minister before God on behalf of all the people, so they were given cities scattered throughout the land. Although Jerusalem was far away from the homes of many Israelites, almost no-one lived more than a day's journey from a Levitical city.

20The rest of the Kohathite clans of the Levites were allotted towns from the tribe of
Ephraim:
21In the hill country of Ephraim they were given Shechem[q] (a city of refuge
for one accused of murder) and Gezer, 22Kibzaim and Beth Horon,[r] together
with their pasture-lands — four towns.[s]
23Also from the tribe of Dan they received Eltekeh, Gibbethon, 24Aijalon and
Gath Rimmon,[t] together with their pasture-lands — four towns.
25From half the tribe of Manasseh they received Taanach and Gath Rimmon,
together with their pasture-lands — two towns.
26All these ten towns and their pasture-lands were given to the rest of the Kohathite
clans.

27The Levite clans of the Gershonites were given:
from the half-tribe of Manasseh,
Golan in Bashan[u] (a city of refuge for one accused of murder[v]) and Be Eshtarah,
together with their pasture-lands — two towns;
28from the tribe of Issachar,[w]
Kishion, Daberath, 29Jarmuth and En Gannim, together with their pasture-
lands — four towns;
30from the tribe of Asher,[x]
Mishal, Abdon, 31Helkath and Rehob, together with their pasture-lands — four
towns;
32from the tribe of Naphtali,
Kedesh[y] in Galilee (a city of refuge for one accused of murder[z]), Hammoth
Dor and Kartan, together with their pasture-lands — three towns.
33All the towns of the Gershonite[a] clans were thirteen, together with their pasture-
lands.

34The Merarite clans (the rest of the Levites) were given:
from the tribe of Zebulun,[b]
Jokneam, Kartah, 35Dimnah and Nahalal, together with their pasture-
lands — four towns;
36from the tribe of Reuben,
Bezer,[c] Jahaz, 37Kedemoth and Mephaath, together with their pasture-
lands — four towns;
38from the tribe of Gad,
Ramoth[d] in Gilead (a city of refuge for one accused of murder), Mahanaim,[e]
39Heshbon and Jazer, together with their pasture-lands — four towns in all.
40All the towns allotted to the Merarite clans, who were the rest of the Levites, were
twelve.
41The towns of the Levites in the territory held by the Israelites were forty-eight
in all, together with their pasture-lands.[f] 42Each of these towns had pasture-lands
surrounding it; this was true for all these towns.

43So the LORD gave Israel all the land he had sworn to give their forefathers,[g] and
they took possession[h] of it and settled there.[i] 44The LORD gave them rest[j] on every
side, just as he had sworn to their forefathers. Not one of their enemies[k] withstood
them; the LORD handed all their enemies[l] over to them.[m] 45Not one of all the LORD's
good promises[n] to the house of Israel failed; every one was fulfilled.

21:21 [q]Jos 17:7; 20:7
21:22 [r]Jos 10:10 [s]1Sa 1:1
21:24 [t]Jos 19:45
21:27 [u]Jos 12:5 [v]Nu 35:6
21:28 [w]Ge 30:18
21:30 [x]Jos 17:7
21:32 [y]Jos 12:22 [z]Nu 35:6; Jos 20:7
21:33 [a]ver 6
21:34 [b]Jos 19:10; 1Ch 6:77
21:36 [c]Jos 20:8
21:38 [d]Dt 4:43 [e]Ge 32:2
21:41 [f]Nu 35:7
21:43 [g]Dt 34:4 [h]Dt 11:31 [i]Dt 17:14
21:44 [j]Ex 33:14; Jos 1:13 [k]Dt 6:19 [l]Ex 23:31 [m]Dt 7:24; 21:10
21:45 [n]Jos 23:14; Ne 9:8

21:43–45 God proved faithful in fulfilling every promise he had given to Israel. Fulfilment of some promises took several years, but "every one was fulfilled". His promises will be fulfilled according to his timetable, not ours, but we know that his word is sure. The more we learn of those promises God has fulfilled and continues to fulfil, the easier it is to hope for those yet to come. Sometimes we become impatient, wanting God to act in a certain way *now*. Instead, we should faithfully do what we know he wants us to do and trust him for the future.

3. Eastern tribes return home

22 Then Joshua summoned the Reubenites, the Gadites and the half-tribe of
Manasseh 2and said to them, "You have done all that Moses the servant of the
LORD commanded,[a] and you have obeyed me in everything I commanded. 3For a
long time now—to this very day—you have not deserted your brothers but have
carried out the mission the LORD your God gave you. 4Now that the LORD your God
has given your brothers rest as he promised, return to your homes[b] in the land that
Moses the servant of the LORD gave you on the other side of the Jordan.[c] 5But be
very careful to keep the commandment[d] and the law that Moses the servant of the
LORD gave you: to love the LORD your God, to walk in all his ways, to obey his
commands,[e] to hold fast to him and to serve him with all your heart and all your
soul.[f]"
6Then Joshua blessed[g] them and sent them away, and they went to their homes.
7(To the half-tribe of Manasseh Moses had given land in Bashan,[h] and to the other
half of the tribe Joshua gave land on the west side[i] of the Jordan with their brothers.)
When Joshua sent them home, he blessed them, 8saying, "Return to your homes with
your great wealth—with large herds of livestock,[j] with silver, gold, bronze and iron,
and a great quantity of clothing—and divide[k] with your brothers the plunder[l] from
your enemies."
9So the Reubenites, the Gadites and the half-tribe of Manasseh left the Israelites
at Shiloh in Canaan to return to Gilead,[m] their own land, which they had acquired
in accordance with the command of the LORD through Moses.
10When they came to Geliloth near the Jordan in the land of Canaan, the Reubenites,
the Gadites and the half-tribe of Manasseh built an imposing altar there by the Jordan.
11And when the Israelites heard that they had built the altar on the border of Canaan
at Geliloth near the Jordan on the Israelite side, 12the whole assembly of Israel
gathered at Shiloh[n] to go to war against them.
13So the Israelites sent Phinehas[o] son of Eleazar,[p] the priest, to the land of
Gilead—to Reuben, Gad and the half-tribe of Manasseh. 14With him they sent ten
of the chief men, one for each of the tribes of Israel, each the head of a family division
among the Israelite clans.[q]
15When they went to Gilead—to Reuben, Gad and the half-tribe of Manasseh—they said to them: 16"The whole assembly of the LORD says: 'How could you
break faith[r] with the God of Israel like this? How could you turn away from the LORD
and build yourselves an altar in rebellion[s] against him now? 17Was not the sin of
Peor[t] enough for us? Up to this very day we have not cleansed ourselves from that
sin, even though a plague fell on the community of the LORD! 18And are you now
turning away from the LORD?
" 'If you rebel against the LORD today, tomorrow he will be angry with the whole
community[u] of Israel. 19If the land you possess is defiled, come over to the LORD's
land, where the LORD's tabernacle stands, and share the land with us. But do not rebel

22:2 [a]Nu 32:25
22:4 [b]Nu 32:22; Dt 3:20 [c]Nu 32:18; Jos 1:13-15
22:5 [d]Isa 43:22 [e]Dt 5:29 [f]Dt 6:6, 17
22:6 [g]Ex 39:43
22:7 [h]Nu 32:33; Jos 12:5 [i]Jos 17:2, 5
22:8 [j]Dt 20:14 [k]Nu 31:27 [l]Ge 49:27; 1Sa 30:16; Isa 9:3
22:9 [m]Nu 32:26, 29
22:12 [n]Jos 18:1
22:13 [o]Nu 25:7 [p]Nu 3:32; Jos 24:33
22:14 [q]Nu 1:4
22:16 [r]Dt 13:14 [s]Dt 12:13-14
22:17 [t]Nu 25:1-9
22:18 [u]Lev 10:6; Nu 16:22

22:2-4 Before the conquest had begun, these tribes were given land on the east side of the Jordan River. But before they could settle down, they had to first promise to help the other tribes conquer the land on the west side (Numbers 32:20–22). They had patiently and diligently carried out their promised duties. Joshua commended them for doing just that. At last they were permitted to return to their families and build their cities. Follow-through is vital in God's work. Beware of the temptation to quit early and leave God's work undone.

22:5 Here Joshua briefly restated the central message Moses gave the people in Deuteronomy: Obedience should be based on love for God. Although the Israelites had completed their military responsibility, Joshua reminded them of their spiritual responsibility. Sometimes we think so much about what we are to do that we neglect thinking about who we are to be. If we know we are God's children, we will love him and joyfully serve him. We must not let daily service take away from our love for God.

22:11-34 When the tribes of Reuben and Gad and the half-tribe of Manasseh built an altar at the Jordan River, the rest of Israel feared that these tribes were starting their own religion and rebelling against God. But before beginning an all-out war, Phinehas led a delegation to learn the truth, following the principle taught in Deuteronomy 13:12–19. He was prepared to negotiate rather than fight if a battle was not necessary. When he learned that the altar was for a memorial rather than for pagan sacrifice, war was averted and unity restored.

As nations and as individuals, we would benefit from a similar approach to resolving conflicts. Assuming the worst about the intentions of others only brings trouble. Israel averted the threat of civil war by asking before assaulting. Beware of reacting before you hear the whole story.

22:17 For the story of how Israel turned away from God and began to worship Baal at Peor, see Numbers 25:1–18.

22:20 [v]Jos 7:1 [w]Ps 7:11 [x]Jos 7:5
22:22 [y]Dt 10:17 [z]Ps 50:1 [a]1Ki 8:39; Job 10:7; Ps 44:21; Jer 17:10
22:23 [b]Jer 41:5 [c]Dt 12:11; 18:19; 1Sa 20:16
22:27 [d]Ge 21:30; Jos 24:27 [e]Dt 12:6
22:29 [f]Jos 24:16 [g]Dt 12:13-14
22:31 [h]Lev 26:11-12; 2Ch 15:2
22:33 [i]1Ch 29:20; Da 2:19; Lk 2:28
22:34 [j]Ge 21:30
23:1 [a]Dt 12:9; Jos 21:44 [b]Jos 13:1
23:2 [c]Jos 7:6 [d]Jos 24:1
23:3 [e]Ex 14:14
23:4 [f]Jos 19:51 [g]Nu 34:6

against the LORD or against us by building an altar for yourselves, other than the altar of the LORD our God.
20When Achan son of Zerah acted unfaithfully regarding the devoted things,[a][v] did not wrath[w] come upon the whole community of Israel? He was not the only one who died for his sin.' "[x]
21Then Reuben, Gad and the half-tribe of Manasseh replied to the heads of the clans of Israel:
22"The Mighty One, God, the LORD! The Mighty One, God,[y] the LORD![z] He knows![a] And let Israel know! If this has been in rebellion or disobedience to the LORD, do not spare us this day.
23If we have built our own altar to turn away from the LORD and to offer burnt offerings and grain offerings,[b] or to sacrifice fellowship offerings[b] on it, may the LORD himself call us to account.[c]
24"No! We did it for fear that some day your descendants might say to ours, 'What do you have to do with the LORD, the God of Israel?
25The LORD has made the Jordan a boundary between us and you—you Reubenites and Gadites! You have no share in the LORD.' So your descendants might cause ours to stop fearing the LORD.
26"That is why we said, 'Let us get ready and build an altar—but not for burnt offerings or sacrifices.'
27On the contrary, it is to be a witness[d] between us and you and the generations that follow, that we will worship the LORD at his sanctuary with our burnt offerings, sacrifices and fellowship offerings.[e] Then in the future your descendants will not be able to say to ours, 'You have no share in the LORD.'
28"And we said, 'If they ever say this to us, or to our descendants, we will answer: Look at the replica of the LORD's altar, which our fathers built, not for burnt offerings and sacrifices, but as a witness between us and you.'
29"Far be it from us to rebel[f] against the LORD and turn away from him today by building an altar for burnt offerings, grain offerings and sacrifices, other than the altar of the LORD our God that stands before his tabernacle.[g]"
30When Phinehas the priest and the leaders of the community—the heads of the clans of the Israelites—heard what Reuben, Gad and Manasseh had to say, they were pleased.
31And Phinehas son of Eleazar, the priest, said to Reuben, Gad and Manasseh, "Today we know that the LORD is with us,[h] because you have not acted unfaithfully towards the LORD in this matter. Now you have rescued the Israelites from the LORD's hand."
32Then Phinehas son of Eleazar, the priest, and the leaders returned to Canaan from their meeting with the Reubenites and Gadites in Gilead and reported to the Israelites.
33They were glad to hear the report and praised God.[i] And they talked no more about going to war against them to devastate the country where the Reubenites and the Gadites lived.
34And the Reubenites and the Gadites gave the altar this name: A Witness[j] Between Us that the LORD is God.

4. Joshua's farewell to the leaders

23 After a long time had passed and the LORD had given Israel rest[a] from all their enemies around them, Joshua, by then old and well advanced in years,[b]
2summoned all Israel—their elders,[c] leaders, judges and officials[d]—and said to them: "I am old and well advanced in years.
3You yourselves have seen everything the LORD your God has done to all these nations for your sake; it was the LORD your God who fought for you.[e]
4Remember how I have allotted[f] as an inheritance for your tribes all the land of the nations that remain—the nations I conquered—between the Jordan and the Great Sea[a][g] in the west.
5The LORD your God himself will drive

[a] *20* The Hebrew term refers to the irrevocable giving over of things or persons to the LORD, often by totally destroying them. [b] *23* Traditionally *peace offerings*; also in verse 27 [a] *4* That is, the Mediterranean

---

22:20 For the story of Achan, a man who allowed greed to get the best of him, see chapter 7.

22:26–28 The tribes were concerned that, without some visible sign of unity between the people on the two sides of the Jordan, future generations might see conflict between them. The altar, patterned after the altar of the Lord, was to remind these people that they all worshipped the same God. Often we need to be reminded of the faith of our fathers. What actions demonstrate to your children your reliance on God and remind them of what he has done? Take the time to establish family traditions that will help your children remember.

them out of your way. He will push them out before you, and you will take possession
of their land, as the LORD your God promised you.[h]
6"Be very strong; be careful to obey all that is written in the Book of the Law of
Moses, without turning aside to the right or to the left.[i] 7Do not associate with these
nations that remain among you; do not invoke the names of their gods or swear[j] by
them. You must not serve them or bow down[k] to them. 8But you are to hold fast
to the LORD[l] your God, as you have until now.
9"The LORD has driven out before you great and powerful nations;[m] to this day
no-one has been able to withstand you.[n] 10One of you routs a thousand,[o] because
the LORD your God fights for you,[p] just as he promised. 11So be very careful to love
the LORD[q] your God.
12"But if you turn away and ally yourselves with the survivors of these nations that
remain among you and if you intermarry with them[r] and associate with them,[s] 13then
you may be sure that the LORD your God will no longer drive out these nations before
you. Instead, they will become snares[t] and traps for you, whips on your backs and
thorns in your eyes,[u] until you perish from this good land, which the LORD your God
has given you.
14"Now I am about to go the way of all the earth.[v] You know with all your heart
and soul that not one of all the good promises the LORD your God gave you has failed.
Every promise has been fulfilled; not one has failed.[w] 15But just as every good
promise of the LORD your God has come true, so the LORD will bring on you all the
evil he has threatened, until he has destroyed you from this good land he has given
you.[x] 16If you violate the covenant of the LORD your God, which he commanded you,
and go and serve other gods and bow down to them, the LORD's anger will burn against
you, and you will quickly perish from the good land he has given you.[y]"

The Covenant Renewed at Shechem

24 Then Joshua assembled all the tribes of Israel at Shechem. He summoned the
elders, leaders, judges and officials of Israel,[a] and they presented themselves
before God.
2Joshua said to all the people, "This is what the LORD, the God of Israel, says: 'Long
ago your forefathers, including Terah the father of Abraham and Nahor, lived beyond
the River[a] and worshipped other gods.[b] 3But I took your father Abraham from the

a 2 That is, the Euphrates; also in verses 3, 14 and 15

23:5 [h]Ex 23:30; Nu 33:53
23:6 [i]Dt 5:32; Jos 1:7
23:7 [j]Ex 23:13; Ps 16:4; Jer 5:7 [k]Ex 20:5
23:8 [l]Dt 10:20
23:9 [m]Dt 11:23 [n]Dt 7:24
23:10 [o]Lev 26:8 [p]Ex 14:14; Dt 3:22
23:11 [q]Jos 22:5
23:12 [r]Dt 7:3 [s]Ex 34:16; Ps 106:34-35
23:13 [t]Ex 23:33 [u]Nu 33:55
23:14 [v]1Ki 2:2 [w]Jos 21:45
23:15 [x]Lev 26:17; Dt 28:15
23:16 [y]Dt 4:25-26
24:1 [a]Jos 23:2
24:2 [b]Ge 11:32

23:6–13 Joshua knew the nation's weak spots. Before dying, he called the people together and gave commands to help them where they were most likely to slip: (1) follow all that is written in the Book of the Law of Moses without turning aside; (2) don't associate with the pagan nations or worship their gods; (3) don't intermarry with the pagan nations. These temptations were right on their doorstep. Our associations and relationships can be temptations to us as well. It's wise to identify our weak spots *before* we break down. Then we can develop strategies to overcome these temptations instead of being overcome by them.

23:8 Joshua was dying and so he called all the leaders of the nation together to give them his final words of encouragement and instruction. His whole message can be summarised in this verse, "Hold fast to the LORD your God." Joshua had been a living example of those words, and he wanted that to be his legacy. For what do you want to be remembered, and what do you want to pass on to your children and associates? You can leave them nothing better than the admonition to hold on to God and to the memory of a person who did.

23:12–16 This chilling prediction about the consequences of intermarriage with the Canaanite nations eventually became a reality. Numerous stories in the book of Judges show what Israel had to suffer because of failure to follow God wholeheartedly. God was supremely loving and patient with Israel, just as he is today. But we must not confuse his patience with us as approval or indifference to our sin. Beware of demanding your own way because eventually you may get it—along with all its painful consequences.

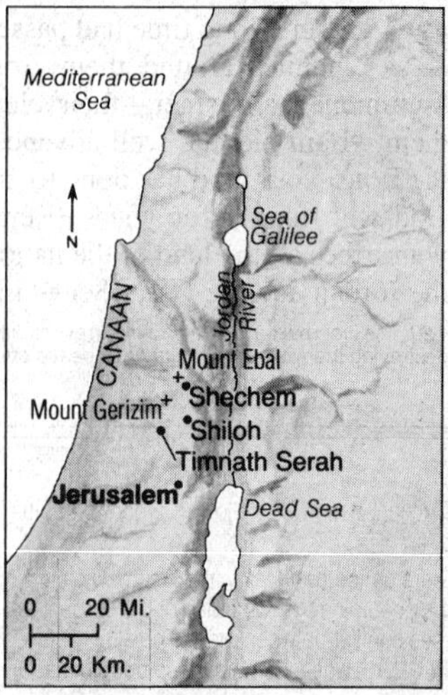

JOSHUA'S FINAL SPEECH
Joshua called all the Israelites to Shechem to hear his final words. He challenged the people to make a conscious choice always to serve God. Soon afterwards, Joshua died and was buried in his home town of Timnath Serah.

land beyond the River and led him throughout Canaan[c] and gave him many descendants.[d] I gave him Isaac,[e] 4and to Isaac I gave Jacob and Esau.[f] I assigned the hill
country of Seir[g] to Esau, but Jacob and his sons went down to Egypt.[h]
5“ ‘Then I sent Moses and Aaron,[i] and I afflicted the Egyptians by what I did there,
and I brought you out. 6When I brought your fathers out of Egypt, you came to the
sea, and the Egyptians pursued them with chariots and horsemen[b][j] as far as the Red
Sea.[c] 7But they cried to the LORD for help, and he put darkness[k] between you and
the Egyptians; he brought the sea over them and covered them.[l] You saw with your
own eyes what I did to the Egyptians. Then you lived in the desert for a long time.[m]
8“ ‘I brought you to the land of the Amorites who lived east of the Jordan. They
fought against you, but I gave them into your hands. I destroyed them from before
you, and you took possession of their land.[n] 9When Balak son of Zippor,[o] the king
of Moab, prepared to fight against Israel, he sent for Balaam son of Beor to put a curse
on you.[p] 10But I would not listen to Balaam, so he blessed you[q] again and again,
and I delivered you out of his hand.
11“ ‘Then you crossed the Jordan[r] and came to Jericho.[s] The citizens of Jericho
fought against you, as did also the Amorites, Perizzites, Canaanites, Hittites, Girgashites, Hivites and Jebusites, but I gave them into your hands.[t] 12I sent the hornet[u]
ahead of you, which drove them out before you—also the two Amorite kings. You
did not do it with your own sword and bow. 13So I gave you a land on which you
did not toil and cities you did not build; and you live in them and eat from vineyards
and olive groves that you did not plant.’[v]
14“Now fear the LORD and serve him with all faithfulness.[w] Throw away the gods[x]
your forefathers worshipped beyond the River and in Egypt,[y] and serve the LORD.
15But if serving the LORD seems undesirable to you, then choose for yourselves this
day whom you will serve, whether the gods your forefathers served beyond the River,
or the gods of the Amorites,[z] in whose land you are living. But as for me and my
household, we will serve the LORD.”[a]
16Then the people answered, “Far be it from us to forsake the LORD to serve other
gods! 17It was the LORD our God himself who brought us and our fathers up out of
Egypt, from that land of slavery, and performed those great signs before our eyes.
He protected us on our entire journey and among all the nations through which we
travelled. 18And the LORD drove out before us all the nations, including the Amorites,
who lived in the land. We too will serve the LORD, because he is our God.”
19Joshua said to the people, “You are not able to serve the LORD. He is a holy God;[b]
he is a jealous God.[c] He will not forgive your rebellion[d] and your sins. 20If you
forsake the LORD[e] and serve foreign gods, he will turn[f] and bring disaster on you
and make an end of you,[g] after he has been good to you.”
21But the people said to Joshua, “No! We will serve the LORD.”
22Then Joshua said, “You are witnesses against yourselves that you have chosen[h]
to serve the LORD.”
“Yes, we are witnesses,” they replied.
23“Now then,” said Joshua, “throw away the foreign gods[i] that are among you and
yield your hearts[j] to the LORD, the God of Israel.”

24:3 [c]Ge 12:1 [d]Ge 15:5 [e]Ge 21:3
24:4 [f]Ge 25:26 [g]Dt 2:5 [h]Ge 46:5-6
24:5 [i]Ex 3:10
24:6 [j]Ex 14:9
24:7 [k]Ex 14:20 [l]Ex 14:28 [m]Dt 1:46
24:8 [n]Nu 21:31
24:9 [o]Nu 22:2 [p]Nu 22:6
24:10 [q]Nu 23:11; Dt 23:5
24:11 [r]Jos 3:16-17 [s]Jos 6:1 [t]Ex 23:23; Dt 7:1
24:12 [u]Ex 23:28; Dt 7:20; Ps 44:3, 6-7
24:13 [v]Dt 6:10-11
24:14 [w]Dt 10:12; 18:13; 1Sa 12:24; 2Co 1:12 [x]ver 23 [y]Eze 23:3
24:15 [z]Jdg 6:10; Ru 1:15 [a]Ru 1:16; 1Ki 18:21
24:19 [b]Lev 19:2; 20:26 [c]Ex 20:5 [d]Ex 23:21
24:20 [e]1Ch 28:9, 20 [f]Ac 7:42 [g]Jos 23:15
24:22 [h]Ps 119:30, 173
24:23 [i]ver 14 [j]1Ki 8:58; Ps 119:36; 141:4

[b] *6* Or *charioteers* [c] *6* Hebrew *Yam Suph*; that is, Sea of Reeds

---

24:15 The people had to decide whether they would obey the Lord, who had proved his trustworthiness, or obey the local gods, which were only man-made idols. It's easy to slip into a quiet rebellion—going about life in your own way. But the time comes when you have to choose who or what will control you. The choice is yours. Will it be God, your own limited personality, or another imperfect substitute? Once you have chosen to be controlled by God's Spirit, reaffirm your choice every day.

24:15 In taking a definite stand for the Lord, Joshua again displayed his spiritual leadership. Regardless of what others decided, Joshua had made a commitment to God, and he was willing to set the example of living by that decision. The way we live shows others the strength of our commitment to serving God.

24:16–18, 21 All the people boldly claimed that they would never forsake the Lord. But they did not keep that promise. Very soon God would charge them with breaking their contract with him (Judges 2:2, 3). Talk is cheap. It is easy to say we will follow God, but it is much more important to live like it. Yet the nation followed God through Joshua's lifetime, a great tribute to Joshua's faith in God and powerful leadership.

24:23 Joshua told the Israelites to throw away their foreign gods, or idols. To follow God requires destroying whatever gets in the way of worshipping him. We have our own form of idols—greed, wrong priorities, jealousies, prejudices—that get in the way of worshipping God. God is not satisfied if we merely hide these idols. We must completely remove them from our lives.

24And the people said to Joshua, "We will serve the LORD our God and obey him."[k]
25On that day Joshua made a covenant[l] for the people, and there at Shechem he
drew up for them decrees and laws.[m] 26And Joshua recorded these things in the Book
of the Law of God.[n] Then he took a large stone[o] and set it up there under the oak
near the holy place of the LORD.
27"See!" he said to all the people. "This stone will be a witness[p] against us. It has
heard all the words the LORD has said to us. It will be a witness against you if you
are untrue to your God."

Buried in the Promised Land

28Then Joshua sent the people away, each to his own inheritance.
29After these things, Joshua son of Nun, the servant of the LORD, died at the age
of a hundred and ten.[q] 30And they buried him in the land of his inheritance, at
Timnath Serah[d][r] in the hill country of Ephraim, north of Mount Gaash.
31Israel served the LORD throughout the lifetime of Joshua and of the elders[s] who
outlived him and who had experienced everything the LORD had done for Israel.
32And Joseph's bones, which the Israelites had brought up from Egypt,[t] were
buried at Shechem in the tract of land[u] that Jacob bought for a hundred pieces of
silver[e] from the sons of Hamor, the father of Shechem. This became the inheritance
of Joseph's descendants.
33And Eleazar son of Aaron[v] died and was buried at Gibeah, which had been
allotted to his son Phinehas[w] in the hill country of Ephraim.

d *30* Also known as *Timnath Heres* (see Judges 2:9) **e** *32* Hebrew *hundred kesitahs*; a kesitah was a unit of money of unknown weight and value.

24:24 [k]Ex 19:8; 24:3, 7; Dt 5:27
24:25 [l]Ex 24:8 [m]Ex 15:25
24:26 [n]Dt 31:24 [o]Ge 28:18
24:27 [p]Jos 22:27
24:29 [q]Jdg 2:8
24:30 [r]Jos 19:50
24:31 [s]Jdg 2:7
24:32 [t]Ge 50:25; Ex 13:19 [u]Ge 33:19; Jn 4:5; Ac 7:16
24:33 [v]Jos 22:13 [w]Ex 6:25

24:24–26 The covenant between Israel and God was that the people would worship and obey the Lord alone. Their purpose was to become a holy nation that would influence the rest of the world for God. The conquest of Canaan was a means to achieve this purpose, but Israel became preoccupied with the land and lost sight of the Lord God.

The same can happen in our lives. We can spend so much time on the means that we forget the end – to glorify God. Churches may make this mistake as well. For example, the congregation may pour all of its energies into a new building extension, only to become self-satisfied or fearful of letting certain groups use it. If this happens, they have focused on the building and lost sight of its purpose – to bring others to God.

24:29–31 The book of Joshua opens with a new leader being handed a seemingly impossible task – to lead the nation in taking over the land of Canaan. By following God closely, Joshua led the people through military victories and faithful spiritual obedience. In 24:16 we read that the people were sure they would never forsake the Lord. The response of the whole nation during these many years is a tribute both to Joshua's leadership and to the God he faithfully served.

24:33 Joshua and Eleazar had died, but not before laying before the people the fundamentals of what it means to have faith in God. We are to fear and serve the Lord alone (24:14). This is based on a choice: to obey him instead of following other gods (24:15). We are incapable, however, of properly worshipping him because of our rebellion and sins (24:19). By choosing God as Lord we enter into a covenant with him (24:25) whereby he promises not only to forgive and love us, but also to enable us by his Spirit to do his work here on earth. This covenant requires us to renounce the principles and practices of the culture around us that are hostile to God's plan (24:23). This is not to be done alone, but by binding ourselves together with others who have faith in God. (See Deuteronomy 30:15–20 for a similar message from Moses.)

NAMES OF GOD

Name of God	Meaning	Reference	Significance
Elohim	God	Genesis 1:1; Numbers 23:19; Psalm 19:1	Refers to God's power and might. He is the only supreme and true God.
Yahweh	The LORD	Genesis 2:4; Exodus 6:2,3	The proper name of the divine person.
El Elyon	God Most High	Genesis 14:17-20; Numbers 24:16; Psalm 7:19; Isaiah 14:13, 14	He is above all gods; nothing in life is more sacred.
El Roi	God Who Sees	Genesis 16:12	God oversees all creation and the affairs of people.
El Shaddai	God Almighty	Genesis 17:1; Psalm 91:1	God is all-powerful.
Yahweh Yireh	The LORD will Provide	Genesis 22:13, 14	God will provide our real needs.
Yahweh Nissi	The LORD is my Banner	Exodus 17:15	We should remember God for helping us.
Adonai	Lord	Deuteronomy 6:4	God alone is the head over all.
Yahweh Elohe Yisrael	LORD God of Israel	Judges 5:3; Psalm 59:5; Isaiah 17:6; Zephaniah 2:9	He is the God of the nation.
Yahweh Shalom	The LORD is Peace	Judges 6:24	God gives us peace, so we need not fear.
Qedosh Yisrael	Holy One of Israel	Isaiah 1:4	God is morally perfect.
Yahweh Sabaoth	LORD of Hosts Host refers to armies but also to all the heavenly powers.	1 Samuel 1:3; Isaiah 6:1-3	God is our saviour and protector.
El Olam	The Everlasting God	Isaiah 40:28-31	God is eternal. He will never die.
Yahweh Tsidkenu	The LORD is Our Righteousness	Jeremiah 23:6; 33:16	God is our standard for right behaviour. He alone can make us righteous.
Yahweh Shammah	The LORD is There	Ezekiel 48:35	God is always present with us.
Attiq Yomin	Ancient of Days	Daniel 7:9; 13:12	God is the ultimate authority. He will one day judge all nations.

JUDGES

Exodus from Egypt 1446 B.C. (1280 B.C.)	*Israelites enter Canaan 1406 (1240)*	*Period of the judges begins 1375 (1220)*	*Othniel 1367–1327 (1202–1162)*	*Ehud 1309–1229 (1184–1104)*	*Deborah 1209–1169 (1192–1152)*

VITAL STATISTICS

PURPOSE:
To show that God's judgment against sin is certain, and his forgiveness of sin and restoration to relationship are just as certain for those who repent

AUTHOR:
Possibly Samuel

SETTING:
The land of Canaan, later called Israel. God had helped the Israelites to conquer Canaan, which had been inhabited by a host of wicked nations. But they were in danger of losing this promised land because they compromised their convictions and disobeyed God.

KEY VERSE:
"In those days Israel had no king; everyone did as he saw fit" (17:6).

KEY PEOPLE:
Othniel, Ehud, Deborah, Gideon, Abimelech, Jephthah, Samson, Delilah

SPECIAL FEATURE:
Records Israel's first civil war

REAL heroes are hard to find these days. Modern research and the media have made the foibles and weaknesses of our leaders very apparent; we search in vain for men and women to emulate. The music, film, and sports industries produce a steady stream of "stars" who shoot to the top and then quickly fade from view.

Judges is a book about heroes—12 men and women who delivered Israel from her oppressors. These judges were not perfect; in fact, they included an assassin, a sexually promiscuous man, and a person who broke all the laws of hospitality. But they were submissive to God, and God used them.

Judges is also a book about sin and its consequences. Like a minor cut or abrasion that becomes infected when left untreated, sin grows and soon poisons the whole body. The book of Joshua ends with the nation taking a stand for God, ready to experience all the blessings of the promised land. After settling in Canaan, however, the Israelites lost their spiritual commitment and motivation. When Joshua and the elders died, the nation experienced a leadership vacuum, leaving them without a strong central government. Instead of enjoying freedom and prosperity in the promised land, Israel entered the dark ages of her history.

Simply stated, the reason for this rapid decline was sin—individual and corporate. The first step away from God was incomplete obedience (1:11—2:5); the Israelites refused to eliminate the enemy completely from the land. This led to intermarriage and idolatry (2:6—3:7) and everyone doing "as he saw fit" (17:6). Before long the Israelites became captives. Out of their desperation they begged God to rescue them. In faithfulness to his promise and out of his loving-kindness, God would raise up a judge to deliver his people and, for a time, there would be peace. Then complacency and disobedience would set in, and the cycle would begin again.

The book of Judges spans a period of over 325 years, recording six successive periods of oppression and deliverance, and the careers of 12 deliverers. Their captors included the Mesopotamians, Moabites, Philistines, Canaanites, Midianites, and Ammonites. A variety of deliverers—from Othniel to Samson—were used by God to lead his people to freedom and true worship. God's deliverance through the judges is a powerful demonstration of his love and mercy towards his people.

As you read the book of Judges, take a good look at these heroes from Jewish history. Take note of their dependence on God and obedience to his commands. Observe Israel's repeated downward spiral into sin, refusing to learn from history and living only for the moment. But most of all, stand in awe of God's mercy as he delivers his people over and over again.

Gideon 1162–1122 (1146–1106)	Samuel born 1105 (1083)	Samson 1075–1055 (1083–1063)	Saul anointed king 1050 (1045)	David becomes king 1010

THE BLUEPRINT

A. THE MILITARY FAILURE OF ISRAEL (1:1—3:6) 1. Incomplete conquest of the land 2. Disobedience and defeat	The tribes had compromised God's command to drive out the inhabitants of the land. Incomplete removal of evil often means disaster in the end. We must beware of compromising with wickedness.
B. THE RESCUE OF ISRAEL BY THE JUDGES (3:7—16:31) 1. First period: Othniel 2. Second period: Ehud and Shamgar 3. Third period: Deborah and Barak 4. Fourth period: Gideon, Tola, and Jair 5. Fifth period: Jephthah, Ibzan, Elon, and Abdon 6. Sixth period: Samson	Repeatedly we see the nation of Israel sinning against God and God allowing suffering to come upon the land and the people. Sin always has its consequences. Where there is sin we can expect suffering to follow. Rather than living in an endless cycle of abandoning God and then crying out to him for rescue, we should seek to live a consistent life of faithfulness.
C. THE MORAL FAILURE OF ISRAEL (17:1—21:25) 1. Idolatry in the tribe of Dan 2. War against the tribe of Benjamin	Despite the efforts of Israel's judges, the people still would not turn wholeheartedly to God. They all did whatever they thought was best for themselves. The result was the spiritual, moral, and political decline of the nation. Our lives will also fall into decline and decay unless we live by the guidelines God has given us.

MEGATHEMES

THEME	EXPLANATION	IMPORTANCE
Decline/ Compromise	Whenever a judge died, the people faced decline and failure because they compromised their high spiritual purpose in many ways. They abandoned their mission to drive all the people out of the land, and they adopted the customs of the people living around them.	Society has many rewards to offer those who compromise their faith: wealth, acceptance, recognition, power, and influence. When God gives us a mission, it must not be polluted by a desire for approval from society. We must keep our eyes on Christ who is our Judge and Deliverer.
Decay/Apostasy	Israel's moral downfall had its roots in the fierce independence that each tribe cherished. It led to everyone doing whatever seemed good in his own eyes. There was no unity in government or in worship. Law and order broke down. Finally idol worship and man-made religion led to the complete abandoning of faith in God.	We can expect decay when we value anything more highly than God. If we value our own independence more than dedication to God, we have placed an idol in our hearts. Soon our lives become temples to that god. We must constantly regard God's first claim on our lives and all our desires.
Defeat/ Oppression	God used evil oppressors to punish the Israelites for their sin, to bring them to the point of repentance, and to test their allegiance to him.	Rebellion against God leads to disaster. God may use defeat to bring wandering hearts back to him. When all else is stripped away, we recognise the importance of serving only him.
Repentance	Decline, decay, and defeat caused the people to cry out to God for help. They vowed to turn from idolatry and to turn to God for mercy and deliverance. When they repented, God delivered them.	Idolatry gains a foothold in our hearts when we make anything more important than God. We must identify modern idols in our hearts, renounce them, and turn to God for his love and mercy.

Deliverance/ Heroes	Because Israel repented, God raised up heroes to deliver his people from their path of sin and the oppression it brought. He used many kinds of people to accomplish this purpose by filling them with his Holy Spirit.	God's Holy Spirit is available to all people. Anyone who is dedicated to God can be used for his service. Real heroes recognise the futility of human effort without God's guidance and power.

KEY PLACES IN JUDGES

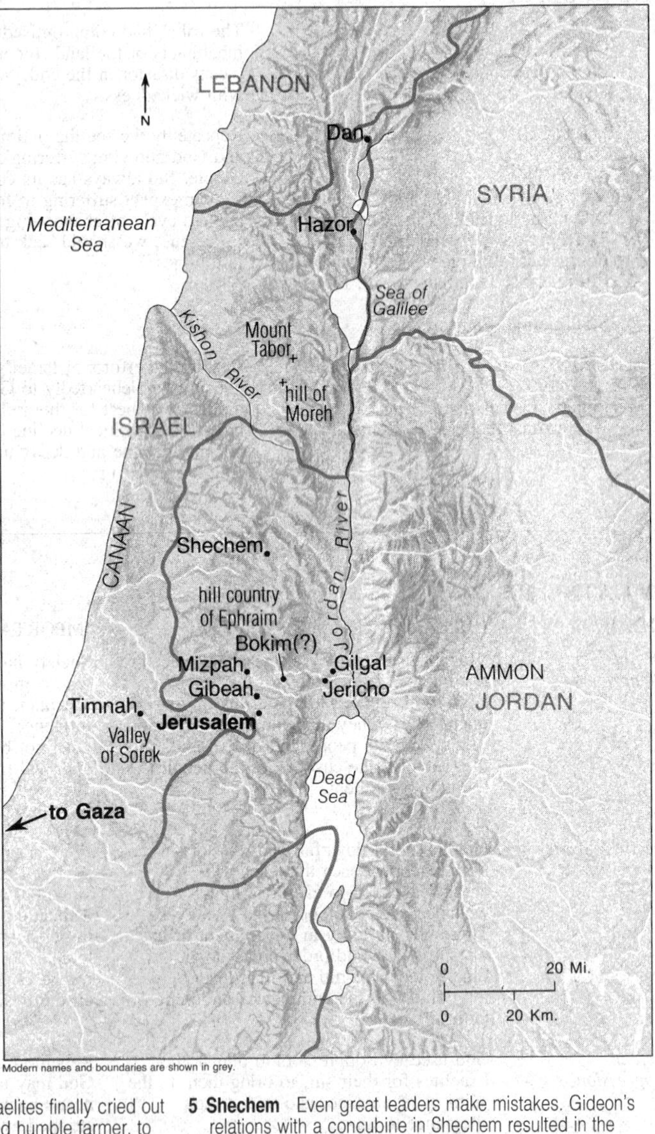

Modern names and boundaries are shown in grey.

1 Bokim The book of Judges opens with the Israelites continuing their conquest of the promised land. Their failure to obey God and destroy all the evil inhabitants soon comes back to haunt them in two ways: (1) the enemies reorganised and counterattacked, and (2) Israel turned away from God, adopting the evil and idolatrous practices of the inhabitants of the land. The angel of the Lord appeared at Bokim to inform the Israelites that their sin and disobedience had broken their agreement with God and would result in punishment through oppression (1:1–3:11).

2 Jericho The nation of Moab was one of the first to oppress Israel. Moab's King Eglon conquered much of Israel—including the city of Jericho ("the City of Palms")—and forced the people to pay unreasonable taxes. The messenger chosen to deliver this tax money to King Eglon was named Ehud. But he had more than money to deliver, for he drew his hidden sword and killed the Moabite king. Ehud then escaped, only to return with an army that chased out the Moabites and freed Israel from its oppressors (3:12–31).

3 Hazor After Ehud's death, King Jabin of Hazor conquered Israel and oppressed the people for 20 years. Then Deborah became Israel's leader. She summoned Barak to fight Commander Sisera, the leader of King Jabin's army. Together Deborah and Barak led their army into battle against Jabin's forces in the land between Mount Tabor and the Kishon River and conquered them (4:1—5:31).

4 Hill of Moreh After 40 years of peace, the Midianites began to harass the Israelites by destroying their flocks and crops. When the Israelites finally cried out to God, he chose Gideon, a poor and humble farmer, to be their deliverer. After struggling with doubt and feelings of inferiority, Gideon took courage and knocked down his town's altar to Baal, causing a great uproar among the citizens. Filled with the Spirit of God, he attacked the vast army of Midian, which was camped near the hill of Moreh. With just a handful of men he sent the enemy running away in confusion (6:1—7:25).

5 Shechem Even great leaders make mistakes. Gideon's relations with a concubine in Shechem resulted in the birth of a son named Abimelech. Abimelech turned out to be treacherous and power hungry—stirring up the people to proclaim him king. To carry out his plan, he went so far as to kill 69 of his 70 half brothers. Eventually some men of Shechem rebelled against Abimelech, but he gathered together an army and defeated them. His lust for power led him to ransack two other cities, but he was killed by a woman who dropped a millstone onto his head (8:28–9:57).

6 Land of Ammon Again Israel turned completely from God; so God turned from them. But when the Ammonites mobilised their army to attack, Israel threw away her idols and called upon God once again. Jephthah, a prostitute's son who had been run out of Israel, was asked to return and lead Israel's forces against the enemy. After defeating the Ammonites, Jephthah became involved in a war with the tribe of Ephraim over a misunderstanding (10:1–12:15).

7 Timnah Israel's next judge, Samson, was a miracle child promised by God to a barren couple. He was the one who would begin to free Israel from their next and most powerful oppressor, the Philistines. According to God's command, Samson was to be a Nazirite—one who took a vow to be set apart for special service to God. One of the stipulations of the vow was that Samson's hair could never be cut. But when Samson grew up, he did not always take his special responsibility to God seriously. He even fell in love with a Philistine girl in Timnah and asked to marry her. Before the wedding, Samson held a party for some men in the city, using a riddle to place a bet with them. The men, however, forced Samson's fiancée into giving away the answer. Furious at being tricked, Samson paid his bet with the lives of 30 Philistines who lived in the nearby city of Ashkelon (13:1–14:20).

8 Valley of Sorek Samson killed thousands of Philistines with his incredible strength. The nation's leaders looked for a way to stop him. They got their chance when another Philistine woman stole Samson's heart. Her name was Delilah, and she lived in the Valley of Sorek. In exchange for a great sum of money, Delilah deceived Samson into confiding in her the secret of his strength. One night while he slept, Delilah cut off his hair. As a result, Samson fell helplessly into the hands of the enemy (15:1–16:20).

9 Gaza Samson was blinded and led captive to a prison in Gaza. There his hair began to grow again. After a while, the Philistines held a great festival to celebrate Samson's imprisonment and to humiliate him before the crowds. When he was brought out as the entertainment, he literally brought down the house when he pushed on the main pillars of the banquet hall and killed the thousands trapped inside. The prophecy that he would begin to free Israel from the Philistines had come true (16:21–31).

10 Hill Country of Ephraim In the hill country of Ephraim lived a man named Micah. Micah employed his own priest to perform priestly duties in the shrine which housed his collection of idols. He thought he was pleasing God with all his religiosity! Like many of the Israelites, Micah assumed that his own opinions of what was right would agree with God's (17:1–13).

11 Dan The tribe of Dan migrated north in order to find new territory. They sent spies ahead of them to scout out the land. One night the spies stopped at Micah's home. Looking for some assurance of victory, the spies stole Micah's idols and priest. Rejoining the tribe, they came upon the city of Laish and slaughtered the unarmed and innocent citizens, renaming the conquered city Dan. Micah's idols were then set up in the city and became the focal point of the tribe's worship for many years (18:1–31).

12 Gibeah The extent to which many people had fallen away from God became clear in Gibeah, a village in the territory of Benjamin. A man and his concubine were travelling north towards the hill country of Ephraim. They stopped for the night in Gibeah, thinking they would be safe. But some perverts in the city gathered around the home where they were staying and demanded that the man come out to have sexual relations with them. Instead, the man and his host pushed the concubine out of the door. She was raped and abused all night. When the man found her lifeless body the next morning, he cut it into 12 pieces and sent one part to each of the Tribes of Israel. This tragic event demonstrated that the nation had sunk to its lowest spiritual level (19:1–30).

13 Mizpah The leaders of Israel came to Mizpah to decide how to punish the wicked men from the city of Gibeah. When the city leaders refused to turn the criminals over, the whole nation of Israel took vengeance upon both Gibeah and the tribe of Benjamin where the city was located. When the battle ended, the entire tribe had been destroyed except for a handful of men who took refuge in the hills. Israel had become morally depraved. The stage was now set for the much-needed spiritual renewal that would come under the prophet Samuel (20:1–21:25).

A. THE MILITARY FAILURE OF ISRAEL (1:1 – 3:6)

By faithfully obeying the Lord, Joshua led the Israelites to military victory. After his death, however, the tribes failed to clear the inhabitants from the land, so the Lord withdrew his promise to help drive the people out and bless the Israelites in battle. The new generation abandoned God and worshipped idols. This part of Judges shows what can happen when we neglect to teach our children to follow the Lord.

1. Incomplete conquest of the land

Israel Fights the Remaining Canaanites

1 After the death[a] of Joshua, the Israelites asked the LORD, "Who will be the first[b]
to go up and fight for us against the Canaanites?[c]"
2The LORD answered, "Judah[d] is to go; I have given the land into their hands.[e]"
3Then the men of Judah said to the Simeonites their brothers, "Come up with us
into the territory allotted to us, to fight against the Canaanites. We in turn will go with
you into yours." So the Simeonites[f] went with them.
4When Judah attacked, the LORD gave the Canaanites and Perizzites[g] into their
hands and they struck down ten thousand men at Bezek.[h] 5It was there that they found
Adoni-Bezek and fought against him, putting to rout the Canaanites and Perizzites.
6Adoni-Bezek fled, but they chased him and caught him, and cut off his thumbs and
big toes.
7Then Adoni-Bezek said, "Seventy kings with their thumbs and big toes cut off have
picked up scraps under my table. Now God has paid me back[i] for what I did to them."
They brought him to Jerusalem, and he died there.
8The men of Judah attacked Jerusalem[j] also and took it. They put the city to the
sword and set it on fire.
9After that, the men of Judah went down to fight against the Canaanites living in
the hill country,[k] the Negev[l] and the western foothills. 10They advanced against the
Canaanites living in Hebron[m] (formerly called Kiriath Arba[n]) and defeated Sheshai,
Ahiman and Talmai.[o]
11From there they advanced against the people living in Debir[p] (formerly called
Kiriath Sepher). 12And Caleb said, "I will give my daughter Acsah in marriage to the
man who attacks and captures Kiriath Sepher." 13Othniel son of Kenaz, Caleb's
younger brother, took it; so Caleb gave his daughter Acsah to him in marriage.

1:1 [a]Jos 24:29 [b]Nu 27:21 [c]ver 27; Jdg 3:1-6
1:2 [d]Ge 49:8 [e]ver 4; Jdg 3:28
1:3 [f]ver 17
1:4 [g]Ge 13:7; Jos 3:10 [h]1Sa 11:8
1:7 [i]Lev 24:19
1:8 [j]ver 21; Jos 15:63
1:9 [k]Nu 13:17 [l]Nu 21:1
1:10 [m]Ge 13:18 [n]Ge 35:27 [o]Jos 15:14
1:11 [p]Jos 15:15

1:1 The people of Israel had finally entered and taken control of the land promised to their ancestors (Genesis 12:7; Exodus 3:16, 17). The book of Judges continues the story of this conquest that began in the book of Joshua. Through God's strength, the Israelites had conquered many enemies and overcome many difficulties, but their work was not yet finished. They had effectively met many political and military challenges, but facing spiritual challenges was more difficult. The unholy but attractive life-style of the Canaanites proved more dangerous than their military might. The Israelites gave in to the pressure and compromised their faith. If we attempt to meet life's challenges with human effort alone, we will find the pressures and temptations around us too great to resist.

1:1 Soon after Joshua died, Israel began to lose its firm grip on the land. Although Joshua was a great commander, the people missed his spiritual leadership even more than his military skill, for he had kept the people focused on God and his purposes. Joshua had been the obvious successor to Moses, but there was no obvious successor to Joshua. During this crisis of leadership, Israel had to learn that no matter how powerful and wise the current leader was, their real leader was God. We often focus our hope and confidence on some influential leader, failing to realise that in reality it is God who is in command. Acknowledge God as your commander in chief, and avoid the temptation of relying too heavily on human leaders, regardless of their spiritual wisdom.

1:1 The Canaanites were all the people who lived in Canaan (the promised land). They lived in city-states where each city had its own government, army, and laws. One reason Canaan was so difficult to conquer was that each city had to be defeated individually. There was no single king who could surrender the entire country into the hands of the Israelites.

Canaan's greatest threat to Israel was not its army, but its religion. Canaanite religion idealised evil traits: cruelty in war, sexual immorality, selfish greed, and materialism. It was a "me first, anything goes" society. Obviously, the religions of Israel and Canaan could not coexist.

1:2 The book of Joshua tells of a swift and thorough conquest of enemy armies and cities, while the book of Judges seems to suggest a more lengthy and gradual conquest. When the Israelites first entered the promised land (Joshua 1 – 12), they united as one army to crush the inhabitants until they were too weak to retaliate. Then, after the land was divided among the 12 tribes (Joshua 13 – 24), each tribe was responsible for driving out the remaining enemy from its own territory. The book of Judges tells of their failure to do this.

Some tribes were more successful than others. Under Joshua, they all began strong, but soon most were sidetracked by fear, weariness, lack of discipline, or pursuit of their own interests. As a result, their faith began to fade away, and "everyone did as he saw fit" (17:6). In order for our faith to survive, it must be practised day by day. It must penetrate every aspect of our lives. Beware of starting out strong and then getting sidetracked from your real purpose – loving God and living for him.

1:6 The Israelites cut off the thumbs and big toes of Adoni-Bezek to humiliate him and make him ineffective in battle. But according to God's instructions for conquering the promised land, he should have been killed.

1:8 Although the Israelites conquered Jerusalem, they did not occupy the city until the days of David (2 Samuel 5:6–10).

1:16 [q]Nu 10:29 [r]Ge 15:19; Jdg 4:11 [s]Dt 34:3; Jdg 3:13 [t]Nu 21:1
1:17 [u]ver 3 [v]Nu 21:3
1:18 [w]Jos 11:22
1:19 [x]ver 2 [y]Jos 17:16
1:20 [z]Jos 14:9; 15:13-14 [a]ver 10; Jos 14:13
1:21 [b]Jos 15:63 [c]ver 8
1:23 [d]Ge 28:19
1:24 [e]Jos 2:12, 14
1:25 [f]Jos 6:25
1:27 [g]Jos 17:11 [h]ver 1

14 One day when she came to Othniel, she urged him[a] to ask her father for a field.
When she got off her donkey, Caleb asked her, "What can I do for you?"
15 She replied, "Do me a special favour. Since you have given me land in the Negev,
give me also springs of water." Then Caleb gave her the upper and lower springs.
16 The descendants of Moses' father-in-law,[q] the Kenite,[r] went up from the City
of Palms[b][s] with the men of Judah to live among the people of the Desert of Judah
in the Negev near Arad.[t]
17 Then the men of Judah went with the Simeonites[u] their brothers and attacked
the Canaanites living in Zephath, and they totally destroyed[c] the city. Therefore it
was called Hormah.[d][v] 18 The men of Judah also took[e] Gaza,[w] Ashkelon and
Ekron—each city with its territory.
19 The LORD was with[x] the men of Judah. They took possession of the hill country,
but they were unable to drive the people from the plains, because they had iron
chariots.[y] 20 As Moses had promised, Hebron[z] was given to Caleb, who drove from
it the three sons of Anak.[a] 21 The Benjamites, however, failed[b] to dislodge the
Jebusites, who were living in Jerusalem;[c] to this day the Jebusites live there with the
Benjamites.
22 Now the house of Joseph attacked Bethel, and the LORD was with them. 23 When
they sent men to spy out Bethel (formerly called Luz),[d] 24 the spies saw a man coming
out of the city and they said to him, "Show us how to get into the city and we will
see that you are treated well.[e]" 25 So he showed them, and they put the city to the
sword but spared[f] the man and his whole family. 26 He then went to the land of the
Hittites, where he built a city and called it Luz, which is its name to this day.
27 But Manasseh did not drive out the people of Beth Shan or Taanach or Dor or
Ibleam[g] or Megiddo and their surrounding settlements, for the Canaanites[h] were
determined to live in that land. 28 When Israel became strong, they pressed the
Canaanites into forced labour but never drove them out completely. 29 Nor did Ephraim

[a] 14 Hebrew; Septuagint and Vulgate *Othniel, he urged her* [b] 16 That is, Jericho [c] 17 The Hebrew term refers to the irrevocable giving over of things or persons to the LORD, often by totally destroying them. [d] 17 *Hormah* means *destruction.* [e] 18 Hebrew; Septuagint *Judah did not take*

JUDAH FIGHTS FOR ITS LAND
The tribe of Judah wasted no time beginning their conquest of the territory allotted to them. With help from the tribe of Simeon, Jerusalem was conquered, as were the Canaanites in the Negev and along the coast. Hebron and Debir fell to Judah, and later Gaza, Ashkelon, and Ekron.

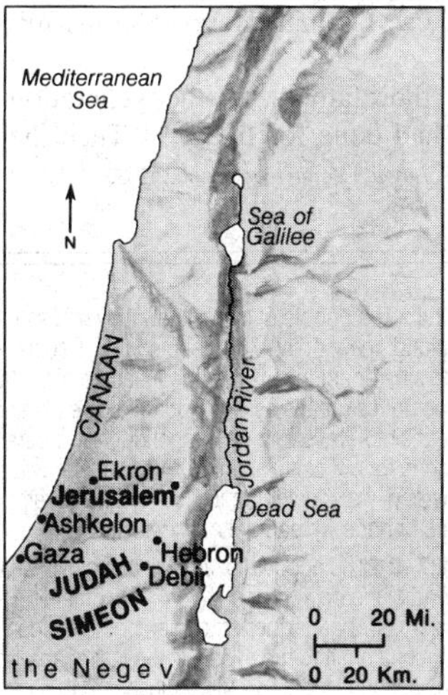

1:12–15 This same event is recorded in Joshua 15:16–19. Caleb was one of the original spies who scouted out the promised land (Numbers 13—14) and, with Joshua, encouraged the people to conquer it. For his faithfulness, he was given the land of his choice.

1:17 Why did God order the Israelites to drive the Canaanites from their land? Although the command seems cruel, the Israelites were under God's order to execute judgment on those wicked people. The other nations were to be judged for their sin as God had judged Israel by forcing them to wander for 40 years before they were allowed to enter the promised land. Over 700 years earlier, God had told Abraham that when the Israelites entered the promised land, the gross evil of the native people would be ready for judgment (Genesis 15:16). But God wasn't playing favourites with the Israelites because eventually they too would be severely punished for becoming as evil as the people they were ordered to drive out (2 Kings 17; 25; Jeremiah 6:18; 19; Ezekiel 8). God is not partial; all people are eligible for God's gracious forgiveness as well as for his firm justice.

1:19 Canaanite chariots pulled by horses were among the most sophisticated weapons of the day. Israelite foot soldiers were absolutely powerless when a speeding iron chariot bore down upon them. This is why Israel preferred to fight in the hills where chariots couldn't venture.

1:21ff Tribe after tribe failed to drive the evil Canaanites from their land. Why didn't they follow through and completely obey God's commands? (1) They had been fighting for a long time and were tired. Although the goal was in sight, they lacked the discipline and energy to reach it. (2) They were afraid the enemy was too strong—the iron chariots seemed invincible. (3) Since Joshua's death, power and authority had been decentralised to the tribal leaders, and the tribes were no longer unified in purpose. (4) Spiritual decay had infected them from within. They thought they could handle the temptation and be more prosperous by doing business with the Canaanites.

We, too, often fail to drive sin from our lives. Often we know what to do but just don't do it. This results in a gradual deterioration of our relationship with God. In our battles, we may grow tired and want rest, but we need more than a break from our work. We need to know that God loves us and has given us a purpose for life. Victory comes from living according to his purpose.

drive out the Canaanites living in Gezer,[i] but the Canaanites continued to live there
among them.[j] 30Neither did Zebulun drive out the Canaanites living in Kitron or
Nahalol, who remained among them; but they did subject them to forced labour. 31Nor
did Asher drive out those living in Acco or Sidon or Ahlab or Aczib[k] or Helbah or
Aphek or Rehob, 32and because of this the people of Asher lived among the Canaanite
inhabitants of the land. 33Neither did Naphtali drive out those living in Beth Shemesh
or Beth Anath[l]; but the Naphtalites too lived among the Canaanite inhabitants of the
land, and those living in Beth Shemesh and Beth Anath became forced labourers for
them. 34The Amorites[m] confined the Danites to the hill country, not allowing them
to come down into the plain. 35And the Amorites were determined also to hold out
in Mount Heres, Aijalon[n] and Shaalbim, but when the power of the house of Joseph
increased, they too were pressed into forced labour. 36The boundary of the Amorites
was from Scorpion[f] Pass[o] to Sela and beyond.

The Angel of the LORD at Bokim

2 The angel of the LORD[a] went up from Gilgal to Bokim[b] and said, "I brought
you up out of Egypt[c] and led you into the land that I swore to give to your
forefathers.[d] I said, 'I will never break my covenant with you,[e] 2and you shall not
make a covenant with the people of this land,[f] but you shall break down their
altars.[g]' Yet you have disobeyed me. Why have you done this? 3Now therefore I tell
you that I will not drive them out before you;[h] they will be ⌞thorns⌟[i] in your sides
and their gods will be a snare[j] to you."

4When the angel of the LORD had spoken these things to all the Israelites, the people
wept aloud, 5and they called that place Bokim.[a] There they offered sacrifices to the
LORD.

2. Disobedience and defeat

6After Joshua had dismissed the Israelites, they went to take possession of the land,
each to his own inheritance. 7The people served the LORD throughout the lifetime of
Joshua and of the elders who outlived him and who had seen all the great things the
LORD had done for Israel.

8Joshua son of Nun, the servant of the LORD, died at the age of a hundred and ten.
9And they buried him in the land of his inheritance, at Timnath Heres[b][k] in the hill
country of Ephraim, north of Mount Gaash.

10After that whole generation had been gathered to their fathers, another generation
grew up, who knew neither the LORD nor what he had done for Israel.[l] 11Then the

[f] *36* Hebrew *Akrabbim* [a] *5* *Bokim* means *weepers.* [b] *9* Also known as *Timnath Serah* (see Joshua 19:50 and 24:30)

1:29 [i]1Ki 9:16 [j]Jos 16:10
1:31 [k]Jdg 10:6
1:33 [l]Jos 19:38
1:34 [m]Ex 3:17
1:35 [n]Jos 19:42
1:36 [o]Jos 15:3
2:1 [a]Jdg 6:11 [b]ver 5 [c]Ex 20:2 [d]Ge 17:8 [e]Lev 26:42-44; Dt 7:9
2:2 [f]Ex 23:32; 34:12; Dt 7:2 [g]Ex 34:13
2:3 [h]Jos 23:13 [i]Nu 33:55 [j]Dt 7:16; Jdg 3:6; Ps 106:36
2:9 [k]Jos 19:50
2:10 [l]Ex 5:2; 1Sa 2:12; 1Ch 28:9; Gal 4:8

2:1–3 This event marks a significant change in Israel's relationship with God. At Mount Sinai, God made a sacred and binding agreement with the Israelites called a covenant (Exodus 19:5–8). God's part was to make Israel a special nation (see the note on Genesis 12:1–3), to protect them, and to give them unique blessings for following him. Israel's part was to love God and obey his laws. But because they rejected and disobeyed God, the agreement to protect them was no longer in effect. But God wasn't going to abandon his people. They would receive wonderful blessings if they asked God to forgive them and sincerely followed him again.

Although God's agreement to help Israel conquer the land was no longer in effect, his promise to make Israel a nation through whom the whole world would be blessed (fulfilled in the Messiah's coming) remained valid. God still wanted the Israelites to be a holy people (just as he wants us to be holy), and he often used oppression to bring them back to him, just as he warned he would (Leviticus 26; Deuteronomy 28). The book of Judges records a number of instances where God allowed his people to be oppressed so that they would repent of their sins and return to him.

Too often people want God to fulfil his promises while excusing themselves from their responsibilities. Before you claim God's promises, ask, "Have I done my part?"

2:4 The people of Israel knew they had sinned, and they wept aloud, responding with deep sorrow. Because we have a tendency to sin, repentance is the true measure of spiritual sensitivity. Repentance means asking God to forgive us, and then abandoning our sinful ways. But we cannot do this sincerely unless we are truly sorry for our sinful actions. When we are aware that we have done wrong, we should admit it plainly to God rather than try to cover it up or hope we can get away with it.

2:7–9 The account of Joshua's death is found here and at the end of the book of Joshua (24:29). Either this account is a summary of what happened earlier, or the account in the book of Joshua omitted the events in the first chapter of Judges. (For more on Joshua, see his Profile in Joshua 2.)

2:10ff One generation died, and the next did not follow God. Judges 2:10 – 3:7 is a brief preview of the cycle of sin, judgment, and repentance that Israel experienced again and again. Each generation failed to teach the next generation to love and follow God. Yet this was at the very centre of God's law (Deuteronomy 6:4–9). It is tempting to leave the job of teaching the Christian faith to the church or Christian school. Yet God says that the responsibility for this task belongs primarily to the family. Because children learn so much by our example, faith must be a family matter.

2:11
[m]Jdg 3:12; 4:1; 6:1
[n]Jdg 3:7; 8:33
2:12
[o]Ps 106:36
[p]Dt 31:16
2:13
[q]Jdg 10:6
2:14
[r]Dt 31:17
[s]Ps 106:41
[t]Dt 32:30;
[u]Dt 28:25
2:16
[v]Ac 13:20
[w]Ps 106:43

Israelites did evil in the eyes of the LORD[m] and served the Baals.[n] 12They forsook
the LORD, the God of their fathers, who had brought them out of Egypt. They followed
and worshipped various gods[o] of the peoples around them.[p] They provoked the LORD
to anger 13because they forsook him and served Baal and the Ashtoreths.[q] 14In his
anger[r] against Israel the LORD handed them over[s] to raiders who plundered them.
He sold them[t] to their enemies all around, whom they were no longer able to resist.[u]
15Whenever Israel went out to fight, the hand of the LORD was against them to defeat
them, just as he had sworn to them. They were in great distress.
16Then the LORD raised up judges,[c][v] who saved[w] them out of the hands of these

c *16* Or *leaders*; similarly in verses 17–19

THE JUDGES OF ISRAEL

Judge	*Years of Judging*	*Memorable Act(s)*	*Reference*
OTHNIEL	40	He captured a powerful Canaanite city	Judges 3:7–11
EHUD	80	He killed Eglon and defeated the Moabites	Judges 3:12–30
SHAMGAR	unrecorded	He killed 600 Philistines with an oxgoad	Judges 3:31
DEBORAH (w/Barak)	40	She defeated Sisera and the Canaanites and later sang a victory song with Barak	Judges 4 and 5
GIDEON	40	He destroyed his family idols, used a fleece to determine God's will, raised an army of 10,000, and defeated 135,000 Midianites with 300 soldiers	Judges 6–8
TOLA	23	He judged Israel for 23 years	Judges 10:1, 2
JAIR	22	He had 30 sons	Judges 10:3–5
JEPHTHAH	6	He made a rash vow, defeated the Ammonites, and later battled against jealous Ephraim	Judges 10:6–12:7
IBZAN	7	He had 30 sons and 30 daughters	Judges 12:8–10
ELON	10	unrecorded	Judges 12:11, 12
ABDON	8	He had 40 sons and 30 grandsons, each of whom had his own donkey	Judges 12:13–15
SAMSON	20	He was a Nazirite, killed a lion with his bare hands, burned the Philistine wheat fields, killed 1,000 Philistines with a donkey's jawbone, tore off an iron gate, was betrayed by Delilah, and destroyed thousands of Philistines in one last mighty act	Judges 13–16

2:11–15 Baal was the god of the storm and rains; therefore, he was thought to control vegetation and agriculture. Ashtoreth was the mother goddess of love, war, and fertility (she was also called Astarte or Ishtar). Temple prostitution and child sacrifice were a part of the worship of these Canaanite idols. This generation of Israelites abandoned the faith of their parents and began worshipping the gods of their neighbours. Many things can tempt us to abandon what we know is right. The desire to be accepted by our neighbours can lead us into behaviour that is unacceptable to God. Don't be pressured into disobedience.

2:12–15 God often saved his harshest criticism and punishment for those who worshipped idols. Why were idols so bad in God's sight? To worship an idol violated the first two of the Ten Commandments (Exodus 20:3–6). The Canaanites had gods for almost every season, activity, or place. To them, the Lord was just another god to add to their collection of gods. Israel, by contrast, was to worship only the Lord. They could not possibly believe that God was the one true God and at the same time bow to an idol. Idol worshippers could not see their god as their creator because they created him. These idols represent sensual, carnal, and immoral aspects of human nature. God's nature is spiritual and moral. Adding the worship of idols to the worship of God could not be tolerated.

2:15, 16 Despite Israel's disobedience, God showed his great mercy by raising up judges to save the people from their oppressors. Mercy has been defined as "not giving a person what he or she deserves". This is exactly what God did for Israel and what he does for us. Our disobedience demands judgment! But God shows mercy towards us by providing an escape from sin's penalty through Jesus Christ, who alone saves us from sin. When we pray for forgiveness, we are asking for what we do not deserve. Yet when we take this step and trust in Christ's saving work on our behalf, we can experience God's forgiveness.

2:16–19 Throughout this period of history Israel went through seven cycles of (1) rebelling against God, (2) being overrun by enemy nations, (3) being delivered by a God-fearing judge, (4) remaining loyal to God under that judge, and (5) again forgetting God when the judge died. We tend to follow the same cycle – remaining loyal to God as long as we are near those who are devoted to him. But when we are on our own, the pressure to be drawn away from God increases. Determine to be faithful to God despite the difficult situations you encounter.

raiders. 17 Yet they would not listen to their judges but prostituted[x] themselves to other
gods and worshipped them. Unlike their fathers, they quickly turned from the way
in which their fathers had walked, the way of obedience to the LORD's commands.[y]
18 Whenever the LORD raised up a judge for them, he was with the judge and saved
them out of the hands of their enemies as long as the judge lived; for the LORD had
compassion[z] on them as they groaned[a] under those who oppressed and afflicted
them. 19 But when the judge died, the people returned to ways even more corrupt[b]
than those of their fathers, following other gods and serving and worshipping them.[c]
They refused to give up their evil practices and stubborn ways.
20 Therefore the LORD was very angry[d] with Israel and said, "Because this nation
has violated the covenant that I laid down for their forefathers and has not listened
to me, 21 I will no longer drive out[e] before them any of the nations Joshua left when
he died. 22 I will use them to test[f] Israel and see whether they will keep the way of
the LORD and walk in it as their forefathers did." 23 The LORD had allowed those nations
to remain; he did not drive them out at once by giving them into the hands of Joshua.
3 These are the nations the LORD left to test[a] all those Israelites who had not
experienced any of the wars in Canaan 2 (he did this only to teach warfare to the
descendants of the Israelites who had not had previous battle experience): 3 the five[b]
rulers of the Philistines, all the Canaanites, the Sidonians, and the Hivites living in
the Lebanon mountains from Mount Baal Hermon to Lebo[a] Hamath. 4 They were left
to test[c] the Israelites to see whether they would obey the LORD's commands, which
he had given their forefathers through Moses.
5 The Israelites lived[d] among the Canaanites, Hittites, Amorites, Perizzites, Hivites
and Jebusites. 6 They took their daughters in marriage and gave their own daughters
to their sons, and served their gods.[e]

B. THE RESCUE OF ISRAEL BY THE JUDGES (3:7–16:31)

The Israelites began a series of cycles of sinning, worshipping idols, being punished, crying out for help, being rescued by a judge sent from God, obeying God for a while, then falling back into idolatry. They were conquered by Syria, Moab, Canaan, Midian, Ammon, and Philistia. They even faced the threat of civil war. Just as God sent help to the people when they cried out to him, he will deliver us when we call on him.

1. First period: Othniel

Othniel

7 The Israelites did evil in the eyes of the LORD; they forgot the LORD[f] their God
and served the Baals and the Asherahs.[g] 8 The anger of the LORD burned against Israel

[a] 3 *Or to the entrance to*

2:17 [x]Ex 34:15 [y]ver 7
2:18 [z]Dt 32:36; Jos 1:5 [a]Ps 106:44
2:19 [b]Jdg 3:12 [c]Jdg 4:1; 8:33
2:20 [d]ver 14; Jos 23:16
2:21 [e]Jos 23:13
2:22 [f]Dt 8:2, 16; Jdg 3:1, 14
3:1 [a]Jdg 2:21-22
3:3 [b]Jos 13:3
3:4 [c]Dt 8:2; Jdg 2:22
3:5 [d]Ps 106:35
3:6 [e]Ex 34:16; Dt 7:3-4
3:7 [f]Dt 4:9 [g]Ex 34:13; Jdg 2:11, 13

2:17 Why would the people of Israel turn so quickly from their faith in God? Simply put, the Canaanite religion appeared more attractive to the sensual nature and offered more short-term benefits (sexual permissiveness and increased fertility in childbearing and farming). One of its most attractive features was that people could remain selfish and yet fulfil their religious requirements. They could do almost anything they wished and still be obeying at least one of the many Canaanite gods. Male and female prostitution were not only allowed, but encouraged as forms of worship.

Faith in the one true God, however, does not offer short-term benefits that appeal to our sinful human nature. The essence of sin is selfishness; the essence of God's way of life is selflessness. We must seek Christ's help to live God's way.

3:1–4 We learn from chapter 1 that these enemy nations were still in the land because the Israelites had failed to obey God and drive them out. Now God would allow the enemies to remain in order to "test" the Israelites; that is, to give them an opportunity to exercise faith and obedience. By now the younger generation that had not fought in the great battles of conquest was coming of age. It was their job to complete the conquest of the land. There were many obstacles yet to be overcome in their new homeland. How they would handle these obstacles would be a test of their faith.

Perhaps God has left obstacles in your life—hostile people, difficult situations, baffling problems—to allow you to develop faith and obedience.

3:5–7 The Israelites discovered that relationships affect faith. The men and women of the surrounding nations were attractive to the Israelites. Soon they intermarried, and the Israelites accepted their pagan gods. This was clearly prohibited by God (Exodus 34:15–17; Deuteronomy 7:1–4). By accepting these gods into their homes, the Israelites gradually began to accept the immoral practices associated with them. Most Israelites didn't start out determined to be idolaters; they just added the idols to the worship of God. But before long they found themselves absorbed in pagan worship.

A similar danger faces us. We want to befriend those who don't know God, but through those friendships we can become entangled in unhealthy practices. Friendships with unbelievers are important, but we must accept people without compromising or adopting their patterns of behaviour.

3:7 Baal was the most worshipped god of the Canaanites. Most often cast in the form of a bull, he symbolised strength and fertility and was considered the god of agriculture. Asherah was Baal's female consort, mother goddess of the sea who was worshipped by

3:8
[h]Jdg 2:14

3:9
[i]ver 15;
Jdg 6:6, 7; 10:10;
Ps 106:44
[j]Jdg 1:13

3:10
[k]Nu 11:25, 29; 24:2;
Jdg 6:34; 11:29;
13:25; 14:6, 19;
1Sa 11:6

3:12
[l]Jdg 2:11, 14
[m]1Sa 12:9

3:13
[n]Jdg 1:16

3:15
[o]ver 9;
Ps 78:34; 107:13

so that he sold[h] them into the hands of Cushan-Rishathaim king of Aram Naharaim,[b]
to whom the Israelites were subject for eight years. 9 But when they cried out[i] to the
LORD, he raised up for them a deliverer, Othniel[j] son of Kenaz, Caleb's younger
brother, who saved them. 10 The Spirit of the LORD came upon him,[k] so that he
became Israel's judge[c] and went to war. The LORD gave Cushan-Rishathaim king of
Aram into the hands of Othniel, who overpowered him. 11 So the land had peace for
forty years, until Othniel son of Kenaz died.

2. Second period: Ehud and Shamgar

Ehud

12 Once again the Israelites did evil in the eyes of the LORD,[l] and because they did
this evil the LORD gave Eglon king of Moab[m] power over Israel. 13 Getting the
Ammonites and Amalekites to join him, Eglon came and attacked Israel, and they took
possession of the City of Palms.[d][n] 14 The Israelites were subject to Eglon king of
Moab for eighteen years.
15 Again the Israelites cried out to the LORD, and he gave them a deliverer[o]—Ehud,

[b] *8* That is, North-west Mesopotamia [c] *10* Or *leader* [d] *13* That is, Jericho

WHY DID ISRAEL WANT TO WORSHIP IDOLS?

Worshipping God	*Worshipping idols*
long-range benefits	short-range benefits
gratification postponed	self-gratification immediate
morality required	sensuality approved
high ethical standards demanded	low ethical standards tolerated
neighbours' sins disapproved	neighbours' sins approved
unseen God worshipped	visible idols worshipped
unselfishness expected	selfishness condoned
business relations hindered	business relations improved
strict religious practices maintained	religious practices loosely regulated
changed life demanded	changed life not demanded
ethical stand expected	compromise and co-operation practised
concern for others taught	no concern for others expected

The temptation to follow false gods because of short-term benefits, good feelings, easy "rules", or convenience was always present. *But the benefits were deceptive because the gods were false.* We worship God because he is the one and only true God.

means of wooden pillars that substituted for sacred trees. In times of famine, the Canaanites believed Baal was angry with them and was withholding rain as punishment. Archaeologists have uncovered many Baal idols in Israel. It is difficult to imagine the people of Israel trading worship of the Lord for worship of idols of wood, stone, and iron, but we do the same when we forsake worshipping God for other activities, hobbies, or priorities. Our idols are not made of wood or stone, but they are every bit as sinful.

3:9 Othniel was Israel's first judge. In 1:13 we read that he volunteered to lead an attack against a fortified city. Here he was to lead the nation back to God. Othniel had a rich spiritual heritage—his uncle was Caleb, a man with unwavering faith in God (Numbers 13:30; 14:24). Othniel's leadership brought the people back to God and freed them from the oppression of the king of Aram, Naharaim. But after Othniel's death, it didn't take the Israelites long to fall back into their neighbours' comfortable but sinful ways.

3:10 This phrase, "The Spirit of the LORD came upon him," was also spoken of the judges Gideon, Jephthah, and Samson, among others. It expresses a temporary and spontaneous increase of physical, spiritual, or mental strength. This was an extraordinary and supernatural occurrence to prepare a person for a special task. The Holy Spirit is available to all believers today, but he will come upon believers in an extraordinary way for special tasks. We should ask the Holy Spirit's help as we face our daily problems as well as life's major challenges.

3:12, 13 The Moabites, Ammonites, and Amalekites were nomadic tribes that lived near each other east and southeast of Canaan. These tribes were notorious raiders, possessing great military skill. This was the first time nations outside Canaan attacked the Israelites in their own land.

3:15 Ehud is called a *deliverer.* In the broadest sense, all the judges can be looked upon as foreshadowing the perfect Deliverer, Jesus Christ. While Ehud delivered Israel from its enemies, Jesus delivers us from sin, our greatest enemy.

3:15–30 This is a strange story, but it teaches us that God can use us just the way he made us. Being left-handed in Ehud's day was considered a handicap. Many Benjaminites were left-handed (see 20:16). But God used Ehud's perceived weakness to give Israel victory. Let God use you the way you are to accomplish his work.

a left-handed man, the son of Gera the Benjamite. The Israelites sent him with tribute
to Eglon king of Moab. 16 Now Ehud had made a double-edged sword about a foot
and a half[e] long, which he strapped to his right thigh under his clothing. 17 He
presented the tribute to Eglon king of Moab, who was a very fat man.[p] 18 After Ehud
had presented the tribute, he sent on their way the men who had carried it. 19 At the
idols[f] near Gilgal he himself turned back and said, "I have a secret message for you,
O king."
The king said, "Quiet!" And all his attendants left him.
20 Ehud then approached him while he was sitting alone in the upper room of his
summer palace[g] and said, "I have a message from God for you." As the king rose
from his seat, 21 Ehud reached with his left hand, drew the sword from his right thigh
and plunged it into the king's belly. 22 Even the handle sank in after the blade, which
came out of his back. Ehud did not pull the sword out, and the fat closed in over it.
23 Then Ehud went out to the porch;[h] he shut the doors of the upper room behind him
and locked them.
24 After he had gone, the servants came and found the doors of the upper room
locked. They said, "He must be relieving himself[q] in the inner room of the house."
25 They waited to the point of embarrassment,[r] but when he did not open the doors
of the room, they took a key and unlocked them. There they saw their lord fallen to
the floor, dead.
26 While they waited, Ehud got away. He passed by the idols and escaped to Seirah.
27 When he arrived there, he blew a trumpet[s] in the hill country of Ephraim, and the
Israelites went down with him from the hills, with him leading them.
28 "Follow me," he ordered, "for the LORD has given Moab, your enemy, into your
hands.[t]" So they followed him down and, taking possession of the fords of the
Jordan[u] that led to Moab, they allowed no-one to cross over. 29 At that time they
struck down about ten thousand Moabites, all vigorous and strong; not a man escaped.
30 That day Moab was made subject to Israel, and the land had peace[v] for eighty years.

Shamgar

31 After Ehud came Shamgar son of Anath,[w] who struck down six hundred[x]
Philistines with an ox-goad. He too saved Israel.

[e] 16 Hebrew *a cubit* (about 0.5 metre) [f] 19 Or *the stone quarries*; also in verse 26 [g] 20 The meaning of the Hebrew for this phrase is uncertain. [h] 23 The meaning of the Hebrew for this word is uncertain.

3:17 [p] ver 12
3:24 [q] 1Sa 24:3
3:25 [r] 2Ki 2:17; 8:11
3:27 [s] Jdg 6:34; 1Sa 13:3
3:28 [t] Jdg 7:9, 15 [u] Jos 2:7; Jdg 7:24; 12:5
3:30 [v] ver 11
3:31 [w] Jdg 5:6 [x] Jos 23:10

3:31 To kill 600 Philistines with an ox-goad was quite a feat. An ox-goad was a long stick with a small flat piece of iron on one side and a sharp point on the other. The sharp side was used to drive the oxen during the times of ploughing, and the flat end was used to clean the mud off the plough. Eight-foot-long ancient ox-goads have been found. In times of crisis they could easily have been used as spears, as in Shamgar's case. Ox-goads are still used in the Middle East to drive oxen.

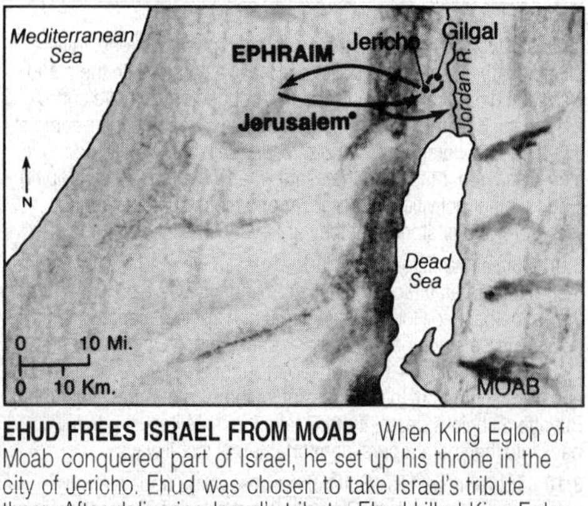

EHUD FREES ISRAEL FROM MOAB When King Eglon of Moab conquered part of Israel, he set up his throne in the city of Jericho. Ehud was chosen to take Israel's tribute there. After delivering Israel's tribute, Ehud killed King Eglon and escaped into the hill country of Ephraim. From there he gathered together an army to cut off any Moabites trying to escape across the Jordan River.

4:1
a Jdg 2:19

4:2
b Jos 11:1
c ver 13, 16; 1Sa 12:9; Ps 83:9

4:3
d Jdg 1:19
e Ps 106:42

3. Third period: Deborah and Barak

Deborah

4 After Ehud died, the Israelites once again did evil[a] in the eyes of the LORD. 2So
the LORD sold them into the hands of Jabin, a king of Canaan, who reigned in
Hazor.[b] The commander of his army was Sisera,[c] who lived in Harosheth Haggoyim. 3Because he had nine hundred iron chariots[d] and had cruelly oppressed[e] the
Israelites for twenty years, they cried to the LORD for help.

EHUD

At first glance, Ehud's career as a judge in Israel may not seem relevant to us. He clearly lived in another time. He took radical and violent action to free his people. His murder of Eglon shocks us. His war on Moab was swift and deadly. His life is difficult to relate to. But our commitment to God's word challenges us not to ignore this leader. As we read about his life, some questions come to mind: (1) When was the last time God showed me something wrong in my life and I took immediate and painful action to correct the error? (2) When was the last time I asked God to show me how he could use something unique about me (as he used Ehud's left-handedness)? (3) When was the last time I made a plan to obey God in some specific area of my life and then followed through with that plan? (4) When was the last time my life was an example to others of obedience to God?

The enemies we face are as real as Ehud's, but they are most often within ourselves. The battles we fight are not against other people but against the power of sin. We need God's help in doing battle against sin. We also need to remember that he has already won the war. He has defeated sin at the cross of his Son, Jesus. His help is the cause of each success, and his forgiveness is sufficient for each failure.

Strengths and accomplishments:
- Second judge of Israel
- A man of direct action, a frontline leader
- Used a perceived weakness (left-handedness) to do a great work for God
- Led the revolt against Moabite domination and gave Israel 80 years of peace

Lessons from his life:
- Some conditions call for radical action
- God responds to the cry of repentance
- God is ready to use our unique qualities to accomplish his work

Vital statistics:
- Where: Born during the last years of the desert wanderings or during Israel's early years in the promised land
- Occupations: Messenger, judge
- Relative: Father: Gera
- Contemporary: Eglon of Moab

Key verse:
"Again the Israelites cried out to the LORD, and he gave them a deliverer—Ehud, a left-handed man, the son of Gera the Benjamite" (Judges 3:15).

His story is told in Judges 3:12–30.

4:1 Israel sinned "in the eyes of the LORD". Our sins harm both ourselves and others, but all sin is ultimately against God because it disregards his commands and his authority over us. When confessing his sin David prayed, "Against you, you only, have I sinned and done what is evil in your sight" (Psalm 51:4). Recognising the seriousness of sin is the first step towards removing it from our lives.

4:2, 3 Nothing more is known about Jabin. Joshua had defeated a king by that name years earlier and burned the city of Hazor to the ground (Joshua 11:1–11). Either the city was rebuilt by this time, or Jabin was hoping to rebuild it.

This is the only time during the period of the judges when the Israelites' enemies came from within their land. The Israelites had failed to drive out all the Canaanites. These Canaanites had regrouped and were attempting to restore their lost power. If the Israelites had obeyed God in the first place and had driven the Canaanites from the land, this incident would not have happened.

4:2, 3 Chariots were the tanks of the ancient world. Made of iron or wood, they were pulled by one or two horses and were the most feared and powerful weapons of the day. Some chariots even had razor-sharp knives extending from the wheels designed to mutilate helpless foot soldiers. The Canaanite army had 900 iron chariots. Israel was not powerful enough to defeat such an invincible army. Therefore, Jabin and Sisera had no trouble oppressing the people – until a faithful woman named Deborah called upon God.

4:3 After 20 years of unbearable circumstances, the Israelites finally cried to the Lord for help. But God should be the first place we turn when we are facing struggles or dilemmas. The Israelites chose to go their own way and got into a mess. We often do the same. Trying to control our own lives without God's help leads to struggle and confusion. By contrast, when we stay in daily contact with the Lord, we are less likely to create painful circumstances for ourselves. This is a lesson the Israelites never fully learned. When struggles come our way, God wants us to come to him first, seeking his strength and guidance.

4Deborah, a prophetess, the wife of Lappidoth, was leading[a] Israel at that time.
5She held court under the Palm of Deborah between Ramah and Bethel[f] in the hill
country of Ephraim, and the Israelites came to her to have their disputes decided. 6She
sent for Barak son of Abinoam[g] from Kedesh in Naphtali and said to him, "The LORD,
the God of Israel, commands you: 'Go, take with you ten thousand men of Naphtali
and Zebulun and lead the way to Mount Tabor. 7I will lure Sisera, the commander
of Jabin's army, with his chariots and his troops to the Kishon River[h] and give him
into your hands.' "
8Barak said to her, "If you go with me, I will go; but if you don't go with me, I
won't go."
9"Very well," Deborah said, "I will go with you. But because of the way you are
going about this,[b] the honour will not be yours, for the LORD will hand Sisera over
to a woman." So Deborah went with Barak to Kedesh,[i] 10where he summoned[j]
Zebulun and Naphtali. Ten thousand men followed him, and Deborah also went with
him.
11Now Heber the Kenite had left the other Kenites,[k] the descendants of Hobab,[l]
Moses' brother-in-law,[c] and pitched his tent by the great tree in Zaanannim[m] near
Kedesh.
12When they told Sisera that Barak son of Abinoam had gone up to Mount Tabor,
13Sisera gathered together his nine hundred iron chariots[n] and all the men with him,
from Harosheth Haggoyim to the Kishon River.
14Then Deborah said to Barak, "Go! This is the day the LORD has given Sisera into
your hands. Has not the LORD gone ahead[o] of you?" So Barak went down Mount
Tabor, followed by ten thousand men. 15At Barak's advance, the LORD routed[p] Sisera
and all his chariots and army by the sword, and Sisera abandoned his chariot and fled
on foot. 16But Barak pursued the chariots and army as far as Harosheth Haggoyim.
All the troops of Sisera fell by the sword; not a man was left.[q]
17Sisera, however, fled on foot to the tent of Jael, the wife of Heber the Kenite,
because there were friendly relations between Jabin king of Hazor and the clan of
Heber the Kenite.
18Jael went out to meet Sisera and said to him, "Come, my lord, come right in.
Don't be afraid." So he entered her tent, and she put a covering over him.

[a] 4 Traditionally *judging* [b] 9 Or *But on the expedition you are undertaking* [c] 11 Or *father-in-law*

4:5 [f] Ge 35:8
4:6 [g] Heb 11:32
4:7 [h] Ps 83:9
4:9 [i] ver 21; Jdg 2:14
4:10 [j] ver 14; Jdg 5:15, 18
4:11 [k] Jdg 1:16 [l] Nu 10:29 [m] Jos 19:33
4:13 [n] ver 3
4:14 [o] Dt 9:3; 2Sa 5:24; Ps 68:7
4:15 [p] Jos 10:10; Ps 83:9-10
4:16 [q] Ex 14:28; Ps 83:9

KING JABIN IS DEFEATED
Deborah travelled from her home between Ramah and Bethel to march with Barak and the Israelite army against Hazor. Sisera, commander of Hazor's army, assembled his men at Harosheth Haggoyim. In spite of Sisera's 900 chariots and expertly trained army, Israel was victorious.

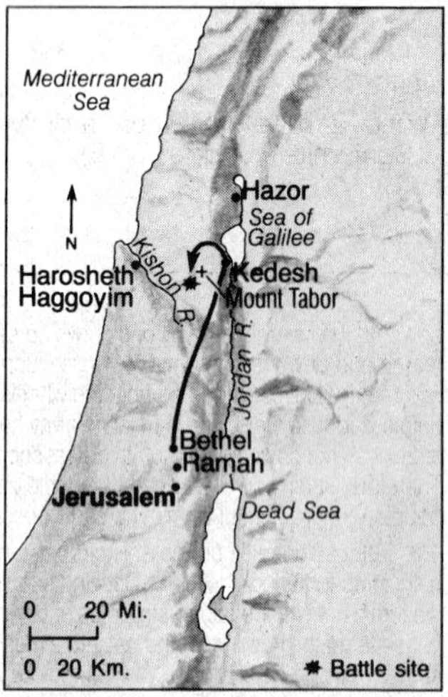

4:4ff The Bible records several women who held national leadership positions, and Deborah was an exceptional woman. Obviously she was the best person for the job, and God chose her to lead Israel. God can choose anyone to lead his people, young or old, man or woman. Don't let your prejudices get in the way of those God may have chosen to lead you.

4:6–8 Was Barak cowardly or just in need of support? We don't know Barak's character, but we see the character of a great leader in Deborah, who took charge as God directed. Deborah told Barak that God would be with him in battle, but that was not enough for Barak. He wanted Deborah to go with him. Barak's request shows that at heart he trusted human strength more than God's promise. A person of real faith steps out at God's command, even if he or she must do so alone.

4:9 How did Deborah command such respect? She was responsible for leading the people into battle, but more than that, she influenced them to live for God after the battle was over. Her personality drew people together and commanded the respect of even Barak, a military general. She was also a prophetess, whose main role was to encourage the people to obey God. Those who lead must not forget about the spiritual condition of those being led. A true leader is concerned for people, not just success.

4:11 Heber was Jael's husband (4:17). He was from the Kenite tribe, a long-standing ally of Israel. But for some reason, Heber decided to side with Jabin, maybe because Jabin's army appeared to have the military advantage. It was probably Heber who told Sisera that the Israelites were camped near Mount Tabor (4:12; see map). Although Heber threw in his lot with Jabin and his forces, his wife, Jael, did not (4:21).

4:18–21 Sisera couldn't have been more pleased when Jael of-

[19]“I’m thirsty,” he said. “Please give me some water.” She opened a skin of milk,[r]
gave him a drink, and covered him up.
[20]“Stand in the doorway of the tent,” he told her. “If someone comes by and asks
you, ‘Is anyone here?’ say ‘No.’ ”
[21]But Jael, Heber’s wife, picked up a tent peg and a hammer and went quietly to
him while he lay fast asleep, exhausted. She drove the peg through his temple into
the ground, and he died.[s]
[22]Barak came by in pursuit of Sisera, and Jael went out to meet him. “Come,” she
said, “I will show you the man you’re looking for.” So he went in with her, and there
lay Sisera with the tent peg through his temple—dead.
[23]On that day God subdued[t] Jabin, the Canaanite king, before the Israelites. [24]And
the hand of the Israelites grew stronger and stronger against Jabin, the Canaanite king,
until they destroyed him.

The Song of Deborah

5 On that day Deborah and Barak son of Abinoam sang this song:[a]

[2]“When the princes in Israel take the lead,
when the people willingly offer[b] themselves—
praise the LORD![c]

[3]“Hear this, you kings! Listen, you rulers!
I will sing to**[a]** the LORD, I will sing;
I will make music to**[b]** the LORD, the God of Israel.[d]

[4]“O LORD, when you went out from Seir,[e]
when you marched from the land of Edom,
the earth shook, the heavens poured,
the clouds poured down water.[f]
[5]The mountains quaked[g] before the LORD, the One of Sinai,
before the LORD, the God of Israel.

[6]“In the days of Shamgar son of Anath,[h]
in the days of Jael,[i] the roads[j] were abandoned;
travellers took to winding paths.

a *3* Or *of* **b** *3* Or */ with song I will praise*

4:19 [r]Jdg 5:25
4:21 [s]Jdg 5:26
4:23 [t]Ne 9:24; Ps 18:47
5:1 [a]Ex 15:1
5:2 [b]2Ch 17:16; Ps 110:3 [c]ver 9
5:3 [d]Ps 27:6
5:4 [e]Dt 33:2 [f]Ps 68:8
5:5 [g]Ex 19:18; Ps 68:8; 97:5; Isa 64:3
5:6 [h]Jdg 3:31 [i]Jdg 4:17 [j]Isa 33:8

THE JUDGES’ FUNCTIONS
Regardless of an individual judge’s leadership style, each one demonstrated that God’s judgment follows apostasy, while repentance brings restoration.

Judges of Israel could be:

saviours (deliverers) and redeemers (Gideon)	or mediators and administrators (Tola)
providers of rest and peace (Ehud and Jair)	or rude, petty dictators (Jephthah)
famous and powerful (Samson)	or hardworking yet unsung (Elon and Abdon)
leaders of the nation (Othniel and Deborah)	or local heroes (Shamgar and Ibzan)

fered him her tent as a hiding place. First, because Jael was the wife of Heber, a man loyal to Sisera’s forces (see the note on 4:11), he thought she certainly could be trusted. Second, because men were never allowed to enter a woman’s tent, no-one would think to look for Sisera there.

Even though her husband, Heber, was loyal to Sisera’s forces, Jael certainly was not. Because women of that day were in charge of pitching the tents, Jael had no problem driving the tent peg into Sisera’s head while he slept. Deborah’s prediction was thus fulfilled: the honour of conquering Sisera went to a brave and resourceful woman (4:9).

5:1ff Music and singing were a cherished part of Israel’s culture. Chapter 5 is a song, possibly composed and sung by Deborah and Barak. It sets to music the story of Israel’s great victory recounted in chapter 4. This victory song was accompanied by joyous celebration. It proclaimed God’s greatness by giving him credit for the victory. It was an excellent way to preserve and retell this wonderful story from generation to generation. (Other songs in the Bible are listed in the chart in Exodus 15.)

5:1ff In victory, Barak and Deborah sang praises to God. Songs of praise focus our attention on God, give us an outlet for spiritual celebration, and remind us of God’s faithfulness and character. Whether you are experiencing a great victory or a major dilemma, singing praises to God can have a positive effect on your attitude.

7 Village life[c] in Israel ceased,
ceased until I,[d] Deborah, arose,
arose a mother in Israel.
8 When they chose new gods,[k]
war came to the city gates,
and not a shield or spear was seen
among forty thousand in Israel.
9 My heart is with Israel's princes,
with the willing volunteers[l] among the people.
Praise the LORD!

10 "You who ride on white donkeys,[m]
sitting on your saddle blankets,
and you who walk along the road,
consider 11 the voice of the singers[e] at the watering places.
They recite the righteous acts[n] of the LORD,
the righteous acts of his warriors[f] in Israel.

"Then the people of the LORD
went down to the city gates.[o]
12 'Wake up,[p] wake up, Deborah!
Wake up, wake up, break out in song!
Arise, O Barak!
Take captive your captives,[q] O son of Abinoam.'

13 "Then the men who were left
came down to the nobles;
the people of the LORD
came to me with the mighty.
14 Some came from Ephraim, whose roots were in Amalek;[r]
Benjamin was with the people who followed you.
From Makir captains came down,
from Zebulun those who bear a commander's staff.
15 The princes of Issachar were with Deborah;[s]
yes, Issachar was with Barak,
rushing after him into the valley.
In the districts of Reuben
there was much searching of heart.
16 Why did you stay among the campfires[g]
to hear the whistling for the flocks?[t]
In the districts of Reuben
there was much searching of heart.
17 Gilead stayed beyond the Jordan.
And Dan, why did he linger by the ships?
Asher remained on the coast[u]
and stayed in his coves.
18 The people of Zebulun risked their very lives;

c 7 Or *Warriors* d 7 Or *you* e 11 Or *archers*; the meaning of the Hebrew for this word is uncertain.
f 11 Or *villagers* g 16 Or *saddlebags*

5:8 k Dt 32:17
5:9 l ver 2
5:10 m Jdg 10:4; 12:14
5:11 n 1Sa 12:7; Mic 6:5 o ver 8
5:12 p Ps 57:8 q Ps 68:18; Eph 4:8
5:14 r Jdg 3:13
5:15 s Jdg 4:10
5:16 t Nu 32:1
5:17 u Jos 19:29

5:8 War was the inevitable result when Israel chose to follow false gods. Although God had given Israel clear directions, the people failed to put his words into practice. Without God at the centre of their national life, pressure from the outside soon became greater than power from within, and they were an easy prey for their enemies. If you are letting a desire for recognition, craving for power, or love of money rule your life, you may find yourself besieged by enemies – stress, anxiety, illness, fatigue. Keep God at the centre of your life, and you will have the power you need to fight these destroyers.

5:15–17 Four tribes – Reuben, Gilead (either Gad or Manasseh), Dan, and Asher – were accused of not lending a helping hand in the battle. No reasons are given for their refusal to help their fellow Israelites, but they may be the same ones that stopped them from driving out the Canaanites in the first place: (1) lack of faith in God to help, (2) lack of effort, (3) fear of the enemy, and (4) fear of antagonising those with whom they did business and thus from whom they prospered. This disobedience showed a lack of enthusiasm for God's plan.

so did Naphtali on the heights of the field.[v]

19 "Kings came[w], they fought;
the kings of Canaan fought
at Taanach by the waters of Megiddo,[x]
but they carried off no silver, no plunder.[y]
20 From the heavens[z] the stars fought,
from their courses they fought against Sisera.
21 The river Kishon[a] swept them away,
the age-old river, the river Kishon.
March on, my soul; be strong!
22 Then thundered the horses' hoofs—
galloping, galloping go his mighty steeds.
23 'Curse Meroz,' said the angel of the LORD.
'Curse its people bitterly,
because they did not come to help the LORD,
to help the LORD against the mighty.'

24 "Most blessed of women be Jael,[b]
the wife of Heber the Kenite,
most blessed of tent-dwelling women.
25 He asked for water, and she gave him milk;[c]
in a bowl fit for nobles she brought him curdled milk.
26 Her hand reached for the tent peg,
her right hand for the workman's hammer.

5:18 [v]Jdg 4:6, 10
5:19 [w]Jos 11:5; Jdg 4:13 [x]Jdg 1:27 [y]ver 30
5:20 [z]Jos 10:11
5:21 [a]Jdg 4:7
5:24 [b]Jdg 4:17
5:25 [c]Jdg 4:19

DEBORAH

Wise leaders are rare. They accomplish great amounts of work without direct involvement because they know how to work through other people. They are able to see the big picture that often escapes those directly involved, so they make good mediators, advisers, and planners. Deborah fitted this description perfectly. She had all these leadership skills, and she had a remarkable relationship with God. The insight and confidence God gave this woman placed her in a unique position in the Old Testament. Deborah is among the outstanding women of history.

Her story shows that she was not power hungry. She wanted to serve God. Whenever praise came her way, she gave God the credit. She didn't deny or resist her position in the culture as a woman and wife, but she never allowed herself to be hindered by it either. Her story shows that God can accomplish great things through people who are willing to be led by him.

Deborah's life challenges us in several ways. She reminds us of the need to be available both to God and to others. She encourages us to spend our efforts on what we can do rather than on worrying about what we can't do. Deborah challenges us to be wise leaders. She demonstrates what a person can accomplish when God is in control.

Strengths and accomplishments:
- Fourth and only female judge of Israel
- Special abilities as a mediator, adviser, and counsellor
- When called on to lead, was able to plan, direct, and delegate
- Known for her prophetic power
- A writer of songs

Lessons from her life:
- God chooses leaders by his standards, not ours
- Wise leaders choose good helpers

Vital statistics:
- Where: Canaan
- Occupations: Prophetess and judge
- Relative: Husband: Lappidoth
- Contemporaries: Barak, Jael, Jabin of Hazor, Sisera

Key verse:
"Deborah, a prophetess, the wife of Lappidoth, was leading Israel at that time" (Judges 4:4).

Her story is told in Judges 4, 5.

She struck Sisera, she crushed his head,
she shattered and pierced his temple.[d]
27 At her feet he sank,
he fell; there he lay.
At her feet he sank, he fell;
where he sank, there he fell—dead.

28 "Through the window peered Sisera's mother;
behind the lattice she cried out,[e]
'Why is his chariot so long in coming?
Why is the clatter of his chariots delayed?'
29 The wisest of her ladies answer her;
indeed, she keeps saying to herself,
30 'Are they not finding and dividing the spoils:[f]
a girl or two for each man,
colourful garments as plunder for Sisera,
colourful garments embroidered,
highly embroidered garments for my neck—
all this as plunder?'

31 "So may all your enemies perish, O LORD!
But may they who love you be like the sun[g]
when it rises in its strength."

Then the land had peace[h] for forty years.

4. Fourth period: Gideon, Tola, and Jair

Gideon

6 Again the Israelites did evil in the eyes of the LORD,[a] and for seven years he
gave them into the hands of the Midianites.[b] 2 Because the power of Midian was
so oppressive,[c] the Israelites prepared shelters for themselves in mountain clefts,
caves and strongholds.[d] 3 Whenever the Israelites planted their crops, the Midianites,
Amalekites[e] and other eastern peoples invaded the country. 4 They camped on the
land and ruined the crops[f] all the way to Gaza and did not spare a living thing for
Israel, neither sheep nor cattle nor donkeys. 5 They came up with their livestock and
their tents like swarms of locusts.[g] It was impossible to count the men and their
camels;[h] they invaded the land to ravage it. 6 Midian so impoverished the Israelites
that they cried out[i] to the LORD for help.
7 When the Israelites cried to the LORD because of Midian, 8 he sent them a prophet,
who said, "This is what the LORD, the God of Israel, says: I brought you up out of
Egypt,[j] out of the land of slavery. 9 I snatched you from the power of Egypt and from
the hand of all your oppressors. I drove them from before you and gave you their
land.[k] 10 I said to you, 'I am the LORD your God; do not worship[l] the gods of the
Amorites,[m] in whose land you live.' But you have not listened to me."
11 The angel of the LORD[n] came and sat down under the oak in Ophrah that belonged

5:26 [d] Jdg 4:21
5:28 [e] Pr 7:6
5:30 [f] Ex 15:9; 1Sa 30:24
5:31 [g] 2Sa 23:4; Ps 19:4; 89:36 [h] Jdg 3:11
6:1 [a] Jdg 2:11 [b] Nu 25:15-18; 31:1-3
6:2 [c] 1Sa 13:6; Isa 8:21 [d] Heb 11:38
6:3 [e] Jdg 3:13
6:4 [f] Lev 26:16; Dt 28:30, 51
6:5 [g] Jdg 7:12 [h] Jdg 8:10
6:6 [i] Jdg 3:9
6:8 [j] Jdg 2:1
6:9 [k] Ps 44:2
6:10 [l] 2Ki 17:35 [m] Jer 10:2
6:11 [n] Ge 16:7

6:2 The Midianites were desert people descended from Abraham's second wife, Keturah (Genesis 25:1, 2). From this relationship came a nation that was always in conflict with Israel. Years earlier the Israelites, while still wandering in the desert, battled the Midianites and almost totally destroyed them (Numbers 31:1–20). Because of their failure to completely destroy them, however, the tribe repopulated. Here they were once again oppressing Israel.

6:6 Again the Israelites hit rock bottom before turning back to God. How much suffering they could have avoided if they had trusted him! Turning to God shouldn't be a last resort; we should look to him for help each day. This isn't to say life will always be easy. There will be struggles, but God will give us the strength to live through them. Don't wait until you're at the end of your tether. Call on God first in every situation.

6:11 The Old Testament records several appearances of the angel of the Lord: Genesis 16:7; 22:11; 31:11; Exodus 3:2; 14:19; Judges 2:1; 13:3; Zechariah 3:1–6. It is not known whether the same angel appeared in each case. The angel mentioned here appears to be separate from God in one place (6:12) and yet the same as God in another place (6:14). This has led some to believe that the angel was a special appearance of Jesus Christ prior to his mission on earth as recorded in the New Testament. It is also possible that as a special messenger from God, the angel had authority to speak for God. In either case, God sent a special messenger to deliver an important message to Gideon.

6:11 Threshing was the process of separating the grains of wheat from the useless outer shell called chaff. This was normally done in a large area, often on a hill, where the wind could blow away the

to Joash the Abiezrite,[o] where his son Gideon[p] was threshing wheat in a winepress
to keep it from the Midianites. 12When the angel of the LORD appeared to Gideon,
he said, "The LORD is with you,[q] mighty warrior."
13"But sir," Gideon replied, "if the LORD is with us, why has all this happened to
us? Where are all his wonders that our fathers told[r] us about when they said, 'Did
not the LORD bring us up out of Egypt?' But now the LORD has abandoned[s] us and
put us into the hand of Midian."
14The LORD turned to him and said, "Go in the strength you have[t] and save Israel
out of Midian's hand. Am I not sending you?"
15"But Lord,"[a] Gideon asked, "how can I save Israel? My clan is the weakest in
Manasseh, and I am the least in my family.[u]"
16The LORD answered, "I will be with you,[v] and you will strike down all the
Midianites together."
17Gideon replied, "If now I have found favour in your eyes, give me a sign[w] that
it is really you talking to me. 18Please do not go away until I come back and bring
my offering and set it before you."
And the LORD said, "I will wait until you return."

a *15* Or *sir*

6:11 [o]Jos 17:2 [p]Heb 11:32
6:12 [q]Jos 1:5; Jdg 13:3; Lk 1:11, 28
6:13 [r]Ps 44:1 [s]2Ch 15:2
6:14 [t]Heb 11:34
6:15 [u]Ex 3:11; 1Sa 9:21
6:16 [v]Ex 3:12; Jos 1:5
6:17 [w]ver 36-37; Ge 24:14; Isa 38:7-8

GOD USES COMMON PEOPLE
God uses all sorts of people to do his work—like you and me!

Person	*Known as*	*Task*	*Reference*
JACOB	A deceiver	To "father" the Israelite nation	Genesis 27
JOSEPH	A slave	To save his family	Genesis 39ff
MOSES	Shepherd in exile (and murderer)	To lead Israel out of bondage, to the promised land	Exodus 3
GIDEON	A farmer	To deliver Israel from Midian	Judges 6:11
JEPHTHAH	Son of a prostitute	To deliver Israel from the Ammonites	Judges 11:1
HANNAH	A housewife	To be the mother of Samuel	1 Samuel 1
DAVID	A shepherd boy and last-born of the family	To be Israel's greatest king	1 Samuel 16
EZRA	A scribe	To lead the return to Judah and to write some of the Bible	Ezra, Nehemiah
ESTHER	A slave girl	To save her people from massacre	Esther
MARY	A peasant girl	To be the mother of Christ	Luke 1:27–38
MATTHEW	A tax collector	To be an apostle and Gospel writer	Matthew 9:9
LUKE	A Greek physician	To be a companion of Paul and a Gospel writer	Colossians 4:14
PETER	A fisherman	To be an apostle, a leader of the early church, and a writer of two New Testament letters	Matthew 4:18–20

lighter chaff when the farmer tossed the beaten wheat into the air. If Gideon had done this, however, he would have been an easy target for the bands of raiders who were overrunning the land. Therefore, he was forced to thresh his wheat in a winepress, a pit that was probably hidden from view and that would not be suspected as a place to find a farmer's crops.

6:13 Gideon questioned God about the problems he and his nation faced and about God's apparent lack of help. What he didn't acknowledge was the fact that the people had brought calamity upon themselves when they decided to disobey and neglect God. How easy it is to overlook personal accountability and blame our problems on God and others. Unfortunately this does not solve our problems. It brings us no closer to God, and it escorts us to the very edge of rebellion and backsliding.

When problems come, the first place to look is within. Our first action should be confession to God of sins that may have created our problems.

6:14–16 "I will be with you," God told Gideon, and God promised to give him the strength he needed to overcome the opposition. In spite of this clear promise of strength, Gideon made excuses. Seeing only his limitations and weaknesses, he failed to see how God could work through him.

Like Gideon, we are called to serve God in specific ways. Although God promises us the tools and strength we need, we often make excuses. But reminding God of our limitations only implies that he does not know all about us or that he has made a mistake in evaluating our character. Don't spend time making excuses. Instead spend it doing what God wants.

19 Gideon went in, prepared a young goat, and from an ephah[b] of flour he made
bread without yeast. Putting the meat in a basket and its broth in a pot, he brought
them out and offered them to him under the oak.[x]
20 The angel of God said to him, "Take the meat and the unleavened bread, place
them on this rock,[y] and pour out the broth." And Gideon did so. 21 With the tip of
the staff that was in his hand, the angel of the LORD touched the meat and the
unleavened bread.[z] Fire flared from the rock, consuming the meat and the bread. And
the angel of the LORD disappeared. 22 When Gideon realised[a] that it was the angel
of the LORD, he exclaimed, "Ah, Sovereign LORD! I have seen the angel of the LORD
face to face!"[b]
23 But the LORD said to him, "Peace! Do not be afraid.[c] You are not going to die."
24 So Gideon built an altar to the LORD there and called[d] it The LORD is Peace. To
this day it stands in Ophrah[e] of the Abiezrites.
25 That same night the LORD said to him, "Take the second bull from your father's
herd, the one seven years old.[c] Tear down your father's altar to Baal and cut down
the Asherah pole[d][f] beside it. 26 Then build a proper kind of[e] altar to the LORD your
God on the top of this height. Using the wood of the Asherah pole that you cut down,
offer the second[f] bull as a burnt offering."
27 So Gideon took ten of his servants and did as the LORD told him. But because
he was afraid of his family and the men of the town, he did it at night rather than in
the daytime.
28 In the morning when the men of the town got up, there was Baal's altar,[g]
demolished, with the Asherah pole beside it cut down and the second bull sacrificed
on the newly-built altar!
29 They asked each other, "Who did this?"
When they carefully investigated, they were told, "Gideon son of Joash did it."
30 The men of the town demanded of Joash, "Bring out your son. He must die,
because he has broken down Baal's altar and cut down the Asherah pole beside it."
31 But Joash replied to the hostile crowd around him, "Are you going to plead Baal's
cause? Are you trying to save him? Whoever fights for him shall be put to death by
morning! If Baal really is a god, he can defend himself when someone breaks down
his altar." 32 So that day they called Gideon "Jerub-Baal,[g][h]" saying, "Let Baal
contend with him," because he broke down Baal's altar.
33 Now all the Midianites, Amalekites and other eastern peoples[i] joined forces and
crossed over the Jordan and camped in the Valley of Jezreel.[j] 34 Then the Spirit of
the LORD came upon[k] Gideon, and he blew a trumpet,[l] summoning the Abiezrites
to follow him. 35 He sent messengers throughout Manasseh, calling them to arms, and
also into Asher, Zebulun and Naphtali,[m] so that they too went up to meet them.
36 Gideon said to God, "If you will save[n] Israel by my hand as you have prom-

6:19 [x]Ge 18:7-8
6:20 [y]Jdg 13:19
6:21 [z]Lev 9:24
6:22 [a]Jdg 13:16, 21 [b]Ge 32:30; Ex 33:20; Jdg 13:22
6:23 [c]Da 10:19
6:24 [d]Ge 22:14 [e]Jdg 8:32
6:25 [f]Ex 34:13; Dt 7:5
6:28 [g]1Ki 16:32
6:32 [h]Jdg 7:1; 8:29, 35; 1Sa 12:11
6:33 [i]ver 3 [j]Jos 17:16
6:34 [k]Jdg 3:10; 1Ch 12:18; 2Ch 24:20 [l]Jdg 3:27
6:35 [m]Jdg 4:6
6:36 [n]ver 14

[b] *19* That is, probably about 3/5 bushel (about 22 litres) [c] *25* Or *Take a full-grown, mature bull from your father's herd* [d] *25* That is, a symbol of the goddess Asherah; here and elsewhere in Judges [e] *26* Or *build with layers of stone an* [f] *26* Or *full-grown*; also in verse 28 [g] *32* *Jerub-Baal* means *let Baal contend.*

6:22, 23 Why was Gideon afraid of seeing an angel? The Israelites believed that no-one could see God and live (see God's words to Moses in Exodus 33:20). Evidently Gideon thought this also applied to angels.

6:25–30 After God called Gideon to be Israel's deliverer, he immediately asked him to tear down the altar of the pagan god, Baal—an act that would test Gideon's faith and commitment. Canaanite religion was very political, so an attack on a god was often seen as an attack on the local government supporting that god. If caught, Gideon would face serious social problems and probable physical attack. (For more on Baal and Asherah, see the notes on 2:11–15 and 3:7.)

Gideon took a great risk by following God's higher law, which specifically forbids idol worship (Exodus 20:1–5). After learning what Gideon had done, the people wanted to kill him. Many of those people were fellow Israelites. This shows how immoral God's people had become. God said in Deuteronomy 13:6–11 that idolaters must be stoned to death, but these Israelites wanted to stone Gideon for tearing down an idol and worshipping God! When you begin to accomplish something for God, you may be criticised by the very people who should support you.

6:33 The armies of Midian and Amalek camped in the Valley of Jezreel, the agricultural centre for the area. Whoever controlled the valley's rich and fertile land controlled the people who lived in and around it. Because of the valley's vast resources, many major trade routes converged at the pass which led into it. This made it the site of many great battles. Gideon's men attacked the enemy armies from the hills, and the only escape route was through the pass towards the Jordan River. That is why Gideon urged some of his troops to take control of the river's crossing points (7:24).

6:37–39 Was Gideon testing God, or was he simply asking God for more encouragement? In either case, though his motive was right (to obey God and defeat the enemy), his method was less than ideal. Gideon seems to have known that his requests might

6:37 [o]Ex 4:3-7 [p]Ge 24:14
ised—37 look, I will place a wool fleece on the threshing-floor.[o] If there is dew only
on the fleece and all the ground is dry, then I will know[p] that you will save Israel
by my hand, as you said." 38 And that is what happened. Gideon rose early the next
day; he squeezed the fleece and wrung out the dew—a bowlful of water.
39 Then Gideon said to God, "Do not be angry with me. Let me make just one more
6:39 [q]Ge 18:32
request.[q] Allow me one more test with the fleece. This time make the fleece dry and
the ground covered with dew." 40 That night God did so. Only the fleece was dry; all
the ground was covered with dew.

Gideon Defeats the Midianites

7:1 [a]Jdg 6:32 [b]Ge 12:6
7 Early in the morning, Jerub-Baal[a] (that is, Gideon) and all his men camped at
the spring of Harod. The camp of Midian was north of them in the valley near
the hill of Moreh.[b] 2 The LORD said to Gideon, "You have too many men for me to
deliver Midian into their hands. In order that Israel may not boast against me that her
7:2 [c]Dt 8:17; 2Co 4:7
own strength[c] has saved her, 3 announce now to the people, 'Anyone who trembles
with fear may turn back and leave Mount Gilead.[d]'" So twenty-two thousand men
left, while ten thousand remained.
4 But the LORD said to Gideon, "There are still too many[e] men. Take them down
to the water, and I will sift them out for you there. If I say, 'This one shall go with
you,' he shall go; but if I say, 'This one shall not go with you,' he shall not go."
7:3 [d]Dt 20:8
5 So Gideon took the men down to the water. There the LORD told him, "Separate
those who lap the water with their tongues like a dog from those who kneel down to
drink." 6 Three hundred men lapped with their hands to their mouths. All the rest got
down on their knees to drink.
7:4 [e]1Sa 14:6
7 The LORD said to Gideon, "With the three hundred men that lapped I will save
you and give the Midianites into your hands. Let all the other men go, each to his
own place."[f] 8 So Gideon sent the rest of the Israelites to their tents but kept the three
hundred, who took over the provisions and trumpets of the others.
Now the camp of Midian lay below him in the valley. 9 During that night the LORD
7:7 [f]1Sa 14:6
said to Gideon, "Get up, go down against the camp, because I am going to give it

---

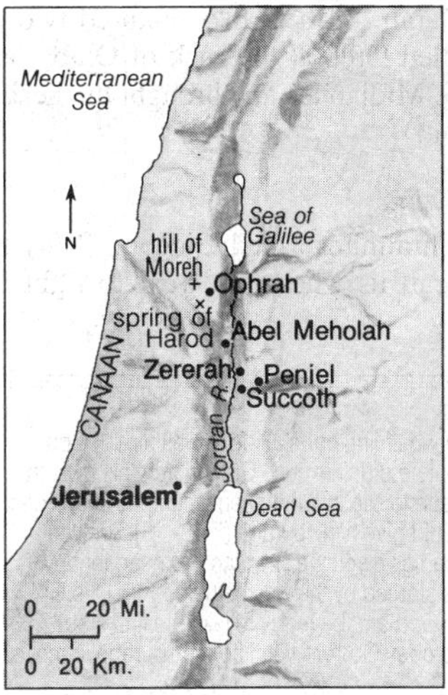

GIDEON'S BATTLE
In spite of Deborah and Barak's victory, the Canaanites still caused trouble in this fertile region. God appeared to Gideon at Ophrah and called him to defeat them. With only 300 fighting men, Gideon routed thousands of Midianites, chasing them to Zererah and Abel Meholah.

displease God (6:39), and yet he demanded two miracles (6:37, 39) even after witnessing the miraculous fire from the rock (6:21). It is true that to make good decisions, we need facts. Gideon had all the facts, but still he hesitated. He delayed obeying God because he wanted even more proof.

Demanding extra signs was an indication of unbelief. Fear often makes us wait for more confirmation when we should be taking action. Visible signs are unnecessary if they only confirm what we already know is true.

Today the greatest means of God's guidance is his word, the Bible. Unlike Gideon, we have God's complete, revealed word. If you want to have more of God's guidance, don't ask for signs; study the Bible (2 Timothy 3:16, 17).

6:39 After seeing the miracle of the wet fleece, why did Gideon ask for another miracle? Perhaps he thought the results of the first test could have happened naturally. A thick fleece could retain moisture long after the sun had dried the surrounding ground. "Putting out fleeces" is a poor decision-making method. Those who do this put limitations on God. They ask him to fit their expectations. The results of such experiments are usually inconclusive and thus fail to make us any more confident about our choices. Don't let a "fleece" become a substitute for God's wisdom that comes through Bible study and prayer.

7:2 Self-sufficiency is an enemy when it causes us to believe we can always do what needs to be done in our own strength. To prevent this attitude among Gideon's soldiers, God reduced their number from 32,000 to 300. With an army this small, there could be no doubt that victory was from God. The men could not take the credit. Like Gideon, we must recognise the danger of fighting in our own strength. We can be confident of victory only if we put our confidence in God and not ourselves.

into your hands.[g] 10If you are afraid to attack, go down to the camp with your servant
Purah 11and listen to what they are saying. Afterwards, you will be encouraged to
attack the camp." So he and Purah his servant went down to the outposts of the camp.
12The Midianites, the Amalekites[h] and all the other eastern peoples had settled in the
valley, thick as locusts.[i] Their camels[j] could no more be counted than the sand on
the seashore.[k]
13Gideon arrived just as a man was telling a friend his dream. "I had a dream," he
was saying. "A round loaf of barley bread came tumbling into the Midianite camp.
It struck the tent with such force that the tent overturned and collapsed."
14His friend responded, "This can be nothing other than the sword of Gideon son
of Joash, the Israelite. God has given the Midianites and the whole camp into his
hands."
15When Gideon heard the dream and its interpretation, he worshipped God.[l] He
returned to the camp of Israel and called out, "Get up! The LORD has given the
Midianite camp into your hands." 16Dividing the three hundred men[m] into three
companies,[n] he placed trumpets and empty jars in the hands of all of them, with
torches inside.
17"Watch me," he told them. "Follow my lead. When I get to the edge of the camp,
do exactly as I do. 18When I and all who are with me blow our trumpets,[o] then from
all around the camp blow yours and shout, 'For the LORD and for Gideon.' "
19Gideon and the hundred men with him reached the edge of the camp at the
beginning of the middle watch, just after they had changed the guard. They blew their
trumpets and broke the jars that were in their hands. 20The three companies blew the
trumpets and smashed the jars. Grasping the torches in their left hands and holding
in their right hands the trumpets they were to blow, they shouted, "A sword[p] for the
LORD and for Gideon!" 21While each man held his position around the camp, all the
Midianites ran, crying out as they fled.[q]
22When the three hundred trumpets sounded,[r] the LORD caused the men throughout
the camp to turn on each other[s] with their swords. The army fled to Beth Shittah
towards Zererah as far as the border of Abel Meholah[t] near Tabbath. 23Israelites from
Naphtali, Asher and all Manasseh were called out,[u] and they pursued the Midianites.
24Gideon sent messengers throughout the hill country of Ephraim, saying, "Come
down against the Midianites and seize the waters of the Jordan[v] ahead of them as
far as Beth Barah."

So all the men of Ephraim were called out and they took the waters of the Jordan
as far as Beth Barah. 25They also captured two of the Midianite leaders, Oreb and
Zeeb[w]. They killed Oreb at the rock of Oreb,[x] and Zeeb at the winepress of Zeeb.
They pursued the Midianites and brought the heads of Oreb and Zeeb to Gideon, who
was by the Jordan.[y]

Zebah and Zalmunna

8 Now the Ephraimites asked Gideon, "Why have you treated us like this? Why
didn't you call us when you went to fight Midian?"[a] And they criticised him
sharply.[b]

7:9 [g]Jos 2:24; 10:8; 11:6
7:12 [h]Jdg 8:10 [i]Jdg 6:5 [j]Jer 49:29 [k]Jos 11:4
7:15 [l]1Sa 15:31
7:16 [m]Ge 14:15 [n]2Sa 18:2
7:18 [o]Jdg 3:27
7:20 [p]ver 14
7:21 [q]2Ki 7:7
7:22 [r]Jos 6:20 [s]1Sa 14:20; 2Ch 20:23 [t]1Ki 4:12; 19:16
7:23 [u]Jdg 6:35
7:24 [v]Jdg 3:28
7:25 [w]Jdg 8:3; Ps 83:11 [x]Isa 10:26 [y]Jdg 8:4
8:1 [a]Jdg 12:1 [b]2Sa 19:41

7:10, 11 Facing overwhelming odds, Gideon was afraid. God understood his fear, but he didn't excuse Gideon from his task. Instead he allowed Gideon to slip into the enemy camp and overhear a conversation that would give him courage (7:12–15). Are you facing a battle? God can give you the strength you need for any situation. And don't be startled by the way he helps you. Like Gideon, you must listen to God and be ready to take the first step. Only after you begin to obey God will you find the courage to move ahead.

7:12 Midianites were camel-riding marauders composed of five families linked to Abraham through Midian, the son of Abraham's second wife, Keturah. They inhabited the desert regions from the Dead Sea to the Red Sea.

7:13 An enemy soldier dreamed of a loaf of barley bread tumbling into camp. Barley grain was only half the value of wheat, and the bread made from it was considered inferior. In the same way, Israel's tiny band of men was considered inferior to the vast forces of Midian and Amalek. But God would make the underdog Israelites seem invincible.

7:19 The night was divided equally into three watches. The beginning of the middle watch would have been around 10:00 p.m. Many in the camp would have still been awake.

7:21 Gideon's army simply watched as the army of Midian fell into panic, confusion, and disordered retreat. Not one man had to draw a sword to defeat the enemy. Gideon's small army could never have brought about such a victory in their own strength. God wanted to demonstrate to Israel that victory depends not on strength or numbers, but on obedience and commitment to him.

GIDEON

Most of us want to know God's plan for our lives, but we're not always sure how to find it. One common misunderstanding is the idea that God's guidance will come to us out of the blue, that it has nothing to do with what we're doing now. But if we're always looking around for God's next assignment, we run the risk of ruining whatever we're working on right now. Fortunately, the Bible points to a kind of guidance that does not put our current projects in jeopardy. In the Bible's descriptions of how God guided many people, we can see that often God's call came while people were completely immersed in the challenge of the moment. A good example of this kind of guidance is seen in Gideon's life.

Gideon had a limited vision, but he was committed to it. His challenge was to obtain food for his family even though hostile invaders were making the growing, gathering, and preparation of the food almost impossible. Gideon was resourceful. He put a winepress to double use by turning it into a sunken threshing floor. It lacked ventilation to blow the chaff away, but at least it was hidden from the Midianites. Gideon was working in his threshing floor when God sent him a messenger with a challenge.

Gideon was surprised by what God told him to do. He did not want to jump into a task for which he was ill prepared. The angel had to overcome three objections before Gideon was convinced: (1) Gideon's feelings of responsibility for his family's welfare, (2) his doubts about the call itself, and (3) his feelings of inadequacy for the job. Once Gideon was convinced, however, he obeyed with zest, resourcefulness, and speed. He dedicated those personality traits to God, with whom he was now personally acquainted.

Gideon had his weak moments and failures, but he was still God's servant. If you can easily see yourself in Gideon's weakness, can you also see yourself in being willing to serve? Remember Gideon as a man who obeyed God by giving his attention to the task at hand. Then give your full attention to believing God will prepare you for tomorrow when it comes.

Strengths and accomplishments:
- Israel's fifth judge. A military strategist who was an expert at surprise
- A member of the Hall of Faith in Hebrews 11
- Defeated the Midianite army
- Was offered a hereditary kingship by the men of Israel
- Though slow to be convinced, acted on his convictions

Weaknesses and mistakes:
- Feared that his own limitations would prevent God from working
- Collected Midianite gold and made a symbol that became an evil object of worship
- Through a concubine, fathered a son who would bring great grief and tragedy to both Gideon's family and the nation of Israel
- Failed to establish the nation in God's ways; after he died they all went back to idol worship

Lessons from his life:
- God calls in the middle of our present obedience. As we are faithful, he gives us more responsibility
- God expands and uses the abilities he has already built into us
- God uses us in spite of our limitations and failures
- Even those who make great spiritual progress can easily fall into sin if they don't consistently follow God

Vital statistics:
- Where: Ophrah, Valley of Jezreel, spring of Harod
- Occupations: Farmer, warrior, and judge
- Relatives: Father: Joash. Son: Abimelech
- Contemporaries: Zebah, Zalmunna

Key verses:
" 'But Lord,' Gideon asked, 'how can I save Israel? My clan is the weakest in Manasseh, and I am the least in my family.' The LORD answered, 'I will be with you, and you will strike down all the Midianites together' " (Judges 6:15, 16).

His story is told in Judges 6–8. He is also mentioned in Hebrews 11:32.

8:1–3 Ephraim's leaders felt left out because Gideon had not called them to join the battle, but had left them in place to "clean up" the escaping Midianites ("the gleanings"), and so they angrily confronted him. Gideon assured the leaders of Ephraim that their accomplishment was even greater than his own clan's (Abiezer). His diplomatic explanation pointed out that this rear guard had managed to capture the enemy's generals, thus cutting off the leaders from their army. Not every necessary job is a highly visible leadership role. Much of the necessary labour of any effective enterprise is considered by many to be dirty work. But such work is

2But he answered them, "What have I accomplished compared to you? Aren't the
gleanings of Ephraim's grapes better than the full grape harvest of Abiezer? 3God gave
Oreb and Zeeb,[c] the Midianite leaders, into your hands. What was I able to do
compared to you?" At this, their resentment against him subsided.
4Gideon and his three hundred men, exhausted yet keeping up the pursuit, came
to the Jordan[d] and crossed it. 5He said to the men of Succoth,[e] "Give my troops
some bread; they are worn out, and I am still pursuing Zebah and Zalmunna,[f] the
kings of Midian."
6But the officials of Succoth said, "Do you already have the hands of Zebah and
Zalmunna in your possession? Why should we give bread[g] to your troops?"[h]
7Then Gideon replied, "Just for that, when the LORD has given Zebah and Zalmunna[i] into my hand, I will tear your flesh with desert thorns and briers."
8From there he went up to Peniel[a][j] and made the same request of them, but they
answered as the men of Succoth had. 9So he said to the men of Peniel, "When I return
in triumph, I will tear down this tower."[k]
10Now Zebah and Zalmunna were in Karkor with a force of about fifteen thousand
men, all that were left of the armies of the eastern peoples; a hundred and twenty
thousand swordsmen had fallen.[l] 11Gideon went up by the route of the nomads east
of Nobah[m] and Jogbehah[n] and fell upon the unsuspecting army. 12Zebah and Zalmunna, the two kings of Midian, fled, but he pursued them and captured them, routing
their entire army.
13Gideon son of Joash then returned from the battle by the Pass of Heres. 14He
caught a young man of Succoth and questioned him, and the young man wrote down
for him the names of the seventy-seven officials of Succoth, the elders of the town.
15Then Gideon came and said to the men of Succoth, "Here are Zebah and Zalmunna,
about whom you taunted me by saying, 'Do you already have the hands of Zebah and
Zalmunna in your possession? Why should we give bread to your exhausted men?[o]' "
16He took the elders of the town and taught the men of Succoth a lesson[p] by punishing
them with desert thorns and briers. 17He also pulled down the tower of Peniel and
killed the men of the town.[q]
18Then he asked Zebah and Zalmunna, "What kind of men did you kill at Tabor?[r]"
"Men like you," they answered, "each one with the bearing of a prince."
19Gideon replied, "Those were my brothers, the sons of my own mother. As surely
as the LORD lives, if you had spared their lives, I would not kill you." 20Turning to
Jether, his oldest son, he said, "Kill them!" But Jether did not draw his sword, because
he was only a boy and was afraid.
21Zebah and Zalmunna said, "Come, do it yourself. 'As is the man, so is his
strength.' " So Gideon stepped forward and killed them, and took the ornaments[s] off
their camels' necks.

[a] 8 Hebrew *Penuel*, a variant of *Peniel*; also in verses 9 and 17

8:3 [c] Jdg 7:25; Pr 15:1
8:4 [d] Jdg 7:25
8:5 [e] Ge 33:17 [f] Ps 83:11
8:6 [g] 1Sa 25:11 [h] ver 15
8:7 [i] Jdg 7:15
8:8 [j] Ge 32:30; 1Ki 12:25
8:9 [k] ver 17
8:10 [l] Jdg 6:5; 7:12; Isa 9:4
8:11 [m] Nu 32:42 [n] Nu 32:35
8:15 [o] ver 6
8:16 [p] ver 7
8:17 [q] ver 9
8:18 [r] Jos 19:22; Jdg 4:6
8:21 [s] ver 26; Ps 83:11

---

vital to getting any big task done. Engineers and millionaires may design and finance an elegant building, but it is the bricklayers who get the work done. Pride causes us to want recognition. Are you content to be God's bricklayer, or do you resent the work God has given you?

8:5, 9 The leaders of Succoth and Peniel refused to help Gideon, probably fearing Midian's revenge should he fail (Gideon's army was 300 men chasing 15,000). They should have realised that victory was certain because God was with Gideon. But they were so worried about saving themselves that they never thought about God's power to save.

Because of fear for ourselves, we may not recognise God's presence in other people and therefore miss God's victory. Then we must face the often bitter consequences of failing to join forces with those God has chosen to do his work. Because God will prevail with or without you, be quick to join others who are engaged in his work. Lend support with your time, money, talents, and prayer.

8:11 The Midianites were escaping into the desert area, where the tent-dwelling nomads lived. They didn't expect Gideon to follow them that far.

8:15–17 Gideon carried out the threat he had made in 8:7. It is difficult to determine whether this act of revenge was justified or whether he should have left the punishment up to God. Gideon was God's appointed leader, but the officials of Succoth and Peniel refused to help him in any way because they feared the enemy. They showed no faith or respect for God or for the man God had chosen to save them. We should help others because it is right, regardless of whether we will benefit personally.

8:20, 21 For a king to be killed by a boy was humiliating because it would look as though he was no match for a boy ("As is the man, so is his strength"). The two men wanted to avoid that disgrace, as well as the slower and more painful death which an inexperienced swordsman might inflict.

Gideon's Ephod

22The Israelites said to Gideon, "Rule over us — you, your son and your grandson — because you have saved us out of the hand of Midian."
23But Gideon told them, "I will not rule over you, nor will my son rule over you.
The LORD will rule[t] over you." 24And he said, "I do have one request, that each of
you give me an ear-ring from your share of the plunder." (It was the custom of the
Ishmaelites[u] to wear gold ear-rings.)
25They answered, "We'll be glad to give them." So they spread out a garment, and
each man threw a ring from his plunder onto it. 26The weight of the gold rings he asked
for came to seventeen hundred shekels,[b] not counting the ornaments, the pendants
and the purple garments worn by the kings of Midian or the chains that were on their
camels' necks. 27Gideon made the gold into an ephod,[v] which he placed in Ophrah,
his town. All Israel prostituted themselves by worshipping it there, and it became a
snare[w] to Gideon and his family.

Gideon's Death

28Thus Midian was subdued before the Israelites and did not raise its head again.
During Gideon's lifetime, the land enjoyed peace[x] for forty years.
29Jerub-Baal[y] son of Joash went back home to live. 30He had seventy sons[z] of
his own, for he had many wives. 31His concubine, who lived in Shechem, also bore
him a son, whom he named Abimelech.[a] 32Gideon son of Joash died at a good old
age[b] and was buried in the tomb of his father Joash in Ophrah of the Abiezrites.
33No sooner had Gideon died than the Israelites again prostituted themselves to the
Baals.[c] They set up Baal-Berith[d] as their god[e] and 34did not remember[f] the LORD
their God, who had rescued them from the hands of all their enemies on every side.
35They also failed to show kindness to the family of Jerub-Baal (that is, Gideon) for
all the good things he had done for them.[g]

Abimelech

9 Abimelech[a] son of Jerub-Baal went to his mother's brothers in Shechem and said
to them and to all his mother's clan, 2"Ask all the citizens of Shechem, 'Which
is better for you: to have all seventy of Jerub-Baal's sons rule over you, or just one
man?' Remember, I am your flesh and blood.[b]"
3When the brothers repeated all this to the citizens of Shechem, they were inclined

b 26 That is, about 43 pounds (about 19.5 kilograms)

8:23 [t]Ex 16:8; 1Sa 8:7; 10:19; 12:12
8:24 [u]Ge 25:13
8:27 [v]Jdg 17:5; 18:14 [w]Dt 7:16; Ps 106:39
8:28 [x]Jdg 5:31
8:29 [y]Jdg 7:1
8:30 [z]Jdg 9:2, 5, 18, 24
8:31 [a]Jdg 9:1
8:32 [b]Ge 25:8
8:33 [c]Jdg 2:11, 13, 19 [d]Jdg 9:4 [e]Jdg 9:27, 46
8:34 [f]Jdg 3:7; Dt 4:9; Ps 78:11, 42
8:35 [g]Jdg 9:16
9:1 [a]Jdg 8:31
9:2 [b]Ge 29:14; Jdg 8:30

8:23 The people wanted to make Gideon their king, but Gideon stressed that the Lord was to rule over them. Despite his inconsistencies, Gideon never lost sight of the importance, for both a nation and an individual, of putting God first. Is God first in your life? If he is, he must affect every dimension of your life, not just what you do in church.

8:26, 27 Those who were very wealthy put ornaments on their camels as a way of displaying their riches. Women wore vast amounts of jewellery as well, often up to 15 pairs of earrings. Jewellery was also worn for good luck. After Gideon's rise to power, he seems to have become carried away with this accumulation of wealth. Eventually it led the Israelites to idolatry.

8:27 An ephod was a linen garment worn by priests over their chests. It was considered holy (Exodus 28:5–35; 39:2–24; Leviticus 8:7, 8). Gideon probably had good motives for making the ephod (a visible remembrance commemorating the victory). Unfortunately, the people began to worship the ephod as an idol. Sadly, many decisions that stem from good motives produce negative results. Perhaps no-one stops to ask, "What might go wrong?" or "Is there a possibility of negative consequences?" In your plans and decisions, take time to anticipate how a good idea might lead to a potential problem.

8:31 This relationship between Gideon and a concubine produced a son who tore apart Gideon's family and caused tragedy for the nation. Gideon's story illustrates the fact that heroes in battle are not always heroes in daily life. Gideon led the nation but could not lead his family. No matter who you are, moral laxness will cause problems. Just because you have won a single battle with temptation does not mean you will automatically win the next one. We need to be constantly watchful against temptation. Sometimes Satan's strongest attacks come after a victory.

8:33 Baal-Berith means "Baal (lord) of the covenant". Worship of the idol may have combined elements of both the Israelites' and Canaanite religions.

9:1–3 With Gideon dead, Abimelech wanted to take his father's place. (Jerub-Baal is another name for Gideon; see 6:32.) To set his plan in motion he went to the city of Shechem, his mother's home town, to drum up support. Here he felt kinship with the residents. These relatives were Canaanites and would be glad to unite against Israel. Shechem was an important city, a crossroads for trade routes and a natural link between the coastal plain and the Jordan Valley. Whoever controlled Shechem would dominate the countryside.

9:2–5 Israel's king was to be the Lord and not a man. But Abimelech wanted to usurp the position reserved for God alone. In his selfish quest, he killed all but one of his 70 half brothers. People with selfish desires often seek to fulfil them in ruthless ways. Examine your ambitions to see if they are self-centred or God-centred. Be sure you always fulfil your desires in ways that God would approve.

to follow Abimelech, for they said, "He is our brother." 4They gave him seventy
shekels[a] of silver from the temple of Baal-Berith,[c] and Abimelech used it to hire
reckless adventurers,[d] who became his followers. 5He went to his father's home in
Ophrah and on one stone murdered his seventy brothers,[e] the sons of Jerub-Baal. But
Jotham, the youngest son of Jerub-Baal, escaped by hiding.[f] 6Then all the citizens
of Shechem and Beth Millo gathered beside the great tree at the pillar in Shechem to
crown Abimelech king.
7When Jotham was told about this, he climbed up on the top of Mount Gerizim[g]
and shouted to them, "Listen to me, citizens of Shechem, so that God may listen to
you. 8One day the trees went out to anoint a king for themselves. They said to the
olive tree, 'Be our king.'
9"But the olive tree answered, 'Should I give up my oil, by which both gods and
men are honoured, to hold sway over the trees?'
10"Next, the trees said to the fig-tree, 'Come and be our king.'
11"But the fig-tree replied, 'Should I give up my fruit, so good and sweet, to hold
sway over the trees?'
12"Then the trees said to the vine, 'Come and be our king.'
13"But the vine answered, 'Should I give up my wine,[h] which cheers both gods
and men, to hold sway over the trees?'
14"Finally all the trees said to the thornbush, 'Come and be our king.'
15"The thornbush said to the trees, 'If you really want to anoint me king over you,
come and take refuge in my shade;[i] but if not, then let fire come out[j] of the
thornbush and consume the cedars of Lebanon!'[k]
16"Now if you have acted honourably and in good faith when you made Abimelech
king, and if you have been fair to Jerub-Baal and his family, and if you have treated
him as he deserves—17and to think that my father fought for you, risked his life to
rescue you from the hand of Midian 18(but today you have revolted against my father's
family, murdered his seventy sons[l] on a single stone, and made Abimelech, the son
of his slave girl, king over the citizens of Shechem because he is your brother)—19if
then you have acted honourably and in good faith towards Jerub-Baal and his family

[a] 4 That is, about 1¾ pounds (about 0.8 kilogram)

9:4 [c] Jdg 8:33 [d] Jdg 11:3; 2Ch 13:7
9:5 [e] ver 2; Jdg 8:30 [f] 2Ki 11:2
9:7 [g] Dt 11:29; 27:12; Jn 4:20
9:13 [h] Ecc 2:3
9:15 [i] Isa 30:2 [j] ver 20 [k] Isa 2:13
9:18 [l] ver 5-6; Jdg 8:30

9:4 Politics played a major part in pagan religions such as the worship of Baal-Berith. Governments often went so far as to employ temple prostitutes to bring in additional money. In many cases a religious system was set up and supported by the government so the offerings could fund community projects. Religion became a profit-making business. In Israel's religion, this was strictly forbidden. God's system of religion was designed to come from an attitude of the heart, not from calculated plans and business opportunities. It was also designed to serve people and help those in need, not to oppress the needy. Is your faith genuine and sincere, or is it based on convenience, comfort, and availability?

9:6 Abimelech was declared ruler of Israel at Shechem, the site of other key Bible events. It was one of Abraham's first stops upon arriving in Canaan (Genesis 12:6, 7). When Jacob lived there, two of his sons killed all the men in Shechem because the prince's son raped their sister (Genesis 34). Joseph's bones were buried in Shechem (Joshua 24:32); Israel renewed its covenant with God there (Joshua 24); and the kingdom of Israel split apart at this same city (1 Kings 12).

9:7–15 In Jotham's parable the trees represented Gideon's 70 sons, and the thornbush represented Abimelech. Jotham's point was this: a productive person would be too busy doing good to want to bother with power politics. A worthless person, on the other hand, would be glad to accept the honour—but he would destroy the people he ruled. Abimelech, like a thornbush, could offer Israel no real protection or security. Jotham's parable came true when Abimelech destroyed the city of Shechem (9:45), burned "the tower of Shechem" (the city of Beth Millo, 9:46–49), and was finally killed at Thebez (9:53, 54).

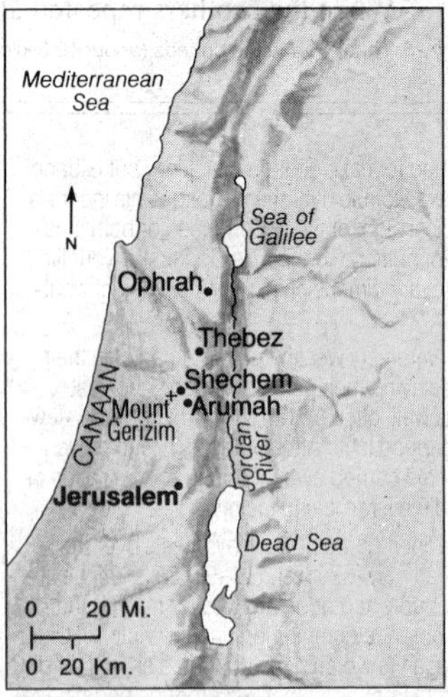

ABIMELECH'S FALL
Gideon's illegitimate son killed 69 of his half brothers in Ophrah and returned to Shechem to be acclaimed king. But three years later, Shechem rebelled. From Arumah, Abimelech attacked Shechem, Beth Millo ("the tower of Shechem"), and Thebez where he was killed.

9:16 Jotham told the story about the trees in order to help the people set good priorities. He did not want them to appoint a leader of dubious character. As we serve in leadership positions, we should examine our motives. Do we just want praise, prestige, or power? In the parable, the good trees chose to be productive and to provide benefits for people. Make sure these are your priorities as you aspire to leadership.

9:20
[m]ver 15

9:23
[n]1Sa 16:14, 23; 18:10; 1Ki 22:22; Isa 19:14; 33:1

9:24
[o]Nu 35:33; 1Ki 2:32
[p]ver 56-57

today, may Abimelech be your joy, and may you be his, too! 20But if you have not,
let fire come out[m] from Abimelech and consume you, citizens of Shechem and Beth
Millo, and let fire come out from you, citizens of Shechem and Beth Millo, and
consume Abimelech!"
21Then Jotham fled, escaping to Beer, and he lived there because he was afraid of
his brother Abimelech.
22After Abimelech had governed Israel for three years, 23God sent an evil spirit[n]
between Abimelech and the citizens of Shechem, who acted treacherously against
Abimelech. 24God did this in order that the crime against Jerub-Baal's seventy sons,
the shedding[o] of their blood, might be avenged[p] on their brother Abimelech and on

ABIMELECH

People who desire power always outnumber those who are able to use power wisely once they have it. Perhaps this is because power has a way of taking over and controlling the person using it. This is especially true in cases of inherited but unmerited power. Abimelech's life shows us what happens when hunger for power corrupts judgment.

Abimelech's position in Gideon's family as the son of a concubine must have created great tension between him and Gideon's many other sons. One against 70: such odds can either crush a person or make him ruthless. It is obvious which direction Abimelech chose. Gideon's position as warrior and judge had placed Abimelech in an environment of power; Gideon's death provided an opportunity for this son to seize power. Once the process began, the disastrous results were inevitable. A person's thirst for power is not satisfied when he gets power—it only becomes more intense. Abimelech's life was consumed by that thirst. Eventually, he could not tolerate any threat to his power.

By this time, ownership had changed: Abimelech no longer had power—power had him. One lesson we can learn from his life is that our goals control our actions. The amount of control is related to the importance of the goal. Abimelech's most important goal was to have power. His lust for power led him to wipe out not only his brothers, but also whole cities that refused to submit to him. Nothing but death could stop his bloodthirsty drive to conquer. How ironic that he was fatally injured by a woman! The contrast between Abimelech and the great people of the Bible is vast. He wanted to control the nation; they were willing to be controlled by God.

Strengths and accomplishments:
- The first self-declared king of Israel
- Qualified tactical planner and organiser

Weaknesses and mistakes:
- Power hungry and ruthless
- Overconfident
- Took advantage of his father's position without imitating his character
- Had 69 of his 70 half brothers killed

Vital statistics:
- Where: Shechem, Arumah, Thebez
- Occupations: Self-acclaimed king, judge, political troublemaker
- Relatives: Father: Gideon. Only surviving brother: Jotham

Key verses:
"Thus God repaid the wickedness that Abimelech had done to his father by murdering his seventy brothers. God also made the men of Shechem pay for all their wickedness. The curse of Jotham son of Jerub-Baal came on them" (Judges 9:56, 57).

His story is told in Judges 8:31—9:57. He is also mentioned in 2 Samuel 11:21.

9:22–24 Abimelech was the opposite of what God wanted in a judge, but it was three years before God moved against him, fulfilling Jotham's parable. Those three years must have seemed like for ever to Jotham. Why wasn't Abimelech punished sooner for his evil ways?

We are not alone when we wonder why evil seems to prevail (Job 10:3; 21:1–18; Jeremiah 12:1; Habakkuk 1:2–4, 12–17). God promises to deal with sin, but in his time, not ours. Actually it is good news that God doesn't punish *us* immediately because we have all sinned and deserve God's punishment. God, in his mercy, often spares us from immediate punishment and allows us time to turn from our sins and turn to him in repentance. Trusting God for justice means (1) we must first recognise our own sins and repent, and (2) we may face a difficult time of waiting for the wicked to be punished. But in God's time, all evil will be destroyed.

9:23 This evil spirit was not just an attitude of strife, it was a demon. It was not Satan himself, but one of the fallen angels under Satan's influence. God used this evil spirit to bring about judgment on Shechem. First Samuel 16:14 records how God judged Saul in a similar way.

the citizens of Shechem, who had helped him[q] murder his brothers. 25 In opposition
to him these citizens of Shechem set men on the hilltops to ambush and rob everyone
who passed by, and this was reported to Abimelech.
26 Now Gaal son of Ebed moved with his brothers into Shechem, and its citizens
put their confidence in him. 27 After they had gone out into the fields and gathered
the grapes and trodden[r] them, they held a festival in the temple of their god.[s] While
they were eating and drinking, they cursed Abimelech. 28 Then Gaal son of Ebed said,
"Who[t] is Abimelech, and who is Shechem, that we should be subject to him? Isn't
he Jerub-Baal's son, and isn't Zebul his deputy? Serve the men of Hamor,[u] Shechem's father! Why should we serve Abimelech? 29 If only this people were under my
command![v] Then I would get rid of him. I would say to Abimelech, 'Call out your
whole army!' "[b]
30 When Zebul the governor of the city heard what Gaal son of Ebed said, he was
very angry. 31 Under cover he sent messengers to Abimelech, saying, "Gaal son of
Ebed and his brothers have come to Shechem and are stirring up the city against you.
32 Now then, during the night you and your men should come and lie in wait[w] in the
fields. 33 In the morning at sunrise, advance against the city. When Gaal and his men
come out against you, do whatever your hand finds to do.[x]"
34 So Abimelech and all his troops set out by night and took up concealed positions
near Shechem in four companies. 35 Now Gaal son of Ebed had gone out and was
standing at the entrance to the city gate just as Abimelech and his soldiers came out
from their hiding-place.[y]
36 When Gaal saw them, he said to Zebul, "Look, people are coming down from
the tops of the mountains!"
Zebul replied, "You mistake the shadows of the mountains for men."
37 But Gaal spoke up again: "Look, people are coming down from the centre of the
land, and a company is coming from the direction of the soothsayers' tree."
38 Then Zebul said to him, "Where is your big talk now, you who said, 'Who is
Abimelech that we should be subject to him?' Aren't these the men you ridiculed?[z]
Go out and fight them!"
39 So Gaal led out[c] the citizens of Shechem and fought Abimelech. 40 Abimelech
chased him, and many fell wounded in the flight—all the way to the entrance to the
gate. 41 Abimelech stayed in Arumah, and Zebul drove Gaal and his brothers out of
Shechem.
42 The next day the people of Shechem went out to the fields, and this was reported
to Abimelech. 43 So he took his men, divided them into three companies[a] and set an
ambush in the fields. When he saw the people coming out of the city, he rose to attack
them. 44 Abimelech and the companies with him rushed forward to a position at the
entrance to the city gate. Then two companies rushed upon those in the fields and
struck them down. 45 All that day Abimelech pressed his attack against the city until
he had captured it and killed its people. Then he destroyed the city[b] and scattered
salt[c] over it.
46 On hearing this, the citizens in the tower of Shechem went into the stronghold
of the temple[d] of El-Berith. 47 When Abimelech heard that they had assembled there,
48 he and all his men went up Mount Zalmon.[e] He took an axe and cut off some
branches, which he lifted to his shoulders. He ordered the men with him, "Quick! Do
what you have seen me do!" 49 So all the men cut branches and followed Abimelech.
They piled them against the stronghold and set it on fire over the people inside. So
all the people in the tower of Shechem, about a thousand men and women, also died.
50 Next Abimelech went to Thebez[f] and besieged it and captured it. 51 Inside the
city, however, was a strong tower, to which all the men and women—all the people
of the city—fled. They locked themselves in and climbed up on the tower roof.

9:24 [q]Dt 27:25
9:27 [r]Am 9:13 [s]Jdg 8:33
9:28 [t]1Sa 25:10; 1Ki 12:16 [u]Ge 34:2, 6
9:29 [v]2Sa 15:4
9:32 [w]Jos 8:2
9:33 [x]1Sa 10:7
9:35 [y]Ps 32:7; Jer 49:10
9:38 [z]ver 28-29
9:43 [a]Jdg 7:16
9:45 [b]ver 20; 2Ki 3:25 [c]Dt 29:23
9:46 [d]Jdg 8:33
9:48 [e]Ps 68:14
9:50 [f]2Sa 11:21

b *29* Septuagint; Hebrew *him." Then he said to Abimelech, "Call out your whole army!"* **c** *39* Or *Gaal went out in the sight of*

9:45 To scatter salt over a conquered city was a ritual to symbolise the perpetual desolation of the city. It would not be rebuilt for 150 years.

9:53
[g]2Sa 11:21

52 Abimelech went to the tower and stormed it. But as he approached the entrance to
the tower to set it on fire, 53 a woman dropped an upper millstone on his head and
cracked his skull.[g]

9:54
[h]1Sa 31:4;
2Sa 1:9

54 Hurriedly he called to his armour-bearer, "Draw your sword and kill me,[h] so that
they can't say, 'A woman killed him.' " So his servant ran him through, and he died.
55 When the Israelites saw that Abimelech was dead, they went home.
56 Thus God repaid the wickedness that Abimelech had done to his father by
murdering his seventy brothers. 57 God also made the men of Shechem pay for all their
wickedness.[i] The curse of Jotham son of Jerub-Baal came on them.

9:57
[i]ver 20

Tola

10:1
[a]Ge 30:18
[b]Ge 46:13
[c]Jdg 2:16; 6:14

10 After the time of Abimelech a man of Issachar,[a] Tola son of Puah,[b] the son
of Dodo, rose to save[c] Israel. He lived in Shamir, in the hill country of
Ephraim. 2 He led[a] Israel for twenty-three years; then he died, and was buried in
Shamir.

Jair

10:4
[d]Nu 32:41

3 He was followed by Jair of Gilead, who led Israel for twenty-two years. 4 He had
thirty sons, who rode thirty donkeys. They controlled thirty towns in Gilead, which
to this day are called Havvoth Jair.[b][d] 5 When Jair died, he was buried in Kamon.

5. Fifth period: Jephthah, Ibzan, Elon, and Abdon

Jephthah

10:6
[e]Jdg 2:11
[f]Jdg 2:13
[g]Jdg 2:12
[h]Dt 32:15

10:7
[i]Dt 31:17
[j]Dt 32:30;
Jdg 2:14;
1Sa 12:9

10:10
[k]1Sa 12:10

6 Again the Israelites did evil in the eyes of the LORD.[e] They served the Baals and
the Ashtoreths,[f] and the gods of Aram, the gods of Sidon, the gods of Moab, the
gods of the Ammonites and the gods of the Philistines.[g] And because the Israelites
forsook the LORD[h] and no longer served him, 7 he became angry[i] with them. He sold
them[j] into the hands of the Philistines and the Ammonites, 8 who that year shattered
and crushed them. For eighteen years they oppressed all the Israelites on the east side
of the Jordan in Gilead, the land of the Amorites. 9 The Ammonites also crossed the
Jordan to fight against Judah, Benjamin and the house of Ephraim; and Israel was in
great distress. 10 Then the Israelites cried out to the LORD, "We have sinned against
you, forsaking our God and serving the Baals."[k]

[a] *2* Traditionally *judged*; also in verse 3 [b] *4* Or *called the settlements of Jair*

9:53 In times of battle, women were sometimes asked to join the men at the city wall to drop heavy objects on the soldiers below. A millstone would have been an ideal object for this purpose. It was a round stone about 18 inches in diameter with a hole in the centre. Millstones were used to grind grain into flour. The grain was placed between two millstones. The top millstone was turned, crushing the grain.

Abimelech's death was especially humiliating: he was killed by a woman, not by fighting; and he was killed by a farm implement instead of a weapon. Abimelech therefore asked his armour-bearer to stab him with his sword before he died from the blow of the millstone.

9:56, 57 Gideon, Abimelech's father, succeeded in military battles, but sometimes failed in his personal struggles. Gideon was not condemned for taking a concubine (8:31), but the family problems that resulted from this relationship are clearly stated.

In the end, Abimelech killed 69 of his 70 half brothers, tore apart a nation, and then was killed himself. From Gideon's life we learn that no matter how much good we do for God's kingdom, sin in our lives will still produce powerful, damaging consequences.

9:56, 57 Jotham's curse is found in 9:16–20.

10:1–5 In five verses we read about two men who judged Israel for a total of 45 years, yet all we know about them besides the length of their rules is that one had 30 sons who rode around on 30 donkeys. What are you doing for God that is worth noting? When your life is over, will people remember more than just what was in your bank account or the number of years you lived?

10:6 Baal and Ashtoreth are explained in the notes on 2:11–15 and 3:7. The gods of Aram and Sidon are very similar. The gods of Moab and Ammon were Chemosh and Molech. The Philistine gods were Dagon, Ashtoreth, Asherah, and Baal-Zebul.

10:9, 10 Once again the Israelites suffered for many years before they gave up their sinful ways and called out to God for help (see 4:1–3; 6:1–7). Notice that when the Israelites were at the end of their tether they did not look to their pagan gods for help, but to the only One who was really able to help.

Is God your last resort? So much unnecessary suffering takes place because we don't call on God until we've used up all other resources. Rather than waiting until the situation becomes desperate, turn to God first. He has the necessary resources to meet every kind of problem.

11 The LORD replied, "When the Egyptians,[l] the Amorites, the Ammonites,[m] the
Philistines,[n] 12 the Sidonians, the Amalekites and the Maonites[c] oppressed you[o] and
you cried to me for help, did I not save you from their hands? 13 But you have forsaken
me and served other gods, so I will no longer save you. 14 Go and cry out to the gods
you have chosen. Let them save you when you are in trouble![p]"
15 But the Israelites said to the LORD, "We have sinned. Do with us whatever you
think best,[q] but please rescue us now." 16 Then they got rid of the foreign gods among
them and served the LORD.[r] And he could bear Israel's misery[s] no longer.[t]
17 When the Ammonites were called to arms and camped in Gilead, the Israelites
assembled and camped at Mizpah.[u] 18 The leaders of the people of Gilead said to each
other, "Whoever will launch the attack against the Ammonites will be the head[v] of
all those living in Gilead."

11 Jephthah[a] the Gileadite was a mighty warrior.[b] His father was Gilead; his
mother was a prostitute. 2 Gilead's wife also bore him sons, and when they were
grown up, they drove Jephthah away. "You are not going to get any inheritance in
our family," they said, "because you are the son of another woman." 3 So Jephthah
fled from his brothers and settled in the land of Tob,[c] where a group of adventurers[d]
gathered around him and followed him.
4 Some time later, when the Ammonites[e] made war on Israel, 5 the elders of Gilead
went to get Jephthah from the land of Tob. 6 "Come," they said, "be our commander,
so we can fight the Ammonites."
7 Jephthah said to them, "Didn't you hate me and drive me from my father's
house?[f] Why do you come to me now, when you're in trouble?"
8 The elders of Gilead said to him, "Nevertheless, we are turning to you now; come
with us to fight the Ammonites, and you will be our head[g] over all who live in
Gilead."
9 Jephthah answered, "Suppose you take me back to fight the Ammonites and the
LORD gives them to me — will I really be your head?"
10 The elders of Gilead replied, "The LORD is our witness;[h] we will certainly do
as you say." 11 So Jephthah went with the elders of Gilead, and the people made him
head and commander over them. And he repeated all his words before the LORD in
Mizpah.[i]
12 Then Jephthah sent messengers to the Ammonite king with the question: "What
do you have against us that you have attacked our country?"
13 The king of the Ammonites answered Jephthah's messengers, "When Israel came
up out of Egypt, they took away my land from the Arnon to the Jabbok,[j] all the way
to the Jordan. Now give it back peaceably."

c *12* Hebrew; some Septuagint manuscripts *Midianites*

10:11 [l] Ex 14:30 [m] Nu 21:21; Jdg 3:13 [n] Jdg 3:31
10:12 [o] Ps 106:42
10:14 [p] Dt 32:37
10:15 [q] 1Sa 3:18; 2Sa 15:26
10:16 [r] Jos 24:23; Jer 18:8 [s] Isa 63:9 [t] Dt 32:36; Ps 106:44-45
10:17 [u] Ge 31:49; Jdg 11:29
10:18 [v] Jdg 11:8, 9
11:1 [a] Heb 11:32 [b] Jdg 6:12
11:3 [c] 2Sa 10:6, 8 [d] Jdg 9:4
11:4 [e] Jdg 10:9
11:7 [f] Ge 26:27
11:8 [g] Jdg 10:18
11:10 [h] Ge 31:50; Jer 42:5
11:11 [i] Jos 11:3; Jdg 10:17; 20:1; 1Sa 10:17
11:13 [j] Ge 32:22; Nu 21:24

10:11–16 These verses show how difficult it can be to follow God long-term. The Israelites always seemed to forget God when all was well. But despite being rejected by his own people, God never failed to rescue them when they called out to him in repentance. God never fails to rescue us either. We act just like the Israelites when we put God outside our daily events instead of at the centre of them. Just as a loving parent feels rejected when a child rebels, so God feels great rejection when we ignore or neglect him (1 Samuel 8:4–9; 10:17–19; John 12:44–50). We should strive to stay close to God rather than see how far we can go before judgment comes.

10:17, 18 The power of the Ammonite nation was at its peak during the period of the judges. The people were descendants of Ammon, conceived when Lot's daughter slept with her drunk father (Genesis 19:30–38). The land of Ammon was located just east of the Jordan River across from Jerusalem. South of Ammon lay the land of Moab, the nation conceived when Lot's other daughter slept with her father. Moab and Ammon were usually allies. It was a formidable task to defeat these nations.

11:1, 2 Jephthah, an illegitimate son of Gilead, was chased out of the country by his half brothers. He suffered as a result of another's decision and not for any wrong he had done. Yet in spite of his brothers' rejection, God used him. If you are suffering from unfair rejection, don't blame others and become discouraged. Remember how God used Jephthah despite his unjust circumstances, and realise that he is able to use you even if you feel rejected by some.

11:3 Circumstances beyond his control forced Jephthah away from his people and into life as an outcast. Today, both believers and non-believers may drive away those who do not fit the norms dictated by our society, neighbourhoods, or churches. Often, as in Jephthah's case, great potential is wasted because of prejudice — a refusal to look beyond ill-conceived stereotypes. Look around you to see if there are potential Jephthahs being kept out due to factors beyond their control. As a Christian you know that everyone can have a place in God's family. Can you do anything to help these people gain acceptance for their character and abilities?

11:11 What does it mean that Jephthah repeated all his words before the Lord? Those making covenants in ancient times often made them at shrines so that they would be witnessed by deities. Often a written copy was also deposited at the shrine. This was much like a coronation ceremony for Jephthah.

11:15
[k]Dt 2:9
[l]Dt 2:19

11:16
[m]Nu 14:25;
Dt 1:40
[n]Nu 20:1

11:17
[o]Nu 20:14
[p]Nu 20:18, 21
[q]Jos 24:9

11:18
[r]Nu 21:4
[s]Dt 2:8
[t]Nu 21:13

11:19
[u]Nu 21:21-22;
Dt 2:26-27

11:20
[v]Nu 21:23;
Dt 2:32

11:22
[w]Dt 2:36

11:24
[x]Nu 21:29;
Jos 3:10;
1Ki 11:7

11:25
[y]Nu 22:2

14 Jephthah sent back messengers to the Ammonite king, 15 saying:

"This is what Jephthah says: Israel did not take the land of Moab[k] or the land
of the Ammonites.[l] 16 But when they came up out of Egypt, Israel went through
the desert to the Red Sea[a][m] and on to Kadesh.[n] 17 Then Israel sent messengers[o]
to the king of Edom, saying, 'Give us permission to go through your country,'[p]
but the king of Edom would not listen. They sent also to the king of Moab, and
he refused.[q] So Israel stayed at Kadesh.
18 "Next they travelled through the desert, skirted the lands of Edom[r] and
Moab, passed along the eastern side[s] of the country of Moab, and camped on
the other side of the Arnon.[t] They did not enter the territory of Moab, for the
Arnon was its border.
19 "Then Israel sent messengers to Sihon king of the Amorites, who ruled in
Heshbon, and said to him, 'Let us pass through your country to our own place.'[u]
20 Sihon, however, did not trust Israel[b] to pass through his territory. He mustered
all his men and encamped at Jahaz and fought with Israel.[v]
21 "Then the LORD, the God of Israel, gave Sihon and all his men into Israel's
hands, and they defeated them. Israel took over all the land of the Amorites who
lived in that country, 22 capturing all of it from the Arnon to the Jabbok and from
the desert to the Jordan.[w]
23 "Now since the LORD, the God of Israel, has driven the Amorites out before
his people Israel, what right have you to take it over? 24 Will you not take what
your god Chemosh[x] gives you? Likewise, whatever the LORD our God has given
us, we will possess. 25 Are you better than Balak son of Zippor,[y] king of Moab?

a *16* Hebrew *Yam Suph*; that is, Sea of Reeds **b** *20* Or *however, would not make an agreement for Israel*

RASH VOWS

Ecclesiastes 5:2 says: "Do not be quick with your mouth, do not be hasty in your heart to utter anything before God." Scripture records the vows of many men and women. Some of these vows proved to be rash and unwise, and others, though extreme, were kept to the letter by those who made them. Let us learn from the examples in God's word not to make rash vows.

Person	*Vow*	*Result*	*Reference*
JACOB	To "choose" the true God and to give back a tenth to him if he kept him safe	God protected Jacob, who kept his vow to follow God	Genesis 28:20
JEPHTHAH	To offer to the Lord whomever came out to meet him after battle (it turned out to be his daughter)	He lost his daughter	Judges 11:30, 31
HANNAH	To give her son back to God, if God would give her a son	When Samuel was born, she dedicated him to God	1 Samuel 1:9–11
SAUL	To kill anyone who ate before evening (Jonathan, his son, had not heard the command and broke it)	Saul would have killed Jonathan if soldiers had not intervened	1 Samuel 14:24–45
DAVID	To be kind to Jonathan's family	Mephibosheth, Jonathan's son, was treated royally by David	2 Samuel 9:7
ITTAI	To remain loyal to David	He became one of the great men in David's army	2 Samuel 15:21
MICAIAH	To say only what God told him to say	He was put in prison	1 Kings 22:14
JOB	That he was not rebelling against God	His fortunes were restored	Job 27:2
HEROD ANTIPAS	To give Herodias' daughter anything she requested	Herod was forced to order John the Baptist's death	Mark 6:22, 23
PAUL	To offer a sacrifice of thanksgiving in Jerusalem	He made the sacrifice despite the danger	Acts 18:18

11:14ff Jephthah sent messengers to the Ammonite king wanting to know why the Israelites in the land of Gilead were being attacked (11:12). The king replied that Israel had stolen this land and he wanted it back (11:13).

Jephthah sent another message to the king (11:14–27). In it he gave three arguments against the king's claim: (1) Gilead was never the king's land in the first place because Israel took it from the Amorites, not the Ammonites (11:16–22); (2) Israel should possess land given by Israel's God, and Ammon should possess land given by Ammon's god; (3) no-one had contested Israel's ownership of the land since its conquest 300 years earlier (11:25, 26).

To Jephthah's credit, he tried to solve the problem without bloodshed. But the king of Ammon ignored his message and prepared his troops for battle.

Did he ever quarrel with Israel or fight with them?[z] 26For three hundred years
Israel occupied[a] Heshbon, Aroer, the surrounding settlements and all the towns
along the Arnon. Why didn't you retake them during that time? 27I have not
wronged you, but you are doing me wrong by waging war against me. Let the
LORD, the Judge,[c][b] decide[c] the dispute this day between the Israelites and the
Ammonites."
28The king of Ammon, however, paid no attention to the message Jephthah sent him.
29Then the Spirit[d] of the LORD came upon Jephthah. He crossed Gilead and
Manasseh, passed through Mizpah of Gilead, and from there he advanced against the
Ammonites. 30And Jephthah made a vow[e] to the LORD: "If you give the Ammonites
into my hands, 31whatever comes out of the door of my house to meet me when I return
in triumph from the Ammonites will be the LORD's, and I will sacrifice it as a burnt
offering."
32Then Jephthah went over to fight the Ammonites, and the LORD gave them into
his hands. 33He devastated twenty towns from Aroer to the vicinity of Minnith,[f] as
far as Abel Keramim. Thus Israel subdued Ammon.
34When Jephthah returned to his home in Mizpah, who should come out to meet
him but his daughter, dancing to the sound of tambourines![g] She was an only child.
Except for her he had neither son nor daughter. 35When he saw her, he tore his clothes
and cried, "Oh! My daughter! You have made me miserable and wretched, because
I have made a vow to the LORD that I cannot break.[h]"
36"My father," she replied, "you have given your word to the LORD. Do to me just
as you promised,[i] now that the LORD has avenged you of your enemies,[j] the
Ammonites. 37But grant me this one request," she said. "Give me two months to roam
the hills and weep with my friends, because I will never marry."
38"You may go," he said. And he let her go for two months. She and the girls went
into the hills and wept because she would never marry. 39After the two months, she
returned to her father and he did to her as he had vowed. And she was a virgin.
From this comes the Israelite custom 40that each year the young women of Israel
go out for four days to commemorate the daughter of Jephthah the Gileadite.

Jephthah and Ephraim

12 The men of Ephraim called out their forces, crossed over to Zaphon and said
to Jephthah, "Why did you go to fight the Ammonites without calling us to go
with you?[a] We're going to burn down your house over your head."

c 27 Or *Ruler*

11:25 [z]Jos 24:9
11:26 [a]Nu 21:25
11:27 [b]Ge 18:25 [c]Ge 16:5; 31:53; 1Sa 24:12, 15
11:29 [d]Nu 11:25; Jdg 3:10; 6:34; 14:6, 19; 15:14; 1Sa 11:6; 16:13; Isa 11:2
11:30 [e]Ge 28:20
11:33 [f]Eze 27:17
11:34 [g]Ex 15:20; Jer 31:4
11:35 [h]Nu 30:2; Ecc 5:2, 4, 5
11:36 [i]Lk 1:38 [j]2Sa 18:19
12:1 [a]Jdg 8:1

11:27 Over the years, Israel had many judges to lead them. But Jephthah recognised the Lord as the people's true Judge, the only One who could really lead them and help them conquer the invading enemies.

11:30, 31 In God's law, a vow was a promise to God that should not be broken (Numbers 30:1, 2; Deuteronomy 23:21–23). It carried as much force as a written contract. Many people made vows in biblical times. Some, like Jephthah's, were very foolish.

11:30, 31 When Jephthah made his vow, did he stop to consider that a person, not a sheep or goat, might come out to meet him? Scholars are divided over the issue. Those who say Jephthah was considering human sacrifice use the following arguments: (1) He was from an area where pagan religion and human sacrifice were common. In his eyes, it may not have seemed like a sin. (2) Jephthah may not have had a background in religious law. Perhaps he was ignorant of God's command against human sacrifice.

Those who say Jephthah could not have been thinking about human sacrifice point to other evidence: (1) As leader of the people, Jephthah must have been familiar with God's laws; human sacrifice was clearly forbidden (Leviticus 18:21; 20:1–5). (2) No legitimate priest would have helped Jephthah carry out his vow if a person was to be the sacrifice.

Whatever Jephthah had in mind when he made the vow, did he or did he not sacrifice his daughter? Some think he did, because his vow was to make a burnt offering. Some think he did not, and they offer several reasons: (1) If the girl was to die, she would not have spent her last two months in the hills. (2) God would not have honoured a vow based on a wicked practice. (3) Verse 39 says that she never married, not that she died, implying that she was set apart for service to God, not killed.

11:34, 35 Jephthah's rash vow brought him unspeakable grief. In the heat of emotion or personal turmoil it is easy to make foolish promises to God. These promises may sound very spiritual when we make them, but they may produce only guilt and frustration when we are forced to fulfil them. Making spiritual "deals" only brings disappointment. God does not want promises for the future, but obedience for today.

JEPHTHAH

It's hard not to admire people whose word can be depended on completely and whose actions are consistent with their words. For such people, talking is not avoiding action; it is the beginning of action. People like this can make excellent negotiators. They approach a conflict with the full intention of settling issues verbally, but they do not hesitate to use other means if verbal attempts fail. Jephthah was this kind of person.

In most of his conflicts, Jephthah's first move was to talk. In the war with the Ammonites, his strategy was negotiation. He clarified the issues so that everyone knew the cause of the conflict. His opponent's response determined his next action.

The fate of Jephthah's daughter is difficult to understand. We are not sure what Jephthah meant by his vow recorded in Judges 11:31. In any case, his vow was unnecessary. We do not know what actually happened to his daughter—whether she was burned as an offering or set apart as a virgin, thus denying Jephthah any hope of descendants since she was his only child. What we do know is that Jephthah was a person of his word, even when it was a word spoken in haste, and even when keeping his word cost him great pain.

How do you approach conflicts? There is a big difference between trying to settle a conflict through words and simply counterattacking someone verbally. How dependable are the statements you make? Do your children, friends, and fellow workers know you to be a person of your word? The measure of your trustworthiness is your willingness to take responsibility, even if you must pay a painful price because of something you said.

Strengths and accomplishments:
- Listed in the Hall of Faith in Hebrews 11
- Controlled by God's Spirit
- Brilliant military strategist who negotiated before fighting

Weaknesses and mistakes:
- Was bitter over the treatment he received from his half brothers
- Made a rash and foolish vow that was costly

Lesson from his life:
- A person's background does not prevent God from working powerfully in his or her life

Vital statistics:
- Where: Gilead
- Occupations: Warrior, judge
- Relative: Father: Gilead

Key verse:
"Then Jephthah went over to fight the Ammonites, and the LORD gave them into his hands" (Judges 11:32).

His story is told in Judges 11:1—12:7. He is also mentioned in 1 Samuel 12:11 and Hebrews 11:32.

JEPHTHAH'S VICTORY
The Ephraimites mobilised an army because they were angry about not being included in the battle against Ammon. They planned to attack Jephthah at his home in Gilead. Jephthah captured the fords of the Jordan at the Jabbok River and killed the Ephraimites who tried to cross.

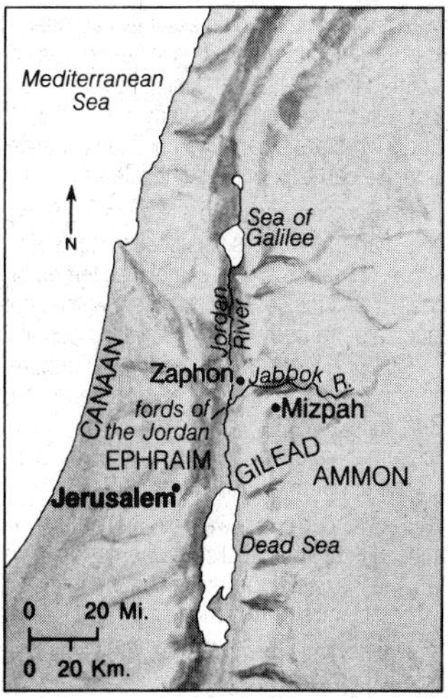

12:1ff Israel had just won a great battle, but instead of joy, there was pettiness and quarrelling. The tribe of Ephraim was angry and jealous that they were not invited to join in the fighting (although Jephthah said he had invited them). The insults of the Ephraimites enraged Jephthah, who called out his troops and killed 42,000 men from Ephraim.

Jephthah usually spoke before he acted, but this time his revenge was swift. It cost Israel dearly, and it might have been avoided. Insulting others and being jealous are not right responses when we feel left out. But seeking revenge for an insult is just as wrong, and very costly.

2Jephthah answered, "I and my people were engaged in a great struggle with the
Ammonites, and although I called, you didn't save me out of their hands. 3When I
saw that you wouldn't help, I took my life in my hands[b] and crossed over to fight
the Ammonites, and the LORD gave me the victory over them. Now why have you
come up today to fight me?"
4Jephthah then called together the men of Gilead and fought against Ephraim. The
Gileadites struck them down because the Ephraimites had said, "You Gileadites are
renegades from Ephraim and Manasseh." 5The Gileadites captured the fords of the
Jordan[c] leading to Ephraim, and whenever a survivor of Ephraim said, "Let me cross
over," the men of Gilead asked him, "Are you an Ephraimite?" If he replied, "No,"
6they said, "All right, say 'Shibboleth'." If he said, "Sibboleth", because he could
not pronounce the word correctly, they seized him and killed him at the fords of the
Jordan. Forty-two thousand Ephraimites were killed at that time.
7Jephthah led[a] Israel for six years. Then Jephthah the Gileadite died, and was
buried in a town in Gilead.

Ibzan, Elon and Abdon

8After him, Ibzan of Bethlehem led Israel. 9He had thirty sons and thirty daughters.
He gave his daughters away in marriage to those outside his clan, and for his sons
he brought in thirty young women as wives from outside his clan. Ibzan led Israel for
seven years. 10Then Ibzan died, and was buried in Bethlehem.
11After him, Elon the Zebulunite led Israel for ten years. 12Then Elon died, and
was buried in Aijalon in the land of Zebulun.
13After him, Abdon son of Hillel, from Pirathon, led Israel. 14He had forty sons
and thirty grandsons,[d] who rode on seventy donkeys.[e] He led Israel for eight years.
15Then Abdon son of Hillel died, and was buried at Pirathon in Ephraim, in the hill
country of the Amalekites.[f]

6. Sixth period: Samson

The Birth of Samson

13 Again the Israelites did evil in the eyes of the LORD, so the LORD delivered them
into the hands of the Philistines[a] for forty years.
2A certain man of Zorah,[b] named Manoah, from the clan of the Danites, had a
wife who was sterile and remained childless. 3The angel of the LORD[c] appeared to
her[d] and said, "You are sterile and childless, but you are going to conceive and have
a son.[e] 4Now see to it that you drink no wine or other fermented drink and that you
do not eat anything unclean,[f] 5because you will conceive and give birth to a son.

12:3 [b] 1Sa 19:5; 28:21; Job 13:14
12:5 [c] Jos 22:11; Jdg 3:28
12:14 [d] Jdg 10:4 [e] Jdg 5:10
12:15 [f] Jdg 5:14
13:1 [a] Jdg 2:11; 1Sa 12:9
13:2 [b] Jos 15:33; 19:41
13:3 [c] ver 6, 8; Jdg 6:12 [d] ver 10 [e] Lk 1:13
13:4 [f] ver 14; Nu 6:2-4; Lk 1:15

[a] 7 Traditionally *judged*; also in verses 8–14

12:4-7 The men of the tribe of Ephraim caused Jephthah trouble just as they had Gideon (8:1–3). Jephthah captured the fords of the Jordan, the boundary of Ephraim, and was able to defeat his countrymen as they crossed the river. He used a pronunciation test. *Shibboleth* is the word for stream. The Ephraimites pronounced "sh" as "s", so Jephthah's army could easily identify them.

12:8-15 There is little else known about these three judges or their importance. The large number of children and cattle are an indication of the wealth of these men.

13:1 The Philistines lived on the west side of Canaan, along the Mediterranean coast. From Samson's day until the time of David they were the major enemy force in the land and a constant threat to Israel. The Philistines were fierce warriors; they had the advantage over Israel in numbers, tactical expertise, and technology. They knew the secret of making weapons out of iron (1 Samuel 13:19–22). But none of that mattered when God was fighting for Israel.

13:1ff Once again the cycle of sin, judgment, and repentance began (3:8, 9, 14, 15; 4:1–4; 6:1–14; 10:6 – 11:11). The Israelites would not turn to God unless they had been stunned by suffering, oppression, and death. This suffering was not caused by God, but resulted from the fact that the people ignored God, their Judge and Ruler. What will it take for you to follow God? The warnings in God's word are clear: if we continue to harden our hearts against God, we can expect the same fate as Israel.

13:5 Samson was to be a Nazirite – a person who took a vow to be set apart for God's service. Samson's parents made the vow for him. A Nazirite vow was sometimes temporary, but in Samson's case, it was for life. As a Nazirite, Samson could not cut his hair, touch a dead body, or drink anything containing alcohol.

Although Samson often used poor judgment and sinned terribly, he accomplished much when he determined to be set apart for God. In this way he was like the nation Israel. As long as the Israelites remained set apart for God, the nation thrived. But they fell into terrible sin when they ignored God.

13:5 Manoah's wife was told that her son would *begin* the deliverance of Israel from Philistine oppression. It wasn't until David's day that the Philistine opposition was completely crushed (2 Samuel 8:1). Samson's part in subduing the Philistines was just the beginning, but it was important nonetheless. It was the task God had given Samson to do. Be faithful in following God even if you

13:5 [g]Nu 6:5; 1Sa 1:11 [h]Nu 6:2, 13 [i]1Sa 7:13

13:6 [j]ver 8; 1Sa 2:27; 9:6 [k]ver 17-18; Mt 28:3

No razor[g] may be used on his head, because the boy is to be a Nazirite,[h] set apart
to God from birth, and he will begin[i] the deliverance of Israel from the hands of the
Philistines."
6Then the woman went to her husband and told him, "A man of God[j] came to
me. He looked like an angel of God,[k] very awesome. I didn't ask him where he came
from, and he didn't tell me his name. 7But he said to me, 'You will conceive and give
birth to a son. Now then, drink no wine or other fermented drink and do not eat
anything unclean, because the boy will be a Nazirite of God from birth until the day
of his death.' "
8Then Manoah prayed to the LORD: "O Lord, I beg you, let the man of God you
sent to us come again to teach us how to bring up the boy who is to be born."
9God heard Manoah, and the angel of God came again to the woman while she was

SAMSON

It is sad to be remembered for what one might have been. Samson had tremendous potential. Not many people have started life with credentials like his. Born as a result of God's plan in the lives of Manoah and his wife, Samson was to do a great work for God—to "begin the deliverance of Israel from the hands of the Philistines". To help him accomplish God's plan, he was given enormous physical strength.

Because Samson wasted his strength on practical jokes and getting out of scrapes, and because he eventually gave it up altogether to satisfy the woman he loved, we tend to see him as a failure. We remember him as the judge in Israel who spent his last days grinding grain in an enemy prison, and we say, "What wasted potential!"

Yes, Samson wasted his life. He could have strengthened his nation. He could have returned his people to the worship of God. He could have wiped out the Philistines. But even though he did none of those things, Samson still accomplished the purpose announced by the angel who visited his parents before his birth. In his final act, Samson began to rescue Israel from the Philistines.

Interestingly, the New Testament does not mention Samson's failures or his heroic feats of strength. In Hebrews, he is simply listed with others "who through faith conquered kingdoms, administered justice, and gained what was promised", and in other ways were given superhuman aid. In the end, Samson recognised his dependence on God. When he died, God turned his failures and defeats into victory. Samson's story teaches us that it is never too late to start again. However badly we may have failed in the past, today is not too late for us to put our complete trust in God.

Strengths and accomplishments:
- Dedicated to God from birth as a Nazirite
- Known for his feats of strength
- Listed in the Hall of Faith in Hebrews 11
- Began to free Israel from Philistine oppression

Weaknesses and mistakes:
- Violated his vow and God's laws on many occasions
- Was controlled by sensuality
- Confided in the wrong people
- Used his gifts and abilities unwisely

Lessons from his life:
- Great strength in one area of life does not make up for great weaknesses in other areas
- God's presence does not overwhelm a person's will
- God can use a person of faith in spite of his or her mistakes

Vital statistics:
- Where: Zorah, Timnah, Ashkelon, Gaza, Valley of Sorek
- Occupation: Judge
- Relative: Father: Manoah
- Contemporaries: Delilah, Samuel (who might have been born while Samson was a judge)

Key verse:
"You will conceive and give birth to a son. No razor may be used on his head, because the boy is to be a Nazirite, set apart to God from birth, and he will begin the deliverance of Israel from the hands of the Philistines" (Judges 13:5).

His story is told in Judges 13—16. He is also mentioned in Hebrews 11:32.

don't see instant results, because you might be beginning an important job that others will finish.

out in the field; but her husband Manoah was not with her. 10 The woman hurried to
tell her husband, "He's here! The man who appeared to me the other day!"
11 Manoah got up and followed his wife. When he came to the man, he said, "Are
you the one who talked to my wife?"
"I am," he said.
12 So Manoah asked him, "When your words are fulfilled, what is to be the rule for
the boy's life and work?"
13 The angel of the LORD answered, "Your wife must do all that I have told her.
14 She must not eat anything that comes from the grapevine, nor drink any wine or
other fermented drink[l] nor eat anything unclean.[m] She must do everything I have
commanded her."
15 Manoah said to the angel of the LORD, "We would like you to stay until we prepare
a young goat[n] for you."
16 The angel of the LORD replied, "Even though you detain me, I will not eat any
of your food. But if you prepare a burnt offering,[o] offer it to the LORD." (Manoah
did not realise that it was the angel of the LORD.)
17 Then Manoah enquired of the angel of the LORD, "What is your name,[p] so that
we may honour you when your word comes true?"
18 He replied, "Why do you ask my name?[q] It is beyond understanding."[a] 19 Then
Manoah took a young goat, together with the grain offering, and sacrificed it on a
rock[r] to the LORD. And the LORD did an amazing thing while Manoah and his wife
watched: 20 As the flame[s] blazed up from the altar towards heaven, the angel of the
LORD ascended in the flame. Seeing this, Manoah and his wife fell with their faces
to the ground.[t] 21 When the angel of the LORD did not show himself again to Manoah
and his wife, Manoah realised[u] that it was the angel of the LORD.
22 "We are doomed[v] to die!" he said to his wife. "We have seen[w] God!"
23 But his wife answered, "If the LORD had meant to kill us, he would not have
accepted a burnt offering and grain offering from our hands, nor shown us all these
things or now told us this."[x]
24 The woman gave birth to a boy and named him Samson.[y] He grew[z] and the
LORD blessed him,[a] 25 and the Spirit of the LORD began to stir[b] him while he was
in Mahaneh Dan,[c] between Zorah and Eshtaol.

Samson's Marriage

14 Samson went down to Timnah[a] and saw there a young Philistine woman.
2 When he returned, he said to his father and mother, "I have seen a Philistine
woman in Timnah; now get her for me as my wife."[b]
3 His father and mother replied, "Isn't there an acceptable woman among your
relatives or among all our people?[c] Must you go to the uncircumcised[d] Philistines
to get a wife?[e]"
But Samson said to his father, "Get her for me. She's the right one for me." 4 (His

a *18 Or is wonderful*

13:14 [l]Nu 6:4 [m]ver 4
13:15 [n]ver 3; Jdg 6:19
13:16 [o]Jdg 6:20
13:17 [p]Ge 32:29
13:18 [q]Isa 9:6
13:19 [r]Jdg 6:20
13:20 [s]Lev 9:24 [t]1Ch 21:16; Eze 1:28; Mt 17:6
13:21 [u]ver 16; Jdg 6:22
13:22 [v]Dt 5:26 [w]Ge 32:30; Jdg 6:22
13:23 [x]Ps 25:14
13:24 [y]Heb 11:32 [z]1Sa 3:19 [a]Lk 1:80
13:25 [b]Jdg 3:10 [c]Jdg 18:12
14:1 [a]Ge 38:12
14:2 [b]Ge 21:21; 34:4
14:3 [c]Ge 24:4 [d]Dt 7:3 [e]Ex 34:16

13:18 Why did the angel keep his name a secret? In those days people believed that if they knew someone's name, they knew his character and how to control him. By not giving his name, the angel was not allowing himself to be controlled by Manoah. He was also saying that his name was a mystery beyond understanding and too wonderful to imagine. Manoah asked the angel for an answer that he wouldn't have understood. Sometimes we ask God questions and then receive no answer. This may not be because God is saying no. We may have asked for knowledge beyond our ability to understand or accept.

13:19 Manoah sacrificed a grain offering to the Lord. A grain offering was grain, oil, and flour shaped into a cake and burned on the altar along with the *burnt offering* (the young goat). The grain offering, described in Leviticus 2, was offered to God as a sign of honour, respect, and worship. It was an acknowledgment that because the Israelites' food came from God, they owed their lives to him. With the grain offering, Manoah showed his desire to serve God and demonstrated his respect.

13:25 Samson's tribe, Dan, continued to wander in their inherited land (18:1), which was as yet unconquered (Joshua 19:47, 48). Samson must have grown up with his warlike tribe's yearnings for a permanent and settled territory. Thus his visits to the tribal army camp stirred his heart, and God's Spirit began preparing him for his role as judge and leader against the Philistines.

Perhaps there are things that stir your heart. These may indicate areas where God wants to use you. God uses a variety of means to develop and prepare us: hereditary traits, environmental influences, and personal experiences. As with Samson, this preparation often begins long before adulthood. Work at being sensitive to the Holy Spirit's leading and the tasks God has prepared for you. Your past may be more useful to you than you imagine.

14:4
[f]Jos 11:20
[g]Jdg 13:1

parents did not know that this was from the LORD, who was seeking an occasion to
confront the Philistines;[f] for at that time they were ruling over Israel.)[g] 5Samson
went down to Timnah together with his father and mother. As they approached the
vineyards of Timnah, suddenly a young lion came roaring towards him. 6The Spirit
of the LORD came upon him in power[h] so that he tore the lion apart with his bare
hands as he might have torn a young goat. But he told neither his father nor his mother
what he had done. 7Then he went down and talked with the woman, and he liked her.

14:6
[h]Jdg 3:10; 13:25

8Some time later, when he went back to marry her, he turned aside to look at the
lion's carcass. In it was a swarm of bees and some honey, 9which he scooped out with
his hands and ate as he went along. When he rejoined his parents, he gave them some,
and they too ate it. But he did not tell them that he had taken the honey from the lion's
carcass.

10Now his father went down to see the woman. And Samson made a feast there,
as was customary for bridegrooms. 11When he appeared, he was given thirty companions.

14:12
[i]1Ki 10:1;
Eze 17:2
[j]Ge 29:27
[k]Ge 45:22;
2Ki 5:5

12"Let me tell you a riddle,[i]" Samson said to them. "If you can give me the answer
within the seven days of the feast,[j] I will give you thirty linen garments and thirty
sets of clothes.[k] 13If you can't tell me the answer, you must give me thirty linen
garments and thirty sets of clothes."

"Tell us your riddle," they said. "Let's hear it."

14He replied,

14:15
[l]Jdg 16:5;
Ecc 7:26
[m]Jdg 15:6

> "Out of the eater, something to eat;
> out of the strong, something sweet."

For three days they could not give the answer.

15On the fourth[a] day, they said to Samson's wife, "Coax[l] your husband into
explaining the riddle for us, or we will burn you and your father's household to
death.[m] Did you invite us here to rob us?"

16Then Samson's wife threw herself on him, sobbing, "You hate me! You don't
really love me.[n] You've given my people a riddle, but you haven't told me the
answer."

14:16
[n]Jdg 16:15

"I haven't even explained it to my father or mother," he replied, "so why should
I explain it to you?" 17She cried the whole seven days[o] of the feast. So on the seventh
day he finally told her, because she continued to press him. She in turn explained the
riddle to her people.

18Before sunset on the seventh day the men of the town said to him,

14:17
[o]Est 1:5

[a] 15 Some Septuagint manuscripts and Syriac; Hebrew *seventh*

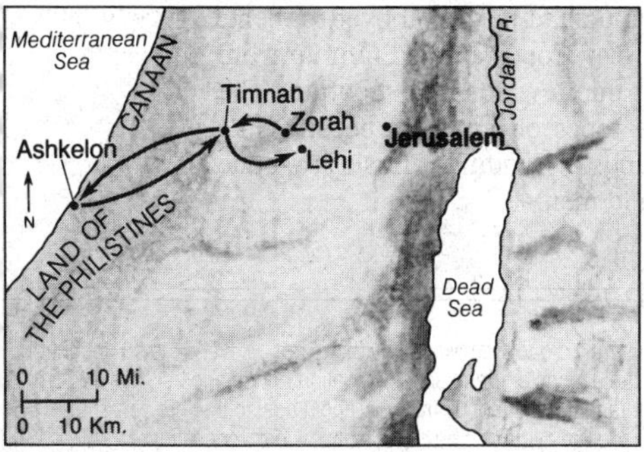

SAMSON'S VENTURES Samson grew up in Zorah and wanted to marry a Philistine girl from Timnah. Tricked at his own wedding feast, he went to Ashkelon and killed some Philistine men and stole their clothes to pay off a bet. Samson then allowed himself to be captured and brought to Lehi where he broke his bonds and killed 1,000 people.

14:3 Samson's parents objected to his marrying the Philistine woman for several reasons: (1) It was against God's law (Exodus 34:15–17; Deuteronomy 7:1–4). A stark example of what happened when the Israelites married pagans can be found in 3:5–7. (2) The Philistines were Israel's greatest enemies. Marriage to a hated Philistine would be a disgrace to Samson's family. But Samson's father gave in to Samson's demand and allowed the marriage, even though he had the right to refuse his son.

14:6 "The Spirit of the LORD came upon him in power" refers to the unusual physical strength given him by the Spirit of the Lord. Samson did not seem to be affected in any other ways than increased physical strength.

14:18 "If you had not ploughed with my heifer" means "If you had not manipulated my wife". If they hadn't threatened his wife, they wouldn't have learned the answer to his riddle.

> "What is sweeter than honey?
> What is stronger than a lion?"[p]

Samson said to them,

> "If you had not ploughed with my heifer,
> you would not have solved my riddle."

19Then the Spirit of the LORD came upon him in power.[q] He went down to Ashkelon, struck down thirty of their men, stripped them of their belongings and gave their clothes to those who had explained the riddle. Burning with anger,[r] he went up to his father's house. 20And Samson's wife was given to the friend[s] who had attended him at his wedding.

Samson's Vengeance on the Philistines

15 Later on, at the time of wheat harvest, Samson took a young goat[a] and went to visit his wife. He said, "I'm going to my wife's room." But her father would not let him go in.

2"I was so sure you thoroughly hated her," he said, "that I gave her to your friend.[b] Isn't her younger sister more attractive? Take her instead."

3Samson said to them, "This time I have a right to get even with the Philistines; I will really harm them." 4So he went out and caught three hundred foxes and tied them tail to tail in pairs. He then fastened a torch to every pair of tails, 5lit the torches and let the foxes loose in the standing corn of the Philistines. He burned up the shocks and standing corn, together with the vineyards and olive groves.

6When the Philistines asked, "Who did this?" they were told, "Samson, the Timnite's son-in-law, because his wife was given to his friend."

So the Philistines went up and burned her and her father to death.[c] 7Samson said to them, "Since you've acted like this, I won't stop until I get my revenge on you." 8He attacked them viciously and slaughtered many of them. Then he went down and stayed in a cave in the rock of Etam.

9The Philistines went up and camped in Judah, spreading out near Lehi.[d] 10The men of Judah asked, "Why have you come to fight us?"

"We have come to take Samson prisoner," they answered, "to do to him as he did to us."

11Then three thousand men from Judah went down to the cave in the rock of Etam and said to Samson, "Don't you realise that the Philistines are rulers over us?[e] What have you done to us?"

He answered, "I merely did to them what they did to me."

12They said to him, "We've come to tie you up and hand you over to the Philistines."

Samson said, "Swear to me that you won't kill me yourselves."

13"Agreed," they answered. "We will only tie you up and hand you over to them. We will not kill you." So they bound him with two new ropes and led him up from the rock. 14As he approached Lehi, the Philistines came towards him shouting. The Spirit of the LORD came upon him in power.[f] The ropes on his arms became like charred flax, and the bindings dropped from his hands. 15Finding a fresh jaw-bone of a donkey, he grabbed it and struck down a thousand men.[g]

16Then Samson said,

14:18 [p]ver 14
14:19 [q]Nu 11:25; Jdg 3:10; 6:34; 11:29; 13:25; 15:14; 1Sa 11:6; 16:13; 1Ki 18:46; 2Ch 24:20; Isa 11:2 [r]1Sa 11:6
14:20 [s]Jdg 15:2, 6; Jn 3:29
15:1 [a]Ge 38:17
15:2 [b]Jdg 14:20
15:6 [c]Jdg 14:15
15:9 [d]ver 14, 17, 19
15:11 [e]Jdg 13:1; 14:4; Ps 106:40-42
15:14 [f]Jdg 3:10; 14:19; 1Sa 11:6
15:15 [g]Lev 26:8; Jos 23:10; Jdg 3:31

14:19 Samson impulsively used the special gift God gave him for selfish purposes. Today, God distributes abilities and skills throughout the church (1 Corinthians 12:1ff). The apostle Paul states that these gifts are to be used "that the body of Christ may be built up"; that is, to build up the church (Ephesians 4:12). To use these abilities for selfish purposes is to rob the church and fellow believers of strength. As you use the gifts God has given you, be sure you are helping others, not just yourself.

15:1ff Samson's reply in 15:11 tells the story of this chapter: "I merely did to them what they did to me." Revenge is an uncontrollable monster. Each act of retaliation brings another. It is a boomerang that cannot be thrown without cost to the thrower. The revenge cycle can be halted only by forgiveness.

15:14–17 The Lord's strength came upon Samson, but he was proud and boasted only of his own strength. "With a donkey's jawbone I have killed a thousand men," he said, and later asked God to refresh him because of *his* accomplishments (15:16–18). Pride can cause us to take credit for work we've done only because of God's strength.

15:18
[h] Jdg 16:28

15:19
[i] Ge 45:27; Isa 40:29

15:20
[j] Jdg 13:1; 16:31; Heb 11:32

16:2
[a] 1Sa 23:26; Ps 118:10-12; Ac 9:24

16:3
[b] Jos 10:36

16:4
[c] Ge 24:67

16:5
[d] Jos 13:3
[e] Ex 10:7; Jdg 14:15
[f] ver 18

16:9
[g] ver 12

"With a donkey's jaw-bone
  I have made donkeys of them.[a]
With a donkey's jaw-bone
  I have killed a thousand men."

17 When he finished speaking, he threw away the jaw-bone; and the place was called Ramath Lehi.[b]

18 Because he was very thirsty, he cried out to the LORD,[h] "You have given your servant this great victory. Must I now die of thirst and fall into the hands of the uncircumcised?" 19 Then God opened up the hollow place in Lehi, and water came out of it. When Samson drank, his strength returned and he revived.[i] So the spring was called En Hakkore,[c] and it is still there in Lehi.

20 Samson led[d] Israel for twenty years[j] in the days of the Philistines.

Samson and Delilah

16 One day Samson went to Gaza, where he saw a prostitute. He went in to spend the night with her. 2 The people of Gaza were told, "Samson is here!" So they surrounded the place and lay in wait for him all night at the city gate.[a] They made no move during the night, saying, "At dawn we'll kill him."

3 But Samson lay there only until the middle of the night. Then he got up and took hold of the doors of the city gate, together with the two posts, and tore them loose, bar and all. He lifted them to his shoulders and carried them to the top of the hill that faces Hebron.[b]

4 Some time later, he fell in love[c] with a woman in the Valley of Sorek whose name was Delilah. 5 The rulers of the Philistines[d] went to her and said, "See if you can lure[e] him into showing you the secret of his great strength and how we can overpower him so that we may tie him up and subdue him. Each one of us will give you eleven hundred shekels[a] of silver."[f]

6 So Delilah said to Samson, "Tell me the secret of your great strength and how you can be tied up and subdued."

7 Samson answered her, "If anyone ties me with seven fresh thongs[b] that have not been dried, I'll become as weak as any other man."

8 Then the rulers of the Philistines brought her seven fresh thongs that had not been dried, and she tied him with them. 9 With men hidden in the room,[g] she called to him, "Samson, the Philistines are upon you!" But he snapped the thongs as easily as a piece

a 16 Or *made a heap or two*; the Hebrew for *donkey* sounds like the Hebrew for *heap.* b 17 *Ramath Lehi* means *jaw-bone hill.* c 19 *En Hakkore* means *caller's spring.* d 20 Traditionally *judged* a 5 That is, about 28 pounds (about 13 kilograms) b 7 Or *bow-strings*; also in verses 8 and 9

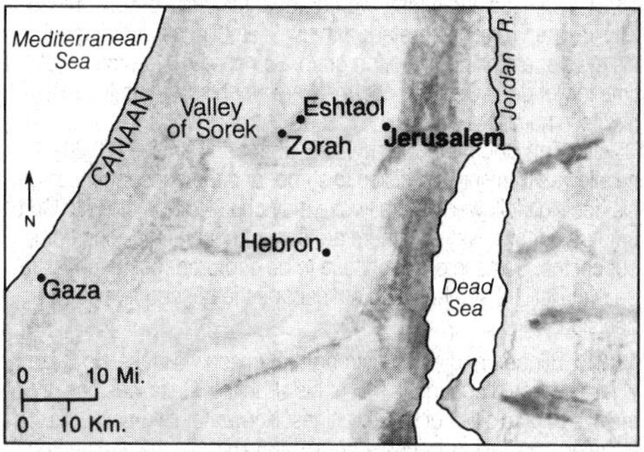

SAMSON AND DELILAH Samson was seduced by a Philistine woman named Delilah who lived in the Valley of Sorek. She betrayed the secret of his strength to the Philistines who captured him and led him away in chains to Gaza. There he died. His relatives buried him between Zorah and Eshtaol.

15:18 Samson was physically and emotionally exhausted. After a great personal victory, his attitude declined quickly into self-pity—"Must I now die of thirst?" Emotionally, we are most vulnerable after a great effort or when faced with real physical needs. Severe depression often follows great achievements, so don't be surprised if you feel drained after a personal victory.

During these times of vulnerability, avoid the temptation to think that God owes you for your efforts. It was *his* strength that gave you victory. Concentrate on keeping your attitudes, actions, and words focused on God instead of yourself.

15:20 Apparently Samson was appointed Israel's judge after this victory over the Philistines.

16:5 The Philistines were ruled by five rulers, not just one. Each ruler ruled from a different city—Ashdod, Ashkelon, Ekron, Gath, or Gaza. Each of these cities was an important centre for trade and commerce. Given Delilah's character, it is little wonder that she betrayed Samson when these rich and powerful men paid her a personal visit.

of string snaps when it comes close to a flame. So the secret of his strength was not
discovered.
10 Then Delilah said to Samson, "You have made a fool of me;[h] you lied to me.
Come now, tell me how you can be tied."
11 He said, "If anyone ties me securely with new ropes[i] that have never been used,
I'll become as weak as any other man."
12 So Delilah took new ropes and tied him with them. Then, with men hidden in
the room, she called to him, "Samson, the Philistines are upon you!" But he snapped
the ropes off his arms as if they were threads.
13 Delilah then said to Samson, "Until now, you have been making a fool of me and
lying to me. Tell me how you can be tied."
He replied, "If you weave the seven braids of my head into the fabric ⌞on the loom⌟
and tighten it with the pin, I'll become as weak as any other man." So while he was
sleeping, Delilah took the seven braids of his head, wove them into the fabric 14 and[c]
tightened it with the pin.
Again she called to him, "Samson, the Philistines are upon you!"[j] He awoke from
his sleep and pulled up the pin and the loom, with the fabric.
15 Then she said to him, "How can you say, 'I love you,'[k] when you won't confide
in me? This is the third time[l] you have made a fool of me and haven't told me the
secret of your great strength.[m]" 16 With such nagging she prodded him day after day
until he was tired to death.
17 So he told her everything.[n] "No razor has ever been used on my head," he said,
"because I have been a Nazirite[o] set apart to God since birth. If my head were shaved,
my strength would leave me, and I would become as weak as any other man."
18 When Delilah saw that he had told her everything, she sent word to the rulers of
the Philistines[p], "Come back once more; he has told me everything." So the rulers
of the Philistines returned with the silver in their hands. 19 Having put him to sleep
on her lap, she called a man to shave off the seven braids of his hair, and so began
to subdue him.[d] And his strength left him.[q]
20 Then she called, "Samson, the Philistines are upon you!"
He awoke from his sleep and thought, "I'll go out as before and shake myself free."
But he did not know that the LORD had left him.[r]
21 Then the Philistines[s] seized him, gouged out his eyes[t] and took him down to

16:10 [h] ver 13
16:11 [i] Jdg 15:13
16:14 [j] ver 9, 20
16:15 [k] Jdg 14:16 [l] Nu 24:10 [m] ver 5
16:17 [n] Mic 7:5 [o] Nu 6:2, 5; Jdg 13:5
16:18 [p] Jos 13:3; 1Sa 5:8
16:19 [q] Pr 7:26-27
16:20 [r] Nu 14:42; Jos 7:12; 1Sa 16:14; 18:12; 28:15
16:21 [s] Jer 47:1 [t] Nu 16:14

c *13,14* Some Septuagint manuscripts; Hebrew "⌞*I can*⌟ *if you weave the seven braids of my head into the fabric* ⌞*on the loom*⌟." 14*So she* d *19* Hebrew; some Septuagint manuscripts *and he began to weaken*

16:15 Samson was deceived because he wanted to believe Delilah's lies. Although he could strangle a lion, he could not smother his burning lust and see Delilah for who she really was. How can you keep your desire for love and sexual pleasure from deceiving you? (1) You must decide what kind of a person you will love *before* passion takes over. Determine whether a person's character and faith in God are as desirable as his or her physical appearance. (2) Because most of the time you spend with your spouse will *not* involve sex, your companion's personality, temperament, and commitment to solve problems must be as gratifying as his or her kisses. (3) Be patient. The second look often reveals what is beneath the pleasant appearance and attentive touch.

16:16, 17 Delilah kept asking Samson for the secret of his strength until he finally grew tired of hearing her nagging and gave in. This was the second time that Samson allowed himself to be worn down by persistent nagging (14:17). What a pitiful excuse for disobedience. Don't allow anyone, no matter how attractive or persuasive, to talk you into doing wrong.

16:19 Delilah was a deceitful woman with honey on her lips and poison in her heart. Cold and calculating, she toyed with Samson, pretending to love him while looking for personal gain. How could Samson be so foolish? Four times Delilah took advantage of him. If he didn't realise what was happening after the first or second experience, surely he should have understood the situation by the fourth time! We think Samson is foolish, but how many times do we allow ourselves to be deceived by flattery and give in to temptation and wrong beliefs? Avoid falling prey to deceit by asking God to help you distinguish between deception and truth.

16:21 Samson, the mighty warrior, became a slave. Rather than kill him, the Philistines preferred to humiliate him by gouging out his eyes and making him grind grain. Samson now had plenty of time to wonder if Delilah's charms were worth spending the rest of his life in humiliation.

Although God did not completely abandon Samson (16:28–30), he allowed Samson's decision to stand, and the consequences of his decision followed naturally. We may choose to be close to God or to go our own way, but there are consequences resulting from our choice. Samson didn't choose to be captured, but he chose to be with Delilah, and he could not escape the consequences of his decision.

16:21 Blinded and without strength, Samson was taken to Gaza where he would spend the rest of his short life. Gaza was one of the five capital cities of the Philistines. Known for its many wells, Gaza was a vital stop along a great caravan route that connected Egypt to the south with Aram to the north. The Philistines probably showed off their prize captive, Samson, to many dignitaries passing through.

Ironically, it was in Gaza that Samson had earlier demonstrated his great strength by uprooting the city gates (16:1–3). Now he was an example of weakness.

16:21 [u]Job 31:10; Isa 47:2
16:23 [v]1Sa 5:2; 1Ch 10:10
16:24 [w]Da 5:4 [x]1Sa 31:9; 1Ch 10:9
16:25 [y]Jdg 9:27; Ru 3:7; Est 1:10
16:27 [z]Dt 22:8; Jos 2:8
16:28 [a]Jdg 15:18

Gaza. Binding him with bronze shackles, they set him to grinding[u] in the prison.
22 But the hair on his head began to grow again after it had been shaved.

The Death of Samson

23 Now the rulers of the Philistines assembled to offer a great sacrifice to Dagon[v]
their god and to celebrate, saying, "Our god has delivered Samson, our enemy, into
our hands."
24 When the people saw him, they praised their god,[w] saying,

"Our god has delivered our enemy
into our hands,[x]
the one who laid waste our land
and multiplied our slain."

25 While they were in high spirits,[y] they shouted, "Bring out Samson to entertain
us." So they called Samson out of the prison, and he performed for them.
When they stood him among the pillars, 26 Samson said to the servant who held his
hand, "Put me where I can feel the pillars that support the temple, so that I may lean
against them." 27 Now the temple was crowded with men and women; all the rulers
of the Philistines were there, and on the roof[z] were about three thousand men and
women watching Samson perform. 28 Then Samson prayed to the LORD,[a] "O Sover-

DELILAH

A person's greatest accomplishment may well be helping others accomplish great things. Likewise, a person's greatest failure may be preventing others from achieving greatness. Delilah played a minor role in Samson's life, but her effect was devastating, for she influenced him to betray his special calling from God. Motivated by greed, Delilah used her persistence to wear down Samson. His infatuation with her made Samson a vulnerable target. For all his physical strength, he was no match for her, and he paid a great price for giving in to her. Delilah is never mentioned again in the Bible. Her unfaithfulness to Samson brought ruin to him and to her people.

Are people helped by knowing you? Do they find that knowing you challenges them to be the best they can be? Even more important, does knowing you help their relationship with God? What do your demands on their time and attention tell them about your real care for them? Are you willing to be God's instrument in the lives of others?

Strength and accomplishment:
- Persistent when faced with obstacles

Weaknesses and mistakes:
- Valued money more than relationships
- Betrayed the man who trusted her

Lesson from her life:
- We need to be careful to place our trust only in people who are trustworthy

Vital statistics:
- Where: Valley of Sorek
- Contemporary: Samson

Key verses:
"With such nagging she prodded him day after day until he was tired to death. So he told her everything" (Judges 16:16, 17).

Her story is told in Judges 16.

16:23, 24 Dagon was the chief god of the Philistines, the god of grain and harvest. Many temples were built to Dagon, and the worship there included human sacrifice. The temples were also the local entertainment centres. Just as people today crowd into theatres, Philistine townspeople crowded into the local temple. They sat on the flat temple roof and looked into the courtyard below. What they often saw was the torture and humiliation of prisoners.

Since the Philistines had control over the Israelites, they thought their god was stronger. But when the ark of God was placed before Dagon in a similar temple, the idol fell over and broke into pieces (1 Samuel 5:1–7). God's strength goes beyond numbers or physical might.

16:28–30 In spite of Samson's past, God still answered his prayer and destroyed the pagan temple and worshippers. God still loved him. He was willing to hear Samson's prayer of confession and repentance and use him one last time. One of the effects of sin in our lives is to keep us from feeling like praying. But perfect moral behaviour is not a condition for prayer. Don't let guilt feelings over sin keep you from your only means of restoration. No matter how long you have been away from God, he is ready to hear from you and restore you to a right relationship. Every situation can be salvaged if you are willing to turn again to him. If God could still work in Samson's situation, he can certainly make something worthwhile out of yours.

eign LORD, remember me. O God, please strengthen me just once more, and let me
with one blow get revenge[b] on the Philistines for my two eyes." 29 Then Samson
reached towards the two central pillars on which the temple stood. Bracing himself
against them, his right hand on the one and his left hand on the other, 30 Samson said,
"Let me die with the Philistines!" Then he pushed with all his might, and down came
the temple on the rulers and all the people in it. Thus he killed many more when he
died than while he lived.
31 Then his brothers and his father's whole family went down to get him. They
brought him back and buried him between Zorah and Eshtaol in the tomb of Manoah[c]
his father. He had led[e][d] Israel for twenty years.[e]

C. THE MORAL FAILURE OF ISRAEL (17:1—21:25)

This section shows Israel falling into idolatry, moral decline, and petty fighting. Israel, the nation that was to set the example for spiritual living, had instead become morally depraved. When Israel did serve God, and that was seldom, it was often from selfish motives. Selfish obedience does not bring us far. Genuine obedience is motivated by a love and reverence for God himself.

1. Idolatry in the tribe of Dan

Micah's Idols

17 Now a man named Micah[a] from the hill country of Ephraim 2 said to his
mother, "The eleven hundred shekels[a] of silver that were taken from you and
about which I heard you utter a curse—I have that silver with me; I took it."
Then his mother said, "The LORD bless you,[b] my son!"
3 When he returned the eleven hundred shekels of silver to his mother, she said, "I
solemnly consecrate my silver to the LORD for my son to make a carved image and
a cast idol.[c] I will give it back to you."
4 So he returned the silver to his mother, and she took two hundred shekels[b] of silver
and gave them to a silversmith, who made them into the image and the idol.[d] And
they were put in Micah's house.
5 Now this man Micah had a shrine,[e] and he made an ephod[f] and some idols[g]
and installed[h] one of his sons as his priest.[i] 6 In those days Israel had no king;[j]
everyone did as he saw fit.[k]
7 A young Levite from Bethlehem in Judah,[l] who had been living within the clan
of Judah, 8 left that town in search of some other place to stay. On his way[c] he came
to Micah's house in the hill country of Ephraim.
9 Micah asked him, "Where are you from?"
"I'm a Levite from Bethlehem in Judah," he said, "and I'm looking for a place to
stay."
10 Then Micah said to him, "Live with me and be my father and priest,[m] and I'll
give you ten shekels[d] of silver a year, your clothes and your food." 11 So the Levite
agreed to live with him, and the young man was to him like one of his sons. 12 Then

16:28 [b] Jer 15:15
16:31 [c] Jdg 13:2 [d] Ru 1:1; 1Sa 4:18 [e] Jdg 15:20
17:1 [a] Jdg 18:2, 13
17:2 [b] Ru 2:20; 1Sa 15:13; 2Sa 2:5
17:3 [c] Ex 20:4, 23; 34:17; Lev 19:4
17:4 [d] Ex 32:4; Isa 17:8
17:5 [e] Isa 44:13; Eze 8:10 [f] Jdg 8:27 [g] Ge 31:19; Jdg 18:14 [h] Nu 16:10 [i] Ex 29:9; Jdg 18:24
17:6 [j] Jdg 18:1; 19:1; 21:25 [k] Dt 12:8
17:7 [l] Jdg 19:1; Ru 1:1-2; Mic 5:2; Mt 2:1
17:10 [m] Jdg 18:19

[e] *31* Traditionally *judged* [a] *2* That is, about 28 pounds (about 13 kilograms) [b] *4* That is, about 5 pounds (about 2.3 kilograms) [c] *8* Or *To carry on his profession* [d] *10* That is, about 4 ounces (about 115 grams)

17:2 Micah and his mother seemed to be good and moral and may have sincerely desired to worship God, but they disobeyed God by following their own desires instead of doing what God wanted. The attitude that prevailed in Micah's day was this: "Everyone did as he saw fit" (17:6). This is remarkably similar to today's prevailing attitudes. But God has given us standards. He has not left our conduct up to us and our opinions. We can avoid conforming to society's low standards by taking God's commands seriously and applying them to life. Independence and self-reliance are positive traits, but only within the framework of God's standards.

17:6 Today, as in Micah's day, everyone seems to put his or her own interests first. Time has not changed human nature. Most people still reject God's right way of living. The people in Micah's time replaced the true worship of God with a homemade version of worship. As a result, justice was soon replaced by revenge and chaos. Ignoring God's direction led to confusion and destruction. Anyone who has not submitted to God will end up doing whatever seems right at the time. This tendency is present in all of us. To know what is really right and to have the strength to do it, we need to draw closer to God and his word.

17:7–12 Apparently the Israelites no longer supported the priests and Levites with their tithes because so many of the people no longer worshipped God. The young Levite in this story probably left his home in Bethlehem because the money he received from the people there was not enough to live on. But Israel's moral decay affected even the priests and Levites. This man accepted money (17:10, 11), idols (18:20), and position (17:12) in a way that was inconsistent with God's laws. While Micah revealed the religious downfall of individual Israelites, this priest illustrated the religious downfall of priests and Levites.

17:12
[n]Nu 16:10

18:1
[a]Jdg 17:6; 19:1
[b]Jos 19:47

18:2
[c]Jdg 13:25
[d]Jos 2:1
[e]Jdg 17:1

18:4
[f]Jdg 17:12

18:5
[g]1Ki 22:5

18:6
[h]1Ki 22:6

18:7
[i]Jos 19:47
[j]ver 28

18:9
[k]Nu 13:30; 1Ki 22:3

18:10
[l]ver 7, 27; Dt 8:9
[m]1Ch 4:40

18:11
[n]ver 16, 17
[o]Jdg 13:2

18:12
[p]Jdg 13:25

Micah installed[n] the Levite, and the young man became his priest and lived in his
house. 13 And Micah said, "Now I know that the LORD will be good to me, since this
Levite has become my priest."

Danites Settle in Laish

18 In those days Israel had no king.[a]
And in those days the tribe of the Danites was seeking a place of their own
where they might settle, because they had not yet come into an inheritance among the
tribes of Israel.[b] 2 So the Danites[c] sent five warriors from Zorah and Eshtaol to spy
out the land and explore it. These men represented all their clans. They told them,
"Go, explore the land."[d]
The men entered the hill country of Ephraim and came to the house of Micah,[e]
where they spent the night. 3 When they were near Micah's house, they recognised
the voice of the young Levite; so they turned in there and asked him, "Who brought
you here? What are you doing in this place? Why are you here?"
4 He told them what Micah had done for him, and said, "He has hired me and I am
his priest.[f]"
5 Then they said to him, "Please enquire of God[g] to learn whether our journey will
be successful."
6 The priest answered them, "Go in peace[h]. Your journey has the LORD's approval."
7 So the five men left and came to Laish,[i] where they saw that the people were
living in safety, like the Sidonians, unsuspecting and secure. And since their land
lacked nothing, they were prosperous.[a] Also, they lived a long way from the Sidonians[j] and had no relationship with anyone else.[b]
8 When they returned to Zorah and Eshtaol, their brothers asked them, "How did
you find things?"
9 They answered, "Come on, let's attack them! We have seen that the land is very
good. Aren't you going to do something? Don't hesitate to go there and take it over.[k]
10 When you get there, you will find an unsuspecting people and a spacious land that
God has put into your hands, a land that lacks nothing[l] whatever.[m]"
11 Then six hundred men[n] from the clan of the Danites,[o] armed for battle, set out
from Zorah and Eshtaol. 12 On their way they set up camp near Kiriath Jearim in Judah.
This is why the place west of Kiriath Jearim is called Mahaneh Dan[c][p] to this day.

[a] 7 The meaning of the Hebrew for this clause is uncertain. [b] 7 Hebrew; some Septuagint manuscripts *with the Arameans* [c] 12 *Mahaneh Dan* means *Dan's camp.*

18:1 The Danites had been assigned enough land to meet their needs (Joshua 19:40–48). However, because they failed to trust God to help them conquer their territory, the Amorites forced them into the hill country and wouldn't let them settle in the plains (1:34). Rather than fight for their allotted territory, they preferred to look for new land in the north where resistance from the enemy wouldn't be so tough. It was while they were travelling north that some of their men passed Micah's home and stole some of his idols.

18:4–6 Priests and their assistants were all members of the tribe of Levi (Numbers 3:5–13). They were to serve the people, teach them how to worship God, and perform the rituals involved in the worship services both at the tabernacle in Shiloh and in the designated cities throughout the land. But this disobedient priest showed disrespect for God because (1) he performed his duties in a house. Priestly duties were to be performed only in the tabernacle or a designated city. This requirement was intended to prevent God's laws from being changed. (2) He carried idols with him (18:20). (3) He claimed to speak for God when God had not spoken through him (18:6).

18:11–26 Through this entire incident, no-one desired to worship God; instead, they wanted to use God for selfish gain. Today some people go to church to feel better, be accepted, relieve guilt, and gain business contacts or friends. Beware of following God for selfish gain rather than selfless service.

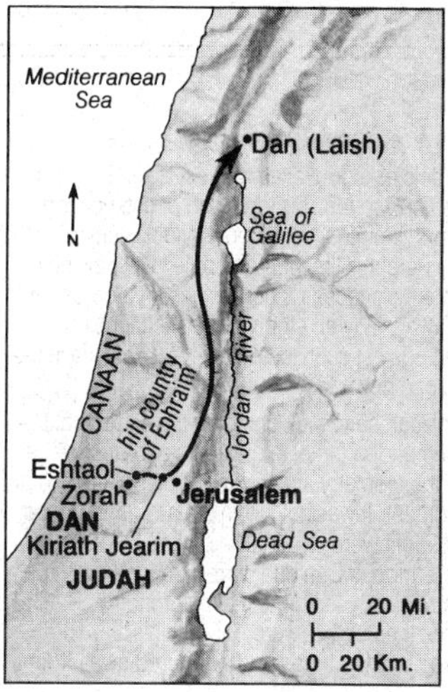

THE TRIBE OF DAN MOVES NORTH
Troops from the tribe of Dan travelled from Zorah and Eshtaol into the hill country of Ephraim where they persuaded Micah's priest to come with them. They continued north to Laish where they ruthlessly butchered its citizens. The city was renamed Dan and the priest's idols became the focus of their worship.

13 From there they went on to the hill country of Ephraim and came to Micah's house.
14 Then the five men who had spied out the land of Laish said to their brothers, "Do
you know that one of these houses has an ephod, other household gods, a carved image
and a cast idol?[q] Now you know what to do." 15 So they turned in there and went
to the house of the young Levite at Micah's place and greeted him. 16 The six hundred
Danites,[r] armed for battle, stood at the entrance to the gate. 17 The five men who had
spied out the land went inside and took the carved image, the ephod, the other
household gods[s] and the cast idol while the priest and the six hundred armed men
stood at the entrance to the gate.
18 When these men went into Micah's house and took[t] the carved image, the ephod,
the other household gods and the cast idol, the priest said to them, "What are you
doing?"
19 They answered him, "Be quiet![u] Don't say a word. Come with us, and be our
father and priest.[v] Isn't it better that you serve a tribe and clan in Israel as priest rather
than just one man's household?" 20 Then the priest was glad. He took the ephod, the
other household gods and the carved image and went along with the people. 21 Putting
their little children, their livestock and their possessions in front of them, they turned
away and left.
22 When they had gone some distance from Micah's house, the men who lived near
Micah were called together and overtook the Danites. 23 As they shouted after them,
the Danites turned and said to Micah, "What's the matter with you that you called
out your men to fight?"
24 He replied, "You took the gods I made, and my priest, and went away. What else
do I have? How can you ask, 'What's the matter with you?' "
25 The Danites answered, "Don't argue with us, or some hot-tempered men will
attack you, and you and your family will lose your lives." 26 So the Danites went their
way, and Micah, seeing that they were too strong for him,[w] turned round and went
back home.
27 Then they took what Micah had made, and his priest, and went on to Laish,
against a peaceful and unsuspecting people.[x] They attacked them with the sword and
burned down their city.[y] 28 There was no-one to rescue them because they lived a long
way from Sidon[z] and had no relationship with anyone else. The city was in a valley
near Beth Rehob.[a]
The Danites rebuilt the city and settled there. 29 They named it Dan[b] after their
forefather Dan, who was born to Israel—though the city used to be called Laish.[c]
30 There the Danites set up for themselves the idols, and Jonathan son of Gershom,[d]
the son of Moses,**d** and his sons were priests for the tribe of Dan until the time of

18:14 [q] Ge 31:19; Jdg 17:5
18:16 [r] ver 11
18:17 [s] Ge 31:19; Mic 5:13
18:18 [t] Isa 46:2; Jer 43:11; Hos 10:5
18:19 [u] Job 21:5; 29:9; 40:4; Mic 7:16 [v] Jdg 17:10
18:26 [w] Ps 18:17; 35:10
18:27 [x] ver 7, 10 [y] Ge 49:17; Jos 19:47
18:28 [z] ver 7 [a] Nu 13:21; 2Sa 10:6
18:29 [b] Ge 14:14 [c] Jos 19:47; 1Ki 15:20
18:30 [d] Ex 2:22; Jdg 17:3, 5

d *30* An ancient Hebrew scribal tradition, some Septuagint manuscripts and Vulgate; Masoretic Text *Manasseh*

18:14 An ephod was a ceremonial vest worn by a priest.

18:24 Micah made idols and employed a priest to run his personal religion. When the men of Dan took his idols and priest, nothing remained. What an empty spiritual condition! An idol is anything that takes God's place in a person's life. Some people invest all their energy in pursuit of money, success, possessions, or a career. If these idols are taken away, only an empty shell is left. The only way to protect yourself against such loss is to invest your life in the living God, whom you can never lose.

18:27 Did the tribe of Dan have the right to kill the citizens of Laish? No. God had commanded Israel to clean out and destroy certain cities because of their idolatry and wickedness, but Laish did not fall under that judgment. It was not within the assigned boundaries of Dan, and its people were peaceful in contrast to the warlike Canaanites. But the tribe of Dan had no regard for God's law. God's law said to destroy a city for idolatry (Deuteronomy 13:12–15). The Danites themselves were guilty of this sin. This story shows how far some of the tribes had wandered away from God.

18:27 Just because the Danites successfully defeated Laish doesn't mean their actions were right. Their idolatry showed that God was not guiding them. Today many justify their wrong actions by outward signs of success. They think that wealth, popularity, or lack of suffering is an indication of God's blessing. But many stories in the Bible indicate that evil and earthly success can go hand in hand (see, for example, 2 Kings 14:23–29). Success doesn't indicate God's approval. Don't allow personal success to become a measuring rod of whether or not you are pleasing God.

18:30, 31 The tribe of Dan had stolen Micah's idols, and now they set them up in Laish. Although the Danites were actually denying God by worshipping these images (Exodus 20:1–5), they probably assumed they were worshipping God through them (see the note on Exodus 32:4, 5). Worshipping images of God is *not* worshipping God, even if it resembles true worship in some ways. People repeat the same mistake today when they claim to be Christians without really believing in God's power or changing their conduct to conform to his expectations. Godliness cannot be merely a claim. It must be a reality in our motives and in our actions.

18:31 [e]Jdg 19:18 [f]Jos 18:1; Jer 7:14

the captivity of the land. 31They continued to use the idols Micah had made, all the
time the house of God[e] was in Shiloh.[f]

2. War against the tribe of Benjamin

A Levite and His Concubine

19:1 [a]Jdg 18:1 [b]Ru 1:1

19 In those days Israel had no king.
Now a Levite who lived in a remote area in the hill country of Ephraim[a] took
a concubine from Bethlehem in Judah.[b] 2But she was unfaithful to him. She left him
and went back to her father's house in Bethlehem, Judah. After she had been there
for four months, 3her husband went to her to persuade her to return. He had with him
his servant and two donkeys. She took him into her father's house, and when her father
saw him, he gladly welcomed him. 4His father-in-law, the girl's father, prevailed upon
him to stay; so he remained with him three days, eating and drinking,[c] and sleeping
there.
5On the fourth day they got up early and he prepared to leave, but the girl's father
said to his son-in-law, "Refresh yourself[d] with something to eat; then you can go."
6So the two of them sat down to eat and drink together. Afterwards the girl's father
said, "Please stay tonight and enjoy yourself.[e]" 7And when the man got up to go,
his father-in-law persuaded him, so he stayed there that night. 8On the morning of
the fifth day, when he rose to go, the girl's father said, "Refresh yourself. Wait till
afternoon!" So the two of them ate together.
9Then when the man, with his concubine and his servant, got up to leave, his
father-in-law, the girl's father, said, "Now look, it's almost evening. Spend the night
here; the day is nearly over. Stay and enjoy yourself. Early tomorrow morning you
can get up and be on your way home." 10But, unwilling to stay another night, the man
left and went towards Jebus[f] (that is, Jerusalem), with his two saddled donkeys and
his concubine.
11When they were near Jebus and the day was almost gone, the servant said to his
master, "Come, let's stop at this city of the Jebusites[g] and spend the night."
12His master replied, "No. We won't go into an alien city, whose people are not
Israelites. We will go on to Gibeah." 13He added, "Come, let's try to reach Gibeah
or Ramah[h] and spend the night in one of those places." 14So they went on, and the
sun set as they neared Gibeah in Benjamin.[i] 15There they stopped to spend the night.
They went and sat in the city square,[j] but no-one took them into his home for the
night.
16That evening[k] an old man from the hill country of Ephraim,[l] who was living
in Gibeah (the men of the place were Benjamites), came in from his work in the fields.

19:4 [c]Ex 32:6
19:5 [d]ver 8; Ge 18:5
19:6 [e]ver 9, 22; Jdg 16:25
19:10 [f]Ge 10:16; Jos 15:8; 1Ch 11:4-5
19:11 [g]Jos 3:10
19:13 [h]Jos 18:25
19:14 [i]1Sa 10:26; Isa 10:29
19:15 [j]Ge 19:2
19:16 [k]Ps 104:23 [l]ver 1

18:31 Shiloh was probably destroyed during the events reported in 1 Samuel 4 and 5, not long after the time described here. Because Shiloh was the religious centre for Israel, all adult males were required to travel there for certain religious feasts. The tribe of Dan, however, set up idols and priests in the new territory they conquered. The fact that they were over 80 miles away from Shiloh may have been their excuse for not fulfilling the law's requirements. This act was a further demonstration of their disregard for God.

18:31 The true worship of God should have been maintained through the Levitical priests scattered throughout the land and the influence of the tabernacle in Shiloh. This story shows how pagan influences and moral depravity had crept into every corner of Israelite culture. Although 300 years had passed since they entered the promised land, they had still not destroyed the idolatry and evil practices within it.

There may be a tendency in your life to allow "harmless" habits to have their own small corners, but they can become dominating forces. The values, attitudes, and practices you have adopted from the world's system can be exposed by applying the light of God's truth to them. Once you see them for what they are, you can begin to uproot them.

19:1 – 21:25 What is the significance of this tragic story? When the Israelites' faith in God disintegrated, their unity as a nation also disintegrated. They could have taken complete possession of the land if they had obeyed God and trusted him to keep his promises. But when they forgot him, they lost their purpose, and soon "everyone did as he saw fit" (21:25). When they stopped letting God lead them, they became no better than the evil people around them. When they made laws for their own benefit, they set standards far below God's. When you leave God out of your life you may be shocked at what you are capable of doing (19:30).

19:1 Having concubines was an accepted part of Israelite society although this is not what God intended (Genesis 2:24). A concubine had most of the duties but only some of the privileges of a wife. Although she was legally attached to one man, she and her children did not usually have the inheritance rights of the legal wife and legitimate children. Her primary purpose was giving the man sexual pleasure, bearing additional children, and contributing more help to the household or estate. Concubines were often foreign prisoners of war. But they could also be Israelites, as was probably the case in this story.

17 When he looked and saw the traveller in the city square, the old man asked, "Where
are you going? Where did you come from?"[m]
18 He answered, "We are on our way from Bethlehem in Judah to a remote area in
the hill country of Ephraim where I live. I have been to Bethlehem in Judah and now
I am going to the house of the LORD.[n] No-one has taken me into his house. 19 We
have both straw and fodder[o] for our donkeys and bread and wine[p] for ourselves your
servants—me, your maidservant, and the young man with us. We don't need anything."
20 "You are welcome at my house," the old man said. "Let me supply whatever you
need. Only don't spend the night in the square." 21 So he took him into his house and
fed his donkeys. After they had washed their feet, they had something to eat and
drink.[q]
22 While they were enjoying themselves,[r] some of the wicked men[s] of the city
surrounded the house. Pounding on the door, they shouted to the old man who owned
the house, "Bring out the man who came to your house so we can have sex with
him.[t]"
23 The owner of the house went outside[u] and said to them, "No, my friends, don't
be so vile. Since this man is my guest, don't do this disgraceful thing.[v] 24 Look, here
is my virgin daughter,[w] and his concubine. I will bring them out to you now, and
you can use them and do to them whatever you wish. But to this man, don't do such
a disgraceful thing."
25 But the men would not listen to him. So the man took his concubine and sent her
outside to them, and they raped her and abused her[x] throughout the night, and at dawn
they let her go. 26 At daybreak the woman went back to the house where her master
was staying, fell down at the door and lay there until daylight.
27 When her master got up in the morning and opened the door of the house and
stepped out to continue on his way, there lay his concubine, fallen in the doorway
of the house, with her hands on the threshold. 28 He said to her, "Get up; let's go."
But there was no answer. Then the man put her on his donkey and set out for home.
29 When he reached home, he took a knife[y] and cut up his concubine, limb by limb,
into twelve parts and sent them into all the areas of Israel.[z] 30 Everyone who saw it
said, "Such a thing has never been seen or done, not since the day the Israelites came
up out of Egypt.[a] Think about it! Consider it! Tell us what to do![b]"

Israelites Fight the Benjamites

20 Then all the Israelites[a] from Dan to Beersheba[b] and from the land of Gilead
came out as one man[c] and assembled[d] before the LORD in Mizpah. 2 The
leaders of all the people of the tribes of Israel took their places in the assembly of the
people of God, four hundred thousand soldiers[e] armed with swords. 3 (The Benjamites heard that the Israelites had gone up to Mizpah.) Then the Israelites said, "Tell
us how this awful thing happened."

19:17 [m]Ge 29:4
19:18 [n]Jdg 18:31
19:19 [o]Ge 24:25 [p]Ge 14:18
19:21 [q]Ge 24:32-33; Lk 7:44
19:22 [r]Jdg 16:25 [s]Dt 13:13 [t]Ge 19:4-5; Jdg 20:5; Ro 1:26-27
19:23 [u]Ge 19:6 [v]Ge 34:7; Lev 19:29; Dt 22:21; Jdg 20:6; 2Sa 13:12; Ro 1:27
19:24 [w]Ge 19:8; Dt 21:14
19:25 [x]1Sa 31:4
19:29 [y]Ge 22:6 [z]Jdg 20:6; 1Sa 11:7
19:30 [a]Hos 9:9 [b]Jdg 20:7; Pr 13:10
20:1 [a]Jdg 21:5 [b]1Sa 3:20; 2Sa 3:10; 1Ki 4:25 [c]1Sa 11:7 [d]1Sa 7:5
20:2 [e]Jdg 8:10

19:24 Nowhere is the unwritten law of hospitality stronger than in the Middle East. Protecting a guest at any cost ranked at the top of a man's code of honour. But here the hospitality code turned to fanaticism. The rape and abuse of a daughter and companion was preferable to the *possibility* of a conflict between a guest and a neighbour. The two men were selfish (they didn't want to get hurt themselves); they lacked courage (they didn't want to face a conflict even when lives were at stake); and they disobeyed God's law (they allowed deliberate abuse and murder). What drastic consequences can result when social protocol carries more authority than moral convictions!

19:29, 30 Although this was a terrible way to spread the news, it effectively communicated the horror of the crime and called the people to action. Saul used a similar method in 1 Samuel 11:7. Ironically, the man who alerted Israel to the murder of his concubine was just as guilty for her death as the men who actually killed her.

19:30 The horrible crime described in this chapter wasn't Israel's worst offence. Even worse was the nation's failure to establish a government based upon God's moral principles, where the law of God was the law of the land. As a result, laws were usually unenforced and crime was ignored. Sexual perversion and lawlessness were a by-product of Israel's disobedience to God. The Israelites weren't willing to speak up until events had gone too far.

Whenever we get away from God and his word, all sorts of evil can follow. Our drifting away from God may be slow and almost imperceptible, with the ultimate results affecting a future generation. We must continually call our nation back to God and work towards the establishment of God's moral and spiritual reign in the heart of every person.

20:1 Dan was the northernmost city in Israel, and Beersheba, the southernmost. The two were often mentioned together as a reference to the entire nation.

[4]So the Levite, the husband of the murdered woman, said, "I and my concubine
came to Gibeah[f] in Benjamin to spend the night.[g] [5]During the night the men of
Gibeah came after me and surrounded the house, intending to kill me.[h] They raped
my concubine, and she died.[i] [6]I took my concubine, cut her into pieces and sent one
piece to each region of Israel's inheritance,[j] because they committed this lewd and
disgraceful act[k] in Israel. [7]Now, all you Israelites, speak up and give your verdict.[l]"
[8]All the people rose as one man, saying, "None of us will go home. No, not one
of us will return to his house. [9]But now this is what we'll do to Gibeah: We'll go up
against it as the lot directs.[m] [10]We'll take ten men out of every hundred from all the
tribes of Israel, and a hundred from a thousand, and a thousand from ten thousand,
to get provisions for the army. Then, when the army arrives at Gibeah[a] in Benjamin,
it can give them what they deserve for all this vileness done in Israel." [11]So all the
men of Israel got together and united as one man[n] against the city.
[12]The tribes of Israel sent men throughout the tribe of Benjamin, saying, "What
about this awful crime that was committed among you? [13]Now surrender those wicked
men[o] of Gibeah so that we may put them to death and purge the evil from Israel.[p]"
But the Benjamites would not listen to their fellow Israelites. [14]From their towns
they came together at Gibeah to fight against the Israelites. [15]At once the Benjamites
mobilised twenty-six thousand swordsmen from their towns, in addition to seven
hundred chosen men from those living in Gibeah. [16]Among all these soldiers there
were seven hundred chosen men who were left-handed,[q] each of whom could sling
a stone at a hair and not miss.
[17]Israel, apart from Benjamin, mustered four hundred thousand swordsmen, all of
them fighting men.
[18]The Israelites went up to Bethel[b] and enquired of God.[r] They said, "Who of
us shall go first to fight[s] against the Benjamites?"
The LORD replied, "Judah shall go first."
[19]The next morning the Israelites got up and pitched camp near Gibeah. [20]The men
of Israel went out to fight the Benjamites and took up battle positions against them
at Gibeah. [21]The Benjamites came out of Gibeah and cut down twenty-two thousand
Israelites[t] on the battlefield that day. [22]But the men of Israel encouraged one another
and again took up their positions where they had stationed themselves the first day.
[23]The Israelites went up and wept before the LORD until evening,[u] and they enquired
of the LORD. They said, "Shall we go up again to battle[v] against the Benjamites, our
brothers?"
The LORD answered, "Go up against them."
[24]Then the Israelites drew near to Benjamin the second day. [25]This time, when the
Benjamites came out from Gibeah to oppose them, they cut down another eighteen
thousand Israelites,[w] all of them armed with swords.
[26]Then the Israelites, all the people, went up to Bethel, and there they sat weeping
before the LORD.[x] They fasted that day until evening and presented burnt offerings
and fellowship offerings[c] to the LORD.[y] [27]And the Israelites enquired of the LORD.
(In those days the ark of the covenant of God[z] was there, [28]with Phinehas son of
Eleazar,[a] the son of Aaron, ministering before it.)[b] They asked, "Shall we go up
again to battle with Benjamin our brother, or not?"

20:4 [f]Jos 15:57 [g]Jdg 19:15
20:5 [h]Jdg 19:22 [i]Jdg 19:25-26
20:6 [j]Jdg 19:29 [k]Jos 7:15; Jdg 19:23
20:7 [l]Jdg 19:30
20:9 [m]Lev 16:8
20:11 [n]ver 1
20:13 [o]Dt 13:13; Jdg 19:22 [p]Dt 17:12
20:16 [q]Jdg 3:15; 1Ch 12:2
20:18 [r]ver 26-27; Nu 27:21 [s]ver 23, 28
20:21 [t]ver 25
20:23 [u]Jos 7:6 [v]ver 18
20:25 [w]ver 21
20:26 [x]ver 23 [y]Jdg 21:4
20:27 [z]Jos 18:1
20:28 [a]Jos 24:33 [b]Dt 18:5

a *10* One Hebrew manuscript; most Hebrew manuscripts *Geba*, a variant of *Gibeah* **b** *18* Or *to the house of God*; also in verse 26 **c** *26* Traditionally *peace offerings*

20:13 Perhaps the Benjamite leaders had been given distorted facts about the serious crime in their territory, or perhaps they were too proud to admit that some of their people had stooped so low. In either case, they would not listen to the rest of Israel and hand over the accused criminals. They were more loyal to their own tribe than to God's law.

By covering for their kinsmen, the entire tribe of Benjamin sank to a level of immorality as low as the criminals'. Through this act, we get a glimpse of how thoroughly the nation's moral fabric had unravelled. The time period of the judges ends in a bloody civil war that sets the stage for the spiritual renewal to come under Samuel (see 1 Samuel).

20:27, 28 This is the only place in Judges where the ark of the covenant is mentioned. This probably indicates how seldom the people consulted God.

Phinehas, the high priest, was also the high priest under Joshua (Joshua 22:13). The reference to Phinehas as high priest and the location of the tabernacle in Bethel instead of Shiloh probably indicate that the events of this story occurred during the early years of the judges.

The LORD responded, "Go, for tomorrow I will give them into your hands.[c]"
29Then Israel set an ambush[d] around Gibeah. 30They went up against the Benjamites on the third day and took up positions against Gibeah as they had done before.
31The Benjamites came out to meet them and were drawn away[e] from the city. They
began to inflict casualties on the Israelites as before, so that about thirty men fell in
the open field and on the roads—the one leading to Bethel and the other to Gibeah.
32While the Benjamites were saying, "We are defeating them as before,"[f] the
Israelites were saying, "Let's retreat and draw them away from the city to the roads."
33All the men of Israel moved from their places and took up positions at Baal Tamar,
and the Israelite ambush charged out of its place[g] on the west**d** of Gibeah.**e** 34Then
ten thousand of Israel's finest men made a frontal attack on Gibeah. The fighting was
so heavy that the Benjamites did not realise[h] how near disaster was.[i] 35The LORD
defeated Benjamin[j] before Israel, and on that day the Israelites struck down 25,100
Benjamites, all armed with swords. 36Then the Benjamites saw that they were beaten.
Now the men of Israel had given way[k] before Benjamin, because they relied on
the ambush they had set near Gibeah. 37The men who had been in ambush made a
sudden dash into Gibeah, spread out and put the whole city to the sword.[l] 38The men
of Israel had arranged with the ambush that they should send up a great cloud of
smoke[m] from the city, 39and then the men of Israel would turn in the battle.
The Benjamites had begun to inflict casualties on the men of Israel (about thirty),
and they said, "We are defeating them as in the first battle."[n] 40But when the column
of smoke began to rise from the city, the Benjamites turned and saw the smoke of
the whole city going up into the sky.[o] 41Then the men of Israel turned on them, and
the men of Benjamin were terrified, because they realised that disaster had come upon
them. 42So they fled before the Israelites in the direction of the desert, but they could
not escape the battle. And the men of Israel who came out of the towns cut them down
there. 43They surrounded the Benjamites, chased them and easily**f** overran them in
the vicinity of Gibeah on the east. 44Eighteen thousand Benjamites fell, all of them
valiant fighters.[p] 45As they turned and fled towards the desert to the rock of Rimmon,[q] the Israelites cut down five thousand men along the roads. They kept pressing
after the Benjamites as far as Gidom and struck down two thousand more.
46On that day twenty-five thousand Benjamite swordsmen fell, all of them valiant
fighters. 47But six hundred men turned and fled into the desert to the rock of Rimmon,
where they stayed for four months. 48The men of Israel went back to Benjamin and
put all the towns to the sword, including the animals and everything else they found.
All the towns they came across they set on fire.[r]

Wives for the Benjamites

21 The men of Israel had taken an oath[a] at Mizpah:[b] "Not one of us will give[c]
his daughter in marriage to a Benjamite."
2The people went to Bethel,**a** where they sat before God until evening, raising their
voices and weeping bitterly. 3"O LORD, the God of Israel," they cried, "why has this
happened to Israel? Why should one tribe be missing from Israel today?"
4Early the next day the people built an altar and presented burnt offerings and
fellowship offerings.**b**[d]
5Then the Israelites asked, "Who from all the tribes of Israel[e] has failed to assemble

d *33* Some Septuagint manuscripts and Vulgate; the meaning of the Hebrew for this word is uncertain.
e *33* Hebrew *Geba*, a variant of *Gibeah* **f** *43* The meaning of the Hebrew for this word is uncertain. **a** *2* Or *to the house of God* **b** *4* Traditionally *peace offerings*

20:28 [c]Jdg 7:9
20:29 [d]Jos 8:2, 4
20:31 [e]Jos 8:16
20:32 [f]ver 39
20:33 [g]Jos 8:19
20:34 [h]Jos 8:14 [i]Isa 47:11
20:35 [j]1Sa 9:21
20:36 [k]Jos 8:15
20:37 [l]Jos 8:19
20:38 [m]Jos 8:20
20:39 [n]ver 32
20:40 [o]Jos 8:20
20:44 [p]Ps 76:5
20:45 [q]Jos 15:32; Jdg 21:13
20:48 [r]Jdg 21:23
21:1 [a]Jos 9:18 [b]Jdg 20:1 [c]ver 7, 18
21:4 [d]Jdg 20:26; 2Sa 24:25
21:5 [e]Jdg 5:23; 20:1

20:46–48 The effects of the horrible rape and murder should never have been felt outside the community where the crime happened. The local people should have brought the criminals to justice and corrected the laxness that originally permitted the crime. Instead, first the town and then the entire tribe defended this wickedness, even going to war over it.

To prevent unresolved problems from turning into major conflicts, firm action must be taken quickly, wisely, and forcefully *before* the situation gets out of hand.

20:48 The tribe of Benjamin eventually recovered from this slaughter. Saul, Israel's first king, was from this tribe (1 Samuel 9:21). So were Queen Esther (Esther 2:5–7) and the apostle Paul (Romans 11:1). But the tribe was always known for being smaller than the rest (as in Psalm 68:27).

21:7 [f]ver 1
21:8 [g]1Sa 11:1; 31:11
21:11 [h]Nu 31:17-18
21:12 [i]Jos 18:1
21:13 [j]Dt 20:10 [k]Jdg 20:47
21:15 [l]ver 6
21:18 [m]ver 1
21:19 [n]Jos 18:1; Jdg 18:31; 1Sa 1:3
21:21 [o]Ex 15:20; Jdg 11:34
21:22 [p]ver 1, 18
21:23 [q]Jdg 20:48
21:25 [r]Dt 12:8; Jdg 17:6; 18:1; 19:1

before the LORD?" For they had taken a solemn oath that anyone who failed to
assemble before the LORD at Mizpah should certainly be put to death.
6Now the Israelites grieved for their brothers, the Benjamites. "Today one tribe is
cut off from Israel," they said. 7"How can we provide wives for those who are left,
since we have taken an oath[f] by the LORD not to give them any of our daughters in
marriage?" 8Then they asked, "Which one of the tribes of Israel failed to assemble
before the LORD at Mizpah?" They discovered that no-one from Jabesh Gilead[g] had
come to the camp for the assembly. 9For when they counted the people, they found
that none of the people of Jabesh Gilead were there.
10So the assembly sent twelve thousand fighting men with instructions to go to
Jabesh Gilead and put to the sword those living there, including the women and
children. 11"This is what you are to do," they said. "Kill every male and every woman
who is not a virgin.[h]" 12They found among the people living in Jabesh Gilead four
hundred young women who had never slept with a man, and they took them to the
camp at Shiloh[i] in Canaan.
13Then the whole assembly sent an offer of peace[j] to the Benjamites at the rock
of Rimmon.[k] 14So the Benjamites returned at that time and were given the women
of Jabesh Gilead who had been spared. But there were not enough for all of them.
15The people grieved for Benjamin,[l] because the LORD had made a gap in the tribes
of Israel. 16And the elders of the assembly said, "With the women of Benjamin
destroyed, how shall we provide wives for the men who are left? 17The Benjamite
survivors must have heirs," they said, "so that a tribe of Israel will not be wiped out.
18We can't give them our daughters as wives, since we Israelites have taken this oath:
'Cursed be anyone who gives[m] a wife to a Benjamite.' 19But look, there is the annual
festival of the LORD in Shiloh,[n] to the north of Bethel, and east of the road that goes
from Bethel to Shechem, and to the south of Lebonah."
20So they instructed the Benjamites, saying, "Go and hide in the vineyards 21and
watch. When the girls of Shiloh come out to join in the dancing,[o] then rush from
the vineyards and each of you seize a wife from the girls of Shiloh and go to the land
of Benjamin. 22When their fathers or brothers complain to us, we will say to them,
'Do us a kindness by helping them, because we did not get wives for them during the
war, and you are innocent, since you did not give[p] your daughters to them.' "
23So that is what the Benjamites did. While the girls were dancing, each man caught
one and carried her off to be his wife. Then they returned to their inheritance and
rebuilt the towns and settled in them.[q]
24At that time the Israelites left that place and went home to their tribes and clans,
each to his own inheritance.
25In those days Israel had no king; everyone did as he saw fit.[r]

21:8–12 The Israelites moved from one mess to another. Because of a rash vow made in the heat of emotion (21:5), here they destroyed another town. Israel probably justified their action with the following arguments: (1) An oath could not be broken, and Israel had vowed that anyone who did not help them fight the Benjamites would be killed. (2) Because all the women from Benjamin had been killed, the few remaining men needed wives to prevent the tribe from disappearing. To spare the unmarried women from Jabesh Gilead seemed the right solution.

We do not know all the circumstances behind the brutal massacre at Jabesh Gilead, but it seems that the rest of Israel followed Benjamin's pattern. They put tribal loyalties above God's commands, and they justified wrong actions to correct past mistakes.

21:25 During the time of the judges, the people of Israel experienced trouble because everyone became his own authority and acted on his own opinions of right and wrong. This produced horrendous results. Our world is similar. Individuals, groups, and societies have made themselves the final authorities without reference to God. When people selfishly satisfy their personal desires at all costs, everyone pays the price.

It is the ultimate heroic act to submit all our plans, desires, and motives to God. Men like Gideon, Jephthah, and Samson are known for their heroism in battle. But their personal lives were far from heroic.

To be truly heroic, we must go into battle each day in our home, job, church, and society to make God's kingdom a reality. Our weapons are the standards, morals, truths, and convictions we receive from God's word. We will lose the battle if we gather the spoils of earthly treasures rather than seeking the treasures of heaven.

RUTH

VITAL STATISTICS

PURPOSE:
To show how three people remained strong in character and true to God even when the society around them was collapsing

AUTHOR:
Unknown. Some think it was Samuel, but internal evidence suggests that it was written after Samuel's death.

DATE WRITTEN:
Some time after the period of the judges (1375–1050 B.C.)

SETTING:
A dark time in Israel's history when people lived to please themselves, not God (Judges 17:6)

KEY VERSE:
"But Ruth replied, 'Don't urge me to leave you or to turn back from you. Where you go I will go, and where you stay I will stay. Your people will be my people and your God my God' " (1:16).

KEY PEOPLE:
Ruth, Naomi, Boaz

KEY PLACES:
Moab, Bethlehem

WHEN someone says, "Let me tell you about my mother-in-law," we expect some kind of negative statement or humorous anecdote because the mother-in-law caricature has been a standard subject for ridicule or comedy. The book of Ruth, however, tells a different story. Ruth loved her mother-in-law, Naomi. Recently widowed, Ruth begged to stay with Naomi wherever she went, even though it would mean leaving her homeland. In heartfelt words Ruth said, "Your people will be my people and your God my God" (1:16). Naomi agreed, and Ruth travelled with her to Bethlehem.

Not much is said about Naomi except that she loved and cared for Ruth. Obviously, Naomi's life was a powerful witness to the reality of God. Ruth was drawn to her—and to the God she worshipped. In the succeeding months and years, God led this young Moabite widow to a man named Boaz, whom she eventually married. As a result, she became the great-grandmother of David and an ancestor in the line of the Messiah. What a profound impact Naomi's life made!

The book of Ruth is also the story of God's grace in the midst of difficult circumstances. Ruth's story occurred during the time of the judges—a period of disobedience, idolatry, and violence. Even in times of crisis and deepest despair, there are those who follow God and through whom God works. No matter how discouraging or antagonistic the world may seem, there are always people who follow God. He will use anyone who is open to him to achieve his purposes. Ruth was a Moabitess and Boaz was a descendant of Rahab, a former prostitute from Jericho. Nevertheless, their offspring continued the family line through which the Messiah came into our world.

Read this book and be encouraged. God is at work in the world, and he wants to use you. God could use you, as he used Naomi, to bring family and friends to him.

THE BLUEPRINT

1. Ruth remains loyal to Naomi (1:1–22)
2. Ruth gleans in Boaz's field (2:1–23)
3. Ruth follows Naomi's plan (3:1–18)
4. Ruth and Boaz are married (4:1–22)

When we first meet Ruth, she is a destitute widow. We follow her as she joins God's people, gleans in the grainfields, and risks her honour at the threshing floor of Boaz. In the end, we see Ruth becoming the wife of Boaz. What a picture of how we come to faith in Christ. We begin with no hope and are rebellious aliens with no part in the kingdom of God. Then as we risk everything by putting our faith in Christ, God saves us, forgives us, rebuilds our lives, and gives us blessings that will last throughout eternity. Boaz's redeeming of Ruth is a picture of Christ redeeming us.

MEGATHEMES

THEME	EXPLANATION	IMPORTANCE
Faithfulness	Ruth's faithfulness to Naomi as a daughter-in-law and friend is a great example of love and loyalty. Ruth, Naomi, and Boaz are also faithful to God and his laws. Throughout the story we see God's faithfulness to his people.	Ruth's life was guided by faithfulness towards God and showed itself in loyalty towards the people she knew. To be loyal and loving in relationships, we must imitate God's faithfulness in our relationships with others.
Kindness	Ruth showed great kindness to Naomi. In turn, Boaz showed kindness to Ruth—a despised Moabite woman with no money. God showed his kindness to Ruth, Naomi, and Boaz by bringing them together for his purposes.	Just as Boaz showed his kindness by buying back land to guarantee Ruth and Naomi's inheritance, so Christ showed his kindness by dying for us to guarantee our eternal life. God's kindness should motivate us to love and honour him.
Integrity	Ruth showed high moral character by being loyal to Naomi, by her clean break from her former land and customs, and by her hard work in the fields. Boaz showed integrity in his moral standards, his honesty, and by following through on his commitments.	When we have experienced God's faithfulness and kindness, we should respond by showing integrity. Just as the values by which Ruth and Boaz lived were in sharp contrast to those of the culture portrayed in Judges, so our lives should stand out from the world around us.
Protection	We see God's care and protection over the lives of Naomi and Ruth. His supreme control over circumstances brings them safety and security. He guides the minds and activities of people to fulfil his purpose.	No matter how devastating our present situation may be, our hope is in God. His resources are infinite. We must believe that he can work in the life of any person—whether that person is a king or a stranger in a foreign land. Trust his protection.
Prosperity/Blessing	Ruth and Naomi came to Bethlehem as poor widows, but they soon became prosperous through Ruth's marriage to Boaz. Ruth became the great-grandmother of King David. Yet the greatest blessing was not the money, the marriage, or the child; it was the quality of love and respect between Ruth, Boaz, and Naomi.	We tend to think of blessings in terms of prosperity rather than the high-quality relationships God makes possible for us. No matter what our economic situation, we can love and respect the people God has brought into our lives. In so doing, we give and receive blessings. Love is the greatest blessing.

1. Ruth remains loyal to Naomi

Naomi and Ruth

1 In the days when the judges ruled,[a][a] there was a famine in the land,[b] and a
man from Bethlehem in Judah, together with his wife and two sons, went to live
for a while in the country of Moab.[c] 2The man's name was Elimelech, his wife's
name Naomi, and the names of his two sons were Mahlon and Kilion. They were
Ephrathites from Bethlehem,[d] Judah. And they went to Moab and lived there.
3Now Elimelech, Naomi's husband, died, and she was left with her two sons. 4They
married Moabite women, one named Orpah and the other Ruth.[e] After they had lived
there about ten years, 5both Mahlon and Kilion also died, and Naomi was left without
her two sons and her husband.
6When she heard in Moab that the LORD had come to the aid of his people[f] by
providing food[g] for them, Naomi and her daughters-in-law prepared to return home
from there. 7With her two daughters-in-law she left the place where she had been
living and set out on the road that would take them back to the land of Judah.
8Then Naomi said to her two daughters-in-law, "Go back, each of you, to your
mother's home. May the LORD show kindness[h] to you, as you have shown to your
dead[i] and to me. 9May the LORD grant that each of you will find rest[j] in the home
of another husband."
Then she kissed them and they wept aloud 10and said to her, "We will go back with
you to your people."
11But Naomi said, "Return home, my daughters. Why would you come with me?
Am I going to have any more sons, who could become your husbands?[k] 12Return
home, my daughters; I am too old to have another husband. Even if I thought there
was still hope for me—even if I had a husband tonight and then gave birth to

1:1 [a]Jdg 2:16-18 [b]Ge 12:10; Ps 105:16 [c]Jdg 3:30
1:2 [d]Ge 35:19
1:4 [e]Mt 1:5
1:6 [f]Ex 4:31; Jer 29:10; Zep 2:7 [g]Ps 132:15; Mt 6:11
1:8 [h]Ru 2:20; 2Ti 1:16 [i]ver 5
1:9 [j]Ru 3:1
1:11 [k]Ge 38:11; Dt 25:5

a *1* Traditionally *judged*

1:1 The story of Ruth takes place sometime during the period of the rule of the judges. These were dark days for Israel, when "everyone did as he saw fit" (Judges 17:6; 21:25). But during those dark and evil times, there were still some who followed God. Naomi and Ruth are beautiful examples of loyalty, friendship, and commitment—to God and to each other.

1:1, 2 Moab was the land east of the Dead Sea. It was one of the nations that oppressed Israel during the period of the judges (Judges 3:12ff), so there was hostility between the two nations. The famine must have been quite severe in Israel for Elimelech to move his family here. They were called Ephrathites because Ephrath was an earlier name for Bethlehem. Even if Israel had already defeated Moab, there would still have been tensions between them.

1:4, 5 Friendly relations with the Moabites were discouraged (Deuteronomy 23:3–6) but probably not forbidden, since the Moabites lived outside the promised land. Marrying a Canaanite (and all those living within the borders of the promised land), however, was against God's law (Deuteronomy 7:1–4). Moabites were not allowed to worship at the tabernacle because they had not let the Israelites pass through their land during the exodus from Egypt.

As God's chosen nation, Israel should have set the standards of high moral living for the other nations. Ironically it was Ruth, a Moabitess, whom God used as an example of genuine spiritual character. This shows just how bleak life had become in Israel during those days.

1:8, 9 There was almost nothing worse than being a widow in the ancient world. Widows were taken advantage of or ignored. They were almost always poverty stricken. God's law, therefore, provided that the nearest relative of the dead husband should care for the widow; but Naomi had no relatives in Moab, and she did not know if any of her relatives were alive in Israel.

Even in her desperate situation, Naomi had a selfless attitude. Although she had decided to return to Israel, she encouraged Ruth and Orpah to stay in Moab and start their lives again, even though this would mean hardship for her. Like Naomi, we must consider the needs of others and not just our own. As Naomi discovered, when you act selflessly, others are encouraged to follow your example.

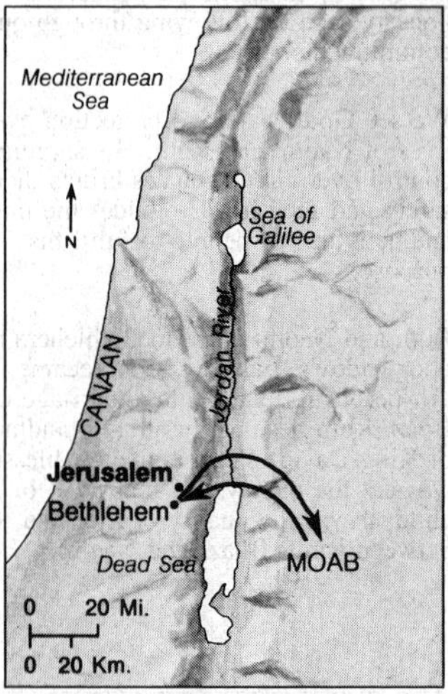

SETTING FOR THE STORY
Elimelech, Naomi, and their sons travelled from Bethlehem to Moab because of a famine. After her husband and sons died, Naomi returned to Bethlehem with her daughter-in-law Ruth.

1:11 Naomi's comment here ("sons, who could become your husbands") refers to *levirate marriage,* the obligation of a dead man's brother to care for the widow (Deuteronomy 25:5–10). This law kept the widow from poverty and provided a way for the family name of the dead husband to continue.

Naomi, however, had no other sons for Ruth or Orpah to marry, so she encouraged them to remain in their homeland and remarry. Orpah agreed, which was her right. But Ruth was willing to give up the possibility of security and children in order to care for Naomi.

1:13 [l]Jdg 2:15; Job 4:5; 19:21; Ps 32:4
1:14 [m]Ru 2:11 [n]Pr 17:17; 18:24
1:15 [o]Jos 24:14; Jdg 11:24
1:16 [p]2Ki 2:2 [q]Ru 2:11, 12
1:17 [r]1Sa 3:17; 25:22; 2Sa 19:13; 2Ki 6:31
1:18 [s]Ac 21:14
1:19 [t]Mt 21:10

sons — 13would you wait until they grew up? Would you remain unmarried for them?
No, my daughters. It is more bitter for me than for you, because the LORD's hand has
gone out against me![l]"
14At this they wept again. Then Orpah kissed her mother-in-law[m] good-bye, but
Ruth clung to her.[n]
15"Look," said Naomi, "your sister-in-law is going back to her people and her
gods.[o] Go back with her."
16But Ruth replied, "Don't urge me to leave you[p] or to turn back from you. Where
you go I will go, and where you stay I will stay. Your people will be my people and
your God my God.[q] 17Where you die I will die, and there I will be buried. May the
LORD deal with me, be it ever so severely,[r] if anything but death separates you and
me." 18When Naomi realised that Ruth was determined to go with her, she stopped
urging her.[s]
19So the two women went on until they came to Bethlehem. When they arrived in
Bethlehem, the whole town was stirred[t] because of them, and the women exclaimed,
"Can this be Naomi?"

RUTH & NAOMI

The stories of several people in the Bible are woven together so closely that they are almost inseparable. We know more about their relationship than we know about them as individuals. And in an age that worships individualism, their stories become helpful models of good relationships. Naomi and Ruth are beautiful examples of this blending of lives. Their cultures, family backgrounds, and ages were very different. As mother-in-law and daughter-in-law, they probably had as many opportunities for tension as for tenderness. And yet they were bound to each other.

They shared deep sorrow, great affection for each other, and an overriding commitment to the God of Israel. And yet as much as they depended on each other, they also gave each other freedom in their commitment to one another. Naomi was willing to let Ruth return to her family. Ruth was willing to leave her homeland to go to Israel. Naomi even helped arrange Ruth's marriage to Boaz although it would change their relationship.

God was at the centre of their intimate communication. Ruth came to know the God of Israel through Naomi. The older woman allowed Ruth to see, hear, and feel all the joy and anguish of her relationship to God. How often do you feel that your thoughts and questions about God should be left out of a close relationship? How often do you share your unedited thoughts about God with your spouse or friends? Sharing openly about our relationship with God can bring depth and intimacy to our relationships with others.

Strengths and accomplishments:
- A relationship where the greatest bond was faith in God
- A relationship of strong mutual commitment
- A relationship in which each person tried to do what was best for the other

Lesson from their lives:
- God's living presence in a relationship overcomes differences that might otherwise create division and disharmony

Vital statistics:
- Where: Moab, Bethlehem
- Occupation: Wives, widows
- Relatives: Elimelech, Mahlon, Kilion, Orpah, Boaz

Key verses:
"But Ruth replied, 'Don't urge me to leave you or to turn back from you. Where you go I will go, and where you stay I will stay. Your people will be my people and your God my God. Where you die I will die, and there I will be buried. May the LORD deal with me, be it ever so severely, if anything but death separates you and me' " (Ruth 1:16, 17).

Their story is told in the book of Ruth. Ruth is also mentioned in Matthew 1:5.

1:16 Ruth was a Moabitess, but that didn't stop her from worshipping the true God, nor did it stop God from accepting her worship and blessing her greatly. The Jews were not the only people God loved. God chose the Jews to be the people through whom the rest of the world would come to know him. This was fulfilled when Jesus Christ was born as a Jew. Through him, the entire world can come to know God. Acts 10:35 says that "[God] accepts men from every nation who fear him and do what is right." God accepts all who worship him; he works through people regardless of their race, sex, or nationality. The book of Ruth is a perfect example of God's impartiality. Although Ruth belonged to a race often despised by Israel, she was blessed because of her faithfulness. She became a great-grandmother of King David and a direct ancestor of Jesus. No-one should feel disqualified from serving God because of race, sex, or national background. And God can use every circumstance to build his kingdom.

20“Don’t call me Naomi,”[b] she told them. “Call me Mara,[c] because the
Almighty[d][u] has made my life very bitter.[v] 21I went away full, but the LORD has
brought me back empty.[w] Why call me Naomi? The LORD has afflicted[e] me; the
Almighty has brought misfortune upon me.”
22So Naomi returned from Moab accompanied by Ruth the Moabitess, her
daughter-in-law, arriving in Bethlehem as the barley harvest[x] was beginning.[y]

2. Ruth gleans in Boaz’s field

Ruth Meets Boaz

2 Now Naomi had a relative[a] on her husband’s side, from the clan of Elimelech,[b]
a man of standing, whose name was Boaz.[c]
2And Ruth the Moabitess said to Naomi, “Let me go to the fields and pick up the
leftover grain[d] behind anyone in whose eyes I find favour.”
Naomi said to her, “Go ahead, my daughter.” 3So she went out and began to glean
in the fields behind the harvesters. As it turned out, she found herself working in a
field belonging to Boaz, who was from the clan of Elimelech.
4Just then Boaz arrived from Bethlehem and greeted the harvesters, “The LORD be
with you![e]”
“The LORD bless you![f]” they called back.
5Boaz asked the foreman of his harvesters, “Whose young woman is that?”
6The foreman replied, “She is the Moabitess[g] who came back from Moab with
Naomi. 7She said, ‘Please let me glean and gather among the sheaves behind the
harvesters.’ She went into the field and has worked steadily from morning till now,
except for a short rest in the shelter.”
8So Boaz said to Ruth, “My daughter, listen to me. Don’t go and glean in another
field and don’t go away from here. Stay here with my servant girls. 9Watch the field
where the men are harvesting, and follow along after the girls. I have told the men
not to touch you. And whenever you are thirsty, go and get a drink from the water
jars the men have filled.”

b *20 Naomi* means *pleasant*; also in verse 21. c *20 Mara* means *bitter*. d *20* Hebrew *Shaddai*; also in verse 21
e *21* Or *has testified against*

1:20 *u*Ex 6:3 *v*ver 13; Job 6:4
1:21 *w*Job 1:21
1:22 *x*Ex 9:31; Ru 2:23 *y*2Sa 21:9
2:1 *a*Ru 3:2, 12 *b*Ru 1:2 *c*Ru 4:21
2:2 *d*ver 7; Lev 19:9; 23:22; Dt 24:19
2:4 *e*Jdg 6:12; Lk 1:28; 2Th 3:16 *f*Ps 129:7-8
2:6 *g*Ru 1:22

1:20, 21 Naomi had experienced severe hardships. She had left Israel married and secure; she returned widowed and poor. Naomi changed her name to express the bitterness and pain she felt. Naomi was not rejecting God by openly expressing her pain. However, she seems to have lost sight of the tremendous resources she had in her relationship with Ruth and with God. When you face bitter times, God welcomes your honest prayers, but be careful not to overlook the love, strength, and resources that he provides in your present relationships. And don't allow bitterness and disappointment to blind you to your opportunities.

1:22 Bethlehem was about five miles southwest of Jerusalem. The town was surrounded by lush fields and olive groves. Its harvests were abundant.

Ruth and Naomi's return to Bethlehem was certainly part of God's plan because in this town David would be born (1 Samuel 16:1), and, as predicted by the prophet Micah (Micah 5:2), Jesus Christ would also be born there. This move, then, was more than merely convenient for Ruth and Naomi. It led to the fulfilment of Scripture.

1:22 Because Israel's climate is quite moderate, there are two harvests each year, in the spring and in the autumn. The barley harvest took place in the spring, and it was during this time of hope and plenty that Ruth and Naomi returned to Bethlehem. Bethlehem was a farming community, and because it was the time of the harvest, there was plenty of leftover grain in the fields. This grain could be collected, or *gleaned,* and then made into food. (See the note on 2:2 for more information on gleaning.)

2:1 A clan is a group of families with a common ancestor.

2:2 When the wheat and barley were ready to be harvested, reapers were employed to cut down the stalks and tie them into bundles. Israelite law demanded that the corners of the fields should not be harvested. In addition, any grain that was dropped was to be left for poor people who picked it up (this was called *gleaning*) and used it for food (Leviticus 19:9; 23:22; Deuteronomy 24:19). The purpose of this law was to feed the poor and to prevent the owners from hoarding. This law served as a type of welfare scheme in Israel. Because she was a widow with no means of providing for herself, Ruth went into the fields to glean the grain.

2:2, 3 Ruth made her home in a foreign land. Instead of depending on Naomi or waiting for good fortune to happen, she took the initiative. She went to work. She was not afraid of admitting her need or working hard to supply it. When Ruth went out to the fields, God provided for her. If you are waiting for God to provide, consider this: He may be waiting for you to take the first step to demonstrate just how important your need is.

10At this, she bowed down with her face to the ground.[h] She exclaimed, "Why
have I found such favour in your eyes that you notice me[i] — a foreigner?[j]"
11Boaz replied, "I've been told all about what you have done for your mother-in-
law[k] since the death of your husband — how you left your father and mother and your
homeland and came to live with a people you did not know before.[l] 12May the LORD
repay you for what you have done. May you be richly rewarded by the LORD,[m] the
God of Israel, under whose wings[n] you have come to take refuge.[o]"
13"May I continue to find favour in your eyes, my lord," she said. "You have given
me comfort and have spoken kindly to your servant — though I do not have the standing
of one of your servant girls."
14At mealtime Boaz said to her, "Come over here. Have some bread and dip it in
the wine vinegar."
When she sat down with the harvesters, he offered her some roasted grain. She ate
all she wanted and had some left over.[p] 15As she got up to glean, Boaz gave orders
to his men, "Even if she gathers among the sheaves, don't embarrass her. 16Rather,
pull out some stalks for her from the bundles and leave them for her to pick up, and
don't rebuke her."
17So Ruth gleaned in the field until evening. Then she threshed the barley she had
gathered, and it amounted to about an ephah.[a] 18She carried it back to town, and her
mother-in-law saw how much she had gathered. Ruth also brought out and gave her
what she had left over[q] after she had eaten enough.
19Her mother-in-law asked her, "Where did you glean today? Where did you work?
Blessed be the man who took notice of you![r]"
Then Ruth told her mother-in-law about the one at whose place she had been
working. "The name of the man I worked with today is Boaz," she said.
20"The LORD bless him!" Naomi said to her daughter-in-law. "He has not stopped
showing his kindness[s] to the living and the dead." She added, "That man is our close
relative; he is one of our kinsman-redeemers.[t]"
21Then Ruth the Moabitess said, "He even said to me, 'Stay with my workers until
they finish harvesting all my grain.' "
22Naomi said to Ruth her daughter-in-law, "It will be good for you, my daughter,
to go with his girls, because in someone else's field you might be harmed."
23So Ruth stayed close to the servant girls of Boaz to glean until the barley and
wheat harvests[u] were finished. And she lived with her mother-in-law.

[a] *17* That is, probably about 3/5 bushel (about 22 litres)

2:10 [h] 1Sa 25:23 [i] Ps 41:1 [j] Dt 15:3
2:11 [k] Ru 1:14 [l] Ru 1:16-17
2:12 [m] 1Sa 24:19 [n] Ps 17:8; 36:7; 57:1; 61:4; 63:7; 91:4 [o] Ru 1:16
2:14 [p] ver 18
2:18 [q] ver 14
2:19 [r] ver 10; Ps 41:1
2:20 [s] Ru 3:10; 2Sa 2:5; Pr 17:17 [t] Ru 3:9, 12; 4:1, 14
2:23 [u] Dt 16:9

2:7 Ruth's task, though menial, tiring, and perhaps degrading, was done faithfully. What is your attitude when the task you have been given is not up to your true potential? The task at hand may be all you can do, or it may be the work God wants you to do. Or, as in Ruth's case, it may be a test of your character that can open up new doors of opportunity.

2:10–12 Ruth's life exhibited admirable qualities: she was hard-working, loving, kind, faithful, and brave. These qualities gained for her a good reputation, but only because she displayed them *consistently* in all areas of her life. Wherever Ruth went or whatever she did, her character remained the same.

Your reputation is formed by the people who watch you at work, in town, at home, in church. A good reputation comes by *consistently* living out the qualities you believe in — no matter what group of people or surroundings you are in.

2:15, 16 The characters in the book of Ruth are classic examples of good people in action. Boaz went far beyond the intent of the gleaners' law in demonstrating his kindness and generosity. Not only did he let Ruth glean in his field, he also told his workers to let some of the grain fall in her path. Out of his abundance, he provided for the needy. How often do you go beyond the accepted patterns of providing for those less fortunate? Do more than the minimum for others.

2:19, 20 Naomi had felt bitter (1:20, 21), but her faith in God was still alive, and she praised God for Boaz's kindness to Ruth. In her sorrows, she still trusted God and acknowledged his goodness. We may feel bitter about a situation, but we must never despair. Today is always a new opportunity for experiencing God's care. (For more on kinsman-redeemer, see the note on 3:1–9.)

2:20 Though Ruth may not have always recognised God's guidance, he had been with her every step of the way. She went to glean and "just happened" to end up in the field owned by Boaz who "just happened" to be a close relative. This was more than mere coincidence. As you go about your daily tasks, God is working in your life in ways you may not even notice. We must not close the door on what God can do. Events do not occur by luck or coincidence. We should have faith that God is directing our lives for his purpose.

3. Ruth follows Naomi's plan

Ruth and Boaz at the Threshing Floor

3 One day Naomi her mother-in-law said to her, "My daughter, should I not try
to find a home[a][a] for you, where you will be well provided for? 2 Is not Boaz,
with whose servant girls you have been, a kinsman[b] of ours? Tonight he will be
winnowing barley on the threshing-floor. 3 Wash and perfume yourself,[c] and put on
your best clothes. Then go down to the threshing-floor, but don't let him know you
are there until he has finished eating and drinking. 4 When he lies down, note the place
where he is lying. Then go and uncover his feet and lie down. He will tell you what
to do."
5 "I will do whatever you say,"[d] Ruth answered. 6 So she went down to the
threshing-floor and did everything her mother-in-law told her to do.
7 When Boaz had finished eating and drinking and was in good spirits,[e] he went
over to lie down at the far end of the grain pile. Ruth approached quietly, uncovered
his feet and lay down. 8 In the middle of the night something startled the man, and
he turned and discovered a woman lying at his feet.
9 "Who are you?" he asked.
"I am your servant Ruth," she said. "Spread the corner of your garment[f] over me,
since you are a kinsman-redeemer.[g]"
10 "The LORD bless you, my daughter," he replied. "This kindness is greater than
that which you showed earlier: You have not run after the younger men, whether rich
or poor. 11 And now, my daughter, don't be afraid. I will do for you all you ask. All
my fellow townsmen know that you are a woman of noble character.[h] 12 Although
it is true that I am near of kin, there is a kinsman-redeemer[i] nearer than[j] I. 13 Stay
here for the night, and in the morning if he wants to redeem,[k] good; let him redeem.
But if he is not willing, as surely as the LORD lives[l] I will do it. Lie here until
morning."
14 So she lay at his feet until morning, but got up before anyone could be recog-

3:1 [a] Ru 1:9
3:2 [b] Dt 25:5-10; Ru 2:1
3:3 [c] 2Sa 14:2
3:5 [d] Eph 6:1; Col 3:20
3:7 [e] Jdg 19:6, 9, 22; 2Sa 13:28; 1Ki 21:7; Est 1:10
3:9 [f] Eze 16:8 [g] ver 12; Ru 2:20
3:11 [h] Pr 12:4; 31:10
3:12 [i] ver 9 [j] Ru 4:1
3:13 [k] Dt 25:5; Ru 4:5; Mt 22:24 [l] Jdg 8:19; Jer 4:2

a *1* Hebrew *find rest* (see Ruth 1:9)

3:1–9 As widows, Ruth and Naomi could only look forward to difficult times. (See the note on 1:8, 9 for more on a widow's life.) But when Naomi heard the news about Boaz, her hope for the future was renewed (2:20). Typical of her character, she thought first of Ruth, encouraging her to see if Boaz would take the responsibility of being a "kinsman-redeemer" to her (2:20).

A kinsman-redeemer was a relative who volunteered to take responsibility for the extended family. When a woman's husband died, the law (Deuteronomy 25:5–10) provided that she could marry a brother of her dead husband. But Naomi had no more sons. In such a case, the nearest relative to the deceased husband could become a kinsman-redeemer and marry the widow. The nearest relative did not have to marry the widow. If he chose not to, the next nearest relative could take his place. If no-one chose to help the widow, she would probably live in poverty for the rest of her life because in Israelite culture the inheritance was passed on to the son or nearest male relative, not to the wife. To take the sting out of these inheritance rules, there were laws for gleaning and kinsman-redeemers.

We have a kinsman-redeemer in Jesus Christ, who though he was God, came to earth as a man in order to save us. By his death on the cross, he has redeemed us from sin and hopelessness and thereby purchased us to be his own possession (1 Peter 1:18, 19). This guarantees our eternal inheritance.

3:2 The threshing floor was the place where the grain was separated from the harvested wheat. The wheat stalks were crushed, either by hand or by oxen, and the valuable grain (inner kernels) separated from the worthless chaff (the outside shell). The floor was made from rock or soil and located outside the village, usually on an elevated site where the winds would blow away the lighter chaff when the crushed wheat was thrown into the air (or winnowed). Boaz spent the night beside the threshing floor for two reasons: (1) to prevent theft and (2) to wait for his turn to thresh grain. (Threshing was often done at night because daylight hours were spent harvesting.)

3:4 Naomi's advice seems strange, but she was not suggesting a seductive act. In reality, Naomi was telling Ruth to act in accordance with Israelite custom and law. It was common for a servant to lie at the feet of his master and even share a part of his covering. By observing this custom, Ruth would inform Boaz that he could be her kinsman-redeemer – that he could find someone to marry her or marry her himself. It was family business, nothing romantic. But the story later became beautifully romantic as Ruth and Boaz developed an unselfish love and deep respect for each other.

3:5 As a foreigner, Ruth may have thought that Naomi's advice was odd. But Ruth followed the advice because she knew Naomi was kind, trustworthy, and filled with moral integrity. Each of us knows a parent, older friend, or relative who is always looking out for our best interests. Be willing to listen to the advice of those older and wiser than you are. The experience and knowledge of such a person can be invaluable. Imagine what Ruth's life would have been like had she ignored her mother-in-law.

3:12 Ruth and Naomi must have assumed that Boaz was their closest relative. Boaz, too, must have already considered marrying Ruth because his answer to her shows he had been thinking about it. He couldn't have considered marrying Naomi because she was probably too old to bear any more children (1:11, 12). One man in the city was a nearer relative than Boaz, and this man had the first right to take Ruth as his wife. If he chose not to, then Boaz could marry Ruth (3:13).

3:14
[m] Ro 14:16; 2Co 8:21

nised; and he said, "Don't let it be known that a woman came to the threshing-
floor."[m]
15He also said, "Bring me the shawl you are wearing and hold it out." When she
did so, he poured into it six measures of barley and put it on her. Then he[b] went back
to town.
16When Ruth came to her mother-in-law, Naomi asked, "How did it go, my
daughter?"
Then she told her everything Boaz had done for her 17and added, "He gave me these
six measures of barley, saying, 'Don't go back to your mother-in-law empty-
handed.' "
18Then Naomi said, "Wait, my daughter, until you find out what happens. For the
man will not rest until the matter is settled today."[n]

3:18
[n] Ps 37:3-5

b *15* Most Hebrew manuscripts; many Hebrew manuscripts, Vulgate and Syriac *she*

BOAZ

Heroes are easier to admire than to define. They are seldom conscious of their moments of heroism, and others may not recognise their acts as heroic. Heroes simply do the right thing at the right time, whether or not they realise the impact their action will have. Perhaps the one quality they share is a tendency to think of others before they think of themselves. Boaz was a hero.

In his dealings with other people, he was always sensitive to their needs. His words to his employees, relatives, and others were coloured with kindness. He offered help openly, not grudgingly. When he discovered who Ruth was, he took several steps to help her because she had been faithful to his relative Naomi. When Naomi advised Ruth to request his protection, he was ready to marry her if the legal complications could be worked out.

Boaz not only did what was right; he also did it right away. Of course he could not foresee all that his actions would accomplish. He could not have known that the child he would have by Ruth would be an ancestor of both David and Jesus. He only met the challenge of taking the right action in the situation facing him.

We are faced with this challenge in our daily choices. Like Naomi's nearer relative, we are often more concerned with making the easy choice than with making the right one. Yet more often than not, the right choice is clear. Ask God to give you a special awareness in your choices today as well as renewed commitment to make the right ones.

Strengths and accomplishments:
- A man of his word
- Sensitive to those in need, caring for his workers
- A keen sense of responsibility, integrity
- A successful and shrewd businessman

Lessons from his life:
- It can be heroic to do what must be done and to do it right
- God often uses little decisions to carry out his big plan

Vital statistics:
- Where: Bethlehem
- Occupation: Wealthy farmer
- Relatives: Elimelech, Naomi, Ruth

Key verse:
"I have also acquired Ruth the Moabitess, Mahlon's widow, as my wife, in order to maintain the name of the dead with his property, so that his name will not disappear from among his family or from the town records. Today you are witnesses!" (Ruth 4:10).

His story is told in the book of Ruth. He is also mentioned in Matthew 1:5.

3:18 Naomi implied that Boaz would follow through with his promise at once. He obviously had a reputation for keeping his word and would not rest until his task was completed. Such reliable people stand out in any age and culture. Do others regard you as one who will do what you say? Keeping your word and following through on commitments should be high on anyone's priority list. Building a reputation for integrity, however, must be done one brick, one act, at a time.

4. Ruth and Boaz are married

Boaz Marries Ruth

4 Meanwhile Boaz went up to the town gate and sat there. When the kinsman-
redeemer he had mentioned[a] came along, Boaz said, "Come over here, my
friend, and sit down." So he went over and sat down.
2Boaz took ten of the elders[b] of the town and said, "Sit here," and they did so.
3Then he said to the kinsman-redeemer, "Naomi, who has come back from Moab,
is selling the piece of land that belonged to our brother Elimelech. 4I thought I should
bring the matter to your attention and suggest that you buy it in the presence of these
seated here and in the presence of the elders of my people. If you will redeem it, do
so. But if you**[a]** will not, tell me, so I will know. For no-one has the right to do it
except you,[c] and I am next in line."
"I will redeem it," he said.
5Then Boaz said, "On the day you buy the land from Naomi and from Ruth the
Moabitess, you acquire**[b]** the dead man's widow, in order to maintain the name of
the dead with his property."[d]
6At this, the kinsman-redeemer said, "Then I cannot redeem[e] it because I might
endanger my own estate. You redeem it yourself. I cannot do it."
7(Now in earlier times in Israel, for the redemption and transfer of property to
become final, one party took off his sandal and gave it to the other. This was the
method of legalising transactions in Israel.)[f]
8So the kinsman-redeemer said to Boaz, "Buy it yourself." And he removed his
sandal.
9Then Boaz announced to the elders and all the people, "Today you are witnesses
that I have bought from Naomi all the property of Elimelech, Kilion and Mahlon. 10I
have also acquired Ruth the Moabitess, Mahlon's widow, as my wife, in order to
maintain the name of the dead with his property, so that his name will not disappear
from among his family or from the town records.[g] Today you are witnesses!"
11Then the elders and all those at the gate said, "We are witnesses.[h] May the LORD
make the woman who is coming into your home like Rachel and Leah,[i] who together
built up the house of Israel. May you have standing in Ephrathah[j] and be famous
in Bethlehem. 12Through the offspring the LORD gives you by this young woman, may
your family be like that of Perez,[k] whom Tamar bore to Judah."

The Genealogy of David

13So Boaz took Ruth and she became his wife. Then he went to her, and the LORD
enabled her to conceive,[l] and she gave birth to a son. 14The women[m] said to Naomi:
"Praise be to the LORD, who this day has not left you without a kinsman-redeemer.
May he become famous throughout Israel! 15He will renew your life and sustain you

4:1 [a]Ru 3:12
4:2 [b]1Ki 21:8; Pr 31:23
4:4 [c]Lev 25:25; Jer 32:7-8
4:5 [d]Ge 38:8; Dt 25:5-6; Ru 3:13; Mt 22:24
4:6 [e]Lev 25:25; Ru 3:13
4:7 [f]Dt 25:7-9
4:10 [g]Dt 25:6
4:11 [h]Dt 25:9 [i]Ps 127:3; 128:3 [j]Ge 35:16
4:12 [k]ver 18; Ge 38:29
4:13 [l]Ge 29:31; 33:5; Ru 3:11
4:14 [m]Lk 1:58

a *4* Many Hebrew manuscripts, Septuagint, Vulgate and Syriac; most Hebrew manuscripts *he* **b** *5* Hebrew; Vulgate and Syriac *Naomi, you acquire Ruth the Moabitess,*

4:1 Boaz knew he could find his relative at the town gate. This was the centre of activity. No-one could enter or leave the town without travelling through the gate. Merchants set up their temporary shops near the gate, which also served as the town hall. Here city officials gathered to transact business. Because there was so much activity, it was a good place to find witnesses (4:2) and an appropriate place for Boaz to make his transaction.

4:3 Boaz cleverly presented his case to the relative. First he brought in new information not yet mentioned in the story—Elimelech, Naomi's former husband, still had some property in the area that was now for sale. As the nearest relative, this man had the first right to buy the land, which he agreed to do (Leviticus 25:25). But then Boaz said that according to the law, if the relative bought the property he also had to marry the widow (probably because Mahlon, Ruth's former husband and Elimelech's son, had inherited the property). At this stipulation, the relative backed down. He did not want to complicate his inheritance. He may have feared that if he had a son through Ruth, some of his estate would transfer away from his family to the family of Elimelech. Whatever his reason, the way was now clear for Boaz to marry Ruth.

4:15 Ruth's love for her mother-in-law was known and recognised throughout the town. From the beginning of the book of Ruth to the end, her kindness towards others remained unchanged.

4:15 God brought great blessings out of Naomi's tragedy, even greater than "seven sons", or an abundance of heirs. Throughout her tough times, Naomi continued to trust God. And God, in his time, blessed her greatly. Even in our sorrow and calamity, God can bring great blessings. Be like Naomi, and don't turn your back on God when tragedy strikes. Instead of asking "How can God allow this to happen to me?" trust him. He will be with you in the hard times.

4:15 [n]Ru 1:16-17; 2:11-12; 1Sa 1:8

4:17 [o]ver 22; 1Sa 16:1, 18; 1Ch 2:12, 13

4:18 [p]Mt 1:3-6

4:19 [q]Ex 6:23

4:21 [r]Ru 2:1

in your old age. For your daughter-in-law, who loves you and who is better to you
than seven sons,[n] has given him birth."
16Then Naomi took the child, laid him in her lap and cared for him. 17The women
living there said, "Naomi has a son." And they named him Obed. He was the father
of Jesse,[o] the father of David.
18This, then, is the family line of Perez[p]:

Perez was the father of Hezron,
19Hezron the father of Ram,
Ram the father of Amminadab,[q]
20Amminadab the father of Nahshon,
Nahshon the father of Salmon,[c]
21Salmon the father of Boaz,[r]
Boaz the father of Obed,
22Obed the father of Jesse,
and Jesse the father of David.

[c] *20* A few Hebrew manuscripts, some Septuagint manuscripts and Vulgate (see also verse 21 and Septuagint of 1 Chron. 2:11); most Hebrew manuscripts *Salma*

4:16, 17 To some, the book of Ruth may be just a nice story about a girl who was fortunate. But in reality, the events recorded in Ruth were part of God's preparations for the births of David and of Jesus, the promised Messiah. Just as Ruth was unaware of this larger purpose in her life, we will not know the full purpose and importance of our lives until we are able to look back from the perspective of eternity. We must make our choices with God's eternal values in mind. Taking moral shortcuts and living for short-term pleasures are not good ways to move ahead. Because of Ruth's faithful obedience, her life and legacy were significant even though she couldn't see all the results. Live in faithfulness to God, knowing that the significance of your life will extend beyond your lifetime. The rewards will outweigh any sacrifice you may have made.

1 SAMUEL

Judges begin to rule 1375 B.C. (1220 B.C.)

Samuel born 1105 (1083)

VITAL STATISTICS

PURPOSE:
To record the life of Samuel, Israel's last judge; the reign and decline of Saul, the first king; and the choice and preparation of David, Israel's greatest king

AUTHOR:
Possibly Samuel, but also includes writings from the prophets Nathan and Gad (1 Chronicles 29:29)

SETTING:
The book begins in the days of the judges and describes Israel's transition from a theocracy (led by God) to a monarchy (led by a king)

KEY VERSES:
"And the LORD told him: 'Listen to all that the people are saying to you; it is not you they have rejected, but they have rejected me as their king . . . Now listen to them; but warn them solemnly and let them know what the king who will reign over them will do' " (8:7, 9).

KEY PEOPLE:
Eli, Hannah, Samuel, Saul, Jonathan, David

"RUNNERS take your marks," the starter barks his signal, and the crowd turns quiet attention to the athletes walking towards the line. "Get set" . . . in position now, muscles tense, nervously anticipating the sound of the gun. It resounds! And the race begins. In any contest, the start is important, but the finish is even more crucial. Often a front-runner will lose strength and fade to the middle of the pack. And there is the tragedy of the brilliant beginner who sets the pace for a time, but does not even finish. He abandons the race burned out, exhausted, or injured.

The book of 1 Samuel is about great beginnings . . . and tragic endings. It begins with Eli as high priest during the time of the judges. As a religious leader, Eli certainly must have begun his life with a close relationship to God. In his communication with Hannah, and in his training of her son Samuel, he demonstrated a clear understanding of God's purposes and call (chapters 1, 3). But his life ended in ignominy as his sacrilegious sons were judged by God and the sacred ark of the covenant fell into enemy hands (chapter 4). Eli's death marked the decline of the influence of the priesthood and the rise of the prophets in Israel.

Samuel was dedicated to God's service by his mother, Hannah. He became one of Israel's greatest prophets. He was a man of prayer who finished the work of the judges, began the school of the prophets, and anointed Israel's first kings. But even Samuel was not immune to finishing poorly. Like Eli's family, Samuel's sons turned away from God; they took bribes and perverted justice. The people rejected the leadership of the judges and priests and clamoured for a king "as all the other nations have" (8:5).

Saul also started quickly. A striking figure, this handsome (9:2) and humble (9:21; 10:22) man was God's choice as Israel's first king (10:24). His early reign was marked by leadership (chapter 11) and bravery (14:46–48). But he disobeyed God (chapter 15), became jealous and paranoid (chapters 18, 19), and finally had his kingship taken away from him by God (chapter 16). Saul's life continued steadily downwards. Obsessed with killing David (chapters 20—30), he consulted a medium (chapter 28) and finally committed suicide (chapter 31).

Among the events of Saul's life is another great beginner—David. A man who followed God (13:14; 16:7), David ministered to Saul (chapter 16), killed Goliath (chapter 17), and became a great warrior. But we'll have to wait until the book of 2 Samuel to see how David finished.

As you read 1 Samuel, note the transition from theocracy to monarchy, exult in the classic stories of David and Goliath, David and Jonathan, David and Abigail, and watch the rise of the influence of the prophets. But in the midst of reading all the history and adventure, determine to run your race as God's person from start to finish.

Samson becomes judge 1075 (1083)	*Saul becomes king 1050 (1045)*	*David born 1040*	*David anointed; Goliath slain 1025*	*David becomes king over Judah 1010*	*David becomes king over all Israel 1003*	*Solomon becomes king 970*	*The kingdom is divided 930*

THE BLUEPRINT

A. ELI AND SAMUEL
(1:1—7:17)
1. Samuel's birth and childhood
2. War with the Philistines

We see a vivid contrast between young Samuel and Eli's sons. Eli's sons were selfish, but Samuel was helpful. Eli's sons defrauded people, but Samuel grew in wisdom and gave the people messages from God. As an adult, Samuel became a prophet, priest, and judge over Israel. A person's actions reflect his character. This was true of Samuel and Eli's sons. It is also true of us. Strive, like Samuel, to keep your heart pure before God.

B. SAMUEL AND SAUL
(8:1—15:35)
1. Saul becomes king of Israel
2. God rejects Saul for disobedience

Saul showed great promise. He was strong, tall, and modest. God's Spirit came upon him, and Samuel was his counsellor. But Saul deliberately disobeyed God and became an evil king. We must not base our hopes or future on our potential. Instead, we must consistently obey God in all areas of life. God evaluates obedience, not potential.

C. SAUL AND DAVID
(16:1—31:13)
1. Samuel anoints David
2. David and Goliath
3. David and Jonathan become friends
4. Saul pursues David
5. Saul's defeat and death

David quickly killed Goliath, but waited patiently for God to deal with Saul. Although David was anointed to be Israel's next king, he had to wait years to realise this promise. The difficult circumstances in life and the times of waiting often refine, teach, and prepare us for the future responsibilities God has for us.

MEGATHEMES

THEME	EXPLANATION	IMPORTANCE
King	Because Israel suffered from corrupt priests and judges, the people wanted a king. They wanted to be organised like the surrounding nations. Though it was against his original purpose, God chose a king for them.	Establishing a monarchy did not solve Israel's problems. What God desires is the genuine devotion of each person's mind and heart to him. No government or set of laws can substitute for the rule of God in your heart and life.
God's Control	Israel prospered as long as the people regarded God as their true king. When the leaders strayed from God's law, God intervened in their personal lives and overruled their actions. In this way, God maintained ultimate control over Israel's history.	God is always at work in this world, even when we can't see what he is doing. No matter what kinds of pressures we must endure or how many changes we must face, God is ultimately in control of our situation. Being confident of God's sovereignty, we can face the difficult situations in our lives with boldness.
Leadership	God guided his people using different forms of leadership: judges, priests, prophets, kings. Those whom he chose for these different offices, such as Eli, Samuel, Saul, and David, portrayed different styles of leadership. Yet the success of each leader depended on his devotion to God, not his position, leadership style, wisdom, age, or strength.	When Eli, Samuel, Saul, and David disobeyed God, they faced tragic consequences. Sin affected what they accomplished for God and how some of them brought up their children. Being a real leader means letting God guide all aspects of your activities, values, and goals, including the way you bring up your children.
Obedience	For God, "to obey is better than sacrifice" (15:22). God wanted his people to obey, serve, and follow him with a whole heart rather than to maintain a superficial commitment based on tradition or ceremonial systems.	Although we are free from the sacrificial system of the Jewish law, we may still rely on outward observances to substitute for inward commitment. God desires that all our work and worship be motivated by genuine, heartfelt devotion to him.

God's Faithfulness	God faithfully kept the promises he made to Israel. He responded to his people with tender mercy and swift justice. In showing mercy, he faithfully acted in the best interests of his people. In showing justice, he was faithful to his word and perfect moral nature.	Because God is faithful, he can be counted on to be merciful towards us. Yet God is also just, and he will not tolerate rebellion against him. His faithfulness and unselfish love should inspire us to dedicate ourselves to him completely. We must never take his mercy for granted.

KEY PLACES IN 1 SAMUEL

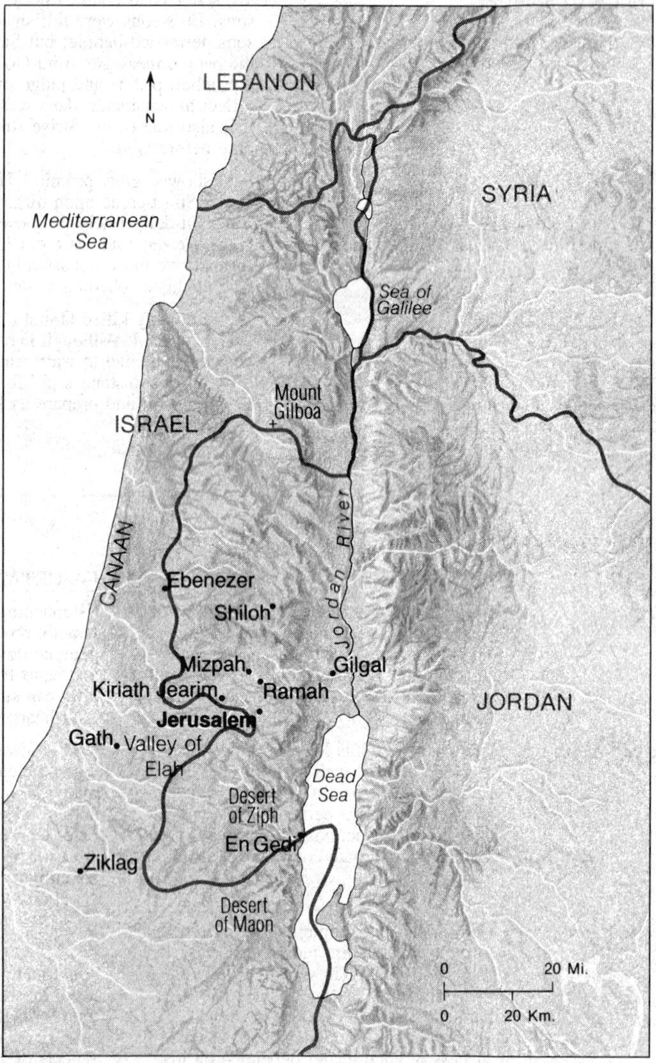

Modern names and boundaries are shown in grey.

1 Ramah Samuel was born in Ramah. Before his birth, Samuel's mother Hannah made a promise to God that she would dedicate her son to serve God alongside the priests in the tabernacle at Shiloh (1:1–2:11).

2 Shiloh The focal point of Israel's worship was at Shiloh, where the tabernacle and the ark of the covenant resided. Eli was the high priest, but his sons, Hophni and Phinehas, were evil men who took advantage of the people. Samuel, however, served God faithfully, and God blessed him as he grew (2:12–3:21).

3 Kiriath Jearim Israel was constantly at odds with the Philistines, and another battle was brewing. Hophni and Phinehas brought the ark of the covenant from Shiloh to the battlefield, believing that its mere presence would bring the Israelites victory. The Israelites were defeated by the Philistines at Ebenezer, and the ark was captured. However, the Philistines soon found out that the ark was not quite the great battle trophy they had expected. For God sent plagues upon every Philistine city into which the ark was brought. Finally, the Philistines sent it back to Kiriath Jearim in Israel (4:1–7:1).

4 Mizpah The Israelites' defeat made them realise that God was no longer blessing them. Samuel called the people together at Mizpah and asked them to fast and pray in sorrow for their sins. The assembly at Mizpah was a tempting target for the confident Philistines who advanced for an attack. But God intervened and routed their mighty army. Meanwhile, Samuel was judging cases throughout Israel. But as Samuel grew old, the people came to him at Ramah (his home base) demanding a king in order to be like the other nations. At Mizpah, Saul was chosen by sacred appointment to be Israel's first king with the blessing, but not the approval, of God and Samuel (7:2–10:27).

5 Gilgal A battle with the Ammonites proved Saul's leadership abilities to the people of Israel. He protected the people of Jabesh Gilead and scattered the Ammonite army. Samuel and the people crowned Saul as king of Israel at Gilgal (11:1–15).

6 Valley of Elah Saul won many other battles, but with time he proved to be arrogant, sinful, and rebellious until God finally rejected him as king. Unknown to Saul, a young shepherd and musician named David was anointed to be Israel's next king. But it would be many years before David sat upon the throne. Ironically, Saul asked David to play the harp in his palace. Saul grew to like David so much that he made him his personal armour-bearer. In one particular battle with the Philistines in the Valley of Elah, David killed Goliath, the Philistines' mightiest soldier. But this victory was the beginning of the end of Saul's love for David. The Israelites praised David more than Saul, causing Saul to become so jealous that he plotted to kill David (12:1–22:23).

7 The Desert Even anointed kings are not exempt from troubles. David literally ran for his life from King Saul, hiding with his band of followers in the Desert of Ziph (where the men of Ziph constantly betrayed him), the Desert of Maon, and the Desert of En Gedi. Though he had opportunities to kill Saul, David refused to do so because Saul was God's anointed king (23:1–26:25).

8 Gath David moved his men and family to Gath, the Philistine city where King Achish lived. Saul then stopped chasing him. The Philistines seemed to welcome this famous fugitive from Israel (27:1–4).

9 Ziklag Desiring privacy in return for his pretended loyalty to King Achish, David asked for a city in which to house his men and family. Achish gave him Ziklag. From there David conducted raids against the cities of the Geshurites, Girzites, and Amalekites, making sure no-one escaped to tell the tale (27:5–12). David later conquered the Amalekites after they raided Ziklag (30:1–31).

10 Mount Gilboa War with the Philistines broke out again in the north, near Mount Gilboa. Saul, who no longer relied on God, consulted a witch in a desperate attempt to contact Samuel for help. In the meantime, David was sent back to Ziklag because the Philistine commanders did not trust his loyalty in battle against Israel. The Philistines slaughtered the Israelites on Mount Gilboa, killing King Saul and his three sons, including David's loyal friend Jonathan. Without God, Saul led a bitter and misguided life. The consequences of his sinful actions affected not only him, but hurt his family and the entire nation as well (28:1–31:13).

1:1
[a]Jos 17:17-18
[b]1Ch 6:27, 34

1:2
[c]Dt 21:15-17; Lk 2:36

1:3
[d]ver 21; Ex 23:14; 34:23; Lk 2:41
[e]Dt 12:5-7

A. ELI AND SAMUEL (1:1–7:17)

Israel has been ruled by judges for over 200 years. Eli and Samuel are the last of those judges. Samuel is born near the end of Eli's life. He grows up in the tabernacle as a priest-in-training under Eli and is well qualified to serve Israel as both a priest and a judge. Although the nation has fallen away from God, it is clear that God is preparing Samuel from the very beginning to lead the nation back to right living. God is always in control; he is able to bring his people back to him.

1. Samuel's birth and childhood

The Birth of Samuel

1 There was a certain man from Ramathaim, a Zuphite[a] from the hill country[a]
of Ephraim, whose name was Elkanah[b] son of Jeroham, the son of Elihu, the
son of Tohu, the son of Zuph, an Ephraimite. 2He had two wives;[c] one was called
Hannah and the other Peninnah. Peninnah had children, but Hannah had none.
3Year after year[d] this man went up from his town to worship[e] and sacrifice to

a *1* Or *from Ramathaim Zuphim*

1:1 The book of 1 Samuel begins in the days when the judges still ruled Israel, possibly during the closing years of Samson's life. Samuel was Israel's last judge and the first priest and prophet to serve during the time of a king. He was the best example of what a good judge should be, governing the people by God's word and not by his own impulses. Samuel was the man who anointed Saul as Israel's first king.

1:2 Although many great Old Testament leaders (such as Abraham, Jacob, and David) had more than one wife, this was not God's original intention for marriage. Genesis 2:24 states that in marriage, two people become one flesh. Why then did polygamy exist among God's people? First, it was to produce more offspring to help in the man's work and to assure the continuation of the man's family line. Numerous children were a symbol of status and wealth. Second, in societies where many young men were killed in battle, polygamy became an accepted way of supporting women who otherwise would have remained unmarried and, very likely, destitute. Nevertheless, polygamy often caused serious family problems, as we see in this story of Hannah and Peninnah.

1:3 The tabernacle (Tent of Meeting) was located at Shiloh, the religious centre of the nation (see Joshua 18:1). Three times a year all Israelite men were required to attend a religious feast held at the tabernacle: the Passover with the Feast of Unleavened Bread, the Feast of Weeks, and the Feast of Tabernacles (Deuteronomy 16:16). Elkanah made this pilgrimage regularly to fulfil God's commands. (See Exodus 23:14–17 for the regulations concerning the pilgrimage, and see the note on Exodus 40:34 for more on the tabernacle.)

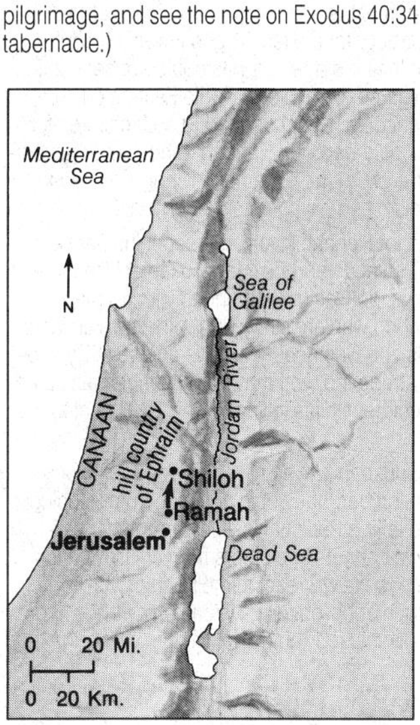

THE JOURNEY TO SHILOH Each year Elkanah and his family travelled from their home at Ramah to Shiloh, where they worshipped and sacrificed at God's tabernacle.

the LORD Almighty at Shiloh,[f] where Hophni and Phinehas, the two sons of Eli, were
priests of the LORD. 4Whenever the day came for Elkanah to sacrifice,[g] he would
give portions of the meat to his wife Peninnah and to all her sons and daughters. 5But
to Hannah he gave a double portion because he loved her, and the LORD had closed
her womb.[h] 6And because the LORD had closed her womb, her rival kept provoking
her in order to irritate her.[i] 7This went on year after year. Whenever Hannah went
up to the house of the LORD, her rival provoked her till she wept and would not eat.
8Elkanah her husband would say to her, "Hannah, why are you weeping? Why don't
you eat? Why are you downhearted? Don't I mean more to you than ten sons?[j]"
9Once when they had finished eating and drinking in Shiloh, Hannah stood up. Now
Eli the priest was sitting on a chair by the doorpost of the LORD's temple.[b][k] 10In
bitterness of soul[l] Hannah wept much and prayed to the LORD. 11And she made a
vow, saying, "O LORD Almighty, if you will only look upon your servant's misery
and remember[m] me, and not forget your servant but give her a son, then I will give
him to the LORD for all the days of his life, and no razor[n] will ever be used on his
head."
12As she kept on praying to the LORD, Eli observed her mouth. 13Hannah was
praying in her heart, and her lips were moving but her voice was not heard. Eli thought
she was drunk 14and said to her, "How long will you keep on getting drunk? Get rid
of your wine."
15"Not so, my lord," Hannah replied, "I am a woman who is deeply troubled. I have
not been drinking wine or beer; I was pouring[o] out my soul to the LORD. 16Do not
take your servant for a wicked woman; I have been praying here out of my great
anguish and grief."
17Eli answered, "Go in peace,[p] and may the God of Israel grant you what you have
asked of him.[q]"
18She said, "May your servant find favour in your eyes.[r]" Then she went her way
and ate something, and her face was no longer downcast.[s]
19Early the next morning they arose and worshipped before the LORD and then went
back to their home at Ramah. Elkanah lay with Hannah his wife, and the LORD

[b] 9 That is, tabernacle

1:3 [f] Jos 18:1
1:4 [g] Dt 12:17-18
1:5 [h] Ge 16:1; 30:2
1:6 [i] Job 24:21
1:8 [j] Ru 4:15
1:9 [k] 1Sa 3:3
1:10 [l] Job 7:11
1:11 [m] Ge 8:1; 28:20; 29:32 [n] Nu 6:1-21; Jdg 13:5
1:15 [o] Ps 42:4; 62:8; La 2:19
1:17 [p] Jdg 18:6; 1Sa 25:35; 2Ki 5:19; Mk 5:34 [q] Ps 20:3-5
1:18 [r] Ru 2:13 [s] Ecc 9:7; Ro 15:13

1:6 Hannah had been unable to conceive children, and in Old Testament times, a childless woman was considered a failure. Her barrenness was a social embarrassment for her husband. Children were a very important part of the society's economic structure. They were a source of labour for the family, and it was their duty to care for their parents in their old age. If a wife could not bear children she was often obligated, by ancient Middle Eastern custom, to give one of her servant girls to her husband to bear children for her. Although Elkanah could have left Hannah (a husband was permitted to divorce a barren wife), he remained lovingly devoted to her despite social criticism and his rights under civil law.

1:7 Part of God's plan for Hannah involved postponing her years of childbearing. While Peninnah and Elkanah looked at Hannah's outward circumstances, God was moving ahead with his plan. Think of those in your world who are struggling with God's timing in answering their prayers and who need your love and help. By supporting those who are struggling, you may help them remain steadfast in their faith and confident in his timing to bring fulfilment to their lives.

1:8 Hannah knew her husband loved her, but even his encouragement could not comfort her. She could not keep from listening to Peninnah's jeers and letting Peninnah's words erode her self-confidence. Although we cannot keep others from unjustly criticising us, we can choose how we will react to their hurtful words. Rather than dwelling upon our problems, we can enjoy the loving relationships God has given us. By so doing, we can exchange self-pity for hope.

1:10 Hannah had good reason to feel discouraged and bitter. She was unable to bear children; she shared her husband with a woman who ridiculed her (1:7); her loving husband could not solve her problem (1:8); and even the high priest misunderstood her motives (1:14). But instead of retaliating or giving up hope, Hannah prayed. She brought her problem honestly before God.

Each of us may face times of barrenness when nothing "comes to birth" in our work, service, or relationships. It is difficult to pray in faith when we feel so ineffective. But, as Hannah discovered, prayer opens the way for God to work (1:19, 20).

1:11 Be careful what you promise in prayer because God may take you up on it. Hannah so desperately wanted a child that she was willing to strike a bargain with God. God took her up on her promise, and to Hannah's credit, she did her part, even though it was painful (1:27, 28).

Although we are not in a position to barter with God, he may still choose to answer a prayer that has an attached promise. When you pray, ask yourself, "Will I follow through on any promises I make to God if he grants my request?" It is dishonest and dangerous to ignore a promise, especially to God. God keeps his promises, and he expects you to keep yours.

1:18 Earlier Hannah had been discouraged to the point of being physically sick and unable to eat. At this point, she returned home well and happy. The change in her attitude may be attributed to three factors: (1) she honestly prayed to God (1:11); (2) she received encouragement from Eli (1:17); (3) she resolved to leave the problem with God (1:18). This is the antidote for discouragement: tell God how you really feel and leave your problems with him. Then rely upon the support of good friends and counsellors.

remembered[t] her. 20So in the course of time Hannah conceived and gave birth to a
son. She named[u] him Samuel,[c] saying, "Because I asked the LORD for him."

Hannah Dedicates Samuel

21When the man Elkanah went up with all his family to offer the annual[v] sacrifice
to the LORD and to fulfil his vow,[w] 22Hannah did not go. She said to her husband,
"After the boy is weaned, I will take him and present[x] him before the LORD, and he
will live there always."
23"Do what seems best to you," Elkanah her husband told her. "Stay here until you
have weaned him; only may the LORD make good[y] his[d] word." So the woman stayed
at home and nursed her son until she had weaned him.
24After he was weaned, she took the boy with her, young as he was, along with
a three-year-old bull,[e][z] an ephah[f] of flour and a skin of wine, and brought him to
the house of the LORD at Shiloh. 25When they had slaughtered the bull, they brought
the boy to Eli, 26and she said to him, "As surely as you live, my lord, I am the woman
who stood here beside you praying to the LORD. 27I prayed[a] for this child, and the
LORD has granted me what I asked of him. 28So now I give him to the LORD. For his
whole life[b] he shall be given over to the LORD." And he worshipped the LORD there.

Hannah's Prayer

2 Then Hannah prayed and said:[a]

"My heart rejoices[b] in the LORD;
in the LORD my horn[a][c] is lifted high.
My mouth boasts over my enemies,
for I delight in your deliverance.

2"There is no-one holy[b][d] like the LORD;
there is no-one besides you;
there is no Rock[e] like our God.

3"Do not keep talking so proudly
or let your mouth speak such arrogance,[f]
for the LORD is a God who knows,
and by him deeds[g] are weighed.[h]

4"The bows of the warriors are broken,[i]
but those who stumbled are armed with strength.

1:19 [t]Ge 4:1; 30:22
1:20 [u]Ge 41:51-52; Ex 2:10, 22; Mt 1:21
1:21 [v]ver 3 [w]Dt 12:11
1:22 [x]ver 11, 28; Lk 2:22
1:23 [y]ver 17; Nu 30:7
1:24 [z]Nu 15:8-10; Dt 12:5; Jos 18:1
1:27 [a]ver 11-13; Ps 66:19-20
1:28 [b]ver 11, 22; Ge 24:26, 52
2:1 [a]Lk 1:46-55 [b]Ps 9:14; 13:5 [c]Ps 89:17, 24; 92:10; Isa 12:2-3
2:2 [d]Ex 15:11; Lev 19:2 [e]Dt 32:30-31; 2Sa 22:2, 32
2:3 [f]Pr 8:13 [g]1Sa 16:7; 1Ki 8:39 [h]Pr 16:2; 24:11-12
2:4 [i]Ps 37:15

[c] *20 Samuel* sounds like the Hebrew for *heard of God.* [d] *23* Masoretic Text; Dead Sea Scrolls, Septuagint and Syriac *your* [e] *24* Dead Sea Scrolls, Septuagint and Syriac; Masoretic Text *with three bulls* [f] *24* That is, probably about 3/5 bushel (about 22 litres) [a] *1 Horn* here symbolises strength; also in verse 10. [b] *2* Or *no Holy One*

1:26–28 To do what she promised (1:11), Hannah gave up what she wanted most – her son – and presented him to Eli to serve in the house of the Lord. In dedicating her only son to God, Hannah was dedicating her entire life and future to God. Because Samuel's life was from God, Hannah was not really giving him up. Rather, she was returning him to God who had given Samuel to Hannah in the first place. These verses illustrate the kind of gifts we should give to God. Do your gifts cost you little (Sunday mornings, a comfortable tithe), or are they gifts of sacrifice? Are you presenting God with tokens, or are you presenting him with your entire life?

1:28 Samuel was probably three years old – the customary age for weaning – when his mother left him at the tabernacle. By saying, "I give him to the LORD," Hannah meant that she was dedicating Samuel to God for lifetime service. She did not, of course, forget her much-wanted son. She visited him regularly. And each year she brought him a robe just like Eli's (2:19). In later years, Samuel lived in Ramah (7:17), his parents' hometown (1:19, 20).

2:1–10 Hannah praised God for his answer to her prayer for a son. The theme of her poetic prayer is her confidence in God's sovereignty and her thankfulness for everything he had done. Mary, the mother of Jesus, modelled her own praise song, called the Magnificat, after Hannah's prayer (Luke 1:46–55). Like Hannah and Mary, we should be confident of God's ultimate control over the events in our lives, and we should be thankful for the ways God has blessed us. By praising God for all good gifts, we acknowledge his ultimate control over all the affairs of life.

2:2 Hannah praised God for being a Rock – firm, strong, and unchanging. In our fast-paced world, friends come and go, and circumstances change. It's difficult to find a solid foundation that will not change. Those who devote their lives to achievements, causes, or possessions have as their security that which is finite and changeable. The possessions that we work so hard to obtain will all pass away. But God is always present. Hope in him. He will never fail.

2:3 No doubt as Hannah said these words, she was thinking of Peninnah's arrogance and chiding. Hannah did not have to get even with Peninnah. She knew that God is all-knowing, and that he will judge all sin and pride. Hannah wisely left judgment up to God. Resist the temptation to take justice into your own hands. God will weigh your deeds as well as those who have wronged you.

5 Those who were full hire themselves out for food,
but those who were hungry hunger no more.
She who was barren[j] has borne seven children,
but she who has had many sons pines away.

6 "The LORD brings death and makes alive;[k]
he brings down to the grave[c] and raises up.[l]
7 The LORD sends poverty and wealth;[m]
he humbles and he exalts.[n]
8 He raises[o] the poor from the dust
and lifts the needy from the ash heap;
he seats them with princes
and has them inherit a throne of honour.[p]

"For the foundations[q] of the earth are the LORD's;
upon them he has set the world.
9 He will guard the feet[r] of his saints,
but the wicked will be silenced in darkness.[s]

"It is not by strength[t] that one prevails;
10 those who oppose the LORD will be shattered.[u]
He will thunder[v] against them from heaven;
the LORD will judge[w] the ends of the earth.

"He will give strength[x] to his king
and exalt the horn[y] of his anointed."

11 Then Elkanah went home to Ramah, but the boy ministered[z] before the LORD
under Eli the priest.

Eli's Wicked Sons

12 Eli's sons were wicked men; they had no regard[a] for the LORD. 13 Now it was
the practice of the priests with the people that whenever anyone offered a sacrifice
and while the meat[b] was being boiled, the servant of the priest would come with a
three-pronged fork in his hand. 14 He would plunge it into the pan or kettle or cauldron

c 6 Hebrew *Sheol*

2:5 [j]Ps 113:9; Jer 15:9
2:6 [k]Dt 32:39 [l]Isa 26:19
2:7 [m]Dt 8:18 [n]Job 5:11; Ps 75:7
2:8 [o]Ps 113:7-8 [p]Job 36:7 [q]Job 38:4
2:9 [r]Ps 91:12 [s]Mt 8:12 [t]Ps 33:16-17
2:10 [u]Ps 2:9 [v]Ps 18:13 [w]Ps 96:13 [x]Ps 21:1 [y]Ps 89:24
2:11 [z]ver 18; 1Sa 3:1
2:12 [a]Jer 2:8; 9:6
2:13 [b]Lev 7:29-34

2:10 Because we live in a world where evil abounds and a nuclear holocaust always threatens, we may forget that God is in control. Hannah saw God as (1) solid as a rock (2:2), (2) the one who knows what we do (2:3), (3) sovereign over all the affairs of people (2:4–8), and (4) the supreme judge who administers perfect justice (2:10). Remembering God's sovereign control helps us put both world and personal events in perspective.

2:11 Samuel "ministered before the LORD under Eli the priest". In other words, Samuel was Eli's helper or assistant. In this role, Samuel's responsibilities would have included opening the tabernacle doors each morning (3:15), cleaning the furniture, and sweeping the floors. As he grew older, Samuel would have assisted Eli in offering sacrifices. The fact that he was wearing a linen ephod (a garment worn only by priests) shows that he was a priest-in-training (2:18). Because Samuel was Eli's helper, he was God's helper too. When you serve others – even in carrying out ordinary tasks – you are serving God. Because ultimately we serve God, every job has dignity.

2:12ff The law stipulated that the needs of all the Levites were to be met through the people's tithes (Numbers 18:20–24; Joshua 13:14, 33). Because Eli's sons were priests, they were to be taken care of this way. But Eli's sons took advantage of their position to satisfy their lust for power, possessions, and control. Their contempt and arrogance towards both people and worship undermined the integrity of the whole priesthood.

Eli knew that his sons were evil, but he did little to correct or stop them, even when the integrity of God's sanctuary was threatened. As the high priest, Eli should have responded by executing his sons (Numbers 15:22–31). No wonder he chose not to confront the situation. But by ignoring their selfish actions, Eli let his sons ruin their own lives and the lives of many others. There are times when serious problems must be confronted, even if the process and consequences could be painful.

2:13, 14 This fork was a utensil used in the tabernacle for offering sacrifices. Made of bronze (Exodus 27:3), it usually had three prongs to hook the meat that was to be offered on the altar. Eli's sons used the fork to take more meat from the pot than was due to them.

2:13–17 What were Eli's sons doing wrong? They were taking parts of the sacrifices *before* they were offered to God on the altar. They were also eating meat before the fat was burned off. This was against God's laws (Leviticus 3:3–5). In effect, Eli's sons were treating God's offerings with contempt. Offerings were given to show honour and respect to God while seeking forgiveness for sins, but through their irreverence, Eli's sons were actually sinning while making the offerings. To add to their sins, they were also sleeping with the women who served there (2:22).

Like Eli's sons, some religious leaders look down on the faith of ordinary people and treat their offerings to God casually or even with contempt. God harshly judges those who lead his people astray or scorn what is devoted to him (Numbers 18:32).

2:17 [c]Mal 2:7-9
2:18 [d]ver 11; 1Sa 3:1 [e]ver 28
2:19 [f]1Sa 1:3
2:20 [g]1Sa 1:11, 27-28; Lk 2:34
2:21 [h]Ge 21:1

or pot, and the priest would take for himself whatever the fork brought up. This is
how they treated all the Israelites who came to Shiloh. 15 But even before the fat was
burned, the servant of the priest would come and say to the man who was sacrificing,
"Give the priest some meat to roast; he won't accept boiled meat from you, but only
raw."
16 If the man said to him, "Let the fat be burned up first, and then take whatever
you want," the servant would then answer, "No, hand it over now; if you don't, I'll
take it by force."
17 This sin of the young men was very great in the LORD's sight, for they[d] were
treating the LORD's offering with contempt.[c]
18 But Samuel was ministering[d] before the LORD—a boy wearing a linen ephod.[e]
19 Each year his mother made him a little robe and took it to him when she went up
with her husband to offer the annual[f] sacrifice. 20 Eli would bless Elkanah and his
wife, saying, "May the LORD give you children by this woman to take the place of
the one she prayed[g] for and gave to the LORD." Then they would go home. 21 And
the LORD was gracious to Hannah;[h] she conceived and gave birth to three sons and

d *17 Or men*

HANNAH

Hannah's prayer shows us that all we have and receive is on loan from God. Hannah might have had many excuses for being a possessive mother. But when God answered her prayer, she kept her promise to dedicate Samuel to God's service.

She discovered that the greatest joy in having a child is to give that child fully and freely back to God. She entered motherhood prepared to do what all mothers must eventually do—let go of their children.

When children are born, they are completely dependent upon their parents for all their basic necessities. This causes some parents to forget that those same children will grow towards independence within the space of a few short years. Being sensitive to the different stages of that healthy process will greatly strengthen family relationships; resisting or denying that process will cause great pain. We must gradually let go of our children in order to allow them to become mature, interdependent adults.

Strengths and accomplishments:
- Mother of Samuel, Israel's greatest judge
- Fervent in worship; effective in prayer
- Willing to go through with even a costly commitment

Weakness and mistake:
- Struggled with her sense of self-worth because she was unable to have children

Lessons from her life:
- God hears and answers prayer
- Our children are gifts from God
- God is concerned for the oppressed and afflicted

Vital statistics:
- Where: Ephraim
- Occupation: Housewife
- Relatives: Husband: Elkanah. Son: Samuel. Later, three other sons and two daughters
- Contemporary: Eli, the priest

Key verses:
"And she said to him, 'As surely as you live, my lord, I am the woman who stood here beside you praying to the LORD. I prayed for this child, and the LORD has granted me what I asked of him. So now I give him to the LORD. For his whole life he shall be given over to the LORD' " (1 Samuel 1:26–28).

Her story is told in 1 Samuel 1, 2.

2:18 Samuel wore a linen ephod. *Ephods,* long sleeveless vests made of plain linen, were worn by all priests. The high priest's ephod carried special significance. It was embroidered with a variety of bright colours. Attached to it was the breastplate, a bib-like garment with gold embroidered shoulder straps. Twelve precious gemstones were attached to the breastplate, each stone representing one of the tribes of Israel. A pouch on the ephod held the Urim and the Thummim, two small objects used to determine God's will in certain national matters.

2:21 God honoured the desires of faithful Hannah. We never hear about Peninnah or her children again, but Samuel was used mightily by God. God also gave Hannah five children in addition to Samuel. God often blesses us in ways we do not expect. Hannah never expected to have a child at her age, much less six children! Don't resent God's timing. His blessings might not be immediate, but they will come if we are faithful to do what he says in his word.

two daughters. Meanwhile, the boy Samuel grew[i] up in the presence of the LORD.
22Now Eli, who was very old, heard about everything his sons were doing to all
Israel and how they slept with the women[j] who served at the entrance to the Tent
of Meeting. 23So he said to them, "Why do you do such things? I hear from all the
people about these wicked deeds of yours. 24No, my sons; it is not a good report that
I hear spreading among the LORD's people. 25If a man sins against another man, God[e]
may mediate for him; but if a man sins against the LORD, who will[k] intercede[l] for
him?" His sons, however, did not listen to their father's rebuke, for it was the LORD's
will to put them to death.
26And the boy Samuel continued to grow[m] in stature and in favour with the LORD
and with men.

Prophecy Against the House of Eli

27Now a man of God[n] came to Eli and said to him, "This is what the LORD says:
'Did I not clearly reveal myself to your father's house when they were in Egypt under
Pharaoh? 28I chose[o] your father out of all the tribes of Israel to be my priest, to go
up to my altar, to burn incense, and to wear an ephod[p] in my presence. I also gave
your father's house all the offerings made with fire by the Israelites. 29Why do you[f]
scorn my sacrifice and offering[q] that I prescribed for my dwelling?[r] Why do you
honour your sons more than me by fattening yourselves on the choice parts of every
offering made by my people Israel?'
30"Therefore the LORD, the God of Israel, declares: 'I promised that your house and
your father's house would minister before me for ever.[s]' But now the LORD declares:
'Far be it from me! Those who honour me I will honour,[t] but those who despise[u]
me will be disdained. 31The time is coming when I will cut short your strength and
the strength of your father's house, so that there will not be an old man in your family
line[v] 32and you will see distress in my dwelling. Although good will be done to Israel,
in your family line there will never be an old man.[w] 33Every one of you that I do
not cut off from my altar will be spared only to blind your eyes with tears and to grieve
your heart, and all your descendants will die in the prime of life.
34" 'And what happens to your two sons, Hophni and Phinehas, will be a sign to
you—they will both die[x] on the same day.[y] 35I will raise up for myself a faithful
priest,[z] who will do according to what is in my heart and mind. I will firmly establish
his house, and he will minister before my anointed[a] one always. 36Then everyone
left in your family line will come and bow down before him for a piece of silver and
a crust of bread and plead, "Appoint me to some priestly office so that I can have food
to eat.[b]" ' "

[e] 25 Or *the judges* [f] 29 The Hebrew is plural.

2:21 [i] ver 26; Jdg 13:24; 1Sa 3:19; Lk 2:40
2:22 [j] Ex 38:8
2:25 [k] Nu 15:30; Jos 11:20 [l] Dt 1:17; 1Sa 3:14; Heb 10:26
2:26 [m] ver 21; Lk 2:52
2:27 [n] Ex 4:14-16; 1Ki 13:1
2:28 [o] Ex 28:1 [p] Lev 8:7-8
2:29 [q] ver 12-17 [r] Dt 12:5; Mt 10:37
2:30 [s] Ex 29:9 [t] Ps 50:23; 91:15 [u] Mal 2:9
2:31 [v] 1Sa 4:11-18; 22:16-20
2:32 [w] 1Ki 2:26-27; Zec 8:4
2:34 [x] 1Sa 4:11 [y] 1Ki 13:3
2:35 [z] 1Sa 12:3; 1Ki 2:35 [a] 1Sa 16:13; 2Sa 7:11, 27; 1Ki 11:38
2:36 [b] 1Ki 2:27

2:23–25 Eli's sons knew better, but they continued to disobey God deliberately by cheating, seducing, and robbing the people. Therefore, God planned to kill them. Any sin is wrong, but sin carried out deliberately and deceitfully is the worst kind. When we sin out of ignorance, we deserve punishment. But when we sin intentionally, the consequences will be more severe. Don't ignore God's warnings about sin. Abandon sin before it becomes a way of life.

2:25 Does a loving God really will or want to put people to death? Consider the situation in the tabernacle. A person made an offering in order to have his sins forgiven, and Eli's sons stole the offering and made a sham of the person's repentant attitude. God, in his love for Israel, could not permit this situation to continue. He allowed Eli's sons to die as a result of their own boastful presumption. They took the ark into battle, thinking it would protect them. But God withdrew his protection, and the wicked sons of Eli were killed (4:10, 11).

2:29 Eli had a difficult time rearing his sons. He apparently did not take any strong disciplinary action with them when he became aware of their wrongdoing. But Eli was not just a father trying to handle his rebellious sons; he was the high priest ignoring the sins of priests under his jurisdiction. As a result, the Lord took the necessary disciplinary action that Eli would not.

Eli was guilty of honouring his sons above God by letting them continue in their sinful ways. Is there a situation in your life, family, or work that you allow to continue even though you know it is wrong? If so, you may become as guilty as those engaged in the wrong act.

2:31, 35, 36 For the fulfilment of this prediction see 1 Kings 2:26, 27. This is where Solomon removed Abiathar from his position, thus ending Eli's line. Then God raised up Zadok, a priest under David and then high priest under Solomon. Zadok's line was probably still in place as late as the days of Ezra.

2:35 "My anointed one" refers to the king (see 2:10). God was saying that his faithful priest would serve his king for ever.

The LORD *Calls Samuel*

3 The boy Samuel ministered[a] before the LORD under Eli. In those days the word
of the LORD was rare;[b] there were not many visions.[c]
2 One night Eli, whose eyes[d] were becoming so weak that he could barely see, was
lying down in his usual place. 3 The lamp[e] of God had not yet gone out, and Samuel
was lying down in the temple[a] of the LORD, where the ark of God was. 4 Then the
LORD called Samuel.
Samuel answered, "Here I am.[f]" 5 And he ran to Eli and said, "Here I am; you
called me."
But Eli said, "I did not call; go back and lie down." So he went and lay down.
6 Again the LORD called, "Samuel!" And Samuel got up and went to Eli and said,
"Here I am; you called me."
"My son," Eli said, "I did not call; go back and lie down."
7 Now Samuel did not yet know the LORD: The word of the LORD had not yet been
revealed[g] to him.
8 The LORD called Samuel a third time, and Samuel got up and went to Eli and said,
"Here I am; you called me."
Then Eli realised that the LORD was calling the boy. 9 So Eli told Samuel, "Go and
lie down, and if he calls you, say, 'Speak, LORD, for your servant is listening.' " So
Samuel went and lay down in his place.
10 The LORD came and stood there, calling as at the other times, "Samuel! Samuel!"
Then Samuel said, "Speak, for your servant is listening."
11 And the LORD said to Samuel: "See, I am about to do something in Israel that
will make the ears of everyone who hears of it tingle.[h] 12 At that time I will carry
out against Eli everything[i] I spoke against his family—from beginning to end. 13 For
I told him that I would judge his family for ever because of the sin he knew about;
his sons made themselves contemptible,[b] and he failed to restrain[j] them. 14 Therefore, I swore to the house of Eli, 'The guilt of Eli's house will never be atoned[k] for
by sacrifice or offering.' "
15 Samuel lay down until morning and then opened the doors of the house of the
LORD. He was afraid to tell Eli the vision, 16 but Eli called him and said, "Samuel,
my son."
Samuel answered, "Here I am."
17 "What was it he said to you?" Eli asked. "Do not hide it from me. May God deal
with you, be it ever so severely,[l] if you hide from me anything he told you." 18 So
Samuel told him everything, hiding nothing from him. Then Eli said, "He is the LORD;
let him do what is good in his eyes."[m]
19 The LORD was with[n] Samuel as he grew[o] up, and he let none[p] of his words

[a] *3* That is, tabernacle [b] *13* Masoretic Text; an ancient Hebrew scribal tradition and Septuagint *sons blasphemed God*

3:1 [a] 1Sa 2:11 [b] Ps 74:9 [c] Am 8:11
3:2 [d] 1Sa 4:15
3:3 [e] Lev 24:1-4
3:4 [f] Isa 6:8
3:7 [g] Ac 19:12
3:11 [h] 2Ki 21:12; Jer 19:3
3:12 [i] 1Sa 2:27-36
3:13 [j] 1Sa 2:12, 17, 22, 29-31
3:14 [k] Lev 15:30-31; 1Sa 2:25; Isa 22:14
3:17 [l] Ru 1:17; 2Sa 3:35
3:18 [m] Job 2:10; Isa 39:8
3:19 [n] Ge 21:22; 39:2 [o] 1Sa 2:21 [p] 1Sa 9:6

3:1-5 Although God had spoken directly and audibly with Moses and Joshua, his word became rare during the three centuries of rule by judges. By Eli's time, no prophets were speaking God's messages to Israel. Why? Look at the attitude of Eli's sons. They either refused to listen to God or allowed greed to get in the way of any communication with him.

Listening and responding is vital in a relationship with God. Although God does not always use the sound of a human voice, he always speaks clearly through his word. To receive his messages, we must be ready to listen and to act upon what he tells us. Like Samuel, be ready to say "Here I am" when God calls you to action.

3:2, 3 The ark of God was kept in the Most Holy Place, the innermost room of the tabernacle where only the high priest could enter once a year. In front of the Most Holy Place was the Holy Place, a small room where the other sacred furniture of the tabernacle was kept (the altar of incense, the bread of the Presence, the lampstand). Just outside the Holy Place was a court with small rooms where the priests were to stay. Samuel probably slept here with the other priests, only a few yards away from the ark.

3:8, 9 One would naturally expect an audible message from God to be given to the priest Eli and not to the child Samuel. Eli was older and more experienced, and he held the proper position. But God's chain of command is based on faith, not on age or position. In finding faithful followers, God may use unexpected channels. Be prepared for the Lord to work at any place, at any time, and through anyone he chooses.

3:13 Eli had spent his entire life in service to God. His responsibility was to oversee all the worship in Israel. But in pursuing this great mission he neglected the responsibilities in his own home. Don't let your desire to do God's work cause you to neglect your family. If you do, your mission may degenerate into a quest for personal importance, and your family will suffer the consequences of your neglect.

3:14 *Atoned for* means "forgiven". God was saying that the sin of Eli's sons could not be covered by sacrifice and that they would be punished.

fall to the ground. 20And all Israel from Dan to Beersheba[q] recognised that Samuel 3:20 q Jdg 20:1
was attested as a prophet of the LORD. 21The LORD continued to appear at Shiloh, and
there he revealed[r] himself to Samuel through his word.
4 And Samuel's word came to all Israel. 3:21 r ver 10

2. War with the Philistines

The Philistines Capture the Ark

4:1 a 1Sa 7:12; b Jos 12:18; 1Sa 29:1
Now the Israelites went out to fight against the Philistines. The Israelites camped
at Ebenezer,[a] and the Philistines at Aphek.[b] 2The Philistines deployed their forces
to meet Israel, and as the battle spread, Israel was defeated by the Philistines, who
killed about four thousand of them on the battlefield. 3When the soldiers returned to 4:3
camp, the elders of Israel asked, "Why[c] did the LORD bring defeat upon us today c Jos 7:7
before the Philistines? Let us bring the ark[d] of the LORD's covenant from Shiloh, so d Nu 10:35; Jos 6:7
that it[a] may go with us and save us from the hand of our enemies."
4So the people sent men to Shiloh, and they brought back the ark of the covenant
of the LORD Almighty, who is enthroned between the cherubim.[e] And Eli's two sons, 4:4 e Ex 25:22;
Hophni and Phinehas, were there with the ark of the covenant of God. 2Sa 6:2
5When the ark of the LORD's covenant came into the camp, all Israel raised such
a great shout[f] that the ground shook. 6Hearing the uproar, the Philistines asked,
"What's all this shouting in the Hebrew camp?" 4:5 f Jos 6:5, 10
When they learned that the ark of the LORD had come into the camp, 7the Philistines
were afraid.[g] "A god has come into the camp," they said. "We're in trouble! Nothing
like this has happened before. 8Woe to us! Who will deliver us from the hand of these 4:7 g Ex 15:14
mighty gods? They are the gods who struck the Egyptians with all kinds of plagues
in the desert. 9Be strong, Philistines! Be men, or you will be subject to the Hebrews,
as they[h] have been to you. Be men, and fight!" 4:9 h Jdg 13:1;

a 3 Or he 1Co 16:13

3:20 The phrase "from Dan to Beersheba" was often used to describe the boundaries of the promised land. Dan was one of the northernmost cities in the land, and Beersheba one of the cities farthest south. In this context, it was a way of emphasising that *everyone* in Israel knew that Samuel was called to be a prophet.

4:1 The Philistines, descendants of Noah's son Ham, settled along the southeastern Mediterranean coast between Egypt and Gaza. They were originally one of the "Sea Peoples" who had migrated to the Middle East in ships from Greece and Crete. By Samuel's time, these warlike people were well established in five of Gaza's cities in southwest Canaan and were constantly pressing inland against the Israelites. Throughout this time, the Philistines were Israel's major enemy.

4:3 The ark of the covenant contained the Ten Commandments given by God to Moses. The ark was supposed to be kept in the Most Holy Place, a sacred part of the tabernacle that only the high priest could enter once a year. Hophni and Phinehas desecrated the room by unlawfully entering it and removing the ark.

The Israelites rightly recognised the great holiness of the ark, but they thought that the ark itself – the wood and metal box – was their source of power. They began to use it as a good luck charm, expecting it to protect them from their enemies. A symbol of God does not guarantee his presence and power. Their attitude towards the ark came perilously close to idol worship. When the ark was captured by their enemies, they thought that Israel's glory was gone (4:19–22) and that God had deserted them (7:1, 2). God uses his power according to his own wisdom and will. He responds to the faith of those who seek him.

4:4 "The LORD Almighty, who is enthroned between the cherubim" conveys that God's presence rested on the ark of the covenant between the two golden cherubim (or angels) attached to its lid. The people believed that the ark would bring victory when Hophni and Phinehas carried it into battle.

4:5–8 The Philistines were afraid because they remembered stories about God's intervention for Israel when they left Egypt. But Israel had turned away from God and was clinging to only a form of godliness, a symbol of former victories.

People (and churches) often try to live on the memories of God's blessings. The Israelites wrongly assumed that because God had given them victory in the past, he would do it again, even though they had strayed far from him. Today, as in Bible times, spiritual victories come through a continually renewed relationship with God. Don't live off the past. Keep your relationship with God new and fresh.

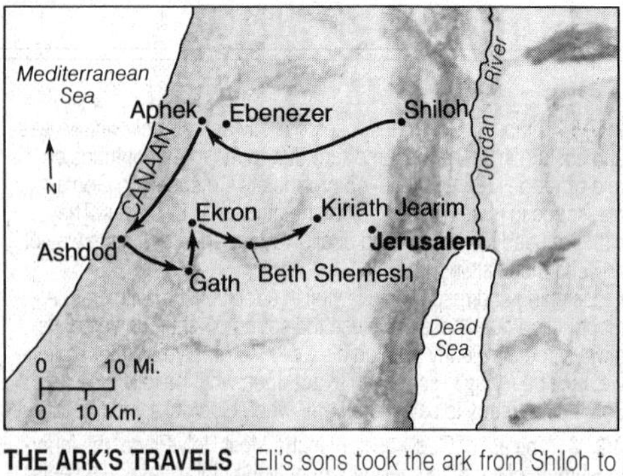

THE ARK'S TRAVELS Eli's sons took the ark from Shiloh to the battlefield on the lower plains at Ebenezer and Aphek. The Philistines captured the ark and took it to Ashdod, Gath, and Ekron. Plagues forced the people to send the ark back to Israel, where it was finally taken by cattle-driven carts to Beth Shemesh and on to the home of Eleazar in Kiriath Jearim.

4:10 [i]ver 2; Dt 28:25; 2Sa 18:17; 2Ki 14:12

4:11 [j]1Sa 2:34; Ps 78:61, 64

4:12 [k]Jos 7:6; 2Sa 1:2; 15:32; Ne 9:1; Job 2:12

4:13 [l]ver 18; 1Sa 1:9

4:15 [m]1Sa 3:2

10So the Philistines fought, and the Israelites were defeated[i] and every man fled
to his tent. The slaughter was very great; Israel lost thirty thousand foot soldiers. 11The
ark of God was captured, and Eli's two sons, Hophni and Phinehas, died.[j]

Death of Eli

12That same day a Benjamite ran from the battle line and went to Shiloh, his clothes
torn and dust[k] on his head. 13When he arrived, there was Eli[l] sitting on his chair
by the side of the road, watching, because his heart feared for the ark of God. When
the man entered the town and told what had happened, the whole town sent up a cry.
14Eli heard the outcry and asked, "What is the meaning of this uproar?"
The man hurried over to Eli, 15who was ninety-eight years old and whose eyes[m]
were set so that he could not see. 16He told Eli, "I have just come from the battle line;
I fled from it this very day."
Eli asked, "What happened, my son?"
17The man who brought the news replied, "Israel fled before the Philistines, and
the army has suffered heavy losses. Also your two sons, Hophni and Phinehas, are
dead, and the ark of God has been captured."

ISRAELITES VERSUS PHILISTINES

The Israelites and Philistines were arch-enemies and constantly fought. Here are some of their confrontations, found in 1 and 2 Samuel. When Israel trusted God for the victory, they always won.

Location of the Battle	*Winner*	*Comments*	*Reference*
Aphek to Ebenezer	Philistines	The ark was captured and Eli's sons killed	1 Samuel 4:1–11
Mizpah	Israelites	After the ark was returned, the Philistines planned to attack again, but God confused them. Israel chased the Philistines back to Beth Car	1 Samuel 7:7–14
Geba	Israelites under Jonathan	One detachment destroyed	1 Samuel 13:3, 4
Gilgal	A draw	The Israelites lost their nerve and hid	1 Samuel 13:6–17
Micmash	Israelites	Jonathan and his armour-bearer said it didn't matter how many enemies there were. If God was with them, they would win. They began the battle, and the army completed it	1 Samuel 13:23–14:23
Valley of Elah	Israelites	David and Goliath	1 Samuel 17:1–58
?	Israelites	David killed 200 Philistines to earn a wife	1 Samuel 18:17–30
Keilah	Israelites under David	David protected the threshing floors from Philistine looters	1 Samuel 23:1–5
Aphek, Jezreel, to Mount Gilboa	Philistines	Saul and Jonathan killed	1 Samuel 29:1; 31:1–13
Baal Perazim	Israelites	The Philistines tried to capture King David	2 Samuel 5:17–25
Metheg Ammah (possibly near Gath)	Israelites	There was very little trouble with the Philistines after this defeat	2 Samuel 8:1
?	Israelites	Abishai saved David from a Philistine giant	2 Samuel 21:15–17
Gob	Israelites	Other giants were killed, including Goliath's brother (See NIV text note)	2 Samuel 21:18–22

4:11 This event fulfils the prophecy in 2:34 stating that Eli's sons, Hophni and Phinehas, would die "on the same day".

4:12 At this time, the city of Shiloh was Israel's religious centre (Joshua 18:1; 1 Samuel 4:3). The tabernacle was permanently set up there. Because Israel did not have a civil capital—a seat of national government—Shiloh was the natural place for a messenger to deliver the sad news from the battle. Many scholars believe that it was during this battle that Shiloh was destroyed (Jeremiah 7:12; 26:2–6; also see the note on 7:1).

18 When he mentioned the ark of God, Eli fell backwards off his chair by the side
of the gate. His neck was broken and he died, for he was an old man and heavy. He
had led[b][n] Israel for forty years.
19 His daughter-in-law, the wife of Phinehas, was pregnant and near the time of
delivery. When she heard the news that the ark of God had been captured and that
her father-in-law and her husband were dead, she went into labour and gave birth,
but was overcome by her labour pains. 20 As she was dying, the women attending her
said, "Don't despair; you have given birth to a son." But she did not respond or pay
any attention.
21 She named the boy Ichabod,[c][o] saying, "The glory[p] has departed from Israel"—because of the capture of the ark of God and the deaths of her father-in-law
and her husband. 22 She said, "The glory has departed from Israel, for the ark of God
has been captured."

The Ark in Ashdod and Ekron

5 After the Philistines had captured the ark of God, they took it from Ebenezer[a]
to Ashdod.[b] 2 Then they carried the ark into Dagon's temple and set it beside
Dagon.[c] 3 When the people of Ashdod rose early the next day, there was Dagon,
fallen[d] on his face on the ground before the ark of the LORD! They took Dagon and
put him back in his place. 4 But the following morning when they rose, there was
Dagon, fallen on his face on the ground before the ark of the LORD! His head and hands
had been broken[e] off and were lying on the threshold; only his body remained. 5 That
is why to this day neither the priests of Dagon nor any others who enter Dagon's temple
at Ashdod step on the threshold.[f]
6 The LORD's hand[g] was heavy upon the people of Ashdod and its vicinity; he
brought devastation[h] upon them and afflicted them with tumours.[a][i] 7 When the men
of Ashdod saw what was happening, they said, "The ark of the god of Israel must
not stay here with us, because his hand is heavy upon us and upon Dagon our god."
8 So they called together all the rulers of the Philistines and asked them, "What shall
we do with the ark of the god of Israel?"
They answered, "Have the ark of the god of Israel moved to Gath.[j]" So they moved
the ark of the God of Israel.
9 But after they had moved it, the LORD's hand was against that city, throwing it
into a great panic.[k] He afflicted the people of the city, both young and old, with an
outbreak of tumours.[b] 10 So they sent the ark of God to Ekron.
As the ark of God was entering Ekron, the people of Ekron cried out, "They have
brought the ark of the god of Israel round to us to kill us and our people." 11 So they
called together all the rulers[l] of the Philistines and said, "Send the ark of the god

4:18 [n] ver 13
4:21 [o] Ge 35:18 [p] Ps 26:8; Jer 2:11
5:1 [a] 1Sa 4:1; 7:12 [b] Jos 13:3
5:2 [c] Jdg 16:23
5:3 [d] Isa 19:1; 46:7
5:4 [e] Eze 6:6; Mic 1:7
5:5 [f] Zep 1:9
5:6 [g] ver 7; Ex 9:3; Ps 32:4; Ac 13:11 [h] ver 11; Ps 78:66 [i] Dt 28:27; 1Sa 6:5
5:8 [j] ver 11
5:9 [k] ver 6, 11; Dt 2:15; 1Sa 7:13; Ps 78:66
5:11 [l] ver 6, 8-9

b *18* Traditionally *judged* **c** *21 Ichabod* means *no glory.* **a** *6* Hebrew; Septuagint and Vulgate *tumours. And rats appeared in their land, and death and destruction were throughout the city* **b** *9* Or *with tumours in the groin* (see Septuagint)

4:18 Eli was Israel's judge and high priest. His death marked the end of the dark period of the judges when most of the nation ignored God. Although Samuel was also a judge, his career saw the transition from Israel's rule by judges to the nation's monarchy. He began the great revival that Israel would experience for the next century. The Bible does not say who became the next high priest (Samuel was not eligible because he was not a direct descendant of Aaron), but Samuel acted as high priest at this time by offering the important sacrifices throughout Israel.

4:19–22 This incident illustrates the spiritual darkness and decline of Israel. This young boy, Ichabod, was supposed to succeed his father Phinehas in the priesthood, but his father had been killed because he was an evil man who desecrated the tabernacle. The terror of God's leaving his people overshadowed the joy of childbirth. When sin dominates our lives, even God-given joys and pleasures seem empty.

5:1ff Dagon was the chief god of the Philistines, whom they believed sent rain and assured a bountiful harvest. But the Philistines, like most of their pagan neighbours, worshipped many gods. The more gods they could have on their side, the more secure they felt. That was why they wanted the ark, thinking that if it helped the Israelites, it could help them too. But when the people living nearby began to get sick and die, the Philistines realised that the ark was not a good omen. It was a source of greater power than they had ever seen—power they could not control.

5:6, 7 Although the Philistines had just witnessed a great victory by Israel's God over their god, Dagon, they didn't act upon that insight until they were afflicted with tumours (possibly bubonic plague). Similarly, today many people don't respond to biblical truth until they experience pain. Are you willing to listen to God for truth's sake, or do you turn to him only when you are hurting?

5:8 The Philistines were governed by five rulers, or lords. Each lord lived in a different city—Gath, Ekron, Ashdod, Ashkelon, Gaza. The ark was taken to three of these capital cities, and each time it brought great trouble and chaos to the citizens.

6:2
[a]Ge 41:8; Ex 7:11; Isa 2:6

of Israel away; let it go back to its own place, or it[c] will kill us and our people."
For death had filled the city with panic; God's hand was very heavy upon it. 12Those
who did not die were afflicted with tumours, and the outcry of the city went up to
heaven.

The Ark Returned to Israel

6 When the ark of the LORD had been in Philistine territory for seven months, 2the
Philistines called for the priests and the diviners[a] and said, "What shall we do
with the ark of the LORD? Tell us how we should send it back to its place."

[c] *11* Or *he*

ELI

Eli was one Old Testament person with a very modern problem. The recognition and respect he earned in public did not extend to his handling of his private affairs. He may have been an excellent priest, but he was a poor parent. His sons brought him grief and ruin. He lacked two important qualities needed for effective parental discipline: firm resolve and corrective action.

Eli responded to situations rather than solving them. But even his responses tended to be weak. God pointed out his sons' errors, but Eli did little to correct them. The contrast between God's dealing with Eli and Eli's dealing with his sons is clear—God gave warning, spelled out the consequences of disobedience, and then acted. Eli only warned. Children need to learn that their parents' words and actions go together. Both love and discipline must be spoken as well as acted out.

But Eli had another problem. He was more concerned with the symbols of his religion than with the God they represented. For Eli, the ark of the covenant had become a relic to be protected rather than a reminder of the Protector. His faith shifted from the Creator to the created.

It may be easier to worship things we can see, whether buildings, people, or Scripture itself, but such tangible things have no power in themselves. This book you hold is either merely a respectable religious relic, or it is the sharp and effective word of God. Your attitude towards it is largely shaped by your relationship to the God from whom it comes. A relic or antique has to be carefully stored away; God's word has to be used and obeyed. Which attitude accurately describes your approach to the word of God?

Strengths and accomplishments:
- Judged Israel for 40 years
- Spoke with Hannah, the mother of Samuel, and assured her of God's blessing
- Brought up and trained Samuel, the greatest judge of Israel

Weaknesses and mistakes:
- Failed to discipline his sons or correct them when they sinned
- Tended to react to situations rather than take decisive action
- Saw the ark of the covenant as a relic to be cherished rather than as a symbol of God's presence with Israel

Lessons from his life:
- Parents need to discipline their children responsibly
- Life is more than simply reacting; it demands action
- Past victories cannot substitute for present trust

Vital statistics:
- Where: Shiloh
- Occupations: High priest and judge of Israel
- Relatives: Sons: Hophni and Phinehas
- Contemporary: Samuel

Key verses:
"And the LORD said to Samuel: 'See, I am about to do something in Israel that will make the ears of everyone who hears of it tingle. At that time I will carry out against Eli everything I spoke against his family—from beginning to end. For I told him that I would judge his family for ever because of the sin he knew about; his sons made themselves contemptible, and he failed to restrain them. Therefore, I swore to the house of Eli, "The guilt of Eli's house will never be atoned for by sacrifice or offering" ' " (1 Samuel 3:11–14).

His story is told in 1 Samuel 1—4. He is also mentioned in 1 Kings 2:26, 27.

3 They answered, "If you return the ark of the god of Israel, do not send it away
empty,[b] but by all means send a guilt offering[c] to him. Then you will be healed,
and you will know why his hand[d] has not been lifted from you."
4 The Philistines asked, "What guilt offering should we send to him?"
They replied, "Five gold tumours and five gold rats, according to the number[e] of
the Philistine rulers, because the same plague has struck both you and your rulers.
5 Make models of the tumours[f] and of the rats that are destroying the country, and
pay honour[g] to Israel's god. Perhaps he will lift his hand from you and your gods
and your land. 6 Why do you harden[h] your hearts as the Egyptians and Pharaoh did?
When he[a] treated them harshly, did they[i] not send the Israelites out so that they could
go on their way?
7 "Now then, get a new cart[j] ready, with two cows that have calved and have never
been yoked.[k] Hitch the cows to the cart, but take their calves away and pen them
up. 8 Take the ark of the LORD and put it on the cart, and in a chest beside it put the
gold objects you are sending back to him as a guilt offering. Send it on its way, 9 but
keep watching it. If it goes up to its own territory, towards Beth Shemesh,[l] then the
LORD has brought this great disaster on us. But if it does not, then we shall know that
it was not his hand that struck us and that it happened to us by chance."
10 So they did this. They took two such cows and hitched them to the cart and penned
up their calves. 11 They placed the ark of the LORD on the cart and along with it the
chest containing the gold rats and the models of the tumours. 12 Then the cows went
straight up towards Beth Shemesh, keeping on the road and lowing all the way; they
did not turn to the right or to the left. The rulers of the Philistines followed them as
far as the border of Beth Shemesh.
13 Now the people of Beth Shemesh were harvesting their wheat in the valley, and
when they looked up and saw the ark, they rejoiced at the sight. 14 The cart came to
the field of Joshua of Beth Shemesh, and there it stopped beside a large rock. The
people chopped up the wood of the cart and sacrificed the cows as a burnt offering[m]
to the LORD. 15 The Levites[n] took down the ark of the LORD, together with the chest
containing the gold objects, and placed them on the large rock. On that day the people
of Beth Shemesh offered burnt offerings and made sacrifices to the LORD. 16 The five
rulers of the Philistines saw all this and then returned that same day to Ekron.
17 These are the gold tumours the Philistines sent as a guilt offering to the
LORD—one each[o] for Ashdod, Gaza, Ashkelon, Gath and Ekron. 18 And the number
of the gold rats was according to the number of Philistine towns belonging to the five
rulers—the fortified towns with their country villages. The large rock, on which[b] they
set the ark of the LORD, is a witness to this day in the field of Joshua of Beth Shemesh.
19 But God struck down[p] some of the men of Beth Shemesh, putting seventy[c] of

6:3 [b] Ex 23:15; Dt 16:16 [c] Lev 5:15 [d] ver 9
6:4 [e] ver 17-18; Jos 13:3; Jdg 3:3
6:5 [f] 1Sa 5:6-11 [g] Jos 7:19; Isa 42:12; Jn 9:24; Rev 14:7
6:6 [h] Ex 7:13; 8:15; 9:34; 14:17 [i] Ex 12:31, 33
6:7 [j] 2Sa 6:3 [k] Nu 19:2
6:9 [l] ver 3; Jos 15:10; 21:16
6:14 [m] 2Sa 24:22; 1Ki 19:21
6:15 [n] Jos 3:3
6:17 [o] ver 4
6:19 [p] 2Sa 6:7

[a] *6* That is, God [b] *18* A few Hebrew manuscripts (see also Septuagint); most Hebrew manuscripts *villages as far as Greater Abel, where* [c] *19* A few Hebrew manuscripts; most Hebrew manuscripts and Septuagint *50,070*

6:3 What was this guilt offering supposed to accomplish? This was a normal reaction to trouble in the Canaanite religion. The Philistines thought their problems were the result of their gods being angry. They recognised their guilt in taking the ark and now were trying everything they could to placate Israel's God. The diviners (6:2) probably helped choose the gift they thought would placate Yahweh. But the offering consisted of images of tumours and rats, not the kind of guilt offering prescribed in God's laws (Leviticus 5:14–6:7; 7:1–10). How easy it is to design our own methods of acknowledging God rather than serving him in the way he requires.

6:7-12 The Philistine priests and diviners devised a test to see if God was really the one who had caused all their recent troubles. Two cows who had just given birth were hitched to a cart and sent towards Israel's border carrying the ark of the covenant. For a cow to leave her nursing calf, she would have to go against all her motherly instincts. Only God, who has power over the natural order, could cause this to happen. God sent the cows to Israel, not to pass the Philistines' test, but to show them his mighty power.

6:9 The Philistines acknowledged the existence of the Hebrew God, but only as one of many deities whose favour they sought. Thinking of God in this way made it easy for them to ignore his demand that people worship him alone. Many people "worship" God this way. They see God as just one ingredient in a successful life. But God is far more than an ingredient—he is the source of life itself. Are you a "Philistine", seeing God's favour as only an ingredient of the good life?

6:19 Why were people killed for looking into the ark? The Israelites had made an idol of the ark. They had tried to harness God's power, to use it for their own purposes (victory in battle). But the Lord of the universe cannot be controlled by humans. To protect the Israelites from his power, he had warned them not even to look at the sacred sanctuary objects in the Most Holy Place or they would die (Numbers 4:20). Only Levites were allowed to move the ark. Because of their disobedience, God carried out his promised judgment.

God could not allow the people to think they could use his power for their own ends. He could not permit them to disregard his warnings and come into his presence lightly. He did not want

them to death because they had looked[q] into the ark of the LORD. The people mourned
because of the heavy blow the LORD had dealt them, 20and the men of Beth Shemesh
asked, "Who can stand[r] in the presence of the LORD, this holy[s] God? To whom will
the ark go up from here?"
21Then they sent messengers to the people of Kiriath Jearim,[t] saying, "The
Philistines have returned the ark of the LORD. Come down and take it up to your
7 place." 1So the men of Kiriath Jearim came and took up the ark of the LORD. They
took it to Abinadab's[a] house on the hill and consecrated Eleazar his son to guard
the ark of the LORD.

Samuel Subdues the Philistines at Mizpah

2It was a long time, twenty years in all, that the ark remained at Kiriath Jearim,
and all the people of Israel mourned and sought after the LORD. 3And Samuel said
to the whole house of Israel, "If you are returning[b] to the LORD with all your hearts,
then rid[c] yourselves of the foreign gods and the Ashtoreths[d] and commit[e] yourselves to the LORD and serve him only,[f] and he will deliver you out of the hand of
the Philistines." 4So the Israelites put away their Baals and Ashtoreths, and served
the LORD only.
5Then Samuel said, "Assemble all Israel at Mizpah[g] and I will intercede with the
LORD for you." 6When they had assembled at Mizpah, they drew water and poured[h]
it out before the LORD. On that day they fasted and there they confessed, "We have
sinned against the LORD." And Samuel was leader[a][i] of Israel at Mizpah.
7When the Philistines heard that Israel had assembled at Mizpah, the rulers of the
Philistines came up to attack them. And when the Israelites heard of it, they were
afraid[j] because of the Philistines. 8They said to Samuel, "Do not stop crying[k] out
to the LORD our God for us, that he may rescue us from the hand of the Philistines."
9Then Samuel[l] took a suckling lamb and offered it up as a whole burnt offering to
the LORD. He cried out to the LORD on Israel's behalf, and the LORD answered him.[m]
10While Samuel was sacrificing the burnt offering, the Philistines drew near to

[a] 6 Traditionally *judge*

6:19 [q]Ex 19:21; Nu 4:5, 15, 20
6:20 [r]2Sa 6:9; Mal 3:2; Rev 6:17 [s]Lev 11:45
6:21 [t]Jos 9:17; 15:9, 60; 1Ch 13:5-6
7:1 [a]2Sa 6:3
7:3 [b]Dt 30:10; Isa 55:7; Hos 6:1 [c]Ge 35:2; Jos 24:14 [d]Jdg 2:12-13; 1Sa 31:10 [e]Joel 2:12 [f]Dt 6:13; Mt 4:10; Lk 4:8
7:5 [g]Jdg 20:1
7:6 [h]Ps 62:8; La 2:19 [i]Jdg 10:10; Ne 9:1; Ps 106:6
7:7 [j]1Sa 17:11
7:8 [k]1Sa 12:19, 23; Isa 37:4; Jer 15:1
7:9 [l]Ps 99:6 [m]Jer 15:1

---

the cycle of disrespect, disobedience, and defeat to start all over again. God did not kill the men of Beth Shemesh to be cruel. He killed them because overlooking their presumptuous sin would encourage the whole nation of Israel to ignore God.

7:1 The ark was taken to Kiriath Jearim, a city near the battlefield, for safekeeping, and Eleazar was given the task of caring for it. Why wasn't it taken back to the tabernacle at Shiloh? Shiloh had probably been defeated and destroyed by the Philistines in an earlier battle (4:1–18; Jeremiah 26:2–6) because of the evil deeds of its priests (2:12–17). Apparently, the tabernacle and its furniture were saved because we read that the tabernacle was set up in Nob during Saul's reign (21:1–6) and in Gibeon during the reigns of David and Solomon (1 Chronicles 16:39; 21:29, 30; 2 Chronicles 1). Shiloh, however, is never again mentioned in the historical books of the Old Testament. Samuel's new home became Ramah (7:15–17; 8:4), his birthplace (further evidence of Shiloh's destruction).

7:2, 3 Israel mourned and sorrow gripped the nation for 20 years. The ark was put away like an unwanted box in an attic, and it seemed as if the Lord had abandoned his people. Samuel, now a grown man, roused them to action by saying that if they were truly sorry, they should do something about it. How easy it is for us to complain about our problems, even to God, while we refuse to act, change, and do what he requires. We don't even take the advice he has already given us. Do you ever feel as if God has abandoned you? Check to see if there is anything he has already told you to do. You may not receive new guidance from God until you have acted on his previous directions.

7:3 Samuel urged the Israelites to get rid of their foreign gods. Idols today are much more subtle than gods of wood and stone, but they are just as dangerous. Whatever holds first place in our lives or controls us is our god. Money, success, material goods, pride, or anything else can be an idol if it takes the place of God in our lives. The Lord alone is worthy of our service and worship, and we must let nothing rival him. If we have "foreign gods", we need to ask God to help us dethrone them, making the true God our first priority.

7:4 Baal was believed to be the son of El, chief deity of the Canaanites. Baal was regarded as the god of thunder and rain, thus he controlled vegetation and agriculture. Ashtoreth was a goddess of love and war (she was called Ishtar in Babylon and Astarte or Aphrodite in Greece). She represented fertility. The Canaanites believed that by the sexual union of Baal and Ashtoreth, the earth would be magically rejuvenated and made fertile.

7:5 Mizpah held special significance for the Israelite nation. It was there that the Israelites had gathered to mobilise against the tribe of Benjamin (Judges 20:1). Samuel was appointed to be leader (7:6), and Saul, Israel's first king, was identified and presented to the people (10:17ff).

7:6 Pouring water on the ground "before the LORD" was a sign of repenting from sin, turning from idols, and determining to obey God alone.

7:6 Samuel became the last in the long line of Israel's judges (leaders), a line that began when Israel first conquered the promised land. For a list of these judges, see the chart in Judges 2. A judge was both a political and a religious leader. God was Israel's true leader, while the judge was to be God's spokesman to the people and administrator of justice throughout the land. While some of Israel's judges relied more on their own judgment than on God's, Samuel's obedience and dedication to God made him one of the greatest judges in Israel's history. (For more on Samuel as a judge, see the note on 4:18.)

engage Israel in battle. But that day the LORD thundered[n] with loud thunder against
the Philistines and threw them into such a panic[o] that they were routed before the
Israelites. 11The men of Israel rushed out of Mizpah and pursued the Philistines,
slaughtering them along the way to a point below Beth Car.
12Then Samuel took a stone[p] and set it up between Mizpah and Shen. He named
it Ebenezer,[b] saying, "Thus far has the LORD helped us." 13So the Philistines were
subdued[q] and did not invade Israelite territory again.
Throughout Samuel's lifetime, the hand of the LORD was against the Philistines.
14The towns from Ekron to Gath that the Philistines had captured from Israel were
restored to her, and Israel delivered the neighbouring territory from the power of the
Philistines. And there was peace between Israel and the Amorites.
15Samuel[r] continued as judge over Israel all the days of his life. 16From year to
year he went on a circuit from Bethel to Gilgal to Mizpah, judging Israel in all those
places. 17But he always went back to Ramah,[s] where his home was, and there he
also judged Israel. And he built an altar[t] there to the LORD.

7:10 [n]1Sa 2:10; 2Sa 22:14-15 [o]Jos 10:10
7:12 [p]Ge 35:14; Jos 4:9
7:13 [q]Jdg 13:1, 5; 1Sa 13:5
7:15 [r]ver 6; 1Sa 12:11
7:17 [s]1Sa 1:19; 8:4 [t]Jdg 21:4

B. SAMUEL AND SAUL (8:1—15:35)

Samuel judges Israel well, saves them from the Philistines, and leads them back to God. But when he retires, the nation does not want another judge. Instead they demand to be given a king in order to be like the nations around them. Although God is unhappy with their request, he tells Samuel to anoint Saul as Israel's first king. Saul is a skilful soldier who successfully leads the nation into many battles against their enemies. But in God's eyes Saul is a failure because he constantly disobeys and does things his own way. God eventually rejected Saul as king. Sometimes we want to go our own way rather than follow the ways of God. This will always end in ruin as it did for Saul.

1. Saul becomes king of Israel

Israel Asks for a King

8 When Samuel grew old, he appointed[a] his sons as judges for Israel. 2The name
of his firstborn was Joel and the name of his second was Abijah, and they served
at Beersheba.[b] 3But his sons did not walk in his ways. They turned aside after

8:1 [a]Dt 16:18-19
8:2 [b]Ge 22:19; 1Ki 19:3; Am 5:4-5

[b] 12 *Ebenezer* means *stone of help.*

7:12 The Israelites had great difficulty with the Philistines, but God rescued them. In response, the people set up a stone as a memorial of God's great help and deliverance. During tough times, we may need to remember the crucial turning points in our past to help us through the present. Memorials can help us remember God's past victories and gain confidence and strength for the present.

7:14 In Joshua's time, the Amorites were a powerful tribe scattered throughout the hill country on both sides of the Jordan with a heavy concentration occupying the east side of the Jordan River opposite the Dead Sea. In the context of this verse, however, *Amorites* is another general name for all the inhabitants of Canaan who were not Israelites.

8:1–3 As an old man, Samuel appointed his sons to be judges over Israel in his place. But they turned out to be corrupt, much like Eli's sons (2:12). We don't know why Samuel's sons went wrong, but we do know that Eli was held responsible for his own sons' corruption (2:29–34).

It is impossible to know if Samuel was a bad parent. His children were old enough to be on their own. We must be careful not to blame ourselves for the sins of our children. On the other hand, parenthood is an awesome responsibility, and nothing is more important than moulding and shaping our children's lives.

If your grown children are not following God, realise that you can't control them any longer. Don't blame yourself for something that is no longer your responsibility. But if your children are still in your care, know that what you do and teach can profoundly affect your children and lasts a lifetime.

8:4–9 Israel wanted a king for several reasons: (1) Samuel's sons were not fit to lead Israel. (2) The 12 tribes of Israel continually had problems working together because each tribe had its own leader and territory. It was hoped that a king would unite the tribes into one nation and one army. (3) The people wanted to be like the neighbouring nations. This is exactly what God didn't want. Having a king would make it easy to forget that God was their real leader. It was not wrong for Israel to want a king; God had mentioned the possibility in Deuteronomy 17:14–20. Yet, in reality, the people were rejecting God as their leader. The Israelites wanted laws, an army, and a human monarch in the place of God. They wanted to run the nation through human strength, even though only God's strength could make them flourish in the hostile land of Canaan.

8:5, 6 The people clamoured for a king, thinking that a new system of government would bring about a change in the nation. But because their basic problem was disobedience to God, their other problems would only continue under the new administration. What they needed was a unified faith, not a uniform rule.

Had the Israelites submitted to God's leadership, they would have thrived beyond their expectations (Deuteronomy 28:1). Our obedience is weak if we ask God to lead our family or personal life but continue to live by the world's standards and values. Faith in God must touch all the practical areas of life.

dishonest gain and accepted bribes[c] and perverted justice.
4So all the elders of Israel gathered together and came to Samuel at Ramah.[d] 5They
said to him, "You are old, and your sons do not walk in your ways; now appoint a
king[e] to lead[a] us, such as all the other nations have."
6But when they said, "Give us a king to lead us," this displeased[f] Samuel; so he
prayed to the LORD. 7And the LORD told him: "Listen to all that the people are saying
to you; it is not you they have rejected, but they have rejected me as their king.[g] 8As
they have done from the day I brought them up out of Egypt until this day, forsaking
me and serving other gods, so they are doing to you. 9Now listen to them; but warn
them solemnly and let them know[h] what the king who will reign over them will do."
10Samuel told all the words of the LORD to the people who were asking him for
a king. 11He said, "This is what the king who will reign over you will do: He will
take[i] your sons and make them serve with his chariots and horses, and they will run
in front of his chariots.[j] 12Some he will assign to be commanders[k] of thousands and

[a] 5 Traditionally *judge*; also in verses 6 and 20

8:3 [c] Ex 23:8; Dt 16:19; Ps 15:5
8:4 [d] 1Sa 7:17
8:5 [e] Dt 17:14-20
8:6 [f] 1Sa 15:11
8:7 [g] Ex 16:8; 1Sa 10:19
8:9 [h] ver 11-18; 1Sa 10:25
8:11 [i] 1Sa 10:25; 14:52 [j] Dt 17:16; 2Sa 15:1
8:12 [k] 1Sa 22:7

SAMUEL

We often wonder about the childhoods of great people. We have little information about the early years of most of the people mentioned in the Bible. One delightful exception is Samuel; he came as a result of God's answer to Hannah's fervent prayer for a child. (In fact, the name *Samuel* comes from the Hebrew expression, "heard of God".) God shaped Samuel from the start. Like Moses, Samuel was called to fill many different roles: judge, priest, prophet, counsellor, and God's man at a turning point in the history of Israel. God worked through Samuel because Samuel was willing to be one thing: God's servant.

Samuel showed that those whom God finds faithful in small things will be trusted with greater things. He grew up assisting the high priest (Eli) in the tabernacle until God directed him to other responsibilities. God was able to use Samuel because he was genuinely dedicated to God.

Samuel moved ahead because he was listening to God's directions. Too often we ask God to control our lives without making us give up the goals for which we strive. We ask God to help us get where *we* want to go. The first step in correcting this tendency is to turn over both the control and destination of our lives to him. The second step is to do what we *already know* God requires of us. The third step is to listen for further direction from his word—God's map for life.

Strengths and accomplishments:
- Used by God to assist Israel's transition from a loosely governed tribal people to a monarchy
- Anointed the first two kings of Israel
- Was the last and most effective of Israel's judges
- Is listed in the Hall of Faith in Hebrews 11

Weakness and mistake:
- Was unable to lead his sons into a close relationship with God

Lessons from his life:
- The significance of what people accomplish is directly related to their relationship with God
- The kind of person we are is more important than anything we might do

Vital statistics:
- Where: Ephraim
- Occupations: Judge, prophet, priest
- Relatives: Mother: Hannah. Father: Elkanah. Sons: Joel and Abijah
- Contemporaries: Eli, Saul, David

Key verses:
"The LORD was with Samuel as he grew up, and he let none of his words fall to the ground. And all Israel from Dan to Beersheba recognised that Samuel was attested as a prophet of the LORD" (1 Samuel 3:19, 20).

His story is told in 1 Samuel 1—28. He is also mentioned in Psalm 99:6; Jeremiah 15:1; Acts 3:24; 13:20; Hebrews 11:32.

commanders of fifties, and others to plough his ground and reap his harvest, and still
others to make weapons of war and equipment for his chariots. 13He will take your
daughters to be perfumers and cooks and bakers. 14He will take the best of your[l]
fields and vineyards[m] and olive groves and give them to his attendants. 15He will take
a tenth of your grain and of your vintage and give it to his officials and attendants.
16Your menservants and maidservants and the best of your cattle[b] and donkeys he
will take for his own use. 17He will take a tenth of your flocks, and you yourselves
will become his slaves. 18When that day comes, you will cry out for relief from the
king you have chosen, and the LORD will not answer[n] you in that day."
19But the people refused[o] to listen to Samuel. "No!" they said. "We want a king
over us. 20Then we shall be like all the other nations,[p] with a king to lead us and
to go out before us and fight our battles."
21When Samuel heard all that the people said, he repeated[q] it before the LORD.
22The LORD answered, "Listen[r] to them and give them a king."
Then Samuel said to the men of Israel, "Everyone is to go back to his town."

Samuel Anoints Saul

9 There was a Benjamite, a man of standing, whose name was Kish[a] son of Abiel,
the son of Zeror, the son of Becorath, the son of Aphiah of Benjamin. 2He had
a son named Saul, an impressive young man without equal[b] among the Israelites—a
head taller[c] than any of the others.
3Now the donkeys belonging to Saul's father Kish were lost, and Kish said to his
son Saul, "Take one of the servants with you and go and look for the donkeys." 4So
he passed through the hill[d] country of Ephraim and through the area around Shali-
sha,[e] but they did not find them. They went on into the district of Shaalim, but the
donkeys were not there. Then he passed through the territory of Benjamin, but they
did not find them.
5When they reached the district of Zuph,[f] Saul said to the servant who was with
him, "Come, let's go back, or my father will stop thinking about the donkeys and start
worrying[g] about us."

b *16* Septuagint; Hebrew *young men*

8:14 [l]Eze 46:18 [m]1Ki 21:7, 15
8:18 [n]Pr 1:28; Isa 1:15; Mic 3:4
8:19 [o]Isa 66:4; Jer 44:16
8:20 [p]ver 5
8:21 [q]Jdg 11:11
8:22 [r]ver 7
9:1 [a]1Sa 14:51; 1Ch 8:33; 9:39
9:2 [b]1Sa 10:24 [c]1Sa 10:23
9:4 [d]Jos 24:33 [e]2Ki 4:42
9:5 [f]1Sa 1:1 [g]1Sa 10:2

8:19, 20 Samuel carefully explained all the negative consequences of having a king, but the Israelites refused to listen. When you have an important decision to make, weigh the positives and negatives carefully, considering everyone who might be affected by your choice. When you want something badly enough, it is difficult to see the potential problems. But don't discount the negatives. Unless you have a plan to handle each one, they will cause you great difficulty later.

8:19, 20 Israel was called to be a holy nation, separate from and unique among all others (Leviticus 20:26). The Israelites' motive in asking for a king was to be like the nations around them. This was in total opposition to God's original plan. It was not their desire for a king that was wrong, but their reasons for wanting a king.

Often we let others' values and actions dictate our attitudes and behaviour. Have you ever made a wrong choice because you wanted to be like everyone else? Be careful that the values of your friends or "heroes" don't pull you away from what God says is right. When God's people want to be like unbelievers, they are heading for spiritual disaster.

9:3 Saul was sent by his father on an important mission—to find their stray donkeys. Donkeys were all-purpose animals, the "pick-up trucks" of Bible times. Used for transportation, hauling, and farming, they were considered necessities. Even the poorest family owned one. To own many donkeys was a sign of wealth, and to lose them was a disaster. Saul's father was wealthy, and his many donkeys were evidence of that wealth.

9:3ff Often we think that events just happen to us, but as we learn from this story about Saul, God may use common occurrences to lead us where he wants. It is important to evaluate all situations as potential "divine appointments" designed to shape our lives. Think of all the good and bad circumstances that have affected you lately. Can you see God's purpose in them? Perhaps he is building a certain quality in you or leading you to serve him in a new area.

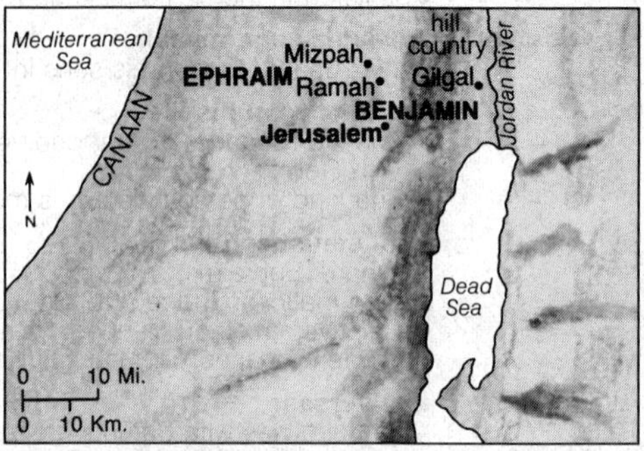

SAUL CHOSEN AS KING Saul and a servant searched for their lost donkeys in the hill country of Ephraim and the territory of Benjamin. They went to Ramah, looking for help from Samuel the prophet. While Saul was there, he found himself unexpectedly anointed by Samuel as Israel's first king. Samuel called Israel together at Mizpah to tell them God's choice for their king.

[6]But the servant replied, "Look, in this town there is a man of God;[h] he is highly
respected, and everything[i] he says comes true. Let's go there now. Perhaps he will
tell us what way to take."
[7]Saul said to his servant, "If we go, what can we give the man? The food in our
sacks is gone. We have no gift[j] to take to the man of God. What do we have?"
[8]The servant answered him again. "Look," he said, "I have a quarter of a shekel[a]
of silver. I will give it to the man of God so that he will tell us what way to take."
[9](Formerly in Israel, if a man went to enquire of God, he would say, "Come, let us
go to the seer," because the prophet of today used to be called a seer.)[k]
[10]"Good," Saul said to his servant. "Come, let's go." So they set out for the town
where the man of God was.
[11]As they were going up the hill to the town, they met some girls coming out to
draw[l] water, and they asked them, "Is the seer here?"
[12]"He is," they answered. "He's ahead of you. Hurry now; he has just come to our
town today, for the people have a sacrifice[m] at the high place.[n] [13]As soon as you
enter the town, you will find him before he goes up to the high place to eat. The people
will not begin eating until he comes, because he must bless the sacrifice; afterwards,
those who are invited will eat. Go up now; you should find him about this time."
[14]They went up to the town, and as they were entering it, there was Samuel, coming
towards them on his way up to the high place.
[15]Now the day before Saul came, the LORD had revealed this to Samuel: [16]"About
this time tomorrow I will send you a man from the land of Benjamin. Anoint[o] him
leader over my people Israel; he will deliver[p] my people from the hand of the
Philistines. I have looked upon my people, for their cry has reached me."
[17]When Samuel caught sight of Saul, the LORD said to him, "This[q] is the man I
spoke to you about; he will govern my people."
[18]Saul approached Samuel in the gateway and asked, "Would you please tell me
where the seer's house is?"
[19]"I am the seer," Samuel replied. "Go up ahead of me to the high place, for today
you are to eat with me, and in the morning I will let you go and will tell you all that
is in your heart. [20]As for the donkeys[r] you lost three days ago, do not worry about
them; they have been found. And to whom is all the desire[s] of Israel turned, if not
to you and all your father's family?"

[a] *8* That is, about 1/10 ounce (about 3 grams)

9:6 [h]Dt 33:1; 1Ki 13:1 [i]1Sa 3:19
9:7 [j]1Ki 14:3; 2Ki 5:5, 15; 8:8
9:9 [k]2Sa 24:11; 2Ki 17:13; 1Ch 9:22; 26:28; 29:29; Isa 30:10; Am 7:12
9:11 [l]Ge 24:11, 13
9:12 [m]Nu 28:11-15; 1Sa 7:17 [n]Ge 31:54; 1Sa 10:5; 1Ki 3:2
9:16 [o]1Sa 10:1 [p]Ex 3:7-9
9:17 [q]1Sa 16:12
9:20 [r]ver 3 [s]1Sa 8:5; 12:13

THE PROBLEMS WITH HAVING A KING

Problems (warned by Samuel)	*Reference*	*Fulfilment*
Drafting young men into the army	8:11, 12	14:52—"Whenever Saul saw a mighty or brave man, he took him into his service."
Having the young men "run in front of his [the king's] chariots"	8:11	2 Samuel 15:1—"Absalom provided himself with a chariot and horses and with fifty men to run ahead of him."
Making slave labourers	8:12, 17	2 Chronicles 2:17, 18—Solomon assigned labourers to build the temple.
Taking the best of your fields and vineyards	8:14	1 Kings 21:5–16—Jezebel stole Naboth's vineyard.
Using your property for his personal gain	8:14–16	1 Kings 9:10–15—Solomon gave away 20 cities to Hiram of Tyre.
Demanding a tenth of your harvest and flocks	8:15, 17	1 Kings 12:1–16—Rehoboam was going to demand heavier taxation than Solomon.

9:6 The city where the servant said the prophet lived was probably Ramah, where Samuel moved after the Philistine battle near Shiloh (7:17). Saul's lack of knowledge about Samuel showed his ignorance of spiritual matters. Saul and Samuel even lived in the same territory, Benjamin.

21 Saul answered, "But am I not a Benjamite, from the smallest tribe[t] of Israel,
and is not my clan the least of all the clans of the tribe of Benjamin?[u] Why do you
say such a thing to me?"
22 Then Samuel brought Saul and his servant into the hall and seated them at the
head of those who were invited — about thirty in number. 23 Samuel said to the cook,
"Bring the piece of meat I gave you, the one I told you to lay aside."
24 So the cook took up the leg[v] with what was on it and set it in front of Saul. Samuel
said, "Here is what has been kept for you. Eat, because it was set aside for you for
this occasion, from the time I said, 'I have invited guests.' " And Saul dined with
Samuel that day.
25 After they came down from the high place to the town, Samuel talked with Saul
on the roof[w] of his house. 26 They rose about daybreak and Samuel called to Saul on
the roof, "Get ready, and I will send you on your way." When Saul got ready, he and
Samuel went outside together. 27 As they were going down to the edge of the town,
Samuel said to Saul, "Tell the servant to go on ahead of us" — and the servant did
so — "but you stay here awhile, so that I may give you a message from God."

10

Then Samuel took a flask[a] of oil and poured it on Saul's head and kissed him,
saying, "Has not the LORD anointed[b] you leader over his inheritance?[a][c]
2 When you leave me today, you will meet two men near Rachel's tomb,[d] at Zelzah
on the border of Benjamin. They will say to you, 'The donkeys[e] you set out to look
for have been found. And now your father has stopped thinking about them and is
worried[f] about you. He is asking, "What shall I do about my son?" '
3 "Then you will go on from there until you reach the great tree of Tabor. Three
men going up to God at Bethel[g] will meet you there. One will be carrying three young
goats, another three loaves of bread, and another a skin of wine. 4 They will greet you
and offer you two loaves of bread, which you will accept from them.
5 "After that you will go to Gibeah of God, where there is a Philistine outpost.[h]
As you approach the town, you will meet a procession of prophets coming down from
the high place[i] with lyres, tambourines, flutes and harps[j] being played before them,
and they will be prophesying.[k] 6 The Spirit[l] of the LORD will come upon you in
power, and you will prophesy with them; and you will be changed into a different
person. 7 Once these signs are fulfilled, do whatever[m] your hand finds to do, for God
is with[n] you.
8 "Go down ahead of me to Gilgal.[o] I will surely come down to you to sacrifice

[a] 1 Hebrew; Septuagint and Vulgate *over his people Israel? You will reign over the LORD's people and save them from the power of their enemies round about. And this will be a sign to you that the LORD has anointed you leader over his inheritance:*

9:21 [t] 1Sa 15:17 [u] Jdg 20:35, 46
9:24 [v] Lev 7:32-34; Nu 18:18
9:25 [w] Dt 22:8; Ac 10:9
10:1 [a] 1Sa 16:13; 2Ki 9:1, 3, 6 [b] Ps 2:12 [c] Dt 32:9; Ps 78:62, 71
10:2 [d] Ge 35:20 [e] 1Sa 9:4 [f] 1Sa 9:5
10:3 [g] Ge 28:22; 35:7-8
10:5 [h] 1Sa 13:3 [i] 1Sa 9:12 [j] 2Ki 3:15 [k] 1Sa 19:20; 1Co 14:1
10:6 [l] ver 10; Nu 11:25; 1Sa 19:23-24
10:7 [m] Ecc 9:10 [n] Jos 1:5; Jdg 6:12; Heb 13:5
10:8 [o] 1Sa 11:14-15

9:21 "Why do you say such a thing to me?" Saul's outburst reveals a problem he would face repeatedly — feeling inferior. Like a leaf tossed about by the wind, Saul vacillated between his feelings and his convictions. Everything he said and did was selfish because he was worried about himself. For example, Saul said his clan was "the least" in the smallest tribe in Israel, but 9:1 says his father was "a man of standing". (The tribe of Benjamin was the smallest because they were nearly wiped out as punishment for their immorality — see Judges 19 – 21.) Saul didn't want to face the responsibility God had given him. Later, Saul kept some war plunder that he shouldn't have and then tried to blame his soldiers (15:21) while claiming that they had really taken it to sacrifice to God (15:15).

Although Saul had been called by God and had a mission in life, he struggled constantly with jealousy, insecurity, arrogance, impulsiveness, and deceit. He did not decide to be wholeheartedly committed to God. Because Saul would not let God's love give rest to his heart, he never became God's man.

10:1 When an Israelite king took office he was not only crowned, he was anointed. The coronation was the political act of establishing the king as ruler; the anointing was the religious act of making the king God's representative to the people. A king was always anointed by a priest or prophet. The special anointing oil was a mixture of olive oil, myrrh, and other expensive spices. It was poured over the king's head to symbolise the presence and power of the Holy Spirit of God in his life. This anointing ceremony was to remind the king of his great responsibility to lead his people by God's wisdom and not his own.

10:6 How could Saul be so filled with the Spirit and yet later commit such evil acts? Throughout the Old Testament, God's Spirit "came upon" a person temporarily so that God could use him or her for great acts. This happened frequently to Israel's judges when they were called by God to rescue the nation (Judges 3:8–10). This was not always a permanent, abiding influence, but sometimes a temporary manifestation of the Holy Spirit. Yet, at times in the Old Testament, the Spirit even came upon unbelievers to enable them to do unusual tasks (Numbers 24; 2 Chronicles 36:22, 23). The Holy Spirit gave the person power to do what God asked, but it did not always produce the other fruits of the Spirit, such as self-control. Saul, in his early years as king, was a different person (10:1–10) as a result of the Holy Spirit's work in him. But as Saul's power grew, so did his pride. After a while he refused to seek God; the Spirit left him (16:14); and his good attitude melted away.

10:9 [p]ver 6
10:10 [q]ver 5-6; 1Sa 19:20
10:11 [r]Mt 13:54; Jn 7:15 [s]1Sa 19:24
10:14 [t]1Sa 14:50
10:16 [u]1Sa 9:20
10:17 [v]Jdg 20:1; 1Sa 7:5
10:18 [w]Jdg 6:8-9
10:19 [x]1Sa 8:5-7; 12:12 [y]Jos 7:14; 24:1

burnt offerings and fellowship offerings,[b] but you must wait seven days until I come
to you and tell you what you are to do."

Saul Made King

9As Saul turned to leave Samuel, God changed[p] Saul's heart, and all these signs
were fulfilled that day. 10When they arrived at Gibeah, a procession of prophets met
him; the Spirit of God came upon him in power, and he joined in their prophesying.[q]
11When all those who had formerly known him saw him prophesying with the
prophets, they asked each other, "What is this[r] that has happened to the son of Kish?
Is Saul also among the prophets?"[s]
12A man who lived there answered, "And who is their father?" So it became a
saying: "Is Saul also among the prophets?" 13After Saul stopped prophesying, he went
to the high place.
14Now Saul's uncle[t] asked him and his servant, "Where have you been?"
"Looking for the donkeys," he said. "But when we saw they were not to be found,
we went to Samuel."
15Saul's uncle said, "Tell me what Samuel said to you."
16Saul replied, "He assured us that the donkeys[u] had been found." But he did not
tell his uncle what Samuel had said about the kingship.
17Samuel summoned the people of Israel to the LORD at Mizpah[v] 18and said to
them, "This is what the LORD, the God of Israel, says: 'I brought Israel up out of
Egypt, and I delivered you from the power of Egypt and all the kingdoms that
oppressed[w] you.' 19But you have now rejected your God, who saves you out of all
your calamities and distresses. And you have said, 'No, set a king[x] over us.' So now
present[y] yourselves before the LORD by your tribes and clans."

b *8* Traditionally *peace offerings*

RELIGIOUS AND POLITICAL CENTRES OF ISRAEL

GILGAL	Joshua 4:19; Judges 2:1; Hosea 4:15; Micah 6:5
SHILOH	Joshua 18:1–10; 19:51; Judges 18:31; 1 Samuel 1:3; Jeremiah 7:12–14
SHECHEM	Joshua 24:1
RAMAH	1 Samuel 7:17; 8:4
MIZPAH	Judges 11:11; 20:1; 1 Samuel 10:17
BETHEL	Judges 20:18, 26; 1 Samuel 10:3
GIBEAH (political centre only)	1 Samuel 10:26
GIBEON (religious centre only)	1 Kings 3:4; 2 Chronicles 1:2, 3
JERUSALEM	1 Kings 8:1ff; Psalm 51:16–19

During the period of the judges, Israel may have had more than one capital. This may explain why the Scriptures overlap with reference to some cities.

Samuel called the Israelites together at Mizpah, where he would anoint Saul as their first king. Up to this point, the political seat of the nation seems to have been the religious centre of the nation as well. Above are the cities which probably served as both the religious and political centres of Israel since the days of Joshua. Saul may have been the first Israelite leader to separate the nation's religious centre (probably Mizpah at this time) from its political centre (Gibeah—1 Samuel 11:4; 26:1). Politically, the nation grew strong for a while. But when Saul and his officials stopped seeking God's will, internal jealousies and strife soon began to decay the nation from within. When David became king he brought the ark of the covenant back to Jerusalem, his capital. King Solomon then completely united the religious and political centres at Jerusalem.

10:10, 11 A prophet is someone who speaks God's words. While God told many prophets to predict certain events, what God wanted most was for them to instruct and inspire people to live in faithfulness to God. When Saul's friends heard inspired words coming from Saul they exclaimed, "Is Saul also among the prophets?" This was an expression of surprise at worldly Saul's becoming religious. It is equivalent to "What? Has he got religion?"

10:19 Israel's true king was God, but the nation demanded another. Imagine wanting a human being instead of God as guide and leader! Throughout history, men and women have rejected God, and they continue to do it today. Are you rejecting God by pushing him aside and acknowledging someone or something else as your "king" or top priority? Learn from these stories of Israel's kings, and don't push God aside.

20 When Samuel brought all the tribes of Israel near, the tribe of Benjamin was
chosen. 21 Then he brought forward the tribe of Benjamin, clan by clan, and Matri's
clan was chosen. Finally Saul son of Kish was chosen. But when they looked for him,
he was not to be found. 22 So they enquired[z] further of the LORD, "Has the man come
here yet?"
And the LORD said, "Yes, he has hidden himself among the baggage."
23 They ran and brought him out, and as he stood among the people he was a head
taller[a] than any of the others. 24 Samuel said to all the people, "Do you see the man
the LORD has chosen?[b] There is no-one like him among all the people."
Then the people shouted, "Long live[c] the king!"
25 Samuel explained to the people the regulations[d] of the kingship. He wrote them
down on a scroll and deposited it before the LORD. Then Samuel dismissed the people,
each to his own home.
26 Saul also went to his home in Gibeah,[e] accompanied by valiant men whose hearts
God had touched. 27 But some troublemakers[f] said, "How can this fellow save us?"
They despised him and brought him no gifts.[g] But Saul kept silent.

Saul Rescues the City of Jabesh

11 Nahash[a] the Ammonite went up and besieged Jabesh Gilead.[b] And all the men
of Jabesh said to him, "Make a treaty[c] with us, and we will be subject to you."
2 But Nahash the Ammonite replied, "I will make a treaty with you only on the
condition that I gouge[d] out the right eye of every one of you and so bring disgrace[e]
on all Israel."
3 The elders of Jabesh said to him, "Give us seven days so that we can send
messengers throughout Israel; if no-one comes to rescue us, we will surrender to you."

10:22 [z] 1Sa 23:2, 4, 9-11
10:23 [a] 1Sa 9:2
10:24 [b] Dt 17:15; 2Sa 21:6 [c] 1Ki 1:25, 34, 39
10:25 [d] Dt 17:14-20; 1Sa 8:11-18
10:26 [e] 1Sa 11:4
10:27 [f] Dt 13:13 [g] 1Ki 10:25; 2Ch 17:5
11:1 [a] 1Sa 12:12 [b] Jdg 21:8 [c] 1Ki 20:34; Eze 17:13
11:2 [d] Nu 16:14 [e] 1Sa 17:26

10:20 The Israelites chose their first king by casting lots or by using the Urim and Thummim, two plates or flat stones carried by the high priest. The fact that Saul was chosen may seem like luck, but it was really the opposite. God had instructed the Israelites to make the Urim and Thummim for the specific purpose of consulting him in times such as this (Exodus 28:30; Numbers 27:12–21). By using the Urim and Thummim, the Israelites were taking the decision out of their own hands and turning it over to God.

Only the high priest could use the Urim and Thummim, which were designed to give only yes or no answers.

10:22 When the Israelites assembled to choose a king, Saul already knew he was the one (10:1). Instead of coming forward, however, he hid among the baggage. Often we hide from important responsibilities because we are afraid of failure, afraid of what others will think, or perhaps unsure about how to proceed. Prepare now to step up to your future responsibilities. Count on God's provision rather than your feelings of adequacy.

10:25 The kings of Israel, unlike kings of other nations, had specific regulations outlined for them (Deuteronomy 17:14–20). Pagan kings were considered gods; they made their own laws and answered to no-one. By contrast, Israel's king had to answer to a higher authority—the Lord of heaven and earth. The Israelites now had a king like everyone else, just as they wanted. But Samuel, in his charge to both the king and the people, wanted to make sure that the rule of Israel's king would be different from that of his pagan counterparts. "Deposited it before the LORD" means that Samuel put the book, as a witness to the agreement, in a special place at Mizpah.

10:26, 27 Some men became Saul's constant companions, while others despised him. Criticism will always be directed towards those who lead because they are out in front. At this time, Saul took no notice of those who seemed to be against him, although later he would become consumed with jealousy (19:1–3; 26:17–21). As you lead, listen to constructive criticism, but don't spend valuable time and energy worrying about those who may oppose you. Instead, focus your attention on those who are ready and willing to help.

11:1ff At this time, Israel was very susceptible to invasion by marauding tribes such as these Ammonites from east of the Jordan River. Saul's leadership in battle against this warlike tribe helped unify the nation and proved that he was a worthy military ruler. Saul's kingship was solidified when he saved the nation from disgrace and spared the people who had criticised him.

11:3 Why would Nahash give the city of Jabesh Gilead seven days to find an army to help them? Because Israel was still disorganised, Nahash was betting that no-one would come to the city's aid. He was hoping to take the city without a fight and avoid a battle. He also may not have been prepared to attack the city because a siege against its walls could last weeks or months.

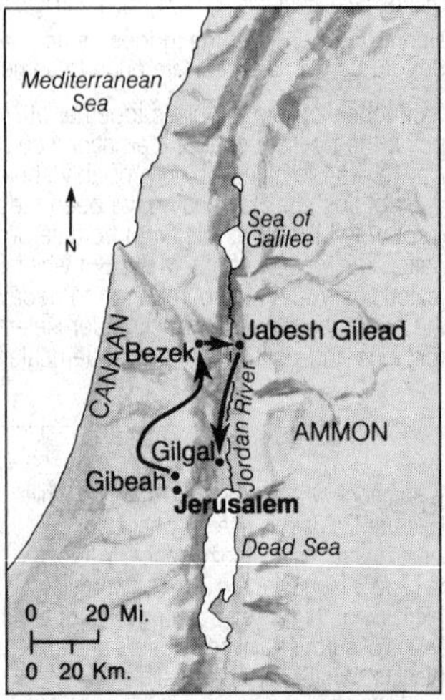

SAUL DEFEATS THE AMMONITES
The Ammonites prepared to attack Jabesh Gilead. The people of Jabesh sent messengers to Saul in Gibeah asking for help. Saul mobilised an army at Bezek and then attacked the Ammonites. After the battle, the Israelites returned to Gilgal to crown Saul as king.

4When the messengers came to Gibeah[f] of Saul and reported these terms to the
people, they all wept[g] aloud. 5Just then Saul was returning from the fields, behind
his oxen, and he asked, "What is wrong with the people? Why are they weeping?"
Then they repeated to him what the men of Jabesh had said.
6When Saul heard their words, the Spirit[h] of God came upon him in power, and
he burned with anger. 7He took a pair of oxen, cut them into pieces, and sent the pieces
by messengers throughout Israel,[i] proclaiming, "This is what will be done to the oxen
of anyone[j] who does not follow Saul and Samuel." Then the terror of the LORD fell
on the people, and they turned out as one man. 8When Saul mustered[k] them at
Bezek,[l] the men of Israel numbered three hundred thousand and the men of Judah
thirty thousand.
9They told the messengers who had come, "Say to the men of Jabesh Gilead, 'By
the time the sun is hot tomorrow, you will be delivered.' " When the messengers went
and reported this to the men of Jabesh, they were elated. 10They said to the Ammonites, "Tomorrow we will surrender[m] to you, and you can do to us whatever seems
good to you."
11The next day Saul separated his men into three divisions;[n] during the last watch
of the night they broke into the camp of the Ammonites and slaughtered them until
the heat of the day. Those who survived were scattered, so that no two of them were
left together.

Saul Confirmed as King

12The people then said to Samuel, "Who[o] was it that asked, 'Shall Saul reign over
us?' Bring these men to us and we will put them to death."
13But Saul said, "No-one shall be put to death today,[p] for this day the LORD has
rescued[q] Israel."
14Then Samuel said to the people, "Come, let us go to Gilgal[r] and there reaffirm
the kingship.[s]" 15So all the people went to Gilgal[t] and confirmed Saul as king in
the presence of the LORD. There they sacrificed fellowship offerings**[a]** before the
LORD, and Saul and all the Israelites held a great celebration.

Samuel's Farewell Speech

12 Samuel said to all Israel, "I have listened[a] to everything you said to me and
have set a king[b] over you. 2Now you have a king as your leader.[c] As for me,
I am old and grey, and my sons are here with you. I have been your leader from my
youth until this day. 3Here I stand. Testify against me in the presence of the LORD
and his anointed.[d] Whose ox have I taken? Whose donkey[e] have I taken? Whom
have I cheated? Whom have I oppressed? From whose hand have I accepted a bribe[f]

a *15* Traditionally *peace offerings*

11:4 [f] 1Sa 10:5, 26; 15:34 [g] Jdg 2:4; 1Sa 30:4
11:6 [h] Jdg 3:10; 6:34; 13:25; 14:6; 1Sa 10:10; 16:13
11:7 [i] Jdg 19:29 [j] Jdg 21:5
11:8 [k] Jdg 20:2 [l] Jdg 1:4
11:10 [m] ver 3
11:11 [n] Jdg 7:16
11:12 [o] 1Sa 10:27; Lk 19:27
11:13 [p] 2Sa 19:22 [q] Ex 14:13; 1Sa 19:5
11:14 [r] 1Sa 10:8 [s] 1Sa 10:25
11:15 [t] 1Sa 10:8, 17
12:1 [a] 1Sa 8:7 [b] 1Sa 10:24; 11:15
12:2 [c] 1Sa 8:5
12:3 [d] 1Sa 10:1; 24:6; 2Sa 1:14 [e] Nu 16:15 [f] Dt 16:19

11:6 Anger is a powerful emotion. Often it may drive people to hurt others with words or physical violence. But anger directed at sin and the mistreatment of others is not wrong. Saul was angered by the Ammonites' threat to humiliate and mistreat his fellow Israelites. The Holy Spirit used Saul's anger to bring justice and freedom. When injustice or sin makes you angry, ask God how you can channel that anger in constructive ways to help bring about a positive change.

11:8 Judah, one of the 12 tribes of Israel, is often mentioned separately from the other 11. There are several reasons for this. Judah was the largest tribe (Numbers 1:20–46), and it was the tribe from which most of Israel's kings would come (Genesis 49:8–12). Later, Judah would be one of the few tribes to return to God after a century of captivity under a hostile foreign power. Judah would also be the tribe through which the Messiah would come (Micah 5:2).

11:14 Saul had been anointed by Samuel at Ramah (10:1); then Saul was publically chosen at Mizpah (10:17–27); his defeat of the Ammonites confirmed his kingship in the people's minds; at this time, all the people confirm his rule.

11:15 The Israelites sacrificed fellowship offerings to God as they made Saul their first king. The instructions for giving these offerings are given in Leviticus 3. The fellowship offering was an expression of gratitude and thanksgiving to God, symbolising the peace that comes to those who know him and who live in accordance with his commands. Although God did not want his people to have a human king, the people were demonstrating through their offerings that he was still their true King. Unfortunately, this attitude did not last, just as God had predicted (8:7–19).

12:1ff Samuel continued to serve the people as their priest, prophet, and judge, but Saul exercised more and more political and military control over the tribes (see 7:15).

12:1–3 In his farewell speech, Samuel asked the Israelites to point out any wrongs he had committed during his time as Israel's judge. By doing so, Samuel was reminding them that he could be trusted to tell the truth. He was also reminding them that having a king was their idea, not his. Samuel was setting the stage for the miraculous thunderstorm recorded in 12:16–19, so that the people could not blame him when God punished them for their selfish motives.

to make me shut my eyes? If I have done[g] any of these, I will make it right."
4"You have not cheated or oppressed us," they replied. "You have not taken
anything from anyone's hand."
5Samuel said to them, "The LORD is witness against you, and also his anointed is
witness this day, that you have not found anything[h] in my hand.[i]"
"He is witness," they said.
6Then Samuel said to the people, "It is the LORD who appointed Moses and Aaron
and brought[j] your forefathers up out of Egypt. 7Now then, stand here, because I am
going to confront[k] you with evidence before the LORD as to all the righteous acts
performed by the LORD for you and your fathers.
8"After Jacob entered Egypt, they cried[l] to the LORD for help, and the LORD sent[m]
Moses and Aaron, who brought your forefathers out of Egypt and settled them in this
place.
9"But they forgot[n] the LORD their God; so he sold them into the hands of Sisera,[o]
the commander of the army of Hazor, and into the hands of the Philistines[p] and the
king of Moab,[q] who fought against them. 10They cried out to the LORD and said, 'We
have sinned; we have forsaken[r] the LORD and served the Baals and the Ashtoreths.[s]
But now deliver us from the hands of our enemies, and we will serve you.' 11Then
the LORD sent Jerub-Baal,[a][t] Barak,[b][u] Jephthah[v] and Samuel,[c] and he delivered
you from the hands of your enemies on every side, so that you lived securely.
12"But when you saw that Nahash[w] king[x] of the Ammonites was moving against
you, you said to me, 'No, we want a king to rule[y] over us'—even though the LORD
your God was your king. 13Now here is the king[z] you have chosen, the one you
asked[a] for; see, the LORD has set a king over you. 14If you fear[b] the LORD and serve
and obey him and do not rebel against his commands, and if both you and the king
who reigns over you follow the LORD your God—good! 15But if you do not obey the
LORD, and if you rebel against[c] his commands, his hand will be against you, as it
was against your fathers.
16"Now then, stand still and see[d] this great thing the LORD is about to do before
your eyes! 17Is it not wheat harvest[e] now? I will call[f] upon the LORD to send thunder
and rain.[g] And you will realise what an evil[h] thing you did in the eyes of the LORD
when you asked for a king."
18Then Samuel called upon the LORD, and that same day the LORD sent thunder and
rain. So all the people stood in awe[i] of the LORD and of Samuel.
19The people all said to Samuel, "Pray[j] to the LORD your God for your servants
so that we will not die, for we have added to all our other sins the evil of asking for
a king."
20"Do not be afraid," Samuel replied. "You have done all this evil; yet do not turn
away from the LORD, but serve the LORD with all your heart. 21Do not turn away after
useless[k] idols.[l] They can do you no good, nor can they rescue you, because they
are useless. 22For the sake[m] of his great name[n] the LORD will not reject[o] his people,
because the LORD was pleased to make[p] you his own. 23As for me, far be it from

a 11 Also called *Gideon* b 11 Some Septuagint manuscripts and Syriac; Hebrew *Bedan* c 11 Hebrew; some Septuagint manuscripts and Syriac *Samson*

12:3 [g]Ac 20:33
12:5 [h]Ac 23:9; 24:20 [i]Ex 22:4
12:6 [j]Ex 6:26; Mic 6:4
12:7 [k]Isa 1:18; Mic 6:1-5
12:8 [l]Ex 2:23 [m]Ex 3:10; 4:16
12:9 [n]Jdg 3:7 [o]Jdg 4:2 [p]Jdg 10:7; 13:1 [q]Jdg 3:12
12:10 [r]Jdg 10:10, 15 [s]Jdg 2:13
12:11 [t]Jdg 6:14, 32 [u]Jdg 4:6 [v]Jdg 11:1
12:12 [w]1Sa 11:1 [x]1Sa 8:5 [y]Jdg 8:23; 1Sa 8:6, 19
12:13 [z]1Sa 8:5; Hos 13:11 [a]1Sa 10:24
12:14 [b]Jos 24:14
12:15 [c]ver 9; Jos 24:20; Isa 1:20
12:16 [d]Ex 14:13
12:17 [e]1Sa 7:9-10 [f]Jas 5:18 [g]Pr 26:1 [h]1Sa 8:6-7
12:18 [i]Ex 14:31
12:19 [j]ver 23; Ex 9:28; Jas 5:18; 1Jn 5:16
12:21 [k]Isa 41:24, 29; Jer 16:19; Hab 2:18 [l]Dt 11:16
12:22 [m]Ps 106:8 [n]Jos 7:9 [o]1Ki 6:13 [p]Dt 7:7; 1Pe 2:9

12:10 "The Baals and the Ashtoreths" were pagan gods. See the note on 7:4 for more information.

12:11 Jerub-Baal was the name given to Gideon when he demolished the altar of Baal (see Judges 6:32).

12:12–15 God granted the nation's request for a king, but his commands and requirements remained the same. God was to be their true King, and both Saul and the people were to be subject to his laws. No person is ever exempt from God's laws. No human action is outside his jurisdiction. God is the true King of every area of life. We must recognise his kingship and pattern our relationships, worklife, and homelife according to his principles.

12:17 The wheat harvest came near the end of the dry season during the months of May and June. Because rain rarely fell during this period, a great thunderstorm was considered a miraculous event. It was not a beneficial miracle, however, because rain during the wheat harvest could damage the crops and cause them to rot quickly. This unusual occurrence showed God's displeasure with Israel's demand for a king.

12:22 Why did God make Israel "his people"? God did not choose them because they deserved it (Deuteronomy 7:7, 8), but in order that they might become his channel of blessing to all people through the Messiah (Genesis 12:1–3). Because God chose the people of Israel, he would never abandon them; but because they were his special nation, he would often punish them for their disobedience in order to bring them back to a right relationship with him.

12:23 Is failing to pray for others a sin? Samuel's words seem to indicate that it is. His actions illustrate two of God's people's re-

12:23 [q]Ro 1:9-10; Col 1:9; 2Ti 1:3 [r]1Ki 8:36; Ps 34:11; Pr 4:11
12:24 [s]Ecc 12:13 [t]Isa 5:12 [u]Dt 10:21
12:25 [v]1Sa 31:1-5 [w]Jos 24:20
13:2 [a]1Sa 10:26
13:3 [b]1Sa 10:5
13:4 [c]Ge 34:30
13:5 [d]Jos 11:4
13:6 [e]Jdg 6:2
13:7 [f]Nu 32:33
13:8 [g]1Sa 10:8
13:9 [h]2Sa 24:25; 1Ki 3:4
13:10 [i]1Sa 15:13

me that I should sin against the LORD by failing to pray[q] for you. And I will teach[r]
you the way that is good and right. 24 But be sure to fear[s] the LORD and serve him
faithfully with all your heart; consider[t] what great[u] things he has done for you. 25 Yet
if you persist[v] in doing evil, both you and your king will be swept[w] away."

2. God rejects Saul for disobedience

Samuel Rebukes Saul

13 Saul was ⌊thirty⌋ **[a]** years old when he became king, and he reigned over Israel
for ⌊forty-⌋ **[b]** two years.
2 Saul **[c]** chose three thousand men from Israel; two thousand were with him at
Michmash and in the hill country of Bethel, and a thousand were with Jonathan at
Gibeah[a] in Benjamin. The rest of the men he sent back to their homes.
3 Jonathan attacked the Philistine outpost[b] at Geba, and the Philistines heard about
it. Then Saul had the trumpet blown throughout the land and said, "Let the Hebrews
hear!" 4 So all Israel heard the news: "Saul has attacked the Philistine outpost, and now
Israel has become an offence[c] to the Philistines." And the people were summoned
to join Saul at Gilgal.
5 The Philistines assembled to fight Israel, with three thousand **[d]** chariots, six
thousand charioteers, and soldiers as numerous as the sand[d] on the seashore. They
went up and camped at Michmash, east of Beth Aven. 6 When the men of Israel saw
that their situation was critical and that their army was hard pressed, they hid in caves
and thickets, among the rocks, and in pits and cisterns.[e] 7 Some Hebrews even crossed
the Jordan to the land of Gad[f] and Gilead.
Saul remained at Gilgal, and all the troops with him were quaking with fear. 8 He
waited for seven[g] days, the time set by Samuel; but Samuel did not come to Gilgal,
and Saul's men began to scatter. 9 So he said, "Bring me the burnt offering and the
fellowship offerings." **[e]** And Saul offered[h] up the burnt offering. 10 Just as he finished
making the offering, Samuel[i] arrived, and Saul went out to greet him.
11 "What have you done?" asked Samuel.
Saul replied, "When I saw that the men were scattering, and that you did not come

a *1* A few late manuscripts of the Septuagint; Hebrew does not have *thirty*. **b** *1* See the round number in Acts 13:21; Hebrew does not have *forty-*. **c** *1,2* Or *and when he had reigned over Israel for two years, 2he* **d** *5* Some Septuagint manuscripts and Syriac; Hebrew *thirty thousand* **e** *9* Traditionally *peace offerings*

---

sponsibilities: (1) they should pray consistently for others (Ephesians 6:18), and (2) they should teach others the right way to God (2 Timothy 2:2). Samuel disagreed with the Israelites' demand for a king, but he assured them that he would continue to pray for them and teach them. We may disagree with others, but we shouldn't stop praying for them.

12:24 This is the second time in his farewell speech that Samuel reminded the people to take time to consider what great things God had done for them (see 12:7). Taking time for reflection allows us to focus our attention upon God's goodness and strengthens our faith. Sometimes we are so progress- and future-oriented that we fail to take time to recall all that God has already done. Remember what God has done for you so that you may move ahead with gratitude.

13:3, 4 Jonathan attacked and destroyed the Philistine outpost, but Saul took all the credit for it. Although this was normal in that culture, it didn't make his action right. Saul's growing pride started out small—taking credit for a battle that was won by his son. Left unchecked, his pride grew into an ugly obsession; thus it destroyed him, tore his family apart, and threatened the well-being of the nation. Taking credit for the accomplishments of others indicates that pride is controlling your life. When you notice pride taking a foothold, take immediate steps to put it in check by giving credit to those who deserve it.

13:6 When we forget who is on our side or see only our own resources, we tend to panic at the sight of the opposition. The Israelites became terrified and hid when they saw the mighty Philistine army. They forgot that God was on their side and that he couldn't be defeated. As you face problems and temptations, focus your attention on God and his resources, trusting him to help you (Romans 8:31–37).

13:9 Rather than waiting for a priest, Saul offered the sacrifice himself. This was against God's laws (Deuteronomy 12:5–14) and against the specific instructions of Samuel (10:8). Under pressure from the approaching Philistines, he took matters into his own hands and disobeyed God. He was doing a good thing (offering a sacrifice to God before a crucial battle), but he did it in the wrong way. Like Saul, our true spiritual character is revealed under pressure. The methods we use to accomplish our goals are as important as the attainment of those goals.

13:11, 12 It is difficult to trust God when you feel your resources slipping away. When Saul felt that time was running out, he became impatient with God's timing. In thinking that the ritual was all he needed, he substituted the ritual for faith in God.

When faced with a difficult decision, don't allow impatience to drive you to disobey God. When you know what God wants, follow his plan regardless of the consequences. God often uses delays to test our obedience and patience.

at the set time, and that the Philistines were assembling at Michmash,[j] 12I thought,
'Now the Philistines will come down against me at Gilgal, and I have not sought the
LORD's favour.[k]' So I felt compelled to offer the burnt offering."
13"You acted foolishly,[l]" Samuel said. "You have not kept[m] the command the
LORD your God gave you; if you had, he would have established your kingdom over
Israel for all time. 14But now your kingdom[n] will not endure; the LORD has sought
out a man after his own heart[o] and appointed[p] him leader of his people, because you
have not kept the LORD's command."
15Then Samuel left Gilgal[f] and went up to Gibeah[q] in Benjamin, and Saul counted
the men who were with him. They numbered about six hundred.

Israel Without Weapons

16Saul and his son Jonathan and the men with them were staying in Gibeah[g] of
Benjamin, while the Philistines camped at Michmash. 17Raiding[r] parties went out
from the Philistine camp in three detachments. One turned towards Ophrah[s] in the
vicinity of Shual, 18another towards Beth Horon,[t] and the third towards the border-
land overlooking the Valley of Zeboim[u] facing the desert.
19Not a blacksmith[v] could be found in the whole land of Israel, because the
Philistines had said, "Otherwise the Hebrews will make swords or spears!" 20So all
Israel went down to the Philistines to have their ploughshares, mattocks, axes and
sickles[h] sharpened. 21The price was two thirds of a shekel[i] for sharpening ploughshares and mattocks, and a third of a shekel[j] for sharpening forks and axes and for
repointing goads.
22So on the day of the battle not a soldier with Saul and Jonathan[w] had a sword
or spear[x] in his hand; only Saul and his son Jonathan had them.

Jonathan Attacks the Philistines

23Now a detachment of Philistines had gone out to the pass[y] at Michmash.
14 1One day Jonathan son of Saul said to the young man bearing his armour,
"Come, let's go over to the Philistine outpost on the other side." But he did
not tell his father.

f *15* Hebrew; Septuagint *Gilgal and went his way; the rest of the people went after Saul to meet the army, and they went out of Gilgal* **g** *16* Two Hebrew manuscripts; most Hebrew manuscripts *Geba,* a variant of *Gibeah* **h** *20* Septuagint; Hebrew *ploughshares* **i** *21* Hebrew *pim*; that is, about ¼ ounce (about 8 grams) **j** *21* That is, about ⅛ ounce (about 4 grams)

13:11 [j]ver 2, 5, 16, 23
13:12 [k]Jer 26:19
13:13 [l]2Ch 16:9 [m]1Sa 15:23, 24
13:14 [n]1Sa 15:28 [o]Ac 7:46; 13:22 [p]2Sa 6:21
13:15 [q]1Sa 14:2
13:17 [r]1Sa 14:15 [s]Jos 18:23
13:18 [t]Jos 18:13-14 [u]Ne 11:34
13:19 [v]2Ki 24:14; Jer 24:1
13:22 [w]1Ch 9:39 [x]Jdg 5:8
13:23 [y]1Sa 14:4

13:12, 13 Saul had plenty of excuses for his disobedience. But Samuel homed in on the real issue: "You have not kept the command the LORD your God gave you." Like Saul, we often gloss over our mistakes and sins, trying to justify and spiritualise our actions because of our "special" circumstances. Our excuses, however, are nothing more than disobedience. God knows our true motives. He forgives, restores, and blesses only when we are honest about our sins. By trying to hide his sins behind excuses, Saul lost his kingship (13:14).

13:19–22 Israel was in no position to conquer anyone. The army had no iron weapons, and there were no facilities for turning their tools into weapons. In fact, if an Israelite wanted to sharpen his tools, he had to pay a Philistine blacksmith to do it because the Philistines had a carefully guarded monopoly on iron and blacksmithing. And they charged high prices for sharpening farm implements. The Philistines' tight control over the technology, along with their surprise raids, demoralised the Israelites and kept them in subjection.

Against such superiority, the Israelites were at a serious disadvantage. How could they hope to rout their oppressors? Only with God's help. God wanted to give Israel victory without swords, so they would realise their true source of strength.

14:1ff In this chapter we read about the miserable job Saul did as leader: he had no communication with Jonathan (14:1, 17); he made a foolish curse (14:24); and he ignored the well-being of his own soldiers (14:31). Saul's poor leadership was not a result of personality traits but of decaying spiritual character. What we do is often a direct result of our spiritual condition. We cannot ignore the importance of spiritual character in effective leadership.

14:1 Why would Jonathan go alone to attack the Philistines? Jonathan may have been weary of the long, hopeless deadlock in the battle; he trusted God to give the victory and wanted to act on that trust. He also knew that the number of Philistines was no problem for God. Perhaps he didn't tell his father about his mission because he thought Saul would not let him go.

14:2
[a] 1Sa 13:15
[b] Isa 10:28

14:3
[c] 1Sa 4:21
[d] 1Sa 22:11, 20
[e] 1Sa 2:28

14:4
[f] 1Sa 13:23

2Saul was staying on the outskirts of Gibeah[a] under a pomegranate tree in Migron.[b] With him were about six hundred men, 3among whom was Ahijah, who was
wearing an ephod. He was a son of Ichabod's[c] brother Ahitub[d] son of Phinehas,
the son of Eli,[e] the LORD's priest in Shiloh. No-one was aware that Jonathan had left.
4On each side of the pass[f] that Jonathan intended to cross to reach the Philistine
outpost was a cliff; one was called Bozez, and the other Seneh. 5One cliff stood to
the north towards Michmash, the other to the south towards Geba.

SAUL

First impressions can be deceiving, especially when the image created by a person's appearance is contradicted by his or her qualities and abilities. Saul presented the ideal visual image of a king, but the tendencies of his character often went contrary to God's commands for a king. Saul was God's chosen leader, but this did not mean he was capable of being king on his own.

During his reign, Saul had his greatest successes when he obeyed God. His greatest failures resulted from acting on his own. Saul had the raw materials to be a good leader—appearance, courage, and action. Even his weaknesses could have been used by God if Saul had recognised them and left them in God's hands. His own choices cut him off from God and eventually alienated him from his own people.

From Saul we learn that while our strengths and abilities make us useful, it is our weaknesses that make us usable. Our skills and talents make us tools, but our failures and shortcomings remind us that we need a Craftsman in control of our lives. Whatever we accomplish on our own is only a hint of what God could do through our lives. Does he control your life?

Strengths and accomplishments:
- First God-appointed king of Israel
- Known for his personal courage and generosity
- Stood tall, with a striking appearance

Weaknesses and mistakes:
- His leadership abilities did not match the expectations created by his appearance
- Impulsive by nature, he tended to overstep the mark
- Jealous of David, he tried to kill him
- He specifically disobeyed God on several occasions

Lessons from his life:
- God wants obedience from the heart, not mere acts of religious ritual
- Obedience always involves sacrifice; but sacrifice is not always obedience
- God wants to make use of our strengths and weaknesses
- Weaknesses should help us remember our need for God's guidance and help

Vital statistics:
- Where: The land of Benjamin
- Occupation: King of Israel
- Relatives: Father: Kish. Sons: Jonathan and Ish-Bosheth. Wife: Ahinoam. Daughters: Merab and Michal

Key verses:
"But Samuel replied: 'Does the LORD delight in burnt offerings and sacrifices as much as in obeying the voice of the LORD? To obey is better than sacrifice, and to heed is better than the fat of rams. For rebellion is like the sin of divination, and arrogance like the evil of idolatry. Because you have rejected the word of the LORD, he has rejected you as king' " (1 Samuel 15:22, 23).

His story is told in 1 Samuel 9—31. He is also mentioned in Acts 13:21.

6Jonathan said to his young armour-bearer, "Come, let's go over to the outpost of
those uncircumcised[g] fellows. Perhaps the LORD will act on our behalf. Nothing[h]
can hinder the LORD from saving, whether by many[i] or by few.[j]"
7"Do all that you have in mind," his armour-bearer said. "Go ahead; I am with you
heart and soul."
8Jonathan said, "Come, then; we will cross over towards the men and let them see
us. 9If they say to us, 'Wait there until we come to you,' we will stay where we are
and not go up to them. 10But if they say, 'Come up to us,' we will climb up, because
that will be our sign[k] that the LORD has given them into our hands."
11So both of them showed themselves to the Philistine outpost. "Look!" said the
Philistines. "The Hebrews are crawling out of the holes they were hiding[l] in." 12The
men of the outpost shouted to Jonathan and his armour-bearer, "Come up to us and
we'll teach you a lesson.[m]"
So Jonathan said to his armour-bearer, "Climb up after me; the LORD has given them
into the hand[n] of Israel."
13Jonathan climbed up, using his hands and feet, with his armour-bearer right
behind him. The Philistines fell before Jonathan, and his armour-bearer followed and
killed behind him. 14In that first attack Jonathan and his armour-bearer killed some
twenty men in an area of about half an acre.[a]

Israel Routs the Philistines

15Then panic[o] struck the whole army—those in the camp and field, and those in
the outposts and raiding[p] parties—and the ground shook. It was a panic sent by
God.[b]
16Saul's lookouts[q] at Gibeah in Benjamin saw the army melting away in all
directions. 17Then Saul said to the men who were with him, "Muster the forces and
see who has left us." When they did, it was Jonathan and his armour-bearer who were
not there.
18Saul said to Ahijah, "Bring[r] the ark of God." (At that time it was with the
Israelites.)[c] 19While Saul was talking to the priest, the tumult in the Philistine camp
increased more and more. So Saul said to the priest,[s] "Withdraw your hand."
20Then Saul and all his men assembled and went to the battle. They found the
Philistines in total confusion, striking[t] each other with their swords. 21Those He-

a 14 Hebrew *half a yoke*; a "yoke" was the land ploughed by a yoke of oxen in one day. b 15 Or *a terrible panic*
c 18 Hebrew; Septuagint *"Bring the ephod." (At that time he wore the ephod before the Israelites.)*

14:6 g1Sa 17:26, 36; Jer 9:26 hHeb 11:34 iJdg 7:4 j1Sa 17:46-47
14:10 kGe 24:14; Jdg 6:36-37
14:11 l1Sa 13:6
14:12 m1Sa 17:43-44 n2Sa 5:24
14:15 oGe 35:5; 2Ki 7:5-7 p1Sa 13:17
14:16 q2Sa 18:24
14:18 r1Sa 30:7
14:19 sNu 27:21
14:20 tJdg 7:22; 2Ch 20:23

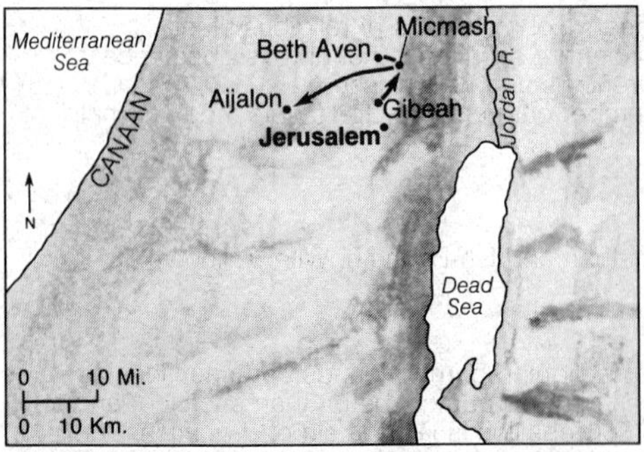

JONATHAN'S BRAVERY Jonathan, Saul's son, left the camp at Gibeah and crept to the Philistine camp at Micmash. With God's help, Jonathan and his armour-bearer surprised the Philistines, who panicked and began killing each other! Saul's army heard the commotion and chased the Philistines as far as Beth Aven and Aijalon.

14:6 Jonathan and his armour-bearer weren't much of a force to attack the huge Philistine army. But while everyone else was afraid, they trusted God, knowing that the size of the enemy army would not restrict God's ability to help them. God honoured the faith and brave action of these two men with a tremendous victory.

Have you ever felt surrounded by the "enemy" or faced overwhelming odds? God is never intimidated by the size of the enemy or the complexity of a problem. With him, there are always enough resources to resist the pressures and win the battle. If God has called you to action, then bravely commit what resources you have to God, and rely upon him to lead you to victory.

14:12 Jonathan did not have the authority to lead all the troops into battle, but he could start a small skirmish in one corner of the enemy camp. When he did, panic broke out among the Philistines, the Hebrews who had been drafted into the Philistine army revolted, and the men who were hiding in the hills regained their courage and returned to fight.

When you are facing a difficult situation that is beyond your control, ask yourself, "What steps can I take now to work towards a solution?" A few small steps may be just what is needed to begin the chain of events leading to eventual victory.

14:19 "Withdraw your hand" refers to the use of the Urim and Thummim. They were withdrawn from the linen ephod (vest) as a way to determine God's will (see the note on 10:20). Saul was rushing the formalities of getting an answer from God so he could hurry and get into battle to take advantage of the confusion of the Philistines.

brews who had previously been with the Philistines and had gone up with them to their
camp went[u] over to the Israelites who were with Saul and Jonathan. 22 When all the
Israelites who had hidden[v] in the hill country of Ephraim heard that the Philistines
were on the run, they joined the battle in hot pursuit. 23 So the LORD rescued[w] Israel
that day, and the battle moved on beyond Beth Aven.[x]

Jonathan Eats Honey

24 Now the men of Israel were in distress that day, because Saul had bound the
people under an oath,[y] saying, "Cursed be any man who eats food before evening
comes, before I have avenged myself on my enemies!" So none of the troops tasted
food.
25 The entire army[d] entered the woods, and there was honey on the ground. 26 When
they went into the woods, they saw the honey oozing out, yet no-one put his hand
to his mouth, because they feared the oath. 27 But Jonathan had not heard that his father
had bound the people with the oath, so he reached out the end of the staff that was
in his hand and dipped it into the honeycomb.[z] He raised his hand to his mouth, and
his eyes brightened.[e] 28 Then one of the soldiers told him, "Your father bound the
army under a strict oath, saying, 'Cursed be any man who eats food today!' That is
why the men are faint."
29 Jonathan said, "My father has made trouble[a] for the country. See how my eyes
brightened[f] when I tasted a little of this honey. 30 How much better it would have
been if the men had eaten today some of the plunder they took from their enemies.
Would not the slaughter of the Philistines have been even greater?"
31 That day, after the Israelites had struck down the Philistines from Michmash to
Aijalon,[b] they were exhausted. 32 They pounced on the plunder[c] and, taking sheep,
cattle and calves, they butchered them on the ground and ate them, together with the
blood.[d] 33 Then someone said to Saul, "Look, the men are sinning against the LORD
by eating meat that has blood in it."
"You have broken faith," he said. "Roll a large stone over here at once." 34 Then
he said, "Go out among the men and tell them, 'Each of you bring me your cattle and
sheep, and slaughter them here and eat them. Do not sin against the LORD by eating
meat with blood still in it.' "

14:21 u 1Sa 29:4
14:22 v 1Sa 13:6
14:23 w Ex 14:30; Ps 44:6-7 x 1Sa 13:5
14:24 y Jos 6:26
14:27 z ver 43; 1Sa 30:12
14:29 a Jos 7:25; 1Ki 18:18
14:31 b Jos 10:12
14:32 c 1Sa 15:19 d Ge 9:4; Lev 3:17; 7:26; 17:10-14; 19:26; Dt 12:16, 23-24

d *25* Or *Now all the people of the land* **e** *27* Or *his strength was renewed* **f** *29* Or *my strength was renewed*

GLOOM AND DOOM

Reference	*Message*
3:11–14	Judgment will come to the house of Eli.
7:1–4	The nation must turn from idol worship.
8:10–22	Your kings will bring you nothing but trouble.
12:25	If you continue in sin, you will be destroyed by God.
13:13, 14	Saul's kingdom will not continue.
15:17–31	Saul, you have sinned before God.

It wasn't easy being a prophet. Most of the messages they had to give were very unpleasant to hear. They preached of repentance, judgment, impending destruction, sin, and in general, how displeased God was with the behaviour of his people. Prophets were not the most popular people in town (unless they were *false* prophets and said just what the people wanted to hear). But popularity was not the bottom line for true prophets of God—it was obedience to God and faithfully proclaiming his word. Samuel is a good example of a faithful prophet.

God has words for us to proclaim as well. And although his messages are loaded with "good news", there is also "bad news" to give. May we, like true prophets, faithfully deliver *all* God's words, regardless of their popularity or lack of it.

14:24 Saul made an oath without thinking through the implications. The results? (1) His men were too tired to fight; (2) they were so hungry they ate meat that still contained blood, which was against God's law (14:32); (3) Saul almost killed his own son (14:42–44).

Saul's impulsive oath sounded heroic, but it had disastrous side effects. If you are in the middle of a conflict, guard against impulsive statements that you may be forced to honour.

14:32–34 One of the oldest and strongest Hebrew food laws was the prohibition against eating meat containing the animal's blood (Leviticus 7:26, 27). This law began in Noah's day (Genesis 9:4) and was still observed by the early Christians (Acts 15:27–29). It was wrong to eat blood because blood represented life and life belonged to God. (For a further explanation, see Leviticus 17:10–14.)

So everyone brought his ox that night and slaughtered it there. 35Then Saul built
an altar[e] to the LORD; it was the first time he had done this.
36Saul said, "Let us go down after the Philistines by night and plunder them till
dawn, and let us not leave one of them alive."
"Do whatever seems best to you," they replied.
But the priest said, "Let us enquire of God here."
37So Saul asked God, "Shall I go down after the Philistines? Will you give them
into Israel's hand?" But God did not answer[f] him that day.
38Saul therefore said, "Come here, all you who are leaders of the army, and let us
find out what sin has been committed[g] today. 39As surely as the LORD who rescues
Israel lives,[h] even if it lies with my son Jonathan, he must die." But not one of the
men said a word.
40Saul then said to all the Israelites, "You stand over there; I and Jonathan my son
will stand over here."
"Do what seems best to you," the men replied.
41Then Saul prayed to the LORD, the God of Israel, "Give[i] me the right[j] answer."**[g]** And Jonathan and Saul were taken by lot, and the men were cleared. 42Saul
said, "Cast the lot between me and Jonathan my son." And Jonathan was taken.
43Then Saul said to Jonathan, "Tell me what you have done."[k]
So Jonathan told him, "I merely tasted a little honey[l] with the end of my staff.
And now must I die?"
44Saul said, "May God deal with me, be it ever so severely,[m] if you do not die,
Jonathan.[n]"
45But the men said to Saul, "Should Jonathan die – he who has brought about this
great deliverance in Israel? Never! As surely as the LORD lives, not a hair[o] of his head
shall fall to the ground, for he did this today with God's help." So the men rescued[p]
Jonathan, and he was not put to death.
46Then Saul stopped pursuing the Philistines, and they withdrew to their own land.
47After Saul had assumed rule over Israel, he fought against their enemies on every
side: Moab, the Ammonites,[q] Edom, the kings**[h]** of Zobah,[r] and the Philistines.
Wherever he turned, he inflicted punishment on them.**[i]** 48He fought valiantly and

g *41* Hebrew; Septuagint *"Why have you not answered your servant today? If the fault is in me or my son Jonathan, respond with Urim, but if the men of Israel are at fault, respond with Thummim."* **h** *47* Masoretic Text; Dead Sea Scrolls and Septuagint *king* **i** *47* Hebrew; Septuagint *he was victorious*

14:35 [e] 1Sa 7:17
14:37 [f] 1Sa 10:22; 28:6, 15
14:38 [g] Jos 7:11; 1Sa 10:19
14:39 [h] 2Sa 12:5
14:41 [i] Ac 1:24 [j] Pr 16:33
14:43 [k] Jos 7:19 [l] ver 27
14:44 [m] Ru 1:17 [n] ver 39
14:45 [o] 1Ki 1:52; Lk 21:18; Ac 27:34 [p] 2Sa 14:11
14:47 [q] 1Sa 11:1-13 [r] ver 52; 2Sa 10:6

14:35, 36 After being king for several years, Saul finally built his first altar to God, but only as a last resort. Throughout Saul's reign he consistently approached God only after he had tried everything else. This was in sharp contrast to the priest, who suggested that God be consulted *first.* How much better if Saul had gone to God first, building an altar as his first official act as king. God is too great to be an afterthought. When we turn to him first, we will never have to turn to him as a last resort.

14:39 This is the second of Saul's foolish curses. Saul made the first of his two oaths (14:24–26) because he was overly anxious to defeat the Philistines and wanted to give his soldiers an incentive to finish the battle quickly. In the Bible, God never asked people to make oaths or vows, but if they did, he expected them to keep them (Leviticus 5:4; Numbers 30).

Saul's curse was not something God would have condoned, but still it was an oath. And Jonathan, although he didn't know about Saul's oath, was nevertheless guilty of breaking it. Like Jephthah (Judges 11), Saul made an oath that risked the life of his own child. Fortunately, the people intervened and spared Jonathan's life.

14:39 Saul had issued a ridiculous command and had driven his men to sin, but still he wouldn't back down even if he had to kill his son. When we make ridiculous statements, it is difficult to admit we are wrong. Sticking to the story, just to save face, only compounds the problem. It takes more courage to admit a mistake than to hold resolutely to an error.

14:43 Jonathan's spiritual character was in striking contrast to Saul's. Jonathan admitted what he had done; he did not try to make excuses. Even though he was unaware of Saul's oath, Jonathan was willing to accept the consequences of his actions. When you do wrong, even unintentionally, respond like Jonathan, not like Saul.

14:44, 45 Saul made another foolish statement, this time because he was more concerned about saving face than being right. To spare Jonathan's life would require him to admit he had acted foolishly, an embarrassment for a king. Saul was really more interested in protecting his image than in enforcing his vow. Fortunately, the people came to Jonathan's rescue. Don't be like Saul. Admit your mistakes, and show that you are more interested in doing what is right than in looking good.

14:47 Why was Saul so successful right after he had disobeyed God and been told that his reign would end (13:13, 14)? Sometimes ungodly people win battles. Victory is neither guaranteed nor limited to the righteous. God provides according to his will. God might have given Saul success for the sake of the people, not for Saul. He may have left Saul on the throne for a while to utilise his military talents so that David, Israel's next king, could spend more time focusing on the nation's spiritual battles. Regardless of God's reasons for delaying Saul's demise, his reign ended exactly the way God had foretold. The timing of God's plans and promises are known only to him. Our task is to commit our ways to God and then trust him for the outcome.

14:48
[s]1Sa 15:2, 7

14:49
[t]1Sa 31:2; 1Ch 8:33
[u]1Sa 18:17-20

14:51
[v]1Sa 9:1

14:52
[w]1Sa 8:11

15:1
[a]1Sa 9:16

15:2
[b]Ex 17:8-14; Nu 24:20; Dt 25:17-19

15:3
[c]Nu 24:20; Dt 20:16-18; Jos 6:17; 1Sa 22:19

15:6
[d]Ex 18:10, 19; Nu 10:29-32; 24:22; Jdg 1:16; 4:1

15:7
[e]1Sa 14:48
[f]Ge 16:7; 25:17-18; Ex 15:22

15:8
[g]1Sa 30:1

15:9
[h]ver 3, 15

15:11
[i]Ge 6:6; 2Sa 24:16
[j]Jos 22:16
[k]1Sa 13:13; 1Ki 9:6-7
[l]ver 35

15:12
[m]Jos 15:55

defeated the Amalekites,[s] delivering Israel from the hands of those who had plundered them.

Saul's Family

49Saul's sons were Jonathan, Ishvi and Malki-Shua.[t] The name of his older
daughter was Merab, and that of the younger was Michal.[u] 50His wife's name was
Ahinoam daughter of Ahimaaz. The name of the commander of Saul's army was
Abner son of Ner, and Ner was Saul's uncle. 51Saul's father Kish[v] and Abner's father
Ner were sons of Abiel.
52All the days of Saul there was bitter war with the Philistines, and whenever Saul
saw a mighty or brave man, he took[w] him into his service.

The Lord Rejects Saul as King

15 Samuel said to Saul, "I am the one the LORD sent to anoint[a] you king over
his people Israel; so listen now to the message from the LORD. 2This is what
the LORD Almighty says: 'I will punish the Amalekites[b] for what they did to Israel
when they waylaid them as they came up from Egypt. 3Now go, attack the Amalekites
and totally[c] destroy**[a]** everything that belongs to them. Do not spare them; put to death
men and women, children and infants, cattle and sheep, camels and donkeys.' "
4So Saul summoned the men and mustered them at Telaim—two hundred thousand
foot soldiers and ten thousand men from Judah. 5Saul went to the city of Amalek and
set an ambush in the ravine. 6Then he said to the Kenites,[d] "Go away, leave the
Amalekites so that I do not destroy you along with them; for you showed kindness
to all the Israelites when they came up out of Egypt." So the Kenites moved away
from the Amalekites.
7Then Saul attacked the Amalekites[e] all the way from Havilah to Shur,[f] to the
east of Egypt. 8He took Agag king of the Amalekites alive,[g] and all his people he
totally destroyed with the sword. 9But Saul and the army spared[h] Agag and the best
of the sheep and cattle, the fat calves**[b]** and lambs—everything that was good. These
they were unwilling to destroy completely, but everything that was despised and weak
they totally destroyed.
10Then the word of the LORD came to Samuel: 11"I am grieved[i] that I have made
Saul king, because he has turned[j] away from me and has not carried out my
instructions."[k] Samuel was troubled,[l] and he cried out to the LORD all that night.
12Early in the morning Samuel got up and went to meet Saul, but he was told, "Saul
has gone to Carmel.[m] There he has set up a monument in his own honour and has
turned and gone on down to Gilgal."

a *3* The Hebrew term refers to the irrevocable giving of things or persons to the LORD, often by totally destroying them; also in verses 8, 9, 15, 18, 20 and 21. **b** *9* Or *the grown bulls*; the meaning of the Hebrew for this phrase is uncertain.

15:2, 3 Why did God command such utter destruction? The Amalekites were a band of guerrilla terrorists. They lived by attacking other nations and carrying off their wealth and their families. They were the first to attack the Israelites as they entered the promised land, and they continued to raid Israelite camps at every opportunity. God knew that the Israelites could never live peacefully in the promised land as long as the Amalekites existed. He also knew that their corrupt, idolatrous religious practices threatened Israel's relationship with him. The only way to protect the Israelites' bodies and souls was to utterly destroy the people of this warlike nation and all their possessions, including their idols.

15:9 Saul and his men did not destroy all the plunder from the battle as God commanded (15:3). The law of devoting something—setting it aside—entirely for destruction was well known to the Israelites. Anything under God's ban was to be completely destroyed (Deuteronomy 20:16–18). This was set up in order to prevent idolatry from taking hold in Israel because many of the valuables were idols. To break this law was punishable by death (Joshua 7). It showed disrespect and disregard for God because it directly violated his command.

When we gloss over sin in order to protect what we have or for material gain, we aren't being shrewd; we are disobeying God's law. Selective obedience is just another form of disobedience.

15:11 When God said he was grieved that he had made Saul king, was he saying he had made a mistake? God's comment was an expression of sorrow, not an admission of error (Genesis 6:5–7). An omniscient God cannot make a mistake; therefore, God did not change his mind. He did, however, change his attitude towards Saul when Saul changed. Saul's heart no longer belonged to God, but to his own interests.

15:12 Saul built a monument in honour of himself. What a contrast to Moses and Joshua, who gave all the credit to God.

13When Samuel reached him, Saul said, "The LORD bless you! I have carried out
the LORD's instructions."
14But Samuel said, "What then is this bleating of sheep in my ears? What is this
lowing of cattle that I hear?"
15Saul answered, "The soldiers brought them from the Amalekites; they spared the
best of the sheep and cattle to sacrifice to the LORD your God, but we totally destroyed
the rest."
16"Stop!" Samuel said to Saul. "Let me tell you what the LORD said to me last
night."
"Tell me," Saul replied.
17Samuel said, "Although you were once small[n] in your own eyes, did you not
become the head of the tribes of Israel? The LORD anointed you king over Israel. 18And
he sent you on a mission, saying, 'Go and completely destroy those wicked people,
the Amalekites; make war on them until you have wiped them out.' 19Why did you
not obey the LORD? Why did you pounce on the plunder[o] and do evil in the eyes of
the LORD?"
20"But I did obey[p] the LORD," Saul said. "I went on the mission the LORD assigned
me. I completely destroyed the Amalekites and brought back Agag their king. 21The
soldiers took sheep and cattle from the plunder, the best of what was devoted to God,
in order to sacrifice them to the LORD your God at Gilgal."
22But Samuel replied:

"Does the LORD delight in burnt offerings and sacrifices
as much as in obeying the voice of the LORD?
To obey is better than sacrifice,[q]
and to heed is better than the fat of rams.
23For rebellion is like the sin of divination,[r]
and arrogance like the evil of idolatry.
Because you have rejected[s] the word of the LORD,
he has rejected you as king."

24Then Saul said to Samuel, "I have sinned.[t] I violated the LORD's command and
your instructions. I was afraid[u] of the people and so I gave in to them. 25Now I beg
you, forgive[v] my sin and come back with me, so that I may worship the LORD."
26But Samuel said to him, "I will not go back with you. You have rejected[w] the
word of the LORD, and the LORD has rejected you as king over Israel!"
27As Samuel turned to leave, Saul caught hold of the hem of his robe, and it tore.[x]
28Samuel said to him, "The LORD has torn[y] the kingdom of Israel from you today
and has given it to one of your neighbours—to one better than you. 29He who is the

15:17 [n]1Sa 9:21
15:19 [o]1Sa 14:32
15:20 [p]ver 13
15:22 [q]Ps 40:6-8; 51:16; Isa 1:11-15; Jer 7:22; Hos 6:6; Mic 6:6-8; Mt 12:7; Mk 12:33; Heb 10:6-9
15:23 [r]Dt 18:10 [s]1Sa 13:13
15:24 [t]2Sa 12:13 [u]Pr 29:25; Isa 51:12-13
15:25 [v]Ex 10:17
15:26 [w]1Sa 13:14
15:27 [x]1Ki 11:11, 31
15:28 [y]1Sa 28:17; 1Ki 11:31

15:13, 14 Saul thought he had won a great victory over the Amalekites, but God saw it as a great failure because Saul had disobeyed him and then lied to Samuel about the results of the battle. Saul may have thought his lie wouldn't be detected, or that what he did was not wrong. Saul was deceiving himself.

Dishonest people soon begin to believe the lies they construct around themselves. Then they lose the ability to tell the difference between truth and lies. By believing your own lies you deceive yourself, you will alienate yourself from God, and you will lose credibility in all your relationships. In the long run, honesty wins out.

15:22, 23 This is the first of numerous places in the Bible where the theme "to obey is better than sacrifice" is stated (Psalms 40:6–8; 51:16, 17; Proverbs 21:3; Isaiah 1:11–17; Jeremiah 7:21–23; Hosea 6:6; Micah 6:6–8; Matthew 12:7; Mark 12:33; Hebrews 10:8, 9). Was Samuel saying that sacrifice is unimportant? No, he was urging Saul to look at his reasons for making the sacrifice rather than at the sacrifice itself. A sacrifice was a ritual transaction between man and God that physically demonstrated a relationship between them. But if the person's heart was not truly repentant or if he did not truly love God, the sacrifice was a hollow ritual. Religious ceremonies or rituals are empty unless they are performed with an attitude of love and obedience. "Being religious" (going to church, serving on a committee, giving to charity) is not enough if we do not act out of devotion and obedience to God.

15:23 Rebellion and arrogance are serious sins. They involve far more than being independent and strong-minded. Scripture equates them with divination (witchcraft) and idolatry, sins worthy of death (Exodus 22:18; Leviticus 20:6; Deuteronomy 13:12–15; 18:10; Micah 5:10–14).

Saul became both rebellious and arrogant, so it is little wonder that God finally rejected him and took away his kingdom. Rebellion against God is perhaps the most serious sin of all because as long as a person rebels, he or she closes the door to forgiveness and restoration with God.

15:26 Saul's excuses had come to an end. It was the time of reckoning. God wasn't rejecting Saul as a person; the king could still seek forgiveness and restore his relationship with God, but it was too late to get his kingdom back. If you do not act responsibly with what God has entrusted to you, eventually you will run out of excuses. All of us must one day give an account for our actions (Romans 14:12; Revelation 22:12).

15:29 [z]1Ch 29:11; Tit 1:2 [a]Nu 23:19; Eze 24:14
15:30 [b]Isa 29:13; Jn 5:44; 12:43
15:33 [c]Ge 9:6; Jdg 1:7
15:34 [d]1Sa 7:17 [e]1Sa 11:4
15:35 [f]1Sa 19:24 [g]1Sa 16:1
16:1 [a]1Sa 15:35 [b]1Sa 15:23 [c]2Ki 9:1 [d]Ru 4:17; 1Sa 9:16 [e]Ps 78:70; Ac 13:22
16:3 [f]Ex 4:15 [g]Dt 17:15; 1Sa 9:16
16:4 [h]Ge 48:7; Lk 2:4 [i]1Ki 2:13; 2Ki 9:17
16:5 [j]Ex 19:10, 22
16:6 [k]1Sa 17:13
16:7 [l]Ps 147:10 [m]1Ki 8:39; 1Ch 28:9; Isa 55:8
16:8 [n]1Sa 17:13

Glory of Israel does not lie[z] or change[a] his mind; for he is not a man, that he should
change his mind."
30Saul replied, "I have sinned. But please honour[b] me before the elders of my
people and before Israel; come back with me, so that I may worship the LORD your
God." 31So Samuel went back with Saul, and Saul worshipped the LORD.
32Then Samuel said, "Bring me Agag king of the Amalekites."
Agag came to him confidently,[c] thinking, "Surely the bitterness of death is past."
33But Samuel said,

> "As your sword has made women childless,
> so will your mother be childless among women."[c]

And Samuel put Agag to death before the LORD at Gilgal.
34Then Samuel left for Ramah,[d] but Saul went up to his home in Gibeah[e] of Saul.
35Until the day Samuel[f] died, he did not go to see Saul again, though Samuel
mourned[g] for him. And the LORD was grieved that he had made Saul king over Israel.

C. SAUL AND DAVID (16:1—31:13)

While Saul is still on the throne, Samuel anoints David as Israel's next king. Young David then bravely conquers Goliath, the Philistine champion, and establishes a lifelong friendship with Jonathan, Saul's son. When Saul realises that David will become king one day, he grows very jealous and tries to kill David on several occasions. David escapes into Philistine territory until Saul is killed in battle. When treated unjustly, we should not take matters into our own hands. God, who is faithful and just, sees all that is happening and will judge all evil.

1. Samuel anoints David

16 The LORD said to Samuel, "How long will you mourn[a] for Saul, since I have
rejected[b] him as king over Israel? Fill your horn with oil[c] and be on your way;
I am sending you to Jesse[d] of Bethlehem. I have chosen[e] one of his sons to be king."
2But Samuel said, "How can I go? Saul will hear about it and kill me."
The LORD said, "Take a heifer with you and say, 'I have come to sacrifice to the
LORD.' 3Invite Jesse to the sacrifice, and I will show[f] you what to do. You are to
anoint[g] for me the one I indicate."
4Samuel did what the LORD said. When he arrived at Bethlehem,[h] the elders of
the town trembled when they met him. They asked, "Do you come in peace?[i]"
5Samuel replied, "Yes, in peace; I have come to sacrifice to the LORD. Consecrate[j]
yourselves and come to the sacrifice with me." Then he consecrated Jesse and his sons
and invited them to the sacrifice.
6When they arrived, Samuel saw Eliab[k] and thought, "Surely the LORD's anointed
stands here before the LORD."
7But the LORD said to Samuel, "Do not consider his appearance or his height, for
I have rejected him. The LORD does not look at the things man looks at. Man looks
at the outward appearance,[l] but the LORD looks at the heart."[m]
8Then Jesse called Abinadab[n] and made him pass in front of Samuel. But Samuel
said, "The LORD has not chosen this one either." 9Jesse then made Shammah pass by,
but Samuel said, "Nor has the LORD chosen this one." 10Jesse made seven of his sons

[c] 32 Or *him trembling, yet*

15:30 Saul was more concerned about what others would think of him than he was about the status of his relationship with God (15:24). He begged Samuel to go with him to worship as a public demonstration that Samuel still supported him. If Samuel had refused, the people probably would have lost all confidence in Saul.

16:5 Samuel "consecrated" Jesse and his sons to prepare them to come before God in worship or to offer a sacrifice. For more on this ceremony, see Genesis 35:2; Exodus 19:10, 14; and the note on Joshua 3:5.

16:7 Saul was tall and handsome; he was an impressive-looking man. Samuel may have been trying to find someone who looked like Saul to be Israel's next king, but God warned him against judging by appearance alone. When people judge by outward appearance, they may overlook quality individuals who lack the particular physical qualities society currently admires. Appearance doesn't reveal what people are really like or what their true value is.

Fortunately, God judges by faith and character, not appearances. And because only God can see on the inside, only he can accurately judge people. Most people spend hours each week maintaining their outward appearance; they should do even more to develop their inner character. While everyone can see your face, only you and God know what your heart really looks like. What steps are you taking to improve your heart's attitude?

pass before Samuel, but Samuel said to him, "The LORD has not chosen these." 11So
he asked Jesse, "Are these all[o] the sons you have?"
"There is still the youngest," Jesse answered, "but he is tending the sheep."
Samuel said, "Send for him; we will not sit down[a] until he arrives."
12So he[p] sent and had him brought in. He was ruddy, with a fine appearance and
handsome[q] features.
Then the LORD said, "Rise and anoint him; he is the one."
13So Samuel took the horn of oil and anointed him in the presence of his brothers,
and from that day on the Spirit of the LORD[r] came upon David in power.[s] Samuel
then went to Ramah.

David in Saul's Service

14Now the Spirit of the LORD had departed[t] from Saul, and an evil[b] spirit[u] from
the LORD tormented him.
15Saul's attendants said to him, "See, an evil spirit from God is tormenting you.
16Let our lord command his servants here to search for someone who can play the
harp.[v] He will play when the evil spirit from God comes upon you, and you will feel
better."
17So Saul said to his attendants, "Find someone who plays well and bring him to
me."
18One of the servants answered, "I have seen a son of Jesse of Bethlehem who
knows how to play the harp. He is a brave man and a warrior. He speaks well and
is a fine-looking man. And the LORD is with[w] him."
19Then Saul sent messengers to Jesse and said, "Send me your son David, who is
with the sheep." 20So Jesse took a donkey loaded with bread,[x] a skin of wine and
a young goat and sent them with his son David to Saul.
21David came to Saul and entered his service.[y] Saul liked him very much, and
David became one of his armour-bearers. 22Then Saul sent word to Jesse, saying,
"Allow David to remain in my service, for I am pleased with him."
23Whenever the spirit from God came upon Saul, David would take his harp and
play. Then relief would come to Saul; he would feel better, and the evil spirit[z] would
leave him.

2. David and Goliath

17 Now the Philistines gathered their forces for war and assembled[a] at Socoh in
Judah. They pitched camp at Ephes Dammim, between Socoh[b] and Azekah.
2Saul and the Israelites assembled and camped in the Valley of Elah[c] and drew up
their battle line to meet the Philistines. 3The Philistines occupied one hill and the
Israelites another, with the valley between them.

[a] *11* Some Septuagint manuscripts; Hebrew *not gather round* [b] *14* Or *injurious*; also in verses 15, 16 and 23

16:11 [o] 1Sa 17:12
16:12 [p] 1Sa 9:17 [q] Ge 39:6; 1Sa 17:42
16:13 [r] Nu 27:18; Jdg 11:29 [s] 1Sa 10:1, 6, 9-10; 11:6
16:14 [t] Jdg 16:20 [u] Jdg 9:23; 1Sa 18:10
16:16 [v] ver 23; 1Sa 18:10; 19:9; 2Ki 3:15
16:18 [w] 1Sa 3:19; 17:32-37
16:20 [x] 1Sa 10:27; Pr 18:16
16:21 [y] Ge 41:46; Pr 22:29
16:23 [z] ver 14-16
17:1 [a] 1Sa 13:5 [b] Jos 15:35; 2Ch 28:18
17:2 [c] 1Sa 21:9

16:13 David was anointed king, but it was done in secret; he was not publicly anointed until much later (2 Samuel 2:4; 5:3). Saul was still legally the king, but God was preparing David for his future responsibilities. The anointing oil poured over David's head stood for holiness. It was used to set people or objects apart for God's service. Each king and high priest of Israel was anointed with oil. This commissioned him as God's representative to the nation. Although God rejected Saul's kingship by not allowing any of his descendants to sit on Israel's throne, Saul himself remained in his position until his death.

16:14 What was this evil spirit the Lord sent? Perhaps Saul was simply depressed. Or perhaps the Holy Spirit had left Saul, and God allowed an evil spirit (a demon) to torment him as judgment for his disobedience (this would demonstrate God's power over the spirit world – 1 Kings 22:19–23). Either way, Saul was driven to insanity, which led him to attempt to murder David.

16:15, 16 Harps were popular musical instruments in Saul's day, and their music is still known for its soothing qualities. The simplest harps were merely two pieces of wood fastened at right angles to each other. The strings were stretched across the wood to give the harp a triangular shape. Simple strings could be made of twisted grasses, but better strings were made of dried animal intestine. Harps could have up to 40 strings and were louder than the smaller three- or four-stringed instruments called lyres. David, known for his shepherding skills and bravery, was also an accomplished harpist and musician who would eventually write many of the psalms found in the Bible.

16:19–21 When Saul asked David to be in his service, he obviously did not know that David had been secretly anointed king (16:12). Saul's invitation presented an excellent opportunity for the young man and future king to gain firsthand information about leading a nation ("David went back and forth from Saul", 17:15).

Sometimes our plans – even the ones we think God has approved – have to be put on hold indefinitely. Like David, we can use this waiting time profitably. We can choose to learn and grow in our present circumstances, whatever they may be.

4A champion named Goliath,[d] who was from Gath, came out of the Philistine
camp. He was over nine feet[a] tall. 5He had a bronze helmet on his head and wore
a coat of scale armour of bronze weighing five thousand shekels;[b] 6on his legs he
wore bronze greaves, and a bronze javelin[e] was slung on his back. 7His spear shaft
was like a weaver's rod,[f] and its iron point weighed six hundred shekels.[c] His
shield-bearer[g] went ahead of him.
8Goliath stood and shouted to the ranks of Israel, "Why do you come out and line
up for battle? Am I not a Philistine, and are you not the servants of Saul? Choose[h]
a man and have him come down to me. 9If he is able to fight and kill me, we will
become your subjects; but if I overcome him and kill him, you will become our
subjects and serve us." 10Then the Philistine said, "This day I defy[i] the ranks of
Israel! Give me a man and let us fight each other." 11On hearing the Philistine's words,
Saul and all the Israelites were dismayed and terrified.
12Now David was the son of an Ephrathite named Jesse,[j] who was from Bethlehem[k] in Judah. Jesse had eight[l] sons, and in Saul's time he was old and well
advanced in years. 13Jesse's three oldest sons had followed Saul to the war: The
firstborn was Eliab;[m] the second, Abinadab; and the third, Shammah.[n] 14David was
the youngest. The three oldest followed Saul, 15but David went back and forth from
Saul to tend his father's sheep[o] at Bethlehem.
16For forty days the Philistine came forward every morning and evening and took
his stand.
17Now Jesse said to his son David, "Take this ephah[d] of roasted grain[p] and these
ten loaves of bread for your brothers and hurry to their camp. 18Take along these ten
cheeses to the commander of their unit.[e] See how your brothers[q] are and bring back
some assurance[f] from them. 19They are with Saul and all the men of Israel in the
Valley of Elah, fighting against the Philistines."
20Early in the morning David left the flock with a shepherd, loaded up and set out,
as Jesse had directed. He reached the camp as the army was going out to its battle
positions, shouting the war cry. 21Israel and the Philistines were drawing up their lines
facing each other. 22David left his things with the keeper of supplies, ran to the battle
lines and greeted his brothers. 23As he was talking with them, Goliath, the Philistine
champion from Gath, stepped out from his lines and shouted his usual[r] defiance, and
David heard it. 24When the Israelites saw the man, they all ran from him in great fear.
25Now the Israelites had been saying, "Do you see how this man keeps coming out?
He comes out to defy Israel. The king will give great wealth to the man who kills him.

17:4 [d]Jos 11:21-22; 2Sa 21:19
17:6 [e]ver 45
17:7 [f]2Sa 21:19 [g]ver 41
17:8 [h]1Sa 8:17
17:10 [i]ver 26, 45; 2Sa 21:21
17:12 [j]Ru 4:17; 1Ch 2:13-15 [k]Ge 35:19 [l]1Sa 16:11
17:13 [m]1Sa 16:6 [n]1Sa 16:9
17:15 [o]1Sa 16:19
17:17 [p]1Sa 25:18
17:18 [q]Ge 37:14
17:23 [r]ver 8-10

a *4* Hebrew *was six cubits and a span* (about 3 metres) b *5* That is, about 125 pounds (about 57 kilograms)
c *7* That is, about 15 pounds (about 7 kilograms) d *17* That is, probably about 3/5 bushel (about 22 litres)
e *18* Hebrew *thousand* f *18* Or *some token*; or *some pledge of spoils*

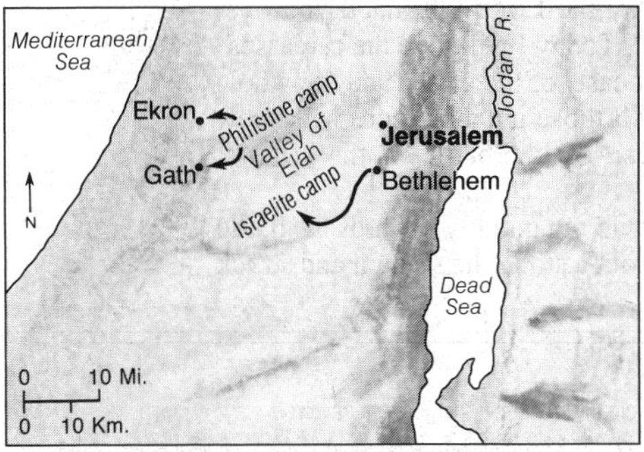

DAVID AND GOLIATH The armies of Israel and Philistia faced each other across the Valley of Elah. David arrived from Bethlehem and offered to fight the giant Goliath. After David defeated Goliath, the Israelite army chased the Philistines to Ekron and Gath (Goliath's home town).

17:4–7 In the days of the exodus, most of the Israelites had been afraid to enter the promised land because of the giants living there (Numbers 13:32, 33). King Og of Bashan needed a bed over 13 feet long (Deuteronomy 3:11). Now Goliath, over nine feet tall, taunted Israel's soldiers and appeared invincible to them. Saul, the tallest of the Israelites, may have been especially worried because he was obviously the best match for Goliath. In God's eyes, however, Goliath was no different than anyone else.

17:9 An army often avoided the high cost of battle by pitting its strongest warrior against the strongest warrior of the enemy. This avoided great bloodshed because the winner of the fight was considered the winner of the battle. Goliath had the definite advantage against David from a human standpoint. But Goliath didn't realise that in fighting David, he also had to fight God.

17:16 Why would this go on for 40 days without one side attacking the other? They were camped on opposite sides of a valley with steep walls. Whoever would rush down the valley and up the steep cliffs would be at a disadvantage at the beginning of the battle and probably suffer great casualties. Each side was waiting for the other to attack first.

He will also give him his daughter[s] in marriage and will exempt his father's family
from taxes in Israel."
26 David asked the men standing near him, "What will be done for the man who
kills this Philistine and removes this disgrace[t] from Israel? Who is this uncircumcised[u] Philistine that he should defy[v] the armies of the living[w] God?"
27 They repeated to him what they had been saying and told him, "This is what will
be done for the man who kills him."
28 When Eliab, David's oldest brother, heard him speaking with the men, he burned
with anger[x] at him and asked, "Why have you come down here? And with whom
did you leave those few sheep in the desert? I know how conceited you are and how
wicked your heart is; you came down only to watch the battle."
29 "Now what have I done?" said David. "Can't I even speak?" 30 He then turned
away to someone else and brought up the same matter, and the men answered him
as before. 31 What David said was overheard and reported to Saul, and Saul sent for
him.
32 David said to Saul, "Let no-one lose heart[y] on account of this Philistine; your
servant will go and fight him."
33 Saul replied,[z] "You are not able to go out against this Philistine and fight him;
you are only a boy, and he has been a fighting man from his youth."
34 But David said to Saul, "Your servant has been keeping his father's sheep. When
a lion[a] or a bear came and carried off a sheep from the flock, 35 I went after it, struck
it and rescued the sheep from its mouth. When it turned on me, I seized it by its hair,
struck it and killed it. 36 Your servant has killed both the lion and the bear; this
uncircumcised Philistine will be like one of them, because he has defied the armies
of the living God. 37 The LORD who delivered[b] me from the paw of the lion[c] and
the paw of the bear will deliver me from the hand of this Philistine."
Saul said to David, "Go, and the LORD be with[d] you."
38 Then Saul dressed David in his own tunic. He put a coat of armour on him and
a bronze helmet on his head. 39 David fastened on his sword over the tunic and tried
walking around, because he was not used to them.
"I cannot go in these," he said to Saul, "because I am not used to them." So he
took them off. 40 Then he took his staff in his hand, chose five smooth stones from
the stream, put them in the pouch of his shepherd's bag and, with his sling in his hand,
approached the Philistine.
41 Meanwhile, the Philistine, with his shield-bearer in front of him, kept coming
closer to David. 42 He looked David over and saw that he was only a boy, ruddy and
handsome,[e] and he despised[f] him. 43 He said to David, "Am I a dog,[g] that you come
at me with sticks?" And the Philistine cursed David by his gods. 44 "Come here," he
said, "and I'll give your flesh to the birds of the air and the beasts of the field![h]"
45 David said to the Philistine, "You come against me with sword and spear and
javelin, but I come against you in the name[i] of the LORD Almighty, the God of the
armies of Israel, whom you have defied.[j] 46 This day the LORD will hand you over
to me, and I'll strike you down and cut off your head. Today I will give the carcasses[k]
of the Philistine army to the birds of the air and the beasts of the earth, and the whole
world[l] will know that there is a God in Israel.[m] 47 All those gathered here will know
that it is not by sword[n] or spear that the LORD saves;[o] for the battle[p] is the LORD's,
and he will give all of you into our hands."
48 As the Philistine moved closer to attack him, David ran quickly towards the battle
line to meet him. 49 Reaching into his bag and taking out a stone, he slung it and struck

17:25 [s] Jos 15:16; 1Sa 18:17
17:26 [t] 1Sa 11:2 [u] 1Sa 14:6 [v] ver 10 [w] Dt 5:26
17:28 [x] Ge 37:4, 8, 11; Pr 18:19; Mt 10:36
17:32 [y] Dt 20:3; 1Sa 16:18
17:33 [z] Nu 13:31
17:34 [a] Jer 49:19; Am 3:12
17:37 [b] 2Co 1:10 [c] 2Ti 4:17 [d] 1Sa 20:13; 1Ch 22:11, 16
17:42 [e] 1Sa 16:12 [f] Ps 123:3-4; Pr 16:18
17:43 [g] 1Sa 24:14; 2Sa 3:8; 9:8; 2Ki 8:13
17:44 [h] 1Ki 20:10-11
17:45 [i] 2Sa 22:33, 35; 2Ch 32:8; Ps 124:8; Heb 11:32-34 [j] ver 10
17:46 [k] Dt 28:26 [l] Jos 4:24; 1Ki 8:43; Isa 52:10 [m] 1Ki 18:36; 2Ki 19:19; Isa 37:20
17:47 [n] Hos 1:7; Zec 4:6 [o] 1Sa 14:6; 2Ch 14:11 [p] 2Ch 20:15; Ps 44:6-7

17:26 What a difference perspective can make. Most of the onlookers saw only a giant. David, however, saw a mortal man defying Almighty God. He knew he would not be alone when he faced Goliath; God would fight with him. He looked at his situation from God's point of view. Viewing impossible situations from God's point of view helps us put giant problems in perspective. Once we see clearly, we can fight more effectively.

17:28–32 Criticism couldn't stop David. While the rest of the army stood around, he knew the importance of taking action. With God to fight for him, there was no reason to wait. People may try to discourage you with negative comments or mockery, but continue to do what you know is right. By doing what is right, you will be pleasing God, whose opinion matters most.

17:50 [q]2Sa 23:21
17:51 [r]Heb 11:34 [s]1Sa 21:9
17:52 [t]Jos 15:11 [u]Jos 15:36

the Philistine on the forehead. The stone sank into his forehead, and he fell face down
on the ground.
50 So David triumphed over the Philistine with a sling[q] and a stone; without a sword
in his hand he struck down the Philistine and killed him.
51 David ran and stood over him. He took hold of the Philistine's sword and drew
it from the scabbard. After he killed him, he cut[r] off his head with the sword.[s]
When the Philistines saw that their hero was dead, they turned and ran. 52 Then the
men of Israel and Judah surged forward with a shout and pursued the Philistines to
the entrance of Gath[g] and to the gates of Ekron.[t] Their dead were strewn along the
Shaaraim[u] road to Gath and Ekron. 53 When the Israelites returned from chasing the

[g] 52 Some Septuagint manuscripts; Hebrew *a valley*

DAVID

When we think of David, we think: shepherd, poet, giant-killer, king, ancestor of Jesus—in short, one of the greatest men in the Old Testament. But alongside that list stands another: betrayer, liar, adulterer, murderer. The first list gives qualities we all might like to have; the second, qualities that might be true of any one of us. The Bible makes no effort to hide David's failures. Yet he is remembered and respected for his heart for God. Knowing how much more we share in David's failures than in his greatness, we should be curious to find out what made God refer to David as "a man after my own heart" (Acts 13:22).

David, more than anything else, had an unchangeable belief in the faithful and forgiving nature of God. He was a man who lived with great zest. He sinned many times, but he was quick to confess his sins. His confessions were from the heart, and his repentance was genuine. David never took God's forgiveness lightly or his blessing for granted. In return, God never held back from David either his forgiveness or the consequences of his actions. David experienced the joy of forgiveness even when he had to suffer the consequences of his sins.

We tend to get these two reversed. Too often we would rather avoid the consequences than experience forgiveness. Another big difference between us and David is that while he sinned greatly, he did not sin repeatedly. He learned from his mistakes because he accepted the suffering they brought. Often we don't seem to learn from our mistakes or the consequences that result from those mistakes. What changes would it take for God to find this kind of obedience in you?

Strengths and accomplishments:
- Greatest king of Israel
- Ancestor of Jesus Christ
- Listed in the Hall of Faith in Hebrews 11
- A man described by God himself as a man after his own heart

Weaknesses and mistakes:
- Committed adultery with Bathsheba
- Arranged the murder of Uriah, Bathsheba's husband
- Directly disobeyed God in taking a census of the people
- Did not deal decisively with the sins of his children

Lessons from his life:
- Willingness to admit our mistakes honestly is the first step in dealing with them
- Forgiveness does not remove the consequences of sin
- God greatly desires our complete trust and worship

Vital statistics:
- Where: Bethlehem, Jerusalem
- Occupations: Shepherd, musician, poet, soldier, king
- Relatives: Father: Jesse. Wives: included Michal, Ahinoam, Bathsheba, Abigail. Sons: included Absalom, Amnon, Solomon, Adonijah. Daughters: included Tamar. Seven brothers
- Contemporaries: Saul, Jonathan, Samuel, Nathan

Key verses:
"O Sovereign LORD, you are God! Your words are trustworthy, and you have promised these good things to your servant. Now be pleased to bless the house of your servant, that it may continue for ever in your sight; for you, O Sovereign LORD, have spoken, and with your blessing the house of your servant will be blessed for ever" (2 Samuel 7:28, 29).

His story is told in 1 Samuel 16—1 Kings 2. He is also mentioned in Amos 6:5; Matthew 1:1, 6; 22:43–45; Luke 1:32; Acts 13:22; Romans 1:3; Hebrews 11:32.

Philistines, they plundered their camp. 54 David took the Philistine's head and brought
it to Jerusalem, and he put the Philistine's weapons in his own tent.
55 As Saul watched David[v] going out to meet the Philistine, he said to Abner,
commander of the army, "Abner, whose son is that young man?"
Abner replied, "As surely as you live, O king, I don't know."
56 The king said, "Find out whose son this young man is."
57 As soon as David returned from killing the Philistine, Abner took him and brought
him before Saul, with David still holding the Philistine's head.
58 "Whose son are you, young man?" Saul asked him.
David said, "I am the son of your servant Jesse[w] of Bethlehem."

3. David and Jonathan become friends

Saul's Jealousy of David

18 After David had finished talking with Saul, Jonathan became one in spirit with
David, and he loved[a] him as himself.[b] 2 From that day Saul kept David with
him and did not let him return to his father's house. 3 And Jonathan made a covenant[c]
with David because he loved him as himself. 4 Jonathan took off the robe[d] he was
wearing and gave it to David, along with his tunic, and even his sword, his bow and
his belt.
5 Whatever Saul sent him to do, David did it so successfully[a] that Saul gave him
a high rank in the army. This pleased all the people, and Saul's officers as well.
6 When the men were returning home after David had killed the Philistine, the
women came out from all the towns of Israel to meet King Saul with singing and
dancing,[e] with joyful songs and with tambourines[f] and lutes. 7 As they danced, they
sang:[g]

> "Saul has slain his thousands,
> and David his tens[h] of thousands."

8 Saul was very angry; this refrain galled him. "They have credited David with tens
of thousands," he thought, "but me with only thousands. What more can he get but
the kingdom?[i]" 9 And from that time on Saul kept a jealous eye on David.
10 The next day an evil[b] spirit[j] from God came forcefully upon Saul. He was
prophesying in his house, while David was playing the harp, as he usually[k] did. Saul
had a spear in his hand 11 and he hurled it, saying to himself,[l] "I'll pin David to the
wall." But David eluded[m] him twice.
12 Saul was afraid[n] of David, because the LORD[o] was with[p] David but had left
Saul. 13 So he sent David away from him and gave him command over a thousand men,
and David led[q] the troops in their campaigns.[r] 14 In everything he did he had great
success,[c][s] because the LORD was with[t] him. 15 When Saul saw how successful[d]

a 5 *Or wisely* b 10 *Or injurious* c 14 *Or he was very wise* d 15 *Or wise*

17:55 v 1Sa 16:21
17:58 w ver 12
18:1 a 2Sa 1:26 b Ge 44:30
18:3 c 1Sa 20:8, 16, 17, 42
18:4 d Ge 41:42
18:6 e Ex 15:20 f Jdg 11:34; Ps 68:25
18:7 g Ex 15:21 h 1Sa 21:11; 29:5
18:8 i 1Sa 15:8
18:10 j 1Sa 16:14 k 1Sa 19:7
18:11 l 1Sa 20:7, 33 m 1Sa 19:10
18:12 n ver 15, 29 o 1Sa 16:13 p 1Sa 28:15
18:13 q ver 16; Nu 27:17 r 2Sa 5:2
18:14 s Ge 39:3 t Ge 39:2, 23; Jos 6:27; 1Sa 16:18

17:55–58 Although David had played his harp many times in front of Saul, Saul's question to Abner seems to show he didn't know David very well. Perhaps, since David was expected to marry Saul's daughter if he was successful (17:25), Saul wanted to know more about his family. Or possibly Saul's unstable mental condition (16:14) may have prevented him from recognising David.

18:1–4 When David and Jonathan met, they became close friends at once. Their friendship is one of the deepest and closest recorded in the Bible: (1) they based their friendship on commitment to God, not just each other; (2) they let nothing come between them, not even career or family problems; (3) they drew closer together when their friendship was tested; (4) they remained friends to the end.

Jonathan, the prince of Israel, later realised that David, and not he, would be the next king (23:17). But that did not weaken his love for David. Jonathan would much rather lose the throne of Israel than lose his closest friend.

18:8 Saul's appreciation for David turned to jealousy as people began to applaud David's exploits. In a jealous rage, Saul attempted to murder David by hurling his spear at him (18:11, 12).

Jealousy may not seem to be a major sin, but in reality, it is one step short of murder. Jealousy starts as you resent a rival; it leads to your wishing he or she were removed; then it manifests itself in your seeking ways to harm that person in word or action. Beware of letting jealousy get a foothold in your life.

18:10 The note on 16:14 explains what this evil spirit might have been.

18:11, 12 Saul tried to kill David because he was jealous of David's popularity, yet David continued to protect and comfort Saul. Perhaps people have been jealous of you and have even attacked you in some way. They may be intimidated by your strengths, which make them conscious of their own shortcomings. It would be natural to strike back or to avoid them. A better response is to befriend them (Matthew 5:43, 44) and to ask God for the strength to continue to love them, as David kept on loving Saul.

18:15–18 While Saul's popularity made him proud and arrogant,

he was, he was afraid of him. 16But all Israel and Judah loved David, because he led
them in their campaigns.[u]
17Saul said to David, "Here is my older daughter[v] Merab. I will give her to you
in marriage; only serve me bravely and fight the battles[w] of the LORD." For Saul said
to himself,[x] "I will not raise a hand against him. Let the Philistines do that!"
18But David said to Saul, "Who am I,[y] and what is my family or my father's clan
in Israel, that I should become the king's son-in-law?[z]" 19So[e] when the time came
for Merab,[a] Saul's daughter, to be given to David, she was given in marriage to
Adriel of Meholah.[b]
20Now Saul's daughter Michal[c] was in love with David, and when they told Saul
about it, he was pleased. 21"I will give her to him," he thought, "so that she may be
a snare[d] to him and so that the hand of the Philistines may be against him." So Saul
said to David, "Now you have a second opportunity to become my son-in-law."
22Then Saul ordered his attendants: "Speak to David privately and say, 'Look, the
king is pleased with you, and his attendants all like you; now become his son-in-law.' "
23They repeated these words to David. But David said, "Do you think it is a small
matter to become the king's son-in-law? I'm only a poor man and little known."
24When Saul's servants told him what David had said, 25Saul replied, "Say to
David, 'The king wants no other price[e] for the bride than a hundred Philistine
foreskins, to take revenge on his enemies.' " Saul's plan[f] was to have David fall by
the hands of the Philistines.
26When the attendants told David these things, he was pleased to become the king's
son-in-law. So before the allotted time elapsed, 27David and his men went out and
killed two hundred Philistines. He brought their foreskins and presented the full
number to the king so that he might become the king's son-in-law. Then Saul gave
him his daughter Michal[g] in marriage.
28When Saul realised that the LORD was with David and that his daughter Michal
loved David, 29Saul became still more afraid of him, and he remained his enemy for
the rest of his days.
30The Philistine commanders continued to go out to battle, and as often as they did,

18:16 [u]ver 5
18:17 [v]1Sa 17:25 [w]Nu 21:14; 1Sa 25:28 [x]ver 25
18:18 [y]1Sa 9:21; 2Sa 7:18 [z]ver 23
18:19 [a]2Sa 21:8 [b]Jdg 7:22
18:20 [c]ver 28
18:21 [d]ver 17, 26
18:25 [e]Ge 34:12; Ex 22:17; 1Sa 14:24 [f]ver 17
18:27 [g]ver 13; 2Sa 3:14

e *19 Or However,*

SIMPLE OBJECTS
God often uses simple, ordinary objects to accomplish his tasks in the world. It is important only that they be dedicated to him for his use. What do you have that God can use? Anything and everything is a possible "instrument" for him.

Object	*Reference*	*Who used it?*	*How was it used?*
a staff	Exodus 4:2–4	Moses	To work miracles before Pharaoh
trumpets	Joshua 6:3–5	Joshua	To flatten the walls of Jericho
a fleece	Judges 6:36–40	Gideon	To confirm God's will
trumpets, jars, and torches	Judges 7:19–22	Gideon	To defeat the Midianites
jawbone	Judges 15:15	Samson	To kill 1,000 Philistines
small stone	1 Samuel 17:40	David	To kill Goliath
oil	2 Kings 4:1–7	Elisha	To demonstrate God's power to provide
a river	2 Kings 5:9–14	Elisha	To heal a man of leprosy
linen belt	Jeremiah 13:1–11	Jeremiah	As an object lesson of God's wrath
pottery	Jeremiah 19:1–13	Jeremiah	As an object lesson of God's wrath
iron pan, water, and food	Ezekiel 4:1–17	Ezekiel	As an object lesson of judgment
five loaves and two fish	Mark 6:30–44	Jesus	To feed a crowd of over 5,000 people

David remained humble (18:23), even when the entire nation praised him. Although David succeeded in almost everything he tried and became famous throughout the land, he refused to use his popular support to his advantage against Saul. Don't allow popularity to twist your perception of your own importance. It's comparatively easy to be humble when you're not on centre stage, but how will you react to praise and honour?

David met with more success[f][h] than the rest of Saul's officers, and his name became
well known.

Saul Tries to Kill David

19 Saul told his son Jonathan[a] and all the attendants to kill[b] David. But Jonathan
was very fond of David 2and warned him, "My father Saul is looking for a
chance to kill you. Be on your guard tomorrow morning; go into hiding and stay there.
3I will go out and stand with my father in the field where you are. I'll speak[c] to him
about you and will tell you what I find out."
4Jonathan spoke[d] well of David to Saul his father and said to him, "Let not the
king do wrong[e] to his servant David; he has not wronged you, and what he has done
has benefited you greatly. 5He took his life in his hands when he killed the Philistine.
The LORD won a great victory[f] for all Israel, and you saw it and were glad. Why
then would you do wrong to an innocent[g] man like David by killing him for no
reason?"
6Saul listened to Jonathan and took this oath: "As surely as the LORD lives, David
will not be put to death."
7So Jonathan called David and told him the whole conversation. He brought him
to Saul, and David was with Saul as before.[h]
8Once more war broke out, and David went out and fought the Philistines. He struck
them with such force that they fled before him.
9But an evil[a] spirit[i] from the LORD came upon Saul as he was sitting in his house
with his spear in his hand. While David was playing the harp, 10Saul tried to pin him
to the wall with his spear, but David eluded[j] him as Saul drove the spear into the
wall. That night David made good his escape.
11Saul sent men to David's house to watch[k] it and to kill him in the morning. But
Michal, David's wife, warned him, "If you don't run for your life tonight, tomorrow
you'll be killed." 12So Michal let David down through a window,[l] and he fled and
escaped. 13Then Michal took an idol[b] and laid it on the bed, covering it with a
garment and putting some goats' hair at the head.
14When Saul sent the men to capture David, Michal said,[m] "He is ill."
15Then Saul sent the men back to see David and told them, "Bring him up to me
in his bed so that I may kill him." 16But when the men entered, there was the idol
in the bed, and at the head was some goats' hair.
17Saul said to Michal, "Why did you deceive me like this and send my enemy away
so that he escaped?"
Michal told him, "He said to me, 'Let me get away. Why should I kill you?' "
18When David had fled and made his escape, he went to Samuel at Ramah[n] and
told him all that Saul had done to him. Then he and Samuel went to Naioth and stayed
there. 19Word came to Saul: "David is in Naioth at Ramah"; 20so he sent men to
capture him. But when they saw a group of prophets[o] prophesying, with Samuel
standing there as their leader, the Spirit of God came upon[p] Saul's men and they also
prophesied.[q] 21Saul was told about it, and he sent more men, and they prophesied
too. Saul sent men a third time, and they also prophesied. 22Finally, he himself left
for Ramah and went to the great cistern at Secu. And he asked, "Where are Samuel
and David?"
"Over in Naioth at Ramah," they said.
23So Saul went to Naioth at Ramah. But the Spirit of God came even upon him,

18:30 [h]ver 5; 2Sa 11:1
19:1 [a]1Sa 18:1 [b]1Sa 18:9
19:3 [c]1Sa 20:12
19:4 [d]1Sa 20:32; Pr 31:8, 9; Jer 18:20 [e]Ge 42:22; Pr 17:13
19:5 [f]1Sa 11:13; 17:49-50; 1Ch 11:14 [g]Dt 19:10-13; 1Sa 20:32; Mt 27:4
19:7 [h]1Sa 16:21; 18:2, 13
19:9 [i]1Sa 16:14; 18:10-11
19:10 [j]1Sa 18:11
19:11 [k]Ps 59 Title
19:12 [l]Jos 2:15; Ac 9:25
19:14 [m]Jos 2:4
19:18 [n]1Sa 7:17
19:20 [o]ver 11, 14; Jn 7:32, 45 [p]Nu 11:25 [q]1Sa 10:5; Joel 2:28

[f] *30* Or *David acted more wisely* [a] *9* Or *injurious* [b] *13* Hebrew *teraphim*; also in verse 16

19:1, 2 Is it ever right to disobey your father, as Jonathan did here? It is clearly a principle of Scripture that when a father instructs a son to break God's laws, the son should obey God rather than man. This principle assumes that the son is old enough to be accountable and to see through any deception. A son's role is to be respectful, helpful, and obedient to his father (Ephesians 6:1–3), but not to follow commands or advice that violate God's laws.

19:20–24 This was the second time that Saul surprised everyone by joining a group of prophets and prophesying. The first time (chapter 10) happened right after he was anointed king and did not want to accept the responsibility. This time Saul was consumed with jealousy over David's growing popularity, but the Spirit of God immobilised him so he was unable to harm David. In both cases, Saul spoke God's words (he "prophesied"), although he was far from thinking God's thoughts.

19:23 [r] 1Sa 10:13
19:24 [s] 2Sa 6:20; Isa 20:2; Mic 1:8 [t] 1Sa 10:11
20:1 [a] 1Sa 24:9
20:3 [b] Dt 6:13
20:5 [c] Nu 10:10; 28:11 [d] 1Sa 19:2
20:6 [e] 1Sa 17:58 [f] Dt 12:5
20:7 [g] 1Sa 25:17
20:8 [h] 1Sa 18:3; 23:18 [i] 2Sa 14:32
20:13 [j] Ru 1:17; 1Sa 3:17 [k] Jos 1:5; 1Sa 17:37; 18:12; 1Ch 22:11, 16
20:15 [l] 2Sa 9:7

and he walked along prophesying[r] until he came to Naioth. 24He stripped[s] off his
robes and also prophesied in Samuel's presence. He lay that way all that day and night.
This is why people say, "Is Saul also among the prophets?"[t]

David and Jonathan

20 Then David fled from Naioth at Ramah and went to Jonathan and asked, "What
have I done? What is my crime? How have I wronged[a] your father, that he
is trying to take my life?"
2"Never!" Jonathan replied. "You are not going to die! Look, my father doesn't
do anything, great or small, without confiding in me. Why should he hide this from
me? It's not so!"
3But David took an oath[b] and said, "Your father knows very well that I have found
favour in your eyes, and he has said to himself, 'Jonathan must not know this or he
will be grieved.' Yet as surely as the LORD lives and as you live, there is only a step
between me and death."
4Jonathan said to David, "Whatever you want me to do, I'll do for you."
5So David said, "Look, tomorrow is the New Moon festival,[c] and I am supposed
to dine with the king; but let me go and hide[d] in the field until the evening of the
day after tomorrow. 6If your father misses me at all, tell him, 'David earnestly asked
my permission to hurry to Bethlehem,[e] his home town, because an annual[f] sacrifice
is being made there for his whole clan.' 7If he says, 'Very well,' then your servant
is safe. But if he loses his temper,[g] you can be sure that he is determined to harm
me. 8As for you, show kindness to your servant, for you have brought him into a
covenant[h] with you before the LORD. If I am guilty, then kill[i] me yourself! Why
hand me over to your father?"
9"Never!" Jonathan said. "If I had the least inkling that my father was determined
to harm you, wouldn't I tell you?"
10David asked, "Who will tell me if your father answers you harshly?"
11"Come," Jonathan said, "let's go out into the field." So they went there together.
12Then Jonathan said to David: "By the LORD, the God of Israel, I will surely sound
out my father by this time the day after tomorrow! If he is favourably disposed towards
you, will I not send you word and let you know? 13But if my father is inclined to harm
you, may the LORD deal with me, be it ever so severely,[j] if I do not let you know
and send you away safely. May the LORD be with[k] you as he has been with my father.
14But show me unfailing kindness like that of the LORD as long as I live, so that I
may not be killed, 15and do not ever cut off your kindness from my family[l]—not

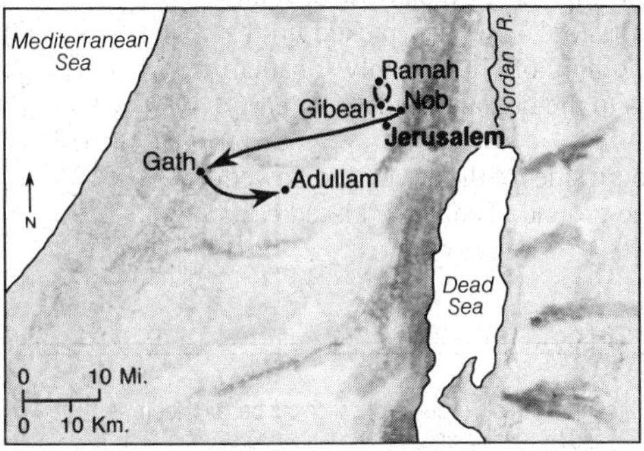

DAVID'S ESCAPE David learned of Saul's plans to kill him and fled to Samuel at Ramah. Returning to Gibeah to say good-bye to Jonathan, he then escaped to Nob, where he received food and a sword from the priest. He then fled to Gath in Philistine territory. When the Philistines became suspicious, he escaped to the cave of Adullam, where many men joined him.

20:5 At the beginning of each month, the Israelites gathered to celebrate the New Moon festival. While this was mainly a time to be enjoyed, it was also a way to dedicate the next month to God. Other nations had celebrations during the full moon and worshipped the moon itself. The Israelites, however, celebrated their festival at the time of the new moon, when the moon was not visible in the sky. This was an added precaution against false worship. Nothing in the creation is to be worshipped – only the Creator.

20:15 Jonathan asked David to keep a promise to treat his children kindly in the future. Years later David took great pains to fulfil this promise: he invited Jonathan's son Mephibosheth into his palace to live (2 Samuel 9).

even when the LORD has cut off every one of David's enemies from the face of the
earth."
16 So Jonathan made a covenant[m] with the house of David, saying, "May the LORD
call David's enemies to account." 17 And Jonathan made David reaffirm his oath[n] out
of love for him, because he loved him as he loved himself.
18 Then Jonathan said to David: "Tomorrow is the New Moon festival. You will be
missed, because your seat will be empty.[o] 19 The day after tomorrow, towards
evening, go to the place where you hid[p] when this trouble began, and wait by the
stone Ezel. 20 I will shoot three arrows to the side of it, as though I were shooting at
a target. 21 Then I will send a boy and say, 'Go, find the arrows.' If I say to him, 'Look,
the arrows are on this side of you; bring them here,' then come, because, as surely
as the LORD lives, you are safe; there is no danger. 22 But if I say to the boy, 'Look,
the arrows are beyond[q] you,' then you must go, because the LORD has sent you away.
23 And about the matter you and I discussed—remember, the LORD is witness[r]
between you and me for ever."
24 So David hid in the field, and when the New Moon festival came, the king sat
down to eat. 25 He sat in his customary place by the wall, opposite Jonathan,[a] and
Abner sat next to Saul, but David's place was empty.[s] 26 Saul said nothing that day,
for he thought, "Something must have happened to David to make him ceremonially
unclean—surely he is unclean.[t]" 27 But the next day, the second day of the month,
David's place was empty again. Then Saul said to his son Jonathan, "Why hasn't the
son of Jesse come to the meal, either yesterday or today?"
28 Jonathan answered, "David earnestly asked me for permission[u] to go to Bethlehem. 29 He said, 'Let me go, because our family is observing a sacrifice in the town
and my brother has ordered me to be there. If I have found favour in your eyes, let
me go to see my brothers.' That is why he has not come to the king's table."
30 Saul's anger flared up at Jonathan and he said to him, "You son of a perverse
and rebellious woman! Don't I know that you have sided with the son of Jesse to your
own shame and to the shame of the mother who bore you? 31 As long as the son of
Jesse lives on this earth, neither you nor your kingdom will be established. Now send
and bring him to me, for he must die!"
32 "Why[v] should he be put to death? What[w] has he done?" Jonathan asked his
father. 33 But Saul hurled his spear at him to kill him. Then Jonathan knew that his
father intended[x] to kill David.
34 Jonathan got up from the table in fierce anger; on that second day of the month
he did not eat, because he was grieved at his father's shameful treatment of David.
35 In the morning Jonathan went out to the field for his meeting with David. He had
a small boy with him, 36 and he said to the boy, "Run and find the arrows I shoot."
As the boy ran, he shot an arrow beyond him. 37 When the boy came to the place where
Jonathan's arrow had fallen, Jonathan called out after him, "Isn't the arrow beyond[y]
you?" 38 Then he shouted, "Hurry! Go quickly! Don't stop!" The boy picked up the
arrow and returned to his master. 39 (The boy knew nothing of all this; only Jonathan
and David knew.) 40 Then Jonathan gave his weapons to the boy and said, "Go, carry
them back to town."
41 After the boy had gone, David got up from the south side ⌞of the stone⌟ and bowed
down before Jonathan three times, with his face to the ground. Then they kissed each
other and wept together—but David wept the most.

[a] *25* Septuagint; Hebrew *wall. Jonathan arose*

20:16 [m] 1Sa 25:22
20:17 [n] 1Sa 18:3
20:18 [o] ver 5, 25
20:19 [p] 1Sa 19:2
20:22 [q] ver 37
20:23 [r] ver 14-15; Ge 31:50
20:25 [s] ver 18
20:26 [t] Lev 7:20-21; 15:5; 1Sa 16:5
20:28 [u] ver 6
20:32 [v] 1Sa 19:4; Mt 27:23 [w] Ge 31:36; Lk 23:22
20:33 [x] ver 7; 1Sa 18:11, 17
20:37 [y] ver 22

20:26 Because the New Moon festival involved making a sacrifice to God (Numbers 28:11–15), those attending the feast had to be ceremonially clean according to God's laws (Exodus 19:10; Leviticus 15; Numbers 19:11–22; also see the note on Joshua 3:5). This cleansing involved washing the body and clothes before approaching God to offer a sacrifice. The outward cleansing was a symbol of the inward desire for a purified heart and right relationship with God. Today our hearts are purified by faith in God through the death of Jesus Christ on our behalf (Hebrews 10:10, 22) and by reading and heeding God's word (John 17:17).

20:31, 32 Saul was still trying to secure his throne for future generations even though he had already been told his dynasty would end with him (13:13, 14). Even worse, he was trying to do this by sinful human means, because he knew he would get no help from God. Jonathan could have made a move to become the next king by killing his rival, but he bypassed this opportunity because of his love for both God and David (23:16–18).

20:42
[z]ver 22; 1Sa 1:17
[a]2Sa 1:26; Pr 18:24

42Jonathan said to David, "Go in peace,[z] for we have sworn friendship[a] with each
other in the name of the LORD, saying, 'The LORD is witness between you and me,
and between your descendants and my descendants for ever.' " Then David left, and
Jonathan went back to the town.

4. Saul pursues David

David at Nob

21:1
[a]1Sa 14:3; 22:9, 19; Ne 11:32; Isa 10:32
[b]1Sa 16:4

21:4
[c]Lev 24:8-9

21 David went to Nob,[a] to Ahimelech the priest. Ahimelech trembled[b] when he
met him, and asked, "Why are you alone? Why is no-one with you?"
2David answered Ahimelech the priest, "The king charged me with a certain matter
and said to me, 'No-one is to know anything about your mission and your instructions.' As for my men, I have told them to meet me at a certain place. 3Now then,
what have you to hand? Give me five loaves of bread, or whatever you can find."
4But the priest answered David, "I don't have any ordinary bread[c] to hand;

JONATHAN

Loyalty is one of life's most costly qualities; it is the most selfless part of love. To be loyal, you cannot live only for yourself. Loyal people not only stand by their commitments, they are willing to suffer for them. Jonathan is a shining example of loyalty. Sometimes he was forced to deal with conflicting loyalties: to his father, Saul, and to his friend David. His solution to that conflict teaches us both how to be loyal and what must guide loyalty. In Jonathan, truth always guided loyalty.

Jonathan realised that the source of truth was God, who demanded his ultimate loyalty. It was his relationship with God that gave Jonathan the ability to deal effectively with the complicated situations in his life. He was loyal to Saul because Saul was his father and the king. He was loyal to David because David was his friend. His loyalty to God guided him through the conflicting demands of his human relationships.

The conflicting demands of our relationships challenge us as well. If we attempt to settle these conflicts only at the human level, we will be constantly dealing with a sense of betrayal. But if we communicate to our friends that our ultimate loyalty is to God and his truth, many of our choices will be much clearer. The truth in his word, the Bible, will bring light to our decisions. Do those closest to you know who has your greatest loyalty?

Strengths and accomplishments:
- Brave, loyal, and a natural leader
- The closest friend David ever had
- Did not put his personal well-being before those he loved
- Depended on God

Lessons from his life:
- Loyalty is one of the strongest parts of courage
- An allegiance to God puts all other relationships into perspective
- Great friendships are costly

Vital statistics:
- Occupation: Military leader
- Relatives: Father: Saul. Mother: Ahinoam. Brothers: Abinadab and Malki-Shua. Sisters: Merab and Michal. Son: Mephibosheth

Key verse:
"I grieve for you, Jonathan my brother; you were very dear to me. Your love for me was wonderful, more wonderful than that of women" (2 Samuel 1:26).

His story is told in 1 Samuel 13—31. He is also mentioned in 2 Samuel 9.

21:1ff This is the first time Ahimelech is mentioned. Either he was the Ahijah mentioned in 14:3, 18, or, more likely, he was Ahijah's successor. In either case, Ahimelech had to go against the law to give the consecrated bread to David because the bread was supposed to be given only to the priests (Leviticus 24:5–9). But Ahimelech put David's need and life ahead of religious ceremony and fed him the consecrated food. This upheld a higher law of love (Leviticus 19:18). Centuries later, Jesus would refer to this incident to show that God's laws should not be applied without compassion. To do good and to save life is God's greater law (Matthew 12:1–8; Luke 6:1–5).

21:2 David lied to protect himself from Saul (21:10). Some excuse this lie because a war was going on, and it is the duty of a good soldier to deceive the enemy. But nowhere is David's lie condoned. In fact, the opposite is true because his lie led to the death of 85 priests (22:9–19). David's small lie seemed harmless enough, but it led to tragedy. The Bible makes it very clear that lying is wrong (Leviticus 19:11). Lying, like every other sin, is serious in God's sight and may lead to all sorts of harmful consequences. Don't minimise or categorise sins. All sins must be avoided whether or not we can foresee their potential consequences.

however, there is some consecrated[d] bread here—provided the men have kept[e]
themselves from women."
5David replied, "Indeed women have been kept from us, as usual whenever[a] I set
out. The men's things[b] are holy[f] even on missions that are not holy. How much more
so today!" 6So the priest gave him the consecrated bread,[g] since there was no bread
there except the bread of the Presence that had been removed from before the LORD
and replaced by hot bread on the day it was taken away.
7Now one of Saul's servants was there that day, detained before the LORD; he was
Doeg[h] the Edomite,[i] Saul's head shepherd.
8David asked Ahimelech, "Don't you have a spear or sword here? I haven't brought
my sword or any other weapon, because the king's business was urgent."
9The priest replied, "The sword[j] of Goliath the Philistine, whom you killed in the
Valley of Elah,[k] is here; it is wrapped in a cloth behind the ephod. If you want it,
take it; there is no sword here but that one."
David said, "There is none like it; give it to me."

David at Gath

10That day David fled from Saul and went[l] to Achish king of Gath. 11But the
servants of Achish said to him, "Isn't this David, the king of the land? Isn't he the
one they sing about in their dances:

> " 'Saul has slain his thousands,
> and David his tens of thousands'?"[m]

12David took these words to heart and was very much afraid of Achish king of Gath.
13So he feigned insanity[n] in their presence; and while he was in their hands he acted
like a madman, making marks on the doors of the gate and letting saliva run down
his beard.
14Achish said to his servants, "Look at the man! He is insane! Why bring him to
me? 15Am I so short of madmen that you have to bring this fellow here to carry on
like this in front of me? Must this man come into my house?"

David at Adullam and Mizpah

22 David left Gath and escaped to the cave[a] of Adullam. When his brothers and
his father's household heard about it, they went down to him there. 2All those
who were in distress or in debt or discontented gathered[b] round him, and he became
their leader. About four hundred men were with him.
3From there David went to Mizpah in Moab and said to the king of Moab, "Would
you let my father and mother come and stay with you until I learn what God will do
for me?" 4So he left them with the king of Moab, and they stayed with him as long
as David was in the stronghold.

[a] 5 Or *from us in the past few days since* [b] 5 Or *bodies*

21:4 [d] Ex 25:30; Mt 12:4 [e] Ex 19:15
21:5 [f] 1Th 4:4
21:6 [g] Lev 24:8-9; Mt 12:3-4; Mk 2:25-28; Lk 6:1-5
21:7 [h] 1Sa 22:9, 22 [i] 1Sa 14:47; Ps 52 Title
21:9 [j] 1Sa 17:51 [k] 1Sa 17:2
21:10 [l] 1Sa 27:2
21:11 [m] 1Sa 18:7; 29:5; Ps 56 Title
21:13 [n] Ps 34 Title
22:1 [a] 2Sa 23:13; Ps 57 Title; 142 Title
22:2 [b] 1Sa 23:13; 25:13; 2Sa 15:20

21:5 The men's bodies were ceremonially clean because they had not had sexual intercourse during this journey. Therefore, the priest allowed them to eat the consecrated bread.

21:6 Once a week on the Sabbath, a priest entered the Holy Place in the tabernacle and placed 12 freshly baked loaves of bread on a small table. This bread, called the bread of the Presence, symbolised God's presence among his people as well as his loving care that met their physical needs. The bread that was replaced was to be eaten only by the priests on duty.

21:9 An ephod was a vest worn by the priest (see the second note on 2:18 for a more detailed explanation). David didn't know Goliath's sword was there probably because David was a young man when he killed the giant and he had spent much of his time at home.

21:10–15 Gath was one of the five major Philistine cities. Why did the Philistines accept their archenemy, David, into their camp? The Philistines may have been initially happy to accept a defector who was a high military leader. Any enemy of Saul would have been a friend of theirs. They could not have known that David had been anointed Israel's next king (16:13). Soon, however, the Philistines became nervous about David's presence. After all, he had slain thousands of their own people (18:7). David then protected himself by acting insane because it was the custom not to harm mentally unstable people.

5 But the prophet Gad[c] said to David, "Do not stay in the stronghold. Go into the
land of Judah." So David left and went to the forest of Hereth.

Saul Kills the Priests of Nob

6 Now Saul heard that David and his men had been discovered. And Saul, spear in
hand, was seated[d] under the tamarisk[e] tree on the hill at Gibeah, with all his officials
standing round him. 7 Saul said to them, "Listen, men of Benjamin! Will the son of
Jesse give all of you fields and vineyards? Will he make all of you commanders[f] of
thousands and commanders of hundreds? 8 Is that why you have all conspired against
me? No-one tells me when my son makes a covenant[g] with the son of Jesse. None
of you is concerned[h] about me or tells me that my son has incited my servant to lie
in wait for me, as he does today."
9 But Doeg[i] the Edomite, who was standing with Saul's officials, said, "I saw the
son of Jesse come to Ahimelech son of Ahitub at Nob.[j] 10 Ahimelech enquired[k] of
the LORD for him; he also gave him provisions[l] and the sword of Goliath the
Philistine."
11 Then the king sent for the priest Ahimelech son of Ahitub and his father's whole
family, who were the priests at Nob, and they all came to the king. 12 Saul said, "Listen
now, son of Ahitub."
"Yes, my lord," he answered.
13 Saul said to him, "Why have you conspired[m] against me, you and the son of
Jesse, giving him bread and a sword and enquiring of God for him, so that he has
rebelled against me and lies in wait for me, as he does today?"
14 Ahimelech answered the king, "Who[n] of all your servants is as loyal as David,
the king's son-in-law, captain of your bodyguard and highly respected in your household? 15 Was that day the first time I enquired of God for him? Of course not! Let not
the king accuse your servant or any of his father's family, for your servant knows
nothing at all about this whole affair."
16 But the king said, "You shall surely die, Ahimelech, you and your father's whole
family."
17 Then the king ordered the guards at his side: "Turn and kill the priests of the LORD,
because they too have sided with David. They knew he was fleeing, yet they did not
tell me."
But the king's officials were not willing[o] to raise a hand to strike the priests of
the LORD.

22:5 [c] 2Sa 24:11; 1Ch 21:9; 29:29; 2Ch 29:25
22:6 [d] Jdg 4:5 [e] Ge 21:33
22:7 [f] 1Sa 8:14
22:8 [g] 1Sa 18:3; 20:16 [h] 1Sa 23:21
22:9 [i] 1Sa 21:7; Ps 52 Title [j] 1Sa 21:1
22:10 [k] Nu 27:21; 1Sa 10:22 [l] 1Sa 21:6
22:13 [m] ver 8
22:14 [n] 1Sa 19:4
22:17 [o] Ex 1:17

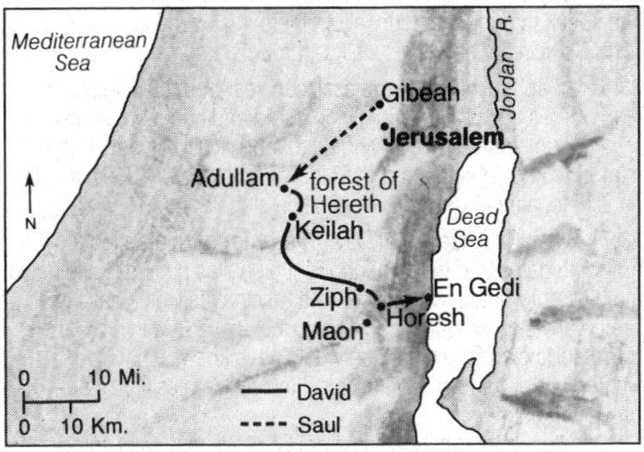

DAVID FLEES FROM SAUL David and his men attacked the Philistines at Keilah from the forest of Hereth. Saul came from Gibeah to attack David, but David escaped into the Desert of Ziph. At Horesh he met Jonathan, who encouraged him. Then he fled into the Desert of Maon and into the strongholds of En Gedi.

22:2 Those in distress, in debt, or discontented joined David, who himself was an outlaw. These people were outcasts themselves and could only improve their lot by helping David become king. David's control over this band of men again shows his resourcefulness and ability to lead and motivate others. It is difficult enough to build an army out of good men, but it takes even greater leadership to build one out of the kind of men that followed David. This group eventually formed the core of his military leadership and produced several "mighty men" (2 Samuel 23:8ff).

22:7, 8 Apparently Saul's key officers were from the tribe of Benjamin, just as he was. David was from the neighbouring tribe of Judah. Saul was appealing to tribal loyalty to maintain his hold on the throne.

18 The king then ordered Doeg, "You turn and strike down the priests." So Doeg
the Edomite turned and struck them down. That day he killed eighty-five men who
wore the linen ephod.[p] 19 He also put to the sword[q] Nob, the town of the priests,
with its men and women, its children and infants, and its cattle, donkeys and sheep.
20 But Abiathar,[r] son of Ahimelech son of Ahitub, escaped and fled to join
David.[s] 21 He told David that Saul had killed the priests of the LORD. 22 Then David
said to Abiathar: "That day, when Doeg[t] the Edomite was there, I knew he would
be sure to tell Saul. I am responsible for the death of your father's whole family. 23 Stay
with me; don't be afraid; the man who is seeking your life[u] is seeking mine also. You
will be safe with me."

David Saves Keilah

23 When David was told, "Look, the Philistines are fighting against Keilah[a] and
are looting the threshing-floors," 2 he enquired[b] of the LORD, saying, "Shall
I go and attack these Philistines?"
The LORD answered him, "Go, attack the Philistines and save Keilah."
3 But David's men said to him, "Here in Judah we are afraid. How much more, then,
if we go to Keilah against the Philistine forces!"
4 Once again David enquired of the LORD, and the LORD answered him, "Go down
to Keilah, for I am going to give the Philistines into your hand.[c]" 5 So David and his
men went to Keilah, fought the Philistines and carried off their livestock. He inflicted
heavy losses on the Philistines and saved the people of Keilah. 6 (Now Abiathar[d] son
of Ahimelech had brought the ephod down with him when he fled to David at Keilah.)

Saul Pursues David

7 Saul was told that David had gone to Keilah, and he said, "God has handed him
over to me, for David has imprisoned himself by entering a town with gates and bars."
8 And Saul called up all his forces for battle, to go down to Keilah to besiege David
and his men.
9 When David learned that Saul was plotting against him, he said to Abiathar[e] the

22:18 [p] 1Sa 2:18, 31
22:19 [q] 1Sa 15:3
22:20 [r] 1Sa 23:6, 9; 30:7; 1Ki 2:22, 26, 27 [s] 1Sa 2:32
22:22 [t] 1Sa 21:7
22:23 [u] 1Ki 2:26
23:1 [a] Jos 15:44
23:2 [b] ver 4, 12; 1Sa 30:8; 2Sa 5:19, 23
23:4 [c] Jos 8:7; Jdg 7:7
23:6 [d] 1Sa 22:20
23:9 [e] ver 6; 1Sa 22:20; 30:7

22:18 Why would Saul have his own priests killed? Saul suspected a conspiracy among Jonathan, David, and the priests. His suspicion came from Doeg's report of seeing David talking to Ahimelech, the high priest, and receiving food and a weapon from him (22:9, 10). Saul's action showed his mental and emotional instability and how far he had strayed from God.

By destroying everything in Nob, Saul was placing the city under the ban (declaring it to be utterly destroyed) described in Deuteronomy 13:12–17, which was supposed to be used only in cases of idolatry and rebellion against God. But it was Saul, not the priests, who had rebelled against God.

22:18, 19 Why did God allow 85 innocent priests to be killed? Their deaths served to dramatise to the nation how a king could become an evil tyrant. Where were Saul's advisers? Where were the elders of Israel? Sometimes God allows evil to develop to teach us not to let evil systems flourish. Serving God is not a ticket to wealth, success, or health. God does not promise to protect good people from evil in this world, but he does promise that ultimately all evil will be abolished. Those who have remained faithful through their trials will experience great rewards in the age to come (Matthew 5:11, 12; Revelation 21:1–7; 22:1–21).

22:20 Abiathar escaped to David with an ephod (23:6), a priestly garment containing the Urim and Thummim, two objects David used to consult God. The ephod was probably the only symbol of the priesthood that survived Saul's raid and made it into David's camp (23:6). Saul destroyed Israel's priesthood, but when David became king, he installed Abiathar as the new high priest. Abiathar remained in that position during David's entire reign.

23:1 Threshing floors were open, circular areas where the grain kernels were separated from their husks. (In order to separate the grain from the husk, farmers would toss their grain into the air. The wind would blow the husks away, leaving only the grain. This process is called *winnowing.*) By looting the threshing floors, the Philistines were robbing Keilah's citizens of all their food supplies. (For more on threshing, see the note on Ruth 3:2.)

23:2 Through the Urim and Thummim that Abiathar the priest brought (23:6), David sought the Lord's guidance *before* he took action. He listened to God's directions and then proceeded accordingly. Rather than trying to find God's will *after* the fact or having to ask God to undo the results of our hasty decisions, we should take time to discern God's will beforehand. We can hear him speak through the counsel of others, his word, and the leading of his Spirit in our hearts, as well as through circumstances.

23:6 An ephod was a sleeveless linen vest worn by priests. The high priest's ephod was brightly coloured and had a breastplate with 12 gemstones representing each tribe. The Urim and Thummim were kept in a pouch of the high priest's ephod. (See the note on 2:18 for a more detailed explanation of the ephod.)

23:7 When Saul heard that David was trapped in a walled town (one with gates and bars), he thought God was putting David at his mercy. Saul wanted to kill David so badly that he would have interpreted any sign as God's approval to move ahead with his plan. Had Saul known God better, he would have known what God wanted and would not have misread the situation as God's approval for murder.

Not every opportunity is sent from God. We may want something so much that we assume any opportunity to obtain it is of divine origin. As we see from Saul's case, however, this may not be true. An opportunity to do something against God's will can never be from God because God does not tempt us. When opportunities come your way, double-check your motives. Make sure you are following God's desires, and not just your own.

23:12 [f]ver 20
23:13 [g]1Sa 22:2; 25:13
23:14 [h]Jos 15:24, 55 [i]Ps 54:3-4 [j]Ps 32:7
23:16 [k]1Sa 30:6
23:17 [l]1Sa 20:31; 24:20
23:18 [m]1Sa 18:3; 20:16, 42; 2Sa 9:1; 21:7
23:19 [n]1Sa 26:1 [o]Ps 54 Title [p]1Sa 26:3
23:20 [q]ver 12
23:21 [r]1Sa 22:8
23:24 [s]Jos 15:55; 1Sa 25:2
23:26 [t]Ps 17:9
23:29 [u]2Ch 20:2
24:1 [a]1Sa 23:28-29
24:2 [b]1Sa 26:2
24:3 [c]Ps 57 Title; 142 Title [d]Jdg 3:24
24:4 [e]1Sa 25:28-30

priest, "Bring the ephod." 10David said, "O LORD, God of Israel, your servant has
heard definitely that Saul plans to come to Keilah and destroy the town on account
of me. 11Will the citizens of Keilah surrender me to him? Will Saul come down, as
your servant has heard? O LORD, God of Israel, tell your servant."
And the LORD said, "He will."
12Again David asked, "Will the citizens of Keilah surrender[f] me and my men to
Saul?"
And the LORD said, "They will."
13So David and his men,[g] about six hundred in number, left Keilah and kept
moving from place to place. When Saul was told that David had escaped from Keilah,
he did not go there.
14David stayed in the desert strongholds and in the hills of the Desert of Ziph.[h]
Day after day Saul searched[i] for him, but God did not[j] give David into his hands.
15While David was at Horesh in the Desert of Ziph, he learned that Saul had come
out to take his life. 16And Saul's son Jonathan went to David at Horesh and helped
him to find strength[k] in God. 17"Don't be afraid," he said. "My father Saul will not
lay a hand on you. You shall be king[l] over Israel, and I will be second to you. Even
my father Saul knows this." 18The two of them made a covenant[m] before the LORD.
Then Jonathan went home, but David remained at Horesh.
19The Ziphites[n] went up to Saul at Gibeah and said, "Is not David hiding among
us[o] in the strongholds at Horesh, on the hill of Hakilah,[p] south of Jeshimon? 20Now,
O king, come down whenever it pleases you to do so, and we will be responsible for
handing[q] him over to the king."
21Saul replied, "The LORD bless you for your concern[r] for me. 22Go and make
further preparation. Find out where David usually goes and who has seen him there.
They tell me he is very crafty. 23Find out about all the hiding-places he uses and come
back to me with definite information.[a] Then I will go with you; if he is in the area,
I will track him down among all the clans of Judah."
24So they set out and went to Ziph ahead of Saul. Now David and his men were
in the Desert of Maon,[s] in the Arabah south of Jeshimon. 25Saul and his men began
the search, and when David was told about it, he went down to the rock and stayed
in the Desert of Maon. When Saul heard this, he went into the Desert of Maon in
pursuit of David.
26Saul[t] was going along one side of the mountain, and David and his men were
on the other side, hurrying to get away from Saul. As Saul and his forces were closing
in on David and his men to capture them, 27a messenger came to Saul, saying, "Come
quickly! The Philistines are raiding the land." 28Then Saul broke off his pursuit of
David and went to meet the Philistines. That is why they call this place Sela Hammahlekoth.[b] 29And David went up from there and lived in the strongholds of En Gedi.[u]

David Spares Saul's Life

24 After Saul returned from pursuing the Philistines, he was told, "David is in the
Desert of En Gedi.[a]" 2So Saul took three thousand chosen men from all Israel
and set out to look[b] for David and his men near the Crags of the Wild Goats.
3He came to the sheep pens along the way; a cave[c] was there, and Saul went in
to relieve[d] himself. David and his men were far back in the cave. 4The men said,
"This is the day the LORD spoke[e] of when he said[a] to you, 'I will give your enemy

a 23 Or *me at Nacon* b 28 *Sela Hammahlekoth* means *rock of parting.* a 4 Or *"Today the LORD is saying*

23:16–18 This may have been the last time David and Jonathan were together. As true friends they were more than just companions who enjoyed each other's company. They encouraged each other's faith in God and trusted each other with their deepest thoughts and closest confidences. These are the marks of true friendship.

24:3 David and his 600 men found the Desert of En Gedi a good place to hide because of the many caves in the area. These caves were used by local people for housing and as tombs. For David's men they were places of refuge. These caves can still be seen today. Some are large enough to hold thousands of people.

24:4 Scripture does not record that God made any such statement to David or his men. The men were probably offering their own interpretation of some previous event such as David's anointing (16:13) or Jonathan's prediction that David would become king (23:17). When David's men saw Saul entering their cave, they wrongly assumed that this was an indication from God that they should act.

into your hands for you to deal with as you wish.' "[f] Then David crept up unnoticed
and cut off a corner of Saul's robe.
5 Afterwards, David was conscience-stricken[g] for having cut off a corner of his
robe. 6 He said to his men, "The LORD forbid that I should do such a thing to my master,
the LORD's anointed,[h] or lift my hand against him; for he is the anointed of the LORD."
7 With these words David rebuked his men and did not allow them to attack Saul. And
Saul left the cave and went his way.
8 Then David went out of the cave and called out to Saul, "My lord the king!" When
Saul looked behind him, David bowed down and prostrated himself with his face to
the ground.[i] 9 He said to Saul, "Why do you listen when men say, 'David is bent
on harming you'? 10 This day you have seen with your own eyes how the LORD gave
you into my hands in the cave. Some urged me to kill you, but I spared you; I said,
'I will not lift my hand against my master, because he is the LORD's anointed.' 11 See,
my father, look at this piece of your robe in my hand! I cut off the corner of your
robe but did not kill you. Now understand and recognise that I am not guilty[j] of
wrongdoing or rebellion. I have not wronged you, but you are hunting[k] me down
to take my life. 12 May the LORD judge[l] between you and me. And may the LORD
avenge[m] the wrongs you have done to me, but my hand will not touch you. 13 As the
old saying goes, 'From evildoers come evil deeds,[n]' so my hand will not touch you.
14 "Against whom has the king of Israel come out? Whom are you pursuing? A dead
dog?[o] A flea?[p] 15 May the LORD be our judge[q] and decide between us. May he
consider my cause and uphold[r] it; may he vindicate[s] me by delivering[t] me from
your hand."
16 When David finished saying this, Saul asked, "Is that your voice,[u] David my
son?" And he wept aloud. 17 "You are more righteous than I,"[v] he said. "You have
treated me well,[w] but I have treated you badly. 18 You have just now told me of the
good you did to me; the LORD gave[x] me into your hands, but you did not kill me.
19 When a man finds his enemy, does he let him get away unharmed? May the LORD
reward you well for the way you treated me today. 20 I know that you will surely be
king[y] and that the kingdom[z] of Israel will be established in your hands. 21 Now
swear[a] to me by the LORD that you will not cut off my descendants or wipe out my
name from my father's family.[b]"
22 So David gave his oath to Saul. Then Saul returned home, but David and his men
went up to the stronghold.[c]

David, Nabal and Abigail

25 Now Samuel died,[a] and all Israel assembled and mourned[b] for him; and they
buried him at his home in Ramah.[c]
Then David moved down into the Desert of Maon.[a] 2 A certain man in Maon,[d]

[a] 1 Some Septuagint manuscripts; Hebrew *Paran*

24:4 [f] 1Sa 23:17; 26:8
24:5 [g] 2Sa 24:10
24:6 [h] 1Sa 26:11
24:8 [i] 1Sa 25:23-24
24:11 [j] Ps 7:3 [k] 1Sa 23:14, 23; 1Sa 26:20
24:12 [l] Ge 16:5; 31:53; Job 5:8 [m] Jdg 11:27; 1Sa 26:10
24:13 [n] Mt 7:20
24:14 [o] 1Sa 17:43; 2Sa 9:8 [p] 1Sa 26:20
24:15 [q] ver 12 [r] Ps 35:1, 23; Mic 7:9 [s] Ps 43:1 [t] Ps 119:134, 154
24:16 [u] 1Sa 26:17
24:17 [v] Ge 38:26; 1Sa 26:21 [w] Mt 5:44
24:18 [x] 1Sa 26:23
24:20 [y] 1Sa 23:17 [z] 1Sa 13:14
24:21 [a] Ge 21:23; 2Sa 21:1-9 [b] 1Sa 20:14-15
24:22 [c] 1Sa 23:29
25:1 [a] 1Sa 28:3 [b] Nu 20:29; Dt 34:8 [c] Ge 21:21; 2Ch 33:20
25:2 [d] Jos 15:55; 1Sa 23:24

24:5, 6 David had great respect for Saul, in spite of the fact that Saul was trying to kill him. Although Saul was sinning and rebelling against God, David still respected the position he held as God's anointed king. David knew he would one day be king, and he also knew it was not right to strike down the man God had placed on the throne. If he assassinated Saul, he would be setting a precedent for his own opponents to remove him some day.

Romans 13:1–7 teaches that God has placed the government and its leaders in power. We may not know why, but, like David, we are to respect the positions and roles of those to whom God has given authority. There is one exception, however. Because God is our highest authority, we should not allow a leader to pressure us to violate God's law.

24:16–19 The means we use to accomplish a goal are just as important as the goal we are trying to accomplish. David's goal was to become king, so his men urged him to kill Saul when he had the chance. David's refusal was not an example of cowardice but of courage – the courage to stand against the group and do what he knew was right. Don't compromise your moral standards by giving in to group pressure or taking the easy way out.

24:21, 22 David kept his promise – he never took revenge on Saul's family or descendants. Most of Saul's sons were killed later, however, by the Philistines (31:2) and the Gibeonites (2 Samuel 21:1–14). David had promised to be kind to the descendants of Saul's son Jonathan (20:14, 15), and he kept this promise when he invited Mephibosheth to live in his palace (2 Samuel 9).

25:1 Saul was king, but Samuel had been the nation's spiritual leader. As a young boy and an older man, Samuel was always careful to listen to (3:10; 9:14–17) and obey (3:21; 10:1, 2) the Lord. With Samuel gone, Israel would be without this spiritual leadership until David became king. (For more on Samuel, read his Profile in chapter 8.)

25:2–11 Nabal rudely refused David's request to feed his 600 men. If we sympathise with Nabal, it is because customs are so different today. First, simple hospitality demanded that travellers – any number of them – be fed. Nabal was very rich and could have

who had property there at Carmel, was very wealthy. He had a thousand goats and
three thousand sheep, which he was shearing in Carmel. 3 His name was Nabal and
his wife's name was Abigail.[e] She was an intelligent and beautiful woman, but her
husband, a Calebite,[f] was surly and mean in his dealings.
4 While David was in the desert, he heard that Nabal was shearing sheep. 5 So he
sent ten young men and said to them, "Go up to Nabal at Carmel and greet him in
my name. 6 Say to him: 'Long life to you! Good health[g] to you and your household!
And good health to all that is yours![h]
7 " 'Now I hear that it is sheep-shearing time. When your shepherds were with us,
we did not ill-treat[i] them, and the whole time they were at Carmel nothing of theirs
was missing. 8 Ask your own servants and they will tell you. Therefore be favourable
towards my young men, since we come at a festive time. Please give your servants
and your son David whatever[j] you can find for them.' "
9 When David's men arrived, they gave Nabal this message in David's name. Then
they waited.
10 Nabal answered David's servants, "Who[k] is this David? Who is this son of Jesse?
Many servants are breaking away from their masters these days. 11 Why should I take
my bread[l] and water, and the meat I have slaughtered for my shearers, and give it
to men coming from who knows where?"
12 David's men turned round and went back. When they arrived, they reported every
word. 13 David said to his men, "Put on your swords!" So they put on their swords,
and David put on his. About four hundred men went[m] up with David, while two
hundred stayed with the supplies.[n]
14 One of the servants told Nabal's wife Abigail: "David sent messengers from the
desert to give our master his greetings,[o] but he hurled insults at them. 15 Yet these
men were very good to us. They did not ill-treat[p] us, and the whole time we were
out in the fields near them nothing was missing.[q] 16 Night and day they were a wall[r]
around us all the time we were herding our sheep near them. 17 Now think it over and
see what you can do, because disaster is hanging over our master and his whole
household. He is such a wicked[s] man that no-one can talk to him."
18 Abigail lost no time. She took two hundred loaves of bread, two skins of wine,
five dressed sheep, five seahs[b] of roasted grain, a hundred cakes of raisins[t] and two
hundred cakes of pressed figs, and loaded them on donkeys.[u] 19 Then she told her
servants, "Go on ahead;[v] I'll follow you." But she did not tell her husband Nabal.

25:3 [e]Pr 31:10 [f]Jos 15:13
25:6 [g]Ps 122:7; Lk 10:5 [h]1Ch 12:18
25:7 [i]ver 15
25:8 [j]Ne 8:10
25:10 [k]Jdg 9:28
25:11 [l]Jdg 8:6
25:13 [m]1Sa 23:13 [n]1Sa 30:24
25:14 [o]1Sa 13:10
25:15 [p]ver 7 [q]ver 21
25:16 [r]Ex 14:22; Job 1:10
25:17 [s]1Sa 20:7
25:18 [t]1Ch 12:40 [u]2Sa 16:1
25:19 [v]Ge 32:20

[b] *18* That is, probably about a bushel (about 37 litres)

LIFE OF DAVID VERSUS LIFE OF SAUL

Life of David	*Life of Saul*
David was God's kind of king (2 Samuel 7:8–16)	Saul was man's kind of king (1 Samuel 10:23, 24)
David was a man after God's heart (Acts 13:22)	Saul was a man after people's praise (1 Samuel 18:6–8)
David's kingship was eternal (through Jesus) (2 Samuel 7:29)	Saul's kingship was rejected (1 Samuel 15:23)
David was kind and benevolent (2 Samuel 9; 1 Chronicles 19:2)	Saul was cruel (1 Samuel 20:30–34; 22:11–19)
David was forgiving (1 Samuel 26)	Saul was unforgiving (1 Samuel 14:44; 18:9)
David repented (2 Samuel 12:13; 24:10)	When confronted, Saul lied (1 Samuel 15:10–31)
David was courageous (1 Samuel 17; 1 Chronicles 18)	Saul was fearful (1 Samuel 17:11; 18:12)
David was at peace with God (Psalms 4:8; 37:11)	Saul was separated from God (1 Samuel 16:14)

easily afforded to meet David's request. Second, David wasn't asking for a handout. He and his men had been protecting Nabal's work force, and part of Nabal's prosperity was due to David's vigilance. We should be generous with those who protect us and help us prosper, even if we are not obligated to do so by law or custom.

20 As she came riding her donkey into a mountain ravine, there were David and his
men descending towards her, and she met them. 21 David had just said, "It's been
useless — all my watching over this fellow's property in the desert so that nothing of
his was missing. He has paid[w] me back evil for good. 22 May God deal with David,[c]
be it ever so severely,[x] if by morning I leave alive one male[y] of all who belong to
him!"

23 When Abigail saw David, she quickly got off her donkey and bowed down before
David with her face to the ground.[z] 24 She fell at his feet and said: "My lord, let the
blame be on me alone. Please let your servant speak to you; hear what your servant
has to say. 25 May my lord pay no attention to that wicked man Nabal. He is just like
his name — his name is Fool,[a] and folly goes with him. But as for me, your servant,
I did not see the men my master sent.

26 "Now since the LORD has kept you, my master, from bloodshed[b] and from
avenging[c] yourself with your own hands, as surely as the LORD lives and as you live,
may your enemies and all who intend to harm my master be like Nabal.[d] 27 And let
this gift,[e] which your servant has brought to my master, be given to the men who
follow you. 28 Please forgive[f] your servant's offence, for the LORD will certainly
make a lasting[g] dynasty for my master, because he fights the LORD's battles.[h] Let
no wrongdoing[i] be found in you as long as you live. 29 Even though someone is
pursuing you to take your life, the life of my master will be bound securely in the
bundle of the living by the LORD your God. But the lives of your enemies he will hurl[j]
away as from the pocket of a sling. 30 When the LORD has done for my master every
good thing he promised concerning him and has appointed him leader[k] over Israel,
31 my master will not have on his conscience the staggering burden of needless
bloodshed or of having avenged himself. And when the LORD has brought my master
success, remember[l] your servant."

32 David said to Abigail, "Praise[m] be to the LORD, the God of Israel, who has sent
you today to meet me. 33 May you be blessed for your good judgment and for keeping
me from bloodshed[n] this day and from avenging myself with my own hands. 34 Otherwise, as surely as the LORD, the God of Israel, lives, who has kept me from harming
you, if you had not come quickly to meet me, not one male belonging to Nabal would
have been left alive by daybreak."

35 Then David accepted from her hand what she had brought to him and said, "Go
home in peace. I have heard your words and granted[o] your request."

36 When Abigail went to Nabal, he was in the house holding a banquet like that of
a king. He was in high[p] spirits and very drunk.[q] So she told[r] him nothing until
daybreak. 37 Then in the morning, when Nabal was sober, his wife told him all these

25:21 [w]Ps 109:5
25:22 [x]1Sa 3:17; 20:13 [y]1Ki 14:10; 21:21; 2Ki 9:8
25:23 [z]1Sa 20:41
25:25 [a]Pr 14:16
25:26 [b]ver 33 [c]Heb 10:30 [d]2Sa 18:32
25:27 [e]Ge 33:11; 1Sa 30:26
25:28 [f]ver 24 [g]2Sa 7:11, 26 [h]1Sa 18:17 [i]1Sa 24:11
25:29 [j]Jer 10:18
25:30 [k]1Sa 13:14
25:31 [l]Ge 40:14
25:32 [m]Ge 24:27; Ex 18:10; Lk 1:68
25:33 [n]ver 26
25:35 [o]Ge 19:21; 1Sa 20:42; 2Ki 5:19
25:36 [p]2Sa 13:23 [q]Pr 20:1; Isa 5:11, 22; Hos 4:11 [r]ver 19

c 22 Some Septuagint manuscripts; Hebrew *with David's enemies*

25:24 David was in no mood to listen when he set out for Nabal's property (25:13, 22). Nevertheless, he stopped to hear what Abigail had to say. If he had ignored her, he would have been guilty of taking vengeance into his own hands. No matter how right we think we are, we must always be careful to stop and listen to others. The extra time and effort can save us pain and trouble in the long run.

25:36 Because Nabal was drunk, Abigail waited until morning to tell him what she had done. Abigail knew that Nabal, in his drunkenness, may not have understood her or may have reacted foolishly. When discussing difficult matters with people, especially family members, timing is everything. Ask God for wisdom to know the best time for confrontation and for bringing up touchy subjects.

25:44 The story of David and Michal does not end here. (See 2 Samuel 3:12–16 for the next episode.)

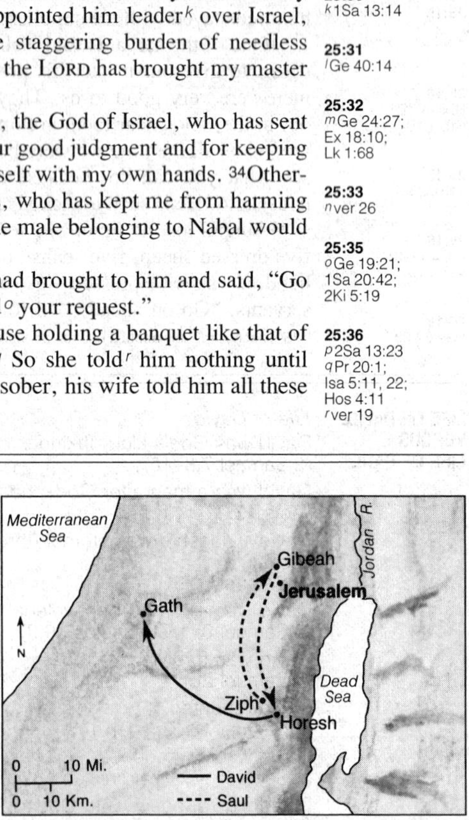

SAUL CHASES DAVID The men of Ziph again betrayed David to Saul, who was in his palace in Gibeah. Saul took 3,000 troops to the area around Horesh in order to find David. David could have killed Saul, but he refused. Saul, feeling foolish at David's kindness, returned to Gibeah, and David went to Gath.

25:38 [s]1Sa 26:10; 2Sa 6:7
25:42 [t]Ge 24:61-67
25:43 [u]Jos 15:56 [v]1Sa 27:3; 30:5
25:44 [w]2Sa 3:15 [x]Isa 10:30
26:1 [a]1Sa 23:19 [b]Ps 54 Title
26:2 [c]1Sa 13:2; 24:2

things, and his heart failed him and he became like a stone. 38About ten days later,
the LORD struck[s] Nabal and he died.
39When David heard that Nabal was dead, he said, "Praise be to the LORD, who
has upheld my cause against Nabal for treating me with contempt. He has kept his
servant from doing wrong and has brought Nabal's wrongdoing down on his own
head."
Then David sent word to Abigail, asking her to become his wife. 40His servants
went to Carmel and said to Abigail, "David has sent us to you to take you to become
his wife."
41She bowed down with her face to the ground and said, "Here is your maidservant,
ready to serve you and wash the feet of my master's servants." 42Abigail[t] quickly
got on a donkey and, attended by her five maids, went with David's messengers and
became his wife. 43David had also married Ahinoam[u] of Jezreel, and they both were
his wives.[v] 44But Saul had given his daughter Michal, David's wife, to Paltiel[d][w]
son of Laish, who was from Gallim.[x]

David Again Spares Saul's Life

26 The Ziphites[a] went to Saul at Gibeah and said, "Is not David hiding[b] on the
hill of Hakilah, which faces Jeshimon?"
2So Saul went down to the Desert of Ziph, with his three thousand chosen men of
Israel, to search[c] there for David. 3Saul made his camp beside the road on the hill
of Hakilah facing Jeshimon, but David stayed in the desert. When he saw that Saul
had followed him there, 4he sent out scouts and learned that Saul had definitely
arrived.[a]

[d] 44 Hebrew *Palti*, a variant of *Paltiel* [a] 4 Or *had come to Nacon*

ABIGAIL

Some men don't deserve their wives. Abigail was probably the best woman Nabal could afford, and he got even more than he bargained for when he arranged to marry her. She was beautiful and more suited than he was to manage his wealth. But Nabal took this wife for granted.

In spite of his shortcomings, Nabal's household did what they could to keep him out of trouble. This loyalty must have been inspired by Abigail. Although her culture and her husband placed a low value on her, she made the most of her skills and opportunities. David was impressed with her abilities, and when Nabal died, he married her.

Abigail was an effective counsellor to both of the men in her life, working hard to prevent them from making rash moves. By her swift action and skilful negotiation, she kept David from taking vengeance upon Nabal. She saw the whole picture and left plenty of room for God to get involved.

Do you, like Abigail, look beyond the present crisis to the whole picture? Do you use your skills to promote peace? Are you loyal without being blind? What challenge or responsibility do you face today that needs a person under God's control?

Strengths and accomplishments:
- Sensible and capable
- A persuasive speaker, able to see beyond herself

Lessons from her life:
- Life's tough situations can bring out the best in people
- One does not need a prestigious title to play a significant role

Vital statistics:
- Where: Carmel
- Occupation: Housewife
- Relatives: First husband: Nabal. Second husband: David. Son: Kileab (Daniel)
- Contemporaries: Saul, Michal, Ahinoam

Key verses:
"David said to Abigail, 'Praise be to the LORD, the God of Israel, who has sent you today to meet me. May you be blessed for your good judgment and for keeping me from bloodshed this day and from avenging myself with my own hands' " (1 Samuel 25:32, 33).

Her story is told in 1 Samuel 25—2 Samuel 2. She is also mentioned in 1 Chronicles 3:1.

5 Then David set out and went to the place where Saul had camped. He saw where
Saul and Abner[d] son of Ner, the commander of the army, had lain down. Saul was
lying inside the camp, with the army encamped around him.
6 David then asked Ahimelech the Hittite and Abishai son of Zeruiah,[e] Joab's
brother, "Who will go down into the camp with me to Saul?"
"I'll go with you," said Abishai.
7 So David and Abishai went to the army by night, and there was Saul, lying asleep
inside the camp with his spear stuck in the ground near his head. Abner and the soldiers
were lying round him.
8 Abishai said to David, "Today God has given your enemy into your hands. Now
let me pin him to the ground with one thrust of my spear; I won't strike him twice."
9 But David said to Abishai, "Don't destroy him! Who can lay a hand on the LORD's
anointed[f] and be guiltless?[g] 10 As surely as the LORD lives," he said, "the LORD
himself will strike[h] him; either his time[i] will come and he will die,[j] or he will go
into battle and perish. 11 But the LORD forbid that I should lay a hand on the LORD's
anointed. Now get the spear and water jug that are near his head, and let's go."
12 So David took the spear and water jug near Saul's head, and they left. No-one
saw or knew about it, nor did anyone wake up. They were all sleeping, because the
LORD had put them into a deep sleep.[k]
13 Then David crossed over to the other side and stood on top of the hill some
distance away; there was a wide space between them. 14 He called out to the army and
to Abner son of Ner, "Aren't you going to answer me, Abner?"
Abner replied, "Who are you who calls to the king?"
15 David said, "You're a man, aren't you? And who is like you in Israel? Why didn't
you guard your lord the king? Someone came to destroy your lord the king. 16 What
you have done is not good. As surely as the LORD lives, you and your men deserve
to die, because you did not guard your master, the LORD's anointed. Look around you.
Where are the king's spear and water jug that were near his head?"
17 Saul recognised David's voice and said, "Is that your voice,[l] David my son?"
David replied, "Yes it is, my lord the king." 18 And he added, "Why is my lord
pursuing his servant? What have I done, and what wrong[m] am I guilty of? 19 Now let
my lord the king listen to his servant's words. If the LORD has incited you against me,
then may he accept an offering.[n] If, however, men have done it, may they be cursed
before the LORD! They have now driven me from my share in the LORD's inheritance[o]
and have said, 'Go, serve other gods.' 20 Now do not let my blood fall to the ground
far from the presence of the LORD. The king of Israel has come out to look for a
flea[p]—as one hunts a partridge in the mountains."
21 Then Saul said, "I have sinned.[q] Come back, David my son. Because you
considered my life precious[r] today, I will not try to harm you again. Surely I have
acted like a fool and have erred greatly."
22 "Here is the king's spear," David answered. "Let one of your young men come

26:5 [d] 1Sa 14:50; 17:55
26:6 [e] Jdg 7:10-11; 1Ch 2:16
26:9 [f] 2Sa 1:14 [g] 1Sa 24:5
26:10 [h] 1Sa 25:38; Ro 12:19 [i] Ge 47:29; Dt 31:14; Ps 37:13 [j] 1Sa 31:6; 2Sa 1:1
26:12 [k] Ge 2:21; 15:12
26:17 [l] 1Sa 24:16
26:18 [m] 1Sa 24:9, 11-14
26:19 [n] 2Sa 16:11 [o] 2Sa 14:16
26:20 [p] 1Sa 24:14
26:21 [q] Ex 9:27; 1Sa 15:24 [r] 1Sa 24:17

26:5–9 Abishai showed great courage when he volunteered to go into Saul's camp with David. In the heat of emotion, Abishai wanted to kill Saul, but David restrained him. Although Abishai was only trying to protect David, his leader, David could not hurt Saul because of his respect for Saul's authority and position as God's anointed king. Abishai may have disagreed with David, but he also respected the one in authority over him. Eventually he became the greatest warrior in David's army (2 Samuel 23:18, 19).

26:8ff The strongest moral decisions are the ones we make before temptation strikes. David was determined to follow God and this carried over into his decision not to murder God's anointed king, Saul, even when his men and the circumstances seemed to make it a feasible option. Who would you have been like in such a situation—David or David's men? To be like David and follow God, we must realise that we can't do wrong in order to execute justice. Even when our closest friends counsel us to do something that seems right, we must always put God's commands first.

26:9 Why did David refuse to kill Saul? God had placed Saul in power and had not yet removed him. David did not want to run ahead of God's timing. We are in similar situations when we have leaders in church or government who are unfaithful or incompetent. It may be easy for us to criticise or move against a leader oblivious to God's hidden purposes and timing. Determining not to do wrong, David left Saul's destiny in God's hands. While we should not ignore sin or sit back and allow evil leaders to carry on their wickedness, neither should we take actions that are against God's laws. We should work for righteousness while trusting God.

26:15, 16 David could have killed Saul and Abner, but he would have disobeyed God and set into motion unknown consequences. Instead, he took a spear and water jug, showing that he could have killed the king, but had not done it. And he made the point that he had great respect for both God and God's anointed king. When you need to make a point, look for creative, God-honouring ways to do so. It will have a more significant impact.

26:23
[s]Ps 62:12
[t]Ps 7:8; 18:20, 24

26:24
[u]Ps 54:7

27:2
[a]1Sa 25:13
[b]1Sa 21:10
[c]1Ki 2:39

27:3
[d]1Sa 25:43; 30:3

27:6
[e]Jos 15:31; 19:5;
Ne 11:28

27:7
[f]1Sa 29:3

27:8
[g]Jos 13:2, 13
[h]Ex 17:8;
1Sa 15:7-8
[i]Ex 15:22

27:9
[j]1Sa 15:3

over and get it. 23 The LORD rewards[s] every man for his righteousness[t] and faithfulness. The LORD gave you into my hands today, but I would not lay a hand on the
LORD's anointed. 24 As surely as I valued your life today, so may the LORD value my
life and deliver[u] me from all trouble."
25 Then Saul said to David, "May you be blessed, my son David; you will do great
things and surely triumph."
So David went on his way, and Saul returned home.

5. Saul's defeat and death

David Among the Philistines

27 But David thought to himself, "One of these days I shall be destroyed by the
hand of Saul. The best thing I can do is to escape to the land of the Philistines.
Then Saul will give up searching for me anywhere in Israel, and I will slip out of his
hand."
2 So David and the six hundred men[a] with him left and went[b] over to Achish[c]
son of Maoch king of Gath. 3 David and his men settled in Gath with Achish. Each
man had his family with him, and David had his two wives:[d] Ahinoam of Jezreel
and Abigail of Carmel, the widow of Nabal. 4 When Saul was told that David had fled
to Gath, he no longer searched for him.
5 Then David said to Achish, "If I have found favour in your eyes, let a place be
assigned to me in one of the country towns, that I may live there. Why should your
servant live in the royal city with you?"
6 So on that day Achish gave him Ziklag,[e] and it has belonged to the kings of Judah
ever since. 7 David lived[f] in Philistine territory for a year and four months.
8 Now David and his men went up and raided the Geshurites,[g] the Girzites and the
Amalekites.[h] (From ancient times these peoples had lived in the land extending to
Shur[i] and Egypt.) 9 Whenever David attacked an area, he did not leave a man or
woman alive,[j] but took sheep and cattle, donkeys and camels, and clothes. Then he
returned to Achish.
10 When Achish asked, "Where did you go raiding today?" David would say,

26:25 Saul had opportunities to kill David, but he never did. Why? First, every time David and Saul were face to face, David did something generous for Saul. The king did not want to respond to David's kindness with cruelty in front of all his men. Second, David had a large following in Israel. By killing him, Saul would risk his hold on the kingdom. Third, God had appointed David to become king of Israel and was protecting him.

27:1-3 For the second time, David sought refuge from Saul in Philistine territory (21:10-15). The once-great conqueror of Philistines now had permission to live under the protection of King Achish of Gath. Previously David had acted as if insane in front of this king. Evidently Achish had forgotten that incident or had overlooked it in the light of David's current situation. Achish certainly would have known about the split between Saul and David and would have been glad to shelter this Israelite traitor. In return, Achish would have expected military support from David and his 600 warriors. David further strengthened his position with Achish by leading Achish to believe that he was conducting raids on Israel and by pretending loyalty to the Philistine ruler.

27:4 Saul finally stopped pursuing David. His army was not strong enough to invade Philistine territory just to seek one man. Besides, the immediate threat to Saul's throne was gone while David was out of the country.

27:5-7 Gath was one of five principal cities in Philistia, and Achish was one of five co-rulers. David may have wanted to move out of this important city to avoid potential skirmishes or attacks upon his family. He may also have wanted to escape the close scrutiny of the Philistine officials. Achish let David move to Ziklag, where he lived until Saul's death (2 Samuel 2:1).

27:8, 9 David probably conducted these guerrilla-style raids because these three tribes were known for their surprise attacks and cruel treatment of innocent people. These desert tribes were a danger not just to the Philistines, but especially to the Israelites, the people David would one day lead.

27:10-12 Was David wrong in falsely reporting his activities to Achish? No doubt David was lying, but he may have felt his strategy was justified in a time of war against a pagan enemy. David knew he would one day be Israel's king. The Philistines were still his enemies, but this was an excellent place to hide from Saul.

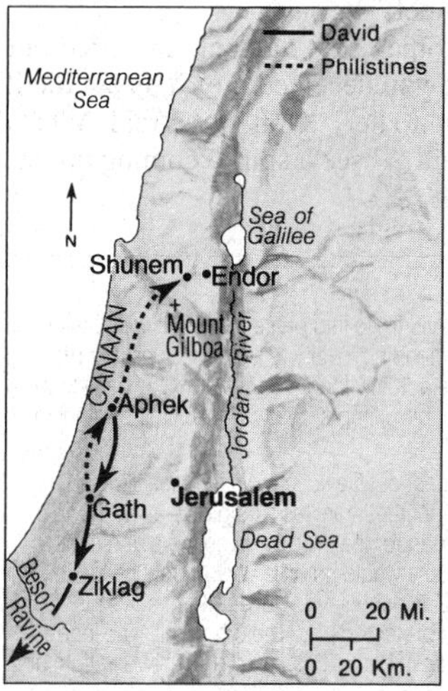

THE BATTLE AT GILBOA David pretended loyalty to Achish, but when war broke out with Israel, he was sent to Ziklag from Aphek. The Philistines defeated the Israelites at Mount Gilboa. David returned to Ziklag to find that the Amalekites had destroyed Ziklag. So David and his men pursued the Amalekite raiders and slaughtered them, recovering all that was taken.

"Against the Negev of Judah" or "Against the Negev of Jerahmeel[k]" or "Against the
Negev of the Kenites.[l]" 11He did not leave a man or woman alive to be brought to
Gath, for he thought, "They might inform on us and say, 'This is what David did.' "
And such was his practice as long as he lived in Philistine territory. 12Achish trusted
David and said to himself, "He has become so odious to his people, the Israelites,
that he will be my servant for ever."

Saul and the Witch of Endor

28 In those days the Philistines gathered[a] their forces to fight against Israel.
Achish said to David, "You must understand that you and your men will
accompany me in the army."
2David said, "Then you will see for yourself what your servant can do."
Achish replied, "Very well, I will make you my bodyguard for life."
3Now Samuel was dead,[b] and all Israel had mourned for him and buried him in
his own town of Ramah.[c] Saul had expelled the mediums and spiritists[d] from the
land.
4The Philistines assembled and came and set up camp at Shunem,[e] while Saul
gathered all the Israelites and set up camp at Gilboa.[f] 5When Saul saw the Philistine
army, he was afraid; terror filled his heart. 6He enquired[g] of the LORD, but the LORD
did not answer him by dreams[h] or Urim[i] or prophets. 7Saul then said to his
attendants, "Find me a woman who is a medium,[j] so that I may go and enquire of
her."
"There is one in Endor,[k]" they said.
8So Saul disguised[l] himself, putting on other clothes, and at night he and two men
went to the woman. "Consult[m] a spirit for me," he said, "and bring up for me the
one I name."
9But the woman said to him, "Surely you know what Saul has done. He has cut
off[n] the mediums and spiritists from the land. Why have you set a trap for my life
to bring about my death?"
10Saul swore to her by the LORD, "As surely as the LORD lives, you will not be
punished for this."
11Then the woman asked, "Whom shall I bring up for you?"
"Bring up Samuel," he said.
12When the woman saw Samuel, she cried out at the top of her voice and said to
Saul, "Why have you deceived me? You are Saul!"
13The king said to her, "Don't be afraid. What do you see?"
The woman said, "I see a spirit[a] coming up out of the ground."

a 13 Or *see spirits*; or *see gods*

27:10 [k]1Sa 30:29; 1Ch 2:9, 25 [l]Jdg 1:16
28:1 [a]1Sa 29:1
28:3 [b]1Sa 25:1 [c]1Sa 7:17 [d]Ex 22:18; Lev 19:31; 20:27; Dt 18:10-11; 1Sa 15:23
28:4 [e]Jos 19:18; 2Ki 4:8 [f]1Sa 31:1, 3
28:6 [g]1Sa 14:37; 1Ch 10:13-14; Pr 1:28 [h]Nu 12:6 [i]Ex 28:30; Nu 27:21
28:7 [j]Ac 16:16 [k]Jos 17:11
28:8 [l]2Ch 18:29; 35:22 [m]Dt 18:10-11; 1Ch 10:13; Isa 8:19
28:9 [n]ver 3

When Achish asked David to go into battle against Israel, David agreed, once again pretending loyalty to the Philistines (28:1ff). Whether he would have actually fought Saul's army we can't know, but we can be sure that his ultimate loyalty was to God and not to Achish or Saul.

28:1, 2 Achish's request put David in a difficult position. To refuse to help Achish fight the Israelites would give away David's loyalty to Israel and endanger the lives of his soldiers and family. But to fight his own people would hurt the very people he loved and would soon lead. David, however, never had to solve his dilemma because God protected him. The other Philistine leaders objected to his presence in battle; thus, he did not have to fight his countrymen.

28:3–8 It was Saul who had banned all mediums and spiritists (those who consult with the dead) from Israel, but in desperation he turned to one for counsel. Although he had removed the sin of witchcraft from the land, he did not remove it from his heart. We may make a great show of denouncing sin, but if our hearts do not change, the sins will return. Knowing what is right and condemning what is wrong does not take the place of *doing* what is right.

28:5, 6 The Urim, along with the Thummim, was used by the high priest to determine God's guidance in certain matters. (See the notes on 2:18 and 10:20 for further information on the use of the Urim and Thummim.)

28:5–7 Saul was overwhelmed at the sight of the Philistine army, and so he turned to the occult. Let life's difficulties and obstacles push you in God's direction and make you depend upon him. As we see from Saul's story, turning to anything or anyone else leads only to disaster.

28:7, 8 God had strictly forbidden the Israelites to have anything to do with divination, sorcery, witchcraft, mediums, spiritists, or anyone who consults the dead (Deuteronomy 18:9–14). In fact, sorcerers were to be put to death (Exodus 22:18). Occult practices were carried on in the name of pagan gods, and people turned to the occult for answers that God would not give.

Practitioners of the occult have Satan and demons as the source of their information; God does not reveal his will to them. Instead he speaks through his own channels: the Bible, his Son Jesus Christ, and the Holy Spirit.

28:12 Did Samuel really come back from the dead at the medium's call? The medium shrieked at the appearance of Samuel—

28:14 [o]1Sa 15:27; 24:8
28:15 [p]ver 6; 1Sa 18:12
28:17 [q]1Sa 15:28
28:18 [r]1Sa 15:20 [s]1Ki 20:42
28:19 [t]1Sa 31:2
28:21 [u]Jdg 12:3; 1Sa 19:5; Job 13:14
28:23 [v]2Ki 5:13
29:1 [a]1Sa 28:1 [b]Jos 12:18; 1Sa 4:1 [c]2Ki 9:30
29:2 [d]1Sa 28:2
29:3 [e]1Sa 27:7; Da 6:5
29:4 [f]1Ch 12:19 [g]1Sa 14:21
29:5 [h]1Sa 18:7; 21:11

14 “What does he look like?” he asked.
“An old man wearing a robe[o] is coming up,” she said.
Then Saul knew it was Samuel, and he bowed down and prostrated himself with
his face to the ground.
15 Samuel said to Saul, “Why have you disturbed me by bringing me up?”
“I am in great distress,” Saul said. “The Philistines are fighting against me, and
God has turned[p] away from me. He no longer answers me, either by prophets or by
dreams. So I have called on you to tell me what to do.”
16 Samuel said, “Why do you consult me, now that the LORD has turned away from
you and become your enemy? 17 The LORD has done what he predicted through me.
The LORD has torn[q] the kingdom out of your hands and given it to one of your
neighbours—to David. 18 Because you did not obey[r] the LORD or carry out his fierce
wrath[s] against the Amalekites, the LORD has done this to you today. 19 The LORD will
hand over both Israel and you to the Philistines, and tomorrow you and your sons[t]
will be with me. The LORD will also hand over the army of Israel to the Philistines.”
20 Immediately Saul fell full length on the ground, filled with fear because of
Samuel's words. His strength was gone, for he had eaten nothing all that day and night.
21 When the woman came to Saul and saw that he was greatly shaken, she said,
“Look, your maidservant has obeyed you. I took my life[u] in my hands and did what
you told me to do. 22 Now please listen to your servant and let me give you some food
so that you may eat and have the strength to go on your way.”
23 He refused[v] and said, “I will not eat.”
But his men joined the woman in urging him, and he listened to them. He got up
from the ground and sat on the couch.
24 The woman had a fattened calf at the house, which she slaughtered at once. She
took some flour, kneaded it and baked bread without yeast. 25 Then she set it before
Saul and his men, and they ate. That same night they got up and left.

Achish Sends David Back to Ziklag

29 The Philistines gathered[a] all their forces at Aphek,[b] and Israel camped by the
spring in Jezreel.[c] 2 As the Philistine rulers marched with their units of hundreds and thousands, David and his men were marching at the rear[d] with Achish.
3 The commanders of the Philistines asked, “What about these Hebrews?”
Achish replied, “Is this not David, who was an officer of Saul king of Israel? He
has already been with me for over a year,[e] and from the day he left Saul until now,
I have found no fault in him.”
4 But the Philistine commanders were angry with him and said, “Send[f] the man
back, that he may return to the place you assigned him. He must not go with us into
battle, or he will turn[g] against us during the fighting. How better could he regain his
master's favour than by taking the heads of our own men? 5 Isn't this the David they
sang about in their dances:

> “ ‘Saul has slain his thousands,
> and David his tens of thousands’?”[h]

6 So Achish called David and said to him, “As surely as the LORD lives, you have
been reliable, and I would be pleased to have you serve with me in the army. From

---

she knew too well that the spirits she usually contacted were either contrived or satanic. Somehow Samuel's appearance revealed to her that she was dealing with a power far greater than she had known. She did not call up Samuel by trickery or by the power of Satan; God brought Samuel back to give Saul a prediction regarding his fate, a message Saul already knew. This in no way justifies efforts to contact the dead or communicate with persons or spirits from the past. God is against all such practices (Galatians 5:19–21).

28:15 God did not answer Saul's appeals because Saul had not followed God's previous directions. Sometimes people wonder why their prayers are not answered. But if they don't fulfil the responsibilities God has already given them, they should not be surprised when he does not give further guidance.

29:4 The other Philistine commanders knew that David was the one who, as a young man, had killed their champion, Goliath (17:32–54), had killed hundreds of Philistine soldiers (18:27), and was the hero of Israelite victory songs (21:11). They were afraid that, in the heat of battle, David might turn against them. Although David was upset at this at first, God used the commanders' suspicion to keep him from having to fight against Saul and his countrymen.

the day[i] you came to me until now, I have found no fault in you, but the rulers[j]
don't approve of you. 7 Turn back and go in peace; do nothing to displease the
Philistine rulers."
8 "But what have I done?" asked David. "What have you found against your servant
from the day I came to you until now? Why can't I go and fight against the enemies
of my lord the king?"
9 Achish answered, "I know that you have been as pleasing in my eyes as an angel[k]
of God; nevertheless, the Philistine commanders[l] have said, 'He must not go up with
us into battle.' 10 Now get up early, along with your master's servants who have come
with you, and leave[m] in the morning as soon as it is light."
11 So David and his men got up early in the morning to go back to the land of the
Philistines, and the Philistines went up to Jezreel.

David Destroys the Amalekites

30 David and his men reached Ziklag[a] on the third day. Now the Amalekites[b]
had raided the Negev and Ziklag. They had attacked Ziklag and burned it, 2 and
had taken captive the women and all who were in it, both young and old. They killed
none of them, but carried them off as they went on their way.
3 When David and his men came to Ziklag, they found it destroyed by fire and their
wives and sons and daughters taken captive. 4 So David and his men wept aloud until
they had no strength left to weep. 5 David's two wives[c] had been captured—Ahinoam
of Jezreel and Abigail, the widow of Nabal of Carmel. 6 David was greatly distressed
because the men were talking of stoning[d] him; each one was bitter in spirit because
of his sons and daughters. But David found strength[e] in the LORD his God.
7 Then David said to Abiathar[f] the priest, the son of Ahimelech, "Bring me the
ephod.[g]" Abiathar brought it to him, 8 and David enquired[h] of the LORD, "Shall I
pursue this raiding party? Will I overtake them?"
"Pursue them," he answered. "You will certainly overtake them and succeed[i] in
the rescue."
9 David and the six hundred men[j] with him came to the Besor Ravine, where some
stayed behind, 10 for two hundred men were too exhausted[k] to cross the ravine. But
David and four hundred men continued the pursuit.
11 They found an Egyptian in a field and brought him to David. They gave him water
to drink and food to eat—12 part of a cake of pressed figs and two cakes of raisins.
He ate and was revived,[l] for he had not eaten any food or drunk any water for three
days and three nights.
13 David asked him, "To whom do you belong, and where do you come from?"
He said, "I am an Egyptian, the slave of an Amalekite. My master abandoned me
when I became ill three days ago. 14 We raided the Negev of the Kerethites[m] and the
territory belonging to Judah and the Negev of Caleb.[n] And we burned[o] Ziklag."
15 David asked him, "Can you lead me down to this raiding party?"
He answered, "Swear to me before God that you will not kill me or hand me over
to my master, and I will take you down to them."
16 He led David down, and there they were, scattered over the countryside, eating,
drinking and revelling[p] because of the great amount of plunder[q] they had taken from

29:6 [i]1Sa 27:8-12 [j]ver 3
29:9 [k]2Sa 14:17, 20; 19:27 [l]ver 4
29:10 [m]1Ch 12:19
30:1 [a]1Sa 29:4, 11 [b]1Sa 15:7; 27:8
30:5 [c]1Sa 25:43; 2Sa 2:2
30:6 [d]Ex 17:4; Jn 8:59 [e]Ps 27:14; 56:3-4, 11; Ro 4:20
30:7 [f]1Sa 22:20 [g]1Sa 23:9
30:8 [h]1Sa 23:2 [i]ver 18
30:9 [j]1Sa 27:2
30:10 [k]ver 9, 21
30:12 [l]Jdg 15:19
30:14 [m]2Sa 8:18; 1Ki 1:38, 44; Eze 25:16; Zep 2:5 [n]ver 16; Jos 14:13; 15:13 [o]ver 1
30:16 [p]Lk 12:19 [q]ver 14

30:6 Faced with the tragedy of losing their families, David's soldiers began to turn against him and even talked about killing him. Instead of planning a rescue, they looked for someone to blame. But David found his strength in God and began looking for a solution instead of a scapegoat. When facing problems, remember that it is useless to look for someone to blame or criticise. Instead, consider how you can help find a solution.

30:7 David couldn't go to the tabernacle to ask the Lord for guidance because it was in Saul's territory. Therefore he called for the ephod, the only tabernacle-related object he possessed. In the presence of the priest and this priestly garment, he asked God for direction. When David called for the ephod, he was really asking the priest to bring him the Urim and Thummim, which were kept in a pouch attached to the ephod. Only the high priest could carry and use the Urim and Thummim. (For more information on the ephod and its contents, see the note on Exodus 39:1–21.)

30:11–15 The Amalekites cruelly left this slave to die, but God used him to lead David and his men to the Amalekite camp. David and his men treated the young man kindly, and he returned the kindness by leading them to the enemy. Treat those you meet with respect and dignity no matter how insignificant they may seem. You never know how God will use them to help you or haunt you, depending upon your response to them.

the land of the Philistines and from Judah. 17David fought[r] them from dusk until the
evening of the next day, and none of them got away, except four hundred young men
who rode off on camels and fled.[s] 18David recovered[t] everything the Amalekites
had taken, including his two wives. 19Nothing was missing: young or old, boy or girl,
plunder or anything else they had taken. David brought everything back. 20He took
all the flocks and herds, and his men drove them ahead of the other livestock, saying,
"This is David's plunder."
21Then David came to the two hundred men who had been too exhausted[u] to follow
him and who were left behind at the Besor Ravine. They came out to meet David and
the people with him. As David and his men approached, he greeted them. 22But all
the evil men and troublemakers among David's followers said, "Because they did not
go out with us, we will not share with them the plunder we recovered. However, each
man may take his wife and children and go."
23David replied, "No, my brothers, you must not do that with what the LORD has
given us. He has protected us and handed over to us the forces that came against us.
24Who will listen to what you say? The share of the man who stayed with the supplies
is to be the same as that of him who went down to the battle. All shall share alike.[v]"
25David made this a statute and ordinance for Israel from that day to this.
26When David arrived in Ziklag, he sent some of the plunder to the elders of Judah,
who were his friends, saying, "Here is a present for you from the plunder of the LORD's
enemies."
27He sent it to those who were in Bethel,[w] Ramoth[x] Negev and Jattir;[y] 28to those
in Aroer,[z] Siphmoth, Eshtemoa[a] 29and Racal; to those in the towns of the Jerahmee-
lites[b] and the Kenites;[c] 30to those in Hormah,[d] Bor Ashan,[e] Athach 31and Hebron;[f] and to those in all the other places where David and his men had roamed.

Saul Takes His Life

31 Now the Philistines fought against Israel; the Israelites fled before them, and
many fell slain on Mount Gilboa.[a] 2The Philistines pressed hard after Saul and
his sons, and they killed his sons Jonathan, Abinadab and Malki-Shua. 3The fighting
grew fierce around Saul, and when the archers overtook him, they wounded[b] him
critically.
4Saul said to his armour-bearer, "Draw your sword and run me through,[c] or these
uncircumcised[d] fellows will come and run me through and abuse me."
But the armour-bearer was terrified and would not do it; so Saul took his own sword
and fell on it. 5When the armour-bearer saw that Saul was dead, he too fell on his

30:17 [r]1Sa 11:11 [s]1Sa 15:3
30:18 [t]Ge 14:16
30:21 [u]ver 10
30:24 [v]Nu 31:27; Jos 22:8
30:27 [w]Jos 7:2 [x]Jos 19:8 [y]Jos 15:48
30:28 [z]Jos 13:16 [a]Jos 15:50
30:29 [b]1Sa 27:10 [c]Jdg 1:16; 1Sa 15:6
30:30 [d]Nu 14:45; Jdg 1:17 [e]Jos 15:42
30:31 [f]Jos 14:13; 2Sa 2:1, 4
31:1 [a]1Sa 28:4; 1Ch 10:1-12
31:3 [b]2Sa 1:6
31:4 [c]Jdg 9:54; 2Sa 1:6, 10 [d]1Sa 14:6

30:24, 25 David made a law that those who stayed with the supplies were to be treated equally with those who fought in battle. Today it takes several people to provide the support services needed for every soldier in battle. In the church and other organisations, we need to treat those who provide support services equally with those on the front line. Without bookkeepers, secretaries, trainers, and administrators, those with a public ministry would be unable to do their jobs. Are you on the front line? Don't forget those who are backing you up. Are you in the support group? Realise that your position, although it may be less glamorous or exciting, is vital to the work of the entire group.

31:3, 4 The Philistines had a well-earned reputation for torturing their captives. Saul no doubt knew about Samson's fate (Judges 16:18–31) and did not want to risk physical mutilation or other abuse. When his armour-bearer refused to kill him, he took his own life.

31:3, 4 Saul was tall, handsome, strong, rich, and powerful, but all of this was not enough to make him someone we should emulate. He was tall physically, but he was small in God's eyes. He was handsome, but his sin made him ugly. He was strong, but his lack of faith made him weak. He was rich, but he was spiritually bankrupt. He could give orders to many, but he couldn't command their respect or allegiance. Saul looked good on the outside, but he was decaying on the inside. A right relationship with God and a strong character are much more valuable than a good-looking exterior.

31:3, 4 Saul's armour-bearer faced a moral dilemma – should he carry out a sinful order from a man he was supposed to obey? He knew he should obey his master, the king, but he also knew murder was wrong. He decided not to kill Saul.

There is a difference between following an order with which you don't agree and following one you know is wrong. It is never right or ethical to carry out a wrong act, no matter who gives the order or what the consequences for disobedience may be. What shapes your choice when you face a moral dilemma? Have the courage to follow God's law above human commands.

31:4 Saul faced death the same way he faced life. He took matters into his own hands without thinking of God or asking for his guidance. If our lives aren't the way we would like them to be now, we can't assume that change will come more easily later. When nearing death, we will respond to God the same way we have been responding all along. Coming face to face with death only shows us what we are *really* like. How do you want to face death? Start facing life that way right now.

sword and died with him. 6So Saul and his three sons and his armour-bearer and all
his men died together that same day.
7When the Israelites along the valley and those across the Jordan saw that the
Israelite army had fled and that Saul and his sons had died, they abandoned their towns
and fled. And the Philistines came and occupied them.
8The next day, when the Philistines came to strip the dead, they found Saul and
his three sons fallen on Mount Gilboa. 9They cut off his head and stripped off his
armour, and they sent messengers throughout the land of the Philistines to proclaim
the news[e] in the temple of their idols and among their people.[f] 10They put his armour
in the temple of the Ashtoreths[g] and fastened his body to the wall of Beth Shan.[h]
11When the people of Jabesh Gilead[i] heard of what the Philistines had done to
Saul, 12all their valiant men journeyed through the night to Beth Shan. They took down
the bodies of Saul and his sons from the wall of Beth Shan and went to Jabesh, where
they burned[j] them. 13Then they took their bones[k] and buried them under a tamarisk[l] tree at Jabesh, and they fasted[m] seven days.[n]

31:9 [e]2Sa 1:20 [f]Jdg 16:24
31:10 [g]Jdg 2:12-13 [h]2Sa 21:12
31:11 [i]1Sa 11:1
31:12 [j]2Sa 2:4-7; Am 6:10
31:13 [k]2Sa 21:12-14 [l]1Sa 22:6 [m]2Sa 1:12 [n]Ge 50:10

31:10 To put Saul's armour in the Philistine temple gave credit to a pagan goddess for victory over Saul. Ashtoreth was a goddess of fertility and sex. Beth Shan was a town on the eastern slopes of Mount Gilboa, overlooking the Jordan Valley.

31:13 Consider the difference between the last judge of Israel and its first king. Saul, the king, was characterised by inconsistency, disobedience, and self-will. He did not have a heart for God. Samuel, the judge, was characterised by consistency, obedience, and a deep desire for God's will. He had a genuine desire for God.

When God called Samuel, he said, "Speak, LORD, for your servant is listening" (3:9). But when God, through Samuel, called Saul, Saul replied, "Why do you say such a thing to me?" (9:21). Saul was dedicated to himself; Samuel was dedicated to God.

31:13 Saul's death was also the death of an ideal – Israel could no longer believe that having a king like the other nations would solve all their troubles. The real problem was not the form of government, but the sinful king. Saul tried to please God by spurts of religiosity, but real spirituality takes a lifetime of consistent obedience.

Heroic spiritual lives are built by stacking days of obedience one on top of the other. Like a brick, each obedient act is small in itself, but in time the acts will pile up, and a huge wall of strong character will be built – a great defence against temptation. We should strive for consistent obedience each day.

KEY PLACES IN 2 SAMUEL

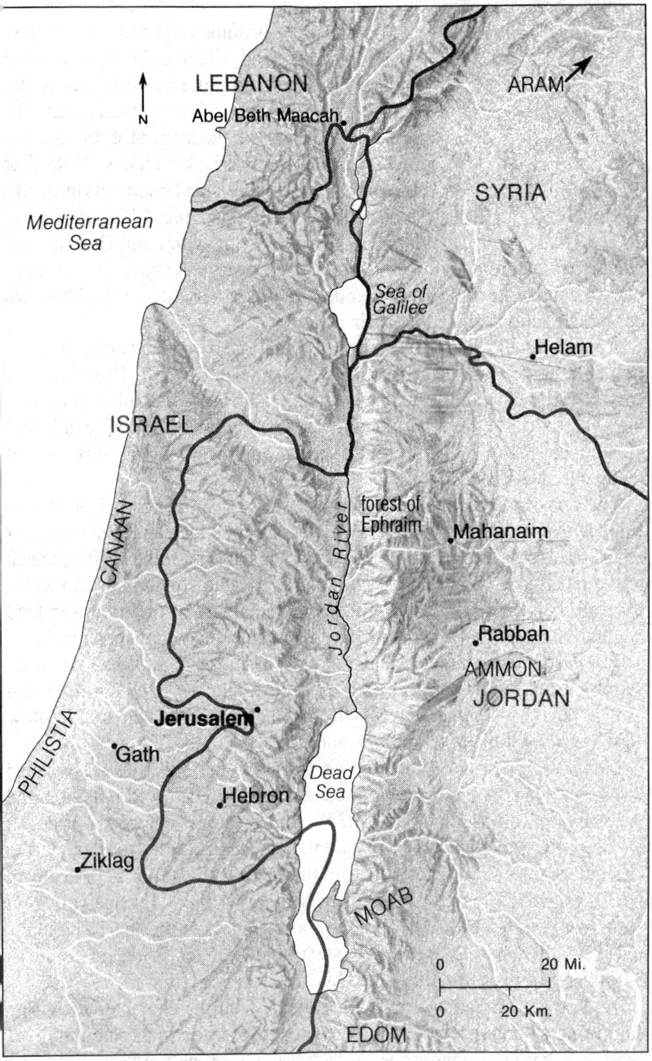

Modern names and boundaries are shown in grey.

1 Hebron After Saul's death, David moved from the Philistine city of Ziklag to Hebron, where the tribe of Judah crowned him king. But the rest of Israel's tribes backed Saul's son Ish-Bosheth and crowned him king at Mahanaim. As a result, there was war between Judah and the rest of the tribes of Israel until Ish-Bosheth was assassinated. Then all of Israel pledged loyalty to David as their king (1:1–5:5).

2 Jerusalem One of David's first battles as king occurred at the fortress city of Jerusalem. David and his troops took the city by surprise, and it became his capital. It was here that David brought the ark of the covenant and made a special agreement with God (5:6–7:29).

3 Gath The Philistines were Israel's constant enemy, though they did give David sanctuary when he was hiding from Saul (1 Samuel 27). But when Saul died and David became king, the Philistines planned to defeat him. In a battle near Jerusalem, David and his troops routed the Philistines (5:17–25), but they were not completely subdued until David conquered Metheg Ammah (possibly near Gath) (8:1).

4 Moab During the time of the judges, Moab controlled many cities in Israel and demanded heavy taxes (Judges 3:12–30). David conquered Moab and, in turn, levied tribute from them (8:2).

5 Edom Though the Edomites and the Israelites traced their ancestry back to the same man, Isaac (Genesis 25:19–23), they were long-standing enemies. David defeated Edom and forced them to pay tribute also (8:14).

6 Rabbah The Ammonites insulted David's delegation and turned a peacemaking mission into angry warfare. The Ammonites called troops from Aram, but David defeated this alliance first at Helam, then at Rabbah, the capital city (9:1–12:31).

7 Mahanaim David had victory in the field, but problems at home. His son, Absalom, incited a rebellion and crowned himself king at Hebron. David and his men fled to Mahanaim. Acting on bad advice, Absalom mobilised his army to fight David (13:1–17:29).

8 Forest of Ephraim The armies of Absalom and David fought in the forest of Ephraim. Absalom's hair got caught in a tree, and Joab, David's general, found and killed him. With Absalom's death, the rebellion died and David was welcomed back to Jerusalem (18:1–19:43).

9 Abel Beth Maacah A man named Sheba also incited a rebellion against David. He fled to Abel Beth Maacah, but Joab and a small troop besieged the city. The citizens of Abel Beth Maacah killed Sheba themselves (20:1–26). David's victories laid the foundation for the peaceful reign of his son, Solomon.

2 SAMUEL

Judges begin to rule 1375 B.C. (1220 B.C.)

Saul becomes king 1050 (1045)

VITAL STATISTICS

PURPOSES:
(1) to record the history of David's reign;
(2) to demonstrate effective leadership under God;
(3) to reveal that one person can make a difference;
(4) to show the personal qualities that please God;
(5) to depict David as an ideal leader of an imperfect kingdom, and to foreshadow Christ, who will be the ideal leader of a new and perfect kingdom (chapter 7)

AUTHOR:
Unknown. Some have suggested that Nathan's son Zabud may have been the author (1 Kings 4:5). The book also includes the writings of Nathan and Gad (1 Chronicles 29:29).

DATE WRITTEN:
930 B.C.; written soon after David's reign, 1050–970 B.C.

SETTING:
The land of Israel under David's rule

KEY VERSE:
"And David knew that the LORD had established him as king over Israel and had exalted his kingdom for the sake of his people Israel" (5:12).

SPECIAL FEATURES:
This book was named after the prophet who anointed David and guided him in living for God.

THE CHILD enters the room with long gown flowing, trailing well behind her high-heeled shoes. The wide-brimmed hat rests precariously on top of her head, tilted to the right, and the long necklace swings like a pendulum as she walks. Following close is the "man". His fingernails peep out of the coat sleeves that are already pushed upwards six inches. With feet shuffling in the double-sized boots, his unsteady steps belie his confident smile. Children at play, dressing up—they copy Mum and Dad, having watched them dress and walk. Models . . . everyone has them . . . people we emulate, people who are our ideals. Unconsciously, perhaps, we copy their actions and adopt their ideas.

Among all the godly role models mentioned in the Bible, there is probably no-one who stands out more than King David. Born halfway between Abraham and Jesus, he became God's leader for all of Israel and the ancestor of the Messiah. David was "a man after [God's] own heart" (1 Samuel 13:14). What are the personal qualities that David possessed that pleased God?

The book of 2 Samuel tells David's story. As you read, you will be filled with excitement as he is crowned king over Judah and then king over all of Israel (5:1–5), praising God as he brings the ark of the covenant back to the tabernacle (6:1–23) and exulting as he leads his armies to victory over all their enemies and completes the conquest of the promised land begun by Joshua (8—10). David was a man who accomplished much.

But David was human, and there were those dark times when he stumbled and fell into sin. The record of lust, adultery, and murder is not easy to read (11—13) and reveals that even great people who try to follow God are susceptible to temptation and sin.

Godliness does not guarantee an easy and carefree life. David had family problems—his own son incited the entire nation to rebellion and crowned himself king (14:1—18:33). And greatness can cause pride, as we see in David's sinful act of taking a census in order to glory in the strength of his nation (24:1–25). But the story of this fallen hero does not end in tragedy. Through repentance, his fellowship and peace with God were restored, but he had to face the consequences of the sins he committed (12—20). These consequences stayed with him for the rest of his life as a reminder of his sinful deeds and his need for God.

As you read 2 Samuel, look for David's Godlike characteristics—his faithfulness, patience, courage, generosity, commitment, honesty—as well as other God-honouring characteristics such as modesty and penitence. Valuable lessons can be learned from his sins and from his repentance. You, like David, can become a person after God's own heart.

Saul dies; David is king over Judah 1010	*David becomes king over all Israel 1003*	*David and Bathsheba sin 997(?)*	*Solomon born 991*	*David's census 980(?)*	*David dies; Solomon made king 970*	*The kingdom is divided 930*

THE BLUEPRINT

A. DAVID'S SUCCESSES (1:1—10:19)
1. David becomes king over Judah
2. David becomes king over Israel
3. David conquers the surrounding nations

David took the fractured kingdom that Saul had left behind and built a strong, united power. Forty years later, David would turn this kingdom over to his son Solomon. David had a heart for God. He was a king who governed God's people by God's principles, and God blessed him greatly. We may not have David's earthly success, but following God is, ultimately, the most successful decision we can make.

B. DAVID'S STRUGGLES (11:1—24:25)
1. David and Bathsheba
2. Turmoil in David's family
3. National rebellion against David
4. The later years of David's rule

David sinned with Bathsheba and then tried to cover his sin by having her husband killed. Although he was forgiven for his sin, the consequences remained—he experienced trouble and distress, both with his family and with the nation. God is always ready to forgive, but we must live with the consequences of our actions. Covering up our sin will only multiply sin's painful consequences.

MEGATHEMES

THEME	EXPLANATION	IMPORTANCE
Kingdom Growth	Under David's leadership, Israel's kingdom grew rapidly. With the growth came many changes: from tribal independence to centralised government, from the leadership of judges to a monarchy, from decentralised worship to worship at Jerusalem.	No matter how much growth or how many changes we experience, God provides for us if we love him and regard his principles highly. God's work done in God's way never lacks God's supply of wisdom and energy.
Personal Greatness	David's popularity and influence increased greatly. He realised that the Lord was behind his success because he wanted to pour out his kindness on Israel. David regarded God's interests as more important than his own.	God graciously pours out his favour on us because of what Christ has done. God does not regard personal greatness as something to be used selfishly, but as an instrument to carry out his work among his people. The greatness we should desire is to love others as God loves us.
Justice	King David showed justice, mercy, and fairness to Saul's family, enemies, rebels, allies, and close friends alike. His just rule was grounded in his faith in and knowledge of God. God's perfect moral nature is the standard for justice.	Although David was the most just of all Israel's kings, he was still imperfect. His use of justice offered hope for a heavenly, ideal kingdom. This hope will never be satisfied in the heart of man until Christ, the Son of David, comes to rule in perfect justice for ever.
Consequences of Sin	David abandoned his purpose as leader and king in time of war. His desire for prosperity and ease led him from triumph to trouble. Because David committed adultery with Bathsheba, he experienced consequences of his sin that ruined both his family and the nation.	Temptation quite often comes when a person's life is aimless. We sometimes think that sinful pleasures and freedom from God's restraint will bring us a feeling of vitality; but sin creates a cycle of suffering that is not worth the fleeting pleasures it offers.
Feet of Clay	David not only sinned with Bathsheba, he murdered an innocent man. He neglected to discipline his sons when they got involved in rape and murder. This great hero showed a lack of character in some of his most important personal decisions. The man of iron had feet of clay.	Sin should never be considered as a mere weakness or flaw. Sin is fatal and must be eradicated from our lives. David's life teaches us to have compassion for all people, including those whose sinful nature leads them into sinful acts. It serves as a warning to us not to excuse sin in our own lives, even in times of success.

A. DAVID'S SUCCESSES (1:1 – 10:19)

After years of running from Saul, David is finally crowned king over the tribe of Judah. The rest of Israel, however, followed Ish-Bosheth, Saul's son. David did not attempt to take the tribes by force, but placed the matter in God's hands. After a few years Ish-Bosheth was assassinated and the rest of the tribes finally put their support behind David. David moved the capital to Jerusalem, defeated the surrounding nations, and even showed kindness to Saul's family. We may not understand why God seems to move slowly at times, but we must trust him and be faithful with what he has given us.

1. David becomes king over Judah

David Hears of Saul's Death

1 After the death[a] of Saul, David returned from defeating[b] the Amalekites and
stayed in Ziklag two days. 2 On the third day a man[c] arrived from Saul's camp,
with his clothes torn and with dust on his head.[d] When he came to David, he fell
to the ground to pay him honour.
3 "Where have you come from?" David asked him.
He answered, "I have escaped from the Israelite camp."
4 "What happened?" David asked. "Tell me."
He said, "The men fled from the battle. Many of them fell and died. And Saul and
his son Jonathan are dead."
5 Then David said to the young man who brought him the report, "How do you know
that Saul and his son Jonathan are dead?"
6 "I happened to be on Mount Gilboa,[e]" the young man said, "and there was Saul,
leaning on his spear, with the chariots and riders almost upon him. 7 When he turned
round and saw me, he called out to me, and I said, 'What can I do?'
8 "He asked me, 'Who are you?'
" 'An Amalekite,[f]' I answered.
9 "Then he said to me, 'Stand over me and kill me! I am in the throes of death, but
I'm still alive.'
10 "So I stood over him and killed him, because I knew that after he had fallen he
could not survive. And I took the crown[g] that was on his head and the band on his
arm and have brought them here to my lord."
11 Then David and all the men with him took hold of their clothes and tore[h] them.
12 They mourned and wept and fasted till evening for Saul and his son Jonathan, and
for the army of the LORD and the house of Israel, because they had fallen by the sword.
13 David said to the young man who brought him the report, "Where are you from?"

1:1 [a] 1Sa 31:6 [b] 1Sa 30:17
1:2 [c] 2Sa 4:10 [d] 1Sa 4:12
1:6 [e] 1Sa 28:4; 31:2-4
1:8 [f] 1Sa 15:2; 30:13, 17
1:10 [g] Jdg 9:54; 2Ki 11:12
1:11 [h] Ge 37:29; 2Sa 3:31; 13:31

1:1 David was a man who had great faith in God. He waited for God to fulfil his promises. The book of 1 Samuel tells of David's struggles as he waited to become king of Israel (Samuel had anointed David as king of Israel many years earlier). King Saul became jealous of David because the people were praising him for his accomplishments. Eventually, Saul's jealousy became so intense that he tried to kill David. As a result, David had to run and hide. For many years David hid from Saul in enemy territory and in the barren desert south and east of Jerusalem. David may have wondered when God's promise that he would be king would come true, but his struggles prepared him for the great responsibilities he would later face. The book of 2 Samuel tells how David was finally rewarded for his patience and consistent faith in God.

1:1 When Saul died, David and his men were still living in Ziklag, a Philistine city. Because Saul had driven him out of Israel, David had pretended to be loyal to Achish, a Philistine ruler (1 Samuel 27). There he was safe from Saul.

1:11, 12 "They mourned and wept and fasted till evening." David and his men were visibly shaken over Saul's death. Their actions showed their genuine sorrow over the loss of their king, their friend Jonathan, and the other soldiers of Israel who died that day. They were not ashamed to grieve. Today, some people consider expressing emotions to be a sign of weakness. Those who wish to appear strong try to hide their feelings. But expressing our grief can help us deal with our intense sorrow when a loved one dies.

1:13 The man identified himself as an Amalekite from Saul's camp (1:2). He may have been an Amalekite under Israelite jurisdiction, but more likely he was a battlefield scavenger. Obviously the man was lying both about his identity and about what happened on the battlefield. (Compare his story with the account in 1 Samuel 31:3, 4.) Because he had Saul's crown with him, something the Philistines wouldn't have left behind, we can infer that he found Saul dead on the battlefield before the Philistines arrived (1 Samuel 31:8).

A life of deceit leads to disaster. The man lied to gain some personal reward for killing David's rival, but he misread David's character. If David had rewarded him for murdering the king, David would have shared his guilt. Instead, David had the messenger killed. Lying can bring disaster upon the liar, even for something he or she has not done.

1:13 The Amalekites were a fierce nomadic tribe that frequently conducted surprise raids on Canaanite villages. They had been Israel's enemies since Moses' time. David had just destroyed an Amalekite band of raiders who had burned his city and kidnapped its women and children (1 Samuel 30:1–20). This man was probably unaware of David's recent confrontations with Amalekites, or he may not have come. Instead, he incurred David's wrath by posing as an enemy of Israel and claiming to have killed God's chosen king.

"I am the son of an alien, an Amalekite,[i]" he answered.
14David asked him, "Why were you not afraid to lift your hand to destroy the
LORD's anointed?[j]"
15Then David called one of his men and said, "Go, strike him down!"[k] So he struck
him down, and he died.[l] 16For David had said to him, "Your blood be on your own
head.[m] Your own mouth testified against you when you said, 'I killed the LORD's
anointed.' "

David's Lament for Saul and Jonathan

17David took up this lament[n] concerning Saul and his son Jonathan, 18and ordered
that the men of Judah be taught this lament of the bow (it is written in the Book of
Jashar):[o]

19"Your glory, O Israel, lies slain on your heights.
How the mighty have fallen![p]

20"Tell it not in Gath,[q]
proclaim it not in the streets of Ashkelon,
lest the daughters of the Philistines[r] be glad,
lest the daughters of the uncircumcised rejoice.[s]

21"O mountains of Gilboa,[t]
may you have neither dew nor rain,
nor fields that yield offerings[u] ⌞of grain⌟.
For there the shield of the mighty was defiled,
the shield of Saul—no longer rubbed with oil.[v]
22From the blood[w] of the slain,
from the flesh of the mighty,
the bow[x] of Jonathan did not turn back,
the sword of Saul did not return unsatisfied.

23"Saul and Jonathan—
in life they were loved and gracious,
and in death they were not parted.
They were swifter than eagles,[y]
they were stronger than lions.[z]

24"O daughters of Israel,
weep for Saul,
who clothed you in scarlet and finery,
who adorned your garments with ornaments of gold.

25"How the mighty have fallen in battle!
Jonathan lies slain on your heights.
26I grieve for you, Jonathan my brother;[a]
you were very dear to me.

1:13 [i]ver 8
1:14 [j]1Sa 24:6; 26:9
1:15 [k]2Sa 4:12 [l]2Sa 4:10
1:16 [m]Lev 20:9; 2Sa 3:28-29; 1Ki 2:32; Mt 27:24-25; Ac 18:6
1:17 [n]2Ch 35:25
1:18 [o]Jos 10:13; 1Sa 31:3
1:19 [p]ver 27
1:20 [q]Mic 1:10 [r]1Sa 31:8 [s]Ex 15:20; 1Sa 18:6
1:21 [t]ver 6; 1Sa 31:1 [u]Eze 31:15 [v]Isa 21:5
1:22 [w]Isa 34:3, 7 [x]Dt 32:42; 1Sa 18:4
1:23 [y]Dt 28:49; Jer 4:13 [z]Jdg 14:18
1:26 [a]1Sa 20:42

1:15, 16 Why did David consider it a crime to kill the king, even though Saul was his enemy? David believed that God anointed Saul, and only God could remove him from office. If it became casual or commonplace to assassinate the king, the whole society would become chaotic. It was God's job, not David's, to judge Saul's sins (Leviticus 19:18). We must realise that God has placed rulers in authority over us, and we should respect their positions (Romans 13:1–5).

1:17, 18 David was a talented musician. He played the harp (1 Samuel 16:23), he brought music into the worship services of the temple (1 Chronicles 25), and he wrote many of the psalms. Here we are told that he wrote a lament in memory of Saul and his son Jonathan, David's closest friend. Music played an important role in Israel's history. (For other famous songs in the Bible, see the chart in Exodus 15.)

1:17–27 Saul had caused much trouble for David, but when he died, David composed a lament for the king and his son. David had every reason to hate Saul, but he chose not to. Instead, he chose to look at the good Saul had done and to ignore the times when Saul had attacked him. It takes courage to lay aside hatred and hurt and to respect the positive side of another person, especially an enemy.

1:26 By saying that Jonathan's love was "more wonderful than that of women", David was not implying that he had a sexual relationship with Jonathan. Homosexual acts were absolutely forbidden in Israel. Leviticus 18:22 calls homosexuality "detestable", and Leviticus 20:13 decrees the death penalty for those who practise homosexuality. David was simply restating the deep brotherhood and faithful friendship he had with Jonathan. (For more on their friendship, see the note on 1 Samuel 18:1–4.)

Your love for me was wonderful,[b]
more wonderful than that of women.

27"How the mighty have fallen!
The weapons of war have perished!"[c]

David Anointed King Over Judah

2 In the course of time, David enquired[a] of the LORD. "Shall I go up to one of
the towns of Judah?" he asked.
The LORD said, "Go up."
David asked, "Where shall I go?"
"To Hebron,"[b] the LORD answered.
2So David went up there with his two wives,[c] Ahinoam of Jezreel and Abigail,[d]
the widow of Nabal of Carmel. 3David also took the men who were with him,[e] each
with his family, and they settled in Hebron and its towns. 4Then the men of Judah
came to Hebron[f] and there they anointed[g] David king over the house of Judah.
When David was told that it was the men of Jabesh Gilead[h] who had buried Saul,
5he sent messengers to the men of Jabesh Gilead to say to them, "The LORD bless[i]
you for showing this kindness to Saul your master by burying him. 6May the LORD
now show you kindness and faithfulness,[j] and I too will show you the same favour
because you have done this. 7Now then, be strong and brave, for Saul your master
is dead, and the house of Judah has anointed me king over them."

War Between the Houses of David and Saul

8Meanwhile, Abner[k] son of Ner, the commander of Saul's army, had taken
Ish-Bosheth son of Saul and brought him over to Mahanaim.[l] 9He made him king
over Gilead,[m] Ashuri[a][n] and Jezreel, and also over Ephraim, Benjamin and all
Israel.[o]
10Ish-Bosheth son of Saul was forty years old when he became king over Israel,

[a] 9 *Or Asher*

1:26 [b]1Sa 18:1
1:27 [c]ver 19, 25; 1Sa 2:4
2:1 [a]1Sa 23:2, 11-12 [b]Ge 13:18; 1Sa 30:31
2:2 [c]1Sa 25:43; 30:5 [d]1Sa 25:42
2:3 [e]1Sa 27:2; 30:9
2:4 [f]1Sa 30:31 [g]1Sa 2:35; 2Sa 5:3-5 [h]1Sa 31:11-13
2:5 [i]1Sa 23:21
2:6 [j]Ex 34:6; 1Ti 1:16
2:8 [k]1Sa 14:50 [l]Ge 32:2
2:9 [m]Nu 32:26 [n]Jdg 1:32 [o]1Ch 12:29

2:1 Although David knew he would become king (1 Samuel 16:13; 23:17; 24:20), and although the time seemed right now that Saul was dead, David still asked God if he should move back to Judah, the home territory of his tribe. Before moving ahead with what seems obvious, first bring the matter to God, who alone knows the best timing.

2:1 God told David to return to Hebron, where he would soon be crowned king of Judah. David made Hebron his capital because (1) it was the largest city in Judah at that time; (2) it was secure against attack; (3) it was located near the centre of Judah's territory, an ideal location for a capital city; (4) many key trade routes converged at Hebron, making it difficult for supply lines to be cut off in wartime.

2:4 The men of Judah publicly anointed David as their king. David had been anointed king by Samuel years earlier (1 Samuel 16:13), but that ceremony had taken place in private. This one was like inaugurating a public official who has already been elected to office. The rest of Israel, however, didn't accept David's kingship for seven and a half years (2:10, 11).

2:4–7 David sent a message thanking the men of Jabesh Gilead who had risked their lives to bury Saul's body (1 Samuel 31:11–13). Saul had rescued Jabesh Gilead from certain defeat when Nahash the Ammonite surrounded the city (1 Samuel 11), so these citizens showed their gratitude and kindness. In his message, he also suggested that they follow Judah's lead and acknowledge him as their king. Jabesh Gilead was to the north in the land of Gilead, and David was seeking to gain support among the 10 remaining tribes who had not yet recognised him as king.

2:10, 11 David ruled over Judah for seven and a half years, while Ish-Bosheth reigned in Israel for only two years. The five-year gap may be due to Ish-Bosheth's not assuming the throne immediately after Saul's death. Because of constant danger from the Philistines in the northern part of Israel, five years may have passed before Ish-Bosheth could begin his reign. During that time, Abner, commander of his army, probably played a principal role in driving out the Philistines and leading the northern confederacy. Regardless of when Ish-Bosheth began to rule, his control was weak and limited. The Philistines still dominated the area, and Ish-Bosheth was intimidated by Abner (3:11).

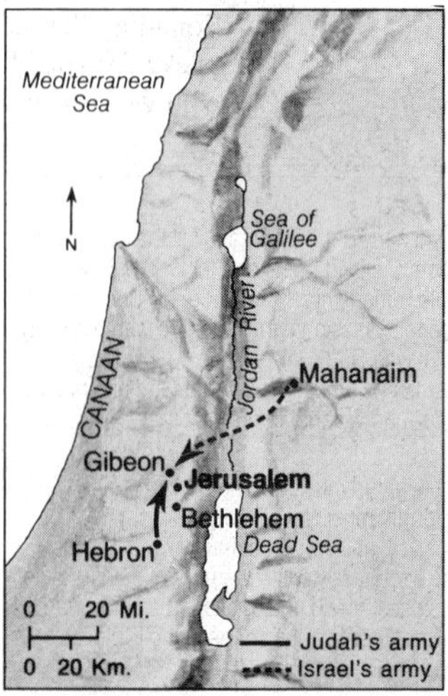

JOAB VERSUS ABNER
David was crowned king of Judah in Hebron; Ish-Bosheth was crowned king of Israel in Mahanaim. The opposing armies of Judah and Israel met at Gibeon for battle—Judah under Joab, Israel under Abner.

and he reigned two years. The house of Judah, however, followed David. 11 The length
of time David was king in Hebron over the house of Judah was seven years and six
months.[p]
12 Abner son of Ner, together with the men of Ish-Bosheth son of Saul, left Mahanaim and went to Gibeon.[q] 13 Joab[r] son of Zeruiah and David's men went out and
met them at the pool of Gibeon. One group sat down on one side of the pool and one
group on the other side.
14 Then Abner said to Joab, "Let's have some of the young men get up and fight
hand to hand in front of us."
"All right, let them do it," Joab said.
15 So they stood up and were counted off—twelve men for Benjamin and Ish-
Bosheth son of Saul, and twelve for David. 16 Then each man grabbed his opponent
by the head and thrust his dagger into his opponent's side, and they fell down together.
So that place in Gibeon was called Helkath Hazzurim.**[b]**
17 The battle that day was very fierce, and Abner and the men of Israel were
defeated[s] by David's men.
18 The three sons of Zeruiah[t] were there: Joab,[u] Abishai[v] and Asahel.[w] Now
Asahel was as fleet-footed as a wild gazelle.[x] 19 He chased Abner, turning neither
to the right nor to the left as he pursued him. 20 Abner looked behind him and asked,
"Is that you, Asahel?"
"It is," he answered.
21 Then Abner said to him, "Turn aside to the right or to the left; take on one of
the young men and strip him of his weapons." But Asahel would not stop chasing him.
22 Again Abner warned Asahel, "Stop chasing me! Why should I strike you down?
How could I look your brother Joab in the face?"[y]
23 But Asahel refused to give up the pursuit; so Abner thrust the butt of his spear
into Asahel's stomach,[z] and the spear came out through his back. He fell there and
died on the spot. And every man stopped when he came to the place where Asahel
had fallen and died.[a]
24 But Joab and Abishai pursued Abner, and as the sun was setting, they came to
the hill of Ammah, near Giah on the way to the wasteland of Gibeon. 25 Then the men

b *16 Helkath Hazzurim* means *field of daggers* or *field of hostilities.*

2:11 [p] 2Sa 5:5
2:12 [q] Jos 18:25
2:13 [r] 2Sa 8:16; 1Ch 2:16; 11:6
2:17 [s] 2Sa 3:1
2:18 [t] 2Sa 3:39 [u] 2Sa 3:30 [v] 1Sa 26:6 [w] 1Ch 2:16 [x] 1Ch 12:8
2:22 [y] 2Sa 3:27
2:23 [z] 2Sa 3:27; 4:6 [a] 2Sa 20:12

CHARACTERS IN THE DRAMA
It can be confusing to keep track of all the characters introduced in the first few chapters of 2 Samuel. Here is some help.

Character	*Relation*	*Position*	*Whose side?*
Joab	Son of Zeruiah, David's half sister	One of David's military leaders and, later, commander in chief	David's
Abner	Saul's cousin	Saul's commander in chief	Saul and Ish-Bosheth's, but made overtures to David
Abishai	Joab's brother	High officer in David's army—chief of "the Three"	Joab and David's
Asahel	Joab and Abishai's brother	High officer—one of David's 30 select warriors ("mighty men")	Joab and David's
Ish-Bosheth	Saul's son	Saul and Abner's selection as king	Saul's

2:12ff With Israel divided, there was constant tension between north and south. David's true rival in the north, however, was not Ish-Bosheth but Abner. In this incident, Abner suggested a "dagger match" between the champions of his army and the champions of David's army, led by Joab. The fact that this confrontation occurred at the pool of Gibeon (located in Saul's home territory of Benjamin) suggests that Joab's men were pushing northwards, gaining more territory. Abner may have suggested this confrontation in hopes of stopping Joab's advance.

Twelve men from each side were supposed to fight each other, and the side with the most survivors would be declared the winner. The confrontation between David and Goliath (1 Samuel 17) was a similar battle strategy—a way to avoid terrible bloodshed from an all-out war. In this case, however, all 24 champions were killed before either side could claim victory. Nothing was accomplished, and the civil war continued.

2:21–23 Abner repeatedly warned Asahel to turn back or risk losing his life, but Asahel refused to turn from his self-imposed duty. Persistence is a good trait if it is for a worthy cause. But if the goal is only personal honour or gain, persistence may be no more than stubbornness. Asahel's stubbornness not only cost his life, but it also spurred unfortunate disunity in David's army for years to come (3:26, 27; 1 Kings 2:28–35). Before you decide to pursue a goal, make sure it is worthy of your devotion.

of Benjamin rallied behind Abner. They formed themselves into a group and took their
stand on top of a hill.
26Abner called out to Joab, "Must the sword devour[b] for ever? Don't you realise
that this will end in bitterness? How long before you order your men to stop pursuing
their brothers?"
27Joab answered, "As surely as God lives, if you had not spoken, the men would
have continued the pursuit of their brothers until morning."[c]
28So Joab[c] blew the trumpet,[d] and all the men came to a halt; they no longer
pursued Israel, nor did they fight any more.
29All that night Abner and his men marched through the Arabah. They crossed the
Jordan, continued through the whole Bithron[d] and came to Mahanaim.[e]
30Then Joab returned from pursuing Abner and assembled all his men. Besides
Asahel, nineteen of David's men were found missing. 31But David's men had killed
360 Benjamites who were with Abner. 32They took Asahel and buried him in his
father's tomb[f] at Bethlehem. Then Joab and his men marched all night and arrived
at Hebron by daybreak.

3 The war between the house of Saul and the house of David lasted a long time.[a]
David grew stronger and stronger,[b] while the house of Saul grew weaker and
weaker.[c]
2Sons were born to David in Hebron:

His firstborn was Amnon the son of Ahinoam[d] of Jezreel;
3his second, Kileab the son of Abigail[e] the widow of Nabal of Carmel;
the third, Absalom[f] the son of Maacah daughter of Talmai king of Geshur;[g]
4the fourth, Adonijah[h] the son of Haggith;
the fifth, Shephatiah the son of Abital;
5and the sixth, Ithream the son of David's wife Eglah.
These were born to David in Hebron.

Abner Goes Over to David

6During the war between the house of Saul and the house of David, Abner had been
strengthening his own position in the house of Saul. 7Now Saul had had a concubine[i]
named Rizpah[j] daughter of Aiah. And Ish-Bosheth said to Abner, "Why did you
sleep with my father's concubine?"
8Abner was very angry because of what Ish-Bosheth said and he answered, "Am I

2:26 [b]Dt 32:42; Jer 46:10, 14
2:28 [c]2Sa 18:16 [d]Jdg 3:27
2:29 [e]ver 8
2:32 [f]Ge 49:29
3:1 [a]1Ki 14:30 [b]2Sa 5:10 [c]2Sa 2:17
3:2 [d]1Sa 25:43; 1Ch 3:1-3
3:3 [e]1Sa 25:42 [f]2Sa 13:1, 28 [g]1Sa 27:8; 2Sa 13:37; 14:32; 15:8
3:4 [h]1Ki 1:5, 11
3:7 [i]2Sa 16:21-22 [j]2Sa 21:8-11

[c] *27* Or *spoken this morning, the men would not have taken up the pursuit of their brothers*; or *spoken, the men would have given up the pursuit of their brothers by morning* [d] *29* Or *morning*; or *ravine*; the meaning of the Hebrew for this word is uncertain.

2:28 This battle ended with a victory for Joab's troops (2:17), but war in the divided nation continued until David was finally crowned king over all Israel (5:1–5).

3:1 The events recorded in chapter 2 led to a long war between David's followers and the troops loyal to Abner and Ish-Bosheth. Civil war rocked the country at great cost to both sides. This war occurred because Israel and Judah had lost sight of God's vision and purpose: to settle the land (Genesis 12:7), to drive out the Canaanites (Deuteronomy 7:1–4), and to obey God's laws (Deuteronomy 8:1). Instead of uniting to accomplish these goals, they fought each other. When you face conflict, step back from the hostilities and consider whether you and your enemy have common goals that are bigger than your differences. Appeal to those interests as you work for a settlement.

3:2–5 David suffered much heartache because of his many wives. Polygamy was a socially acceptable practice for kings at this time, although God specifically warned against it (Deuteronomy 17:14–17). Sadly, the numerous sons born to David's wives caused him great trouble. Rape (13:14), murder (13:28), rebellion (15:13), and greed (1 Kings 1:5, 6) all resulted from the jealous rivalries among the half brothers. Solomon, one of David's sons and his successor to the throne, also took many wives who eventually turned him away from God (1 Kings 11:3, 4).

3:6, 7 To sleep with any of the king's wives or concubines was to make a claim to the throne, and it was considered treason. Because Ish-Bosheth was a weak ruler, Abner was running the country; thus he may have felt justified in sleeping with Saul's concubine. Ish-Bosheth, however, saw that Abner's power was becoming too great.

3:7 Ish-Bosheth may have been right to speak out against Abner's behaviour, but he didn't have the moral strength to maintain his authority (3:11). Lack of moral backbone became the root of Israel's troubles over the next four centuries. Only 4 of the next 40 kings of Israel were called "good". It takes courage and strength to stand firm in your convictions and to confront wrongdoing in the face of opposition. When you believe something is wrong, do not let yourself be talked out of your position. Firmly attack the wrong and uphold the right.

3:8 By saying, "Am I a dog's head?" Abner meant, "Am I a traitor for Judah?" He may have been refuting the accusation that he was trying to take over the throne, or he may have been angry that Ish-Bosheth scolded him after Abner had helped put him on the throne in the first place. Prior to this conversation, Abner realised that he could not keep David from eventually taking over Israel. Because he was angry at Ish-Bosheth, Abner devised a plan to turn over the kingdom of Israel to David.

3:8 [k]1Sa 24:14; 2Sa 9:8; 16:9
3:9 [l]1Sa 15:28; 1Ki 19:2
3:10 [m]Jdg 20:1; 1Sa 3:20
3:13 [n]Ge 43:5; 1Sa 18:20

a dog's head[k]—on Judah's side? This very day I am loyal to the house of your father
Saul and to his family and friends. I haven't handed you over to David. Yet now you
accuse me of an offence involving this woman! 9 May God deal with Abner, be it ever
so severely, if I do not do for David what the LORD promised[l] him on oath 10 and
transfer the kingdom from the house of Saul and establish David's throne over Israel
and Judah from Dan to Beersheba."[m] 11 Ish-Bosheth did not dare to say another word
to Abner, because he was afraid of him.
12 Then Abner sent messengers on his behalf to say to David, "Whose land is it?
Make an agreement with me, and I will help you bring all Israel over to you."
13 "Good," said David. "I will make an agreement with you. But I demand one thing
of you: Do not come into my presence unless you bring Michal daughter of Saul when
you come to see me."[n] 14 Then David sent messengers to Ish-Bosheth son of Saul,

ABNER

The honest compliments of an opponent are often the best measure of someone's greatness. Although Abner and David frequently saw each other across battle lines, the Bible gives a glimpse of the respect they had for each other. As a young man, David had served under Abner. But later, Saul's campaign to kill David was carried out by Abner. After Saul's death, Abner temporarily upheld the power of the king's family. But the struggle between Abner and Saul's heir, Ish-Bosheth, brought about Abner's decision to support David's claim to the throne. It was during his efforts to unite the kingdom that Abner was murdered by Joab.

Several years earlier, in a battle between Ish-Bosheth's army under Abner and David's forces under Joab, Abner fled and was pursued by Joab's brother, Asahel. Abner told Asahel twice to stop following him. But the eager young soldier refused, so Abner killed him. Joab was determined to avenge his brother.

Abner realised Saul's family was doomed to defeat and that David would be the next king, so he decided to change sides. He hoped that in exchange for his delivering Saul's kingdom, David would make him commander in chief of his army. David's willingness to accept this proposal was probably another reason for Joab's action.

Abner lived by his wits and his will. To him, God was someone with whom he would co-operate if it suited his plans. Otherwise he did what seemed best for him at the time. We can identify with Abner's tendency to give God conditional co-operation. Obedience is easy when the instructions in God's word fit in with our plans. But our allegiance to God is tested when his plans are contrary to ours. What action should you take today in obedience to God's word?

Strengths and accomplishments:
- Commander in chief of Saul's army and a capable military leader
- Held Israel together for several years under the weak king Ish-Bosheth
- Recognised and accepted God's plan to make David king over all Israel and Judah

Weaknesses and mistakes:
- He had selfish motives in his effort to reunite Judah and Israel rather than godly conviction
- He slept with one of the royal concubines after Saul's death

Lesson from his life:
- God requires more than conditional, half-hearted co-operation

Vital statistics:
- Where: Territory of Benjamin
- Occupation: Commander of the armies under Saul and Ish-Bosheth
- Relatives: Father: Ner. Cousin: Saul. Son: Jaasiel
- Contemporaries: David, Asahel, Joab, Abishai

Key verse:
"Then the king said to his men, 'Do you not realise that a prince and a great man has fallen in Israel this day?' " (2 Samuel 3:38).

Abner's story is told in 1 Samuel 14:50—2 Samuel 4:12. He is also mentioned in 1 Kings 2:5, 32; 1 Chronicles 26:28; 27:16–22.

3:13, 14 Michal had been married to David. Saul had arranged the marriage as a reward for David's acts of bravery (1 Samuel 17:25; 18:24–27). Later, however, in one of his jealous fits, Saul took Michal away from David and forced her to marry Paltiel (1 Samuel 25:44). Now David wanted his wife back before he would begin to negotiate peace with the northern tribes. Perhaps David still loved her (but see 6:20–23 for the tension in their relationship). More likely, he thought that marriage to Saul's daughter would strengthen his claim to rule all Israel and demonstrate that he had no animosity towards Saul's house. Paltiel was the unfortunate victim caught in the web of Saul's jealousy.

demanding, "Give me my wife Michal,[o] whom I betrothed to myself for the price
of a hundred Philistine foreskins."
15So Ish-Bosheth gave orders and had her taken away from her husband[p] Paltiel[q]
son of Laish. 16Her husband, however, went with her, weeping behind her all the way
to Bahurim.[r] Then Abner said to him, "Go back home!" So he went back.
17Abner conferred with the elders[s] of Israel and said, "For some time you have
wanted to make David your king. 18Now do it! For the LORD promised David, 'By
my servant David I will rescue my people Israel from the hand of the Philistines[t]
and from the hand of all their enemies.[u]' "
19Abner also spoke to the Benjamites in person. Then he went to Hebron to tell
David everything that Israel and the whole house of Benjamin[v] wanted to do. 20When
Abner, who had twenty men with him, came to David at Hebron, David prepared a
feast for him and his men. 21Then Abner said to David, "Let me go at once and
assemble all Israel for my lord the king, so that they may make a compact[w] with you,
and that you may rule over all that your heart desires."[x] So David sent Abner away,
and he went in peace.

Joab Murders Abner

22Just then David's men and Joab returned from a raid and brought with them a great
deal of plunder. But Abner was no longer with David in Hebron, because David had
sent him away, and he had gone in peace. 23When Joab and all the soldiers with him
arrived, he was told that Abner son of Ner had come to the king and that the king
had sent him away and that he had gone in peace.
24So Joab went to the king and said, "What have you done? Look, Abner came to
you. Why did you let him go? Now he is gone! 25You know Abner son of Ner; he
came to deceive you and observe your movements and find out everything you are
doing."
26Joab then left David and sent messengers after Abner, and they brought him back
from the well of Sirah. But David did not know it. 27Now when Abner[y] returned to
Hebron, Joab took him aside into the gateway, as though to speak with him privately.
And there, to avenge the blood of his brother Asahel, Joab stabbed him in the stomach,
and he died.[z]
28Later, when David heard about this, he said, "I and my kingdom are for ever
innocent[a] before the LORD concerning the blood of Abner son of Ner. 29May his
blood[b] fall upon the head of Joab and upon all his father's house![c] May Joab's house
never be without someone who has a running sore[d] or leprosy**[a]** or who leans on a
crutch or who falls by the sword or who lacks food."
30(Joab and his brother Abishai murdered Abner because he had killed their brother
Asahel in the battle of Gibeon.)
31Then David said to Joab and all the people with him, "Tear your clothes and put

a *29* The Hebrew word was used for various diseases affecting the skin—not necessarily leprosy.

3:14 [o]1Sa 18:27
3:15 [p]Dt 24:1-4 [q]1Sa 25:44
3:16 [r]2Sa 16:5; 19:16
3:17 [s]Jdg 11:11
3:18 [t]1Sa 9:16 [u]1Sa 15:28; 2Sa 8:6
3:19 [v]1Sa 10:20-21; 1Ch 12:2, 16, 29
3:21 [w]ver 10, 12 [x]1Ki 11:37
3:27 [y]2Sa 2:8 [z]2Sa 2:22; 20:9-10; 1Ki 2:5
3:28 [a]ver 37; Dt 21:9
3:29 [b]Lev 20:9 [c]1Ki 2:31-33 [d]Lev 15:2

3:19 Because Saul, Ish-Bosheth, and Abner were all from the tribe of Benjamin, the support of the elders of that tribe meant that Abner was serious about his offer. There was a strong possibility of overcoming tribal jealousies and uniting the kingdom.

3:26–29 Joab took revenge for the death of his brother instead of leaving justice to God. But that revenge backfired on him (1 Kings 2:31–34). God will repay those who deserve it (Romans 12:19). Refuse to rejoice when your enemies suffer, and don't try to get revenge. Seeking revenge will ruin your own peace of mind and increase the chances of further retaliation.

3:27 Abner killed Joab's brother Asahel in self-defence. Joab then killed Abner to avenge his brother's death and also to save his position of military leadership. People who killed in self-defence were supposed to be safe in cities of refuge (Numbers 35:22–25). Joab showed his disrespect for God's laws by killing Abner out of revenge in Hebron, a city of refuge (Joshua 20:7).

3:29 David was saying that Joab's descendants would be unclean, unhealthy, and in want. Why did David say such harsh words about Joab? David was upset over Abner's death for several reasons. (1) He was grieved over the loss of a skilled military officer. (2) He wanted to place the guilt of Abner's murder on Joab, not himself. (3) He was on the verge of becoming king over the entire nation, and utilising Abner was the key to winning over the northern tribes. Abner's death could have revived the civil war. (4) Joab violated David's agreement to protect Abner. Joab's murderous act ruined David's plans, and David was especially angry that his own commander had committed the crime.

3:31 By walking behind the bier, or coffin, David was leading the mourning.

3:31ff David ordered Joab to mourn, possibly because few people were aware that Joab had committed the crime and because David did not want any further trouble. If this is true, David was thinking more about strengthening his kingdom than about justice.

on sackcloth[e] and walk in mourning[f] in front of Abner." King David himself walked
behind the bier. 32They buried Abner in Hebron, and the king wept[g] aloud at Abner's
tomb. All the people wept also.
33The king sang this lament[h] for Abner:

"Should Abner have died as the lawless die?
34 Your hands were not bound,
your feet were not fettered.
You fell as one falls before wicked men."

And all the people wept over him again.
35Then they all came and urged David to eat something while it was still day; but
David took an oath, saying, "May God deal with me, be it ever so severely,[i] if I
taste bread[j] or anything else before the sun sets!"
36All the people took note and were pleased; indeed, everything the king did pleased
them. 37So on that day all the people and all Israel knew that the king had no part[k]
in the murder of Abner son of Ner.
38Then the king said to his men, "Do you not realise that a prince and a great man
has fallen[l] in Israel this day? 39And today, though I am the anointed king, I am weak,
and these sons of Zeruiah[m] are too strong for me.[n] May the LORD repay[o] the evildoer
according to his evil deeds!"

Ish-Bosheth Murdered

4 When Ish-Bosheth son of Saul heard that Abner[a] had died in Hebron, he lost
courage, and all Israel became alarmed. 2Now Saul's son had two men who were
leaders of raiding bands. One was named Baanah and the other Recab; they were sons
of Rimmon the Beerothite from the tribe of Benjamin—Beeroth[b] is considered part
of Benjamin, 3because the people of Beeroth fled to Gittaim[c] and have lived there
as aliens to this day.
4(Jonathan[d] son of Saul had a son who was lame in both feet. He was five years
old when the news[e] about Saul and Jonathan came from Jezreel. His nurse picked
him up and fled, but as she hurried to leave, he fell and became crippled.[f] His name
was Mephibosheth.)[g]
5Now Recab and Baanah, the sons of Rimmon the Beerothite, set out for the house
of Ish-Bosheth,[h] and they arrived there in the heat of the day while he was taking
his noonday rest. 6They went into the inner part of the house as if to get some wheat,
and they stabbed[i] him in the stomach. Then Recab and his brother Baanah slipped
away.
7They had gone into the house while he was lying on the bed in his bedroom. After
they stabbed and killed him, they cut off his head. Taking it with them, they travelled
all night by way of the Arabah. 8They brought the head of Ish-Bosheth to David at
Hebron and said to the king, "Here is the head of Ish-Bosheth son of Saul,[j] your
enemy, who tried to take your life. This day the LORD has avenged my lord the king
against Saul and his offspring."
9David answered Recab and his brother Baanah, the sons of Rimmon the Beerothite, "As surely as the LORD lives, who has delivered[k] me out of all trouble, 10when
a man told me, 'Saul is dead,' and thought he was bringing good news, I seized him

3:31 [e]2Sa 1:2, 11; Ps 30:11; Isa 20:2 [f]Ge 37:34
3:32 [g]Nu 14:1; Pr 24:17
3:33 [h]2Sa 1:17
3:35 [i]Ru 1:17; 1Sa 3:17 [j]1Sa 31:13; 2Sa 1:12; 12:17; Jer 16:7
3:37 [k]ver 28
3:38 [l]2Sa 1:19
3:39 [m]2Sa 2:18 [n]2Sa 19:5-7 [o]1Ki 2:5-6, 33-34; Ps 41:10; 101:8
4:1 [a]2Sa 3:27; Ezr 4:4
4:2 [b]Jos 9:17; 18:25
4:3 [c]Ne 11:33
4:4 [d]1Sa 18:1 [e]1Sa 31:1-4 [f]Lev 21:18 [g]2Sa 9:3, 6; 1Ch 8:34; 9:40
4:5 [h]2Sa 2:8
4:6 [i]2Sa 2:23
4:8 [j]1Sa 24:4; 25:29
4:9 [k]Ge 48:16; 1Ki 1:29

3:39 Joab and Abishai were the two sons of Zeruiah David mentioned. David had an especially hard time controlling Joab because, although he was intensely loyal, he was strong willed, preferring to do things his own way. In exchange for his loyalty, however, David was willing to give him the flexibility he craved.

Joab's murder of Abner is an example of his fierce independence. While David opposed the murder, he allowed it to remain unpunished because (1) to punish Joab could cause the troops to rebel; (2) Joab was David's nephew, and any harsh treatment could cause family problems; (3) Joab was from the tribe of Judah, and David didn't want rebellion from his own tribe; (4) to get rid of Joab would mean losing a skilled and competent commander who had been invaluable in strengthening his army.

4:1 Ish-Bosheth was a man who took his courage from another man (Abner) rather than from God. When Abner died, Ish-Bosheth was left with nothing. In crisis and under pressure, he collapsed in fear. Fear can paralyse us, but faith and trust in God can overcome fear (2 Timothy 1:6–8; Hebrews 13:6). If we trust in God, we will be free to respond boldly to the events around us.

4:4 The rest of Mephibosheth's story is told in chapters 9; 16:1–4; and 19:24–30.

and put him to death in Ziklag.[l] That was the reward I gave him for his news! 11 How
much more — when wicked men have killed an innocent man in his own house and
on his own bed — should I not now demand his blood[m] from your hand and rid the
earth of you!"
12 So David gave an order to his men, and they killed them.[n] They cut off their
hands and feet and hung the bodies by the pool in Hebron. But they took the head
of Ish-Bosheth and buried it in Abner's tomb at Hebron.

2. David becomes king over Israel

5 All the tribes of Israel[a] came to David at Hebron and said, "We are your own
flesh and blood.[b] 2 In the past, while Saul was king over us, you were the one
who led Israel on their military campaigns.[c] And the LORD said to you, 'You shall
shepherd[d] my people Israel, and you shall become their ruler.[e]' "
3 When all the elders of Israel had come to King David at Hebron, the king made
a compact[f] with them at Hebron before the LORD, and they anointed[g] David king
over Israel.
4 David was thirty years old[h] when he became king, and he reigned[i] for forty[j]
years. 5 In Hebron he reigned over Judah for seven years and six months,[k] and in
Jerusalem he reigned over all Israel and Judah for thirty-three years.

David Conquers Jerusalem

6 The king and his men marched to Jerusalem[l] to attack the Jebusites,[m] who lived
there. The Jebusites said to David, "You will not get in here; even the blind and the
lame can ward you off." They thought, "David cannot get in here." 7 Nevertheless,
David captured the fortress of Zion, the City of David.[n]
8 On that day, David said, "Anyone who conquers the Jebusites will have to use the

4:10 [l]2Sa 1:2-16
4:11 [m]Ge 9:5; Ps 9:12
4:12 [n]2Sa 1:15
5:1 [a]2Sa 19:43 [b]1Ch 11:1
5:2 [c]1Sa 18:5, 13, 16 [d]1Sa 16:1; 2Sa 7:7 [e]1Sa 25:30
5:3 [f]2Sa 3:21 [g]2Sa 2:4
5:4 [h]Lk 3:23 [i]1Ki 2:11; 1Ch 3:4 [j]1Ch 26:31; 29:27
5:5 [k]2Sa 2:11; 1Ch 3:4
5:6 [l]Jdg 1:8 [m]Jos 15:8
5:7 [n]2Sa 6:12, 16; 1Ki 2:10

4:11 David called Ish-Bosheth an "innocent man". As Saul's son, Ish-Bosheth had reason to think he was in line for the throne. He was not wicked for wanting to be king; rather, he was simply too weak to stand against injustice. Although David knew Ish-Bosheth was not the strong leader needed to unite Israel, he had no intention of killing him. God had promised the kingdom to David, and he knew that God would fulfil his promise.

When David learned of Ish-Bosheth's death, he was angry. He had never harmed Saul, and he thought the assassins' method was cowardly. David wanted to unite Israel, not drive a permanent wedge between him and Ish-Bosheth's supporters. To show that he had nothing to do with the extermination of Saul's royal line, he ordered the assassins killed and gave Ish-Bosheth a proper burial. All the tribes of Israel, recognising in David the strong leader they needed, pledged their loyalty to him. No doubt the Philistine threat and David's military reputation (1 Samuel 18:7) also helped unify the people.

5:3–5 This was the third time David was anointed king. First he was privately anointed by Samuel (1 Samuel 16:13). Then he was made king over the tribe of Judah (2:4). Finally he was crowned king over all Israel. As an outlaw, life had looked bleak, but God's promise to make him king over all Israel was now being fulfilled. Although the kingdom would be divided again in less than 75 years, David's dynasty would reign over Judah, the southern kingdom, for over 400 years.

5:4, 5 David did not become king over all Israel until he was 37 years old, although he had been promised the kingdom many years earlier (1 Samuel 16:13). During those years, David had to wait patiently for the fulfilment of God's promise. If you feel pressured to achieve instant results and success, remember David's patience. Just as his time of waiting prepared him for his important task, a waiting period may help prepare you by strengthening your character.

5:6 The fortress city of Jerusalem was located on a high ridge near the centre of the united Israelite kingdom. It was considered neutral territory because it stood on the border of the territory of the tribes of Benjamin and Judah and it was still occupied by the Jebusites, a Canaanite tribe that had never been expelled from the land (Judges 1:21). Because of its strategic advantages, David made Jerusalem his capital.

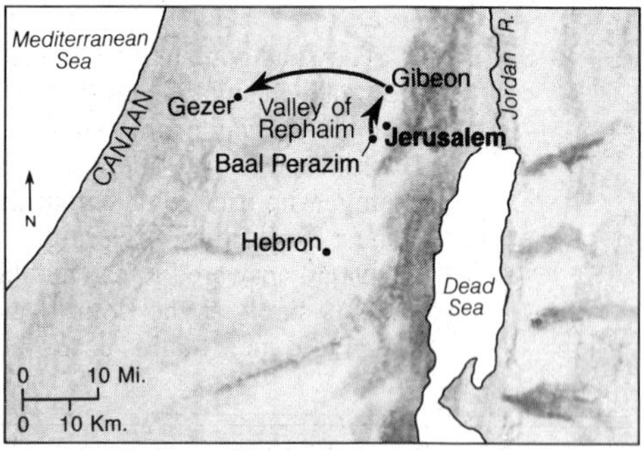

DAVID DEFEATS THE PHILISTINES The Philistines camped in the Valley of Rephaim. David defeated them at Baal Perazim, but they remained in the valley. He attacked again, and chased them from Gibeon to Gezer.

5:6, 7 The Jebusites had a clear military advantage, and they boasted of their security behind the impregnable walls of Jerusalem, also called Zion. But they soon discovered that their walls would not protect them. David caught them by surprise by entering the city through the water tunnel.

Only in God are we truly safe and secure. Anything else is false security. Whether you are surrounded by mighty walls of stone, a

water shaft[a] to reach those 'lame and blind' who are David's enemies."[b] That is why
they say, "The 'blind and lame' will not enter the palace."
9David then took up residence in the fortress and called it the City of David. He
built up the area around it, from the supporting terraces[c][o] inward. 10And he became
more and more powerful,[p] because the LORD God Almighty was with him.
11Now Hiram[q] king of Tyre sent messengers to David, along with cedar logs and
carpenters and stonemasons, and they built a palace for David. 12And David knew
that the LORD had established him as king over Israel and had exalted his kingdom
for the sake of his people Israel.
13After he left Hebron, David took more concubines and wives[r] in Jerusalem, and
more sons and daughters were born to him. 14These are the names of the children born
to him there:[s] Shammua, Shobab, Nathan, Solomon, 15Ibhar, Elishua, Nepheg,
Japhia, 16Elishama, Eliada and Eliphelet.

David Defeats the Philistines

17When the Philistines heard that David had been anointed king over Israel, they
went up in full force to search for him, but David heard about it and went down to
the stronghold.[t] 18Now the Philistines had come and spread out in the Valley of
Rephaim;[u] 19so David enquired[v] of the LORD, "Shall I go and attack the Philistines?
Will you hand them over to me?"
The LORD answered him, "Go, for I will surely hand the Philistines over to you."
20So David went to Baal Perazim, and there he defeated them. He said, "As waters
break out, the LORD has broken out against my enemies before me." So that place was
called Baal Perazim.[d][w] 21The Philistines abandoned their idols there, and David and
his men carried them off.[x]
22Once more the Philistines came up and spread out in the Valley of Rephaim; 23so
David enquired of the LORD, and he answered, "Do not go straight up, but circle round
behind them and attack them in front of the balsam trees. 24As soon as you hear the
sound[y] of marching in the tops of the balsam trees, move quickly, because that will
mean the LORD has gone out in front[z] of you to strike the Philistine army." 25So David
did as the LORD commanded him, and he struck down the Philistines all the way from
Gibeon[e][a] to Gezer.[b]

a *8* Or *use scaling hooks* **b** *8* Or *are hated by David* **c** *9* Or *the Millo* **d** *20* *Baal Perazim* means *the lord who breaks out.* **e** *25* Septuagint (see also 1 Chron. 14:16); Hebrew *Geba*

5:9 *o* ver 7; 1Ki 9:15, 24
5:10 *p* 2Sa 3:1
5:11 *q* 1Ki 5:1, 18; 1Ch 14:1
5:13 *r* Dt 17:17; 1Ch 3:9
5:14 *s* 1Ch 3:5
5:17 *t* 2Sa 23:14; 1Ch 11:16
5:18 *u* Jos 15:8; 17:15; 18:16
5:19 *v* 1Sa 23:2; 2Sa 2:1
5:20 *w* Isa 28:21
5:21 *x* Dt 7:5; 1Ch 14:12; Isa 46:2
5:24 *y* 2Ki 7:6 *z* Jdg 4:14
5:25 *a* Isa 28:21 *b* 1Ch 14:16

---

comfortable home, or a secure job, no-one can predict what tomorrow may bring. Our relationship with God is the only security that cannot be taken away.

5:12 "David knew that the LORD had established him . . ." Although the pagan kingdoms based their greatness on conquest, power, armies, and wealth, David knew that his greatness came only from God. To be great means keeping a close relationship with God personally and nationally. To do this, David had to keep his ambition under control. Although he was famous, successful, and well liked, he gave God first place in his life and served the people according to God's purposes. Do you seek greatness from God or from people? In the drive for success, remember to keep your ambition under God's control.

5:17 "The stronghold" is the mountain stronghold in the Desert of Judah that David used when defending himself against Saul (see 23:14 and 1 Chronicles 12:8).

5:17 The Philistine oppression of Israel began in the days of Samson (Judges 13–16). The Philistines were still Israel's most powerful enemy although David was once considered a friend and ally (1 Samuel 27; 29). Because they occupied much of Israel's northern territory, they apparently did not bother David while he was king of Judah to the south. But when they learned that David was planning to unite all Israel, they tried to stop him.

5:19 How could David get such a clear message from God? He may have prayed and been urged to action by the Holy Spirit. He may have asked God through a prophet. Most likely, however, he went to the high priest, who consulted God through the Urim and Thummim that God had told the Israelites to use for just such a purpose. (For more on the Urim and Thummim, see the notes on Leviticus 8:8 and 1 Samuel 10:20.)

5:19–25 David fought his battles the way God instructed him. In each instance he (1) asked if he should fight or not, (2) followed instructions carefully, and (3) gave God the glory. We can err in our "battles" by ignoring these steps and instead: (1) do what we want without considering God's will, (2) do things our way and ignore advice in the Bible or from other wise people, and (3) take the glory ourselves or give it to someone else without acknowledging the help we received from God. All these responses are sinful.

5:25 After David became king, his first order of business was to subdue his enemies – a task the nation had failed to complete when they first entered the land (Judges 2:1–4). David knew this had to be done in order to (1) protect the nation, (2) unify the kingdom, and (3) prepare for building the temple (which would unify religion under God and help abolish idolatrous influences).

The Ark Brought to Jerusalem

6 David again brought together out of Israel chosen men, thirty thousand in all. 2 He
and all his men set out from Baalah[a] of Judah[a] to bring up from there the ark[b]
of God, which is called by the Name,[b][c] the name of the LORD Almighty, who is
enthroned[d] between the cherubim[e] that are on the ark. 3 They set the ark of God on
a new cart[f] and brought it from the house of Abinadab, which was on the hill. Uzzah
and Ahio, sons of Abinadab, were guiding the new cart 4 with the ark of God on it,[c]
and Ahio was walking in front of it. 5 David and the whole house of Israel were
celebrating with all their might before the LORD, with songs[d] and with harps, lyres,
tambourines, sistrums and cymbals.[g]
6 When they came to the threshing-floor of Nacon, Uzzah reached out and took hold
of[h] the ark of God, because the oxen stumbled. 7 The LORD's anger burned against
Uzzah because of his irreverent act;[i] therefore God struck him down[j] and he died
there beside the ark of God.
8 Then David was angry because the LORD's wrath[k] had broken out against Uzzah,
and to this day that place is called Perez Uzzah.[e][l]
9 David was afraid of the LORD that day and said, "How[m] can the ark of the LORD
ever come to me?" 10 He was not willing to take the ark of the LORD to be with him
in the City of David. Instead, he took it aside to the house of Obed-Edom[n] the Gittite.
11 The ark of the LORD remained in the house of Obed-Edom the Gittite for three
months, and the LORD blessed him and his entire household.[o]
12 Now King David[p] was told, "The LORD has blessed the household of Obed-Edom
and everything he has, because of the ark of God." So David went down and brought
up the ark of God from the house of Obed-Edom to the City of David with rejoicing.
13 When those who were carrying the ark of the LORD had taken six steps, he sacrificed[q] a bull and a fattened calf. 14 David, wearing a linen ephod,[r] danced[s] before
the LORD with all his might, 15 while he and the entire house of Israel brought up the
ark of the LORD with shouts and the sound of trumpets.[t]
16 As the ark of the LORD was entering the City of David,[u] Michal daughter of Saul
watched from a window. And when she saw King David leaping and dancing before
the LORD, she despised him in her heart.
17 They brought the ark of the LORD and set it in its place inside the tent that David

[a] 2 That is, Kiriath Jearim; Hebrew *Baale Judah*, a variant of *Baalah of Judah* [b] 2 Hebrew; Septuagint and Vulgate do not have *the Name.* [c] 3,4 Dead Sea Scrolls and some Septuagint manuscripts; Masoretic Text *cart 4and they brought it with the ark of God from the house of Abinadab, which was on the hill* [d] 5 See Dead Sea Scrolls, Septuagint and 1 Chron. 13:8; Masoretic Text *celebrating before the LORD with all kinds of instruments made of pine.* [e] 8 *Perez Uzzah* means *the outbreak against Uzzah.*

6:2 [a]Jos 15:9 [b]1Sa 4:4; 7:1 [c]Lev 24:16; Isa 63:14 [d]Ps 99:1 [e]Ex 25:22; 1Ch 13:5-6
6:3 [f]Nu 7:4-9; 1Sa 6:7
6:5 [g]1Sa 18:6-7; Ezr 3:10; Ps 150:5
6:6 [h]Nu 4:15, 19-20; 1Ch 13:9
6:7 [i]1Ch 15:13-15 [j]Ex 19:22; 1Sa 6:19
6:8 [k]Ps 7:11 [l]Ge 38:29
6:9 [m]Ps 119:120
6:10 [n]1Ch 13:13; 26:4-5
6:11 [o]Ge 30:27; 39:5
6:12 [p]1Ki 8:1; 1Ch 15:25
6:13 [q]1Ki 8:5, 62
6:14 [r]Ex 19:6; 1Sa 2:18 [s]Ex 15:20
6:15 [t]Ps 47:5; 98:6
6:16 [u]2Sa 5:7

6:3 The ark of God was Israel's national treasure and was ordinarily kept in the tabernacle. When the ark was returned to Israel after a brief Philistine captivity (1 Samuel 4:1 – 7:2), it was kept in Abinadab's home for 20 years. David saw how God blessed Abinadab, and he wanted to bring the ark to Jerusalem to ensure God's blessing on the entire nation. (See the notes on Exodus 37:1 and Joshua 3:2–4 for more information on the ark.)

6:6, 7 Uzzah was only trying to protect the ark, so was God's anger against Uzzah just? According to Numbers 4:5–15, the ark was to be moved only by the Levites, who were to carry it using the carrying poles – they were *never* to touch the ark itself. To touch it was a capital offence under Hebrew law (Numbers 4:15). God's action was directed against both David and Uzzah. David placed the ark on a cart, following the Philistines' example (1 Samuel 6:7, 8) rather than God's commands. Uzzah, though sincere in his desire to protect the ark, had to face the consequences of the sin of touching it. Also, Uzzah may not have been a Levite. As David sought to bring Israel back into a relationship with God, God had to remind the nation dramatically that enthusiasm must be accompanied by obedience to his laws. The next time David tried to bring the ark to Jerusalem, he was careful to handle it correctly (1 Chronicles 15:1–15).

6:8–12 David was angry that a well-meaning man had been killed and that his plans for a joyous return of the ark had been spoiled (6:8). He undoubtedly knew that the fault was his own for transporting the ark carelessly. After cooling down, he had the ark put into temporary storage while he waited to see if the Lord would allow him to bring it to Jerusalem. This also gave David time to consider the right way to transport the ark. The fact that God blessed the home of Obed-Edom was a sign to David that he could try once again to move the ark to Jerusalem.

6:14 David wore a linen ephod, the priest's apron, possibly because it was a religious celebration.

6:16ff Michal was David's first wife, but here she is called daughter of Saul, possibly to show how similar her attitude was to her father's. Her contempt for David probably did not start with David's grand entrance into the city. Perhaps she thought it was undignified to be so concerned with public worship at a time when it was so unimportant in the kingdom. Or maybe she thought it was not fitting for a king to display such emotion. She may have resented David's taking her from Paltiel (see the note on 3:13, 14). Whatever the reason, this contempt she felt towards her husband escalated into a difficult confrontation, and Michal ended up childless for life. Feelings of bitterness and resentment that go unchecked will destroy a relationship. Deal with your feelings before they escalate into open warfare.

6:17 Only a priest could place the sacrifices on the altar. Leviticus 1:2–13 indicates that anyone who was ceremonially clean

6:17 [v]1Ch 15:1; 2Ch 1:4 [w]Lev 1:1-17; 1Ki 8:62-64
6:18 [x]1Ki 8:22
6:19 [y]Hos 3:1 [z]Ne 8:10
6:20 [a]ver 14, 16
6:21 [b]1Sa 13:14; 15:28

had pitched for it,[v] and David sacrificed burnt offerings[w] and fellowship offerings[f]
before the LORD. 18After he had finished sacrificing[x] the burnt offerings and fellowship offerings, he blessed the people in the name of the LORD Almighty. 19Then he
gave a loaf of bread, a cake of dates and a cake of raisins[y] to each person in the whole
crowd of Israelites, both men and women.[z] And all the people went to their homes.
20When David returned home to bless his household, Michal daughter of Saul came
out to meet him and said, "How the king of Israel has distinguished himself today,
disrobing[a] in the sight of the slave girls of his servants as any vulgar fellow would."
21David said to Michal, "It was before the LORD, who chose me rather than your
father or anyone from his house when he appointed[b] me ruler over the LORD's people
Israel—I will celebrate before the LORD. 22I will become even more undignified than
this, and I will be humiliated in my own eyes. But by these slave girls you spoke of,
I will be held in honour."

[f] *17* Traditionally *peace offerings*; also in verse 18

MICHAL

Sometimes love is not enough—especially if that love is little more than the strong emotional attraction that grows between a hero and an admirer. To Michal, Saul's daughter, the courageous young David must have seemed like a dream come true. Her feelings about this hero gradually became obvious to others, and eventually, her father heard about her love for David. He saw this as an opportunity to get rid of his rival for the people's loyalty. He promised Michal's hand in marriage in exchange for David's success in the impossible task of killing 100 Philistines. But David was victorious, and so Saul lost a daughter and saw his rival become even more popular with the people.

Michal's love for David did not have time to be tested by the realities of marriage. Instead, she became involved in saving David's life. Her quick thinking helped him escape, but it cost her Saul's anger and her separation from David. Her father gave her to another man, Paltiel, but David eventually took her back.

Unlike her brother Jonathan, Michal did not have the kind of deep relationship with God that would have helped her through the difficulties in her life. Instead she became bitter. She could not share David's joyful worship of God, so she hated it. As a result, she never bore David any children.

Beyond feeling sorry for her, we need to see Michal as a person mirroring our own tendencies. How quickly and easily we become bitter with life's unexpected turns. But bitterness cannot remove or change the bad things that have happened. Often bitterness only makes a bad situation worse. On the other hand, a willingness to respond to God gives him the opportunity to bring good out of the difficult situations. That willingness has two parts: asking God for his guidance and looking for that guidance in his word.

Strengths and accomplishments:
- Loved David and became his first wife
- Saved David's life
- Could think and act quickly when it was needed

Weaknesses and mistakes:
- Lied under pressure
- Allowed herself to become bitter over her circumstances
- In her unhappiness, she hated David for loving God

Lessons from her life:
- We are not as responsible for what happens to us as we are for how we respond to our circumstances
- Disobedience to God almost always harms us as well as others

Vital statistics:
- Occupations: Daughter of one king, Saul, and wife of another, David
- Relatives: Parents: Saul and Ahinoam. Brothers: Abinadab, Jonathan, Malki-Shua. Sister: Merab. Husbands: David and Paltiel

Key verse:
"As the ark of the LORD was entering the City of David, Michal daughter of Saul watched from a window. And when she saw King David leaping and dancing before the LORD, she despised him in her heart" (2 Samuel 6:16).

Michal's story is told in 1 Samuel 14—2 Samuel 6. She is also mentioned in 1 Chronicles 15:29.

---

could assist a priest in offering the sacrifice (see the notes on Joshua 3:5; 1 Samuel 20:26). So David probably offered these sacrifices to God with the aid of a priest. Solomon did the same (1 Kings 8:62–65).

23 And Michal daughter of Saul had no children to the day of her death.

God's Promise to David

7 After the king was settled in his palace[a] and the LORD had given him rest from
all his enemies around him, 2 he said to Nathan the prophet, "Here I am, living
in a palace[b] of cedar, while the ark of God remains in a tent."[c]
3 Nathan replied to the king, "Whatever you have in mind, go ahead and do it, for
the LORD is with you."
4 That night the word of the LORD came to Nathan, saying:

5 "Go and tell my servant David, 'This is what the LORD says: Are you[d] the
one to build me a house to dwell in?[e] 6 I have not dwelt in a house from the day
I brought the Israelites up out of Egypt to this day. I have been moving from place
to place with a tent[f] as my dwelling.[g] 7 Wherever I have moved with all the
Israelites,[h] did I ever say to any of their rulers whom I commanded to shepherd[i]
my people Israel, "Why have you not built me a house of cedar?[j]" '
8 "Now then, tell my servant David, 'This is what the LORD Almighty says:
I took you from the pasture and from following the flock[k] to be ruler[l] over my
people Israel.[m] 9 I have been with you wherever you have gone,[n] and I have cut
off all your enemies from before you.[o] Now I will make your name great, like
the names of the greatest men of the earth. 10 And I will provide a place for my
people Israel and will plant[p] them so that they can have a home of their own
and no longer be disturbed. Wicked[q] people shall not oppress them any more,[r]
as they did at the beginning 11 and have done ever since the time I appointed
leaders**[a]**[s] over my people Israel. I will also give you rest from all your enemies.[t]
" 'The LORD declares to you that the LORD himself will establish[u] a house[v]
for you: 12 When your days are over and you rest[w] with your fathers, I will raise
up your offspring to succeed you, who will come from your own body,[x] and
I will establish his kingdom. 13 He is the one who will build a house for my
Name,[y] and I will establish the throne of his kingdom for ever.[z] 14 I will be his
father, and he shall be my son.[a] When he does wrong, I will punish him with
the rod[b] of men, with floggings inflicted by men. 15 But my love will never be
taken away from him, as I took it away from Saul,[c] whom I removed from before
you. 16 Your house and your kingdom shall endure for ever before me;**[b]** your
throne[d] shall be established for ever.[e]' "

17 Nathan reported to David all the words of this entire revelation.

a *11* Traditionally *judges* **b** *16* Some Hebrew manuscripts and Septuagint; most Hebrew manuscripts *you*

7:1 [a] 1Ch 17:1
7:2 [b] 2Sa 5:11 [c] Ex 26:1; Ac 7:45-46
7:5 [d] 1Ki 8:19; 1Ch 22:8 [e] 1Ki 5:3-5
7:6 [f] Ex 40:18, 34 [g] 1Ki 8:16
7:7 [h] Dt 23:14 [i] 2Sa 5:2 [j] Lev 26:11-12
7:8 [k] 1Sa 16:11 [l] 2Sa 6:21 [m] Ps 78:70-72; 2Co 6:18*
7:9 [n] 2Sa 5:10 [o] Ps 18:37-42
7:10 [p] Ex 15:17; Isa 5:1-7 [q] Ps 89:22-23 [r] Isa 60:18
7:11 [s] Jdg 2:16; 1Sa 12:9-11 [t] ver 1 [u] 1Sa 25:28 [v] ver 27
7:12 [w] 1Ki 2:1 [x] Ps 132:11-12
7:13 [y] 1Ki 5:5; 8:19, 29 [z] Isa 9:7
7:14 [a] Ps 89:26; Heb 1:5* [b] Ps 89:30-33
7:15 [c] 1Sa 15:23, 28
7:16 [d] Ps 89:36-37 [e] ver 13

7:1ff This chapter records the covenant God made with David, promising to carry on David's line for ever. This promise would be fully realised in the birth of Jesus Christ. Although the word *covenant* is not specifically stated here, it is used elsewhere to describe this occasion (23:5; Psalm 89:3, 4, 28, 34–37).

7:2 This is the first time Nathan the prophet is mentioned. God made certain that a prophet was living during the reign of each of the kings of Israel. The prophet's main tasks were to urge the people to follow God and to communicate God's laws and plans to the king. Most of the kings rejected the prophets God sent. But at least God had given them the opportunity to listen and obey. In earlier years, judges and priests had the role of prophets. Samuel served as judge, priest, and prophet, bridging the gap between the period of the judges and the monarchy.

7:5 In this message from Nathan, God is saying that he doesn't want David to build a "house" for him. Why didn't God want David to build the temple? God told David that his job was to unify and lead Israel and to destroy its enemies. This huge task would require David to shed a great deal of blood. In 1 Chronicles 28:3, we learn that God did not want his temple built by a warrior. Therefore, David made the plans and collected the materials so that his son Solomon could begin work on the temple as soon as he became king (1 Kings 5 – 7). David accepted his part in God's plan and did not try to go beyond it. Sometimes God says no to our plans. When he does, we should utilise the other opportunities he gives us.

7:8–16 David's request was good, but God said no. This does not mean that God rejected David. In fact, God was planning to do something even greater in David's life than allowing him the prestige of building the temple. Although God turned down David's request, he promised to continue the house (or dynasty) of David for ever. David's earthly dynasty ended four centuries later, but Jesus Christ, a direct descendant of David, was the ultimate fulfilment of this promise (Acts 2:22–36). Christ will reign for eternity – now in his spiritual kingdom and in heaven, and later, on earth, in the new Jerusalem (Luke 1:30–33; Revelation 21). Have you prayed with good intentions, only to have God say no? This is God's way of directing you to a greater purpose in your life. Accepting God's no requires as great a faith as carrying out his yes.

7:18 [f]Ex 3:11; 1Sa 18:18
7:19 [g]Isa 55:8-9
7:20 [h]Jn 21:17 [i]1Sa 16:7
7:22 [j]Ps 48:1; 86:10; Jer 10:6 [k]Dt 3:24 [l]Ex 15:11 [m]Ex 10:2; Ps 44:1
7:23 [n]Dt 4:32-38 [o]Dt 10:21 [p]Dt 9:26; 15:15
7:24 [q]Dt 26:18 [r]Ex 6:6-7; Ps 48:14
7:28 [s]Ex 34:6; Jn 17:17
7:29 [t]Nu 6:23-27

David's Prayer

18 Then King David went in and sat before the LORD, and he said:

"Who am I,[f] O Sovereign LORD, and what is my family, that you have
brought me this far? 19 And as if this were not enough in your sight, O Sovereign
LORD, you have also spoken about the future of the house of your servant. Is this
your usual way of dealing with man,[g] O Sovereign LORD?
20 "What more can David say to you? For you know[h] your servant,[i] O
Sovereign LORD. 21 For the sake of your word and according to your will, you
have done this great thing and made it known to your servant.
22 "How great[j] you are,[k] O Sovereign LORD! There is no-one like you, and
there is no God[l] but you, as we have heard with our own ears.[m] 23 And who
is like your people Israel[n]—the one nation on earth that God went out to redeem
as a people for himself, and to make a name for himself, and to perform great
and awesome wonders[o] by driving out nations and their gods from before your
people, whom you redeemed[p] from Egypt?[c] 24 You have established your
people Israel as your very own[q] for ever, and you, O LORD, have become their
God.[r]
25 "And now, LORD God, keep for ever the promise you have made concerning
your servant and his house. Do as you promised, 26 so that your name will be great
for ever. Then men will say, 'The LORD Almighty is God over Israel!' And the
house of your servant David will be established before you.
27 "O LORD Almighty, God of Israel, you have revealed this to your servant,
saying, 'I will build a house for you.' So your servant has found courage to offer
you this prayer. 28 O Sovereign LORD, you are God! Your words are trustworthy,[s] and you have promised these good things to your servant. 29 Now be
pleased to bless the house of your servant, that it may continue for ever in your
sight; for you, O Sovereign LORD, have spoken, and with your blessing[t] the
house of your servant will be blessed for ever."

c 23 See Septuagint and 1 Chron. 17:21; Hebrew *wonders for your land and before your people, whom you redeemed from Egypt, from the nations and their gods.*

CRITICISING GOD'S LEADERS
It is dangerous to criticise God's leaders. Consider the consequences for these men and women.

Person/Situation	*Result*	*Reference*
Miriam: Mocked Moses because he had a Cushite wife	Stricken with leprosy	Numbers 12
Korah and followers: Led the people of Israel to rebel against Moses' leadership	Swallowed by the earth	Numbers 16
Michal: Despised David because he danced before the Lord	Remained childless	2 Samuel 6
Shimei: Cursed and threw stones at David	Executed at Solomon's order	2 Samuel 16 1 Kings 2
Youths: Mocked Elisha and laughed at his baldness	Killed by bears	2 Kings 2
Sanballat and Tobiah: Spread rumours and lies to stop the building of Jerusalem's walls	Frightened and humiliated	Nehemiah 2, 4, 6
Hananiah: Contradicted Jeremiah's prophecies with false predictions	Died two months later	Jeremiah 28
Bar-Jesus, a sorcerer: Lied about Paul in an attempt to turn the proconsul against him	Stricken with blindness	Acts 13

7:18ff This section records David's prayer expressing his humble acceptance of God's promise to extend his dynasty for ever. David realised that these blessings were given to him and his descendants in order that Israel might benefit from them. They would help fulfil God's greater purpose and promises that through the nation the whole world would be blessed (Genesis 12:1–3).

3. David conquers the surrounding nations

David's Victories

8 In the course of time, David defeated the Philistines and subdued them, and he
took Metheg Ammah from the control of the Philistines.
2 David also defeated the Moabites.[a] He made them lie down on the ground and
measured them off with a length of cord. Every two lengths of them were put to death,
and the third length was allowed to live. So the Moabites became subject to David
and brought tribute.
3 Moreover, David fought Hadadezer[b] son of Rehob, king of Zobah,[c] when he
went to restore his control along the Euphrates River. 4 David captured a thousand of
his chariots, seven thousand charioteers[a] and twenty thousand foot soldiers. He
hamstrung[d] all but a hundred of the chariot horses.
5 When the Arameans of Damascus[e] came to help Hadadezer king of Zobah, David
struck down twenty-two thousand of them. 6 He put garrisons in the Aramean kingdom
of Damascus, and the Arameans became subject to him and brought tribute. The LORD
gave David victory wherever he went.[f]
7 David took the gold shields[g] that belonged to the officers of Hadadezer and
brought them to Jerusalem. 8 From Tebah[b] and Berothai,[h] towns that belonged to
Hadadezer, King David took a great quantity of bronze.
9 When Tou[c] king of Hamath[i] heard that David had defeated the entire army of
Hadadezer, 10 he sent his son Joram[d] to King David to greet him and congratulate
him on his victory in battle over Hadadezer, who had been at war with Tou. Joram
brought with him articles of silver and gold and bronze.
11 King David dedicated[j] these articles to the LORD, as he had done with the silver
and gold from all the nations he had subdued: 12 Edom[e] and Moab,[k] the Ammonites[l]
and the Philistines,[m] and Amalek.[n] He also dedicated the plunder taken from Hadadezer son of Rehob, king of Zobah.
13 And David became famous[o] after he returned from striking down eighteen
thousand Edomites[f] in the Valley of Salt.[p]
14 He put garrisons throughout Edom, and all the Edomites[q] became subject to
David.[r] The LORD gave David victory wherever he went.[s]

a *4* Septuagint (see also Dead Sea Scrolls and 1 Chron. 18:4); Masoretic Text *captured seventeen hundred of his charioteers* **b** *8* See some Septuagint manuscripts (see also 1 Chron. 18:8); Hebrew *Betah.* **c** *9* Hebrew *Toi,* a variant of *Tou;* also in verse 10 **d** *10* A variant of *Hadoram* **e** *12* Some Hebrew manuscripts, Septuagint and Syriac (see also 1 Chron. 18:11); most Hebrew manuscripts *Aram* **f** *13* A few Hebrew manuscripts, Septuagint and Syriac (see also 1 Chron. 18:12); most Hebrew manuscripts *Aram* (that is, Arameans)

8:2 [a]Ge 19:37; Nu 24:17
8:3 [b]2Sa 10:16, 19 [c]1Sa 14:47
8:4 [d]Jos 11:9
8:5 [e]1Ki 11:24
8:6 [f]ver 14; 2Sa 3:18; 7:9
8:7 [g]1Ki 10:16
8:8 [h]Eze 47:16
8:9 [i]1Ki 8:65; 2Ch 8:4
8:11 [j]1Ki 7:51; 1Ch 26:26
8:12 [k]ver 2 [l]2Sa 10:14 [m]2Sa 5:25 [n]1Sa 27:8
8:13 [o]2Sa 7:9 [p]2Ki 14:7; 1Ch 18:12
8:14 [q]Nu 24:17-18 [r]Ge 27:29, 37-40 [s]ver 6

8:1–5 Part of God's covenant with David included the promise that the Israelites' enemies would be defeated and would no longer oppress them (7:10, 11). God fulfilled this promise by helping David defeat the opposing nations. Several enemies are listed in this chapter: (1) *The Moabites,* descendants of Lot who lived east of the Dead Sea. They posed a constant military and religious threat to Israel (Numbers 25:1–3; Judges 3:12–30; 1 Samuel 14:47). David seemed to have a good relationship with the Moabites at one time. (2) *King Hadadezer of Zobah.* His defeat at David's hands fulfilled God's promise to Abraham that Israel would control the land as far north as the Euphrates River (Genesis 15:18). (3) *The Edomites,* descendants of Esau (Genesis 36:1) who were also archenemies of Israel (see 2 Kings 8:20; Jeremiah 49:7–22; Ezekiel 25:12–14; and the note on Genesis 36:9).

8:6 The *tribute* was the tax levied on conquered nations. The tax helped to support Israel's government and demonstrated that the conquered nation was under Israel's control.

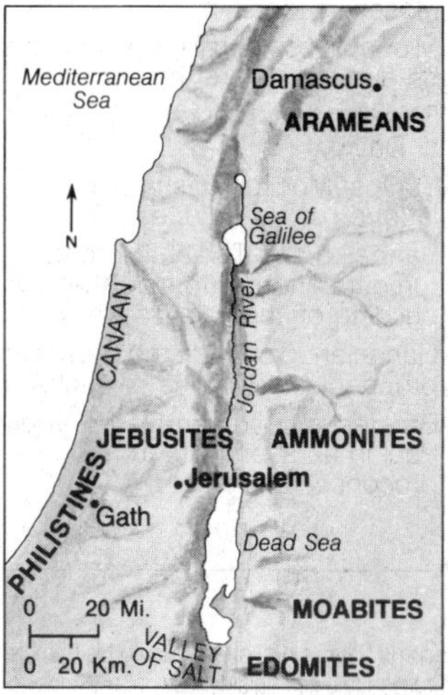

DAVID'S ENEMIES
David wanted to complete the conquest of Canaan begun by Joshua. He defeated the Jebusites at Jerusalem and the Philistines in the vicinity of Gath. The Ammonites, Arameans, and Moabites became his subjects. He put garrisons in Edom and levied a tax upon them.

8:16
[t]2Sa 19:13; 1Ch 11:6
[u]2Sa 20:24; 1Ki 4:3

8:17
[v]2Sa 15:24, 29; 1Ch 16:39; 24:3
[w]1Ki 4:3; 2Ki 12:10

8:18
[x]2Sa 20:23; 1Ki 1:8, 38; 1Ch 18:17
[y]1Sa 30:14

9:1
[a]1Sa 20:14-17, 42

9:2
[b]2Sa 16:1-4; 19:17, 26, 29

9:3
[c]1Sa 20:14
[d]2Sa 4:4

9:4
[e]2Sa 17:27-29

David's Officials

15David reigned over all Israel, doing what was just and right for all his people.
16Joab[t] son of Zeruiah was over the army; Jehoshaphat[u] son of Ahilud was recorder;
17Zadok[v] son of Ahitub and Ahimelech son of Abiathar were priests; Seraiah was
secretary;[w] 18Benaiah[x] son of Jehoiada was over the Kerethites[y] and Pelethites; and
David's sons were royal advisers.[g]

David and Mephibosheth

9 David asked, "Is there anyone still left of the house of Saul to whom I can show
kindness for Jonathan's sake?"[a]
2Now there was a servant of Saul's household named Ziba.[b] They called him to
appear before David, and the king said to him, "Are you Ziba?"
"Your servant," he replied.
3The king asked, "Is there no-one still left of the house of Saul to whom I can show
God's kindness?"
Ziba answered the king, "There is still a son of Jonathan;[c] he is crippled[d] in both
feet."
4"Where is he?" the king asked.
Ziba answered, "He is at the house of Makir[e] son of Ammiel in Lo Debar."

[g] 18 Or *were priests*

COVENANTS

A covenant is a legally binding obligation (promise). Throughout history God has made covenants with his people—he would keep his side if they would keep theirs. Here are seven covenants found in the Bible.

Name and Reference	*God's Promise*	*Sign*
In Eden Genesis 3:15	Satan and mankind will be enemies	Pain of childbirth
Noah Genesis 9:8–17	God would never again destroy the earth with a flood	Rainbow
Abraham Genesis 15:12–21; 17:1–14	Abraham's descendants would become a great nation if they obeyed God. God would be their God for ever	Smoking firepot and blazing torch
At Mount Sinai Exodus 19:5, 6	Israel would be God's special people, a holy nation. But they would have to keep their part of the covenant—obedience	The exodus
The Priesthood Numbers 25:10–13	Aaron's descendants would be priests for ever	The Aaronic priesthood
David 2 Samuel 7:13; 23:5	Salvation would come through David's line through the birth of the Messiah	David's line continued and the Messiah was born a descendant of David
New Covenant Hebrews 8:6–13	Forgiveness and salvation are available through faith in Christ	Christ's resurrection

8:15 David pleased the people (3:36), not because he tried to please them, but because he tried to please God. Often those who try the hardest to become popular never make it. But the praise of people is not that important. Don't spend your time devising ways to become accepted in the public eye. Instead strive to do what is right, and both God and people will respect your convictions.

8:15 King David's reign was characterised by doing what was "just and right". Justice means fairness in interpreting the law, administering punishment with mercy, respect for people's rights, and recognition of people's duty towards God. Is it any wonder that almost everyone trusted and followed David? Why was it good for David to pursue justice? (1) It was God's command (Deuteronomy 16:18–20) and his character (Deuteronomy 32:4). God's laws were meant to establish a just society. (2) It was in the nation's best interest because times would arise when each individual would need justice. Justice should characterise the way you relate to people. Make sure you are fair in the way you treat them.

9:1ff Most kings in David's day tried to wipe out the families of their rivals in order to prevent any descendants from seeking the throne. But David showed kindness to Mephibosheth, whose father was Jonathan and whose grandfather was King Saul. David was kind, partly because of his loyalty to God's previously anointed king (see the note on 1 Samuel 24:5, 6); partly for political reasons—to unite Judah and Israel (see the notes on 3:13, 14 and 3:29); and mainly because of his vow to show kindness to all of Jonathan's descendants (1 Samuel 20:14–17).

9:3 How Mephibosheth became crippled is recorded in 4:4. Mephibosheth was five years old when Saul and Jonathan died.

5 So King David had him brought from Lo Debar, from the house of Makir son of
Ammiel.
6 When Mephibosheth son of Jonathan, the son of Saul, came to David, he bowed
down to pay him honour.[f]
David said, "Mephibosheth!"
"Your servant," he replied.
7 "Don't be afraid," David said to him, "for I will surely show you kindness for the
sake of your father Jonathan. I will restore to you all the land that belonged to your
grandfather Saul, and you will always eat at my table.[g]"
8 Mephibosheth bowed down and said, "What is your servant, that you should notice
a dead dog[h] like me?"
9 Then the king summoned Ziba, Saul's servant, and said to him, "I have given your
master's grandson everything that belonged to Saul and his family. 10 You and your
sons and your servants are to farm the land for him and bring in the crops, so that
your master's grandson[i] may be provided for. And Mephibosheth, grandson of your
master, will always eat at my table." (Now Ziba had fifteen sons and twenty servants.)
11 Then Ziba said to the king, "Your servant will do whatever my lord the king
commands his servant to do." So Mephibosheth ate at David's[a] table like one of the
king's sons.[j]
12 Mephibosheth had a young son named Mica, and all the members of Ziba's
household were servants of Mephibosheth.[k] 13 And Mephibosheth lived in Jerusalem,
because he always ate at the king's table, and he was crippled in both feet.

David Defeats the Ammonites

10 In the course of time, the king of the Ammonites died, and his son Hanun
succeeded him as king. 2 David thought, "I will show kindness to Hanun son
of Nahash,[a] just as his father showed kindness to me." So David sent a delegation
to express his sympathy to Hanun concerning his father.
When David's men came to the land of the Ammonites, 3 the Ammonite nobles said

a 11 Septuagint; Hebrew *my*

9:6 [f] 2Sa 16:4; 19:24-30
9:7 [g] ver 1, 3; 2Sa 12:8; 19:28; 1Ki 2:7; 2Ki 25:29
9:8 [h] 2Sa 16:9
9:10 [i] ver 7, 11, 13; 2Sa 19:28
9:11 [j] Job 36:7; Ps 113:8
9:12 [k] 1Ch 8:34
10:2 [a] 1Sa 11:1

9:5, 6 Mephibosheth was afraid to visit the king, who wanted to treat him like a prince. Although Mephibosheth feared for his life and may have felt unworthy, that didn't mean he should refuse David's gifts. When God graciously offers us forgiveness of sins and a place in heaven, we may feel unworthy, but we will receive these gifts if we accept them. A reception even warmer than the one David gave Mephibosheth waits for all who receive God's gifts through trusting Jesus Christ, not because we deserve it, but because of God's promise (Ephesians 2:8, 9).

9:7 His treatment of Mephibosheth shows David's integrity as a leader who accepted his obligation to show love and mercy. His generous provision for Jonathan's son goes beyond any political benefit he might have received. Are you able to forgive those who have wronged you? Can you be generous with those less deserving? Each time we show compassion, our character is strengthened.

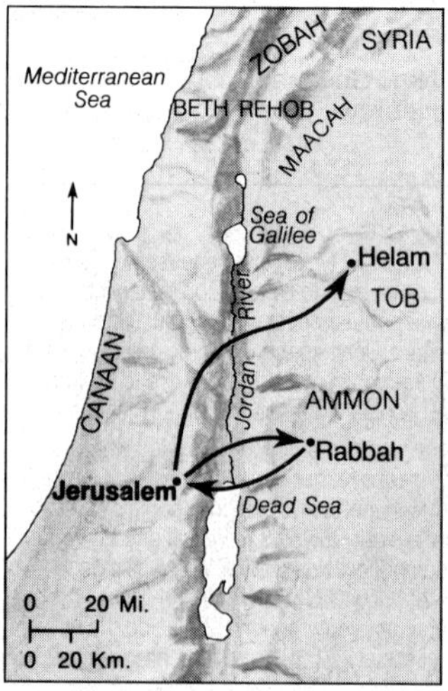

DAVID AND THE AMMONITES Ammon gathered together its troops from the north; Joab brought the Israelite army to attack them near Rabbah. Joab returned to Jerusalem victorious, but the enemy recruited additional forces and regrouped at Helam. David himself led the next victorious attack.

10:4
[b] Lev 19:27; Isa 15:2; Jer 48:37
[c] Isa 20:4

to Hanun their lord, "Do you think David is honouring your father by sending men
to you to express sympathy? Hasn't David sent them to you to explore the city and
spy it out and overthrow it?" 4 So Hanun seized David's men, shaved off half of each
man's beard,[b] cut off their garments in the middle at the buttocks,[c] and sent them
away.
5 When David was told about this, he sent messengers to meet the men, for they
were greatly humiliated. The king said, "Stay at Jericho till your beards have grown,
and then come back."
6 When the Ammonites realised that they had become an offence to[d] David's
nostrils, they hired twenty thousand Aramean[e] foot soldiers from Beth Rehob[f] and
Zobah, as well as the king of Maacah[g] with a thousand men, and also twelve thousand
men from Tob.

10:6
[d] Ge 34:30
[e] 2Sa 8:5
[f] Jdg 18:28
[g] Dt 3:14

7 On hearing this, David sent Joab out with the entire army of fighting men. 8 The
Ammonites came out and drew up in battle formation at the entrance to their city gate,
while the Arameans of Zobah and Rehob and the men of Tob and Maacah were by
themselves in the open country.
9 Joab saw that there were battle lines in front of him and behind him; so he selected
some of the best troops in Israel and deployed them against the Arameans. 10 He put
the rest of the men under the command of Abishai his brother and deployed them
against the Ammonites. 11 Joab said, "If the Arameans are too strong for me, then you
are to come to my rescue; but if the Ammonites are too strong for you, then I will
come to rescue you. 12 Be strong[h] and let us fight bravely for our people and the cities
of our God. The LORD will do what is good in his sight."[i]

10:12
[h] Dt 31:6; 1Co 16:13; Eph 6:10
[i] Jdg 10:15; 1Sa 3:18; Ne 4:14

13 Then Joab and the troops with him advanced to fight the Arameans, and they fled
before him. 14 When the Ammonites saw that the Arameans were fleeing, they fled
before Abishai and went inside the city. So Joab returned from fighting the Ammonites
and came to Jerusalem.
15 After the Arameans saw that they had been routed by Israel, they regrouped.
16 Hadadezer had Arameans brought from beyond the River;[a] they went to Helam,
with Shobach the commander of Hadadezer's army leading them.
17 When David was told of this, he gathered all Israel, crossed the Jordan and went
to Helam. The Arameans formed their battle lines to meet David and fought against
him. 18 But they fled before Israel, and David killed seven hundred of their charioteers
and forty thousand of their foot soldiers.[b] He also struck down Shobach the commander of their army, and he died there. 19 When all the kings who were vassals of
Hadadezer saw that they had been defeated by Israel, they made peace with the
Israelites and became subject[j] to them.
So the Arameans[k] were afraid to help the Ammonites any more.

10:19
[j] 2Sa 8:6
[k] 1Ki 11:25; 2Ki 5:1

a *16* That is, the Euphrates b *18* Some Septuagint manuscripts (see also 1 Chron. 19:18); Hebrew *horsemen*

10:4, 5 In Israelite culture, all men wore full beards. It was a sign of maturity and authority. Thus when these ambassadors had their beards half shaved, they suffered great indignity. Cutting off their garments also exposed them to ridicule.

10:6 Because Hanun took the wrong advice, he suspected the motives of the ambassadors and humiliated them. Then he realised that David was angry and immediately marshalled his forces for battle. Hanun should have thought through the advice more carefully; but even if he had not, he should have tried to negotiate with David. Instead, he refused to admit any fault and got ready for war. Often we respond angrily and defensively rather than admitting our mistakes, apologising, and trying to diffuse the other person's anger. Instead of fighting, we should seek peace.

10:12 There must be a balance in life between our actions and our faith in God. Joab said, "Let us fight bravely." In other words, they should do what they could, using their minds to figure out the best techniques and using their resources. But he also said, "The LORD will do what is good in his sight." He knew that the outcome was in God's hands. We should use our minds and our resources to obey God, while at the same time trusting God for the outcome.

B. DAVID'S STRUGGLES (11:1 – 24:25)

After restoring the nation to peace and great military power, David's personal life becomes entangled in sin. He commits adultery with Bathsheba and then orders her husband killed in an attempted cover-up. David deeply regretted what he had done and sought God's forgiveness, but the child of his sinful act died. We may be forgiven by God for our sins, but we will often experience harsh consequences.

1. David and Bathsheba

11 In the spring,[a] at the time when kings go off to war, David sent Joab[b] out
with the king's men and the whole Israelite army.[c] They destroyed the Ammonites and besieged Rabbah.[d] But David remained in Jerusalem.
2One evening David got up from his bed and walked around on the roof[e] of the
palace. From the roof he saw[f] a woman bathing. The woman was very beautiful,
3and David sent someone to find out about her. The man said, "Isn't this Bathsheba,[g]
the daughter of Eliam[h] and the wife of Uriah[i] the Hittite?" 4Then David sent
messengers to get her.[j] She came to him, and he slept[k] with her. (She had purified
herself from her uncleanness.)[l] Then**[a]** she went back home. 5The woman conceived
and sent word to David, saying, "I am pregnant."
6So David sent this word to Joab: "Send me Uriah[m] the Hittite." And Joab sent
him to David. 7When Uriah came to him, David asked him how Joab was, how the
soldiers were and how the war was going. 8Then David said to Uriah, "Go down to
your house and wash your feet."[n] So Uriah left the palace, and a gift from the king
was sent after him. 9But Uriah slept at the entrance to the palace with all his master's
servants and did not go down to his house.
10When David was told, "Uriah did not go home," he asked him, "Haven't you just
come from a distance? Why didn't you go home?"
11Uriah said to David, "The ark[o] and Israel and Judah are staying in tents, and my
master Joab and my lord's men are camped in the open fields. How could I go to my
house to eat and drink and lie with my wife? As surely as you live, I will not do such
a thing!"
12Then David said to him, "Stay here one more day, and tomorrow I will send you
back." So Uriah remained in Jerusalem that day and the next. 13At David's invitation,
he ate and drank with him, and David made him drunk. But in the evening Uriah went
out to sleep on his mat among his master's servants; he did not go home.
14In the morning David wrote a letter[p] to Joab and sent it with Uriah. 15In it he

a *4 Or with her. When she purified herself from her uncleanness,*

11:1 [a]1Ki 20:22, 26 [b]2Sa 2:18 [c]1Ch 20:1 [d]2Sa 12:26-28

11:2 [e]Dt 22:8; Jos 2:8 [f]Mt 5:28

11:3 [g]1Ch 3:5 [h]2Sa 23:34 [i]2Sa 23:39

11:4 [j]Lev 20:10; Ps 51 Title; Jas 1:14-15 [k]Dt 22:22 [l]Lev 15:25-30; 18:19

11:6 [m]1Ch 11:41

11:8 [n]Ge 18:4; 43:24; Lk 7:44

11:11 [o]2Sa 7:2

11:14 [p]1Ki 21:8

11:1 Winter is the rainy season in Israel, the time when crops are planted. Spring was a good time to go to war because the roads were dry, making travel easier for troop movements, supply wagons, and chariots. In Israel, wheat and barley were ready to be harvested in the spring. These crops were an important food source for travelling armies.

11:1 This successful siege (see 12:26, 27) put an end to the Ammonites' power. From this time on, the Ammonites were subject to Israel.

11:1ff In the episode with Bathsheba, David allowed himself to fall deeper and deeper into sin. (1) David abandoned his purpose by staying home from war (11:1). (2) He focused on his own desires (11:3). (3) When temptation came, he looked into it instead of turning away from it (11:4). (4) He sinned deliberately (11:4). (5) He tried to cover up his sin by deceiving others (11:6–15). (6) He committed murder to continue the cover-up (11:15, 17). Eventually David's sin was exposed (12:9) and punished (12:10–14). (7) The consequences of David's sin were far-reaching, affecting many others (11:17; 12:11, 14, 15).

David could have chosen to stop and turn from evil at any stage along the way. But once sin gets started, it is difficult to stop (James 1:14, 15). The deeper the mess, the less we want to admit having caused it. It's much easier to stop sliding down a hill when you are near the top than when you are halfway down. The best solution is to stop sin before it starts.

11:3 See 1 Kings 1 for Bathsheba's Profile.

11:3, 4 As David looked from the roof of the palace, he saw a beautiful woman bathing, and he was filled with lust. David should have left the roof and fled the temptation. Instead, he entertained the temptation by inquiring about Bathsheba. The results were devastating.

To flee temptation, (1) ask God in earnest prayer to help you stay away from people, places, and situations that may tempt you. (2) Memorise and meditate on portions of Scripture that combat your specific weaknesses. At the root of most temptation is a real need or desire that God can fill, but we must trust in his timing. (3) Find another believer with whom you can openly share your struggles, and call this person for help when temptation strikes.

11:4 The phrase "she had purified herself from her uncleanness" means that Bathsheba had just completed the purification rites following menstruation. Thus she could not have already been pregnant by her own husband when David slept with her. Leviticus 15:19–30 gives more information on the purification rites Bathsheba had to perform.

11:15 David put both Bathsheba and Joab in difficult situations. Bathsheba knew it was wrong to commit adultery, but to refuse a king's request could mean punishment or death. Joab did not know why Uriah had to die, but it was obvious the king wanted him killed. We sometimes face situations with only two apparent choices, and both seem wrong. When that happens, we must not

11:15
[q] 2Sa 12:9
[r] 2Sa 12:12

wrote, "Put Uriah in the front line where the fighting is fiercest. Then withdraw from
him so that he will be struck down[q] and die.[r]"
16 So while Joab had the city under siege, he put Uriah at a place where he knew
the strongest defenders were. 17 When the men of the city came out and fought against
Joab, some of the men in David's army fell; moreover, Uriah the Hittite died.
18 Joab sent David a full account of the battle. 19 He instructed the messenger: "When
you have finished giving the king this account of the battle, 20 the king's anger may
flare up, and he may ask you, 'Why did you get so close to the city to fight? Didn't
you know they would shoot arrows from the wall? 21 Who killed Abimelech[s] son of
Jerub-Besheth?[b] Didn't a woman throw an upper millstone on him from the wall,[t]
so that he died in Thebez? Why did you get so close to the wall?' If he asks you this,
then say to him, 'Also, your servant Uriah the Hittite is dead.' "
22 The messenger set out, and when he arrived he told David everything Joab had
sent him to say. 23 The messenger said to David, "The men overpowered us and came
out against us in the open, but we drove them back to the entrance to the city gate.
24 Then the archers shot arrows at your servants from the wall, and some of the king's
men died. Moreover, your servant Uriah the Hittite is dead."
25 David told the messenger, "Say this to Joab: 'Don't let this upset you; the sword
devours one as well as another. Press the attack against the city and destroy it.' Say
this to encourage Joab."
26 When Uriah's wife heard that her husband was dead, she mourned for him.
27 After the time of mourning was over, David had her brought to his house, and she

11:21
[s] Jdg 8:31
[t] Jdg 9:50-54

b *21* Also known as *Jerub-Baal* (that is, Gideon)

DAVID'S FAMILY TROUBLES
David's many wives caused him much grief. And as a result of David's sin with Bathsheba, God said that murder would be a constant threat in his family, his family would rebel, and someone else would sleep with his wives. All this happened as the prophet Nathan had predicted. The consequences of sin affect not only us, but those we know and love. Remember that the next time you are tempted to sin.

Wife	*Children*	*What happened*
Michal (Saul's daughter)	She was childless	David gave her five nephews to the Gibeonites to be killed because of Saul's sins
Ahinoam (from Jezreel)	Amnon, David's firstborn	He raped Tamar, his half sister, and was later murdered by Absalom in revenge
Maacah (daughter of King Talmai of Geshur)	Absalom, third son Tamar, the only daughter mentioned by name	Absalom killed Amnon for raping Tamar, and then fled to Geshur. Later he returned, only to rebel against David. He set up a tent on his roof and slept with ten of his father's concubines there. His pride led to his death
Haggith	Adonijah, fourth son. He was very handsome, but it is recorded that he was never disciplined	He set himself up as king before David's death. His plot was exposed and David spared his life, but his half brother Solomon later had him executed
Bathsheba	Unnamed son	Died in fulfilment of God's punishment for David and Bathsheba's adultery
Bathsheba	Solomon	Became the next king of Israel. Ironically, Solomon's many wives caused his downfall

lose sight of what God wants. The answer may be to seek out more choices. By doing this, we are likely to find a choice that honours God.

11:25 David's response to Uriah's death seems flippant and insensitive. While he grieved deeply for Saul and Abner, his rivals (chapter 1; 3:31–39), he showed no grief for Uriah, a good man with strong spiritual character. Why? David had become callous to his own sin. The only way he could cover up his first sin (adultery) was to sin again, and soon he no longer felt guilty for what he had done. Feelings are not reliable guides for determining right and wrong. Deliberate, repeated sinning had dulled David's sensitivity to God's laws and others' rights. The more you try to cover up a sin, the more insensitive you become towards it. Don't become hardened to sin, as David did. Confess your wrong actions to God before you forget they are sins.

became his wife and bore him a son. But the thing David had done displeased[u] the
LORD.

Nathan Rebukes David

12 The LORD sent Nathan[a] to David.[b] When he came to him,[c] he said, "There
were two men in a certain town, one rich and the other poor. 2 The rich man
had a very large number of sheep and cattle, 3 but the poor man had nothing except
one little ewe lamb that he had bought. He raised it, and it grew up with him and his
children. It shared his food, drank from his cup and even slept in his arms. It was
like a daughter to him.
4 "Now a traveller came to the rich man, but the rich man refrained from taking one
of his own sheep or cattle to prepare a meal for the traveller who had come to him.
Instead, he took the ewe lamb that belonged to the poor man and prepared it for the
one who had come to him."
5 David[d] burned with anger against the man and said to Nathan, "As surely as the
LORD lives, the man who did this deserves to die! 6 He must pay for that lamb four
times over,[e] because he did such a thing and had no pity."
7 Then Nathan said to David, "You are the man! This is what the LORD, the God
of Israel, says: 'I anointed[f] you[g] king over Israel, and I delivered you from the hand
of Saul. 8 I gave your master's house to you,[h] and your master's wives into your arms.
I gave you the house of Israel and Judah. And if all this had been too little, I would
have given you even more. 9 Why did you despise[i] the word of the LORD by doing
what is evil in his eyes? You struck down[j] Uriah the Hittite with the sword and took
his wife to be your own. You killed him with the sword of the Ammonites. 10 Now,
therefore, the sword[k] shall never depart from your house, because you despised me
and took the wife of Uriah the Hittite to be your own.'
11 "This is what the LORD says: 'Out of your own household I am going to bring
calamity upon you.[l] Before your very eyes I will take your wives and give them to
one who is close to you, and he will lie with your wives in broad daylight. 12 You did
it in secret,[m] but I will do this thing in broad daylight[n] before all Israel.' "
13 Then David said to Nathan, "I have sinned[o] against the LORD."
Nathan replied, "The LORD has taken away[p] your sin.[q] You are not going to die.[r]
14 But because by doing this you have made the enemies of the LORD show utter
contempt,[a][s] the son born to you will die."

a *14* Masoretic Text; an ancient Hebrew scribal tradition *this you have shown utter contempt for the LORD*

11:27 [u]2Sa 12:9; Ps 51:4-5
12:1 [a]2Sa 7:2; 1Ki 20:35-41 [b]Ps 51 Title [c]2Sa 14:4
12:5 [d]1Ki 20:40
12:6 [e]Ex 22:1; Lk 19:8
12:7 [f]1Sa 16:13 [g]1Ki 20:42
12:8 [h]2Sa 9:7
12:9 [i]Nu 15:31; 1Sa 15:19 [j]2Sa 11:15
12:10 [k]2Sa 13:28; 18:14-15; 1Ki 2:25
12:11 [l]Dt 28:30; 2Sa 16:21-22
12:12 [m]2Sa 11:4-15 [n]2Sa 16:22
12:13 [o]Ge 13:13; Nu 22:34; 1Sa 15:24; 2Sa 24:10 [p]Ps 32:1-5; 51:1, 9; 103:12; Zec 3:4, 9 [q]Pr 28:13; Mic 7:18-19 [r]Lev 20:10; 24:17
12:14 [s]Isa 52:5; Ro 2:24

12:1ff As a prophet, Nathan was required to confront sin, even the sin of a king. It took great courage, skill, and tact to speak to David in a way that would make him aware of his wrong actions. When you have to confront someone with unpleasant news, pray for courage, skill, and tact. If you want that person to respond constructively, think through what you are going to say. How you present your message may be as important as what you say. Season your words with wisdom.

12:5, 6 It was a year later, and by then David had become so insensitive to his own sins that he didn't realise he was the villain in Nathan's story. The qualities we condemn in others are often our own character flaws. Which friends, associates, or family members do you find easy to criticise and hard to accept? Instead of trying to change them, ask God to help you understand their feelings and see your own flaws more clearly. You may discover that in condemning others, you have been condemning yourself.

12:10–14 The predictions in these verses came true. Because David murdered Uriah and stole his wife, (1) murder was a constant threat in his family (13:26–30; 18:14, 15; 1 Kings 2:23–25); (2) his household rebelled against him (15:13); (3) his wives were given to another in public view (16:20–23); (4) his first child by Bathsheba died (12:18). If David had known the painful consequences of his sin, he might not have pursued the pleasures of the moment.

12:13 During this incident, David wrote Psalm 51, giving valuable insight into his character and offering hope for us as well. No matter how miserable guilt makes you feel or how terribly you have sinned, you can pour out your heart to God and seek his forgiveness as David did. There is forgiveness for us when we sin. David also wrote Psalm 32 to express the joy he felt after he was forgiven.

12:14 David confessed and repented of his sin (12:13), but God's judgment was that his child would die. The consequences of David's sin were irreversible. Sometimes an apology isn't enough. When God forgives us and restores our relationship with him, he doesn't eliminate all the consequences of our wrongdoing. We may be tempted to say, "If this is wrong, I can always apologise to God," but we must remember that we may set into motion events with irreversible consequences.

12:14 Why did this child have to die? This was not a judgment on the child for being conceived out of wedlock, but a judgment on David for his sin. David and Bathsheba deserved to die, but God spared their lives and took the child instead. God still had work for David to do in building the kingdom. Perhaps the child's death was a greater punishment for David than his own death would have been.

It is also possible that had the child lived, God's name would have been dishonoured among Israel's pagan neighbours. What would they have thought of a God who rewards murder and adultery by giving a king a new heir? A baby's death is tragic, but despising God brings death to entire nations. While God readily

[15]After Nathan had gone home, the LORD struck[t] the child that Uriah's wife had
borne to David, and he became ill. [16]David pleaded with God for the child. He fasted
and went into his house and spent the nights lying[u] on the ground. [17]The elders of
his household stood beside him to get him up from the ground, but he refused, and
he would not eat any food with them.[v]
[18]On the seventh day the child died. David's servants were afraid to tell him that
the child was dead, for they thought, "While the child was still living, we spoke to
David but he would not listen to us. How can we tell him the child is dead? He may
do something desperate."
[19]David noticed that his servants were whispering among themselves and he realised
that the child was dead. "Is the child dead?" he asked.
"Yes," they replied, "he is dead."
[20]Then David got up from the ground. After he had washed,[w] put on lotions and
changed his clothes,[x] he went into the house of the LORD and worshipped. Then he
went to his own house, and at his request they served him food, and he ate.
[21]His servants asked him, "Why are you acting in this way? While the child was
alive, you fasted and wept,[y] but now that the child is dead, you get up and eat!"
[22]He answered, "While the child was still alive, I fasted and wept. I thought, 'Who

12:15 [t] 1Sa 25:38
12:16 [u] 2Sa 13:31; Ps 5:7
12:17 [v] 2Sa 3:35
12:20 [w] Mt 6:17 [x] Job 1:20
12:21 [y] Jdg 20:26

NATHAN

This prophet lived up to the meaning of his name, "he [God] has given". He was a necessary and helpful gift from God to David. He served as God's spokesman to David and proved himself a fearless friend and counsellor, always willing to speak the truth, even when he knew great pain would result.

In confronting David's multiple sin of coveting, theft, adultery, and murder in his affair with Bathsheba, Nathan was able to help David see his own wrongdoing by showing that he would not have tolerated such actions from anyone else. David's repentance allowed Nathan to comfort him with the reality of God's forgiveness, and at the same time remind him of the painful consequences his sin would bring.

Nathan's approach helps us to judge our actions. How often do we make choices that we would condemn others for making? It is helpful to ask ourselves how God and others see our actions. Unfortunately, we have a huge capacity to lie to ourselves. God still provides two safeguards against self-deception: his word and true friends. In each case, we get a view beyond ourselves. You are holding God's word. Let it speak to you about yourself, even if the truth is painful. If you don't have a friend like Nathan, ask God for one. And ask God to use you as a suitable Nathan for someone else.

Strengths and accomplishments:
- A trusted adviser to David
- A prophet of God
- A fearless, but careful confronter
- One of God's controls in David's life

Weakness and mistake:
- His eagerness to see David build a temple for God in Jerusalem made him speak without God's instruction

Lessons from his life:
- We should not be afraid to tell the truth to those we care about
- A trustworthy companion is one of God's greatest gifts
- God cares enough to find a way to communicate to us when we are in the wrong

Vital statistics:
- Occupations: Prophet, royal adviser
- Contemporaries: David, Bathsheba, Solomon, Zadok, Adonijah

Key verse:
"Nathan reported to David all the words of this entire revelation" (2 Samuel 7:17).

Nathan's story is told in 2 Samuel 7—1 Kings 1. He is also mentioned in 1 Chronicles 17:15; 2 Chronicles 9:29; 29:25.

forgave David's sin, he did not negate all its consequences.

12:20–24 David did not continue to dwell on his sin. He returned to God, and God forgave him, opening the way to begin life anew. Even the name God gave Solomon (*Jedidiah,* "loved by the LORD"; 12:25) was a reminder of God's grace. When we return to God, accept his forgiveness, and change our ways, he gives us a fresh start. To feel forgiven as David did, admit your sins to God and turn to him. Then move ahead with a new and fresh approach to life.

12:22, 23 Perhaps the most bitter experience in life is the death of one's child. For comfort in such difficult circumstances, see Psalms 16:9–11; 17:15; 139; Isaiah 40:11.

knows?[z] The LORD may be gracious to me and let the child live.'[a] 23But now that
he is dead, why should I fast? Can I bring him back again? I will go to him,[b] but
he will not return to me."[c]
24Then David comforted his wife Bathsheba,[d] and he went to her and lay with her.
She gave birth to a son, and they named him Solomon.[e] The LORD loved him; 25and
because the LORD loved him, he sent word through Nathan the prophet to name him
Jedidiah.[b][f]
26Meanwhile Joab fought against Rabbah[g] of the Ammonites and captured the
royal citadel. 27Joab then sent messengers to David, saying, "I have fought against
Rabbah and taken its water supply. 28Now muster the rest of the troops and besiege
the city and capture it. Otherwise I shall take the city, and it will be named after me."
29So David mustered the entire army and went to Rabbah, and attacked and captured
it. 30He took the crown[h] from the head of their king[c]—its weight was a talent[d] of
gold, and it was set with precious stones—and it was placed on David's head. He took
a great quantity of plunder from the city 31and brought out the people who were there,
consigning them to labour with saws and with iron picks and axes, and he made them
work at brickmaking.[e] He did this to all the Ammonite[i] towns. Then David and his
entire army returned to Jerusalem.

2. Turmoil in David's family

Amnon and Tamar

13 In the course of time, Amnon[a] son of David fell in love with Tamar,[b] the
beautiful sister of Absalom[c] son of David.
2Amnon became frustrated to the point of illness on account of his sister Tamar,
for she was a virgin, and it seemed impossible for him to do anything to her.
3Now Amnon had a friend named Jonadab son of Shimeah,[d] David's brother.
Jonadab was a very shrewd man. 4He asked Amnon, "Why do you, the king's son,
look so haggard morning after morning? Won't you tell me?"
Amnon said to him, "I'm in love with Tamar, my brother Absalom's sister."
5"Go to bed and pretend to be ill," Jonadab said. "When your father comes to see
you, say to him, 'I would like my sister Tamar to come and give me something to
eat. Let her prepare the food in my sight so that I may watch her and then eat it from
her hand.' "
6So Amnon lay down and pretended to be ill. When the king came to see him,
Amnon said to him, "I would like my sister Tamar to come and make some special
bread in my sight, so that I may eat from her hand."
7David sent word to Tamar at the palace: "Go to the house of your brother Amnon
and prepare some food for him." 8So Tamar went to the house of her brother Amnon,
who was lying down. She took some dough, kneaded it, made the bread in his sight
and baked it. 9Then she took the pan and served him the bread, but he refused to eat.
"Send everyone out of here,"[e] Amnon said. So everyone left him. 10Then Amnon
said to Tamar, "Bring the food here into my bedroom so that I may eat from your
hand." And Tamar took the bread she had prepared and brought it to her brother
Amnon in his bedroom. 11But when she took it to him to eat, he grabbed[f] her and
said, "Come to bed with me, my sister."[g]
12"Don't, my brother!" she said to him. "Don't force me. Such a thing should not
be done in Israel![h] Don't do this wicked thing.[i] 13What about me?[j] Where could
I get rid of my disgrace? And what about you? You would be like one of the wicked
fools in Israel. Please speak to the king; he will not keep me from being married to

12:22 [z]Jnh 3:9 [a]Isa 38:1-5
12:23 [b]Ge 37:35 [c]1Sa 31:13; 2Sa 13:39; Job 7:10; 10:21
12:24 [d]1Ki 1:11 [e]1Ki 1:10; 1Ch 22:9; 28:5; Mt 1:6
12:25 [f]Ne 13:26
12:26 [g]Dt 3:11; 1Ch 20:1-3
12:30 [h]1Ch 20:2; Est 8:15; Ps 21:3; 132:18
12:31 [i]1Sa 14:47
13:1 [a]2Sa 3:2 [b]2Sa 14:27; 1Ch 3:9 [c]2Sa 3:3
13:3 [d]1Sa 16:9
13:9 [e]Ge 45:1
13:11 [f]Ge 39:12 [g]Ge 38:16
13:12 [h]Lev 20:17; Jdg 20:6 [i]Ge 34:7; Jdg 19:23
13:13 [j]Ge 20:12; Lev 18:9; Dt 22:21, 23-24

[b] *25 Jedidiah* means *loved by the LORD.* [c] *30* Or *of Milcom* (that is, Molech) [d] *30* That is, about 75 pounds (about 34 kilograms) [e] *31* The meaning of the Hebrew for this clause is uncertain.

12:24 Solomon was the fourth son of David and Bathsheba (1 Chronicles 3:5). Therefore several years passed between the death of their first child and Solomon's birth. Bathsheba may still have been grieving over the child's death.

13:3–5 Amnon was encouraged by his cousin Jonadab to commit sexual sin. We may be more vulnerable to the advice of our relatives because we are close to them. However, we must make sure to evaluate every piece of advice by God's standards, even when it comes from relatives.

you." 14But he refused to listen to her, and since he was stronger than she, he raped
her.[k]
15Then Amnon hated her with intense hatred. In fact, he hated her more than he
had loved her. Amnon said to her, "Get up and get out!"
16"No!" she said to him. "Sending me away would be a greater wrong than what
you have already done to me."
But he refused to listen to her. 17He called his personal servant and said, "Get this
woman out of here and bolt the door after her." 18So his servant put her out and bolted
the door after her. She was wearing a richly ornamented[a] robe,[l] for this was the
kind of garment the virgin daughters of the king wore. 19Tamar put ashes[m] on her
head and tore the ornamented robe she was wearing. She put her hand on her head
and went away, weeping aloud as she went.
20Her brother Absalom said to her, "Has that Amnon, your brother, been with you?
Be quiet now, my sister; he is your brother. Don't take this thing to heart." And Tamar
lived in her brother Absalom's house, a desolate woman.
21When King David heard all this, he was furious.[n] 22Absalom never said a word
to Amnon, either good or bad;[o] he hated[p] Amnon because he had disgraced his sister
Tamar.

Absalom Kills Amnon

23Two years later, when Absalom's sheep-shearers[q] were at Baal Hazor near the
border of Ephraim, he invited all the king's sons to come there. 24Absalom went to
the king and said, "Your servant has had shearers come. Will the king and his officials
please join me?"
25"No, my son," the king replied. "All of us should not go; we would only be a
burden to you." Although Absalom urged him, he still refused to go, but gave him
his blessing.
26Then Absalom said, "If not, please let my brother Amnon come with us."
The king asked him, "Why should he go with you?" 27But Absalom urged him,
so he sent with him Amnon and the rest of the king's sons.
28Absalom[r] ordered his men, "Listen! When Amnon is in high[s] spirits from
drinking wine and I say to you, 'Strike Amnon down,' then kill him. Don't be afraid.
Have not I given you this order? Be strong and brave.[t]" 29So Absalom's men did
to Amnon what Absalom had ordered. Then all the king's sons got up, mounted their
mules and fled.
30While they were on their way, the report came to David: "Absalom has struck
down all the king's sons; not one of them is left." 31The king stood up, tore[u] his
clothes and lay down on the ground; and all his servants stood by with their clothes
torn.
32But Jonadab son of Shimeah, David's brother, said, "My lord should not think
that they killed all the princes; only Amnon is dead. This has been Absalom's
expressed intention ever since the day that Amnon raped his sister Tamar. 33My lord

a *18* The meaning of the Hebrew for this phrase is uncertain; also in verse 19.

13:14 [k]Ge 34:2; Dt 22:25; Eze 22:11
13:18 [l]Ge 37:23; Jdg 5:30
13:19 [m]Jos 7:6; 1Sa 4:12; 2Sa 1:2; Est 4:1; Da 9:3
13:21 [n]Ge 34:7
13:22 [o]Ge 31:24 [p]Lev 19:17-18; 1Jn 2:9-11
13:23 [q]1Sa 25:7
13:28 [r]2Sa 3:3 [s]Jdg 19:6, 9, 22; Ru 3:7; 1Sa 25:36 [t]2Sa 12:10
13:31 [u]Nu 14:6; 2Sa 1:11; 12:16

13:14, 15 Love and lust are very different. After Amnon raped his half sister, his "love" turned to hate. Although he had claimed to be in love, he was actually overcome by lust. Love is patient; lust requires immediate satisfaction. Love is kind; lust is harsh. Love does not demand its own way; lust does. You can read about the characteristics of real love in 1 Corinthians 13. Lust may feel like love at first, but when physically expressed, it results in self-disgust and hatred of the other person. If you just can't wait, what you feel is not true love.

13:16 Rape was strictly forbidden by God (Deuteronomy 22:28, 29). Why was sending Tamar away an even greater crime? By throwing her out, Amnon made it look as if Tamar had made a shameful proposition to him, and there were no witnesses on her behalf because he had got rid of the servants. His crime destroyed her chances of marriage—because she was no longer a virgin, she could not be given in marriage.

13:20 Absalom tried to comfort Tamar and persuade her not to turn the incident into a public scandal. Secretly, he planned to take revenge against Amnon himself. This he did two years later (13:23–33). Absalom told Tamar the crime was only a family matter. But God's standards for moral conduct are not suspended when we deal with family matters.

13:21–24 David was angry with Amnon for raping Tamar, but David did not punish him. David probably hesitated because (1) he didn't want to cross Amnon, who was his firstborn son (1 Chronicles 3:1) and therefore next in line to be king, and (2) David was guilty of a similar sin himself in his adultery with Bathsheba. While David was unsurpassed as a king and military leader, he lacked skill and sensitivity as a husband and father.

the king should not be concerned about the report that all the king's sons are dead.
Only Amnon is dead."
34Meanwhile, Absalom had fled.
Now the man standing watch looked up and saw many people on the road west of
him, coming down the side of the hill. The watchman went and told the king, "I see
men in the direction of Horonaim, on the side of the hill."[b]
35Jonadab said to the king, "See, the king's sons are here; it has happened just as
your servant said."
36As he finished speaking, the king's sons came in, wailing loudly. The king, too,
and all his servants wept very bitterly.
37Absalom fled and went to Talmai[v] son of Ammihud, the king of Geshur. But
King David mourned for his son every day.
38After Absalom fled and went to Geshur, he stayed there for three years. 39And
the spirit of the king[c] longed to go to Absalom,[w] for he was consoled[x] concerning
Amnon's death.

Absalom Returns to Jerusalem

14 Joab[a] son of Zeruiah knew that the king's heart longed for Absalom. 2So Joab
sent someone to Tekoa[b] and had a wise woman[c] brought from there. He said
to her, "Pretend you are in mourning. Dress in mourning clothes, and don't use any
cosmetic lotions.[d] Act like a woman who has spent many days grieving for the dead.
3Then go to the king and speak these words to him." And Joab[e] put the words in
her mouth.
4When the woman from Tekoa went[a] to the king, she fell with her face to the
ground to pay him honour, and she said, "Help me, O king!"
5The king asked her, "What is troubling you?"
She said, "I am indeed a widow; my husband is dead. 6I your servant had two sons.
They got into a fight with each other in the field, and no-one was there to separate
them. One struck the other and killed him. 7Now the whole clan has risen up against
your servant; they say, 'Hand over the one who struck his brother down, so that we
may put him to death[f] for the life of his brother whom he killed; then we will get
rid of the heir[g] as well.' They would put out the only burning coal I have left,[h]
leaving my husband neither name nor descendant on the face of the earth."
8The king said to the woman, "Go home,[i] and I will issue an order on your behalf."
9But the woman from Tekoa said to him, "My lord the king, let the blame[j] rest
on me and on my father's family,[k] and let the king and his throne be without guilt.[l]"
10The king replied, "If anyone says anything to you, bring him to me, and he will
not bother you again."
11She said, "Then let the king invoke the LORD his God to prevent the avenger[m]
of blood from adding to the destruction, so that my son shall not be destroyed."
"As surely as the LORD lives," he said, "not one hair[n] of your son's head will fall
to the ground.[o]"
12Then the woman said, "Let your servant speak a word to my lord the king."
"Speak," he replied.
13The woman said, "Why then have you devised a thing like this against the people
of God? When the king says this, does he not convict himself,[p] for the king has not
brought back his banished son?[q] 14Like water[r] spilled on the ground, which cannot
be recovered, so we must die.[s] But God does not take away life; instead, he devises
ways so that a banished person[t] may not remain estranged from him.
15"And now I have come to say this to my lord the king because the people have

[b] *34* Septuagint; Hebrew does not have this sentence. [c] *39* Dead Sea Scrolls and some Septuagint manuscripts; Masoretic Text *But the spirit of* David the king [a] *4* Many Hebrew manuscripts, Septuagint, Vulgate and Syriac; most Hebrew manuscripts *spoke*

13:37 [v]ver 34; 2Sa 3:3; 14:23, 32
13:39 [w]2Sa 14:13 [x]2Sa 12:19-23
14:1 [a]2Sa 2:18
14:2 [b]2Ch 11:6; Ne 3:5; Jer 6:1; Am 1:1 [c]2Sa 20:16 [d]Ru 3:3; 2Sa 12:20; Isa 1:6
14:3 [e]ver 19
14:7 [f]Nu 35:19 [g]Mt 21:38 [h]Dt 19:10-13
14:8 [i]1Sa 25:35
14:9 [j]1Sa 25:24 [k]Mt 27:25 [l]1Sa 25:28; 1Ki 2:33
14:11 [m]Nu 35:12, 21 [n]Mt 10:30 [o]1Sa 14:45
14:13 [p]2Sa 12:7; 1Ki 20:40 [q]2Sa 13:38-39
14:14 [r]Job 14:11; Ps 58:7; Isa 19:5 [s]Job 10:8; 17:13; 30:23; Ps 22:15; Heb 9:27 [t]Nu 35:15, 25-28; Job 34:15

13:37–39 Absalom fled to Geshur because King Talmai was his grandfather (1 Chronicles 3:2), and he would be welcomed.

14:11 The law provided for a way to avenge murder. Numbers 35:9–21 records how cities of refuge protected people from revenge and how blood avengers were to pursue murderers. This woman was asking for the king's protection against any claim against her.

made me afraid. Your servant thought, 'I will speak to the king; perhaps he will do
what his servant asks. 16Perhaps the king will agree to deliver his servant from the
hand of the man who is trying to cut off both me and my son from the inheritance[u]
God gave us.'
17"And now your servant says, 'May the word of my lord the king bring me rest,
for my lord the king is like an angel[v] of God in discerning[w] good and evil. May the
LORD your God be with you.' "
18Then the king said to the woman, "Do not keep from me the answer to what I
am going to ask you."
"Let my lord the king speak," the woman said.
19The king asked, "Isn't the hand of Joab[x] with you in all this?"
The woman answered, "As surely as you live, my lord the king, no-one can turn
to the right or to the left from anything my lord the king says. Yes, it was your servant
Joab who instructed me to do this and who put all these words into the mouth of your
servant. 20Your servant Joab did this to change the present situation. My lord has
wisdom[y] like that of an angel of God—he knows everything that happens in the
land.[z]"
21The king said to Joab, "Very well, I will do it. Go, bring back the young man
Absalom."
22Joab fell with his face to the ground to pay him honour, and he blessed the king.[a]
Joab said, "Today your servant knows that he has found favour in your eyes, my lord
the king, because the king has granted his servant's request."
23Then Joab went to Geshur and brought Absalom back to Jerusalem. 24But the king
said, "He must go to his own house; he must not see my face." So Absalom went to
his own house and did not see the face of the king.
25In all Israel there was not a man so highly praised for his handsome appearance
as Absalom. From the top of his head to the sole of his foot there was no blemish
in him. 26Whenever he cut the hair of his head[b]—he used to cut his hair from time
to time when it became too heavy for him—he would weigh it, and its weight was
two hundred shekels**[b]** by the royal standard.
27Three sons[c] and a daughter were born to Absalom. The daughter's name was
Tamar,[d] and she became a beautiful woman.
28Absalom lived for two years in Jerusalem without seeing the king's face. 29Then
Absalom sent for Joab in order to send him to the king, but Joab refused to come to
him. So he sent a second time, but he refused to come. 30Then he said to his servants,
"Look, Joab's field is next to mine, and he has barley[e] there. Go and set it on fire."
So Absalom's servants set the field on fire.
31Then Joab did go to Absalom's house and he said to him, "Why have your
servants set my field on fire?[f]"
32Absalom said to Joab, "Look, I sent word to you and said, 'Come here so that
I can send you to the king to ask, "Why have I come from Geshur?[g] It would be better
for me if I were still there!" ' Now then, I want to see the king's face, and if I am
guilty of anything, let him put me to death."[h]
33So Joab went to the king and told him this. Then the king summoned Absalom,
and he came in and bowed down with his face to the ground before the king. And
the king kissed[i] Absalom.

b *26* That is, about 5 pounds (about 2.3 kilograms)

14:16 [u]Ex 34:9; 1Sa 26:19
14:17 [v]ver 20; 1Sa 29:9; 2Sa 19:27 [w]1Ki 3:9; Da 2:21
14:19 [x]ver 3
14:20 [y]1Ki 3:12, 28; Isa 28:6 [z]ver 17; 2Sa 18:13; 19:27
14:22 [a]Ge 47:7
14:26 [b]2Sa 18:9; Eze 44:20
14:27 [c]2Sa 18:18 [d]2Sa 13:1
14:30 [e]Ex 9:31
14:31 [f]Jdg 15:5
14:32 [g]2Sa 3:3 [h]1Sa 20:8
14:33 [i]Ge 33:4; Lk 15:20

14:27 By naming his daughter Tamar, Absalom was showing his love and respect for his sister Tamar. This was also a reminder to everyone of the Amnon/Tamar incident.

14:30 Already we can see the seeds of rebellion in Absalom. As an independent and scheming young man, he took matters into his own hands and killed his brother (13:22–29). Without his father or anyone else to keep him in check, he probably did whatever he wanted, as evidenced by his setting Joab's field on fire to get his attention (14:30). Undoubtedly his good looks also added to his self-centredness (14:25). Children need discipline, especially those with natural abilities and beauty. Otherwise, like Absalom, they will grow up thinking they can do whatever they want whenever they want to.

14:33 David only made halfhearted efforts to correct his children. He did not punish Amnon for his sin against Tamar, nor did he deal decisively with Absalom's murder of Amnon. Such indecisiveness became David's undoing. When we ignore sin, we experience greater pain than if we deal with it immediately.

3. National rebellion against David

Absalom's Conspiracy

15 In the course of time,[a] Absalom provided himself with a chariot[b] and horses
and with fifty men to run ahead of him. 2He would get up early and stand by
the side of the road leading to the city gate.[c] Whenever anyone came with a complaint
to be placed before the king for a decision, Absalom would call out to him, "What
town are you from?" He would answer, "Your servant is from one of the tribes of
Israel." 3Then Absalom would say to him, "Look, your claims are valid and proper,
but there is no representative of the king to hear you."[d] 4And Absalom would add,
"If only I were appointed judge in the land![e] Then everyone who has a complaint
or case could come to me and I would see that he receives justice."
5Also, whenever anyone approached him to bow down before him, Absalom would
reach out his hand, take hold of him and kiss him. 6Absalom behaved in this way
towards all the Israelites who came to the king asking for justice, and so he stole the
hearts[f] of the men of Israel.
7At the end of four[a] years, Absalom said to the king, "Let me go to Hebron and
fulfil a vow I made to the LORD. 8While your servant was living at Geshur[g] in Aram,
I made this vow:[h] 'If the LORD takes me back to Jerusalem, I will worship the LORD
in Hebron.' "[b]
9The king said to him, "Go in peace." So he went to Hebron.
10Then Absalom sent secret messengers throughout the tribes of Israel to say, "As
soon as you hear the sound of the trumpets,[i] then say, 'Absalom is king in Hebron.' "
11Two hundred men from Jerusalem had accompanied Absalom. They had been
invited as guests and went quite innocently, knowing nothing about the matter.
12While Absalom was offering sacrifices, he also sent for Ahithophel[j] the Gilonite,
David's counsellor,[k] to come from Giloh,[l] his home town. And so the conspiracy
gained strength, and Absalom's following kept on increasing.[m]

David Flees

13A messenger came and told David, "The hearts of the men of Israel are with
Absalom."
14Then David said to all his officials who were with him in Jerusalem, "Come! We

15:1 [a]2Sa 12:11 [b]1Sa 8:11; 1Ki 1:5
15:2 [c]Ge 23:10; 2Sa 19:8
15:3 [d]Pr 12:2
15:4 [e]Jdg 9:29
15:6 [f]Ro 16:18
15:8 [g]2Sa 3:3; 13:37-38 [h]Ge 28:20
15:10 [i]1Ki 1:34, 39; 2Ki 9:13
15:12 [j]ver 31, 34; 2Sa 16:15, 23; 1Ch 27:33 [k]Job 19:14; Ps 41:9; 55:13; Jer 9:4 [l]Jos 15:51 [m]Ps 3:1

a *7* Some Septuagint manuscripts, Syriac and Josephus; Hebrew *forty* **b** *8* Some Septuagint manuscripts; Hebrew does not have *in Hebron.*

15:1ff David wrote several psalms during the days of Absalom's rebellion. Some of them are Psalms 39, 41, 55, 61, and 63.

15:2 The city gate was like city hall and a shopping centre combined. Because Jerusalem was the nation's capital, both local and national leaders met there daily to transact business and conduct government affairs. The city gate was the perfect spot for this because government and business transactions needed witnesses to be legitimate, and anyone entering or leaving the city had to enter through the gate. Merchants set up their tent-shops near the gate for the same reason. Absalom, therefore, went to the city gate to win the hearts of Israel's leaders as well as those of the common people.

15:5, 6 Absalom's political strategy was to steal the hearts of the people with his good looks, grand entrances, apparent concern for justice, and friendly embraces. Many were fooled and switched their allegiance. Later, however, Absalom proved to be an evil ruler.

We need to evaluate our leaders to make sure their charisma is not a mask covering graft, deception, or hunger for power. Make sure that underneath their style and charm, they are able to make good decisions and handle people wisely.

15:9 Absalom went to Hebron because it was his hometown (3:2, 3). Hebron was David's first capital as well, and there Absalom could expect to find loyal friends who would be proud of him.

15:14 Had David not escaped from Jerusalem, the ensuing fight might have killed both him and many innocent inhabitants of the city. Some fights that we think necessary can be costly and destructive to those around us. In such cases, it may be wise to back down and save the fight for another day – even if doing so hurts

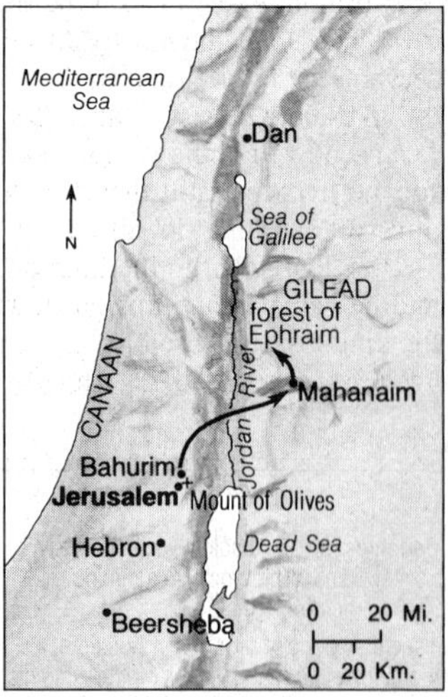

ABSALOM'S REBELLION
Absalom crowned himself king in Hebron. David and his men fled from Jerusalem, crossed the Jordan, and went to Mahanaim. Absalom and his army followed, only to be defeated in the forest of Ephraim, where Absalom was killed.

15:14 [n]2Sa 12:11; 1Ki 2:26; Ps 132:1; Ps 3 Title [o]2Sa 19:9
15:16 [p]2Sa 16:21-22; 20:3
15:18 [q]1Sa 30:14; 2Sa 8:18; 20:7, 23; 1Ki 1:38, 44; 1Ch 18:17
15:19 [r]2Sa 18:2 [s]Ge 31:15

must flee,[n] or none of us will escape from Absalom.[o] We must leave immediately,
or he will move quickly to overtake us and bring ruin upon us and put the city to the
sword."
15The king's officials answered him, "Your servants are ready to do whatever our
lord the king chooses."
16The king set out, with his entire household following him; but he left ten concubines[p] to take care of the palace. 17So the king set out, with all the people following
him, and they halted at a place some distance away. 18All his men marched past him,
along with all the Kerethites[q] and Pelethites; and all the six hundred Gittites who had
accompanied him from Gath marched before the king.
19The king said to Ittai[r] the Gittite, "Why should you come along with us? Go back
and stay with King Absalom. You are a foreigner,[s] an exile from your homeland.

ABSALOM

A father's mistakes are often reflected in the lives of his children. In Absalom, David saw a bitter replay and amplification of many of his own past sins. God had predicted that David's family would suffer because of his sin against Bathsheba and Uriah. David's heart was broken as he realised that God's predictions were coming true. God forgave David, but he did not cancel the consequences of his sin. David was horrified as he saw his son's strengths run wild without the controls God had built into his own life.

By most casual evaluations, Absalom would have made an excellent king, and the people loved him. But he lacked the inner character and control needed in a good leader. His appearance, skill, and position did not make up for his lack of personal integrity.

David's sins took him away from God, but repentance brought him back. In contrast, Absalom sinned and kept on sinning. Although he relied heavily on the advice of others, he was not wise enough to evaluate the counsel he received.

Can you identify with Absalom? Do you find yourself on a fast track towards self-destruction? Absalom wasn't able to say, "I was wrong. I need forgiveness." God offers forgiveness, but we will not experience that forgiveness until we genuinely admit our sins and confess them to God. Absalom rejected his father's love and ultimately God's love. How often do you miss entering back into God's love through the door of forgiveness?

Strength and accomplishment:
- Was handsome and charismatic like his father, David

Weaknesses and mistakes:
- Avenged the rape of his sister Tamar by killing his half brother Amnon
- Plotted against his father to take away the throne
- Consistently listened to the wrong advice

Lessons from his life:
- The sins of parents are often repeated and amplified in the children
- A smart man gets a lot of advice; a wise man evaluates the advice he gets
- Actions against God's plans will fail, sooner or later

Vital statistics:
- Where: Hebron
- Occupation: Prince
- Relatives: Father: David. Mother: Maacah. Brothers: Amnon, Kileab, Solomon, and others. Sister: Tamar
- Contemporaries: Nathan, Jonadab, Joab, Ahithophel, Hushai

Key verse:
"Then Absalom sent secret messengers throughout the tribes of Israel to say, 'As soon as you hear the sound of the trumpets, then say, "Absalom is king in Hebron" ' " (2 Samuel 15:10).

Absalom's story is told in 2 Samuel 3:3; 13—19.

---

our pride. It takes courage to stand and fight, but it also takes courage to back down for the sake of others.

15:14 Why couldn't David just crush this rebellion? There were several reasons he chose to flee: (1) The rebellion was widespread (15:10–13) and would not have been easily suppressed; (2) David did not want the city of Jerusalem to be destroyed; (3) David still cared for his son and did not want to hurt him. We know that David expected to return to Jerusalem soon because he left ten of his concubines to take care of the palace (15:16).

15:17, 18 David had many loyal non-Israelites in his armed forces. The Gittites, from the Philistine city of Gath, were apparently friends David had acquired while hiding from Saul. The Kerethites and Pelethites were also from Philistine territory. Although Israel was supposed to destroy wicked enemies, the nation was to welcome foreigners who came on friendly terms (Exodus 23:9; Deuteronomy 10:19) and to try to show them the importance of obeying God.

20You came only yesterday. And today shall I make you wander[t] about with us, when
I do not know where I am going? Go back, and take your countrymen. May kindness
and faithfulness[u] be with you."
21But Ittai replied to the king, "As surely as the LORD lives, and as my lord the
king lives, wherever my lord the king may be, whether it means life or death, there
will your servant be."[v]
22David said to Ittai, "Go ahead, march on." So Ittai the Gittite marched on with
all his men and the families that were with him.
23The whole countryside wept aloud as all the people passed by. The king also
crossed the Kidron Valley,[w] and all the people moved on towards the desert.
24Zadok[x] was there, too, and all the Levites who were with him were carrying the
ark[y] of the covenant of God. They set down the ark of God, and Abiathar[z] offered
sacrifices[c] until all the people had finished leaving the city.
25Then the king said to Zadok, "Take the ark of God back into the city. If I find
favour in the LORD's eyes, he will bring me back and let me see it and his dwelling-
place[a] again. 26But if he says, 'I am not pleased with you,' then I am ready; let him
do to me whatever seems good to him.[b]"
27The king also said to Zadok the priest, "Aren't you a seer?[c] Go back to the city
in peace, with your son Ahimaaz and Jonathan[d] son of Abiathar. You and Abiathar
take your two sons with you. 28I will wait at the fords[e] in the desert until word comes
from you to inform me." 29So Zadok and Abiathar took the ark of God back to
Jerusalem and stayed there.
30But David continued up the Mount of Olives, weeping[f] as he went; his head[g]
was covered and he was barefoot. All the people with him covered their heads too
and were weeping as they went up. 31Now David had been told, "Ahithophel[h] is
among the conspirators with Absalom." So David prayed, "O LORD, turn Ahithophel's counsel into foolishness."
32When David arrived at the summit, where people used to worship God, Hushai
the Arkite[i] was there to meet him, his robe torn and dust[j] on his head. 33David said
to him, "If you go with me, you will be a burden[k] to me. 34But if you return to the
city and say to Absalom, 'I will be your servant, O king; I was your father's servant
in the past, but now I will be your servant,'[l] then you can help me by frustrating
Ahithophel's advice. 35Won't the priests Zadok and Abiathar be there with you? Tell
them anything you hear in the king's palace.[m] 36Their two sons, Ahimaaz son of
Zadok and Jonathan[n] son of Abiathar, are there with them. Send them to me with
anything you hear."
37So David's friend Hushai[o] arrived at Jerusalem as Absalom[p] was entering the
city.

David and Ziba

16 When David had gone a short distance beyond the summit, there was Ziba,[a]
the steward of Mephibosheth, waiting to meet him. He had a string of donkeys
saddled and loaded with two hundred loaves of bread, a hundred cakes of raisins, a
hundred cakes of figs and a skin of wine.[b]
2The king asked Ziba, "Why have you brought these?"
Ziba answered, "The donkeys are for the king's household to ride on, the bread and
fruit are for the men to eat, and the wine is to refresh[c] those who become exhausted
in the desert."
3The king then asked, "Where is your master's grandson?"[d]

c 24 Or *Abiathar went up*

15:20 [t]1Sa 23:13 [u]2Sa 2:6
15:21 [v]Ru 1:16-17; Pr 17:17
15:23 [w]2Ch 29:16
15:24 [x]2Sa 8:17 [y]Nu 4:15 [z]1Sa 22:20
15:25 [a]Ex 15:13; Ps 43:3; Jer 25:30
15:26 [b]1Sa 3:18; 2Sa 22:20; 1Ki 10:9
15:27 [c]1Sa 9:9 [d]2Sa 17:17
15:28 [e]2Sa 17:16
15:30 [f]2Sa 19:4; Ps 126:6 [g]Est 6:12; Isa 20:2-4
15:31 [h]ver 12; 2Sa 16:23; 17:14, 23
15:32 [i]Jos 16:2 [j]2Sa 1:2
15:33 [k]2Sa 19:35
15:34 [l]2Sa 16:19
15:35 [m]2Sa 17:15-16
15:36 [n]ver 27; 2Sa 17:17
15:37 [o]2Sa 16:16-17; 1Ch 27:33 [p]2Sa 16:15
16:1 [a]2Sa 9:1-13 [b]1Sa 25:18
16:2 [c]2Sa 17:27-29
16:3 [d]2Sa 9:9-10; 19:26-27

15:24, 25 The priests and Levites were also loyal to David.

15:27–37 David needed spies in Absalom's court to inform him of Absalom's decisions. By sending Hushai to Absalom as a supposed traitor to David, Hushai could offer advice contradictory to Ahithophel's advice. Ahithophel was Absalom's adviser (he was also Bathsheba's grandfather).

16:3 Saul was Mephibosheth's grandfather. Most likely Ziba was lying, hoping to receive a reward from David. (See 19:24–30 for Mephibosheth's side of the story.) For the story of Mephibosheth, see chapter 9.

16:5
[e] 2Sa 3:16
[f] 2Sa 19:16-23; 1Ki 2:8-9, 36, 44
[g] Ex 22:28

16:8
[h] 2Sa 21:9

16:9
[i] 2Sa 9:8
[j] Ex 22:28; Lk 9:54

16:10
[k] 2Sa 19:22
[l] Ro 9:20

16:11
[m] 2Sa 12:11
[n] Ge 45:5

16:12
[o] Ps 4:1; 25:18
[p] Dt 23:5; Ro 8:28
[q] Ps 109:28

16:14
[r] 2Sa 17:2

Ziba said to him, "He is staying in Jerusalem, because he thinks, 'Today the house
of Israel will give me back my grandfather's kingdom.' "
4Then the king said to Ziba, "All that belonged to Mephibosheth is now yours."
"I humbly bow," Ziba said. "May I find favour in your eyes, my lord the king."

Shimei Curses David

5As King David approached Bahurim,[e] a man from the same clan as Saul's family
came out from there. His name was Shimei[f] son of Gera, and he cursed[g] as he came
out. 6He pelted David and all the king's officials with stones, though all the troops
and the special guard were on David's right and left. 7As he cursed, Shimei said, "Get
out, get out, you man of blood, you scoundrel! 8The LORD has repaid you for all the
blood you shed in the household of Saul, in whose place you have reigned.[h] The LORD
has handed the kingdom over to your son Absalom. You have come to ruin because
you are a man of blood!"
9Then Abishai[i] son of Zeruiah said to the king, "Why should this dead dog curse
my lord the king? Let me go over and cut off his head."[j]
10But the king said, "What do you and I have in common, you sons of Zeruiah?[k]
If he is cursing because the LORD said to him, 'Curse David,' who can ask, 'Why do
you do this?' "[l]
11David then said to Abishai and all his officials, "My son,[m] who is of my own
flesh, is trying to take my life. How much more, then, this Benjamite! Leave him
alone; let him curse, for the LORD has told him to.[n] 12It may be that the LORD will
see my distress[o] and repay me with good[p] for the cursing I am receiving today.[q]"
13So David and his men continued along the road while Shimei was going along
the hillside opposite him, cursing as he went and throwing stones at him and showering
him with dirt. 14The king and all the people with him arrived at their destination
exhausted.[r] And there he refreshed himself.

HIGHS AND LOWS OF DAVID'S LIFE

The Bible calls David a man after God's own heart (1 Samuel 13:14; Acts 13:22), but that didn't mean his life was free of troubles. David's life was full of highs and lows. Some of David's troubles were a result of his sins; some were a result of the sins of others. We can't always control our ups and downs, but we can trust God every day. We can be certain that he will help us through our trials, just as he helped David. In the end, he will reward us for our consistent faith.

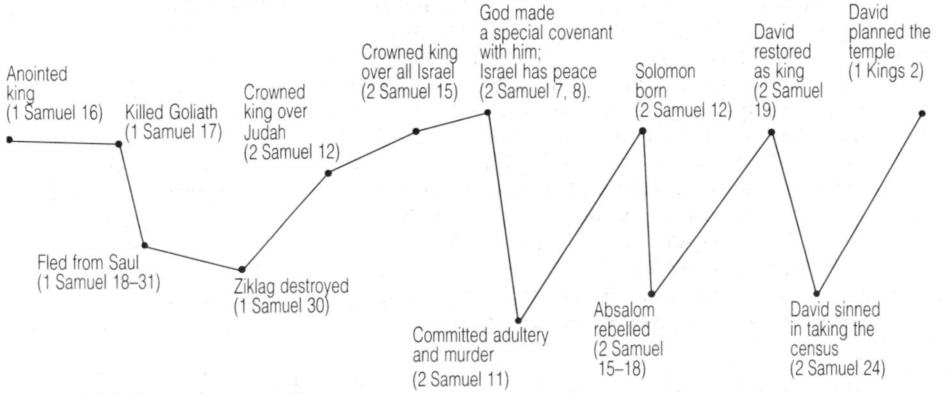

16:4 David believed Ziba's charge against Mephibosheth without checking into it or even being sceptical. Don't be hasty to accept someone's condemnation of another, especially when the accuser may profit from the other's downfall. David should have been sceptical of Ziba's comments until he checked them out for himself.

16:5–14 Shimei kept up a steady tirade against David. Although his curses were unjustified because David had had no part in Saul's death, David and his followers quietly tolerated the abuse. Maintaining your composure in the face of unjustified criticism can be a trying experience and an emotional drain, but if you can't stop criticism, it is best just to ignore it. Remember that God knows what you are enduring, and he will vindicate you if you are in the right.

The Advice of Hushai and Ahithophel

15Meanwhile, Absalom[s] and all the men of Israel came to Jerusalem, and Ahithophel[t] was with him. 16Then Hushai[u] the Arkite, David's friend, went to Absalom
and said to him, "Long live the king! Long live the king!"
17Absalom asked Hushai, "Is this the love you show your friend? Why didn't you
go with your friend?"[v]
18Hushai said to Absalom, "No, the one chosen by the LORD, by these people and
by all the men of Israel—his I will be, and I will remain with him. 19Furthermore,
whom should I serve? Should I not serve the son? Just as I served your father, so I
will serve you."[w]
20Absalom said to Ahithophel, "Give us your advice. What should we do?"
21Ahithophel answered, "Lie with your father's concubines whom he left to take
care of the palace. Then all Israel will hear that you have made yourself an offence
to your father's nostrils, and the hands of everyone with you will be strengthened."
22So they pitched a tent for Absalom on the roof, and he lay with his father's
concubines in the sight of all Israel.[x]
23Now in those days the advice[y] Ahithophel gave was like that of one who enquires
of God. That was how both David[z] and Absalom regarded all of Ahithophel's advice.
17 Ahithophel said to Absalom, "I would**[a]** choose twelve thousand men and set
out tonight in pursuit of David. 2I would**[b]** attack him while he is weary and
weak.[a] I would**[b]** strike him with terror, and then all the people with him will flee.
I would**[b]** strike down only the king[b] 3and bring all the people back to you. The death
of the man you seek will mean the return of all; all the people will be unharmed."
4This plan seemed good to Absalom and to all the elders of Israel.
5But Absalom said, "Summon also Hushai[c] the Arkite, so that we can hear what
he has to say." 6When Hushai came to him, Absalom said, "Ahithophel has given this
advice. Should we do what he says? If not, give us your opinion."
7Hushai replied to Absalom, "The advice Ahithophel has given is not good this
time. 8You know your father and his men; they are fighters, and as fierce as a wild
bear robbed of her cubs.[d] Besides, your father is an experienced fighter;[e] he will
not spend the night with the troops. 9Even now, he is hidden in a cave or some other
place.[f] If he should attack your troops first,**[c]** whoever hears about it will say, 'There
has been a slaughter among the troops who follow Absalom.' 10Then even the bravest
soldier, whose heart is like the heart of a lion,[g] will melt[h] with fear, for all Israel
knows that your father is a fighter and that those with him are brave.[i]
11"So I advise you: Let all Israel, from Dan to Beersheba[j]—as numerous as the
sand[k] on the seashore—be gathered to you, with you yourself leading them into
battle. 12Then we will attack him wherever he may be found, and we will fall on him
as dew settles on the ground. Neither he nor any of his men will be left alive. 13If
he withdraws into a city, then all Israel will bring ropes to that city, and we will drag
it down to the valley[l] until not even a piece of it can be found."
14Absalom and all the men of Israel said, "The advice[m] of Hushai the Arkite is
better than that of Ahithophel."[n] For the LORD had determined to frustrate[o] the good
advice of Ahithophel in order to bring disaster[p] on Absalom.[q]
15Hushai told Zadok and Abiathar, the priests, "Ahithophel has advised Absalom
and the elders of Israel to do such and such, but I have advised them to do so and
so. 16Now send a message immediately and tell David, 'Do not spend the night at the

a *1* Or *Let me* **b** *2* Or *will* **c** *9* Or *When some of the men fall at the first attack*

16:15 [s]2Sa 15:37 [t]2Sa 15:12
16:16 [u]2Sa 15:37
16:17 [v]2Sa 19:25
16:19 [w]2Sa 15:34
16:22 [x]2Sa 12:11-12; 15:16
16:23 [y]2Sa 17:14, 23 [z]2Sa 15:12
17:2 [a]2Sa 16:14 [b]1Ki 22:31; Zec 13:7
17:5 [c]2Sa 15:32
17:8 [d]Hos 13:8 [e]1Sa 16:18
17:9 [f]Jer 41:9
17:10 [g]1Ch 12:8 [h]Jos 2:9, 11; Eze 21:15 [i]2Sa 23:8; 1Ch 11:11
17:11 [j]Jdg 20:1 [k]Ge 12:2; 22:17; Jos 11:4
17:13 [l]Mic 1:6
17:14 [m]2Sa 16:23 [n]2Sa 15:12 [o]2Sa 15:34; Ne 4:15 [p]Ps 9:16 [q]2Ch 10:8

16:21, 22 This incident fulfilled Nathan's prediction that because of David's sin, another man would sleep with his wives (12:11, 12). (See the note on 3:6, 7 for the cultural significance of this act.)

16:23 Ahithophel was an adviser to Absalom. Most rulers had advisers to help them make decisions about governmental and political matters. They probably arranged the king's marriages as well because these were usually politically motivated unions. But God made Ahithophel's advice seem foolish, just as David had prayed (15:31).

17:11 Hushai appealed to Absalom through flattery, and Absalom's vanity became his own trap. Hushai predicted great glory for Absalom if he personally led the entire army against David. "Pride goes before destruction" (Proverbs 16:18) is an appropriate comment on Absalom's ambitions.

fords in the desert;[r] cross over without fail, or the king and all the people with him
will be swallowed up.[s]' "
17 Jonathan[t] and Ahimaaz were staying at En Rogel.[u] A servant girl was to go
and inform them, and they were to go and tell King David, for they could not risk
being seen entering the city. 18 But a young man saw them and told Absalom. So the
two of them left quickly and went to the house of a man in Bahurim.[v] He had a well
in his courtyard, and they climbed down into it. 19 His wife took a covering and spread
it out over the opening of the well and scattered grain over it. No-one knew anything
about it.[w]
20 When Absalom's men came to the woman[x] at the house, they asked, "Where
are Ahimaaz and Jonathan?"
The woman answered them, "They crossed over the brook."[d] The men searched
but found no-one, so they returned to Jerusalem.
21 After the men had gone, the two climbed out of the well and went to inform King
David. They said to him, "Set out and cross the river at once; Ahithophel has advised
such and such against you." 22 So David and all the people with him set out and crossed
the Jordan. By daybreak, no-one was left who had not crossed the Jordan.
23 When Ahithophel saw that his advice[y] had not been followed, he saddled his
donkey and set out for his house in his home town. He put his house in order[z] and
then hanged himself. So he died and was buried in his father's tomb.
24 David went to Mahanaim,[a] and Absalom crossed the Jordan with all the men
of Israel. 25 Absalom had appointed Amasa[b] over the army in place of Joab. Amasa
was the son of a man named Jether,[e][c] an Israelite[f] who had married Abigail,[g] the
daughter of Nahash and sister of Zeruiah the mother of Joab. 26 The Israelites and
Absalom camped in the land of Gilead.
27 When David came to Mahanaim, Shobi son of Nahash[d] from Rabbah[e] of the
Ammonites, and Makir[f] son of Ammiel from Lo Debar, and Barzillai[g] the Gileadite[h] from Rogelim 28 brought bedding and bowls and articles of pottery. They also
brought wheat and barley, flour and roasted grain, beans and lentils,[h] 29 honey and
curds, sheep, and cheese from cows' milk for David and his people to eat.[i] For they
said, "The people have become hungry and tired and thirsty in the desert.[j]"

Absalom's Death

18 David mustered the men who were with him and appointed over them commanders of thousands and commanders of hundreds. 2 David sent the troops
out[a]—a third under the command of Joab, a third under Joab's brother Abishai[b] son
of Zeruiah, and a third under Ittai[c] the Gittite. The king told the troops, "I myself
will surely march out with you."
3 But the men said, "You must not go out; if we are forced to flee, they won't care
about us. Even if half of us die, they won't care; but you are worth ten[d] thousand
of us.[a] It would be better now for you to give us support from the city."[e]
4 The king answered, "I will do whatever seems best to you."
So the king stood beside the gate while all the men marched out in units of hundreds
and of thousands. 5 The king commanded Joab, Abishai and Ittai, "Be gentle with the
young man Absalom for my sake." And all the troops heard the king giving orders
concerning Absalom to each of the commanders.
6 The army marched into the field to fight Israel, and the battle took place in the
forest[f] of Ephraim. 7 There the army of Israel was defeated by David's men, and the

[d] 20 Or *"They passed by the sheep pen towards the water."* [e] 25 Hebrew *Ithra*, a variant of *Jether* [f] 25 Hebrew and some Septuagint manuscripts; other Septuagint manuscripts (see also 1 Chron. 2:17) *Ishmaelite* or *Jezreelite* [g] 25 Hebrew *Abigal*, a variant of *Abigail* [h] 28 Most Septuagint manuscripts and Syriac; Hebrew *lentils, and roasted grain* [a] 3 Two Hebrew manuscripts, some Septuagint manuscripts and Vulgate; most Hebrew manuscripts *care; for now there are ten thousand like us*

17:16 [r] 2Sa 15:28 [s] 2Sa 15:35
17:17 [t] 2Sa 15:27, 36 [u] Jos 15:7; 18:16
17:18 [v] 2Sa 3:16; 16:5
17:19 [w] Jos 2:6
17:20 [x] Ex 1:19; Jos 2:3-5; 1Sa 19:12-17
17:23 [y] 2Sa 15:12; 16:23 [z] 2Ki 20:1; Mt 27:5
17:24 [a] Ge 32:2; 2Sa 2:8
17:25 [b] 2Sa 19:13; 20:4, 9-12; 1Ki 2:5, 32; 1Ch 12:18 [c] 1Ch 2:13-17
17:27 [d] 1Sa 11:1 [e] Dt 3:11; 2Sa 10:1-2; 12:26, 29 [f] 2Sa 9:4 [g] 2Sa 19:31-39; 1Ki 2:7 [h] 2Sa 19:31; Ezr 2:61
17:29 [i] 1Ch 12:40 [j] 2Sa 16:2; Ro 12:13
18:2 [a] Jdg 7:16; 1Sa 11:11 [b] 1Sa 26:6 [c] 2Sa 15:19
18:3 [d] 1Sa 18:7 [e] 2Sa 21:17
18:6 [f] Jos 17:18

17:25 Joab and Amasa were David's nephews and Absalom's cousins. Because Joab had left Jerusalem with David (see 18:5, 10ff), Amasa took his place as commander of Israel's troops.

18:1 David took command as he had in former days. In recent years, his life had been characterised by indecisiveness and moral paralysis. At this time he began to take charge and do his duty.

casualties that day were great—twenty thousand men. 8The battle spread out over the
whole countryside, and the forest claimed more lives that day than the sword.
9Now Absalom happened to meet David's men. He was riding his mule, and as the
mule went under the thick branches of a large oak, Absalom's head[g] got caught in
the tree. He was left hanging in mid-air, while the mule he was riding kept on going.
10When one of the men saw this, he told Joab, "I have just seen Absalom hanging
in an oak tree."
11Joab said to the man who had told him this, "What! You saw him? Why didn't
you strike[h] him to the ground right there? Then I would have had to give you ten
shekels[b] of silver and a warrior's belt.[i]"
12But the man replied, "Even if a thousand shekels[c] were weighed out into my
hands, I would not lift my hand against the king's son. In our hearing the king
commanded you and Abishai and Ittai, 'Protect the young man Absalom for my
sake.'[d] 13And if I had put my life in jeopardy[e]—and nothing is hidden from the
king[j]—you would have kept your distance from me."
14Joab[k] said, "I am not going to wait like this for you." So he took three javelins
in his hand and plunged them into Absalom's heart while Absalom was still alive in
the oak tree. 15And ten of Joab's armour-bearers surrounded Absalom, struck him and
killed him.[l]
16Then Joab[m] sounded the trumpet, and the troops stopped pursuing Israel, for Joab
halted them. 17They took Absalom, threw him into a big pit in the forest and piled
up[n] a large heap of rocks[o] over him. Meanwhile, all the Israelites fled to their homes.
18During his life-time Absalom had taken a pillar and erected it in the King's
Valley[p] as a monument[q] to himself, for he thought, "I have no son[r] to carry on
the memory of my name." He named the pillar after himself, and it is called Absalom's
Monument to this day.

David Mourns

19Now Ahimaaz[s] son of Zadok said, "Let me run and take the news to the king
that the LORD has delivered him from the hand of his enemies.[t]"
20"You are not the one to take the news today," Joab told him. "You may take the
news another time, but you must not do so today, because the king's son is dead."
21Then Joab said to a Cushite, "Go, tell the king what you have seen." The Cushite
bowed down before Joab and ran off.
22Ahimaaz son of Zadok again said to Joab, "Come what may, please let me run
behind the Cushite."
But Joab replied, "My son, why do you want to go? You don't have any news that
will bring you a reward."
23He said, "Come what may, I want to run."
So Joab said, "Run!" Then Ahimaaz ran by way of the plain[f] and outran the
Cushite.
24While David was sitting between the inner and outer gates, the watchman[u] went
up to the roof of the gateway by the wall. As he looked out, he saw a man running
alone. 25The watchman called out to the king and reported it.
The king said, "If he is alone, he must have good news." And the man came closer
and closer.

b *11* That is, about 4 ounces (about 115 grams) c *12* That is, about 25 pounds (about 11 kilograms) d *12* A few Hebrew manuscripts, Septuagint, Vulgate and Syriac; most Hebrew manuscripts may be translated *Absalom, whoever you may be.* e *13* Or *Otherwise, if I had acted treacherously towards him* f *23* That is, the plain of the Jordan

18:9 g2Sa 14:26
18:11 h2Sa 3:39 i1Sa 18:4
18:13 j2Sa 14:19-20
18:14 k2Sa 2:18; 14:30
18:15 l2Sa 12:10
18:16 m2Sa 2:28; 20:22
18:17 nJos 7:26 oJos 8:29
18:18 pGe 14:17 qGe 50:5; Nu 32:42; 1Sa 15:12 r2Sa 14:27
18:19 s2Sa 15:36 tver 31; Jdg 11:36
18:24 u1Sa 14:16; 2Sa 19:8; 2Ki 9:17; Jer 51:12

18:12–14 This man had caught Joab in his hypocrisy. He knew Joab would have turned on him for killing the man if the king had found out about it. Joab could not answer, but only dismissed him. Those about to do evil often do not take the time to consider what they are about to do. They don't care whether or not it is right or lawful. Don't rush into action without thinking. Consider whether what you are about to do is right or wrong.

18:26
[v] 1Ki 1:42; Isa 52:7; 61:1

26Then the watchman saw another man running, and he called down to the gatekeeper, "Look, another man running alone!"
The king said, "He must be bringing good news,[v] too."

REBELLION
The Bible records many rebellions. Many were against God's chosen leaders. They were doomed to failure. Others were begun by wicked men against wicked men. While these were sometimes successful, the rebel's life usually came to a violent end. Still other rebellions were made by good people against the wicked or unjust actions of others. This kind of rebellion is sometimes good in freeing the common people from oppression and giving them the freedom to turn back to God.

Who rebelled?	*Who they rebelled against*	*What happened*	*Reference*
Adam and Eve	God	Expelled from Eden	Genesis 3
Israelites	God, Moses	Forced to wander in desert for 40 years	Numbers 14
Korah	Moses	Swallowed by the earth	Numbers 16
Israelites	God	God took away his special promise of protection	Judges 2
Absalom (David's son)	David	Killed in battle	2 Samuel 15—18
Sheba	David	Killed in battle	2 Samuel 20
Adonijah (David's son)	David, Solomon	Killed for treason	1 Kings 1, 2
Joab	David, Solomon	Supported Adonijah's kingship without seeking God's choice. Killed for treason	1 Kings 1, 2
Ten tribes of Israel	Rehoboam	The kingdom was divided. The ten tribes forgot about God, sinned, and were eventually taken into captivity	1 Kings 12:16–20
Baasha king of Israel	Nadab king of Israel	Overthrew the throne and became king. God destroyed his descendants	1 Kings15:27—16:7
Zimri king of Israel	Elah king of Israel	Overthrew the throne, but killed himself when his rule was not accepted	1 Kings 16:9–16
Jehu king of Israel	Joram king of Israel Ahaziah king of Judah	Killed both kings. Later turned from God and his dynasty was wiped out	2 Kings 9, 10
Joash king of Judah Jehoiada, a priest	Athaliah queen of Judah	Athaliah, a wicked queen, was overthrown. This was a "good" rebellion	2 Kings 11
Shallum king of Israel	Zechariah king of Israel	Overthrew the throne, but then was assassinated	2 Kings 15:8–15
Menahem king of Israel	Shallum king of Israel	Overthrew the throne, but then was invaded by Assyrian army	2 Kings 15:16–22
Hoshea king of Israel	Assyria	The city of Samaria was destroyed, the nation of Israel taken into captivity	2 Kings 17
Zedekiah king of Judah	Nebuchadnezzar king of Babylon	The city of Jerusalem destroyed, the nation of Judah taken into captivity	2 Kings 24, 25

27The watchman said, "It seems to me that the first one runs like[w] Ahimaaz son
of Zadok."
"He's a good man," the king said. "He comes with good news."
28Then Ahimaaz called out to the king, "All is well!" He bowed down before the
king with his face to the ground and said, "Praise be to the LORD your God! He has
delivered up the men who lifted their hands against my lord the king."
29The king asked, "Is the young man Absalom safe?"
Ahimaaz answered, "I saw great confusion just as Joab was about to send the king's
servant and me, your servant, but I don't know what it was."
30The king said, "Stand aside and wait here." So he stepped aside and stood there.
31Then the Cushite arrived and said, "My lord the king, hear the good news! The
LORD has delivered you today from all who rose up against you."
32The king asked the Cushite, "Is the young man Absalom safe?"
The Cushite replied, "May the enemies of my lord the king and all who rise up to
harm you be like that young man."[x]
33The king was shaken. He went up to the room over the gateway and wept. As
he went, he said: "O my son Absalom! My son, my son Absalom! If only I had died[y]
instead of you—O Absalom, my son, my son!"[z]

19 Joab was told, "The king is weeping and mourning for Absalom." 2And for the
whole army the victory that day was turned into mourning, because on that day
the troops heard it said, "The king is grieving for his son." 3The men stole into the
city that day as men steal in who are ashamed when they flee from battle. 4The king
covered his face and cried aloud, "O my son Absalom! O Absalom, my son, my son!"
5Then Joab went into the house to the king and said, "Today you have humiliated
all your men, who have just saved your life and the lives of your sons and daughters
and the lives of your wives and concubines. 6You love those who hate you and hate
those who love you. You have made it clear today that the commanders and their men
mean nothing to you. I see that you would be pleased if Absalom were alive today
and all of us were dead. 7Now go out and encourage your men. I swear by the LORD
that if you don't go out, not a man will be left with you by nightfall. This will be worse
for you than all the calamities that have come upon you from your youth till now."[a]
8So the king got up and took his seat in the gateway. When the men were told, "The
king is sitting in the gateway,[b]" they all came before him.

David Returns to Jerusalem

Meanwhile, the Israelites had fled to their homes. 9Throughout the tribes of Israel,
the people were all arguing with each other, saying, "The king delivered us from the
hand of our enemies; he is the one who rescued us from the hand of the Philistines.[c]
But now he has fled the country because of Absalom;[d] 10and Absalom, whom we
anointed to rule over us, has died in battle. So why do you say nothing about bringing
the king back?"
11King David sent this message to Zadok[e] and Abiathar, the priests: "Ask the
elders of Judah, 'Why should you be the last to bring the king back to his palace, since
what is being said throughout Israel has reached the king at his quarters? 12You are

18:27 [w]2Ki 9:20
18:32 [x]Jdg 5:31; 1Sa 25:26
18:33 [y]Ex 32:32 [z]Ge 43:14; 2Sa 19:4; Ro 9:3
19:7 [a]Pr 14:28
19:8 [b]2Sa 15:2
19:9 [c]2Sa 8:1-14 [d]2Sa 15:14
19:11 [e]2Sa 15:24

18:29 Although he reached the city first, Ahimaaz was afraid to tell the king the truth about the death of his son Absalom.

18:33 Why was David so upset over the death of his rebel son? (1) David realised that he, in part, was responsible for Absalom's death. Nathan, the prophet, had said that because David had killed Uriah, his own sons would rebel against him. (2) David was angry at Joab and his officers for killing Absalom against his wishes. (3) David truly loved his son, even though Absalom did nothing to deserve his love. It would have been kinder and more loving to deal with Absalom and his runaway ego when he was younger.

19:4–7 At times we must reprove those in authority over us. Joab knew he was risking the king's displeasure by confronting him, but he saw what had to be done. Joab told David that there would be dreadful consequences if he didn't commend the troops for their victory. Joab's actions are a helpful example to us when personal confrontation is necessary.

19:8 David sat at the gateway (city gate) because that was where business was conducted and judgment rendered. His presence there showed that he was over his mourning and back in control.

19:8–10 Just a few days before, most of Israel was supporting the rebel ruler Absalom. Now the people wanted David back as their king. Because crowds are often fickle, there must be a higher moral code to follow than the pleasure of the majority. Following the moral principles given in God's word will help you avoid being swayed by the popular opinions of the crowd.

19:13
[f]2Sa 17:25
[g]Ge 29:14
[h]Ru 1:17; 1Ki 19:2; 8:16
[i]2Sa 2:13

19:15
[j]Jos 5:9; 1Sa 11:15

19:16
[k]2Sa 16:5-13; 1Ki 2:8

my brothers, my own flesh and blood. So why should you be the last to bring back
the king?' 13 And say to Amasa,[f] 'Are you not my own flesh and blood?[g] May God
deal with me, be it ever so severely,[h] if from now on you are not the commander
of my army in place of Joab.[i]' "
14 He won over the hearts of all the men of Judah as though they were one man.
They sent word to the king, "Return, you and all your men." 15 Then the king returned
and went as far as the Jordan.
Now the men of Judah had come to Gilgal[j] to go out and meet the king and bring
him across the Jordan. 16 Shimei[k] son of Gera, the Benjamite from Bahurim, hurried
down with the men of Judah to meet King David. 17 With him were a thousand

JOAB

Joab, the great military leader, had two brothers who were also famous soldiers: Abishai and Asahel. Joab proved to be the greatest leader of the three and was the commander of David's army throughout most of David's reign. There is no record that his troops ever lost a battle.

Joab was a fearless fighter like his brothers. Unlike them, he was also a brilliant and ruthless strategist. His plans usually worked, but he was seldom concerned about those hurt or killed by them. He did not hesitate to use treachery or murder to achieve his goals. His career is a story of great accomplishments and shameful acts. He conquered Jerusalem and the surrounding nations, defeated Abner, and reconciled Absalom and David. But he also murdered Abner, Amasa, and Absalom, took part in Uriah's murder, and plotted with Adonijah against Solomon. That plot led to his execution.

Joab set his own standards—he lived by them and died because of them. There is little evidence that Joab ever acknowledged God's standards. On one occasion he confronted David about the danger of taking a census without God's command, but this may have been little more than a move to protect himself. Joab's self-centredness eventually destroyed him. He was loyal only to himself, even willing to betray his lifelong relationship with David to preserve his power.

Joab's life illustrates the disastrous results of having no source of direction outside oneself. Brilliance and power are self-destructive without God's guidance. Only God can give the direction we need. For that reason, he has made available his word, the Bible, and he is willing to be personally present in the lives of those who admit their need for him.

Strengths and accomplishments:
- Brilliant planner and strategist
- Fearless fighter and resourceful commander
- Confident leader who did not hesitate to confront even the king
- Helped reconcile David and Absalom
- Masterminded the conquest of Jerusalem

Weaknesses and mistakes:
- Was repeatedly ruthless, violent, and vengeful
- Carried out David's scheme to have Uriah, Bathsheba's husband, killed
- Avenged his brother's murder by murdering Abner
- Killed Absalom against David's orders
- Plotted with Adonijah against David and Solomon

Lessons from his life:
- Those who live by violence often die by violence
- Even brilliant leaders need guidance

Vital statistics:
- Occupation: Commander in chief of David's army
- Relatives: Mother: Zeruiah. Brothers: Abishai, Asahel. Uncle: David
- Contemporaries: Saul, Abner, Absalom

Key verse:
"Then the king commanded Benaiah, 'Do as he says. Strike him down and bury him, and so clear me and my father's house of the guilt of the innocent blood that Joab shed' " (1 Kings 2:31).

Joab's story is told in 2 Samuel 2—1 Kings 2. He is also mentioned in 1 Chronicles 2:16; 11:5–9, 20, 26; 19:8–15; 20:1; 21:2–6; 26:28; and in the title of Psalm 60.

19:13 David's appointment of Amasa was a shrewd political move. First, Amasa had been commander of Absalom's army; by making Amasa his commander, David would secure the allegiance of the rebel army. Second, by replacing Joab as commander in chief, David punished him for his previous crimes (3:26–29). Third, Amasa had a great deal of influence over the leaders of Judah (19:14). All of these moves would help to unite the kingdom.

Benjamites, along with Ziba,[l] the steward of Saul's household,[m] and his fifteen sons
and twenty servants. They rushed to the Jordan, where the king was. 18 They crossed
at the ford to take the king's household over and to do whatever he wished.
When Shimei son of Gera crossed the Jordan, he fell prostrate before the king 19 and
said to him, "May my lord not hold me guilty. Do not remember how your servant
did wrong on the day my lord the king left Jerusalem.[n] May the king put it out of
his mind. 20 For I your servant know that I have sinned, but today I have come here
as the first of the whole house of Joseph to come down and meet my lord the king."
21 Then Abishai[o] son of Zeruiah said, "Shouldn't Shimei be put to death for this?
He cursed[p] the LORD's anointed."[q]
22 David replied, "What do you and I have in common, you sons of Zeruiah?[r] This
day you have become my adversaries! Should anyone be put to death in Israel today?[s]
Do I not know that today I am king over Israel?" 23 So the king said to Shimei, "You
shall not die." And the king promised him on oath.[t]
24 Mephibosheth,[u] Saul's grandson, also went down to meet the king. He had not
taken care of his feet or trimmed his moustache or washed his clothes from the day
the king left until the day he returned safely. 25 When he came from Jerusalem to meet
the king, the king asked him, "Why didn't you go with me,[v] Mephibosheth?"
26 He said, "My lord the king, since I your servant am lame,[w] I said, 'I will have
my donkey saddled and will ride on it, so that I can go with the king.' But Ziba[x]
my servant betrayed me. 27 And he has slandered your servant to my lord the king.
My lord the king is like an angel[y] of God; so do whatever pleases you. 28 All my
grandfather's descendants deserved nothing but death[z] from my lord the king, but
you gave your servant a place among those who eat at your table.[a] So what right do
I have to make any more appeals to the king?"
29 The king said to him, "Why say more? I order you and Ziba to divide the fields."
30 Mephibosheth said to the king, "Let him take everything, now that my lord the
king has arrived home safely."
31 Barzillai[b] the Gileadite also came down from Rogelim to cross the Jordan with
the king and to send him on his way from there. 32 Now Barzillai was a very old man,
eighty years of age. He had provided for the king during his stay in Mahanaim, for
he was a very wealthy[c] man. 33 The king said to Barzillai, "Cross over with me and
stay with me in Jerusalem, and I will provide for you."
34 But Barzillai answered the king, "How many more years shall I live, that I should
go up to Jerusalem with the king? 35 I am now eighty[d] years old. Can I tell the
difference between what is good and what is not? Can your servant taste what he eats
and drinks? Can I still hear the voices of men and women singers?[e] Why should your
servant be an added[f] burden to my lord the king? 36 Your servant will cross over the
Jordan with the king for a short distance, but why should the king reward me in this
way? 37 Let your servant return, that I may die in my own town near the tomb of my
father[g] and mother. But here is your servant Kimham.[h] Let him cross over with my
lord the king. Do for him whatever pleases you."
38 The king said, "Kimham shall cross over with me, and I will do for him whatever
pleases you. And anything you desire from me I will do for you."
39 So all the people crossed the Jordan, and then the king crossed over. The king
kissed Barzillai and gave him his blessing,[i] and Barzillai returned to his home.
40 When the king crossed over to Gilgal, Kimham crossed with him. All the troops
of Judah and half the troops of Israel had taken the king over.
41 Soon all the men of Israel were coming to the king and saying to him, "Why did

19:17 [l] 2Sa 9:2; 16:1-2 [m] Ge 43:16
19:19 [n] 1Sa 22:15; 2Sa 16:6-8
19:21 [o] 1Sa 26:6 [p] Ex 22:28 [q] 1Sa 12:3; 26:9; 2Sa 16:7-8
19:22 [r] 2Sa 2:18; 16:10 [s] 1Sa 11:13
19:23 [t] 1Ki 2:8, 42
19:24 [u] 2Sa 4:4; 9:6-10
19:25 [v] 2Sa 16:17
19:26 [w] Lev 21:18 [x] 2Sa 9:2
19:27 [y] 1Sa 29:9; 2Sa 14:17, 20
19:28 [z] 2Sa 16:8; 21:6-9 [a] 2Sa 9:7, 13
19:31 [b] 2Sa 17:27-29, 27; 1Ki 2:7
19:32 [c] 1Sa 25:2; 2Sa 17:27
19:35 [d] Ps 90:10 [e] 2Ch 35:25; Ezr 2:65; Ecc 2:8; 12:1; Isa 5:11-12 [f] 2Sa 15:33
19:37 [g] Ge 49:29; 1Ki 2:7 [h] ver 40; Jer 41:17
19:39 [i] Ge 31:55; Ge 47:7

19:19, 20 By admitting his wrong and asking David's forgiveness, Shimei was trying to save his own life. His plan worked for a while. This was a day of celebration, not execution. But we read in 1 Kings 2:8, 9 that David advised Solomon to execute Shimei.

19:21ff David showed tremendous mercy and generosity as he returned to Jerusalem. He spared Shimei, restored Mephibosheth, and rewarded faithful Barzillai. David's fairness sets a standard for government that will be fully realised in Christ's righteous rule in the coming kingdom.

19:24–30 David could not be certain if Mephibosheth or Ziba was in the right, and Scripture leaves the question unanswered. (For the whole story on Mephibosheth, see also 9:1–13 and 16:1–4.)

19:41 [j]Jdg 8:1; 12:1
19:43 [k]2Sa 5:1

our brothers, the men of Judah, steal the king away and bring him and his household
across the Jordan, together with all his men?"[j]
42 All the men of Judah answered the men of Israel, "We did this because the king
is closely related to us. Why are you angry about it? Have we eaten any of the king's
provisions? Have we taken anything for ourselves?"
43 Then the men of Israel[k] answered the men of Judah, "We have ten shares in the
king; and besides, we have a greater claim on David than you have. So why do you
treat us with contempt? Were we not the first to speak of bringing back our king?"
But the men of Judah responded even more harshly than the men of Israel.

20:1 [a]Ge 31:14 [b]Ge 29:14; 1Ki 12:16 [c]1Sa 22:7-8; 2Ch 10:16

Sheba Rebels Against David

20 Now a troublemaker named Sheba son of Bicri, a Benjamite, happened to be
there. He sounded the trumpet and shouted,

> "We have no share[a] in David,[b]
> no part in Jesse's son![c]
> Every man to his tent, O Israel!"

20:3 [d]2Sa 15:16; 16:21-22
20:4 [e]2Sa 17:25; 19:13

2 So all the men of Israel deserted David to follow Sheba son of Bicri. But the men
of Judah stayed by their king all the way from the Jordan to Jerusalem.
3 When David returned to his palace in Jerusalem, he took the ten concubines[d] he
had left to take care of the palace and put them in a house under guard. He provided
for them, but did not lie with them. They were kept in confinement till the day of their
death, living as widows.
4 Then the king said to Amasa,[e] "Summon the men of Judah to come to me within
three days, and be here yourself." 5 But when Amasa went to summon Judah, he took
longer than the time the king had set for him.

20:6 [f]2Sa 21:17
20:7 [g]1Sa 30:14; 2Sa 8:18; 15:18; 1Ki 1:38
20:8 [h]Jos 9:3 [i]2Sa 2:18

6 David said to Abishai,[f] "Now Sheba son of Bicri will do us more harm than
Absalom did. Take your master's men and pursue him, or he will find fortified cities
and escape from us." 7 So Joab's men and the Kerethites[g] and Pelethites and all the
mighty warriors went out under the command of Abishai. They marched out from
Jerusalem to pursue Sheba son of Bicri.
8 While they were at the great rock in Gibeon,[h] Amasa came to meet them. Joab[i]
was wearing his military tunic, and strapped over it at his waist was a belt with a dagger
in its sheath. As he stepped forward, it dropped out of its sheath.
9 Joab said to Amasa, "How are you, my brother?" Then Joab took Amasa by the
beard with his right hand to kiss him. 10 Amasa was not on his guard against the

---

SHEBA'S REBELLION
After defeating Absalom, David returned to Jerusalem from Mahanaim. But Sheba incited a rebellion against David, so David sent Joab, Abishai, and a small army after him. Joab and his troops besieged Abel Beth Maacah, Sheba's hideout, until the people of Abel Beth Maacah killed Sheba themselves.

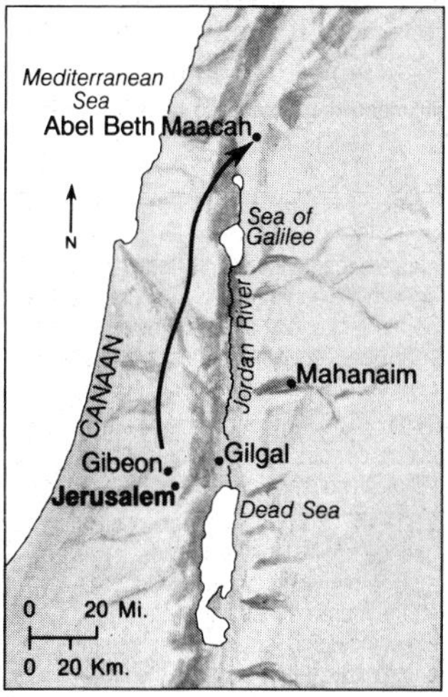

20:1 Although Israel was a united kingdom, it was still made up of 12 separate tribes. These tribes often had difficulty agreeing on the goals of the nation as a whole. Tribal jealousies had originally kept Israel from completely conquering the promised land (read the book of Joshua), and now tribal jealousies were threatening the stability of David's reign by giving Sheba an opportunity to rebel (20:1ff).

20:7–10 Once again Joab's murderous act went unpunished, just as it did when he killed Abner (3:26, 27). Eventually, however, justice caught up with him (1 Kings 2:28–35). It may seem that sin and treachery often go unpunished, but God's justice is not limited to this life's rewards. Even if Joab had died of old age, he would have to face the day of judgment.

dagger[j] in Joab[k]'s hand, and Joab plunged it into his belly, and his intestines spilled
out on the ground. Without being stabbed again, Amasa died. Then Joab and his
brother Abishai pursued Sheba son of Bicri.
11One of Joab's men stood beside Amasa and said, "Whoever favours Joab, and
whoever is for David, let him follow Joab!" 12Amasa lay wallowing in his blood in
the middle of the road, and the man saw that all the troops came to a halt[l] there.
When he realised that everyone who came up to Amasa stopped, he dragged him from
the road into a field and threw a garment over him. 13After Amasa had been removed
from the road, all the men went on with Joab to pursue Sheba son of Bicri.
14Sheba passed through all the tribes of Israel to Abel Beth Maacah[a] and through
the entire region of the Berites,[m] who gathered together and followed him. 15All the
troops with Joab came and besieged Sheba in Abel Beth Maacah.[n] They built a siege
ramp[o] up to the city, and it stood against the outer fortifications. While they were
battering the wall to bring it down, 16a wise woman[p] called from the city, "Listen!
Listen! Tell Joab to come here so that I can speak to him." 17He went towards her,
and she asked, "Are you Joab?"
"I am," he answered.
She said, "Listen to what your servant has to say."
"I'm listening," he said.
18She continued, "Long ago they used to say, 'Get your answer at Abel,' and that
settled it. 19We are the peaceful[q] and faithful in Israel. You are trying to destroy a
city that is a mother in Israel. Why do you want to swallow up the LORD's inheritance?"[r]
20"Far be it from me!" Joab replied, "Far be it from me to swallow up or destroy!
21That is not the case. A man named Sheba son of Bicri, from the hill country of
Ephraim, has lifted up his hand against the king, against David. Hand over this one
man, and I'll withdraw from the city."
The woman said to Joab, "His head[s] will be thrown to you from the wall."
22Then the woman went to all the people with her wise advice,[t] and they cut off
the head of Sheba son of Bicri and threw it to Joab. So he sounded the trumpet, and
his men dispersed from the city, each returning to his home. And Joab went back to
the king in Jerusalem.
23Joab[u] was over Israel's entire army; Benaiah son of Jehoiada was over the
Kerethites and Pelethites; 24Adoniram[b][v] was in charge of forced labour; Jehoshaphat[w] son of Ahilud was recorder; 25Sheva was secretary; Zadok[x] and Abiathar were
priests; 26and Ira the Jairite was David's priest.

4. The later years of David's rule

The Gibeonites Avenged

21 During the reign of David, there was a famine[a] for three successive years; so
David sought[b] the face of the LORD. The LORD said, "It is on account of Saul
and his blood-stained house; it is because he put the Gibeonites to death."

a *14* Or *Abel, even Beth Maacah*; also in verse 15 **b** *24* Some Septuagint manuscripts (see also 1 Kings 4:6 and 5:14); Hebrew *Adoram*

20:10 [j]Jdg 3:21; 2Sa 2:23; 3:27 [k]1Ki 2:5
20:12 [l]2Sa 2:23
20:14 [m]Nu 21:16
20:15 [n]1Ki 15:20; 2Ki 15:29 [o]2Ki 19:32; Isa 37:33; Jer 6:6; 32:24
20:16 [p]2Sa 14:2
20:19 [q]Dt 2:26 [r]1Sa 26:19; 2Sa 21:3
20:21 [s]2Sa 4:8
20:22 [t]Ecc 9:13
20:23 [u]2Sa 2:28; 8:16-18; 24:2
20:24 [v]1Ki 4:6; 5:14; 12:18; 2Ch 10:18 [w]2Sa 8:16; 1Ki 4:3
20:25 [x]1Sa 2:35; 2Sa 8:17
21:1 [a]Ge 12:10; Dt 32:24 [b]Ex 32:11

20:16ff Joab's men were attacking the city, and it looked as if it would be destroyed. Though women in that society were usually quiet in public, this woman spoke out. She stopped Joab's attack, not with weapons, but with wise words and a plan of action. Often the courage to speak a few sensible words can prevent great disaster.

20:23 Benaiah was the captain of David's bodyguard and a famous member of that special group of mighty men called "the Thirty" (23:24). He remained loyal to David during Absalom's rebellion. Later he helped establish Solomon as king (1 Kings 1:32–40; 2:28–34) and eventually replaced Joab as commander of Israel's army (1 Kings 2:35).

21:1 Farmers relied heavily on spring and autumn rains for their crops. If the rains stopped or came at the wrong time, or if the plants became insect infested, there would be drastic food shortages in the coming year. Agriculture at that time was completely dependent upon natural conditions. There were no irrigation sprinklers, fertilisers, or pesticides. Even moderate variations in rainfall or insect activity could destroy an entire harvest.

21:1ff The next four chapters are an appendix to the book. The events described are not presented in chronological order. They tell of David's exploits at various times during his reign.

21:1–14 Although the Bible does not record Saul's act of vengeance against the Gibeonites, it was apparently a serious crime making him guilty of their blood. Still, why were Saul's sons killed for the murders their father committed? In many Near Eastern cultures, including Israel's, an entire family was held guilty for the crime of the father because the family was considered an indis-

2The king summoned the Gibeonites[c] and spoke to them. (Now the Gibeonites
were not a part of Israel but were survivors of the Amorites; the Israelites had sworn
to ⌞spare⌟ them, but Saul in his zeal for Israel and Judah had tried to annihilate them.)
3David asked the Gibeonites, "What shall I do for you? How shall I make amends
so that you will bless the LORD's inheritance?"[d]
4The Gibeonites answered him, "We have no right to demand silver or gold from
Saul or his family, nor do we have the right to put anyone in Israel to death."[e]
"What do you want me to do for you?" David asked.
5They answered the king, "As for the man who destroyed us and plotted against
us so that we have been decimated and have no place anywhere in Israel, 6let seven
of his male descendants be given to us to be killed and exposed[f] before the LORD
at Gibeah of Saul—the LORD's chosen[g] one."
So the king said, "I will give them to you."
7The king spared Mephibosheth[h] son of Jonathan, the son of Saul, because of the
oath[i] before the LORD between David and Jonathan son of Saul. 8But the king took
Armoni and Mephibosheth, the two sons of Aiah's daughter Rizpah,[j] whom she had
borne to Saul, together with the five sons of Saul's daughter Merab,[a] whom she had

[a] *8* Two Hebrew manuscripts, some Septuagint manuscripts and Syriac (see also 1 Samuel 18:19); most Hebrew and Septuagint manuscripts *Michal*

21:2 [c] Jos 9:15
21:3 [d] 1Sa 26:19; 2Sa 20:19
21:4 [e] Nu 35:33-34
21:6 [f] Nu 25:4 [g] 1Sa 10:24
21:7 [h] 2Sa 4:4 [i] 1Sa 18:3; 20:8, 15; 2Sa 9:7
21:8 [j] 2Sa 3:7

ABISHAI

Most great leaders struggle with a few followers who try too hard. For David, Abishai was that kind of follower. His fierce loyalty to David had to be kept from becoming destructive—he was too willing to leap to his leader's defence. David never put down Abishai's eager loyalty. Instead, he patiently tried to direct its powerful energy. This approach, while not completely successful, saved David's life on at least one occasion. At three other times, however, Abishai would have killed for the king if David had not stopped him.

Abishai was an excellent soldier, but he was better at taking orders than giving them. When he wasn't carrying out David's orders, Abishai was usually under the command of his younger brother Joab. The two brothers helped each other accomplish great military feats as well as shameful acts of violence—Abishai helped Joab murder Abner and Amasa. When he was effective as a leader, he led mostly by example. But all too often he did not think before he acted.

We should be challenged by Abishai's admirable qualities of fearlessness and loyalty, but we should be warned by his tendency to act without thinking. It is not enough to be strong and effective; we must also have the self-control and wisdom that God can give us. We are to follow and obey with our hearts and our minds.

Strengths and accomplishments:
- Known as one of the heroes among David's fighting men
- A fearless and willing volunteer, fiercely loyal to David
- Saved David's life

Weaknesses and mistakes:
- Tended to act without thinking
- Helped Joab murder Abner and Amasa

Lessons from his life:
- The most effective followers combine careful thought and action
- Blind loyalty can cause great evil

Vital statistics:
- Occupation: Soldier
- Relatives: Mother: Zeruiah. Brothers: Joab and Asahel. Uncle: David

Key verses:
"Abishai the brother of Joab son of Zeruiah was chief of the Three. He raised his spear against three hundred men, whom he killed, and so he became as famous as the Three. Was he not held in greater honour than the Three? He became their commander, even though he was not included among them" (2 Samuel 23:18, 19).

Abishai's story is told in 2 Samuel 2:18—23:19. He is also mentioned in 1 Samuel 26:1–13; 1 Chronicles 2:16; 11:20; 18:12; 19:11, 15.

soluble unit. Saul broke the vow that the Israelites made to the Gibeonites (Joshua 9:16–20). This was a serious offence against God's law (Numbers 30:1, 2). Either David was following the custom of treating the family as a unit, or Saul's sons were guilty of helping Saul kill the Gibeonites.

borne to Adriel son of Barzillai the Meholathite.[k] 9He handed them over to the
Gibeonites, who killed and exposed them on a hill before the LORD. All seven of them
fell together; they were put to death[l] during the first days of harvest, just as the barley
harvest was beginning.[m]
10Rizpah daughter of Aiah took sackcloth and spread it out for herself on a rock.
From the beginning of the harvest till the rain poured down from the heavens on the
bodies, she did not let the birds of the air touch them by day or the wild animals by
night.[n] 11When David was told what Aiah's daughter Rizpah, Saul's concubine, had
done, 12he went and took the bones of Saul[o] and his son Jonathan from the citizens
of Jabesh Gilead. (They had taken them secretly from the public square at Beth Shan,[p]
where the Philistines had hung[q] them after they struck Saul down on Gilboa.) 13David
brought the bones of Saul and his son Jonathan from there, and the bones of those
who had been killed and exposed were gathered up.
14They buried the bones of Saul and his son Jonathan in the tomb of Saul's father
Kish, at Zela[r] in Benjamin, and did everything the king commanded. After that,[s]
God answered prayer[t] on behalf of the land.

Wars Against the Philistines

15Once again there was a battle between the Philistines[u] and Israel. David went
down with his men to fight against the Philistines, and he became exhausted. 16And
Ishbi-Benob, one of the descendants of Rapha, whose bronze spearhead weighed three
hundred shekels**b** and who was armed with a new ⌞sword⌟, said he would kill David.
17But Abishai[v] son of Zeruiah came to David's rescue; he struck the Philistine down
and killed him. Then David's men swore to him, saying, "Never again will you go
out with us to battle, so that the lamp[w] of Israel will not be extinguished.[x]"
18In the course of time, there was another battle with the Philistines, at Gob. At
that time Sibbecai[y] the Hushathite killed Saph, one of the descendants of Rapha.
19In another battle with the Philistines at Gob, Elhanan son of Jaare-Oregim**c** the
Bethlehemite killed Goliath**d** the Gittite, who had a spear with a shaft like a weaver's
rod.[z]
20In still another battle, which took place at Gath, there was a huge man with six
fingers on each hand and six toes on each foot—twenty-four in all. He also was
descended from Rapha. 21When he taunted Israel, Jonathan son of Shimeah,[a] David's
brother, killed him.
22These four were descendants of Rapha in Gath, and they fell at the hands of David
and his men.

David's Song of Praise

22 David sang[a] to the LORD the words of this song when the LORD delivered him
from the hand of all his enemies and from the hand of Saul. 2He said:

"The LORD is my rock,[b] my fortress[c] and my deliverer;[d]
3 my God is my rock, in whom I take refuge,[e]
my shield[f] and the horn**a**[g] of my salvation.
He is my stronghold,[h] my refuge and my saviour—
from violent men you save me.
4I call to the LORD, who is worthy[i] of praise,
and I am saved from my enemies.

b *16* That is, about 7½ pounds (about 3.5 kilograms) **c** *19* Or *son of Jair the weaver* **d** *19* Hebrew and Septuagint; 1 Chron. 20:5 *son of Jair killed Lahmi the brother of Goliath* **a** *3* *Horn* here symbolises strength.

21:8 [k]1Sa 18:19
21:9 [l]2Sa 16:8 [m]Ru 1:22
21:10 [n]ver 8; Dt 21:23; 1Sa 17:44
21:12 [o]1Sa 31:11-13 [p]Jos 17:11 [q]1Sa 31:10
21:14 [r]Jos 18:28 [s]Jos 7:26 [t]2Sa 24:25
21:15 [u]2Sa 5:25
21:17 [v]2Sa 20:6 [w]1Ki 11:36 [x]2Sa 18:3
21:18 [y]1Ch 11:29; 20:4; 27:11
21:19 [z]1Sa 17:7
21:21 [a]1Sa 16:9
22:1 [a]Ex 15:1; Jdg 5:1; Ps 18:2-50
22:2 [b]Dt 32:4; Ps 71:3 [c]Ps 31:3; 91:2 [d]Ps 144:2
22:3 [e]Dt 32:37; Jer 16:19 [f]Ge 15:1 [g]Lk 1:69 [h]Ps 9:9
22:4 [i]Ps 48:1; 96:4

21:9, 10 The barley harvest was in late April and early May. Barley was similar to wheat but less suitable for breadmaking. Rizpah guarded the men's bodies during the entire harvest season, which lasted from April to October.

21:16–18 By calling these men "descendants of Rapha", the writer was saying that they were giants. For more information on giants, see 1 Samuel 17:4–7 and the note on Genesis 6:4.

22:1ff David was a skilled musician who played his harp for Saul (1 Samuel 16:23), instituted the music programmes in the temple (1 Chronicles 25), and wrote more of the book of Psalms than anyone else. Writing a song like this was not unusual for David. This royal hymn of thanksgiving is almost identical to Psalm 18. (For other songs in the Bible, see the chart in Exodus 15.)

22:3 David calls God "the horn of my salvation", referring to the strength and defensive protection animals have in their horns. God

5"The waves[j] of death swirled about me;
the torrents of destruction overwhelmed me.
6The cords of the grave[b][k] coiled around me;
the snares of death confronted me.
7In my distress[l] I called[m] to the LORD;
I called out to my God.
From his temple he heard my voice;
my cry came to his ears.

8"The earth[n] trembled and quaked,[o]
the foundations[p] of the heavens[c] shook;
they trembled because he was angry.
9Smoke rose from his nostrils;
consuming fire[q] came from his mouth,
burning coals blazed out of it.
10He parted the heavens and came down;
dark clouds[r] were under his feet.
11He mounted the cherubim and flew;
he soared[d] on the wings of the wind.[s]
12He made darkness his canopy around him—
the dark[e] rain clouds of the sky.
13Out of the brightness of his presence
bolts of lightning[t] blazed forth.
14The LORD thundered[u] from heaven;
the voice of the Most High resounded.
15He shot arrows[v] and scattered ⌊the enemies⌋,
bolts of lightning and routed them.
16The valleys of the sea were exposed
and the foundations of the earth laid bare
at the rebuke[w] of the LORD,
at the blast of breath from his nostrils.

17"He reached down from on high[x] and took hold of me;
he drew[y] me out of deep waters.
18He rescued me from my powerful enemy,
from my foes, who were too strong for me.
19They confronted me in the day of my disaster,
but the LORD was my support.[z]
20He brought me out into a spacious[a] place;
he rescued[b] me because he delighted[c] in me.[d]

21"The LORD has dealt with me according to my righteousness;[e]
according to the cleanness of my hands[f] he has rewarded me.

22:5 [j]Ps 69:14-15; 93:4; Jnh 2:3
22:6 [k]Ps 116:3
22:7 [l]Ps 120:1 [m]Ps 34:6, 15; 116:4
22:8 [n]Jdg 5:4; Ps 97:4 [o]Ps 77:18 [p]Job 26:11
22:9 [q]Ps 97:3; Heb 12:29
22:10 [r]1Ki 8:12; Na 1:3
22:11 [s]Ps 104:3
22:13 [t]ver 9
22:14 [u]1Sa 2:10
22:15 [v]Dt 32:23
22:16 [w]Na 1:4
22:17 [x]Ps 144:7 [y]Ex 2:10
22:19 [z]Ps 23:4
22:20 [a]Ps 31:8 [b]Ps 118:5 [c]Ps 22:8 [d]2Sa 15:26
22:21 [e]1Sa 26:23 [f]Ps 24:4

b *6* Hebrew *Sheol* **c** *8* Hebrew; Vulgate and Syriac (see also Psalm 18:7) *mountains* **d** *11* Many Hebrew manuscripts (see also Psalm 18:10); most Hebrew manuscripts *appeared* **e** *12* Septuagint and Vulgate (see also Psalm 18:11); Hebrew *massed*

David reveals many truths about God in his song of praise	*David says, "The LORD is my . . ."*	Rock, Fortress, Deliverer, Refuge, Shield, Horn of Salvation, Stronghold, Saviour, Lamp
	David names these characteristics of God. He is:	Saving, Worthy of praise, Hearing, Angry (against enemies), Rescuing, Rewarding, Seeing, Faithful, Showing (revealing) himself, Shrewd, Powerful, Strong, Perfect, Pure, Flawless, Shielding (us from enemies), Giving, Gentle, Preserving, Living

had helped David overcome his enemies and rescued him from his foes.

22:11 Cherubim are mighty angels.

22 For I have kept[g] the ways of the LORD;
I have not done evil by turning from my God.
23 All his laws are before me;[h]
I have not turned[i] away from his decrees.
24 I have been blameless[j] before him
and have kept myself from sin.
25 The LORD has rewarded me according to my righteousness,[k]
according to my cleanness[f] in his sight.

26 "To the faithful you show yourself faithful,
to the blameless you show yourself blameless,
27 to the pure[l] you show yourself pure,
but to the crooked you show yourself shrewd.[m]
28 You save the humble,[n]
but your eyes are on the haughty to bring them low.[o]
29 You are my lamp,[p] O LORD;
the LORD turns my darkness into light.
30 With your help I can advance against a troop;[g]
with my God I can scale a wall.

31 "As for God, his way is perfect;[q]
the word of the LORD is flawless.[r]
He is a shield
for all who take refuge in him.
32 For who is God besides the LORD?
And who is the Rock[s] except our God?
33 It is God who arms me with strength[h]
and makes my way perfect.
34 He makes my feet like the feet of a deer;[t]
he enables me to stand on the heights.[u]
35 He trains my hands[v] for battle;
my arms can bend a bow of bronze.
36 You give me your shield[w] of victory;
you stoop down to make me great.
37 You broaden the path[x] beneath me,
so that my ankles do not turn over.

38 "I pursued my enemies and crushed them;
I did not turn back till they were destroyed.
39 I crushed[y] them completely, and they could not rise;
they fell beneath my feet.
40 You armed me with strength for battle;
you made my adversaries bow at my feet.[z]
41 You made my enemies turn their backs[a] in flight,
and I destroyed my foes.
42 They cried for help,[b] but there was no-one to save them —[c]
to the LORD, but he did not answer.
43 I beat them as fine as the dust of the earth;
I pounded and trampled[d] them like mud[e] in the streets.

22:22 [g]Ge 18:19; Ps 128:1; Pr 8:32
22:23 [h]Dt 6:4-9; Ps 119:30-32 [i]Ps 119:102
22:24 [j]Ge 6:9; Eph 1:4
22:25 [k]ver 21
22:27 [l]Mt 5:8 [m]Lev 26:23-24
22:28 [n]Ex 3:8; Ps 72:12-13 [o]Isa 2:12, 17; 5:15
22:29 [p]Ps 27:1
22:31 [q]Dt 32:4; Mt 5:48 [r]Ps 12:6; 119:140; Pr 30:5-6
22:32 [s]1Sa 2:2
22:34 [t]Hab 3:19 [u]Dt 32:13
22:35 [v]Ps 144:1
22:36 [w]Eph 6:16
22:37 [x]Pr 4:11
22:39 [y]Mal 4:3
22:40 [z]Ps 44:5
22:41 [a]Ex 23:27
22:42 [b]Isa 1:15 [c]Ps 50:22
22:43 [d]Mic 7:10 [e]Isa 10:6; Mic 7:10

f 25 Hebrew; Septuagint and Vulgate (see also Psalm 18:24) *to the cleanness of my hands* g 30 Or *can run through a barricade* h 33 Dead Sea Scrolls, some Septuagint manuscripts, Vulgate and Syriac (see also Psalm 18:32); Masoretic Text *who is my strong refuge*

22:22–24 David was not denying that he had ever sinned. Psalm 51 shows his tremendous anguish over his sin against Uriah and Bathsheba. But David understood God's faithfulness and was writing this hymn from God's perspective. He knew that God had made him clean again — "whiter than snow", (Psalm 51:7) with a "pure heart" (Psalm 51:10). Through the death and resurrection of Jesus Christ, we also are made clean and perfect. God replaces our sin with his purity, and he no longer sees our sin.

22:27 "To the crooked you show yourself shrewd" means that to those who sin, God is a judge who will punish them for their sins. God destroys those who are evil.

44"You have delivered[f] me from the attacks of my people;
you have preserved[g] me as the head of nations.
People[h] I did not know are subject to me,
45 and foreigners come cringing[i] to me;
as soon as they hear me, they obey me.
46They all lose heart;
they come trembling[i][j] from their strongholds.

47"The LORD lives! Praise be to my Rock!
Exalted be God, the Rock, my Saviour![k]
48He is the God who avenges me,[l]
who puts the nations under me,
49 who sets me free from my enemies.[m]
You exalted me above my foes;
from violent men you rescued me.
50Therefore I will praise you, O LORD, among the nations;
I will sing praises to your name.[n]
51He gives his king great victories;[o]
he shows unfailing kindness to his anointed,[p]
to David[q] and his descendants for ever."[r]

The Last Words of David

23 These are the last words of David:

"The oracle of David son of Jesse,
the oracle of the man exalted[a] by the Most High,
the man anointed[b] by the God of Jacob,
Israel's singer of songs:[a]

2"The Spirit[c] of the LORD spoke through me;
his word was on my tongue.
3The God of Israel spoke,
the Rock[d] of Israel said to me:
'When one rules over men in righteousness,[e]
when he rules in the fear of God,[f]
4he is like the light of morning at sunrise[g]
on a cloudless morning,
like the brightness after rain
that brings the grass from the earth.'

5"Is not my house right with God?
Has he not made with me an everlasting covenant,[h]
arranged and secured in every part?
Will he not bring to fruition my salvation
and grant me my every desire?
6But evil men are all to be cast aside like thorns,[i]
which are not gathered with the hand.
7Whoever touches thorns
uses a tool of iron or the shaft of a spear;
they are burned up where they lie."

i *46* Some Septuagint manuscripts and Vulgate (see also Psalm 18:45); Masoretic Text *they arm themselves.*
a *1* Or *Israel's beloved singer*

22:44 [f]2Sa 3:1 [g]Dt 28:13 [h]2Sa 8:1-14; Isa 55:3-5
22:45 [i]Ps 66:3; 81:15
22:46 [j]Mic 7:17
22:47 [k]Ps 89:26
22:48 [l]Ps 94:1; 144:2; 1Sa 25:39
22:49 [m]Ps 140:1, 4
22:50 [n]Ro 15:9*
22:51 [o]Ps 144:9-10 [p]Ps 89:20 [q]2Sa 7:13 [r]Ps 89:24, 29
23:1 [a]2Sa 7:8-9; Ps 78:70-71; 89:27 [b]1Sa 16:12-13; Ps 89:20
23:2 [c]Mt 22:43; 2Pe 1:21
23:3 [d]Dt 32:4; 2Sa 22:2, 32 [e]Ps 72:3 [f]2Ch 19:7, 9; Isa 11:1-5
23:4 [g]Jdg 5:31; Ps 89:36
23:5 [h]Ps 89:29; Isa 55:3
23:6 [i]Mt 13:40-41

23:3 In the style of a prophet, David spoke of a just and righteous ruler. This will be fulfilled in Jesus Christ when he returns to rule in perfect justice and peace. For similar prophecies, see Isaiah 11:1–10; Jeremiah 23:5, 6; 33:15–18; Zechariah 9:9, 10. For the fulfilment of some of these prophecies, see Matthew 4:14–16; Luke 24:25–27, 44–49; John 5:45–47; 8:28, 29.

David's Mighty Men

8These are the names of David's mighty men:
Josheb-Basshebeth,[b] a Tahkemonite,[c] was chief of the Three; he raised his spear
against eight hundred men, whom he killed[d] in one encounter.
9Next to him was Eleazar son of Dodai[j] the Ahohite.[k] As one of the three mighty
men, he was with David when they taunted the Philistines gathered ⌊at Pas Dammim⌋[e]
for battle. Then the men of Israel retreated, 10but he stood his ground and struck down
the Philistines till his hand grew tired and froze to the sword. The LORD brought about
a great victory that day. The troops returned to Eleazar, but only to strip the dead.
11Next to him was Shammah son of Agee the Hararite. When the Philistines banded
together at a place where there was a field full of lentils, Israel's troops fled from them.
12But Shammah took his stand in the middle of the field. He defended it and struck
the Philistines down, and the LORD brought about a great victory.
13During harvest time, three of the thirty chief men came down to David at the cave
of Adullam,[l] while a band of Philistines was encamped in the Valley of Rephaim.[m]
14At that time David was in the stronghold,[n] and the Philistine garrison was at
Bethlehem.[o] 15David longed for water and said, "Oh, that someone would get me
a drink of water from the well near the gate of Bethlehem!" 16So the three mighty
men broke through the Philistine lines, drew water from the well near the gate of
Bethlehem and carried it back to David. But he refused to drink it; instead, he poured[p]
it out before the LORD. 17"Far be it from me, O LORD, to do this!" he said. "Is it not
the blood[q] of men who went at the risk of their lives?" And David would not drink
it.
Such were the exploits of the three mighty men.
18Abishai[r] the brother of Joab son of Zeruiah was chief of the Three.[f] He raised
his spear against three hundred men, whom he killed, and so he became as famous
as the Three. 19Was he not held in greater honour than the Three? He became their
commander, even though he was not included among them.
20Benaiah[s] son of Jehoiada was a valiant fighter from Kabzeel,[t] who performed
great exploits. He struck down two of Moab's best men. He also went down into a
pit on a snowy day and killed a lion. 21And he struck down a huge Egyptian. Although
the Egyptian had a spear in his hand, Benaiah went against him with a club. He
snatched the spear from the Egyptian's hand and killed him with his own spear. 22Such
were the exploits of Benaiah son of Jehoiada; he too was as famous as the three mighty
men. 23He was held in greater honour than any of the Thirty, but he was not included
among the Three. And David put him in charge of his bodyguard.

24Among the Thirty were:
Asahel[u] the brother of Joab,
Elhanan son of Dodo from Bethlehem,
25Shammah the Harodite,[v]
Elika the Harodite,
26Helez[w] the Paltite,
Ira son of Ikkesh from Tekoa,
27Abiezer from Anathoth,[x]

23:9 [j]1Ch 27:4 [k]1Ch 8:4
23:13 [l]1Sa 22:1 [m]2Sa 5:18
23:14 [n]1Sa 22:4-5 [o]Ru 1:19
23:16 [p]Ge 35:14
23:17 [q]Lev 17:10-12
23:18 [r]2Sa 10:10, 14; 1Ch 11:20
23:20 [s]2Sa 8:18; 20:23 [t]Jos 15:21
23:24 [u]2Sa 2:18
23:25 [v]Jdg 7:1; 1Ch 11:27
23:26 [w]1Ch 27:10
23:27 [x]Jos 21:18

[b] *8* Hebrew; some Septuagint manuscripts suggest *Ish-Bosheth*, that is, *Esh-Baal* (see also 1 Chron. 11:11 *Jashobeam*). [c] *8* Probably a variant of *Hacmonite* (see 1 Chron. 11:11) [d] *8* Some Septuagint manuscripts (see also 1 Chron. 11:11); Hebrew and other Septuagint manuscripts *Three; it was Adino the Eznite who killed eight hundred men* [e] *9* See 1 Chron. 11:13; Hebrew *gathered there.* [f] *18* Most Hebrew manuscripts (see also 1 Chron. 11:20); two Hebrew manuscripts and Syriac *Thirty*

23:8–39 These verses tell of some of the exploits that the special corps of David's army carried out. There were two elite groups of men: "the Thirty" and "the Three" (23:18, 23; 1 Chronicles 11:11–25). To become a member of such a group a man had to show unparalleled courage in battle as well as wisdom in leadership. "The Three" was the most elite group. The list of "the Thirty" actually contains 37 names, but it mentions some warriors known to be dead (Uriah, for example, in 23:39). Apparently, new members were appointed to replace those who had fallen in battle.

23:16 David poured out the water as an offering to God because he was so moved by the sacrifice it represented. When Hebrews offered sacrifices, they never consumed the blood. It represented life, and they poured it out before God. David would not drink this water that represented the lives of his soldiers. Instead, he offered it to God.

23:28 [y]1Ch 27:13 [z]2Ki 25:23; Ne 7:26
23:29 [a]Jos 15:57
23:30 [b]Jdg 12:13 [c]Jos 24:30
23:31 [d]2Sa 3:16
23:34 [e]2Sa 11:3 [f]2Sa 15:12
23:35 [g]Jos 12:22
23:36 [h]1Sa 14:47

Mebunnai[g] the Hushathite,
28 Zalmon the Ahohite,
Maharai[y] the Netophathite,[z]
29 Heled[h] son of Baanah the Netophathite,
Ithai son of Ribai from Gibeah[a] in Benjamin,
30 Benaiah the Pirathonite,[b]
Hiddai[i] from the ravines of Gaash,[c]
31 Abi-Albon the Arbathite,
Azmaveth the Barhumite,[d]
32 Eliahba the Shaalbonite,
the sons of Jashen,
Jonathan 33 son of[j] Shammah the Hararite,
Ahiam son of Sharar[k] the Hararite,
34 Eliphelet son of Ahasbai the Maacathite,
Eliam[e] son of Ahithophel[f] the Gilonite,
35 Hezro the Carmelite,[g]
Paarai the Arbite,
36 Igal son of Nathan from Zobah,[h]

g *27* Hebrew; some Septuagint manuscripts (see also 1 Chron. 11:29) *Sibbecai* h *29* Some Hebrew manuscripts and Vulgate (see also 1 Chron. 11:30); most Hebrew manuscripts *Heleb* i *30* Hebrew; some Septuagint manuscripts (see also 1 Chron. 11:32) *Hurai* j *33* Some Septuagint manuscripts (see also 1 Chron. 11:34); Hebrew does not have *son of.* k *33* Hebrew; some Septuagint manuscripts (see also 1 Chron. 11:35) *Sacar*

DAVID'S MIGHTY MEN

One way to understand David's success is to notice the kind of men who followed him. During the time he was being hunted by Saul, David gradually built a fighting force of several hundred men. Some were relatives, others were outcasts of society, many were in trouble with the law. They all had at least one trait in common—complete devotion to David. Their achievements made them famous. Among these men were elite military groups like "the Three" and "the Thirty". They were true heroes.

Scripture gives the impression that these men were motivated to greatness by the personal qualities of their leader. David inspired them to achieve beyond their goals and meet their true potential. Likewise, the leaders we follow and the causes to which we commit ourselves will affect our lives. David's effectiveness was clearly connected with his awareness of God's leading. He was a good leader when he was following *his* Leader. Do you know whom the people you respect most are following? Your answer should help you decide whether they deserve your loyalty. Do you also recognise God's leading in your life? No-one can lead you to excellence as your Creator can.

Strengths and accomplishments:
- Able soldiers and military leaders
- Shared many special skills
- Though frequently outnumbered, were consistently victorious
- Loyal to David

Weakness and mistake:
- Often had little in common beyond their loyalty to David and their military expertise

Lessons from their lives:
- Greatness is often inspired by the quality and character of leadership
- Even a small force of able and loyal men can accomplish great feats

Vital statistics:
- Where: They came from all over Israel (primarily Judah and Benjamin), and from some of the other surrounding nations as well
- Occupations: Various backgrounds—almost all were fugitives

Key verses:
"David left Gath and escaped to the cave of Adullam. When his brothers and his father's household heard about it, they went down to him there. All those who were in distress or in debt or discontented gathered round him, and he became their leader. About four hundred men were with him" (1 Samuel 22:1, 2).

Their stories are told in 1 Samuel 22—2 Samuel 23:39. They are also mentioned in 1 Chronicles 11, 12.

the son of Hagri,[l]
37Zelek the Ammonite,
Naharai the Beerothite, the armour-bearer of Joab son of Zeruiah,
38Ira the Ithrite,[i]
Gareb the Ithrite
39and Uriah[j] the Hittite.
There were thirty-seven in all.

David Counts the Fighting Men

24 Again[a] the anger of the LORD burned against Israel, and he incited David
against them, saying, "Go and take a census of[b] Israel and Judah."
2So the king said to Joab[c] and the army commanders[a] with him, "Go throughout
the tribes of Israel from Dan to Beersheba[d] and enrol the fighting men, so that I may
know how many there are."
3But Joab replied to the king, "May the LORD your God multiply the troops a
hundred times over,[e] and may the eyes of my lord the king see it. But why does my
lord the king want to do such a thing?"
4The king's word, however, overruled Joab and the army commanders; so they left
the presence of the king to enrol the fighting men of Israel.
5After crossing the Jordan, they camped near Aroer,[f] south of the town in the
gorge, and then went through Gad and on to Jazer.[g] 6They went to Gilead and the
region of Tahtim Hodshi, and on to Dan Jaan and around towards Sidon.[h] 7Then they
went towards the fortress of Tyre[i] and all the towns of the Hivites and Canaanites.
Finally, they went on to Beersheba[j] in the Negev[k] of Judah.
8After they had gone through the entire land, they came back to Jerusalem at the
end of nine months and twenty days.
9Joab reported the number of the fighting men to the king: In Israel there were eight
hundred thousand able-bodied men who could handle a sword, and in Judah five
hundred thousand.[l]
10David was conscience-stricken[m] after he had counted the fighting men, and he
said to the LORD, "I have sinned[n] greatly in what I have done. Now, O LORD, I beg
you, take away the guilt of your servant. I have done a very foolish thing.[o]"
11Before David got up the next morning, the word of the LORD had come to Gad[p]
the prophet, David's seer:[q] 12"Go and tell David, 'This is what the LORD says: I am
giving you three options. Choose one of them for me to carry out against you.' "
13So Gad went to David and said to him, "Shall there come upon you three[b] years
of famine[r] in your land? Or three months of fleeing from your enemies while they

[l] *36* Some Septuagint manuscripts (see also 1 Chron. 11:38); Hebrew *Haggadi* [a] *2* Septuagint (see also verse 4 and 1 Chron. 21:2); Hebrew *Joab the army commander* [b] *13* Septuagint (see also 1 Chron. 21:12); Hebrew *seven*

23:38 [i]2Sa 20:26; 1Ch 2:53
23:39 [j]2Sa 11:3
24:1 [a]Jos 9:15 [b]1Ch 27:23
24:2 [c]2Sa 20:23 [d]Jdg 20:1; 2Sa 3:10
24:3 [e]Dt 1:11
24:5 [f]Dt 2:36; Jos 13:9 [g]Nu 21:32
24:6 [h]Ge 10:19; Jos 19:28; Jdg 1:31
24:7 [i]Jos 19:29 [j]Ge 21:22-33 [k]Dt 1:7; Jos 11:3
24:9 [l]Nu 1:44-46; 1Ch 21:5
24:10 [m]1Sa 24:5 [n]2Sa 12:13 [o]Nu 12:11; 1Sa 13:13
24:11 [p]1Sa 22:5 [q]1Sa 9:9; 1Ch 29:29
24:13 [r]Dt 28:38-42, 48; Eze 14:21

24:1 Did God cause David to sin? God does not cause people to sin, but he does allow sinners to reveal the sinfulness of their hearts by their actions. God presented the opportunity to David in order to deal with a disastrous national tendency, and he wanted this desire to show itself. First Chronicles 21:1 says Satan incited David to do it. Hebrew writers do not always distinguish between primary and secondary causes. So if God allowed Satan to tempt David, to them it is as if God did it.

24:1–3 What was wrong with taking a census? A census was commanded in Numbers to prepare an army for conquering the promised land (Numbers 1:2; 26:2). A census amounted to a draft or conscription for the army. The land was now at peace, so there was no need to enlist troops. Israel had extended its borders and become a recognised power. David's sin was pride and ambition in counting the people so that he could glory in the size of his nation and army, its power and defences. By doing this, he put his faith in the size of his army rather than in God's ability to protect them regardless of their number. Even Joab knew a census was wrong, but David did not heed his advice. We sin in a similar way when we place our security in money, possessions, or the might of our nation.

24:12–14 Both David and the Israelites were guilty of sin (24:1). David's sin was pride, but the Bible does not say why God was angry with the people of Israel. Perhaps it was due to their support of the rebellions of Absalom (chapters 15–18) and Sheba (chapter 20), or perhaps they put their security in military and financial prosperity rather than God, as David did. God dealt with the whole nation through David who exemplified the national sin of pride.

God gave David three choices. Each was a form of punishment God had told the people they could expect if they disobeyed his laws (disease – Deuteronomy 28:20–22; famine – 28:23, 24; war – 28:25, 26). David wisely chose the form of punishment that came most directly from God. He knew how brutal and harsh men in war could be, and he also knew God's great mercy. When you sin greatly, turn back to God. To be punished by him is far better than to take your chances without him.

pursue you? Or three days of plague[s] in your land? Now then, think it over and decide
how I should answer the one who sent me."
14 David said to Gad, "I am in deep distress. Let us fall into the hands of the LORD,
for his mercy[t] is great; but do not let me fall into the hands of men."
15 So the LORD sent a plague on Israel from that morning until the end of the time
designated, and seventy thousand of the people from Dan to Beersheba died.[u]
16 When the angel stretched out his hand to destroy Jerusalem, the LORD was grieved[v]
because of the calamity and said to the angel who was afflicting the people, "Enough!
Withdraw your hand." The angel of the LORD[w] was then at the threshing-floor of
Araunah the Jebusite.
17 When David saw the angel who was striking down the people, he said to the
LORD, "I am the one who has sinned and done wrong. These are but sheep.[x] What
have they done? Let your hand fall upon me and my family."[y]

David Builds an Altar

18 On that day Gad went to David and said to him, "Go up and build an altar to the
LORD on the threshing-floor of Araunah the Jebusite." 19 So David went up, as the
LORD had commanded through Gad. 20 When Araunah looked and saw the king and
his men coming towards him, he went out and bowed down before the king with his
face to the ground.
21 Araunah said, "Why has my lord the king come to his servant?"
"To buy your threshing-floor," David answered, "so that I can build an altar to the
LORD, that the plague on the people may be stopped."[z]
22 Araunah said to David, "Let my lord the king take whatever pleases him and offer
it up. Here are oxen[a] for the burnt offering, and here are threshing-sledges and ox
yokes for the wood. 23 O king, Araunah gives[b] all this to the king." Araunah also said
to him, "May the LORD your God accept you."
24 But the king replied to Araunah, "No, I insist on paying you for it. I will not
sacrifice to the LORD my God burnt offerings that cost me nothing."[c]
So David bought the threshing-floor and the oxen and paid fifty shekels[c] of silver
for them. 25 David built an altar[d] to the LORD there and sacrificed burnt offerings and
fellowship offerings.[d] Then the LORD answered prayer[e] on behalf of the land, and
the plague on Israel was stopped.

c *24* That is, about 1¼ pounds (about 0.6 kilogram) d *25* Traditionally *peace offerings*

24:13 s Lev 26:25
24:14 t Ne 9:28; Ps 51:1; 103:8, 13; 130:4
24:15 u 1Ch 27:24
24:16 v Ge 6:6; 1Sa 15:11 w Ex 12:23; Ac 12:23
24:17 x Ps 74:1 y Jnh 1:12
24:21 z Nu 16:44-50
24:22 a 1Sa 6:14; 1Ki 19:21
24:23 b Eze 20:40-41
24:24 c Mal 1:13-14
24:25 d 1Sa 7:17 e 2Sa 21:14

24:18 Many believe that this threshing floor where David built the altar is the location where Abraham nearly sacrificed his son Isaac (Genesis 22:1–18). After David's death, Solomon built the temple on this spot. Centuries later, Jesus would teach and preach here.

24:25 The book of 2 Samuel describes David's reign. Since the Israelites first entered the promised land under Joshua, they had been struggling to unite the nation and drive out the wicked inhabitants. Now, after more than 400 years, Israel was finally at peace. David had accomplished what no leader before him, judge or king, had done. His administration was run on the principle of dedication to God and to the well-being of the people. Yet David also sinned. Despite his sins, however, the Bible calls David a man after God's own heart (1 Samuel 13:14; Acts 13:22) because when he sinned, he recognised it and confessed his sins to God. David committed his life to God and remained loyal to him throughout his lifetime. Psalms gives an even deeper insight into David's love for God.

1 KINGS

David becomes king 1010 B.C.	Solomon becomes king 970	Temple completed 959	The kingdom divides 930	Shish invac Jerus 925

VITAL STATISTICS

PURPOSE:
To contrast the lives of those who live for God and those who refuse to do so through the history of the kings of Israel and Judah

AUTHOR:
Unknown. Possibly Jeremiah or a group of prophets

SETTING:
The once great nation of Israel turned into a land divided, not only physically, but also spiritually.

KEY VERSES:
"As for you, if you walk before me in integrity of heart and uprightness, as David your father did, and do all I command and observe my decrees and laws, I will establish your royal throne over Israel for ever, as I promised David your father when I said, 'You shall never fail to have a man on the throne of Israel' " (9:4, 5).

KEY PEOPLE:
David, Solomon, Rehoboam, Jeroboam, Elijah, Ahab, Jezebel

SPECIAL FEATURE:
The books of 1 and 2 Kings were originally one book.

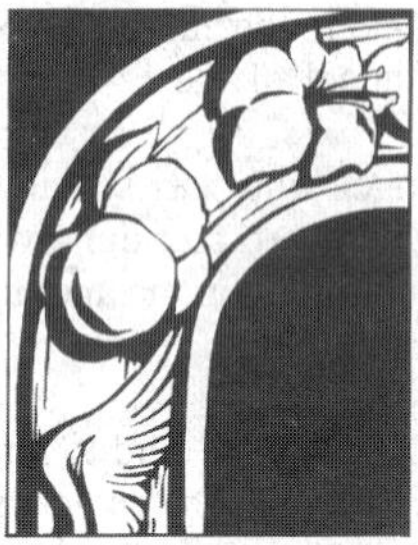

"I DON'T CARE what anyone says, I'm going to do it!" he yells at his mother as he storms out of the house.

This is a familiar scene in our society. The words change, but the essential message is the same . . . the person is *not* open to advice because his mind is closed. Some advice may be sought, but it is heeded only if it reinforces the decision already made or is an easier path to take. It is human nature to reject help and to do things *our* way.

A much wiser approach is to seek, hear, and heed the advice of good counsellors. Solomon, the world's wisest man, urges this in Proverbs (see 11:14; 15:22; 24:6). How ironic that his son and successor, Rehoboam, listened instead to foolish advice, with devastating results. At Rehoboam's inauguration, he was petitioned by the people to be a kind and generous ruler. The older men counselled him to "be a servant to these people and serve them and give them a favourable answer" (12:7). But Rehoboam agrees to the cruel words of his peers who urge him to be harsh. As a result, Rehoboam split the kingdom. Learn from Rehoboam's mistake. Commit yourself to seeking and following wise counsel.

The main events of 1 Kings are David's death, Solomon's reign, the division of the kingdom, and Elijah's ministry. As Solomon ascended the throne, David charged him to obey God's laws and to walk "in his ways" (2:3). This Solomon did; and when given the choice of gifts from God, he humbly asked for discernment (3:9). As a result, Solomon's reign began with great success, including the construction of the temple—his greatest achievement. Unfortunately, Solomon took many pagan wives and concubines who eventually turned his heart away from the Lord to their false gods (11:1–4).

Rehoboam succeeded Solomon and had the opportunity to be a wise, compassionate, and just king. Instead, he accepted the poor advice of his young friends and attempted to rule with an iron hand. But the people rebelled, and the kingdom split with ten tribes in the north (Israel) ruled by Jeroboam, and only Judah and Benjamin remaining with Rehoboam. Both kingdoms wove a path through the reigns of corrupt and idolatrous kings with only the clear voice of the prophets continuing to warn and call the nation back to God.

Elijah is surely one of the greatest prophets, and chapters 17–22 feature his conflict with wicked Ahab and Jezebel in Israel. In one of the most dramatic confrontations in history, Elijah defeated the prophets of Baal at Mount Carmel. In spite of incredible opposition, Elijah stood for God and proves that *one plus God* is a majority. If God is on our side, no-one can stand against us (Romans 8:31).

Asa becomes king of Judah 910	*Elijah begins his ministry 875*	*Ahab becomes king of Israel 874*	*Jehoshaphat becomes king of Judah 872*	*Ben-Hadad attacks Samaria 857*	*Ahab dies in battle 853*

THE BLUEPRINT

A. THE UNITED KINGDOM (1:1—11:43)
1. Solomon becomes king
2. Solomon's wisdom
3. Solomon builds the temple
4. Solomon's greatness and downfall

Solomon was a botanist, zoologist, architect, poet, and philosopher. He was the wisest king in the history of Israel, but his wives led to the introduction of false gods and false worship in Israel. It is good for us to have wisdom, but that is not enough. The highest goal in life is to obey the Lord. Patient obedience to God should characterise our lives.

B. THE DIVIDED KINGDOM (12:1—22:53)
1. Revolt of the northern tribes
2. Kings of Israel and Judah
3. Elijah's ministry
4. Kings of Israel and Judah

When the northern kingdom of Israel was being led by wicked kings, God raised up a prophet to proclaim his messages. Elijah single-handedly challenged the priesthood of the state religion and had them removed in one day. Through the dividing of the kingdom and the sending of Elijah, God dealt with the people's sin in powerful ways. Sin in our lives is graciously forgiven by God. However, the sin of an unrepentant person will be handled harshly. We must turn from sin and turn to God to be saved from judgment.

MEGATHEMES

THEME	EXPLANATION	IMPORTANCE
The King	Solomon's wisdom, power, and achievements brought honour to the Israelite nation and to God. All the kings of Israel and Judah were told to obey God and to govern according to his laws. But their tendency to abandon God's commands and to worship other gods led them to change the religion and government to meet their personal desires. This neglect of God's law led to their downfall.	Wisdom, power, and achievement do not ultimately come from any human source; they are from God. No matter what we lead or govern, we can't do well when we ignore God's guidelines. Whether or not we are leaders, effectiveness depends upon listening and obeying God's word. Don't let your personal desires distort God's word.
The Temple	Solomon's temple was a beautiful place of worship and prayer. This sanctuary was the centre of Jewish religion. It was the place of God's special presence and housed the ark of the covenant containing the Ten Commandments.	A beautiful house of worship doesn't always guarantee heartfelt worship of God. Providing opportunities for true worship doesn't ensure that it will happen. God wants to live in our hearts, not just meet us in a sanctuary.
Other Gods	Although the Israelites had God's law and experienced his presence among them, they became attracted to other gods. When this happened, their hearts became cold to God's law, resulting in the ruin of families and government, and eventually leading to the destruction of the nation.	Through the years, the people took on the false qualities of the false gods they worshipped. They became cruel, power-hungry, and sexually perverse. We tend to become what we worship. Unless we serve the true God, we will become slaves to whatever takes his place.
The Prophet's Message	The prophet's responsibility was to confront and correct any deviation from God's law. Elijah was a bolt of judgment against Israel. His messages and miracles were a warning to the evil and rebellious kings and people.	The Bible, the truth in sermons, and the wise counsel of believers are warnings to us. Anyone who points out how we deviate from obeying God's word is a blessing to us. Changing our lives in order to obey God and get back on track often takes painful discipline and hard work.
Sin and Repentance	Each king had God's commands, a priest or prophet, and the lessons of the past to draw him back to God. All the people had the same resources. Whenever they repented and returned to God, God heard their prayers and forgave them.	God hears and forgives us when we pray—if we are willing to trust him and turn from sin. Our desire to forsake our sin must be heartfelt and sincere. Then he will give us a fresh start and a desire to live for him.

KEY PLACES IN 1 KINGS

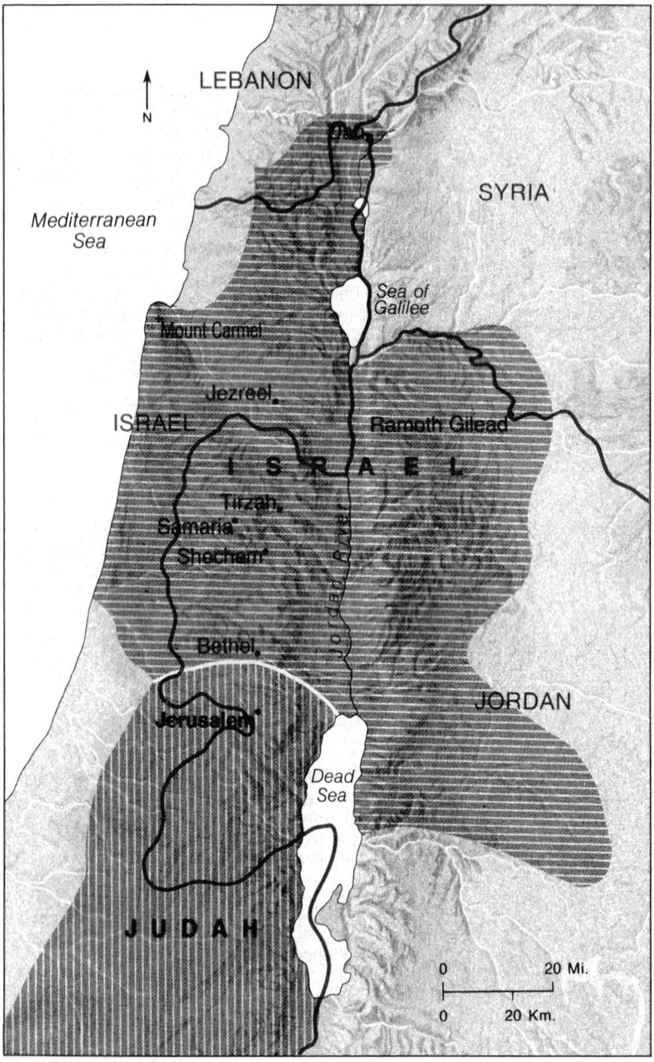

Modern names and boundaries are shown in grey.

Solomon, David's son, brought Israel into its golden age. His wealth and wisdom were acclaimed worldwide. But he ignored God in his later years (1:1–11:25).

1 **Shechem** After Solomon's death, Israel assembled at Shechem to inaugurate his son Rehoboam. However, Rehoboam foolishly angered the people by threatening even heavier burdens, causing a revolt (11:26–12:19).

2 **Israel** Jeroboam, leader of the rebels, was made king of Israel, now called the northern kingdom. Jeroboam made Shechem his capital city (12:20, 25).

3 **Judah** Only the tribes of Judah and part of Benjamin remained loyal to Rehoboam. These two tribes became the southern kingdom. Rehoboam returned to Judah from Shechem and prepared to force the rebels into submission, but a prophet's message halted these plans (12:21–24).

4 **Jerusalem** Jerusalem was the capital city of Judah. Its temple, built by Solomon, was the focal point of Jewish worship. This worried Jeroboam. How could he keep his people loyal if they were constantly going to Rehoboam's capital to worship (12:26, 27)?

5 **Dan** Jeroboam's solution was to set up his own worship centres. Two golden calves were made and proclaimed to be Israel's gods. One was placed in Dan, and the people were told that they could go there instead of to Jerusalem to worship (12:28, 29).

6 **Bethel** The other golden calf was placed in Bethel. The people of the northern kingdom had two convenient locations for worship in their own country, but their sin displeased God. In Jerusalem, meanwhile, Rehoboam was also allowing idolatry to creep in. The two nations were constantly at war (12:29–15:26).

7 **Tirzah** Jeroboam had moved the capital city to Tirzah (1 Kings 14:17). Next, Baasha became king of Israel after assassinating Nadab (15:27–16:22).

8 **Samaria** Israel continued to gain and lose kings through plots, assassinations, and warfare. When Omri became king, he bought a hill on which he built a new capital city, Samaria. Omri's son, Ahab, became the most wicked king of Israel. His wife Jezebel worshipped Baal. Ahab erected a temple to Baal in Samaria (16:23–34).

9 **Mount Carmel** Great evil often brings great people who oppose it. Elijah challenged the prophets of Baal and Asherah at Mount Carmel, where he would prove that they were false prophets. There Elijah humiliated these prophets and then executed them (17:1–18:46).

10 **Jezreel** Elijah returned to Jezreel. But Queen Jezebel, furious at the execution of her prophets, vowed to kill Elijah. He ran for his life, but God cared for and encouraged him. During his travels he anointed the future kings of Aram and Israel, as well as Elisha, his own replacement (19:1–21).

11 **Ramoth Gilead** The king of Aram declared war on Israel and was defeated in two battles. But the Arameans occupied Ramoth Gilead. Ahab and Jehoshaphat joined forces to recover the city. In this battle, Ahab was killed. Jehoshaphat later died (20:1–22:53).

A. THE UNITED KINGDOM (1:1—11:43)

When Solomon is anointed king, he eliminates all opposition to the throne, builds the temple, establishes a strong army, and becomes the richest and wisest king in the history of Israel. But his pagan wives lead him into idolatry and, as a result, he leads the nation into spiritual decline. No matter what position in life we attain, we are always ripe for a downfall and must never let our guard down against sin and temptation.

1. Solomon becomes king

Adonijah Sets Himself Up as King

1:3 [a]Jos 19:18 1 When King David was old and well advanced in years, he could not keep warm
even when they put covers over him. 2So his servants said to him, "Let us look
for a young virgin to attend the king and take care of him. She can lie beside him so
that our lord the king may keep warm."
3Then they searched throughout Israel for a beautiful girl and found Abishag, a
Shunammite,[a] and brought her to the king. 4The girl was very beautiful; she took
care of the king and waited on him, but the king had no intimate relations with her.
5Now Adonijah,[b] whose mother was Haggith, put himself forward and said, "I will
1:5 [b]2Sa 3:4 [c]2Sa 15:1 be king." So he got chariots[c] and horses[a] ready, with fifty men to run ahead of him.

[a] 5 Or *charioteers*

1:1 Israel was near the end of the golden years of David's reign. The book of 1 Kings begins with a unified kingdom, glorious and God-centred; it ends with a divided kingdom, degraded and idolatrous. The reason for Israel's decline appears simple to us—they failed to obey God. But we are vulnerable to the same forces that brought about Israel's decay—greed, jealousy, lust for power, weakening of marriage vows, and superficiality in our devotion to God. As we read about these tragic events in Israel's history, we must see ourselves in the mirror of their experiences.

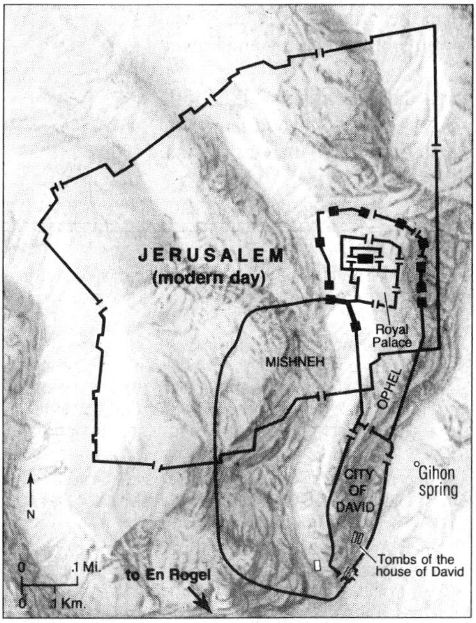

TWO CORONATIONS As David lay on his deathbed, his son Adonijah crowned himself king at En Rogel outside Jerusalem. When the news reached David, he declared that Solomon was to be the next ruler. Solomon was anointed at Gihon. It may have been more than coincidence that Gihon was not only within shouting distance of En Rogel, but also closer to the royal palace.

1:4 David was about 70 years old. His health had deteriorated from years of hardship. Abishag served as his nurse and to help keep him warm. In times when polygamy was accepted and kings had harems, this action was not considered offensive.

1:5 Adonijah was David's fourth son and the logical choice to succeed him as king. David's first son, Amnon, had been killed by Absalom for having raped his sister (2 Samuel 13:20–33). His second son, Daniel, is mentioned only in the genealogy of 1 Chronicles 3:1 and had probably died by this time. David's third son, Absalom, died in an earlier rebellion (2 Samuel 18:1–18). Although many people expected Adonijah to be the next king (2:13–25), David (and God) had other plans (1:29, 30).

1:5 Adonijah decided to seize the throne without David's knowledge. He knew that Solomon, not he, was David's first choice to be the next king (1:17). This was why he did not invite Solomon and David's loyal advisers when he declared himself king (1:9, 10). But his deceptive plans to gain the throne were unsuccessful. The proud Adonijah was self-exalted and self-defeated.

6(His father had never interfered[d] with him by asking, "Why do you behave as you
do?" He was also very handsome and was born next after Absalom.)
7Adonijah conferred with Joab[e] son of Zeruiah and with Abiathar[f] the priest, and
they gave him their support. 8But Zadok[g] the priest, Benaiah[h] son of Jehoiada,
Nathan[i] the prophet, Shimei[j] and Rei[b] and David's special guard[k] did not join
Adonijah.
9Adonijah then sacrificed sheep, cattle and fattened calves at the Stone of Zoheleth
near En Rogel.[l] He invited all his brothers, the king's sons, and all the men of Judah
who were royal officials, 10but he did not invite Nathan the prophet or Benaiah or the
special guard or his brother Solomon.[m]
11Then Nathan asked Bathsheba,[n] Solomon's mother, "Have you not heard that
Adonijah,[o] the son of Haggith, has become king without our lord David's knowing
it? 12Now then, let me advise[p] you how you can save your own life and the life of
your son Solomon. 13Go in to King David and say to him, 'My lord the king, did you
not swear[q] to me your servant: "Surely Solomon your son shall be king after me, and
he will sit on my throne"? Why then has Adonijah become king?' 14While you are
still there talking to the king, I will come in and confirm what you have said."
15So Bathsheba went to see the aged king in his room, where Abishag[r] the
Shunammite was attending him. 16Bathsheba bowed low and knelt before the king.
"What is it you want?" the king asked.
17She said to him, "My lord, you yourself swore[s] to me your servant by the LORD
your God: 'Solomon your son shall become king after me, and he will sit on my
throne.' 18But now Adonijah has become king, and you, my lord the king, do not
know about it. 19He has sacrificed[t] great numbers of cattle, fattened calves, and
sheep, and has invited all the king's sons, Abiathar the priest and Joab the commander
of the army, but he has not invited Solomon your servant. 20My lord the king, the
eyes of all Israel are on you, to learn from you who will sit on the throne of my lord
the king after him. 21Otherwise, as soon as my lord the king is laid to rest[u] with his
fathers, I and my son Solomon will be treated as criminals."
22While she was still speaking with the king, Nathan the prophet arrived. 23And
they told the king, "Nathan the prophet is here." So he went before the king and bowed
with his face to the ground.
24Nathan said, "Have you, my lord the king, declared that Adonijah shall be king
after you, and that he will sit on your throne? 25Today he has gone down and sacrificed
great numbers of cattle, fattened calves, and sheep. He has invited all the king's sons,

[b] 8 Or *and his friends*

1:6 [d] 2Sa 3:3-4
1:7 [e] 1Ki 2:22, 28; 1Ch 11:6 [f] 1Sa 22:20; 2Sa 20:25
1:8 [g] 2Sa 20:25 [h] 2Sa 8:18 [i] 2Sa 12:1 [j] 1Ki 4:18 [k] 2Sa 23:8
1:9 [l] 2Sa 17:17
1:10 [m] 2Sa 12:24
1:11 [n] 2Sa 12:24 [o] 2Sa 3:4
1:12 [p] Pr 15:22
1:13 [q] ver 30; 1Ch 22:9-13
1:15 [r] ver 1
1:17 [s] ver 13, 30
1:19 [t] ver 9
1:21 [u] Dt 31:16; 1Ki 2:10

1:6 God-fearing people like David and Samuel were used by God to lead nations, but nevertheless they had problems in family relationships. God-fearing leaders cannot take for granted the spiritual well-being of their children. They are used to having others follow their orders, but they cannot expect their children to manufacture faith upon request. Moral and spiritual character takes years to build, and it requires constant attention and patient discipline.

David served God well as a king, but as a parent he often failed both God and his children. Don't let your service to God even in leadership positions take up so much of your time and energy that you neglect your other God-given responsibilities.

1:6 Because David had never interfered by opposing or even questioning his son, Adonijah did not know how to work within limits. The result was that he always wanted his own way, regardless of how it affected others. Adonijah did whatever he wanted and paid no respect to God's wishes. An undisciplined child may look cute to his or her parents, but an undisciplined adult destroys himself and others. As you set limits for your children, you make it possible for them to develop the self-restraint they will need in order to control themselves later. Discipline your children carefully while they are young, so that they will grow into self-disciplined adults.

1:7 See Joab's Profile in 2 Samuel 19 for a more complete picture of his life. For more information on Abiathar, see the note on 1 Samuel 22:20.

1:9 When Saul was anointed king, fellowship offerings were sacrificed as a reminder of the nation's covenant with God given at Mount Sinai. Adonijah wanted sacrifices offered, perhaps hoping to legitimise his takeover. But Adonijah was not God's choice to succeed David. Sealing an action with religious ceremony does not make it God's will.

1:11 For more on Bathsheba, David's wife, read 2 Samuel 11; 12. As mother of the king, Bathsheba was highly influential in the royal palace.

1:11–14 When Nathan learned of Adonijah's conspiracy, he immediately tried to stop it. He was a man of both faith and action. He knew that Solomon should rightly be king, and he moved quickly when he saw someone else trying to take the throne. We often know what is right but don't act on it. Perhaps we don't want to get involved, or maybe we are fearful or lazy. Don't stop with prayer, good intentions, or angry feelings. Take the action needed to correct the situation.

1:13 The Bible does not record David's promise that Solomon would be Israel's next king, but it is clear that Solomon was the choice of both David (1:17, 30) and God (1 Chronicles 22:9, 10).

1:26 [v]ver 8, 10
the commanders of the army and Abiathar the priest. At this very moment they are
eating and drinking with him and saying, 'Long live King Adonijah!' 26But me your
servant, and Zadok the priest, and Benaiah son of Jehoiada, and your servant Solomon
he did not invite.[v] 27Is this something my lord the king has done without letting his
servants know who should sit on the throne of my lord the king after him?"

1:29 [w]2Sa 4:9

David Makes Solomon King

28Then King David said, "Call in Bathsheba." So she came into the king's presence
and stood before him.
29The king then took an oath: "As surely as the LORD lives, who has delivered me
out of every trouble,[w] 30I will surely carry out today what I swore[x] to you by the
1:30 [x]ver 13, 17
LORD, the God of Israel: Solomon your son shall be king after me, and he will sit on
my throne in my place."
31Then Bathsheba bowed low with her face to the ground and, kneeling before the
king, said, "May my lord King David live for ever!"
32King David said, "Call in Zadok the priest, Nathan the prophet and Benaiah son
of Jehoiada." When they came before the king, 33he said to them: "Take your lord's
1:33 [y]2Sa 20:6-7
servants with you and set Solomon my son on my own mule[y] and take him down

BATHSHEBA

Bathsheba was the unlikely link between Israel's two most famous kings—David and Solomon. She was lover and wife to one, mother to the other. Her adultery with David almost brought an end to the family through which God planned physically to enter his world. Out of the ashes of that sin, however, God brought good. Eventually Jesus Christ, the salvation of mankind, was born to a descendant of David and Bathsheba.

David and Bathsheba's story shows that little wrong decisions often lead to big mistakes. It is likely that neither was where he or she should have been. Bathsheba may have been rash in bathing where she might be seen; David should have been at war with his army. Each decision contributed to the beginning of a very sad series of events.

Bathsheba must have been devastated by the chain of events—unfaithfulness to her husband, discovery of pregnancy, death of her husband, death of her child. We are told that David comforted her (2 Samuel 12:24), and she lived to see another son, Solomon, sit on the throne.

From her life we see that the little, day-to-day choices we make are very important. They prepare us to make the right choices when the big decisions come. The wisdom to make right choices in small and large matters is a gift from God. Understanding this should make us more conscious of the decisions we make and more willing to include God in our decision making. Have you asked for his help with today's decisions?

Strengths and accomplishments:
- Became influential in the palace alongside her son, Solomon
- Was the mother of Israel's wisest king and an ancestor of Jesus Christ

Weakness and mistake:
- Committed adultery

Lessons from her life:
- Although we may feel caught up in a chain of events, we are still responsible for the way we participate in those events
- A sin may seem like one small seed, but the harvest of consequences is beyond measure
- In the worst possible situations, God is still able to bring about good when people truly turn to him
- While we must live with the natural consequences of our sins, God's forgiveness of sin is total

Vital statistics:
- Where: Jerusalem
- Occupations: Queen and queen mother
- Relatives: Father: Elim. Husbands: Uriah and David. Son: Solomon
- Contemporaries: Nathan, Joab, Adonijah

Key verses:
"When Uriah's wife heard that her husband was dead, she mourned for him. After the time of mourning was over, David had her brought to his house, and she became his wife and bore him a son. But the thing David had done displeased the LORD" (2 Samuel 11:26, 27).

Her story is told in 2 Samuel 11, 12 and 1 Kings 1, 2. A related passage is Psalm 51.

to Gihon.[z] 34There shall Zadok the priest and Nathan the prophet anoint[a] him king
over Israel. Blow the trumpet[b] and shout, 'Long live King Solomon!' 35Then you
are to go up with him, and he is to come and sit on my throne and reign in my place.
I have appointed him ruler over Israel and Judah."
36Benaiah son of Jehoiada answered the king, "Amen! May the LORD, the God of
my lord the king, so declare it. 37As the LORD was with my lord the king, so may
he be with[c] Solomon to make his throne even greater[d] than the throne of my lord
King David!"
38So Zadok[e] the priest, Nathan the prophet, Benaiah son of Jehoiada, the Kerethites[f] and the Pelethites went down and put Solomon on King David's mule and
escorted him to Gihon.[g] 39Zadok the priest took the horn of oil[h] from the sacred tent
and anointed Solomon. Then they sounded the trumpet and all the people shouted,[i]
"Long live King Solomon!" 40And all the people went up after him, playing flutes
and rejoicing greatly, so that the ground shook with the sound.
41Adonijah and all the guests who were with him heard it as they were finishing
their feast. On hearing the sound of the trumpet, Joab asked, "What's the meaning
of all the noise in the city?"
42Even as he was speaking, Jonathan[j] son of Abiathar the priest arrived. Adonijah
said, "Come in. A worthy man like you must be bringing good news."[k]
43"Not at all!" Jonathan answered. "Our lord King David has made Solomon king.
44The king has sent with him Zadok the priest, Nathan the prophet, Benaiah son of
Jehoiada, the Kerethites and the Pelethites, and they have put him on the king's mule,
45and Zadok the priest and Nathan the prophet have anointed him king at Gihon. From
there they have gone up cheering, and the city resounds[l] with it. That's the noise
you hear. 46Moreover, Solomon has taken his seat on the royal throne. 47Also, the
royal officials have come to congratulate our lord King David, saying, 'May your God
make Solomon's name more famous than yours and his throne greater[m] than yours!'
And the king bowed in worship on his bed 48and said, 'Praise be to the LORD, the
God of Israel, who has allowed my eyes to see a successor[n] on my throne today.' "
49At this, all Adonijah's guests rose in alarm and dispersed. 50But Adonijah, in fear
of Solomon, went and took hold of the horns[o] of the altar. 51Then Solomon was told,
"Adonijah is afraid of King Solomon and is clinging to the horns of the altar. He says,
'Let King Solomon swear to me today that he will not put his servant to death with
the sword.' "
52Solomon replied, "If he shows himself to be a worthy man, not a hair[p] of his
head will fall to the ground; but if evil is found in him, he will die." 53Then King
Solomon sent men, and they brought him down from the altar. And Adonijah came
and bowed down to King Solomon, and Solomon said, "Go to your home."

1:33
[z] 2Ch 32:30; 33:14

1:34
[a] 1Sa 10:1; 16:3, 12; 1Ki 19:16; 2Ki 9:3, 13
[b] ver 25; 2Sa 5:3; 15:10

1:37
[c] Jos 1:5, 17; 1Sa 20:13
[d] ver 47

1:38
[e] ver 8
[f] 2Sa 8:18
[g] ver 33

1:39
[h] Ex 30:23-32; Ps 89:20
[i] ver 34; 1Sa 10:24

1:42
[j] 2Sa 15:27, 36
[k] 2Sa 18:26

1:45
[l] ver 40

1:47
[m] ver 37; Ge 47:31

1:48
[n] 2Sa 7:12; 1Ki 3:6

1:50
[o] 1Ki 2:28

1:52
[p] 1Sa 14:45; 2Sa 14:11

1:39 The sacred anointing oil was used to anoint Israel's kings and high priests, as well as to dedicate certain objects to God. The sacred tent where the oil was kept was probably the tent David set up to shelter the ark of the covenant (2 Samuel 6:17). It was not the tabernacle Moses carried in the desert; that tabernacle was still at Gibeon (see the note on 1 Samuel 7:1 for more details). The recipe and uses for the sacred oil are found in Exodus 30:22–33. For more on anointing, see the notes on 1 Samuel 10:1 and 16:13.

1:49, 50 Sometimes it takes getting caught before someone is willing to give up his scheme. When Adonijah learned that his plans were doomed to fail, he ran in panic to the altar, the place of God's mercy and forgiveness. He went there, however, *after* his plans for treason were exposed. If Adonijah had first considered what God wanted, he might have avoided trouble. Don't wait until you have made a mess of your life before you run to God. Seek God's guidance *before* you act.

1:49–51 Both Adonijah and his commander, Joab, thought they would be safe by clutching the horns (or corner posts) of the sacred altar of burnt offering in the tabernacle court. They hoped to place themselves under God's protection. Solomon granted Adonijah a reprieve, but later he had Joab killed right at the altar (2:28–34). This punishment was appropriate justice for a cold-blooded murderer such as Joab (Exodus 21:14).

1:52, 53 While Adonijah feared for his life and expected the severest punishment, Solomon simply dismissed his brother and sent him home. As a new king, Solomon had the power to kill his rivals, something Adonijah would have done had his conspiracy succeeded. But Solomon acted as if he had nothing to prove, thus demonstrating his authority and power. Sometimes forgiving a personal attack shows more strength than lashing out in revenge. Trying to prove one's power and authority often proves only one's fear and self-doubt. Only after Adonijah made another attempt to secure royal power was Solomon forced to have him executed (2:13–25).

2:1 [a]Ge 47:29; Dt 31:14
2:2 [b]Jos 23:14
[c]Dt 31:7, 23; Jos 1:6
2:3 [d]Dt 17:14-20; Jos 1:7
[e]1Ch 22:13
2:4 [f]2Sa 7:13, 25; 1Ki 8:25
[g]2Ki 20:3; Ps 132:12
2:5 [h]2Sa 2:18; 18:5, 12, 14
[i]2Sa 3:27
[j]2Sa 20:10

David's Charge to Solomon

2 When the time drew near for David to die,[a] he gave a charge to Solomon his
son.
2"I am about to go the way of all the earth,"[b] he said. "So be strong,[c] show
yourself a man, 3and observe[d] what the LORD your God requires: Walk in his ways,
and keep his decrees and commands, his laws and requirements, as written in the Law
of Moses, so that you may prosper[e] in all you do and wherever you go, 4and that
the LORD may keep his promise[f] to me: 'If your descendants watch how they live,
and if they walk faithfully[g] before me with all their heart and soul, you will never
fail to have a man on the throne of Israel.'
5"Now you yourself know what Joab[h] son of Zeruiah did to me—what he did to
the two commanders of Israel's armies, Abner[i] son of Ner and Amasa[j] son of Jether.
He killed them, shedding their blood in peacetime as if in battle, and with that blood

Who joined Adonijah's conspiracy and who remained loyal to David? Contrast the fate of those who rebelled and those who remained loyal to David, God's appointed leader. Adonijah, the leader of the conspiracy, met a violent death (2:25). Those who rebel against God's leaders rebel against God.

Joined Adonijah

JOAB (1:7)
Brilliant military general and commander of David's army. He continually demonstrated his belief that cold-blooded murder was as acceptable as a fairly fought battle. Solomon later had him executed.

ABIATHAR (1:7)
One of two high priests under David. He was a son of Ahimelech who had helped David, and David promised to protect him. Abiathar repaid David with his treachery. Solomon later had him banished, fulfilling the prophecy that Eli's priestly line would end (1 Samuel 2:31).

JONATHAN (1:42)
Abiathar's son. He helped David stop Absalom's rebellion (2 Samuel 17:17–22), but supported this rebellion by another of David's sons.

CHARIOTEERS (1:5)
Hired by Adonijah, apparently more loyal to money than to their king.

50 RUNNERS (1:5)
Recruited to give Adonijah a "royal" appearance.

Remained with David

ZADOK (1:8)
The other high priest under David. His loyalty gave him the privilege of crowning Solomon. He became the sole high priest under King Solomon.

BENAIAH (1:8)
Distinguished himself as a great warrior. Commanded a division of David's army—over 24,000 men. One of the Thirty, he was also placed in charge of David's bodyguard. Solomon later made him chief commander of the army.

NATHAN (1:8)
God's prominent prophet during David's reign. The Bible says he wrote a history of David and Solomon.

SHIMEI (1:8)
This man was probably the Shimei who was rewarded by Solomon and appointed district governor in Benjamin (4:18). (He was not the same person who cursed David at Bahurim and brought on his own death under Solomon.)

REI (1:8)
Only mentioned here. Possibly he was an army officer. The word means "and his friends".

MIGHTY MEN (1:8, 10)
David's army was highly organised with several different divisions of troops. It is enough to know that many of his leaders remained true to their king.

2:3, 4 David stressed to Solomon the need to make God and his laws the centre of personal life and government in order to preserve the kingdom, as God had promised to do (2 Samuel 7). This promise from God had two parts. One part was conditional and depended upon the kings' actions. The other part was unconditional.

God's conditional promise was that David and his descendants would remain in office as kings *only* when they honoured and obeyed him. When David's descendants failed to do this, they lost the throne (2 Kings 25). God's unconditional promise was that David's line would go on for ever. This was fulfilled in the birth of Jesus Christ, a descendant of David who was also the eternal Son of God (Romans 1:3, 4). David, whose life exemplified obedience, gave well-seasoned advice to his son, the next king. It would be up to Solomon to follow it.

2:5–7 Joab epitomises those who are ruthless in accomplishing their goals. His strength was his only code, and winning the battle his only law. He wanted to get power for himself and protect it. In contrast, Barzillai stands for those who are loyal to God and live by his standards. When offered glory, for example, he unselfishly asked that it be given to his son. Is your leadership self-serving or God-serving?

2:5–9 David had some harsh advice for Solomon concerning his enemies. This advice was designed to help the young king establish and secure his throne, and it was directed only towards blatant enemies—those who opposed God by opposing God's appointed king. Legally, David was asking Solomon to give his enemies the punishment they deserved. It was against both civil law and God's laws for Shimei to curse a king (Exodus 22:28).

stained the belt round his waist and the sandals on his feet. 6 Deal with him according
to your wisdom,[k] but do not let his grey head go down to the grave[a] in peace.
7 "But show kindness to the sons of Barzillai[l] of Gilead and let them be among
those who eat at your table.[m] They stood by me when I fled from your brother
Absalom.
8 "And remember, you have with you Shimei[n] son of Gera, the Benjamite from
Bahurim, who called down bitter curses on me the day I went to Mahanaim. When
he came down to meet me at the Jordan, I swore[o] to him by the LORD: 'I will not
put you to death by the sword.' 9 But now, do not consider him innocent. You are a
man of wisdom;[p] you will know what to do to him. Bring his grey head down to the
grave in blood."
10 Then David rested with his fathers and was buried[q] in the City of David.[r] 11 He
had reigned[s] for forty years over Israel—seven years in Hebron and thirty-three in
Jerusalem. 12 So Solomon sat on the throne[t] of his father David, and his rule was
firmly established.[u]

Solomon's Throne Established

13 Now Adonijah, the son of Haggith, went to Bathsheba, Solomon's mother.
Bathsheba asked him, "Do you come peacefully?"[v]
He answered, "Yes, peacefully." 14 Then he added, "I have something to say to
you."
"You may say it," she replied.
15 "As you know," he said, "the kingdom was mine. All Israel looked to me as their
king. But things changed, and the kingdom has gone to my brother; for it has come
to him from the LORD. 16 Now I have one request to make of you. Do not refuse me."
"You may make it," she said.
17 So he continued, "Please ask King Solomon—he will not refuse you—to give
me Abishag[w] the Shunammite as my wife."
18 "Very well," Bathsheba replied, "I will speak to the king for you."
19 When Bathsheba went to King Solomon to speak to him for Adonijah, the king
stood up to meet her, bowed down to her and sat down on his throne. He had a throne
brought for the king's mother,[x] and she sat down at his right hand.[y]
20 "I have one small request to make of you," she said. "Do not refuse me."
The king replied, "Make it, my mother; I will not refuse you."
21 So she said, "Let Abishag[z] the Shunammite be given in marriage to your brother
Adonijah."
22 King Solomon answered his mother, "Why do you request Abishag[a] the Shunammite for Adonijah? You might as well request the kingdom for him—after all,
he is my older brother[b]—yes, for him and for Abiathar the priest and Joab son of
Zeruiah!"
23 Then King Solomon swore by the LORD: "May God deal with me, be it ever so
severely,[c] if Adonijah does not pay with his life for this request! 24 And now, as surely
as the LORD lives—he who has established me securely on the throne of my father
David and has founded a dynasty for me as he promised[d]—Adonijah shall be put
to death today!" 25 So King Solomon gave orders to Benaiah[e] son of Jehoiada, and
he struck down Adonijah and he died.
26 To Abiathar[f] the priest the king said, "Go back to your fields in Anathoth.[g] You

2:6 [k]ver 9
2:7 [l]2Sa 17:27; 19:31-39 [m]2Sa 9:7
2:8 [n]2Sa 16:5-13 [o]2Sa 19:18-23
2:9 [p]ver 6
2:10 [q]Ac 2:29; 13:36 [r]2Sa 5:7
2:11 [s]2Sa 5:4, 5
2:12 [t]1Ch 29:23 [u]2Ch 1:1
2:13 [v]1Sa 16:4
2:17 [w]1Ki 1:3
2:19 [x]1Ki 15:13 [y]Ps 45:9
2:21 [z]1Ki 1:3
2:22 [a]2Sa 12:8; 1Ki 1:3 [b]1Ch 3:2
2:23 [c]Ru 1:17
2:24 [d]2Sa 7:11; 1Ch 22:10
2:25 [e]2Sa 8:18
2:26 [f]1Sa 22:20 [g]Jos 21:18

[a] *6* Hebrew *Sheol*; also in verse 9

2:10 David died at about the age of 70 (2 Samuel 5:4, 5). See David's Profile in 1 Samuel 17 for more on his life.

2:15–22 This was not a case of thwarted love, although Adonijah probably hoped Bathsheba would think so. Although she was still a virgin, Abishag was considered part of David's harem. Adonijah wanted Abishag because possessing the king's harem was equivalent to claiming the throne. Absalom had done the same thing in his rebellion against David (2 Samuel 16:20–23). Solomon well understood what Adonijah was trying to do.

2:26, 27 As a young man, Abiathar was the only one to escape when King Saul massacred all the priests in the city of Nob (1 Samuel 22:11–23). Abiathar then became the high priest under David and remained loyal to David throughout his reign. When he supported Adonijah's wrongful claim to the throne after David's death (1:7), Solomon forced him to give up the priesthood, fulfilling the prophecy of 1 Samuel 2:27–36 that Eli's descendants would not continue to serve as priests.

deserve to die, but I will not put you to death now, because you carried the ark[h] of
the Sovereign LORD before my father David and shared all my father's hardships."[i]
27So Solomon removed Abiathar from the priesthood of the LORD, fulfilling[j] the
word the LORD had spoken at Shiloh about the house of Eli.
28When the news reached Joab, who had conspired with Adonijah though not with
Absalom, he fled to the tent of the LORD and took hold of the horns[k] of the altar.
29King Solomon was told that Joab had fled to the tent of the LORD and was beside
the altar. Then Solomon ordered Benaiah[l] son of Jehoiada, "Go, strike him down!"
30So Benaiah entered the tent of the LORD and said to Joab, "The king says, 'Come
out![m]' "
But he answered, "No, I will die here."
Benaiah reported to the king, "This is how Joab answered me."
31Then the king commanded Benaiah, "Do as he says. Strike him down and bury
him, and so clear me and my father's house of the guilt of the innocent blood[n] that
Joab shed. 32The LORD will repay[o] him for the blood he shed,[p] because without the
knowledge of my father David he attacked two men and killed them with the sword.
Both of them—Abner son of Ner, commander of Israel's army, and Amasa[q] son of
Jether, commander of Judah's army—were better[r] men and more upright than he.
33May the guilt of their blood rest on the head of Joab and his descendants for ever.
But on David and his descendants, his house and his throne, may there be the LORD's
peace for ever."
34So Benaiah son of Jehoiada went up and struck down Joab and killed him, and
he was buried on his own land**b** in the desert. 35The king put Benaiah[s] son of
Jehoiada over the army in Joab's position and replaced Abiathar with Zadok[t] the
priest.
36Then the king sent for Shimei[u] and said to him, "Build yourself a house in
Jerusalem and live there, but do not go anywhere else. 37The day you leave and cross
the Kidron Valley,[v] you can be sure you will die; your blood will be on your own
head."[w]
38Shimei answered the king, "What you say is good. Your servant will do as my
lord the king has said." And Shimei stayed in Jerusalem for a long time.
39But three years later, two of Shimei's slaves ran off to Achish[x] son of Maacah,
king of Gath, and Shimei was told, "Your slaves are in Gath." 40At this, he saddled
his donkey and went to Achish at Gath in search of his slaves. So Shimei went away
and brought the slaves back from Gath.
41When Solomon was told that Shimei had gone from Jerusalem to Gath and had
returned, 42the king summoned Shimei and said to him, "Did I not make you swear
by the LORD and warn you, 'On the day you leave to go anywhere else, you can be
sure you will die'? At that time you said to me, 'What you say is good. I will obey.'
43Why then did you not keep your oath to the LORD and obey the command I gave
you?"
44The king also said to Shimei, "You know in your heart all the wrong[y] you did
to my father David. Now the LORD will repay you for your wrongdoing. 45But King
Solomon will be blessed, and David's throne will remain secure[z] before the LORD
for ever."

b *34* Or *buried in his tomb*

2:26 [h]2Sa 15:24 [i]1Sa 23:6
2:27 [j]1Sa 2:27-36
2:28 [k]1Ki 1:7, 50
2:29 [l]ver 25
2:30 [m]Ex 21:14
2:31 [n]Nu 35:33; Dt 19:13; 21:8-9
2:32 [o]Jdg 9:57; Ps 7:16 [p]Jdg 9:24 [q]2Sa 3:27; 20:10 [r]2Ch 21:13
2:35 [s]1Ki 4:4 [t]ver 27; 1Ch 29:22
2:36 [u]ver 8; 2Sa 16:5
2:37 [v]2Sa 15:23 [w]Lev 20:9; Jos 2:19; 2Sa 1:16
2:39 [x]1Sa 27:2
2:44 [y]1Sa 25:39; 2Sa 16:5-13; Eze 17:19
2:45 [z]2Sa 7:13; Pr 25:5

2:31 Joab had spent his life trying to defend his position as David's commander. Twice David tried to replace him, and both times Joab treacherously killed his rivals before they could assume command (2 Samuel 3:17–30; 19:13; 20:4–10). Because Joab was in his service, David was ultimately responsible for these senseless deaths. But for political and military reasons (see the note on 2 Samuel 3:39), David decided not to publicly punish Joab. Instead he put a curse on Joab and his family (2 Samuel 3:29). Solomon, in punishing Joab, was publicly declaring that David was not part of Joab's crimes, thus removing the guilt from David and placing it on Joab where it belonged.

2:35 Abiathar the high priest and Joab the army commander were key men in David's kingdom. But when they conspired against Solomon, they were replaced with Zadok and Benaiah. Zadok, a descendant of Aaron, had been a prominent priest during David's reign, and he was also loyal to Solomon after David's death. He was put in charge of the ark of the covenant (2 Samuel 15:24ff). His descendants were in charge of the temple until its destruction. At one time, Benaiah was one of David's mighty men (2 Samuel 23:20–23) and the captain of David's bodyguard.

46 Then the king gave the order to Benaiah son of Jehoiada, and he went out and
struck Shimei down and killed him.
The kingdom was now firmly established[a] in Solomon's hands.

2. Solomon's wisdom

Solomon Asks for Wisdom

3 Solomon made an alliance with Pharaoh king of Egypt and married[a] his daughter.[b] He brought her to the City of David[c] until he finished building his palace[d]
and the temple of the LORD, and the wall around Jerusalem. 2 The people, however,
were still sacrificing at the high places,[e] because a temple had not yet been built for
the Name of the LORD. 3 Solomon showed his love[f] for the LORD by walking
according to the statutes[g] of his father David, except that he offered sacrifices and
burned incense on the high places.
4 The king went to Gibeon[h] to offer sacrifices, for that was the most important high
place, and Solomon offered a thousand burnt offerings on that altar. 5 At Gibeon the
LORD appeared[i] to Solomon during the night in a dream,[j] and God said, "Ask for
whatever you want me to give you."
6 Solomon answered, "You have shown great kindness to your servant, my father
David, because he was faithful[k] to you and righteous and upright in heart. You have
continued this great kindness to him and have given him a son[l] to sit on his throne
this very day.
7 "Now, O LORD my God, you have made your servant king in place of my father
David. But I am only a little child[m] and do not know how to carry out my duties.
8 Your servant is here among the people you have chosen,[n] a great people, too
numerous to count or number.[o] 9 So give your servant a discerning[p] heart to govern
your people and to distinguish[q] between right and wrong. For who is able[r] to govern
this great people of yours?"
10 The Lord was pleased that Solomon had asked for this. 11 So God said to him,
"Since you have asked[s] for this and not for long life or wealth for yourself, nor have
asked for the death of your enemies but for discernment in administering justice, 12 I
will do what you have asked.[t] I will give you a wise[u] and discerning heart, so that
there will never have been anyone like you, nor will there ever be. 13 Moreover, I will

2:46 [a] ver 12; 2Ch 1:1
3:1 [a] 1Ki 7:8 [b] 1Ki 9:24 [c] 2Sa 5:7 [d] 1Ki 7:1; 9:15, 19
3:2 [e] Lev 17:3-5; Dt 12:2, 4-5; 1Ki 22:43
3:3 [f] Dt 6:5; Ps 31:23; 1Co 8:3 [g] 1Ki 2:3; 9:4; 11:4, 6, 38
3:4 [h] 1Ch 16:39
3:5 [i] 1Ki 9:2 [j] Nu 12:6; Mt 1:20
3:6 [k] 1Ki 2:4; 9:4 [l] 1Ki 1:48
3:7 [m] Nu 27:17; 1Ch 29:1
3:8 [n] Dt 7:6 [o] Ge 15:5
3:9 [p] 2Sa 14:17; Jas 1:5 [q] Pr 2:3-9; Heb 5:14 [r] Ps 72:1-2
3:11 [s] Jas 4:3
3:12 [t] 1Jn 5:14-15 [u] 1Ki 4:29, 30, 31; 5:12; 10:23; Ecc 1:16

2:46 Solomon ordered the executions of Adonijah, Joab, and Shimei, forced Abiathar out as priest, and then appointed new men to take their places. He did these things swiftly, securing his grip on the kingdom. By executing justice and tying up loose ends that could affect the future stability of his kingdom, Solomon was promoting peace, not bloodshed. He was a man of peace in two ways: he did not go to war, and he put an end to internal rebellion.

3:1 Marriage between royal families was a common practice in the ancient Near East because it secured peace. Although Solomon's marital alliances built friendships with surrounding nations, they were also the beginning of his downfall. These relationships became inroads for pagan ideas and practices. Solomon's foreign wives brought their gods to Jerusalem and eventually lured him into idolatry (11:1–6).

It is easy to minimise religious differences in order to encourage the development of a friendship, but seemingly small differences can have an enormous impact upon a relationship. God gives us standards to follow for all our relationships, including marriage. If we follow God's will, we will not be lured away from our true focus.

3:2, 3 God's laws said that the Israelites could make sacrifices only in specified places (Deuteronomy 12:13, 14). This was to prevent the people from instituting their own methods of worship and allowing pagan practices to creep into their worship. But many Israelites, including Solomon, made sacrifices in the surrounding hills. Solomon loved God, but this act was sin. It took the offerings out of the watchful care of priests and ministers loyal to God and opened the way for false teaching to be tied to these sacrifices. God appeared to Solomon to grant him wisdom, but at night, not during the sacrifice. God honoured his prayer but did not condone the sacrifice.

3:6–9 When given a chance to have anything in the world, Solomon asked for wisdom – "a discerning heart" – in order to lead well and to make right decisions. We can ask God for this same wisdom (James 1:5). Notice that Solomon asked for discernment to carry out his job; he did not ask God to do the job for him. We should not ask God to do *for* us what he wants to do *through* us. Instead we should ask God to give us the wisdom to know what to do and the courage to follow through on it.

3:11–14 Solomon asked for wisdom ("discernment"), not wealth, but God gave him riches and long life as well. While God does not promise riches to those who follow him, he gives us what we need if we put his kingdom, his interests, and his principles first (Matthew 6:31–33). Setting your sights on riches will only leave you dissatisfied because even if you get the riches you crave, you will still want something more. But if you put God and his work first, he will satisfy your deepest needs.

3:12 Solomon received "a wise and discerning heart" from God, but it was up to Solomon to apply that wisdom to all areas of his life. Solomon was obviously wise in governing the nation, but he was foolish in running his household. Wisdom is both the ability to discern what is best and the strength of character to act upon that knowledge. While Solomon remained wise all his life, he did not always act upon his wisdom (11:6).

3:13–18 Solomon's settlement of this dispute was a classic example of his wisdom. This wise ruling was verification that God had answered Solomon's prayer and given him a discerning heart. We

3:13
[v]Mt 6:33
[w]1Ki 4:21-24
[x]1Ki 10:23
3:14
[y]Pr 3:1-2, 16
[z]Ps 61:6; 91:16
3:15
[a]Ge 41:7
[b]1Ki 8:65
[c]Mk 6:21
[d]Est 1:3, 9

give you what you have not[v] asked for—both riches and honour[w]—so that in your
lifetime you will have no equal[x] among kings. 14And if you walk[y] in my ways and
obey my statutes and commands as David your father did, I will give you a long
life."[z] 15Then Solomon awoke[a]—and he realised it had been a dream.
He returned to Jerusalem, stood before the ark of the Lord's covenant and sacrificed
burnt offerings[b] and fellowship offerings.[a][c] Then he gave a feast[d] for all his court.

a *15* Traditionally *peace offerings*

SOLOMON

Wisdom is only effective when it is put into action. Early in his life, Solomon had the sense to recognise his need for wisdom. But by the time Solomon asked for wisdom to rule his kingdom, he had already started a habit that would make his wisdom ineffective for his own life—he sealed a pact with Egypt by marrying Pharaoh's daughter. She was the first of hundreds of wives married for political reasons. In doing this, Solomon went against not only his father's last words, but also God's direct commands. His action reminds us how easy it is to know what is right and yet not do it.

It is clear that God's gift of wisdom to Solomon did not mean that he couldn't make mistakes. He had been given great possibilities as the king of God's chosen people, but with them came great responsibilities; unfortunately, he tended to pursue the former and neglect the latter. While becoming famous as the builder of the temple and the palace, he became infamous as a leader who excessively taxed and worked his people. Visitors from distant lands came to admire this wise king, while his own people were gradually alienated from him.

Little is mentioned in the Bible about the last decade of Solomon's reign. Ecclesiastes probably records his last reflections on life. In that book we find a man proving through bitter experience that finding meaning in life apart from God is a vain pursuit. Security and contentment are found only in a personal relationship with God. The contentment we find in the opportunities and successes of this life is temporary. The more we expect our successes to be permanent, the more quickly they are gone. Be sure to balance your pursuit of life's possibilities with reliable fulfilment of your responsibilities.

Strengths and accomplishments:
- Third king of Israel, David's chosen heir
- The wisest man who ever lived
- Author of Ecclesiastes and Song of Songs, as well as many of the proverbs and a couple of the psalms
- Built God's temple in Jerusalem
- Diplomat, trader, collector, patron of the arts

Weaknesses and mistakes:
- Sealed many foreign agreements by marrying pagan women
- Allowed his wives to affect his loyalty to God
- Excessively taxed his people and drafted them into a labour and military force

Lessons from his life:
- Effective leadership can be nullified by an ineffective personal life
- Solomon failed to obey God, but did not learn the lesson of repentance until late in life
- Knowing what actions are required of us means little without the will to do those actions

Vital statistics:
- Where: Jerusalem
- Occupation: King of Israel
- Relatives: Father: David. Mother: Bathsheba. Brothers: Absalom, Adonijah. Sister: Tamar. Son: Rehoboam

Key verse:
"Was it not because of marriages like these that Solomon king of Israel sinned? Among the many nations there was no king like him. He was loved by his God, and God made him king over all Israel, but even he was led into sin by foreign women" (Nehemiah 13:26).

Solomon's story is told in 2 Samuel 12:24—1 Kings 11:43. He is also mentioned in 1 Chronicles 28, 29; 2 Chronicles 1—10; Nehemiah 13:26; Psalm 72; and Matthew 6:29; 12:42.

---

have God's wisdom available to us as we pray and request it. But, like Solomon, we must put it into action. Applying wisdom to life demonstrates our discernment.

A Wise Ruling

16Now two prostitutes came to the king and stood before him. 17One of them said,
"My lord, this woman and I live in the same house. I had a baby while she was there
with me. 18The third day after my child was born, this woman also had a baby. We
were alone; there was no-one in the house but the two of us.
19"During the night this woman's son died because she lay on him. 20So she got
up in the middle of the night and took my son from my side while I your servant was
asleep. She put him by her breast and put her dead son by my breast. 21The next
morning, I got up to nurse my son — and he was dead! But when I looked at him closely
in the morning light, I saw that it wasn't the son I had borne."
22The other woman said, "No! The living one is my son; the dead one is yours."
But the first one insisted, "No! The dead one is yours; the living one is mine." And
so they argued before the king.
23The king said, "This one says, 'My son is alive and your son is dead,' while that
one says, 'No! Your son is dead and mine is alive.' "
24Then the king said, "Bring me a sword." So they brought a sword for the king.
25He then gave an order: "Cut the living child in two and give half to one and half
to the other."
26The woman whose son was alive was filled with compassion[e] for her son and
said to the king, "Please, my lord, give her the living baby! Don't kill him!"
But the other said, "Neither I nor you shall have him. Cut him in two!"
27Then the king gave his ruling: "Give the living baby to the first woman. Do not
kill him; she is his mother."
28When all Israel heard the verdict the king had given, they held the king in awe,
because they saw that he had wisdom[f] from God to administer justice.

Solomon's Officials and Governors

4 So King Solomon ruled over all Israel. 2And these were his chief officials:

Azariah[a] son of Zadok — the priest;
3Elihoreph and Ahijah, sons of Shisha — secretaries;
Jehoshaphat[b] son of Ahilud — recorder;
4Benaiah[c] son of Jehoiada — commander-in-chief;
Zadok[d] and Abiathar — priests;
5Azariah son of Nathan — in charge of the district officers;
Zabud son of Nathan — a priest and personal adviser to the king;
6Ahishar — in charge of the palace;
Adoniram son of Abda — in charge of forced labour.

7Solomon also had twelve district governors over all Israel, who supplied provisions
for the king and the royal household. Each one had to provide supplies for one month
in the year. 8These are their names:

Ben-Hur — in the hill country[e] of Ephraim;
9Ben-Deker — in Makaz, Shaalbim,[f] Beth Shemesh[g] and Elon Bethhanan;
10Ben-Hesed — in Arubboth (Socoh[h] and all the land of Hepher[i] were his);
11Ben-Abinadab — in Naphoth Dor[a][j] (he was married to Taphath daughter of Solomon);
12Baana son of Ahilud — in Taanach and Megiddo, and in all of Beth Shan[k] next to Zarethan[l] below Jezreel, from Beth Shan to Abel Meholah[m] across to Jokmeam;[n]
13Ben-Geber — in Ramoth Gilead (the settlements of Jair[o] son of Manasseh in

a 11 *Or in the heights of Dor*

3:26 [e]Ge 43:30; Isa 49:15; Jer 31:20; Hos 11:8
3:28 [f]ver 9, 11-12; Col 2:3
4:2 [a]1Ch 6:10
4:3 [b]2Sa 8:16
4:4 [c]1Ki 2:35 [d]1Ki 2:27
4:8 [e]Jos 24:33
4:9 [f]Jdg 1:35 [g]Jos 21:16
4:10 [h]Jos 15:35 [i]Jos 12:17
4:11 [j]Jos 11:2
4:12 [k]Jos 17:11; Jdg 5:19 [l]Jos 3:16 [m]1Ki 19:16 [n]1Ch 6:68
4:13 [o]Nu 32:41

4:1ff Solomon was well organised, with 11 chief officials with specific responsibilities, 12 district governors, and a manager in charge of the district officers. Each person had a specific responsibility or territory to manage. This organisation was essential to maintain the government's effectiveness: it was a wise move by a wise man. It is good stewardship to be well organised. Good organisation helps people work together in harmony and ensures that the desired goal will be reached.

Gilead were his, as well as the district of Argob in Bashan and its sixty large
walled cities[p] with bronze gate bars);
14 Ahinadab son of Iddo — in Mahanaim;[q]
15 Ahimaaz[r] — in Naphtali (he had married Basemath daughter of Solomon);
16 Baana son of Hushai[s] — in Asher and in Aloth;
17 Jehoshaphat son of Paruah — in Issachar;
18 Shimei[t] son of Ela — in Benjamin;
19 Geber son of Uri — in Gilead (the country of Sihon king of the Amorites and
the country of Og[u] king of Bashan). He was the only governor over the
district.

Solomon's Daily Provisions

20 The people of Judah and Israel were as numerous as the sand[v] on the seashore;
they ate, they drank and they were happy. 21 And Solomon ruled[w] over all the
kingdoms from the River[b][x] to the land of the Philistines, as far as the border of
Egypt.[y] These countries brought tribute[z] and were Solomon's subjects all his life.
22 Solomon's daily provisions were thirty cors[c] of fine flour and sixty cors[d] of
meal, 23 ten head of stall-fed cattle, twenty of pasture-fed cattle and a hundred sheep
and goats, as well as deer, gazelles, roebucks and choice fowl. 24 For he ruled over
all the kingdoms west of the River, from Tiphsah[a] to Gaza, and had peace[b] on all
sides. 25 During Solomon's lifetime Judah and Israel, from Dan to Beersheba,[c] lived
in safety,[d] each man under his own vine and fig-tree.[e]
26 Solomon had four[e] thousand stalls for chariot horses,[f] and twelve thousand
horses.[f]
27 The district officers,[g] each in his month, supplied provisions for King Solomon
and all who came to the king's table. They saw to it that nothing was lacking. 28 They
also brought to the proper place their quotas of barley and straw for the chariot horses
and the other horses.

Solomon's Wisdom

29 God gave Solomon wisdom[h] and very great insight, and a breadth of understanding as measureless as the sand on the seashore. 30 Solomon's wisdom was greater than
the wisdom of all the men of the East,[i] and greater than all the wisdom of Egypt.[j]
31 He was wiser[k] than any other man, including Ethan the Ezrahite — wiser than
Heman, Calcol and Darda, the sons of Mahol. And his fame spread to all the
surrounding nations. 32 He spoke three thousand proverbs[l] and his songs[m] numbered
a thousand and five. 33 He described plant life, from the cedar of Lebanon to the hyssop

4:13 [p] Dt 3:4
4:14 [q] Jos 13:26
4:15 [r] 2Sa 15:27
4:16 [s] 2Sa 15:32
4:18 [t] 1Ki 1:8
4:19 [u] Dt 3:8-10
4:20 [v] Ge 22:17; 32:12; 1Ki 3:8
4:21 [w] 2Ch 9:26; Ps 72:11 [x] Jos 1:4; Ps 72:8 [y] Ge 15:18 [z] Ps 68:29
4:24 [a] Ps 72:11 [b] 1Ch 22:9
4:25 [c] Jdg 20:1 [d] Jer 23:6 [e] Mic 4:4; Zec 3:10
4:26 [f] 1Ki 10:26; 2Ch 1:14
4:27 [g] ver 7
4:29 [h] 1Ki 3:12
4:30 [i] Ge 25:6 [j] Ac 7:22
4:31 [k] 1Ki 3:12; 1Ch 2:6; 6:33; 15:19; Ps 89 Title
4:32 [l] Pr 1:1; Ecc 12:9 [m] SS 1:1

b *21* That is, the Euphrates; also in verse 24 **c** *22* That is, probably about 180 bushels (about 6.6 kilolitres) **d** *22* That is, probably about 365 bushels (about 13.2 kilolitres) **e** *26* Some Septuagint manuscripts (see also 2 Chron. 9:25); Hebrew *forty* **f** *26* Or *charioteers*

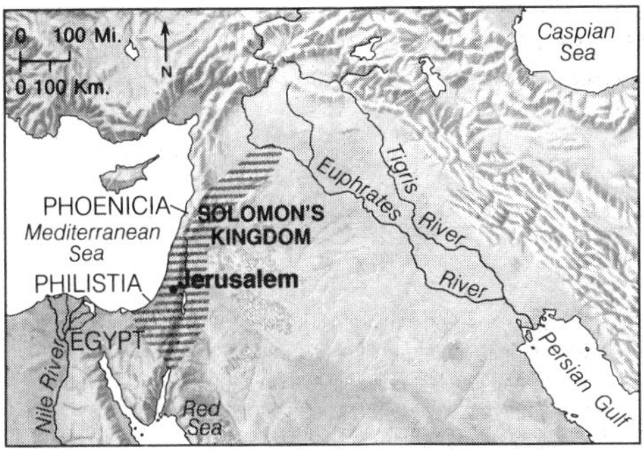

SOLOMON'S KINGDOM Solomon's kingdom spread from the Euphrates River in the north to the borders of Egypt. The entire land was at peace under his rule.

4:20–25 Throughout most of his reign, Solomon applied his wisdom well because he sought God. The fruits of this wisdom were peace, security, and prosperity for the nation. Solomon's era is often looked upon as the ideal of what any nation can become when united in trust and in obedience to God.

4:32 The book of Proverbs records many of these 3,000 wise proverbs. Other biblical writings of Solomon include Psalms 72 and 127, and the books of Ecclesiastes and Song of Songs. Solomon's wisdom was known throughout the world.

that grows out of walls. He also taught about animals and birds, reptiles and fish.
34 Men of all nations came to listen to Solomon's wisdom, sent by all the kings[n] of
the world, who had heard of his wisdom.

3. Solomon builds the temple

Preparations for Building the Temple

5 When Hiram[a] king of Tyre heard that Solomon had been anointed king to
succeed his father David, he sent his envoys to Solomon, because he had always
been on friendly terms with David. 2 Solomon sent back this message to Hiram:

> 3 "You know that because of the wars[b] waged against my father David from
> all sides, he could not build a temple for the Name of the LORD his God until
> the LORD put his enemies under his feet. 4 But now the LORD my God has given
> me rest[c] on every side, and there is no adversary or disaster. 5 I intend, therefore,
> to build a temple[d] for the Name of the LORD my God, as the LORD told my father
> David, when he said, 'Your son whom I will put on the throne in your place will
> build the temple for my Name.'[e]
>
> 6 "So give orders that cedars of Lebanon be cut for me. My men will work with
> yours, and I will pay you for your men whatever wages you set. You know that
> we have no-one so skilled in felling timber as the Sidonians."

7 When Hiram heard Solomon's message, he was greatly pleased and said, "Praise
be to the LORD today, for he has given David a wise son to rule over this great nation."
8 So Hiram sent word to Solomon:

> "I have received the message you sent me and will do all you want in providing
> the cedar and pine logs. 9 My men will haul them down from Lebanon to the sea[f],
> and I will float them in rafts by sea to the place you specify. There I will separate
> them and you can take them away. And you are to grant my wish by providing
> food[g] for my royal household."

10 In this way Hiram kept Solomon supplied with all the cedar and pine logs he
wanted, 11 and Solomon gave Hiram twenty thousand cors**a** of wheat as food for his
household, in addition to twenty thousand baths**b,c** of pressed olive oil. Solomon
continued to do this for Hiram year after year. 12 The LORD gave Solomon wisdom,[h]
just as he had promised him. There were peaceful relations between Hiram and
Solomon, and the two of them made a treaty.[i]
13 King Solomon conscripted labourers[j] from all Israel—thirty thousand men.
14 He sent them off to Lebanon in shifts of ten thousand a month, so that they spent
one month in Lebanon and two months at home. Adoniram[k] was in charge of the
forced labour. 15 Solomon had seventy thousand carriers and eighty thousand stonecutters in the hills, 16 as well as thirty-three hundred**d** foremen[l] who supervised the
project and directed the workmen. 17 At the king's command they removed from the
quarry[m] large blocks of quality stone[n] to provide a foundation of dressed stone for
the temple. 18 The craftsmen of Solomon and Hiram and the men of Gebal**e**[o] cut and
prepared the timber and stone for the building of the temple.

a *11* That is, probably about 121,000 bushels (about 4,400 kilolitres) **b** *11* Septuagint (see also 2 Chron. 2:10); Hebrew *twenty cors* **c** *11* That is, about 97,000 gallons (about 440 kilolitres) **d** *16* Hebrew; some Septuagint manuscripts (see also 2 Chron. 2:2, 18) *thirty-six hundred* **e** *18* That is, Byblos

4:34 [n]1Ki 10:1; 2Ch 9:23
5:1 [a]ver 10, 18; 2Sa 5:11; 1Ch 14:1
5:3 [b]1Ch 22:8; 28:3
5:4 [c]1Ki 4:24; 1Ch 22:9
5:5 [d]1Ch 17:12 [e]2Sa 7:13; 1Ch 22:10
5:9 [f]Ezr 3:7 [g]Eze 27:17; Ac 12:20
5:12 [h]1Ki 3:12 [i]Am 1:9
5:13 [j]1Ki 9:15
5:14 [k]1Ki 4:6; 2Ch 10:18
5:16 [l]1Ki 9:23
5:17 [m]1Ki 6:7 [n]1Ch 22:2
5:18 [o]Jos 13:5

5:2, 3 When David offered to build a temple, God said no through the prophet Nathan (2 Samuel 7:1–17). God wanted a peacemaker, not a warrior, to build his house of prayer (1 Chronicles 28:2, 3).

5:13, 14 Solomon drafted three times the number of workers needed for the temple project and then arranged their schedules so they didn't have to be away from home for long periods of time. This showed his concern for the welfare of his workers and the importance he placed on family life. The strength of a nation is in direct proportion to the strength of its families. Solomon wisely recognised that family should always be a top priority. As you structure your own work or arrange the schedules of others, watch for the impact of your plans on families.

5:18 Gebal, also called Byblos, was located north of what is now Beirut, near the cedar forest. These men were Phoenicians, probably skilled as shipbuilders, but employed for this project.

Solomon Builds the Temple

6 In the four hundred and eightieth[a] year after the Israelites had come out of Egypt,
in the fourth year of Solomon's reign over Israel, in the month of Ziv, the second
month, he began to build the temple of the LORD.[a]
2 The temple[b] that King Solomon built for the LORD was sixty cubits long, twenty
wide and thirty high.[b] 3 The portico at the front of the main hall of the temple extended
the width of the temple, that is twenty cubits,[c] and projected ten cubits[d] from the
front of the temple. 4 He made narrow clerestory windows[c] in the temple. 5 Against
the walls of the main hall and inner sanctuary he built a structure around the building,
in which there were side rooms.[d] 6 The lowest floor was five cubits[e] wide, the middle
floor six cubits[f] and the third floor seven.[g] He made offset ledges around the outside
of the temple so that nothing would be inserted into the temple walls.
7 In building the temple, only blocks dressed[e] at the quarry were used, and no
hammer, chisel or any other iron tool[f] was heard at the temple site while it was being
built.
8 The entrance to the lowest[h] floor was on the south side of the temple; a stairway
led up to the middle level and from there to the third. 9 So he built the temple and
completed it, roofing it with beams and cedar[g] planks. 10 And he built the side rooms
all along the temple. The height of each was five cubits, and they were attached to
the temple by beams of cedar.
11 The word of the LORD came to Solomon: 12 "As for this temple you are building,
if you follow my decrees, carry out my regulations and keep all my commands and
obey them, I will fulfil through you the promise[h] I gave to David your father. 13 And
I will live among the Israelites and will not abandon[i] my people Israel."
14 So Solomon built the temple and completed[j] it. 15 He lined its interior walls with
cedar boards, panelling them from the floor of the temple to the ceiling,[k] and covered
the floor of the temple with planks of pine. 16 He partitioned off twenty cubits[i] at the
rear of the temple with cedar boards from floor to ceiling to form within the temple
an inner sanctuary, the Most Holy Place.[l] 17 The main hall in front of this room was
forty cubits[j] long. 18 The inside of the temple was cedar,[m] carved with gourds and
open flowers. Everything was cedar; no stone was to be seen.
19 He prepared the inner sanctuary[n] within the temple to set the ark of the covenant[o] of the LORD there. 20 The inner sanctuary[p] was twenty cubits long, twenty
wide and twenty high.[k] He overlaid the inside with pure gold, and he also overlaid
the altar of cedar. 21 Solomon covered the inside of the temple with pure gold, and
he extended gold chains across the front of the inner sanctuary, which was overlaid
with gold. 22 So he overlaid the whole interior with gold. He also overlaid with gold
the altar that belonged to the inner sanctuary.

a *1* Hebrew; Septuagint *four hundred and fortieth* **b** *2* That is, about 90 feet (about 27 metres) long and 30 feet (about 9 metres) wide and 45 feet (about 13.5 metres) high **c** *3* That is, about 30 feet (about 9 metres) **d** *3* That is, about 15 feet (about 4.5 metres) **e** *6* That is, about 7½ feet (about 2.3 metres); also in verses 10 and 24 **f** *6* That is, about 9 feet (about 2.7 metres) **g** *6* That is, about 10½ feet (about 3.2 metres) **h** *8* Septuagint; Hebrew *middle* **i** *16* That is, about 30 feet (about 9 metres) **j** *17* That is, about 60 feet (about 18 metres) **k** *20* That is, about 30 feet (about 9 metres) long, wide and high

6:1 *a* Ac 7:47
6:2 *b* Eze 41:1
6:4 *c* Eze 40:16; 41:16
6:5 *d* ver 16, 19-21; Eze 41:5-6
6:7 *e* Ex 20:25 *f* Dt 27:5
6:9 *g* ver 14, 38
6:12 *h* 2Sa 7:12-16; 1Ki 2:4; 9:5
6:13 *i* Ex 25:8; Lev 26:11; Dt 31:6; Heb 13:5
6:14 *j* ver 9, 38
6:15 *k* 1Ki 7:7
6:16 *l* Ex 26:33; Lev 16:2; 1Ki 8:6
6:18 *m* 1Ki 7:24; Ps 74:6
6:19 *n* 1Ki 8:6 *o* 1Sa 3:3
6:20 *p* Eze 41:3-4

6:1ff For more information on the purpose of the temple, see the note on 2 Chronicles 5:1ff.

6:3 The portico was like a large porch.

6:4 Clerestory windows were windows near the tops of the walls to help light the centre of the temple.

6:7 In honour of God, the temple in Jerusalem was built without the sound of a hammer or any other tool at the building site. This meant that the stone had to be "dressed" (cut and shaped) miles away at the quarry. The people's honour and respect for God extended to every aspect of constructing this house of worship. This detail is recorded not to teach us how to build a church, but to show us the importance of demonstrating care, concern, honour, and respect for God and his sanctuary.

6:13 This verse summarises the temple's main purpose. God promised that his eternal presence would never leave the temple as long as one condition was met: the Israelites had to obey God's law. Knowing how many laws they had to follow, we may think this condition was difficult. But the Israelites' situation was much like ours today: they were not cut off from God for failing to keep some small subpoint of a law. Forgiveness was amply provided for all their sins, no matter how large or small. As you read the history of the kings, you will see that lawbreaking was the result, not the cause, of estrangement from God. The kings abandoned God in their hearts first and *then* failed to keep his laws. When we close our hearts to God, his power and presence soon leave us.

6:14 The concept of Solomon's temple was more like a palace for God than a place of worship. As a dwelling place for God, it was fitting for it to be ornate and beautiful. It had small inside dimensions because most worshippers gathered outside.

23In the inner sanctuary he made a pair of cherubim[q] of olive wood, each ten
cubits[l] high. 24One wing of the first cherub was five cubits long, and the other wing
five cubits—ten cubits from wing tip to wing tip. 25The second cherub also measured
ten cubits, for the two cherubim were identical in size and shape. 26The height of each
cherub was ten cubits. 27He placed the cherubim[r] inside the innermost room of the
temple, with their wings spread out. The wing of one cherub touched one wall, while
the wing of the other touched the other wall, and their wings touched each other in
the middle of the room. 28He overlaid the cherubim with gold.
29On the walls all round the temple, in both the inner and outer rooms, he carved
cherubim,[s] palm trees and open flowers. 30He also covered the floors of both the
inner and outer rooms of the temple with gold.
31For the entrance of the inner sanctuary he made doors of olive wood with
five-sided jambs. 32And on the two olive wood doors he carved cherubim, palm trees
and open flowers, and overlaid the cherubim and palm trees with beaten gold. 33In
the same way he made four-sided jambs of olive wood for the entrance to the main
hall. 34He also made two pine doors, each having two leaves that turned in sockets.
35He carved cherubim, palm trees and open flowers on them and overlaid them with
gold hammered evenly over the carvings.
36And he built the inner courtyard of three courses[t] of dressed stone and one course
of trimmed cedar beams.
37The foundation of the temple of the LORD was laid in the fourth year, in the month
of Ziv. 38In the eleventh year in the month of Bul, the eighth month, the temple was
finished in all its details according to its specifications.[u] He had spent seven years
building it.

Solomon Builds His Palace

7 It took Solomon thirteen years, however, to complete the construction of his
palace.[a] 2He built the Palace[b] of the Forest of Lebanon[c] a hundred cubits long,
fifty wide and thirty high,[a] with four rows of cedar columns supporting trimmed cedar
beams. 3It was roofed with cedar above the beams that rested on the columns—forty-
five beams, fifteen to a row. 4Its windows were placed high in sets of three, facing
each other. 5All the doorways had rectangular frames; they were in the front part in
sets of three, facing each other.[b]
6He made a colonnade fifty cubits long and thirty wide.[c] In front of it was a portico,
and in front of that were pillars and an overhanging roof.
7He built the throne hall, the Hall of Justice, where he was to judge,[d] and he
covered it with cedar from floor to ceiling.[d][e] 8And the palace in which he was to
live, set farther back, was similar in design. Solomon also made a palace like this hall
for Pharaoh's daughter, whom he had married.[f]
9All these structures, from the outside to the great courtyard and from foundation
to eaves, were made of blocks of high-grade stone cut to size and trimmed with a saw
on their inner and outer faces. 10The foundations were laid with large stones of good
quality, some measuring ten cubits[e] and some eight.[f] 11Above were high-grade
stones, cut to size, and cedar beams. 12The great courtyard was surrounded by a wall
of three courses[g] of dressed stone and one course of trimmed cedar beams, as was
the inner courtyard of the temple of the LORD with its portico.

The Temple's Furnishings

13King Solomon sent to Tyre and brought Huram,[g][h] 14whose mother was a widow
from the tribe of Naphtali and whose father was a man of Tyre and a craftsman in

6:23 [q]Ex 37:1-9
6:27 [r]Ex 25:20; 37:9; 1Ki 8:7; 2Ch 5:8
6:29 [s]ver 32, 35
6:36 [t]1Ki 7:12; Ezr 6:4
6:38 [u]Heb 8:5
7:1 [a]1Ki 9:10; 2Ch 8:1
7:2 [b]2Sa 7:2 [c]1Ki 10:17; 2Ch 9:16
7:7 [d]Ps 122:5; Pr 20:8 [e]1Ki 6:15
7:8 [f]1Ki 3:1; 2Ch 8:11
7:12 [g]1Ki 6:36
7:13 [h]2Ch 2:13

[l] *23* That is, about 15 feet (about 4.5 metres) **a** *2* That is, about 150 feet (about 46 metres) long, 75 feet (about 23 metres) wide and 45 feet (about 13.5 metres) high **b** *5* The meaning of the Hebrew for this verse is uncertain. **c** *6* That is, about 75 feet (about 23 metres) long and 45 feet (about 13.5 metres) wide **d** *7* Vulgate and Syriac; Hebrew *floor* **e** *10* That is, about 15 feet (about 4.5 metres) **f** *10* That is, about 12 feet (about 3.7 metres) **g** *13* Hebrew *Hiram*, a variant of *Huram*; also in verses 40 and 45

7:1 That Solomon took longer to build his palace than to build the temple is not a comment on his priorities. His palace project took longer because it was part of a huge civic building project including barracks and housing for his harem.

bronze. Huram was highly skilled[i] and experienced in all kinds of bronze work. He
came to King Solomon and did all[j] the work assigned to him.
15He cast two bronze pillars,[k] each eighteen cubits high and twelve cubits round,[h]
by line. 16He also made two capitals[l] of cast bronze to set on the tops of the pillars;
each capital was five cubits[i] high. 17A network of interwoven chains festooned the
capitals on top of the pillars, seven for each capital. 18He made pomegranates in two
rows[j] encircling each network to decorate the capitals on top of the pillars.[k] He did
the same for each capital. 19The capitals on top of the pillars in the portico were in
the shape of lilies, four cubits[l] high. 20On the capitals of both pillars, above the
bowl-shaped part next to the network, were the two hundred pomegranates[m] in rows
all around. 21He erected the pillars at the portico of the temple. The pillar to the south
he named Jakin[m] and the one to the north Boaz.[n][n] 22The capitals on top were in
the shape of lilies. And so the work on the pillars was completed.
23He made the Sea[o] of cast metal, circular in shape, measuring ten cubits[o] from
rim to rim and five cubits high. It took a line of thirty cubits[p] to measure round it.
24Below the rim, gourds encircled it—ten to a cubit. The gourds were cast in two rows
in one piece with the Sea.
25The Sea stood on twelve bulls,[p] three facing north, three facing west, three facing
south and three facing east. The Sea rested on top of them, and their hindquarters were
towards the centre. 26It was a handbreadth[q] in thickness, and its rim was like the rim
of a cup, like a lily blossom. It held two thousand baths.[r]
27He also made ten movable stands[q] of bronze; each was four cubits long, four
wide and three high.[s] 28This is how the stands were made: They had side panels
attached to uprights. 29On the panels between the uprights were lions, bulls and
cherubim—and on the uprights as well. Above and below the lions and bulls were
wreaths of hammered work. 30Each stand[r] had four bronze wheels with bronze axles,
and each had a basin resting on four supports, cast with wreaths on each side. 31On
the inside of the stand there was an opening that had a circular frame one cubit[t] deep.
This opening was round, and with its basework it measured a cubit and a half.[u]
Around its opening there was engraving. The panels of the stands were square, not
round. 32The four wheels were under the panels, and the axles of the wheels were
attached to the stand. The diameter of each wheel was a cubit and a half. 33The wheels
were made like chariot wheels; the axles, rims, spokes and hubs were all of cast metal.
34Each stand had four handles, one on each corner, projecting from the stand. 35At
the top of the stand there was a circular band half a cubit[v] deep. The supports and
panels were attached to the top of the stand. 36He engraved cherubim, lions and palm
trees on the surfaces of the supports and on the panels, in every available space, with
wreaths all around. 37This is the way he made the ten stands. They were all cast in
the same moulds and were identical in size and shape.
38He then made ten bronze basins,[s] each holding forty baths[w] and measuring four
cubits across, one basin to go on each of the ten stands. 39He placed five of the stands
on the south side of the temple and five on the north. He placed the Sea on the south

7:14 [i]Ex 31:2-5; 35:31; 36:1; 2Ch 2:14 [j]2Ch 4:11, 16
7:15 [k]2Ki 25:17; 2Ch 3:15; 4:12; 52:17, 21
7:16 [l]2Ki 25:17
7:20 [m]2Ch 3:16; 4:13; Jer 52:23
7:21 [n]1Ki 6:3; 2Ch 3:17
7:23 [o]2Ki 25:13; 1Ch 18:8; Jer 52:17
7:25 [p]2Ch 4:4-5; Jer 52:20
7:27 [q]ver 38; 2Ch 4:14
7:30 [r]2Ki 16:17
7:38 [s]Ex 30:18; 2Ch 4:6

h *15* That is, about 27 feet (about 8.2 metres) high and 18 feet (about 5.5 metres) round **i** *16* That is, about 7½ feet (about 2.3 metres); also in verse 23 **j** *18* Two Hebrew manuscripts and Septuagint; most Hebrew manuscripts *made the pillars, and there were two rows* **k** *18* Many Hebrew manuscripts and Syriac; most Hebrew manuscripts *pomegranates* **l** *19* That is, about 6 feet (about 1.8 metres); also in verse 38 **m** *21* *Jakin* probably means *he establishes.* **n** *21* *Boaz* probably means *in him is strength.* **o** *23* That is, about 15 feet (about 4.5 metres) **p** *23* That is, about 45 feet (about 13.7 metres) **q** *26* That is, about 3 inches (about 8 centimetres) **r** *26* That is, probably about 9,700 gallons (about 44 kilolitres); the Septuagint does not have this sentence. **s** *27* That is, about 6 feet (about 1.8 metres) long and wide and about 4½ feet (about 1.4 metres) high **t** *31* That is, about 1½ feet (about 0.5 metre) **u** *31* That is, about 2¼ feet (about 0.7 metre); also in verse 32 **v** *35* That is, about ¾ foot (about 0.2 metre) **w** *38* That is, about 195 gallons (about 880 litres)

7:14 Huram was an expert craftsman. Solomon chose only the best.

7:23 The "Sea" was an enormous tank. Designed and used for the priests' ceremonial washings, it was placed in the temple court near the altar of burnt offering. There the priests washed themselves before offering sacrifices or entering the temple (Exodus 30:17–21).

7:27–39 These 10 "movable stands" held basins of water. The basins were used for washing the various parts of the animal sacrifices. The basins were movable so they could be used where needed.

side, at the south-east corner of the temple. 40He also made the basins and shovels
and sprinkling bowls.
So Huram finished all the work he had undertaken for King Solomon in the temple
of the LORD:

41the two pillars;
the two bowl-shaped capitals on top of the pillars;
the two sets of network decorating the two bowl-shaped capitals on top of the
pillars;
42the four hundred pomegranates for the two sets of network (two rows of
pomegranates for each network, decorating the bowl-shaped capitals[t] on top
of the pillars);
43the ten stands with their ten basins;
44the Sea and the twelve bulls under it;
45the pots, shovels and sprinkling bowls.[u]

All these objects that Huram made for King Solomon for the temple of the LORD
were of burnished bronze. 46The king had them cast in clay moulds in the plain[v] of
the Jordan between Succoth[w] and Zarethan.[x] 47Solomon left all these things un-
weighed,[y] because there were so many; the weight of the bronze was not determined.
48Solomon also made all the furnishings that were in the LORD's temple:

the golden altar;
the golden table[z] on which was the bread of the Presence;[a]
49the lampstands[b] of pure gold (five on the right and five on the left, in front
of the inner sanctuary);
the gold floral work and lamps and tongs;
50the pure gold dishes, wick trimmers, sprinkling bowls, dishes and censers;[c]
and the gold sockets for the doors of the innermost room, the Most Holy Place,
and also for the doors of the main hall of the temple.

51When all the work King Solomon had done for the temple of the LORD was
finished, he brought in the things his father David had dedicated[d]—the silver and
gold and the furnishings—and he placed them in the treasuries of the LORD's temple.

The Ark Brought to the Temple

8 Then King Solomon summoned into his presence at Jerusalem the elders of Israel,
all the heads of the tribes and the chiefs[a] of the Israelite families, to bring up
the ark[b] of the LORD's covenant from Zion, the City of David.[c] 2All the men of Israel
came together to King Solomon at the time of the festival[d] in the month of Ethanim,
the seventh month.[e]
3When all the elders of Israel had arrived, the priests[f] took up the ark, 4and they
brought up the ark of the LORD and the Tent of Meeting[g] and all the sacred furnishings
in it. The priests and Levites carried them up, 5and King Solomon and the entire
assembly of Israel that had gathered about him were before the ark, sacrificing[h] so
many sheep and cattle that they could not be recorded or counted.
6The priests then brought the ark of the LORD's covenant[i] to its place in the inner
sanctuary of the temple, the Most Holy Place, and put it beneath the wings of the
cherubim.[j] 7The cherubim spread their wings over the place of the ark and overshad-

7:42 [t]ver 20
7:45 [u]Ex 27:3
7:46 [v]2Ch 4:17 [w]Ge 33:17; Jos 13:27 [x]Jos 3:16
7:47 [y]1Ch 22:3
7:48 [z]Ex 37:10 [a]Ex 25:30
7:49 [b]Ex 25:31-38
7:50 [c]2Ki 25:13
7:51 [d]2Sa 8:11
8:1 [a]Nu 7:2 [b]2Sa 6:17 [c]2Sa 5:7
8:2 [d]2Ch 7:8 [e]Lev 23:34
8:3 [f]Nu 7:9; Jos 3:3
8:4 [g]1Ki 3:4; 2Ch 1:3
8:5 [h]2Sa 6:13
8:6 [i]2Sa 6:17 [j]1Ki 6:19, 27

7:40–47 Huram's items of bronze would look strange in today's churches, but we use other articles to enhance worship. Stained-glass windows, crosses, pulpits, hymnbooks, and communion tables serve as aids to worship. While the instruments of worship may change, the purpose of worship should never change—to give honour and praise to God.

8:1ff Solomon gathered the people not just to dedicate the temple, but to rededicate themselves to God's service. Solomon could well be speaking these words to us today: "But your hearts must be fully committed to the LORD our God, to live by his decrees and obey his commands, as at this time" (8:61).

8:1ff What was the difference between the tabernacle and the temple, and why did the Israelites change from one to the other? As a tent, the tabernacle was a portable place of worship designed for the people as they were travelling towards the promised land. The temple was a permanent place to worship God after the Israelites were at peace in their land. To bring the ark of the Lord's covenant to the temple signified God's actual presence there.

8:6 Cherubim are mighty angels.

8:8
[k]Ex 25:13-15
8:9
[l]Ex 24:7-8; 25:21; 40:20;
Dt 10:2-5;
Heb 9:4
8:10
[m]Ex 40:34-35;
2Ch 7:1-2
8:12
[n]Ps 18:11; 97:2
8:13
[o]Ex 15:17;
2Sa 7:13;
Ps 132:13

owed the ark and its carrying poles. 8These poles were so long that their ends could
be seen from the Holy Place in front of the inner sanctuary, but not from outside the
Holy Place; and they are still there today.[k] 9There was nothing in the ark except the
two stone tablets[l] that Moses had placed in it at Horeb, where the LORD made a
covenant with the Israelites after they came out of Egypt.
10When the priests withdrew from the Holy Place, the cloud[m] filled the temple of
the LORD. 11And the priests could not perform their service because of the cloud, for
the glory of the LORD filled his temple.
12Then Solomon said, "The LORD has said that he would dwell in a dark cloud;[n]
13I have indeed built a magnificent temple for you, a place for you to dwell[o] for ever."

SOLOMON'S TEMPLE 960–586 B.C.

Solomon's temple was a beautiful sight. It took over seven years to build and was a magnificent building containing gold, silver, bronze, and cedar. This house for God was without equal. The description is found in 2 Chronicles 2–4.

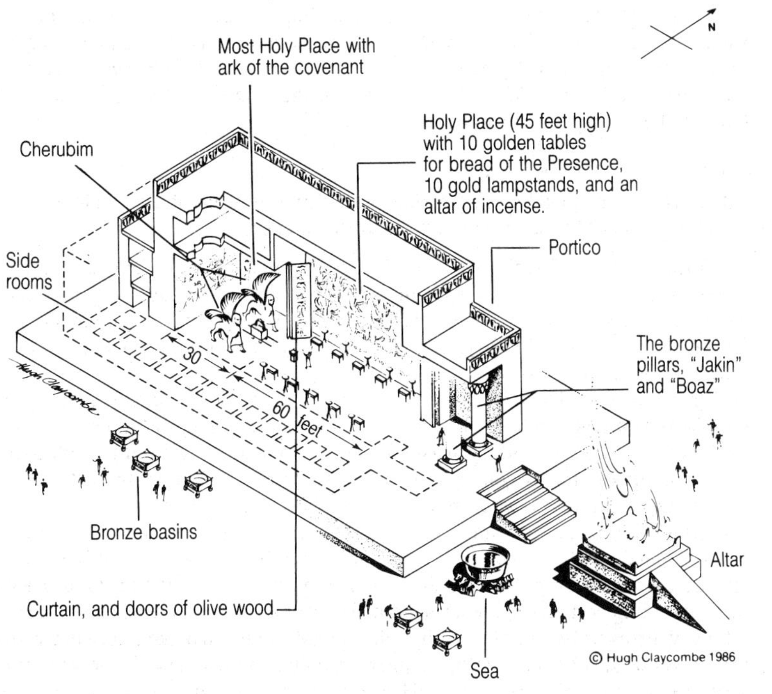

FURNISHINGS

Cherubim: represented heavenly beings, symbolised God's presence and holiness (gold-plated, 15 feet wide)

Ark of the covenant: contained the law written on two tablets, symbolised God's presence with Israel (wood overlaid with gold)

Curtain: separated the Holy Place from the Most Holy Place (blue, purple, and crimson yarn and fine linen, with cherubim worked into it)

Doors: between Holy Place and Most Holy Place (wood overlaid with gold)

Golden tables (wood overlaid with gold), *gold lampstands* (with seven lamps on each stand), and *altar of incense* (wood overlaid with gold): instruments for priestly functions in the Holy Place

Bronze pillars: named Jakin (meaning "he establishes") and Boaz (meaning "in him is strength")—taken together they could mean "God provides the strength"

Altar: for burning of sacrifices (bronze)

Sea: for priests' washing (had 12,000 gallon capacity)

Bronze basins: for washing the sacrifices (water basins on wheeled bases)

This reconstruction uses known archaeological parallels to supplement the text, and assumes interior dimensions from 1 Kings 6:17–20. © Hugh Claycombe.

[14]While the whole assembly of Israel was standing there, the king turned round and
blessed[p] them. [15]Then he said:

"Praise be to the LORD,[q] the God of Israel, who with his own hand has fulfilled
what he promised with his own mouth to my father David. For he said, [16]'Since
the day I brought my people Israel out of Egypt, I have not chosen a city in any
tribe of Israel to have a temple built for my Name[r] to be there, but I have
chosen[s] David[t] to rule my people Israel.'
[17]"My father David had it in his heart to build a temple[u] for the Name of the
LORD, the God of Israel. [18]But the LORD said to my father David, 'Because it
was in your heart to build a temple for my Name, you did well to have this in
your heart. [19]Nevertheless, you[v] are not the one to build the temple, but your
son, who is your own flesh and blood—he is the one who will build the temple
for my Name.'[w]
[20]"The LORD has kept the promise he made: I have succeeded David my father
and now I sit on the throne of Israel, just as the LORD promised, and I have built[x]
the temple for the Name of the LORD, the God of Israel. [21]I have provided a place
there for the ark, in which is the covenant of the LORD that he made with our
fathers when he brought them out of Egypt."

Solomon's Prayer of Dedication

[22]Then Solomon stood before the altar of the LORD in front of the whole assembly
of Israel, spread out his hands[y] towards heaven [23]and said:

"O LORD, God of Israel, there is no God like[z] you in heaven above or on earth
below—you who keep your covenant of love[a] with your servants who continue
wholeheartedly in your way. [24]You have kept your promise to your servant David
my father; with your mouth you have promised and with your hand you have
fulfilled it—as it is today.
[25]"Now LORD, God of Israel, keep for your servant David my father the
promises[b] you made to him when you said, 'You shall never fail to have a man
to sit before me on the throne of Israel, if only your sons are careful in all they
do to walk before me as you have done.' [26]And now, O God of Israel, let your
word that you promised[c] your servant David my father come true.
[27]"But will God really dwell[d] on earth? The heavens, even the highest heaven,
cannot contain[e] you. How much less this temple I have built! [28]Yet give
attention to your servant's prayer and his plea for mercy, O LORD my God. Hear
the cry and the prayer that your servant is praying in your presence this day.
[29]May your eyes be open[f] towards[g] this temple night and day, this place of
which you said, 'My Name[h] shall be there,' so that you will hear the prayer your
servant prays towards this place. [30]Hear the supplication of your servant and of
your people Israel when they pray towards this place. Hear from heaven, your
dwelling-place, and when you hear, forgive.[i]
[31]"When a man wrongs his neighbour and is required to take an oath and he
comes and swears the oath[j] before your altar in this temple, [32]then hear from
heaven and act. Judge between your servants, condemning the guilty and bringing down on his own head what he has done. Declare the innocent not guilty,
and so establish his innocence.[k]
[33]"When your people Israel have been defeated[l] by an enemy because they

8:14 [p]2Sa 6:18
8:15 [q]2Sa 7:12-13; 1Ch 29:10, 20; Ne 9:5; Lk 1:68
8:16 [r]Dt 12:5 [s]1Sa 16:1 [t]2Sa 7:4-6, 8
8:17 [u]2Sa 7:2; 1Ch 17:1
8:19 [v]2Sa 7:5 [w]2Sa 7:13; 1Ki 5:3, 5
8:20 [x]1Ch 28:6
8:22 [y]Ex 9:29; Ezr 9:5
8:23 [z]1Sa 2:2; 2Sa 7:22 [a]Dt 7:9, 12; Ne 1:5; 9:32; Da 9:4
8:25 [b]1Ki 2:4
8:26 [c]2Sa 7:25
8:27 [d]Ac 7:48 [e]2Ch 2:6; Ps 139:7-16; Isa 66:1; Jer 23:24
8:29 [f]2Ch 7:15; Ne 1:6 [g]Da 6:10 [h]Dt 12:11
8:30 [i]Ps 85:2
8:31 [j]Ex 22:11
8:32 [k]Dt 25:1
8:33 [l]Lev 26:17; Dt 28:25

8:15–21 For 480 years after Israel's escape from Egypt, God did not ask them to build a temple for him. Instead he emphasised the importance of his presence among them and their need for spiritual leaders. It is easy to think of a building as the focus of God's presence and power, but God chooses and uses *people* to do his work. He can use you more than he can use a building of wood and stone. Building or enlarging our place of worship may be necessary, but it should never take priority over developing spiritual leaders.

8:24 Solomon was referring to the promise God made to David in 2 Samuel 7:12–15 that one of David's sons would build the temple.

8:27 In his prayer of dedication, Solomon declared that even the highest heaven cannot contain God. Isn't it amazing that, though the heavens can't contain God, he is willing to live in the hearts of those who love him? The God of the universe takes up residence in his people.

8:33, 34 After Solomon's reign, the people continually turned away from God. The rest of the kingdom era is a vivid fulfilment of

8:33 [m]Lev 26:39
8:35 [n]Lev 26:19; Dt 28:24
8:36 [o]1Sa 12:23; Ps 25:4; 94:12 [p]Ps 5:8; 27:11; Jer 6:16
8:37 [q]Lev 26:26 [r]Dt 28:22
8:39 [s]1Sa 16:7; 1Ch 28:9; Ps 11:4; Jer 17:10; Jn 2:24; Ac 1:24
8:40 [t]Ps 130:4
8:42 [u]Dt 3:24
8:43 [v]1Sa 17:46; 2Ki 19:19 [w]Ps 102:15
8:46 [x]Pr 20:9; Ecc 7:20; Ro 3:9; 1Jn 1:8-10 [y]Lev 26:33-39; Dt 28:64
8:47 [z]Lev 26:40; Ne 1:6 [a]Ps 106:6; Da 9:5
8:48 [b]Dt 4:29; Jer 29:12-14 [c]Da 6:10 [d]Jnh 2:4
8:50 [e]2Ch 30:9; Ps 106:46
8:51 [f]Dt 4:20; 9:29; Ne 1:10 [g]Jer 11:4
8:53 [h]Ex 19:5; Dt 9:26-29

have sinned[m] against you, and when they turn back to you and confess your
name, praying and making supplication to you in this temple, 34then hear from
heaven and forgive the sin of your people Israel and bring them back to the land
you gave to their fathers.
35"When the heavens are shut up and there is no rain[n] because your people
have sinned against you, and when they pray towards this place and confess your
name and turn from their sin because you have afflicted them, 36then hear from
heaven and forgive the sin of your servants, your people Israel. Teach[o] them
the right way[p] to live, and send rain on the land you gave your people for an
inheritance.
37"When famine[q] or plague comes to the land, or blight[r] or mildew, locusts
or grasshoppers, or when an enemy besieges them in any of their cities, whatever
disaster or disease may come, 38and when a prayer or plea is made by any of
your people Israel—each one aware of the afflictions of his own heart, and
spreading out his hands towards this temple—39then hear from heaven, your
dwelling-place. Forgive and act; deal with each man according to all he does,
since you know[s] his heart (for you alone know the hearts of all men), 40so that
they will fear[t] you all the time they live in the land you gave our fathers.
41"As for the foreigner who does not belong to your people Israel but has come
from a distant land because of your name—42for men will hear of your great
name and your mighty hand[u] and your outstretched arm—when he comes and
prays towards this temple, 43then hear from heaven, your dwelling-place, and
do whatever the foreigner asks of you, so that all the peoples of the earth may
know[v] your name and fear[w] you, as do your own people Israel, and may know
that this house I have built bears your Name.
44"When your people go to war against their enemies, wherever you send
them, and when they pray to the LORD towards the city you have chosen and the
temple I have built for your Name, 45then hear from heaven their prayer and their
plea, and uphold their cause.
46"When they sin against you—for there is no-one who does not sin[x]—and
you become angry with them and give them over to the enemy, who takes them
captive[y] to his own land, far away or near; 47and if they have a change of heart
in the land where they are held captive, and repent and plead[z] with you in the
land of their conquerors and say, 'We have sinned, we have done wrong, we have
acted wickedly';[a] 48and if they turn back to you with all their heart[b] and soul
in the land of their enemies who took them captive, and pray[c] to you towards
the land you gave their fathers, towards the city you have chosen and the temple[d]
I have built for your Name; 49then from heaven, your dwelling-place, hear their
prayer and their plea, and uphold their cause. 50And forgive your people, who
have sinned against you; forgive all the offences they have committed against
you, and cause their conquerors to show them mercy;[e] 51for they are your people
and your inheritance,[f] whom you brought out of Egypt, out of that iron-smelting
furnace.[g]
52"May your eyes be open to your servant's plea and to the plea of your people
Israel, and may you listen to them whenever they cry out to you. 53For you
singled them out from all the nations of the world to be your own inheritance,[h]

Solomon's description in these verses. As a result of the people's sin, God let them be overrun by enemies several times. Then, in desperation, they cried out to God for forgiveness, and God restored them.

8:41–43 God chose Israel to be a blessing to the whole world (Genesis 12:1–3). This blessing found its fulfilment in Jesus—a descendant of Abraham and David (Galatians 3:8, 9)—who became the Messiah for all people, Jews and non-Jews. When the Israelites first entered the promised land, they were ordered to clear out several wicked nations; thus we read in the Old Testament of many wars. But we should not conclude that war was Israel's first duty. After subduing the evil people, Israel was to become a light to the surrounding nations. Sadly, Israel's own sin and spiritual blindness prevented them from reaching out to the rest of the world with God's love. Jesus came to do what the nation of Israel failed to do.

8:46–53 Solomon, who seemed to have prophetic insight into the future captivities of his people (2 Kings 17; 25), asked God to be merciful to them when they cried out to him, to forgive them, and to return them to their homeland. Reference to their return is made in Ezra 1; 2; Nehemiah 1; 2.

just as you declared through your servant Moses when you, O Sovereign LORD,
brought our fathers out of Egypt."

54When Solomon had finished all these prayers and supplications to the LORD, he
rose from before the altar of the LORD, where he had been kneeling with his hands
spread out towards heaven. 55He stood and blessed[i] the whole assembly of Israel in
a loud voice, saying:

56"Praise be to the LORD, who has given rest[j] to his people Israel just as he
promised. Not one word has failed of all the good promises[k] he gave through
his servant Moses. 57May the LORD our God be with us as he was with our fathers;
may he never leave us nor forsake[l] us. 58May he turn our hearts[m] to him, to
walk in all his ways and to keep the commands, decrees and regulations he gave
our fathers. 59And may these words of mine, which I have prayed before the
LORD, be near to the LORD our God day and night, that he may uphold the cause
of his servant and the cause of his people Israel according to each day's need,
60so that all the peoples[n] of the earth may know that the LORD is God and that
there is no other.[o] 61But your hearts must be fully committed[p] to the LORD our
God, to live by his decrees and obey his commands, as at this time."

The Dedication of the Temple

62Then the king and all Israel with him offered sacrifices before the LORD. 63Solo-
mon offered a sacrifice of fellowship offerings[a] to the LORD: twenty-two thousand
cattle and a hundred and twenty thousand sheep and goats. So the king and all the
Israelites dedicated the temple of the LORD.
64On that same day the king consecrated the middle part of the courtyard in front
of the temple of the LORD, and there he offered burnt offerings, grain offerings and
the fat of the fellowship offerings, because the bronze altar[q] before the LORD was
too small to hold the burnt offerings, the grain offerings and the fat of the fellowship
offerings.
65So Solomon observed the festival[r] at that time, and all Israel with him—a vast
assembly, people from Lebo[b] Hamath[s] to the Wadi of Egypt.[t] They celebrated it
before the LORD our God for seven days and seven days more, fourteen days in all.
66On the following day he sent the people away. They blessed the king and then went
home, joyful and glad in heart for all the good things the LORD had done for his servant
David and his people Israel.

4. Solomon's greatness and downfall

The LORD Appears to Solomon

9 When Solomon had finished[a] building the temple of the LORD and the royal
palace, and had achieved all he had desired to do, 2the LORD appeared[b] to him
a second time, as he had appeared to him at Gibeon. 3The LORD said to him:

"I have heard[c] the prayer and plea you have made before me; I have consecrated this temple, which you have built, by putting my Name there for ever.
My eyes[d] and my heart will always be there.
4"As for you, if you walk before me in integrity of heart[e] and uprightness,
as David[f] your father did, and do all I command and observe my decrees and
laws, 5I will establish[g] your royal throne over Israel for ever, as I promised

[a] 63 Traditionally *peace offerings*; also in verse 64 [b] 65 Or *from the entrance to*

8:55 [i]ver 14; 2Sa 6:18
8:56 [j]Dt 12:10 [k]Jos 21:45; 23:15
8:57 [l]Dt 31:6; Jos 1:5; Heb 13:5
8:58 [m]Ps 119:36
8:60 [n]Jos 4:24; 1Sa 17:46 [o]Dt 4:35; 1Ki 18:39; Jer 10:10-12
8:61 [p]1Ki 11:4; 15:3, 14; 2Ki 20:3
8:64 [q]2Ch 4:1
8:65 [r]ver 2; Lev 23:34 [s]Nu 34:8; Jos 13:5; Jdg 3:3; 2Ki 14:25 [t]Ge 15:18
9:1 [a]1Ki 7:1; 2Ch 8:6
9:2 [b]1Ki 3:5
9:3 [c]2Ki 20:5; Ps 10:17 [d]Dt 11:12; 1Ki 8:29
9:4 [e]Ge 17:1 [f]1Ki 15:5
9:5 [g]1Ch 22:10

8:56–60 Solomon praised the Lord and prayed for the people. His prayer can be a pattern for our prayers. He had five basic requests: (1) for God's presence (8:57); (2) for the desire to do God's will in everything; ("turn our hearts to him", 8:58); (3) for help with each day's need (8:59); (4) for the desire and ability to obey God's decrees and commands (8:58); (5) for the spread of God's kingdom to the entire world (8:60). These prayer requests are just as important today. When you pray for your church or family, you can make these same requests to God.

8:65 A wadi is a stream or dry stream bed.

9:4–9 God appeared to Solomon a second time; the first was at Gibeon (3:4–15). For more on the conditions of God's great promise to David and his descendants, see the note on 2:3, 4.

David your father when I said, 'You shall never fail[h] to have a man on the throne
of Israel.'
6"But if you[a] or your sons turn away[i] from me and do not observe the
commands and decrees I have given you[a] and go off to serve other gods and
worship them, 7then I will cut off Israel from the land[j] I have given them and
will reject this temple I have consecrated for my Name.[k] Israel will then become
a byword[l] and an object of ridicule[m] among all peoples. 8And though this
temple is now imposing, all who pass by will be appalled and will scoff and say,
'Why has the LORD done such a thing to this land and to this temple?'[n] 9People
will answer, 'Because they have forsaken the LORD their God, who brought their
fathers out of Egypt, and have embraced other gods, worshipping and serving
them — that is why the LORD brought all this disaster on them.' "

Solomon's Other Activities

10At the end of twenty years, during which Solomon built these two buildings — the
temple of the LORD and the royal palace — 11King Solomon gave twenty towns in
Galilee to Hiram king of Tyre, because Hiram had supplied him with all the cedar
and pine and gold[o] he wanted. 12But when Hiram went from Tyre to see the towns
that Solomon had given him, he was not pleased with them. 13"What kind of towns
are these you have given me, my brother?" he asked. And he called them the Land
of Cabul,[b][p] a name they have to this day. 14Now Hiram had sent to the king 120
talents[c] of gold.
15Here is the account of the forced labour King Solomon conscripted[q] to build the
LORD's temple, his own palace, the supporting terraces,[d][r] the wall of Jerusalem,
and Hazor,[s] Megiddo and Gezer.[t] 16(Pharaoh king of Egypt had attacked and
captured Gezer. He had set it on fire. He killed its Canaanite inhabitants and then gave
it as a wedding gift to his daughter, Solomon's wife. 17And Solomon rebuilt Gezer.)
He built up Lower Beth Horon,[u] 18Baalath,[v] and Tadmor[e] in the desert, within his
land, 19as well as all his store cities[w] and the towns for his chariots[x] and for his
horses[f] — whatever he desired to build in Jerusalem, in Lebanon and throughout all
the territory he ruled.
20All the people left from the Amorites, Hittites, Perizzites, Hivites and Jebusites
(these peoples were not Israelites), 21that is, their descendants[y] remaining in the land,

a *6* The Hebrew is plural. b *13* *Cabul* sounds like the Hebrew for *good-for-nothing.* c *14* That is, about 4 tons (about 4 metric tons) d *15* Or *the Millo*; also in verse 24 e *18* The Hebrew may also be read *Tamar.* f *19* Or *charioteers*

9:5 h2Sa 7:15; 1Ki 2:4
9:6 i2Sa 7:14
9:7 j2Ki 17:23; 25:21 kJer 7:14 lPs 44:14 mDt 28:37
9:8 nDt 29:24; Jer 22:8-9
9:11 o2Ch 8:2
9:13 pJos 19:27
9:15 qJos 16:10; 1Ki 5:13 rver 24; 2Sa 5:9 sJos 19:36 tJos 17:11
9:17 uJos 16:3; 2Ch 8:5
9:18 vJos 19:44
9:19 wver 1 x1Ki 4:26
9:21 yGe 9:25-26

SOLOMON'S BUILDING PROJECTS
Solomon became known as one of the great builders in Israel's history. He built Hazor, Megiddo, and Gezer as fortress cities at key points during his reign. He also rebuilt the cities of Lower Beth Horon, Baalath, and Tadmor.

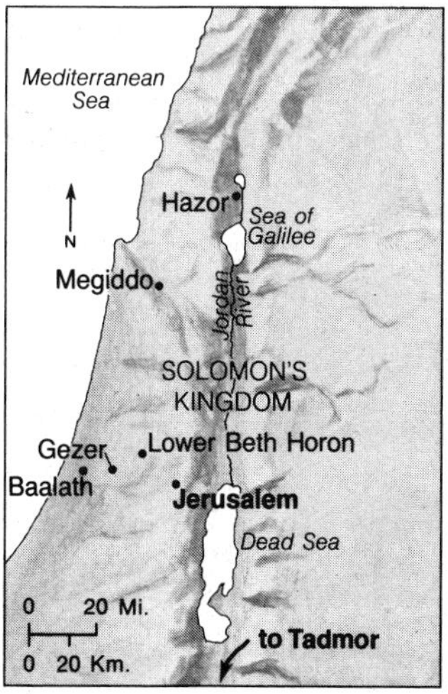

9:11–14 Was Solomon being unfair to Hiram? It is not clear from these verses whether Solomon gave these towns to Hiram, or whether they were collateral until he could repay Hiram for the gold he had borrowed. Second Chronicles 8:1, 2 implies that the towns were returned to Solomon. In either case, Hiram probably preferred a piece of land on the coast more suitable for trade (the name he gave these cities, *Cabul,* sounds like the Hebrew word for "good-for-nothing"). In the end, Hiram was repaid many times over through his trade partnerships with Solomon (2 Chronicles 9:10, 21). Because Phoenicia was on friendly terms with Israel and dependent on it for grain and oil, Hiram's relationship with Solomon was more important than a feud over some cities.

9:16 At this time, Israel and Egypt were the major powers in the Near East. For many years Egypt had retained control of Gezer, even though it was in Israelite territory. In Solomon's time the Pharaoh gave the city to his daughter, whom Solomon married, putting Gezer under Israelite control. Intermarriage among royal families was common, but it was not endorsed by God (Deuteronomy 17:17).

whom the Israelites could not exterminate[g][z]—these Solomon conscripted for his
slave labour force,[a] as it is to this day. 22But Solomon did not make slaves[b] of any
of the Israelites; they were his fighting men, his government officials, his officers,
his captains, and the commanders of his chariots and charioteers. 23They were also
the chief officials[c] in charge of Solomon's projects—550 officials supervising the
men who did the work.
24After Pharaoh's daughter[d] had come up from the City of David to the palace
Solomon had built for her, he constructed the supporting terraces.[e]
25Three[f] times a year Solomon sacrificed burnt offerings and fellowship offerings[h] on the altar he had built for the LORD, burning incense before the LORD along
with them, and so fulfilled the temple obligations.
26King Solomon also built ships[g] at Ezion Geber,[h] which is near Elath in Edom,
on the shore of the Red Sea.[i] 27And Hiram sent his men—sailors[i] who knew the
sea—to serve in the fleet with Solomon's men. 28They sailed to Ophir[j] and brought
back 420 talents[j] of gold, which they delivered to King Solomon.

The Queen of Sheba Visits Solomon

10 When the queen of Sheba[a] heard about the fame of Solomon and his relation
to the name of the LORD, she came to test him with hard questions.[b] 2Arriving
at Jerusalem with a very great caravan—with camels carrying spices, large quantities
of gold, and precious stones—she came to Solomon and talked with him about all
that she had on her mind. 3Solomon answered all her questions; nothing was too hard
for the king to explain to her. 4When the queen of Sheba saw all the wisdom of
Solomon and the palace he had built, 5the food on his table,[c] the seating of his
officials, the attending servants in their robes, his cupbearers, and the burnt offerings
he made at[a] the temple of the LORD, she was overwhelmed.
6She said to the king, "The report I heard in my own country about your achievements and your wisdom is true. 7But I did not believe these things until I came and
saw with my own eyes. Indeed, not even half was told me; in wisdom and wealth[d]
you have far exceeded the report I heard. 8How happy your men must be! How happy
your officials, who continually stand before you and hear[e] your wisdom! 9Praise[f]
be to the LORD your God, who has delighted in you and placed you on the throne of
Israel. Because of the LORD's eternal love for Israel, he has made you king, to maintain
justice[g] and righteousness."
10And she gave the king 120 talents[b] of gold,[h] large quantities of spices, and
precious stones. Never again were so many spices brought in as those the queen of
Sheba gave to King Solomon.
11(Hiram's ships brought gold from Ophir;[i] and from there they brought great
cargoes of almug-wood[c] and precious stones. 12The king used the almug-wood to
make supports for the temple of the LORD and for the royal palace, and to make harps
and lyres for the musicians. So much almug-wood has never been imported or seen
since that day.)
13King Solomon gave the queen of Sheba all she desired and asked for, besides what
he had given her out of his royal bounty. Then she left and returned with her retinue
to her own country.

9:21 [z]Jos 15:63; 17:12; Jdg 1:21, 27, 29 [a]Ezr 2:55, 58
9:22 [b]Lev 25:39
9:23 [c]1Ki 5:16
9:24 [d]1Ki 3:1; 7:8 [e]2Sa 5:9; 1Ki 11:27; 2Ch 32:5
9:25 [f]Ex 23:14; 2Ch 8:12-13, 16
9:26 [g]1Ki 22:48 [h]Nu 33:35; Dt 2:8
9:27 [i]1Ki 10:11; Eze 27:8
9:28 [j]1Ch 29:4
10:1 [a]Ge 10:7, 28; Mt 12:42; Lk 11:31 [b]Jdg 14:12
10:5 [c]1Ch 26:16
10:7 [d]1Ch 29:25
10:8 [e]Pr 8:34
10:9 [f]1Ki 5:7 [g]2Sa 8:15; Ps 33:5; 72:2
10:10 [h]ver 2
10:11 [i]Ge 10:29; 1Ki 9:27-28

[g] *21* The Hebrew term refers to the irrevocable giving over of things or persons to the LORD, often by totally destroying them. [h] *25* Traditionally *peace offerings* [i] *26* Hebrew *Yam Suph*; that is, Sea of Reeds [j] *28* That is, about 14 tons (about 14.5 metric tons) [a] *5* Or *the ascent by which he went up to* [b] *10* That is, about 4 tons (about 4 metric tons) [c] *11* Probably a variant of *algum-wood*; also in verse 12

10:1–5 The queen of Sheba came to see for herself if everything she had heard about Solomon was true. Contests using riddles or proverbs were often used to test wisdom. The queen may have used some of these as she questioned Solomon (10:1, 3). When she realised the extent of his riches and wisdom, "she was overwhelmed" and no longer questioned his power or wisdom. No longer a competitor, she became an admirer. Her experience was repeated by many kings and foreign dignitaries who paid honour to Solomon (4:34).

10:14 [j]1Ki 9:28
10:16 [k]1Ki 14:26-28
10:17 [l]1Ki 7:2
10:22 [m]1Ki 9:26
10:23 [n]1Ki 3:13 [o]1Ki 4:30
10:24 [p]1Ki 3:9, 12, 28

Solomon's Splendour

14 The weight of the gold[j] that Solomon received yearly was 666 talents,[d] 15 not
including the revenues from merchants and traders and from all the Arabian kings and
the governors of the land.
16 King Solomon made two hundred large shields[k] of hammered gold; six hundred
bekas[e] of gold went into each shield. 17 He also made three hundred small shields
of hammered gold, with three minas[f] of gold in each shield. The king put them in
the Palace of the Forest of Lebanon.[l]
18 Then the king made a great throne inlaid with ivory and overlaid with fine gold.
19 The throne had six steps, and its back had a rounded top. On both sides of the seat
were armrests, with a lion standing beside each of them. 20 Twelve lions stood on the
six steps, one at either end of each step. Nothing like it had ever been made for any
other kingdom. 21 All King Solomon's goblets were gold, and all the household articles
in the Palace of the Forest of Lebanon were pure gold. Nothing was made of silver,
because silver was considered of little value in Solomon's days. 22 The king had a fleet
of trading ships[g][m] at sea along with the ships of Hiram. Once every three years it
returned carrying gold, silver and ivory, and apes and baboons.
23 King Solomon was greater in riches[n] and wisdom[o] than all the other kings of
the earth. 24 The whole world sought audience with Solomon to hear the wisdom[p] God
had put in his heart. 25 Year after year, everyone who came brought a gift—articles
of silver and gold, robes, weapons and spices, and horses and mules.

[d] *14* That is, about 22½ tons (about 23 metric tons) [e] *16* That is, about 7½ pounds (about 3.5 kilograms)
[f] *17* That is, about 3¾ pounds (about 1.7 kilograms) [g] *22* Hebrew *of ships of Tarshish*

FRIENDS AND ENEMIES Solomon's reputation brought acclaim and riches from many nations, but he disobeyed God, marrying pagan women and worshipping their gods. So God raised up enemies like Hadad from Edom and Rezon from Zobah (modern-day Syria). Jeroboam from Zeredah was another enemy who would eventually divide this mighty kingdom.

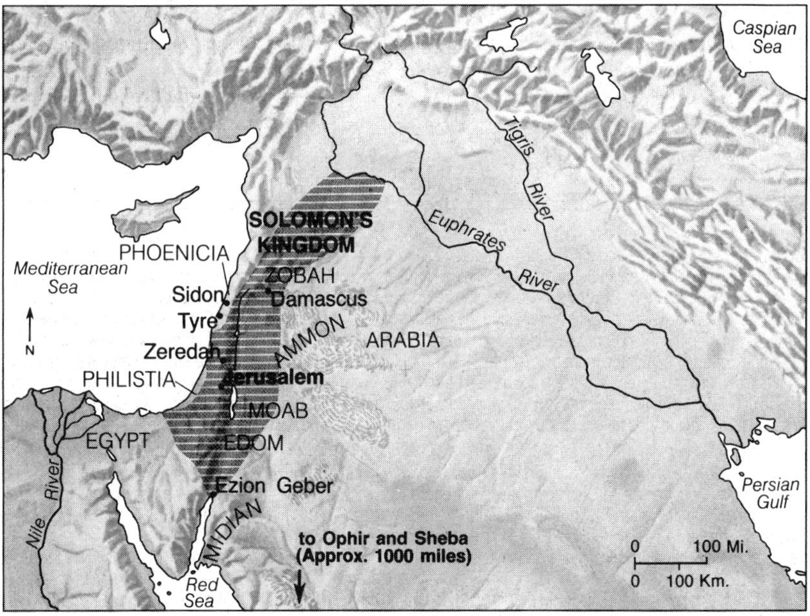

10:14ff When Solomon asked for wisdom, God promised him riches and honour as well (3:13). These verses show just how extensive his wealth became. Israel was no longer a second-rate nation, but at the height of its power and wealth. Solomon's riches became legendary. Great men came from many nations to listen to Israel's powerful king. Jesus would later refer to "Solomon in all his splendour" (Matthew 6:29).

10:23 Why does the Bible place so much emphasis on Solomon's material possessions? In the Old Testament, riches were considered tangible evidence of God's blessing. Prosperity was seen as a proof of right living. In the books of Ecclesiastes and Job this concept is placed in a broader perspective. In ideal conditions, people prosper when God runs their lives, but prosperity is not guaranteed. Wealth does not prove that a person is living rightly before God, and poverty does not indicate sin.

In fact, a greater evidence that a person is living for God is the presence of suffering and persecution (Mark 10:29–31; 13:13). The most important "treasure" is not earthly, but heavenly (Matthew 6:19–21; 19:21; 1 Timothy 6:17–19). The gift of greatest worth has no price tag—it is the gift of salvation freely offered by God.

26Solomon accumulated chariots and horses;[q] he had fourteen hundred chariots and
twelve thousand horses,[h] which he kept in the chariot cities and also with him in
Jerusalem. 27The king made silver as common[r] in Jerusalem as stones, and cedar
as plentiful as sycamore-fig trees in the foothills. 28Solomon's horses were imported
from Egypt[i] and from Kue[j]—the royal merchants purchased them from Kue.[j]
29They imported a chariot from Egypt for six hundred shekels[k] of silver, and a horse
for a hundred and fifty.[l] They also exported them to all the kings of the Hittites[s]
and of the Arameans.

Solomon's Wives

11 King Solomon, however, loved many foreign women[a] besides Pharaoh's
daughter—Moabites, Ammonites, Edomites, Sidonians and Hittites. 2They
were from nations about which the LORD had told the Israelites, "You must not
intermarry[b] with them, because they will surely turn your hearts after their gods."
Nevertheless, Solomon held fast to them in love. 3He had seven hundred wives of
royal birth and three hundred concubines, and his wives led him astray. 4As Solomon
grew old, his wives turned his heart after other gods, and his heart was not fully
devoted[c] to the LORD his God, as the heart of David his father had been. 5He followed
Ashtoreth[d] the goddess of the Sidonians, and Molech[a][e] the detestable god of the
Ammonites. 6So Solomon did evil in the eyes of the LORD; he did not follow the LORD
completely, as David his father had done.
7On a hill east[f] of Jerusalem, Solomon built a high place for Chemosh[g] the
detestable god of Moab, and for Molech[h] the detestable god of the Ammonites. 8He
did the same for all his foreign wives, who burned incense and offered sacrifices to
their gods.
9The LORD became angry with Solomon because his heart had turned away from
the LORD, the God of Israel, who had appeared[i] to him twice. 10Although he had
forbidden Solomon to follow other gods,[j] Solomon did not keep the LORD's command.[k] 11So the LORD said to Solomon, "Since this is your attitude and you have

10:26 [q]Dt 17:16; 1Ki 4:26; 9:19; 2Ch 1:14; 9:25
10:27 [r]Dt 17:17
10:29 [s]2Ki 7:6-7
11:1 [a]Dt 17:17; Ne 13:26
11:2 [b]Ex 34:16; Dt 7:3-4
11:4 [c]1Ki 8:61; 9:4
11:5 [d]ver 33; Jdg 2:13; 2Ki 23:13 [e]ver 7
11:7 [f]2Ki 23:13 [g]Nu 21:29; Jdg 11:24 [h]Lev 20:2-5; Ac 7:43
11:9 [i]ver 2-3; 1Ki 3:5; 9:2
11:10 [j]1Ki 9:6 [k]1Ki 6:12

[h] *26* Or *charioteers* [i] *28* Or possibly *Muzur*, a region in Cilicia; also in verse 29 [j] *28* Probably *Cilicia*
[k] *29* That is, about 15 pounds (about 7 kilograms) [l] *29* That is, about 3¾ pounds (about 1.7 kilograms)
[a] *5* Hebrew *Milcom*; also in verse 33

10:26–11:3 In accumulating chariots and horses, a huge harem, and incredible wealth, Solomon was violating God's commands for a king (Deuteronomy 17:14–20). Why were they prohibited? God knew how these activities would hurt the nation both politically and spiritually (1 Samuel 8:11–18). The more luxurious Solomon's court became, the more the people were taxed. Excessive taxation created unrest, and soon conditions became ripe for a revolution. With everything he wanted, Solomon forgot God and allowed pagan influences to enter his court through his pagan wives, thus accelerating the spiritual corruption of the nation.

11:2 Although Solomon had clear instructions from God *not* to marry women from foreign nations, he chose to disregard God's commands. He married not one, but many foreign women, who subsequently led him away from God. God knows our strengths and weaknesses, and his commands are always for our good. When people ignore God's commands, negative consequences inevitably result. It is not enough to know God's word or even to believe it; we must follow it and apply it to our daily activities and decisions. Take God's commands seriously. Like Solomon, the wisest man who ever lived, we are not as strong as we may think.

11:3 For all his wisdom, Solomon had some weak spots. He could not say no to compromise or to lustful desires. Whether he married to strengthen political alliances or to gain personal pleasure, these foreign wives led him into idolatry. You may have strong faith, but you also have weak spots—and that is where temptation usually strikes. Strengthen and protect your weaker areas because a chain is only as strong as its weakest link. If Solomon, the wisest man, could fall, so can you.

11:4 Solomon handled great pressures in running the government, but he could not handle the pressure from his wives who wanted him to worship their gods. In marriage and close friendships, it is difficult to resist pressure to compromise. Our love leads us to identify with the desires of those we care about.

Faced with such pressure, Solomon at first *resisted* it, maintaining pure faith. Then he *tolerated* a more widespread practice of idolatry. Finally he became involved in idolatrous worship, *rationalising* away the potential danger to himself and to the kingdom. It is because we want to please and identify with our loved ones that God asks us not to marry those who do not share our commitment to him.

11:5–8 Ashtoreth was a goddess that symbolised reproductive power—a mistress of the god Baal. Molech was the national god of the Ammonites, called "detestable" because its worship rites included child sacrifice. Chemosh was the Moabites' national god. The Israelites were warned against worshipping all other gods in general and Molech in particular (Exodus 20:1–6; Leviticus 18:21; 20:1–5).

11:9, 10 Solomon didn't turn away from God all at once or in a brief moment. His spiritual coldness started with a minor departure from God's laws (3:1). Over the years, that little sin grew until it resulted in Solomon's downfall. A little sin can be the first step in turning away from God. It is not the sins we don't know about, but the sins we excuse, that cause us the greatest trouble. We must never let any sin go unchallenged. In your life, is an unchallenged sin spreading like a deadly cancer? Don't excuse it. Confess this sin to God and ask him for strength to resist temptation.

11:11–13 Solomon's powerful and glorious kingdom could have been blessed for all time; instead, it was approaching its end. Sol-

not kept my covenant and my decrees, which I commanded you, I will most certainly
tear[l] the kingdom away from you and give it to one of your subordinates. 12Neverthe-
less, for the sake of David your father, I will not do it during your lifetime. I will
tear it out of the hand of your son. 13Yet I will not tear the whole kingdom from him,
but will give him one tribe[m] for the sake[n] of David my servant and for the sake of
Jerusalem, which I have chosen."[o]

Solomon's Adversaries

14Then the LORD raised up against Solomon an adversary, Hadad the Edomite, from
the royal line of Edom. 15Earlier when David was fighting with Edom, Joab the
commander of the army, who had gone up to bury the dead, had struck down all the
men in Edom.[p] 16Joab and all the Israelites stayed there for six months, until they
had destroyed all the men in Edom. 17But Hadad, still only a boy, fled to Egypt with
some Edomite officials who had served his father. 18They set out from Midian and
went to Paran.[q] Then taking men from Paran with them, they went to Egypt, to
Pharaoh king of Egypt, who gave Hadad a house and land and provided him with food.
19Pharaoh was so pleased with Hadad that he gave him a sister of his own wife,
Queen Tahpenes, in marriage. 20The sister of Tahpenes bore him a son named
Genubath, whom Tahpenes brought up in the royal palace. There Genubath lived with
Pharaoh's own children.
21While he was in Egypt, Hadad heard that David rested with his fathers and that
Joab the commander of the army was also dead. Then Hadad said to Pharaoh, "Let
me go, so that I may return to my own country."
22"What have you lacked here that you want to go back to your own country?"
Pharaoh asked.
"Nothing," Hadad replied, "but do let me go!"
23And God raised up against Solomon another adversary,[r] Rezon son of Eliada,
who had fled from his master, Hadadezer[s] king of Zobah. 24He gathered men around
him and became the leader of a band of rebels when David destroyed the forces[b] ⌞of
Zobah⌟; the rebels went to Damascus,[t] where they settled and took control. 25Rezon
was Israel's adversary as long as Solomon lived, adding to the trouble caused by
Hadad. So Rezon ruled in Aram[u] and was hostile towards Israel.

Jeroboam Rebels Against Solomon

26Also, Jeroboam son of Nebat rebelled[v] against the king. He was one of Solomon's officials, an Ephraimite from Zeredah, and his mother was a widow named
Zeruah.
27Here is the account of how he rebelled against the king: Solomon had built the
supporting terraces[c][w] and had filled in the gap in the wall of the city of David his
father. 28Now Jeroboam was a man of standing,[x] and when Solomon saw how well[y]
the young man did his work, he put him in charge of the whole labour force of the
house of Joseph.
29About that time Jeroboam was going out of Jerusalem, and Ahijah[z] the prophet
of Shiloh met him on the way, wearing a new cloak. The two of them were alone out

11:11 [l]ver 31; 1Ki 12:15-16; 2Ki 17:21
11:13 [m]1Ki 12:20 [n]2Sa 7:15 [o]Dt 12:11
11:15 [p]Dt 20:13; 2Sa 8:14; 1Ch 18:12
11:18 [q]Nu 10:12
11:23 [r]ver 14 [s]2Sa 8:3
11:24 [t]2Sa 8:5; 10:8, 18
11:25 [u]2Sa 10:19
11:26 [v]2Sa 20:21; 1Ki 12:2; 2Ch 13:6
11:27 [w]1Ki 9:24
11:28 [x]Ru 2:1 [y]Pr 22:29
11:29 [z]1Ki 12:15; 14:2; 2Ch 9:29

[b] 24 Hebrew *destroyed them* [c] 27 Or *the Millo*

omon had God's promises, guidance, and answers to prayer, and yet he allowed sin to remain all around him. Eventually it corrupted him so much that he was no longer interested in God. Psalm 127, written by Solomon, says, "Unless the LORD builds the house, its builders labour in vain." Solomon had begun by laying the foundation with God, but he did not build on this in his later years. As a result, he lost everything. It is not enough to get off to a right start in building our marriage, career, or church on God's principles; we must remain faithful to God to the end (Mark 13:13). God must be in control of our lives from start to finish.

11:14–22 Edom was the kingdom southeast of the Dead Sea. David had added this nation to his empire (2 Samuel 8:13, 14). It was of strategic importance because it controlled the route to the Red Sea. Edom's revolt was disturbing the peace of Solomon's kingdom.

11:29–39 The prophet Ahijah predicted the division of the kingdom of Israel. After Solomon's death, 10 of Israel's 12 tribes would follow Jeroboam. The other two tribes, Judah and the area of Benjamin around Jerusalem, would remain loyal to David. Judah, the largest tribe, and Benjamin, the smallest, were often mentioned as one tribe because they shared the same border. Both Jeroboam and Ahijah were from Ephraim, the most prominent of the 10 rebel tribes. (For more on the divided kingdom, see the note on 12:20.)

in the country, 30 and Ahijah took hold of the new cloak he was wearing and tore[a]
it into twelve pieces. 31 Then he said to Jeroboam, "Take ten pieces for yourself, for
this is what the LORD, the God of Israel, says: 'See, I am going to tear[b] the kingdom
out of Solomon's hand and give you ten tribes. 32 But for the sake of my servant David
and the city of Jerusalem, which I have chosen out of all the tribes of Israel, he will
have one tribe. 33 I will do this because they have[d] forsaken me and worshipped[c]
Ashtoreth the goddess of the Sidonians, Chemosh the god of the Moabites, and
Molech the god of the Ammonites, and have not walked in my ways, nor done what
is right in my eyes, nor kept my statutes[d] and laws as David, Solomon's father, did.
34 " 'But I will not take the whole kingdom out of Solomon's hand; I have made
him ruler all the days of his life for the sake of David my servant, whom I chose and
who observed my commands and statutes. 35 I will take the kingdom from his son's
hands and give you ten tribes. 36 I will give one tribe[e] to his son so that David my
servant may always have a lamp[f] before me in Jerusalem, the city where I chose to
put my Name. 37 However, as for you, I will take you, and you will rule over all that
your heart desires;[g] you will be king over Israel. 38 If you do whatever I command
you and walk in my ways and do what is right in my eyes by keeping my statutes[h]
and commands, as David my servant did, I will be with you. I will build you a
dynasty[i] as enduring as the one I built for David and will give Israel to you. 39 I will
humble David's descendants because of this, but not for ever.' "
40 Solomon tried to kill Jeroboam, but Jeroboam fled to Egypt, to Shishak[j] the
king, and stayed there until Solomon's death.

Solomon's Death

41 As for the other events of Solomon's reign—all he did and the wisdom he
displayed—are they not written in the book of the annals of Solomon? 42 Solomon
reigned in Jerusalem over all Israel for forty years. 43 Then he rested with his fathers
and was buried in the city of David his father. And Rehoboam[k] his son succeeded
him as king.

B. THE DIVIDED KINGDOM (12:1—22:53)

After Solomon's death, the northern tribes revolt, forming two separate nations. Each nation experiences disastrous consequences from having evil kings. Elijah appears on the scene, confronting these kings for their sin. God deals with sin in powerful ways. Although judgment may appear to be slow, God will judge evil harshly.

1. Revolt of the northern tribes

Israel Rebels Against Rehoboam

12 Rehoboam went to Shechem, for all the Israelites had gone there to make him
king. 2 When Jeroboam son of Nebat heard this (he was still in Egypt, where
he had fled[a] from King Solomon), he returned from[a] Egypt. 3 So they sent for
Jeroboam, and he and the whole assembly of Israel went to Rehoboam and said to
him: 4 "Your father put a heavy yoke[b] on us, but now lighten the harsh labour and
the heavy yoke he put on us, and we will serve you."
5 Rehoboam answered, "Go away for three days and then come back to me." So
the people went away.
6 Then King Rehoboam consulted the elders[c] who had served his father Solomon
during his lifetime. "How would you advise me to answer these people?" he asked.
7 They replied, "If today you will be a servant to these people and serve them and
give them a favourable answer,[d] they will always be your servants."
8 But Rehoboam rejected the advice the elders gave him and consulted the young

d 33 Hebrew; Septuagint, Vulgate and Syriac *because he has* **a** 2 Or *he remained in*

11:30 a 1Sa 15:27
11:31 b ver 11
11:33 c ver 5-7; d 1Ki 3:3
11:36 e ver 13; 1Ki 12:17; f 1Ki 15:4; 2Ki 8:19
11:37 g 2Sa 3:21
11:38 h Dt 17:19; i Jos 1:5; 2Sa 7:11, 27
11:40 j 2Ch 12:2
11:43 k 1Ki 14:21; Mt 1:7
12:2 a 1Ki 11:40
12:4 b 1Sa 8:11-18; 1Ki 4:20-28
12:6 c 1Ki 4:2
12:7 d Pr 15:1

11:41 Nothing is known of "the book of the annals of Solomon". See also the note on 14:19.

12:1 Rehoboam was made king at Shechem, about 35 miles north of Jerusalem. It would have been normal to anoint the new king in Jerusalem, the capital city, but Rehoboam saw trouble brewing with Jeroboam and went north to try to maintain good relations with the northern tribes. He probably chose Shechem because it was an ancient location for making covenants (Joshua 24:1). When the kingdom divided, Shechem became the capital of the northern kingdom for a short time (12:25).

12:14 [e]Ex 1:14; 5:5-9, 16-18
12:15 [f]ver 24; Dt 2:30; Jdg 14:4; 2Ch 22:7; 25:20 [g]1Ki 11:29
12:16 [h]2Sa 20:1
12:17 [i]1Ki 11:13, 36
12:18 [j]2Sa 20:24; 1Ki 4:6; 5:14
12:19 [k]2Ki 17:21
12:20 [l]1Ki 11:13, 32

men who had grown up with him and were serving him. 9He asked them, "What is
your advice? How should we answer these people who say to me, 'Lighten the yoke
your father put on us'?"
10The young men who had grown up with him replied, "Tell these people who have
said to you, 'Your father put a heavy yoke on us, but make our yoke lighter'—tell
them, 'My little finger is thicker than my father's waist. 11My father laid on you a
heavy yoke; I will make it even heavier. My father scourged you with whips; I will
scourge you with scorpions.' "
12Three days later Jeroboam and all the people returned to Rehoboam, as the king
had said, "Come back to me in three days." 13The king answered the people harshly.
Rejecting the advice given him by the elders, 14he followed the advice of the young
men and said, "My father made your yoke heavy; I will make it even heavier. My
father scourged[e] you with whips; I will scourge you with scorpions." 15So the king
did not listen to the people, for this turn of events was from the LORD,[f] to fulfil the
word the LORD had spoken to Jeroboam son of Nebat through Ahijah[g] the Shilonite.
16When all Israel saw that the king refused to listen to them, they answered the king:

> "What share do we have in David,
> what part in Jesse's son?
> To your tents, O Israel![h]
> Look after your own house, O David!"

So the Israelites went home. 17But as for the Israelites who were living in the towns
of Judah,[i] Rehoboam still ruled over them.
18King Rehoboam sent out Adoniram,[b][j] who was in charge of forced labour, but
all Israel stoned him to death. King Rehoboam, however, managed to get into his
chariot and escape to Jerusalem. 19So Israel has been in rebellion against the house
of David[k] to this day.
20When all the Israelites heard that Jeroboam had returned, they sent and called him
to the assembly and made him king over all Israel. Only the tribe of Judah remained
loyal to the house of David.[l]
21When Rehoboam arrived in Jerusalem, he mustered the whole house of Judah and

b *18* Some Septuagint manuscripts and Syriac (see also 1 Kings 4:6 and 5:14); Hebrew *Adoram*

THE KINGDOM DIVIDES
Rehoboam's threat of heavier burdens caused a rebellion and divided the nation. Rehoboam ruled the southern kingdom; Jeroboam ruled the northern kingdom. Jeroboam set up idols in Dan and Bethel to discourage worship in Jerusalem. At the same time Aram, Ammon, Moab, and Edom claimed independence from the divided nation.

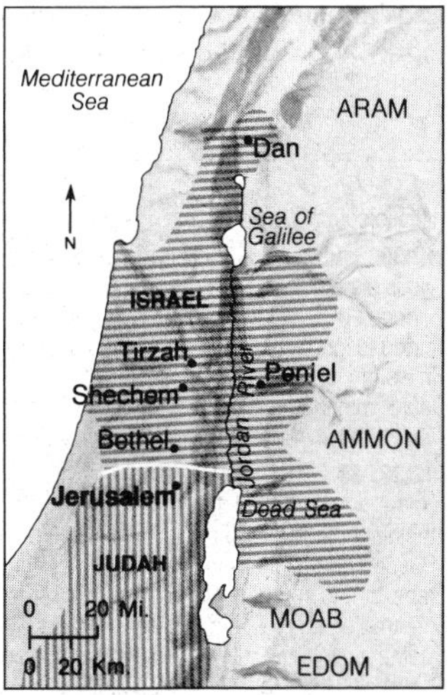

12:6–14 Rehoboam asked for advice, but he didn't carefully evaluate what he was told. If he had, he would have realised that the advice offered by the elders was wiser than that of his peers. To evaluate advice, ask if it is realistic, workable, and consistent with biblical principles. Determine if the results of following the advice will be fair, make improvements, and give a positive solution or direction. Seek counsel from those more experienced and wiser. Advice is helpful only if it is consistent with God's standards.

12:15–19 Both Jeroboam and Rehoboam did what was good for themselves, not what was good for their people. Rehoboam was harsh and did not listen to what the people said; Jeroboam established new places of worship to keep his people from travelling to Jerusalem, Rehoboam's capital. Both actions backfired. Rehoboam's move divided the nation, and Jeroboam's turned the people from God. Good leaders put the best interests of the "followers" above their own. Making decisions only for yourself will backfire and cause you to lose more than if you had kept the welfare of others in mind.

12:20 This marks the beginning of the division of the kingdom that lasted for centuries. Ten of Israel's 12 tribes followed Jeroboam and called their new nation Israel (the northern kingdom). The other two tribes remained loyal to Rehoboam and called their nation Judah (the southern kingdom). The kingdom did not split overnight. It was already dividing as early as the days of the judges because of tribal jealousies, especially between Ephraim, the most influential tribe of the north, and Judah, the chief tribe of the south.

Before the days of Saul and David, the religious centre of Israel was located, for the most part, in the territory of Ephraim. When Solomon built the temple, he moved the religious centre of Israel to Jerusalem. This eventually brought tribal rivalries to the breaking point. (For more information on tribal jealousies and how they affected Israel, see Judges 12:1ff; 2 Samuel 2:4ff; 19:41–43.)

the tribe of Benjamin—a hundred and eighty thousand fighting men—to make war[m]
against the house of Israel and to regain the kingdom for Rehoboam son of Solomon.
22 But this word of God came to Shemaiah[n] the man of God: 23 "Say to Rehoboam
son of Solomon king of Judah, to the whole house of Judah and Benjamin, and to the
rest of the people, 24 'This is what the LORD says: Do not go up to fight against your
brothers, the Israelites. Go home, every one of you, for this is my doing.' " So they
obeyed the word of the LORD and went home again, as the LORD had ordered.

Golden Calves at Bethel and Dan

25 Then Jeroboam fortified Shechem[o] in the hill country of Ephraim and lived there.
From there he went out and built up Peniel.[c][p]
26 Jeroboam thought to himself, "The kingdom is now likely to revert to the house
of David. 27 If these people go up to offer sacrifices at the temple of the LORD in
Jerusalem,[q] they will again give their allegiance to their lord, Rehoboam king of
Judah. They will kill me and return to King Rehoboam."
28 After seeking advice, the king made two golden calves.[r] He said to the people,
"It is too much for you to go up to Jerusalem. Here are your gods, O Israel, who
brought you up out of Egypt."[s] 29 One he set up in Bethel,[t] and the other in Dan.[u]
30 And this thing became a sin;[v] the people went even as far as Dan to worship the
one there.
31 Jeroboam built shrines[w] on high places and appointed priests[x] from all sorts of
people, even though they were not Levites. 32 He instituted a festival on the fifteenth
day of the eighth[y] month, like the festival held in Judah, and offered sacrifices on
the altar. This he did in Bethel, sacrificing to the calves he had made. And at Bethel
he also installed priests at the high places he had made. 33 On the fifteenth day of the
eighth month, a month of his own choosing, he offered sacrifices on the altar he had
built at Bethel.[z] So he instituted the festival for the Israelites and went up to the altar
to make offerings.

2. Kings of Israel and Judah

The Man of God From Judah

13 By the word of the LORD a man of God[a] came from Judah to Bethel,[b] as
Jeroboam was standing by the altar to make an offering. 2 He cried out against
the altar by the word of the LORD: "O altar, altar! This is what the LORD says: 'A son
named Josiah[c] will be born to the house of David. On you he will sacrifice the priests
of the high places who now make offerings here, and human bones will be burned
on you.' " 3 That same day the man of God gave a sign:[d] "This is the sign the LORD

[c] 25 Hebrew *Penuel,* a variant of *Peniel*

12:21 [m] 2Ch 11:1
12:22 [n] 2Ch 12:5-7
12:25 [o] Jdg 9:45 [p] Jdg 8:8, 17
12:27 [q] Dt 12:5-6
12:28 [r] Ex 32:4; 2Ki 10:29; 17:16 [s] Ex 32:8
12:29 [t] Ge 28:19 [u] Jdg 18:27-31
12:30 [v] 1Ki 13:34; 2Ki 17:21
12:31 [w] 1Ki 13:32 [x] Nu 3:10; 1Ki 13:33; 2Ki 17:32; 2Ch 11:14-15; 13:9
12:32 [y] Lev 23:33-34; Nu 29:12
12:33 [z] Nu 15:39; 1Ki 13:1; Am 7:13
13:1 [a] 2Ki 23:17 [b] 1Ki 12:32-33
13:2 [c] 2Ki 23:15-16, 20
13:3 [d] Jdg 6:17; Isa 7:14; Jn 2:11; 1Co 1:22

12:28 All Jewish men were required to travel to the temple three times each year (Deuteronomy 16:16), but Jeroboam set up his own worship centres and told his people it was too much trouble to travel all the way to Jerusalem. Those who obeyed Jeroboam were disobeying God. Some ideas, though practical, may include suggestions that lead you away from God. Don't let anyone talk you out of doing what is right by telling you that moral actions are not worth the effort. Do what God wants, no matter what the cost in time, energy, reputation, or resources.

12:28, 29 Calves were used as idols to symbolise fertility and strength. Pagan gods of the Canaanites were often depicted as standing on calves or bulls. Jeroboam shrewdly placed the golden calves in Bethel and Dan, strategic locations. Bethel was just 10 miles north of Jerusalem on the main road, enticing the citizens from the north to stop there instead of travelling the rest of the way to Jerusalem. Dan was the northernmost city in Israel, so people living in the north far from Jerusalem were attracted to its convenient location. As leader of the northern kingdom, Jeroboam wanted to establish his own worship centres; otherwise his people would make regular trips to Jerusalem, and his authority would be undermined. Soon this substitute religion had little in common with true faith in God.

12:30 Jeroboam and his advisers did not learn from Israel's previous disaster with a golden calf (Exodus 32). Perhaps they were ignorant of Scripture, or maybe they knew about the event and decided to ignore it. Study the Bible to become aware of God's acts in history, and then apply the important lessons to your life. If you learn from the past, you will not face disaster as a result of repeating others' mistakes (Isaiah 42:23; 1 Corinthians 10:11).

12:32, 33 In the days of Israel's founding fathers, the city of Bethel was a symbol of commitment to God because it was there that Jacob had rededicated himself to God (Genesis 28:16–22). But Jeroboam turned the city into Israel's chief religious centre, intending it to compete with Jerusalem. Bethel's religion, however, centred on an idol, and this led to Israel's eventual downfall. Bethel developed a reputation as a wicked and idolatrous city. The prophets Hosea and Amos recognised the sins of Bethel and condemned the city for its godless ways (Hosea 4:15–17; 10:8; Amos 5:4–6).

13:2 Three hundred years later, this prophecy was fulfilled in every detail when Josiah killed the pagan priests at their own altars. The story is found in 2 Kings 23:1–20.

13:6 [e]Ex 8:8; 9:28; 10:17; Lk 6:27-28; Ac 8:24; Jas 5:16

has declared: The altar will be split apart and the ashes on it will be poured out."
4When King Jeroboam heard what the man of God cried out against the altar at
Bethel, he stretched out his hand from the altar and said, "Seize him!" But the hand
he stretched out towards the man shrivelled up, so that he could not pull it back. 5Also,
the altar was split apart and its ashes poured out according to the sign given by the
man of God by the word of the LORD.
6Then the king said to the man of God, "Intercede[e] with the LORD your God and
pray for me that my hand may be restored." So the man of God interceded with the
LORD, and the king's hand was restored and became as it was before.

13:7 [f]1Sa 9:7; 2Ki 5:15

7The king said to the man of God, "Come home with me and have something to
eat, and I will give you a gift."[f]
8But the man of God answered the king, "Even if you were to give me half your
possessions,[g] I would not go with you, nor would I eat bread[h] or drink water here.
9For I was commanded by the word of the LORD: 'You must not eat bread or drink
water or return by the way you came.' " 10So he took another road and did not return
by the way he had come to Bethel.

13:8 [g]Nu 22:18; 24:13 [h]ver 16

11Now there was a certain old prophet living in Bethel, whose sons came and told
him all that the man of God had done there that day. They also told their father what
he had said to the king. 12Their father asked them, "Which way did he go?" And his
sons showed him which road the man of God from Judah had taken. 13So he said to
his sons, "Saddle the donkey for me." And when they had saddled the donkey for him,
he mounted it 14and rode after the man of God. He found him sitting under an oak
tree and asked, "Are you the man of God who came from Judah?"
"I am," he replied.
15So the prophet said to him, "Come home with me and eat."

13:16 [i]ver 8

16The man of God said, "I cannot turn back and go with you, nor can I eat bread[i]
or drink water with you in this place. 17I have been told by the word of the LORD:
'You must not eat bread or drink water there or return by the way you came.' "
18The old prophet answered, "I too am a prophet, as you are. And an angel said
to me by the word of the LORD: 'Bring him back with you to your house so that he
may eat bread and drink water.' " (But he was lying[j] to him.) 19So the man of God
returned with him and ate and drank in his house.

13:18 [j]Dt 13:3

20While they were sitting at the table, the word of the LORD came to the old prophet

---

TRIBAL JEALOUSIES

Although the kingdom of Israel was "united" under David and Solomon, the tensions between north and south were never resolved. The jealousy and animosity behind this civil war didn't begin with Rehoboam and Jeroboam, but had its roots in the days of the judges, when the people were more interested in tribal loyalty than in national unity. Note how easily tension arose between Ephraim, the most prominent tribe in the north, and Judah, the prominent tribe of the south.

- Ephraim claimed the promises in Genesis 48:17–22 and 49:22–26 for its leadership role.
- Joshua, who conquered the promised land, was an Ephraimite (Numbers 13:8).
- Samuel, Israel's greatest judge, was from Ephraim (1 Samuel 1:1ff).
- Ephraim allied with Ish-Bosheth in revolt against David, who was from the tribe of Judah (2 Samuel 2:8–11).
- David, a shepherd from the tribe of Judah, became king over all Israel, including Ephraim, which no longer had a claim to leadership.
- Although David helped to smooth over the bad feelings, the heavy yoke under Solomon and Rehoboam led the northern tribes to breaking point.

Such tension developed because Ephraim was the key tribe in the north. They resented Judah's role in leadership under David and resented that the nation's capital and centre of worship were located in Jerusalem.

13:7–32 This prophet had been given strict orders from God not to eat or drink anything while on his mission (13:9). He died because he listened to a man who claimed to have a message from God, rather than to God himself. This prophet should have followed God's word instead of hearsay. Trust what God's word says rather than what someone claims is true. And disregard what others claim to be messages from God if their words contradict the Bible.

who had brought him back. 21He cried out to the man of God who had come from
Judah, "This is what the LORD says: 'You have defied[k] the word of the LORD and
have not kept the command the LORD your God gave you. 22You came back and ate
bread and drank water in the place where he told you not to eat or drink. Therefore
your body will not be buried in the tomb of your fathers.' "
23When the man of God had finished eating and drinking, the prophet who had
brought him back saddled his donkey for him. 24As he went on his way, a lion[l] met
him on the road and killed him, and his body was thrown down on the road, with both
the donkey and the lion standing beside it. 25Some people who passed by saw the body
thrown down there, with the lion standing beside the body, and they went and reported
it in the city where the old prophet lived.
26When the prophet who had brought him back from his journey heard of it, he said,
"It is the man of God who defied the word of the LORD. The LORD has given him over
to the lion, which has mauled him and killed him, as the word of the LORD had warned
him."
27The prophet said to his sons, "Saddle the donkey for me," and they did so. 28Then
he went out and found the body thrown down on the road, with the donkey and the
lion standing beside it. The lion had neither eaten the body nor mauled the donkey.
29So the prophet picked up the body of the man of God, laid it on the donkey, and
brought it back to his own city to mourn for him and bury him. 30Then he laid the
body in his own tomb, and they mourned over him and said, "Oh, my brother!"[m]
31After burying him, he said to his sons, "When I die, bury me in the grave where
the man of God is buried; lay my bones[n] beside his bones. 32For the message he
declared by the word of the LORD against the altar in Bethel and against all the shrines
on the high places[o] in the towns of Samaria[p] will certainly come true."[q]
33Even after this, Jeroboam did not change his evil ways, but once more appointed
priests for the high places from all sorts[r] of people. Anyone who wanted to become
a priest he consecrated for the high places. 34This was the sin[s] of the house of
Jeroboam that led to its downfall and to its destruction[t] from the face of the earth.

Ahijah's Prophecy Against Jeroboam

14 At that time Abijah son of Jeroboam became ill, 2and Jeroboam said to his wife,
"Go, disguise yourself, so that you won't be recognised as the wife of Jeroboam. Then go to Shiloh. Ahijah[a] the prophet is there — the one who told me I would
be king over this people. 3Take ten loaves of bread[b] with you, some cakes and a jar
of honey, and go to him. He will tell you what will happen to the boy." 4So Jeroboam's
wife did what he said and went to Ahijah's house in Shiloh.
Now Ahijah could not see; his sight was gone because of his age. 5But the LORD
had told Ahijah, "Jeroboam's wife is coming to ask you about her son, for he is ill,
and you are to give her such and such an answer. When she arrives, she will pretend
to be someone else."
6So when Ahijah heard the sound of her footsteps at the door, he said, "Come in,
wife of Jeroboam. Why this pretence? I have been sent to you with bad news. 7Go,
tell Jeroboam that this is what the LORD, the God of Israel, says: 'I raised you up from
among the people and made you a leader[c] over my people Israel. 8I tore[d] the
kingdom away from the house of David and gave it to you, but you have not been
like my servant David, who kept my commands and followed me with all his heart,
doing only what was right[e] in my eyes. 9You have done more evil than all who lived

13:21 [k] ver 26
13:24 [l] 1Ki 20:36
13:30 [m] Jer 22:18
13:31 [n] 2Ki 23:18
13:32 [o] ver 2; Lev 26:30 [p] 1Ki 16:24, 28 [q] 2Ki 23:16
13:33 [r] 1Ki 12:31; 2Ch 11:15; 13:9
13:34 [s] 1Ki 12:30 [t] 1Ki 14:10
14:2 [a] 1Sa 28:8; 2Sa 14:2; 1Ki 11:29
14:3 [b] 1Sa 9:7
14:7 [c] 2Sa 12:7-8; 1Ki 16:2
14:8 [d] 1Ki 11:31, 33, 38 [e] 1Ki 15:5

13:24, 25 Lions are mentioned frequently in the Old Testament. They were common enough to be a threat both to people and to their flocks. Samson (Judges 14:5, 6), David (1 Samuel 17:34–37), and Benaiah (2 Samuel 23:20) all faced wild lions. The fact that the lion and the donkey were standing by the prophet's body showed that this was a divine judgment. Normally, the lion would have attacked the donkey and/or devoured the man.

13:33, 34 Under penalty of death, God had forbidden anyone to be a priest who was not from the tribe of Levi (Numbers 3:10). Levites were assured of lifetime support from the tithe, so they did not have to spend time farming, worrying about tribal interests, or fearing for their financial futures. Jeroboam's new priests were financed by the king and his fees. They had to mix priestly and secular duties, and they quickly fell into party politics. Because they didn't have job security, they were easily corrupted by bribes. Jeroboam's disobedience was the downfall of true religion in the northern kingdom.

14:9
1Ki 12:28;
Ps 50:17

14:10
[h]Dt 32:36;
1Ki 21:21;
2Ki 9:8-9; 14:26
[i]1Ki 15:29

14:11
[j]1Ki 16:4; 21:24

before you. You have made for yourself other gods, idols[f] made of metal; you have
provoked me to anger and thrust me behind your back.[g]
10“ ‘Because of this, I am going to bring disaster on the house of Jeroboam. I will
cut off from Jeroboam every last male in Israel—slave or free.[h] I will burn up the
house of Jeroboam as one burns dung, until it is all gone.[i] 11Dogs[j] will eat those
belonging to Jeroboam who die in the city, and the birds of the air will feed on those
who die in the country. The LORD has spoken!’

JEROBOAM

Even clear warnings are hard to obey. The Bible is filled with stories of people who had direction from God and yet chose their own way. Their disobedience was rarely due to ignorance of what God wanted; rather, it grew out of stubborn selfishness. Jeroboam was a consistent example of this all-too-human trait.

During his construction activities, Solomon noticed young Jeroboam’s natural leadership skills and made him a special project foreman. Shortly after this, God contacted Jeroboam through the prophet Ahijah. He told Jeroboam that God would punish David’s dynasty by tearing the kingdom from Solomon’s son and that Jeroboam would rule the ten northern tribes. And God made it clear that the same fate would destroy Jeroboam’s family if they refused to obey God. Apparently Solomon heard about these events and tried to have Jeroboam killed. The future king escaped to Egypt, where he stayed until Solomon died.

When Rehoboam, Solomon’s heir, took the throne, Jeroboam returned. He represented the people in demanding that the new king be more lenient than his father. Rehoboam’s unwise choice to reject his people’s request led to their rejecting him as king. Only Judah and the annexed tribe of Benjamin remained loyal to David’s dynasty. The other ten tribes made Jeroboam king.

Rather than seeing this fulfilment of God’s promise as motivation to obey God, Jeroboam decided to do whatever he could to secure his position. He led his kingdom away from the God who had allowed him to reign. God had already warned him of the consequences of this action—his family was eventually wiped out. And Jeroboam set into motion events that would lead to the destruction of the northern kingdom.

Sin’s consequences are guaranteed in God’s word, but the timing of those consequences is hard to predict. When we do something directly opposed to God’s commands and there isn’t immediate disaster, we are often fooled into believing we have got away with disobedience. But that is a dangerous assumption. Jeroboam’s life should make us recognise our frequent need to admit our disobedience and ask God to forgive us.

Strengths and accomplishments:
- An effective leader and organiser
- First king of the ten tribes of Israel in the divided kingdom
- A charismatic leader with much popular support

Weaknesses and mistakes:
- Erected idols in Israel to keep people away from the temple in Jerusalem
- Appointed priests from outside the tribe of Levi
- Depended more on his own cunning than on God’s promises

Lessons from his life:
- Great opportunities are often destroyed by small decisions
- Careless efforts to correct another’s errors often lead to the same errors
- Mistakes always occur when we attempt to take over God’s role in a situation

Vital statistics:
- Where: The northern kingdom of Israel
- Occupations: Project foreman, king of Israel
- Relatives: Father: Nebat. Mother: Zeruah. Sons: Abijah, Nadab
- Contemporaries: Solomon, Nathan, Ahijah, Rehoboam

Key verses:
“Even after this, Jeroboam did not change his evil ways, but once more appointed priests for the high places from all sorts of people. Anyone who wanted to become a priest he consecrated for the high places. This was the sin of the house of Jeroboam that led to its downfall and to its destruction from the face of the earth” (1 Kings 13:33, 34).

Jeroboam’s story is told in 1 Kings 11:26—14:20. He is also mentioned in 2 Chronicles 10—13.

14:10, 11 These disasters were practical applications to Israel of the specific teachings of Deuteronomy (see Deuteronomy 28:15–19, 36–68; 30:15–20). Ahijah is prophesying the downfall of Israel for its flagrant violation of God’s commands.

12"As for you, go back home. When you set foot in your city, the boy will die.
13All Israel will mourn for him and bury him. He is the only one belonging to
Jeroboam who will be buried, because he is the only one in the house of Jeroboam
in whom the LORD, the God of Israel, has found anything good.[k]
14"The LORD will raise up for himself a king over Israel who will cut off the family
of Jeroboam. This is the day! What? Yes, even now.[a] 15And the LORD will strike
Israel, so that it will be like a reed swaying in the water. He will uproot[l] Israel from
this good land that he gave to their forefathers and scatter them beyond the River,[b]
because they provoked[m] the LORD to anger by making Asherah[n] poles.[c] 16And he
will give Israel up because of the sins[o] Jeroboam has committed and has caused Israel
to commit."
17Then Jeroboam's wife got up and left and went to Tirzah.[p] As soon as she stepped
over the threshold of the house, the boy died. 18They buried him, and all Israel
mourned for him, as the LORD had said through his servant the prophet Ahijah.
19The other events of Jeroboam's reign, his wars and how he ruled, are written in
the book of the annals of the kings of Israel. 20He reigned for twenty-two years and
then rested with his fathers. And Nadab his son succeeded him as king.

Rehoboam King of Judah

21Rehoboam son of Solomon was king in Judah. He was forty-one years old when
he became king, and he reigned for seventeen years in Jerusalem, the city the LORD
had chosen out of all the tribes of Israel in which to put his Name. His mother's name
was Naamah; she was an Ammonite.[q]
22Judah[r] did evil in the eyes of the LORD. By the sins they committed they stirred
up his jealous anger[s] more than their fathers had done. 23They also set up for
themselves high places, sacred stones[t] and Asherah poles on every high hill and
under every spreading tree.[u] 24There were even male shrine-prostitutes[v] in the land;
the people engaged in all the detestable practices of the nations the LORD had driven
out before the Israelites.
25In the fifth year of King Rehoboam, Shishak king of Egypt attacked[w] Jerusalem.
26He carried off the treasures of the temple[x] of the LORD and the treasures of the royal
palace. He took everything, including all the gold shields[y] Solomon had made. 27So
King Rehoboam made bronze shields to replace them and assigned these to the
commanders of the guard on duty at the entrance to the royal palace. 28Whenever the
king went to the LORD's temple, the guards bore the shields, and afterwards they
returned them to the guardroom.
29As for the other events of Rehoboam's reign, and all he did, are they not written
in the book of the annals of the kings of Judah? 30There was continual warfare[z]
between Rehoboam and Jeroboam. 31And Rehoboam rested with his fathers and was

14:13 [k]2Ch 12:12; 19:3
14:15 [l]Dt 29:28; 2Ki 15:29; 17:6; Ps 52:5 [m]Jos 23:15-16 [n]Ex 34:13; Dt 12:3
14:16 [o]1Ki 12:30; 13:34; 15:30, 34; 16:2
14:17 [p]ver 12; 1Ki 15:33; 16:6-9
14:21 [q]ver 31; 1Ki 11:1; 2Ch 12:13
14:22 [r]2Ch 12:1 [s]Dt 32:21; Ps 78:58; 1Co 10:22
14:23 [t]Dt 16:22; 2Ki 17:9-10; Eze 16:24-25 [u]Dt 12:2; Isa 57:5
14:24 [v]Dt 23:17; 1Ki 15:12; 2Ki 23:7
14:25 [w]1Ki 11:40; 2Ch 12:2
14:26 [x]1Ki 15:15, 18 [y]1Ki 10:17
14:30 [z]1Ki 12:21; 15:6

[a] *14* The meaning of the Hebrew for this sentence is uncertain. [b] *15* That is, the Euphrates [c] *15* That is, symbols of the goddess Asherah; here and elsewhere in 1 Kings

14:14 Who was this king who would "cut off the family of Jeroboam"? His name was Baasha, and he would kill all of Jeroboam's descendants (15:27–30).

14:15 "Asherah poles" refers to idol worship. Wooden images were made for the worship of Asherah, a Canaanite mother-goddess.

14:19 Three books are mentioned in 1 and 2 Kings – the book of the annals of the kings of Israel (14:19), the book of the annals of the kings of Judah (14:29), and the book of the annals of Solomon (11:41). These historical records of Israel and Judah were the main sources of material God directed the author to use to write 1 and 2 Kings. No copies of these books have been found.

14:23 "Sacred stones" were pillars of stone placed next to pagan altars. These pillars were supposed to represent deity.

14:25 When Rehoboam came to power, he inherited a mighty kingdom. Everything he could ever want was given to him. But apparently he did not recognise why he had so much or how it had been obtained. To teach Rehoboam a lesson, God allowed Shishak of Egypt to invade Judah and Israel. Egypt was no longer the world power it had once been, and Shishak, possibly resenting Solomon's enormous success, was determined to change that. Shishak's army was not strong enough to destroy Judah and Israel, but he weakened them so much that they were never the same again.

14:25, 26 Just five years after Solomon died, the temple and palace were ransacked by foreign invaders. How quickly the glory, power, and money disappeared! When the people became spiritually corrupt and immoral (14:24), it was just a short time until they lost everything. Wealth, idol worship, and immorality had become more important to them than God. When God is gone from our

14:31 [a]ver 21; 2Ch 12:16

buried with them in the City of David. His mother's name was Naamah; she was an
Ammonite.[a] And Abijah[d] his son succeeded him as king.

Abijah King of Judah

15:2 [a]2Ch 11:20; 13:2
15:3 [b]1Ki 11:4; Ps 119:80
15:4 [c]2Sa 21:17; 1Ki 11:36; 2Ch 21:7
15:5 [d]1Ki 9:4; 14:8 [e]2Sa 11:2-27; 12:9
15:6 [f]1Ki 14:30
15:10 [g]ver 2

15 In the eighteenth year of the reign of Jeroboam son of Nebat, Abijah[a] became
king of Judah, 2 and he reigned in Jerusalem for three years. His mother's name
was Maacah[a] daughter of Abishalom.[b]
3 He committed all the sins his father had done before him; his heart was not fully
devoted[b] to the LORD his God, as the heart of David his forefather had been.
4 Nevertheless, for David's sake the LORD his God gave him a lamp[c] in Jerusalem
by raising up a son to succeed him and by making Jerusalem strong. 5 For David had
done what was right in the eyes of the LORD and had not failed to keep[d] any of the
LORD's commands all the days of his life—except in the case of Uriah[e] the Hittite.
6 There was war[f] between Rehoboam[c] and Jeroboam throughout ⌞Abijah's⌟ lifetime. 7 As for the other events of Abijah's reign, and all he did, are they not written
in the book of the annals of the kings of Judah? There was war between Abijah and
Jeroboam. 8 And Abijah rested with his fathers and was buried in the City of David.
And Asa his son succeeded him as king.

Asa King of Judah

9 In the twentieth year of Jeroboam king of Israel, Asa became king of Judah, 10 and
he reigned in Jerusalem for forty-one years. His grandmother's name was Maacah[g]
daughter of Abishalom.

d *31* Some Hebrew manuscripts and Septuagint (see also 2 Chron. 12:16); most Hebrew manuscripts *Abijam*
a *1* Some Hebrew manuscripts and Septuagint (see also 2 Chron. 12:16); most Hebrew manuscripts *Abijam*; also in verses 7 and 8 **b** *2* A variant of *Absalom*; also in verse 10 **c** *6* Most Hebrew manuscripts; some Hebrew manuscripts and Syriac *Abijam* (that is, Abijah)

THE APPEAL OF IDOLS
On the surface, the lives of the kings don't make sense. How could they run to idolatry so fast when they had God's word (at least some of it), prophets, and the example of David? Here are some of the reasons for the enticement of idols:

	The appeal of Idols	*Modern parallel*
POWER	The people wanted freedom from the authority of both God and the priests. They wanted their religion to fit their lifestyle, not their lifestyle to fit their religion.	People do not want to answer to a greater authority. Instead of having power *over* others, God wants us to have the Holy Spirit's power to *help* others.
PLEASURE	Idol worship exalted sensuality without responsibility or guilt. People acted out the vicious and sensuous personalities of the gods they worshipped, thus gaining approval for their degraded lives.	People deify pleasure, seeking it at the expense of everything else. Instead of seeking pleasure that leads to long-term disaster, God calls us to seek the kind of pleasure that leads to long-term rewards.
PASSION	Mankind was reduced to little more than animals. The people did not have to be viewed as unique individuals, but could be exploited sexually, politically, and economically.	Like animals, people let physical drives and passion rule them. Instead of seeking passion that exploits others, God calls us to redirect our passions to areas that build others up.
PRAISE AND POPULARITY	The high and holy nature of God was replaced by gods who were more a reflection of human nature, thus more culturally suitable to the people. These gods no longer required sacrifice, just a token of appeasement.	Sacrifice is seen as self-inflicted punishment, making no sense. Success is to be sought at all costs. Instead of seeking praise for ourselves, God calls us to praise him and those who honour him.

As societies change, they often throw out norms and values no longer considered necessary or acceptable. Believers must be careful not to follow society's example if it discards God's word. When society does that, only godlessness and evil remain.

lives, everything else becomes useless, no matter how valuable it seems.

15:5 See 2 Samuel 11 for the story of David and Uriah the Hittite.

15:9 See Asa's Profile in 2 Chronicles 14 for more information on this king.

11Asa did what was right in the eyes of the LORD, as his father David had done.
12He expelled the male shrine-prostitutes[h] from the land and got rid of all the idols
his fathers had made. 13He even deposed his grandmother Maacah from her position
as queen mother, because she had made a repulsive Asherah pole. Asa cut the pole
down[i] and burned it in the Kidron Valley. 14Although he did not remove the high
places, Asa's heart was fully committed[j] to the LORD all his life. 15He brought into
the temple of the LORD the silver and gold and the articles that he and his father had
dedicated.[k]
16There was war[l] between Asa and Baasha king of Israel throughout their reigns.
17Baasha king of Israel went up against Judah and fortified Ramah[m] to prevent anyone
from leaving or entering the territory of Asa king of Judah.
18Asa then took all the silver and gold that was left in the treasuries of the LORD's
temple[n] and of his own palace. He entrusted it to his officials and sent[o] them to
Ben-Hadad[p] son of Tabrimmon, the son of Hezion, the king of Aram, who was ruling
in Damascus. 19"Let there be a treaty between me and you," he said, "as there was
between my father and your father. See, I am sending you a gift of silver and gold.
Now break your treaty with Baasha king of Israel so that he will withdraw from me."
20Ben-Hadad agreed with King Asa and sent the commanders of his forces against
the towns of Israel. He conquered[q] Ijon, Dan, Abel Beth Maacah and all Kinnereth
in addition to Naphtali. 21When Baasha heard this, he stopped building Ramah and
withdrew to Tirzah. 22Then King Asa issued an order to all Judah—no-one was
exempt—and they carried away from Ramah the stones and timber Baasha had been
using there. With them King Asa built up Geba[r] in Benjamin, and also Mizpah.
23As for all the other events of Asa's reign, all his achievements, all he did and
the cities he built, are they not written in the book of the annals of the kings of Judah?
In his old age, however, his feet became diseased. 24Then Asa rested with his fathers
and was buried with them in the city of his father David. And Jehoshaphat[s] his son
succeeded him as king.

Nadab King of Israel

25Nadab son of Jeroboam became king of Israel in the second year of Asa king of
Judah, and he reigned over Israel for two years. 26He did evil in the eyes of the LORD,
walking in the ways of his father[t] and in his sin, which he had caused Israel to
commit.
27Baasha son of Ahijah of the house of Issachar plotted against him, and he struck
him down[u] at Gibbethon,[v] a Philistine town, while Nadab and all Israel were
besieging it. 28Baasha killed Nadab in the third year of Asa king of Judah and
succeeded him as king.
29As soon as he began to reign, he killed Jeroboam's whole family.[w] He did not
leave Jeroboam anyone that breathed, but destroyed them all, according to the word
of the LORD given through his servant Ahijah the Shilonite—30because of the sins[x]
Jeroboam had committed and had caused Israel to commit, and because he provoked
the LORD, the God of Israel, to anger.
31As for the other events of Nadab's reign, and all he did, are they not written in
the book of the annals of the kings of Israel? 32There was war[y] between Asa and
Baasha king of Israel throughout their reigns.

15:12 [h] 1Ki 14:24; 22:46
15:13 [i] Ex 32:20
15:14 [j] ver 3; 1Ki 8:61; 22:43
15:15 [k] 1Ki 7:51
15:16 [l] ver 32
15:17 [m] Jos 18:25; 1Ki 12:27
15:18 [n] ver 15; 1Ki 14:26 [o] 2Ki 12:18 [p] 1Ki 11:23-24
15:20 [q] Jdg 18:29; 2Sa 20:14; 2Ki 15:29
15:22 [r] Jos 18:24; 21:17
15:24 [s] Mt 1:8
15:26 [t] 1Ki 12:30; 14:16
15:27 [u] 1Ki 14:14 [v] Jos 19:44; 21:23
15:29 [w] 1Ki 14:10, 14
15:30 [x] 1Ki 14:9, 16
15:32 [y] ver 16

15:15 These gifts for the temple were articles devoted to God as sacred offerings that Abijah had taken in his war with Jeroboam (2 Chronicles 13:16, 17) and Asa had taken when he defeated the Cushites (2 Chronicles 14:12, 13).

15:16 Baasha seized the throne from Nadab (15:27, 28), who had replaced his father, Jeroboam, as king.

15:29 See 1 Kings 14:12–14 for Ahijah's prediction of this event.

15:30 All the descendants of Jeroboam were killed because Jeroboam had led Israel into sin. Sin is always judged harshly, but the worst sinners are those who lead others into doing wrong. Jesus said it would be better if such people had millstones tied around their necks and were thrown into the sea (Mark 9:42). If you have taken the responsibility for leading others, remember the consequences of leading them astray. Teaching the truth is a responsibility that goes with the privilege of leadership.

15:34
[z]ver 26;
1Ki 12:28-29; 13:33; 14:16

16:1
[a]ver 7;
2Ch 19:2; 20:34
[b]2Ch 16:7

16:2
[c]1Sa 2:8
[d]1Ki 14:7-9
[e]1Ki 15:34

16:3
[f]ver 11;
1Ki 14:10; 15:29; 21:22

16:4
[g]1Ki 14:11

16:5
[h]1Ki 14:19; 15:31

16:6
[i]1Ki 14:17; 15:33

16:7
[j]1Ki 15:27, 29
[k]ver 1

16:9
[l]2Ki 9:30-33
[m]1Ki 18:3

Baasha King of Israel

33 In the third year of Asa king of Judah, Baasha son of Ahijah became king of all
Israel in Tirzah, and he reigned for twenty-four years. 34 He did evil[z] in the eyes of
the LORD, walking in the ways of Jeroboam and in his sin, which he had caused Israel
to commit.

16 Then the word of the LORD came to Jehu[a] son of Hanani[b] against Baasha:
2 "I lifted you up from the dust[c] and made you leader[d] of my people Israel,
but you walked in the ways of Jeroboam and caused[e] my people Israel to sin and to
provoke me to anger by their sins. 3 So I am about to consume Baasha and his house,[f]
and I will make your house like that of Jeroboam son of Nebat. 4 Dogs[g] will eat those
belonging to Baasha who die in the city, and the birds of the air will feed on those
who die in the country."

5 As for the other events of Baasha's reign, what he did and his achievements, are
they not written in the book of the annals[h] of the kings of Israel? 6 Baasha rested with
his fathers and was buried in Tirzah.[i] And Elah his son succeeded him as king.
7 Moreover, the word of the LORD came[j] through the prophet Jehu[k] son of Hanani
to Baasha and his house, because of all the evil he had done in the eyes of the LORD,
provoking him to anger by the things he did, and becoming like the house of Jeroboam—and also because he destroyed it.

Elah King of Israel

8 In the twenty-sixth year of Asa king of Judah, Elah son of Baasha became king
of Israel, and he reigned in Tirzah for two years.
9 Zimri, one of his officials, who had command of half his chariots, plotted against
him. Elah was in Tirzah at the time, getting drunk[l] in the home of Arza, the man
in charge[m] of the palace at Tirzah. 10 Zimri came in, struck him down and killed him

KINGS TO DATE AND THEIR ENEMIES

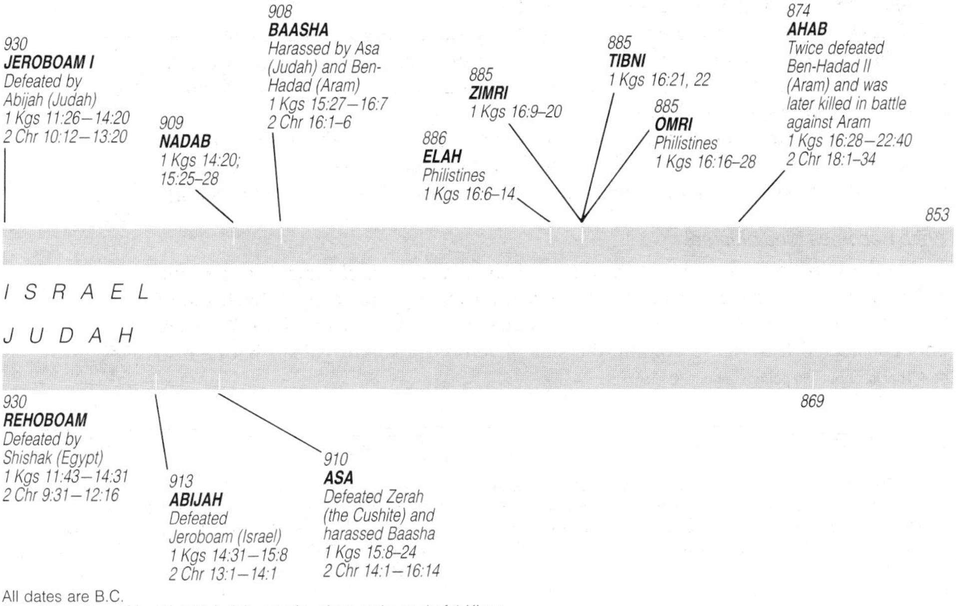

All dates are B.C.
For all the kings of Israel and Judah, see the chart at the end of 1 Kings.

16:1–7 God destroyed Jeroboam's descendants for their flagrant sins, and yet Baasha repeated the same mistakes. He did not learn from the example of those who went before him; he did not stop to think that his sin would be punished. Make sure you learn from your past, the experiences of others, and the lives of those whose stories are told in the Bible. Don't repeat mistakes.

in the twenty-seventh year of Asa king of Judah. Then he succeeded him as king.
11 As soon as he began to reign and was seated on the throne, he killed off Baasha's
whole family.[n] He did not spare a single male, whether relative or friend. 12 So Zimri
destroyed the whole family of Baasha, in accordance with the word of the LORD
spoken against Baasha through the prophet Jehu— 13 because of all the sins Baasha and
his son Elah had committed and had caused Israel to commit, so that they provoked
the LORD, the God of Israel, to anger by their worthless idols.[o]
14 As for the other events of Elah's reign, and all he did, are they not written in the
book of the annals of the kings of Israel?

Zimri King of Israel

15 In the twenty-seventh year of Asa king of Judah, Zimri reigned in Tirzah for seven
days. The army was encamped near Gibbethon,[p] a Philistine town. 16 When the
Israelites in the camp heard that Zimri had plotted against the king and murdered him,
they proclaimed Omri, the commander of the army, king over Israel that very day there
in the camp. 17 Then Omri and all the Israelites with him withdrew from Gibbethon
and laid siege to Tirzah. 18 When Zimri saw that the city was taken, he went into the
citadel of the royal palace and set the palace on fire around him. So he died, 19 because
of the sins he had committed, doing evil in the eyes of the LORD and walking in the
ways of Jeroboam and in the sin he had committed and had caused Israel to commit.
20 As for the other events of Zimri's reign, and the rebellion he carried out, are they
not written in the book of the annals of the kings of Israel?

Omri King of Israel

21 Then the people of Israel were split into two factions; half supported Tibni son
of Ginath for king, and the other half supported Omri. 22 But Omri's followers proved
stronger than those of Tibni son of Ginath. So Tibni died and Omri became king.
23 In the thirty-first year of Asa king of Judah, Omri became king of Israel, and he
reigned for twelve years, six of them in Tirzah.[q] 24 He bought the hill of Samaria from
Shemer for two talents[a] of silver and built a city on the hill, calling it Samaria,[r] after
Shemer, the name of the former owner of the hill.
25 But Omri did evil[s] in the eyes of the LORD and sinned more than all those before
him. 26 He walked in all the ways of Jeroboam son of Nebat and in his sin, which he
had caused[t] Israel to commit, so that they provoked the LORD, the God of Israel,
to anger by their worthless idols.[u]
27 As for the other events of Omri's reign, what he did and the things he achieved,
are they not written in the book of the annals of the kings of Israel? 28 Omri rested
with his fathers and was buried in Samaria. And Ahab his son succeeded him as king.

Ahab Becomes King of Israel

29 In the thirty-eighth year of Asa king of Judah, Ahab son of Omri became king
of Israel, and he reigned in Samaria over Israel for twenty-two years. 30 Ahab son of
Omri did more[v] evil in the eyes of the LORD than any of those before him. 31 He not
only considered it trivial to commit the sins of Jeroboam son of Nebat, but he also

16:11 [n] ver 3
16:13 [o] Dt 32:21; 1Sa 12:21; Isa 41:29
16:15 [p] Jos 19:44; 1Ki 15:27
16:23 [q] 1Ki 15:21
16:24 [r] 1Ki 13:32; Jn 4:4
16:25 [s] Dt 4:25; Mic 6:16
16:26 [t] ver 19 [u] Dt 32:21
16:30 [v] ver 25; 1Ki 14:9

[a] *24* That is, about 150 pounds (about 70 kilograms)

16:21, 22 Omri began his reign as political dissension brewed in Israel. After Zimri killed himself, the Israelite army chose Omri, their commander, as the next ruler. Tibni, Omri's chief rival to the throne, died, and Omri then began his evil reign. During his 12-year rule over Israel, he was a shrewd and capable leader. He organised the building of his new capital city, Samaria, while strengthening the nation politically and militarily. But he did not care about the nation's spiritual condition (Micah 6:16), and he purposely led Israel farther from God in order to put more power in his own hands.

16:24 Omri's new capital, Samaria, offered some political advantages. The city was his personal property, so he had total control over it. Samaria also commanded a hilltop position, which made it easy to defend. Omri died before completing the city. So his son, Ahab, completed it, building not only the beautiful ivory palace (1 Kings 22:39; Amos 3:13–15), but also a temple to the god Baal. Samaria served as the capital city for the rest of Israel's dynasties until it fell to the Assyrians in 722 B.C. (2 Kings 17:5).

16:31 Ahab's evil wife, Jezebel, came from the Phoenician city of Tyre where her father had been a high priest and eventually king. Jezebel worshipped the god Baal. In order to please her, Ahab built a temple and an altar for Baal (16:32), thus promoting idolatry and leading the entire nation into sin. (For more about Baal, see the note on 18:18.)

married[w] Jezebel daughter[x] of Ethbaal king of the Sidonians, and began to serve
Baal[y] and worship him. 32He set up an altar for Baal in the temple[z] of Baal that
he built in Samaria. 33Ahab also made an Asherah pole[a] and did more[b] to provoke
the LORD, the God of Israel, to anger than did all the kings of Israel before him.
34In Ahab's time, Hiel of Bethel rebuilt Jericho. He laid its foundations at the cost
of his firstborn son Abiram, and he set up its gates at the cost of his youngest son
Segub, in accordance with the word of the LORD spoken by Joshua son of Nun.[c]

3. Elijah's ministry

Elijah Fed by Ravens

17 Now Elijah[a] the Tishbite, from Tishbe[a] in Gilead,[b] said to Ahab, "As the
LORD, the God of Israel, lives, whom I serve, there will be neither dew nor
rain[c] in the next few years except at my word."
2Then the word of the LORD came to Elijah: 3"Leave here, turn eastward and hide
in the Kerith Ravine, east of the Jordan. 4You will drink from the brook, and I have
ordered the ravens[d] to feed you there."
5So he did what the LORD had told him. He went to the Kerith Ravine, east of the
Jordan, and stayed there. 6The ravens brought him bread and meat in the morning[e]
and bread and meat in the evening, and he drank from the brook.

The Widow at Zarephath

7Some time later the brook dried up because there had been no rain in the land.
8Then the word of the LORD came to him: 9"Go at once to Zarephath[f] of Sidon and
stay there. I have commanded a widow[g] in that place to supply you with food." 10So
he went to Zarephath. When he came to the town gate, a widow was there gathering
sticks. He called to her and asked, "Would you bring me a little water in a jar so I
may have a drink?"[h] 11As she was going to get it, he called, "And bring me, please,
a piece of bread."
12"As surely as the LORD your God lives," she replied, "I don't have any
bread—only a handful of flour in a jar and a little oil[i] in a jug. I am gathering a few
sticks to take home and make a meal for myself and my son, that we may eat it—and
die."

a 1 Or *Tishbite, of the settlers*

16:31 [w]Dt 7:3; 1Ki 11:2 [x]Jdg 18:7; 2Ki 9:34 [y]2Ki 10:18; 17:16
16:32 [z]2Ki 10:21, 27; 11:18
16:33 [a]2Ki 13:6 [b]ver 29, 30; 1Ki 14:9; 21:25
16:34 [c]Jos 6:26
17:1 [a]Mal 4:5; Jas 5:17 [b]Jdg 12:4 [c]Dt 10:8; 1Ki 18:1; 2Ki 3:14; Lk 4:25
17:4 [d]Ge 8:7
17:6 [e]Ex 16:8
17:9 [f]Ob 1:20 [g]Lk 4:26
17:10 [h]Ge 24:17; Jn 4:7
17:12 [i]ver 1; 2Ki 4:2

17:1 Elijah was the first in a long line of important prophets God sent to Israel and Judah. Israel, the northern kingdom, had no faithful kings throughout its history. Each king was wicked, actually leading the people in worshipping pagan gods. There were few priests left from the tribe of Levi (most had gone to Judah), and the priests appointed by Israel's kings were corrupt and ineffective. With no king or priests to bring God's word to the people, God called prophets to try to rescue Israel from its moral and spiritual decline. For the next 300 years these men and women would play vital roles in both nations, encouraging the people and leaders to turn back to God.

17:1 Those who worshipped Baal believed he was the god who brought the rains and bountiful harvests. So when Elijah walked into the presence of this Baal-worshipping king and told him there would be no rain for several years, Ahab was shocked. Ahab had built a strong military defence, but it would be no help against drought. He had many priests of Baal, but they could not bring rain. Elijah bravely confronted the man who led his people into evil, and he told of a power far greater than any pagan god—the Lord God of Israel. When rebellion and heresy were at an all-time high in Israel, God responded not only with words but with action.

17:10ff In a nation that was required by law to care for its prophets, it is ironic that God turned to ravens (unclean birds) and a widow (a foreigner from Jezebel's home territory) to care for Elijah. God has help where we least expect it. He provides for us in ways that go beyond our narrow definitions or expectations. No matter how bitter our trials or how seemingly hopeless our situation, we should look for God's caring touch. We may find his providence in some strange places!

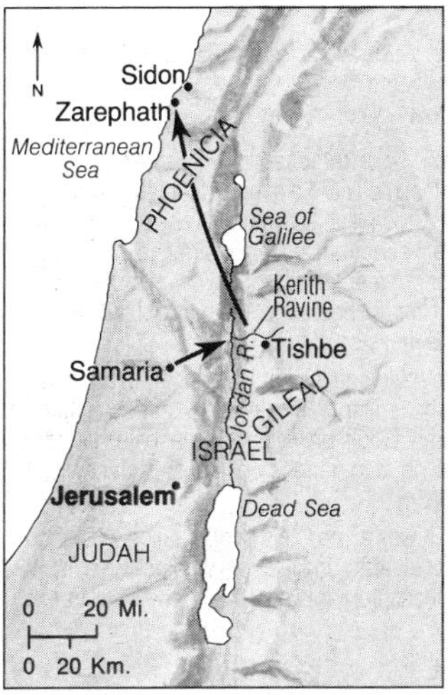

ELIJAH HIDES FROM AHAB
Elijah prophesied a drought and then hid from King Ahab by the Kerith Ravine where he was fed by ravens. When the brook in the ravine dried up, God sent him to Zarephath in Phoenicia where a widow and her son fed him and gave him lodging.

[13]Elijah said to her, "Don't be afraid. Go home and do as you have said. But first
make a small cake of bread for me from what you have and bring it to me, and then
make something for yourself and your son. [14]For this is what the LORD, the God of
Israel, says: 'The jar of flour will not be used up and the jug of oil will not run dry
until the day the LORD gives rain on the land.' "
[15]She went away and did as Elijah had told her. So there was food every day for
Elijah and for the woman and her family. [16]For the jar of flour was not used up and
the jug of oil did not run dry, in keeping with the word of the LORD spoken by Elijah.
[17]Some time later the son of the woman who owned the house became ill. He grew
worse and worse, and finally stopped breathing. [18]She said to Elijah, "What do you
have against me, man of God? Did you come to remind me of my sin[j] and kill my
son?"
[19]"Give me your son," Elijah replied. He took him from her arms, carried him to
the upper room where he was staying, and laid him on his bed. [20]Then he cried out
to the LORD, "O LORD my God, have you brought tragedy also upon this widow I am
staying with, by causing her son to die?" [21]Then he stretched[k] himself out on the boy
three times and cried to the LORD, "O LORD my God, let this boy's life return to him!"
[22]The LORD heard Elijah's cry, and the boy's life returned to him, and he lived.
[23]Elijah picked up the child and carried him down from the room into the house. He
gave him to his mother and said, "Look, your son is alive!"
[24]Then the woman said to Elijah, "Now I know[l] that you are a man of God and
that the word of the LORD from your mouth is the truth."[m]

Elijah and Obadiah

18 After a long time, in the third[a] year, the word of the LORD came to Elijah: "Go
and present yourself to Ahab, and I will send rain[b] on the land." [2]So Elijah
went to present himself to Ahab.
Now the famine was severe in Samaria, [3]and Ahab had summoned Obadiah, who
was in charge[c] of his palace. (Obadiah was a devout believer[d] in the LORD. [4]While
Jezebel[e] was killing off the LORD's prophets, Obadiah had taken a hundred prophets
and hidden[f] them in two caves, fifty in each, and had supplied them with food and
water.) [5]Ahab had said to Obadiah, "Go through the land to all the springs and valleys.
Maybe we can find some grass to keep the horses and mules alive so we will not have
to kill any of our animals." [6]So they divided the land they were to cover, Ahab going
in one direction and Obadiah in another.

17:18 [j]2Ki 3:13; Lk 5:8

17:21 [k]2Ki 4:34; Ac 20:10

17:24 [l]Jn 3:2; 16:30 [m]Ps 119:43; Jn 17:17

18:1 [a]1Ki 17:1; Lk 4:25; Jas 5:17 [b]Dt 28:12

18:3 [c]1Ki 16:9 [d]Ne 7:2

18:4 [e]2Ki 9:7 [f]ver 13; Isa 16:3

17:13–16 When the widow of Zarephath met Elijah, she thought she was preparing her last meal. But a simple act of faith produced a miracle. She trusted Elijah and gave all she had to eat to him. Faith is the step between promise and assurance. Miracles seem so out of reach for our feeble faith. But every miracle, large or small, begins with an act of obedience. We may not see the solution until we take the first step of faith.

17:17 Even when God has done a miracle in our lives, our troubles may not be over. The famine was a terrible experience, but the worst was yet to come. God's provision is never given in order to let us rest upon it. We need to depend on him as each new trial faces us.

18:3, 4 Although Elijah was alone in his confrontation with Ahab and Jezebel, he was not the only one in Israel who believed in God. Obadiah had been faithful in hiding 100 prophets still true to the Lord.

THE SHOWDOWN AT CARMEL
In a showdown with the false prophets of Baal at Mount Carmel, Elijah set out to prove to evil Ahab that only the Lord is God. Elijah then killed the false prophets in the Kishon Valley and fled back to Jezreel.

18:7 [g]2Ki 1:8
7 As Obadiah was walking along, Elijah met him. Obadiah recognised[g] him, bowed
down to the ground, and said, "Is it really you, my lord Elijah?"
8 "Yes," he replied. "Go tell your master, 'Elijah is here.' "
18:10 [h]1Ki 17:3
9 "What have I done wrong," asked Obadiah, "that you are handing your servant
over to Ahab to be put to death? 10 As surely as the LORD your God lives, there is not
a nation or kingdom where my master has not sent someone to look[h] for you. And
18:12 [i]2Ki 2:16; Eze 3:14; Ac 8:39
whenever a nation or kingdom claimed you were not there, he made them swear they
could not find you. 11 But now you tell me to go to my master and say, 'Elijah is here.'
12 I don't know where the Spirit[i] of the LORD may carry you when I leave you. If

ELIJAH

Elijah's single-minded commitment to God shocks and challenges us. He was sent to confront, not comfort, and he spoke God's words to a king who often rejected his message just because he brought it. Elijah chose to carry out his ministry for God alone and paid for that decision by experiencing isolation from others who were also faithful to God.

It is interesting to think about the amazing miracles God accomplished through Elijah, but we would do well to focus on the relationship they shared. All that happened in Elijah's life began with the same miracle that is available to us—he responded to the miracle of being able to know God.

For example, after God worked an overwhelming miracle through Elijah in defeating the prophets of Baal, Queen Jezebel retaliated by threatening Elijah's life. And Elijah ran. He felt afraid, depressed, and abandoned. Despite God's provision of food and shelter in the desert, Elijah wanted to die. So God presented Elijah with an "audio-visual display" and a message he needed to hear. Elijah witnessed a hurricane, an earthquake, and fire. But the Lord was not in any of those powerful things. Instead, God displayed his presence in a gentle whisper.

Elijah, like us, struggled with his feelings even after this comforting message from God. So God confronted Elijah's emotions and commanded action. He told Elijah what to do next and informed him that part of his loneliness was based on ignorance: 7,000 others in Israel were still faithful to God.

Even today, God often speaks through the gentle and obvious rather than the spectacular and unusual. God has work for us to do even when we feel fear and failure. And God always has more resources and people than we know about. Although we might wish to do amazing miracles for God, we should instead focus on developing a relationship with him. The real miracle of Elijah's life was his very personal relationship with God. And that miracle is available to us.

Strengths and accomplishments:
- Was the most famous and dramatic of Israel's prophets
- Predicted the beginning and end of a three-year drought
- Was used by God to restore a dead child to his mother
- Represented God in a showdown with priests of Baal and Asherah
- Appeared with Moses and Jesus in the New Testament transfiguration scene

Weaknesses and mistakes:
- Chose to work alone and paid for it with isolation and loneliness
- Fled in fear from Jezebel when she threatened his life

Lessons from his life:
- We are never closer to defeat than in our moments of greatest victory
- We are never as alone as we may feel; God is always there
- God speaks more frequently in persistent whispers than in shouts

Vital statistics:
- Where: Gilead
- Occupation: Prophet
- Contemporaries: Ahab, Jezebel, Ahaziah, Obadiah, Jehu, Hazael

Key verses:
"At the time of sacrifice, the prophet Elijah stepped forward and prayed: 'O LORD, God of Abraham, Isaac and Israel, let it be known today that you are God in Israel and that I am your servant and have done all these things at your command. Answer me, O LORD, answer me, so these people will know that you, O LORD, are God, and that you are turning their hearts back again.' Then the fire of the LORD fell and burned up the sacrifice, the wood, the stones and the soil, and also licked up the water in the trench" (1 Kings 18:36–38).

Elijah's story is told in 1 Kings 17:1—2 Kings 2:11. He is also mentioned in 2 Chronicles 21:12–15; Malachi 4:5, 6; Matthew 11:14; 16:14; 17:3–13; 27:47–49; Luke 1:17; 4:25, 26; John 1:19–25; Romans 11:2–4; James 5:17, 18.

I go and tell Ahab and he doesn't find you, he will kill me. Yet I your servant have
worshipped the LORD since my youth. 13 Haven't you heard, my lord, what I did while
Jezebel was killing the prophets of the LORD? I hid a hundred of the LORD's prophets
in two caves, fifty in each, and supplied them with food and water. 14 And now you
tell me to go to my master and say, 'Elijah is here.' He will kill me!"
15 Elijah said, "As the LORD Almighty lives, whom I serve, I will surely present[j]
myself to Ahab today."

Elijah on Mount Carmel

16 So Obadiah went to meet Ahab and told him, and Ahab went to meet Elijah.
17 When he saw Elijah, he said to him, "Is that you, you troubler[k] of Israel?"
18 "I have not made trouble for Israel," Elijah replied. "But you[l] and your father's
family have. You have abandoned[m] the LORD's commands and have followed the
Baals. 19 Now summon the people from all over Israel to meet me on Mount Carmel.[n]
And bring the four hundred and fifty prophets of Baal and the four hundred prophets
of Asherah, who eat at Jezebel's table."
20 So Ahab sent word throughout all Israel and assembled the prophets on Mount
Carmel. 21 Elijah went before the people and said, "How long will you waver[o]
between two opinions? If the LORD is God, follow him; but if Baal is God, follow
him."
But the people said nothing.
22 Then Elijah said to them, "I am the only one of the LORD's prophets left,[p] but
Baal has four hundred and fifty prophets.[q] 23 Get two bulls for us. Let them choose
one for themselves, and let them cut it into pieces and put it on the wood but not set
fire to it. I will prepare the other bull and put it on the wood but not set fire to it.
24 Then you call on the name of your god, and I will call on the name of the LORD.
The god who answers by fire[r]—he is God."
Then all the people said, "What you say is good."
25 Elijah said to the prophets of Baal, "Choose one of the bulls and prepare it first,
since there are so many of you. Call on the name of your god, but do not light the
fire." 26 So they took the bull given them and prepared it.
Then they called on the name of Baal from morning till noon. "O Baal, answer us!"
they shouted. But there was no response;[s] no-one answered. And they danced around
the altar they had made.
27 At noon Elijah began to taunt them. "Shout louder!" he said. "Surely he is a god!
Perhaps he is deep in thought, or busy, or travelling. Maybe he is sleeping and must
be awakened."[t] 28 So they shouted louder and slashed[u] themselves with swords and
spears, as was their custom, until their blood flowed. 29 Midday passed, and they
continued their frantic prophesying until the time for the evening sacrifice.[v] But there
was no response, no-one answered, no-one paid attention.[w]
30 Then Elijah said to all the people, "Come here to me." They came to him, and
he repaired the altar[x] of the LORD, which was in ruins. 31 Elijah took twelve stones,

18:15 [j]1Ki 17:1
18:17 [k]Jos 7:25; 1Ki 21:20; Ac 16:20
18:18 [l]1Ki 16:31, 33; 21:25 [m]2Ch 15:2
18:19 [n]Jos 19:26
18:21 [o]Jos 24:15; 2Ki 17:41; Mt 6:24
18:22 [p]1Ki 19:10 [q]ver 19
18:24 [r]ver 38; 1Ch 21:26
18:26 [s]Ps 115:4-5; Jer 10:5; 1Co 8:4; 12:2
18:27 [t]Hab 2:19
18:28 [u]Lev 19:28; Dt 14:1
18:29 [v]Ex 29:41 [w]ver 26
18:30 [x]1Ki 19:10

18:18 Instead of worshipping the true God, Ahab and his wife Jezebel worshipped Baal, the most popular Canaanite god. Baal idols were often made in the shape of a bull, representing strength and fertility and reflecting lust for power and sexual pleasure.

18:19 Ahab brought 850 pagan prophets to Mount Carmel to match wits and power with Elijah. Evil kings hated God's prophets because they spoke against sin and idolatry and undermined their control over the people. With the wicked kings' backing, many pagan prophets sprang up to counter the words of God's prophets. But Elijah showed the people that speaking a prophecy wasn't enough. One needed the power of a living God to fulfil it.

18:21 Elijah challenged the people to take a stand—to follow whoever was the true God. Why did so many people waver between the two choices? Perhaps some were not sure. Many, however, knew that the Lord was God, but they enjoyed the sinful pleasures and other benefits that came with following Ahab in his idolatrous worship. It is important to take a stand for the Lord. If we just drift along with whatever is pleasant and easy, we will someday discover that we have been worshipping a false god—ourselves.

18:29 Although the prophets of Baal raved all afternoon, no-one answered them. Their god was silent because it was not real. The gods we may be tempted to follow are not idols of wood or stone, but they are just as false and dangerous because they cause us to depend on something other than God. Power, status, appearance, or material possessions can become our gods if we devote our lives to them. But when we reach times of crisis and desperately call out to these gods, there will only be silence. They can offer no true answers, no guidance, and no wisdom.

18:31 Using 12 stones to build the altar took courage. This would have angered some of the people because it was a silent reminder of the split between the tribes. While the 10 tribes of the north

one for each of the tribes descended from Jacob, to whom the word of the LORD had
come, saying, "Your name shall be Israel."[y] 32With the stones he built an altar in
the name[z] of the LORD, and he dug a trench round it large enough to hold two seahs[a]
of seed. 33He arranged[a] the wood, cut the bull into pieces and laid it on the wood.
Then he said to them, "Fill four large jars with water and pour it on the offering and
on the wood."
34"Do it again," he said, and they did it again.
"Do it a third time," he ordered, and they did it the third time. 35The water ran down
around the altar and even filled the trench.
36At the time of sacrifice, the prophet Elijah stepped forward and prayed: "O LORD,
God of Abraham,[b] Isaac and Israel, let it be known[c] today that you are God in Israel
and that I am your servant and have done all these things at your command.[d]
37Answer me, O LORD, answer me, so these people will know that you, O LORD, are
God, and that you are turning their hearts back again."
38Then the fire[e] of the LORD fell and burned up the sacrifice, the wood, the stones
and the soil, and also licked up the water in the trench.
39When all the people saw this, they fell prostrate and cried, "The LORD—he is
God! The LORD—he is God!"[f]
40Then Elijah commanded them, "Seize the prophets of Baal. Don't let anyone get
away!" They seized them, and Elijah had them brought down to the Kishon Valley[g]
and slaughtered[h] there.
41And Elijah said to Ahab, "Go, eat and drink, for there is the sound of a heavy
rain." 42So Ahab went off to eat and drink, but Elijah climbed to the top of Carmel,
bent down to the ground and put his face between his knees.[i]
43"Go and look towards the sea," he told his servant. And he went up and looked.
"There is nothing there," he said.
Seven times Elijah said, "Go back."
44The seventh time the servant reported, "A cloud[j] as small as a man's hand is
rising from the sea."
So Elijah said, "Go and tell Ahab, 'Hitch up your chariot and go down before the
rain stops you.' "
45Meanwhile, the sky grew black with clouds, the wind rose, a heavy rain came
on and Ahab rode off to Jezreel. 46The power[k] of the LORD came upon Elijah and,
tucking his cloak into his belt,[l] he ran ahead of Ahab all the way to Jezreel.

[a] *32* That is, probably about 26 pints (about 15 litres)

18:31 [y]Ge 32:28; 35:10; 2Ki 17:34
18:32 [z]Col 3:17
18:33 [a]Ge 22:9; Lev 1:6-8
18:36 [b]Ex 3:6; Mt 22:32 [c]1Ki 8:43; 2Ki 19:19 [d]Nu 16:28
18:38 [e]Lev 9:24; Jdg 6:21; 1Ch 21:26; 2Ch 7:1; Job 1:16
18:39 [f]ver 24
18:40 [g]Jdg 4:7 [h]Dt 13:5; 18:20; 2Ki 10:24-25
18:42 [i]ver 19-20; Jas 5:18
18:44 [j]Lk 12:54
18:46 [k]2Ki 3:15 [l]2Ki 4:29; 9:1

PROPHETS—FALSE AND TRUE

False Prophets	*True Prophets*
Worked for political purposes to benefit themselves	Worked for spiritual purposes to serve God and the people
Held positions of great wealth	Owned little or nothing
Gave false messages	Spoke only true messages
Spoke only what the people wanted to hear	Spoke only what God told them to say—no matter how unpopular

The false prophets were an obstacle to bringing God's word to the people. They would bring messages that contradicted the words of the true prophets. They gave "messages" that appealed to the people's sinful natures and comforted their fears. False prophets told people what they wanted to hear. True prophets told God's truth.

called themselves Israel, it was a name originally given to all 12 of the tribes together.

18:36–38 God flashed fire from heaven for Elijah, and he will help us accomplish what he commands us to do. The proof may not be as dramatic in our lives as in Elijah's, but God will make resources available to us in creative ways to accomplish his purposes. He will give us the wisdom to raise a family, the courage to take a stand for truth, or the means to provide help for someone in need. Like Elijah, we can have faith that whatever God commands us to do, he will provide what we need to carry it through.

18:46 Elijah ran the six miles back to the city in order to give Ahab a last chance to turn from his sin before joining Jezebel in Jezreel. His run also ensured that the correct story of what happened would reach Jezreel.

Elijah Flees to Horeb

19 Now Ahab told Jezebel everything Elijah had done and how he had killed[a] all
the prophets with the sword. 2So Jezebel sent a messenger to Elijah to say,
"May the gods deal with me, be it ever so severely,[b] if by this time tomorrow I do
not make your life like that of one of them."
3Elijah was afraid[a] and ran[c] for his life. When he came to Beersheba in Judah,
he left his servant there, 4while he himself went a day's journey into the desert. He
came to a broom tree, sat down under it and prayed that he might die. "I have had
enough, LORD," he said. "Take my life;[d] I am no better than my ancestors." 5Then
he lay down under the tree and fell asleep.[e]
All at once an angel touched him and said, "Get up and eat." 6He looked around,
and there by his head was a cake of bread baked over hot coals, and a jar of water.
He ate and drank and then lay down again.
7The angel of the LORD came back a second time and touched him and said, "Get
up and eat, for the journey is too much for you." 8So he got up and ate and drank.
Strengthened by that food, he travelled for forty[f] days and forty nights until he
reached Horeb,[g] the mountain of God. 9There he went into a cave[h] and spent the
night.

The LORD Appears to Elijah

And the word of the LORD came to him: "What are you doing here, Elijah?"
10He replied, "I have been very zealous[i] for the LORD God Almighty. The
Israelites have rejected your covenant, broken down your altars, and put your prophets
to death with the sword. I am the only one left,[j] and now they are trying to kill me
too."
11The LORD said, "Go out and stand on the mountain[k] in the presence of the LORD,
for the LORD is about to pass by."

[a] 3 Or *Elijah saw*

19:1 [a]1Ki 18:40
19:2 [b]1Ki 20:10; 2Ki 6:31; Ru 1:17
19:3 [c]Ge 31:21
19:4 [d]Nu 11:15; Jer 20:18; Jnh 4:8
19:5 [e]Ge 28:11
19:8 [f]Ex 24:18; 34:28; Dt 9:9-11, 18; Mt 4:2 [g]Ex 3:1
19:9 [h]Ex 33:22
19:10 [i]Nu 25:13 [j]1Ki 18:4, 22; Ro 11:3*
19:11 [k]Ex 24:12

19:2 Jezebel was enraged about the death of her prophets because they had told her everything *she* wanted to hear, prophesying her future power and glory. Their job was to deify the king and queen and help perpetuate their kingdom. Jezebel was also angry because her supporters had been eliminated and her pride and authority damaged. The money she had invested in these prophets was now lost.

Elijah, who caused the prophets' deaths, was a constant thorn in Jezebel's side because he was always predicting gloom and doom. Because she could not control his actions, she vowed to kill him. As long as God's prophet was around, she could not carry out all the evil she wanted.

19:3ff Elijah experienced the depths of fatigue and discouragement just after his two great spiritual victories: the defeat of the prophets of Baal and the answered prayer for rain. Often discouragement sets in after great spiritual experiences, especially those requiring physical effort or involving great emotion. To lead him out of depression, God first let Elijah rest and eat. Then God confronted him with the need to return to his mission—to speak God's words in Israel. Elijah's battles were not over; there was still work for him to do. When you feel let down after a great spiritual experience, remember that God's purpose for your life is not yet over.

19:8 When Elijah fled to Mount Horeb, he was returning to the sacred place where God had met Moses and had given his laws to the people. Obviously, God gave Elijah special strength to travel this great distance—over 200 miles—without additional food. Like Moses before him and Jesus after him, Elijah fasted for 40 days and 40 nights (Deuteronomy 9:9; Matthew 4:1, 2). Centuries later, Moses, Elijah, and Jesus would meet together on a mountaintop (Luke 9:28–36).

19:10 Elijah thought he was the only person left who was still true to God. He had seen both the king's court and the priesthood become corrupt. After experiencing great victory at Mount Carmel, he

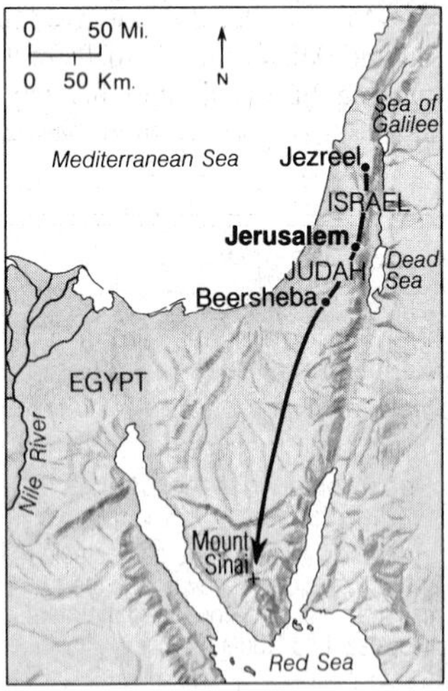

ELIJAH FLEES FROM JEZEBEL
After killing Baal's prophets, Elijah ran from the furious Queen Jezebel. He fled to Beersheba, then into the desert, and finally to Mount Horeb (Sinai). There, like Moses centuries earlier, he talked with God.

had to run for his life. Lonely and discouraged, he forgot that others had remained faithful during the nation's wickedness. When you are tempted to think that you are the only one remaining faithful to a task, don't stop to feel sorry for yourself. Self-pity will dilute the good you are doing. Be assured that even if you don't know who they are, others are faithfully obeying God and fulfilling their duties.

19:11–13 Elijah knew that the sound of gentle whisper was God's voice. He realised that God doesn't reveal himself only in powerful, miraculous ways. To look for God only in something big (rallies,

19:11 [l]Eze 1:4; 37:7
19:12 [m]Job 4:16; Zec 4:6
19:13 [n]ver 9; Ex 3:6

Then a great and powerful wind[l] tore the mountains apart and shattered the rocks
before the LORD, but the LORD was not in the wind. After the wind there was an
earthquake, but the LORD was not in the earthquake. 12 After the earthquake came a
fire, but the LORD was not in the fire. And after the fire came a gentle whisper.[m]
13 When Elijah heard it, he pulled his cloak over his face[n] and went out and stood
at the mouth of the cave.

Then a voice said to him, "What are you doing here, Elijah?"

AHAB

The kings of Israel and Judah, both good and evil, had prophets sent by God to advise, confront, and aid them. King David had a faithful friend in God's prophet, Nathan; Ahab could have had an equally faithful friend in Elijah. But while David listened to Nathan and was willing to repent of his sins, Ahab saw Elijah as his enemy. Why? Because Elijah always brought bad news to Ahab, and Ahab refused to acknowledge that it was his own constant disobedience to God and persistent idol worship, not Elijah's prophecies, that brought the evil on his nation. He blamed Elijah for bringing the prophecies of judgment, rather than taking his advice and changing his evil ways.

Ahab was trapped by his own choices, and he was unwilling to take the right action. As king, he was responsible to God and his prophet Elijah, but he was married to an evil woman who drew him into idol worship. He was a childish man who brooded for days if unable to get his own way. He took his evil wife's advice, listened only to the "prophets" who gave good news, and surrounded himself with people who encouraged him to do whatever he wanted. But the value of advice cannot be judged by the number of people for or against it. Ahab consistently chose to follow the majority opinion of those who surrounded him, and that led to his death.

It may seem nice to have someone encourage us to do whatever we want because advice that goes against our wishes is difficult to accept. However, our decisions must be based on the quality of the advice, not its attractiveness or the majority opinion of our peers. God encourages us to seek advice from wise counsellors, but how can we test the advice we receive? Advice that agrees with the principles in God's word is reliable. We must always separate advice from our own desires, the majority opinion, or whatever seems best in our limited perspective, and weigh it against God's commands. He will never lead us to do what he has forbidden in his word—even in principle. Unlike Ahab, we should trust godly counsellors and have the courage to stand against those who would have us do otherwise.

Strengths and accomplishments:
- Eighth king of Israel
- Capable leader and military strategist

Weaknesses and mistakes:
- Was the most evil king of Israel
- Married Jezebel, a pagan woman, and allowed her to promote Baal worship
- Brooded about not being able to get a piece of land, and so his wife had its owner, Naboth, killed
- Was used to getting his own way, and felt depressed when he didn't

Lessons from his life:
- The choice of a partner will have a significant effect on life—physically, spiritually, and emotionally
- Selfishness, left unchecked, can lead to great evil

Vital statistics:
- Where: Northern kingdom of Israel
- Occupation: King
- Relatives: Wife: Jezebel. Father: Omri. Sons: Ahaziah, Joram
- Contemporaries: Elijah, Naboth, Jehu, Ben-Hadad, Jehoshaphat

Key verses:
"Ahab son of Omri did more evil in the eyes of the LORD than any of those before him. . . . He also married Jezebel daughter of Ethbaal king of the Sidonians, and began to serve Baal and worship him. He set up an altar for Baal in the temple of Baal that he built in Samaria. Ahab also made an Asherah pole and did more to provoke the LORD, the God of Israel, to anger than did all the kings of Israel before him" (1 Kings 16:30–33).

Ahab's story is told in 1 Kings 16:28—22:40. He is also mentioned in 2 Chronicles 18—22; Micah 6:16.

churches, conferences, highly visible leaders) may be to miss him because he is often found gently whispering in the quietness of a humbled heart. Are you listening for God? Step back from the noise and activity of your busy life and listen humbly and quietly for his guidance. It may come when you least expect it.

14He replied, "I have been very zealous for the LORD God Almighty. The Israelites
have rejected your covenant, broken down your altars, and put your prophets to death
with the sword. I am the only one left,[o] and now they are trying to kill me too."
15The LORD said to him, "Go back the way you came, and go to the Desert of
Damascus. When you get there, anoint Hazael[p] king over Aram. 16Also, anoint[q]
Jehu son of Nimshi king over Israel, and anoint Elisha[r] son of Shaphat from Abel
Meholah to succeed you as prophet. 17Jehu will put to death any who escape the sword
of Hazael,[s] and Elisha will put to death any who escape the sword of Jehu. 18Yet
I reserve[t] seven thousand in Israel—all whose knees have not bowed down to Baal
and all whose mouths have not kissed[u] him."

The Call of Elisha

19So Elijah went from there and found Elisha son of Shaphat. He was ploughing
with twelve yoke of oxen, and he himself was driving the twelfth pair. Elijah went
up to him and threw his cloak[v] around him. 20Elisha then left his oxen and ran after
Elijah. "Let me kiss my father and mother good-bye,"[w] he said, "and then I will come
with you."
"Go back," Elijah replied. "What have I done to you?"
21So Elisha left him and went back. He took his yoke of oxen[x] and slaughtered
them. He burned the ploughing equipment to cook the meat and gave it to the people,
and they ate. Then he set out to follow Elijah and became his attendant.[y]

Ben-Hadad Attacks Samaria

20 Now Ben-Hadad[a] king of Aram mustered his entire army. Accompanied by
thirty-two kings with their horses and chariots, he went up and besieged
Samaria and attacked it. 2He sent messengers into the city to Ahab king of Israel,
saying, "This is what Ben-Hadad says: 3'Your silver and gold are mine, and the best
of your wives and children are mine.' "
4The king of Israel answered, "Just as you say, my lord the king. I and all I have
are yours."
5The messengers came again and said, "This is what Ben-Hadad says: 'I sent to

19:14 [o]ver 10
19:15 [p]2Ki 8:7-15
19:16 [q]2Ki 9:1-3, 6 [r]ver 21; 2Ki 2:9, 15
19:17 [s]2Ki 8:12, 29; 9:14; 13:3, 7, 22
19:18 [t]Ro 11:4* [u]Hos 13:2
19:19 [v]2Ki 2:8, 14
19:20 [w]Mt 8:21-22; Lk 9:61
19:21 [x]2Sa 24:22 [y]ver 16
20:1 [a]1Ki 15:18; 22:31; 2Ki 6:24

19:15, 16 God asked Elijah to anoint three different people. The first was Hazael, as king of Aram. Elijah was told to anoint an enemy king because God was going to use Aram as his instrument to punish Israel for its sin. Aram brought Israel's *external* punishment.

Israel's *internal* punishment came from Jehu, the next man Elijah was to anoint. As king of Israel, Jehu would destroy those who worshipped the false god Baal (2 Kings 9; 10).

The third person Elijah was told to anoint was Elisha, the prophet who would succeed him. Elisha's job was to work in Israel, the northern kingdom, to help point the people back to God. At this time, the southern kingdom was ruled by Jehoshaphat, a king devoted to God.

19:18 Kissing Baal meant kissing some object representing him to show loyalty to him.

19:19 The cloak was the most important article of clothing a person could own. It was used as protection against the weather, as bedding, as a place to sit, and as luggage. It could be given as a pledge for a debt or torn into pieces to show grief. Elijah put his cloak on Elisha's shoulders to show that he would become Elijah's successor. Later, when the transfer of authority was complete, Elijah left his cloak for Elisha (2 Kings 2:11–14).

19:21 By killing his oxen, Elisha made a strong commitment to follow Elijah. Without them, he could not return to his life as a wealthy farmer. This meal was more than a feast among farmers. It was an offering of thanks to the Lord who chose Elisha to be his prophet.

20:1ff With two evil and two good kings up to this point, the southern kingdom, Judah, wavered between godly and ungodly living. But the northern kingdom, Israel, had eight evil kings in succession. To punish both kingdoms for living their own way instead of following God, God allowed other nations to gain strength and become their enemies. Three main enemies threatened Israel and Judah during the next two centuries—Aram, Assyria, and Babylon. Aram, the first to rise to power, presented an immediate threat to Ahab and Israel.

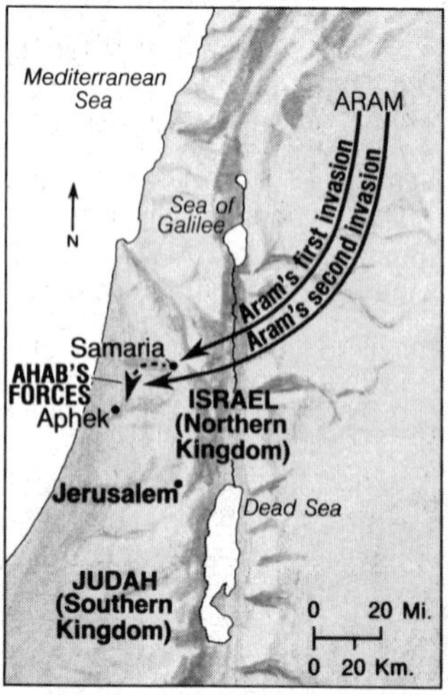

GOD DELIVERS AHAB
Despite Ahab's wickedness, God approached him in love. When Samaria was surrounded by Aramean forces, God miraculously delivered the city. But Ahab refused to give God credit. A year later, the Arameans attacked near Aphek. Again God gave Ahab victory, but again the king refused to acknowledge God's help.

demand your silver and gold, your wives and your children. 6But about this time
tomorrow I am going to send my officials to search your palace and the houses of your
officials. They will seize everything you value and carry it away.' "
7The king of Israel summoned all the elders of the land and said to them, "See how
this man is looking for trouble![b] When he sent for my wives and my children, my
silver and my gold, I did not refuse him."
8The elders and the people all answered, "Don't listen to him or agree to his
demands."
9So he replied to Ben-Hadad's messengers, "Tell my lord the king, 'Your servant
will do all you demanded the first time, but this demand I cannot meet.' " They left
and took the answer back to Ben-Hadad.
10Then Ben-Hadad sent another message to Ahab: "May the gods deal with me,
be it ever so severely, if enough dust[c] remains in Samaria to give each of my men
a handful."
11The king of Israel answered, "Tell him: 'One who puts on his armour should not
boast[d] like one who takes it off.' "
12Ben-Hadad heard this message while he and the kings were drinking[e] in their
tents,[a] and he ordered his men: "Prepare to attack." So they prepared to attack the
city.

Ahab Defeats Ben-Hadad

13Meanwhile a prophet came to Ahab king of Israel and announced, "This is what
the LORD says: 'Do you see this vast army? I will give it into your hand today, and
then you will know[f] that I am the LORD.' "
14"But who will do this?" asked Ahab.
The prophet replied, "This is what the LORD says: 'The young officers of the
provincial commanders will do it.' "
"And who will start[g] the battle?" he asked.
The prophet answered, "You will."
15So Ahab summoned the young officers of the provincial commanders, 232 men.
Then he assembled the rest of the Israelites, 7,000 in all. 16They set out at noon while
Ben-Hadad and the 32 kings allied with him were in their tents getting drunk.[h] 17The
young officers of the provincial commanders went out first.
Now Ben-Hadad had dispatched scouts, who reported, "Men are advancing from
Samaria."
18He said, "If they have come out for peace, take them alive; if they have come
out for war, take them alive."
19The young officers of the provincial commanders marched out of the city with
the army behind them 20and each one struck down his opponent. At that, the Arameans
fled, with the Israelites in pursuit. But Ben-Hadad king of Aram escaped on horseback
with some of his horsemen. 21The king of Israel advanced and overpowered the horses
and chariots and inflicted heavy losses on the Arameans.
22Afterwards, the prophet[i] came to the king of Israel and said, "Strengthen your
position and see what must be done, because next spring[j] the king of Aram will attack
you again."
23Meanwhile, the officials of the king of Aram advised him, "Their gods are gods[k]
of the hills. That is why they were too strong for us. But if we fight them on the plains,
surely we will be stronger than they. 24Do this: Remove all the kings from their
commands and replace them with other officers. 25You must also raise an army like
the one you lost—horse for horse and chariot for chariot—so we can fight Israel on

[a] 12 Or *in Succoth*; also in verse 16

20:7 [b] 2Ki 5:7
20:10 [c] 2Sa 22:43; 1Ki 19:2
20:11 [d] Pr 27:1; Jer 9:23
20:12 [e] ver 16; 1Ki 16:9
20:13 [f] ver 28; Ex 6:7
20:14 [g] Jdg 1:1
20:16 [h] ver 12; 1Ki 16:9
20:22 [i] ver 13 [j] ver 26; 2Sa 11:1
20:23 [k] 1Ki 14:23; Ro 1:21-23

20:23 Since the days of Joshua, Israel's soldiers had a reputation for being superior fighters in the hills, but ineffective in the open plains and valleys because they did not use chariots in battle. Horse-drawn chariots, useless in hilly terrain and dense forests, could easily run down great numbers of foot soldiers on the plains. What Ben-Hadad's officers did not understand was that it was God, not chariots, that made the difference in battle.

the plains. Then surely we will be stronger than they." He agreed with them and acted
accordingly.
26The next spring[l] Ben-Hadad mustered the Arameans and went up to Aphek[m]
to fight against Israel. 27When the Israelites were also mustered and given provisions,
they marched out to meet them. The Israelites camped opposite them like two small
flocks of goats, while the Arameans covered the countryside.[n]
28The man of God came up and told the king of Israel, "This is what the LORD says:
'Because the Arameans think the LORD is a god of the hills and not a god[o] of the
valleys, I will deliver this vast army into your hands, and you will know[p] that I am
the LORD.' "
29For seven days they camped opposite each other, and on the seventh day the battle
was joined. The Israelites inflicted a hundred thousand casualties on the Aramean foot
soldiers in one day. 30The rest of them escaped to the city of Aphek,[q] where the wall
collapsed on twenty-seven thousand of them. And Ben-Hadad fled to the city and hid[r]
in an inner room.
31His officials said to him, "Look, we have heard that the kings of the house of
Israel are merciful. Let us go to the king of Israel with sackcloth[s] round our waists
and ropes round our heads. Perhaps he will spare your life."
32Wearing sackcloth round their waists and ropes round their heads, they went to
the king of Israel and said, "Your servant Ben-Hadad says: 'Please let me live.' "
The king answered, "Is he still alive? He is my brother."
33The men took this as a good sign and were quick to pick up his word. "Yes, your
brother Ben-Hadad!" they said.
"Go and get him," the king said. When Ben-Hadad came out, Ahab had him come
up into his chariot.
34"I will return the cities[t] my father took from your father," Ben-Hadad offered.
"You may set up your own market areas in Damascus,[u] as my father did in Samaria."
⌞Ahab said,⌟ "On the basis of a treaty[v] I will set you free." So he made a treaty
with him, and let him go.

A Prophet Condemns Ahab

35By the word of the LORD one of the sons of the prophets said to his companion,
"Strike me with your weapon," but the man refused.[w]
36So the prophet said, "Because you have not obeyed the LORD, as soon as you leave
me a lion[x] will kill you." And after the man went away, a lion found him and killed
him.
37The prophet found another man and said, "Strike me, please." So the man struck
him and wounded him. 38Then the prophet went and stood by the road waiting for
the king. He disguised himself with his headband down over his eyes. 39As the king
passed by, the prophet called out to him, "Your servant went into the thick of the
battle, and someone came to me with a captive and said, 'Guard this man. If he is
missing, it will be your life for his life,[y] or you must pay a talent[b] of silver.' 40While
your servant was busy here and there, the man disappeared."
"That is your sentence," the king of Israel said. "You have pronounced it yourself."
41Then the prophet quickly removed the headband from his eyes, and the king of
Israel recognised him as one of the prophets. 42He said to the king, "This is what the

b *39* That is, about 75 pounds (about 34 kilograms)

20:26 [l]ver 22 [m]2Ki 13:17
20:27 [n]Jdg 6:6; 1Sa 13:6
20:28 [o]ver 23 [p]ver 13
20:30 [q]ver 26 [r]1Ki 22:25; 2Ch 18:24
20:31 [s]Ge 37:34
20:34 [t]1Ki 15:20 [u]Jer 49:23-27 [v]Ex 23:32
20:35 [w]1Ki 13:21; 2Ki 2:3-7
20:36 [x]1Ki 13:24
20:39 [y]2Ki 10:24

20:31 Sackcloth was coarse cloth usually made of goat's hair and was worn as a symbol of mourning for the dead or for natural disaster. Wearing ropes around the head may have been a symbol of putting oneself at another's disposal. In other words, Ahab could have hung them if he wished. Wearing ropes around the head, therefore, was a sign of submission.

20:35, 36 The prophet needed a wound so he would look like an injured soldier and could effectively deliver his prophecy to Ahab. The first man was killed by a lion because he refused to obey the Lord's instructions through the prophet.

20:41, 42 It is difficult to explain why Ahab let Ben-Hadad go, especially after all the trouble the Arameans had caused him. God helped Ahab destroy the Aramean army to prove to Ahab and to Aram that he alone was God. But Ahab failed to destroy the king, his greatest enemy. Ben-Hadad was under God's judgment to die, and Ahab had no authority to let him live. For this, God told Ahab that he must now die instead. This prophet's message soon came true when Ahab was killed on the battlefield (22:35).

20:42 [z]Jer 48:10 [a]ver 39; Jos 2:14; 1Ki 22:31-37

LORD says: 'You have set free a man I had determined should die.[c][z] Therefore it
is your life for his life,[a] your people for his people.' " 43Sullen and angry,[b] the king
of Israel went to his palace in Samaria.

20:43 [b]1Ki 21:4

Naboth's Vineyard

21:1 [a]2Ki 9:21 [b]1Ki 18:45-46

21 Some time later there was an incident involving a vineyard belonging to
Naboth[a] the Jezreelite. The vineyard was in Jezreel,[b] close to the palace of
Ahab king of Samaria. 2Ahab said to Naboth, "Let me have your vineyard to use for
a vegetable garden, since it is close to my palace. In exchange I will give you a better
vineyard or, if you prefer, I will pay you whatever it is worth."
3But Naboth replied, "The LORD forbid that I should give you the inheritance[c] of
my fathers."

21:3 [c]Lev 25:23; Nu 36:7; Eze 46:18

c *42* The Hebrew term refers to the irrevocable giving over of things or persons to the LORD, often by totally destroying them.

JEZEBEL

The Bible is as honest about the lives of its heroes as it is about those who rejected God. Some Bible characters found out what God can do with failures when they turned to him. Many, however, neither admitted their failures nor turned to God.

Jezebel ranks as the most evil woman in the Bible. The Bible even uses her name as an example of people who completely reject God (Revelation 2:20, 21). Many pagan women married into Israel without acknowledging the God their husbands worshipped. They brought their religions with them. But no-one was as determined as Jezebel to make all Israel worship *her* gods. To the prophet Elijah, she seemed to have succeeded. He felt he was the only one still faithful to God until God told him there were still 7,000 who had not turned from the faith. Jezebel's one outstanding "success" was in contributing to the cause of the eventual downfall of the northern kingdom—idolatry. God punished the northern tribes for their idolatry by having them carried off into captivity.

Jezebel held great power. She not only managed her husband, Ahab, but she also had 850 assorted pagan priests under her control. She was committed to her gods and to getting what she wanted. She believed that the king had the right to possess anything he wanted. When Naboth refused to sell Ahab his vineyard, Jezebel ruthlessly had Naboth killed and took ownership of the land. Jezebel's plan to wipe out worship of God in Israel led to painful consequences. Before she died, Jezebel suffered the loss of her husband in combat and her son at the hand of Jehu, who took the throne by force. She died in the defiant and scornful way she had lived.

When comparing Jezebel and Elijah, we have to admire each one's strength of commitment. The big difference was *to whom* they were committed. Jezebel was committed to herself and her false gods; Elijah was totally committed to the one true God. In the end, God proved Elijah right. To what or to whom are you most committed? How would God evaluate your commitment?

Weaknesses and mistakes:
- Systematically eliminated the representatives of God in Israel
- Promoted and funded Baal worship
- Threatened to have Elijah killed
- Believed kings and queens could rightfully do or have anything they wanted
- Used her strong convictions to get her own way

Lessons from her life:
- It is not enough to be committed or sincere. Where our commitment lies makes a great difference
- Rejecting God always leads to disaster

Vital statistics:
- Where: Sidon, Samaria
- Occupation: Queen of Israel
- Relatives: Husband: Ahab. Father: Ethbaal. Sons: Joram, Ahaziah
- Contemporaries: Elijah, Jehu

Key verse:
"There was never a man like Ahab, who sold himself to do evil in the eyes of the LORD, urged on by Jezebel his wife" (1 Kings 21:25).

Jezebel's story is told in 1 Kings 16:31—2 Kings 9:37. Her name is used as a synonym for great evil in Revelation 2:20.

4So Ahab went home, sullen and angry[d] because Naboth the Jezreelite had said,
"I will not give you the inheritance of my fathers." He lay on his bed sulking and
refused to eat.
5His wife Jezebel came in and asked him, "Why are you so sullen? Why won't you
eat?"
6He answered her, "Because I said to Naboth the Jezreelite, 'Sell me your vineyard;
or if you prefer, I will give you another vineyard in its place.' But he said, 'I will
not give you my vineyard.' "
7Jezebel his wife said, "Is this how you act as king over Israel? Get up and eat!
Cheer up. I'll get you the vineyard[e] of Naboth the Jezreelite."
8So she wrote letters in Ahab's name, placed his seal[f] on them, and sent them to
the elders and nobles who lived in Naboth's city with him. 9In those letters she wrote:

> "Proclaim a day of fasting and seat Naboth in a prominent place among the
> people. 10But seat two scoundrels[g] opposite him and have them testify that he
> has cursed[h] both God and the king. Then take him out and stone him to death."

11So the elders and nobles who lived in Naboth's city did as Jezebel directed in the
letters she had written to them. 12They proclaimed a fast[i] and seated Naboth in a
prominent place among the people. 13Then two scoundrels came and sat opposite him
and brought charges against Naboth before the people, saying, "Naboth has cursed
both God and the king." So they took him outside the city and stoned him to death.[j]
14Then they sent word to Jezebel: "Naboth has been stoned and is dead."
15As soon as Jezebel heard that Naboth had been stoned to death, she said to Ahab,
"Get up and take possession of the vineyard[k] of Naboth the Jezreelite that he refused
to sell you. He is no longer alive, but dead." 16When Ahab heard that Naboth was
dead, he got up and went down to take possession of Naboth's vineyard.
17Then the word of the LORD came to Elijah the Tishbite: 18"Go down to meet Ahab
king of Israel, who rules in Samaria. He is now in Naboth's vineyard, where he has
gone to take possession of it. 19Say to him, 'This is what the LORD says: Have you
not murdered a man and seized his property?' Then say to him, 'This is what the LORD
says: In the place where dogs licked up Naboth's blood,[l] dogs[m] will lick up your
blood—yes, yours!' "
20Ahab said to Elijah, "So you have found me, my enemy!"[n]
"I have found you," he answered, "because you have sold[o] yourself to do evil in
the eyes of the LORD. 21'I am going to bring disaster on you. I will consume your
descendants and cut off from Ahab every last male[p] in Israel—slave or free. 22I will
make your house[q] like that of Jeroboam son of Nebat and that of Baasha son of
Ahijah, because you have provoked me to anger and have caused Israel to sin.'[r]
23"And also concerning Jezebel the LORD says: 'Dogs[s] will devour Jezebel by the
wall of[a] Jezreel.'
24"Dogs[t] will eat those belonging to Ahab who die in the city, and the birds of
the air will feed on those who die in the country."
25(There was never[u] a man like Ahab, who sold himself to do evil in the eyes of

[a] *23* Most Hebrew manuscripts; a few Hebrew manuscripts, Vulgate and Syriac (see also 2 Kings 9:26) *the plot of ground at*

21:4 [d]1Ki 20:43
21:7 [e]1Sa 8:14
21:8 [f]Ge 38:18; Est 3:12; 8:8, 10
21:10 [g]Ac 6:11 [h]Ex 22:28; Lev 24:15-16
21:12 [i]Isa 58:4
21:13 [j]2Ki 9:26
21:15 [k]1Sa 8:14
21:19 [l]2Ki 9:26; Ps 9:12; Isa 14:20 [m]1Ki 22:38
21:20 [n]1Ki 18:17 [o]ver 25; 2Ki 17:17; Ro 7:14
21:21 [p]1Ki 14:10; 2Ki 9:8
21:22 [q]1Ki 15:29; 16:3 [r]1Ki 12:30
21:23 [s]2Ki 9:10, 34-36
21:24 [t]1Ki 14:11; 16:4
21:25 [u]ver 20; 1Ki 16:33

21:4 After hearing God's judgment (20:42), Ahab went home to pout. Driven by anger and rebellion against God, he had a fit of rage when Naboth refused to sell his vineyard. The same feelings that led him to a career of power grabbing drove him to resent Naboth. Rage turned to hatred and led to murder. Naboth, however, wanted to uphold God's laws: it was considered a duty to keep ancestral land in the family. This incident shows the cruel interplay between Ahab and Jezebel, two of the most wicked leaders in Israel's history.

21:13 Jezebel devised a scheme that appeared legal to get the land for her husband. Two witnesses were required to establish guilt, and the punishment for blasphemy was death by stoning. Those who twist the law and legal procedures to get what they want today may be more sophisticated in how they go about it, but they are still guilty of the same sin.

21:19, 23 For the fulfilment of these verses, see 22:38 where dogs licked Ahab's blood, and 2 Kings 9:30—10:28 where Jezebel and the rest of Ahab's family were destroyed.

21:20 Ahab still refused to admit his sin against God. Instead he accused Elijah of being his enemy. When we are blinded by envy and hatred, it is almost impossible to see our own sin.

21:26 [v] Ge 15:16; Lev 18:25-30; 2Ki 21:11
21:27 [w] Ge 37:34; 2Sa 3:31; 2Ki 6:30
21:29 [x] 2Ki 9:26
22:3 [a] Dt 4:43; Jos 21:38
22:4 [b] 2Ki 3:7
22:5 [c] Ex 33:7; 2Ki 3:11
22:6 [d] 1Ki 18:19

the LORD, urged on by Jezebel his wife. 26He behaved in the vilest manner by going
after idols, like the Amorites[v] the LORD drove out before Israel.)
27When Ahab heard these words, he tore his clothes, put on sackcloth[w] and fasted.
He lay in sackcloth and went around meekly.
28Then the word of the LORD came to Elijah the Tishbite: 29"Have you noticed how
Ahab has humbled himself before me? Because he has humbled himself, I will not
bring this disaster in his day, but I will bring it on his house in the days of his son."[x]

4. Kings of Israel and Judah

Micaiah Prophesies Against Ahab

22 For three years there was no war between Aram and Israel. 2But in the third
year Jehoshaphat king of Judah went down to see the king of Israel. 3The king
of Israel had said to his officials, "Don't you know that Ramoth Gilead[a] belongs to
us and yet we are doing nothing to retake it from the king of Aram?"
4So he asked Jehoshaphat, "Will you go with me to fight[b] against Ramoth Gilead?"
Jehoshaphat replied to the king of Israel, "I am as you are, my people as your
people, my horses as your horses." 5But Jehoshaphat also said to the king of Israel,
"First seek the counsel[c] of the LORD."
6So the king of Israel brought together the prophets — about four hundred men — and
asked them, "Shall I go to war against Ramoth Gilead, or shall I refrain?"
"Go,"[d] they answered, "for the Lord will give it into the king's hand."

KINGS TO DATE AND THEIR ENEMIES

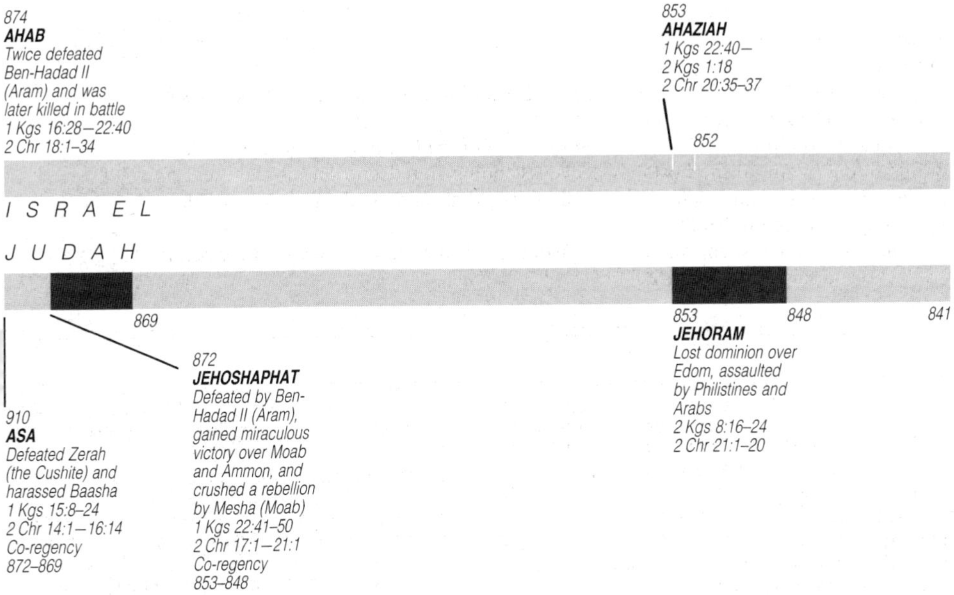

All dates are B.C.
Solid section of the timeline indicates co-regency.
For all the kings of Israel and Judah, see the chart at the end of 1 Kings.

21:29 Ahab was more wicked than any other king of Israel (16:30; 21:25), but when he repented in deep humility, God took notice and reduced his punishment. The same Lord who was merciful to Ahab wants to be merciful to you. No matter how evil you have been, it is never too late to humble yourself, turn to God, and ask for forgiveness.

22:6 These 400 prophets may have been the 400 Asherah priests left alive by Elijah at Carmel, although 450 prophets of Baal were killed (see 18:19–40).

7But Jehoshaphat asked, "Is there not a prophet[e] of the LORD here whom we can
enquire of?"
8The king of Israel answered Jehoshaphat, "There is still one man through whom
we can enquire of the LORD, but I hate[f] him because he never prophesies anything
good[g] about me, but always bad. He is Micaiah son of Imlah."
"The king should not say that," Jehoshaphat replied.
9So the king of Israel called one of his officials and said, "Bring Micaiah son of
Imlah at once."
10Dressed in their royal robes, the king of Israel and Jehoshaphat king of Judah were
sitting on their thrones at the threshing-floor[h] by the entrance of the gate of Samaria,
with all the prophets prophesying before them. 11Now Zedekiah son of Kenaanah had
made iron horns[i] and he declared, "This is what the LORD says: 'With these you will
gore the Arameans until they are destroyed.' "
12All the other prophets were prophesying the same thing. "Attack Ramoth Gilead
and be victorious," they said, "for the LORD will give it into the king's hand."
13The messenger who had gone to summon Micaiah said to him, "Look, as one man
the other prophets are predicting success for the king. Let your word agree with theirs,
and speak favourably."
14But Micaiah said, "As surely as the LORD lives, I can tell him only what the LORD
tells me."[j]
15When he arrived, the king asked him, "Micaiah, shall we go to war against
Ramoth Gilead, or shall I refrain?"
"Attack and be victorious," he answered, "for the LORD will give it into the king's
hand."
16The king said to him, "How many times must I make you swear to tell me nothing
but the truth in the name of the LORD?"
17Then Micaiah answered, "I saw all Israel scattered on the hills like sheep without
a shepherd,[k] and the LORD said, 'These people have no master. Let each one go home
in peace.' "
18The king of Israel said to Jehoshaphat, "Didn't I tell you that he never prophesies
anything good about me, but only bad?"
19Micaiah continued, "Therefore hear the word of the LORD: I saw the LORD sitting
on his throne[l] with all the host[m] of heaven standing round him on his right and on
his left. 20And the LORD said, 'Who will entice Ahab into attacking Ramoth Gilead
and going to his death there?'
"One suggested this, and another that. 21Finally, a spirit came forward, stood before
the LORD and said, 'I will entice him.'

22:7 [e]2Ki 3:11
22:8 [f]Am 5:10 [g]Isa 5:20
22:10 [h]ver 6
22:11 [i]Dt 33:17; Zec 1:18-21
22:14 [j]Nu 22:18; 24:13; 1Ki 18:10, 15
22:17 [k]ver 34-36; Nu 27:17; Mt 9:36
22:19 [l]Isa 6:1; Eze 1:26; Da 7:9 [m]Job 1:6; 2:1; Ps 103:20-21; Mt 18:10; Heb 1:7, 14

22:7 Jehoshaphat knew there was a difference between these pagan prophets and the "prophet of the LORD", so he asked if one was available. Evidently Jehoshaphat wanted to do what was right although Ahab didn't. However, both kings disregarded God's message and listened only to the pagan prophets.

22:10 Threshing floors were placed in elevated areas to allow the wind to blow away the discarded husks of grain.

22:15, 16 Why did Micaiah tell Ahab to attack when he had previously vowed to speak only what God had told him? Perhaps he was speaking sarcastically, making fun of the messages from the pagan prophets by showing that they were telling the king only what he wanted to hear. Somehow, Micaiah's tone of voice let everyone know he was mocking the pagan prophets. When confronted, he predicted that the king would die and the battle would be lost. Although Ahab repented temporarily (21:27), he still maintained the system of false prophets. These false prophets would be instrumental in leading him to his own ruin.

22:19–22 The vision Micaiah saw was either a picture of a real incident in heaven, or a parable of what was happening on earth, illustrating that the seductive influence of the false prophets would be part of God's judgment upon Ahab (22:23). Whether or not God sent an angel in disguise, he used the system of false prophets to snare Ahab in his sin. The lying spirit (22:22) symbolised the way of life for these prophets, who told the king only what he wanted to hear.

22:20–22 Does God allow angels to entice people to do evil? To understand evil one must first understand God. (1) God himself is good (Psalm 11:7). (2) God created a good world that fell because of man's sin (Romans 5:12). (3) Someday God will recreate the world and it will be good again (Revelation 21:1). (4) God is stronger than evil (Matthew 13:41–43; Revelation 19:11–21). (5) God allows evil, and thus he has control over it. God did not create evil, and he offers help to those who wish to overcome it (Matthew 11:28–30). (6) God uses everything – both good and evil – for his good purposes (Genesis 50:20; Romans 8:28).

The Bible shows us a God who hates all evil and will one day do away with it completely and for ever (Revelation 20:10–15). God does not entice anyone to become evil. Those committed to evil, however, may be used by God to sin even more in order to hurry their deserved judgment (Exodus 11:10). We don't need to understand every detail of how God works in order to have perfect confidence in his absolute power over evil and his total goodness towards us.

22“ ‘By what means?’ the LORD asked.
“ ‘I will go out and be a lying[n] spirit in the mouths of all his prophets,’ he said.
“ ‘You will succeed in enticing him,’ said the LORD. ‘Go and do it.’
23“So now the LORD has put a lying spirit in the mouths of all these prophets[o] of
yours. The LORD has decreed disaster for you.”
24Then Zedekiah[p] son of Kenaanah went up and slapped[q] Micaiah in the face.
“Which way did the spirit from[a] the LORD go when he went from me to speak to you?”
he asked.
25Micaiah replied, “You will find out on the day you go to hide[r] in an inner room.”
26The king of Israel then ordered, “Take Micaiah and send him back to Amon the
ruler of the city and to Joash the king’s son 27and say, ‘This is what the king says:
Put this fellow in prison[s] and give him nothing but bread and water until I return
safely.’ ”
28Micaiah declared, “If you ever return safely, the LORD has not spoken[t] through
me.” Then he added, “Mark my words, all you people!”

Ahab Killed at Ramoth Gilead

29So the king of Israel and Jehoshaphat king of Judah went up to Ramoth Gilead.
30The king of Israel said to Jehoshaphat, “I will enter the battle in disguise,[u] but you
wear your royal robes.” So the king of Israel disguised himself and went into battle.
31Now the king of Aram had ordered his thirty-two chariot commanders, “Do not
fight with anyone, small or great, except the king[v] of Israel.” 32When the chariot
commanders saw Jehoshaphat, they thought, “Surely this is the king of Israel.” So
they turned to attack him, but when Jehoshaphat cried out, 33the chariot commanders
saw that he was not the king of Israel and stopped pursuing him.
34But someone drew his bow[w] at random and hit the king of Israel between the
sections of his armour. The king told his chariot driver, “Wheel round and get me out
of the fighting. I’ve been wounded.” 35All day long the battle raged, and the king was
propped up in his chariot facing the Arameans. The blood from his wound ran onto
the floor of the chariot, and that evening he died. 36As the sun was setting, a cry spread
through the army: “Every man to his town; everyone to his land!”[x]
37So the king died and was brought to Samaria, and they buried him there. 38They
washed the chariot at a pool in Samaria (where the prostitutes bathed),[b] and the dogs[y]
licked up his blood, as the word of the LORD had declared.
39As for the other events of Ahab’s reign, including all he did, the palace he built
and inlaid with ivory,[z] and the cities he fortified, are they not written in the book
of the annals of the kings of Israel? 40Ahab rested with his fathers. And Ahaziah his
son succeeded him as king.

Jehoshaphat King of Judah

41Jehoshaphat son of Asa became king of Judah in the fourth year of Ahab king
of Israel. 42Jehoshaphat was thirty-five years old when he became king, and he reigned
in Jerusalem for twenty-five years. His mother’s name was Azubah daughter of Shilhi.
43In everything he walked in the ways of his father Asa[a] and did not stray from them;

[a] *24* Or *Spirit of* [b] *38* Or *Samaria and cleaned the weapons*

22:22 [n]Jdg 9:23; 1Sa 16:14; 18:10; 19:9; Eze 14:9; 2Th 2:11
22:23 [o]Eze 14:9
22:24 [p]ver 11 [q]Ac 23:2
22:25 [r]1Ki 20:30
22:27 [s]2Ch 16:10
22:28 [t]Dt 18:22
22:30 [u]2Ch 35:32
22:31 [v]2Sa 17:2
22:34 [w]2Ch 35:23
22:36 [x]2Ki 14:12
22:38 [y]1Ki 21:19
22:39 [z]2Ch 9:17; Am 3:15
22:43 [a]2Ch 17:3

22:34 Ahab could not escape God’s judgment. The king of Aram sent 32 of his best chariot commanders with the sole purpose of killing Ahab. Thinking he could escape, Ahab tried a disguise, but a random arrow struck him while the chariots chased the wrong king, Jehoshaphat. It was foolish for Ahab to think he could escape by wearing a disguise. Sometimes people try to escape reality by disguising themselves – changing jobs, moving to a new town, even changing spouses. But God sees and evaluates the motives of each person. Any attempted disguise is futile.

22:35 Just as the prophet had predicted (20:42), Ahab was killed. See Ahab’s Profile in chapter 19 for more of Ahab’s sad story.

22:41–50 For more details on Jehoshaphat, see the other account of his reign in 2 Chronicles 17 – 20.

22:43 Just like his ancestors Solomon and Asa, Jehoshaphat followed God, but he didn’t remove the high places – the pagan shrines in the hills (2 Chronicles 20:33). It was against God’s laws to worship idols in the shrines (Numbers 33:52), and at first Jehoshaphat attempted to remove them (2 Chronicles 17:6). They were so popular, however, that this proved difficult. In spite of Jehoshaphat’s many contributions to the spiritual, moral, and material health of his country, he did not succeed in eradicating the hill shrines.

he did what was right in the eyes of the LORD. The high places,[b] however, were not
removed, and the people continued to offer sacrifices and burn incense there. 44 Jehoshaphat was also at peace with the king of Israel.
45 As for the other events of Jehoshaphat's reign, the things he achieved and his
military exploits, are they not written in the book of the annals of the kings of Judah?
46 He rid the land of the rest of the male shrine-prostitutes[c] who remained there even
after the reign of his father Asa. 47 There was then no king[d] in Edom; a deputy ruled.
48 Now Jehoshaphat built a fleet of trading ships[c][e] to go to Ophir for gold, but
they never set sail—they were wrecked at Ezion Geber. 49 At that time Ahaziah son
of Ahab said to Jehoshaphat, "Let my men sail with your men," but Jehoshaphat
refused.
50 Then Jehoshaphat rested with his fathers and was buried with them in the city of
David his father. And Jehoram his son succeeded him.

Ahaziah King of Israel

51 Ahaziah son of Ahab became king of Israel in Samaria in the seventeenth year
of Jehoshaphat king of Judah, and he reigned over Israel for two years. 52 He did evil[f]
in the eyes of the LORD, because he walked in the ways of his father and mother and
in the ways of Jeroboam son of Nebat, who caused Israel to sin. 53 He served and
worshipped Baal[g] and provoked the LORD, the God of Israel, to anger, just as his
father[h] had done.

22:43 [b] 1Ki 3:2; 15:14; 2Ki 12:3
22:46 [c] Dt 23:17; 1Ki 14:24; 15:12
22:47 [d] 2Sa 8:14; 2Ki 3:9; 8:20
22:48 [e] 1Ki 9:26; 10:22
22:52 [f] 1Ki 15:26; 21:25
22:53 [g] Jdg 2:11 [h] 1Ki 16:30-32

c *48* Hebrew *of ships of Tarshish*

22:52, 53 The book of 1 Kings begins with a nation united under David, the most devout king in Israel's history. The book ends with a divided kingdom and the death of Ahab, the most wicked king of all. What happened? The people forgot to acknowledge God as their ultimate leader; they appointed human leaders who ignored God; and then they conformed to the life-styles of these evil leaders. Occasional wrongdoing gradually turned into a way of life. Their blatant wickedness could be met only with judgment from God, who allowed enemy nations to arise and defeat Israel and Judah in battle as punishment for their sins. Failing to acknowledge God as our ultimate leader is the first step towards ruin.

TEMPLE INVADERS

Who?	*Reference*	*What happened*
Shishak king of Egypt	1 Kings 14:25, 26	Ransacked the temple, carried away certain treasures
Asa king of Judah	1 Kings 15:18, 19	Took temple treasures and money to buy an alliance with King Ben-Hadad of Aram
Athaliah queen of Judah	2 Kings 11:13–15 2 Chronicles 24:7	Ravaged the temple; later ran into the temple only to discover that her wicked reign had come to an end
Joash king of Judah	2 Kings 12:18	Took gold and sacred objects from the temple to stop King Hazael of Aram from attacking
Jehoash king of Israel	2 Kings 14:14	Entered the temple, taking gold and silver to get back at Amaziah
Ahaz king of Judah	2 Kings 16:8–18	Took silver, gold, and various furnishings from the temple to send sufficient tribute to appease Assyria's king
Hezekiah king of Judah	2 Kings 18:13–16	Took all the silver from the temple and stripped the gold from its doors to persuade Sennacherib king of Assyria to call off his attack
Manasseh king of Judah	2 Kings 21:4–8	Placed pagan altars in the temple
Nebuchadnezzar king of Babylon	2 Kings 24:13 2 Chronicles 36:10 2 Kings 25:1–17 2 Chronicles 36:18, 19	Nebuchadnezzar raided the temple during his second and third invasions of Judah. In his third invasion, he destroyed the temple and carried away all its treasures.

DIVIDED KINGDOM OF ISRAEL

AHIJAH 934–909

ELIJAH 875–

930
JEROBOAM I
(22 years)
Fortified a capital city (Shechem), set up two golden calf-idols, led the nation into sin, allowed anyone to be a priest
1 Kgs 11:26–14:34
2 Chr 10:12–13:20

909
NADAB
(2 years)
1 Kgs 15:25–28

908
BAASHA
(24 years)
Led people in idol worship
1 Kgs 15:27–16:7
2 Chr 16:1–6

886
ELAH
(2 years)
Continued idol worship
1 Kgs 16:6–14

885
ZIMRI
(7 days)
1 Kgs 16:9–20

885
TIBNI
1 Kgs 16:21, 22

885
OMRI
(12 years)
Built the capital city of Samaria, had great military power, but continued to lead Israel into idolatry
1 Kgs 16:16–28

874
AHAB
(22 years)
Married Jezebel (a non-Jew and extremely wicked woman), worshipped Baal, and suffered three years of famine caused by his consistent disobedience to God
1 Kgs 16:28–22:40
2 Chr 18:1–34

CAPITAL: SHECHEM, THEN TIRZAH, THEN SAMARIA
THE NORTHERN KINGDOM OF ISRAEL (TEN TRIBES)

THE SOUTHERN KINGDOM OF JUDAH (TWO TRIBES)
CAPITAL: JERUSALEM

930
REHOBOAM
(17 years)
Built many fortified cities, strengthened the economy (despite the tribute paid to Egypt), followed God for three years, but then set up idols and shrines to foreign gods
1 Kgs 11:43–14:31
2 Chr 9:31–12:16

913
ABIJAH
(3 years)
Despite his wickedness, he called for God's help to win the battle against Israel
1 Kgs 14:31–15:8
2 Chr 13:1–14:1

910
ASA
(41 years)
Destroyed pagan altars and rebuilt altar of God, built fortified cities, gained much wealth from plunder of foreign conquest, removed the queen mother for worshipping Asherah, led the people to worship God with their hearts, provided peace on home soil, was greatly loved, and given a beautiful funeral
1 Kgs 15:8–24
2 Chr 14:1–16:14

872
JEHOSHAPHAT
(25 years)
Arranged for the marriage of his son to a daughter of Ahab (who made trouble later on), had a strong military (kept troops in cities of Israel his father had conquered), collected tribute from the Philistines, worshipped the Lord and destroyed idols, established education, and appointed judges and courts
1 Kgs 15:24; 22:41–50
2 Chr 17:1–21:1

All dates are B.C. The total years of reign sometimes include years of co-regency.
(See charts, "Kings to Date", throughout 1 and 2 Kings.)

ELISHA 848–797

JONAH
793–753(?)

853
AHAZIAH
(2 years)
Proposed a joint trade venture with Judah
1 Kgs 22:40–2 Kgs 1:18
2 Chr 20:35–37

852
JORAM
(12 years)
Suffered famine and war during most of his reign
2 Kgs 3:1–8:25
2 Chr 22:5–7

841
JEHU
(28 years)
Was responsible for the deaths of Joram (king of Israel), Ahaziah (king of Judah), Jezebel (wicked mother of Joram); destroyed the priests and temples of Baal, but did not consistently follow God
2 Kgs 9:1–10:36
2 Chr 22:7–12

814
JEHOAHAZ
(17 years)
Evil reign included worship of Asherah, usually called "detestable"
2 Kgs 13:1–9

798
JEHOASH
(16 years)
Even though he was evil, he recognised the authority of Elisha as a prophet of God
2 Kgs 13:10–14:16
2 Chr 25:17–24

793
JEROBOAM II
(41 years)
Very evil but politically powerful, his nation enjoyed economic prosperity and military peace
2 Kgs 14:16–29

853
JEHORAM
(8 years)
Married a wicked daughter of Ahab, compelled the people to worship idols, and killed all his brothers
2 Kgs 8:16–24
2 Chr 21:1–20

841
AHAZIAH
(1 year)
Friend of Joram of Israel
2 Kgs 8:24–9:29
2 Chr 22:1–10

841
ATHALIAH (QUEEN)
(6 years)
Killed all her grandchildren except Joash who was hidden by his nurse for six years, and ravaged the temple to furnish Baal's temple
2 Kgs 11:1–20
2 Chr 22:10–23:21

835
JOASH
(40 years)
Was crowned king at the age of seven by Jehoiada (the high priest), promoted peace and prosperity, repaired the temple and smashed the altars to Baal—but after Jehoiada died, Joash abandoned God, and even had Jehoiada's son killed
2 Kgs 11:2–12:21
2 Chr 22:11–24:27

796
AMAZIAH
(29 years)
Was basically good but did not completely wipe out idol worship, organised and mustered the army 2 Kgs 14:1–20
2 Chr 25:1–28

792
AZARIAH (UZZIAH)
(52 years)
Rebuilt a city named Elath, owned many farms and vineyards, constructed water reservoirs and fortified towers, reorganised the army (so powerful that his fame spread to Egypt), but violated God's laws for priestly function—so God struck him with leprosy
2 Kgs 15:1–17
2 Chr 26:1–23

OBADIAH 855–840(?)

JOEL 835–796(?)

HOSEA 753–715

AMOS 760–750

753
ZECHARIAH
(6 months)
Encouraged idol worship
2 Kgs 14:29—15:11

752
SHALLUM
(1 month)
2 Kgs 15:10–15

752
MENAHEM
(10 years)
Imposed heavy taxes and oppressed his people
2 Kgs 15:14–22

742
PEKAHIAH
(2 years)
Continued idol worship
2 Kgs 15:22–26

740
PEKAH
(8 years)
During his reign many of the people were taken captive to Assyria
2 Kgs 15:25–31
2 Chr 28:5–8

732
HOSHEA
(9 years)
Suffered heavy taxation by Assyria and eventual conquest–bringing about Israelite captivity and resettlement of foreigners in Israel 2 Kgs 15:30; 17:1–6

722
END OF THE NORTHERN KINGDOM–
Israel taken to Assyria by Shalmaneser

ISRAEL

JUDAH

750
JOTHAM
(16 years)
Rebuilt the Upper Gate of the temple, rebuilt walls and cities, but still permitted idol worship
2 Kgs 15:32–38
2 Chr 27:1–9

735
AHAZ
(16 years)
Sacrificed his own son to pagan gods, nailed the temple doors shut
2 Kgs 16:1–20
2 Chr 28:1–27

715
HEZEKIAH
(29 years)
Was a devoted follower of God, reopened the temple doors, purified the temple, reinstated priests and their duties, organised an orchestra to aid worship, destroyed idols (including the bronze snake of Moses because people had begun to worship it), celebrated the Passover and even invited people who were living in the north to participate, constructed large public waterworks, was given 15 extra years of life, foolishly showed messengers the wealth in the temple
2 Kgs 16:20; 18:1—20:21
2 Chr 29:1—32:33

697
MANASSEH
(55 years)
Rebuilt all the pagan shrines, sacrificed one of his own sons, practised sorcery, set up an idol right in the temple, murdered many of his own people, but repented during his Assyrian captivity
2 Kgs 21:1–18
2 Chr 33:1–20

MICAH 742–687

ISAIAH 740–681

586
END OF THE SOUTHERN KINGDOM—
carried off captive to Babylon by Nebuchadnezzar

42
MON
? years)
Kgs 21:18–26
Chr 33:20–25

640
JOSIAH
(31 years)
Loved God with all his heart, repaired the temple, found a lost scroll of the law (he promised to obey it, thus God delayed destruction of Judah until after his death), personally oversaw the major project of destroying idol shrines, reinstated the priests of God, celebrated the Passover with greater zeal than had been since Samuel's day, was greatly loved by his people
2 Kgs 21:26–23:30
2 Chr 33:25–35:27

609
JEHOAHAZ
(3 months)
Jailed and taken to Egypt where he died
2 Kgs 23:30–34
2 Chr 36:1–4

609
JEHOIAKIM
(11 years)
Burned part of God's words given to Jeremiah, was a puppet king for Egypt and then Babylon, watched gold and articles taken from the temple to Babylon, saw first exile (in which Daniel was taken)
2 Kgs 23:34–24:6
2 Chr 36:5–8

598
JEHOIACHIN
(3 months)
Saw next exile to Babylon
2 Kgs 24:6–15; 25:27–30
2 Chr 36:8–10

597
ZEDEKIAH
(11 years)
Saw the temple burned and Jerusalem destroyed, was tortured and carried away in the final exile to Babylon
2 Kgs 24:17–25:21
2 Chr 36:10–21

HABAKKUK 612—589

AHUM 663—654

ZEPHANIAH 640—621

HULDAH 632

JEREMIAH 627—586

2 KINGS

Kingdom divides 930 B.C.	Ahab dies in battle 853	Elijah's ministry transfers to Elisha 848	Jehu becomes king of Israel 841	Joash becomes king of Judah 835	Elisha's ministry ends 797	Jeroboam II becomes king of Israel 793	Amos' ministry begins 760	Hosea ministr begins 753

VITAL STATISTICS

PURPOSE:
To demonstrate the fate that awaits all who refuse to make God their true leader

AUTHOR:
Unknown. Possibly Jeremiah or a group of prophets

SETTING:
The once-united nation of Israel has been divided into two kingdoms, Israel and Judah, for over a century.

KEY VERSES:
"The LORD warned Israel and Judah through all his prophets and seers: 'Turn from your evil ways. Observe my commands and decrees, in accordance with the entire Law that I commanded your fathers to obey and that I delivered to you through my servants the prophets.' But they would not listen and were as stiff-necked as their fathers, who did not trust in the LORD their God" (17:13, 14).

KEY PEOPLE:
Elijah, Elisha, Shunammite woman, Naaman, Jezebel, Jehu, Joash, Hezekiah, Sennacherib, Isaiah, Manasseh, Josiah, Jehoiakim, Zedekiah, Nebuchadnezzar

SPECIAL FEATURES:
The 17 prophetic books at the end of the Old Testament give great insights into the time period of 2 Kings.

SPARKLING as it crashes against boulders alon its banks, the river swiftly cascades towards th sea. The current grabs, pushes, and tugs at leave and logs, carrying them along for the ride. Her and there a sportsman is spotted in a canoe, goin with the flow. Gravity pulls the water, and th river pulls the rest . . . downwards. Suddenly, silver missile breaks the surface and darts up stream, and then another. Oblivious to the swir ing opposition, the shining salmon swim again the stream. They must go upstream, and nothin will stop them from reaching their destination.

The current of society's river is flowing fast and furious, pulling dowr wards everything in its way. It would be easy to float along with th current. But God calls us to swim against the flow. It will not be easy, an we may be alone, but it will be right.

In the book of 2 Kings, we read of evil rulers, rampant idolatry, and complacent populace—certainly pulling downwards. Despite the pressu to conform, to turn from the Lord and to serve only self, a minority chosen people moved in the opposite direction, towards God. The Beth prophets and others, as well as two righteous kings, spoke God's word an stood for him. As you read 2 Kings, watch these courageous individual Catch the strength and force of Elijah and Elisha and the commitment Hezekiah and Josiah, and determine to be one who swims against th current!

The book continues the history of Israel, halfway between the death David and the death of the nation. Israel had been divided (1 Kings 12 and the two kingdoms had begun to slide into idolatry and corruptic towards collapse and captivity. Second Kings relates the sordid stories the 12 kings of the northern kingdom (called Israel) and the 16 kings of th southern kingdom (called Judah). For 130 years, Israel endures the suc cession of evil rulers until they were conquered by Shalmaneser of Assyri and led into captivity in 722 B.C. (17:6). Of all the kings in both the nort and south, only two—Hezekiah and Josiah—were called good. Becaus of their obedience to God and the spiritual revivals during their reign Judah stood for an additional 136 years until falling to Nebuchadnezz and the Babylonians in 586 B.C.

Throughout this dark period, the Bible mentions 30 prophets wh proclaimed God's message to the people and their leaders. Most notable these fearless people of God are Elijah and Elisha. As Elijah neared th end of his earthly ministry, Elisha asked for a double portion of h beloved mentor's spirit (2:9). Soon after, Elijah was taken to heaven in whirlwind (2:11), and Elisha became God's spokesman to the norther kingdom. Elisha's life was filled with signs, proclamations, warning and miracles. Four of the most memorable are the flowing oil (4:1–7), th healing of the Shunammite woman's son (4:8–37), the healing of Na man's leprosy (5:1–27), and the floating axe-head (6:1–7).

Even in the midst of terrible situations, God will have his faithf minority, his remnant (19:31). He desires courageous men and women proclaim his truth.

Micah's ministry begins 742	*Isaiah's ministry begins 740*	*Israel (northern kingdom) falls 722*	*Hezekiah becomes king of Judah 715*	*Josiah becomes king of Judah 640*	*Jeremiah's ministry begins 627*	*Book of the Law found in the temple 622*	*First captivity of Judah; Daniel taken 605*	*Second captivity of Judah; Ezekiel taken 597*	*Judah (southern kingdom) falls 586*

THE BLUEPRINT

A. THE DIVIDED KINGDOM (1:1—17:41)
1. Elisha's ministry
2. Kings of Israel and Judah
3. Israel is exiled to Assyria

Although Israel had the witness and power of Elisha, the nation turned from God and was exiled to Assyria. Assyria filled the northern kingdom with people from other lands. There has been no return from this captivity—it was permanent. Such is the end of all who shut God out of their lives.

B. THE SURVIVING KINGDOM (18:1—25:30)
1. Kings of Judah
2. Judah is exiled to Babylon

The northern kingdom was destroyed, and prophets were predicting the same fate for Judah. What more could cause the nation to repent? Hezekiah and Josiah were able to stem the tide of evil. They both repaired the temple and gathered the people for the Passover. Josiah eradicated idolatry from the land, but as soon as these good kings were gone, the people returned again to living their own way instead of God's way. Each individual must believe and live for God in his or her family, church, and nation.

MEGATHEMES

THEME	EXPLANATION	IMPORTANCE
Elisha	The purpose of Elisha's ministry was to restore respect for God and his message, and he stood firmly against the evil kings of Israel. By faith, with courage and prayer, he revealed not only God's judgment on sin, but also his mercy, love, and tenderness towards faithful people.	Elisha's mighty miracles showed that God controls not only great armies, but also events in everyday life. When we listen to and obey God, he shows us his power to transform any situation. God's care is for all who are willing to follow him. He can perform miracles in our lives.
Idolatry	Every evil king in both Israel and Judah encouraged idolatry. These false gods represented war, cruelty, power, and sex. Although they had God's law, priests, and prophets to guide them, these kings sought priests and prophets whom they could manipulate to their own advantage.	An idol is any idea, ability, possession, or person that we regard more highly than God. We condemn Israel and Judah for foolishly worshipping idols, but we also worship other gods—power, money, physical attractiveness. Those who believe in God must resist the lure of these attractive idols.
Evil Kings/ Good Kings	Only 20 per cent of Israel and Judah's kings followed God. The evil kings were short-sighted. They thought they could control their nations' destinies by importing other religions, forming alliances with pagan nations, and enriching themselves. The good kings had to spend most of their time undoing the evil done by their predecessors.	Although the evil kings led the people into sin, the priests, princes, heads of families, and military leaders all had to co-operate with the evil plans and practices in order for them to be carried out. We cannot discharge our responsibility to obey God by blaming our leaders. We are responsible to know God's word and obey it.
God's Patience	God told his people that if they obeyed him they would live successfully; if they disobeyed, they would be judged and destroyed. God had been patient with the people for hundreds of years. He sent many prophets to guide them. And he gave ample warning of coming destruction. But even God's patience has limits.	God is patient with us. He gives us many chances to hear his message, to turn from sin, and to believe him. His patience does not mean he is indifferent to how we live, nor does it mean we can ignore his warnings. His patience should make us want to come to him now.
Judgment	After King Solomon's reign, Israel lasted 209 years before the Assyrians destroyed it; Judah lasted 345 years before the Babylonians took Jerusalem. After repeated warnings to his people, God used these evil nations as instruments for his justice.	The consequences of rejecting God's commands and purpose for our lives are severe. He will not ignore unbelief or rebellion. We must believe in him and accept Christ's sacrificial death on our behalf, or we will be judged also.

KEY PLACES IN 2 KINGS

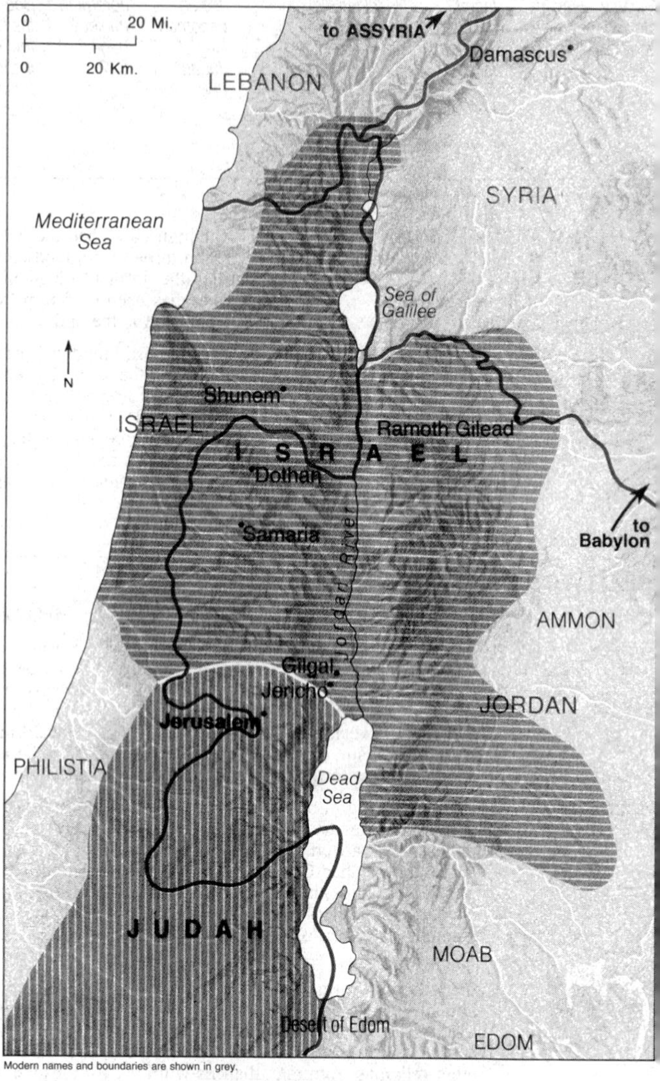

Modern names and boundaries are shown in grey.

The history of both Israel and Judah was much affected by the prophet Elisha's ministry. He served Israel for 50 years, fighting the idolatry of its kings and calling its people back to God.

1 **Jericho** Elijah's ministry had come to an end. He touched his cloak to the Jordan River, and he and Elisha crossed on dry ground. Elijah was taken by God in a whirlwind, and Elisha returned alone with the cloak. The prophets in Jericho realised that Elisha was Elijah's replacement (1:1–2:25).

2 **Desert of Edom** The king of Moab rebelled against Israel, so the nations of Israel, Judah, and Edom decided to attack from the Desert of Edom, but ran out of water. The kings consulted Elisha, who said God would send both water and victory (3:1–27).

3 **Shunem** Elisha cared for individuals and their needs. He helped a woman clear a debt by giving her a supply of oil to sell. For another family in Shunem, he raised a son from the dead (4:1–37).

4 **Gilgal** Elisha cared for the young prophets in Gilgal—he removed poison from a stew, made a small amount of food feed everyone, and even caused an axe-head to float so it could be retrieved. It was to Elisha that Naaman, a commander in the Aramean army, came to be healed of leprosy (4:38–6:7).

5 **Dothan** Although he cured an Aramean commander's leprosy, Elisha was loyal to Israel. He knew the Aramean army's battle plans and kept Israel's king informed. The Aramean king tracked Elisha down in Dothan and surrounded the city, hoping to kill him. But Elisha prayed that the Arameans would be blinded, then he led the blinded army into Samaria, Israel's capital city (6:8–23).

6 **Samaria** But the Arameans didn't learn their lesson. They later besieged Samaria. Ironically, Israel's king thought it was Elisha's fault, but Elisha said food would be available in abundance the next day. True to Elisha's word, the Lord caused panic in the Aramean camp, and the enemy ran, leaving their supplies to Samaria's starving people (6:24–7:20).

7 **Damascus** Despite Elisha's loyalty to Israel, he obeyed God and travelled to Damascus, the capital of Aram. King Ben-Hadad was sick, and he sent Hazael to ask Elisha if he would recover. Elisha knew the king would die, and told this to Hazael. But Hazael then murdered Ben-Hadad, making himself king. Later, Israel and Judah joined forces to fight this new Aramean threat (8:1–29).

8 **Ramoth Gilead** As Israel and Judah warred with Aram, Elisha sent a young prophet to Ramoth Gilead to anoint Jehu as Israel's next king. Jehu set out to destroy the wicked dynasties of Israel and Judah, killing kings Joram and Ahaziah, and wicked Queen Jezebel. He then destroyed King Ahab's family, and all the Baal worshippers in Israel (9:1–11:1).

9 **Jerusalem** Power-hungry Athaliah became queen of Judah when her son Ahaziah was killed. She had all her grandsons killed except Joash who was hidden by his aunt. Joash was crowned king at the age of seven and overthrew Athaliah. Meanwhile in Samaria, the Arameans continued to harass Israel. Israel's new king met with Elisha and was told that he would be victorious over Aram three times (11:2–13:19).

Following Elisha's death came a series of evil kings in Israel. Their idolatry and rejection of God caused their downfall. The Assyrian empire captured Samaria and took most of the Israelites into captivity (13:20–17:41). Judah had a short reprieve because of a few good kings who destroyed idols and worshipped God. But many strayed from God. So Jerusalem fell to the next world power, Babylon (18:1–25:30).

1:1
[a]Ge 19:37;
2Sa 8:2;
2Ki 3:5

1:2
[b]ver 16
[c]Mk 3:22
[d]1Sa 6:2;
Isa 2:6; 14:29;
Mt 10:25
[e]Jdg 18:5;
2Ki 8:7-10

1:3
[f]ver 15;
Ge 16:7
[g]1Ki 17:1
[h]1Sa 28:8

1:4
[i]ver 6, 16;
Ps 41:8

1:8
[j]1Ki 18:7;
Zec 13:4;
Mt 3:4;
Mk 1:6

1:9
[k]2Ki 6:14
[l]Ex 18:25;
Isa 3:3

1:10
[m]1Ki 18:38;
Lk 9:54;
Rev 11:5; 13:13

1:13
[n]1Sa 26:21;
Ps 72:14

A. THE DIVIDED KINGDOM (1:1—17:41)

Elisha begins his ministry to the northern kingdom after Elijah is taken away by a chariot of fire. Elisha performs many miracles and calls Israel to return to God, but they persist in their wickedness. Israel is defeated by Assyria and the people of the northern kingdom are exiled, never to return. Such is the end of all those who ignore God's warnings and demand their own way in their desire to sin.

The LORD's Judgment on Ahaziah

1 After Ahab's death, Moab[a] rebelled against Israel. 2Now Ahaziah had fallen
through the lattice of his upper room in Samaria and injured himself. So he sent
messengers,[b] saying to them, "Go and consult Baal-Zebub,[c] the god of Ekron,[d]
to see if I will recover[e] from this injury."
3But the angel[f] of the LORD said to Elijah[g] the Tishbite, "Go up and meet the
messengers of the king of Samaria and ask them, 'Is it because there is no God in
Israel[h] that you are going off to consult Baal-Zebub, the god of Ekron?' 4Therefore
this is what the LORD says: 'You will not leave[i] the bed you are lying on. You will
certainly die!' " So Elijah went.
5When the messengers returned to the king, he asked them, "Why have you come
back?"
6"A man came to meet us," they replied. "And he said to us, 'Go back to the king
who sent you and tell him, "This is what the LORD says: Is it because there is no God
in Israel that you are sending men to consult Baal-Zebub, the god of Ekron? Therefore
you will not leave the bed you are lying on. You will certainly die!" ' "
7The king asked them, "What kind of man was it who came to meet you and told
you this?"
8They replied, "He was a man with a garment of hair[j] and with a leather belt round
his waist."
The king said, "That was Elijah the Tishbite."
9Then he sent[k] to Elijah a captain[l] with his company of fifty men. The captain
went up to Elijah, who was sitting on the top of a hill, and said to him, "Man of God,
the king says, 'Come down!' "
10Elijah answered the captain, "If I am a man of God, may fire come down from
heaven and consume you and your fifty men!" Then the fire[m] fell from heaven and
consumed the captain and his men.
11At this the king sent to Elijah another captain with his fifty men. The captain said
to him, "Man of God, this is what the king says, 'Come down at once!' "
12"If I am a man of God," Elijah replied, "may fire come down from heaven and
consume you and your fifty men!" Then the fire of God fell from heaven and consumed
him and his fifty men.
13So the king sent a third captain with his fifty men. This third captain went up and
fell on his knees before Elijah. "Man of God," he begged, "please have respect for
my life[n] and the lives of these fifty men, your servants! 14See, fire has fallen from

---

1:1 Because 1 and 2 Kings were originally one book, 2 Kings continues where 1 Kings ended. The once great nation of Israel was split in two because the people forgot God. The book begins with Elijah, a prophet of God, being carried away to heaven. It ends with the people of Israel and Judah being carried away into captivity. In 1 Kings, the beautiful temple of God was built. In 2 Kings, it is desecrated and destroyed.

Our world is strikingly similar to the world described in 2 Kings. National and local governments do not seek God, and countries are tormented by war. Many people follow the false gods of technology, materialism, and war. True worship of God is rare on the earth.

In our chaotic and corrupt world, we can turn to examples such as David, Elijah, and Elisha, who were devoted to God's high honour and moral law and who brought about renewal and change in their society. More important, we can look to Jesus Christ, the perfect example. For nations to do God's will, they need individuals who will do God's work. If your heart is committed to God, he can work through you to accomplish the work he has called you to do.

1:2 Baal-Zebub was not the same god as Baal, the Canaanite god worshipped by Ahab and Jezebel (1 Kings 16:31–33). Baal-Zebub was another popular god whose temple was located in the city of Ekron. Because this god was thought to have the power of prophecy, King Ahaziah sent messengers to Ekron to learn of his fate. Supernatural power and mystery were associated with this god. Ahaziah's action showed the king's disrespect for God.

1:8 For more information on Elijah, see his Profile in 1 Kings 18.

1:13–15 Notice how the third captain went to Elijah. Although the first two captains called Elijah "man of God", they were not being genuine—God was not in their hearts. The third captain also called him "man of God", but he humbly begged for mercy. His attitude showed respect for God and his power and saved the lives of his men. Effective living begins with a right attitude towards God. Before religious words come to your mouth, make sure they are from your heart. Let respect, humility, and servanthood characterise your attitude towards God and others.

heaven and consumed the first two captains and all their men. But now have respect
for my life!"
15 The angel[o] of the LORD said to Elijah, "Go down with him; do not be afraid[p]
of him." So Elijah got up and went down with him to the king.
16 He told the king, "This is what the LORD says: Is it because there is no God in
Israel for you to consult that you have sent messengers[q] to consult Baal-Zebub, the
god of Ekron? Because you have done this, you will never leave[r] the bed you are
lying on. You will certainly die!" 17 So he died,[s] according to the word of the LORD
that Elijah had spoken.
Because Ahaziah had no son, Joram[a][t] succeeded him as king in the second year
of Jehoram son of Jehoshaphat king of Judah. 18 As for all the other events of Ahaziah's
reign, and what he did, are they not written in the book of the annals of the kings of
Israel?

1. Elisha's ministry

Elijah Taken Up to Heaven

2 When the LORD was about to take[a] Elijah up to heaven in a whirlwind,[b] Elijah
and Elisha[c] were on their way from Gilgal.[d] 2 Elijah said to Elisha, "Stay here;[e]
the LORD has sent me to Bethel."
But Elisha said, "As surely as the LORD lives and as you live, I will not leave you."[f]
So they went down to Bethel.
3 The company[g] of the prophets at Bethel came out to Elisha and asked, "Do you
know that the LORD is going to take your master from you today?"
"Yes, I know," Elisha replied, "but do not speak of it."
4 Then Elijah said to him, "Stay here, Elisha; the LORD has sent me to Jericho.[h]"
And he replied, "As surely as the LORD lives and as you live, I will not leave you."
So they went to Jericho.
5 The company[i] of the prophets at Jericho went up to Elisha and asked him, "Do
you know that the LORD is going to take your master from you today?"
"Yes, I know," he replied, "but do not speak of it."
6 Then Elijah said to him, "Stay here;[j] the LORD has sent me to the Jordan."[k]
And he replied, "As surely as the LORD lives and as you live, I will not leave you."[l]
So the two of them walked on.
7 Fifty men of the company of the prophets went and stood at a distance, facing the
place where Elijah and Elisha had stopped at the Jordan. 8 Elijah took his cloak,[m]
rolled it up and struck[n] the water with it. The water divided[o] to the right and to the
left, and the two of them crossed over on dry[p] ground.
9 When they had crossed, Elijah said to Elisha, "Tell me, what can I do for you
before I am taken from you?"
"Let me inherit a double[q] portion of your spirit,"[r] Elisha replied.
10 "You have asked a difficult thing," Elijah said, "yet if you see me when I am
taken from you, it will be yours—otherwise not."

[a] 17 Hebrew *Jehoram*, a variant of *Joram*

1:15 [o]ver 3 [p]Isa 51:12; 57:11; Jer 1:17; Eze 2:6
1:16 [q]ver 2 [r]ver 4
1:17 [s]2Ki 8:15; Jer 20:6; 28:17 [t]2Ki 3:1; 8:16
2:1 [a]Ge 5:24; Heb 11:5 [b]ver 11; 1Ki 19:11; Isa 5:28; 66:15; Jer 4:13; Na 1:3 [c]1Ki 19:16, 21 [d]Dt 11:30; 2Ki 4:38
2:2 [e]ver 6 [f]Ru 1:16; 1Sa 1:26; 2Ki 4:30
2:3 [g]1Sa 10:5; 2Ki 4:1, 38
2:4 [h]Jos 3:16; 6:26
2:5 [i]ver 3
2:6 [j]ver 2 [k]Jos 3:15 [l]Ru 1:16
2:8 [m]1Ki 19:19 [n]ver 14 [o]Ex 14:21 [p]Ex 14:22, 29
2:9 [q]Dt 21:17 [r]Nu 11:17

1:18 The book of the annals of the kings of Israel and the book of the annals of the kings of Judah (8:23) were history books. The inspired writer of 2 Kings selected facts from these books to retell the story of Israel and Judah from God's perspective. God directed the writer's thoughts and selection process to make sure that the truth, God's word, would be written.

2:3 A "company of the prophets" was like a school, a gathering of disciples around a recognised prophet, such as Elijah or Elisha. These companies of prophets, located throughout the country, helped stem the tide of spiritual and moral decline in the nation begun under Jeroboam. The students at Bethel were eyewitnesses to the succession of the prophetic ministry from Elijah to Elisha.

2:8 Elijah's cloak was a symbol of his authority as a prophet.

2:9 Elisha asked for a double portion of Elijah's spirit (prophetic ministry). Deuteronomy 21:17 helps explain Elisha's request. According to custom, the firstborn son received a double portion of the father's inheritance (see the note on Genesis 25:31). He was asking to be Elijah's heir, or successor, the one who would continue Elijah's work as leader of the prophets. But the decision to grant Elisha's request was up to God. Elijah only told him how he would know if his request had been granted.

2:9 God granted Elisha's request because Elisha's motives were pure. His main goal was not to be better or more powerful than Elijah, but to accomplish more for God. If our motives are pure, we don't have to be afraid to ask great things from God. When we ask God for great power or ability, we need to examine our desires and get rid of any selfishness we find. To have the Holy Spirit's help, we must be willing to ask.

2:11 [s]2Ki 6:17; Ps 68:17; 104:3, 4; Isa 66:15; Hab 3:8; Zec 6:1 [t]Ge 5:24 [u]ver 1
2:12 [v]2Ki 6:17; 13:14 [w]Ge 37:29
2:14 [x]1Ki 19:19 [y]ver 8
2:15 [z]ver 7; 1Sa 10:5 [a]Nu 11:17
2:16 [b]1Ki 18:12 [c]Ac 8:39
2:17 [d]2Ki 8:11

11 As they were walking along and talking together, suddenly a chariot of fire[s] and
horses of fire appeared and separated the two of them, and Elijah went up to heaven[t]
in a whirlwind.[u] 12 Elisha saw this and cried out, "My father! My father! The
chariots[v] and horsemen of Israel!" And Elisha saw him no more. Then he took hold
of his own clothes and tore[w] them apart.
13 He picked up the cloak that had fallen from Elijah and went back and stood on
the bank of the Jordan. 14 Then he took the cloak[x] that had fallen from him and
struck[y] the water with it. "Where now is the LORD, the God of Elijah?" he asked.
When he struck the water, it divided to the right and to the left, and he crossed over.
15 The company[z] of the prophets from Jericho, who were watching, said, "The
spirit[a] of Elijah is resting on Elisha." And they went to meet him and bowed to the
ground before him. 16 "Look," they said, "we your servants have fifty able men. Let
them go and look for your master. Perhaps the Spirit[b] of the LORD has picked him
up[c] and set him down on some mountain or in some valley."
"No," Elisha replied, "do not send them."
17 But they persisted until he was too ashamed[d] to refuse. So he said, "Send them."
And they sent fifty men, who searched for three days but did not find him. 18 When
they returned to Elisha, who was staying in Jericho, he said to them, "Didn't I tell
you not to go?"

KINGS TO DATE AND THEIR ENEMIES

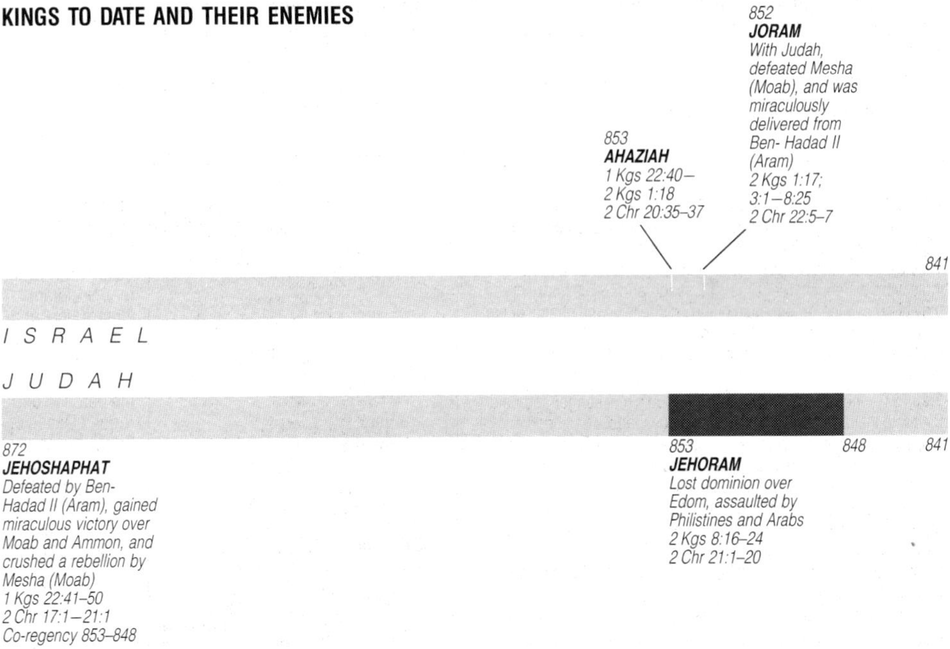

All dates are B.C.
Solid section of the timeline indicates co-regency.
For all the kings of Israel and Judah, see the chart at the end of 1 Kings.

2:11 Elijah was taken to heaven without dying. He is the second person mentioned in Scripture to do so. Enoch was the first (Genesis 5:21–24). The other prophets may not have seen God take Elijah, or they may have had a difficult time believing what they saw. In either case, they wanted to search for Elijah (2:16–18). Finding no physical trace of him would confirm what had happened and strengthen their faith. The only other person taken to heaven in bodily form was Jesus after his resurrection from the dead (Acts 1:9).

2:13–25 These three incidents were testimonies to Elisha's commission as a prophet of God. They are recorded to demonstrate Elisha's new power and authority as Israel's chief prophet under God's ultimate power and authority.

2:14 When Elisha struck the water, it was not out of disrespect to God or Elijah. It was a plea by Elisha to God to confirm his appointment as Elijah's successor.

Healing of the Water

19The men of the city said to Elisha, "Look, our lord, this town is well situated,
as you can see, but the water is bad and the land is unproductive."
20"Bring me a new bowl," he said, "and put salt in it." So they brought it to him.
21Then he went out to the spring and threw[e] the salt into it, saying, "This is what
the LORD says: 'I have healed this water. Never again will it cause death or make the
land unproductive.' " 22And the water has remained wholesome[f] to this day, according to the word Elisha had spoken.

Elisha Is Jeered

23From there Elisha went up to Bethel. As he was walking along the road, some
youths came out of the town and jeered[g] at him. "Go on up, you baldhead!" they
said. "Go on up, you baldhead!" 24He turned round, looked at them and called down
a curse[h] on them in the name[i] of the LORD. Then two bears came out of the woods
and mauled forty-two of the youths. 25And he went on to Mount Carmel[j] and from
there returned to Samaria.

Moab Revolts

3 Joram[a][a] son of Ahab became king of Israel in Samaria in the eighteenth year
of Jehoshaphat king of Judah, and he reigned for twelve years. 2He did evil[b] in
the eyes of the LORD, but not as his father[c] and mother had done. He got rid of the
sacred stone[d] of Baal that his father had made. 3Nevertheless he clung to the sins[e]
of Jeroboam son of Nebat, which he had caused Israel to commit; he did not turn away
from them.
4Now Mesha king of Moab[f] raised sheep, and he had to supply the king of Israel

a *1* Hebrew *Jehoram,* a variant of *Joram;* also in verse 6

2:21 [e]Ex 15:25; 2Ki 4:41; 6:6
2:22 [f]Ex 15:25
2:23 [g]Ex 22:28; 2Ch 36:16; Job 19:18; Ps 31:18
2:24 [h]Ge 4:11; Ne 13:25-27 [i]Dt 18:19
2:25 [j]1Ki 18:20; 2Ki 4:25
3:1 [a]2Ki 1:17
3:2 [b]1Ki 15:26 [c]1Ki 16:30-32 [d]Ex 23:24; 2Ki 10:18, 26-28
3:3 [e]1Ki 12:28-32; 14:9, 16
3:4 [f]Ge 19:37; 2Ki 1:1

2:23, 24 This mob of youths was from Bethel, the religious centre of idolatry in the northern kingdom, and they were probably warning Elisha not to speak against their immorality as Elijah had done. They were not merely teasing Elisha about his baldness, but showing severe disrespect for Elisha's message and God's power. They may also have jeered because of their disbelief in the chariot of fire that had taken Elijah. When Elisha cursed them, he did not call out the bears himself. God sent them as a judgment for their callous unbelief.

2:23, 24 These young men jeered at God's messenger and paid for it with their lives. Making fun of religious leaders has been a popular sport through the ages. To take a stand for God is to be different from the world and vulnerable to verbal abuse. When we are cynical and sarcastic towards religious leaders, we are in danger of mocking not just the person, but also the spiritual message. While we are not to condone the sin that some leaders commit, we need to pray for them, not laugh at them. True leaders, those who follow God, need to be heard with respect and encouraged in their ministry.

3:1 Although 1:17 says that Jehoram was king of Judah, 3:1 says that Jehoshaphat was Judah's king. As a king grew older, it was common for his son to rule beside him. Jehoshaphat, nearing the end of his reign, appointed his son Jehoram to rule with him. Jehoram served as co-ruler with Jehoshaphat for five years (853–848 B.C.; he is mentioned again in 8:16–24). Joram, king of Israel, was Ahab's son and Ahaziah's brother (1:17). Both Ahab (1 Kings 16:29 – 22:40) and Ahaziah (1:2–18) served as kings of Israel before Joram.

3:3 The sins of Israel's kings are often compared to "the sins of Jeroboam", the first ruler of the northern kingdom of Israel. His great sin was to institute idol worship throughout his kingdom, causing people to turn away from God (1 Kings 12:25–33). By ignoring God and allowing idol worship, Joram clung to Jeroboam's sins.

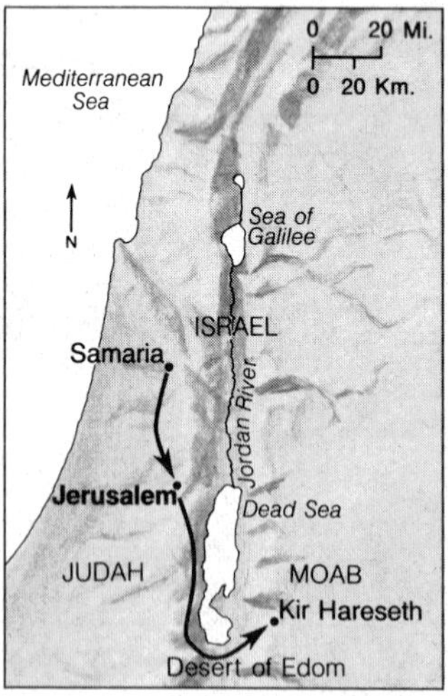

WAR AGAINST MOAB
Moab's king rebelled against Israel. So Joram, Israel's king, and Jehoshaphat, Judah's king, attacked Moab. In the parched and rugged Desert of Edom, the armies ran out of water, but Elisha promised that both water and victory would soon come.

3:4, 5 Israel and Judah held some of the most fertile land and strategic positions in the ancient Near East. It is no wonder that neighbouring nations like Moab envied them and constantly attempted to seize the land. Moab lay just southeast of Israel. The country had been under Israel's control for some time due to Ahab's strong military leadership. When Ahab died, Mesha, the Moabite king, took the opportunity to rebel. While Israel's next king, Ahaziah, did nothing about the revolt, his successor, Joram, decided to take action. He joined forces with Jehoshaphat, king of Judah, and went to fight the Moabites. Together, Israel and Judah brought the Moabites to the brink of surrender. But when they saw the Moabite king sacrifice his own son and successor (3:27), they withdrew even though they had won the battle. Moab fought many

with a hundred thousand lambs[g] and with the wool of a hundred thousand rams. 5But
after Ahab died, the king of Moab rebelled[h] against the king of Israel. 6So at that
time King Joram set out from Samaria and mobilised all Israel. 7He also sent this
message to Jehoshaphat king of Judah: "The king of Moab has rebelled against me.
Will you go with me to fight[i] against Moab?"
"I will go with you," he replied. "I am as you are, my people as your people, my
horses as your horses."
8"By what route shall we attack?" he asked.
"Through the Desert of Edom," he answered.
9So the king of Israel set out with the king of Judah and the king of Edom.[j] After
a roundabout march of seven days, the army had no more water for themselves or for
the animals with them.
10"What!" exclaimed the king of Israel. "Has the LORD called us three kings
together only to hand us over to Moab?"
11But Jehoshaphat asked, "Is there no prophet of the LORD here, that we may
enquire[k] of the LORD through him?"
An officer of the king of Israel answered, "Elisha[l] son of Shaphat is here. He used
to pour water on the hands of Elijah."[b][m]
12Jehoshaphat said, "The word[n] of the LORD is with him." So the king of Israel
and Jehoshaphat and the king of Edom went down to him.
13Elisha said to the king of Israel, "What do we have to do with each other? Go
to the prophets of your father and the prophets of your mother."
"No," the king of Israel answered, "because it was the LORD who called us three
kings together to hand us over to Moab."
14Elisha said, "As surely as the LORD Almighty lives, whom I serve, if I did not

3:4 [g]Ezr 7:17; Isa 16:1
3:5 [h]2Ki 1:1
3:7 [i]1Ki 22:4
3:9 [j]1Ki 22:47
3:11 [k]Ge 25:22; 1Ki 22:7 [l]Ge 20:7 [m]1Ki 19:16
3:12 [n]Nu 11:17

b *11* That is, he was Elijah's personal servant.

MIRACLES OF ELIJAH & ELISHA
Baal, the false god worshipped by many Israelites, was the god of rain, fire, and farm crops. He also demanded child sacrifice. Elijah's and Elisha's miracles repeatedly show the power of the true God over the purported realm of Baal, as well as the value God places on the life of a child.

Miracle	*Found where?*	*Factors*
E L I J A H		
1. Food brought by ravens	1 Kings 17:5, 6	Food
2. Widow's food multiplied	1 Kings 17:12–16	Flour and oil
3. Widow's son raised to life	1 Kings 17:17–24	Life of a child
4. Altar and sacrifice consumed	1 Kings 18:16–46	Fire and water
5. Ahaziah's soldiers consumed	2 Kings 1:9–14	Fire
6. Jordan River parted	2 Kings 2:6–8	Water
7. Transported to heaven	2 Kings 2:11, 12	Fire and wind
E L I S H A		
1. Jordan River parted	2 Kings 2:13, 14	Water
2. Spring purified at Jericho	2 Kings 2:19–22	Water
3. Widow's oil multiplied	2 Kings 4:1–7	Oil
4. Dead boy raised to life	2 Kings 4:18–37	Life of a child
5. Poison in stew purified	2 Kings 4:38–41	Flour
6. Prophets' food multiplied	2 Kings 4:42–44	Bread and grain
7. Naaman healed of leprosy	2 Kings 5:1–14	Water
8. Gehazi became leprous	2 Kings 5:15–27	Words alone
9. Axe-head floated	2 Kings 6:1–7	Water
10. Aramean army blinded	2 Kings 6:8–23	Elisha's prayer

other battles with both Israel and Judah. Some of them, in fact, were recorded by Mesha (c. 840 B.C.), who carved his exploits on a plaque called the Moabite Stone (discovered in 1868).

3:10 Edom was under Judah's control; thus they marched with them, making three kings.

3:11–20 Jehoshaphat's request for "a prophet of the LORD" shows how true worship and religious experience in both Israel and Judah had declined. In David's day, both the high priest and the prophets gave the king advice. But most of the priests had left Israel (see the first note on 1 Kings 17:1), and God's prophets were seen as messengers of doom (1 Kings 22:18). This miracle predicted by Elisha affirmed God's power and authority and validated Elisha's ministry. In 2 Chronicles 18, King Jehoshaphat of Judah and King Ahab of Israel gave the prophet Micaiah a similar request. But they ignored God's advice – with disastrous results.

have respect for the presence of Jehoshaphat king of Judah, I would not look at you
or even notice you. 15But now bring me a harpist."[o]
While the harpist was playing, the hand[p] of the LORD came upon Elisha 16and he
said, "This is what the LORD says: Make this valley full of ditches. 17For this is what
the LORD says: You will see neither wind nor rain, yet this valley will be filled with
water,[q] and you, your cattle and your other animals will drink. 18This is an easy[r]
thing in the eyes of the LORD; he will also hand Moab over to you. 19You will
overthrow every fortified city and every major town. You will cut down every good
tree, stop up all the springs, and ruin every good field with stones."
20The next morning, about the time[s] for offering the sacrifice, there it was—water
flowing from the direction of Edom! And the land was filled with water.[t]
21Now all the Moabites had heard that the kings had come to fight against them;
so every man, young and old, who could bear arms was called up and stationed on
the border. 22When they got up early in the morning, the sun was shining on the water.
To the Moabites across the way, the water looked red—like blood. 23"That's blood!"
they said. "Those kings must have fought and slaughtered each other. Now to the
plunder, Moab!"
24But when the Moabites came to the camp of Israel, the Israelites rose up and
fought them until they fled. And the Israelites invaded the land and slaughtered the
Moabites. 25They destroyed the towns, and each man threw a stone on every good
field until it was covered. They stopped up all the springs and cut down every good
tree. Only Kir Hareseth[u] was left with its stones in place, but men armed with slings
surrounded it and attacked it as well.
26When the king of Moab saw that the battle had gone against him, he took with
him seven hundred swordsmen to break through to the king of Edom, but they failed.
27Then he took his firstborn[v] son, who was to succeed him as king, and offered him
as a sacrifice on the city wall. The fury against Israel was great; they withdrew and
returned to their own land.

The Widow's Oil

4 The wife of a man from the company[a] of the prophets cried out to Elisha, "Your
servant my husband is dead, and you know that he revered the LORD. But now
his creditor[b] is coming to take my two boys as his slaves."
2Elisha replied to her, "How can I help you? Tell me, what do you have in your
house?"
"Your servant has nothing there at all," she said, "except a little oil."[c]
3Elisha said, "Go round and ask all your neighbours for empty jars. Don't ask for
just a few. 4Then go inside and shut the door behind you and your sons. Pour oil into
all the jars, and as each is filled, put it to one side."
5She left him and afterwards shut the door behind her and her sons. They brought
the jars to her and she kept pouring. 6When all the jars were full, she said to her son,
"Bring me another one."

3:15 [o]1Sa 16:23 [p]Jer 15:17; Eze 1:3
3:17 [q]Ps 107:35; Isa 32:2; 35:6; 41:18
3:18 [r]Ge 18:14; 2Ki 20:10; Isa 49:6; Jer 32:17, 27; Mk 10:27
3:20 [s]Ex 29:39-40 [t]Ex 17:6
3:25 [u]ver 19; Isa 15:1; 16:7; Jer 48:31, 36
3:27 [v]Dt 12:31; 2Ki 16:3; 21:6; 2Ch 28:3; Ps 106:38; Jer 19:4-5; Am 2:1; Mic 6:7
4:1 [a]1Sa 10:5; 2Ki 2:3 [b]Ex 22:26; Lev 25:39-43; Ne 5:3-5; Job 22:6; 24:9
4:2 [c]1Ki 17:12

3:15 In Old Testament times music often accompanied prophecy (1 Chronicles 25:1).

3:20 The morning sacrifice was one of two sacrifices that the priests were required to offer each day.

4:1 Poor people and debtors were allowed to pay their debts by selling themselves or their children as slaves. God ordered rich people and creditors not to take advantage of these people during their time of extreme need (see Deuteronomy 15:1–18 for an explanation of these practices). This woman's creditor was not acting in the spirit of God's law. Elisha's kind deed demonstrates that God wants us to go beyond simply keeping the law. We must also show compassion.

4:1ff This chapter records four of God's miracles through Elisha: providing money for a poverty-stricken widow (4:1–7); raising a dead boy to life (4:32–37); purifying poisonous food (4:38–41); and providing food for 100 men (4:42–44). These miracles show God's tenderness and care for those who are faithful to him.

When reading the Old Testament, it is easy to focus on God's harsh judgment of the rebellious and to minimise his tender care for those who love and serve him. To see him at work providing for his followers helps us keep his severe justice towards the unrepentant in proper perspective.

4:6 The woman and her sons collected jars from their neighbours, pouring oil into them from their one pot. The oil was probably olive oil and was used for cooking, for lamps, and for fuel. The oil stopped pouring only when they ran out of containers. The number of jars they gathered was an indication of their faith. God's provision was as large as their faith and willingness to obey. Beware of limiting God's blessings by a lack of faith and obedience. God is able to do immeasurably more than all we ask or imagine (Ephesians 3:20).

4:7 [d]1Ki 12:22

But he replied, "There is not a jar left." Then the oil stopped flowing.
7She went and told the man of God,[d] and he said, "Go, sell the oil and pay your
debts. You and your sons can live on what is left."

4:8 [e]Jos 19:18

The Shunammite's Son Restored to Life

8One day Elisha went to Shunem.[e] And a well-to-do woman was there, who urged
him to stay for a meal. So whenever he came by, he stopped there to eat. 9She said
to her husband, "I know that this man who often comes our way is a holy man of God.
10Let's make a small room on the roof and put in it a bed and a table, a chair and
a lamp for him. Then he can stay[f] there whenever he comes to us."
11One day when Elisha came, he went up to his room and lay down there. 12He
said to his servant Gehazi, "Call the Shunammite."[g] So he called her, and she stood
before him. 13Elisha said to him, "Tell her, 'You have gone to all this trouble for us.
Now what can be done for you? Can we speak on your behalf to the king or the
commander of the army?' "
She replied, "I have a home among my own people."
14"What can be done for her?" Elisha asked.
Gehazi said, "Well, she has no son and her husband is old."
15Then Elisha said, "Call her." So he called her, and she stood in the doorway.
16"About this time[h] next year," Elisha said, "you will hold a son in your arms."
"No, my lord," she objected. "Don't mislead your servant, O man of God!"
17But the woman became pregnant, and the next year about that same time she gave
birth to a son, just as Elisha had told her.
18The child grew, and one day he went out to his father, who was with the reapers.[i]
19"My head! My head!" he said to his father.
His father told a servant, "Carry him to his mother." 20After the servant had lifted
him up and carried him to his mother, the boy sat on her lap until noon, and then he
died. 21She went up and laid him on the bed[j] of the man of God, then shut the door
and went out.
22She called her husband and said, "Please send me one of the servants and a donkey
so I can go to the man of God quickly and return."
23"Why go to him today?" he asked. "It's not the New Moon[k] or the Sabbath."
"It's all right," she said.
24She saddled the donkey and said to her servant, "Lead on; don't slow down for
me unless I tell you." 25So she set out and came to the man of God at Mount Carmel.[l]
When he saw her in the distance, the man of God said to his servant Gehazi, "Look!

4:10 [f]Mt 10:41; Ro 12:13

4:12 [g]2Ki 8:1

4:16 [h]Ge 18:10

4:18 [i]Ru 2:3

4:21 [j]ver 32

4:23 [k]Nu 10:10; 1Ch 23:31; Ps 81:3

4:25 [l]1Ki 18:20; 2Ki 2:25

THE FAMILY IN SHUNEM
Elisha often stayed with a kind family in Shunem. When the son suddenly died, his mother travelled to Mount Carmel to find Elisha. He returned with her, and raised the boy from the dead. Elisha then went to his home in Gilgal.

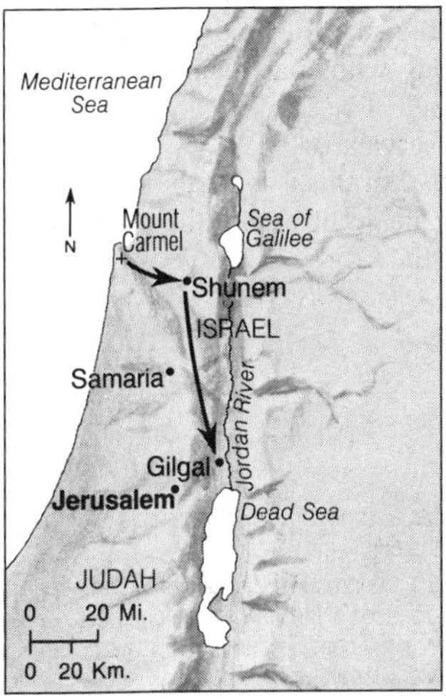

4:9 The Shunammite woman realised that Elisha was a man of God, and so she prepared a room for him to use whenever he was in town. She did this out of kindness and because she sensed a need, not for any selfish motives. Soon, however, her kindness would be rewarded far beyond her wildest dreams. How sensitive are you to those who pass by your home and flow through your life – especially those who teach and preach God's word? What special needs do they have that you could meet? Look for ways to serve and help.

There's the Shunammite! 26 Run to meet her and ask her, 'Are you all right? Is your
husband all right? Is your child all right?' "
"Everything is all right," she said.
27 When she reached the man of God at the mountain, she took hold of his feet.
Gehazi came over to push her away, but the man of God said, "Leave her alone! She
is in bitter distress,[m] but the LORD has hidden it from me and has not told me why."
28 "Did I ask you for a son, my lord?" she said. "Didn't I tell you, 'Don't raise my
hopes'?"
29 Elisha said to Gehazi, "Tuck your cloak into your belt,[n] take my staff[o] in your
hand and run. If you meet anyone, do not greet him, and if anyone greets you, do
not answer. Lay my staff on the boy's face."
30 But the child's mother said, "As surely as the LORD lives and as you live, I will
not leave you." So he got up and followed her.
31 Gehazi went on ahead and laid the staff on the boy's face, but there was no sound
or response. So Gehazi went back to meet Elisha and told him, "The boy has not
awakened."
32 When Elisha reached the house, there was the boy lying dead on his couch.[p] 33 He
went in, shut the door on the two of them and prayed[q] to the LORD. 34 Then he got
on the bed and lay upon the boy, mouth to mouth, eyes to eyes, hands to hands. As
he stretched[r] himself out upon him, the boy's body grew warm. 35 Elisha turned away
and walked back and forth in the room and then got onto the bed and stretched out
upon him once more. The boy sneezed seven times[s] and opened his eyes.[t]
36 Elisha summoned Gehazi and said, "Call the Shunammite." And he did. When
she came, he said, "Take your son."[u] 37 She came in, fell at his feet and bowed to
the ground. Then she took her son and went out.

Death in the Pot

38 Elisha returned to Gilgal[v] and there was a famine[w] in that region. While the
company of the prophets was meeting with him, he said to his servant, "Put on the
large pot and cook some stew for these men."
39 One of them went out into the fields to gather herbs and found a wild vine. He
gathered some of its gourds and filled the fold of his cloak. When he returned, he cut
them up into the pot of stew, though no-one knew what they were. 40 The stew was
poured out for the men, but as they began to eat it, they cried out, "O man of God,
there is death in the pot!" And they could not eat it.
41 Elisha said, "Get some flour." He put it into the pot and said, "Serve it to the
people to eat." And there was nothing harmful in the pot.[x]

Feeding of a Hundred

42 A man came from Baal Shalishah,[y] bringing the man of God twenty loaves[z]
of barley bread[a] baked from the first ripe corn, along with some ears of new corn.
"Give it to the people to eat," Elisha said.
43 "How can I set this before a hundred men?" his servant asked.
But Elisha answered, "Give it to the people to eat.[b] For this is what the LORD says:
'They will eat and have some left over.[c]' " 44 Then he set it before them, and they
ate and had some left over, according to the word of the LORD.

4:27 [m] 1Sa 1:15
4:29 [n] 1Ki 18:46; 2Ki 2:8, 14; 9:1 [o] Ex 4:2; 7:19; 14:16
4:32 [p] ver 21
4:33 [q] 1Ki 17:20; Mt 6:6
4:34 [r] 1Ki 17:21; Ac 20:10
4:35 [s] Jos 6:15 [t] 2Ki 8:5
4:36 [u] Heb 11:35
4:38 [v] 2Ki 2:1 [w] Lev 26:26; 2Ki 8:1
4:41 [x] Ex 15:25; 2Ki 2:21
4:42 [y] 1Sa 9:4 [z] Mt 14:17; 15:36 [a] 1Sa 9:7
4:43 [b] Lk 9:13 [c] Mt 14:20; Jn 6:12

4:32–36 Elisha's prayer and method of raising the dead boy show God's personal care for hurting people. We must express genuine concern for others as we carry God's message to them. Only then will we faithfully represent our compassionate Father in heaven.

4:40 "Death in the pot" means that the food was poisonous. Perhaps a poisonous wild vegetable or herb had been mixed in with the edible plants.

5:1 Leprosy, much like AIDS today, was one of the most feared diseases of the time. Some forms were extremely contagious and, in many cases, incurable. In its worst forms, leprosy led to death. Many lepers were forced out of the cities into quarantined camps.

Naaman Healed of Leprosy

5 Now Naaman was commander of the army of the king of Aram.[a] He was a great
man in the sight of his master and highly regarded, because through him the LORD
had given victory to Aram. He was a valiant soldier, but he had leprosy.[a][b]
[2]Now bands[c] from Aram had gone out and had taken captive a young girl from
Israel, and she served Naaman's wife. [3]She said to her mistress, "If only my master
would see the prophet[d] who is in Samaria! He would cure him of his leprosy."
[4]Naaman went to his master and told him what the girl from Israel had said. [5]"By
all means, go," the king of Aram replied. "I will send a letter to the king of Israel."
So Naaman left, taking with him ten talents[b] of silver, six thousand shekels[c] of gold
and ten sets of clothing.[e] [6]The letter that he took to the king of Israel read: "With
this letter I am sending my servant Naaman to you so that you may cure him of his
leprosy."
[7]As soon as the king of Israel read the letter,[f] he tore his robes and said, "Am I
God?[g] Can I kill and bring back to life?[h] Why does this fellow send someone to me
to be cured of his leprosy? See how he is trying to pick a quarrel[i] with me!"
[8]When Elisha the man of God heard that the king of Israel had torn his robes, he
sent him this message: "Why have you torn your robes? Make the man come to me
and he will know that there is a prophet[j] in Israel." [9]So Naaman went with his horses
and chariots and stopped at the door of Elisha's house. [10]Elisha sent a messenger to
say to him, "Go, wash[k] yourself seven times[l] in the Jordan, and your flesh will be
restored and you will be cleansed."
[11]But Naaman went away angry and said, "I thought that he would surely come
out to me and stand and call on the name of the LORD his God, wave his hand[m] over
the spot and cure me of my leprosy. [12]Are not Abana and Pharpar, the rivers of
Damascus, better than any of the waters[n] of Israel? Couldn't I wash in them and be
cleansed?" So he turned and went off in a rage.[o]
[13]Naaman's servants went to him and said, "My father,[p] if the prophet had told
you to do some great thing, would you not have done it? How much more, then, when
he tells you, 'Wash and be cleansed'?" [14]So he went down and dipped himself in the
Jordan seven times,[q] as the man of God had told him, and his flesh was restored[r]
and became clean like that of a young boy.[s]
[15]Then Naaman and all his attendants went back to the man of God[t]. He stood

a *1* The Hebrew word was used for various diseases affecting the skin—not necessarily leprosy; also in verses 3, 6, 7, 11 and 27. b *5* That is, about 750 pounds (about 340 kilograms) c *5* That is, about 150 pounds (about 70 kilograms)

5:1 [a]Ge 10:22; 2Sa 10:19 [b]Ex 4:6; Nu 12:10; Lk 4:27
5:2 [c]2Ki 6:23; 13:20; 24:2
5:3 [d]Ge 20:7
5:5 [e]ver 22; Ge 24:53; Jdg 14:12; 1Sa 9:7
5:7 [f]2Ki 19:14 [g]Ge 30:2 [h]Dt 32:39; 1Sa 2:6 [i]1Ki 20:7
5:8 [j]1Ki 22:7
5:10 [k]Jn 9:7 [l]Ge 33:3; Lev 14:7
5:11 [m]Ex 7:19
5:12 [n]Isa 8:6 [o]Pr 14:17, 29; 19:11; 29:11
5:13 [p]2Ki 6:21; 13:14
5:14 [q]Ge 33:3; Lev 14:7; Jos 6:15 [r]Ex 4:7 [s]Job 33:25; Lk 4:27
5:15 [t]Jos 2:11

Because Naaman still held his post, he probably had a mild form of the disease, or perhaps it was still in the early stages. In either case, his life would have been tragically shortened by his disease. (For more about leprosy in Bible times, see the note on Leviticus 13:1ff.)

5:2 Aram was Israel's neighbour to the northeast, but the two nations were rarely on friendly terms. Under David, Aram paid tribute to Israel. In Elisha's day, Aram was growing in power and frequently conducted raids on Israel, trying to frustrate the people and bring about political confusion. Israelite captives were often taken back to Aram after successful raids. Naaman's servant girl was an Israelite, kidnapped from her home and family. Ironically, Naaman's only hope of being cured came from Israel.

5:3, 4 The little girl's faith and Naaman's quest contrast with the stubbornness of Israel's king (5:7). A leader in mighty Aram sought the God of Israel; Israel's own king would not. We don't know the little girl's name or much about her, but her brief word to her mistress brought healing and faith in God to a powerful Aramean captain. God had placed her for a purpose, and she was faithful. Where has God put you? No matter how humble or small your position, God can use you to spread his word. Look for opportunities to tell others what God can do. There's no telling who will hear your message!

5:9–15 Naaman, a great hero, was used to getting respect, and he was outraged when Elisha treated him like an ordinary person. A proud man, he expected royal treatment. To wash in a great river would be one thing, but the Jordan was small and dirty. To wash in the Jordan, Naaman thought, was beneath a man of his position. But Naaman had to humble himself and obey Elisha's commands in order to be healed.

Obedience to God begins with humility. We must believe that his way is better than our own. We may not always understand his ways of working, but by humbly obeying, we will receive his blessings. We must remember that (1) God's ways are best; (2) God wants our obedience more than anything else; (3) God can use anything to accomplish his purposes.

5:12 Naaman left in a rage because the cure for his disease seemed too simple. He was a hero, and he expected a heroic cure. Full of pride and self-will, he could not accept the simple cure of faith. Sometimes people react to God's offer of forgiveness in the same way. Just to *believe* in Jesus Christ somehow doesn't seem significant enough to bring eternal life. To obey God's commands doesn't seem heroic. What Naaman had to do to have his leprosy washed away is similar to what we must do to have our sin washed away—humbly accept God's mercy. Don't let your reaction to the way of faith keep you from the cure you need the most.

before him and said, "Now I know[u] that there is no God in all the world except in
Israel. Please accept now a gift[v] from your servant."
16 The prophet answered, "As surely as the LORD lives, whom I serve, I will not
accept a thing." And even though Naaman urged him, he refused.[w]
17 "If you will not," said Naaman, "please let me, your servant, be given as much
earth[x] as a pair of mules can carry, for your servant will never again make burnt
offerings and sacrifices to any other god but the LORD. 18 But may the LORD forgive
your servant for this one thing: When my master enters the temple of Rimmon to bow
down and he is leaning[y] on my arm and I bow there also—when I bow down in the
temple of Rimmon, may the LORD forgive your servant for this."
19 "Go in peace,"[z] Elisha said.
After Naaman had travelled some distance, 20 Gehazi, the servant of Elisha the man
of God, said to himself, "My master was too easy on Naaman, this Aramean, by not
accepting from him what he brought. As surely as the LORD[a] lives, I will run after
him and get something from him."
21 So Gehazi hurried after Naaman. When Naaman saw him running towards him,
he got down from the chariot to meet him. "Is everything all right?" he asked.
22 "Everything is all right," Gehazi answered. "My master sent me to say, 'Two
young men from the company of the prophets have just come to me from the hill
country of Ephraim. Please give them a talent[d] of silver and two sets of clothing.' "[b]
23 "By all means, take two talents," said Naaman. He urged Gehazi to accept them,
and then tied up the two talents of silver in two bags, with two sets of clothing. He
gave them to two of his servants, and they carried them ahead of Gehazi. 24 When
Gehazi came to the hill, he took the things from the servants and put them away in
the house. He sent the men away and they left. 25 Then he went in and stood before
his master Elisha.
"Where have you been, Gehazi?" Elisha asked.
"Your servant didn't go anywhere," Gehazi answered.
26 But Elisha said to him, "Was not my spirit with you when the man got down from
his chariot to meet you? Is this the time[c] to take money, or to accept clothes, olive
groves, vineyards, flocks, herds, or menservants and maidservants?[d] 27 Naaman's
leprosy[e] will cling to you and to your descendants for ever." Then Gehazi[f] went
from Elisha's presence and he was leprous, as white as snow.[g]

An Axhead Floats

6 The company[a] of the prophets said to Elisha, "Look, the place where we meet
with you is too small for us. 2 Let us go to the Jordan, where each of us can get
a pole; and let us build a place there for us to live."
And he said, "Go."

5:15 [u]Jos 4:24; 1Sa 17:46; Da 2:47 [v]1Sa 9:7; 25:27
5:16 [w]ver 20, 26; Ge 14:23; Da 5:17
5:17 [x]Ex 20:24
5:18 [y]2Ki 7:2
5:19 [z]1Sa 1:17; Ac 15:33
5:20 [a]Ex 20:7
5:22 [b]ver 5; Ge 45:22
5:26 [c]ver 16 [d]Jer 45:5
5:27 [e]Nu 12:10; 2Ki 15:5 [f]Col 3:5 [g]Ex 4:6
6:1 [a]1Sa 10:5; 2Ki 4:38

d *22* That is, about 75 pounds (about 34 kilograms)

5:16 Elisha refused Naaman's money to show that God's favour cannot be purchased. Our money, like Naaman's, is useless when we face death. No matter how much wealth we accumulate in this life, it will evaporate when we stand before God, our Creator. It will be our faith in Jesus Christ that saves us, not our bank accounts.

5:18, 19 How could Naaman be forgiven for bowing to a pagan idol? Naaman was not asking for permission to worship the god Rimmon, but to do his civil duty, helping the king get down and up as he bowed. Also known as Hadad, Rimmon, the god of Damascus, was believed to be a god of rain and thunder. Naaman, unlike most of his contemporaries, showed a keen awareness of God's power. Instead of adding God to his nation's collection of idols, he acknowledged that there was only one true God. He did not intend to worship other gods. His asking for pardon in this one area shows the marked contrast between Naaman and the Israelites, who were continually worshipping many idols.

5:20–27 Gehazi saw a perfect opportunity to get rich by selfishly asking for the reward Elisha had refused. Unfortunately, there were three problems with his plan: (1) he willingly accepted money that had been offered to someone else; (2) he wrongly implied that money could be exchanged for God's free gift of healing and mercy; (3) he lied and tried to cover up his motives for accepting the money. Although Gehazi had been a helpful servant, personal gain had become more important to him than serving God.

This passage is not teaching that money is evil or that ministers should not get paid; instead, it is warning against greed and deceit. True service is motivated by love and devotion to God and seeks no personal gain. As you serve God, check your motives—you can't serve both God and money (Matthew 6:24).

6:1–7 The incident of the floating axe head is recorded to show God's care and provision for those who trust him, even in the insignificant events of everyday life. God is always present. Placed in the Bible between the healing of an Aramean general and the deliverance of Israel's army, this miracle also shows Elisha's personal contact with the students in the companies of the prophets. Although he had the respect of kings, Elisha never forgot to care for the faithful. Don't let the importance of your work drive out your concern for human need.

6:6 [b]Ex 15:25; 2Ki 2:21
6:9 [c]ver 12
6:10 [d]Jer 11:18

3Then one of them said, "Won't you please come with your servants?"
"I will," Elisha replied. 4And he went with them.
They went to the Jordan and began to cut down trees. 5As one of them was cutting
down a tree, the iron axe-head fell into the water. "Oh, my lord," he cried out, "it
was borrowed!"
6The man of God asked, "Where did it fall?" When he showed him the place, Elisha
cut a stick and threw[b] it there, and made the iron float. 7"Lift it out," he said. Then
the man reached out his hand and took it.

Elisha Traps Blinded Arameans

8Now the king of Aram was at war with Israel. After conferring with his officers,
he said, "I will set up my camp in such and such a place."
9The man of God sent word to the king[c] of Israel: "Beware of passing that place,
because the Arameans are going down there." 10So the king of Israel checked on the
place indicated by the man of God. Time and again Elisha warned[d] the king, so that
he was on his guard in such places.
11This enraged the king of Aram. He summoned his officers and demanded of them,
"Will you not tell me which of us is on the side of the king of Israel?"

ELISHA

Few "replacements" in Scripture were as effective as Elisha, who was Elijah's replacement as God's prophet to Israel. But Elisha had a great example to follow in the prophet Elijah. He remained with Elijah until the last moments of his teacher's life on earth. He was willing to follow and learn in order to gain power to do the work to which God had called him.

Both Elijah and Elisha concentrated their efforts on the particular needs of the people around them. The fiery Elijah confronted and exposed idolatry, helping to create an atmosphere where people could freely and publicly worship God. Elisha then moved in to demonstrate God's powerful, yet caring, nature to all who came to him for help. He spent less time in conflict with evil and more in compassionate care of people. The Bible records 18 encounters between Elisha and needy people.

Elisha saw more *in* life than most people because he recognised that with God there was more *to* life. He knew that all we are and have comes to us from God. The miracles that occurred during Elisha's ministry put people in touch with the personal and all-powerful God. Elijah would have been proud of his replacement's work.

We too have great examples to follow—both people in Scripture and those who have positively influenced our lives. We must resist the tendency to think about the limitations that our family background or environment create for us. Instead, we should ask God to use us for his purposes—perhaps, like Elijah, to take a stand against great wrongs or, like Elisha, to show compassion for the daily needs of those around us. Ask him to use you as only he can.

Strengths and accomplishments:
- Was Elijah's successor as a prophet of God
- Had a ministry that lasted over 50 years
- Had a major impact on four nations: Israel, Judah, Moab, and Aram
- Was a man of integrity who did not try to enrich himself at others' expense
- Did many miracles to help those in need

Lessons from his life:
- In God's eyes, one measure of greatness is the willingness to serve the poor as well as the powerful
- An effective replacement not only learns from his master, but also builds upon his master's achievements

Vital statistics:
- Where: Prophesied to the northern kingdom
- Occupations: Farmer, prophet
- Relative: Father: Shaphat
- Contemporaries: Elijah, Ahab, Jezebel, Jehu

Key verse:
"When they had crossed, Elijah said to Elisha, 'Tell me, what can I do for you before I am taken from you?'

" 'Let me inherit a double portion of your spirit,' Elisha replied" (2 Kings 2:9).

Elisha's story is told in 1 Kings 19:16—2 Kings 13:20. He is also mentioned in Luke 4:27.

[12]"None of us, my lord the king[e]," said one of his officers, "but Elisha, the prophet
who is in Israel, tells the king of Israel the very words you speak in your bedroom."
[13]"Go, find out where he is," the king ordered, "so that I can send men and capture
him." The report came back: "He is in Dothan."[f] [14]Then he sent[g] horses and chariots
and a strong force there. They went by night and surrounded the city.
[15]When the servant of the man of God got up and went out early the next morning,
an army with horses and chariots had surrounded the city. "Oh, my lord, what shall
we do?" the servant asked.
[16]"Don't be afraid,"[h] the prophet answered. "Those who are with us are more[i]
than those who are with them."
[17]And Elisha prayed, "O LORD, open his eyes so that he may see." Then the LORD
opened the servant's eyes, and he looked and saw the hills full of horses and chariots[j]
of fire all round Elisha.
[18]As the enemy came down towards him, Elisha prayed to the LORD, "Strike these
people with blindness."[k] So he struck them with blindness, as Elisha had asked.
[19]Elisha told them, "This is not the road and this is not the city. Follow me, and
I will lead you to the man you are looking for." And he led them to Samaria.
[20]After they entered the city, Elisha said, "LORD, open the eyes of these men so
that they can see." Then the LORD opened their eyes and they looked, and there they
were, inside Samaria.
[21]When the king of Israel saw them, he asked Elisha, "Shall I kill them, my
father?[l] Shall I kill them?"
[22]"Do not kill them," he answered. "Would you kill men you have captured[m] with
your own sword or bow? Set food and water before them so that they may eat and
drink and then go back to their master." [23]So he prepared a great feast for them, and
after they had finished eating and drinking, he sent them away, and they returned to
their master. So the bands[n] from Aram stopped raiding Israel's territory.

Famine in Besieged Samaria

[24]Some time later, Ben-Hadad[o] king of Aram mobilised his entire army and
marched up and laid siege[p] to Samaria. [25]There was a great famine[q] in the city; the
siege lasted so long that a donkey's head sold for eighty shekels[a] of silver, and a
quarter of a cab[b] of seed pods[c][r] for five shekels.[d]

[a] *25* That is, about 2 pounds (about 1 kilogram) [b] *25* That is, probably about ½ pint (about 0.3 litre) [c] *25* Or *of dove's dung* [d] *25* That is, about 2 ounces (about 55 grams)

6:12 [e]ver 9
6:13 [f]Ge 37:17
6:14 [g]2Ki 1:9
6:16 [h]Ge 15:1 [i]2Ch 32:7; Ps 55:18; Ro 8:31; 1Jn 4:4
6:17 [j]2Ki 2:11, 12; Ps 68:17; Zec 6:1-7
6:18 [k]Ge 19:11; Ac 13:11
6:21 [l]2Ki 5:13
6:22 [m]Dt 20:11; 2Ch 28:8-15; Ro 12:20
6:23 [n]2Ki 5:2
6:24 [o]1Ki 15:18; 20:1; 2Ki 8:7 [p]Dt 28:52
6:25 [q]Lev 26:26; Ru 1:1 [r]Isa 36:12

ELISHA AND THE ARAMEANS
Elisha knew Aram's battle plans and kept Israel's king informed. The Aramean king tracked down Elisha at Dothan, but Elisha prayed that the Aramean army would be blinded. He then led the blind army into Samaria, Israel's capital city!

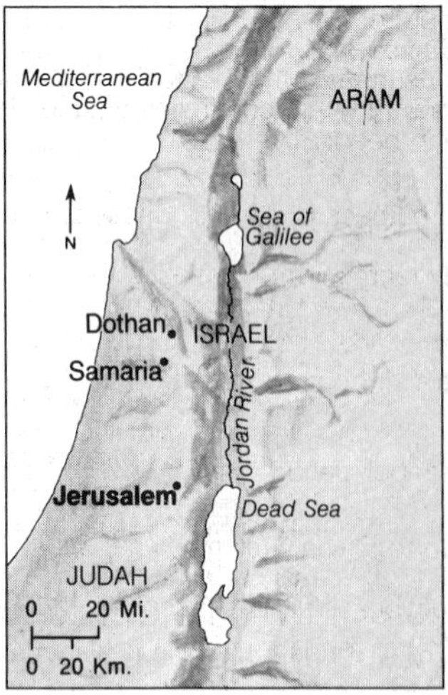

6:16, 17 Elisha's servant was no longer afraid when he saw God's mighty heavenly army. Faith reveals that God is doing more for his people than we can ever realise through sight alone. When you face difficulties that seem insurmountable, remember that spiritual resources are there even if you can't see them. Look through the eyes of faith and let God show you his resources. If you don't see God working in your life, the problem may be your spiritual eyesight, not God's power.

6:21, 22 Elisha told the king not to kill the Arameans. The king was not to take credit for what God alone had done. In setting food and water before them, he was heaping "burning coals" on their heads (Proverbs 25:21, 22).

6:23 How long the Arameans stayed away from Israel is not known, but a number of years probably passed before the invasion recorded in 6:24 occurred. The Arameans must have forgotten the time their army was supernaturally blinded and sent home.

6:24 This was probably Ben-Hadad II, whose father ruled Aram in the days of Baasha (1 Kings 15:18). Elisha constantly frustrated Ben-Hadad II in his attempts to take control of Israel.

6:25 When a city like Samaria faced famine, it was no small matter. Although its farmers grew enough food to feed the people for a specific season, they did not have enough to maintain them in prolonged times of emergency when all supplies were cut off. This famine was so severe that mothers resorted to eating their children

6:29 [s]Lev 26:29; Dt 28:53-55
6:30 [t]2Ki 18:37; Isa 22:15 [u]Ge 37:34; 1Ki 21:27
6:32 [v]Eze 8:1; 14:1; 20:1 [w]1Ki 18:4 [x]ver 31
6:33 [y]Lev 24:11; Job 2:9; 14:14; Isa 40:31
7:1 [a]ver 16
7:2 [b]2Ki 5:18 [c]ver 19; Ge 7:11; Ps 78:23; Mal 3:10 [d]ver 17

26 As the king of Israel was passing by on the wall, a woman cried to him, "Help
me, my lord the king!"
27 The king replied, "If the LORD does not help you, where can I get help for you?
From the threshing-floor? From the winepress?" 28 Then he asked her, "What's the
matter?"
She answered, "This woman said to me, 'Give up your son so that we may eat him
today, and tomorrow we'll eat my son.' 29 So we cooked my son and ate[s] him. The
next day I said to her, 'Give up your son so that we may eat him,' but she had hidden
him."
30 When the king heard the woman's words, he tore[t] his robes. As he went along
the wall, the people looked, and there, underneath, he had sackcloth[u] on his body.
31 He said, "May God deal with me, be it ever so severely, if the head of Elisha son
of Shaphat remains on his shoulders today!"
32 Now Elisha was sitting in his house, and the elders[v] were sitting with him. The
king sent a messenger ahead, but before he arrived, Elisha said to the elders, "Don't
you see how this murderer[w] is sending someone to cut off my head?[x] Look, when
the messenger comes, shut the door and hold it shut against him. Is not the sound of
his master's footsteps behind him?"
33 While he was still talking to them, the messenger came down to him. And ⌞the
king⌟ said, "This disaster is from the LORD. Why should I wait[y] for the LORD any
longer?"

7 Elisha said, "Hear the word of the LORD. This is what the LORD says: About this
time tomorrow, a seah[a] of flour will sell for a shekel[b] and two seahs[c] of barley
for a shekel[a] at the gate of Samaria."
2 The officer on whose arm the king was leaning[b] said to the man of God, "Look,
even if the LORD should open the floodgates[c] of the heavens, could this happen?"
"You will see it with your own eyes," answered Elisha, "but you will not eat[d] any
of it!"

a *1* That is, probably about 13 pints (about 7.3 litres); also in verses 16 and 18 b *1* That is, about 2/5 ounce (about 11 grams); also in verses 16 and 18 c *1* That is, probably about 13 quarts (about 15 litres); also in verses 16 and 18

PEOPLE RAISED FROM THE DEAD
God is all-powerful. Nothing in life is beyond his control, not even death.

Elijah raised a boy from the dead	1 Kings 17:22
Elisha raised a boy from the dead	2 Kings 4:34–35
Elisha's bones raised a man from the dead	2 Kings 13:20–21
Jesus raised a boy from the dead	Luke 7:14, 15
Jesus raised a girl from the dead	Luke 8:52–56
Jesus raised Lazarus from the dead	John 11:38–44
Peter raised a woman from the dead	Acts 9:40, 41
Paul raised a man from the dead	Acts 20:9–20

(6:26–30). Deuteronomy 28:49–57 predicted that this would happen when the people of Israel rejected God's leadership.

6:31–33 Why did the king blame Elisha for the famine and troubles of the siege? Here are some possible reasons: (1) Some commentators say that Elisha must have told the king to trust God for deliverance. The king did this and even wore sackcloth (6:30), but at this point the situation seemed hopeless. Apparently the king thought Elisha had given him bad advice and not even God could help them. (2) For years there was conflict between the kings of Israel and the prophets of God. The prophets often predicted doom because of the kings' evil, so the kings saw them as trouble-makers. Thus Israel's king was striking out in frustration at Elisha. (3) The king may have remembered when Elijah helped bring an end to a famine (1 Kings 18:41–46). Knowing Elisha was a man of God, perhaps the king thought he could do any miracle he wanted and was angry that he had not come to Israel's rescue.

7:1, 2 When Elisha prophesied God's deliverance, the king's officer said it couldn't happen. The officer's faith and hope were gone, but God's words came true anyway (7:14–16)! Sometimes we become preoccupied with problems when we should be looking for opportunities. Instead of focusing on the negatives, develop an attitude of expectancy. To say that God *cannot* rescue someone or that a situation is *impossible* demonstrates a lack of faith.

The Siege Lifted

3Now there were four men with leprosy[d][e] at the entrance of the city gate. They
said to each other, "Why stay here until we die? 4If we say, 'We'll go into the
city' — the famine is there, and we will die. And if we stay here, we will die. So let's
go over to the camp of the Arameans and surrender. If they spare us, we live; if they
kill us, then we die."
5At dusk they got up and went to the camp of the Arameans. When they reached
the edge of the camp, not a man was there, 6for the Lord had caused the Arameans
to hear the sound[f] of chariots and horses and a great army, so that they said to one
another, "Look, the king of Israel has hired[g] the Hittite[h] and Egyptian kings to attack
us!" 7So they got up and fled[i] in the dusk and abandoned their tents and their horses
and donkeys. They left the camp as it was and ran for their lives.
8The men who had leprosy[j] reached the edge of the camp and entered one of the
tents. They ate and drank, and carried away silver, gold and clothes, and went off
and hid them. They returned and entered another tent and took some things from it
and hid them also.
9Then they said to each other, "We're not doing right. This is a day of good news
and we are keeping it to ourselves. If we wait until daylight, punishment will overtake
us. Let's go at once and report this to the royal palace."
10So they went and called out to the city gatekeepers and told them, "We went into
the Aramean camp and not a man was there — not a sound of anyone — only tethered
horses and donkeys, and the tents left just as they were." 11The gatekeepers shouted
the news, and it was reported within the palace.
12The king got up in the night and said to his officers, "I will tell you what the
Arameans have done to us. They know we are starving; so they have left the camp
to hide[k] in the countryside, thinking, 'They will surely come out, and then we will
take them alive and get into the city.' "
13One of his officers answered, "Make some men take five of the horses that are
left in the city. Their plight will be like that of all the Israelites left here — yes, they
will only be like all these Israelites who are doomed. So let us send them to find out
what happened."
14So they selected two chariots with their horses, and the king sent them after the
Aramean army. He commanded the drivers, "Go and find out what has happened."
15They followed them as far as the Jordan, and they found the whole road strewn with
the clothing and equipment the Arameans had thrown away in their headlong flight.
So the messengers returned and reported to the king. 16Then the people went out and
plundered[l] the camp of the Arameans. So a seah of flour sold for a shekel, and two
seahs of barley sold for a shekel,[m] as the LORD had said.
17Now the king had put the officer on whose arm he leaned in charge of the gate,
and the people trampled him in the gateway, and he died,[n] just as the man of God
had foretold when the king came down to his house. 18It happened as the man of God
had said to the king: "About this time tomorrow, a seah of flour will sell for a shekel
and two seahs of barley for a shekel at the gate of Samaria."
19The officer had said to the man of God, "Look, even if the LORD should open
the floodgates[o] of the heavens, could this happen?" The man of God had replied,
"You will see it with your own eyes, but you will not eat any of it!" 20And that is

[d] 3 The Hebrew word is used for various diseases affecting the skin — not necessarily leprosy; also in verse 8.

7:3 [e] Lev 13:45-46; Nu 5:1-4
7:6 [f] Ex 14:24; 2Sa 5:24; Eze 1:24 [g] 2Sa 10:6; Jer 46:21 [h] Nu 13:29
7:7 [i] Jdg 7:21; Ps 48:4-6; Pr 28:1; Isa 30:17
7:8 [j] Isa 33:23; 35:6
7:12 [k] Jos 8:4; 2Ki 6:25-29
7:16 [l] Isa 33:4, 23 [m] ver 1
7:17 [n] ver 2; 2Ki 6:32
7:19 [o] ver 2

7:3 According to the law, lepers were not allowed in the city, but were to depend on charity outside the gate (Leviticus 13:45, 46; Numbers 5:1–4). Because of the famine and the presence of the Aramean army, their situation was desperate.

7:3–10 The lepers discovered the deserted camp and realised their lives had been spared. At first they kept the good news to themselves, forgetting their fellow citizens who were starving in the city. The Good News about Jesus Christ must be shared too, for no news is more important. We must not forget those who are dying without it. We must not become so preoccupied with our own faith that we neglect sharing it with those around us. Our "good news", like that of the lepers, will not "wait until daylight".

7:19, 20 It is God, not worthless idols, who provides our daily food. Although our faith may be weak or very small, we must avoid becoming sceptical of God's provision. When our resources are low and our doubts are the strongest, remember God can open the floodgates of heaven.

exactly what happened to him, for the people trampled him in the gateway, and he
died.

The Shunammite's Land Restored

8 Now Elisha had said to the woman[a] whose son he had restored to life, "Go away
with your family and stay for a while wherever you can, because the LORD has
decreed a famine[b] in the land that will last seven years."[c] 2 The woman proceeded
to do as the man of God said. She and her family went away and stayed in the land
of the Philistines for seven years.
3 At the end of the seven years she came back from the land of the Philistines and
went to the king to beg for her house and land. 4 The king was talking to Gehazi, the
servant of the man of God, and had said, "Tell me about all the great things Elisha
has done." 5 Just as Gehazi was telling the king how Elisha had restored[d] the dead
to life, the woman whose son Elisha had brought back to life came to beg the king
for her house and land.
Gehazi said, "This is the woman, my lord the king, and this is her son whom Elisha
restored to life." 6 The king asked the woman about it, and she told him.
Then he assigned an official to her case and said to him, "Give back everything
that belonged to her, including all the income from her land from the day she left the
country until now."

Hazael Murders Ben-Hadad

7 Elisha went to Damascus,[e] and Ben-Hadad[f] king of Aram was ill. When the king
was told, "The man of God has come all the way up here," 8 he said to Hazael,[g] "Take
a gift[h] with you and go to meet the man of God. Consult[i] the LORD through him;
ask him, 'Will I recover from this illness?' "
9 Hazael went to meet Elisha, taking with him as a gift forty camel-loads of all the
finest wares of Damascus. He went in and stood before him, and said, "Your son
Ben-Hadad king of Aram has sent me to ask, 'Will I recover from this illness?' "
10 Elisha answered, "Go and say to him, 'You will certainly recover';[j] but**a** the
LORD has revealed to me that he will in fact die." 11 He stared at him with a fixed gaze
until Hazael felt ashamed.[k] Then the man of God began to weep.[l]
12 "Why is my lord weeping?" asked Hazael.
"Because I know the harm[m] you will do to the Israelites," he answered. "You will
set fire to their fortified places, kill their young men with the sword, dash[n] their little
children[o] to the ground, and rip open[p] their pregnant women."
13 Hazael said, "How could your servant, a mere dog,[q] accomplish such a feat?"
"The LORD has shown me that you will become king[r] of Aram," answered Elisha.
14 Then Hazael left Elisha and returned to his master. When Ben-Hadad asked,
"What did Elisha say to you?" Hazael replied, "He told me that you would certainly
recover." 15 But the next day he took a thick cloth, soaked it in water and spread it
over the king's face, so that he died.[s] Then Hazael succeeded him as king.

a *10* The Hebrew may also be read *Go and say, 'You will certainly not recover,' for.*

8:1 [a]2Ki 4:8-37 [b]Lev 26:26; Dt 28:22; Ru 1:1 [c]Ge 12:10; Ps 105:16; Hag 1:11
8:5 [d]2Ki 4:35
8:7 [e]2Sa 8:5; 1Ki 11:24 [f]2Ki 6:24
8:8 [g]1Ki 19:15 [h]Ge 32:20; 1Sa 9:7; 2Ki 1:2 [i]Jdg 18:5
8:10 [j]Isa 38:1
8:11 [k]Jdg 3:25 [l]Lk 19:41
8:12 [m]1Ki 19:17; 2Ki 10:32; 12:17; 13:3, 7 [n]Ps 137:9; Isa 13:16; Hos 13:16; Na 3:10; Lk 19:44 [o]Ge 34:29 [p]2Ki 15:16; Am 1:13
8:13 [q]1Sa 17:43; 2Sa 3:8 [r]1Ki 19:15
8:15 [s]2Ki 1:17

8:1–6 This story must have happened before the events recorded in chapter 5, because the seven-year famine must have ended before Gehazi was struck with leprosy. This shows Elijah's long-term concern for this widow and contrasts his miraculous public ministry with his private ministry to this family. Elisha's life exemplifies the kind of concern we should have for others.

8:12, 13 When Elisha told Hazael he would sin greatly, Hazael protested that he would never do that sort of thing. He did not acknowledge his personal potential for evil. In our enlightened society, it is easy to think we are above gross sin and can control our actions. We think that we would never sink so low. Instead, we should take a more biblical and realistic look at ourselves and admit our sinful potential. Then we will ask for God's strength to resist such evil.

8:12–15 Elisha's words about Hazael's treatment of Israel were partially fulfilled in 10:32, 33. Apparently Hazael had known he would be king because Elijah had anointed him (1 Kings 19:15). But he was impatient and, instead of waiting for God's timing, took matters into his own hands, killing Ben-Hadad. God used Hazael as an instrument of judgment against the disobedient Israelites.

2. Kings of Israel and Judah

Jehoram King of Judah

16 In the fifth year of Joram[t] son of Ahab king of Israel, when Jehoshaphat was
king of Judah, Jehoram[u] son of Jehoshaphat began his reign as king of Judah. 17 He
was thirty-two years old when he became king, and he reigned in Jerusalem for eight
years. 18 He walked in the ways of the kings of Israel, as the house of Ahab had done,
for he married a daughter[v] of Ahab. He did evil in the eyes of the LORD. 19 Nevertheless, for the sake of his servant David, the LORD was not willing to destroy[w] Judah.
He had promised to maintain a lamp[x] for David and his descendants for ever.
20 In the time of Jehoram, Edom rebelled against Judah and set up its own king.[y]
21 So Jehoram[b] went to Zair with all his chariots. The Edomites surrounded him and
his chariot commanders, but he rose up and broke through by night; his army,
however, fled back home. 22 To this day Edom has been in rebellion[z] against Judah.
Libnah[a] revolted at the same time.
23 As for the other events of Jehoram's reign, and all he did, are they not written
in the book of the annals of the kings of Judah? 24 Jehoram rested with his fathers and
was buried with them in the City of David. And Ahaziah his son succeeded him as
king.

Ahaziah King of Judah

25 In the twelfth[b] year of Joram son of Ahab king of Israel, Ahaziah son of Jehoram
king of Judah began to reign. 26 Ahaziah was twenty-two years old when he became
king, and he reigned in Jerusalem for one year. His mother's name was Athaliah,[c]
a granddaughter of Omri[d] king of Israel. 27 He walked in the ways of the house of
Ahab[e] and did evil[f] in the eyes of the LORD, as the house of Ahab had done, for
he was related by marriage to Ahab's family.
28 Ahaziah went with Joram son of Ahab to war against Hazael king of Aram at
Ramoth Gilead.[g] The Arameans wounded Joram; 29 so King Joram returned to Jezreel[h] to recover from the wounds the Arameans had inflicted on him at Ramoth[c] in
his battle with Hazael[i] king of Aram.
Then Ahaziah son of Jehoram king of Judah went down to Jezreel to see Joram son
of Ahab, because he had been wounded.

Jehu Anointed King of Israel

9 The prophet Elisha summoned a man from the company[a] of the prophets and
said to him, "Tuck your cloak into your belt,[b] take this flask of oil[c] with you
and go to Ramoth Gilead.[d] 2 When you get there, look for Jehu son of Jehoshaphat,
the son of Nimshi. Go to him, get him away from his companions and take him into
an inner room. 3 Then take the flask and pour the oil[e] on his head and declare, 'This

b 21 Hebrew *Joram*, a variant of *Jehoram*; also in verses 23 and 24 c 29 Hebrew *Ramah*, a variant of *Ramoth*

8:16 [t]2Ki 1:17; 3:1 [u]2Ch 21:1-4
8:18 [v]ver 26; 2Ki 11:1
8:19 [w]Ge 6:13 [x]2Sa 21:17; 7:13; 1Ki 11:36; Rev 21:23
8:20 [y]1Ki 22:47
8:22 [z]Ge 27:40 [a]Nu 33:20; Jos 21:13; 2Ki 19:8
8:25 [b]2Ki 9:29
8:26 [c]ver 18 [d]1Ki 16:23
8:27 [e]1Ki 16:30 [f]1Ki 15:26
8:28 [g]Dt 4:43; 1Ki 22:3, 29
8:29 [h]2Ki 9:15 [i]1Ki 19:15, 17
9:1 [a]1Sa 10:5 [b]2Ki 4:29 [c]1Sa 10:1 [d]2Ki 8:28
9:3 [e]1Ki 19:16

8:18 King Jehoshaphat arranged the marriage between Jehoram, his son, and Athaliah, the daughter of wicked Ahab and Jezebel. Athaliah followed the idolatrous ways of the northern kingdom, bringing Baal worship into Judah and starting the southern kingdom's decline. When Jehoram died, his son Ahaziah became king. Then, when Ahaziah was killed in battle, Athaliah murdered all her grandsons except Joash and made herself queen (11:1–3). Jehoram's marriage may have been politically advantageous, but spiritually it was deadly.

8:20–22 Although Judah and Edom shared a common border and a common ancestor (Isaac), the two nations fought continually. Edom had been a vassal of the united kingdom of Israel and then the southern kingdom of Judah since the days of David (2 Samuel 8:13, 14). Here Edom rebelled against Jehoram and declared independence. Immediately Jehoram marched out to attack Edom, but his ambush failed. Thus Jehoram lost some of his borderlands as punishment for his failure to honour God.

8:26 Ahaziah was the only remaining son of Jehoram of Judah. Although he was the youngest son, he took the throne because the rest of his brothers had been taken captive in a raid by the Philistines and Arabs (2 Chronicles 21:16, 17).

8:26, 27 Ahaziah's mother was Athaliah, daughter of Ahab and Jezebel, former king and queen of Israel, and granddaughter of Omri, Ahab's father and predecessor. The evil of Ahab and Jezebel spread to Judah through Athaliah.

8:29 Jezreel was the location of the summer palace of the kings of Israel.

9:1 Tucking the cloak into the belt made it easier to run.

9:3 Elijah had prophesied that many people would be killed when Jehu became king (1 Kings 19:16, 17). Thus Elisha advised the young prophet to get out of the area as soon as he delivered his message, before the slaughter began. Jehu's actions seem harsh, as he hunted down relatives and friends of Ahab (2 Chronicles 22:8, 9), but unchecked Baal worship was destroying the nation. If Israel was to survive, the followers of Baal had to be eliminated. Jehu fulfilled the need of the hour – justice.

9:6
[f]1Ki 19:16; 2Ch 22:7

9:7
[g]Ge 4:24; Rev 6:10
[h]Dt 32:43
[i]1Ki 18:4; 21:15

9:8
[j]2Ki 10:17
[k]Dt 32:36; 1Sa 25:22; 1Ki 21:21; 2Ki 14:26

is what the LORD says: I anoint you king over Israel.' Then open the door and run;
don't delay!"
4So the young man, the prophet, went to Ramoth Gilead. 5When he arrived, he
found the army officers sitting together. "I have a message for you, commander," he
said.
"For which of us?" asked Jehu.
"For you, commander," he replied.
6Jehu got up and went into the house. Then the prophet poured the oil[f] on Jehu's
head and declared, "This is what the LORD, the God of Israel, says: 'I anoint you king
over the LORD's people Israel. 7You are to destroy the house of Ahab your master,
and I will avenge[g] the blood of my servants[h] the prophets and the blood of all the
LORD's servants shed by Jezebel.[i] 8The whole house[j] of Ahab will perish. I will
cut off from Ahab every last male[k] in Israel—slave or free. 9I will make the house

JEHU

Jehu had the basic qualities that could have made him a great success. From a human perspective, in fact, he was a successful king. His family ruled the northern kingdom longer than any other. He was used by God as an instrument of punishment to Ahab's evil dynasty, and he fiercely attacked Baal worship. He came close to being God's kind of king, but he recklessly went beyond God's commands and failed to continue with the obedient actions that began his reign. Within sight of victory, he settled for mediocrity.

Jehu was a man of immediate action but without ultimate purpose. His kingdom moved, but its destination was unclear. He eliminated one form of idolatry, Baal worship, only to uphold another by continuing to worship the golden calves Jeroboam had set up. He could have accomplished much for God if he had been obedient to the One who made him king. Even when he was carrying out God's directions, Jehu's style showed he was not fully aware of who was directing him.

As he did with Jehu, God gives each person strengths and abilities that will find their greatest usefulness only under his control. Outside that control, however, they don't accomplish what they could and often become tools for evil. One way to make sure this does not happen is to tell God of your willingness to be under his control. With his presence in your life, your natural strengths and abilities will be used to their greatest potential for the greatest good.

Strengths and accomplishments:
- Took the throne from Ahab's family and destroyed his evil influence
- Founded the longest-lived dynasty of the northern kingdom
- Was anointed by Elijah and confirmed by Elisha
- Destroyed Baal worship

Weaknesses and mistakes:
- Had a reckless outlook on life that made him bold and prone to error
- Worshipped Jeroboam's golden calves
- Was devoted to God only to the point that obedience served his own interests

Lessons from his life:
- Fierce commitment needs control because it can result in recklessness
- Obedience involves both action and direction

Vital statistics:
- Where: The northern kingdom of Israel
- Occupations: Commander in the army of Joram, king of Israel
- Relatives: Grandfather: Nimshi. Father: Jehoshaphat. Son: Jehoahaz
- Contemporaries: Elijah, Elisha, Ahab, Jezebel, Joram, Ahaziah

Key verse:
"Yet Jehu was not careful to keep the law of the LORD, the God of Israel, with all his heart. He did not turn away from the sins of Jeroboam, which he had caused Israel to commit" (2 Kings 10:31).

Jehu's story is told in 1 Kings 19:16—2 Kings 10:36. He is also mentioned in 2 Kings 15:12; 2 Chronicles 22:7–9; Hosea 1:4, 5.

9:7 Elisha's statement fulfilled Elijah's prophecy made 20 years earlier: all of Ahab's family would be killed (1 Kings 21:17–24). Jezebel's death, predicted by Elijah, is described in 9:30–37.

9:9 Ahab's dynasty would end as had those of Jeroboam and Baasha. Ahijah had prophesied the end of Jeroboam's dynasty (1 Kings 14:1–11), and this was fulfilled by Baasha (1 Kings 15:29). The prophet Jehu—not King Jehu—then foretold the end of Baasha's family (1 Kings 16:1–7), and this too was fulfilled (1 Kings 16:11, 12). The end of Ahab's family, therefore, was certain—Elijah had predicted it (1 Kings 21:17–24), and God brought it to pass.

of Ahab like the house of Jeroboam[l] son of Nebat and like the house of Baasha[m]
son of Ahijah. 10As for Jezebel, dogs[n] will devour her on the plot of ground at Jezreel,
and no-one will bury her.' " Then he opened the door and ran.
11When Jehu went out to his fellow officers, one of them asked him, "Is everything
all right? Why did this madman[o] come to you?"
"You know the man and the sort of things he says," Jehu replied.
12"That's not true!" they said. "Tell us."
Jehu said, "Here is what he told me: 'This is what the LORD says: I anoint you king
over Israel.' "
13They hurried and took their cloaks and spread[p] them under him on the bare steps.
Then they blew the trumpet[q] and shouted, "Jehu is king!"

Jehu Kills Joram and Ahaziah

14So Jehu son of Jehoshaphat, the son of Nimshi, conspired against Joram. (Now
Joram and all Israel had been defending Ramoth Gilead[r] against Hazael king of
Aram, 15but King Joram[a] had returned to Jezreel to recover[s] from the wounds the
Arameans had inflicted on him in the battle with Hazael king of Aram.) Jehu said,
"If this is the way you feel, don't let anyone slip out of the city to go and tell the news
in Jezreel." 16Then he got into his chariot and rode to Jezreel, because Joram was
resting there and Ahaziah[t] king of Judah had gone down to see him.
17When the lookout[u] standing on the tower in Jezreel saw Jehu's troops approaching, he called out, "I see some troops coming."
"Get a horseman," Joram ordered. "Send him to meet them and ask, 'Do you come
in peace?[v]' "
18The horseman rode off to meet Jehu and said, "This is what the king says: 'Do
you come in peace?' "
"What do you have to do with peace?" Jehu replied. "Fall in behind me."
The lookout reported, "The messenger has reached them, but he isn't coming back."
19So the king sent out a second horseman. When he came to them he said, "This
is what the king says: 'Do you come in peace?' "
Jehu replied, "What do you have to do with peace? Fall in behind me."
20The lookout reported, "He has reached them, but he isn't coming back either. The
driving is like[w] that of Jehu son of Nimshi—he drives like a madman."
21"Hitch up my chariot," Joram ordered. And when it was hitched up, Joram king
of Israel and Ahaziah king of Judah rode out, each in his own chariot, to meet Jehu.

[a] 15 Hebrew *Jehoram*, a variant of *Joram*; also in verses 17 and 21–24

9:9 [l]1Ki 14:10; 15:29; 16:3, 11 [m]1Ki 16:3
9:10 [n]ver 35-36; 1Ki 21:23
9:11 [o]Jer 29:26; Jn 10:20; Ac 26:24
9:13 [p]Mt 21:8; Lk 19:36 [q]2Sa 15:10; 1Ki 1:34, 39
9:14 [r]Dt 4:43; 2Ki 8:28
9:15 [s]2Ki 8:29
9:16 [t]2Ch 22:7
9:17 [u]Isa 21:6 [v]1Sa 16:4
9:20 [w]2Sa 18:27

9:18, 19 The horsemen met Jehu and asked if he came in peace. But Jehu responded, "What do you have to do with peace?" Peace, properly understood, comes from God. It is not genuine except when rooted in belief in God and love for him. Jehu knew the men represented a disobedient, wicked king. Don't seek peace and friendship with those who are enemies of the good and the true. Lasting peace can come only from knowing God who gives it to us.

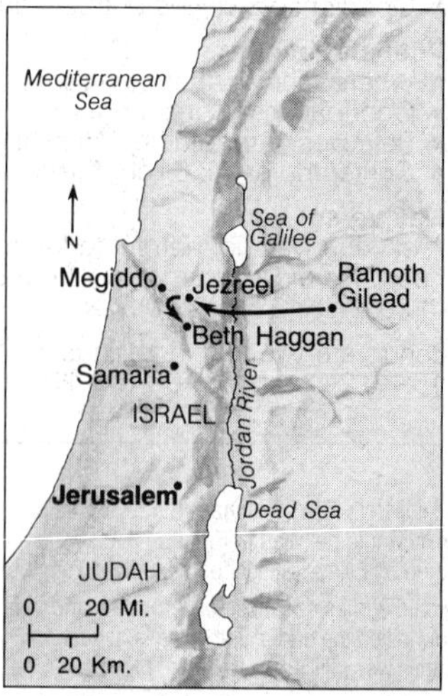

JEHU TAKES OVER ISRAEL
Elisha sent a prophet to Ramoth Gilead to anoint Jehu as Israel's new king. Jehu immediately rode to Jezreel to find and kill King Joram of Israel and King Ahaziah of Judah. Jehu killed Joram; Ahaziah fled towards Beth Haggan where he was wounded. He later died at Megiddo. Back in Jezreel, Jehu had Jezebel killed.

They met him at the plot of ground that had belonged to Naboth[x] the Jezreelite.
22When Joram saw Jehu he asked, "Have you come in peace, Jehu?"
"How can there be peace," Jehu replied, "as long as all the idolatry and witchcraft
of your mother Jezebel[y] abound?"
23Joram turned about and fled, calling out to Ahaziah, "Treachery,[z] Ahaziah!"
24Then Jehu drew his bow[a] and shot Joram between the shoulders. The arrow
pierced his heart and he slumped down in his chariot. 25Jehu said to Bidkar, his chariot
officer, "Pick him up and throw him on the field that belonged to Naboth the Jezreelite.
Remember how you and I were riding together in chariots behind Ahab his father when
the LORD made this prophecy[b] about him: 26'Yesterday I saw the blood of Naboth[c]
and the blood of his sons, declares the LORD, and I will surely make you pay for it
on this plot of ground, declares the LORD.'**b** Now then, pick him up and throw him
on that plot, in accordance with the word of the LORD."[d]
27When Ahaziah king of Judah saw what had happened, he fled up the road to Beth
Haggan.**c** Jehu chased him, shouting, "Kill him too!" They wounded him in his
chariot on the way up to Gur near Ibleam,[e] but he escaped to Megiddo[f] and died
there. 28His servants took him by chariot[g] to Jerusalem and buried him with his
fathers in his tomb in the City of David. 29(In the eleventh[h] year of Joram son of
Ahab, Ahaziah had become king of Judah.)

Jezebel Killed

30Then Jehu went to Jezreel. When Jezebel heard about it, she painted[i] her eyes,
arranged her hair and looked out of a window. 31As Jehu entered the gate, she asked,
"Have you come in peace, Zimri,[j] you murderer of your master?"**d**
32He looked up at the window and called out, "Who is on my side? Who?" Two
or three eunuchs looked down at him. 33"Throw her down!" Jehu said. So they threw
her down, and some of her blood spattered the wall and the horses as they trampled
her underfoot.[k]
34Jehu went in and ate and drank. "Take care of that cursed woman," he said, "and
bury her, for she was a king's daughter."[l] 35But when they went out to bury her,
they found nothing except her skull, her feet and her hands. 36They went back and
told Jehu, who said, "This is the word of the LORD that he spoke through his servant
Elijah the Tishbite: On the plot of ground at Jezreel dogs[m] will devour Jezebel's
flesh.**e**[n] 37Jezebel's body will be like refuse[o] on the ground in the plot at Jezreel,
so that no-one will be able to say, 'This is Jezebel.' "

Ahab's Family Killed

10 Now there were in Samaria[a] seventy sons[b] of the house of Ahab. So Jehu
wrote letters and sent them to Samaria: to the officials of Jezreel,**a**[c] to the
elders and to the guardians[d] of Ahab's children. He said, 2"As soon as this letter
reaches you, since your master's sons are with you and you have chariots and horses,
a fortified city and weapons, 3choose the best and most worthy of your master's sons
and set him on his father's throne. Then fight for your master's house."
4But they were terrified and said, "If two kings could not resist him, how can we?"
5So the palace administrator, the city governor, the elders and the guardians sent

9:21 [x]ver 26; 1Ki 21:1-7, 15-19
9:22 [y]1Ki 16:30-33; 18:19; 2Ch 21:13; Rev 2:20
9:23 [z]2Ki 11:14
9:24 [a]1Ki 22:34
9:25 [b]1Ki 21:19-22, 24-29
9:26 [c]1Ki 21:19 [d]1Ki 21:29
9:27 [e]Jdg 1:27 [f]2Ki 23:29
9:28 [g]2Ki 14:20; 23:30
9:29 [h]2Ki 8:25
9:30 [i]Jer 4:30; Eze 23:40
9:31 [j]1Ki 16:9-10
9:33 [k]Ps 7:5
9:34 [l]1Ki 16:31; 21:25
9:36 [m]Ps 68:23; Jer 15:3 [n]1Ki 21:23
9:37 [o]Ps 83:10; Isa 5:25; Jer 8:2; 9:22; 16:4; 25:33; Zep 1:17
10:1 [a]1Ki 13:32 [b]Jdg 8:30 [c]1Ki 21:1 [d]ver 5

b *26* See 1 Kings 21:19. **c** *27* Or *fled by way of the garden house* **d** *31* Or *"Did Zimri have peace, who murdered his master?"* **e** *36* See 1 Kings 21:23. **a** *1* Hebrew; some Septuagint manuscripts and Vulgate *of the city*

9:26 Joram of Israel was wicked like his father and mother, Ahab and Jezebel; therefore, his body was thrown into the field that his parents had unlawfully taken. Jezebel had arranged the murder of Naboth, the previous owner, because he would not sell his vineyard – which Ahab wanted for a garden (1 Kings 21:1–24). Little did Ahab know that it would become a burial plot for his evil son.

9:31 Why did Jezebel refer to Zimri? Zimri was an army commander who, some 40 years earlier, had killed Elah and then had declared himself king of Israel (1 Kings 16:8–10). Jezebel was accusing Jehu of trying the same treachery.

9:35 Jezebel's skull, feet, and hands were all that remained of her evil life – no power, no money, no prestige, no royal finery, no family, no spiritual heritage. In the end, her life of luxury and treachery amounted to nothing. Power, health, and wealth may make you feel as if you can live for ever. But death strips everyone of all external security. The time to set your life's course is now, while you still have time and before you heart becomes hardened. The end will come soon enough.

this message to Jehu: "We are your servants[e] and we will do anything you say. We
will not appoint anyone as king; you do whatever you think best."
6Then Jehu wrote them a second letter, saying, "If you are on my side and will obey
me, take the heads of your master's sons and come to me in Jezreel by this time
tomorrow."
Now the royal princes, seventy of them, were with the leading men of the city, who
were bringing them up. 7When the letter arrived, these men took the princes and
slaughtered all seventy[f] of them. They put their heads[g] in baskets and sent them to
Jehu in Jezreel. 8When the messenger arrived, he told Jehu, "They have brought the
heads of the princes."
Then Jehu ordered, "Put them in two piles at the entrance of the city gate until
morning."
9The next morning Jehu went out. He stood before all the people and said, "You
are innocent. It was I who conspired against my master and killed him, but who killed
all these? 10Know then, that not a word the LORD has spoken against the house of Ahab
will fail. The LORD has done what he promised[h] through his servant Elijah."[i] 11So
Jehu[j] killed everyone in Jezreel who remained of the house of Ahab, as well as all
his chief men, his close friends and his priests, leaving him no survivor.[k]
12Jehu then set out and went towards Samaria. At Beth Eked of the Shepherds, 13he
met some relatives of Ahaziah king of Judah and asked, "Who are you?"
They said, "We are relatives of Ahaziah,[l] and we have come down to greet the
families of the king and of the queen mother.[m]"
14"Take them alive!" he ordered. So they took them alive and slaughtered them by
the well of Beth Eked—forty-two men. He left no survivor.
15After he left there, he came upon Jehonadab[n] son of Recab,[o] who was on his
way to meet him. Jehu greeted him and said, "Are you in accord with me, as I am
with you?"
"I am," Jehonadab answered.
"If so," said Jehu, "give me your hand."[p] So he did, and Jehu helped him up into
the chariot. 16Jehu said, "Come with me and see my zeal[q] for the LORD." Then he
made him ride in his chariot.
17When Jehu came to Samaria, he killed all who were left there of Ahab's family;[r]
he destroyed them, according to the word of the LORD spoken to Elijah.

Ministers of Baal Killed

18Then Jehu brought all the people together and said to them, "Ahab served[s] Baal
a little; Jehu will serve him much. 19Now summon[t] all the prophets of Baal, all his
ministers and all his priests. See that no-one is missing, because I am going to hold
a great sacrifice for Baal. Anyone who fails to come will no longer live." But Jehu
was acting deceptively in order to destroy the ministers of Baal.
20Jehu said, "Call an assembly[u] in honour of Baal." So they proclaimed it. 21Then
he sent word throughout Israel, and all the ministers of Baal came; not one stayed
away. They crowded into the temple of Baal until it was full from one end to the other.
22And Jehu said to the keeper of the wardrobe, "Bring robes for all the ministers of
Baal." So he brought out robes for them.
23Then Jehu and Jehonadab son of Recab went into the temple of Baal. Jehu said
to the ministers of Baal, "Look around and see that no servants of the LORD are here

10:5 [e]Jos 9:8; 1Ki 20:4, 32
10:7 [f]1Ki 21:21 [g]2Sa 4:8
10:10 [h]2Ki 9:7-10 [i]1Ki 21:29
10:11 [j]Hos 1:4 [k]ver 14; Job 18:19
10:13 [l]2Ki 8:24, 29; 2Ch 22:8 [m]1Ki 2:19
10:15 [n]Jer 35:6, 14-19 [o]1Ch 2:55; Jer 35:2 [p]Ezr 10:19; Eze 17:18
10:16 [q]Nu 25:13; 1Ki 19:10
10:17 [r]2Ki 9:8
10:18 [s]Jdg 2:11; 1Ki 16:31-32
10:19 [t]1Ki 18:19; 22:6
10:20 [u]Ex 32:5; Joel 1:14

10:7 This fulfilled Elijah's prophecy that not one of Ahab's male descendants would survive (1 Kings 21:17–24).

10:11 In his zeal, Jehu went far beyond the Lord's command with this bloodbath. The prophet Hosea later announced punishment upon Jehu's dynasty for this senseless slaughter (Hosea 1:4, 5). Many times in history, "religious" people have mixed faith with personal ambition, power, or cruelty, without God's consent or blessing. To use God or the Bible to condone oppression is wrong. When people attack Christianity because of atrocities that "Christians" carried out, help them to see that these men and women were using faith to their own political ends and not following Christ.

10:15 Jehonadab was a man who, like Jehu, was zealous in following God. Jehonadab, however, demonstrated his zeal by separating himself and his family from the materialistic, idol-worshipping culture. He founded a group called the Recabites (named after his father Recab), who strove to keep their lives pure by living apart from society's pressures and temptations. Jeremiah 35 gives us an example of their dedication to God. Because of their dedication, God promised that they would always have descendants who would worship him.

with you—only ministers of Baal." 24So they went in to make sacrifices and burnt
offerings. Now Jehu had posted eighty men outside with this warning: "If one of you
lets any of the men I am placing in your hands escape, it will be your life for his life."[v]
25As soon as Jehu had finished making the burnt offering, he ordered the guards
and officers: "Go in and kill[w] them; let no-one escape."[x] So they cut them down with
the sword. The guards and officers threw the bodies out and then entered the inner
shrine of the temple of Baal. 26They brought the sacred stone[y] out of the temple of
Baal and burned it. 27They demolished the sacred stone of Baal and tore down the
temple[z] of Baal, and people have used it for a latrine to this day.
28So Jehu[a] destroyed Baal worship in Israel. 29However, he did not turn away from
the sins[b] of Jeroboam son of Nebat, which he had caused Israel to commit—the
worship of the golden calves[c] at Bethel[d] and Dan.
30The LORD said to Jehu, "Because you have done well in accomplishing what is
right in my eyes and have done to the house of Ahab all I had in mind to do, your
descendants will sit on the throne of Israel to the fourth generation."[e] 31Yet Jehu was
not careful[f] to keep the law of the LORD, the God of Israel, with all his heart. He
did not turn away from the sins[g] of Jeroboam, which he had caused Israel to commit.
32In those days the LORD began to reduce[h] the size of Israel. Hazael[i] overpowered
the Israelites throughout their territory 33east of the Jordan in all the land of Gilead
(the region of Gad, Reuben and Manasseh), from Aroer[j] by the Arnon Gorge through
Gilead to Bashan.
34As for the other events of Jehu's reign, all he did, and all his achievements, are
they not written in the book of the annals[k] of the kings of Israel?
35Jehu rested with his fathers and was buried in Samaria. And Jehoahaz his son
succeeded him as king. 36The time that Jehu reigned over Israel in Samaria was
twenty-eight years.

Athaliah and Joash

11 When Athaliah[a] the mother of Ahaziah saw that her son was dead, she
proceeded to destroy the whole royal family. 2But Jehosheba, the daughter of
King Jehoram[a] and sister of Ahaziah, took Joash[b] son of Ahaziah and stole him away
from among the royal princes, who were about to be murdered. She put him and his
nurse in a bedroom to hide him from Athaliah; so he was not killed.[c] 3He remained
hidden with his nurse at the temple of the LORD for six years while Athaliah ruled the
land.
4In the seventh year Jehoiada sent for the commanders of units of a hundred, the

a *2* Hebrew *Joram*, a variant of *Jehoram*

10:24 v 1Ki 20:39
10:25 w Ex 22:20; 2Ki 11:18 x 1Ki 18:40
10:26 y 1Ki 14:23
10:27 z 1Ki 16:32
10:28 a 1Ki 19:17
10:29 b 1Ki 12:30 c 1Ki 12:28-29 d 1Ki 12:32
10:30 e ver 35; 2Ki 15:12
10:31 f Pr 4:23 g 1Ki 12:30
10:32 h 2Ki 13:25 i 1Ki 19:17; 2Ki 8:12
10:33 j Nu 32:34; Dt 2:36; Jdg 11:26; Isa 17:2
10:34 k 1Ki 15:31
11:1 a 2Ki 8:18
11:2 b ver 21; 2Ki 12:1 c Jdg 9:5

10:24 Israel was supposed to be intolerant of any religion that did not worship the true God. The religions of surrounding nations were evil and corrupt. They were designed to destroy life, not uphold it. Israel was God's special nation, chosen to be an example of what was right. But Israel's kings, priests, and elders first tolerated, then incorporated surrounding pagan beliefs, and thus became apathetic to God's way. We are to be completely intolerant of sin and remove it from our lives. We should be tolerant of people who hold differing views, but we should not condone beliefs or practices that lead people away from God's standards of living.

10:28, 29 Why did Jehu destroy the idols of Baal but not the golden calves in Bethel and Dan? Jehu's motives may have been more political than spiritual. (1) If Jehu had destroyed the golden calves, his people would have travelled to the temple in Jerusalem, in the rival southern kingdom, and worshipped there (which is why Jeroboam set them up in the first place; see 1 Kings 12:25–33). (2) Baal worship was associated with the dynasty of Ahab, so it was politically advantageous to destroy Baal. The golden calves, on the other hand, had a longer history in the northern kingdom and were valued by all political factions. (3) Baal worship was anti-God, but the golden calves were thought by many to be visible representations of God himself, even though God's law stated clearly that such worship was idolatrous (Exodus 20:3–6). Like Jehu, it is easy for us to denounce the sins of others while excusing sin in our own lives.

10:30, 31 Jehu did much of what the Lord told him to, but he did not obey him with all his heart. He had become God's *instrument* for carrying out justice, but he had not become God's *servant.* As a result, he gave only lip service to God while permitting the worship of the golden calves. Check the condition of your heart towards God. We can be very active in our work for God and still not give the heartfelt obedience he desires.

11:1 This story is continued from 9:27, where Ahaziah, Athaliah's son, had been killed by Jehu. Athaliah's attempt to kill all of Ahaziah's sons was futile because God had promised that the Messiah would be born through David's descendants (2 Samuel 7).

11:2, 3 Jehosheba was the wife of Jehoiada, the high priest, so the temple was a practical and natural place to hide baby Joash. Athaliah, who loved idolatry, would have had no interest in the temple.

11:4 The Carites were mercenary troops possibly associated with the Philistines. Some scholars believe they settled in southern Palestine from Crete.

Carites[d] and the guards and had them brought to him at the temple of the LORD. He
made a covenant with them and put them under oath at the temple of the LORD. Then
he showed them the king's son. 5He commanded them, saying, "This is what you are
to do: You who are in the three companies that are going on duty on the Sabbath[e]—a
third of you guarding the royal palace,[f] 6a third at the Sur Gate, and a third at the
gate behind the guard, who take turns guarding the temple—7and you who are in the
other two companies that normally go off Sabbath duty are all to guard the temple
for the king. 8Station yourselves round the king, each man with his weapon in his
hand. Anyone who approaches your ranks[b] must be put to death. Stay close to the
king wherever he goes."
9The commanders of units of a hundred did just as Jehoiada the priest ordered. Each
one took his men—those who were going on duty on the Sabbath and those who were
going off duty—and came to Jehoiada the priest. 10Then he gave the commanders the
spears and shields[g] that had belonged to King David and that were in the temple of
the LORD. 11The guards, each with his weapon in his hand, stationed themselves round
the king—near the altar and the temple, from the south side to the north side of the
temple.
12Jehoiada brought out the king's son and put the crown on him; he presented him
with a copy of the covenant[h] and proclaimed him king. They anointed[i] him, and
the people clapped their hands[j] and shouted, "Long live the king!"[k]
13When Athaliah heard the noise made by the guards and the people, she went to
the people at the temple of the LORD. 14She looked and there was the king, standing
by the pillar,[l] as the custom was. The officers and the trumpeters were beside the
king, and all the people of the land were rejoicing and blowing trumpets.[m] Then
Athaliah tore[n] her robes and called out, "Treason! Treason!"[o]
15Jehoiada the priest ordered the commanders of units of a hundred, who were in
charge of the troops: "Bring her out between the ranks[c] and put to the sword anyone
who follows her." For the priest had said, "She must not be put to death in the temple[p]
of the LORD." 16So they seized her as she reached the place where the horses enter[q]
the palace grounds, and there she was put to death.[r]
17Jehoiada then made a covenant[s] between the LORD and the king and people that
they would be the LORD's people. He also made a covenant between the king and the
people.[t] 18All the people of the land went to the temple[u] of Baal and tore it down.
They smashed[v] the altars and idols to pieces and killed Mattan the priest[w] of Baal
in front of the altars.
Then Jehoiada the priest posted guards at the temple of the LORD. 19He took with
him the commanders of hundreds, the Carites,[x] the guards and all the people of the
land, and together they brought the king down from the temple of the LORD and went
into the palace, entering by way of the gate of the guards. The king then took his place
on the royal throne, 20and all the people of the land rejoiced.[y] And the city was quiet,
because Athaliah had been slain with the sword at the palace.
21Joash[d] was seven years old when he began his reign.

Joash Repairs the Temple

12 In the seventh year of Jehu, Joash[a][a] became king, and he reigned in Jerusalem
for forty years. His mother's name was Zibiah; she was from Beersheba. 2Joash
did what was right in the eyes of the LORD all the years Jehoiada the priest instructed

11:4 [d]ver 19
11:5 [e]1Ch 9:25 [f]1Ki 14:27
11:10 [g]2Sa 8:7; 1Ch 18:7
11:12 [h]Ex 25:16; 2Ki 23:3 [i]1Sa 9:16; 1Ki 1:39 [j]Ps 47:1; 98:8; Isa 55:12 [k]1Sa 10:24
11:14 [l]1Ki 7:15; 2Ki 23:3; 2Ch 34:31 [m]1Ki 1:39 [n]Ge 37:29 [o]2Ki 9:23
11:15 [p]1Ki 2:30
11:16 [q]Ne 3:28; Jer 31:40 [r]Ge 4:14
11:17 [s]Ex 24:8; 2Sa 5:3; 2Ch 15:12; 23:3; 29:10; 34:31; Ezr 10:3 [t]2Ki 23:3; Jer 34:8
11:18 [u]1Ki 16:32 [v]Dt 12:3 [w]1Ki 18:40; 2Ki 10:25; 23:20
11:19 [x]ver 4
11:20 [y]Pr 11:10; 28:12; 29:2
12:1 [a]2Ki 11:2

b *8* Or *approaches the precincts* c *15* Or *out from the precincts* d *21* Hebrew *Jehoash*, a variant of *Joash*
a *1* Hebrew *Jehoash*, a variant of *Joash*; also in verses 2, 4, 6, 7 and 18

11:17 This covenant was in fact a recommitment to a very old covenant—the one set up in the book of Deuteronomy for the righteous rule of the nation. It was meant to function as a constitution for the people. This covenant, however, had been virtually ignored for over 100 years. Unfortunately, with Jehoiada's death, the reforms were discontinued.

11:21 If Joash became king at only seven years of age, who really ran the country? Although the answer is not spelled out in the Bible, Judah was probably run during the first seven years of Joash's reign by the king's mother, the high priest Jehoiada, and other advisers.

12:2ff Joash didn't go far enough in removing sin from the nation, but he did much that was good and right. When we aren't sure if we've gone far enough in correcting our actions, we can ask: (1) Does the Bible expressly prohibit this action? (2) Does this action take me away from loving, worshipping, or serving God?

him. 3The high places,[b] however, were not removed; the people continued to offer
sacrifices and burn incense there.
4Joash said to the priests, "Collect[c] all the money that is brought as sacred
offerings[d] to the temple of the LORD—the money collected in the census,[e] the money
received from personal vows and the money brought voluntarily[f] to the temple. 5Let
every priest receive the money from one of the treasurers, and let it be used to repair
whatever damage is found in the temple."
6But by the twenty-third year of King Joash the priests still had not repaired the
temple. 7Therefore King Joash summoned Jehoiada the priest and the other priests and
asked them, "Why aren't you repairing the damage done to the temple? Take no more
money from your treasurers, but hand it over for repairing the temple." 8The priests
agreed that they would not collect any more money from the people and that they
would not repair the temple themselves.
9Jehoiada the priest took a chest and bored a hole in its lid. He placed it beside the
altar, on the right side as one enters the temple of the LORD. The priests who guarded
the entrance[g] put into the chest all the money[h] that was brought to the temple of the
LORD. 10Whenever they saw that there was a large amount of money in the chest, the
royal secretary[i] and the high priest came, counted the money that had been brought
into the temple of the LORD and put it into bags. 11When the amount had been
determined, they gave the money to the men appointed to supervise the work on the
temple. With it they paid those who worked on the temple of the LORD—the carpenters
and builders, 12the masons and stonecutters.[j] They purchased timber and dressed
stone for the repair of the temple of the LORD, and met all the other expenses of
restoring the temple.
13The money brought into the temple was not spent for making silver basins, wick
trimmers, sprinkling bowls, trumpets or any other articles of gold[k] or silver for the
temple of the LORD; 14it was paid to the workmen, who used it to repair the temple.
15They did not require an accounting from those to whom they gave the money to pay
the workers, because they acted with complete honesty.[l] 16The money from the guilt
offerings[m] and sin offerings[n] was not brought into the temple of the LORD; it
belonged[o] to the priests.
17About this time Hazael[p] king of Aram went up and attacked Gath and captured
it. Then he turned to attack Jerusalem. 18But Joash king of Judah took all the sacred
objects dedicated by his fathers—Jehoshaphat, Jehoram and Ahaziah, the kings of
Judah—and the gifts he himself had dedicated and all the gold found in the treasuries
of the temple of the LORD and of the royal palace, and he sent[q] them to Hazael king
of Aram, who then withdrew[r] from Jerusalem.
19As for the other events of the reign of Joash, and all he did, are they not written
in the book of the annals of the kings of Judah? 20His officials[s] conspired against

12:3 [b] 1Ki 3:3; 2Ki 14:4; 15:35; 18:4
12:4 [c] 2Ki 22:4 [d] Ex 35:5 [e] Ex 30:12 [f] Ex 35:29; 1Ch 29:3-9
12:9 [g] Jer 35:4 [h] 2Ch 24:8; Mk 12:41; Lk 21:1
12:10 [i] 2Sa 8:17
12:12 [j] 2Ki 22:5-6
12:13 [k] 1Ki 7:48-51; 2Ch 24:14
12:15 [l] 2Ki 22:7; 1Co 4:2
12:16 [m] Lev 5:14-19; Nu 18:9 [n] Lev 4:1-35 [o] Lev 7:7
12:17 [p] 2Ki 8:12
12:18 [q] 1Ki 15:18; 2Ch 21:16-17 [r] 1Ki 15:21
12:20 [s] 2Ki 14:5

---

(3) Does it make me its slave? (4) Is it bringing out the best in me, consistent with God's purpose? (5) Does it benefit other believers?

12:3 The Israelites were supposed to offer sacrifices to God only in designated areas under supervision of the priests, not just anywhere (Deuteronomy 12:13, 14). Making sacrifices on the hilltops (high places) copied pagan customs and encouraged other pagan practices to enter into their worship. By blending in these beliefs, people were custom-making their religion, and it led them far away from God. (For more information on these high places, see the note on 1 Kings 22:43.)

12:4, 5 The temple needed repair because it had been damaged and neglected by previous evil leaders, especially Athaliah (2 Chronicles 24:7). The temple was to be a holy place, set apart for worship of God. Thanks to Joash's fund-raising programme, it could be restored. The dirt and filth that had collected inside over the years were cleaned out; joints were remortared; pagan idols and other traces of idol worship were removed; and the gold and bronze were polished. The neglected condition of the temple reveals how far the people had strayed from God.

12:15 What a contrast between the workmen who needed no accounting of their use of the money, and the priests who couldn't be trusted to handle their funds well enough to set some aside for the temple (12:8). As trained men of God, the Levites should have been responsible and concerned. After all, the temple was their life's work. Though the priests were not dishonest, they did not have the commitment or energy needed to finish the work. Sometimes God's work is better accomplished by devoted laypeople. Don't let your lack of training or position stop you from contributing to God's kingdom. Everyone's energy is needed to carry out God's work.

12:16 To read more about guilt and sin offerings, see Leviticus 4; 5; 6:24–7:10.

12:20 The reasons for the officials' plot against Joash are listed in 2 Chronicles 24:17–26. Joash had begun to worship idols, had killed the prophet Zechariah, and had been conquered by the Arameans. When Joash turned away from God, his life began to unravel. The officials didn't kill Joash because he turned from God; they killed him because his kingdom was out of control. In the end he became an evil man and was killed by evil people.

him and assassinated[t] him at Beth Millo,[u] on the road down to Silla. 21The officials
who murdered him were Jozabad son of Shimeath and Jehozabad son of Shomer. He
died and was buried with his fathers in the City of David. And Amaziah his son
succeeded him as king.

Jehoahaz King of Israel

13 In the twenty-third year of Joash son of Ahaziah king of Judah, Jehoahaz son
of Jehu became king of Israel in Samaria, and he reigned for seventeen years.
2He did evil[a] in the eyes of the LORD by following the sins of Jeroboam son of Nebat,
which he had caused Israel to commit, and he did not turn away from them. 3So the
LORD's anger[b] burned against Israel, and for a long time he kept them under the
power[c] of Hazael king of Aram and Ben-Hadad[d] his son.

4Then Jehoahaz sought[e] the LORD's favour, and the LORD listened to him, for he
saw[f] how severely the king of Aram was oppressing[g] Israel. 5The LORD provided
a deliverer[h] for Israel, and they escaped from the power of Aram. So the Israelites
lived in their own homes as they had before. 6But they did not turn away from the
sins[i] of the house of Jeroboam, which he had caused Israel to commit; they continued
in them. Also, the Asherah pole**[a]**[j] remained standing in Samaria.

7Nothing had been left[k] of the army of Jehoahaz except fifty horsemen, ten chariots
and ten thousand foot soldiers, for the king of Aram had destroyed the rest and made
them like the dust[l] at threshing time.

8As for the other events of the reign of Jehoahaz, all he did and his achievements,
are they not written in the book of the annals of the kings of Israel? 9Jehoahaz rested
with his fathers and was buried in Samaria. And Jehoash**[b]** his son succeeded him as
king.

Jehoash King of Israel

10In the thirty-seventh year of Joash king of Judah, Jehoash son of Jehoahaz became
king of Israel in Samaria, and he reigned for sixteen years. 11He did evil in the eyes
of the LORD and did not turn away from any of the sins of Jeroboam son of Nebat,
which he had caused Israel to commit; he continued in them.

12As for the other events of the reign of Jehoash, all he did and his achievements,
including his war against Amaziah[m] king of Judah, are they not written in the book
of the annals[n] of the kings of Israel? 13Jehoash rested with his fathers, and Jeroboam[o]
succeeded him on the throne. Jehoash was buried in Samaria with the kings of Israel.

14Now Elisha was suffering from the illness from which he died. Jehoash king of
Israel went down to see him and wept over him. "My father! My father!" he cried.
"The chariots[p] and horsemen of Israel!"

15Elisha said, "Get a bow and some arrows,"[q] and he did so. 16"Take the bow in

[a] *6* That is, a symbol of the goddess Asherah; here and elsewhere in 2 Kings [b] *9* Hebrew *Joash*, a variant of *Jehoash*; also in verses 12–14 and 25

12:20 [t] 2Ch 24:25 [u] Jdg 9:6
13:2 [a] 1Ki 12:26-33
13:3 [b] Dt 31:17; Jdg 2:14 [c] 1Ki 8:12; 12:17; 19:17 [d] ver 24
13:4 [e] Dt 4:29; Ps 78:34 [f] Ex 3:7; Dt 26:7 [g] 2Ki 14:26
13:5 [h] ver 25; 2Ki 14:25, 27
13:6 [i] 1Ki 12:30 [j] 1Ki 16:33
13:7 [k] 2Ki 10:32-33 [l] 2Sa 22:43
13:12 [m] 2Ki 14:15 [n] 1Ki 15:31
13:13 [o] 2Ki 14:23; Hos 1:1
13:14 [p] 2Ki 2:12
13:15 [q] 1Sa 20:20

13:4–6 The Lord heard Jehoahaz's prayer for help. God delayed his judgment on Israel when they turned to him for help, but they did not sustain their dependence on God for long. Although there were periodic breaks in their idol worship, there was rarely evidence of genuine faith. It is not enough to say no to sin; we must also say yes to a life of commitment to God. An occasional call for help is not a substitute for a daily life of trust in God.

13:5 Aram, which lay to the north of Israel, was always Israel's enemy. This was partly because Israel blocked most of Aram's trade from the south, and Aram cut off most of Israel's from the north. If one nation could conquer the other, all its trade routes would be open and its economy would flourish. Israel and Aram were so busy fighting each other that they didn't notice the rapidly growing strength of the Assyrians to the far north. Soon both nations would be surprised (16:9; 17:6).

13:9, 10 Jehoash assumed the throne of Israel in 798 B.C. At that time, the king of Judah, Joash, was nearing the end of his reign. In Hebrew, Jehoash and Joash were two forms of the same name. Thus two kings named with the same name, one in the south and one in the north, reigned at approximately the same time. While Joash of Judah began as a good king, Jehoash of Israel was evil.

13:14 Elisha was highly regarded for his prophetic powers and miracles on Israel's behalf. Jehoash called him, "The chariots and horsemen of Israel"! This recalls the title Elisha gave to Elijah in 2:12. Jehoash feared Elisha's death because he ascribed the nation's well-being to Elisha rather than to God. Jehoash's fear reveals his lack of spiritual understanding. At least 43 years had passed since Elisha was last mentioned in Scripture (9:1), when he anointed Jehu king (841 B.C.). Jehoash's reign began in 798 B.C.

13:15–19 When Jehoash was told to strike the ground with the arrows, he did it only halfheartedly. As a result, Elisha told the king that his victory over Aram would not be complete. Receiving the full benefits of God's plan for our lives requires us to receive and obey God's commands fully. If we don't follow God's complete in-

your hands," he said to the king of Israel. When he had taken it, Elisha put his hands
on the king's hands.
17"Open the east window," he said, and he opened it. "Shoot!"[r] Elisha said, and
he shot. "The LORD's arrow of victory, the arrow of victory over Aram!" Elisha
declared. "You will completely destroy the Arameans at Aphek."[s]
18Then he said, "Take the arrows," and the king took them. Elisha told him, "Strike
the ground." He struck it three times and stopped. 19The man of God was angry with
him and said, "You should have struck the ground five or six times; then you would
have defeated Aram and completely destroyed it. But now you will defeat it only three
times."[t]
20Elisha died and was buried.
Now Moabite raiders[u] used to enter the country every spring. 21Once while some
Israelites were burying a man, suddenly they saw a band of raiders; so they threw the
man's body into Elisha's tomb. When the body touched Elisha's bones, the man came
to life[v] and stood up on his feet.
22Hazael king of Aram oppressed[w] Israel throughout the reign of Jehoahaz. 23But
the LORD was gracious to them and had compassion and showed concern for them
because of his covenant[x] with Abraham, Isaac and Jacob. To this day he has been
unwilling to destroy[y] them or banish them from his presence.[z]
24Hazael king of Aram died, and Ben-Hadad[a] his son succeeded him as king.
25Then Jehoash son of Jehoahaz recaptured from Ben-Hadad son of Hazael the towns
he had taken in battle from his father Jehoahaz. Three times[b] Jehoash defeated him,
and so he recovered[c] the Israelite towns.

Amaziah King of Judah

14 In the second year of Jehoash[a] son of Jehoahaz king of Israel, Amaziah son
of Joash king of Judah began to reign. 2He was twenty-five years old when he
became king, and he reigned in Jerusalem for twenty-nine years. His mother's name
was Jehoaddin; she was from Jerusalem. 3He did what was right in the eyes of the
LORD, but not as his father David had done. In everything he followed the example
of his father Joash. 4The high places,[a] however, were not removed; the people
continued to offer sacrifices and burn incense there.
5After the kingdom was firmly in his grasp, he executed[b] the officials[c] who had
murdered his father the king. 6Yet he did not put the sons of the assassins to death,
in accordance with what is written in the Book of the Law[d] of Moses where the LORD
commanded: "Fathers shall not be put to death for their children, nor children put to
death for their fathers; each is to die for his own sins."[b][e]

a *1* Hebrew *Joash*, a variant of *Jehoash*; also in verses 13, 23 and 27 b *6* Deut. 24:16

13:17 r Jos 8:18; s 1Ki 20:26
13:19 t ver 25
13:20 u 2Ki 3:7; 24:2
13:21 v Mt 27:52
13:22 w 1Ki 19:17; 2Ki 8:12
13:23 x Ge 13:16-17; Ex 2:24; y Dt 29:20; z Ex 33:15; 2Ki 14:27; 17:18; 24:3, 20
13:24 a ver 3
13:25 b ver 18, 19; c 2Ki 10:32
14:4 a 2Ki 12:3; 16:4
14:5 b 2Ki 21:24; c 2Ki 12:20
14:6 d Dt 28:61; e Nu 26:11; Job 21:20; Jer 31:30; 44:3; Eze 18:4, 20

GOD OR IDOLS
Why did people continually turn to idols instead of to God?

Idols were:	*God is:*
Tangible	Intangible—no physical form
Morally similar—had human characteristics	Morally dissimilar—has divine characteristics
Comprehensible	Incomprehensible
Able to be manipulated	Not able to be manipulated
Worshipping idols involved:	*Worshipping God involved:*
Materialism	Sacrifice
Sexual immorality	Purity and commitment
Doing whatever a person wanted	Doing what God wants
Focusing on self	Focusing on others

---

structions, we should not be surprised that his full benefits and blessings are not present.

13:20, 21 Elisha was dead, but his good influence remained, even causing miracles. This demonstrated that Elisha was indeed a prophet of God. It also attested to God's power—no pagan idol ever raised anyone from the dead. This miracle served as one more reminder to Israel that it had rejected God's word as given through Elisha.

7He was the one who defeated ten thousand Edomites in the Valley of Salt[f] and
captured Sela[g] in battle, calling it Joktheel, the name it has to this day.
8Then Amaziah sent messengers to Jehoash son of Jehoahaz, the son of Jehu, king
of Israel, with the challenge: "Come, meet me face to face."
9But Jehoash king of Israel replied to Amaziah king of Judah: "A thistle[h] in
Lebanon sent a message to a cedar in Lebanon, 'Give your daughter to my son in
marriage.' Then a wild beast in Lebanon came along and trampled the thistle underfoot. 10You have indeed defeated Edom and now you are arrogant.[i] Glory in your
victory, but stay at home! Why ask for trouble and cause your own downfall and that
of Judah also?"
11Amaziah, however, would not listen, so Jehoash king of Israel attacked. He and
Amaziah king of Judah faced each other at Beth Shemesh[j] in Judah. 12Judah was
routed by Israel, and every man fled to his home.[k] 13Jehoash king of Israel captured
Amaziah king of Judah, the son of Joash, the son of Ahaziah, at Beth Shemesh. Then
Jehoash went to Jerusalem and broke down the wall[l] of Jerusalem from the Ephraim
Gate[m] to the Corner Gate[n]—a section about six hundred feet long.[c] 14He took all
the gold and silver and all the articles found in the temple of the LORD and in the
treasuries of the royal palace. He also took hostages and returned to Samaria.
15As for the other events of the reign of Jehoash, what he did and his achievements,
including his war[o] against Amaziah king of Judah, are they not written in the book
of the annals of the kings of Israel? 16Jehoash rested with his fathers and was buried
in Samaria with the kings of Israel. And Jeroboam his son succeeded him as king.
17Amaziah son of Joash king of Judah lived for fifteen years after the death of
Jehoash son of Jehoahaz king of Israel. 18As for the other events of Amaziah's reign,
are they not written in the book of the annals of the kings of Judah?
19They conspired[p] against him in Jerusalem, and he fled to Lachish,[q] but they
sent men after him to Lachish and killed him there. 20He was brought back by horse[r]
and was buried in Jerusalem with his fathers, in the City of David.
21Then all the people of Judah took Azariah,[d][s] who was sixteen years old, and
made him king in place of his father Amaziah. 22He was the one who rebuilt Elath[t]
and restored it to Judah after Amaziah rested with his fathers.

Jeroboam II King of Israel

23In the fifteenth year of Amaziah son of Joash king of Judah, Jeroboam[u] son of
Jehoash king of Israel became king in Samaria, and he reigned for forty-one years.
24He did evil in the eyes of the LORD and did not turn away from any of the sins of
Jeroboam son of Nebat, which he had caused Israel to commit.[v] 25He was the one
who restored the boundaries of Israel from Lebo[e] Hamath[w] to the Sea of the
Arabah,[f][x] in accordance with the word of the LORD, the God of Israel, spoken
through his servant Jonah[y] son of Amittai, the prophet from Gath Hepher.
26The LORD had seen how bitterly everyone in Israel, whether slave or free,[z] was
suffering;[a] there was no-one to help them.[b] 27And since the LORD had not said he
would blot out[c] the name of Israel from under heaven, he saved[d] them by the hand
of Jeroboam son of Jehoash.

c *13* Hebrew *four hundred cubits* (about 180 metres) **d** *21* Also called *Uzziah* **e** *25* Or *from the entrance to*
f *25* That is, the Dead Sea

14:7 [f]2Sa 8:13; 2Ch 25:11 [g]Jdg 1:36
14:9 [h]Jdg 9:8-15
14:10 [i]Dt 8:14; 2Ch 26:16; 32:25
14:11 [j]Jos 15:10
14:12 [k]2Sa 18:17
14:13 [l]1Ki 3:1; 2Ch 33:14; 36:19; Jer 39:2 [m]Ne 8:16; 12:39 [n]2Ch 25:23; Jer 31:38; Zec 14:10
14:15 [o]2Ki 13:12
14:19 [p]2Ki 12:20 [q]Jos 10:3; 2Ki 18:14, 17
14:20 [r]2Ki 9:28
14:21 [s]2Ki 15:1; 2Ch 26:23
14:22 [t]1Ki 9:26; 2Ki 16:6
14:23 [u]2Ki 13:13
14:24 [v]1Ki 15:30
14:25 [w]Nu 13:21; 1Ki 8:65 [x]Dt 3:17 [y]Jnh 1:1; Mt 12:39
14:26 [z]Dt 32:36 [a]2Ki 13:4 [b]Ps 18:41; 22:11; 72:12; 107:12; Isa 63:5; La 1:7
14:27 [c]2Ki 13:23 [d]Jdg 6:14

14:7 Sela was the ancient stronghold of Petra, a city carved into a rock cliff. It was not only a stronghold for Edom, but also a wealthy outpost for trade with India.

14:9, 10 In this parable, Judah is compared to a small thistle. King Amaziah of Judah had become proud after defeating the Edomites. Here he was trying to pick a fight with Israel because he was sure his army was stronger. Jehoash tried to warn Amaziah not to attack by comparing his army to a thistle and Israel's army to a cedar tree. Amaziah had overrated his strength; his ambition was greater than his ability. He didn't listen to Jehoash and was soundly defeated.

14:13 A broken-down city wall disgraced the citizens and left them defenceless against future invasions.

14:25 During this period of history, many prophets—such as Hosea, Amos, Jonah, Micah, and Isaiah—began collecting their prophecies and writing them under God's direction. They continued to preach about the worldwide significance of God's work as they looked forward to the future spiritual kingdom. God would use Israel's moral and spiritual decline to prepare the way for the Messiah's coming. Because the kingdom and military power of Israel was stripped away, many people would be ready to turn to the Good News that Jesus would bring.

14:25 For more information about the prophet Jonah, see the book of Jonah.

14:28
[e]2Sa 8:5;
1Ki 11:24
[f]2Ch 8:3
[g]1Ki 15:31

28 As for the other events of Jeroboam's reign, all he did, and his military achievements, including how he recovered for Israel both Damascus[e] and Hamath,[f] which
had belonged to Yaudi,[g] are they not written in the book of the annals[g] of the kings
of Israel? 29 Jeroboam rested with his fathers, the kings of Israel. And Zechariah his
son succeeded him as king.

Azariah King of Judah

15 In the twenty-seventh year of Jeroboam king of Israel, Azariah[a] son of Amaziah king of Judah began to reign. 2 He was sixteen years old when he became
king, and he reigned in Jerusalem for fifty-two years. His mother's name was Jecoliah;
she was from Jerusalem. 3 He did what was right in the eyes of the LORD, just as his

15:1
[a]ver 32;
2Ki 14:21

[g] *28* Or *Judah*

KINGS TO DATE AND THEIR ENEMIES

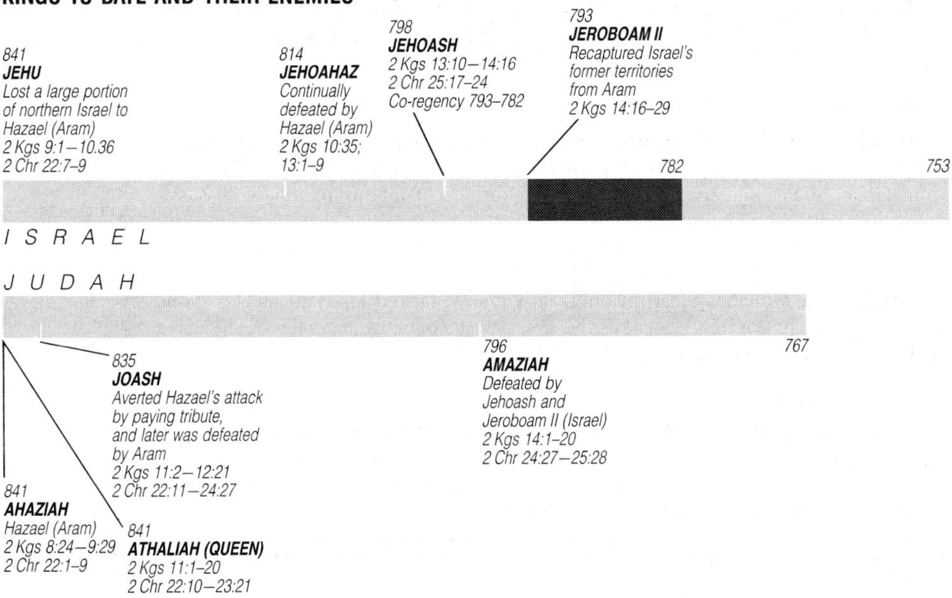

All dates are B.C.
Solid section of the timeline indicates co-regency.
For all the kings of Israel and Judah, see the chart at the end of 1 Kings.

14:28 Jeroboam II had no devotion to God, yet under his warlike policies and skilful administration Israel enjoyed more national power and material prosperity than at any time since the days of Solomon. The prophets Amos and Hosea, however, tell us what was really happening within the kingdom (Hosea 13:4–8; Amos 6:11–14). Jeroboam's administration ignored policies of justice and fairness. As a result, the rich became richer, and the poor, poorer. The people became self-centred, relying more on their power, security, and possessions than on God. The poor were so oppressed that it was hard for them to believe God noticed their plight. Material prosperity is not always an indication of God's blessing. It can also be a result of self-centredness. If you are experiencing prosperity, remember that God holds us accountable for how we attain success and how we use our wealth. Everything we have really belongs to him. We must use God's gifts with his interests in mind.

15:1 Azariah was also known as Uzziah. His story is given in greater detail in 2 Chronicles 26. He is also mentioned in Isaiah 1:1 and 6:1. Before the beginning of Azariah's reign, Israel broke down 200 yards of Jerusalem's walls after defeating Judah and carrying off their king, Amaziah (14:13; 2 Chronicles 25:23, 24). But during Azariah's 52-year reign, Judah rebuilt the wall, refortified the city with anti-siege weapons, and gained independence from Israel. Azariah's devotion to God helped Judah enjoy peace and prosperity such as it had not experienced since the days of Solomon. During this time, however, Israel declined drastically and would soon be overthrown.

father Amaziah had done. 4The high places, however, were not removed; the people
continued to offer sacrifices and burn incense there.
5The LORD afflicted[b] the king with leprosy[a] until the day he died, and he lived
in a separate house.[b][c] Jotham[d] the king's son had charge of the palace[e] and
governed the people of the land.
6As for the other events of Azariah's reign, and all he did, are they not written in
the book of the annals of the kings of Judah? 7Azariah rested[f] with his fathers and
was buried near them in the City of David. And Jotham[g] his son succeeded him as
king.

Zechariah King of Israel

8In the thirty-eighth year of Azariah king of Judah, Zechariah son of Jeroboam
became king of Israel in Samaria, and he reigned for six months. 9He did evil[h] in
the eyes of the LORD, as his fathers had done. He did not turn away from the sins of
Jeroboam son of Nebat, which he had caused Israel to commit.
10Shallum son of Jabesh conspired against Zechariah. He attacked him in front of
the people,[c] assassinated[i] him and succeeded him as king. 11The other events of
Zechariah's reign are written in the book of the annals[j] of the kings of Israel. 12So
the word of the LORD spoken to Jehu was fulfilled:[k] "Your descendants will sit on
the throne of Israel to the fourth generation."[d]

Shallum King of Israel

13Shallum son of Jabesh became king in the thirty-ninth year of Uzziah king of
Judah, and he reigned in Samaria[l] for one month. 14Then Menahem son of Gadi went
from Tirzah[m] up to Samaria. He attacked Shallum son of Jabesh in Samaria, assassinated[n] him and succeeded him as king.
15The other events of Shallum's reign, and the conspiracy he led, are written in the
book of the annals[o] of the kings of Israel.
16At that time Menahem, starting out from Tirzah, attacked Tiphsah[p] and everyone
in the city and its vicinity, because they refused to open[q] their gates. He sacked
Tiphsah and ripped open all the pregnant women.

Menahem King of Israel

17In the thirty-ninth year of Azariah king of Judah, Menahem son of Gadi became
king of Israel, and he reigned in Samaria for ten years. 18He did evil in the eyes of
the LORD. During his entire reign he did not turn away from the sins of Jeroboam son
of Nebat, which he had caused Israel to commit.

a *5* The Hebrew word was used for various diseases affecting the skin—not necessarily leprosy. **b** *5* Or *in a house where he was relieved of responsibility* **c** *10* Hebrew; some Septuagint manuscripts *in Ibleam*
d *12* 2 Kings 10:30

15:5 [b]Ge 12:17 [c]Lev 13:46 [d]2Ch 27:1 [e]Ge 41:40
15:7 [f]Isa 6:1; 14:28 [g]ver 5
15:9 [h]1Ki 15:26
15:10 [i]2Ki 12:20
15:11 [j]1Ki 15:31
15:12 [k]2Ki 10:30
15:13 [l]ver 1, 8
15:14 [m]1Ki 14:17 [n]2Ki 12:20
15:15 [o]1Ki 15:31
15:16 [p]1Ki 4:24 [q]2Ki 8:12; Hos 13:16

15:4 Although Azariah accomplished a great deal, he failed to destroy the high places, the location of pagan shrines in Judah, just as his father Amaziah and grandfather Joash had failed to do. Azariah imitated the kings he had heard stories about and had watched while growing up. Although Azariah's father and grandfather were basically good kings, they were poor models in some important areas. To rise above the influence of poor models, we must seek better ones. Christ provides a perfect model. No matter how you were raised or who has influenced your life, you can move beyond those limitations by taking Christ as your example and consciously trying to live as he did.

15:5 For 10 years Jotham was the co-ruler with his father, Azariah. A father and son would rule together for any of the following reasons: (1) the father was very old and needed help; (2) the father wanted to train his son in leading the nation; (3) the father was sick or exiled. There were many co-regents during the period of the kings—Asa/Jehoshaphat; Jehoshaphat/Jehoram; Azariah/Jotham; Jehoash/Jeroboam II; Hezekiah/Manasseh.

15:8 Zechariah was an evil king because he encouraged Israel to sin by worshipping idols. Sin in our lives is serious. But it is even more serious to encourage others to disobey God. We are responsible for the way we influence others. Beware of double sins: ones that not only hurt us, but also hurt others by encouraging them to sin.

15:10 Zechariah was warned by the prophet Amos of his impending death and the subsequent end of Jeroboam's dynasty (Amos 7:9).

15:14 Ancient historical documents say that Menahem was the commander in chief of Jeroboam's army (see 14:23–29 for an account of Jeroboam II's reign). After Jeroboam's son was assassinated (15:8–10), Menahem probably saw himself, and not Shallum, as the rightful successor to Israel's throne.

15:18 Menahem, like the kings before him, led his people into sin—"He did evil in the eyes of the LORD." What a horrible epitaph for a leader! Leaders profoundly affect the people they serve. They can either encourage or discourage devotion to God both by their example and by the structure they give their organisation. Good leaders put up no obstacles to faith in God or to right living.

19 Then Pul[e][r] king of Assyria invaded the land, and Menahem gave him a thousand
talents[f] of silver to gain his support and strengthen his own hold on the kingdom.
20 Menahem exacted this money from Israel. Every wealthy man had to contribute fifty
shekels[g] of silver to be given to the king of Assyria. So the king of Assyria withdrew[s]
and stayed in the land no longer.
21 As for the other events of Menahem's reign, and all he did, are they not written
in the book of the annals of the kings of Israel? 22 Menahem rested with his fathers.
And Pekahiah his son succeeded him as king.

Pekahiah King of Israel

23 In the fiftieth year of Azariah king of Judah, Pekahiah son of Menahem became
king of Israel in Samaria, and he reigned for two years. 24 Pekahiah did evil in the
eyes of the LORD. He did not turn away from the sins of Jeroboam son of Nebat, which
he had caused Israel to commit. 25 One of his chief officers, Pekah[t] son of Remaliah,
conspired against him. Taking fifty men of Gilead with him, he assassinated[u] Pekahiah, along with Argob and Arieh, in the citadel of the royal palace at Samaria. So
Pekah killed Pekahiah and succeeded him as king.
26 The other events of Pekahiah's reign, and all he did, are written in the book of
the annals of the kings of Israel.

Pekah King of Israel

27 In the fifty-second year of Azariah king of Judah, Pekah[v] son of Remaliah[w]
became king of Israel in Samaria, and he reigned for twenty years. 28 He did evil in
the eyes of the LORD. He did not turn away from the sins of Jeroboam son of Nebat,
which he had caused Israel to commit.
29 In the time of Pekah king of Israel, Tiglath-Pileser[x] king of Assyria came and
took Ijon,[y] Abel Beth Maacah, Janoah, Kedesh and Hazor. He took Gilead and
Galilee, including all the land of Naphtali,[z] and deported[a] the people to Assyria.
30 Then Hoshea[b] son of Elah conspired against Pekah son of Remaliah. He attacked
and assassinated[c] him, and then succeeded him as king in the twentieth year of Jotham
son of Uzziah.
31 As for the other events of Pekah's reign, and all he did, are they not written in
the book of the annals of the kings of Israel?

Jotham King of Judah

32 In the second year of Pekah son of Remaliah king of Israel, Jotham[d] son of
Uzziah king of Judah began to reign. 33 He was twenty-five years old when he became
king, and he reigned in Jerusalem for sixteen years. His mother's name was Jerusha
daughter of Zadok. 34 He did what was right[e] in the eyes of the LORD, just as his father
Uzziah had done. 35 The high places,[f] however, were not removed; the people
continued to offer sacrifices and burn incense there. Jotham rebuilt the Upper Gate[g]
of the temple of the LORD.
36 As for the other events of Jotham's reign, and what he did, are they not written
in the book of the annals of the kings of Judah? 37 (In those days the LORD began to
send Rezin[h] king of Aram and Pekah son of Remaliah against Judah.) 38 Jotham rested

15:19 [r] 1Ch 5:6, 26
15:20 [s] 2Ki 12:18
15:25 [t] 2Ch 28:6; Isa 7:1 [u] 2Ki 12:20
15:27 [v] 2Ch 28:6; Isa 7:1 [w] Isa 7:4
15:29 [x] 2Ki 16:7; 17:6; 1Ch 5:26; 2Ch 28:20; Jer 50:17 [y] 1Ki 15:20 [z] 2Ki 16:9; 17:24; 2Ch 16:4; Isa 9:1 [a] 2Ki 24:14-16; 1Ch 5:22; Isa 14:6, 17; 36:17; 45:13
15:30 [b] 2Ki 17:1 [c] 2Ki 12:20
15:32 [d] 1Ch 5:17
15:34 [e] ver 3; 1Ki 14:8; 2Ch 26:4-5
15:35 [f] 2Ki 12:3 [g] 2Ch 23:20
15:37 [h] 2Ki 16:5; Isa 7:1

e *19* Also called *Tiglath-Pileser* f *19* That is, about 34 tons (about 34 metric tons) g *20* That is, about 1¼ pounds (about 0.6 kilogram)

15:19, 20 When King Pul of Assyria (also called Tiglath-Pileser in 15:29) took the throne, the Assyrian empire was becoming a world power, and the nations of Aram, Israel, and Judah were in decline. This is the first mention of Assyria in 2 Kings. Pul's invasion occurred in 743 B.C. Assyria made Israel a vassal, and Menahem was forced to pay tribute to Assyria. This was the first of three Assyrian invasions (15:29 and 17:6 tell of the other ones).

15:30 Hoshea was Israel's last king.

15:32 A year after Pekah became king, Uzziah (also called Azariah) of Judah died, and Isaiah the prophet had a vision of God's holiness and Israel's future destruction. See Isaiah 6 for more details on what Isaiah saw.

15:34, 35 Much good can be said of Jotham and his reign as king of Judah, but he failed in a most important area: he didn't destroy the high places, although leaving them clearly violated the first commandment (Exodus 20:3). Like Jotham, we may live basically good lives and yet miss doing what is most important. A lifetime of doing good is not enough if we make the crucial mistake of not following God with all our hearts. A true follower of God puts God first in all areas of life.

with his fathers and was buried with them in the City of David, the city of his father.
And Ahaz his son succeeded him as king.

Ahaz King of Judah

16 In the seventeenth year of Pekah son of Remaliah, Ahaz[a] son of Jotham king
of Judah began to reign. 2Ahaz was twenty years old when he became king,
and he reigned in Jerusalem for sixteen years. Unlike David his father, he did not do
what was right[b] in the eyes of the LORD his God. 3He walked in the ways of the kings
of Israel and even sacrificed his son[c] in[a] the fire, following the detestable[d] ways
of the nations the LORD had driven out before the Israelites. 4He offered sacrifices and
burned incense at the high places, on the hilltops and under every spreading tree.[e]
5Then Rezin[f] king of Aram and Pekah son of Remaliah king of Israel marched
up to fight against Jerusalem and besieged Ahaz, but they could not overpower him.
6At that time, Rezin[g] king of Aram recovered Elath[h] for Aram by driving out the
men of Judah. Edomites then moved into Elath and have lived there to this day.
7Ahaz sent messengers to say to Tiglath-Pileser[i] king of Assyria, "I am your
servant and vassal. Come up and save[j] me out of the hand of the king of Aram and
of the king of Israel who are attacking me." 8And Ahaz took the silver and gold found
in the temple of the LORD and in the treasuries of the royal palace and sent it as a gift[k]
to the king of Assyria. 9The king of Assyria complied by attacking Damascus[l] and
capturing it. He deported its inhabitants to Kir[m] and put Rezin to death.
10Then King Ahaz went to Damascus to meet Tiglath-Pileser king of Assyria. He
saw an altar in Damascus and sent to Uriah[n] the priest a sketch of the altar, with
detailed plans for its construction. 11So Uriah the priest built an altar in accordance
with all the plans that King Ahaz had sent from Damascus and finished it before King
Ahaz returned. 12When the king came back from Damascus and saw the altar, he
approached it and presented offerings[b][o] on it. 13He offered up his burnt offering[p]
and grain offering, poured out his drink offering, and sprinkled the blood of his
fellowship offerings[c][q] on the altar. 14The bronze altar[r] that stood before the LORD
he brought from the front of the temple—from between the new altar and the temple
of the LORD—and put it on the north side of the new altar.
15King Ahaz then gave these orders to Uriah the priest: "On the large new altar,
offer the morning[s] burnt offering and the evening grain offering, the king's burnt
offering and his grain offering, and the burnt offering of all the people of the land,
and their grain offering and their drink offering. Sprinkle on the altar all the blood
of the burnt offerings and sacrifices. But I will use the bronze altar for seeking
guidance."[t] 16And Uriah the priest did just as King Ahaz had ordered.
17King Ahaz took away the side panels and removed the basins from the movable
stands. He removed the Sea from the bronze bulls that supported it and set it on a stone

a *3* Or *even made his son pass through* **b** *12* Or *and went up* **c** *13* Traditionally *peace offerings*

16:1 [a]Isa 1:1; 14:28
16:2 [b]1Ki 14:8
16:3 [c]Lev 18:21; 2Ki 21:6 [d]Lev 18:3; Dt 9:4; 12:31
16:4 [e]Dt 12:2; Eze 6:13
16:5 [f]2Ki 15:37; Isa 7:1, 4
16:6 [g]Isa 9:12 [h]2Ki 14:22; 2Ch 26:2
16:7 [i]2Ki 15:29 [j]Isa 2:6; Jer 2:18; Eze 16:28; Hos 10:6
16:8 [k]2Ki 12:18
16:9 [l]2Ki 15:29 [m]Isa 22:6; Am 1:5; 9:7
16:10 [n]Isa 8:2
16:12 [o]2Ch 26:16
16:13 [p]Lev 6:8-13 [q]Lev 7:11-21
16:14 [r]2Ch 4:1
16:15 [s]Ex 29:38-41 [t]1Sa 9:9

16:3 Ahaz was so depraved that he sacrificed his own son to the pagan gods. This was a practice of the Canaanites whom the Israelites were supposed to drive out of the land.

16:5 Israel and Aram were both under Assyria's control. They joined forces against Judah, hoping to force the southern kingdom to join their revolt against Assyria and strengthen their western alliance. But the plan backfired when King Ahaz of Judah unexpectedly asked Assyria to come to his aid (16:8, 9).

16:10 Ahaz went to Damascus to express gratitude and loyalty to Tiglath-Pileser. Because the Assyrians had captured Damascus, the capital of Aram (732 B.C.), Ahaz was afraid of a southern sweep. But he was relying more on money than on God to keep the powerful king out of his land, and his plan failed. Although Tiglath-Pileser did not conquer Judah, he caused much trouble, and Ahaz regretted asking for his help (2 Chronicles 28:20, 21).

16:10–16 Evil King Ahaz copied pagan religious customs, changed the temple services, and used the temple altar for his personal benefit. In so doing, he demonstrated a callous disregard for God's commands. We condemn Ahaz for his action, but we act the same way if we try to mould God's message to fit our personal preferences. We must worship God for who he is, not what we would selfishly like him to be.

16:14–18 Ahaz replaced the altar of burnt offering with a replica of the pagan altar he had seen in Damascus. (The original bronze altar was not thrown out, but was kept for use in divination. The basins were where the sacrifices were washed. The Sea was a huge reservoir of water for temple use.) This was extremely serious because God had given specific directions on how the altar should look and be used (Exodus 27:1–8). Building this new altar was like installing an idol. But because Judah was Assyria's vassal, Ahaz was eager to please the Assyrian king. Sadly, Ahaz allowed the king of Assyria to replace God as Judah's leader. No-one, no matter how attractive or powerful, should replace God's leadership in our lives.

16:17
[u]1Ki 7:27

base.[u] 18He took away the Sabbath canopy[d] that had been built at the temple and
removed the royal entrance outside the temple of the LORD, in deference to the king
of Assyria.[v]
19As for the other events of the reign of Ahaz, and what he did, are they not written
in the book of the annals of the kings of Judah? 20Ahaz rested with his fathers and
was buried with them in the City of David. And Hezekiah his son succeeded him as
king.

16:18
[v]Eze 16:28

3. Israel is exiled to Assyria

Hoshea Last King of Israel

17 In the twelfth year of Ahaz king of Judah, Hoshea[a] son of Elah became king
of Israel in Samaria, and he reigned for nine years. 2He did evil in the eyes
of the LORD, but not like the kings of Israel who preceded him.

17:1
[a]2Ki 15:30

d 18 Or *the dais of his throne* (see Septuagint)

KINGS TO DATE AND THEIR ENEMIES

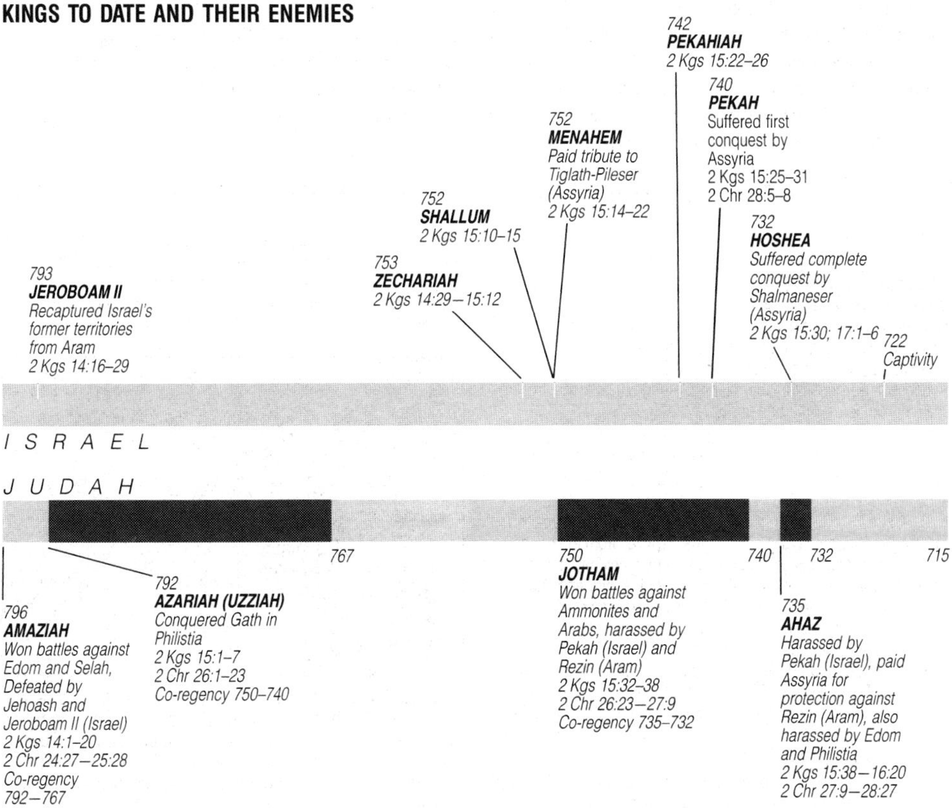

All dates are B.C.
Solid section of the timeline indicates co-regency.
For all the kings of Israel and Judah, see the chart at the end of 1 Kings.

16:18 Ahaz had become a weak king with a weak and compromising high priest. Judah's religious system was in shambles. It was now built on pagan customs, and its chief aim was only to please those in power. If we are quick to copy others in order to please them, we risk making them more important than God in our lives.

3 Shalmaneser[b] king of Assyria came up to attack Hoshea, who had been Shalmaneser's vassal and had paid him tribute. 4 But the king of Assyria discovered that Hoshea
was a traitor, for he had sent envoys to So[a] king of Egypt, and he no longer paid
tribute to the king of Assyria, as he had done year by year. Therefore Shalmaneser
seized him and put him in prison. 5 The king of Assyria invaded the entire land,
marched against Samaria and laid siege[c] to it for three years. 6 In the ninth year of
Hoshea, the king of Assyria captured Samaria[d] and deported[e] the Israelites to
Assyria. He settled them in Halah, in Gozan[f] on the Habor River and in the towns
of the Medes.

Israel Exiled Because of Sin

7 All this took place because the Israelites had sinned[g] against the LORD their God,
who had brought them up out of Egypt[h] from under the power of Pharaoh king of
Egypt. They worshipped other gods 8 and followed the practices of the nations[i] the
LORD had driven out before them, as well as the practices that the kings of Israel had
introduced. 9 The Israelites secretly did things against the LORD their God that were
not right. From watchtower to fortified city[j] they built themselves high places in all
their towns. 10 They set up sacred stones and Asherah poles[k] on every high hill and
under every spreading tree.[l] 11 At every high place they burned incense, as the nations
whom the LORD had driven out before them had done. They did wicked things that
provoked the LORD to anger. 12 They worshipped idols,[m] though the LORD had said,
"You shall not do this."[b] 13 The LORD warned Israel and Judah through all his prophets
and seers:[n] "Turn from your evil ways.[o] Observe my commands and decrees, in

a *4* Or *to Sais, to the*; *So* is possibly an abbreviation for *Osorkon*. **b** *12* Exodus 20:4, 5

17:3 [b] 2Ki 18:9-12; Hos 10:14
17:5 [c] Hos 13:16
17:6 [d] Hos 13:16 [e] Dt 28:36, 64; 2Ki 18:10-11 [f] 1Ch 5:26
17:7 [g] Jos 23:16; Jdg 6:10 [h] Ex 14:15-31
17:8 [i] Lev 18:3; Dt 18:9; 2Ki 16:3
17:9 [j] 2Ki 18:8
17:10 [k] Ex 34:13; Mic 5:14 [l] 1Ki 14:23
17:12 [m] Ex 20:4
17:13 [n] 1Sa 9:9 [o] Jer 18:11; 25:5; 35:15

17:3 This was probably Shalmaneser V, who became king of Assyria after Tiglath-Pileser (727–722 B.C.). He continued to demand heavy tribute from Israel. Israel's King Hoshea decided to rebel against Assyria and join forces with King So of Egypt (17:4). This was not only foolish, but also against God's commands. To destroy this conspiracy, Shalmaneser attacked and besieged Samaria for three years. But just before Samaria fell, Shalmaneser died. His successor, Sargon II, took credit for capturing the city, destroying the nation of Israel, and carrying away its people.

17:5, 6 This was the third and final invasion of Assyria into Israel. (The first two invasions are recorded in 15:19 and 15:29.) The first wave was merely a warning to Israel—to avoid further attack, pay money and not rebel. The people should have learned their lesson and returned to God. When they didn't, God allowed Assyria to invade again, this time carrying off some captives from the northern border. But the people still did not realise that they had caused their own troubles. Thus Assyria invaded for the third and final time, destroying Israel completely, carrying away most of the people, and resettling the land with foreigners.

God was doing what he had said he would do (Deuteronomy 28). He had given Israel ample warning; they knew what would come, but they still ignored God. Israel was now no better than the pagan nations it had destroyed in the days of Joshua. The nation had turned sour and rejected its original purpose—to honour God and be a light to the world.

17:7–17 The Lord judged the people of Israel because they copied the evil customs of the surrounding nations, worshipping false gods, accommodating pagan customs, and following their own desires. It is not safe to create your own religion because people who do tend to live selfishly. And to live for yourself, as Israel learned, brings serious consequences from God. Sometimes it is difficult and painful to follow God, but consider the alternative. You can live for God or die for yourself. Determine to be God's person and do what he says regardless of the cost. What God thinks of you is infinitely more important than what those around you think. (See Romans 12:1, 2; 1 John 2:15–17.)

17:9 Ruin came upon Israel for both their public sins and their secret sins. Not only did they condone wickedness and idolatry in public, but they committed even worse sins in private. Secret sins are the ones we don't want others to know about because they are embarrassing or incriminating. Sins done in private are not secret to God, and secret defiance of him is just as damaging as open rebellion.

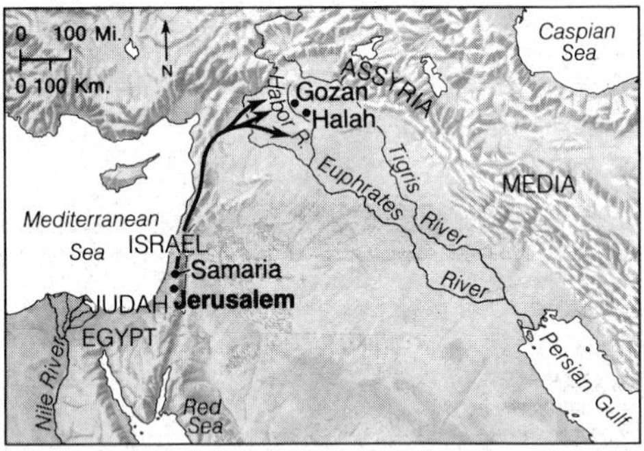

ISRAEL TAKEN CAPTIVE Finally the sins of Israel's people caught up with them. God allowed Assyria to defeat and disperse the people. They were led into captivity, swallowed up by the mighty, evil Assyrian empire. Sin always brings discipline, and the consequences of that sin are sometimes irreversible.

17:13–15 The people took on the characteristics of the idols and imitated the godless nations around them. Israel had forgotten the importance and benefits of obeying God's word. The king and the people were mired in wickedness. Time and again God had sent prophets to warn them of how far they had turned away from him and to call them to turn back.

God's patience and mercy are beyond our ability to understand. He will pursue us until we either respond to him or, by our own choice and hardness of heart, make ourselves unreachable. Then God's judgment is swift and sure. The only safe course is to turn to God before our stubbornness puts us out of his reach.

accordance with the entire Law that I commanded your fathers to obey and that I
delivered to you through my servants the prophets."
14 But they would not listen and were as stiff-necked[p] as their fathers, who did not
trust in the LORD their God. 15 They rejected his decrees and the covenant[q] he had
made with their fathers and the warnings he had given them. They followed worthless
idols[r] and themselves became worthless. They imitated the nations[s] around them
although the LORD had ordered them, "Do not do as they do," and they did the things
the LORD had forbidden them to do.
16 They forsook all the commands of the LORD their God and made for themselves
two idols cast in the shape of calves,[t] and an Asherah[u] pole. They bowed down to
all the starry hosts,[v] and they worshipped Baal.[w] 17 They sacrificed[x] their sons and
daughters in[c] the fire. They practised divination and sorcery[y] and sold[z] themselves
to do evil in the eyes of the LORD, provoking him to anger.
18 So the LORD was very angry with Israel and removed them from his presence.
Only the tribe of Judah was left, 19 and even Judah did not keep the commands of the
LORD their God. They followed the practices Israel had introduced.[a] 20 Therefore the
LORD rejected all the people of Israel; he afflicted them and gave them into the hands
of plunderers,[b] until he thrust them from his presence.
21 When he tore[c] Israel away from the house of David, they made Jeroboam son
of Nebat their king.[d] Jeroboam enticed Israel away from following the LORD and
caused them to commit a great sin. 22 The Israelites persisted in all the sins of Jeroboam
and did not turn away from them 23 until the LORD removed them from his presence,
as he had warned through all his servants the prophets. So the people of Israel were
taken from their homeland into exile in Assyria, and they are still there.

Samaria Resettled

24 The king of Assyria[e] brought people from Babylon, Cuthah, Avva, Hamath and
Sepharvaim[f] and settled them in the towns of Samaria to replace the Israelites. They
took over Samaria and lived in its towns. 25 When they first lived there, they did not
worship the LORD; so he sent lions[g] among them and they killed some of the people.
26 It was reported to the king of Assyria: "The people you deported and resettled in
the towns of Samaria do not know what the god of that country requires. He has sent
lions among them, which are killing them off, because the people do not know what
he requires."

c 17 Or *They made their sons and daughters pass through*

17:14 [p]Ex 32:9; Dt 31:27; Ac 7:51
17:15 [q]Dt 29:25 [r]Dt 32:21; Ro 1:21-23 [s]Dt 12:30-31
17:16 [t]1Ki 12:28 [u]1Ki 14:15, 23 [v]2Ki 21:3 [w]1Ki 16:31
17:17 [x]Dt 18:10-12; 2Ki 16:3 [y]Lev 19:26 [z]1Ki 21:20
17:19 [a]1Ki 14:22-23; 2Ki 16:3
17:20 [b]2Ki 15:29
17:21 [c]1Ki 11:11 [d]1Ki 12:20
17:24 [e]Ezr 4:2, 10 [f]2Ki 18:34
17:25 [g]Ge 37:20

17:16 The "starry hosts" refers to the Canaanite practice of worshipping the sun, moon, and constellations. These were Assyrian gods that were being added to their religion. (See also 21:1–6; 23:4, 5.)

17:17 Divination means witchcraft, and sorcery is consulting evil spirits. Forms of witchcraft, fortune-telling, and black magic were forbidden by God (Deuteronomy 18:9–14). They were wrong because they sought power and guidance totally apart from God, his law, and his word. Isaiah echoed this law and prophesied of the complete destruction these occult practices would bring to those who participated in them (Isaiah 8:19–22).

17:23 Israel was taken into exile, just as God's prophets had warned. Whatever God predicts will come to pass. This, of course, is good news to those who trust and obey him—they can be confident of his promises; but it is bad news to those who ignore or disobey him. Both the promises and warnings God has given in his word will surely come true.

17:24 Moving the Israelites out and moving foreigners in was Assyria's resettlement policy to prevent revolt. Spreading the captives across Assyria prevented their uniting, and repopulating Israel with foreign captives made it difficult for the remaining Israelites to unite as well. This mixture of peoples resettled in Israel came to be known as *Samaritans.* They were despised by the Jews, even through the time of Christ (John 4:9).

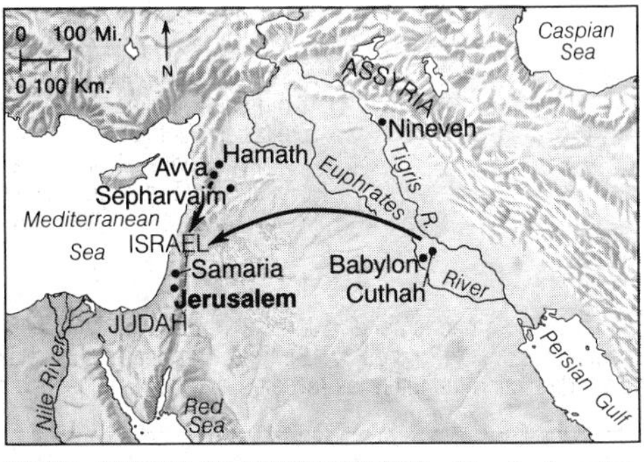

ISRAEL RESETTLED BY FOREIGNERS After the Israelites were deported, foreigners from the Assyrian empire were sent to resettle the land. This policy helped Assyria to keep peace in conquered territories.

27Then the king of Assyria gave this order: "Make one of the priests
you took captive from Samaria go back to live there and teach the people what
the god of the land requires." 28So one of the priests who had been exiled from

WHO WERE

Who?	When? (B.C.)	Ministered during the reign of these kings:	Main message	Significance
AHIJAH	934–909	Jeroboam I of Israel (1 Kings 11:29–39)	Said Israel would split in two and stated that God had chosen Jeroboam to lead the ten tribes. Warned that he should remain obedient to God.	We should not take lightly our God-given responsibilities. Jeroboam did and lost his kingdom.
ELIJAH	875–848	Ahab of Israel (1 Kings 17:1—2 Kings 2:11)	In fiery style, urged wicked Ahab to turn back to God. On Mount Carmel, he proved who is the one true God (1 Kings 18).	Even giants of faith can't force sinners to change. But those who remain faithful to God have a great impact for him.
MICAIAH	865–853	Ahab of Israel Jehoshaphat of Judah (1 Kings 22:8; 2 Chronicles 18:28)	Ahab would be unsuccessful in fighting the Arameans.	It is foolish to move ahead with plans that are contrary to God's word.
JEHU	853	Jehoshaphat of Judah (2 Chronicles 19:1–3)	Jehoshaphat should never have allied himself with wicked Ahab.	Partnerships with immoral people can lead us into trouble.
OBADIAH	855–840(?)	Jehoram of Judah (The book of Obadiah)	God would judge the Edomites for taking advantage of God's people.	Pride is one of the most dangerous sins because it causes us to take advantage of others.
ELISHA	848–797	Joram, Jehu, Jehoahaz, and Jehoash, all of Israel (2 Kings 2:1—9:1; 13:10–21)	Expressed by his actions the importance of helping ordinary people in need.	God is concerned about the everyday needs of his people.
JOEL	835–796(?)	Joash of Judah (The book of Joel)	Because a plague of locusts had come to punish the nation, he called the people to turn back to God before an even greater judgment occurred.	While God judges all people for their sins, he gives eternal salvation only to those who have turned to him.
JONAH	793–753	Jeroboam II of Israel (2 Kings 14:25; the book of Jonah)	Nineveh, the capital of Assyria, should repent of its sins.	God wants all nations to turn to him. His love reaches out to all peoples.
AMOS	760–750	Jeroboam II of Israel (The book of Amos)	Warned against those who exploited or ignored the needy. (In Amos' day, Israel was an affluent and materialistic society.)	Believing in God is more than a personal matter. God calls all believers to work against injustices in society and to aid those less fortunate.
HOSEA	753–715	The last seven kings of Israel; Azariah (Uzziah), Jotham, Ahaz, and Hezekiah of Judah (The book of Hosea)	Condemned the people of Israel because they had sinned against God as an adulterous woman sins against her husband.	When we sin, we sever our relationship with God, breaking our commitment to him. While all must answer to God for their sins, those who seek God's forgiveness are spared from eternal judgment.

"The LORD warned Israel and Judah through all his prophets and seers: 'Turn from your evil ways. Observe my commands . . . .'" (2 Kings 17:13). Who were these prophets? Here are some of those who tried to turn their nations back to God. Predicting the future as revealed by God was just one part of a prophet's job; his main role was to preach God's word

17:27–29 The new settlers in Israel worshipped God without giving up their pagan customs. They worshipped God to appease him rather than to please him, treating him as a good luck charm or just another idol to add to their collection. A similar attitude is common today. Many people claim to believe in God while refusing to give up attitudes and actions that God denounces. God cannot be added to the values we already have. He must come first, and his

17:29
h Jer 2:28
i 1Ki 12:31

Samaria came to live in Bethel and taught them how to worship the LORD.
29 Nevertheless, each national group made its own gods in the several towns[h] where
they settled, and set them up in the shrines[i] the people of Samaria had made at the

THESE PROPHETS?

Who?	*When? (B.C.)*	*Ministered during the reign of these kings:*	*Main message*	*Significance*
MICAH	742–687	Jotham, Ahaz, and Hezekiah of Judah (The book of Micah)	Predicted the fall of both the northern and southern kingdoms. This was God's discipline on the people, actually showing how much he cared for them.	Choosing to live a life apart from God is making a commitment to sin. Sin leads to judgment and death. God alone shows us the way to eternal peace. His discipline often keeps us on the right path.
ISAIAH	740–681	Azariah (Uzziah), Jotham, Ahaz, Hezekiah, and Manasseh of Judah (The book of Isaiah)	Called the people back to a special relationship with God—although judgment through other nations was inevitable.	Sometimes we must suffer judgment and discipline before we are restored to God.
NAHUM	663–654	Manasseh of Judah (The book of Nahum)	The mighty empire of Assyria that oppressed God's people would soon tumble.	Those who do evil and oppress others will one day meet a bitter end.
ZEPHANIAH	640–621	Josiah of Judah (The book of Zephaniah)	A day will come when God, as Judge, will severely punish all nations; but afterwards, he will show mercy to his people.	We will all be judged for our disobedience to God, but if we remain faithful to him, he will show us mercy.
JEREMIAH	627–586	Josiah, Jehoahaz, Jehoiakim, Jehoiachin, Zedekiah of Judah (The book of Jeremiah)	Repentance would postpone Judah's coming judgment at the hands of Babylon.	Repentance is one of the greatest needs in our world of immorality. God's promises to the faithful shine brightly.
HABAKKUK	612–589	Josiah, Jehoahaz, Jehoiakim, Jehoiachin, Zedekiah of Judah (The book of Habakkuk)	Habakkuk couldn't understand why God seemed to do nothing about the wickedness in society. Then he realised that faith in God alone would one day supply the answer.	Instead of questioning the ways of God, we should realise that he is completely just, and we should have faith that he is in control and that one day evil will be utterly destroyed.
DANIEL	605–536	Prophesied as an exile in Babylon during the reigns of Nebuchadnezzar, Darius the Mede, and Cyrus of Persia (The book of Daniel)	Describes both near and distant future events—throughout it all, God is sovereign and triumphant.	We should spend less time wondering when these events will happen and more time learning how we should live *now* so we won't be victims of those events.
EZEKIEL	593–571	Prophesied as an exile in Babylon during the reign of Nebuchadnezzar (The book of Ezekiel)	Sent messages back to Jerusalem urging the people to turn back to God before they were all forced to join him in exile. After Jerusalem fell, Ezekiel urged his fellow exiles to turn back to God so they could eventually return to their homeland.	God disciplines his people to draw them closer to him.

to the people—warning, instructing, and encouraging them to live as they ought.

The prophets Haggai, Zechariah, and Malachi were prophets to the people of Judah after they returned from exile. For more information, see the chart in Ezra 5.

word must shape all our actions and attitudes.

17:29–31 Israel was conquered because it had lost sight of the only true God and why it was important to follow him. When conquering the land, the Israelites were told to destroy the pagan influences that could lead them away from God. Their failure to do so brought about their ruin. Here they faced an even greater influx of gods from the many pagan peoples moving into the land.

high places.[j] 30The men from Babylon made Succoth Benoth, the men from Cuthah
made Nergal, and the men from Hamath made Ashima; 31the Avvites made Nibhaz
and Tartak, and the Sepharvites burned their children in the fire as sacrifices to
Adrammelech[k] and Anammelech, the gods of Sepharvaim.[l] 32They worshipped the
LORD, but they also appointed all sorts[m] of their own people to officiate for them as
priests in the shrines at the high places. 33They worshipped the LORD, but they also
served their own gods in accordance with the customs of the nations from which they
had been brought.

34To this day they persist in their former practices. They neither worship the LORD
nor adhere to the decrees and ordinances, the laws and commands that the LORD gave
the descendants of Jacob, whom he named Israel.[n] 35When the LORD made a covenant
with the Israelites, he commanded them: "Do not worship[o] any other gods or bow
down to them, serve them or sacrifice to them. 36But the LORD, who brought you up
out of Egypt with mighty power and outstretched arm,[p] is the one you must worship.
To him you shall bow down and to him offer sacrifices. 37You must always be
careful[q] to keep the decrees and ordinances, the laws and commands he wrote for
you. Do not worship other gods. 38Do not forget[r] the covenant I have made with you,
and do not worship other gods. 39Rather, worship the LORD your God; it is he who
will deliver you from the hand of all your enemies."

40They would not listen, however, but persisted in their former practices. 41Even
while these people were worshipping the LORD,[s] they were serving their idols. To
this day their children and grandchildren continue to do as their fathers did.

B. THE SURVIVING KINGDOM (18:1–25:30)

After seeing their brothers and sisters carried away into exile, Judah still lapses into sin. Hezekiah and Josiah begin many reforms, but this is not enough to turn the nation permanently back to God. Judah is defeated by the Babylonians, who exile many of them, but they are not scattered and the land is not repopulated. Sometimes we do not learn from the examples of sin and foolishness around us.

1. Kings of Judah

Hezekiah King of Judah

18 In the third year of Hoshea son of Elah king of Israel, Hezekiah[a] son of Ahaz
king of Judah began to reign. 2He was twenty-five years old when he became
king, and he reigned in Jerusalem for twenty-nine years.[b] His mother's name was
Abijah[a] daughter of Zechariah. 3He did what was right in the eyes of the LORD, just
as his father David[c] had done. 4He removed[d] the high places, smashed the sacred
stones[e] and cut down the Asherah poles. He broke into pieces the bronze snake[f]
Moses had made, for up to that time the Israelites had been burning incense to it. (It
was called[b] Nehushtan.[c])

5Hezekiah trusted[g] in the LORD, the God of Israel. There was no-one like him
among all the kings of Judah, either before him or after him. 6He held fast[h] to the
LORD and did not cease to follow him; he kept the commands the LORD had given
Moses. 7And the LORD was with him; he was successful[i] in whatever he undertook.
He rebelled[j] against the king of Assyria and did not serve him. 8From watch-

[a] *2* Hebrew *Abi*, a variant of *Abijah* [b] *4* Or *He called it* [c] *4* *Nehushtan* sounds like the Hebrew for *bronze* and *snake* and *unclean thing*.

17:29 [j]Mic 4:5
17:31 [k]2Ki 19:37 [l]ver 24
17:32 [m]1Ki 12:31
17:34 [n]Ge 32:28; 35:10; 1Ki 18:31
17:35 [o]Ex 20:5; Jdg 6:10
17:36 [p]Ex 3:20; 6:6; Ps 136:12
17:37 [q]Dt 5:32
17:38 [r]Dt 4:23; 6:12
17:41 [s]ver 32-33; 1Ki 18:21; Mt 6:24
18:1 [a]Isa 1:1; 2Ch 28:27
18:2 [b]Isa 38:5
18:3 [c]Isa 38:5
18:4 [d]2Ch 31:1 [e]Ex 23:24 [f]Nu 21:9
18:5 [g]2Ki 19:10; 23:25
18:6 [h]Dt 10:20; Jos 23:8; Dt
18:7 [i]Ge 39:3; 1Sa 18:14 [j]2Ki 16:7

18:4 The bronze snake had been made to cure the Israelites of the bite of venomous snakes (Numbers 21:4–9). It demonstrated God's presence and power and reminded the people of his mercy and forgiveness. But it had become an object of worship instead of a reminder of *whom* to worship, so Hezekiah was forced to destroy it. We must be careful that aids to our worship don't become objects of worship themselves. Most objects are not made to be idols—they become idols by the way people use them.

18:5 "There was no-one like him . . . ." In dramatic contrast with his father, Ahaz, Hezekiah followed God more closely and sincerely than any other king of Judah or Israel. This statement refers to the kings after the division of the kingdom and so does not include David, considered the king most devoted to God.

18:7 Judah was sandwiched between two world powers, Egypt and Assyria. Both wanted to control Judah and Israel because they lay at the vital crossroads of all ancient Near East trade. The nation who controlled Judah would have a military and economic advantage over its rivals. When Hezekiah became king, Assyria controlled Judah. Acting with great courage, Hezekiah rebelled against this mighty empire to whom his father had submitted. He placed his faith in God's strength rather than his own, and he obeyed God's commands in spite of the obstacles and dangers that, from a purely human standpoint, looked overwhelming.

18:8 [k]2Ki 17:9; Isa 14:29
18:9 [l]Isa 1:1

tower to fortified city,[k] he defeated the Philistines, as far as Gaza and its
territory.
9In King Hezekiah's fourth year,[l] which was the seventh year of Hoshea son of

HEZEKIAH

The past is an important part of today's actions and tomorrow's plans. The people and kings of Judah had a rich past, filled with God's action, guidance, and commands. But with each passing generation, they also had a growing list of tragedies that occurred when the people forgot that their God, who had cared for them in the past, also cared about the present and the future—and demanded their continued obedience. Hezekiah was one of the few kings of Judah who was constantly aware of God's acts in the past and his interest in the events of every day. The Bible describes him as a king who had a close relationship with God.

As a reformer, Hezekiah was most concerned with present obedience. Judah was filled with visual reminders of the people's lack of trust in God, and Hezekiah boldly began cleaning up. Altars, idols, and pagan temples were destroyed. Even the bronze snake Moses had made in the desert was not spared because it had ceased to point the people to God and had also become an idol. The temple in Jerusalem, whose doors had been nailed shut by Hezekiah's own father, was cleaned out and reopened. The Passover was reinstituted as a national holiday, and there was revival in Judah.

Although he had a natural inclination to respond to present problems, Hezekiah's life shows little evidence of concern about the future. He took few actions to preserve the effects of his sweeping reforms. His successful efforts made him proud. His unwise display of wealth to the Babylonian delegation caused Judah to be included on Babylon's "Nations to Conquer" list. When Isaiah informed Hezekiah of the foolishness of his act, the king's answer displayed his persistent lack of foresight—he was thankful that any evil consequences would be delayed until after he died. And the lives of three kings who followed him—Manasseh, Amon, and Josiah—were deeply affected by both Hezekiah's accomplishments *and* his weaknesses.

The past affects your decisions and actions today, and these, in turn, affect the future. There are lessons to learn and errors to avoid repeating. Remember that part of the success of your past will be measured by what you do with it now and how well you use it to prepare for the future.

Strengths and accomplishments:
- Was the king of Judah who instigated civil and religious reforms
- Had a personal, growing relationship with God
- Developed a powerful prayer life
- Noted as the author of several chapters in the book of Proverbs (Proverbs 25:1)

Weaknesses and mistakes:
- Showed little interest or wisdom in planning for the future and protecting for others the spiritual heritage he enjoyed
- Rashly showed all his wealth to messengers from Babylon

Lessons from his life:
- Sweeping reforms are short-lived when little action is taken to preserve them for the future
- Past obedience to God does not remove the possibility of present disobedience
- Complete dependence on God yields amazing results

Vital statistics:
- Where: Jerusalem
- Occupation: 13th king of Judah, the southern kingdom
- Relatives: Father: Ahaz. Mother: Abijah. Son: Manasseh
- Contemporaries: Isaiah, Hoshea, Micah, Sennacherib

Key verses:
"Hezekiah trusted in the LORD, the God of Israel. There was no-one like him among all the kings of Judah, either before him or after him. He held fast to the LORD and did not cease to follow him; he kept the commands the LORD had given Moses" (2 Kings 18:5, 6).

Hezekiah's story is told in 2 Kings 16:20—20:21; 2 Chronicles 28:27—32:33; Isaiah 36:1—39:8. He is also mentioned in Proverbs 25:1; Isaiah 1:1; Jeremiah 15:4; 26:18, 19; Hosea 1:1; Micah 1:1.

18:9–12 These verses flash back to the days just before Israel's destruction. Hezekiah reigned with his father Ahaz for 14 years (729–715 B.C.), by himself for 18 years (715–697 B.C.), and with his son Manasseh for 11 years (697–686 B.C.), a total of 43 years. The 29 years listed in 18:2 indicate only those years in which Hezekiah had complete control of the kingdom. While Hezekiah was on the throne, the nation of Israel to the north was destroyed (722 B.C.). Knowing Israel's fate probably caused Hezekiah to reform his own nation. (For more on Hezekiah, see 2 Chronicles 29—32 and Isaiah 36—39.)

Elah king of Israel, Shalmaneser king of Assyria marched against Samaria and laid
siege to it. 10 At the end of three years the Assyrians took it. So Samaria was captured
in Hezekiah's sixth year, which was the ninth year of Hoshea king of Israel. 11 The
king[m] of Assyria deported Israel to Assyria and settled them in Halah, in Gozan on
the Habor River, and in towns of the Medes. 12 This happened because they had not
obeyed the LORD their God, but had violated his covenant[n]—all that Moses the
servant of the LORD commanded.[o] They neither listened to the commands[p] nor
carried them out.

13 In the fourteenth year of King Hezekiah's reign, Sennacherib king of Assyria
attacked all the fortified cities of Judah[q] and captured them. 14 So Hezekiah king of
Judah sent this message to the king of Assyria at Lachish: "I have done wrong.[r]
Withdraw from me, and I will pay whatever you demand of me." The king of Assyria
exacted from Hezekiah king of Judah three hundred talents[d] of silver and thirty
talents[e] of gold. 15 So Hezekiah gave[s] him all the silver that was found in the temple
of the LORD and in the treasuries of the royal palace.

16 At this time Hezekiah king of Judah stripped off the gold with which he had
covered the doors and doorposts of the temple of the LORD, and gave it to the king
of Assyria.

Sennacherib Threatens Jerusalem

17 The king of Assyria sent his supreme commander,[t] his chief officer and his field
commander with a large army, from Lachish to King Hezekiah at Jerusalem. They
came up to Jerusalem and stopped at the aqueduct of the Upper Pool,[u] on the road
to the Washerman's Field. 18 They called for the king; and Eliakim[v] son of Hilkiah
the palace administrator, Shebna[w] the secretary, and Joah son of Asaph the recorder
went out to them.

19 The field commander said to them, "Tell Hezekiah:

> " 'This is what the great king, the king of Assyria, says: On what are you
> basing this confidence of yours? 20 You say you have strategy and military
> strength—but you speak only empty words. On whom are you depending, that
> you rebel against me? 21 Look now, you are depending on Egypt,[x] that splintered
> reed of a staff,[y] which pierces a man's hand and wounds him if he leans on it!
> Such is Pharaoh king of Egypt to all who depend on him. 22 And if you say to
> me, "We are depending on the LORD our God"—isn't he the one whose high
> places and altars Hezekiah removed, saying to Judah and Jerusalem, "You must
> worship before this altar in Jerusalem"?
>
> 23 " 'Come now, make a bargain with my master, the king of Assyria: I will
> give you two thousand horses—if you can put riders on them! 24 How can you
> repulse one officer[z] of the least of my master's officials, even though you are
> depending on Egypt for chariots and horsemen?[f] 25 Furthermore, have I come
> to attack and destroy this place without word from the LORD?[a] The LORD himself
> told me to march against this country and destroy it.' "

26 Then Eliakim son of Hilkiah, and Shebna and Joah said to the field commander,
"Please speak to your servants in Aramaic,[b] since we understand it. Don't speak to
us in Hebrew in the hearing of the people on the wall."

[d] *14* That is, about 10 tons (about 10 metric tons) [e] *14* That is, about 1 ton (about 1 metric ton)
[f] *24* Or *charioteers*

18:11 [m] Isa 37:12
18:12 [n] 2Ki 17:15 [o] Da 9:6, 10 [p] 1Ki 9:6
18:13 [q] 2Ch 32:1; Isa 1:7; Mic 1:9
18:14 [r] Isa 24:5
18:15 [s] 1Ki 15:18; 2Ki 16:8
18:17 [t] Isa 20:1 [u] 2Ki 20:20; 2Ch 32:4, 30; Isa 7:3
18:18 [v] 2Ki 19:2; Isa 22:20 [w] Isa 22:15
18:21 [x] Isa 20:5; Eze 29:6 [y] Isa 30:5, 7
18:24 [z] Isa 10:8
18:25 [a] 2Ki 19:6, 22
18:26 [b] Ezr 4:7

18:13 This event occurred in 701 B.C., four years after Sennacherib had become Assyria's king. Sennacherib was the son of Sargon II, the king who had deported Israel's people into captivity (see the note on 17:3). To keep Assyria from attacking, the southern kingdom paid tribute annually. But when Sennacherib became king, Hezekiah stopped paying this money, hoping Assyria would ignore him. When Sennacherib and his army retaliated, Hezekiah realised his mistake and paid the tribute money (18:14), but Sennacherib attacked anyway (18:19ff). Although Sennacherib attacked Judah, he was not as war-hungry as the previous Assyrian kings, preferring to spend most of his time building and beautifying his capital city, Nineveh. With less frequent invasions, Hezekiah was able to institute many reforms and strengthen the nation.

18:17 Sending the supreme commander, the chief officer, and the field commander was like sending the prime minister, foreign secretary and chief of stalt to speak to the enemy prior to a battle. All of these men were sent in an effort to impress and discourage the Israelites.

27But the commander replied, "Was it only to your master and you that my master sent me to say these things, and not to the men sitting on the wall — who, like you, will have to eat their own filth and drink their own urine?"

28Then the commander stood and called out in Hebrew: "Hear the word of the great king, the king of Assyria! 29This is what the king says: Do not let Hezekiah deceive[c] you. He cannot deliver you from my hand. 30Do not let Hezekiah persuade you to trust in the LORD when he says, 'The LORD will surely deliver us; this city will not be given into the hand of the king of Assyria.'

31"Do not listen to Hezekiah. This is what the king of Assyria says: Make peace with me and come out to me. Then every one of you will eat from his own vine and fig-tree[d] and drink water from his own cistern,[e] 32until I come and take you to a land like your own, a land of grain and new wine, a land of bread and vineyards, a land of olive trees and honey. Choose life[f] and not death!

"Do not listen to Hezekiah, for he is misleading you when he says, 'The LORD will deliver us.' 33Has the god[g] of any nation ever delivered his land from the hand of the king of Assyria? 34Where are the gods of Hamath[h] and Arpad?[i] Where are the gods of Sepharvaim, Hena and Ivvah? Have they rescued Samaria from my hand? 35Who of all the gods of these countries has been able to save his land from me? How then can the LORD deliver Jerusalem from my hand?"[j]

36But the people remained silent and said nothing in reply, because the king had commanded, "Do not answer him."

37Then Eliakim son of Hilkiah the palace administrator, Shebna the secretary and Joah son of Asaph the recorder went to Hezekiah, with their clothes torn,[k] and told him what the field commander had said.

Jerusalem's Deliverance Foretold

19 When King Hezekiah heard this, he tore[a] his clothes and put on sackcloth and went into the temple of the LORD. 2He sent Eliakim the palace administrator, Shebna the secretary and the leading priests, all wearing sackcloth, to the prophet Isaiah[b] son of Amoz. 3They told him, "This is what Hezekiah says: This day is a day of distress and rebuke and disgrace, as when children come to the point of birth and there is no strength to deliver them. 4It may be that the LORD your God will hear all the words of the field commander, whom his master, the king of Assyria, has sent to ridicule[c] the living God, and that he will rebuke[d] him for the words the LORD your God has heard. Therefore pray for the remnant that still survives."

5When King Hezekiah's officials came to Isaiah, 6Isaiah said to them, "Tell your master, 'This is what the LORD says: Do not be afraid of what you have heard — those words with which the underlings of the king of Assyria have blasphemed[e] me. 7Listen! I am going to put such a spirit in him that when he hears a certain report, he will return to his own country, and there I will have him cut down with the sword.[f] "

8When the field commander heard that the king of Assyria had left Lachish,[g] he withdrew and found the king fighting against Libnah.

9Now Sennacherib received a report that Tirhakah, the Cushite[a] king ⌞of Egypt⌟, was marching out to fight against him. So he again sent messengers to Hezekiah with this word: 10"Say to Hezekiah king of Judah: Do not let the god you depend[h] on deceive[i] you when he says, 'Jerusalem will not be handed over to the king of Assyria.' 11Surely you have heard what the kings of Assyria have done to all the

18:29 [c] 2Ki 19:10
18:31 [d] Nu 13:23; 1Ki 4:25 [e] Jer 14:3; La 4:4
18:32 [f] Dt 8:7-9; 30:19
18:33 [g] 2Ki 19:12; Isa 10:10-11
18:34 [h] 2Ki 17:24; 19:13 [i] Isa 10:9
18:35 [j] Ps 2:1-2
18:37 [k] 2Ki 6:30
19:1 [a] Ge 37:34; 1Ki 21:27; 2Ch 32:20-22
19:2 [b] Isa 1:1
19:4 [c] 2Ki 18:35 [d] 2Sa 16:12
19:6 [e] 2Ki 18:25
19:7 [f] ver 37
19:8 [g] 2Ki 18:14
19:10 [h] 2Ki 18:5 [i] 2Ki 18:29

a *9* That is, from the upper Nile region

19:1–7 Sennacherib, whose armies had captured all the fortified cities of Judah, sent a message to Hezekiah to surrender. Realising the situation was hopeless, Hezekiah went to the temple and prayed. God answered Hezekiah's prayer and delivered Judah by sending an army to attack the Assyrian camp, forcing Sennacherib to leave at once. Prayer should be our first response in any crisis. Don't wait until things are hopeless. Pray daily for his guidance. Our problems are God's opportunities.

19:2 Isaiah the prophet had been working for God since the days of Uzziah — 40 years (Isaiah 6:1). Although Assyria was a world power, it could not conquer Judah as long as Isaiah counselled the kings. Isaiah prophesied during the reigns of Uzziah (Azariah), Jotham, Ahaz, and Hezekiah. Ahaz ignored Isaiah, but Hezekiah listened to his advice. To read his prophecies, see the book of Isaiah.

countries, destroying them completely. And will you be delivered? 12Did the gods of
the nations that were destroyed by my forefathers deliver[j] them: the gods of Gozan,[k]
Haran,[l] Rezeph and the people of Eden who were in Tel Assar? 13Where is the king
of Hamath, the king of Arpad, the king of the city of Sepharvaim, or of Hena or
Ivvah?"[m]

Hezekiah's Prayer

14Hezekiah received the letter from the messengers and read it. Then he went up
to the temple of the LORD and spread it out before the LORD. 15And Hezekiah prayed
to the LORD: "O LORD, God of Israel, enthroned between the cherubim,[n] you alone
are God over all the kingdoms of the earth. You have made heaven and earth. 16Give
ear,[o] O LORD, and hear;[p] open your eyes,[q] O LORD, and see; listen to the words
Sennacherib has sent to insult the living God.
17"It is true, O LORD, that the Assyrian kings have laid waste these nations and their
lands. 18They have thrown their gods into the fire and destroyed them, for they were
not gods[r] but only wood and stone, fashioned by men's hands.[s] 19Now, O LORD
our God, deliver us from his hand, so that all kingdoms[t] on earth may know[u] that
you alone, O LORD, are God."

Isaiah Prophesies Sennacherib's Fall

20Then Isaiah son of Amoz sent a message to Hezekiah: "This is what the LORD,
the God of Israel, says: I have heard[v] your prayer concerning Sennacherib king of
Assyria. 21This is the word that the LORD has spoken against him:

" 'The Virgin Daughter[w] of Zion
despises you and mocks[x] you.
The Daughter of Jerusalem
tosses her head[y] as you flee.
22Who is it you have insulted and blasphemed?
Against whom have you raised your voice
and lifted your eyes in pride?
Against the Holy One[z] of Israel!
23By your messengers
you have heaped insults on the Lord.
And you have said,[a]
"With my many chariots[b]
I have ascended the heights of the mountains,
the utmost heights of Lebanon.
I have cut down its tallest cedars,
the choicest of its pines.
I have reached its remotest parts,
the finest of its forests.
24I have dug wells in foreign lands
and drunk the water there.
With the soles of my feet
I have dried up all the streams of Egypt."

25" 'Have you not heard?[c]
Long ago I ordained it.
In days of old I planned[d] it;

19:12 [j]2Ki 18:33 [k]2Ki 17:6 [l]Ge 11:31
19:13 [m]2Ki 18:34
19:15 [n]Ex 25:22
19:16 [o]Ps 31:2 [p]1Ki 8:29 [q]ver 4; 2Ch 6:40
19:18 [r]Isa 44:9-11; Jer 10:3-10 [s]Ps 115:4; Ac 17:29
19:19 [t]1Ki 8:43 [u]Ps 83:18
19:20 [v]2Ki 20:5
19:21 [w]Jer 14:17; La 2:13 [x]Ps 22:7-8 [y]Job 16:4; Ps 109:25
19:22 [z]Ps 71:22; Isa 5:24
19:23 [a]Isa 10:18 [b]Ps 20:7
19:25 [c]Isa 40:21, 28 [d]Isa 10:5; 45:7

19:15 Cherubim are mighty angels.

19:15–19 Although Hezekiah came boldly to God, he did not take God for granted or approach him flippantly. Instead, Hezekiah acknowledged God's sovereignty and Judah's total dependence on him. Hezekiah's prayer provides a good model for us. We should not be afraid to approach God with our prayers, but we must come to him with respect for who he is and what he can do.

19:21–34 God replied to Sennacherib's taunting words (18:19–25), indicting him for arrogance. Sennacherib believed his kingdom had grown because of his own efforts and strength. In reality, said God, he succeeded only because of what God had allowed and caused. It is arrogance to think we are solely responsible for our achievements. God, as Creator, rules over nations and people.

19:25 [e]Mic 1:6
19:26 [f]Ps 6:10 [g]Isa 4:2 [h]Ps 129:6
19:27 [i]Ps 139:1-4
19:28 [j]Eze 19:9; 29:4 [k]Isa 30:28 [l]ver 33
19:29 [m]2Ki 20:8-9; Lk 2:12 [n]Lev 25:5 [o]Ps 107:37
19:30 [p]2Ch 32:22-23
19:31 [q]Isa 9:7
19:33 [r]ver 28
19:34 [s]2Ki 20:6 [t]1Ki 11:12-13
19:35 [u]Ex 12:23 [v]Job 24:24
19:36 [w]Ge 10:11; Jnh 1:2
19:37 [x]ver 7 [y]Ge 8:4 [z]Ezr 4:2

now I have brought it to pass,
that you have turned fortified cities
into piles of stone.[e]
26 Their people, drained of power,
are dismayed[f] and put to shame.
They are like plants in the field,
like tender green shoots,[g]
like grass sprouting on the roof,
scorched[h] before it grows up.

27 " 'But I know[i] where you stay
and when you come and go
and how you rage against me.
28 Because you rage against me
and your insolence has reached my ears,
I will put my hook[j] in your nose
and my bit[k] in your mouth,
and I will make you return[l]
by the way you came.'

29 "This will be the sign[m] for you, O Hezekiah:

This year you will eat what grows by itself,[n]
and the second year what springs from that.
But in the third year sow and reap,
plant vineyards[o] and eat their fruit.
30 Once more a remnant of the house of Judah
will take root[p] below and bear fruit above.
31 For out of Jerusalem will come a remnant,
and out of Mount Zion a band of survivors.

The zeal[q] of the LORD Almighty will accomplish this.

32 "Therefore this is what the LORD says concerning the king of Assyria:

"He will not enter this city
or shoot an arrow here.
He will not come before it with shield
or build a siege ramp against it.
33 By the way that he came he will return;[r]
he will not enter this city,
declares the LORD.
34 I will defend[s] this city and save it,
for my sake and for the sake of David[t] my servant."

35 That night the angel of the LORD[u] went out and put to death a hundred and
eighty-five thousand men in the Assyrian camp. When the people got up the next
morning—there were all the dead bodies![v] 36 So Sennacherib king of Assyria broke
camp and withdrew. He returned to Nineveh[w] and stayed there.
37 One day, while he was worshipping in the temple of his god Nisroch, his sons
Adrammelech and Sharezer cut him down with the sword,[x] and they escaped to the
land of Ararat.[y] And Esarhaddon[z] his son succeeded him as king.

19:28 The Assyrians treated captives with cruelty. They tortured them for entertainment by blinding them, cutting them, or pulling off strips of their skin until they died. If they wished to make a captive a slave, they would often put a hook in his nose. God was saying that the Assyrians would be treated the way they had treated others.

19:31 As long as a tiny spark remains, a fire can be rekindled and fanned into a roaring blaze. Similarly, if just the smallest remnant of true believers retains the spark of faith, God can rebuild it into a strong nation. And if only a glimmer of faith remains in a heart, God can use it to restore blazing faith in that believer. If you feel that only a spark of faith remains in you, ask God to use it to rekindle a blazing fire of commitment to him.

Hezekiah's Illness

20 In those days Hezekiah became ill and was at the point of death. The prophet
Isaiah son of Amoz went to him and said, "This is what the LORD says: Put
your house in order, because you are going to die; you will not recover."
2Hezekiah turned his face to the wall and prayed to the LORD, 3"Remember,[a]
O LORD, how I have walked before you faithfully[b] and with wholehearted devotion
and have done what is good in your eyes." And Hezekiah wept bitterly.
4Before Isaiah had left the middle court, the word of the LORD came to him: 5"Go
back and tell Hezekiah, the leader of my people, 'This is what the LORD, the God of
your father David, says: I have heard[c] your prayer and seen your tears;[d] I will heal
you. On the third day from now you will go up to the temple of the LORD. 6I will
add fifteen years to your life. And I will deliver you and this city from the hand of
the king of Assyria. I will defend[e] this city for my sake and for the sake of my servant
David.' "
7Then Isaiah said, "Prepare a poultice of figs." They did so and applied it to the
boil,[f] and he recovered.
8Hezekiah had asked Isaiah, "What will be the sign that the LORD will heal me and
that I will go up to the temple of the LORD on the third day from now?"
9Isaiah answered, "This is the LORD's sign[g] to you that the LORD will do what he
has promised: Shall the shadow go forward ten steps, or shall it go back ten steps?"
10"It is a simple matter for the shadow to go forward ten steps," said Hezekiah.
"Rather, have it go back ten steps."
11Then the prophet Isaiah called upon the LORD, and the LORD made the shadow
go back[h] the ten steps it had gone down on the stairway of Ahaz.

Envoys From Babylon

12At that time Merodach-Baladan son of Baladan king of Babylon sent Hezekiah
letters and a gift, because he had heard of Hezekiah's illness. 13Hezekiah received
the messengers and showed them all that was in his storehouses — the silver, the gold,
the spices and the fine oil — his armoury and everything found among his treasures.
There was nothing in his palace or in all his kingdom that Hezekiah did not show them.
14Then Isaiah the prophet went to King Hezekiah and asked, "What did those men
say, and where did they come from?"
"From a distant land," Hezekiah replied. "They came from Babylon."
15The prophet asked, "What did they see in your palace?"
"They saw everything in my palace," Hezekiah said. "There is nothing among my
treasures that I did not show them."
16Then Isaiah said to Hezekiah, "Hear the word of the LORD: 17The time will surely
come when everything in your palace, and all that your fathers have stored up until
this day, will be carried off to Babylon.[i] Nothing will be left, says the LORD. 18And
some of your descendants,[j] your own flesh and blood, that will be born to you, will
be taken away, and they will become eunuchs in the palace of the king of Babylon."

20:3 [a]Ne 13:22 [b]2Ki 18:3-6
20:5 [c]1Sa 9:16; 1Ki 9:3; 2Ki 19:20 [d]Ps 39:12; 56:8
20:6 [e]2Ki 19:34
20:7 [f]Isa 38:21
20:9 [g]Dt 13:2; Jer 44:29
20:11 [h]Jos 10:13
20:17 [i]2Ki 24:13; 25:13; 2Ch 36:10; Jer 27:22; 52:17-23
20:18 [j]2Ki 24:15; 2Ch 33:11; Da 1:3

20:5, 6 Over a 100-year period of Judah's history (732–640 B.C.), Hezekiah was the only faithful king; but what a difference he made! Because of Hezekiah's faith and prayer, God healed him and saved his city from the Assyrians. You can make a difference too, even if your faith puts you in the minority. Faith and prayer, if they are sincere and directed toward the one true God, can change any situation.

20:11 The stairway of Ahaz was a sundial. Egyptian sundials in this period were sometimes made in the form of miniature staircases so that the shadows moved up and down the steps.

20:12–19 Hezekiah had been a good and faithful king. But when Isaiah asked him what he had shown the messengers from Babylon, he replied, "They saw everything in my palace." From the account in 2 Chronicles 32:24–31, it appears that Hezekiah's prosperity, success, and deliverance from sickness had made him proud. Rather than giving credit to God for all his blessings, he tried to impress the foreigners. When God helps us, we must not use his blessings to impress others. A testimony of victory can quickly degenerate into vanity and self-congratulations.

20:14 Babylon, a city that had rebelled against the Assyrian empire, was destroyed by Sennacherib in 689 B.C. This story probably occurred shortly before that date. When Sennacherib died in 681 B.C., his son, Esarhaddon, foolishly rebuilt the city of Babylon. Assyria, whose rulers at that time were weak, allowed Babylon plenty of opportunity to become strong. As the Assyrian army marched off to conquer and oppress faraway lands, the city of Babylon grew and expanded into a small nation. After some years, Babylon was strong enough to rebel again. It eventually crushed Assyria (612 B.C.) and became the next world power.

20:20 [k]Ne 3:16
21:1 [a]Isa 62:4
21:2 [b]Jer 15:4 [c]2Ki 16:3
21:3 [d]2Ki 18:4 [e]Jdg 6:28; 1Ki 16:32 [f]Dt 17:3; 2Ki 17:16
21:4 [g]Jer 32:34 [h]2Sa 7:13; 1Ki 8:29
21:5 [i]1Ki 7:12; 2Ki 23:12
21:6 [j]Lev 18:21; Dt 18:10; 2Ki 16:3; 17:17 [k]Lev 19:31
21:7 [l]Dt 16:21; 2Ki 23:4 [m]2Sa 7:13; 1Ki 8:29; 9:3; 2Ki 23:27; Jer 32:34
21:8 [n]2Sa 7:10 [o]2Ki 18:12
21:9 [p]Pr 29:12 [q]Dt 9:4
21:11 [r]2Ki 24:3-4 [s]Ge 15:16; 1Ki 21:26
21:12 [t]2Ki 23:26; 24:3; Jer 15:4 [u]1Sa 3:11; Jer 19:3
21:13 [v]Isa 34:11; La 2:8; Am 7:7-9 [w]2Ki 23:27
21:14 [x]Ps 78:58-60 [y]2Ki 19:4; Mic 2:12
21:15 [z]Ex 32:22 [a]Jer 25:7

19“The word of the LORD you have spoken is good,” Hezekiah replied. For he
thought, “Will there not be peace and security in my lifetime?”
20As for the other events of Hezekiah’s reign, all his achievements and how he made
the pool[k] and the tunnel by which he brought water into the city, are they not written
in the book of the annals of the kings of Judah? 21Hezekiah rested with his fathers.
And Manasseh his son succeeded him as king.

Manasseh King of Judah

21 Manasseh was twelve years old when he became king, and he reigned in
Jerusalem for fifty-five years. His mother’s name was Hephzibah.[a] 2He did
evil[b] in the eyes of the LORD, following the detestable practices[c] of the nations the
LORD had driven out before the Israelites. 3He rebuilt the high places[d] his father
Hezekiah had destroyed; he also erected altars to Baal[e] and made an Asherah pole,
as Ahab king of Israel had done. He bowed down to all the starry hosts[f] and
worshipped them. 4He built altars[g] in the temple of the LORD, of which the LORD
had said, “In Jerusalem I will put my Name.”[h] 5In both courts[i] of the temple of the
LORD, he built altars to all the starry hosts. 6He sacrificed his own son[j] in**[a]** the fire,
practised sorcery and divination, and consulted mediums and spiritists.[k] He did much
evil in the eyes of the LORD, provoking him to anger.
7He took the carved Asherah pole[l] he had made and put it in the temple, of which
the LORD had said to David and to his son Solomon, “In this temple and in Jerusalem,
which I have chosen out of all the tribes of Israel, I will put my Name[m] for ever. 8I
will not again[n] make the feet of the Israelites wander from the land I gave their
forefathers, if only they will be careful to do everything I commanded them and will
keep the whole Law that my servant Moses[o] gave them.” 9But the people did not
listen. Manasseh led them astray, so that they did more evil[p] than the nations[q] the
LORD had destroyed before the Israelites.
10The LORD said through his servants the prophets: 11“Manasseh king of Judah has
committed these detestable sins. He has done more evil[r] than the Amorites[s] who
preceded him and has led Judah into sin with his idols. 12Therefore this is what the
LORD, the God of Israel, says: I am going to bring such disaster[t] on Jerusalem and
Judah that the ears of everyone who hears of it will tingle.[u] 13I will stretch out over
Jerusalem the measuring line used against Samaria and the plumb-line[v] used against
the house of Ahab. I will wipe[w] out Jerusalem as one wipes out a dish, wiping it and
turning it upside-down. 14I will forsake[x] the remnant[y] of my inheritance and hand
them over to their enemies. They will be looted and plundered by all their foes,
15because they have done evil[z] in my eyes and have provoked[a] me to anger from
the day their forefathers came out of Egypt until this day.”

a *6* Or *He made his own son pass through*

20:19 Hezekiah was saying that it was good that these terrible events foretold by Isaiah wouldn’t happen during his lifetime. Hezekiah’s statement seems selfish, shortsighted, and proud. However, he knew that his nation would be punished for its sins, so he may have been acknowledging and thanking God for choosing not to destroy Judah during his lifetime.

20:20 The pool and the tunnel refer to a 1,777 foot tunnel built from the Gihon spring to the Pool of Siloam (see 2 Chronicles 32:30). It was from a water source outside the wall of Jerusalem to a secure reservoir inside the city. This was done so the Assyrian army would not cut off the city’s water supply.

21:1ff Manasseh followed the example of his grandfather Ahaz more than that of his father. He adopted the wicked practices of the Babylonians and Canaanites including sacrificing his own son (21:6). He did not listen to the words of God’s prophets, but wilfully led his people into sin. (See his Profile in 2 Chronicles 33 for more information about his life. The “high places” were shrines in the hills for worshipping idols.)

21:6 Manasseh was an evil king, and he angered God with his sin. Listed among his sins are occult practices—sorcery and divination, and consulting mediums and spiritists. These acts were strictly forbidden by God (Leviticus 19:31; Deuteronomy 18:9–13) because they demonstrate a lack of faith in him, involve sinful actions, and open the door to demonic influences. Today, many books, television shows, and games emphasise fortune-telling, séances, and other occult practices. Don’t let desire to know the future or the belief that superstition is harmless lead you into condoning occult practices. They are counterfeits of God’s power and have as their root a system of beliefs totally opposed to God.

21:7 Asherah was a Canaanite mother-goddess, a mistress of Baal. Her images were made of wood. In Exodus 34:13 and Deuteronomy 12:3, the Israelites were expressly forbidden to associate with Asherah practices in any way.

21:13 The measuring line and the plumb line symbolise the judgment process. These measuring instruments used in construction measured Jerusalem and the city was found lacking. God was saying that he would destroy Jerusalem as he did Samaria and the house of Ahab.

16 Moreover, Manasseh also shed so much innocent blood[b] that he filled Jerusalem
from end to end—besides the sin that he had caused Judah to commit, so that they
did evil in the eyes of the LORD.
17 As for the other events of Manasseh's reign, and all he did, including the sin he
committed, are they not written in the book of the annals of the kings of Judah?
18 Manasseh rested with his fathers and was buried in his palace garden,[c] the garden
of Uzza. And Amon his son succeeded him as king.

Amon King of Judah

19 Amon was twenty-two years old when he became king, and he reigned in
Jerusalem for two years. His mother's name was Meshullemeth daughter of Haruz;
she was from Jotbah. 20 He did evil[d] in the eyes of the LORD, as his father Manasseh
had done. 21 He walked in all the ways of his father; he worshipped the idols his father
had worshipped, and bowed down to them. 22 He forsook the LORD, the God of his
fathers, and did not walk[e] in the way of the LORD.
23 Amon's officials conspired against him and assassinated[f] the king in his palace.
24 Then the people of the land killed[g] all who had plotted against King Amon, and
they made Josiah his son king in his place.
25 As for the other events of Amon's reign, and what he did, are they not written
in the book of the annals of the kings of Judah? 26 He was buried in his grave in the
garden[h] of Uzza. And Josiah his son succeeded him as king.

The Book of the Law Found

22 Josiah was eight years old when he became king, and he reigned in Jerusalem
for thirty-one years. His mother's name was Jedidah daughter of Adaiah; she
was from Bozkath.[a] 2 He did what was right[b] in the eyes of the LORD and walked
in all the ways of his father David, not turning aside to the right[c] or to the left.
3 In the eighteenth year of his reign, King Josiah sent the secretary, Shaphan[d] son
of Azaliah, the son of Meshullam, to the temple of the LORD. He said: 4 "Go up to
Hilkiah the high priest and make him get ready the money that has been brought into
the temple of the LORD, which the doorkeepers have collected[e] from the people.
5 Make them entrust it to the men appointed to supervise the work on the temple. And
make these men pay the workers who repair[f] the temple of the LORD—6 the carpenters, the builders and the masons. Also make them purchase timber and dressed stone
to repair the temple.[g] 7 But they need not account for the money entrusted to them,
because they are acting faithfully."[h]
8 Hilkiah the high priest said to Shaphan the secretary, "I have found the Book of
the Law[i] in the temple of the LORD." He gave it to Shaphan, who read it. 9 Then
Shaphan the secretary went to the king and reported to him: "Your officials have paid
out the money that was in the temple of the LORD and have entrusted it to the workers
and supervisors at the temple." 10 Then Shaphan the secretary informed the king,
"Hilkiah the priest has given me a book." And Shaphan read from it in the presence
of the king.[j]
11 When the king heard the words of the Book of the Law, he tore his robes. 12 He

21:16 [b] 2Ki 24:4
21:18 [c] ver 26
21:20 [d] ver 2-6
21:22 [e] 1Ki 11:33
21:23 [f] 2Ki 12:20; 2Ch 33:24-25
21:24 [g] 2Ki 14:5
21:26 [h] ver 18
22:1 [a] Jos 15:39
22:2 [b] Dt 17:19 [c] Dt 5:32
22:3 [d] 2Ch 34:20; Jer 39:14
22:4 [e] 2Ki 12:4-5
22:5 [f] 2Ki 12:5, 11-14
22:6 [g] 2Ki 12:11-12
22:7 [h] 2Ki 12:15
22:8 [i] Dt 31:24
22:10 [j] Jer 36:21

21:16 Tradition says that during Manasseh's massive slaughter, Isaiah was sawn in two when trying to hide in a hollow log (see Hebrews 11:37, 38). Other prophets may also have been killed at this time.

22:1, 2 In reading the biblical lists of kings, it is rare to find one who obeyed God completely. Josiah was such a person, and he was only eight years old when he began to reign. For 18 years he reigned obediently; then, when he was 26, he began the reforms based on God's laws. Children are the future leaders of our churches and our world. A person's major work for God may have to wait until he is an adult, but no-one is ever too young to take God seriously and obey him. Josiah's early years laid the base for his later task of reforming Judah.

22:4 The doorkeepers controlled who entered the temple and supervised the collection of the money.

22:8 This book may have been the entire Pentateuch (Genesis—Deuteronomy) or just the book of Deuteronomy. Because of the long line of evil kings, the record of God's laws had been lost. Josiah, who was about 26 years old at this time, wanted religious reform throughout the nation. When God's word was found, drastic changes had to be made to bring the kingdom in line with God's commands. Today you have God's word at your fingertips. How much change must you make in order to bring your life into line with God's word?

22:11ff When Josiah heard the law, he tore his robes in grief. He immediately instituted reforms. With just one reading of God's law, he changed the course of the nation. Today many people own Bibles, but few are affected by the truths found in God's word. The

gave these orders to Hilkiah the priest, Ahikam[k] son of Shaphan, Acbor son of
Micaiah, Shaphan the secretary and Asaiah the king's attendant: 13"Go and enquire
of the LORD for me and for the people and for all Judah about what is written in this
book that has been found. Great is the LORD's anger[l] that burns against us because
our fathers have not obeyed the words of this book; they have not acted in accordance
with all that is written there concerning us."
14Hilkiah the priest, Ahikam, Acbor, Shaphan and Asaiah went to speak to the
prophetess Huldah, who was the wife of Shallum son of Tikvah, the son of Harhas,
keeper of the wardrobe. She lived in Jerusalem, in the Second District.
15She said to them, "This is what the LORD, the God of Israel, says: Tell the man
who sent you to me, 16'This is what the LORD says: I am going to bring disaster[m]
on this place and its people, according to everything written in the book[n] the king
of Judah has read. 17Because they have forsaken[o] me and burned incense to other
gods and provoked me to anger by all the idols their hands have made,[a] my anger
will burn against this place and will not be quenched.' 18Tell the king of Judah, who
sent you to enquire[p] of the LORD, 'This is what the LORD, the God of Israel, says
concerning the words you heard: 19Because your heart was responsive and you
humbled[q] yourself before the LORD when you heard what I have spoken against this
place and its people, that they would become accursed[r] and laid waste,[s] and because
you tore your robes and wept in my presence, I have heard you, declares the LORD.
20Therefore I will gather you to your fathers, and you will be buried in peace.[t] Your
eyes will not see all the disaster I am going to bring on this place.' "
So they took her answer back to the king.

Josiah Renews the Covenant

23 Then the king called together all the elders of Judah and Jerusalem. 2He went
up to the temple of the LORD with the men of Judah, the people of Jerusalem,
the priests and the prophets—all the people from the least to the greatest. He read[a]
in their hearing all the words of the Book of the Covenant, which had been found in
the temple of the LORD. 3The king stood by the pillar and renewed the covenant[b] in
the presence of the LORD—to follow[c] the LORD and keep his commands, regulations
and decrees with all his heart and all his soul, thus confirming the words of the
covenant written in this book. Then all the people pledged themselves to the covenant.
4The king ordered Hilkiah the high priest, the priests next in rank and the doorkeepers[d] to remove[e] from the temple of the LORD all the articles made for Baal and
Asherah and all the starry hosts. He burned them outside Jerusalem in the fields of
the Kidron Valley and took the ashes to Bethel. 5He did away with the pagan priests
appointed by the kings of Judah to burn incense on the high places of the towns of
Judah and on those around Jerusalem—those who burned incense to Baal, to the sun
and moon, to the constellations and to all the starry hosts.[f] 6He took the Asherah
pole from the temple of the LORD to the Kidron Valley outside Jerusalem and burned
it there. He ground it to powder and scattered the dust over the graves of the common

22:12 [k]2Ki 25:22; Jer 26:24
22:13 [l]Dt 29:24-28; 31:17
22:16 [m]Dt 31:29; Jos 23:15 [n]Dt 29:27; Da 9:11
22:17 [o]Dt 29:25-27
22:18 [p]2Ch 34:26; Jer 21:2
22:19 [q]Ex 10:3; 1Ki 21:29; Ps 51:17; Isa 57:15; Mic 6:8 [r]Jer 26:6 [s]Lev 26:31
22:20 [t]Isa 57:1
23:2 [a]Dt 31:11; 2Ki 22:8
23:3 [b]2Ki 11:14, 17 [c]Dt 13:4
23:4 [d]2Ki 25:18 [e]2Ki 21:7
23:5 [f]2Ki 21:3; Jer 8:2

a *17 Or by everything they have done*

---

word of God should cause us, like Josiah, to take action immediately to reform our lives and bring them into harmony with God's will.

22:14 Huldah was a prophetess, as were Miriam (Exodus 15:20) and Deborah (Judges 4:4). God freely selects his servants to carry out his will—rich or poor, male or female, king or slave (Joel 2:28–30). Huldah was obviously highly regarded by the people of her time.

22:19 When Josiah realised how corrupt his nation had become, he tore his robes and wept before God. Then God had mercy on him. Josiah used the customs of his day to show his repentance. When we repent today, we are unlikely to tear our clothing, but weeping, fasting, making restitution or apologies (if our sin has involved others) demonstrate our sincerity when we repent. The hardest part of repentance is changing the attitudes that originally produced the sinful behaviour.

23:1, 2 For more about the importance and operation of the temple, see 1 Kings 5–8 and 2 Chronicles 2–7.

23:4–8 When Josiah realised the terrible state of Judah's religious life, he did something about it. It is not enough to say we believe what is right; we must respond with action, doing what faith requires. This is what James was emphasising when he wrote, "faith without deeds is useless" (James 2:20). This means acting differently at home, school, work, and church. Simply talking about obedience is not enough.

23:6 This shameful Asherah pole had been set up in God's temple by the evil King Manasseh (21:7). Asherah is most often identified as a sea goddess and the mistress of Baal. She was a chief goddess of the Canaanites. Her worship glorified sex and war and was accompanied by male prostitution.

people.[g] 7He also tore down the quarters of the male shrine-prostitutes,[h] which were
in the temple of the LORD and where women did weaving for Asherah.
8Josiah brought all the priests from the towns of Judah and desecrated the high
places, from Geba[i] to Beersheba, where the priests had burned incense. He broke
down the shrines[a] at the gates—at the entrance to the Gate of Joshua, the city
governor, which is on the left of the city gate. 9Although the priests of the high places
did not serve[j] at the altar of the LORD in Jerusalem, they ate unleavened bread with
their fellow priests.
10He desecrated Topheth,[k] which was in the Valley of Ben Hinnom,[l] so no-one
could use it to sacrifice his son[m] or daughter in[b] the fire to Molech. 11He removed
from the entrance to the temple of the LORD the horses that the kings of Judah had
dedicated to the sun. They were in the court near the room of an official named
Nathan-Melech. Josiah then burned the chariots dedicated to the sun.[n]
12He pulled down the altars the kings of Judah had erected on the roof[o] near the
upper room of Ahaz, and the altars Manasseh had built in the two courts[p] of the
temple of the LORD. He removed them from there, smashed them to pieces and threw
the rubble into the Kidron Valley. 13The king also desecrated the high places that were
east of Jerusalem on the south of the Hill of Corruption—the ones Solomon[q] king
of Israel had built for Ashtoreth the vile goddess of the Sidonians, for Chemosh the
vile god of Moab, and for Molech[c] the detestable god of the people of Ammon.
14Josiah smashed[r] the sacred stones and cut down the Asherah poles and covered the
sites with human bones.
15Even the altar[s] at Bethel, the high place made by Jeroboam[t] son of Nebat, who
had caused Israel to sin—even that altar and high place he demolished. He burned
the high place and ground it to powder, and burned the Asherah pole also. 16Then
Josiah[u] looked around, and when he saw the tombs that were there on the hillside,
he had the bones removed from them and burned on the altar to defile it, in accordance
with the word of the LORD proclaimed by the man of God who foretold these things.
17The king asked, "What is that tombstone I see?"
The men of the city said, "It marks the tomb of the man of God who came from
Judah and pronounced against the altar of Bethel the very things you have done to
it."
18"Leave it alone," he said. "Don't let anyone disturb his bones[v]." So they spared
his bones and those of the prophet who had come from Samaria.
19Just as he had done at Bethel, Josiah removed and defiled all the shrines at the
high places that the kings of Israel had built in the towns of Samaria that had provoked
the LORD to anger. 20Josiah slaughtered[w] all the priests of those high places on the
altars and burned human bones[x] on them. Then he went back to Jerusalem.
21The king gave this order to all the people: "Celebrate the Passover[y] to the LORD
your God, as it is written in this Book of the Covenant." 22Not since the days of the
judges who led Israel, nor throughout the days of the kings of Israel and the kings
of Judah, had any such Passover been observed. 23But in the eighteenth year of King
Josiah, this Passover was celebrated to the LORD in Jerusalem.
24Furthermore, Josiah got rid of the mediums and spiritists,[z] the household gods,[a]
the idols and all the other detestable things seen in Judah and Jerusalem. This he did

[a] 8 Or *high places* [b] 10 Or *to make his son or daughter pass through* [c] 13 Hebrew *Milcom*

23:6 [g] Jer 26:23
23:7 [h] 1Ki 14:24; 15:12; Eze 16:16
23:8 [i] 1Ki 15:22
23:9 [j] Eze 44:10-14
23:10 [k] Isa 30:33; Jer 7:31, 32; 19:6 [l] Jos 15:8 [m] Lev 18:21; Dt 18:10
23:11 [n] Dt 4:19
23:12 [o] Jer 19:13; Zep 1:5 [p] 2Ki 21:5
23:13 [q] 1Ki 11:7
23:14 [r] Ex 23:24; Dt 7:5, 25
23:15 [s] 1Ki 13:1-3 [t] 1Ki 12:33
23:16 [u] 1Ki 13:2
23:18 [v] 1Ki 13:31
23:20 [w] Ex 22:20; 2Ki 10:25; 11:18 [x] 1Ki 13:2
23:21 [y] Ex 12:11; Nu 9:2; Dt 16:1-8
23:24 [z] Lev 19:31; Dt 18:11; 2Ki 21:6 [a] Ge 31:19

23:11 These horses were used in processions honouring the sun.

23:13 The Mount of Olives is here called the Hill of Corruption because it had become a favourite spot to build pagan shrines. Solomon built a pagan shrine and other kings built places of idol worship there. But God-fearing kings such as Hezekiah and Josiah destroyed these pagan worship centres. In New Testament times, Jesus often sat on the Mount of Olives and taught his disciples about serving only God (Matthew 24:3). For more background on Ashtoreth, Chemosh, and Molech, see the note on 1 Kings 11:5–8.

23:16–18 The prophecies mentioned in this passage appear in 1 Kings 13:20–32.

23:21–23 When Josiah rediscovered the Passover in the Book of the Covenant, he ordered everyone to observe the ceremonies exactly as prescribed. This Passover celebration was to have been a yearly holiday celebrated in remembrance of the entire nation's deliverance from slavery in Egypt (Exodus 12), but it had not been kept for many years. As a result, "not since the days of the judges who led Israel, nor throughout the days of the kings of Israel and the kings of Judah, had any such Passover been observed". It is a common misconception that God is against celebration, wanting to take all the fun out of life. In reality, God wants to give us life in its fullness (John 10:10), and those who love him have the most to celebrate.

23:25 [b]2Ki 18:5
23:26 [c]2Ki 21:12; Jer 15:4
23:27 [d]2Ki 21:13 [e]2Ki 18:11

to fulfil the requirements of the law written in the book that Hilkiah the priest had
discovered in the temple of the LORD. 25Neither before nor after Josiah was there a
king like him who turned[b] to the LORD as he did—with all his heart and with all his
soul and with all his strength, in accordance with all the Law of Moses.
26Nevertheless, the LORD did not turn away from the heat of his fierce anger, which
burned against Judah because of all that Manasseh[c] had done to provoke him to anger.
27So the LORD said, "I will remove[d] Judah also from my presence[e] as I removed

JOSIAH

Josiah never knew his great-grandfather Hezekiah, but they were alike in many ways. Both had close, personal relationships with God. Both were passionate reformers, making valiant efforts to lead their people back to God. Both were bright flashes of obedience to God among kings with darkened consciences, who seemed bent on outdoing each other in disobedience and evil.

Although Josiah's father and grandfather were exceptionally wicked, his life is an example of God's willingness to provide ongoing guidance to those who set out to be obedient. At a young age, Josiah already understood that there was spiritual sickness in his land. Idols were sprouting in the countryside faster than crops. In a sense, Josiah began his search for God by destroying and cleaning up whatever he recognised as not belonging to the worship of the true God. In the process, God's word was rediscovered. The king's intentions and the power of God's written revelation were brought together.

As the Book of God's Law was read to Josiah, he was shocked, frightened, and humbled. He realised what a great gap existed between his efforts to lead his people to God and God's expectations for his chosen nation. He was overwhelmed by God's holiness and immediately tried to expose his people to that holiness. The people did respond, but the Bible makes it clear that their renewed worship of God was much more out of respect for Josiah than out of personal understanding of their own guilt before God.

How would you describe your relationship with God? Are your feeble efforts at holiness based mostly on a desire to "go along" with a well-liked leader or popular opinion? Or are you, like Josiah, deeply humbled by God's word, realising that great gap between your life and the kind of life God expects, realising your deep need to be cleansed and renewed by him? Humble obedience pleases God. Good intentions, even reforms, are not enough. You must allow God's word to truly humble you and change your life.

Strengths and accomplishments:
- Was king of Judah
- Sought after God and was open to him
- Was a reformer like his great-grandfather Hezekiah
- Cleaned out the temple and revived obedience to God's law

Weakness and mistake:
- Became involved in a military conflict that he had been warned against

Lessons from his life:
- God consistently responds to those with repentant and humble hearts
- Even sweeping outward reforms are of little lasting value if there are no changes in people's lives

Vital statistics:
- Where: Jerusalem
- Occupation: 16th king of Judah, the southern kingdom
- Relatives: Father: Amon. Mother: Jedidah. Son: Jehoahaz
- Contemporaries: Jeremiah, Huldah, Hilkiah, Zephaniah

Key verse:
"Neither before nor after Josiah was there a king like him who turned to the LORD as he did—with all his heart and with all his soul and with all his strength, in accordance with all the Law of Moses" (2 Kings 23:25).

Josiah's story is told in 2 Kings 21:24—23:30; 2 Chronicles 33:25—35:26. He is also mentioned in Jeremiah 1:1–3; 22:11, 18.

23:25 Josiah is remembered as Judah's most obedient king. His obedience followed this pattern: (1) he recognised sin; (2) he eliminated sinful practices; (3) he attacked the causes of sin. This approach for dealing with sin is still effective today. Not only must we remove sinful actions, we must also eliminate causes for sin—those situations, relationships, routines, and patterns of life that lead us to the door of temptation.

23:25 Both Josiah and Hezekiah (18:5) are praised for their reverence towards God. Hezekiah was said to be greatest in trusting God (faith), while Josiah is said to be greatest in following the law of God (obedience). May we follow their example through our trust in God and our obedient actions.

Israel, and I will reject Jerusalem, the city I chose, and this temple, about which I
said, 'There shall my Name be.'[d]"
28 As for the other events of Josiah's reign, and all he did, are they not written in
the book of the annals of the kings of Judah?
29 While Josiah was king, Pharaoh Neco[f] king of Egypt went up to the Euphrates
River to help the king of Assyria. King Josiah marched out to meet him in battle, but
Neco faced him and killed him at Megiddo.[g] 30 Josiah's servants brought his body
in a chariot[h] from Megiddo to Jerusalem and buried him in his own tomb. And the
people of the land took Jehoahaz son of Josiah and anointed him and made him king
in place of his father.

Jehoahaz King of Judah

31 Jehoahaz[i] was twenty-three years old when he became king, and he reigned in
Jerusalem for three months. His mother's name was Hamutal[j] daughter of Jeremiah;
she was from Libnah. 32 He did evil in the eyes of the LORD, just as his fathers had
done. 33 Pharaoh Neco put him in chains at Riblah[k] in the land of Hamath[e][l] so that
he might not reign in Jerusalem, and he imposed on Judah a levy of a hundred talents[f]
of silver and a talent[g] of gold. 34 Pharaoh Neco made Eliakim[m] son of Josiah king
in place of his father Josiah and changed Eliakim's name to Jehoiakim. But he took
Jehoahaz and carried him off to Egypt, and there he died.[n] 35 Jehoiakim paid Pharaoh
Neco the silver and gold he demanded. In order to do so, he taxed the land and exacted
the silver and gold from the people of the land according to their assessments.[o]

2. Judah is exiled to Babylon

Jehoiakim King of Judah

36 Jehoiakim[p] was twenty-five years old when he became king, and he reigned in
Jerusalem for eleven years. His mother's name was Zebidah daughter of Pedaiah; she
was from Rumah. 37 And he did evil in the eyes of the LORD, just as his fathers had
done.

24 During Jehoiakim's reign, Nebuchadnezzar[a] king of Babylon invaded the
land, and Jehoiakim became his vassal for three years. But then he changed
his mind and rebelled against Nebuchadnezzar. 2 The LORD sent Babylonian,[a] Ara-

[d] *27* 1 Kings 8:29 [e] *33* Hebrew; Septuagint (see also 2 Chron. 36:3) *Neco at Riblah in Hamath removed him*
[f] *33* That is, about 3½ tons (about 3.4 metric tons) [g] *33* That is, about 75 pounds (about 34 kilograms)
[a] *2* Or *Chaldean*

23:29 [f] Jer 46:2 [g] Zec 12:11
23:30 [h] 2Ki 9:28
23:31 [i] 1Ch 3:15; Jer 22:11 [j] 2Ki 24:18
23:33 [k] 2Ki 25:6 [l] 1Ki 8:65
23:34 [m] 1Ch 3:15; 2Ch 36:5-8 [n] Jer 22:12; Eze 19:3-4
23:35 [o] ver 33
23:36 [p] Jer 26:1
24:1 [a] Jer 25:1, 9; Da 1:1

23:29 Pharaoh Neco of Egypt was marching through Judah to Assyria. Egypt and Assyria had formed an alliance to battle Babylon, which was threatening to become the dominant world power. Josiah may have thought that both nations would turn on him after the battle with Babylon, so he tried to stop Egypt's army from marching through his land. But Josiah was killed, his army was defeated, and the nation of Judah became a vassal of Egypt (609 B.C.). A more detailed account of this story is found in 2 Chronicles 35:20–25.

23:31–34 The people appointed Jehoahaz, one of Josiah's sons, to be Judah's next king. But Neco was not happy with their choice, and he exiled Jehoahaz to Egypt, where he died. Neco then appointed Eliakim, another of Josiah's sons, king of Judah, changing his name to Jehoiakim. Jehoiakim was little more than a puppet ruler. In 605 B.C., Egypt was defeated by Babylon. Judah then became a vassal of Babylon (24:1).

23:36, 37 Josiah followed God, but Jehoiakim, his son, was evil. He killed the prophet Uriah (Jeremiah 26:20–23) and was dishonest, greedy, and unjust with the people (Jeremiah 22:13–19). Jehoiakim also rebelled against Babylon, switching his allegiance to Egypt. This proved to be a crucial mistake. Nebuchadnezzar crushed Jehoiakim's rebellion and took him to Babylon (2 Chronicles 36:6), but he was eventually allowed to return to Jerusalem, where he died. The Bible does not record the cause of Jehoiakim's death.

23:37 Many good kings had children who did not turn out to follow God. Perhaps it was because of neglect or preoccupation with political and military affairs or because these kings delegated the religious education to others. No doubt many of the children simply rebelled at the way they were raised. Being a strong believer as a parent doesn't guarantee that your children will pick up your beliefs. Children must be taught about faith, and parents dare not leave that task for others to do. Make sure you practise, explain, and teach what you preach.

24:1 Babylon became the new world power after overthrowing Assyria in 612 B.C. and defeating Egypt at the battle of Carchemish in 605 B.C. After defeating Egypt, the Babylonians invaded Judah and brought it under their control. This was the first of three Babylonian invasions of Judah over the next 20 years. The other two invasions occurred in 597 and 586 B.C. With each invasion, captives were taken back to Babylon. Daniel, who wrote the book of Daniel, was one of the captives taken during this first invasion (605 B.C.; Daniel 1:1–6).

24:1 For more information on Nebuchadnezzar, see his Profile in Daniel 3.

24:1–4 Nebuchadnezzar took control as king of Babylon in 605 B.C. Earlier that year Nebuchadnezzar had defeated the Egyptians led by Pharaoh Neco at Carchemish. Thus Babylon took control of

24:2 [b]Jer 35:11 [c]Jer 25:9
24:3 [d]2Ki 18:25 [e]2Ki 21:12; 23:26
24:4 [f]2Ki 21:16
24:6 [g]Jer 22:19
24:7 [h]Ge 15:18 [i]Jer 37:5-7; 46:2
24:8 [j]1Ch 3:16
24:10 [k]Da 1:1
24:12 [l]2Ki 25:27; Jer 22:24-30; 24:1; 25:1; 29:2; 52:28
24:13 [m]2Ki 20:17 [n]2Ki 25:15; Isa 39:6 [o]2Ki 25:14; Jer 20:5 [p]1Ki 7:51
24:14 [q]Jer 24:1; 52:28 [r]2Ki 25:12; Jer 40:7; 52:16
24:15 [s]Jer 22:24-28 [t]Est 2:6; Eze 17:12-14
24:16 [u]Jer 52:28
24:17 [v]1Ch 3:15; 2Ch 36:11; Jer 37:1
24:18 [w]Jer 52:1 [x]2Ki 23:31
24:20 [y]Dt 4:26; 29:27

mean,[b] Moabite and Ammonite raiders against him. He sent them to destroy[c] Judah,
in accordance with the word of the LORD proclaimed by his servants the prophets.
3 Surely these things happened to Judah according to the LORD's command,[d] in order
to remove them from his presence because of the sins of Manasseh[e] and all he had
done, 4 including the shedding of innocent blood.[f] For he had filled Jerusalem with
innocent blood, and the LORD was not willing to forgive.
5 As for the other events of Jehoiakim's reign, and all he did, are they not written
in the book of the annals of the kings of Judah? 6 Jehoiakim rested[g] with his fathers.
And Jehoiachin his son succeeded him as king.
7 The king of Egypt[h] did not march out from his own country again, because the
king of Babylon[i] had taken all his territory, from the Wadi of Egypt to the Euphrates
River.

Jehoiachin King of Judah

8 Jehoiachin[j] was eighteen years old when he became king, and he reigned in
Jerusalem for three months. His mother's name was Nehushta daughter of Elnathan;
she was from Jerusalem. 9 He did evil in the eyes of the LORD, just as his father had
done.
10 At that time the officers of Nebuchadnezzar[k] king of Babylon advanced on
Jerusalem and laid siege to it, 11 and Nebuchadnezzar himself came up to the city while
his officers were besieging it. 12 Jehoiachin king of Judah, his mother, his attendants,
his nobles and his officials all surrendered[l] to him.
In the eighth year of the reign of the king of Babylon, he took Jehoiachin prisoner.
13 As the LORD had declared,[m] Nebuchadnezzar removed all the treasures[n] from the
temple of the LORD and from the royal palace, and took away all the gold articles[o]
that Solomon[p] king of Israel had made for the temple of the LORD. 14 He carried
into exile[q] all Jerusalem: all the officers and fighting men, and all the craftsmen
and artisans—a total of ten thousand. Only the poorest[r] people of the land were
left.
15 Nebuchadnezzar took Jehoiachin captive to Babylon. He also took from Jerusalem to Babylon the king's mother,[s] his wives, his officials and the leading men[t]
of the land. 16 The king of Babylon also deported to Babylon the entire force of seven
thousand fighting men, strong and fit for war, and a thousand craftsmen and artisans.[u]
17 He made Mattaniah, Jehoiachin's uncle, king in his place and changed his name to
Zedekiah.[v]

Zedekiah King of Judah

18 Zedekiah[w] was twenty-one years old when he became king, and he reigned in
Jerusalem for eleven years. His mother's name was Hamutal[x] daughter of Jeremiah;
she was from Libnah. 19 He did evil in the eyes of the LORD, just as Jehoiakim had
done. 20 It was because of the LORD's anger that all this happened to Jerusalem and
Judah, and in the end he thrust[y] them from his presence.

---

all Egypt's vassals (including Judah). Nebuchadnezzar invaded the land later in order to establish his rule by force.

24:10 Babylonian troops were already on the march to crush Jehoiakim's rebellion when he died. After Jehoiakim's death, his son Jehoiachin became king of Judah, only to face the mightiest army on earth just weeks after he was crowned (597 B.C.). During this second of three invasions, the Babylonians looted the temple and took most of the leaders captive, including the king. Then Nebuchadnezzar placed Zedekiah, another son of Josiah, on the throne. The Jews, however, didn't recognise him as their true king as long as Jehoiachin was still alive, even though he was a captive in Babylon.

24:14 The Babylonian policy for taking captives was different from that of the Assyrians who moved most of the people out and resettled the land with foreigners (see the note on 17:24). The Babylonians took only the strong and skilled, leaving the poor and weak to rule the land, thus elevating them to positions of authority and winning their loyalty. The leaders were taken to Babylonian cities where they were permitted to live together, find jobs, and become an important part of the society. This policy kept the Jews united and faithful to God throughout the captivity and made it possible for their return in the days of Zerubbabel and Ezra as recorded in the book of Ezra.

The Fall of Jerusalem

Now Zedekiah rebelled against the king of Babylon.
25 So in the ninth year of Zedekiah's reign, on the tenth day of the tenth month,
Nebuchadnezzar[a] king of Babylon marched against Jerusalem with his whole
army. He encamped outside the city and built siege works[b] all around it. 2The city
was kept under siege until the eleventh year of King Zedekiah. 3By the ninth day of
the ⌞fourth⌟ **[a]** month the famine[c] in the city had become so severe that there was no
food for the people to eat. 4Then the city wall was broken through,[d] and the whole
army fled at night through the gate between the two walls near the king's garden,
though the Babylonians**[b]** were surrounding[e] the city. They fled towards the Arabah,**[c]** 5but the Babylonian**[d]** army pursued the king and overtook him in the plains
of Jericho. All his soldiers were separated from him and scattered,[f] 6and he was
captured.[g] He was taken to the king of Babylon at Riblah,[h] where sentence was
pronounced on him. 7They killed the sons of Zedekiah before his eyes. Then they put
out his eyes, bound him with bronze shackles and took him to Babylon.[i]
8On the seventh day of the fifth month, in the nineteenth year of Nebuchadnezzar
king of Babylon, Nebuzaradan commander of the imperial guard, an official of the
king of Babylon, came to Jerusalem. 9He set fire[j] to the temple of the LORD, the
royal palace and all the houses of Jerusalem. Every important building he burned
down.[k] 10The whole Babylonian army, under the commander of the imperial guard,
broke down the walls[l] around Jerusalem. 11Nebuzaradan the commander of the guard
carried into exile[m] the people who remained in the city, along with the rest of the
populace and those who had gone over to the king of Babylon.[n] 12But the commander
left behind some of the poorest people[o] of the land to work the vineyards and fields.
13The Babylonians broke up the bronze pillars, the movable stands and the bronze
Sea that were at the temple of the LORD and they carried the bronze to Babylon. 14They
also took away the pots, shovels, wick trimmers, dishes and all the bronze articles[p]
used in the temple service. 15The commander of the imperial guard took away the
censers and sprinkling bowls—all that were made of pure gold or silver.
16The bronze from the two pillars, the Sea and the movable stands, which Solomon
had made for the temple of the LORD, was more than could be weighed. 17Each pillar[q]
was twenty-seven feet**[e]** high. The bronze capital on top of one pillar was four and
a half feet**[f]** high and was decorated with a network and pomegranates of bronze all
around. The other pillar, with its network, was similar.

a *3* See Jer. 52:6. **b** *4* Or *Chaldeans*; also in verses 13, 25 and 26 **c** *4* Or *the Jordan Valley* **d** *5* Or *Chaldean*; also in verses 10 and 24 **e** *17* Hebrew *eighteen cubits* (about 8.2 metres) **f** *17* Hebrew *three cubits* (about 1.4 metres)

25:1 [a]Jer 34:1-7 [b]Eze 24:2
25:3 [c]Jer 14:18; La 4:9
25:4 [d]Eze 33:21 [e]Jer 4:17
25:5 [f]Eze 12:14
25:6 [g]Jer 34:21-22 [h]2Ki 23:33
25:7 [i]Jer 21:7; 32:4-5; Eze 12:11
25:9 [j]Isa 60:7 [k]Ps 74:3-8; Jer 2:15; Am 2:5; Mic 3:12
25:10 [l]Ne 1:3
25:11 [m]2Ki 24:14 [n]2Ki 24:1
25:12 [o]2Ki 24:14
25:14 [p]Ex 27:3; 1Ki 7:47-50
25:17 [q]1Ki 7:15-22

25:1 Judah was invaded by the Babylonians three times (24:1; 24:10; 25:1), just as Israel was invaded by the Assyrians three times. Once again, God demonstrated his mercy in the face of deserved judgment by giving the people repeated opportunities to repent.

25:13 The bronze Sea was used to contain the huge reservoir of water for ritual cleansing for the priests. The bronze was so valuable that it was broken up and carried off to Babylon.

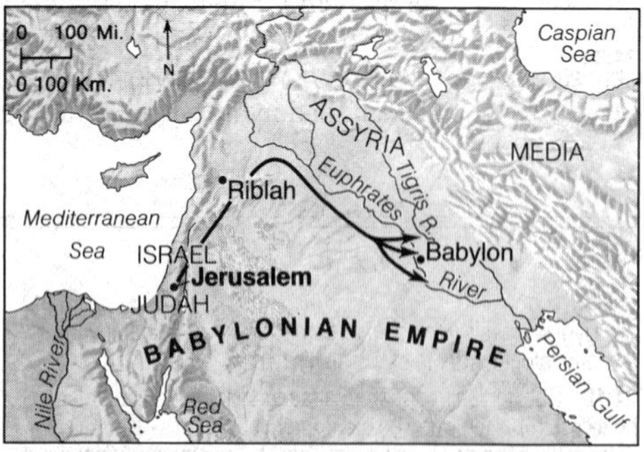

JUDAH EXILED Evil permeated Judah, and God's anger flared against his rebellious people. Babylon conquered Assyria and became the new world power. The Babylonian army marched into Jerusalem, burned the temple, tore down the city's massive walls, and carried off the people into captivity.

25:18
[r] 1Ch 6:14; Ezr 7:1; Ne 11:11
[s] Jer 21:1; 29:25

25:21
[t] Ge 12:7; Dt 28:64; Jos 23:13; 2Ki 23:27

25:22
[u] Jer 39:14; 40:5, 7

18The commander of the guard took as prisoners Seraiah[r] the chief priest, Zephaniah[s] the priest next in rank and the three doorkeepers. 19Of those still in the city,
he took the officer in charge of the fighting men and five royal advisers. He also took
the secretary who was chief officer in charge of conscripting the people of the land
and sixty of his men who were found in the city. 20Nebuzaradan the commander took
them all and brought them to the king of Babylon at Riblah. 21There at Riblah, in the
land of Hamath, the king had them executed.
So Judah went into captivity, away from her land.[t]
22Nebuchadnezzar king of Babylon appointed Gedaliah[u] son of Ahikam, the son
of Shaphan, to be over the people he had left behind in Judah. 23When all the army
officers and their men heard that the king of Babylon had appointed Gedaliah as
governor, they came to Gedaliah at Mizpah—Ishmael son of Nethaniah, Johanan son
of Kareah, Seraiah son of Tanhumeth the Netophathite, Jaazaniah the son of the
Maacathite, and their men. 24Gedaliah took an oath to reassure them and their men.
"Do not be afraid of the Babylonian officials," he said. "Settle down in the land and
serve the king of Babylon, and it will go well with you."
25In the seventh month, however, Ishmael son of Nethaniah, the son of Elishama,
who was of royal blood, came with ten men and assassinated Gedaliah and also the

KINGS TO DATE AND THEIR ENEMIES

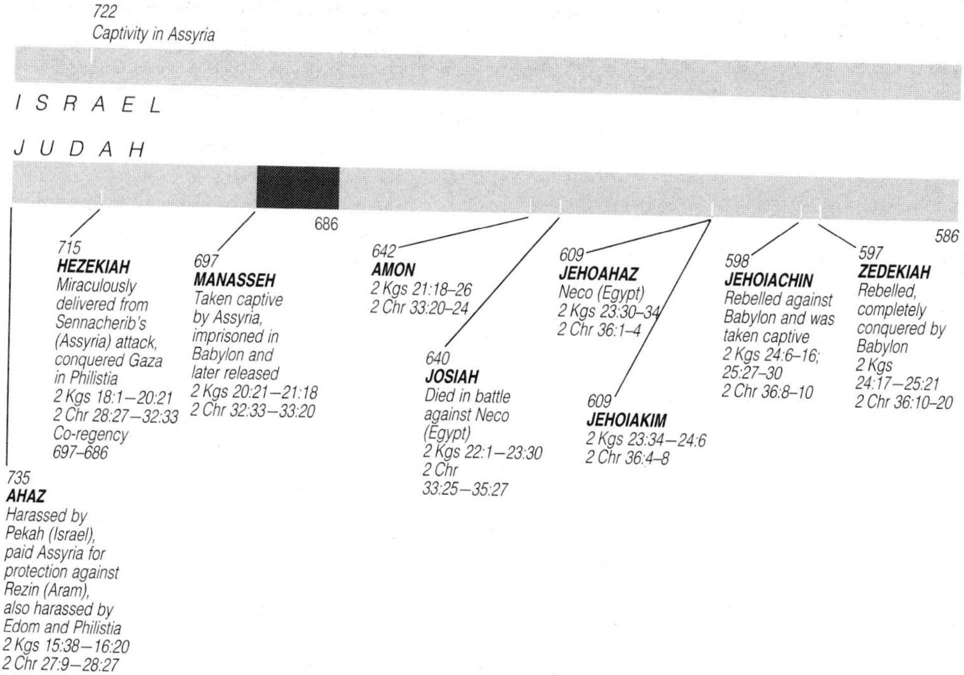

All dates are B.C.
Solid section of the timeline indicates co-regency.
For all the kings of Israel and Judah, see the chart at the end of 1 Kings.

25:21 Judah, like Israel, was unfaithful to God. So God, as he had warned, allowed Judah to be destroyed and taken away (Deuteronomy 28). The book of Lamentations records the prophet Jeremiah's sorrow at seeing Jerusalem destroyed.

25:22 In place of the king (Zedekiah) who was deported to Babylon, Nebuchadnezzar appointed a governor (Gedaliah) who would faithfully administer the Babylonian policies.

25:22–30 This story shows that Israel's last hope of gaining back its land was gone—even the army officers (now guerrilla rebels) had fled. Judah's earthly kingdom was absolutely demolished. But through prophets like Ezekiel and Daniel, who were also captives, God was able to keep his spiritual kingdom alive in the hearts of many of the exiles.

men of Judah and the Babylonians who were with him at Mizpah. 26At this, all the
people from the least to the greatest, together with the army officers, fled to Egypt[v]
for fear of the Babylonians.

Jehoiachin Released

27In the thirty-seventh year of the exile of Jehoiachin king of Judah, in the year
Evil-Merodach[g] became king of Babylon, he released Jehoiachin[w] from prison on
the twenty-seventh day of the twelfth month. 28He spoke kindly to him and gave him
a seat of honour[x] higher than those of the other kings who were with him in Babylon.
29So Jehoiachin put aside his prison clothes and for the rest of his life ate regularly
at the king's table.[y] 30Day by day the king gave Jehoiachin a regular allowance as
long as he lived.[z]

g *27* Also called *Amel-Marduk*

25:26 [v]Isa 30:2; Jer 43:7
25:27 [w]2Ki 24:12; Jer 52:31-34
25:28 [x]Ezr 5:5; Ne 2:1; Da 2:48
25:29 [y]2Sa 9:7
25:30 [z]Est 2:9; Jer 28:4

25:27 Evil-Merodach, the son of Nebuchadnezzar, became king of the Babylonian empire in 562 B.C., 24 years after the beginning of the general captivity and 37 years after Jehoiachin was removed from Jerusalem. The new king treated Jehoiachin with kindness, even allowing him to eat at his table (25:29). Evil-Merodach was later killed in a plot by his brother-in-law, Nergal-Sharezer, who succeeded him to the throne.

25:30 The book of 2 Kings opens with Elijah being carried to heaven – the destination awaiting those who follow God. But the book ends with the people of Judah being carried off to foreign lands as humiliated slaves – the result of failing to follow God.

Second Kings is an illustration of what happens when we make anything more important than God, when we make ruinous alliances, when our consciences become desensitised to right and wrong, and when we are no longer able to discern God's purpose for our lives. We may fail, like the people of Judah and Israel, but God's promises do not. He is always there to help us straighten out our lives and start again. And that is just what would happen in the book of Ezra. When the people acknowledged their sins, God was ready and willing to help them return to their land and start again.

KEY PLACES IN 1 CHRONICLES

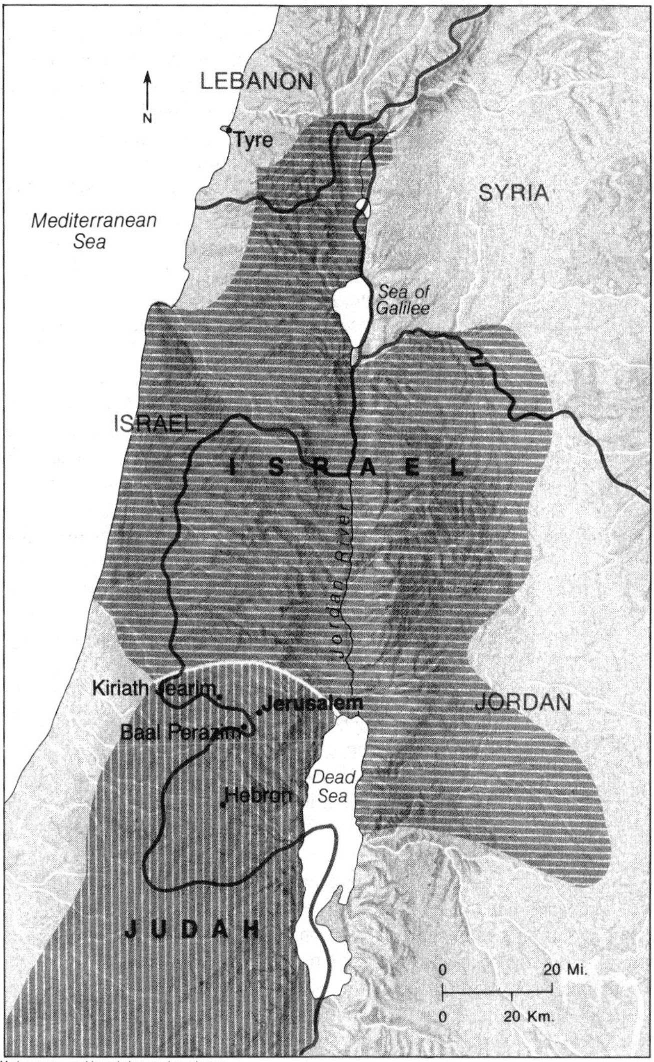

Modern names and boundaries are shown in grey.

1 Hebron Although David had been anointed king years earlier, his reign began when the leaders of Israel accepted him as king at Hebron (11:1–3).

2 Jerusalem David set out to complete the conquest of the land begun by Joshua. He attacked Jerusalem, captured it, and made it his capital (11:4—12:40).

3 Kiriath Jearim The ark of the covenant, which had been captured by the Philistines in battle and returned (1 Samuel 4—6), was in safekeeping in Kiriath Jearim. David summoned all Israel to this city to join in bringing the ark to Jerusalem. Unfortunately, it was not moved according to God's instructions, and as a result one man died. David left the ark in the home of Obed-Edom until he could discover how to transport it correctly (13:1–14).

4 Tyre David did much building in Jerusalem. King Hiram of Tyre sent workers and supplies to help build David's palace. Cedar, abundant in the mountains north of Israel, was a valuable and hardy wood for the beautiful buildings in Jerusalem (14:1—17:27).

5 Baal Perazim David was not very popular with the Philistines because he had slain Goliath, one of their greatest warriors (1 Samuel 17). When David began to rule over a united Israel, the Philistines set out to capture him. But David and his army attacked the Philistines at Baal Perazim as they approached Jerusalem. His army defeated the mighty Philistines twice, causing all the surrounding nations to fear David's power (14:11–17). After this battle, David moved the ark to Jerusalem (this time in accordance with God's instructions for the transportation of the ark). There was great celebration as the ark was brought into Jerusalem (15:1—17:27). David spent the remainder of his life making preparations for the building of the temple, a central place for the worship of God (18:1—29:30).

The genealogies of 1 Chronicles present an overview of Israel's history. The first nine chapters are filled with genealogies tracing the lineages of people from the creation to the exile in Babylon. Saul's death is recorded in chapter 10. Chapter 11 begins the history of David's reign over Israel.

1 CHRONICLES

Saul becomes king 1050 B.C. (1045 B.C.)

Saul dies; David becomes king over Judah 1010

David becomes king over all Israel 1003

David captures Jerusalem 1000

Dav capt Rab 997

VITAL STATISTICS

PURPOSE:
To unify God's people, to trace the Davidic line, and to teach that genuine worship ought to be the centre of individual and national life

AUTHOR:
Ezra, according to Jewish tradition

TO WHOM WRITTEN:
All Israel

DATE WRITTEN:
Approximately 430 B.C., recording events that occurred from about 1000–960 B.C.

SETTING:
1 Chronicles parallels 2 Samuel and serves as a commentary on it. Written after the exile from a priestly point of view, 1 Chronicles emphasises the religious history of Judah and Israel.

KEY VERSE:
"And David knew that the LORD had established him as king over Israel and that his kingdom had been highly exalted for the sake of his people Israel" (14:2).

KEY PEOPLE:
David, Solomon

KEY PLACES:
Hebron, Jerusalem, the temple

IN THE WIDE shade of the ageless oak, a mother watches her toddler discover acorns, leaves, and dandelions. Nearby, her mother, aunt, and uncle spread the tablecloth over a park bench and cover it with plates and bowls of fried chicken, potato salad, baked beans, and assorted family recipes. The clanging of Grandpa's and Dad's horseshoes against stakes regularly pierces the air and mixes with cheers, laughs, and shouts of the teenagers' game of football. A family reunion—a sunny afternoon filled with four generations and miscellaneous kids, parents, and second cousins once-removed.

These meetings are important . . . touching and connecting with other branches of the family tree, tracing one's personal history back through time and culture, seeing physical reflections (her eyes, his nose), remembering warm traditions. Knowing one's genetical and relational path provides a sense of identity, heritage, and destiny.

It is with this same high purpose that the writer of Chronicles begins his unifying work with an extensive genealogy. He traces the roots of the nation in a literary family reunion from Adam onwards, recounting its royal line and the loving plan of a personal God. We read 1 Chronicles and gain a glimpse of God at work through his people for generations. If you are a believer, these people are your ancestors too. As you approach this part of God's word, read their names with awe and respect, and gain new security and identity in your relationship with God.

The previous book, 2 Kings, ends with both Israel and Judah in captivity, surely a dark age for God's people. Then follows Chronicles (1 and 2 Chronicles were originally one book). Written after the captivity, it summarises Israel's history, emphasising the Jewish people's spiritual heritage in an attempt to unify the nation. The chronicler is selective in his history telling. Instead of writing an exhaustive work, he carefully weaves the narrative, highlighting spiritual lessons and teaching moral truths. In Chronicles the northern kingdom is virtually ignored, David's triumphs—not his sins—are recalled, and the temple is given great prominence as the vital centre of national life.

The book begins with Adam, and, for nine chapters, the writer gives us a "Who's Who" of Israel's history with special emphasis on David's royal line. The rest of the book tells the story of David—the great man of God, Israel's king—who served God and laid out the plans for the construction of and worship in the temple.

This account is an invaluable supplement to 2 Samuel and a strong reminder of the necessity for tracing our roots, and thus rediscovering our foundation. As you read 1 Chronicles, trace your own godly heritage, thank God for your spiritual forefathers, and recommit yourself to passing on God's truth to the next generation.

David's census 980(?)	*Solomon becomes king 970*	*The kingdom divides 930*

THE BLUEPRINT

A. THE GENEALOGIES OF ISRAEL (1:1—9:44) 1. Ancestry of the nation 2. The tribes of Israel 3. Those returned from exile in Babylon	The long list of names that follows presents a history of God's work in the world from Adam to Zerubbabel. Some of these names remind us of stories of great faith, and others of tragic failure. About most of the people named, however, we know nothing. But those who died unknown to us are known by God. God will also remember us when we die.
B. THE REIGN OF DAVID (10:1—29:30) 1. David becomes king over all of Israel 2. David brings the ark to Jerusalem 3. David's military exploits 4. David arranges for the building of the temple	David loved the Lord and wanted to build a temple to replace the tabernacle, but God denied his request. David's greatest contribution to the temple would not be the construction, but the preparation. We may be unable to see the results of our labours for God in our lifetime, but David's example helps us to understand that we serve God so *he* will see *his* results, not so we will see ours.

MEGATHEMES

THEME	EXPLANATION	IMPORTANCE
Israel's History	By retelling Israel's history in the genealogies and the stories of the kings, the writer laid down the true spiritual foundation for the nation. God kept his promises and we are reminded of them in the historical record of his people, leaders, prophets, priests, and kings.	Israel's past formed a reliable basis for reconstructing the nation after the exile. Because God's promises are revealed in the Bible, we can know God and trust him to keep his word. Like Israel, we should have no higher goal in life than devoted service to God.
God's People	By listing the names of people in Israel's past, God established Israel's true heritage. They were all one family in Adam, one nation in Abraham, one priesthood under Levi, and one kingdom under David. The national and spiritual unity of the people were important to the rebuilding of the nation.	God is always faithful to his people. He protects them in every generation and provides leaders to guide them. Because God has been at work throughout the centuries, his people can trust him to work in the present. You can rely on his presence today.
David, the King	The story of David's life and his relationship with God showed that he was God's appointed leader. David's devotion to God, the law, the temple, true worship, the people, and justice sets the standard for what God's chosen king should be.	Jesus Christ came to earth as a descendant of David. One day he will rule as king over all the earth. His strength and justice will fulfil God's ideal for the king. He is our hope. We can experience God's kingdom now by giving Christ complete control of our lives.
True Worship	David brought the ark of the covenant to the tabernacle at Jerusalem to restore true worship to the people. God gave the plans for building the temple, and David organised the priests to make worship central to all Israel.	The temple stood as the throne of God on earth, the place of true worship. God's true throne is in the hearts of his people. When we acknowledge him as the true king over our lives, true worship takes place.
The Priests	God ordained the priests and Levites to guide the people in faithful worship according to his law. By leading the people in worship according to God's design, the priests and Levites were an important safeguard to Israel's faith.	For true worship to remain central in our lives, God's people need to take a firm stand for the ways of God recorded in the Bible. Today, all believers are priests for one another, and we should encourage each other to faithful worship.

A. THE GENEALOGIES OF ISRAEL (1:1—9:44)

These genealogies are the official family records of the nation of Israel. They give us an overview of the history of God's work from creation through to the captivity of his people. These records served to teach the exiles returning from Babylon about their spiritual heritage as a nation and to inspire them to renew their faithfulness to God. Although these lists show the racial heritage of the Jews, they contain the spiritual heritage for every believer. We are a part of the community of faith that has existed from generation to generation since the dawn of man.

1. Ancestry of the nation

Historical Records From Adam to Abraham

To Noah's Sons

1 Adam,[a] Seth, Enosh, 2Kenan,[b] Mahalalel,[c] Jared,[d] 3Enoch,[e] Methuselah,[f]
Lamech,[g] Noah.[h]

4The sons of Noah:[a][i]
Shem, Ham and Japheth.[j]

The Japhethites

5The sons[b] of Japheth:
Gomer, Magog, Madai, Javan, Tubal, Meshech and Tiras.
6The sons of Gomer:
Ashkenaz, Riphath[c] and Togarmah.
7The sons of Javan:
Elishah, Tarshish, the Kittim and the Rodanim.

The Hamites

8The sons of Ham:
Cush, Mizraim,[d] Put and Canaan.
9The sons of Cush:
Seba, Havilah, Sabta, Raamah and Sabteca.
The sons of Raamah:
Sheba and Dedan.
10Cush was the father[e] of
Nimrod, who grew to be a mighty warrior on earth.
11Mizraim was the father of

1:1 [a]Ge 5:1-32; Lk 3:36-38
1:2 [b]Ge 5:9 [c]Ge 5:12 [d]Ge 5:15
1:3 [e]Ge 5:18; Jude 1:14 [f]Ge 5:21 [g]Ge 5:25 [h]Ge 5:29
1:4 [i]Ge 6:10; 10:1 [j]Ge 5:32

a 4 Septuagint; Hebrew does not have *The sons of Noah:* b 5 *Sons* may mean *descendants* or *successors* or *nations*; also in verses 6–10, 17 and 20. c 6 Many Hebrew manuscripts and Vulgate (see also Septuagint and Gen. 10:3); most Hebrew manuscripts *Diphath* d 8 That is, Egypt; also in verse 11 e 10 *Father* may mean *ancestor* or *predecessor* or *founder*, also in verses 11, 13, 18 and 20.

1:1 This record of names demonstrates that God is interested not only in nations, but also in individuals. Although billions of people have lived since Adam, God knows and remembers the face and name of each person. Each of us is more than a name on a list; we are special persons whom God knows and loves. As we recognise and accept his love, we discover both our uniqueness as individuals and our solidarity with the rest of his family.

1:1ff This long list of names was compiled after the people of Judah, the southern kingdom, were taken captive to Babylon. As the exiles looked forward to the day when they would return to their homeland, one of their biggest fears was that the records of their heritage would be lost. The Jews placed great importance upon their heritage because each person wanted to be able to prove that he was a descendant of Abraham, the father of the Jewish people. Only then could he enjoy the benefits of the special blessings God promised to Abraham and his descendants (see the notes on Genesis 12:1–3 and 17:2–8 for what these special blessings were).

This list reconstructed the family tree for both Judah, the southern kingdom, and Israel, the northern kingdom, before their captivities and served as proof for those who claimed to be Abraham's descendants. (For more information about why the Bible includes genealogies, read the notes on Genesis 5:1ff, Matthew 1:1, and Luke 3:23–38.)

1:1ff There is more to this long genealogy than meets the eye. It holds importance for us today because it supports the Old Testament promise that Jesus the Messiah would be a descendant of Abraham and David. This promise is recorded in Genesis 12:1–3 and 2 Samuel 7:12, 13.

1:1, 4 Adam's story and Profile are found in Genesis 1—5. Noah's story and Profile are found in Genesis 6—9.

1:5–9 *Sons* can also mean *descendants;* thus a biblical genealogy may skip several generations. These lists were not meant to be exhaustive, but to give adequate information about the various family lines.

1:10 Nimrod is also mentioned in Genesis 10:8, 9.

1:11, 12 The Philistines had been Israel's constant enemy from the days of the judges. King David finally weakened them, and by this time they were no longer a threat. (For more information on the Philistines, see the notes on Judges 13:1 and 1 Samuel 4:1.)

1:24
[k]Ge 10:21-25;
Lk 3:34-36

the Ludites, Anamites, Lehabites, Naphtuhites, 12Pathrusites, Casluhites
(from whom the Philistines came) and Caphtorites.
13Canaan was the father of
Sidon his firstborn,[f] and of the Hittites, 14Jebusites, Amorites, Girgashites,
15Hivites, Arkites, Sinites, 16Arvadites, Zemarites and Hamathites.

The Semites

17The sons of Shem:
Elam, Asshur, Arphaxad, Lud and Aram.
The sons of Aram:[g]
Uz, Hul, Gether and Meshech.
18Arphaxad was the father of Shelah, and Shelah the father of Eber.
19Two sons were born to Eber:
One was named Peleg,[h] because in his time the earth was divided; his brother
was named Joktan.
20Joktan was the father of
Almodad, Sheleph, Hazarmaveth, Jerah, 21Hadoram, Uzal, Diklah,
22Obal,[i] Abimael, Sheba, 23Ophir, Havilah and Jobab. All these were sons
of Joktan.

24Shem,[k] Arphaxad,[j] Shelah,
25Eber, Peleg, Reu,
26Serug, Nahor, Terah
27and Abram (that is, Abraham).

The Family of Abraham

28The sons of Abraham:
Isaac and Ishmael.

Descendants of Hagar

29These were their descendants:
Nebaioth the firstborn of Ishmael, Kedar, Adbeel, Mibsam, 30Mishma, Dumah, Massa, Hadad, Tema, 31Jetur, Naphish and Kedemah. These were the
sons of Ishmael.

Descendants of Keturah

32The sons born to Keturah, Abraham's concubine:[l]
Zimran, Jokshan, Medan, Midian, Ishbak and Shuah.
The sons of Jokshan:
Sheba and Dedan.[m]
33The sons of Midian:
Ephah, Epher, Hanoch, Abida and Eldaah.
All these were descendants of Keturah.

1:32
[l]Ge 22:24
[m]Ge 10:7

[f] 13 Or *of the Sidonians, the foremost* [g] 17 One Hebrew manuscript and some Septuagint manuscripts (see also Gen. 10:23); most Hebrew manuscripts do not have this line. [h] 19 *Peleg* means *division.* [i] 22 Some Hebrew manuscripts and Syriac (see also Gen. 10:28); most Hebrew manuscripts *Ebal* [j] 24 Hebrew; some Septuagint manuscripts *Arphaxad, Cainan* (see also note at Gen. 11:10)

1:13–16 Canaan was the ancestor of the Canaanites, who inhabited the promised land (also called Canaan) before the Israelites entered under Joshua's leadership. God helped the Israelites drive out the Canaanites, a wicked and idolatrous people. The land's name was then changed to Israel. The book of Joshua tells that story.

1:19 'The earth was divided' refers to when the earth was divided into different language groups. At one time, everyone spoke a single language. But some people became proud of their accomplishments and gathered to build a monument to themselves—the tower of Babel. The building project was brought to an abrupt conclusion when God caused the people to speak different languages. Without the ability to communicate with one another, the people could not be unified. God showed them that their great efforts were useless without him. Pride in our achievements must not lead us to conclude that we no longer need God. This story is told in Genesis 11:1–9.

1:24–27 Abraham's story and Profile are found in Genesis 11:26–25:10.

1:28–31 Ishmael's story and Profile are found in Genesis 17 and 21.

Descendants of Sarah

34 Abraham[n] was the father of Isaac.[o]
The sons of Isaac:
Esau and Israel.[p]

Esau's Sons

35 The sons of Esau:[q]
Eliphaz, Reuel,[r] Jeush, Jalam and Korah.
36 The sons of Eliphaz:
Teman, Omar, Zepho,[k] Gatam and Kenaz;
by Timna: Amalek.[l][s]
37 The sons of Reuel:[t]
Nahath, Zerah, Shammah and Mizzah.

The People of Seir in Edom

38 The sons of Seir:
Lotan, Shobal, Zibeon, Anah, Dishon, Ezer and Dishan.
39 The sons of Lotan:
Hori and Homam. Timna was Lotan's sister.
40 The sons of Shobal:
Alvan,[m] Manahath, Ebal, Shepho and Onam.
The sons of Zibeon:
Aiah and Anah.[u]
41 The son of Anah:
Dishon.
The sons of Dishon:
Hemdan,[n] Eshban, Ithran and Keran.
42 The sons of Ezer:
Bilhan, Zaavan and Akan.[o]
The sons of Dishan:[p]
Uz and Aran.

The Rulers of Edom

43 These were the kings who reigned in Edom before any Israelite king reigned:[q]
Bela son of Beor, whose city was named Dinhabah.
44 When Bela died, Jobab son of Zerah from Bozrah succeeded him as king.
45 When Jobab died, Husham from the land of the Temanites[v] succeeded him as king.
46 When Husham died, Hadad son of Bedad, who defeated Midian in the country of Moab, succeeded him as king. His city was named Avith.
47 When Hadad died, Samlah from Masrekah succeeded him as king.
48 When Samlah died, Shaul from Rehoboth on the river[r] succeeded him as king.

1:34 [n] Lk 3:34 [o] Ge 21:2-3; Mt 1:2; Ac 7:8 [p] Ge 17:5; 25:25-26
1:35 [q] Ge 36:19 [r] Ge 36:4
1:36 [s] Ex 17:14
1:37 [t] Ge 36:17
1:40 [u] Ge 36:2
1:45 [v] Ge 36:11

k *36* Many Hebrew manuscripts, some Septuagint manuscripts and Syriac (see also Gen. 36:11); most Hebrew manuscripts *Zephi* l *36* Some Septuagint manuscripts (see also Gen. 36:12); Hebrew *Gatam, Kenaz, Timna and Amalek* m *40* Many Hebrew manuscripts and some Septuagint manuscripts (see also Gen. 36:23); most Hebrew manuscripts *Alian* n *41* Many Hebrew manuscripts and some Septuagint manuscripts (see also Gen. 36:26); most Hebrew manuscripts *Hamran* o *42* Many Hebrew and Septuagint manuscripts (see also Gen. 36:27); most Hebrew manuscripts *Zaavan, Jaakan* p *42* Hebrew *Dishon*, a variant of *Dishan* q *43* Or *before an Israelite king reigned over them* r *48* Possibly the Euphrates

1:34 Israel is another name for Jacob because Jacob's 12 sons became the nation of Israel. Esau's descendants became the nation of Edom, a constant enemy of Israel. To learn more about the lives of Isaac and his two sons, Jacob and Esau, read their stories and Profiles in Genesis 21 – 36 and 46 – 49.

1:36 Amalek, Esau's grandson, was the son of his father's concubine (Genesis 36:12). He was the ancestor of the wicked tribe known as Amalekites, the first people to attack the Israelites on their way to the promised land. (For more about the Amalekites, read the note on Exodus 17:8.)

1:43–54 Why are we given information in this genealogy about the descendants of Edom who were Israel's enemies? Esau, ancestor of the Edomites, was Isaac's oldest son and thus a direct descendant of Abraham. As Abraham's first grandson, he deserved a place in the Jewish records. It was through Esau's marriages to pagan women, however, that the nation of Edom began. This genealogy shows the ancestry of enemy nations; they were *not* a part of the direct lineage of King David, and thus of the Messiah. This listing further identified Israel's special identity and role.

49 When Shaul died, Baal-Hanan son of Acbor succeeded him as king.
50 When Baal-Hanan died, Hadad succeeded him as king. His city was named
Pau,[s] and his wife's name was Mehetabel daughter of Matred, the daughter
of Me-Zahab. 51 Hadad also died.

The chiefs of Edom were:
Timna, Alvah, Jetheth, 52 Oholibamah, Elah, Pinon, 53 Kenaz, Teman, Mibzar, 54 Magdiel and Iram. These were the chiefs of Edom.

Israel's Sons

2 These were the sons of Israel:
Reuben, Simeon, Levi, Judah, Issachar, Zebulun, 2 Dan, Joseph, Benjamin,
Naphtali, Gad and Asher.

Judah

To Hezron's Sons

3 The sons of Judah:[a]
Er, Onan and Shelah.[b] These three were born to him by a Canaanite woman,
the daughter of Shua.[c] Er, Judah's firstborn, was wicked in the LORD's sight;
so the LORD put him to death.[d] 4 Tamar,[e] Judah's daughter-in-law,[f] bore
him Perez[g] and Zerah. Judah had five sons in all.

5 The sons of Perez:[h]
Hezron[i] and Hamul.
6 The sons of Zerah:
Zimri, Ethan, Heman, Calcol and Darda[a]—five in all.
7 The son of Carmi:
Achar,[b][j] who brought trouble on Israel by violating the ban on taking
devoted things.[c][k]
8 The son of Ethan:
Azariah.
9 The sons born to Hezron[l] were:
Jerahmeel, Ram and Caleb.[d]

From Ram Son of Hezron

10 Ram[m] was the father of
Amminadab[n], and Amminadab the father of Nahshon,[o] the leader of the
people of Judah. 11 Nahshon was the father of Salmon,[e] Salmon the father
of Boaz, 12 Boaz[p] the father of Obed and Obed the father of Jesse.[q]
13 Jesse[r] was the father of
Eliab[s] his firstborn; the second son was Abinadab, the third Shimea, 14 the

[s] *50* Many Hebrew manuscripts, some Septuagint manuscripts, Vulgate and Syriac (see also Gen. 36:39); most Hebrew manuscripts *Pai* [a] *6* Many Hebrew manuscripts, some Septuagint manuscripts and Syriac (see also 1 Kings 4:31); most Hebrew manuscripts *Dara* [b] *7* *Achar* means *trouble*; *Achar* is called *Achan* in Joshua. [c] *7* The Hebrew term refers to the irrevocable giving over of things or persons to the LORD, often by totally destroying them. [d] *9* Hebrew *Kelubai*, a variant of *Caleb* [e] *11* Septuagint (see also Ruth 4:21); Hebrew *Salma*

2:3 [a] Ge 29:35; 38:2-10 [b] Ge 38:5 [c] Ge 38:2 [d] Nu 26:19
2:4 [e] Ge 38:11-30 [f] Ge 11:31 [g] Ge 38:29
2:5 [h] Ge 46:12 [i] Nu 26:21
2:7 [j] Jos 7:1 [k] Jos 6:18
2:9 [l] Nu 26:21
2:10 [m] Lk 3:32-33 [n] Ex 6:23 [o] Nu 1:7
2:12 [p] Ru 2:1 [q] Ru 4:17
2:13 [r] Ru 4:17 [s] 1Sa 16:6

2:1, 2 The story of Israel's (Jacob's) sons is found in Genesis 29:32–50:26. Profiles of Reuben, Judah, and Joseph are found in the same section.

2:3 This long genealogy not only lists names, but gives us insights into some of the people. Here, almost as an epitaph, the genealogy states that Er "was wicked in the LORD's sight; so the LORD put him to death". Now, thousands of years later, this is all we know of the man. Each of us is forging a reputation, developing personal qualities by which we will be remembered. How would God summarise your life up to now? Some defiantly claim that how they live is their own business. But Scripture teaches that the way you live today will determine how you will be remembered by others and how you will be judged by God. What you do now *does* matter.

2:7 Achar is called Achan in Joshua 7. This is the man who kept for himself some of the plunder that was devoted to the Lord for destruction.

2:12 Boaz was Ruth's husband and an ancestor of both David and Jesus. Boaz's story and Profile are found in the book of Ruth.

fourth Nethanel, the fifth Raddai, 15the sixth Ozem and the seventh David.
16Their sisters were Zeruiah[t] and Abigail. Zeruiah's[u] three sons were
Abishai, Joab[v] and Asahel. 17Abigail was the mother of Amasa,[w] whose
father was Jether the Ishmaelite.

Caleb Son of Hezron

18Caleb son of Hezron had children by his wife Azubah (and by Jerioth). These
were her sons: Jesher, Shobab and Ardon. 19When Azubah died, Caleb[x]
married Ephrath, who bore him Hur. 20Hur was the father of Uri, and Uri
the father of Bezalel.[y]
21Later, Hezron lay with the daughter of Makir the father of Gilead[z] (he had
married her when he was sixty years old), and she bore him Segub. 22Segub
was the father of Jair, who controlled twenty-three towns in Gilead. 23(But
Geshur and Aram captured Havvoth Jair,[f][a] as well as Kenath[b] with its
surrounding settlements—sixty towns.) All these were descendants of Makir
the father of Gilead.

24After Hezron died in Caleb Ephrathah, Abijah the wife of Hezron bore him
Ashhur[c] the father[g] of Tekoa.

Jerahmeel Son of Hezron

25The sons of Jerahmeel the firstborn of Hezron:
Ram his firstborn, Bunah, Oren, Ozem and[h] Ahijah. 26Jerahmeel had an-
other wife, whose name was Atarah; she was the mother of Onam.
27The sons of Ram the firstborn of Jerahmeel:
Maaz, Jamin and Eker.
28The sons of Onam:
Shammai and Jada.
The sons of Shammai:
Nadab and Abishur.
29Abishur's wife was named Abihail, who bore him Ahban and Molid.
30The sons of Nadab:
Seled and Appaim. Seled died without children.
31The son of Appaim:
Ishi, who was the father of Sheshan.
Sheshan was the father of Ahlai.
32The sons of Jada, Shammai's brother:
Jether and Jonathan. Jether died without children.
33The sons of Jonathan:
Peleth and Zaza.
These were the descendants of Jerahmeel.
34Sheshan had no sons—only daughters.
He had an Egyptian servant named Jarha. 35Sheshan gave his daughter in
marriage to his servant Jarha, and she bore him Attai.
36Attai was the father of Nathan,
Nathan the father of Zabad,[d]
37Zabad the father of Ephlal,

f 23 Or *captured the settlements of Jair* g 24 *Father* may mean *civic leader* or *military leader*; also in verses 42, 45, 49–52 and possibly elsewhere. h 25 Or *Oren and Ozem, by*

2:16 [t] 1Sa 26:6 [u] 2Sa 2:18 [v] 2Sa 2:13
2:17 [w] 2Sa 17:25
2:19 [x] ver 42, 50
2:20 [y] Ex 31:2
2:21 [z] Nu 27:1
2:23 [a] Nu 32:41; Dt 3:14; Jos 13:30 [b] Nu 32:42
2:24 [c] 1Ch 4:5
2:36 [d] 1Ch 11:41

2:15 David is one of the best-known people of the Bible. He was certainly not perfect, but he exemplified what it means to seek God first in all areas of life. God called David "a man after my own heart" (Acts 13:22) because David's greatest desire was to serve and worship God. We can please God in the same way by making God our first consideration in all our desires and plans. David's story is found in 1 Samuel 16:1–1 Kings 2:10 and 1 Chronicles 10:14–29:30. David's Profile is found in 1 Samuel 17.

2:16 Joab's story is found in 2 Samuel 2; 3; 10–20; 24; 1 Kings 1–3; 1 Chronicles 11:4–9; 19–21. His Profile is found in 2 Samuel 18. Abishai's story is found in 1 Samuel 26; 2 Samuel 2;

Ephlal the father of Obed,
38 Obed the father of Jehu,
Jehu the father of Azariah,
39 Azariah the father of Helez,
Helez the father of Eleasah,
40 Eleasah the father of Sismai,
Sismai the father of Shallum,
41 Shallum the father of Jekamiah, and Jekamiah the father of Elishama.

The Clans of Caleb

42 The sons of Caleb[e] the brother of Jerahmeel:
Mesha his firstborn, who was the father of Ziph, and his son Mareshah,[i] who was the father of Hebron.
43 The sons of Hebron:
Korah, Tappuah, Rekem and Shema. 44 Shema was the father of Raham, and
Raham the father of Jorkeam. Rekem was the father of Shammai. 45 The son
of Shammai was Maon[f], and Maon was the father of Beth Zur.[g]
46 Caleb's concubine Ephah was the mother of Haran, Moza and Gazez. Haran was the father of Gazez.
47 The sons of Jahdai:
Regem, Jotham, Geshan, Pelet, Ephah and Shaaph.
48 Caleb's concubine Maacah was the mother of Sheber and Tirhanah. 49 She also
gave birth to Shaaph the father of Madmannah[h] and to Sheva the father of
Macbenah and Gibea. Caleb's daughter was Acsah.[i] 50 These were the
descendants of Caleb.

The sons of Hur[j] the firstborn of Ephrathah:
Shobal the father of Kiriath Jearim,[k] 51 Salma the father of Bethlehem, and
Hareph the father of Beth Gader.
52 The descendants of Shobal the father of Kiriath Jearim were:
Haroeh, half the Manahathites, 53 and the clans of Kiriath Jearim: the Ith-
rites,[l] Puthites, Shumathites and Mishraites. From these descended the
Zorathites and Eshtaolites.
54 The descendants of Salma:
Bethlehem, the Netophathites,[m] Atroth Beth Joab, half the Manahathites, the
Zorites, 55 and the clans of scribes[j] who lived at Jabez: the Tirathites,
Shimeathites and Sucathites. These are the Kenites[n] who came from Hammath,[o] the father of the house of Recab.[k][p]

The Sons of David

3 These were the sons of David[a] born to him in Hebron:
The firstborn was Amnon the son of Ahinoam of Jezreel;[b]
the second, Daniel the son of Abigail[c] of Carmel;
2 the third, Absalom the son of Maacah daughter of Talmai king of Geshur;
the fourth, Adonijah[d] the son of Haggith;
3 the fifth, Shephatiah the son of Abital;
and the sixth, Ithream, by his wife Eglah.
4 These six were born to David in Hebron,[e] where he reigned for seven years and six months.[f]

[i] *42* The meaning of the Hebrew for this phrase is uncertain. [j] *55* Or *of the Sopherites* [k] *55* Or *father of Beth Recab*

2:42 [e] ver 19
2:45 [f] Jos 15:55 [g] Jos 15:58
2:49 [h] Jos 15:31 [i] Jos 15:16
2:50 [j] 1Ch 4:4 [k] ver 19
2:53 [l] 2Sa 23:38
2:54 [m] Ezr 2:22; Ne 7:26; 12:28
2:55 [n] Ge 15:19; Jdg 1:16; Jdg 4:11 [o] Jos 19:35 [p] 2Ki 10:15, 23; Jer 35:2-19
3:1 [a] 1Ch 14:3; 28:5 [b] Jos 15:56 [c] 1Sa 25:42
3:2 [d] 1Ki 2:22
3:4 [e] 2Sa 5:4; 1Ch 29:27 [f] 2Sa 2:11; 5:5

3; 10; 15 – 21; 23; 1 Chronicles 18:12; 19. Abishai's Profile is found in 2 Samuel 21.

2:18 This is not the Caleb who spied out the promised land with Joshua. Caleb, the spy, is listed in 4:15.

3:1 Abigail's story is found in 1 Samuel 25; her Profile is in 1 Samuel 26.

3:2 Absalom's story and Profile are found in 2 Samuel 13 – 18.

David reigned in Jerusalem for thirty-three years, 5 and these were the children born
to him there:

Shammua,[a] Shobab, Nathan and Solomon. These four were by Bathsheba[b][g] daughter of Ammiel. 6 There were also Ibhar, Elishua,[c] Eliphelet,
7 Nogah, Nepheg, Japhia, 8 Elishama, Eliada and Eliphelet—nine in all. 9 All
these were the sons of David, besides his sons by his concubines. And
Tamar[h] was their sister.[i]

The Kings of Judah

10 Solomon's son was Rehoboam,[j]
Abijah his son,
Asa his son,
Jehoshaphat[k] his son,
11 Jehoram[d][l] his son,
Ahaziah[m] his son,
Joash[n] his son,
12 Amaziah[o] his son,
Azariah his son,
Jotham[p] his son,
13 Ahaz[q] his son,
Hezekiah[r] his son,
Manasseh[s] his son,
14 Amon[t] his son,
Josiah[u] his son.
15 The sons of Josiah:
Johanan the firstborn,
Jehoiakim[v] the second son,
Zedekiah[w] the third,
Shallum[x] the fourth.
16 The successors of Jehoiakim:
Jehoiachin[e][y] his son,
and Zedekiah.[z]

The Royal Line After the Exile

17 The descendants of Jehoiachin the captive:
Shealtiel[a] his son, 18 Malkiram, Pedaiah, Shenazzar,[b] Jekamiah, Hoshama
and Nedabiah.[c]
19 The sons of Pedaiah:
Zerubbabel[d] and Shimei.
The sons of Zerubbabel:
Meshullam and Hananiah.
Shelomith was their sister.
20 There were also five others:
Hashubah, Ohel, Berekiah, Hasadiah and Jushab-Hesed.
21 The descendants of Hananiah:

a *5* Hebrew *Shimea*, a variant of *Shammua* **b** *5* One Hebrew manuscript and Vulgate (see also Septuagint and 2 Sam. 11:3); most Hebrew manuscripts *Bathshua* **c** *6* Two Hebrew manuscripts (see also 2 Sam. 5:15 and 1 Chron. 14:5); most Hebrew manuscripts *Elishama* **d** *11* Hebrew *Joram*, a variant of *Jehoram* **e** *16* Hebrew *Jeconiah*, a variant of *Jehoiachin*; also in verse 17

3:5 [g] 2Sa 11:3; 12:24
3:9 [h] 2Sa 13:1 [i] 1Ch 14:4
3:10 [j] 1Ki 11:43; 14:21-31; 2Ch 12:16 [k] 2Ch 17:1-21:3
3:11 [l] 2Ki 8:16-24; 2Ch 21:1 [m] 2Ch 22:1-10 [n] 2Ki 11:1-12:21
3:12 [o] 2Ki 14:1-22; 2Ch 25:1-28 [p] Isa 1:1; Hos 1:1; Mic 1:1
3:13 [q] 2Ki 16:1-20; 2Ch 28:1; Isa 7:1 [r] 2Ki 18:1-20:21; 2Ch 29:1; Jer 26:19 [s] 2Ch 33:1
3:14 [t] 2Ki 21:19-26; 2Ch 33:21; Zep 1:1 [u] 2Ch 34:1; Jer 1:2; 3:6; 25:3
3:15 [v] 2Ki 23:34 [w] Jer 37:1 [x] 2Ki 23:31
3:16 [y] 2Ki 24:6, 8; Mt 1:11 [z] 2Ki 24:18
3:17 [a] Ezr 3:2
3:18 [b] Ezr 1:8; 5:14 [c] Jer 22:30
3:19 [d] Ezr 2:2; 3:2; 5:2; Ne 7:7; 12:1; Hag 1:1; 2:2; Zec 4:6

3:5 Bathsheba's story is found in 2 Samuel 11; 12; 1 Kings 1, and her Profile is in 1 Kings 1. The story of her son, Solomon, who became Israel's third king, is found in 1 Kings 1–11 and 2 Chronicles 1–9. Solomon's Profile is found in 1 Kings 4.

3:9 The tragic story of Tamar, David's daughter, is found in 2 Samuel 13; 14.

3:10–14 Many of Solomon's descendants ruled the nation of Judah. For Rehoboam's story and Profile, see 2 Chronicles 10–12. For Jehoshaphat's story and Profile, see 2 Chronicles 17–20. Azariah's (Uzziah's) story and Profile are found in 2 Chronicles 26. Hezekiah's story and Profile are in 2 Kings 18–20. For Josiah's story, see 2 Kings 22; 23. His Profile is in 2 Kings 24.

3:15 Jehoiakim's story is found in Jeremiah 22–28; 35; 36. Zedekiah's story is found in Jeremiah 21–39.

3:19, 20 Zerubbabel was the leader of the first exiles to return from Babylon. His story and Profile are found in the book of Ezra.

3:22
[e]Ezr 8:2-3

Pelatiah and Jeshaiah, and the sons of Rephaiah, of Arnan, of Obadiah and of Shecaniah.
22The descendants of Shecaniah:
Shemaiah and his sons:
Hattush,[e] Igal, Bariah, Neariah and Shaphat—six in all.
23The sons of Neariah:
Elioenai, Hizkiah and Azrikam—three in all.
24The sons of Elioenai:
Hodaviah, Eliashib, Pelaiah, Akkub, Johanan, Delaiah and Anani—seven in all.

4:1
[a]Ge 29:35; 46:12; 1Ch 2:3
[b]Nu 26:21

2. The tribes of Israel

Other Clans of Judah

4 The descendants of Judah:[a]
Perez, Hezron,[b] Carmi, Hur and Shobal.
2Reaiah son of Shobal was the father of Jahath, and Jahath the father of Ahumai and Lahad. These were the clans of the Zorathites.
3These were the sons**[a]** of Etam:
Jezreel, Ishma and Idbash. Their sister was named Hazzelelponi. 4Penuel was the father of Gedor, and Ezer the father of Hushah.
These were the descendants of Hur,[c] the firstborn of Ephrathah and father**[b]** of Bethlehem.[d]

4:4
[c]1Ch 2:50
[d]Ru 1:19

5Ashhur[e] the father of Tekoa had two wives, Helah and Naarah.
6Naarah bore him Ahuzzam, Hepher, Temeni and Haahashtari. These were the descendants of Naarah.
7The sons of Helah:
Zereth, Zohar, Ethnan, 8and Koz, who was the father of Anub and Hazzobebah and of the clans of Aharhel son of Harum.

9Jabez was more honourable than his brothers. His mother had named him Jabez,**[c]**
saying, "I gave birth to him in pain." 10Jabez cried out to the God of Israel, "Oh, that
you would bless me and enlarge my territory! Let your hand be with me, and keep
me from harm so that I will be free from pain." And God granted his request.

4:5
[e]1Ch 2:24

11Kelub, Shuhah's brother, was the father of Mehir, who was the father of Eshton.
12Eshton was the father of Beth Rapha, Paseah and Tehinnah the father of Ir Nahash.**[d]** These were the men of Recah.

13The sons of Kenaz:
Othniel[f] and Seraiah.
The sons of Othniel:
Hathath and Meonothai.**[e]** 14Meonothai was the father of Ophrah.
Seraiah was the father of Joab,
the father of Ge Harashim.**[f]** It was called this because its people were craftsmen.

a *3* Some Septuagint manuscripts (see also Vulgate); Hebrew *father* **b** *4* *Father* may mean *civic leader* or *military leader*; also in verses 12, 14, 17, 18 and possibly elsewhere. **c** *9* *Jabez* sounds like the Hebrew for *pain.* **d** *12* Or *of the city of Nahash* **e** *13* Some Septuagint manuscripts and Vulgate; Hebrew does not have *and Meonothai.* **f** *14* *Ge Harashim* means *valley of craftsmen.*

4:13
[f]Jos 15:17

4:9, 10 Jabez is remembered for a prayer request rather than a heroic act. In his prayer, he asked God to (1) bless him, (2) help him in his work ("enlarge my territory"), (3) be with him in all he did, and (4) keep him from evil and harm. Jabez acknowledged God as the true centre of his work. When we pray for God's blessing, we should also pray that he will take his rightful position as Lord over our work, our family time, and our recreation. Obeying him in daily responsibilities *is* heroic living.

4:10 Jabez prayed specifically to be protected from harm and pain. We live in a fallen world filled with sin, and it is important to ask God to keep us safe from the unavoidable evil that comes our way. But we must also avoid evil motives, desires, and actions that begin within us. Therefore, not only must we seek God's protection from evil, but we must also ask God to guard our thoughts and actions. We can begin to utilise his protection by filling our minds with positive thoughts and attitudes.

4:13 Othniel was Israel's first judge. He reformed the nation and brought peace to the land. His story is found in Judges 1:9–15 and 3:5–14.

15 The sons of Caleb son of Jephunneh:
Iru, Elah and Naam.
The son of Elah:
Kenaz.
16 The sons of Jehallelel:
Ziph, Ziphah, Tiria and Asarel.
17 The sons of Ezrah:
Jether, Mered, Epher and Jalon. One of Mered's wives gave birth to Miriam,[g] Shammai and Ishbah the father of Eshtemoa. 18 (His Judean wife gave
birth to Jered the father of Gedor, Heber the father of Soco, and Jekuthiel
the father of Zanoah.[h]) These were the children of Pharaoh's daughter
Bithiah, whom Mered had married.
19 The sons of Hodiah's wife, the sister of Naham:
the father of Keilah[i] the Garmite, and Eshtemoa the Maacathite.[j]
20 The sons of Shimon:
Amnon, Rinnah, Ben-Hanan and Tilon.
The descendants of Ishi:
Zoheth and Ben-Zoheth.
21 The sons of Shelah[k] son of Judah:
Er the father of Lecah, Laadah the father of Mareshah and the clans of the
linen workers at Beth Ashbea, 22 Jokim, the men of Cozeba, and Joash and
Saraph, who ruled in Moab and Jashubi Lehem. (These records are from
ancient times.) 23 They were the potters who lived at Netaim and Gederah;
they stayed there and worked for the king.

Simeon

24 The descendants of Simeon:[l]
Nemuel, Jamin, Jarib,[m] Zerah and Shaul;
25 Shallum was Shaul's son, Mibsam his son and Mishma his son.
26 The descendants of Mishma:
Hammuel his son, Zaccur his son and Shimei his son.
27 Shimei had sixteen sons and six daughters, but his brothers did not have many
children; so their entire clan did not become as numerous as the people of Judah.
28 They lived in Beersheba,[n] Moladah,[o] Hazar Shual, 29 Bilhah, Ezem,[p] Tolad,
30 Bethuel, Hormah,[q] Ziklag, 31 Beth Marcaboth, Hazar Susim, Beth Biri and Shaaraim.[r] These were their towns until the reign of David. 32 Their surrounding villages
were Etam, Ain,[s] Rimmon, Token and Ashan[t]—five towns— 33 and all the villages
around these towns as far as Baalath.**[g]** These were their settlements. And they kept
a genealogical record.

34 Meshobab, Jamlech, Joshah son of Amaziah, 35 Joel, Jehu son of Joshibiah, the
son of Seraiah, the son of Asiel, 36 also Elioenai, Jaakobah, Jeshohaiah, Asaiah,
Adiel, Jesimiel, Benaiah, 37 and Ziza son of Shiphi, the son of Allon, the son of
Jedaiah, the son of Shimri, the son of Shemaiah.

38 The men listed above by name were leaders of their clans. Their families increased
greatly, 39 and they went to the outskirts of Gedor[u] to the east of the valley in search
of pasture for their flocks. 40 They found rich, good pasture, and the land was spacious,
peaceful and quiet.[v] Some Hamites had lived there formerly.
41 The men whose names were listed came in the days of Hezekiah king of Judah.
They attacked the Hamites in their dwellings and also the Meunites[w] who were there
and completely destroyed**[h]** them, as is evident to this day. Then they settled in their

g *33* Some Septuagint manuscripts (see also Joshua 19:8); Hebrew *Baal* **h** *41* The Hebrew term refers to the irrevocable giving over of things or persons to the LORD, often by totally destroying them.

4:17 [g] Ex 15:20
4:18 [h] Jos 15:34
4:19 [i] Jos 15:44 [j] Dt 3:14
4:21 [k] Ge 38:5
4:24 [l] Ge 29:33 [m] Nu 26:12
4:28 [n] Ge 21:14 [o] Jos 15:26
4:29 [p] Jos 15:29
4:30 [q] Nu 14:45
4:31 [r] Jos 15:36
4:32 [s] Nu 34:11 [t] Jos 15:42
4:39 [u] Jos 15:58
4:40 [v] Jdg 18:7-10
4:41 [w] 2Ch 20:1; 26:7

4:15 Caleb was one of the 12 spies sent into the promised land by Moses. He and Joshua were the only two spies to return with a positive report, believing in God's promise to help the Israelites conquer the land. Caleb's story is told in Numbers 13; 14 and Joshua 14; 15. His Profile is found in Numbers 15.

WHO'S WHO IN THE BIBLE

Here are some of the people mentioned in this genealogy who are also mentioned elsewhere in the Bible. The writer of Chronicles reproduced a thorough history of Israel in one list of people. Many of the people in this list have exciting stories that can be traced through the Bible. Look up some of the names below that intrigue you. You may be surprised what you discover!

Name	*Key life lesson*	*Story told in:*
Adam (1:1)	Our sins have far greater implications than we realise.	Genesis 2, 3
Noah (1:4)	Great rewards come from obeying God.	Genesis 6—9
Abraham (1:27)	Faith alone makes one right in God's eyes.	Genesis 11:26—25:10
Isaac (1:28)	Seeking peace brings true respect.	Genesis 21—35
Esau (1:35)	It is never too late to put away bitterness and forgive.	Genesis 25:20—36:43
Amalek (1:36)	There are evil men and nations who seek to harm God's people.	Exodus 17:8–16
Israel (Jacob) (2:1)	While our sins may haunt us, God will honour our faith.	Genesis 25:20—50:13
Judah (2:3)	God can change the hearts of even the most wicked people.	Genesis 37—50
Tamar (2:4)	God works his purposes even through sinful events.	Genesis 38
Perez (2:5)	Your background does not matter to God.	Genesis 38:27–30
Boaz (2:12)	Those who are kind to others will receive kindness themselves.	The book of Ruth
Jesse (2:13)	Never take lightly the impact you may have on your children.	1 Samuel 16
David (2:15)	True greatness is having a heart for God.	The books of 1 and 2 Samuel
Joab (2:16)	Those who seek power die with nothing.	2 Samuel 2:13—1 Kings 2:34
Amnon (3:1)	Giving in to lust leads only to tragedy.	2 Samuel 13
Absalom (3:2)	Those seeking to oust a God-appointed leader will have a difficult battle.	2 Samuel 13—18
Adonijah (3:2)	God must determine what is rightfully ours.	1 Kings 1—2
Bathsheba (3:5)	One wrong act does not disqualify us from accomplishing things for God.	2 Samuel 11, 12; 1 Kings 1, 2
Solomon (3:5)	Man's wisdom is foolishness without God.	1 Kings 1—11
Reuben (5:1)	What is gained from a moment of passion is only perceived; what is lost is real and permanent.	Genesis 35:22; 37; 49:3, 4
Aaron (6:3)	Don't expect God's leaders to be perfect, but don't let them get away with sin either.	Exodus 4—Numbers 20
Nadab (6:3)	Pretending to be God's representative is a dangerous business.	Leviticus 10
Eleazar (6:3)	Those who are consistent in their faith are the best models to follow.	Numbers 20:25–29; 26—34; Joshua 24:33
Korah (6:22)	Rebelling against God's leaders is rebelling against God and will always be unsuccessful.	Numbers 16
Joshua (7:27)	Real courage comes from God.	The book of Joshua
Saul (8:33)	Those who say they follow God but don't live like it waste their God-given potential.	1 Samuel 8—31
Jonathan (8:33)	True friends always think of the other person, not just themselves.	1 Samuel 14—31

place, because there was pasture for their flocks. 42And five hundred of these Simeonites, led by Pelatiah, Neariah, Rephaiah and Uzziel, the sons of Ishi, invaded the hill
country of Seir.[x] 43They killed the remaining Amalekites[y] who had escaped, and
they have lived there to this day.

Reuben

5 The sons of Reuben[a] the firstborn of Israel (he was the firstborn, but when he
defiled his father's marriage bed,[b] his rights as firstborn were given to the sons
of Joseph[c] son of Israel;[d] so he could not be listed in the genealogical record in
accordance with his birthright,[e] 2and though Judah[f] was the strongest of his brothers
and a ruler[g] came from him, the rights of the firstborn[h] belonged to Joseph)—3the
sons of Reuben[i] the firstborn of Israel:

Hanoch, Pallu,[j] Hezron and Carmi.

4The descendants of Joel:

Shemaiah his son, Gog his son,
Shimei his son, 5Micah his son,
Reaiah his son, Baal his son,
6and Beerah his son, whom Tiglath-Pileser[a][k] king of Assyria took into exile.
Beerah was a leader of the Reubenites.

7Their relatives by clans,[l] listed according to their genealogical records:

Jeiel the chief, Zechariah, 8and Bela son of Azaz, the son of Shema, the son
of Joel. They settled in the area from Aroer[m] to Nebo and Baal Meon.[n] 9To
the east they occupied the land up to the edge of the desert that extends to
the Euphrates River, because their livestock had increased in Gilead.[o]
10During Saul's reign they waged war against the Hagrites[p], who were
defeated at their hands; they occupied the dwellings of the Hagrites throughout the entire region east of Gilead.

Gad

11The Gadites[q] lived next to them in Bashan, as far as Salecah:[r]
12Joel was the chief, Shapham the second, then Janai and Shaphat, in Bashan.
13Their relatives, by families, were:
Michael, Meshullam, Sheba, Jorai, Jacan, Zia and Eber—seven in all.
14These were the sons of Abihail son of Huri, the son of Jaroah, the son of
Gilead, the son of Michael, the son of Jeshishai, the son of Jahdo, the son
of Buz.
15Ahi son of Abdiel, the son of Guni, was head of their family.
16The Gadites lived in Gilead, in Bashan and its outlying villages, and on all the
pasture-lands of Sharon as far as they extended.
17All these were entered in the genealogical records during the reigns of Jotham[s]
king of Judah and Jeroboam[t] king of Israel.

18The Reubenites, the Gadites and the half-tribe of Manasseh had 44,760 men ready
for military service[u]—able-bodied men who could handle shield and sword, who
could use a bow, and who were trained for battle. 19They waged war against the
Hagrites, Jetur,[v] Naphish and Nodab. 20They were helped[w] in fighting them, and

a 6 Hebrew *Tilgath-Pilneser,* a variant of *Tiglath-Pileser,* also in verse 26

4:42 [x]Ge 14:6
4:43 [y]1Sa 15:8; 30:17; 2Sa 8:12; Est 3:1; 9:16
5:1 [a]Ge 29:32 [b]Ge 35:22; 49:4 [c]Ge 48:16, 22; 49:26 [d]Ge 48:5 [e]1Ch 26:10
5:2 [f]Ge 49:10, 12 [g]1Sa 9:16; 12:12; 2Sa 6:21; 1Ch 11:2; 2Ch 7:18; Ps 60:7; Mic 5:2; Mt 2:6 [h]Ge 25:31
5:3 [i]Ge 29:32; 46:9; Ex 6:14; Nu 26:5-11 [j]Nu 26:5
5:6 [k]ver 26; 2Ki 15:19; 16:10; 2Ch 28:20
5:7 [l]ver 17
5:8 [m]Nu 32:34 [n]Jos 13:17
5:9 [o]Nu 32:26; Jos 22:9
5:10 [p]ver 18-21
5:11 [q]Jos 13:24-28 [r]Dt 3:10; Jos 13:11
5:17 [s]2Ki 15:32 [t]2Ki 14:16, 28
5:18 [u]Nu 1:3
5:19 [v]ver 10; Ge 25:15; 1Ch 1:31
5:20 [w]Ps 37:40

5:1 Reuben's sin of incest was recorded for all future generations to read. The purpose of this epitaph was not to smear Reuben's name, but to show that painful memories aren't the only results of sin. The real consequences of sin are ruined lives. As the oldest son, Reuben was the rightful heir to both a double portion of his father's estate and the leadership of Abraham's descendants, who had grown into a large tribe. But his sin stripped away his rights and privileges and ruined his family. Before you give in to temptation, take a close look at the disastrous consequences sin may produce in your life and the lives of others.

5:2 This ruler from the tribe of Judah refers to David and his royal line, and to Jesus the Messiah, David's greatest descendant.

5:18–22 The armies of Reuben, Gad, and Manasseh succeeded in battle because they trusted God. Although they had instinct and skill as soldiers, they prayed and sought God's direction. The natural and developed abilities God gives us are meant to be used for him, but they should never replace our dependence on him. When we trust in our own cleverness, skill, and strength rather than in God, we open the door for pride. When facing difficult situations, seek God's purpose and ask for his guidance and strength. Psalm 20:7 says, "Some trust in chariots and some in horses, but we trust in the name of the LORD our God."

God handed the Hagrites and all their allies over to them, because they cried[x] out
to him during the battle. He answered their prayers, because they trusted[y] in him.
21 They seized the livestock of the Hagrites—fifty thousand camels, two hundred and
fifty thousand sheep and two thousand donkeys. They also took one hundred thousand
people captive, 22 and many others fell slain, because the battle[z] was God's. And they
occupied the land until the exile.[a]

The Half-Tribe of Manasseh

23 The people of the half-tribe of Manasseh were numerous; they settled in the land
from Bashan to Baal Hermon, that is, to Senir (Mount Hermon).[b]
24 These were the heads of their families: Epher, Ishi, Eliel, Azriel, Jeremiah,
Hodaviah and Jahdiel. They were brave warriors, famous men, and heads of their
families. 25 But they were unfaithful[c] to the God of their fathers and prostituted[d]
themselves to the gods of the peoples of the land, whom God had destroyed before
them. 26 So the God of Israel stirred up the spirit of Pul[e] king of Assyria (that is,
Tiglath-Pileser[f] king of Assyria), who took the Reubenites, the Gadites and the
half-tribe of Manasseh into exile. He took them to Halah,[g] Habor, Hara and the river
of Gozan, where they are to this day.

Levi

6 The sons of Levi:[a]
Gershon, Kohath and Merari.
2 The sons of Kohath:
Amram, Izhar, Hebron and Uzziel.
3 The children of Amram:
Aaron, Moses and Miriam.
The sons of Aaron:
Nadab, Abihu,[b] Eleazar and Ithamar.
4 Eleazar was the father of Phinehas,
Phinehas the father of Abishua,
5 Abishua the father of Bukki,
Bukki the father of Uzzi,
6 Uzzi the father of Zerahiah,
Zerahiah the father of Meraioth,
7 Meraioth the father of Amariah,
Amariah the father of Ahitub,
8 Ahitub the father of Zadok,[c]
Zadok the father of Ahimaaz,
9 Ahimaaz the father of Azariah,
Azariah the father of Johanan,
10 Johanan the father of Azariah[d] (it was he who served as priest in the temple
Solomon built in Jerusalem),
11 Azariah the father of Amariah,

5:20 [x]1Ki 8:44; 2Ch 13:14; 14:11; Ps 20:7-9; 22:5 [y]Ps 26:1; Da 6:23
5:22 [z]2Ch 32:8 [a]2Ki 15:29; 17:6
5:23 [b]Dt 3:8, 9; SS 4:8
5:25 [c]Dt 32:15-18; 2Ki 17:7; 1Ch 9:1; 2Ch 26:16 [d]Ex 34:15
5:26 [e]2Ki 15:19 [f]2Ki 15:29 [g]2Ki 17:6; 18:11
6:1 [a]Ge 46:11; Ex 6:16; Nu 26:57; 1Ch 23:6
6:3 [b]Lev 10:1
6:8 [c]2Sa 8:17; 15:27; Ezr 7:2
6:10 [d]1Ki 4:2; 6:1; 2Ch 3:1; 26:17-18

5:22 The exile mentioned here refers to the exile of the ten northern tribes (the northern kingdom of Israel) to Assyria in 722 B.C. These tribes never returned to their homeland. This story is found in 2 Kings 15:29–17:41.

5:24, 25 As warriors and leaders, these men had established excellent reputations for their great skill and leadership qualities. But in God's eyes they failed in the most important quality—being faithful to God. If you try to measure up to society's standards for fame and success, you may neglect your true purpose—to please and obey God. In the end, God alone examines our hearts and determines our final standing.

6:1ff The tribe of Levi was set apart to serve God in the tabernacle (Numbers 3; 4), and later in the temple (1 Chronicles 23–26). Aaron, Levi's descendant (6:3), became Israel's first high priest. God required all future priests to be descendants of Aaron. The rest of the Levites assisted the priests in the various tabernacle or temple duties and assisted the people by teaching them God's word and encouraging them to obey it.

6:3 The people listed here played major roles in the drama of the exodus. Aaron's story is found in the books of Exodus, Leviticus, and Numbers. His Profile is found in Exodus 32. Moses was one of the greatest prophets and leaders in Israel's history. His story is found in the books of Exodus, Leviticus, Numbers, and Deuteronomy. His Profile is found in Exodus 14. The story of Miriam, Moses' and Aaron's sister, is found in Exodus 2; 15:20, 21; and Numbers 12; 20:1. Her Profile is found in Numbers 13. Nadab and Abihu were killed for disobeying God (Leviticus 10). Eleazar became Israel's high priest after Aaron (Numbers 20:24–28), and Ithamar played an important role in organising the worship services of the tabernacle (Numbers 4:28, 33; 7:8).

Amariah the father of Ahitub,
12 Ahitub the father of Zadok,
Zadok the father of Shallum,
13 Shallum the father of Hilkiah,[e]
Hilkiah the father of Azariah,
14 Azariah the father of Seraiah,[f]
and Seraiah the father of Jehozadak.
15 Jehozadak[g] was deported when the LORD sent Judah and Jerusalem into exile
by the hand of Nebuchadnezzar.

16 The sons of Levi:[h]
Gershon,[a] Kohath and Merari.[i]
17 These are the names of the sons of Gershon:
Libni and Shimei.
18 The sons of Kohath:
Amram, Izhar, Hebron and Uzziel.
19 The sons of Merari:[j]
Mahli and Mushi.
These are the clans of the Levites listed according to their fathers:
20 Of Gershon:
Libni his son, Jehath his son,
Zimmah his son, 21 Joah his son,
Iddo his son, Zerah his son
and Jeatherai his son.
22 The descendants of Kohath:
Amminadab his son, Korah[k] his son,
Assir his son, 23 Elkanah his son,
Ebiasaph his son, Assir his son,
24 Tahath his son, Uriel[l] his son,
Uzziah his son and Shaul his son.
25 The descendants of Elkanah:
Amasai, Ahimoth,
26 Elkanah his son,[b] Zophai his son,
Nahath his son, 27 Eliab his son,
Jeroham his son, Elkanah[m] his son
and Samuel[n] his son.[c]
28 The sons of Samuel:
Joel[d][o] the firstborn
and Abijah the second son.
29 The descendants of Merari:
Mahli, Libni his son,
Shimei his son, Uzzah his son,
30 Shimea his son, Haggiah his son
and Asaiah his son.

The Temple Musicians

31 These are the men[p] David put in charge of the music[q] in the house of the LORD
after the ark came to rest there. 32 They ministered with music before the tabernacle,

6:13 [e] 2Ki 22:1-20; 2Ch 34:9; 35:8
6:14 [f] 2Ki 25:18; Ezr 2:2; Ne 11:11
6:15 [g] 2Ki 25:18; Ne 12:1; Hag 1:1, 14; 2:2, 4; Zec 6:11
6:16 [h] Ge 29:34; Ex 6:16; Nu 3:17-20 [i] Nu 26:57
6:19 [j] Ge 46:11; 1Ch 23:21; 24:26
6:22 [k] Ex 6:24
6:24 [l] 1Ch 15:5
6:27 [m] 1Sa 1:1 [n] 1Sa 1:20
6:28 [o] ver 33; 1Sa 8:2
6:31 [p] 1Ch 25:1; 2Ch 29:25-26; Ne 12:45 [q] 1Ch 9:33; 15:19; Ezr 3:10; Ps 68:25

a *16* Hebrew *Gershom*, a variant of *Gershon*; also in verses 17, 20, 43, 62 and 71 b *26* Some Hebrew manuscripts, Septuagint and Syriac; most Hebrew manuscripts *Ahimoth* [26]*and Elkanah. The sons of Elkanah:* c *27* Some Septuagint manuscripts (see also 1 Sam. 1:19, 20 and 1 Chron. 6:33, 34); Hebrew does not have *and Samuel his son.* d *28* Some Septuagint manuscripts and Syriac (see also 1 Sam. 8:2 and 1 Chron. 6:33); Hebrew does not have *Joel.*

6:28 When Samuel became God's leader and spokesman, Israel was on the brink of collapse. The last few chapters of the book of Judges give a vivid picture of the moral decay and the resulting decline of the nation. But with God's help, Samuel almost single-handedly brought the nation from ruin to revival. He unified the people by showing them that God was their common Leader and that any nation that focused on him would find and fulfil its true purpose. For the rest of Samuel's story, and to see how he set up rules for governing a nation based on spiritual principles, read the book of 1 Samuel and his Profile in chapter 7.

6:31 David did much to bring music into worship. He established songleaders and choirs to perform regularly at the temple (chapter

6:33
[r] 1Ki 4:31; 1Ch 15:17; 25:1
[s] ver 28

the Tent of Meeting, until Solomon built the temple of the LORD in Jerusalem. They performed their duties according to the regulations laid down for them.

33 Here are the men who served, together with their sons:

From the Kohathites:
Heman,[r] the musician,
the son of Joel,[s] the son of Samuel,
34 the son of Elkanah,[t] the son of Jeroham,
the son of Eliel, the son of Toah,
35 the son of Zuph, the son of Elkanah,
the son of Mahath, the son of Amasai,
36 the son of Elkanah, the son of Joel,
the son of Azariah, the son of Zephaniah,
37 the son of Tahath, the son of Assir,
the son of Ebiasaph, the son of Korah,[u]
38 the son of Izhar,[v] the son of Kohath,
the son of Levi, the son of Israel;
39 and Heman's associate Asaph,[w] who served at his right hand:
Asaph son of Berekiah, the son of Shimea,[x]
40 the son of Michael, the son of Baaseiah,[e]
the son of Malkijah, 41 the son of Ethni,
the son of Zerah, the son of Adaiah,
42 the son of Ethan, the son of Zimmah,
the son of Shimei, 43 the son of Jahath,
the son of Gershon, the son of Levi;
44 and from their associates, the Merarites, at his left hand:
Ethan son of Kishi, the son of Abdi,
the son of Malluch, 45 the son of Hashabiah,
the son of Amaziah, the son of Hilkiah,
46 the son of Amzi, the son of Bani,
the son of Shemer, 47 the son of Mahli,
the son of Mushi, the son of Merari,
the son of Levi.

6:34
[t] 1Sa 1:1

6:37
[u] Ex 6:24

6:38
[v] Ex 6:21

6:39
[w] 1Ch 25:1, 9; 2Ch 29:13; Ne 11:17
[x] 1Ch 15:17

6:48
[y] 1Ch 23:32

48 Their fellow Levites[y] were assigned to all the other duties of the tabernacle, the house of God. 49 But Aaron and his descendants were the ones who presented offerings on the altar[z] of burnt offering and on the altar of incense[a] in connection with all that was done in the Most Holy Place, making atonement for Israel, in accordance with all that Moses the servant of God had commanded.

6:49
[z] Ex 27:1-8
[a] Ex 30:1-7, 10; 2Ch 26:18

50 These were the descendants of Aaron:
Eleazar his son, Phinehas his son,
Abishua his son, 51 Bukki his son,
Uzzi his son, Zerahiah his son,
52 Meraioth his son, Amariah his son,
Ahitub his son, 53 Zadok[b] his son
and Ahimaaz his son.

6:53
[b] 2Sa 8:17

[e] *40* Most Hebrew manuscripts; some Hebrew manuscripts, one Septuagint manuscript and Syriac *Maaseiah*

---

25). As a young man, David was hired to play the harp for King Saul (1 Samuel 16:15–23). He also wrote many of the songs found in the book of Psalms.

6:31ff The builders and craftsmen had completed the temple, and the priests and Levites had been given their responsibilities for taking care of it. Then it was time for another group of people – the musicians – to exercise their talents for God. Some of those who served with music are recorded here. You don't have to be an ordained minister to have an important place in the body of believers. Builders, craftsmen, worship assistants, choir members, and songleaders all have significant contributions to make. God has given you a unique combination of talents. Use them to serve and honour him.

6:49 Aaron and his descendants strictly followed the details of worship commanded by God through Moses. They did not choose only those commands they *wanted* to obey. Note what happened to Uzzah when important details in handling the ark of the covenant were neglected (13:6–10). We should not try to obey God selectively, choosing those commands we will obey and those we will ignore. God's word has authority over every aspect of our lives, not just selected portions.

6:49 For more information on priests, see the note on Leviticus 8:1ff.

54 These were the locations of their settlements[c] allotted as their territory (they were
assigned to the descendants of Aaron who were from the Kohathite clan, because the
first lot was for them):

55 They were given Hebron in Judah with its surrounding pasture-lands. 56 But
the fields and villages around the city were given to Caleb son of Jephunneh.[d]
57 So the descendants of Aaron were given Hebron (a city of refuge), and
Libnah,[f][e] Jattir,[f] Eshtemoa, 58 Hilen, Debir,[g] 59 Ashan,[h] Juttah[g] and Beth
Shemesh, together with their pasture-lands. 60 And from the tribe of Benjamin
they were given Gibeon,[h] Geba, Alemeth and Anathoth,[i] together with their
pasture-lands.

These towns, which were distributed among the Kohathite clans, were thirteen
in all.

61 The rest of Kohath's descendants were allotted ten towns from the clans of half
the tribe of Manasseh.
62 The descendants of Gershon, clan by clan, were allotted thirteen towns from the
tribes of Issachar, Asher and Naphtali, and from the part of the tribe of Manasseh that
is in Bashan.
63 The descendants of Merari, clan by clan, were allotted twelve towns from the
tribes of Reuben, Gad and Zebulun.
64 So the Israelites gave the Levites these towns[j] and their pasture-lands. 65 From
the tribes of Judah, Simeon and Benjamin they allotted the previously named towns.
66 Some of the Kohathite clans were given as their territory towns from the tribe of
Ephraim.

67 In the hill country of Ephraim they were given Shechem (a city of refuge),
and Gezer,[i][k] 68 Jokmeam,[l] Beth Horon,[m] 69 Aijalon[n] and Gath Rimmon,[o]
together with their pasture-lands.
70 And from half the tribe of Manasseh the Israelites gave Aner and Bileam,
together with their pasture-lands, to the rest of the Kohathite clans.

71 The Gershonites[p] received the following:
From the clan of the half-tribe of Manasseh
they received Golan in Bashan[q] and also Ashtaroth, together with their
pasture-lands;
72 from the tribe of Issachar
they received Kedesh, Daberath,[r] 73 Ramoth and Anem, together with their
pasture-lands;
74 from the tribe of Asher
they received Mashal, Abdon,[s] 75 Hukok[t] and Rehob,[u] together with their
pasture-lands;
76 and from the tribe of Naphtali
they received Kedesh in Galilee, Hammon[v] and Kiriathaim,[w] together with
their pasture-lands.

77 The Merarites (the rest of the Levites) received the following:

f *57* See Joshua 21:13; Hebrew *given the cities of refuge: Hebron, Libnah.* **g** *59* Syriac (see also Septuagint and Joshua 21:16); Hebrew does not have *Juttah.* **h** *60* See Joshua 21:17; Hebrew does not have *Gibeon.* **i** *67* See Joshua 21:21; Hebrew *given the cities of refuge: Shechem, Gezer.*

6:54 [c]Nu 31:10
6:56 [d]Jos 14:13; 15:13
6:57 [e]Nu 33:20 [f]Jos 15:48
6:58 [g]Jos 10:3
6:59 [h]Jos 15:42
6:60 [i]Jer 1:1
6:64 [j]Nu 35:1-8; Jos 21:3, 41-42
6:67 [k]Jos 10:33
6:68 [l]1Ki 4:12 [m]Jos 10:10
6:69 [n]Jos 10:12 [o]Jos 19:45
6:71 [p]1Ch 23:7 [q]Jos 20:8
6:72 [r]Jos 19:12
6:74 [s]Jos 19:28
6:75 [t]Jos 19:34 [u]Nu 13:21
6:76 [v]Jos 19:28 [w]Nu 32:37

6:54 The tribe of Levi was not given a specific area of land as were the other tribes. Instead, the Levites were to live throughout the land in order to aid the people of *every* tribe in their worship of God. Thus the Levites were given towns or pasturelands within the allotted areas of the other tribes (Joshua 13:14, 33).

6:57ff God had told the tribes to designate specific cities to be cities of refuge (Numbers 35). These cities were to provide refuge for a person who accidentally killed someone. This instruction may have seemed unimportant when it was given—the Israelites hadn't even entered the promised land. Sometimes God gives us instructions that do not seem relevant to us at the moment. But later we can see the importance of those instructions. Don't discard the lessons of the Bible because certain details seem irrelevant. Obey God now—in the future you will have a clearer understanding of the reasons for his instructions.

6:61 The Israelites cast lots in order to take the decision-making process out of man's hands and put it into God's hands. Casting lots was like drawing straws or throwing dice. Lots were cast only after seeking God's guidance in prayer. (For more information on casting lots, see the note on Joshua 18:8.)

From the tribe of Zebulun
they received Jokneam, Kartah,[j] Rimmono and Tabor, together with their pasture-lands;
78from the tribe of Reuben across the Jordan east of Jericho
they received Bezer[x] in the desert, Jahzah, 79Kedemoth[y] and Mephaath, together with their pasture-lands;
80and from the tribe of Gad
they received Ramoth in Gilead,[z] Mahanaim,[a] 81Heshbon and Jazer,[b] together with their pasture-lands.[c]

Issachar

7 The sons of Issachar:[a]
Tola, Puah,[b] Jashub and Shimron — four in all.
2The sons of Tola:
Uzzi, Rephaiah, Jeriel, Jahmai, Ibsam and Samuel — heads of their families. During the reign of David, the descendants of Tola listed as fighting men in their genealogy numbered 22,600.
3The son of Uzzi:
Izrahiah.
The sons of Izrahiah:
Michael, Obadiah, Joel and Isshiah. All five of them were chiefs. 4According
to their family genealogy, they had 36,000 men ready for battle, for they had many wives and children.
5The relatives who were fighting men belonging to all the clans of Issachar, as listed in their genealogy, were 87,000 in all.

Benjamin

6Three sons of Benjamin:[c]
Bela, Beker and Jediael.
7The sons of Bela:
Ezbon, Uzzi, Uzziel, Jerimoth and Iri, heads of families — five in all. Their genealogical record listed 22,034 fighting men.
8The sons of Beker:
Zemirah, Joash, Eliezer, Elioenai, Omri, Jeremoth, Abijah, Anathoth and
Alemeth. All these were the sons of Beker. 9Their genealogical record listed
the heads of families and 20,200 fighting men.
10The son of Jediael:
Bilhan.
The sons of Bilhan:
Jeush, Benjamin, Ehud, Kenaanah, Zethan, Tarshish and Ahishahar. 11All
these sons of Jediael were heads of families. There were 17,200 fighting men ready to go out to war.
12The Shuppites and Huppites were the descendants of Ir, and the Hushites the descendants of Aher.

Naphtali

13The sons of Naphtali:[d]
Jahziel, Guni, Jezer and Shillem[a] — the descendants of Bilhah.

Manasseh

14The descendants of Manasseh:[e]
Asriel was his descendant through his Aramean concubine. She gave birth to
Makir the father of Gilead.[f] 15Makir took a wife from among the Huppites and
Shuppites. His sister's name was Maacah.
Another descendant was named Zelophehad,[g] who had only daughters.

6:78 [x]Jos 20:8
6:79 [y]Dt 2:26
6:80 [z]Jos 20:8 [a]Ge 32:2
6:81 [b]Nu 21:32 [c]2Ch 11:14
7:1 [a]Ge 30:18; Nu 26:23 [b]Ge 46:13
7:6 [c]Ge 46:21; Nu 26:38; 1Ch 8:1-40
7:13 [d]Ge 30:8; 46:24
7:14 [e]Ge 41:51; Jos 17:1; 1Ch 5:23 [f]Nu 26:30
7:15 [g]Nu 26:33; 36:1-12

[j] *77* See Septuagint and Joshua 21:34; Hebrew does not have *Jokneam, Kartah.* [a] *13* Some Hebrew and Septuagint manuscripts (see also Gen. 46:24 and Num. 26:49); most Hebrew manuscripts *Shallum*

16 Makir's wife Maacah gave birth to a son and named him Peresh. His brother
was named Sheresh, and his sons were Ulam and Rakem.
17 The son of Ulam:
Bedan.
These were the sons of Gilead[h] son of Makir, the son of Manasseh. 18 His sister
Hammoleketh gave birth to Ishhod, Abiezer[i] and Mahlah.
19 The sons of Shemida were:
Ahian, Shechem, Likhi and Aniam.

Ephraim

20 The descendants of Ephraim:[j]
Shuthelah, Bered his son,
Tahath his son, Eleadah his son,
Tahath his son, 21 Zabad his son
and Shuthelah his son.
Ezer and Elead were killed by the native-born men of Gath, when they went
down to seize their livestock. 22 Their father Ephraim mourned for them many
days, and his relatives came to comfort him. 23 Then he lay with his wife again,
and she became pregnant and gave birth to a son. He named him Beriah,[b]
because there had been misfortune in his family. 24 His daughter was Sheerah,
who built Lower and Upper Beth Horon[k] as well as Uzzen Sheerah.
25 Rephah was his son, Resheph his son,[c]
Telah his son, Tahan his son,
26 Ladan his son, Ammihud his son,
Elishama his son, 27 Nun his son
and Joshua his son.
28 Their lands and settlements included Bethel and its surrounding villages, Naaran
to the east, Gezer[l] and its villages to the west, and Shechem and its villages all the
way to Ayyah and its villages. 29 Along the borders of Manasseh were Beth Shan,[m]
Taanach, Megiddo and Dor,[n] together with their villages. The descendants of Joseph
son of Israel lived in these towns.

Asher

30 The sons of Asher:[o]
Imnah, Ishvah, Ishvi and Beriah. Their sister was Serah.
31 The sons of Beriah:
Heber and Malkiel, who was the father of Birzaith.
32 Heber was the father of Japhlet, Shomer and Hotham and of their sister Shua.
33 The sons of Japhlet:
Pasach, Bimhal and Ashvath.
These were Japhlet's sons.
34 The sons of Shomer:
Ahi, Rohgah,[d] Hubbah and Aram.
35 The sons of his brother Helem:
Zophah, Imna, Shelesh and Amal.
36 The sons of Zophah:
Suah, Harnepher, Shual, Beri, Imrah, 37 Bezer, Hod, Shamma, Shilshah,
Ithran[e] and Beera.
38 The sons of Jether:
Jephunneh, Pispah and Ara.
39 The sons of Ulla:
Arah, Hanniel and Rizia.

7:17 [h] Nu 26:30; 1Sa 12:11
7:18 [i] Jos 17:2
7:20 [j] Ge 41:52; Nu 1:33; 26:35
7:24 [k] Jos 10:10; 16:3, 5
7:28 [l] Jos 10:33; 16:7
7:29 [m] Jos 17:11 [n] Jos 11:2
7:30 [o] Ge 46:17; Nu 1:40; 26:44

b 23 *Beriah* sounds like the Hebrew for *misfortune.* c 25 Some Septuagint manuscripts; Hebrew does not have *his son.* d 34 Or *of his brother Shomer: Rohgah* e 37 Possibly a variant of *Jether*

7:27 Joshua was one of Israel's great leaders, leading the people into the promised land. His story is told in the book of Joshua. His Profile is found in Joshua 2.

40All these were descendants of Asher—heads of families, choice men, brave
warriors and outstanding leaders. The number of men ready for battle, as listed in their
genealogy, was 26,000.

The Genealogy of Saul the Benjamite

8 Benjamin[a] was the father of Bela his firstborn,
Ashbel the second son, Aharah the third,
2Nohah the fourth and Rapha the fifth.
3The sons of Bela were:
Addar,[b] Gera, Abihud,[a] 4Abishua, Naaman, Ahoah,[c] 5Gera, Shephuphan
and Huram.
6These were the descendants of Ehud,[d] who were heads of families of those
living in Geba and were deported to Manahath:
7Naaman, Ahijah and Gera, who deported them and who was the father of
Uzza and Ahihud.
8Sons were born to Shaharaim in Moab after he had divorced his wives Hushim
and Baara. 9By his wife Hodesh he had Jobab, Zibia, Mesha, Malcam,
10Jeuz, Sakia and Mirmah. These were his sons, heads of families. 11By
Hushim he had Abitub and Elpaal.
12The sons of Elpaal:
Eber, Misham, Shemed (who built Ono[e] and Lod with its surrounding
villages), 13and Beriah and Shema, who were heads of families of those living
in Aijalon[f] and who drove out the inhabitants of Gath.[g]
14Ahio, Shashak, Jeremoth, 15Zebadiah, Arad, Eder, 16Michael, Ishpah and Joha
were the sons of Beriah.
17Zebadiah, Meshullam, Hizki, Heber, 18Ishmerai, Izliah and Jobab were the sons
of Elpaal.
19Jakim, Zicri, Zabdi, 20Elienai, Zillethai, Eliel, 21Adaiah, Beraiah and Shimrath
were the sons of Shimei.
22Ishpan, Eber, Eliel, 23Abdon, Zicri, Hanan, 24Hananiah, Elam, Anthothijah,
25Iphdeiah and Penuel were the sons of Shashak.
26Shamsherai, Shehariah, Athaliah, 27Jaareshiah, Elijah and Zicri were the sons
of Jeroham.
28All these were heads of families, chiefs as listed in their genealogy, and they lived
in Jerusalem.

29Jeiel[b] the father[c] of Gibeon lived in Gibeon.[h]
His wife's name was Maacah, 30and his firstborn son was Abdon, followed
by Zur, Kish, Baal, Ner,[d] Nadab, 31Gedor, Ahio, Zeker 32and Mikloth, who
was the father of Shimeah. They too lived near their relatives in Jerusalem.
33Ner[i] was the father of Kish,[j] Kish the father of Saul[k], and Saul the father
of Jonathan, Malki-Shua, Abinadab and Esh-Baal.[e][l]
34The son of Jonathan:[m]
Merib-Baal,[f][n] who was the father of Micah.
35The sons of Micah:

8:1 [a]Ge 46:21; 1Ch 7:6
8:3 [b]Ge 46:21
8:4 [c]2Sa 23:9
8:6 [d]Jdg 3:12-30; 1Ch 2:52
8:12 [e]Ezr 2:33; Ne 6:2; 7:37; 11:35
8:13 [f]Jos 10:12 [g]Jos 11:22
8:29 [h]Jos 9:3
8:33 [i]1Sa 28:19 [j]1Sa 9:1 [k]1Sa 14:49 [l]2Sa 2:8
8:34 [m]2Sa 9:12 [n]2Sa 4:4

[a] *3* Or *Gera the father of Ehud* [b] *29* Some Septuagint manuscripts (see also 1 Chron. 9:35); Hebrew does not have *Jeiel.* [c] *29* *Father* may mean *civic leader* or *military leader.* [d] *30* Some Septuagint manuscripts (see also 1 Chron. 9:36); Hebrew does not have *Ner.* [e] *33* Also known as *Ish-Bosheth* [f] *34* Also known as *Mephibosheth*

8:8–10 These verses list Shaharaim's children by Hodesh after he had divorced his first two wives, Hushim and Baara. Divorce and polygamy are sometimes recorded in the Old Testament without critical comments. This does not mean that God takes divorce lightly. Malachi 2:15, 16 says, "... do not break faith with the wife of your youth. 'I hate divorce,' says the LORD God of Israel ..." Jesus explained that although divorce was allowed, it was not God's will: " 'Moses permitted you to divorce your wives because your hearts were hard. But it was not this way from the beginning' " (Matthew 19:8). Don't assume that God approves of an act because it isn't vigorously condemned in every related Bible reference.

8:33 Saul, Israel's first king, was very inconsistent. His story is found in 1 Samuel 9–31, and his Profile is in 1 Samuel 13. Saul's son Jonathan was the opposite. Although Jonathan was the rightful heir to the throne, he realised that David was God's choice to be Israel's next king. Instead of being jealous, Jonathan was David's friend and even helped him escape from Saul's attempts at murder. Jonathan's story is told in 1 Samuel 14–31. His Profile is found in 1 Samuel 20.

Pithon, Melech, Tarea and Ahaz.
36 Ahaz was the father of Jehoaddah, Jehoaddah was the father of Alemeth,
Azmaveth and Zimri, and Zimri was the father of Moza. 37 Moza was the
father of Binea; Raphah was his son, Eleasah his son and Azel his son.
38 Azel had six sons, and these were their names:
Azrikam, Bokeru, Ishmael, Sheariah, Obadiah and Hanan. All these were the
sons of Azel.
39 The sons of his brother Eshek:
Ulam his firstborn, Jeush the second son and Eliphelet the third. 40 The sons
of Ulam were brave warriors who could handle the bow. They had many sons
and grandsons—150 in all.
All these were the descendants of Benjamin.[o]

9 All Israel was listed in the genealogies in the book of the kings of Israel.

3. Those returned from exile in Babylon

The People in Jerusalem

The people of Judah were taken captive to Babylon because of their unfaithfulness.[a] 2 Now the first to resettle on their own property in their own towns[b] were some
Israelites, priests, Levites and temple servants.[c]
3 Those from Judah, from Benjamin, and from Ephraim and Manasseh who lived
in Jerusalem were:
4 Uthai son of Ammihud, the son of Omri, the son of Imri, the son of Bani, a
descendant of Perez son of Judah.[d]
5 Of the Shilonites:
Asaiah the firstborn and his sons.
6 Of the Zerahites:
Jeuel.
The people from Judah numbered 690.
7 Of the Benjamites:
Sallu son of Meshullam, the son of Hodaviah, the son of Hassenuah;
8 Ibneiah son of Jeroham; Elah son of Uzzi, the son of Micri; and Meshullam
son of Shephatiah, the son of Reuel, the son of Ibnijah.
9 The people from Benjamin, as listed in their genealogy, numbered 956. All
these men were heads of their families.
10 Of the priests:
Jedaiah; Jehoiarib; Jakin;
11 Azariah son of Hilkiah, the son of Meshullam, the son of Zadok, the son of
Meraioth, the son of Ahitub, the official in charge of the house of God;
12 Adaiah son of Jeroham, the son of Pashhur,[e] the son of Malkijah; and Maasai
son of Adiel, the son of Jahzerah, the son of Meshullam, the son of Meshille-
mith, the son of Immer.
13 The priests, who were heads of families, numbered 1,760. They were able
men, responsible for ministering in the house of God.
14 Of the Levites:
Shemaiah son of Hasshub, the son of Azrikam, the son of Hashabiah, a
Merarite; 15 Bakbakkar, Heresh, Galal and Mattaniah[f] son of Mica, the son
of Zicri, the son of Asaph; 16 Obadiah son of Shemaiah, the son of Galal, the

8:40 [o]Nu 26:38
9:1 [a]1Ch 5:25
9:2 [b]Jos 9:27; Ezr 2:70 [c]Ezr 2:43, 58; 8:20; Ne 7:60
9:4 [d]Ge 38:29; 46:12
9:12 [e]Ezr 2:38; 10:22; Ne 10:3; Jer 21:1; 38:1
9:15 [f]2Ch 20:14; Ne 11:22

9:1 Although not every person in Judah was unfaithful, the entire nation was carried away into captivity. Everyone was affected by the sin of some. Even if we don't participate in a certain widespread wrongdoing, we will still be affected by those who do. It is not enough to say, "I didn't do it." We must speak out against the sins of our society.

9:1ff Chronologically, this chapter could be placed at the end of 2 Chronicles because it records the names of the exiles who returned from the Babylonian captivity. The writer included it here to show his concern for their need, as a nation, to return to what made them great in the first place—obedience to God.

9:10, 11 When we think of doing God's work, usually preaching, teaching, singing, and other kinds of up-front leadership come to mind. Azariah, however, was in charge of the house of God, and he was singled out for special mention. Whatever role you have in church, it is important to God. He appreciates your service and the attitude you have as you do it.

son of Jeduthun; and Berekiah son of Asa, the son of Elkanah, who lived in
the villages of the Netophathites.[g]
[17]The gatekeepers:[h]
Shallum, Akkub, Talmon, Ahiman and their brothers, Shallum their chief
[18]being stationed at the King's Gate[i] on the east, up to the present time.
These were the gatekeepers belonging to the camp of the Levites. [19]Shallum[j]
son of Kore, the son of Ebiasaph, the son of Korah, and his fellow gatekeepers
from his family (the Korahites) were responsible for guarding the thresholds
of the Tent[a] just as their fathers had been responsible for guarding the
entrance to the dwelling of the LORD. [20]In earlier times Phinehas[k] son of
Eleazar was in charge of the gatekeepers, and the LORD was with him.
[21]Zechariah[l] son of Meshelemiah was the gatekeeper at the entrance to the
Tent of Meeting.
[22]Altogether, those chosen to be gatekeepers[m] at the thresholds numbered 212.
They were registered by genealogy in their villages. The gatekeepers had been
assigned to their positions of trust by David and Samuel the seer.[n] [23]They and their
descendants were in charge of guarding the gates of the house of the LORD — the house
called the Tent. [24]The gatekeepers were on the four sides: east, west, north and south.
[25]Their brothers in their villages had to come from time to time and share their duties
for seven-day[o] periods. [26]But the four principal gatekeepers, who were Levites, were
entrusted with the responsibility for the rooms and treasuries[p] in the house of God.
[27]They would spend the night stationed round the house of God,[q] because they had
to guard it; and they had charge of the key[r] for opening it each morning.
[28]Some of them were in charge of the articles used in the temple service; they
counted them when they were brought in and when they were taken out. [29]Others were
assigned to take care of the furnishings and all the other articles of the sanctuary,[s]
as well as the flour and wine, and the oil, incense and spices. [30]But some[t] of the
priests took care of mixing the spices. [31]A Levite named Mattithiah, the firstborn son
of Shallum the Korahite, was entrusted with the responsibility for baking the offering
bread. [32]Some of their Kohathite brothers were in charge of preparing for every
Sabbath the bread set out on the table.[u]
[33]Those who were musicians,[v] heads of Levite families, stayed in the rooms of
the temple and were exempt from other duties because they were responsible for the
work day and night.[w]
[34]All these were heads of Levite families, chiefs as listed in their genealogy, and
they lived in Jerusalem.

The Genealogy of Saul

[35]Jeiel[x] the father[b] of Gibeon lived in Gibeon.
His wife's name was Maacah, [36]and his firstborn son was Abdon, followed
by Zur, Kish, Baal, Ner, Nadab, [37]Gedor, Ahio, Zechariah and Mikloth.

a *19* That is, the temple; also in verses 21 and 23 b *35* *Father* may mean *civic leader* or *military leader.*

9:16 [g]Ne 12:28
9:17 [h]ver 22; 1Ch 26:1; 2Ch 8:14; 31:14; Ezr 2:42; Ne 7:45
9:18 [i]1Ch 26:14; Eze 43:1; 46:1
9:19 [j]Jer 35:4
9:20 [k]Nu 25:7-13
9:21 [l]1Ch 26:2, 14
9:22 [m]ver 17; 1Ch 26:1-2; 2Ch 31:15, 18 [n]1Sa 9:9
9:25 [o]2Ki 11:5; 2Ch 23:8
9:26 [p]1Ch 26:22
9:27 [q]Nu 3:38; 1Ch 23:30-32 [r]Isa 22:22
9:29 [s]Nu 3:28; 1Ch 23:29
9:30 [t]Ex 30:23-25
9:32 [u]Lev 24:5-8; 1Ch 23:29; 2Ch 13:11
9:33 [v]1Ch 6:31; 25:1-31 [w]Ps 134:1
9:35 [x]1Ch 8:29

9:17, 18 Gatekeepers guarded the four main entrances to the temple and opened the gates each morning for those who wanted to worship. In addition, they did other day-to-day chores to keep the temple running smoothly — cleaning, preparing the offerings for sacrifice, and accounting for the gifts designated to the temple (9:22–32).

Gatekeepers had to be reliable, honest, and trustworthy. The people in our churches who handle the offerings and care for the materials and functions of the building follow in a great tradition and we should honour them for their reliability and service.

9:22–32 The priests and Levites put a great deal of time and care into worship. Not only did they perform rather complicated tasks (described in Leviticus 1 – 9), they also took care of many pieces of equipment. Everything relating to worship was carefully prepared and maintained so they and all the people could enter worship with their minds and hearts focused on God.

In our busy world, it is easy to rush into our one-hour-a-week worship services without preparing ourselves for worship beforehand. We reflect and worry about the week's problems; we pray about whatever comes into our minds; and we do not meditate on the words we are singing. But God wants our worship to be conducted "in a fitting and orderly way" (1 Corinthians 14:40). Just as we prepare to meet a business associate or invited guests, we should carefully prepare to meet our King in worship.

9:33, 34 Worship was the primary focus of many Israelites, whose vocation centred on the house of the Lord. Worship (appreciating God for his nature and worth) should occupy the core of our lives and not just a few minutes once a week. We too can worship at all hours if we stay aware of God's presence and guidance in all situations and if we maintain an attitude of serving him. Build your life around the worship of God rather than making worship just another activity in a busy schedule.

38Mikloth was the father of Shimeam. They too lived near their relatives in
Jerusalem.
39Ner[y] was the father of Kish,[z] Kish the father of Saul, and Saul the father of
Jonathan,[a] Malki-Shua, Abinadab and Esh-Baal.[c][b]
40The son of Jonathan:
Merib-Baal,[d][c] who was the father of Micah.
41The sons of Micah:
Pithon, Melech, Tahrea and Ahaz.[e]
42Ahaz was the father of Jadah, Jadah[f] was the father of Alemeth, Azmaveth
and Zimri, and Zimri was the father of Moza. 43Moza was the father of Binea;
Rephaiah was his son, Eleasah his son and Azel his son.
44Azel had six sons, and these were their names:
Azrikam, Bokeru, Ishmael, Sheariah, Obadiah and Hanan. These were the
sons of Azel.

9:39
y 1Ch 8:33
z 1Sa 9:1
a 1Sa 13:22
b 2Sa 2:8

B. THE REIGN OF DAVID (10:1 – 29:30)

David becomes king over all Israel and captures the city of Jerusalem. God promises blessings to him and the nation, but David is not allowed to build the temple. Instead, he begins to make preparations for its construction. Although stumbling and falling occasionally, David walks step by step with God, sincerely wanting to be obedient. Through David's successes and his failures, we learn the importance of giving our whole heart to God and letting him be the focus of our lives, striving each day to be consistent in our obedience to his will.

9:40
c 2Sa 4:4

1. David becomes king over all of Israel

Saul Takes His Life

10 Now the Philistines fought against Israel; the Israelites fled before them, and
many fell slain on Mount Gilboa. 2The Philistines pressed hard after Saul and
his sons, and they killed his sons Jonathan, Abinadab and Malki-Shua. 3The fighting
grew fierce around Saul, and when the archers overtook him, they wounded him.
4Saul said to his armour-bearer, "Draw your sword and run me through, or these
uncircumcised fellows will come and abuse me."
But his armour-bearer was terrified and would not do it; so Saul took his own sword
and fell on it. 5When the armour-bearer saw that Saul was dead, he too fell on his
sword and died. 6So Saul and his three sons died, and all his house died together.
7When all the Israelites in the valley saw that the army had fled and that Saul and
his sons had died, they abandoned their towns and fled. And the Philistines came and
occupied them.
8The next day, when the Philistines came to strip the dead, they found Saul and
his sons fallen on Mount Gilboa. 9They stripped him and took his head and his armour,
and sent messengers throughout the land of the Philistines to proclaim the news among
their idols and their people. 10They put his armour in the temple of their gods and
hung up his head in the temple of Dagon.[a]
11When all the inhabitants of Jabesh Gilead[b] heard of everything the Philistines
had done to Saul, 12all their valiant men went and took the bodies of Saul and his sons

10:10
a Jdg 16:23

c *39* Also known as *Ish-Bosheth* d *40* Also known as *Mephibosheth* e *41* Vulgate and Syriac (see also Septuagint and 1 Chron. 8:35); Hebrew does not have *and Ahaz.* f *42* Some Hebrew manuscripts and Septuagint (see also 1 Chron. 8:36); most Hebrew manuscripts *Jarah, Jarah*

10:11
b Jdg 21:8

10:1 The chronology of chapters 1 – 9 covers Israelite history from creation to the exile in Babylon (586 B.C.). At this point, the narrative goes back to the beginning of Israel's kingdom period, picking up with Israel's first king, Saul. 1 Chronicles begins with Saul's death; to learn about his reign, read 1 Samuel.

10:10 Dagon, the most important god of the Philistines, was believed to bring rain and provide rich harvests. The Philistines built temples to him when they settled in the grain-producing land of Canaan. In times of drought, people begged Dagon for pity, even to the point of sacrificing their children in his temples. In times of plenty, the temples were used for twisted forms of entertainment, such as the humiliation of captives (see Judges 16:23–30). But Dagon, like the other pagan gods, was powerless against the one true God (1 Samuel 5:1–7).

10:11, 12 The actions of the valiant warriors who brought back and buried the bodies of King Saul and his sons should encourage us to respect our God-given leaders. David showed respect for Saul's position, even when Saul was chasing him to kill him (1 Samuel 26). How easy it is to be critical of those in authority over us, focusing only on their weaknesses. We cannot excuse sin, but we should respect the positions of those in authority, whether at work, at church, or in government. First Thessalonians 5:12, 13 gives instructions for honouring church leaders. Romans 13:1ff gives instructions for relating to government leaders.

and brought them to Jabesh. Then they buried their bones under the great tree in
Jabesh, and they fasted seven days.
13Saul died[c] because he was unfaithful[d] to the LORD; he did not keep[e] the word
of the LORD, and even consulted a medium[f] for guidance, 14and did not enquire of
the LORD. So the LORD put him to death and turned[g] the kingdom[h] over to David
son of Jesse.

David Becomes King Over Israel

11 All Israel[a] came together to David at Hebron[b] and said, "We are your own
flesh and blood. 2In the past, even while Saul was king, you were the one who
led Israel on their military campaigns.[c] And the LORD your God said to you, 'You
will shepherd[d] my people Israel, and you will become their ruler.[e]' "
3When all the elders of Israel had come to King David at Hebron, he made a
compact with them at Hebron before the LORD, and they anointed[f] David king over
Israel, as the LORD had promised through Samuel.

David Conquers Jerusalem

4David and all the Israelites marched to Jerusalem (that is, Jebus). The Jebusites[g]
who lived there 5said to David, "You will not get in here." Nevertheless, David
captured the fortress of Zion, the City of David.
6David had said, "Whoever leads the attack on the Jebusites will become
commander-in-chief." Joab[h] son of Zeruiah went up first, and so he received the
command.
7David then took up residence in the fortress, and so it was called the City of David.
8He built up the city around it, from the supporting terraces[a][i] to the surrounding
wall, while Joab restored the rest of the city. 9And David became more and more
powerful,[j] because the LORD Almighty was with him.

[a] 8 Or *the Millo*

10:13 [c]2Sa 1:1 [d]1Sa 15:23; 1Ch 5:25 [e]1Sa 13:13 [f]Lev 19:31; 20:6; Dt 18:9-14; 1Sa 28:7

10:14 [g]1Ch 12:23 [h]1Sa 13:14; 15:28

11:1 [a]1Ch 9:1 [b]Ge 13:18; 23:19

11:2 [c]1Sa 18:5, 16 [d]Ps 78:71; Mt 2:6 [e]1Ch 5:2

11:3 [f]1Sa 16:1-13

11:4 [g]Ge 10:16; 15:18-21; Jos 3:10; 15:8; Jdg 1:21; 19:10

11:6 [h]2Sa 2:13; 8:16

11:8 [i]2Sa 5:9; 2Ch 32:5

11:9 [j]2Sa 3:1; Est 9:4

10:13, 14 Saul's unfaithfulness was both active and passive; he not only did wrong, but he also *failed to do right.* He actively disobeyed by attempting murder, ignoring God's instructions, and seeking guidance from a witch. He passively disobeyed by neglecting to ask God for guidance as he ran the kingdom. Obedience, too, is both passive and active. It is not enough just to avoid what is wrong, we need to actively pursue what is right.

10:13, 14 In the account in 1 Samuel 28, Saul asked the Lord for guidance but received no answer; this account says he "did not inquire of the LORD". The answer to this apparent contradiction lies in understanding Saul's motives and the timing of his request to God. His frantic requests came only when he had tried everything his own way. He never went to God unless there was nowhere else to turn. When he finally asked, God refused to answer. Saul sought God only when it suited him, and God rejected him for his constant stubbornness and rebellion.

10:14 Throughout much of Saul's reign, David was forced to hide from him (1 Samuel 19 – 30). During this time David had opportunities to kill Saul (1 Samuel 24; 26) and to assume the throne that God had promised him (1 Samuel 16:1–13). But David trusted in God's promise that he would be king in God's good timing. It was not up to David to decide when Saul's reign would end. During this battle, God ended Saul's reign just as he had promised.

10:14 Why does this verse say that the Lord put Saul to death, when Saul took his own life (1 Samuel 31:3, 4)? God had rejected Saul because of his stubbornness and rebellion (1 Samuel 15:22–26) and had judged him for his sins (1 Samuel 28:16–19). God arranged a defeat in battle so that Saul would die and his kingdom would be taken from his family. If Saul had not taken his own life, the Philistine soldiers would have killed him.

11:1, 2 The details of how David came to power are given more completely in 2 Samuel. Chronicles emphasises that *God* declared David to be the ruler although he used the efforts of many people, even some of Saul's own family. God is still sovereign over history, directing events to accomplish his will. The books of Chronicles demonstrate that no matter what people may do to try to hinder God's work, God still controls all events and works his will in them.

11:3, 4 David was king over Judah for seven and a half years before he captured Jerusalem. When David was finally anointed king over all Israel, 20 years had passed since Samuel had anointed him (1 Samuel 16:1–13). God's promises are worth waiting for, even when his timetable doesn't match our expectations or desires.

11:4 David chose Jerusalem as his capital for both political and military reasons. Jerusalem was near the centre of the kingdom and, because it rested on a tribal border, was in neutral territory. Thus its location decreased tribal jealousies. Jerusalem also sat on a high ridge, making it difficult to attack. (For more information on the city of Jerusalem, see the note on 2 Samuel 5:6.)

11:9 David's power increased as a direct result of his consistent trust in God. In contrast, Saul's power decreased because he wanted all the credit for himself and ignored God (1 Samuel 15:17–26). Those who are concerned about building a name for themselves risk losing the very recognition they crave. Like David, we should be concerned for righteousness, honesty, and excellence, and leave the results to God.

David's Mighty Men

10 These were the chiefs of David's mighty men—they, together with all Israel,[k]
gave his kingship strong support to extend it over the whole land, as the LORD had
promised[l]— 11 this is the list of David's mighty men:[m]
Jashobeam,[b] a Hacmonite, was chief of the officers;[c] he raised his spear against
three hundred men, whom he killed in one encounter.
12 Next to him was Eleazar son of Dodai the Ahohite, one of the three mighty men.
13 He was with David at Pas Dammim when the Philistines gathered there for battle.
At a place where there was a field full of barley, the troops fled from the Philistines.
14 But they took their stand in the middle of the field. They defended it and struck the
Philistines down, and the LORD brought about a great victory.[n]
15 Three of the thirty chiefs came down to David to the rock at the cave of Adullam,
while a band of Philistines was encamped in the Valley[o] of Rephaim. 16 At that time
David was in the stronghold,[p] and the Philistine garrison was at Bethlehem. 17 David
longed for water and said, "Oh, that someone would get me a drink of water from
the well near the gate of Bethlehem!" 18 So the Three broke through the Philistine lines,
drew water from the well near the gate of Bethlehem and carried it back to David.
But he refused to drink it; instead, he poured[q] it out before the LORD. 19 "God forbid
that I should do this!" he said. "Should I drink the blood of these men who went at
the risk of their lives?" Because they risked their lives to bring it back, David would
not drink it.
Such were the exploits of the three mighty men.
20 Abishai[r] the brother of Joab was chief of the Three. He raised his spear against
three hundred men, whom he killed, and so he became as famous as the Three. 21 He
was doubly honoured above the Three and became their commander, even though he
was not included among them.
22 Benaiah son of Jehoiada was a valiant fighter from Kabzeel,[s] who performed
great exploits. He struck down two of Moab's best men. He also went down into a
pit on a snowy day and killed a lion.[t] 23 And he struck down an Egyptian who was
seven and a half feet[d] tall. Although the Egyptian had a spear like a weaver's rod[u]
in his hand, Benaiah went against him with a club. He snatched the spear from the
Egyptian's hand and killed him with his own spear. 24 Such were the exploits of
Benaiah son of Jehoiada; he too was as famous as the three mighty men. 25 He was
held in greater honour than any of the Thirty, but he was not included among the
Three. And David put him in charge of his bodyguard.

26 The mighty men were:
Asahel[v] the brother of Joab,
Elhanan son of Dodo from Bethlehem,
27 Shammoth[w] the Harorite,
Helez the Pelonite,
28 Ira son of Ikkesh from Tekoa,
Abiezer[x] from Anathoth,
29 Sibbecai[y] the Hushathite,
Ilai the Ahohite,
30 Maharai the Netophathite,
Heled son of Baanah the Netophathite,

[b] 11 Possibly a variant of *Jashob-Baal* [c] 11 Or *Thirty*; some Septuagint manuscripts *Three* (see also 2 Sam. 23:8) [d] 23 Hebrew *five cubits* (about 2.3 metres)

11:10 [k] ver 1 [l] ver 3 1Ch 12:23
11:11 [m] 2Sa 17:10
11:14 [n] Ex 14:30; 1Sa 11:13
11:15 [o] 1Ch 14:9; Isa 17:5
11:16 [p] 2Sa 5:17
11:18 [q] Dt 12:16
11:20 [r] 1Sa 26:6
11:22 [s] Jos 15:21 [t] 1Sa 17:36
11:23 [u] 1Sa 17:7
11:26 [v] 2Sa 2:18
11:27 [w] 1Ch 27:8
11:28 [x] 1Ch 27:12
11:29 [y] 2Sa 21:18

11:12–14 Eleazar's action changed the course of a battle. When everyone around him ran, he held his ground and was saved by the Lord. In any struggle, fear can keep us from taking a stand for God and from participating in God's victories. Face your fear head on. If you are grounded in God, victory will come when you hold that ground.

11:15 The 30 chiefs were the most courageous and highest-ranking officers of David's army.

11:15–19 These three men risked their lives just to serve and please David. David recognised that their devotion to him was inspired by their devotion to God, so he poured out the water as a drink offering, demonstrating that only God is worthy of such devotion. They gave the water to David and he, in turn, gave it to God. Just as these men gave of themselves to serve David, we should put aside our own interests to serve other Christians (Romans 12:10). When we serve others, we are also serving God.

11:31
[z] 1Ch 27:14
[a] Jdg 12:13

11:41
[b] 2Sa 11:6
[c] 1Ch 2:36

11:44
[d] Dt 1:4

12:1
[a] Jos 15:31; 1Sa 27:2-6

12:2
[b] Jdg 3:15; 20:16
[c] 2Sa 3:19

31 Ithai son of Ribai from Gibeah in Benjamin,
Benaiah[z] the Pirathonite,[a]
32 Hurai from the ravines of Gaash,
Abiel the Arbathite,
33 Azmaveth the Baharumite,
Eliahba the Shaalbonite,
34 the sons of Hashem the Gizonite,
Jonathan son of Shagee the Hararite,
35 Ahiam son of Sacar the Hararite,
Eliphal son of Ur,
36 Hepher the Mekerathite,
Ahijah the Pelonite,
37 Hezro the Carmelite,
Naarai son of Ezbai,
38 Joel the brother of Nathan,
Mibhar son of Hagri,
39 Zelek the Ammonite,
Naharai the Berothite, the armour-bearer of Joab son of Zeruiah,
40 Ira the Ithrite,
Gareb the Ithrite,
41 Uriah[b] the Hittite,
Zabad[c] son of Ahlai,
42 Adina son of Shiza the Reubenite, who was chief of the Reubenites, and the thirty with him,
43 Hanan son of Maacah,
Joshaphat the Mithnite,
44 Uzzia the Ashterathite,[d]
Shama and Jeiel the sons of Hotham the Aroerite,
45 Jediael son of Shimri,
his brother Joha the Tizite,
46 Eliel the Mahavite,
Jeribai and Joshaviah the sons of Elnaam,
Ithmah the Moabite,
47 Eliel, Obed and Jaasiel the Mezobaite.

Warriors Join David

12 These were the men who came to David at Ziklag,[a] while he was banished
from the presence of Saul son of Kish (they were among the warriors who
helped him in battle; 2 they were armed with bows and were able to shoot arrows or
to sling stones right-handed or left-handed;[b] they were kinsmen of Saul[c] from the
tribe of Benjamin):

3 Ahiezer their chief and Joash the sons of Shemaah the Gibeathite; Jeziel and

---

12:1 Ziklag was a city in Philistia where David had escaped to hide from Saul. Achish, the Philistine ruler of the area, was happy to have a famous Israelite warrior defect to his land. He did not know, however, that David was only pretending loyalty. Achish gave the city of Ziklag to David, his family, and his army (1 Samuel 27:5–7). David's whereabouts were not a great secret, and many loyal followers joined him there.

12:1ff David surrounded himself with great warriors, the best of the Israelite army. What qualities made them worthy to be David's warriors and servants? (1) They had practised long and hard to perfect their skills (with bow, sling, and spear); (2) they were mentally tough and determined ("Their faces were the faces of lions", 12:8); (3) they were physically in shape ("as swift as gazelles", 12:8); (4) they were dedicated to serving God and David. Weak leaders are easily threatened by competent subordinates, but strong leaders surround themselves with the best. They are not intimidated by able and competent followers.

12:1–7 All the warriors mentioned here were from the tribe of Benjamin. Even members of Saul's own tribe (1 Samuel 9:1, 2) were deserting him to help David become king over all Israel. It was clear to them that God had chosen David to be Israel's next leader.

12:2 Archers and slingers had special weapons. The sling was unassuming in appearance but deadly in battle. A shallow leather pouch with a cord of leather or goat's hair attached to each side, the sling was whirled around the head. When one side was released, it sent a stone to its target. The bow and arrow had been in use for thousands of years. Arrowheads were made of stone, wood, or bone because the Philistines still had a monopoly on metalworking (1 Samuel 13:19, 20). Arrow shafts were made of reed or wood, and bowstrings were made of animal gut.

Pelet the sons of Azmaveth; Beracah, Jehu the Anathothite, 4and Ishmaiah the
Gibeonite, a mighty man among the Thirty, who was a leader of the Thirty;
Jeremiah, Jahaziel, Johanan, Jozabad the Gederathite,[d] 5Eluzai, Jerimoth, Beal-
iah, Shemariah and Shephatiah the Haruphite; 6Elkanah, Isshiah, Azarel, Joezer
and Jashobeam the Korahites; 7and Joelah and Zebadiah the sons of Jeroham from
Gedor.[e]

8Some Gadites[f] defected to David at his stronghold in the desert. They were brave
warriors, ready for battle and able to handle the shield and spear. Their faces were
the faces of lions,[g] and they were as swift as gazelles[h] in the mountains.

9Ezer was the chief,
Obadiah the second in command, Eliab the third,
10Mishmannah the fourth, Jeremiah the fifth,
11Attai the sixth, Eliel the seventh,
12Johanan the eighth, Elzabad the ninth,
13Jeremiah the tenth and Macbannai the eleventh.

14These Gadites were army commanders; the least was a match for a hundred,[i]
and the greatest for a thousand.[j] 15It was they who crossed the Jordan in the first
month when it was overflowing all its banks,[k] and they put to flight everyone living
in the valleys, to the east and to the west.

16Other Benjamites[l] and some men from Judah also came to David in his stronghold. 17David went out to meet them and said to them, "If you have come to me in
peace, to help me, I am ready to have you unite with me. But if you have come to
betray me to my enemies when my hands are free from violence, may the God of our
fathers see it and judge you."

18Then the Spirit[m] came upon Amasai,[n] chief of the Thirty, and he said:

"We are yours, O David!
We are with you, O son of Jesse!
Success,[o] success to you,
and success to those who help you,
for your God will help you."

So David received them and made them leaders of his raiding bands.

19Some of the men of Manasseh defected to David when he went with the Philistines
to fight against Saul. (He and his men did not help the Philistines because, after
consultation, their rulers sent him away. They said, "It will cost us our heads if he
deserts to his master Saul.")[p] 20When David went to Ziklag,[q] these were the men
of Manasseh who defected to him: Adnah, Jozabad, Jediael, Michael, Jozabad, Elihu
and Zillethai, leaders of units of a thousand in Manasseh. 21They helped David against
raiding bands, for all of them were brave warriors, and they were commanders in his
army. 22Day after day men came to help David, until he had a great army, like the
army of God.[a]

[a] *22* Or *a great and mighty army*

12:4 [d] Jos 15:36
12:7 [e] Jos 15:58
12:8 [f] Ge 30:11 [g] 2Sa 17:10 [h] 2Sa 2:18
12:14 [i] Lev 26:8 [j] Dt 32:30
12:15 [k] Jos 3:15
12:16 [l] 2Sa 3:19
12:18 [m] Jdg 3:10; 6:34; 1Ch 28:12; 2Ch 15:1; 20:14; 24:20 [n] 2Sa 17:25 [o] 1Sa 25:5-6
12:19 [p] 1Sa 29:2-11
12:20 [q] 1Sa 27:6

12:8 While the men of Benjamin were expert archers and slingers, the warriors of Gad were experts with the shield and spear. Israelite spears had wood shafts and spearheads of bone or stone and were often thrown through the air toward their mark. Philistine spears had bronze shafts and iron spearheads, and their shields were made of wood and overlaid with leather. Large shields were often carried by an armour-bearer, whose main task was to protect the warrior.

12:18 How did the Holy Spirit work in Old Testament times? When there was an important job to be done, God chose a person to do it, and the Spirit gave that person the needed power and ability. The Spirit gave Bezalel artistic ability (Exodus 31:1–5), Jephthah military prowess (Judges 11:29), David power to rule (1 Samuel 16:13), and Zechariah an authoritative word of prophecy (2 Chronicles 24:20). Here the Holy Spirit came upon David's warriors. The Spirit came upon individuals in order to accomplish specific goals. Beginning at Pentecost, however, the Spirit came upon all believers, not only to empower them to do God's will, but also to dwell in them day by day (Acts 2:14–21).

12:22 David "had a great army, like the army of God". Men were drawn to David by the reputation of his great warriors, the news of their victories, and their desire to see God's will done in making David king. People are often drawn to a great cause and the brave, determined people who support it. As believers, we have the greatest cause – the salvation of mankind. If we are brave, determined, and faithful, others will be drawn to work with us.

12:23
r2Sa 2:3-4
s1Ch 10:14
t1Sa 16:1;
1Ch 11:10

12:28
u2Sa 8:17;
1Ch 6:8; 15:11;
16:39; 27:17

12:29
v2Sa 3:19
w2Sa 2:8-9

12:32
xEst 1:13

12:38
y2Sa 5:1-3;
1Ch 9:1

12:39
z2Sa 3:20;
Isa 25:6-8

12:40
a2Sa 16:1; 17:29
b1Sa 25:18
c1Ch 29:22

Others Join David at Hebron

23 These are the numbers of the men armed for battle who came to David at Hebron[r]
to turn[s] Saul's kingdom over to him, as the LORD had said:[t]

24 men of Judah, carrying shield and spear—6,800 armed for battle;
25 men of Simeon, warriors ready for battle—7,100;
26 men of Levi—4,600, 27 including Jehoiada, leader of the family of Aaron with
3,700 men, 28 and Zadok,[u] a brave young warrior, with 22 officers from his
family;
29 men of Benjamin,[v] Saul's kinsmen—3,000, most[w] of whom had remained
loyal to Saul's house until then;
30 men of Ephraim, brave warriors, famous in their own clans—20,800;
31 men of half the tribe of Manasseh, designated by name to come and make David
king—18,000;
32 men of Issachar, who understood the times and knew what Israel should
do[x]—200 chiefs, with all their relatives under their command;
33 men of Zebulun, experienced soldiers prepared for battle with every type of
weapon, to help David with undivided loyalty—50,000;
34 men of Naphtali—1,000 officers, together with 37,000 men carrying shields
and spears;
35 men of Dan, ready for battle—28,600;
36 men of Asher, experienced soldiers prepared for battle—40,000;
37 and from east of the Jordan, men of Reuben, Gad, and the half-tribe of Manasseh, armed with every type of weapon—120,000.

38 All these were fighting men who volunteered to serve in the ranks. They came
to Hebron fully determined to make David king over all Israel.[y] All the rest of the
Israelites were also of one mind to make David king. 39 The men spent three days there
with David, eating and drinking,[z] for their families had supplied provisions for them.
40 Also, their neighbours from as far away as Issachar, Zebulun and Naphtali came
bringing food on donkeys, camels, mules and oxen. There were plentiful supplies[a]
of flour, fig cakes, raisin[b] cakes, wine, oil, cattle and sheep, for there was joy[c] in
Israel.

2. David brings the ark to Jerusalem

Bringing Back the Ark

13 David conferred with each of his officers, the commanders of thousands and
commanders of hundreds. 2 He then said to the whole assembly of Israel, "If
it seems good to you and if it is the will of the LORD our God, let us send word far
and wide to the rest of our brothers throughout the territories of Israel, and also to
the priests and Levites who are with them in their towns and pasture-lands, to come

---

12:26–29 In Numbers 1:47–50, God said that the Levites were to be exempt from military service. Why then are they listed as part of David's army? Although they were exempt from the draft, they strongly supported David and volunteered their services to help install him as king.

12:32 The 200 chiefs from the tribe of Issachar "understood the times". As a result, their knowledge and judgment provided needed help in making decisions for the nation. For leaders today, it is equally necessary to know what is happening in society in order to plan the best course of action for the church. Knowledge of current events, trends, and needs helps us understand people's thoughts and attitudes. This gives leaders information to help them make wise decisions for the church and make God's message relevant to people's lives.

12:40 The people were ready for change. They had suffered under Saul's leadership because of his disobedience to God (see 10:13). They were so overjoyed with David's coronation that they contributed lavishly to the celebration. It is right and proper to give generously for celebration and joyous worship. God is the author of joy, and he will join us in our celebrations.

13:1 David took time to confer with all his officers. As king, he had ultimate authority and could have given orders on his own, but he chose to involve others in leadership. Perhaps this is why there was unanimous support for his decisions (13:1–5). When we are in charge, it is tempting to make unilateral decisions, pushing through our own opinions. But effective leaders listen carefully to others' opinions, and they encourage others to participate in making decisions. Of course, we should always consult God first. We can run into big problems if we don't talk to him (see the note on 13:10).

13:1ff The parallel account of moving the ark (2 Samuel 5; 6) shows that David's building projects were completed *before* he brought the ark to Jerusalem. The writer of Chronicles puts the moving of the ark first in order to highlight David's spiritual accomplishments and relationship to God.

and join us. 3Let us bring the ark of our God back to us,[a] for we did not enquire[b]
of[a] it[b] during the reign of Saul." 4The whole assembly agreed to do this, because
it seemed right to all the people.
5So David assembled all the Israelites,[c] from the Shihor River[d] in Egypt to Lebo[c]
Hamath,[e] to bring the ark of God from Kiriath Jearim.[f] 6David and all the Israelites
with him went to Baalah[g] of Judah (Kiriath Jearim) to bring up from there the ark
of God the LORD, who is enthroned between the cherubim[h]—the ark that is called
by the Name.
7They moved the ark of God from Abinadab's[i] house on a new cart, with Uzzah
and Ahio guiding it. 8David and all the Israelites were celebrating with all their might
before God, with songs and with harps, lyres, tambourines, cymbals and trumpets.[j]
9When they came to the threshing-floor of Kidon, Uzzah reached out his hand to
steady the ark, because the oxen stumbled. 10The LORD's anger[k] burned against
Uzzah, and he struck him down[l] because he had put his hand on the ark. So he died
there before God.
11Then David was angry because the LORD's wrath had broken out against Uzzah,
and to this day that place is called Perez Uzzah.[d][m]
12David was afraid of God that day and asked, "How can I ever bring the ark of
God to me?" 13He did not take the ark to be with him in the City of David. Instead,
he took it aside to the house of Obed-Edom[n] the Gittite. 14The ark of God remained
with the family of Obed-Edom in his house for three months, and the LORD blessed
his household[o] and everything he had.

David's House and Family

14 Now Hiram king of Tyre sent messengers to David, along with cedar logs,[a]
stonemasons and carpenters to build a palace for him. 2And David knew that
the LORD had established him as king over Israel and that his kingdom had been highly
exalted[b] for the sake of his people Israel.

[a] 3 Or *we neglected* [b] 3 Or *him* [c] 5 Or *to the entrance to* [d] 11 *Perez Uzzah* means *outbreak against Uzzah.*

13:3 [a] 1Sa 7:1-2 [b] 2Ch 1:5
13:5 [c] 1Ch 11:1; 15:3 [d] Jos 13:3 [e] Nu 13:21 [f] 1Sa 6:21; 7:2
13:6 [g] Jos 15:9; 2Sa 6:2 [h] Ex 25:22; 2Ki 19:15
13:7 [i] Nu 4:15; 1Sa 7:1
13:8 [j] 2Sa 6:5; 1Ch 15:16, 19, 24; 2Ch 5:12; Ps 92:3
13:10 [k] 1Ch 15:13, 15 [l] Lev 10:2
13:11 [m] 1Ch 15:13; Ps 7:11
13:13 [n] 1Ch 15:18, 24; 16:38; 26:4-5, 15
13:14 [o] 2Sa 6:11; 1Ch 26:4-5
14:1 [a] 2Ch 2:3; Ezr 3:7
14:2 [b] Nu 24:7; Dt 26:19

13:3 The ark of God is also called the ark of the covenant. The most sacred object of the Hebrew faith, it was a large box containing the stone tablets on which God had written the Ten Commandments (Exodus 25:10–22). David had already made Jerusalem his political capital (11:4–9). At this time, David brought the ark there in order to make Jerusalem the nation's centre for worship.

13:3 The ark of God had been in Kiriath Jearim for many years. The neglect of the ark symbolised Israel's neglect of God. Bringing the ark back to the centre of Israel's life reflected David's desire to remind the nation of its true foundation – God. Neglecting those things that remind us of God – the Bible, the church, and contact with Christians – will cause us also to neglect God. We must keep God at the centre of our lives.

13:6 Cherubim are mighty angels.

13:8 Worship in the Old Testament was more than a sober religious exercise. David's exuberance as he worshipped God with dancing and music is approved in Scripture. Our worship should reflect a healthy balance: sometimes we should be reflective and serious (see Exodus 19:14ff), and sometimes we should show enthusiasm and jubilation. What do you need – more serious reflection or more joyous celebration?

13:10 Why did Uzzah die? He touched the ark, and that offence was punishable by death. God had given specific instructions about how the ark was to be moved and carried (Numbers 4:5–15), and those instructions were neglected. The Levites were responsible to move the ark (there is no record that Uzzah was a Levite), and it was to be carried on their shoulders with poles through its rings (Numbers 7:9). It was *never* to be touched. Bringing the ark on a cart followed the Philistines' example (1 Samuel 6:1ff). Uzzah, though sincere in his desire to protect the ark, had to face the consequences of his sin, and David was reminded that his obedience to God's laws was more important than his enthusiasm. Also David had "conferred with each of his officers" (13:1), but he neglected to ask God. The advice of our friends and colleagues is no substitute for God's direction.

13:10–14 Uzzah died instantly for touching the ark, but God blessed Obed-Edom's home where the ark was stored. This demonstrates the two-edged aspect of God's power: he is perfectly loving and perfectly just. Great blessings come to those who obey his commands, but severe punishment comes to those who disobey him. This punishment may come swiftly or over time, but it will come. Sometimes we focus only on the blessings God gives us, while forgetting that when we sin, "It is a dreadful thing to fall into the hands of the living God" (Hebrews 10:31). At other times, however, we concentrate so much on judgment that we miss his blessings. Don't fall into a one-sided view of God. Along with God's blessings comes the responsibility to live up to his demands for fairness, honesty, and justice.

13:11 David was angry at both God and himself. David knew that he had done something wrong in transporting the ark, and he was angry that his plans for the joyous return of the ark had ended in a man's death. But David's anger cooled, and he left the ark in Obed-Edom's home until he could consider how to get it to Jerusalem. This allowed David to discover God's instructions for transporting the ark. The next trip would be carried out according to God's commands.

14:1 King Hiram also sent lumber and craftsmen to help Solomon build the temple (2 Chronicles 2:1ff).

14:2 God gave David honour and success ("his kingdom had been highly exalted"), but not simply for David's personal gain. David realised that God had prospered him for a special reason – for the sake of God's people! Often we are tempted to use our position or possessions only for our own good. Instead, we must remember that God has placed us where we are and given us all

3In Jerusalem David took more wives and became the father of more sons[c] and
daughters. 4These are the names of the children born to him there:[d] Shammua,
Shobab, Nathan, Solomon, 5Ibhar, Elishua, Elpelet, 6Nogah, Nepheg, Japhia, 7Eli-
shama, Beeliada[a] and Eliphelet.

David Defeats the Philistines

8When the Philistines heard that David had been anointed king over all Israel,[e]
they went up in full force to search for him, but David heard about it and went out
to meet them. 9Now the Philistines had come and raided the Valley[f] of Rephaim;
10so David enquired of God: "Shall I go and attack the Philistines? Will you hand them
over to me?"
The LORD answered him, "Go, I will hand them over to you."
11So David and his men went up to Baal Perazim,[g] and there he defeated them.
He said, "As waters break out, God has broken out against my enemies by my hand."
So that place was called Baal Perazim.[b] 12The Philistines had abandoned their gods
there, and David gave orders to burn[h] them in the fire.[i]
13Once more the Philistines raided the valley;[j] 14so David enquired of God again,
and God answered him, "Do not go straight up, but circle round them and attack them
in front of the balsam trees. 15As soon as you hear the sound of marching in the tops
of the balsam trees, move out to battle, because that will mean God has gone out in
front of you to strike the Philistine army." 16So David did as God commanded him,
and they struck down the Philistine army, all the way from Gibeon[k] to Gezer.[l]
17So David's fame[m] spread throughout every land, and the LORD made all the
nations fear[n] him.

The Ark Brought to Jerusalem

15 After David had constructed buildings for himself in the City of David, he
prepared[a] a place for the ark of God and pitched[b] a tent for it. 2Then David
said, "No-one but the Levites[c] may carry[d] the ark of God, because the LORD chose
them to carry the ark of the LORD and to minister[e] before him for ever."
3David assembled all Israel[f] in Jerusalem to bring up the ark of the LORD to the
place he had prepared for it. 4He called together the descendants of Aaron and the
Levites:

5From the descendants of Kohath,
Uriel the leader and 120 relatives;
6from the descendants of Merari,
Asaiah the leader and 220 relatives;
7from the descendants of Gershon,[a]
Joel the leader and 130 relatives;
8from the descendants of Elizaphan,[g]
Shemaiah the leader and 200 relatives;

[a] 7 A variant of *Eliada* [b] 11 *Baal Perazim* means *the lord who breaks out.* [a] 7 Hebrew *Gershom*, a variant of *Gershon*

14:3 [c]1Ch 3:1
14:4 [d]1Ch 3:9
14:8 [e]1Ch 11:1
14:9 [f]ver 13; Jos 15:8; 1Ch 11:15
14:11 [g]Isa 28:21
14:12 [h]Ex 32:20 [i]Jos 7:15
14:13 [j]ver 9
14:16 [k]Jos 9:3 [l]Jos 10:33
14:17 [m]Jos 6:27; 2Ch 26:8 [n]Ex 15:14-16; Dt 2:25
15:1 [a]Ps 132:1-18 [b]1Ch 16:1; 17:1
15:2 [c]Nu 4:15; Dt 10:8; 2Ch 5:5 [d]Dt 31:9 [e]1Ch 23:13
15:3 [f]1Ki 8:1; 1Ch 13:5
15:8 [g]Ex 6:22

---

we have so that we may encourage others and give to those in need.

14:3 Accumulating wives and concubines in a harem was the custom of the day among Middle Eastern royalty, but it was not God's ideal (Genesis 2:24). David's marriages brought him greater power and influence, but they also caused strife, jealousy, and even murder within his family. (See the chart in 2 Samuel 11 for other consequences of polygamy.)

14:8–16 A map of this battle is in 2 Samuel 5.

14:10 Before David went to battle, he inquired of God first, asking for his presence and guidance. Too often we wait until we are in trouble before turning to God. By then the consequences of our actions are already unfolding. Do you ask for God's help only as a desperate last resort? Instead, go to him first! Like David, you may receive incredible help and avoid serious trouble.

14:12 David's quick and decisive action against idols helped unify his kingdom and focus the people on worshipping the one true God. He was obeying the law that said, "This is what you are to do to them: Break down their altars, smash their sacred stones, cut down their Asherah poles and burn their idols in the fire" (Deuteronomy 7:5). Most of David's successors failed to destroy idols, and this led to unbelievable moral corruption in Israel.

14:12 Often the soldiers wanted to keep souvenirs from the battle (and 2 Samuel 5:21 states that some of the men kept some of these idols), but David ordered them to burn the idols. The only proper response to sin is to get rid of it completely. You cannot be a follower of God while continuing to hold on to parts of your past life that push God out of the centre of your thoughts and actions. Eliminate whatever takes God's rightful place in your life, and follow him with complete devotion.

9 from the descendants of Hebron,[h]
Eliel the leader and 80 relatives;
10 from the descendants of Uzziel,
Amminadab the leader and 112 relatives.
11 Then David summoned Zadok[i] and Abiathar[j] the priests, and Uriel, Asaiah,
Joel, Shemaiah, Eliel and Amminadab the Levites. 12 He said to them, "You are the
heads of the Levitical families; you and your fellow Levites are to consecrate[k]
yourselves and bring up the ark of the LORD, the God of Israel, to the place I have
prepared for it. 13 It was because you, the Levites,[l] did not bring it up the first time
that the LORD our God broke out in anger against us.[m] We did not enquire of him
about how to do it in the prescribed way." 14 So the priests and Levites consecrated
themselves in order to bring up the ark of the LORD, the God of Israel. 15 And the
Levites carried the ark of God with the poles on their shoulders, as Moses had
commanded[n] in accordance with the word of the LORD.
16 David told the leaders of the Levites to appoint their brothers as singers[o] to sing
joyful songs, accompanied by musical instruments: lyres, harps and cymbals.[p]
17 So the Levites appointed Heman[q] son of Joel; from his brothers, Asaph[r] son
of Berekiah; and from their brothers the Merarites,[s] Ethan son of Kushaiah; 18 and
with them their brothers next in rank: Zechariah,[b] Jaaziel, Shemiramoth, Jehiel,
Unni, Eliab, Benaiah, Maaseiah, Mattithiah, Eliphelehu, Mikneiah, Obed-Edom[t]
and Jeiel,[c] the gatekeepers.
19 The musicians Heman,[u] Asaph and Ethan were to sound the bronze cymbals;
20 Zechariah, Aziel, Shemiramoth, Jehiel, Unni, Eliab, Maaseiah and Benaiah were
to play the lyres according to *alamoth*,[d] 21 and Mattithiah, Eliphelehu, Mikneiah,
Obed-Edom, Jeiel and Azaziah were to play the harps, directing according to *sheminith*.[e] 22 Kenaniah the head Levite was in charge of the singing; that was his responsibility because he was skilful at it.
23 Berekiah and Elkanah were to be doorkeepers for the ark. 24 Shebaniah, Joshaphat, Nethanel, Amasai, Zechariah, Benaiah and Eliezer the priests were to blow
trumpets[v] before the ark of God. Obed-Edom and Jehiah were also to be doorkeepers
for the ark.
25 So David and the elders of Israel and the commanders of units of a thousand went
to bring up the ark[w] of the covenant of the LORD from the house of Obed-Edom, with
rejoicing. 26 Because God had helped the Levites who were carrying the ark of the
covenant of the LORD, seven bulls and seven rams[x] were sacrificed. 27 Now David
was clothed in a robe of fine linen, as were all the Levites who were carrying the ark,
and as were the singers, and Kenaniah, who was in charge of the singing of the choirs.

b *18* Three Hebrew manuscripts and most Septuagint manuscripts (see also verse 20 and 1 Chron. 16:5); most Hebrew manuscripts *Zechariah son and* or *Zechariah, Ben and* **c** *18* Hebrew; Septuagint (see also verse 21) *Jeiel and Azaziah* **d** *20* Probably a musical term **e** *21* Probably a musical term

15:9 [h]Ex 6:18
15:11 [i]1Ch 12:28 [j]1Sa 22:20
15:12 [k]Ex 19:14-15; Lev 11:44; 2Ch 35:6
15:13 [l]1Ki 8:4 [m]2Sa 6:3; 1Ch 13:7-10
15:15 [n]Ex 25:14; Nu 4:5, 15
15:16 [o]Ps 68:25 [p]1Ch 13:8; 25:1; Ne 12:27, 36
15:17 [q]1Ch 6:33 [r]1Ch 6:39 [s]1Ch 6:44
15:18 [t]1Ch 26:4-5
15:19 [u]1Ch 25:6
15:24 [v]ver 28; 1Ch 16:6; 2Ch 7:6
15:25 [w]1Ch 13:13; 2Ch 1:4
15:26 [x]Nu 23:1-4, 29

15:12 The priests consecrated themselves so they would be prepared to carry the ark. To *consecrate* literally means to separate, to set apart for sacred purposes, to purify. The priests symbolically separated themselves from sin and evil. This was done by washing themselves and their clothing in a special ceremony (Numbers 8:5–8). While we are not required to carry out this ceremony today, we can purify ourselves by reading God's word and preparing our hearts to participate in worship.

15:13 David refers to the incident recorded in 13:8–11 and 2 Samuel 6:1–11. As the ark was being brought back to Israel on an oxcart, the oxen stumbled. Uzzah, trying to steady the ark with his hand, was killed instantly for touching it. The mistake was not in David's desire to move the ark, but in his method for its return. David either ignored or was unaware of the specific instructions in God's law about how the ark was to be moved. Obviously he had discovered his mistake and was now preparing to correct it. This incident was a divine object lesson to all Israel that God governed the king and not the other way around. If David had been allowed to handle the ark of God carelessly, what would that have said to the people about their faith?

15:13–15 When David's first attempt to move the ark failed (13:8–14), he learned an important lesson: when God gives specific instructions, it is wise to follow them precisely. This time David saw to it that the Levites carried the ark (Numbers 4:5–15). We may not fully understand the reasons behind God's instructions, but we do know that his wisdom is complete and his judgment infallible. The way to know God's instructions is to know his word. But just as children do not understand the reasons for all their parents' instructions until they are older, we may not understand all of God's reasons in this life. It is far better to obey God first, and then discover the reasons. We are never free to disobey God just because we don't understand.

15:16–25 The great musical procession was designed as a worthy accompaniment to the great occasion. It heightened the excitement, elevated the people's hearts and minds, and focused their attention on the event. It also helped seal it in their memory for years to come. Beginning any task by praising God can inspire us to give him our best. Develop the practice of giving praise to God, and you will experience greater joy and strength to face anything.

15:28
[y]1Ch 13:8

16:1
[a]1Ch 15:1

16:2
[b]Ex 39:43

16:4
[c]1Ch 15:2

16:7
[d]2Sa 23:1

16:8
[e]ver 34;
Ps 136:1
[f]2Ki 19:19

16:9
[g]Ex 15:1

16:11
[h]1Ch 28:9;
2Ch 7:14;
Ps 24:6; 119:2, 58

16:12
[i]Ps 77:11
[j]Ps 78:43

16:14
[k]Isa 26:9

16:16
[l]Ge 12:7; 15:18;
17:2; 22:16-18;
26:3; 28:13; 35:11

16:17
[m]Ge 35:9-12

David also wore a linen ephod. 28So all Israel brought up the ark of the covenant of
the LORD with shouts, with the sounding of rams' horns[y] and trumpets, and of
cymbals, and the playing of lyres and harps.
29As the ark of the covenant of the LORD was entering the City of David, Michal
daughter of Saul watched from a window. And when she saw King David dancing
and celebrating, she despised him in her heart.

16 They brought the ark of God and set it inside the tent that David had pitched[a]
for it, and they presented burnt offerings and fellowship offerings[a] before God.
2After David had finished sacrificing the burnt offerings and fellowship offerings, he
blessed[b] the people in the name of the LORD. 3Then he gave a loaf of bread, a cake
of dates and a cake of raisins to each Israelite man and woman.
4He appointed some of the Levites to minister[c] before the ark of the LORD, to make
petition, to give thanks, and to praise the LORD, the God of Israel: 5Asaph was the
chief, Zechariah second, then Jeiel, Shemiramoth, Jehiel, Mattithiah, Eliab, Benaiah,
Obed-Edom and Jeiel. They were to play the lyres and harps, Asaph was to sound
the cymbals, 6and Benaiah and Jahaziel the priests were to blow the trumpets regularly
before the ark of the covenant of God.

David's Psalm of Thanks

7That day David first committed to Asaph and his associates this psalm[d] of thanks
to the LORD:

8Give thanks[e] to the LORD, call on his name;
make known among the nations[f] what he has done.
9Sing to him, sing praise[g] to him;
tell of all his wonderful acts.
10Glory in his holy name;
let the hearts of those who seek the LORD rejoice.
11Look to the LORD and his strength;
seek[h] his face always.
12Remember[i] the wonders he has done,
his miracles,[j] and the judgments he pronounced,
13O descendants of Israel his servant,
O sons of Jacob, his chosen ones.

14He is the LORD our God;
his judgments[k] are in all the earth.
15He remembers[b] his covenant for ever,
the word he commanded, for a thousand generations,
16the covenant[l] he made with Abraham,
the oath he swore to Isaac.
17He confirmed it to Jacob[m] as a decree,
to Israel as an everlasting covenant:

a *1* Traditionally *peace offerings*; also in verse 2 **b** *15* Some Septuagint manuscripts (see also Psalm 105:8); Hebrew *Remember*

15:29 David was willing to look foolish in the eyes of some people in order to express his thankfulness to God fully and honestly. In contrast, Michal was so disgusted by his "undignified" actions that she could not rejoice in the ark's return to Jerusalem. Worship had so deteriorated under her father Saul's reign that it had become stilted and ritualistic. Michal could accept David as a military conqueror and as a king, but she could not accept his free and spontaneous expression of praise to God. Some devoted people may look foolish to us in their heartfelt expressions of worship, but we must accept them. In the same way, we should not be afraid to worship God with whatever expressions seem appropriate.

16:4 Certain Levites were appointed to give continual praise and thanks to God. Praise and thanksgiving should be a regular part of our routine, not reserved only for celebrations. Praise God continually, and you will find that you won't take his blessings for granted.

16:7–36 Four elements of true thanksgiving are found in this song (psalm): (1) *remembering* what God has done, (2) *telling* others about it, (3) *showing* God's glory to others, and (4) *offering* gifts of self, time, and resources. If you are truly thankful, your life will show it.

16:8ff Several parts of this psalm are parallel to songs in the book of Psalms: 16:8–22 with Psalm 105:1–15; 16:23–33 with Psalm 96; 16:34–36 with Psalm 106:1, 47, 48.

16:15–18 This covenant was given to Abraham (Genesis 15:18–21), and then passed on to Isaac (Genesis 26:24, 25) and Jacob (Genesis 28:13–15). God promised to give the land of Canaan (present-day Israel) to their descendants. He also promised that the Messiah would come from their line.

18"To you I will give the land of Canaan[n]
as the portion you will inherit."

19When they were but few in number,[o]
few indeed, and strangers in it,
20they[c] wandered from nation to nation,
from one kingdom to another.
21He allowed no man to oppress them;
for their sake he rebuked kings:[p]
22"Do not touch my anointed ones;
do my prophets[q] no harm."

23Sing to the LORD, all the earth;
proclaim his salvation day after day.
24Declare his glory among the nations,
his marvellous deeds among all peoples.
25For great is the LORD and most worthy of praise;[r]
he is to be feared[s] above all gods.[t]
26For all the gods of the nations are idols,
but the LORD made the heavens.[u]
27Splendour and majesty are before him;
strength and joy in his dwelling-place.
28Ascribe to the LORD, O families of nations,
ascribe to the LORD glory and strength,[v]
29 ascribe to the LORD the glory due to his name.
Bring an offering and come before him;
worship the LORD in the splendour of his[d] holiness.[w]
30Tremble[x] before him, all the earth!
The world is firmly established; it cannot be moved.
31Let the heavens rejoice, let the earth be glad;[y]
let them say among the nations, "The LORD reigns![z]"
32Let the sea resound, and all that is in it;[a]
let the fields be jubilant, and everything in them!
33Then the trees[b] of the forest will sing,
they will sing for joy before the LORD,
for he comes to judge[c] the earth.

34Give thanks[d] to the LORD, for he is good;[e]
his love endures for ever.[f]
35Cry out, "Save us, O God our Saviour;[g]
gather us and deliver us from the nations,
that we may give thanks to your holy name,
that we may glory in your praise."
36Praise be to the LORD, the God of Israel,[h]
from everlasting to everlasting.

Then all the people said "Amen" and "Praise the LORD."

37David left Asaph and his associates before the ark of the covenant of the LORD
to minister there regularly, according to each day's requirements.[i] 38He also left

c *18–20* One Hebrew manuscript, Septuagint and Vulgate (see also Psalm 105:12); most Hebrew manuscripts *inherit, / 19though you are but few in number, / few indeed, and strangers in it." / 20They* d *29* Or LORD *with the splendour of*

16:18 [n]Ge 13:14-17
16:19 [o]Ge 34:30; Dt 7:7
16:21 [p]Ge 12:17; 20:3; Ex 7:15-18
16:22 [q]Ge 20:7
16:25 [r]Ps 48:1 [s]Ps 76:7; 89:7 [t]Dt 32:39
16:26 [u]Lev 19:4; Ps 102:25
16:28 [v]Ps 29:1-2
16:29 [w]Ps 29:1-2
16:30 [x]Ps 114:7
16:31 [y]Isa 44:23; 49:13 [z]Ps 93:1
16:32 [a]Ps 98:7
16:33 [b]Isa 55:12 [c]Ps 96:10; 98:9
16:34 [d]ver 8 [e]Na 1:7 [f]2Ch 5:13; 7:3; Ezr 3:11; Ps 136:1-26; Jer 33:11
16:35 [g]Mic 7:7
16:36 [h]Dt 27:15; 1Ki 8:15; Ps 72:18-19
16:37 [i]2Ch 8:14

16:25 The basis of praise is declaring God's character and attributes in the presence of others. When we recognise and affirm his goodness we are holding up his perfect moral nature for all to see. Praise benefits us because it takes our minds off our problems and needs and focuses on God's power, mercy, majesty, and love.

16:29 Genuine praise also involves ascribing glory to God. Remember this in your worship – give God all the glory.

16:37 Asaph and his fellow Levites ministered in the temple, doing each day whatever was needed. To carry out God's work is not merely to engage in religious exercises. It includes other necessary tasks. Even if you don't have the opportunity to teach or preach, God can use you in the ministry. What needs to be done? Cleaning, serving, singing, planning, administering? Look for ways to minister each day.

Obed-Edom[j] and his sixty-eight associates to minister with them. Obed-Edom son
of Jeduthun, and also Hosah,[k] were gatekeepers.
39David left Zadok[l] the priest and his fellow priests before the tabernacle of the
LORD at the high place in Gibeon[m] 40to present burnt offerings to the LORD on the
altar of burnt offering regularly, morning and evening, in accordance with everything
written in the Law[n] of the LORD, which he had given Israel. 41With them were
Heman[o] and Jeduthun and the rest of those chosen and designated by name to give
thanks to the LORD, "for his love endures for ever." 42Heman and Jeduthun were
responsible for the sounding of the trumpets and cymbals and for the playing of the
other instruments for sacred song.[p] The sons of Jeduthun were stationed at the gate.
43Then all the people left, each for his own home, and David returned home to bless
his family.

God's Promise to David

17 After David was settled in his palace, he said to Nathan the prophet, "Here I
am, living in a palace of cedar, while the ark of the covenant of the LORD is
under a tent.[a]"
2Nathan replied to David, "Whatever you have in mind,[b] do it, for God is with
you."
3That night the word of God came to Nathan, saying:

4"Go and tell my servant David, 'This is what the LORD says: You[c] are not
the one to build me a house to dwell in. 5I have not dwelt in a house from the
day I brought Israel up out of Egypt to this day. I have moved from one tent site
to another, from one dwelling-place to another. 6Wherever I have moved with
all the Israelites, did I ever say to any of their leaders[a] whom I commanded to
shepherd my people, "Why have you not built me a house of cedar?" '
7"Now then, tell my servant David, 'This is what the LORD Almighty says:
I took you from the pasture and from following the flock, to be ruler[d] over my
people Israel. 8I have been with you wherever you have gone, and I have cut
off all your enemies from before you. Now I will make your name like the names
of the greatest men of the earth. 9And I will provide a place for my people Israel
and will plant them so that they can have a home of their own and no longer be
disturbed. Wicked people will not oppress them any more, as they did at the
beginning 10and have done ever since the time I appointed leaders[e] over my
people Israel. I will also subdue all your enemies.
" 'I declare to you that the LORD will build a house for you: 11When your days
are over and you go to be with your fathers, I will raise up your offspring to
succeed you, one of your own sons, and I will establish his kingdom. 12He is
the one who will build[f] a house for me, and I will establish his throne for ever.[g]
13I will be his father,[h] and he will be my son.[i] I will never take my love away

a 6 Traditionally *judges*; also in verse 10

16:38 [j]1Ch 13:13 [k]1Ch 26:10
16:39 [l]2Sa 8:17; 1Ch 15:11 [m]1Ki 3:4; 2Ch 1:3
16:40 [n]Ex 29:38; Nu 28:1-8
16:41 [o]1Ch 6:33; 25:1-6; 2Ch 5:13
16:42 [p]2Ch 7:6
17:1 [a]1Ch 15:1
17:2 [b]2Ch 6:7
17:4 [c]1Ch 28:3
17:7 [d]2Sa 6:21
17:10 [e]Jdg 2:16
17:12 [f]1Ki 5:5 [g]2Ch 7:18
17:13 [h]2Co 6:18 [i]Lk 1:32; Heb 1:5

16:39 David brought the ark to Jerusalem although the tabernacle was still at Gibeon. His plan was to reunite the tabernacle and ark in a new temple at Jerusalem that would then become Israel's only worship centre. The temple, however, was not built until Solomon's time. In the meantime, Israel had two worship centres and two high priests (15:11), one at Gibeon and one at Jerusalem.

17:1 David felt disturbed that the ark, the symbol of God's presence, sat in a tent while he lived in a beautiful palace. David's desire was right, but his timing was wrong. God told David *not* to build a temple (17:3, 4), and David was willing to abide by God's timing. If you live in comparative luxury while God's work, house, or ministers go lacking, perhaps God wants you to change the situation. Like David, take action to correct the imbalance, but be willing to move according to God's timing.

17:3–14 God did not want a warrior to build his temple (28:3; 1 Kings 5:3), and David had shed much blood in unifying the nation. So the honour of building the temple would go to David's son Solomon. David would pass on to Solomon a peaceful and united kingdom, ready to begin work on a beautiful temple.

17:10 God promised to subdue David's enemies. Chapters 18 – 20 tell how God kept that promise.

17:12–14 Why, after this eternal promise, were the Israelites eventually taken from the promised land into captivity? The promise to David had two parts. The first part was conditional: as long as David's descendants followed God's laws and honoured him, they would continually be on the throne of Israel. The second part was unconditional: a son of David would occupy his throne for ever. This was Jesus the Messiah. The first part of the promise was based on the faithful obedience of David's descendants. The second part would come true regardless of the way his descendants acted.

from him, as I took it away from your predecessor. 14 I will set him over my house
and my kingdom for ever; his throne[j] will be established for ever.[k]' "
15 Nathan reported to David all the words of this entire revelation.

David's Prayer

16 Then King David went in and sat before the LORD, and he said:

"Who am I, O LORD God, and what is my family, that you have brought me
this far? 17 And as if this were not enough in your sight, O God, you have spoken
about the future of the house of your servant. You have looked on me as though
I were the most exalted of men, O LORD God.
18 "What more can David say to you for honouring your servant? For you know
your servant, 19 O LORD. For the sake[l] of your servant and according to your
will, you have done this great thing and made known all these great promises.[m]
20 "There is no-one like you, O LORD, and there is no God but you,[n] as we
have heard with our own ears. 21 And who is like your people Israel—the one
nation on earth whose God went out to redeem[o] a people for himself, and to
make a name for yourself, and to perform great and awesome wonders by driving
out nations from before your people, whom you redeemed from Egypt? 22 You
made your people Israel your very own for ever,[p] and you, O LORD, have
become their God.
23 "And now, LORD, let the promise[q] you have made concerning your servant
and his house be established for ever. Do as you promised, 24 so that it will be
established and that your name will be great for ever. Then men will say, 'The
LORD Almighty, the God over Israel, is Israel's God!' And the house of your
servant David will be established before you.
25 "You, my God, have revealed to your servant that you will build a house
for him. So your servant has found courage to pray to you. 26 O LORD, you are
God! You have promised these good things to your servant. 27 Now you have been
pleased to bless the house of your servant, that it may continue for ever in your
sight;[r] for you, O LORD, have blessed it, and it will be blessed for ever."

3. David's military exploits

David's Victories

18 In the course of time, David defeated the Philistines and subdued them, and
he took Gath and its surrounding villages from the control of the Philistines.
2 David also defeated the Moabites,[a] and they became subject to him and brought
tribute.
3 Moreover, David fought Hadadezer king of Zobah,[b] as far as Hamath, when he
went to establish his control along the Euphrates River.[c] 4 David captured a thousand
of his chariots, seven thousand charioteers and twenty thousand foot soldiers. He
hamstrung[d] all but a hundred of the chariot horses.
5 When the Arameans of Damascus[e] came to help Hadadezer king of Zobah, David
struck down twenty-two thousand of them. 6 He put garrisons in the Aramean kingdom

17:14 [j]1Ki 2:12; 1Ch 28:5 [k]Ps 132:11; Jer 33:17
17:19 [l]2Sa 7:16-17; 2Ki 20:6; Isa 9:7; 37:35; 55:3 [m]2Sa 7:25
17:20 [n]Ex 8:10; 9:14; 15:11; Isa 44:6; 46:9
17:21 [o]Ex 6:6
17:22 [p]Ex 19:5-6
17:23 [q]1Ki 8:25
17:27 [r]Ps 16:11; 21:6
18:2 [a]Nu 21:29
18:3 [b]1Ch 19:6 [c]Ge 2:14
18:4 [d]Ge 49:6
18:5 [e]2Ki 16:9; 1Ch 19:6

17:16–20 God told David that Solomon would be given the honour of building the temple. David responded with deep humility, not resentment. This king who had conquered his enemies and was loved by his people said, "Who am I . . . that you have brought me this far"? David recognised that God was the *true* king. God has done just as much for us, and he plans to do even more! Like David, we should humble ourselves and give glory to God, saying, "There is no-one like you, O LORD." When God chooses someone else to implement your ideas, will you respond with such humility?

17:16–27 David prayed by humbling himself (17:16–18), praising God (17:19, 20), recognising God's blessings (17:21, 22), and accepting God's decisions, promises, and commands (17:23, 24). Sometimes we are quick to make requests to God and to tell him our troubles, but these other dimensions of prayer can deepen our spiritual life. Take time to praise God, to count his blessings, and to affirm your commitment to do what he has already said to do.

17:21 David's reference to Israel's exodus from Egypt would have had special significance to the original readers of 1 Chronicles who were either beginning or had just completed a second great exodus back to Israel from captivity in Babylon. Remembering God's promises, mercy, and protection during the first exodus would have encouraged the exiles returning once again to Israel, just as God had promised.

18:8
[f]1Ki 7:23; 2Ch 4:12, 15-16

18:11
[g]Nu 24:18
[h]Nu 24:20

18:12
[i]1Ki 11:15

18:14
[j]1Ch 29:26
[k]1Ch 11:1

18:15
[l]2Sa 5:6-8; 1Ch 11:6

18:16
[m]2Sa 8:17; 1Ch 6:8
[n]1Ch 24:6

18:17
[o]1Sa 30:14; 2Sa 8:18; 15:18

of Damascus, and the Arameans became subject to him and brought tribute. The LORD
gave David victory everywhere he went.
7 David took the gold shields carried by the officers of Hadadezer and brought them
to Jerusalem. 8 From Tebah[a] and Cun, towns that belonged to Hadadezer, David took
a great quantity of bronze, which Solomon used to make the bronze Sea,[f] the pillars
and various bronze articles.
9 When Tou king of Hamath heard that David had defeated the entire army of
Hadadezer king of Zobah, 10 he sent his son Hadoram to King David to greet him and
congratulate him on his victory in battle over Hadadezer, who had been at war with
Tou. Hadoram brought all kinds of articles of gold and silver and bronze.
11 King David dedicated these articles to the LORD, as he had done with the silver
and gold he had taken from all these nations: Edom[g] and Moab, the Ammonites and
the Philistines, and Amalek.[h]
12 Abishai son of Zeruiah struck down eighteen thousand Edomites[i] in the Valley
of Salt. 13 He put garrisons in Edom, and all the Edomites became subject to David.
The LORD gave David victory everywhere he went.

David's Officials

14 David reigned[j] over all Israel,[k] doing what was just and right for all his people.
15 Joab[l] son of Zeruiah was over the army; Jehoshaphat son of Ahilud was recorder;
16 Zadok[m] son of Ahitub and Ahimelech[b][n] son of Abiathar were priests; Shavsha
was secretary; 17 Benaiah son of Jehoiada was over the Kerethites and Pelethites;[o] and
David's sons were chief officials at the king's side.

[a] 8 Hebrew *Tibhath*, a variant of *Tebah* [b] 16 Some Hebrew manuscripts, Vulgate and Syriac (see also 2 Sam. 8:17); most Hebrew manuscripts *Abimelech*

DAVID SUBDUES HIS ENEMIES
David expanded his kingdom as the Lord continued to give him victory. He subdued the Philistines by taking Gath, conquered Moab, won battles as far north as Zobah and Hamath (conquering Aram when they came to help these enemy nations), and subdued the other surrounding nations of Ammon and Amalek.

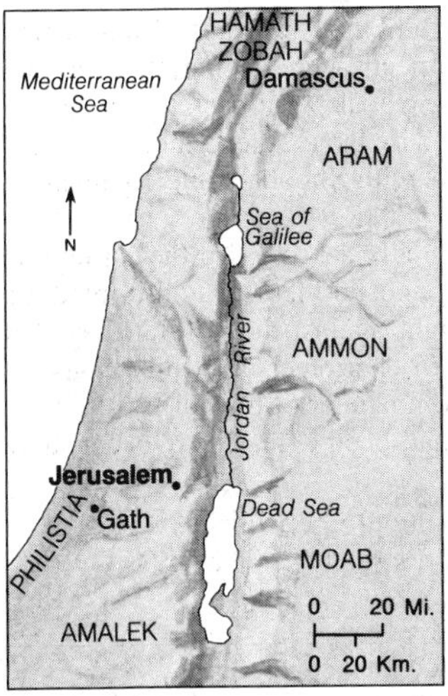

18:2 In 2 Samuel 8:1, 2, it is recorded that David killed two-thirds of the people of Moab. His ancestor Ruth was originally from the land of Moab.

18:6, 14 David was a victorious and just ruler. We see in David's glowing success a hint of what Christ's reign will be like – complete victory and justice. If David's glory was great, how much greater will Christ's glory be! The great news for us is that we can be rightly related to Jesus Christ through faith. One day we will share in his glory as we reign with him.

18:9–11 When David received gifts from King Tou, he dedicated them to God, realising that all had come from God and was to be used for him. It is easy to think that our financial and material blessings are the result of our own skill and hard work rather than coming from a loving God (James 1:17). What has God given you? Dedicate all your gifts and resources to him, and use them for his service. He will lead you in the method you should use. The first step is to be willing.

18:13 The list of battles in this chapter shows how God gave David victory after victory. Unbelieving people think that victory comes from their own skill plus a little luck. Just as David acknowledged God's role in his success, so should we. Don't take credit for the work God does.

18:17 The Kerethites and Pelethites were probably a group of foreign soldiers who had joined David during his flight from Saul. They remained loyal to David throughout his reign (2 Samuel 15:17, 18) and became part of his bodyguard.

The Battle Against the Ammonites

19 In the course of time, Nahash king of the Ammonites[a] died, and his son succeeded him as king. [2]David thought, "I will show kindness to Hanun son of Nahash, because his father showed kindness to me." So David sent a delegation to express his sympathy to Hanun concerning his father.

When David's men came to Hanun in the land of the Ammonites to express sympathy to him, [3]the Ammonite nobles said to Hanun, "Do you think David is honouring your father by sending men to you to express sympathy? Haven't his men come to you to explore and spy out[b] the country and overthrow it?" [4]So Hanun seized David's men, shaved them, cut off their garments in the middle at the buttocks, and sent them away.

[5]When someone came and told David about the men, he sent messengers to meet them, for they were greatly humiliated. The king said, "Stay at Jericho till your beards have grown, and then come back."

[6]When the Ammonites realised that they had become an offence to[c] David's nostrils, Hanun and the Ammonites sent a thousand talents[a] of silver to hire chariots and charioteers from Aram Naharaim,[b] Aram Maacah and Zobah.[d] [7]They hired thirty-two thousand chariots and charioteers, as well as the king of Maacah with his troops, who came and camped near Medeba,[e] while the Ammonites were mustered from their towns and moved out for battle.

[8]On hearing this, David sent Joab out with the entire army of fighting men. [9]The Ammonites came out and drew up in battle formation at the entrance to their city, while the kings who had come were by themselves in the open country.

[10]Joab saw that there were battle lines in front of him and behind him; so he selected some of the best troops in Israel and deployed them against the Arameans. [11]He put the rest of the men under the command of Abishai[f] his brother, and they were deployed against the Ammonites. [12]Joab said, "If the Arameans are too strong for me, then you are to rescue me; but if the Ammonites are too strong for you, then I will rescue you. [13]Be strong and let us fight bravely for our people and the cities of our God. The LORD will do what is good in his sight."

[14]Then Joab and the troops with him advanced to fight the Arameans, and they fled before him. [15]When the Ammonites saw that the Arameans were fleeing, they too fled before his brother Abishai and went inside the city. So Joab went back to Jerusalem.

[16]After the Arameans saw that they had been routed by Israel, they sent messengers and had Arameans brought from beyond the River,[c] with Shophach the commander of Hadadezer's army leading them.

[17]When David was told of this, he gathered all Israel[g] and crossed the Jordan; he advanced against them and formed his battle lines opposite them. David formed his lines to meet the Arameans in battle, and they fought against him. [18]But they fled before Israel, and David killed seven thousand of their charioteers and forty thousand of their foot soldiers. He also killed Shophach the commander of their army.

[19]When the vassals of Hadadezer saw that they had been defeated by Israel, they made peace with David and became subject to him.

So the Arameans were not willing to help the Ammonites any more.

19:1 [a]Ge 19:38; Jdg 10:17-11:33; 2Ch 20:1-2; Zep 2:8-11
19:3 [b]Nu 21:32
19:6 [c]Ge 34:30 [d]1Ch 18:3, 5, 9
19:7 [e]Nu 21:30; Jos 13:9, 16
19:11 [f]1Sa 26:6
19:17 [g]1Ch 9:1

a *6* That is, about 34 tons (about 34 metric tons) b *6* That is, North-west Mesopotamia c *16* That is, the Euphrates

19:1 The land of Ammon bordered Israel to the east. The nation had a sordid beginning—its founding ancestor, Ben-Ammi, was conceived through incest between Lot and his daughter (Genesis 19:30–38). The Ammonites, who were constant enemies of Israel, reached their greatest strength in the days of the judges. David was the first military leader of Israel to crush them. They were unable to cause further trouble for many years.

19:2, 3 Hanun misread David's intentions. Because he was overly suspicious, he brought disaster upon himself. Because of past experiences, it is easy to be overly suspicious of others, questioning every move and querying their motives. But while we should be cautious and wise as we deal with others, we should not assume their every action is ill-intended.

19:4, 5 Israelite men always wore beards. To be forcibly shaven was embarrassing enough, but these men were also left half naked. Hanun's actions humiliated these men and insulted Israel.

19:6 Rather than admit his mistake and seek forgiveness and reconciliation, Hanun spent an enormous amount of money to cover up his error. His cover-up cost him dearly (20:1–4). It often costs more to cover up an error than to admit it honestly. Rather than compound an error through defensiveness, seek forgiveness and reconciliation as soon as you realise your mistake. You will save yourself and others a lot of pain and trouble.

20:1 [a]Dt 3:11; 2Sa 12:26 [b]Am 1:13-15

The Capture of Rabbah

20 In the spring, at the time when kings go off to war, Joab led out the armed
forces. He laid waste the land of the Ammonites and went to Rabbah[a] and
besieged it, but David remained in Jerusalem. Joab attacked Rabbah and left it in
ruins.[b] 2David took the crown from the head of their king[a]—its weight was found
to be a talent[b] of gold, and it was set with precious stones—and it was placed on
David's head. He took a great quantity of plunder from the city 3and brought out the
people who were there, consigning them to labour with saws and with iron picks and
axes.[c] David did this to all the Ammonite towns. Then David and his entire army
returned to Jerusalem.

20:3 [c]Dt 29:11

War With the Philistines

20:4 [d]Jos 10:33 [e]Ge 14:5

4In the course of time, war broke out with the Philistines, at Gezer.[d] At that time
Sibbecai the Hushathite killed Sippai, one of the descendants of the Rephaites,[e] and
the Philistines were subjugated.
5In another battle with the Philistines, Elhanan son of Jair killed Lahmi the brother
of Goliath the Gittite, who had a spear with a shaft like a weaver's rod.[f]
6In still another battle, which took place at Gath, there was a huge man with six
fingers on each hand and six toes on each foot—twenty-four in all. He also was
descended from Rapha. 7When he taunted Israel, Jonathan son of Shimea, David's
brother, killed him.
8These were descendants of Rapha in Gath, and they fell at the hands of David and
his men.

20:5 [f]1Sa 17:7

21:1 [a]2Ch 18:21; Ps 109:6 [b]2Ch 14:8; 25:5

David Numbers the Fighting Men

21 Satan[a] rose up against Israel and incited David to take a census[b] of Israel.
2So David said to Joab and the commanders of the troops, "Go and count[c]
the Israelites from Beersheba to Dan. Then report back to me so that I may know how
many there are."
3But Joab replied, "May the LORD multiply his troops a hundred times over.[d] My
lord the king, are they not all my lord's subjects? Why does my lord want to do this?
Why should he bring guilt on Israel?"
4The king's word, however, overruled Joab; so Joab left and went throughout Israel
and then came back to Jerusalem. 5Joab reported the number of the fighting men to

21:2 [c]1Ch 27:23-24

21:3 [d]Dt 1:11

[a] *2* Or *of Milcom*, that is, Molech [b] *2* That is, about 75 pounds (about 34 kilograms)

20:1 David's adultery occurred at this time, while he remained in Jerusalem instead of going to battle (2 Samuel 11, 12). This story may have been excluded from 1 Chronicles because the book was written to focus on God's long-term interest in Israel and on the temple as a symbol of God's presence among them. The story of David and Bathsheba did not fit this purpose. The story of Absalom's rebellion, which occurred between this chapter and the next, was probably omitted for the same reason (2 Samuel 15–18).

20:1 Kings went out to battle following the spring harvest. At this time, farm work eased off, and the armies could live off the land. During the winter, they plotted and planned future conquests. Then, when the fair weather permitted it, their armies went into war. But David ignored this opportunity. He stayed home and sent Joab out to lead the army. It was during this time of inactivity that he sinned with Bathsheba. Look for the "springs" in your life, the times when God wants you to respond, take the initiative, and move out to do his will. It is during these critical times that we may be most sensitive to temptation. Resolve to take the action God has prescribed. Don't give temptation a foothold in your inactivity.

20:1 Rabbah was the capital of the Ammonites and is the site of modern Amman in Jordan.

21:1 David's census brought disaster because, unlike the census taken in the book of Numbers (Numbers 1; 2) that God had ordered, this census was taken so David could take pride in the strength of his army. In determining his military strength, he was beginning to trust more in military power than in God. There is a thin line between feeling confident because you rely on God's power and becoming proud because you have been used by God for great purposes.

21:1 The Bible text says Satan *incited* David to take a census. Can Satan force people to do wrong? No, Satan only *tempted* David with the idea, but David *decided to act* on the temptation. Ever since the Garden of Eden, Satan has been tempting people to sin. David's census was not against God's law, but his reason for the census was wrong—pride in his mighty army while forgetting that his real strength came from God. Even Joab, not known for his high moral ideals, recognised the census as sin. From David's example we learn that an action that may not be wrong in itself can be sinful if it is motivated by greed, arrogance, or selfishness. Often our motives, not the action itself, contain the sin. We must constantly weigh our motives before we act.

21:1–3 David fell to Satan's temptation. God provided a way out in Joab's counsel, but David's curiosity was spurred on by arrogance. His faith was in his own strength rather than in God's. If we feel self-sufficient and put confidence in ourselves apart from God, we soon fall to Satan's schemes. Self-sufficiency pulls us away from God. When you are tempted, examine your inner desires to understand why the external temptation is so appealing. (See 1 Corinthians 10:13 for more about escaping temptation.)

David: In all Israel[e] there were one million one hundred thousand men who could
handle a sword, including four hundred and seventy thousand in Judah.
6 But Joab did not include Levi and Benjamin in the numbering, because the king's
command was repulsive to him. 7 This command was also evil in the sight of God;
so he punished Israel.
8 Then David said to God, "I have sinned greatly by doing this. Now, I beg you,
take away the guilt of your servant. I have done a very foolish thing."
9 The LORD said to Gad,[f] David's seer,[g] 10 "Go and tell David, 'This is what the
LORD says: I am giving you three options. Choose one of them for me to carry out
against you.' "
11 So Gad went to David and said to him, "This is what the LORD says: 'Take your
choice: 12 three years of famine,[h] three months of being swept away[a] before your
enemies, with their swords overtaking you, or three days of the sword[i] of the
LORD[j]—days of plague in the land, with the angel of the LORD ravaging every part
of Israel.' Now then, decide how I should answer the one who sent me."
13 David said to Gad, "I am in deep distress. Let me fall into the hands of the LORD,
for his mercy[k] is very great; but do not let me fall into the hands of men."
14 So the LORD sent a plague on Israel, and seventy thousand men of Israel fell
dead.[l] 15 And God sent an angel[m] to destroy Jerusalem.[n] But as the angel was doing
so, the LORD saw it and was grieved[o] because of the calamity and said to the angel
who was destroying[p] the people, "Enough! Withdraw your hand." The angel of the
LORD was then standing at the threshing-floor of Araunah[b] the Jebusite.
16 David looked up and saw the angel of the LORD standing between heaven and
earth, with a drawn sword in his hand extended over Jerusalem. Then David and the
elders, clothed in sackcloth, fell face down.[q]
17 David said to God, "Was it not I who ordered the fighting men to be counted?
I am the one who has sinned and done wrong. These are but sheep.[r] What have they
done? O LORD my God, let your hand fall upon me and my family,[s] but do not let
this plague remain on your people."
18 Then the angel of the LORD ordered Gad to tell David to go up and build an altar
to the LORD on the threshing-floor[t] of Araunah the Jebusite. 19 So David went up in
obedience to the word that Gad had spoken in the name of the LORD.
20 While Araunah was threshing wheat,[u] he turned and saw the angel; his four sons
who were with him hid themselves. 21 Then David approached, and when Araunah
looked and saw him, he left the threshing-floor and bowed down before David with
his face to the ground.
22 David said to him, "Let me have the site of your threshing-floor so that I can build

[a] *12* Hebrew; Septuagint and Vulgate (see also 2 Sam. 24:13) *of fleeing* [b] *15* Hebrew *Ornan*, a variant of *Araunah*; also in verses 18–28

21:5 [e] 1Ch 9:1
21:9 [f] 1Sa 22:5 [g] 1Sa 9:9
21:12 [h] Dt 32:24 [i] Eze 30:25 [j] Ge 19:13
21:13 [k] Ps 6:4; 86:15; 130:4, 7
21:14 [l] 1Ch 27:24
21:15 [m] Ge 32:1 [n] Ps 125:2 [o] Ge 6:6; Ex 32:14 [p] Ge 19:13
21:16 [q] Nu 14:5; Jos 7:6
21:17 [r] 2Sa 7:8; Ps 74:1 [s] Jnh 1:12
21:18 [t] 2Ch 3:1
21:20 [u] Jdg 6:11

21:8 When David realised his sin, he took full responsibility, admitted he was wrong, and asked God to forgive him. Many people want to add God and the benefits of Christianity to their lives without acknowledging their personal sin and guilt. But confession and repentance must come before receiving forgiveness. Like David, we must take full responsibility for our actions and confess them to God before we can expect him to forgive us and continue his work in us.

21:13, 14 Sin has a domino effect; once a sin is committed, a series of consequences follows. God will forgive our sin if we ask him, but the consequences of that sin have already been set in motion. David pled for mercy, and God responded by stopping the angel before his mission of death was complete. The consequences of David's sin, however, had already caused severe damage. God will always forgive our sins and will often intervene to make their bitter consequences less severe, but the scars will remain. Thinking through the possible consequences before we act can stop us and thus save us much sorrow and suffering.

21:14 Why did 70,000 innocent people die for David's sin? Our society places great emphasis upon the individual. In ancient times, however, the family leaders, tribal leaders, and kings represented the people they led, and all expected to share in their successes as well as in their failures and punishments. David deserved punishment for his sin, but his death could have resulted in political chaos and invasion by enemy armies, leaving hundreds of thousands dead. Instead, God graciously spared David's life. He also put a stop to the plague so that most of the people of Jerusalem were spared.

God made us to work together interdependently. Whether we think it is fair or not, the group usually suffers because of the sins of its leaders. Similarly, our actions always affect other people whether we want them to or not. We cannot fully know the mind of God in this severe judgment. We don't know where the prophets, the tribal leaders, and the other advisers were during this incident and whether or not they chose to go along with the king. We do know that putting confidence in military might alone is idolatry. To allow anything to take God's place is sinful, and it may cause disastrous consequences.

21:22–24 When David wanted to buy Araunah's land to build an altar, Araunah generously offered it as a gift. But David refused, saying, "I will not take for the LORD what is yours, or sacrifice a

an altar to the LORD, that the plague on the people may be stopped. Sell it to me at
the full price."
23 Araunah said to David, "Take it! Let my lord the king do whatever pleases him.
Look, I will give the oxen for the burnt offerings, the threshing-sledges for the wood,
and the wheat for the grain offering. I will give all this."
24 But King David replied to Araunah, "No, I insist on paying the full price. I will
not take for the LORD what is yours, or sacrifice a burnt offering that costs me
nothing."
25 So David paid Araunah six hundred shekels[c] of gold for the site. 26 David built
an altar to the LORD there and sacrificed burnt offerings and fellowship offerings.[d]
He called on the LORD, and the LORD answered him with fire[v] from heaven on the
altar of burnt offering.
27 Then the LORD spoke to the angel, and he put his sword back into its sheath. 28 At
that time, when David saw that the LORD had answered him on the threshing-floor
of Araunah the Jebusite, he offered sacrifices there. 29 The tabernacle of the LORD,
which Moses had made in the desert, and the altar of burnt offering were at that time
on the high place at Gibeon.[w] 30 But David could not go before it to enquire of God,
because he was afraid of the sword of the angel of the LORD.

22 Then David said, "The house of the LORD God[a] is to be here, and also the
altar of burnt offering for Israel."

4. David arranges for the building of the temple

Preparations for the Temple

2 So David gave orders to assemble the aliens[b] living in Israel, and from among
them he appointed stonecutters[c] to prepare dressed stone for building the house of
God. 3 He provided a large amount of iron to make nails for the doors of the gateways
and for the fittings, and more bronze than could be weighed.[d] 4 He also provided more
cedar logs[e] than could be counted, for the Sidonians and Tyrians had brought large
numbers of them to David.
5 David said, "My son Solomon is young[f] and inexperienced, and the house to be
built for the LORD should be of great magnificence and fame and splendour in the sight
of all the nations. Therefore I will make preparations for it." So David made extensive
preparations before his death.
6 Then he called for his son Solomon and charged him to build[g] a house for the
LORD, the God of Israel. 7 David said to Solomon: "My son, I had it in my heart[h]
to build[i] a house for the Name[j] of the LORD my God. 8 But this word of the LORD
came to me: 'You have shed much blood and have fought many wars.[k] You are not
to build a house for my Name,[l] because you have shed much blood on the earth in
my sight. 9 But you will have a son who will be a man of peace[m] and rest, and I will
give him rest from all his enemies on every side. His name will be Solomon,[a][n] and
I will grant Israel peace and quiet[o] during his reign. 10 He is the one who will build

21:26 [v] Lev 9:24; Jdg 6:21
21:29 [w] 1Ki 3:4; 1Ch 16:39
22:1 [a] Ge 28:17; 1Ch 21:18-29; 2Ch 3:1
22:2 [b] 1Ki 9:21; Isa 56:6 [c] 1Ki 5:17-18
22:3 [d] ver 14; 1Ki 7:47; 1Ch 29:2-5
22:4 [e] 1Ki 5:6
22:5 [f] 1Ki 3:7; 1Ch 29:1
22:6 [g] Ac 7:47
22:7 [h] 1Ch 17:2 [i] 2Sa 7:2; 1Ki 8:17 [j] Dt 12:5, 11
22:8 [k] 1Ki 5:3 [l] 1Ch 28:3
22:9 [m] 1Ki 5:4 [n] 2Sa 12:24 [o] 1Ki 4:20

c *25* That is, about 15 pounds (about 7 kilograms) d *26* Traditionally *peace offerings* a *9* *Solomon* sounds like and may be derived from the Hebrew for *peace.*

---

burnt offering that costs me nothing." David wanted to offer a sacrifice to God. The word *sacrifice* implies giving something that costs the giver in terms of self, time, or money. To give sacrificially requires more than a token effort or gift. God wants us to give voluntarily, but he wants it to mean something. Giving to God what costs you nothing does not demonstrate commitment.

21:29 – 22:1 Gibeon was a Benjamite city. After the defeat of Nob by Saul, who was a Benjamite, Saul moved the tabernacle to Gibeon. Gibeon was about two hours journey northwest of Jerusalem.

22:1 Out of David's tragic mistake came the purchase of a plot of land that would become the site of God's temple, the symbol of God's presence among his people. Every time the people went to the temple they would remember that God is their true King and that everyone, including their human king, is fallible and subject to sin. God can use our sins for good purposes if we are sorry for them and seek his forgiveness. When we confess our sins, the way is opened for God to bring good from a bad situation.

22:7–10 God told David he would not be the one to build the temple. Instead the task would be left to his son Solomon. David graciously accepted this "no" from God. He was not jealous of the fact that his son would have the honour of building God's temple, but instead made preparations for Solomon to carry out his task. Similarly, we should take steps now to prepare the way for our children to find and fulfil God's purpose. Sooner or later our children will have to make their own decisions, but we can help by supplying them with the proper tools: showing them how to pray and study God's word, the difference between right and wrong, and the importance of church involvement.

a house for my Name.[p] He will be my son,[q] and I will be his father. And I will
establish the throne of his kingdom over Israel for ever.'[r]
11 "Now, my son, the LORD be with[s] you, and may you have success and build
the house of the LORD your God, as he said you would. 12 May the LORD give you
discretion and understanding[t] when he puts you in command over Israel, so that you
may keep the law of the LORD your God. 13 Then you will have success if you are
careful to observe the decrees and laws[u] that the LORD gave to Moses for Israel. Be
strong and courageous.[v] Do not be afraid or discouraged.
14 "I have taken great pains to provide for the temple of the LORD a hundred thousand
talents[b] of gold, a million talents[c] of silver, quantities of bronze and iron too great
to be weighed, and wood and stone. And you may add to them.[w] 15 You have many
workmen: stonecutters, masons and carpenters, as well as men skilled in every kind
of work 16 in gold and silver, bronze and iron—craftsmen[x] beyond number. Now
begin the work, and the LORD be with you."
17 Then David ordered[y] all the leaders of Israel to help his son Solomon. 18 He said
to them, "Is not the LORD your God with you? And has he not granted you rest[z] on
every side?[a] For he has handed the inhabitants of the land over to me, and the land
is subject to the LORD and to his people. 19 Now devote your heart and soul to seeking
the LORD your God.[b] Begin to build the sanctuary of the LORD God, so that you may
bring the ark of the covenant of the LORD and the sacred articles belonging to God
into the temple that will be built for the Name of the LORD."

The Levites

23 When David was old and full of years, he made his son Solomon[a] king over
Israel.[b]
2 He also gathered together all the leaders of Israel, as well as the priests and Levites.
3 The Levites thirty years old or more[c] were counted, and the total number of men
was thirty-eight thousand.[d] 4 David said, "Of these, twenty-four thousand are to
supervise[e] the work of the temple of the LORD and six thousand are to be officials
and judges.[f] 5 Four thousand are to be gatekeepers and four thousand are to praise
the LORD with the musical instruments[g] I have provided for that purpose."[h]
6 David divided[i] the Levites into groups corresponding to the sons of Levi: Gershon, Kohath and Merari.

Gershonites

7 Belonging to the Gershonites:
Ladan and Shimei.
8 The sons of Ladan:
Jehiel the first, Zetham and Joel—three in all.
9 The sons of Shimei:
Shelomoth, Haziel and Haran—three in all.
These were the heads of the families of Ladan.
10 And the sons of Shimei:
Jahath, Ziza,[a] Jeush and Beriah.
These were the sons of Shimei—four in all.
11 Jahath was the first and Ziza the second, but Jeush and Beriah did not have
many sons; so they were counted as one family with one assignment.

22:10 [p] 1Ch 17:12 [q] 2Sa 7:13 [r] 2Sa 7:14; 2Ch 6:15
22:11 [s] ver 16
22:12 [t] 1Ki 3:9-12; 2Ch 1:10
22:13 [u] 1Ch 28:7 [v] Dt 31:6; Jos 1:6-9; 1Ch 28:20
22:14 [w] ver 3; 1Ch 29:2-5, 19
22:16 [x] ver 11; 2Ch 2:7
22:17 [y] 1Ch 28:1-6
22:18 [z] ver 9; 1Ch 23:25 [a] 2Sa 7:1
22:19 [b] ver 7; 1Ki 8:6; 1Ch 28:9; 2Ch 5:7; 7:14
23:1 [a] 1Ki 1:33-39; 1Ch 28:5 [b] 1Ki 1:30; 1Ch 29:28
23:3 [c] ver 24; Nu 8:24 [d] Nu 4:3-49
23:4 [e] Ezr 3:8 [f] 1Ch 26:29; 2Ch 19:8
23:5 [g] 1Ch 15:16 [h] Ne 12:45
23:6 [i] 2Ch 8:14; 29:25

b *14* That is, about 3,395 tons (about 3,450 metric tons) **c** *14* That is, about 33,950 tons (about 34,500 metric tons) **a** *10* One Hebrew manuscript, Septuagint and Vulgate (see also verse 11); most Hebrew manuscripts *Zina*

23:1 For more information on Solomon's coronation and the attempts to seize his throne, see 1 Kings 1; 2.

23:1ff Although David couldn't build the temple, he could make preparations, and he took that job seriously. He not only gathered funds and materials for God's house, he also planned much of the administration and arranged the worship services. The original readers of Chronicles were rebuilding the temple after it had been destroyed by invading armies, and this information about its procedures was invaluable to them. The next five chapters demonstrate that organisation is essential for smooth and effective service.

23:3 Why was this census acceptable when the other was not (chapter 21)? This census counted only the Levites—those set apart to serve God—and was used to organise the work in the temple. The census was not based on pride or self-sufficiency as was the previous census of fighting men.

23:12 [j]Ex 6:18
23:13 [k]Ex 6:20; 28:1 [l]Ex 30:7-10; Dt 21:5 [m]Nu 6:23
23:14 [n]Dt 33:1
23:15 [o]Ex 18:4
23:16 [p]1Ch 26:24-28
23:19 [q]1Ch 24:23
23:21 [r]1Ch 24:26

Kohathites

12 The sons of Kohath:[j]
Amram, Izhar, Hebron and Uzziel—four in all.
13 The sons of Amram:[k]
Aaron and Moses.
Aaron was set apart,[l] he and his descendants for ever, to consecrate the most
holy things, to offer sacrifices before the LORD, to minister before him and
to pronounce blessings[m] in his name for ever.
14 The sons of Moses the man[n]
of God were counted as part of the tribe of Levi.
15 The sons of Moses:
Gershom and Eliezer.[o]
16 The descendants of Gershom:[p]
Shubael was the first.
17 The descendants of Eliezer:
Rehabiah was the first.
Eliezer had no other sons, but the sons of Rehabiah were very numerous.
18 The sons of Izhar:
Shelomith was the first.
19 The sons of Hebron:[q]
Jeriah the first, Amariah the second, Jahaziel the third and Jekameam the fourth.
20 The sons of Uzziel:
Micah the first and Isshiah the second.

Merarites

21 The sons of Merari:[r]
Mahli and Mushi.

DUTIES ASSIGNED IN THE TEMPLE
King David charged all these people to do their jobs "for the Name of the LORD" (1 Chronicles 22:17–19). God needs people of every talent—not just prophets and priests—to obey him.

Administrative Duties	Supervisors	1 Chronicles 23:4, 5
	Officials	1 Chronicles 23:4, 5
	Judges	1 Chronicles 23:4, 5
	Public administrators	1 Chronicles 26:29, 30
Ministerial Duties	Priests	1 Chronicles 24:1
	Prophets	1 Chronicles 25:1
	Assistants for sacrifices	1 Chronicles 23:29–31
	Assistants for purification ceremonies	1 Chronicles 23:28
Service Duties	Bakers of the bread of the Presence	1 Chronicles 23:29
	Those who made the measurements	1 Chronicles 23:29
	Caretakers	1 Chronicles 23:28
Financial Duties	Those who cared for the treasuries	1 Chronicles 26:20
	Those who cared for the dedicated things	1 Chronicles 26:26–28
Artistic Duties	Musicians	1 Chronicles 25:6
	Singers	1 Chronicles 25:7
Protective Duties	Gatekeepers	1 Chronicles 26:12–18
Individual Assignments	Chief of the gatekeepers	1 Chronicles 9:19–21
	Scribe	1 Chronicles 24:6
	Seer	1 Chronicles 25:5
	Prophet under the king	1 Chronicles 25:2
	Chief officer of the treasuries	1 Chronicles 26:23, 24

23:14 All that is stated here about Moses is that he was "the man of God". What a profound description of a person! A man or woman of God is one whose life reflects God's presence, priorities, and power.

The sons of Mahli:
Eleazar and Kish.
22Eleazar died without having sons: he had only daughters. Their cousins, the
sons of Kish, married them.
23The sons of Mushi:
Mahli, Eder and Jerimoth — three in all.

24These were the descendants of Levi by their families — the heads of families as
they were registered under their names and counted individually, that is, the workers
twenty years old or more[s] who served in the temple of the LORD. 25For David had
said, "Since the LORD, the God of Israel, has granted rest[t] to his people and has come
to dwell in Jerusalem for ever, 26the Levites no longer need to carry the tabernacle
or any of the articles used in its service."[u] 27According to the last instructions of
David, the Levites were counted from those twenty years old or more.
28The duty of the Levites was to help Aaron's descendants in the service of the
temple of the LORD: to be in charge of the courtyards, the side rooms, the purification[v]
of all sacred things and the performance of other duties at the house of God. 29They
were in charge of the bread set out on the table,[w] the flour for the grain offerings,[x]
the unleavened wafers, the baking and the mixing, and all measurements of quantity
and size.[y] 30They were also to stand every morning to thank and praise the LORD.
They were to do the same in the evening[z] 31and whenever burnt offerings were
presented to the LORD on Sabbaths and at New Moon[a] festivals and at appointed
feasts.[b] They were to serve before the LORD regularly in the proper number and in
the way prescribed for them.
32And so the Levites[c] carried out their responsibilities for the Tent of Meeting,[d]
for the Holy Place and, under their brothers the descendants of Aaron, for the service
of the temple of the LORD.[e]

The Divisions of Priests

24 These were the divisions[a] of the sons of Aaron:[b]
The sons of Aaron were Nadab, Abihu, Eleazar and Ithamar.[c] 2But Nadab
and Abihu died before their father did,[d] and they had no sons; so Eleazar and Ithamar
served as the priests. 3With the help of Zadok[e] a descendant of Eleazar and Ahimelech a descendant of Ithamar, David separated them into divisions for their appointed
order of ministering. 4A larger number of leaders were found among Eleazar's
descendants than among Ithamar's, and they were divided accordingly: sixteen heads
of families from Eleazar's descendants and eight heads of families from Ithamar's
descendants. 5They divided them impartially by drawing lots,[f] for there were officials of the sanctuary and officials of God among the descendants of both Eleazar and
Ithamar.

23:24 [s]Nu 4:3; 10:17, 21
23:25 [t]1Ch 22:9
23:26 [u]Nu 4:5, 15; 7:9; Dt 10:8
23:28 [v]2Ch 29:15; Ne 13:9; Mal 3:3
23:29 [w]Ex 25:30 [x]Lev 2:4-7; 6:20-23 [y]Lev 19:35-36; 1Ch 9:29, 32
23:30 [z]1Ch 9:33; Ps 134:1
23:31 [a]2Ki 4:23 [b]Lev 23:4; Nu 28:9-29:39; Isa 1:13-14; Col 2:16
23:32 [c]Nu 1:53; 1Ch 6:48 [d]Nu 3:6-8, 38 [e]2Ch 23:18; 31:2; Eze 44:14
24:1 [a]1Ch 23:6; 28:13; 2Ch 5:11; 8:14; 23:8; 31:2; 35:4, 5; Ezr 6:18 [b]Nu 3:2-4 [c]Ex 6:23
24:2 [d]Lev 10:1-2; Nu 3:4
24:3 [e]2Sa 8:17
24:5 [f]ver 31; 1Ch 25:8

23:28–32 Priests and Levites had different jobs in and around the temple. Priests were authorised to perform the sacrifices. Levites were set apart to help the priests. They did the work of elders, deacons, custodians, assistants, musicians, removal men, and repairmen. Both priests and Levites came from the tribe of Levi, but priests also had to be descendants of Aaron, Israel's first high priest (Exodus 28:1–3). Priests and Levites were supported by Israel's tithes and by revenues from certain cities that had been given to them. Worship in the temple could not have taken place without the combined efforts of the priests and Levites. Their responsibilities were different, but they were equally important to God's plan. No matter what place of service you have in the church, you are important to the healthy functioning of the congregation.

24:1ff The temple service was highly structured, but this did not hinder the Spirit of God. Rather, it provided an orderly context for worship. (Compare 1 Corinthians 14:40.) Sometimes we feel that planning and structure are unspiritual activities that may hinder spontaneity in worship. But order and structure can free us to respond to God. Order brings glory to God as we experience the joy, freedom, and calm that come when we have wisely prepared in advance.

24:3 This Ahimelech was the son of Abiathar and the grandson of another Ahimelech, one of the priests massacred by Saul (1 Samuel 22:11–18). Abiathar and Zadok were co–high priests under David: one was at Jerusalem where the ark of God was kept, and one was at Gibeon serving at the tabernacle. It appears from this verse and 18:16 that Ahimelech began to assume some of Abiathar's duties as his father grew old.

24:4 Eleazar's descendants were divided into 16 groups (as opposed to Ithamar's eight) for three reasons. (1) Eleazar had received the birthright since his two older brothers, Nadab and Abihu, had been killed (Leviticus 10). The birthright included a double portion of the father's estate. (2) His descendants were greater in number than Ithamar's. (3) His descendants had greater leadership ability. These 24 groups gave order to the functioning of the temple.

24:6 [g]1Ch 18:16

6The scribe Shemaiah son of Nethanel, a Levite, recorded their names in the presence of the king and of the officials: Zadok the priest, Ahimelech[g] son of Abiathar and the heads of families of the priests and of the Levites—one family being taken from Eleazar and then one from Ithamar.

7The first lot fell to Jehoiarib,
the second to Jedaiah,[h]
8the third to Harim,[i]
the fourth to Seorim,
9the fifth to Malkijah,
the sixth to Mijamin,
10the seventh to Hakkoz,
the eighth to Abijah,[j]
11the ninth to Jeshua,
the tenth to Shecaniah,
12the eleventh to Eliashib,
the twelfth to Jakim,
13the thirteenth to Huppah,
the fourteenth to Jeshebeab,
14the fifteenth to Bilgah,
the sixteenth to Immer,[k]
15the seventeenth to Hezir,[l]
the eighteenth to Happizzez,
16the nineteenth to Pethahiah,
the twentieth to Jehezkel,
17the twenty-first to Jakin,
the twenty-second to Gamul,
18the twenty-third to Delaiah
and the twenty-fourth to Maaziah.

24:7 [h]Ezr 2:36; Ne 12:6
24:8 [i]Ezr 2:39; Ne 10:5
24:10 [j]Ne 12:4, 17; Lk 1:5
24:14 [k]Jer 20:1
24:15 [l]Ne 10:20

19This was their appointed order of ministering when they entered the temple of the LORD, according to the regulations prescribed for them by their forefather Aaron, as the LORD, the God of Israel, had commanded him.

The Rest of the Levites

20As for the rest of the descendants of Levi:[m]
from the sons of Amram: Shubael;
from the sons of Shubael: Jehdeiah.
21As for Rehabiah,[n] from his sons:
Isshiah was the first.
22From the Izharites: Shelomoth;
from the sons of Shelomoth: Jahath.
23The sons of Hebron:[o] Jeriah the first,[a] Amariah the second, Jahaziel the third and Jekameam the fourth.
24The son of Uzziel: Micah;
from the sons of Micah: Shamir.
25The brother of Micah: Isshiah;
from the sons of Isshiah: Zechariah.
26The sons of Merari:[p] Mahli and Mushi.
The son of Jaaziah: Beno.
27The sons of Merari:
from Jaaziah: Beno, Shoham, Zaccur and Ibri.

24:20 [m]1Ch 23:6
24:21 [n]1Ch 23:17
24:23 [o]1Ch 23:19
24:26 [p]1Ch 6:19; 23:21

[a] *23* Two Hebrew manuscripts and some Septuagint manuscripts (see also 1 Chron. 23:19); most Hebrew manuscripts *The sons of Jeriah:*

24:7–18 Each of these 24 groups of priests served two-week shifts each year at the temple. The rest of the time they served in their hometowns. This system was still in place in Jesus' day (Luke 1:5–9). Zechariah was a member of the Abijah division. During his shift at the temple, an angel appeared to him and predicted that he would have a son, John.

28 From Mahli: Eleazar, who had no sons.
29 From Kish: the son of Kish:
Jerahmeel.
30 And the sons of Mushi: Mahli, Eder and Jerimoth.

These were the Levites, according to their families. 31 They also cast lots,[q] just as
their brothers the descendants of Aaron did, in the presence of King David and of
Zadok, Ahimelech, and the heads of families of the priests and of the Levites. The
families of the oldest brother were treated the same as those of the youngest.

The Singers

25 David, together with the commanders of the army, set apart some of the sons
of Asaph,[a] Heman[b] and Jeduthun[c] for the ministry of prophesying,[d] accompanied by harps, lyres and cymbals.[e] Here is the list of the men[f] who performed
this service:[g]

2 From the sons of Asaph:
Zaccur, Joseph, Nethaniah and Asarelah. The sons of Asaph were under the supervision of Asaph, who prophesied under the king's supervision.
3 As for Jeduthun, from his sons:[h]
Gedaliah, Zeri, Jeshaiah, Shimei,[a] Hashabiah and Mattithiah, six in all, under the supervision of their father Jeduthun, who prophesied, using the harp[i] in thanking and praising the LORD.
4 As for Heman, from his sons:
Bukkiah, Mattaniah, Uzziel, Shubael and Jerimoth; Hananiah, Hanani,
Eliathah, Giddalti and Romamti-Ezer; Joshbekashah, Mallothi, Hothir and
Mahazioth. 5 All these were sons of Heman the king's seer. They were given to
him through the promises of God to exalt him.[b] God gave Heman fourteen
sons and three daughters.

6 All these men were under the supervision of their fathers[j] for the music of the
temple of the LORD, with cymbals, lyres and harps, for the ministry at the house of
God. Asaph, Jeduthun and Heman[k] were under the supervision of the king.[l] 7 Along
with their relatives—all of them trained and skilled in music for the LORD—they
numbered 288. 8 Young and old alike, teacher as well as student, cast lots[m] for their
duties.

9 The first lot, which was for Asaph,[n] fell to Joseph,	
his sons and relatives,[c]	12[d]
the second to Gedaliah,	
he and his relatives and sons,	12
10 the third to Zaccur,	
his sons and relatives,	12
11 the fourth to Izri,[e]	
his sons and relatives,	12
12 the fifth to Nethaniah,	

[a] 3 One Hebrew manuscript and some Septuagint manuscripts (see also verse 17); most Hebrew manuscripts do not have *Shimei.* [b] 5 Hebrew *exalt the horn* [c] 9 See Septuagint; Hebrew does not have *his sons and relatives.* [d] 9 See the total in verse 7; Hebrew does not have *twelve.* [e] 11 A variant of *Zeri*

24:31 [q] ver 5

25:1 [a] 1Ch 6:39 [b] 1Ch 6:33 [c] 1Ch 16:41, 42; Ne 11:17 [d] 1Sa 10:5; 2Ki 3:15 [e] 1Ch 15:16 [f] 1Ch 6:31 [g] 2Ch 5:12; 8:14; 34:12; 35:15; Ezr 3:10

25:3 [h] 1Ch 16:41-42 [i] Ge 4:21; Ps 33:2

25:6 [j] 1Ch 15:16 [k] 1Ch 15:19 [l] 2Ch 23:18; 29:25

25:8 [m] 1Ch 26:13

25:9 [n] 1Ch 6:39

25:1 There is more to prophesying than predicting the future. Prophecy also involves singing God's praises and preaching God's messages (1 Corinthians 14:1ff). Prophets could be musicians, farmers (Amos 1:1), wives (2 Kings 22:14), or leaders (Deuteronomy 34:10)—anyone who boldly and accurately spoke out for God and tried to bring people back to worshipping him. From a large group of musicians David chose those who showed an unusual ability to tell about God and to encourage others in song.

25:1–7 There were many ways to contribute to the worship in the tabernacle. Some prophesied (25:1), some led in thanksgiving and praise (25:3), and others played instruments (25:6, 7). God wants all his people to participate in worship. You may not be a master musician, a prophet, or a teacher, but God appreciates whatever you have to offer. Develop your special gifts to offer in service to God (Romans 12:3–8; 1 Corinthians 12:29–31).

25:9–31 The musicians were divided into 24 groups to match the 24 groups of Levites (24:7–25). This division of labour gave order to the planning of temple work, promoted excellence by making training easier, gave variety to worship because each group worked a term, and provided opportunities for many to be involved.

his sons and relatives,	12
13 the sixth to Bukkiah,	
his sons and relatives,	12
14 the seventh to Jesarelah,[f]	
his sons and relatives,	12
15 the eighth to Jeshaiah,	
his sons and relatives,	12
16 the ninth to Mattaniah,	
his sons and relatives,	12
17 the tenth to Shimei,	
his sons and relatives,	12
18 the eleventh to Azarel,[g]	
his sons and relatives,	12
19 the twelfth to Hashabiah,	
his sons and relatives,	12
20 the thirteenth to Shubael,	
his sons and relatives,	12
21 the fourteenth to Mattithiah,	
his sons and relatives,	12
22 the fifteenth to Jerimoth,	
his sons and relatives,	12
23 the sixteenth to Hananiah,	
his sons and relatives,	12
24 the seventeenth to Joshbekashah,	
his sons and relatives,	12
25 the eighteenth to Hanani,	
his sons and relatives,	12
26 the nineteenth to Mallothi,	
his sons and relatives,	12
27 the twentieth to Eliathah,	

f *14* A variant of *Asarelah* g *18* A variant of *Uzziel*

MUSIC IN BIBLE TIMES

Paul clearly puts forth the Christian's view that things are not good or bad in and of themselves (see Romans 14 and 1 Corinthians 14:7, 8, 26). The point should always be to worship the Lord or help others by means of the things of this world, including music. Music was created by God and can be returned to him in praise. Does the music you play or listen to have a negative or positive impact upon your relationship with God?

Highlights of musical use in Scripture	*References*
Jubal was father of all musicians	Genesis 4:21
Miriam and other women sang and danced to praise God	Exodus 15:1–21
The priest was to have bells on his robes	Exodus 28:34, 35
Jericho fell to the sound of trumpets	Joshua 6:4-20
Saul experienced the soothing effect of music	1 Samuel 16:14–23
The king's coronation was accompanied by music	1 Kings 1:39, 40
The ark was accompanied by trumpeters	1 Chronicles 16:6
There were musicians for the king's court	Ecclesiastes 2:8
From David's time on, the use of music in worship was much more organised. Music for the temple became refined.	1 Chronicles 15:16–24 1 Chronicles 16:4–7 2 Chronicles 5:11–14
Everything was to be used by everyone to praise the Lord	Psalm 150
In the New Testament, worship continued in the synagogues until the Christians became unwelcome there, so there was a rich musical heritage already established. The fact that music is mentioned less often in the New Testament does not mean it was less important.	
Jesus and the disciples sang a hymn	Matthew 26:30
Paul and Silas sang in jail	Acts 16:25
We are to sing to the Lord as a response to what he has done in our lives	Ephesians 5:19, 20 Colossians 3:16 James 5:13

his sons and relatives, 12
28the twenty-first to Hothir,
his sons and relatives, 12
29the twenty-second to Giddalti,
his sons and relatives, 12
30the twenty-third to Mahazioth,
his sons and relatives, 12
31the twenty-fourth to Romamti-Ezer,
his sons and relatives. 12[o]

The Gatekeepers

26 The divisions of the gatekeepers:[a]

From the Korahites: Meshelemiah son of Kore, one of the sons of Asaph.
2Meshelemiah had sons:
Zechariah[b] the firstborn,
Jediael the second,
Zebadiah the third,
Jathniel the fourth,
3Elam the fifth,
Jehohanan the sixth
and Eliehoenai the seventh.
4Obed-Edom also had sons:
Shemaiah the firstborn,
Jehozabad the second,
Joah the third,
Sacar the fourth,
Nethanel the fifth,
5Ammiel the sixth,
Issachar the seventh
and Peullethai the eighth.
(For God had blessed Obed-Edom.[c])

6His son Shemaiah also had sons, who were leaders in their father's family
because they were very capable men. 7The sons of Shemaiah: Othni, Re-
phael, Obed and Elzabad; his relatives Elihu and Semakiah were also able
men. 8All these were descendants of Obed-Edom; they and their sons and
their relatives were capable men with the strength to do the
work—descendants of Obed-Edom, 62 in all.
9Meshelemiah had sons and relatives, who were able men—18 in all.

10Hosah the Merarite had sons: Shimri the first (although he was not the firstborn,
his father had appointed him the first),[d] 11Hilkiah the second, Tabaliah the
third and Zechariah the fourth. The sons and relatives of Hosah were 13 in
all.
12These divisions of the gatekeepers, through their chief men, had duties for
ministering[e] in the temple of the LORD, just as their relatives had. 13Lots[f] were cast
for each gate, according to their families, young and old alike.
14The lot for the East Gate[g] fell to Shelemiah.**a** Then lots were cast for his son

a *14* A variant of *Meshelemiah*

25:31 [o] 1Ch 9:33
26:1 [a] 1Ch 9:17
26:2 [b] 1Ch 9:21
26:5 [c] 2Sa 6:10; 1Ch 13:13; 16:38
26:10 [d] Dt 21:16; 1Ch 5:1
26:12 [e] 1Ch 9:22
26:13 [f] 1Ch 24:5, 31; 25:8
26:14 [g] 1Ch 9:18

26:1 There were 4,000 gatekeepers (23:4, 5). They were all Levites and did many other jobs as well. Some of their duties included (1) checking out the equipment and utensils used each day and making sure they were returned, (2) storing, ordering, and maintaining the food supplies for the priests and sacrifices, (3) caring for the furniture, (4) mixing the incense that was burned daily, and (5) accounting for the gifts brought. (For more on gatekeepers, see the note on 9:17, 18.)

26:5 "God had blessed Obed-Edom." The status of children in society has fluctuated throughout history; sometimes they are highly esteemed, and sometimes abused and cheated. But Scripture shows no such vacillation—children are called a blessing from God, and God never views them as a burden (Psalm 127:3–5; Mark 10:13–15).

Zechariah,[h] a wise counsellor, and the lot for the North Gate fell to him. 15The lot
for the South Gate fell to Obed-Edom,[i] and the lot for the storehouse fell to his sons.
16The lots for the West Gate and the Shalleketh Gate on the upper road fell to Shuppim
and Hosah.
Guard was alongside guard: 17There were six Levites a day on the east, four a day
on the north, four a day on the south and two at a time at the storehouse. 18As for
the court to the west, there were four at the road and two at the court itself.
19These were the divisions of the gatekeepers who were descendants of Korah and
Merari.[j]

The Treasurers and Other Officials

20Their fellow Levites[k] were[b] in charge of the treasuries of the house of God and
the treasuries for the dedicated things.[l]
21The descendants of Ladan, who were Gershonites through Ladan and who were
heads of families belonging to Ladan the Gershonite,[m] were Jehieli, 22the sons of
Jehieli, Zetham and his brother Joel. They were in charge of the treasuries[n] of the
temple of the LORD.
23From the Amramites, the Izharites, the Hebronites and the Uzzielites:[o]

24Shubael,[p] a descendant of Gershom son of Moses, was the officer in charge
of the treasuries. 25His relatives through Eliezer: Rehabiah his son, Jeshaiah
his son, Joram his son, Zicri his son and Shelomith[q] his son. 26Shelomith
and his relatives were in charge of all the treasuries for the things dedicated[r]
by King David, by the heads of families who were the commanders of
thousands and commanders of hundreds, and by the other army commanders.
27Some of the plunder taken in battle they dedicated for the repair of the
temple of the LORD. 28And everything dedicated by Samuel the seer[s] and
by Saul son of Kish, Abner son of Ner and Joab son of Zeruiah, and all the
other dedicated things were in the care of Shelomith and his relatives.
29From the Izharites: Kenaniah and his sons were assigned duties away from the
temple, as officials and judges[t] over Israel.
30From the Hebronites: Hashabiah[u] and his relatives—seventeen hundred able
men—were responsible in Israel west of the Jordan for all the work of the
LORD and for the king's service. 31As for the Hebronites,[v] Jeriah was their
chief according to the genealogical records of their families. In the fortieth[w]
year of David's reign a search was made in the records, and capable men
among the Hebronites were found at Jazer in Gilead. 32Jeriah had two
thousand seven hundred relatives, who were able men and heads of families,
and King David put them in charge of the Reubenites, the Gadites and the
half-tribe of Manasseh for every matter pertaining to God and for the affairs
of the king.

Army Divisions

27 This is the list of the Israelites—heads of families, commanders of thousands
and commanders of hundreds, and their officers, who served the king in all that
concerned the army divisions that were on duty month by month throughout the year.
Each division consisted of 24,000 men.

2In charge of the first division, for the first month, was Jashobeam[a] son of Zabdiel.
There were 24,000 men in his division. 3He was a descendant of Perez and chief
of all the army officers for the first month.
4In charge of the division for the second month was Dodai[b] the Ahohite; Mikloth
was the leader of his division. There were 24,000 men in his division.

26:14 [h]1Ch 9:21
26:15 [i]1Ch 13:13; 2Ch 25:24
26:19 [j]2Ch 35:15; Ne 7:1; Eze 44:11
26:20 [k]2Ch 24:5 [l]1Ch 28:12
26:21 [m]1Ch 23:7; 29:8
26:22 [n]1Ch 9:26
26:23 [o]Nu 3:27
26:24 [p]1Ch 23:16
26:25 [q]1Ch 23:18
26:26 [r]2Sa 8:11
26:28 [s]1Sa 9:9
26:29 [t]Dt 17:8-13; 1Ch 23:4; Ne 11:16
26:30 [u]1Ch 27:17
26:31 [v]1Ch 23:19 [w]2Sa 5:4
27:2 [a]2Sa 23:8; 1Ch 11:11
27:4 [b]2Sa 23:9

b *20* Septuagint; Hebrew *As for the Levites, Ahijah was*

26:27 War plunder rightfully belonged to the victorious army. These soldiers, however, gave their portion of all the plunder to the temple to express their dedication to God. Like these commanders, we should think of what we *can* give, rather than what we are obligated to give. Is your giving a matter of rejoicing rather than duty? Give as a response of joy and love for God.

5The third army commander, for the third month, was Benaiah[c] son of Jehoiada
the priest. He was chief and there were 24,000 men in his division. 6This was
the Benaiah who was a mighty man among the Thirty and was over the Thirty.
His son Ammizabad was in charge of his division.
7The fourth, for the fourth month, was Asahel[d] the brother of Joab; his son
Zebadiah was his successor. There were 24,000 men in his division.
8The fifth, for the fifth month, was the commander Shamhuth[e] the Izrahite. There
were 24,000 men in his division.
9The sixth, for the sixth month, was Ira[f] the son of Ikkesh the Tekoite. There were
24,000 men in his division.
10The seventh, for the seventh month, was Helez[g] the Pelonite, an Ephraimite.
There were 24,000 men in his division.
11The eighth, for the eighth month, was Sibbecai[h] the Hushathite, a Zerahite. There
were 24,000 men in his division.
12The ninth, for the ninth month, was Abiezer[i] the Anathothite, a Benjamite. There
were 24,000 men in his division.
13The tenth, for the tenth month, was Maharai[j] the Netophathite, a Zerahite. There
were 24,000 men in his division.
14The eleventh, for the eleventh month, was Benaiah[k] the Pirathonite, an Ephraimite. There were 24,000 men in his division.
15The twelfth, for the twelfth month, was Heldai[l] the Netophathite, from the family
of Othniel.[m] There were 24,000 men in his division.

Officers of the Tribes

16The officers over the tribes of Israel:

over the Reubenites: Eliezer son of Zicri;
over the Simeonites: Shephatiah son of Maacah;
17over Levi: Hashabiah[n] son of Kemuel;
over Aaron: Zadok;[o]
18over Judah: Elihu, a brother of David;
over Issachar: Omri son of Michael;
19over Zebulun: Ishmaiah son of Obadiah;
over Naphtali: Jerimoth son of Azriel;
20over the Ephraimites: Hoshea son of Azaziah;
over half the tribe of Manasseh: Joel son of Pedaiah;
21over the half-tribe of Manasseh in Gilead: Iddo son of Zechariah;
over Benjamin: Jaasiel son of Abner;
22over Dan: Azarel son of Jeroham.
These were the officers over the tribes of Israel.

23David did not take the number of the men twenty years old or less,[p] because the
LORD had promised to make Israel as numerous as the stars[q] in the sky. 24Joab son
of Zeruiah began to count the men but did not finish. Wrath came on Israel on account
of this numbering,[r] and the number was not entered in the book[a] of the annals of
King David.

The King's Overseers

25Azmaveth son of Adiel was in charge of the royal storehouses.
Jonathan son of Uzziah was in charge of the storehouses in the outlying districts,
in the towns, the villages and the watchtowers.
26Ezri son of Kelub was in charge of the field workers who farmed the land.
27Shimei the Ramathite was in charge of the vineyards.
Zabdi the Shiphmite was in charge of the produce of the vineyards for the wine vats.

a 24 Septuagint; Hebrew *number*

27:5 c2Sa 23:20
27:7 d2Sa 2:18; 1Ch 11:26
27:8 e1Ch 11:27
27:9 f2Sa 23:26; 1Ch 11:28
27:10 g2Sa 23:26; 1Ch 11:27
27:11 h2Sa 21:18
27:12 i2Sa 23:27; 1Ch 11:28
27:13 j2Sa 23:28; 1Ch 11:30
27:14 k1Ch 11:31
27:15 l2Sa 23:29 mJos 15:17
27:17 n1Ch 26:30 o2Sa 8:17; 1Ch 12:28
27:23 p1Ch 21:2-5 qGe 15:5
27:24 r2Sa 24:15; 1Ch 21:7

27:24 The book of the annals of King David was a historical document kept in the royal archives with other official records. It no longer exists. See 1 Kings 14:19.

28Baal-Hanan the Gederite was in charge of the olive and sycamore-fig[s] trees in
the western foothills.
Joash was in charge of the supplies of olive oil.
29Shitrai the Sharonite was in charge of the herds grazing in Sharon.
Shaphat son of Adlai was in charge of the herds in the valleys.
30Obil the Ishmaelite was in charge of the camels.
Jehdeiah the Meronothite was in charge of the donkeys.
31Jaziz the Hagrite[t] was in charge of the flocks.
All these were the officials in charge of King David's property.

32Jonathan, David's uncle, was a counsellor, a man of insight and a scribe. Jehiel
son of Hacmoni took care of the king's sons.
33Ahithophel[u] was the king's counsellor.
Hushai[v] the Arkite was the king's friend. 34Ahithophel was succeeded by Jehoiada
son of Benaiah and by Abiathar.[w]
Joab[x] was the commander of the royal army.

David's Plans for the Temple

28 David summoned all the officials[a] of Israel to assemble at Jerusalem: the
officers over the tribes, the commanders of the divisions in the service of the
king, the commanders of thousands and commanders of hundreds, and the officials
in charge of all the property and livestock belonging to the king and his sons, together
with the palace officials, the mighty men and all the brave warriors.
2King David rose to his feet and said: "Listen to me, my brothers and my people.
I had it in my heart[b] to build a house as a place of rest for the ark of the covenant
of the LORD, for the footstool[c] of our God, and I made plans to build it. 3But God
said to me,[d] 'You are not to build a house for my Name,[e] because you are a warrior
and have shed blood.'[f]
4"Yet the LORD, the God of Israel, chose me[g] from my whole family[h] to be king
over Israel for ever. He chose Judah[i] as leader, and from the house of Judah he chose
my family, and from my father's sons he was pleased to make me king over all Israel.
5Of all my sons—and the LORD has given me many[j]—he has chosen my son
Solomon[k] to sit on the throne of the kingdom of the LORD over Israel. 6He said to
me, 'Solomon your son is the one who will build my house and my courts, for I have
chosen him to be my son,[l] and I will be his father. 7I will establish his kingdom for
ever if he is unswerving in carrying out my commands and laws,[m] as is being done
at this time.'
8"So now I charge you in the sight of all Israel and of the assembly of the LORD,
and in the hearing of our God: Be careful to follow all the commands[n] of the LORD
your God, that you may possess this good land and pass it on as an inheritance to your
descendants for ever.[o]
9"And you, my son Solomon, acknowledge the God of your father, and serve him

27:28 [s] 1Ki 10:27; 2Ch 1:15
27:31 [t] 1Ch 5:10
27:33 [u] 2Sa 15:12 [v] 2Sa 15:37
27:34 [w] 1Ki 1:7 [x] 1Ch 11:6
28:1 [a] 1Ch 11:10; 27:1-31
28:2 [b] 1Ch 17:2 [c] Ps 99:5; 132:7
28:3 [d] 2Sa 7:5 [e] 1Ch 22:8 [f] 1Ki 5:3; 1Ch 17:4
28:4 [g] 1Ch 17:23, 27; 2Ch 6:6 [h] 1Sa 16:1-13 [i] Ge 49:10; 1Ch 5:2
28:5 [j] 1Ch 3:1 [k] 1Ch 22:9; 23:1
28:6 [l] 2Sa 7:13; 1Ch 22:9-10
28:7 [m] 1Ch 22:13
28:8 [n] Dt 6:1 [o] Dt 4:1

27:33, 34 When Absalom rebelled against David, Ahithophel betrayed David and joined the rebellion. Hushai pretended loyalty to Absalom, and his advice caused Absalom's downfall (2 Samuel 15:31–17:23).

28:1 The last two chapters of 1 Chronicles present the transition from David to Solomon as king of Israel. The writer doesn't mention Adonijah's conspiracy or David's frailty (1 Kings 1; 2). Instead, he focuses on the positive—God's plans for Israel and his promise to David's descendants.

28:5 The kingdom of Israel belonged to the Lord, not to David or anyone else. Israel's king, then, was God's deputy, commissioned to carry out God's will for the nation. Thus God could choose the person he wanted as king without following customary lines of succession. David was not Saul's heir, and Solomon was not David's oldest son, but this did not matter because God appointed them.

28:8 David told Solomon to be careful to follow every one of God's commands to ensure Israel's prosperity and the continuation of David's descendants upon the throne. It was the king's solemn duty to study and obey God's laws. The teachings of Scripture are the keys to security, happiness, and justice, but you'll never discover them unless you search God's word. If we ignore God's will and neglect his teaching, anything we attempt to build, even if it has God's name on it, will be heading for collapse. Get to know God's commands through regular Bible study, and find ways to apply them consistently.

28:9 "The LORD searches every heart . . . ." Nothing can be hidden from God. He sees and understands everything in our hearts. David found this out the hard way when God sent Nathan to expose David's sins of adultery and murder (2 Samuel 12). David told Solomon to be completely open with God and dedicated to him. It makes no sense to try to hide any thoughts or actions from an all-knowing God. This should cause us joy, not fear, because God knows even the worst about us and loves us anyway.

with wholehearted devotion[p] and with a willing mind, for the LORD searches every
heart[q] and understands every motive behind the thoughts. If you seek him,[r] he will
be found by you; but if you forsake[s] him, he will reject[t] you for ever. 10Consider
now, for the LORD has chosen you to build a temple as a sanctuary. Be strong and
do the work."
11Then David gave his son Solomon the plans[u] for the portico of the temple, its
buildings, its storerooms, its upper parts, its inner rooms and the place of atonement.
12He gave him the plans of all that the Spirit[v] had put in his mind for the courts of
the temple of the LORD and all the surrounding rooms, for the treasuries of the temple
of God and for the treasuries for the dedicated things.[w] 13He gave him instructions
for the divisions[x] of the priests and Levites, and for all the work of serving in the
temple of the LORD, as well as for all the articles to be used in its service. 14He
designated the weight of gold for all the gold articles to be used in various kinds of
service, and the weight of silver for all the silver articles to be used in various kinds
of service: 15the weight of gold for the gold lampstands[y] and their lamps, with the
weight for each lampstand and its lamps; and the weight of silver for each silver
lampstand and its lamps, according to the use of each lampstand; 16the weight of gold
for each table[z] for consecrated bread; the weight of silver for the silver tables; 17the
weight of pure gold for the forks, sprinkling bowls[a] and pitchers; the weight of gold
for each gold dish; the weight of silver for each silver dish; 18and the weight of the
refined gold for the altar of incense.[b] He also gave him the plan for the chariot,[c]
that is, the cherubim of gold that spread their wings and shelter[d] the ark of the
covenant of the LORD.
19"All this," David said, "I have in writing from the hand of the LORD upon me,
and he gave me understanding in all the details[e] of the plan.[f]"
20David also said to Solomon his son, "Be strong and courageous,[g] and do the
work. Do not be afraid or discouraged, for the LORD God, my God, is with you. He
will not fail you or forsake[h] you until all the work for the service of the temple of
the LORD is finished.[i] 21The divisions of the priests and Levites are ready for all the
work on the temple of God, and every willing man skilled[j] in any craft will help you
in all the work. The officials and all the people will obey your every command."

Gifts for Building the Temple

29 Then King David said to the whole assembly: "My son Solomon, the one whom
God has chosen, is young and inexperienced.[a] The task is great, because this
palatial structure is not for man but for the LORD God. 2With all my resources I have
provided for the temple of my God—gold[b] for the gold work, silver for the silver,
bronze for the bronze, iron for the iron and wood for the wood, as well as onyx for
the settings, turquoise,**[a]**[c] stones of various colours, and all kinds of fine stone and
marble—all of these in large quantities.[d] 3Besides, in my devotion to the temple of
my God I now give my personal treasures of gold and silver for the temple of my God,
over and above everything I have provided[e] for this holy temple: 4three thousand
talents**[b]** of gold (gold of Ophir)[f] and seven thousand talents**[c]** of refined silver,[g]

a *2* The meaning of the Hebrew for this word is uncertain. **b** *4* That is, about 100 tons (about 100 metric tons)
c *4* That is, about 240 tons (about 240 metric tons)

28:9 [p]1Ch 29:19 [q]1Sa 16:7; Ps 7:9 [r]Ps 40:16; Jer 29:13 [s]Jos 24:20; 2Ch 15:2 [t]Ps 44:23
28:11 [u]Ex 25:9
28:12 [v]1Ch 12:18 [w]1Ch 26:20
28:13 [x]1Ch 24:1
28:15 [y]Ex 25:31
28:16 [z]Ex 25:23
28:17 [a]Ex 27:3
28:18 [b]Ex 30:1-10 [c]Ex 25:18-22 [d]Ex 25:20
28:19 [e]1Ki 6:38 [f]Ex 25:9
28:20 [g]Dt 31:6; 1Ch 22:13; 2Ch 19:11; Hag 2:4 [h]Dt 4:31; Jos 24:20 [i]1Ki 6:14; 2Ch 7:11
28:21 [j]Ex 35:25-36:5
29:1 [a]1Ki 3:7; 1Ch 22:5; 2Ch 13:7
29:2 [b]ver 7, 14, 16; Ezr 1:4; 6:5; Hag 2:8 [c]Isa 54:11 [d]1Ch 22:2-5
29:3 [e]2Ch 24:10; 31:3; 35:8
29:4 [f]Ge 10:29 [g]1Ch 22:14

28:13 Some of the instructions about the work of the priests and Levites are in chapters 23 and 24.

28:20 David advised Solomon not to be frightened about the size of his task as king and builder of the temple. Fear can immobilise us. The size of a job, its risks, or the pressure of the situation can cause us to freeze and do nothing. One remedy for fear is found here—don't focus on the fear; instead, get to work. Getting started is often the most difficult and frightening part of a job.

29:1 Solomon became king in 970 B.C.

29:1 It is possible to be obsessed with a church building to the neglect of the real church—the people of God. But the opposite response, neglecting the church building, is also wrong. David makes this point when he says that the temple is not "for man but for the LORD God". Although we should avoid wasteful extravagance, we must remember that every church building can be a visible witness for God. How can your church building be better used to tell the world about God?

29:3–5 David gave from his personal fortune for the temple. He encouraged others to follow his example, and they willingly did. Both the tabernacle (Exodus 35:5–36:7) and the temple were built from the voluntary gifts of the people. Like David, we can acknowledge that all we have comes from God (29:14–16). We may not have David's wealth, but we can develop his willingness to give. It is not what we have that counts with God, but our willingness to give it.

for the overlaying of the walls of the buildings, 5for the gold work and the silver work,
and for all the work to be done by the craftsmen. Now, who is willing to consecrate
himself today to the LORD?"
6Then the leaders of families, the officers of the tribes of Israel, the commanders
of thousands and commanders of hundreds, and the officials[h] in charge of the king's
work gave willingly.[i] 7They[j] gave towards the work on the temple of God five
thousand talents[d] and ten thousand darics[e] of gold, ten thousand talents[f] of silver,
eighteen thousand talents[g] of bronze and a hundred thousand talents[h] of iron. 8Any
who had precious stones[k] gave them to the treasury of the temple of the LORD in the
custody of Jehiel the Gershonite.[l] 9The people rejoiced at the willing response of their
leaders, for they had given freely and wholeheartedly[m] to the LORD. David the king
also rejoiced greatly.

David's Prayer

10David praised the LORD in the presence of the whole assembly, saying,

"Praise be to you, O LORD,
God of our father Israel,
from everlasting to everlasting.
11Yours, O LORD, is the greatness and the power[n]
and the glory and the majesty and the splendour,
for everything in heaven and earth is yours.[o]
Yours, O LORD, is the kingdom;
you are exalted as head over all.[p]
12Wealth and honour[q] come from you;
you are the ruler[r] of all things.
In your hands are strength and power
to exalt and give strength to all.
13Now, our God, we give you thanks,
and praise your glorious name.

14"But who am I, and who are my people, that we should be able to give as
generously as this? Everything comes from you, and we have given you only what
comes from your hand. 15We are aliens and strangers[s] in your sight, as were all our
forefathers. Our days on earth are like a shadow,[t] without hope. 16O LORD our God,
as for all this abundance that we have provided for building you a temple for your
Holy Name, it comes from your hand, and all of it belongs to you. 17I know, my God,
that you test the heart[u] and are pleased with integrity. All these things have I given

29:6 [h]1Ch 27:1; 28:1 [i]ver 9; Ex 25:1-8; 35:20-29; 36:2; 2Ch 24:10; Ezr 7:15
29:7 [j]Ex 25:2; Ne 7:70-71
29:8 [k]Ex 35:27 [l]1Ch 26:21
29:9 [m]1Ki 8:61; 2Co 9:7
29:11 [n]Ps 24:8; 59:17; 62:11 [o]Ps 89:11 [p]Rev 5:12-13
29:12 [q]2Ch 1:12 [r]2Ch 20:6; Ro 11:36
29:15 [s]Ps 39:12; Heb 11:13 [t]Job 14:2
29:17 [u]Ps 139:23; Pr 15:11; 17:3; Jer 11:20; 17:10

[d] *7* That is, about 170 tons (about 170 metric tons) [e] *7* That is, about 185 pounds (about 84 kilograms) [f] *7* That is, about 340 tons (about 345 metric tons) [g] *7* That is, about 610 tons (about 620 metric tons) [h] *7* That is, about 3,400 tons (about 3,450 metric tons)

PRINCIPLES TO LIVE BY

King David gave his son Solomon principles to guide him through life (see 1 Chronicles 28:9, 10). These same ideas are ones that any Christian parent would want to present to a child:

1. Get to know God personally.
2. Learn God's commands and discover what he wants you to do.
3. Worship God with wholehearted devotion.
4. Serve God with a willing mind.
5. Be faithful.
6. Don't become discouraged.

29:6–9 These leaders displayed a right attitude towards their money by giving willingly to God's work. This attitude is described by Paul in 2 Corinthians 9:7: "Each man should give what he has decided in his heart to give, not reluctantly or under compulsion, for God loves a cheerful giver." When we are generous because we are thankful, our attitude can inspire others. Give generously to God's work.

29:15 David contrasts God's everlasting nature with the fleeting lives of his people. Nothing lasts unless it is rooted in God's unchanging character. If our most impressive deeds fade as dust before God, where should we place our confidence? Only in a relationship with God can we find anything permanent. His love never fades and nothing can take it away.

willingly and with honest intent. And now I have seen with joy how willingly your
people who are here have given to you.[v] 18 O LORD, God of our fathers Abraham,
Isaac and Israel, keep this desire in the hearts of your people for ever, and keep their
hearts loyal to you. 19 And give my son Solomon the wholehearted devotion[w] to keep
your commands, requirements and decrees[x] and to do everything to build the palatial
structure for which I have provided."[y]

20 Then David said to the whole assembly, "Praise the LORD your God." So they
all praised the LORD, the God of their fathers; they bowed low and fell prostrate before
the LORD and the king.

Solomon Acknowledged as King

21 The next day they made sacrifices to the LORD and presented burnt offerings to
him:[z] a thousand bulls, a thousand rams and a thousand male lambs, together with
their drink offerings, and other sacrifices in abundance for all Israel. 22 They ate and
drank with great joy[a] in the presence of the LORD that day.

Then they acknowledged Solomon son of David as king a second time, anointing
him before the LORD to be ruler and Zadok[b] to be priest. 23 So Solomon sat on the
throne[c] of the LORD as king in place of his father David. He prospered and all Israel
obeyed him. 24 All the officers and mighty men, as well as all of King David's sons,
pledged their submission to King Solomon.

25 The LORD highly exalted Solomon in the sight of all Israel and bestowed on him
royal splendour[d] such as no king over Israel ever had before.[e]

The Death of David

26 David son of Jesse was king[f] over all Israel. 27 He ruled over Israel for forty
years—seven in Hebron and thirty-three in Jerusalem.[g] 28 He died[h] at a good old
age, having enjoyed long life, wealth and honour. His son Solomon succeeded him
as king.[i]

29 As for the events of King David's reign, from beginning to end, they are written
in the records of Samuel the seer,[j] the records of Nathan[k] the prophet and the records
of Gad[l] the seer, 30 together with the details of his reign and power, and the circumstances that surrounded him and Israel and the kingdoms of all the other lands.

29:17 [v] 1Ch 28:9; Ps 15:1-5
29:19 [w] 1Ch 28:9 [x] Ps 72:1 [y] 1Ch 22:14
29:21 [z] 1Ki 8:62
29:22 [a] 1Ch 23:1 [b] 1Ki 1:33-39
29:23 [c] 1Ki 2:12
29:25 [d] 2Ch 1:1, 12 [e] 1Ki 3:13; Ecc 2:9
29:26 [f] 1Ch 18:14
29:27 [g] 2Sa 5:4-5; 1Ki 2:11; 1Ch 3:4
29:28 [h] Ge 15:15; Ac 13:36 [i] 1Ch 23:1
29:29 [j] 1Sa 9:9 [k] 2Sa 7:2 [l] 1Sa 22:5

29:19 "Wholehearted devotion" means to be entirely dedicated to God. This is what David wished for Solomon—that he would desire, above all else, to serve God. Do you find it hard to do what God wants, or even harder to want to do it? God can give you wholehearted devotion. If you believe in Jesus Christ, this is already happening in you. Paul wrote that God works within us "to will and to act according to his good purpose" (Philippians 2:13).

29:21 Drink offerings of wine were poured out as sacrifices to God to acknowledge his role in providing for his people.

29:25 Solomon surpassed his father's wealth and splendour. David's legacy resulted from his vital relationship with the Lord, and he passed his spiritual values on to Solomon. Any money or power we leave to our children are far less valuable than the spiritual legacy we pass on. What spiritual inheritance will your children receive?

29:29 A seer was someone who received messages from God for the nation in visions or dreams.

29:30 First Chronicles vividly illustrates the importance of maintaining a relationship with God. The genealogies in chapters 1–9 emphasise the importance of a spiritual heritage. The second part of the book details the life of David. Few men or women in the Bible were as close to God as David was. His daily contact with God increased his capacity to worship and strengthened his desire to build God's temple. David's life shows us the importance of staying close to God—through studying and obeying his word and communicating with him daily. Second Chronicles, on the other hand, reveals how quickly our lives can deteriorate (spiritually, mentally, and socially) when we fail to stay well grounded in God.

KEY PLACES IN 2 CHRONICLES

1 Gibeon David's son Solomon became king over Israel. He summoned the nation's leaders to a ceremony in Gibeon. Here God told Solomon to ask for whatever he desired. Solomon asked for wisdom and knowledge to rule Israel (1:1–12).

2 Jerusalem After the ceremony in Gibeon, Solomon returned to the capital city, Jerusalem. His reign began a golden age for Israel. Solomon implemented the plans for the temple which had been drawn up by his father, Da- vid. It was a magnificent con- struction. It symbolised Solomon's wealth and wisdom, which became known worldwide (1:13–9:31).

3 Shechem After Solomon's death, his son Rehoboam was ready to be crowned in Shechem. However, his promise of higher taxes and harder work for the people led to rebellion. Everyone but the tribes of Judah and Benjamin deserted Rehoboam and set up their own kingdom to the north called Israel. Reho- boam returned to Jerusalem as ruler over the southern kingdom called Judah (10:1–12:16). The remainder of 2 Chronicles records the history of Judah.

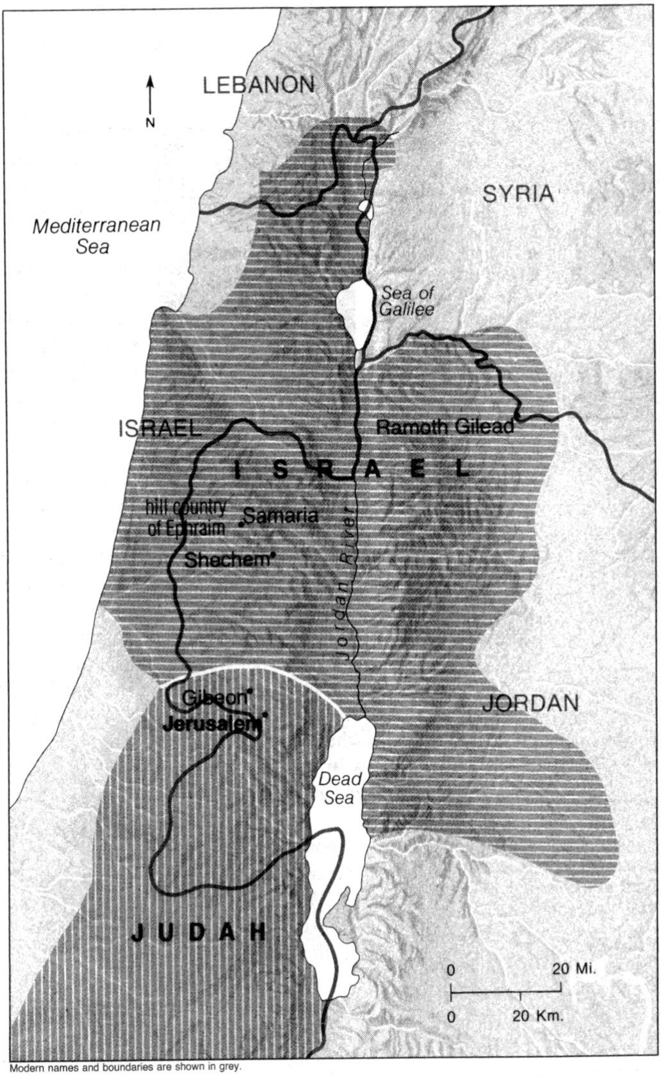

Modern names and boundaries are shown in grey.

4 Hill Country of Ephraim Abijah became the next king of Judah, and soon war broke out between Israel and Judah. When the ar- mies of the two nations arrived for battle in the hill country of Ephraim, Israel had twice as many troops as Judah. It looked like Judah's defeat was certain. But they cried out to God, and God gave them victory over Israel. In their history as separate nations, Judah had a few godly kings who instituted reforms and brought the people back to God. Israel, however, had a succession of only evil kings (13:1–22).

5 Aram Asa, a godly king, removed every trace of pagan worship from Judah and renewed the people's covenant with God in Jerusalem. But King Baasha of Israel built a fortress to control traffic into Judah. Instead of looking to God for guidance, Asa took the silver and gold from the temple and sent it to the king of Aram requesting his help against King Baasha. As a result, God became angry with Judah (14:1–16:14).

6 Samaria Although Jehoshaphat was a godly king, he allied himself with Israel's most evil king, Ahab. Ahab's capital was in Samaria. Ahab wanted help fighting against Ramoth Gilead. Jehoshaphat wanted advice, but rather than listening to God's prophet who had promised defeat, he joined Ahab in battle (17:1–18:27).

7 Ramoth Gilead The alliance with Israel against Ramoth Gilead ended in defeat and Ahab's death. Although shaken by his defeat, Jehoshaphat returned to Jerusalem and to God. But his son Jehoram was a wicked king, as was his son Ahaziah, and history repeated itself. Ahaziah formed an alliance with Israel's King Joram to do battle with the Arameans at Ramoth Gilead. This led to the death of both kings (18:28–22:9).

8 Jerusalem The rest of Judah's history recorded in 2 Chronicles centres on Jerusalem. Some kings caused Judah to sin by bringing idol worship into their midst. Others did away with idol worship, reopened and restored the temple and, in the case of Josiah, tried to follow God's laws as they were written by Moses. In spite of the few good influences, a series of evil kings sent Judah into a downward spiral that ended with the Babylonian empire overrunning the country. The temple was burned, the walls of the city were broken down, and the people were deported to Babylon.

2 CHRONICLES

Solomon becomes king 970 B.C.	Temple built 966–959	The kingdom divides 930	Asa becomes king of Judah 910	Jehoshaphat becomes king of Judah 872	Ahab killed in battle 853	Athaliah seizes the throne 841	Uz be kir Ju 79

VITAL STATISTICS

PURPOSE:
To unify the nation around true worship of God by showing his standard for judging kings. The righteous kings of Judah and the religious revivals under their rule are highlighted, and the sins of the evil kings are exposed.

AUTHOR:
Ezra, according to Jewish tradition

TO WHOM WRITTEN:
All Israel

DATE WRITTEN:
Approximately 430 B.C., recording events from the beginning of Solomon's reign (970 B.C.) to the beginning of the Babylonian captivity (586 B.C.)

SETTING:
2 Chronicles parallels 1 and 2 Kings and serves as their commentary. Originally 1 and 2 Chronicles were one book. It was written after the exile from a priestly perspective, highlighting the importance of the temple and the religious revivals in Judah. The northern kingdom, Israel, is virtually ignored in this history.

KEY VERSE:
"If my people who are called by my name, will humble themselves and pray and seek my face and turn from their wicked ways, then will I hear from heaven and will forgive their sin and will heal their land" (7:14).

KEY PEOPLE:
Solomon, the queen of Sheba, Rehoboam, Asa, Jehoshaphat, Jehoram, Joash, Uzziah (Azariah), Ahaz, Hezekiah, Manasseh, Josiah

KEY PLACES:
Jerusalem, the temple

SPECIAL FEATURES:
Includes a detailed record of the temple's construction

THE slide clicks, and our eyes focus on the image flashed onto the screen in the darkened sanctuary. "This idol," explains the missionary, "is made of stone and is worshipped daily. The natives believe that this will guarantee good crops and healthy children." With condescending smiles, we wonder at their ignorance. How could anyone worship an object? Idols are for the naive and the superstitious! But after the presentation we return home to *our* idols of wealth, prestige, or self-fulfilment. If we put anything in God's place, we worship it, despite what we profess with our lips.

Our experience parallels Israel's. They were chosen by God to represent him on earth. But too often they forgot the truth and their calling, stumbling blindly after idols as the neighbouring nations did. Then prophets, priests, and judgment would push them abruptly back to God, the one true God. The book of 2 Chronicles relates this sordid history of Judah's corrupt and idolatrous kings. Here and there a good king would arise in Judah, and for a time there would be revival, but the downward spiral would continue—ending in chaos, destruction, and captivity.

The chronicler writes this volume to bring the nation back to God by reminding them of their past. Only by following God would they prosper! As you read 2 Chronicles you will catch a vivid glimpse of Judah's history (the history of Israel, the northern kingdom, is virtually ignored), and you will see the tragic results of idolatry. Learn the lessons of the past: determine to get rid of any idols in your life and to worship God alone.

This account continues the history of 1 Chronicles. David's son, Solomon, was inaugurated as king. Solomon built the magnificent temple in Jerusalem, thus fulfilling his father's wish and last request (chapters 2—5). Solomon enjoyed a peaceful and prosperous reign of 40 years that made him world famous. After Solomon died, his son Rehoboam assumed the throne, and his immaturity divided the kingdom.

In Judah, there were a few good kings and many evil ones. The writer of Chronicles faithfully records their achievements and failures, noting how each king measured up to God's standard for success. Clearly a good king obeyed God's laws, eliminated the places of idol worship, and made no alliances with other nations. Judah's good kings include Asa, Jehoshaphat, Uzziah (Azariah), Hezekiah, and Josiah. Of its many evil ones, Ahaz and Manasseh were perhaps the worst. Eventually the nation was conquered and taken captive, and the temple was destroyed.

The writer's purpose was to reunite the nation around the true worship of God after the captivity. In these pages, he reminds the people of their past. He clearly broadcasts his message through one of the best-known verses in Scripture, "If my people, who are called by my name, will humble themselves and pray and seek my face and turn from their wicked ways, then will I hear from heaven and will forgive their sin and will heal their land" (7:14). As you read 2 Chronicles, listen to God's voice and obey him; and receive his redemptive, healing touch.

Israel (northern kingdom) falls 722	*Hezekiah becomes king of Judah 715*	*Sennacherib taunts Hezekiah 701*	*Josiah becomes king 640*	*Book of the Law found 622*	*Judah (southern kingdom) falls 586*	*Cyrus' decree 538*

THE BLUEPRINT

A. THE REIGN OF SOLOMON (1:1—9:31)
1. Solomon asks for wisdom
2. Solomon builds the temple
3. Solomon dedicates the temple
4. Solomon's riches and wisdom

Solomon achieved much in business and government, but most important, he was the man God used to build the glorious temple. This beautiful building was the religious centre of the nation. It symbolised the unity of all the tribes, the presence of God among them, and the nation's high calling. We may achieve great things in life, but we must not neglect any effort that will help nurture God's people or bring others into God's kingdom. It is easy for us to get the wrong perspective on what's really important in life.

B. THE KINGDOM OF JUDAH (10:1—36:23)
1. The northern tribes revolt
2. History of apostasy and reform
3. Judah is exiled to Babylon

Throughout the reigns of 20 kings, the nation of Judah wavered between obedience to God and apostasy. The reigning king's response to God determined the spiritual climate of the nation and whether or not God would send judgment upon his people. Our personal history is shaped by our response to God. Just as Judah's failure to repent brought them captivity in Babylon, so the abuse of our high calling by sinful living will ultimately bring us catastrophe and destruction.

MEGATHEMES

THEME	EXPLANATION	IMPORTANCE
Temple	The temple was the symbol of God's presence and the place set aside for worship and prayer. Built by Solomon from the plans God gave to David, the temple was the spiritual centre of the nation.	As Christians meet together to worship God, they experience the presence of God in a way that no individual believer could. For the dwelling place of God is the people of God. The body of Christ is God's temple.
Peace	As Solomon and his descendants were faithful to God, they experienced victory in battle, success in government, and peace with other nations. Peace was the result of the people being unified and loyal to God and his law.	Only God can bring true peace. God is greater than any enemy, army, or nation. Just as Israel's faithful response was the key to her peace and survival as a nation, so our obedience to God as individuals and nations is vital to peace today.
Prayer	After Solomon died, David's kingdom was divided. When a king led the Israelites into idolatry, the nation suffered. When the king and his people prayed to God for deliverance and they turned from their sinful ways, God delivered them.	God still answers prayer today. We have God's promise that if we humble ourselves, seek him, turn from our sin, and pray, God will hear, heal, and forgive us. If we are alert, we can pray for God's guidance before we get into trouble.
Reform	Although idolatry and injustice were common, some kings turned to God and led the people in spiritual revival—renewing their commitment to God and reforming their society. Revival included the destruction of idols, obedience to the law, and the restoration of the priesthood.	We must constantly commit ourselves to obeying God. We are never secure in what others have done before us. Each generation of believers must rededicate themselves to the task of carrying out God's will in their own lives as well as in society.
National Collapse	In 586 B.C. the Babylonians completely destroyed Solomon's beautiful temple. The formal worship of God was ended. The Israelites had abandoned God. As a result, God brought judgment upon his people and they were carried off into captivity.	Although our disobedience may not be as blatant as Israel's, quite often our commitment to God is insincere and casual. When we forget that all our power, wisdom, and wealth come from God and not ourselves, we are in danger of the same spiritual and moral collapse that Israel experienced.

A. THE REIGN OF SOLOMON (1:1 – 9:31)

In response to Solomon's request, God gives to Solomon great wisdom. Solomon launches extensive building programmes, including the temple, his greatest achievement. In the midst of the celebration dedicating the temple, fire flashes down from heaven and God's glory fills the temple. God wants to live among his people and to be central in their lives. Today, our bodies are God's temple, the place where God, through his Holy Spirit, lives and reigns.

1. Solomon asks for wisdom

1 Solomon son of David established[a] himself firmly over his kingdom, for the
LORD his God was with[b] him and made him exceedingly great.[c]
2Then Solomon spoke to all Israel[d]—to the commanders of thousands and commanders of hundreds, to the judges and to all the leaders in Israel, the heads of
families—3and Solomon and the whole assembly went to the high place at Gibeon,
for God's Tent of Meeting[e] was there, which Moses[f] the LORD's servant had made
in the desert. 4Now David had brought up the ark[g] of God from Kiriath Jearim to
the place he had prepared for it, because he had pitched a tent[h] for it in Jerusalem.
5But the bronze altar[i] that Bezalel[j] son of Uri, the son of Hur, had made was in
Gibeon in front of the tabernacle of the LORD; so Solomon and the assembly enquired[k]
of him there. 6Solomon went up to the bronze altar before the LORD in the Tent of
Meeting and offered a thousand burnt offerings on it.
7That night God appeared[l] to Solomon and said to him, "Ask for whatever you
want me to give you."
8Solomon answered God, "You have shown great kindness to David my father and
have made me[m] king in his place. 9Now, LORD God, let your promise[n] to my father
David be confirmed, for you have made me king over a people who are as numerous
as the dust of the earth.[o] 10Give me wisdom and knowledge, that I may lead[p] this
people, for who is able to govern this great people of yours?"
11God said to Solomon, "Since this is your heart's desire and you have not asked
for wealth,[q] riches or honour, nor for the death of your enemies, and since you have
not asked for a long life but for wisdom and knowledge to govern my people over
whom I have made you king, 12therefore wisdom and knowledge will be given you.
And I will also give you wealth, riches and honour,[r] such as no king who was before
you ever had and none after you will have.[s]"
13Then Solomon went to Jerusalem from the high place at Gibeon, from before the
Tent of Meeting. And he reigned over Israel.

1:1 [a] 1Ki 2:12, 26; 2Ch 12:1 [b] Ge 21:22; 39:2; Nu 14:43 [c] 1Ch 29:25
1:2 [d] 1Ch 9:1; 28:1
1:3 [e] Ex 36:8 [f] Ex 40:18
1:4 [g] 2Sa 6:2; 1Ch 15:25 [h] 2Sa 6:17; 1Ch 15:1
1:5 [i] Ex 38:2 [j] Ex 31:2 [k] 1Ch 13:3
1:7 [l] 2Ch 7:12
1:8 [m] 1Ch 23:1; 28:5
1:9 [n] 2Sa 7:25; 1Ki 8:25 [o] Ge 12:2
1:10 [p] Nu 27:17; 2Sa 5:2; Pr 8:15-16
1:11 [q] Dt 17:17
1:12 [r] 1Ch 29:12 [s] 1Ch 29:25; 2Ch 9:22; Ne 13:26

1:1 While the book of 1 Chronicles focuses mainly on David's life, 2 Chronicles focuses on the lives of the rest of the kings of Judah, the southern kingdom. Very little is mentioned about Israel, the northern kingdom, because (1) Chronicles was written for Judeans who had returned from captivity in Babylon, and (2) Judah represented David's family, from which the Messiah would come. Israel was in a state of constant turmoil, anarchy, and rebellion against God, but Judah, at least, made sporadic efforts to follow God.

1:1 More details about Solomon's rise to the throne can be read in 1 Kings 1; 2. Solomon's Profile is found in 1 Kings 4.

1:2–5 The Tent of Meeting, or tabernacle, that Moses had built centuries earlier (Exodus 35 – 40) was still in operation although it had been moved several times. When Solomon became king, the tabernacle was located at Gibeon, a town about six miles north-west of Jerusalem. All the tabernacle furniture was kept at Gibeon except the ark of God, which David had moved to Jerusalem (1 Chronicles 13; 15; 16). David wanted the ark, the symbol of God's presence, to reside in the city where he ruled the people. The tabernacle at Gibeon, however, was still considered Israel's main religious centre until Solomon built the temple in Jerusalem.

1:10 Wisdom is the ability to make good decisions based on proper discernment and judgment. Knowledge, in this verse, refers to the practical know-how necessary for handling everyday matters. Solomon used his wisdom and knowledge not only to build the temple from his father's plans, but also to put the nation on a firm economic footing.

1:10 God's offer to Solomon stretches the imagination: "Ask for whatever you want me to give you" (1:7). But Solomon put the needs of his people first and asked for wisdom rather than riches. He realised that wisdom would be the most valuable asset he could have as king. Later he wrote, wisdom "is more precious than rubies; nothing you desire can compare with her" (Proverbs 3:15). The same wisdom that was given to Solomon is available to us; the same God offers it. How can we acquire wisdom? First, we must ask God, who "gives generously to all without finding fault" (James 1:5). Second, we must devote ourselves wholeheartedly to studying and applying God's word, the source of divine wisdom. (For more on Solomon's wisdom, read the notes on 1 Kings 3:6–9 and 3:12.)

1:11, 12 Solomon could have had anything, but he asked for wisdom to rule the nation. Because God approved of the way Solomon ordered his priorities, he gave Solomon wealth, riches, and honour as well. Jesus also spoke about priorities. He said that when we put God first, everything we really need will be given to us as well (Matthew 6:33). This does not guarantee that we will be wealthy and famous like Solomon, but it means that when we put God first, the wisdom he gives will enable us to have richly rewarding lives. When we have a purpose for living and learn to be content with what we have, we will have greater wealth than we could ever accumulate.

1:14 [t]1Sa 8:11; 1Ki 4:26; 9:19
1:15 [u]1Ki 9:28; Isa 60:5
1:17 [v]SS 1:9
2:1 [a]Dt 12:5 [b]Ecc 2:4
2:2 [c]ver 18; 2Ch 10:4
2:3 [d]2Sa 5:11 [e]1Ch 14:1
2:4 [f]ver 1; Dt 12:5 [g]Ex 30:7 [h]Ex 25:30 [i]Ex 29:42; 2Ch 13:11 [j]Nu 28:9-10
2:5 [k]1Ch 22:5; Ps 135:5 [l]1Ch 16:25
2:6 [m]1Ki 8:27; 2Ch 6:18; Jer 23:24 [n]Ex 3:11
2:7 [o]ver 13-14; Ex 35:31; 1Ch 22:16

14 Solomon accumulated chariots[t] and horses; he had fourteen hundred chariots and twelve thousand horses,[a] which he kept in the chariot cities and also with him in Jerusalem. 15 The king made silver and gold[u] as common in Jerusalem as stones, and cedar as plentiful as sycamore-fig trees in the foothills. 16 Solomon's horses were imported from Egypt[b] and from Kue[c] — the royal merchants purchased them from Kue. 17 They imported a chariot[v] from Egypt for six hundred shekels[d] of silver, and a horse for a hundred and fifty.[e] They also exported them to all the kings of the Hittites and of the Arameans.

2. Solomon builds the temple

Preparations for Building the Temple

2 Solomon gave orders to build a temple[a] for the Name of the LORD and a royal palace for himself.[b] 2 He conscripted seventy thousand men as carriers and eighty thousand as stonecutters in the hills and thirty-six hundred as foremen over them.[c]

3 Solomon sent this message to Hiram[a][d] king of Tyre:

"Send me cedar logs[e] as you did for my father David when you sent him cedar to build a palace to live in. 4 Now I am about to build a temple[f] for the Name of the LORD my God and to dedicate it to him for burning fragrant incense[g] before him, for setting out the consecrated bread[h] regularly, and for making burnt offerings[i] every morning and evening and on Sabbaths[j] and New Moons and at the appointed feasts of the LORD our God. This is a lasting ordinance for Israel.

5 "The temple I am going to build will be great,[k] because our God is greater than all other gods.[l] 6 But who is able to build a temple for him, since the heavens, even the highest heavens, cannot contain him?[m] Who then am I[n] to build a temple for him, except as a place to burn sacrifices before him?

7 "Send me, therefore, a man skilled to work in gold and silver, bronze and iron, and in purple, crimson and blue yarn, and experienced in the art of engraving, to work in Judah and Jerusalem with my skilled craftsmen,[o] whom my father David provided.

a 14 Or *charioteers* b 16 Or possibly *Muzur*, a region in Cilicia; also in verse 17 c 16 Probably Cilicia
d 17 That is, about 15 pounds (about 7 kilograms) e 17 That is, about 3¾ pounds (about 1.7 kilograms)
a 3 Hebrew *Huram*, a variant of *Hiram*; also in verses 11 and 12

2:1 David had wanted to build a temple for God (2 Samuel 7). God denied his request because David had been a warrior, but God said that David's son Solomon would build the temple. God allowed David to make the plans and preparations for the temple (1 Chronicles 23–26; 28:11–13). David bought the land (2 Samuel 24:18–25; 1 Chronicles 22:1), gathered most of the construction materials (1 Chronicles 22:14–16), and received the plans from God (1 Chronicles 28:11, 12). It was Solomon's responsibility to make the plans a reality. His job was made easier by his father's exhaustive preparations. God's work can be moved forward when the older generation paves the way for the younger.

2:3–12 Although Hiram was one of David's and Solomon's friendly allies, he was the ruler of a nation that worshipped many different gods. Hiram was happy to send materials for the temple, and both David and Solomon used this occasion to testify about the one true God.

2:5, 6 We should try our best to build beautiful and helpful places of worship to be a testimony and credit to God. In so doing, however, we must remember that God cannot be contained in our building or beautiful setting. He is far greater than any building, so we must focus our praise on him and not merely on the place of worship.

2:7 Why use foreign craftsmen? The Israelites had great knowledge of agriculture, but knew little about metalworking. So they found people who were experts in this area. It is not a sin to obtain secular expertise for God's work. He distributes natural talents as he chooses, and he often decides to give skill to non-Christians.

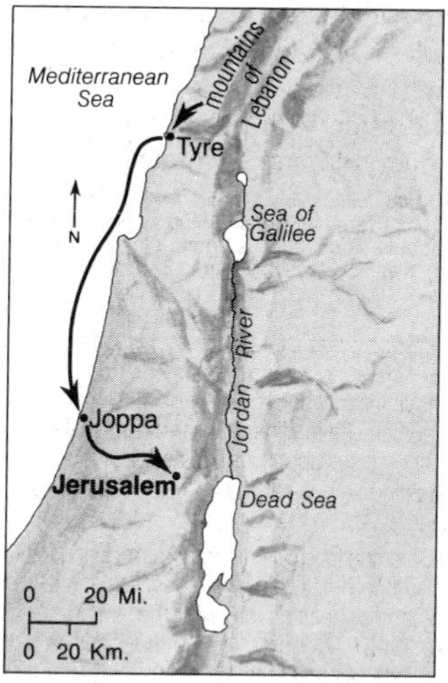

SHIPPING RESOURCES FOR THE TEMPLE
Solomon asked King Hiram of Tyre to provide supplies and skilled workmen to help build God's temple in Jerusalem. The plan was to cut the cedar logs in the mountains of Lebanon, float them by sea to Joppa, then bring them inland to Jerusalem by the shortest and easiest route.

When we hire secular contractors to build or repair our church buildings, we are recognising that God gives gifts liberally. We may also be gaining an opportunity to tell the workers about God.

8"Send me also cedar, pine and algum[b] logs from Lebanon, for I know that
your men are skilled in cutting timber there. My men shall work with yours 9to
provide me with plenty of timber, because the temple I build must be large and
magnificent. 10I will give your servants, the woodsmen who cut the timber,
twenty thousand cors[c] of ground wheat, twenty thousand cors of barley, twenty
thousand baths[d] of wine and twenty thousand baths of olive oil.[p]"

11Hiram king of Tyre replied by letter to Solomon:

"Because the LORD loves[q] his people, he has made you their king."

12And Hiram added:

"Praise be to the LORD, the God of Israel, who made heaven and earth![r] He
has given King David a wise son, endowed with intelligence and discernment,
who will build a temple for the LORD and a palace for himself.
13"I am sending you Huram-Abi,[s] a man of great skill, 14whose mother was
from Dan[t] and whose father was from Tyre. He is trained[u] to work in gold and
silver, bronze and iron, stone and wood, and with purple and blue[v] and crimson
yarn and fine linen. He is experienced in all kinds of engraving and can execute
any design given to him. He will work with your craftsmen and with those of
my lord, David your father.
15"Now let my lord send his servants the wheat and barley and the olive oil[w]
and wine he promised, 16and we will cut all the logs from Lebanon that you need
and will float them in rafts by sea down to Joppa.[x] You can then take them up
to Jerusalem."

17Solomon took a census of all the aliens[y] who were in Israel, after the census[z]
his father David had taken; and they were found to be 153,600. 18He assigned[a]
70,000 of them to be carriers and 80,000 to be stonecutters in the hills, with 3,600
foremen over them to keep the people working.

Solomon Builds the Temple

3 Then Solomon began to build[a] the temple of the LORD[b] in Jerusalem on Mount
Moriah, where the LORD had appeared to his father David. It was on the threshing-
floor of Araunah[a][c] the Jebusite, the place provided by David. 2He began building
on the second day of the second month in the fourth year of his reign.[d]
3The foundation Solomon laid for building the temple of God was sixty cubits long
and twenty cubits wide[b][e] (using the cubit of the old standard). 4The portico at the
front of the temple was twenty cubits[c] long across the width of the building and
twenty cubits[d] high.
He overlaid the inside with pure gold. 5He panelled the main hall with pine and
covered it with fine gold and decorated it with palm tree[f] and chain designs. 6He

b *8* Probably a variant of *almug*; possibly juniper **c** *10* That is, probably about 120,000 bushels (about 4,400 kilolitres) **d** *10* That is, probably about 95,000 gallons (about 440 kilolitres) **a** *1* Hebrew *Ornan*, a variant of *Araunah* **b** *3* That is, about 90 feet (about 27 metres) long and 30 feet (about 9 metres) wide **c** *4* That is, about 30 feet (about 9 metres); also in verses 8, 11 and 13 **d** *4* Some Septuagint and Syriac manuscripts; Hebrew *and a hundred and twenty*

2:10 [p]Ezr 3:7
2:11 [q]1Ki 10:9; 2Ch 9:8
2:12 [r]Ne 9:6; Ps 8:3; 33:6; 102:25
2:13 [s]1Ki 7:13
2:14 [t]Ex 31:6 [u]Ex 35:31 [v]Ex 35:35
2:15 [w]ver 10; Ezr 3:7
2:16 [x]Jos 19:46; Jnh 1:3
2:17 [y]1Ch 22:2 [z]2Sa 24:2
2:18 [a]ver 2; 1Ch 22:2; 2Ch 8:8
3:1 [a]Ac 7:47 [b]Ge 28:17 [c]2Sa 24:18; 1Ch 21:18
3:2 [d]Ezr 5:11
3:3 [e]Eze 41:2
3:5 [f]Eze 40:16

2:8, 9 Israel did not have much wood, but Lebanon, a small nation on the seacoast, had some of the finest cedar forests in the ancient Near East. Lebanon also imported a great deal of food from Israel. Thus the two kings made a trade agreement that was beneficial to both nations.

2:17, 18 Why would Solomon force aliens (foreigners) living in Israel to do the work of slaves? These aliens were descendants of the pagan nations who had not been driven out of the land in Joshua's day (Joshua 9:23–27; Judges 1:21–33; 1 Kings 9:20, 21). Scripture has specific laws about treating slaves fairly (Leviticus 25:39–55), so Solomon would not have treated them harshly as other nations might. Solomon's action was probably only in force during the construction of the temple.

3:1 Solomon built a permanent temple on Mount Moriah to replace the movable tabernacle (now at Gibeon) that had accompanied Israel in the desert. Mount Moriah was also the place where God had stopped Abraham from sacrificing Isaac (Genesis 22:1–18). David purchased the land when it was a threshing floor (see 2 Samuel 24:15–25 and the note on 1 Chronicles 21:22–24).

3:1ff Why was the temple decorated so ornately? Although no-one can build God a worthy home (2:6), this temple was going to be the best that humans could design. The care and craftsmanship were acts of worship in themselves. Although a simple chapel is an adequate place to pray and meet God, it is not wrong to want to make a beautiful place of worship.

3:3 The "cubit of the old standard" was equal to 20.5 inches and was the one used by Ezekiel in the temple he envisioned.

3:10 Cherubim are mighty angels.

adorned the temple with precious stones. And the gold he used was gold of Parvaim.
[7]He overlaid the ceiling beams, door-frames, walls and doors of the temple with gold,
and he carved cherubim[g] on the walls.
[8]He built the Most Holy Place,[h] its length corresponding to the width of the
temple—twenty cubits long and twenty cubits wide. He overlaid the inside with six
hundred talents[e] of fine gold. [9]The gold nails[i] weighed fifty shekels.[f] He also
overlaid the upper parts with gold.
[10]In the Most Holy Place he made a pair[j] of sculptured cherubim and overlaid them
with gold. [11]The total wing-span of the cherubim was twenty cubits. One wing of the
first cherub was five cubits[g] long and touched the temple wall, while its other wing,
also five cubits long, touched the wing of the other cherub. [12]Similarly one wing of
the second cherub was five cubits long and touched the other temple wall, and its other
wing, also five cubits long, touched the wing of the first cherub. [13]The wings of these
cherubim[k] extended twenty cubits. They stood on their feet, facing the main hall.[h]
[14]He made the curtain[l] of blue, purple and crimson yarn and fine linen, with
cherubim[m] worked into it.
[15]In the front of the temple he made two pillars,[n] which ⌞together⌟ were thirty-five
cubits[i] long, each with a capital[o] on top measuring five cubits. [16]He made interwoven chains[j][p] and put them on top of the pillars. He also made a hundred
pomegranates[q] and attached them to the chains. [17]He erected the pillars in the front
of the temple, one to the south and one to the north. The one to the south he named
Jakin[k] and the one to the north Boaz.[l]

The Temple's Furnishings

4 He made a bronze altar[a] twenty cubits long, twenty cubits wide and ten cubits
high.[a] [2]He made the Sea[b] of cast metal, circular in shape, measuring ten cubits
from rim to rim and five cubits[b] high. It took a line of thirty cubits[c] to measure round

3:7 [g]Ge 3:24; 1Ki 6:29-35; Eze 41:18
3:8 [h]Ex 26:33
3:9 [i]Ex 26:32
3:10 [j]Ex 25:18
3:13 [k]Ex 25:18
3:14 [l]Ex 26:31, 33; Heb 9:3 [m]Ge 3:24
3:15 [n]1Ki 7:15; Rev 3:12 [o]1Ki 7:22
3:16 [p]1Ki 7:17 [q]1Ki 7:20
4:1 [a]Ex 20:24; 27:1-2; 40:6; 1Ki 8:64; 2Ki 16:14
4:2 [b]Rev 4:6; 15:2

[e] *8* That is, about 20 tons (about 21 metric tons) [f] *9* That is, about 1¼ pounds (about 0.6 kilogram) [g] *11* That is, about 7½ feet (about 2.3 metres); also in verse 15 [h] *13* Or *facing inward* [i] *15* That is, about 52 feet (about 16 metres) [j] *16* Or possibly *made chains in the inner sanctuary*; the meaning of the Hebrew for this phrase is uncertain. [k] *17* *Jakin* probably means *he establishes.* [l] *17* *Boaz* probably means *in him is strength.*
[a] *1* That is, about 30 feet (about 9 metres) long and wide, and about 15 feet (about 4.5 metres) high [b] *2* That is, about 7½ feet (about 2.3 metres) [c] *2* That is, about 45 feet (about 13.5 metres)

CAREFUL OBEDIENCE
Solomon and his workers carefully followed God's instructions. As a result, the temple work was blessed by God and completed in every detail. Here are a few examples of people in the Bible who did *not* carefully follow one of God's instructions, and the resulting consequences. It is not enough to obey God half-heartedly.

Who?	*God's instruction*	*Disobedience*	*Result*
Adam and Eve	Don't eat fruit from the tree of the knowledge of good and evil (Genesis 2:16, 17)	Satan tempted them, and they ate (Genesis 3:1–6)	They were banished from the Garden of Eden; pain and death were inflicted on all mankind (Genesis 3:24; Romans 5:12)
Nadab and Abihu	Fire for the sacrifice must come from the proper source (Leviticus 6:12, 13)	They used unauthorised fire for their sacrifice (Leviticus 10:1)	They were struck dead (Leviticus 10:2)
Moses	"Speak to that rock before their eyes and it will pour out its water " (Numbers 20:8)	He spoke to the rock, but also struck it with his staff (Numbers 20:11)	He was not allowed to enter the promised land (Numbers 20:12)
Saul	Completely destroy the evil Amalekites (1 Samuel 15:3)	He spared the king and kept some of the plunder (1 Samuel 15:8, 9)	God promised to end his reign (1 Samuel 15:16–26)
Uzzah	Only a priest can touch the holy furnishings and articles (Numbers 4:15)	He touched the ark of the covenant (2 Samuel 6:6)	He died instantly (2 Samuel 6:7)
Uzziah	Only the priests could offer incense in the temple or tabernacle sanctuary (Numbers 16:39, 40; 18:7)	He entered the Holy Place in the temple where only priests were allowed to go (2 Chronicles 26:16–18)	He became a leper (2 Chronicles 26:19)

it. 3Below the rim, figures of bulls encircled it—ten to a cubit.[d] The bulls were cast
in two rows in one piece with the Sea.
4The Sea stood on twelve bulls, three facing north, three facing west, three facing
south and three facing east.[c] The Sea rested on top of them, and their hindquarters
were towards the centre. 5It was a handbreadth[e] in thickness, and its rim was like
the rim of a cup, like a lily blossom. It held three thousand baths.[f]
6He then made ten basins[d] for washing and placed five on the south side and five
on the north. In them the things to be used for the burnt offerings[e] were rinsed, but
the Sea was to be used by the priests for washing.
7He made ten gold lampstands[f] according to the specifications[g] for them and
placed them in the temple, five on the south side and five on the north.
8He made ten tables[h] and placed them in the temple, five on the south side and
five on the north. He also made a hundred gold sprinkling bowls.[i]
9He made the courtyard[j] of the priests, and the large court and the doors for the
court, and overlaid the doors with bronze. 10He placed the Sea on the south side, at
the south-east corner.
11He also made the pots and shovels and sprinkling bowls.
So Huram finished[k] the work he had undertaken for King Solomon in the temple
of God:

12the two pillars;
the two bowl-shaped capitals on top of the pillars;
the two sets of network decorating the two bowl-shaped capitals on top of the pillars;
13the four hundred pomegranates for the two sets of network (two rows of pomegranates for each network, decorating the bowl-shaped capitals on top of the pillars);
14the stands[l] with their basins;
15the Sea and the twelve bulls under it;
16the pots, shovels, meat forks and all related articles.

All the objects that Huram-Abi[m] made for King Solomon for the temple of the LORD
were of polished bronze. 17The king had them cast in clay moulds in the plain of the
Jordan between Succoth[n] and Zarethan.[g] 18All these things that Solomon made
amounted to so much that the weight of the bronze[o] was not determined.
19Solomon also made all the furnishings that were in God's temple:

the golden altar;
the tables[p] on which was the bread of the Presence;
20the lampstands[q] of pure gold with their lamps, to burn in front of the inner sanctuary as prescribed;
21the gold floral work and lamps and tongs (they were solid gold);
22the pure gold wick trimmers, sprinkling bowls, dishes[r] and censers;[s] and the gold doors of the temple: the inner doors to the Most Holy Place and the doors of the main hall.

[d] *3* That is, about 1½ feet (about 0.5 metre) [e] *5* That is, about 3 inches (about 8 centimetres) [f] *5* That is, about 14,500 gallons (about 66 kilolitres) [g] *17* Hebrew *Zeredatha*, a variant of *Zarethan*

4:4 [c] Nu 2:3-25; Eze 48:30-34; Rev 21:13
4:6 [d] Ex 30:18 [e] Ne 13:5, 9; Eze 40:38
4:7 [f] Ex 25:31 [g] Ex 25:40
4:8 [h] Ex 25:23 [i] Nu 4:14
4:9 [j] 1Ki 6:36; 2Ki 21:5; 2Ch 33:5
4:11 [k] 1Ki 7:14
4:14 [l] 1Ki 7:27-30
4:16 [m] 1Ki 7:13
4:17 [n] Ge 33:17
4:18 [o] 1Ki 7:23
4:19 [p] Ex 25:23, 30
4:20 [q] Ex 25:31
4:22 [r] Nu 7:14 [s] Lev 10:1

4:6 Why was everything in the temple built on such a grand scale? The great size and numbers were necessary to accommodate the huge crowds that would visit for the feasts, such as the Passover (30:13). The numerous daily sacrifices (5:6) required many priests and much equipment.

4:7 The craftsmen followed God's specifications carefully—with spectacular results. When God gives specific instructions, they must be followed to the letter. There is a time to be creative and to put forth our own ideas, but not when the ideas add to, alter, or contradict any specific directions God has already given to us in the Bible. For best results in your spiritual life, carefully seek and follow God's instructions.

4:11–16 Pots, shovels, and bowls—these are implements of worship unfamiliar to us. Although the articles we use to aid our worship have changed, the purpose of worship remains the same—to give honour and praise to God. We must never let our worship of God be overshadowed by things we use to help us worship him.

4:22 All these details about the temple demonstrated the care Israel gave to acts of worship (see the note on 3:1ff). The instructions also served as a manual to the original readers of 2 Chronicles, those who would rebuild a new temple on its original site (Ezra 3:8–6:15) after Solomon's temple was destroyed by the Babylonians (2 Kings 25).

5:1 [a]1Ki 6:14 [b]2Sa 8:11
5:2 [c]Nu 3:31; 2Sa 6:12; 1Ch 15:25
5:3 [d]1Ch 9:1; 2Ch 7:8-10
5:5 [e]Nu 3:31; 1Ch 15:2
5:7 [f]Rev 11:19
5:8 [g]Ge 3:24
5:10 [h]Heb 9:4 [i]Ex 16:34; Dt 10:2
5:11 [j]1Ch 24:1
5:12 [k]1Ki 10:12; 1Ch 25:1; Ps 68:25 [l]1Ch 13:8; 15:24

5 When all the work Solomon had done for the temple of the LORD was finished,[a]
he brought in the things his father David had dedicated[b]—the silver and gold
and all the furnishings—and he placed them in the treasuries of God's temple.

3. Solomon dedicates the temple

The Ark Brought to the Temple

2Then Solomon summoned to Jerusalem the elders of Israel, all the heads of the
tribes and the chiefs of the Israelite families, to bring up the ark[c] of the LORD's
covenant from Zion, the City of David. 3And all the men of Israel[d] came together
to the king at the time of the festival in the seventh month.
4When all the elders of Israel had arrived, the Levites took up the ark, 5and they
brought up the ark and the Tent of Meeting and all the sacred furnishings in it. The
priests, who were Levites,[e] carried them up; 6and King Solomon and the entire
assembly of Israel that had gathered about him were before the ark, sacrificing so many
sheep and cattle that they could not be recorded or counted.
7The priests then brought the ark[f] of the LORD's covenant to its place in the inner
sanctuary of the temple, the Most Holy Place, and put it beneath the wings of the
cherubim. 8The cherubim[g] spread their wings over the place of the ark and covered
the ark and its carrying poles. 9These poles were so long that their ends, extending
from the ark, could be seen from in front of the inner sanctuary, but not from outside
the Holy Place; and they are still there today. 10There was nothing in the ark except[h]
the two tablets[i] that Moses had placed in it at Horeb, where the LORD made a
covenant with the Israelites after they came out of Egypt.
11The priests then withdrew from the Holy Place. All the priests who were there
had consecrated themselves, regardless of their divisions.[j] 12All the Levites who
were musicians[k]—Asaph, Heman, Jeduthun and their sons and relatives—stood on
the east side of the altar, dressed in fine linen and playing cymbals, harps and lyres.
They were accompanied by 120 priests sounding trumpets.[l] 13The trumpeters and

---

5:1ff Why is there so much emphasis on the temple in the Old Testament?

(1) *It was a symbol of religious authority.* The temple was God's way of centralising worship at Jerusalem in order to insure that correct belief would be kept intact through many generations.

(2) *It was a symbol of God's holiness.* The temple's beautiful atmosphere inspired respect and awe for God; it was the setting for many of the great visions of the prophets.

(3) *It was a symbol of God's covenant with Israel.* The temple kept the people focused upon God's law (the tablets of the Ten Commandments were kept in the temple) rather than on the kings' exploits. It was a place where God was especially present to his people.

(4) *It was a symbol of forgiveness.* The temple's design, furniture, and customs were great object lessons for all the people, reminding them of the seriousness of sin, the penalty that sin incurred, and their need of forgiveness.

(5) *It prepared the people for the Messiah.* In the New Testament, Christ said he came to fulfil the law, not destroy it. Hebrews 8:1, 2 and 9:11, 12 use temple customs to explain what Christ did when he died for us.

(6) *It was a testimony to human effort and creativity.* Inspired by the beauty of God's character, people devoted themselves to high achievements in engineering, science, and art in order to praise him.

(7) *It was a place of prayer.* In the temple, people could spend time in prayer to God.

5:1–3 The temple took seven years to build. 1 Kings 6:38 says that the temple was completed in the eighth month (November) of Solomon's eleventh year as king (959 B.C.). Because 5:3 states that the dedication ceremonies were held in the seventh month, they must have occurred either one month before or eleven months after the temple's completion.

5:3 The festival in the seventh month was the Feast of Tabernacles, celebrating God's protection of Israel as they wandered in the desert before entering the promised land. The purpose of this annual festival was to renew Israel's commitment to God and their trust in his guidance and protection. The festival beautifully coincided with the dedication of the temple. As the people remembered the wanderings in the desert when their ancestors had lived in tents, they were even more thankful for the permanence of this glorious temple.

5:9 Under God's inspiration, some books of the Bible were compiled and edited from other sources. Because 1 and 2 Chronicles cover many centuries, they were compiled from several sources by a single person. The phrase "they are still there today" (see also 1 Kings 8:8) was taken from material written before Judah's exile in 586 B.C. Although 1 and 2 Chronicles were compiled after the exile and after Solomon's temple was destroyed, the writer thought it best to leave this phrase in the narrative.

5:7–12 The priests came out of the Holy Place after having placed the ark in the Most Holy Place of the temple. The Holy Place is the outer room, where the bread of the Presence, altar of incense, and lampstand were kept. Ordinarily the Most Holy Place could be entered only once a year by the high priest on the Day of Atonement. On this unique occasion, however, several priests had to enter the Most Holy Place to carry the ark to its new resting place. The Levites praised God when these priests emerged from the Holy Place because they then knew God had accepted this new home for the ark (5:13).

5:13 The first service at the temple began with honouring God and acknowledging his presence and goodness. In the same way, our worship should begin by acknowledging God's love. Praise God first; then you will be prepared to present your needs to him. Recalling God's love and mercy will inspire you to worship him daily. Psalm 107 is an example of how David recalled God's enduring love.

singers joined in unison, as with one voice, to give praise and thanks to the LORD.
Accompanied by trumpets, cymbals and other instruments, they raised their voices
in praise to the LORD and sang:

> "He is good;
> his love endures for ever."[m]

Then the temple of the LORD was filled with a cloud, 14and the priests could not
perform[n] their service because of the cloud,[o] for the glory[p] of the LORD filled the
temple of God.

6 Then Solomon said, "The LORD has said that he would dwell in a dark cloud;[a]
2I have built a magnificent temple for you, a place for you to dwell for ever.[b]"
3While the whole assembly of Israel was standing there, the king turned round and
blessed them. 4Then he said:

"Praise be to the LORD, the God of Israel, who with his hands has fulfilled what
he promised with his mouth to my father David. For he said, 5'Since the day I
brought my people out of Egypt, I have not chosen a city in any tribe of Israel
to have a temple built for my Name to be there, nor have I chosen anyone to be
the leader over my people Israel. 6But now I have chosen Jerusalem[c] for my
Name[d] to be there, and I have chosen David[e] to rule my people Israel.'
7"My father David had it in his heart[f] to build a temple for the Name of the
LORD, the God of Israel. 8But the LORD said to my father David, 'Because it was
in your heart to build a temple for my Name, you did well to have this in your
heart. 9Nevertheless, you are not the one to build the temple, but your son, who
is your own flesh and blood—he is the one who will build the temple for my
Name.'
10"The LORD has kept the promise he made. I have succeeded David my father
and now I sit on the throne of Israel, just as the LORD promised, and I have built
the temple for the Name of the LORD, the God of Israel. 11There I have placed
the ark, in which is the covenant[g] of the LORD that he made with the people of
Israel."

Solomon's Prayer of Dedication

12Then Solomon stood before the altar of the LORD in front of the whole assembly
of Israel and spread out his hands. 13Now he had made a bronze platform,[h] five
cubits**a** long, five cubits wide and three cubits**b** high, and had placed it in the centre
of the outer court. He stood on the platform and then knelt down[i] before the whole
assembly of Israel and spread out his hands towards heaven. 14He said:

"O LORD, God of Israel, there is no God like you[j] in heaven or on earth—you
who keep your covenant of love[k] with your servants who continue wholeheartedly in your way. 15You have kept your promise to your servant David my
father; with your mouth you have promised[l] and with your hand you have
fulfilled it—as it is today.
16"Now LORD, God of Israel, keep for your servant David my father the
promises you made to him when you said, 'You shall never fail[m] to have a man
to sit before me on the throne of Israel, if only your sons are careful in all they
do to walk before me according to my law,[n] as you have done.' 17And now,

a *13* That is, about 7½ feet (about 2.3 metres) **b** *13* That is, about 4½ feet (about 1.4 metres)

5:13 [m] 1Ch 16:34, 41; 2Ch 7:3; 20:21; Ezr 3:11; Ps 100:5; 136:1; Jer 33:11
5:14 [n] Ex 40:35; Rev 15:8 [o] Ex 19:16 [p] Ex 29:43; 2Ch 7:2
6:1 [a] Ex 19:9; 1Ki 8:12-50
6:2 [b] Ezr 6:12; 7:15; Ps 135:21
6:6 [c] Dt 12:5; Isa 14:1 [d] Ex 20:24; 2Ch 12:13 [e] 1Ch 28:4
6:7 [f] 1Sa 10:7; 1Ch 17:2; 28:2; Ac 7:46
6:11 [g] Dt 10:2; 2Ch 5:10; Ps 25:10; 50:5
6:13 [h] Ne 8:4 [i] Ps 95:6
6:14 [j] Ex 8:10; 15:11 [k] Dt 7:9
6:15 [l] 1Ch 22:10
6:16 [m] 2Sa 7:13, 15; 1Ki 2:4; 2Ch 7:18; 23:3 [n] Ps 132:12

6:3 As the people received Solomon's blessing, they stood; as Solomon prayed, he knelt (6:13). Both standing and kneeling are acts of reverence. Acts of reverence make us feel more worshipful, and they let others see that we are honouring God. When you stand or kneel in church or at prayer, make these actions more than mere forms prescribed by tradition. Let them indicate your love for God.

6:12, 13 It was unusual for a king to kneel before someone else in front of his own people because kneeling meant submitting to a higher authority. Solomon demonstrated his great love and respect for God by kneeling before him. His action showed that he acknowledged God as the ultimate king and authority, and it encouraged the people to do the same.

O LORD, God of Israel, let your word that you promised your servant David come
true.
18"But will God really dwell[o] on earth with men? The heavens,[p] even the
highest heavens, cannot contain you. How much less this temple that I have built!
19Yet give attention to your servant's prayer and his plea for mercy, O LORD my
God. Hear the cry and the prayer that your servant is praying in your presence.
20May your eyes[q] be open towards this temple day and night, this place of which
you said you would put your Name[r] there. May you hear[s] the prayer your
servant prays towards this place. 21Hear the supplications of your servant and of
your people Israel when they pray towards this place. Hear from heaven, your
dwelling-place; and when you hear, forgive.[t]
22"When a man wrongs his neighbour and is required to take an oath[u] and
he comes and swears the oath before your altar in this temple, 23then hear from
heaven and act. Judge between your servants, repaying[v] the guilty by bringing
down on his own head what he has done. Declare the innocent not guilty and
so establish his innocence.
24"When your people Israel have been defeated[w] by an enemy because they
have sinned against you and when they turn back and confess your name, praying
and making supplication before you in this temple, 25then hear from heaven and
forgive the sin of your people Israel and bring them back to the land you gave
to them and their fathers.
26"When the heavens are shut up and there is no rain[x] because your people
have sinned against you, and when they pray towards this place and confess your
name and turn from their sin because you have afflicted them, 27then hear from
heaven and forgive[y] the sin of your servants, your people Israel. Teach them
the right way to live, and send rain on the land that you gave your people for
an inheritance.
28"When famine[z] or plague comes to the land, or blight or mildew, locusts
or grasshoppers, or when enemies besiege them in any of their cities, whatever
disaster or disease may come, 29and when a prayer or plea is made by any of
your people Israel—each one aware of his afflictions and pains, and spreading
out his hands towards this temple—30then hear from heaven, your dwelling-
place. Forgive,[a] and deal with each man according to all he does, since you
know his heart (for you alone know the hearts of men),[b] 31so that they will fear
you[c] and walk in your ways all the time they live in the land that you gave our
fathers.
32"As for the foreigner who does not belong to your people Israel but has
come[d] from a distant land because of your great name and your mighty hand[e]
and your outstretched arm—when he comes and prays towards this temple,
33then hear from heaven, your dwelling-place, and do whatever the foreigner[f]
asks of you, so that all the peoples of the earth may know your name and fear
you, as do your own people Israel, and may know that this house that I have built
bears your Name.

6:18 [o]Rev 21:3 [p]2Ch 2:6; Ps 11:4; Isa 40:22; 66:1; Ac 7:49

6:20 [q]Ex 3:16; Ps 34:15 [r]Dt 12:11 [s]2Ch 7:14; 30:20

6:21 [t]Ps 51:1; Isa 33:24; 40:2; 43:25; 44:22; 55:7; Mic 7:18

6:22 [u]Ex 22:11

6:23 [v]Isa 3:11; 65:6; Mt 16:27

6:24 [w]Lev 26:17

6:26 [x]Lev 26:19; Dt 11:17; 28:24; 2Sa 1:21; 1Ki 17:1

6:27 [y]ver 30, 39; 2Ch 7:14

6:28 [z]2Ch 20:9

6:30 [a]ver 27 [b]1Sa 16:7; 1Ch 28:9; Ps 7:9; 44:21; Pr 16:2; 17:3

6:31 [c]Ps 103:11, 13; Pr 8:13

6:32 [d]2Ch 9:6; Jn 12:20; Ac 8:27 [e]Ex 3:19, 20

6:33 [f]2Ch 7:14

6:18 Solomon marvelled that the temple could contain the power of God and that God would be willing to live on earth among sinful people. We marvel that God, through his Son, Jesus, lived among us in human form to reveal his eternal purposes to us. In doing so, God was reaching out to us in love. God wants us to reach out to him in return in order to know him and to love him with all our hearts. Don't simply marvel at his power; take time to get to know him.

6:19–42 As Solomon led the people in prayer, he asked God to hear their prayers concerning a variety of situations: (1) crime (6:22, 23); (2) enemy attacks (6:24, 25); (3) drought (6:26, 27); (4) famine (6:28–31); (5) the influx of foreigners (6:32, 33); (6) war (6:34, 35); (7) sin (6:36–39). God is concerned with whatever we face, even the difficult consequences we bring upon ourselves. He wants us to turn to him in prayer. When you pray, remember that God hears you. Don't let the extremity of your situation cause you to doubt his care for you.

6:26 Why would Solomon assume that drought would come as a result of sin? Sin is not necessarily the direct cause of natural disasters today, but this was a special case. God had made a specific agreement with the Israelites that drought could be a consequence of their sins (Deuteronomy 28:20–24).

6:30 Have you ever felt far from God, separated by feelings of failure and personal problems? In his prayer, Solomon underscored the fact that God stands ready to hear his people, to forgive their sins, and to restore their relationship with him. God is waiting and listening for our confessions of guilt and our recommitment to obey him. He hears us when we pour out our needs and problems to him and is ready to forgive us and restore us to fellowship with him. Don't wait to experience his loving forgiveness.

34"When your people go to war against their enemies,[g] wherever you send
them, and when they pray[h] to you towards this city you have chosen and the
temple I have built for your Name, 35then hear from heaven their prayer and their
plea, and uphold their cause.
36"When they sin against you—for there is no-one who does not sin[i]—and
you become angry with them and give them over to the enemy, who takes them
captive[j] to a land far away or near; 37and if they have a change of heart[k] in
the land where they are held captive, and repent and plead with you in the land
of their captivity and say, 'We have sinned, we have done wrong and acted
wickedly'; 38and if they turn back to you with all their heart and soul in the land
of their captivity where they were taken, and pray towards the land that you gave
their fathers, towards the city you have chosen and towards the temple that I have
built for your Name; 39then from heaven, your dwelling-place, hear their prayer
and their pleas, and uphold their cause. And forgive your people, who have
sinned against you.
40"Now, my God, may your eyes be open and your ears attentive[l] to the
prayers offered in this place.

41"Now arise,[m] O LORD God, and come to your resting
place,[n]
you and the ark of your might.
May your priests,[o] O LORD God, be clothed with salvation,
may your saints rejoice in your goodness.[p]
42O LORD God, do not reject your anointed one.
Remember the great love[q] promised to David your
servant."

The Dedication of the Temple

7 When Solomon finished praying, fire[a] came down from heaven and consumed
the burnt offering and the sacrifices, and the glory of the LORD filled[b] the
temple.[c] 2The priests could not enter[d] the temple of the LORD because the glory[e]
of the LORD filled it. 3When all the Israelites saw the fire coming down and the glory
of the LORD above the temple, they knelt on the pavement with their faces to the
ground, and they worshipped and gave thanks to the LORD, saying,

"He is good;
his love endures for ever."[f]

4Then the king and all the people offered sacrifices before the LORD. 5And King
Solomon offered a sacrifice of twenty-two thousand head of cattle and a hundred and
twenty thousand sheep and goats. So the king and all the people dedicated the temple
of God. 6The priests took their positions, as did the Levites[g] with the LORD's musical
instruments,[h] which King David had made for praising the LORD and which were used
when he gave thanks, saying, "His love endures for ever." Opposite the Levites, the
priests blew their trumpets, and all the Israelites were standing.
7Solomon consecrated the middle part of the courtyard in front of the temple of the
LORD, and there he offered burnt offerings and the fat of the fellowship offerings,[a]

6:34 [g]Dt 28:7 [h]1Ch 5:20
6:36 [i]Job 15:14; Ps 143:2; Ecc 7:20; Jer 17:9; Jas 3:1; 1Jn 1:8-10 [j]Lev 26:44
6:37 [k]2Ch 7:14; 33:12, 19, 23; Jer 29:13
6:40 [l]2Ch 7:15; Ne 1:6, 11; Ps 17:1, 6
6:41 [m]Isa 33:10 [n]1Ch 28:2 [o]Ps 132:16 [p]Ps 116:12
6:42 [q]Ps 89:24, 28; Isa 55:3
7:1 [a]Lev 9:24; 1Ki 18:38 [b]Ex 16:10 [c]Ps 26:8
7:2 [d]1Ki 8:11 [e]Ex 29:43; 40:35; 2Ch 5:14
7:3 [f]1Ch 16:34; 2Ch 5:13; 20:21
7:6 [g]1Ch 15:16 [h]2Ch 5:12

a 7 Traditionally *peace offerings*

6:36 "For there is no-one who does not sin"—the Bible makes it clear that no-one is exempt from sin, not even God's appointed kings. Sin is a condition we all share, and we all should acknowledge it as Solomon did. When we realise we have sinned, we should quickly ask God for forgiveness and restoration. Knowing we have a tendency to sin should keep us close to God, seeking his guidance and strength. This truth is also mentioned in Psalm 14:3, Ecclesiastes 7:20, and Romans 3:23.

7:1, 2 God sent fire from heaven to consume the offering and to begin the fire that was to burn continuously under the altar of burnt offering (see Leviticus 6:8–13). This perpetual fire symbolised God's presence. God also sent fire when inaugurating the tabernacle (Leviticus 9:22–24). This was the real dedication of the temple because only God's purifying power can make something holy.

7:4, 5 The temple was dedicated to God, and Solomon and the people prepared to worship him. Dedication means setting apart a place, an object, or a person for an exclusive purpose. The purpose of this dedication was to set apart the temple as a place to worship God. Today, our bodies are God's temple (2 Corinthians 6:16). Solomon's dedication of the temple shows us that we should dedicate ourselves to carry out God's special purpose (Ephesians 1:11, 12).

7:8 [i]2Ch 30:26 [j]Ge 15:18
7:9 [k]Lev 23:36
7:12 [l]Dt 12:5
7:13 [m]2Ch 6:26-28; Am 4:7
7:14 [n]Lev 26:41; 2Ch 6:37; Jas 4:10 [o]1Ch 16:11 [p]Isa 55:7; Zec 1:4 [q]2Ch 6:27 [r]2Ch 30:20; Isa 30:26; 57:18
7:15 [s]2Ch 6:40
7:16 [t]ver 12; 2Ch 6:6
7:17 [u]1Ki 9:4
7:18 [v]2Ch 6:16 [w]2Sa 7:13; 2Ch 13:5
7:19 [x]Dt 28:15 [y]Lev 26:14, 33
7:20 [z]Dt 29:28 [a]1Ki 14:15 [b]Dt 28:37
7:21 [c]Dt 29:24

because the bronze altar he had made could not hold the burnt offerings, the grain
offerings and the fat portions.
8 So Solomon observed the festival[i] at that time for seven days, and all Israel with
him—a vast assembly, people from Lebo[b] Hamath to the Wadi of Egypt.[j] 9 On the
eighth day they held an assembly, for they had celebrated the dedication of the altar
for seven days and the festival[k] for seven days more. 10 On the twenty-third day of
the seventh month he sent the people to their homes, joyful and glad in heart for the
good things the LORD had done for David and Solomon and for his people Israel.

The LORD Appears to Solomon

11 When Solomon had finished the temple of the LORD and the royal palace, and
had succeeded in carrying out all he had in mind to do in the temple of the LORD and
in his own palace, 12 the LORD appeared to him at night and said:

"I have heard your prayer and have chosen this place for myself[l] as a temple
for sacrifices.
13 "When I shut up the heavens so that there is no rain,[m] or command locusts
to devour the land or send a plague among my people, 14 if my people, who are
called by my name, will humble[n] themselves and pray and seek my face[o] and
turn[p] from their wicked ways, then will I hear from heaven and will forgive[q]
their sin and will heal[r] their land. 15 Now my eyes will be open and my ears
attentive to the prayers offered in this place.[s] 16 I have chosen[t] and consecrated
this temple so that my Name may be there for ever. My eyes and my heart will
always be there.
17 "As for you, if you walk before me[u] as David your father did, and do all
I command, and observe my decrees and laws, 18 I will establish your royal
throne, as I covenanted with David your father when I said, 'You shall never fail
to have a man[v] to rule over Israel.'[w]
19 "But if you[c] turn away[x] and forsake[y] the decrees and commands I have
given you[c] and go off to serve other gods and worship them, 20 then I will
uproot[z] Israel from my land,[a] which I have given them, and will reject this
temple which I have consecrated for my Name. I will make it a byword and an
object of ridicule[b] among all peoples. 21 And though this temple is now so
imposing, all who pass by will be appalled and say,[c] 'Why has the LORD done
such a thing to this land and to this temple?' 22 People will answer, 'Because they
have forsaken the LORD, the God of their fathers, who brought them out of Egypt,
and have embraced other gods, worshipping and serving them—that is why he
brought all this disaster on them.' "

b *8* Or *from the entrance to* **c** *19* The Hebrew is plural.

7:8 A wadi is a stream or dry streambed.

7:12 Months, maybe years, had passed since Solomon's prayer of dedication (chapter 6). Several other building projects had been completed after the temple (7:11; 8:1). Then after all this time, God told Solomon that he had heard Solomon's prayer. How often do we look for immediate answers to our prayers and, when nothing happens, wonder if God has heard us? God does hear, and he will provide for us. We must trust that God will answer at the proper time.

7:14 In chapter 6, Solomon asked God to make provisions for the people when they sinned. God answered with four conditions for forgiveness: (1) humble yourself by admitting your sins, (2) pray to God, asking for forgiveness, (3) seek God continually, and (4) turn from sinful behaviour. True repentance is more than talk—it is changed behaviour. Whether we sin individually, as a group, or as a nation, following these steps will lead to forgiveness. God will answer our earnest prayers.

7:17–22 God plainly set forth certain conditions for Solomon to meet if he wanted the kingdom to continue. If Solomon followed God, he and his descendants would prosper; if Solomon did not, he and the nation would be destroyed. In Deuteronomy 27 and 28, these conditions were outlined before all the people.

But sin is deceptively attractive, and Solomon eventually turned from God. As a result, his son and heir lost most of the kingdom. Following God brings benefits and rewards (not necessarily material). Turning away from God brings suffering, punishment, and ultimately destruction. Today, God's conditions are just as clear as they were in Solomon's day. Choose to obey God and live.

7:21, 22 Soon after Solomon's reign, the temple was ransacked (12:9). It is difficult for us to imagine that such a great and wise king could become corrupted by idols—symbols of power, prosperity, and sexuality. But even today these idols lure us into their traps. When we allow any desire to rival God's proper place, we have taken the first step towards moral and spiritual decay.

4. Solomon's riches and wisdom

Solomon's Other Activities

8 At the end of twenty years, during which Solomon built the temple of the LORD
and his own palace, 2 Solomon rebuilt the villages that Hiram[a] had given him,
and settled Israelites in them. 3 Solomon then went to Hamath Zobah and captured it.
4 He also built up Tadmor in the desert and all the store cities he had built in Hamath.
5 He rebuilt Upper Beth Horon[a] and Lower Beth Horon as fortified cities, with walls
and with gates and bars, 6 as well as Baalath and all his store cities, and all the cities
for his chariots and for his horses[b]—whatever he desired to build in Jerusalem, in
Lebanon and throughout all the territory that he ruled.
7 All the people left from the Hittites, Amorites, Perizzites, Hivites and Jebusites[b]
(these peoples were not Israelites), 8 that is, their descendants remaining in the land,
whom the Israelites had not destroyed—these Solomon conscripted[c] for his slave
labour force, as it is to this day. 9 But Solomon did not make slaves of the Israelites
for his work; they were his fighting men, commanders of his captains, and commanders of his chariots and charioteers. 10 They were also King Solomon's chief officials—two hundred and fifty officials supervising the men.
11 Solomon brought Pharaoh's daughter[d] up from the City of David to the palace
he had built for her, for he said, "My wife must not live in the palace of David king
of Israel, because the places the ark of the LORD has entered are holy."
12 On the altar[e] of the LORD that he had built in front of the portico, Solomon
sacrificed burnt offerings to the LORD, 13 according to the daily requirement[f] for
offerings commanded by Moses for Sabbaths,[g] New Moons and the three[h] annual
feasts—the Feast of Unleavened Bread, the Feast of Weeks[i] and the Feast of
Tabernacles. 14 In keeping with the ordinance of his father David, he appointed the
divisions[j] of the priests for their duties and the Levites[k] to lead the praise and to
assist the priests according to each day's requirement. He also appointed the gatekeepers[l] by divisions for the various gates, because this was what David the man
of God[m] had ordered.[n] 15 They did not deviate from the king's commands to the
priests or to the Levites in any matter, including that of the treasuries.
16 All Solomon's work was carried out, from the day the foundation of the temple
of the LORD was laid until its completion. So the temple of the LORD was finished.
17 Then Solomon went to Ezion Geber and Elath on the coast of Edom. 18 And Hiram
sent him ships commanded by his own officers, men who knew the sea. These, with
Solomon's men, sailed to Ophir and brought back four hundred and fifty talents[c] of
gold,[o] which they delivered to King Solomon.

The Queen of Sheba Visits Solomon

9 When the queen of Sheba[a] heard of Solomon's fame, she came to Jerusalem to
test him with hard questions. Arriving with a very great caravan—with camels
carrying spices, large quantities of gold, and precious stones—she came to Solomon
and talked with him about all she had on her mind. 2 Solomon answered all her
questions; nothing was too hard for him to explain to her. 3 When the queen of Sheba
saw the wisdom of Solomon,[b] as well as the palace he had built, 4 the food on his

[a] *2* Hebrew *Huram*, a variant of *Hiram*; also in verse 18 [b] *6* Or *charioteers* [c] *18* That is, about 17 tons (about 16 metric tons)

8:5 [a] 1Ch 7:24; 2Ch 14:7
8:7 [b] Ge 10:16
8:8 [c] 1Ki 4:6; 9:21
8:11 [d] 1Ki 3:1; 7:8
8:12 [e] 1Ki 8:64; 2Ch 4:1; 15:8
8:13 [f] Ex 29:38; Nu 28:3 [g] Nu 28:9 [h] Ex 23:14; Dt 16:16 [i] Ex 23:16
8:14 [j] 1Ch 24:1 [k] 1Ch 25:1 [l] 1Ch 9:17; 26:1 [m] Ne 12:24, 36 [n] 1Ch 23:6; Ne 12:45
8:18 [o] 2Ch 9:9
9:1 [a] Ge 10:7; Eze 23:42; Mt 12:42; Lk 11:31
9:3 [b] 1Ki 5:12

8:11 Solomon married Pharaoh's daughter to secure a military alliance with Egypt. He did not let the woman live in David's palace, however, where the ark of God had once been kept. This implies that Solomon knew his pagan marriage would not please God. Solomon married many other foreign women, and this was contrary to God's law (Deuteronomy 7:3, 4). These women worshipped false gods and were certain to contaminate Israel with their beliefs and practices. Eventually Solomon's pagan wives caused his downfall (1 Kings 11:1–11).

8:15 Although Solomon carefully followed God's instructions for building the temple and offering sacrifices (8:13), he paid no attention to what God said about marrying pagan women. His sin in marrying a foreign wife (8:11) began his slide away from God. No matter how good or spiritual we are in most areas of life, one unsurrendered area can begin a downfall. Guard carefully *every* area of your life, especially your relationships. Don't give sin any foothold.

9:1–8 The queen of Sheba had heard about Solomon's wisdom, but she was overwhelmed when she saw for herself the fruits of that wisdom. Although Solomon had married Pharaoh's daughter, he still sincerely tried to follow God at this stage in his life. When people get to know you and ask hard questions, will your responses reflect God? Your life can be a powerful witness; let others see God at work in you.

table, the seating of his officials, the attending servants in their robes, the cupbearers in their robes and the burnt offerings he made at[a] the temple of the LORD, she was overwhelmed.

5She said to the king, "The report I heard in my own country about your achievements and your wisdom is true. 6But I did not believe what they said until I came[c] and saw with my own eyes. Indeed, not even half the greatness of your wisdom was told me; you have far exceeded the report I heard. 7How happy your men must be! How happy your officials, who continually stand before you and hear your wisdom! 8Praise be to the LORD your God, who has delighted in you and placed you on his throne[d] as king to rule for the LORD your God. Because of the love of your God for Israel and his desire to uphold them for ever, he has made you king[e] over them, to maintain justice and righteousness."

9Then she gave the king 120 talents[b] of gold,[f] large quantities of spices, and precious stones. There had never been such spices as those the queen of Sheba gave to King Solomon.

10(The men of Hiram and the men of Solomon brought gold from Ophir;[g] they also brought algum-wood[c] and precious stones. 11The king used the algum-wood to make steps for the temple of the LORD and for the royal palace, and to make harps and lyres for the musicians. Nothing like them had ever been seen in Judah.)

12King Solomon gave the queen of Sheba all she desired and asked for; he gave her more than she had brought to him. Then she left and returned with her retinue to her own country.

Solomon's Splendour

13The weight of the gold that Solomon received yearly was 666 talents,[d] 14not including the revenues brought in by merchants and traders. Also all the kings of Arabia[h] and the governors of the land brought gold and silver to Solomon.

15King Solomon made two hundred large shields of hammered gold; six hundred bekas[e] of hammered gold went into each shield. 16He also made three hundred small shields[i] of hammered gold, with three hundred bekas[f] of gold in each shield. The king put them in the Palace of the Forest of Lebanon.[j]

17Then the king made a great throne inlaid with ivory[k] and overlaid with pure gold. 18The throne had six steps, and a footstool of gold was attached to it. On both sides of the seat were armrests, with a lion standing beside each of them. 19Twelve lions stood on the six steps, one at either end of each step. Nothing like it had ever been made for any other kingdom. 20All King Solomon's goblets were gold, and all the household articles in the Palace of the Forest of Lebanon were pure gold. Nothing was made of silver, because silver was considered of little value in Solomon's day. 21The king had a fleet of trading ships[g] manned by Hiram's[h] men. Once every three years it returned, carrying gold, silver and ivory, and apes and baboons.

22King Solomon was greater in riches and wisdom than all the other kings of the earth.[l] 23All the kings[m] of the earth sought audience with Solomon to hear the wisdom God had put in his heart. 24Year after year, everyone who came brought a gift[n]—articles of silver and gold, and robes, weapons and spices, and horses and mules.

25Solomon had four thousand stalls for horses and chariots,[o] and twelve thousand horses,[i] which he kept in the chariot cities and also with him in Jerusalem. 26He ruled[p] over all the kings from the River[j][q] to the land of the Philistines, as far as

9:6 *c* 2Ch 6:32
9:8 *d* 1Ki 2:12; 1Ch 17:14; 28:5; 29:23; 2Ch 13:8 *e* 2Ch 2:11
9:9 *f* 2Ch 8:18
9:10 *g* 2Ch 8:18
9:14 *h* 2Ch 17:11; Isa 21:13; Jer 25:24; Eze 27:21; 30:5
9:16 *i* 2Ch 12:9 *j* 1Ki 7:2
9:17 *k* 1Ki 22:39
9:22 *l* 1Ki 3:13; 2Ch 1:12
9:23 *m* 1Ki 4:34
9:24 *n* 2Ch 32:23; Ps 45:12; 68:29; 72:10; Isa 18:7
9:25 *o* 1Sa 8:11; 1Ki 4:26
9:26 *p* 1Ki 4:21 *q* Ps 72:8-9

a *4* Or *the ascent by which he went up to* b *9* That is, about 4 tons (about 4 metric tons) c *10* Probably a variant of *almug-wood* d *13* That is, about 23 tons (about 23 metric tons) e *15* That is, about 7½ pounds (about 3.5 kilograms) f *16* That is, about 3¾ pounds (about 1.7 kilograms) g *21* Hebrew *of ships that could go to Tarshish* h *21* Hebrew *Huram*, a variant of *Hiram* i *25* Or *charioteers* j *26* That is, the Euphrates

9:8 The queen of Sheba marvelled at Solomon, claiming that God must love his people greatly to give them such a king. Israel greatly prospered during Solomon's reign, witnessing to God's power and love for his people. The good times show God's love and faithfulness. But hard times come to believers, too, and our perseverance and steadfast hope during those times will demonstrate our love and faithfulness to God. How we live will help others see our love for God.

9:11 Algumwood was probably sandalwood, a smooth, red-coloured wood that accepts a high polish. This beautiful wood was extremely expensive.

the border of Egypt.[r] 27 The king made silver as common in Jerusalem as stones, and
cedar as plentiful as sycamore-fig trees in the foothills. 28 Solomon's horses were
imported from Egypt[k] and from all other countries.

Solomon's Death

29 As for the other events of Solomon's reign, from beginning to end, are they not
written in the records of Nathan[s] the prophet, in the prophecy of Ahijah[t] the
Shilonite and in the visions of Iddo the seer concerning Jeroboam[u] son of Nebat?
30 Solomon reigned in Jerusalem over all Israel for forty years. 31 Then he rested with
his fathers and was buried in the city of David[v] his father. And Rehoboam his son
succeeded him as king.

B. THE KINGDOM OF JUDAH (10:1 – 36:23)

After Solomon's death, the northern tribes revolt, and we read little more about them in 2 Chronicles. The remainder of 2 Chronicles recounts the alternating periods of apostasy and reform in Judah. In the end, Judah would not turn from its sin, and the tragic result was a 70-year captivity in Babylon. Sin in our lives will also lead to judgment and devastation. Although God's judgment may seem slow, it is nevertheless certain.

1. The northern tribes revolt

Israel Rebels Against Rehoboam

10 Rehoboam went to Shechem, for all the Israelites had gone there to make him
king. 2 When Jeroboam[a] son of Nebat heard this (he was in Egypt, where he
had fled[b] from King Solomon), he returned from Egypt. 3 So they sent for Jeroboam,
and he and all Israel[c] went to Rehoboam and said to him: 4 "Your father put a heavy
yoke on us,[d] but now lighten the harsh labour and the heavy yoke he put on us, and
we will serve you."

5 Rehoboam answered, "Come back to me in three days." So the people went away.
6 Then King Rehoboam consulted the elders[e] who had served his father Solomon
during his lifetime. "How would you advise me to answer these people?" he asked.
7 They replied, "If you will be kind to these people and please them and give them
a favourable answer,[f] they will always be your servants."
8 But Rehoboam rejected[g] the advice the elders[h] gave him and consulted the young
men who had grown up with him and were serving him. 9 He asked them, "What is
your advice? How should we answer these people who say to me, 'Lighten the yoke
your father put on us'?"
10 The young men who had grown up with him replied, "Tell the people who have
said to you, 'Your father put a heavy yoke on us, but make our yoke lighter' – tell
them, 'My little finger is thicker than my father's waist. 11 My father laid on you a
heavy yoke; I will make it even heavier. My father scourged you with whips; I will
scourge you with scorpions.' "
12 Three days later Jeroboam and all the people returned to Rehoboam, as the king
had said, "Come back to me in three days." 13 The king answered them harshly.
Rejecting the advice of the elders, 14 he followed the advice of the young men and said,

k 28 Or possibly *Muzur*, a region in Cilicia

9:26 [r] Ge 15:18-21
9:29 [s] 2Sa 7:2; 1Ch 29:29 [t] 1Ki 11:29 [u] 2Ch 10:2
9:31 [v] 1Ki 2:10
10:2 [a] 2Ch 9:29 [b] 1Ki 11:40
10:3 [c] 1Ch 9:1
10:4 [d] 2Ch 2:2
10:6 [e] Job 8:8-9; 12:12; 15:10; 32:7
10:7 [f] Pr 15:1
10:8 [g] 2Sa 17:14 [h] Pr 13:20

9:29 For the rest of Solomon's story, see 1 Kings 10:26 – 11:43. In his later years, Solomon turned away from God and led the nation into worshipping idols.

10:1 The crowning of an Israelite king would normally have taken place in Jerusalem, the capital city. But Rehoboam saw that there was the possibility of trouble in the north; so to maintain his hold on the country, he chose Shechem, a city about 35 miles north of Jerusalem. Shechem was an ancient site for making covenants (Joshua 24:1).

10:1-15 Following bad advice can cause disaster. Rehoboam lost the chance to rule a peaceful, united kingdom because he rejected the advice of Solomon's older counsellors, preferring the counsel of his peers. Rehoboam made two errors in seeking advice: (1) he did not give extra consideration to the suggestions of those who knew the situation better than he, and (2) he did not ask God for wisdom to discern which was the better option.

It is easy to follow the advice of our peers because they often feel as we do. But their view may be limited. It is important to listen carefully to those who have more experience than we do – they can see the bigger picture.

10:2, 3 Why was Jeroboam in Egypt? Ahijah the prophet had predicted that Israel would split in two and that Jeroboam would become king of the northern section. When Solomon learned of this prophecy, he tried to kill Jeroboam, and Jeroboam was forced to flee to Egypt (1 Kings 11:26-40).

10:14 Rehoboam must have gotten an unbalanced picture of

10:15
[i] 2Ch 11:4; 25:16-20
[j] 1Ki 11:29

"My father made your yoke heavy; I will make it even heavier. My father scourged
you with whips; I will scourge you with scorpions." 15So the king did not listen to
the people, for this turn of events was from God,[i] to fulfil the word that the LORD
had spoken to Jeroboam son of Nebat through Ahijah the Shilonite.[j]
16When all Israel[k] saw that the king refused to listen to them, they answered the
king:

10:16
[k] 1Ch 9:1
[l] ver 19;
2Sa 20:1

"What share do we have in David,[l]
what part in Jesse's son?

REHOBOAM

Settling for cheap imitations in exchange for the real thing is a poor way to live. In every area of his life, Rehoboam consistently traded what was real for what was counterfeit. Given wise and unwise counsel by his advisers at his coronation, he chose to grab for power and control rather than to take patiently the counsel of those older and wiser than he and treat his people with kindness. Although his position came from God, he chose to abandon God. These unwise decisions made him weaker rather than stronger. As a result, he was invaded by the Egyptians and stripped of the riches he inherited from David and Solomon. To replace them, he had cheap bronze copies made.

Throughout the early part of his reign, Rehoboam fluctuated between obeying God and going his own way. Outward appearances were kept up, but his inward attitudes were evil. Following in the tradition of David gave Rehoboam many opportunities for real greatness. Instead, he ended up with a divided and broken kingdom.

How much of real living have we exchanged for the things that do not last? We trade healthy bodies for momentary excitement, personal integrity for fast-fading wealth, honesty for lies, God's wise guidance for our selfish ways. We sin when we willingly give little value to "the real thing" God has already given us.

Our counterfeit lives may fool some people, but they never fool God. Yet in spite of what he sees in us, God offers mercy. Are you a self-managed enterprise, counterfeit at best? Or have you placed yourself in God's care? Do the decisions you must make today need a second consideration in the light of Rehoboam's example?

Strengths and accomplishments:
- Fourth and last king of the united nation of Israel, but only for a short time
- Fortified his kingdom and achieved a measure of popularity

Weaknesses and mistakes:
- Followed unwise advice and divided his kingdom
- Married foreign women, as his father Solomon had done
- Abandoned the worship of God and allowed idolatry to flourish

Lessons from his life:
- Thoughtless decisions often lead to exchanging what is most valuable for something of far less value
- Every choice we make has real and long-lasting consequences

Vital statistics:
- Where: Jerusalem
- Occupation: King of the united kingdom of Israel, and later of the southern kingdom of Judah
- Relatives: Father: Solomon. Mother: Naamah. Son: Abijah. Wife: Maacah
- Contemporaries: Jeroboam, Shishak, Shemaiah

Key verse:
"After Rehoboam's position as king was established and he had become strong, he and all Israel with him abandoned the law of the LORD" (2 Chronicles 12:1).

Rehoboam's story is told in 1 Kings 11:43—14:31 and 2 Chronicles 9:31—13:7. He is also mentioned in Matthew 1:7.

---

leadership from his father, Solomon. Apparently Rehoboam saw only the difficulty of leading the nation, not the opportunities. He mentioned only the harsher aspects of Solomon's rule, and he himself decided to be very harsh towards the people. As you discuss your responsibilities with your children, be sure that you temper words of complaint with words of joy. Otherwise you may sour their attitudes toward the work you do and those you serve.

10:16–19 In trying to have it all, Rehoboam lost almost everything. Motivated by greed and power, he pressed too hard and divided his kingdom. He didn't need more money or power because he had inherited the richest kingdom in the world. He didn't need more control because he was the king. His demands were based on selfishness rather than reason or spiritual discernment. Those who insist on having it all often wind up with little or nothing.

10:16–19 This is the beginning of the divided kingdom. The peaceful united kingdom under Solomon divided into two parts. Ten of the tribes followed Jeroboam and called their nation Israel, or the northern kingdom. The other two tribes, Judah and Benjamin, remained loyal to David's line and accepted Rehoboam's rule. They called their nation Judah, or the southern kingdom.

To your tents, O Israel!
Look after your own house, O David!"

So all the Israelites went home. 17 But as for the Israelites who were living in the towns
of Judah, Rehoboam still ruled over them.
18 King Rehoboam sent out Adoniram,[a][m] who was in charge of forced labour, but
the Israelites stoned him to death. King Rehoboam, however, managed to get into his
chariot and escape to Jerusalem. 19 So Israel has been in rebellion against the house
of David to this day.

11 When Rehoboam arrived in Jerusalem,[a] he mustered the house of Judah and
Benjamin—a hundred and eighty thousand fighting men—to make war against
Israel and to regain the kingdom for Rehoboam.
2 But this word of the LORD came to Shemaiah[b] the man of God: 3 "Say to Rehoboam son of Solomon king of Judah and to all the Israelites in Judah and Benjamin,
4 'This is what the LORD says: Do not go up to fight against your brothers.[c] Go home,
every one of you, for this is my doing.' " So they obeyed the words of the LORD and
turned back from marching against Jeroboam.

Rehoboam Fortifies Judah

5 Rehoboam lived in Jerusalem and built up towns for defence in Judah: 6 Bethlehem,
Etam, Tekoa, 7 Beth Zur, Soco, Adullam, 8 Gath, Mareshah, Ziph, 9 Adoraim, Lachish, Azekah, 10 Zorah, Aijalon and Hebron. These were fortified cities in Judah and
Benjamin. 11 He strengthened their defences and put commanders in them, with
supplies of food, olive oil and wine. 12 He put shields and spears in all the cities, and
made them very strong. So Judah and Benjamin were his.
13 The priests and Levites from all their districts throughout Israel sided with him.
14 The Levites[d] even abandoned their pasture-lands and property,[e] and came to Judah
and Jerusalem because Jeroboam and his sons had rejected them as priests of the LORD.
15 And he appointed[f] his own priests[g] for the high places and for the goat[h] and calf[i]
idols he had made. 16 Those from every tribe of Israel[j] who set their hearts on seeking
the LORD, the God of Israel, followed the Levites to Jerusalem to offer sacrifices to
the LORD, the God of their fathers. 17 They strengthened[k] the kingdom of Judah and
supported Rehoboam son of Solomon for three years, walking in the ways of David
and Solomon during this time.

2. History of apostasy and reform

Rehoboam's Family

18 Rehoboam married Mahalath, who was the daughter of David's son Jerimoth and
of Abihail, the daughter of Jesse's son Eliab. 19 She bore him sons: Jeush, Shemariah
and Zaham. 20 Then he married Maacah[l] daughter of Absalom, who bore him

a *18* Hebrew *Hadoram*, a variant of *Adoniram*

10:18 [m] 1Ki 5:14
11:1 [a] 1Ki 12:21
11:2 [b] 2Ch 12:5-7, 15
11:4 [c] 2Ch 28:8-11
11:14 [d] Nu 35:2-5 [e] 2Ch 13:9
11:15 [f] 1Ki 13:33 [g] 1Ki 12:31 [h] Lev 17:7 [i] 1Ki 12:28; 2Ch 13:8
11:16 [j] 2Ch 15:9
11:17 [k] 2Ch 12:1
11:20 [l] 1Ki 15:2

11:1 Rehoboam's foolishness divided his kingdom, and he tried to reunite it by force. True unity, however, cannot be forced—it must be the free response of willing hearts. If you want the loyalty of employees, children, or anyone else in your charge, win their respect through love instead of trying to gain their submission through force.

11:4 Why would God support this rebellion? It was part of the nation's punishment for turning away from God (1 Kings 11:11). It may also have been God's way of saving Rehoboam's smaller kingdom from defeat. In doing so, God preserved David's line and kept intact his plan for the Messiah to be a descendant of David (see 2 Samuel 7:16). When we see division, especially in a church that splits, we wonder what God would have us do. God desires unity, but while we should always work toward reconciliation, we must recognise that only God knows the future. He may allow a division in order to fulfil his greater purposes.

11:13, 14 Before the nation split, the centre of worship was in Jerusalem, and people flocked there for the three great annual religious festivals. During the rest of the year, other worship services and rituals were conducted in the tribal territories by priests and Levites who lived throughout the land. They offered sacrifices, taught God's laws, and encouraged the people to continue to follow God and avoid pagan influences.

After the nation split, Jeroboam, the new king of Israel, saw these priests and Levites as threats to his new government because they retained loyalty to Jerusalem, now the capital of Judah. So he appointed his own priests, effectively banning the Levites from their duties and forcing them to move to the southern kingdom. Jeroboam's pagan priests encouraged idol worship. With the absence of spiritual leaders, the new northern kingdom was in danger of abandoning God.

11:16 These people obeyed God rather than Jeroboam. By their actions, they preserved their integrity and strengthened the southern kingdom. In the future, most of the people in the northern kingdom would go along with the evil designs of the kings, hoping to

Abijah,[m] Attai, Ziza and Shelomith. 21Rehoboam loved Maacah daughter of Absalom
more than any of his other wives and concubines. In all he had eighteen wives[n] and
sixty concubines, twenty-eight sons and sixty daughters.
22Rehoboam appointed Abijah[o] son of Maacah to be the chief prince among his
brothers, in order to make him king. 23He acted wisely, dispersing some of his sons
throughout the districts of Judah and Benjamin, and to all the fortified cities. He gave
them abundant provisions and took many wives for them.

Shishak Attacks Jerusalem

12 After Rehoboam's position as king was established[a] and he had become
strong,[b] he and all Israel[**a**] with him abandoned the law of the LORD. 2Because
they had been unfaithful[c] to the LORD, Shishak[d] king of Egypt attacked Jerusalem
in the fifth year of King Rehoboam. 3With twelve hundred chariots and sixty thousand
horsemen and the innumerable troops of Libyans, Sukkites and Cushites[**b**][e] that came
with him from Egypt, 4he captured the fortified cities[f] of Judah and came as far as
Jerusalem.
5Then the prophet Shemaiah[g] came to Rehoboam and to the leaders of Judah who
had assembled in Jerusalem for fear of Shishak, and he said to them, "This is what
the LORD says: 'You have abandoned me; therefore I now abandon[h] you to Shishak.' "
6The leaders of Israel and the king humbled themselves and said, "The LORD is
just."[i]
7When the LORD saw that they humbled themselves, this word of the LORD came
to Shemaiah: "Since they have humbled themselves, I will not destroy them but will
soon give them deliverance.[j] My wrath will not be poured out on Jerusalem through
Shishak. 8They will, however, become subject[k] to him, so that they may learn the
difference between serving me and serving the kings of other lands."
9When Shishak king of Egypt attacked Jerusalem, he carried off the treasures of
the temple of the LORD and the treasures of the royal palace. He took everything,
including the gold shields[l] that Solomon had made. 10So King Rehoboam made
bronze shields to replace them and assigned these to the commanders of the guard on
duty at the entrance to the royal palace. 11Whenever the king went to the LORD's
temple, the guards went with him, bearing the shields, and afterwards they returned
them to the guardroom.
12Because Rehoboam humbled himself, the LORD's anger turned from him, and he
was not totally destroyed. Indeed, there was some good[m] in Judah.
13King Rehoboam established himself firmly in Jerusalem and continued as king.
He was forty-one years old when he became king, and he reigned for seventeen years
in Jerusalem, the city the LORD had chosen out of all the tribes of Israel in which to

a *1* That is, Judah, as frequently in 2 Chronicles **b** *3* That is, people from the upper Nile region

11:20 [m]2Ch 13:2
11:21 [n]Dt 17:17
11:22 [o]Dt 21:15-17
12:1 [a]ver 13 [b]2Ch 11:17
12:2 [c]1Ki 14:22-24 [d]1Ki 11:40
12:3 [e]2Ch 16:8; Na 3:9
12:4 [f]2Ch 11:10
12:5 [g]2Ch 11:2 [h]Dt 28:15; 2Ch 15:2
12:6 [i]Ex 9:27; Da 9:14
12:7 [j]1Ki 21:29; Ps 78:38
12:8 [k]Dt 28:48
12:9 [l]2Ch 9:16
12:12 [m]1Ki 14:13; 2Ch 19:3

---

benefit by cooperating. Don't follow their example and rationalise away God's teachings in order to gain earthly reward.

12:1, 2 Here "Israel" refers to Judah, the southern kingdom. During his first three years on the throne, Rehoboam made an attempt to obey God, and as a result Judah prospered. But then, at his peak of popularity and power, he abandoned God. The result was destruction because God allowed Judah to be conquered by Egypt. How could this happen? Often it is more difficult to be a believer in good times than in bad. Tough times push us towards God; but easy times can make us feel self-sufficient and self-satisfied. When everything is going right, guard your faith closely.

12:2 A record of this invasion has been found on an Egyptian stone that says Shishak's army penetrated as far north as the Sea of Galilee, in the northern kingdom. Egypt was not the world power it had once been, and Shishak wanted to restore his nation to its former greatness. He was not strong enough to conquer both Israel and Judah, but he managed to destroy key cities in Judah in an effort to regain control of the trade routes and create dissension among the people.

12:6–8 God eased his judgment when Israel's leaders confessed their sins, humbled themselves, and recognised God's justice in punishing them. It's never too late to repent, even in the midst of punishment. Regardless of what we have done, God is willing to receive us back into fellowship. Are you struggling and alone because sin has broken your fellowship with God? Confession and humility will open the door to receiving God's mercy.

12:8 "Serving the kings of other lands" was the price Judah had to pay for disobeying God. The nation's leaders thought they could succeed in their own strength, but they were wrong. When we rebel against God, we always pay for it. When we leave God out of our lives, we lose more spiritually than we ever gain financially.

12:10, 11 How ironic that the pure gold of Solomon's temple was replaced by cheaper bronze. Rehoboam tried to maintain the trappings and appearance of former glory, but he couldn't measure up. When God is no longer central in our lives, maintaining the appearance of a Christian life becomes superficial. Outer beauty must come from inner strength.

put his Name.[n] His mother's name was Naamah; she was an Ammonite. 14He did
evil because he had not set his heart on seeking the LORD.
15As for the events of Rehoboam's reign, from beginning to end, are they not
written in the records of Shemaiah[o] the prophet and of Iddo the seer that deal with
genealogies? There was continual warfare between Rehoboam and Jeroboam. 16Reho-
boam rested with his fathers and was buried in the City of David. And Abijah[p] his
son succeeded him as king.

Abijah King of Judah

13 In the eighteenth year of the reign of Jeroboam, Abijah became king of Judah,
2and he reigned in Jerusalem for three years. His mother's name was Maacah,[a]
a daughter[b] of Uriel of Gibeah.
There was war between Abijah[a] and Jeroboam.[b] 3Abijah went into battle with a
force of four hundred thousand able fighting men, and Jeroboam drew up a battle line
against him with eight hundred thousand able troops.
4Abijah stood on Mount Zemaraim,[c] in the hill country of Ephraim, and said,
"Jeroboam and all Israel,[d] listen to me! 5Don't you know that the LORD, the God
of Israel, has given the kingship of Israel to David and his descendants for ever[e] by
a covenant of salt?[f] 6Yet Jeroboam son of Nebat, an official of Solomon son of
David, rebelled[g] against his master. 7Some worthless scoundrels[h] gathered around
him and opposed Rehoboam son of Solomon when he was young and indecisive and
not strong enough to resist them.
8"And now you plan to resist the kingdom of the LORD, which is in the hands of
David's descendants. You are indeed a vast army and have with you the golden
calves[i] that Jeroboam made to be your gods. 9But didn't you drive out the priests
of the LORD,[j] the sons of Aaron, and the Levites, and make priests of your own as
the peoples of other lands do? Whoever comes to consecrate himself with a young
bull[k] and seven rams may become a priest of what are not gods.[l]
10"As for us, the LORD is our God, and we have not forsaken him. The priests who
serve the LORD are sons of Aaron, and the Levites assist them. 11Every morning and
evening[m] they present burnt offerings and fragrant incense to the LORD. They set out
the bread on the ceremonially clean table[n] and light the lamps on the gold lampstand
every evening. We are observing the requirements of the LORD our God. But you have
forsaken him. 12God is with us; he is our leader. His priests with their trumpets will
sound the battle cry against you.[o] Men of Israel, do not fight against the LORD,[p]
the God of your fathers, for you will not succeed."
13Now Jeroboam had sent troops round to the rear, so that while he was in front
of Judah the ambush[q] was behind them. 14Judah turned and saw that they were being
attacked at both front and rear. Then they cried out[r] to the LORD. The priests blew
their trumpets 15and the men of Judah raised the battle cry. At the sound of their battle
cry, God routed Jeroboam and all Israel[s] before Abijah and Judah. 16The Israelites
fled before Judah, and God delivered[t] them into their hands. 17Abijah and his men
inflicted heavy losses on them, so that there were five hundred thousand casualties

12:13 [n]Dt 12:5; 2Ch 6:6
12:15 [o]2Ch 9:29; 11:2
12:16 [p]2Ch 11:20
13:2 [a]2Ch 11:20 [b]1Ki 15:6
13:4 [c]Jos 18:22 [d]1Ch 11:1
13:5 [e]2Sa 7:13 [f]Lev 2:13; Nu 18:19
13:6 [g]1Ki 11:26
13:7 [h]Jdg 9:4
13:8 [i]1Ki 12:28; 2Ch 11:15
13:9 [j]2Ch 11:14-15 [k]Ex 29:35-36 [l]Jer 2:11
13:11 [m]Ex 29:39; 2Ch 2:4 [n]Lev 24:5-9
13:12 [o]Nu 10:8-9 [p]Ac 5:39
13:13 [q]Jos 8:9
13:14 [r]2Ch 14:11
13:15 [s]2Ch 14:12
13:16 [t]2Ch 16:8

[a] 2 Most Septuagint manuscripts and Syriac (see also 2 Chron. 11:20 and 1 Kings 15:2); Hebrew *Micaiah*
[b] 2 Or *granddaughter*

12:14 Rehoboam's story is tragic because he "had not set his heart on seeking the LORD". It is dangerous to put off responding to God. God asks us for a firm commitment, and unless we respond by trusting him completely, we will find ourselves alienated from him.

13:1ff 1 Kings 15:3 says Abijah committed many sins, but the Chronicles account has only positive comments about him. For the most part, Abijah was, no doubt, a wicked king. The writer of Chronicles chose to highlight the little good he did in order to show that he was still under God's covenant promise to David. Because of Abijah's fiery speech to Jeroboam (13:4–12), he was spared the immediate consequences of his sin.

13:8 Jeroboam's army was cursed because of the golden calves they carried with them. It was as though they had put sin into a physical form so they could haul it around. Consider carefully the things you cherish. If you value anything more than God, it becomes your golden calf and will one day drag you down. Let go of anything that interferes with your relationship with God.

13:9 Abijah criticised Jeroboam's low standards in appointing priests. Anyone is qualified to represent a god that is worthless. To represent the Lord God Almighty, however, a person must live by God's standards, not man's. Those appointed to positions of responsibility in your church should not be selected merely because they volunteer, are influential, or are highly educated. Instead they should demonstrate sound doctrine, dedication to God, and strong spiritual character (see 2 Timothy 3).

among Israel's able men. 18The men of Israel were subdued on that occasion, and the
men of Judah were victorious because they relied[u] on the LORD, the God of their
fathers.
19Abijah pursued Jeroboam and took from him the towns of Bethel, Jeshanah and
Ephron, with their surrounding villages. 20Jeroboam did not regain power during the
time of Abijah. And the LORD struck him down and he died.
21But Abijah grew in strength. He married fourteen wives and had twenty-two sons
and sixteen daughters.
22The other events of Abijah's reign, what he did and what he said, are written in
the annotations of the prophet Iddo.

14 And Abijah rested with his fathers and was buried in the City of David. Asa
his son succeeded him as king, and in his days the country was at peace for
ten years.

Asa King of Judah

2Asa did what was good and right in the eyes of the LORD his God. 3He removed
the foreign altars and the high places, smashed the sacred stones and cut down the
Asherah poles.[a][a] 4He commanded Judah to seek the LORD, the God of their fathers,
and to obey his laws and commands. 5He removed the high places and incense altars[b]
in every town in Judah, and the kingdom was at peace under him. 6He built up the
fortified cities of Judah, since the land was at peace. No-one was at war with him
during those years, for the LORD gave him rest.[c]
7"Let us build up these towns," he said to Judah, "and put walls round them, with
towers, gates and bars. The land is still ours, because we have sought the LORD our
God; we sought him and he has given us rest on every side." So they built and
prospered.
8Asa had an army of three hundred thousand men from Judah, equipped with large
shields and with spears, and two hundred and eighty thousand from Benjamin, armed
with small shields and with bows. All these were brave fighting men.
9Zerah the Cushite[d] marched out against them with a vast army[b] and three hundred
chariots, and came as far as Mareshah.[e] 10Asa went out to meet him, and they took
up battle positions in the Valley of Zephathah near Mareshah.
11Then Asa called[f] to the LORD his God and said, "LORD, there is no-one like you
to help the powerless against the mighty. Help us, O LORD our God, for we rely[g]

13:18 [u]1Ch 5:20; 2Ch 14:11; Ps 22:5
14:3 [a]Ex 34:13; Dt 7:5; 1Ki 15:12-14
14:5 [b]2Ch 34:4, 7
14:6 [c]1Ch 22:9; 2Ch 15:15
14:9 [d]2Ch 12:3; 16:8 [e]2Ch 11:8
14:11 [f]2Ch 13:14 [g]2Ch 13:18

a *3* That is, symbols of the goddess Asherah; here and elsewhere in 2 Chronicles b *9* Hebrew *with an army of a thousand thousands* or *with an army of thousands upon thousands*

13:18, 19 Although outnumbered by Israel, Judah won this conflict by depending on God's help. Some kings in Judah's history focused on God, but not one Israelite king consistently followed God – all followed Jeroboam's idolatry or served Baal. As a result, Israel experienced God's punishment many years before Judah did.

Judah had an advantage – the temple, with its sacrifices and the loyal priests and prophets, was in the southern kingdom. Many of Judah's kings were good, at least for parts of their reigns. Whenever an idolatrous king reigned, his rule was followed by that of a God-honouring king who reformed religious life. Also, the idolatrous kings usually served for a much shorter time than the good ones. The result was that true faith in God ran stronger and deeper in Judah than in Israel, but it was still not up to God's standards.

14:1–6 Asa's reign was marked by peace because he "did what was good and right in the eyes of the LORD his God". This refrain is often repeated in Chronicles – *obedience* to God leads to *peace* with God and others. In the case of Judah's kings, obedience to God led to national peace, just as God had promised centuries earlier. In our case, obedience may not always bring peace with our enemies, but it will bring peace with God and complete peace in his future kingdom. Obeying God is the first step on the path to peace.

14:3–5 Simply attending worship services is not enough to secure God's peace. Like Asa, we must also actively remove anything that is offensive to God. Becoming more active in church attendance or good deeds will still leave us in turmoil if we have failed to eliminate sinful practices from our lives. We should continually ask God to help us remove any source of temptation from our lives.

14:7 "Rest on every side" means that Judah had peace with all her neighbours. Times of peace are not just for resting. They allow us to prepare for times of trouble. King Asa recognised the period of peace as the right time to build his defences – the moment of attack would be too late. It is also difficult to withstand spiritual attack unless defences are prepared beforehand. Decisions about how to face temptations must be made with cool heads long before we feel the heat of temptation. Build your defences now before temptation strikes.

14:11 If you are facing battles you feel you can't possibly win, don't give up. In the face of vast hordes of enemy soldiers, Asa prayed for God's help, recognising his powerlessness against such a mighty army. The secret of victory is first to admit the futility of unaided human effort and then to trust God to save. His power works best through those who recognise their limitations (2 Corinthians 12:9). It is those who think they can do it all on their own who are in the greatest danger.

on you, and in your name[h] we have come against this vast army. O LORD, you are
our God; do not let man prevail[i] against you."
12 The LORD struck down[j] the Cushites before Asa and Judah. The Cushites fled,
13 and Asa and his army pursued them as far as Gerar.[k] Such a great number of
Cushites fell that they could not recover; they were crushed before the LORD and his
forces. The men of Judah carried off a large amount of plunder. 14 They destroyed all
the villages around Gerar, for the terror[l] of the LORD had fallen upon them. They
plundered all these villages, since there was much booty there. 15 They also attacked
the camps of the herdsmen and carried off droves of sheep and goats and camels. Then
they returned to Jerusalem.

Asa's Reform

15 The Spirit of God came upon[a] Azariah son of Oded. 2 He went out to meet
Asa and said to him, "Listen to me, Asa and all Judah and Benjamin. The LORD
is with you[b] when you are with him.[c] If you seek[d] him, he will be found by you,
but if you forsake him, he will forsake you.[e] 3 For a long time Israel was without the
true God, without a priest to teach[f] and without the law.[g] 4 But in their distress they
turned to the LORD, the God of Israel, and sought him,[h] and he was found by them.
5 In those days it was not safe to travel about,[i] for all the inhabitants of the lands were
in great turmoil. 6 One nation was being crushed by another and one city by another,[j]
because God was troubling them with every kind of distress. 7 But as for you, be
strong[k] and do not give up, for your work will be rewarded."[l]
8 When Asa heard these words and the prophecy of Azariah son of[a] Oded the
prophet, he took courage. He removed the detestable idols from the whole land of
Judah and Benjamin and from the towns he had captured[m] in the hills of Ephraim.
He repaired the altar[n] of the LORD that was in front of the portico of the LORD's
temple.
9 Then he assembled all Judah and Benjamin and the people from Ephraim, Manasseh and Simeon who had settled among them, for large numbers[o] had come over to
him from Israel when they saw that the LORD his God was with him.
10 They assembled at Jerusalem in the third month of the fifteenth year of Asa's
reign. 11 At that time they sacrificed to the LORD seven hundred head of cattle and
seven thousand sheep and goats from the plunder[p] they had brought back. 12 They
entered into a covenant[q] to seek the LORD,[r] the God of their fathers, with all their
heart and soul. 13 All who would not seek the LORD, the God of Israel, were to be put

a *8* Vulgate and Syriac (see also Septuagint and verse 1); Hebrew does not have *Azariah son of.*

14:11 [h] 1Sa 17:45 [i] 1Sa 14:6; Ps 9:19
14:12 [j] 2Ch 13:15
14:13 [k] Ge 10:19
14:14 [l] Ge 35:5; 2Ch 17:10
15:1 [a] Nu 11:25, 26; 24:2; 2Ch 20:14; 24:20
15:2 [b] ver 4, 15; 2Ch 20:17 [c] Jas 4:8 [d] Jer 29:13 [e] 1Ch 28:9; 2Ch 24:20
15:3 [f] Lev 10:11 [g] 2Ch 17:9; La 2:9
15:4 [h] Dt 4:29
15:5 [i] Jdg 5:6
15:6 [j] Mt 24:7
15:7 [k] Jos 1:7, 9 [l] Ps 58:11
15:8 [m] 2Ch 13:19 [n] 2Ch 8:12
15:9 [o] 2Ch 11:16-17
15:11 [p] 2Ch 14:13
15:12 [q] 2Ki 11:17; 2Ch 23:16; 34:31 [r] 1Ch 16:11

ASA'S BATTLES
A huge army from Cush under Zerah advanced towards Mareshah, greatly outnumbering King Asa's army. Asa sent his troops to meet them, and the battle took place in the Valley of Zephathah. Asa prayed to God, and the Cushites were defeated and chased as far as Gerar.

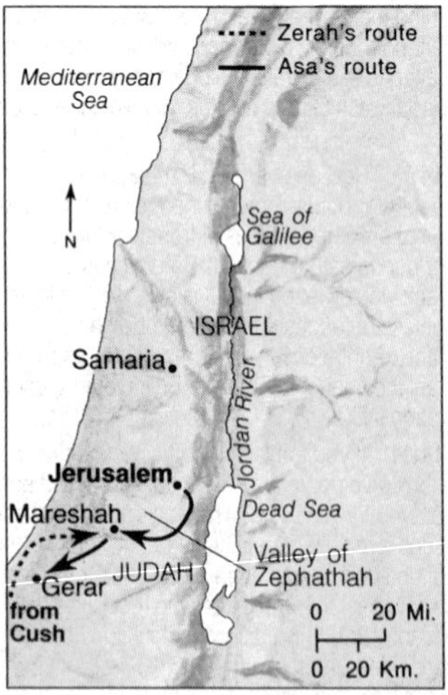

15:1, 2 Asa wisely welcomed people who had a close relationship with God, and he listened to their messages. Azariah gave the armies an important warning and encouraged them to stay close to God. Keep in contact with people who are filled with God's Spirit, and you will learn God's counsel. Spend regular time in discussion and prayer with those who can help explain and apply God's message.

15:3 Azariah said that Israel, the northern kingdom, was "without the true God". Eight kings reigned in Israel during the 41-year rule of Asa in Judah, and all eight were evil. Jeroboam, the first ruler of Israel, began this wicked trend by setting up idols and expelling God's priests (11:13–15). Azariah used Israel's problems as an example of the evil that would come to Judah if they turned away from God as their northern brothers and sisters had.

15:7 Azariah encouraged the men of Judah to keep up the good work, "for your work will be rewarded". This is an inspiration for us too. Recognition and reward are great motivators that have two dimensions: (1) *The temporal dimension.* Living by God's standards may result in acclaim here on earth. (2) *The eternal dimension.* Permanent recognition and reward will be given in the next life. Don't be discouraged if you feel your faith in God is going unrewarded here on earth. The best rewards are not in this life but in the life to come.

15:13 [s]Ex 22:20; Dt 13:9-16 — to death,[s] whether small or great, man or woman. 14They took an oath to the LORD
with loud acclamation, with shouting and with trumpets and horns. 15All Judah
15:15 [t]Dt 4:29 [u]1Ch 22:9; 2Ch 14:7 — rejoiced about the oath because they had sworn it wholeheartedly. They sought God[t]
eagerly, and he was found by them. So the LORD gave them rest[u] on every side.
16King Asa also deposed his grandmother Maacah from her position as queen
15:16 [v]Ex 34:13; 2Ch 14:2-5 — mother, because she had made a repulsive Asherah pole.[v] Asa cut the pole down,
broke it up and burned it in the Kidron Valley. 17Although he did not remove the high

---

ASA

God has never accepted the idea that "the ends justify the means". He is just and perfect in all his ways. People, on the other hand, are far from perfect. That a bond can exist between a loving and merciful Creator and a resisting and rebellious creation is as great a miracle as creation itself! As a king, Asa came very close to being good. He travelled a long way with God before going off course. His sin was not so much deliberate disobedience as choosing the *easy* way rather than the *right* way.

When the odds seemed impossible in the battle with the Cushites, Asa recognised his need to depend on God. Following that victory, God's promise of peace based on obedience spurred the king and people to many years of right living. But Asa was to face a tougher test.

Years of animosity between Asa and Israel's king Baasha took an ugly turn. Baasha, king of the rival northern kingdom, was building a fort that threatened both the peace and the economy of Judah. Asa thought he saw a way out—he bribed King Ben-Hadad of Aram to break his alliance with King Baasha. The plan worked brilliantly, but it wasn't God's way. When Asa was confronted by God's prophet Hanani, he flew into a rage, jailed Hanani, and took out his anger on his people. Asa rejected correction and refused to admit his error to God. His greatest failure was missing what God could have done with his life if he had been willing to be humble. His pride ruined the health of his reign. He stubbornly held on to his failure until his death.

Does this attitude sound familiar? Can you identify failures in your life that you have continued to rationalise rather than admit them to God and accept his forgiveness? The ends do not justify the means. Such a belief leads to sin and failure. The stubborn refusal to admit a failure due to sin can become a big problem because it makes you spend time rationalising rather than learning from your mistakes and moving on.

Strengths and accomplishments:
- Obeyed God during the first ten years of his reign
- Carried out a partially successful effort to abolish idolatry
- Deposed his idolatrous mother Maacah
- Defeated Cush's mighty army

Weaknesses and mistakes:
- Responded with rage when confronted about his sin
- Made alliances with foreign nations and evil people

Lessons from his life:
- God not only reinforces good, he confronts evil
- Efforts to follow God's plans and rules yield positive results
- How well a plan works is no measure of its rightness or approval by God

Vital statistics:
- Where: Jerusalem
- Occupation: King of Judah
- Relatives: Mother: Maacah. Father: Abijah. Son: Jehoshaphat
- Contemporaries: Hanani, Ben-Hadad, Zerah, Azariah, Baasha

Key verse:
"For the eyes of the LORD range throughout the earth to strengthen those whose hearts are fully committed to him. You have done a foolish thing, and from now on you will be at war" (2 Chronicles 16:9).

Asa's story is told in 1 Kings 15:8–24 and 2 Chronicles 14—16. He is also mentioned in Jeremiah 41:9; Matthew 1:7.

15:14, 15 Many people find it difficult to commit themselves to anything. They are tentative, indecisive, and afraid of responsibility. Asa and his people were different—they had clearly declared themselves for God. Their oath of allegiance was punctuated with shouts and trumpet blasts! This decisive and wholehearted commitment pleased God and resulted in peace for the nation. If you want peace, check to see if there is some area where you lack total commitment to God. Peace comes as a by-product of giving your life wholeheartedly to God.

15:16 The Ten Commandments tell us to honour our fathers and mothers, and yet Asa removed his mother from the throne. While honouring parents is God's command, maintaining loyalty to God is an even higher priority. Jesus warned that respect for parents should never keep us from following him (Luke 14:26). If you have unbelieving parents, you must respect and honour them, but you must make devotion to God an even higher priority.

places from Israel, Asa's heart was fully committed ⌞to the LORD⌟ all his life. 18 He
brought into the temple of God the silver and gold and the articles that he and his father
had dedicated.
19 There was no more war until the thirty-fifth year of Asa's reign.

Asa's Last Years

16 In the thirty-sixth year of Asa's reign Baasha[a] king of Israel went up against
Judah and fortified Ramah to prevent anyone from leaving or entering the
territory of Asa king of Judah.
2 Asa then took the silver and gold out of the treasuries of the LORD's temple and
of his own palace and sent it to Ben-Hadad king of Aram, who was ruling in
Damascus. 3 "Let there be a treaty[b] between me and you," he said, "as there was
between my father and your father. See, I am sending you silver and gold. Now break
your treaty with Baasha king of Israel so that he will withdraw from me."
4 Ben-Hadad agreed with King Asa and sent the commanders of his forces against
the towns of Israel. They conquered Ijon, Dan, Abel Maim**a** and all the store cities
of Naphtali. 5 When Baasha heard this, he stopped building Ramah and abandoned his
work. 6 Then King Asa brought all the men of Judah, and they carried away from
Ramah the stones and timber Baasha had been using. With them he built up Geba and
Mizpah.
7 At that time Hanani[c] the seer came to Asa king of Judah and said to him: "Because
you relied on the king of Aram and not on the LORD your God, the army of the king
of Aram has escaped from your hand. 8 Were not the Cushites**b**[d] and Libyans a
mighty army with great numbers of chariots and horsemen**c**? Yet when you relied
on the LORD, he delivered[e] them into your hand. 9 For the eyes[f] of the LORD range
throughout the earth to strengthen those whose hearts are fully committed to him. You
have done a foolish[g] thing, and from now on you will be at war."
10 Asa was angry with the seer because of this; he was so enraged that he put him
in prison. At the same time Asa brutally oppressed some of the people.
11 The events of Asa's reign, from beginning to end, are written in the book of the
kings of Judah and Israel. 12 In the thirty-ninth year of his reign Asa was afflicted with
a disease in his feet. Though his disease was severe, even in his illness he did not
seek help from the LORD,[h] but only from the physicians. 13 Then in the forty-first year
of his reign Asa died and rested with his fathers. 14 They buried him in the tomb that
he had cut out for himself in the City of David. They laid him on a bier covered with
spices and various blended perfumes,[i] and they made a huge fire[j] in his honour.

Jehoshaphat King of Judah

17 Jehoshaphat his son succeeded him as king and strengthened himself against
Israel. 2 He stationed troops in all the fortified cities of Judah and put garrisons
in Judah and in the towns of Ephraim that his father Asa had captured.[a]
3 The LORD was with Jehoshaphat because in his early years he walked in the ways
that his father David[b] had followed. He did not consult the Baals 4 but sought[c] the
God of his father and followed his commands rather than the practices of Israel. 5 The
LORD established the kingdom under his control; and all Judah brought gifts[d] to

a *4* Also known as *Abel Beth Maacah* **b** *8* That is, people from the upper Nile region **c** *8* Or *charioteers*

16:1 [a]Jer 41:9
16:3 [b]2Ch 20:35
16:7 [c]1Ki 16:1
16:8 [d]2Ch 12:3; 14:9 [e]2Ch 13:16
16:9 [f]Pr 15:3; Jer 16:17; Zec 4:10 [g]1Sa 13:13
16:12 [h]Jer 17:5-6
16:14 [i]Ge 50:2; Jn 19:39-40 [j]2Ch 21:19; Jer 34:5
17:2 [a]2Ch 15:8
17:3 [b]1Ki 22:43
17:4 [c]1Ki 12:28; 2Ch 22:9
17:5 [d]1Sa 10:27

16:7–10 Judah and Israel never learned! Although God had delivered them even when they were outnumbered (13:3ff; 14:9ff), they repeatedly sought help from pagan nations rather than from God. That Asa sought help from Aram was evidence of national spiritual decline. With help from God alone, Asa had defeated the Cushites in open battle. But his confidence in God had slipped, and now he sought only a human solution to his problem. When confronted by the prophet Hanani, Asa threw him in prison, revealing the true condition of his heart. It is not sin to use human means to solve our problems, but it is sin to trust them more than God, to think they are better than God's ways, or to leave God completely out of the problem-solving process.

16:12 The criticism of Asa's visit to the physicians was not a general indictment of medicine. Asa's problem was that he completely ignored God's help. The medicine practised at this time was a mixture of superstition and folk remedies. We should certainly avoid any pseudo-medical treatment derived from occult sources. Asa's experience should also encourage us to follow the New Testament practice of receiving prayer for our sickness (James 5:14) as we seek responsible medical help.

16:14 A bier is the stand or platform on which a coffin or corpse is placed.

17:5 [e]2Ch 18:1
17:6 [f]1Ki 8:61 [g]1Ki 15:14; [h]Ex 34:13 [i]2Ch 21:12
17:7 [j]Lev 10:11
17:8 [k]2Ch 19:8

Jehoshaphat, so that he had great wealth and honour.[e] 6His heart was devoted[f] to
the ways of the LORD; furthermore, he removed the high places[g] and the Asherah
poles[h] from Judah.[i]
7In the third year of his reign he sent his officials Ben-Hail, Obadiah, Zechariah,
Nethanel and Micaiah to teach[j] in the towns of Judah. 8With them were certain
Levites[k]—Shemaiah, Nethaniah, Zebadiah, Asahel, Shemiramoth, Jehonathan,
Adonijah, Tobijah and Tob-Adonijah—and the priests Elishama and Jehoram. 9They

---

JEHOSHAPHAT

Are children more likely to learn from their parents' mistakes or to simply repeat them? In the lives of the people in the Bible, we find that the effects of parental examples are powerful and long-lasting. For much of his life, Jehoshaphat seems to have been a son who learned from his father Asa's mistakes and followed his positive actions. But on several occasions, his decisions reveal the negative aspects of his father's example.

When the challenges were obvious, like the need for religious education of the people or the threat of war with a vast army, Jehoshaphat turned to God for guidance and made the right choices. His dependence on God was consistent when the odds were clearly against him. It was in depending on God for the day-to-day plans and actions that Jehoshaphat was weak. He allowed his son to marry Athaliah, the daughter of the wicked Ahab and Jezebel of Israel, who did her best to be as evil as her parents. Jehoshaphat was almost killed when, without asking God, he made an alliance with Ahab. Later, he became involved in an unwise shipbuilding venture with Ahab's son, Ahaziah—a venture that was shipwrecked by God.

God's faithfulness when the issues are clear and the enemy overwhelming is more than enough reason to seek his guidance when the issues are unclear and the enemy unseen. Jehoshaphat knew this, yet he made little use of that knowledge.

We repeat Jehoshaphat's error when we relegate God to the background in the "easy" decisions of life. Then, when things get out of hand, we want him to get us out of the mess we got ourselves into. God wants us to give him not only the major decisions, but also our daily lives—the things we are most often fooled into believing we can control. Perhaps there is nothing major facing you today. Have you paused long enough to give your day to God anyway?

Strengths and accomplishments:
- A bold follower of God, he reminded the people of the early years of his father, Asa
- Carried out a national programme of religious education
- Had many military victories
- Developed an extensive legal structure throughout the kingdom

Weaknesses and mistakes:
- Failed to recognise the long-term results of his decisions
- Did not completely destroy idolatry in the land
- Became entangled with evil King Ahab through alliances
- Allowed his son Jehoram to marry Athaliah, Ahab's daughter
- Became Ahaziah's business partner in an ill-fated shipping venture

Vital statistics:
- Where: Jerusalem
- Occupation: King of Judah
- Relatives: Father: Asa. Mother: Azubah. Son: Jehoram. Daughter-in-law: Athaliah
- Contemporaries: Ahab, Jezebel, Micaiah, Ahaziah, Jehu

Key verses:
"He walked in the ways of his father Asa and did not stray from them; he did what was right in the eyes of the LORD. The high places, however, were not removed, and the people still had not set their hearts on the God of their fathers" (2 Chronicles 20:32, 33).

Jehoshaphat's story is told in 1 Kings 15:24—22:50 and 2 Chronicles 17:1—21:1. He is also mentioned in 2 Kings 3:1–14 and Joel 3:2, 12.

17:7–9 The people of Judah were biblically illiterate. They had never taken time to listen to and discuss God's law and understand how it could change them. Jehoshaphat realised that knowing God's commands was the first step to getting people to live as they should, so he initiated a nationwide religious education programme. He reversed the religious decline that had occurred at the end of Asa's reign by putting God first in the people's minds and instilling in them a sense of commitment and mission. Because of this action, the nation began to follow God. Churches and Christian schools today need solid Christian education programmes. Exposure to good Bible teaching through Sunday school, church, Bible study, and personal and family devotions is essential for living as God intended.

taught throughout Judah, taking with them the Book of the Law[l] of the LORD; they
went round to all the towns of Judah and taught the people.
10 The fear[m] of the LORD fell on all the kingdoms of the lands surrounding Judah,
so that they did not make war with Jehoshaphat. 11 Some Philistines brought Jehoshaphat gifts and silver as tribute, and the Arabs[n] brought him flocks:[o] seven thousand
seven hundred rams and seven thousand seven hundred goats.
12 Jehoshaphat became more and more powerful; he built forts and store cities in
Judah 13 and had large supplies in the towns of Judah. He also kept experienced
fighting men in Jerusalem. 14 Their enrolment[p] by families was as follows:

From Judah, commanders of units of 1,000:
Adnah the commander, with 300,000 fighting men;
15 next, Jehohanan the commander, with 280,000;
16 next, Amasiah son of Zicri, who volunteered[q] himself for the service of the LORD, with 200,000.
17 From Benjamin:[r]
Eliada, a valiant soldier, with 200,000 men armed with bows and shields;
18 next, Jehozabad, with 180,000 men armed for battle.

19 These were the men who served the king, besides those he stationed in the fortified
cities[s] throughout Judah.[t]

Micaiah Prophesies Against Ahab

18 Now Jehoshaphat had great wealth and honour,[a] and he allied[b] himself with
Ahab[c] by marriage. 2 Some years later he went down to visit Ahab in Samaria.
Ahab slaughtered many sheep and cattle for him and the people with him and urged
him to attack Ramoth Gilead. 3 Ahab king of Israel asked Jehoshaphat king of Judah,
"Will you go with me against Ramoth Gilead?"
Jehoshaphat replied, "I am as you are, and my people as your people; we will join
you in the war." 4 But Jehoshaphat also said to the king of Israel, "First seek the counsel
of the LORD."
5 So the king of Israel brought together the prophets—four hundred men—and
asked them, "Shall we go to war against Ramoth Gilead, or shall I refrain?"

17:9 [l]Dt 6:4-9; 28:61
17:10 [m]Ge 35:5; Dt 2:25; 2Ch 14:14
17:11 [n]2Ch 9:14; 26:8 [o]2Ch 21:16
17:14 [p]2Sa 24:2
17:16 [q]Jdg 5:9; 1Ch 29:9
17:17 [r]Nu 1:36
17:19 [s]2Ch 11:10 [t]2Ch 25:5
18:1 [a]2Ch 17:5 [b]2Ch 19:1-3; 22:3 [c]2Ch 21:6

18:1ff Although Jehoshaphat was deeply committed to God, he arranged for his son to marry Athaliah, the daughter of wicked King Ahab of Israel, and then made a military alliance with him. Jehoshaphat's popularity and power made him attractive to the cunning and opportunistic Ahab. This alliance had three devastating consequences: (1) Jehoshaphat incurred God's wrath (19:2); (2) when Jehoshaphat died and Athaliah became queen, she seized the throne and almost destroyed all of David's descendants (22:10–12); (3) Athaliah brought the evil practices of Israel into Judah, which eventually led to the nation's downfall.

When believers in leadership positions become allied with unbelievers, values can be compromised and spiritual awareness dulled. The Bible often warns against teaming with unbelievers (2 Corinthians 6:14). (See the note on 20:37 for more on alliances.)

18:3–8 Evil kings did not like God's prophets bringing messages of doom (18:17; Jeremiah 5:13). Many, therefore, hired prophets who told them only what they wanted to hear (Isaiah 30:10, 11; Jeremiah 14:13–16; 23:16, 21, 30–36). These men were false prophets because they extolled the greatness of the king and predicted victory regardless of the real situation.

18:3–8 Wicked Ahab asked Jehoshaphat to join forces with him in battle (18:2, 3). Before making that commitment, Jehoshaphat rightly sought God's advice. However, when God gave his answer through the prophet Micaiah (18:16), Jehoshaphat ignored it (18:28). It does us no good to seek God's advice if we ignore it when it is given. Real love for God is shown not by merely asking for direction, but by following that direction once it is given.

18:5–16 When you want to please or impress someone, it is

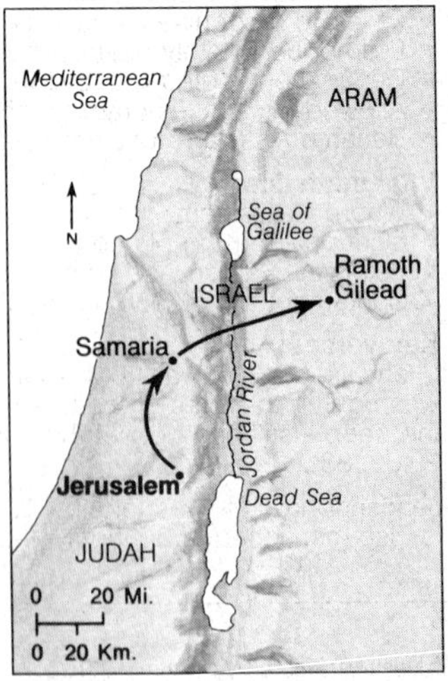

BATTLE WITH ARAM
King Jehoshaphat made an alliance with evil King Ahab of Israel. Together they decided to attack Ramoth Gilead and rout the Arameans who had occupied the city. But Jehoshaphat first wanted to seek the advice of a prophet. Ahab's prophets predicted victory; but Micaiah predicted defeat. The two kings were defeated, and Ahab was killed.

tempting to lie to make yourself look good. Ahab's 400 prophets did just that, telling Ahab only what he wanted to hear. They were then rewarded for making Ahab happy. Micaiah, however, told the truth and got arrested (18:25, 26). Obeying God doesn't always protect us from evil consequences. Obedience may, in fact, pro-

18:11
[d]2Ch 22:5

"Go," they answered, "for God will give it into the king's hand."
6But Jehoshaphat asked, "Is there not a prophet of the LORD here whom we can
enquire of?"
7The king of Israel answered Jehoshaphat, "There is still one man through whom
we can enquire of the LORD, but I hate him because he never prophesies anything good
about me, but always bad. He is Micaiah son of Imlah."
"The king should not say that," Jehoshaphat replied.

18:13
[e]Nu 22:18, 20, 35

8So the king of Israel called one of his officials and said, "Bring Micaiah son of
Imlah at once."
9Dressed in their royal robes, the king of Israel and Jehoshaphat king of Judah were
sitting on their thrones at the threshing-floor by the entrance to the gate of Samaria,
with all the prophets prophesying before them. 10Now Zedekiah son of Kenaanah had
made iron horns, and he declared, "This is what the LORD says: 'With these you will
gore the Arameans until they are destroyed.' "

18:16
[f]1Ch 9:1
[g]Nu 27:17;
Eze 34:5-8

11All the other prophets were prophesying the same thing. "Attack Ramoth Gilead[d]
and be victorious," they said, "for the LORD will give it into the king's hand."
12The messenger who had gone to summon Micaiah said to him, "Look, as one man
the other prophets are predicting success for the king. Let your word agree with theirs,
and speak favourably."
13But Micaiah said, "As surely as the LORD lives, I can tell him only what my God
says."[e]
14When he arrived, the king asked him, "Micaiah, shall we go to war against

18:18
[h]Da 7:9

Ramoth Gilead, or shall I refrain?"
"Attack and be victorious," he answered, "for they will be given into your hand."
15The king said to him, "How many times must I make you swear to tell me nothing
but the truth in the name of the LORD?"
16Then Micaiah answered, "I saw all Israel[f] scattered on the hills like sheep
without a shepherd,[g] and the LORD said, 'These people have no master. Let each one
go home in peace.' "

18:21
[i]1Ch 21:1;
Job 1:6;
Zec 3:1;
Jn 8:44

17The king of Israel said to Jehoshaphat, "Didn't I tell you that he never prophesies
anything good about me, but only bad?"
18Micaiah continued, "Therefore hear the word of the LORD: I saw the LORD sitting
on his throne[h] with all the host of heaven standing on his right and on his left. 19And
the LORD said, 'Who will entice Ahab king of Israel into attacking Ramoth Gilead
and going to his death there?'
"One suggested this, and another that. 20Finally, a spirit came forward, stood before
the LORD and said, 'I will entice him.'
" 'By what means?' the LORD asked.

18:22
[j]Job 12:16;
Isa 19:14;
Eze 14:9

21" 'I will go and be a lying spirit[i] in the mouths of all his prophets,' he said.
" 'You will succeed in enticing him,' said the LORD. 'Go and do it.'
22"So now the LORD has put a lying spirit in the mouths of these prophets of yours.[j]
The LORD has decreed disaster for you."
23Then Zedekiah son of Kenaanah went up and slapped[k] Micaiah in the face.
"Which way did the spirit from[a] the LORD go when he went from me to speak to you?"
he asked.
24Micaiah replied, "You will find out on the day you go to hide in an inner room."

18:23
[k]Jer 20:2;
Mk 14:65;
Ac 23:2

25The king of Israel then ordered, "Take Micaiah and send him back to Amon the
ruler of the city and to Joash the king's son, 26and say, 'This is what the king says:

[a] 23 Or *Spirit of*

---

voke them. But it is better to suffer from man's displeasure than from God's wrath (Matthew 10:28). If you are ridiculed for being honest, remember that this can be a sign that you are indeed doing what is right in God's eyes (Matthew 5:10–12; Romans 8:17, 35–39).

18:22 God used the seductive influence of false prophets to judge Ahab. They were determined to tell Ahab what he wanted to hear. God confirmed their plans to lie as a means to remove Ahab from the throne. These prophets, supported by Ahab, snared him in his sin. Because he listened to them instead of God, he was killed in battle. The lying spirit is a picture of the prophets' entire way of life – telling the king only what he wanted to hear, not what he needed to hear. Leaders will only find trouble if they surround themselves with advisers whose only thought is to please them.

Put this fellow in prison[l] and give him nothing but bread and water until I return safely.' "
27Micaiah declared, "If you ever return safely, the LORD has not spoken through
me." Then he added, "Mark my words, all you people!"

18:26 [l]2Ch 16:10; Heb 11:36

Ahab Killed at Ramoth Gilead

28So the king of Israel and Jehoshaphat king of Judah went up to Ramoth Gilead.
29The king of Israel said to Jehoshaphat, "I will enter the battle in disguise, but you wear your royal robes." So the king of Israel disguised[m] himself and went into battle.
30Now the king of Aram had ordered his chariot commanders, "Do not fight with anyone, small or great, except the king of Israel." 31When the chariot commanders
saw Jehoshaphat, they thought, "This is the king of Israel." So they turned to attack

18:29 [m]1Sa 28:8

BIBLE

The Persecuted	*The Persecutors*	*Why the Persecution*	*Result*	*Reference*
Isaac	The Philistines	God was blessing Isaac, and they envied him	The Philistines could not subdue Isaac, so they made peace with him	Genesis 26:12–33
Moses	Israelites	The Israelites wanted water	God provided water, thanks to Moses' prayer	Exodus 17:1–7
David	Saul and others	David was becoming a powerful leader, threatening Saul's position as king	David endured the persecution and became king	1 Samuel 20—27 Psalms 31:13; 59:1–4
Priests of Nob	Saul and Doeg	Saul and Doeg thought the priests helped David escape	85 priests were killed	1 Samuel 22
Prophets	Jezebel	Jezebel didn't like to have her evil ways pointed out	Many prophets were killed	1 Kings 18:3, 4
Elijah	Ahab and Jezebel	Elijah confronted their sins	Elijah had to flee for his life	1 Kings 18:10—19:2
Micaiah	Ahab	Ahab thought Micaiah was stirring up trouble rather than prophesying from God	Micaiah was thrown into prison	2 Chronicles 18:12–26
Elisha	A king of Israel (Probably Joram)	The king thought Elisha had caused the famine	Elisha ignored the threatened persecution and prophesied the famine's end	2 Kings 6:31
Hanani	Asa	Hanani criticised Asa for trusting in Aram's help more than in God's help	Hanani was thrown into prison	2 Chronicles 16:7–10
Zechariah	Joash	Zechariah confronted the people of Judah for disregarding God's commands	Zechariah was executed	2 Chronicles 24:20–22
Uriah	Jehoiakim	Uriah confronted Jehoiakim about his evil ways	Uriah was butchered to death	Jeremiah 26:20–23
Jeremiah	Zedekiah	Zedekiah thought Jeremiah was a traitor for prophesying Jerusalem's fall	Jeremiah was thrown into prison, then into a muddy cistern	Jeremiah 37:1—38:13
Shadrach, Meshach, Abednego	Nebuchadnezzar	The three men refused to bow down to anyone but God	They were thrown into a fiery furnace, but God miraculously saved them	Daniel 3

18:31 Jehoshaphat's troubles began when he joined forces with the evil King Ahab. Almost at once he found himself the target for soldiers who mistakenly identified him as Ahab. He could have accepted this fate because he deserved it, but instead he cried out to God, who miraculously saved him. When we sin and the inevitable consequences follow, we may be tempted to give up. "I chose to sin," we may think, "it's my fault, and I must accept the consequences." While we may deserve what comes to us, that is no reason to avoid calling on God for urgent help. Had Jehoshaphat given up, he might have died. No matter how greatly you have sinned, you can still call upon God.

18:31 [n]2Ch 13:14
18:34 [o]2Ch 22:5
19:2 [a]1Ki 16:1 [b]2Ch 16:2-9 [c]Ps 139:21-22 [d]2Ch 24:18; 32:25; Ps 7:11
19:3 [e]1Ki 14:13; 2Ch 12:12

him, but Jehoshaphat cried out,[n] and the LORD helped him. God drew them away
from him, 32for when the chariot commanders saw that he was not the king of Israel,
they stopped pursuing him.
33But someone drew his bow at random and hit the king of Israel between the
sections of his armour. The king told the chariot driver, "Wheel around and get me
out of the fighting. I've been wounded." 34All day long the battle raged, and the king
of Israel propped himself up in his chariot facing the Arameans until evening. Then
at sunset he died.[o]

19 When Jehoshaphat king of Judah returned safely to his palace in Jerusalem,
2Jehu[a] the seer, the son of Hanani, went out to meet him and said to the king,
"Should you help the wicked[b] and love[a] those who hate the LORD?[c] Because of
this, the wrath[d] of the LORD is upon you. 3There is, however, some good[e] in you,

[a] 2 Or *and make alliances with*

PERSECUTIONS

The Persecuted	*The Persecutors*	*Why the Persecution*	*Result*	*Reference*
Daniel	National leaders	Daniel was praying	Daniel was thrown into a den of lions, but God miraculously saved him	Daniel 6
Job	Satan	Satan wanted to prove that pain and suffering would make a person abandon God	Job remained faithful to God and was restored	Job 1:8–12; 2:3–7
John the Baptist	Herod and Herodias	John confronted King Herod's adultery	John was beheaded	Matthew 14:3–13
Jesus	Religious leaders	Jesus exposed their sinful motives	Jesus was crucified, but rose again from the dead to show his authority over all evil	Mark 7:1–16; Luke 22:63–24:7
Peter and John	Religious leaders	Peter and John preached that Jesus was God's Son and the only way to salvation	They were thrown into prison, but later released	Acts 4:1–31
Stephen	Religious leaders	Stephen exposed their guilt in crucifying Jesus	Stephen was stoned to death	Acts 6–7
The church	Paul and others	The Christians preached Jesus as the Messiah	Believers faced death, prison, torture, exile	Acts 8:1–3; 9:1–9
James	Herod Agrippa I	To please the Jewish leaders	James was executed	Acts 12:1–2
Peter	Herod Agrippa I	To please the Jewish leaders	Peter was thrown into prison	Acts 12:3–17
Paul	Jews, city officials	Paul preached about Jesus and confronted those who made money by manipulating others	Paul was stoned; thrown into prison	Acts 14:19; 16:16–24
Timothy	Unknown	Unknown	Timothy was thrown into prison	Hebrews 13:23
John	Probably the Romans	John told others about Jesus	John was sent into exile on a remote island	Revelation 1:9

Micaiah, like thousands of believers before and after him, was persecuted for his faith. The chart shows that persecution comes from a variety of people and is given in a variety of ways. Sometimes God protects us from it, sometimes he doesn't. But as long as we remain faithful to God *alone*, we must expect persecution (see also Luke 6:22; 2 Corinthians 6:4–10; 2 Timothy 2:9–12; Revelation 2:10). God also seems to have a special reward for those who endure such persecution (Revelation 6:9–11; 20:4).

18:33 Micaiah prophesied death for Ahab (18:16, 27), so Ahab disguised himself to fool the enemy. Apparently the disguise worked, but that didn't change the prophecy. A random Aramean arrow found a crack in his armour and killed him. God fulfils his will despite the defences people try to erect. God can use anything, even an error, to bring his will to pass. This is good news for God's followers because we can trust him to work his plans and keep his promises no matter how desperate our circumstances are.

for you have rid the land of the Asherah poles[f] and have set your heart on seeking
God.[g]"

Jehoshaphat Appoints Judges

4 Jehoshaphat lived in Jerusalem, and he went out again among the people from
Beersheba to the hill country of Ephraim and turned them back to the LORD, the God
of their fathers. 5 He appointed judges[h] in the land, in each of the fortified cities of
Judah. 6 He told them, "Consider carefully what you do,[i] because you are not judging
for man[j] but for the LORD, who is with you whenever you give a verdict. 7 Now let
the fear of the LORD be upon you. Judge carefully, for with the LORD our God there
is no injustice[k] or partiality[l] or bribery."
8 In Jerusalem also, Jehoshaphat appointed some of the Levites, priests and heads
of Israelite families to administer[m] the law of the LORD and to settle disputes. And
they lived in Jerusalem. 9 He gave them these orders: "You must serve faithfully and
wholeheartedly in the fear of the LORD. 10 In every case that comes before you from
your fellow countrymen who live in the cities—whether bloodshed or other concerns
of the law, commands, decrees or ordinances—you are to warn them not to sin against
the LORD;[n] otherwise his wrath will come on you and your brothers. Do this, and
you will not sin.
11 "Amariah the chief priest will be over you in any matter concerning the LORD,
and Zebadiah son of Ishmael, the leader of the tribe of Judah, will be over you in any
matter concerning the king, and the Levites will serve as officials before you. Act with
courage,[o] and may the LORD be with those who do well."

Jehoshaphat Defeats Moab and Ammon

20 After this, the Moabites and Ammonites with some of the Meunites[a][a] came
to make war on Jehoshaphat.
2 Some men came and told Jehoshaphat, "A vast army is coming against you from
Edom,[b] from the other side of the Sea.[c] It is already in Hazezon Tamar[b]" (that is,
En Gedi). 3 Alarmed, Jehoshaphat resolved to enquire of the LORD, and he proclaimed
a fast[c] for all Judah. 4 The people of Judah came together to seek help from the LORD;
indeed, they came from every town in Judah to seek him.
5 Then Jehoshaphat stood up in the assembly of Judah and Jerusalem at the temple
of the LORD in the front of the new courtyard 6 and said:

"O LORD, God of our fathers,[d] are you not the God who is in heaven?[e] You
rule over all the kingdoms[f] of the nations. Power and might are in your hand,
and no-one can withstand you. 7 O our God, did you not drive out the inhabitants
of this land before your people Israel and give it for ever to the descendants of
Abraham your friend?[g] 8 They have lived in it and have built in it a sanctuary[h]

a *1* Some Septuagint manuscripts; Hebrew *Ammonites* **b** *2* One Hebrew manuscript; most Hebrew manuscripts, Septuagint and Vulgate *Aram* **c** *2* That is, the Dead Sea

19:3 *f* 2Ch 17:6 *g* 2Ch 18:1; 20:35; 25:7; Ezr 7:10
19:5 *h* Ge 47:6; Ex 18:26
19:6 *i* Lev 19:15 *j* Dt 1:17; 16:18-20; 17:8-13
19:7 *k* Ge 18:25; Dt 32:4 *l* Dt 10:17; Job 34:19; Ro 2:11; Col 3:25
19:8 *m* 2Ch 17:8-9
19:10 *n* Dt 17:8-13
19:11 *o* 1Ch 28:20
20:1 *a* 1Ch 4:41
20:2 *b* Ge 14:7
20:3 *c* 1Sa 7:6; 2Ch 19:3; Ezr 8:21; Jer 36:9; Jnh 3:5, 7
20:6 *d* Mt 6:9 *e* Dt 4:39 *f* 1Ch 29:11-12
20:7 *g* Isa 41:8; Jas 2:23
20:8 *h* 2Ch 6:20

19:5–10 Jehoshaphat delegated some of the responsibilities for ruling and judging the people, but he warned his appointees that they were accountable to God for the standards they used to judge others. Jehoshaphat's advice is helpful for all leaders: (1) realise you are judging for God (19:6); (2) be impartial and honest (19:7); (3) be faithful (19:9); (4) act only out of fear of God, not men (19:9). God holds us accountable for the authority we exercise.

19:8 Jehoshaphat appointed priests and Levites to help in administering civil laws. Many years earlier, Moses had chosen men who were capable, faithful, and honest to help him judge disputes among the people (Exodus 18:21, 22). Obviously the best kind of leader is one who always acts with reverence for God. Effective leaders get the job done; faithful leaders make sure the job is done in God's way with God's timing. They are careful to instil God's wisdom in future leaders and build God's values into the entire community.

20:3 When the nation was faced with disaster, Jehoshaphat called upon the people to get serious with God by going without food (fasting) for a designated time. By separating themselves from the daily routine of food preparation and eating, they could devote that extra time to considering their sin and praying to God for help. Hunger pangs would reinforce their feelings of penitence and remind them of their weakness and their dependence upon God. Fasting still can be helpful today as we seek God's will in special situations.

20:6ff Jehoshaphat's prayer had several essential ingredients. (1) He committed the situation to God, acknowledging that only God could save the nation. (2) He sought God's favour because his people were God's people. (3) He acknowledged God's sovereignty over the current situation. (4) He praised God's glory and took comfort in his promises. (5) He professed complete dependence on God, not himself, for deliverance. To be God's kind of leader today, follow Jehoshaphat's example—focus entirely on God's power rather than your own.

for your Name, saying, [9]'If calamity comes upon us, whether the sword of judgment, or plague or famine,[i] we will stand in your presence before this temple that bears your Name and will cry out to you in our distress, and you will hear us and save us.'

[10]"But now here are men from Ammon, Moab and Mount Seir, whose territory you would not allow Israel to invade when they came from Egypt;[j] so they turned away from them and did not destroy them. [11]See how they are repaying us by coming to drive us out of the possession[k] you gave us as an inheritance. [12]O our God, will you not judge them?[l] For we have no power to face this vast army that is attacking us. We do not know what to do, but our eyes are upon you.[m]"

[13]All the men of Judah, with their wives and children and little ones, stood there before the LORD.

[14]Then the Spirit[n] of the LORD came upon Jahaziel son of Zechariah, the son of Benaiah, the son of Jeiel, the son of Mattaniah, a Levite and descendant of Asaph, as he stood in the assembly.

[15]He said: "Listen, King Jehoshaphat and all who live in Judah and Jerusalem! This is what the LORD says to you: 'Do not be afraid or discouraged[o] because of this vast army. For the battle[p] is not yours, but God's. [16]Tomorrow march down against them. They will be climbing up by the Pass of Ziz, and you will find them at the end of the gorge in the Desert of Jeruel. [17]You will not have to fight this battle. Take up your positions; stand firm and see[q] the deliverance the LORD will give you, O Judah and Jerusalem. Do not be afraid; do not be discouraged. Go out to face them tomorrow, and the LORD will be with you.' "

[18]Jehoshaphat bowed[r] with his face to the ground, and all the people of Judah and Jerusalem fell down in worship before the LORD. [19]Then some Levites from the Kohathites and Korahites stood up and praised the LORD, the God of Israel, with a very loud voice.

[20]Early in the morning they left for the Desert of Tekoa. As they set out, Jehoshaphat stood and said, "Listen to me, Judah and people of Jerusalem! Have faith[s] in the LORD your God and you will be upheld; have faith in his prophets and you will be successful.[t]" [21]After consulting the people, Jehoshaphat appointed men to sing to the LORD and to praise him for the splendour of his[d] holiness[u] as they went out at the head of the army, saying:

"Give thanks to the LORD,
for his love endures for ever."[v]

[22]As they began to sing and praise, the LORD set ambushes[w] against the men of Ammon and Moab and Mount Seir who were invading Judah, and they were defeated. [23]The men of Ammon[x] and Moab rose up against the men from Mount Seir[y] to destroy and annihilate them. After they finished slaughtering the men from Seir, they helped to destroy one another.[z]

[24]When the men of Judah came to the place that overlooks the desert and looked towards the vast army, they saw only dead bodies lying on the ground; no-one had escaped. [25]So Jehoshaphat and his men went to carry off their plunder, and they found among them a great amount of equipment and clothing[e] and also articles of value—more than they could take away. There was so much plunder that it took three days to collect it. [26]On the fourth day they assembled in the Valley of Beracah, where

20:9 [i]2Ch 6:28
20:10 [j]Nu 20:14-21; Dt 2:4-6, 9, 18-19
20:11 [k]Ps 83:1-12
20:12 [l]Jdg 11:27 [m]Ps 25:15; 121:1-2
20:14 [n]2Ch 15:1
20:15 [o]2Ch 32:7 [p]Ex 14:13-14; 1Sa 17:47
20:17 [q]Ex 14:13; 2Ch 15:2
20:18 [r]Ex 4:31
20:20 [s]Isa 7:9 [t]Ge 39:3; Pr 16:3
20:21 [u]1Ch 16:29; Ps 29:2 [v]2Ch 5:13; Ps 136:1
20:22 [w]Jdg 7:22; 2Ch 13:13
20:23 [x]Ge 19:38 [y]2Ch 21:8 [z]Jdg 7:22; 1Sa 14:20; Eze 38:21

d *21* Or *him with the splendour of* **e** *25* Some Hebrew manuscripts and Vulgate; most Hebrew manuscripts *corpses*

20:15 As the enemy bore down on Judah, God spoke through Jahaziel: "Do not be afraid or discouraged . . . . For the battle is not yours, but God's." We may not fight an enemy army, but every day we battle temptation, pressure, and "rulers . . . of this dark world" (Ephesians 6:12) who want us to rebel against God. Remember, as believers, we have God's Spirit in us. If we ask for God's help when we face struggles, God will fight for us. And God always triumphs.

How do we let God fight for us? (1) By realising the battle is not ours, but God's; (2) by recognising human limitations and allowing God's strength to work through our fears and weaknesses; (3) by making sure we are pursuing God's interests and not just our own selfish desires; (4) by asking God for help in our daily battles.

they praised the LORD. This is why it is called the Valley of Beracah[f] to this day.
27Then, led by Jehoshaphat, all the men of Judah and Jerusalem returned joyfully
to Jerusalem, for the LORD had given them cause to rejoice over their enemies. 28They
entered Jerusalem and went to the temple of the LORD with harps and lutes and
trumpets.
29The fear[a] of God came upon all the kingdoms of the countries when they heard
how the LORD had fought[b] against the enemies of Israel. 30And the kingdom of
Jehoshaphat was at peace, for his God had given him rest[c] on every side.

The End of Jehoshaphat's Reign

31So Jehoshaphat reigned over Judah. He was thirty-five years old when he became
king of Judah, and he reigned in Jerusalem for twenty-five years. His mother's name
was Azubah daughter of Shilhi. 32He walked in the ways of his father Asa and did
not stray from them; he did what was right in the eyes of the LORD. 33The high
places,[d] however, were not removed, and the people still had not set their hearts on
the God of their fathers.
34The other events of Jehoshaphat's reign, from beginning to end, are written in
the annals of Jehu[e] son of Hanani, which are recorded in the book of the kings of
Israel.
35Later, Jehoshaphat king of Judah made an alliance[f] with Ahaziah king of Israel,
who was guilty of wickedness.[g] 36He agreed with him to construct a fleet of trading
ships.[g] After these were built at Ezion Geber, 37Eliezer son of Dodavahu of Mareshah
prophesied against Jehoshaphat, saying, "Because you have made an alliance with
Ahaziah, the LORD will destroy what you have made." The ships[h] were wrecked and
were not able to set sail to trade.[h]

21 Then Jehoshaphat rested with his fathers and was buried with them in the City
of David. And Jehoram[a] his son succeeded him as king. 2Jehoram's brothers,
the sons of Jehoshaphat, were Azariah, Jehiel, Zechariah, Azariahu, Michael and
Shephatiah. All these were sons of Jehoshaphat king of Israel.[a] 3Their father had
given them many gifts[b] of silver and gold and articles of value, as well as fortified
cities[c] in Judah, but he had given the kingdom to Jehoram because he was his firstborn
son.

Jehoram King of Judah

4When Jehoram established[d] himself firmly over his father's kingdom, he put all
his brothers[e] to the sword along with some of the princes of Israel. 5Jehoram was
thirty-two years old when he became king, and he reigned in Jerusalem for eight years.
6He walked in the ways of the kings of Israel,[f] as the house of Ahab had done, for
he married a daughter of Ahab.[g] He did evil in the eyes of the LORD. 7Nevertheless,

20:29 [a]Ge 35:5; Dt 2:25; 2Ch 14:14; 17:10 [b]Ex 14:14
20:30 [c]1Ch 22:9; 2Ch 14:6-7; 15:15
20:33 [d]2Ch 17:6; 19:3
20:34 [e]1Ki 16:1
20:35 [f]2Ch 16:3 [g]2Ch 19:1-3
20:37 [h]1Ki 9:26; 2Ch 9:21
21:1 [a]1Ch 3:11
21:3 [b]2Ch 11:23 [c]2Ch 11:10
21:4 [d]1Ki 2:12 [e]Jdg 9:5
21:6 [f]1Ki 12:28-30 [g]2Ch 18:1; 22:3

[f] 26 *Beracah* means *praise.* [g] 36 Hebrew *of ships that could go to Tarshish* [h] 37 Hebrew *sail for Tarshish*
[a] 2 That is, Judah, as frequently in 2 Chronicles

20:33 This verse says that Jehoshaphat did not remove the corrupt high places (idol shrines), while 17:6 and 19:3 say he did remove them. Jehoshaphat destroyed most of the Baal and Asherah idols, but he did not succeed in wiping out the corrupt religions practised at the high places.

20:37 Jehoshaphat met disaster when he joined forces with wicked King Ahaziah. He did not learn from his disastrous alliance with Ahab (18:28–34) or from his father's alliance with Aram (16:2–9). The partnership stood on unequal footing because one man served the Lord and the other worshipped idols. We court disaster when we enter into partnership with unbelievers, because our very foundations differ (2 Corinthians 6:14–18). While one serves the Lord, the other does not recognise God's authority. Inevitably, the one who serves God is faced with the temptation to compromise values. When that happens, spiritual disaster results.

Before entering into partnerships, ask: (1) What are my motives? (2) What problems am I avoiding by seeking this partnership? (3) Is this partnership the best solution, or is it only a quick solution to my problem? (4) Have I prayed or asked others to pray for guidance? (5) Are my partner and I really working towards the same goals? (6) Am I willing to settle for less financial gain in order to do what God wants?

21:6 Jehoram, the new king of Judah, married Athaliah, one of the daughters of King Ahab of Israel. She became the mother of Judah's next king, Ahaziah (22:2). Athaliah's mother was Jezebel, the most wicked woman Israel had ever known. Jehoram's marriage to Athaliah was Judah's downfall, for Athaliah brought her mother's wicked influence into Judah, causing the nation to forget God and turn to Baal worship (22:3).

21:7 God promised that a descendant of David would always sit on the throne (2 Samuel 7:8–16). What happened to this promise when the nation was destroyed and carried away? There were two parts to God's promise. (1) In the physical sense, as long as there was an actual throne in Judah, a descendant of David would sit upon it. But this part of the promise depended on the obedience of these kings. When they disobeyed, God was not bound to continue

because of the covenant the LORD had made with David,[h] the LORD was not willing to destroy the house of David.[i] He had promised to maintain a lamp[j] for him and his descendants for ever.

8In the time of Jehoram, Edom[k] rebelled against Judah and set up its own king. 9So Jehoram went there with his officers and all his chariots. The Edomites surrounded him and his chariot commanders, but he rose up and broke through by night. 10To this day Edom has been in rebellion against Judah.

Libnah[l] revolted at the same time, because Jehoram had forsaken the LORD, the God of his fathers. 11He had also built high places on the hills of Judah and had caused the people of Jerusalem to prostitute themselves and had led Judah astray.

12Jehoram received a letter from Elijah[m] the prophet, which said:

"This is what the LORD, the God of your father[n] David, says: 'You have not walked in the ways of your father Jehoshaphat or of Asa[o] king of Judah. 13But you have walked in the ways of the kings of Israel, and you have led Judah and the people of Jerusalem to prostitute themselves, just as the house of Ahab did.[p] You have also murdered your own brothers, members of your father's house, men who were better[q] than you. 14So now the LORD is about to strike your people, your sons, your wives and everything that is yours, with a heavy blow. 15You yourself will be very ill with a lingering disease[r] of the bowels, until the disease causes your bowels to come out.' "

16The LORD aroused against Jehoram the hostility of the Philistines and of the Arabs[s] who lived near the Cushites. 17They attacked Judah, invaded it and carried off all the goods found in the king's palace, together with his sons and wives. Not a son was left to him except Ahaziah,**b** the youngest.[t]

18After all this, the LORD afflicted Jehoram with an incurable disease of the bowels. 19In the course of time, at the end of the second year, his bowels came out because of the disease, and he died in great pain. His people made no fire in his honour,[u] as they had for his fathers.

20Jehoram was thirty-two years old when he became king, and he reigned in Jerusalem for eight years. He passed away, to no-one's regret, and was buried[v] in the City of David, but not in the tombs of the kings.

Ahaziah King of Judah

22 The people[a] of Jerusalem[b] made Ahaziah, Jehoram's youngest son, king in his place, since the raiders,[c] who came with the Arabs into the camp, had killed all the older sons. So Ahaziah son of Jehoram king of Judah began to reign.

2Ahaziah was twenty-two**a** years old when he became king, and he reigned in Jerusalem for one year. His mother's name was Athaliah, a granddaughter of Omri.

3He too walked[d] in the ways of the house of Ahab,[e] for his mother encouraged him in doing wrong. 4He did evil in the eyes of the LORD, as the house of Ahab had done, for after his father's death they became his advisers, to his undoing. 5He also followed their counsel when he went with Joram**b** son of Ahab king of Israel to war against Hazael king of Aram at Ramoth Gilead.[f] The Arameans wounded Joram; 6so

21:7 [h]2Sa 7:13 [i]2Sa 7:15; 2Ch 23:3 [j]2Sa 21:17; 1Ki 11:36
21:8 [k]2Ch 20:22-23
21:10 [l]Nu 33:20
21:12 [m]2Ki 1:16-17 [n]2Ch 17:3-6 [o]2Ch 14:2
21:13 [p]ver 6, 11; 1Ki 16:29-33 [q]ver 4; 1Ki 2:32
21:15 [r]ver 18-19; Nu 12:10
21:16 [s]2Ch 17:10-11; 22:1; 26:7
21:17 [t]2Ki 12:18; 2Ch 22:1; 25:23; Joel 3:5
21:19 [u]2Ch 16:14
21:20 [v]2Ch 24:25; 28:27; 33:20; Jer 22:18, 28
22:1 [a]2Ch 33:25; 36:1 [b]2Ch 23:20-21; 26:1 [c]2Ch 21:16-17
22:3 [d]2Ch 18:1 [e]2Ch 21:6
22:5 [f]2Ch 18:11, 34

b *17* Hebrew *Jehoahaz*, a variant of *Ahaziah* **a** *2* Some Septuagint manuscripts and Syriac (see also 2 Kings 8:26); Hebrew *forty-two* **b** *5* Hebrew *Jehoram*, a variant of *Joram*; also in verses 6 and 7

David's temporal line. (2) In the spiritual sense, this promise was completely fulfilled in the coming of Jesus the Messiah, a descendant of David, who would sit on the throne of David for ever.

21:8–11 Jehoram's reign was marked by sin and cruelty. He married a woman who worshipped idols; he killed his six brothers; he allowed and even promoted idol worship. Yet he was not killed in battle or by treachery – he died by a lingering and painful disease (21:18, 19). Punishment for sin is not always immediate or dramatic. But if we ignore God's laws, we will eventually suffer the consequences of our sin.

21:12 Chronicles mentions Elijah only here. Much more about this great prophet can be found in 1 Kings 17:1 – 2 Kings 2:11. Elijah's Profile is found in 1 Kings 18.

22:4, 5 Although it is wise to seek advice, we must also carefully weigh the advice we receive. Ahaziah had advisers, but they were wicked and led him to ruin. When you seek advice, listen carefully and use God's word to "test everything. Hold on to the good" (1 Thessalonians 5:21).

he returned to Jezreel to recover from the wounds they had inflicted on him at
Ramoth[c] in his battle with Hazael[g] king of Aram.
Then Ahaziah[d] son of Jehoram king of Judah went down to Jezreel to see Joram
son of Ahab because he had been wounded.
7Through Ahaziah's[h] visit to Joram, God brought about Ahaziah's downfall. When
Ahaziah arrived, he went out with Joram to meet Jehu son of Nimshi, whom the LORD
had anointed to destroy the house of Ahab. 8While Jehu was executing judgment on
the house of Ahab,[i] he found the princes of Judah and the sons of Ahaziah's relatives,
who had been attending Ahaziah, and he killed them. 9He then went in search of
Ahaziah, and his men captured him while he was hiding[j] in Samaria. He was brought
to Jehu and put to death. They buried him, for they said, "He was a son of Jehoshaphat,
who sought[k] the LORD with all his heart." So there was no-one in the house of Ahaziah
powerful enough to retain the kingdom.

Athaliah and Joash

10When Athaliah the mother of Ahaziah saw that her son was dead, she proceeded
to destroy the whole royal family of the house of Judah. 11But Jehosheba,[e] the
daughter of King Jehoram, took Joash son of Ahaziah and stole him away from among
the royal princes who were about to be murdered and put him and his nurse in a
bedroom. Because Jehosheba,[e] the daughter of King Jehoram and wife of the priest
Jehoiada, was Ahaziah's sister, she hid the child from Athaliah so that she could not
kill him. 12He remained hidden with them at the temple of God for six years while
Athaliah ruled the land.

23 In the seventh year Jehoiada showed his strength. He made a covenant with
the commanders of units of a hundred: Azariah son of Jeroham, Ishmael son
of Jehohanan, Azariah son of Obed, Maaseiah son of Adaiah, and Elishaphat son of
Zicri. 2They went throughout Judah and gathered the Levites[a] and the heads of
Israelite families from all the towns. When they came to Jerusalem, 3the whole
assembly made a covenant[b] with the king at the temple of God.
Jehoiada said to them, "The king's son shall reign, as the LORD promised concerning the descendants of David.[c] 4Now this is what you are to do: A third of you priests
and Levites who are going on duty on the Sabbath are to keep watch at the doors,
5a third of you at the royal palace and a third at the Foundation Gate, and all the other
men are to be in the courtyards of the temple of the LORD. 6No-one is to enter the
temple of the LORD except the priests and Levites on duty; they may enter because
they are consecrated, but all the other men are to guard[d] what the LORD has assigned
to them.[a] 7The Levites are to station themselves round the king, each man with his
weapons in his hand. Anyone who enters the temple must be put to death. Stay close
to the king wherever he goes."
8The Levites and all the men of Judah did just as Jehoiada the priest ordered.[e] Each
one took his men—those who were going on duty on the Sabbath and those who were
going off duty—for Jehoiada the priest had not released any of the divisions.[f] 9Then
he gave the commanders of units of a hundred the spears and the large and small
shields that had belonged to King David and that were in the temple of God. 10He
stationed all the men, each with his weapon in his hand, round the king—near the
altar and the temple, from the south side to the north side of the temple.
11Jehoiada and his sons brought out the king's son and put the crown on him; they

22:6 [g]1Ki 19:15; 2Ki 8:13-15; 9:15
22:7 [h]2Ki 9:16; 2Ch 10:15
22:8 [i]2Ki 10:13
22:9 [j]Jdg 9:5 [k]2Ch 17:4
23:2 [a]Nu 35:2-5
23:3 [b]2Ki 11:17 [c]2Sa 7:12; 1Ki 2:4; 2Ch 6:16; 7:18; 21:7
23:6 [d]1Ch 23:28-29; Zec 3:7
23:8 [e]2Ki 11:9 [f]1Ch 24:1

[c] 6 Hebrew *Ramah*, a variant of *Ramoth* [d] 6 Some Hebrew manuscripts, Septuagint, Vulgate and Syriac (see also 2 Kings 8:29); most Hebrew manuscripts *Azariah* [e] 11 Hebrew *Jehoshabeath*, a variant of *Jehosheba*
[a] 6 Or *to observe the LORD's command* ⌞*not to enter*⌟

22:7 Jehu's Profile and a more complete story of his reign are found in 2 Kings 9:1–10:36.

23:1 After seven years of rule by Athaliah, the queen mother, Jehoiada the priest finally got up his courage and took action to get rid of the idolatrous ruler. To confront the king (or queen) with the demands of God's law was supposed to be the role of every priest in every generation. Tragically, many priests shied away from this duty, and thus only a few made a difference in the nation.

23:1 Although it could have cost him his life, this priest did what was right, restoring the temple worship and anointing the new king. There are times when we must correct a wrong or speak out for what is right. When such a situation arises, gather up your courage and act.

presented him with a copy[g] of the covenant and proclaimed him king. They anointed
him and shouted, "Long live the king!"
12When Athaliah heard the noise of the people running and cheering the king, she
went to them at the temple of the LORD. 13She looked, and there was the king,[h]
standing by his pillar[i] at the entrance. The officers and the trumpeters were beside
the king, and all the people of the land were rejoicing and blowing trumpets, and
singers with musical instruments were leading the praises. Then Athaliah tore her
robes and shouted, "Treason! Treason!"
14Jehoiada the priest sent out the commanders of units of a hundred, who were in
charge of the troops, and said to them: "Bring her out between the ranks[b] and put
to the sword anyone who follows her." For the priest had said, "Do not put her to
death at the temple of the LORD." 15So they seized her as she reached the entrance
of the Horse Gate[j] on the palace grounds, and there they put her to death.
16Jehoiada then made a covenant[k] that he and the people and the king[c] would be
the LORD's people. 17All the people went to the temple of Baal and tore it down. They
smashed the altars and idols and killed[l] Mattan the priest of Baal in front of the altars.
18Then Jehoiada placed the oversight of the temple of the LORD in the hands of the
priests, who were Levites,[m] to whom David had made assignments in the temple,[n]
to present the burnt offerings of the LORD as written in the Law of Moses, with
rejoicing and singing, as David had ordered. 19He also stationed doorkeepers[o] at the
gates of the LORD's temple so that no-one who was in any way unclean might enter.
20He took with him the commanders of hundreds, the nobles, the rulers of the people
and all the people of the land and brought the king down from the temple of the LORD.
They went into the palace through the Upper Gate[p] and seated the king on the royal
throne, 21and all the people of the land rejoiced. And the city was quiet, because
Athaliah had been slain with the sword.[q]

Joash Repairs the Temple

24 Joash was seven years old when he became king, and he reigned in Jerusalem
for forty years. His mother's name was Zibiah; she was from Beersheba. 2Joash
did what was right in the eyes of the LORD[a] all the years of Jehoiada the priest.
3Jehoiada chose two wives for him, and he had sons and daughters.
4Some time later Joash decided to restore the temple of the LORD. 5He called
together the priests and Levites and said to them, "Go to the towns of Judah and collect
the money[b] due annually from all Israel,[c] to repair the temple of your God. Do it
now." But the Levites[d] did not act at once.
6Therefore the king summoned Jehoiada the chief priest and said to him, "Why
haven't you required the Levites to bring in from Judah and Jerusalem the tax imposed
by Moses the servant of the LORD and by the assembly of Israel for the Tent of the
Testimony?"[e]
7Now the sons of that wicked woman Athaliah had broken into the temple of God
and had used even its sacred objects for the Baals.
8At the king's command, a chest was made and placed outside, at the gate of the
temple of the LORD. 9A proclamation was then issued in Judah and Jerusalem that they
should bring to the LORD the tax that Moses the servant of God had required of Israel

23:11 [g]Ex 25:16; Dt 17:18; 1Sa 10:24
23:13 [h]1Ki 1:41 [i]1Ki 7:15
23:15 [j]Ne 3:28; Jer 31:40
23:16 [k]2Ch 29:10; 34:31; Ne 9:38
23:17 [l]Dt 13:6-9
23:18 [m]1Ch 23:28-32; 2Ch 5:5 [n]1Ch 23:6; 25:6
23:19 [o]1Ch 9:22
23:20 [p]2Ki 15:35
23:21 [q]2Ch 22:1
24:2 [a]2Ch 25:2; 26:5
24:5 [b]Ex 30:16; Ne 10:32-33; Mt 17:24 [c]1Ch 11:1 [d]1Ch 26:20
24:6 [e]Ex 30:12-16; Nu 1:50

b *14* Or *out from the precincts* c *16* Or *covenant between ˻the LORD˼ and the people and the king that they* (see 2 Kings 11:17)

23:12–15 Athaliah thought she had it made. After assuming the throne, she killed all potential heirs to it—so she thought. But even the best plans for evil go sour. When the truth was revealed, she was overthrown immediately. It is much safer to live according to the truth, even if it means not obtaining everything you want.

23:15–17 Athaliah's life ended as her mother Jezebel's had—by execution. Her life of idolatry and treachery was cut short by God's judgment of her sin. By this time Judah had slipped so far away from God that Baal was worshipped in Jerusalem.

23:18 Jehoiada restored the temple procedures and its worship services according to David's original plans, recorded in 1 Chronicles 24; 25.

24:5 The Levites took their time carrying out the king's order, even though he told them not to delay. A tax for keeping the temple in order was not just the king's wish, but God's command (Exodus 30:11–16). The Levites, therefore, were not only disregarding the king, but disregarding God. When it comes to following God's commands, a slow response may be little better than disobedience. Obey God willingly and immediately.

in the desert. 10All the officials and all the people brought their contributions gladly,[f]
dropping them into the chest until it was full. 11Whenever the chest was brought in
by the Levites to the king's officials and they saw that there was a large amount of
money, the royal secretary and the officer of the chief priest would come and empty
the chest and carry it back to its place. They did this regularly and collected a great
amount of money. 12The king and Jehoiada gave it to the men who carried out the
work required for the temple of the LORD. They hired[g] masons and carpenters to
restore the LORD's temple, and also workers in iron and bronze to repair the temple.
13The men in charge of the work were diligent, and the repairs progressed under
them. They rebuilt the temple of God according to its original design and reinforced
it. 14When they had finished, they brought the rest of the money to the king and
Jehoiada, and with it were made articles for the LORD's temple: articles for the service
and for the burnt offerings, and also dishes and other objects of gold and silver. As
long as Jehoiada lived, burnt offerings were presented continually in the temple of the
LORD.
15Now Jehoiada was old and full of years, and he died at the age of a hundred and
thirty. 16He was buried with the kings in the City of David, because of the good he
had done in Israel for God and his temple.

The Wickedness of Joash

17After the death of Jehoiada, the officials of Judah came and paid homage to the
king, and he listened to them. 18They abandoned[h] the temple of the LORD, the God
of their fathers, and worshipped Asherah poles and idols.[i] Because of their guilt,
God's anger[j] came upon Judah and Jerusalem. 19Although the LORD sent prophets
to the people to bring them back to him, and though they testified against them, they
would not listen.[k]
20Then the Spirit[l] of God came upon Zechariah[m] son of Jehoiada the priest. He
stood before the people and said, "This is what God says: 'Why do you disobey the
LORD's commands? You will not prosper.[n] Because you have forsaken the LORD, he
has forsaken[o] you.' "
21But they plotted against him, and by order of the king they stoned[p] him to death[q]
in the courtyard of the LORD's temple.[r] 22King Joash did not remember the kindness
Zechariah's father Jehoiada had shown him but killed his son, who said as he lay
dying, "May the LORD see this and call you to account."[s]
23At the turn of the year,[a] the army of Aram marched against Joash; it invaded
Judah and Jerusalem and killed all the leaders of the people.[t] They sent all the plunder
to their king in Damascus. 24Although the Aramean army had come with only a few
men,[u] the LORD delivered into their hands a much larger army.[v] Because Judah had
forsaken the LORD, the God of their fathers, judgment was executed on Joash. 25When
the Arameans withdrew, they left Joash severely wounded. His officials conspired
against him for murdering the son of Jehoiada the priest, and they killed him in his

a *23* Probably in the spring

24:10 [f]Ex 25:2; 1Ch 29:3, 6, 9
24:12 [g]2Ch 34:11
24:18 [h]ver 4; Jos 24:20; 2Ch 7:19 [i]Ex 34:13; 1Ki 14:23; 2Ch 33:3; Jer 17:2 [j]Jos 22:20; 2Ch 19:2
24:19 [k]Nu 11:29; Jer 7:25; Zec 1:4
24:20 [l]Jdg 3:10; 1Ch 12:18; 2Ch 20:14 [m]Mt 23:35; Lk 11:51 [n]Nu 14:41 [o]Dt 31:17; 2Ch 15:2
24:21 [p]Jos 7:25; Ac 7:58-59 [q]Ne 9:26; Jer 26:21 [r]Jer 20:2; Mt 23:35
24:22 [s]Ge 9:5
24:23 [t]2Ki 12:17-18
24:24 [u]2Ch 14:9; 16:8; 20:2, 12 [v]Lev 26:23-25; Dt 28:25

24:10 Evidently the Levites weren't convinced that the people would want to contribute to the rebuilding of the temple (24:5), but the people were glad to give of what they had for this project. Don't underestimate people's desire to be faithful to God. When challenged to do God's work, they will often respond willingly and generously.

24:18 If everything went so well in Judah when the people worshipped God, why did they turn away from him? Prosperity can be both a blessing and a curse. While it can be a sign of God's blessing to those who follow him, it carries with it the potential for moral and spiritual decline. Prosperous people are tempted to become self-sufficient and proud – to take God for granted. In our prosperity, we must not forget that God is the source of our blessings. See Deuteronomy 6:10–12; 8:11–14.

24:18–20 When King Joash and the nation of Judah abandoned God, God sent Zechariah to call them to repentance. Before dispensing judgment and punishment, God gave them another chance. In the same way, God does not abandon us or lash out in revenge when we sin. Instead, he aggressively pursues us through his word, his Spirit in us, the words of others, and sometimes discipline. He does not intend to destroy us, but to urge us to return to him. When you are moving away from God, remember that he is pursuing you. Stop and listen. Allow him to point out your sin so you can repent and follow him again.

24:19 God sent many prophets to Joash and the people to warn them that they were headed for destruction. Joel may have been one of these prophets. Read the book of Joel for more information about the political and spiritual climate of the times.

24:22 Zechariah asked God to call the people to account for their sins. He was not seeking revenge, but pleading for justice. When we feel like despairing over the wickedness around us, we can rest assured that in the end God will bring complete justice to the earth.

24:25 [w]2Ch 21:20

bed. So he died and was buried[w] in the City of David, but not in the tombs of the
kings.
26Those who conspired against him were Zabad,[b] son of Shimeath an Ammonite
woman, and Jehozabad, son of Shimrith[c][x] a Moabite woman.[y] 27The account of
his sons, the many prophecies about him, and the record of the restoration of the
temple of God are written in the annotations on the book of the kings. And Amaziah
his son succeeded him as king.

24:26 [x]2Ki 12:21 [y]Ru 1:4

[b] 26 A variant of *Jozabad* [c] 26 A variant of *Shomer*

JOASH

All parents want their children to make the right decisions. But to do this, children must first learn to make *their own* decisions. Making bad ones helps them learn to make good ones. If parents make all the decisions for their children, they leave their children without the skills for wise decision making when they are on their own. This problem seriously affected Joash. He had great advice, but he never grew up. He became so dependent on what he was told that his effectiveness was limited to the quality of his advisers.

When Joash was one year old, his grandmother Athaliah decided to slaughter all her descendants in a desperate bid for power. Joash was the only survivor, rescued and hidden by his aunt and uncle, Jehosheba and Jehoiada. Jehoiada's work as a priest made it possible to keep Joash hidden in the temple for six years. At that point, Jehoiada arranged for the overthrow of Athaliah and the crowning of Joash. For many years following, Jehoiada made most of the kingdom's decisions for Joash. When the old priest died, he was buried in the royal cemetery as a tribute to his role.

But after Jehoiada's death, Joash didn't know what to do. He listened to counsel that carried him into evil. Within a short time he even ordered the death of Jehoiada's son Zechariah. After a few months, Joash's army had been soundly defeated by the Arameans. Jerusalem was saved only because Joash stripped the temple of its treasures as a bribe. Finally, the king's own officials assassinated him. In contrast to Jehoiada, Joash was not buried among the kings; he is not even listed in Jesus' genealogy in the New Testament.

As dependent as Joash was on Jehoiada, there is little evidence that he ever established a real dependence on the God Jehoiada obeyed. Like many children, Joash's knowledge of God was secondhand. It was a start, but the king needed his own relationship with God that would outlast and overrule the changes in the advice he received.

It would be easy to criticise Joash's failure were it not for the fact that we often fall into the same traps. How often have we acted on poor advice without considering God's word?

Strengths and accomplishments:
- Carried out extensive repairs on the temple
- Was faithful to God as long as Jehoiada lived

Weaknesses and mistakes:
- Allowed idolatry to continue among his people
- Used the temple treasures to bribe King Hazael of Aram
- Killed Jehoiada's son Zechariah
- Allowed his advisers to lead the people away from God

Lessons from his life:
- A good and hopeful start can be ruined by an evil end
- Even the best counsel is ineffective if it does not help us to make wise decisions
- As helpful or hurtful as others may be, we are individually responsible for what we do

Vital statistics:
- Where: Jerusalem
- Occupation: King of Judah
- Relatives: Father: Ahaziah. Mother: Zibiah. Grandmother: Athaliah. Aunt: Jehosheba. Uncle: Jehoiada. Son: Amaziah. Cousin: Zechariah
- Contemporaries: Jehu, Hazael

Key verses:
"After the death of Jehoiada, the officials of Judah came and paid homage to the king, and he listened to them. They abandoned the temple of the LORD, the God of their fathers, and worshipped Asherah poles and idols. Because of their guilt, God's anger came upon Judah and Jerusalem" (2 Chronicles 24:17, 18).

Joash's story is told in 2 Kings 11:1—14:23 and 2 Chronicles 22:11—25:25.

Amaziah King of Judah

25 Amaziah was twenty-five years old when he became king, and he reigned in
Jerusalem for twenty-nine years. His mother's name was Jehoaddin;[a] she was
from Jerusalem. 2He did what was right in the eyes of the LORD, but not wholeheartedly.[a] 3After the kingdom was firmly in his control, he executed the officials
who had murdered his father the king. 4Yet he did not put their sons to death, but
acted in accordance with what is written in the Law, in the Book of Moses,[b] where
the LORD commanded: "Fathers shall not be put to death for their children, nor children
put to death for their fathers; each is to die for his own sins."[b][c]
5Amaziah called the people of Judah together and assigned them according to their
families to commanders of thousands and commanders of hundreds for all Judah and
Benjamin. He then mustered[d] those twenty years old[e] or more and found that there
were three hundred thousand men ready for military service,[f] able to handle the spear
and shield. 6He also hired a hundred thousand fighting men from Israel for a hundred
talents[c] of silver.
7But a man of God came to him and said, "O king, these troops from Israel[g] must
not march with you, for the LORD is not with Israel—not with any of the people of
Ephraim. 8Even if you go and fight courageously in battle, God will overthrow you
before the enemy, for God has the power to help or to overthrow."[h]
9Amaziah asked the man of God, "But what about the hundred talents I paid for
these Israelite troops?"
The man of God replied, "The LORD can give you much more than that."[i]
10So Amaziah dismissed the troops who had come to him from Ephraim and sent
them home. They were furious with Judah and left for home in a great rage.[j]
11Amaziah then marshalled his strength and led his army to the Valley of Salt, where
he killed ten thousand men of Seir. 12The army of Judah also captured ten thousand
men alive, took them to the top of a cliff and threw them down so that all were dashed
to pieces.[k]
13Meanwhile the troops that Amaziah had sent back and had not allowed to take
part in the war raided Judean towns from Samaria to Beth Horon. They killed three
thousand people and carried off great quantities of plunder.
14When Amaziah returned from slaughtering the Edomites, he brought back the
gods of the people of Seir. He set them up as his own gods,[l] bowed down to them
and burned sacrifices to them. 15The anger of the LORD burned against Amaziah, and
he sent a prophet to him, who said, "Why do you consult this people's gods, which
could not save[m] their own people from your hand?"
16While he was still speaking, the king said to him, "Have we appointed you an
adviser to the king? Stop! Why be struck down?"
So the prophet stopped but said, "I know that God has determined to destroy you,
because you have done this and have not listened to my counsel."
17After Amaziah king of Judah consulted his advisers, he sent this challenge to

a *1* Hebrew *Jehoaddan*, a variant of *Jehoaddin* b *4* Deut. 24:16 c *6* That is, about 3 1/3 tons (about 3.4 metric tons); also in verse 9

25:2 [a]ver 14; 1Ki 8:61; 2Ch 24:2
25:4 [b]Dt 28:61 [c]Nu 26:11; Dt 24:16
25:5 [d]2Sa 24:2 [e]Ex 30:14 [f]Nu 1:3; 1Ch 21:1; 2Ch 17:14-19
25:7 [g]2Ch 16:2-9; 19:1-3
25:8 [h]2Ch 14:11; 20:6
25:9 [i]Dt 8:18; Pr 10:22
25:10 [j]ver 13
25:12 [k]Ps 141:6; Ob 1:3
25:14 [l]Ex 20:3; 2Ch 28:23; Isa 44:15
25:15 [m]Ps 96:5; Isa 36:20

25:2 Amaziah did what was right on the outside, but inside he often resented what he had to do. His obedience was at best half-hearted. When the prophet promised God's deliverance, Amaziah first complained about the money that had been lost (25:9). And he valued military success more than God's will. We must search our own hearts and root out any resistance to obeying God. Grudging compliance is not true obedience.

25:9, 10 Amaziah made a financial agreement with Israelite soldiers, offering to pay them to fight for him (25:6). But before they could go to battle, Amaziah sent them home with their pay because of the prophet's warning. Although it cost him plenty, he wisely realised that the money was not worth the ruin the alliance could cause. How would you have reacted? Money must never stand in the way of making right decisions. The Lord's favour is priceless, worth more than any amount of money.

25:14 After the victory, Amaziah returned and sacrificed to idols. We are very susceptible to sin after great victories. It is then that we feel confident, relaxed, and ready to celebrate. If, in that excitement, we let our defences down, Satan can attack with all sorts of temptations. When you win, watch out. After the mountain peaks come the valleys.

25:15 Amaziah made a foolish mistake by worshipping the gods of the nation he had just conquered. Impressed by the accomplishments of the Edomites, Amaziah worshipped their idols! How foolish to serve the gods of a defeated enemy. We make the same mistake as Amaziah when we run after money, power, or recognition. By recognising the emptiness of these worldly pursuits, we can free ourselves from the desire to follow them.

Jehoash[d] son of Jehoahaz, the son of Jehu, king of Israel: "Come, meet me face to
face."
18But Jehoash king of Israel replied to Amaziah king of Judah, "A thistle[n] in
Lebanon sent a message to a cedar in Lebanon, 'Give your daughter to my son in
marriage.' Then a wild beast in Lebanon came along and trampled the thistle underfoot. 19You say to yourself that you have defeated Edom, and now you are arrogant
and proud. But stay at home! Why ask for trouble and cause your own downfall and
that of Judah also?"
20Amaziah, however, would not listen, for God so worked that he might hand them
over to ⌞Jehoash⌟, because they sought the gods of Edom.[o] 21So Jehoash king of Israel
attacked. He and Amaziah king of Judah faced each other at Beth Shemesh in Judah.
22Judah was routed by Israel, and every man fled to his home. 23Jehoash king of Israel
captured Amaziah king of Judah, the son of Joash, the son of Ahaziah,[e] at Beth
Shemesh. Then Jehoash brought him to Jerusalem and broke down the wall of
Jerusalem from the Ephraim Gate[p] to the Corner Gate[q]—a section about six hundred
feet[f] long. 24He took all the gold and silver and all the articles found in the temple
of God that had been in the care of Obed-Edom,[r] together with the palace treasures
and the hostages, and returned to Samaria.
25Amaziah son of Joash king of Judah lived for fifteen years after the death of
Jehoash son of Jehoahaz king of Israel. 26As for the other events of Amaziah's reign,
from beginning to end, are they not written in the book of the kings of Judah and Israel?
27From the time that Amaziah turned away from following the LORD, they conspired
against him in Jerusalem and he fled to Lachish[s], but they sent men after him to
Lachish and killed him there. 28He was brought back by horse and was buried with
his fathers in the City of Judah.

Uzziah King of Judah

26 Then all the people of Judah[a] took Uzziah,[a] who was sixteen years old, and
made him king in place of his father Amaziah. 2He was the one who rebuilt
Elath and restored it to Judah after Amaziah rested with his fathers.
3Uzziah was sixteen years old when he became king, and he reigned in Jerusalem
for fifty-two years. His mother's name was Jecoliah; she was from Jerusalem. 4He
did what was right in the eyes of the LORD, just as his father Amaziah had done. 5He
sought God during the days of Zechariah, who instructed him in the fear[b] of God.[b]
As long as he sought the LORD, God gave him success.[c]
6He went to war against the Philistines[d] and broke down the walls of Gath, Jabneh
and Ashdod.[e] He then rebuilt towns near Ashdod and elsewhere among the Philistines. 7God helped him against the Philistines and against the Arabs[f] who lived in
Gur Baal and against the Meunites.[g] 8The Ammonites[h] brought tribute to Uzziah,
and his fame spread as far as the border of Egypt, because he had become very
powerful.
9Uzziah built towers in Jerusalem at the Corner Gate,[i] at the Valley Gate[j] and
at the angle of the wall, and he fortified them. 10He also built towers in the desert
and dug many cisterns, because he had much livestock in the foothills and in the plain.
He had people working his fields and vineyards in the hills and in the fertile lands,
for he loved the soil.
11Uzziah had a well-trained army, ready to go out by divisions according to their
numbers as mustered by Jeiel the secretary and Maaseiah the officer under the
direction of Hananiah, one of the royal officials. 12The total number of family leaders
over the fighting men was 2,600. 13Under their command was an army of 307,500
men trained for war, a powerful force to support the king against his enemies. 14Uzziah

25:18 [n] Jdg 9:8-15
25:20 [o] 1Ki 12:15; 2Ch 10:15; 22:7
25:23 [p] 2Ki 14:13; Ne 8:16; 12:39 [q] 2Ch 26:9; Jer 31:38
25:24 [r] 1Ch 26:15
25:27 [s] Jos 10:3
26:1 [a] 2Ch 22:1
26:5 [b] 2Ch 15:2; 24:2; Da 1:17 [c] 2Ch 27:6
26:6 [d] Isa 2:6; 11:14; 14:29; Jer 25:20 [e] Am 1:8; 3:9
26:7 [f] 2Ch 21:16 [g] 2Ch 20:1
26:8 [h] Ge 19:38; 2Ch 17:11
26:9 [i] 2Ki 14:13; 2Ch 25:23 [j] Ne 2:13; 3:13

d *17* Hebrew *Joash*, a variant of *Jehoash*; also in verses 18, 21, 23 and 25 **e** *23* Hebrew *Jehoahaz*, a variant of *Ahaziah* **f** *23* Hebrew *four hundred cubits* (about 180 metres) **a** *1* Also called *Azariah* **b** *5* Many Hebrew manuscripts, Septuagint and Syriac; other Hebrew manuscripts *vision*

25:18 In this parable, Judah is the thistle and Israel's army is the cedar. Ahaziah was proud after defeating Edom. He wanted to defeat Israel, but Jehoash warned him not to attack. Ahaziah had more ambition than ability, and he paid for it when he was soundly defeated. Don't let ambition and pride into your life, for they will cause you to forget God.

provided shields, spears, helmets, coats of armour, bows and slingstones for the entire
army.[k] 15In Jerusalem he made machines designed by skilful men for use on the
towers and on the corner defences to shoot arrows and hurl large stones. His fame
spread far and wide, for he was greatly helped until he became powerful.
16But after Uzziah became powerful, his pride[l] led to his downfall.[m] He was
unfaithful[n] to the LORD his God, and entered the temple of the LORD to burn incense[o]
on the altar of incense. 17Azariah[p] the priest with eighty other courageous priests of
the LORD followed him in. 18They confronted him and said, "It is not right for you,
Uzziah, to burn incense to the LORD. That is for the priests,[q] the descendants[r] of
Aaron,[s] who have been consecrated to burn incense.[t] Leave the sanctuary, for you
have been unfaithful; and you will not be honoured by the LORD God."
19Uzziah, who had a censer in his hand ready to burn incense, became angry. While
he was raging at the priests in their presence before the incense altar in the LORD's
temple, leprosy**c**[u] broke out on his forehead. 20When Azariah the chief priest and
all the other priests looked at him, they saw that he had leprosy on his forehead, so
they hurried him out. Indeed, he himself was eager to leave, because the LORD had
afflicted him.
21King Uzziah had leprosy until the day he died. He lived in a separate house**d**[v]
—leprous, and excluded from the temple of the LORD. Jotham his son had charge of
the palace and governed the people of the land.
22The other events of Uzziah's reign, from beginning to end, are recorded by the
prophet Isaiah[w] son of Amoz. 23Uzziah[x] rested with his fathers and was buried near
them in a field for burial that belonged to the kings, for people said, "He had leprosy."
And Jotham his son succeeded him as king.[y]

Jotham King of Judah

27 Jotham[a] was twenty-five years old when he became king, and he reigned in
Jerusalem for sixteen years. His mother's name was Jerusha daughter of Zadok.
2He did what was right in the eyes of the LORD, just as his father Uzziah had done,
but unlike him he did not enter the temple of the LORD. The people, however,
continued their corrupt practices. 3Jotham rebuilt the Upper Gate of the temple of the
LORD and did extensive work on the wall at the hill of Ophel.[b] 4He built towns in
the Judean hills and forts and towers in the wooded areas.
5Jotham made war on the king of the Ammonites[c] and conquered them. That year
the Ammonites paid him a hundred talents**a** of silver, ten thousand cors**b** of wheat
and ten thousand cors of barley. The Ammonites brought him the same amount also
in the second and third years.
6Jotham grew powerful[d] because he walked steadfastly before the LORD his God.
7The other events in Jotham's reign, including all his wars and the other things he
did, are written in the book of the kings of Israel and Judah. 8He was twenty-five years

c *19* The Hebrew word was used for various diseases affecting the skin—not necessarily leprosy; also in verses 20, 21 and 23. **d** *21* Or *in a house where he was relieved of responsibilities* **a** *5* That is, about 3 1/3 tons (about 3.4 metric tons) **b** *5* That is, probably about 60,500 bushels (about 2,200 kilolitres)

26:14 [k]Jer 46:4
26:16 [l]2Ki 14:10 [m]Dt 32:15; 2Ch 25:19 [n]1Ch 5:25 [o]2Ki 16:12
26:17 [p]1Ki 4:2; 1Ch 6:10
26:18 [q]Nu 16:39 [r]Nu 18:1-7 [s]Ex 30:7 [t]1Ch 6:49
26:19 [u]Nu 12:10; 2Ki 5:25-27
26:21 [v]Ex 4:6; Lev 13:46; 14:8; Nu 5:2; 19:12
26:22 [w]2Ki 15:1; Isa 1:1; 6:1
26:23 [x]Isa 1:1; 6:1 [y]2Ki 14:21; 15:7; Am 1:1
27:1 [a]2Ki 15:5, 32; 1Ch 3:12
27:3 [b]2Ch 33:14; Ne 3:26
27:5 [c]Ge 19:38
27:6 [d]2Ch 26:5

26:15 These machines were similar to the catapults later used by the Romans and were capable of slinging stones or arrows a great distance.

26:16 After God gave Uzziah great prosperity and power, he became proud and corrupt. It is true that "pride goes before destruction" (Proverbs 16:18). If God has given you wealth, influence, popularity, and power, be thankful, but be careful. God hates pride. While it is normal to feel elation when we accomplish something, it is wrong to be disdainful of God or to look down on others. Check your attitudes and remember to give God the credit for what you have. Use your gifts in ways that please him.

26:17–21 When people have power, they often think they can live above the law. But even rulers are subject to God, as Uzziah discovered. No matter what your position in society, God expects you to honour, worship, and obey him.

26:21 For much of his life, Uzziah "did what was right in the eyes of the LORD" (26:4). But Uzziah turned away from God, and he was struck with leprosy and remained leprous until his death. He is remembered more for his arrogant act and subsequent punishment than for his great reforms. God requires lifelong obedience. Spurts of obedience are not enough. Only "he who stands firm to the end" will be rewarded (Mark 13:13). Be remembered for your consistent faith; otherwise you, too, may become more famous for your downfall than for your success.

26:23 This was the year that God called Isaiah to be a prophet (Isaiah 6:1).

27:2 Jotham was generally a good king (27:6), but his people became corrupt. Those you lead will not always follow your example, but that should not affect the way you live for God. This sinfulness of Jotham's kingdom is vividly portrayed in Isaiah 1–5.

27:5 The tribute he received amounted to 3 3/4 tons of silver and 62,000 bushels each of wheat and barley.

old when he became king, and he reigned in Jerusalem for sixteen years. 9Jotham
rested with his fathers and was buried in the City of David. And Ahaz his son
succeeded him as king.

Ahaz King of Judah

28 Ahaz[a] was twenty years old when he became king, and he reigned in Jerusalem for sixteen years. Unlike David his father, he did not do what was right
in the eyes of the LORD. 2He walked in the ways of the kings of Israel and also made
cast idols[b] for worshipping the Baals. 3He burned sacrifices in the Valley of Ben
Hinnom[c] and sacrificed his sons[d] in the fire, following the detestable[e] ways of the
nations that the LORD had driven out before the Israelites. 4He offered sacrifices and
burned incense at the high places, on the hilltops and under every spreading tree.
5Therefore the LORD his God handed him over to the king of Aram.[f] The Arameans
defeated him and took many of his people as prisoners and brought them to Damascus.

28:1 [a]1Ch 3:13; Isa 1:1
28:2 [b]Ex 34:17; 2Ch 22:3
28:3 [c]Jos 15:8; 2Ki 23:10 [d]Lev 18:21; 2Ki 3:27; 2Ch 33:6; Eze 20:26 [e]Dt 18:9; 2Ch 33:2
28:5 [f]Isa 7:1

UZZIAH

We are never closer to failure than during our greatest successes. If we fail to recognise God's part in our achievements, they are no better than failures. Uzziah (also called Azariah) was a remarkably successful king. His achievements brought him fame. He was successful in war and peace, in planning and execution, in building and planting.

Uzziah overestimated his own importance in bringing about the great achievements he experienced. He did so many things well that a consuming pride gradually invaded his life like the leprous disease that finally destroyed his body. In trying to act like a priest, he took on a role that God did not mean him to have. He had forgotten not only how much God had given him, but also that God had certain roles for others that he needed to respect.

Uzziah's pride was rooted in his lack of thankfulness. We have no accounts of this king ever showing appreciation to God for the marvellous gifts he received. Our accomplishments may not compare with Uzziah's, but we still owe a debt of thanksgiving to God for our very lives. If God is not getting the credit for your successes, shouldn't you start looking at your life differently?

Strengths and accomplishments:
- Pleased God during his early years as king
- Successful warrior and city builder
- Skilful in organising and delegating
- Reigned for 52 years

Weaknesses and mistakes:
- Developed a proud attitude due to his great success
- Tried to perform the priests' duties, in direct disobedience to God
- Failed to remove many of the symbols of idolatry in the land

Lessons from his life:
- Lack of thankfulness to God can lead to pride
- Even successful people must acknowledge the role God has for others in their lives

Vital statistics:
- Where: Jerusalem
- Occupation: King of Judah
- Relatives: Father: Amaziah. Mother: Jecoliah. Son: Jotham
- Contemporaries: Isaiah, Amos, Hosea, Jeroboam, Zechariah, Azariah

Key verses:
"In Jerusalem he made machines designed by skilful men for use on the towers and on the corner defences to shoot arrows and hurl large stones. His fame spread far and wide, for he was greatly helped until he became powerful. But after Uzziah became powerful, his pride led to his downfall. He was unfaithful to the LORD his God, and entered the temple of the LORD to burn incense on the altar of incense" (2 Chronicles 26:15, 16).

Uzziah's story is told in 2 Kings 15:1–7 (where he is called Azariah), and in 2 Chronicles 26:1–23. He is also mentioned in Isaiah 1:1; 6:1; 7:1; Hosea 1:1; Amos 1:1; Zechariah 14:5.

28:3 Imagine the monstrous evil of a religion that offers young children as sacrifices. God allowed the nation to be conquered in response to Ahaz's evil practices. Even today the practice hasn't abated. The sacrifice of children to the harsh gods of convenience, economy, and whim continues in sterile medical institutions in numbers that would astound the wicked Ahaz. If we are to allow children to come to Christ (Matthew 19:14), we must first allow them to come into the world.

He was also given into the hands of the king of Israel, who inflicted heavy casualties
on him. 6In one day Pekah[g] son of Remaliah killed a hundred and twenty thousand
soldiers in Judah[h]—because Judah had forsaken the LORD, the God of their fathers.
7Zicri, an Ephraimite warrior, killed Maaseiah the king's son, Azrikam the officer in
charge of the palace, and Elkanah, second to the king. 8The Israelites took captive
from their kinsmen[i] two hundred thousand wives, sons and daughters. They also took
a great deal of plunder, which they carried back to Samaria.[j]
9But a prophet of the LORD named Oded was there, and he went out to meet the
army when it returned to Samaria. He said to them, "Because the LORD, the God of
your fathers, was angry[k] with Judah, he gave them into your hand. But you have
slaughtered them in a rage that reaches to heaven.[l] 10And now you intend to make
the men and women of Judah and Jerusalem your slaves.[m] But aren't you also guilty
of sins against the LORD your God? 11Now listen to me! Send back your fellow
countrymen that you have taken as prisoners, for the LORD's fierce anger rests on
you.[n]"
12Then some of the leaders in Ephraim—Azariah son of Jehohanan, Berekiah son
of Meshillemoth, Jehizkiah son of Shallum, and Amasa son of Hadlai—confronted
those who were arriving from the war. 13"You must not bring those prisoners here,"
they said, "or we will be guilty before the LORD. Do you intend to add to our sin and
guilt? For our guilt is already great, and his fierce anger rests on Israel."
14So the soldiers gave up the prisoners and plunder in the presence of the officials
and all the assembly. 15The men designated by name took the prisoners, and from the
plunder they clothed all who were naked. They provided them with clothes and
sandals, food and drink,[o] and healing balm. All those who were weak they put on
donkeys. So they took them back to their fellow countrymen at Jericho, the City of
Palms,[p] and returned to Samaria.
16At that time King Ahaz sent to the king[a] of Assyria[q] for help. 17The Edomites[r]
had again come and attacked Judah and carried away prisoners,[s] 18while the Philistines[t] had raided towns in the foothills and in the Negev of Judah. They captured
and occupied Beth Shemesh, Aijalon[u] and Gederoth, as well as Soco, Timnah and
Gimzo, with their surrounding villages. 19The LORD had humbled Judah because of
Ahaz king of Israel,[b] for he had promoted wickedness in Judah and had been most
unfaithful[v] to the LORD. 20Tiglath-Pileser[c][w] king of Assyria came to him, but gave
him trouble instead of help.[x] 21Ahaz took some of the things from the temple of the
LORD and from the royal palace and from the princes and presented them to the king
of Assyria, but that did not help him.
22In his time of trouble King Ahaz became even more unfaithful[y] to the LORD. 23He
offered sacrifices to the gods[z] of Damascus, who had defeated him; for he thought,
"Since the gods of the kings of Aram have helped them, I will sacrifice to them so
that they will help me."[a] But they were his downfall and the downfall of all Israel.
24Ahaz gathered together the furnishings from the temple of God[b] and took them
away.[d] He shut the doors[c] of the LORD's temple and set up altars[d] at every street
corner in Jerusalem. 25In every town in Judah he built high places to burn sacrifices
to other gods and provoked the LORD, the God of his fathers, to anger.
26The other events of his reign and all his ways, from beginning to end, are written
in the book of the kings of Judah and Israel. 27Ahaz rested[e] with his fathers and was
buried[f] in the city of Jerusalem, but he was not placed in the tombs of the kings of
Israel. And Hezekiah his son succeeded him as king.

a *16* One Hebrew manuscript, Septuagint and Vulgate (see also 2 Kings 16:7); most Hebrew manuscripts *kings*
b *19* That is, Judah, as frequently in 2 Chronicles c *20* Hebrew *Tilgath-Pilneser,* a variant of *Tiglath-Pileser*
d *24* Or *and cut them up*

28:6
g 2Ki 15:25, 27
h ver 8; Isa 9:21; 11:13

28:8
i Dt 28:25-41; 2Ch 11:4
j 2Ch 29:9

28:9
k 2Ch 25:15; Isa 10:6; 47:6; Zec 1:15
l Ezr 9:6; Rev 18:5

28:10
m Lev 25:39-46

28:11
n 2Ch 11:4; Jas 2:13

28:15
o 2Ki 6:22; Pr 25:21-22
p Dt 34:3; Jdg 1:16

28:16
q 2Ki 16:7

28:17
r Ps 137:7; Isa 34:5
s 2Ch 29:9

28:18
t Eze 16:27, 57
u Jos 10:12

28:19
v 2Ch 21:2

28:20
w 2Ki 15:29; 1Ch 5:6
x 2Ki 16:7

28:22
y Jer 5:3

28:23
z 2Ch 25:14
a Jer 44:17-18

28:24
b 2Ki 16:18
c 2Ch 29:7
d 2Ch 30:14

28:27
e Isa 14:28-32
f 2Ch 21:20; 24:25

28:22 Difficulties and struggles can devastate people, or they can stimulate growth and maturity. For Ahaz, deep troubles led to spiritual collapse. We do not need to respond like Ahaz. When facing problems or tragedy, we must remember that rough times give us a chance to grow (James 1:2–4). When you are facing trials, don't turn away from God; turn *to* him. See these times as an opportunity for you to claim God's help.

Hezekiah Purifies the Temple

29 Hezekiah[a] was twenty-five years old when he became king, and he reigned
in Jerusalem for twenty-nine years. His mother's name was Abijah daughter
of Zechariah. 2He did what was right in the eyes of the LORD, just as his father David[b]
had done.
3In the first month of the first year of his reign, he opened the doors of the temple
of the LORD and repaired[c] them. 4He brought in the priests and the Levites, assembled
them in the square on the east side 5and said, "Listen to me, Levites! Consecrate[d]
yourselves now and consecrate the temple of the LORD, the God of your fathers.
Remove all defilement from the sanctuary. 6Our fathers[e] were unfaithful;[f] they did
evil in the eyes of the LORD our God and forsook him. They turned their faces away
from the LORD's dwelling-place and turned their backs on him. 7They also shut the
doors of the portico and put out the lamps. They did not burn incense or present any
burnt offerings at the sanctuary to the God of Israel. 8Therefore, the anger of the LORD
has fallen on Judah and Jerusalem; he has made them an object of dread and horror[g]
and scorn,[h] as you can see with your own eyes. 9This is why our fathers have fallen
by the sword and why our sons and daughters and our wives are in captivity.[i] 10Now
I intend to make a covenant[j] with the LORD, the God of Israel, so that his fierce anger
will turn away from us. 11My sons, do not be negligent now, for the LORD has chosen
you to stand before him and serve him,[k] to minister[l] before him and to burn
incense."
12Then these Levites[m] set to work:
from the Kohathites,
Mahath son of Amasai and Joel son of Azariah;
from the Merarites,
Kish son of Abdi and Azariah son of Jehallelel;
from the Gershonites,
Joah son of Zimmah and Eden[n] son of Joah;

29:1 [a] 1Ch 3:13
29:2 [b] 2Ch 28:1; 34:2
29:3 [c] 2Ch 28:24
29:5 [d] 2Ch 35:6
29:6 [e] Ps 106:6-47; Jer 2:27 [f] 1Ch 5:25; Eze 8:16
29:8 [g] Dt 28:25; 2Ch 24:18 [h] Jer 18:16; 19:8; 25:9, 18
29:9 [i] 2Ch 28:5-8, 17
29:10 [j] 2Ch 15:12; 23:16
29:11 [k] Nu 3:6; 8:6, 14 [l] 1Ch 15:2
29:12 [m] Nu 3:17-20 [n] 2Ch 31:15

GREAT REVIVALS IN THE BIBLE

The Bible records several great revivals where people in great numbers turned to God and gave up their sinful ways of living. Each revival was characterised by a *leader* who recognised his nation's spiritual dryness. And in each case, the leader *took action* and was not afraid to make his desires known to the people.

Leader	*Reference*	*How the People Responded*
Moses	Exodus 32, 33	Accepted God's laws and built the tabernacle
Samuel	1 Samuel 7:2–13	Promised to make God first in their lives by destroying their idols
David	2 Samuel 6	Brought the ark of the covenant to Jerusalem; praised God with singing and musical instruments
Jehoshaphat	2 Chronicles 20	Decided to trust in God alone to help them, and their discouragement turned to joy
Hezekiah	2 Chronicles 29—31	Purified the temple; did away with idols; brought tithes to God's house
Josiah	2 Chronicles 34, 35	Made a commitment to obey God's commands and remove sinful influences from their lives
Ezra	Ezra 9, 10 Haggai 1	Stopped associating with those who caused them to compromise their faith; renewed their commitment to God's commands; began rebuilding the temple
Nehemiah (with Ezra)	Nehemiah 8—10	Fasted, confessed their sins, read God's word publicly, and promised in writing to serve God wholeheartedly again

29:1 Hezekiah's Profile is found in 2 Kings 18.

29:11 The Levites, chosen by God to serve in the temple, had been kept from their duties by Ahaz's wickedness (28:24). But Hezekiah called them back into service, reminding them that the Lord had chosen them to minister.

We may not have to face a wicked king, but pressures or responsibilities can render us inactive and ineffective. When you have been given the responsibility to minister, don't neglect your duty. If you have become inactive in Christian service, either by choice or by circumstance, look for opportunities (and listen to the "Hezekiahs") God will send your way to help you resume your responsibilities. Then, like the Levites, be ready for action (29:12–15).

13 from the descendants of Elizaphan,
Shimri and Jeiel;
from the descendants of Asaph,[o]
Zechariah and Mattaniah;
14 from the descendants of Heman,
Jehiel and Shimei;
from the descendants of Jeduthun,
Shemaiah and Uzziel.

15 When they had assembled their brothers and consecrated themselves, they went
in to purify[p] the temple of the LORD, as the king had ordered, following the word
of the LORD. 16 The priests went into the sanctuary of the LORD to purify it. They
brought out to the courtyard of the LORD's temple everything unclean that they found
in the temple of the LORD. The Levites took it and carried it out to the Kidron Valley.[q]
17 They began the consecration on the first day of the first month, and by the eighth
day of the month they reached the portico of the LORD. For eight more days they
consecrated the temple of the LORD itself, finishing in the sixteenth day of the first
month.

18 Then they went in to King Hezekiah and reported: "We have purified the entire
temple of the LORD, the altar of burnt offering with all its utensils, and the table for
setting out the consecrated bread, with all its articles. 19 We have prepared and
consecrated all the articles[r] that King Ahaz removed in his unfaithfulness while he
was king. They are now in front of the LORD's altar."

20 Early the next morning King Hezekiah gathered the city officials together and
went up to the temple of the LORD. 21 They brought seven bulls, seven rams, seven
male lambs and seven male goats as a sin offering[s] for the kingdom, for the sanctuary
and for Judah. The king commanded the priests, the descendants of Aaron, to offer
these on the altar of the LORD. 22 So they slaughtered the bulls, and the priests took
the blood and sprinkled it on the altar; next they slaughtered the rams and sprinkled
their blood on the altar; then they slaughtered the lambs and sprinkled their blood[t]
on the altar. 23 The goats for the sin offering were brought before the king and the
assembly, and they laid their hands[u] on them. 24 The priests then slaughtered the goats
and presented their blood on the altar for a sin offering to atone[v] for all Israel, because
the king had ordered the burnt offering and the sin offering for all Israel.

25 He stationed the Levites in the temple of the LORD with cymbals, harps and lyres
in the way prescribed by David[w] and Gad[x] the king's seer and Nathan the prophet;
this was commanded by the LORD through his prophets. 26 So the Levites stood ready
with David's instruments,[y] and the priests with their trumpets.[z]

27 Hezekiah gave the order to sacrifice the burnt offering on the altar. As the offering
began, singing to the LORD began also, accompanied by trumpets and the instruments[a] of David king of Israel. 28 The whole assembly bowed in worship, while the
singers sang and the trumpeters played. All this continued until the sacrifice of the
burnt offering was completed.

29 When the offerings were finished, the king and everyone present with him knelt
down and worshipped.[b] 30 King Hezekiah and his officials ordered the Levites to
praise the LORD with the words of David and of Asaph the seer. So they sang praises
with gladness and bowed their heads and worshipped.

31 Then Hezekiah said, "You have now dedicated yourselves to the LORD. Come

29:13 [o] 1Ch 6:39
29:15 [p] ver 5; 1Ch 23:28; 2Ch 30:12
29:16 [q] 2Sa 15:23
29:19 [r] 2Ch 28:24
29:21 [s] Lev 4:13-14
29:22 [t] Lev 4:18
29:23 [u] Lev 4:15
29:24 [v] Ex 29:36; Lev 4:26
29:25 [w] 1Ch 25:6; 2Ch 8:14 [x] 1Sa 22:5; 2Sa 24:11
29:26 [y] 1Ch 15:16 [z] 1Ch 15:24; 23:5; 2Ch 5:12
29:27 [a] 2Ch 23:18
29:29 [b] 2Ch 20:18

29:21 Throughout the Old Testament, the sacrifice was God's appointed way of approaching him and restoring a right relationship with him. The sin offering made by Hezekiah was one such sacrifice, given to ask God's forgiveness for unintentional sins. (For more information on why God required sacrifices and how they were carried out, see the notes in Leviticus 1.)

29:22 The blood sprinkled on the altar represented the innocence of the sacrificed animal taking the place of the guilt of the person making the offering. The animal died so the sinner could live. This ritual looked forward to the day when Jesus Christ, God's perfect Son, would sacrifice his innocent life on the cross in order that the sinful and guilty human race might be spared the punishment it deserves (Hebrews 10:1–14).

29:30 A seer was someone who received messages from God for the nation through visions or dreams.

29:31 A thank offering, one type of fellowship offering (see Leviticus 7:12–15), was given as an expression of gratitude towards God. As a fellowship offering, it symbolised restored peace and fellowship with God.

29:31 [c]Heb 13:15-16 [d]Ex 25:2; 35:22

29:34 [e]2Ch 35:11 [f]2Ch 30:3, 15

29:35 [g]Ex 29:13; Lev 3:16 [h]Lev 7:11-21 [i]Nu 15:5-10

30:1 [a]Ge 41:52 [b]Ex 12:11; Nu 28:16

30:2 [c]Nu 9:10

30:3 [d]2Ch 29:34

30:5 [e]Jdg 20:1

30:7 [f]Ps 78:8, 57; 106:6; Eze 20:18 [g]2Ch 29:8

30:8 [h]Ex 32:9 [i]Nu 25:4; 2Ch 29:10

30:9 [j]Dt 30:2-5; Isa 1:16; 55:7 [k]1Ki 8:50; Ps 106:46 [l]Ex 34:6-7; Dt 4:31; Mic 7:18

and bring sacrifices[c] and thank-offerings to the temple of the LORD." So the assembly
brought sacrifices and thank-offerings, and all whose hearts were willing[d] brought
burnt offerings.
32The number of burnt offerings the assembly brought was seventy bulls, a hundred
rams and two hundred male lambs—all of them for burnt offerings to the LORD. 33The
animals consecrated as sacrifices amounted to six hundred bulls and three thousand
sheep and goats. 34The priests, however, were too few to skin all the burnt offerings;[e]
so their kinsmen the Levites helped them until the task was finished and until other
priests had been consecrated,[f] for the Levites had been more conscientious in
consecrating themselves than the priests had been. 35There were burnt offerings in
abundance, together with the fat[g] of the fellowship offerings[a][h] and the drink
offerings[i] that accompanied the burnt offerings.
So the service of the temple of the LORD was re-established. 36Hezekiah and all the
people rejoiced at what God had brought about for his people, because it was done
so quickly.

Hezekiah Celebrates the Passover

30 Hezekiah sent word to all Israel and Judah and also wrote letters to Ephraim
and Manasseh,[a] inviting them to come to the temple of the LORD in Jerusalem
and celebrate the Passover[b] to the LORD, the God of Israel. 2The king and his officials
and the whole assembly in Jerusalem decided to celebrate[c] the Passover in the second
month. 3They had not been able to celebrate it at the regular time because not enough
priests had consecrated[d] themselves and the people had not assembled in Jerusalem.
4The plan seemed right both to the king and to the whole assembly. 5They decided
to send a proclamation throughout Israel, from Beersheba to Dan,[e] calling the people
to come to Jerusalem and celebrate the Passover to the LORD, the God of Israel. It
had not been celebrated in large numbers according to what was written.
6At the king's command, couriers went throughout Israel and Judah with letters
from the king and from his officials, which read:

> "People of Israel, return to the LORD, the God of Abraham, Isaac and Israel,
> that he may return to you who are left, who have escaped from the hand of the
> kings of Assyria. 7Do not be like your fathers[f] and brothers, who were unfaithful
> to the LORD, the God of their fathers, so that he made them an object of horror,[g]
> as you see. 8Do not be stiff-necked,[h] as your fathers were; submit to the LORD.
> Come to the sanctuary, which he has consecrated for ever. Serve the LORD your
> God, so that his fierce anger[i] will turn away from you. 9If you return[j] to the
> LORD, then your brothers and your children will be shown compassion[k] by their
> captors and will come back to this land, for the LORD your God is gracious and
> compassionate.[l] He will not turn his face from you if you return to him."

10The couriers went from town to town in Ephraim and Manasseh, as far as

[a] *35* Traditionally *peace offerings*

30:1 The Passover celebration commemorated the time that God spared the lives of Israel's firstborn sons in Egypt. God had promised to send a plague to kill all the firstborn sons except in those homes where the blood of a slain lamb had been painted on the doorframes. The Israelites obeyed, and when the destroyer saw the blood, he "passed over" the house and did not harm anyone in it (Exodus 12:23). After this plague, Pharaoh freed the Israelites from slavery. This celebration was to be a yearly reminder of how God delivered his people. The careful preparations, both in the temple and for the feast, show that this was not a temporary or impulsive revival, but a deep-seated change of heart and life.

30:2, 3 God's law had a provision that, under certain circumstances, the Passover could be celebrated one month later (Numbers 9:10, 11).

30:6–9 Hezekiah was a king dedicated to God and to the spiritual progress of the nation. He sent letters throughout Judah and Israel urging everyone to return to God. He told them not to be stubborn, but to submit to the Lord. To submit means to obey him first, yielding our bodies, minds, wills, and emotions to him. His Holy Spirit must guide and renew every part of us. Only then will we be able to temper our stubborn selfishness.

30:10 The northern kingdom of Israel had recently been conquered by Assyria, and most of the people had been carried away to foreign lands. Hezekiah sent a proclamation to the few people who remained, inviting them to come to the Passover (30:1), but most responded with scorn and ridicule. People may mock you when you try to promote spiritual renewal and growth. Are you prepared to be ridiculed for your faith? When it comes your way, do not waver. Stand strong in your faith, as Hezekiah did, and God will honour you.

Zebulun, but the people scorned and ridiculed[m] them. 11 Nevertheless, some men of
Asher, Manasseh and Zebulun humbled themselves and went to Jerusalem.[n] 12 Also
in Judah the hand of God was on the people to give them unity[o] of mind to carry
out what the king and his officials had ordered, following the word of the LORD.
13 A very large crowd of people assembled in Jerusalem to celebrate the Feast of
Unleavened Bread[p] in the second month. 14 They removed the altars[q] in Jerusalem
and cleared away the incense altars and threw them into the Kidron Valley.[r]
15 They slaughtered the Passover lamb on the fourteenth day of the second month.
The priests and the Levites were ashamed and consecrated[s] themselves and brought
burnt offerings to the temple of the LORD. 16 Then they took up their regular positions[t]
as prescribed in the Law of Moses the man of God. The priests sprinkled the blood
handed to them by the Levites. 17 Since many in the crowd had not consecrated
themselves, the Levites had to kill[u] the Passover lambs for all those who were not
ceremonially clean and could not consecrate ⌞their lambs⌟ to the LORD. 18 Although
most of the many people who came from Ephraim, Manasseh, Issachar and Zebulun
had not purified themselves,[v] yet they ate the Passover, contrary to what was written.
But Hezekiah prayed for them, saying, "May the LORD, who is good, pardon everyone
19 who sets his heart on seeking God—the LORD, the God of his fathers—even if he
is not clean according to the rules of the sanctuary." 20 And the LORD heard[w] Hezekiah
and healed[x] the people.[y]
21 The Israelites who were present in Jerusalem celebrated the Feast of Unleavened
Bread[z] for seven days with great rejoicing, while the Levites and priests sang to the
LORD every day, accompanied by the LORD's instruments of praise.[a]
22 Hezekiah spoke encouragingly to all the Levites, who showed good understanding
of the service of the LORD. For the seven days they ate their assigned portion and
offered fellowship offerings[b] and praised the LORD, the God of their fathers.
23 The whole assembly then agreed to celebrate[a] the festival seven more days; so
for another seven days they celebrated joyfully. 24 Hezekiah king of Judah provided[b]
a thousand bulls and seven thousand sheep and goats for the assembly, and the officials
provided them with a thousand bulls and ten thousand sheep and goats. A great number
of priests consecrated themselves. 25 The entire assembly of Judah rejoiced, along with
the priests and Levites and all who had assembled from Israel[c], including the aliens
who had come from Israel and those who lived in Judah. 26 There was great joy in
Jerusalem, for since the days of Solomon[d] son of David king of Israel there had been
nothing like this in Jerusalem. 27 The priests and the Levites stood to bless[e] the people,
and God heard them, for their prayer reached heaven, his holy dwelling-place.

31 When all this had ended, the Israelites who were there went out to the towns
of Judah, smashed the sacred stones and cut down[a] the Asherah poles. They
destroyed the high places and the altars throughout Judah and Benjamin and in

a 21 *Or priests praised the LORD every day with resounding instruments belonging to the LORD.* b 22 Traditionally *peace offerings*

30:10 m 2Ch 36:16
30:11 n ver 25
30:12 o Jer 32:39; Eze 11:19; Php 2:13
30:13 p Nu 28:16
30:14 q 2Ch 28:24; r 2Sa 15:23
30:15 s 2Ch 29:34
30:16 t 2Ch 35:10
30:17 u 2Ch 29:34
30:18 v Ex 12:43-49; Nu 9:6-10
30:20 w 2Ch 6:20; x 2Ch 7:14; Mal 4:2; y Jas 5:16
30:21 z Ex 12:15, 17; 13:6
30:23 a 1Ki 8:65; 2Ch 7:9
30:24 b 1Ki 8:5; 2Ch 29:34; 35:7; Ezr 6:17; 8:35
30:25 c ver 11
30:26 d 2Ch 7:8
30:27 e Ex 39:43; Nu 6:23; Dt 26:15; 2Ch 23:18; Ps 68:5
31:1 a 2Ki 18:4; 2Ch 32:12; Isa 36:7

30:11 These people invited to the Passover scorned Hezekiah's messengers, but some accepted the invitation. Our efforts to tell others about God often meet with similar reactions. Many people will laugh at an invitation to accept Christ. But this must not stop us from reaching out. If you know and understand that rejecting the gospel is common, you can guard against feelings of personal rejection. Remember that the Holy Spirit convicts and convinces. Our task is to invite others to consider God's actions, his claims, and his promises.

30:14 Just as the priests had consecrated the temple (29:4, 5), so the people cleared the city of pagan idols and then consecrated themselves to prepare for worship (30:17–19). Even the good kings of Judah found it difficult to get rid of the pagan idols and altars in the high places (2 Kings 14:4; 2 Chronicles 20:33). Finally Hezekiah, with the help of his people, completed this task.

30:15 The people were so zealous to celebrate the Passover and bring offerings to the temple that the priests and Levites were ashamed they did not share the same enthusiasm. The zeal of common people's faith motivated the ministers to take action. The devoted faith of laypersons today should motivate professional church staff to rekindle their enthusiasm for God's work. Laypersons should never be shut out of church government or decision making. The church needs their good examples of faith.

30:22 One important purpose of the fellowship offering was to express gratitude to God for health or for safety in times of crisis.

30:26 It had been more than 200 years since there had been such a celebration in Jerusalem.

31:1ff Why was idol worship so bad? The Israelites had access to the one true God, but they constantly fell into worshipping lifeless idols made of wood or stone. They put aside worshipping the Creator in order to worship the creation. We are just as guilty when God no longer holds first place in our lives. When we think more about wealth, pleasure, prestige, or material possessions than about God, we are actually worshipping them as gods. Because of idol worship, the people of Judah were eventually sent into captivity in foreign lands (36:14–17). We may not be sent into captivity,

Ephraim and Manasseh. After they had destroyed all of them, the Israelites returned
to their own towns and to their own property.

Contributions for Worship

2Hezekiah[b] assigned the priests and Levites to divisions[c]—each of them according to their duties as priests or Levites—to offer burnt offerings and fellowship
offerings,[a] to minister,[d] to give thanks and to sing praises[e] at the gates of the LORD's
dwelling.[f] 3The king contributed[g] from his own possessions for the morning and
evening burnt offerings and for the burnt offerings on the Sabbaths, New Moons and
appointed feasts as written in the Law of the LORD.[h] 4He ordered the people living
in Jerusalem to give the portion[i] due to the priests and Levites so that they could
devote themselves to the Law of the LORD. 5As soon as the order went out, the
Israelites generously gave the firstfruits[j] of their grain, new wine,[k] oil and honey
and all that the fields produced. They brought a great amount, a tithe of everything.
6The men of Israel and Judah who lived in the towns of Judah also brought a tithe[l]
of their herds and flocks and a tithe of the holy things dedicated to the LORD their God,
and they piled them in heaps.[m] 7They began doing this in the third month and finished
in the seventh month.[n] 8When Hezekiah and his officials came and saw the heaps,
they praised the LORD and blessed[o] his people Israel.
9Hezekiah asked the priests and Levites about the heaps; 10and Azariah the chief
priest, from the family of Zadok,[p] answered, "Since the people began to bring their
contributions to the temple of the LORD, we have had enough to eat and plenty to spare,
because the LORD has blessed his people, and this great amount is left over."[q]
11Hezekiah gave orders to prepare storerooms in the temple of the LORD, and this
was done. 12Then they faithfully brought in the contributions, tithes and dedicated
gifts. Conaniah,[r] a Levite, was in charge of these things, and his brother Shimei was

[a] 2 Traditionally *peace offerings*

31:2 [b] 2Ch 29:9 [c] 1Ch 24:1 [d] 1Ch 15:2 [e] Ps 7:17; 9:2; 47:6; 71:22 [f] 1Ch 23:28-32
31:3 [g] 1Ch 29:3; 2Ch 35:7; Eze 45:17 [h] Nu 28:1-29:40
31:4 [i] Nu 18:8; Dt 18:8; Ne 13:10; Mal 2:7
31:5 [j] Nu 18:12, 24; Ne 13:12; Eze 44:30 [k] Dt 12:17
31:6 [l] Lev 27:30; Ne 13:10-12 [m] Dt 14:28; Ru 3:7
31:7 [n] Ex 23:16
31:8 [o] Ps 144:13-15
31:10 [p] 2Sa 8:17 [q] Ex 36:5; Eze 44:30; Mal 3:10-12
31:12 [r] 2Ch 35:9

THE DAVIDIC DYNASTY

The Lord promised David that his kingdom would endure and his throne would be established for ever (2 Samuel 7:16). As a partial fulfilment of this promise, David and his descendants ruled Judah for over 400 years. Jesus Christ was a direct descendant of David, and was the ultimate fulfilment of this promise (Acts 2:22–36).

David (40 years, 1 Chr. 10—29)
Solomon (40 years, 2 Chr. 1—9)
Rehoboam (17 years, 2 Chr. 10—12)
Abijah (3 years, 2 Chr. 13)
Asa (41 years, 2 Chr. 14—16)
Jehoshaphat (25 years, 2 Chr. 17—20)
Jehoram (8 years, 2 Chr. 21)
Ahaziah (1 years, 2 Chr. 22:1–9)
Athaliah (6 years, 2 Chr. 22:10—23:21)
Joash (40 years, 2 Chr. 24)
Amaziah (29 years, 2 Chr. 25)
Uzziah (Azariah) (52 years, 2 Chr. 26)
Jotham (16 years, 2 Chr. 27)
Ahaz (16 years, 2 Chr. 28)
Hezekiah (29 years, 2 Chr. 29—32)
Manasseh (55 years, 2 Chr. 33:1–20)
Amon (2 years, 2 Chr. 33:21–25)
Josiah (31 years, 2 Chr. 34—35)
Jehoahaz (3 months, 2 Chr. 36:1–4)
Jehoiakim (11 years, 2 Chr. 36:5–8)
Jehoiachin (3 months, 2 Chr. 36:9–10)
Zedekiah (11 years, 2 Chr. 36:11–16)

but discipline awaits all those who continually put earthly desires above spiritual priorities.

31:2–21 The priests had not been supported by the government during the evil kings' reigns. Now that the temple was repaired, Hezekiah organised the priests and resumed the work of the temple according to a plan originally set up by David (1 Chronicles 23:6–23; 24:3–19).

31:4–8 Hezekiah reinstated the practice of tithing—giving a tenth of one's income to the priests and Levites so they could be free to serve God and minister to the people. The people responded immediately and generously. God's work needs the support of God's people. Does God receive a regular percentage of your income? Generosity makes our giving delightful to us and to God (2 Corinthians 8; 9). How different the church would be today if all believers consistently followed this pattern.

next in rank. 13Jehiel, Azaziah, Nahath, Asahel, Jerimoth, Jozabad,[s] Eliel, Isma-
kiah, Mahath and Benaiah were supervisors under Conaniah and Shimei his brother,
by appointment of King Hezekiah and Azariah the official in charge of the temple of
God.
14Kore son of Imnah the Levite, keeper of the East Gate, was in charge of the
freewill offerings given to God, distributing the contributions made to the LORD and
also the consecrated gifts. 15Eden,[t] Miniamin, Jeshua, Shemaiah, Amariah and
Shecaniah assisted him faithfully in the towns[u] of the priests, distributing to their
fellow priests according to their divisions, old and young alike.
16In addition, they distributed to the males three years old or more whose names
were in the genealogical records[v]—all who would enter the temple of the LORD to
perform the daily duties of their various tasks, according to their responsibilities and
their divisions. 17And they distributed to the priests enrolled by their families in the
genealogical records and likewise to the Levites twenty years old or more, according
to their responsibilities and their divisions. 18They included all the little ones, the
wives, and the sons and daughters of the whole community listed in these genealogical
records. For they were faithful in consecrating themselves.
19As for the priests, the descendants of Aaron, who lived on the farm lands around
their towns or in any other towns,[w] men were designated by name to distribute
portions to every male among them and to all who were recorded in the genealogies
of the Levites.
20This is what Hezekiah did throughout Judah, doing what was good and right and
faithful[x] before the LORD his God. 21In everything that he undertook in the service
of God's temple and in obedience to the law and the commands, he sought his God
and worked wholeheartedly. And so he prospered.[y]

31:13 [s]2Ch 35:9
31:15 [t]2Ch 29:12 [u]Jos 21:9-19
31:16 [v]1Ch 23:3; Ezr 3:4
31:19 [w]ver 12-15; Lev 25:34; Nu 35:2-5
31:20 [x]2Ki 20:3; 22:2
31:21 [y]Dt 29:9

Sennacherib Threatens Jerusalem

32 After all that Hezekiah had so faithfully done, Sennacherib[a] king of Assyria
came and invaded Judah. He laid siege to the fortified cities, thinking to
conquer them for himself. 2When Hezekiah saw that Sennacherib had come and that

32:1 [a]2Ki 18:13-19; Isa 36:1; 37:9, 17, 37

31:20, 21 Because Hezekiah did "what was good and right and faithful before the LORD," he led the people of Judah in spiritual renewal. His actions serve as a model of renewal for us: (1) he remembered God's compassion (30:9); (2) he kept going despite ridicule (30:10); (3) he aggressively removed evil influences from his life (30:14; 31:1); (4) he interceded for the people, asking for the Lord's pardon (30:15–20); (5) he was open to spontaneity in worship (30:23); (6) he contributed generously to God's work (31:3). If any of these are lacking in your life, consider how they might apply, and renew your commitment to God.

32:1 Assyria was a great empire by Hezekiah's time, controlling most of the Middle East. From a small strip of land located in present-day Iran and Iraq, it began to establish its power under Ashurnasirpal II (883–859 B.C.) and his son Shalmaneser III (859–824). Under Tiglath-Pileser III (745–727), Assyria's boundaries extended to the borders of Israel, making it one of the largest empires in ancient history. Shalmaneser V destroyed the northern kingdom in 722, and his grandson, Sennacherib (705–681), tried to bring Judah, the southern kingdom, under his control. Less than a century later, Assyria would lie in ruins (612).

32:1 Sennacherib wanted to "conquer them for himself" so he could force the cities to pay tribute. Forcing captured cities to pay tribute was a way for kings to build their income base. Often Assyria would require an oath of allegiance from a country, including the promise to pay taxes in the form of livestock, wine, battle equipment (horses, chariots, weapons), gold, silver, and anything else that pleased the invading king. Tribute was more important to Assyria than captives because captives cost money. Thus captives were taken only in cases of extreme rebellion or to repopulate cities that had been destroyed.

32:1ff When Hezekiah was confronted with the frightening prospect of an Assyrian invasion, he made two important decisions. He did everything he could to deal with the situation, and he trusted God for the outcome. That is exactly what we must do when faced with difficult or frightening situations. Take all the steps you possibly can to solve the problem or improve the situation. But also commit the situation to God in prayer, trusting him for the solution.

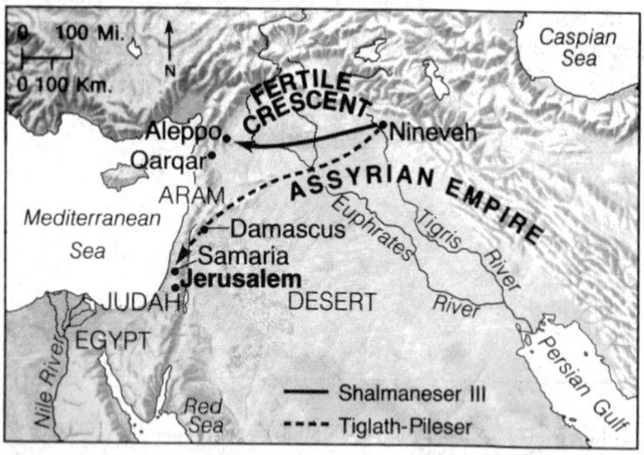

THE ASSYRIAN EMPIRE The mighty Assyrian empire extended from the Persian Gulf, across the Fertile Crescent, and south to Egypt. Shalmaneser III extended the empire towards the Mediterranean Sea by conquering cities as far west as Qarqar. Tiglath-Pileser extended the empire south into Aram, Israel, Judah, and Philistia. It was Shalmaneser V who destroyed Samaria, Israel's capital.

he intended to make war on Jerusalem,[b] 3 he consulted with his officials and military
staff about blocking off the water from the springs outside the city, and they helped
him. 4 A large force of men assembled, and they blocked all the springs[c] and the
stream that flowed through the land. "Why should the kings[a] of Assyria come and
find plenty of water?" they said. 5 Then he worked hard repairing all the broken
sections of the wall[d] and building towers on it. He built another wall outside that one
and reinforced the supporting terraces[b][e] of the City of David. He also made large
numbers of weapons[f] and shields.
6 He appointed military officers over the people and assembled them before him in
the square at the city gate and encouraged them with these words: 7 "Be strong and
courageous.[g] Do not be afraid or discouraged[h] because of the king of Assyria and
the vast army with him, for there is a greater power with us than with him.[i] 8 With
him is only the arm of flesh,[j] but with us[k] is the LORD our God to help us and to
fight our battles."[l] And the people gained confidence from what Hezekiah the king
of Judah said.
9 Later, when Sennacherib king of Assyria and all his forces were laying siege to
Lachish,[m] he sent his officers to Jerusalem with this message for Hezekiah king of
Judah and for all the people of Judah who were there:

> 10 "This is what Sennacherib king of Assyria says: On what are you basing your
> confidence,[n] that you remain in Jerusalem under siege? 11 When Hezekiah says,
> 'The LORD our God will save us from the hand of the king of Assyria,' he is
> misleading[o] you, to let you die of hunger and thirst. 12 Did not Hezekiah himself
> remove this god's high places and altars, saying to Judah and Jerusalem, 'You
> must worship before one altar[p] and burn sacrifices on it'?
> 13 "Do you not know what I and my fathers have done to all the peoples of the
> other lands? Were the gods of those nations ever able to deliver their land from
> my hand?[q] 14 Who of all the gods of these nations that my fathers destroyed has
> been able to save his people from me? How then can your god deliver you from
> my hand? 15 Now do not let Hezekiah deceive[r] you and mislead you like this.
> Do not believe him, for no god of any nation or kingdom has been able to
> deliver[s] his people from my hand or the hand of my fathers.[t] How much less
> will your god deliver you from my hand!"

16 Sennacherib's officers spoke further against the LORD God and against his servant
Hezekiah. 17 The king also wrote letters[u] insulting[v] the LORD, the God of Israel, and
saying this against him: "Just as the gods[w] of the peoples of the other lands did not
rescue their people from my hand, so the god of Hezekiah will not rescue his people
from my hand." 18 Then they called out in Hebrew to the people of Jerusalem who
were on the wall, to terrify them and make them afraid in order to capture the city.
19 They spoke about the God of Jerusalem as they did about the gods of the other
peoples of the world—the work of men's hands.[x]
20 King Hezekiah and the prophet Isaiah son of Amoz cried out in prayer to heaven
about this. 21 And the LORD sent an angel,[y] who annihilated all the fighting men and
the leaders and officers in the camp of the Assyrian king. So he withdrew to his own
land in disgrace. And when he went into the temple of his god, some of his sons cut
him down with the sword.[z]
22 So the LORD saved Hezekiah and the people of Jerusalem from the hand of

a 4 Hebrew; Septuagint and Syriac *king* b 5 Or *the Millo*

32:2 b Isa 22:7; Jer 1:15
32:4 c 2Ki 18:17; 20:20; Isa 22:9, 11; Na 3:14
32:5 d 2Ch 25:23; Isa 22:10 e 1Ki 9:24; 1Ch 11:8 f Isa 22:8
32:7 g Dt 31:6; 1Ch 22:13 h 2Ch 20:15 i Nu 14:9; 2Ki 6:16
32:8 j Job 40:9; Isa 52:10; Jer 17:5; 32:21 k Dt 3:22; 1Sa 17:45; 2Ch 13:12 l 1Ch 5:22; 2Ch 20:17; Ps 20:7; Isa 28:6
32:9 m Jos 10:3, 31
32:10 n Eze 29:16
32:11 o Isa 37:10
32:12 p 2Ch 31:1
32:13 q ver 15
32:15 r Isa 37:10 s Da 3:15 t Ex 5:2
32:17 u Isa 37:14 v Ps 74:22; Isa 37:4, 17 w 2Ki 19:12
32:19 x 2Ki 19:18; Ps 115:4, 4-8; Isa 2:8; 17:8
32:21 y Ge 19:13 z 2Ki 19:7

32:3, 4 Cities had to be built near reliable water sources. Natural springs were some of Jerusalem's major sources of water. In a brilliant military move, Hezekiah plugged the springs outside the city and channelled the water through an underground tunnel (32:30); therefore, Jerusalem would have water even through a long siege. Hezekiah's tunnel has been discovered along with an inscription describing how it was built: two groups of workers started digging underground, one in Jerusalem and one at the Gihon spring, and they met in the middle.

32:7, 8 Hezekiah could see with eyes of faith. The number of his opponents meant nothing as long as he was on the Lord's side. Victory is "not by might nor by power, but by my Spirit, says the LORD Almighty" (Zechariah 4:6). Hezekiah could confidently encourage his men because he had no doubt about where he stood with God. Are you on the Lord's side? You may never face an enemy army, but the battles you face every day can be won with God's strength.

Sennacherib king of Assyria and from the hand of all others. He took care of them[c]
on every side. 23 Many brought offerings to Jerusalem for the LORD and valuable gifts[a]
for Hezekiah king of Judah. From then on he was highly regarded by all the nations.

Hezekiah's Pride, Success and Death

24 In those days Hezekiah became ill and was at the point of death. He prayed to
the LORD, who answered him and gave him a miraculous sign. 25 But Hezekiah's heart
was proud[b] and he did not respond to the kindness shown him; therefore the LORD's
wrath[c] was on him and on Judah and Jerusalem. 26 Then Hezekiah repented[d] of the
pride of his heart, as did the people of Jerusalem; therefore the LORD's wrath did not
come upon them during the days of Hezekiah.[e]
27 Hezekiah had very great riches and honour,[f] and he made treasuries for his silver
and gold and for his precious stones, spices, shields and all kinds of valuables. 28 He
also made buildings to store the harvest of grain, new wine and oil; and he made stalls
for various kinds of cattle, and pens for the flocks. 29 He built villages and acquired
great numbers of flocks and herds, for God had given him very great riches.[g]
30 It was Hezekiah who blocked[h] the upper outlet of the Gihon[i] spring and
channelled the water down to the west side of the City of David. He succeeded in
everything he undertook. 31 But when envoys were sent by the rulers of Babylon[j] to
ask him about the miraculous sign[k] that had occurred in the land, God left him to
test[l] him and to know everything that was in his heart.
32 The other events of Hezekiah's reign and his acts of devotion are written in the
vision of the prophet Isaiah son of Amoz in the book of the kings of Judah and Israel.
33 Hezekiah rested with his fathers and was buried on the hill where the tombs of
David's descendants are. All Judah and the people of Jerusalem honoured him when
he died. And Manasseh his son succeeded him as king.

Manasseh King of Judah

33 Manasseh[a] was twelve years old when he became king, and he reigned in
Jerusalem for fifty-five years. 2 He did evil in the eyes of the LORD,[b] following
the detestable[c] practices of the nations the LORD had driven out before the Israelites.
3 He rebuilt the high places his father Hezekiah had demolished; he also erected altars
to the Baals and made Asherah poles.[d] He bowed down[e] to all the starry hosts and
worshipped them. 4 He built altars in the temple of the LORD, of which the LORD had
said, "My Name[f] will remain in Jerusalem for ever." 5 In both courts of the temple
of the LORD,[g] he built altars to all the starry hosts. 6 He sacrificed his sons[h] in[a] the
fire in the Valley of Ben Hinnom, practised sorcery, divination and witchcraft, and
consulted mediums[i] and spiritists.[j] He did much evil in the eyes of the LORD,
provoking him to anger.
7 He took the carved image he had made and put it in God's temple,[k] of which God

c *22* Hebrew; Septuagint and Vulgate *He gave them rest* a *6* Or *He made his sons pass through*

32:23 a 2Ch 9:24; 17:5; Isa 45:14; Zec 14:16-17
32:25 b 2Ki 14:10; 2Ch 26:16 c 2Ch 19:2; 24:18
32:26 d Jer 26:18-19 e 2Ch 34:27, 28; Isa 39:8
32:27 f 1Ch 29:12
32:29 g 1Ch 29:12
32:30 h 2Ki 18:17 i 1Ki 1:33
32:31 j Isa 39:1 k ver 24; Isa 38:7 l Ge 22:1; Dt 8:16
33:1 a 1Ch 3:13
33:2 b Jer 15:4 c Dt 18:9; 2Ch 28:3
33:3 d Dt 16:21-22 e Dt 17:3; 2Ch 31:1
33:4 f 2Ch 7:16
33:5 g 2Ch 4:9
33:6 h Lev 18:21; Dt 18:10; 2Ch 28:3 i Lev 19:31 j 1Sa 28:13
33:7 k 2Ch 7:16

32:31 A test can bring out a person's true character. God tested Hezekiah to see what he was really like and to show him his own shortcomings and the attitude of his heart. God did not totally abandon Hezekiah, nor did he tempt him to sin or trick him. The test was meant to strengthen Hezekiah, develop his character, and prepare him for the tasks ahead. In times of success, most of us can live good lives. But pressure, trouble, or pain will quickly remove our thin veneer of goodness unless our strength comes from God. What are you like under pressure or when everything is going wrong? Do you give in or turn to God? Those who are consistently in touch with God don't have to worry about what pressure may reveal about them.

32:31 Babylon was slowly and quietly rising to become a world power. At the same time, the Assyrian empire was slowly declining due to internal strife and a succession of weak kings. When Assyria was finally crushed in 612 B.C., Babylon under Nebuchadnezzar moved into its place of prominence. (For more information on Babylon, see the note on 2 Kings 20:14.)

32:31 Why did God leave Hezekiah to himself? After Hezekiah was healed of his sickness, he developed excessive pride. When envoys came to inquire about his miraculous healing, God stepped back to see how Hezekiah would respond. Unfortunately, Hezekiah's actions revealed his runaway pride. He pointed to his own accomplishments rather than to God (see 2 Kings 20:12–19). Pride is any attitude that elevates our effort or abilities above God's, or treats with disdain his work in us. It causes us to congratulate ourselves for our successes and to look down on other people. God does not object to self-confidence, healthy self-esteem, or good feelings about our accomplishments. He objects to the foolish attitude of taking full credit for what he has done or for setting ourselves up as superior to others.

33:6 Sorcery is using power gained from evil spirits. Divination is predicting the future through omens.

33:8 [l]2Sa 7:10
33:9 [m]Jer 15:4
33:11 [n]Dt 28:36 [o]Ps 149:8
33:12 [p]2Ch 6:37; 32:26; 1Pe 5:6
33:14 [q]1Ki 1:33 [r]Ne 3:3; 12:39; Zep 1:10

had said to David and to his son Solomon, "In this temple and in Jerusalem, which
I have chosen out of all the tribes of Israel, I will put my Name for ever. 8I will not
again make the feet of the Israelites leave the land[l] I assigned to your forefathers,
if only they will be careful to do everything that I commanded them concerning all
the laws, decrees and ordinances given through Moses." 9But Manasseh led Judah and
the people of Jerusalem astray, so that they did more evil than the nations the LORD
had destroyed before the Israelites.[m]
10The LORD spoke to Manasseh and his people, but they paid no attention. 11So
the LORD brought against them the army commanders of the king of Assyria, who took
Manasseh prisoner,[n] put a hook in his nose, bound him with bronze shackles[o] and
took him to Babylon. 12In his distress he sought the favour of the LORD his God and
humbled[p] himself greatly before the God of his fathers. 13And when he prayed to
him, the LORD was moved by his entreaty and listened to his plea; so he brought him
back to Jerusalem and to his kingdom. Then Manasseh knew that the LORD is God.
14Afterwards he rebuilt the outer wall of the City of David, west of the Gihon[q]
spring in the valley, as far as the entrance of the Fish Gate[r] and encircling the hill

MANASSEH

Even a brief outline of King Manasseh's evil sickens us, and we wonder how God could ever forgive him. Not only did he intentionally offend God by desecrating Solomon's temple with idols, but he also worshipped pagan gods and even sacrificed his children to them! Child sacrifice is a vile act of pagan idolatry, an act against both God and people. Such blatant sins require severe correction.

God showed justice to Manasseh in warning and punishing him. He showed mercy in responding to Manasseh's heartfelt repentance by forgiving and restoring him. Given the nature of Manasseh's rebellion, we are not surprised by God's punishment—defeat and exile at the hands of the Assyrians. But Manasseh's repentance and God's forgiveness are unexpected. Manasseh's life was changed. He was given a new start.

How far has God gone to gain your attention? Have you ever, like Manasseh, come to your senses and cried out to God for help? Only your repentance and a prayer for a new attitude stand between you and God's complete forgiveness.

Strengths and accomplishments:
- Despite the bitter consequences of his sins, he learned from them
- Humbly repented of his sins before God

Weaknesses and mistakes:
- Challenged God's authority and was defeated
- Reversed many of the positive effects of his father Hezekiah's rule
- Sacrificed his children to idols

Lessons from his life:
- God will go a long way to gain someone's attention
- Forgiveness is limited not by the amount of sin, but by our willingness to repent

Vital statistics:
- Where: Jerusalem
- Occupation: King of Judah
- Relatives: Father: Hezekiah. Mother: Hephzibah. Son: Amon

Key verses:
"In his distress he sought the favour of the LORD his God and humbled himself greatly before the God of his fathers. And when he prayed to him, the LORD was moved by his entreaty and listened to his plea; so he brought him back to Jerusalem and to his kingdom. Then Manasseh knew that the LORD is God" (2 Chronicles 33:12, 13).

Manasseh's story is told in 2 Kings 21:1–18 and 2 Chronicles 32:33—33:20. He is also mentioned in Jeremiah 15:4.

33:11 Between 652 and 648 B.C., the city of Babylon rebelled against Assyria. The rebellion was crushed, but Assyria may have suspected that Manasseh supported it. That may explain why Manasseh was taken to Babylon for trial rather than to the Assyrian capital of Nineveh.

33:12, 13 In a list of corrupt kings, Manasseh would rank near the top. His life was a catalogue of evil deeds including idol worship, sacrificing his own children, and temple desecration. Eventually, however, he realised his sins and cried out to God for forgiveness. And God listened. If God can forgive Manasseh, surely he can forgive anyone. Are you burdened by overpowering guilt? Do you doubt that anyone could forgive what you have done? Take heart—until death, no-one is beyond the reach of God's forgiveness.

of Ophel;[s] he also made it much higher. He stationed military commanders in all the
fortified cities in Judah.
15He got rid of the foreign gods and removed[t] the image from the temple of the
LORD, as well as all the altars he had built on the temple hill and in Jerusalem; and
he threw them out of the city. 16Then he restored the altar of the LORD and sacrificed
fellowship offerings[b] and thank-offerings[u] on it, and told Judah to serve the LORD,
the God of Israel. 17The people, however, continued to sacrifice at the high places,
but only to the LORD their God.
18The other events of Manasseh's reign, including his prayer to his God and the
words the seers spoke to him in the name of the LORD, the God of Israel, are written
in the annals of the kings of Israel.[c] 19His prayer and how God was moved by his
entreaty, as well as all his sins and unfaithfulness, and the sites where he built high
places and set up Asherah poles and idols before he humbled[v] himself—all are
written in the records of the seers.[d][w] 20Manasseh rested with his fathers and was
buried[x] in his palace. And Amon his son succeeded him as king.

Amon King of Judah

21Amon[y] was twenty-two years old when he became king, and he reigned in
Jerusalem for two years. 22He did evil in the eyes of the LORD, as his father Manasseh
had done. Amon worshipped and offered sacrifices to all the idols Manasseh had
made. 23But unlike his father Manasseh, he did not humble[z] himself before the LORD;
Amon increased his guilt.
24Amon's officials conspired against him and assassinated him in his palace. 25Then
the people[a] of the land killed all who had plotted against King Amon, and they made
Josiah his son king in his place.

Josiah's Reforms

34 Josiah[a] was eight years old when he became king,[b] and he reigned in
Jerusalem for thirty-one years. 2He did what was right in the eyes of the LORD
and walked in the ways of his father David,[c] not turning aside to the right or to the
left.
3In the eighth year of his reign, while he was still young, he began to seek the God[d]
of his father David. In his twelfth year he began to purge Judah and Jerusalem of high
places, Asherah poles, carved idols and cast images. 4Under his direction the altars
of the Baals were torn down; he cut to pieces the incense altars that were above them,
and smashed the Asherah poles,[e] the idols and the images. These he broke to pieces
and scattered over the graves of those who had sacrificed to them.[f] 5He burned[g] the
bones of the priests on their altars, and so he purged Judah and Jerusalem. 6In the
towns of Manasseh, Ephraim and Simeon, as far as Naphtali, and in the ruins around
them, 7he tore down the altars and the Asherah poles and crushed the idols to powder[h]
and cut to pieces all the incense altars throughout Israel. Then he went back to
Jerusalem.
8In the eighteenth year of Josiah's reign, to purify the land and the temple, he sent
Shaphan son of Azaliah and Maaseiah the ruler of the city, with Joah son of Joahaz,
the recorder, to repair the temple of the LORD his God.
9They went to Hilkiah[i] the high priest and gave him the money that had been

b *16* Traditionally *peace offerings* c *18* That is, Judah, as frequently in 2 Chronicles d *19* One Hebrew manuscript and Septuagint; most Hebrew manuscripts *of Hozai*

33:14 [s]2Ch 27:3; Ne 3:26
33:15 [t]ver 3-7; 2Ki 23:12
33:16 [u]Lev 7:11-18
33:19 [v]2Ch 6:37 [w]2Ki 21:17
33:20 [x]2Ki 21:18; 2Ch 21:20
33:21 [y]1Ch 3:14
33:23 [z]ver 12; Ex 10:3; 2Ch 7:14; Ps 18:27; 147:6; Pr 3:34
33:25 [a]2Ch 22:1
34:1 [a]1Ch 3:14 [b]Zep 1:1
34:2 [c]2Ch 29:2
34:3 [d]1Ki 13:2; 1Ch 16:11; 2Ch 15:2; 33:17, 22
34:4 [e]Ex 34:13 [f]Ex 32:20; Lev 26:30; 2Ki 23:11; Mic 1:5
34:5 [g]1Ki 13:2
34:7 [h]Ex 32:20; 2Ch 31:1
34:9 [i]1Ch 6:13; 2Ch 35:8

33:17 Although the people worshipped God alone, they worshipped him in the wrong way. God had told them to make their sacrifices only in certain places (Deuteronomy 12:13, 14). This kept them from changing their way of worship and protected them against the dangerous influence of pagan religious practices. Unfortunately, the people continued to use these places of worship, not realising that (1) they were adopting practices God opposed, and (2) these places were against God's law. They were mixing pagan beliefs with worship of God. Blending religious ideas leads to confusion about who God really is. We must take care that subtle secular influences do not distort our worship practices.

34:1 Josiah's Profile is found in 2 Kings 24.

34:3 In Josiah's day, boys were considered men at age 12. By 16, Josiah understood the responsibility of his office. Even at this young age, he showed greater wisdom than many of the older kings who came before him because he had decided to seek the Lord God and his wisdom. Don't let your age disqualify you from serving God.

brought into the temple of God, which the Levites who were the doorkeepers had
collected from the people of Manasseh, Ephraim and the entire remnant of Israel and
from all the people of Judah and Benjamin and the inhabitants of Jerusalem. 10Then
they entrusted it to the men appointed to supervise the work on the LORD's temple.
These men paid the workers who repaired and restored the temple. 11They also gave
money[j] to the carpenters and builders to purchase dressed stone, and timber for joists
and beams for the buildings that the kings of Judah had allowed to fall into ruin.[k]
12The men did the work faithfully.[l] Over them to direct them were Jahath and
Obadiah, Levites descended from Merari, and Zechariah and Meshullam, descended
from Kohath. The Levites—all who were skilled in playing musical instruments—[m]13had charge of the labourers[n] and supervised all the workers from job to
job. Some of the Levites were secretaries, scribes and doorkeepers.

The Book of the Law Found

14While they were bringing out the money that had been taken into the temple of
the LORD, Hilkiah the priest found the Book of the Law of the LORD that had been
given through Moses. 15Hilkiah said to Shaphan the secretary, "I have found the Book
of the Law[o] in the temple of the LORD." He gave it to Shaphan.
16Then Shaphan took the book to the king and reported to him: "Your officials are
doing everything that has been committed to them. 17They have paid out the money
that was in the temple of the LORD and have entrusted it to the supervisors and
workers." 18Then Shaphan the secretary informed the king, "Hilkiah the priest has
given me a book." And Shaphan read from it in the presence of the king.
19When the king heard the words of the Law,[p] he tore[q] his robes. 20He gave these
orders to Hilkiah, Ahikam son of Shaphan[r], Abdon son of Micah,[a] Shaphan the
secretary and Asaiah the king's attendant: 21"Go and enquire of the LORD for me and
for the remnant in Israel and Judah about what is written in this book that has been
found. Great is the LORD's anger that is poured out[s] on us because our fathers have
not kept the word of the LORD; they have not acted in accordance with all that is written
in this book."
22Hilkiah and those the king had sent with him[b] went to speak to the prophetess[t]
Huldah, who was the wife of Shallum son of Tokhath,[c] the son of Hasrah,[d] keeper
of the wardrobe. She lived in Jerusalem, in the Second District.
23She said to them, "This is what the LORD, the God of Israel, says: Tell the man
who sent you to me, 24'This is what the LORD says: I am going to bring disaster[u]
on this place and its people[v]—all the curses[w] written in the book that has been read
in the presence of the king of Judah. 25Because they have forsaken me[x] and burned
incense to other gods and provoked me to anger by all that their hands have made,[e]
my anger will be poured out on this place and will not be quenched.' 26Tell the king
of Judah, who sent you to enquire of the LORD, 'This is what the LORD, the God of
Israel, says concerning the words you heard: 27Because your heart was responsive[y]
and you humbled[z] yourself before God when you heard what he spoke against this
place and its people, and because you humbled yourself before me and tore your robes
and wept in my presence, I have heard you, declares the LORD. 28Now I will gather
you to your fathers,[a] and you will be buried in peace. Your eyes will not see all the
disaster I am going to bring on this place and on those who live here.' "[b]

a *20* Also called *Acbor son of Micaiah* **b** *22* One Hebrew manuscript, Vulgate and Syriac; most Hebrew manuscripts do not have *had sent with him.* **c** *22* Also called *Tikvah* **d** *22* Also called *Harhas* **e** *25* Or *by everything they have done*

34:11 j2Ch 24:12 k2Ch 33:4-7
34:12 l2Ki 12:15
34:13 m1Ch 25:1 n1Ch 23:4
34:15 o2Ki 22:8; Ezr 7:6; Ne 8:1
34:19 pDt 28:3-68 qJos 7:6; Isa 36:22; 37:1
34:20 r2Ki 22:3
34:21 s2Ch 29:8; La 2:4; 4:11; Eze 36:18
34:22 tEx 15:20; Ne 6:14
34:24 uPr 16:4; Isa 3:9; Jer 40:2; 42:10; 44:2, 11 v2Ch 36:14-20 wDt 28:15-68
34:25 x2Ch 33:3-6; Jer 22:9
34:27 y2Ch 12:7; 32:26 zEx 10:3; 2Ch 6:37
34:28 a2Ch 35:20-25 b2Ch 32:26

34:14, 15 The Book of the Law of the Lord that Hilkiah found was probably the book of Deuteronomy that had been lost during the reigns of the evil kings. Now that it was found, Josiah realised that drastic changes had to be made in order to bring the nation back in line with God's commands. This account is also recorded in 2 Kings 22:8–13.

34:19 It is human nature to treat sin lightly—to make excuses, blame somebody else, or minimise the harm done. Not so with Josiah. He was so appalled at the people's neglect of the law that he tore his clothing to express his grief. True understanding of our sins should lead to "godly sorrow" that "brings repentance that leads to salvation" (2 Corinthians 7:10). Are you always excusing your sin, blaming others, and pretending that it's not so bad? God does not take sin lightly, and he wants us to respond with true remorse as Josiah did.

So they took her answer back to the king.
29Then the king called together all the elders of Judah and Jerusalem. 30He went
up to the temple of the LORD[c] with the men of Judah, the people of Jerusalem, the
priests and the Levites — all the people from the least to the greatest. He read in their
hearing all the words of the Book of the Covenant, which had been found in the temple
of the LORD. 31The king stood by his pillar[d] and renewed the covenant[e] in the
presence of the LORD — to follow[f] the LORD and keep his commands, regulations and
decrees with all his heart and all his soul, and to obey the words of the covenant written
in this book.
32Then he made everyone in Jerusalem and Benjamin pledge themselves to it; the
people of Jerusalem did this in accordance with the covenant of God, the God of their
fathers.
33Josiah removed all the detestable[g] idols from all the territory belonging to the
Israelites, and he made all who were present in Israel serve the LORD their God. As
long as he lived, they did not fail to follow the LORD, the God of their fathers.

Josiah Celebrates the Passover

35 Josiah celebrated the Passover[a] to the LORD in Jerusalem, and the Passover
lamb was slaughtered on the fourteenth day of the first month. 2He appointed
the priests to their duties and encouraged them in the service of the LORD's temple.
3He said to the Levites, who instructed[b] all Israel and who had been consecrated to
the LORD: "Put the sacred ark in the temple that Solomon son of David king of Israel
built. It is not to be carried about on your shoulders. Now serve the LORD your God
and his people Israel. 4Prepare yourselves by families in your divisions,[c] according
to the directions written by David king of Israel and by his son Solomon.
5"Stand in the holy place with a group of Levites for each sub-division of the
families of your fellow countrymen, the lay people. 6Slaughter the Passover lambs,
consecrate yourselves[d] and prepare ⌞the lambs⌟ for your fellow countrymen, doing
what the LORD commanded through Moses."
7Josiah provided for all the lay people who were there a total of thirty thousand
sheep and goats for the Passover offerings,[e] and also three thousand cattle — all from
the king's own possessions.[f]
8His officials also contributed[g] voluntarily to the people and the priests and
Levites. Hilkiah,[h] Zechariah and Jehiel, the administrators of God's temple, gave the
priests two thousand six hundred Passover offerings and three hundred cattle. 9Also
Conaniah[i] along with Shemaiah and Nethanel, his brothers, and Hashabiah, Jeiel and
Jozabad,[j] the leaders of the Levites, provided five thousand Passover offerings and
five hundred head of cattle for the Levites.
10The service was arranged and the priests stood in their places with the Levites
in their divisions[k] as the king had ordered.[l] 11The Passover lambs were slaughtered,[m] and the priests sprinkled the blood handed to them, while the Levites skinned
the animals. 12They set aside the burnt offerings to give them to the sub-divisions of
the families of the people to offer to the LORD, as is written in the Book of Moses.
They did the same with the cattle. 13They roasted the Passover animals over the fire
as prescribed,[n] and boiled the holy offerings in pots, cauldrons and pans and served
them quickly to all the people. 14After this, they made preparations for themselves
and for the priests, because the priests, the descendants of Aaron, were sacrificing the

34:30 [c]2Ki 23:2; Ne 8:1-3
34:31 [d]1Ki 7:15; 2Ki 11:14 [e]2Ki 11:17; 2Ch 23:16; 29:10 [f]Dt 13:4
34:33 [g]ver 3-7; Dt 18:9
35:1 [a]Ex 12:1-30; Nu 9:3; 28:16
35:3 [b]Dt 33:10; 1Ch 23:26; 2Ch 5:7; 17:7
35:4 [c]ver 10; 1Ch 9:10-13; 24:1; 2Ch 8:14; Ezr 6:18
35:6 [d]Lev 11:44; 2Ch 29:5, 15
35:7 [e]2Ch 30:24 [f]2Ch 31:3
35:8 [g]1Ch 29:3; 2Ch 29:31-36 [h]1Ch 6:13
35:9 [i]2Ch 31:12 [j]2Ch 31:13
35:10 [k]ver 4; Ezr 6:18 [l]2Ch 30:16
35:11 [m]2Ch 29:22, 34; 30:17
35:13 [n]Ex 12:2-11; Lev 6:25; 1Sa 2:13-15

34:31 When Josiah read the book that Hilkiah discovered (34:14), he responded with repentance and humility and promised to follow God's commands as written in the book. The Bible is God's word to us, "living and active" (Hebrews 4:12), but we cannot know what God wants us to do if we do not read it. And even reading God's word is not enough; we must be willing to do what it says. There is not much difference between the book hidden in the temple and the Bible hidden on the bookshelf. An unread Bible is as useless as a lost one.

35:3 In Moses' day, one of the duties of the Levites was to carry the ark of the covenant whenever Israel travelled. "Put the sacred ark in the temple" implies that it may have been moved during the reigns of the previous evil kings, Manasseh and Amon. The ark was now permanently housed in the temple and would no longer be carried about in procession as it was in the desert. Josiah was telling the Levites that they were now free to take on other responsibilities (1 Chronicles 24).

burnt offerings and the fat portions[o] until nightfall. So the Levites made preparations
for themselves and for the Aaronic priests.
15The musicians,[p] the descendants of Asaph, were in the places prescribed by
David, Asaph, Heman and Jeduthun the king's seer. The gatekeepers at each gate did
not need to leave their posts, because their fellow Levites made the preparations for
them.
16So at that time the entire service of the LORD was carried out for the celebration
of the Passover and the offering of burnt offerings on the altar of the LORD, as King
Josiah had ordered. 17The Israelites who were present celebrated the Passover at that
time and observed the Feast of Unleavened Bread for seven days. 18The Passover had
not been observed like this in Israel since the days of the prophet Samuel; and none
of the kings of Israel had ever celebrated such a Passover as did Josiah, with the
priests, the Levites and all Judah and Israel who were there with the people of
Jerusalem. 19This Passover was celebrated in the eighteenth year of Josiah's reign.

The Death of Josiah

20After all this, when Josiah had set the temple in order, Neco king of Egypt went
up to fight at Carchemish[q] on the Euphrates,[r] and Josiah marched out to meet him
in battle. 21But Neco sent messengers to him saying, "What quarrel is there between
you and me, O king of Judah? It is not you I am attacking at this time, but the house
with which I am at war. God has told[s] me to hurry; so stop opposing God, who is
with me, or he will destroy you."
22Josiah, however, would not turn away from him, but disguised[t] himself to
engage him in battle. He would not listen to what Neco had said at God's command
but went to fight him on the plain of Megiddo.
23Archers[u] shot King Josiah, and he told his officers, "Take me away; I am badly
wounded." 24So they took him out of his chariot, put him in the other chariot he had
and brought him to Jerusalem, where he died. He was buried in the tombs of his
fathers, and all Judah and Jerusalem mourned for him.

35:14 [o]Ex 29:13
35:15 [p]1Ch 25:1; 26:12-19; 2Ch 29:30; Ne 12:46; Ps 68:25
35:20 [q]Isa 10:9; Jer 46:2 [r]Ge 2:14
35:21 [s]1Ki 13:18; 2Ki 18:25
35:22 [t]Jdg 5:19; 1Sa 28:8; 2Ch 18:29
35:23 [u]1Ki 22:34

35:15 The temple gatekeepers, who were all Levites, guarded the four main entrances to the temple and opened the gates each morning. They also did other day-to-day chores such as cleaning and preparing the offerings for sacrifice and accounting for the gifts given to the temple. (For more on gatekeepers, see 1 Chronicles 26:1ff.)

35:17 The Feast of Unleavened Bread was a seven-day celebration beginning the day after Passover. Like Passover, it commemorated the exodus from Egypt. For seven days the people ate bread without yeast, just as their ancestors did while leaving Egypt because it could be made quickly in preparation for their swift departure (Exodus 12:14–20). This feast reminded the people that they had left slavery behind and had come to the land God promised them.

35:20 This event occurred in 609 B.C. Nineveh, the Assyrian capital, had been destroyed three years earlier by the Babylonians. The defeated Assyrians regrouped at Haran and Carchemish, but Babylon sent its army to destroy them once and for all. Pharaoh Neco, who wanted to make Egypt a world power, was worried about Babylon's growing strength, so he marched his army north through Judah to help the Assyrians at Carchemish. But King Josiah of Judah tried to prevent Neco from passing through his land on his way to Carchemish. Josiah was killed, and Judah became subject to Egypt. (2 Kings 23:25–30 helps explain the tragedy. Even though Josiah followed the Lord, God did not turn from his judgment on Judah because of Manasseh's sin and Israel's superficial repentance.) Neco went on to Carchemish and held off the Babylonians for four years, but in 605 he was soundly defeated, and Babylon moved into the spotlight as the dominant world power.

35:21–24 Josiah ignored Neco's message because of who Neco was—king of a pagan nation. The mistaken assumption that Neco could not be part of God's larger plan cost Josiah his life. While not everyone who claims to have a message from God really does, God's messages may come in unexpected ways. God had spoken to pagan kings in the past (Genesis 12:17–20; 20:3–7; see also Daniel 4:1–3). Don't let prejudice or false assumptions blind you to God's message.

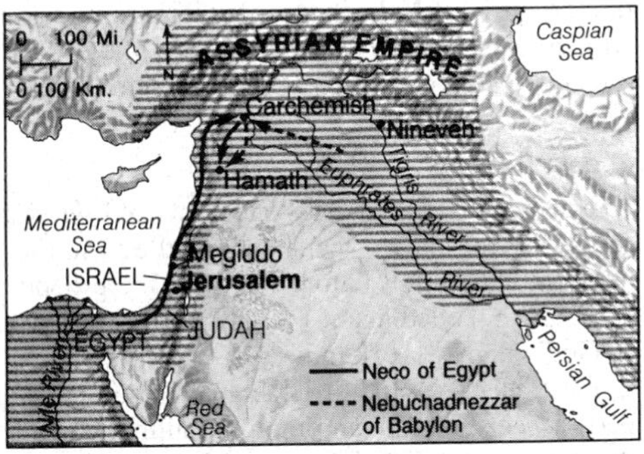

THE BATTLE AT CARCHEMISH A world war was brewing in 609 B.C. when Pharaoh Neco of Egypt set out for the city of Carchemish to join the Assyrians in an attempt to defeat the Babylonians, who were rising to great power. Neco marched his armies through Judah, where King Josiah tried to stop him at Megiddo, but was killed. The battle began at Carchemish in 605 B.C., and the Egyptians and Assyrians were soundly defeated, chased to Hamath, and defeated again. Babylon was now the new world power.

25 Jeremiah composed laments for Josiah, and to this day all the men and women
singers commemorate Josiah in the laments.[v] These became a tradition in Israel and
are written in the Laments.
26 The other events of Josiah's reign and his acts of devotion, according to what is
written in the Law of the LORD—27 all the events, from beginning to end, are written
36 in the book of the kings of Israel and Judah. 1 And the people of the land took
Jehoahaz son of Josiah and made him king in Jerusalem in place of his father.

3. Judah is exiled to Babylon

Jehoahaz King of Judah

2 Jehoahaz[a] was twenty-three years old when he became king, and he reigned in
Jerusalem for three months. 3 The king of Egypt dethroned him in Jerusalem and
imposed on Judah a levy of a hundred talents[b] of silver and a talent[c] of gold. 4 The
king of Egypt made Eliakim, a brother of Jehoahaz, king over Judah and Jerusalem
and changed Eliakim's name to Jehoiakim. But Neco[a] took Eliakim's brother Jehoahaz and carried him off to Egypt.

Jehoiakim King of Judah

5 Jehoiakim[b] was twenty-five years old when he became king, and he reigned in
Jerusalem for eleven years. He did evil in the eyes of the LORD his God. 6 Nebuchadnezzar[c] king of Babylon attacked him and bound him with bronze shackles to take
him to Babylon.[d] 7 Nebuchadnezzar also took to Babylon articles from the temple of
the LORD and put them in his temple[d] there.[e]
8 The other events of Jehoiakim's reign, the detestable things he did and all that was
found against him, are written in the book of the kings of Israel and Judah. And
Jehoiachin his son succeeded him as king.

Jehoiachin King of Judah

9 Jehoiachin[f] was eighteen[e] years old when he became king, and he reigned in
Jerusalem for three months and ten days. He did evil in the eyes of the LORD. 10 In
the spring, King Nebuchadnezzar sent for him and brought him to Babylon,[g] together
with articles of value from the temple of the LORD, and he made Jehoiachin's uncle,[f]
Zedekiah, king over Judah and Jerusalem.

Zedekiah King of Judah

11 Zedekiah[h] was twenty-one years old when he became king, and he reigned in
Jerusalem for eleven years. 12 He did evil in the eyes of the LORD[i] his God and did
not humble[j] himself before Jeremiah the prophet, who spoke the word of the LORD.
13 He also rebelled against King Nebuchadnezzar, who had made him take an oath[k]
in God's name. He became stiff-necked[l] and hardened his heart and would not turn
to the LORD, the God of Israel. 14 Furthermore, all the leaders of the priests and the
people became more and more unfaithful,[m] following all the detestable practices of
the nations and defiling the temple of the LORD, which he had consecrated in Jerusalem.

[a] 2 Hebrew *Joahaz*, a variant of *Jehoahaz*; also in verse 4 [b] 3 That is, about 3 1/3 tons (about 3.4 metric tons) [c] 3 That is, about 75 pounds (about 34 kilograms) [d] 7 Or *palace* [e] 9 One Hebrew manuscript, some Septuagint manuscripts and Syriac (see also 2 Kings 24:8); most Hebrew manuscripts *eight* [f] 10 Hebrew *brother*, that is, relative (see 2 Kings 24:17)

35:25 [v] Jer 22:10, 15-16
36:4 [a] Jer 22:10-12
36:5 [b] Jer 22:18; 26:1; 35:1
36:6 [c] Jer 25:9; 27:6; Eze 29:18 [d] 2Ch 33:11; Eze 19:9; Da 1:1
36:7 [e] 2Ki 24:13; Ezr 1:7; Da 1:2
36:9 [f] Jer 22:24-28; 52:31
36:10 [g] ver 18; 2Ki 20:17; Ezr 1:7; Jer 22:25; 24:1; 29:1; 37:1; Eze 17:12
36:11 [h] 2Ki 24:17; Jer 27:1; 28:1
36:12 [i] Jer 37:1-39:18 [j] Dt 8:3; 2Ch 7:14; 2Ch 33:23; Jer 21:3-7
36:13 [k] Eze 17:13 [l] 2Ki 17:14; 2Ch 30:8
36:14 [m] 1Ch 5:25

35:25 Though Jeremiah recorded these laments for the death of Josiah, they are not the same as the book of Lamentations.

36:6 Nebuchadnezzar was the son of the founder of the new Babylonian empire. In 605 B.C., the year he became king, Nebuchadnezzar won the battle of Carchemish. That loss crushed Assyria (see the note on 35:20). (For more information about Nebuchadnezzar, read his Profile in Daniel 3.)

36:9, 10 In 2 Kings 24:8, Jehoiachin is listed as 18 years old. Many Hebrew manuscripts list him as eight years old. The age given in 2 Kings 24:8 is most likely accurate because he had wives at that time (see 2 Kings 24:15).

36:15
[n]Isa 5:4; 44:26; Mal 2:7; 3:1
[o]Jer 7:13, 25; 25:3-4; 35:14, 15; 44:4-6
36:16
[p]2Ki 2:23; Jer 5:13
[q]Ezr 5:12; Pr 1:30-31
[r]Pr 29:1
36:17
[s]Jer 6:11
[t]Ezr 5:12; Jer 32:28
36:18
[u]ver 7, 10
36:19
[v]Jer 11:16; 17:27; 21:10, 14; 22:7; 32:29; 39:8; Eze 20:47; Am 2:5; Zec 11:1
[w]1Ki 9:8-9
[x]2Ki 14:13
[y]La 2:6
[z]Ps 79:1-3
36:20
[a]2Ki 24:14; Ezr 2:1
[b]Jer 27:7
36:21
[c]Lev 25:4; 26:34
[d]1Ch 22:9
[e]Jer 1:1; 25:11; 27:22; 29:10; 40:1; Da 9:2; Zec 1:12; 7:5
36:22
[f]Isa 44:28; 45:1, 13
36:23
[g]Jdg 4:10

The Fall of Jerusalem

15 The LORD, the God of their fathers, sent word to them through his messengers[n]
again and again,[o] because he had pity on his people and on his dwelling-place. 16 But
they mocked God's messengers, despised his words and scoffed[p] at his prophets until
the wrath[q] of the LORD was aroused against his people and there was no remedy.[r]
17 He brought up against them the king of the Babylonians,[g] who killed their young
men with the sword in the sanctuary, and spared neither young man[s] nor young
woman, old man or aged. God handed all of them over to Nebuchadnezzar.[t] 18 He
carried to Babylon all the articles[u] from the temple of God, both large and small,
and the treasures of the LORD's temple and the treasures of the king and his officials.
19 They set fire[v] to God's temple[w] and broke down the wall[x] of Jerusalem; they
burned all the palaces and destroyed[y] everything of value there.[z]
20 He carried into exile[a] to Babylon the remnant who escaped from the sword, and
they became servants[b] to him and his sons until the kingdom of Persia came to power.
21 The land enjoyed its sabbath rests;[c] all the time of its desolation it rested,[d] until
the seventy years[e] were completed in fulfilment of the word of the LORD spoken by
Jeremiah.
22 In the first year of Cyrus[f] king of Persia, in order to fulfil the word of the LORD
spoken by Jeremiah, the LORD moved the heart of Cyrus king of Persia to make a
proclamation throughout his realm and to put it in writing:

23 "This is what Cyrus king of Persia says:
" 'The LORD, the God of heaven, has given me all the kingdoms of the earth
and he has appointed[g] me to build a temple for him at Jerusalem in Judah.
Anyone of his people among you—may the LORD his God be with him, and let
him go up.' "

g *17* Or *Chaldeans*

36:16 God warned Judah about its sin and continually restored the people to his favour, only to have them turn away. Eventually the situation was beyond remedy. Beware of harbouring sin in your heart. The day will come when remedy is no longer possible and God's judgment replaces his mercy. Sin often repeated, but never repented of, invites disaster.

36:21 Leviticus 26:27–45 strikingly predicts the captivity, telling how God's people would be torn from their land for disobeying him. One of the laws they had ignored stated that one year in every seven the land should lie fallow, resting from producing crops (Exodus 23:10, 11). The 70-year captivity allowed the land to rest, making up for all the years the Israelites had not observed this law. We know that God keeps all his promises—not only his promises of blessing, but also his promises of judgment.

36:22, 23 Cyrus made this proclamation 48 years after the temple was destroyed (36:18, 19), the year after he conquered Babylon. The book of Ezra tells the story of this proclamation and the return of the exiles to Judah.

36:22, 23 Second Chronicles focuses on the rise and fall of the worship of God as symbolised by the Jerusalem temple. David planned the temple; Solomon built it and then put on the greatest dedication service the world had ever seen. Worship in the temple was superbly organised.

But several evil kings defiled the temple and degraded worship so that the people revered idols more highly than God. Finally, King Nebuchadnezzar of Babylon destroyed the temple (36:19). The kings were gone, the temple was destroyed, and the people were removed. The nation was stripped to its very foundation. But fortunately there was a greater foundation—God himself. When everything in life seems stripped away from us, we too still have God—his word, his presence, and his promises.

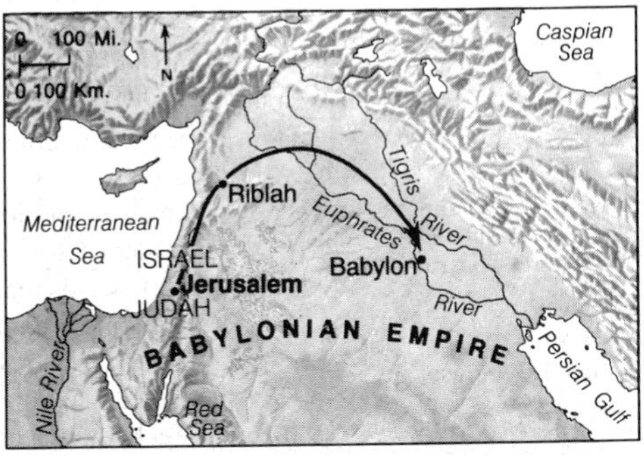

EXILE TO BABYLON Despite Judah's few good kings and timely reforms, the people never truly changed. Their evil continued, and finally God used the Babylonian empire, under Nebuchadnezzar, to conquer Judah, destroy Jerusalem, and take the people captive to Babylon.

EZRA

Jerusalem destroyed; exiles go to Babylon 586 B.C.

Babylon overthrown by Cyrus 539

Exiles return to Jerusalem 538

Temple construction begins 536

Temple work halted 530

VITAL STATISTICS

PURPOSE:
To show God's faithfulness and the way he kept his promise to restore his people to their land

AUTHOR:
Not stated, but probably Ezra

DATE WRITTEN:
Around 450 B.C., recording events from about 538–450 B.C. (omitting 516–458 B.C.); possibly begun earlier in Babylon and finished in Jerusalem

SETTING:
Ezra follows 2 Chronicles as a history of the Jewish people, recording their return to the land after the captivity.

KEY VERSES:
"So the Israelites who had returned from the exile ate it, together with all who had separated themselves from the unclean practices of their Gentile neighbours in order to seek the LORD, the God of Israel. For seven days they celebrated with joy the Feast of Unleavened Bread, because the LORD had filled them with joy by changing the attitude of the king of Assyria, so that he assisted them in the work on the house of God, the God of Israel" (6:21, 22).

KEY PEOPLE:
Cyrus, Zerubbabel, Haggai, Zechariah, Darius, Artaxerxes I, Ezra

KEY PLACES:
Babylon, Jerusalem

SPECIAL FEATURES:
Ezra and Nehemiah were one book in the Hebrew Bible, and, with Esther, they comprise the post-captivity historical books. The post-captivity prophetic books are Haggai, Zechariah, and Malachi. Haggai and Zechariah should be studied with Ezra because they prophesied during the period of the reconstruction.

NAME the truly great men and women of your lifetime. Celebrities, including politicians, war heroes, sports figures, and maybe your parents and special friends come to mind. You remember them because of certain acts or character qualities. Now, name some biblical heroes—figures etched into your life through countless sermons and Sunday school lessons. This list undoubtedly includes many who served God faithfully and courageously. Does your list include Ezra? Far from being well known, this unheralded man of God deserves to be mentioned in any discussion of greatness.

Ezra was a priest, a scribe, and a great leader. His name means "help", and his whole life was dedicated to serving God and God's people. Tradition says that Ezra wrote most of 1 and 2 Chronicles, Ezra, Nehemiah, and Psalm 119, and that he led the council of 120 men who formed the Old Testament canon. He centres the narrative of the book of Ezra around God and his promise that the Jews would return to their land, as promised by Jeremiah (see the note on 1:1). This message formed the core of Ezra's life. The last half of the book gives a very personal glimpse of Ezra. His knowledge of Scripture and his God-given wisdom were so obvious to the king that he appointed Ezra to lead the second emigration to Jerusalem, to teach the people God's word, and to administer national life (7:14–26).

Ezra not only knew God's word, he believed and obeyed it. Upon learning of the Israelites' sins of intermarriage and idolatry, Ezra fell in humility before God and prayed for the nation (9:1–15). Their disobedience touched him deeply (10:1). His response helped lead the people back to God.

2 Chronicles finishes with Cyrus, king of Persia, asking for volunteers to return to Jerusalem to build a house for God. Ezra continues this account (1:1–3 is almost identical to 2 Chronicles 36:22, 23) as two caravans of God's people were returning to Jerusalem. Zerubbabel, the leader of the first trip, was joined by 42,360 pilgrims who journeyed homewards (chapter 2). After arriving, they began to build the altar and the temple foundations (chapter 3). But opposition arose from the local inhabitants, and a campaign of accusations and rumours temporarily halted the project (chapter 4). During this time, the prophets Haggai and Zechariah encouraged the people (chapter 5). Finally, Darius decreed that the work should proceed unhindered (chapter 6).

After a 58-year gap, Ezra led a group of Jews from Persia. Armed with decrees and authority from Artaxerxes I, Ezra's task was to administer the affairs of the land (chapters 7, 8). Upon arrival, he learned of intermarriage between God's people and their pagan neighbours. He wept and prayed for the nation (chapter 9). Ezra's example of humble confession led to national revival (chapter 10). Ezra, a man of God and a true hero, was a model for Israel, and he is a fitting model for us.

Read Ezra, the book, and remember Ezra, the man—a humble, obedient helper. Commit yourself to serving God as he did, with your whole life.

Darius I becomes king of Persia 522	Temple work resumed/ messages of Haggai, Zechariah 520	Temple completed 516	Ezra comes to Jerusalem 458	Nehemiah comes to Jerusalem 445

THE BLUEPRINT

A. THE RETURN LED BY ZERUBBABEL (1:1—6:22)
1. The first group of exiles returns to the land
2. The people rebuild the temple

Finally given the chance to return to their homeland, the people started to rebuild the temple, only to be stopped by opposition from their enemies. God's work in the world is not without opposition. We must not become discouraged and give up, as the returning people did at first, but continue boldly in the face of difficulties, as they did later with encouragement from the prophets.

B. THE RETURN LED BY EZRA (7:1—10:44)
1. The second group of exiles returns to the land
2. Ezra opposes intermarriage

Ezra returned to Jerusalem almost 80 years after Zerubbabel, only to discover that the people had married pagan or foreign spouses. This polluted the religious purity of the people and endangered the future of the nation. Believers today must be careful not to threaten their walk with God by taking on the practices of unbelievers.

MEGATHEMES

THEME	EXPLANATION	IMPORTANCE
The Jews Return	By returning to the land of Israel from Babylon, the Jews showed their faith in God's promise to restore them as a people. They returned not only to their homeland, but also to the place where their forefathers had promised to follow God.	God shows his mercy to every generation. He compassionately restores his people. No matter how difficult our present "captivity", we are never far from his love and mercy. He restores us when we return to him.
Rededication	In 536 B.C., Zerubbabel led the people in rebuilding the altar and laying the temple foundations. They reinstated daily sacrifices and annual feasts, and rededicated themselves to a new spiritual worship of God.	In rededicating the altar, the people were recommitting themselves to God and his service. To grow spiritually, our commitment must be reviewed and renewed often. As we rededicate ourselves to God, our lives become altars to him.
Opposition	Opposition came soon after the altar was built and the temple foundations laid. Enemies of the Jews used deceit to hinder the building for over six years. Finally, there was a decree to stop the building altogether. This opposition severely tested their wavering faith.	There will always be adversaries who oppose God's work. The life of faith is never easy. But God can overrule all opposition to his service. When we face opposition, we must not falter or withdraw, but keep active and patient.
God's Word	When the people returned to the land, they were also returning to the influence of God's word. The prophets Haggai and Zechariah helped to encourage them while Ezra's preaching of Scripture built them up. God's word gave them what they needed to do God's work.	We also need the encouragement and direction of God's word. We must make it the basis for our faith and actions to finish God's work and fulfil our obligations. We must never waver in our commitment to hear and obey his word.
Faith and Action	The urging of Israel's leaders motivated the people to complete the temple. Over the years, they had intermarried with idol-worshippers and adopted their pagan practices. Their faith, tested and revived, also led them to remove these sins from their lives.	Faith led them to complete the temple and to remove sin from their society. As we trust God with our hearts and minds, we must also act by completing our daily responsibilities. It is not enough to say we believe; we must make the changes God requires.

A. THE RETURN LED BY ZERUBBABEL (1.1 – 6.22)

After 70 years in exile, the captives from Judah were allowed to return to their homeland. Nearly 50,000 people made this journey. Upon arrival they began to rebuild the temple, but became discouraged by opposition. After encouragement from Haggai and Zechariah, they returned to the task and completed the temple. The message of the prophets still speaks to us today, encouraging us to continue building up God's church.

1. The first group of exiles returns to the land

Cyrus Helps the Exiles to Return

1 In the first year of Cyrus king of Persia, in order to fulfil the word of the LORD
spoken by Jeremiah,[a] the LORD moved the heart[b] of Cyrus king of Persia to
make a proclamation throughout his realm and to put it in writing:

2"This is what Cyrus king of Persia says:
" 'The LORD, the God of heaven, has given me all the kingdoms of the earth
and he has appointed[c] me to build[d] a temple for him at Jerusalem in Judah.
3Anyone of his people among you — may his God be with him, and let him go
up to Jerusalem in Judah and build the temple of the LORD, the God of Israel,
the God who is in Jerusalem. 4And the people of any place where survivors[e]
may now be living are to provide him with silver and gold, with goods and
livestock, and with freewill offerings[f] for the temple of God in Jerusalem.' "[g]

5Then the family heads of Judah and Benjamin,[h] and the priests and Le-

1:1 [a]Jer 25:11-12; 29:10-14 [b]2Ch 36:22, 23
1:2 [c]Isa 44:28; 45:13 [d]Ezr 5:13
1:4 [e]Isa 10:20-22 [f]Nu 15:3; Ps 50:14; 54:6; 116:17 [g]Ezr 4:3; 5:13; 6:3, 14
1:5 [h]Ezr 4:1; Ne 11:4

1:1 The book of Ezra opens in 538 B.C., 48 years after Nebuchadnezzar destroyed Jerusalem, defeated the southern kingdom of Judah, and carried the Jews away to Babylon as captives (2 Kings 25; 2 Chronicles 36). Nebuchadnezzar died in 562, and because his successors were not strong, Babylon was overthrown by Persia in 539, just prior to the events recorded in this book. Both the Babylonians and the Persians had a relaxed policy towards their captives, allowing them to own land and homes and to take ordinary jobs. Many Jews such as Daniel, Mordecai, and Esther rose to prominent positions within the nation. King Cyrus of Persia went a step further: he allowed many groups of exiles, including the Jews, to return to their homelands. By doing this, he hoped to win their loyalty and thus provide buffer zones around the borders of his empire. For the Jews this was a day of hope, a new beginning.

1:1 Cyrus, king of Persia (559–530 B.C.), had already begun his rise to power in the Near East by unifying the Medes and Persians into a strong empire. As he conquered cities, he treated the inhabitants with mercy. Although not a servant of Yahweh, Cyrus was used by God to return the Jews to their homeland. Cyrus may have been shown the prophecy of Isaiah 44:28 – 45:6, written over a century earlier, which predicted that Cyrus himself would help the Jews return to Jerusalem. Daniel, a prominent government official (Daniel 5:29; 6:28), would have been familiar with the prophecy. The book of Daniel has more to say about Cyrus.

1:1 Jeremiah prophesied that the Jews would remain in captivity for 70 years (Jeremiah 25:11; 29:10). The 70-year period has been calculated two different ways: (1) from the first captivity in 605 B.C. (2 Kings 24:1) until the altar was rebuilt by the returned exiles in 536 (Ezra 3:1–6), or (2) from the destruction of the temple in 586 until the exiles finished rebuilding it in 516. Many scholars prefer the second approach because the temple was the focus and heartbeat of the nation. Without the temple, the Jews did not consider themselves re-established as a nation.

1:2 Cyrus was not a Jew, but God worked through him to return the exiled Jews to their homeland. Cyrus gave the proclamation allowing their return, and he gave them protection, money, and the temple articles taken by Nebuchadnezzar. When you face difficult situations and feel surrounded, outnumbered, overpowered, or outclassed, remember that God's power is not limited to your resources. He is able to use anyone to carry out his plans.

1:2-4 This proclamation permitted the Jews to work together to accomplish the huge task of rebuilding the temple. Some did the actual building, while others operated the supply lines. Significant ventures require teamwork, with certain people serving in the forefront and others providing support. Each function is vital to accomplishing the task. When you're asked to serve, do so faithfully as a team member, no matter who gets the credit.

1:5 Cyrus was king over the entire region that had once been Assyria and Babylon. Assyria had deported the Israelites from the northern kingdom (Israel) in 722 B.C. Babylon, the next world power, had taken Israelites captive from the southern kingdom (Judah) in 586 B.C. Therefore, when the Medo-Persian empire came to power, King Cyrus's proclamation of freedom went to all the original 12 tribes, but only Judah and Benjamin responded and returned to rebuild God's temple. The ten tribes of the northern kingdom had been so fractured and dispersed by Assyria, and so much time had elapsed since their captivity, that many may have been unsure of their real heritage. Thus they were unwilling to share in the vision of rebuilding the temple.

1:5 God moved the hearts of the leaders, family heads, priests, and Levites and gave them a great desire to return to Jerusalem to rebuild the temple. Major changes begin on the inside as God works on our attitudes, beliefs, and desires. These inner changes lead to faithful actions. After 48 years of captivity, the arrogant Jewish nation had been humbled. When the people's attitudes and desires changed, God ended their punishment and gave them another opportunity to go home and try again. Paul reminds us that "for it is God who works in you to will and to act according to his good purpose" (Philippians 2:13). Doing God's will begins with your desires. Are you willing to be humble, to be open to his opportunities, and to move at his direction? Ask God to give you the desire to follow him more closely.

1:5, 6 Many Jews chose to go to Jerusalem, but many more chose to remain in Babylon rather than return to their homeland. The journey back to Jerusalem was difficult, dangerous, and expensive, lasting over four months. Travel conditions were poor; Jerusalem and the surrounding countryside were in ruins; and the people living in the area were hostile.

Persian records indicate that many Jews in captivity had accumulated great wealth. Returning to Jerusalem would have meant giving up everything they had and starting again. Many people couldn't bring themselves to do that; they preferred wealth and security to the sacrifice that God's work would require. Their priorities

1:5
[i]ver 1; Ex 35:20-22; 2Ch 36:22; Hag 1:14; Php 2:13
[j]Ps 127:1

vites—everyone whose heart God had moved[i]—prepared to go up and build the
house[j] of the LORD in Jerusalem. 6All their neighbours assisted them with articles
of silver and gold, with goods and livestock, and with valuable gifts, in addition to
all the freewill offerings. 7Moreover, King Cyrus brought out the articles belonging
to the temple of the LORD, which Nebuchadnezzar had carried away from Jerusalem
and had placed in the temple of his god.[a][k] 8Cyrus king of Persia had them brought
by Mithredath the treasurer, who counted them out to Sheshbazzar[l] the prince of
Judah.

9This was the inventory:

gold dishes	30
silver dishes	1,000
silver pans[b]	29
10gold bowls	30
matching silver bowls	410
other articles	1,000

11In all, there were 5,400 articles of gold and of silver. Sheshbazzar brought all
these along when the exiles came up from Babylon to Jerusalem.

1:7
[k]2Ki 24:13; 2Ch 36:7, 10; Ezr 5:14; 6:5

1:8
[l]Ezr 5:14

[a] 7 Or *gods* [b] 9 The meaning of the Hebrew for this word is uncertain.

PROPHECIES FULFILLED BY THE RETURN OF ISRAEL FROM EXILE

Reference	*Prophecy*	*Approximate Date*	*Fulfilment Date*	*Significance*
Isaiah 44:28	Cyrus would be used by God to guarantee the return of a remnant. Jerusalem would be rebuilt and the temple restored.	688 B.C.	539 B.C.	As God named Cyrus even before he was born, God knows what will happen—he is in control.
Jeremiah 25:12	Babylon would be punished for destroying Jerusalem and exiling God's people.	605 B.C.	539 B.C.	Babylon was conquered by Cyrus the Great. God may seem to allow evil to go unpunished, but consequences for wrongdoing are inevitable. God will punish evil.
Jeremiah 29:10	The people would spend 70 years in Babylon, then God would bring them back to their homeland.	594 B.C.	538 B.C.	The 70 years of captivity passed (see the third note on 1:1), and God provided the opportunity for Zerubbabel to lead the first group of captives home. God's plans may allow for hardship, but his desire is for our good.
Daniel 5:17–30	God had judged the Babylonian empire. It would be given to the Medes and the Persians, forming a new world power.	539 B.C.	539 B.C.	Belshazzar was killed and Babylon was conquered the same night. God's judgment is accurate and swift. God knows the point of no return in each of our lives. Until then, he allows the freedom for us to repent and seek his forgiveness.

God, through his faithful prophets, predicted that the people of Judah would be taken into captivity because of their sinfulness. But he also predicted that they would return to Jerusalem and rebuild the city, the temple, and the nation.

were upside down (Mark 4:18, 19). We must not let our comfort, security, or material possessions prevent us from doing what God wants.

1:7 When King Nebuchadnezzar ransacked the temple, he took many of the valuable furnishings with him. What he did not take, he burned (2 Chronicles 36:18, 19). Most of the captured items were made of solid gold (1 Kings 7:48–50), and Cyrus kindly returned them to the Jews for the temple they would soon rebuild.

1:8 Either Sheshbazzar was the Babylonian name for Zerubbabel, one of the Jewish leaders during the first return (2:2; 3:8; 4:3), or he was a government official with responsibility for the returning party. The reasons Sheshbazzar may be identified with Zerubbabel are as follows: (1) both were called governors (5:14; Haggai 1:1); (2) both laid the temple foundation (3:8; 5:16); (3) Jews in exile were often given Babylonian names (see Daniel 1:7 where Daniel and his companions were given new names).

1:9–11 Every article of gold and silver was a witness to God's protection and care. Although many years had passed, God delivered these temple articles back to his people. We may be discouraged by events in life, but we must never give up our hope in God's promises to us. The turning point may be just ahead.

The List of the Exiles Who Returned

2 Now these are the people of the province who came up from the captivity of the
exiles,[a] whom Nebuchadnezzar king of Babylon[b] had taken captive to Babylon
(they returned to Jerusalem and Judah, each to his own town,[c]
2in company with
Zerubbabel,[d] Jeshua,[e] Nehemiah, Seraiah,[f] Reelaiah, Mordecai, Bilshan, Mispar,
Bigvai, Rehum and Baanah):

The list of the men of the people of Israel:

3the descendants of Parosh[g]	2,172
4of Shephatiah	372
5of Arah	775
6of Pahath-Moab (through the line of Jeshua and Joab)	2,812
7of Elam	1,254
8of Zattu	945
9of Zaccai	760
10of Bani	642
11of Bebai	623
12of Azgad	1,222
13of Adonikam[h]	666
14of Bigvai	2,056
15of Adin	454
16of Ater (through Hezekiah)	98
17of Bezai	323
18of Jorah	112
19of Hashum	223
20of Gibbar	95
21the men of Bethlehem[i]	123
22of Netophah	56
23of Anathoth	128
24of Azmaveth	42
25of Kiriath Jearim,[a] Kephirah and Beeroth	743
26of Ramah[j] and Geba	621
27of Michmash	122
28of Bethel and Ai[k]	223
29of Nebo	52

a *25* See Septuagint (see also Neh. 7:29); Hebrew *Kiriath Arim.*

2:1 [a]2Ch 36:20; Ne 7:6 [b]2Ki 24:16; 25:12 [c]Ne 7:73
2:2 [d]1Ch 3:19 [e]Ezr 3:2 [f]Ne 10:2
2:3 [g]Ezr 8:3
2:13 [h]Ezr 8:13
2:21 [i]Mic 5:2
2:26 [j]Jos 18:25
2:28 [k]Ge 12:8

2:2 The Nehemiah listed here is a different person from the one who rebuilt Jerusalem's walls 80 years later, and the Mordecai listed here is not the one who appears in the book of Esther.

2:2 This first list is made up of men who were leaders. The same list occurs in Nehemiah 7:7.

2:2–35 These people were from the tribes of Judah and Benjamin (1:5).

2:3–35 This list is the major group of those returning, divided by families (2:3–20) or by cities (2:21–35). Verse 36 begins listing priests, Levites, and other temple servants.

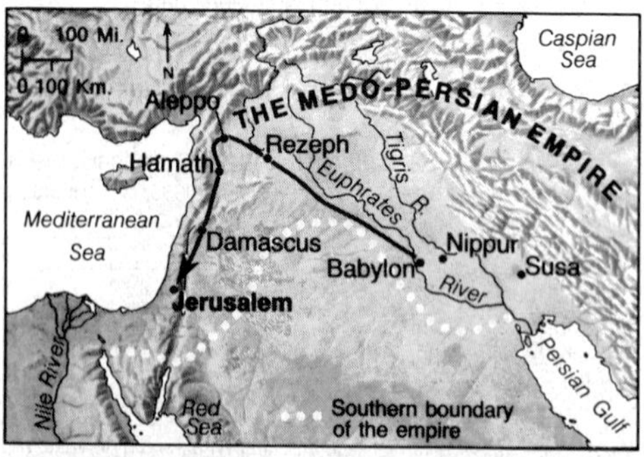

THE JOURNEY HOME The vast Medo-Persian empire included all the area on this map and more. A group of exiles began the long trip back to their homeland. Many exiles, however, preferred the comfort and security they had in Babylon to the dangerous trip back to Jerusalem, and so they decided to stay in Babylon.

30of Magbish	156
31of the other Elam	1,254
32of Harim	320
33of Lod, Hadid and Ono	725
34of Jericho[l]	345
35of Senaah	3,630

36The priests:

the descendants of Jedaiah[m] (through the family of Jeshua)	973
37of Immer[n]	1,052
38of Pashhur[o]	1,247
39of Harim[p]	1,017

40The Levites:[q]

the descendants of Jeshua[r] and Kadmiel (through the line of Hodaviah)	74

41The singers:[s]

the descendants of Asaph	128

42The gatekeepers[t] of the temple:

the descendants of Shallum, Ater, Talmon, Akkub, Hatita and Shobai	139

43The temple servants:[u]

the descendants of
Ziha, Hasupha, Tabbaoth,
44Keros, Siaha, Padon,
45Lebanah, Hagabah, Akkub,
46Hagab, Shalmai, Hanan,

2:34 [l]1Ki 16:34; 2Ch 28:15
2:36 [m]1Ch 24:7
2:37 [n]1Ch 24:14
2:38 [o]1Ch 9:12
2:39 [p]1Ch 24:8
2:40 [q]Ge 29:34; Nu 3:9; Dt 18:6-7; 1Ch 16:4; Ezr 7:7; 8:15; Ne 12:24 [r]Ezr 3:9
2:41 [s]1Ch 15:16
2:42 [t]1Sa 3:15; 1Ch 9:17
2:43 [u]1Ch 9:2; Ne 11:21

THE RETURN FROM EXILE

Year	*Number of People Returned*	*Persian King*	*Jewish Leader*	*Main Accomplishment*
538 B.C.	50,000	Cyrus	Zerubbabel	They rebuilt the temple, but only after a 20-year struggle. The work was halted for several years but was finally finished.
458 B.C.	2,000 men and their families	Artaxerxes	Ezra	Ezra confronted the spiritual disobedience of the people, and they repented and established worship at the temple. But the wall of Jerusalem remained in ruins.
445 B.C.	Small group	Artaxerxes	Nehemiah	The city was rebuilt, and a spiritual awakening followed. But the people still struggled with ongoing disobedience.

Babylon, the once-mighty nation that had destroyed Jerusalem and carried the people of Judah into captivity, had itself become a defeated nation. Persia was the new world power, and under its new foreign policy, captured peoples were allowed to return to their homelands. The people of Judah and Israel returned to their land in three successive waves.

47 Giddel, Gahar, Reaiah,
48 Rezin, Nekoda, Gazzam,
49 Uzza, Paseah, Besai,
50 Asnah, Meunim, Nephussim,
51 Bakbuk, Hakupha, Harhur,
52 Bazluth, Mehida, Harsha,
53 Barkos, Sisera, Temah,
54 Neziah and Hatipha

55 The descendants of the servants of Solomon:

the descendants of
Sotai, Hassophereth, Peruda,
56 Jaala, Darkon, Giddel,
57 Shephatiah, Hattil,
Pokereth-Hazzebaim and Ami

58 The temple servants[v] and the descendants of the servants
of Solomon 392

59 The following came up from the towns of Tel Melah, Tel Harsha, Kerub,
Addon and Immer, but they could not show that their families were descended[w]
from Israel:

60 The descendants of
Delaiah, Tobiah and Nekoda 652

61 And from among the priests:

The descendants of
Hobaiah, Hakkoz and Barzillai (a man who had married
a daughter of Barzillai the Gileadite[x] and was called by
that name).
62 These searched for their family records, but they could not find them and
so were excluded from the priesthood[y] as unclean. 63 The governor ordered them
not to eat any of the most sacred food[z] until there was a priest ministering with
the Urim and Thummim.[a]

64 The whole company numbered 42,360, 65 besides their 7,337 menservants
and maidservants; and they also had 200 men and women singers.[b] 66 They had
736 horses,[c] 245 mules, 67 435 camels and 6,720 donkeys.

68 When they arrived at the house of the LORD in Jerusalem, some of the heads of
the families[d] gave freewill offerings towards the rebuilding of the house of God on
its site. 69 According to their ability they gave to the treasury for this work 61,000
drachmas[b] of gold, 5,000 minas[c] of silver and 100 priestly garments.

b *69* That is, about 1,100 pounds (about 500 kilograms) **c** *69* That is, about 2-⅘ tons (about 2.9 metric tons)

2:58 [v] 1Ki 9:21; 1Ch 9:2
2:59 [w] Nu 1:18
2:61 [x] 2Sa 17:27
2:62 [y] Nu 3:10; 16:39-40
2:63 [z] Lev 2:3, 10 [a] Ex 28:30; Nu 27:21
2:65 [b] 2Sa 19:35
2:66 [c] Isa 66:20
2:68 [d] Ex 25:2

2:59–63 Genealogies were very important credentials to the Hebrew people. If they could not prove they had descended from Abraham, they were not considered true Jews and were excluded from full participation in Jewish community life. In addition, some privileges were restricted to members of certain tribes. For example, only descendants of Levi (Abraham's great-grandson) could serve in the temple.

2:63 The governor mentioned here was probably Zerubbabel. The Urim and Thummim were two objects, probably shaped like flat stones, originally carried in the garment worn by the high priest. They were used to determine God's will in important matters. (For more on the Urim and Thummim, see the note on Leviticus 8:8.) The "most sacred food" was the food that only the priests could eat. It was their allotted portion of meat that was sacrificed on the altar.

2:68, 69 As the temple reconstruction progressed, everyone contributed freewill offerings according to his or her ability. Some were able to give huge gifts and did so generously. Everyone's effort and co-operation were required, and the people gave as much as they could. Often we limit our giving to ten per-cent of our income. The Bible, however, emphasises that we should give from the heart *all* that we are able (2 Corinthians 8:12; 9:6). Let the amount of your gift be decided by God's call to give generously, not by the amount of your leftovers.

2:69 Drachmas and minas were gold and silver coins. The money given was enough to start rebuilding the temple. The people put what resources they had to their best use. They were enthusiastic and sincere, but this temple would never match the splendour of Solomon's. The money David gathered to start the building of Solomon's temple was a thousand times more (1 Chronicles 22:14). Some people wept as they remembered the glorious

2:70
[e] ver 1; 1Ch 9:2; Ne 11:3-4

3:1
[a] Ne 7:73; 8:1
[b] Lev 23:24

3:2
[c] Ezr 2:2; Ne 12:1, 8; Hag 2:2
[d] Hag 1:1; Zec 6:11
[e] 1Ch 3:17
[f] Ex 20:24; Dt 12:5-6

3:3
[g] Ezr 4:4; Da 9:25
[h] Ex 29:39; Nu 28:1-8

3:4
[i] Ex 23:16; Nu 29:12-38; Ne 8:14-18; Zec 14:16-19

3:5
[j] Nu 28:3, 11, 14; Col 2:16
[k] Lev 23:1-44; Nu 29:39

3:7
[l] 1Ch 14:1
[m] Isa 35:2
[n] Ezr 1:2-4; 6:3

3:8
[o] Zec 4:9
[p] 1Ch 23:24

3:9
[q] Ezr 2:40

70The priests, the Levites, the singers, the gatekeepers and the temple servants
settled in their own towns, along with some of the other people, and the rest of the
Israelites settled in their towns.[e]

2. The people rebuild the temple

Rebuilding the Altar

3 When the seventh month came and the Israelites had settled in their towns,[a] the
people assembled[b] as one man in Jerusalem. 2Then Jeshua[c] son of Jozadak[d]
and his fellow priests and Zerubbabel son of Shealtiel[e] and his associates began to
build the altar of the God of Israel to sacrifice burnt offerings on it, in accordance with
what is written in the Law of Moses[f] the man of God. 3Despite their fear[g] of the
peoples around them, they built the altar on its foundation and sacrificed burnt
offerings on it to the LORD, both the morning and evening sacrifices.[h] 4Then in
accordance with what is written, they celebrated the Feast of Tabernacles[i] with the
required number of burnt offerings prescribed for each day. 5After that, they presented
the regular burnt offerings, the New Moon[j] sacrifices and the sacrifices for all the
appointed sacred feasts of the LORD,[k] as well as those brought as freewill offerings
to the LORD. 6On the first day of the seventh month they began to offer burnt offerings
to the LORD, though the foundation of the LORD's temple had not yet been laid.

Rebuilding the Temple

7Then they gave money to the masons and carpenters, and gave food and drink and
oil to the people of Sidon and Tyre, so that they would bring cedar logs[l] by sea from
Lebanon[m] to Joppa, as authorised by Cyrus[n] king of Persia.
8In the second month of the second year after their arrival at the house of God in
Jerusalem, Zerubbabel[o] son of Shealtiel, Jeshua son of Jozadak and the rest of their
brothers (the priests and the Levites and all who had returned from the captivity to
Jerusalem) began the work, appointing Levites twenty[p] years of age and older to
supervise the building of the house of the LORD. 9Jeshua[q] and his sons and brothers
and Kadmiel and his sons (descendants of Hodaviah[a]) and the sons of Henadad and

[a] 9 Hebrew *Yehudah,* probably a variant of *Hodaviah*

temple that had been destroyed (3:12).

3:2, 3 The Jews built the altar as one of their first official acts. It symbolised God's presence and protection. It also demonstrated their purpose as a nation and their commitment to serve God alone. Zerubbabel sacrificed burnt offerings as the Law of Moses instructed (Leviticus 1–7). The sacrifices were essential because they demonstrated that the people were seeking God's guidance, rededicating themselves to living as he commanded, and daily asking him to forgive their sins.

3:3 The Jews were afraid they were going to be attacked by the surrounding people—a mixed group whose ancestors had been conquered by the Assyrians. Foreigners had been forced to resettle in the northern kingdom of Israel after Israel was defeated and her people taken captive in 722 B.C. (4:1, 2). This resettlement procedure was a common tactic of the Assyrians to prevent strong nationalistic uprisings by conquered peoples. Some of the resettled people in Israel had migrated south near Jerusalem, and they may have thought the returning exiles threatened their claim on the land.

3:4 The Feast of Tabernacles lasted seven days. During this time the people lived in temporary dwellings (tents, booths, lean-tos) as their ancestors had done years before as they journeyed through the desert on their way to the promised land. The Feast reminded the people of God's past protection and guidance in the desert and of his continued love for them. The Feast of Tabernacles is described in detail in Leviticus 23:33–36.

3:5 Almost immediately after arriving in the new land, the returning exiles built an altar. The people began worshipping God through sacrifices even before the temple foundations were laid. After many years in captivity, they had learned their lesson—they knew that God does not offer special protection to people who ignore him. They had been carried off by the Babylonians when they were relatively strong; here they were few, weak, and surrounded by enemies. If ever they needed to rely on God's power, it was at this time. They realised the importance of obeying God from the heart, and not merely out of habit. If we want God's help when we undertake large tasks, we must make staying close to him our top priority.

3:5 These sacrifices were originally set up under the Law of Moses in Leviticus 1 and 6:8–13. The feasts are described in Leviticus 23. Every month on the day of the New Moon, they held a special observance (Numbers 10:10).

3:7 When Solomon built the first temple (2 Chronicles 2), he also exchanged food and olive oil—plentiful resources in Israel—for wood, a resource Israel lacked. The wood came from Sidon and Tyre that time too.

3:8 Why was the Lord's temple begun first, even before the city wall? The temple was used for spiritual purposes; the wall, for military and political purposes. God had always been the nation's protector, and the Jews knew that the strongest stone wall would not protect them if God was not with them. They knew that putting their spiritual lives in order was a far higher priority than assuring the national defence.

3:8 It took from September (3:1; September was the seventh month because the year began in March) to June just to *prepare* to build the temple. The exiles took time to make plans because the project was important to them. Preparation may not feel heroic or spiritual, but it is vital to any project meant to be done well.

their sons and brothers—all Levites—joined together in supervising those working
on the house of God.
10When the builders laid[r] the foundation of the temple of the LORD, the priests
in their vestments and with trumpets,[s] and the Levites (the sons of Asaph) with
cymbals, took their places to praise[t] the LORD, as prescribed by David[u] king of
Israel.[v] 11With praise and thanksgiving they sang to the LORD:

> "He is good;
> his love to Israel endures for ever."[w]

And all the people gave a great shout[x] of praise to the LORD, because the foundation
of the house of the LORD was laid. 12But many of the older priests and Levites and
family heads, who had seen the former temple,[y] wept aloud when they saw the
foundation of this temple being laid, while many others shouted for joy. 13No-one
could distinguish the sound of the shouts of joy[z] from the sound of weeping, because
the people made so much noise. And the sound was heard far away.

Opposition to the Rebuilding

4 When the enemies of Judah and Benjamin heard that the exiles were building a
temple for the LORD, the God of Israel, 2they came to Zerubbabel and to the heads
of the families and said, "Let us help you build because, like you, we seek your God
and have been sacrificing to him since the time of Esarhaddon[a] king of Assyria, who
brought us here."[b]
3But Zerubbabel, Jeshua and the rest of the heads of the families of Israel answered,
"You have no part with us in building a temple to our God. We alone will build it

3:10
[r] Ezr 5:16
[s] Nu 10:2; 1Ch 16:6
[t] 1Ch 25:1
[u] 1Ch 6:31
[v] Zec 6:12

3:11
[w] 1Ch 16:34, 41; 2Ch 7:3; Ps 107:1; 118:1
[x] Ne 12:24

3:12
[y] Hag 2:3, 9

3:13
[z] Job 8:21; Ps 27:6; Isa 16:9

4:2
[a] 2Ki 17:24; 19:37
[b] 2Ki 17:41

3:10, 11 David had given clear instructions concerning the use of music in worship services in the temple (1 Chronicles 16; 25).

3:10, 11 Completing the foundation for the temple required great effort on the part of all involved. But no-one tried to get praise for himself and his own hard work. Instead, everyone praised God for what had been done. All good gifts come from God—talents, abilities, strength, and leadership. We should thank God for what has been done in and through us!

3:11 The Bible records many songs and musical events. For a list of such events, see the chart in Exodus 16.

3:12 Fifty years after its destruction, the temple was being rebuilt (536 B.C.). Some of the older people remembered Solomon's temple, and they wept because the new temple would not be as glorious as the first one. But the beauty of the building was not nearly as important to God as were the attitudes of the builders and worshippers. God cares more about who we are than what we accomplish. Our world is always changing, and once-magnificent accomplishments decay and disappear. Seek to serve God wholeheartedly. Then you won't need to compare your work with anyone else's.

3:12 Because the new temple was built on the foundation of Solomon's temple, the two structures were not that different in size. But the old temple was far more elaborate and ornate, and was surrounded by many buildings and a vast courtyard. Both temples were constructed of imported cedar wood, but Solomon's was decorated with vast amounts of gold and precious stones. Solomon's temple took over seven years to build; Zerubbabel's took about four years. Solomon's temple was at the hub of a thriving city; Zerubbabel's was surrounded by ruins. No wonder the people wept.

3:13 The celebration after laying the temple foundation was marked by contrasts of emotion—shouts of joy and sounds of weeping. Both were appropriate. The Holy Spirit can stimulate us both to rejoice over the goodness of his grace and to grieve over the sins that required him to correct us. When we come into the presence of Almighty God, we may feel full of joy and thanksgiving, yet at the same time feel sobered by our shortcomings.

4:1–3 The enemies of Judah and Benjamin were people who had been relocated in the northern kingdom when Assyria conquered Israel (see 2 Kings 17 and the note on 3:3). In an attempt to infiltrate and disrupt the project, these people offered to help in the rebuilding project. They wanted to keep a close eye on what the Jews were doing. They were hoping to keep Jerusalem from becoming strong again. The Jews, however, saw through their ploy. Such a partnership with unbelievers would have led God's people to compromise their faith.

4:1–6 Believers can expect opposition when they do God's work (2 Timothy 3:12). Unbelievers and evil spiritual forces are always working against God and his people. The opposition may offer compromising alliances (4:2), attempt to discourage and intimidate us (4:4, 5), or accuse us unjustly (4:6). If you expect these tactics, you won't be halted by them. Move ahead with the work God has planned for you, and trust him to show you how to overcome the obstacles.

4:2 These enemies claimed to worship the same God as Zerubbabel and the rest of the Jews. In one sense, this was true; they worshipped God, but they also worshipped many other gods (see 2 Kings 17:27–29, 32–34, 41). In God's eyes, this was not worship—it was sin and rebellion. True worship involves devotion to God alone (Exodus 20:3–5). To these foreigners, God was just another "idol" to be added to their collection. Their real motive was to disrupt the temple project. Believers today must beware of those who claim to be Christians but whose actions clearly reveal they are using Christianity to serve their own interests.

4:4, 5 Discouragement and fear are two of the greatest obstacles to completing God's work. Most often they come where and when you least expect them. Discouragement eats away at our motivation and fear paralyses us so we don't act at all. Recognise these common barriers. Remember that God's people in every age have faced these problems and with God's help overcame them. By standing together with other believers, you can overcome fear and discouragement and complete God's will.

4:3 [c]Ezr 1:1-4; Ne 2:20
4:4 [d]Ezr 3:3

for the LORD, the God of Israel, as King Cyrus, the king of Persia, commanded us."[c]
4Then the peoples around them set out to discourage the people of Judah and make
them afraid to go on building.[a][d] 5They hired counsellors to work against them and

[a] 4 Or *and troubled them as they built*

ZERUBBABEL

Sometimes God's ownership of a project is only recognised after *our* best efforts have failed. It is dangerous to think of God as responsible for the insignificant details while we take charge of the larger aspects of a project. Instead, it is God who is in control, and we only play a part in his overall plan. When God gives us important jobs to do, it isn't because he needs our help. Zerubbabel learned this lesson.

God's people had been exiled in Babylon for many years. Many had settled into comfortable lifestyles there and wanted to stay. There were, however, almost 60,000 who had not forgotten Judah. When Babylon was defeated in 539 B.C., the Persian ruler, Cyrus, allowed the Jews to return to Jerusalem and rebuild their temple. Zerubbabel led the first and largest group back to the promised land.

Zerubbabel's leadership was by right and recognition. Not only was he a descendant of David, he also had personal leadership qualities. When the people arrived in Judah, they were given time to establish living quarters, and then were called to begin the work. They began not by laying the city walls or constructing government buildings, but by rebuilding the altar, worshipping God together, and celebrating a feast. Under Zerubbabel's leadership, they established a spiritual foundation for their building efforts.

The temple foundation was then quickly completed, and another round of celebration followed. But soon, two problems arose. A few old men remembered Solomon's glorious temple and were saddened by how much smaller and less glorious this one was. Also, some enemies of the Jews tried to infiltrate the workforce and stop the building with political pressure. Fear caused the work to grind to a halt. The people went to their homes, and 16 years passed.

We do not know what Zerubbabel did during this time. His discouragement, following those first months of excitement and accomplishment, must have been deep. Those feelings eventually hardened into hopelessness. So God sent the prophets Haggai and Zechariah to be Zerubbabel's encouraging companions. They confronted the people's reluctance and comforted their fears. The work began once again with renewed energy and was completed in four years.

Zerubbabel, like many of us, knew how to start well but found it hard to keep going. His successes depended on the quality of encouragement he received. Zerubbabel let discouragement get the better of him. But when he let God take control, the work was finished. God is always in control. We must not let circumstances or lack of encouragement deter us from doing the tasks God has given us.

Strengths and accomplishments:
- Led the first group of Jewish exiles back to Jerusalem from Babylon
- Completed the rebuilding of God's temple
- Demonstrated wisdom in the help he accepted and refused
- Started his building project with worship as the focal point

Weaknesses and mistakes:
- Needed constant encouragement
- Allowed problems and resistance to stop the rebuilding work

Lessons from his life:
- A leader needs to provide not only the initial motivation for a project, but the continued encouragement necessary to keep the project going
- A leader must find his/her own dependable source of encouragement
- God's faithfulness is shown in the way he preserved David's line

Vital statistics:
- Where: Babylon, Jerusalem
- Occupation: Recognised leader of the exiles
- Relatives: Father: Shealtiel. Grandfather: Jehoiachin
- Contemporaries: Cyrus, Darius, Zechariah, Haggai

Key verses:
"This is the word of the LORD to Zerubbabel: 'Not by might nor by power, but by my Spirit,' says the LORD Almighty. 'What are you, O mighty mountain? Before Zerubbabel you will become level ground. Then he will bring out the capstone to shouts of "God bless it! God bless it!" ' " (Zechariah 4:6, 7).

Zerubbabel's story is told in Ezra 2:2—5:2. He is also mentioned in 1 Chronicles 3:19; Nehemiah 7:7; 12:1, 47; Haggai 1:1, 12, 14; 2:4, 21, 23; Zechariah 4:6–10; Matthew 1:12, 13; Luke 3:27.

frustrate their plans during the entire reign of Cyrus king of Persia and down to the
reign of Darius king of Persia.

Later Opposition Under Xerxes and Artaxerxes

6 At the beginning of the reign of Xerxes,[b][e] they lodged an accusation against the
people of Judah and Jerusalem.[f]
7 And in the days of Artaxerxes[g] king of Persia, Bishlam, Mithredath, Tabeel and
the rest of his associates wrote a letter to Artaxerxes. The letter was written in Aramaic
script and in the Aramaic[h] language.[c,d]
8 Rehum the commanding officer and Shimshai the secretary wrote a letter against
Jerusalem to Artaxerxes the king as follows:

9 Rehum the commanding officer and Shimshai the secretary, together with the
rest of their associates[i]—the judges and officials over the men from Tripolis,
Persia,[e] Erech and Babylon, the Elamites of Susa,
10 and the other people whom
the great and honourable Ashurbanipal[f] deported and settled in the city of
Samaria and elsewhere in Trans-Euphrates.[j]

11 (This is a copy of the letter they sent him.)

To King Artaxerxes,

From your servants, the men of Trans-Euphrates:

12 The king should know that the Jews who came up to us from you have gone
to Jerusalem and are rebuilding that rebellious and wicked city. They are restoring
the walls and repairing the foundations.[k]
13 Furthermore, the king should know that if this city is built and its walls are
restored, no more taxes, tribute or duty[l] will be paid, and the royal revenues
will suffer.
14 Now since we are under obligation to the palace and it is not proper
for us to see the king dishonoured, we are sending this message to inform the
king,
15 so that a search may be made in the archives[m] of your predecessors. In
these records you will find that this city is a rebellious city, troublesome to kings
and provinces, a place of rebellion from ancient times. That is why this city was
destroyed.[n]
16 We inform the king that if this city is built and its walls are
restored, you will be left with nothing in Trans-Euphrates.

17 The king sent this reply:

To Rehum the commanding officer, Shimshai the secretary and the rest of their
associates living in Samaria and elsewhere in Trans-Euphrates:[o]

Greetings.

18 The letter you sent us has been read and translated in my presence.
19 I issued
an order and a search was made, and it was found that this city has a long history
of revolt[p] against kings and has been a place of rebellion and sedition.
20 Jerusalem has had powerful kings ruling over the whole of Trans-Euphrates,[q] and

4:6 [e]Est 1:1; Da 9:1 [f]Est 3:13; 9:5
4:7 [g]Ezr 7:1; Ne 2:1 [h]2Ki 18:26; Isa 36:11; Da 2:4
4:9 [i]Ezr 5:6; 6:6, 13
4:10 [j]ver 17; Ne 4:2
4:12 [k]Ezr 5:3, 9
4:13 [l]Ezr 7:24; Ne 5:4
4:15 [m]Ezr 5:17; 6:1 [n]Est 3:8
4:17 [o]ver 10
4:19 [p]2Ki 18:7
4:20 [q]Ge 15:18-21; Ex 23:31; Jos 1:4; 1Ki 4:21; 1Ch 18:3; Ps 72:8-11

[b] *6* Hebrew *Ahasuerus,* a variant of Xerxes' Persian name [c] *7* Or *written in Aramaic and translated* [d] *7* The text of Ezra 4:8–6:18 is in Aramaic. [e] *9* Or *officials, magistrates and governors over the men from* [f] *10* Aramaic *Osnappar,* a variant of *Ashurbanipal*

4:6–23 In these verses, Ezra summarises the entire story of the opposition to building the temple, the walls, and other important buildings in Jerusalem. Chronologically, 4:6 fits between chapters 6 and 7; 4:7–23 refers to the events between Ezra 7 and Nehemiah 1. Ezra grouped them here to highlight the persistent opposition to God's people over the years and God's ability to overcome it.

4:7 This letter sent to King Artaxerxes may have been inscribed on a clay tablet, a fragment of pottery, or sheets of parchment.

4:10 Ashurbanipal (669–627 B.C.) was the Assyrian king who completed the relocation of Israelite captives. He was the last of the strong Assyrian kings. After his death the nation quickly declined. Assyria was conquered by Babylon in 612.

4:19, 20 Artaxerxes said that Jerusalem "has a long history of revolt against kings and has been a place of rebellion and sedition". By reading the historical records, he learned that mighty kings had come from Jerusalem, and he may have feared that another would arise if the city were rebuilt. Solomon had ruled a huge empire (1 Kings 4:21), and Jerusalem's kings had rebelled against mighty powers—for example, Zedekiah rebelled against Nebuchadnezzar despite his oath of loyalty (2 Chronicles 36:13). Artaxerxes did not want to aid the rebuilding of a rebellious city and nation.

4:22 [r]Da 6:2

4:23 [s]ver 9

4:24 [t]Ne 2:1-8; Da 9:25; Hag 1:1, 15; Zec 1:1

5:1 [a]Ezr 6:14; Hag 1:1, 3, 12; 2:1, 10, 20 [b]Zec 1:1; 7:1 [c]Hag 1:14-2:9; Zec 4:9-10; 8:9

5:2 [d]1Ch 3:19; Hag 1:14; 2:21; Zec 4:6-10 [e]Ezr 2:2; 3:2 [f]ver 8; Hag 2:2-5

5:3 [g]Ezr 6:6 [h]Ezr 6:6 [i]ver 9; Ezr 1:3; 4:12

5:5 [j]2Ki 25:28; Ezr 7:6, 9, 28; 8:18, 22, 31; Ne 2:8, 18; Ps 33:18; Isa 66:14

taxes, tribute and duty were paid to them. 21Now issue an order to these men
to stop work, so that this city will not be rebuilt until I so order. 22Be careful
not to neglect this matter. Why let this threat grow, to the detriment of the royal
interests?[r]

23As soon as the copy of the letter of King Artaxerxes was read to Rehum and
Shimshai the secretary and their associates,[s] they went immediately to the Jews in
Jerusalem and compelled them by force to stop.

24Thus the work on the house of God in Jerusalem came to a standstill until the
second year of the reign of Darius[t] king of Persia.

Tattenai's Letter to Darius

5 Now Haggai[a] the prophet and Zechariah[b] the prophet, a descendant of Iddo,
prophesied[c] to the Jews in Judah and Jerusalem in the name of the God of Israel,
who was over them. 2Then Zerubbabel[d] son of Shealtiel and Jeshua[e] son of Jozadak
set to work[f] to rebuild the house of God in Jerusalem. And the prophets of God were
with them, helping them.
3At that time Tattenai,[g] governor of Trans-Euphrates, and Shethar-Bozenai[h] and
their associates went to them and asked, "Who authorised you to rebuild this temple
and restore this structure?"[i] 4They also asked, "What are the names of the men
constructing this building?"[a] 5But the eye of their God[j] was watching over the elders
of the Jews, and they were not stopped until a report could go to Darius and his written
reply be received.
6This is a copy of the letter that Tattenai, governor of Trans-Euphrates, and
Shethar-Bozenai and their associates, the officials of Trans-Euphrates, sent to King
Darius. 7The report they sent him read as follows:

a *4* See Septuagint; Aramaic 4*We told them the names of the men constructing this building.*

THE PERSIAN KINGS OF EZRA'S DAY

Name	*Date of Reign*	*Relationship to Israel*
Cyrus	559–530 B.C.	Conquered Babylon. Established a policy of returning exiles to their homelands. Sent Zerubbabel to Jerusalem, financed his project, and returned the gold and silver articles that Nebuchadnezzar had taken from the temple. He probably knew Daniel.
Darius	522–486 B.C.	Stopped construction of the temple in Jerusalem.
Xerxes (Ahasuerus)	486–465 B.C.	Was Esther's husband. Allowed the Jews to protect themselves against Haman's attempt to eliminate their people.
Artaxerxes	465–424 B.C.	Had Nehemiah as his cupbearer. Allowed both Ezra and Nehemiah to return to Jerusalem.

4:23 Setbacks and standstills are painful and discouraging to God's workers. These exiles had received a double dose (see 4:1–5 and 4:6–22). Leaders should do everything to keep work from grinding to a halt; yet circumstances sometimes really are beyond our control. When you have been brought to a standstill, remember to still stand strong in the Lord.

4:24 Ezra resumes his chronological account here. It may have been ten years since the Israelites had worked on the temple. It did not begin again until 520 B.C., the second year of Darius's reign (5:1ff).

5:1 More details about the work and messages of Haggai and Zechariah are found in the books of the Bible that bear their names.

5:1, 2 "The prophets of God were with them, helping them." God sometimes sends prophets to encourage and strengthen his people. To accomplish this, Haggai and Zechariah not only preached, but also got involved in the labour. In the church today, God appoints prophetic voices to help us with our work (Ephesians 4:11–13). Their ministry should have the same effect upon us as Haggai's and Zechariah's had on Israel. "But everyone who prophesies speaks to men for their strengthening, encouragement and comfort" (1 Corinthians 14:3). In turn, we should encourage those who bring God's words to us.

5:3–5 The non-Jews who lived nearby attempted to hinder the construction of the temple. But while the legal debate went on and the decision was under appeal, the Jews continued to rebuild. When we are doing God's work, others may try to delay, confuse, or frustrate us, but we can proceed confidently. God will accomplish his purposes in our world, no matter who attempts to block them. Just as he watched over the Jewish elders, he watches over you. Concentrate on God's purpose, and don't be sidetracked by intrigues or slander.

To King Darius:

Cordial greetings.

8The king should know that we went to the district of Judah, to the temple of
the great God. The people are building it with large stones and placing the timbers
in the walls. The work[k] is being carried on with diligence and is making rapid
progress under their direction.
9We questioned the elders and asked them, "Who authorised you to rebuild
this temple and restore this structure?"[l] 10We also asked them their names, so
that we could write down the names of their leaders for your information.
11This is the answer they gave us:

"We are the servants of the God of heaven and earth, and we are rebuilding
the temple[m] that was built many years ago, one that a great king of Israel built
and finished. 12But because our fathers angered[n] the God of heaven, he handed
them over to Nebuchadnezzar the Chaldean, king of Babylon, who destroyed this
temple and deported the people to Babylon.[o]
13"However, in the first year of Cyrus king of Babylon, King Cyrus issued
a decree[p] to rebuild this house of God. 14He even removed from the temple**b**
of Babylon the gold and silver articles of the house of God, which Nebuchadnezzar had taken from the temple in Jerusalem and brought to the temple**b** in
Babylon.[q]
"Then King Cyrus gave them to a man named Sheshbazzar,[r] whom he had
appointed governor, 15and he told him, 'Take these articles and go and deposit
them in the temple in Jerusalem. And rebuild the house of God on its site.' 16So
this Sheshbazzar came and laid the foundations of the house of God[s] in Jerusalem. From that day to the present it has been under construction but is not yet
finished."

17Now if it pleases the king, let a search be made in the royal archives[t] of
Babylon to see if King Cyrus did in fact issue a decree to rebuild this house of
God in Jerusalem. Then let the king send us his decision in this matter.

The Decree of Darius

6 King Darius then issued an order, and they searched in the archives[a] stored in
the treasury at Babylon. 2A scroll was found in the citadel of Ecbatana in the
province of Media, and this was written on it:

Memorandum:

3In the first year of King Cyrus, the king issued a decree concerning the temple
of God in Jerusalem:

Let the temple be rebuilt as a place to present sacrifices, and let its foundations
be laid.[b] It is to be ninety feet**a** high and ninety feet wide, 4with three courses[c]
of large stones and one of timbers. The costs are to be paid by the royal treasury.[d]
5Also, the gold[e] and silver articles of the house of God, which Nebuchadnezzar
took from the temple in Jerusalem and brought to Babylon, are to be returned

b *14* Or *palace* **a** *3* Aramaic *sixty cubits* (about 27 metres)

5:8 [k]ver 2
5:9 [l]Ezr 4:12
5:11 [m]1Ki 6:1; 2Ch 3:1-2
5:12 [n]2Ch 36:16 [o]Dt 21:10; 28:36; 2Ki 24:1; 25:8, 9, 11; Jer 1:3
5:13 [p]Ezr 1:1
5:14 [q]Ezr 1:7; 6:5; Da 5:2 [r]1Ch 3:18
5:16 [s]Ezr 3:10; 6:15
5:17 [t]Ezr 4:15; 6:1, 2
6:1 [a]Ezr 4:15; 5:17
6:3 [b]Ezr 3:10; Hag 2:3
6:4 [c]1Ki 6:36 [d]ver 8; Ezr 7:20
6:5 [e]1Ch 29:2

5:11 While rebuilding the temple, the workers were confronted by the Persia-appointed governor, demanding to know who gave permission for their construction project (5:3). This could have been intimidating, but, as we learn from the letter, they boldly replied, "We are the servants of the God of heaven and earth."

It is not always easy to speak up for our faith in an unbelieving world, but we must. The way to deal with pressure and intimidation is to recognise that we are workers for God. Our allegiance is to him first, people second. When we contemplate the reactions and criticisms of hostile people, we can become paralysed with fear. If we try to offend no-one or to please everyone, we won't be effective. God is our leader, and his rewards are most important. So don't be intimidated. Let others know by your words and actions whom you really serve.

5:13–17 Cyrus is called king of Persia in 1:1 and king of Babylon in 5:13. Because Persia had just conquered Babylon, Cyrus was king of both nations. Babylon is more important to this story because it was the location of the Hebrews' 70-year captivity. The Babylon in 5:17 may refer to the city of Babylon, which was the capital of the nation of Babylon.

6:1, 2 Many clay and papyrus documents recording business transactions and historical data have been discovered in this area (near present-day Syria). A great library and archives with thousands of such records have been discovered at Ebla in Syria.

6:5 [f]Ezr 1:7; 5:14
6:6 [g]Ezr 5:3 [h]Ezr 5:3
6:8 [i]ver 4 [j]1Sa 9:20
6:9 [k]Lev 1:3, 10
6:10 [l]Ezr 7:23; 1Ti 2:1-2
6:11 [m]Dt 21:22-23; Est 2:23; 5:14; 9:14 [n]Ezr 7:26; Da 2:5; 3:29
6:12 [o]Ex 20:24; Dt 12:5; 1Ki 9:3; 2Ch 6:2 [p]ver 14
6:13 [q]Ezr 4:9
6:14 [r]Ezr 5:1 [s]Ezr 1:1-4 [t]ver 12 [u]Ezr 7:1; Ne 2:1
6:15 [v]Zec 1:1; 4:9

to their places in the temple in Jerusalem; they are to be deposited in the house
of God.[f]

6 Now then, Tattenai,[g] governor of Trans-Euphrates, and Shethar-Bozenai[h]
and you, their fellow officials of that province, stay away from there. 7 Do not
interfere with the work on this temple of God. Let the governor of the Jews and
the Jewish elders rebuild this house of God on its site.

8 Moreover, I hereby decree what you are to do for these elders of the Jews
in the construction of this house of God:

The expenses of these men are to be fully paid out of the royal treasury,[i] from
the revenues[j] of Trans-Euphrates, so that the work will not stop. 9 Whatever is
needed—young bulls, rams, male lambs for burnt offerings[k] to the God of
heaven, and wheat, salt, wine and oil, as requested by the priests in Jerusalem—must be given them daily without fail, 10 so that they may offer sacrifices
pleasing to the God of heaven and pray for the well-being of the king and his
sons.[l]

11 Furthermore, I decree that if anyone changes this edict, a beam is to be pulled
from his house and he is to be lifted up and impaled[m] on it. And for this crime
his house is to be made a pile of rubble.[n] 12 May God, who has caused his Name
to dwell there,[o] overthrow any king or people who lifts a hand to change this
decree or to destroy this temple in Jerusalem.

I Darius[p] have decreed it. Let it be carried out with diligence.

Completion and Dedication of the Temple

13 Then, because of the decree King Darius had sent, Tattenai, governor of Trans-
Euphrates, and Shethar-Bozenai and their associates[q] carried it out with diligence.
14 So the elders of the Jews continued to build and prosper under the preaching[r] of
Haggai the prophet and Zechariah, a descendant of Iddo. They finished building the
temple according to the command of the God of Israel and the decrees of Cyrus,[s]
Darius[t] and Artaxerxes,[u] kings of Persia. 15 The temple was completed on the third
day of the month Adar, in the sixth year of the reign of King Darius.[v]

THE POST-EXILIC PROPHETS

God used these men to confront and comfort his people after their return to their homeland from exile in Babylon.

Who?	*When?*	*Ministered to These Contemporary Leaders*	*Main Message*	*Significance*
Haggai	520 B.C.	Zerubbabel Joshua	• Encouraged the leaders and the people to continue rebuilding the temple, which God would bless • Challenged the people's careless worship, which God would not bless	Disobedience and careless obedience of God's commands lead to judgment.
Zechariah	520 B.C.	Zerubbabel Joshua	• Emphasised God's command to rebuild his temple • Gave the people another look at God's plan to bless the world through Israel and its coming king—the Messiah (9:9, 10)	Encouragement for today's effort sometimes requires that we remember God has a plan and purpose for tomorrow. Meanwhile, the challenge is to live for him today.
Malachi	430 B.C.	The priests are the only leaders mentioned	• Confronted the people and priests with God's promises of judgment on those who reject him and God's blessing on those who live as he desires	God expects our obedience to him to affect our attitude towards him and our treatment of one another.

6:14 Ezra carefully pointed out that rebuilding the temple was commanded first by God and then by the kings, who were his instruments. How ironic and wonderful that God's work was carried on by the discovery of a lost paragraph in a pagan library. All the opposition of powerful forces was stopped by a clause in a legal document. God's will is supreme over all rulers, all historical events, and all hostile forces. He can deliver us in ways we can't imagine. If we trust in his power and love, no opposition can stop us.

6:15 The temple was completed in 516 B.C.

16Then the people of Israel—the priests, the Levites and the rest of the ex-
les—celebrated the dedication[w] of the house of God with joy. 17For the dedication
of this house of God they offered[x] a hundred bulls, two hundred rams, four hundred
male lambs and, as a sin offering for all Israel, twelve male goats, one for each of
he tribes of Israel. 18And they installed the priests in their divisions[y] and the Levites
n their groups[z] for the service of God at Jerusalem, according to what is written in
he Book of Moses.[a]

The Passover

19On the fourteenth day of the first month, the exiles celebrated the Passover.[b]
20The priests and Levites had purified themselves and were all ceremonially clean.
The Levites slaughtered[c] the Passover lamb for all the exiles, for their brothers the
priests and for themselves. 21So the Israelites who had returned from the exile ate it,
together with all who had separated themselves[d] from the unclean practices[e] of their
Gentile neighbours in order to seek the LORD,[f] the God of Israel. 22For seven days
they celebrated with joy the Feast of Unleavened Bread,[g] because the LORD had filled
them with joy by changing the attitude[h] of the king of Assyria, so that he assisted
them in the work on the house of God, the God of Israel.

B. THE RETURN LED BY EZRA (7.1—10.44)

Ezra returned to the land with a second group of exiles, 80 years after Zerubbabel. Ezra found the temple rebuilt, but the lives of the people in shambles. Intermarriage with foreigners opposed to God threatened the spiritual future of the nation. So Ezra prayed for guidance and then followed this through with action. Christians today must also strive to keep their lives pure, refusing to let the sinful allurements of the world around them compromise their lifestyle.

1. The second group of exiles returns to the land

Ezra Comes to Jerusalem

7 After these things, during the reign of Artaxerxes[a] king of Persia, Ezra son of
Seraiah, the son of Azariah, the son of Hilkiah,[b] 2the son of Shallum, the son
of Zadok,[c] the son of Ahitub,[d] 3the son of Amariah, the son of Azariah, the son
of Meraioth, 4the son of Zerahiah, the son of Uzzi, the son of Bukki, 5the son of
Abishua, the son of Phinehas, the son of Eleazar, the son of Aaron the chief
priest—6this Ezra[e] came up from Babylon. He was a teacher well versed in the Law
of Moses, which the LORD, the God of Israel, had given. The king had granted him

6:16 [w] 1Ki 8:63; 2Ch 7:5

6:17 [x] 2Sa 6:13; 2Ch 29:21; 30:24; Ezr 8:35

6:18 [y] 1Ch 23:6; 2Ch 35:4; Lk 1:5 [z] 1Ch 24:1 [a] Nu 3:6-9; 8:9-11; 18:1-32

6:19 [b] Ex 12:11; Nu 28:16

6:20 [c] 2Ch 30:15, 17; 35:11

6:21 [d] Ezr 9:1; Ne 9:2 [e] Dt 18:9; Ezr 9:11; Eze 36:25 [f] 1Ch 22:19; Ps 14:2

6:22 [g] Ex 12:17 [h] Ezr 1:1

7:1 [a] Ezr 4:7; 6:14; Ne 2:1 [b] 2Ki 22:4

7:2 [c] 1Ki 1:8; 1Ch 6:8 [d] Ne 11:11

7:6 [e] Ne 12:36

6:16–22 Feasting and celebration were in order at the great temple dedication. This celebration was similar to the one that Solomon had when he dedicated the temple in 1 Kings 8:63, although Solomon offered more than 200 times as many cattle and sheep. This Book of Moses was probably Leviticus. The priests and Levites were organised into groups in order to do "the service of God, . . . according to what is written in the Book of Moses". There is time to celebrate, but there is also a time to work. Both are proper and necessary when worshipping God, and both are pleasing to him.

6:19 The Passover was an annual celebration commemorating Israel's deliverance from Egypt. After a series of plagues failed to convince Pharaoh to free the Israelites, God said that he would send the destroying angel to kill the firstborn in every household. But the angel would pass over every home that had the blood of a specified type of lamb on the sides and top of the doorframe. See Exodus 12:1–30 for the story of this event and the establishment of the Passover celebration.

6:22 There are many ways to pray for God's help. Have you ever considered that God would change the attitude of a person or group of people? God is infinitely powerful, his insight and wisdom transcend the laws of human nature. While you must always change your attitude as a first step, remember that he can change the attitude of others.

7:1 There is a gap of almost 60 years between the events of chapters six and seven. The story in the book of Esther occurred during this time, in the reign of Xerxes, who ruled from 486–465 B.C. Artaxerxes, his son, became king in 465, and Ezra returned to Jerusalem in 458.

7:6 Eighty years after the first exiles returned to Jerusalem (2:1), Ezra himself returned. This was his first trip, and it took four months. The temple had been standing for about 58 years. Up to this point in the narrative, Ezra had remained in Babylon, probably compiling a record of the events that had taken place.

Why did he have to ask the king if he could return? Ezra wanted to lead many Jews back to Jerusalem, and he needed a decree from the king stating that any Jew who wanted to return could do so. This decree would be like a passport in case they ran into opposition along the way. The king's generous decree showed that God was blessing Ezra (7:6, 28). It also indicated that Ezra was probably a prominent man in Artaxerxes' kingdom. He was willing to give up this position in order to return to his homeland and teach the Israelites God's laws.

7:6–10 Ezra demonstrates how a gifted Bible teacher can move God's people forward. He was effective because he was a well-versed student of the Law of the Lord and because he was determined to obey those laws. He taught through both his speaking and his example. Like Ezra, we should determine both to study and to obey God's word.

7:6 [f]Ezr 5:5; Isa 41:20
7:7 [g]Ezr 8:1
7:9 [h]ver 6
7:10 [i]ver 25; Dt 33:10; Ne 8:1-8
7:12 [j]Eze 26:7; Da 2:37
7:14 [k]Est 1:14
7:15 [l]1Ch 29:6 [m]1Ch 29:6, 9; 2Ch 6:2
7:16 [n]Ezr 8:25

everything he asked, for the hand of the LORD his God was on him.[f] 7Some of the
Israelites, including priests, Levites, singers, gatekeepers and temple servants, also
came up to Jerusalem in the seventh year of King Artaxerxes.[g]
8Ezra arrived in Jerusalem in the fifth month of the seventh year of the king. 9He
had begun his journey from Babylon on the first day of the first month, and he arrived
in Jerusalem on the first day of the fifth month, for the gracious hand of his God was
on him.[h] 10For Ezra had devoted himself to the study and observance of the Law of
the LORD, and to teaching[i] its decrees and laws in Israel.

King Artaxerxes' Letter to Ezra

11This is a copy of the letter King Artaxerxes had given to Ezra the priest and
teacher, a man learned in matters concerning the commands and decrees of the LORD
for Israel:

12[a]Artaxerxes, king of kings,[j]

To Ezra the priest, a teacher of the Law of the God of heaven:

Greetings.

13Now I decree that any of the Israelites in my kingdom, including priests and
Levites, who wish to go to Jerusalem with you, may go. 14You are sent by the
king and his seven advisers[k] to enquire about Judah and Jerusalem with regard
to the Law of your God, which is in your hand. 15Moreover, you are to take with
you the silver and gold that the king and his advisers have freely given[l] to the
God of Israel, whose dwelling[m] is in Jerusalem, 16together with all the silver
and gold[n] you may obtain from the province of Babylon, as well as the freewill

a *12* The text of Ezra 7:12–26 is in Aramaic.

THE MEDO-PERSIAN EMPIRE
The Medo-Persian empire included the lands of Media and Persia, much of the area shown on this map and more. The Jewish exiles were concentrated in the area around Nippur in the Babylonian province. The decree by King Cyrus that allowed the Israelites to return to their homeland and rebuild the temple was discovered in the palace at Ecbatana.

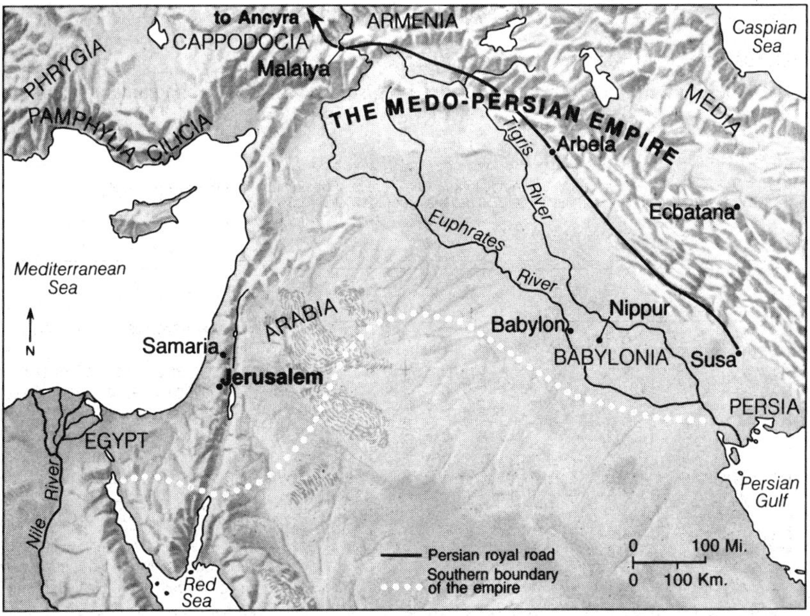

7:14 The seven advisers were Artaxerxes' supreme court (see Esther 1:14).

7:14 When Nebuchadnezzar destroyed the temple, he took a vast amount of plunder that may have included a copy of the Book of the Law (2 Chronicles 36:18). It is also possible that this book was brought by the Jews into exile and was confiscated and read by their conquerors. Foreign leaders who worshipped many gods liked to have records of the gods of other nations for military and political reasons.

offerings of the people and priests for the temple of their God in Jerusalem.[o]
17With this money be sure to buy bulls, rams and male lambs,[p] together with
their grain offerings and drink offerings,[q] and sacrifice[r] them on the altar of
the temple of your God in Jerusalem.
18You and your brother Jews may then do whatever seems best with the rest
of the silver and gold, in accordance with the will of your God. 19Deliver[s] to
the God of Jerusalem all the articles entrusted to you for worship in the temple
of your God. 20And anything else needed for the temple of your God that you
may have occasion to supply, you may provide from the royal treasury.[t]
21Now I, King Artaxerxes, order all the treasurers of Trans-Euphrates to
provide with diligence whatever Ezra the priest, a teacher of the Law of the God
of heaven, may ask of you—22up to a hundred talents**b** of silver, a hundred
cors**c** of wheat, a hundred baths**d** of wine, a hundred baths**d** of olive oil, and
salt without limit. 23Whatever the God of heaven has prescribed, let it be done
with diligence for the temple of the God of heaven. Why should there be wrath
against the realm of the king and of his sons?[u] 24You are also to know that you
have no authority to impose taxes, tribute or duty[v] on any of the priests, Levites,
singers, gatekeepers, temple servants or other workers at this house of God.[w]
25And you, Ezra, in accordance with the wisdom of your God, which you
possess, appoint[x] magistrates and judges to administer justice to all the people
of Trans-Euphrates—all who know the laws of your God. And you are to teach[y]
any who do not know them. 26Whoever does not obey the law of your God and
the law of the king must surely be punished by death, banishment, confiscation
of property, or imprisonment.[z]

27Praise be to the LORD, the God of our fathers, who has put it into the king's heart[a]
to bring honour[b] to the house of the LORD in Jerusalem in this way 28and who has
extended his good favour[c] to me before the king and his advisers and all the king's
powerful officials. Because the hand of the LORD my God was on me,[d] I took courage
and gathered leading men from Israel to go up with me.

List of the Family Heads Returning With Ezra

8 These are the family heads and those registered with them who came up with me
from Babylon during the reign of King Artaxerxes:[a]

2of the descendants of Phinehas, Gershom;

b *22* That is, about 3 ⅓ tons (about 3.4 metric tons) **c** *22* That is, probably about 600 bushels (about 22 kilolitres) **d** *22* That is, probably about 500 gallons (about 2.2 kilolitres)

7:16 [o]Zec 6:10
7:17 [p]2Ki 3:4 [q]Nu 15:5-12 [r]Dt 12:5-11
7:19 [s]Ezr 5:14; Jer 27:22
7:20 [t]Ezr 6:4
7:23 [u]Ezr 6:10
7:24 [v]Ezr 4:13 [w]Ezr 8:36
7:25 [x]Ex 18:21, 26; Dt 16:18 [y]ver 10; Lev 10:11
7:26 [z]Ezr 6:11
7:27 [a]Ezr 1:1; 6:22 [b]1Ch 29:12
7:28 [c]2Ki 25:28 [d]Ezr 5:5; 9:9
8:1 [a]Ezr 7:7

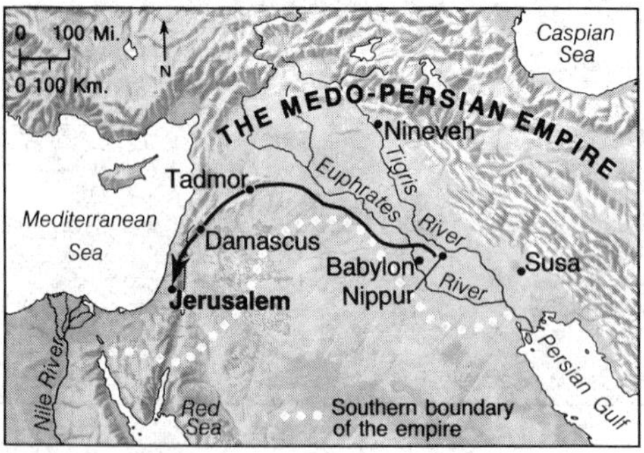

EZRA'S JOURNEY Ezra led a second group of exiles back to Judah and Jerusalem about 80 years after the first group. He travelled the dangerous route without military escort (8:22), but the people prayed and, under Ezra's godly leadership, arrived safely in Jerusalem after several months.

7:24 Why did Artaxerxes exempt temple workers from paying taxes? He recognised that the priests and Levites filled an important role in society as spiritual leaders, so he freed them of tax burdens. While the Bible does not teach tax exemption for religious employees, Artaxerxes, a pagan king, recognised and supported the principle. Today, churches have the responsibility to keep worldly burdens off the shoulders of spiritual workers.

7:27 In Ezra's doxology, he acknowledges that God "put it into the king's heart". God can change a king's heart (see Proverbs 21:1). When we face life's challenges, we often must work diligently and with extraordinary effort, realising that God oversees all our work. Recognise his hand in your success, and remember to praise him for his help and protection.

7:27, 28 Ezra praised God for all that God had done for him and through him. Ezra had honoured God throughout his life, and God chose to honour him. Ezra could have assumed that his own greatness and charisma had won over the king and his princes, but he gave the credit to God. We, too, should be grateful to God for our success and not think that we did it in our own power.

7:28 The speaker here is Ezra. He writes in the first person for the remainder of the book.

8:3 b 1Ch 3:22 c Ezr 2:3

of the descendants of Ithamar, Daniel;
of the descendants of David, Hattush 3of the descendants of Shecaniah;[b]
of the descendants of Parosh,[c] Zechariah, and with him were registered 150 men;
4of the descendants of Pahath-Moab,[d] Eliehoenai son of Zerahiah, and with him 200 men;
5of the descendants of Zattu,[a] Shecaniah son of Jahaziel, and with him 300 men;
6of the descendants of Adin,[e] Ebed son of Jonathan, and with him 50 men;
7of the descendants of Elam, Jeshaiah son of Athaliah, and with him 70 men;
8of the descendants of Shephatiah, Zebadiah son of Michael, and with him 80 men;

8:4 d Ezr 2:6

8:6 e Ezr 2:15; Ne 7:20; 10:16

a *5* Some Septuagint manuscripts (also 1 Esdras 8:32); Hebrew does not have *Zattu.*

EZRA

It is not personal achievement, but personal commitment to live for God, that is important. Achievements are simply examples of what God can do through someone's life. The most effective leaders spoken of in the Bible had little awareness of the impact their lives had on others. They were too busy obeying God to keep track of their successes. Ezra fits that description.

About 80 years after the rebuilding of the temple under Zerubbabel, Ezra returned to Judah with about 2,000 men and their families. He was given a letter from Artaxerxes instructing him to carry out a programme of religious education. Along with the letter came significant power. But long before Ezra's mission began, God had shaped him in three important ways so that he would use the power well. First, as a scribe, Ezra dedicated himself to carefully studying God's word. Second, he intended to apply and obey personally the commands he discovered in God's word. Third, he was committed to teaching others both God's word and its application to life.

Knowing Ezra's priorities, it is not surprising to note his actions when he arrived in Jerusalem. The people had disobeyed God's command not to marry women of foreign nations. On a cold and rainy day, Ezra addressed the people and made it clear they had sinned. Because of the sins of many, all were under God's condemnation. Confession, repentance, and action were needed. The people admitted their sin and devised a plan to deal with the problem.

This initial effort on Ezra's part set the stage for what Nehemiah would later accomplish. Ezra continued his ministry under Nehemiah, and the two were used by God to start a spiritual movement that swept the nation following the rebuilding of Jerusalem.

Ezra achieved great things and made a significant impact because he had the right starting place for his actions and his life: God's word. He studied it seriously and applied it faithfully. He taught others what he learned. He is, therefore, a great model for anyone who wants to live for God.

Strengths and accomplishments:
- Committed to study, follow, and teach God's word
- Led the second group of exiles from Babylon to Jerusalem
- May have written 1 and 2 Chronicles
- Concerned about keeping the details of God's commands
- Sent by King Artaxerxes to Jerusalem to evaluate the situation, set up a religious education system, and return with a firsthand report
- Worked alongside Nehemiah during the last spiritual awakening recorded in the Old Testament

Lessons from his life:
- A person's willingness to know and practise God's word will have a direct effect on how God uses his/her life
- The starting place for serving God is a personal commitment to serve him today, even before knowing what that service will be

Vital statistics:
- Where: Babylon, Jerusalem
- Occupations: Scribe among the exiles in Babylon, king's envoy, teacher
- Relative: Father: Seriah
- Contemporaries: Nehemiah, Artaxerxes

Key verse:
"For Ezra had devoted himself to the study and observance of the Law of the LORD, and to teaching its decrees and laws in Israel" (Ezra 7:10).

Ezra's story is told in Ezra 7:1—10:16 and Nehemiah 8:1—12:36.

9 of the descendants of Joab, Obadiah son of Jehiel, and with him 218 men;
10 of the descendants of Bani,[b] Shelomith son of Josiphiah, and with him 160 men;
11 of the descendants of Bebai, Zechariah son of Bebai, and with him 28 men;
12 of the descendants of Azgad, Johanan son of Hakkatan, and with him 110 men;
13 of the descendants of Adonikam,[f] the last ones, whose names were Eliphelet, Jeuel and Shemaiah, and with them 60 men;
14 of the descendants of Bigvai, Uthai and Zaccur, and with them 70 men.

The Return to Jerusalem

15 I assembled them at the canal that flows towards Ahava,[g] and we camped there
three days. When I checked among the people and the priests, I found no Levites[h]
there. 16 So I summoned Eliezer, Ariel, Shemaiah, Elnathan, Jarib, Elnathan, Nathan,
Zechariah and Meshullam, who were leaders, and Joiarib and Elnathan, who were men
of learning, 17 and I sent them to Iddo, the leader in Casiphia. I told them what to say
to Iddo and his kinsmen, the temple servants[i] in Casiphia, so that they might bring
attendants to us for the house of our God. 18 Because the gracious hand of our God
was on us,[j] they brought us Sherebiah, a capable man, from the descendants of Mahli
son of Levi, the son of Israel, and Sherebiah's sons and brothers, 18 men; 19 and
Hashabiah, together with Jeshaiah from the descendants of Merari, and his brothers
and nephews, 20 men. 20 They also brought 220 of the temple servants[k]—a body that
David and the officials had established to assist the Levites. All were registered by
name.
21 There, by the Ahava Canal,[l] I proclaimed a fast, so that we might humble
ourselves before our God and ask him for a safe journey[m] for us and our children,
with all our possessions. 22 I was ashamed to ask the king for soldiers[n] and horsemen
to protect us from enemies on the road, because we had told the king, "The gracious
hand of our God is on everyone[o] who looks to him, but his great anger is against
all who forsake him.[p]" 23 So we fasted[q] and petitioned our God about this, and he
answered our prayer.
24 Then I set apart twelve of the leading priests, together with Sherebiah,[r] Hashabiah and ten of their brothers, 25 and I weighed out[s] to them the offering of silver and
gold and the articles that the king, his advisers, his officials and all Israel present there
had donated for the house of our God. 26 I weighed out to them 650 talents[c] of silver,
silver articles weighing 100 talents,[d] 100 talents[d] of gold, 27 20 bowls of gold valued
at 1,000 darics,[e] and two fine articles of polished bronze, as precious as gold.
28 I said to them, "You as well as these articles are consecrated to the LORD.[t] The

[b] *10* Some Septuagint manuscripts (also 1 Esdras 8:36); Hebrew does not have *Bani.* [c] *26* That is, about 22 tons (about 22 metric tons) [d] *26* That is, about 3 ⅓ tons (about 3.4 metric tons) [e] *27* That is, about 19 pounds (about 8.5 kilograms)

8:13 [f] Ezr 2:13
8:15 [g] ver 21, 31 [h] Ezr 2:40; 7:7
8:17 [i] Ezr 2:43
8:18 [j] Ezr 5:5
8:20 [k] 1Ch 9:2; Ezr 2:43
8:21 [l] ver 15; 2Ch 20:3 [m] Ps 5:8; 107:7
8:22 [n] Ne 2:9; Ezr 7:6, 9, 28 [o] Ezr 5:5 [p] Dt 31:17; 2Ch 15:2
8:23 [q] 2Ch 20:3; 33:13
8:24 [r] ver 18
8:25 [s] ver 33; Ezr 7:15, 16
8:28 [t] Lev 21:6; 22:2-3

8:15 Ezra's progress back to Jerusalem was halted while he waited to recruit Levites. God had called these men to a special service, and yet few were willing to volunteer when their services were needed. God has gifted each of us with abilities so we can make a contribution to his kingdom work (Romans 12:4–8). Don't wait to be recruited, but look for opportunities to volunteer. Don't hinder God's work by holding back. "Each one should use whatever gift he has received to serve others, faithfully administering God's grace in its various forms" (1 Peter 4:10).

8:21 Ezra and the people travelled approximately 900 miles on foot. The trip took them through dangerous and difficult territory and lasted about four months. They prayed that God would give them a safe journey. Our journeys today may not be as difficult and dangerous as Ezra's, but we should recognise our need to ask God for guidance and protection.

8:21–23 Before making all the physical preparations for the journey, Ezra made spiritual preparations. Their prayers and fasting prepared them spiritually by showing their dependence on God for protection, their faith that God was in control, and their affirmation that they were not strong enough to make the trip without him. When we take time to put God first in any endeavour, we are preparing well for whatever lies ahead.

8:23 Ezra knew God's promises to protect his people, but he didn't take them for granted. He also knew that God's blessings are appropriated through prayer; so Ezra and the people humbled themselves by fasting and praying. And their prayers were answered. Fasting humbled them because going without food was a reminder of their complete dependence on God. Fasting also gave them more time to pray and meditate on God.

Too often we pray glibly and superficially. Serious prayer, by contrast, requires concentration. It puts us in touch with God's will and can really change us. Without serious prayer, we reduce God to a pharmacist with painkillers for our every ailment.

8:26 Six hundred and fifty talents of silver would be about 25 tons. This was a large amount of treasure to transport, with or without a detachment of soldiers for protection.

8:28, 29 Every object used in temple service was consecrated to God; each was considered a holy treasure to be guarded carefully

8:31 [u]ver 15
8:32 [v]Ge 40:13; Ne 2:11
8:33 [w]Ne 3:4, 21 [x]Ne 3:24
8:35 [y]2Ch 29:21; Ezr 6:17
8:36 [z]Ezr 7:21-24 [a]Est 9:3

silver and gold are a freewill offering to the LORD, the God of your fathers. 29Guard
them carefully until you weigh them out in the chambers of the house of the LORD
in Jerusalem before the leading priests and the Levites and the family heads of Israel."
30Then the priests and Levites received the silver and gold and sacred articles that had
been weighed out to be taken to the house of our God in Jerusalem.
31On the twelfth day of the first month we set out from the Ahava Canal[u] to go
to Jerusalem. The hand of our God was on us, and he protected us from enemies and
bandits along the way. 32So we arrived in Jerusalem, where we rested three days.[v]
33On the fourth day, in the house of our God, we weighed out the silver and gold
and the sacred articles into the hands of Meremoth[w] son of Uriah, the priest. Eleazar
son of Phinehas was with him, and so were the Levites Jozabad son of Jeshua and
Noadiah son of Binnui.[x] 34Everything was accounted for by number and weight, and
the entire weight was recorded at that time.
35Then the exiles who had returned from captivity sacrificed burnt offerings to the
God of Israel: twelve bulls for all Israel, ninety-six rams, seventy-seven male lambs
and, as a sin offering, twelve male goats.[y] All this was a burnt offering to the LORD.
36They also delivered the king's orders[z] to the royal satraps and to the governors of
Trans-Euphrates who then gave assistance to the people and to the house of God.[a]

9:1 [a]Ezr 6:21; Ne 9:2 [b]Ge 19:38 [c]Ex 13:5
9:2 [d]Ex 34:16 [e]Ex 22:31 [f]Ezr 10:2
9:4 [g]Ezr 10:3
9:5 [h]Ex 29:41

2. Ezra opposes intermarriage

Ezra's Prayer About Intermarriage

9 After these things had been done, the leaders came to me and said, "The people
of Israel, including the priests and the Levites, have not kept themselves separate[a] from the neighbouring peoples with their detestable practices, like those of the
Canaanites, Hittites, Perizzites, Jebusites, Ammonites,[b] Moabites, Egyptians and
Amorites.[c] 2They have taken some of their daughters[d] as wives for themselves and
their sons, and have mingled the holy race[e] with the peoples around them. And the
leaders and officials have led the way in this unfaithfulness."[f]
3When I heard this, I tore my tunic and cloak, pulled hair from my head and beard
and sat down appalled. 4Then everyone who trembled[g] at the words of the God of
Israel gathered round me because of this unfaithfulness of the exiles. And I sat there
appalled until the evening sacrifice.
5Then, at the evening sacrifice,[h] I rose from my self-abasement, with my tunic

---

and set apart for his special use. Stewardship means taking special care of whatever God has entrusted to you. This means considering what God has given to you as being *from* him and *for* his use. What has God entrusted to your care?

8:36 *Satraps* were the equivalent of provincial governors.

9:1, 2 Since the time of the judges, Israelite men had married pagan women and then adopted their religious practices (Judges 3:5–7). Even Israel's great King Solomon was guilty of this sin (1 Kings 11:1–8). Although this practice was forbidden in God's law (Exodus 34:11–16; Deuteronomy 7:1–4), it happened in Ezra's day, and again only a generation after him (Nehemiah 13:23–27). Opposition to mixed marriage was not racial prejudice because Jews and non-Jews of this area were of the same Semitic background. The reasons were strictly spiritual. A person who married a pagan was inclined to adopt that person's pagan beliefs and practices. If the Israelites were insensitive enough to disobey God in something as important as marriage, they wouldn't be strong enough to stand firm against their spouses' idolatry. Until the Israelites finally stopped this practice, idolatry remained a constant problem.

9:2 Some Israelites had married pagan spouses and lost track of God's purpose for them. The New Testament says that believers should not "be yoked together with" unbelievers (2 Corinthians 6:14). Such marriages cannot have unity in the most important issue in life – commitment and obedience to God. Because marriage involves two people becoming one, faith may become an issue, and one spouse may have to compromise beliefs for the sake of unity. Many people discount this problem only to regret it later. Don't allow emotion or passion to blind you to the ultimate importance of marrying someone with whom you can be united spiritually.

9:3–5 Tearing one's clothes or pulling hair from one's head or beard were signs of self-abasement or humility. They expressed sorrow for sin.

9:5–15 After learning about the sins of the people, Ezra fell to his knees in prayer. His heartfelt prayer provides a good perspective on sin. He recognised: (1) that sin is serious (9:6); (2) that no-one sins without affecting others (9:7); (3) that he was not sinless, although he didn't have a pagan wife (9:10ff); (4) that God's love and mercy had spared the nation when they did nothing to deserve it (9:8, 9, 15). It is easy to view sin lightly in a world that sees sin as inconsequential, but we should view sin as seriously as Ezra did.

9:5–15 Ezra's prayer confessed the sins of his people. Although he had not sinned in the way his people had, he identified with their sins. With weeping, he expressed shame for sin, fear of the consequences, and desire that the people would come to their senses and repent. His prayer moved the people to tears (10:1). Ezra demonstrated the need for a holy community around the rebuilt temple. We need a holy community in our local churches too. Even when we sin in the worst imaginable way, we can turn to God with prayers of repentance.

and cloak torn, and fell on my knees with my hands spread out to the LORD my God
6and prayed:

"O my God, I am too ashamed and disgraced to lift up my face to you, my
God, because our sins are higher than our heads and our guilt has reached to the
heavens.[i] 7From the days of our forefathers[j] until now, our guilt has been
great. Because of our sins, we and our kings and our priests have been subjected
to the sword[k] and captivity,[l] to pillage and humiliation[m] at the hand of foreign
kings, as it is today.
8"But now, for a brief moment, the LORD our God has been gracious[n] in
leaving us a remnant[o] and giving us a firm place[p] in his sanctuary, and so our
God gives light to our eyes[q] and a little relief in our bondage. 9Though we are
slaves,[r] our God has not deserted us in our bondage. He has shown us kindness[s]
in the sight of the kings of Persia: He has granted us new life to rebuild the house
of our God and repair its ruins,[t] and he has given us a wall of protection in Judah
and Jerusalem.
10"But now, O our God, what can we say after this? For we have disregarded
the commands[u] 11you gave through your servants the prophets when you said:
'The land you are entering to possess is a land polluted[v] by the corruption of
its peoples. By their detestable practices[w] they have filled it with their impurity
from one end to the other. 12Therefore, do not give your daughters in marriage
to their sons or take their daughters for your sons. Do not seek a treaty of
friendship with them[x] at any time, that you may be strong and eat the good things
of the land and leave it to your children as an everlasting inheritance.'
13"What has happened to us is a result of our evil deeds and our great guilt,
and yet, our God, you have punished us less than our sins have deserved[y] and
have given us a remnant like this. 14Shall we again break your commands and
intermarry[z] with the peoples who commit such detestable practices? Would you
not be angry enough with us to destroy us,[a] leaving us no remnant[b] or survivor?
15O LORD, God of Israel, you are righteous![c] We are left this day as a remnant.
Here we are before you in our guilt, though because of it not one of us can stand[d]
in your presence.[e]"

The People's Confession of Sin

10 While Ezra was praying and confessing,[a] weeping and throwing himself down
before the house of God, a large crowd of Israelites—men, women and children—gathered round him. They too wept bitterly. 2Then Shecaniah son of Jehiel,
one of the descendants of Elam, said to Ezra, "We have been unfaithful[b] to our God
by marrying foreign women from the peoples around us. But in spite of this, there
is still hope for Israel.[c] 3Now let us make a covenant[d] before our God to send away[e]
all these women and their children, in accordance with the counsel of my lord and
of those who fear the commands of our God. Let it be done according to the Law.

9:6 [i]2Ch 28:9; Job 42:6; Ps 38:4; Rev 18:5
9:7 [j]2Ch 29:6 [k]Eze 21:1-32 [l]Dt 28:64 [m]Dt 28:37
9:8 [n]Ps 25:16; Isa 33:2 [o]Ge 45:7 [p]Ecc 12:11; Isa 22:23 [q]Ps 13:3
9:9 [r]Ex 1:14; Ne 9:36 [s]Ezr 7:28 [t]Ps 69:35; Isa 43:1; Jer 32:44
9:10 [u]Dt 11:8; Isa 1:19-20
9:11 [v]Lev 18:25-28 [w]Dt 9:4
9:12 [x]Ex 34:15; Dt 7:3; 23:6
9:13 [y]Job 11:6; Ps 103:10
9:14 [z]Ne 13:27 [a]Dt 9:8 [b]Dt 9:14
9:15 [c]Ge 18:25; Ps 51:4; Jer 12:1; Da 9:7 [d]Ne 9:33; Ps 130:3; Mal 3:2 [e]1Ki 8:47
10:1 [a]2Ch 20:9; Da 9:20
10:2 [b]Ezr 9:2; Ne 13:27 [c]Dt 30:8-10
10:3 [d]2Ch 34:31 [e]Ex 34:16; Dt 7:2-3; Ezr 9:4

9:9 Building a wall was not only a matter of civic pride or architectural beauty, it was essential for security and defence against robbers and marauders (see 9:7). God in his kindness had given them new life and protection.

9:15 Ezra recognised that if God gave the people the justice they deserved, they would not be able to stand before him. Often we cry out for justice when we feel abused and unfairly treated. In those moments, we forget the reality of our own sin and the righteous judgment we deserve. How fortunate we are that God gives us mercy and grace rather than only justice. The next time you ask God for fair and just treatment, pause to think what would happen if God gave you what you really deserve. Plead instead for his mercy.

10:3 Why were the men commanded to send away their wives and children? Although the measure was extreme, intermarriage to pagans was strictly forbidden (Deuteronomy 7:3, 4), and even the priests and Levites had intermarried. This could be compared today to a Christian marrying a devil worshipper. Although a severe solution, it only involved 113 of the approximately 29,000 families.

Ezra's strong act, though very difficult for some, was necessary to preserve Israel as a nation committed to God. Some of the exiles of the northern kingdom of Israel had lost both their spiritual and physical identity through intermarriage. Their pagan spouses had caused the people to worship idols. Ezra did not want this to happen to the exiles of the southern kingdom of Judah.

10:3, 4, 11 Following Ezra's earnest prayer, the people confessed their sin to God. Then they asked for direction in restoring their relationship with God. True repentance does not end with words of confession—that would be mere lip service. It must lead to corrected behaviour and changed attitudes. When you sin and are truly sorry, confess this to God, ask his forgiveness, and accept his grace and mercy. Then, as an act of thankfulness for your forgiveness, make the needed corrections.

4 Rise up; this matter is in your hands. We will support you, so take courage and do
it."
5 So Ezra rose up and put the leading priests and Levites and all Israel under oath[f]
to do what had been suggested. And they took the oath. 6 Then Ezra withdrew from
before the house of God and went to the room of Jehohanan son of Eliashib. While
he was there, he ate no food and drank no water,[g] because he continued to mourn
over the unfaithfulness of the exiles.
7 A proclamation was then issued throughout Judah and Jerusalem for all the exiles
to assemble in Jerusalem. 8 Anyone who failed to appear within three days would
forfeit all his property, in accordance with the decision of the officials and elders, and
would himself be expelled from the assembly of the exiles.

9 Within the three days, all the men of Judah and Benjamin[h] had gathered in
Jerusalem. And on the twentieth day of the ninth month, all the people were sitting
in the square before the house of God, greatly distressed by the occasion and because
of the rain. 10 Then Ezra the priest stood up and said to them, "You have been
unfaithful; you have married foreign women, adding to Israel's guilt. 11 Now make
confession to the LORD, the God of your fathers, and do his will. Separate yourselves
from the peoples around you and from your foreign wives."[i]
12 The whole assembly responded with a loud voice:[j] "You are right! We must do
as you say. 13 But there are many people here and it is the rainy season; so we cannot
stand outside. Besides, this matter cannot be taken care of in a day or two, because
we have sinned greatly in this thing. 14 Let our officials act for the whole assembly.
Then let everyone in our towns who has married a foreign woman come at a set time,
along with the elders and judges[k] of each town, until the fierce anger[l] of our God
in this matter is turned away from us." 15 Only Jonathan son of Asahel and Jahzeiah
son of Tikvah, supported by Meshullam and Shabbethai[m] the Levite, opposed this.
16 So the exiles did as was proposed. Ezra the priest selected men who were family
heads, one from each family division, and all of them designated by name. On the
first day of the tenth month they sat down to investigate the cases, 17 and by the first
day of the first month they finished dealing with all the men who had married foreign
women.

Those Guilty of Intermarriage

18 Among the descendants of the priests, the following had married foreign
women:[n]

From the descendants of Jeshua[o] son of Jozadak, and his brothers:
Maaseiah, Eliezer, Jarib and Gedaliah. 19 (They all gave their hands[p] in
pledge to put away their wives, and for their guilt they each presented a ram
from the flock as a guilt offering.)[q]
20 From the descendants of Immer:[r]
Hanani and Zebadiah.
21 From the descendants of Harim:[s]
Maaseiah, Elijah, Shemaiah, Jehiel and Uzziah.
22 From the descendants of Pashhur:[t]
Elioenai, Maaseiah, Ishmael, Nethanel, Jozabad and Elasah.

23 Among the Levites:[u]

Jozabad, Shimei, Kelaiah (that is Kelita), Pethahiah, Judah and Eliezer.

10:5 [f] Ne 5:12; 13:25
10:6 [g] Ex 34:28; Dt 9:18
10:9 [h] Ezr 1:5
10:11 [i] ver 3; Dt 24:1; Ne 9:2; Mal 2:10-16
10:12 [j] Jos 6:5
10:14 [k] Dt 16:18 [l] Nu 25:4; 2Ch 29:10; 30:8
10:15 [m] Ne 11:16
10:18 [n] Jdg 3:6 [o] Ezr 2:2
10:19 [p] 2Ki 10:15 [q] Lev 5:15; 6:6
10:20 [r] 1Ch 24:14
10:21 [s] 1Ch 24:8
10:22 [t] 1Ch 9:12
10:23 [u] Ne 8:7; 9:4

10:8 To forfeit one's property meant to be disinherited, to lose one's legal right to own land. This was to ensure that no pagan children would inherit Israel's land. In addition, the person who refused to come to Jerusalem would be expelled from the assembly of the exiles and not allowed to worship in the temple. The Jews considered this a horrible punishment.

10:11 As believers in Christ, all our sins are forgiven. His death cleansed us from all sin. Why do we then still confess our sins? Confession is more than appropriating Christ's forgiveness for what we have done wrong, and we do not have to confess again sins that were previously confessed. Confession is agreeing with God that our thoughts, words, and actions are wrong and contrary to his will. It is recommitting ourselves to do his will and to renounce any acts of disobedience. Confession is turning away from sin and asking God for fresh power to live for him.

[24]From the singers:
Eliashib.[v]
From the gatekeepers:
Shallum, Telem and Uri.

[25]And among the other Israelites:

From the descendants of Parosh:[w]
Ramiah, Izziah, Malkijah, Mijamin, Eleazar, Malkijah and Benaiah.
[26]From the descendants of Elam:[x]
Mattaniah, Zechariah, Jehiel, Abdi, Jeremoth and Elijah.
[27]From the descendants of Zattu:
Elioenai, Eliashib, Mattaniah, Jeremoth, Zabad and Aziza.
[28]From the descendants of Bebai:
Jehohanan, Hananiah, Zabbai and Athlai.
[29]From the descendants of Bani:
Meshullam, Malluch, Adaiah, Jashub, Sheal and Jeremoth.
[30]From the descendants of Pahath-Moab:
Adna, Kelal, Benaiah, Maaseiah, Mattaniah, Bezalel, Binnui and Manasseh.
[31]From the descendants of Harim:
Eliezer, Ishijah, Malkijah, Shemaiah, Shimeon, [32]Benjamin, Malluch and Shemariah.
[33]From the descendants of Hashum:
Mattenai, Mattattah, Zabad, Eliphelet, Jeremai, Manasseh and Shimei.
[34]From the descendants of Bani:
Maadai, Amram, Uel, [35]Benaiah, Bedeiah, Keluhi, [36]Vaniah, Meremoth, Eliashib, [37]Mattaniah, Mattenai and Jaasu.
[38]From the descendants of Binnui:[a]
Shimei, [39]Shelemiah, Nathan, Adaiah, [40]Macnadebai, Shashai, Sharai, [41]Azarel, Shelemiah, Shemariah, [42]Shallum, Amariah and Joseph.
[43]From the descendants of Nebo:
Jeiel, Mattithiah, Zabad, Zebina, Jaddai, Joel and Benaiah.

[44]All these had married foreign women, and some of them had children by these wives.[b]

[a] *37,38* See Septuagint (also 1 Esdras 9:34); Hebrew *Jaasu* [38]*and Bani and Binnui,* [b] *44* Or *and they sent them away with their children*

10:24
[v]Ne 3:1; 12:10; 13:7, 28

10:25
[w]Ezr 2:3

10:26
[x]ver 2

10:44 The book of Ezra opens with God's temple in ruins and the people of Judah captive in Babylon. Ezra tells of the return of God's people, the rebuilding of the temple, and the restoration of the sacrificial worship system. Similarly, God is able to restore and rebuild the lives of people today. No one is so far away from God that he or she cannot be restored. Repentance is all that is required. No matter how far we have strayed or how long it has been since we have worshipped God, he is able to restore our relationship to him and rebuild our lives.

THE MEDO-PERSIAN EMPIRE

The events in the books of Ezra, Nehemiah, and Esther took place during the rule of the Medes and Persians. These two kingdoms came from the northeast of Mesopotamia (present-day Iran) and joined forces to defeat the Babylonians (Daniel 5:30, 31). The Persians ruled until the rise of the Greek empire under Alexander the Great. The Persians had a relaxed policy towards their captives, allowing them to own land and homes. King Cyrus of Persia went a step further, allowing many groups of exiles, including the Jews, to return to their homelands. In the books of Ezra and Nehemiah, groups of Jewish exiles were allowed to return to Palestine to rebuild their capital city and temple. The first group of returnees led by Zerubabbel arrived in 538 B.C. The second group returned with Ezra in 458 B.C. Nehemiah came in 455 B.C. to encourage the rebuilding of Jerusalem's wall. Esther became queen of the kingdom in 479 B.C., between the first and second returns.

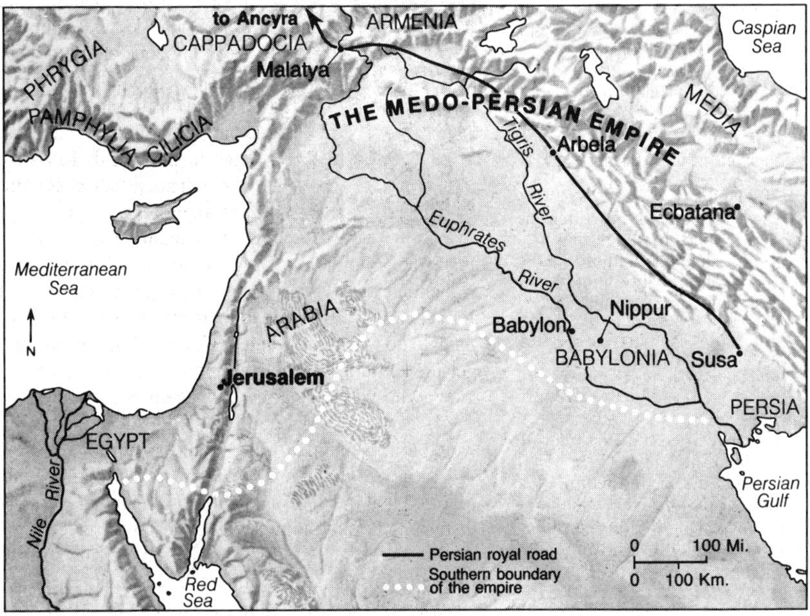

NEHEMIAH

Jerusalem destroyed; exiles go to Babylon 586 B.C.

First exiles return to Jerusalem 538

Temple completed 516

VITAL STATISTICS

PURPOSE:
Nehemiah is the last of the Old Testament historical books. It records the history of the third return to Jerusalem after captivity, telling how the walls were rebuilt and the people were renewed in their faith.

AUTHOR:
Much of the book is written in the first person, suggesting Nehemiah as the author. Nehemiah probably wrote the book with Ezra serving as editor.

DATE WRITTEN:
Approximately 445–432 B.C.

SETTING:
Zerubbabel led the first return to Jerusalem in 538 B.C. In 458, Ezra led the second return. Finally, in 445, Nehemiah returned with the third group of exiles to rebuild the city walls.

KEY VERSES:
"So the wall was completed on the twenty-fifth of Elul, in fifty-two days. When all our enemies heard about this, all the surrounding nations were afraid and lost their self-confidence, because they realised that this work had been done with the help of our God" (6:15, 16).

KEY PEOPLE:
Nehemiah, Ezra, Sanballat, Tobiah

KEY PLACE:
Jerusalem

SPECIAL FEATURES:
The book shows the fulfilment of the prophecies of Zechariah and Daniel concerning the rebuilding of Jerusalem's walls.

"WHAT this church needs is . . . !" "I can't believe our government officials. If I were there I would . . . !" "Our schools are in a really bad way. Someone ought to do something!"

Gripers, complainers, self-proclaimed prophets, and "armchair critics" abound. It is easy to analyse, scrutinise, and *talk* about all the problems in the world. But we really need people who will not just discuss a situation, but who will *do* something about it!

Nehemiah saw a problem and was distressed. Instead of complaining or wallowing in self-pity and grief, he took action. Nehemiah knew that God wanted him to motivate the Jews to rebuild Jerusalem's walls, so he left a responsible position in the Persian government to do what God wanted. Nehemiah knew God could use his talents to get the job done. From the moment he arrived in Jerusalem, everyone knew who was in charge. He organised, managed, supervised, encouraged, met opposition, confronted injustice, and kept going until the walls were built. Nehemiah was a man of action.

As the story begins, Nehemiah was talking with fellow Jews who reported that the walls and gates of Jerusalem were in disrepair. This was disturbing news, and rebuilding those walls became Nehemiah's burden. At the appropriate time, Nehemiah asked King Artaxerxes for permission to go to Jerusalem to rebuild its fallen walls. The king approved.

Armed with royal letters, Nehemiah travelled to Jerusalem. He organised the people into groups and assigned them to specific sections of the wall (chapter 3). The construction project was not without opposition, however. Sanballat, Tobiah, and others tried to halt the work with insults, ridicule, threats, and sabotage. Some of the workers became fearful; others became weary. In each case, Nehemiah employed a strategy to frustrate the enemies—prayer, encouragement, guard duty, consolidation (chapter 4). But a different problem arose—an internal one. Rich Jews were profiteering off the plight of their working countrymen. Hearing of their oppression and greed, Nehemiah confronted the extortioners face to face (chapter 5). Then, with the walls almost complete, Sanballat, Tobiah, and company tried one last time to stop Nehemiah. But Nehemiah stood firm, and the wall was finished in just 52 days. What a tremendous monument to God's love and faithfulness. Enemies and friends alike knew that God had helped (chapter 6).

After building the walls, Nehemiah continued to organise the people, taking a registration and appointing gatekeepers, Levites, and other officials (chapter 7). Ezra led the city in worship and Bible instruction (chapters 8, 9). This led to a reaffirmation of faith and religious revival as the people promised to serve God faithfully (chapters 10, 11).

Nehemiah closes with the listing of the clans and their leaders, the dedication of the new wall of Jerusalem, and the purging of sin from the land (chapters 12, 13). As you read this book, watch Nehemiah in action—and determine to be a person on whom God can depend to *act* for him in the world.

Xerxes becomes king of Persia 486	*Artaxerxes I becomes king of Persia 465*	*Ezra comes to Jerusalem 458*	*Nehemiah comes to Jerusalem; wall completed 445*	*Nehemiah returns to Babylon 433*	*Nehemiah goes back to Jerusalem 432*	*Malachi begins his ministry 430(?)*

THE BLUEPRINT

A. REBUILDING THE WALL (1:1—7:73)
1. Nehemiah returns to Jerusalem
2. Nehemiah leads the people

Nehemiah's life is an example of leadership and organisation. Giving up a comfortable and wealthy position in Persia, he returned to the fractured homeland of his ancestors and rallied the people to rebuild Jerusalem's wall. In the face of opposition, he used wise defence measures to care for the people and to keep the project moving. To accomplish more for the sake of God's kingdom, we must pray, persevere, and sacrifice, as did Nehemiah.

B. REFORMING THE PEOPLE (8:1—13:31)
1. Ezra renews the covenant
2. Nehemiah establishes policies

After the wall was rebuilt, Ezra read the law to the people, bringing about national repentance. Nehemiah and Ezra were very different people, yet God used them both to lead the nation. Remember, there is a place for you in God's work even if you're different from most other people. God uses each person in a unique way to accomplish his purposes.

MEGATHEMES

THEME	EXPLANATION	IMPORTANCE
Vision	Although the Jews completed the temple in 516 B.C., the city walls remained a shambles for the next 70 years. These walls represented power, protection, and beauty to the city of Jerusalem. They were also desperately needed to protect the temple from attack and to ensure the continuity of worship. God put the desire to rebuild the walls in Nehemiah's heart, giving him a vision for the work.	Does God have a vision for us? Are there "walls" that need to be built today? God still wants his people to be united and trained to do his work. As we recognise deep needs in our world, God can give us the vision and desire to "build". With that vision, we can mobilise others to pray and put together an action plan.
Prayer	Both Nehemiah and Ezra responded to problems with prayer. When Nehemiah began his work, he recognised the problem, immediately prayed, and then acted on the problem.	Prayer is still God's mighty force in solving problems today. Prayer and action go hand in hand. Through prayer, God guides our preparation, teamwork, and diligent efforts to carry out his will.
Leadership	Nehemiah demonstrated excellent leadership. He was spiritually ready to heed God's call. He used careful planning, teamwork, problem solving, and courage to get the work done. Although he had tremendous faith, he never avoided the extra work necessary for good leadership.	Being God's leader is not just gaining recognition, holding a position, or being the boss. It requires planning, hard work, courage, and perseverance. Positive expectations are never a substitute for doing the difficult work. And in order to lead others, you need to listen for God's direction in your own life.
Problems	After the work began, Nehemiah faced scorn, slander, and threats from enemies, as well as fear, conflict, and discouragement from his own workers. Although these problems were difficult, they did not stop Nehemiah from finishing the work.	When difficulties come, there is a tendency for conflict and discouragement to set in. We must recognise that there are no triumphs without troubles. When problems arise, we must face them squarely and press on to complete God's work.
Repentance/ Revival	Although God had enabled them to build the wall, the work wasn't complete until the people rebuilt their lives spiritually. Ezra instructed the people in God's word. As they listened, they recognised the sin in their lives, admitted it, and took steps to remove it.	Recognising and admitting sin is not enough; revival must result in reform, or it is merely the expression of enthusiasm. God does not want half-hearted measures. We must not only remove sin from our lives, but also ask God to move into the centre of all we do.

A. REBUILDING THE WALL (1.1 – 7.73)

Despite the fact that the returned exiles had been in Jerusalem for many years, the walls of the city remained unrepaired, leaving its people defenceless and vulnerable. Upon hearing this news, Nehemiah seeks permission from the Persian king to go to Jerusalem. Arriving in Jerusalem, he mobilises the people to begin rebuilding the wall. Faced with opposition, both from without and from within, Nehemiah perseveres until the project is complete and the city is resettled. Seemingly impossible tasks can be accomplished when God is helping those who honour him and when their efforts are united.

1. Nehemiah returns to Jerusalem

Nehemiah's Prayer

1 The words of Nehemiah son of Hacaliah:

In the month of Kislev[a] in the twentieth year, while I was in the citadel of Susa,
2Hanani,[b] one of my brothers, came from Judah with some other men, and I
questioned them about the Jewish remnant[c] that survived the exile, and also about
Jerusalem.
3They said to me, "Those who survived the exile and are back in the province are
in great trouble and disgrace. The wall of Jerusalem is broken down, and its gates have
been burned with fire.[d]"
4When I heard these things, I sat down and wept.[e] For some days I mourned and
fasted[f] and prayed before the God of heaven. 5Then I said:

"O LORD, God of heaven, the great and awesome God,[g] who keeps his
covenant of love[h] with those who love him and obey his commands, 6let your
ear be attentive and your eyes open to hear[i] the prayer[j] your servant is praying
before you day and night for your servants, the people of Israel. I confess the
sins we Israelites, including myself and my father's house, have committed

1:1 [a]Ne 10:1; Zec 7:1
1:2 [b]Ne 7:2 [c]Jer 52:28
1:3 [d]2Ki 25:10; Ne 2:3, 13, 17
1:4 [e]Ps 137:1 [f]Ezr 9:4
1:5 [g]Dt 7:21; Ne 4:14 [h]Ex 20:6; Da 9:4
1:6 [i]1Ki 8:29 [j]Da 9:17

1:1 Nehemiah wasn't the first of the exiles to return to Jerusalem. Zerubbabel had led the first group back in 537 B.C., more than 90 years earlier (Ezra 1, 2). Ezra followed with a second group in 458 B.C. (Ezra 7), and here Nehemiah was ready to lead the third major return to Jerusalem (445 B.C.). When he arrived after a three-month journey, he saw the completed temple and became acquainted with others who had returned to their homeland.

But Nehemiah also found a disorganised group of people and a defenceless city with no walls to protect it. Before the exile, Israel had its own language, king, army, and identity. At this time it had none of these. What the Jews lacked most was leadership; there was no-one to show them where to start and what direction to take as they tried to rebuild their city. As soon as Nehemiah arrived he began a back-to-the-basics programme. He helped care for the people's physical needs by setting up a fair system of government and rebuilding Jerusalem's walls. He also cared for their spiritual needs by rebuilding broken lives. Nehemiah is a model of committed, God-honouring leadership, and his book contains many useful lessons for today.

1:2–4 Nehemiah was concerned about Jerusalem because it was the Jews' holy city. As Judah's capital city, it represented Jewish national identity, and it was blessed with God's special presence in the temple. Jewish history centred around the city from the time of Abraham's gifts to Melchizedek, king of Salem (Genesis 14:17–20), to the days when Solomon built the glorious temple (1 Kings 7:51), and throughout the history of the kings. Nehemiah loved his homeland even though he had lived his whole life in Babylon. He wanted to return to Jerusalem to reunite the Jews and to remove the shame of Jerusalem's broken-down walls. This would bring glory to God and restore the reality and power of God's presence among his people.

1:4 Nehemiah broke down and wept when he heard that Jerusalem's walls still had not been rebuilt. Why did this upset him? Walls mean little in most present-day cities, but in Nehemiah's day they were essential. They offered safety from raids and symbolised strength and peace. Nehemiah also mourned for his people, the Jews, who had been stifled by a previous edict that kept them from rebuilding their walls (Ezra 4:6–23).

1:4 Nehemiah was deeply grieved about the condition of Jerusalem, but he didn't just brood about it. After his initial grief, he prayed, pouring his heart out to God (1:5–11), and he looked for ways to improve the situation. Nehemiah put all his resources of knowledge, experience, and organisation into determining what should be done. When tragic news comes to you, first pray. Then seek ways to move beyond grief to specific action that helps those who need it.

1:5 God's "covenant of love" refers to God's promise to love the descendants of Abraham. It is also mentioned in Deuteronomy 7:7–9.

1:5ff Nehemiah fasted and prayed for several days, expressing his sorrow for Israel's sin and his desire that Jerusalem would again come alive with the worship of the one true God. Nehemiah demonstrated the elements of effective prayer: (1) praise, (2) thanksgiving, (3) repentance, (4) specific request, and (5) commitment.

Heartfelt prayers like Nehemiah's can help clarify (1) any problem you may be facing, (2) God's great power to help you, and (3) the job you have to do. By the end of his prayer time, Nehemiah knew what action he had to take (1:11). When God's people pray, difficult decisions fall into proper perspective, and appropriate actions follow.

1:7 [k]Dt 28:14-15; Ps 106:6
1:8 [l]2Ki 20:3 [m]Lev 26:33
1:9 [n]Dt 30:4 [o]1Ki 8:48; Jer 29:14
1:10 [p]Ex 32:11; Dt 9:29
1:11 [q]ver 6 [r]Ge 40:1

against you. 7We have acted very wickedly[k] towards you. We have not obeyed
the commands, decrees and laws you gave your servant Moses.
8"Remember[l] the instruction you gave your servant Moses, saying, 'If you
are unfaithful, I will scatter[m] you among the nations, 9but if you return to me
and obey my commands, then even if your exiled people are at the farthest
horizon, I will gather[n] them from there and bring them to the place I have chosen
as a dwelling for my Name.'[o]
10"They are your servants and your people, whom you redeemed by your great
strength and your mighty hand.[p] 11O Lord, let your ear be attentive[q] to the
prayer of this your servant and to the prayer of your servants who delight in
revering your name. Give your servant success today by granting him favour in
the presence of this man."

I was cupbearer[r] to the king.

HOW NEHEMIAH USED PRAYER

Reference	*Occasion*	*Summary of his Prayer*	*What Prayer Accomplished*	*Our Prayers*
1:4–11	After receiving the bad news about the state of Jerusalem's walls	Recognised God's holiness. Asked for a hearing. Confessed sin. Asked for specific help in approaching the king	Included God in Nehemiah's plans and concerns. Prepared Nehemiah's heart and gave God room to work	How often do you pour out your heart to God? How often do you give him a specific request to answer?
2:4	During his conversation with the king	"Here's where you can help, God!"	Put the expected results in God's hands	Giving God credit for what happens before it happens keeps us from taking more credit than we should.
4:4, 5	After being taunted and ridiculed by Tobiah and Sanballat	"They're mocking you, God. You decide what to do with them."	Expressed anger to God, but Nehemiah did not take matters into his own hands	We are prone to do exactly the opposite—take matters into our hands and not tell God how we feel.
4:9	After threats of attack by enemies	"We are in your hands, God. We'll keep our weapons handy in case you want us to use them."	Showed trust in God even while taking necessary precautions	Trusting God does not mean we do nothing. Action does not mean we do not trust.
6:9	Responding to threats	"Oh Lord God, please strengthen me!"	Showed Nehemiah's reliance on God for emotional and mental stability	How often do you ask God for help when under pressure?
13:29	Reflecting on the actions of his enemies	Asked God to deal with the enemies and their evil plans	Took away the compulsion to have revenge, and entrusted justice to God	When did you last settle a desire for revenge by turning the matter over to God?
5:19; 13:14, 22, 31	Reflecting on his own efforts to serve God	"Remember me, God."	Kept clear in Nehemiah's mind his own motives for action	How many of your actions today will be done with the purpose of pleasing God?

1:11 Nehemiah was in a unique position to speak to the king. He was the trusted cupbearer who ensured the safety and quality of the king's food and drink. Nehemiah was concerned, prayerful, and prepared as he looked for the right opportunity to tell the king about God's people. Each of us is unique and capable of serving no matter what our position. Just as Nehemiah used his place as the king's trusted servant to intercede for his people, we can use our present positions to serve God.

1:11 Nehemiah prayed for success in this venture, not just for the strength to cope with his problems (see also 2:20). Yet the success he prayed for was not for personal advantage, position, or acclaim. He requested success for God's work. When God's purposes are at work, don't hesitate to ask for success.

Artaxerxes Sends Nehemiah to Jerusalem

2 In the month of Nisan in the twentieth year of King Artaxerxes,[a] when wine was
brought for him, I took the wine and gave it to the king. I had not been sad in
his presence before; 2so the king asked me, "Why does your face look so sad when
you are not ill? This can be nothing but sadness of heart."
I was very much afraid, 3but I said to the king, "May the king live for ever![b] Why
should my face not look sad when the city[c] where my fathers are buried lies in ruins,
and its gates have been destroyed by fire?[d]"
4The king said to me, "What is it you want?"
Then I prayed to the God of heaven, 5and I answered the king, "If it pleases the
king and if your servant has found favour in his sight, let him send me to the city in
Judah where my fathers are buried so that I can rebuild it."
6Then the king[e], with the queen sitting beside him, asked me, "How long will your
journey take, and when will you get back?" It pleased the king to send me; so I set
a time.
7I also said to him, "If it pleases the king, may I have letters to the governors of
Trans-Euphrates,[f] so that they will provide me safe-conduct until I arrive in Judah?
8And may I have a letter to Asaph, keeper of the king's forest, so he will give me
timber to make beams for the gates of the citadel[g] by the temple and for the city wall
and for the residence I will occupy?" And because the gracious hand of my God was
upon me,[h] the king granted my requests. 9So I went to the governors of Trans-

2:1 [a]Ezr 7:1
2:3 [b]1Ki 1:31; Da 2:4; 5:10; 6:6, 21 [c]Ps 137:6 [d]Ne 1:3
2:6 [e]Ne 5:14; 13:6
2:7 [f]Ezr 8:36
2:8 [g]Ne 7:2 [h]ver 18; Ezr 5:5; 7:6

2:2 The king noticed Nehemiah's sad appearance. This frightened Nehemiah because it was dangerous to show sorrow before the king, who could execute anyone who displeased him. Anyone wearing sackcloth (mourning clothes) was barred from the palace (Esther 4:2).

2:2, 3 Nehemiah wasn't ashamed to admit his fear, but he refused to allow fear to stop him from doing what God had called him to do. When we allow our fears to rule us, we make fear more powerful than God. Is there a task God wants you to do, but fear is holding you back? God is greater than all your fears. Recognising why you are afraid is the first step in committing it to God. Realise that if God has called you to a task, he will help you accomplish it.

2:4 With little time to think, Nehemiah immediately prayed. Eight times in this book we read that he prayed spontaneously (2:4; 4:4–5, 9; 5:19; 6:14; 13:14, 22, 29). Nehemiah prayed at any time, even while talking with others. He knew that God is always in charge, is always present, and hears and answers every prayer. Nehemiah could confidently pray throughout the day because he had established an intimate relationship with God during times of extended prayer (1:4–7). If we want to reach God with our emergency prayers, we need to take time to cultivate a strong relationship with God through times of in-depth prayer.

2:6 The king asked Nehemiah how long he would be gone. The Bible does not record Nehemiah's immediate answer, but he ended up staying in Jerusalem 12 years (5:14; 13:6).

2:7, 8 After his prayer, Nehemiah asked the king for permission to go to Judah. As soon as he got a positive answer, he began asking for additional help. Sometimes when we have needs, we hesitate to ask the right people for help because we are afraid to approach them. Not Nehemiah! He went directly to the person who could help him the most. Don't be reluctant to ask those who are most able to help. They may be more interested and approachable than you think. God's answers to prayer may come as a result of our asking others.

2:8 Nehemiah had position, power, and many good organisational skills, but he acknowledged that God's gracious hand was upon him. He knew that without God's strength, his efforts would be in vain. Do you acknowledge God as your power source and the giver of your gifts?

2:9, 10, 19 When Nehemiah arrived in Judah, he was greeted with opposition. Opposition to the rebuilding of Jerusalem had been going on for 90 years by those who settled in the area when the Jews were taken captive. In every generation there are those who hate God's people and try to block God's purpose. When you attempt to do God's work, some will oppose you; some will even hope you fail. If you expect opposition, you will be prepared rather than surprised (1 John 3:13). Knowing that God is behind your task is the best incentive to move ahead in the face of opposition.

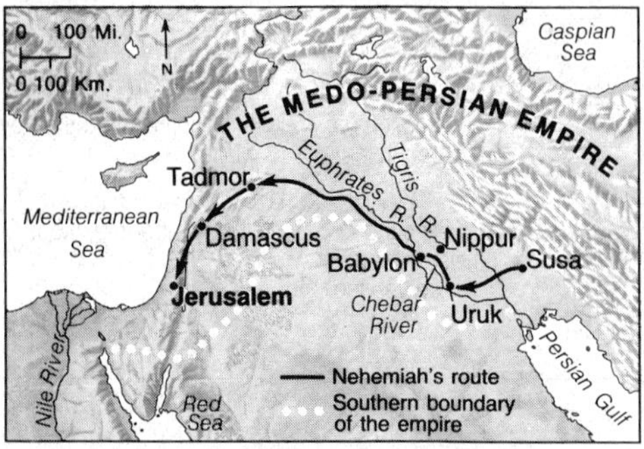

NEHEMIAH GOES TO JERUSALEM Nehemiah worked in Susa as a personal assistant to the king of the vast Medo-Persian empire. When he heard that the rebuilding projects in Jerusalem were progressing slowly, he asked the king if he could go there to help his people complete the task of rebuilding their city's walls. The king agreed to let him go; so he left as soon as possible, travelling along much the same route Ezra had taken.

Euphrates and gave them the king's letters. The king had also sent army officers and
cavalry[i] with me.
10 When Sanballat[j] the Horonite and Tobiah[k] the Ammonite official heard about
this, they were very much disturbed that someone had come to promote the welfare
of the Israelites.[l]

2. Nehemiah leads the people

Nehemiah Inspects Jerusalem's Walls

11 I went to Jerusalem, and after staying there three days[m] 12 I set out during the
night with a few men. I had not told anyone what my God had put in my heart to do
for Jerusalem. There were no mounts with me except the one I was riding on.
13 By night I went out through the Valley Gate[n] towards the Jackal[a] Well and the
Dung Gate,[o] examining the walls[p] of Jerusalem, which had been broken down, and
its gates, which had been destroyed by fire. 14 Then I moved on towards the Fountain
Gate[q] and the King's Pool,[r] but there was not enough room for my mount to get
through; 15 so I went up the valley by night, examining the wall. Finally, I turned back
and re-entered through the Valley Gate. 16 The officials did not know where I had gone
or what I was doing, because as yet I had said nothing to the Jews or the priests or
nobles or officials or any others who would be doing the work.
17 Then I said to them, "You see the trouble we are in: Jerusalem lies in ruins, and
its gates have been burned with fire.[s] Come, let us rebuild the wall[t] of Jerusalem,
and we will no longer be in disgrace.[u]" 18 I also told them about the gracious hand
of my God upon me[v] and what the king had said to me.
They replied, "Let us start rebuilding." So they began this good work.
19 But when Sanballat the Horonite, Tobiah the Ammonite official and Geshem[w]
the Arab heard about it, they mocked and ridiculed us.[x] "What is this you are doing?"
they asked. "Are you rebelling against the king?"
20 I answered them by saying, "The God of heaven will give us success. We his
servants will start rebuilding, but as for you, you have no share[y] in Jerusalem or any
claim or historic right to it."

[a] *13* Or *Serpent* or *Fig*

2:9 [i]Ezr 8:22
2:10 [j]ver 19; Ne 4:1, 7 [k]Ne 4:3; 13:4-7 [l]Est 10:3
2:11 [m]Ge 40:13
2:13 [n]2Ch 26:9 [o]Ne 3:13 [p]Ne 1:3
2:14 [q]Ne 3:15 [r]2Ki 18:17
2:17 [s]Ne 1:3 [t]Ps 102:16; Isa 30:13; 58:12 [u]Eze 5:14
2:18 [v]2Sa 2:7
2:19 [w]Ne 6:1, 2, 6 [x]Ps 44:13-16
2:20 [y]Ezr 4:3

2:10 Sanballat was governor of Samaria, and Tobiah was probably governor of Transjordan under the Persians. Why were these government officials so concerned about the arrival of Nehemiah and his small band of exiles? There are several possible reasons. (1) When Zerubbabel first returned with his group (Ezra 1; 2), his refusal to accept help from the Samaritans had caused bad relations. (2) Nehemiah was no ordinary exile; he was the king's personal adviser and cupbearer, arriving in Jerusalem with the king's approval to build and fortify the city. If anyone could rebuild Jerusalem, he could. A rebuilt Jerusalem was a threat to the authority of the Samaritan officials who had been in charge of the land since Judah's exile. (3) This was the third group to return from exile. The increasing number of people in Jerusalem made Sanballat and Tobiah angry. They did not want returned exiles taking control of the land and threatening their secure position.

2:11–17 Nehemiah arrived quietly in Jerusalem and spent several days carefully observing and assessing the damage to the walls. Following this time of thoughtful consideration, he confidently presented his plan. Nehemiah demonstrated an excellent approach to problem solving. He got firsthand information and carefully considered the situation. Then he presented a realistic strategy. Before jumping into a project, follow Nehemiah's example and plan ahead. Check your information to make sure your ideas will work – be realistic. Then you will be able to present your plan with confidence.

2:14 The walls were so broken down that Nehemiah's mount couldn't get through, so Nehemiah had to inspect that section on foot.

2:15, 16 Nehemiah kept his mission a secret and surveyed the walls by moonlight to avoid unhealthy gossip about his arrival and to prevent enemies from being alerted to his plans. Only after planning carefully would he be ready to go public with his mission from God. A premature announcement could have caused rivalry among the Jews as to the best way to begin. In this case, Nehemiah didn't need tedious planning sessions; he needed one plan that would bring quick action.

2:17, 18 Spiritual renewal often begins with one person's vision. Nehemiah had a vision, and he shared it with enthusiasm, inspiring Jerusalem's leaders to rebuild the walls.

We frequently underestimate people and don't challenge them with our dreams for God's work in the world. When God plants an idea in your mind to accomplish something for him, share it with others and trust the Holy Spirit to impress them with similar thoughts. Don't regard yourself as the only one through whom God is working. Often God uses one person to express the vision and others to turn it into reality. When you encourage and inspire others, you put teamwork into action to accomplish God's goals.

2:19 Sanballat and Tobiah labelled the rebuilding of Jerusalem's walls as rebellion against the king, probably threatening to report the builders as traitors. These enemies also ridiculed Nehemiah, saying that the walls could never be rebuilt because the damage was too extensive. Nehemiah did not tell them he already had permission from the king to rebuild. Instead, he simply said he had God's approval – that was enough.

Builders of the Wall

3 Eliashib[a] the high priest and his fellow priests went to work and rebuilt[b] the
Sheep Gate.[c] They dedicated it and set its doors in place, building as far as the
Tower of the Hundred, which they dedicated, and as far as the Tower of Hananel.[d]
2The men of Jericho[e] built the adjoining section, and Zaccur son of Imri built next
to them.

3The Fish Gate[f] was rebuilt by the sons of Hassenaah. They laid its beams and
put its doors and bolts and bars in place. 4Meremoth son of Uriah, the son of Hakkoz,
repaired the next section. Next to him Meshullam son of Berekiah, the son of
Meshezabel, made repairs, and next to him Zadok son of Baana also made repairs.
5The next section was repaired by the men of Tekoa,[g] but their nobles would not put
their shoulders to the work under their supervisors.[a]

6The Jeshanah[b] Gate[h] was repaired by Joiada son of Paseah and Meshullam son
of Besodeiah. They laid its beams and put its doors and bolts and bars in place. 7Next
to them, repairs were made by men from Gibeon[i] and Mizpah — Melatiah of Gibeon
and Jadon of Meronoth — places under the authority of the governor of Trans-
Euphrates. 8Uzziel son of Harhaiah, one of the goldsmiths, repaired the next section;
and Hananiah, one of the perfume-makers, made repairs next to that. They restored[c]
Jerusalem as far as the Broad Wall.[j] 9Rephaiah son of Hur, ruler of a half-district
of Jerusalem, repaired the next section. 10Adjoining this, Jedaiah son of Harumaph
made repairs opposite his house, and Hattush son of Hashabneiah made repairs next
to him. 11Malkijah son of Harim and Hasshub son of Pahath-Moab repaired another

[a] 5 Or *their Lord* or *the governor* [b] 6 Or *Old* [c] 8 Or *They left out part of*

3:1 [a]Ezr 10:24 [b]Isa 58:12 [c]ver 32; Ne 12:39 [d]Ne 12:39; Jer 31:38; Zec 14:10
3:2 [e]Ne 7:36
3:3 [f]2Ch 33:14; Ne 12:39
3:5 [g]2Sa 14:2
3:6 [h]Ne 12:39
3:7 [i]Jos 9:3; Ne 2:7
3:8 [j]Ne 12:38

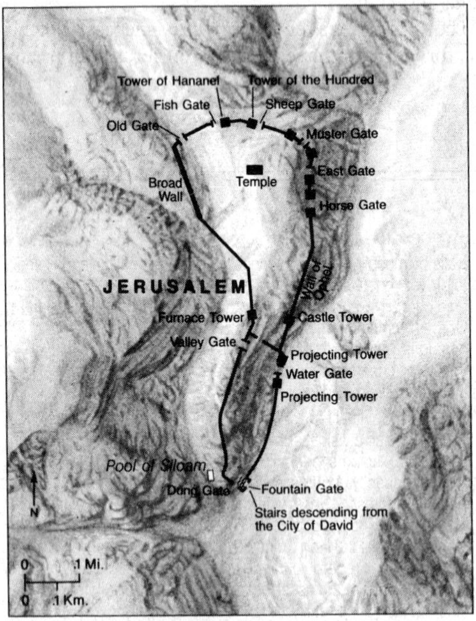

THE RESTORATION OF THE CITY WALLS Nehemiah takes us on an anti-clockwise tour around Jerusalem (beginning with the Sheep Gate). He describes for us each section, gate, and tower on the wall and who worked to rebuild it.

3:1 The high priest is the first person mentioned who pitched in and helped with the work. Spiritual leaders must lead not only by word, but also by action. The Sheep Gate was the gate used to bring sheep into the city to the temple for sacrifices. Nehemiah had the priests repair this gate and section of the wall, respecting the priests' area of interest and at the same time emphasising the priority of worship.

3:1ff All the citizens of Jerusalem did their part on the huge job of rebuilding the city wall. Similarly, the work of the church requires every member's effort in order for the body of Christ to function effectively (1 Corinthians 12:12–27). The body needs you! Are you doing your part? Find a place to serve God, and start contributing whatever time, talent, and money is needed.

3:1ff Jerusalem was a large city, and because many roads converged there, it required many gates. The wall on each side of these heavy wooden gates was taller and thicker so soldiers could stand guard to defend the gates against attack. Sometimes two stone towers guarded the gate. In times of peace, the city gates were hubs of activity – city council was held there, and shopkeepers set up their wares at the entrance. Building the city walls and gates was not only a military priority, but also a boost for trade and commerce.

3:3 One of the main roads through Jerusalem entered the city through the Fish Gate (2 Chronicles 33:14). The fish market was near the gate, and merchants from Tyre, the Sea of Galilee, and other fishing areas entered this gate to sell their goods.

3:5 The nobles of Tekoa were lazy and wouldn't help. These men were the only ones who did not support the building project in Jerusalem. Every group, even churches, will have those who think they are too wise or important to work hard. Gentle encouragement doesn't seem to help. Sometimes the best policy is to ignore them. They may think they are getting away with something, but their inactivity will be remembered by all who worked hard.

3:12 Shallum's daughters helped with the difficult work of repairing the city walls. Rebuilding Jerusalem's walls was a matter of national emergency for the Jews, not just a civic beautification project. Nearly everyone was dedicated to the task and willing to work at it.

section and the Tower of the Ovens.[k] 12 Shallum son of Hallohesh, ruler of a
half-district of Jerusalem, repaired the next section with the help of his daughters.

13 The Valley Gate[l] was repaired by Hanun and the residents of Zanoah.[m] They
rebuilt it and put its doors and bolts and bars in place. They also repaired five hundred
yards[d] of the wall as far as the Dung Gate.[n]

14 The Dung Gate was repaired by Malkijah son of Recab, ruler of the district of
Beth Hakkerem.[o] He rebuilt it and put its doors and bolts and bars in place.

15 The Fountain Gate was repaired by Shallun son of Col-Hozeh, ruler of the district
of Mizpah. He rebuilt it, roofing it over and putting its doors and bolts and bars in
place. He also repaired the wall of the Pool of Siloam,[e][p] by the King's Garden, as
far as the steps going down from the City of David. 16 Beyond him, Nehemiah son
of Azbuk, ruler of a half-district of Beth Zur,[q] made repairs up to a point opposite
the tombs[f][r] of David, as far as the artificial pool and the House of the Heroes.
17 Next to him, the repairs were made by the Levites under Rehum son of Bani.
Beside him, Hashabiah, ruler of half the district of Keilah,[s] carried out repairs for
his district. 18 Next to him, the repairs were made by their countrymen under Binnui[g]
son of Henadad, ruler of the other half-district of Keilah. 19 Next to him, Ezer son of
Jeshua, ruler of Mizpah, repaired another section, from a point facing the ascent to
the armoury as far as the angle. 20 Next to him, Baruch son of Zabbai zealously
repaired another section, from the angle to the entrance of the house of Eliashib the
high priest. 21 Next to him, Meremoth[t] son of Uriah, the son of Hakkoz, repaired
another section, from the entrance of Eliashib's house to the end of it.
22 The repairs next to him were made by the priests from the surrounding region.
23 Beyond them, Benjamin and Hasshub made repairs in front of their house; and next
to them, Azariah son of Maaseiah, the son of Ananiah, made repairs beside his house.
24 Next to him, Binnui[u] son of Henadad repaired another section, from Azariah's
house to the angle and the corner, 25 and Palal son of Uzai worked opposite the angle
and the tower projecting from the upper palace near the court of the guard.[v] Next
to him, Pedaiah son of Parosh[w] 26 and the temple servants[x] living on the hill of
Ophel[y] made repairs up to a point opposite the Water Gate[z] towards the east and
the projecting tower. 27 Next to them, the men of Tekoa[a] repaired another section,
from the great projecting tower[b] to the wall of Ophel.

28 Above the Horse Gate,[c] the priests made repairs, each in front of his own house.
29 Next to them, Zadok son of Immer made repairs opposite his house. Next to him,
Shemaiah son of Shecaniah, the guard at the East Gate, made repairs. 30 Next to him,
Hananiah son of Shelemiah, and Hanun, the sixth son of Zalaph, repaired another
section. Next to them, Meshullam son of Berekiah made repairs opposite his living
quarters. 31 Next to him, Malkijah, one of the goldsmiths, made repairs as far as the
house of the temple servants and the merchants, opposite the Inspection Gate, and as
far as the room above the corner; 32 and between the room above the corner and the
Sheep Gate[d] the goldsmiths and merchants made repairs.

3:11 [k] Ne 12:38
3:13 [l] 2Ch 26:9 [m] Jos 15:34 [n] Ne 2:13
3:14 [o] Jer 6:1
3:15 [p] Isa 8:6; Jn 9:7
3:16 [q] Jos 15:58 [r] Ac 2:29
3:17 [s] Jos 15:44
3:21 [t] Ezr 8:33
3:24 [u] Ezr 8:33
3:25 [v] Jer 32:2; 37:21; 39:14 [w] Ezr 2:3
3:26 [x] Ne 7:46; 11:21 [y] 2Ch 33:14 [z] Ne 8:1, 3, 16; 12:37
3:27 [a] ver 5 [b] Ps 48:12
3:28 [c] 2Ki 11:16; 2Ch 23:15; Jer 31:40
3:32 [d] ver 1; Jn 5:2

d *13* Hebrew *a thousand cubits* (about 450 metres) **e** *15* Hebrew *Shelah*, a variant of *Shiloah*, that is, *Siloam*
f *16* Hebrew; Septuagint, some Vulgate manuscripts and Syriac *tomb* **g** *18* Two Hebrew manuscripts and Syriac (see also Septuagint and verse 24); most Hebrew manuscripts *Bavvai*

3:14 The Dung Gate was the gate through which the people carried their garbage to be burned in the Valley of Hinnom.

3:28 The Horse Gate was at the far eastern point of the wall, facing the Kidron Valley.

3:28 Each priest also repaired the wall in front of his own house, in addition to other sections. If each person was responsible for the part of the wall closest to his own house, (1) he would be more motivated to build it quickly and properly, (2) he wouldn't waste time travelling to more distant parts of the wall, (3) he would defend his own home if the wall were attacked, and (4) he would be able to make the building a family effort. Nehemiah blended self-interest with the group's objectives, helping everyone to feel that the wall project was his own. If you are part of a group working on a large project, make sure each person sees the importance and meaning of the job that he or she has to do. This will ensure high-quality work and personal satisfaction.

3:31 The Inspection Gate was in the northern part of the eastern wall.

Opposition to the Rebuilding

4 When Sanballat[a] heard that we were rebuilding the wall, he became angry and
was greatly incensed. He ridiculed the Jews, 2and in the presence of his associates[b] and the army of Samaria, he said, "What are those feeble Jews doing? Will they
restore their wall? Will they offer sacrifices? Will they finish in a day? Can they bring
the stones back to life from those heaps of rubble[c]—burned as they are?"
3Tobiah[d] the Ammonite, who was at his side, said, "What they are building—if
even a fox climbed up on it, he would break down their wall of stones!"[e]

4Hear us, O our God, for we are despised.[f] Turn their insults back on their own
heads. Give them over as plunder in a land of captivity. 5Do not cover up their guilt[g]
or blot out their sins from your sight,[h] for they have thrown insults in the face of[a]
the builders.

6So we rebuilt the wall till all of it reached half its height, for the people worked
with all their heart.
7But when Sanballat, Tobiah,[i] the Arabs, the Ammonites and the men of Ashdod
heard that the repairs to Jerusalem's walls had gone ahead and that the gaps were being
closed, they were very angry. 8They all plotted together[j] to come and fight against
Jerusalem and stir up trouble against it. 9But we prayed to our God and posted a guard
day and night to meet this threat.
10Meanwhile, the people in Judah said, "The strength of the labourers[k] is giving
out, and there is so much rubble that we cannot rebuild the wall."
11Also our enemies said, "Before they know it or see us, we will be right there
among them and will kill them and put an end to the work."
12Then the Jews who lived near them came and told us ten times over, "Wherever
you turn, they will attack us."
13Therefore I stationed some of the people behind the lowest points of the wall at
the exposed places, posting them by families, with their swords, spears and bows.
14After I looked things over, I stood up and said to the nobles, the officials and the
rest of the people, "Don't be afraid[l] of them. Remember[m] the Lord, who is great
and awesome,[n] and fight[o] for your brothers, your sons and your daughters, your
wives and your homes."
15When our enemies heard that we were aware of their plot and that God had
frustrated it,[p] we all returned to the wall, each to his own work.

a 5 Or *have provoked you to anger before*

4:1 [a]Ne 2:10
4:2 [b]Ezr 4:9-10 [c]Ps 79:1; Jer 26:18
4:3 [d]Ne 2:10 [e]Job 13:12; 15:3
4:4 [f]Ps 44:13; 79:12; 123:3-4; Jer 33:24
4:5 [g]Isa 2:9; La 1:22 [h]2Ki 14:27; Ps 51:1; 69:27-28; 109:14; Jer 18:23
4:7 [i]Ne 2:10
4:8 [j]Ps 2:2; 83:1-18
4:10 [k]1Ch 23:4
4:14 [l]Ge 28:15; Nu 14:9; Dt 1:29 [m]Ne 1:8 [n]Ne 1:5 [o]2Sa 10:12
4:15 [p]2Sa 17:14; Job 5:12

4:1 Sanballat was governor of Samaria, the region just north of Judea where Jerusalem was located. Sanballat may have hoped to become governor of Judea as well, but Nehemiah's arrival spoiled his plans. (For his other reasons for opposing Nehemiah, see the note on 2:10.) Sanballat tried to scare Nehemiah away or at least discourage him by scorn (4:2; 6:6), threats (4:8), and bluffs (6:7).

4:1, 2 Almost 300 years before Nehemiah's time, the northern kingdom of Israel was conquered, and most of the people were carried away captive (722 B.C.). Sargon of Assyria repopulated Israel with captives from other lands. These captives eventually intermarried with the few Israelites who remained in the land to form a mixed race of people who became known as Samaritans. The Jews who returned to Jerusalem and the southern region of Judea during the days of Ezra and Nehemiah would have nothing to do with Samaritans, whom they considered to be racially impure. Relations between both groups grew progressively worse—400 years later, the Jews and Samaritans hated each other (John 4:9).

4:1–5 Ridicule can cut deeply, causing discouragement and despair. Sanballat and Tobiah used ridicule to try to dissuade the Jews from building the wall. Instead of trading insults, however, Nehemiah prayed, and the work continued. When you are mocked for your faith or criticised for doing what you know is right, refuse to respond in the same way or to become discouraged. Tell God how you feel and remember his promise to be with you. This will give you encouragement and strength to carry on.

4:4, 5 Nehemiah is not praying for revenge but that God's justice would be carried out. His prayer is similar to many of David's (see the note in Psalm 7:1–6).

4:6 The work of rebuilding the wall progressed well because the people had set their hearts and minds on accomplishing the task. They did not lose faith or give up, but they persevered in the work. If God has called you to a task, determine to complete it, even if you face opposition or discouragement. The rewards of work well done will be worth the effort.

4:9 Nehemiah constantly combined prayer with preparation and planning. His people trusted God and at the same time kept vigilant watch over what had been entrusted to them. Too often we pray without looking for what God wants us to do. We show God we are serious when we combine prayer with thought, preparation, and effort.

4:10–14 Accomplishing any large task is tiring. There are always pressures that foster discouragement—the task seems impossible, it can never be finished, or too many factors are working against us. The only cure for fatigue and discouragement is focusing on God's purposes. Nehemiah reminded the workers of their calling, their goal, and God's protection. If you are overwhelmed by an assignment, tired, and discouraged, remember God's purpose for your life and his special purpose for the project.

4:17
[q]Ps 149:6

16From that day on, half of my men did the work, while the other half were equipped
with spears, shields, bows and armour. The officers posted themselves behind all the
people of Judah 17who were building the wall. Those who carried materials did their
work with one hand and held a weapon[q] in the other, 18and each of the builders wore

NEHEMIAH

God is in the business of working through his people to accomplish seemingly impossible tasks. God often shapes people with personality traits, experiences, and training that prepare them for his purpose, and usually the people have no idea what God has in store for them. God prepared and positioned Nehemiah to accomplish one of the Bible's "impossible" tasks.

Nehemiah was a common man in a unique position. He was secure and successful as cupbearer to the Persian king Artaxerxes. Nehemiah had little power, but he had great influence. He was trusted by the king. He was also a man of God, concerned about the fate of Jerusalem.

Seventy years earlier, Zerubbabel had managed to rebuild God's temple. Thirteen years had passed since Ezra had returned to Jerusalem and helped the people with their spiritual needs. Now Nehemiah was needed. Jerusalem's wall was still in ruins, and the news broke his heart. As he talked to God, a plan began to take form in Nehemiah's mind about his own role in the rebuilding of the city walls. He willingly left the security of his home and job in Persia to follow God on an "impossible" mission. And the rest is history.

From beginning to end, Nehemiah prayed for God's help. He never hesitated to ask God to remember him, closing his autobiography with these words: "Remember me with favour, O my God." Throughout the "impossible" task, Nehemiah displayed unusual leadership. The wall around Jerusalem was rebuilt in record time, despite resistance. Even Israel's enemies grudgingly and fearfully admitted that God was with these builders. Not only that, but God worked through Nehemiah to bring about a spiritual awakening among the people of Judah.

You may not have Nehemiah's unique abilities or feel that you are in a position where you can do anything great for God, but there are two ways you can become useful to God. First, be a person who *talks* to God. Welcome him into your thoughts and share yourself with him—your concerns, feelings, and dreams. Second, be a person who *walks* with God. Put what you learn from his word into action. God may have an "impossible" mission that he wants to perform through you.

Strengths and accomplishments:
- A man of character, persistence, and prayer
- Brilliant planner, organiser, and motivator
- Under his leadership, the wall around Jerusalem was rebuilt in 52 days
- As political leader, led the nation to religious reform and spiritual awakening
- Was calm under opposition
- Was capable of being bluntly honest with his people when they were sinning

Lessons from his life:
- The first step in any venture is to pray
- People under God's direction can accomplish impossible tasks
- There are two parts to real service for God: talking with him, and walking with him

Vital statistics:
- Where: Persia, Jerusalem
- Occupations: King's cupbearer, city builder, governor of Judah
- Relative: Father: Hacaliah
- Contemporaries: Ezra, Artaxerxes, Tobiah, Sanballat

Key verse:
"I also told them about the gracious hand of my God upon me and what the king had said to me. They replied, 'Let us start rebuilding.' So they began this good work" (Nehemiah 2:18).

Nehemiah's story is told in the book of Nehemiah.

4:16 The workers were spread out along the wall, so Nehemiah devised a plan of defence that would unite and protect his people—half the men worked while the other half stood guard. Christians need to help one another in the same way because we can become so afraid of possible dangers that we can't get anything done. By looking out for each other, we will be free to put forth our best efforts, confident that others are ready to offer help when needed. Don't cut yourself off from others; instead, join together for mutual benefit. You need them as much as they need you.

4:18–20 To further relieve the anxieties of the people, Nehemiah set up a communication system. The man who sounded the trumpet stayed with Nehemiah, and the people knew what to do if they heard it. We have no record that the trumpet was ever used, but simply knowing it would issue a warning when needed was reassuring. The promise of open, immediate communication helped the group accomplish its task.

his sword at his side as he worked. But the man who sounded the trumpet[r] stayed
with me.
19Then I said to the nobles, the officials and the rest of the people, "The work is
extensive and spread out, and we are widely separated from each other along the wall.
20Wherever you hear the sound of the trumpet,[s] join us there. Our God will fight[t]
for us!"
21So we continued the work with half the men holding spears, from the first light
of dawn till the stars came out. 22At that time I also said to the people, "Have every
man and his helper stay inside Jerusalem at night, so that they can serve us as guards
by night and workmen by day." 23Neither I nor my brothers nor my men nor the guards
with me took off our clothes; each had his weapon, even when he went for water.[b]

Nehemiah Helps the Poor

5 Now the men and their wives raised a great outcry against their Jewish brothers.
2Some were saying, "We and our sons and daughters are numerous; in order for
us to eat and stay alive, we must get grain."
3Others were saying, "We are mortgaging our fields,[a] our vineyards and our homes
to get grain during the famine."[b]
4Still others were saying, "We have had to borrow money to pay the king's tax[c]
on our fields and vineyards. 5Although we are of the same flesh and blood[d] as our
countrymen and though our sons are as good as theirs, yet we have to subject our sons
and daughters to slavery.[e] Some of our daughters have already been enslaved, but
we are powerless, because our fields and our vineyards belong to others."[f]
6When I heard their outcry and these charges, I was very angry. 7I pondered them
in my mind and then accused the nobles and officials. I told them, "You are exacting
usury[g] from your own countrymen!" So I called together a large meeting to deal with
them 8and said: "As far as possible, we have bought[h] back our Jewish brothers who
were sold to the Gentiles. Now you are selling your brothers, only for them to be sold
back to us!" They kept quiet, because they could find nothing to say.[i]
9So I continued, "What you are doing is not right. Shouldn't you walk in the fear
of our God to avoid the reproach[j] of our Gentile enemies? 10I and my brothers and
my men are also lending the people money and grain. But let the exacting of usury
stop![k] 11Give back to them immediately their fields, vineyards, olive groves and
houses, and also the usury[l] you are charging them—the hundredth part of the money,
grain, new wine and oil."
12"We will give it back," they said. "And we will not demand anything more from
them. We will do as you say."
Then I summoned the priests and made the nobles and officials take an oath[m] to
do what they had promised. 13I also shook[n] out the folds of my robe and said, "In

b 23 The meaning of the Hebrew for this clause is uncertain.

4:18 [r]Nu 10:2
4:20 [s]Eze 33:3 [t]Ex 14:14; Dt 1:30; 20:4; Jos 10:14
5:3 [a]Ps 109:11 [b]Ge 47:23
5:4 [c]Ezr 4:13
5:5 [d]Ge 29:14 [e]Lev 25:39-43, 47; 2Ki 4:1; Isa 50:1 [f]Dt 15:7-11; 2Ki 4:1
5:7 [g]Ex 22:25-27; Lev 25:35-37; Dt 23:19-20; 24:10-13
5:8 [h]Lev 25:47 [i]Jer 34:8
5:9 [j]Isa 52:5
5:10 [k]Ex 22:25
5:11 [l]Isa 58:6
5:12 [m]Ezr 10:5
5:13 [n]Mt 10:14; Ac 18:6

4:23 Although the exact meaning of the Hebrew phrase, "even when he went for water" is unclear (it has been translated, "in his right hand" or "at his right hand at night"), the point is that each man always had his weapon close at hand. The guards were prepared and took their responsibilities seriously.

5:1–5 Who were these bitterly resented Jews? They were either (1) Jews who had become wealthy in exile and brought this wealth with them to Jerusalem, or (2) descendants of Jews who had arrived almost a century earlier during the first return under Zerubbabel (Ezra 1; 2) and had established lucrative businesses.

5:7–9 Many of the returned exiles were suffering at the hands of some of their rich countrymen. These people would lend large sums of money; then, when the debtors missed a payment, they would take over their fields. Left with no means of income, the debtors were forced to sell their children into slavery, a common practice of this time. Nehemiah was angry with these Jews who were taking advantage of their own people in order to enrich themselves. Usury is the practice of charging excessive interest. These practices violated the law set forth in Exodus 22:25.

5:9–11 God's concern for the poor is revealed in almost every book of the Bible. Here, Nehemiah insisted that fairness to the poor and oppressed was central to following God. The books of Moses clearly spelled out the Israelites' responsibility to care for the poor (Exodus 22:22–27; Leviticus 25:35–37; Deuteronomy 14:28, 29; 15:7–11). The way we help those in need ought to mirror God's love and concern.

5:10 Nehemiah told the rich Jews to stop charging interest ("exacting usury") on their loans to their needy brothers. God never intended people to profit from others' misfortunes. In contrast to the values of this world, God says that caring for one another is more important than personal gain. When a Christian brother or sister suffers, we all suffer (1 Corinthians 12:26). We should help needy believers, not exploit them. The Jerusalem church was praised for working together to eliminate poverty (Acts 4:34, 35). Remember, "He who gives to the poor will lack nothing" (Proverbs 28:27). Make it a practice to help those in need around you.

5:13 This symbolic act was a curse. Nehemiah shook out the fold of his garment and pronounced that anyone who did not keep his

this way may God shake out of his house and possessions every man who does not
keep this promise. So may such a man be shaken out and emptied!"
At this the whole assembly said, "Amen,"[o] and praised the LORD. And the people
did as they had promised.
14Moreover, from the twentieth year of King Artaxerxes,[p] when I was appointed
to be their governor[q] in the land of Judah, until his thirty-second year—twelve
years—neither I nor my brothers ate the food allotted to the governor. 15But the earlier
governors—those preceding me—placed a heavy burden on the people and took forty
shekels[a] of silver from them in addition to food and wine. Their assistants also lorded
it over the people. But out of reverence for God[r] I did not act like that. 16Instead,[s]
I devoted myself to the work on this wall. All my men were assembled there for the
work; we[b] did not acquire any land.
17Furthermore, a hundred and fifty Jews and officials ate at my table, as well as
those who came to us from the surrounding nations. 18Each day one ox, six choice
sheep and some poultry[t] were prepared for me, and every ten days an abundant
supply of wine of all kinds. In spite of all this, I never demanded the food allotted
to the governor, because the demands were heavy on these people.
19Remember[u] me with favour, O my God, for all I have done for these people.

Further Opposition to the Rebuilding

6 When word came to Sanballat, Tobiah,[a] Geshem[b] the Arab and the rest of our
enemies that I had rebuilt the wall and not a gap was left in it—though up to that
time I had not set the doors in the gates—2Sanballat and Geshem sent me this message:
"Come, let us meet together in one of the villages[a] on the plain of Ono.[c]"
But they were scheming to harm me; 3so I sent messengers to them with this reply:
"I am carrying on a great project and cannot go down. Why should the work stop while
I leave it and go down to you?" 4Four times they sent me the same message, and each
time I gave them the same answer.
5Then, the fifth time, Sanballat[d] sent his assistant to me with the same message,
and in his hand was an unsealed letter 6in which was written:

> "It is reported among the nations—and Geshem[b][e] says it is true—that you
> and the Jews are plotting to revolt, and therefore you are building the wall.
> Moreover, according to these reports you are about to become their king 7and
> have even appointed prophets to make this proclamation about you in Jerusalem:
> 'There is a king in Judah!' Now this report will get back to the king; so come,
> let us confer together."

8I sent him this reply: "Nothing like what you are saying is happening; you are just
making it up out of your head."

a *15* That is, about 1 pound (about 0.5 kilogram) **b** *16* Most Hebrew manuscripts; some Hebrew manuscripts, Septuagint, Vulgate and Syriac *I* **a** *2* Or *in Kephirim* **b** *6* Hebrew *Gashmu*, a variant of *Geshem*

5:13 [o]Dt 27:15-26
5:14 [p]Ne 2:6; 13:6 [q]Ge 42:6; Ezr 6:7; Jer 40:7; Hag 1:1
5:15 [r]Ge 20:11
5:16 [s]2Th 3:7-10
5:18 [t]1Ki 4:23
5:19 [u]Ge 8:1; 2Ki 20:3; Ne 1:8; 13:14, 22, 31
6:1 [a]Ne 2:10 [b]Ne 2:19
6:2 [c]1Ch 8:12
6:5 [d]Ne 2:10
6:6 [e]Ne 2:19

promise would likewise be "shaken out and emptied", losing all he had.

5:14, 15 This comment by Nehemiah is a parenthetical statement, comparing his 12 years as governor with the unjust proceedings in the land before he arrived. The governor was appointed by the Persian king, not elected by the people.

5:16 Nehemiah led the entire construction project, but he also worked on the wall alongside the others. He was not a bureaucrat in a well-guarded office, but a leader who got involved in the day-to-day work. He did not use his position to lord it over his people. A good leader keeps in touch with the work to be done. Those who lead best lead by what they *do* as well as by what they say.

6:1ff Sanballat and Tobiah were desperate. The wall was almost complete, and their efforts to stop its construction were failing. So they tried a new approach, centring their attacks on Nehemiah's character. They attacked him personally with rumours (6:6), deceit (6:10–13), and false reports (6:17). Personal attacks hurt, and when the criticism is unjustified, it is easy to despair. When you are doing God's work, you may receive attacks on your character. Follow Nehemiah's example by trusting God to accomplish the task and by overlooking unjustified abuse.

6:2 The plain of Ono was about 20 miles northwest of Jerusalem. If Sanballat and Geshem could get Nehemiah to agree to meet them there, they could ambush him on the way.

6:7 During these days, prophets such as Malachi proclaimed the coming of the Messiah (Malachi 3:1–3). Sanballat, with his usual flair for stirring up trouble, tried to turn Nehemiah's people against him by saying that Nehemiah was trying to set himself up as the king. Sanballat also tried to turn the local officials against Nehemiah by threatening to report to the king of Persia that Nehemiah was starting a revolt. The fact that Sanballat had an open, or unsealed, letter delivered to Nehemiah shows that he wanted to make sure the letter's contents were made public. But Sanballat's accusations were untrue and did not divert Nehemiah from his task.

[9]They were all trying to frighten us, thinking, "Their hands will get too weak for
the work, and it will not be completed."
⌞But I prayed,⌟ "Now strengthen my hands."
[10]One day I went to the house of Shemaiah son of Delaiah, the son of Mehetabel,
who was shut in at his home. He said, "Let us meet in the house of God, inside the
temple[f], and let us close the temple doors, because men are coming to kill you—by
night they are coming to kill you."
[11]But I said, "Should a man like me run away? Or should one like me go into the
temple to save his life? I will not go!" [12]I realised that God had not sent him, but that
he had prophesied against me[g] because Tobiah and Sanballat[h] had hired him. [13]He
had been hired to intimidate me so that I would commit a sin by doing this, and then
they would give me a bad name to discredit me.[i]

[14]Remember[j] Tobiah and Sanballat,[k] O my God, because of what they have done;
remember also the prophetess[l] Noadiah and the rest of the prophets[m] who have been
trying to intimidate me.

The Completion of the Wall

[15]So the wall was completed on the twenty-fifth of Elul, in fifty-two days. [16]When
all our enemies heard about this, all the surrounding nations were afraid and lost their
self-confidence, because they realised that this work had been done with the help of
our God.
[17]Also, in those days the nobles of Judah were sending many letters to Tobiah, and
replies from Tobiah kept coming to them. [18]For many in Judah were under oath to
him, since he was son-in-law to Shecaniah son of Arah, and his son Jehohanan had
married the daughter of Meshullam son of Berekiah. [19]Moreover, they kept reporting
to me his good deeds and then telling him what I said. And Tobiah sent letters to
intimidate me.

7 After the wall had been rebuilt and I had set the doors in place, the gatekeepers[a]
and the singers[b] and the Levites[c] were appointed. [2]I put in charge of Jerusalem
my brother Hanani,[d] along with[a] Hananiah[e] the commander of the citadel,[f]
because he was a man of integrity and feared[g] God more than most men do. [3]I said

[a] 2 Or *Hanani, that is,*

6:10 [f]Nu 18:7
6:12 [g]Eze 13:22-23 [h]Ne 2:10
6:13 [i]Jer 20:10
6:14 [j]Ne 1:8 [k]Ne 2:10 [l]Ex 15:20; Eze 13:17-23; Ac 21:9; Rev 2:20 [m]Ne 13:29; Jer 23:9-40; Zec 13:2-3
7:1 [a]1Ch 9:27; 26:12-19; Ne 6:1, 15 [b]Ps 68:25 [c]Ne 8:9
7:2 [d]Ne 1:2 [e]Ne 10:23 [f]Ne 2:8 [g]1Ki 18:3

6:9 When opposition builds up against you or God's work, it is tempting to pray, "God, get me out of this situation." But Nehemiah prayed, "strengthen my hands." He showed tremendous determination and character to remain steadfast in his responsibility. When we pray for strength, God always answers.

6:10 Shemaiah warned Nehemiah of danger and told him to hide in the temple. Nehemiah wisely tested the message, exposing it as another trick of the enemy. People may misuse God's name by saying they know God's will when they have other motives. Examine self-proclaimed messengers from God to see if they stand up to the test of being consistent with what is revealed in God's word.

6:10–13 Nehemiah did not have the full support of the people. Shemaiah (6:10), Noadiah (6:14), and many of the nobles (6:17) were working against him. When Nehemiah was attacked personally, he refused to give in to fear and flee to the temple. According to God's law, it would have been wrong for Nehemiah to go into the temple to hide because he wasn't a priest (Numbers 18:22). If he had run for his life, he would have undermined the courage he was trying to instil in the people. Leaders are targets for attacks. Make it a practice to pray for those in authority (1 Timothy 2:1, 2). Request God to give them strength to stand against personal attacks and temptation. They need God-given courage to overcome fear.

6:15 Daniel, who was among the first group of captives taken from Jerusalem to Babylon (605 B.C.), predicted the rebuilding of the city (Daniel 9:25). Here his prophecy comes true. He, like Nehemiah, was a Jew who held a prominent position in the kingdom where he had been exiled (Daniel 5:29–6:3).

6:15 They said it couldn't be done. The job was too big, and the problems were too great. But God's men and women, joined together for special tasks, can solve huge problems and accomplish great goals. Don't let the size of a task or the length of time needed to accomplish it keep you from doing it. With God's help, it can be done.

7:2 Integrity and fear of God were the key character traits that qualified these men to govern Jerusalem. People of integrity can be trusted to carry out their work; God-fearing people can be expected to do so in line with God's priorities. These men had both qualities. If you are in a position of selecting leaders, look for integrity and reverence as two of the most important qualifications. Although other qualities may seem more impressive, integrity and reverence pass the test of time.

7:3 City gates were usually opened at sunrise, enabling merchants to enter and set up their tent-stores. Nehemiah didn't want Jerusalem to be caught unprepared by an enemy attack, so he ordered the gates closed until well after sunrise when the people were sure to be awake and alert.

7:3 The wall was complete, but the work was not finished. Nehemiah assigned each family the task of protecting the section of wall next to their home. It is tempting to relax our guard and rest on past accomplishments after we have completed a large task. But we must continue to serve and to take care of all that God has entrusted to us. Following through after a project is completed is as vital as doing the project itself.

7:4 [h]Ne 11:1

to them, "The gates of Jerusalem are not to be opened until the sun is hot. While the gatekeepers are still on duty, make them shut the doors and bar them. Also appoint residents of Jerusalem as guards, some at their posts and some near their own houses."

The List of the Exiles Who Returned

7:6 [i]2Ch 36:20; Ezr 2:1-70; Ne 1:2

4Now the city was large and spacious, but there were few people in it,[h] and the
houses had not yet been rebuilt. 5So my God put it into my heart to assemble the
nobles, the officials and the common people for registration by families. I found the
genealogical record of those who had been the first to return. This is what I found
written there:

7:7 [j]1Ch 3:19; Ezr 2:2

6These are the people of the province who came up from the captivity of the
exiles[i] whom Nebuchadnezzar king of Babylon had taken captive (they returned
to Jerusalem and Judah, each to his own town, 7in company with Zerubbabel,[j]
Jeshua, Nehemiah, Azariah, Raamiah, Nahamani, Mordecai, Bilshan, Mispereth, Bigvai, Nehum and Baanah):

The list of the men of Israel:

7:20 [k]Ezr 8:6

7:26 [l]2Sa 23:28; 1Ch 2:54

7:27 [m]Jos 21:18

7:29 [n]Jos 18:26 [o]Jos 18:25

7:32 [p]Ge 12:8

7:36 [q]Ne 3:2

7:37 [r]1Ch 8:12

8the descendants of Parosh	2,172
9of Shephatiah	372
10of Arah	652
11of Pahath-Moab (through the line of Jeshua and Joab)	2,818
12of Elam	1,254
13of Zattu	845
14of Zaccai	760
15of Binnui	648
16of Bebai	628
17of Azgad	2,322
18of Adonikam	667
19of Bigvai	2,067
20of Adin[k]	655
21of Ater (through Hezekiah)	98
22of Hashum	328
23of Bezai	324
24of Hariph	112
25of Gibeon	95
26the men of Bethlehem and Netophah[l]	188
27of Anathoth[m]	128
28of Beth Azmaveth	42
29of Kiriath Jearim, Kephirah[n] and Beeroth[o]	743
30of Ramah and Geba	621
31of Michmash	122
32of Bethel and Ai[p]	123
33of the other Nebo	52
34of the other Elam	1,254
35of Harim	320
36of Jericho[q]	345
37of Lod, Hadid and Ono[r]	721
38of Senaah	3,930

39The priests:

the descendants of Jedaiah (through the family of Jeshua)	973

7:5ff Nehemiah found the genealogical record. Because this genealogy is almost identical to Ezra's (Ezra 2), most likely Ezra's list was stored in the temple archives and was the one Nehemiah found.

40of Immer	1,052
41of Pashhur	1,247
42of Harim	1,017

43The Levites:

the descendants of Jeshua (through Kadmiel through the line of Hodaviah)	74

44The singers:[s]

the descendants of Asaph	148

45The gatekeepers:[t]

the descendants of Shallum, Ater, Talmon, Akkub, Hatita and Shobai	138

46The temple servants:[u]

the descendants of
Ziha, Hasupha, Tabbaoth,
47Keros, Sia, Padon,
48Lebana, Hagaba, Shalmai,
49Hanan, Giddel, Gahar,
50Reaiah, Rezin, Nekoda,
51Gazzam, Uzza, Paseah,
52Besai, Meunim, Nephussim,
53Bakbuk, Hakupha, Harhur,
54Bazluth, Mehida, Harsha,
55Barkos, Sisera, Temah,
56Neziah and Hatipha

57The descendants of the servants of Solomon:

the descendants of
Sotai, Sophereth, Perida,
58Jaala, Darkon, Giddel,
59Shephatiah, Hattil,
Pokereth-Hazzebaim and Amon

60The temple servants and the descendants of the servants of Solomon[v]	392

61The following came up from the towns of Tel Melah, Tel Harsha, Kerub, Addon and Immer, but they could not show that their families were descended from Israel:

62the descendants of Delaiah, Tobiah and Nekoda	642

63And from among the priests:

the descendants of
Hobaiah, Hakkoz and Barzillai (a man who had married a daughter of Barzillai the Gileadite and was called by that name).

64These searched for their family records, but they could not find them and

7:44 [s]Ne 11:23
7:45 [t]1Ch 9:17
7:46 [u]Ne 3:26
7:60 [v]1Ch 9:2

7:61 Genealogies were greatly valued because it was vitally important for a Jew to be able to prove that he or she was a descendant of Abraham and was, therefore, part of God's people (Genesis 12:1–3; 15; Exodus 19:5, 6; Deuteronomy 11:22–28). A lost genealogy put one's status as a Jew at risk.

7:64, 65 The Urim and Thummim were a means of learning God's will (Exodus 28:30). If someone's name wasn't in the genealogies, he could still be admitted as a priest if the Urim and Thummim proved him to be a Jew and a Levite. It is not clear whether the Urim and Thummim were the originals that had survived the

7:65 [w]Ex 28:30; Ne 8:9
7:71 [x]1Ch 29:7
7:72 [y]Ex 25:2
7:73 [z]Ne 1:10; Ps 34:22; 103:21; 113:1; 135:1 [a]Ezr 3:1; Ne 11:1
7:73 [b]Ezr 3:1
8:1 [a]Ne 3:26 [b]Dt 28:61; 2Ch 34:15; Ezr 7:6
8:2 [c]Lev 23:23-25; Nu 29:1-6 [d]Dt 31:11
8:3 [e]Ne 3:26
8:4 [f]2Ch 6:13
8:5 [g]Jdg 3:20
8:6 [h]Ex 4:31; Ezr 9:5; 1Ti 2:8

so were excluded from the priesthood as unclean. 65The governor, therefore,
ordered them not to eat any of the most sacred food until there should be a priest
ministering with the Urim and Thummim.[w]

66The whole company numbered 42,360, 67besides their 7,337 menservants
and maidservants; and they also had 245 men and women singers. 68There were
736 horses, 245 mules,[b] 69435 camels and 6,720 donkeys.

70Some of the heads of the families contributed to the work. The governor gave
to the treasury 1,000 drachmas[c] of gold, 50 bowls and 530 garments for priests.
71Some of the heads of the families[x] gave to the treasury for the work 20,000
drachmas[d] of gold and 2,200 minas[e] of silver. 72The total given by the rest of
the people was 20,000 drachmas of gold, 2,000 minas[f] of silver and 67 garments
for priests.[y]

73The priests, the Levites, the gatekeepers, the singers and the temple servants,[z] along with certain of the people and the rest of the Israelites, settled in
their own towns.[a]

B. REFORMING THE PEOPLE (8.1—13.31)

When Nehemiah arrived in Jerusalem he found more than just broken walls; he found broken lives. In response, Nehemiah gathers the people together to hear Ezra read God's law. The people repent and promise to change their lives by obeying God's words. No matter where we live, backsliding is an ever-present danger. We must constantly check our behaviour against God's standards in the Bible so that we do not slide back into sinful ways of living.

1. Ezra renews the covenant

Ezra Reads the Law

8 When the seventh month came and the Israelites had settled in their towns,[b] 1all
the people assembled as one man in the square before the Water Gate.[a] They
told Ezra the scribe to bring out the Book of the Law of Moses,[b] which the LORD
had commanded for Israel.

2So on the first day of the seventh month,[c] Ezra the priest brought the Law[d] before
the assembly, which was made up of men and women and all who were able to
understand. 3He read it aloud from daybreak till noon as he faced the square before
the Water Gate[e] in the presence of the men, women and others who could understand.
And all the people listened attentively to the Book of the Law.

4Ezra the scribe stood on a high wooden platform[f] built for the occasion. Beside
him on his right stood Mattithiah, Shema, Anaiah, Uriah, Hilkiah and Maaseiah; and
on his left were Pedaiah, Mishael, Malkijah, Hashum, Hashbaddanah, Zechariah and
Meshullam.

5Ezra opened the book. All the people could see him because he was standing[g]
above them; and as he opened it, the people all stood up. 6Ezra praised the LORD,
the great God; and all the people lifted their hands[h] and responded, "Amen! Amen!"
Then they bowed down and worshipped the LORD with their faces to the ground.

b *68* Some Hebrew manuscripts (see also Ezra 2:66); most Hebrew manuscripts do not have this verse.
c *70* That is, about 19 pounds (about 8.5 kilograms) **d** *71* That is, about 375 pounds (about 170 kilograms); also in verse 72 **e** *71* That is, about 1¼ tons (about 1.3 metric tons) **f** *72* That is, about 1 ton (about 1.1 metric tons)

---

destruction of Jerusalem or if they were new. The "most sacred food" was meat dedicated to God as part of the sacrifice. Only true priests could eat it.

8:1 This is the first mention of Ezra in this book. He had arrived in Jerusalem from Babylon 13 years before Nehemiah (458 B.C., see Ezra 7:6–9).

8:1 Ezra and Nehemiah were contemporaries (8:9), although Ezra was probably much older. Nehemiah, as governor, was the political leader; and Ezra, as priest and scribe, was the religious leader. A scribe in these days was a combination of lawyer, notary public, scholar, and consultant. Scribes were among the most educated people, so they were teachers. No doubt the Jews would have liked to set up the kingdom again as in the days of David, but this would have signalled rebellion against the king of Persia to whom they were subject. The best alternative was to divide the leadership between Nehemiah and Ezra.

8:1–5 The Book of the Law of Moses was probably the Pentateuch, the first five books of the Bible. The people listened attentively to Ezra as he read God's word, and their lives were changed. Because we hear the Bible so often, we can become dulled to its words and immune to its teachings. Instead, we should *listen carefully* to every verse and ask the Holy Spirit to help us answer the question, "How does this apply to *my* life?"

7The Levites[i]—Jeshua, Bani, Sherebiah, Jamin, Akkub, Shabbethai, Hodiah,
Maaseiah, Kelita, Azariah, Jozabad, Hanan and Pelaiah—instructed[j] the people in
the Law while the people were standing there. 8They read from the Book of the Law
of God, making it clear[a] and giving the meaning so that the people could understand
what was being read.
9Then Nehemiah the governor, Ezra the priest and scribe, and the Levites[k] who
were instructing the people said to them all, "This day is sacred to the LORD your God.
Do not mourn or weep."[l] For all the people had been weeping as they listened to
the words of the Law.
10Nehemiah said, "Go and enjoy choice food and sweet drinks, and send some to
those who have nothing[m] prepared. This day is sacred to our Lord. Do not grieve,
for the joy[n] of the LORD is your strength."
11The Levites calmed all the people, saying, "Be still, for this is a sacred day. Do
not grieve."
12Then all the people went away to eat and drink, to send portions of food and to
celebrate with great joy,[o] because they now understood the words that had been made
known to them.
13On the second day of the month, the heads of all the families, along with the
priests and the Levites, gathered round Ezra the scribe to give attention to the words
of the Law. 14They found written in the Law, which the LORD had commanded through
Moses, that the Israelites were to live in booths during the feast of the seventh month
15and that they should proclaim this word and spread it throughout their towns and
in Jerusalem: "Go out into the hill country and bring back branches from olive and
wild olive trees, and from myrtles, palms and shade trees, to make booths"—as it is
written.[b]
16So the people went out and brought back branches and built themselves booths
on their own roofs, in their courtyards, in the courts of the house of God and in the
square by the Water Gate and the one by the Gate of Ephraim.[p] 17The whole company
that had returned from exile built booths and lived in them. From the days of Joshua
son of Nun until that day, the Israelites had not celebrated[q] it like this. And their joy
was very great.
18Day after day, from the first day to the last, Ezra read[r] from the Book of the
Law of God. They celebrated the feast for seven days, and on the eighth day, in
accordance with the regulation,[s] there was an assembly.

The Israelites Confess Their Sins

9 On the twenty-fourth day of the same month, the Israelites gathered together,
fasting and wearing sackcloth and having dust on their heads.[a] 2Those of Israelite
descent had separated themselves from all foreigners.[b] They stood in their places and

[a] 8 Or *God, translating it* [b] 15 See Lev. 23:37–40.

8:7 [i]Ezr 10:23 [j]Lev 10:11; 2Ch 17:7
8:9 [k]Ne 7:1, 65, 70 [l]Dt 12:7, 12; 16:14-15
8:10 [m]1Sa 25:8; Lk 14:12-14 [n]Lev 23:40; Dt 12:18; 16:11, 14-15
8:12 [o]Est 9:22
8:16 [p]2Ki 14:13; Ne 12:39
8:17 [q]2Ch 7:8; 8:13; 30:21
8:18 [r]Dt 31:11 [s]Lev 23:36, 40; Nu 29:35
9:1 [a]Jos 7:6; 1Sa 4:12
9:2 [b]Ne 13:3, 30

8:9 Ezra, not Nehemiah, was the official religious leader. It is significant that Nehemiah was a layman, not a member of the religious establishment or a prophet. He was motivated by his relationship with God, and he devoted his life to doing God's will in a secular world. Such people are crucial to God's work in all aspects of life. No matter what your work or role in life, view it as God's special calling to serve him.

8:9, 10 The people wept openly when they heard God's laws and realised how far they were from obeying them. But Ezra told them they should be filled with joy because the day was holy. It was time to celebrate and to give gifts to those in need.

Celebration is not to be self-centred. Ezra connected celebration with giving. This gave those in need an opportunity to celebrate as well. Often when we celebrate and give to others (even when we don't feel like it), we are strengthened spiritually and filled with joy. Enter into celebrations that honour God, and allow him to fill you with his joy.

8:13ff After Ezra read God's laws to the people, they studied them further and then acted upon them. A careful reading of Scripture always calls for a response to these questions: What should I *do* with this knowledge? How should my life change? We must *do* something about what we have learned if it is to have real significance for our lives.

8:14–17 During the seven-day Feast of Tabernacles, the people lived in booths made of branches. This practice was instituted as a reminder of their rescue from Egypt and the time spent in shelters in the desert (Leviticus 23:43). They were to think about God's protection and guidance during their years of wandering and the fact that God would still protect and guide them if they obeyed him. This was a time to remember their origins, where they came from. It is helpful to remember our beginnings in order to appreciate where we are today. Think back on your life to see where God has led you. Then thank God for his continuing work to protect you and provide for your needs.

9:1 Fasting, wearing sackcloth, and putting dust on the head were public signs of sorrow and repentance.

confessed their sins and the wickedness of their fathers.[c] 3 They stood where they
were and read from the Book of the Law of the LORD their God for a quarter of the
day, and spent another quarter in confession and in worshipping the LORD their God.
4 Standing on the stairs were the Levites[d]—Jeshua, Bani, Kadmiel, Shebaniah,
Bunni, Sherebiah, Bani and Kenani—who called with loud voices to the LORD their
God. 5 And the Levites—Jeshua, Kadmiel, Bani, Hashabneiah, Sherebiah, Hodiah,
Shebaniah and Pethahiah—said: "Stand up and praise the LORD your God,[e] who is
from everlasting to everlasting."[a]

"Blessed be your glorious name, and may it be exalted above all blessing and
praise. 6 You alone are the LORD.[f] You made the heavens,[g] even the highest
heavens, and all their starry host, the earth[h] and all that is on it, the seas[i] and
all that is in them.[j] You give life to everything, and the multitudes of heaven
worship you.

7 "You are the LORD God, who chose Abram and brought him out of Ur of the
Chaldeans[k] and named him Abraham.[l] 8 You found his heart faithful to you,
and you made a covenant with him to give to his descendants the land of the
Canaanites, Hittites, Amorites, Perizzites, Jebusites and Girgashites.[m] You have
kept your promise[n] because you are righteous.[o]

9 "You saw the suffering of our forefathers in Egypt;[p] you heard their cry at
the Red Sea.[b][q] 10 You sent miraculous signs[r] and wonders against Pharaoh,
against all his officials and all the people of his land, for you knew how arrogantly
the Egyptians treated them. You made a name[s] for yourself, which remains to

9:2 [c]Ezr 10:11; Ps 106:6
9:4 [d]Ezr 10:23
9:5 [e]Ps 78:4
9:6 [f]Dt 6:4 [g]2Ki 19:15 [h]Ge 1:1; Isa 37:16 [i]Ps 95:5 [j]Dt 10:14
9:7 [k]Ge 11:31 [l]Ge 17:5
9:8 [m]Ge 15:18-21 [n]Jos 21:45 [o]Ge 15:6; Ezr 9:15
9:9 [p]Ex 3:7 [q]Ex 14:10-30
9:10 [r]Ex 10:1 [s]Jer 32:20; Da 9:15

a 5 Or *God for ever and ever* b 9 Hebrew *Yam Suph*; that is, Sea of Reeds

GOING HOME: TWO GREAT JOURNEYS OF ISRAEL

What about the Journeys?	*The Exodus*	*The Return from Exile*
Where were they?	Egypt (430 years)	Babylon (70 years)
How many?	About 1 million	60,000
How long did the journey take them?	40 years and 2 attempts	100 years and 3 journeys
Who led them?	Moses/Aaron/Joshua	Zerubbabel/Ezra/Nehemiah
What was their purpose?	To reclaim the promised land	To rebuild the temple and city of Jerusalem
What obstacles did they face?	Red Sea/Desert/Enemies	Ruins/Limited Resources/Enemies
What failures did they experience?	Complaining/Disobedience/Retreat—all of which turned a journey of a few weeks into a 40-year ordeal	Fear/Discouragement/Apathy—all of which turned a project of a few months into one that required a century to complete
What successes did they have?	Eventually entered the promised land	Eventually rebuilt Jerusalem's temple and wall
What lessons did they learn?	God will build his nation. God is both faithful and just. God will accomplish great acts to make his promises come true.	God will preserve his nation. God will continue to have a chosen people, a home for them, and a plan to offer himself to mankind.

9:2, 3 The Hebrews practised open confession, admitting their sins to one another. Reading and studying God's word should precede confession (see 8:18) because God can show us where we are sinning. Honest confession should precede worship, because we cannot have a right relationship with God if we hold on to certain sins.

9:7–38 Many prayers and speeches in the Bible include a long summary of Israel's history because individuals did not have their own copies of the Bible as we do today. This summary of God's past works reminded the people of their great heritage and God's promises.

We should also remember our history to avoid repeating our mistakes so that we can serve God better. Reviewing our past helps us understand how to improve our behaviour. It shows us the pattern to our spiritual growth. Learn from your past so that you will become the kind of person God wants you to be.

this day. 11 You divided the sea before them,[t] so that they passed through it on
dry ground, but you hurled their pursuers into the depths, like a stone into mighty
waters.[u] 12 By day you led[v] them with a pillar of cloud,[w] and by night with
a pillar of fire to give them light on the way they were to take.
13 "You came down on Mount Sinai;[x] you spoke[y] to them from heaven. You
gave them regulations and laws that are just[z] and right, and decrees and commands that are good.[a] 14 You made known to them your holy Sabbath[b] and gave
them commands, decrees and laws through your servant Moses. 15 In their hunger
you gave them bread from heaven[c] and in their thirst you brought them water
from the rock;[d] you told them to go in and take possession of the land you had
sworn with uplifted hand to give them.[e]
16 "But they, our forefathers, became arrogant and stiff-necked, and did not
obey your commands.[f] 17 They refused to listen and failed to remember[g] the
miracles you performed among them. They became stiff-necked and in their
rebellion appointed a leader in order to return to their slavery.[h] But you are a
forgiving God, gracious and compassionate, slow to anger[i] and abounding in
love.[j] Therefore you did not desert them,[k] 18 even when they cast for themselves an image of a calf[l] and said, 'This is your god, who brought you up out
of Egypt,' or when they committed awful blasphemies.
19 "Because of your great compassion you did not abandon them in the desert.
By day the pillar of cloud did not cease to guide them on their path, nor the pillar
of fire by night to shine on the way they were to take. 20 You gave your good
Spirit[m] to instruct them. You did not withhold your manna[n] from their mouths,
and you gave them water[o] for their thirst. 21 For forty years you sustained them
in the desert; they lacked nothing,[p] their clothes did not wear out nor did their
feet become swollen.[q]
22 "You gave them kingdoms and nations, allotting to them even the remotest
frontiers. They took over the country of Sihon[c][r] king of Heshbon and the
country of Og king of Bashan.[s] 23 You made their sons as numerous as the stars
in the sky, and you brought them into the land that you told their fathers to enter
and possess. 24 Their sons went in and took possession of the land.[t] You subdued
before them the Canaanites, who lived in the land; you handed the Canaanites
over to them, along with their kings and the peoples of the land, to deal with them
as they pleased. 25 They captured fortified cities and fertile land; they took
possession of houses filled with all kinds of good things, wells already dug,
vineyards, olive groves and fruit trees in abundance. They ate to the full and were
well-nourished;[u] they revelled in your great goodness.[v]
26 "But they were disobedient and rebelled against you; they put your law
behind their backs.[w] They killed your prophets,[x] who had admonished them in
order to turn them back to you; they committed awful blasphemies.[y] 27 So you
handed them over to their enemies,[z] who oppressed them. But when they were
oppressed they cried out to you. From heaven you heard them, and in your great
compassion[a] you gave them deliverers, who rescued them from the hand of their
enemies.
28 "But as soon as they were at rest, they again did what was evil in your sight.
Then you abandoned them to the hand of their enemies so that they ruled over
them. And when they cried out to you again, you heard from heaven, and in your
compassion you delivered them[b] time after time.

c *22* One Hebrew manuscript and Septuagint; most Hebrew manuscripts *Sihon, that is, the country of the*

9:11 [t] Ex 14:21; Ps 78:13 [u] Ex 15:4-5, 10; Heb 11:29
9:12 [v] Ex 15:13 [w] Ex 13:21
9:13 [x] Ex 19:11 [y] Ex 19:19 [z] Ps 119:137 [a] Ex 20:1
9:14 [b] Ge 2:3; Ex 20:8-11
9:15 [c] Ex 16:4; Jn 6:31 [d] Ex 17:6; Nu 20:7-13 [e] Dt 1:8, 21
9:16 [f] Dt 1:26-33; 31:29
9:17 [g] Ps 78:42 [h] Nu 14:1-4 [i] Ex 34:6 [j] Nu 14:17-19 [k] Ps 78:11
9:18 [l] Ex 32:4
9:20 [m] Nu 11:17; Isa 63:11, 14 [n] Ex 16:15 [o] Ex 17:6
9:21 [p] Dt 2:7 [q] Dt 8:4
9:22 [r] Nu 21:21 [s] Nu 21:33
9:24 [t] Jos 11:23
9:25 [u] Dt 6:10-12 [v] Nu 13:27; Dt 32:12-15
9:26 [w] 1Ki 14:9 [x] Mt 21:35-36 [y] Jdg 2:12-13
9:27 [z] Jdg 2:14 [a] Ps 106:45
9:28 [b] Ps 106:43

9:16–21 Seeing how God continued to be with his people shows that his patience is amazing! In spite of our repeated failings, pride, and stubbornness, he is always ready to pardon (9:17), and his Spirit is always ready to instruct (9:20). Realising the extent of God's forgiveness helps us forgive those who fail us, even "seventy-seven times" if necessary (Matthew 18:21, 22).

9:28–31 Israel was devastated by times of intense rebellion and sin. Yet when the people repented and returned to God, he delivered them. God puts no limit on the number of times we can come to him to obtain mercy, but we must *come* in order to obtain it, recognising our need and asking him for help. This miracle of grace should inspire us to say, "You are a gracious and merciful God!" If there is a recurring problem or difficulty in your life, continue to ask God for help, and be willing and ready to make changes in your attitude and behaviour that will correct that situation.

29"You warned them to return to your law, but they became arrogant[c] and
disobeyed your commands. They sinned against your ordinances, by which a man
will live if he obeys them.[d] Stubbornly they turned their backs on you, became
stiff-necked and refused to listen.[e] 30For many years you were patient with
them. By your Spirit you admonished them through your prophets.[f] Yet they
paid no attention, so you handed them over to the neighbouring peoples. 31But
in your great mercy you did not put an end[g] to them or abandon them, for you
are a gracious and merciful God.

32"Now therefore, O our God, the great, mighty[h] and awesome God, who
keeps his covenant of love,[i] do not let all this hardship seem trifling in your
eyes — the hardship that has come upon us, upon our kings and leaders, upon our
priests and prophets, upon our fathers and all your people, from the days of the
kings of Assyria until today. 33In all that has happened to us, you have been
just;[j] you have acted faithfully, while we did wrong.[k] 34Our kings,[l] our
leaders, our priests and our fathers[m] did not follow your law; they did not pay
attention to your commands or the warnings you gave them. 35Even while they
were in their kingdom, enjoying your great goodness[n] to them in the spacious
and fertile land you gave them, they did not serve you[o] or turn from their evil
ways.

36"But see, we are slaves[p] today, slaves in the land you gave our forefathers
so that they could eat its fruit and the other good things it produces. 37Because
of our sins, its abundant harvest goes to the kings you have placed over us. They
rule over our bodies and our cattle as they please. We are in great distress.[q]

The Agreement of the People

38"In view of all this, we are making a binding agreement,[r] putting it in writing,[s]
and our leaders, our Levites and our priests are affixing their seals to it."

10 Those who sealed it were:

Nehemiah the governor, the son of Hacaliah.

Zedekiah, 2Seraiah,[a] Azariah, Jeremiah,
3Pashhur,[b] Amariah, Malkijah,
4Hattush, Shebaniah, Malluch,
5Harim,[c] Meremoth, Obadiah,
6Daniel, Ginnethon, Baruch,
7Meshullam, Abijah, Mijamin,
8Maaziah, Bilgai and Shemaiah.
These were the priests.

9The Levites:[d]

Jeshua son of Azaniah,
Binnui of the sons of Henadad, Kadmiel,
10and their associates:
Shebaniah, Hodiah, Kelita, Pelaiah, Hanan,
11Mica, Rehob, Hashabiah,
12Zaccur, Sherebiah, Shebaniah,

9:29 [c]Ps 5:5; Isa 2:11; Jer 43:2 [d]Dt 30:16 [e]Zec 7:11-12
9:30 [f]2Ki 17:13-18; 2Ch 36:16
9:31 [g]Isa 48:9; Jer 4:27
9:32 [h]Ps 24:8 [i]Dt 7:9
9:33 [j]Ge 18:25 [k]Jer 44:3; Da 9:7-8, 14
9:34 [l]2Ki 23:11 [m]Jer 44:17
9:35 [n]Isa 63:7 [o]Dt 28:45-48
9:36 [p]Dt 28:48; Ezr 9:9
9:37 [q]Dt 28:33; La 5:5
9:38 [r]2Ch 23:16 [s]Isa 44:5
10:2 [a]Ezr 2:2
10:3 [b]1Ch 9:12
10:5 [c]1Ch 24:8
10:9 [d]Ne 12:1

9:35 Sometimes the very blessings God has showered on us make us forget him (9:28). We are often tempted to rely on wealth for security rather than on God. As you see what happened to the Israelites, look at your own life. Do your blessings make you thankful to God and draw you closer to him, or do they make you feel self-sufficient and forgetful of God?

9:36 The Israelites were in the strange position of being slaves in their own land, having to turn over a part of their resources each year to a foreign king. How ironic, since God had given the land to them.

9:38 This binding agreement or covenant between the people and God had six provisions. They agreed to: (1) not marry non-Jewish neighbours (10:30), (2) observe the Sabbath (10:31), (3) observe every seventh year as a sabbath year (10:31), (4) pay a temple tax (10:32, 33), (5) supply wood for the burnt offerings in the temple (10:34), and (6) give dues to the temple (10:35–38). After years of decadence and exile, the people once again took seriously their responsibility to follow God and keep his laws wholeheartedly.

13Hodiah, Bani and Beninu.

14The leaders of the people:

Parosh, Pahath-Moab, Elam, Zattu, Bani,
15Bunni, Azgad, Bebai,
16Adonijah, Bigvai, Adin,[e]
17Ater, Hezekiah, Azzur,
18Hodiah, Hashum, Bezai,
19Hariph, Anathoth, Nebai,
20Magpiash, Meshullam, Hezir,[f]
21Meshezabel, Zadok, Jaddua,
22Pelatiah, Hanan, Anaiah,
23Hoshea, Hananiah,[g] Hasshub,
24Hallohesh, Pilha, Shobek,
25Rehum, Hashabnah, Maaseiah,
26Ahiah, Hanan, Anan,
27Malluch, Harim and Baanah.

28"The rest of the people—priests, Levites, gatekeepers, singers, temple
servants[h] and all who separated themselves from the neighbouring peoples[i] for
the sake of the Law of God, together with their wives and all their sons and
daughters who are able to understand—29all these now join their brothers the
nobles, and bind themselves with a curse and an oath[j] to follow the Law of God
given through Moses the servant of God and to obey carefully all the commands,
regulations and decrees of the LORD our Lord.
30"We promise not to give our daughters in marriage to the peoples around
us or take their daughters for our sons.[k]
31"When the neighbouring peoples bring merchandise or grain to sell on the
Sabbath,[l] we will not buy from them on the Sabbath or on any holy day. Every
seventh year we will forgo working the land[m] and will cancel all debts.[n]
32"We assume the responsibility for carrying out the commands to give a third
of a shekel[a] each year for the service of the house of our God: 33for the bread
set out on the table;[o] for the regular grain offerings and burnt offerings; for the
offerings on the Sabbaths, New Moon[p] festivals and appointed feasts; for the
holy offerings; for sin offerings to make atonement for Israel; and for all the duties
of the house of our God.[q]
34"We—the priests, the Levites and the people—have cast lots[r] to determine
when each of our families is to bring to the house of our God at set times each
year a contribution of wood[s] to burn on the altar of the LORD our God, as it is
written in the Law.

a *32* That is, about ⅛ ounce (about 4 grams)

10:16 [e]Ezr 8:6
10:20 [f]1Ch 24:15
10:23 [g]Ne 7:2
10:28 [h]Ps 135:1 [i]2Ch 6:26; Ne 9:2
10:29 [j]Nu 5:21; Ps 119:106
10:30 [k]Ex 34:16; Dt 7:3; Ne 13:23
10:31 [l]Ne 13:16, 18; Jer 17:27; Eze 23:38; Am 8:5 [m]Ex 23:11; Lev 25:1-7 [n]Dt 15:1
10:33 [o]Lev 24:6 [p]Nu 10:10; Ps 81:3; Isa 1:14 [q]2Ch 24:5
10:34 [r]Lev 16:8 [s]Ne 13:31

10:28ff The wall was completed, and the agreement God made with his people in the days of Moses was restored (Deuteronomy 8). This covenant has principles that are important for us today. Our relationship with God must go far beyond church attendance and regular devotions. It should affect our relationships (10:30), our time (10:31), and our material resources (10:32–39). When you chose to follow God, you promised to serve him in this way. The Israelites had fallen away from their original commitment. We must keep our promise to God in times of adversity or prosperity.

10:30 If God's chosen people were going to witness for him in a pagan world, they needed united, God-fearing families. They also needed to avoid any enticements to worship the idols of the people who lived around them. This was why God prohibited marriage between Israelites and the pagan inhabitants of the land (Deuteronomy 7:3, 4). But Israelites and pagans often intermarried anyway, and the results were disastrous for the families and for the nation. Time after time, marrying foreigners led God's people into idolatry (1 Kings 11:1–11). Whenever the nation turned its back on God, it also lost its prosperity and influence for good.

10:31 God recognised that the lure of money would conflict with the need for a day of rest, so trade was forbidden inside the city on the Sabbath. By deciding to honour God first, the Israelites would be refusing to make money their god. Our culture often makes us choose between convenience and profit on the one hand, and putting God first on the other. Look at your work and worship habits: is God really first?

10:31 Forgoing all debts every seventh year was a part of the law (see Exodus 23:10 and Deuteronomy 15:1, 2). The people were reciting and promising to obey God's law and keep the covenant.

10:32 The temple had been rebuilt under Ezra's leadership about 70 years earlier (Ezra 6:14, 15). So the temple tax, offerings, and feasts had been restored.

35"We also assume responsibility for bringing to the house of the LORD each
year the firstfruits[t] of our crops and of every fruit tree.[u]
36"As it is also written in the Law, we will bring the firstborn[v] of our sons
and of our cattle, of our herds and of our flocks to the house of our God, to the
priests ministering there.[w]
37"Moreover, we will bring to the storerooms of the house of our God, to the
priests, the first of our ground meal, of our ⌊grain⌋ offerings, of the fruit of all
our trees and of our new wine and oil.[x] And we will bring a tithe[y] of our crops
to the Levites,[z] for it is the Levites who collect the tithes in all the towns where
we work.[a] 38A priest descended from Aaron is to accompany the Levites when
they receive the tithes, and the Levites are to bring a tenth of the tithes[b] up to
the house of our God, to the storerooms of the treasury. 39The people of Israel,
including the Levites, are to bring their contributions of grain, new wine and oil
to the storerooms where the articles for the sanctuary are kept and where the
ministering priests, the gatekeepers and the singers stay.
"We will not neglect the house of our God."[c]

2. Nehemiah establishes policies

The New Residents of Jerusalem

11 Now the leaders of the people settled in Jerusalem, and the rest of the people
cast lots to bring one out of every ten to live in Jerusalem,[a] the holy city,[b]
while the remaining nine were to stay in their own towns.[c] 2The people commended
all the men who volunteered to live in Jerusalem.
3These are the provincial leaders who settled in Jerusalem (now some Israelites,
priests, Levites, temple servants and descendants of Solomon's servants lived in the
towns of Judah, each on his own property in the various towns,[d] 4while other people
from both Judah and Benjamin[e] lived in Jerusalem):[f]

From the descendants of Judah:

Athaiah son of Uzziah, the son of Zechariah, the son of Amariah, the son of
Shephatiah, the son of Mahalalel, a descendant of Perez; 5and Maaseiah son of
Baruch, the son of Col-Hozeh, the son of Hazaiah, the son of Adaiah, the son
of Joiarib, the son of Zechariah, a descendant of Shelah. 6The descendants of
Perez who lived in Jerusalem totalled 468 able men.

7From the descendants of Benjamin:

Sallu son of Meshullam, the son of Joed, the son of Pedaiah, the son of Kolaiah,
the son of Maaseiah, the son of Ithiel, the son of Jeshaiah, 8and his followers,
Gabbai and Sallai—928 men. 9Joel son of Zicri was their chief officer, and Judah
son of Hassenuah was over the Second District of the city.

10From the priests:

10:35 [t]Ex 22:29; 23:19; Nu 18:12 [u]Dt 26:1-11
10:36 [v]Ex 13:2; Nu 18:14-16 [w]Ne 13:31
10:37 [x]Lev 23:17; Nu 18:12 [y]Lev 27:30; Nu 18:21 [z]Dt 14:22-29 [a]Eze 44:30
10:38 [b]Nu 18:26
10:39 [c]Dt 12:6; Ne 13:11, 12
11:1 [a]Ne 7:4 [b]ver 18; Isa 48:2; 52:1; 64:10; Zec 14:20-21 [c]Ne 7:73
11:3 [d]1Ch 9:2-3; Ezr 2:1
11:4 [e]Ezr 1:5 [f]Ezr 2:70

10:36 This practice was instituted at the time of the exodus from Egypt (see the note on Exodus 13:12–14). The people needed to relearn the importance of dedicating the firstfruits of their yield to God. Nehemiah was simply reinstating this practice from the early days of the nation (Exodus 13:1, 2; Numbers 3:40–51). Although this principle was not carried over to New Testament times, the concept of giving God the first portion of our time, treasure, and talent still remains. Do you give God your first and best, or merely what is left over?

10:37–39 According to God's law, the people were to give a tenth of their produce to the temple for the support of the Levites (those who cared for the temple and the religious observances). A tenth of what the Levites received or produced went to the priests for their support. The principle at work was to ensure the support of the house of God and his workers. We must not overlook our responsibility to God's workers today.

11:1ff The exiles who returned were few in number compared to Jerusalem's population in the days of the kings. And because the walls had been rebuilt on their original foundations, the city seemed sparsely populated. Nehemiah asked one-tenth of the people from the outlying areas to move inside the city walls to keep large areas of the city from being vacant. Apparently these people did not want to move into the city. Only a few people volunteered (11:1, 2), and Nehemiah cast lots to determine who among the remaining people would have to move.

Many of them may not have wanted to live in the city because (1) non-Jews attached a stigma to Jerusalem residents, often excluding them from trade because of their religious beliefs; (2) moving into the city meant rebuilding their homes and re-establishing their businesses, a major investment of time and money; (3) living in Jerusalem required stricter obedience to God's word because of greater social pressure and proximity to the temple.

Jedaiah; the son of Joiarib; Jakin; 11Seraiah[g] son of Hilkiah, the son of Meshullam, the son of Zadok, the son of Meraioth, the son of Ahitub,[h] supervisor in
the house of God, 12and their associates, who carried on work for the temple—822 men; Adaiah son of Jeroham, the son of Pelaliah, the son of Amzi,
the son of Zechariah, the son of Pashhur, the son of Malkijah, 13and his associates, who were heads of families—242 men; Amashsai son of Azarel, the son
of Ahzai, the son of Meshillemoth, the son of Immer, 14and his[a] associates, who
were able men—128 men. Their chief officer was Zabdiel son of Haggedolim.

15From the Levites:

Shemaiah son of Hasshub, the son of Azrikam, the son of Hashabiah, the son
of Bunni; 16Shabbethai[i] and Jozabad,[j] two of the heads of the Levites, who
had charge of the outside work of the house of God; 17Mattaniah[k] son of Mica,
the son of Zabdi, the son of Asaph,[l] the director who led in thanksgiving and
prayer; Bakbukiah, second among his associates; and Abda son of Shammua, the
son of Galal, the son of Jeduthun.[m] 18The Levites in the holy city[n] totalled 284.

19The gatekeepers:

Akkub, Talmon and their associates, who kept watch at the gates—172 men.

20The rest of the Israelites, with the priests and Levites, were in all the towns of
Judah, each on his ancestral property.
21The temple servants[o] lived on the hill of Ophel, and Ziha and Gishpa were in
charge of them.
22The chief officer of the Levites in Jerusalem was Uzzi son of Bani, the son of
Hashabiah, the son of Mattaniah,[p] the son of Mica. Uzzi was one of Asaph's
descendants, who were the singers responsible for the service of the house of God.
23The singers[q] were under the king's orders, which regulated their daily activity.
24Pethahiah son of Meshezabel, one of the descendants of Zerah[r] son of Judah,
was the king's agent in all affairs relating to the people.
25As for the villages with their fields, some of the people of Judah lived in Kiriath
Arba[s] and its surrounding settlements, in Dibon[t] and its settlements, in Jekabzeel
and its villages, 26in Jeshua, in Moladah, in Beth Pelet,[u] 27in Hazar Shual, in
Beersheba[v] and its settlements, 28in Ziklag,[w] in Meconah and its settlements, 29in
En Rimmon, in Zorah,[x] in Jarmuth,[y] 30Zanoah, Adullam[z] and their villages, in
Lachish[a] and its fields, and in Azekah[b] and its settlements. So they were living all
the way from Beersheba[c] to the Valley of Hinnom.
31The descendants of the Benjamites from Geba[d] lived in Michmash,[e] Aija,
Bethel and its settlements, 32in Anathoth,[f] Nob[g] and Ananiah, 33in Hazor,[h] Ramah
and Gittaim,[i] 34in Hadid, Zeboim[j] and Neballat, 35in Lod and Ono,[k] and in the
Valley of the Craftsmen.
36Some of the divisions of the Levites of Judah settled in Benjamin.

Priests and Levites

12 These were the priests[a] and Levites who returned with Zerubbabel[b] son of
Shealtiel and with Jeshua:[c]
Seraiah,[d] Jeremiah, Ezra,
2Amariah, Malluch, Hattush,
3Shecaniah, Rehum, Meremoth,
4Iddo,[e] Ginnethon,[a] Abijah,[f]
5Mijamin,[b] Moadiah, Bilgah,
6Shemaiah, Joiarib, Jedaiah,[g]
7Sallu, Amok, Hilkiah and Jedaiah.
These were the leaders of the priests and their associates in the days of Jeshua.
8The Levites were Jeshua, Binnui, Kadmiel, Sherebiah, Judah, and also Mattaniah,[h] who, together with his associates, was in charge of the songs of thanksgiving.

a *14* Most Septuagint manuscripts; Hebrew *their* a *4* Many Hebrew manuscripts and Vulgate (see also Neh. 12:16); most Hebrew manuscripts *Ginnethoi* b *5* A variant of *Miniamin*

11:11 g 2Ki 25:18; Ezr 2:2 h Ezr 7:2
11:16 i Ezr 10:15 j Ezr 8:33
11:17 k 1Ch 9:15; Ne 12:8 l 2Ch 5:12 m 1Ch 25:1
11:18 n Rev 21:2
11:21 o Ezr 2:43; Ne 3:26
11:22 p 1Ch 9:15
11:23 q Ne 7:44
11:24 r Ge 38:30
11:25 s Ge 35:27; Jos 14:15 t Nu 21:30
11:26 u Jos 15:27
11:27 v Ge 21:14
11:28 w 1Sa 27:6
11:29 x Jos 15:33 y Jos 10:3
11:30 z Jos 15:35 a Jos 10:3 b Jos 10:10 c Jos 15:28
11:31 d Jos 21:17; Isa 10:29 e 1Sa 13:2
11:32 f Jos 21:18; Isa 10:30 g 1Sa 21:1
11:33 h Jos 11:1 i 2Sa 4:3
11:34 j 1Sa 13:18
11:35 k 1Ch 8:12
12:1 a Ne 10:1-8 b 1Ch 3:19 c Ezr 2:2 d Ezr 2:2
12:4 e Zec 1:1 f Lk 1:5
12:6 g 1Ch 24:7
12:8 h Ne 11:17

9Bakbukiah and Unni, their associates, stood opposite them in the services.
10Jeshua was the father of Joiakim, Joiakim the father of Eliashib,[i] Eliashib the
father of Joiada, 11Joiada the father of Jonathan, and Jonathan the father of Jaddua.
12In the days of Joiakim, these were the heads of the priestly families:
of Seraiah's family, Meraiah;
of Jeremiah's, Hananiah;
13of Ezra's, Meshullam;
of Amariah's, Jehohanan;
14of Malluch's, Jonathan;
of Shecaniah's,[c] Joseph;
15of Harim's, Adna;
of Meremoth's,[d] Helkai;
16of Iddo's,[j] Zechariah;
of Ginnethon's, Meshullam;
17of Abijah's, Zicri;
of Miniamin's and of Moadiah's, Piltai;
18of Bilgah's, Shammua;
of Shemaiah's, Jehonathan;
19of Joiarib's, Mattenai;
of Jedaiah's, Uzzi;
20of Sallu's, Kallai;
of Amok's, Eber;
21of Hilkiah's, Hashabiah;
of Jedaiah's, Nethanel.
22The family heads of the Levites in the days of Eliashib, Joiada, Johanan and
Jaddua, as well as those of the priests, were recorded in the reign of Darius the Persian.
23The family heads among the descendants of Levi up to the time of Johanan son of
Eliashib were recorded in the book of the annals. 24And the leaders of the Levites[k]
were Hashabiah, Sherebiah, Jeshua son of Kadmiel, and their associates, who stood
opposite them to give praise and thanksgiving, one section responding to the other,
as prescribed by David the man of God.
25Mattaniah, Bakbukiah, Obadiah, Meshullam, Talmon and Akkub were gatekeepers who guarded the storerooms at the gates. 26They served in the days of Joiakim
son of Jeshua, the son of Jozadak, and in the days of Nehemiah the governor and of
Ezra the priest and scribe.

Dedication of the Wall of Jerusalem

27At the dedication[l] of the wall of Jerusalem, the Levites were sought out from
where they lived and were brought to Jerusalem to celebrate joyfully the dedication
with songs of thanksgiving and with the music of cymbals,[m] harps and lyres.[n] 28The
singers also were brought together from the region around Jerusalem—from the
villages of the Netophathites,[o] 29from Beth Gilgal, and from the area of Geba and
Azmaveth, for the singers had built villages for themselves around Jerusalem. 30When
the priests and Levites had purified themselves ceremonially, they purified the people,[p] the gates and the wall.
31I had the leaders of Judah go up on top[e] of the wall. I also assigned two large
choirs to give thanks. One was to proceed on top[f] of the wall to the right, towards
the Dung Gate.[q] 32Hoshaiah and half the leaders of Judah followed them, 33along
with Azariah, Ezra, Meshullam, 34Judah, Benjamin,[r] Shemaiah, Jeremiah, 35as well

12:10 [i]Ezr 10:24
12:16 [j]ver 4
12:24 [k]Ezr 2:40
12:27 [l]Dt 20:5 [m]2Sa 6:5 [n]1Ch 15:16, 28; 25:6; Ps 92:3
12:28 [o]1Ch 2:54; 9:16
12:30 [p]Ex 19:10; Job 1:5
12:31 [q]Ne 2:13
12:34 [r]Ezr 1:5

c *14* Very many Hebrew manuscripts, some Septuagint manuscripts and Syriac (see also Neh. 12:3); most Hebrew manuscripts *Shebaniah's* d *15* Some Septuagint manuscripts (see also Neh. 12:3); Hebrew *Meraioth's*
e *31* Or *go alongside* f *31* Or *proceed alongside*

12:35, 36 How could the priests have used musical instruments? David had instituted music as a part of worship in the temple, and so his instruments had probably been stored there. Although Nebuchadnezzar destroyed the temple, he took many temple items back to Babylon with him (2 Chronicles 36:18). These were most likely preserved in Babylon and given back to the Israelites by Cyrus when they returned to their land (Ezra 1:7–11).

as some priests with trumpets,[s] and also Zechariah son of Jonathan, the son of
Shemaiah, the son of Mattaniah, the son of Micaiah, the son of Zaccur, the son of
Asaph, 36and his associates—Shemaiah, Azarel, Milalai, Gilalai, Maai, Nethanel,
Judah and Hanani—with musical instruments[t] ⌞prescribed by⌟ David the man of
God.[u] Ezra[v] the scribe led the procession. 37At the Fountain Gate[w] they continued
directly up the steps of the City of David on the ascent to the wall and passed above
the house of David to the Water Gate[x] on the east.
38The second choir proceeded in the opposite direction. I followed them on top[g]
of the wall, together with half the people—past the Tower of the Ovens[y] to the Broad
Wall,[z] 39over the Gate of Ephraim,[a] the Jeshanah[h] Gate,[b] the Fish Gate,[c] the
Tower of Hananel[d] and the Tower of the Hundred,[e] as far as the Sheep Gate.[f] At
the Gate of the Guard they stopped.
40The two choirs that gave thanks then took their places in the house of God; so
did I, together with half the officials, 41as well as the priests—Eliakim, Maaseiah,
Miniamin, Micaiah, Elioenai, Zechariah and Hananiah with their trumpets—42and
also Maaseiah, Shemaiah, Eleazar, Uzzi, Jehohanan, Malkijah, Elam and Ezer. The
choirs sang under the direction of Jezrahiah. 43And on that day they offered great
sacrifices, rejoicing because God had given them great joy. The women and children
also rejoiced. The sound of rejoicing in Jerusalem could be heard far away.
44At that time men were appointed to be in charge of the storerooms[g] for the
contributions, firstfruits and tithes.[h] From the fields around the towns they were to
bring into the storerooms the portions required by the Law for the priests and the
Levites, for Judah was pleased with the ministering priests and Levites.[i] 45They
performed the service of their God and the service of purification, as did also the
singers and gatekeepers, according to the commands of David[j] and his son Solomon.[k] 46For long ago, in the days of David and Asaph,[l] there had been directors
for the singers and for the songs of praise[m] and thanksgiving to God. 47So in the days
of Zerubbabel and of Nehemiah, all Israel contributed the daily portions for the singers
and gatekeepers. They also set aside the portion for the other Levites, and the Levites
set aside the portion for the descendants of Aaron.[n]

Nehemiah's Final Reforms

13 On that day the Book of Moses was read aloud in the hearing of the people and
there it was found written that no Ammonite or Moabite should ever be admitted
into the assembly of God,[a] 2because they had not met the Israelites with food and
water but had hired Balaam[b] to call a curse down on them.[c] (Our God, however,
turned the curse into a blessing.)[d] 3When the people heard this law, they excluded
from Israel all who were of foreign descent.[e]
4Before this, Eliashib the priest had been put in charge of the storerooms[f] of the
house of our God. He was closely associated with Tobiah,[g] 5and he had provided
him with a large room formerly used to store the grain offerings and incense and temple
articles, and also the tithes[h] of grain, new wine and oil prescribed for the Levites,
singers and gatekeepers, as well as the contributions for the priests.
6But while all this was going on, I was not in Jerusalem, for in the thirty-second

g 38 *Or them alongside* h 39 *Or Old*

12:35 [s]Ezr 3:10
12:36 [t]1Ch 15:16 [u]2Ch 8:14 [v]Ezr 7:6
12:37 [w]Ne 2:14; 3:15 [x]Ne 3:26
12:38 [y]Ne 3:11 [z]Ne 3:8
12:39 [a]2Ki 14:13; Ne 8:16 [b]Ne 3:6 [c]2Ch 33:14; Ne 3:3 [d]Ne 3:1 [e]Ne 3:1 [f]Ne 3:1
12:44 [g]Ne 13:4, 13 [h]Lev 27:30 [i]Dt 18:8
12:45 [j]1Ch 25:1; 2Ch 8:14 [k]1Ch 6:31; 23:5
12:46 [l]2Ch 35:15 [m]2Ch 29:27; Ps 137:4
12:47 [n]Nu 18:21; Dt 18:8
13:1 [a]ver 23; Dt 23:3
13:2 [b]Nu 22:3-11 [c]Nu 23:7; Dt 23:3 [d]Nu 23:11; Dt 23:4-5
13:3 [e]ver 23; Ne 9:2
13:4 [f]Ne 12:44 [g]Ne 2:10
13:5 [h]Lev 27:30; Nu 18:21

12:44 Further arrangements were made for supporting those who served at the temple. The storerooms were administered by men who made sure the tithes and contributions were collected and distributed appropriately. These storerooms had to be large to hold all the grain presented by the people. This storeroom administration was an important responsibility.

12:44–47 The dedication of the city wall was characterised by joy, praise, and singing (12:24, 27–29, 35, 36, 40–43). Nehemiah repeatedly mentioned David, who began the custom of using choirs in worship. In David's day, Israel was a vigorous, God-fearing nation. These exiles who had returned wanted their rebuilt Jerusalem to be the hub of a renewed nation, strengthened by God; therefore, they dedicated themselves and their city to God.

13:3 "All who were of foreign descent" refers to the Moabites and Ammonites, two nations who were bitter enemies of Israel (13:1). God's law clearly stated that these two peoples should never be allowed in the temple (Deuteronomy 23:3–5). This had nothing to do with racial prejudice, because God clearly loved all people, including foreigners (Deuteronomy 10:18). He allowed foreigners to make sacrifices (Numbers 15:15, 16), and he desires all nations to know and love him (Isaiah 42:6). But while God wants all to come to him, he warns believers to stay away from those bent on evil (Proverbs 24:1). The relationships established between Jews and pagans had caused their captivity in the first place. In their celebration and rededication, they had to show they were serious about following God's law.

year of Artaxerxes[i] king of Babylon I had returned to the king. Some time later I
asked his permission 7and came back to Jerusalem. Here I learned about the evil thing
Eliashib[j] had done in providing Tobiah a room in the courts of the house of God.
8I was greatly displeased and threw all Tobiah's household goods out of the room.[k]
9I gave orders to purify the rooms,[l] and then I put back into them the equipment of
the house of God, with the grain offerings and the incense.
10I also learned that the portions assigned to the Levites had not been given to
them,[m] and that all the Levites and singers responsible for the service had gone back
to their own fields. 11So I rebuked the officials and asked them, "Why is the house
of God neglected?"[n] Then I called them together and stationed them at their posts.
12All Judah brought the tithes[o] of grain, new wine and oil into the storerooms.[p]
13I put Shelemiah the priest, Zadok the scribe, and a Levite named Pedaiah in charge
of the storerooms and made Hanan son of Zaccur, the son of Mattaniah, their assistant,
because these men were considered trustworthy. They were made responsible for
distributing the supplies to their brothers.[q]

14Remember[r] me for this, O my God, and do not blot out what I have so faithfully
done for the house of my God and its services.

15In those days I saw men in Judah treading winepresses on the Sabbath and
bringing in grain and loading it on donkeys, together with wine, grapes, figs and all
other kinds of loads. And they were bringing all this into Jerusalem on the Sabbath.[s]
Therefore I warned them against selling food on that day. 16Men from Tyre who lived
in Jerusalem were bringing in fish and all kinds of merchandise and selling them in
Jerusalem on the Sabbath[t] to the people of Judah. 17I rebuked the nobles of Judah
and said to them, "What is this wicked thing you are doing—desecrating the Sabbath
day? 18Didn't your forefathers do the same things, so that our God brought all this
calamity upon us and upon this city? Now you are stirring up more wrath against Israel
by desecrating the Sabbath."[u]
19When evening shadows fell on the gates of Jerusalem before the Sabbath,[v] I
ordered the doors to be shut and not opened until the Sabbath was over. I stationed
some of my own men at the gates so that no load could be brought in on the Sabbath
day. 20Once or twice the merchants and sellers of all kinds of goods spent the night
outside Jerusalem. 21But I warned them and said, "Why do you spend the night by
the wall? If you do this again, I will lay hands on you." From that time on they no
longer came on the Sabbath. 22Then I commanded the Levites to purify themselves
and go and guard the gates in order to keep the Sabbath day holy.

Remember[w] me for this also, O my God, and show mercy to me according to your
great love.

23Moreover, in those days I saw men of Judah who had married[x] women from
Ashdod, Ammon and Moab.[y] 24Half of their children spoke the language of Ashdod

13:6 [i]Ne 2:6; 5:14
13:7 [j]Ezr 10:24
13:8 [k]Mt 21:12-13; Jn 2:13-16
13:9 [l]1Ch 23:28; 2Ch 29:5
13:10 [m]Dt 12:19
13:11 [n]Ne 10:37-39; Hag 1:1-9
13:12 [o]2Ch 31:6 [p]1Ki 7:51; Ne 10:37-39; Mal 3:10
13:13 [q]Ne 12:44; Ac 6:1-5
13:14 [r]Ge 8:1
13:15 [s]Ex 20:8-11; 34:21; Dt 5:12-15; Ne 10:31
13:16 [t]Ne 10:31
13:18 [u]Ne 10:31; Jer 17:21-23
13:19 [v]Lev 23:32
13:22 [w]Ge 8:1; Ne 12:30
13:23 [x]Ezr 9:1-2; Mal 2:11 [y]ver 1; Ne 10:30

13:6, 7 Nehemiah had to return to Babylon in 433 B.C., 12 years after he had arrived in Jerusalem. Either he was recalled by Artaxerxes, or he was fulfilling an agreement to return. It is not known exactly how long he remained in Babylon, but when he returned to Jerusalem (13:7), he found that one of his major opponents in rebuilding the wall, Tobiah, had been given his own room at the temple. He was an Ammonite (4:3), and thus forbidden to enter the temple. Eliashib, the priest, had married Tobiah's daughter, so Tobiah used his influence with his son-in-law to get this special room. Chapters 2, 4, and 6 tell about Tobiah's opposition to Nehemiah and Nehemiah's appropriate action.

13:10 Because the Levites were no longer supported, they had returned to their farms to support themselves, neglecting their temple duties and the spiritual welfare of the people. Spiritual workers deserve their pay, and their support ought to be enough to care for their needs. They shouldn't have to suffer (or leave) because believers don't adequately assess and meet the needs of their ministers.

13:16 Tyre was a large Phoenician city and port on the Mediterranean Sea.

13:17 God had commanded Israel not to work on the Sabbath, but to rest in remembrance of creation and the exodus (Exodus 20:8–11; Deuteronomy 5:12–15). The Sabbath rest, lasting from sunset Friday to sunset Saturday, was to be honoured and observed by all Jews, servants, visiting foreigners, and even farm animals. Jerusalem's busy Sabbath trade directly violated God's law, so Nehemiah commanded that the city gates be shut and traders be sent home every Friday afternoon as the Sabbath hours approached.

13:24 Ashdod was on the Mediterranean coast, in the region controlled by the Philistines. Ammon and Moab were across the Jordan to the east. These nations were abhorrent to those who knew Israel's history.

or the language of one of the other peoples, and did not know how to speak the
language of Judah. 25I rebuked them and called curses down on them. I beat some
of the men and pulled out their hair. I made them take an oath[z] in God's name and
said: "You are not to give your daughters in marriage to their sons, nor are you to
take their daughters in marriage for your sons or for yourselves. 26Was it not because
of marriages like these that Solomon king of Israel sinned? Among the many nations
there was no king like him.[a] He was loved by his God,[b] and God made him king
over all Israel, but even he was led into sin by foreign women.[c] 27Must we hear now
that you too are doing all this terrible wickedness and are being unfaithful to our God
by marrying[d] foreign women?"

28One of the sons of Joiada son of Eliashib[e] the high priest was son-in-law to
Sanballat[f] the Horonite. And I drove him away from me.

29Remember[g] them, O my God, because they defiled the priestly office and the
covenant of the priesthood and of the Levites.

30So I purified the priests and the Levites of everything foreign,[h] and assigned them
duties, each to his own task. 31I also made provision for contributions of wood[i] at
designated times, and for the firstfruits.

Remember[j] me with favour, O my God.

13:25 [z]Ezr 10:5
13:26 [a]1Ki 3:13; 2Ch 1:12 [b]2Sa 12:25 [c]1Ki 11:3
13:27 [d]Ezr 9:14; 10:2
13:28 [e]Ezr 10:24 [f]Ne 2:10
13:29 [g]Ne 6:14
13:30 [h]Ne 10:30
13:31 [i]Ne 10:34 [j]ver 14, 22; Ge 8:1

13:25 Nehemiah was filled with righteous indignation at the blatant way the Jews were breaking God's laws and disregarding the covenant they had previously reaffirmed (10:30). The people had promised not to allow their children to marry pagans. But during Nehemiah's absence, the people had been intermarrying, breaking their solemn covenant with God. Nehemiah's severe treatment of these people shows the contrast between his great faithfulness to God and the people's neglect, disobedience, and disloyalty (see also Ezra 10:3).

13:26 Nehemiah used the example of Solomon's mistakes to teach his people. If one of the greatest kings of Israel fell because of the influence of unbelievers, others could too. Nehemiah saw this principle in Solomon's example: your gifts and strengths won't be of much benefit if you fail to deal with your weaknesses. Although Solomon was a great king, his marriages to foreign women brought tragedy to the whole kingdom. A tendency to sin must be recognised and dealt with swiftly; otherwise, it may overpower you and bring you down. One of the strongest reasons for reading the Bible is to learn from the mistakes of God's people.

13:31 "Remember me with favour" means "look favourably upon me for all that I have done".

13:31 Nehemiah's life story provides many principles of effective leadership that are still valid today. (1) *Have a clear purpose and keep evaluating it in light of God's will.* Nothing prevented Nehemiah from staying on track. (2) *Be straightforward and honest.* Everyone knew exactly what Nehemiah needed, and he spoke the truth even when it made his goal harder to achieve. (3) *Live above reproach.* The accusations against Nehemiah were empty and false. (4) *Be a person of constant prayer,* deriving power and wisdom from your contact with God. Everything Nehemiah did glorified God.

Leadership appears glamorous at times, but it is often lonely, thankless, and filled with pressures to compromise values and standards. Nehemiah was able to accomplish a huge task against incredible odds because he learned that there is no success without risk of failure, no reward without hard work, no opportunity without criticism, and no true leadership without trust in God. This book is about rebuilding the wall of a great city, but it is also about spiritual renewal, rebuilding a people's dependence on God. When we take our eyes off God, our lives begin to crumble.

ESTHER

Jerusalem destroyed/ exiles go to Babylon 586 B.C.	*First exiles return to Jerusalem 538*	*Temple completed 516*	*Xerxes becomes king of Persia 486*	*Esther becomes queen 479*	*Haman's decree to destroy the Jews 474*	*First feast of Purim 473*

DRAMA, power, romance, intrigue—this is the stuff of which best-selling novels are made. But far from a modern piece of fiction, those words describe a true story, lived and written centuries ago. More than entertaining reading, it is a story of the profound interplay of God's sovereignty and human will. God prepared the place and the opportunity, and his people, Esther and Mordecai, chose to act.

The book of Esther begins with Queen Vashti refusing to obey an order from her husband, King Xerxes. She was subsequently banished, and the search began for a new queen. The king sent out a decree to gather together all the beautiful women in the empire and bring them into the royal harem. Esther, a young Jewish woman, was one of those chosen to be in the royal harem. King Xerxes was so pleased with Esther that he made her his queen.

Meanwhile, Mordecai, Esther's older cousin, became a government official and during his tenure foiled an assassination plot. But the ambitious and self-serving Haman was appointed second-in-command in the empire. When Mordecai refused to bow in reverence to him, Haman became furious and determined to destroy Mordecai and all the Jews along with him.

To accomplish his vengeful deed, Haman deceived the king and persuaded him to issue an edict condemning the Jews to death. Mordecai told Queen Esther about this edict, and she decided to risk her life to save her people. Esther asked King Xerxes and Haman to be her guests at a banquet. During the feast, the king asked Esther what she really wanted, and he promised to give her anything. Esther simply invited both men to another banquet the next day.

That night, unable to sleep, the king was flipping through some records in the royal archives when he read of the assassination plot that Mordecai had thwarted. Surprised to learn that Mordecai had never been rewarded for this deed, the king asked Haman what should be done to thank a hero properly. Haman thought the king must be talking about him, and so he described a lavish reward. The king agreed, but to Haman's shock and utter humiliation, he learned that Mordecai was the person to be so honoured.

During the second banquet, the king again asked Esther what she desired. She replied that someone had plotted to destroy her and her people, and she named Haman as the culprit. Immediately the king sentenced Haman to die on the gallows that Haman had built for Mordecai.

In the final act of this true-life drama, Mordecai was appointed to Haman's position, and the Jews were guaranteed protection throughout the land. To celebrate this historic occasion, the feast of Purim was established.

Because of Queen Esther's courageous act, a whole nation was saved. Seeing her God-given opportunity, she seized it! Her life made a difference. Read Esther and watch for God at work in *your* life. Perhaps he has prepared you to act in "such a time as this" (4:14).

VITAL STATISTICS

PURPOSE:
To demonstrate God's sovereignty and his loving care for his people

AUTHOR:
Unknown. Possibly Mordecai (9:29). Some have suggested Ezra or Nehemiah because of the similarity of the writing style.

DATE WRITTEN:
Approximately 483–471 B.C. (Esther became queen in 479)

SETTING:
Although Esther follows Nehemiah in the Bible, its events are about 30 years prior to those recorded in Nehemiah. The story is set in the Persian empire, and most of the action takes place in the king's palace in Susa, the Persian capital.

KEY VERSE:
"For if you remain silent at this time, relief and deliverance for the Jews will arise from another place, but you and your father's family will perish. And who knows but that you have come to royal position for such a time as this?" (4:14).

KEY PEOPLE:
Esther, Mordecai, King Xerxes I, Haman

KEY PLACE:
The king's palace in Susa, Persia

SPECIAL FEATURES:
Esther is one of only two books named after women (Ruth is the other). The book is unusual in that in the original version no name, title, or pronoun for God appears in it (see the note on 4:14). This caused some church fathers to question its inclusion in the canon. But God's presence is clear throughout the book.

THE BLUEPRINT

1. Esther becomes queen (1:1—2:23)
2. The Jews are threatened (3:1—4:17)
3. Esther intercedes for the Jews (5:1—8:17)
4. The Jews are delivered (9:1—10:3)

The book of Esther is an example of God's divine guidance and care over our lives. God's sovereignty and power are seen throughout this book. Although we may question certain circumstances in our lives, we must have faith that God is in control, working through both the pleasant and difficult times so that we can serve him effectively.

MEGATHEMES

THEME	EXPLANATION	IMPORTANCE
God's Sovereignty	The book of Esther tells of the circumstances that were essential to the survival of God's people in Persia. These "circumstances" were not the result of chance, but of God's grand design. God is sovereign over every area of life.	With God in charge, we can take courage. He can guide us through the circumstances we face in our lives. We should expect God to display his power in carrying out his will. As we unite our life's purposes to God's purpose, we benefit from his sovereign care.
Racial Hatred	The Jews in Persia had been a minority since their deportation from Judah 100 years earlier. Haman was a descendant of King Agag, an enemy of the Jews. Lust for power and pride drove Haman to hate Mordecai, Esther's cousin. Haman convinced the king to kill all the Jews.	Racial hatred is always sinful. We must never condone it in any form. Every person on earth has intrinsic worth because God created mankind in his image. Therefore, God's people must stand against racism whenever and wherever it occurs.
Deliverance	On February 28th, the Jews celebrate the feast of Purim, which symbolises God's deliverance. *Purim* means "lots", such as those used by Haman to set the date for the extermination of all Jews from Persia. But God overruled, using Queen Esther to intercede on behalf of the Jews.	Because God is in control of history, he is never frustrated by any turn of events or action of man. He is able to save us from the evil of this world and deliver us from sin and death. Because we trust God, we are not to fear what people may do to us; instead, we are to be confident in God's control.
Action	Faced with death, Esther and Mordecai set aside their own fear and took action. Esther risked her life by asking King Xerxes to save the Jews. They were not paralysed by fear.	When outnumbered and powerless, it is natural for us to feel helpless. Esther and Mordecai resisted this temptation and acted with courage. It is not enough to know that God is in control; we must act with self-sacrifice and courage to follow God's guidance.
Wisdom	The Jews were a minority in a world hostile to them. It took great wisdom for Mordecai to survive. Serving as a faithful official of the king, Mordecai took steps to understand and work with the Persian law. Yet he did not compromise his integrity.	It takes great wisdom to survive in a non-believing world. In a setting which is for the most part hostile to Christianity, we can demonstrate wisdom by giving respect to what is true and good and by humbly standing against what is wrong.

1. Esther becomes queen

Queen Vashti Deposed

1 This is what happened during the time of Xerxes,[a] [a] the Xerxes who ruled over
127 provinces[b] stretching from India to Cush:[b] [c] 2At that time King Xerxes
reigned from his royal throne in the citadel of Susa,[d] 3and in the third year of his

[a] *1* Hebrew *Ahasuerus*, a variant of Xerxes' Persian name; here and throughout Esther [b] *1* That is, the upper Nile region

1:1 [a]Ezr 4:6; Da 9:1 [b]Est 9:30; Da 3:2; 6:1 [c]Est 8:9

1:2 [d]Ezr 4:9; Ne 1:1; Est 2:8

1:1 Esther's story begins in 483 B.C., 103 years after Nebuchadnezzar had taken the Jews into captivity (2 Kings 25), 54 years after Zerubbabel led the first group of exiles back to Jerusalem (Ezra 1; 2), and 25 years before Ezra led the second group to Jerusalem (Ezra 7). Esther lived in the kingdom of Persia, the dominant kingdom in the Middle East after Babylon's fall in 539 B.C. Esther's parents must have been among those exiles who chose not to return to Jerusalem, even though Cyrus, the Persian king, had issued

1:3 [e]1Ki 3:15; Est 2:18

1:5 [f]Jdg 14:17 [g]2Ki 21:18; Est 7:7-8

1:6 [h]Est 7:8; Eze 23:41; Am 3:12; 6:4

1:7 [i]Est 2:18; Da 5:2

1:9 [j]1Ki 3:15

reign he gave a banquet[e] for all his nobles and officials. The military leaders of Persia
and Media, the princes, and the nobles of the provinces were present.
4For a full 180 days he displayed the vast wealth of his kingdom and the splendour
and glory of his majesty. 5When these days were over, the king gave a banquet, lasting
seven days,[f] in the enclosed garden[g] of the king's palace, for all the people from
the least to the greatest, who were in the citadel of Susa. 6The garden had hangings
of white and blue linen, fastened with cords of white linen and purple material to silver
rings on marble pillars. There were couches[h] of gold and silver on a mosaic pavement
of porphyry, marble, mother-of-pearl and other costly stones. 7Wine was served in
goblets of gold, each one different from the other, and the royal wine was abundant,
in keeping with the king's liberality.[i] 8By the king's command each guest was
allowed to drink in his own way, for the king instructed all the wine stewards to serve
each man what he wished.
9Queen Vashti also gave a banquet[j] for the women in the royal palace of King
Xerxes.

THE WORLD OF ESTHER'S DAY
Esther lived in the capital of the vast Medo-Persian empire, which incorporated the provinces of Media and Persia, as well as the previous empires of Assyria and Babylon. Esther, a Jewess, was chosen by King Xerxes to be his queen. The story of how she saved her people takes place in the palace in Susa.

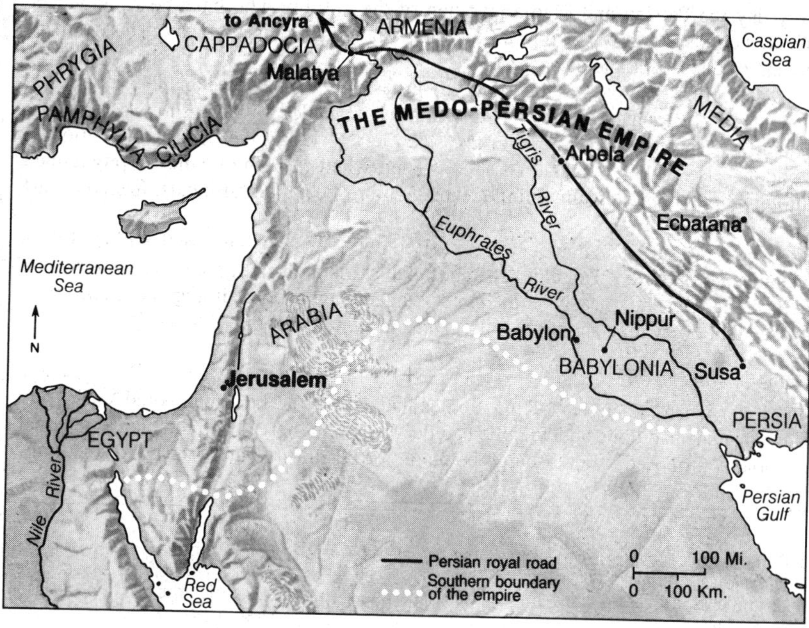

a decree allowing them to do so. The Jewish exiles had great freedom in Persia, and many remained because they had established themselves there or were fearful of the dangerous journey back to their homeland.

1:1 Xerxes the Great was Persia's fifth king (486–465 B.C.). He was proud and impulsive, as we see from the events in chapter 1. His winter palace was in Susa, where he held the banquet described in 1:3–7. Persian kings often held great banquets before going to war. In 481, Xerxes launched an attack against Greece. After his fleet won a great victory at Thermopylae, he was defeated at Salamis in 480 and had to return to Persia. Esther became queen in 479.

1:2 In this context, "citadel" means "palace".

1:4 The celebration lasted 180 days (about six months) because its real purpose was to plan the battle strategy for invading Greece and to demonstrate that the king had sufficient wealth to carry it out. Waging war was not only for survival; it was a means of acquiring more wealth, territory, and power.

1:5–7 Persia was a world power, and the king, as the centre of that power, was one of the wealthiest people in the world. Persian kings loved to flaunt their wealth, even wearing precious gemstones in their beards. Jewellery was a sign of rank for Persian men. Even soldiers wore great amounts of gold jewellery into battle.

1:8 "Each guest was allowed to drink in his own way" means that the guests could drink as much or as little as they wished. (Usually the king controlled how much his guests could drink.)

1:9 Ancient Greek documents call Xerxes' wife Amestris, probably a Greek form of Vashti. Vashti was deposed in 484/483 B.C., but she is mentioned again in ancient records as the queen mother during the reign of her son, Artaxerxes, who succeeded Xerxes. Toward the end of Xerxes' reign, either Esther died or Vashti was able through her son to regain the influence she had lost.

10On the seventh day, when King Xerxes was in high spirits[k] from wine,[l] he
commanded the seven eunuchs who served him—Mehuman, Biztha, Harbona,[m]
Bigtha, Abagtha, Zethar and Carcas—11to bring[n] before him Queen Vashti, wearing
her royal crown, in order to display her beauty[o] to the people and nobles, for she
was lovely to look at. 12But when the attendants delivered the king's command, Queen
Vashti refused to come. Then the king became furious and burned with anger.[p]
13Since it was customary for the king to consult experts in matters of law and justice,
he spoke with the wise men who understood the times[q] 14and were closest to the
king—Carshena, Shethar, Admatha, Tarshish, Meres, Marsena and Memucan, the
seven nobles[r] of Persia and Media who had special access to the king and were
highest in the kingdom.
15"According to law, what must be done to Queen Vashti?" he asked. "She has not
obeyed the command of King Xerxes that the eunuchs have taken to her."
16Then Memucan replied in the presence of the king and the nobles, "Queen Vashti
has done wrong, not only against the king but also against all the nobles and the
peoples of all the provinces of King Xerxes. 17For the queen's conduct will become
known to all the women, and so they will despise their husbands and say, 'King Xerxes
commanded Queen Vashti to be brought before him, but she would not come.' 18This
very day the Persian and Median women of the nobility who have heard about the
queen's conduct will respond to all the king's nobles in the same way. There will be
no end of disrespect and discord.[s]
19"Therefore, if it pleases the king,[t] let him issue a royal decree and let it be written
in the laws of Persia and Media, which cannot be repealed,[u] that Vashti is never again
to enter the presence of King Xerxes. Also let the king give her royal position to
someone else who is better than she. 20Then when the king's edict is proclaimed
throughout all his vast realm, all the women will respect their husbands, from the least
to the greatest."
21The king and his nobles were pleased with this advice, so the king did as
Memucan proposed. 22He sent dispatches to all parts of the kingdom, to each province
in its own script and to each people in its own language,[v] proclaiming in each people's
tongue that every man should be ruler over his own household.

Esther Made Queen

2 Later when the anger of King Xerxes had subsided,[a] he remembered Vashti and
what she had done and what he had decreed about her. 2Then the king's personal
attendants proposed, "Let a search be made for beautiful young virgins for the king.

1:10 [k]Jdg 16:25; Ru 3:7 [l]Ge 14:18; Est 3:15; 5:6; 7:2; Pr 31:4-7; Da 5:1-4 [m]Est 7:9
1:11 [n]SS 2:4 [o]Ps 45:11; Eze 16:14
1:12 [p]Ge 39:19; Est 2:21; 7:7; Pr 19:12
1:13 [q]1Ch 12:32; Jer 10:7; Da 2:12
1:14 [r]2Ki 25:19; Ezr 7:14
1:18 [s]Pr 19:13; 27:15
1:19 [t]Ecc 8:4 [u]Est 8:8; Da 6:8, 12
1:22 [v]Ne 13:24; Est 8:9; Eph 5:22-24; 1Ti 2:12
2:1 [a]Est 1:19-20; 7:10

1:10 Some advisers and government officials were castrated in order to prevent them from having children and then rebelling and trying to establish a dynasty of their own. A castrated official was called a eunuch.

1:10, 11 Xerxes made a rash, half-drunk decision, based purely on feelings. His self-restraint and practical wisdom were weakened by too much wine. Poor decisions are made when people don't think clearly. Base your decisions on careful thinking, not on the emotions of the moment. Impulsive decision making leads to severe complications.

1:12 Queen Vashti refused to parade before the king's all-male party, possibly because it was against Persian custom for a woman to appear before a public gathering of men. This conflict between Persian custom and the king's command put her in a difficult situation, and she chose to refuse her half-drunk husband, hoping he would come to his senses later. Some have suggested that Vashti was pregnant with Artaxerxes, who was born in 483 B.C., and that she did not want to be seen in public in that state.

Whatever the reason, her action was a breach of protocol that also placed Xerxes in a difficult situation. Once he made the command, as a Persian king he could not reverse it (see the note on 1:19). While preparing to invade Greece, Xerxes had invited important officials from all over his land to see his power, wealth, and authority. If it was perceived that he had no authority over his own wife, his military credibility would be damaged—the greatest criterion of success for an ancient king. In addition, King Xerxes was accustomed to getting what he wanted.

1:15 Middle Eastern kings often did not have close personal relationships with their wives. Xerxes demonstrates this because (1) he had a harem (2:3); (2) he showed no respect for Vashti's personhood (1:10–12); (3) Esther, when she became queen, did not see him for long periods of time (4:11).

1:16–21 Perhaps the men's thinking had been clouded by drinking. Obviously this law would not cause the women of the country to respect their husbands. Respect between men and women comes from mutual regard and appreciation for each other as those created in God's image, not from legal pronouncements and orders. Forced obedience is a poor substitute for the love and respect wives and husbands should have for each other.

1:19 A Persian king was thought to be a god by many of his people; therefore, when he issued a law or command, it stood for ever (see the notes on 8:8 and Daniel 6:8). The law could never be cancelled, even if it was ill-advised; but if necessary, a new law could be issued to neutralise the effects of the old law.

2:1 The phrase, "he remembered Vashti", may mean that the king began to miss his queen and what she had done for him. But he

2:5 [b]1Sa 9:1; Est 3:2
2:6 [c]2Ki 24:6, 15; 2Ch 36:10, 20 [d]Da 1:1-5; 5:13
2:7 [e]Ge 41:45 [f]Ge 39:6
2:8 [g]ver 3, 15; Ne 1:1; Est 1:2; Da 8:2
2:9 [h]Ge 39:21 [i]ver 3, 12; Ge 37:3; 1Sa 9:22-24; 2Ki 25:30; Eze 16:9-13; Da 1:5
2:10 [j]ver 20
2:12 [k]Pr 27:9; SS 1:3; Isa 3:24
2:14 [l]1Ki 11:3; SS 6:8; Da 5:2 [m]Est 4:11
2:15 [n]Est 9:29 [o]Ps 45:14 [p]Ge 18:3; 30:27; Est 5:8
2:17 [q]Est 1:11; Eze 16:9-13

3Let the king appoint commissioners in every province of his realm to bring all these
beautiful girls into the harem at the citadel of Susa. Let them be placed under the care
of Hegai, the king's eunuch, who is in charge of the women; and let beauty treatments
be given to them. 4Then let the girl who pleases the king be queen instead of Vashti."
This advice appealed to the king, and he followed it.
5Now there was in the citadel of Susa a Jew of the tribe of Benjamin, named
Mordecai son of Jair, the son of Shimei, the son of Kish,[b] 6who had been carried
into exile from Jerusalem by Nebuchadnezzar king of Babylon, among those taken
captive with Jehoiachin[a][c] king of Judah.[d] 7Mordecai had a cousin named Hadassah,
whom he had brought up because she had neither father nor mother. This girl, who
was also known as Esther,[e] was lovely[f] in form and features, and Mordecai had
taken her as his own daughter when her father and mother died.
8When the king's order and edict had been proclaimed, many girls were brought
to the citadel of Susa[g] and put under the care of Hegai. Esther also was taken to the
king's palace and entrusted to Hegai, who had charge of the harem. 9The girl pleased
him and won his favour.[h] Immediately he provided her with her beauty treatments
and special food.[i] He assigned to her seven maids selected from the king's palace
and moved her and her maids into the best place in the harem.
10Esther had not revealed her nationality and family background, because Mordecai
had forbidden her to do so.[j] 11Every day he walked to and fro near the courtyard
of the harem to find out how Esther was and what was happening to her.
12Before a girl's turn came to go in to King Xerxes, she had to complete twelve
months of beauty treatments prescribed for the women, six months with oil of myrrh
and six with perfumes[k] and cosmetics. 13And this is how she would go to the king:
Anything she wanted was given to her to take with her from the harem to the king's
palace. 14In the evening she would go there and in the morning return to another part
of the harem to the care of Shaashgaz, the king's eunuch who was in charge of the
concubines.[l] She would not return to the king unless he was pleased with her and
summoned her by name.[m]
15When the turn came for Esther (the girl Mordecai had adopted, the daughter of
his uncle Abihail[n]) to go to the king,[o] she asked for nothing other than what Hegai,
the king's eunuch who was in charge of the harem, suggested. And Esther won the
favour[p] of everyone who saw her. 16She was taken to King Xerxes in the royal
residence in the tenth month, the month of Tebeth, in the seventh year of his reign.
17Now the king was attracted to Esther more than to any of the other women, and
she won his favour and approval more than any of the other virgins. So he set a royal
crown on her head and made her queen[q] instead of Vashti. 18And the king gave a

[a] *6* Hebrew *Jeconiah*, a variant of *Jehoiachin*

---

also remembered that in his anger he had banished her from his presence with a decree that couldn't be rescinded.

2:3, 14–17 Persian kings collected not only vast amounts of jewellery, but also great numbers of women. These young virgins were taken from their homes and were required to live in a separate building near the palace, called a harem. Their sole purpose was to serve the king and to await his call for sexual pleasure. They rarely saw the king, and their lives were restricted and boring. If rejected, Esther would be one of many girls the king had seen once and forgotten. But Esther's presence and beauty pleased the king enough that he crowned her queen in place of Vashti. The queen held a more influential position than a concubine, and she was given more freedom and authority than others in the harem. But even as queen, Esther had few rights – especially because she had been chosen to replace a woman who had become too assertive.

2:5, 6 Mordecai was a Jew. The Jewish population had increased since their exile over 100 years earlier. They had been given great freedom and were allowed to run their own businesses and hold positions in government (2:19; Daniel 6:3).

2:6 The Bible says that Mordecai was carried into exile from Jerusalem by Nebuchadnezzar. If this referred to Mordecai himself, he would have been over 100 years old at the time of this story. This difficult phrase can be resolved by understanding that the word "who", referring to Mordecai, can also mean "whose family". It is likely that Mordecai's great-grandparents were carried into captivity rather than Mordecai himself.

2:10 With virtually no rights and little access to the king, it was better for Esther not to reveal her identity. While boldness in stating our identity as God's people is our responsibility, at times a good strategy is to keep quiet until we have won the right to be heard. This is especially true when dealing with those in authority over us. But we can always let them see the difference God makes in our lives.

2:17 God placed Esther on the throne even before the Jews faced the possibility of complete destruction (3:5ff), so that when trouble came, a person would already be in the position to help. No human effort could thwart God's plan to send the Messiah to earth as a Jew. If you are changing jobs, position, or location and can't see God's purpose in your situation, understand that God is in control. He may be placing you in a position so you can help when the need arises.

great banquet,[r] Esther's banquet, for all his nobles and officials.[s] He proclaimed
a holiday throughout the provinces and distributed gifts with royal liberality.[t]

Mordecai Uncovers a Conspiracy

19 When the virgins were assembled a second time, Mordecai was sitting at the
king's gate.[u] 20 But Esther had kept secret her family background and nationality just
as Mordecai had told her to do, for she continued to follow Mordecai's instructions
as she had done when he was bringing her up.[v]
21 During the time Mordecai was sitting at the king's gate, Bigthana[b] and Teresh,
two of the king's officers[w] who guarded the doorway, became angry[x] and conspired
to assassinate King Xerxes. 22 But Mordecai found out about the plot and told Queen
Esther, who in turn reported it to the king, giving credit to Mordecai. 23 And when
the report was investigated and found to be true, the two officials were hanged[y] on
a gallows.[c] All this was recorded in the book of the annals[z] in the presence of the
king.

2. The Jews are threatened

Haman's Plot to Destroy the Jews

3 After these events, King Xerxes honoured Haman son of Hammedatha, the
Agagite,[a] elevating him and giving him a seat of honour higher than that of all
the other nobles. 2 All the royal officials at the king's gate knelt down and paid honour
to Haman, for the king had commanded this concerning him. But Mordecai would
not kneel down or pay him honour.
3 Then the royal officials at the king's gate asked Mordecai, "Why do you disobey
the king's command?"[b] 4 Day after day they spoke to him but he refused to comply.[c]
Therefore they told Haman about it to see whether Mordecai's behaviour would be
tolerated, for he had told them he was a Jew.
5 When Haman saw that Mordecai would not kneel down or pay him honour, he
was enraged.[d] 6 Yet having learned who Mordecai's people were, he scorned the idea
of killing only Mordecai. Instead Haman looked for a way[e] to destroy[f] all Mordecai's people, the Jews,[g] throughout the whole kingdom of Xerxes.
7 In the twelfth year of King Xerxes, in the first month, the month of Nisan, they
cast the *pur*[h] (that is, the lot[i]) in the presence of Haman to select a day and month.
And the lot fell on[a] the twelfth month, the month of Adar.[j]

[b] *21* Hebrew *Bigthan,* a variant of *Bigthana* [c] *23* Or *were hung* (or *impaled*) *on poles*; similarly elsewhere in Esther [a] *7* Septuagint; Hebrew does not have *And the lot fell on.*

2:18 [r] 1Ki 3:15; Est 1:3 [s] Ge 40:20 [t] Est 1:7
2:19 [u] ver 21; Est 3:2; 4:2; 5:13
2:20 [v] ver 10
2:21 [w] Ge 40:2; Est 6:2 [x] Est 1:12; 3:5; 5:9; 7:7
2:23 [y] Ge 40:19; Ps 7:14-16; Pr 26:27 [z] Est 6:1; 10:2
3:1 [a] ver 10; Ex 17:8-16; Nu 24:7; Dt 25:17-19; 1Sa 14:48; Est 5:11
3:3 [b] Est 5:9; Da 3:12
3:4 [c] Ge 39:10
3:5 [d] Est 2:21; 5:9
3:6 [e] Pr 16:25 [f] Ps 74:8; 83:4 [g] Est 9:24
3:7 [h] Est 9:24, 26 [i] Lev 16:8; 1Sa 10:21 [j] ver 13; Ezr 6:15; Est 9:19

3:2 Mordecai's determination came from his faith in God. He did not take a poll first to determine the safest or most popular course of action; he had the courage to stand alone. Doing what is right will not always make you popular. Those who do right will be in the minority, but to obey God is more important than to obey people (Acts 5:29).

3:2–4 Mordecai refused to kneel down before Haman. Jews did bow down to government authorities, at times, as a sign of respect (Genesis 23:7; 1 Samuel 24:8), but Haman's ancestors were ancient enemies of the Jews. Israel had been commanded by God to "blot out the memory of Amalek from under heaven" (Deuteronomy 25:17–19; see also Exodus 17:16). Mordecai was not about to kneel before wicked Haman and, by his act, acknowledge Haman as a god. Daniel's three friends had the same convictions (Daniel 3). We must worship God alone. We should never let any person, institution, or government take God's place. When people demand loyalties or duties from you that do not honour God, don't give in. It may be time to take a stand.

3:5, 6 Why did Haman want to destroy all Jews just because of one man's action? (1) Haman was an Agagite (3:1), a descendant of Agag, king of the Amalekites (1 Samuel 15:20). The Amalekites were ancient enemies of the Israelites (see Exodus 17:16; Deuteronomy 25:17–19). Haman's hatred was directed not just at Mordecai, but at all the Jews. (2) As second-in-command in the Persian empire (3:1), Haman loved his power and authority and the reverence shown him. The Jews, however, looked to God as their final authority, not to any man. Haman realised that the only way to fulfil his self-centred desires was to kill all those who disregarded his authority. His quest for personal power and his hatred of the Jewish race consumed him.

3:5, 6 Haman enjoyed the power and prestige of his position, and he was enraged when Mordecai did not respond with the expected reverential bow. Haman's anger was not directed just toward Mordecai, but towards what Mordecai stood for – the Jews' dedication to God as the only authority worthy of reverence. Haman's attitude was prejudiced: he hated a group of people because of a difference in belief or culture. Prejudice grows out of personal pride – considering oneself better than others. In the end, Haman was punished for his arrogant attitude (7:9, 10). God will harshly judge those who are prejudiced or whose pride causes them to look down on others.

3:7 Haman cast lots to determine the best day to carry out his decree. Little did he know that he was playing into the hands of God, for the day of death was set for almost a year away, giving Esther time to make her plea to the king. The Persian word for lots was *purim,* which became the name for the holiday celebrated by the Jews when they were delivered, not killed, on the day appointed by Haman.

3:8
[k]Ac 16:20-21
[l]Jer 29:7; Da 6:13
[m]Ezr 4:15

3:9
[n]Est 7:4

8Then Haman said to King Xerxes, "There is a certain people dispersed and
scattered among the peoples in all the provinces of your kingdom whose customs[k]
are different from those of all other people and who do not obey[l] the king's laws;
it is not in the king's best interest to tolerate them.[m] 9If it pleases the king, let a decree
be issued to destroy them, and I will put ten thousand talents[b] of silver into the royal
treasury for the men who carry out this business."[n]

b *9* That is, about 340 tons (about 345 metric tons)

MORDECAI

Following Jerusalem's last stand against Nebuchadnezzar, Mordecai's family was deported to the Babylonian empire. He was probably born in Susa, a city that became one of Persia's capitals after Cyrus conquered Babylon, and inherited an official position among the Jewish captives that kept him around the palace even after the Babylonians were driven out. At one time, when he overheard plans to assassinate Xerxes, he reported the plot and saved the king's life.

Mordecai's life was filled with challenges that he turned into opportunities. When his aunt and uncle died, he adopted Esther, their daughter and his young cousin, probably because his own parents were dead and he felt responsible for her. Later, when she was drafted into Xerxes' harem and chosen to be queen, Mordecai continued to advise her. Shortly after this, he found himself in conflict with Xerxes' recently appointed second-in- command, Haman. Although willing to serve the king, Mordecai refused to worship the king's representative. Haman was furious with Mordecai. So he planned to have Mordecai and all the Jews killed. His plan became a law of the Medes and Persians, and it looked as though the Jews were doomed.

Mordecai, willing to be God's servant wherever he was, responded by contacting Esther and telling her that one reason God had allowed her to be queen might well be to save her people from this threat. But God had also placed *him* in the right place years earlier. God revealed to the king through his night-time reading of historical documents that Mordecai had once saved his life, and the king realised he had never thanked Mordecai. The great honour then given to Mordecai ruined Haman's plan to hang him on the gallows. God had woven an effective counter-strategy against which Haman's plan could not stand.

Later, Mordecai instituted the Jewish feast of Purim. He had a lengthy career of service to the king on behalf of the Jews. In Mordecai's life, God blended both character and circumstances to accomplish great things. He has not changed the way he works. God is using the situations you face each day to weave a pattern of godliness into your character. Pause and ask God to help you respond appropriately to the situations you find yourself in today.

Strengths and accomplishments:
- Exposed an assassination plot against the king
- Cared enough to adopt his cousin
- Refused to bow to anyone except God
- Took Haman's place as second-in-command under Xerxes

Lessons from his life:
- The opportunities we have are more important than the ones we wish we had
- We can trust God to weave together the events of life for our best, even though we may not be able to see the overall pattern
- The rewards for doing right are sometimes delayed, but they are guaranteed by God himself

Vital statistics:
- Where: Susa, one of several capital cities in Persia
- Occupation: Jewish official who became second in rank to Xerxes
- Relatives: Adopted daughter: Esther. Father: Jair
- Contemporaries: Xerxes, Haman

Key verse:
"Mordecai the Jew was second in rank to King Xerxes, pre-eminent among the Jews, and held in high esteem by his many fellow Jews, because he worked for the good of his people and spoke up for the welfare of all the Jews" (Esther 10:3).

Mordecai's story is told in the book of Esther.

3:9 Haman must have hoped to acquire this tremendous sum of money by plundering the homes and businesses of the Jews who would be killed through his decree.

10 So the king took his signet ring[o] from his finger and gave it to Haman son of
Hammedatha, the Agagite, the enemy of the Jews. 11 "Keep the money," the king said
to Haman, "and do with the people as you please."
12 Then on the thirteenth day of the first month the royal secretaries were summoned.
They wrote out in the script of each province and in the language[p] of each people
all Haman's orders to the king's satraps, the governors of the various provinces and
the nobles of the various peoples. These were written in the name of King Xerxes
himself and sealed[q] with his own ring. 13 Dispatches were sent by couriers to all the
king's provinces with the order to destroy, kill and annihilate all the Jews[r]—young
and old, women and little children—on a single day, the thirteenth day of the twelfth
month, the month of Adar,[s] and to plunder[t] their goods. 14 A copy of the text of
the edict was to be issued as law in every province and made known to the people
of every nationality so that they would be ready for that day.[u]
15 Spurred on by the king's command, the couriers went out, and the edict was issued
in the citadel of Susa.[v] The king and Haman sat down to drink,[w] but the city of Susa
was bewildered.[x]

Mordecai Persuades Esther to Help

4 When Mordecai learned of all that had been done, he tore his clothes,[a] put on
sackcloth and ashes,[b] and went out into the city, wailing[c] loudly and bitterly.
2 But he went only as far as the king's gate,[d] because no-one clothed in sackcloth was
allowed to enter it. 3 In every province to which the edict and order of the king came,
there was great mourning among the Jews, with fasting, weeping and wailing. Many
lay in sackcloth and ashes.
4 When Esther's maids and eunuchs came and told her about Mordecai, she was in
great distress. She sent clothes for him to put on instead of his sackcloth, but he would
not accept them. 5 Then Esther summoned Hathach, one of the king's eunuchs assigned
to attend her, and ordered him to find out what was troubling Mordecai and why.
6 So Hathach went out to Mordecai in the open square of the city in front of the king's
gate. 7 Mordecai told him everything that had happened to him, including the exact
amount of money Haman had promised to pay into the royal treasury for the destruction of the Jews.[e] 8 He also gave him a copy of the text of the edict for their
annihilation, which had been published in Susa, to show to Esther and explain it to
her, and he told him to urge her to go into the king's presence to beg for mercy and
plead with him for her people.
9 Hathach went back and reported to Esther what Mordecai had said. 10 Then she
instructed him to say to Mordecai, 11 "All the king's officials and the people of the
royal provinces know that for any man or woman who approaches the king in the inner
court without being summoned[f] the king has but one law:[g] that he be put to death.
The only exception to this is for the king to extend the gold sceptre[h] to him and spare
his life. But thirty days have passed since I was called to go to the king."
12 When Esther's words were reported to Mordecai, 13 he sent back this answer: "Do

3:10 [o]Ge 41:42; Est 7:6; 8:2
3:12 [p]Ne 13:24 [q]Ge 38:18; 1Ki 21:8; Est 8:8-10
3:13 [r]1Sa 15:3; Ezr 4:6; Est 8:10-14 [s]ver 7 [t]Est 8:11; 9:10
3:14 [u]Est 8:8; 9:1
3:15 [v]Est 8:14 [w]Est 1:10 [x]Est 8:15
4:1 [a]Nu 14:6 [b]2Sa 13:19; Eze 27:30-31; Jnh 3:5-6 [c]Ex 11:6; Ps 30:11
4:2 [d]Est 2:19
4:7 [e]Est 3:9; 7:4
4:11 [f]Est 2:14 [g]Da 2:9 [h]Est 5:1, 2; 8:4

3:10–12 Officials in the ancient world used signet rings as personal signatures. The ring's surface had a raised imprint made of metal, wood, or bone; Xerxes' was probably made of silver or gold. Each individual had his own imprint. Letters were sealed by pressing the ring into soft wax, and official documents were certified by using the royal signet. By giving Haman his signet ring, Xerxes gave him his personal signature and with it the authority to do whatever he wished. Little did the king realise that his own ring would sign the death warrant for his queen, Esther.

4:11 – 5:2 Esther risked her life by coming before the king. Her courageous act gives us a model to follow in approaching a difficult or dangerous task. Like Esther, we can: (1) *Calculate the cost.* Esther realised her life was at stake. (2) *Set priorities.* She believed that the safety of the Jewish race was more important than her life. (3) *Prepare.* She gathered support and fasted. (4) *Determine a course of action and move ahead boldly.* She didn't think too long about it, allowing the interlude to lessen her commitment to what she had to do.

Do you have to face a hostile audience, confront a friend on a delicate subject, or talk to your family about changes to be made? Rather than dreading difficult situations or putting them off, take action with confidence by following Esther's inspiring example.

4:13 Although Esther was the queen and shared some of the king's power and wealth, she still needed God's protection and wisdom. No one is secure in his or her own strength in any political system. It is foolish to believe that wealth or position can make us impervious to danger. Deliverance only comes from God.

4:13, 14 After the decree to kill the Jews was given, Mordecai and Esther could have despaired, decided to save only themselves, or just waited for God's intervention. Instead, they saw that God had placed them in their positions for a purpose, so they seized the moment and acted. When it is within our reach to save

4:14
[i]Ecc 3:7; Isa 62:1; Am 5:13
[j]Est 9:16, 22
[k]Ge 45:7; Dt 28:29
[l]Ge 50:20

4:16
[m]2Ch 20:3; Est 9:31
[n]Ge 43:14

5:1
[a]Est 4:16; Eze 16:13
[b]Est 6:4; Pr 21:1

5:2
[c]Est 4:11; 8:4; Pr 21:1

5:3
[d]Est 7:2; Da 5:16; Mk 6:23

not think that because you are in the king's house you alone of all the Jews will escape.
14For if you remain silent[i] at this time, relief[j] and deliverance[k] for the Jews will arise from another place, but you and your father's family will perish. And who knows but that you have come to royal position for such a time as this?"[l]
15Then Esther sent this reply to Mordecai:
16"Go, gather together all the Jews who are in Susa, and fast[m] for me. Do not eat or drink for three days, night or day. I and my maids will fast as you do. When this is done, I will go to the king, even though it is against the law. And if I perish, I perish."[n]
17So Mordecai went away and carried out all of Esther's instructions.

3. Esther intercedes for the Jews

Esther's Request to the King

5 On the third day Esther put on her royal robes[a] and stood in the inner court of the palace, in front of the king's[b] hall. The king was sitting on his royal throne in the hall, facing the entrance.
2When he saw Queen Esther standing in the court, he was pleased with her and held out to her the gold sceptre that was in his hand. So Esther approached and touched the tip of the sceptre.[c]
3Then the king asked, "What is it, Queen Esther? What is your request? Even up to half the kingdom,[d] it will be given you."
4"If it pleases the king," replied Esther, "let the king, together with Haman, come today to a banquet I have prepared for him."
5"Bring Haman at once," the king said, "so that we may do what Esther asks."
So the king and Haman went to the banquet Esther had prepared.
6As they were

GOD BEHIND THE SCENES IN ESTHER
Although God's name is not mentioned in the Hebrew text of Esther, he makes himself known in these ways:

Indirect References	2:17	Esther, who worshipped God, became queen
	4:14	God's existence and his power over the affairs of men are assumed.
	4:16	Fasting was a distinct spiritual activity usually connected with prayer.
Divine Incidents The book of Esther is filled with divine interventions	2:21, 23	Mordecai overhears a death plot and saves the king's life
	6:1	Xerxes can't sleep and decides to read a history book
	6:2	Xerxes reads the exact page needed for the moment, reminding him of an unpaid reward to Mordecai
	7:9, 10	Haman's plan is exactly reversed—the intended victims are the victors

Why was God's name hidden in the book of Esther? There were many gods in the Middle East and Persian empire. Usually, their names were mentioned in official documents in order to control the peoples who worshipped those particular gods. The Jews were unique in being the people of one God. A story about them was naturally a story about God, for even the name "Jew" carried with it the connotation of one who worshipped Yahweh.

others, we must do so. In a life-threatening situation, don't withdraw, behave selfishly, wallow in despair, or wait for God to fix everything. Instead, ask God for his direction, and *act!* God may have placed you where you are "for such a time as this".

4:14 God is not specifically mentioned in the book of Esther, but it is obvious that Mordecai expected God to deliver his people. While the book of Esther does not mention God directly, his presence fills the pages. Esther and Mordecai believed in God's care, and because they acted at the right time, God used them to save his people.

4:16 By calling for a fast, Esther was asking the Jews to pray for God's help on her dangerous mission. In the Old Testament, prayer always accompanies fasting (see Exodus 34:28; Deuteronomy 9:9; Ezra 8:21–23). An important function of a community of believers is mutual support in difficult times. When you are experiencing struggles, turn to fellow believers for support by sharing your trials with them and gaining strength from the bond that unites you. Ask them to pray for you. And when others need your support, give it willingly.

4:16 *Save your own skin* and *Watch out for number one* are mottoes that reflect our world's selfish outlook on life. Esther's attitude stands in bold contrast to this. She knew what she had to do, and she knew it could cost her her life. And yet she responded, "If I perish, I perish." We should have the same commitment to do what is right despite the possible consequences. Do you try to save yourself by remaining silent rather than standing up for what is right? Decide to do what God wants, and trust him for the outcome.

4:17–5:1 God was in control, yet Mordecai and Esther had to act. We cannot understand how both can be true at the same time, and yet they are. God chooses to work through those *willing* to act for him. We should pray as if all depended on God and act as if all depended on us. We should avoid two extremes: doing nothing, and feeling that we must do everything.

drinking wine,[e] the king again asked Esther, "Now what is your petition? It will be
given you. And what is your request? Even up to half the kingdom,[f] it will be
granted."[g]
7 Esther replied, "My petition and my request is this: 8 If the king regards me with
favour[h] and if it pleases the king to grant my petition and fulfil my request, let the
king and Haman come tomorrow to the banquet[i] I will prepare for them. Then I will
answer the king's question."

Haman's Rage Against Mordecai

9 Haman went out that day happy and in high spirits. But when he saw Mordecai
at the king's gate and observed that he neither rose nor showed fear in his presence,
he was filled with rage[j] against Mordecai.[k] 10 Nevertheless, Haman restrained
himself and went home.
Calling together his friends and Zeresh,[l] his wife, 11 Haman boasted[m] to them
about his vast wealth, his many sons,[n] and all the ways the king had honoured him
and how he had elevated him above the other nobles and officials. 12 "And that's not
all," Haman added. "I'm the only person[o] Queen Esther invited to accompany the
king to the banquet she gave. And she has invited me along with the king tomorrow.
13 But all this gives me no satisfaction as long as I see that Jew Mordecai sitting at
the king's gate.[p]"
14 His wife Zeresh and all his friends said to him, "Have a gallows built, seventy-five
feet**[a]** high,[q] and ask the king in the morning to have Mordecai hanged[r] on it. Then
go with the king to the dinner and be happy." This suggestion delighted Haman, and
he had the gallows built.

Mordecai Honoured

6 That night the king could not sleep;[a] so he ordered the book of the chronicles,[b]
the record of his reign, to be brought in and read to him. 2 It was found recorded
there that Mordecai had exposed Bigthana and Teresh, two of the king's officers who
guarded the doorway, who had conspired to assassinate King Xerxes.
3 "What honour and recognition has Mordecai received for this?" the king asked.
"Nothing has been done for him,"[c] his attendants answered.
4 The king said, "Who is in the court?" Now Haman had just entered the outer court
of the palace to speak to the king about hanging Mordecai on the gallows he had
erected for him.
5 His attendants answered, "Haman is standing in the court."
"Bring him in," the king ordered.
6 When Haman entered, the king asked him, "What should be done for the man the
king delights to honour?"
Now Haman thought to himself, "Who is there that the king would rather honour
than me?" 7 So he answered the king, "For the man the king delights to honour, 8 have
them bring a royal robe[d] the king has worn and a horse[e] the king has ridden, one

5:6 [e] Est 1:10 [f] Mk 6:23 [g] Est 7:2; 9:12
5:8 [h] Est 2:15; 7:3; 8:5 [i] 1Ki 3:15; Est 6:14
5:9 [j] Est 2:21; Pr 14:17 [k] Est 3:3, 5
5:10 [l] Est 6:13
5:11 [m] Pr 13:16 [n] Est 9:7-10, 13
5:12 [o] Job 22:29; Pr 16:18; 29:23
5:13 [p] Est 2:19
5:14 [q] Est 7:9 [r] Ezr 6:11; Est 6:4
6:1 [a] Da 2:1; 6:18 [b] Est 2:23; 10:2
6:3 [c] Ecc 9:13-16
6:8 [d] Ge 41:42; Isa 52:1 [e] 1Ki 1:33

a *14* Hebrew *fifty cubits* (about 23 metres)

5:9 Hatred and bitterness are like weeds with long roots that grow in the heart and corrupt all of life. Haman was so consumed with hatred towards Mordecai that he could not even enjoy the honour of being invited to Esther's party. Hebrews 12:15 warns us to watch out "that no bitter root grows up to cause trouble and defile many". Don't let hatred and its resulting bitterness build in your heart. Like Haman, you will find it backfiring against you (see 6:13; 7:9, 10). If the mere mention of someone's name provokes you to anger, confess your bitterness as sin. Ignoring bitterness, hiding it from others, or making superficial changes in behaviour is not enough. If bitterness isn't completely removed, it will grow back, making matters worse.

5:14 Haman's family and friends, who were as arrogant as he, suggested that the gallows be 75 feet high, probably built on the city wall or some prominent building. They wanted to make sure that all the people of the city saw Mordecai's death and would be reminded of the consequences of disobeying Haman. Ironically, these high gallows allowed everyone to see Haman's death.

6:1, 2 Unable to sleep, the king decided to review the history of his reign, and his servants read to him about Mordecai's good deed. This seems coincidental, but God is *always* at work. God has been working quietly and patiently throughout your life as well. The events that have come together for good are not mere coincidence; they are the result of God's sovereign control over the course of people's lives (Romans 8:28).

6:7–9 Haman had wealth, but he craved something even his money couldn't buy – respect. He could buy the trappings of success and power, but his lust for popularity had become an obsession. Don't let your desire for approval, applause, and popularity drive you to immoral actions.

6:9 [f]Ge 41:43 with a royal crest placed on its head. 9Then let the robe and horse be entrusted to one
of the king's most noble princes. Let them robe the man the king delights to honour,
and lead him on the horse through the city streets, proclaiming before him, 'This is
what is done for the man the king delights to honour![f]' "
10"Go at once," the king commanded Haman. "Get the robe and the horse and do
just as you have suggested for Mordecai the Jew, who sits at the king's gate. Do not
neglect anything you have recommended."
11So Haman got[g] the robe and the horse. He robed Mordecai, and led him on
horseback through the city streets, proclaiming before him, "This is what is done for
6:11 the man the king delights to honour!"
[g]Ge 41:42 12Afterwards Mordecai returned to the king's gate. But Haman rushed home, with

---

ESTHER

We treasure security, even though we know that security in this life carries no guarantees—possessions can be destroyed, beauty fades, relationships can be broken, death is inevitable. Real security, then, must be found beyond this life. Only when our security rests in God and his unchanging nature can we face the challenges that life is sure to bring our way.

Esther's beauty and character won Xerxes' heart, and he made her his queen. Even in her favoured position, however, she would risk her life if she attempted to see the king when he had not requested her presence. There was no guarantee that the king would even see her. Although she was queen, she was still not secure. But, cautiously and courageously, Esther decided to risk her life by approaching the king on behalf of her people.

She made her plans carefully. The Jews were asked to fast and pray with her before she went to the king. Then on the chosen day she went before him, and he *did* ask her to come forward and speak. But instead of issuing her request directly, she invited him and Haman to a banquet. He was astute enough to realise she had something on her mind, yet she conveyed the importance of the matter by insisting on a second banquet.

In the meantime, God was working behind the scenes. He caused Xerxes to read the historical records of the kingdom late one night, and the king discovered that Mordecai had once saved his life. Xerxes lost no time in honouring Mordecai for that act. During the second banquet, Esther told the king of Haman's plot against the Jews, and Haman was doomed. There is grim justice in Haman's death on the gallows he had built for Mordecai, and it seems fitting that the day on which the Jews were to be slaughtered became the day their enemies died. Esther's risk confirmed that God was the source of her security.

How much of your security lies in your possessions, position, or reputation? God has not placed you in your present position for your own benefit. He put you there *to serve him.* As in Esther's case, this may involve risking your security. Are you willing to let God be your ultimate security?

Strengths and accomplishments:
- Her beauty and character won the heart of Persia's king
- She combined courage with careful planning
- She was open to advice and willing to act
- She was more concerned for others than for her own security

Lessons from her life:
- Serving God often demands that we risk our own security
- God has a purpose for the situations in which he places us
- Courage, while often vital, does not replace careful planning

Vital statistics:
- Where: Persian empire
- Occupation: Xerxes' wife, queen of Persia
- Relatives: Cousin: Mordecai. Husband: Xerxes. Father: Abihail

Key verse:
"Go, gather together all the Jews who are in Susa, and fast for me. Do not eat or drink for three days, night or day. I and my maids will fast as you do. When this is done, I will go to the king, even though it is against the law. And if I perish, I perish" (Esther 4:16).

Esther's story is told in the book of Esther.

6:10–13 Mordecai had exposed a plot to assassinate Xerxes—thus he had saved the king's life (2:21–23). Although his good deed was recorded in the history books, Mordecai had gone unrewarded. But God was saving Mordecai's reward for the right time. Just as Haman was about to hang Mordecai unjustly, the king was ready to give the reward. Although God promises to reward our good deeds, we sometimes feel our "payoff" is too far away. Be patient. God steps in when it will do the most good.

his head covered,[h] in grief, 13and told Zeresh[i] his wife and all his friends everything
that had happened to him.
His advisers and his wife Zeresh said to him, "Since Mordecai, before whom your
downfall[j] has started, is of Jewish origin, you cannot stand against him—you will
surely come to ruin!" 14While they were still talking with him, the king's eunuchs
arrived and hurried Haman away to the banquet[k] Esther had prepared.

Haman Hanged

7 So the king and Haman went to dine[a] with Queen Esther, 2and as they were
drinking wine[b] on that second day, the king again asked, "Queen Esther, what
is your petition? It will be given you. What is your request? Even up to half the
kingdom,[c] it will be granted.[d]"
3Then Queen Esther answered, "If I have found favour[e] with you, O king, and
if it pleases your majesty, grant me my life—this is my petition. And spare my
people—this is my request. 4For I and my people have been sold for destruction and
slaughter and annihilation.[f] If we had merely been sold as male and female slaves,
I would have kept quiet, because no such distress would justify disturbing the king."**a**
5King Xerxes asked Queen Esther, "Who is he? Where is the man who has dared
to do such a thing?"
6Esther said, "The adversary and enemy is this vile Haman."
Then Haman was terrified before the king and queen. 7The king got up in a rage,[g]
left his wine and went out into the palace garden.[h] But Haman, realising that the king
had already decided his fate,[i] stayed behind to beg Queen Esther for his life.
8Just as the king returned from the palace garden to the banquet hall, Haman was
falling on the couch[j] where Esther was reclining.[k]
The king exclaimed, "Will he even molest the queen while she is with me in the
house?"[l]
As soon as the word left the king's mouth, they covered Haman's face.[m] 9Then
Harbona,[n] one of the eunuchs attending the king, said, "A gallows seventy-five feet**b**
high[o] stands by Haman's house. He had it made for Mordecai, who spoke up to help
the king."
The king said, "Hang him on it!"[p] 10So they hanged Haman[q] on the gallows[r]
he had prepared for Mordecai.[s] Then the king's fury subsided.[t]

The King's Edict in Behalf of the Jews

8 That same day King Xerxes gave Queen Esther the estate of Haman,[a] the enemy
of the Jews. And Mordecai came into the presence of the king, for Esther had
told how he was related to her. 2The king took off his signet ring,[b] which he had
reclaimed from Haman, and presented it to Mordecai. And Esther appointed him over
Haman's estate.[c]
3Esther again pleaded with the king, falling at his feet and weeping. She begged
him to put an end to the evil plan of Haman the Agagite, which he had devised against
the Jews. 4Then the king extended the gold sceptre[d] to Esther and she arose and stood
before him.
5"If it pleases the king," she said, "and if he regards me with favour and thinks it
the right thing to do, and if he is pleased with me, let an order be written overruling
the dispatches that Haman son of Hammedatha, the Agagite, devised and wrote to

6:12 [h]2Sa 15:30; Jer 14:3, 4; Mic 3:7
6:13 [i]Est 5:10 [j]Ps 57:6; Pr 26:27; 28:18
6:14 [k]1Ki 3:15; Est 5:8
7:1 [a]Ge 40:20-22; Mt 22:1-14
7:2 [b]Est 1:10 [c]Est 5:3 [d]Est 9:12
7:3 [e]Est 2:15
7:4 [f]Est 3:9
7:7 [g]Ge 34:7; Est 1:12; Pr 19:12; 20:1-2 [h]2Ki 21:18 [i]Est 6:13
7:8 [j]Est 1:6 [k]Ge 39:14 [l]Ge 34:7 [m]Est 6:12
7:9 [n]Est 1:10 [o]Est 5:14 [p]Ps 7:14-16; 9:16; Pr 11:5-6; 26:27; Mt 7:2
7:10 [q]Pr 10:28 [r]Est 9:25 [s]Da 6:24 [t]Est 2:1
8:1 [a]Est 2:7; 7:6; Pr 22:22-23
8:2 [b]Ge 41:42; Est 3:10 [c]Pr 13:22; Da 2:48
8:4 [d]Est 4:11; 5:2

a *4* Or *quiet, but the compensation our adversary offers cannot be compared with the loss the king would suffer*
b *9* Hebrew *fifty cubits* (about 23 metres)

7:6–10 Haman's hatred and evil plotting turned against him when the king discovered his true intentions. He was hanged on the gallows he had built for someone else. Proverbs 26:27 teaches that a person who digs a pit for others will fall into it himself. What happened to Haman shows the often violent results of setting any kind of trap for others.

7:8 "They covered Haman's face". A veil was placed over the face of someone condemned to death because Persian kings refused to look upon the face of a condemned person.

8:1–7 While we should not expect earthly rewards for being faithful to God, they often come. Esther and Mordecai were faithful, even to the point of risking their lives to save others. When they were willing to give up everything, God gave them a reward in proportion to their all-out commitment.

8:6
e Est 7:4; 9:1

8:8
f Est 3:12-14
g Ge 41:42
h Est 1:19; Da 6:15

8:9
i Est 1:1

destroy the Jews in all the king's provinces. 6For how can I bear to see disaster fall
on my people? How can I bear to see the destruction of my family?"[e]
7King Xerxes replied to Queen Esther and to Mordecai the Jew, "Because Haman
attacked the Jews, I have given his estate to Esther, and they have hanged him on the
gallows. 8Now write another decree[f] in the king's name on behalf of the Jews as
seems best to you, and seal it with the king's signet ring[g] — for no document written
in the king's name and sealed with his ring can be revoked."[h]
9At once the royal secretaries were summoned — on the twenty-third day of the third
month, the month of Sivan. They wrote out all Mordecai's orders to the Jews, and
to the satraps, governors and nobles of the 127 provinces stretching from India to
Cush.[a][i] These orders were written in the script of each province and the language

a 9 That is, the upper Nile region

HAMAN

The most arrogant people are often those who must measure their self-worth by the power or influence they think they have over others. Haman was an extremely arrogant leader. He recognised the king as his superior, but could not accept anyone as an equal. When one man, Mordecai, refused to bow in submission to him, Haman wanted to destroy him. He became consumed with hatred for Mordecai. He was already filled with racial hatred for all the Jewish people because of the long-standing hatred between the Jews and Haman's ancestors, the Amalekites. Mordecai's dedication to God and his refusal to give homage to any human person challenged Haman's self-centred religion. Haman saw the Jews as a threat to his power, and he decided to kill them all.

God was preparing Haman's downfall and the protection of his people long before Haman came to power under Xerxes. Esther, a Jew, became queen, and Mordecai's role in exposing an assassination plot indebted the king to him. Not only was Haman prevented from killing Mordecai, he also had to suffer the humiliation of publicly honouring him. Within hours, Haman died on the gallows he had built to hang Mordecai, and his plan to wipe out the Jews was thwarted. In contrast to Esther, who risked everything for God and won, Haman risked everything for an evil purpose and lost.

Our initial response to the story about Haman is to say that he got what he deserved. But the Bible leads us to ask deeper questions: "How much of Haman is in me?" "Do I desire to control others?" "Am I threatened when others don't appreciate me as I think they should?" "Do I want revenge when my pride is attacked?" Confess these attitudes to God, and ask him to replace them with an attitude of forgiveness. Otherwise, God's justice will settle the matter.

Strength and accomplishment:
- Achieved great power, second in rank to Persia's King Xerxes

Weaknesses and mistakes:
- The desire to control others and receive honour was his highest goal
- Was blinded by arrogance and self-importance
- Planned to murder Mordecai and built a gallows for him
- Orchestrated the plan to slaughter God's people throughout the empire

Lessons from his life:
- Hatred will be punished
- God has an amazing record for making evil plans backfire on the planners
- Pride and self-importance will be punished
- An insatiable thirst for power and prestige is self-destructive

Vital statistics:
- Where: Susa, the capital of Persia
- Occupation: Second in rank in the empire
- Relative: Wife: Zeresh
- Contemporaries: Xerxes, Mordecai, Esther

Key verses:
"When Haman saw that Mordecai would not kneel down or pay him honour he was enraged. Yet having learned who Mordecai's people were, he scorned the idea of killing only Mordecai. Instead Haman looked for a way to destroy all Mordecai's people, the Jews, throughout the whole kingdom of Xerxes" (Esther 3:5, 6).

Haman's story is told in the book of Esther.

8:8 Haman's message had been sealed with the king's signet ring and could not be reversed, even by the king. It was part of the famed "law of the Medes and Persians". Now the king gave permission for whatever other decree Mordecai could devise that would offset the first, without actually cancelling it.

of each people and also to the Jews in their own script and language.[j] 10Mordecai
wrote in the name of King Xerxes, sealed the dispatches with the king's signet ring,
and sent them by mounted couriers, who rode fast horses especially bred for the king.
11The king's edict granted the Jews in every city the right to assemble and protect
themselves; to destroy, kill and annihilate any armed force of any nationality or
province that might attack them and their women and children; and to plunder[k] the
property of their enemies. 12The day appointed for the Jews to do this in all the
provinces of King Xerxes was the thirteenth day of the twelfth month, the month of
Adar.[l] 13A copy of the text of the edict was to be issued as law in every province
and made known to the people of every nationality so that the Jews would be ready
on that day[m] to avenge themselves on their enemies.
14The couriers, riding the royal horses, raced out, spurred on by the king's command. And the edict was also issued in the citadel of Susa.
15Mordecai[n] left the king's presence wearing royal garments of blue and white,
a large crown of gold and a purple robe of fine linen.[o] And the city of Susa held a
joyous celebration.[p] 16For the Jews it was a time of happiness and joy,[q] gladness
and honour.[r] 17In every province and in every city, wherever the edict of the king
went, there was joy[s] and gladness among the Jews, with feasting and celebrating.
And many people of other nationalities became Jews because fear[t] of the Jews had
seized them.[u]

4. The Jews are delivered

Triumph of the Jews

9 On the thirteenth day of the twelfth month, the month of Adar,[a] the edict
commanded by the king was to be carried out. On this day the enemies of the
Jews had hoped to overpower them, but now the tables were turned and the Jews got
the upper hand[b] over those who hated them.[c] 2The Jews assembled in their cities[d]
in all the provinces of King Xerxes to attack those seeking their destruction. No-one
could stand against them,[e] because the people of all the other nationalities were afraid
of them. 3And all the nobles of the provinces, the satraps, the governors and the king's
administrators helped the Jews,[f] because fear of Mordecai had seized them. 4Morde-
cai was prominent[g] in the palace; his reputation spread throughout the provinces, and
he became more and more powerful.[h]
5The Jews struck down all their enemies with the sword, killing and destroying
them,[i] and they did what they pleased to those who hated them. 6In the citadel of
Susa, the Jews killed and destroyed five hundred men. 7They also killed Parshandatha,
Dalphon, Aspatha, 8Poratha, Adalia, Aridatha, 9Parmashta, Arisai, Aridai and Vaiza-
tha, 10the ten sons[j] of Haman son of Hammedatha, the enemy of the Jews. But they
did not lay their hands on the plunder.[k]
11The number of those slain in the citadel of Susa was reported to the king that same
day. 12The king said to Queen Esther, "The Jews have killed and destroyed five
hundred men and the ten sons of Haman in the citadel of Susa. What have they done
in the rest of the king's provinces? Now what is your petition? It will be given you.
What is your request? It will also be granted."[l]
13"If it pleases the king," Esther answered, "give the Jews in Susa permission to

8:9 [j]Est 1:22
8:11 [k]Est 9:10, 15, 16
8:12 [l]Est 3:13; 9:1
8:13 [m]Est 3:14
8:15 [n]Est 9:4 [o]Ge 41:42 [p]Est 3:15
8:16 [q]Ps 97:10-12 [r]Ps 112:4
8:17 [s]Est 9:19, 27; Ps 35:27; Pr 11:10 [t]Ex 15:14, 16; Dt 11:25 [u]Est 9:3
9:1 [a]Est 8:12 [b]Jer 29:4-7 [c]Est 3:12-14; Pr 22:22-23
9:2 [d]ver 15-18 [e]Est 8:11, 17; Ps 71:13, 24
9:3 [f]Ezr 8:36
9:4 [g]Ex 11:3 [h]2Sa 3:1; 1Ch 11:9
9:5 [i]Ezr 4:6
9:10 [j]Est 5:11 [k]Ge 14:23; 1Sa 14:32; Est 3:13; 8:11
9:12 [l]Est 5:6; 7:2

8:12 This was the day set by Haman for the extermination of the Jews.

8:15–17 Everyone wants to be a hero and receive praise, honour, and wealth. But few are willing to pay the price. Mordecai served the government faithfully for years, bore Haman's hatred and oppression, and risked his life for his people. The price to be paid by God's heroes is long-term commitment. Are you ready and willing to pay the price?

9:5–16 Haman had decreed that on the 13th day of the 12th month anyone could kill the Jews and take their property. Mordecai's decree could not reverse Haman's because no law signed by the king could be repealed. Instead, Mordecai had the king sign a new law giving Jews the right to fight back. When the dreaded day arrived, there was much fighting, but the Jews killed only those who wanted to kill them, and they did not take their enemies' possessions, even though they could have (8:11; 9:10, 16). There were no additional riots after the two-day slaughter, so obviously selfish gain or revenge were not primary motives of the Jews. They simply wanted to defend themselves and their families from those who hated them.

9:11 Here the word "citadel" seems to refer to the fortified city of Susa. The king appears to be more concerned about Esther's wishes than the slaughter of his subjects.

9:13
m Est 5:11
n Dt 21:22-23

carry out this day's edict tomorrow also, and let Haman's ten sons*m* be hanged*n* on gallows."

¹⁴So the king commanded that this be done. An edict was issued in Susa, and they hanged*o* the ten sons of Haman. ¹⁵The Jews in Susa came together on the fourteenth day of the month of Adar, and they put to death in Susa three hundred men, but they did not lay their hands on the plunder.*p*

9:14
o Ezr 6:11

9:15
p Ge 14:23;
Est 8:11

¹⁶Meanwhile, the remainder of the Jews who were in the king's provinces also assembled to protect themselves and get relief*q* from their enemies.*r* They killed seventy-five thousand of them*s* but did not lay their hands on the plunder. ¹⁷This happened on the thirteenth day of the month of Adar, and on the fourteenth they rested and made it a day of feasting*t* and joy.

9:16
q Est 4:14
r Dt 25:19
s 1Ch 4:43

Purim Celebrated

9:17
t 1Ki 3:15

¹⁸The Jews in Susa, however, had assembled on the thirteenth and fourteenth, and then on the fifteenth they rested and made it a day of feasting and joy.

HOW GOD WORKS IN THE WORLD	*God's will*	*What God wants done—he works through . . .*		
		➡*Natural order*	➡*Miracles*	➡*Providence*
	God's action	➡God set into action through creation a normal working of his universe. He also revealed his expectations of man through his word and man's conscience.	➡God breaks into the natural order to respond to the expressed needs of people.	➡God overrules the natural order to accomplish an act that people may or may not have requested.
	Examples from Esther	➡God gave Esther natural beauty.	➡God allowed Esther to speak to the king.	➡God allowed Mordecai to overhear a plot.
		▲Esther planned a way to save her people.	▲The people prayed and fasted.	▲ Mordecai trusted God to accomplish what was impossible in human terms.
	Man's will	*What man wants done—he either . . .*		
		▲*Plans*	▲*Prays*	▲*Trusts & Obeys*
	Action we can take	▲Can make plans based on the order and dependability of God's creation. Know and obey his words.	▲Can ask God to intervene in certain affairs while realising that our knowledge and perspective are limited.	▲Can trust that God is in control even when the circumstances may not seem to indicate that he is.
		or . . .		
	Mistakes we can make	➡*Disobeys*	➡*Demands*	➡*Despairs*
		➡Can violate the natural order, disobey God's commands.	➡Can assume that we understand what is needed and expect God to agree and answer our prayers that way.	➡Can assume God doesn't answer prayer or respond to our needs and live as though there is nothing but the natural order.

[19]That is why rural Jews—those living in villages—observe the fourteenth of the
month of Adar[u] as a day of joy and feasting, a day for giving presents to each other.[v]
[20]Mordecai recorded these events, and he sent letters to all the Jews throughout the
provinces of King Xerxes, near and far, [21]to have them celebrate annually the
fourteenth and fifteenth days of the month of Adar [22]as the time when the Jews got
relief[w] from their enemies, and as the month when their sorrow was turned into joy
and their mourning into a day of celebration.[x] He wrote to them to observe the days
as days of feasting and joy and giving presents of food[y] to one another and gifts to
the poor.
[23]So the Jews agreed to continue the celebration they had begun, doing what
Mordecai had written to them. [24]For Haman son of Hammedatha, the Agagite,[z] the
enemy of all the Jews, had plotted against the Jews to destroy them and had cast the
pur[a] (that is, the lot[b]) for their ruin and destruction. [25]But when the plot came to
the king's attention,**[a]** he issued written orders that the evil scheme Haman had devised
against the Jews should come back on to his own head,[c] and that he and his sons
should be hanged[d] on the gallows.[e] [26](Therefore these days were called Purim, from
the word *pur*.[f]) Because of everything written in this letter and because of what they
had seen and what had happened to them, [27]the Jews took it upon themselves to
establish the custom that they and their descendants and all who join them should
without fail observe these two days every year, in the way prescribed and at the time
appointed. [28]These days should be remembered and observed in every generation by
every family, and in every province and in every city. And these days of Purim should
never cease to be celebrated by the Jews, nor should the memory of them die out
among their descendants.
[29]So Queen Esther, daughter of Abihail,[g] along with Mordecai the Jew, wrote with
full authority to confirm this second letter concerning Purim. [30]And Mordecai sent
letters to all the Jews in the 127 provinces[h] of the kingdom of Xerxes—words of
goodwill and assurance—[31]to establish these days of Purim at their designated times,
as Mordecai the Jew and Queen Esther had decreed for them, and as they had
established for themselves and their descendants in regard to their times of fasting[i]
and lamentation.[j] [32]Esther's decree confirmed these regulations about Purim, and it
was written down in the records.

The Greatness of Mordecai

10 King Xerxes imposed tribute throughout the empire, to its distant shores.[a]
[2]And all his acts of power and might, together with a full account of the
greatness of Mordecai[b] to which the king had raised him,[c] are they not written in

9:19 [u]Est 3:7 [v]ver 22; Dt 16:11, 14; Ne 8:10, 12; Est 2:9; Rev 11:10
9:22 [w]Est 4:14 [x]Ne 8:12; Ps 30:11-12 [y]2Ki 25:30
9:24 [z]Ex 17:8-16 [a]Est 3:7 [b]Lev 16:8
9:25 [c]Ps 7:16 [d]Dt 21:22-23 [e]Est 7:10
9:26 [f]ver 20; Est 3:7
9:29 [g]Est 2:15
9:30 [h]Est 1:1
9:31 [i]Est 4:16 [j]Est 4:1-3
10:1 [a]Ps 72:10; 97:1; Isa 24:15
10:2 [b]Est 8:15; 9:4 [c]Ge 41:44

a *25* *Or when Esther came before the king*

9:19–22 People tend to have short memories when it comes to God's faithfulness. To help counter this, Mordecai wrote down these events and encouraged an annual holiday to commemorate the historic days of Purim. Jews still celebrate Purim today. Celebrations of feasting, gladness, and gift-giving are important ways to remember God's specific acts. Today the festivities of Christmas and Easter help us remember the birth and resurrection of Jesus Christ. Don't let the celebration or the exchanging of gifts hide the meaning of these great events.

9:29–31 Among Jews, women were expected to be quiet, to serve in the home, and to stay on the fringe of religious and political life. But Esther was a Jewish woman who broke through the cultural norms, stepping outside her expected role to risk her life to help God's people. Whatever your place in life, God can use you. Be open, available, and ready because God may use you to do what others are afraid even to consider.

10:3 Mordecai enjoyed a good reputation among the Jews because he was still their friend when he rose to a place of power. Corruption and abuse of authority often characterise those in power. But power used to lift the fallen and ease the burden of the oppressed is power used well. People placed by God in positions of power or political influence must not turn their backs on those in need.

10:3 No archaeological records of Mordecai's being second-in-command have been discovered, but during this time there is a strange gap in ancient Persian records. The records indicate that another man held that position in 465 B.C., about seven years after Mordecai was first appointed. One tablet has been discovered naming Mardukaya as an official in the early years of Xerxes' reign; some believe this was Mordecai.

10:3 In the book of Esther, we clearly see God at work in the lives of individuals and in the affairs of a nation. Even when it looks as if the world is in the hands of evil people, God is still in control, protecting those who are his. Although we may not understand everything happening around us, we must trust in God's protection and retain our integrity by doing what we know is right. Esther, who

10:2
[d]Est 2:23
10:3
[e]Da 5:7
[f]Ge 41:43
[g]Ge 41:40
[h]Ne 2:10

the book of the annals[d] of the kings of Media and Persia?
3 Mordecai the Jew was second[e] in rank[f] to King Xerxes,[g] pre-eminent among the Jews, and held in high esteem by his many fellow Jews, because he worked for the good of his people and spoke up for the welfare of all the Jews.[h]

risked her life appearing before the king, became a hero. Mordecai, who was effectively condemned to death, rose to become the second highest ranking official in the nation. No matter how hopeless our condition, or how much we would like to give up, we need not despair. God is in control of our world.

JOB

VITAL STATISTICS

PURPOSE:
To demonstrate God's sovereignty and the meaning of true faith. It addresses the question, "Why do the righteous suffer?"

AUTHOR:
Unknown, possibly Job. Some have suggested Moses, Solomon, or Elihu.

DATE WRITTEN:
Unknown. Records events that probably occurred during the time of the patriarchs, approximately 2000–1800 B.C.

SETTING:
The land of Uz, probably located northeast of Palestine, near desert land between Damascus and the Euphrates River.

KEY VERSE:
"Then the LORD said to Satan, 'Have you considered my servant Job? There is no-one on earth like him; he is blameless and upright, a man who fears God and shuns evil. And he still maintains his integrity, though you incited me against him to ruin him without any reason' " (2:3).

KEY PEOPLE:
Job, Eliphaz the Temanite, Bildad the Shuhite, Zophar the Naamathite, Elihu the Buzite

SPECIAL FEATURES:
Job is the first of the poetic books in the Hebrew Bible. Some believe this was the first book of the Bible to be written. The book gives us insights into the work of Satan. Ezekiel 14:14, 20 and James 5:11 mention Job as a historical character.

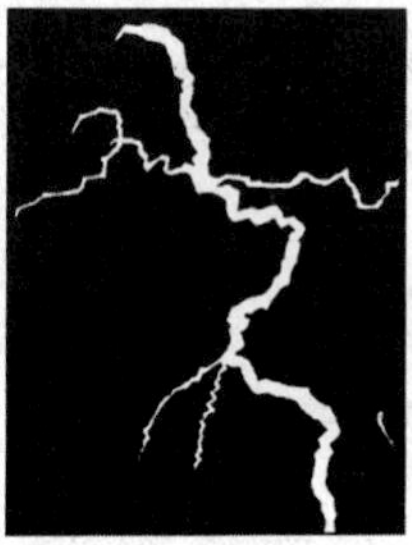

TREES snap like toothpicks or fly upwards, wrenched from the earth. Whole rooftops sail, cars tumble like toys, walls collapse, and a mountain of water crosses the shore and engulfs the land. A hurricane cuts and tears, and only solid foundations survive her unbridled fury. But those foundations can be used for rebuilding after the storm.

For any building, the foundations are critical. They must be deep enough and solid enough to withstand the weight of the building and other stresses. Lives are like buildings, and the quality of their foundations will determine the quality of the whole. Too often inferior materials are used, and when tests come, lives crumble.

Job was tested. With a life filled with prestige, possessions, and people, he was suddenly assaulted on every side, devastated, stripped down to his foundations. But his life was built on God, and he endured.

Job, the book, tells the story of Job, the man of God. It is a gripping drama of riches-to-rags-to-riches, a theological treatise about suffering and divine sovereignty, and a picture of faith that endures. As you read Job, analyse your life and check your foundations. And may you be able to say that when all is gone but God, he is enough.

Job was a prosperous farmer living in the land of Uz. He had thousands of sheep, camels, and other livestock, a large family, and many servants. Suddenly Satan, the accuser, came before God claiming that Job was trusting God only because he was wealthy and everything was going well for him. And so the testing of Job's faith began.

Satan was allowed to destroy Job's children, servants, livestock, herdsmen, and home; but Job continued to trust in God. Next Satan attacked Job physically, covering him with painful sores. Job's wife told him to curse God and die (2:9), but Job suffered in silence.

Three of Job's friends, Eliphaz, Bildad, and Zophar, came to visit him. At first they silently grieved with Job. But when they began to talk about the reasons for Job's tragedies, they told him that sin had caused his suffering. They told him to confess his sins and turn back to God. But Job maintained his innocence.

Unable to convince Job of his sin, the three men fell silent (32:1). At this point, another voice—the young Elihu—entered the debate. Although his argument also failed to convince Job, it prepared the way for God to speak.

Finally, God spoke out of a mighty storm. Confronted with the great power and majesty of God, Job fell in humble reverence before God—speechless. God rebuked Job's friends, and the drama ended with Job restored to happiness and wealth.

It is easy to think that we have all the answers. In reality, only God knows exactly why things happen as they do, and we must submit to him as our Sovereign. As you read this book, emulate Job and decide to trust God no matter what happens.

THE BLUEPRINT

A. JOB IS TESTED (1:1—2:13)	Job, a wealthy and upright man, lost his possessions, his children, and his health. Job did not understand why he was suffering. Why does God allow his children to suffer? Although there is an explanation, we may not know it while we are here on earth. In the meantime, we must always be ready for testing in our lives.
B. THREE FRIENDS ANSWER JOB (3:1—31:40) 1. First round of discussion 2. Second round of discussion 3. Third round of discussion	Job's friends wrongly assumed that suffering always came as a result of sin. With this in mind, they tried to persuade Job to repent of his sin. But the three friends were wrong. Suffering is not always a direct result of personal sin. When we experience severe suffering, it may not be our fault, so we don't have to add to our pain by feeling guilty that some hidden sin is causing our trouble.
C. A YOUNG MAN ANSWERS JOB (32:1—37:24)	A young man named Elihu, who had been listening to the entire conversation, criticised the three friends for being unable to answer Job. He said that although Job was a good man, he had allowed himself to become proud, and God was punishing him in order to humble him. This answer was partially true because suffering does purify our faith. But God is beyond our comprehension and we cannot know why he allows each instance of suffering to come into our lives. Our part is simply to remain faithful.
D. GOD ANSWERS JOB (38:1—41:34)	God himself finally answered Job. God is in control of the world and only he understands why the good are allowed to suffer. This only becomes clear to us when we see God for who he is. We must courageously accept what God allows to happen in our lives and remain firmly committed to him.
E. JOB IS RESTORED (42:1–17)	Job finally learned that when nothing else was left, he had God, and that was enough. Through suffering, we learn that God is enough for our lives and our future. We must love God regardless of whether he allows blessing or suffering to come to us. Testing is difficult, but the result is often a deeper relationship with God. Those who endure the testing of their faith will experience God's great rewards in the end.

MEGATHEMES

THEME	EXPLANATION	IMPORTANCE
Suffering	Through no fault of his own, Job lost his wealth, children, and health. Even his friends were convinced that Job had brought this suffering upon himself. For Job, the greatest trial was not the pain or the loss; it was not being able to understand why God allowed him to suffer.	Suffering can be, but is not always, a penalty for sin. In the same way, prosperity is not always a reward for being good. Those who love God are not exempt from trouble. Although we may not be able to understand fully the pain we experience, it can lead us to rediscover God.
Satan's Attacks	Satan attempted to drive a wedge between Job and God by getting Job to believe that God's governing of the world was not just and good. Satan had to ask God for permission to take Job's wealth, children, and health away. Satan was limited to what God allowed.	We must learn to recognise and not fear Satan's attacks because Satan cannot exceed the limits that God sets. Don't let any experience drive a wedge between you and God. Although you can't control how Satan may attack, you can always choose how you will respond when it happens.

God's Goodness	God is all-wise and all-powerful. His will is perfect, yet he doesn't always act in ways that we understand. Job's suffering didn't make sense because everyone believed good people were supposed to prosper. When Job was at the point of despair, God spoke to him, showing him his great power and wisdom.	Although God is present everywhere, at times he may seem far away. This may cause us to feel alone and to doubt his care for us. We should serve God for who he is, not what we feel. He is never insensitive to our suffering. Because God is sufficient, we must hold on to him.
Pride	Job's friends were certain that they were correct in their judgment of him. God rebuked them for their pride and arrogance. Man's wisdom is always partial and temporary, so undue pride in our own conclusions is sin.	We must be careful not to judge others who are suffering. We may be demonstrating the sin of pride. We must be cautious in maintaining the certainty of our own conclusions about how God treats us. When we congratulate ourselves for being right, we become proud.
Trusting	God alone knew the purpose behind Job's suffering, and yet he never explained it to Job. In spite of this, Job never gave up on God—even in the midst of suffering. He never placed his hope in his experience, his wisdom, his friends, or his wealth. Job focused on God.	Job showed the kind of trust we are to have. When everything is stripped away, we are to recognise that God is all we ever really had. We should not demand that God explain everything. God gives us himself, but not all the details of his plans. We must remember that this life, with all its pain, is not our final destiny.

A. JOB IS TESTED (1:1–2:13)

Job is portrayed as a wealthy man of upright character who loves God. Yet God allows Satan to destroy his flocks, his possessions, his children, and his health. Job refuses to give up on God, even though he does not understand why this is happening to him. We, too, must trust God when we do not understand the difficulties we face.

Prologue

1 In the land of Uz[a] there lived a man whose name was Job.[b] This man was
blameless[c] and upright; he feared God[d] and shunned evil. 2 He had seven sons
and three daughters,[e] 3 and he owned seven thousand sheep, three thousand camels,
five hundred yoke of oxen and five hundred donkeys, and had a large number of
servants. He was the greatest man[f] among all the people of the East.
4 His sons used to take turns holding feasts in their homes, and they would invite
their three sisters to eat and drink with them. 5 When a period of feasting had run its

1:1 [a] Jer 25:20 [b] Eze 14:14, 20; Jas 5:11 [c] Ge 6:9; 17:1 [d] Ge 22:12; Ex 18:21
1:2 [e] Job 42:13
1:3 [f] Job 29:25

1:1 As we read the book of Job, we have information that the characters of the story do not. Job, the main character of the book, lost all he had through no fault of his own. As he struggled to understand why all this was happening to him, it became clear that he was not meant to know the reasons. He would have to face life with the answers and explanations held back. Only then would his faith fully develop.

We must experience life as Job did—one day at a time and without complete answers to all of life's questions. Will we, like Job, trust God no matter what? Or will we give in to the temptation to say that God doesn't really care?

1:1 The location of the land of Uz is uncertain. We only know that Uz had plentiful pastures and crops (1:3), was located near a desert (1:19), and was close enough to the Sabeans and Chaldeans to be raided (1:14–17). Uz is also mentioned in Jeremiah 25:19, 20. Most scholars believe Uz was located east of the Jordan River near Canaan (Israel), where the Jews (those to whom God first revealed himself) lived. Job probably knew about God because he knew God's people.

1:1ff As we see calamity and suffering in the book of Job, we must remember that we live in a fallen world where good behaviour is not always rewarded and bad behaviour is not always punished. When we see a notorious criminal prospering or an innocent child in pain, we say, "That's wrong." And it is. Sin has twisted justice and made our world unpredictable and ugly.

The book of Job shows a good man suffering for no apparent fault of his own. Sadly, our world is like that. But Job's story does not end in despair. Through Job's life we can see that faith in God is justified even when our situations look hopeless. Faith based on rewards or prosperity is hollow. To be unshakable, faith must be built on the confidence that God's ultimate purpose will come to pass.

1:5 It is not known for sure, but Job probably lived during the days of the patriarchs (Abraham, Isaac, Jacob) before God gave his written law or appointed priests to be religious leaders. During Job's day, the father was the family's religious leader. Because there were no priests to instruct him in God's laws, Job acted as the priest and offered sacrifices to God to ask for forgiveness for sins he and his family had committed. This demonstrated that Job did not consider himself sinless. Job did this out of conviction and love for God, not just because it was his role as head of the house. Do you carry out your spiritual duties because they are expected, or spontaneously from a heart of devotion?

1:5 Job showed deep concern for the spiritual welfare of his children. Fearful that they might have sinned unknowingly, he offered sacrifices for them. Parents today can show the same concern by praying for their children. This means "sacrificing" some time each

course, Job would send and have them purified. Early in the morning he would
sacrifice a burnt offering[g] for each of them, thinking, "Perhaps my children have
sinned[h] and cursed God[i] in their hearts." This was Job's regular custom.

Job's First Test

6One day the angels[a][j] came to present themselves before the LORD, and Satan[b]
also came with them.[k] 7The LORD said to Satan, "Where have you come from?"
Satan answered the LORD, "From roaming through the earth and going to and fro
in it."[l]
8Then the LORD said to Satan, "Have you considered my servant Job?[m] There is
no-one on earth like him; he is blameless and upright, a man who fears God and shuns
evil."[n]
9"Does Job fear God for nothing?"[o] Satan replied. 10"Have you not put a hedge
around him and his household and everything he has?[p] You have blessed the work
of his hands, so that his flocks and herds are spread throughout the land.[q] 11But
stretch out your hand and strike everything he has,[r] and he will surely curse you to
your face."[s]
12The LORD said to Satan, "Very well, then, everything he has is in your hands,
but on the man himself do not lay a finger."
Then Satan went out from the presence of the LORD.
13One day when Job's sons and daughters were feasting and drinking wine at the
oldest brother's house, 14a messenger came to Job and said, "The oxen were ploughing
and the donkeys were grazing nearby, 15and the Sabeans[t] attacked and carried them
off. They put the servants to the sword, and I am the only one who has escaped to
tell you!"

1:5 [g]Ge 8:20; Job 42:8 [h]Job 8:4 [i]1Ki 21:10, 13
1:6 [j]Job 38:7 [k]Job 2:1
1:7 [l]1Pe 5:8
1:8 [m]Jos 1:7; Job 42:7-8 [n]ver 1
1:9 [o]1Ti 6:5
1:10 [p]Ps 34:7 [q]ver 3; Job 29:6; 31:25; Ps 128:1-2
1:11 [r]Job 19:21 [s]Job 2:5
1:15 [t]Ge 10:7; Job 6:19

[a] *6* Hebrew *the sons of God* [b] *6* *Satan* means *accuser.*

day to ask God to forgive them, to help them grow, to protect them, and to help them please him.

1:6 The Bible speaks of other heavenly councils where God and the angels plan their activities on earth and where angels are required to give account of themselves (i.e., 1 Kings 22:19–23). Because God is Creator of all angels – both of those who serve him and of those who rebelled – he has complete power and authority over them.

1:6, 7 Satan, originally an angel of God, became corrupt through his own pride. He has been evil since his rebellion against God (1 John 3:8). Satan considers God as his enemy. He tries to hinder God's work in people, but he is limited by God's power and can do only what he is permitted (Luke 22:31, 32; 1 Timothy 1:19, 20; 2 Timothy 2:23–26). Satan is called the enemy because he actively looks for people to attack with temptation (1 Peter 5:8, 9) and because he wants to make people hate God. He does this through lies and deception (Genesis 3:1–6). Job, a blameless and upright man who had been greatly blessed, was a perfect target for Satan. Any person who is committed to God should expect Satan's attacks. Satan, who hates God, also hates God's people.

1:6–12 From this conversation, we learn a great deal about Satan. (1) He is accountable to God. All angelic beings, good and evil, are compelled to present themselves before God (1:6). God knew that Satan was intent on attacking Job. (2) Satan can be at only one place at a time (1:6, 7). His demons aid him in his work; but as a created being, he is limited. (3) Satan cannot see into our minds or foretell the future (1:9–11). If he could, he would have known that Job would not break under pressure. (4) Because Satan can do nothing without God's permission (1:12), God's people can overcome his attacks through God's power. (5) God puts limitations on what Satan can do (1:12; 2:6). Satan's response to the Lord's question (1:7) tells us that Satan is real and active on earth. Knowing this about Satan should cause us to remain close to the One who is greater than Satan – God himself.

1:7ff Some people suggest that this dialogue was made up by the author of this book. Could this conversation between God and Satan really have happened? Other Bible passages tell us that Satan does indeed have access to God (see Revelation 12:10). He even went into God's presence to make accusations against Joshua the high priest (Zechariah 3:1, 2). If this conversation didn't take place, then the reasons for Job's suffering become meaningless and the book of Job is reduced to fiction rather than fact.

1:8, 12 Job was a model of trust and obedience to God, yet God permitted Satan to attack him in an especially harsh manner. Although God loves us, believing and obeying him do not shelter us from life's calamities. Setbacks, tragedies, and sorrows strike Christians and non-Christians alike. But in our tests and trials, God expects us to express our faith to the world. How do you respond to your troubles? Do you ask God, "Why me?" or do you say, "Use me!"?

1:9 Satan attacked Job's motives, saying that Job was blameless and upright only because he had no reason to turn against God. Ever since he had started following God, everything had gone well for Job. Satan wanted to prove that Job worshipped God, not out of love, but because God had given him so much.

Satan accurately analysed why many people trust God. They are fair-weather believers, following God only when everything is going well or for what they can get. Adversity destroys this superficial faith. But adversity strengthens real faith by causing believers to dig their roots deeper into God in order to withstand the storms. How deep does your faith go? Put the roots of your faith down deep into God so that you can withstand any storm you may face.

1:12 This conversation between God and Satan teaches us an important fact about God – he is fully aware of every attempt by Satan to bring suffering and difficulty upon us. While God may allow us to suffer for a reason beyond our understanding, he is never caught by surprise by our troubles and is always compassionate.

1:15–17 The Sabeans were from southwest Arabia, while the Chaldeans were from the region north of the Persian Gulf.

16While he was still speaking, another messenger came and said, "The fire of God
fell from the sky[u] and burned up the sheep and the servants,[v] and I am the only one
who has escaped to tell you!"
17While he was still speaking, another messenger came and said, "The Chaldeans[w]
formed three raiding parties and swept down on your camels and carried them off.
They put the servants to the sword, and I am the only one who has escaped to tell
you!"
18While he was still speaking, yet another messenger came and said, "Your sons
and daughters were feasting and drinking wine at the oldest brother's house, 19when
suddenly a mighty wind[x] swept in from the desert and struck the four corners of the
house. It collapsed on them and they are dead, and I am the only one who has escaped
to tell you!"
20At this, Job got up and tore his robe[y] and shaved his head. Then he fell to the
ground in worship[z] 21and said:

"Naked I came from my mother's womb,
and naked I shall depart.[c][a]
The LORD gave and the LORD has taken away;[b]
may the name of the LORD be praised."[c]

22In all this, Job did not sin by charging God with wrongdoing.[d]

Job's Second Test

2 On another day the angels[a] came to present themselves before the LORD, and
Satan also came with them[a] to present himself before him. 2And the LORD said
to Satan, "Where have you come from?"
Satan answered the LORD, "From roaming through the earth and going to and fro
in it."
3Then the LORD said to Satan, "Have you considered my servant Job? There is
no-one on earth like him; he is blameless and upright, a man who fears God and shuns
evil.[b] And he still maintains his integrity,[c] though you incited me against him to
ruin him without any reason."[d]
4"Skin for skin!" Satan replied. "A man will give all he has for his own life. 5But
stretch out your hand and strike his flesh and bones,[e] and he will surely curse you
to your face."[f]
6The LORD said to Satan, "Very well, then, he is in your hands; but you must spare
his life."[g]
7So Satan went out from the presence of the LORD and afflicted Job with painful
sores from the soles of his feet to the top of his head.[h] 8Then Job took a piece of
broken pottery and scraped himself with it as he sat among the ashes.[i]
9His wife said to him, "Are you still holding on to your integrity? Curse God and
die!"

c 21 Or *shall return there* a 1 Hebrew *the sons of God*

1:16 [u]Ge 19:24 [v]Lev 10:2; Nu 11:1-3
1:17 [w]Ge 11:28, 31
1:19 [x]Jer 4:11; 13:24
1:20 [y]Ge 37:29 [z]1Pe 5:6
1:21 [a]Ecc 5:15; 1Ti 6:7 [b]1Sa 2:7 [c]Job 2:10; Eph 5:20; 1Th 5:18
1:22 [d]Job 2:10
2:1 [a]Job 1:6
2:3 [b]Job 1:1, 8 [c]Job 27:6 [d]Job 9:17
2:5 [e]Job 19:20 [f]Job 1:11
2:6 [g]Job 1:12
2:7 [h]Dt 28:35; Job 7:5
2:8 [i]Job 42:6; Jer 6:26; Eze 27:30; Mt 11:21

1:16 "The fire of God" was a poetic way to describe lightning (1 Kings 18:38; 2 Kings 1:10–14). In this case, it had to be unusually powerful to kill 7,000 sheep.

1:20–22 Job did not hide his overwhelming grief. He had not lost his faith in God; instead, his emotions showed that he was human and that he loved his family. God created our emotions, and it is not sinful or inappropriate to express them as Job did. If you have experienced a deep loss, a disappointment, or a heartbreak, admit your feelings to yourself and others, and grieve.

1:20–22 Job had lost his possessions and family in this first of Satan's tests, but he reacted rightly towards God by acknowledging God's sovereign authority over everything God had given him. Satan lost this first round. Job passed the test and proved that people can love God for who he is, not for what he gives.

2:3–6 Can Satan persuade God to change his plans? At first God said he did not want Job harmed physically, but then he decided to allow it. Satan is unable to persuade God to go against his character: God is completely and eternally good. But God was willing to go along with Satan's plan because God knew the eventual outcome of Job's story. God cannot be fooled by Satan. Job's suffering was a test for Job, Satan, and us—not God.

2:4, 5 "Skin for skin" was Satan's comment concerning Job's response to the loss of his family. Satan still held to his opinion that Job was faithful only because of God's blessings. Satan believed that Job was willing to accept the loss of family and property as long as his own skin was safe. Satan's next step was to inflict physical suffering upon Job to prove his original accusation (1:9).

2:6 Again Satan had to seek permission from God to inflict pain upon Job. God limits Satan, and in this case, he did not allow Satan to destroy Job.

2:9 Why was Job's wife spared when the rest of his family was killed? It is possible that her very presence caused Job even more

2:10
[j] Job 1:21
[k] Job 1:22;
Ps 39:1;
Jas 1:12; 5:11

2:11
[l] Ge 36:11;
Jer 49:7
[m] Ge 25:2
[n] Job 42:11;
Ro 12:15

2:12
[o] Jos 7:6;
Ne 9:1;
La 2:10;
Eze 27:30

2:13
[p] Ge 50:10;
Eze 3:15

10 He replied, "You are talking like a foolish[b] woman. Shall we accept good from
God, and not trouble?"[j]
In all this, Job did not sin in what he said.[k]

Job's Three Friends

11 When Job's three friends, Eliphaz the Temanite,[l] Bildad the Shuhite[m] and
Zophar the Naamathite, heard about all the troubles that had come upon him, they
set out from their homes and met together by agreement to go and sympathise with
him and comfort him.[n] 12 When they saw him from a distance, they could hardly
recognise him; they began to weep aloud, and they tore their robes and sprinkled dust
on their heads.[o] 13 Then they sat on the ground with him for seven days and seven
nights.[p] No-one said a word to him, because they saw how great his suffering was.

b *10* The Hebrew word rendered *foolish* denotes moral deficiency.

THE SOURCES OF SUFFERING

Sources	*Who is Responsible*	*Who is Affected*	*Needed Response*
My sin	I am	Myself and others	Repentance and confession to God
Others' sin	Person who sinned and others who allowed the sin	Probably many people, including those who sinned	Active resistance to the sinful behaviour, while accepting the sinner
Avoidable physical (or natural) disaster	Persons who ignore the facts or refuse to take precautions	Most of those exposed to the cause	Prevent them if possible, be prepared if they can't be prevented
Unavoidable physical (or natural) disaster	God, Satan	Most of those present	Ongoing trust in God's faithfulness

When suffering or troubles happen, do they always come from Satan? In Job's story, his series of tragedies did come from Satan, but this is not always the case. The chart above demonstrates the four main causes of suffering. Any one of these or a combination of them may create suffering. If knowing why we are suffering will teach us to avoid the cause, then the causes are worth knowing. However, it is most important to know how to respond during suffering.

suffering through her chiding or sorrow over all they had lost.

2:10 Many people think that believing in God protects them from trouble, so when calamity comes, they question God's goodness and justice. But the message of Job is that you should not give up on God because he allows you to have bad experiences. Faith in God does not guarantee personal prosperity, and lack of faith does not guarantee troubles in this life. If this were so, people would believe in God simply to get rich. God is capable of rescuing us from suffering, but he may also allow suffering to come for reasons we cannot understand. It is Satan's strategy to get us to doubt God at exactly this moment. Here Job shows a perspective broader than seeking his own personal comfort. If we always knew why we were suffering, our faith would have no room to grow.

2:11 Eliphaz, Bildad, and Zophar were not only Job's friends, they were also known for their wisdom. In the end, however, their wisdom was shown to be narrow-minded and incomplete.

2:11 Upon learning of Job's difficulties, three of his friends came to sympathise with him and and comfort him. Later we learn that their words of comfort were not helpful – but at least they came. While God rebuked them for what they said (42:7), he did not rebuke them for what they did – making the effort to come to someone who was in need. Unfortunately, when they came, they did a poor job of comforting Job because they were proud of their own advice and insensitive to Job's needs. When someone is in need, go to that person, but be sensitive in how you comfort him or her.

2:13 Why did the friends arrive and then just sit quietly? According to Jewish tradition, people who come to comfort someone in mourning should not speak until the mourner speaks. Often the best response to another person's suffering is silence. Job's friends realised that his pain was too deep to be healed with mere words, so they said nothing. (If only they had continued to sit quietly!) Often, we feel we must say something spiritual and insightful to a hurting friend. Perhaps what he or she needs most is just our presence, showing that we care. Pat answers and trite quotations say much less than empathetic silence and loving companionship.

B. THREE FRIENDS ANSWER JOB (3.1 — 31.40)

Job agonises over his situation. His three friends explain that he must be suffering because of some terrible sin he has committed. They try to persuade Job to repent of his sin. When Job argues that he has not sinned enough to deserve such suffering, his friends respond with even harsher accusations. While there are elements of truth in the speeches of Job's three friends, they are based on wrong assumptions. We must be careful what we assume to be true in the lives of others. We cannot assume that suffering is their own fault or a result of their sin.

1. First round of discussion

Job Speaks

3 After this, Job opened his mouth and cursed the day of his birth. 2He said:

3"May the day of my birth perish,
and the night it was said, 'A boy is born!'[a]
4That day — may it turn to darkness;
may God above not care about it;
may no light shine upon it.
5May darkness and deep shadow[a][b] claim it once more;
may a cloud settle over it;
may blackness overwhelm its light.
6That night — may thick darkness[c] seize it;
may it not be included among the days of the year
nor be entered in any of the months.
7May that night be barren;
may no shout of joy be heard in it.
8May those who curse days[b] curse that day,
those who are ready to rouse Leviathan.[d]
9May its morning stars become dark;
may it wait for daylight in vain
and not see the first rays of dawn,[e]
10for it did not shut the doors of the womb on me
to hide trouble from my eyes.

11"Why did I not perish at birth,
and die as I came from the womb?[f]
12Why were there knees to receive me[g]
and breasts that I might be nursed?
13For now I would be lying down[h] in peace;
I would be asleep and at rest[i]
14with kings and counsellors of the earth,[j]
who built for themselves places now lying in ruins,[k]
15with rulers[l] who had gold,
who filled their houses with silver.[m]
16Or why was I not hidden in the ground like a stillborn child,[n]
like an infant who never saw the light of day?
17There the wicked cease from turmoil,
and there the weary are at rest.[o]
18Captives also enjoy their ease;

3:3 [a]Job 10:18-19; Jer 20:14-18
3:5 [b]Job 10:21, 22; Ps 23:4; Jer 2:6; 13:16
3:6 [c]Job 23:17
3:8 [d]Job 41:1, 8, 10, 25
3:9 [e]Job 41:18
3:11 [f]Job 10:18
3:12 [g]Ge 30:3; Isa 66:12
3:13 [h]Job 17:13 [i]Job 7:8-10, 21; 10:22; 14:10-12; 19:27; 21:13, 23
3:14 [j]Job 12:17 [k]Job 15:28
3:15 [l]Job 12:21 [m]Job 27:17
3:16 [n]Ps 58:8; Ecc 6:3
3:17 [o]Job 17:16

[a] 5 *Or and the shadow of death* [b] 8 *Or the sea*

3:1ff Job's response to his second test — physical affliction — contrasts greatly to his attitude after the first test (1:20–22). Job still did not curse God, but he cursed the day of his birth. He felt it would be better never to be born than to be forsaken by God. Job was struggling emotionally, physically, and spiritually; his misery was pervasive and deep. Never underestimate how vulnerable we are during times of suffering and pain. We must hold on to our faith even if there is no relief.

3:8 In Job's day, people were hired to pronounce curses. Job desires that the soothsayers would call up the sea monster, Leviathan, to swallow up the day of Job's birth.

3:11 Job was experiencing extreme physical pain as well as grief over the loss of his family and possessions. He can't be blamed for wishing he were dead. Job's grief placed him at the crossroads of his faith, shattering many misconceptions about God (such as: he makes you rich, always keeps you from trouble and pain, or protects your loved ones). Job was driven back to the basics of his faith in God. He had only two choices: (1) he could curse God and give up, or (2) he could trust God and draw strength from him to continue.

3:18 [p] Job 39:7

3:20 [q] 1Sa 1:10; Jer 20:18; Eze 27:30-31

3:21 [r] Rev 9:6

they no longer hear the slave driver's shout.[p]
19 The small and the great are there,
and the slave is freed from his master.

20 "Why is light given to those in misery,
and life to the bitter of soul,[q]
21 to those who long for death that does not come,[r]

JOB

Children never tire of asking "Why?" Yet the question produces a bitter taste the older we get. Children wonder about everything; adults wonder about suffering. We notice that the world seems to run by a system of cause and effect, yet there are some effects for which we can't find a clear cause, and some causes that don't lead to the expected effects. We would expect Job's wealth and family to give him a very happy life, and, for a while, they did. But the loss and pain he experienced shock us. The first two chapters of his story are more than we can bear. To those so quick to ask "Why?" at the smallest misfortune, Job's faithfulness seems incredible. But even Job had something to learn. We can learn with him.

Our age of "instant" everything has caused us to lose the ability to wait. We expect to learn patience instantly, and in our hurry, we miss the contradiction. Of all that we want now, relief from pain is at the top of our list. We want an instant cure for everything from toothaches to heartbreaks.

Although some pains have been cured, we still live in a world where many people suffer. Job was not expecting instant answers for the intense emotional and physical pain he endured. But in the end, what broke Job's patience was not the suffering, but not knowing *why* he suffered.

When Job expressed his frustration, his friends were ready with their answers. They believed that the law of cause and effect applied to all people's experiences. Their view of life boiled down to this: good things happen to good people, and bad things happen to bad people. Because of this, they felt their role was to help Job admit to whatever sin was causing his suffering.

Job actually looked at life in almost the same way as his friends. What he couldn't understand was why he was suffering so much when he was sure he had done nothing to deserve such punishment. The last friend, Elihu, did offer another explanation for the pain by pointing out that God might be allowing it in order to purify Job. But this was only partly helpful. When God finally spoke, he didn't offer Job an answer. Instead, he drove home the point that it is better to know God than to know answers.

Often we suffer consequences for bad decisions and actions. Job's willingness to repent and confess known wrongs is a good guideline for us. Sometimes suffering shapes us for special service to others. Sometimes suffering is an attack by Satan on our lives. And sometimes we don't know why we suffer. At those times, are we willing to trust God in spite of unanswered questions?

Strengths and accomplishments:
- Was a man of faith, patience, and endurance
- Was known as a generous and caring person
- Was very wealthy

Weakness and mistake:
- Allowed his desire to understand why he was suffering to overwhelm him and make him question God

Lessons from his life:
- Knowing God is better than knowing answers
- God is not arbitrary or uncaring
- Pain is not always punishment

Vital statistics:
- Where: Uz
- Occupation: Wealthy landowner and livestock owner
- Relatives: Wife and first ten children not named. Daughters from the second set of children: Jemimah, Keziah, Keren-Happuch
- Contemporaries: Eliphaz, Bildad, Zophar, Elihu

Key verses:
"Brothers, as an example of patience in the face of suffering, take the prophets who spoke in the name of the Lord. As you know, we consider blessed those who have persevered. You have heard of Job's perseverance and have seen what the Lord finally brought about. The Lord is full of compassion and mercy" (James 5:10, 11).

Job's story is told in the book of Job. He is also referred to in Ezekiel 14:14, 20 and James 5:11.

who search for it more than for hidden treasure,[s]
22 who are filled with gladness
and rejoice when they reach the grave?
23 Why is life given to a man
whose way is hidden,
whom God has hedged in?[t]
24 For sighing comes to me instead of food;[u]
my groans pour out like water.[v]
25 What I feared has come upon me;
what I dreaded[w] has happened to me.
26 I have no peace, no quietness;
I have no rest,[x] but only turmoil."

Eliphaz

4 Then Eliphaz the Temanite replied:

2 "If someone ventures a word with you, will you be impatient?
But who can keep from speaking?[a]
3 Think how you have instructed many,
how you have strengthened feeble hands.[b]
4 Your words have supported those who stumbled;
you have strengthened faltering knees.[c]
5 But now trouble comes to you, and you are discouraged;
it strikes[d] you, and you are dismayed.[e]
6 Should not your piety be your confidence[f]
and your blameless[g] ways your hope?

7 "Consider now: Who, being innocent, has ever perished?[h]
Where were the upright ever destroyed?[i]
8 As I have observed, those who plough evil[j]
and those who sow trouble reap it.[k]
9 At the breath of God[l] they are destroyed;
at the blast of his anger they perish.[m]
10 The lions may roar and growl,
yet the teeth of the great lions are broken.[n]
11 The lion perishes for lack of prey,[o]
and the cubs of the lioness are scattered.

12 "A word was secretly brought to me,

3:21 [s]Pr 2:4
3:23 [t]Job 19:6, 8, 12; Ps 88:8; La 3:7
3:24 [u]Job 6:7; 33:20 [v]Ps 42:3, 4
3:25 [w]Job 30:15
3:26 [x]Job 7:4, 14
4:2 [a]Job 32:20
4:3 [b]Isa 35:3; Heb 12:12
4:4 [c]Isa 35:3; Heb 12:12
4:5 [d]Job 19:21 [e]Job 6:14
4:6 [f]Pr 3:26 [g]Job 1:1
4:7 [h]Job 36:7 [i]Job 8:20; Ps 37:25
4:8 [j]Job 15:35 [k]Pr 22:8; Hos 10:13; Gal 6:7-8
4:9 [l]Job 15:30; Isa 30:33; 2Th 2:8 [m]Job 40:13
4:10 [n]Job 5:15; Ps 58:6
4:11 [o]Job 27:14; Ps 34:10

3:23–26 Job had been careful not to worship material possessions but to worship God alone. Here he was overwhelmed by calamities that mocked his caution, and he complained about trials that came despite his right living. All the principles by which he had lived were crumbling, and Job began to lose his perspective. Trials and grief, whether temporary or enduring, do not destroy the real purpose of life. Life is not given merely for happiness and personal fulfilment, but for us to serve and honour God. The worth and meaning of life is not based on what we feel, but on the one reality no-one can take away—God's love for us. Don't assume that because God truly loves you, he will always prevent suffering. The opposite may be true. God's love cannot be measured or limited by how great or how little we may suffer. Romans 8:38, 39 teaches us that nothing can separate us from God's love.

4:1ff Eliphaz claimed to have been given secret knowledge through a special revelation from God (4:12–16), and that he had learned much from personal experience (4:8). He argued that suffering is a direct result of sin, so if Job would only confess his sin, his suffering would end. Eliphaz saw suffering as God's punishment, which should be welcomed in order to bring a person back to God. In some cases, of course, this may be true (Galatians 6:7, 8), but it was not true with Job. Although Eliphaz had many good and true comments, he made three wrong assumptions: (1) a good and innocent person never suffers; (2) those who suffer are being punished for their past sins; and (3) Job, because he was suffering, had done something wrong in God's eyes. (For more about Eliphaz, see the chart in chapter 28. Teman was a trading city in Edom, noted as a place of wisdom; see Jeremiah 49:7.)

4:7, 8 Part of what Eliphaz said is true, and part is false. It is true that those who promote sin and trouble eventually will be punished; it is false that anyone who is good and innocent will never suffer.

All the material recorded and quoted in the Bible is there by God's choice. Some is a record of what people said and did but is not an example to follow. The sins, the defeats, the evil thoughts, and misconceptions about God are all part of God's divinely inspired word, but we should not follow those wrong examples just because they are in the Bible. The Bible gives us teachings and examples of what we *should* do as well as what we *should not* do. Eliphaz's comments are an example of what we should try to avoid—making false assumptions about others based on our own experiences.

4:12
[p] Job 26:14
[q] Job 33:14

4:13
[r] Job 33:15

4:14
[s] Jer 23:9; Hab 3:16

4:17
[t] Job 9:2
[u] Job 35:10

my ears caught a whisper[p] of it.[q]
13 Amid disquieting dreams in the night,
when deep sleep falls on men,[r]
14 fear and trembling seized me
and made all my bones shake.[s]
15 A spirit glided past my face,
and the hair on my body stood on end.
16 It stopped,
but I could not tell what it was.
A form stood before my eyes,
and I heard a hushed voice:
17 'Can a mortal be more righteous than God?[t]
Can a man be more pure than his Maker?[u]

ADVICE FROM FRIENDS Overwhelmed by suffering, Job was not comforted, but condemned by his friends. Each of their views represents a well-known way to understand suffering. God proves that each explanation given by Job's friends has less than the whole answer.

Who they were	*Where they spoke*	*How they helped*	*How they explained Job's pain*	*Their advice to Job*	*Job's response*	*God's response to Job's friends*
Eliphaz the Temanite	Job 4, 5, 15, 22		Job is suffering because he has sinned	Go to God and lay your cause before him. (5:8)	Take back your false accusations. (6:29)	
Bildad the Shuhite	Job 8, 18, 25	They sat in silence with Job for seven days (2:11–13)	Job won't admit he sinned, so he's still suffering	How long will you go on like this? (8:2)	I will say to God . . . tell me what charges you have against me. (10:2)	God rebukes Job's friends (42:7)
Zophar the Naamathite	Job 11, 20		Job's sin deserves even more suffering than he's experienced	Get rid of your sins. (11:13, 14)	I know that I will be justified. (13:18)	
Elihu the Buzite	Job 32–37		God is using suffering to mould and train Job	Be silent and I will teach you wisdom. (33:33)	No response	God does not directly address Elihu.
God	Job 38–41	Confronted Job with the need to be content without knowing why he was suffering	Did not explain the reason for the pain	Do you still want to argue with the Almighty? (40:2)	I was talking about things I did not understand. (42:3–5)	

4:12, 13 Although Eliphaz claimed that his vision was divinely inspired, it is doubtful that it came from God because later God criticised Eliphaz for misrepresenting him (42:7). Whatever the vision's source, it is summarised in 4:17. On the surface, this statement is completely true – a mere mortal cannot compare to God and should not try to question God's motives and actions. Eliphaz, however, took this thought and expounded on it later, expressing his own opinions. His conclusion (5:8) reveals a very shallow understanding of Job and his suffering. It is easy for teachers, counsellors, and well-meaning friends to begin with a portion of God's truth but then go off on a tangent. Don't limit God to your perspective and finite understanding of life.

18 If God places no trust in his servants,
if he charges his angels with error,[v]
19 how much more those who live in houses of clay,[w]
whose foundations[x] are in the dust,[y]
who are crushed more readily than a moth!
20 Between dawn and dusk they are broken to pieces;
unnoticed, they perish for ever.[z]
21 Are not the cords of their tent pulled up,[a]
so that they die without wisdom?'[a][b]

5 "Call if you will, but who will answer you?
To which of the holy ones[a] will you turn?
2 Resentment kills a fool,
and envy slays the simple.[b]
3 I myself have seen a fool taking root,[c]
but suddenly his house was cursed.[d]
4 His children are far from safety,[e]
crushed in court[f] without a defender.
5 The hungry consume his harvest,[g]
taking it even from among thorns,
and the thirsty pant after his wealth.
6 For hardship does not spring from the soil,
nor does trouble sprout from the ground.
7 Yet man is born to trouble[h]
as surely as sparks fly upward.

8 "But if it were I, I would appeal to God;
I would lay my cause before him.[i]
9 He performs wonders that cannot be fathomed,[j]
miracles that cannot be counted.
10 He bestows rain on the earth;
he sends water upon the countryside.[k]
11 The lowly he sets on high,[l]
and those who mourn are lifted to safety.
12 He thwarts the plans[m] of the crafty,
so that their hands achieve no success.
13 He catches the wise in their craftiness,[n]
and the schemes of the wily are swept away.
14 Darkness[o] comes upon them in the daytime;
at noon they grope as in the night.[p]
15 He saves the needy[q] from the sword in their mouth;
he saves them from the clutches of the powerful.[r]
16 So the poor have hope,
and injustice shuts its mouth.[s]

17 "Blessed is the man whom God corrects;[t]

4:18 [v] Job 15:15
4:19 [w] Job 10:9 [x] Job 22:16 [y] Ge 2:7
4:20 [z] Job 14:2, 20; 20:7; Ps 90:5-6
4:21 [a] Job 8:22 [b] Job 18:21; 36:12
5:1 [a] Job 15:15
5:2 [b] Pr 12:16
5:3 [c] Ps 37:35; Jer 12:2 [d] Job 24:18
5:4 [e] Job 4:11 [f] Am 5:12
5:5 [g] Job 18:8-10
5:7 [h] Job 14:1
5:8 [i] Ps 35:23; 50:15
5:9 [j] Job 42:3; Ps 40:5
5:10 [k] Job 36:28
5:11 [l] Ps 113:7-8
5:12 [m] Ne 4:15; Ps 33:10
5:13 [n] 1Co 3:19*
5:14 [o] Job 12:25 [p] Dt 28:29
5:15 [q] Ps 35:10 [r] Job 4:10
5:16 [s] Ps 107:42
5:17 [t] Jas 1:12

a *21* Some interpreters end the quotation after verse 17.

4:18, 19 Do angels really make errors? Remember that Eliphaz was speaking, not God, so we must be careful about building our knowledge of the spiritual world from Eliphaz's opinions. In addition, the word translated *error* is used only here, and its meaning is unclear. We could save Eliphaz's credibility by saying he meant fallen angels, but this passage is not meant to teach about angels. Eliphaz was saying that sinful human beings are far beneath God and the angels. Eliphaz was right about God's greatness, but he did not understand God's greater purposes concerning suffering.

5:8 All three of Job's friends made the mistake of assuming that Job had committed some great sin that had caused his suffering. Neither they nor Job knew of Satan's conversation with God (1:6–2:8). It is human nature to blame people for their own troubles, but Job's story makes it clear that blame cannot always be attached to those whom trouble strikes.

5:13 Paul later quoted part of this verse (1 Corinthians 3:19)—the only time Job is clearly quoted in the New Testament. Although God rebuked Eliphaz for being wrong in his advice to Job (42:7), not all he said was in error. The part Paul quoted was correct—people are often caught in their own traps ("in their craftiness"). This illustrates how Scripture must be used to explain and comment on itself. We must be familiar with the entire scope of God's word to properly understand the difficult portions of it.

so do not despise the discipline[u] of the Almighty.[a][v]
18For he wounds, but he also binds up;[w]
he injures, but his hands also heal.[x]
19From six calamities he will rescue you;
in seven no harm will befall you.[y]
20In famine[z] he will ransom you from death,
and in battle from the stroke of the sword.[a]
21You will be protected from the lash of the tongue,[b]
and need not fear[c] when destruction comes.
22You will laugh at destruction and famine,
and need not fear the beasts of the earth.[d]
23For you will have a covenant with the stones[e] of the field,
and the wild animals will be at peace with you.[f]
24You will know that your tent is secure;
you will take stock of your property and find nothing missing.[g]
25You will know that your children will be many,[h]
and your descendants like the grass of the earth.[i]
26You will come to the grave in full vigour,[j]
like sheaves gathered in season.

27"We have examined this, and it is true.
So hear it and apply it to yourself."

Job

6 Then Job replied:

2"If only my anguish could be weighed
and all my misery be placed on the scales![a]
3It would surely outweigh the sand[b] of the seas—
no wonder my words have been impetuous.[c]
4The arrows[d] of the Almighty are in me,[e]
my spirit drinks[f] in their poison;
God's terrors[g] are marshalled against me.[h]
5Does a wild donkey bray when it has grass,
or an ox bellow when it has fodder?
6Is tasteless food eaten without salt,
or is there flavour in the white of an egg?[a]
7I refuse to touch it;
such food makes me ill.[i]

8"Oh, that I might have my request,
that God would grant what I hope for,[j]

5:17 [u]Ps 94:12; Pr 3:11 [v]Heb 12:5-11
5:18 [w]Isa 30:26 [x]1Sa 2:6
5:19 [y]Ps 34:19; 91:10
5:20 [z]Ps 33:19 [a]Ps 144:10
5:21 [b]Ps 31:20 [c]Ps 91:5
5:22 [d]Ps 91:13; Eze 34:25
5:23 [e]Ps 91:12 [f]Isa 11:6-9
5:24 [g]Job 8:6
5:25 [h]Ps 112:2 [i]Ps 72:16; Isa 44:3-4
5:26 [j]Ge 15:15
6:2 [a]Job 31:6
6:3 [b]Pr 27:3 [c]Job 23:2
6:4 [d]Ps 38:2 [e]Job 16:12, 13 [f]Job 21:20 [g]Job 30:15 [h]Ps 88:15-18
6:7 [i]Job 3:24
6:8 [j]Job 14:13

a *17* Hebrew *Shaddai*; here and throughout Job **a** *6* The meaning of the Hebrew for this phrase is uncertain.

5:17 Eliphaz was correct—it is a blessing to be disciplined by God when we do wrong. Eliphaz's advice, however, did not apply to Job. As we know from the beginning of the book, Job's suffering was not a result of some great sin. We sometimes give people excellent advice only to learn that it does not apply to them and is therefore not very helpful. All who offer counsel from God's word should take care to thoroughly understand a person's situation *before* giving advice.

5:17–26 Eliphaz's words in 5:17, 18 show a view of discipline that has been almost forgotten: pain can help us grow. These are good words to remember when we face hardship and loss. Because Job did not understand why he suffered, his faith in God had a chance to grow. On the other hand, we must not make Eliphaz's mistake. God does not eliminate all hardship when we are following him closely, and good behaviour is not always rewarded by prosperity. Rewards for good and punishment for evil are in God's hands and given out according to his timetable. Satan's ploy is to get us to doubt God's goodwill towards us.

6:6, 7 Job said that Eliphaz's advice was like eating the tasteless white of an egg. When people are going through severe trials, ill-advised counsel is distasteful. They may listen politely, but inside they are upset. Be slow to give advice to those who are hurting. They often need compassion more than they need advice.

6:8, 9 In his grief, Job wanted to give in, to be freed from his discomfort, and to die. But God did not grant Job's request. He had a greater plan for him. Our tendency, like Job's, is to want to give up and get out when the going gets rough. To trust God in the good times is commendable, but to trust him during the difficult times tests us to our limits and exercises our faith. In your struggles,

9 that God would be willing to crush me,
to let loose his hand and cut me off![k]
10 Then I would still have this consolation —
my joy in unrelenting pain —
that I had not denied the words[l] of the Holy One.[m]

11 "What strength do I have, that I should still hope?
What prospects, that I should be patient?[n]
12 Do I have the strength of stone?
Is my flesh bronze?
13 Do I have any power to help myself,[o]
now that success has been driven from me?

14 "A despairing man[p] should have the devotion[q] of his friends,
even though he forsakes the fear of the Almighty.
15 But my brothers are as undependable as intermittent streams,[r]
as the streams that overflow
16 when darkened by thawing ice
and swollen with melting snow,
17 but that cease to flow in the dry season,
and in the heat[s] vanish from their channels.
18 Caravans turn aside from their routes;
they go up into the wasteland and perish.
19 The caravans of Tema[t] look for water,
the travelling merchants of Sheba look in hope.
20 They are distressed, because they had been confident;
they arrive there, only to be disappointed.[u]
21 Now you too have proved to be of no help;
you see something dreadful and are afraid.[v]
22 Have I ever said, 'Give something on my behalf,
pay a ransom for me from your wealth,
23 deliver me from the hand of the enemy,
ransom me from the clutches of the ruthless'?

24 "Teach me, and I will be quiet;[w]
show me where I have been wrong.
25 How painful are honest words![x]
But what do your arguments prove?
26 Do you mean to correct what I say,
and treat the words of a despairing man as wind?[y]
27 You would even cast lots[z] for the fatherless
and barter away your friend.

28 "But now be so kind as to look at me.
Would I lie to your face?[a]
29 Relent, do not be unjust;
reconsider, for my integrity is at stake.[b][b]
30 Is there any wickedness on my lips?[c]
Can my mouth not discern[d] malice?

6:9 [k] Nu 11:15; 1Ki 19:4
6:10 [l] Job 22:22; 23:12 [m] Lev 19:2; Isa 57:15
6:11 [n] Job 21:4
6:13 [o] Job 26:2
6:14 [p] Job 4:5 [q] Job 15:4
6:15 [r] Ps 38:11; Jer 15:18
6:17 [s] Job 24:19
6:19 [t] Ge 25:15; Isa 21:14
6:20 [u] Jer 14:3
6:21 [v] Ps 38:11
6:24 [w] Ps 39:1
6:25 [x] Ecc 12:11
6:26 [y] Job 8:2; 15:3
6:27 [z] Joel 3:3; Na 3:10; 2Pe 2:3
6:28 [a] Job 27:4; 33:1, 3; 36:3, 4
6:29 [b] Job 23:7, 10; 34:5, 36; 42:6
6:30 [c] Job 27:4 [d] Job 12:11

b *29* Or *my righteousness still stands*

---

large or small, trust that God is in control and that he will take care of you (Romans 8:28).

6:29, 30 Job referred to his own integrity, not because he was sinless, but because he had a right relationship with God. He was not guilty of the sins his friends accused him of (see chapter 31 for his summary of the life he had led). Another rendering of this verse could read, "My righteousness still stands." *Righteousness* is not the same as *sinlessness* (Romans 3:23). No-one but Jesus Christ has ever been sinless — free from all wrong thoughts and actions. Even Job needed to make some changes in his attitude towards God, as we will see by the end of the book. Nevertheless, Job was righteous (1:8). He carefully obeyed God to the best of his ability in all aspects of his life.

7

"Does not man have hard service[a] on earth?[b]
Are not his days like those of a hired man?[c]
2Like a slave longing for the evening shadows,
or a hired man waiting eagerly for his wages,[d]
3so I have been allotted months of futility,
and nights of misery have been assigned to me.[e]
4When I lie down I think, 'How long before I get up?'[f]
The night drags on, and I toss till dawn.
5My body is clothed with worms[g] and scabs,
my skin is broken and festering.

6"My days are swifter than a weaver's shuttle,[h]
and they come to an end without hope.[i]
7Remember, O God, that my life is but a breath;[j]
my eyes will never see happiness again.[k]
8The eye that now sees me will see me no longer;
you will look for me, but I will be no more.[l]
9As a cloud vanishes and is gone,
so he who goes down to the grave[a][m] does not return.[n]
10He will never come to his house again;
his place[o] will know him no more.[p]

11"Therefore I will not keep silent;[q]
I will speak out in the anguish of my spirit,
I will complain in the bitterness of my soul.[r]
12Am I the sea, or the monster of the deep,[s]
that you put me under guard?
13When I think my bed will comfort me
and my couch will ease my complaint,[t]
14even then you frighten me with dreams
and terrify[u] me with visions,
15so that I prefer strangling and death,[v]
rather than this body of mine.
16I despise my life;[w] I would not live for ever.
Let me alone; my days have no meaning.

17"What is man that you make so much of him,
that you give him so much attention,[x]
18that you examine him every morning
and test him every moment?[y]
19Will you never look away from me,
or let me alone even for an instant?[z]
20If I have sinned, what have I done to you,[a]
O watcher of men?
Why have you made me your target?[b]
Have I become a burden to you?[b]

[a] *9* Hebrew *Sheol* [b] *20* A few manuscripts of the Masoretic Text, an ancient Hebrew scribal tradition and Septuagint; most manuscripts of the Masoretic Text *I have become a burden to myself.*

7:1 [a]Job 14:14; Isa 40:2 [b]Job 5:7 [c]Job 14:6
7:2 [d]Lev 19:13
7:3 [e]Job 16:7; Ps 6:6
7:4 [f]Dt 28:67
7:5 [g]Job 17:14; Isa 14:11
7:6 [h]Job 9:25 [i]Job 13:15; 17:11, 15
7:7 [j]Ps 78:39; Jas 4:14 [k]Job 9:25
7:8 [l]Job 20:7, 9, 21
7:9 [m]Job 11:8 [n]2Sa 12:23; Job 30:15
7:10 [o]Job 27:21, 23 [p]Job 8:18
7:11 [q]Ps 40:9 [r]1Sa 1:10
7:12 [s]Eze 32:2-3
7:13 [t]Job 9:27
7:14 [u]Job 9:34
7:15 [v]1Ki 19:4
7:16 [w]Job 9:21; 10:1
7:17 [x]Ps 8:4; 144:3; Heb 2:6
7:18 [y]Job 14:3
7:19 [z]Job 9:18
7:20 [a]Job 35:6 [b]Job 16:12

7:11 Job felt deep anguish and bitterness, and he spoke honestly to God about his feelings to let out his frustrations. If we express our feelings to God, we can deal with them without exploding in harsh words and actions, possibly hurting ourselves and others. The next time strong emotions threaten to overwhelm you, express them openly to God in prayer. This will help you gain an eternal perspective on the situation and give you greater ability to deal with it constructively.

7:12 Job stopped talking to Eliphaz and spoke directly to God. Although Job had lived a blameless life, he was beginning to doubt the value of living in such a way. By doing this, he was coming dangerously close to suggesting that God didn't care about him and was not being fair. Later God reproved Job for this attitude (38:2). Satan always exploits these thoughts to get us to forsake God. Our suffering, like Job's, may not be the result of our sin, but we must be careful not to sin as a result of our suffering.

7:20 Job referred to God as a watcher or observer of humanity. He was expressing his feeling that God seemed like an enemy to him—someone who mercilessly watched him squirm in his misery. We know that God does watch over everything that happens to us. We must never forget that he sees us with compassion, not merely with critical scrutiny. His eyes are eyes of love.

21 Why do you not pardon my offences
and forgive my sins?[c]
For I shall soon lie down in the dust;[d]
you will search for me, but I shall be no more."

Bildad

8 Then Bildad the Shuhite replied:

2 "How long will you say such things?
Your words are a blustering wind.[a]
3 Does God pervert justice?[b]
Does the Almighty pervert what is right?[c]
4 When your children sinned against him,
he gave them over to the penalty of their sin.[d]
5 But if you will look to God
and plead[e] with the Almighty,
6 if you are pure and upright,
even now he will rouse himself on your behalf[f]
and restore you to your rightful place.[g]
7 Your beginnings will seem humble,
so prosperous[h] will your future be.

8 "Ask the former generations[i]
and find out what their fathers learned,
9 for we were born only yesterday and know nothing,[j]
and our days on earth are but a shadow.[k]
10 Will they not instruct you and tell you?
Will they not bring forth words from their understanding?
11 Can papyrus grow tall where there is no marsh?
Can reeds thrive without water?
12 While still growing and uncut,
they wither more quickly than grass.[l]
13 Such is the destiny of all who forget God;[m]
so perishes the hope of the godless.[n]
14 What he trusts in is fragile;[a]
what he relies on is a spider's web.[o]
15 He leans on his web,[p] but it gives way;
he clings to it, but it does not hold.[q]
16 He is like a well-watered plant in the sunshine,
spreading its shoots[r] over the garden;[s]
17 it entwines its roots around a pile of rocks
and looks for a place among the stones.
18 But when it is torn from its spot,
that place disowns it and says, 'I never saw you.'[t]
19 Surely its life withers[u] away,
and[b] from the soil other plants grow.[v]

7:21 [c]Job 10:14 [d]Job 10:9; Ps 104:29
8:2 [a]Job 6:26
8:3 [b]Dt 32:4; 2Ch 19:7; Ro 3:5 [c]Ge 18:25
8:4 [d]Job 1:19
8:5 [e]Job 11:13
8:6 [f]Ps 7:6 [g]Job 5:24
8:7 [h]Job 42:12
8:8 [i]Dt 4:32; 32:7; Job 15:18
8:9 [j]Ge 47:9 [k]1Ch 29:15; Job 7:6
8:12 [l]Ps 129:6; Jer 17:6
8:13 [m]Ps 9:17 [n]Job 11:20; 13:16; 15:34; Pr 10:28
8:14 [o]Isa 59:5
8:15 [p]Job 27:18 [q]Ps 49:11
8:16 [r]Ps 80:11 [s]Ps 37:35; Jer 11:16
8:18 [t]Job 7:8; Ps 37:36
8:19 [u]Job 20:5 [v]Ecc 1:4

a *14* The meaning of the Hebrew for this word is uncertain. **b** *19* Or *Surely all the joy it has / is that*

8:1ff Bildad was upset that Job still claimed innocence while questioning God's justice. The basis of Bildad's argument (the justice of God) was correct, but his idea of God's justice was not. Bildad's argument went like this: God could not be unjust, and God would not punish a just man; therefore Job must be unjust. Bildad felt there were no exceptions to his theory. Like Eliphaz, Bildad wrongly assumed that people suffer only as a result of their sins. Bildad was even less sensitive and compassionate, saying that Job's children died because of *their* wickedness. (For more information about Bildad, see the chart in chapter 28.)

8:14, 15 Bildad wrongly assumed that Job was trusting in something other than God for security, so he pointed out that such supports will collapse ("what he trusts in is fragile"). One of man's basic needs is security, and people will do almost anything to feel secure. Eventually, however, our money, possessions, knowledge, and relationships will fail or be gone. Only God can give lasting security. What have you trusted for your security? How lasting is it? If you have a secure foundation with God, feelings of insecurity will not undermine you.

8:20
[w]Job 1:1
[x]Job 21:30

8:21
[y]Job 5:22
[z]Ps 126:2; 132:16

8:22
[a]Ps 35:26; 109:29; 132:18
[b]Job 18:6, 14, 21

9:2
[a]Job 4:17; Ps 143:2; Ro 3:20

9:3
[b]Job 10:2; 40:2

9:4
[c]Job 11:6
[d]Job 36:5
[e]2Ch 13:12

9:5
[f]Mic 1:4

9:6
[g]Isa 2:21; Hag 2:6; Heb 12:26
[h]Job 26:11

9:7
[i]Isa 13:10; Eze 32:8

9:8
[j]Ge 1:6; Ps 104:2-3
[k]Job 38:16; Ps 77:19

9:9
[l]Ge 1:16; Job 38:31; Am 5:8

9:10
[m]Ps 71:15
[n]Job 5:9

9:11
[o]Job 23:8-9; 35:14

9:12
[p]Job 11:10
[q]Isa 45:9; Ro 9:20

9:13
[r]Job 26:12; Ps 89:10; Isa 30:7; 51:9

9:15
[s]Job 10:15
[t]Job 8:5

9:17
[u]Job 16:12
[v]Job 30:22
[w]Job 16:14
[x]Job 2:3

9:18
[y]Job 7:19; 27:2

20 "Surely God does not reject a blameless[w] man
or strengthen the hands of evildoers.[x]
21 He will yet fill your mouth with laughter[y]
and your lips with shouts of joy.[z]
22 Your enemies will be clothed in shame,[a]
and the tents of the wicked will be no more."[b]

Job

9 Then Job replied:

2 "Indeed, I know that this is true.
But how can a mortal be righteous before God?[a]
3 Though one wished to dispute with him,
he could not answer him one time out of a thousand.[b]
4 His wisdom[c] is profound, his power is vast.[d]
Who has resisted him and come out unscathed?[e]
5 He moves mountains without their knowing it
and overturns them in his anger.[f]
6 He shakes the earth[g] from its place
and makes its pillars tremble.[h]
7 He speaks to the sun and it does not shine;
he seals off the light of the stars.[i]
8 He alone stretches out the heavens[j]
and treads on the waves of the sea.[k]
9 He is the Maker of the Bear and Orion,
the Pleiades and the constellations of the south.[l]
10 He performs wonders[m] that cannot be fathomed,
miracles that cannot be counted.[n]
11 When he passes me, I cannot see him;
when he goes by, I cannot perceive him.[o]
12 If he snatches away, who can stop him?[p]
Who can say to him, 'What are you doing?'[q]
13 God does not restrain his anger;
even the cohorts of Rahab[r] cowered at his feet.

14 "How then can I dispute with him?
How can I find words to argue with him?
15 Though I were innocent, I could not answer him;[s]
I could only plead[t] with my Judge for mercy.
16 Even if I summoned him and he responded,
I do not believe he would give me a hearing.
17 He would crush me[u] with a storm[v]
and multiply[w] my wounds for no reason.[x]
18 He would not let me regain my breath
but would overwhelm me with misery.[y]
19 If it is a matter of strength, he is mighty!
And if it is a matter of justice, who will summon him?[a]

[a] *19* See Septuagint; Hebrew *me.*

9:1ff Bildad said nothing new to Job. Job knew that the wicked ultimately perish, but his situation confused him. Why, then, was *he* perishing? Job didn't think his life warranted such suffering, so he wanted his case presented before God (9:32–35). He recognised, however, that arguing with God would be futile and unproductive (9:4). Job didn't claim to be perfect (7:20, 21; 9:20), but he did claim to be good and faithful (6:29, 30). While Job showed impatience towards God, he did not reject or curse God.

9:9 The Bear, Orion, and Pleiades are constellations of stars.

9:13 Rahab is the name of a legendary sea monster. According to a Babylonian creation myth, Marduk defeated Tiamat (another name for Rahab), then captured her helpers. Job's friends would have known this myth and understood Job's meaning. God is sovereign over all the forces.

20Even if I were innocent, my mouth would condemn me;
if I were blameless, it would pronounce me guilty.

21"Although I am blameless,[z]
I have no concern for myself;
I despise my own life.[a]
22It is all the same; that is why I say,
'He destroys both the blameless and the wicked.'[b]
23When a scourge[c] brings sudden death,
he mocks the despair of the innocent.[d]
24When a land falls into the hands of the wicked,[e]
he blindfolds its judges.[f]
If it is not he, then who is it?

25"My days are swifter than a runner;[g]
they fly away without a glimpse of joy.
26They skim past like boats of papyrus,[h]
like eagles swooping down on their prey.[i]
27If I say, 'I will forget my complaint,[j]
I will change my expression, and smile,'
28I still dread[k] all my sufferings,
for I know you will not hold me innocent.[l]
29Since I am already found guilty,
why should I struggle in vain?[m]
30Even if I washed myself with soap**[b]**
and my hands[n] with washing soda,[o]
31you would plunge me into a slime pit
so that even my clothes would detest me.

32"He is not a man like me that I might answer him,[p]
that we might confront each other in court.[q]
33If only there were someone to arbitrate between us,[r]
to lay his hand upon us both,
34someone to remove God's rod from me,[s]
so that his terror would frighten me no more.
35Then I would speak up without fear of him,
but as it now stands with me, I cannot.[t]

10

"I loathe my very life;[a]
therefore I will give free rein to my complaint
and speak out in the bitterness of my soul.[b]
2I will say to God: Do not condemn me,
but tell me what charges[c] you have against me.
3Does it please you to oppress me,[d]
to spurn the work of your hands,[e]
while you smile on the schemes of the wicked?[f]
4Do you have eyes of flesh?
Do you see as a mortal sees?[g]
5Are your days like those of a mortal

b *30* Or *snow*

9:21 [z]Job 1:1 [a]Job 7:16
9:22 [b]Job 10:8; Ecc 9:2, 3; Eze 21:3
9:23 [c]Heb 11:36 [d]Job 24:1, 12
9:24 [e]Job 10:3; 16:11 [f]Job 12:6
9:25 [g]Job 7:6
9:26 [h]Isa 18:2 [i]Hab 1:8
9:27 [j]Job 7:11
9:28 [k]Job 3:25; Ps 119:120 [l]Job 7:21
9:29 [m]Ps 37:33
9:30 [n]Job 31:7 [o]Jer 2:22
9:32 [p]Ro 9:20 [q]Ps 143:2; Ecc 6:10
9:33 [r]1Sa 2:25
9:34 [s]Job 13:21; Ps 39:10
9:35 [t]Job 13:21
10:1 [a]1Ki 19:4 [b]Job 7:11
10:2 [c]Job 9:29
10:3 [d]Job 9:22 [e]Job 14:15; Ps 138:8; Isa 64:8 [f]Job 21:16; 22:18
10:4 [g]1Sa 16:7

9:20, 21 "Even if I were innocent, my mouth would condemn me." Job was saying, "In spite of my good life, God is determined to condemn me." As his suffering continued, he became more impatient. Although Job remained loyal to God, he made statements he would later regret. In times of extended sickness or prolonged pain, it is natural for people to doubt, to despair, or to become impatient. During those times, people need someone to listen to them, to help them work through their feelings and frustrations. Your patience with their impatience will help them.

10:1 Job began to wallow in self-pity. When we face baffling affliction, our pain lures us towards feeling sorry for ourselves. At this point we are only one step from self-righteousness, where we keep track of life's injustices and say, "Look what happened to me; how unfair it is!" We may feel like blaming God. Remember that life's trials, whether allowed by God or sent by God, can be the means for development and refinement. When facing trials, ask, "What can I learn and how can I grow?" rather than "Who did this to me and how can I get out of it?"

or your years like those of a man,[h]
6that you must search out my faults
and probe after my sin[i]—
7though you know that I am not guilty
and that no-one can rescue me from your hand?

8"Your hands shaped[j] me and made me.
Will you now turn and destroy me?
9Remember that you moulded me like clay.[k]
Will you now turn me to dust again?[l]
10Did you not pour me out like milk
and curdle me like cheese,
11clothe me with skin and flesh
and knit me together[m] with bones and sinews?
12You gave me life[n] and showed me kindness,
and in your providence watched over my spirit.

13"But this is what you concealed in your heart,
and I know that this was in your mind:[o]
14If I sinned, you would be watching me
and would not let my offence go unpunished.[p]
15If I am guilty—woe to me![q]
Even if I am innocent, I cannot lift my head,[r]
for I am full of shame
and drowned in[a] my affliction.
16If I hold my head high, you stalk me like a lion[s]
and again display your awesome power against me.[t]
17You bring new witnesses against me[u]
and increase your anger towards me;[v]
your forces come against me wave upon wave.

18"Why then did you bring me out of the womb?[w]
I wish I had died before any eye saw me.
19If only I had never come into being,
or had been carried straight from the womb to the grave!
20Are not my few days[x] almost over?[y]
Turn away from me[z] so that I can have a moment's joy
21before I go to the place of no return,[a]
to the land of gloom and deep shadow,[b][b]
22to the land of deepest night,
of deep shadow and disorder,
where even the light is like darkness."

Zophar

11 Then Zophar the Naamathite replied:

2"Are all these words to go unanswered?[a]
Is this talker to be vindicated?

a *15* Or *and aware of* **b** *21* Or *and the shadow of death*; also in verse 22

10:5 [h]Ps 90:2, 4; 2Pe 3:8
10:6 [i]Job 14:16
10:8 [j]Ps 119:73
10:9 [k]Isa 64:8 [l]Ge 2:7
10:11 [m]Ps 139:13, 15
10:12 [n]Job 33:4
10:13 [o]Job 23:13
10:14 [p]Job 7:21
10:15 [q]Job 9:13; Isa 3:11 [r]Job 9:15
10:16 [s]Isa 38:13; La 3:10 [t]Job 5:9
10:17 [u]Job 16:8 [v]Ru 1:21
10:18 [w]Job 3:11
10:20 [x]Job 14:1 [y]Job 7:19 [z]Job 7:16
10:21 [a]2Sa 12:23; Job 3:13; 16:22 [b]Ps 23:4; 88:12
11:2 [a]Job 8:2

10:13, 14 In frustration, Job jumped to the false conclusion that God was out to get him. Wrong assumptions lead to wrong conclusions. We dare not take our limited experiences and jump to conclusions about life in general. If you find yourself doubting God, remember that you don't have all the facts. God wants only the very best for your life. Many people endure great pain, but ultimately they find some greater good came from it. When you're struggling, don't assume the worst.

10:20–22 Job was expressing the view of death common in Old Testament times, that the dead went to a joyless, dark place. There was no punishment or reward there, and no escape from it. (See the note on 19:26 for a broader picture of Job's view of death.)

11:1ff Zophar is the third of Job's friends to speak, and the least courteous. Full of anger, he lashed out at Job, saying that Job deserved more punishment, not less. Zophar took the same position as Eliphaz (chapters 4, 5) and Bildad (chapter 8)—that Job was suffering because of sin—but his speech was by far the most arrogant. Zophar was the kind of person who has an answer for everything; he was totally insensitive to Job's unique situation. (For more on Zophar, see the chart in chapter 28.)

3Will your idle talk reduce men to silence?
Will no-one rebuke you when you mock?[b]
4You say to God, 'My beliefs are flawless[c]
and I am pure[d] in your sight.'
5Oh, how I wish that God would speak,
that he would open his lips against you
6and disclose to you the secrets of wisdom,[e]
for true wisdom has two sides.
Know this: God has even forgotten some of your sin.[f]

7"Can you fathom[g] the mysteries of God?
Can you probe the limits of the Almighty?
8They are higher than the heavens[h] — what can you do?
They are deeper than the depths of the grave**a** — what can you know?
9Their measure is longer than the earth
and wider than the sea.

10"If he comes along and confines you in prison
and convenes a court, who can oppose him?[i]
11Surely he recognises deceitful men;
and when he sees evil, does he not take note?[j]
12But a witless man can no more become wise
than a wild donkey's colt can be born a man.**b**

13"Yet if you devote your heart[k] to him
and stretch out your hands to him,[l]
14if you put away the sin that is in your hand
and allow no evil[m] to dwell in your tent,[n]
15then you will lift up your face[o] without shame;
you will stand firm and without fear.
16You will surely forget your trouble,[p]
recalling it only as waters gone by.[q]
17Life will be brighter than noonday,[r]
and darkness will become like morning.
18You will be secure, because there is hope;
you will look about you and take your rest[s] in safety.[t]
19You will lie down, with no-one to make you afraid,[u]
and many will court your favour.[v]
20But the eyes of the wicked will fail,[w]
and escape will elude them;[x]
their hope will become a dying gasp."[y]

Job

12 Then Job replied:

2"Doubtless you are the people,
and wisdom will die with you![a]

a *8* Hebrew *than Sheol* **b** *12* Or *wild donkey can be born tame*

11:3 [b]Job 17:2; 21:3
11:4 [c]Job 6:10 [d]Job 10:7
11:6 [e]Job 9:4 [f]Ezr 9:13; Job 15:5
11:7 [g]Ecc 3:11; Ro 11:33
11:8 [h]Job 22:12
11:10 [i]Job 9:12; Rev 3:7
11:11 [j]Job 34:21-25; Ps 10:14
11:13 [k]1Sa 7:3; Ps 78:8 [l]Ps 88:9
11:14 [m]Ps 101:4 [n]Job 22:23
11:15 [o]Job 22:26; 1Jn 3:21
11:16 [p]Isa 65:16 [q]Job 22:11
11:17 [r]Job 22:28; Ps 37:6; Isa 58:8, 10
11:18 [s]Ps 3:5 [t]Lev 26:6; Pr 3:24
11:19 [u]Lev 26:6 [v]Isa 45:14
11:20 [w]Dt 28:65; Job 17:5 [x]Job 27:22; 34:22 [y]Job 8:13
12:2 [a]Job 17:10

11:11 By calling Job "deceitful", Zophar was accusing Job of hiding secret faults and sins. Although Zophar's assumption was wrong, he explained quite accurately that God knows and sees everything. We are often tempted by the thought, "No one will ever know!" Perhaps we can hide some sin from others, but we can do *nothing* without God knowing about it. Because our very thoughts are known to God, of course he will notice our sins. Job understood this as well as Zophar did, but it didn't apply to his current dilemma.

12:1ff Job answered Zophar's argument with great sarcasm: "Wisdom will die with you." He went on to say that his three friends didn't need to explain God to him – they were saying nothing he didn't already know (12:7–9; 13:1, 2). Job continued to maintain that his friends had completely misunderstood the reason for his suffering. Job did not know it either, but he was certain that his friends' reasons were both narrow-minded and incorrect. Once again Job appealed to God to give him an answer (13:3).

12:3
[b]Job 13:2

12:4
[c]Job 21:3
[d]Ps 91:15
[e]Job 6:29

12:6
[f]Job 22:18
[g]Job 9:24; 21:9

12:9
[h]Isa 41:20

12:10
[i]Job 27:3; 33:4; Ac 17:28

12:11
[j]Job 34:3

12:12
[k]Job 15:10
[l]Job 32:7, 9

12:13
[m]Job 11:6
[n]Job 9:4
[o]Job 32:8; 38:36

12:14
[p]Job 19:10
[q]Job 37:7; Isa 25:2

12:15
[r]1Ki 8:35
[s]1Ki 17:1
[t]Ge 7:11

12:16
[u]Job 13:7, 9

12:17
[v]Job 19:9
[w]Job 3:14

12:18
[x]Ps 116:16

12:19
[y]Job 24:12, 22; 34:20, 28; 35:9

12:20
[z]Job 32:9

12:22
[a]1Co 4:5
[b]Job 3:5
[c]Da 2:22

12:23
[d]Jer 25:9
[e]Ps 107:38; Isa 9:3; 26:15

12:24
[f]Ps 107:40

12:25
[g]Job 5:14
[h]Ps 107:27; Isa 24:20

3 But I have a mind as well as you;
I am not inferior to you.
Who does not know all these things?[b]

4 "I have become a laughing-stock[c] to my friends,
though I called upon God and he answered[d]—
a mere laughing-stock, though righteous and blameless![e]
5 Men at ease have contempt for misfortune
as the fate of those whose feet are slipping.
6 The tents of marauders are undisturbed,[f]
and those who provoke God are secure[g]—
those who carry their god in their hands.[a]

7 "But ask the animals, and they will teach you,
or the birds of the air, and they will tell you;
8 or speak to the earth, and it will teach you,
or let the fish of the sea inform you.
9 Which of all these does not know
that the hand of the LORD has done this?[h]
10 In his hand is the life of every creature
and the breath of all mankind.[i]
11 Does not the ear test words
as the tongue tastes food?[j]
12 Is not wisdom found among the aged?[k]
Does not long life bring understanding?[l]

13 "To God belong wisdom[m] and power;[n]
counsel and understanding are his.[o]
14 What he tears down[p] cannot be rebuilt;[q]
the man he imprisons cannot be released.
15 If he holds back the waters,[r] there is drought;[s]
if he lets them loose, they devastate the land.[t]
16 To him belong strength and victory;
both deceived and deceiver are his.[u]
17 He leads counsellors away stripped[v]
and makes fools of judges.[w]
18 He takes off the shackles[x] put on by kings
and ties a loincloth[b] round their waist.
19 He leads priests away stripped
and overthrows men long established.[y]
20 He silences the lips of trusted advisers
and takes away the discernment of elders.[z]
21 He pours contempt on nobles
and disarms the mighty.
22 He reveals the deep things of darkness[a]
and brings deep shadows[b] into the light.[c]
23 He makes nations great, and destroys them;[d]
he enlarges nations,[e] and disperses them.
24 He deprives the leaders of the earth of their reason;
he sends them wandering through a trackless waste.[f]
25 They grope in darkness with no light;[g]
he makes them stagger like drunkards.[h]

a *6* Or *secure / in what God's hand brings them* **b** *18* Or *shackles of kings / and ties a belt*

12:24, 25 Job affirmed that no leader has any real wisdom apart from God. No research or report can outweigh God's opinion. No scientific discovery or medical advance takes him by surprise. When we look for guidance for our decisions, we must recognise that God's wisdom is superior to any the world has to offer. Don't let earthly advisers dampen your desire to know God better.

13

"My eyes have seen all this,
my ears have heard and understood it.
2 What you know, I also know;
I am not inferior to you.[a]
3 But I desire to speak to the Almighty
and to argue my case with God.[b]
4 You, however, smear me with lies;[c]
you are worthless physicians, all of you!
5 If only you would be altogether silent!
For you, that would be wisdom.[d]
6 Hear now my argument;
listen to the plea of my lips.
7 Will you speak wickedly on God's behalf?
Will you speak deceitfully for him?[e]
8 Will you show him partiality?[f]
Will you argue the case for God?
9 Would it turn out well if he examined you?
Could you deceive him as you might deceive men?[g]
10 He would surely rebuke you
if you secretly showed partiality.
11 Would not his splendour[h] terrify you?
Would not the dread of him fall on you?
12 Your maxims are proverbs of ashes;
your defences are defences of clay.

13 "Keep silent and let me speak;
then let come to me what may.
14 Why do I put myself in jeopardy
and take my life in my hands?
15 Though he slay me, yet will I hope[i] in him;[j]
I will surely[a] defend my ways to his face.[k]
16 Indeed, this will turn out for my deliverance,[l]
for no godless man would dare come before him!
17 Listen carefully to my words;[m]
let your ears take in what I say.
18 Now that I have prepared my case,[n]
I know I will be vindicated.
19 Can anyone bring charges against me?[o]
If so, I will be silent and die.[p]

20 "Only grant me these two things, O God,
and then I will not hide from you:
21 Withdraw your hand[q] far from me,
and stop frightening me with your terrors.
22 Then summon me and I will answer,[r]
or let me speak, and you reply.[s]
23 How many wrongs and sins have I committed?[t]
Show me my offence and my sin.
24 Why do you hide your face[u]
and consider me your enemy?[v]
25 Will you torment a wind-blown leaf?[w]

a 15 *Or He will surely slay me; I have no hope — / yet I will*

13:2 [a]Job 12:3
13:3 [b]Job 23:3-4
13:4 [c]Ps 119:69; Jer 23:32
13:5 [d]Pr 17:28
13:7 [e]Job 36:4
13:8 [f]Lev 19:15
13:9 [g]Job 12:16; Gal 6:7
13:11 [h]Job 31:23
13:15 [i]Job 7:6 [j]Ps 23:4; Pr 14:32 [k]Job 27:5
13:16 [l]Isa 12:1
13:17 [m]Job 21:2
13:18 [n]Job 23:4
13:19 [o]Job 40:4; Isa 50:8 [p]Job 10:8
13:21 [q]Ps 39:10
13:22 [r]Job 14:15 [s]Job 9:16
13:23 [t]1Sa 26:18
13:24 [u]Dt 32:20; Ps 13:1; Isa 8:17 [v]Job 19:11; La 2:5
13:25 [w]Lev 26:36

13:4 Job compared his three friends to physicians who did not know what they were doing. They were like eye surgeons trying to perform open-heart surgery. Many of their ideas about God were true, but they did not apply to Job's situation. They were right to say that God is just. They were right to say God punishes sin. But they were wrong to assume that Job's suffering was a just punishment for his sin. They took a true principle and applied it wrongly, ignoring the vast differences in human circumstances. We must be careful and compassionate in how we apply biblical condemnations to others; we must be slow to judge.

13:25 [x]Job 21:18; Isa 42:3
13:26 [y]Ps 25:7
13:27 [z]Job 33:11
13:28 [a]Isa 50:9; Jas 5:2
14:1 [a]Job 5:7; Ecc 2:23
14:2 [b]Jas 1:10 [c]Ps 90:5-6 [d]Job 8:9
14:3 [e]Ps 8:4; 144:3 [f]Ps 143:2
14:4 [g]Ps 51:10 [h]Eph 2:1-3 [i]Jn 3:6; Ro 5:12
14:5 [j]Job 21:21
14:6 [k]Job 7:19 [l]Job 7:1, 2; Ps 39:13
14:10 [m]Job 13:19
14:11 [n]Isa 19:5
14:12 [o]Rev 20:11; 21:1 [p]Ac 3:21
14:13 [q]Isa 26:20
14:15 [r]Job 13:22
14:16 [s]Ps 139:1-3; Pr 5:21; Jer 32:19

Will you chase after dry chaff?[x]
26 For you write down bitter things against me
and make me inherit the sins of my youth.[y]
27 You fasten my feet in shackles;[z]
you keep close watch on all my paths
by putting marks on the soles of my feet.

28 "So man wastes away like something rotten,
like a garment eaten by moths.[a]

14

"Man born of woman
is of few days and full of trouble.[a]
2 He springs up like a flower[b] and withers away;[c]
like a fleeting shadow,[d] he does not endure.
3 Do you fix your eye on such a one?[e]
Will you bring him[a] before you for judgment?[f]
4 Who can bring what is pure[g] from the impure?[h]
No-one![i]
5 Man's days are determined;
you have decreed the number of his months[j]
and have set limits he cannot exceed.
6 So look away from him and let him alone,[k]
till he has put in his time like a hired man.[l]

7 "At least there is hope for a tree:
If it is cut down, it will sprout again,
and its new shoots will not fail.
8 Its roots may grow old in the ground
and its stump die in the soil,
9 yet at the scent of water it will bud
and put forth shoots like a plant.
10 But man dies and is laid low;
he breathes his last and is no more.[m]
11 As water disappears from the sea
or a river bed becomes parched and dry,[n]
12 so man lies down and does not rise;
till the heavens are no more,[o] men will not awake
or be roused from their sleep.[p]

13 "If only you would hide me in the grave[b]
and conceal me till your anger has passed![q]
If only you would set me a time
and then remember me!
14 If a man dies, will he live again?
All the days of my hard service
I will wait for my renewal[c] to come.
15 You will call and I will answer you;[r]
you will long for the creature your hands have made.
16 Surely then you will count my steps[s]

[a] 3 Septuagint, Vulgate and Syriac; Hebrew *me* [b] 13 Hebrew *Sheol* [c] 14 Or *release*

14:1ff Life is brief and full of trouble, Job laments in his closing remarks. Sickness, loneliness, disappointment, and death cause Job to say that life is not fair. Some understand verses 14 and 15 to mean that, even in his gloom, Job hoped for the resurrection of the dead. If this is true, then Job understood the one truth that could put his suffering in perspective. God's solution to believers who live in an unfair world is to guarantee life with him for ever. No matter how unfair your present world seems, God offers the hope of being in his presence eternally. Have you accepted this offer?

14:7–22 The Old Testament does not say much about the resurrection of the dead. This is not surprising because Jesus had not yet conquered death. Job's pessimism about death is understandable. What is remarkable is his budding hope (14:14). If only God would hide him with the dead and then bring him out again! If only he could die and live again! When we must endure suffering, we have an advantage over Job. We *know* that the dead will rise. Christ arose, and we have hope based on Christ's promise in John 14:19.

but not keep track of my sin.[t]
17My offences will be sealed up in a bag;[u]
you will cover over my sin.[v]

18"But as a mountain erodes and crumbles
and as a rock is moved from its place,
19as water wears away stones
and torrents wash away the soil,
so you destroy man's hope.[w]
20You overpower him once for all, and he is gone;
you change his countenance and send him away.
21If his sons are honoured, he does not know it;
if they are brought low, he does not see it.[x]
22He feels but the pain of his own body
and mourns only for himself."

2. Second round of discussion

Eliphaz

15 Then Eliphaz the Temanite replied:

2"Would a wise man answer with empty notions
or fill his belly with the hot east wind?[a]
3Would he argue with useless words,
with speeches that have no value?
4But you even undermine piety
and hinder devotion to God.
5Your sin prompts your mouth;
you adopt the tongue of the crafty.[b]
6Your own mouth condemns you, not mine;
your own lips testify against you.[c]

7"Are you the first man ever born?[d]
Were you brought forth before the hills?[e]
8Do you listen in on God's council?[f]
Do you limit wisdom to yourself?
9What do you know that we do not know?
What insights do you have that we do not have?[g]
10The grey-haired and the aged[h] are on our side,
men even older than your father.
11Are God's consolations[i] not enough for you,
words[j] spoken gently to you?[k]
12Why has your heart[l] carried you away,
and why do your eyes flash,
13so that you vent your rage against God
and pour out such words from your mouth?

14"What is man, that he could be pure,

14:16 [t]Job 10:6
14:17 [u]Dt 32:34 [v]Hos 13:12
14:19 [w]Job 7:6
14:21 [x]Ecc 9:5; Isa 63:16
15:2 [a]Job 6:26
15:5 [b]Job 5:13
15:6 [c]Lk 19:22
15:7 [d]Job 38:21 [e]Ps 90:2; Pr 8:25
15:8 [f]Ro 11:34; 1Co 2:11
15:9 [g]Job 13:2
15:10 [h]Job 32:6-7
15:11 [i]2Co 1:3-4 [j]Zec 1:13 [k]Job 36:16
15:12 [l]Job 11:13

14:22 Job's profound speech in this chapter illustrates a great truth: to have a right set of doctrines is not enough. To know what to believe is not all that is required to please God. Truth untested by life's experiences may become static and stagnant. Suffering can bring a dynamic quality to life. Just as drought drives the roots of a tree deeper to find water, so suffering can drive us beyond superficial acceptance of truth to dependence on God for hope and life.

15:1ff With the first round of talks concluded, each friend, in the same order, pressed the argument further. Again Job answered each argument (chapters 15–31). This time Eliphaz was more rude, more intense, and more threatening, but he said nothing new. (See his first speech in chapters 4, 5.) He began by saying that Job's words were empty and useless; then he restated his opinion that Job must be a great sinner. According to Eliphaz, the experience and wisdom of their ancestors were more valuable than

15:14 [m]Job 14:4; 25:4 [n]Pr 20:9; Ecc 7:20
15:15 [o]Job 4:18; 25:5
15:16 [p]Ps 14:1 [q]Job 34:7; Pr 19:28
15:18 [r]Job 8:8
15:20 [s]Job 24:1; 27:13-23
15:21 [t]Job 18:11; 20:25 [u]Job 27:20; 1Th 5:3
15:22 [v]Job 19:29; 27:14
15:23 [w]Ps 59:15; 109:10 [x]Job 18:12
15:25 [y]Job 36:9
15:27 [z]Ps 17:10
15:28 [a]Isa 5:9 [b]Job 3:14
15:29 [c]Job 27:16-17
15:30 [d]Job 5:14 [e]Job 22:20 [f]Job 4:9
15:31 [g]Isa 59:4
15:32 [h]Ecc 7:17 [i]Job 22:16; Ps 55:23 [j]Job 18:16
15:33 [k]Hab 3:17
15:34 [l]Job 8:22
15:35 [m]Ps 7:14; Isa 59:4; Hos 10:13

or one born of woman,[m] that he could be righteous?[n]
15 If God places no trust in his holy ones,
if even the heavens are not pure in his eyes,[o]
16 how much less man, who is vile and corrupt,[p]
who drinks up evil like water![q]

17 "Listen to me and I will explain to you;
let me tell you what I have seen,
18 what wise men have declared,
hiding nothing received from their fathers[r]
19 (to whom alone the land was given
when no alien passed among them):
20 All his days the wicked man suffers torment,
the ruthless through all the years stored up for him.[s]
21 Terrifying sounds fill his ears;[t]
when all seems well, marauders attack him.[u]
22 He despairs of escaping the darkness;
he is marked for the sword.[v]
23 He wanders about[w]—food for vultures;[a]
he knows the day of darkness is at hand.[x]
24 Distress and anguish fill him with terror;
they overwhelm him, like a king poised to attack,
25 because he shakes his fist at God
and vaunts himself against the Almighty,[y]
26 defiantly charging against him
with a thick, strong shield.

27 "Though his face is covered with fat
and his waist bulges with flesh,[z]
28 he will inhabit ruined towns
and houses where no-one lives,[a]
houses crumbling to rubble.[b]
29 He will no longer be rich and his wealth will not endure,[c]
nor will his possessions spread over the land.
30 He will not escape the darkness;[d]
a flame[e] will wither his shoots,
and the breath of God's mouth[f] will carry him away.
31 Let him not deceive himself by trusting what is worthless,[g]
for he will get nothing in return.
32 Before his time[h] he will be paid in full,[i]
and his branches will not flourish.[j]
33 He will be like a vine stripped of its unripe grapes,[k]
like an olive tree shedding its blossoms.
34 For the company of the godless will be barren,
and fire will consume the tents of those who love bribes.[l]
35 They conceive trouble and give birth to evil;[m]
their womb fashions deceit."

a *23* Or *about, looking for food*

Job's individual thoughts. Eliphaz assumed that his words were as true as God's. It is easy to spot his arrogance.

15:15, 16 "Even the heavens are not pure in his eyes." Eliphaz was repeating his argument that anything created, whether angels (holy ones) or man, is not a sufficient basis for trust and hope. Only in God can we be sure. (See the note on 4:18, 19.)

16:1ff Job's friends were supposed to be comforting him in his grief. Instead they condemned him for causing his own suffering.

Job

16

Then Job replied:

2"I have heard many things like these;
miserable comforters are you all![a]
3Will your long-winded speeches never end?
What ails you that you keep on arguing?[b]
4I also could speak like you,
if you were in my place;
I could make fine speeches against you
and shake my head[c] at you.
5But my mouth would encourage you;
comfort from my lips would bring you relief.

6"Yet if I speak, my pain is not relieved;
and if I refrain, it does not go away.
7Surely, O God, you have worn me out;[d]
you have devastated my entire household.
8You have bound me—and it has become a witness;
my gauntness[e] rises up and testifies against me.[f]
9God assails me and tears[g] me in his anger
and gnashes his teeth at me;[h]
my opponent fastens on me his piercing eyes.[i]
10Men open their mouths[j] to jeer at me;
they strike my cheek[k] in scorn
and unite together against me.[l]
11God has turned me over to evil men
and thrown me into the clutches of the wicked.[m]
12All was well with me, but he shattered me;
he seized me by the neck and crushed me.[n]
He has made me his target;[o]
13 his archers surround me.
Without pity, he pierces[p] my kidneys
and spills my gall on the ground.
14Again and again[q] he bursts upon me;
he rushes at me like a warrior.[r]

15"I have sewed sackcloth[s] over my skin
and buried my brow in the dust.
16My face is red with weeping,
deep shadows ring my eyes;
17yet my hands have been free of violence[t]
and my prayer is pure.

18"O earth, do not cover my blood;[u]
may my cry never be laid to rest![v]
19Even now my witness[w] is in heaven;
my advocate is on high.

16:2 [a]Job 13:4
16:3 [b]Job 6:26
16:4 [c]Ps 22:7; 109:25; La 2:15; Zep 2:15; Mt 27:39
16:7 [d]Job 7:3
16:8 [e]Job 19:20 [f]Job 10:17
16:9 [g]Hos 6:1 [h]Ps 35:16; La 2:16; Ac 7:54 [i]Job 13:24
16:10 [j]Ps 22:13 [k]Isa 50:6; La 3:30; Mic 5:1; Ac 23:2 [l]Ps 35:15
16:11 [m]Job 1:15, 17
16:12 [n]Job 9:17 [o]La 3:12
16:13 [p]Job 20:24
16:14 [q]Job 9:17 [r]Joel 2:7
16:15 [s]Ge 37:34
16:17 [t]Isa 59:6; Jnh 3:8
16:18 [u]Isa 26:21 [v]Ps 66:18-19
16:19 [w]Ge 31:50; Ro 1:9; 1Th 2:5

Job began his reply to Eliphaz by calling him and his friends "miserable comforters". Job's words reveal several ways to become a better comforter to those in pain: (1) don't talk just for the sake of talking; (2) don't sermonise by giving pat answers; (3) don't accuse or criticise; (4) put yourself in the other person's place; and (5) offer help and encouragement. Try Job's suggestions, knowing that they are given by a person who needed great comfort. The best comforters are those who know something about personal suffering.

16:19 Job was afraid that God had abandoned him. Yet he appealed directly to God (his witness and advocate) and to God's knowledge of his innocence. A *witness* is someone who has seen what has happened, and an *advocate* is like a lawyer who speaks on behalf of the plaintiff. By using these terms, Job showed he had cast all his hope for any fair defence upon God in heaven because he would probably die before it happened on earth. In the New Testament we learn that Jesus Christ intercedes on our behalf (Hebrews 7:25; 1 John 2:1); therefore, we have nothing to fear.

16:20
[x]La 2:19

16:21
[y]Ps 9:4

16:22
[z]Ecc 12:5

17:1
[a]Ps 88:3-4

17:2
[b]1Sa 1:6-7

17:3
[c]Ps 119:122
[d]Pr 6:1
[e]Isa 38:14

17:5
[f]Job 11:20

17:6
[g]Job 30:9

17:7
[h]Job 16:8

17:8
[i]Job 22:19

17:9
[j]Pr 4:18
[k]Job 22:30

17:10
[l]Job 12:2

17:11
[m]Job 7:6

17:13
[n]Job 3:13

17:14
[o]Job 13:28; 30:28, 30;
Ps 16:10
[p]Job 21:26

17:15
[q]Job 7:6

17:16
[r]Job 3:17-19;
Jnh 2:6

20 My intercessor is my friend[a]
as my eyes pour out[x] tears to God;
21 on behalf of a man he pleads[y] with God
as a man pleads for his friend.

22 "Only a few years will pass
before I go on the journey of no return.[z]

17

1 My spirit is broken,
my days are cut short,
the grave awaits me.[a]
2 Surely mockers[b] surround me;
my eyes must dwell on their hostility.

3 "Give me, O God, the pledge you demand.[c]
Who else will put up security[d] for me?[e]
4 You have closed their minds to understanding;
therefore you will not let them triumph.
5 If a man denounces his friends for reward,
the eyes of his children will fail.[f]

6 "God has made me a byword[g] to everyone,
a man in whose face people spit.
7 My eyes have grown dim with grief;[h]
my whole frame is but a shadow.
8 Upright men are appalled at this;
the innocent are aroused[i] against the ungodly.
9 Nevertheless, the righteous[j] will hold to their ways,
and those with clean hands[k] will grow stronger.

10 "But come on, all of you, try again!
I will not find a wise man among you.[l]
11 My days have passed, my plans are shattered,
and so are the desires of my heart.[m]
12 These men turn night into day;
in the face of darkness they say, 'Light is near.'
13 If the only home I hope for is the grave,[a][n]
if I spread out my bed in darkness,
14 if I say to corruption,[o] 'You are my father,'
and to the worm,[p] 'My mother' or 'My sister',
15 where then is my hope?[q]
Who can see any hope for me?
16 Will it go down to the gates of death?[b][r]
Will we descend together into the dust?"

a *20* Or *My friends treat me with scorn* a *13* Hebrew *Sheol* b *16* Hebrew *to Sheol*

17:10 Job's three friends had a reputation for being wise, but Job could not find wisdom in any of them. God backed up Job's claim in 42:7, when he condemned these men for their false portrayal of him. Obviously these men had a faulty view of wisdom. They assumed that because they were prosperous and successful, God must be pleased with the way they were living and thinking. Job, however, told his friends that they were starting with the wrong idea because earthly success and prosperity are not proof of faith in God. Likewise, trouble and affliction do not prove faithlessness. The truly wise man knows that wisdom comes from God alone, not from human successes or failures. And the truly wise man never forsakes God. God's wisdom proved superior to Job and to all his friends.

17:15 Job was giving up hope of any future restoration of wealth and family and wrapping himself in thoughts of death and the rest from grief and pain it promised. The rewards that Job's friends described were all related to this present life. They were silent about the possibility of life after death. We must not evaluate life only in terms of this present world because God promises a never-ending, wonderful future to those who are faithful to him.

Bildad

18 Then Bildad the Shuhite replied:

2"When will you end these speeches?
Be sensible, and then we can talk.
3Why are we regarded as cattle
and considered stupid in your sight?[a]
4You who tear yourself[b] to pieces in your anger,
is the earth to be abandoned for your sake?
Or must the rocks be moved from their place?

5"The lamp of the wicked is snuffed out;[c]
the flame of his fire stops burning.
6The light in his tent becomes dark;
the lamp beside him goes out.
7The vigour of his step is weakened;[d]
his own schemes[e] throw him down.[f]
8His feet thrust him into a net[g]
and he wanders into its mesh.
9A trap seizes him by the heel;
a snare holds him fast.
10A noose is hidden for him on the ground;
a trap lies in his path.
11Terrors startle him on every side[h]
and dog[i] his every step.
12Calamity is hungry[j] for him;
disaster is ready for him when he falls.
13It eats away parts of his skin;
death's firstborn devours his limbs.[k]
14He is torn from the security of his tent[l]
and marched off to the king of terrors.
15Fire resides[a] in his tent;
burning sulphur[m] is scattered over his dwelling.
16His roots dry up below[n]
and his branches wither above.[o]
17The memory of him perishes from the earth;
he has no name in the land.[p]
18He is driven from light into darkness[q]
and is banished from the world.
19He has no offspring[r] or descendants[s] among his people,
no survivor where once he lived.[t]
20Men of the west are appalled at his fate;[u]
men of the east are seized with horror.
21Surely such is the dwelling[v] of an evil man;
such is the place of one who knows not God."[w]

a *15* Or *Nothing he had remains*

18:3 [a]Ps 73:22
18:4 [b]Job 13:14
18:5 [c]Job 21:17; Pr 13:9; 20:20; 24:20
18:7 [d]Pr 4:12 [e]Job 5:13 [f]Job 15:6
18:8 [g]Job 22:10; Ps 9:15; 35:7
18:11 [h]Job 15:21; Jer 6:25; 20:3 [i]Job 20:8
18:12 [j]Isa 8:21
18:13 [k]Zec 14:12
18:14 [l]Job 8:22
18:15 [m]Ps 11:6
18:16 [n]Isa 5:24; Hos 9:1-16; Am 2:9 [o]Job 15:30; Mal 4:1
18:17 [p]Ps 34:16; Pr 2:22; 10:7
18:18 [q]Job 5:14
18:19 [r]Jer 22:30 [s]Isa 14:22 [t]Job 27:14-15
18:20 [u]Ps 37:13; Jer 50:27, 31
18:21 [v]Job 21:28 [w]Jer 9:3; 1Th 4:5

18:1ff Bildad thought he knew how the universe should be run, and he saw Job as an illustration of the consequences of sin. Bildad rejected Job's side of the story because it did not fit in with his outlook on life. It is easy to condemn Bildad because his errors are obvious; unfortunately, however, we often act the same way when our ideas are threatened.

18:14 The "king of terrors" is a figure of speech referring to death. Bildad viewed death as a great devourer (18:13), but the Bible teaches that God has the power to devour even death (Psalm 49:15; Isaiah 25:8; 1 Corinthians 15:54–56).

19:4
[a]Job 6:24
19:5
[b]Ps 35:26; 38:16; 55:12
19:6
[c]Job 27:2
[d]Job 18:8
19:7
[e]Job 30:20
[f]Job 9:24; Hab 1:2-4
19:8
[g]Job 3:23; La 3:7
[h]Job 30:26
19:9
[i]Job 12:17
[j]Ps 89:39, 44; La 5:16
19:10
[k]Job 12:14
[l]Job 7:6
[m]Job 24:20
19:11
[n]Job 16:9
[o]Job 13:24
19:12
[p]Job 16:13
[q]Job 30:12
19:13
[r]Ps 69:8
[s]Job 16:7; Ps 88:8
19:18
[t]2Ki 2:23
19:19
[u]Ps 55:12-13
[v]Ps 38:11
19:20
[w]Job 33:21; Ps 102:5
19:22
[x]Job 13:25; 16:11
[y]Ps 69:26

Job

19 Then Job replied:

2"How long will you torment me
and crush me with words?
3Ten times now you have reproached me;
shamelessly you attack me.
4If it is true that I have gone astray,
my error[a] remains my concern alone.
5If indeed you would exalt yourselves above me[b]
and use my humiliation against me,
6then know that God has wronged me[c]
and drawn his net[d] around me.

7"Though I cry, 'I've been wronged!' I get no response;[e]
though I call for help, there is no justice.[f]
8He has blocked my way so that I cannot pass;[g]
he has shrouded my paths in darkness.[h]
9He has stripped[i] me of my honour
and removed the crown from my head.[j]
10He tears me down[k] on every side till I am gone;
he uproots my hope[l] like a tree.[m]
11His anger[n] burns against me;
he counts me among his enemies.[o]
12His troops advance in force;[p]
they build a siege ramp[q] against me
and encamp around my tent.

13"He has alienated my brothers[r] from me;
my acquaintances are completely estranged from me.[s]
14My kinsmen have gone away;
my friends have forgotten me.
15My guests and my maidservants count me a stranger;
they look upon me as an alien.
16I summon my servant, but he does not answer,
though I beg him with my own mouth.
17My breath is offensive to my wife;
I am loathsome to my own brothers.
18Even the little boys[t] scorn me;
when I appear, they ridicule me.
19All my intimate friends[u] detest me;[v]
those I love have turned against me.
20I am nothing but skin and bones;[w]
I have escaped by only the skin of my teeth.[a]

21"Have pity on me, my friends, have pity,
for the hand of God has struck me.
22Why do you pursue[x] me as God does?
Will you never get enough of my flesh?[y]

[a] *20* Or *only my gums*

19:3–5 It is easy to point out someone else's faults or sins. Job's friends accused him of sin to make him feel guilty, not to encourage or correct him. If we feel we must admonish someone, we should be sure we are confronting that person because we love him, not because we are annoyed, inconvenienced, or seeking to blame him.

19:6 Job felt that God was treating him as an enemy when, in fact, God was his friend and thought highly of him (1:8; 2:3). In his difficulty, Job pointed at the wrong person. It was Satan, not God, who was Job's enemy. Because they stressed ultimate causes, most Israelites believed that both good and evil came from God; they also thought people were responsible for their own destinies. But the evil power loose in this world accounts for much of the suffering we experience. In verse 7, Job continued to cry out to be heard by God.

23"Oh, that my words were recorded,
that they were written on a scroll,[z]
24that they were inscribed with an iron tool on[b] lead,
or engraved in rock for ever!
25I know that my Redeemer[c][a] lives,[b]
and that in the end he will stand upon the earth.[d]
26And after my skin has been destroyed,
yet[e] in[f] my flesh I will see God;[c]
27I myself will see him
with my own eyes—I, and not another.
How my heart yearns[d] within me!

28"If you say, 'How we will hound him,
since the root of the trouble lies in him,'[g]
29you should fear the sword yourselves;
for wrath will bring punishment by the sword,[e]
and then you will know that there is judgment."[h][f]

Zophar

20 Then Zophar the Naamathite replied:

2"My troubled thoughts prompt me to answer
because I am greatly disturbed.
3I hear a rebuke[a] that dishonours me,
and my understanding inspires me to reply.

4"Surely you know how it has been from of old,
ever since man[a] was placed on the earth,
5that the mirth of the wicked is brief,
the joy of the godless lasts but a moment.[b]
6Though his pride reaches to the heavens
and his head touches the clouds,[c]
7he will perish for ever,[d] like his own dung;
those who have seen him will say, 'Where is he?'[e]
8Like a dream[f] he flies away,[g] no more to be found,
banished[h] like a vision of the night.[i]
9The eye that saw him will not see him again;
his place will look on him no more.[j]
10His children[k] must make amends to the poor;

b 24 Or *and* **c** 25 Or *defender* **d** 25 Or *upon my grave* **e** 26 Or *And after I awake, / though this ˌbodyˌ has been destroyed, / then* **f** 26 Or */ apart from* **g** 28 Many Hebrew manuscripts, Septuagint and Vulgate; most Hebrew manuscripts *me* **h** 29 Or */ that you may come to know the Almighty* **a** 4 Or *Adam*

19:23 [z]Isa 30:8
19:25 [a]Ps 78:35; Pr 23:11; Isa 43:14; Jer 50:34 [b]Job 16:19
19:26 [c]Ps 17:15; Mt 5:8; 1Co 13:12; 1Jn 3:2
19:27 [d]Ps 73:26
19:29 [e]Job 15:22 [f]Job 22:4; Ps 1:5; 9:7
20:3 [a]Job 19:3
20:5 [b]Job 8:12; Ps 37:35-36; 73:19
20:6 [c]Isa 14:13-14; Ob 1:3-4
20:7 [d]Job 4:20 [e]Job 7:10; 8:18
20:8 [f]Ps 73:20 [g]Job 27:21-23 [h]Job 18:18 [i]Ps 90:5
20:9 [j]Job 7:8
20:10 [k]Job 5:4

19:25–27 At the heart of the book of Job comes his ringing affirmation of confidence: "I know that my Redeemer lives." In ancient Israel a *redeemer* was a family member who bought a slave's way to freedom or who took care of a widow (see the note on Ruth 3:1). What tremendous faith Job had, especially in light of the fact that he was unaware of the conference between God and Satan. Job thought that God had brought all these disasters upon him! Faced with death and decay, Job still expected to see God—and he expected to do so in his body. When the book of Job was written, Israel did not have a well-developed doctrine of the resurrection. Although Job struggled with the idea that God was presently against him, he firmly believed that in the end God would be on his side. This belief was so strong that Job became one of the first to talk about the resurrection of the body (see also Psalm 16:10; Isaiah 26:19; Daniel 12:2, 13).

19:26 Job said: "in my flesh I will see God." In Job's situation, it seemed unlikely to him that he would, in his flesh, see God. And that's just the point of Job's faith! He was confident that God's justice would triumph, even if it would take a miracle like resurrection to accomplish this.

20:1ff Zophar's speech again revealed his false assumption because he based his arguments purely on the idea that Job was an evil hypocrite. Zophar said that although Job had it good for a while, he didn't live righteously, so God took his wealth from him. According to Zophar, Job's calamities *proved* his wickedness.

20:6, 7 Although Zophar was wrong in directing this tirade against Job, he was correct in talking about the final end of evil people. At first, sin seems enjoyable and attractive. Lying, stealing, or oppressing others often brings temporary gain to those who practise these sins. Some live a long time with ill-gotten gain. But in the end, God's justice will prevail. What Zophar missed is that judgment for these sins may not come in the lifetime of the sinner. Punishment may be deferred until the last judgment, when sinners will be eternally cut off from God. We should not be impressed with the success and power of evil people. God's judgment on them is certain.

20:10
[l] Job 27:16-17

20:11
[m] Job 13:26
[n] Job 21:26

20:13
[o] Nu 11:18-20

20:16
[p] Dt 32:32
[q] Dt 32:24

20:17
[r] Dt 32:13
[s] Job 29:6

20:19
[t] Job 24:4, 14; 35:9

20:20
[u] Ecc 5:12-14

20:21
[v] Job 15:29

20:23
[w] Ps 78:30-31

20:24
[x] Isa 24:18; Am 5:19

20:25
[y] Job 18:11
[z] Job 16:13

20:26
[a] Job 18:18
[b] Ps 21:9

20:27
[c] Dt 31:28

20:28
[d] Dt 28:31
[e] Job 21:17, 20, 30

20:29
[f] Job 27:13

21:3
[a] Job 16:10

his own hands must give back his wealth.[l]
11 The youthful vigour[m] that fills his bones
will lie with him in the dust.[n]

12 "Though evil is sweet in his mouth
and he hides it under his tongue,
13 though he cannot bear to let it go
and keeps it in his mouth,[o]
14 yet his food will turn sour in his stomach;
it will become the venom of serpents within him.
15 He will spit out the riches he swallowed;
God will make his stomach vomit them up.
16 He will suck the poison[p] of serpents;
the fangs of an adder will kill him.[q]
17 He will not enjoy the streams,
the rivers flowing with honey[r] and cream.[s]
18 What he toiled for he must give back uneaten;
he will not enjoy the profit from his trading.
19 For he has oppressed the poor and left them destitute;[t]
he has seized houses he did not build.

20 "Surely he will have no respite from his craving;[u]
he cannot save himself by his treasure.
21 Nothing is left for him to devour;
his prosperity will not endure.[v]
22 In the midst of his plenty, distress will overtake him;
the full force of misery will come upon him.
23 When he has filled his belly,
God will vent his burning anger against him
and rain down his blows upon him.[w]
24 Though he flees[x] from an iron weapon,
a bronze-tipped arrow pierces him.
25 He pulls it out of his back,
the gleaming point out of his liver.
Terrors[y] will come over him;[z]
26 total darkness[a] lies in wait for his treasures.
A fire unfanned will consume him[b]
and devour what is left in his tent.
27 The heavens will expose his guilt;
the earth will rise up against him.[c]
28 A flood will carry off his house,[d]
rushing waters**[b]** on the day of God's wrath.[e]
29 Such is the fate God allots the wicked,
the heritage appointed for them by God."[f]

Job

21

Then Job replied:

2 "Listen carefully to my words;
let this be the consolation you give me.
3 Bear with me while I speak,
and after I have spoken, mock on.[a]

b *28* Or *The possessions in his house will be carried off, / washed away*

21:1ff Job refuted Zophar's idea that evil people never experience wealth and happiness, pointing out that in the real world the wicked do indeed prosper. God does as he wills to individuals (21:22–25), and people cannot use their circumstances to measure their own goodness or God's—they are sometimes (but not always) related. Success to Job's friends was based on outward performance; success to God, however, is based on a person's heart.

4 "Is my complaint directed to man?
Why should I not be impatient?[b]
5 Look at me and be astonished;
clap your hand over your mouth.[c]
6 When I think about this, I am terrified;
trembling seizes my body.
7 Why do the wicked live on,
growing old and increasing in power?[d]
8 They see their children established around them,
their offspring before their eyes.[e]
9 Their homes are safe and free from fear;[f]
the rod of God is not upon them.
10 Their bulls never fail to breed;
their cows calve and do not miscarry.[g]
11 They send forth their children as a flock;
their little ones dance about.
12 They sing to the music of tambourine and harp;
they make merry to the sound of the flute.[h]
13 They spend their years in prosperity[i]
and go down to the grave**[a]** in peace.**[b]**
14 Yet they say to God, 'Leave us alone![j]
We have no desire to know your ways.[k]
15 Who is the Almighty, that we should serve him?
What would we gain by praying to him?'[l]
16 But their prosperity is not in their own hands,
so I stand aloof from the counsel of the wicked.

17 "Yet how often is the lamp of the wicked snuffed out?[m]
How often does calamity come upon them,
the fate God allots in his anger?
18 How often are they like straw before the wind,
like chaff[n] swept away by a gale?
19 ⌊It is said,⌋ 'God stores up a man's punishment for his sons.'[o]
Let him repay the man himself, so that he will know it!
20 Let his own eyes see his destruction;
let him drink[p] of the wrath of the Almighty.**[c]**[q]
21 For what does he care about the family he leaves behind
when his allotted months[r] come to an end?

22 "Can anyone teach knowledge to God,[s]
since he judges even the highest?[t]
23 One man dies in full vigour,
completely secure and at ease,
24 his body**[d]** well nourished,
his bones rich with marrow.[u]
25 Another man dies in bitterness of soul,
never having enjoyed anything good.
26 Side by side they lie in the dust,
and worms cover them both.[v]

27 "I know full well what you are thinking,
the schemes by which you would wrong me.

a *13* Hebrew *Sheol* **b** *13* Or *in an instant* **c** *17–20* Verses 17 and 18 may be taken as exclamations and 19 and 20 as declarations. **d** *24* The meaning of the Hebrew for this word is uncertain.

21:4 *b* Job 6:11
21:5 *c* Jdg 18:19; Job 29:9; 40:4
21:7 *d* Job 12:6; Ps 73:3; Jer 12:1; Hab 1:13
21:8 *e* Ps 17:14
21:9 *f* Ps 73:5
21:10 *g* Ex 23:26
21:12 *h* Ps 81:2
21:13 *i* Job 36:11
21:14 *j* Job 22:17 *k* Pr 1:29
21:15 *l* Ex 5:2; Job 34:9; Mal 3:14
21:17 *m* Job 18:5
21:18 *n* Job 13:25; Ps 1:4
21:19 *o* Ex 20:5; Jer 31:29; Eze 18:2
21:20 *p* Ps 75:8; Isa 51:17 *q* Jer 25:15; Rev 14:10
21:21 *r* Job 14:5
21:22 *s* Job 35:11; 36:22; Isa 40:13-14; Ro 11:34 *t* Ps 82:1
21:24 *u* Pr 3:8
21:26 *v* Job 24:20; Ecc 9:2-3; Isa 14:11

21:22 Although baffled by the reasons for his suffering, Job affirmed God's superior understanding by asking, "Can anyone teach knowledge to God?" The way you respond to your personal struggles shows your attitude towards God. Rather than becoming angry with God, continue to trust him, no matter what your circumstances may be. Although it is sometimes difficult to see, God *is* in control. We must commit ourselves to him so we will not resent his timing.

21:28 [w]Job 1:3; 12:21; 31:37 [x]Job 8:22
21:30 [y]Pr 16:4 [z]Job 20:22, 28; 2Pe 2:9
21:33 [a]Job 3:22; 17:16; 24:24 [b]Job 3:19
21:34 [c]Job 16:2
22:2 [a]Lk 17:10
22:4 [b]Job 14:3; 19:29; Ps 143:2
22:5 [c]Job 11:6; 15:5
22:6 [d]Ex 22:26; Dt 24:6, 17; Eze 18:12, 16
22:7 [e]Job 31:17, 21, 31
22:8 [f]Isa 3:3; 9:15
22:9 [g]Job 24:3, 21
22:11 [h]Job 5:14 [i]Ps 69:1-2; 124:4-5; La 3:54
22:12 [j]Job 11:8
22:13 [k]Ps 10:11; Isa 29:15 [l]Eze 8:12

28 You say, 'Where now is the great man's[w] house,
the tents where wicked men lived?'[x]
29 Have you never questioned those who travel?
Have you paid no regard to their accounts—
30 that the evil man is spared from the day of calamity,[y]
that he is delivered from[e] the day of wrath?[z]
31 Who denounces his conduct to his face?
Who repays him for what he has done?
32 He is carried to the grave,
and watch is kept over his tomb.
33 The soil in the valley is sweet to him;[a]
all men follow after him,
and a countless throng goes[f] before him.[b]

34 "So how can you console me[c] with your nonsense?
Nothing is left of your answers but falsehood!"

3. Third round of discussion

Eliphaz

22 Then Eliphaz the Temanite replied:

2 "Can a man be of benefit to God?[a]
Can even a wise man benefit him?
3 What pleasure would it give the Almighty if you were righteous?
What would he gain if your ways were blameless?

4 "Is it for your piety that he rebukes you
and brings charges against you?[b]
5 Is not your wickedness great?
Are not your sins[c] endless?
6 You demanded security[d] from your brothers for no reason;
you stripped men of their clothing, leaving them naked.
7 You gave no water to the weary
and you withheld food from the hungry,[e]
8 though you were a powerful man, owning land—
an honoured man,[f] living on it.
9 And you sent widows away empty-handed[g]
and broke the strength of the fatherless.
10 That is why snares are all around you,
why sudden peril terrifies you,
11 why it is so dark[h] that you cannot see,
and why a flood of water covers you.[i]

12 "Is not God in the heights of heaven?[j]
And see how lofty are the highest stars!
13 Yet you say, 'What does God know?[k]
Does he judge through such darkness?[l]

[e] *30* Or *man is reserved for the day of calamity, / that he is brought forth to* [f] *33* Or / *as a countless throng went*

21:29–33 If wicked people become wealthy despite their sin, why should we try to be good? The wicked may *seem* to get away with sin, but there is a higher Judge and a future judgment (Revelation 20:11–15). The final settlement of justice will come not in this life, but in the next. What is important is how a person views God in prosperity or poverty, not the prosperity or poverty itself.

22:1ff This is Eliphaz's third and final speech to Job. When he first spoke to Job (chapters 4, 5), he commended Job's good deeds and gently suggested that Job might need to repent of some sin. While he said nothing new in this speech, he did get more specific. He couldn't shake his belief that suffering is God's punishment for evil deeds, so he suggested several possible sins that Job might have committed. Eliphaz wasn't trying to destroy Job; at the end of his speech he promised that Job would receive peace and restoration if he would only admit his sin and repent.

22:12–14 Eliphaz declared that Job's view of God was too small, and he criticised Job for thinking that God was too far removed from earth to care about him. If Job knew of God's intense, personal interest in him, Eliphaz said, he wouldn't dare take his sins so lightly. Eliphaz had a point—some people do take sin lightly because they think God is far away and doesn't notice all we do. But his point did not apply to Job.

14Thick clouds[m] veil him, so he does not see us
as he goes about in the vaulted heavens.'
15Will you keep to the old path
that evil men have trod?
16They were carried off before their time,[n]
their foundations washed away by a flood.[o]
17They said to God, 'Leave us alone!
What can the Almighty do to us?'[p]
18Yet it was he who filled their houses with good things,[q]
so I stand aloof from the counsel of the wicked.[r]

19"The righteous see their ruin and rejoice;[s]
the innocent mock[t] them, saying,
20'Surely our foes are destroyed,
and fire[u] devours their wealth.'

21"Submit to God and be at peace with him;
in this way prosperity will come to you.[v]
22Accept instruction from his mouth
and lay up his words in your heart.
23If you return[w] to the Almighty, you will be restored:[x]
If you remove wickedness far from your tent[y]
24and assign your nuggets to the dust,
your gold of Ophir to the rocks in the ravines,[z]
25then the Almighty will be your gold,
the choicest silver for you.[a]
26Surely then you will find delight in the Almighty[b]
and will lift up your face to God.
27You will pray to him,[c] and he will hear you,
and you will fulfil your vows.
28What you decide on will be done,
and light will shine on your ways.
29When men are brought low and you say, 'Lift them up!'
then he will save the downcast.[d]
30He will deliver even one who is not innocent,
who will be delivered through the cleanness of your hands."[e]

Job

23 Then Job replied:

2"Even today my complaint[a] is bitter;[b]
his hand**[a]** is heavy in spite of**[b]** my groaning.
3If only I knew where to find him;
if only I could go to his dwelling!
4I would state my case[c] before him
and fill my mouth with arguments.
5I would find out what he would answer me,
and consider what he would say.

[a] *2* Septuagint and Syriac; Hebrew / *the hand on me* [b] *2* Or *heavy on me in*

22:14 [m]Job 26:9
22:16 [n]Job 15:32 [o]Job 14:19; Mt 7:26-27
22:17 [p]Job 21:15
22:18 [q]Job 12:6 [r]Job 21:16
22:19 [s]Ps 58:10; 107:42 [t]Ps 52:6
22:20 [u]Job 15:30
22:21 [v]Ps 34:8-10
22:23 [w]Job 8:5; Isa 31:6; Zec 1:3 [x]Isa 19:22; Ac 20:32 [y]Job 11:14
22:24 [z]Job 31:25
22:25 [a]Isa 33:6
22:26 [b]Job 27:10; Isa 58:14
22:27 [c]Job 33:26; 34:28; Isa 58:9
22:29 [d]Mt 23:12; 1Pe 5:5
22:30 [e]Job 42:7-8
23:2 [a]Job 7:11 [b]Job 6:3
23:4 [c]Job 13:18

22:21–30 Several times Job's friends showed a partial knowledge of God's truth and character, but they had trouble accurately applying this truth to life. Such was the case with Eliphaz, who gave a beautiful summary of repentance. He was correct in saying that we must ask for God's forgiveness when we sin, but his statement did not apply to Job who had already sought God's forgiveness (7:20, 21; 9:20; 13:23) and had lived closely in touch with God all along.

23:1–24:25 Job continued his questioning, saying that his suffering would be more bearable if only he knew why it was happening. If there was sin for which he could repent, he would! He knew about the wicked and the fact that they would be punished; he knew God could vindicate him if he so chose. In all his examples of the wicked in the world, his overriding desire was for God to clear his name, prove his righteousness, and explain why he was chosen to receive all this calamity. Job tried to make his friends see that questions about God, life, and justice are not as simple as they assumed.

23:6 [d]Job 9:4
23:7 [e]Job 13:3
23:9 [f]Job 9:11
23:10 [g]Ps 66:10; 139:1-3 [h]1Pe 1:7
23:11 [i]Ps 17:5 [j]Ps 44:18
23:12 [k]Job 6:10 [l]Jn 4:32, 34
23:13 [m]Ps 115:3
23:14 [n]1Th 3:3
23:16 [o]Dt 20:3; Ps 22:14; Jer 51:46 [p]Job 27:2
23:17 [q]Job 19:8
24:1 [a]Jer 46:10 [b]Ac 1:7
24:2 [c]Dt 19:14; 27:17; Pr 23:10
24:3 [d]Dt 24:6, 10, 12, 17; Job 22:6
24:4 [e]Job 29:12; 30:25; Ps 41:1 [f]Pr 28:28
24:5 [g]Ps 104:23
24:7 [h]Ex 22:27; Job 22:6
24:8 [i]La 4:5
24:9 [j]Dt 24:17

6 Would he oppose me with great power?[d]
No, he would not press charges against me.
7 There an upright man could present his case before him,[e]
and I would be delivered for ever from my judge.

8 "But if I go to the east, he is not there;
if I go to the west, I do not find him.
9 When he is at work in the north, I do not see him;
when he turns to the south, I catch no glimpse of him.[f]
10 But he knows the way that I take;
when he has tested me,[g] I shall come forth as gold.[h]
11 My feet have closely followed his steps;[i]
I have kept to his way without turning aside.[j]
12 I have not departed from the commands of his lips;[k]
I have treasured the words of his mouth more than my daily bread.[l]

13 "But he stands alone, and who can oppose him?
He does whatever he pleases.[m]
14 He carries out his decree against me,
and many such plans he still has in store.[n]
15 That is why I am terrified before him;
when I think of all this, I fear him.
16 God has made my heart faint;[o]
the Almighty[p] has terrified me.
17 Yet I am not silenced by the darkness,[q]
by the thick darkness that covers my face.

24

"Why does the Almighty not set times for judgment?[a]
Why must those who know him look in vain for such days?[b]
2 Men move boundary stones;[c]
they pasture flocks they have stolen.
3 They drive away the orphan's donkey
and take the widow's ox in pledge.[d]
4 They thrust the needy from the path
and force all the poor[e] of the land into hiding.[f]
5 Like wild donkeys in the desert,
the poor go about their labour[g] of foraging food;
the wasteland provides food for their children.
6 They gather fodder in the fields
and glean in the vineyards of the wicked.
7 Lacking clothes, they spend the night naked;
they have nothing to cover themselves in the cold.[h]
8 They are drenched by mountain rains
and hug[i] the rocks for lack of shelter.
9 The fatherless[j] child is snatched from the breast;
the infant of the poor is seized for a debt.
10 Lacking clothes, they go about naked;
they carry the sheaves, but still go hungry.

23:10 In chapter 22, Eliphaz had tried to condemn Job by identifying some secret sin which he may have committed. Here Job declares his confidence in his integrity and God's justice. We are always likely to have hidden sin in our lives, sin we don't even know about because God's standards are so high and our performance is so imperfect. If we are true believers, however, all our sins are forgiven because of what Christ did on the cross in our behalf (Romans 5:1; 8:1). The Bible also teaches that even if our hearts condemn us, God is greater than our hearts (1 John 3:20). His forgiveness and cleansing are sufficient; they overrule our nagging doubts. The Holy Spirit in us is our proof that we are forgiven in God's eyes even though we may *feel* guilty. If we, like Job, are truly seeking God, we can stand up to others' accusations as well as our own nagging doubts. If God has forgiven and accepted us, we are forgiven indeed.

11 They crush olives among the terraces;[a]
they tread the winepresses, yet suffer thirst.
12 The groans of the dying rise from the city,
and the souls of the wounded cry out for help.[k]
But God charges no-one with wrongdoing.[l]

13 "There are those who rebel against the light,[m]
who do not know its ways
or stay in its paths.[n]
14 When daylight is gone, the murderer rises up
and kills the poor and needy;
in the night he steals forth like a thief.[o]
15 The eye of the adulterer watches for dusk;[p]
he thinks, 'No eye will see me,'[q]
and he keeps his face concealed.
16 In the dark, men break into houses,[r]
but by day they shut themselves in;
they want nothing to do with the light.[s]
17 For all of them, deep darkness is their morning;[b]
they make friends with the terrors of darkness.[c]

18 "Yet they are foam[t] on the surface of the water;[u]
their portion of the land is cursed,
so that no-one goes to the vineyards.
19 As heat and drought snatch away the melted snow,[v]
so the grave[d][w] snatches away those who have sinned.
20 The womb forgets them,
the worm feasts on them;
evil men are no longer remembered[x]
but are broken like a tree.[y]
21 They prey on the barren and childless woman,
and to the widow show no kindness.[z]
22 But God drags away the mighty by his power;
though they become established, they have no assurance of
life.[a]
23 He may let them rest in a feeling of security,[b]
but his eyes are on their ways.[c]
24 For a little while they are exalted, and then they are gone;[d]
they are brought low and gathered up like all others;
they are cut off like ears of corn.[e]

25 "If this is not so, who can prove me false
and reduce my words to nothing?"[f]

Bildad

25

Then Bildad the Shuhite replied:

2 "Dominion and awe belong to God;[a]
he establishes order in the heights of heaven.
3 Can his forces be numbered?

24:12 [k]Eze 26:15 [l]Job 9:23
24:13 [m]Jn 3:19-20 [n]Isa 5:20
24:14 [o]Ps 10:9
24:15 [p]Pr 7:8-9 [q]Ps 10:11
24:16 [r]Ex 22:2; Mt 6:19 [s]Jn 3:20
24:18 [t]Job 9:26 [u]Job 22:16
24:19 [v]Job 6:17 [w]Job 21:13
24:20 [x]Job 18:17; Pr 10:7 [y]Ps 31:12; Da 4:14
24:21 [z]Job 22:9
24:22 [a]Dt 28:66
24:23 [b]Job 12:6 [c]Job 11:11
24:24 [d]Job 14:21; Ps 37:10 [e]Isa 17:5
24:25 [f]Job 6:28; 27:4
25:2 [a]Job 9:4; Rev 1:6

a *11* Or *olives between the millstones*; the meaning of the Hebrew for this word is uncertain. **b** *17* Or *them, their morning is like the shadow of death* **c** *17* Or *of the shadow of death* **d** *19* Hebrew *Sheol*

24:18–21 Job suddenly seemed to be arguing on his friends' side. For this reason, some commentators think one of Job's friends said these words. But we shouldn't expect Job to present a unified argument. He was confused. He was not arguing that, in every case, God rewards the wicked and punishes the righteous; he was simply asserting that in his case, a righteous man was suffering.

25:1ff Bildad's final reply was weak. It ignored Job's examples of the prosperity of the wicked. Instead of attempting to refute Job, Bildad accused Job of pride because he was claiming that his suffering was not the result of sin. Job never claimed to be without sin, but only that his sin could not have caused his present trouble.

Upon whom does his light not rise?[b]
4How then can a man be righteous before God?
How can one born of woman be pure?[c]
5If even the moon[d] is not bright
and the stars are not pure in his eyes,[e]
6how much less man, who is but a maggot—
a son of man,[f] who is only a worm!"[g]

Job

26 Then Job replied:

2"How you have helped the powerless![a]
How you have saved the arm that is feeble![b]
3What advice you have offered to one without wisdom!
And what great insight you have displayed!
4Who has helped you utter these words?
And whose spirit spoke from your mouth?

5"The dead are in deep anguish,[c]
those beneath the waters and all that live in them.
6Death[a][d] is naked before God;
Destruction[b] lies uncovered.[e]
7He spreads out the northern ⌞skies⌟[f] over empty space;
he suspends the earth over nothing.
8He wraps up the waters[g] in his clouds,[h]
yet the clouds do not burst under their weight.
9He covers the face of the full moon,
spreading his clouds[i] over it.
10He marks out the horizon on the face of the waters[j]
for a boundary between light and darkness.[k]
11The pillars of the heavens quake,
aghast at his rebuke.
12By his power he churned up the sea;[l]
by his wisdom[m] he cut Rahab to pieces.
13By his breath the skies became fair;
his hand pierced the gliding serpent.[n]
14And these are but the outer fringe of his works;
how faint the whisper we hear of him!
Who then can understand the thunder of his power?"[o]

27 And Job continued his discourse:[a]

2"As surely as God lives, who has denied me justice,[b]
the Almighty, who has made me taste bitterness of soul,[c]
3as long as I have life within me,

25:3 [b]Jas 1:17
25:4 [c]Job 4:17; 14:4
25:5 [d]Job 31:26 [e]Job 15:15
25:6 [f]Job 7:17 [g]Ps 22:6
26:2 [a]Job 6:12 [b]Ps 71:9
26:5 [c]Ps 88:10
26:6 [d]Ps 139:8 [e]Job 41:11; Pr 15:11; Heb 4:13
26:7 [f]Job 9:8
26:8 [g]Pr 30:4 [h]Job 37:11
26:9 [i]Job 22:14; Ps 97:2
26:10 [j]Pr 8:27, 29 [k]Job 38:8-11
26:12 [l]Ex 14:21; Isa 51:15; Jer 31:35 [m]Job 12:13
26:13 [n]Isa 27:1
26:14 [o]Job 36:29
27:1 [a]Job 29:1
27:2 [b]Job 34:5 [c]Job 9:18

[a]*6* Hebrew *Sheol* [b]*6* Hebrew *Abaddon*

25:6 It is important to understand that Bildad, not God, was calling man a worm. Human beings are created in God's image (Genesis 1:26, 27). Psalm 8:5 says that man is "a little lower than the heavenly beings". Bildad may have simply been using a poetic description to contrast our worth to the worth and power of God. To come to God, we need not crawl like worms. We can approach him boldly in faith (Hebrews 4:16).

26:1ff Job has the distinction of giving the longest speech in the book—six chapters—weaving together pictures of God's mystery and power in a beautiful poem of trust. Beginning by brushing off Bildad's latest reply as irrelevant (chapter 25), Job then told Bildad and his friends that they could not possibly know everything about God. Wisdom does not originate from this life or from the human mind—it comes from God (28:27, 28). Job then defended his upright and honest life. He had effectively sought to follow God's way of living. While admitting that he was not perfect, Job maintained that his motives were right.

26:2–4 With great sarcasm, Job attacked Bildad's comments. Their theological explanations failed to bring any relief because they were unable to turn their knowledge into helpful counsel. When dealing with people, it is more important to love and understand them than to analyse them or give advice. Compassion produces greater results than criticism or blame.

the breath of God[d] in my nostrils,
4my lips will not speak wickedness,
and my tongue will utter no deceit.[e]
5I will never admit you are in the right;
till I die, I will not deny my integrity.[f]
6I will maintain my righteousness and never let go of it;
my conscience will not reproach me as long as I live.[g]

7"May my enemies be like the wicked,
my adversaries like the unjust!
8For what hope has the godless[h] when he is cut off,
when God takes away his life?[i]
9Does God listen to his cry
when distress comes upon him?[j]
10Will he find delight in the Almighty?[k]
Will he call upon God at all times?

11"I will teach you about the power of God;
the ways of the Almighty I will not conceal.
12You have all seen this yourselves.
Why then this meaningless talk?

13"Here is the fate God allots to the wicked,
the heritage a ruthless man receives from the Almighty:[l]
14However many his children, their fate is the sword;[m]
his offspring will never have enough to eat.[n]
15The plague will bury those who survive him,
and their widows will not weep for them.[o]
16Though he heaps up silver like dust
and clothes like piles of clay,[p]
17what he lays up the righteous will wear,[q]
and the innocent will divide his silver.
18The house he builds is like a moth's cocoon,[r]
like a hut[s] made by a watchman.
19He lies down wealthy, but will do so no more;[t]
when he opens his eyes, all is gone.
20Terrors overtake him like a flood;[u]
a tempest snatches him away in the night.[v]
21The east wind carries him off, and he is gone;
it sweeps him out of his place.[w]
22It hurls itself against him without mercy[x]
as he flees headlong from its power.[y]
23It claps its hands in derision
and hisses him out of his place.[z]

28 "There is a mine for silver
and a place where gold is refined.
2Iron is taken from the earth,
and copper is smelted from ore.[a]
3Man puts an end to the darkness;[b]
he searches the farthest recesses

27:3 [d]Job 32:8; 33:4
27:4 [e]Job 6:28
27:5 [f]Job 2:9; 13:15
27:6 [g]Job 2:3
27:8 [h]Job 8:13 [i]Job 11:20; Lk 12:20
27:9 [j]Job 35:12; Pr 1:28; Isa 1:15; Jer 14:12; Mic 3:4
27:10 [k]Job 22:26
27:13 [l]Job 15:20; 20:29
27:14 [m]Dt 28:41; Job 15:22; Hos 9:13 [n]Job 20:10
27:15 [o]Ps 78:64
27:16 [p]Zec 9:3
27:17 [q]Pr 28:8; Ecc 2:26
27:18 [r]Job 8:14 [s]Isa 1:8
27:19 [t]Job 7:8
27:20 [u]Job 15:21 [v]Job 20:8
27:21 [w]Job 7:10; 21:18
27:22 [x]Jer 13:14; Eze 5:11; 24:14 [y]Job 11:20
27:23 [z]Job 18:18
28:2 [a]Dt 8:9
28:3 [b]Ecc 1:13

27:6 In the midst of all the accusations, Job was able to declare that his conscience was clear. Only God's forgiveness and the determination to live rightly before God can bring a clear conscience. How important Job's record became as he was being accused. Like Job, we can't claim sinless lives, but we *can* claim forgiven lives. When we confess our sins to God, he forgives us. Then we can live with clear consciences (1 John 1:9).

27:13–23 Job agreed with his friends that the end of the wicked will be disaster, but he did not agree that *he* was wicked and deserving of punishment. Most of the punishments Job listed never happened to him. So he wasn't including himself as one of the wicked. On the contrary, he continually pleaded for God to vindicate him.

28:5 [c]Ps 104:14
28:12 [d]Ecc 7:24
28:13 [e]Pr 3:15; Mt 13:44-46
28:15 [f]Pr 3:13-14; 8:10-11; 16:16
28:17 [g]Pr 16:16

for ore in the blackest darkness.
4Far from where people dwell he cuts a shaft,
in places forgotten by the foot of man;
far from men he dangles and sways.
5The earth, from which food comes,[c]
is transformed below as by fire;
6sapphires[a] come from its rocks,
and its dust contains nuggets of gold.
7No bird of prey knows that hidden path,
no falcon's eye has seen it.
8Proud beasts do not set foot on it,
and no lion prowls there.
9Man's hand assaults the flinty rock
and lays bare the roots of the mountains.
10He tunnels through the rock;
his eyes see all its treasures.
11He searches[b] the sources of the rivers
and brings hidden things to light.

12"But where can wisdom be found?[d]
Where does understanding dwell?
13Man does not comprehend its worth;[e]
it cannot be found in the land of the living.
14The deep says, 'It is not in me';
the sea says, 'It is not with me.'
15It cannot be bought with the finest gold,
nor can its price be weighed in silver.[f]
16It cannot be bought with the gold of Ophir,
with precious onyx or sapphires.
17Neither gold nor crystal can compare with it,
nor can it be had for jewels of gold.[g]
18Coral and jasper are not worthy of mention;

[a] *6* Or *lapis lazuli*; also in verse 16 [b] *11* Septuagint, Aquila and Vulgate; Hebrew *He dams up*

WHERE CAN WISDOM BE FOUND?
Job and his friends differed in their ideas of how people become wise.

Person	*His source of wisdom*	*Attitude towards God*
Eliphaz	Wisdom is learned by observing and experiencing life. He based his advice to Job on his confident, firsthand knowledge (4:7, 8; 5:3, 27).	"I have personally observed how God works and have figured him out."
Bildad	Wisdom is inherited from the past. Trustworthy knowledge is secondhand. He based his advice to Job on traditional proverbs and sayings that he frequently quoted (8:8, 9; 18:5–21).	"Those who have gone before us figured God out and all we have to do is use that knowledge."
Zophar	Wisdom belongs to the wise. He based his advice on his wisdom that had no other source than himself (11:6; 20:1–29).	"The wise know what God is like, but there aren't many of us around."
Job	God is the source of wisdom, and the first step towards wisdom is to fear God (28:20–28).	"God reveals his wisdom to those who humbly trust him."

28:13 Job stated that wisdom cannot be found among the living. It is natural for people who do not understand the importance of God's word to seek wisdom here on earth. They look to philosophers and other leaders to give them direction for living. Yet Job said that wisdom is not found there. No leader or group of leaders can produce enough knowledge or insight to explain the totality of human experience. The ultimate interpretation of life, of who we are and where we are going, must come from outside and above our mortal life. When looking for guidance, seek God's wisdom as revealed in the Bible. To be lifted above and beyond the boundaries of life, we must know and trust the Lord of life.

28:16 Gold of Ophir was considered the finest gold available. Ophir may have been located in Africa, along the Arabian coast, or in India. Wherever it was, it was a good distance from Israel, for it took Solomon's ships three years to make the voyage (1 Kings 9:28; 10:22).

the price of wisdom is beyond rubies.[h]
19 The topaz of Cush cannot compare with it;
it cannot be bought with pure gold.[i]

20 "Where then does wisdom come from?
Where does understanding dwell?[j]
21 It is hidden from the eyes of every living thing,
concealed even from the birds of the air.
22 Destruction[c][k] and Death say,
'Only a rumour of it has reached our ears.'
23 God understands the way to it
and he alone knows where it dwells,[l]
24 for he views the ends of the earth[m]
and sees everything under the heavens.[n]
25 When he established the force of the wind
and measured out the waters,[o]
26 when he made a decree for the rain
and a path for the thunderstorm,[p]
27 then he looked at wisdom and appraised it;
he confirmed it and tested it.
28 And he said to man,
'The fear of the Lord—that is wisdom,
and to shun evil is understanding.[q]' "

29 Job continued his discourse:[a]

2 "How I long for the months gone by,
for the days when God watched over me,[b]
3 when his lamp shone upon my head
and by his light I walked through darkness![c]
4 Oh, for the days when I was in my prime,
when God's intimate friendship blessed my house,[d]
5 when the Almighty was still with me
and my children were around me,
6 when my path was drenched with cream[e]
and the rock[f] poured out for me streams of olive oil.[g]

7 "When I went to the gate[h] of the city
and took my seat in the public square,
8 the young men saw me and stepped aside
and the old men rose to their feet;
9 the chief men refrained from speaking
and covered their mouths with their hands;[i]
10 the voices of the nobles were hushed,
and their tongues stuck to the roof of their mouths.[j]
11 Whoever heard me spoke well of me,

c 22 Hebrew *Abaddon*

28:18 h Pr 3:15
28:19 i Pr 8:19
28:20 j ver 23, 28
28:22 k Job 26:6
28:23 l Pr 8:22-31
28:24 m Ps 33:13-14; n Pr 15:3
28:25 o Job 12:15; Ps 135:7
28:26 p Job 37:3, 8, 11; 38:25, 27
28:28 q Dt 4:6; Ps 111:10; Pr 1:7; 9:10
29:1 a Job 13:12; 27:1
29:2 b Jer 31:28
29:3 c Job 11:17
29:4 d Ps 25:14; Pr 3:32
29:6 e Job 20:17; f Ps 81:16; g Dt 32:13
29:7 h Job 31:21
29:9 i Job 21:5
29:10 j Ps 137:6

28:28 "The fear of the Lord" is a key theme in the wisdom literature of the Bible (Job through Song of Songs). It means to have respect and reverence for God and to be in awe of his majesty and power. This is the starting point to finding real wisdom (see Proverbs 1:7–9).

29:6 Cream and olive oil were symbols of material prosperity in an agricultural society. Job's flocks and olive trees were so plentiful that everything seemed to overflow.

29:7ff Job was walking a fine line between bragging about past accomplishments and recalling good deeds in order to answer the charges against him. Job's one weakness throughout his conversations is that he came dangerously close to pride. Pride is especially deceptive when we are doing right. But it separates us from God by making us think we're better than we really are. Then comes the tendency to trust our own opinions, which leads to other kinds of sin. While it is not wrong to recount past deeds, it is far better to recount God's blessings to us. This will help keep us from inadvertently falling into pride.

29:7–17 Because of this description of Job's work, many commentators believe that Job was a judge. In Job's day, a judge served as both a city councillor and a magistrate, helping to manage the community and settle disputes. In most cases, this was not a full-time position but a part-time post held on the basis of one's respect and standing in the area.

and those who saw me commended me,
12because I rescued the poor[k] who cried for help,
and the fatherless[l] who had none to assist him.[m]
13The man who was dying blessed me;[n]
I made the widow's[o] heart sing.
14I put on righteousness[p] as my clothing;
justice was my robe and my turban.
15I was eyes[q] to the blind
and feet to the lame.
16I was a father to the needy;[r]
I took up the case of the stranger.
17I broke the fangs of the wicked
and snatched the victims from their teeth.[s]

18"I thought, 'I shall die in my own house,
my days as numerous as the grains of sand.[t]
19My roots will reach to the water,[u]
and the dew will lie all night on my branches.
20My glory will remain fresh in me,
the bow[v] ever new in my hand.'[w]

21"Men listened to me expectantly,
waiting in silence for my counsel.
22After I had spoken, they spoke no more;
my words fell gently on their ears.[x]
23They waited for me as for showers
and drank in my words as the spring rain.
24When I smiled at them, they scarcely believed it;
the light of my face was precious to them.[a]
25I chose the way for them and sat as their chief;
I dwelt as a king[y] among his troops;
I was like one who comforts mourners.[z]

30 "But now they mock me,[a]
men younger than I,
whose fathers I would have disdained
to put with my sheep dogs.
2Of what use was the strength of their hands to me,
since their vigour had gone from them?
3Haggard from want and hunger,
they roamed[a] the parched land
in desolate wastelands at night.
4In the brush they gathered salt herbs,
and their food[b] was the root of the broom tree.
5They were banished from their fellow-men,
shouted at as if they were thieves.
6They were forced to live in the dry stream beds,
among the rocks and in holes in the ground.
7They brayed among the bushes
and huddled in the undergrowth.
8A base and nameless brood,
they were driven out of the land.

29:12 [k]Job 24:4 [l]Job 31:17, 21 [m]Ps 72:12; Pr 21:13
29:13 [n]Job 31:20 [o]Job 22:9
29:14 [p]Job 27:6; Ps 132:9; Isa 59:17; 61:10; Eph 6:14
29:15 [q]Nu 10:31
29:16 [r]Job 24:4; Pr 29:7
29:17 [s]Ps 3:7
29:18 [t]Ps 30:6
29:19 [u]Job 18:16; Jer 17:8
29:20 [v]Ps 18:34 [w]Ge 49:24
29:22 [x]Dt 32:2
29:25 [y]Job 1:3; 31:37 [z]Job 4:4
30:1 [a]Job 12:4

a *24* The meaning of the Hebrew for this clause is uncertain. a *3* Or *gnawed* b *4* Or *fuel*

30:1ff To suffer extreme loss, as Job did, was humiliating. But to face abuse at the hands of young upstarts added insult to injury. Job had lost his family, possessions, health, position, and good name. He was not even respected for suffering bravely. Unfortunately, young people sometimes mock and take advantage of older people and those who are limited in some way. Instead, they should realise that their own physical abilities and attributes are short-lived and that God loves all people equally.

9"And now their sons mock me[b] in song;[c]
I have become a byword[d] among them.
10They detest me and keep their distance;
they do not hesitate to spit in my face.[e]
11Now that God has unstrung my bow and afflicted me,[f]
they throw off restraint[g] in my presence.
12On my right the tribe[c] attacks;
they lay snares for my feet,[h]
they build their siege ramps against me.[i]
13They break up my road;[j]
they succeed in destroying me—
without anyone's helping them.[d]
14They advance as through a gaping breach;
amid the ruins they come rolling in.
15Terrors overwhelm me;[k]
my dignity is driven away as by the wind,
my safety vanishes like a cloud.[l]

16"And now my life ebbs away;[m]
days of suffering grip me.
17Night pierces my bones;
my gnawing pains never rest.
18In his great power ⌞God⌟ becomes like clothing to me;[e]
he binds me like the neck of my garment.
19He throws me into the mud,[n]
and I am reduced to dust and ashes.

20"I cry out to you, O God, but you do not answer;[o]
I stand up, but you merely look at me.
21You turn on me ruthlessly;[p]
with the might of your hand[q] you attack me.[r]
22You snatch me up and drive me before the wind;[s]
you toss me about in the storm.[t]
23I know you will bring me down to death,[u]
to the place appointed for all the living.[v]

24"Surely no-one lays a hand on a broken man
when he cries for help in his distress.[w]
25Have I not wept for those in trouble?
Has not my soul grieved for the poor?[x]
26Yet when I hoped for good, evil came;
when I looked for light, then came darkness.[y]
27The churning inside me never stops;[z]
days of suffering confront me.
28I go about blackened,[a] but not by the sun;
I stand up in the assembly and cry for help.[b]
29I have become a brother of jackals,[c]
a companion of owls.[d]
30My skin grows black and peels;[e]
my body burns with fever.[f]
31My harp is tuned to mourning,[g]
and my flute to the sound of wailing.

31 "I made a covenant with my eyes
not to look lustfully at a girl.[a]
2For what is man's lot from God above,
his heritage from the Almighty on high?[b]
3Is it not ruin[c] for the wicked,

c *12* The meaning of the Hebrew for this word is uncertain. **d** *13* Or *me.* / *'No-one can help him,'* ⌞they say⌟.
e *18* Hebrew; Septuagint ⌞*God*⌟ *grasps my clothing*

30:9 [b]Ps 69:11 [c]Job 12:4; La 3:14, 63 [d]Job 17:6
30:10 [e]Nu 12:14; Dt 25:9; Isa 50:6; Mt 26:67
30:11 [f]Ru 1:21 [g]Ps 32:9
30:12 [h]Ps 140:4-5 [i]Job 19:12
30:13 [j]Isa 3:12
30:15 [k]Job 31:23; Ps 55:4-5 [l]Job 3:25; Hos 13:3
30:16 [m]Job 3:24; Ps 22:14; 42:4
30:19 [n]Ps 69:2, 14
30:20 [o]Job 19:7
30:21 [p]Job 19:6, 22 [q]Job 16:9, 14 [r]Job 10:3
30:22 [s]Job 27:21 [t]Job 9:17
30:23 [u]Job 9:22; 10:8 [v]Job 3:19
30:24 [w]Job 19:7
30:25 [x]Job 24:4; Ps 35:13-14; Ro 12:15
30:26 [y]Job 3:25-26; 19:8; Jer 8:15
30:27 [z]La 2:11
30:28 [a]Ps 38:6; 42:9; 43:2 [b]Job 19:7
30:29 [c]Ps 44:19 [d]Ps 102:6; Mic 1:8
30:30 [e]La 4:8 [f]Ps 102:3
30:31 [g]Isa 24:8
31:1 [a]Mt 5:28
31:2 [b]Job 20:29
31:3 [c]Job 21:30

disaster for those who do wrong?[d]
4Does he not see my ways[e]
and count my every step?[f]

5"If I have walked in falsehood
or my foot has hurried after deceit[g]—
6let God weigh me in honest scales[h]
and he will know that I am blameless—
7if my steps have turned from the path,[i]
if my heart has been led by my eyes,
or if my hands[j] have been defiled,
8then may others eat what I have sown,[k]
and may my crops be uprooted.[l]

9"If my heart has been enticed[m] by a woman,
or if I have lurked at my neighbour's door,
10then may my wife grind another man's grain,
and may other men sleep with her.[n]
11For that would have been shameful,
a sin to be judged.[o]
12It is a fire[p] that burns to Destruction;[a][q]
it would have uprooted my harvest.[r]

13"If I have denied justice to my menservants and maidservants
when they had a grievance against me,[s]
14what will I do when God confronts me?
What will I answer when called to account?
15Did not he who made me in the womb make them?
Did not the same one form us both within our mothers?[t]

16"If I have denied the desires of the poor[u]
or let the eyes of the widow[v] grow weary,
17if I have kept my bread to myself,
not sharing it with the fatherless[w]—
18but from my youth I reared him as would a father,
and from my birth I guided the widow—
19if I have seen anyone perishing for lack of clothing,[x]
or a needy[y] man without a garment,
20and his heart did not bless me
for warming him with the fleece from my sheep,
21if I have raised my hand against the fatherless,[z]
knowing that I had influence in court,
22then let my arm fall from the shoulder,
let it be broken off at the joint.[a]
23For I dreaded destruction from God,
and for fear of his splendour[b] I could not do such things.

24"If I have put my trust in gold[c]
or said to pure gold, 'You are my security,'[d]
25if I have rejoiced over my great wealth,[e]

31:3 [d]Job 34:22
31:4 [e]2Ch 16:9 [f]Pr 5:21
31:5 [g]Mic 2:11
31:6 [h]Job 6:2; 27:5-6
31:7 [i]Job 23:11 [j]Job 9:30
31:8 [k]Lev 26:16; Job 20:18 [l]Mic 6:15
31:9 [m]Job 24:15
31:10 [n]Dt 28:30; Jer 8:10
31:11 [o]Ge 38:24; Lev 20:10; Dt 22:22-24
31:12 [p]Job 15:30 [q]Job 26:6 [r]Job 20:28
31:13 [s]Dt 24:14-15
31:15 [t]Job 10:3
31:16 [u]Job 5:16; 20:19 [v]Job 22:9
31:17 [w]Job 22:7; 29:12
31:19 [x]Job 22:6 [y]Job 24:4
31:21 [z]Job 22:9
31:22 [a]Job 38:15
31:23 [b]Job 13:11
31:24 [c]Job 22:25 [d]Mt 6:24; Mk 10:24
31:25 [e]Ps 62:10

a *12* Hebrew *Abaddon*

31:1–4 Job had not only avoided committing the great sin of adultery; he had not even taken the first step towards that sin by looking at a woman with lust. Job said he was innocent of both outward and inward sins. In chapter 29, Job reviewed his good deeds. Here in chapter 31 he listed sins he had not committed—in his heart (31:1–12), against his neighbours (31:13–23), or against God (31:24–34).

31:24–28 Job affirmed that depending on wealth for happiness is idolatry and denies the God of heaven. We excuse our society's obsession with money and possessions as a necessary evil or "the way it works" in the modern world. But every society in every age has valued the power and prestige that money brings. True believers must purge themselves of the deep-seated desire for more power, prestige, and possessions. They must also not withhold their resources from neighbours near and far who have desperate physical needs.

the fortune my hands had gained,
26if I have regarded the sun[f] in its radiance
or the moon moving in splendour,
27so that my heart was secretly enticed
and my hand offered them a kiss of homage,
28then these also would be sins to be judged,[g]
for I would have been unfaithful to God on high.

29"If I have rejoiced at my enemy's misfortune[h]
or gloated over the trouble that came to him[i]—
30I have not allowed my mouth to sin
by invoking a curse against his life—
31if the men of my household have never said,
'Who has not had his fill of Job's meat?'[j]—
32but no stranger had to spend the night in the street,
for my door was always open to the traveller[k]—
33if I have concealed[l] my sin as men do,[b]
by hiding[m] my guilt in my heart
34because I so feared the crowd[n]
and so dreaded the contempt of the clans
that I kept silent and would not go outside—

35("Oh, that I had someone to hear me![o]
I sign now my defence—let the Almighty answer me;
let my accuser[p] put his indictment in writing.
36Surely I would wear it on my shoulder,
I would put it on like a crown.
37I would give him an account of my every step;
like a prince[q] I would approach him.)—

38"if my land cries out against me[r]
and all its furrows are wet with tears,
39if I have devoured its yield without payment[s]
or broken the spirit of its tenants,[t]
40then let briers[u] come up instead of wheat
and weeds instead of barley."

The words of Job are ended.

C. A YOUNG MAN ANSWERS JOB (32:1—37:24)

Young Elihu rebukes the three friends for being unable to give Job a reasonable answer for why he is suffering. But he only gives a partial answer to Job's question by saying that man cannot understand all that God allows, but must trust him. This was the best answer that man could give, yet it was incomplete. Often the best human answers are incomplete because we do not have all the facts.

Elihu

32 So these three men stopped answering Job, because he was righteous in his own
eyes.[a] 2But Elihu son of Barakel the Buzite,[b] of the family of Ram, became
very angry with Job for justifying himself rather than God.[c] 3He was also angry with

[b] 33 *Or as Adam did*

31:26 [f]Eze 8:16
31:28 [g]Dt 17:2-7
31:29 [h]Ob 1:12 [i]Pr 17:5; 24:17-18
31:31 [j]Job 22:7
31:32 [k]Ge 19:2-3; Ro 12:13
31:33 [l]Pr 28:13 [m]Ge 3:8
31:34 [n]Ex 23:2
31:35 [o]Job 19:7; 30:28 [p]Job 27:7; 35:14
31:37 [q]Job 1:3; 29:25
31:38 [r]Ge 4:10
31:39 [s]1Ki 21:19 [t]Lev 19:13; Jas 5:4
31:40 [u]Ge 3:18
32:1 [a]Job 10:7; 33:9
32:2 [b]Ge 22:21 [c]Job 27:5; 30:21

31:33, 34 Job declared that he did not try to hide his sin as men often do. The fear that our sins will be discovered leads us to patterns of deception. We cover up with lies so that we will appear good to others. But we cannot hide from God. Do you try to keep people from seeing the real you? When you acknowledge your sins, you free yourself to receive forgiveness and a new life.

32:1 If Job was really a good man, his three friends would have to drop their theory that suffering is always God's punishment for evil actions. Instead of considering another viewpoint, however, they cut off the discussion. They were convinced that Job had some hidden fault or sin, so there was no point in talking if Job would not confess it. But Job knew he had lived uprightly before God and others (chapter 29) and had avoided wrong thoughts and actions (chapter 31). He wasn't about to invent a sin to satisfy his friends!

32:2ff When Eliphaz, Bildad, and Zophar had nothing more to say, Elihu became the fourth person to speak to Job. This was the first and only time he spoke. Apparently he was a bystander and much younger than the others (32:6, 7), but he introduced a new viewpoint. While Job's three friends said he was suffering from

32:6 [d]Job 15:10

the three friends, because they had found no way to refute Job, and yet had condemned
him.[a] 4Now Elihu had waited before speaking to Job because they were older than
he. 5But when he saw that the three men had nothing more to say, his anger was
aroused.
6So Elihu son of Barakel the Buzite said:

"I am young in years,
and you are old;[d]
that is why I was fearful,
not daring to tell you what I know.
7I thought, 'Age should speak;
advanced years should teach wisdom.'
8But it is the spirit[b] in a man,
the breath of the Almighty,[e] that gives him understanding.[f]
9It is not only the old[c] who are wise,[g]
not only the aged who understand what is right.

10"Therefore I say: Listen to me;
I too will tell you what I know.
11I waited while you spoke,
I listened to your reasoning;
while you were searching for words,
12 I gave you my full attention.
But not one of you has proved Job wrong;
none of you has answered his arguments.
13Do not say, 'We have found wisdom;[h]
let God refute him, not man.'
14But Job has not marshalled his words against me,
and I will not answer him with your arguments.

15"They are dismayed and have no more to say;
words have failed them.
16Must I wait, now that they are silent,
now that they stand there with no reply?
17I too will have my say;
I too will tell what I know.
18For I am full of words,
and the spirit within me compels me;
19inside I am like bottled-up wine,
like new wineskins ready to burst.
20I must speak and find relief;
I must open my lips and reply.
21I will show partiality[i] to no-one,[j]
nor will I flatter any man;
22for if I were skilled in flattery,
my Maker would soon take me away.

32:8 [e]Job 27:3; 33:4 [f]Pr 2:6

32:9 [g]1Co 1:26

32:13 [h]Jer 9:23

32:21 [i]Lev 19:15; Job 13:10 [j]Mt 22:16

[a] *3* Masoretic Text; an ancient Hebrew scribal tradition *Job, and so had condemned God* [b] *8* Or *Spirit*; also in verse 18 [c] *9* Or *many*; or *great*

---

some past sins, Elihu said Job's suffering would not go away until he realised his *present* sin. He maintained that Job wasn't suffering because of sin, he was sinning because of suffering. Elihu pointed out that Job's attitude had become arrogant as he tried to defend his innocence. Elihu also said that suffering is not meant to punish us as much as it is meant to correct and restore us, to keep us on the right path.

There is much truth in Elihu's speech. He was urging Job to look at his suffering from a different perspective and with a greater purpose in mind. While his speech is on a higher spiritual plateau than the others, Elihu still wrongly assumed that a correct response to suffering always brings healing and restoration (33:23–30) and that suffering is always in some way connected to sin (34:11).

32:7–9 "The breath of the Almighty, that gives him understanding." It is not enough to recognise a great truth; it must be lived out each day. Elihu recognised the truth that God was the only source of real wisdom, but he did not use God's wisdom to help Job. While he recognised where wisdom came from, he did not seek to acquire it. Becoming wise is an ongoing, lifelong pursuit. Don't be content just to know about wisdom; make it part of your life.

33

"But now, Job, listen to my words;
pay attention to everything I say.[a]
2I am about to open my mouth;
my words are on the tip of my tongue.
3My words come from an upright heart;
my lips sincerely speak what I know.[b]
4The Spirit of God has made me;[c]
the breath of the Almighty[d] gives me life.
5Answer me[e] then, if you can;
prepare[f] yourself and confront me.
6I am just like you before God;
I too have been taken from clay.[g]
7No fear of me should alarm you,
nor should my hand be heavy upon you.[h]

8"But you have said in my hearing—
I heard the very words—
9'I am pure[i] and without sin;[j]
I am clean and free from guilt.
10Yet God has found fault with me;
he considers me his enemy.[k]
11He fastens my feet in shackles;[l]
he keeps close watch on all my paths.'[m]

12"But I tell you, in this you are not right,
for God is greater than man.[n]
13Why do you complain to him[o]
that he answers none of man's words?**a**
14For God does speak[p]—now one way, now another—
though man may not perceive it.
15In a dream,[q] in a vision of the night,
when deep sleep falls on men
as they slumber in their beds,
16he may speak[r] in their ears
and terrify them with warnings,
17to turn man from wrongdoing
and keep him from pride,
18to preserve his soul from the pit,**b**[s]
his life from perishing by the sword.**c**[t]
19Or a man may be chastened on a bed of pain
with constant distress in his bones,[u]
20so that his very being finds food[v] repulsive
and his soul loathes the choicest meal.[w]
21His flesh wastes away to nothing,
and his bones, once hidden, now stick out.[x]
22His soul draws near to the pit,**d**

a *13 Or that he does not answer for any of his actions* **b** *18 Or preserve him from the grave* **c** *18 Or from crossing the River* **d** *22 Or He draws near to the grave*

33:1 [a]Job 13:6
33:3 [b]Job 6:28; 27:4; 36:4
33:4 [c]Ge 2:7; Job 10:3 [d]Job 27:3
33:5 [e]ver 32 [f]Job 13:18
33:6 [g]Job 4:19
33:7 [h]Job 9:34; 13:21; 2Co 2:4
33:9 [i]Job 10:7 [j]Job 13:23; 16:17
33:10 [k]Job 13:24
33:11 [l]Job 13:27 [m]Job 14:16
33:12 [n]Ecc 7:20
33:13 [o]Job 40:2; Isa 45:9
33:14 [p]Ps 62:11
33:15 [q]Job 4:13
33:16 [r]Job 36:10, 15
33:18 [s]ver 22, 24, 28, 30 [t]Job 15:22
33:19 [u]Job 30:17
33:20 [v]Ps 107:18 [w]Job 3:24; 6:6
33:21 [x]Job 16:8; 19:20

33:13 Being informed brings a sense of security. It's natural to want to know what's happening in our lives. Job wanted to know what was going on, why he was suffering. In previous chapters, we sense his frustration. Elihu claimed to have the answer for Job's biggest question, "Why doesn't God tell me what is happening?" Elihu told Job that God was trying to answer him, but he was not listening. Elihu misjudged God on this point. If God were to answer all our questions, we would not be adequately tested. What if God had said, "Job, Satan's going to test you and afflict you, but in the end you'll be healed and get everything back?" Job's greatest test was not the pain, but that he did not know *why* he was suffering. Our greatest test may be that we must trust God's goodness even though we don't understand why our lives are going a certain way. We must learn to trust in *God* who is good and not in the goodness of life.

33:14–24 Elihu's point was that God had spoken again and again. He spoke in dreams and visions (33:15–18), through suffering (33:19–22), and by mediating angels (33:23, 24). Job already knew that. Elihu accused Job of not listening to God, which was not true.

and his life to the messengers of death.[e] [y]

23"Yet if there is an angel on his side
as a mediator, one out of a thousand,
to tell a man what is right for him,[z]
24to be gracious to him and say,
'Spare him from going down to the pit;[f] [a]
I have found a ransom for him'—
25then his flesh is renewed like a child's;
it is restored as in the days of his youth.[b]
26He prays to God and finds favour with him,[c]
he sees God's face and shouts for joy;[d]
he is restored by God to his righteous state.[e]
27Then he comes to men and says,
'I have sinned,[f] and perverted what was right,[g]
but I did not get what I deserved.[h]
28He redeemed my soul from going down to the pit,[g]
and I shall live to enjoy the light.'[i]

29"God does all these things to a man[j]—
twice, even three times—
30to turn back his soul from the pit,[h]
that the light of life[k] may shine on him.

31"Pay attention, Job, and listen to me;
be silent, and I will speak.
32If you have anything to say, answer me;
speak up, for I want you to be cleared.
33But if not, then listen to me;
be silent, and I will teach you wisdom.[l]"

34

Then Elihu said:

2"Hear my words, you wise men;
listen to me, you men of learning.
3For the ear tests words
as the tongue tastes food.[a]
4Let us discern for ourselves what is right;

33:22 [y]Ps 88:3
33:23 [z]Mic 6:8
33:24 [a]Isa 38:17
33:25 [b]2Ki 5:14
33:26 [c]Job 34:28 [d]Job 22:26 [e]Ps 50:15; 51:12
33:27 [f]2Sa 12:13 [g]Lk 15:21 [h]Ro 6:21
33:28 [i]Job 22:28
33:29 [j]1Co 12:6; Eph 1:11; Php 2:13
33:30 [k]Ps 56:13
33:33 [l]Ps 34:11
34:3 [a]Job 12:11

[e] *22* Or *to the dead* [f] *24* Or *grave* [g] *28* Or *redeemed me from going down to the grave* [h] *30* Or *turn him back from the grave*

HOW SUFFERING AFFECTS US

Suffering is helpful when:	*Suffering is harmful when:*
We turn to God for understanding, endurance, and deliverance	We become hardened and reject God
We ask important questions we might not take time to think about in our normal routine	We refuse to ask any questions and miss any lessons that might be good for us
We are prepared by it to identify with and comfort others who suffer	We allow it to make us self-centred and selfish
We are open to being helped by others who are obeying God	We withdraw from the help others can give
We are ready to learn from a trustworthy God	We reject the fact that God can bring good out of calamity
We realise we can identify with what Christ suffered on the cross for us	We accuse God of being unjust and perhaps lead others to reject him
We are sensitised to the amount of suffering in the world	We refuse to be open to any changes in our lives

let us learn together what is good.[b]

5"Job says, 'I am innocent,[c]
but God denies me justice.[d]
6Although I am right,
I am considered a liar;
although I am guiltless,
his arrow inflicts an incurable wound.'[e]
7What man is like Job,
who drinks scorn like water?[f]
8He keeps company with evildoers;
he associates with wicked men.[g]
9For he says, 'It profits a man nothing
when he tries to please God.'[h]

10"So listen to me, you men of understanding.
Far be it from God to do evil,[i]
from the Almighty to do wrong.[j]
11He repays a man for what he has done;[k]
he brings upon him what his conduct deserves.[l]
12It is unthinkable that God would do wrong,
that the Almighty would pervert justice.[m]
13Who appointed him over the earth?
Who put him in charge of the whole world?[n]
14If it were his intention
and he withdrew his spirit[a] and breath,[o]
15all mankind would perish together
and man would return to the dust.[p]

16"If you have understanding, hear this;
listen to what I say.
17Can he who hates justice govern?[q]
Will you condemn the just and mighty One?[r]
18Is he not the One who says to kings, 'You are worthless,'
and to nobles, 'You are wicked,'[s]
19who shows no partiality[t] to princes
and does not favour the rich over the poor,[u]
for they are all the work of his hands?[v]
20They die in an instant, in the middle of the night;[w]
the people are shaken and they pass away;
the mighty are removed without human hand.[x]

21"His eyes are on the ways of men;
he sees their every step.[y]
22There is no dark place,[z] no deep shadow,[a]
where evildoers can hide.
23God has no need to examine men further,
that they should come before him for judgment.[b]
24Without enquiry he shatters the mighty[c]
and sets up others in their place.[d]
25Because he takes note of their deeds,
he overthrows them in the night and they are crushed.
26He punishes them for their wickedness

a *14* Or *Spirit*

34:4 [b]1Th 5:21
34:5 [c]Job 33:9 [d]Job 27:2
34:6 [e]Job 6:4
34:7 [f]Job 15:16
34:8 [g]Job 22:15; Ps 50:18
34:9 [h]Job 21:15; 35:3
34:10 [i]Ge 18:25 [j]Dt 32:4; Job 8:3; Ro 9:14
34:11 [k]Ps 62:12; Mt 16:27; Ro 2:6; 2Co 5:10 [l]Jer 32:19; Eze 33:20
34:12 [m]Job 8:3
34:13 [n]Job 38:4, 6
34:14 [o]Ps 104:29
34:15 [p]Ge 3:19; Job 9:22
34:17 [q]2Sa 23:3-4 [r]Job 40:8
34:18 [s]Ex 22:28
34:19 [t]Dt 10:17; Ac 10:34 [u]Lev 19:15 [v]Job 10:3
34:20 [w]Ex 12:29 [x]Job 12:19
34:21 [y]Job 31:4; Pr 15:3
34:22 [z]Ps 139:12 [a]Am 9:2-3
34:23 [b]Job 11:11
34:24 [c]Job 12:19 [d]Da 2:21

34:10–15 God doesn't sin and is never unjust, Elihu claimed. Throughout this book, Eliphaz, Bildad, Zophar, and Elihu all have elements of truth in their speeches. Unfortunately, the nuggets of truth are buried under layers of false assumptions and conclusions. Although we might have a wealth of Bible knowledge and life experiences, we must make sure our conclusions are consistent with all of God's word, not just parts of it.

where everyone can see them,
27 because they turned from following him[e]
and had no regard for any of his ways.[f]
28 They caused the cry of the poor to come before him,
so that he heard the cry of the needy.[g]
29 But if he remains silent, who can condemn him?
If he hides his face, who can see him?
Yet he is over man and nation alike,
30 to keep a godless man from ruling,
from laying snares for the people.[h]

31 "Suppose a man says to God,
'I am guilty but will offend no more.
32 Teach me what I cannot see;[i]
if I have done wrong, I will not do so again.'[j]
33 Should God then reward you on your terms,
when you refuse to repent?[k]
You must decide, not I;
so tell me what you know.

34 "Men of understanding declare,
wise men who hear me say to me,
35 'Job speaks without knowledge;[l]
his words lack insight.'
36 Oh, that Job might be tested to the utmost
for answering like a wicked man![m]
37 To his sin he adds rebellion;
scornfully he claps his hands[n] among us
and multiplies his words against God."[o]

35

Then Elihu said:

2 "Do you think this is just?
You say, 'I shall be cleared by God.'[a]
3 Yet you ask him, 'What profit is it to me,[b]
and what do I gain by not sinning?'[a]

4 "I would like to reply to you
and to your friends with you.
5 Look up at the heavens[b] and see;
gaze at the clouds so high above you.[c]
6 If you sin, how does that affect him?
If your sins are many, what does that do to him?[d]
7 If you are righteous, what do you give to him,[e]
or what does he receive[f] from your hand?[g]
8 Your wickedness affects only a man like yourself,
and your righteousness only the sons of men.

9 "Men cry out[h] under a load of oppression;
they plead for relief from the arm of the powerful.[i]
10 But no-one says, 'Where is God my Maker,[j]
who gives songs in the night,[k]
11 who teaches[l] more to us than to[c] the beasts of the earth
and makes us wiser than[d] the birds of the air?'

34:27 [e]Ps 28:5; Isa 5:12 [f]1Sa 15:11
34:28 [g]Ex 22:23; Job 35:9; Jas 5:4
34:30 [h]Pr 29:2-12
34:32 [i]Job 35:11; Ps 25:4 [j]Job 33:27
34:33 [k]Job 41:11
34:35 [l]Job 35:16; 38:2
34:36 [m]Job 22:15
34:37 [n]Job 27:23 [o]Job 23:2
35:3 [a]Job 9:29-31; 34:9
35:5 [b]Ge 15:5 [c]Job 22:12
35:6 [d]Pr 8:36
35:7 [e]Ro 11:35 [f]Pr 9:12 [g]Job 22:2-3; Lk 17:10
35:9 [h]Ex 2:23 [i]Job 12:19
35:10 [j]Job 27:10; Isa 51:13 [k]Ps 42:8; 149:5; Ac 16:25
35:11 [l]Ps 94:12

a *2* Or *My righteousness is more than God's* **b** *3* Or *you* **c** *11* Or *teaches us by* **d** *11* Or *us wise by*

35:1ff Sometimes we wonder if being faithful to our convictions really does any good at all. Elihu spoke to this very point. His conclusion was that God is still concerned even though he doesn't intervene immediately in every situation. In the broad scope of time God executes justice. We have his promise on that. Don't lose hope. Wait upon God. He notices your right living and your faith.

12 He does not answer[m] when men cry out
because of the arrogance of the wicked.
13 Indeed, God does not listen to their empty plea;
the Almighty pays no attention to it.[n]
14 How much less, then, will he listen
when you say that you do not see him,[o]
that your case[p] is before him
and you must wait for him,
15 and further, that his anger never punishes
and he does not take the least notice of wickedness.[e]
16 So Job opens his mouth with empty talk;
without knowledge he multiplies words."[q]

36

Elihu continued:

2 "Bear with me a little longer and I will show you
that there is more to be said on God's behalf.
3 I get my knowledge from afar;
I will ascribe justice to my Maker.[a]
4 Be assured that my words are not false;[b]
one perfect in knowledge[c] is with you.

5 "God is mighty, but does not despise men;[d]
he is mighty, and firm in his purpose.[e]
6 He does not keep the wicked alive[f]
but gives the afflicted their rights.[g]
7 He does not take his eyes off the righteous;[h]
he enthrones them with kings[i]
and exalts them for ever.
8 But if men are bound in chains,[j]
held fast by cords of affliction,
9 he tells them what they have done—
that they have sinned arrogantly.[k]
10 He makes them listen[l] to correction
and commands them to repent of their evil.[m]
11 If they obey and serve him,[n]
they will spend the rest of their days in prosperity
and their years in contentment.
12 But if they do not listen,
they will perish by the sword[a][o]
and die without knowledge.[p]

13 "The godless in heart[q] harbour resentment;
even when he fetters them, they do not cry for help.
14 They die in their youth,
among male prostitutes of the shrines.[r]
15 But those who suffer he delivers in their suffering;
he speaks to them in their affliction.

16 "He is wooing[s] you from the jaws of distress
to a spacious place free from restriction,
to the comfort of your table[t] laden with choice food.
17 But now you are laden with the judgment due to the wicked;
judgment and justice have taken hold of you.[u]
18 Be careful that no-one entices you by riches;
do not let a large bribe turn you aside.[v]
19 Would your wealth

35:12 [m]Pr 1:28
35:13 [n]Job 27:9; Pr 15:29; Isa 1:15; Jer 11:11
35:14 [o]Job 9:11 [p]Ps 37:6
35:16 [q]Job 34:35, 37
36:3 [a]Job 8:3; 37:23
36:4 [b]Job 33:3 [c]Job 37:5, 16, 23
36:5 [d]Ps 22:24 [e]Job 12:13
36:6 [f]Job 8:22 [g]Job 5:15
36:7 [h]Ps 33:18 [i]Ps 113:8
36:8 [j]Ps 107:10, 14
36:9 [k]Job 15:25
36:10 [l]Job 33:16 [m]2Ki 17:13
36:11 [n]Isa 1:19
36:12 [o]Job 15:22 [p]Job 4:21
36:13 [q]Ro 2:5
36:14 [r]Dt 23:17
36:16 [s]Hos 2:14 [t]Ps 23:5
36:17 [u]Job 22:11
36:18 [v]Job 34:33

[e] *15* Symmachus, Theodotion and Vulgate; the meaning of the Hebrew for this word is uncertain. [a] *12* Or *will cross the River*

36:20
[w] Job 34:20, 25

36:21
[x] Ps 66:18
[y] Heb 11:25

36:22
[z] Isa 40:13;
1Co 2:16

36:23
[a] Job 34:13
[b] Job 8:3

36:24
[c] Ps 92:5; 138:5
[d] Ps 59:16;
Rev 15:3

36:26
[e] 1Co 13:12
[f] Job 10:5;
Ps 90:2; 102:24;
Heb 1:12

36:27
[g] Job 38:28;
Ps 147:8

36:28
[h] Job 5:10

36:29
[i] Job 26:14; 37:16

36:31
[j] Job 37:13
[k] Ps 136:25;
Ac 14:17

36:32
[l] Job 37:12, 15

37:2
[a] Ps 29:3-9

37:5
[b] Job 5:9

37:6
[c] Job 38:22
[d] Job 36:27

or even all your mighty efforts
sustain you so you would not be in distress?
20 Do not long for the night,[w]
to drag people away from their homes.[b]
21 Beware of turning to evil,[x]
which you seem to prefer to affliction.[y]

22 "God is exalted in his power.
Who is a teacher like him?[z]
23 Who has prescribed his ways for him,[a]
or said to him, 'You have done wrong'?[b]
24 Remember to extol his work,[c]
which men have praised in song.[d]
25 All mankind has seen it;
men gaze on it from afar.
26 How great is God—beyond our understanding![e]
The number of his years is past finding out.[f]

27 "He draws up the drops of water,
which distil as rain to the streams;[c][g]
28 the clouds pour down their moisture
and abundant showers fall on mankind.[h]
29 Who can understand how he spreads out the clouds,
how he thunders from his pavilion?[i]
30 See how he scatters his lightning about him,
bathing the depths of the sea.
31 This is the way he governs[d] the nations[j]
and provides food in abundance.[k]
32 He fills his hands with lightning
and commands it to strike its mark.[l]
33 His thunder announces the coming storm;
even the cattle make known its approach.[e]

37 "At this my heart pounds
and leaps from its place.
2 Listen! Listen to the roar of his voice,
to the rumbling that comes from his mouth.[a]
3 He unleashes his lightning beneath the whole heaven
and sends it to the ends of the earth.
4 After that comes the sound of his roar;
he thunders with his majestic voice.
When his voice resounds,
he holds nothing back.
5 God's voice thunders in marvellous ways;
he does great things beyond our understanding.[b]
6 He says to the snow,[c] 'Fall on the earth,'
and to the rain shower, 'Be a mighty downpour.'[d]
7 So that all men he has made may know his work,

[b] *20* The meaning of the Hebrew for verses 18–20 is uncertain. [c] *27* Or *distil from the mist as rain*
[d] *31* Or *nourishes* [e] *33* Or *announces his coming— / the One zealous against evil*

36:26 One theme in the poetic literature of the Bible is that God is incomprehensible; we cannot know him completely. We can have some knowledge about him, for the Bible is full of details about who God is, how we can know him, and how we can have an eternal relationship with him. But we can never know enough to answer all of life's questions (Ecclesiastes 3:11), to predict our own future, or to manipulate God for our own ends. Life always creates more questions than we have answers, and we must constantly go to God for fresh insights into life's dilemmas. (See 37:19–24.)

37:2 Nothing can compare to God. His power and presence are awesome, and when he speaks, we must listen. Too often we presume to speak for God (as did Job's friends), to put words in his mouth, to take him for granted, or to interpret his silence to mean that he is absent or unconcerned. But God cares. He is in control, and he will speak. Be ready to hear his message—in the Bible, in your life through the Holy Spirit, and through circumstances and relationships.

he stops every man from his labour.[a] [e]
8The animals take cover;
they remain in their dens.[f]
9The tempest comes out from its chamber,
the cold from the driving winds.
10The breath of God produces ice,
and the broad waters become frozen.[g]
11He loads the clouds with moisture;
he scatters his lightning through them.[h]
12At his direction they swirl around
over the face of the whole earth
to do whatever he commands them.[i]
13He brings the clouds to punish men,[j]
or to water his earth[b] and show his love.[k]

14"Listen to this, Job;
stop and consider God's wonders.
15Do you know how God controls the clouds
and makes his lightning flash?
16Do you know how the clouds hang poised,
those wonders of him who is perfect in knowledge?[l]
17You who swelter in your clothes
when the land lies hushed under the south wind,
18can you join him in spreading out the skies,[m]
hard as a mirror of cast bronze?

19"Tell us what we should say to him;
we cannot draw up our case because of our darkness.
20Should he be told that I want to speak?
Would any man ask to be swallowed up?
21Now no-one can look at the sun,
bright as it is in the skies
after the wind has swept them clean.
22Out of the north he comes in golden splendour;
God comes in awesome majesty.
23The Almighty is beyond our reach and exalted in power;[n]
in his justice[o] and great righteousness, he does not oppress.[p]
24Therefore, men revere him,[q]
for does he not have regard for all the wise[r] in heart?"[c]

37:7 [e]Job 12:14
37:8 [f]Job 38:40; Ps 104:22
37:10 [g]Job 38:29-30; Ps 147:17
37:11 [h]Job 36:27, 29
37:12 [i]Ps 148:8
37:13 [j]1Sa 12:17 [k]Ex 9:18; 1Ki 18:45; Job 38:27
37:16 [l]Job 36:4
37:18 [m]Job 9:8; Ps 104:2; Isa 44:24
37:23 [n]Job 9:4; 36:4; 1Ti 6:16 [o]Job 8:3 [p]Isa 63:9; Eze 18:23, 32
37:24 [q]Mt 10:28 [r]Mt 11:25

D. GOD ANSWERS JOB (38:1—41:34)

Instead of answering Job's question directly, God asks Job a series of questions which no human could possibly answer. Job responds by recognising that God's ways are best. During difficult times we too must humbly remember our position before the eternal, holy, incomprehensible God.

The LORD Speaks

38 Then the LORD answered Job out of the storm.[a] He said:

2"Who is this that darkens my counsel
with words without knowledge?[b]

38:1 [a]Job 40:6
38:2 [b]Job 35:16; 42:3; 1Ti 1:7

[a] 7 Or *I he fills all men with fear by his power* [b] 13 Or *to favour them* [c] 24 Or *for he does not have regard for any who think they are wise.*

37:21–24 Elihu concluded his speech with the tremendous truth that faith in God is far more important than Job's desire for an explanation for his suffering. He came so close to helping Job but then went down the wrong path. Significantly, it is here that God himself breaks into the discussion to draw the right conclusions from this important truth (38:1ff).

37:23 Elihu stressed God's sovereignty over all of nature as a reminder of his sovereignty over our lives. God is in control – he directs, preserves, and maintains his created order. Although we can't see it, God is divinely governing the moral and political affairs of people as well. By spending time observing the majestic and intricate parts of God's creation, we can be reminded of his power in every aspect of our lives.

38:1ff Out of a mighty storm, God spoke. Surprisingly, he didn't

3Brace yourself like a man;
I will question you,
and you shall answer me.[c]

4"Where were you when I laid the earth's foundation?[d]
Tell me, if you understand.
5Who marked off its dimensions?[e] Surely you know!
Who stretched a measuring line across it?
6On what were its footings set,
or who laid its cornerstone[f]—
7while the morning stars sang together
and all the angels[a] shouted for joy?

8"Who shut up the sea behind doors[g]
when it burst forth from the womb,[h]
9when I made the clouds its garment
and wrapped it in thick darkness,
10when I fixed limits for it[i]
and set its doors and bars in place,[j]
11when I said, 'This far you may come and no farther;
here is where your proud waves halt'?[k]

12"Have you ever given orders to the morning,
or shown the dawn its place,
13that it might take the earth by the edges
and shake the wicked[l] out of it?
14The earth takes shape like clay under a seal;
its features stand out like those of a garment.
15The wicked are denied their light,[m]

38:3 [c]Job 40:7
38:4 [d]Ps 104:5; Pr 8:29
38:5 [e]Pr 8:29; Isa 40:12
38:6 [f]Job 26:7
38:8 [g]Jer 5:22 [h]Ge 1:9-10
38:10 [i]Ps 33:7; 104:9 [j]Job 26:10
38:11 [k]Ps 89:9
38:13 [l]Ps 104:35
38:15 [m]Job 18:5

[a] 7 Hebrew *the sons of God*

GOD SPEAKS
On various occasions in the Old Testament, God chose to communicate audibly with individuals. God will always find a way to make contact with those who want to know him. Some of those occasions are listed here.

Whom he spoke to	*What he said*	*Reference*
Adam and Eve	Confronted them about sin	Genesis 3:8–13
Noah	Gave him directions about building the ark	Genesis 6:13–22; 7:1; 8:15–17
Abraham	Commanded him to follow God's leading and promised to bless him	Genesis 12:1–9
	Tested his obedience by commanding him to sacrifice his son	Genesis 22:1–14
Jacob	Permitted him to go to Egypt	Genesis 46:1–4
Moses	Sent him to lead the people out of Egypt	Exodus 3:1–10
	Gave him the Ten Commandments	Exodus 19:1—20:20
Moses, Aaron, Miriam	Pronounced judgment on a family conflict	Numbers 12:1–15
Joshua	Promised to be with him as he was with Moses	Joshua 1:1–9
Samuel	Chose him to be his spokesman	1 Samuel 3:1–18
Isaiah	Sent him to the people with his message	Isaiah 6:1–13
Jeremiah	Encouraged him to be his prophet	Jeremiah 1:4–10
Ezekiel	Sent him to Israel to warn them of coming judgment	Ezekiel 2:1–8

answer any of Job's questions; Job's questions were not at the heart of the issue. Instead, God used Job's ignorance of the earth's natural order to reveal his ignorance of God's moral order. If Job did not understand the workings of God's physical creation, how could he possibly understand God's mind and character? There is no standard or criterion higher than God himself by which to judge. God himself is the standard. Our only option is to submit to his authority and rest in his care.

and their upraised arm is broken.[n]

16"Have you journeyed to the springs of the sea
or walked in the recesses of the deep?[o]
17Have the gates of death[p] been shown to you?
Have you seen the gates of the shadow of death?[b]
18Have you comprehended the vast expanses of the earth?[q]
Tell me, if you know all this.

19"What is the way to the abode of light?
And where does darkness reside?
20Can you take them to their places?
Do you know the paths[r] to their dwellings?
21Surely you know, for you were already born![s]
You have lived so many years!

22"Have you entered the storehouses of the snow[t]
or seen the storehouses of the hail,
23which I reserve for times of trouble,[u]
for days of war and battle?[v]
24What is the way to the place where the lightning is dispersed,
or the place where the east winds are scattered over the earth?
25Who cuts a channel for the torrents of rain,
and a path for the thunderstorm,[w]
26to water[x] a land where no man lives,
a desert with no-one in it,
27to satisfy a desolate wasteland
and make it sprout with grass?[y]
28Does the rain have a father?[z]
Who fathers the drops of dew?
29From whose womb comes the ice?
Who gives birth to the frost from the heavens[a]
30when the waters become hard as stone,
when the surface of the deep is frozen?[b]

31"Can you bind the beautiful[c] Pleiades?
Can you loose the cords of Orion?[c]
32Can you bring forth the constellations in their seasons[d]
or lead out the Bear[e] with its cubs?
33Do you know the laws[d] of the heavens?
Can you set up ⌊God's[f]⌋ dominion over the earth?

34"Can you raise your voice to the clouds
and cover yourself with a flood of water?[e]
35Do you send the lightning bolts on their way?[f]
Do they report to you, 'Here we are'?
36Who endowed the heart[g] with wisdom[g]
or gave understanding[h] to the mind?[h]

38:15 [n]Ps 10:15
38:16 [o]Ps 77:19
38:17 [p]Ps 9:13
38:18 [q]Job 28:24
38:20 [r]Job 26:10
38:21 [s]Job 15:7
38:22 [t]Job 37:6
38:23 [u]Isa 30:30; Eze 13:11 [v]Ex 9:18; Jos 10:11; Rev 16:21
38:25 [w]Job 28:26
38:26 [x]Job 36:27
38:27 [y]Ps 104:14; 107:35
38:28 [z]Ps 147:8; Jer 14:22
38:29 [a]Ps 147:16-17
38:30 [b]Job 37:10
38:31 [c]Job 9:9; Am 5:8
38:33 [d]Ps 148:6; Jer 31:36
38:34 [e]Job 22:11; 36:27-28
38:35 [f]Job 36:32; 37:3
38:36 [g]Job 9:4 [h]Job 32:8; Ps 51:6; Ecc 2:26

b *17* Or *gates of deep shadows* **c** *31* Or *the twinkling*; or *the chains of the* **d** *32* Or *the morning star in its season* **e** *32* Or *out Leo* **f** *33* Or *his*; or *their* **g** *36* The meaning of the Hebrew for this word is uncertain. **h** *36* The meaning of the Hebrew for this word is uncertain.

38:22, 23 God said he was reserving the storehouses of the snow and hail for times of trouble. God used hail to help Joshua and the Israelites win a battle (Joshua 10:11). Just as armies keep weapons in the armoury, God has all the forces of nature in his control. Sometimes he uses them to confound those opposed to him or his people. Job couldn't even begin to know all of God's resources.

38:22–35 God stated that he has all the forces of nature at his command and that he can unleash or restrain them at will. No-one completely understands such common occurrences as rain or snow, and no-one can command them – only God who created them has that power. God's point was that if Job could not explain such common events in nature, how could he possibly explain or question God? And if nature is beyond our grasp, God's moral purposes may not be what we imagine either.

38:31, 32 These are star constellations, and they are all under God's control.

37 Who has the wisdom to count the clouds?
Who can tip over the water jars of the heavens
38 when the dust becomes hard
and the clods of earth stick together?

39 "Do you hunt the prey for the lioness
and satisfy the hunger of the lions[i]
40 when they crouch in their dens[j]
or lie in wait in a thicket?
41 Who provides food for the raven[k]
when its young cry out to God
and wander about for lack of food?[l]

39 "Do you know when the mountain goats[a] give birth?
Do you watch when the doe bears her fawn?
2 Do you count the months till they bear?
Do you know the time they give birth?
3 They crouch down and bring forth their young;
their labour pains are ended.
4 Their young thrive and grow strong in the wilds;
they leave and do not return.

5 "Who let the wild donkey[b] go free?
Who untied his ropes?
6 I gave him the wasteland[c] as his home,
the salt flats as his habitat.[d]
7 He laughs at the commotion in the town;
he does not hear a driver's shout.[e]
8 He ranges the hills for his pasture
and searches for any green thing.

9 "Will the wild ox[f] consent to serve you?
Will he stay by your manger at night?
10 Can you hold him to the furrow with a harness?
Will he till the valleys behind you?
11 Will you rely on him for his great strength?
Will you leave your heavy work to him?
12 Can you trust him to bring in your grain
and gather it to your threshing-floor?

13 "The wings of the ostrich flap joyfully,

38:39 [i]Ps 104:21
38:40 [j]Job 37:8
38:41 [k]Lk 12:24 [l]Ps 147:9; Mt 6:26
39:1 [a]Dt 14:5
39:5 [b]Job 6:5; 11:12; 24:5
39:6 [c]Job 24:5; Ps 107:34; Jer 2:24 [d]Hos 8:9
39:7 [e]Job 3:18
39:9 [f]Nu 23:22; Dt 33:17

GOD'S JUSTICE

Wrong view

LAW OF FAIRNESS

GOD

There is a law of fairness or justice that is higher and more absolute than God. It is binding even for God. God must act in response to that law in order to be fair. Our response is to appeal to that law.

Correct view

GOD

JUSTICE

God himself is the standard of justice. He uses his power according to his own moral perfection. Thus, whatever he does is fair, even if we don't understand it. Our response is to appeal directly to him.

39:1ff God asked Job several questions about the animal kingdom in order to demonstrate how limited Job's knowledge really was. God was not seeking answers from Job. Instead, he was getting Job to recognise and submit to God's power and sovereignty. Only then could he hear what God was really saying to him.

but they cannot compare with the pinions and feathers of the
stork.
14She lays her eggs on the ground
and lets them warm in the sand,
15unmindful that a foot may crush them,
that some wild animal may trample them.
16She treats her young harshly,[g] as if they were not hers;
she cares not that her labour was in vain,
17for God did not endow her with wisdom
or give her a share of good sense.[h]
18Yet when she spreads her feathers to run,
she laughs at horse and rider.

19"Do you give the horse his strength
or clothe his neck with a flowing mane?
20Do you make him leap like a locust,[i]
striking terror with his proud snorting?[j]
21He paws fiercely, rejoicing in his strength,
and charges into the fray.[k]
22He laughs at fear, afraid of nothing;
he does not shy away from the sword.
23The quiver rattles against his side,
along with the flashing spear and lance.
24In frenzied excitement he eats up the ground;
he cannot stand still when the trumpet sounds.[l]
25At the blast of the trumpet[m] he snorts, 'Aha!'
He catches the scent of battle from afar,
the shout of commanders and the battle cry.[n]

26"Does the hawk take flight by your wisdom
and spread his wings towards the south?
27Does the eagle soar at your command
and build his nest on high?[o]
28He dwells on a cliff and stays there at night;
a rocky crag is his stronghold.
29From there he seeks out his food;[p]
his eyes detect it from afar.
30His young ones feast on blood,
and where the slain are, there is he."[q]

39:16 [g]La 4:3
39:17 [h]Job 35:11
39:20 [i]Joel 2:4-5 [j]Jer 8:16
39:21 [k]Jer 8:6
39:24 [l]Jer 4:5, 19; Eze 7:14; Am 3:6
39:25 [m]Jos 6:5 [n]Am 1:14; 2:2
39:27 [o]Jer 49:16; Ob 1:4
39:29 [p]Job 9:26
39:30 [q]Mt 24:28; Lk 17:37

40

The LORD said to Job:[a]

2"Will the one who contends with the Almighty correct him?
Let him who accuses God answer him!"

3Then Job answered the LORD:

4"I am unworthy[b] — how can I reply to you?
I put my hand over my mouth.[c]

40:1 [a]Job 10:2; 13:3; 23:4; 31:35; 33:13
40:4 [b]Job 42:6 [c]Job 29:9

40:2–5 How do you contend with or accuse Almighty God? Do you demand answers when things don't go your way, you lose a job, someone close to you is ill or dies, finances are tight, you fail, or unexpected changes occur? The next time you are tempted to complain to God, consider how much he loves you. And remember Job's reaction when he had his chance to speak. Are you worse off than Job or more righteous than he? Give God a chance to reveal his greater purposes for you, but remember that they may unfold over the course of your life and not at the moment you desire.

40:4 Throughout his time of suffering, Job longed to have an opportunity to plead his innocence before God. Here God appeared to Job and gave him that opportunity. But Job decided to remain quiet because it was no longer necessary for him to speak. God had shown Job that, as a limited human being, he had neither the ability to judge the God who created the universe nor the right to ask why. God's actions do not depend on ours. He will do what he knows is best, regardless of what we think is fair. It is important to

5I spoke once, but I have no answer[d]—
twice, but I will say no more."[e]

6Then the LORD spoke to Job out of the storm:[f]

7"Brace yourself like a man;
I will question you,
and you shall answer me.[g]

8"Would you discredit my justice?[h]
Would you condemn me to justify yourself?
9Do you have an arm like God's,[i]
and can your voice thunder like his?[j]
10Then adorn yourself with glory and splendour,
and clothe yourself in honour and majesty.[k]
11Unleash the fury of your wrath,[l]
look at every proud man and bring him low,[m]
12look at every proud man and humble him,[n]
crush[o] the wicked where they stand.
13Bury them all in the dust together;
shroud their faces in the grave.
14Then I myself will admit to you
that your own right hand can save you.[p]

15"Look at the behemoth,**[a]**
which I made along with you
and which feeds on grass like an ox.
16What strength he has in his loins,
what power in the muscles of his belly!
17His tail**[b]** sways like a cedar;
the sinews of his thighs are close-knit.
18His bones are tubes of bronze,
his limbs like rods of iron.
19He ranks first among the works of God,[q]
yet his Maker can approach him with his sword.
20The hills bring him their produce,[r]
and all the wild animals play[s] nearby.
21Under the lotus plant he lies,
hidden among the reeds in the marsh.
22The lotuses conceal him in their shadow;
the poplars by the stream[t] surround him.
23When the river rages, he is not alarmed;
he is secure, though the Jordan should surge against his mouth.
24Can anyone capture him by the eyes,**[c]**
or trap him and pierce his nose?[u]

40:5 [d]Job 9:3 [e]Job 9:15
40:6 [f]Job 38:1
40:7 [g]Job 38:3; 42:4
40:8 [h]Job 27:2; Ro 3:3
40:9 [i]2Ch 32:8 [j]Job 37:5; Ps 29:3-4
40:10 [k]Ps 93:1; 104:1
40:11 [l]Isa 42:25; Na 1:6 [m]Isa 2:11, 12, 17; Da 4:37
40:12 [n]1Sa 2:7 [o]Isa 13:11; 63:2-3, 6
40:14 [p]Ps 20:6; 60:5; 108:6
40:19 [q]Job 41:33
40:20 [r]Ps 104:14 [s]Ps 104:26
40:22 [t]Isa 44:4
40:24 [u]Job 41:2, 7, 26

a *15* Possibly the hippopotamus or the elephant **b** *17* Possibly trunk **c** *24* Or *by a water hole*

FOUR VIEWS OF SUFFERING		
	Satan's view	People believe in God only when they are prospering and not suffering. This is wrong.
	The view of Job's three friends	Suffering is God's judgment for sin. This is not always true.
	Elihu's view	Suffering is God's way to teach, discipline, and refine. This is true, but an incomplete explanation.
	God's view	Suffering causes us to trust God for who he is, not what he does.

note, however, that God came to Job, demonstrating his love and care for him.

40:15 The behemoth was a large land animal, possibly an elephant or hippopotamus.

41 "Can you pull in the leviathan[a] [a] with a fishhook
or tie down his tongue with a rope?
2 Can you put a cord through his nose
or pierce his jaw with a hook? [b]
3 Will he keep begging you for mercy?
Will he speak to you with gentle words?
4 Will he make an agreement with you
for you to take him as your slave for life? [c]
5 Can you make a pet of him like a bird
or put him on a leash for your girls?
6 Will traders barter for him?
Will they divide him up among the merchants?
7 Can you fill his hide with harpoons
or his head with fishing spears?
8 If you lay a hand on him,
you will remember the struggle and never do it again!
9 Any hope of subduing him is false;
the mere sight of him is overpowering.
10 No-one is fierce enough to rouse him. [d]
Who then is able to stand against me? [e]
11 Who has a claim against me that I must pay? [f]
Everything under heaven belongs to me. [g]

12 "I will not fail to speak of his limbs,
his strength and his graceful form.
13 Who can strip off his outer coat?
Who would approach him with a bridle?
14 Who dares open the doors of his mouth,
ringed about with his fearsome teeth?
15 His back has[b] rows of shields
tightly sealed together;
16 each is so close to the next
that no air can pass between.
17 They are joined fast to one another;
they cling together and cannot be parted.
18 His snorting throws out flashes of light;
his eyes are like the rays of dawn. [h]
19 Firebrands stream from his mouth;
sparks of fire shoot out.
20 Smoke pours from his nostrils
as from a boiling pot over a fire of reeds.
21 His breath [i] sets coals ablaze,
and flames dart from his mouth. [j]
22 Strength resides in his neck;
dismay goes before him.
23 The folds of his flesh are tightly joined;
they are firm and immovable.
24 His chest is hard as rock,

41:1 [a] Job 3:8; Ps 104:26; Isa 27:1
41:2 [b] Isa 37:29
41:4 [c] Ex 21:6
41:10 [d] Job 3:8 [e] Jer 50:44
41:11 [f] Ro 11:35 [g] Ex 19:5; Dt 10:14; Ps 24:1; 50:12; 1Co 10:26
41:18 [h] Job 3:9
41:21 [i] Isa 40:7 [j] Ps 18:8

a *1* Possibly the crocodile **b** *15* Or *His pride is his*

41:1 While *leviathan* usually refers to a seven-headed sea monster in old Canaanite myths, it probably means crocodile here.

41:9–11 It is foolish for people to think they can stand up against God when they are afraid to confront even a crocodile. How much more powerful is God!

41:30
[k] Isa 41:15

41:33
[l] Job 40:19

41:34
[m] Job 28:8

hard as a lower millstone.
25 When he rises up, the mighty are terrified;
they retreat before his thrashing.
26 The sword that reaches him has no effect,
nor does the spear or the dart or the javelin.
27 Iron he treats like straw
and bronze like rotten wood.
28 Arrows do not make him flee;
slingstones are like chaff to him.
29 A club seems to him but a piece of straw;
he laughs at the rattling of the lance.
30 His undersides are jagged potsherds,
leaving a trail in the mud like a threshing-sledge.[k]
31 He makes the depths churn like a boiling cauldron
and stirs up the sea like a pot of ointment.
32 Behind him he leaves a glistening wake;
one would think the deep had white hair.
33 Nothing on earth is his equal[l]—
a creature without fear.
34 He looks down on all that are haughty;
he is king over all that are proud.[m]"

E. JOB IS RESTORED (42:1–17)

In response to God's speech, Job humbles himself. God rebukes the three friends for adding to Job's suffering by their false assumptions and critical attitudes. Job's material possessions and family are restored, and he receives even greater blessings than he had before. Those who persist in trusting God will be rewarded.

Job

42 Then Job replied to the LORD:

42:2
[a] Ge 18:14; Mt 19:26
[b] 2Ch 20:6

2 "I know that you can do all things;[a]
no plan of yours can be thwarted.[b]

JOB AND JESUS
The book of Job is intimately tied to the New Testament because Job's questions and problems are answered perfectly in Jesus Christ.

Subject	*Reference in Job*	*How Jesus is the Answer*
Someone must help us approach God	9:32, 33	1 Timothy 2:5
Is there life after death?	14:14	John 11:25
There is one in heaven working on our behalf	16:19	Hebrews 9:24
There is one who can save us from judgment	19:25	Hebrews 7:24, 25
Where do we find God?	23:3–5	John 14:9
What is important in life?	21:7–15	Matthew 16:26; John 3:16

42:1ff Throughout the book, Job's friends had asked him to admit his sin and ask for forgiveness, and eventually Job did indeed repent. Ironically, Job's repentance was not the kind called for by his friends. He did not ask for forgiveness for committing secret sins, but for questioning God's sovereignty and justice. Job repented of his attitude and acknowledged God's great power and perfect justice. We sin when we angrily ask, "If God is in control, how could he let this happen?" Because we are locked into time, unable to see beyond today, we cannot know the reasons for everything that happens. Thus we must often choose between doubt and trust. Will you trust God with your unanswered questions?

42:2–4 Job was quoting the Lord's earlier questions to him (38:2, 3). He openly and honestly faced God and admitted that he was the one who had been foolish. Are you using what you can't understand as an excuse for your lack of trust? Admit to God that you don't even have enough faith to trust him. True faith begins in such humility.

3 ⌞You asked,⌟ 'Who is this that obscures my counsel without
knowledge?'[c]
Surely I spoke of things I did not understand,
things too wonderful for me to know.[d]

4 ⌞"You said,⌟ 'Listen now, and I will speak;
I will question you,
and you shall answer me.'[e]
5 My ears had heard of you[f]
but now my eyes have seen you.[g]
6 Therefore I despise myself[h]
and repent in dust and ashes."[i]

Epilogue

7 After the LORD had said these things to Job, he said to Eliphaz the Temanite, "I
am angry with you and your two friends,[j] because you have not spoken of me what
is right, as my servant Job has. 8 So now take seven bulls and seven rams[k] and go
to my servant Job and sacrifice a burnt offering[l] for yourselves. My servant Job will
pray for you, and I will accept his prayer[m] and not deal with you according to your
folly.[n] You have not spoken of me what is right, as my servant Job has." 9 So Eliphaz
the Temanite, Bildad the Shuhite and Zophar the Naamathite did what the LORD told
them; and the LORD accepted Job's prayer.
10 After Job had prayed for his friends, the LORD made him prosperous again[o] and
gave him twice as much as he had before.[p] 11 All his brothers and sisters and everyone
who had known him before[q] came and ate with him in his house. They comforted
and consoled him over all the trouble the LORD had brought upon him, and each one
gave him a piece of silver[a] and a gold ring.
12 The LORD blessed the latter part of Job's life more than the first. He had fourteen
thousand sheep, six thousand camels, a thousand yoke of oxen and a thousand
donkeys. 13 And he also had seven sons and three daughters. 14 The first daughter he
named Jemimah, the second Keziah and the third Keren-Happuch. 15 Nowhere in all

[a] *11* Hebrew *him a kesitah*; a kesitah was a unit of money of unknown weight and value.

42:3
[c] Job 38:2
[d] Ps 40:5; 131:1; 139:6

42:4
[e] Job 38:3; 40:7

42:5
[f] Job 26:14; Ro 10:17
[g] Jdg 13:22; Isa 6:5; Eph 1:17-18

42:6
[h] Job 40:4
[i] Ezr 9:6

42:7
[j] Job 32:3

42:8
[k] Nu 23:1, 29
[l] Job 1:5
[m] Ge 20:17; Jas 5:15-16; 1Jn 5:16
[n] Job 22:30

42:10
[o] Dt 30:3; Ps 14:7
[p] Job 1:3; Ps 85:1-3; 126:5-6

42:11
[q] Job 19:13

42:7, 8 God made it clear that Job's friends were wrong. The fact that God did not mention any specific sins shows that God confirmed Job's claim to have led a devout and obedient life. Job's friends had made the error of assuming that Job's suffering was caused by some great sin. They were judging Job without knowing what God was doing. We must be careful to avoid making judgments about a person because God may be working in ways we know nothing about.

42:8–10 After receiving much criticism, Job was still able to pray for his three friends. It is difficult to forgive someone who has accused us of wrongdoing, but Job did. Are you praying for those who have hurt you? Can you forgive them? Follow the actions of Job, whom God called a good man, and pray for those who have wronged you.

42:10, 11 Would the message of the book of Job change if God had not restored to Job his former blessings? No. God is still sovereign. Jesus said that anyone who gives up something for the kingdom of God will be repaid (Luke 18:29, 30). Our restoration may or may not be the same kind as Job's, which was both spiritual and material. Our complete restoration may not be in this life—but it *will* happen. God loves us, and he is just. He not only will restore whatever we have lost unjustly, but he also will give us more than we can imagine as we live with him in eternity. Cling tightly to your faith through all your trials, and you too will be rewarded by God—if not now, in the life to come.

42:17 The main question in the book of Job is timely: Why do believers experience troubles and suffering? Through a long debate, Job's supposedly wise friends were unable to answer this question. Job's friends made a serious error for which God rebuked them. They assumed that trouble comes only because people sin. People make the same mistake today when they assert that sickness or lack of material blessing is a sign of unconfessed sin or lack of faith. Though normally (but not always) following God leads to a happier life, and rebelling against God normally (but not always) leads to an unhappy life, *God is in control.* In our world invaded by sin, calamity and suffering may come to good and bad alike.

This does not mean that God is indifferent, uncaring, unjust, or powerless to protect us. Bad things happen because we live in a fallen world where both believers and unbelievers are hit with the tragic consequences of sin. God allows evil for a time although he often turns it around for our good (Romans 8:28). We may have no answers as to why God allows evil, but we can be sure he is all-powerful and knows what he is doing. The next time you face trials

42:17
[r] Ge 15:15; 25:8

the land were there found women as beautiful as Job's daughters, and their father granted them an inheritance along with their brothers.
16 After this, Job lived a hundred and forty years; he saw his children and their children to the fourth generation.
17 And so he died, old and full of years.[r]

WHEN WE SUFFER
Here are six questions to ask ourselves when we suffer, and what to do if the answer is yes.

Questions	*Our response*
Am I being punished by God for sin?	Confess known sin.
Is Satan attacking me as I try to survive as a Christian?	Call on God for strength.
Am I being prepared for a special service, learning to be compassionate to those who suffer?	Resist self-pity. Ask God to open up doors of opportunity and help you discover others who suffer as you do.
Am I specifically selected for testing, like Job?	Accept help from the body of believers. Trust God to work his purpose through you.
Is my suffering a result of natural consequences for which I am not directly responsible?	Recognise that in a sinful world, both good and evil people will suffer. But the good person has a promise from God that his or her suffering will one day come to an end.
Is my suffering due to some unknown reason?	Don't withdraw inwards from the pain. Proclaim your faith in God, know that he cares, and wait patiently for his aid.

and dilemmas, see them as opportunities to turn to God for strength. You will find a God who only desires to show his love and compassion to you. If you can trust him in pain, confusion, and loneliness, you will win the victory and eliminate doubt, one of Satan's greatest footholds in your life. Make God your foundation. You can never be separated from his love.

PSALMS

VITAL STATISTICS

PURPOSE:
To provide poetry for the expression of praise, worship, and confession to God

AUTHORS:
David wrote 73 psalms; Asaph wrote 12; the sons of Korah wrote nine; Solomon wrote two; Heman (with the sons of Korah), Ethan, and Moses each wrote one; and 51 psalms are anonymous. The New Testament ascribes two of the anonymous psalms (Psalms 2 and 95) to David (see Acts 4:25; Hebrews 4:7).

DATE WRITTEN:
Between the time of Moses (around 1440 B.C.) and the Babylonian captivity (586 B.C.)

SETTING:
For the most part, the psalms were not intended to be narrations of historical events. However, they often parallel events in history, such as David's flight from Saul and his sin with Bathsheba.

KEY VERSE:
"Let everything that has breath praise the LORD. Praise the LORD" (150:6).

KEY PERSON:
David

KEY PLACE:
God's holy temple

"HELLO, how are you?" "Fine." Not exactly an "in-depth" discussion, this brief interchange is normal as friends and acquaintances pass and briefly touch each other with a cliché or two. Actually, clichés are a way of life, saturating sentences and permeating paragraphs. But if this is the essence of their communication, the relationship will stall on a superficial plateau. Facts and opinions also fill our verbiage. These words go deeper, but the true person still lies hidden beneath them. In reality, it is only when honest feelings and emotions are shared that real people can be known, loved, and helped.

Often, patterns of superficial communication spill over into our talks with God. We easily slide through well-worn lines recited for decades, or we quickly toss a cliché or two at God and call it prayer. There is no doubt that God hears and understands these feeble attempts, but by limiting the depth of our communication, we become shallow in our relationship with him. But God knows us, and he wants to have genuine communication with us.

At the centre of the Bible is the book of Psalms. This great collection of songs and prayers expresses the heart and soul of humanity. In them, the whole range of human experiences is expressed. There are no clichés in this book. Instead, David and the other writers honestly pour out their true feelings, reflecting a dynamic, powerful, and life-changing friendship with God. The psalmists confess their sins, express their doubts and fears, ask God for help in times of trouble, and praise and worship him.

As you read the book of Psalms, you will hear believers crying out to God from the depths of despair, and you will hear them singing to him in the heights of celebration. But whether despairing or rejoicing, you will always hear them sharing honest feelings with their God. Because of the honesty expressed by the psalmists, men and women throughout history have come, again and again, to the book of Psalms for comfort during times of struggle and distress. And with the psalmists, they have risen from the depths of despair to new heights of joy and praise as they also discovered the power of God's everlasting love and forgiveness. Let the honesty of the psalmists guide you into a deep and genuine relationship with God.

THE BLUEPRINT

BOOK I
PSALMS 1:1—41:13

While the psalms are not organised by topic, it is helpful to compare the dominant themes in each section of the psalms to the five books of Moses. This first collection of psalms, mainly written by David, is similar to the book of Genesis. Just as Genesis tells how mankind was created, fell into sin, and was then promised redemption, many of these psalms discuss humans as blessed, fallen, and redeemed by God.

BOOK II PSALMS 42:1—72:20	This collection of psalms, mainly written by David and the sons of Korah, is similar to the book of Exodus. Just as Exodus describes the nation of Israel, many of these psalms describe the nation as ruined and then recovered. As God rescued the nation of Israel, he also rescues us. We do not have to work out solutions first, but we can go to God with our problems and ask him to help.
BOOK III PSALMS 73:1—89:52	This collection of psalms, mainly written by Asaph or Asaph's descendants, is similar to the book of Leviticus. Just as Leviticus discusses the tabernacle and God's holiness, many of these psalms discuss the temple and God's enthronement. Because God is almighty, we can turn to him for deliverance. These psalms praise God because he is holy, and his perfect holiness deserves our worship and reverence.
BOOK IV PSALMS 90:1—106:48	This collection of psalms, mainly written by unknown authors, is similar to the book of Numbers. Just as Numbers discusses the relationship of the nation of Israel to surrounding nations, these psalms often mention the relationship of God's overruling kingdom to the other nations. Because we are citizens of the kingdom of God, we can keep the events and troubles of earth in their proper perspective.
BOOK V PSALMS 107:1—150:6	This collection of psalms, mainly written by David, is similar to the book of Deuteronomy. Just as Deuteronomy was concerned with God and his word, these psalms are anthems of praise and thanksgiving for God and his word. Most of the psalms were originally set to music and used in worship. We can use these psalms today as they were used in the past, as a hymnbook of praise and worship. This is a book that ought to make our hearts sing.

MEGATHEMES

THEME	EXPLANATION	IMPORTANCE
Praise	Psalms are songs of praise to God as our Creator, Sustainer, and Redeemer. Praise is recognising, appreciating, and expressing God's greatness.	Focusing our thoughts on God moves us to praise him. The more we know him, the more we can appreciate what he has done for us.
God's Power	God is all-powerful; and he always acts at the right time. He is sovereign over every situation. God's power is shown by the ways he reveals himself in creation, history, and his word.	When we feel powerless, God can help us. His strength can overcome the despair of any pain or trial. We can always pray that he will deliver, protect, and sustain us.
Forgiveness	Many psalms are intense prayers asking God for forgiveness. God forgives us when we confess our sin and turn from it.	Because God forgives us, we can pray to him honestly and directly. When we receive his forgiveness, we move from alienation to intimacy, from guilt to love.
Thankfulness	We are grateful to God for his personal concern, help, and mercy. Not only does he protect, guide, and forgive us, but his creation provides everything we need.	When we realise how we benefit from knowing God, we can fully express our thanks to him. By thanking him often, we develop spontaneity in our prayer life.
Trust	God is faithful and just. When we put our trust in him, he quiets our hearts. Because he has been faithful throughout history, we can trust him in times of trouble.	People can be unfair and friends may desert us. But we can trust God. Knowing God intimately drives away doubt, fear, and loneliness.

BOOK I
PSALMS 1:1—41:13

In this book, the psalmists praise God for his justice, express confidence in God's compassion, recount the depravity of man, plead for vindication, ask God to deliver them from their enemies, speak of the blessedness of the forgiven sinner, and portray God as a shepherd. We should worship God with the same sense of adoration found in these psalms.

PSALM 1

Theme: Life's two roads. The life of the faithful person is contrasted with the life of the faithless person.
Author: Anonymous

1 Blessed is the man
who does not walk[a] in the counsel of the wicked
or stand in the way of sinners
or sit[b] in the seat of mockers.
2 But his delight[c] is in the law of the LORD,[d]
and on his law he meditates[e] day and night.
3 He is like a tree[f] planted by streams of water,[g]
which yields its fruit[h] in season
and whose leaf does not wither.
Whatever he does prospers.[i]

4 Not so the wicked!
They are like chaff[j]
that the wind blows away.
5 Therefore the wicked will not stand[k] in the judgment,[l]
nor sinners in the assembly of the righteous.

6 For the LORD watches over[m] the way of the righteous,
but the way of the wicked will perish.[n]

1:1 [a]Pr 4:14 [b]Ps 26:4; Jer 15:17
1:2 [c]Ps 119:16, 35 [d]Ps 119:1 [e]Jos 1:8
1:3 [f]Ps 128:3 [g]Jer 17:8 [h]Eze 47:12 [i]Ge 39:3
1:4 [j]Job 21:18; Isa 17:13
1:5 [k]Ps 5:5 [l]Ps 9:7-8, 16
1:6 [m]Ps 37:18; 2Ti 2:19 [n]Ps 9:6

1:1 The writer begins his psalm extolling the joys of obeying God and refusing to listen to those who discredit or ridicule him. Our friends and associates can have a profound influence on us, often in very subtle ways. If we insist on friendships with those who mock what God considers important, we might sin by becoming indifferent to God's will. This attitude is the same as mocking. Do your friends build up your faith, or do they tear it down? True friends should help, not hinder, you to draw closer to God.

1:1ff God doesn't judge people on the basis of race, sex, or national origin. He judges them on the basis of their faith in him and their response to his revealed will. Those who diligently try to obey God's will are blessed. Their happy condition is like healthy, fruit-bearing trees with strong roots (Jeremiah 17:5–8), and God promises to watch over them. God's wisdom guides their lives. In contrast, those who don't trust and obey God have meaningless lives that blow away like dust.

There are only two paths of life before us—God's way of obedience or the way of rebellion and destruction. Be sure to choose God's path because the path you choose determines how you will spend eternity.

1:2 You can learn how to follow God by meditating on his word. Meditating means spending time reading and thinking about what you have read. It means asking yourself how you should change so you're living as God wants. Knowing and meditating on God's word are the first steps towards applying it to your everyday life. If you want to follow God more closely, you must know what he says.

1:2 This "law of the LORD" means all of Scripture: the first five books of Moses, the Prophets, and the other writings. The more we know of the whole scope of God's word, the more resources we will have to guide us in our daily decisions.

1:2, 3 There is simple wisdom in these two verses—the more we delight in God's presence, the more fruitful we are. On the other hand, the more we allow those who ridicule God to affect our thoughts and attitudes, the more we separate ourselves from our source of nourishment. We must have contact with unbelievers if we are to witness to them, but we must not join in or imitate their sinful behaviour. If you want despair, spend time with mocking sinners; but if you want God's happiness, make friends with those who love God and his word.

1:3 When Scripture says, "Whatever he does prospers," it does not mean immunity from failure or difficulties. Nor is it a guarantee of health, wealth, and happiness. What the Bible means by prosperity is this: when we apply God's wisdom, the fruit (results or by-products) we bear will be good and receive God's approval. Just as a tree soaks up water and bears luscious fruit, we also are to soak up God's word, producing actions and attitudes that honour God. To achieve anything worthwhile, we must have God's word in our hearts.

1:4 Chaff is the outer shell (or husk) that must be removed to get at the valuable kernels of grain inside. Chaff was removed by a process called threshing and winnowing. After the plants were cut, they were crushed, and then the pieces were thrown into the air. Chaff is very light and is carried away by even the slightest wind, while the good grain falls back to the earth. Chaff is a symbol of a faithless life that drifts along without direction. Good grain is a symbol of a faithful life that can be used by God. Unlike grain, however, we can choose the direction we will take.

2:1
[a] Ps 21:11

PSALM 2

Theme: God's ultimate rule. A psalm written to celebrate the coronation of an Israelite king, but also written for the coronation of Christ, the eternal King.
Author: David (see Acts 4:25, 26)

2:2
[b] Ps 48:4
[c] Jn 1:41
[d] Ps 74:18, 23; Ac 4:25-26*

1 Why do the nations conspire[a]
and the peoples plot[a] in vain?
2 The kings[b] of the earth take their stand
and the rulers gather together against the LORD
and against his Anointed[c] One.[b d]
3 "Let us break their chains," they say,
"and throw off their fetters."[e]

2:3
[e] Jer 5:5

[a] *1* Hebrew; Septuagint *rage* [b] *2* Or *anointed one*

REASONS TO READ PSALMS

When you want . . .	*Read . . .*
to find comfort	Psalm 23
to meet God intimately	Psalm 103
to learn a new prayer	Psalm 136
to learn a new song	Psalm 92
to learn more about God	Psalm 24
to understand yourself more clearly	Psalm 8
to know how to come to God each day	Psalm 5
to be forgiven for your sins	Psalm 51
to feel worthwhile	Psalm 139
to understand why you should read the Bible	Psalm 119
to give praise to God	Psalm 145
to know that God is in control	Psalm 146
to give thanks to God	Psalm 136
to please God	Psalm 15
to know why you should worship God	Psalm 104

God's word was written to be studied, understood, and applied, and the book of Psalms lends itself most directly to application. We understand the psalms best when we "stand under" them and allow them to flow over us like a shower of rain. We may turn to Psalms looking for something, but sooner or later we will meet Someone. As we read and memorise the psalms, we will gradually discover how much they are already part of us. They put into words our deepest hurts, longings, thoughts, and prayers. They gently push us towards being what God designed us to be—people loving and living for him.

2:1ff Several psalms are called *Messianic* because of their prophetic descriptions of Jesus the Messiah (Christ)—his life, death, resurrection, and future reign. David, who may have been the author of this psalm, was a shepherd, soldier, and king. We can see that he was also a prophet (Acts 2:29, 30) because this psalm describes the rebellion of the nations and the coming of Christ to establish his eternal reign. This psalm is often mentioned in the New Testament (see Acts 4:25, 26; 13:33; Hebrews 1:5, 6; 5:5; Revelation 2:26, 27; 12:5; 19:15).

2:1ff David may have written these words during a conspiracy against Israel by some of the surrounding pagan nations. Chosen and anointed by God, David knew that God would fulfil his promise to bring the Messiah into the world through his bloodline (2 Samuel 7:16; 1 Chronicles 17:11, 12).

2:3 People often think they will be free if they can get away from God. Yet we all inevitably serve somebody or something, whether a human king, an organisation, or even our own selfish desires. Just as a fish is not free when it leaves the water and a tree is not free when it leaves the soil, we are not free when we leave the Lord. We can find the one sure route to freedom by wholeheartedly serving God the Creator. God can set you free to be the person he created you to be.

4The One enthroned in heaven laughs;[f]
the Lord scoffs at them.
5Then he rebukes them in his anger
and terrifies them in his wrath,[g] saying,
6"I have installed my King[c]
on Zion, my holy hill."

7I will proclaim the decree of the LORD:

He said to me, "You are my Son;[d]
today I have become your Father.[e][h]
8Ask of me,
and I will make the nations your inheritance,
the ends of the earth[i] your possession.
9You will rule them with an iron sceptre;[f][j]
you will dash them to pieces[k] like pottery.[l]"

10Therefore, you kings, be wise;
be warned, you rulers of the earth.
11Serve the LORD with fear
and rejoice[m] with trembling.[n]
12Kiss the Son,[o] lest he be angry
and you be destroyed in your way,
for his wrath[p] can flare up in a moment.
Blessed are all who take refuge[q] in him.

PSALM 3

A psalm of David. When he fled from his son Absalom.[a]

Theme: Confidently trusting God for protection and peace.
Author: David

1O LORD, how many are my foes!
How many rise up against me!
2Many are saying of me,
"God will not deliver him.[b]" *Selah*[a]

[c] *6* Or *king* [d] *7* Or *son*; also in verse 12 [e] *7* Or *have begotten you* [f] *9* Or *will break them with a rod of iron*
[a] *2* A word of uncertain meaning, occurring frequently in the Psalms; possibly a musical term

2:4 [f]Ps 37:13; 59:8; Pr 1:26
2:5 [g]Ps 21:9; 78:49-50
2:7 [h]Ac 13:33*; Heb 1:5*
2:8 [i]Ps 22:27
2:9 [j]Rev 12:5 [k]Ps 89:23 [l]Rev 2:27*
2:11 [m]Heb 12:28 [n]Ps 119:119-120
2:12 [o]Jn 5:23 [p]Rev 6:16 [q]Ps 34:8; Ro 9:33
3 Title [a]2Sa 15:14
3:2 [b]Ps 71:11

2:4 God laughs, not at the nations, but at their confused thoughts about power. It is the laughter of a father when his three-year-old boasts that he or she can outrun him or beat him in a wrestling match. The father knows the boundaries of power of his little child, and God knows the boundaries of power of the nations. Every nation is limited, but God is transcendent. If you have to choose between confidence in God and confidence in any nation, choose God!

2:4 God is all-powerful. He created the world, and knew about the empires of the earth long before they came into being (Daniel 2:26–45). But pride and power cause nations and leaders to rebel against God and try to break free of him. Our world has many leaders who boast of their power, who rant and rave against God and his people, who promise to take over and form their own empires. But God laughs because any power they have comes from him, and he can also take it from them. We need not fear the boasts of tyrants – they are in God's hands.

2:11, 12 To "kiss the Son" means to surrender fully and submit to him. Christ is not only God's chosen King, he is also the rightful King of our hearts and lives. To be ready for his coming, we must submit to his leadership every day.

3:1, 2 David felt like he was in the minority. There may have been as many as 10,000 soldiers surrounding him at this time (3:6). Not only did David's enemies view life differently, they actively sought to harm him. As king, David could have trusted his army to defeat Absalom. Instead, he depended upon God's mercy (3:4); therefore, he was at peace with whatever outcome occurred, knowing that God's great purposes would prevail. We can overcome fear by trusting God for his protection in our darkest hour.

3:1–3 David was not sitting on his throne in a place of power, but he was running for his life from his rebellious son Absalom and a host of traitors. When circumstances go against us, it is tempting to think that God is also against us. But David reminds us that the opposite is true. When everything seems to go against us, God is still for us. If circumstance has turned against you, don't blame God – seek him!

3:2 The word *Selah* occurs 71 times in Psalms and three times in Habakkuk (3:3, 9, 13). Though its precise use is unknown, it was most likely a musical sign. Three suggestions are: (1) It was a musical direction to the singers and orchestra to play *forte* or *crescendo.* (2) It was a signal to lift up the hands or voice in worship, or to the priest to give a benediction. (3) It was a phrase like "Amen" meaning "so be it", or "Hallelujah" meaning "Praise the Lord".

3:3 [c]Ge 15:1; Ps 28:7 [d]Ps 27:6
3:4 [e]Ps 2:6
3:5 [f]Lev 26:6; Pr 3:24
3:6 [g]Ps 27:3
3:7 [h]Ps 7:6 [i]Ps 6:4

3But you are a shield[c] around me, O LORD;
you bestow glory on me and lift[b] up my head.[d]
4To the LORD I cry aloud,
and he answers me from his holy hill.[e] *Selah*

5I lie down and sleep;[f]
I wake again, because the LORD sustains me.
6I will not fear[g] the tens of thousands
drawn up against me on every side.

7Arise,[h] O LORD!
Deliver me,[i] O my God!

b 3 Or *LORD, / my Glorious One, who lifts*

PSALMS FROM DAVID'S LIFE
Of the more than 70 psalms attributed to David, at least 14 of them are connected with specific events in his life. From them we see an outline of a growing relationship with God. They are listed here, roughly in chronological order.

Event in David's life	*Reference*	*Psalm*	*What David learned about God*
When Saul sent men to David's home to kill him	1 Samuel 19	59	God is my fortress.
While running from Saul	1 Samuel 21	34	I will glorify the Lord at all times.
While running from Saul	1 Samuel 21	56	When I am afraid, I will trust in God.
While hiding in the cave of Adullam	1 Samuel 22	142	God is my refuge.
After learning that Doeg had murdered 85 priests and their families	1 Samuel 22	52	God will bring evil people down to everlasting ruin.
When the Ziphites tried to betray him	1 Samuel 23	54	Surely God is my help.
While hiding in a cave	1 Samuel 24	57	I will take refuge in the shadow of God's wings until the disaster has passed.
While hiding in the Desert of En Gedi	1 Samuel 24	63	My soul clings to God; his right hand upholds me.
When Saul's pursuit was over	2 Samuel 22	18	To the faithful God shows himself faithful.
After being confronted about his adultery with Bathsheba	2 Samuel 12	51	The sacrifices of God are a broken spirit; a broken and contrite heart he will not despise.
During Absalom's rebellion	2 Samuel 15	3	From the Lord comes deliverance.
During Absalom's rebellion	2 Samuel 15	7	He is a righteous God who searches minds and hearts and can bring to an end the violence of the wicked and make the righteous secure.

3:4 God's holy hill was Mount Moriah in Jerusalem, the place where David's son Solomon would build the temple (2 Chronicles 3:1). David knew that God could not be confined to any space, but he wrote poetically, expressing confidence that God would hear him when he prayed. God responds to us when we urgently pray to him.

3:5 Sleep does not come easily during a crisis. David could have had sleepless nights when his son Absalom rebelled and gathered an army to kill him. But he slept peacefully, even during the rebellion. What made the difference? David cried out to the Lord, and the Lord heard him. The assurance of answered prayer brings peace. It is easier to sleep well when we have full assurance that God is in control of circumstances. If you are lying awake at night worrying about circumstances you can't change, pour out your heart to God, and thank him that he is in control. Then sleep will come.

3:7 This description of God's anger reveals David's desire for justice against his persecutors. David himself was slapped and insulted, and here he simply asked for equal treatment for his enemies. He did this, not out of personal revenge, but for the sake of God's justice. Verse 8 shows the humility behind David's words – he realised that faith in God's timing was the answer to his question about the success the wicked had unfairly achieved.

Strike[j] all my enemies on the jaw;
  break the teeth[k] of the wicked.

8From the LORD comes deliverance.[l]
  May your blessing be on your people. *Selah*

3:7 [j]Job 16:10 [k]Ps 58:6

3:8 [l]Isa 43:3, 11

PSALM 4

For the director of music. With stringed instruments. A psalm of David.

4:1 [a]Ps 25:16 [b]Ps 17:6

Theme: Rejoicing in God's protection and peace. We can place our confidence in God because he will listen when we call on him.
Author: David

4:2 [c]Ps 31:6

1Answer me when I call to you,
  O my righteous God.
 Give me relief from my distress;
  be merciful[a] to me and hear my prayer.[b]

2How long, O men, will you turn my glory into shame?[a]
  How long will you love delusions and seek false gods?[b][c] *Selah*

3Know that the LORD has set apart the godly[d] for himself;
  the LORD will hear[e] when I call to him.

4In your anger do not sin;[f]
  when you are on your beds,[g]
  search your hearts and be silent. *Selah*

5Offer right sacrifices
  and trust in the LORD.[h]

6Many are asking, "Who can show us any good?"
  Let the light of your face shine upon us,[i] O LORD.

7You have filled my heart[j] with greater joy[k]
  than when their grain and new wine abound.

8I will lie down and sleep[l] in peace,
  for you alone, O LORD,
  make me dwell in safety.[m]

a 2 Or *you dishonour my Glorious One* b 2 Or *seek lies*

4:3 [d]Ps 31:23 [e]Ps 6:8

4:4 [f]Eph 4:26* [g]Ps 77:6

4:5 [h]Dt 33:19; Ps 37:3

4:6 [i]Nu 6:25

4:7 [j]Ac 14:17 [k]Isa 9:3

4:8 [l]Ps 3:5 [m]Lev 25:18

4:1ff This psalm may have been written as David was asking his enemies to reconsider their support of Absalom. Others see this psalm as a prayer for relief from a calamity such as a drought (see 4:7). It was probably written shortly after Psalm 3.

4:3 The godly are those who are faithful and devoted to God. David knew that God would hear him when he called and would answer him. We too can be confident that God listens to our prayers and answers when we call on him. Sometimes we think that God will not hear us because we have fallen short of his high standards for holy living. But if we have trusted Christ for salvation, God has forgiven us, and he will listen to us. When you feel as though your prayers are bouncing off the ceiling, remember that as a believer you have been set apart by God and that he loves you. He hears and answers, although his answers may not be what you expect. Look at your problems in the light of God's power instead of looking at God in the shadow of your problems.

4:5 Worship in David's day included animal sacrifices by the priests in the tabernacle. The animal's blood covered the sins of the one who offered the animal. There were specific rules for offering sacrifices, but more important to God than ceremony was the offerer's attitude of submission and obedience (1 Samuel 15:22, 23). Today, a "right sacrifice", one that is pleasing to God, is still the same. He wants our obedience and our praise before our gifts (Hebrews 13:15). Offer God your sacrifice of total obedience and heartfelt praise.

4:7 Two kinds of joy are contrasted here – inward joy that comes from knowing and trusting God and happiness that comes as a result of pleasant circumstances. Inward joy is steady as long as we trust God; happiness is unpredictable. Inward joy defeats discouragement; happiness covers it up. Inward joy is lasting; happiness is temporary.

5:2 [a]Ps 3:4 [b]Ps 84:3
5:3 [c]Ps 88:13
5:4 [d]Ps 11:5; 92:15
5:5 [e]Ps 73:3 [f]Ps 1:5 [g]Ps 11:5
5:6 [h]Ps 55:23; Rev 21:8
5:7 [i]Ps 138:2
5:8 [j]Ps 31:1 [k]Ps 27:11
5:9 [l]Lk 11:44 [m]Ro 3:13*
5:10 [n]Ps 9:16 [o]Ps 107:11
5:11 [p]Ps 2:12 [q]Ps 69:36 [r]Isa 65:13
5:12 [s]Ps 32:7

PSALM 5

For the director of music. For flutes. A psalm of David.

Theme: The lies of enemies. God is able to defend us from lies spoken against us.
Author: David

1 Give ear to my words, O LORD,
consider my sighing.
2 Listen to my cry for help,[a]
my King and my God,[b]
for to you I pray.
3 In the morning,[c] O LORD, you hear my voice;
in the morning I lay my requests before you
and wait in expectation.

4 You are not a God who takes pleasure in evil;
with you the wicked[d] cannot dwell.
5 The arrogant[e] cannot stand[f] in your presence;
you hate[g] all who do wrong.
6 You destroy those who tell lies;[h]
bloodthirsty and deceitful men
the LORD abhors.

7 But I, by your great mercy,
will come into your house;
in reverence will I bow down[i]
towards your holy temple.
8 Lead me, O LORD, in your righteousness[j]
because of my enemies—
make straight your way[k] before me.

9 Not a word from their mouth can be trusted;
their heart is filled with destruction.
Their throat is an open grave;[l]
with their tongue they speak deceit.[m]
10 Declare them guilty, O God!
Let their intrigues be their downfall.
Banish them for their many sins,[n]
for they have rebelled[o] against you.

11 But let all who take refuge in you be glad;
let them ever sing for joy.[p]
Spread your protection over them,
that those who love your name[q] may rejoice in you.[r]
12 For surely, O LORD, you bless the righteous;
you surround them[s] with your favour as with a shield.

5:1–3 The secret of a close relationship with God is to pray to him earnestly *each morning.* In the morning, our minds are more free from problems and then we can commit the whole day to God. Regular communication helps any friendship and is certainly necessary for a strong relationship with God. We need to communicate with him daily. Do you have a regular time to pray and read God's word?

5:5 God cannot condone or excuse even the smallest sin. Therefore we cannot excuse ourselves for sinning only a little bit. As we grow spiritually, our sensitivity to sin increases. What is your reaction to sin in your life? Are you insensitive, unconcerned, disappointed, or comfortable? As God makes us aware of sin, we must be intolerant towards it and be willing to change. All believers should strive to be more tolerant of people but less tolerant of the sin in others and in themselves.

PSALM 6

For the director of music. With stringed instruments. According to *sheminith*.[a] A psalm of David.

Theme: Deliverance in trouble. God is able to rescue us.
Author: David

1O LORD, do not rebuke me in your anger[a]
or discipline me in your wrath.
2Be merciful to me, LORD, for I am faint;
O LORD, heal me,[b] for my bones are in agony.[c]
3My soul is in anguish.[d]
How long,[e] O LORD, how long?

4Turn, O LORD, and deliver me;
save me because of your unfailing love.[f]
5No-one remembers you when he is dead.
Who praises you from his grave?[b][g]

6I am worn out[h] from groaning;
all night long I flood my bed with weeping
and drench my couch with tears.[i]
7My eyes grow weak[j] with sorrow;
they fail because of all my foes.

8Away from me,[k] all you who do evil,[l]
for the LORD has heard my weeping.
9The LORD has heard my cry for mercy;[m]
the LORD accepts my prayer.
10All my enemies will be ashamed and dismayed;
they will turn back in sudden disgrace.[n]

PSALM 7

A *shiggaion*[a] of David, which he sang to the LORD concerning Cush, a Benjamite.

Theme: A request for justice against those who make slanderous comments. God is the perfect judge and will punish those who persecute the innocent.
Author: David

1O LORD my God, I take refuge in you;
save and deliver me from all who pursue me,[a]

[a] Title: Probably a musical term [b] 5 Hebrew *Sheol* [a] Title: Probably a literary or musical term

6:1 [a]Ps 38:1
6:2 [b]Hos 6:1 [c]Ps 22:14; 31:10
6:3 [d]Jn 12:27 [e]Ps 90:13
6:4 [f]Ps 17:13
6:5 [g]Ps 30:9; 88:10-12; Ecc 9:10; Isa 38:18
6:6 [h]Ps 69:3 [i]Ps 42:3
6:7 [j]Ps 31:9
6:8 [k]Ps 119:115 [l]Mt 7:23; Lk 13:27
6:9 [m]Ps 116:1
6:10 [n]Ps 71:24; 73:19
7:1 [a]Ps 31:15

6:1ff This is the first of seven "penitential" psalms, where the writer humbly realises his predicament (usually the result of sin), expresses sorrow over it, and demonstrates a fresh commitment to remain close to God. We don't know the cause of David's pain, but whatever the cause, he sought God for the remedy.

6:1–3 David accepted God's punishment, but he begged God not to discipline him in anger. Jeremiah also asked God to correct him gently and not in anger (Jeremiah 10:24). David recognised that if God treated him with justice alone and not with mercy, he would be wiped out by God's wrath. Often we want God to show mercy to us and justice to everyone else. God in his kindness forgives us instead of giving us what we deserve.

6:6 Pouring out his heart with tears, David was completely honest with God. We can be honest with God even when we are filled with anger or despair because God knows us thoroughly and wants the very best for us. Anger may result in rash outward acts or turning inward in depression. But because we trust in our all-powerful God, we don't have to be victims of circumstance or be weighed down by the guilt of sin. Be honest with God, and he will help you turn your attention from yourself to him and his mercy.

7:1 *Shiggaion* may be a term derived from the verb "to err" or "to wander"; it might also mean "wild" or "ecstatic". It is a poem written with intense feeling, a lament to stir the emotions.

7:1–6 Have you ever been falsely accused or so badly hurt that you wanted revenge? David wrote this psalm in response to the slanderous accusations of those who claimed he was trying to kill Saul and seize the throne (1 Samuel 24:9–11). Instead of taking matters into his own hands and striking back, David cried out to God for justice. The proper response to slander is prayer, not revenge, because God says, "It is mine to avenge; I will repay" (Romans 12:19; see also Deuteronomy 32:35, 36; Hebrews 10:30). Instead of striking back, ask God to take your case, bring justice, and restore your reputation.

7:2 [b]Isa 38:13 [c]Ps 50:22

2or they will tear me like a lion[b]
and rip me to pieces with no-one to rescue[c] me.

3O LORD my God, if I have done this
and there is guilt on my hands[d]—
4if I have done evil to him who is at peace with me
or without cause have robbed my foe—
5then let my enemy pursue and overtake me;
let him trample my life to the ground
and make me sleep in the dust. *Selah*

7:3 [d]1Sa 24:11; Isa 59:3

6Arise,[e] O LORD, in your anger;
rise up against the rage of my enemies.[f]
Awake,[g] my God; decree justice.
7Let the assembled peoples gather round you.
Rule over them from on high;
8 let the LORD judge the peoples.
Judge me, O LORD, according to my righteousness,[h]
according to my integrity, O Most High.
9O righteous God,[i]
who searches minds and hearts,[j]
bring to an end the violence of the wicked
and make the righteous secure.[k]

7:6 [e]Ps 94:2 [f]Ps 138:7 [g]Ps 44:23

7:8 [h]Ps 18:20; 96:13

7:9 [i]Jer 11:20 [j]1Ch 28:9; Ps 26:2; Rev 2:23 [k]Ps 37:23

10My shield[b] is God Most High,
who saves the upright in heart.[l]
11God is a righteous judge,[m]
a God who expresses his wrath every day.
12If he does not relent,
he[c] will sharpen his sword;[n]
he will bend and string his bow.
13He has prepared his deadly weapons;
he makes ready his flaming arrows.

7:10 [l]Ps 125:4

7:11 [m]Ps 50:6

7:12 [n]Dt 32:41

14He who is pregnant with evil
and conceives trouble gives birth[o] to disillusionment.
15He who digs a hole and scoops it out
falls into the pit he has made.[p]
16The trouble he causes recoils on himself;
his violence comes down on his own head.

7:14 [o]Job 15:35; Isa 59:4; Jas 1:15

7:15 [p]Job 4:8

17I will give thanks to the LORD because of his righteousness[q]
and will sing praise[r] to the name of the LORD Most High.

7:17 [q]Ps 71:15-16 [r]Ps 9:2

b *10* Or *sovereign* **c** *12* Or *If a man does not repent, / God*

7:9 God "searches minds and hearts". Nothing is hidden from God—this can be either terrifying or comforting. Our thoughts are an open book to him. Because he knows even our motives, we have no place to hide, no way to pretend we can get away with sin. But that very knowledge also gives us great comfort. We don't have to impress God or put up a false front. Instead, we can trust God to help us work through our weaknesses in order to serve him as he has planned. When we truly follow God, he rewards our effort.

7:14–16 When allowed to run its course, evil destroys itself. Violent people become victims of violence, and liars become victims of others' deceit (9:15, 16). But in the process, innocent people are hurt. Sometimes God intervenes and stops evildoers in their tracks in order to protect his followers. At other times, for reasons known only to him, God allows evil to continue even though innocent people are hurt. It is during these times that we must ask God to protect us. Remember that God will execute final justice, even if it is not during our lifetime.

7:17 During a time of great evil and injustice, David was grateful that God is righteous (see also 7:11). When we wonder if anyone is honest or fair, we can be assured that God will continue to bring justice and fairness when we involve him in our activities. If you ever feel that you are being treated unfairly, ask the One who is always fair and just to be with you. Then thank him for his presence (see Isaiah 42:1–6).

PSALM 8

For the director of music. According to *gittith*.[a] A psalm of David.

Theme: The greatness of God assures the worth of mankind. God, the all-powerful Creator, cares for his most valuable creation — people.
Author: David

1O LORD, our Lord,
how majestic is your name in all the earth!

You have set your glory
above the heavens.[a]
2From the lips of children and infants
you have ordained praise[b][b]
because of your enemies,
to silence the foe[c] and the avenger.

3When I consider your heavens,[d]
the work of your fingers,
the moon and the stars,[e]
which you have set in place,
4what is man that you are mindful of him,
the son of man that you care for him?[f]
5You made him a little lower than the heavenly beings[c]
and crowned him with glory and honour.[g]

6You made him ruler[h] over the works of your hands;
you put everything under his feet:[i][j]
7all flocks and herds,
and the beasts of the field,
8the birds of the air,
and the fish of the sea,
all that swim the paths of the seas.

9O LORD, our Lord,
how majestic is your name in all the earth![k]

a Title: Probably a musical term b 2 Or *strength* c 5 Or *than God*

8:1
a Ps 57:5; 113:4; 148:13

8:2
b Mt 21:16*
c Ps 44:16; 1Co 1:27

8:3
d Ps 89:11
e Ps 136:9

8:4
f Job 7:17; Ps 144:3; Heb 2:6

8:5
g Ps 21:5; 103:4

8:6
h Ge 1:28
i Heb 2:6-8*
j 1Co 15:25, 27*; Eph 1:22

8:9
k ver 1

8:1ff Portions of this psalm are quoted in the New Testament and applied to Christ (1 Corinthians 15:27; Hebrews 2:6–8). Jesus became human, just a little lower than the heavenly beings (8:5), and he will raise all who belong to him above the heavenly beings when he comes to reign over the new heaven and new earth. Jesus is the only person who perfectly reflects God's image (Galatians 2:20; Colossians 1:15).

8:2 Children are able to trust and praise God without doubts or reservations. As we get older, many of us find this more and more difficult to do. Ask God to give you childlike faith, removing any barriers to having a closer walk with him. Get in touch with this childlike quality in yourself so that you can be more expressive.

8:3, 4 To respect God's majesty, we must compare ourselves to his greatness. When we look at creation, we often feel small by comparison. To feel small is a healthy way to get back to reality, but God does not want us to dwell on our smallness. Humility means proper respect for God, not self-depreciation.

8:3–5 When we look at the vast expanse of creation, we wonder how God could be concerned for people who constantly disappoint him. Yet God created us only a little lower than himself or the angels! The next time you question your worth as a person, remember that God considers you highly valuable. We have great worth because we bear the stamp of the Creator. (See Genesis 1:26, 27 for the extent of worth God places on all people.) Because God has already declared how valuable we are to him, we can be set free from feelings of worthlessness.

8:6 God gave human beings tremendous authority — to be in charge of the whole earth. But with great authority comes great responsibility. If we own a pet, we have the legal authority to do with it as we wish, but we also have the responsibility to feed and care for it. How do you treat God's creation? Use your resources wisely because God holds you accountable for your stewardship.

9:1 [a]Ps 86:12 [b]Ps 26:7
9:2 [c]Ps 5:11 [d]Ps 92:1; 83:18
9:4 [e]Ps 140:12 [f]1Pe 2:23
9:5 [g]Pr 10:7
9:6 [h]Ps 34:16
9:7 [i]Ps 89:14
9:8 [j]Ps 96:13
9:9 [k]Ps 32:7
9:10 [l]Ps 91:14 [m]Ps 37:28
9:11 [n]Ps 76:2 [o]Ps 107:22 [p]Ps 105:1
9:12 [q]Ge 9:5
9:13 [r]Ps 38:19
9:14 [s]Ps 106:2 [t]Ps 13:5; 51:12

PSALM 9[a]

For the director of music. To ⌊the tune of⌋ "The Death of the Son". A psalm of David.

Theme: God never ignores our cries for help.
Author: David, probably written after a victory over the Philistines

1 I will praise you, O LORD, with all my heart;[a]
I will tell of all your wonders.[b]
2 I will be glad and rejoice[c] in you;
I will sing praise to your name,[d] O Most High.

3 My enemies turn back;
they stumble and perish before you.
4 For you have upheld my right and my cause;[e]
you have sat on your throne, judging righteously.[f]
5 You have rebuked the nations and destroyed the wicked;
you have blotted out their name[g] for ever and ever.
6 Endless ruin has overtaken the enemy,
you have uprooted their cities;
even the memory of them[h] has perished.

7 The LORD reigns for ever;
he has established his throne[i] for judgment.
8 He will judge the world in righteousness;[j]
he will govern the peoples with justice.
9 The LORD is a refuge for the oppressed,
a stronghold in times of trouble.[k]
10 Those who know your name[l] will trust in you,
for you, LORD, have never forsaken[m] those who seek you.

11 Sing praises to the LORD, enthroned in Zion;[n]
proclaim among the nations[o] what he has done.[p]
12 For he who avenges blood[q] remembers;
he does not ignore the cry of the afflicted.

13 O LORD, see how my enemies[r] persecute me!
Have mercy and lift me up from the gates of death,
14 that I may declare your praises[s]
in the gates of the Daughter of Zion
and there rejoice in your salvation.[t]

[a] Psalms 9 and 10 may have been originally a single acrostic poem, the stanzas of which begin with the successive letters of the Hebrew alphabet. In the Septuagint they constitute one psalm.

9:1ff Praise is expressing to God our appreciation and understanding of his worth. It is saying "thank you" for each aspect of his divine nature. Our inward attitude becomes outward expression. When we praise God, we help ourselves by expanding our awareness of who he is. In each psalm you read, look for an attribute or characteristic of God for which you can thank him.

9:4 God upholds our just cause; he is our vindicator (one who clears us from criticism and justifies us before others). In this life, we may face many injustices: (1) we may be falsely accused and misunderstood by friends and enemies; (2) we may not be truly appreciated by others for the love we show; (3) the true value of our work and service may not be duly rewarded; (4) our ideas may be ignored. But God is to be praised, for he sees and remembers all the good we do, and it is up to him to decide the timing and the appropriateness of our rewards. If we do not trust him to vindicate us, then we will be susceptible to hatred and self-pity. If we do trust him, we can experience God's peace and be free from the worry of how others perceive us and treat us.

9:10 God will never forsake those who seek him. To forsake someone is to abandon that person. God's promise does not mean that if we trust in him we will escape loss or suffering; it means that God himself will never leave us no matter what we face.

9:11 God does not live only in Zion (another name for Mount Moriah, the hill on which the temple was built); he is everywhere all the time. The focal point of Israelite worship, however, came to be Jerusalem and its beautiful temple. God was present in the tabernacle (Exodus 25:8, 9) and in the temple built by Solomon (2 Chronicles 7:16). From this central place of worship, the Jews were to tell the world about the one true God.

9:13, 14 All of us want God to help us when we are in trouble, but often for different reasons. Some want God's help so that they will be successful and other people will like them. Others want God's help so that they will be comfortable and feel good about themselves. David, however, wanted help from God so that justice would be restored to Israel and so that he could show others God's power. When you call to God for help, consider your motive. Is it to save yourself pain and embarrassment or to bring God glory and honour?

15 The nations have fallen into the pit they have dug;[u]
their feet are caught in the net they have hidden.[v]
16 The LORD is known by his justice;
the wicked are ensnared by the work of their hands.
Higgaion.[b] *Selah*

17 The wicked return to the grave,[c][w]
all the nations that forget God.[x]
18 But the needy will not always be forgotten,
nor the hope[y] of the afflicted[z] ever perish.

19 Arise, O LORD, let not man triumph;
let the nations be judged in your presence.
20 Strike them with terror, O LORD;
let the nations know they are but men.[a]
Selah

PSALM 10[a]

Theme: Why do the wicked succeed? Although God may seem to be hidden at times, we can be assured that he is aware of every injustice.
Author: Anonymous, but probably David. Many ancient manuscripts combine Psalms 9 and 10, and Psalm 9 was written by David.

1 Why, O LORD, do you stand far off?[a]
Why do you hide yourself[b] in times of trouble?

2 In his arrogance the wicked man hunts down the weak,
who are caught in the schemes he devises.
3 He boasts[c] of the cravings of his heart;
he blesses the greedy and reviles the LORD.
4 In his pride the wicked does not seek him;
in all his thoughts there is no room for God.[d]
5 His ways are always prosperous;
he is haughty and your laws are far from him;
he sneers at all his enemies.
6 He says to himself, "Nothing will shake me;
I'll always be happy[e] and never have trouble."
7 His mouth is full of curses[f] and lies and threats;[g]
trouble and evil are under his tongue.[h]
8 He lies in wait near the villages;
from ambush he murders the innocent,[i]
watching in secret for his victims.
9 He lies in wait like a lion in cover;

9:15 [u]Ps 7:15-16 [v]Ps 35:8; 57:6
9:17 [w]Ps 49:14 [x]Job 8:13; Ps 50:22
9:18 [y]Ps 71:5; Pr 23:18 [z]Ps 12:5
9:20 [a]Ps 62:9; Isa 31:3
10:1 [a]Ps 22:1, 11 [b]Ps 13:1
10:3 [c]Ps 94:4
10:4 [d]Ps 14:1; 36:1
10:6 [e]Rev 18:7
10:7 [f]Ro 3:14* [g]Ps 73:8 [h]Ps 140:3
10:8 [i]Ps 94:6

b *16* Or *Meditation*; possibly a musical notation c *17* Hebrew *Sheol* a Psalms 9 and 10 may have been originally a single acrostic poem, the stanzas of which begin with the successive letters of the Hebrew alphabet. In the Septuagint they constitute one psalm.

9:16 *Higgaion* is a musical direction and probably means to use the quieter instruments.

9:18 The world may ignore the plight of the needy, crushing any earthly hope they may have. But God, the champion of the weak, promises that this will not be the case for ever. The wicked nations who forget the Lord and refuse to help their people will be judged by God. He knows our needs, he knows our tendency to despair, and he has promised to care for us (see also 9:9, 12). Even when others forget us, he will remember.

10:1 "Why do you hide yourself in times of trouble?" To the psalmist, God seemed far away. But even though the writer had honest doubts, he did not stop praying or conclude that God no longer cared. He was not complaining, but simply asking God to hurry to his aid. It is during those times when we feel most alone or oppressed that we need to keep praying, telling God about our troubles.

10:4–6 Some people succeed in everything they do, and they brag that no-one, not even God, can keep them down. We may wonder why God allows these people to amass great wealth while they despise him as they do. But why are we upset when the wicked prosper? Are we angry about the damage they are doing or just jealous of their success? To answer these questions we must gain the right perspective on wickedness and wealth. The wicked will surely be punished because God hates their evil deeds. Wealth is only temporary. It is not necessarily a sign of God's approval on a person's life; nor is lack of it a sign of God's disapproval. Don't let wealth or lack of it become your obsession. See Proverbs 30:7, 8 for a prayer you can pray.

he lies in wait to catch the helpless;[j]
he catches the helpless and drags them off in his net.
10His victims are crushed, they collapse;
they fall under his strength.
11He says to himself, "God has forgotten;[k]
he covers his face and never sees."

12Arise, LORD! Lift up your hand,[l] O God.
Do not forget the helpless.[m]
13Why does the wicked man revile God?
Why does he say to himself,
"He won't call me to account"?
14But you, O God, do see trouble[n] and grief;
you consider it to take it in hand.
The victim commits himself to you;[o]
you are the helper[p] of the fatherless.
15Break the arm of the wicked and evil man;[q]
call him to account for his wickedness
that would not be found out.

16The LORD is King for ever and ever;[r]
the nations[s] will perish from his land.
17You hear, O LORD, the desire of the afflicted;[t]
you encourage them, and you listen to their cry,
18defending the fatherless[u] and the oppressed,[v]
in order that man, who is of the earth, may terrify no more.

PSALM 11

For the director of music. Of David.

Theme: God's rule provides stability in the midst of panic. Because we can trust him, we can face our problems.
Author: David

1In the LORD I take refuge.[a]
How then can you say to me:
"Flee like a bird to your mountain.
2For look, the wicked bend their bows;
they set their arrows[b] against the strings
to shoot from the shadows
at the upright in heart.[c]
3When the foundations[d] are being destroyed,
what can the righteous do?"[a]

a 3 Or *what is the Righteous One doing*

10:9 [j]Ps 17:12; 59:3; 140:5
10:11 [k]Job 22:13
10:12 [l]Ps 17:7; Mic 5:9 [m]Ps 9:12
10:14 [n]Ps 22:11 [o]Ps 37:5 [p]Ps 68:5
10:15 [q]Ps 37:17
10:16 [r]Ps 29:10 [s]Dt 8:20
10:17 [t]1Ch 29:18; Ps 34:15
10:18 [u]Ps 82:3 [v]Ps 9:9
11:1 [a]Ps 56:11
11:2 [b]Ps 7:13 [c]Ps 64:3-4
11:3 [d]Ps 82:5

10:11 There is an incompatibility between blind arrogance and the presence of God in our hearts. The proud person depends on himself rather than on God. This causes God's guiding influences to leave his life. When God's presence is welcome, there is no room for pride because he makes us aware of our true selves.

10:14 God sees and takes note of each evil deed, encourages us, and listens to our cries (10:17). He is always with us. We can face the wicked because we do not face them alone. God is by our side.

11:1–4 David was forced to flee for safety several times. Being God's anointed king did not make him immune to injustice and hatred from others. This psalm may have been written when he was being hunted by Saul (1 Samuel 18 – 31) or during the days of Absalom's rebellion (2 Samuel 15 – 18). In both instances, David fled, but not as if all was lost. He knew God was in control. While David wisely avoided trouble, he did not fearfully run away from his troubles.

11:1–4 David seems to be speaking to those who are advising him to run from his enemies. David's faith contrasted dramatically with the fear of the advisers who tell him to flee. Faith in God keeps us from losing hope and helps us resist fear. David's advisers were afraid because they saw only frightening circumstances and crumbling foundations. David was comforted and optimistic because he knew God was greater than anything his enemies could bring against him (7:10; 16:1; 31:2, 3).

4The LORD is in his holy temple;[e]
the LORD is on his heavenly throne.[f]
He observes the sons of men;[g]
his eyes examine[h] them.
5The LORD examines the righteous,[i]
but the wicked[b] and those who love violence
his soul hates.[j]
6On the wicked he will rain
fiery coals and burning sulphur;[k]
a scorching wind[l] will be their lot.

7For the LORD is righteous,[m]
he loves justice;[n]
upright men will see his face.[o]

11:4
[e]Ps 18:6
[f]Ps 103:19
[g]Ps 33:13
[h]Ps 34:15-16

11:5
[i]Ge 22:1;
Jas 1:12
[j]Ps 5:5

11:6
[k]Eze 38:22
[l]Jer 4:11-12

11:7
[m]Ps 7:9, 11; 45:7
[n]Ps 33:5
[o]Ps 17:15

PSALM 12

For the director of music. According to *sheminith*.[a] A psalm of David.

Theme: The proud and lying words of people versus the true and pure words of God. A call for protection against those who try to manipulate us.
Author: David

1Help, LORD, for the godly are no more;[a]
the faithful have vanished from among men.
2Everyone lies to his neighbour;
their flattering lips speak with deception.[b]

3May the LORD cut off all flattering lips
and every boastful tongue[c]
4that says, "We will triumph with our tongues;
we own our lips[b] — who is our master?"

5"Because of the oppression of the weak
and the groaning of the needy,
I will now arise," says the LORD.
"I will protect them[d] from those who malign them."
6And the words of the LORD are flawless,[e]
like silver refined in a furnace of clay,
purified seven times.

12:1
[a]Isa 57:1

12:2
[b]Ps 10:7; 41:6;
55:21;
Ro 16:18

12:3
[c]Da 7:8;
Rev 13:5

12:5
[d]Ps 10:18; 34:6

12:6
[e]2Sa 22:31;
Ps 18:30;
Pr 30:5

b 5 Or *The LORD, the Righteous One, examines the wicked, /* a Title: Probably a musical term b 4 Or */ our lips are our ploughshares*

11:4 When the foundations are shaking and you wish you could hide, remember that God is still in control. His power is not diminished by any turn of events. Nothing happens without his knowledge and permission. When you feel like running away – run to God. He will restore justice and goodness on the earth in his good time.

11:5 God does not preserve believers from difficult circumstances, but he tests both the righteous and the wicked. For some, God's tests become a refining fire, while for others, they become an incinerator for destruction. Don't ignore or defy the tests and challenges that come your way. Use them as opportunities for you to grow.

12:1 Living for God in a deceitful world can be a difficult and lonely battle. At one time the great prophet Elijah felt so lonely he wanted to die. But God told him that there were 7,000 other faithful servants (1 Kings 19:4, 14, 18). We are never alone in our battle against evil. When you feel alone, seek out other believers for strength and support.

12:2–4 We may be tempted to believe that lies are relatively harmless, even useful at times. But God does not overlook lies, flattery, deception, or boasting. Each of these sins originates from a bad attitude that is eventually expressed in our speech. The tongue can be our greatest enemy because, though small, it can do great damage (James 3:5). Be careful how you use yours.

12:5 God cares for the weak and the needy. Here he promises to protect the downtrodden and confront their oppressors. We should identify with God's attitude. His work is not done until we care for the needs of the poor.

12:6 Sincerity and truth are extremely valuable because they are so rare. Many people are deceivers, liars, flatterers; they think they will get what they want by deception. As a king, David certainly faced his share of such people, who hoped to win his favour and gain advancement through flattery. When we feel as though sincerity and truth have nearly gone out of existence, we have one hope – the word of God. God's words are as flawless as refined silver. So listen carefully when he speaks.

[7]O LORD, you will keep us safe
and protect us from such people for ever.[f]
[8]The wicked freely strut[g] about
when what is vile is honoured among men.

PSALM 13

For the director of music. A psalm of David.

Theme: Praying for relief from despair. We must continue to trust God even when he doesn't answer us immediately.
Author: David

[1]How long, O LORD? Will you forget me for ever?
How long will you hide your face[a] from me?
[2]How long must I wrestle with my thoughts[b]
and every day have sorrow in my heart?
How long will my enemy triumph over me?[c]

[3]Look on me and answer,[d] O LORD my God.
Give light to my eyes,[e] or I will sleep in death;[f]
[4]my enemy will say, "I have overcome him,[g]"
and my foes will rejoice when I fall.

[5]But I trust in your unfailing love;[h]
my heart rejoices in your salvation.[i]
[6]I will sing[j] to the LORD,
for he has been good to me.

12:7 [f]Ps 37:28
12:8 [g]Ps 55:10-11
13:1 [a] Job 13:24; Ps 44:24
13:2 [b]Ps 42:4 [c]Ps 42:9
13:3 [d]Ps 5:1 [e]Ezr 9:8 [f]Jer 51:39
13:4 [g]Ps 25:2
13:5 [h]Ps 52:8 [i]Ps 9:14
13:6 [j]Ps 116:7

TROUBLES AND COMPLAINTS IN PSALMS

We can relate to the psalms because they express our feelings. We all face troubles, as did the psalm writers hundreds of years ago, and we often respond as they did. In Psalm 3, David told God how he felt about the odds against him. But within three verses, the king realised that God's presence and care made the odds meaningless. This experience is repeated in many of the psalms. Usually, the hope and confidence in God outweigh the fear and suffering; sometimes they do not. Still, the psalm writers consistently poured out their thoughts and emotions to God. When they felt abandoned by God, they told him so. When they were impatient with how slowly God seemed to be answering their prayers, they also told him so. Because they recognised the difference between themselves and God, they were free to be men and to be honest with their Creator. That is why so many of the dark psalms end in the light. The psalmists started by expressing their feelings and ended up remembering to whom they were speaking!

Although we have much in common with the psalmists, we may differ in two ways: we might not tell God what we are really thinking and feeling; and therefore we also might not recognise, even faintly, who is listening to our prayers!

Notice this pattern as you read Psalms, and put the psalmists' insight to the test. You may well find that your awareness and appreciation of God will grow as you are honest with him. (See Psalms 3; 6; 13; 31; 37; 64; 77; 102; 121; 142.)

13:1 Sometimes all we need to do is talk over a problem with a friend to help put it in perspective. In this psalm, the phrase "how long" occurs four times in the first two verses, indicating the depth of David's distress. David expressed his feelings to God and found strength. By the end of his prayer, he was able to express hope and trust in God. Through prayer we can express our feelings and talk our problems out with God. He helps us regain the right perspective, and this gives us peace (Habakkuk 3:17–19).

13:1–5 David frequently claimed that God was slow to act on his behalf. We often feel this same impatience. It seems that evil and suffering go unchecked, and we wonder when God is going to stop them. David affirmed that he would continue to trust God no matter how long he had to wait for God's justice to be realised. When you feel impatient, remember David's steadfast faith in God's unfailing love.

PSALM 14
For the director of music. Of David.

Theme: Only the fool denies God. How foolish it must seem to God when people say there is no God.
Author: David

1 The fool[a] says in his heart,
"There is no God."[a]
They are corrupt, their deeds are vile;
there is no-one who does good.

2 The LORD looks down from heaven[b]
on the sons of men
to see if there are any who understand,[c]
any who seek God.
3 All have turned aside,
they have together become corrupt;[d]
there is no-one who does good,[e]
not even one.[f]

4 Will evildoers never learn—[g]
those who devour my people[h] as men eat bread
and who do not call on the LORD?[i]
5 There they are, overwhelmed with dread,
for God is present in the company of the righteous.
6 You evildoers frustrate the plans of the poor,
but the LORD is their refuge.[j]

7 Oh, that salvation for Israel would come out of Zion!
When the LORD restores the fortunes[k] of his people,
let Jacob rejoice and Israel be glad!

PSALM 15
A psalm of David.

Theme: Guidelines for living a blameless life.
Author: David

1 LORD, who may dwell in your sanctuary?[a]
Who may live on your holy hill?[b]

14:1 [a]Ps 10:4
14:2 [b]Ps 33:13 [c]Ps 92:6
14:3 [d]Ps 58:3 [e]Ps 143:2 [f]Ro 3:10-12*
14:4 [g]Ps 82:5 [h]Ps 27:2 [i]Ps 79:6; Isa 64:7
14:6 [j]Ps 9:9; 40:17
14:7 [k]Ps 53:6
15:1 [a]Ps 27:5-6 [b]Ps 24:3-5

a *1* The Hebrew words rendered *fool* in Psalms denote one who is morally deficient.

14:1–3 The true atheist is either foolish or wicked—foolish because he ignores the evidence that God exists or wicked because he refuses to live by God's truths. We become atheists in practice when we rely more on ourselves than on God. The fool mentioned here is someone who is aggressively perverse in his actions. To speak in direct defiance of God is utterly foolish according to the Bible.

14:3 No-one but God is perfect; all of us stand guilty before him (see Romans 3:23) and need his forgiveness. No matter how well we perform or how much we achieve compared to others, none of us can boast of his or her goodness when compared to God's standard. God not only expects us to obey his guidelines, but he wants us to love him with all our heart. No-one except Jesus Christ has done that perfectly. Because we all fall short we must turn to Christ to save us (Romans 10:9–11). Have you asked him to save you?

14:3, 4 David applies these observations to his enemies when he says the evildoers "devour my people as men eat bread": "They have together become corrupt; there is no-one who does good, not even one." By contrast, David said, "Though you probe my heart, . . . you will find nothing" (17:3).

There is a clear distinction between those who worship God and those who refuse to worship him. David worshipped God, and under his leadership Israel obeyed God and prospered. Several hundred years later, however, Israel forgot God, and it became difficult to distinguish between God's followers and those who worshipped idols. When Isaiah called Israel to repentance, he, like David, spoke of people who had gone astray (Isaiah 53:6). But Isaiah was talking about the Israelites themselves. Paul quoted Psalm 14 in Romans 3:10–12. He made the image of straying sheep even more general, referring to all people. The whole human race—Jew and Gentile alike—has turned away from God.

14:5 If God is "in the company of the righteous", then those who attack God's followers may be attacking God. To attack God is utterly futile (see 2:4, 5, 10–12). Thus, while we may feel we are losing the battle, there can be absolutely no doubt that our ultimate victory is in God.

15:1 *Sanctuary* and *holy hill* are interchangeable words describ-

2He whose walk is blameless
and who does what is righteous,
who speaks the truth[c] from his heart
3 and has no slander[d] on his tongue,
who does his neighbour no wrong
and casts no slur on his fellow-man,
4who despises a vile man
but honours[e] those who fear the LORD,
who keeps his oath[f]
even when it hurts,
5who lends his money without usury[g]
and does not accept a bribe[h] against the innocent.

He who does these things
will never be shaken.[i]

PSALM 16

A *miktam*[a] of David.

Theme: The joys and benefits of a life lived in companionship with God. We enjoy these benefits now and eternally.
Author: David

1Keep me safe,[a] O God,
for in you I take refuge.[b]

2I said to the LORD, "You are my Lord;
apart from you I have no good thing."[c]
3As for the saints who are in the land,[d]
they are the glorious ones in whom is all my delight.[b]
4The sorrows[e] of those will increase
who run after other gods.[f]
I will not pour out their libations of blood
or take up their names[g] on my lips.

5LORD, you have assigned me my portion[h] and my cup;[i]
you have made my lot secure.
6The boundary lines have fallen for me in pleasant places;
surely I have a delightful inheritance.[j]

7I will praise the LORD, who counsels me;[k]

15:2 [c]Ps 24:4; Zec 8:3, 16; Eph 4:25
15:3 [d]Ex 23:1
15:4 [e]Ac 28:10 [f]Jdg 11:35
15:5 [g]Ex 22:25 [h]Ex 23:8; Dt 16:19 [i]2Pe 1:10
16:1 [a]Ps 17:8 [b]Ps 7:1
16:2 [c]Ps 73:25
16:3 [d]Ps 101:6
16:4 [e]Ps 32:10 [f]Ps 106:37-38 [g]Ex 23:13
16:5 [h]Ps 73:26 [i]Ps 23:5
16:6 [j]Ps 78:55; Jer 3:19
16:7 [k]Ps 73:24

[a] Title: Probably a literary or musical term [b] 3 Or *As for the pagan priests who are in the land / and the nobles in whom all delight, I said:*

ing the focal point of Israelite worship – the dwelling place of God. In Hebrew poetry the repeating pattern is found more in the thought than in the sound or rhythm.

15:1ff God calls his people to be morally upright, and, in this psalm, he gives us ten standards to determine how we are doing. We live among evil people whose standards and morals are eroding. Our standards for living should not come from our evil society, but from God. For other references where righteous conduct is summarised, see Isaiah 33:15; 56:1; Micah 6:8; Habakkuk 2:4; and Mark 12:29–31.

15:3, 4 Words are powerful, and how you use them reflects on your relationship with God. Perhaps nothing so identifies Christians as their ability to control their speech – speaking the truth, refusing to slander, and keeping oaths (promises). Watch out for what you say. (See James 3:1–12 for more on the importance of controlling your tongue.)

15:5 God was against the Jews' charging interest (usury) or making a profit on loans to needy, fellow Jews (see also Exodus 22:25; Leviticus 25:35–37), although charging interest on loans to foreigners was allowed (Deuteronomy 23:20). Interest was also allowable for business purposes, as long as it wasn't exorbitant (Proverbs 28:8).

15:5 Some people are so obsessed with money that they will change their God-given standards and life-style to get it. If money is a controlling force in your life, it must be curbed, or it will harm others and destroy your relationship with God.

16:1 *Miktam* comes from a term that may mean "to cover". It could mean a covering of the lips (a silent prayer), or a prayer that someone might be covered with protection. *Cover* can also mean "atone for". *Miktam* may mean a psalm of atonement.

16:7, 8 It is human nature to make our own plans and *then* ask God to bless them. Instead, we should seek God's will first. By constantly thinking about the Lord and his way of living, we will gain insights that will help us make right decisions and live the way God desires. Communicating with God allows him to counsel us and give us wisdom.

even at night[l] my heart instructs me.
8 I have set the LORD always before me.
Because he is at my right hand,[m]
I shall not be shaken.

9 Therefore my heart is glad[n] and my tongue rejoices;
my body also will rest secure,[o]
10 because you will not abandon me to the grave,[c]
nor will you let your Holy One[d] see decay.[p]
11 You have made known[e] to me the path of life;[q]
you will fill me with joy in your presence,[r]
with eternal pleasures[s] at your right hand.

PSALM 17

A prayer of David.

Theme: A plea for justice in the face of false accusations and persecution. David urges us to realise the true goal of life—to know God—and the true reward of life—to see God one day.
Author: David, written while he was being persecuted by Saul

1 Hear, O LORD, my righteous plea;
listen to my cry.[a]
Give ear to my prayer—
it does not rise from deceitful lips.[b]
2 May my vindication come from you;
may your eyes see what is right.

3 Though you probe my heart and examine me at night,
though you test me,[c] you will find nothing;[d]
I have resolved that my mouth will not sin.[e]
4 As for the deeds of men—
by the word of your lips
I have kept myself
from the ways of the violent.
5 My steps have held to your paths;[f]
my feet have not slipped.[g]

6 I call on you, O God, for you will answer me;[h]
give ear to me[i] and hear my prayer.[j]
7 Show the wonder of your great love,[k]

[c] *10* Hebrew *Sheol* [d] *10* Or *your faithful one* [e] *11* Or *You will make known*

16:7 [l]Ps 77:6
16:8 [m]Ps 73:23
16:9 [n]Ps 4:7; 30:11 [o]Ps 4:8
16:10 [p]Ac 13:35*
16:11 [q]Mt 7:14 [r]Ac 2:25-28* [s]Ps 36:7-8
17:1 [a]Ps 61:1 [b]Isa 29:13
17:3 [c]Ps 26:2; 66:10 [d]Job 23:10; Jer 50:20 [e]Ps 39:1
17:5 [f]Ps 44:18; 119:133 [g]Ps 18:36
17:6 [h]Ps 86:7 [i]Ps 116:2 [j]Ps 88:2
17:7 [k]Ps 31:21

16:8 By saying that he "will not be shaken", David was talking about the unique sense of security felt by believers. God does not exempt believers from the day-to-day circumstances of life. Believers and unbelievers alike experience pain, trouble, and failure at times (Matthew 5:45). Unbelievers have a sense of hopelessness about life and confusion over their true purpose on earth. Those who seek God, however, can move ahead confidently with what they know is right and important in God's eyes. They know that God will keep them from being moved off of his chosen path.

16:8–11 This psalm is often called a Messianic psalm because it is quoted in the New Testament as referring to the resurrection of Jesus Christ. Both Peter and Paul quoted from this psalm when speaking of Christ's bodily resurrection (see Acts 2:25–28, 31; 13:35–37).

16:9 David's heart was glad—he had found the secret to joy. True joy is far deeper than happiness; we can feel joy in spite of our deepest troubles. Happiness is temporary because it is based on external circumstances, but joy is lasting because it is based on God's presence within us. As we contemplate his daily presence, we will find contentment. As we understand the future he has for us, we will experience joy. Don't base your life on circumstances, but on God.

16:10 David stated confidently that God would not leave him in the grave. Many people fear death because they can neither control nor understand it. As believers, we can be assured that God will not forget us when we die. He will bring us to life again to live with him for ever. This provides *real* security. For other passages about resurrection, see Job 19:25, 26; Isaiah 26:19; Daniel 12:2, 13; Mark 13:27; 1 Corinthians 15:12–58; 1 Thessalonians 4:13–18; Revelation 20:11–21:4.

17:3 Was David saying he was sinless? Far from a proud assumption of purity, David's claim was an understanding of his relationship with God. In Psalms 32 and 51, David freely acknowledged his own sins. Nevertheless, his relationship with God was one of close fellowship and constant repentance and forgiveness. His claim to goodness, therefore, was based on his continual seeking after God.

17:7 [l]Ps 20:6

you who save by your right hand[l]
those who take refuge in you from their foes.
8Keep me as the apple of your eye;[m]
hide me in the shadow of your wings
9from the wicked who assail me,
from my mortal enemies who surround me.[n]

17:8 [m]Dt 32:10

17:9 [n]Ps 31:20; 109:3

10They close up their callous hearts,[o]
and their mouths speak with arrogance.[p]
11They have tracked me down, they now surround me,[q]
with eyes alert, to throw me to the ground.
12They are like a lion[r] hungry for prey,
like a great lion crouching in cover.

17:10 [o]Ps 73:7 [p]1Sa 2:3

17:11 [q]Ps 37:14; 88:17

13Rise up, O LORD, confront them, bring them down;[s]
rescue me from the wicked by your sword.
14O LORD, by your hand save me from such men,
from men of this world[t] whose reward is in this life.

17:12 [r]Ps 7:2; 10:9

You still the hunger of those you cherish;
their sons have plenty,
and they store up wealth[u] for their children.
15And I—in righteousness I shall see your face;
when I awake, I shall be satisfied with seeing your likeness.[v]

17:13 [s]Ps 7:12; 22:20; 73:18

17:14 [t]Lk 16:8 [u]Ps 73:3-7

17:15 [v]Nu 12:8; Ps 4:6-7; 16:11; 1Jn 3:2

PSALM 18

For the director of music. Of David the servant of the LORD. He sang to the LORD the words of this song when the LORD delivered him from the hand of all his enemies and from the hand of Saul. He said:

Theme: Gratitude for deliverance and victory. The only sure way to be delivered from surrounding evil is to call upon God for help and strength.
Author: David

1I love you, O LORD, my strength.

2The LORD is my rock,[a] my fortress and my deliverer;
my God is my rock, in whom I take refuge.
He is my shield[b] and the horn[a] of my salvation,[c] my
stronghold.

18:2 [a]Ps 19:14 [b]Ps 59:11 [c]Ps 75:10

[a] 2 *Horn* here symbolises strength.

17:8 Just as we protect the pupils ("apples") of our eyes, so God will protect us. We must not conclude, however, that we have somehow missed God's protection if we experience troubles. God's protection has far greater purposes than helping us avoid pain; it is to make us better servants for him. God also protects us by guiding us through painful circumstances, not only by helping us escape them.

17:8 The "shadow of your wings" is a figure of speech symbolising God's protection. He guards us just as a mother bird protects her young by covering them with her wings. Moses used this same metaphor in Deuteronomy 32:11.

17:13–15 We deceive ourselves when we measure our happiness or contentment in life by the amount of wealth we possess. When we put riches at the top of our value system, we let power, pleasure, and financial security overshadow the eternal value of our relationship with God. We think we will be happy or content when we get riches, only to discover that they don't really satisfy, and the pleasures fade away. The true measurement of happiness or contentment is found in God's love and in doing his will. You will find true happiness if you put your relationship with God above earthly riches.

17:15 The word *awake* shows that David believed in life after death. Although belief in resurrection was not widespread in Old Testament times, several verses show that it was partially understood. Some of these are Job 19:25–27; Psalms 16:10; 49:15; 139:17, 18; Isaiah 26:19; and Daniel 12:2, 13.

18:1ff This psalm is almost a duplicate of 2 Samuel 22. It may have been written towards the end of David's life when there was peace. God is praised for his glorious works and blessings through the years.

18:2, 3 God's protection of his people is limitless and can take many forms. David characterised God's care with five military symbols. God is like (1) a *rock* that can't be moved by any who would harm us, (2) a *fortress* or place of safety where the enemy can't follow, (3) a *shield* that comes between us and harm, (4) a *horn* of salvation, a symbol of might and power, (5) a *stronghold* high above our enemies. If you need protection, look to God.

3I call to the LORD, who is worthy of praise,[d]
and I am saved from my enemies.

4The cords of death[e] entangled me;
the torrents[f] of destruction overwhelmed me.
5The cords of the grave[b] coiled around me;
the snares of death[g] confronted me.
6In my distress I called to the LORD;
I cried to my God for help.
From his temple he heard my voice;[h]
my cry came before him, into his ears.

7The earth trembled and quaked,[i]
and the foundations of the mountains shook;
they trembled because he was angry.[j]
8Smoke rose from his nostrils;
consuming fire[k] came from his mouth,
burning coals blazed out of it.
9He parted the heavens and came down;[l]
dark clouds were under his feet.
10He mounted the cherubim[m] and flew;
he soared on the wings of the wind.[n]
11He made darkness his covering,[o] his canopy around him—
the dark rain clouds of the sky.
12Out of the brightness of his presence[p] clouds advanced,
with hailstones and bolts of lightning.[q]
13The LORD thundered[r] from heaven;
the voice of the Most High resounded.[c]
14He shot his arrows and scattered ⌞the enemies⌟,
great bolts of lightning and routed them.[s]
15The valleys of the sea were exposed
and the foundations of the earth laid bare
at your rebuke,[t] O LORD,
at the blast of breath from your nostrils.

16He reached down from on high and took hold of me;
he drew me out of deep waters.[u]
17He rescued me from my powerful enemy,
from my foes, who were too strong for me.[v]
18They confronted me in the day of my disaster,
but the LORD was my support.[w]
19He brought me out into a spacious place;[x]
he rescued me because he delighted in me.[y]

20The LORD has dealt with me according to my righteousness;
according to the cleanness of my hands[z] he has rewarded me.
21For I have kept the ways of the LORD;[a]

18:3 [d]Ps 48:1
18:4 [e]Ps 116:3 [f]Ps 124:4
18:5 [g]Ps 116:3
18:6 [h]Ps 34:15
18:7 [i]Jdg 5:4 [j]Ps 68:7-8
18:8 [k]Ps 50:3
18:9 [l]Ps 144:5
18:10 [m]Ps 80:1 [n]Ps 104:3
18:11 [o]Dt 4:11; Ps 97:2
18:12 [p]Ps 104:2 [q]Ps 97:3
18:13 [r]Ps 29:3; 104:7
18:14 [s]Ps 144:6
18:15 [t]Ps 76:6; 106:9
18:16 [u]Ps 144:7
18:17 [v]Ps 35:10
18:18 [w]Ps 59:16
18:19 [x]Ps 31:8 [y]Ps 118:5
18:20 [z]Ps 24:4
18:21 [a]2Ch 34:33

[b] *5* Hebrew *Sheol* [c] *13* Some Hebrew manuscripts and Septuagint (see also 2 Samuel 22:14); most Hebrew manuscripts *resounded, / amid hailstones and bolts of lightning*

18:10 Cherubim are mighty angels. One of the functions of the cherubim was to serve as guardians. These angels guarded the entrances to both the tree of life (Genesis 3:24) and the Most Holy Place (Exodus 26:31–33). Two cherubim of hammered gold were part of the ark of the covenant (Exodus 25:18–22). The living creatures carrying God's throne in Ezekiel 1 may have been cherubim.

18:13 The "Most High" was an important designation for David to make. Pagan idol worship was deeply rooted in the land, and each region had its own deity. But these images of wood and stone were powerless. David was placing the Lord alone in a superior category: he is by far the Most High.

18:16 Do your troubles, like "deep waters", threaten to drown you? David, helpless and weak, knew that God alone had rescued him from his enemies when he was defenceless. When you wish that God would quickly rescue you from your troubles, remember that he can either deliver you or be your support as you go through them (18:18). Either way, his protection is best for you. When you feel like you're drowning in troubles, ask God to help you, hold you steady, and protect you. In his care, you are never helpless.

18:21 [b]Ps 119:102
18:22 [c]Ps 119:30
18:24 [d]1Sa 26:23
18:25 [e]1Ki 8:32; Ps 62:12; Mt 5:7
18:26 [f]Pr 3:34
18:27 [g]Pr 6:17
18:28 [h]Job 18:6; 29:3
18:29 [i]Heb 11:34
18:30 [j]Dt 32:4; Rev 15:3 [k]Ps 12:6 [l]Ps 17:7
18:31 [m]Dt 32:39; 86:8; Isa 45:5, 6, 14, 18, 21 [n]Dt 32:31; 1Sa 2:2
18:32 [o]Isa 45:5
18:33 [p]Hab 3:19 [q]Dt 32:13
18:34 [r]Ps 144:1
18:35 [s]Ps 119:116
18:37 [t]Ps 37:20; 44:5
18:38 [u]Ps 36:12 [v]Ps 47:3
18:40 [w]Ps 21:12 [x]Ps 94:23
18:41 [y]Ps 50:22 [z]Job 27:9; Pr 1:28

I have not done evil by turning[b] from my God.
22 All his laws are before me;[c]
I have not turned away from his decrees.
23 I have been blameless before him
and have kept myself from sin.
24 The LORD has rewarded me according to my righteousness,[d]
according to the cleanness of my hands in his sight.

25 To the faithful[e] you show yourself faithful,
to the blameless you show yourself blameless,
26 to the pure you show yourself pure,
but to the crooked you show yourself shrewd.[f]
27 You save the humble
but bring low those whose eyes are haughty.[g]
28 You, O LORD, keep my lamp burning;
my God turns my darkness into light.[h]
29 With your help[i] I can advance against a troop;**[d]**
with my God I can scale a wall.

30 As for God, his way is perfect;[j]
the word of the LORD is flawless.[k]
He is a shield
for all who take refuge[l] in him.
31 For who is God besides the LORD?[m]
And who is the Rock[n] except our God?
32 It is God who arms me with strength[o]
and makes my way perfect.
33 He makes my feet like the feet of a deer;[p]
he enables me to stand on the heights.[q]
34 He trains my hands for battle;[r]
my arms can bend a bow of bronze.
35 You give me your shield of victory,
and your right hand sustains[s] me;
you stoop down to make me great.
36 You broaden the path beneath me,
so that my ankles do not turn over.

37 I pursued my enemies[t] and overtook them;
I did not turn back till they were destroyed.
38 I crushed them so that they could not rise;[u]
they fell beneath my feet.[v]
39 You armed me with strength for battle;
you made my adversaries bow at my feet.
40 You made my enemies turn their backs[w] in flight,
and I destroyed[x] my foes.
41 They cried for help, but there was no-one to save them[y]—
to the LORD, but he did not answer.[z]

d *29 Or can run through a barricade*

18:30 Some people think that belief in God is a crutch for weak people who cannot make it on their own. God is indeed a shield to protect us when we are too weak to face certain trials by ourselves, but he does not want us to remain weak. He strengthens, protects, and guides us in order to send us back into an evil world to fight for him. And then he continues to work with us because the strongest person on earth is infinitely weaker than God and needs his help. David was not a coward; he was a mighty warrior who, even with all his armies and weapons, knew that only God could ultimately protect and save him.

18:32–34 God promises to give us strength to meet challenges, but he doesn't promise to eliminate them. If he gave us no rough roads to walk, no mountains to climb, and no battles to fight, we would not grow. He does not leave us alone with our challenges, however. Instead he stands beside us, teaches us, and strengthens us to face them.

18:40–42 David was a merciful man. He spared the lives of Saul (1 Samuel 24:1–8), Nabal (1 Samuel 25:21–35), and Shimei (2 Samuel 16:5–12) and showed great kindness to Mephibosheth (2 Samuel 9). In asking God to destroy his enemies, David was simply asking him to give the wicked the punishment they deserved.

42 I beat them as fine as dust borne on the wind;
I poured them out like mud in the streets.

43 You have delivered me from the attacks of the people;
you have made me the head of nations;[a]
people I did not know[b] are subject to me.
44 As soon as they hear me, they obey me;
foreigners[c] cringe before me.
45 They all lose heart;
they come trembling from their strongholds.[d]

46 The LORD lives! Praise be to my Rock!
Exalted be God my Saviour![e]
47 He is the God who avenges me,
who subdues nations[f] under me,
48 who saves[g] me from my enemies.
You exalted me above my foes;
from violent men you rescued me.
49 Therefore I will praise you among the nations, O LORD;
I will sing[h] praises to your name.[i]
50 He gives his king great victories;
he shows unfailing kindness to his anointed,
to David[j] and his descendants for ever.[k]

18:43 [a] 2Sa 8:1-14 [b] Isa 52:15; 55:5
18:44 [c] Ps 66:3
18:45 [d] Mic 7:17
18:46 [e] Ps 51:14
18:47 [f] Ps 47:3
18:48 [g] Ps 59:1
18:49 [h] Ps 108:1 [i] Ro 15:9*
18:50 [j] Ps 144:10 [k] Ps 89:4

PSALM 19

For the director of music. A psalm of David.

Theme: Both God's creation and his word reveal his greatness.
Author: David

1 The heavens[a] declare[b] the glory of God;
the skies proclaim the work of his hands.
2 Day after day they pour forth speech;
night after night they display knowledge.[c]
3 There is no speech or language
where their voice is not heard.**[a]**
4 Their voice**[b]** goes out into all the earth,
their words to the ends of the world.[d]

In the heavens he has pitched a tent[e] for the sun,

19:1 [a] Isa 40:22 [b] Ps 50:6; Ro 1:19
19:2 [c] Ps 74:16
19:4 [d] Ro 10:18* [e] Ps 104:2

a 3 Or *They have no speech, there are no words; / no sound is heard from them* **b** 4 Septuagint, Jerome and Syriac; Hebrew *line*

18:43–45 David's great power had become legendary. God gave him victory in every battle. The book of 2 Samuel records victories over the Jebusites (5:6–10), the Philistines (5:17–25; 8:1, 2), Hadadezer of Zobah (8:3, 4), the Arameans (8:5, 6; 10), the Edomites (8:13, 14), and the Ammonites (12:26–31). In addition, the king of Tyre sent supplies and workmen to help David build his palace (5:11). But David did not attribute his victories to himself. He fully realised that the purpose of his position was to bless God's people (1 Chronicles 14:2).

19:1ff In this psalm, David's steps of meditation take him from creation, through God's word, through David's own sinfulness, to salvation. As God reveals himself through nature (19:1–6), we learn about his power and our finiteness. As God reveals himself through Scripture (19:7–11), we learn about his holiness and our sinfulness. As God reveals himself through daily experiences (19:12–14), we learn about his gracious forgiveness and our salvation.

19:1–6 We are surrounded by fantastic displays of God's craftsmanship—the heavens give dramatic evidence of his existence, his power, his love, his care. To say that the universe happened by chance is absurd. Its design, intricacy, and orderliness point to a personally involved Creator. As you look at God's handiwork in nature and the heavens, thank him for such magnificent beauty and the truth it reveals about the Creator.

19:3, 4 The apostle Paul referred to this psalm when he explained that everyone knows about God because nature proclaims God's existence and power (Romans 1:19, 20). This does not cancel the need for missions because the message of God's salvation found in his word, the Bible, must still be told to the ends of the earth. While nature points to the existence of God, the Bible tells us about salvation. God's people must explain to others how they can have a relationship with God. Although people everywhere should already believe in a Creator by just looking at the evidence of nature around them, God needs us to explain his love, mercy, and grace. What are you doing to take God's message to the world?

19:6 [f]Ps 113:3; Ecc 1:5

5 which is like a bridegroom coming forth from his pavilion,
like a champion rejoicing to run his course.
6 It rises at one end of the heavens
and makes its circuit to the other;[f]
nothing is hidden from its heat.

19:7 [g]Ps 23:3 [h]Ps 93:5; 111:7 [i]Ps 119:98-100

7 The law of the LORD is perfect,
reviving the soul.[g]
The statutes of the LORD are trustworthy,[h]
making wise the simple.[i]
8 The precepts of the LORD are right,[j]
giving joy to the heart.

19:8 [j]Ps 12:6; 119:128

The commands of the LORD are radiant,
giving light to the eyes.
9 The fear of the LORD is pure,
enduring for ever.

19:9 [k]Ps 119:138, 142

The ordinances of the LORD are sure
and altogether righteous.[k]
10 They are more precious than gold,[l]
than much pure gold;

19:10 [l]Pr 8:10

they are sweeter than honey,
than honey from the comb.
11 By them is your servant warned;
in keeping them there is great reward.

19:12 [m]Ps 51:2; 90:8; 139:6

12 Who can discern his errors?
Forgive my hidden faults.[m]
13 Keep your servant also from wilful sins;
may they not rule over me.
Then will I be blameless,
innocent of great transgression.

19:14 [n]Ps 104:34 [o]Ps 18:2 [p]Isa 47:4

14 May the words of my mouth and the meditation of my heart
be pleasing[n] in your sight,
O LORD, my Rock[o] and my Redeemer.[p]

20:1 [a]Ps 46:7, 11 [b]Ps 91:14

PSALM 20

For the director of music. A psalm of David.

Theme: A prayer for victory in battle. Such a prayer can help us prepare for any great challenge. David knew that trust should be placed in the Lord more than in human power.
Author: David. The events in 2 Samuel 10 may have prompted this prayer.

20:2 [c]Ps 3:4

1 May the LORD answer you when you are in distress;
may the name of the God of Jacob[a] protect you.[b]
2 May he send you help from the sanctuary[c]
and grant you support from Zion.

20:3 [d]Ac 10:4 [e]Ps 51:19

3 May he remember[d] all your sacrifices
and accept your burnt offerings.[e] *Selah*

19:7-11 When we think of the law, we often think of something that keeps us from having fun. But here we see the opposite – law that revives us, makes us wise, gives joy to the heart, gives light to the eyes, warns us, and rewards us. That's because God's laws are guidelines and lights for our path, rather than chains on our hands and feet. They point at danger and warn us, then point at success and guide us.

19:12, 13 Many Christians are plagued by guilt. They worry that they may have committed a sin unknowingly, done something good with selfish intentions, failed to put their whole heart into a task, or neglected what they should have done. Guilt can play an important role in bringing us to Christ and in keeping us behaving properly, but it should not cripple us or make us fearful. God fully and completely forgives us – even for those sins we do unknowingly.

19:14 Would you change the way you live if you knew that every word and thought would be examined by God first? David asks that God approve his words and thoughts as though they were offerings brought to the altar. As you begin each day, determine that God's love will guide what you say and how you think.

4May he give you the desire of your heart[f]
and make all your plans succeed.
5We will shout for joy when you are victorious
and will lift up our banners[g] in the name of our God.
May the LORD grant all your requests.[h]

6Now I know that the LORD saves his anointed;[i]
he answers him from his holy heaven
with the saving power of his right hand.
7Some trust in chariots and some in horses,[j]
but we trust in the name of the LORD our God.[k]
8They are brought to their knees and fall,
but we rise up[l] and stand firm.[m]

9O LORD, save the king!
Answer[a] us[n] when we call!

PSALM 21

For the director of music. A psalm of David.

Theme: Praising God after victory in battle. When God answers our prayers for victory, we must quickly and openly thank him for his help.
Author: David

1O LORD, the king rejoices in your strength.
How great is his joy in the victories you give![a]
2You have granted him the desire of his heart[b]
and have not withheld the request of his lips. *Selah*
3You welcomed him with rich blessings
and placed a crown of pure gold[c] on his head.
4He asked you for life, and you gave it to him—
length of days, for ever and ever.[d]
5Through the victories[e] you gave, his glory is great;
you have bestowed on him splendour and majesty.
6Surely you have granted him eternal blessings
and made him glad with the joy[f] of your presence.[g]
7For the king trusts in the LORD;
through the unfailing love of the Most High
he will not be shaken.

8Your hand will lay hold[h] on all your enemies;
your right hand will seize your foes.
9At the time of your appearing
you will make them like a fiery furnace.
In his wrath the LORD will swallow them up,

a 9 Or *save! / O King, answer*

20:4 [f]Ps 21:2; 145:16, 19
20:5 [g]Ps 9:14; 60:4 [h]1Sa 1:17
20:6 [i]Ps 28:8; 41:11; Isa 58:9
20:7 [j]Ps 33:17; Isa 31:1 [k]2Ch 32:8
20:8 [l]Mic 7:8 [m]Ps 37:23
20:9 [n]Ps 3:7; 17:6
21:1 [a]Ps 59:16-17
21:2 [b]Ps 37:4
21:3 [c]2Sa 12:30
21:4 [d]Ps 61:5-6; 91:16; 133:3
21:5 [e]Ps 18:50
21:6 [f]Ps 43:4 [g]1Ch 17:27
21:8 [h]Isa 10:10

20:6–8 As long as there have been armies and weapons, nations have boasted of their power, but such power does not last. Throughout history, empires and kingdoms have risen to great power only to vanish in the dust. David, however, knew that the true might of his nation was not in weaponry but in worship; not in firepower but in God's power. Because God alone can preserve a nation or an individual, be sure your confidence is in God, who gives eternal victory. Whom do you trust?

21:1–6 David described all that he had as gifts from God: "the desire of his heart", rich blessings, a crown of pure gold, long life, splendour and majesty, eternal blessings, gladness. We too must look upon all we have—position, family, wealth, talent—as gifts from God. Only then will we use them to give glory back to him.

21:7 A good leader trusts the Lord and depends upon his unfailing love. Too often leaders trust in their own cleverness, popular support, or military power. But God is above all these "gods". If you aspire to leadership, keep the Lord God at the centre of your life and depend on him. His wisdom is the best strength you can have.

21:7 Because David trusted in God, God would not let him be shaken (removed from the throne). When we trust in God, we have permanence and stability. We may lose a great deal—families, jobs, material possessions—but we cannot be shaken from God's favour. He will be our foundation of solid rock. He will never leave or desert us.

21:9 [i]Ps 50:3; La 2:2; Mal 4:1
21:10 [j]Dt 28:18; Ps 37:28
21:11 [k]Ps 2:1 [l]Ps 10:2
21:12 [m]Ps 7:12-13; 18:40
22:1 [a]Mt 27:46*; Mk 15:34* [b]Ps 10:1
22:2 [c]Ps 42:3
22:3 [d]Ps 99:9 [e]Dt 10:21
22:5 [f]Isa 49:23
22:6 [g]Job 25:6; Isa 41:14 [h]Ps 31:11 [i]Isa 49:7; 53:3
22:7 [j]Mt 27:39, 44 [k]Mk 15:29
22:8 [l]Ps 91:14 [m]Mt 27:43
22:9 [n]Ps 71:6
22:10 [o]Isa 46:3

and his fire will consume them.[i]
10 You will destroy their descendants from the earth,
their posterity from mankind.[j]
11 Though they plot evil[k] against you
and devise wicked schemes,[l] they cannot succeed;
12 for you will make them turn their backs[m]
when you aim at them with drawn bow.

13 Be exalted, O LORD, in your strength;
we will sing and praise your might.

PSALM 22

For the director of music. To ⌞the tune of⌟ "The Doe of the Morning". A psalm of David.

Theme: A prayer that carries us from great suffering to great joy. Despite apparent rejection by his friends and God, David believed that God would lead him out of despair. He looked forward to that future day when God would rule over the entire earth.
Author: David

1 My God, my God, why have you forsaken me?[a]
Why are you so far[b] from saving me,
so far from the words of my groaning?
2 O my God, I cry out by day, but you do not answer,
by night,[c] and am not silent.

3 Yet you are enthroned as the Holy One;[d]
you are the praise[e] of Israel.[a]
4 In you our fathers put their trust;
they trusted and you delivered them.
5 They cried to you and were saved;
in you they trusted and were not disappointed.[f]

6 But I am a worm[g] and not a man,
scorned by men[h] and despised[i] by the people.
7 All who see me mock me;
they hurl insults,[j] shaking their heads:[k]
8 "He trusts in the LORD;
let the LORD rescue him.[l]
Let him deliver him,
since he delights[m] in him."

9 Yet you brought me out of the womb;[n]
you made me trust in you
even at my mother's breast.
10 From birth[o] I was cast upon you;

a 3 Or *Yet you are holy, / enthroned on the praises of Israel*

21:11 When you see people succeeding with evil acts, remember that they will not succeed for ever. Their power is only temporary, and God's very presence would send them scattering in a moment. God, according to his plan and purpose, will intervene for his people and give the wicked the judgment they deserve. We should not be dismayed when we see the temporary advantage God's enemies have.

22:1 David gave an amazingly accurate description of the suffering the Messiah would endure hundreds of years later. David was obviously enduring some great trial, but through his suffering he, like the Messiah to come, gained victory. Jesus, the Messiah, quoted this verse while hanging on the cross carrying our burden of sin (Matthew 27:46). It was not a cry of doubt, but an urgent appeal to God.

22:6 When others despise us and heap scorn upon us, they treat us as less than human. After much degradation, we, like David, could begin to feel like worms. When we feel the sting of rejection, we must keep in mind the hope and victory that God promises us (22:22ff).

22:9–11 God's loving concern does not begin on the day we are born and conclude on the day we die. It reaches back to those days before we were born, and reaches ahead along the unending path of eternity. Our only sure help comes from a God whose concern for us reaches beyond our earthly existence. When faced with such love, how could anyone reject it?

from my mother's womb you have been my God.
11 Do not be far from me,
for trouble is near
and there is no-one to help.[p]

12 Many bulls[q] surround me;
strong bulls of Bashan[r] encircle me.
13 Roaring lions[s] tearing their prey
open their mouths wide[t] against me.
14 I am poured out like water,
and all my bones are out of joint.[u]
My heart has turned to wax;
it has melted away[v] within me.
15 My strength is dried up like a potsherd,
and my tongue sticks to the roof of my mouth;[w]
you lay me[b] in the dust[x] of death.
16 Dogs[y] have surrounded me;
a band of evil men has encircled me,
they have pierced[c][z] my hands and my feet.
17 I can count all my bones;
people stare[a] and gloat over me.[b]
18 They divide my garments among them
and cast lots[c] for my clothing.

19 But you, O LORD, be not far off;
O my Strength, come quickly[d] to help me.
20 Deliver my life from the sword,
my precious life[e] from the power of the dogs.
21 Rescue me from the mouth of the lions;
save[d] me from the horns of the wild oxen.

22 I will declare your name to my brothers;
in the congregation I will praise you.[f]
23 You who fear the LORD, praise him![g]
All you descendants of Jacob, honour him!
Revere him,[h] all you descendants of Israel!
24 For he has not despised or disdained
the suffering of the afflicted one;
he has not hidden his face[i] from him
but has listened to his cry for help.[j]

25 From you comes the theme of my praise in the great assembly;[k]
before those who fear you[e] will I fulfil my vows.[l]
26 The poor will eat[m] and be satisfied;
they who seek the LORD will praise him —[n]
may your hearts live for ever!
27 All the ends of the earth[o]
will remember and turn to the LORD,
and all the families of the nations
will bow down before him,[p]

22:11 [p]Ps 72:12
22:12 [q]Ps 68:30 [r]Dt 32:14
22:13 [s]Ps 17:12 [t]Ps 35:21
22:14 [u]Ps 31:10 [v]Job 30:16; Da 5:6
22:15 [w]Ps 38:10; Jn 19:28 [x]Ps 104:29
22:16 [y]Ps 59:6 [z]Isa 53:5; Zec 12:10; Jn 19:34
22:17 [a]Lk 23:35 [b]Lk 23:27
22:18 [c]Mt 27:35*; Lk 23:34; Jn 19:24*
22:19 [d]Ps 70:5
22:20 [e]Ps 35:17
22:22 [f]Heb 2:12*
22:23 [g]Ps 86:12; 135:19 [h]Ps 33:8
22:24 [i]Ps 69:17 [j]Heb 5:7
22:25 [k]Ps 35:18 [l]Ecc 5:4
22:26 [m]Ps 107:9 [n]Ps 40:16
22:27 [o]Ps 2:8 [p]Ps 86:9

b *15* Or / *I am laid* **c** *16* Some Hebrew manuscripts, Septuagint and Syriac; most Hebrew manuscripts / *like the lion,* **d** *21* Or / *you have heard* **e** *25* Hebrew *him*

22:12 The land of Bashan, located east of the Sea of Galilee, was known for its strong and well-fed cattle (Amos 4:1). Because of its grain fields, it was often called the breadbasket of Palestine.

22:15 A "potsherd" is a pottery fragment or a piece of sun-baked clay.

22:22 David would praise God in the congregation because his private deliverance deserved a public testimony. God wonderfully delivers us in the quiet moments when we are hurting, and we must be prepared to offer public praise for his care.

22:28 [q]Ps 47:7-8

28 for dominion belongs to the LORD[q]
and he rules over the nations.

22:29 [r]Ps 45:12 [s]Isa 26:19

29 All the rich[r] of the earth will feast and worship;
all who go down to the dust[s] will kneel before him—
those who cannot keep themselves alive.

22:30 [t]Ps 102:28

30 Posterity[t] will serve him;
future generations will be told about the Lord.

22:31 [u]Ps 78:6

31 They will proclaim his righteousness
to a people yet unborn[u]—
for he has done it.

CHRIST IN THE PSALMS

Both the Jewish and Christian faiths have long believed that many psalms referred as much to the promised Messiah as they did to events at the time. Because the Messiah was to be a descendant of David, it was expected that many of the royal psalms would apply to him. Christians noted how many of the passages seemed to describe in detail events from Christ's life and death. Jesus himself frequently quoted from Psalms. Almost everything that happened at the crucifixion and most of Jesus' words during his final hours are prophesied in Psalms.

The following is a list of the main references in Psalms pertaining to Christ.

Reference in Psalms	*Reference to Christ*	*Fulfilment in the New Testament*
2:7	The Messiah will be God's Son	Hebrews 1:5, 6
16:8–10	He will rise from the dead	Luke 24:5–7
22:1–21	He will experience agony on the cross	Matthew 26, 27
22:18	Evil men cast lots for his clothing	Matthew 27:35; John 19:23, 24
22:15	He thirsts while on the cross	John 19:28
22:22	He will declare God's name	Hebrews 2:12
34:20	His bones would not be broken	John 19:36, 37
40:6–8	He came to do God's will	Hebrews 10:5–7
41:9	His close friend would betray him	Luke 22:48
45:6, 7	His throne will last for ever	Hebrews 1:8, 9
68:18	He ascended into heaven	Ephesians 4:8–10
69:9	He is zealous for God	John 2:17
69:21	He was offered vinegar for his thirst on the cross	Matthew 27:48
89:3, 4, 35, 36	He will be a descendant of David	Luke 1:31–33
96:13	He will return to judge the world	1 Thessalonians 1:10
110:1	He is David's son and David's Lord	Matthew 22:44
110:4	He is the eternal priest-king	Hebrews 6:20
118:22	He is rejected by many but accepted by God	1 Peter 2:7, 8

22:30, 31 Unborn generations are depending on our faithfulness today. As we teach our children about the Lord, so they will teach their children and their children's children. If we fail to tell our children about the Lord, we may well be breaking the chain of God's influence in generations to come. We must view our children and all the young people we meet as God's future leaders. If we are faithful in opportunities today, we may well be affecting the future.

22:30, 31 If we want our children to serve the Lord, they must hear about him from us. It is not enough to rely on the church or those with more knowledge to provide all their Christian education. We must reinforce the lessons of the Bible in our homes.

PSALM 23

A psalm of David.

Theme: God is seen as a caring shepherd and a dependable guide. We must follow God and obey his commands. He is our only hope for eternal life and security.
Author: David

1 The LORD is my shepherd,[a] I shall not be in want.[b]
2 He makes me lie down in green pastures,
he leads me beside quiet waters,[c]
3 he restores my soul.[d]
He guides me in paths of righteousness[e]
for his name's sake.
4 Even though I walk
through the valley of the shadow of death,[a][f]
I will fear no evil,[g]
for you are with me;[h]
your rod and your staff,
they comfort me.

5 You prepare a table before me
in the presence of my enemies.
You anoint my head with oil;[i]
my cup[j] overflows.
6 Surely goodness and love will follow me
all the days of my life,
and I will dwell in the house of the LORD
for ever.

PSALM 24

Of David. A psalm.

Theme: Everything belongs to God — the glorious eternal King. Let us worship him and welcome his glorious reign.
Author: David

1 The earth is the LORD's,[a] and everything in it,
the world, and all who live in it;[b]

a 4 Or *through the darkest valley*

23:1 [a] Isa 40:11; Jn 10:11; 1Pe 2:25 [b] Php 4:19
23:2 [c] Eze 34:14; Rev 7:17
23:3 [d] Ps 19:7 [e] Ps 5:8; 85:13
23:4 [f] Job 10:21-22 [g] Ps 3:6; 27:1 [h] Isa 43:2
23:5 [i] Ps 92:10 [j] Ps 16:5
24:1 [a] Ex 9:29; Job 41:11; Ps 89:11 [b] 1Co 10:26*

23:1 In describing the Lord as a shepherd, David wrote out of his own experience because he had spent his early years caring for sheep (1 Samuel 16:10, 11). Sheep are completely dependent on the shepherd for provision, guidance, and protection. The New Testament calls Jesus the good shepherd (John 10:11); the great Shepherd (Hebrews 13:20); and the Chief Shepherd (1 Peter 5:4). As the Lord is the good shepherd, so we are his sheep — not frightened, passive animals, but obedient followers, wise enough to follow one who will lead us in the right places and in right ways. This psalm does not focus on the animal-like qualities of sheep, but on the discipleship qualities of those who follow. When you recognise the good shepherd, follow him!

23:2, 3 When we allow God our shepherd to guide us, we have contentment. When we choose to sin, however, we go our own way and cannot blame God for the environment we create for ourselves. Our shepherd knows the "green pastures" and "quiet waters" that will restore us. We will reach these places only by following him obediently. Rebelling against the shepherd's leading is actually rebelling against our own best interests. We must remember this the next time we are tempted to go our own way rather than the shepherd's way.

23:4 Death casts a frightening shadow over us because we are entirely helpless in its presence. We can struggle with other enemies — pain, suffering, disease, injury — but strength and courage cannot overcome death. It has the final word. Only one person can walk with us through death's dark valley and bring us safely to the other side — the God of life, our shepherd. Because life is uncertain, we should follow this shepherd who offers us eternal comfort.

23:5, 6 In ancient Near Eastern culture, at a banquet it was customary to anoint a person with fragrant oil as a lotion. Hosts were also expected to protect their guests at all costs. God offers the protection of a host even when enemies surround us. In the final scene of this psalm, we see that believers will dwell with God. God, the perfect shepherd and host, promises to guide and protect us through life to bring us into his house for ever.

24:1 Because "the earth is the LORD's", all of us are stewards, or caretakers. We should be committed to the proper management of this world and its resources, but we are not to become devoted to anything created or act as sole proprietors because this world will pass away (1 John 2:17).

24:1ff This psalm may have been written to celebrate the moving of the ark of the covenant from Obed-Edom's house to Jerusalem (2 Samuel 6:10–12). Tradition says that this psalm was sung on

24:3
c Ps 2:6
d Ps 15:1; 65:4

24:4
e Job 17:9
f Mt 5:8

24:6
g Ps 27:8

24:7
h Isa 26:2
i Ps 97:6; 1Co 2:8

24:8
j Ps 76:3-6

2 for he founded it upon the seas
and established it upon the waters.

3 Who may ascend the hill[c] of the LORD?
Who may stand in his holy place?[d]
4 He who has clean hands[e] and a pure heart,[f]
who does not lift up his soul to an idol
or swear by what is false.[a]
5 He will receive blessing from the LORD
and vindication from God his Saviour.
6 Such is the generation of those who seek him,
who seek your face,[g] O God of Jacob.[b] *Selah*

7 Lift up your heads, O you gates;[h]
be lifted up, you ancient doors,
that the King of glory[i] may come in.
8 Who is this King of glory?
The LORD strong and mighty,
the LORD mighty in battle.[j]
9 Lift up your heads, O you gates;
lift them up, you ancient doors,
that the King of glory may come in.
10 Who is he, this King of glory?
The LORD Almighty—
he is the King of glory. *Selah*

a *4* Or *swear falsely* b *6* Two Hebrew manuscripts and Syriac (see also Septuagint); most Hebrew manuscripts *face, Jacob*

PSALMS TO LEARN AND LOVE

Almost everyone, whether religious or not, has heard Psalm 23 because it is quoted so frequently. Many other psalms are also familiar because they are quoted in music, in literature, or in the words of the worship service.

The psalms we know and love are the ones that come into our minds when we need them. They inspire us, comfort us, correct us just when we need a word from the Lord. If you want to begin memorising psalms, start with some of these favourites. Memorise the whole psalm or just the verses that speak most directly to you. Or read the psalm aloud several times a day until it is part of you.

Psalms to bring us into God's presence	29; 95:1–7a; 96; 100
Psalms about goodness	1; 19; 24; 133; 136; 139
Psalms of praise	8; 97; 103; 107; 113; 145; 150
Psalms of repentance and forgiveness	32:1–5; 51; 103
Psalms for times of trouble	3; 14; 22; 37:1–11; 42; 46; 53; 116:1–7
Psalms of confidence and trust	23; 40:1–4; 91; 119:11; 121; 127

the first day of each week in the temple services. Verses 1–6 tell who is worthy to join in such a celebration of worship.

24:4 Swearing by what is false means telling lies under oath. How greatly God values honesty! Dishonesty comes easily, especially when complete truthfulness could cost us something, make us uncomfortable, or put us in an unfavourable light. Dishonest communication hinders relationships. Without honesty, a relationship with God is impossible. If we lie to others, we will begin to deceive ourselves. God cannot hear us or speak to us if we are building a wall of self-deception.

24:7 Who is this King of glory? The King of glory, identified also as the Lord of hosts, or the commander of heaven's armies, is the Messiah himself, eternal, holy, and mighty. This psalm is not only a battle cry for the church, it also looks forward to Christ's future entry into the new Jerusalem to reign for ever (Revelation 19:11–21).

24:7–10 This psalm, often set to music, was probably used in corporate worship. It may have been re-enacted many times at the temple. The people outside would call out to the temple gates to open up and let the King of glory in. From inside, the priests or another group would ask, "Who is this King of glory?" Outside, the people would respond in unison, "The LORD strong and mighty, the LORD mighty in battle," proclaiming his great power and strength. The exchange was then repeated (24:9, 10), and the temple gates would swing open, symbolising the people's desire to have God's presence among them. This would have been an important lesson for children who were participating.

PSALM 25[a]
Of David.

eme: A prayer for defence, guidance, and pardon. As we trust in God, grants these same requests to us.
thor: David

1To you, O LORD, I lift up my soul;[a]
2 in you I trust,[b] O my God.
Do not let me be put to shame,
nor let my enemies triumph over me.
3No-one whose hope is in you
will ever be put to shame,[c]
but they will be put to shame
who are treacherous without excuse.

4Show me your ways, O LORD,
teach me your paths;[d]
5guide me in your truth and teach me,
for you are God my Saviour,
and my hope is in you all day long.
6Remember, O LORD, your great mercy and love,[e]
for they are from of old.
7Remember not the sins of my youth[f]
and my rebellious ways;
according to your love[g] remember me,
for you are good, O LORD.

8Good and upright[h] is the LORD;
therefore he instructs[i] sinners in his ways.
9He guides[j] the humble in what is right
and teaches them[k] his way.
10All the ways of the LORD are loving and faithful[l]
for those who keep the demands of his covenant.[m]
11For the sake of your name,[n] O LORD,
forgive my iniquity, though it is great.
12Who, then, is the man that fears the LORD?
He will instruct him in the way[o] chosen for him.
13He will spend his days in prosperity,[p]
and his descendants will inherit the land.[q]
14The LORD confides[r] in those who fear him;

a This psalm is an acrostic poem, the verses of which begin with the successive letters of the Hebrew alphabet.

25:1 [a]Ps 86:4
25:2 [b]Ps 41:11
25:3 [c]Isa 49:23
25:4 [d]Ex 33:13
25:6 [e]Ps 103:17; Isa 63:7, 15
25:7 [f]Job 13:26; Jer 3:25 [g]Ps 51:1
25:8 [h]Ps 92:15 [i]Ps 32:8
25:9 [j]Ps 23:3 [k]Ps 27:11
25:10 [l]Ps 40:11 [m]Ps 103:18
25:11 [n]Ps 31:3; 79:9
25:12 [o]Ps 37:23
25:13 [p]Pr 19:23 [q]Ps 37:11
25:14 [r]Pr 3:32

25:2 Seventy-two psalms – almost half the book – speak about enemies. Enemies are those who oppose not only us, but also God's way of living. We can view temptations – money, success, prestige, lust – as our enemies. And our greatest enemy is Satan. David asked God to keep his enemies from overcoming him because they opposed what God stood for. If his enemies succeeded, David feared that many would think that living for God was futile. David did not question his own faith – he knew that God would triumph. But he didn't want his enemies' success to be an obstacle to the faith of others.

25:4 David expressed his desire for guidance. How do we receive God's guidance? The first step is to *want* to be guided and to realise that God's primary guidance system is in his word, the Bible. Psalm 119 tells of the endless knowledge found in God's word. By reading it and constantly learning from it, we will gain the wisdom to perceive God's direction for our lives. We may be tempted to demand answers from God, but David asked for direction. When we are willing to seek God, learn from his word, and obey his commands, then will we receive his specific guidance.

25:8–11 We are bombarded today with relentless appeals to go in various directions. Television advertising alone places hundreds of options before us, in addition to appeals made by political parties, cults, false religions, and dozens of other groups. Numerous organisations, including Christian organisations, seek to motivate us to support a cause. Add to that the dozens of decisions we must make concerning our job, our family, our money, our society, and we become desperate for someone to show us the right way. If you find yourself pulled in several directions, remember that God teaches the humble his way.

25:12 To fear the Lord is to recognise God for who he is: holy, almighty, righteous, pure, all-knowing, all-powerful, and all-wise. When we regard God correctly, we gain a clearer picture of ourselves: sinful, weak, frail, and needy. When we recognise who God is and who we are, we will fall at his feet in humble respect. Only then will he show us how to choose his way.

25:14 "The LORD confides in those who fear him." God offers intimate and lasting friendship to those who revere him, who hold him in highest honour. What relationship could ever compare with hav-

he makes his covenant known[s] to them.
15My eyes are ever on the LORD,[t]
for only he will release my feet from the snare.

16Turn to me[u] and be gracious to me,
for I am lonely and afflicted.
17The troubles of my heart have multiplied;
free me from my anguish.[v]
18Look upon my affliction and my distress[w]
and take away all my sins.
19See how my enemies[x] have increased
and how fiercely they hate me!
20Guard my life[y] and rescue me;
let me not be put to shame,
for I take refuge in you.
21May integrity[z] and uprightness protect me,
because my hope is in you.

22Redeem Israel,[a] O God,
from all their troubles!

PSALM 26

Of David.

Theme: Declaring loyalty to God. If we are genuinely committed to God, we can stand up to opposition and examination.
Author: David, possibly written during the days of Absalom's rebellion

1Vindicate me, O LORD,
for I have led a blameless life;[a]
I have trusted[b] in the LORD
without wavering.[c]
2Test me,[d] O LORD, and try me,
examine my heart and my mind;[e]
3for your love is ever before me,
and I walk continually[f] in your truth.
4I do not sit[g] with deceitful men,
nor do I consort with hypocrites;
5I abhor[h] the assembly of evildoers
and refuse to sit with the wicked.
6I wash my hands in innocence,[i]
and go about your altar, O LORD,

25:14 [s]Jn 7:17
25:15 [t]Ps 141:8
25:16 [u]Ps 69:16
25:17 [v]Ps 107:6
25:18 [w]2Sa 16:12
25:19 [x]Ps 3:1
25:20 [y]Ps 86:2
25:21 [z]Ps 41:12
25:22 [a]Ps 130:8
26:1 [a]Ps 7:8; Pr 20:7 [b]Ps 28:7 [c]2Ki 20:3; Heb 10:23
26:2 [d]Ps 17:3 [e]Ps 7:9
26:3 [f]2Ki 20:3
26:4 [g]Ps 1:1
26:5 [h]Ps 31:6; 139:21
26:6 [i]Ps 73:13

---

ing the Lord of all creation for a friend? Your everlasting friendship with God will grow as you revere him.

25:16, 17 Do life's problems always seem to go from bad to worse? God is the only one who can reverse this downward spiral. He can take our problems and turn them into glorious victories. There is one necessary requirement – we, like David, must cry out, "Turn to me and be gracious to me." When you are willing to do that, God can turn the worst into something wonderful. The next step is yours – God has already made his offer.

25:21 If ever we needed two powerful forces to preserve us along life's way, they are integrity and uprightness. The psalmist asks for these to protect him step by step. Uprightness makes us learn God's requirements and strive to fulfil them. Integrity – being what we say we are – keeps us from claiming to be upright while living as if we do not know God. Uprightness says, "This is the Shepherd's way," and integrity says, "I will walk consistently in it."

26:1–3 By saying that he was "blameless", David was not claiming to be sinless – that is impossible for any human being to achieve. But he was consistently in fellowship with God, clearing his record when he sinned by asking for forgiveness. Here he pleads with God to clear his name of the false charges made against him by his enemies. We also can ask God to examine us, trusting him to forgive our sins and clear our record according to his mercy.

26:4, 5 Should we stay away from unbelievers? No. Although there are some places Christians should avoid, Jesus demonstrated that we must go among unbelievers to help them. But there is a difference between being *with* unbelievers and being *one of* them. Trying to be one of them harms our witness for God. Ask about the people you enjoy, "If I am with them often, will I become less obedient to God in outlook or action?" If the answer is yes, carefully monitor how you spend your time with these people and what effect it has on you.

7proclaiming aloud your praise
and telling of all your wonderful deeds.[j]
8I love[k] the house where you live, O LORD,
the place where your glory dwells.

9Do not take away my soul along with sinners,
my life with bloodthirsty men,[l]
10in whose hands are wicked schemes,
whose right hands are full of bribes.[m]
11But I lead a blameless life;
redeem me[n] and be merciful to me.

12My feet stand on level ground;[o]
in the great assembly[p] I will praise the LORD.

PSALM 27
Of David.

Theme: God offers help for today and hope for the future. Unwavering confidence in God is our antidote to fear and loneliness.
Author: David

1The LORD is my light[a] and my salvation[b]—
whom shall I fear?
The LORD is the stronghold of my life—
of whom shall I be afraid?[c]
2When evil men advance against me
to devour my flesh,[a]
when my enemies and my foes attack me,
they will stumble and fall.[d]
3Though an army besiege me,
my heart will not fear;[e]
though war break out against me,
even then will I be confident.[f]

4One thing[g] I ask of the LORD,
this is what I seek:
that I may dwell in the house of the LORD
all the days of my life,[h]
to gaze upon the beauty of the LORD
and to seek him in his temple.
5For in the day of trouble
he will keep me safe in his dwelling;
he will hide me[i] in the shelter of his tabernacle
and set me high upon a rock.[j]

a 2 Or *to slander me*

26:7 [j]Ps 9:1
26:8 [k]Ps 27:4
26:9 [l]Ps 28:3
26:10 [m]1Sa 8:3
26:11 [n]Ps 69:18
26:12 [o]Ps 27:11; 40:2 [p]Ps 22:22
27:1 [a]Isa 60:19 [b]Ex 15:2 [c]Ps 118:6
27:2 [d]Ps 9:3; 14:4
27:3 [e]Ps 3:6 [f]Job 4:6
27:4 [g]Ps 90:17 [h]Ps 23:6; 26:8
27:5 [i]Ps 17:8; 31:20 [j]Ps 40:2

26:8 God's house in this verse can mean either the tabernacle in Gibeon (the one constructed in the days of Moses; see Exodus 40:35) or the temporary dwelling David built to house the ark of the covenant (2 Samuel 6:17). David exclaimed how he loved to worship God at this place. We should worship God with the same love and reverence as David did.

26:12 Too often we complain about our problems to anyone who will listen and praise God only in private. How much better it would be for us to complain privately and to praise God publicly.

27:1 Fear is a dark shadow that envelops us and ultimately imprisons us within ourselves. Each of us has been a prisoner of fear at one time or another—fear of rejection, misunderstanding, uncertainty, sickness, or even death. But we can conquer fear by using the bright liberating light of the Lord who brings salvation. If we want to dispel the darkness of fear, let us remember with the psalmist that "the LORD is my light and my salvation".

27:4 By the "house of the LORD" and "his temple", David could be referring to the tabernacle in Gibeon, to the sanctuary he had put up to house the ark of the covenant, or to the temple that his son Solomon was to build. David probably had the temple in mind because he made many of the plans for it (1 Chronicles 22). But David may also have used the word *temple* to mean "the presence of the LORD". His greatest desire was to live in God's presence each day of his life. Sadly, this is not the greatest desire of many who claim to be believers. But those who desire to live in God's presence each day will be able to enjoy that relationship for ever.

27:6
[k]Ps 3:3
[l]Ps 107:22

6Then my head will be exalted[k]
above the enemies who surround me;
at his tabernacle will I sacrifice[l] with shouts of joy;
I will sing and make music to the LORD.

27:7
[m]Ps 13:3

7Hear my voice when I call, O LORD;
be merciful to me and answer me.[m]
8My heart says of you, "Seek his[b] face!"
Your face, LORD, I will seek.

27:9
[n]Ps 69:17

9Do not hide your face[n] from me,
do not turn your servant away in anger;
you have been my helper.
Do not reject me or forsake me,
O God my Saviour.
10Though my father and mother forsake me,
the LORD will receive me.

27:11
[o]Ps 5:8; 25:4; 86:11

11Teach me your way, O LORD;
lead me in a straight path[o]
because of my oppressors.

27:12
[p]Mt 26:60; Ac 9:1

12Do not hand me over to the desire of my foes,
for false witnesses[p] rise up against me,
breathing out violence.

27:13
[q]Ps 31:19
[r]Jer 11:19; Eze 26:20

13I am still confident of this:
I will see the goodness of the LORD[q]
in the land of the living.[r]

27:14
[s]Ps 40:1

14Wait[s] for the LORD;
be strong and take heart
and wait for the LORD.

PSALM 28

Of David.

Theme: Prayer when surrounded by trouble or wickedness. God is our only real source of safety. Prayer is our best help when trials come our way because it keeps us in communion with God.
Author: David

28:1
[a]Ps 83:1
[b]Ps 88:4

1To you I call, O LORD my Rock;
do not turn a deaf ear to me.
For if you remain silent,[a]
I shall be like those who have gone down to the pit.[b]

28:2
[c]Ps 138:2; 140:6

2Hear my cry for mercy[c]
as I call to you for help,
as I lift up my hands

b *8* Or *To you, O my heart, he has said, "Seek my*

27:10 Many have had the sad experience of being forsaken by father or mother. Broken homes, differences of belief, addiction to drugs or alcohol, even psychological isolation can leave children crippled by this loss. Even as adults, the pain may linger. God can take that place in our life, fill that void, and heal that hurt. He can direct us to adults who may take the role of father or mother for us. His love is sufficient for all our needs.

27:13 The "land of the living" simply means "this life". David was obviously going through a trial, but he was confident that in this present life God would see him through it.

27:14 David knew from experience what it meant to wait for the Lord. He had been anointed king at the age of 16, but didn't become king until he was 30. During the interim, he was chased through the desert by jealous King Saul. David had to wait on God for the fulfilment of his promise to reign. Later, after becoming king, he was chased by his rebellious son, Absalom.

Waiting for God is not easy. Often it seems that he isn't answering our prayers or doesn't understand the urgency of our situation. That kind of thinking implies that God is not in control or is not fair. But God is worth waiting for. Lamentations 3:24–26 calls us to hope in and wait for the Lord because often God uses waiting to refresh, renew, and teach us. Make good use of your waiting times by discovering what God may be trying to teach you in them.

towards your Most Holy Place.[d]

3Do not drag me away with the wicked,
with those who do evil,
who speak cordially with their neighbours
but harbour malice in their hearts.[e]
4Repay them for their deeds
and for their evil work;
repay them for what their hands have done[f]
and bring back upon them what they deserve.[g]
5Since they show no regard for the works of the LORD
and what his hands have done,[h]
he will tear them down
and never build them up again.

6Praise be to the LORD,
for he has heard my cry for mercy.
7The LORD is my strength[i] and my shield;
my heart trusts[j] in him, and I am helped.
My heart leaps for joy
and I will give thanks to him in song.[k]

8The LORD is the strength of his people,
a fortress of salvation for his anointed one.[l]
9Save your people and bless your inheritance;[m]
be their shepherd[n] and carry them[o] for ever.

28:2 [d]Ps 5:7
28:3 [e]Ps 12:2; Ps 26:9; Jer 9:8
28:4 [f]2Ti 4:14; Rev 22:12 [g]Rev 18:6
28:5 [h]Isa 5:12
28:7 [i]Ps 18:1 [j]Ps 13:5 [k]Ps 40:3; 69:30
28:8 [l]Ps 20:6
28:9 [m]Dt 9:29; Ezr 1:4 [n]Isa 40:11 [o]Dt 1:31; 32:11

PSALM 29

A psalm of David.

Theme: God reveals his great power in nature. We can trust God to give us both the peace and the strength to weather the storms of life.
Author: David

1Ascribe to the LORD,[a] O mighty ones,
ascribe to the LORD glory[b] and strength.
2Ascribe to the LORD the glory due to his name;
worship the LORD in the splendour of his[a] holiness.[c]

3The voice[d] of the LORD is over the waters;
the God of glory thunders,[e]
the LORD thunders over the mighty waters.
4The voice of the LORD is powerful;[f]
the voice of the LORD is majestic.
5The voice of the LORD breaks the cedars;
the LORD breaks in pieces the cedars of Lebanon.[g]
6He makes Lebanon skip[h] like a calf,
Sirion[b][i] like a young wild ox.
7The voice of the LORD strikes
with flashes of lightning.
8The voice of the LORD shakes the desert;

29:1 [a]1Ch 16:28 [b]Ps 96:7-9
29:2 [c]2Ch 20:21
29:3 [d]Job 37:5 [e]Ps 18:13
29:4 [f]Ps 68:33
29:5 [g]Jdg 9:15
29:6 [h]Ps 114:4 [i]Dt 3:9

a *2* Or *LORD with the splendour of* **b** *6* That is, Mount Hermon

28:3–5 It's easy to feign friendship. Wicked people often put on a show of kindness or friendship in order to gain their own ends. David, in his royal position, may have met many who pretended friendship only to meet their own goals. David knew that God would punish them eventually, but he prayed that their punishment would come swiftly. True believers should be straightforward and sincere in all their relationships.

29:5, 6 The cedars of Lebanon were giant trees that could grow to 120 feet tall and 30 feet in circumference. A voice that could break the cedars of Lebanon would be a truly powerful voice – the voice of God. *Sirion* means Mount Hermon. All that was impressive to people was under God's complete control.

the LORD shakes the Desert of Kadesh.[j]
9 The voice of the LORD twists the oaks[c]
and strips the forests bare.
And in his temple all cry, "Glory!"[k]

10 The LORD sits[d] enthroned over the flood;[l]
the LORD is enthroned as King for ever.[m]
11 The LORD gives strength to his people;[n]
the LORD blesses his people with peace.[o]

PSALM 30

A psalm. A song. For the dedication of the temple.[a] Of David.

Theme: A celebration of God's deliverance.
Earthly security is uncertain, but God is always faithful.
Author: David

1 I will exalt you, O LORD,
for you lifted me out of the depths
and did not let my enemies gloat over me.[a]
2 O LORD my God, I called to you for help[b]
and you healed me.[c]
3 O LORD, you brought me up from the grave;[b]
you spared me from going down into the pit.[d]

4 Sing to the LORD, you saints[e] of his;
praise his holy name.[f]
5 For his anger[g] lasts only a moment,
but his favour lasts a lifetime;
weeping may remain for a night,
but rejoicing comes in the morning.[h]

6 When I felt secure, I said,
"I shall never be shaken."
7 O LORD, when you favoured me,
you made my mountain[c] stand firm;
but when you hid your face,[i]
I was dismayed.

8 To you, O LORD, I called;
to the Lord I cried for mercy:
9 "What gain is there in my destruction,[d]
in my going down into the pit?
Will the dust praise you?
Will it proclaim your faithfulness?[j]

29:8 [j]Nu 13:26
29:9 [k]Ps 26:8
29:10 [l]Ge 6:17 [m]Ps 10:16
29:11 [n]Ps 28:8 [o]Ps 37:11
30:1 [a]Ps 25:2; 28:9
30:2 [b]Ps 88:13 [c]Ps 6:2
30:3 [d]Ps 28:1; 86:13
30:4 [e]Ps 149:1 [f]Ps 97:12
30:5 [g]Ps 103:9 [h]2Co 4:17
30:7 [i]Dt 31:17; Ps 104:29
30:9 [j]Ps 6:5

[c] *9* Or *LORD makes the deer give birth* [d] *10* Or *sat* [a] Title: Or *palace* [b] *3* Hebrew *Sheol* [c] *7* Or *hill country*
[d] *9* Or *there if I am silenced*

29:10, 11 Throughout history, God has revealed his power through mighty miracles over nature, such as the great flood (Genesis 6–9). He promises to continue to reveal his power. Paul urged us to understand how great God's power is (Ephesians 1:18–23). The same power that raised Christ from the dead is available to help us with our daily problems. When you feel weak and limited, don't despair. Remember that God can give you strength. The power that controls creation and raises the dead is available to you.

30:1ff David may have written this psalm when he dedicated Araunah's threshing floor (which became the future site of the temple) and after God stopped the great plague he had used to discipline David (1 Chronicles 21:1 – 22:6). The serious illness mentioned in 30:2, 3 may refer to an illness David experienced or to the plague itself.

30:5 Like a shot given by a doctor, the discomfort of God's anger lasts only a moment, but the good effects go on for a long time. Let God's anger be a sharp pain that warns you to turn from sin.

30:6, 7 Security had made David feel invincible. Although he knew that his riches and power had come from God, they had gone to his head, making him proud. Wealth, power, and fame have an intoxicating effect on people, making them feel self-reliant, self-secure, and independent of God. But this false security can be easily shattered. Don't be trapped by the false security of prosperity. Depend on God for your security, and you won't be shaken when worldly possessions disappear.

10Hear, O LORD, and be merciful to me;
O LORD, be my help."

11You turned my wailing into dancing;
you removed my sackcloth and clothed me with joy,[k]
12that my heart may sing to you and not be silent.
O LORD my God, I will give you thanks[l] for ever.[m]

30:11 [k]Ps 4:7; Jer 31:4, 13
30:12 [l]Ps 16:9 [m]Ps 44:8

PSALM 31

For the director of music. A psalm of David.

Theme: In times of stress, depending upon God requires complete commitment.
Author: David, although some say Jeremiah

1In you, O LORD, I have taken refuge;
let me never be put to shame;
deliver me in your righteousness.
2Turn your ear to me,
come quickly to my rescue;[a]
be my rock of refuge,[b]
a strong fortress to save me.
3Since you are my rock and my fortress,[c]
for the sake of your name[d] lead and guide me.
4Free me from the trap that is set for me,
for you are my refuge.[e]
5Into your hands I commit my spirit;[f]
redeem me, O LORD, the God of truth.

6I hate those who cling to worthless idols;
I trust in the LORD.[g]
7I will be glad and rejoice in your love,
for you saw my affliction[h]
and knew the anguish[i] of my soul.
8You have not handed me over[j] to the enemy
but have set my feet in a spacious place.

9Be merciful to me, O LORD, for I am in distress;
my eyes grow weak with sorrow,[k]
my soul and my body with grief.

31:2 [a]Ps 71:2 [b]Ps 18:2
31:3 [c]Ps 18:2 [d]Ps 23:3
31:4 [e]Ps 25:15
31:5 [f]Lk 23:46; Ac 7:59
31:6 [g]Jnh 2:8
31:7 [h]Ps 90:14 [i]Ps 10:14; Jn 10:27
31:8 [j]Dt 32:30
31:9 [k]Pns 6:7

30:11 *Sackcloth* refers to clothes worn as a sign of mourning.

31:1 David called upon God to deliver him. He wanted God to stop those who were unjustly causing trouble. Therefore, David made his request based upon what he knew of God's name, or character. Because God is righteous and loving, he loves to deliver his people.

31:1–6 We say we have faith in God, but do we really trust him? David's words, "Into your hands I commit my spirit," convey his complete trust in God. Jesus used this phrase as he was dying on the cross – showing his absolute dependence on God the Father (Luke 23:46). Stephen repeated these words as he was being stoned to death (Acts 7:59), confident that in death he was simply passing from God's earthly care to God's eternal care. We should commit our possessions, our families, and our vocations to God. But first and foremost, we should commit *ourselves* completely to him.

31:6 Why did David suddenly bring up the subject of idol worship? He wanted to contrast his total devotion to God with the diluted worship offered by many Israelites. Pagan religious rituals were never completely banished from Israel and Judah, despite the efforts of David and a few other kings. Obviously a person who clung to idols could not commit his spirit into God's hands. When we put today's idols (wealth, material possessions, success) first in our lives, we cannot expect God's Spirit to guide us. God is our highest authority and requires our first allegiance.

31:8 In David's day, armies needed large areas of land for their military manoeuvres. David praised God for the "spacious place" – the open spaces that gave him the freedom to move within God's boundaries. If you feel restrained by God's moral boundaries, remember that God has given you much freedom, far more than you need, to move within those boundaries. Use the opportunities he gives you to make wise decisions. Use them wisely and they will lead to victory.

31:9–13 In describing his own feelings, David writes of the helplessness and hopelessness everyone feels when hated or rejected. But adversity is easier to accept when we recognise our true relationship with the sovereign God (31:14–18). Although our enemies may seem to have the upper hand, they are ultimately the helpless and hopeless ones. Those who know God will be victorious in the end (31:23). We can have courage today because God will preserve us.

31:10 [l]Ps 13:2 [m]Ps 38:3; 39:11
31:11 [n]Job 19:13; Ps 38:11; 64:8; Isa 53:4
31:12 [o]Ps 88:4
31:13 [p]Jer 20:3, 10; La 2:22 [q]Mt 27:1
31:14 [r]Ps 140:6
31:15 [s]Job 24:1; Ps 143:9
31:16 [t]Nu 6:25; Ps 4:6
31:17 [u]Ps 25:2-3 [v]Ps 115:17
31:18 [w]Ps 120:2 [x]Ps 94:4
31:19 [y]Ro 11:22 [z]Isa 64:4
31:20 [a]Ps 27:5 [b]Job 5:21
31:21 [c]Ps 17:7 [d]1Sa 23:7
31:22 [e]Ps 116:11 [f]La 3:54
31:23 [g]Ps 34:9 [h]Ps 145:20 [i]Ps 94:2
31:24 [j]Ps 27:14

10 My life is consumed by anguish
and my years by groaning;[l]
my strength fails because of my affliction,[a]
and my bones grow weak.[m]
11 Because of all my enemies,
I am the utter contempt of my neighbours;[n]
I am a dread to my friends —
those who see me on the street flee from me.
12 I am forgotten by them as though I were dead;[o]
I have become like broken pottery.
13 For I hear the slander of many;
there is terror on every side;[p]
they conspire against me
and plot to take my life.[q]

14 But I trust[r] in you, O LORD;
I say, "You are my God."
15 My times[s] are in your hands;
deliver me from my enemies
and from those who pursue me.
16 Let your face shine[t] on your servant;
save me in your unfailing love.
17 Let me not be put to shame,[u] O LORD,
for I have cried out to you;
but let the wicked be put to shame
and lie silent[v] in the grave.[b]
18 Let their lying lips[w] be silenced,
for with pride and contempt
they speak arrogantly[x] against the righteous.

19 How great is your goodness,[y]
which you have stored up for those who fear you,
which you bestow in the sight of men[z]
on those who take refuge in you.
20 In the shelter of your presence you hide[a] them
from the intrigues of men;[b]
in your dwelling you keep them safe
from accusing tongues.

21 Praise be to the LORD,
for he showed his wonderful love[c] to me
when I was in a besieged city.[d]
22 In my alarm[e] I said,
"I am cut off from your sight!"
Yet you heard my cry[f] for mercy
when I called to you for help.

23 Love the LORD, all his saints![g]
The LORD preserves the faithful,[h]
but the proud he pays back[i] in full.
24 Be strong and take heart,[j]
all you who hope in the LORD.

[a] *10* Or *guilt* [b] *17* Hebrew *Sheol*

31:14, 15 In saying, "My times are in your hands," David was expressing his belief that all of life's circumstances are under God's control. Knowing that God loves and cares for us enables us to keep steady in our faith regardless of our circumstances. It keeps us from sinning foolishly by taking matters into our own hands or resenting God's timetable.

PSALM 32

Of David. A *maskil*.[a]

Theme: Forgiveness brings true joy. Only when we ask God to forgive our sins will he give us real happiness and relief from guilt.
Author: David

1Blessed is he
whose transgressions are forgiven,
whose sins are covered.[a]
2Blessed is the man
whose sin the LORD does not count against him[b]
and in whose spirit is no deceit.[c]

3When I kept silent,
my bones wasted away[d]
through my groaning all day long.
4For day and night
your hand was heavy[e] upon me;
my strength was sapped
as in the heat of summer. *Selah*
5Then I acknowledged my sin to you
and did not cover up my iniquity.
I said, "I will confess[f]
my transgressions[g] to the LORD"—
and you forgave
the guilt of my sin.[h] *Selah*

6Therefore let everyone who is godly pray to you
while you may be found;[i]
surely when the mighty waters rise,
they will not reach him.[j]
7You are my hiding-place;
you will protect me from trouble[k]
and surround me with songs of deliverance.[l] *Selah*

8I will instruct[m] you and teach you in the way you should go;
I will counsel you and watch over[n] you.
9Do not be like the horse or the mule,
which have no understanding
but must be controlled by bit and bridle[o]
or they will not come to you.
10Many are the woes of the wicked,[p]
but the LORD's unfailing love
surrounds the man who trusts[q] in him.

[a] Title: Probably a literary or musical term

32:1 [a]Ps 85:2
32:2 [b]Ro 4:7-8*; 2Co 5:19 [c]Jn 1:47
32:3 [d]Ps 31:10
32:4 [e]Job 33:7
32:5 [f]Pr 28:13 [g]Ps 103:12 [h]Lev 26:40
32:6 [i]Ps 69:13; Isa 55:6 [j]Isa 43:2
32:7 [k]Ps 9:9 [l]Ex 15:1
32:8 [m]Ps 25:8 [n]Ps 33:18
32:9 [o]Pr 26:3
32:10 [p]Ro 2:9 [q]Pr 16:20

32:1 *Maskil* is a term perhaps denoting psalms written to make a person wise or prudent, to increase a person's success or skill.

32:1ff Read this psalm in conjunction with Psalm 51 – both are penitential psalms. Here David expresses the joy of forgiveness. God had forgiven him for the sins he had committed against Bathsheba and Uriah (2 Samuel 11, 12). This is another of the penitential (repentance) psalms where the writer confesses his sin to God.

32:1, 2 God *wants* to forgive sinners. Forgiveness has always been part of his loving nature. He announced this to Moses (Exodus 34:7); he revealed it to David; and he dramatically showed it to the world through Jesus Christ. These verses convey several aspects of God's forgiveness: forgives transgression, covers sin, doesn't count our sins against us. Paul quoted these verses in Romans 4:7, 8 and showed that we can have this joyous experience of forgiveness through faith in Christ.

32:5 What is confession? To confess our sin is to agree with God, acknowledging that he is right to declare what we have done as sinful, and that we are wrong to desire or to do it. It is to affirm our intention of abandoning that sin in order to follow him more faithfully.

32:8, 9 God describes some people as being like horses or mules that have to be controlled by bits and bridles. Rather than letting God guide them step by step, they stubbornly leave God only one option. If God wants to keep them useful for him, he must use discipline and punishment. God longs to guide us with love and wisdom rather than punishment. He offers to teach us the *best* way to go. Accept the advice written in God's word and don't let your stubbornness keep you from obeying God.

32:11
[r]Ps 64:10

[11]Rejoice in the LORD[r] and be glad, you righteous;
sing, all you who are upright in heart!

33:1
[a]Ps 147:1
[b]Ps 32:11

PSALM 33

33:2
[c]Ps 92:3

Theme: Because God is Creator, Lord, Saviour, and Deliverer, he is worthy of our trust and praise. Because he is faithful and his word is dependable, we can rejoice and sing, giving thanks and praise.
Author: Anonymous

33:3
[d]Ps 96:1

33:4
[e]Ps 19:8

[1]Sing joyfully to the LORD, you righteous;
it is fitting[a] for the upright[b] to praise him.
[2]Praise the LORD with the harp;
make music to him on the ten-stringed lyre.[c]
[3]Sing to him a new song;[d]
play skilfully, and shout for joy.

33:5
[f]Ps 11:7
[g]Ps 119:64

[4]For the word of the LORD is right[e] and true;
he is faithful in all he does.
[5]The LORD loves righteousness and justice;[f]
the earth is full of his unfailing love.[g]

33:6
[h]Heb 11:3

33:8
[i]Ps 67:7; 96:9

33:9
[j]Ge 1:3;
Ps 148:5

33:10
[k]Isa 8:10

[6]By the word[h] of the LORD were the heavens made,
their starry host by the breath of his mouth.
[7]He gathers the waters of the sea into jars;[a]
he puts the deep into storehouses.
[8]Let all the earth fear the LORD;
let all the people of the world revere him.[i]
[9]For he spoke, and it came to be;
he commanded,[j] and it stood firm.
[10]The LORD foils the plans of the nations;[k]
he thwarts the purposes of the peoples.

a 7 Or *sea as into a heap*

CONFESSION, REPENTANCE, AND FORGIVENESS IN PSALMS

Over the centuries, many believers, overcome by an awareness of their own sins, have found in the words of the penitential (confession) psalms a ray of hope. The psalmists shared with God both the depth of their sorrow and repentance, as well as the height of joy at being forgiven. They rejoiced in the knowledge that God would respond to confession and repentance with complete forgiveness. We, who live on the other side of the cross of Christ, can rejoice even more because we understand more. God has shown us that he is willing to forgive because his judgment on sin was satisfied by Christ's death on the cross.

As you read these psalms, note the pattern followed by the psalmists in responding to God: (1) they recognised their sinfulness and tendency to do wrong; (2) they realised that sin was rebellion against God himself; (3) they admitted their sins to God; (4) they trusted in God's willingness to forgive; and (5) they accepted his forgiveness. Use these psalms as a reminder of how easy it is to drift away from God and fall into sin, and what is needed to re-establish that fellowship.

Selected psalms that emphasise these themes are 6; 14; 31; 32; 38; 41; 51; 102; 130; 143.

33:2, 3 David, who some believe wrote this psalm, was an accomplished harpist (1 Samuel 16:15–25). He frequently spoke about musical instruments throughout his psalms. He undoubtedly composed music for many of the psalms, and he commissioned music for temple worship (1 Chronicles 25).

33:4 All God's words are right and true – they can be trusted. The Bible is reliable because, unlike people, God does not lie, forget, change his words, or leave his promises unfulfilled. We can trust the Bible because it contains the words of a holy, trustworthy, and unchangeable God.

33:6–9 This is a poetic summary of the first chapter of Genesis. God is not just the co-ordinator of natural forces, he is the Lord of creation, the almighty God. Because he is all-powerful, we should revere him in all we do.

11 But the plans of the LORD stand firm for ever,
the purposes[l] of his heart through all generations.

12 Blessed is the nation whose God is the LORD,[m]
the people he chose[n] for his inheritance.
13 From heaven the LORD looks down
and sees all mankind;[o]
14 from his dwelling-place[p] he watches
all who live on earth—
15 he who forms[q] the hearts of all,
who considers everything they do.[r]
16 No king is saved by the size of his army;[s]
no warrior escapes by his great strength.
17 A horse[t] is a vain hope for deliverance;
despite all its great strength it cannot save.
18 But the eyes[u] of the LORD are on those who fear him,
on those whose hope is in his unfailing love,[v]
19 to deliver them from death
and keep them alive in famine.[w]

20 We wait[x] in hope for the LORD;
he is our help and our shield.
21 In him our hearts rejoice,[y]
for we trust in his holy name.
22 May your unfailing love rest upon us, O LORD,
even as we put our hope in you.

PSALM 34[a]

Of David. When he pretended to be insane before Abimelech,
who drove him away, and he left.

Theme: God pays attention to those who call on him. Whether God offers escape from trouble or help in times of trouble, we can be certain that he always hears and acts on behalf of those who love him.
Author: David, after pretending to be insane in order to escape from King Achish (1 Samuel 21:10–15)

1 I will extol the LORD at all times;[a]
his praise will always be on my lips.
2 My soul will boast[b] in the LORD;
let the afflicted hear and rejoice.[c]
3 Glorify the LORD with me;
let us exalt[d] his name together.

[a] This psalm is an acrostic poem, the verses of which begin with the successive letters of the Hebrew alphabet.

33:11 [l]Job 23:13
33:12 [m]Ps 144:15 [n]Ex 19:5; Dt 7:6
33:13 [o]Job 28:24; Ps 11:4
33:14 [p]1Ki 8:39
33:15 [q]Job 10:8 [r]Jer 32:19
33:16 [s]Ps 44:6
33:17 [t]Ps 20:7; Pr 21:31
33:18 [u]Job 36:7; Ps 34:15 [v]Ps 147:11
33:19 [w]Job 5:20
33:20 [x]Ps 130:6
33:21 [y]Zec 10:7; Jn 16:22
34:1 [a]Ps 71:6; Eph 5:20
34:2 [b]Jer 9:24; 1Co 1:31 [c]Ps 119:74
34:3 [d]Lk 1:46

33:11 "The plans of the LORD stand firm for ever." Are you frustrated by inconsistencies you see in others, or even in yourself? God is completely trustworthy—his intentions never change. There is a promise that good and perfect gifts come to us from the Creator who never changes (James 1:17). When you wonder if there is anyone in whom you can trust, remember that God is completely consistent. Let him counsel you.

33:16, 17 *Horse* refers to military strength. Because God rules and overrules every nation, leaders should never put their trust in their physical power. Military might is not the ground of our hope. Our hope is in God and in his gracious offer to save us if we will trust in him.

33:18, 19 This is not a cast-iron guarantee that all believers will be delivered from death and starvation. Thousands of Christian saints have been beaten to death, whipped, fed to lions, or executed (Romans 8:35, 36; Hebrews 11:32–40). God can (and often miraculously does) deliver his followers from pain and death, though sometimes, for purposes known only to him, he chooses not to. When faced with these harsh realities, we must focus on the wise judgments of God. The writer was pleading for God's watchful care and protection. In times of crisis, we can place our hope in God.

34:1ff God promises great blessings to his people, but many of these blessings require our active participation. He will deliver us from fear (34:4), save us out of our troubles (34:6), guard and deliver us (34:7), show us goodness (34:8), supply our needs (34:9), listen when we talk to him (34:15), and redeem us (34:22), but we must do our part. We can appropriate his blessings when we seek him (34:4, 10), cry out to him (34:6, 17), trust him (34:8), fear him (34:7, 9), refrain from lying (34:13), turn from evil, do good and seek peace (34:14), are humble (34:18), and serve him (34:22).

34:4
[e] Mt 7:7

34:5
[f] Ps 36:9
[g] Ps 25:3

34:7
[h] 2Ki 6:17; Da 6:22

34:8
[i] 1Pe 2:3
[j] Ps 2:12

34:9
[k] Ps 23:1

34:10
[l] Ps 84:11

34:11
[m] Ps 32:8

34:12
[n] 1Pe 3:10

34:13
[o] 1Pe 2:22

34:14
[p] Ps 37:27
[q] Heb 12:14

34:15
[r] Ps 33:18
[s] Job 36:7

34:16
[t] Lev 17:10; Jer 44:11
[u] 1Pe 3:10-12*
[v] Pr 10:7

34:17
[w] Ps 145:19

34:18
[x] Ps 145:18
[y] Isa 57:15

34:19
[z] ver 17
[a] ver 4, 6; Pr 24:16

4 I sought the LORD,[e] and he answered me;
he delivered me from all my fears.
5 Those who look to him are radiant;[f]
their faces are never covered with shame.[g]
6 This poor man called, and the LORD heard him;
he saved him out of all his troubles.
7 The angel of the LORD[h] encamps around those who fear him,
and he delivers them.

8 Taste and see that the LORD is good;[i]
blessed is the man who takes refuge[j] in him.
9 Fear the LORD, you his saints,
for those who fear him lack nothing.[k]
10 The lions may grow weak and hungry,
but those who seek the LORD lack no good thing.[l]

11 Come, my children, listen to me;
I will teach you[m] the fear of the LORD.
12 Whoever of you loves life[n]
and desires to see many good days,
13 keep your tongue from evil
and your lips from speaking lies.[o]
14 Turn from evil and do good;[p]
seek peace[q] and pursue it.

15 The eyes of the LORD[r] are on the righteous[s]
and his ears are attentive to their cry;
16 the face of the LORD is against[t] those who do evil,[u]
to cut off the memory[v] of them from the earth.

17 The righteous cry out, and the LORD hears[w] them;
he delivers them from all their troubles.
18 The LORD is close[x] to the broken-hearted[y]
and saves those who are crushed in spirit.

19 A righteous man may have many troubles,[z]
but the LORD delivers him from them all;[a]

34:8 "Taste and see" does not mean, "Check out God's credentials." Instead it is a warm invitation: "Try this; I know you'll like it." When we take that first step of obedience in following God, we cannot help discovering that he is good and kind. When we begin the Christian life, our knowledge of God is partial and incomplete. As we trust him daily, we experience how good he is.

34:9 You say you belong to the Lord, but do you fear him? To fear the Lord means to show deep respect and honour to him. We demonstrate true reverence by our humble attitude and genuine worship. Reverence was shown by Abraham (Genesis 17:2–4), Moses (Exodus 3:5, 6), and the Israelites (Exodus 19:16–24). Their reactions to God's presence varied, but all deeply respected him.

34:9, 10 At first we may question David's statement, because we seem to lack many good things. This is not a blanket promise that all Christians will have everything they want. Instead, this is David's praise for God's goodness – all those who call upon God in their need will be answered, sometimes in unexpected ways.

Remember, God knows what we need, and our deepest needs are spiritual. Many Christians, even though they face unbearable poverty and hardship, still have enough spiritual nourishment to live for God. David was saying that to have God is to have all you really need. God is enough.

If you feel you don't have everything you need, ask: (1) Is this really a need? (2) Is this really good for me? (3) Is this the best time for me to have what I desire? Even if you answer yes to all three questions, God may allow you to go without to help you grow more dependent on him. He may want you to learn that you need *him* more than your immediate desires.

34:11–14 The Bible often connects the fear of the Lord (love and reverence for him) with obedience. "Fear God and keep his commandments" (Ecclesiastes 12:13); "If anyone loves me, he will obey my teaching" (John 14:23). David said that a person who fears the Lord doesn't lie, turns from evil, does good, and promotes peace. Reverence is much more than sitting quietly in church. It includes obeying God in the way we speak and the way we treat others.

34:14 Somehow we think that peace should come to us with no effort. But David explained that we are to seek and pursue peace. Paul echoed this thought in Romans 12:18. A person who wants peace cannot be argumentative and contentious. Because peaceful relationships come from our efforts at peacemaking, work hard at living in peace with others each day.

34:18, 19 We often wish we could escape troubles – the pain of grief, loss, sorrow, and failure; or even the small daily frustrations that constantly wear us down. God promises to be "close to the brokenhearted", to be our source of power, courage, and wisdom, helping us through our problems. Sometimes he chooses to deliver us from those problems. When trouble strikes, don't get frustrated with God. Instead, admit that you need God's help and thank him for being by your side.

20he protects all his bones,
not one of them will be broken.[b]

21Evil will slay the wicked;[c]
the foes of the righteous will be condemned.
22The LORD redeems[d] his servants;
no-one will be condemned who takes refuge in him.

34:20 [b]Jn 19:36*
34:21 [c]Ps 94:23
34:22 [d]1Ki 1:29; Ps 71:23

PSALM 35
Of David.

Theme: A prayer to God for help against those who try to inflict injury for no reason. When our enemies are unjust and lie about us, even when we do good to them, we can appeal to God who is always just.
Author: David, possibly written when he was being hunted by Saul (1 Samuel 24)

1Contend, O LORD, with those who contend with me;
fight[a] against those who fight against me.
2Take up shield and buckler;
arise[b] and come to my aid.
3Brandish spear and javelin[a]
against those who pursue me.
Say to my soul,
"I am your salvation."

4May those who seek my life
be disgraced[c] and put to shame;
may those who plot my ruin
be turned back in dismay.
5May they be like chaff[d] before the wind,
with the angel of the LORD driving them away;
6may their path be dark and slippery,
with the angel of the LORD pursuing them.
7Since they hid their net for me without cause
and without cause dug a pit for me,
8may ruin overtake them by surprise—[e]
may the net they hid entangle them,
may they fall into the pit,[f] to their ruin.
9Then my soul will rejoice[g] in the LORD
and delight in his salvation.[h]
10My whole being will exclaim,
"Who is like you,[i] O LORD?
You rescue the poor from those too strong[j] for them,
the poor and needy[k] from those who rob them."

11Ruthless witnesses[l] come forward;
they question me on things I know nothing about.

35:1 [a]Ps 43:1
35:2 [b]Ps 62:2
35:4 [c]Ps 70:2
35:5 [d]Job 21:18; Ps 1:4; Isa 29:5
35:8 [e]1Th 5:3 [f]Ps 9:15
35:9 [g]Lk 1:47 [h]Isa 61:10
35:10 [i]Ex 15:11 [j]Ps 18:17 [k]Ps 37:14
35:11 [l]Ps 27:12

a 3 *Or and block the way*

34:20 This is a prophecy about Christ when he was crucified. Although it was the Roman custom to break the legs of the victim to speed death, not one of Jesus' bones was broken (John 19:32–37). In addition to the prophetic meaning, David was pleading for God's protection in times of crisis.

35:1ff This is one of the "imprecatory" (cursing) psalms that call upon God to deal with enemies. These psalms sound extremely harsh, but we must remember: (1) David could not understand why he was forced to flee from men who were unjustly seeking to kill him. He was God's anointed king over a nation called to annihilate the evil people of the land. (2) David's call for justice was sincere; it was not a cover for his own personal vengeance. He truly wanted to seek God's perfect ideal for his nation. (3) David did not say that *he* would take revenge, but he gave the matter to God. These are merely his suggestions. (4) These psalms use hyperbole (or overstatement). They were meant to motivate others to take a strong stand against sin and evil.

Cruelty may be far removed from some people's experience, but it is a daily reality to others. God promises to help the persecuted and to bring judgment on unrepentant sinners. When we pray for justice to be done, we are praying as David did. When Christ returns, the wicked will be punished.

12They repay me evil for good[m]
and leave my soul forlorn.
13Yet when they were ill, I put on sackcloth
and humbled myself with fasting.[n]
When my prayers returned to me unanswered,
14 I went about mourning
as though for my friend or brother.
I bowed my head in grief
as though weeping for my mother.
15But when I stumbled, they gathered in glee;
attackers gathered against me when I was unaware.
They slandered[o] me without ceasing.
16Like the ungodly they maliciously mocked;[b]
they gnashed their teeth[p] at me.
17O Lord, how long[q] will you look on?
Rescue my life from their ravages,
my precious life[r] from these lions.
18I will give you thanks in the great assembly;[s]
among throngs of people I will praise you.[t]

19Let not those gloat over me
who are my enemies without cause;
let not those who hate me without reason[u]
maliciously wink the eye.[v]
20They do not speak peaceably,
but devise false accusations
against those who live quietly in the land.
21They gape[w] at me and say, "Aha! Aha![x]
With our own eyes we have seen it."

22O LORD, you have seen[y] this; be not silent.
Do not be far[z] from me, O Lord.
23Awake,[a] and rise to my defence!
Contend for me, my God and Lord.
24Vindicate me in your righteousness, O LORD my God;
do not let them gloat over me.
25Do not let them think, "Aha, just what we wanted!"
or say, "We have swallowed him up."[b]

26May all who gloat over my distress
be put to shame[c] and confusion;
may all who exalt themselves over me[d]
be clothed with shame and disgrace.
27May those who delight in my vindication[e]
shout for joy[f] and gladness;
may they always say, "The LORD be exalted,
who delights[g] in the well-being of his servant."
28My tongue will speak of your righteousness[h]
and of your praises all day long.

35:12 [m]Jn 10:32
35:13 [n]Job 30:25; Ps 69:10
35:15 [o]Job 30:1, 8
35:16 [p]Job 16:9; La 2:16
35:17 [q]Hab 1:13 [r]Ps 22:20
35:18 [s]Ps 22:25 [t]Ps 22:22
35:19 [u]Ps 38:19; 69:4; Jn 15:25* [v]Ps 13:4; Pr 6:13
35:21 [w]Ps 22:13 [x]Ps 40:15
35:22 [y]Ex 3:7 [z]Ps 10:1; 28:1
35:23 [a]Ps 44:23
35:25 [b]La 2:16
35:26 [c]Ps 40:14; 109:29 [d]Ps 38:16
35:27 [e]Ps 9:4 [f]Ps 32:11 [g]Ps 40:16; 147:11
35:28 [h]Ps 51:14

b *16* Septuagint; Hebrew may mean *ungodly circle of mockers.*

35:13 David was sad when his prayers seemed "unanswered". When our deliverance is delayed, it is easy to assume that God hasn't answered our prayers. God hears every prayer, but he answers according to his wisdom. Don't let the absence of an immediate answer cause you to doubt or resent God. Instead let it be an occasion to deepen your faith.

35:21–23 David cried out to God to defend him when people wrongly accused him. If you are unjustly accused, your natural reaction may be to lash out in revenge or to give a detailed defence of your every move. Instead, ask God to fight the battle for you. He will clear your name in the eyes of those who really matter.

PSALM 36

For the director of music. Of David the servant of the LORD.

Theme: God's faithfulness, justice, and love are contrasted with the sinful hearts of men and women. In spite of our fallen condition, God pours out his love on those who know him.
Author: David

1 An oracle is within my heart
concerning the sinfulness of the wicked:[a]
There is no fear of God
before his eyes.[a]
2 For in his own eyes he flatters himself
too much to detect or hate his sin.
3 The words of his mouth[b] are wicked and deceitful;
he has ceased to be wise[c] and to do good.[d]
4 Even on his bed he plots evil;[e]
he commits himself to a sinful course[f]
and does not reject what is wrong.[g]

5 Your love, O LORD, reaches to the heavens,
your faithfulness to the skies.
6 Your righteousness is like the mighty mountains,
your justice like the great deep.[h]
O LORD, you preserve both man and beast.
7 How priceless is your unfailing love!
Both high and low among men
find[b] refuge in the shadow of your wings.[i]
8 They feast in the abundance of your house;[j]
you give them drink from your river[k] of delights.
9 For with you is the fountain of life;[l]
in your light[m] we see light.

10 Continue your love to those who know you,
your righteousness to the upright in heart.
11 May the foot of the proud not come against me,
nor the hand of the wicked drive me away.
12 See how the evildoers lie fallen—
thrown down, not able to rise![n]

PSALM 37[a]

Of David.

Theme: Trust in the Lord and wait patiently for him to act.
This psalm vividly contrasts the wicked person with the righteous.
Author: David

1 Do not fret because of evil men
or be envious[a] of those who do wrong;[b]

[a] *1* Or *heart: / Sin proceeds from the wicked.* [b] *7* Or *love, O God! / Men find*; or *love! / Both heavenly beings and men / find* [a] This psalm is an acrostic poem, the stanzas of which begin with the successive letters of the Hebrew alphabet.

36:1 [a]Ro 3:18*
36:3 [b]Ps 10:7 [c]Ps 94:8 [d]Jer 4:22
36:4 [e]Pr 4:16; Mic 2:1 [f]Isa 65:2 [g]Ps 52:3; Ro 12:9
36:6 [h]Job 11:8; Ps 77:19; Ro 11:33
36:7 [i]Ru 2:12; Ps 17:8
36:8 [j]Ps 65:4 [k]Job 20:17; Rev 22:1
36:9 [l]Jer 2:13 [m]1Pe 2:9
36:12 [n]Ps 140:10
37:1 [a]Pr 23:17-18 [b]Ps 73:3

36:1 Because the wicked have no fear of God, nothing restrains them from sinning. They plunge ahead as if nothing will happen to them. But God is just and is only delaying their punishment. This knowledge should hold us back from sinning. Let the fear of God do its work in you to keep you from sin. In your gratitude for God's love, don't ignore his justice.

36:5–8 In contrast to evil people and their wicked plots that end in failure, God is faithful, righteous, and just. His love reaches to the heavens; his faithfulness reaches to the skies; his righteousness is as solid as mighty mountains; and his judgments are as full of wisdom as the oceans with water ("the great deep"). We need not fear evil people because we know God loves us, judges evil, and will care for us throughout eternity.

36:9 This vivid image—"fountain of life"—gives us a sense of fresh, cleansing water that gives life to the spiritually thirsty. This same picture is used in Jeremiah 2:13, where God is called the "spring of living water". Jesus spoke of himself as living water that could quench thirst for ever and give eternal life (John 4:14).

37:2
[c]Ps 90:6

37:3
[d]Dt 30:20
[e]Isa 40:11; Jn 10:9

37:4
[f]Isa 58:14

37:5
[g]Ps 4:5; Ps 55:22; Pr 16:3; 1Pe 5:7

37:6
[h]Mic 7:9
[i]Job 11:17

37:7
[j]Ps 62:5; La 3:26
[k]Ps 40:1

37:8
[l]Eph 4:31; Col 3:8

37:9
[m]Isa 57:13; 60:21

37:10
[n]Job 7:10; 24:24

37:11
[o]Mt 5:5

37:12
[p]Ps 35:16

37:13
[q]1Sa 26:10; Ps 2:4

37:14
[r]Ps 11:2
[s]Ps 35:10

37:15
[t]Ps 9:16

37:16
[u]Pr 15:16

37:17
[v]Job 38:15; Ps 10:15

37:18
[w]Ps 1:6

2for like the grass they will soon wither,
like green plants they will soon die away.[c]

3Trust in the LORD and do good;
dwell in the land[d] and enjoy safe pasture.[e]
4Delight[f] yourself in the LORD
and he will give you the desires of your heart.

5Commit your way to the LORD;
trust in him[g] and he will do this:
6He will make your righteousness[h] shine like the dawn,[i]
the justice of your cause like the noonday sun.

7Be still[j] before the LORD and wait patiently[k] for him;
do not fret when men succeed in their ways,
when they carry out their wicked schemes.

8Refrain from anger[l] and turn from wrath;
do not fret—it leads only to evil.
9For evil men will be cut off,
but those who hope in the LORD will inherit the land.[m]

10A little while, and the wicked will be no more;[n]
though you look for them, they will not be found.
11But the meek will inherit the land[o]
and enjoy great peace.

12The wicked plot against the righteous
and gnash their teeth[p] at them;
13but the Lord laughs at the wicked,
for he knows their day is coming.[q]

14The wicked draw the sword
and bend the bow[r]
to bring down the poor and needy,[s]
to slay those whose ways are upright.
15But their swords will pierce their own hearts,[t]
and their bows will be broken.

16Better the little that the righteous have
than the wealth[u] of many wicked;
17for the power of the wicked will be broken,[v]
but the LORD upholds the righteous.

18The days of the blameless are known to the LORD,[w]
and their inheritance will endure for ever.
19In times of disaster they will not wither;

37:1 We should never envy evil people, even though some may be extremely popular or excessively rich. No matter how much they have, it will fade and vanish like grass that withers and dies. Those who follow God live differently from the wicked and, in the end, will have far greater treasures in heaven. What the unbeliever gets may last a lifetime, if he is lucky. What you get from following God lasts for ever.

37:4, 5 David calls us to take delight in the Lord and to commit everything we have and do (our "way") to him. But how do we do this? To *delight* in someone means to experience great pleasure and joy in his or her presence. This happens only when we know that person well. Thus, to delight in the Lord, we must know him better. Knowledge of God's great love for us will indeed give us delight.

To *commit* ourselves to the Lord means entrusting everything—our lives, families, jobs, possessions—to his control and guidance. To commit ourselves to the Lord means to trust in him (37:5), believing that he can care for us better than we can ourselves. We should be willing to wait patiently (37:7) for him to work out what is best for us.

37:8, 9 Anger and worry (fretting) are two very destructive emotions. They reveal a lack of faith that God loves us and is in control. We should not worry; instead, we should trust in God, giving ourselves to him for his use and safekeeping. When you dwell on your problems, you will become anxious and angry. But if you concentrate on God and his goodness, you will find peace. Where do you focus your attention?

37:11 Meekness hardly seems the proper weapon to deal with enemies. God's warfare must be carried out with calm faith, humility before God, and hope in his deliverance. Jesus also promises a sure reward for those with humble attitudes (Matthew 5:5).

in days of famine they will enjoy plenty.

20 But the wicked will perish:
The LORD's enemies will be like the beauty of the fields,
they will vanish—vanish like smoke.[x]

21 The wicked borrow and do not repay,
but the righteous give generously;[y]
22 those the LORD blesses will inherit the land,
but those he curses[z] will be cut off.

23 If the LORD delights[a] in a man's way,
he makes his steps firm;[b]
24 though he stumble, he will not fall,[c]
for the LORD upholds[d] him with his hand.

25 I was young and now I am old,
yet I have never seen the righteous forsaken[e]
or their children begging bread.
26 They are always generous and lend freely;
their children will be blessed.[f]

27 Turn from evil and do good;[g]
then you will dwell in the land for ever.
28 For the LORD loves the just
and will not forsake his faithful ones.

They will be protected for ever,
but the offspring of the wicked will be cut off;[h]
29 the righteous will inherit the land[i]
and dwell in it for ever.

30 The mouth of the righteous man utters wisdom,
and his tongue speaks what is just.
31 The law of his God is in his heart;[j]
his feet do not slip.[k]

32 The wicked lie in wait[l] for the righteous,
seeking their very lives;
33 but the LORD will not leave them in their power
or let them be condemned when brought to trial.[m]

34 Wait for the LORD[n]
and keep his way.
He will exalt you to inherit the land;
when the wicked are cut off, you will see[o] it.

37:20 [x]Ps 102:3
37:21 [y]Ps 112:5
37:22 [z]Job 5:3; Pr 3:33
37:23 [a]Ps 147:11 [b]1Sa 2:9
37:24 [c]Pr 24:16 [d]Ps 145:14; 147:6
37:25 [e]Heb 13:5
37:26 [f]Ps 147:13
37:27 [g]Ps 34:14
37:28 [h]Ps 21:10; Isa 14:20
37:29 [i]ver 9; Pr 2:21
37:31 [j]Dt 6:6; Ps 40:8; Isa 51:7 [k]ver 23
37:32 [l]Ps 10:8
37:33 [m]Ps 109:31; 2Pe 2:9
37:34 [n]Ps 27:14 [o]Ps 52:6

37:21 You can tell a lot about a person's character by the way he or she handles money. The wicked person steals under the guise of borrowing. The righteous person gives generously to the needy. The wicked person, therefore, focuses on himself, while the righteous person looks to the welfare of others.

37:23, 24 The person in whom God delights is one who follows God, trusts him, and tries to do his will. God watches over and makes firm every step that person takes. If you would like to have God direct your way, then seek his advice before you step out.

37:25 Because children starve today, as they did in David's time, what did David mean by these words? David is observing God's provision over a lifetime. Though there are unfortunate exceptions to this general principle, God provides for his own people. The children of the righteous need not go hungry because other believers can help out in their time of need. In David's day, Israel obeyed God's laws that ensured that the poor were treated fairly and mercifully. As long as Israel was obedient, there was enough food for everyone. When Israel forgot God, the rich took care only of themselves, and the poor suffered (Amos 2:6, 7).

When we see a Christian brother or sister suffering today, we can respond in one of three ways. (1) We can say, as Job's friends did, that the afflicted person brought this on himself. (2) We can say that this is a test to help the poor develop more patience and trust in God. (3) We can help the person in need. David would approve of only the last option. Although many governments today have their own schemes for helping those in need, this is no excuse for ignoring the poor and needy within our reach.

37:34 It is difficult to wait patiently for God to act when we want change right away. But God promises that if we submit to his timing, he will honour us. Peter said, "Humble yourselves, therefore, under God's mighty hand, that he may lift you up in due time" (1 Peter 5:6). Be patient, steadily doing the work God has given you to do, and allow God to choose the best time to change your circumstances.

37:35 [p]Job 5:3
37:36 [q]Job 20:5
37:37 [r]Isa 57:1-2
37:38 [s]Ps 1:4
37:39 [t]Ps 3:8 [u]Ps 9:9
37:40 [v]1Ch 5:20 [w]Isa 31:5

35I have seen a wicked and ruthless man
flourishing[p] like a green tree in its native soil,
36but he soon passed away and was no more;
though I looked for him, he could not be found.[q]

37Consider the blameless, observe the upright;
there is a future[b] for the man of peace.[r]
38But all sinners will be destroyed;
the future[c] of the wicked will be cut off.[s]

39The salvation[t] of the righteous comes from the LORD;
he is their stronghold in time of trouble.[u]
40The LORD helps[v] them and delivers[w] them;
he delivers them from the wicked and saves them,
because they take refuge in him.

PSALM 38

A psalm of David. A petition.

Theme: Sorrow for sin brings hope. God alone is the true source of healing and protection for those who confess their sins to him.
Author: David

38:1 [a]Ps 6:1
38:2 [b]Job 6:4; Ps 32:4
38:3 [c]Ps 6:2; Isa 1:6
38:4 [d]Ezr 9:6
38:5 [e]Ps 69:5
38:6 [f]Job 30:28; Ps 35:14; 42:9
38:7 [g]Ps 102:3
38:8 [h]Ps 22:1
38:9 [i]Job 3:24; Ps 6:6; 10:17
38:10 [j]Ps 31:10 [k]Ps 6:7
38:11 [l]Ps 31:11

1O LORD, do not rebuke me in your anger
or discipline me in your wrath.[a]
2For your arrows[b] have pierced me,
and your hand has come down upon me.
3Because of your wrath there is no health in my body;
my bones[c] have no soundness because of my sin.
4My guilt has overwhelmed me
like a burden too heavy to bear.[d]

5My wounds fester and are loathsome
because of my sinful folly.[e]
6I am bowed down and brought very low;
all day long I go about mourning.[f]
7My back is filled with searing pain;[g]
there is no health in my body.
8I am feeble and utterly crushed;
I groan[h] in anguish of heart.

9All my longings lie open before you, O Lord:
my sighing[i] is not hidden from you.
10My heart pounds, my strength fails[j] me;
even the light has gone from my eyes.[k]
11My friends and companions avoid me because of my wounds;[l]
my neighbours stay far away.

b *37 Or there will be posterity* c *38 Or posterity*

38:1 As a child might cry to his father, so David cried to God. David was not saying, "Don't punish me," but, "Don't punish me while you are angry." He acknowledged that he deserved to be punished, but he asked that God temper his discipline with mercy. Like children, we are free to ask for mercy, but we should not deny that we deserve punishment.

38:1ff This is called a penitential psalm because David expressed sorrow for his sin (38:18). He stated that his sin led to health problems (38:1–8) and separated him from God and others, causing extreme loneliness (38:9–14). He then confessed his sin and repented (38:15–22).

38:2–4 David saw his anguish as judgment from God for his sins. Although God does not always send physical illness to punish us for sin, this verse and others in Scripture (Acts 12:21–23; 1 Corinthians 11:30–32) indicate that he does in certain circumstances. Our sin can have physical or mental side effects that can cause great suffering. Sometimes God has to punish his children in order to bring them back to himself (Hebrews 12:5–11). When we repent of our sin, God promises to forgive us. He delivers us from sin's eternal consequences although he does not promise to undo all of sin's earthly consequences.

12Those who seek my life set their traps,[m]
those who would harm me talk of my ruin;[n]
all day long they plot deception.[o]

13I am like a deaf man, who cannot hear,
like a mute, who cannot open his mouth;
14I have become like a man who does not hear,
whose mouth can offer no reply.
15I wait[p] for you, O LORD;
you will answer,[q] O Lord my God.
16For I said, "Do not let them gloat[r]
or exalt themselves over me when my foot slips."[s]

17For I am about to fall,
and my pain is ever with me.
18I confess my iniquity;[t]
I am troubled by my sin.
19Many are those who are my vigorous enemies;[u]
those who hate me without reason[v] are numerous.
20Those who repay my good with evil[w]
slander me when I pursue what is good.

21O LORD, do not forsake me;
be not far[x] from me, O my God.
22Come quickly to help me,[y]
O Lord my Saviour.[z]

PSALM 39

For the director of music. For Jeduthun. A psalm of David.

Theme: Apart from God, life is fleeting and empty.
This is an appeal for God's mercy because life is so brief.
Author: David

1I said, "I will watch my ways[a]
and keep my tongue from sin;[b]
I will put a muzzle on my mouth
as long as the wicked are in my presence."
2But when I was silent[c] and still,
not even saying anything good,
my anguish increased.
3My heart grew hot within me,
and as I meditated, the fire burned;
then I spoke with my tongue:

4"Show me, O LORD, my life's end
and the number of my days;[d]

38:12 [m]Ps 140:5 [n]Ps 35:4; 54:3 [o]Ps 35:20
38:15 [p]Ps 39:7 [q]Ps 17:6
38:16 [r]Ps 35:26 [s]Ps 13:4
38:18 [t]Ps 32:5
38:19 [u]Ps 18:17 [v]Ps 35:19
38:20 [w]Ps 35:12; 1Jn 3:12
38:21 [x]Ps 35:22
38:22 [y]Ps 40:13 [z]Ps 27:1
39:1 [a]1Ki 2:4 [b]Job 2:10; Jas 3:2
39:2 [c]Ps 38:13
39:4 [d]Ps 90:12

38:13, 14 It is extremely difficult to be silent when others tear us down because we want to protect our reputation. We find it difficult to do nothing while they assault something so precious to us. But we don't need to lash out in revenge or justify our position; we can trust God to protect our reputation. Jesus was silent before his accusers (Luke 23:9, 10); he left his case in God's hands (1 Peter 2:21–24). That is a good place to leave our case too!

39:1–3 David resolved to keep his tongue from sin; that is, he decided not to complain to other people about God's treatment of him. David certainly had reason to complain. David was the anointed king of Israel, but he had to wait many years before taking the throne. Then one of his sons tried to kill him and become king instead. But when David could not keep still any longer, he took his complaints directly to God. We all have complaints about our job, money, or situations, but complaining to others may make them think that God cannot take care of us. It may also look as if we blame God for our troubles. Instead, like David, we should take our complaints directly to God.

39:4 Life is short no matter how long we live. If there is something important we want to do, we must not put it off for a better day. Ask yourself, "If I had only six months to live, what would I do?" Tell someone that you love him or her? Deal with an undisciplined area in your life? Tell someone about Jesus? Because life is short, don't neglect what is truly important.

let me know how fleeting is my life.[e]
5You have made my days[f] a mere handbreadth;
the span of my years is as nothing before you.
Each man's life is but a breath.[g] *Selah*
6Man is a mere phantom[h] as he goes to and fro:
He bustles about, but only in vain;[i]
he heaps up wealth, not knowing who will get it.[j]

7"But now, Lord, what do I look for?
My hope is in you.[k]
8Save me[l] from all my transgressions;[m]
do not make me the scorn of fools.
9I was silent; I would not open my mouth,[n]
for you are the one who has done this.
10Remove your scourge from me;
I am overcome by the blow of your hand.[o]
11You rebuke[p] and discipline men for their sin;
you consume their wealth like a moth[q]—
each man is but a breath. *Selah*

12"Hear my prayer, O LORD,
listen to my cry for help;
be not deaf to my weeping.
For I dwell with you as an alien,[r]
a stranger,[s] as all my fathers were.
13Look away from me, that I may rejoice again
before I depart and am no more."[t]

PSALM 40

For the director of music. Of David. A psalm.

Theme: Doing God's will sometimes means waiting patiently. While we wait, we can love God, serve others, and tell others about him.
Author: David

1I waited patiently[a] for the LORD;
he turned to me and heard my cry.[b]
2He lifted me out of the slimy pit,
out of the mud and mire;[c]
he set my feet on a rock[d]
and gave me a firm place to stand.
3He put a new song[e] in my mouth,
a hymn of praise to our God.
Many will see and fear
and put their trust in the LORD.

4Blessed is the man[f]
who makes the LORD his trust,[g]
who does not look to the proud,

9:4 Ps 103:14
9:5 Ps 89:45; Ps 62:9
9:6 1Pe 1:24; Ps 127:2; Lk 12:20
9:7 Ps 38:15
9:8 Ps 51:9; Ps 44:13
9:9 Job 2:10
9:10 Job 9:34; Ps 32:4
9:11 2Pe 2:16; Job 13:28
9:12 1Pe 2:11; Heb 11:13
9:13 Job 10:21; 14:10
0:1 Ps 27:14; Ps 34:15
0:2 Ps 69:14; Ps 27:5
0:3 Ps 33:3
0:4 Ps 34:8; Ps 84:12

9:5, 6 The brevity of life is a theme throughout the books of salms, Proverbs, and Ecclesiastes. Jesus also spoke about it Luke 12:20). It is ironic that people spend so much time securing heir lives on earth and spend little or no thought about where they will spend eternity. David realised that amassing riches and busily ccomplishing worldly tasks would make no difference in eternity. ew people understand that their only hope is in the Lord. (For ther verses on the brevity of life, see Ecclesiastes 2:18 and James :14.)

9:10 What did David mean when he asked God to remove the "scourge" because he was overcome by the "blow" of God's hand? It may be a picture of the difficulties David was facing that caused him to feel as if he were being struck. Just as a loving father carefully disciplines his children, so God corrects us (Hebrews 12:5–9).

40:1–4 Waiting for God to help us is not easy, but David received four benefits from waiting: God (1) lifted him out of his despair, (2) set his feet on a rock, (3) gave him a firm place to stand, and (4) put a new song of praise in his mouth. Often blessings cannot be received unless we go through the trial of waiting.

to those who turn aside to false gods.[a]
5Many, O LORD my God,
are the wonders[h] you have done.
The things you planned for us
no-one can recount[i] to you;
were I to speak and tell of them,
they would be too many to declare.

6Sacrifice and offering you did not desire,[j]
but my ears you have pierced;[b,c]
burnt offerings[k] and sin offerings
you did not require.
7Then I said, "Here I am, I have come—
it is written about me in the scroll.[d]
8I desire to do your will,[l] O my God;
your law is within my heart."[m]

9I proclaim righteousness in the great assembly;[n]
I do not seal my lips,
as you know,[o] O LORD.
10I do not hide your righteousness in my heart;
I speak of your faithfulness[p] and salvation.
I do not conceal your love and your truth
from the great assembly.[q]

11Do not withhold your mercy from me, O LORD;
may your love[r] and your truth[s] always protect me.
12For troubles[t] without number surround me;
my sins have overtaken me, and I cannot see.[u]
They are more than the hairs of my head,[v]
and my heart fails[w] within me.

13Be pleased, O LORD, to save me;
O LORD, come quickly to help me.[x]
14May all who seek to take my life
be put to shame and confusion;
may all who desire my ruin[y]
be turned back in disgrace.
15May those who say to me, "Aha! Aha!"
be appalled at their own shame.
16But may all who seek you
rejoice and be glad in you;
may those who love your salvation always say,

a *4* Or *to falsehood* b *6* Hebrew; Septuagint *but a body you have prepared for me* (see also Symmachus and Theodotion) c *6* Or *opened* d *7* Or *come / with the scroll written for me*

40:5 [h]Ps 136:4 [i]Ps 139:18; Isa 55:8
40:6 [j]1Sa 15:22; Am 5:22 [k]Isa 1:11
40:8 [l]Jn 4:34 [m]Ps 37:31
40:9 [n]Ps 22:25 [o]Jos 22:22; Ps 119:13
40:10 [p]Ps 89:1 [q]Ac 20:20
40:11 [r]Pr 20:28 [s]Ps 43:3
40:12 [t]Ps 116:3 [u]Ps 38:4 [v]Ps 69:4 [w]Ps 73:26
40:13 [x]Ps 70:1
40:14 [y]Ps 35:4

40:6 "Sacrifice and offering you did not desire." The religious ritual of David's day involved sacrificing animals in the tabernacle. David says these acts were meaningless unless done for the right reasons. Today we often make rituals of going to church, taking communion, or paying tithes. These activities are also empty if our reasons for doing them are selfish. God doesn't want these sacrifices and offerings without an attitude of devotion to him. The prophet Samuel told Saul, "To obey is better than sacrifice" (1 Samuel 15:22). Make sure that you give God the obedience and lifelong service he desires from you.

40:7, 8 "I desire to do your will, O my God." Jesus portrayed this attitude of obeying and serving God (John 4:34; 5:30). He came as the prophets foretold, proclaiming the Good News of God's righteousness and forgiveness of sins. In Hebrews 10:5–10, verses 6–8 are applied to Jesus.

40:9, 10 David said he would speak of God's faithfulness and salvation to those around him. When we feel the impact of God's righteousness on our lives, we cannot keep it hidden. We want to tell other people what God has done for us. If God's faithfulness has changed your life, don't be timid. It is natural to share a good bargain with others or recommend a skilful doctor, so it should also feel natural to share what God has done for us.

40:10 When we think of faithfulness, a friend or a spouse may come to mind. People who are faithful to us accept and love us, even when we are unlovable. Faithful people keep their promises, whether promises of support or promises made in our marriage vows. God's faithfulness is like human faithfulness, only perfect. His love is absolute, and his promises are irrevocable. He loves us in spite of our constant bent towards sin, and he keeps all the promises he has made to us, even when we break our promises to him.

"The LORD be exalted!"[z]

17 Yet I am poor and needy;
may the Lord think of me.
You are my help and my deliverer;
O my God, do not delay.[a]

PSALM 41

For the director of music. A psalm of David.

Theme: A prayer for God's mercy when feeling sick or abandoned. When we're sick or when everyone deserts us, God remains at our side.
Author: David

1 Blessed is he who has regard for the weak;[a]
the LORD delivers him in times of trouble.
2 The LORD will protect him and preserve his life;
he will bless him in the land[b]
and not surrender him to the desire of his foes.[c]
3 The LORD will sustain him on his sick-bed
and restore him from his bed of illness.

4 I said, "O LORD, have mercy[d] on me;
heal me, for I have sinned[e] against you."
5 My enemies say of me in malice,
"When will he die and his name perish?[f]"
6 Whenever one comes to see me,
he speaks falsely,[g] while his heart gathers slander;[h]
then he goes out and spreads it abroad.

7 All my enemies whisper together[i] against me;
they imagine the worst for me, saying,
8 "A vile disease has beset him;
he will never get up from the place where he lies."
9 Even my close friend,[j] whom I trusted,
he who shared my bread,
has lifted up his heel against me.[k]

10 But you, O LORD, have mercy on me;
raise me up,[l] that I may repay them.
11 I know that you are pleased with me,[m]
for my enemy does not triumph over me.[n]
12 In my integrity you uphold me[o]
and set me in your presence for ever.[p]

13 Praise be to the LORD, the God of Israel,[q]
from everlasting to everlasting.
Amen and Amen.[r]

40:16 [z]Ps 35:27
40:17 [a]Ps 70:5
41:1 [a]Ps 82:3-4; Pr 14:21
41:2 [b]Ps 37:22 [c]Ps 27:12
41:4 [d]Ps 6:2 [e]Ps 51:4
41:5 [f]Ps 38:12
41:6 [g]Ps 12:2 [h]Pr 26:24
41:7 [i]Ps 56:5; 71:10-11
41:9 [j]2Sa 15:12; Ps 55:12 [k]Job 19:19; Ps 55:20; Mt 26:23; Jn 13:18*
41:10 [l]Ps 3:3
41:11 [m]Ps 147:11 [n]Ps 25:2
41:12 [o]Ps 37:17 [p]Job 36:7
41:13 [q]Ps 72:18 [r]Ps 89:52; 106:48

41:1 The Bible often speaks of God's care for the weak, poor, and needy, and of his blessing on those who share this concern. God wants our generosity to reflect his own free giving. As he has blessed us, we should bless others.

41:9 This verse is viewed in the New Testament as a prophecy of Christ's betrayal (John 13:18). Judas, one of Jesus' 12 disciples, had spent three years learning from Jesus, travelling and eating with him (Mark 3:14–19), and handling the finances for the group. Eventually Judas, who knew Jesus extremely well, betrayed him (Matthew 26:14–16, 20–25).

41:13 Psalms is divided into five books, and each one ends with a doxology or an expression of praise to God. The first book of the psalms, chapters 1–41, takes us on a journey through suffering, sorrow, and great joy. It teaches us much about God's eternal love and care for us and how we should trust him even in the day-to-day experiences of life.

BOOK II
PSALMS 42:1—72:20

These psalms include a prayer for rescue, a call to worship, a confession of sin, an encouragement to trust God, a psalm for those hurt by friends, a prayer for those who have been slandered, and a missionary psalm. These psalms can help us to retain a sense of wonder in our worship.

PSALM 42[a]

For the director of music. A *maskil*[b] of the Sons of Korah.

Theme: A thirst for God. When you feel lonely or depressed, meditate on God's kindness and love.
Authors: The sons of Korah, who were temple musicians and assistants

1 As the deer pants for streams of water,
so my soul pants[a] for you, O God.
2 My soul thirsts[b] for God, for the living God.[c]
When can I go[d] and meet with God?
3 My tears[e] have been my food
day and night,
while men say to me all day long,
"Where is your God?"[f]
4 These things I remember
as I pour out my soul:
how I used to go with the multitude,
leading the procession to the house of God,[g]
with shouts of joy and thanksgiving[h]
among the festive throng.

5 Why are you downcast,[i] O my soul?
Why so disturbed within me?
Put your hope in God,[j]
for I will yet praise him,
my Saviour[k] and 6 my God.

My[c] soul is downcast within me;
therefore I will remember you
from the land of the Jordan,
the heights of Hermon—from Mount Mizar.
7 Deep calls to deep
in the roar of your waterfalls;
all your waves and breakers
have swept over me.[l]

42:1 [a]Ps 119:131
42:2 [b]Ps 63:1 [c]Jer 10:10 [d]Ps 43:4
42:3 [e]Ps 80:5 [f]Ps 79:10
42:4 [g]Isa 30:29 [h]Ps 100:4
42:5 [i]Ps 38:6; 77:3 [j]La 3:24 [k]Ps 44:3
42:7 [l]Ps 88:7; Jnh 2:3

[a] In many Hebrew manuscripts Psalms 42 and 43 constitute one psalm. [b] Title: Probably a literary or musical term [c] *5,6* A few Hebrew manuscripts, Septuagint and Syriac; most Hebrew manuscripts *praise him for his saving help. / 6O my God, my*

42:1ff Psalms 42—49 were written by the sons of Korah. Korah was a Levite who led a rebellion against Moses (Numbers 16:1–35). He was killed, but his descendants remained faithful to God and continued to serve God in the temple. David appointed men from the clan of Korah to serve as choir leaders (1 Chronicles 6:31–38), and they continued to be temple musicians for hundreds of years (2 Chronicles 20:18, 19).

42:1, 2 As the life of a deer depends upon water, so our lives depend upon God. Those who seek him and long to understand him find never-ending life. Feeling separated from God, this psalmist wouldn't rest until he restored his relationship with God because he knew that his very life depended on it.

42:4, 5 The writer of this psalm was discouraged because he was exiled to a place far from Jerusalem and could not worship in the temple. During these God-given holidays, the nation was to remember all that God had done for them. Many of these festivals are explained in the chart in Exodus 23.

42:5, 6 Depression is one of the most common emotional ailments. One antidote for depression is to meditate on the record of God's goodness to his people. This will take your mind off the present situation and give hope that it will improve. It will focus your thoughts on God's ability to help you rather than on your inability to help yourself. When you feel depressed, take advantage of this psalm's antidepressant. Read the Bible's accounts of God's goodness, and meditate on them.

42:6 Hermon refers to Mount Hermon. *Mizar* means smallness, so Mount Mizar could be a smaller mountain in that mountain range.

42:8
[m] Ps 57:3
[n] Job 35:10
[o] Ps 63:6; 149:5

42:9
[p] Ps 38:6

42:11
[q] Ps 43:5

43:1
[a] 1Sa 24:15; Ps 26:1; 35:1
[b] Ps 5:6

43:2
[c] Ps 44:9
[d] Ps 42:9

43:3
[e] Ps 36:9
[f] Ps 42:4
[g] Ps 84:1

43:4
[h] Ps 26:6
[i] Ps 33:2

43:5
[j] Ps 42:6

8 By day the LORD directs his love,[m]
at night[n] his song[o] is with me—
a prayer to the God of my life.

9 I say to God my Rock,
"Why have you forgotten me?
Why must I go about mourning,[p]
oppressed by the enemy?"
10 My bones suffer mortal agony
as my foes taunt me,
saying to me all day long,
"Where is your God?"

11 Why are you downcast, O my soul?
Why so disturbed within me?
Put your hope in God,
for I will yet praise him,
my Saviour and my God.[q]

PSALM 43[a]

Theme: Hope in a time of discouragement. In the face of discouragement, our only hope is in God.
Authors: The sons of Korah (temple assistants) Psalms 42 and 43 are one psalm in many Hebrew manuscripts

1 Vindicate me, O God,
and plead my cause[a] against an ungodly nation;
rescue me from deceitful and wicked men.[b]
2 You are God my stronghold.
Why have you rejected[c] me?
Why must I go about mourning,
oppressed by the enemy?[d]
3 Send forth your light[e] and your truth,
let them guide me;
let them bring me to your holy mountain,[f]
to the place where you dwell.[g]
4 Then will I go to the altar[h] of God,
to God, my joy and my delight.
I will praise you with the harp,[i]
O God, my God.

5 Why are you downcast, O my soul?
Why so disturbed within me?
Put your hope in God,
for I will yet praise him,
my Saviour and my God.[j]

[a] In many Hebrew manuscripts Psalms 42 and 43 constitute one psalm.

43:3 The "holy mountain" is Mount Zion, in Jerusalem, the city that David named as Israel's capital. The temple was built there as the place for the people to meet God in worship and prayer.

43:3, 4 The psalmist asked God to send his light and truth to guide him to the holy mountain, the temple, where he would meet God. God's truth (see 1 John 2:27) provides the right path to follow, and God's light (see 1 John 1:5) provides the clear vision to follow it. If you feel surrounded by darkness and uncertainty, follow God's light and truth. He will guide you.

PSALM 44

For the director of music. Of the Sons of Korah. A *maskil.* [a]

Theme: A plea for victory by the battle-weary and defeated. When it seems that God has let you down, don't despair. Instead, remember God's past deliverance and be confident that he will restore you.
Authors: The sons of Korah (temple assistants)

1 We have heard with our ears, O God;
our fathers have told us[a]
what you did in their days,
in days long ago.
2 With your hand you drove out[b] the nations
and planted[c] our fathers;
you crushed the peoples
and made our fathers flourish.[d]
3 It was not by their sword[e] that they won the land,
nor did their arm bring them victory;
it was your right hand, your arm,[f]
and the light of your face, for you loved[g] them.

4 You are my King[h] and my God,
who decrees[b] victories for Jacob.
5 Through you we push back our enemies;
through your name we trample[i] our foes.
6 I do not trust in my bow,[j]
my sword does not bring me victory;
7 but you give us victory[k] over our enemies,
you put our adversaries to shame.[l]
8 In God we make our boast[m] all day long,
and we will praise your name for ever.[n] *Selah*

9 But now you have rejected[o] and humbled us;
you no longer go out with our armies.[p]
10 You made us retreat[q] before the enemy,
and our adversaries have plundered us.
11 You gave us up to be devoured like sheep[r]
and have scattered us among the nations.[s]
12 You sold your people for a pittance,[t]
gaining nothing from their sale.

13 You have made us a reproach to our neighbours,[u]
the scorn[v] and derision of those around us.
14 You have made us a byword among the nations;
the peoples shake their heads[w] at us.
15 My disgrace is before me all day long,
and my face is covered with shame

a Title: Probably a literary or musical term b *4* Septuagint, Aquila and Syriac; Hebrew *King, O God; / command*

44:1 aEx 12:26; Ps 78:3
44:2 bPs 78:55 cEx 15:17 dPs 80:9
44:3 eDt 8:17; Jos 24:12 fPs 77:15 gDt 4:37; 7:7-8
44:4 hPs 74:12
44:5 iPs 108:13
44:6 jPs 33:16
44:7 kPs 136:24 lPs 53:5
44:8 mPs 34:2 nPs 30:12
44:9 oPs 74:1 pPs 60:1, 10
44:10 qLev 26:17; Jos 7:8; Ps 89:41
44:11 rRo 8:36 sDt 4:27; 28:64; Ps 106:27
44:12 tIsa 52:3; Jer 15:13
44:13 uPs 79:4; 80:6 vDt 28:37
44:14 wPs 109:25; Jer 24:9

44:1ff This psalm may have been sung at an occasion like the one in 2 Chronicles 20:18, 19, where the faithful Jehoshaphat was surrounded by enemies and the Levites sang to the Lord before the battle.

44:1–3 Driving out the nations refers to the conquest of Canaan (the promised land) described in the book of Joshua. God gave the land to Israel – they were supposed to enter and drive out anyone who was wicked and opposed to God. Israel was told to settle in the land and to be a witness to the world of God's power and love. Surrounded by enemies, the psalmist remembered what God had done for his people and took heart. We can have this same confidence in God when we feel attacked.

44:6, 7 In whom or in what do you trust? Only God is trustworthy – he will never let you down.

44:9–22 Israel had been defeated despite their faith (44:17) and obedience (44:18) to God. The psalmist could not understand why God allowed this to happen, but he did not give up hope of discovering the answer (44:17–22). Although he felt his suffering was undeserved, he revealed the real reason for it: he suffered because he was *committed to the Lord.* Paul quoted the psalmist's complaint (Romans 8:36) to show that we must always be ready to face death for the cause of Christ. Thus, our suffering may not be a punishment, but a battle scar that demonstrates our loyalty.

44:16
[x]Ps 74:10

44:17
[y]Ps 78:7, 57; Da 9:13

44:18
[z]Job 23:11

44:19
[a]Ps 51:8
[b]Job 3:5

44:20
[c]Ps 78:11
[d]Dt 6:14; Ps 81:9

44:21
[e]Ps 139:1-2; Jer 17:10

44:22
[f]Isa 53:7; Ro 8:36*

44:23
[g]Ps 7:6
[h]Ps 78:65
[i]Ps 77:7

44:24
[j]Job 13:24
[k]Ps 42:9

44:25
[l]Ps 119:25

44:26
[m]Ps 35:2
[n]Ps 25:22

45:2
[a]Lk 4:22

45:3
[b]Heb 4:12; Rev 1:16
[c]Isa 9:6

45:4
[d]Rev 6:2

16 at the taunts of those who reproach and revile[x] me,
because of the enemy, who is bent on revenge.

17 All this happened to us,
though we had not forgotten[y] you
or been false to your covenant.
18 Our hearts had not turned[z] back;
our feet had not strayed from your path.
19 But you crushed[a] us and made us a haunt for jackals
and covered us over with deep darkness.[b]

20 If we had forgotten[c] the name of our God
or spread out our hands to a foreign god,[d]
21 would not God have discovered it,
since he knows the secrets of the heart?[e]
22 Yet for your sake we face death all day long;
we are considered as sheep to be slaughtered.[f]

23 Awake,[g] O Lord! Why do you sleep?[h]
Rouse yourself! Do not reject us for ever.[i]
24 Why do you hide your face[j]
and forget our misery and oppression?[k]

25 We are brought down to the dust;[l]
our bodies cling to the ground.
26 Rise up[m] and help us;
redeem[n] us because of your unfailing love.

PSALM 45

For the director of music. To ⌊the tune of⌋ "Lilies". Of the Sons of Korah. A *maskil*.[a] A wedding song.

Theme: A poem to the king (possibly Solomon) on the occasion of his wedding. While this psalm was written for an historic occasion, it is also seen as a prophecy about Christ and his bride, the church, who will praise him throughout all generations.
Authors: The sons of Korah (temple assistants)

1 My heart is stirred by a noble theme
as I recite my verses for the king;
my tongue is the pen of a skilful writer.

2 You are the most excellent of men
and your lips have been anointed with grace,[a]
since God has blessed you for ever.
3 Gird your sword[b] upon your side, O mighty one;[c]
clothe yourself with splendour and majesty.
4 In your majesty ride forth victoriously[d]
on behalf of truth, humility and righteousness;
let your right hand display awesome deeds.
5 Let your sharp arrows pierce the hearts of the king's enemies;

a Title: Probably a literary or musical term

44:22–26 The writer cried out to God to redeem his people because of his unfailing love. Nothing can separate us from God's love, not even death (Romans 8:36–39). When you fear for your life, ask God for deliverance, and remember that even death cannot separate you from him.

44:23–25 The psalmist's words suggest that he did not believe God had left him. God was still the Ruler, but he seemed to be asleep, and the psalmist wondered why. In the New Testament, the disciples wondered why Jesus was asleep when they needed his help during a storm (Mark 4:35–41). In both cases, of course, God was ready to help, but he wished first to build faith in his followers.

45:1ff This is called a *Messianic* psalm because it prophetically describes the Messiah's future relationship to the church, his body of believers. Verse 2 expresses God's abundant blessing on his Messiah; verses 6–8 find their true fulfilment in Christ (Hebrews 1:8, 9). The church is described as the bride of Christ in Revelation 19:7, 8; 21:9; 22:17.

let the nations fall beneath your feet.
6Your throne, O God, will last for ever and ever;[e]
a sceptre of justice will be the sceptre of your kingdom.
7You love righteousness[f] and hate wickedness;
therefore God, your God, has set you above your companions
by anointing[g] you with the oil of joy.[h]
8All your robes are fragrant[i] with myrrh and aloes and cassia;
from palaces adorned with ivory
the music of the strings makes you glad.
9Daughters of kings[j] are among your honoured women;
at your right hand[k] is the royal bride in gold of Ophir.

10Listen, O daughter, consider and give ear:
Forget your people[l] and your father's house.
11The king is enthralled by your beauty;
honour[m] him, for he is your lord.[n]
12The Daughter of Tyre will come with a gift,[b][o]
men of wealth will seek your favour.

13All glorious[p] is the princess within ⌊her chamber⌋;
her gown is interwoven with gold.
14In embroidered garments she is led to the king;[q]
her virgin companions follow her
and are brought to you.
15They are led in with joy and gladness;
they enter the palace of the king.

16Your sons will take the place of your fathers;
you will make them princes throughout the land.
17I will perpetuate your memory through all generations;[r]
therefore the nations will praise you[s] for ever and ever.

PSALM 46

For the director of music. Of the Sons of Korah. According to *alamoth*.[a] A song.

Theme: God is always there to help, providing refuge, security, and peace. God's power is complete and his ultimate victory is certain. He will not fail to rescue those who love him.
Authors: The sons of Korah (temple assistants)

1God is our refuge[a] and strength,
an ever-present[b] help in trouble.
2Therefore we will not fear,[c] though the earth give way[d]
and the mountains fall[e] into the heart of the sea,
3though its waters roar[f] and foam
and the mountains quake with their surging. *Selah*

b *12 Or A Tyrian robe is among the gifts* **a** Title: Probably a musical term

45:6 [e]Ps 93:2; 98:9
45:7 [f]Ps 33:5 [g]Isa 61:1 [h]Ps 21:6; Heb 1:8-9*
45:8 [i]SS 1:3
45:9 [j]SS 6:8 [k]1Ki 2:19
45:10 [l]Dt 21:13
45:11 [m]Ps 95:6 [n]Isa 54:5
45:12 [o]Ps 22:29; Isa 49:23
45:13 [p]Isa 61:10
45:14 [q]SS 1:4
45:17 [r]Mal 1:11 [s]Ps 138:4
46:1 [a]Ps 9:9; 14:6 [b]Dt 4:7
46:2 [c]Ps 23:4 [d]Ps 82:5 [e]Ps 18:7
46:3 [f]Ps 93:3

45:8, 9 Myrrh is a fragrant gum of an Arabian tree, generally used in perfumes. Aloes, a spice, may have come from sandalwood, a close-grained and fragrant wood often used for storage boxes or chests (see also Proverbs 7:14–17; Song of Songs 4:13, 14). Cassia was probably made from flowers of the cinnamon tree. These expensive fragrances were appropriate for a king's wedding. The location of Ophir is unknown, but believed to be in either Arabia or Africa. It was famous as a source of gold.

45:13–17 This beautiful section of poetry pictures Christ's bride, the church, with the richest blessings as she unites for ever with him (see Revelation 19:6–8; 21:2).

46–48 Psalms 46–48 are hymns of praise, celebrating deliverance from some great foe. Psalm 46 may have been written when the Assyrian army invaded the land and surrounded Jerusalem (2 Kings 18:13–19:37).

46:1–3 The fear of mountains or cities suddenly crumbling into the sea as the result of a nuclear blast haunts many people today. But the psalmist says that even if the world ends, we need not fear. In the face of utter destruction, the writer expressed a quiet confidence in God's ability to save him. It seems impossible to consider the end of the world without becoming consumed by fear, but the Bible is clear – God is our refuge even in the face of total destruction. He is not merely a temporary retreat; he is our eternal refuge and can provide strength in any circumstances.

46:4 [g] Ps 48:1, 8; Isa 60:14
46:5 [h] Isa 12:6; Eze 43:7 [i] Ps 37:40
46:6 [j] Ps 2:1 [k] Ps 68:32 [l] Mic 1:4
46:7 [m] 2Ch 13:12 [n] Ps 9:9
46:8 [o] Ps 66:5 [p] Isa 61:4
46:9 [q] Isa 2:4 [r] Ps 76:3 [s] Eze 39:9
46:10 [t] Ps 100:3 [u] Isa 2:11
47:1 [a] Ps 98:8; Isa 55:12 [b] Ps 106:47
47:2 [c] Dt 7:21

4There is a river whose streams make glad the city of God,[g]
the holy place where the Most High dwells.
5God is within her,[h] she will not fall;
God will help[i] her at break of day.
6Nations[j] are in uproar, kingdoms[k] fall;
he lifts his voice, the earth melts.[l]

7The LORD Almighty is with us;[m]
the God of Jacob is our fortress.[n] *Selah*

8Come and see the works of the LORD,[o]
the desolations[p] he has brought on the earth.
9He makes wars[q] cease to the ends of the earth;
he breaks the bow[r] and shatters the spear,
he burns the shields[b] with fire.[s]
10"Be still, and know that I am God;[t]
I will be exalted[u] among the nations,
I will be exalted in the earth."

11The LORD Almighty is with us;
the God of Jacob is our fortress. *Selah*

PSALM 47

For the director of music. Of the Sons of Korah. A psalm.

Theme: God is still King of the world. All nations of the earth will eventually recognise his lordship.
Authors: The sons of Korah (temple assistants)

1Clap your hands,[a] all you nations;
shout to God with cries of joy.[b]
2How awesome[c] is the LORD Most High,

[b] 9 Or *chariots*

PSALMS THAT HAVE INSPIRED HYMNS

Psalm 23	The King of Love My Shepherd Is My Shepherd Shall Supply My Need The Lord Is My Shepherd
Psalm 46	A Mighty Fortress Is Our God
Psalm 61	Hiding in Thee (O Safe to the Rock That Is Higher Than I . . .)
Psalm 87	Glorious Things of Thee Are Spoken
Psalm 90	O God, Our Help in Ages Past
Psalm 100	All People That on Earth Do Dwell Before Jehovah's Awful Throne
Psalm 103	Praise to the Lord, the Almighty
Psalm 104	O Worship the King, All Glorious Above
Psalm 126	Bringing in the Sheaves

46:4, 5 Many great cities have rivers flowing through them, sustaining people's lives by making agriculture possible and facilitating trade with other cities. Jerusalem had no river, but it had God who, like a river, sustained the people's lives. As long as God lived among the people, the city was invincible. But when the people abandoned him, God no longer protected them, and Jerusalem fell to the Babylonian army.

46:10 War and destruction are inevitable, but so is God's final victory. At that time, all will stand quietly before the Lord Almighty. How proper, then, for us to be still now, reverently honouring him and his power and majesty. Take time each day to be still and to exalt God.

47:1ff This psalm may have been written about the same event as Psalm 46—the Assyrian invasion of Judah by Sennacherib (2 Kings 18:13—19:37).

47:2 The Lord Most High is awesome beyond words, but this didn't keep Bible writers from trying to describe him. And it shouldn't keep us from talking about him either. We can't describe God completely, but we can tell others what he has done for us. Don't let the indescribable aspects of God's greatness prevent you from telling others what you know about him.

the great King[d] over all the earth!
3He subdued[e] nations under us,
peoples under our feet.
4He chose our inheritance[f] for us,
the pride of Jacob, whom he loved. *Selah*

5God has ascended amid shouts of joy,
the LORD amid the sounding of trumpets.[g]
6Sing praises[h] to God, sing praises;
sing praises to our King, sing praises.

7For God is the King of all the earth;[i]
sing to him a psalm[a][j] of praise.
8God reigns[k] over the nations;
God is seated on his holy throne.
9The nobles of the nations assemble
as the people of the God of Abraham,
for the kings[b] of the earth belong to God;[l]
he is greatly exalted.[m]

PSALM 48

A song. A psalm of the Sons of Korah.

Theme: God's presence is our joy, security, and salvation. God is praised as the defender of Jerusalem, the holy city of the Jews. He is also our defender and guide for ever.
Authors: The sons of Korah (temple assistants)

1Great is the LORD,[a] and most worthy of praise,
in the city of our God,[b] his holy mountain.[c]
2It is beautiful[d] in its loftiness,
the joy of the whole earth.
Like the utmost heights of Zaphon[a] is Mount Zion,
the[b] city of the Great King.[e]
3God is in her citadels;
he has shown himself to be her fortress.[f]

4When the kings joined forces,
when they advanced together,[g]
5they saw ⌊her⌋ and were astounded;
they fled in terror.[h]
6Trembling seized them there,
pain like that of a woman in labour.
7You destroyed them like ships of Tarshish
shattered by an east wind.[i]

8As we have heard,
so have we seen
in the city of the LORD Almighty,
in the city of our God:

a *7* Or *a maskil* (probably a literary or musical term) **b** *9* Or *shields* **a** *2* *Zaphon* can refer to a sacred mountain or the direction north. **b** *2* Or *earth, / Mount Zion, on the northern side / of the*

47:2 [d]Mal 1:14
47:3 [e]Ps 18:39, 47
47:4 [f]1Pe 1:4
47:5 [g]Ps 68:33; 98:6
47:6 [h]Ps 68:4; 89:18
47:7 [i]Zec 14:9 [j]Col 3:16
47:8 [k]1Ch 16:31
47:9 [l]Ps 72:11; 89:18 [m]Ps 97:9
48:1 [a]Ps 96:4 [b]Ps 46:4 [c]Isa 2:2-3; Mic 4:1; Zec 8:3
48:2 [d]Ps 50:2; La 2:15 [e]Mt 5:35
48:3 [f]Ps 46:7
48:4 [g]2Sa 10:1-19
48:5 [h]Ex 15:16
48:7 [i]Jer 18:17; Eze 27:26

47:9 Abraham was the father of the Israelite nation. The one true God was sometimes called the "God of Abraham" (Exodus 3:6; 1 Kings 18:36). In a spiritual sense, God's promises to Abraham apply to all who believe in God, Jew or Gentile (Romans 4:11, 12; Galatians 3:7–9). Thus the God of Abraham is our God too.

48:2 Why is Mount Zion – Jerusalem – "the city of the Great King"? Because the temple was located in Jerusalem, the city was seen as the centre of God's presence in the world. The Bible pictures Jerusalem as the place where believers will gather in the "last days" (Isaiah 2:2ff), and as the spiritual home of all believers where God will live among them (Revelation 21:2, 3).

48:8 Because Jerusalem has been destroyed several times since this psalm was written, the phrase, "God makes her secure for ever" may refer prophetically to the new Jerusalem where God will judge all nations and live with all believers (Revelation 21).

48:8 [j]Ps 87:5

God makes her secure for ever.[j] *Selah*

9Within your temple, O God,
we meditate on your unfailing love.[k]
10Like your name,[l] O God,
your praise reaches to the ends of the earth;[m]
your right hand is filled with righteousness.
11Mount Zion rejoices,
the villages of Judah are glad
because of your judgments.[n]

12Walk about Zion, go round her,
count her towers,
13consider well her ramparts,
view her citadels,[o]
that you may tell of them to the next generation.[p]
14For this God is our God for ever and ever;
he will be our guide[q] even to the end.

48:9 [k]Ps 26:3
48:10 [l]Dt 28:58; Jos 7:9 [m]Isa 41:10
48:11 [n]Ps 97:8
48:13 [o]ver 3; Ps 122:7 [p]Ps 78:6
48:14 [q]Ps 23:4

PSALM 49

For the director of music. Of the Sons of Korah. A psalm.

Theme: Trusting in worldly possessions is futile. You cannot take possessions with you when you die, and they cannot buy forgiveness from sin.
Authors: The sons of Korah (temple assistants)

1Hear this, all you peoples;[a]
listen, all who live in this world,[b]
2both low and high,
rich and poor alike:
3My mouth will speak words of wisdom;[c]
the utterance from my heart will give understanding.[d]
4I will turn my ear to a proverb;[e]
with the harp I will expound my riddle:[f]

5Why should I fear[g] when evil days come,
when wicked deceivers surround me—
6those who trust in their wealth[h]
and boast of their great riches?
7No man can redeem the life of another
or give to God a ransom for him—
8the ransom for a life is costly,

49:1 [a]Ps 78:1 [b]Ps 33:8
49:3 [c]Ps 37:30 [d]Ps 119:130
49:4 [e]Ps 78:2 [f]Nu 12:8
49:5 [g]Ps 23:4
49:6 [h]Job 31:24

48:11 The people of Judah were from Israel's largest tribe, which settled in the southern part of Canaan where Jerusalem was located (Joshua 15:1–12). David was from Judah, and he made Jerusalem his capital and the centre of the nation's worship. Jesus was also a member of the tribe of Judah. The psalmist was saying that the day would come when God would bring justice to the land, and God's people would get the respect they deserved.

48:12, 13 After an enemy army had unsuccessfully besieged Jerusalem, it was important for the people to make a tour of the city, inspecting its defences and praising God for the protection they had offered. In times of great joy or after God has brought us through some great trial, we ought to inspect our defences to make sure that the foundations—faith in God, knowledge of his word, and the fellowship and prayers of the body of believers—remain strong (Ephesians 2:20–22). Then we should praise God for his protection!

48:14 We often pray for God's guidance as we struggle with decisions. What we need is both guidance and a guide—a map that gives us landmarks and directions and a constant companion who has an intimate knowledge of the way and will make sure we interpret the map correctly. The Bible will be such a map, and the Holy Spirit will be the constant companion and guide. As you make your way through life, use both the map and your Guide.

49:1ff The futility of worldliness—riches, pride, fame—resounds from this psalm. Comparable in form to the book of Ecclesiastes, this psalm is one of the few written more to instruct than to give praise.

49:7, 8, 15 In the slave market of the ancient world, a slave had to be redeemed or ransomed (someone had to pay the price) in order to go free. In Mark 10:45, Ephesians 1:7, and Hebrews 9:12, we learn that Jesus paid such a price so that we could be set free from slavery to sin in order to begin a new life with him.

There is no way for a person to buy eternal life with God. God alone can redeem a soul. Don't count on wealth and physical comforts to keep you happy because you will never have enough wealth to keep from dying.

no payment is ever enough—[i]
9that he should live on[j] for ever
and not see decay.

10For all can see that wise men die;[k]
the foolish and the senseless alike perish
and leave their wealth to others.[l]
11Their tombs will remain their houses[a] for ever,
their dwellings for endless generations,
though they had[b] named[m] lands after themselves.

12But man, despite his riches, does not endure;
he is[c] like the beasts that perish.

13This is the fate of those who trust in themselves,[n]
and of their followers, who approve their sayings. *Selah*
14Like sheep they are destined for the grave,[d][o]
and death will feed on them.
The upright will rule[p] over them in the morning;
their forms will decay in the grave,[d]
far from their princely mansions.
15But God will redeem my life[e] from the grave;[q]
he will surely take me to himself.[r] *Selah*

16Do not be overawed when a man grows rich,
when the splendour of his house increases;
17for he will take nothing with him when he dies,
his splendour will not descend with him.[s]
18Though while he lived he counted himself blessed—[t]
and men praise you when you prosper—
19he will join the generation of his fathers,[u]
who will never see the light[v] ⌞of life⌟.

20A man who has riches without understanding
is like the beasts that perish.[w]

PSALM 50

A psalm of Asaph.

Theme: The contrast between true and false faith. God desires sincere thanks, trust, and praise.
Author: Asaph, one of David's chief musicians

1The Mighty One, God, the LORD,[a]
speaks and summons the earth

49:8 [i]Mt 16:26
49:9 [j]Ps 22:29; 89:48
49:10 [k]Ecc 2:16 [l]Ecc 2:18, 21
49:11 [m]Ge 4:17; Dt 3:14
49:13 [n]Lk 12:20
49:14 [o]Job 24:19; Ps 9:17 [p]Da 7:18; Mal 4:3; 1Co 6:2; Rev 2:26
49:15 [q]Ps 56:13; Hos 13:14 [r]Ps 73:24
49:17 [s]Ps 17:14; 1Ti 6:7
49:18 [t]Dt 29:19; Lk 12:19
49:19 [u]Ge 15:15 [v]Job 33:30
49:20 [w]Ecc 3:19
50:1 [a]Jos 22:22

a *11* Septuagint and Syriac; Hebrew *In their thoughts their houses will remain* b *11* Or */ for they have*
c *12* Hebrew; Septuagint and Syriac read verse 12 the same as verse 20. d *14* Hebrew *Sheol*; also in verse 15
e *15* Or *soul*

49:10–14 The rich and poor have one similarity – when they die, they leave all they own here on earth. At the moment of death (and all of us will face that moment), both rich and poor are naked and empty-handed before God. The only riches we have at that time are those we have already invested in our eternal heritage. At the time of death, each of us will wish we had invested less on earth, where we must leave it, and more in heaven, where we will retain it for ever. To have treasure in heaven, we must place our faith in God, pledge ourselves to obey him, and utilise our resources for the good of his kingdom. This is a good time to check up on your investments and see where you have invested the most. Then do whatever it takes to place your investments where they really count.

50:1ff God judges people for treating him lightly. First, he speaks to the superficially religious people who bring their sacrifices but are only going through the motions (50:1–15). They do not honour God with true praise and thankfulness. Second, he chides wicked, hardhearted people for their evil words and immoral lives (50:16–22). He asks the superficially religious for genuine thanksgiving and trust, and he warns the evil people to consider their deeds, lest he destroy them in his anger.

50:1–4 This psalm begins as though God is finally ready to judge the evil people on earth. But surprisingly, we read that God's great fury is levelled against his own people (or at least those who claim to be his). God's judgment must begin with his own people (1 Peter 4:17).

from the rising of the sun to the place where it sets.[b]
2From Zion, perfect in beauty,[c]
God shines forth.[d]
3Our God comes[e] and will not be silent;
a fire devours before him,[f]
and around him a tempest rages.
4He summons the heavens above,
and the earth,[g] that he may judge his people:
5"Gather to me my consecrated ones,[h]
who made a covenant[i] with me by sacrifice."
6And the heavens proclaim[j] his righteousness,
for God himself is judge.[k] *Selah*

7"Hear, O my people, and I will speak,
O Israel, and I will testify[l] against you:
I am God, your God.[m]
8I do not rebuke you for your sacrifices
or your burnt offerings,[n] which are ever before me.
9I have no need of a bull[o] from your stall
or of goats from your pens,
10for every animal of the forest is mine,
and the cattle on a thousand hills.[p]
11I know every bird in the mountains,
and the creatures of the field are mine.
12If I were hungry I would not tell you,
for the world[q] is mine, and all that is in it.
13Do I eat the flesh of bulls
or drink the blood of goats?
14Sacrifice thank-offerings[r] to God,
fulfil your vows[s] to the Most High,
15and call[t] upon me in the day of trouble;
I will deliver you, and you will honour[u] me."

16But to the wicked, God says:

"What right have you to recite my laws
or take my covenant on your lips?[v]
17You hate my instruction
and cast my words behind[w] you.
18When you see a thief, you join[x] with him;
you throw in your lot with adulterers.
19You use your mouth for evil
and harness your tongue to deceit.[y]
20You speak continually against your brother[z]
and slander your own mother's son.
21These things you have done and I kept silent;[a]
you thought I was altogether**a** like you.

a *21* Or *thought the 'I AM' was*

50:1 [b]Ps 113:3
50:2 [c]Ps 48:2 [d]Dt 33:2; Ps 80:1
50:3 [e]Ps 96:13 [f]Ps 97:3; Da 7:10
50:4 [g]Dt 4:26; Isa 1:2
50:5 [h]Ps 30:4 [i]Ex 24:7
50:6 [j]Ps 89:5 [k]Ps 75:7
50:7 [l]Ps 81:8 [m]Ex 20:2
50:8 [n]Ps 40:6; Hos 6:6
50:9 [o]Ps 69:31
50:10 [p]Ps 104:24
50:12 [q]Ex 19:5
50:14 [r]Heb 13:15 [s]Dt 23:21
50:15 [t]Ps 81:7 [u]Ps 22:23
50:16 [v]Isa 29:13
50:17 [w]Ne 9:26; Ro 2:21-22
50:18 [x]Ro 1:32; 1Ti 5:22
50:19 [y]Ps 10:7; 52:2
50:20 [z]Mt 10:21
50:21 [a]Ecc 8:11; Isa 42:14

50:5–9 God's perfect moral nature demands that the penalty for sin be death; however, a person could offer an animal to God as a substitute for himself, symbolising the person's faith in the merciful, forgiving God. But, the people were offering sacrifices and forgetting their significance! The very act of sacrifice showed that they had once agreed to follow God wholeheartedly. But at this time their hearts were not in it. We may fall into the same pattern when we participate in religious activities, tithe, or attend church out of habit or conformity rather than out of heartfelt love and obedience. God wants righteousness, not empty ritual. (See the note on 40:6.)

50:16–22 Some people glibly recite God's laws but are filled with deceit and evil. They claim his promises but refuse to obey him. This is sin, and God will judge people for it. We too are hypocrites when we are not what we claim to be. To let this inconsistency remain shows that we are not true followers of God.

50:21 At times God seems silent. By his silence he is not condoning sin, nor is he indifferent to it. Instead, he is withholding deserved punishment, giving time for people to repent (2 Peter 3:9). God takes no pleasure in the death of the wicked and wants them to turn from evil (Ezekiel 33:11). But his silence does not last for ever—a time of punishment will surely come.

But I will rebuke you
and accuse[b] you to your face.

22"Consider this, you who forget God,[c]
or I will tear you to pieces, with none to rescue:[d]
23He who sacrifices thank-offerings honours me,
and he prepares the way[e]
so that I may show him**b** the salvation of God.[f]"

50:21 [b]Ps 90:8

50:22 [c]Job 8:13; Ps 9:17 [d]Ps 7:2

50:23 [e]Ps 85:13 [f]Ps 91:16

PSALM 51

For the director of music. A psalm of David. When the prophet Nathan came to him after David had committed adultery with Bathsheba.

Theme: David's plea for mercy, forgiveness, and cleansing. God wants our hearts to be right with him.
Author: David

1Have mercy on me, O God,
according to your unfailing love;
according to your great compassion
blot out[a] my transgressions.[b]
2Wash away[c] all my iniquity
and cleanse[d] me from my sin.

3For I know my transgressions,
and my sin is always before me.[e]
4Against you, you only, have I sinned
and done what is evil in your sight,[f]
so that you are proved right when you speak
and justified when you judge.[g]
5Surely I was sinful[h] at birth,
sinful from the time my mother conceived me.
6Surely you desire truth in the inner parts;**a**
you teach**b** me wisdom[i] in the inmost place.[j]

7Cleanse me with hyssop,[k] and I shall be clean;
wash me, and I shall be whiter than snow.[l]
8Let me hear joy and gladness;[m]
let the bones you have crushed rejoice.
9Hide your face from my sins[n]
and blot out all my iniquity.

10Create in me a pure heart,[o] O God,

51:1 [a]Ac 3:19 [b]Isa 43:25; Col 2:14

51:2 [c]1Jn 1:9 [d]Heb 9:14

51:3 [e]Isa 59:12

51:4 [f]Ge 20:6; Lk 15:21 [g]Ro 3:4*

51:5 [h]Job 14:4

51:6 [i]Pr 2:6 [j]Ps 15:2

51:7 [k]Lev 14:4; Heb 9:19 [l]Isa 1:18

51:8 [m]Isa 35:10

51:9 [n]Jer 16:17

51:10 [o]Ps 78:37; Ac 15:9

b *23* Or *and to him who considers his way / I will show* **a** *6* The meaning of the Hebrew for this phrase is uncertain. **b** *6* Or *you desired . . . ; / you taught*

51:1–7 David was truly sorry for his adultery with Bathsheba and for murdering her husband to cover it up. He knew that his actions had hurt many people. But because David repented of those sins, God mercifully forgave him. No sin is too great to be forgiven! Do you feel that you could never come close to God because you have done something terrible? God can and will forgive you of any sin. While God forgives us, however, he does not always erase the natural consequences of our sin—David's life and family were never the same as a result of what he had done (see 2 Samuel 12:1–23).

51:4 Although David had sinned with Bathsheba, David said that he had sinned against God. When someone steals, murders, or slanders, it is against someone else—a victim. According to the world's standards, extramarital sex between two consenting adults is acceptable if nobody gets hurt. But people *do* get hurt—in David's case, a man was murdered, and a baby died. All sin hurts us and others, but ultimately it offends God because sin in any form is a rebellion against God's way of living. When tempted to do wrong, remember that you will be sinning against God. That may help you stay on the right track.

51:7 Hyssop branches were used by the Israelites in Egypt to place the blood of a lamb on the door frames of their homes. This would keep them safe from death (Exodus 12:22). This act demonstrated the Israelites' faith and secured their release from slavery in Egypt. This verse calls for cleansing from sin and readiness to serve the Lord.

51:10 Because we are born as sinners (51:5), our natural inclination is to please ourselves rather than God. David followed that in-

51:10 [p]Eze 18:31
51:11 [q]Eph 4:30
51:12 [r]Ps 13:5
51:13 [s]Ac 9:21-22 [t]Ps 22:27
51:14 [u]2Sa 12:9 [v]Ps 25:5 [w]Ps 35:28
51:15 [x]Ps 9:14
51:16 [y]1Sa 15:22; Ps 40:6
51:17 [z]Ps 34:18
51:18 [a]Ps 102:16; Isa 51:3
51:19 [b]Ps 4:5 [c]Ps 66:13 [d]Ps 66:15
52:Title [a]1Sa 22:9
52:1 [b]Ps 94:4
52:2 [c]Ps 57:4 [d]Ps 50:19

and renew a steadfast spirit within me.[p]
11 Do not cast me from your presence
or take your Holy Spirit[q] from me.
12 Restore to me the joy of your salvation[r]
and grant me a willing spirit, to sustain me.

13 Then I will teach transgressors your ways,[s]
and sinners will turn back to you.[t]
14 Save me from bloodguilt,[u] O God,
the God who saves me,[v]
and my tongue will sing of your righteousness.[w]
15 O Lord, open my lips,[x]
and my mouth will declare your praise.
16 You do not delight in sacrifice,[y] or I would bring it;
you do not take pleasure in burnt offerings.
17 The sacrifices of God are[c] a broken spirit;
a broken and contrite heart,[z]
O God, you will not despise.

18 In your good pleasure make Zion[a] prosper;
build up the walls of Jerusalem.
19 Then there will be righteous sacrifices,[b]
whole burnt offerings[c] to delight you;
then bulls[d] will be offered on your altar.

PSALM 52

For the director of music. A *maskil*[a] of David. When Doeg the Edomite[a] had gone to Saul and told him: "David has gone to the house of Ahimelech."

Theme: God will judge the evil-doer. Our anger must not block our confidence in God's ability to defeat evil.
Author: David

1 Why do you boast of evil, you mighty man?
Why do you boast[b] all day long,
you who are a disgrace in the eyes of God?
2 Your tongue plots destruction;
it is like a sharpened razor,[c]
you who practise deceit.[d]
3 You love evil rather than good,

[c] *17* Or *My sacrifice, O God, is* [a] Title: Probably a literary or musical term

clination when he took another man's wife. We also follow it when we sin in any way. Like David, we must ask God to cleanse us from within (51:7), clearing our hearts and spirits for new thoughts and desires. Right conduct can come only from a clean heart and spirit. Ask God to create a pure heart and spirit in you.

51:12 Do you ever feel stagnant in your faith, as though you are just going through the motions? Has sin ever driven a wedge between you and God, making him seem distant? David felt this way. He had sinned with Bathsheba and had just been confronted by Nathan the prophet. In his prayer he cried, "Restore to me the joy of your salvation." God wants us to be close to him and to experience his full and complete life. But sin that remains unconfessed makes such intimacy impossible. Confess your sin to God. You may still have to face some earthly consequences, as David did, but God will give back the joy of your relationship with him.

51:13 When God forgives our sin and restores us to a relationship with him, we want to reach out to others who need this forgiveness and reconciliation. The more you have felt God's forgiveness, the more you will desire to tell others about it.

51:17 God wants a broken spirit and a broken and contrite heart. You can never please God by outward actions – no matter how good – if your inward heart attitude is not right. Are you sorry for your sin? Do you genuinely intend to stop? God is pleased by this kind of humility.

52:1 This psalm was written about Doeg, the Edomite who had betrayed Ahimelech and David and then killed God's priests (see 1 Samuel 21:7; 22:9–23). Doeg thought he was a great hero – even boasting about his deed. In reality, his deed was evil, an offence to God. It is easy to equate "accomplishment" with goodness. Just because something is done well or thoroughly doesn't mean it is good (for example, someone may be a great gambler or a skilful liar). Measure all you do by the rule of God's word, not by how proficiently you do it.

falsehood[e] rather than speaking the truth. *Selah*
4 You love every harmful word,
O you deceitful tongue![f]

5 Surely God will bring you down to everlasting ruin:
He will snatch you up and tear[g] you from your tent;
he will uproot[h] you from the land of the living.[i] *Selah*
6 The righteous will see and fear;
they will laugh[j] at him, saying,
7 "Here now is the man
who did not make God his stronghold
but trusted in his great wealth[k]
and grew strong by destroying others!"

8 But I am like an olive tree[l]
flourishing in the house of God;
I trust[m] in God's unfailing love
for ever and ever.
9 I will praise you for ever[n] for what you have done;
in your name I will hope, for your name is good.[o]
I will praise you in the presence of your saints.

PSALM 53

For the director of music. According to *mahalath*.[a] A *maskil*[b] of David.

Theme: All have sinned. Because of sin, no person can find God on his own. Only God can save us.
Author: David

1 The fool[a] says in his heart,
"There is no God."[b]
They are corrupt, and their ways are vile;
there is no-one who does good.

2 God looks down from heaven[c]
on the sons of men
to see if there are any who understand,
any who seek God.[d]
3 Everyone has turned away,
they have together become corrupt;
there is no-one who does good,
not even one.[e]

4 Will the evildoers never learn—
those who devour my people as men eat bread
and who do not call on God?
5 There they were, overwhelmed with dread,
where there was nothing to dread.[f]
God scattered the bones[g] of those who attacked you;
you put them to shame, for God despised them.

a Title: Probably a musical term b Title: Probably a literary or musical term

52:3 e Jer 9:5
52:4 f Ps 120:2, 3
52:5 g Isa 22:19 h Pr 2:22 i Ps 27:13
52:6 j Job 22:19; Ps 37:34; 40:3
52:7 k Ps 49:6
52:8 l Jer 11:16 m Ps 13:5
52:9 n Ps 30:12 o Ps 54:6
53:1 a Ps 14:1-7; Ro 3:10 b Ps 10:4
53:2 c Ps 33:13 d 2Ch 15:2
53:3 e Ro 3:10-12*
53:5 f Lev 26:17 g Eze 6:5

52:8 With God by his side, David compared himself to an olive tree flourishing in the house of God. Not only is an olive tree one of the longest-living trees, but a flourishing tree has even greater longevity. David was contrasting God's eternal protection of his faithful servants with the sudden destruction of the wicked (52:5–7).

53:1 Echoing the message of Psalm 14, this psalm proclaims the foolishness of atheism (see also Romans 3:10). People may say there is no God in order to cover their sin, to have an excuse to continue in sin, and/or to ignore the Judge in order to avoid the judgment. A "fool" does not necessarily lack intelligence; many atheists and unbelievers are highly educated. Fools are people who reject God, the only one who can save them.

6Oh, that salvation for Israel would come out of Zion!
When God restores the fortunes of his people,
let Jacob rejoice and Israel be glad!

PSALM 54

For the director of music. With stringed instruments. A *maskil*[a] of David. When the Ziphites had gone to Saul and said, "Is not David hiding among us?"

Theme: A call for God to overcome enemies. God is our helper, even in times of hurt and betrayal.
Author: David

1Save me, O God, by your name;[a]
vindicate me by your might.[b]
2Hear my prayer, O God;[c]
listen to the words of my mouth.

3Strangers are attacking me;[d]
ruthless men seek my life[e]—
men without regard for God.[f] *Selah*

4Surely God is my help;[g]
the Lord is the one who sustains me.[h]

5Let evil recoil[i] on those who slander me;
in your faithfulness[j] destroy them.

6I will sacrifice a freewill offering[k] to you;
I will praise your name, O LORD,
for it is good.[l]
7For he has delivered me[m] from all my troubles,
and my eyes have looked in triumph on my foes.[n]

PSALM 55

For the director of music. With stringed instruments. A *maskil*[a] of David.

Theme: Expressing deep dismay over the treachery of a close friend. When friends hurt us, the burden is too difficult to carry alone.
Author: David

1Listen to my prayer, O God,
do not ignore my plea;[a]
2 hear me and answer me.[b]
My thoughts trouble me and I am distraught[c]
3 at the voice of the enemy,
at the stares of the wicked;
for they bring down suffering upon me[d]
and revile me in their anger.[e]

[a] Title: Probably a literary or musical term [a] Title: Probably a literary or musical term

54:1 [a]Ps 20:1 [b]2Ch 20:6
54:2 [c]Ps 5:1; 55:1
54:3 [d]Ps 86:14 [e]Ps 40:14 [f]Ps 36:1
54:4 [g]Ps 118:7 [h]Ps 41:12
54:5 [i]Ps 94:23 [j]Ps 89:49; 143:12
54:6 [k]Ps 50:14 [l]Ps 52:9
54:7 [m]Ps 34:6 [n]Ps 59:10
55:1 [a]Ps 27:9; 61:1
55:2 [b]Ps 66:19 [c]Ps 77:3; Isa 38:14
55:3 [d]2Sa 16:6-8; Ps 17:9 [e]Ps 71:11

54:3, 4 Many of David's psalms follow the pattern found in these two verses—a transition from prayer to praise. David was not afraid to come to God and express his true feelings and needs. Thus his spirit was lifted, and he praised God, his helper, protector, and friend.

54:5 David said that God repays evil to his enemies. Proverbs 26:27 warns that those who cause trouble will reap trouble. What we have intended for others may blow up in our own faces. To be honest and straightforward before God and others is simpler, easier, and safer in the long run.

55:1ff This psalm was most likely written during the time of Absalom's rebellion and Ahithophel's betrayal (2 Samuel 15—17). Some say verses 12–14 are Messianic because they also describe Judas' betrayal of Christ (Matthew 26:14–16, 20–25).

4My heart is in anguish within me;
the terrors[f] of death assail me.
5Fear and trembling[g] have beset me;
horror has overwhelmed me.
6I said, "Oh, that I had the wings of a dove!
I would fly away and be at rest—
7I would flee far away
and stay in the desert; *Selah*
8I would hurry to my place of shelter,
far from the tempest and storm.[h]"

9Confuse the wicked, O Lord, confound their speech,
for I see violence and strife[i] in the city.
10Day and night they prowl about on its walls;
malice and abuse are within it.
11Destructive forces[j] are at work in the city;
threats and lies[k] never leave its streets.

12If an enemy were insulting me,
I could endure it;
if a foe were raising himself against me,
I could hide from him.
13But it is you, a man like myself,
my companion, my close friend,[l]
14with whom I once enjoyed sweet fellowship
as we walked with the throng at the house of God.[m]

15Let death take my enemies by surprise;[n]
let them go down alive to the grave,[b][o]
for evil finds lodging among them.

16But I call to God,
and the LORD saves me.
17Evening,[p] morning[q] and noon
I cry out in distress,
and he hears my voice.
18He ransoms me unharmed
from the battle waged against me,
even though many oppose me.
19God, who is enthroned for ever,[r]
will hear[s] them and afflict them— *Selah*
men who never change their ways
and have no fear of God.

20My companion attacks his friends;[t]
he violates his covenant.[u]
21His speech is smooth as butter,
yet war is in his heart;

55:4 [f]Ps 116:3
55:5 [g]Job 21:6; Ps 119:120
55:8 [h]Isa 4:6
55:9 [i]Jer 6:7
55:11 [j]Ps 5:9 [k]Ps 10:7
55:13 [l]2Sa 15:12; Ps 41:9
55:14 [m]Ps 42:4
55:15 [n]Ps 64:7 [o]Nu 16:30, 33
55:17 [p]Ps 141:2; Ac 3:1 [q]Ps 5:3
55:19 [r]Dt 33:27 [s]Ps 78:59
55:20 [t]Ps 7:4 [u]Ps 89:34

[b] 15 Hebrew *Sheol*

55:6–8 Even those who are especially close to God, as David was, have moments when they want to escape from their problems and pressures.

55:9–11 The city that was supposed to be holy was plagued by internal problems: violence, strife, malice, abuse, destruction, threats, and lies. External enemies, though a constant threat, were not nearly as dangerous as the corruption inside. Even today, churches often look to defend themselves against troubles from the sinful world while failing to see that their own sins are causing their troubles.

55:12–14 Nothing hurts more than a wound from a friend. There may be times when friends will lovingly confront you in order to help you. Real friends stick by you in times of trouble and bring healing, love, acceptance, and understanding. What kind of friend are you? Don't betray those you love.

55:17 Praying evening, morning, and noon is certainly an excellent way to maintain correct priorities throughout every day. Daniel followed this pattern (Daniel 6:10), as did Peter (Acts 10:9, 10). The prayers of God's people are effective against the overwhelming evil in the world.

55:21 [v] Pr 5:3 [w] Ps 28:3; Ps 57:4; 59:7
55:22 [x] Ps 37:5; Mt 6:25-34; 1Pe 5:7 [y] Ps 37:24
55:23 [z] Ps 73:18 [a] Ps 5:6 [b] Job 15:32; Pr 10:27 [c] Ps 25:2

his words are more soothing than oil,[v]
yet they are drawn swords.[w]

22 Cast your cares on the LORD
and he will sustain you;[x]
he will never let the righteous fall.[y]
23 But you, O God, will bring down the wicked
into the pit[z] of corruption;
bloodthirsty and deceitful men[a]
will not live out half their days.[b]

But as for me, I trust in you.[c]

PSALM 56

For the director of music. To ⌊the tune of⌋ "A Dove on Distant Oaks". Of David. A *miktam*.[a] When the Philistines had seized him in Gath.

Theme: Trusting in God's care in the midst of fear. When all seems dark, one truth still shines bright: when God is for us, those against us will never succeed.
Author: David

56:1 [a] Ps 57:1-3
56:2 [b] Ps 57:3 [c] Ps 35:1
56:3 [d] Ps 55:4-5
56:4 [e] Ps 118:6; Heb 13:6
56:5 [f] Ps 41:7
56:6 [g] Ps 59:3 [h] Ps 71:10
56:7 [i] Ps 36:12; 55:23
56:8 [j] Mal 3:16
56:9 [k] Ps 9:3 [l] Ps 102:2 [m] Ro 8:31

1 Be merciful to me, O God, for men hotly pursue me;[a]
all day long they press their attack.
2 My slanderers pursue me all day long;[b]
many are attacking me in their pride.[c]

3 When I am afraid,[d]
I will trust in you.
4 In God, whose word I praise,
in God I trust; I will not be afraid.
What can mortal man do to me?[e]

5 All day long they twist my words;[f]
they are always plotting to harm me.
6 They conspire,[g] they lurk,
they watch my steps,
eager to take my life.[h]

7 On no account let them escape;
in your anger, O God, bring down the nations.[i]
8 Record my lament;
list my tears on your scroll[b] —
are they not in your record?[j]

9 Then my enemies will turn back[k]
when I call for help.[l]
By this I will know that God is for me.[m]

[a] Title: Probably a literary or musical term [b] *8* Or *I put my tears in your wineskin*

55:22 God wants us to cast our cares on him, but often we continue to bear them ourselves even when we say we are trusting in him. Trust the same strength that sustains you to carry your cares also.

56:1ff This was probably written on the same occasion as Psalm 34, when David fled from Saul to Philistine territory. He had to pretend insanity before Achish when some servants grew suspicious of him (1 Samuel 21:10–15).

56:3, 4 David stated, "What can mortal man do to me?" How much harm can people do to us? They can inflict pain, suffering, and death. But no person can rob us of our souls or our future beyond this life. How much harm can we do to ourselves? The worst thing we can do is to reject God and lose our eternal future. Jesus said, "Do not be afraid of those who kill the body but cannot kill the soul" (Matthew 10:28). Instead, we should fear God, who controls this life and the next.

56:8 Even in our deepest sorrow, God cares! Jesus reminded us further of how much God understands us – he knows even the number of hairs on our heads (Matthew 10:30). Often we waver between faith and fear. When you feel so discouraged that you are sure no-one understands, remember that God knows every problem and sees every tear.

10In God, whose word I praise,
in the LORD, whose word I praise—
11in God I trust; I will not be afraid.
What can man do to me?

12I am under vows[n] to you, O God;
I will present my thank-offerings to you.
13For you have delivered me[c] from death[o]
and my feet from stumbling,
that I may walk before God
in the light of life.[d][p]

56:12 [n]Ps 50:14
56:13 [o]Ps 116:8 [p]Job 33:30

PSALM 57

For the director of music. To the tune of "Do Not Destroy". Of David. A *miktam*.[a] When he had fled from Saul into the cave.

Theme: God's faithful help and love in times of trouble. When we face trials, God will quieten our hearts and give us confidence.
Author: David

1Have mercy on me, O God, have mercy on me,
for in you my soul takes refuge.[a]
I will take refuge in the shadow of your wings[b]
until the disaster has passed.[c]

2I cry out to God Most High,
to God, who fulfils his purpose for me.[d]
3He sends from heaven and saves me,[e]
rebuking those who hotly pursue me;[f] *Selah*
God sends his love and his faithfulness.[g]

4I am in the midst of lions;[h]
I lie among ravenous beasts—
men whose teeth are spears and arrows,
whose tongues are sharp swords.[i]

5Be exalted, O God, above the heavens;
let your glory be over all the earth.[j]

6They spread a net for my feet—
I was bowed down[k] in distress.
They dug a pit[l] in my path—
but they have fallen into it themselves.[m] *Selah*

7My heart is steadfast, O God,
my heart is steadfast;[n]
I will sing and make music.
8Awake, my soul!
Awake, harp and lyre![o]
I will awaken the dawn.

9I will praise you, O Lord, among the nations;
I will sing of you among the peoples.

c 13 Or *my soul* d 13 Or *the land of the living* a Title: Probably a literary or musical term

57:1 [a]Ps 2:12 [b]Ps 17:8 [c]Isa 26:20
57:2 [d]Ps 138:8
57:3 [e]Ps 18:9, 16 [f]Ps 56:1 [g]Ps 40:11
57:4 [h]Ps 35:17 [i]Ps 55:21; Pr 30:14
57:5 [j]Ps 108:5
57:6 [k]Ps 145:14 [l]Ps 35:7 [m]Ps 7:15; Pr 28:10
57:7 [n]Ps 108:1
57:8 [o]Ps 16:9; 30:12; 150:3

57:1ff This psalm was probably written when David was hiding in a cave from Saul (see 1 Samuel 22–24).

57:4 At times, we may be surrounded by people who gossip about us or criticise us. Verbal cruelty can damage us as badly as physical abuse. Rather than answering with hateful words, we, like David, can talk with God about the problem.

57:7 David's firm faith in God contrasted sharply with his enemies' loud lying and boasting. When confronted with verbal attacks, the best defence is simply to be quiet and praise God, realising that our confidence is in his love and faithfulness (57:10). In times of great suffering, don't turn inward to self-pity or outward to revenge, but upward to God.

57:10
[p] Ps 36:5; 103:11

57:11
[q] ver 5

10 For great is your love, reaching to the heavens;
your faithfulness reaches to the skies.[p]

11 Be exalted, O God, above the heavens;
let your glory be over all the earth.[q]

58:1
[a] Ps 82:2

58:2
[b] Ps 94:20; Mal 3:15

58:4
[c] Ps 140:3; Ecc 10:11

58:6
[d] Ps 3:7
[e] Job 4:10

58:7
[f] Jos 7:5; Ps 112:10
[g] Ps 64:3

58:8
[h] Job 3:16

58:9
[i] Ps 118:12
[j] Pr 10:25

58:10
[k] Ps 64:10; 91:8
[l] Ps 68:23

58:11
[m] Ps 9:8; 18:20

PSALM 58

For the director of music. ⌞To the tune of⌟ "Do Not Destroy".
Of David. A *miktam*.[a]

Theme: A prayer for God's justice. When no justice can be found, rejoice in knowing that justice will triumph because there is a God who will judge with complete fairness.
Author: David, at a time when men in authority were twisting justice

1 Do you rulers indeed speak justly?[a]
Do you judge uprightly among men?
2 No, in your heart you devise injustice,
and your hands mete out violence on the earth.[b]
3 Even from birth the wicked go astray;
from the womb they are wayward and speak lies.
4 Their venom is like the venom of a snake,[c]
like that of a cobra that has stopped its ears,
5 that will not heed the tune of the charmer,
however skilful the enchanter may be.

6 Break the teeth in their mouths, O God;[d]
tear out, O LORD, the fangs of the lions![e]
7 Let them vanish like water that flows away;[f]
when they draw the bow, let their arrows be blunted.[g]
8 Like a slug melting away as it moves along,
like a stillborn child,[h] may they not see the sun.

9 Before your pots can feel ⌞the heat of⌟ the thorns[i]—
whether they be green or dry—the wicked will be swept away.[b][j]
10 The righteous will be glad when they are avenged,[k]
when they bathe their feet in the blood of the wicked.[l]
11 Then men will say,
"Surely the righteous still are rewarded;
surely there is a God who judges the earth."[m]

a Title: Probably a literary or musical term b 9 The meaning of the Hebrew for this verse is uncertain.

58:1ff This is called an imprecatory psalm (see the note on 35:1ff). It is a cry for justice so intense that it seems, at first glance, to be a call for revenge.

58:1ff The Old Testament is filled with references to justice, and it is a key topic in the psalms. Unfortunately, many judges and rulers in ancient times took justice into their own hands. They had complete authority with no accountability and the power to make their own laws. When earth's judges are corrupt, there is little hope of justice in this life. But God loves justice, and those who obey him will experience perfect justice in eternity.

58:11 Of all people, our national leaders should be just and fair. When they are unjust and unfair, people suffer. The rich get richer, the poor get poorer, politicians wrest power from the people, national morality deteriorates, and God is ignored. When right triumphs at last, "the righteous will be glad" (58:10). Be assured that there will be a day of accountability and that God judges fairly. Be careful never to side with injustice, lest you find yourself standing before an angry Judge.

PSALM 59

For the director of music. To the tune of "Do Not Destroy". Of David. A *miktam*.[a] When Saul had sent men to watch David's house in order to kill him.

Theme: Prayer and praise for God's saving help.
God's constant love is our place of safety in a wicked world.
Author: David

1 Deliver me from my enemies, O God;[a]
protect me from those who rise up against me.
2 Deliver me from evildoers
and save me from bloodthirsty men.[b]

3 See how they lie in wait for me!
Fierce men conspire[c] against me
for no offence or sin of mine, O LORD.
4 I have done no wrong, yet they are ready to attack me.[d]
Arise to help me; look on my plight!
5 O LORD God Almighty, the God of Israel,
rouse yourself to punish all the nations;
show no mercy to wicked traitors.[e] *Selah*

6 They return at evening,
snarling like dogs,[f]
and prowl about the city.
7 See what they spew from their mouths —
they spew out swords[g] from their lips,
and they say, "Who can hear us?"[h]
8 But you, O LORD, laugh at them;[i]
you scoff at all those nations.[j]

9 O my Strength, I watch for you;
you, O God, are my fortress,[k] 10 my loving God.

God will go before me
and will let me gloat over those who slander me.
11 But do not kill them, O Lord our shield,[b][l]
or my people will forget.[m]
In your might make them wander about,
and bring them down.[n]
12 For the sins of their mouths,[o]
for the words of their lips,[p]
let them be caught in their pride.[q]
For the curses and lies they utter,
13 consume them in wrath,
consume them till they are no more.[r]
Then it will be known to the ends of the earth
that God rules over Jacob.[s] *Selah*

14 They return at evening,
snarling like dogs,

a Title: Probably a literary or musical term b *11* Or *sovereign*

59:1 [a]Ps 143:9
59:2 [b]Ps 139:19
59:3 [c]Ps 56:6
59:4 [d]Ps 35:19, 23
59:5 [e]Jer 18:23
59:6 [f]ver 14
59:7 [g]Ps 57:4 [h]Ps 10:11
59:8 [i]Ps 37:13; Pr 1:26 [j]Ps 2:4
59:9 [k]Ps 9:9; 62:2
59:11 [l]Ps 84:9 [m]Dt 4:9 [n]Ps 106:27
59:12 [o]Ps 10:7 [p]Pr 12:13 [q]Zep 3:11
59:13 [r]Ps 104:35 [s]Ps 83:18

59:7, 8 Vile men curse God as if he cannot hear and will not respond. But God scoffs at them. Evil people live as if God cannot see and will not punish. But God watches patiently until that day when their deeds will rise up to accuse them. As believers we must be careful not to follow the same foolish practices as evil people. We must remember that God hears and sees all we do.

59:10 David was hunted by those whose love had turned to jealousy, and this was driving them to try to murder him. Trusted friends, and even his son, had turned against him. What changeable love! But David knew that God's love for him was *changeless.* "His love endures for ever" (100:5). God's mercy to all who trust him is just as permanent as his mercy to David. When the love of others fails or disappoints us, we can rest in God's enduring love.

and prowl about the city.
15They wander about for food[t]
and howl if not satisfied.
16But I will sing of your strength,[u]
in the morning[v] I will sing of your love;[w]
for you are my fortress,
my refuge in times of trouble.[x]

17O my Strength, I sing praise to you;
you, O God, are my fortress, my loving God.

PSALM 60

For the director of music. To ⌊the tune of⌋ "The Lily of the Covenant". A *miktam*[a] of David. For teaching. When he fought Aram Naharaim[b] and Aram Zobah,[c] and when Joab returned and struck down twelve thousand Edomites in the Valley of Salt.

Theme: Real help comes from God alone. When a situation seems out of control, we can trust God to do mighty things.
Author: David, when Israel was away at war with Aram in the north, and Edom invaded Judah from the south (2 Samuel 8)

1You have rejected us,[a] O God, and burst forth upon us;
you have been angry[b]—now restore us![c]
2You have shaken the land[d] and torn it open;
mend its fractures,[e] for it is quaking.
3You have shown your people desperate times;[f]
you have given us wine that makes us stagger.[g]

4But for those who fear you, you have raised a banner
to be unfurled against the bow. *Selah*

5Save us and help us with your right hand,[h]
that those you love[i] may be delivered.
6God has spoken from his sanctuary:
"In triumph I will parcel out Shechem[j]
and measure off the Valley of Succoth.
7Gilead[k] is mine, and Manasseh is mine;
Ephraim is my helmet,
Judah[l] my sceptre.[m]
8Moab is my washbasin,
upon Edom I toss my sandal;
over Philistia I shout in triumph.[n]"

9Who will bring me to the fortified city?
Who will lead me to Edom?
10Is it not you, O God, you who have rejected us
and no longer go out with our armies?[o]

59:15 [t]Job 15:23
59:16 [u]Ps 21:13 [v]Ps 88:13 [w]Ps 101:1 [x]Ps 46:1
60:1 [a]2Sa 5:20; Ps 44:9 [b]Ps 79:5 [c]Ps 80:3
60:2 [d]Ps 18:7 [e]2Ch 7:14
60:3 [f]Ps 71:20 [g]Isa 51:17; Jer 25:16
60:5 [h]Ps 17:7; 108:6 [i]Ps 127:2
60:6 [j]Ge 12:6
60:7 [k]Jos 13:31 [l]Dt 33:17 [m]Ge 49:10
60:8 [n]2Sa 8:1
60:10 [o]Jos 7:12; Ps 44:9; 108:11

a Title: Probably a literary or musical term **b** Title: That is, Arameans of North-west Mesopotamia **c** Title: That is, Arameans of central Syria

60:1ff This psalm gives us information about David's reign not found in the books of 1 and 2 Samuel or 1 and 2 Chronicles. Although the setting of the psalm is found in 2 Samuel 8, that passage makes no reference to the fact that David's forces had met stiff resistance (60:1–3) and apparently even a temporary defeat (60:9, 10). The closer we get to God, the more our enemies will attack us because we threaten their evil and selfish way of living.

60:3 Instead of the wine of blessing God had given them the cup of his judgment. God's rejection was intended to bring them back to himself.

60:6–10 God said the cities and territories of Israel were his, and he knew the future of each of the nations. When the world seems out of control, we must remind ourselves that God owns the cities and knows the future of every nation. God is in control. In and through him we will gain the victory.

60:8 David mentioned the enemy nations that surrounded Israel. Moab lay directly to the east, Edom to the south, and Philistia to the west. At the time this psalm was written, David was fighting Aram to the north. Although he was surrounded by enemies, David believed that God would help him triumph.

11Give us aid against the enemy,
for the help of man is worthless.[p]
12With God we shall gain the victory,
and he will trample down our enemies.[q]

60:11 [p]Ps 146:3
60:12 [q]Nu 24:18; Ps 44:5

PSALM 61

For the director of music. With stringed instruments. Of David.

Theme: Prayer for security and assurance. Wherever we are, we can trust that God will be there to answer our cries for help.
Author: David, written when he was forced to escape during the days of Absalom's rebellion (2 Samuel 15—18), or after he had narrowly escaped one of Saul's efforts to kill him while hiding in the desert

1Hear my cry, O God;[a]
listen to my prayer.[b]

2From the ends of the earth I call to you,
I call as my heart grows faint;[c]
lead me to the rock[d] that is higher than I.
3For you have been my refuge,[e]
a strong tower against the foe.[f]

4I long to dwell[g] in your tent for ever
and take refuge in the shelter of your wings.[h] *Selah*
5For you have heard my vows,[i] O God;
you have given me the heritage of those who fear your name.[j]

6Increase the days of the king's life,
his years for many generations.[k]
7May he be enthroned in God's presence for ever;[l]
appoint your love and faithfulness to protect him.[m]

8Then will I ever sing praise to your name[n]
and fulfil my vows day after day.

61:1 [a]Ps 64:1 [b]Ps 86:6
61:2 [c]Ps 77:3 [d]Ps 18:2
61:3 [e]Ps 62:7 [f]Pr 18:10
61:4 [g]Ps 23:6 [h]Ps 91:4
61:5 [i]Ps 56:12 [j]Ps 86:11
61:6 [k]Ps 21:4
61:7 [l]Ps 41:12 [m]Ps 40:11
61:8 [n]Ps 65:1; 71:22

PSALM 62

For the director of music. For Jeduthun. A psalm of David.

Theme: Placing all hope in God. Knowing that God is in control allows us to wait patiently for him to rescue us. True relief does not come when the problem is resolved because more problems are on the way! True relief comes from an enduring hope in God's ultimate salvation. Only then will all trials be resolved.
Author: David, written during the days of Absalom's rebellion (2 Samuel 15—18)

1My soul finds rest[a] in God alone;
my salvation comes from him.
2He alone is my rock[b] and my salvation;
he is my fortress, I shall never be shaken.

3How long will you assault a man?

62:1 [a]Ps 33:20
62:2 [b]Ps 89:26

61:1, 2 David must have been far from home when he wrote this psalm. Fortunately, God is not limited to any geographic location. Even when we are among unknown people and surroundings, God never abandons us. A "higher" rock would be a plain of refuge and safety. God's all-surpassing strength is always with us.

61:8 David made a vow to praise God each day. David continually praised God through both the good and difficult times of his life. Do you find something to praise God for each day? As you do, you will find your heart elevated from daily distractions to lasting confidence.

62:3–6 David expressed his feelings to God and then reaffirmed his faith. Prayer can release our tensions in times of emotional stress. Trusting God to be our rock, salvation, and fortress (62:2) will change our entire outlook on life. No longer must we be held captive by resentment towards others when they hurt us. When we are resting in God's strength, nothing can shake us.

62:3
[c]Isa 30:13

Would all of you throw him down —
this leaning wall,[c] this tottering fence?
4They fully intend to topple him
from his lofty place;
they take delight in lies.
With their mouths they bless,
but in their hearts they curse.[d] *Selah*

62:4
[d]Ps 28:3

5Find rest, O my soul, in God alone;
my hope comes from him.
6He alone is my rock and my salvation;
he is my fortress, I shall not be shaken.
7My salvation and my honour depend on God;[a]
he is my mighty rock, my refuge.[e]
8Trust in him at all times, O people;
pour out your hearts to him,[f]
for God is our refuge. *Selah*

62:7
[e]Ps 46:1; 85:9;
Jer 3:23

62:8
[f]1Sa 1:15;
Ps 42:4;
La 2:19

9Lowborn men are but a breath,[g]
the highborn are but a lie;
if weighed on a balance,[h] they are nothing;
together they are only a breath.
10Do not trust in extortion
or take pride in stolen goods;[i]
though your riches increase,
do not set your heart on them.[j]

62:9
[g]Ps 39:5, 11
[h]Isa 40:15

11One thing God has spoken,
two things have I heard:
that you, O God, are strong,
12 and that you, O Lord, are loving.
Surely you will reward each person
according to what he has done.[k]

62:10
[i]Isa 61:8
[j]Job 31:25;
1Ti 6:6-10

PSALM 63

A psalm of David. When he was in the Desert of Judah.

62:12
[k]Job 34:11;
Mt 16:27

Theme: A desire for God's presence, provision, and protection. No matter where we are, our desire should be for God because only he satisfies fully.
Author: David

1O God, you are my God,
earnestly I seek you;
my soul thirsts for you,[a]
my body longs for you,
in a dry and weary land
where there is no water.

63:1
[a]Ps 42:2; 84:2

2I have seen you in the sanctuary[b]
and beheld your power and your glory.

63:2
[b]Ps 27:4

a 7 Or / *God Most High is my salvation and my honour*

62:9–12 It is tempting to use honour, power, wealth, or prestige to measure people. We may even think that such people are really getting ahead in life. But on God's scales, these people are a "breath", a puff of air. What, then, can tilt the scales when God weighs us? Trusting God and working for him (62:12). Wealth, honour, power, or prestige add nothing to our value in God's eyes, but the faithful work we do for him has eternal value.

63:1ff Psalms 61, 62, and 63 were probably written when David was seeking refuge during Absalom's rebellion (2 Samuel 15 — 18).

63:1–5 Hiding from his enemies in the barren Desert of Judah, David was intensely lonely. He longed for a friend he could trust to ease his loneliness. No wonder he cried out, "O God. . . my soul thirsts for you. . . in a dry and weary land." If you are lonely or thirsty for something lasting in your life, remember David's prayer. God alone can satisfy our deepest longings!

3Because your love is better than life,[c]
my lips will glorify you.
4I will praise you as long as I live,[d]
and in your name I will lift up my hands.[e]
5My soul will be satisfied as with the richest of foods;[f]
with singing lips my mouth will praise you.

6On my bed I remember you;
I think of you through the watches of the night.[g]
7Because you are my help,[h]
I sing in the shadow of your wings.
8My soul clings to you;
your right hand upholds me.[i]

9They who seek my life will be destroyed;[j]
they will go down to the depths of the earth.[k]
10They will be given over to the sword
and become food for jackals.

11But the king will rejoice in God;
all who swear by God's name will praise him,[l]
while the mouths of liars will be silenced.

PSALM 64

For the director of music. A psalm of David.

Theme: A complaint against conspiracy. When others conspire against us, we can ask God for protection because he knows everything.
Author: David

1Hear me, O God, as I voice my complaint;[a]
protect my life from the threat of the enemy.[b]
2Hide me from the conspiracy of the wicked,[c]
from that noisy crowd of evildoers.

3They sharpen their tongues like swords
and aim their words like deadly arrows.[d]
4They shoot from ambush at the innocent man;[e]
they shoot at him suddenly, without fear.[f]

5They encourage each other in evil plans,
they talk about hiding their snares;
they say, "Who will see them?"[a][g]
6They plot injustice and say,
"We have devised a perfect plan!"
Surely the mind and heart of man are cunning.

7But God will shoot them with arrows;

[a] 5 Or *us*

63:3 [c]Ps 69:16
63:4 [d]Ps 104:33 [e]Ps 28:2
63:5 [f]Ps 36:8
63:6 [g]Ps 42:8
63:7 [h]Ps 27:9
63:8 [i]Ps 18:35
63:9 [j]Ps 40:14 [k]Ps 55:15
63:11 [l]Dt 6:13; Ps 21:1; Isa 45:23
64:1 [a]Ps 55:2 [b]Ps 140:1
64:2 [c]Ps 56:6; 59:2
64:3 [d]Ps 58:7
64:4 [e]Ps 11:2 [f]Ps 55:19
64:5 [g]Ps 10:11

63:6 The night was divided into three watches. Someone aware of all three would be having a sleepless night. A cure for sleepless nights is to turn our thoughts to God. There are many reasons we can't sleep – illness, stress, worry – but sleepless nights can be turned into quiet times of reflection and worship. Use them to review how God has guided and helped you.

64:1ff Evil can come in the form of a secret conspiracy or an ambush because Satan wants to catch us unprepared. He tempts us in our weakest areas when we least expect it. But God himself will strike down our enemies (64:7), whether they are physical or spiritual. Wickedness is widespread and affects us in many ways, but the final victory already belongs to God and those who trust and believe in him.

64:1, 2 We may believe that God wants to hear only certain requests from us. While it is true that we should offer praise, confession, and respectful petitions, it is also true that God is willing to listen to *anything* we want to tell him. David expressed himself honestly, knowing that God would hear his voice. God will always listen to us, and he will fully understand what we say.

64:3–10 The words spoken against us are among the most painful attacks we may have to face. If we trust in God, these attacks will not hurt us.

64:8 [h]Ps 9:3; Pr 18:7 [i]Ps 22:7

suddenly they will be struck down.
8He will turn their own tongues against them[h]
and bring them to ruin;
all who see them will shake their heads[i] in scorn.

64:9 [j]Jer 51:10

9All mankind will fear;
they will proclaim the works of God
and ponder what he has done.[j]
10Let the righteous rejoice in the LORD
and take refuge in him;[k]
let all the upright in heart praise him![l]

64:10 [k]Ps 25:20 [l]Ps 32:11

PSALM 65

For the director of music. A psalm of David. A song.

65:1 [a]Ps 116:18

Theme: God provides abundantly. We can be thankful to God for his many blessings.
Author: David

65:2 [b]Isa 66:23

1Praise awaits**a** you, O God, in Zion;
to you our vows will be fulfilled.[a]
2O you who hear prayer,
to you all men will come.[b]
3When we were overwhelmed by sins,[c]
you forgave**b** our transgressions.[d]
4Blessed are those you choose[e]
and bring near to live in your courts!
We are filled with the good things of your house,[f]
of your holy temple.

65:3 [c]Ps 38:4 [d]Heb 9:14

65:4 [e]Ps 4:3; 33:12 [f]Ps 36:8

5You answer us with awesome deeds of righteousness,
O God our Saviour,[g]
the hope of all the ends of the earth
and of the farthest seas,[h]
6who formed the mountains by your power,
having armed yourself with strength,[i]
7who stilled the roaring of the seas,[j]
the roaring of their waves,
and the turmoil of the nations.[k]
8Those living far away fear your wonders;
where morning dawns and evening fades
you call forth songs of joy.

65:5 [g]Ps 85:4 [h]Ps 107:23

65:6 [i]Ps 93:1

65:7 [j]Mt 8:26 [k]Isa 17:12-13

9You care for the land and water it;[l]
you enrich it abundantly.
The streams of God are filled with water

65:9 [l]Ps 68:9-10

a *1* Or *befits*; the meaning of the Hebrew for this word is uncertain. **b** *3* Or *made atonement for*

65:1, 2 In Old Testament times, vows were taken seriously and fulfilled completely. No-one had to make a vow, but once made, it was binding (Deuteronomy 23:21–23). The vow that is being fulfilled here is the promise to praise God for his answers to prayer.

65:3 Although we may feel overwhelmed by the multitude of our sins, God will forgive them all if we ask sincerely. Do you feel as though God could never forgive you, that your sins are too many, or that some of them are too great? The good news is that God can and will forgive them all. Nobody is beyond redemption, and nobody is so full of sin that he or she cannot be made clean.

65:4 Access to God, the joy of living in the temple courts, was a great honour. God had chosen a special group of Israelites, the tribe of Levi, to serve as priests in the tabernacle (Numbers 3:5–51). They were the only ones who could enter the sacred rooms where God's presence resided. Because of Jesus' death on the cross, all believers today have personal access to God's presence everywhere and at any time.

65:6–13 This harvest psalm glorifies God the Creator as reflected in the beauty of nature. Nature helps us understand something of God's character. The Jews believed that God's care of nature was a sign of his love and provision for them. Nature shows God's generosity—giving us more than we need or deserve. Understanding God's abundant generosity should make us grateful to God and generous to others.

to provide the people with corn,[m]
for so you have ordained it.[c]
10 You drench its furrows
and level its ridges;
you soften it with showers
and bless its crops.
11 You crown the year with your bounty,
and your carts overflow with abundance.
12 The grasslands of the desert overflow;[n]
the hills are clothed with gladness.
13 The meadows are covered with flocks[o]
and the valleys are mantled with corn;[p]
they shout for joy and sing.[q]

PSALM 66

For the director of music. A song. A psalm.

Theme: God answers prayer. Individually and as a body of believers, we should praise and worship God.
Author: Anonymous, written after a great victory in battle

1 Shout with joy to God, all the earth![a]
2 Sing the glory of his name;[b]
make his praise glorious!
3 Say to God, "How awesome are your deeds![c]
So great is your power
that your enemies cringe[d] before you.
4 All the earth bows down[e] to you;
they sing praise[f] to you,
they sing praise to your name." *Selah*

5 Come and see what God has done,
how awesome his works[g] on man's behalf!
6 He turned the sea into dry land,[h]
they passed through the waters on foot—
come, let us rejoice in him.
7 He rules for ever[i] by his power,
his eyes watch[j] the nations—
let not the rebellious[k] rise up against him. *Selah*

8 Praise[l] our God, O peoples,
let the sound of his praise be heard;
9 he has preserved our lives
and kept our feet from slipping.[m]
10 For you, O God, tested us;
you refined us like silver.[n]
11 You brought us into prison
and laid burdens[o] on our backs.
12 You let men ride over our heads;[p]
we went through fire and water,
but you brought us to a place of abundance.[q]

c 9 Or *for that is how you prepare the land*

65:9 m Ps 46:4; 104:14
65:12 n Job 28:26
65:13 o Ps 144:13 p Ps 72:16 q Ps 98:8; Isa 55:12
66:1 a Ps 100:1
66:2 b Ps 79:9
66:3 c Ps 65:5 d Ps 18:44
66:4 e Ps 22:27 f Ps 67:3
66:5 g Ps 106:22
66:6 h Ex 14:22
66:7 i Ps 145:13 j Ps 11:4 k Ps 140:8
66:8 l Ps 98:4
66:9 m Ps 121:3
66:10 n Ps 17:3; Isa 48:10; Zec 13:9; 1Pe 1:6-7
66:11 o La 1:13
66:12 p Isa 51:23 q Isa 43:2

66:5–7 The writer was remembering the famous story about God's rescue of the Israelites by parting the Red Sea. God saved the Israelites then, and he continues to save his people today.

66:10–12 Just as fire refines silver in the smelting process, trials refine our character. They bring us a new and deeper wisdom, helping us discern truth from falsehood and giving us the discipline to do what we know is right. Above all, these trials help us realise that life is a gift from God to be cherished, not a right to be taken for granted.

13I will come to your temple with burnt offerings
and fulfil my vows[r] to you—
14vows my lips promised and my mouth spoke
when I was in trouble.
15I will sacrifice fat animals to you
and an offering of rams;
I will offer bulls and goats.[s] *Selah*

16Come and listen,[t] all you who fear God;
let me tell[u] you what he has done for me.
17I cried out to him with my mouth;
his praise was on my tongue.
18If I had cherished sin in my heart,
the Lord would not have listened;[v]
19but God has surely listened
and heard my voice[w] in prayer.
20Praise be to God,
who has not rejected[x] my prayer
or withheld his love from me!

PSALM 67

For the director of music. With stringed instruments. A psalm.
A song.

Theme: Joy comes from spreading the news about God around the world.
Author: Anonymous, possibly written for one of the harvest festivals

1May God be gracious to us and bless us
and make his face shine upon us,[a] *Selah*
2that your ways may be known on earth,
your salvation[b] among all nations.[c]

3May the peoples praise you, O God;
may all the peoples praise you.
4May the nations be glad and sing for joy,
for you rule the peoples justly[d]
and guide the nations of the earth. *Selah*
5May the peoples praise you, O God;
may all the peoples praise you.

6Then the land will yield its harvest,[e]
and God, our God, will bless us.
7God will bless us,
and all the ends of the earth will fear him.[f]

66:13 [r]Ecc 5:4
66:15 [s]Nu 6:14; Ps 51:19
66:16 [t]Ps 34:11 [u]Ps 71:15, 24
66:18 [v]Job 36:21; Isa 1:15; Jas 4:3
66:19 [w]Ps 116:1-2
66:20 [x]Ps 22:24; 68:35
67:1 [a]Nu 6:24-26; Ps 4:6
67:2 [b]Isa 52:10 [c]Tit 2:11
67:4 [d]Ps 96:10-13
67:6 [e]Lev 26:4; Ps 85:12; Eze 34:27
67:7 [f]Ps 33:8

66:13–15 People sometimes make bargains with God, saying, "If you heal me (or get me out of this mess), I'll obey you for the rest of my life." However, soon after they recover, the vow is forgotten and the old life-style is resumed. This writer made a promise to God, but he remembered the promise and was prepared to carry it out. God always keeps his promises and wants us to follow his example. Be careful to follow through on whatever you promise to do.

66:18 Our confession of sin must be continual because we continue to do wrong. But true confession requires us to listen to God and to want to stop doing what is wrong. David confessed his sin and prayed, "Forgive my hidden faults. Keep your servant also from wilful sins" (19:12, 13). When we *refuse* to repent or when we harbour and cherish certain sins, we place a wall between us and God. We may not be able to remember *every* sin we have ever committed, but our attitude should be one of confession and obedience.

67:2 Could the psalmist have looked across the years to see the gospel go throughout the earth? This psalm surely speaks of the fulfilment of the Great Commission (Matthew 28:18–20), when Jesus commanded that the gospel be taken to all nations. Count yourself among that great crowd of believers worldwide who know the Saviour; praise him for his Good News; and share that gospel so that the harvest will be abundant.

PSALM 68

For the director of music. Of David. A psalm. A song.

Theme: Remembering God's glory and power. Times and cultures change, but God is always majestically present as defender and provider.
Author: David

1May God arise, may his enemies be scattered;
may his foes flee[a] before him.
2As smoke[b] is blown away by the wind,
may you blow them away;
as wax melts[c] before the fire,
may the wicked perish before God.
3But may the righteous be glad
and rejoice[d] before God;
may they be happy and joyful.

4Sing to God, sing praise to his name,[e]
extol him who rides on the clouds[a][f]—
his name is the LORD[g]—
and rejoice before him.
5A father to the fatherless,[h] a defender of widows,[i]
is God in his holy dwelling.[j]
6God sets the lonely in families,[b][k]
he leads forth the prisoners[l] with singing;
but the rebellious live in a sun-scorched land.[m]

7When you went out[n] before your people, O God,
when you marched through the wasteland, *Selah*
8the earth shook,
the heavens poured down rain,[o]
before God, the One of Sinai,[p]
before God, the God of Israel.
9You gave abundant showers,[q] O God;
you refreshed your weary inheritance.
10Your people settled in it,
and from your bounty, O God, you provided[r] for the poor.

11The Lord announced the word,
and great was the company of those who proclaimed it:
12"Kings and armies flee[s] in haste;
in the camps men divide the plunder.
13Even while you sleep among the campfires,[c][t]
the wings of ⌊my⌋ dove are sheathed with silver,
its feathers with shining gold."

a *4* Or *I prepare the way for him who rides through the deserts* b *6* Or *the desolate in a homeland*
c *13* Or *saddlebags*

68:1 [a]Nu 10:35; Isa 33:3
68:2 [b]Hos 13:3 [c]Isa 9:18; Mic 1:4
68:3 [d]Ps 32:11
68:4 [e]Ps 66:2 [f]Dt 33:26 [g]Ex 6:3; Ps 83:18
68:5 [h]Ps 10:14 [i]Dt 10:18 [j]Dt 26:15
68:6 [k]Ps 113:9 [l]Ac 12:6 [m]Ps 107:34
68:7 [n]Ex 13:21; Jdg 4:14
68:8 [o]Jdg 5:4 [p]Ex 19:16, 18
68:9 [q]Dt 11:11
68:10 [r]Ps 74:19
68:12 [s]Jos 10:16
68:13 [t]Ge 49:14

68:1ff This psalm begins just like Moses' cry in Numbers 10:35 as the Israelites followed the ark of the covenant. It undoubtedly brought to mind the time when David led a joyous procession that brought the ark from the house of Obed-Edom to Jerusalem (2 Samuel 6:11–15).

68:3–6 With shouts of praise and the sound of trumpets, David and his people took the holy ark towards Mount Zion (2 Samuel 6:15). It was a time to sing praises to the Lord, whose presence brings great joy. Only in God is there hope for the orphans, widows, prisoners, and all other lonely people. If you are lonely or disadvantaged, join David in praise, and discover great joy from loving and praising God.

68:4–6 David praised God for his protection and provision. When we see God's true majesty, our response should be to praise him. This was a song of faith because many of these benefits had not yet come true in David's time. It should also be our song of faith. We must continue to trust God because, in time, he will fulfil all his promises.

68:8 Mount Sinai had a prominent role in Israelite history. It was at Mount Sinai that God met Moses and commissioned him to lead Israel out of Egypt (Exodus 3:1–10). It was to Mount Sinai that the nation of Israel returned and received God's laws (Exodus 19:1–3), and God's presence made the entire mountain tremble (Exodus 19:18). This sacred mountain was a constant reminder of God's words and promises.

68:13 The dove is a symbol of God's beloved Israel, who is so protected and blessed that it has taken silver and gold from its enemies, even though it stayed in camp.

14 When the Almighty[d] scattered[u] the kings in the land,
it was like snow fallen on Zalmon.

15 The mountains of Bashan are majestic mountains;
rugged are the mountains of Bashan.
16 Why gaze in envy, O rugged mountains,
at the mountain where God chooses[v] to reign,
where the LORD himself will dwell for ever?
17 The chariots of God are tens of thousands
and thousands of thousands;[w]
the Lord ⌞has come⌟ from Sinai into his sanctuary.
18 When you ascended on high,
you led captives[x] in your train;
you received gifts from men,[y]
even from[e] the rebellious—
that you,[f] O LORD God, might dwell there.

19 Praise be to the Lord, to God our Saviour,[z]
who daily bears our burdens.[a] *Selah*
20 Our God is a God who saves;
from the Sovereign LORD comes escape from death.[b]

21 Surely God will crush the heads[c] of his enemies,
the hairy crowns of those who go on in their sins.
22 The Lord says, "I will bring them from Bashan;
I will bring them from the depths of the sea,[d]
23 that you may plunge your feet in the blood of your foes,[e]
while the tongues of your dogs[f] have their share."

24 Your procession has come into view, O God,
the procession of my God and King into the sanctuary.[g]
25 In front are the singers, after them the musicians;
with them are the maidens playing tambourines.[h]
26 Praise God in the great congregation;
praise the LORD in the assembly of Israel.[i]
27 There is the little tribe[j] of Benjamin, leading them,
there the great throng of Judah's princes,
and there the princes of Zebulun and of Naphtali.

28 Summon your power, O God;[g]
show us your strength, O God, as you have done before.
29 Because of your temple at Jerusalem
kings will bring you gifts.[k]
30 Rebuke the beast among the reeds,
the herd of bulls[l] among the calves of the nations.
Humbled, may it bring bars of silver.
Scatter the nations[m] who delight in war.
31 Envoys will come from Egypt;[n]

68:14 [u] Jos 10:10
68:16 [v] Dt 12:5
68:17 [w] Dt 33:2; Da 7:10
68:18 [x] Jdg 5:12 [y] Eph 4:8*
68:19 [z] Ps 65:5 [a] Ps 55:22
68:20 [b] Ps 56:13
68:21 [c] Ps 110:5; Hab 3:13
68:22 [d] Nu 21:33
68:23 [e] Ps 58:10 [f] 1Ki 21:19
68:24 [g] Ps 63:2
68:25 [h] Jdg 11:34; 1Ch 13:8
68:26 [i] Ps 26:12; Isa 48:1
68:27 [j] 1Sa 9:21
68:29 [k] Ps 72:10
68:30 [l] Ps 22:12 [m] Ps 89:10
68:31 [n] Isa 19:19; 45:14

[d] *14* Hebrew *Shaddai* [e] *18* Or *gifts for men, / even* [f] *18* Or *they* [g] *28* Many Hebrew manuscripts, Septuagint and Syriac; most Hebrew manuscripts *Your God has summoned power for you*

68:15, 16 Bashan, the land northeast of Israel, was the home of mighty mountains, including Mount Hermon, the tallest and most awesome mountain in the region. God's choice of Mount Zion, a foothill by comparison, for the site of the temple led the psalmist to write poetically of the envy of the mountains of Bashan.

68:17 This psalm celebrates the final stages of a journey that began at Mount Sinai with the construction of the ark of the covenant and finally ended at Mount Zion (site of the sanctuary), the chosen dwelling place of God among his people. It may describe the moving of the ark of the covenant into Jerusalem.

68:18 This verse, quoted in Ephesians 4:8, is applied to the ministry of the ascended Christ. It celebrates his victory over evil. It assures all of us who believe in Christ that by trusting him, we can overcome evil.

68:19–21 God sets his people free and crushes his enemies. Salvation is freedom from sin and death. Those who refuse to turn to God will be crushed by sin and death. They will be trapped by the sin they loved and destroyed by the death they feared. How much better it will be for those who love God and fear the consequences of sin.

Cush[h] will submit herself to God.

32 Sing to God, O kingdoms of the earth,
sing praise to the Lord, *Selah*
33 to him who rides[o] the ancient skies above,
who thunders with mighty voice.[p]
34 Proclaim the power[q] of God,
whose majesty is over Israel,
whose power is in the skies.
35 You are awesome, O God, in your sanctuary;
the God of Israel gives power and strength to his people.[r]

Praise be to God![s]

PSALM 69

For the director of music. To ⌊the tune of⌋ "Lilies". Of David.

Theme: A cry of distress in a sea of trouble. We may have to suffer severely for our devotion to God, but that should cause us to look forward with joy to the day when evil and injustice will be gone for ever.
Author: David

1 Save me, O God,
for the waters have come up to my neck.[a]
2 I sink in the miry depths,[b]
where there is no foothold.
I have come into the deep waters;
the floods engulf me.
3 I am worn out calling for help;[c]
my throat is parched.
My eyes fail,[d]
looking for my God.
4 Those who hate me without reason[e]
outnumber the hairs of my head;
many are my enemies without cause,[f]
those who seek to destroy me.
I am forced to restore
what I did not steal.

5 You know my folly,[g] O God;
my guilt is not hidden from you.[h]

6 May those who hope in you
not be disgraced because of me,
O Lord, the LORD Almighty;
may those who seek you
not be put to shame because of me,

68:33 [o]Ps 18:10 [p]Ps 29:4
68:34 [q]Ps 29:1
68:35 [r]Ps 29:11 [s]Ps 66:20
69:1 [a]Jnh 2:5
69:2 [b]Ps 40:2
69:3 [c]Ps 6:6 [d]Ps 119:82; Isa 38:14
69:4 [e]Jn 15:25* [f]Ps 35:19; 38:19
69:5 [g]Ps 38:5 [h]Ps 44:21

h *31* That is, the upper Nile region

68:34, 35 When we consider all God has done for us, we should feel an overwhelming sense of awe as we kneel before the Lord in his sanctuary. Nature surrounds us with countless signs of God's wonderful power. His unlimited power and unspeakable majesty leave us breathless in his presence. How fortunate we are that God cares for us.

69:1ff This is one of the most quoted psalms in the New Testament, and it is often applied to the ministry and suffering of Jesus. Verse 4, like John 15:25, speaks of Jesus' many enemies. The experience of being scorned by his brothers (69:8) is expressed in John 7:5. Verse 9 portrays David's zeal for God; Christ showed great zeal when he threw the money changers out of the temple (John 2:14–17). Paul quoted part of 69:9 in Romans 15:3. Christ's great suffering is portrayed in 69:20, 21 (Matthew 27:24; Mark 15:23; Luke 23:36; John 19:28–30). Verses 22–28 are quoted in Romans 11:9, 10; and Peter applied 69:25 to Judas (Acts 1:20).

69:3 David cried out until he was physically exhausted, with a parched throat and blurred vision. Yet he still trusted God to save him. When devastated by death or tragedy, we need not collapse or despair because we can turn to God and ask him to save us and help us. The tears will still come, but we will not be crying in vain.

O God of Israel.
7For I endure scorn for your sake,[i]
and shame covers my face.[j]
8I am a stranger to my brothers,
an alien to my own mother's sons;[k]
9for zeal for your house consumes me,[l]
and the insults of those who insult you fall on me.[m]
10When I weep and fast,[n]
I must endure scorn;
11when I put on sackcloth,[o]
people make sport of me.
12Those who sit at the gate mock me,
and I am the song of the drunkards.[p]

13But I pray to you, O LORD,
in the time of your favour;[q]
in your great love,[r] O God,
answer me with your sure salvation.
14Rescue me from the mire,
do not let me sink;
deliver me from those who hate me,
from the deep waters.[s]
15Do not let the floodwaters[t] engulf me
or the depths swallow me up[u]
or the pit close its mouth over me.
16Answer me, O LORD, out of the goodness of your love;[v]
in your great mercy turn to me.
17Do not hide your face[w] from your servant;
answer me quickly, for I am in trouble.[x]
18Come near and rescue me;
redeem[y] me because of my foes.

19You know how I am scorned,[z] disgraced and shamed;
all my enemies are before you.
20Scorn has broken my heart
and has left me helpless;
I looked for sympathy, but there was none,
for comforters,[a] but I found none.[b]
21They put gall in my food
and gave me vinegar for my thirst.[c]

22May the table set before them become a snare;
may it become retribution and[a] a trap.
23May their eyes be darkened so that they cannot see,
and their backs be bent for ever.[d]
24Pour out your wrath[e] on them;
let your fierce anger overtake them.
25May their place be deserted;[f]
let there be no-one to dwell in their tents.[g]
26For they persecute those you wound
and talk about the pain of those you hurt.[h]
27Charge them with crime upon crime;[i]

69:7 [i]Jer 15:15 [j]Ps 44:15
69:8 [k]Ps 31:11; Isa 53:3
69:9 [l]Jn 2:17* [m]Ps 89:50-51; Ro 15:3
69:10 [n]Ps 35:13
69:11 [o]Ps 35:13
69:12 [p]Job 30:9
69:13 [q]Isa 49:8; 2Co 6:2 [r]Ps 51:1
69:14 [s]ver 2; Ps 144:7
69:15 [t]Ps 124:4-5 [u]Nu 16:33
69:16 [v]Ps 63:3
69:17 [w]Ps 27:9 [x]Ps 66:14
69:18 [y]Ps 49:15
69:19 [z]Ps 22:6
69:20 [a]Job 16:2 [b]Isa 63:5
69:21 [c]Mt 27:34; Mk 15:23; Jn 19:28-30
69:23 [d]Isa 6:9-10; Ro 11:9-10*
69:24 [e]Ps 79:6
69:25 [f]Mt 23:38 [g]Ac 1:20*
69:26 [h]Isa 53:4; Zec 1:15
69:27 [i]Ne 4:5

a *22* Or *snare / and their fellowship become*

69:13 What problems David faced! He was scoffed at, mocked, insulted, humiliated, and made the object of city-wide gossip. But still he prayed. When we are completely beaten down, we are tempted to turn from God, give up, and stop trusting him. When your situation seems hopeless, determine that no matter how bad things become you will continue to pray. God will hear your prayer, and he will rescue you. When others reject us, we need God most. Don't turn from your most faithful friend.

do not let them share in your salvation.[j]
28 May they be blotted out of the book of life[k]
and not be listed with the righteous.[l]

29 I am in pain and distress;
may your salvation, O God, protect me.[m]

30 I will praise God's name in song[n]
and glorify him[o] with thanksgiving.
31 This will please the LORD more than an ox,
more than a bull with its horns and hoofs.[p]
32 The poor will see and be glad[q]—
you who seek God, may your hearts live![r]
33 The LORD hears the needy[s]
and does not despise his captive people.

34 Let heaven and earth praise him,
the seas and all that move in them,[t]
35 for God will save Zion[u]
and rebuild the cities of Judah.[v]
Then people will settle there and possess it;
36 the children of his servants will inherit it,
and those who love his name will dwell there.[w]

69:27 [j]Ps 109:14; Isa 26:10
69:28 [k]Ex 32:32-33; Lk 10:20; Php 4:3 [l]Eze 13:9
69:29 [m]Ps 59:1; 70:5
69:30 [n]Ps 28:7 [o]Ps 34:3
69:31 [p]Ps 50:9-13
69:32 [q]Ps 34:2 [r]Ps 22:26
69:33 [s]Ps 12:5; 68:6
69:34 [t]Ps 96:11; 148:1; Isa 44:23; 49:13; 55:12
69:35 [u]Ob 1:17 [v]Ps 51:18; Isa 44:26
69:36 [w]Ps 37:29; 102:28

PSALM 70

For the director of music. Of David. A petition.

Theme: An urgent prayer for help. It can be your prayer when you're short on time and long on need.
Author: David

1 Hasten, O God, to save me;
O LORD, come quickly to help me.[a]
2 May those who seek my life[b]
be put to shame and confusion;
may all who desire my ruin
be turned back in disgrace.[c]
3 May those who say to me, "Aha! Aha!"
turn back because of their shame.
4 But may all who seek you
rejoice and be glad in you;
may those who love your salvation always say,
"Let God be exalted!"

5 Yet I am poor and needy;[d]
come quickly to me,[e] O God.

70:1 [a]Ps 40:13
70:2 [b]Ps 35:4 [c]Ps 35:26
70:5 [d]Ps 40:17 [e]Ps 141:1

69:28 The book of life is God's list of those who are in right relationship with him and who remain faithful (1:3; 7:9; 11:7; 34:12; 37:17, 29; 55:22; 75:10; 92:12–14; 140:13). The New Testament use of "book of life" indicates those who will receive eternal life (see Philippians 4:3; Revelation 3:5; 13:8; 20:15).

69:32 When David says, "May your hearts live!" he means, "You will feel glad and joyful." Most people want lasting joy and will try almost anything to obtain it, from scrambling for more money to being involved in sexual escapades. The only genuine source of happiness is God, and we receive lasting joy only by seeking him. How are you trying to find happiness? Seek God and live as he directs you (Matthew 6:33, 34), and true joy will soon follow.

70:1–5 When others disappoint and threaten us, we feel empty, as though a vital part of ourselves has been stolen. When others break the trust we have placed in them, they also break our spirits. At those empty, broken moments, we must join the psalmist in begging God to rush to our aid. He alone can fill our lives with his joy (70:4). With the psalmist we should cry out, "O LORD, do not delay!"

70:4 This short psalm (similar in content to 40:13–17) was David's plea for God to come quickly with his help. Yet even in his moment of panic, he did not forget praise. Praise is important because it helps us remember who God is. Often our prayers are filled with requests for ourselves and others, and we forget to thank God for what he has done and to worship him for who he is. Don't take God for granted and treat him as a vending machine. Even when David was afraid, he praised God.

71:1 [a]Ps 25:2-3; 31:1
71:2 [b]Ps 17:6
71:3 [c]Ps 18:2; 31:2-3; 44:4
71:4 [d]Ps 140:4
71:5 [e]Job 4:6; Jer 17:7
71:6 [f]Ps 22:10 [g]Ps 22:9; Isa 46:3 [h]Ps 9:1; 34:1; 52:9; 119:164; 145:2
71:7 [i]Isa 8:18; 1Co 4:9 [j]2Sa 22:3; Ps 61:3
71:8 [k]Ps 51:15; 63:5 [l]Ps 35:28; 96:6; 104:1
71:9 [m]Ps 51:11 [n]ver 18; Ps 92:14; Isa 46:4
71:10 [o]Ps 10:8; 59:3; Pr 1:18 [p]Ps 31:13; 56:6; Mt 12:14
71:11 [q]Ps 7:2
71:12 [r]Ps 35:22; 38:21 [s]Ps 38:22; 70:1
71:13 [t]ver 24
71:14 [u]Ps 130:7
71:15 [v]Ps 35:28; 40:5
71:16 [w]Ps 106:2
71:17 [x]Dt 4:5 [y]Ps 26:7

You are my help and my deliverer;
O LORD, do not delay.

PSALM 71

Theme: God's constant help—from childhood to old age. Our lives are a testimony of what God has done for us.
Author: Anonymous

1 In you, O LORD, I have taken refuge;
let me never be put to shame.[a]
2 Rescue me and deliver me in your righteousness;
turn your ear[b] to me and save me.
3 Be my rock of refuge,
to which I can always go;
give the command to save me,
for you are my rock and my fortress.[c]
4 Deliver me, O my God, from the hand of the wicked,[d]
from the grasp of evil and cruel men.

5 For you have been my hope, O Sovereign LORD,
my confidence[e] since my youth.
6 From my birth[f] I have relied on you;
you brought me forth from my mother's womb.[g]
I will ever praise[h] you.
7 I have become like a portent[i] to many,
but you are my strong refuge.[j]
8 My mouth[k] is filled with your praise,
declaring your splendour[l] all day long.

9 Do not cast[m] me away when I am old;[n]
do not forsake me when my strength is gone.
10 For my enemies speak against me;
those who wait to kill[o] me conspire[p] together.
11 They say, "God has forsaken him;
pursue him and seize him,
for no-one will rescue[q] him."
12 Be not far[r] from me, O God;
come quickly, O my God, to help[s] me.
13 May my accusers perish in shame;
may those who want to harm me
be covered with scorn and disgrace.[t]

14 But as for me, I shall always have hope;[u]
I will praise you more and more.
15 My mouth will tell[v] of your righteousness,
of your salvation all day long,
though I know not its measure.
16 I will come and proclaim your mighty acts,[w] O Sovereign LORD;
I will proclaim your righteousness, yours alone.
17 Since my youth, O God, you have taught[x] me,
and to this day I declare your marvellous deeds.[y]

71:1ff The psalmist was old and saw his life as a "portent", a solemn sign or testimony to others of all God had done for him (71:7, 18). Remembering God's lifetime of blessing will help us see the consistency of his grace throughout the years, trust him for the future, and share with others the benefits of following him.

71:14 As we face the sunset years, we recognise that God has been our constant help in the past. As physical powers wane, we need God even more, and we realise he is still our constant help. We must never despair, but keep on expecting his help no matter how severe our limitations. Hope in him helps us to keep going, to keep serving him.

18Even when I am old and grey,[z]
do not forsake me, O God,
till I declare your power to the next generation,
your might to all who are to come.[a]

19Your righteousness reaches to the skies,[b] O God,
you who have done great things.[c]
Who, O God, is like you?[d]
20Though you have made me see troubles,[e] many and bitter,
you will restore[f] my life again;
from the depths of the earth
you will again bring me up.
21You will increase my honour[g]
and comfort[h] me once again.

22I will praise you with the harp[i]
for your faithfulness, O my God;
I will sing praise to you with the lyre,[j]
O Holy One of Israel.[k]
23My lips will shout for joy
when I sing praise to you—
I, whom you have redeemed.[l]
24My tongue will tell of your righteous acts
all day long,[m]
for those who wanted to harm me[n]
have been put to shame and confusion.

PSALM 72

Of Solomon.

Theme: The perfect king. In this psalm, a king asks God to help his son rule the nation justly and wisely. It looks forward to the endless reign of the Messiah, who alone can rule with perfect justice and whose citizens will enjoy perfect peace.
Author: Solomon

1Endow the king with your justice, O God,
the royal son with your righteousness.
2He will**a** judge your people in righteousness,[a]
your afflicted ones with justice.
3The mountains will bring prosperity to the people,
the hills the fruit of righteousness.
4He will defend the afflicted among the people
and save the children of the needy;[b]
he will crush the oppressor.

5He will endure**b** as long as the sun,
as long as the moon, through all generations.
6He will be like rain[c] falling on a mown field,
like showers watering the earth.

a *2* Or *May he*; similarly in verses 3–11 and 17 **b** *5* Septuagint; Hebrew *You will be feared*

71:18 [z]ver 9 [a]Ps 22:30, 31; 78:4
71:19 [b]Ps 36:5; 57:10 [c]Ps 126:2; Lk 1:49 [d]Ps 35:10
71:20 [e]Ps 60:3 [f]Hos 6:2
71:21 [g]Ps 18:35 [h]Ps 23:4; 86:17; Isa 12:1; 49:13
71:22 [i]Ps 33:2 [j]Ps 92:3; 144:9 [k]2Ki 19:22
71:23 [l]Ps 103:4
71:24 [m]Ps 35:28 [n]ver 13
72:2 [a]Isa 9:7; 11:4-5; 32:1
72:4 [b]Isa 11:4
72:6 [c]Dt 32:2; Hos 6:3

71:18 A person is never too old to serve God, never too old to pray. Though age may stop us from certain physical activities, it need not end our desire to tell others (especially children) about all we have seen God do in the many years we've lived.

72:1, 2 What qualities do we want most in our leaders? God desires all who rule under him to be righteous and just. Think how the

72:7
[d]Ps 92:12; Isa 2:4

7In his days the righteous will flourish;[d]
prosperity will abound till the moon is no more.

8He will rule from sea to sea
and from the River[c][e] to the ends of the earth.[d][f]
9The desert tribes will bow before him
and his enemies will lick the dust.
10The kings of Tarshish and of distant shores
will bring tribute to him;
the kings of Sheba[g] and Seba
will present him gifts.[h]
11All kings will bow down to him
and all nations will serve him.

12For he will deliver the needy who cry out,
the afflicted who have no-one to help.
13He will take pity on the weak and the needy
and save the needy from death.
14He will rescue[i] them from oppression and violence,
for precious[j] is their blood in his sight.

15Long may he live!
May gold from Sheba[k] be given to him.
May people ever pray for him
and bless him all day long.
16Let corn abound throughout the land;
on the tops of the hills may it sway.
Let its fruit flourish like Lebanon;[l]
let it thrive like the grass of the field.
17May his name endure for ever;[m]
may it continue as long as the sun.[n]

All nations will be blessed through him,
and they will call him blessed.[o]

18Praise be to the LORD God, the God of Israel,[p]
who alone does marvellous deeds.[q]
19Praise be to his glorious name for ever;
may the whole earth be filled with his glory.[r]
Amen and Amen.[s]

20This concludes the prayers of David son of Jesse.

72:8
[e]Ex 23:31
[f]Zec 9:10

72:10
[g]Ge 10:7
[h]2Ch 9:24

72:14
[i]Ps 69:18
[j]1Sa 26:21; Ps 116:15

72:15
[k]Isa 60:6

72:16
[l]Ps 104:16

72:17
[m]Ex 3:15
[n]Ps 89:36
[o]Ge 12:3; Lk 1:48

72:18
[p]1Ch 29:10; Ps 41:13; 106:48
[q]Job 5:9

72:19
[r]Nu 14:21; Ne 9:5
[s]Ps 41:13

[c] *8* That is, the Euphrates [d] *8* Or *the end of the land*

world would change if world leaders would commit themselves to these two qualities. Let us pray that they will (see 1 Timothy 2:1, 2).

72:12–14 God cares for the needy, the afflicted, and the weak because they are precious to him. If God feels so strongly about these needy ones and loves them so deeply, how can we ignore their plight? Examine what you are doing to reach out with God's love – are you ignoring their plight or are you meeting their needs?

72:17 Solomon, David's son, reigned in Israel's golden age. He built the magnificent temple, and the land rested in peace. This psalm, though written by Solomon, looks beyond Solomon's reign to that of Jesus the Messiah, whose kingdom extends "to the ends of the earth" (72:8) and is greater than any human empire. This will be fulfilled when Christ returns to reign for ever (Revelation 11:15). When we anticipate his worldwide rule, it fills our hearts with hope.

72:19, 20 Book II ends with "Amen and Amen", as did Psalm 41, which closed Book I. This last verse does not mean that David wrote this psalm, but that he wrote most of the psalms in Book II.

BOOK III
PSALMS 73:1 – 89:52

These psalms celebrate the sovereignty of God, God's hand in history, God's faithfulness, and God's covenant with David. These psalms remind us that our worship of the almighty God should be continual.

PSALM 73

A psalm of Asaph.

Theme: The temporary prosperity of the wicked and the lasting rewards of the righteous. We should live holy lives and trust God for our future rewards.
Author: Asaph, a leader of one of the temple choirs (see 1 Chronicles 25:1)

1 Surely God is good to Israel,
to those who are pure in heart.[a]

2 But as for me, my feet had almost slipped;
I had nearly lost my foothold.
3 For I envied[b] the arrogant
when I saw the prosperity of the wicked.[c]

4 They have no struggles;
their bodies are healthy and strong.[a]
5 They are free[d] from the burdens common to man;
they are not plagued by human ills.
6 Therefore pride is their necklace;[e]
they clothe themselves with violence.[f]
7 From their callous hearts[g] comes iniquity;[b]
the evil conceits of their minds know no limits.
8 They scoff, and speak with malice;
in their arrogance[h] they threaten oppression.
9 Their mouths lay claim to heaven,
and their tongues take possession of the earth.
10 Therefore their people turn to them
and drink up waters in abundance.[c]
11 They say, "How can God know?
Does the Most High have knowledge?"

12 This is what the wicked are like –
always carefree, they increase in wealth.[i]

13 Surely in vain[j] have I kept my heart pure;
in vain have I washed my hands in innocence.[k]
14 All day long I have been plagued;
I have been punished every morning.

15 If I had said, "I will speak thus,"
I would have betrayed your children.
16 When I tried to understand[l] all this,
it was oppressive to me

73:1 [a]Mt 5:8
73:3 [b]Ps 37:1; Pr 23:17 [c]Job 21:7; Jer 12:1
73:5 [d]Job 21:9
73:6 [e]Ge 41:42 [f]Ps 109:18
73:7 [g]Ps 17:10
73:8 [h]Ps 17:10; Jude 16
73:12 [i]Ps 49:6
73:13 [j]Job 21:15; 34:9 [k]Ps 26:6
73:16 [l]Ecc 8:17

a *4* With a different word division of the Hebrew; Masoretic Text *struggles at their death; / their bodies are healthy* **b** *7* Syriac (see also Septuagint); Hebrew *Their eyes bulge with fat* **c** *10* The meaning of the Hebrew for this verse is uncertain.

73:1ff Asaph was the leader of one of David's Levitical choirs. He collected Psalms 73 – 83 but may not have written all of them. In this psalm, Asaph explains that until he entered God's sanctuary, he could not understand the justice in allowing the wicked to thrive while the righteous endured hardship. But when he saw that one day justice would be done, he acknowledged God's wisdom.

73:1-20 Two strong themes wind their way through these verses: (1) the wicked prosper, leaving faithful people wondering why they bother to be good, and (2) the wealth of the wicked looks so inviting that faithful people may wish they could trade places. But these two themes come to unexpected ends, for the wealth of the wicked suddenly loses its power at death and the rewards for the good suddenly take on eternal value. What seemed like wealth is now waste, and what seemed worthless now lasts for ever. Don't wish you could trade places with evil people to get their wealth. One day they will wish they could trade places with you and have your eternal wealth.

73:17
[m] Ps 77:13
[n] Ps 37:38

[17]till I entered the sanctuary[m] of God;
then I understood their final destiny.[n]

[18]Surely you place them on slippery ground;[o]
you cast them down to ruin.
[19]How suddenly[p] are they destroyed,
completely swept away by terrors!
[20]As a dream[q] when one awakes,[r]
so when you arise, O Lord,
you will despise them as fantasies.

[21]When my heart was grieved
and my spirit embittered,
[22]I was senseless[s] and ignorant;
I was a brute beast[t] before you.

[23]Yet I am always with you;
you hold me by my right hand.
[24]You guide[u] me with your counsel,[v]
and afterwards you will take me into glory.
[25]Whom have I in heaven but you?
And earth has nothing I desire besides you.[w]
[26]My flesh and my heart[x] may fail,[y]
but God is the strength of my heart
and my portion for ever.

[27]Those who are far from you will perish;[z]
you destroy all who are unfaithful to you.
[28]But as for me, it is good to be near God.[a]
I have made the Sovereign LORD my refuge;
I will tell of all your deeds.[b]

73:18
[o] Ps 35:6
73:19
[p] Isa 47:11
73:20
[q] Job 20:8
[r] Ps 78:65
73:22
[s] Ps 49:10; 92:6
[t] Ecc 3:18
73:24
[u] Ps 48:14
[v] Ps 32:8
73:25
[w] Php 3:8
73:26
[x] Ps 84:2
[y] Ps 40:12
73:27
[z] Ps 119:155
73:28
[a] Heb 10:22; Jas 4:8
[b] Ps 40:5

PSALM 74

A *maskil*[a] of Asaph.

Theme: A plea for God to help his people defend his cause and remember his promises. When we feel devastated or forgotten, we can plead with God for help, knowing that he hears.
Author: Asaph (or one of his descendants, since many believe this to be written after Jerusalem's fall in 586 B.C.)

[1]Why have you rejected us for ever,[a] O God?
Why does your anger smoulder against the sheep of your
pasture?[b]
[2]Remember the people you purchased[c] of old,[d]
the tribe of your inheritance, whom you redeemed[e]—
Mount Zion, where you dwelt.[f]
[3]Turn your steps towards these everlasting ruins,

74:1
[a] Dt 29:20; Ps 44:23
[b] Ps 79:13; 95:7; 100:3
74:2
[c] Ex 15:16
[d] Dt 32:7
[e] Ex 15:13
[f] Ps 68:16

a Title: Probably a literary or musical term

73:20 Asaph realised that the rich who put their hope, joy, and confidence in their wealth live in a dreamworld. A dream exists only in the mind of the dreamer. Don't let your life's goals be so unreal that you awaken too late and miss the reality of God's truth. Happiness and hope can be a reality, but only when they are based on God, not on riches. Because reality is in God, we should get as close to him as we can in order to be realistic about life.

73:23, 24 Asaph declares his confidence in God's presence and guidance. From birth to death God has us continually in his grip. But far more, we have the hope of the resurrection. Though our courage and strength may fail, we know that one day we will be raised to life to serve him for ever. He is our security, and we must cling to him.

74:1, 2 God's anger against Israel had grown hot during the many years of their sin and idolatry. His patience endured for generations, but at last it was set aside for judgment. If you fall into sin and quickly seek God's forgiveness, his mercy may come quickly and his anger may leave quickly. If you persist in sinning against him, don't be surprised when his patience runs out.

all this destruction the enemy has brought on the sanctuary.
4 Your foes roared[g] in the place where you met with us;
they set up their standards[h] as signs.
5 They behaved like men wielding axes
to cut through a thicket of trees.[i]
6 They smashed all the carved[j] panelling
with their axes and hatchets.
7 They burned your sanctuary to the ground;
they defiled the dwelling-place of your Name.
8 They said in their hearts, "We will crush[k] them completely!"
They burned every place where God was worshipped in the land.
9 We are given no miraculous signs;
no prophets[l] are left,
and none of us knows how long this will be.

10 How long will the enemy mock you, O God?
Will the foe revile[m] your name for ever?
11 Why do you hold back your hand, your right hand?[n]
Take it from the folds of your garment and destroy them!

12 But you, O God, are my king[o] from of old;
you bring salvation upon the earth.
13 It was you who split open the sea[p] by your power;
you broke the heads of the monster[q] in the waters.
14 It was you who crushed the heads of Leviathan
and gave him as food to the creatures of the desert.
15 It was you who opened up springs[r] and streams;
you dried up[s] the ever-flowing rivers.
16 The day is yours, and yours also the night;
you established the sun and moon.[t]
17 It was you who set all the boundaries[u] of the earth;
you made both summer and winter.[v]

18 Remember how the enemy has mocked you, O LORD,
how foolish people[w] have reviled your name.
19 Do not hand over the life of your dove to wild beasts;
do not forget the lives of your afflicted[x] people for ever.
20 Have regard for your covenant,[y]
because haunts of violence fill the dark places of the land.
21 Do not let the oppressed[z] retreat in disgrace;
may the poor and needy[a] praise your name.

22 Rise up, O God, and defend your cause;
remember how fools[b] mock you all day long.
23 Do not ignore the clamour of your adversaries,[c]
the uproar of your enemies, which rises continually.

74:4 [g]La 2:7 [h]Nu 2:2
74:5 [i]Jer 46:22
74:6 [j]1Ki 6:18
74:8 [k]Ps 83:4
74:9 [l]1Sa 3:1
74:10 [m]Ps 44:16
74:11 [n]La 2:3
74:12 [o]Ps 44:4
74:13 [p]Ex 14:21 [q]Isa 51:9; Eze 29:3
74:15 [r]Ex 17:6; Nu 20:11 [s]Jos 2:10; 3:13
74:16 [t]Ge 1:16; Ps 136:7-9
74:17 [u]Dt 32:8; Ac 17:26 [v]Ge 8:22
74:18 [w]Dt 32:6; Ps 39:8
74:19 [x]Ps 9:18
74:20 [y]Ge 17:7; Ps 106:45
74:21 [z]Ps 103:6 [a]Ps 35:10
74:22 [b]Ps 53:1
74:23 [c]Ps 65:7

74:8 When enemy armies defeated Israel, they sacked and burned Jerusalem, trying to wipe out every trace of God. This has often been the response of people who hate God. Today many are trying to erase God from traditions in our society and from subjects taught in our schools. Do what you can to maintain a Christian influence, but don't become discouraged when others appear to make great strides in eliminating all traces of God – they cannot eliminate his presence among believers.

74:10–18 From our perspective, God sometimes seems slow to intervene on our behalf. But what might appear slow to us is good timing from God's perspective. It's easy to become impatient while waiting for God to act, but we must never give up on him. When God is silent and you are in deep anguish, follow the method in this psalm. Review the great acts of God throughout biblical history; then review what he has done for you. This will remind you that God is at work, not only in history, but also in your life today.

74:13, 14 "The monster in the waters" recalls the Lord's words to Egypt (Ezekiel 32:2ff). "Leviathan" refers to the Canaanite seven-headed serpent, Lotan. In their legends, Baal defeated these creatures. This psalm praised God for doing in reality what the Canaanite gods could only do in legends.

75:1
[a]Ps 145:18
[b]Ps 44:1; 71:16

PSALM 75

For the director of music. ⌞To the tune of⌟ "Do Not Destroy". A psalm of Asaph. A song.

Theme: Because God is the final judge, the tables will be turned upon the wicked. When arrogant people threaten our security, we can be confident that God will ultimately overrule and destroy them.
Author: Asaph

75:3
[c]Isa 24:19
[d]1Sa 2:8

1 We give thanks to you, O God,
we give thanks, for your Name is near;[a]
men tell of your wonderful deeds.[b]

75:4
[e]Zec 1:21

2 You say, "I choose the appointed time;
it is I who judge uprightly.
3 When the earth and all its people quake,[c]
it is I who hold its pillars[d] firm. *Selah*
4 To the arrogant I say, 'Boast no more,'
and to the wicked, 'Do not lift up your horns.[e]
5 Do not lift your horns against heaven;
do not speak with outstretched neck.' "

75:7
[f]Ps 50:6
[g]1Sa 2:7; Ps 147:6; Da 2:21

6 No-one from the east or the west
or from the desert can exalt a man.
7 But it is God who judges:[f]
He brings one down, he exalts another.[g]
8 In the hand of the LORD is a cup
full of foaming wine mixed[h] with spices;
he pours it out, and all the wicked of the earth
drink it down to its very dregs.[i]

75:8
[h]Pr 23:30
[i]Job 21:20; Jer 25:15

9 As for me, I will declare[j] this for ever;
I will sing praise to the God of Jacob.
10 I will cut off the horns of all the wicked,
but the horns of the righteous shall be lifted up.[k]

75:9
[j]Ps 40:10

75:10
[k]Ps 89:17; 92:10; 148:14

PSALM 76

For the director of music. With stringed instruments. A psalm of Asaph. A song.

Theme: A call for God to punish evil-doers. Even man's angry revolt will be used by God to bring glory to himself.
Author: Asaph

76:2
[a]Ge 14:18

1 In Judah God is known;
his name is great in Israel.
2 His tent is in Salem,[a]
his dwelling-place in Zion.
3 There he broke the flashing arrows,
the shields and the swords, the weapons of war.[b] *Selah*

76:3
[b]Ps 46:9

75:2 God will act when he is ready. Children have difficulty grasping the concept of time. "It's not time yet" is not a reason they easily understand because they only comprehend the present. As limited human beings, we can't understand God's perspective about time. We want everything now, unaware that God's timing is better. When God is ready, he will do what needs to be done, not what we would like him to do. We may be as impatient as children, but we must not doubt the wisdom of God's timing. Wait for God to reveal his plan. Don't take matters into your own hands.

75:8 The cup of wine represents God's judgment. The judgment of God is coming against the wicked. God will pour out his fury on his enemies, and they will be forced to drink it. Drinking the cup of God's judgment is a picture used frequently in Scripture (Isaiah 51:17, 22; Jeremiah 25:15; 49:12; Habakkuk 2:16; Revelation 14:10; 16:19; 18:6). It gives the impression of taking a dose of one's own medicine. To drink it down to the dregs means to be punished completely.

76:1ff This psalm praises God for his awesome power. It was most likely written to celebrate the defeat of Sennacherib's army after he invaded Judah (see 2 Kings 18:13–19, 37).

4 You are resplendent with light,
more majestic than mountains rich with game.
5 Valiant men lie plundered,
they sleep their last sleep;[c]
not one of the warriors
can lift his hands.
6 At your rebuke, O God of Jacob,
both horse and chariot[d] lie still.
7 You alone are to be feared.[e]
Who can stand[f] before you when you are angry?[g]
8 From heaven you pronounced judgment,
and the land feared[h] and was quiet—
9 when you, O God, rose up to judge,[i]
to save all the afflicted of the land. *Selah*
10 Surely your wrath against men brings you praise,[j]
and the survivors of your wrath are restrained.[a]

11 Make vows to the LORD your God and fulfil them;[k]
let all the neighbouring lands
bring gifts[l] to the One to be feared.
12 He breaks the spirit of rulers;
he is feared by the kings of the earth.

PSALM 77

For the director of music. For Jeduthun. Of Asaph. A psalm.

Theme: We are comforted through the hard times by remembering God's help in the past. Recalling God's miracles and previous works can give us courage to continue.
Author: Asaph

1 I cried out to God[a] for help;
I cried out to God to hear me.
2 When I was in distress,[b] I sought the Lord;
at night I stretched out untiring hands[c]
and my soul refused to be comforted.[d]

3 I remembered you, O God, and I groaned;
I mused, and my spirit grew faint.[e] *Selah*
4 You kept my eyes from closing;
I was too troubled to speak.
5 I thought about the former days,[f]
the years of long ago;
6 I remembered my songs in the night.
My heart mused and my spirit enquired:

7 "Will the Lord reject for ever?
Will he never show his favour[g] again?
8 Has his unfailing love vanished for ever?

a *10* Or *Surely the wrath of men brings you praise, / and with the remainder of wrath you arm yourself*

76:5 [c]Ps 13:3
76:6 [d]Ex 15:1
76:7 [e]1Ch 16:25 [f]Ezr 9:15; Rev 6:17 [g]Ps 2:5; Na 1:6
76:8 [h]1Ch 16:30; 2Ch 20:29-30
76:9 [i]Ps 9:8
76:10 [j]Ex 9:16; Ro 9:17
76:11 [k]Ps 50:14; Ecc 5:4-5 [l]2Ch 32:23; Ps 68:29
77:1 [a]Ps 3:4
77:2 [b]Ps 50:15; Isa 26:9, 16 [c]Job 11:13 [d]Ge 37:35
77:3 [e]Ps 143:4
77:5 [f]Dt 32:7; Ps 44:1; 143:5; Isa 51:9
77:7 [g]Ps 85:1

76:10 How can wrath bring praise to God? Hostility to God and his people gives God the opportunity to do great deeds. For example, the Pharaoh of Egypt refused to free the Hebrew slaves (Exodus 5:1, 2) and thus allowed God to work mighty miracles for his people (Exodus 11:9). God turns the tables on evildoers and brings glory to himself from the foolishness of those who deny him or revolt against him. God's wrath expressed in judgment brings praise from those who have been delivered.

77:1–12 Asaph cried out to God for courage during a time of deep distress. The source of Asaph's distress (77:4) was his doubt (77:7–9). He pleaded, "I cried out to God for help." But in 77:13–20, the "I" is gone. As Asaph expressed his requests to God, his focus changed from thinking of himself to worshipping God: "You are the God who performs miracles" (77:14). Only after he put aside his doubts about God's holiness and care for him (77:13, 14) did he eliminate his distress (77:20). As we pray to God, he shifts our focus from ourselves to him.

Has his promise[h] failed for all time?
9Has God forgotten to be merciful?[i]
Has he in anger withheld his compassion?[j]" *Selah*

10Then I thought, "To this I will appeal:
the years of the right hand[k] of the Most High."
11I will remember the deeds of the LORD;
yes, I will remember your miracles[l] of long ago.
12I will meditate on all your works
and consider all your mighty deeds.

13Your ways, O God, are holy.
What god is so great as our God?[m]
14You are the God who performs miracles;
you display your power among the peoples.
15With your mighty arm you redeemed your people,[n]
the descendants of Jacob and Joseph. *Selah*

16The waters[o] saw you, O God,
the waters saw you and writhed;[p]
the very depths were convulsed.
17The clouds poured down water,[q]
the skies resounded with thunder;
your arrows flashed back and forth.
18Your thunder was heard in the whirlwind,
your lightning lit up the world;
the earth trembled and quaked.[r]
19Your path led through the sea,[s]
your way through the mighty waters,
though your footprints were not seen.

20You led your people[t] like a flock[u]
by the hand of Moses and Aaron.

PSALM 78

A *maskil*[a] of Asaph.

Theme: Lessons from history. Asaph retells the history of the Jewish nation from the time of slavery in Egypt to David's reign. It was told over and over to each generation so they would not forget God and make the same mistakes as their ancestors.
Author: Asaph

1O my people, hear my teaching;[a]
listen to the words of my mouth.
2I will open my mouth in parables,[b]
I will utter hidden things, things from of old—
3what we have heard and known,
what our fathers have told us.[c]
4We will not hide them from their children;[d]

[a] Title: Probably a literary or musical term

77:8 [h] 2Pe 3:9
77:9 [i] Ps 25:6; 40:11; 51:1 [j] Isa 49:15
77:10 [k] Ps 31:22
77:11 [l] Ps 143:5
77:13 [m] Ex 15:11; Ps 71:19; 86:8
77:15 [n] Ex 6:6; Dt 9:29
77:16 [o] Ex 14:21, 28; Hab 3:8 [p] Ps 114:4; Hab 3:10
77:17 [q] Jdg 5:4
77:18 [r] Jdg 5:4
77:19 [s] Hab 3:15
77:20 [t] Ex 13:21 [u] Ps 78:52; Isa 63:11
78:1 [a] Isa 51:4; 55:3
78:2 [b] Ps 49:4; Mt 13:35*
78:3 [c] Ps 44:1
78:4 [d] Dt 11:19

77:11, 12 Memories of God's miracles and faithfulness sustained Israel through their difficulties. They knew that God was capable and trustworthy. When you meet new trials, review how good God has been to you, and this will strengthen your faith.

77:16 This statement refers to the miraculous parting of the Red Sea. This great event is mentioned many times in the Old Testament (Exodus 14:21, 22; Joshua 24:6; Nehemiah 9:9; Psalm 74:13; 106:9; 136:13–15). The story of this incredible miracle was handed down from generation to generation, reminding the Israelites of God's power, protection, and love.

78:1ff The people of Israel rebelled and were not faithful to God (78:8); forgot about the wonders God had done (78:11, 12); put God to the test by making demands on him (78:18); lied to him and tried to flatter him (78:36); and continued to turn away from him even after he did great works on their behalf (78:42–56). This is recorded in God's word so that we can avoid the same errors. In 1 Corinthians 10:5–12, Paul used this classic story of Israel's unfaithfulness to warn the early Christians to be faithful.

we will tell the next generation
the praiseworthy deeds[e] of the LORD,
his power, and the wonders he has done.
5He decreed statutes[f] for Jacob[g]
and established the law in Israel,
which he commanded our forefathers
to teach their children,
6so that the next generation would know them,
even the children yet to be born,[h]
and they in turn would tell their children.
7Then they would put their trust in God
and would not forget[i] his deeds
but would keep his commands.[j]
8They would not be like their forefathers[k]—
a stubborn[l] and rebellious[m] generation,
whose hearts were not loyal to God,
whose spirits were not faithful to him.

9The men of Ephraim, though armed with bows,[n]
turned back on the day of battle;[o]
10they did not keep God's covenant[p]
and refused to live by his law.
11They forgot what he had done,[q]
the wonders he had shown them.
12He did miracles[r] in the sight of their fathers
in the land of Egypt,[s] in the region of Zoan.[t]
13He divided the sea[u] and led them through;
he made the water stand firm like a wall.[v]
14He guided them with the cloud by day
and with light from the fire all night.[w]
15He split the rocks[x] in the desert
and gave them water as abundant as the seas;
16he brought streams out of a rocky crag
and made water flow down like rivers.

17But they continued to sin[y] against him,
rebelling in the desert against the Most High.
18They wilfully put God to the test[z]
by demanding the food they craved.[a]
19They spoke against God,[b] saying,
"Can God spread a table in the desert?
20When he struck the rock, water gushed out,[c]
and streams flowed abundantly.
But can he also give us food?
Can he supply meat[d] for his people?"
21When the LORD heard them, he was very angry;
his fire broke out[e] against Jacob,
and his wrath rose against Israel,

78:4 [e]Ps 26:7; 71:17
78:5 [f]Ps 19:7; 81:5 [g]Ps 147:19
78:6 [h]Ps 22:31; 102:18
78:7 [i]Dt 6:12 [j]Dt 5:29
78:8 [k]2Ch 30:7 [l]Ex 32:9 [m]ver 37; Isa 30:9
78:9 [n]ver 57; 1Ch 12:2 [o]Jdg 20:39
78:10 [p]2Ki 17:15
78:11 [q]Ps 106:13
78:12 [r]Ps 106:22 [s]Ex 7-12 [t]Nu 13:22
78:13 [u]Ex 14:21; Ps 136:13 [v]Ex 15:8
78:14 [w]Ex 13:21; Ps 105:39
78:15 [x]Nu 20:11; 1Co 10:4
78:17 [y]Dt 9:22; Isa 63:10; Heb 3:16
78:18 [z]1Co 10:9 [a]Ex 16:2; Nu 11:4
78:19 [b]Nu 21:5
78:20 [c]Nu 20:11 [d]Nu 11:18
78:21 [e]Nu 11:1

78:5 God commanded that the stories of his mighty acts in Israel's history and his laws be passed on from parents to children. This shows the purpose and importance of religious education—to help each generation obey God and set their hope on him. It is important to keep children from repeating the same mistakes as their ancestors. What are you doing to pass on the history of God's work to the next generation?

78:9, 10 Ephraim was the most prominent tribe of Israel from the days of Moses to Saul's time. The tabernacle was set up in its territory. There is no other biblical record of Ephraim's soldiers turning back from battle, so this is probably a metaphor referring to Ephraim's failure to provide strong leadership during those years. When David became king, the tribe of Judah gained prominence. Because of David's faith and obedience, God chose Jerusalem in Judah to be the place for the new temple and rejected Ephraim (78:67). This caused tension between the two tribes. This psalm may have been written because of that tension in order to demonstrate once again why God chose Judah. God works through those who are faithful to him.

22 for they did not believe in God
or trust[f] in his deliverance.
23 Yet he gave a command to the skies above
and opened the doors of the heavens;[g]
24 he rained down manna[h] for the people to eat,
he gave them the grain of heaven.
25 Men ate the bread of angels;
he sent them all the food they could eat.
26 He let loose the east wind[i] from the heavens
and led forth the south wind by his power.
27 He rained meat down on them like dust,
flying birds like sand on the seashore.
28 He made them come down inside their camp,
all around their tents.
29 They ate till they had more than enough,[j]
for he had given them what they craved.
30 But before they turned from the food they craved,
even while it was still in their mouths,[k]
31 God's anger rose against them;
he put to death the sturdiest[l] among them,
cutting down the young men of Israel.

32 In spite of all this, they kept on sinning;
in spite of his wonders,[m] they did not believe.[n]
33 So he ended their days in futility[o]
and their years in terror.
34 Whenever God slew them, they would seek[p] him;
they eagerly turned to him again.
35 They remembered that God was their Rock,[q]
that God Most High was their Redeemer.[r]
36 But then they would flatter him with their mouths,[s]
lying to him with their tongues;
37 their hearts were not loyal[t] to him,
they were not faithful to his covenant.
38 Yet he was merciful;[u]
he forgave[v] their iniquities[w]
and did not destroy them.
Time after time he restrained his anger
and did not stir up his full wrath.
39 He remembered that they were but flesh,[x]
a passing breeze[y] that does not return.

40 How often they rebelled[z] against him in the desert[a]
and grieved him[b] in the wasteland!
41 Again and again they put God to the test;[c]
they vexed the Holy One of Israel.[d]
42 They did not remember his power—
the day he redeemed them from the oppressor,
43 the day he displayed his miraculous signs in Egypt,
his wonders in the region of Zoan.
44 He turned their rivers to blood;[e]
they could not drink from their streams.
45 He sent swarms of flies[f] that devoured them,
and frogs[g] that devastated them.

78:22 [f]Dt 1:32; Heb 3:19
78:23 [g]Ge 7:11; Mal 3:10
78:24 [h]Ex 16:4; Jn 6:31*
78:26 [i]Nu 11:31
78:29 [j]Nu 11:20
78:30 [k]Nu 11:33
78:31 [l]Isa 10:16
78:32 [m]ver 11 [n]ver 22
78:33 [o]Nu 14:29, 35
78:34 [p]Hos 5:15
78:35 [q]Dt 32:4 [r]Dt 9:26
78:36 [s]Eze 33:31
78:37 [t]ver 8; Ac 8:21
78:38 [u]Ex 34:6 [v]Isa 48:10 [w]Nu 14:18, 20
78:39 [x]Ge 6:3; Ps 103:14 [y]Job 7:7; Jas 4:14
78:40 [z]Heb 3:16 [a]Ps 95:8; 106:14 [b]Eph 4:30
78:41 [c]Nu 14:22 [d]2Ki 19:22; Ps 89:18
78:44 [e]Ex 7:20-21; Ps 105:29
78:45 [f]Ex 8:24; Ps 105:31 [g]Ex 8:2, 6

78:36, 37 Over and over the children of Israel claimed that they would follow God, but then they turned away from him. The problem was that they followed God with words and not with their hearts; thus their repentance was empty. Talk is cheap. God wants our conduct to back up our spiritual claims and promises.

46He gave their crops to the grasshopper,
their produce to the locust.[h]
47He destroyed their vines with hail[i]
and their sycamore-figs with sleet.
48He gave over their cattle to the hail,
their livestock[j] to bolts of lightning.
49He unleashed against them his hot anger,[k]
his wrath, indignation and hostility—
a band of destroying angels.
50He prepared a path for his anger;
he did not spare them from death
but gave them over to the plague.
51He struck down all the firstborn of Egypt,[l]
the firstfruits of manhood in the tents of Ham.[m]
52But he brought his people out like a flock;[n]
he led them like sheep through the desert.
53He guided them safely, so they were unafraid;
but the sea engulfed[o] their enemies.[p]
54Thus he brought them to the border of his holy land,
to the hill country his right hand[q] had taken.
55He drove out nations[r] before them
and allotted their lands to them as an inheritance;[s]
he settled the tribes of Israel in their homes.

56But they put God to the test
and rebelled against the Most High;
they did not keep his statutes.
57Like their fathers[t] they were disloyal and faithless,
as unreliable as a faulty bow.[u]
58They angered him[v] with their high places;[w]
they aroused his jealousy with their idols.[x]
59When God heard them, he was very angry;
he rejected Israel[y] completely.
60He abandoned the tabernacle of Shiloh,[z]
the tent he had set up among men.
61He sent ⌊the ark of⌋ his might[a] into captivity,[b]
his splendour into the hands of the enemy.
62He gave his people over to the sword;
he was very angry with his inheritance.
63Fire consumed[c] their young men,
and their maidens had no wedding songs;[d]
64their priests were put to the sword,[e]
and their widows could not weep.

65Then the Lord awoke as from sleep,[f]
as a man wakes from the stupor of wine.
66He beat back his enemies;
he put them to everlasting shame.[g]
67Then he rejected the tents of Joseph,
he did not choose the tribe of Ephraim;
68but he chose the tribe of Judah,
Mount Zion,[h] which he loved.
69He built his sanctuary like the heights,
like the earth that he established for ever.
70He chose David[i] his servant

78:46 [h]Ex 10:13
78:47 [i]Ex 9:23; Ps 105:32
78:48 [j]Ex 9:25
78:49 [k]Ex 15:7
78:51 [l]Ex 12:29; Ps 135:8 [m]Ps 105:23; 106:22
78:52 [n]Ps 77:20
78:53 [o]Ex 14:28 [p]Ps 106:10
78:54 [q]Ex 15:17; Ps 44:3
78:55 [r]Ps 44:2 [s]Jos 13:7
78:57 [t]Eze 20:27 [u]Hos 7:16
78:58 [v]Jdg 2:12 [w]Lev 26:30 [x]Ex 20:4; Dt 32:21
78:59 [y]Dt 32:19
78:60 [z]Jos 18:1
78:61 [a]Ps 132:8 [b]1Sa 4:17
78:63 [c]Nu 11:1 [d]Jer 7:34; 16:9
78:64 [e]1Sa 4:17; 22:18
78:65 [f]Ps 44:23
78:66 [g]1Sa 5:6
78:68 [h]Ps 87:2
78:70 [i]1Sa 16:1

78:51 This was the Passover described in Exodus 12:29, 30 when all the firstborn of the Egyptians were slain. The "tents of Ham" refers to Noah's second son, who was the ancestor of the Egyptians. Ham is sometimes used as a synonym for Egypt.

78:71
[j]2Sa 5:2;
Ps 28:9

78:72
[k]1Ki 9:4

and took him from the sheep pens;
71 from tending the sheep he brought him
to be the shepherd[j] of his people Jacob,
of Israel his inheritance.
72 And David shepherded them with integrity of heart;[k]
with skilful hands he led them.

79:1
[a]Ps 74:2
[b]2Ki 25:9

79:2
[c]Dt 28:26;
Jer 7:33

79:3
[d]Jer 16:4

79:4
[e]Ps 44:13; 80:6

79:5
[f]Ps 74:10
[g]Ps 74:1; 85:5

PSALM 79

A psalm of Asaph.

Theme: When outraged by injustice, cry out to God, not against him. In times of disaster, our mood may be anger, but our trust must remain in God.
Author: Asaph (or one of his descendants), probably written after the Babylonians had levelled Jerusalem (see 2 Kings 25)

1 O God, the nations have invaded your inheritance;[a]
they have defiled your holy temple,
they have reduced Jerusalem to rubble.[b]
2 They have given the dead bodies of your servants
as food to the birds of the air,
the flesh of your saints to the beasts of the earth.[c]
3 They have poured out blood like water
all around Jerusalem,
and there is no-one to bury the dead.[d]
4 We are objects of reproach to our neighbours,
of scorn and derision to those around us.[e]

5 How long,[f] O LORD? Will you be angry[g] for ever?

PRAYER IN THE BOOK OF PSALMS

Prayer is human communication with God. Psalms could be described as a collection of song-prayers. Probably the most striking feature of these prayers is their unedited honesty. The words often express our own feelings—feelings that we would prefer no-one, much less God, ever knew. Making these psalms our prayers can teach us a great deal about how God wants us to communicate with him. Too often we give God a watered-down version of our feelings, hoping we won't offend him or make him curious about our motives. As we use the psalms to express our feelings, we learn that honesty, openness, and sincerity are valuable to God.

Below are several types of prayers with examples from Psalms. Note that the psalm writers communicated with God in a variety of ways for a variety of reasons. Each of us is invited to communicate with God. Using the psalms will enrich your personal prayer life.

Prayers of:	*Psalms:*
Praise to God	100; 113; 117
Thanksgiving by a community	67; 75; 136
Thanksgiving by an individual	18; 30; 32
Request by the community	79; 80; 123
Request by an individual	3; 55; 86
Sorrow by the community	44; 74; 137
Sorrow by an individual	5; 6; 120
Anger	35; 109; 140
Confession	6; 32; 51
Faith	11; 16; 23

78:71, 72 Although David had been on the throne when this psalm was written, he is called a shepherd and not a king. Shepherding, a common profession in biblical times, was a highly responsible job. The flocks were completely dependent upon shepherds for guidance, provision, and protection. David had spent his early years as a shepherd (1 Samuel 16:10, 11). This was a training ground for the future responsibilities God had in store for him. When he was ready, God took him from caring for sheep to caring for Israel, God's people. Don't treat your present situation lightly or irresponsibly; it may be God's training ground for your future.

How long will your jealousy burn like fire?[h]
6Pour out your wrath[i] on the nations
that do not acknowledge[j] you,
on the kingdoms
that do not call on your name;[k]
7for they have devoured Jacob
and destroyed his homeland.
8Do not hold against us the sins of the fathers;[l]
may your mercy come quickly to meet us,
for we are in desperate need.[m]

9Help us,[n] O God our Saviour,
for the glory of your name;
deliver us and forgive our sins
for your name's sake.[o]
10Why should the nations say,
"Where is their God?"[p]
Before our eyes, make known among the nations
that you avenge[q] the outpoured blood of your servants.
11May the groans of the prisoners come before you;
by the strength of your arm
preserve those condemned to die.

12Pay back into the laps[r] of our neighbours seven times[s]
the reproach they have hurled at you, O Lord.
13Then we your people, the sheep of your pasture,[t]
will praise you for ever;[u]
from generation to generation
we will recount your praise.

PSALM 80

For the director of music. To ⌞the tune of⌟ "The Lilies of the Covenant". Of Asaph. A psalm.

Theme: A prayer for revival and restoration after experiencing destruction. God is our only hope for salvation.
Author: Asaph (or one of his descendants), probably written after the northern kingdom of Israel was defeated and its people deported to Assyria

1Hear us, O Shepherd of Israel,
you who lead Joseph like a flock;[a]
you who sit enthroned between the cherubim,[b] shine forth
2 before Ephraim, Benjamin and Manasseh.[c]
Awaken[d] your might;
come and save us.

79:5 [h]Dt 29:20; Ps 89:46; Zep 3:8
79:6 [i]Ps 69:24; Rev 16:1 [j]Jer 10:25; 2Th 1:8 [k]Ps 14:4
79:8 [l]Isa 64:9 [m]Ps 116:6; 142:6
79:9 [n]2Ch 14:11 [o]Ps 25:11; 31:3; Jer 14:7
79:10 [p]Ps 42:10 [q]Ps 94:1
79:12 [r]Isa 65:6; Jer 32:18 [s]Ge 4:15
79:13 [t]Ps 74:1; 95:7 [u]Ps 44:8
80:1 [a]Ps 77:20 [b]Ex 25:22
80:2 [c]Nu 2:18-24 [d]Ps 35:23

79:6 According to the Old Testament, God's wrath and judgment often fell on entire nations because of the sins of people within those nations. Here Asaph pleaded for judgment on kingdoms that refused to acknowledge God's authority. Ironically, Asaph's own nation of Judah was being judged by God for refusing to do this very thing (2 Chronicles 36:14–20). These were people who had sworn allegiance to God but were now rejecting him. This made their judgment even worse.

79:10 In the end, God's glory will be evident to all people, but in the meantime, we must endure suffering with patience and allow God to strengthen our character through it. For reasons that we do not know, pagan people are often allowed to scoff at believers. We should be prepared for criticism, jokes, and unkind remarks because God does not place us beyond the attacks of scoffers.

[3]Restore[e] us,[f] O God;
make your face shine upon us,
that we may be saved.

[4]O LORD God Almighty,
how long will your anger smoulder
against the prayers of your people?
[5]You have fed them with the bread of tears;
you have made them drink tears by the bowlful.[g]
[6]You have made us a source of contention to our neighbours,
and our enemies mock us.[h]

[7]Restore us, O God Almighty;
make your face shine upon us,
that we may be saved.

[8]You brought a vine[i] out of Egypt;
you drove out[j] the nations and planted it.
[9]You cleared the ground for it,
and it took root and filled the land.
[10]The mountains were covered with its shade,
the mighty cedars with its branches.
[11]It sent out its boughs to the Sea,[a]
its shoots as far as the River.[b][k]

[12]Why have you broken down its walls[l]
so that all who pass by pick its grapes?
[13]Boars from the forest ravage[m] it
and the creatures of the field feed on it.
[14]Return to us, O God Almighty!
Look down from heaven and see![n]
Watch over this vine,
[15] the root your right hand has planted,
the son[c] you have raised up for yourself.

[16]Your vine is cut down, it is burned with fire;
at your rebuke[o] your people perish.
[17]Let your hand rest on the man at your right hand,
the son of man you have raised up for yourself.
[18]Then we will not turn away from you;
revive us, and we will call on your name.

[19]Restore us, O LORD God Almighty;
make your face shine upon us,
that we may be saved.

80:3 [e]Ps 85:4; La 5:21 [f]Nu 6:25
80:5 [g]Ps 42:3; Isa 30:20
80:6 [h]Ps 79:4
80:8 [i]Isa 5:1-2; Jer 2:21 [j]Jos 13:6; Ac 7:45
80:11 [k]Ps 72:8
80:12 [l]Ps 89:40; Isa 5:5
80:13 [m]Jer 5:6
80:14 [n]Isa 63:15
80:16 [o]Ps 39:11; 76:6

[a] *11* Probably the Mediterranean [b] *11* That is, the Euphrates [c] *15* Or *branch*

80:1 Cherubim are mighty angels.

80:3, 7, 19 Three times the writer calls on God to "restore us". Before restoration must come repentance, turning away from sin. Repentance involves humbling ourselves and turning to God to receive his forgiveness. As we turn to God, he helps us see ourselves, including our sin, more clearly. Then, as we see our sin, we must repeat the process of repentance. Only then can we constantly be restored to fellowship with God.

80:17 "The man at your right hand" is probably not the Messiah, but Israel, whom God calls elsewhere his "firstborn son" (Exodus 4:22). The psalmist is making a plea that God would restore his mercy to Israel, the people he chose to bring his message into the world.

PSALM 81

For the director of music. According to *gittith*.[a] Of Asaph.

Theme: A holiday hymn. This hymn celebrates the exodus from Egypt—God's goodness versus Israel's waywardness. God is our deliverer in spite of our wanderings.
Author: Asaph, probably written to be used during the Feasts of Tabernacles

1 Sing for joy to God our strength;
shout aloud to the God of Jacob![a]
2 Begin the music, strike the tambourine,[b]
play the melodious harp[c] and lyre.
3 Sound the ram's horn at the New Moon,
and when the moon is full, on the day of our Feast;
4 this is a decree for Israel,
an ordinance of the God of Jacob.
5 He established it as a statute for Joseph
when he went out against Egypt,[d]
where we heard a language we did not understand.[b][e]

6 He says, "I removed the burden from their shoulders;[f]
their hands were set free from the basket.
7 In your distress you called[g] and I rescued you,
I answered[h] you out of a thundercloud;
I tested you at the waters of Meribah.[i] *Selah*

8 "Hear, O my people,[j] and I will warn you—
if you would but listen to me, O Israel!
9 You shall have no foreign god[k] among you;
you shall not bow down to an alien god.
10 I am the LORD your God,
who brought you up out of Egypt.[l]
Open wide your mouth and I will fill[m] it.

11 "But my people would not listen to me;
Israel would not submit to me.[n]
12 So I gave them over[o] to their stubborn hearts
to follow their own devices.

13 "If my people would but listen to me,[p]
if Israel would follow my ways,
14 how quickly would I subdue[q] their enemies
and turn my hand against[r] their foes!
15 Those who hate the LORD would cringe before him,
and their punishment would last for ever.
16 But you would be fed with the finest of wheat;[s]
with honey from the rock I would satisfy you."

a Title: Probably a musical term b 5 Or / *and we heard a voice we had not known*

81:1 [a]Ps 66:1
81:2 [b]Ex 15:20 [c]Ps 92:3
81:5 [d]Ex 11:4 [e]Ps 114:1
81:6 [f]Isa 9:4
81:7 [g]Ex 2:23; Ps 50:15 [h]Ex 19:19 [i]Ex 17:7
81:8 [j]Ps 50:7
81:9 [k]Ex 20:3; Dt 32:12; Isa 43:12
81:10 [l]Ex 20:2 [m]Ps 107:9
81:11 [n]Ex 32:1-6
81:12 [o]Ac 7:42; Ro 1:24
81:13 [p]Dt 5:29; Isa 48:18
81:14 [q]Ps 47:3 [r]Am 1:8
81:16 [s]Dt 32:14

81:1–5 Israel's holidays reminded the nation of God's great miracles. They were times of rejoicing and times to renew one's strength for life's daily struggles. At Christmas, do your thoughts revolve mostly around presents? Is Easter only a warm anticipation of spring? Remember the spiritual origins of these special days, and use them as opportunities to worship God for his goodness to you, your family, and your nation.

81:2–4 David instituted music for the temple worship services (1 Chronicles 25). Music and worship go hand in hand. Worship should involve the whole person, and music helps lift a person's thoughts and emotions to God. Through music we can reflect upon our needs and shortcomings as well as celebrate God's greatness.

81:11, 12 God let the Israelites go on blindly, stubbornly, and selfishly, when they should have been obeying and pursuing God's desires. God sometimes lets us continue in our stubbornness to bring us to our senses. He does not keep us from rebelling because he wants us to learn the consequences of sin. He uses these experiences to turn people away from greater sin to faith in him.

81:13–16 God had provided in his covenant that he would restore his people if they would listen to him and return to him (Exodus 23:22–27; Leviticus 26:3–13; Deuteronomy 7:12–26; 28:1–14).

PSALM 82

A psalm of Asaph.

Theme: A fair judge. God will judge the wicked who have unfairly treated others.
Author: Asaph

1 God presides in the great assembly;
he gives judgment[a] among the "gods":

2 "How long will you[a] defend the unjust
and show partiality[b] to the wicked?[c] *Selah*
3 Defend the cause of the weak and fatherless;[d]
maintain the rights of the poor[e] and oppressed.
4 Rescue the weak and needy;
deliver them from the hand of the wicked.

5 "They know nothing, they understand nothing.[f]
They walk about in darkness;[g]
all the foundations[h] of the earth are shaken.

6 "I said, 'You are "gods";[i]
you are all sons of the Most High.'
7 But you will die[j] like mere men;
you will fall like every other ruler."

8 Rise up,[k] O God, judge the earth,
for all the nations are your inheritance.[l]

82:1 [a]Ps 58:11; Isa 3:13
82:2 [b]Dt 1:17 [c]Ps 58:1-2; Pr 18:5
82:3 [d]Dt 24:17 [e]Jer 22:16
82:5 [f]Ps 14:4; Mic 3:1 [g]Isa 59:9 [h]Ps 11:3
82:6 [i]Jn 10:34*
82:7 [j]Ps 49:12; Eze 31:14
82:8 [k]Ps 12:5 [l]Ps 2:8; Rev 11:15

PSALM 83

A song. A psalm of Asaph.

Theme: Combating God's enemies. This psalm is a prayer for God to do whatever it takes to convince the world that he is indeed God. Oneday all will recognise and admit that God is in charge.
Author: Asaph (or one of his descendants)

1 O God, do not keep silent;[a]
be not quiet, O God, be not still.
2 See how your enemies are astir,[b]
how your foes rear their heads.[c]
3 With cunning they conspire[d] against your people;
they plot against those you cherish.
4 "Come," they say, "let us destroy[e] them as a nation,
that the name of Israel be remembered[f] no more."

5 With one mind they plot together;[g]
they form an alliance against you—
6 the tents of Edom[h] and the Ishmaelites,
of Moab[i] and the Hagrites,[j]
7 Gebal,[a][k] Ammon and Amalek,

83:1 [a]Ps 28:1; 35:22
83:2 [b]Ps 2:1; Isa 17:12 [c]Jdg 8:28; Ps 81:15
83:3 [d]Ps 31:13
83:4 [e]Est 3:6 [f]Jer 11:19
83:5 [g]Ps 2:2
83:6 [h]Ps 137:7 [i]2Ch 20:1 [j]Ge 25:16
83:7 [k]Jos 13:5

[a] *2* The Hebrew is plural. [a] *7* That is, Byblos

82:6 This psalm calls the rulers and judges of Israel "gods" and "sons of the Most High". They were called gods because they represented God in executing judgment. John 10:34–36 records Jesus using this passage to defend his claims to be God. His argument was as follows: if God would call mere men "gods", why was it blasphemous for him, the true Son of God, to declare himself equal with God?

83:5–8 This alliance against God may refer to the gathering of certain kings to fight against Jehoshaphat and the people of Judah (2 Chronicles 20). The psalm's author is called Asaph, but this can mean Asaph or one of his descendants. A descendant of Asaph named Jahaziel prophesied victory for Judah in the battle against Jehoshaphat (2 Chronicles 20:13–17). The psalmist says the alliance against Judah is really against God. Thus Jahaziel exclaimed, "The battle is not yours, but God's" (2 Chronicles 20:15). God is "the Most High over all the earth" (83:18), and the enemies of Israel were considered God's enemies.

83:6 The Hagrites may have been the descendants of Hagar (Genesis 21:8–21).

Philistia, with the people of Tyre.[l]
8Even Assyria has joined them
to lend strength to the descendants of Lot.[m] *Selah*
9Do to them as you did to Midian,[n]
as you did to Sisera and Jabin at the river Kishon,[o]
10who perished at Endor
and became like refuse[p] on the ground.
11Make their nobles like Oreb and Zeeb,[q]
all their princes like Zebah and Zalmunna,[r]
12who said, "Let us take possession[s]
of the pasture-lands of God."

13Make them like tumble-weed, O my God,
like chaff[t] before the wind.
14As fire consumes the forest
or a flame sets the mountains ablaze,[u]
15so pursue them with your tempest
and terrify them with your storm.[v]
16Cover their faces with shame[w]
so that men will seek your name, O LORD.

17May they ever be ashamed and dismayed;
may they perish in disgrace.[x]
18Let them know that you, whose name is the LORD—
that you alone are the Most High over all the earth.[y]

PSALM 84

For the director of music. According to *gittith*.[a] Of the Sons of Korah. A psalm.

Theme: God's living presence is our greatest joy. His radiant presence helps us to grow in strength, grace, and glory.
Authors: The sons of Korah (temple assistants)

1How lovely is your dwelling-place,[a]
O LORD Almighty!
2My soul yearns,[b] even faints,
for the courts of the LORD;
my heart and my flesh cry out
for the living God.

3Even the sparrow has found a home,
and the swallow a nest for herself,
where she may have her young—
a place near your altar,[c]
O LORD Almighty, my King and my God.[d]

[a] Title: Probably a musical term

83:7 [l]Eze 27:3
83:8 [m]Dt 2:9
83:9 [n]Jdg 7:1-23 [o]Jdg 4:23-24
83:10 [p]Zep 1:17
83:11 [q]Jdg 7:25 [r]Jdg 8:12, 21
83:12 [s]2Ch 20:11
83:13 [t]Ps 35:5; Isa 17:13
83:14 [u]Dt 32:22; Isa 9:18
83:15 [v]Job 9:17
83:16 [w]Ps 109:29; 132:18
83:17 [x]Ps 35:4
83:18 [y]Ps 59:13
84:1 [a]Ps 27:4; 43:3; 132:5
84:2 [b]Ps 42:1-2
84:3 [c]Ps 43:4 [d]Ps 5:2

83:8–11 The "descendants of Lot" refers to the Moabites and Ammonites (Genesis 19:36–38). Sisera was the commander of the army of the oppressive Canaanite King Jabin. He was killed by a woman (see Judges 4 for the complete story). (For the story of Oreb and Zeeb, see Judges 7:25; for Zebah and Zalmunna, see Judges 8:21.)

83:13–18 Surrounding Judah were pagan nations that sought Judah's downfall. The psalmist prayed that God would blow these nations away like chaff before the wind until they recognised that the Lord is above all rulers of the earth. Sometimes we must be humbled by adversity before we will look up and see the Lord; we must be defeated before we can have the ultimate victory. Wouldn't it be better to seek the Lord in times of prosperity than to wait until his judgment is upon us?

84:1, 4 The writer longed to get away from the bustling world to meet God inside his dwelling place, his holy temple. We can meet God anywhere, at any time. But we know that going into a church building can help us step aside from the busy mainstream of life so we can quietly meditate and pray. We find joy not only in the beautiful building but also in the prayers, music, lessons, sermons, and fellowship.

84:5
[e]Ps 81:1
[f]Jer 31:6

84:6
[g]Joel 2:23

84:7
[h]Pr 4:18
[i]Dt 16:16

84:9
[j]Ps 59:11
[k]1Sa 16:6; Ps 2:2; 132:17

84:10
[l]1Ch 23:5

84:11
[m]Isa 60:19; Rev 21:23
[n]Ge 15:1
[o]Ps 34:10

84:12
[p]Ps 2:12

85:1
[a]Ps 14:7; Jer 30:18; Eze 39:25

85:2
[b]Nu 14:19
[c]Ps 78:38

85:3
[d]Ps 106:23
[e]Ex 32:12; Dt 13:17; Ps 78:38; Jnh 3:9

85:4
[f]Ps 80:3, 7

85:5
[g]Ps 79:5

85:6
[h]Ps 80:18; Hab 3:2

4 Blessed are those who dwell in your house;
they are ever praising you. *Selah*

5 Blessed are those whose strength[e] is in you,
who have set their hearts on pilgrimage.[f]
6 As they pass through the Valley of Baca,
they make it a place of springs;
the autumn[g] rains also cover it with pools.[b]
7 They go from strength to strength,[h]
till each appears[i] before God in Zion.

8 Hear my prayer, O LORD God Almighty;
listen to me, O God of Jacob. *Selah*
9 Look upon our shield,[c][j] O God;
look with favour on your anointed one.[k]

10 Better is one day in your courts
than a thousand elsewhere;
I would rather be a doorkeeper[l] in the house of my God
than dwell in the tents of the wicked.
11 For the LORD God is a sun[m] and shield;[n]
the LORD bestows favour and honour;
no good thing does he withhold[o]
from those whose walk is blameless.

12 O LORD Almighty,
blessed[p] is the man who trusts in you.

PSALM 85

For the director of music. Of the Sons of Korah. A psalm.

Theme: From reverence to restoration. Reverence leads to forgiveness, restoring our love and joy for God.
Authors: The sons of Korah (temple assistants)

1 You showed favour to your land, O LORD;
you restored the fortunes[a] of Jacob.
2 You forgave[b] the iniquity[c] of your people
and covered all their sins. *Selah*
3 You set aside all your wrath[d]
and turned from your fierce anger.[e]

4 Restore[f] us again, O God our Saviour,
and put away your displeasure towards us.
5 Will you be angry with us for ever?[g]
Will you prolong your anger through all generations?
6 Will you not revive[h] us again,
that your people may rejoice in you?

b 6 Or *blessings* **c** 9 Or *sovereign*

84:5–7 The pilgrimage to the temple passed through the barren Valley of Baca. No specific valley has been identified with Baca. Because *Baca* can mean "weeping", it may have been a symbolic reference to the times of struggles and tears through which people must pass on their way to meet God. Growing strong in God's presence is often preceded by a journey through barren places in our lives. The person who loves to spend time with God will see his or her adversity as an opportunity to re-experience God's faithfulness. If you are walking through your own Valley of Baca today, be sure your pilgrimage leads towards God, not away from him.

84:11 God does not promise to give us everything *we* think is good, but he will not withhold what is permanently good. He will give us the means to walk along his paths, but we must do the walking. When we obey him, he will not hold anything back that will help us serve him.

85:6, 7 The psalmist was asking God to revive his people, bringing them back to spiritual life. God is capable of reviving both churches and individuals. He can pour out his love on us, renewing our love for him. If you need revival in your church, family, or personal spiritual life, ask God to give you a fresh touch of his love.

7Show us your unfailing love, O LORD,
and grant us your salvation.

8I will listen to what God the LORD will say;
he promises peace[i] to his people, his saints—
but let them not return to folly.
9Surely his salvation[j] is near those who fear him,
that his glory[k] may dwell in our land.

10Love and faithfulness[l] meet together;
righteousness[m] and peace kiss each other.
11Faithfulness springs forth from the earth,
and righteousness[n] looks down from heaven.
12The LORD will indeed give what is good,[o]
and our land will yield[p] its harvest.
13Righteousness goes before him
and prepares the way for his steps.

PSALM 86

A prayer of David.

Theme: Devoted trust in times of deep trouble
Author: David

1Hear, O LORD, and answer[a] me,
for I am poor and needy.
2Guard my life, for I am devoted to you.
You are my God; save your servant
who trusts in you.[b]
3Have mercy[c] on me, O Lord,
for I call[d] to you all day long.
4Bring joy to your servant,
for to you, O Lord,
I lift[e] up my soul.

5You are forgiving and good, O Lord,
abounding in love[f] to all who call to you.
6Hear my prayer, O LORD;
listen to my cry for mercy.
7In the day of my trouble[g] I will call to you,
for you will answer me.

8Among the gods there is none like you,[h] O Lord;
no deeds can compare with yours.
9All the nations you have made
will come and worship[i] before you, O Lord;
they will bring glory[j] to your name.
10For you are great and do marvellous deeds;[k]
you alone[l] are God.

11Teach me your way,[m] O LORD,
and I will walk in your truth;

85:8 [i]Zec 9:10
85:9 [j]Isa 46:13 [k]Zec 2:5
85:10 [l]Ps 89:14; Pr 3:3 [m]Ps 72:2-3; Isa 32:17
85:11 [n]Isa 45:8
85:12 [o]Ps 84:11; Jas 1:17 [p]Lev 26:4; Ps 67:6; Zec 8:12
86:1 [a]Ps 17:6
86:2 [b]Ps 25:2; 31:14
86:3 [c]Ps 4:1; 57:1 [d]Ps 88:9
86:4 [e]Ps 25:1; 143:8
86:5 [f]Ex 34:6; Ne 9:17; Ps 103:8; 145:8; Joel 2:13; Jnh 4:2
86:7 [g]Ps 50:15
86:8 [h]Ex 15:11; Dt 3:24; Ps 89:6
86:9 [i]Ps 66:4; Rev 15:4 [j]Isa 43:7
86:10 [k]Ps 72:18 [l]Dt 6:4; Mk 12:29; 1Co 8:4
86:11 [m]Ps 25:5

86:7 Sometimes our trouble or pain is so great that all we can do is cry out to God, "Guard my life" (86:2). And often, when there is no relief in sight, all we can do is acknowledge the greatness of God and wait for better days ahead. The conviction that God answers prayer will sustain us in such difficult times.

86:8–10 "There is none like you, O LORD." The God of the Bible is unique! He is alive and able to do mighty deeds for those who love him. All man-created deities are powerless because they are merely inventions of the mind, not living beings. The Lord alone is "worthy . . . to receive glory and honour and power" (Revelation 4:11). Although people believe in many gods, you need never fear that God is only one among many or that you may be worshipping the wrong God. The Lord alone is God.

give me an undivided[n] heart,
that I may fear your name.
12 I will praise you, O Lord my God, with all my heart;
I will glorify your name for ever.
13 For great is your love towards me;
you have delivered me from the depths of the grave.[a]

14 The arrogant are attacking me, O God;
a band of ruthless men seeks my life —
men without regard for you.[o]
15 But you, O Lord, are a compassionate and gracious[p] God,
slow to anger, abounding in love and faithfulness.[q]
16 Turn to me and have mercy on me;
grant your strength to your servant
and save the son of your maidservant.[b][r]
17 Give me a sign of your goodness,
that my enemies may see it and be put to shame,
for you, O LORD, have helped me and comforted me.

PSALM 87

Of the Sons of Korah. A psalm. A song.

Theme: The city of God, where all believers will one day gather
Authors: The sons of Korah (temple assistants)

1 He has set his foundation on the holy mountain;
2 the LORD loves the gates of Zion[a]
more than all the dwellings of Jacob.
3 Glorious things are said of you,
O city of God:[b] *Selah*
4 "I will record Rahab[a][c] and Babylon
among those who acknowledge me —
Philistia too, and Tyre[d], along with Cush[b] —
and will say, 'This[c] one was born in Zion.[e]' "

5 Indeed, of Zion it will be said,
"This one and that one were born in her,
and the Most High himself will establish her."
6 The LORD will write in the register[f] of the peoples:
"This one was born in Zion." *Selah*
7 As they make music[g] they will sing,
"All my fountains[h] are in you."

86:11 [n]Jer 32:39
86:14 [o]Ps 54:3
86:15 [p]Ps 103:8 [q]Ex 34:6; Ne 9:17; Joel 2:13
86:16 [r]Ps 116:16
87:2 [a]Ps 78:68
87:3 [b]Ps 46:4; Isa 60:1
87:4 [c]Job 9:13 [d]Ps 45:12 [e]Isa 19:25
87:6 [f]Ps 69:28; Isa 4:3; Eze 13:9
87:7 [g]Ps 149:3 [h]Ps 36:9

a *13* Hebrew *Sheol* b *16* Or *save your faithful son* a *4* A poetic name for Egypt b *4* That is, the upper Nile region c *4* Or *"O Rahab and Babylon, / Philistia, Tyre and Cush, / I will record concerning those who acknowledge me: / 'This*

86:17 It is right to pray for a sign of God's goodness. As David found, it may be just what we need. But let us not overlook the signs he has already given: the support of family and friends, the fellowship of other Christians, the light of each new day. And we can be confident that he knows our situation no matter how desperate it becomes, and he cares.

87:1ff Zion (the holy mountain, Jerusalem) and its temple here represent the future community of all believers. This psalm looks ahead to the Holy City of God described in Revelation 21:10–27. The honour of living there will be granted to all whose names are recorded in the Lamb's book of life (Revelation 21:27). It is God's grace that forms and sustains this wonderful community. How could anyone refuse God's offer to be part of this celebration?

87:4 Rahab is a name for a monster known in ancient Near Eastern poetry as an enemy of God. Here the name is used to represent Egypt, a traditional enemy of God's people.

PSALM 88

A song. A psalm of the Sons of Korah. For the director of music. According to *mahalath leannoth*.[a] A *maskil*[b] of Heman the Ezrahite.

Theme: When there is no relief in sight. God understands even our deepest misery.
Author: Heman, one of the sons of Korah (possibly the same man mentioned in 1 Chronicles 15:19; 16:41; 25:4, 5 as a musician and the king's seer)

1 O LORD, the God who saves me,[a]
day and night I cry out[b] before you.
2 May my prayer come before you;
turn your ear to my cry.

3 For my soul is full of trouble
and my life draws near the grave.[c][c]
4 I am counted among those who go down to the pit;[d]
I am like a man without strength.
5 I am set apart with the dead,
like the slain who lie in the grave,
whom you remember no more,
who are cut off[e] from your care.

6 You have put me in the lowest pit,
in the darkest depths.[f]
7 Your wrath lies heavily upon me;
you have overwhelmed me with all your waves.[g] *Selah*
8 You have taken from me my closest friends[h]
and have made me repulsive to them.
I am confined[i] and cannot escape;
9 my eyes[j] are dim with grief.

I call[k] to you, O LORD, every day;
I spread out my hands[l] to you.
10 Do you show your wonders to the dead?
Do those who are dead rise up and praise you?[m] *Selah*
11 Is your love declared in the grave,
your faithfulness[n] in Destruction?[d]
12 Are your wonders known in the place of darkness,
or your righteous deeds in the land of oblivion?

13 But I cry to you for help,[o] O LORD;
in the morning[p] my prayer comes before you.[q]
14 Why, O LORD, do you reject[r] me
and hide your face[s] from me?

15 From my youth I have been afflicted and close to death;
I have suffered your terrors[t] and am in despair.
16 Your wrath has swept over me;
your terrors have destroyed me.
17 All day long they surround me like a flood;[u]
they have completely engulfed me.

[a] Title: Possibly a tune, "The Suffering of Affliction" [b] Title: Probably a literary or musical term [c] *3* Hebrew *Sheol* [d] *11* Hebrew *Abaddon*

88:1 [a]Ps 51:14 [b]Ps 22:2; 27:9; Lk 18:7
88:3 [c]Ps 107:18, 26
88:4 [d]Ps 28:1
88:5 [e]Ps 31:22; Isa 53:8
88:6 [f]Ps 69:15; La 3:55
88:7 [g]Ps 42:7
88:8 [h]Job 19:13; Ps 31:11 [i]Jer 32:2
88:9 [j]Ps 38:10 [k]Ps 86:3 [l]Job 11:13; Ps 143:6
88:10 [m]Ps 6:5
88:11 [n]Ps 30:9
88:13 [o]Ps 30:2 [p]Ps 5:3 [q]Ps 119:147
88:14 [r]Ps 43:2 [s]Job 13:24; Ps 13:1
88:15 [t]Job 6:4
88:17 [u]Ps 22:16; 124:4

88:1ff Have you ever felt as though you have hit rock bottom? The psalmist is so low that he even despairs of life itself. Although everything is bad and getting worse, he is able to tell it all to God. This is one of the few psalms that gives no answer or expression of hope. Don't think that you must always be cheerful and positive. Grief and depression take time to heal. No matter how low we feel, we can always take our problems to God and express our anguish to him.

88:13, 14 When writing this, the psalmist was close to death, perhaps debilitated by disease, and forsaken by friends. But he could still pray. Perhaps you are not so afflicted, but you know someone who is. Consider being a prayer companion for that person. This psalm can be a prayer you can lift to God on his or her behalf.

[18]You have taken my companions[v] and loved ones from me;
the darkness is my closest friend.

PSALM 89

A *maskil*[a] of Ethan the Ezrahite.

Theme: God's promise to preserve David's descendants. God's promise is fulfilled in Jesus Christ, who will reign for eternity. The love and kindness promised to David is ours in Christ.
Author: Ethan (a Levite leader and possibly one of the head musicians in the temple, 1 Chronicles 15:17, 19), or one of his descendants

[1]I will sing[a] of the LORD's great love for ever;
with my mouth I will make your faithfulness known[b] through
all generations.
[2]I will declare that your love stands firm for ever,
that you established your faithfulness in heaven itself.[c]

[3]You said, "I have made a covenant with my chosen one,
I have sworn to David my servant,
[4]'I will establish your line for ever
and make your throne firm through all generations.' "[d] *Selah*

[5]The heavens[e] praise your wonders, O LORD,
your faithfulness too, in the assembly of the holy ones.
[6]For who in the skies above can compare with the LORD?
Who is like the LORD among the heavenly beings?[f]
[7]In the council of the holy ones God is greatly feared;
he is more awesome than all who surround him.[g]
[8]O LORD God Almighty, who is like you?[h]
You are mighty, O LORD, and your faithfulness surrounds you.

[9]You rule over the surging sea;
when its waves mount up, you still them.[i]
[10]You crushed Rahab[j] like one of the slain;
with your strong arm you scattered[k] your enemies.
[11]The heavens are yours, and yours also the earth;[l]
you founded the world and all that is in it.[m]
[12]You created the north and the south;
Tabor[n] and Hermon[o] sing for joy[p] at your name.
[13]Your arm is endued with power;
your hand is strong, your right hand exalted.

[14]Righteousness and justice are the foundation of your throne;[q]
love and faithfulness go before you.
[15]Blessed are those who have learned to acclaim you,
who walk in the light[r] of your presence, O LORD.

a Title: Probably a literary or musical term

88:18 v ver 8; Job 19:13; Ps 38:11
89:1 a Ps 59:16; Ps 101:1 b Ps 36:5; 40:10
89:2 c Ps 36:5
89:4 d 2Sa 7:12-16; 1Ki 8:16; Ps 132:11-12; Isa 9:7; Lk 1:33
89:5 e Ps 19:1
89:6 f Ps 113:5
89:7 g Ps 47:2
89:8 h Ps 71:19
89:9 i Ps 65:7
89:10 j Ps 87:4 k Ps 68:1
89:11 l 1Ch 29:11; Ps 24:1 m Ge 1:1
89:12 n Jos 19:22 o Dt 3:8; Jos 12:1 p Ps 98:8
89:14 q Ps 97:2
89:15 r Ps 44:3

89:1ff This psalm was written to describe the glorious reign of David. God had promised to make David the mightiest king on earth and to keep his descendants on the throne for ever (2 Samuel 7:8–16). But Jerusalem was destroyed, and kings no longer reign there. So these verses can only look forward, prophetically, to the future reign of Jesus Christ, David's descendant. Verse 27 is a prophecy concerning David's never-ending dynasty, which will reach its fulfilment and highest expression in Christ's future reign over the world (see Revelation 22:5).

89:5 The "assembly of the holy ones" generally refers to angels. In the courts of heaven, a host of angels praise the Lord. This scene is one of majesty and grandeur to show that God is beyond compare. His power and purity place him high above nature and angels. See Deuteronomy 33:2, Luke 2:13, and Hebrews 12:22 for more about angels.

89:12 This refers to Mount Tabor and Mount Hermon. Mount Tabor, though low in elevation (1,900 feet), was the scene of Deborah's victory in Judges 4. Mount Hermon (9,000 feet) was tall and majestic.

89:14, 15 Righteousness, justice, love, and faithfulness are the foundation of God's throne; they are fundamental aspects of the way God rules. As God's ambassadors, we should deal with people similarly. Make sure your actions flow out of righteousness, justice, love, and faithfulness because any unfair, unloving, or dishonest action cannot come from God.

16They rejoice in your name[s] all day long;
they exult in your righteousness.
17For you are their glory and strength,
and by your favour you exalt our horn.[b][t]
18Indeed, our shield[c] belongs to the LORD,
our king[u] to the Holy One of Israel.

19Once you spoke in a vision,
to your faithful people you said:
"I have bestowed strength on a warrior;
I have exalted a young man from among the people.
20I have found David[v] my servant;[w]
with my sacred oil I have anointed[x] him.
21My hand will sustain him;
surely my arm will strengthen him.[y]
22No enemy will subject him to tribute;
no wicked man will oppress[z] him.
23I will crush his foes before him[a]
and strike down his adversaries.[b]
24My faithful love will be with him,[c]
and through my name his horn[d] will be exalted.
25I will set his hand over the sea,
his right hand over the rivers.[d]
26He will call out to me, 'You are my Father,[e]
my God, the Rock my Saviour.'[f]
27I will also appoint him my firstborn,[g]
the most exalted[h] of the kings[i] of the earth.
28I will maintain my love to him for ever,
and my covenant with him will never fail.[j]
29I will establish his line for ever,
his throne as long as the heavens endure.[k]

30"If his sons forsake my law
and do not follow my statutes,
31if they violate my decrees
and fail to keep my commands,
32I will punish their sin with the rod,
their iniquity with flogging;[l]
33but I will not take my love from him,[m]
nor will I ever betray my faithfulness.
34I will not violate my covenant
or alter what my lips have uttered.[n]
35Once for all, I have sworn by my holiness —
and I will not lie to David —
36that his line will continue for ever

b 17 *Horn* here symbolises strong one. **c** 18 Or *sovereign* **d** 24 *Horn* here symbolises strength.

89:16 [s]Ps 105:3
89:17 [t]Ps 75:10; 92:10; 148:14
89:18 [u]Ps 47:9
89:20 [v]Ac 13:22 [w]Ps 78:70 [x]1Sa 16:1, 12
89:21 [y]Ps 18:35
89:22 [z]2Sa 7:10
89:23 [a]Ps 18:40 [b]2Sa 7:9
89:24 [c]2Sa 7:15
89:25 [d]Ps 72:8
89:26 [e]2Sa 7:14 [f]2Sa 22:47
89:27 [g]Col 1:18 [h]Nu 24:7 [i]Rev 1:5; 19:16
89:28 [j]ver 33-34; Isa 55:3
89:29 [k]ver 4, 36; Dt 11:21; Jer 33:17
89:32 [l]2Sa 7:14
89:33 [m]2Sa 7:15
89:34 [n]Nu 23:19

89:17, 24 *Horn* refers to the horn of an animal, the symbol of its power. In verse 17, *horn* means our strong one, our hope for the Messiah. In verse 24, David is promised God's power to accomplish God's will. Without God's help, we are weak and powerless, inadequate for even the simplest spiritual tasks. But when we are filled with God's Spirit, his power flows through us and our accomplishments will exceed our expectations.

89:34–37 In light of Israel's continual disobedience throughout history, this is an amazing promise. God promised that David's descendants would always sit on the throne (89:29), but that if the people disobeyed, they would be punished (89:30–32). Yet, even through their disobedience and punishment, God would never break faith with them (89:33). Israel *did* disobey, evil ran rampant, the nation was divided, exile came — but through it all, a remnant of God's people remained faithful. Centuries later, the Messiah arrived, the eternal King from David's line, just as God had promised. All that God promises, he fulfils. He will not take back even one word of what he says. God can also be trusted to save us as he promised he would (Hebrews 6:13–18). God is completely reliable.

and his throne endure before me like the sun;
37 it will be established for ever like the moon,
the faithful witness in the sky." *Selah*

38 But you have rejected,[o] you have spurned,
you have been very angry with your anointed one.
39 You have renounced the covenant with your servant
and have defiled his crown in the dust.[p]
40 You have broken through all his walls[q]
and reduced his strongholds[r] to ruins.
41 All who pass by have plundered him;
he has become the scorn of his neighbours.[s]
42 You have exalted the right hand of his foes;
you have made all his enemies rejoice.[t]
43 You have turned back the edge of his sword
and have not supported him in battle.[u]
44 You have put an end to his splendour
and cast his throne to the ground.
45 You have cut short the days of his youth;
you have covered him with a mantle of shame.[v] *Selah*

46 How long, O LORD? Will you hide yourself for ever?
How long will your wrath burn like fire?[w]
47 Remember how fleeting is my life.[x]
For what futility you have created all men!
48 What man can live and not see death,
or save himself from the power of the grave?[e][y] *Selah*
49 O Lord, where is your former great love,
which in your faithfulness you swore to David?
50 Remember, Lord, how your servant has[f] been mocked,[z]
how I bear in my heart the taunts of all the nations,
51 the taunts with which your enemies have mocked, O LORD,
with which they have mocked every step of your anointed one.[a]

52 Praise be to the LORD for ever!
Amen and Amen.[b]

89:38 [o]Dt 32:19; 1Ch 28:9; Ps 44:9
89:39 [p]La 5:16
89:40 [q]Ps 80:12 [r]La 2:2
89:41 [s]Ps 44:13
89:42 [t]Ps 13:2; 80:6
89:43 [u]Ps 44:10
89:45 [v]Ps 44:15; 109:29
89:46 [w]Ps 79:5
89:47 [x]Job 7:7; Ps 39:5
89:48 [y]Ps 22:29; 49:9
89:50 [z]Ps 69:19
89:51 [a]Ps 74:10
89:52 [b]Ps 41:13; 72:19

BOOK IV
PSALMS 90:1 — 106:48

These psalms include a prayer of Moses, a psalm about oppressors, and a psalm praising God as our King. These psalms remind us that we should remember our place and be submissive before the almighty God.

PSALM 90

A prayer of Moses the man of God.

Theme: God's eternal nature is contrasted with man's frailty. Our time on earth is limited and we are to use it wisely, not living for the moment, but with our eternal home in mind.
Author: Moses, making this the oldest of the psalms

1 Lord, you have been our dwelling-place[a]
throughout all generations.
2 Before the mountains were born[b]
or you brought forth the earth and the world,
from everlasting to everlasting you are God.[c]

3 You turn men back to dust,
saying, "Return to dust, O sons of men."[d]

90:1 [a]Dt 33:27; Eze 11:16
90:2 [b]Job 15:7; Pr 8:25 [c]Ps 102:24-27
90:3 [d]Ge 3:19; Job 34:15

[e] *48* Hebrew *Sheol* [f] *50* Or *your servants have*

4For a thousand years in your sight
are like a day that has just gone by,
or like a watch in the night.[e]
5You sweep men away[f] in the sleep of death;
they are like the new grass of the morning—
6though in the morning it springs up new,
by evening it is dry and withered.[g]

7We are consumed by your anger
and terrified by your indignation.
8You have set our iniquities before you,
our secret sins[h] in the light of your presence.
9All our days pass away under your wrath;
we finish our years with a moan.[i]
10The length of our days is seventy years—
or eighty, if we have the strength;
yet their span[a] is but trouble and sorrow,
for they quickly pass, and we fly away.[j]

11Who knows the power of your anger?
For your wrath is as great as the fear that is due to you.[k]
12Teach us to number our days[l] aright,
that we may gain a heart of wisdom.[m]

13Relent, O LORD! How long[n] will it be?
Have compassion on your servants.[o]
14Satisfy[p] us in the morning with your unfailing love,
that we may sing for joy[q] and be glad all our days.[r]
15Make us glad for as many days as you have afflicted us,
for as many years as we have seen trouble.
16May your deeds be shown to your servants,
your splendour to their children.[s]

17May the favour[b] of the Lord our God rest upon us;
establish the work of our hands for us—
yes, establish the work of our hands.[t]

PSALM 91

Theme: God's protection in the midst of danger. God doesn't promise a world free from danger, but he does promise his help whenever we face danger.
Author: Anonymous

1He who dwells in the shelter[a] of the Most High
will rest in the shadow[b] of the Almighty.[a]

[a] *10* Or *yet the best of them* [b] *17* Or *beauty* [a] *1* Hebrew *Shaddai*

90:4 [e]2Pe 3:8
90:5 [f]Ps 73:20; Isa 40:6
90:6 [g]Mt 6:30; Jas 1:10
90:8 [h]Ps 19:12
90:9 [i]Ps 78:33
90:10 [j]Job 20:8
90:11 [k]Ps 76:7
90:12 [l]Ps 39:4 [m]Dt 32:29
90:13 [n]Ps 6:3 [o]Dt 32:36; Ps 135:14
90:14 [p]Ps 103:5 [q]Ps 85:6 [r]Ps 31:7
90:16 [s]Ps 44:1; Hab 3:2
90:17 [t]Isa 26:12
91:1 [a]Ps 31:20 [b]Ps 17:8

90:4 Moses reminds us that a thousand years are like a day to the Lord. God is not limited by time. It's easy to get discouraged when years pass and the world doesn't get better. We sometimes wonder if God is able to see the future. But don't assume that God has our limitations. God is completely unrestricted by time. Because he is eternal, we can depend on him.

90:8 God knows all our sins as if they were spread out before him, even the secret ones. We don't need to cover up our sins before him because we can talk openly and honestly with him. But while he knows all that terrible information about us, God still loves us and wants to forgive us. This should encourage us to come to him rather than frighten us into covering up our sin.

90:12 Realising that life is short helps us use the little time we have more wisely and for eternal good. Take time to number your days by asking, "What do I want to see happen in my life before I die? What small step could I take towards that purpose today?"

90:17 Because our days are numbered, we want our work to count, to be effective and productive. We desire to see God's eternal plan revealed now and for our work to reflect his permanence. If we feel dissatisfied with this life and all its imperfections, remember our desire to see our work established is placed there by God (see the note on Ecclesiastes 3:11). But our desire can only be satisfied in eternity. Until then we must apply ourselves to loving and serving God.

91:1–6 God is a shelter, a refuge when we are afraid. The writer's faith in the Almighty God as Protector would carry him through all the dangers and fears of life. This should be a picture of our trust—trading all our fears for faith in him, no matter how in-

91:2
^{c}Ps 142:5

91:3
^{d}Ps 124:7; Pr 6:5
^{e}1Ki 8:37

91:4
^{f}Ps 17:8
^{g}Ps 35:2

91:5
^{h}Job 5:21

91:8
^{i}Ps 37:34; 58:10; Mal 1:5

91:10
^{j}Pr 12:21

91:11
^{k}Heb 1:14
^{l}Ps 34:7

91:12
^{m}Mt 4:6*; Lk 4:10-11*

91:13
^{n}Da 6:22; Lk 10:19

91:15
^{o}1Sa 2:30; Ps 50:15; Jn 12:26

91:16
^{p}Dt 6:2; Ps 21:4
^{q}Ps 50:23

92:1
^{a}Ps 147:1
^{b}Ps 135:3

92:2
^{c}Ps 89:1

2 I will say[b] of the LORD, "He is my refuge[c] and my fortress,
my God, in whom I trust."

3 Surely he will save you from the fowler's snare[d]
and from the deadly pestilence.[e]
4 He will cover you with his feathers,
and under his wings you will find refuge;[f]
his faithfulness will be your shield[g] and rampart.
5 You will not fear[h] the terror of night,
nor the arrow that flies by day,
6 nor the pestilence that stalks in the darkness,
nor the plague that destroys at midday.
7 A thousand may fall at your side,
ten thousand at your right hand,
but it will not come near you.
8 You will only observe with your eyes
and see the punishment of the wicked.[i]

9 If you make the Most High your dwelling—
even the LORD, who is my refuge—
10 then no harm[j] will befall you,
no disaster will come near your tent.
11 For he will command his angels[k] concerning you
to guard you in all your ways;[l]
12 they will lift you up in their hands,
so that you will not strike your foot against a stone.[m]
13 You will tread upon the lion and the cobra;
you will trample the great lion and the serpent.[n]

14 "Because he loves me," says the LORD, "I will rescue him;
I will protect him, for he acknowledges my name.
15 He will call upon me, and I will answer him;
I will be with him in trouble,
I will deliver him and honour him.[o]
16 With long life[p] will I satisfy him
and show him my salvation.[q]"

PSALM 92

A psalm. A song. For the Sabbath day.

Theme: Be thankful and faithful every day.
This psalm was used in temple services on the Sabbath.
Author: Anonymous

1 It is good to praise the LORD
and make music to your name,[a] O Most High,[b]
2 to proclaim your love in the morning[c]

b *2 Or He says*

---

tense our fears. To do this we must "dwell" and "rest" with him (91:1). By entrusting ourselves to his protection and pledging our daily devotion to him, we will be kept safe.

91:11 One of the functions of angels is to watch over believers (Hebrews 1:14). There are examples of guardian angels in Scripture (1 Kings 19:5; Daniel 6:22; Matthew 18:10; Luke 16:22; Acts 12:7), although there is no indication that one angel is assigned to each believer. Angels can also be God's messengers (Matthew 2:13; Acts 27:23, 24). Angels are not visible, except on special occasions (Numbers 22:31; Luke 2:9). Verses 11 and 12 were quoted by Satan when he tempted Jesus (Matthew 4:6; Luke 4:10, 11). It is comforting to know that God watches over us even in times of great stress and fear.

92:1, 2 When things are going well, we focus on our blessings and express our gratitude to God for them. But thanks should be on our lips every day. We can never say thank you enough to parents, friends, leaders, and especially to God. When thanksgiving becomes an integral part of your life, you will find that your attitude towards life will change. You will become more positive, gracious, loving, and humble.

and your faithfulness at night,
3 to the music of the ten-stringed lyre
and the melody of the harp.[d]

4 For you make me glad by your deeds, O LORD;
I sing for joy at the work of your hands.[e]
5 How great are your works,[f] O LORD,
how profound your thoughts![g]
6 The senseless man[h] does not know,
fools do not understand,
7 that though the wicked spring up like grass
and all evildoers flourish,
they will be for ever destroyed.

8 But you, O LORD, are exalted for ever.

9 For surely your enemies, O LORD,
surely your enemies will perish;
all evildoers will be scattered.[i]
10 You have exalted my horn[a][j] like that of a wild ox;
fine oils[k] have been poured upon me.
11 My eyes have seen the defeat of my adversaries;
my ears have heard the rout of my wicked foes.[l]

12 The righteous will flourish like a palm tree,
they will grow like a cedar of Lebanon;[m]
13 planted in the house of the LORD,
they will flourish in the courts of our God.[n]
14 They will still bear fruit[o] in old age,
they will stay fresh and green,
15 proclaiming, "The LORD is upright;
he is my Rock, and there is no wickedness in him.[p]"

PSALM 93

Theme: God's unchanging and almighty nature. His creation reminds us of his great power.
Author: Anonymous

1 The LORD reigns,[a] he is robed in majesty;[b]
the LORD is robed in majesty
and is armed with strength.[c]
The world is firmly established;
it cannot be moved.[d]
2 Your throne was established long ago;
you are from all eternity.[e]

3 The seas[f] have lifted up, O LORD,
the seas have lifted up their voice;

a *10 Horn* here symbolises strength.

92:3 [d] 1Sa 10:5; Ne 12:27; Ps 33:2
92:4 [e] Ps 8:6; 143:5
92:5 [f] Rev 15:3 [g] Ps 40:5; 139:17; Isa 28:29; Ro 11:33
92:6 [h] Ps 73:22
92:9 [i] Ps 68:1; 89:10
92:10 [j] Ps 89:17 [k] Ps 23:5
92:11 [l] Ps 54:7; 91:8
92:12 [m] Ps 1:3; 52:8; Jer 17:8; Hos 14:6
92:13 [n] Ps 100:4
92:14 [o] Jn 15:2
92:15 [p] Job 34:10
93:1 [a] Ps 97:1 [b] Ps 104:1 [c] Ps 65:6 [d] Ps 96:10
93:2 [e] Ps 45:6
93:3 [f] Ps 96:11

92:12, 13 Palm trees are known for their long life. To flourish like palm trees means to stand tall and to live long. The cedars of Lebanon grew to 120 feet in height and up to 30 feet in circumference; thus, they were solid, strong, and immovable. The psalmist saw believers as upright, strong, and unmoved by the winds of circumstance. Those who place their faith firmly in God can have this strength and vitality.

92:14 Honouring God is not limited to young people who seem to have unlimited strength and energy. Even in old age, devoted believers can produce spiritual fruit. There are many faithful older people who continue to have a fresh outlook and can teach us from a lifetime's experience of serving God. Seek out an elderly friend or relative to tell you about his or her experiences with the Lord and challenge you to new heights of spiritual growth.

93:1ff Jewish tradition claims that the next seven psalms (93–99) anticipated some of the works of the Messiah. Psalm 93 is said to have been used in post-captivity temple services and may have been written during Sennacherib's invasion (2 Kings 18:13–19:37).

93:4 [g]Ps 65:7
93:5 [h]Ps 29:2
94:1 [a]Na 1:2; Ro 12:19 [b]Ps 80:1
94:2 [c]Ge 18:25 [d]Ps 31:23
94:4 [e]Ps 31:18 [f]Ps 52:1
94:5 [g]Isa 3:15
94:7 [h]Job 22:14; Ps 10:11
94:8 [i]Ps 92:6
94:9 [j]Ex 4:11; Pr 20:12
94:10 [k]Job 35:11; Isa 28:26
94:11 [l]1Co 3:20*

the seas have lifted up their pounding waves.
4 Mightier than the thunder[g] of the great waters,
mightier than the breakers of the sea—
the LORD on high is mighty.

5 Your statutes stand firm;
holiness[h] adorns your house
for endless days, O LORD.

PSALM 94

Theme: God will keep his people from the severe punishment awaiting the wicked. Since God is holy and just, we can be certain that the wicked will not prevail.
Author: Anonymous

1 O LORD, the God who avenges,[a]
O God who avenges, shine forth.[b]
2 Rise up, O Judge[c] of the earth;
pay back[d] to the proud what they deserve.
3 How long will the wicked, O LORD,
how long will the wicked be jubilant?

4 They pour out arrogant[e] words;
all the evildoers are full of boasting.[f]
5 They crush your people,[g] O LORD;
they oppress your inheritance.
6 They slay the widow and the alien;
they murder the fatherless.
7 They say, "The LORD does not see;[h]
the God of Jacob pays no heed."

8 Take heed, you senseless ones[i] among the people;
you fools, when will you become wise?
9 Does he who implanted the ear not hear?
Does he who formed the eye not see?[j]
10 Does he who disciplines nations not punish?
Does he who teaches[k] man lack knowledge?
11 The LORD knows the thoughts of man;
he knows that they are futile.[l]

JUSTICE IN THE BOOK OF PSALMS

Justice is a major theme in Psalms. The psalmists praise God because he is just; they plead with him to intervene and bring justice where there is oppression and wickedness; they condemn the wicked who trust in their wealth; they extol the righteous who are just towards their neighbours.

Justice in Psalms is more than honesty. It is active intervention on behalf of the helpless, especially the poor. The psalmists do not merely wish the poor could be given what they need, but they plead with God to destroy those nations that are subverting justice and oppressing God's people.

Here are some examples of psalms that speak about justice. As you read them, ask yourself, "Who is my neighbour? Does my lifestyle—my work, my play, my buying habits, my giving—help or hurt people who have less than I do? What one thing could I do this week to help a helpless person?"

Selected psalms that emphasise this theme are 7; 9; 15; 37; 50; 72; 75; 82; 94; 145.

93:5 The key to God's eternal reign is his holiness. God's glory is seen not only in his strength but in his perfect moral character as well. God will never do anything that is not morally perfect. This reassures us that we can trust him, yet it places a demand on us. Our desire to be holy (dedicated to God and morally clean) is our only suitable response. We must never use unholy means to reach a holy goal because God says, "Be holy because I, the LORD your God, am holy" (Leviticus 19:1, 2).

12Blessed is the man you discipline,[m] O LORD,
the man you teach[n] from your law;
13you grant him relief from days of trouble,
till a pit[o] is dug for the wicked.
14For the LORD will not reject his people;[p]
he will never forsake his inheritance.
15Judgment will again be founded on righteousness,[q]
and all the upright in heart will follow it.

16Who will rise up[r] for me against the wicked?
Who will take a stand for me against evildoers?[s]
17Unless the LORD had given me help,[t]
I would soon have dwelt in the silence of death.
18When I said, "My foot is slipping,[u]"
your love, O LORD, supported me.
19When anxiety was great within me,
your consolation brought joy to my soul.

20Can a corrupt throne be allied with you—
one that brings on misery by its decrees?[v]
21They band together[w] against the righteous
and condemn the innocent[x] to death.
22But the LORD has become my fortress,
and my God the rock in whom I take refuge.[y]
23He will repay[z] them for their sins
and destroy them for their wickedness;
the LORD our God will destroy them.

PSALM 95

Theme: An invitation to worship God
Author: Anonymous

1Come, let us sing for joy to the LORD;
let us shout aloud[a] to the Rock[b] of our salvation.
2Let us come before him[c] with thanksgiving
and extol him with music[d] and song.

3For the LORD is the great God,[e]
the great King above all gods.[f]
4In his hand are the depths of the earth,
and the mountain peaks belong to him.
5The sea is his, for he made it,
and his hands formed the dry land.[g]

6Come, let us bow down[h] in worship,
let us kneel[i] before the LORD our Maker;[j]
7for he is our God
and we are the people of his pasture,[k]
the flock under his care.

Today, if you hear his voice,
8 do not harden your hearts as you did at Meribah,[a][l]

[a] 8 *Meribah* means *quarrelling.*

94:12 [m]Job 5:17; Heb 12:5 [n]Dt 8:3
94:13 [o]Ps 55:23
94:14 [p]1Sa 12:22; Ps 37:28; Ro 11:2
94:15 [q]Ps 97:2
94:16 [r]Nu 10:35; Ps 17:13 [s]Ps 59:2
94:17 [t]Ps 124:2
94:18 [u]Ps 38:16
94:20 [v]Ps 58:2
94:21 [w]Ps 56:6 [x]Ps 106:38; Pr 17:15, 26
94:22 [y]Ps 18:2; 59:9
94:23 [z]Ps 7:16
95:1 [a]Ps 81:1 [b]2Sa 22:47
95:2 [c]Mic 6:6 [d]Ps 81:2; Eph 5:19
95:3 [e]Ps 48:1; 145:3 [f]Ps 96:4; 97:9
95:5 [g]Ge 1:9; Ps 146:6
95:6 [h]Php 2:10 [i]2Ch 6:13 [j]Ps 100:3; 149:2; Isa 17:7; Da 6:10-11; Hos 8:14
95:7 [k]Ps 74:1; 79:13
95:8 [l]Ex 17:7

94:12, 13 At times, God must discipline us to help us. This is similar to a loving parent's disciplining his child. The discipline is not very enjoyable to the child, but it is essential to teach him right from wrong. The Bible says that "no discipline seems pleasant at the time, but painful. Later on, however, it produces a harvest of righteousness and peace for those who have been trained by it" (Hebrews 12:11). When you feel God's hand of correction, accept it as proof of his love. Realise that God is urging you to follow his

95:9 [m]Nu 14:22; Ps 78:18; 1Co 10:9
95:10 [n]Ac 7:36; Heb 3:17
95:11 [o]Nu 14:23 [p]Dt 1:35; Heb 4:3, 5*

as you did that day at Massah[b] in the desert,
9 where your fathers tested[m] and tried me,
though they had seen what I did.
10 For forty years[n] I was angry with that generation;
I said, "They are a people whose hearts go astray,
and they have not known my ways."
11 So I declared on oath[o] in my anger,
"They shall never enter my rest."[p]

PSALM 96

96:1 [a]1Ch 16:23
96:2 [b]Ps 71:15
96:4 [c]Ps 18:3; 145:3 [d]Ps 89:7 [e]Ps 95:3
96:5 [f]Ps 115:15
96:6 [g]Ps 29:1
96:7 [h]Ps 29:1 [i]Ps 22:27
96:8 [j]Ps 45:12; 72:10
96:9 [k]Ps 29:2 [l]Ps 114:7 [m]Ps 33:8
96:10 [n]Ps 97:1 [o]Ps 93:1 [p]Ps 67:4
96:11 [q]Ps 97:1; 98:7; Isa 49:13

Theme: How to praise God. We can sing about him, tell others about him, worship him, give him glory, bring offerings to him, and live holy lives.
Author: Possibly David because this psalm closely resembles David's hymn of praise in 1 Chronicles 16:23–36

1 Sing to the LORD[a] a new song;
sing to the LORD, all the earth.
2 Sing to the LORD, praise his name;
proclaim his salvation[b] day after day.
3 Declare his glory among the nations,
his marvellous deeds among all peoples.

4 For great is the LORD and most worthy of praise;[c]
he is to be feared[d] above all gods.[e]
5 For all the gods of the nations are idols,
but the LORD made the heavens.[f]
6 Splendour and majesty are before him;
strength and glory[g] are in his sanctuary.

7 Ascribe to the LORD,[h] O families of nations,[i]
ascribe to the LORD glory and strength.
8 Ascribe to the LORD the glory due to his name;
bring an offering[j] and come into his courts.
9 Worship the LORD in the splendour of his[a] holiness;[k]
tremble[l] before him, all the earth.[m]

10 Say among the nations, "The LORD reigns.[n]"
The world is firmly established, it cannot be moved;[o]
he will judge the peoples with equity.[p]
11 Let the heavens rejoice, let the earth be glad;[q]
let the sea resound, and all that is in it;
12 let the fields be jubilant, and everything in them.

b *8 Massah* means *testing.* **a** *9* Or *LORD with the splendour of*

paths instead of stubbornly going your own way.

95:8 A hardened heart is as useless as a hardened lump of clay or a hardened loaf of bread. Nothing can restore it and make it useful. The psalmist warns against hardening our hearts as Israel did in the desert by continuing to resist God's will (Exodus 17:7). They were so convinced that God couldn't deliver them that they simply lost their faith in him. When someone's heart becomes hardened, that person is so stubbornly set in his ways that he or she cannot turn to God. This does not happen all at once; it is the result of a series of choices to disregard God's will. If you resist God long enough, God may toss you aside like hardened bread, useless and worthless.

95:8 *Meribah* means "quarrelling", and *Massah* means "testing". This refers to the incident at Rephidim (Exodus 17:1–7) when the Israelites complained to Moses because they had no water (see also Numbers 20:1–13).

95:11 What keeps us from God's ultimate blessings (entering his "rest")? Ungrateful hearts (95:2), not worshipping or submitting to him (95:6), hardening our hearts (95:8), testing God because of stubborn doubts (95:9). In Hebrews 4:5–11, we are warned not to harden our hearts, but to reject the glamour of sin and anything else that would lead us away from God.

96:1–4 The psalmist sings out his praises to God, overwhelmed by all that God has done. If we believe God is great, we cannot help telling others about him. The best witnessing happens when our hearts are full of appreciation for what he has done. God has chosen to use us to "declare . . . his marvellous deeds among all peoples". Praise for our great God overflows from his creation and should overflow from our lips. How well are you doing at telling others about God's greatness?

Then all the trees of the forest[r] will sing for joy;[s]
13 they will sing before the LORD, for he comes,
he comes to judge[t] the earth.
He will judge the world in righteousness
and the peoples in his truth.

PSALM 97

Theme: God, our awesome Conqueror, is righteous and just.
Author: Anonymous

1 The LORD reigns,[a] let the earth be glad;[b]
let the distant shores rejoice.

2 Clouds and thick darkness[c] surround him;
righteousness and justice are the foundation of his throne.[d]
3 Fire[e] goes before[f] him
and consumes[g] his foes on every side.
4 His lightning lights up the world;
the earth sees and trembles.[h]
5 The mountains melt[i] like wax before the LORD,
before the Lord of all the earth.[j]
6 The heavens proclaim his righteousness,[k]
and all the peoples see his glory.[l]

7 All who worship images[m] are put to shame,[n]
those who boast in idols—
worship him,[o] all you gods!

8 Zion hears and rejoices
and the villages of Judah are glad
because of your judgments,[p] O LORD.
9 For you, O LORD, are the Most High over all the earth;[q]
you are exalted[r] far above all gods.

10 Let those who love the LORD hate evil,[s]
for he guards the lives of his faithful ones[t]
and delivers[u] them from the hand of the wicked.[v]
11 Light is shed[w] upon the righteous
and joy on the upright in heart.
12 Rejoice in the LORD, you who are righteous,
and praise his holy name.[x]

96:12 [r]Isa 44:23 [s]Ps 65:13
96:13 [t]Rev 19:11
97:1 [a]Ps 96:10 [b]Ps 96:11
97:2 [c]Ex 19:9; Ps 18:11 [d]Ps 89:14
97:3 [e]Da 7:10 [f]Hab 3:5 [g]Ps 18:8
97:4 [h]Ps 104:32
97:5 [i]Ps 46:2, 6; Mic 1:4 [j]Jos 3:11
97:6 [k]Ps 50:6 [l]Ps 19:1
97:7 [m]Lev 26:1 [n]Jer 10:14 [o]Heb 1:6
97:8 [p]Ps 48:11
97:9 [q]Ps 83:18; 95:3 [r]Ex 18:11
97:10 [s]Ps 34:14; Am 5:15; Ro 12:9 [t]Pr 2:8 [u]Da 3:28 [v]Ps 37:40; Jer 15:21
97:11 [w]Job 22:28
97:12 [x]Ps 30:4

97:2 The clouds and thick darkness that surround God symbolise his unapproachable holiness and the inability of people to find him on their own. If he were uncovered, no-one could stand before his blazing holiness and glory.

97:7 People worship all kinds of images and idols. Although God reveals himself and his love through nature and the Bible, there are many who decide to ignore or reject him and pursue goals they believe are more important. The Bible makes it clear that these people are idol worshippers because they give their highest loyalty to something other than God. One day we will stand before God in all his glory and power. Then we will see all our goals and accomplishments for what they really are. How foolish our earthly pursuits will seem then!

97:10 A sincere desire to please God will result in an alignment of your desires with God's desires. You will love what God loves and hate what God hates. If you love the Lord, you will hate evil. If you do not despise the actions of people who take advantage of others, if you admire people who only look out for themselves, or if you envy those who get ahead using any means to accomplish their ends, then your primary desire in life is not to please God. Learn to love God's ways and hate evil in every form—not only the obvious sins but also the socially acceptable ones.

98:1
[a]Ps 96:1
[b]Ps 96:3
[c]Ex 15:6
[d]Isa 52:10

98:2
[e]Isa 52:10

98:3
[f]Lk 1:54

98:4
[g]Isa 44:23

98:5
[h]Ps 92:3
[i]Isa 51:3

98:6
[j]Nu 10:10
[k]Ps 47:7

98:7
[l]Ps 24:1

98:8
[m]Isa 55:12

98:9
[n]Ps 96:10

PSALM 98

A psalm.

Theme: A song of joy and victory. Because God is victorious over evil, all those who follow him will be victorious with him when he judges the earth.
Author: Anonymous

1 Sing to the LORD a new song,[a]
for he has done marvellous things;[b]
his right hand[c] and his holy arm[d]
have worked salvation for him.
2 The LORD has made his salvation known[e]
and revealed his righteousness to the nations.
3 He has remembered[f] his love
and his faithfulness to the house of Israel;
all the ends of the earth have seen
the salvation of our God.

4 Shout for joy[g] to the LORD, all the earth,
burst into jubilant song with music;
5 make music to the LORD with the harp,[h]
with the harp and the sound of singing,[i]
6 with trumpets[j] and the blast of the ram's horn—
shout for joy before the LORD, the King.[k]

7 Let the sea resound, and everything in it,
the world, and all who live in it.[l]
8 Let the rivers clap their hands,
let the mountains[m] sing together for joy;
9 let them sing before the LORD,
for he comes to judge the earth.
He will judge the world in righteousness
and the peoples with equity.[n]

99:1
[a]Ps 97:1
[b]Ex 25:22

99:2
[c]Ps 48:1
[d]Ps 97:9; 113:4

99:3
[e]Ps 76:1

99:4
[f]Ps 11:7
[g]Ps 98:9

PSALM 99

Theme: Praise for God's fairness and holiness. Because God is perfectly just and fair, we can trust him completely.
Author: Anonymous

1 The LORD reigns,[a]
let the nations tremble;
he sits enthroned between the cherubim,[b]
let the earth shake.
2 Great is the LORD[c] in Zion;
he is exalted[d] over all the nations.
3 Let them praise your great and awesome name[e]—
he is holy.

4 The King is mighty, he loves justice[f]—
you have established equity;[g]

98:1ff This is a psalm of praise anticipating the coming of God to rule his people. Jesus fulfilled this anticipation when he came to save all people from their sins (98:2, 3), and he will come again to judge the world (98:8, 9). God is both perfectly loving and perfectly just. He is merciful when he punishes, and he overlooks no sin when he loves. Praise him for his promise to save you and to return again.

99:1 Cherubim are mighty angels that comprise one of several ranks of angels. (For more on angels, see the note on 91:11.)

99:3 Everyone should praise God's great and awesome name because his name symbolises his nature, his personage, and his reputation. But the name of God is used so often in vulgar conversation that we have lost sight of its holiness. How easy it is to treat God lightly in everyday life. If you claim him as your Father, live worthy of the family name. Respect God's name and give him praise by both your *words* and your *life.*

in Jacob you have done
what is just and right.
5 Exalt[h] the LORD our God
and worship at his footstool;
he is holy.

6 Moses[i] and Aaron were among his priests,
Samuel[j] was among those who called on his name;
they called on the LORD
and he answered[k] them.
7 He spoke to them from the pillar of cloud;[l]
they kept his statutes and the decrees he gave them.

8 O LORD our God,
you answered them;
you were to Israel[a] a forgiving God,[m]
though you punished their misdeeds.[b]
9 Exalt the LORD our God
and worship at his holy mountain,
for the LORD our God is holy.

PSALM 100

A psalm. For giving thanks.

Theme: An invitation to enter joyfully into God's presence. His faithfulness extends to our generation and beyond.
Author: Anonymous

1 Shout for joy[a] to the LORD, all the earth.
2 Worship the LORD with gladness;
come before him[b] with joyful songs.
3 Know that the LORD is God.[c]
It is he who made us,[d] and we are his;[a]
we are his people, the sheep of his pasture.[e]

4 Enter his gates with thanksgiving
and his courts with praise;
give thanks to him and praise his name.[f]
5 For the LORD is good[g] and his love endures for ever;[h]
his faithfulness[i] continues through all generations.

a 8 Hebrew *them* b 8 Or / *an avenger of the wrongs done to them* a 3 Or *and not we ourselves*

99:5 [h]Ps 132:7
99:6 [i]Ex 24:6 [j]Jer 15:1 [k]1Sa 7:9
99:7 [l]Ex 33:9
99:8 [m]Nu 14:20
100:1 [a]Ps 98:4
100:2 [b]Ps 95:2
100:3 [c]Ps 46:10 [d]Job 10:3 [e]Ps 74:1; Eze 34:31
100:4 [f]Ps 116:17
100:5 [g]1Ch 16:34; Ps 25:8 [h]Ezr 3:11; Ps 106:1 [i]Ps 119:90

99:5 God's holiness is terribly frightening for sinners, but a wonderful comfort for believers. God is morally perfect and is set apart from people and sin. He has no weaknesses or shortcomings. For sinners, this is frightening because all their inadequacies and evil are exposed by the light of God's holiness. God cannot tolerate, ignore, or excuse sin. For believers, God's holiness gives comfort because, as we worship him, we are lifted from the mire of sin. As we believe in him, we are made holy.

99:6 The Bible records several instances where Moses, Aaron, and Samuel cried out to God for help (Exodus 15:25; 17:4; Numbers 11:11–15; 12:13; 14:13ff; 16:44–48; 1 Samuel 7:5, 9; 15:11).

100:3 God is our Creator; we did not create ourselves. Many people live as though they are the creator and centre of their own little world. This mind-set leads to a greedy possessiveness and, if everything should be taken away, a loss of hope itself. But when we realise that God created us and gives us all we have, we will want to give to others as God gave to us (2 Corinthians 9:8). Then, if all is lost, we still have God and all he gives us.

100:4 God alone is worthy of being worshipped. What is your attitude towards worship? Do you willingly and joyfully come into God's presence, or are you just going through the motions, reluctantly going to church? This psalm tells us to remember God's goodness and dependability, and then to worship with thanksgiving and praise!

101:1
[a] Ps 51:14; 89:1; 145:7

PSALM 101
Of David. A psalm.

Theme: A prayer for help to walk a blameless path. To live with integrity, both our efforts and God's help are necessary.
Author: David

1 I will sing of your love[a] and justice;
to you, O LORD, I will sing praise.
2 I will be careful to lead a blameless life—
when will you come to me?

I will walk in my house
with blameless heart.
3 I will set before my eyes
no vile thing.[b]

The deeds of faithless men I hate;[c]
they shall not cling to me.
4 Men of perverse heart[d] shall be far from me;
I will have nothing to do with evil.

5 Whoever slanders his neighbour[e] in secret,
him will I put to silence;
whoever has haughty eyes[f] and a proud heart,
him will I not endure.

6 My eyes will be on the faithful in the land,
that they may dwell with me;
he whose walk is blameless[g]
will minister to me.

7 No-one who practises deceit
will dwell in my house;
no-one who speaks falsely
will stand in my presence.

8 Every morning[h] I will put to silence
all the wicked[i] in the land;
I will cut off every evildoer[j]
from the city of the LORD.[k]

101:3
[b] Dt 15:9
[c] Ps 40:4

101:4
[d] Pr 11:20

101:5
[e] Ps 50:20
[f] Ps 10:5; Pr 6:17

101:6
[g] Ps 119:1

101:8
[h] Jer 21:12
[i] Ps 75:10
[j] Ps 118:10-12
[k] Ps 46:4

PSALM 102
A prayer of an afflicted man. When he is faint and pours out his lament before the LORD.

Theme: The cure for distress. Because God is living, eternal, and unchanging, we can trust him to help his people in this generation just as he helped his people in past generations.
Author: Anonymous

1 Hear my prayer, O LORD;
let my cry for help[a] come to you.
2 Do not hide your face[b] from me
when I am in distress.

102:1
[a] Ex 2:23

102:2
[b] Ps 69:17

101:1ff David may have written this psalm early in his reign as king as he set down the standards he wanted to follow. David knew that to lead a blameless life he would need God's help (101:2). We can lead blameless lives if we avoid (1) looking at wickedness ("I will set before my eyes no vile thing", 101:3), (2) evil associates ("men of perverse heart", 101:4), (3) slander (101:5), and (4) pride (101:5). While avoiding the wrongs listed above, we must also let God's word show us the standards by which to live.

101:6 David said that he would keep his eyes "on the faithful in the land". In other words, he would choose as models and as friends those who are godly and truthful. Our friends and associates can have a profound influence on our lives. Make sure you keep your eyes on those who are faithful to God and his word.

Turn your ear to me;
when I call, answer me quickly.

3For my days vanish like smoke;[c]
my bones burn like glowing embers.
4My heart is blighted and withered like grass;[d]
I forget to eat my food.
5Because of my loud groaning
I am reduced to skin and bones.
6I am like a desert owl,[e]
like an owl among the ruins.
7I lie awake;[f] I have become
like a bird alone[g] on a roof.
8All day long my enemies taunt me;
those who rail against me use my name as a curse.
9For I eat ashes as my food
and mingle my drink with tears[h]
10because of your great wrath,[i]
for you have taken me up and thrown me aside.
11My days are like the evening shadow;[j]
I wither away like grass.

12But you, O LORD, sit enthroned for ever;[k]
your renown endures[l] through all generations.
13You will arise and have compassion[m] on Zion,
for it is time to show favour to her;
the appointed time has come.
14For her stones are dear to your servants;
her very dust moves them to pity.
15The nations will fear[n] the name of the LORD,
all the kings[o] of the earth will revere your glory.
16For the LORD will rebuild Zion
and appear in his glory.[p]
17He will respond to the prayer[q] of the destitute;
he will not despise their plea.

18Let this be written[r] for a future generation,
that a people not yet created[s] may praise the LORD:
19"The LORD looked down[t] from his sanctuary on high,
from heaven he viewed the earth,
20to hear the groans of the prisoners[u]
and release those condemned to death."
21So the name of the LORD will be declared[v] in Zion
and his praise in Jerusalem
22when the peoples and the kingdoms
assemble to worship the LORD.

23In the course of my life[a] he broke my strength;
he cut short my days.
24So I said:

[a] *23* Or *By his power*

102:3 [c]Jas 4:14
102:4 [d]Ps 37:2
102:6 [e]Job 30:29; Isa 34:11
102:7 [f]Ps 77:4 [g]Ps 38:11
102:9 [h]Ps 42:3
102:10 [i]Ps 38:3
102:11 [j]Job 14:2
102:12 [k]Ps 9:7 [l]Ps 135:13
102:13 [m]Isa 60:10
102:15 [n]1Ki 8:43 [o]Ps 138:4
102:16 [p]Isa 60:1-2
102:17 [q]Ne 1:6
102:18 [r]Ro 15:4 [s]Ps 22:31
102:19 [t]Dt 26:15
102:20 [u]Ps 79:11
102:21 [v]Ps 22:22

102:3, 4 The psalmist felt so bad that he forgot to eat. When we face sickness and despair, our days pass blindly and we don't care about even our basic needs. In these times, God alone is our comfort and strength. Even when we are too weak to fight, we can lean on him. It is often when we recognise our weaknesses that God's greatest strength becomes available.

102:6, 7 These birds are pictures of loneliness and desolation. At times we may need to be alone, and solitude may comfort us. But we must be careful not to spurn those who reach out to us. Don't reject help and conversation. Suffering silently is neither Christian nor particularly healthy. Instead, accept graciously the support and help from family and friends.

102:16–22 Christ's future reign on earth will encompass two events mentioned in these verses. Jerusalem (Zion) will be restored, and the entire world will worship God (Revelation 11:15; 21:1–27).

102:24
[w] Ps 90:2; Isa 38:10

102:25
[x] Ge 1:1; Heb 1:10-12*

102:26
[y] Isa 34:4; Mt 24:35; 2Pe 3:7-10; Rev 20:11

102:27
[z] Mal 3:6; Heb 13:8; Jas 1:17

102:28
[a] Ps 69:36
[b] Ps 89:4

"Do not take me away, O my God, in the midst of my days;
your years go on[w] through all generations.
25 In the beginning[x] you laid the foundations of the earth,
and the heavens are the work of your hands.
26 They will perish,[y] but you remain;
they will all wear out like a garment.
Like clothing you will change them
and they will be discarded.
27 But you remain the same,[z]
and your years will never end.
28 The children of your servants[a] will live in your presence;
their descendants[b] will be established before you."

PSALM 103

Of David.

Theme: God's great love for us. What God does for us tells us what he is really like.
Author: David

103:1
[a] Ps 104:1

103:3
[b] Ps 130:8
[c] Ex 15:26

103:5
[d] Isa 40:31

103:7
[e] Ps 99:7; 147:19
[f] Ex 33:13
[g] Ps 106:22

103:8
[h] Ex 34:6; Ps 86:15; Jas 5:11

103:9
[i] Ps 30:5; Isa 57:16; Jer 3:5, 12; Mic 7:18

103:10
[j] Ezr 9:13

103:11
[k] Ps 57:10

1 Praise the LORD, O my soul;[a]
all my inmost being, praise his holy name.
2 Praise the LORD, O my soul,
and forget not all his benefits—
3 who forgives all your sins[b]
and heals[c] all your diseases,
4 who redeems your life from the pit
and crowns you with love and compassion,
5 who satisfies your desires with good things
so that your youth is renewed like the eagle's.[d]

6 The LORD works righteousness
and justice for all the oppressed.

7 He made known[e] his ways[f] to Moses,
his deeds[g] to the people of Israel:
8 The LORD is compassionate and gracious,[h]
slow to anger, abounding in love.
9 He will not always accuse,
nor will he harbour his anger for ever;[i]
10 he does not treat us as our sins deserve[j]
or repay us according to our iniquities.
11 For as high as the heavens are above the earth,
so great is his love[k] for those who fear him;
12 as far as the east is from the west,

102:25–27 The writer of this psalm felt rejected and tossed aside because of his great troubles (102:9, 10). Problems and heartaches can overwhelm us and cause us to feel that God has rejected us. But God our Creator is eternally with us and will keep all his promises, even though we may feel alone. The world will perish, but God will remain. Hebrews 1:10–12 quotes these verses to show that Jesus Christ, God's Son, was also present and active at the creation of the world.

103:1ff David's praise focused on God's glorious deeds. It is easy to complain about life, but David's list gives us plenty for which to praise God—he forgives our sins, heals our diseases, redeems us from death, crowns us with love and compassion, satisfies our desires, and gives righteousness and justice. We receive all of these without deserving any of them. No matter how difficult your life's journey, you can always count your blessings—past, present, and future. When you feel as though you have nothing for which to praise God, read David's list.

103:7 God's law was given first to Moses and the people of Israel. God's law presents a clear picture of God's nature and will. It was God's training manual to prepare his people to serve him and to follow his ways. Review the Ten Commandments (Exodus 20) and the history of how they were given, asking God to show you his will and his ways through them.

103:12 East and west can never meet. This is a symbolic portrait of God's forgiveness—when he forgives our sin, he separates it from us and doesn't even remember it. We need never wallow in the past, for God forgives and forgets. We tend to dredge up the ugly past, but God has wiped our record clean. If we are to follow God, we must model his forgiveness. When we forgive another, we must also forget the sin. Otherwise, we have not truly forgiven.

so far has he removed our transgressions[l] from us.
13 As a father has compassion[m] on his children,
so the LORD has compassion on those who fear him;
14 for he knows how we are formed,[n]
he remembers that we are dust.
15 As for man, his days are like grass,[o]
he flourishes like a flower[p] of the field;
16 the wind blows[q] over it and it is gone,
and its place[r] remembers it no more.
17 But from everlasting to everlasting
the LORD's love is with those who fear him,
and his righteousness with their children's children—
18 with those who keep his covenant
and remember to obey his precepts.[s]

19 The LORD has established his throne in heaven,
and his kingdom rules[t] over all.

20 Praise the LORD, you his angels,[u]
you mighty ones[v] who do his bidding,
who obey his word.
21 Praise the LORD, all his heavenly hosts,[w]
you his servants who do his will.
22 Praise the LORD, all his works[x]
everywhere in his dominion.

Praise the LORD, O my soul.

PSALM 104

Theme: Appreciating God through his creation. He not only creates, but maintains his creation. The Lord's care is the source of our joy.
Author: Anonymous

1 Praise the LORD, O my soul.[a]

O LORD my God, you are very great;
you are clothed with splendour and majesty.
2 He wraps[b] himself in light as with a garment;
he stretches out the heavens[c] like a tent
3 and lays the beams[d] of his upper chambers on their waters.
He makes the clouds[e] his chariot
and rides on the wings of the wind.[f]
4 He makes winds his messengers,[a][g]
flames of fire[h] his servants.

5 He set the earth[i] on its foundations;

103:12 [l] 2Sa 12:13
103:13 [m] Mal 3:17
103:14 [n] Isa 29:16
103:15 [o] Ps 90:5 [p] Job 14:2; Jas 1:10; 1Pe 1:24
103:16 [q] Isa 40:7 [r] Job 7:10
103:18 [s] Dt 7:9
103:19 [t] Ps 47:2
103:20 [u] Ps 148:2; Heb 1:14 [v] Ps 29:1
103:21 [w] 1Ki 22:19
103:22 [x] Ps 145:10
104:1 [a] Ps 103:22
104:2 [b] Da 7:9 [c] Isa 40:22
104:3 [d] Am 9:6 [e] Isa 19:1 [f] Ps 18:10
104:4 [g] Ps 148:8; Heb 1:7* [h] 2Ki 2:11
104:5 [i] Job 26:7; Ps 24:1-2

[a] 4 Or *angels*

103:13, 14 We are fragile, but God's care is eternal. Too often we focus on God as Judge and Lawgiver, ignoring his compassion and concern for us. When God examines our lives, he remembers our human condition. Our weakness should never be used as a justification for sin. His mercy takes everything into account. God will deal with you compassionately. Trust him.

103:20–22 Everything everywhere is to praise the Lord: all angels—mighty ones and heavenly hosts—and all his works! Praising God means remembering all he has done for us (103:2), fearing him and obeying his commands (103:17, 18), and doing his will (103:21). Does your life praise the Lord?

104:1ff This psalm is a poetic summary of God's creation of the world as found in the first chapter of Genesis. What God created each day is mentioned by the psalmist as a reason to praise God. On day one, God created light (104:1, 2; Genesis 1:3); day two, the heavens and the waters (104:2, 3; Genesis 1:6); day three, land and vegetation (104:6–18; Genesis 1:9–13); day four, the sun, moon, and stars (104:19–23; Genesis 1:14–16); day five, fish and birds (104:25, 26; Genesis 1:20–23); and on day six, animals, man, and food to sustain them (104:21–24, 27–30; Genesis 1:24–31). God's act of creation deserves the praise of all people.

104:5 The earth is built on God's foundations, and he guarantees its permanence. "It can never be moved" by anyone other than God. Even though one day the heavens and the earth will be de-

104:6 [j]Ge 7:19 [k]Ge 1:2
104:7 [l]Ps 18:15
104:8 [m]Ps 33:7
104:10 [n]Ps 107:33; Isa 41:18
104:12 [o]Mt 8:20
104:13 [p]Ps 147:8; Jer 10:13
104:14 [q]Job 38:27; Ps 147:8 [r]Ge 1:30; Job 28:5
104:15 [s]Jdg 9:13 [t]Ps 23:5; 92:10; Lk 7:46
104:17 [u]ver 12
104:18 [v]Pr 30:26
104:19 [w]Ge 1:14 [x]Ps 19:6
104:20 [y]Isa 45:7 [z]Ps 74:16

it can never be moved.
6 You covered it[j] with the deep[k] as with a garment;
the waters stood above the mountains.
7 But at your rebuke[l] the waters fled,
at the sound of your thunder they took to flight;
8 they flowed over the mountains,
they went down into the valleys,
to the place you assigned[m] for them.
9 You set a boundary they cannot cross;
never again will they cover the earth.

10 He makes springs[n] pour water into the ravines;
it flows between the mountains.
11 They give water to all the beasts of the field;
the wild donkeys quench their thirst.
12 The birds of the air[o] nest by the waters;
they sing among the branches.
13 He waters the mountains[p] from his upper chambers;
the earth is satisfied by the fruit of his work.
14 He makes grass grow[q] for the cattle,
and plants for man to cultivate—
bringing forth food[r] from the earth:
15 wine[s] that gladdens the heart of man,
oil[t] to make his face shine,
and bread that sustains his heart.
16 The trees of the LORD are well watered,
the cedars of Lebanon that he planted.
17 There the birds[u] make their nests;
the stork has its home in the pine trees.
18 The high mountains belong to the wild goats;
the crags are a refuge for the conies.[b][v]

19 The moon marks off the seasons,[w]
and the sun[x] knows when to go down.
20 You bring darkness,[y] it becomes night,[z]

b *18* That is, the hyrax or rock badger

HOW GOD IS DESCRIBED IN PSALMS

Most of the psalms speak to God or about God. Because they were composed in a variety of situations, various facets of God's character are mentioned. Here is a sample of God's characteristics as understood and experienced by the psalm writers. As you read these psalms, ask yourself if this is the God you know.

God is . . .	*References*
All-knowing and ever-present	Psalm 139
Beautiful and desirable	Psalms 27; 36; 45
Creator	Psalms 8; 104; 148
Good and generous	Psalms 34; 81; 107
Great and sovereign	Psalms 33; 89; 96
Holy	Psalms 66; 99; 145
Loving and faithful	Psalms 23; 42; 51
Merciful and forgiving	Psalms 32; 111; 130
Powerful	Psalms 76; 89; 93
Willing to reveal his will, law, and direction	Psalms 1; 19; 119
Righteous and just	Psalms 71; 97; 113
Spirit	Psalms 104; 139; 143

stroyed (2 Peter 3:10), he will create a new heaven and a new earth that will last for ever (Isaiah 65:17; Revelation 21:1). The same power that undergirds the world also provides a firm foundation for believers.

and all the beasts of the forest[a] prowl.
21 The lions roar for their prey
and seek their food from God.[b]
22 The sun rises, and they steal away;
they return and lie down in their dens.[c]
23 Then man goes out to his work,[d]
to his labour until evening.

24 How many are your works,[e] O LORD!
In wisdom you made[f] them all;
the earth is full of your creatures.
25 There is the sea,[g] vast and spacious,
teeming with creatures beyond number—
living things both large and small.
26 There the ships[h] go to and fro,
and the leviathan,[i] which you formed to frolic there.

27 These all look to you
to give them their food[j] at the proper time.
28 When you give it to them,
they gather it up;
when you open your hand,
they are satisfied[k] with good things.
29 When you hide your face,[l]
they are terrified;
when you take away their breath,
they die and return to the dust.[m]
30 When you send your Spirit,
they are created,
and you renew the face of the earth.

31 May the glory of the LORD endure for ever;
may the LORD rejoice in his works[n]—
32 he who looks at the earth, and it trembles,[o]
who touches the mountains,[p] and they smoke.[q]

33 I will sing[r] to the LORD all my life;
I will sing praise to my God as long as I live.
34 May my meditation be pleasing to him,
as I rejoice[s] in the LORD.
35 But may sinners vanish[t] from the earth
and the wicked be no more.

Praise the LORD, O my soul.

Praise the LORD.[c][u]

[c] 35 Hebrew *Hallelu Yah*; in the Septuagint this line stands at the beginning of Psalm 105.

104:20 [a] Ps 50:10
104:21 [b] Job 38:39; Ps 145:15; Joel 1:20
104:22 [c] Job 37:8
104:23 [d] Ge 3:19
104:24 [e] Ps 40:5 [f] Pr 3:19
104:25 [g] Ps 69:34
104:26 [h] Ps 107:23; Eze 27:9 [i] Job 41:1
104:27 [j] Job 36:31; Ps 136:25; 145:15; 147:9
104:28 [k] Ps 145:16
104:29 [l] Dt 31:17 [m] Job 34:14; Ecc 12:7
104:31 [n] Ge 1:31
104:32 [o] Ps 97:4 [p] Ex 19:18 [q] Ps 144:5
104:33 [r] Ps 63:4
104:34 [s] Ps 9:2
104:35 [t] Ps 37:38 [u] Ps 105:45; 106:48

104:24 Creation is filled with stunning variety, revealing the rich creativity, goodness, and wisdom of our loving God. As you observe your natural surroundings, thank God for his creativity. Take a fresh look at people, seeing each one as God's unique creation, each with his or her own special talents, abilities, and gifts.

104:26 Here *leviathan* simply means a large and active sea creature.

104:28–30 Psalm 105 expresses God's sovereignty in history; this psalm tells of his sovereignty over all creation. God has supreme, unlimited power over the entire universe. He creates; he preserves; he governs. As we understand God's power, we realise that he is sufficient to handle our lives.

104:29 Today many people are arrogant enough to think they don't need God. But our every breath depends on the spirit he has breathed into us (Genesis 2:7; 3:19; Job 33:4; 34:14, 15; Daniel 5:23). Not only do we depend on God for our very lives, but he wants the best for us. We should also desire to learn more of his plans for us each day.

105:1
[a]1Ch 16:34
[b]Ps 99:6

105:2
[c]Ps 96:1

105:4
[d]Ps 27:8

105:5
[e]Ps 40:5
[f]Ps 77:11

105:6
[g]ver 42
[h]Ps 106:5

105:8
[i]Ps 106:45;
Lk 1:72

105:9
[j]Ge 12:7; 17:2;
22:16-18;
Gal 3:15-18

105:10
[k]Ge 28:13-15

105:11
[l]Ge 13:15; 15:18

105:12
[m]Ge 34:30;
Dt 7:7
[n]Ge 23:4;
Heb 11:9

105:14
[o]Ge 35:5
[p]Ge 12:17-20

105:15
[q]Ge 26:11

PSALM 105

Theme: God's mighty deeds in bringing Israel to the promised land. Remembering his miracles encourages us to keep living close to him.
Author: David

1Give thanks to the LORD,[a] call on his name;[b]
make known among the nations what he has done.
2Sing to him,[c] sing praise to him;
tell of all his wonderful acts.
3Glory in his holy name;
let the hearts of those who seek the LORD rejoice.
4Look to the LORD and his strength;
seek his face[d] always.

5Remember the wonders[e] he has done,
his miracles, and the judgments he pronounced,[f]
6O descendants of Abraham his servant,[g]
O sons of Jacob, his chosen[h] ones.
7He is the LORD our God;
his judgments are in all the earth.

8He remembers his covenant[i] for ever,
the word he commanded, for a thousand generations,
9the covenant he made with Abraham,[j]
the oath he swore to Isaac.
10He confirmed it[k] to Jacob as a decree,
to Israel as an everlasting covenant:
11"To you I will give the land of Canaan[l]
as the portion you will inherit."

12When they were but few in number,[m]
few indeed, and strangers in it,[n]
13they wandered from nation to nation,
from one kingdom to another.
14He allowed no-one to oppress[o] them;
for their sake he rebuked kings:[p]
15"Do not touch[q] my anointed ones;
do my prophets no harm."

HISTORY IN THE BOOK OF PSALMS

For the original hearers, the historical psalms were vivid reminders of God's past acts on behalf of Israel. These history songs were written for passing on important lessons to succeeding generations. They celebrated the many promises God had made and faithfully kept; they also recounted the faithlessness of the people.

We cannot read this ancient history without reflecting on how consistently God's people failed to learn from the past. They repeatedly turned from fresh examples of God's faithfulness and forgiveness only to plunge back into sin. God can use these psalms to remind us how often we do exactly the same thing: having every reason to live for God, we choose instead to live for everything but God. If we paid more attention to "his story" we wouldn't make so many mistakes in our own stories.

Selected historical psalms include: 68; 78; 95; 105; 106; 111; 114; 135; 136; 149.

105:1ff The first 15 verses of this psalm are also found in 1 Chronicles 16:8–22, where they are sung as part of the celebration of David's bringing the ark of the covenant to Jerusalem. Three other psalms are also hymns recounting Israel's history—78, 106, and 136.

105:4, 5 If God seems far away, persist in your search for him. God rewards those who sincerely look for him (Hebrews 11:6). Jesus promised, "Seek and you will find" (Matthew 7:7). The psalmist suggested a valuable way to find God—become familiar with the way he has helped his people in the past. The Bible records the history of God's people. In searching its pages we will discover a loving God who is waiting for us to find him.

105:6–11 The nation Israel, the people through whom God revealed his laws to mankind, is descended from Abraham. God chose Abraham and promised that his descendants would live in the land of Canaan (now called Israel), and that they would be too numerous to count (Genesis 17:6–8). Abraham's son was Isaac; Isaac's son was Jacob. These three men are considered the patriarchs or founders of Israel. God blessed them because of their faith (see Hebrews 11:8–21).

16 He called down famine[r] on the land
and destroyed all their supplies of food;
17 and he sent a man before them—
Joseph, sold as a slave.[s]
18 They bruised his feet with shackles,[t]
his neck was put in irons,
19 till what he foretold[u] came to pass,
till the word of the LORD proved him true.
20 The king sent and released him,
the ruler of peoples set him free.[v]
21 He made him master of his household,
ruler over all he possessed,
22 to instruct his princes[w] as he pleased
and teach his elders wisdom.

23 Then Israel entered Egypt;[x]
Jacob lived as an alien in the land of Ham.
24 The LORD made his people very fruitful;
he made them too numerous[y] for their foes,
25 whose hearts he turned[z] to hate his people,
to conspire[a] against his servants.
26 He sent Moses[b] his servant,
and Aaron, whom he had chosen.[c]
27 They performed[d] his miraculous signs among them,
his wonders in the land of Ham.
28 He sent darkness[e] and made the land dark—
for had they not rebelled against his words?
29 He turned their waters into blood,[f]
causing their fish to die.[g]
30 Their land teemed with frogs,[h]
which went up into the bedrooms of their rulers.
31 He spoke, and there came swarms of flies,[i]
and gnats[j] throughout their country.
32 He turned their rain into hail,[k]
with lightning throughout their land;
33 he struck down their vines[l] and fig-trees
and shattered the trees of their country.
34 He spoke, and the locusts came,[m]
grasshoppers without number;
35 they ate up every green thing in their land,
ate up the produce of their soil.
36 Then he struck down all the firstborn[n] in their land,
the firstfruits of all their manhood.

37 He brought out Israel, laden with silver and gold,[o]
and from among their tribes no-one faltered.
38 Egypt was glad when they left,
because dread of Israel[p] had fallen on them.
39 He spread out a cloud[q] as a covering,
and a fire to give light at night.[r]
40 They asked,[s] and he brought them quail[t]
and satisfied them with the bread of heaven.[u]
41 He opened the rock,[v] and water gushed out;

105:16 [r]Ge 41:54; Lev 26:26; Isa 3:1; Eze 4:16
105:17 [s]Ge 37:28; 45:5; Ac 7:9
105:18 [t]Ge 40:15
105:19 [u]Ge 40:20-22
105:20 [v]Ge 41:14
105:22 [w]Ge 41:43-44
105:23 [x]Ge 46:6; Ac 13:17
105:24 [y]Ex 1:7, 9
105:25 [z]Ex 4:21 [a]Ex 1:6-10; Ac 7:19
105:26 [b]Ex 3:10 [c]Nu 16:5; 17:5-8
105:27 [d]Ex 7:8-12:51
105:28 [e]Ex 10:22
105:29 [f]Ps 78:44 [g]Ex 7:21
105:30 [h]Ex 8:2, 6
105:31 [i]Ex 8:21-24 [j]Ex 8:16-18
105:32 [k]Ex 9:22-25
105:33 [l]Ps 78:47
105:34 [m]Ex 10:4, 12-15
105:36 [n]Ex 12:29
105:37 [o]Ex 12:35
105:38 [p]Ex 12:33; 15:16
105:39 [q]Ex 13:21 [r]Ne 9:12; Ps 78:14
105:40 [s]Ps 78:18, 24 [t]Ex 16:13 [u]Jn 6:31
105:41 [v]Ex 17:6; Nu 20:11; Ps 78:15-16; 1Co 10:4

105:23–25 Did God cause the Egyptians to hate the Israelites? God is not the author of evil, but the Bible writers don't always distinguish between God's ultimate action and the intermediate steps. Thus by God blessing the Israelites, the Egyptians came to hate them (Exodus 1:8–22). Because God caused the Israelites' blessing, he is also said to have caused the Egyptians to hate them. God used their animosity as a means to lead the Israelites out of Egypt.

like a river it flowed in the desert.

42 For he remembered his holy promise[w]
given to his servant Abraham.
43 He brought out his people with rejoicing,[x]
his chosen ones with shouts of joy;
44 he gave them the lands of the nations,[y]
and they fell heir to what others had toiled for—
45 that they might keep his precepts
and observe his laws.[z]

Praise the LORD.[a]

PSALM 106

Theme: A song of national repentance as the people return from captivity. God patiently delivers us, in spite of our forgetfulness and self-willed rebellion.
Author: Anonymous

1 Praise the LORD.[a]

Give thanks to the LORD, for he is good;[a]
his love endures for ever.
2 Who can proclaim the mighty acts[b] of the LORD
or fully declare his praise?
3 Blessed are they who maintain justice,
who constantly do what is right.[c]
4 Remember me,[d] O LORD, when you show favour to your people,
come to my aid when you save them,
5 that I may enjoy the prosperity[e] of your chosen ones,
that I may share in the joy[f] of your nation
and join your inheritance in giving praise.

6 We have sinned,[g] even as our fathers did;
we have done wrong and acted wickedly.
7 When our fathers were in Egypt,
they gave no thought to your miracles;
they did not remember[h] your many kindnesses,
and they rebelled by the sea,[i] the Red Sea.[b]
8 Yet he saved them for his name's sake,[j]
to make his mighty power known.
9 He rebuked[k] the Red Sea, and it dried up;[l]
he led them through[m] the depths as through a desert.
10 He saved them[n] from the hand of the foe;
from the hand of the enemy he redeemed them.[o]
11 The waters covered[p] their adversaries;

105:42 [w]Ge 15:13-16
105:43 [x]Ex 15:1-18; Ps 106:12
105:44 [y]Jos 13:6-7
105:45 [z]Dt 4:40; 6:21-24
106:1 [a]Ps 100:5; 105:1
106:2 [b]Ps 145:4, 12
106:3 [c]Ps 15:2
106:4 [d]Ps 119:132
106:5 [e]Ps 1:3 [f]Ps 118:15
106:6 [g]Da 9:5
106:7 [h]Ps 78:11, 42 [i]Ex 14:11-12
106:8 [j]Ex 9:16
106:9 [k]Ps 18:15 [l]Ex 14:21; Na 1:4 [m]Isa 63:11-14
106:10 [n]Ex 14:30 [o]Ps 107:2
106:11 [p]Ex 14:28; 15:5

[a] *45* Hebrew *Hallelu Yah* [a] *1* Hebrew *Hallelu Yah*; also in verse 48 [b] *7* Hebrew *Yam Suph*; that is, Sea of Reeds; also in verses 9 and 22

105:45 God's purpose for saving the Israelites was that they would "keep his precepts and observe his laws". Too often we use our lives and freedom to please ourselves, but we should honour God. That is God's purpose for our lives and why he gave us his word.

106:1ff While Psalm 105 is a summary of God's faithfulness, Psalm 106 is a summary of man's sinfulness. Psalm 105 covers events up to the exodus from Egypt (Exodus 5 – 14), and Psalm 106 covers events from the exodus up to what appears to be the Babylonian captivity (2 Kings 25).

106:2 If we ever stopped to list all the mighty acts or miracles in the Bible, we would be astounded. They cover every aspect of life. The more we think about what God has done, the more we can appreciate the miracles he has done for us individually – birth, personality development, loving friends and family, specific guidance, healing, salvation – the list goes on and on. If you think you have never seen a miracle, look closer – you will see God's power and loving intervention on your behalf. God still performs great miracles!

not one of them survived.
12 Then they believed his promises
and sang his praise.[q]

13 But they soon forgot[r] what he had done
and did not wait for his counsel.
14 In the desert they gave in to their craving;
in the wasteland they put God to the test.[s]
15 So he gave them[t] what they asked for,
but sent a wasting disease[u] upon them.

16 In the camp they grew envious[v] of Moses
and of Aaron, who was consecrated to the LORD.
17 The earth opened[w] up and swallowed Dathan;
it buried the company of Abiram.
18 Fire blazed[x] among their followers;
a flame consumed the wicked.

19 At Horeb they made a calf[y]
and worshipped an idol cast from metal.
20 They exchanged their Glory[z]
for an image of a bull, which eats grass.
21 They forgot the God[a] who saved them,
who had done great things[b] in Egypt,
22 miracles in the land of Ham[c]
and awesome deeds by the Red Sea.
23 So he said he would destroy[d] them—
had not Moses, his chosen one,
stood in the breach[e] before him
to keep his wrath from destroying them.

24 Then they despised the pleasant land;[f]
they did not believe[g] his promise.
25 They grumbled[h] in their tents
and did not obey the LORD.
26 So he swore[i] to them with uplifted hand
that he would make them fall in the desert,[j]
27 make their descendants fall among the nations
and scatter[k] them throughout the lands.

28 They yoked themselves to the Baal of Peor[l]
and ate sacrifices offered to lifeless gods;
29 they provoked the LORD to anger by their wicked deeds,
and a plague broke out among them.
30 But Phinehas stood up and intervened,
and the plague was checked.[m]
31 This was credited to him[n] as righteousness
for endless generations to come.

32 By the waters of Meribah[o] they angered the LORD,
and trouble came to Moses because of them;
33 for they rebelled against the Spirit of God,

106:12 [q] Ex 15:1-21
106:13 [r] Ex 15:24
106:14 [s] 1Co 10:9
106:15 [t] Nu 11:31 [u] Isa 10:16
106:16 [v] Nu 16:1-3
106:17 [w] Dt 11:6
106:18 [x] Nu 16:35
106:19 [y] Ex 32:4
106:20 [z] Jer 2:11; Ro 1:23
106:21 [a] Ps 78:11 [b] Dt 10:21
106:22 [c] Ps 105:27
106:23 [d] Ex 32:10 [e] Ex 32:11-14
106:24 [f] Dt 8:7; Eze 20:6 [g] Heb 3:18-19
106:25 [h] Nu 14:2
106:26 [i] Eze 20:15; Heb 3:11 [j] Nu 14:28-35
106:27 [k] Lev 26:33; Ps 44:11
106:28 [l] Nu 25:2-3; Hos 9:10
106:30 [m] Nu 25:8
106:31 [n] Nu 25:11-13
106:32 [o] Nu 20:2-13; Ps 81:7

106:13–15 In the desert, Israel was so intent on getting the food and water *they* wanted that they became blind to what God wanted. They were more concerned about immediate physical gratification than lasting spiritual satisfaction. They did not want what was best for them, and they refused to trust in God's care and provision (Numbers 11:18–33). If you complain enough, God may give you what you ask for, even if it is not the best for you. If you're not getting what you want, perhaps God knows it is not in your best interest. Trust in his care and provision.

106:22 The land of Ham is Egypt.

106:23 "Stood in the breach" means that Moses served as the people's intercessor. This refers to the time when the Lord wanted to destroy the people for worshipping the golden calf (Exodus 32:7–14).

106:33 [p]Nu 20:8-12
106:34 [q]Jdg 1:21 [r]Dt 7:16
106:35 [s]Jdg 3:5-6
106:36 [t]Jdg 2:12
106:37 [u]2Ki 16:3; 17:17
106:38 [v]Nu 35:33
106:39 [w]Eze 20:18 [x]Lev 17:7; Nu 15:39
106:40 [y]Jdg 2:14; Ps 78:59 [z]Dt 9:29
106:41 [a]Jdg 2:14; Ne 9:27
106:43 [b]Jdg 2:16-19
106:44 [c]Jdg 3:9; 10:10
106:45 [d]Lev 26:42; Ps 105:8 [e]Jdg 2:18
106:46 [f]Ezr 9:9; Jer 42:12
106:47 [g]Ps 147:2
106:48 [h]Ps 41:13

and rash words came from Moses' lips.[c][p]

34 They did not destroy[q] the peoples
as the LORD had commanded[r] them,
35 but they mingled[s] with the nations
and adopted their customs.
36 They worshipped their idols,[t]
which became a snare to them.
37 They sacrificed their sons[u]
and their daughters to demons.
38 They shed innocent blood,
the blood of their sons[v] and daughters,
whom they sacrificed to the idols of Canaan,
and the land was desecrated by their blood.
39 They defiled themselves[w] by what they did;
by their deeds they prostituted[x] themselves.

40 Therefore the LORD was angry[y] with his people
and abhorred his inheritance.[z]
41 He handed them over[a] to the nations,
and their foes ruled over them.
42 Their enemies oppressed them
and subjected them to their power.
43 Many times he delivered them,
but they were bent on rebellion[b]
and they wasted away in their sin.

44 But he took note of their distress
when he heard their cry;[c]
45 for their sake he remembered his covenant[d]
and out of his great love[e] he relented.
46 He caused them to be pitied[f]
by all who held them captive.

47 Save us, O LORD our God,
and gather us[g] from the nations,
that we may give thanks to your holy name
and glory in your praise.

48 Praise be to the LORD, the God of Israel,
from everlasting to everlasting.
Let all the people say, "Amen!"[h]

Praise the LORD.

[c] 33 Or *against his spirit, / and rash words came from his lips*

106:34–39 Israel constantly turned away from God. How, after the great miracles they saw, could they turn from God and worship the idols of the land? We too have seen God's great miracles, but sometimes find ourselves enticed by the world's gods – power, convenience, fame, sex, and pleasure. As Israel forgot God, so we are susceptible to forgetting him and giving in to the pressures of an evil world. Remember all that God has done for you so you won't be drawn away from him by the world's pleasures.

106:40–42 God allowed trouble to come to the Israelites in order to help them. Our troubles can be helpful because they (1) humble us, (2) wean us from the allurements of the world and drive us back to God, (3) vitalise our prayers, (4) allow us to experience more of God's faithfulness, (5) make us more dependent upon God, (6) encourage us to submit to God's purpose for our lives, and (7) make us more compassionate towards others in trouble.

106:44–46 This is a beautiful picture of God's great love for his people who deserved only judgment. Fortunately, God's compassion and mercy towards us are not limited by our faithfulness to him. God was merciful to us in sending his Son to die for our sins. If he did this while we were captive to sin, how much more merciful will he be now that we are his children?

OOK V
SALMS 107:1—150:6

hese psalms praise God's works, recount the blessings of righteous living, thank od for deliverance, and praise God for his wonderful word. These psalms remind s that the best sacrifice we can offer to God is a faithful and obedient life.

PSALM 107

heme: Thankfulness to God should constantly be on the lips of those whom he has saved. his psalm was written to celebrate the Jews' return from their exile in Babylon.
uthor: Anonymous

1Give thanks to the LORD,[a] for he is good;
his love endures for ever.
2Let the redeemed[b] of the LORD say this—
those he redeemed from the hand of the foe,
3those he gathered[c] from the lands,
from east and west, from north and south.[a]

4Some wandered in desert[d] wastelands,
finding no way to a city where they could settle.
5They were hungry and thirsty,
and their lives ebbed away.
6Then they cried out[e] to the LORD in their trouble,
and he delivered them from their distress.
7He led them by a straight way[f]
to a city where they could settle.
8Let them give thanks to the LORD for his unfailing love
and his wonderful deeds for men,
9for he satisfies[g] the thirsty
and fills the hungry with good things.[h]

10Some sat in darkness[i] and the deepest gloom,
prisoners suffering in iron chains,[j]
11for they had rebelled[k] against the words of God
and despised the counsel[l] of the Most High.
12So he subjected them to bitter labour;
they stumbled, and there was no-one to help.[m]
13Then they cried to the LORD in their trouble,
and he saved them from their distress.
14He brought them out of darkness and the deepest gloom
and broke away their chains.[n]
15Let them give thanks to the LORD for his unfailing love
and his wonderful deeds for men,
16for he breaks down gates of bronze
and cuts through bars of iron.

17Some became fools through their rebellious ways

107:1 [a]Ps 106:1
107:2 [b]Ps 106:10
107:3 [c]Ps 106:47; Isa 43:5-6
107:4 [d]Nu 14:33; 32:13
107:6 [e]Ps 50:15
107:7 [f]Ezr 8:21
107:9 [g]Ps 22:26; Lk 1:53 [h]Ps 34:10
107:10 [i]Lk 1:79 [j]Job 36:8
107:11 [k]Ps 106:7; La 3:42 [l]2Ch 36:16
107:12 [m]Ps 22:11
107:14 [n]Ps 116:16; Lk 13:16; Ac 12:7

a 3 Hebrew *north and the sea*

107:1ff This psalm speaks of four different types of people in distress and how God rescues them: wanderers (107:4–9), prisoners (107:10–16), the sick (107:17–20), and the storm-tossed (107:23–30). No matter how extreme our calamity, God is able to break through to help us. He is loving and kind to those who are distressed.

107:1, 2 "Let the redeemed of the LORD say . . ." God has done so much for us, and we have so much for which to thank him (see Psalm 103). He wants us to tell everyone all that he has done. These verses are not so much a mandate to witness as a declaration that when we live in God's presence we will not be able to keep this glorious experience to ourselves (see also Acts 1:8; 2 Corinthians 5:18–20). What has God done for you? Is there someone you can tell?

107:5–9 Lost, hungry, thirsty, and exhausted, these wanderers typify the Israelites in exile. But they also typify anyone who has not found the satisfaction that comes from knowing God. Anyone who recognises his or her own lostness can receive the offer of Jesus to satisfy these needs. Jesus is the way (John 14:6), the bread from heaven (John 6:33, 35), the living water (John 4:10–14), and the giver of rest (Matthew 11:28–30). Have you received his life-giving offer?

107:17
[o] Isa 65:6-7; La 3:39

107:18
[p] Job 33:20
[q] Job 33:22; Ps 9:13; 88:3

107:20
[r] Mt 8:8
[s] Ps 103:3
[t] Job 33:28
[u] Ps 30:3; 49:15

107:22
[v] Lev 7:12; Ps 50:14; 116:17
[w] Ps 9:11; 73:28; 118:17

107:25
[x] Ps 105:31
[y] Jnh 1:4
[z] Ps 93:3

107:26
[a] Ps 22:14

107:29
[b] Mt 8:26
[c] Ps 89:9

107:32
[d] Ps 22:22, 25; 35:18

107:33
[e] 1Ki 17:1; Ps 74:15

107:34
[f] Ge 13:10; 14:3; 19:25

107:35
[g] Ps 114:8; Isa 41:18

107:37
[h] Isa 65:21

107:38
[i] Ge 12:2; 17:16, 20; Ex 1:7

107:39
[j] 2Ki 10:32; Eze 5:12

107:40
[k] Job 12:21
[l] Job 12:24

107:41
[m] 1Sa 2:8; Ps 113:7-9

107:42
[n] Job 22:19
[o] Job 5:16; Ps 63:11; Ro 3:19

and suffered affliction[o] because of their iniquities.
18 They loathed all food[p]
and drew near the gates of death.[q]
19 Then they cried to the LORD in their trouble,
and he saved them from their distress.
20 He sent forth his word[r] and healed them;[s]
he rescued[t] them from the grave.[u]
21 Let them give thanks to the LORD for his unfailing love
and his wonderful deeds for men.
22 Let them sacrifice thank-offerings[v]
and tell of his works[w] with songs of joy.

23 Others went out on the sea in ships;
they were merchants on the mighty waters.
24 They saw the works of the LORD,
his wonderful deeds in the deep.
25 For he spoke[x] and stirred up a tempest[y]
that lifted high the waves.[z]
26 They mounted up to the heavens and went down to the depths;
in their peril their courage melted[a] away.
27 They reeled and staggered like drunken men;
they were at their wits' end.
28 Then they cried out to the LORD in their trouble,
and he brought them out of their distress.
29 He stilled the storm[b] to a whisper;
the waves[c] of the sea were hushed.
30 They were glad when it grew calm,
and he guided them to their desired haven.
31 Let them give thanks to the LORD for his unfailing love
and his wonderful deeds for men.
32 Let them exalt him in the assembly[d] of the people
and praise him in the council of the elders.

33 He turned rivers into a desert,[e]
flowing springs into thirsty ground,
34 and fruitful land into a salt waste,[f]
because of the wickedness of those who lived there.
35 He turned the desert into pools of water[g]
and the parched ground into flowing springs;
36 there he brought the hungry to live,
and they founded a city where they could settle.
37 They sowed fields and planted vineyards[h]
that yielded a fruitful harvest;
38 he blessed them, and their numbers greatly increased,[i]
and he did not let their herds diminish.

39 Then their numbers decreased,[j] and they were humbled
by oppression, calamity and sorrow;
40 he who pours contempt on nobles[k]
made them wander in a trackless waste.[l]
41 But he lifted the needy[m] out of their affliction
and increased their families like flocks.
42 The upright see and rejoice,[n]
but all the wicked shut their mouths.[o]

107:32 Those who have never truly suffered may not appreciate God as much as those who have matured under hardship. Those who have seen God work in times of distress have a deeper insight into his loving-kindness. If you have experienced great trials, you have the potential for great praise.

43 Whoever is wise,[p] let him heed these things
and consider the great love[q] of the LORD.

107:43 [p]Jer 9:12; Hos 14:9 [q]Ps 64:9

PSALM 108

A song. A psalm of David.

Theme: Victory in God's strength. With God's help, we can do more than we think.
Author: David

1 My heart is steadfast, O God;
I will sing and make music with all my soul.
2 Awake, harp and lyre!
I will awaken the dawn.
3 I will praise you, O LORD, among the nations;
I will sing of you among the peoples.
4 For great is your love, higher than the heavens;
your faithfulness reaches to the skies.
5 Be exalted, O God, above the heavens,
and let your glory be over all the earth.[a]

108:5 [a]Ps 57:5

6 Save us and help us with your right hand,
that those you love may be delivered.
7 God has spoken from his sanctuary:
"In triumph I will parcel out Shechem
and measure off the Valley of Succoth.
8 Gilead is mine, Manasseh is mine;
Ephraim is my helmet,
Judah[b] my sceptre.
9 Moab is my washbasin,
upon Edom I toss my sandal;
over Philistia I shout in triumph."

108:8 [b]Ge 49:10

10 Who will bring me to the fortified city?
Who will lead me to Edom?
11 Is it not you, O God, you who have rejected us
and no longer go out with our armies?[c]
12 Give us aid against the enemy,
for the help of man is worthless.
13 With God we shall gain the victory,
and he will trample down our enemies.

108:11 [c]Ps 44:9

PSALM 109

For the director of music. Of David. A psalm.

Theme: Righteous indignation against liars and slanderers.
We can tell God our true feelings and desires.
Author: David

1 O God, whom I praise,
do not remain silent,[a]

109:1 [a]Ps 83:1

108:1ff The conclusions from two previous psalms have been put together to make this psalm. The first five verses are quoted from Psalm 57:7–11, and the next eight verses (108:6–13) are from Psalm 60:5–12.

108:9 Moab, Edom, and Philistia were Israel's enemies to the east, south, and west, respectively. They despised the Israelites and Israel's God.

108:13 Do our prayers end with requests for help to make it through stressful situations? David prayed not merely for rescue, but for victory. With God's help we can claim more than mere survival, we can claim victory! Look for ways God can use your distress as an opportunity to show his mighty power.

109:1ff David endured many false accusations (1 Samuel 22:7–13; 2 Samuel 15:3, 4), as did Christ centuries later (Matthew

109:2 [b]Ps 52:4; 120:2
109:3 [c]Ps 69:4 [d]Ps 35:7; Jn 15:25
109:4 [e]Ps 69:13
109:5 [f]Ps 35:12; 38:20
109:6 [g]Zec 3:1
109:7 [h]Pr 28:9
109:8 [i]Ac 1:20*
109:9 [j]Ex 22:24
109:11 [k]Job 5:5
109:12 [l]Isa 9:17
109:13 [m]Job 18:19; Ps 37:28 [n]Pr 10:7
109:14 [o]Ex 20:5; Ne 4:5; Jer 18:23
109:15 [p]Job 18:17; Ps 34:16
109:16 [q]Ps 37:14, 32 [r]Ps 34:18
109:17 [s]Pr 14:14; Eze 35:6
109:18 [t]Ps 73:6 [u]Nu 5:22
109:20 [v]Ps 94:23; 2Ti 4:14 [w]Ps 71:10

2 for wicked and deceitful men
have opened their mouths against me;
they have spoken against me with lying tongues.[b]
3 With words of hatred[c] they surround me;
they attack me without cause.[d]
4 In return for my friendship they accuse me,
but I am a man of prayer.[e]
5 They repay me evil for good,[f]
and hatred for my friendship.

6 Appoint[a] an evil man[b] to oppose him;
let an accuser[c][g] stand at his right hand.
7 When he is tried, let him be found guilty,
and may his prayers condemn[h] him.
8 May his days be few;
may another take his place[i] of leadership.
9 May his children be fatherless
and his wife a widow.[j]
10 May his children be wandering beggars;
may they be driven[d] from their ruined homes.
11 May a creditor seize all he has;
may strangers plunder the fruits of his labour.[k]
12 May no-one extend kindness to him
or take pity[l] on his fatherless children.
13 May his descendants be cut off,[m]
their names blotted out[n] from the next generation.
14 May the iniquity of his fathers[o] be remembered before the
LORD;
may the sin of his mother never be blotted out.
15 May their sins always remain before the LORD,
that he may cut off the memory[p] of them from the earth.

16 For he never thought of doing a kindness,
but hounded to death the poor
and the needy[q] and the broken-hearted.[r]
17 He loved to pronounce a curse—
may it[e] come on him;[s]
he found no pleasure in blessing—
may it be[f] far from him.
18 He wore cursing[t] as his garment;
it entered into his body like water,[u]
into his bones like oil.
19 May it be like a cloak wrapped about him,
like a belt tied for ever round him.
20 May this be the LORD's payment[v] to my accusers,
to those who speak evil[w] of me.

[a] 6 Or ⌞They say:⌟ *"Appoint* (with quotation marks at the end of verse 19) [b] 6 Or *the Evil One* [c] 6 Or *let Satan* [d] 10 Septuagint; Hebrew *sought* [e] 17 Or *curse, / and it has* [f] 17 Or *blessing, / and it is*

26:59–61; 27:39–44). Verse 8 is quoted in Acts 1:20 as being fulfilled in Judas' death.

109:4 David was angry at being attacked by evil people who slandered him and lied. Yet David remained a friend and a man of prayer. While we must hate evil and work to overcome it, we must love everyone, including those who do evil, because God loves them. We are called to hate the sin, but love the person. Only through God's strength will we be able to follow David's example.

109:6–20 This is another of the imprecatory psalms, a call for God to judge the wicked. (For an explanation of imprecatory psalms, see the note on 35:1ff.) David was not taking vengeance into his own hands, but was asking that God be swift in his promised judgment of evil people. David's words depict the eventual doom of all God's enemies.

21But you, O Sovereign LORD,
deal well with me for your name's sake;[x]
out of the goodness of your love,[y] deliver me.
22For I am poor and needy,
and my heart is wounded within me.
23I fade away like an evening shadow;[z]
I am shaken off like a locust.
24My knees give[a] way from fasting;
my body is thin and gaunt.
25I am an object of scorn[b] to my accusers;
when they see me, they shake their heads.[c]

26Help me,[d] O LORD my God;
save me in accordance with your love.
27Let them know[e] that it is your hand,
that you, O LORD, have done it.
28They may curse,[f] but you will bless;
when they attack they will be put to shame,
but your servant will rejoice.[g]
29My accusers will be clothed with disgrace
and wrapped in shame[h] as in a cloak.

30With my mouth I will greatly extol the LORD;
in the great throng[i] I will praise him.
31For he stands at the right hand[j] of the needy one,
to save his life from those who condemn him.

109:21 [x]Ps 79:9 [y]Ps 69:16
109:23 [z]Ps 102:11
109:24 [a]Heb 12:12
109:25 [b]Ps 22:6 [c]Mt 27:39; Mk 15:29
109:26 [d]Ps 119:86
109:27 [e]Job 37:7
109:28 [f]2Sa 16:12 [g]Isa 65:14
109:29 [h]Ps 35:26; 132:18
109:30 [i]Ps 35:18; 111:1
109:31 [j]Ps 16:8; 73:23; 121:5

PSALM 110
Of David. A psalm.

Theme: The credentials for the Messiah. Jesus is the Messiah.
Author: David

1The LORD says[a] to my Lord:
"Sit at my right hand
until I make your enemies
a footstool for your feet."[b]

2The LORD will extend your mighty sceptre[c] from Zion;
you will rule in the midst of your enemies.
3Your troops will be willing
on your day of battle.
Arrayed in holy majesty,[d]
from the womb of the dawn
you will receive the dew of your youth.[a]

[a] 3 Or / *your young men will come to you like the dew*

110:1 [a]Mt 22:44*; Mk 12:36*; Lk 20:42*; Ac 2:34* [b]1Co 15:25
110:2 [c]Ps 45:6
110:3 [d]Jdg 5:2; Ps 96:9

109:21 A name is more than a label; it is a representation of character and reputation. David is pleading for God to live up to his name – to his character of love and mercy. "For your name's sake", then, means "in accordance with your character".

110:1 This is one of the most-quoted psalms in the New Testament because of its clear references to the Messiah. In Matthew 22:41–45, Jesus recited the words of this verse and applied them to himself. Verses 1 and 6 look forward to Christ's final and total destruction of the wicked (Revelation 6 – 9); 110:2 prophesies Christ's reign on the earth (Revelation 20:1–7); 110:3, 4 tell of Christ's priestly work for his people (Hebrews 5 – 8); and 110:5, 6 look forward to the final battle on earth when Christ will overcome the forces of evil (Revelation 19:11–21).

110:1–7 Many people have a vague belief in God, but refuse to accept Jesus as anything more than a great human teacher. But the Bible does not allow that option. Both the Old and New Testaments proclaim the deity of the One who came to save and to reign. Jesus explained that this psalm spoke of the Messiah as greater than David, Israel's greatest king (Mark 12:35–37). Peter used this psalm to show that Jesus, the Messiah, sits at God's right hand and is Lord over all (Acts 2:32–35). You can't straddle the fence, calling Jesus "just a good teacher" because the Bible clearly calls him Lord.

110:4 [e]Nu 23:19 [f]Heb 5:6*; 7:21* [g]Heb 7:15-17*

4The LORD has sworn
and will not change his mind:[e]
"You are a priest for ever,[f]
in the order of Melchizedek.[g]"

110:5 [h]Ps 16:8 [i]Ps 2:12 [j]Ps 2:5; Ro 2:5

5The Lord is at your right hand;[h]
he will crush kings[i] on the day of his wrath.[j]
6He will judge nations,[k] heaping up the dead[l]
and crushing the rulers[m] of the whole earth.
7He will drink from a brook beside the way;[b]
therefore he will lift up his head.[n]

110:6 [k]Isa 2:4 [l]Isa 66:24 [m]Ps 68:21

110:7 [n]Ps 27:6

PSALM 111[a]

Theme: All that God does is good. Reverence for God is the beginning of wisdom.
Author: Anonymous

1Praise the LORD.[b]

I will extol the LORD with all my heart
in the council of the upright and in the assembly.

111:2 [a]Ps 92:5; 143:5

2Great are the works[a] of the LORD;
they are pondered by all who delight in them.
3Glorious and majestic are his deeds,
and his righteousness endures for ever.
4He has caused his wonders to be remembered;
the LORD is gracious and compassionate.[b]
5He provides food[c] for those who fear him;
he remembers his covenant for ever.
6He has shown his people the power of his works,
giving them the lands of other nations.
7The works of his hands are faithful and just;
all his precepts are trustworthy.[d]
8They are steadfast for ever[e] and ever,
done in faithfulness and uprightness.
9He provided redemption[f] for his people;
he ordained his covenant for ever—
holy and awesome[g] is his name.

111:4 [b]Ps 103:8

111:5 [c]Mt 6:26, 31-33

111:7 [d]Ps 19:7; Rev 15:3

111:8 [e]Isa 40:8; Mt 5:18

111:9 [f]Lk 1:68 [g]Ps 99:3; Lk 1:49

10The fear of the LORD is the beginning of wisdom;[h]
all who follow his precepts have good understanding.[i]
To him belongs eternal praise.[j]

111:10 [h]Pr 9:10 [i]Ecc 12:13 [j]Ps 145:2

b *7* Or / *The One who grants succession will set him in authority* **a** This psalm is an acrostic poem, the lines of which begin with the successive letters of the Hebrew alphabet. **b** *1* Hebrew *Hallelu Yah*

110:4 For more about Melchizedek, see his Profile at the end of Genesis 14. As a priest like Melchizedek, Christ will never abuse his divine position, and his reign will be for ever. Jesus is more fully described as our High Priest in Hebrews 5.

111–118 Psalms 111–118 are called hallelujah psalms. *Hallelujah* means "praise the LORD" and expresses the uplifting and optimistic tone of these songs.

111:9 The redemption here pictures the rescue by God of the Israelites from Egypt and the future return from captivity in Babylon (see Deuteronomy 7:8; Jeremiah 31:11). *Redemption* means recovery of something or someone upon payment of a ransom. All people were being held in slavery by sin, until Jesus paid the price to free us—giving his life as a perfect sacrifice. Before Jesus offered himself as a sacrifice for sin, people were not permitted into God's presence (the Most Holy Place); now, all believers can freely approach God's throne through prayer and have God in their lives through the Holy Spirit.

111:10 The only way to become truly wise is to fear (revere) God. This same thought is expressed in Proverbs 1:7–9. Too often people want to skip this step, thinking they can become wise by life experience and academic knowledge alone. But if we do not acknowledge God as the source of wisdom, then our foundation for making wise decisions is shaky, and we are prone to mistakes and foolish choices.

PSALM 112[a]

Theme: The advantages of having faith in God. God guards the minds and actions of those who follow his commands.
Author: Anonymous

1 Praise the LORD.[b]

Blessed is the man who fears the LORD,[a]
who finds great delight[b] in his commands.

2 His children will be mighty in the land;
the generation of the upright will be blessed.
3 Wealth and riches are in his house,
and his righteousness endures for ever.
4 Even in darkness light dawns[c] for the upright,
for the gracious and compassionate and righteous[d] man.[c]
5 Good will come to him who is generous and lends freely,[e]
who conducts his affairs with justice.
6 Surely he will never be shaken;
a righteous man will be remembered[f] for ever.
7 He will have no fear of bad news;
his heart is steadfast,[g] trusting in the LORD.
8 His heart is secure, he will have no fear;
in the end he will look in triumph on his foes.[h]
9 He has scattered abroad his gifts to the poor,[i]
his righteousness endures for ever;
his horn[d] will be lifted[j] high in honour.

10 The wicked man will see[k] and be vexed,
he will gnash his teeth[l] and waste away;[m]
the longings of the wicked will come to nothing.[n]

PSALM 113

Theme: The scope of God's care. God's great mercy is demonstrated by his concern for the poor and the oppressed.
Author: Anonymous

1 Praise the LORD.[a]

Praise, O servants of the LORD,[a]
praise the name of the LORD.
2 Let the name of the LORD be praised,
both now and for evermore.[b]

[a] This psalm is an acrostic poem, the lines of which begin with the successive letters of the Hebrew alphabet.
[b] *1* Hebrew *Hallelu Yah* [c] *4* Or / *for* ⌞*the* LORD⌟ *is gracious and compassionate and righteous* [d] *9* *Horn* here symbolises dignity. [a] *1* Hebrew *Hallelu Yah*; also in verse 9

112:1 [a]Ps 128:1 [b]Ps 119:14, 16, 47, 92
112:4 [c]Job 11:17 [d]Ps 97:11
112:5 [e]Ps 37:21, 26
112:6 [f]Pr 10:7
112:7 [g]Ps 57:7; Pr 1:33
112:8 [h]Ps 59:10
112:9 [i]2Co 9:9* [j]Ps 75:10
112:10 [k]Ps 86:17 [l]Ps 37:12 [m]Ps 58:7-8 [n]Pr 11:7
113:1 [a]Ps 135:1
113:2 [b]Da 2:20

112:1 Many blessings are available to us – honour, prosperity, security, freedom from fear (112:2–9) – if we *fear* the Lord and *delight* in obeying his commands. If you expect God's blessings, you must revere him and gladly obey him.

112:5 Generosity will cure two problems that money can create. The rich man may abuse others in his desire to accumulate wealth. Generosity will eliminate that abuse. Also, the fear of losing money can be a snare. Generosity and respect for God place our trust in him, not our money, for justice and security.

112:7, 8 We all want to live without fear; our heroes are fearless people who take on all dangers and overcome them. The psalmist teaches us that *fear* of God can lead to a *fearless* life. To fear God means to respect and revere him as the almighty Lord. When we trust God completely to take care of us, we will find that our other fears – even of death itself – will subside.

113:3 [c] Isa 59:19; Mal 1:11
113:4 [d] Ps 99:2 [e] Ps 8:1; 97:9
113:5 [f] Ps 89:6 [g] Ps 103:19
113:6 [h] Ps 11:4; 138:6; Isa 57:15
113:7 [i] 1Sa 2:8 [j] Ps 107:41
113:8 [k] Job 36:7
113:9 [l] 1Sa 2:5; Ps 68:6; Isa 54:1
114:1 [a] Ex 13:3
114:3 [b] Ex 14:21; Ps 77:16 [c] Jos 3:16
114:7 [d] Ps 96:9
114:8 [e] Ex 17:6; Nu 20:11; Ps 107:35

3 From the rising of the sun[c] to the place where it sets,
the name of the LORD is to be praised.
4 The LORD is exalted[d] over all the nations,
his glory above the heavens.[e]
5 Who is like the LORD our God,[f]
the One who sits enthroned[g] on high,
6 who stoops down to look[h]
on the heavens and the earth?

7 He raises the poor[i] from the dust
and lifts the needy[j] from the ash heap;
8 he seats them[k] with princes,
with the princes of their people.
9 He settles the barren[l] woman in her home
as a happy mother of children.

Praise the LORD.

PSALM 114

Theme: The mighty God who delivered Israel from Egypt. We can celebrate God's great work in our lives.
Author: Anonymous

1 When Israel came out of Egypt,[a]
the house of Jacob from a people of foreign tongue,
2 Judah became God's sanctuary,
Israel his dominion.

3 The sea looked and fled,[b]
the Jordan turned back;[c]
4 the mountains skipped like rams,
the hills like lambs.

5 Why was it, O sea, that you fled,
O Jordan, that you turned back,
6 you mountains, that you skipped like rams,
you hills, like lambs?

7 Tremble, O earth,[d] at the presence of the Lord,
at the presence of the God of Jacob,
8 who turned the rock into a pool,
the hard rock into springs of water.[e]

112:9 "His horn will be lifted high in honour" means that God's dignity will be uplifted and those faithful to God will be honoured. The horn was a symbol of power and dignity just as the horns of animals represent their strength.

113:5–9 In God's eyes, a person's value has no relationship to his or her wealth or position on the social ladder. Many people who have excelled in God's work began in poverty or humble beginnings. God supersedes the social orders of this world, often choosing his future leaders and ambassadors from among social outcasts. Do you treat the unwanted in society as though they have value? Demonstrate by your actions that all people are valuable and useful in God's eyes.

114:7 When God gave the law at Mount Sinai, the mountain trembled in God's presence. Even with our great technology, the seas, rivers, and mountains still present us with formidable challenges. But to God, who controls nature, they are as nothing. When observing the power of an ocean wave or the majesty of a mountain peak, think of God's greatness and glory, which are far more awesome than the natural wonders you can see. To tremble at God's presence means to recognise God's complete power and authority and our frailty by comparison.

PSALM 115

Theme: God is alive. He is thinking about us and caring for us, and we should put him first in our lives.
Author: Anonymous

1Not to us, O LORD, not to us
but to your name be the glory,[a]
because of your love and faithfulness.

2Why do the nations say,
"Where is their God?"[b]
3Our God is in heaven;[c]
he does whatever pleases him.[d]
4But their idols are silver and gold,
made by the hands of men.[e]
5They have mouths, but cannot speak,[f]
eyes, but they cannot see;
6they have ears, but cannot hear,
noses, but they cannot smell;
7they have hands, but cannot feel,
feet, but they cannot walk;
nor can they utter a sound with their throats.
8Those who make them will be like them,
and so will all who trust in them.

9O house of Israel, trust in the LORD—
he is their help and shield.
10O house of Aaron,[g] trust in the LORD—
he is their help and shield.
11You who fear him, trust in the LORD—
he is their help and shield.

12The LORD remembers us and will bless us:
He will bless the house of Israel,
he will bless the house of Aaron,
13he will bless those who fear[h] the LORD—
small and great alike.

14May the LORD make you increase,[i]
both you and your children.
15May you be blessed by the LORD,
the Maker of heaven[j] and earth.

16The highest heavens belong to the LORD,[k]
but the earth he has given[l] to man.
17It is not the dead[m] who praise the LORD,
those who go down to silence;

115:1 [a]Ps 96:8; Isa 48:11; Eze 36:32
115:2 [b]Ps 42:3; 79:10
115:3 [c]Ps 103:19 [d]Ps 135:6; Da 4:35
115:4 [e]Dt 4:28; Jer 10:3-5
115:5 [f]Jer 10:5
115:10 [g]Ps 118:3
115:13 [h]Ps 128:1, 4
115:14 [i]Dt 1:11
115:15 [j]Ge 1:1; 14:19; Ps 96:5
115:16 [k]Ps 89:11 [l]Ps 8:6-8
115:17 [m]Ps 6:5; 88:10-12; Isa 38:18

115–118 Psalms 115–118 were traditionally sung at the Passover meal, commemorating Israel's escape from slavery in Egypt (Exodus 11, 12).

115:1 The psalmist asked that God's name, not the nation's, be glorified. Too often we ask God to glorify his name *with* ours. For example, we may pray for help to do a good job so that our work will be noticed. Or we may ask that a presentation go well so we will get applause. There is nothing wrong with looking good or impressing others; the problem comes when we want to look good no matter what happens to God's reputation in the process. Before you pray, ask yourself, "Who will get the credit if God answers my prayer?"

115:4–8 When the psalms were written, many people worshipped idols—statues of wood, stone, or metal. They took pride in what they could see and had contempt for what they couldn't see. Today, we may still value tangible objects (home, clothing, possessions) rather than intangible realities (spiritual growth, salvation, giving to those in need, spending time with loved ones). Those who spend their time obtaining tangible objects are as foolish and empty as the idols themselves. (For more on the foolishness of idols, see Isaiah 44:9–20.)

115:12 "The LORD remembers us," says the psalm writer. What a fantastic truth! There are many times when we feel isolated, alone, and abandoned, even by God. In reality, he sees, understands, and thinks about us. When depressed by problems or struggling with self-worth, be encouraged that God keeps you in his thoughts. If he thinks about you, surely his help is near.

115:18
[n]Ps 113:2; Da 2:20

18it is we who extol the LORD,
both now and for evermore.[n]

Praise the LORD.[a]

116:1
[a]Ps 18:1
[b]Ps 66:19

116:2
[c]Ps 40:1

116:3
[d]Ps 18:4-5

116:4
[e]Ps 118:5
[f]Ps 22:20

116:5
[g]Ezr 9:15; Ne 9:8; Ps 103:8; 145:17

116:6
[h]Ps 19:7; 79:8

116:7
[i]Jer 6:16; Mt 11:29
[j]Ps 13:6

116:8
[k]Ps 56:13

116:9
[l]Ps 27:13

116:10
[m]2Co 4:13*

116:11
[n]Ro 3:4

116:13
[o]Ps 16:5; 80:18

116:14
[p]Ps 22:25; Jnh 2:9

116:15
[q]Ps 72:14

116:16
[r]Ps 119:125; 143:12
[s]Ps 86:16

PSALM 116

Theme: Praise for being saved from certain death. Worship is a thankful response and not a repayment for what God has done.
Author: Anonymous

1I love the LORD,[a] for he heard my voice;
he heard my cry[b] for mercy.
2Because he turned his ear[c] to me,
I will call on him as long as I live.

3The cords of death[d] entangled me,
the anguish of the grave[a] came upon me;
I was overcome by trouble and sorrow.
4Then I called on the name[e] of the LORD:
"O LORD, save me![f]"

5The LORD is gracious and righteous;[g]
our God is full of compassion.
6The LORD protects the simple-hearted;
when I was in great need,[h] he saved me.

7Be at rest[i] once more, O my soul,
for the LORD has been good[j] to you.

8For you, O LORD, have delivered my soul[k] from death,
my eyes from tears,
my feet from stumbling,
9that I may walk before the LORD
in the land of the living.[l]
10I believed;[m] therefore[b] I said,
"I am greatly afflicted."
11And in my dismay I said,
"All men are liars."[n]

12How can I repay the LORD
for all his goodness to me?
13I will lift up the cup of salvation
and call on the name[o] of the LORD.
14I will fulfil my vows[p] to the LORD
in the presence of all his people.

15Precious in the sight[q] of the LORD
is the death of his saints.
16O LORD, truly I am your servant;[r]
I am your servant, the son of your maidservant;[c][s]
you have freed me from my chains.

[a] *18* Hebrew *Hallelu Yah* [a] *3* Hebrew *Sheol* [b] *10* Or *believed even when* [c] *16* Or *servant, your faithful son*

116:1, 2 God is so responsive that you can always reach him. He bends down and listens to your voice. This writer's love for the Lord had grown because he had experienced answers to his prayers. If you are discouraged, remember that God is near, listening carefully to every prayer and answering each prayer in order to give you his best.

116:15 God stays close to us even in death. When someone we love is nearing death, we may become angry and feel abandoned. But believers (saints) are precious to God, and he carefully chooses the time when they will be called into his presence. Let this truth provide comfort when you've lost a loved one. God sees, and each life is valuable to him (see Jesus' statement in Matthew 10:29).

17I will sacrifice a thank-offering[t] to you
and call on the name of the LORD.
18I will fulfil my vows to the LORD
in the presence of all his people,
19in the courts[u] of the house of the LORD—
in your midst, O Jerusalem.

Praise the LORD.[d]

116:17 [t]Lev 7:12; Ps 50:14
116:19 [u]Ps 96:8; 135:2

PSALM 117

Theme: Another reason for praise—God's love for the whole world. We should praise God for his unlimited love.
Author: Anonymous

1Praise the LORD, all you nations;[a]
extol him, all you peoples.
2For great is his love towards us,
and the faithfulness of the LORD[b] endures for ever.

Praise the LORD.[d]

117:1 [a]Ro 15:11*
117:2 [b]Ps 100:5

PSALM 118

Theme: Confidence in God's eternal love. God's love is unchanging in the midst of changing situations. This gives us security.
Author: Anonymous

1Give thanks to the LORD,[a] for he is good;
his love endures for ever.[b]

2Let Israel say:[c]
"His love endures for ever."
3Let the house of Aaron say:
"His love endures for ever."
4Let those who fear the LORD say:
"His love endures for ever."

5In my anguish[d] I cried to the LORD,
and he answered[e] by setting me free.
6The LORD is with me;[f] I will not be afraid.
What can man do to me?[g]
7The LORD is with me; he is my helper.[h]
I will look in triumph on my enemies.[i]

8It is better to take refuge in the LORD[j]
than to trust in man.[k]
9It is better to take refuge in the LORD
than to trust in princes.[l]

10All the nations surrounded me,

118:1 [a]1Ch 16:8 [b]Ps 106:1; 136:1
118:2 [c]Ps 115:9
118:5 [d]Ps 120:1 [e]Ps 18:19
118:6 [f]Heb 13:6* [g]Ps 27:1; 56:4
118:7 [h]Ps 54:4 [i]Ps 59:10
118:8 [j]Ps 40:4 [k]Jer 17:5
118:9 [l]Ps 146:3

d *19* Hebrew *Hallelu Yah*

117:1, 2 Not only is Psalm 117 the shortest chapter in the Bible, it is also the middle chapter. Paul quotes from this psalm in Romans 15:11 to show that God's salvation is for *all* people, not just the Jews.

117:1, 2 Have you ever said, "I can't think of anything God has done for me. How can I praise him?" This psalm gives two reasons for praising God: his great love towards us, and his faithfulness that endures for ever. If he did nothing else for us, he would still be worthy of our highest praise.

118:8 Pilots put confidence in their planes. Commuters place confidence in trains, cars, or buses. Each day we must put our confidence in something or someone. If you are willing to trust a plane or car to get you to your destination, are you willing to trust God to guide you here on earth and to your eternal destination? Do you trust him more than any human being? How futile it is to trust anything or anyone more than God.

118:10 [m]Ps 18:40
118:11 [n]Ps 88:17 [o]Ps 3:6
118:12 [p]Dt 1:44 [q]Ps 58:9
118:13 [r]Ps 86:17; 140:4
118:14 [s]Ex 15:2 [t]Isa 12:2
118:15 [u]Ps 68:3 [v]Ps 89:13
118:17 [w]Ps 6:5; Hab 1:12 [x]Ex 15:6; Ps 73:28
118:18 [y]2Co 6:9
118:19 [z]Isa 26:2
118:20 [a]Ps 24:7; Isa 35:8; Rev 22:14
118:21 [b]Ps 116:1
118:22 [c]Mt 21:42; Mk 12:10; Lk 20:17*; Ac 4:11*; 1Pe 2:7*
118:26 [d]Mt 21:9*; Mk 11:9*; Lk 13:35*; 19:38*; Jn 12:13*
118:27 [e]1Pe 2:9
118:28 [f]Isa 25:1 [g]Ex 15:2

but in the name of the LORD I cut them off.[m]
11 They surrounded me[n] on every side,[o]
but in the name of the LORD I cut them off.
12 They swarmed around me like bees,[p]
but they died out as quickly as burning thorns;[q]
in the name of the LORD I cut them off.

13 I was pushed back and about to fall,
but the LORD helped me.[r]
14 The LORD is my strength[s] and my song;
he has become my salvation.[t]

15 Shouts of joy[u] and victory
resound in the tents of the righteous:
"The LORD's right hand[v] has done mighty things!
16 The LORD's right hand is lifted high;
the LORD's right hand has done mighty things!"

17 I will not die[w] but live,
and will proclaim[x] what the LORD has done.
18 The LORD has chastened me severely,
but he has not given me over to death.[y]

19 Open for me the gates[z] of righteousness;
I will enter and give thanks to the LORD.
20 This is the gate of the LORD
through which the righteous may enter.[a]
21 I will give you thanks, for you answered me;[b]
you have become my salvation.

22 The stone the builders rejected
has become the capstone;[c]
23 the LORD has done this,
and it is marvellous in our eyes.
24 This is the day the LORD has made;
let us rejoice and be glad in it.

25 O LORD, save us;
O LORD, grant us success.
26 Blessed is he who comes[d] in the name of the LORD.
From the house of the LORD we bless you.**[a]**
27 The LORD is God,
and he has made his light shine[e] upon us.
With boughs in hand, join in the festal procession
up**[b]** to the horns of the altar.

28 You are my God, and I will give thanks;
you are my God,[f] and I will exalt[g] you.

29 Give thanks to the LORD, for he is good;
his love endures for ever.

a *26* The Hebrew is plural. **b** *27* Or *Bind the festal sacrifice with ropes / and take it*

118:22, 23 Jesus referred to this verse when he spoke of being rejected by his own people (Matthew 21:42; Mark 12:10, 11; Luke 20:17). Although he was rejected, Jesus is now the "capstone", the most important part of the church (Acts 4:11; Ephesians 2:20; 1 Peter 2:6, 7). The capstone is the centre stone in the top of an arch, holding the whole arch together.

118:24 There are days when the last thing we want to do is rejoice. Our mood is down, our situation is out of hand, and our sorrow or guilt is overwhelming. We can relate to the writers of the psalms who often felt this way. But no matter how low the psalmists felt, they were always honest with God. And as they talked to God, their prayers ended in praise. When you don't feel like rejoicing, tell God how you truly feel. You will find that God will give you a reason to rejoice. God has given you this day to live and to serve him – be glad!

118:27 The "horns of the altar" were the projections from the four corners of the altar.

PSALM 119[a]

Theme: God's word is true and wonderful. Stay true to God and his word no matter how bad the world becomes. Obedience to God's laws is the only way to achieve real happiness.
Author: Anonymous, some suggest Ezra the priest

א Aleph

1 Blessed are they whose ways are blameless,
who walk[a] according to the law of the LORD.
2 Blessed are they who keep his statutes
and seek him with all their heart.[b]
3 They do nothing wrong;[c]
they walk in his ways.
4 You have laid down precepts
that are to be fully obeyed.
5 Oh, that my ways were steadfast
in obeying your decrees!
6 Then I would not be put to shame
when I consider all your commands.
7 I will praise you with an upright heart
as I learn your righteous laws.
8 I will obey your decrees;
do not utterly forsake me.

ב Beth

9 How can a young man keep his way pure?
By living according to your word.[d]
10 I seek you with all my heart;[e]
do not let me stray from your commands.[f]
11 I have hidden your word in my heart[g]
that I might not sin against you.
12 Praise be to you, O LORD;
teach me your decrees.[h]
13 With my lips I recount
all the laws that come from your mouth.[i]
14 I rejoice in following your statutes
as one rejoices in great riches.
15 I meditate on your precepts[j]
and consider your ways.
16 I delight[k] in your decrees;
I will not neglect your word.

[a] This psalm is an acrostic poem; the verses of each stanza begin with the same letter of the Hebrew alphabet.

119:1 [a]Ps 128:1
119:2 [b]Dt 6:5
119:3 [c]1Jn 3:9; 5:18
119:9 [d]2Ch 6:16
119:10 [e]2Ch 15:15 [f]ver 21, 118
119:11 [g]Ps 37:31; Lk 2:19, 51
119:12 [h]ver 26
119:13 [i]Ps 40:9
119:15 [j]Ps 1:2
119:16 [k]Ps 1:2

119:1ff This is both the longest psalm and the longest chapter in the Bible. It may have been written by Ezra after the temple was rebuilt (Ezra 6:14, 15) as a repetitive meditation on the beauty of God's word and how it helps us stay pure and grow in faith. Psalm 119 has 22 carefully constructed sections, each corresponding to a different letter in the Hebrew alphabet and each verse beginning with the letter of its section. Almost every verse mentions God's word. Such repetition was common in the Hebrew culture. People did not have personal copies of the Scriptures to read as we do, so God's people memorised his word and passed it on orally. The structure of this psalm allowed for easy memorisation. Remember, God's word, the Bible, is the only sure guide for living a pure life.

119:9 We are drowning in a sea of impurity. Everywhere we look we find temptation to lead impure lives. The psalmist asked a question that troubles us all: how do we stay pure in a filthy environment? We cannot do this on our own, but must have counsel and strength more dynamic than the tempting influences around us. Where can we find that strength and wisdom? By reading God's word and doing what it says.

119:11 Hiding (keeping) God's word in our hearts is a deterrent to sin. This alone should inspire us to memorise Scripture. But memorization alone will not keep us from sin; we must also put God's word to work in our lives, making it a vital guide for everything we do.

119:12–24 Most of us chafe under rules, for we think they restrict us from doing what we want. At first glance, then, it may seem strange to hear the psalmist talk of rejoicing in following God's statutes as much as in great riches. But God's laws were given to free us to be all he wants us to be. They restrict us from doing what might cripple us and keep us from being our best. God's guidelines help us follow his path and avoid paths that lead to destruction.

119:17
[l]Ps 13:6; 116:7

119:19
[m]1Ch 29:15; Ps 39:12; 2Co 5:6; Heb 11:13

119:20
[n]Ps 42:2; 84:2
[o]Ps 63:1

119:21
[p]ver 10

119:22
[q]Ps 39:8

119:25
[r]Ps 44:25
[s]Ps 143:11

119:26
[t]Ps 25:4; 27:11; 86:11

119:27
[u]Ps 145:5

119:28
[v]Ps 107:26
[w]Ps 20:2; 1Pe 5:10

119:31
[x]Dt 11:22

119:33
[y]ver 12

119:36
[z]1Ki 8:58

ג Gimel

17 Do good to your servant,[l] and I will live;
I will obey your word.
18 Open my eyes that I may see
wonderful things in your law.
19 I am a stranger on earth;[m]
do not hide your commands from me.
20 My soul is consumed[n] with longing
for your laws[o] at all times.
21 You rebuke the arrogant, who are cursed
and who stray[p] from your commands.
22 Remove from me scorn[q] and contempt,
for I keep your statutes.
23 Though rulers sit together and slander me,
your servant will meditate on your decrees.
24 Your statutes are my delight;
they are my counsellors.

ד Daleth

25 I am laid low in the dust;[r]
preserve my life[s] according to your word.
26 I recounted my ways and you answered me;
teach me your decrees.[t]
27 Let me understand the teaching of your precepts;
then I will meditate on your wonders.[u]
28 My soul is weary with sorrow;[v]
strengthen me[w] according to your word.
29 Keep me from deceitful ways;
be gracious to me through your law.
30 I have chosen the way of truth;
I have set my heart on your laws.
31 I hold fast[x] to your statutes, O LORD;
do not let me be put to shame.
32 I run in the path of your commands,
for you have set my heart free.

ה He

33 Teach me,[y] O LORD, to follow your decrees;
then I will keep them to the end.
34 Give me understanding, and I will keep your law
and obey it with all my heart.
35 Direct me in the path of your commands,
for there I find delight.
36 Turn my heart[z] towards your statutes

119:19 The psalmist says that he is a "stranger on earth", and so he needed guidance. Almost any long trip requires a map or guide. As we travel through life, the Bible should be our road map, pointing out safe routes, obstacles to avoid, and our final destination. We must recognise ourselves as pilgrims, travellers here on earth who need to study God's map to learn the way. If we ignore the map, we will wander aimlessly through life and risk missing our real destination.

119:27, 28 Our lives are cluttered with rule books, but the authors never come with us to help us follow the rules. But God does. That is the uniqueness of our Bible. God not only provides the rules and guidelines, but comes with us personally each day to strengthen us so that we can live according to those rules. All we must do is invite him and respond to his direction.

119:36 In today's world, people most often covet financial gain. Money represents power, influence, and success. For many people, money is a god. They think about little else. True, money can buy certain comforts and offer some security. But far more valuable than wealth is obedience to God because it is a heavenly treasure rather than an earthly one (Luke 12:33). We should do what God wants, regardless of the financial implications. Make the psalmist's prayer your own, asking God to turn your heart towards his statutes and not towards making money; it's in your own best interest in the long run.

and not towards selfish gain.[a]
37Turn my eyes away from worthless things;
preserve my life[b] according to your word.[b]
38Fulfil your promise[c] to your servant,
so that you may be feared.
39Take away the disgrace I dread,
for your laws are good.
40How I long[d] for your precepts!
Preserve my life in your righteousness.

ו Waw

41May your unfailing love come to me, O LORD,
your salvation according to your promise;
42then I will answer[e] the one who taunts me,
for I trust in your word.
43Do not snatch the word of truth from my mouth,
for I have put my hope in your laws.
44I will always obey your law,
for ever and ever.
45I will walk about in freedom,
for I have sought out your precepts.
46I will speak of your statutes before kings[f]
and will not be put to shame,
47for I delight in your commands
because I love them.
48I lift up my hands to[c] your commands, which I love,
and I meditate on your decrees.

ז Zayin

49Remember your word to your servant,
for you have given me hope.
50My comfort in my suffering is this:
Your promise preserves my life.[g]
51The arrogant mock me[h] without restraint,
but I do not turn[i] from your law.
52I remember[j] your ancient laws, O LORD,
and I find comfort in them.
53Indignation grips me[k] because of the wicked,
who have forsaken your law.[l]
54Your decrees are the theme of my song
wherever I lodge.
55In the night I remember[m] your name, O LORD,
and I will keep your law.
56This has been my practice:
I obey your precepts.

ח Heth

57You are my portion,[n] O LORD;
I have promised to obey your words.
58I have sought your face with all my heart;

119:36 [a]Eze 33:31; Mk 7:21-22; Lk 12:15; Heb 13:5
119:37 [b]Ps 71:20; Isa 33:15
119:38 [c]2Sa 7:25
119:40 [d]ver 20
119:42 [e]Pr 27:11
119:46 [f]Mt 10:18; Ac 26:1-2
119:50 [g]Ro 15:4
119:51 [h]Jer 20:7 [i]ver 157; Job 23:11; Ps 44:18
119:52 [j]Ps 103:18
119:53 [k]Ezr 9:3 [l]Ps 89:30
119:55 [m]Ps 63:6
119:57 [n]Ps 16:5; La 3:24

b *37* Two manuscripts of the Masoretic Text and Dead Sea Scrolls; most manuscripts of the Masoretic Text *life in your way* **c** *48* Or *for*

119:44–46 The psalmist talks about keeping the laws and yet being free. Contrary to what we often expect, obeying God's laws does not inhibit or restrain us. Instead it frees us to be what God designed us to be. By seeking God's salvation and forgiveness, we have freedom from sin and the resulting oppressive guilt. By living God's way, we have freedom to fulfil God's plan for our lives.

be gracious to me[o] according to your promise.[p]
59 I have considered my ways[q]
and have turned my steps to your statutes.
60 I will hasten and not delay
to obey your commands.
61 Though the wicked bind me with ropes,
I will not forget[r] your law.
62 At midnight[s] I rise to give you thanks
for your righteous laws.
63 I am a friend to all who fear you,[t]
to all who follow your precepts.
64 The earth is filled with your love,[u] O LORD;
teach me your decrees.

ט Teth

65 Do good to your servant
according to your word, O LORD.
66 Teach me knowledge and good judgment,
for I believe in your commands.
67 Before I was afflicted I went astray,[v]
but now I obey your word.
68 You are good,[w] and what you do is good;
teach me your decrees.[x]
69 Though the arrogant have smeared me with lies,[y]
I keep your precepts with all my heart.
70 Their hearts are callous[z] and unfeeling,
but I delight in your law.
71 It was good for me to be afflicted
so that I might learn your decrees.
72 The law from your mouth is more precious to me
than thousands of pieces of silver and gold.[a]

י Yodh

73 Your hands made me[b] and formed me;
give me understanding to learn your commands.
74 May those who fear you rejoice[c] when they see me,
for I have put my hope in your word.
75 I know, O LORD, that your laws are righteous,
and in faithfulness[d] you have afflicted me.
76 May your unfailing love be my comfort,
according to your promise to your servant.
77 Let your compassion[e] come to me that I may live,
for your law is my delight.
78 May the arrogant[f] be put to shame for wronging me without cause;[g]
but I will meditate on your precepts.
79 May those who fear you turn to me,
those who understand your statutes.
80 May my heart be blameless towards your decrees,
that I may not be put to shame.

כ Kaph

81 My soul faints[h] with longing for your salvation,
but I have put my hope in your word.
82 My eyes fail,[i] looking for your promise;
I say, "When will you comfort me?"
83 Though I am like a wineskin in the smoke,

119:58 [o] 1Ki 13:6 [p] ver 41
119:59 [q] Lk 15:17-18
119:61 [r] Ps 140:5
119:62 [s] Ac 16:25
119:63 [t] Ps 101:6-7
119:64 [u] Ps 33:5
119:67 [v] Jer 31:18-19; Heb 12:11
119:68 [w] Ps 106:1; 107:1; Mt 19:17 [x] ver 12
119:69 [y] Job 13:4; Ps 109:2
119:70 [z] Ps 17:10; Isa 6:10; Ac 28:27
119:72 [a] Ps 19:10; Pr 8:10-11, 19
119:73 [b] Job 10:8; Ps 100:3; 138:8; 139:13-16
119:74 [c] Ps 34:2
119:75 [d] Heb 12:5-11
119:77 [e] ver 41
119:78 [f] Jer 50:32 [g] ver 86, 161
119:81 [h] Ps 84:2
119:82 [i] Ps 69:3; La 2:11

I do not forget your decrees.
84 How long[j] must your servant wait?
When will you punish my persecutors?
85 The arrogant dig pitfalls[k] for me,
contrary to your law.
86 All your commands are trustworthy;[l]
help me,[m] for men persecute me without cause.[n]
87 They almost wiped me from the earth,
but I have not forsaken[o] your precepts.
88 Preserve my life according to your love,
and I will obey the statutes of your mouth.

ל Lamedh

89 Your word, O LORD, is eternal;[p]
it stands firm in the heavens.
90 Your faithfulness[q] continues through all generations;
you established the earth, and it endures.[r]
91 Your laws endure[s] to this day,
for all things serve you.
92 If your law had not been my delight,
I would have perished in my affliction.
93 I will never forget your precepts,
for by them you have preserved my life.
94 Save me, for I am yours;
I have sought out your precepts.
95 The wicked are waiting to destroy me,
but I will ponder your statutes.
96 To all perfection I see a limit;
but your commands are boundless.

מ Mem

97 Oh, how I love your law!
I meditate[t] on it all day long.
98 Your commands make me wiser[u] than my enemies,
for they are ever with me.
99 I have more insight than all my teachers,
for I meditate on your statutes.
100 I have more understanding than the elders,
for I obey your precepts.[v]
101 I have kept my feet[w] from every evil path
so that I might obey your word.
102 I have not departed from your laws,
for you yourself have taught me.
103 How sweet are your words to my taste,
sweeter than honey[x] to my mouth![y]
104 I gain understanding from your precepts;
therefore I hate every wrong path.[z]

נ Nun

105 Your word is a lamp to my feet
and a light[a] for my path.

119:84 [j]Ps 39:4; Rev 6:10
119:85 [k]Ps 35:7; Jer 18:20, 22
119:86 [l]Ps 35:19 [m]Ps 109:26 [n]ver 78
119:87 [o]Isa 58:2
119:89 [p]Mt 24:34-35; 1Pe 1:25
119:90 [q]Ps 36:5 [r]Ps 148:6; Ecc 1:4
119:91 [s]Jer 33:25
119:97 [t]Ps 1:2
119:98 [u]Dt 4:6
119:100 [v]Job 32:7-9
119:101 [w]Pr 1:15
119:103 [x]Ps 19:10; Pr 8:11 [y]Pr 24:13-14
119:104 [z]ver 128
119:105 [a]Pr 6:23

119:97–104 God's word makes us wise—wiser than our enemies and wiser than any teachers who ignore it. True wisdom goes beyond amassing knowledge; it is *applying* knowledge in a life-changing way. Intelligent or experienced people are not necessarily wise. Wisdom comes from allowing what God teaches to guide us.

119:105 To walk safely in the woods at night we need a light so we don't trip over tree roots or fall into holes. In this life, we walk

119:106 [b]Ne 10:29
119:108 [c]Hos 14:2; Heb 13:15
119:109 [d]Jdg 12:3; Job 13:14
119:110 [e]Ps 140:5; 141:9 [f]ver 10
119:112 [g]ver 33
119:113 [h]Jas 1:8
119:114 [i]Ps 32:7; 91:1 [j]ver 74
119:115 [k]Ps 6:8; 139:19; Mt 7:23
119:116 [l]Ps 54:4 [m]Ps 25:2; Ro 5:5; 9:33
119:119 [n]Eze 22:18, 19
119:120 [o]Hab 3:16
119:122 [p]Job 17:3
119:123 [q]ver 82
119:124 [r]ver 12
119:125 [s]Ps 116:16

106 I have taken an oath[b] and confirmed it,
that I will follow your righteous laws.
107 I have suffered much;
preserve my life, O LORD, according to your word.
108 Accept, O LORD, the willing praise of my mouth,[c]
and teach me your laws.
109 Though I constantly take my life in my hands,[d]
I will not forget your law.
110 The wicked have set a snare[e] for me,
but I have not strayed[f] from your precepts.
111 Your statutes are my heritage for ever;
they are the joy of my heart.
112 My heart is set on keeping your decrees
to the very end.[g]

ס Samekh

113 I hate double-minded men,[h]
but I love your law.
114 You are my refuge and my shield;[i]
I have put my hope[j] in your word.
115 Away from me,[k] you evildoers,
that I may keep the commands of my God!
116 Sustain me[l] according to your promise, and I shall live;
do not let my hopes be dashed.[m]
117 Uphold me, and I shall be delivered;
I shall always have regard for your decrees.
118 You reject all who stray from your decrees,
for their deceitfulness is in vain.
119 All the wicked of the earth you discard like dross;[n]
therefore I love your statutes.
120 My flesh trembles[o] in fear of you;
I stand in awe of your laws.

ע Ayin

121 I have done what is righteous and just;
do not leave me to my oppressors.
122 Ensure your servant's well-being;[p]
let not the arrogant oppress me.
123 My eyes fail, looking for your salvation,
looking for your righteous promise.[q]
124 Deal with your servant according to your love
and teach me your decrees.[r]
125 I am your servant;[s] give me discernment
that I may understand your statutes.
126 It is time for you to act, O LORD;
your law is being broken.
127 Because I love your commands

---

through a dark forest of evil. But the Bible can be our light to show us the way ahead so we won't stumble as we walk. It reveals the entangling roots of false values and philosophies. Study the Bible so you will be able to see your way clear enough to stay on the right path.

119:113 Double-minded people cannot make up their minds between good and evil. But when it comes to obeying God, there is no middle ground; you must take a stand. Either you are obeying him or you are not. Either you are doing what he wants or you are undecided. Choose to obey God, and say with the psalmist, "I love your law."

119:125 The psalmist asked God for discernment. Faith comes alive when we apply Scripture to our daily tasks and concerns. We need discernment so we can understand, and we need the desire to apply Scripture where we need help. The Bible is like medicine—it goes to work only when we apply it to the affected areas. As you read the Bible, be alert for lessons, commands, or examples that you can put into practice.

more than gold,[t] more than pure gold,
128 and because I consider all your precepts right,
I hate every wrong path.[u]

פ Pe

129 Your statutes are wonderful;
therefore I obey them.
130 The unfolding of your words gives light;[v]
it gives understanding to the simple.[w]
131 I open my mouth and pant,[x]
longing for your commands.[y]
132 Turn to me and have mercy[z] on me,
as you always do to those who love your name.
133 Direct my footsteps according to your word;[a]
let no sin rule[b] over me.
134 Redeem me from the oppression of men,[c]
that I may obey your precepts.
135 Make your face shine[d] upon your servant
and teach me your decrees.
136 Streams of tears[e] flow from my eyes,
for your law is not obeyed.[f]

צ Tsadhe

137 Righteous are you,[g] O LORD,
and your laws are right.[h]
138 The statutes you have laid down are righteous;[i]
they are fully trustworthy.
139 My zeal wears me out,[j]
for my enemies ignore your words.
140 Your promises have been thoroughly tested,[k]
and your servant loves them.
141 Though I am lowly and despised,[l]
I do not forget your precepts.
142 Your righteousness is everlasting
and your law is true.[m]
143 Trouble and distress have come upon me,
but your commands are my delight.
144 Your statutes are for ever right;
give me understanding[n] that I may live.

ק Qoph

145 I call with all my heart; answer me, O LORD,
and I will obey your decrees.
146 I call out to you; save me
and I will keep your statutes.
147 I rise before dawn[o] and cry for help;
I have put my hope in your word.
148 My eyes stay open through the watches of the night,[p]
that I may meditate on your promises.
149 Hear my voice in accordance with your love;
preserve my life, O LORD, according to your laws.
150 Those who devise wicked schemes are near,
but they are far from your law.
151 Yet you are near,[q] O LORD,
and all your commands are true.[r]
152 Long ago I learned from your statutes
that you established them to last for ever.[s]

119:127 [t]Ps 19:10
119:128 [u]ver 104, 163
119:130 [v]Pr 6:23 [w]Ps 19:7
119:131 [x]Ps 42:1 [y]ver 20
119:132 [z]Ps 25:16; 106:4
119:133 [a]Ps 17:5 [b]Ps 19:13; Ro 6:12
119:134 [c]Ps 142:6; Lk 1:74
119:135 [d]Nu 6:25; Ps 4:6
119:136 [e]Jer 9:1, 18 [f]Eze 9:4
119:137 [g]Ezr 9:15; Jer 12:1 [h]Ne 9:13
119:138 [i]Ps 19:7
119:139 [j]Ps 69:9; Jn 2:17
119:140 [k]Ps 12:6
119:141 [l]Ps 22:6
119:142 [m]Ps 19:7
119:144 [n]Ps 19:9
119:147 [o]Ps 5:3; 57:8; 108:2
119:148 [p]Ps 63:6
119:151 [q]Ps 34:18; 145:18 [r]ver 142
119:152 [s]Lk 21:33

119:153 [t]La 5:1 [u]Pr 3:1
119:154 [v]Mic 7:9 [w]1Sa 24:15
119:155 [x]Job 5:4
119:156 [y]2Sa 24:14
119:157 [z]Ps 7:1
119:158 [a]Ps 139:21
119:161 [b]1Sa 24:11
119:162 [c]1Sa 30:16
119:165 [d]Pr 3:2; Isa 26:3, 12; 32:17
119:166 [e]Ge 49:18
119:168 [f]Pr 5:21
119:169 [g]Ps 18:6
119:170 [h]Ps 28:2 [i]Ps 31:2
119:171 [j]Ps 51:15 [k]Ps 94:12
119:173 [l]Ps 37:24 [m]Jos 24:22
119:174 [n]ver 166
119:175 [o]Isa 55:3

ר Resh

153 Look upon my suffering[t] and deliver me,
for I have not forgotten[u] your law.
154 Defend my cause[v] and redeem me;[w]
preserve my life according to your promise.
155 Salvation is far from the wicked,
for they do not seek out[x] your decrees.
156 Your compassion is great, O LORD;
preserve my life[y] according to your laws.
157 Many are the foes who persecute me,[z]
but I have not turned from your statutes.
158 I look on the faithless with loathing,[a]
for they do not obey your word.
159 See how I love your precepts;
preserve my life, O LORD, according to your love.
160 All your words are true;
all your righteous laws are eternal.

ש Sin and Shin

161 Rulers persecute me[b] without cause,
but my heart trembles at your word.
162 I rejoice in your promise
like one who finds great spoil.[c]
163 I hate and abhor falsehood
but I love your law.
164 Seven times a day I praise you
for your righteous laws.
165 Great peace[d] have they who love your law,
and nothing can make them stumble.
166 I wait for your salvation,[e] O LORD,
and I follow your commands.
167 I obey your statutes,
for I love them greatly.
168 I obey your precepts and your statutes,
for all my ways are known[f] to you.

ת Taw

169 May my cry come[g] before you, O LORD;
give me understanding according to your word.
170 May my supplication come[h] before you;
deliver me[i] according to your promise.
171 May my lips overflow with praise,[j]
for you teach me[k] your decrees.
172 May my tongue sing of your word,
for all your commands are righteous.
173 May your hand be ready to help[l] me,
for I have chosen[m] your precepts.
174 I long for your salvation,[n] O LORD,
and your law is my delight.
175 Let me live[o] that I may praise you,
and may your laws sustain me.

119:160 One of God's characteristics is truthfulness. He embodies perfect truth; therefore, his word cannot lie. It is true and dependable for guidance and help (see John 17:14–17). The Bible is completely true and trustworthy.

119:165 Modern society longs for peace of mind. Here is clear-cut instruction on how to attain this: if we love God and obey his laws, we will have "great peace". Trust in God, who alone stands above the pressures of daily life and gives us full assurance.

176I have strayed like a lost sheep.[p]
Seek your servant,
for I have not forgotten your commands.

119:176 [p]Isa 53:6

PSALM 120

A song of ascents.

Theme: A prayer for deliverance from false accusers. All believers must live with the tension of being in the world but not belonging to it.
Author: Anonymous, some suggest Hezekiah

1I call on the LORD in my distress,[a]
and he answers me.
2Save me, O LORD, from lying lips[b]
and from deceitful tongues.[c]

3What will he do to you,
and what more besides, O deceitful tongue?
4He will punish you with a warrior's sharp arrows,[d]
with burning coals of the broom tree.

5Woe to me that I dwell in Meshech,
that I live among the tents of Kedar![e]
6Too long have I lived
among those who hate peace.
7I am a man of peace;
but when I speak, they are for war.

120:1 [a]Ps 102:2; Jnh 2:2
120:2 [b]Pr 12:22 [c]Ps 52:4
120:4 [d]Ps 45:5
120:5 [e]Ge 25:13; Jer 49:28

PSALM 121

A song of ascents.

Theme: We can depend upon God for help. Pilgrims must travel through lonely country to their destination; they are protected, not by anything created, but by the Creator of everything.
Author: Anonymous, some suggest Hezekiah

1I lift up my eyes to the hills—
where does my help come from?
2My help comes from the LORD,
the Maker of heaven and earth.[a]

3He will not let your foot slip—
he who watches over you will not slumber;
4indeed, he who watches over Israel
will neither slumber nor sleep.

121:2 [a]Ps 115:15; 124:8

120–134 Psalms 120–134 are called "Pilgrim Psalms" or "Songs of Ascent". They were sung by those who journeyed (and thus "ascended") to the temple for the annual feasts. Each psalm is a "step" along the journey. Psalm 120 begins the journey in a distant land in hostile surroundings; Psalm 122 pictures the pilgrims arriving in Jerusalem; and the rest of the psalms move towards the temple, mentioning various characteristics of God.

120:5, 6 Meshech was a nation far to the north of Israel; Kedar a nation to the southeast. Both were known for being warlike and barbarian. Because the psalmist couldn't have been in two places at one time, he was lamenting that he felt far from home and surrounded by pagan people.

120:7 Peacemaking is not always popular. Some people prefer to fight for what they believe in. The glory of battle is in the hope of winning, but someone must be a loser. The glory of peacemaking is that it may actually produce two winners. Peacemaking is God's way, so we should carefully and prayerfully attempt to be peacemakers.

121:1ff This song expresses assurance and hope in God's protection day and night. He not only made the hills but heaven and earth as well. We should never trust a lesser power than God him-

121:5
[b] Isa 25:4

121:6
[c] Ps 91:5; Isa 49:10; Rev 7:16

121:7
[d] Ps 41:2; 91:10-12

121:8
[e] Dt 28:6

5The LORD watches over[b] you—
the LORD is your shade at your right hand;
6the sun[c] will not harm you by day,
nor the moon by night.

7The LORD will keep you from all harm[d]—
he will watch over your life;
8the LORD will watch over your coming and going
both now and for evermore.[e]

PSALM 122

A song of ascents. Of David.

Theme: Stepping into the presence of God. What Jerusalem was for the Israelites, the church is to the believer.
Author: David

122:6
[a] Ps 51:18

122:9
[b] Ne 2:10

1I rejoiced with those who said to me,
"Let us go to the house of the LORD."
2Our feet are standing
in your gates, O Jerusalem.

3Jerusalem is built like a city
that is closely compacted together.
4That is where the tribes go up,
the tribes of the LORD,
to praise the name of the LORD
according to the statute given to Israel.
5There the thrones for judgment stand,
the thrones of the house of David.

6Pray for the peace of Jerusalem:
"May those who love[a] you be secure.
7May there be peace within your walls
and security within your citadels."
8For the sake of my brothers and friends,
I will say, "Peace be within you."
9For the sake of the house of the LORD our God,
I will seek your prosperity.[b]

self. But not only is he all-powerful, he also watches over us. Nothing diverts or deters him. We are safe. We never outgrow our need for God's untiring watch over our lives.

122:1 Going to God's house can be a chore or a delight. For the psalmist, it was a delight. As a pilgrim attending one of the three great religious festivals, he rejoiced to worship with God's people in God's house. We may find worship a chore if we have unconfessed sin or if our love for God has cooled. But if we are close to God and enjoy his presence, we will be eager to worship and praise him. Our attitude towards God will determine our view of worship.

122:5 The "thrones for judgment" are the courts of justice by the town gate. In Bible times, the elders in a town sat to hear cases and administer justice at the gate (Ruth 4:1, 2). Sometimes the king himself would sit at the gate to meet his subjects and make legal decisions (2 Samuel 19:8). Speeches and prophecies were also made at the city gate (Nehemiah 8:1; Jeremiah 17:19, 20).

122:6–9 The psalmist was not praying for his own peace and prosperity, but for that of his brothers and friends in Jerusalem. This is intercessory prayer, prayer on behalf of others. Too often we are quick to pray for our own needs and desires, and omit interceding for others. Will you intercede for someone in need today?

122:6–9 The peace sought in these verses is much more than the mere absence of conflict. It suggests completeness, health, justice, prosperity, and protection. The world cannot provide this peace. Real peace comes from faith in God because he alone embodies all the characteristics of peace. To find peace of mind and peace with others, you must find peace with God.

PSALM 123

A song of ascents.

Theme: Look to God for mercy. We are encouraged to be attentive to God's leading.
Author: Anonymous, some suggest Hezekiah

1 I lift up my eyes to you,
to you whose throne[a] is in heaven.
2 As the eyes of slaves look to the hand of their master,
as the eyes of a maid look to the hand of her mistress,
so our eyes look to the LORD[b] our God,
till he shows us his mercy.

3 Have mercy on us, O LORD, have mercy on us,
for we have endured much contempt.
4 We have endured much ridicule from the proud,
much contempt from the arrogant.

123:1
[a] Ps 11:4; 121:1; 141:8

123:2
[b] Ps 25:15

PSALM 124

A song of ascents. Of David.

Theme: God delivers us from those who seek to destroy us. God is on the side of those who seek him.
Author: David, probably written after his defeat of the Philistines (2 Samuel 5:17–25)

1 If the LORD had not been on our side—
let Israel say[a]—
2 if the LORD had not been on our side
when men attacked us,
3 when their anger flared against us,
they would have swallowed us alive;
4 the flood would have engulfed us,
the torrent would have swept over us,
5 the raging waters
would have swept us away.

6 Praise be to the LORD,
who has not let us be torn by their teeth.
7 We have escaped like a bird
out of the fowler's snare;[b]
the snare has been broken,
and we have escaped.
8 Our help is in the name of the LORD,
the Maker of heaven[c] and earth.

124:1
[a] Ps 129:1

124:7
[b] Ps 91:3; Pr 6:5

124:8
[c] Ge 1:1; Ps 121:2; 134:3

123:1ff The psalmist lifted his eyes to God, waiting and watching for God to send his mercy. The more he waited, the more he cried out to God because he knew that the evil and proud offered no help—they had only contempt for God.

124:7, 8 Do you ever feel trapped by overwhelming odds? With God, there is always a way out because he is the Creator of all that exists. No problem is beyond his ability to solve; no circumstance is too difficult for him. We can turn to the Creator for help in our time of need, for he is on our side. God will provide a way out; we need only trust him and look for it. David compared this to a bird escaping the fowler's snare (trap).

125:1 Have you ever known people who were drawn to every new fad or idea? Such people are inconsistent and therefore unreliable. The secret of consistency is to trust in God, because he never changes. He cannot be shaken by the changes in our world, and he endures for ever. The fads and ideas of our world, and our world itself, will not.

125:3 Although the psalmist wrote, "The sceptre of the wicked will not remain over the land allotted to the righteous," often Israel had to put up with evil rulers. The psalmist was expressing what will ultimately happen when God executes his final judgment. Hu-

PSALM 125

A song of ascents.

Theme: God is our Protector. The mountains around Jerusalem symbolise God's protection for his people.
Author: Anonymous, some suggest Hezekiah

1 Those who trust in the LORD are like Mount Zion,
which cannot be shaken[a] but endures for ever.
2 As the mountains surround Jerusalem,
so the LORD surrounds[b] his people
both now and for evermore.

3 The sceptre of the wicked will not remain[c]
over the land allotted to the righteous,
for then the righteous might use
their hands to do evil.[d]

4 Do good, O LORD,[e] to those who are good,
to those who are upright in heart.[f]
5 But those who turn[g] to crooked ways[h]
the LORD will banish with the evildoers.

Peace be upon Israel.[i]

125:1 [a]Ps 46:5
125:2 [b]Ps 121:8; Zec 2:4-5
125:3 [c]Ps 89:22; Pr 22:8; Isa 14:5 [d]1Sa 24:10; Ps 55:20
125:4 [e]Ps 119:68 [f]Ps 7:10; 36:10; 94:15
125:5 [g]Job 23:11 [h]Pr 2:15; Isa 59:8 [i]Ps 128:6

PSALM 126

A song of ascents.

Theme: God does great things. His power not only releases us from sin's captive hold, but brings us back to him.
Author: Anonymous, possibly written to celebrate the exiles' return from captivity (Ezra 1)

1 When the LORD brought back[a] the captives to[a] Zion,
we were like men who dreamed.[b]
2 Our mouths were filled with laughter,
our tongues with songs of joy.[b]
Then it was said among the nations,
"The LORD has done great things[c] for them."
3 The LORD has done great things for us,
and we are filled with joy.[d]

4 Restore our fortunes,[c] O LORD,
like streams in the Negev.[e]
5 Those who sow in tears
will reap with songs of joy.[f]
6 He who goes out weeping,
carrying seed to sow,
will return with songs of joy,
carrying sheaves with him.

a *1* Or *LORD restored the fortunes of* **b** *1* Or *men restored to health* **c** *4* Or *Bring back our captives*

126:1 [a]Ps 85:1; Hos 6:11
126:2 [b]Job 8:21; Ps 51:14 [c]Ps 71:19
126:3 [d]Isa 25:9
126:4 [e]Isa 35:6; 43:19
126:5 [f]Isa 35:10

---

man sinfulness often ruins God's ideal on earth, but that doesn't mean God has lost control. Evil prevails only as long as God allows.

126:5, 6 God's ability to restore life is beyond our understanding. Forests burn down and are able to grow back. Broken bones heal. Even grief is not a permanent condition. Our tears can be seeds that will grow into a harvest of joy because God is able to bring good out of tragedy. When burdened by sorrow, know that your times of grief will end and that you will again find joy. We must be patient as we wait. God's great harvest of joy is coming!

PSALM 127

A song of ascents. Of Solomon.

127:1
[a]Ps 78:69
[b]Ps 121:4

Theme: Life without God is senseless. All of life's work—building a home, establishing a career, and raising a family—must have God as the foundation.
Author: Solomon

1Unless the LORD builds[a] the house,
its builders labour in vain.
Unless the LORD watches[b] over the city,
the watchmen stand guard in vain.
2In vain you rise early
and stay up late,
toiling for food[c] to eat—
for he grants sleep[d] to[a] those he loves.

127:2
[c]Ge 3:17
[d]Job 11:18

3Sons are a heritage from the LORD,
children a reward[e] from him.
4Like arrows in the hands of a warrior
are sons born in one's youth.
5Blessed is the man
whose quiver is full of them.
They will not be put to shame
when they contend with their enemies[f] in the gate.

127:3
[e]Ge 33:5

127:5
[f]Pr 27:11

PSALM 128

A song of ascents.

128:1
[a]Ps 112:1
[b]Ps 119:1-3

Theme: God, the true head of the home. [This is called the marriage prayer because it was often sung at Israelite marriages.] God will reward your devotion to him with inner peace.
Author: Anonymous, some suggest Hezekiah

1Blessed are all who fear the LORD,[a]
who walk in his ways.[b]
2You will eat the fruit of your labour;[c]
blessings and prosperity[d] will be yours.
3Your wife will be like a fruitful vine[e]
within your house;
your sons will be like olive shoots[f]
round your table.
4Thus is the man blessed
who fears the LORD.

128:2
[c]Isa 3:10
[d]Ecc 8:12

128:3
[e]Eze 19:10
[f]Ps 52:8; 144:12

5May the LORD bless you from Zion[g]
all the days of your life;

128:5
[g]Ps 20:2; 134:3

a 2 Or *eat— / for while they sleep he provides for*

127:1 Families establish homes and watchmen guard cities, but both these activities are futile unless God is with them. A family without God can never experience the spiritual bond God brings to relationships. A city without God will crumble from evil and corruption on the inside. Don't make the mistake of leaving God out of your life—if you do, all your accomplishments will be futile. Make God your highest priority, and let him do the building.

127:2 God is not against human effort. Hard work honours God (Proverbs 31:10–29). But working to the exclusion of rest or to the neglect of family may be a cover-up for an inability to trust God to provide for our needs. We all need adequate rest and times of spiritual refreshment. On the other hand, this verse is not an excuse to be lazy (Proverbs 18:9). Be careful to maintain a balance: work while trusting God, and also rest while trusting him.

127:3–5 Too often children are seen as liabilities rather than assets. But the Bible calls children "a heritage from the LORD", a reward. We can learn valuable lessons from their inquisitive minds and trusting spirits. Those who view children as a distraction or nuisance should instead see them as an opportunity to shape the future. We dare not treat children as an inconvenience when God values them so highly.

128:1ff The psalmist wrote that a good family life is a reward for following God. The values outlined in God's word include love, service, honesty, integrity, and prayer. These help all relationships, and they are especially vital to home life. Is your home life heavenly or hectic? Reading and obeying God's word is a good place to start to make your family all that it should be.

128:6
[h] Ge 50:23; Job 42:16
[i] Ps 125:5

may you see the prosperity of Jerusalem,
6 and may you live to see your children's children.[h]

Peace be upon Israel.[i]

129:1 [a] Ps 88:15; Hos 2:15 [b] Ps 124:1
129:2 [c] Mt 16:18
129:4 [d] Ps 119:137
129:5 [e] Mic 4:11 [f] Ps 71:13
129:6 [g] Ps 37:2
129:8 [h] Ru 2:4; Ps 118:26

PSALM 129

A song of ascents.

Theme: Confidence in times of persecution. God will bring us through the tough times.
Author: Anonymous, some suggest Hezekiah

1 They have greatly oppressed me from my youth[a]—
let Israel say[b]—
2 they have greatly oppressed me from my youth,
but they have not gained the victory[c] over me.
3 Ploughmen have ploughed my back
and made their furrows long.
4 But the LORD is righteous;[d]
he has cut me free from the cords of the wicked.

5 May all who hate Zion[e]
be turned back in shame.[f]
6 May they be like grass on the roof,
which withers[g] before it can grow;
7 with it the reaper cannot fill his hands,
nor the one who gathers fill his arms.
8 May those who pass by not say,
"The blessing of the LORD be upon you;
we bless you[h] in the name of the LORD."

130:1 [a] Ps 42:7; 69:2; La 3:55
130:2 [b] Ps 28:2 [c] 2Ch 6:40; Ps 64:1
130:3 [d] Ps 76:7; 143:2
130:4 [e] Ex 34:7; Isa 55:7; Jer 33:8

PSALM 130

A song of ascents.

Theme: Assurance of the Lord's forgiveness.
God will surely forgive us if we confess our sins to him.
Author: Anonymous, some suggest Hezekiah

1 Out of the depths[a] I cry to you, O LORD;
2 O Lord, hear my voice.[b]
Let your ears be attentive[c]
to my cry for mercy.

3 If you, O LORD, kept a record of sins,
O Lord, who could stand?[d]
4 But with you there is forgiveness;[e]

129:2 The people of Israel were persecuted from their earliest days, but never destroyed completely. The same is true of the church. Christians have faced times of severe persecution, but the church has never been destroyed. As Jesus said to Peter, "On this rock I will build my church, and the gates of Hades will not overcome it" (Matthew 16:18). When you face persecution and discrimination, take courage—the church will never be destroyed.

129:3 This verse foreshadowed Jesus' unjust punishment before his death. He endured horrible lashes from the whip of his tormentors, which indeed made "furrows" on his back (John 19:1).

130:1, 2 In the depths of despair, the psalmist cried out to God. Despair makes us feel isolated and distant from God, but this is precisely when we need God most. Despair over sin should not lead to self-pity, causing us to think more about ourselves than God. Instead, it should lead to confession and then to God's mercy, forgiveness, and redemption. When we feel overwhelmed by a problem, feeling sorry for ourselves will only increase feelings of hopelessness; but crying out to God will turn our attention to the only One who can really help.

130:3, 4 Keeping a record of sins (or holding a grudge) is like building a wall between you and another person, and it is nearly impossible to talk openly while the wall is there. God doesn't keep a record of our sins; when he forgives, he forgives completely, tearing down any wall between us and him. Therefore, we fear (revere) God, yet we can talk to him about anything. When you pray, realise that God is holding nothing against you. His lines of communication are completely open.

therefore you are feared.[f]

5I wait for the LORD,[g] my soul waits,
and in his word[h] I put my hope.
6My soul waits for the Lord
more than watchmen[i] wait for the morning,
more than watchmen wait for the morning.[j]

7O Israel, put your hope[k] in the LORD,
for with the LORD is unfailing love
and with him is full redemption.
8He himself will redeem[l] Israel
from all their sins.

PSALM 131

A song of ascents. Of David.

Theme: Trust and contentment. Quiet trust in God is the basis for our contentment.
Author: David

1My heart is not proud,[a] O LORD,
my eyes are not haughty;
I do not concern myself with great matters
or things too wonderful for me.
2But I have stilled and quietened my soul;
like a weaned child with its mother,
like a weaned child is my soul[b] within me.

3O Israel, put your hope[c] in the LORD
both now and for evermore.

PSALM 132

A song of ascents.

Theme: Honour God and he will honour you. The psalmist reflects upon that great day when the ark of the covenant was brought to Jerusalem and praises God for his promise to perpetuate David's line.
Author: Anonymous

1O LORD, remember David
and all the hardships he endured.

2He swore an oath to the LORD
and made a vow to the Mighty One of Jacob:[a]
3"I will not enter my house
or go to my bed—
4I will allow no sleep to my eyes,
no slumber to my eyelids,
5till I find a place[b] for the LORD,
a dwelling for the Mighty One of Jacob."

130:4 [f]1Ki 8:40
130:5 [g]Ps 27:14; 33:20; Isa 8:17 [h]Ps 119:81
130:6 [i]Ps 63:6 [j]Ps 119:147
130:7 [k]Ps 131:3
130:8 [l]Lk 1:68
131:1 [a]Ps 101:5; Ro 12:16
131:2 [b]Mt 18:3; 1Co 14:20
131:3 [c]Ps 130:7
132:2 [a]Ge 49:24
132:5 [b]Ac 7:46

131:1, 2 Pride results from overvaluing ourselves and undervaluing others. It leads to restlessness because it makes us dissatisfied with what we have and concerned about what everyone else is doing. It keeps us always hungering for more attention and adoration. By contrast, humility puts others first and allows us to be content with God's leading in our lives. Such contentment gives us security so that we no longer have to prove ourselves to others. Let humility and trust affect your perspective and give you the strength and freedom to serve God and others.

132:2–5 This refers to David's desire to build the temple. When David became king, he built a beautiful palace, but he was troubled that the ark of the covenant, the symbol of God's presence among his people (Exodus 25:10–22), remained in a tent (2 Samuel 6:17; 7:1–17). This so bothered David that he couldn't sleep until he corrected the situation. He began to lay the plans for the temple to house the ark. (Eventually the temple was built by his son, Solomon.) We must live so close to God that we become restless until God's will is accomplished through us.

6We heard it in Ephrathah,[c]
we came upon it in the fields of Jaar:[a,b][d]
7"Let us go to his dwelling-place;[e]
let us worship at his footstool[f]—
8arise, O LORD,[g] and come to your resting place,
you and the ark of your might.
9May your priests be clothed with righteousness;[h]
may your saints sing for joy."

10For the sake of David your servant,
do not reject your anointed one.

11The LORD swore an oath to David,[i]
a sure oath that he will not revoke:
"One of your own descendants[j]
I will place on your throne—
12if your sons keep my covenant
and the statutes I teach them,
then their sons shall sit
on your throne[k] for ever and ever."

13For the LORD has chosen Zion,[l]
he has desired it for his dwelling:
14"This is my resting place for ever and ever;[m]
here I will sit enthroned, for I have desired it—
15I will bless her with abundant provisions;
her poor will I satisfy with food.[n]
16I will clothe her priests[o] with salvation,
and her saints shall ever sing for joy.

17"Here I will make a horn[c] grow[p] for David
and set up a lamp[q] for my anointed one.
18I will clothe his enemies with shame,[r]
but the crown on his head shall be resplendent."

PSALM 133

A song of ascents. Of David.

Theme: The joy of harmonious relationships
Author: David

1How good and pleasant it is
when brothers live together[a] in unity!

a *6* That is, Kiriath Jearim b *6* Or *heard of it in Ephrathah, / we found it in the fields of Jaar.* (and no quotation marks around verses 7–9) c *17* *Horn* here symbolises strong one, that is, king.

132:6 [c]1Sa 17:12 [d]1Sa 7:2
132:7 [e]Ps 5:7 [f]Ps 99:5
132:8 [g]Nu 10:35; Ps 78:61
132:9 [h]Job 29:14; Isa 61:3, 10
132:11 [i]Ps 89:3-4, 35 [j]2Sa 7:12
132:12 [k]Lk 1:32; Ac 2:30
132:13 [l]Ps 48:1-2
132:14 [m]Ps 68:16
132:15 [n]Ps 107:9; 147:14
132:16 [o]2Ch 6:41
132:17 [p]Eze 29:21; Lk 1:69 [q]1Ki 11:36; 2Ch 21:7
132:18 [r]Ps 35:26; 109:29
133:1 [a]Ge 13:8; Heb 13:1

132:11, 12 The promise that David's sons would sit on Israel's throne for ever is found in 2 Samuel 7:8–29. This promise had two parts: (1) David's descendants would perpetually rule over Israel as long as they followed God, and (2) David's royal line would never end. The first part was conditional; as long as the kings obeyed God ("keep my covenant and the statutes I teach them"), their dynasty continued. The second part of the promise was unconditional. It was fulfilled in Jesus Christ, a descendant of David, who reigns for ever.

132:17, 18 The horn to "grow for David" refers to one of his mighty descendants. David's son, Solomon, was indeed a glorious king (1 Kings 3:10–14); but these verses look ahead even further to another descendant of David, Jesus the Messiah (Matthew 1:17). The power, might, and glory of the Messiah will last for ever.

133:1–3 David stated that unity is pleasant and precious. Unfortunately, unity does not abound in the church as it should. People disagree and cause division over unimportant issues. Some delight in causing tension by discrediting others. Unity is important because (1) it makes the church a positive example to the world and helps draw others to us; (2) it helps us co-operate as a body of believers as God meant us to, giving us a foretaste of heaven; (3) it renews and revitalises ministry because there is less tension to sap our energy.

Living in unity does not mean that we will agree on everything; there will be many opinions just as there are many notes in a musical chord. But we must agree on our purpose in life—to work together for God. Our outward expression of unity will reflect our inward unity of purpose.

2It is like precious oil poured on the head,[b]
running down on the beard,
running down on Aaron's beard,
down upon the collar of his robes.
3It is as if the dew of Hermon[c]
were falling on Mount Zion.
For there the LORD bestows his blessing,[d]
even life for evermore.[e]

PSALM 134

A song of ascents.

Theme: Worship God and experience the joy of his blessings
Author: Anonymous, some suggest Hezekiah

1Praise the LORD, all you servants[a] of the LORD
who minister by night[b] in the house of the LORD.
2Lift up your hands[c] in the sanctuary
and praise the LORD.

3May the LORD, the Maker of heaven[d] and earth,
bless you from Zion.[e]

PSALM 135

Theme: A hymn of praise. This psalm contrasts the greatness of God with the powerlessness of idols. Pagan worship idols while God's people worship the living God.
Author: Anonymous

1Praise the LORD.[a]

Praise the name of the LORD;
praise him, you servants[a] of the LORD,
2you who minister in the house[b] of the LORD,
in the courts[c] of the house of our God.

3Praise the LORD, for the LORD is good;[d]
sing praise to his name, for that is pleasant.[e]
4For the LORD has chosen Jacob[f] to be his own,
Israel to be his treasured possession.[g]

5I know that the LORD is great,[h]
that our Lord is greater than all gods.[i]
6The LORD does whatever pleases him,[j]
in the heavens and on the earth,
in the seas and all their depths.
7He makes clouds rise from the ends of the earth;

a *1* Hebrew *Hallelu Yah*; also in verses 3 and 21

133:2 [b]Ex 30:25
133:3 [c]Dt 4:48 [d]Lev 25:21; Dt 28:8 [e]Ps 42:8
134:1 [a]Ps 135:1-2 [b]1Ch 9:33
134:2 [c]Ps 28:2; 1Ti 2:8
134:3 [d]Ps 124:8 [e]Ps 128:5
135:1 [a]Ps 113:1; 134:1
135:2 [b]Lk 2:37 [c]Ps 116:19
135:3 [d]Ps 119:68 [e]Ps 147:1
135:4 [f]Dt 10:15; 1Pe 2:9 [g]Ex 19:5; Dt 7:6
135:5 [h]Ps 48:1 [i]Ps 97:9
135:6 [j]Ps 115:3

133:2 Expensive oil was used by Moses to anoint Aaron as the first high priest of Israel (Exodus 29:7) and to dedicate all the priests to God's service. Brotherly unity, like the anointing oil, shows that we are dedicated to serving God wholeheartedly.

133:3 Mount Hermon is the tallest mountain in Palestine, located northeast of the Sea of Galilee.

134:1–3 This psalm is about a very small group—the Levites who served as temple watchmen ("you servants of the LORD who minister by night"). Singing this psalm, the last of the "songs of ascent" (Psalms 120–134), the worshippers would ascend the hill where the temple sits and see the watchmen who protect it day and night. They saw the watchmen's work as an act of praise to God, done reverently and responsibly. Make your job or your responsibility in the church an act of praise by doing it with reverence to God. Honour him by the quality of your work and the attitude of service you bring to it.

134:3 Zion is another name for Jerusalem.

135:4 That the descendants of Jacob, Israel, were a chosen people reflects God's commission to the nation in Deuteronomy 7:6–8 and in Peter's sermon to the church in 1 Peter 2:9. God treasures us. He gives love and mercy to all those who believe in him.

he sends lightning with the rain[k]
and brings out the wind[l] from his storehouses.[m]

8He struck down the firstborn[n] of Egypt,
the firstborn of men and animals.
9He sent his signs[o] and wonders into your midst, O Egypt,
against Pharaoh and all his servants.[p]
10He struck down many[q] nations
and killed mighty kings—
11Sihon[r] king of the Amorites,
Og king of Bashan
and all the kings of Canaan[s]—
12and he gave their land as an inheritance,[t]
an inheritance to his people Israel.

13Your name, O LORD, endures for ever,[u]
your renown,[v] O LORD, through all generations.
14For the LORD will vindicate his people
and have compassion on his servants.[w]

15The idols of the nations are silver and gold,
made by the hands of men.
16They have mouths, but cannot speak,
eyes, but they cannot see;
17they have ears, but cannot hear,
nor is there breath in their mouths.
18Those who make them will be like them,
and so will all who trust in them.

19O house of Israel, praise the LORD;
O house of Aaron, praise the LORD;
20O house of Levi, praise the LORD;
you who fear him, praise the LORD.
21Praise be to the LORD from Zion,[x]
to him who dwells in Jerusalem.

Praise the LORD.

135:7 [k]Jer 10:13; Zec 10:1 [l]Job 28:25 [m]Job 38:22
135:8 [n]Ex 12:12; Ps 78:51
135:9 [o]Dt 6:22 [p]Ps 136:10-15
135:10 [q]Nu 21:21-25; Ps 136:17-21
135:11 [r]Nu 21:21 [s]Jos 12:7-24
135:12 [t]Ps 78:55
135:13 [u]Ex 3:15 [v]Ps 102:12
135:14 [w]Dt 32:36
135:21 [x]Ps 134:3

PSALM 136

Theme: The never-ending story of God's love.
God deserves our praise because his endless love never fails.
Author: Anonymous

1Give thanks to the LORD, for he is good.[a]
His love endures for ever.[b]
2Give thanks to the God of gods.[c]
His love endures for ever.
3Give thanks to the Lord of lords:
His love endures for ever.

4to him who alone does great wonders,[d]
His love endures for ever.

136:1 [a]Ps 106:1 [b]1Ch 16:34; 2Ch 20:21
136:2 [c]Dt 10:17
136:4 [d]Ps 72:18

135:15–18 Those who worshipped idols were as blind and insensitive as the idols themselves. They couldn't see or hear what God had to say. In subtle, imperceptible ways we become like the idols we worship. If the true God is your God, you will become more like him as you worship him. What are your goals? What takes priority in your life? Choose carefully because you will take on the characteristics of whatever you worship.

136:1ff Repeated throughout this psalm is the phrase, "His love endures for ever." This psalm may have been a responsive reading, with the congregation saying these words in unison after each sentence. The repetition made this important lesson sink in. God's love includes aspects of love, kindness, mercy, and faithfulness. We never have to worry that God will run out of love because it flows from a well that will never run dry.

5who by his understanding[e] made the heavens,[f]
His love endures for ever.
6who spread out the earth[g] upon the waters,[h]
His love endures for ever.
7who made the great lights[i]—
His love endures for ever.
8the sun to govern[j] the day,
His love endures for ever.
9the moon and stars to govern the night;
His love endures for ever.

10to him who struck down the firstborn[k] of Egypt
His love endures for ever.
11and brought Israel out[l] from among them
His love endures for ever.
12with a mighty hand and outstretched arm;[m]
His love endures for ever.

13to him who divided the Red Sea[a][n] asunder
His love endures for ever.
14and brought Israel through[o] the midst of it,
His love endures for ever.
15but swept Pharaoh and his army into the Red Sea;[p]
His love endures for ever.

16to him who led his people through the desert,[q]
His love endures for ever.
17who struck down great kings,[r]
His love endures for ever.
18and killed mighty kings[s]—
His love endures for ever.
19Sihon king of the Amorites[t]
His love endures for ever.
20and Og king of Bashan—
His love endures for ever.
21and gave their land[u] as an inheritance,
His love endures for ever.
22an inheritance to his servant Israel;
His love endures for ever.

23to the One who remembered us[v] in our low estate
His love endures for ever.
24and freed us from our enemies,[w]
His love endures for ever.
25and who gives food[x] to every creature.
His love endures for ever.

26Give thanks to the God of heaven.
His love endures for ever.

PSALM 137

Theme: A person in exile weeps over the bitterness of captivity. Our sorrow can make it difficult to imagine singing joyful songs again.
Author: Anonymous

1By the rivers of Babylon[a] we sat and wept[b]
when we remembered Zion.
2There on the poplars

a *13* Hebrew *Yam Suph*; that is, Sea of Reeds; also in verse 15

136:5 [e]Pr 3:19; Jer 51:15 [f]Ge 1:1
136:6 [g]Ge 1:9; Jer 10:12 [h]Ps 24:2
136:7 [i]Ge 1:14, 16
136:8 [j]Ge 1:16
136:10 [k]Ex 12:29; Ps 135:8
136:11 [l]Ex 6:6; 12:51
136:12 [m]Dt 4:34; Ps 44:3
136:13 [n]Ex 14:21; Ps 78:13
136:14 [o]Ex 14:22
136:15 [p]Ex 14:27; Ps 135:9
136:16 [q]Ex 13:18
136:17 [r]Ps 135:9-12
136:18 [s]Dt 29:7
136:19 [t]Nu 21:21-25
136:21 [u]Jos 12:1
136:23 [v]Ps 113:7
136:24 [w]Ps 107:2
136:25 [x]Ps 104:27; 145:15
137:1 [a]Eze 1:1, 3 [b]Ne 1:4

137:3
[c]Ps 80:6

we hung our harps,
3for there our captors asked us for songs,
our tormentors demanded[c] songs of joy;
they said, "Sing us one of the songs of Zion!"

137:6
[d]Eze 3:26

4How can we sing the songs of the LORD
while in a foreign land?
5If I forget you, O Jerusalem,
may my right hand forget ⌞its skill⌟.

137:7
[e]Jer 49:7;
La 4:21-22;
Eze 25:12
[f]Ob 1:11

6May my tongue cling to the roof[d] of my mouth
if I do not remember you,
if I do not consider Jerusalem
my highest joy.

7Remember, O LORD, what the Edomites[e] did

137:8
[g]Isa 13:1, 19;
Jer 25:12, 26;
Jer 50:15;
Rev 18:6

on the day Jerusalem fell.[f]
"Tear it down," they cried,
"tear it down to its foundations!"

8O Daughter of Babylon, doomed to destruction,[g]
happy is he who repays you
for what you have done to us—

137:9
[h]2Ki 8:12;
Isa 13:16

9he who seizes your infants
and dashes them[h] against the rocks.

PSALM 138

138:1
[a]Ps 95:3; 96:4

Of David.

Theme: Thanksgiving for answered prayer. God works out his plans for our lives and will bring us through the difficulties we face.
Author: David

138:2
[b]1Ki 8:29;
Ps 5:7; 28:2
[c]Isa 42:21

1I will praise you, O LORD, with all my heart;
before the "gods"[a] I will sing your praise.
2I will bow down towards your holy temple[b]
and will praise your name

138:3
[d]Ps 28:7

for your love and your faithfulness,
for you have exalted above all things
your name and your word.[c]
3When I called, you answered me;
you made me bold and stout-hearted.[d]

138:4
[e]Ps 102:15

4May all the kings of the earth[e] praise you, O LORD,
when they hear the words of your mouth.
5May they sing of the ways of the LORD,
for the glory of the LORD is great.

138:6
[f]Ps 113:6;
Isa 57:15

6Though the LORD is on high, he looks upon the lowly,[f]

137:7 The Edomites were related to the Israelites, both nations having descended from Isaac and his father Abraham. Although Israel shared its southern border with Edom, there was bitter hatred between the two nations. The Edomites did not come to help when the city of Jerusalem was besieged by the Babylonian army. In fact, they rejoiced when the city was destroyed (Jeremiah 49:7–22; Joel 3:19; Obadiah 1:1–20).

137:8, 9 God destroyed Babylon and its offspring for their proud assault against God and his kingdom. The Medes and Persians destroyed Babylon in 539 B.C. Many of those who were oppressed lived to see the victory. The phrase about the infants is harsh because the psalmist is crying out for judgment: "Treat the Babylonians the way they treated us."

138:1 "Before the 'gods' " may mean in the presence of subordinate heavenly beings (angels), or, more likely, it may be a statement ridiculing the kings or gods of the pagan nations. God is the highest in the whole earth.

138:1–3 Thanksgiving should be an integral part of our praise to God. This theme is woven throughout the psalms. As we praise and thank God for material and spiritual blessings, we should also thank him for answered prayer. Remember when you asked God for protection, strength, comfort, patience, love, or other special needs, and he supplied them? Beware of taking God's provision and answered prayer for granted.

but the proud[g] he knows from afar.
7Though I walk[h] in the midst of trouble,
you preserve my life;
you stretch out your hand against the anger of my foes,[i]
with your right hand[j] you save me.[k]
8The LORD will fulfil ⌞his purpose⌟[l] for me;
your love, O LORD, endures for ever—
do not abandon the works of your hands.[m]

PSALM 139

For the director of music. Of David. A psalm.

Theme: God is all-seeing, all-knowing, all-powerful, and everywhere present. God knows us, God is with us, and his greatest gift is to allow us to know him.
Author: David

1O LORD, you have searched me[a]
and you know[b] me.
2You know when I sit and when I rise;[c]
you perceive my thoughts[d] from afar.
3You discern my going out and my lying down;
you are familiar with all my ways.[e]
4Before a word is on my tongue
you know it completely,[f] O LORD.

5You hem me in[g]—behind and before;
you have laid your hand upon me.
6Such knowledge is too wonderful for me,
too lofty[h] for me to attain.

7Where can I go from your Spirit?
Where can I flee[i] from your presence?
8If I go up to the heavens,[j] you are there;
if I make my bed[k] in the depths,[a] you are there.
9If I rise on the wings of the dawn,
if I settle on the far side of the sea,
10even there your hand will guide me,[l]
your right hand will hold me fast.

11If I say, "Surely the darkness will hide me
and the light become night around me,"
12even the darkness will not be dark[m] to you;
the night will shine like the day,
for darkness is as light to you.

13For you created my inmost being;[n]

[a] 8 Hebrew *Sheol*

138:6 [g] Pr 3:34; Jas 4:6
138:7 [h] Ps 23:4 [i] Jer 51:25 [j] Ps 20:6 [k] Ps 71:20
138:8 [l] Ps 57:2; Php 1:6 [m] Job 10:3, 8; 14:15
139:1 [a] Ps 17:3 [b] Jer 12:3
139:2 [c] 2Ki 19:27 [d] Mt 9:4; Jn 2:24
139:3 [e] Job 31:4
139:4 [f] Heb 4:13
139:5 [g] Ps 34:7
139:6 [h] Job 42:3; Ro 11:33
139:7 [i] Jer 23:24; Jnh 1:3
139:8 [j] Am 9:2-3 [k] Pr 15:11
139:10 [l] Ps 23:3
139:12 [m] Job 34:22; Da 2:22
139:13 [n] Ps 119:73

138:8 Every person dreams and makes plans for the future. Then they work hard to see those dreams and plans come true. But to make the most of life, we must include God's plan in our plans. He alone knows what is best for us; he alone can fulfil his purpose for us. As you make plans and dream dreams, talk with God about them.

139:1–5 Sometimes we don't let people get to know us completely because we are afraid they will discover something about us that they won't like. But God already knows everything about us, even to the number of hairs on our heads (Matthew 10:30), and still he accepts and loves us. God is with us through every situation, in every trial—protecting, loving, guiding. He knows and loves us completely.

139:7 God is omnipresent—he is present everywhere. Because this is so, you can never be lost to his Spirit. This is good news to those who know and love God, because no matter what we do or where we go, we can never be far from God's comforting presence (see Romans 8:35–39).

139:13–15 God's character goes into the creation of every person. When you feel worthless or even begin to hate yourself, remember that God's Spirit is ready and willing to work within you. We should have as much respect for ourselves as our Maker has for us.

139:13
[o] Job 10:11

you knit me together[o] in my mother's womb.
14 I praise you because I am fearfully and wonderfully made;
your works are wonderful,[p]
I know that full well.

139:14
[p] Ps 40:5

15 My frame was not hidden from you
when I was made in the secret place.
When I was woven together[q] in the depths of the earth,[r]
16 your eyes saw my unformed body.
All the days ordained for me
were written in your book
before one of them came to be.

139:15
[q] Job 10:11
[r] Ps 63:9

17 How precious to[b] me are your thoughts, O God![s]
How vast is the sum of them!
18 Were I to count them,
they would outnumber the grains of sand.
When I awake,
I am still with you.

139:17
[s] Ps 40:5

19 If only you would slay the wicked,[t] O God!
Away from me,[u] you bloodthirsty men!
20 They speak of you with evil intent;
your adversaries misuse your name.[v]

139:19
[t] Isa 11:4
[u] Ps 119:115

139:20
[v] Jude 15

b 17 *Or concerning*

ANGER AND VENGEANCE IN THE BOOK OF PSALMS

Several psalms shock those familiar with New Testament teachings. The psalmists didn't hesitate to demand God's justice and make vivid suggestions as to how he might carry it out. Apparently, no subject was unsuitable for discussion with God, but our tendency is to avoid the subjects of anger and vengeance in the psalms.

To understand the words of anger and vengeance, we need to understand several things:

(1) The judgments asked for are to be carried out by God, and are written out of intense personal and national suffering. The people are unable or unwilling to take revenge themselves and are asking God to intervene. Because few of us have suffered intense cruelty on a personal or national level, we find it difficult to grasp these outbursts.

(2) These writers were intimately aware of God's justice. Some of their words are efforts to vividly imagine what God might allow to happen to those who had harmed his people.

(3) If we dared to write down our thoughts while unjustly attacked or suffering cruelty, we might be shocked at our own bold desire for vengeance. We would be surprised at how much we have in common with these men of old. The psalmists did not have Jesus' command to pray for one's enemies, but they did point to the right place to start. We are challenged to pay back good for evil, but until we respond to this challenge, we will not know how much we need God's help in order to forgive others.

(4) There is a helpful parallel between the psalms of anger and the psalms of vengeance. The "angry" psalms are intense and graphic, but they are directed at God. He is boldly told how disappointing it is when he turns his back on his people or acts too slowly. But while these thoughts and feelings were sincerely expressed, we know from the psalms themselves that these passing feelings were followed by renewed confidence in God's faithfulness. It is reasonable to expect the same of the "vengeance" psalms. We read, for example, David's angry outburst against Saul's pursuit in Psalm 59, yet we know that David never took personal revenge on Saul. The psalmists freely spoke their minds to God, having confidence that he could sort out what was meant and what was felt. Pray with that same confidence—God can be trusted with your heart.

Selected psalms that emphasise these themes are 10; 23; 28; 35; 59; 69; 109; 137; 139; 140.

21Do I not hate those[w] who hate you, O LORD,
and abhor those who rise up against you?
22I have nothing but hatred for them;
I count them my enemies.

23Search me,[x] O God, and know my heart;[y]
test me and know my anxious thoughts.
24See if there is any offensive way in me,
and lead me[z] in the way everlasting.

139:21 [w]2Ch 19:2; Ps 31:6; 119:113; Ps 119:158
139:23 [x]Job 31:6; Ps 26:2 [y]Jer 11:20
139:24 [z]Ps 5:8; 143:10; Pr 15:9

PSALM 140

For the director of music. A psalm of David.

Theme: Prayer for protection against those who slander or threaten you. Deliverance begins with concentrating on our future life with God.
Author: David

1Rescue me,[a] O LORD, from evil men;
protect me from men of violence,[b]
2who devise evil plans[c] in their hearts
and stir up war every day.
3They make their tongues as sharp as[d] a serpent's;
the poison of vipers[e] is on their lips. *Selah*

4Keep me,[f] O LORD, from the hands of the wicked;[g]
protect me from men of violence
who plan to trip my feet.
5Proud men have hidden a snare for me;
they have spread out the cords of their net
and have set traps[h] for me along my path. *Selah*

6O LORD, I say to you, "You are my God."[i]
Hear, O LORD, my cry for mercy.[j]
7O Sovereign LORD,[k] my strong deliverer,
who shields my head in the day of battle—
8do not grant the wicked[l] their desires, O LORD;
do not let their plans succeed,
or they will become proud. *Selah*

9Let the heads of those who surround me
be covered with the trouble their lips have caused.[m]
10Let burning coals fall upon them;
may they be thrown into the fire,[n]
into miry pits, never to rise.
11Let slanderers not be established in the land;
may disaster hunt down men of violence.[o]

12I know that the LORD secures justice for the poor

140:1 [a]Ps 17:13 [b]Ps 18:48
140:2 [c]Ps 36:4; 56:6
140:3 [d]Ps 57:4 [e]Ps 58:4; Jas 3:8
140:4 [f]Ps 141:9 [g]Ps 71:4
140:5 [h]Ps 31:4; 35:7
140:6 [i]Ps 16:2 [j]Ps 116:1; 143:1
140:7 [k]Ps 28:8
140:8 [l]Ps 10:2-3
140:9 [m]Ps 7:16
140:10 [n]Ps 11:6; 21:9
140:11 [o]Ps 34:21

139:21–24 David's hatred for his enemies came from his zeal for God. David regarded his enemies as God's enemies, so his hatred was a desire for God's righteous justice and not for personal vengeance. Is it all right to be angry at people who hate God? Yes, but we must remember that it is God who will deal with them, not us. If we truly love God, then we will be deeply hurt if someone hates him. David asked God to search his heart and mind and point out any wrong motives that may have been behind his strong words. But while we seek justice against evil, we must also pray that God's enemies will turn to him before he judges them (see Matthew 5:44).

139:23, 24 David asked God to search for sin and point it out, even to the level of testing his thoughts. This is exploratory surgery for sin. How are we to recognise sin unless God points it out? Then, when God shows us, we can repent and be forgiven. Make this verse your prayer. If you ask the Lord to search your heart and your thoughts and to reveal your sin, you will be continuing on God's "way everlasting".

140:12 To whom can the poor turn when they are persecuted? They lack the money to get professional help; they may be unable to defend themselves. But there is always someone on their side—the Lord will stand by them and ultimately bring about justice. This should be a comfort for us all. No matter what our situation may be, the Lord is with us. But this truth should also call us to responsibil-

140:12
[p]Ps 9:4
[q]Ps 35:10

and upholds the cause[p] of the needy.[q]
13 Surely the righteous will praise your name[r]
and the upright will live[s] before you.

140:13
[r]Ps 97:12
[s]Ps 11:7

PSALM 141

A psalm of David.

Theme: A prayer for help when facing temptation. David asks God to protect him and to give him wisdom in accepting criticism. Be open to honest criticism — God may be speaking to you through others.
Author: David

141:1
[a]Ps 22:19; 70:5
[b]Ps 143:1

1 O LORD, I call to you; come quickly[a] to me.
Hear my voice[b] when I call to you.

141:2
[c]Rev 5:8; 8:3
[d]1Ti 2:8
[e]Ex 29:39, 41

2 May my prayer be set before you like incense;[c]
may the lifting up of my hands[d] be like the evening sacrifice.[e]

3 Set a guard over my mouth, O LORD;
keep watch over the door of my lips.

141:4
[f]Pr 23:6

4 Let not my heart be drawn to what is evil,
to take part in wicked deeds
with men who are evildoers;
let me not eat of their delicacies.[f]

141:5
[g]Pr 9:8
[h]Ps 23:5

5 Let a righteous man[a] strike me — it is a kindness;
let him rebuke me[g] — it is oil on my head.[h]
My head will not refuse it.

141:7
[i]Ps 53:5

Yet my prayer is ever against the deeds of evildoers;
6 their rulers will be thrown down from the cliffs,
and the wicked will learn that my words were well spoken.
7 ⌞They will say,⌟ "As one ploughs and breaks up the earth,
so our bones have been scattered at the mouth[i] of the grave."[b]

141:8
[j]Ps 25:15
[k]Ps 2:12

8 But my eyes are fixed[j] on you, O Sovereign LORD;
in you I take refuge[k] — do not give me over to death.

141:9
[l]Ps 140:4
[m]Ps 38:12

9 Keep me[l] from the snares they have laid for me,
from the traps set[m] by evildoers.
10 Let the wicked fall[n] into their own nets,
while I pass by in safety.

141:10
[n]Ps 35:8

[a] 5 Or *Let the Righteous One* [b] 7 Hebrew *Sheol*

---

ity. As God's people, we are required to defend the rights of the powerless.

141:3 James wrote that "the tongue is a small part of the body, but it makes great boasts" (James 3:5). On average, a person opens his or her mouth approximately 700 times a day to speak. David wisely asked God to help keep him from speaking evil — sometimes even as he underwent persecution. Jesus himself was silent before his accusers (Matthew 26:63). Knowing the power of the tongue, we would do well to ask God to guard what we say so that our words will bring honour to his name.

141:4 David asked God to guard his heart. Evil acts begin with evil desires. It isn't enough to ask God to keep you away from temptation, make you stronger, or change your circumstances. You must ask him to change you on the inside — at the level of your desires.

141:5 David says that being rebuked by a righteous person is a kindness. Nobody really likes criticism, but everybody can benefit from it when it is given wisely and taken humbly. David suggested how to accept criticism: (1) don't refuse it, (2) consider it a kindness, and (3) keep quiet (don't fight back). Putting these suggestions into practice will help you control how you react to criticism, making it productive rather than destructive, no matter how it was originally intended.

PSALM 142

A *maskil*[a] of David. When he was in the cave. A prayer.

Theme: A prayer when overwhelmed and desperate.
When we feel cornered by our enemies, only God can keep us safe.
Author: David

1I cry aloud to the LORD;
I lift up my voice to the LORD for mercy.[a]
2I pour out my complaint[b] before him;
before him I tell my trouble.

3When my spirit grows faint[c] within me,
it is you who know my way.
In the path where I walk
men have hidden a snare for me.
4Look to my right and see;
no-one is concerned for me.
I have no refuge;
no-one cares[d] for my life.

5I cry to you, O LORD;
I say, "You are my refuge,[e]
my portion[f] in the land of the living."[g]
6Listen to my cry,[h]
for I am in desperate need;[i]
rescue me from those who pursue me,
for they are too strong for me.
7Set me free from my prison,[j]
that I may praise your name.

Then the righteous will gather about me
because of your goodness to me.[k]

PSALM 143

A psalm of David.

Theme: A prayer in the midst of hopelessness and depression. Our prayers should fit into what we know is consistent with God's character and plans.
Author: David

1O LORD, hear my prayer,
listen to my cry for mercy;[a]
in your faithfulness[b] and righteousness[c]
come to my relief.
2Do not bring your servant into judgment,
for no-one living is righteous[d] before you.

3The enemy pursues me,
he crushes me to the ground;
he makes me dwell in darkness
like those long dead.
4So my spirit grows faint within me;
my heart within me is dismayed.[e]

a Title: Probably a literary or musical term

142:1 aPs 30:8
142:2 bIsa 26:16
142:3 cPs 140:5; 143:4, 7
142:4 dPs 31:11; Jer 30:17
142:5 ePs 46:1 fPs 16:5 gPs 27:13
142:6 hPs 17:1 iPs 79:8; 116:6
142:7 jPs 146:7 kPs 13:6
143:1 aPs 140:6 bPs 89:1-2 cPs 71:2
143:2 dPs 14:3; Ecc 7:20; Ro 3:20
143:4 ePs 142:3

142:4, 5 Have you ever felt that no-one cared what happened to you? David had good reason to feel that way, and he wrote, "I cry to you, O LORD." Through prayer we can pull out of our tailspin and be reminded that God cares for us deeply.

142:7 This psalm was written when David was hiding from Saul in caves like the ones at Adullam (1 Samuel 22) or En Gedi (1 Samuel 24). These may have seemed like prisons to him because of the confinement.

143:5 [f]Ps 77:6

143:6 [g]Ps 63:1; 88:9

143:7 [h]Ps 69:17 [i]Ps 27:9; 28:1

143:8 [j]Ps 46:5; 90:14 [k]Ps 27:11 [l]Ps 25:1-2

143:9 [m]Ps 31:15

143:10 [n]Ne 9:20; Ps 23:3; 25:4-5

143:11 [o]Ps 119:25 [p]Ps 31:1

143:12 [q]Ps 52:5; 54:5 [r]Ps 116:16

5 I remember[f] the days of long ago;
I meditate on all your works
and consider what your hands have done.
6 I spread out my hands[g] to you;
my soul thirsts for you like a parched land. *Selah*

7 Answer me quickly,[h] O LORD;
my spirit fails.
Do not hide your face[i] from me
or I will be like those who go down to the pit.
8 Let the morning bring me word of your unfailing love,[j]
for I have put my trust in you.
Show me the way[k] I should go,
for to you I lift up my soul.[l]
9 Rescue me from my enemies,[m] O LORD,
for I hide myself in you.
10 Teach me to do your will,
for you are my God;
may your good Spirit
lead[n] me on level ground.

11 For your name's sake, O LORD, preserve my life;[o]
in your righteousness,[p] bring me out of trouble.
12 In your unfailing love, silence my enemies;
destroy all my foes,[q]
for I am your servant.[r]

PSALM 144

Of David.

Theme: Rejoicing in God's care. Whether in times of prosperity or adversity, blessed are those whose God is the Lord.
Author: David

144:1 [a]Ps 18:2, 34

144:2 [b]Ps 59:9; 91:2 [c]Ps 84:9

144:3 [d]Ps 8:4; Heb 2:6

144:4 [e]Ps 39:11; 102:11

144:5 [f]Ps 18:9; Isa 64:1

1 Praise be to the LORD my Rock,[a]
who trains my hands for war,
my fingers for battle.
2 He is my loving God and my fortress,[b]
my stronghold and my deliverer,
my shield,[c] in whom I take refuge,
who subdues peoples[a] under me.

3 O LORD, what is man[d] that you care for him,
the son of man that you think of him?
4 Man is like a breath;
his days are like a fleeting shadow.[e]

5 Part your heavens,[f] O LORD, and come down;

[a] 2 Many manuscripts of the Masoretic Text, Dead Sea Scrolls, Aquila, Jerome and Syriac; most manuscripts of the Masoretic Text *subdues my people*

143:7 David was losing hope, caught in paralysing fear and deep depression. At times, we feel caught in deepening depression, and we are unable to pull ourselves out. At those times, we can come to the Lord and, like David, express our true feelings. Then he will help us as we remember his works (143:5), reach out to him in prayer (143:6), trust him (143:8), and decide to do his will (143:10).

143:10 David's prayer was to be taught to do God's will, not his own. A prayer for guidance is self-centred if it doesn't recognise God's power to redirect our lives. Asking God to restructure our priorities awakens our minds and stirs our wills.

144:3, 4 Life is short. David reminds us that it is "like a breath" and that our "days are like a fleeting shadow". James says that our lives are "a mist that appears for a little while and then vanishes" (James 4:14). Because life is short, we should live for God while we have the time. Don't waste your life by selecting an inferior purpose that has no lasting value. Live for God – he alone can make your life worthwhile, purposeful, and meaningful.

touch the mountains, so that they smoke.[g]
6Send forth lightning and scatter ⌞the enemies⌟;
shoot your arrows[h] and rout them.
7Reach down your hand from on high;
deliver me and rescue me
from the mighty waters,[i]
from the hands of foreigners[j]
8whose mouths are full of lies,[k]
whose right hands are deceitful.

9I will sing a new song to you, O God;
on the ten-stringed lyre[l] I will make music to you,
10to the One who gives victory to kings,
who delivers his servant David[m] from the deadly sword.

11Deliver me and rescue me
from the hands of foreigners
whose mouths are full of lies,
whose right hands are deceitful.[n]

12Then our sons in their youth
will be like well-nurtured plants,[o]
and our daughters will be like pillars
carved to adorn a palace.
13Our barns will be filled
with every kind of provision.
Our sheep will increase by thousands,
by tens of thousands in our fields;
14 our oxen will draw heavy loads.[b]
There will be no breaching of walls,
no going into captivity,
no cry of distress in our streets.

15Blessed are the people[p] of whom this is true;
blessed are the people whose God is the LORD.

PSALM 145[a]

A psalm of praise. Of David.

Theme: A time will come when all people will join together in recognising and worshipping God. Because God is full of love, he satisfies all who trust in him.
Author: David

1I will exalt you,[a] my God the King;[b]
I will praise your name for ever and ever.
2Every day I will praise[c] you
and extol your name for ever and ever.

3Great is the LORD and most worthy of praise;
his greatness no-one can fathom.[d]
4One generation[e] will commend your works to another;
they will tell of your mighty acts.
5They will speak of the glorious splendour of your majesty,
and I will meditate on your wonderful works.[b][f]
6They will tell of the power of your awesome works,[g]
and I will proclaim[h] your great deeds.
7They will celebrate your abundant goodness[i]

b *14 Or our chieftains will be firmly established* **a** This psalm is an acrostic poem, the verses of which (including verse 13b) begin with the successive letters of the Hebrew alphabet. **b** *5* Dead Sea Scrolls and Syriac (see also Septuagint); Masoretic Text *On the glorious splendour of your majesty / and on your wonderful works I will meditate*

144:5 [g]Ps 104:32
144:6 [h]Ps 7:12-13; 18:14
144:7 [i]Ps 69:2 [j]Ps 18:44
144:8 [k]Ps 12:2
144:9 [l]Ps 33:2-3
144:10 [m]Ps 18:50
144:11 [n]Ps 12:2; Isa 44:20
144:12 [o]Ps 128:3
144:15 [p]Ps 33:12
145:1 [a]Ps 30:1; 34:1 [b]Ps 5:2
145:2 [c]Ps 71:6
145:3 [d]Job 5:9; Ps 147:5; Ro 11:33
145:4 [e]Isa 38:19
145:5 [f]Ps 119:27
145:6 [g]Ps 66:3 [h]Dt 32:3
145:7 [i]Isa 63:7

145:7 [j]Ps 51:14
145:8 [k]Ps 86:15 [l]Ex 34:6; Nu 14:18
145:9 [m]Ps 100:5
145:10 [n]Ps 19:1 [o]Ps 68:26
145:12 [p]Ps 105:1
145:13 [q]1Ti 1:17; 2Pe 1:11
145:14 [r]Ps 37:24 [s]Ps 146:8
145:15 [t]Ps 104:27; 136:25
145:16 [u]Ps 104:28
145:18 [v]Dt 4:7 [w]Jn 4:24
145:19 [x]Ps 37:4 [y]Pr 15:29
145:20 [z]Ps 31:23; 97:10 [a]Ps 9:5
145:21 [b]Ps 71:8 [c]Ps 65:2

and joyfully sing of your righteousness.[j]

8 The LORD is gracious and compassionate,[k]
slow to anger and rich in love.[l]
9 The LORD is good[m] to all;
he has compassion on all he has made.
10 All you have made will praise you,[n] O LORD;
your saints will extol you.[o]
11 They will tell of the glory of your kingdom
and speak of your might,
12 so that all men may know of your mighty acts[p]
and the glorious splendour of your kingdom.
13 Your kingdom is an everlasting kingdom,[q]
and your dominion endures through all generations.

The LORD is faithful to all his promises
and loving towards all he has made.[c]
14 The LORD upholds[r] all those who fall
and lifts up all[s] who are bowed down.
15 The eyes of all look to you,
and you give them their food[t] at the proper time.
16 You open your hand
and satisfy the desires[u] of every living thing.

17 The LORD is righteous in all his ways
and loving towards all he has made.
18 The LORD is near[v] to all who call on him,[w]
to all who call on him in truth.
19 He fulfils the desires[x] of those who fear him;
he hears their cry[y] and saves them.
20 The LORD watches over all who love him,[z]
but all the wicked he will destroy.[a]

21 My mouth will speak[b] in praise of the LORD.
Let every creature[c] praise his holy name
for ever and ever.

c *13* One manuscript of the Masoretic Text, Dead Sea Scrolls and Syriac (see also Septuagint); most manuscripts of the Masoretic Text do not have the last two lines of verse 13.

PRAISE IN THE BOOK OF PSALMS

Most of the psalms are prayers, and most of the prayers include praise to God. Praise expresses admiration, appreciation, and thanks. Praise in the book of Psalms is often directed to God, and just as often the praise is shared with others. Considering all that God has done and does for us, what could be more natural than outbursts of heartfelt praise?

As you read Psalms, note the praise given to God, not only for what he does—his creation, his blessings, his forgiveness—but also for who he is—loving, just, faithful, forgiving, patient. Note also those times when the praise of God is shared with others, and they too are encouraged to praise him. In what ways have you recently praised God or told others all that he has done for you?

Selected psalms that emphasise this theme are 8; 19; 30; 65; 84; 96; 100; 136; 145; 150.

145:14 Sometimes our burdens seem more than we can bear, and we wonder how we can go on. David stands at this bleak intersection of life's road and points towards the Lord, the great burden-bearer. God is able to lift us up because (1) his greatness is unfathomable (145:3); (2) he does mighty acts across many generations (145:4); (3) he is full of glorious splendour and majesty (145:5); (4) he does wonderful and awesome works (145:5, 6); (5) he is righteous (145:7); (6) he is gracious, compassionate, patient, and loving (145:8, 9); (7) he rules over an everlasting kingdom (145:13); (8) he is the source of all our daily needs (145:15, 16); (9) he is righteous and loving in all his dealings (145:17); (10) he remains near to those who call on him (145:18); (11) he hears our cries and saves us (145:19, 20). If you are bending under a burden and feel that you are about to fall, turn to God for help. He is ready to lift you up and bear your burden.

PSALM 146

Theme: The help of man versus the help of God. Help from man is temporal and unstable, but help from God is lasting and complete.
Author: Anonymous

1 Praise the LORD.[a]

Praise the LORD,[a] O my soul.
2 I will praise the LORD all my life;[b]
I will sing praise to my God as long as I live.

3 Do not put your trust in princes,[c]
in mortal men,[d] who cannot save.
4 When their spirit departs, they return to the ground;[e]
on that very day their plans come to nothing.[f]

5 Blessed is he[g] whose help[h] is the God of Jacob,
whose hope is in the LORD his God,
6 the Maker of heaven[i] and earth,
the sea, and everything in them—
the LORD, who remains faithful[j] for ever.
7 He upholds the cause of the oppressed[k]
and gives food to the hungry.[l]
The LORD sets prisoners free,[m]
8 the LORD gives sight to the blind,[n]
the LORD lifts up those who are bowed down,
the LORD loves the righteous.
9 The LORD watches over the alien
and sustains the fatherless and the widow,[o]
but he frustrates the ways of the wicked.

10 The LORD reigns[p] for ever,
your God, O Zion, for all generations.

Praise the LORD.

PSALM 147

Theme: What gives God joy. Although God created everything, his greatest joy comes from our genuine worship and trust.
Author: Anonymous, written when the exiles returned to Jerusalem

1 Praise the LORD.[a]

How good it is to sing praises to our God,
how pleasant[a] and fitting to praise him![b]

2 The LORD builds up Jerusalem;[c]
he gathers the exiles[d] of Israel.

146:1 [a]Ps 103:1
146:2 [b]Ps 104:33
146:3 [c]Ps 118:9 [d]Isa 2:22
146:4 [e]Ps 104:29; Ecc 12:7 [f]Ps 33:10; 1Co 2:6
146:5 [g]Ps 144:15; Jer 17:7 [h]Ps 71:5
146:6 [i]Ps 115:15; Ac 14:15; Rev 14:7 [j]Ps 117:2
146:7 [k]Ps 103:6 [l]Ps 107:9 [m]Ps 68:6
146:8 [n]Mt 9:30
146:9 [o]Ex 22:22; Dt 10:18; Ps 68:5
146:10 [p]Ex 15:18; Ps 10:16
147:1 [a]Ps 135:3 [b]Ps 33:1
147:2 [c]Ps 102:16 [d]Dt 30:3

a *1* Hebrew *Hallelu Yah*; also in verse 10 **a** *1* Hebrew *Hallelu Yah*; also in verse 20

146–150 These last five psalms overflow with praise. Each begins and ends with "Praise the LORD". They show us where, why, and how to praise God. What does praise do? (1) Praise takes our minds off our problems and shortcomings, and focuses them on God. (2) Praise leads us from individual meditation to corporate worship. (3) Praise causes us to consider and appreciate God's character. (4) Praise lifts our perspective from the earthly to the heavenly.

146:3–8 The psalmist portrays man as an inadequate saviour, a false hope; even princes cannot deliver (146:3). God is the hope and the help of the needy. Jesus affirms his concern for the poor and afflicted in Luke 4:18–21; 7:21–23. He does not separate the social and spiritual needs of people, but attends to both. While God, not the government, is the hope of the needy, *we* are his instruments to help here on earth.

146:9 God's plans frustrate the "ways of the wicked" because his values are the opposite of society's. Jesus turned society's values upside down when he proclaimed that "many who are first will be last, and many who are last will be first" (Matthew 19:30), and that "whoever wants to save his life will lose it, but whoever loses his life for me will find it" (Matthew 16:25). Don't be surprised when others don't understand your Christian values, but don't give in to theirs.

147:4
[e] Isa 40:26

147:5
[f] Ps 48:1
[g] Isa 40:28

147:6
[h] Ps 146:8-9

147:7
[i] Ps 33:3

147:8
[j] Job 38:26
[k] Ps 104:14

147:9
[l] Ps 104:27-28; Mt 6:26
[m] Job 38:41

147:10
[n] 1Sa 16:7
[o] Ps 33:16-17

147:14
[p] Isa 60:17-18
[q] Ps 132:15

147:15
[r] Job 37:12

147:16
[s] Job 37:6
[t] Job 38:29

147:18
[u] Ps 33:9

147:19
[v] Dt 33:4; Mal 4:4

147:20
[w] Dt 4:7-8, 32-34

3 He heals the broken-hearted
and binds up their wounds.

4 He determines the number of the stars[e]
and calls them each by name.
5 Great is our Lord[f] and mighty in power;
his understanding has no limit.[g]
6 The LORD sustains the humble[h]
but casts the wicked to the ground.

7 Sing to the LORD[i] with thanksgiving;
make music to our God on the harp.
8 He covers the sky with clouds;
he supplies the earth with rain[j]
and makes grass grow[k] on the hills.
9 He provides food[l] for the cattle
and for the young ravens[m] when they call.

10 His pleasure is not in the strength[n] of the horse,[o]
nor his delight in the legs of a man;
11 the LORD delights in those who fear him,
who put their hope in his unfailing love.

12 Extol the LORD, O Jerusalem;
praise your God, O Zion,
13 for he strengthens the bars of your gates
and blesses your people within you.
14 He grants peace[p] to your borders
and satisfies you[q] with the finest of wheat.

15 He sends his command[r] to the earth;
his word runs swiftly.
16 He spreads the snow[s] like wool
and scatters the frost[t] like ashes.
17 He hurls down hail like pebbles.
Who can withstand his icy blast?
18 He sends his word[u] and melts them;
he stirs up his breezes, and the waters flow.

19 He has revealed his word to Jacob,
his laws and decrees[v] to Israel.
20 He has done this for no other nation;[w]
they do not know his laws.

Praise the LORD.

147:5 Sometimes we feel as if we don't understand ourselves—what we want, how we feel, what's wrong with us, or what we should do about it. But God's understanding has no limit, and therefore he understands us fully. If you feel troubled and don't understand yourself, remember that God understands you perfectly. Take your mind off yourself and focus it on God. Strive to become more and more like him. The more you learn about God and his ways, the better you will understand yourself.

147:10, 11 We spend much effort trying to sharpen our skills or increase our strength. There is nothing wrong with doing so, and, in fact, our gifts can be used to glorify God. But when we use our skills with no regard for God, they are indeed worth little. It is our *fear* (reverence) and trust that God desires. When he has those, then he will use our skills and strengths in ways far greater than we can imagine.

147:19, 20 The nation of Israel (the descendants of Jacob) was special to God because to its people God brought his laws, and through its people he sent his Son, Jesus Christ. Now any individual who follows God is just as special to him. In fact, the Bible says that the real nation of Israel is not a specific people or geographic place, but the community of all who believe in and obey God (see Galatians 3:28, 29).

PSALM 148

Theme: Let all creation praise and worship the Lord.
Author: Anonymous

1Praise the LORD.[a]

Praise the LORD from the heavens,
praise him in the heights above.
2Praise him, all his angels,[a]
praise him, all his heavenly hosts.
3Praise him, sun and moon,
praise him, all you shining stars.
4Praise him, you highest heavens
and you waters above the skies.[b]
5Let them praise the name of the LORD,
for he commanded[c] and they were created.
6He set them in place for ever and ever;
he gave a decree[d] that will never pass away.

7Praise the LORD from the earth,
you great sea creatures[e] and all ocean depths,
8lightning and hail, snow and clouds,
stormy winds that do his bidding,[f]
9you mountains and all hills,[g]
fruit trees and all cedars,
10wild animals and all cattle,
small creatures and flying birds,
11kings of the earth and all nations,
you princes and all rulers on earth,
12young men and maidens,
old men and children.

13Let them praise the name of the LORD,[h]
for his name alone is exalted;
his splendour is above the earth and the heavens.[i]
14He has raised up for his people a horn,[b][j]
the praise of all his saints,
of Israel, the people close to his heart.

Praise the LORD.

PSALM 149

Theme: A victory celebration. We have the assurance that God truly enjoys his people.
Author: Anonymous

1Praise the LORD.[a][a]

Sing to the LORD a new song,
his praise in the assembly[b] of the saints.

2Let Israel rejoice in their Maker;[c]
let the people of Zion be glad in their King.[d]

a *1* Hebrew *Hallelu Yah*; also in verse 14 **b** *14* *Horn* here symbolises strong one, that is, king. **a** *1* Hebrew *Hallelu Yah*; also in verse 9

148:2 [a]Ps 103:20
148:4 [b]Ge 1:7; 1Ki 8:27
148:5 [c]Ge 1:1, 6; Ps 33:6, 9
148:6 [d]Job 38:33; Ps 89:37; Jer 33:25
148:7 [e]Ps 74:13-14
148:8 [f]Ps 147:15-18
148:9 [g]Isa 44:23; 49:13; 55:12
148:13 [h]Isa 12:4 [i]Ps 8:1; 113:4
148:14 [j]Ps 75:10
149:1 [a]Ps 33:2 [b]Ps 35:18
149:2 [c]Ps 95:6 [d]Ps 47:6; Zec 9:9

148:5-14 All creation is like a majestic symphony or a great choir composed of many harmonious parts that together offer up songs of praise. Each part (independent, yet part of the whole) is caught up and carried along in the swelling tides of praise. This is a picture of how we as believers should praise God – individually, yet as part of the great choir of believers worldwide. Are you singing your part well in the worldwide choir of praise?

[3]Let them praise his name with dancing
and make music to him with tambourine and harp.[e]
[4]For the LORD takes delight[f] in his people;
he crowns the humble with salvation.[g]
[5]Let the saints rejoice[h] in this honour
and sing for joy on their beds.[i]

[6]May the praise of God be in their mouths[j]
and a double-edged[k] sword in their hands,
[7]to inflict vengeance on the nations
and punishment on the peoples,
[8]to bind their kings with fetters,
their nobles with shackles of iron,
[9]to carry out the sentence written against them.[l]
This is the glory of all his saints.[m]

Praise the LORD.

PSALM 150

Theme: A closing hymn of praise. God's creation praises him everywhere in every way. We should join this rejoicing song of praise.
Author: Anonymous

[1]Praise the LORD.[a]

Praise God in his sanctuary;[a]
praise him in his mighty heavens.[b]
[2]Praise him for his acts of power;[c]
praise him for his surpassing greatness.[d]
[3]Praise him with the sounding of the trumpet,
praise him with the harp and lyre,[e]
[4]praise him with tambourine and dancing,[f]
praise him with the strings[g] and flute,
[5]praise him with the clash of cymbals,[h]
praise him with resounding cymbals.

[6]Let everything[i] that has breath praise the LORD.

Praise the LORD.

a *1* Hebrew *Hallelu Yah*; also in verse 6

149:3 [e]Ps 81:2; 150:4
149:4 [f]Ps 35:27 [g]Ps 132:16
149:5 [h]Ps 132:16 [i]Job 35:10
149:6 [j]Ps 66:17 [k]Heb 4:12; Rev 1:16
149:9 [l]Dt 7:1; Eze 28:26 [m]Ps 148:14
150:1 [a]Ps 102:19 [b]Ps 19:1
150:2 [c]Dt 3:24 [d]Ps 145:5-6
150:3 [e]Ps 149:3
150:4 [f]Ex 15:20 [g]Isa 38:20
150:5 [h]1Ch 13:8; 15:16
150:6 [i]Ps 145:21

149:3–5 Although the Bible invites us to praise God, we are often unsure how to go about it. Here, several ways are suggested—in the dance, with the voice, with musical instruments. God enjoys his people, and we should enjoy praising him.

149:6, 7 The double-edged sword symbolises the completeness of judgment that will be executed by the Messiah when he returns to punish all evildoers (Revelation 1:16).

150:3–5 Music and song were an integral part of Old Testament worship. David introduced music into the tabernacle and temple services (1 Chronicles 16:4–7). The music must have been loud and joyous as evidenced by the list of instruments and the presence of choirs and songleaders. Music was also important in New Testament worship (Ephesians 5:19; Colossians 3:16).

150:6 How could the message be more clear? The writer was telling the individual listeners to praise God. What a fitting way to end this book of praise—with a direct encouragement for *you* to praise God too. Remember to praise him every day!

150:6 In a way, the book of Psalms parallels our spiritual journey through life. It begins by presenting us with two roads—the way to life and the way to death. If we choose God's way to life, we still face both blessings and troubles, joy and grief, successes and obstacles. Throughout it all, God is at our side, guiding, encouraging, comforting, and caring. As the wise and faithful person's life draws to an end, he or she realises clearly that God's road is the right road. Knowing this will cause us to praise God for leading us in the right direction and for assuring our place in the perfect world God has in store for those who have faithfully followed him.

WHERE TO GET HELP IN THE BOOK OF PSALMS

When you feel . . .

Afraid: 3; 4; 27; 46; 49; 56; 91; 118
Alone: 9; 10; 12; 13; 27; 40; 43
"Burned out": 6; 63
Cheated: 41
Confused: 10; 12; 73
Depressed: 27; 34; 42; 43; 88; 143
Distressed: 13; 25; 31; 40; 107
Elated: 19; 96
Guilty: 19; 32; 38; 51
Hateful: 11
Impatient: 13; 27; 37; 40
Insecure: 3; 5; 12; 91
Insulted: 41; 70
Jealous: 37
Like giving up: 29; 43; 145
Lost: 23; 139
Overwhelmed: 25; 69; 142
Penitent/Sorry: 32; 51; 66
Proud: 14; 30; 49
Purposeless: 14; 25; 39; 49; 90
Sad: 13
Self-confident: 24
Tense: 4
Thankful: 118; 136; 138
Threatened: 3; 11; 17
Tired/Weak: 6; 13; 18; 28; 29; 40; 86
Trapped: 7; 17; 42; 88; 142
Unimportant: 8; 90; 139
Vengeful: 3; 7; 109
Worried: 37
Worshipful: 8; 19; 27; 29; 150

When you're facing . . .

Atheists: 10; 14; 19; 52; 53; 115
Competition: 133
Criticism: 35; 56; 120
Danger: 11
Death: 6; 71; 90
Decisions: 1; 119
Discrimination: 54
Doubts: 34; 37; 94
Evil people: 10; 35; 36; 49; 52; 109; 140
Enemies: 3; 25; 35; 41; 56; 59
Heresy: 14
Hypocrisy: 26; 28; 40; 50
Illness: 6; 139
Lies: 5; 12; 120
Old Age: 71; 92
Persecution: 1; 3; 7; 56
Poverty: 9; 10; 12
Punishment: 6; 38; 39
Slander/Insults: 7; 15; 35; 43; 120
Slaughter: 6; 46; 83
Sorrow: 23; 34
Success: 18; 112; 127; 128
Temptation: 38; 141
Troubles: 34; 55; 86; 102; 142; 145
Verbal Cruelty: 35; 120

When you want . . .

Acceptance: 139
Answers: 4; 17
Confidence: 46; 71
Courage: 11; 42
Fellowship with God: 5; 16; 25; 27; 37; 133
Forgiveness: 32; 38; 40; 51; 69; 86; 103; 130
Friendship: 16
Godliness: 15; 25
Guidance: 1; 5; 15; 19; 25; 32; 48
Healing: 6; 41
Hope: 16; 17; 18; 23; 27
Humility: 19; 147
Illumination: 19
Integrity: 24; 25
Joy: 9; 16; 28; 126
Justice: 2; 7; 14; 26; 37; 49; 58; 82
Knowledge: 2; 8; 18; 19; 25; 29; 97; 103
Leadership: 72
Miracles: 60; 111
Money: 15; 16; 17; 49
Peace: 3; 4
Perspective: 2; 11
Prayer: 5; 17; 27; 61
Protection: 3; 4; 7; 16; 17; 18; 23; 27; 31; 91; 121; 125
Provision: 23
Rest: 23; 27
Salvation: 26; 37; 49; 126
Stability: 11; 33; 46
Vindication: 9; 14; 28; 35; 109
Wisdom: 1; 16; 19; 64; 111

PROVERBS

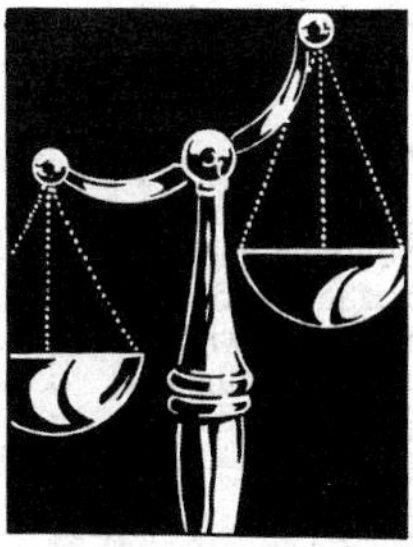

ALPHABET letters, vowels, and consonants, formed into words, sentences, paragraphs, and books—spoken, lectured, signed, whispered, written, and printed. From friendly advice to impassioned speeches and from dusty volumes to daily tabloids, messages are sent and received with each sender trying to impart knowledge . . . and wisdom.

Woven into human fabric is the desire to learn and understand. Our minds set us apart from animals, and we analyse, conceptualise, theorise, discuss, and debate everything from science to the supernatural. And we build schools, institutes, and universities where learned professors can teach us about the world and about life.

Knowledge is good, but there is a vast difference between "knowledge" (having the facts) and "wisdom" (applying those facts to life). We may amass knowledge, but without wisdom, our knowledge is useless. We must learn how to *live out* what we know.

The wisest man who ever lived, Solomon, left us a legacy of written wisdom in three volumes—Proverbs, Ecclesiastes, and Song of Songs. In these books, under the inspiration of the Holy Spirit, he gives practical insights and guidelines for life.

In the first of these three volumes, Solomon passes on his practical advice in the form of proverbs. A proverb is a short, concise sentence that conveys moral truth. The book of Proverbs is a collection of these wise statements. The main theme of Proverbs, as we might expect, is the nature of true wisdom. Solomon writes, "The fear of the LORD is the beginning of knowledge, but fools despise wisdom and discipline" (1:7). He then proceeds to give hundreds of practical examples of how to live according to godly wisdom.

Proverbs covers a wide range of topics, including youth and discipline, family life, self-control and resisting temptation, business matters, words and the tongue, knowing God, marriage, seeking the truth, wealth and poverty, immorality, and, of course, wisdom. These proverbs are short poems (usually in couplet form), containing a holy mixture of common sense and timely warnings. Although they are not meant to teach doctrine, a person who follows their advice will walk closely with God. The word "proverb" comes from a Hebrew word that means "to rule or to govern", and these sayings, reminders, and admonitions provide profound advice for governing our lives.

As you read Proverbs, understand that knowing God is the key to wisdom. Listen to thoughts and lessons from the world's wisest man, and apply these truths to your life. Don't just read these proverbs; act on them!

VITAL STATISTICS

PURPOSE:
To teach people how to attain wisdom and discipline and a prudent life, and how to do what is right and just and fair (see 1:2, 3)—in short, to apply divine wisdom to daily life and to provide moral instruction

AUTHOR:
Solomon wrote most of this book, with Agur and Lemuel contributing some of the later sections

DATE WRITTEN:
Solomon wrote and compiled most of these proverbs early in his reign

SETTING:
This is a book of wise sayings, a textbook for teaching people how to live godly lives through the repetition of wise thoughts

KEY VERSE:
"The fear of the LORD is the beginning of knowledge, but fools despise wisdom and discipline" (1:7).

SPECIAL FEATURES:
The book uses varied *literary forms:* poems, brief parables, pointed questions, and couplets. Other *literary devices* include antithesis, comparison, and personification

THE BLUEPRINT

A. WISDOM FOR YOUNG PEOPLE (1:1–9:18)	Solomon instructed the young people of his day like a father giving advice to his child. While many of these proverbs are directed towards young people, the principles supporting them are helpful to all believers, male and female, young and old. Anyone beginning his or her journey to discover more of wisdom will benefit greatly from these wise sayings.
B. WISDOM FOR ALL PEOPLE (10:1–24:34)	Solomon wanted to impart wisdom to all people, regardless of their age, sex, or position in society. These short, wise sayings give us practical wisdom for daily living. We should study them diligently and integrate them into our life.
C. WISDOM FOR THE LEADERS (25:1–31:31)	In addition to the proverbs that Solomon collected, the men of Hezekiah collected many proverbs that Solomon and others wrote. While most of these are general in nature, many are directed specifically to the king and those who dealt with the king. These are particularly useful for those who are leaders or aspire to be leaders.

MEGATHEMES

THEME	EXPLANATION	IMPORTANCE
Wisdom	God wants his people to be wise. Two kinds of people portray two contrasting paths of life. The fool is the wicked, stubborn person who hates or ignores God. The wise person seeks to know and love God.	When we choose God's way, he grants us wisdom. His word, the Bible, leads us to live rightly, have right relationships, and make right decisions.
Relationships	Proverbs gives us advice for developing our personal relationships with friends, family members, and co-workers. In every relationship, we must show love, dedication, and high moral standards.	To relate to people, we need consistency, tact, and discipline to use the wisdom God gives us. If we don't treat others according to the wisdom God gives, our relationships will suffer.
Speech	What we say shows our real attitude towards others. How we talk reveals what we're really like. Our speech is a test of how wise we have become.	To be wise in our speech we need to use self-control. Our words should be honest and well-chosen.
Work	God controls the final outcome of all we do. We are accountable to carry out our work with diligence and discipline, not laziness.	Because God evaluates how we live, we should work purposefully. We must never be lax or self-satisfied in using our skills.
Success	Although people work very hard for money and fame, God views success as having a good reputation, moral character, and the spiritual devotion to obey him.	A successful relationship with God counts for eternity. Everything else is perishable. All our resources, time, and talents come from God. We should strive to use them wisely.

A. WISDOM FOR YOUNG PEOPLE (1:1–9:18)

Proverbs begins with a clear statement of its purpose—to impart wisdom for godly living. The first few chapters are Solomon's fatherly advice to young people. Although most of the material in this section is directed towards young people, all who seek wisdom will greatly benefit from these wise words. This is where one can discover the source of wisdom, the value of wisdom, and the benefits of wisdom.

Prologue: Purpose and Theme

1 The proverbs of Solomon[a] son of David, king of Israel:[b]

2for attaining wisdom and discipline;
for understanding words of insight;
3for acquiring a disciplined and prudent life,

1:1
[a] 1Ki 4:29-34
[b] Pr 10:1; 25:1; Ecc 1:1

doing what is right and just and fair;
4for giving prudence to the simple,[c]
knowledge and discretion[d] to the young —
5let the wise listen and add to their learning,[e]
and let the discerning get guidance —
6for understanding proverbs and parables,[f]
the sayings and riddles[g] of the wise.

7The fear of the LORD[h] is the beginning of knowledge,
but fools[a] despise wisdom and discipline.

Exhortations to Embrace Wisdom

Warning Against Enticement

8Listen, my son,[i] to your father's instruction
and do not forsake your mother's teaching.[j]
9They will be a garland to grace your head
and a chain to adorn your neck.[k]

10My son, if sinners entice[l] you,
do not give in[m] to them.[n]
11If they say, "Come along with us;
let's lie in wait[o] for someone's blood,
let's waylay some harmless soul;

1:4 [c]Pr 8:5 [d]Pr 2:10-11; 8:12
1:5 [e]Pr 9:9
1:6 [f]Ps 49:4; 78:2 [g]Nu 12:8
1:7 [h]Job 28:28; Ps 111:10; Pr 9:10; 15:33; Ecc 12:13
1:8 [i]Pr 4:1 [j]Pr 6:20
1:9 [k]Pr 4:1-9
1:10 [l]Ge 39:7 [m]Dt 13:8 [n]Pr 16:29; Eph 5:11
1:11 [o]Ps 10:8

a *7* The Hebrew words rendered *fool* in Proverbs, and often elsewhere in the Old Testament, denote one who is morally deficient.

UNDERSTANDING PROVERBS Usually, proverbs are written in the form of couplets. These are constructed in three ways:

Type	*Description*	*Key Word(s)*	*Examples*
Contrasting	Meaning and application come from the differences or contrast between the two statements of the proverb	"but"	10:6; 15:25, 27
Comparing	Meaning and application come from the similarities or comparison between the two statements of the proverb	"as/so" "better/than"	10:26; 15:16, 17; 25:25
Complementing	Meaning and application come from the way the second statement complements the first	"and"	10:18; 15:23

1:1 What the book of Psalms is to prayer and devotional life, the book of Proverbs is to everyday life. Proverbs gives practical suggestions for effective living. This book is not just a collection of homespun sayings; it contains deep spiritual insights drawn from experience. A *proverb* is a short, wise, easy-to-learn saying that calls a person to action. It doesn't argue about basic spiritual and moral beliefs; it assumes we already hold them. The book of Proverbs focuses on God – his character, works, and blessings – and it tells how we can live in close relationship to him.

1:1 Solomon, the third king of Israel, son of the great King David, reigned during Israel's golden age. When God said he would give him whatever he wanted, he asked for a discerning heart (1 Kings 3:5–14). God was pleased with this request, and he not only made Solomon wise but also gave him great riches and power and an era of peace. Solomon built the glorious temple in Jerusalem (1 Kings 6) and wrote most of the book of Proverbs. His Profile is found in 1 Kings 4.

1:6 Riddles were thought-provoking questions.

1:7 One of the most annoying types of people is a know-it-all, a person who has a dogmatic opinion about everything, is closed to anything new, resents discipline, and refuses to learn. Solomon calls this kind of person a fool. Don't be a know-it-all. Instead, be open to the advice of others, especially those who know you well and can give valuable insight and counsel. Learn how to learn from others. Remember, only God knows it all.

1:7–9 In this age of information, knowledge is plentiful, but wisdom is scarce. Wisdom means far more than simply knowing a lot. It is a basic attitude that affects every aspect of life. The foundation of knowledge is to fear the Lord – to honour and respect God, to live in awe of his power, and to obey his word. Faith in God should be the controlling principle for your understanding of the world, your attitudes, and your actions. Trust in God – he will make you truly wise.

1:8 Our actions speak louder than our words. This is especially true in the home. Children learn values, morals, and priorities by observing how their parents act and react every day. If parents exhibit a deep reverence for and dependence on God, the children will catch these attitudes. Let them see your reverence for God. Teach them right living by giving worship an important place in your family life and by reading the Bible together.

1:10–19 Sin is enticing because it offers a quick route to prosperity and makes us feel like one of the crowd. But when we go along with others and refuse to listen to the truth, our own appetites become our masters, and we'll do anything to satisfy them. Sin, even when attractive, is deadly. We must learn to make choices, not on the basis of flashy appeal or short-term pleasure, but in view of the long-term effects. Sometimes this means steering clear of people who want to entice us into activities that we know are wrong. We can't be friendly with sin and expect our lives to remain unaffected.

12let's swallow them alive, like the grave,[b]
and whole, like those who go down to the pit;[p]
13we will get all sorts of valuable things
and fill our houses with plunder;
14throw in your lot with us,
and we will share a common purse" —
15my son, do not go along with them,
do not set foot[q] on their paths;[r]
16for their feet rush into sin,
they are swift to shed blood.[s]
17How useless to spread a net
in full view of all the birds!
18These men lie in wait for their own blood;
they waylay only themselves!
19Such is the end of all who go after ill-gotten gain;
it takes away the lives of those who get it.[t]

Warning Against Rejecting Wisdom

20Wisdom calls aloud[u] in the street,
she raises her voice in the public squares;
21at the head of the noisy streets[c] she cries out,
in the gateways of the city she makes her speech:

22"How long will you simple ones[d][v] love your simple ways?
How long will mockers delight in mockery
and fools hate knowledge?
23If you had responded to my rebuke,
I would have poured out my heart to you
and made my thoughts known to you.
24But since you rejected me when I called[w]
and no-one gave heed when I stretched out my hand,
25since you ignored all my advice
and would not accept my rebuke,
26I in turn will laugh[x] at your disaster;
I will mock when calamity overtakes you[y]—
27when calamity overtakes you like a storm,
when disaster sweeps over you like a whirlwind,
when distress and trouble overwhelm you.

28"Then they will call to me but I will not answer;[z]
they will look for me but will not find me.[a]
29Since they hated knowledge
and did not choose to fear the LORD,[b]
30since they would not accept my advice

1:12 [p]Ps 28:1
1:15 [q]Ps 119:101 [r]Ps 1:1; Pr 4:14
1:16 [s]Pr 6:18; Isa 59:7
1:19 [t]Pr 15:27
1:20 [u]Pr 8:1; 9:1-3, 13-15
1:22 [v]Pr 8:5; 9:4, 16
1:24 [w]Isa 65:12; 66:4; Jer 7:13; Zec 7:11
1:26 [x]Ps 2:4 [y]Pr 6:15; 10:24
1:28 [z]1Sa 8:18; Isa 1:15; Jer 11:11; Mic 3:4 [a]Job 27:9; Pr 8:17; Eze 8:18; Zec 7:13
1:29 [b]Job 21:14

b *12* Hebrew *Sheol* **c** *21* Hebrew; Septuagint */ on the tops of the walls* **d** *22* The Hebrew word rendered *simple* in Proverbs generally denotes one without moral direction and inclined to evil.

1:19 Going after "ill-gotten gain" is one of Satan's surest traps. It begins when he plants the suggestion that we can't live without some possession or more money. Then that desire fans its own fire until it becomes an all-consuming obsession. Ask God for wisdom to recognise any greedy desire before it destroys you. God will help you overcome it.

1:20 The picture of wisdom calling aloud in the streets is a personification—a literary device to make wisdom come alive for us. Wisdom is not a separate being; it is the mind of God revealed. By reading about Jesus Christ's earthly ministry, we can see wisdom in action. In order to understand how to become wise, we can listen to wisdom calling and instructing us in the book of Proverbs (see the chart in chapter 14). For New Testament calls to wisdom, see 2 Timothy 1:7 and James 1:5. Make sure you don't reject God's offer of wisdom to you.

1:22 In the book of Proverbs, a "simple one" or a fool is not someone with a *mental* deficiency but someone with a *character* deficiency (such as rebellion, laziness, or anger). The fool is not stupid, but he or she is unable to tell right from wrong or good from bad.

1:23–28 God is more than willing to pour out his heart and make known his thoughts to us. To receive his advice, we must be willing to listen, refusing to let pride stand in our way. Pride is thinking more highly of our own wisdom and desires than of God's. If we think we know better than God or feel we have no need of God's direction, we have fallen into foolish and disastrous pride.

1:30 [c]ver 25; Ps 81:11
1:31 [d]Job 4:8; Pr 14:14; Isa 3:11; Jer 6:19
1:32 [e]Jer 2:19
1:33 [f]Ps 25:12; Pr 3:23 [g]Ps 112:8
2:2 [a]Pr 22:17
2:4 [b]Job 3:21; Pr 3:14; Mt 13:44
2:5 [c]Pr 1:7

and spurned my rebuke,[c]
31 they will eat the fruit of their ways
and be filled with the fruit of their schemes.[d]
32 For the waywardness of the simple will kill them,
and the complacency of fools will destroy them;[e]
33 but whoever listens to me will live in safety[f]
and be at ease, without fear of harm."[g]

Moral Benefits of Wisdom

2 My son, if you accept my words
and store up my commands within you,
2 turning your ear to wisdom
and applying your heart to understanding,[a]
3 and if you call out for insight
and cry aloud for understanding,
4 and if you look for it as for silver
and search for it as for hidden treasure,[b]
5 then you will understand the fear of the LORD
and find the knowledge of God.[c]

PEOPLE CALLED "WISE" IN THE BIBLE

The special description "wise" is used for 12 significant people in the Bible. They can be helpful models in our own pursuit of wisdom.

The Person	*Their Role*	*Reference*	*How they practised wisdom*
Joseph	Wise leader	Acts 7:10	Prepared for a major famine. Helped rule Egypt.
Moses	Wise leader	Acts 7:20–22	Learned all the Egyptian wisdom, then graduated to God's lessons in wisdom to lead Israel out of Egypt.
Bezalel	Wise artist	Exodus 31:1–5	Designed and supervised the construction of the tabernacle and its utensils in the desert.
Joshua	Wise leader	Deuteronomy 34:9	Learned by observing Moses, obeyed God, led the people into the promised land.
David	Wise leader	2 Samuel 14:20	Never let his failures keep him from the source of wisdom—reverence for God.
Abigail	Wise wife	1 Samuel 25:3	Managed her household well in spite of a surly and mean husband.
Solomon	Wise leader	1 Kings 3:5–14; 4:29–34	Knew what to do even though he often failed to put his own wisdom into action.
Daniel	Wise counsellor	Daniel 5:11, 12	Known as a man in touch with God. A solver of complex problems with God's help
Magi	Wise learners	Matthew 2:1–12	Not only received special knowledge of God's visit to earth, but checked it personally.
Stephen	Wise leader	Acts 6:8–10	Organised the distribution of food to the Grecian widows. Preached the gospel to the Jews.
Paul	Wise messenger	2 Peter 3:15, 16	Spent his life communicating God's love to all who would listen.
Christ	Wise youth Wise Saviour Wisdom of God	Luke 2:40, 52; 1 Corinthians 1:20–25	Not only lived a perfect life, but died on the cross to save us and make God's wise plan of eternal life available to us.

1:31, 32 Many proverbs point out that the "fruit of their ways" will be the consequences people will experience in this life. Faced with either choosing God's wisdom or persisting in rebellious independence, many decide to go it alone. The problems such people create for themselves will destroy them. Don't ignore God's advice even if it is painful for the present. It will keep you from greater pain in the future.

2:3–6 Wisdom comes in two ways: it is a God-given gift and also the result of an energetic search. Wisdom's starting point is God and his revealed word, the source of "knowledge and understanding" (2:6). In that sense, wisdom is his gift to us. But he gives it only to those who earnestly seek it. But because God's wisdom is hidden from the rebellious and foolish, it takes effort to find it and use it. The pathway to wisdom is strenuous. When we are on the path, we discover that true wisdom is God's and that he will guide us and reward our sincere and persistent search.

6For the LORD gives wisdom,[d]
and from his mouth come knowledge and understanding.
7He holds victory in store for the upright,
he is a shield[e] to those whose walk is blameless,[f]
8for he guards the course of the just
and protects the way of his faithful ones.[g]

9Then you will understand what is right and just
and fair—every good path.
10For wisdom will enter your heart,[h]
and knowledge will be pleasant to your soul.
11Discretion will protect you,
and understanding will guard you.[i]

12Wisdom will save you from the ways of wicked men,
from men whose words are perverse,
13who leave the straight paths
to walk in dark ways,[j]
14who delight in doing wrong
and rejoice in the perverseness of evil,[k]
15whose paths are crooked[l]
and who are devious in their ways.[m]

16It will save you also from the adulteress,[n]
from the wayward wife with her seductive words,
17who has left the partner of her youth
and ignored the covenant she made before God.[a][o]
18For her house leads down to death
and her paths to the spirits of the dead.[p]
19None who go to her return
or attain the paths of life.[q]

20Thus you will walk in the ways of good men
and keep to the paths of the righteous.
21For the upright will live in the land,[r]
and the blameless will remain in it;
22but the wicked will be cut off from the land,[s]
and the unfaithful will be torn from it.[t]

Further Benefits of Wisdom

3 My son, do not forget my teaching,[a]
but keep my commands in your heart,
2for they will prolong your life many years[b]

a 17 Or *covenant of her God*

2:6 [d] 1Ki 3:9, 12; Jas 1:5
2:7 [e] Pr 30:5-6 [f] Ps 84:11
2:8 [g] 1Sa 2:9; Ps 66:9
2:10 [h] Pr 14:33
2:11 [i] Pr 4:6; 6:22
2:13 [j] Pr 4:19; Jn 3:19
2:14 [k] Pr 10:23; Jer 11:15
2:15 [l] Ps 125:5 [m] Pr 21:8
2:16 [n] Pr 5:1-6; 6:20-29; 7:5-27
2:17 [o] Mal 2:14
2:18 [p] Pr 7:27
2:19 [q] Ecc 7:26
2:21 [r] Ps 37:29
2:22 [s] Job 18:17; Ps 37:38 [t] Dt 28:63; Pr 10:30
3:1 [a] Pr 4:5
3:2 [b] Pr 4:10

2:6, 7 God gives us wisdom and victory but not for drifting through life or acting irresponsibly with his gifts and resources. If we are faithful and keep our purpose in life clearly in mind, he will keep us from pride and greed.

2:9, 10 We gain wisdom through a constant process of growing. First, we must trust and honour God. Second, we must realise that the Bible reveals God's wisdom to us. Third, we must make a life-long series of right choices and avoid moral pitfalls. Fourth, when we make sinful or mistaken choices, we must learn from our errors and recover. People don't develop all aspects of wisdom at once. For example, some people have more insight than discretion; others have more knowledge than common sense. But we can pray for all aspects of wisdom and take the steps to develop them in our lives.

2:11 Discretion is the ability to tell right from wrong. It enables the believer to detect evil motives in men (2:12) and women (2:16). With practice it helps us evaluate courses of action and consequences. For some it is a gift; for most it is developed by using God's truth to make wise choices day by day. Hebrews 5:14 emphasises that we must train ourselves in order to have discretion.

2:16, 17 An *adulteress* is a seductive woman or a prostitute. Two of the most difficult sins to resist are pride and sexual immorality. Both are seductive. Pride says, "I deserve it"; sexual desire says, "I need it." In combination, their appeal is deadly. In fact, says Solomon, only by relying on God's strength can we overcome them. Pride appeals to the empty head; sexual enticement to the empty heart. By looking to God, we can fill our heads with his wisdom and our hearts with his love. Don't be fooled—remember what God says about who you are and what you were meant to be. Ask him for strength to resist these temptations.

3:3 [c]Ex 13:9; Pr 6:21; 7:3; 2Co 3:3
3:4 [d]1Sa 2:26; Lk 2:52
3:5 [e]Ps 37:3, 5
3:6 [f]1Ch 28:9 [g]Pr 16:3; Isa 45:13
3:7 [h]Ro 12:16 [i]Job 1:1; Pr 16:6
3:8 [j]Pr 4:22 [k]Job 21:24
3:9 [l]Ex 22:29; 23:19; Dt 26:1-15
3:10 [m]Dt 28:8

and bring you prosperity.

3 Let love and faithfulness never leave you;
bind them around your neck,
write them on the tablet of your heart.[c]
4 Then you will win favour and a good name
in the sight of God and man.[d]

5 Trust in the LORD[e] with all your heart
and lean not on your own understanding;
6 in all your ways acknowledge him,
and he will make your paths[f] straight.[a][g]

7 Do not be wise in your own eyes;[h]
fear the LORD and shun evil.[i]
8 This will bring health to your body[j]
and nourishment to your bones.[k]

9 Honour the LORD with your wealth,
with the firstfruits[l] of all your crops;
10 then your barns will be filled[m] to overflowing,

a *6* Or *will direct your paths.*

WISDOM: APPLIED TRUTH
The book of Proverbs tells us about people who have wisdom and enjoy its benefits.

Reference	*The Person Who Has Wisdom*	*Benefits of Wisdom*
Proverbs 3; 4 A father's instructions	Is loving Is faithful Trusts in the Lord Puts God first Turns away from evil Knows right from wrong Listens and learns Does what is right	Long, prosperous life Favour with God and people Reputation for good judgment Success Health, vitality Riches, honour, pleasure, peace Protection
Proverbs 8; 9 Wisdom speaks	Possesses knowledge and discretion Hates pride, arrogance, and evil behaviour Respects and fears God Gives good advice and has common sense Loves correction and is teachable Knows God	Riches, honour Justice Righteousness Life God's favour Constant learning Understanding

3:3 Love and faithfulness are important character qualities. Both involve actions as well as attitudes. A loving person not only feels love; he or she also acts loyally and responsibly. A faithful person not only believes the truth; he or she also works for justice for others. Thoughts and words are not enough – our lives reveal whether we are truly loving and faithful. Do your actions measure up to your attitudes?

3:5, 6 *Leaning* has the sense of putting your whole weight on something, resting on and trusting in that person or thing. When we have an important decision to make, we sometimes feel that we can't trust anyone – not even God. But God knows what is best for us. He is a better judge of what we want than even we are! We must trust him completely in every choice we make. We should not omit careful thinking or belittle our God-given ability to reason; but we should not trust our own ideas to the exclusion of all others. We must not be wise in our own eyes. We should always be willing to listen to and be corrected by God's word and wise counsellors. Bring your decisions to God in prayer; use the Bible as your guide; and then follow God's leading. He will make your paths straight by both guiding and protecting you.

3:6 To receive God's guidance, said Solomon, we must acknowledge God in all our ways. This means turning every area of life over to him. About a thousand years later, Jesus emphasised this same truth (Matthew 6:33). Look at your values and priorities. What is important to you? In what areas have you not acknowledged him? What is his advice? In many areas of your life you may already acknowledge God, but it is in the areas where you attempt to restrict or ignore his influence that will cause you grief. Make him a vital part of everything you do; then he will guide you because you will be working to accomplish his purposes.

3:9, 10 The *firstfruits* refers to the practice of giving to God's use the first and best portion of the harvest (Deuteronomy 26:9–11). Many people give God their leftovers. If they can afford to donate anything, they do so. These people may be sincere and contribute willingly, but their attitude is nonetheless backward. It is better to give God the first part of our income. This demonstrates that God, not possessions, has first place in our lives and that our resources belong to him (we are only managers of God's resources). Giving to God first helps us conquer greed, helps us properly manage God's resources, and opens us up to receive God's special blessings.

and your vats will brim over with new wine.[n]

11 My son, do not despise the LORD's discipline[o]
and do not resent his rebuke,
12 because the LORD disciplines those he loves,[p]
as a father[b] the son he delights in.[q]

13 Blessed is the man who finds wisdom,
the man who gains understanding,
14 for she is more profitable than silver
and yields better returns than gold.[r]
15 She is more precious than rubies;[s]
nothing you desire can compare with her.[t]
16 Long life is in her right hand;
in her left hand are riches and honour.[u]
17 Her ways are pleasant ways,
and all her paths are peace.[v]
18 She is a tree of life[w] to those who embrace her;
those who lay hold of her will be blessed.

19 By wisdom the LORD laid the earth's foundations,[x]
by understanding he set the heavens[y] in place;
20 by his knowledge the deeps were divided,
and the clouds let drop the dew.

21 My son, preserve sound judgment and discernment,
do not let them out of your sight;[z]
22 they will be life for you,
an ornament to grace your neck.[a]
23 Then you will go on your way in safety,
and your foot will not stumble;[b]
24 when you lie down,[c] you will not be afraid;
when you lie down, your sleep[d] will be sweet.
25 Have no fear of sudden disaster
or of the ruin that overtakes the wicked,
26 for the LORD will be your confidence
and will keep your foot[e] from being snared.

27 Do not withhold good from those who deserve it,
when it is in your power to act.

b *12* Hebrew; Septuagint / *and he punishes*

3:10 [n]Joel 2:24
3:11 [o]Job 5:17
3:12 [p]Pr 13:24; Rev 3:19 [q]Dt 8:5; Heb 12:5-6*
3:14 [r]Job 28:15; Pr 8:19; 16:16
3:15 [s]Job 28:18 [t]Pr 8:11
3:16 [u]Pr 8:18
3:17 [v]Pr 16:7; Mt 11:28-30
3:18 [w]Ge 2:9; Pr 11:30; Rev 2:7
3:19 [x]Ps 104:24 [y]Pr 8:27-29
3:21 [z]Pr 4:20-22
3:22 [a]Pr 1:8-9
3:23 [b]Ps 37:24; Pr 4:12
3:24 [c]Lev 26:6; Ps 3:5 [d]Job 11:18
3:26 [e]1Sa 2:9

3:11, 12 Since righteous people are not always prosperous, we are to regard adversity as discipline. *Discipline* means "to teach and to train". Discipline sounds negative to many people because some disciplinarians are not loving. God, however, is the source of all love. He doesn't punish us because he enjoys inflicting pain but because he is deeply concerned about our development. He knows that in order to become morally strong and good, we must learn the difference between right and wrong. His loving discipline enables us to do that.

3:11, 12 It's difficult to know when God has been disciplining us until we look back on the situation later. Not every calamity comes directly from God, of course. But if we rebel against God and refuse to repent when God has identified some sin in our lives, he may use guilt, crises, or bad experiences to bring us back to him. Sometimes, however, difficult times come even when there is no flagrant sin in our lives. Then, our response should be patience, integrity, and confidence that God will show us what to do.

3:16, 17 Proverbs contains many strong statements about the benefits of wisdom, including long life, wealth, honour, and peace. If you aren't experiencing them, does this mean you are short on wisdom? Not necessarily. Instead of guarantees, these statements are general principles. In a perfect world, wise behaviour would always lead to these benefits. Even in our troubled world, living wisely usually results in obvious blessings – but not always. Sometimes sin intervenes, and some blessings must be delayed until Jesus returns to establish his eternal kingdom. That is why we must "live by faith, not by sight" (2 Corinthians 5:7). We can be sure that wisdom ultimately leads to blessing.

3:21 What is the difference between sound judgment and discernment? Discernment (or discretion) is the ability God gives to many people to think and make correct choices. Sound judgment, however, he gives only to those who follow him. Sound judgment includes discernment, but goes beyond it. It also includes the knowledge that comes from instruction, training, and discipline, and the insight that results from knowing and applying God's truths.

3:27, 28 Delaying to do good is inconsiderate and unfair, whether it is repaying a loan, returning a tool, or fulfilling a promise. Withholding destroys trust and creates a great inconvenience. Be as eager to do good as you are to have good done to you.

3:28 [f]Lev 19:13; Dt 24:15

3:31 [g]Ps 37:1; Pr 24:1-2

3:32 [h]Pr 11:20 [i]Job 29:4; Ps 25:14

3:33 [j]Dt 11:28; Mal 2:2 [k]Zec 5:4 [l]Ps 1:3

3:34 [m]Jas 4:6*; 1Pe 5:5*

4:1 [a]Pr 1:8

4:4 [b]Pr 7:2

4:5 [c]Pr 16:16

4:6 [d]2Th 2:10

28 Do not say to your neighbour,
"Come back later; I'll give it tomorrow" —
when you now have it with you.[f]

29 Do not plot harm against your neighbour,
who lives trustfully near you.
30 Do not accuse a man for no reason —
when he has done you no harm.

31 Do not envy[g] a violent man
or choose any of his ways,
32 for the LORD detests a perverse man[h]
but takes the upright into his confidence.[i]

33 The LORD's curse[j] is on the house of the wicked,[k]
but he blesses the home of the righteous.[l]
34 He mocks proud mockers
but gives grace to the humble.[m]
35 The wise inherit honour,
but fools he holds up to shame.

Wisdom Is Supreme

4 Listen, my sons,[a] to a father's instruction;
pay attention and gain understanding.
2 I give you sound learning,
so do not forsake my teaching.
3 When I was a boy in my father's house,
still tender, and an only child of my mother,
4 he taught me and said,
"Lay hold of my words with all your heart;
keep my commands and you will live.[b]
5 Get wisdom,[c] get understanding;
do not forget my words or swerve from them.
6 Do not forsake wisdom, and she will protect you;[d]
love her, and she will watch over you.

STRATEGY FOR EFFECTIVE LIVING	*Begins with*	God's Wisdom	Respecting and appreciating who God is. Reverence and awe in recognising the almighty God.
	Requires	Moral Application	Trusting in God and his word. Allowing his word to speak to us personally. Willing to obey.
	Requires	Practical Application	Acting on God's direction in daily devotions.
	Results in	Effective Living	Experiencing what God does with our obedience.

4:3, 4 One of the greatest responsibilities of parents is to encourage their children to become wise. Here Solomon tells how his father, David, encouraged him to seek wisdom when he was young ("tender") (see 1 Kings 2:1–9 and 1 Chronicles 28, 29 for David's charge to his son). This encouragement may have prompted Solomon to ask God for a discerning heart above everything else (1 Kings 3:9). Wisdom can be passed on from parents to children, from generation to generation. Ultimately, of course, all wisdom comes from God; parents can only urge their children to turn to him. If your parents never taught you in this way, God's word can function as a loving and compassionate mother or father to you. You can learn from the Scriptures and then create a legacy of wisdom as you teach your own children.

4:5–7 If you want wisdom, you must decide to go after it. It takes resolve — a determination not to abandon the search once you begin no matter how difficult the road may become. This is not a once-in-a-lifetime step, but a daily process of choosing between two paths — the wicked (4:14–17, 19) and the righteous (4:18). Nothing else is more important or more valuable.

7 Wisdom is supreme; therefore get wisdom.
Though it cost all[e] you have,[a] get understanding.[f]
8 Esteem her, and she will exalt you;
embrace her, and she will honour you.[g]
9 She will set a garland of grace on your head
and present you with a crown of splendour.[h]"

10 Listen, my son, accept what I say,
and the years of your life will be many.[i]
11 I guide[j] you in the way of wisdom
and lead you along straight paths.
12 When you walk, your steps will not be hampered;
when you run, you will not stumble.[k]
13 Hold on to instruction, do not let it go;
guard it well, for it is your life.[l]
14 Do not set foot on the path of the wicked
or walk in the way of evil men.[m]
15 Avoid it, do not travel on it;
turn from it and go on your way.
16 For they cannot sleep till they do evil;[n]
they are robbed of slumber till they make someone fall.
17 They eat the bread of wickedness
and drink the wine of violence.

18 The path of the righteous[o] is like the first gleam of dawn,
shining ever brighter till the full light of day.[p]
19 But the way of the wicked is like deep darkness;[q]
they do not know what makes them stumble.

20 My son, pay attention to what I say;
listen closely to my words.[r]
21 Do not let them out of your sight,[s]
keep them within your heart;
22 for they are life to those who find them
and health to a man's whole body.[t]
23 Above all else, guard your heart,
for it is the wellspring of life.[u]
24 Put away perversity from your mouth;
keep corrupt talk far from your lips.
25 Let your eyes look straight ahead,
fix your gaze directly before you.
26 Make level[b] paths for your feet[v]
and take only ways that are firm.
27 Do not swerve to the right or the left;[w]
keep your foot from evil.

[a] 7 Or *Whatever else you get* [b] 26 Or *Consider the*

4:7 [e]Mt 13:44-46 [f]Pr 23:23
4:8 [g]1Sa 2:30; Pr 3:18
4:9 [h]Pr 1:8-9
4:10 [i]Pr 3:2
4:11 [j]1Sa 12:23
4:12 [k]Job 18:7; Pr 3:23
4:13 [l]Pr 3:22
4:14 [m]Ps 1:1; Pr 1:15
4:16 [n]Ps 36:4; Mic 2:1
4:18 [o]Isa 26:7 [p]2Sa 23:4; Da 12:3; Mt 5:14; Php 2:15
4:19 [q]Job 18:5; Pr 2:13; Isa 59:9-10; Jn 12:35
4:20 [r]Pr 5:1
4:21 [s]Pr 3:21; 7:1-2
4:22 [t]Pr 3:8; 12:18
4:23 [u]Mt 12:34; Lk 6:45
4:26 [v]Heb 12:13*
4:27 [w]Dt 5:32; 28:14

4:7 David taught Solomon as a young boy that seeking God's wisdom was the most important choice he could make. Solomon learned the lesson well. When God appeared to the new king to fulfil any request, Solomon chose wisdom above all else. We should also make God's wisdom our first choice. We don't have to wait for God to appear to us. We can boldly ask him for wisdom today through prayer. James 1:5 assures us that God will grant our request.

4:13–17 Even friends can make you fall. It is difficult for people to accept the fact that friends and acquaintances might be luring them to do wrong. Young people want to be accepted, so they would never want to confront or criticise a friend for wrong plans or actions. Many other people can't even see how their friends' actions could lead to trouble. While we should be accepting of others, we need a healthy scepticism about human behaviour. When you feel yourself being heavily influenced, proceed with caution. Don't let your friends cause you to fall into sin.

4:23–27 Our heart – our feelings of love and desire – dictates to a great extent how we live because we always find time to do what we enjoy. Solomon tells us to guard our heart above all else, making sure we concentrate on those desires that will keep us on the right path. Make sure your affections push you in the right direction. Put boundaries on your desires: don't go after everything you see. Look straight ahead, keep your eyes fixed on your goal, and don't get sidetracked on detours that lead to sin.

5:1 [a]Pr 4:20; 22:17
5:3 [b]Ps 55:21; Pr 2:16; 7:5
5:4 [c]Ecc 7:26
5:5 [d]Pr 7:26-27
5:6 [e]Pr 30:20
5:7 [f]Pr 7:24
5:8 [g]Pr 7:1-27
5:12 [h]Pr 1:29; 12:1

Warning Against Adultery

5 My son, pay attention to my wisdom,
listen well to my words[a] of insight,
2that you may maintain discretion
and your lips may preserve knowledge.
3For the lips of an adulteress drip honey,
and her speech is smoother than oil;[b]
4but in the end she is bitter as gall,[c]
sharp as a double-edged sword.
5Her feet go down to death;
her steps lead straight to the grave.[a][d]
6She gives no thought to the way of life;
her paths are crooked, but she knows it not.[e]

7Now then, my sons, listen[f] to me;
do not turn aside from what I say.
8Keep to a path far from her,[g]
do not go near the door of her house,
9lest you give your best strength to others
and your years to one who is cruel,
10lest strangers feast on your wealth
and your toil enrich another man's house.
11At the end of your life you will groan,
when your flesh and body are spent.
12You will say, "How I hated discipline!
How my heart spurned correction![h]
13I would not obey my teachers
or listen to my instructors.
14I have come to the brink of utter ruin
in the midst of the whole assembly."

15Drink water from your own cistern,
running water from your own well.
16Should your springs overflow in the streets,
your streams of water in the public squares?
17Let them be yours alone,
never to be shared with strangers.

[a] 5 Hebrew *Sheol*

5:3 This "adulteress" is a prostitute. Proverbs includes many warnings against illicit sex for several reasons. First, a prostitute's charm is used as an example of any temptation to do wrong or to leave the pursuit of wisdom. Second, sexual immorality of any kind was and still is extremely dangerous. It destroys family life. It erodes a person's ability to love. It degrades human beings and turns them into objects. It can lead to disease. It can result in unwanted children. Third, sexual immorality is against God's law.

5:3–8 Any person should be on guard against those who use flattery and smooth speech (lips that drip honey) that would lead him or her into sin. The best advice is to take a detour and even avoid conversation with such people.

5:11–13 At the end of your life, it will be too late to ask for advice. When desire is fully activated, people don't want advice – they want satisfaction. The best time to learn the dangers and foolishness of going after forbidden sex (or anything else that is harmful) is long before the temptation comes. Resistance is easier if the decision has already been made. Don't wait to see what happens. Prepare for temptation by deciding *now* how you will act when you face it.

5:15 "Drink water from your own cistern" is a picture of faithfulness in marriage. It means to enjoy the spouse God has given you. In desert lands, water is precious, and a well is a family's most important possession. In Old Testament times, it was considered a crime to steal water from someone else's well, just as it was a crime to have intercourse with another man's wife. In both cases, the offender is endangering the health and security of family.

5:15–21 In contrast to much of what we read, see, and hear today, this passage urges couples to look to each other for lifelong satisfaction and companionship. Many temptations entice husbands and wives to desert each other for excitement and pleasures to be found elsewhere when marriage becomes dull. But God designed marriage and sanctified it, and only within this covenant relationship can we find real love and fulfilment. Don't let God's best for you be wasted on the illusion of greener pastures somewhere else. Instead, rejoice with your spouse as you give yourselves to God and to each other.

[18]May your fountain[i] be blessed,
and may you rejoice in the wife of your youth.[j]
[19]A loving doe, a graceful deer[k]—
may her breasts satisfy you always,
may you ever be captivated by her love.
[20]Why be captivated, my son, by an adulteress?
Why embrace the bosom of another man's wife?

[21]For a man's ways are in full view[l] of the LORD,
and he examines all his paths.[m]
[22]The evil deeds of a wicked man ensnare him;[n]
the cords of his sin hold him fast.[o]
[23]He will die for lack of discipline,[p]
led astray by his own great folly.

Warnings Against Folly

6 My son, if you have put up security for your neighbour,[a]
if you have struck hands in pledge[b] for another,
[2]if you have been trapped by what you said,
ensnared by the words of your mouth,
[3]then do this, my son, to free yourself,
since you have fallen into your neighbour's hands:
Go and humble yourself;
press your plea with your neighbour!
[4]Allow no sleep to your eyes,
no slumber to your eyelids.[c]
[5]Free yourself, like a gazelle from the hand of the hunter,
like a bird from the snare of the fowler.[d]

[6]Go to the ant, you sluggard;[e]
consider its ways and be wise!
[7]It has no commander,
no overseer or ruler,
[8]yet it stores its provisions in summer
and gathers its food at harvest.[f]

[9]How long will you lie there, you sluggard?[g]
When will you get up from your sleep?
[10]A little sleep, a little slumber,
a little folding of the hands to rest[h]—
[11]and poverty[i] will come on you like a bandit
and scarcity like an armed man.[a]

[12]A scoundrel and villain,

a 11 *Or like a vagrant / and scarcity like a beggar*

5:18 [i]SS 4:12-15 [j]Ecc 9:9; Mal 2:14
5:19 [k]SS 2:9; 4:5
5:21 [l]Ps 119:168; Hos 7:2 [m]Job 14:16; Job 31:4; 34:21; Pr 15:3; Jer 16:17; 32:19; Heb 4:13
5:22 [n]Ps 9:16 [o]Nu 32:23; Ps 7:15-16; Pr 1:31-32
5:23 [p]Job 4:21; 36:12
6:1 [a]Pr 17:18 [b]Pr 11:15; 22:26-27
6:4 [c]Ps 132:4
6:5 [d]Ps 91:3
6:6 [e]Pr 20:4
6:8 [f]Pr 10:4
6:9 [g]Pr 24:30-34
6:10 [h]Pr 24:33
6:11 [i]Pr 24:30-34

5:18–20 God does not intend faithfulness in marriage to be boring, lifeless, pleasureless, and dull. Sex is a gift God gives to married people for their mutual enjoyment. Real happiness comes when we decide to find pleasure in the relationship God has given or will give us and to commit ourselves to making it pleasurable for our spouse. The real danger is in doubting that God knows and cares for us. We may then resent his timing and carelessly pursue sexual pleasure without his blessing.

5:19 See Song of Songs, chapter 4, for parallels to this frank expression of the joys of sexual pleasure in marriage.

6:1–5 These verses are not a plea against generosity, but against overextending one's financial resources and acting in irresponsible ways that could lead to poverty. It is important to maintain a balance between generosity and good stewardship. God wants us to help our friends and the needy, but he does not promise to cover the costs of every unwise commitment we make. We should also act responsibly so that our family does not suffer.

6:6–11 Those last few moments of sleep are delicious – we savour them as we resist beginning another day's work. But Proverbs warns against giving in to the temptation of laziness, of sleeping instead of working. This does not mean we should never rest: God gave the Jews the Sabbath, a weekly day of rest and restoration. But we should not rest when we should be working. The ant is used as an example because it utilises its energy and resources economically. If laziness turns us from our responsibilities, poverty may soon bar us from the legitimate rest we should enjoy. (See also the chart in chapter 28.)

6:13 [j]Ps 35:19
6:14 [k]Mic 2:1 [l]ver 16-19
6:15 [m]2Ch 36:16
6:17 [n]Ps 120:2; Pr 12:22 [o]Dt 19:10; Isa 1:15; 59:7
6:18 [p]Ge 6:5
6:19 [q]Ps 27:12 [r]ver 12-15
6:20 [s]Pr 1:8
6:21 [t]Pr 3:3; 7:1-3
6:23 [u]Ps 19:8; 119:105
6:24 [v]Pr 2:16; 7:5

who goes about with a corrupt mouth,
13 who winks with his eye,[j]
signals with his feet
and motions with his fingers,
14 who plots evil[k] with deceit in his heart—
he always stirs up dissension.[l]
15 Therefore disaster will overtake him in an instant;
he will suddenly be destroyed—without remedy.[m]

16 There are six things the LORD hates,
seven that are detestable to him:
17 haughty eyes,
a lying tongue,[n]
hands that shed innocent blood,[o]
18 a heart that devises wicked schemes,
feet that are quick to rush into evil,[p]
19 a false witness[q] who pours out lies
and a man who stirs up dissension among brothers.[r]

Warning Against Adultery

20 My son, keep your father's commands
and do not forsake your mother's teaching.[s]
21 Bind them upon your heart for ever;
fasten them around your neck.[t]
22 When you walk, they will guide you;
when you sleep, they will watch over you;
when you awake, they will speak to you.
23 For these commands are a lamp,
this teaching is a light,[u]
and the corrections of discipline
are the way to life,
24 keeping you from the immoral woman,
from the smooth tongue of the wayward wife.[v]
25 Do not lust in your heart after her beauty
or let her captivate you with her eyes,

THINGS GOD HATES
The book of Proverbs notes 14 types of people and actions that God hates. Let these be guidelines of what we are *not* to be and do!

Violent people	Proverbs 3:31
Haughtiness, lying, murdering, scheming, eagerness to do evil, a false witness, stirring up dissension	Proverbs 6:16–19
Those who are untruthful	Proverbs 12:22
The sacrifice of the wicked	Proverbs 15:8
The way of the wicked	Proverbs 15:9
The thoughts of the wicked	Proverbs 15:26
Those who are proud	Proverbs 16:5
Those who judge unjustly	Proverbs 17:15

6:20–23 It is natural and good for children, as they grow towards adulthood, to become increasingly independent of their parents. Young adults, however, should take care not to turn a deaf ear to their parents—to reject their advice just when it is needed most. If you are struggling with a decision or looking for insight, check with your parents or other older adults who know you well. Their extra years of experience may have given them the wisdom you seek.

6:25 Regard lust as a warning sign of danger ahead. When you notice that you are attracted to a person of the opposite sex or preoccupied with thoughts of him or her, your desires may lead you to sin. Ask God to help you change your desires before you are drawn into sin.

6:25–35 Some people argue that it is all right to break God's law against sexual sin if nobody gets hurt. In truth, somebody always gets hurt. Spouses are devastated. Children are scarred. The partners themselves, even if they escape disease and unwanted pregnancy, lose their ability to fulfil commitments, to feel sexual desire, to trust, and to be entirely open with another person. God's laws are not arbitrary. They do not forbid good, clean fun; rather, they warn us against destroying ourselves through unwise actions or running ahead of God's timetable.

26 for the prostitute reduces you to a loaf of bread,
and the adulteress preys upon your very life.[w]
27 Can a man scoop fire into his lap
without his clothes being burned?
28 Can a man walk on hot coals
without his feet being scorched?
29 So is he who sleeps[x] with another man's wife;[y]
no-one who touches her will go unpunished.

30 Men do not despise a thief if he steals
to satisfy his hunger when he is starving.
31 Yet if he is caught, he must pay sevenfold,[z]
though it costs him all the wealth of his house.
32 But a man who commits adultery[a] lacks judgment;[b]
whoever does so destroys himself.
33 Blows and disgrace are his lot,
and his shame will never[c] be wiped away;
34 for jealousy[d] arouses a husband's fury,[e]
and he will show no mercy when he takes revenge.
35 He will not accept any compensation;
he will refuse the bribe, however great it is.[f]

Warning Against the Adulteress

7 My son,[a] keep my words
and store up my commands within you.
2 Keep my commands and you will live;[b]
guard my teachings as the apple of your eye.
3 Bind them on your fingers;
write them on the tablet of your heart.[c]
4 Say to wisdom, "You are my sister,"
and call understanding your kinsman;
5 they will keep you from the adulteress,
from the wayward wife with her seductive words.[d]

6 At the window of my house
I looked out through the lattice.
7 I saw among the simple,
I noticed among the young men,
a youth who lacked judgment.[e]
8 He was going down the street near her corner,
walking along in the direction of her house
9 at twilight,[f] as the day was fading,
as the dark of night set in.

10 Then out came a woman to meet him,
dressed like a prostitute and with crafty intent.
11 (She is loud[g] and defiant,
her feet never stay at home;
12 now in the street, now in the squares,
at every corner she lurks.)[h]
13 She took hold of him[i] and kissed him

6:26 [w]Pr 7:22-23; 29:3
6:29 [x]Ex 20:14 [y]Pr 2:16-19; 5:8
6:31 [z]Ex 22:1-14
6:32 [a]Ex 20:14 [b]Pr 7:7; 9:4, 16
6:33 [c]Pr 5:9-14
6:34 [d]Nu 5:14 [e]Ge 34:7
6:35 [f]Job 31:9-11; SS 8:7
7:1 [a]Pr 1:8; 2:1
7:2 [b]Pr 4:4
7:3 [c]Dt 6:8; Pr 3:3
7:5 [d]ver 21; Job 31:9; Pr 2:16; 6:24
7:7 [e]Pr 1:22; 6:32
7:9 [f]Job 24:15
7:11 [g]Pr 9:13; 1Ti 5:13
7:12 [h]Pr 8:1-36; 23:26-28
7:13 [i]Ge 39:12

7:6–23 Although this advice is directed towards young men, young women should heed it as well. The person who has no purpose in life is simple-minded (7:7). Without aim or direction, an empty life is unstable, vulnerable to many temptations. Even though the young man in this passage doesn't know where he is going, the adulteress knows where she wants him. Notice her strategies: she is dressed to allure men (7:10); her approach is bold (7:13); she invites him over to her place (7:16–18); she cunningly answers his every objection (7:19, 20); she persuades him with smooth talk (7:21); she traps him (7:23). To combat temptation, make sure your life is full of God's word and wisdom (7:4). Recognise the strategies of temptation, and run away from them—fast.

and with a brazen face she said:[j]

14"I have fellowship offerings[a][k] at home;
today I fulfilled my vows.
15So I came out to meet you;
I looked for you and have found you!
16I have covered my bed
with coloured linens from Egypt.
17I have perfumed my bed[l]
with myrrh,[m] aloes and cinnamon.
18Come, let's drink deep of love till morning;
let's enjoy ourselves with love![n]
19My husband is not at home;
he has gone on a long journey.
20He took his purse filled with money
and will not be home till full moon."

21With persuasive words she led him astray;
she seduced him with her smooth talk.[o]
22All at once he followed her
like an ox going to the slaughter,
like a deer[b] stepping into a noose[c][p]
23 till an arrow pierces[q] his liver,
like a bird darting into a snare,
little knowing it will cost him his life.[r]

24Now then, my sons, listen[s] to me;
pay attention to what I say.
25Do not let your heart turn to her ways
or stray into her paths.[t]
26Many are the victims she has brought down;
her slain are a mighty throng.
27Her house is a highway to the grave,[d]
leading down to the chambers of death.[u]

Wisdom's Call

8 Does not wisdom call out?[a]
Does not understanding raise her voice?
2On the heights along the way,
where the paths meet, she takes her stand;
3beside the gates leading into the city,
at the entrances, she cries aloud:[b]
4"To you, O men, I call out;
I raise my voice to all mankind.
5You who are simple,[c] gain prudence;[d]
you who are foolish, gain understanding.
6Listen, for I have worthy things to say;
I open my lips to speak what is right.
7My mouth speaks what is true,[e]

7:13 [j]Pr 1:20
7:14 [k]Lev 7:11-18
7:17 [l]Est 1:6; Isa 57:7; Eze 23:41; Am 6:4 [m]Ge 37:25
7:18 [n]Ge 39:7
7:21 [o]Pr 5:3
7:22 [p]Job 18:10
7:23 [q]Job 15:22; 16:13 [r]Pr 6:26; Ecc 7:26; 9:12
7:24 [s]Pr 1:8-9; 5:7; 8:32
7:25 [t]Pr 5:7-8
7:27 [u]Pr 2:18; 5:5; 9:18; Rev 22:15
8:1 [a]Pr 1:20; 9:3
8:3 [b]Job 29:7
8:5 [c]Pr 1:22 [d]Pr 1:4
8:7 [e]Ps 37:30; Jn 8:14

a *14* Traditionally *peace offerings* **b** *22* Syriac (see also Septuagint); Hebrew *fool* **c** *22* The meaning of the Hebrew for this line is uncertain. **d** *27* Hebrew *Sheol*

7:25–27 There are definite steps you can take to avoid sexual sins. First, guard your mind. Don't read books, look at pictures, or encourage fantasies that stimulate the wrong desires. Second, keep away from settings and friends that tempt you to sin. Third, don't think only of the moment – focus on the future. Today's thrill may lead to tomorrow's ruin.

8:1ff Wisdom's call is contrasted to the call of the adulteress in chapter 7. Wisdom is portrayed as a woman who guides us (8:1–13) and makes us succeed (8:14–21). Wisdom was present at the creation and works with the Creator (8:22–31). God approves of those who listen to wisdom's counsel (8:32–35). Those who hate wisdom love death (8:36). Wisdom should affect every aspect of our entire life, from beginning to end. Be sure to open all corners of your life to God's direction and guidance.

for my lips detest wickedness.
8 All the words of my mouth are just;
none of them is crooked or perverse.
9 To the discerning all of them are right;
they are faultless to those who have knowledge.
10 Choose my instruction instead of silver,
knowledge rather than choice gold,[f]
11 for wisdom is more precious[g] than rubies,
and nothing you desire can compare with her.[h]

12 "I, wisdom, dwell together with prudence;
I possess knowledge and discretion.[i]
13 To fear the LORD is to hate evil;[j]
I hate[k] pride and arrogance,
evil behaviour and perverse speech.
14 Counsel and sound judgment are mine;
I have understanding and power.[l]
15 By me kings reign
and rulers[m] make laws that are just;
16 by me princes govern,
and all nobles who rule on earth.[a]
17 I love those who love me,[n]
and those who seek me find me.[o]
18 With me are riches and honour,[p]
enduring wealth and prosperity.[q]
19 My fruit is better than fine gold;
what I yield surpasses choice silver.[r]
20 I walk in the way of righteousness,
along the paths of justice,
21 bestowing wealth on those who love me
and making their treasuries full.[s]

22 "The LORD brought me forth as the first of his works,[b,c]
before his deeds of old;
23 I was appointed[d] from eternity,
from the beginning, before the world began.
24 When there were no oceans, I was given birth,
when there were no springs abounding with water;[t]
25 before the mountains were settled in place,
before the hills, I was given birth,[u]
26 before he made the earth or its fields
or any of the dust of the world.[v]
27 I was there when he set the heavens in place,[w]
when he marked out the horizon on the face of the deep,
28 when he established the clouds above
and fixed securely the fountains of the deep,
29 when he gave the sea its boundary[x]
so that the waters would not overstep his command,[y]
and when he marked out the foundations of the earth.[z]
30 Then I was the craftsman at his side.[a]

a *16* Many Hebrew manuscripts and Septuagint; most Hebrew manuscripts *and nobles—all righteous rulers*
b *22* Or *way*; or *dominion* c *22* Or *The LORD possessed me at the beginning of his work*; or *The LORD brought me forth at the beginning of his work* d *23* Or *fashioned*

8:10 [f]Pr 3:14-15
8:11 [g]Job 28:17-19 [h]Pr 3:13-15
8:12 [i]Pr 1:4
8:13 [j]Pr 16:6 [k]Jer 44:4
8:14 [l]Pr 21:22; Ecc 7:19
8:15 [m]Da 2:21; Ro 13:1
8:17 [n]1Sa 2:30; Ps 91:14; Jn 14:21-24 [o]Pr 1:28; Jas 1:5
8:18 [p]Pr 3:16 [q]Dt 8:18; Mt 6:33
8:19 [r]Pr 3:13-14; 10:20
8:21 [s]Pr 24:4
8:24 [t]Ge 7:11
8:25 [u]Job 15:7
8:26 [v]Ps 90:2
8:27 [w]Pr 3:19
8:29 [x]Ge 1:9; Job 38:10; Ps 16:6 [y]Ps 104:9 [z]Job 38:5
8:30 [a]Jn 1:1-3

8:13 The more a person fears and respects God, the more he or she will hate evil. Love for God and love for sin cannot coexist. Harbouring secret sins means that you are tolerating evil within yourself. Make a clean break with sin and commit yourself completely to God.

8:22–31 God says wisdom is primary and fundamental. It is the foundation on which all life is built. Paul and John may have alluded to some of Solomon's statements about wisdom to describe Christ's presence at the creation of the world (Colossians 1:15–17; 2:2, 3; Revelation 3:14).

I was filled with delight day after day,
rejoicing always in his presence,
31 rejoicing in his whole world
and delighting in mankind.[b]

32 "Now then, my sons, listen to me;
blessed are[c] those who keep my ways.[d]
33 Listen to my instruction and be wise;
do not ignore it.
34 Blessed is the man who listens[e] to me,
watching daily at my doors,
waiting at my doorway.
35 For whoever finds me[f] finds life
and receives favour from the LORD.[g]
36 But whoever fails to find me harms himself;[h]
all who hate me love death."

Invitations of Wisdom and of Folly

9 Wisdom has built[a] her house;
she has hewn out its seven pillars.
2 She has prepared her meat and mixed her wine;
she has also set her table.[b]
3 She has sent out her maids, and she calls[c]
from the highest point of the city.[d]
4 "Let all who are simple come in here!"
she says to those who lack judgment.[e]
5 "Come, eat my food
and drink the wine I have mixed.[f]
6 Leave your simple ways and you will live;[g]
walk in the way of understanding.

7 "Whoever corrects a mocker invites insult;
whoever rebukes a wicked man incurs abuse.[h]
8 Do not rebuke a mocker[i] or he will hate you;
rebuke a wise man and he will love you.[j]
9 Instruct a wise man and he will be wiser still;
teach a righteous man and he will add to his learning.[k]

10 "The fear of the LORD[l] is the beginning of wisdom,
and knowledge of the Holy One is understanding.
11 For through me your days will be many,
and years will be added to your life.[m]
12 If you are wise, your wisdom will reward you;
if you are a mocker, you alone will suffer."

13 The woman Folly is loud;[n]

8:31 [b]Ps 16:3; 104:1-30
8:32 [c]Lk 11:28 [d]Ps 119:1-2
8:34 [e]Pr 3:13, 18
8:35 [f]Pr 3:13-18 [g]Pr 12:2
8:36 [h]Pr 15:32
9:1 [a]Eph 2:20-22; 1Pe 2:5
9:2 [b]Lk 14:16-23
9:3 [c]Pr 8:1-3 [d]ver 14
9:4 [e]Pr 6:32
9:5 [f]Isa 55:1
9:6 [g]Pr 8:35
9:7 [h]Pr 23:9
9:8 [i]Pr 15:12 [j]Ps 141:5
9:9 [k]Pr 1:5, 7
9:10 [l]Job 28:28; Pr 1:7
9:11 [m]Pr 3:16; 10:27
9:13 [n]Pr 7:11

9:1 The seven pillars are figurative; they do not represent seven principles of wisdom. In the Bible, the number seven represents completeness and perfection. This verse poetically states that wisdom lacks nothing – it is complete and perfect.

9:1ff Wisdom and Folly (foolishness) are portrayed in this chapter as rival young women, each preparing a feast and inviting people to it. But Wisdom is a responsible woman of character, while Folly is a prostitute serving stolen food. Wisdom appeals first to the mind; Folly to the senses. It is easier to excite the senses, but the pleasures of Folly are temporary. By contrast, the satisfaction that wisdom brings lasts for ever.

9:1–5 The banquet described in this chapter has some interesting parallels to the banquet Jesus described in one of his parables (Luke 14:15–24). Many may intend to go, but they never make it because they get sidetracked by other activities that seem more important at the time. Don't let anything become more important than your search for God's wisdom.

9:7–10 Are you a mocker or a wise person? You can tell by the way you respond to criticism. Instead of tossing back a quick put-down or clever retort when rebuked, listen to what is being said. Learn from your critics; this is the path to wisdom. Wisdom begins with knowing God. He gives insight into living because he created life. To know God is not just to know the facts about him, but to stand in awe of him and have a relationship with him. Do you really want to be wise? Get to know God better and better. (See James 1:5, 2 Peter 1:2–4 for more on how to become wise.)

she is undisciplined and without knowledge.[o]
14She sits at the door of her house,
on a seat at the highest point of the city,[p]
15calling out to those who pass by,
who go straight on their way.
16"Let all who are simple come in here!"
she says to those who lack judgment.
17"Stolen water is sweet;
food eaten in secret is delicious![q]"
18But little do they know that the dead are there,
that her guests are in the depths of the grave.[a][r]

9:13 [o]Pr 5:6
9:14 [p]ver 3
9:17 [q]Pr 20:17
9:18 [r]Pr 2:18; 7:26-27

B. WISDOM FOR ALL PEOPLE (10:1–24:34)

These short couplets are what we commonly recognise as proverbs. They cover a wide range of topics. The first section was written by Solomon. The next two sections were written by others, but collected by Solomon. These sayings give people practical wisdom for godly living at every stage of life.

Proverbs of Solomon

10 The proverbs of Solomon:[a]

A wise son brings joy to his father,[b]
but a foolish son grief to his mother.

2Ill-gotten treasures are of no value,[c]
but righteousness delivers from death.[d]

3The LORD does not let the righteous go hungry[e]
but he thwarts the craving of the wicked.

4Lazy hands make a man poor,[f]
but diligent hands bring wealth.[g]

5He who gathers crops in summer is a wise son,
but he who sleeps during harvest is a disgraceful son.

6Blessings crown the head of the righteous,
but violence overwhelms the mouth of the wicked.[a][h]

7The memory of the righteous[i] will be a blessing,
but the name of the wicked[j] will rot.[k]

8The wise in heart accept commands,
but a chattering fool comes to ruin.[l]

9The man of integrity[m] walks securely,[n]

10:1 [a]Pr 1:1 [b]Pr 15:20; 29:3
10:2 [c]Pr 21:6 [d]Pr 11:4, 19
10:3 [e]Mt 6:25-34
10:4 [f]Pr 19:15 [g]Pr 12:24; 13:4; 21:5
10:6 [h]ver 8, 11, 14
10:7 [i]Ps 112:6 [j]Ps 109:13 [k]Ps 9:6
10:8 [l]Mt 7:24-27
10:9 [m]Isa 33:15 [n]Ps 23:4

a 18 Hebrew *Sheol* a 6 Or *but the mouth of the wicked conceals violence*; also in verse 11

9:14–17 There is something hypnotic and intoxicating about wickedness. One sin leads us to want more; sinful behaviour seems more exciting than the Christian life. That is why many people put aside all thought of Wisdom's sumptuous banquet (9:1–5) in order to eat the stolen food of Folly. Don't be deceived – sin is dangerous. Before reaching for forbidden fruit, take a long look at what happens to those who eat it. (See the chart in chapter 22.)

10:2 Some people bring unhappiness on themselves by choosing ill-gotten treasures. For example, craving satisfaction, they may do something that destroys their chances of ever achieving happiness. God's principles for right living bring lasting happiness because they guide us into long-term right behaviour in spite of our ever-changing feelings.

10:3 Proverbs is full of verses contrasting the righteous person with the wicked. These statements are not intended to apply universally to all people in every situation. For example, some good people do go hungry. Rather, they are intended to communicate the general truth that the life of the person who seeks God is better in the long run than the life of the wicked person – a life that leads to ruin. These statements are not cast-iron promises, but general truths. In addition, a proverb like this assumes a just government that cares for the poor and needy – the kind of government Israel was intended to have (see Deuteronomy 24:17–22). A corrupt government often thwarts the plans of righteous men and women.

10:4, 5 Every day has 24 hours filled with opportunities to grow, serve, and be productive. Yet it is so easy to waste time, letting life slip from our grasp. Refuse to be a lazy person, sleeping or frittering away the hours meant for productive work. See time as God's gift and seize your opportunities to live diligently for him.

but he who takes crooked paths will be found out.[o]

10He who winks maliciously[p] causes grief,
and a chattering fool comes to ruin.

11The mouth of the righteous is a fountain of life,[q]
but violence overwhelms the mouth of the wicked.[r]

12Hatred stirs up dissension,
but love covers over all wrongs.[s]

13Wisdom is found on the lips of the discerning,[t]
but a rod is for the back of him who lacks judgment.[u]

14Wise men store up knowledge,
but the mouth of a fool invites ruin.[v]

15The wealth of the rich is their fortified city,[w]
but poverty is the ruin of the poor.[x]

16The wages of the righteous bring them life,
but the income of the wicked brings them punishment.[y]

17He who heeds discipline shows the way to life,[z]
but whoever ignores correction leads others astray.

18He who conceals his hatred has lying lips,
and whoever spreads slander is a fool.

19When words are many, sin is not absent,
but he who holds his tongue is wise.[a]

20The tongue of the righteous is choice silver,
but the heart of the wicked is of little value.

21The lips of the righteous nourish many,
but fools die for lack of judgment.[b]

22The blessing of the LORD brings wealth,[c]
and he adds no trouble to it.

23A fool finds pleasure in evil conduct,[d]
but a man of understanding delights in wisdom.

24What the wicked dreads[e] will overtake him;
what the righteous desire will be granted.[f]

25When the storm has swept by, the wicked are gone,
but the righteous stand firm[g] for ever.[h]

26As vinegar to the teeth and smoke to the eyes,
so is a sluggard to those who send him.[i]

27The fear of the LORD adds length to life,[j]

10:9 [o]Pr 28:18
10:10 [p]Ps 35:19
10:11 [q]Ps 37:30; Pr 13:12, 14, 19 [r]ver 6
10:12 [s]Pr 17:9; 1Co 13:4-7; 1Pe 4:8
10:13 [t]ver 31 [u]Pr 26:3
10:14 [v]Pr 18:6, 7
10:15 [w]Pr 18:11 [x]Pr 19:7
10:16 [y]Pr 11:18-19
10:17 [z]Pr 6:23
10:19 [a]Pr 17:28; Ecc 5:3; Jas 1:19; 3:2-12
10:21 [b]Pr 5:22-23; Hos 4:1, 6, 14
10:22 [c]Ge 24:35; Ps 37:22
10:23 [d]Pr 2:14; 15:21
10:24 [e]Isa 66:4 [f]Ps 145:17-19; Mt 5:6; 1Jn 5:14-15
10:25 [g]Ps 15:5 [h]Pr 12:3, 7; Mt 7:24-27
10:26 [i]Pr 26:6
10:27 [j]Pr 9:10-11

10:18 By hating another person you may become a liar or a fool. If you try to conceal your hatred, you end up lying. If you slander the other person and are proved wrong, you are a fool. The only way out is to admit your hateful feelings to God. Ask him to change your heart, to help you love instead of hate.

10:20 Words from a good person are valuable ("choice silver"). A lot of poor advice is worth less than a little good advice. It is easy to get opinions from people who will tell us only what they think will please us, but such advice is not helpful. Instead we should look for those who will speak the truth, even when it hurts. Think about the people to whom you go for advice. What do you expect to hear from them?

10:22 God supplies most people with the personal and financial abilities to respond to the needs of others. If we all realised how God has blessed us, and if we all used our resources to do God's will, hunger and poverty would be wiped out. Wealth is a blessing only if we use it in the way God intended.

10:24 The wicked person dreads death. Those who do not believe in God usually fear death, and with good reason. By contrast, believers desire eternal life and God's salvation – their hopes will be rewarded. This verse offers a choice: you can have either your fears or your desires come true. You make that choice by rejecting God and living your own way, or by accepting God and following him.

but the years of the wicked are cut short.[k]

28 The prospect of the righteous is joy,
but the hopes of the wicked come to nothing.[l]

29 The way of the LORD is a refuge for the righteous,
but it is the ruin of those who do evil.[m]

30 The righteous will never be uprooted,
but the wicked will not remain in the land.[n]

31 The mouth of the righteous brings forth wisdom,[o]
but a perverse tongue will be cut out.

32 The lips of the righteous know what is fitting,[p]
but the mouth of the wicked only what is perverse.

11 The LORD abhors dishonest scales,[a]
but accurate weights are his delight.[b]

2 When pride comes, then comes disgrace,[c]
but with humility comes wisdom.[d]

3 The integrity of the upright guides them,
but the unfaithful are destroyed by their duplicity.[e]

4 Wealth is worthless in the day of wrath,[f]
but righteousness delivers from death.[g]

5 The righteousness of the blameless makes a straight way for them,
but the wicked are brought down by their own wickedness.[h]

6 The righteousness of the upright delivers them,
but the unfaithful are trapped by evil desires.

7 When a wicked man dies, his hope perishes;
all he expected from his power comes to nothing.[i]

8 The righteous man is rescued from trouble,
and it comes on the wicked instead.[j]

9 With his mouth the godless destroys his neighbour,
but through knowledge the righteous escape.

10 When the righteous prosper, the city rejoices;[k]
when the wicked perish, there are shouts of joy.

11 Through the blessing of the upright a city is exalted,
but by the mouth of the wicked it is destroyed.[l]

12 A man who lacks judgment derides his neighbour,[m]
but a man of understanding holds his tongue.

13 A gossip betrays a confidence,[n]
but a trustworthy man keeps a secret.

10:27 [k]Job 15:32
10:28 [l]Job 8:13; Pr 11:7
10:29 [m]Pr 21:15
10:30 [n]Ps 37:9, 28-29; Pr 2:20-22
10:31 [o]Ps 37:30
10:32 [p]Ecc 10:12
11:1 [a]Lev 19:36; Dt 25:13-16; Pr 20:10, 23 [b]Pr 16:11
11:2 [c]Pr 16:18 [d]Pr 18:12; 29:23
11:3 [e]Pr 13:6
11:4 [f]Eze 7:19; Zep 1:18 [g]Ge 7:1; Pr 10:2
11:5 [h]Pr 5:21-23
11:7 [i]Pr 10:28
11:8 [j]Pr 21:18
11:10 [k]Pr 28:12
11:11 [l]Pr 29:8
11:12 [m]Pr 14:21
11:13 [n]Lev 19:16; Pr 20:19; 1Ti 5:13

11:4 "The day of wrath" refers to when we die or to the time when God settles accounts with all people. On judgment day, each of us will stand alone, accountable for all our deeds. At that time, no amount of riches will buy reconciliation with God. Only our love for God and obedience to him will count.

11:7, 8 These verses, like 10:3, contrast two paths in life, but are not intended to apply universally to all people in all circumstances. God's people are not excluded from problems or struggles. If a person follows God's wisdom, however, God can rescue him or her from trouble. But a wicked person will fall into his or her own traps. Even if good people suffer, they can be sure they will ultimately be rescued from eternal death.

11:9 The mouth can be used either as a weapon or a tool, hurting relationships or building them up. Sadly, it is often easier to destroy than to build, and most people have received more destructive comments than those that build up. Every person you meet today is either a demolition site or a construction opportunity. Your words will make a difference. Will they be weapons for destruction or tools for construction?

14For lack of guidance a nation falls,[o]
but many advisers make victory sure.[p]

15He who puts up security[q] for another will surely suffer,
but whoever refuses to strike hands in pledge is safe.

16A kind-hearted woman gains respect,[r]
but ruthless men gain only wealth.

17A kind man benefits himself,
but a cruel man brings trouble on himself.

18The wicked man earns deceptive wages,
but he who sows righteousness reaps a sure reward.[s]

19The truly righteous man attains life,
but he who pursues evil goes to his death.

20The LORD detests men of perverse heart
but he delights in those whose ways are blameless.[t]

21Be sure of this: The wicked will not go unpunished,
but those who are righteous will go free.[u]

22Like a gold ring in a pig's snout
is a beautiful woman who shows no discretion.

23The desire of the righteous ends only in good,
but the hope of the wicked only in wrath.

24One man gives freely, yet gains even more;
another withholds unduly, but comes to poverty.

25A generous man will prosper;

11:14 [o]Pr 20:18 [p]Pr 15:22; 24:6
11:15 [q]Pr 6:1
11:16 [r]Pr 31:31
11:18 [s]Hos 10:12-13
11:20 [t]1Ch 29:17; Ps 119:1; Pr 12:2, 22
11:21 [u]Pr 16:5

GOD'S ADVICE ABOUT MONEY

Proverbs gives some practical instruction on the use of money, although sometimes it is advice we would rather not hear. It's more comfortable to continue in our habits than to learn how to use money more wisely. The advice includes:

Be generous in giving	11:24, 25; 22:9
Place people's needs ahead of profit	11:26
Be cautious of countersigning for another	17:18; 22:26, 27
Don't accept bribes	17:23
Help the poor	19:17; 21:13
Store up for the future	21:20
Be careful about borrowing	22:7

Other verses to study include: 11:15; 20:16; 25:14; 27:13

11:14 A good leader needs and uses wise advisers. One person's perspective and understanding is severely limited; he or she may not have all the facts or may be blinded by bias, emotions, or wrong impressions. To be a wise leader at home, at church, or at work, seek the counsel of others and be open to their advice. Then, after considering all the facts, make your decision. (See the chart in chapter 30.)

11:19 Righteous people attain life because they live life more fully each day. They also attain life because people usually live longer when they live sensibly, with proper diet, exercise, and rest. In addition, they need not fear death because eternal life is God's gift to them (John 11:25). By contrast, evil people not only find eternal death, but also miss out on real life on earth.

11:22 Physical attractiveness without discretion soon wears thin. We are to seek those character strengths that help us make wise decisions, not just those that make us look good. Not everyone who looks good is pleasant to live or work with. While taking good care of our body and appearance is not wrong, we also need to develop our ability to think.

11:24, 25 These two verses present a paradox: that we become richer by being generous. The world says to hold on to as much as possible, but God blesses those who give freely of their possessions, time, and energy. When we give, God supplies us with more so that we can give more. In addition, giving helps us gain a right perspective on our possessions. We realise they were never really ours to begin with, but they were given to us by God to be used to help others. What then do we gain by giving? Freedom from enslavement to our possessions, the joy of helping others, and God's approval.

he who refreshes others will himself be refreshed.[v]

26 People curse the man who hoards grain,
but blessing crowns him who is willing to sell.

27 He who seeks good finds goodwill,
but evil comes to him who searches for it.[w]

28 Whoever trusts in his riches will fall,[x]
but the righteous will thrive like a green leaf.[y]

29 He who brings trouble on his family will inherit only wind,
and the fool will be servant to the wise.[z]

30 The fruit of the righteous is a tree of life,[a]
and he who wins souls is wise.

31 If the righteous receive their due[b] on earth,
how much more the ungodly and the sinner!

12 Whoever loves discipline loves knowledge,
but he who hates correction is stupid.[a]

2 A good man obtains favour from the LORD,
but the LORD condemns a crafty man.

3 A man cannot be established through wickedness,
but the righteous cannot be uprooted.[b]

4 A wife of noble character is her husband's crown,
but a disgraceful wife is like decay in his bones.[c]

5 The plans of the righteous are just,
but the advice of the wicked is deceitful.

6 The words of the wicked lie in wait for blood,
but the speech of the upright rescues them.[d]

7 Wicked men are overthrown and are no more,[e]
but the house of the righteous stands firm.[f]

8 A man is praised according to his wisdom,
but men with warped minds are despised.

9 Better to be a nobody and yet have a servant
than pretend to be somebody and have no food.

10 A righteous man cares for the needs of his animal,

11:25 [v]Mt 5:7; 2Co 9:6-9
11:27 [w]Est 7:10; Ps 7:15-16
11:28 [x]Job 31:24-28; Ps 49:6; 52:7; Mk 10:25; 1Ti 6:17 [y]Ps 1:3; 92:12-14; Jer 17:8
11:29 [z]Pr 14:19
11:30 [a]Jas 5:20
11:31 [b]Pr 13:21; Jer 25:29; 1Pe 4:18
12:1 [a]Pr 9:7-9; 15:5, 10, 12, 32
12:3 [b]Pr 10:25
12:4 [c]Pr 14:30
12:6 [d]Pr 14:3
12:7 [e]Ps 37:36 [f]Pr 10:25

11:29 One of the greatest resources God gives us is the family. Families provide acceptance, encouragement, guidance, and counsel. Bringing trouble on your family – whether through anger or through an exaggerated desire for independence – is foolish because you cut yourself off from all they provide. In your family, strive for healing, communication, and understanding.

11:30 A wise person is a model of a meaningful life. Like a tree attracts people to its shade, his or her sense of purpose attracts others who want to know how they too can find meaning. Gaining wisdom yourself, then, can be the first step in leading people to God. Leading people to God is important because it keeps us in touch with God while offering others eternal life.

11:31 Contrary to popular opinion, no-one sins and gets away with it. The faithful are rewarded for their faith. The wicked are punished for their sins. Don't think for a moment that "it won't matter" or "nobody will know" or "we won't get caught" (see also 1 Peter 4:18).

12:1 If you don't want to learn, years of schooling will teach you very little. But if you want to be taught, there is no end to what you can learn. This includes being willing to accept discipline and correction and to learn from the wisdom of others. A person who refuses constructive criticism has a problem with pride. Such a person is unlikely to learn very much.

12:3 To be established means to be successful. Real success comes only to those who do what is right. Their efforts stand the test of time. Then, what kind of success does wickedness bring? We all know people who cheated to pass an exam or to get a larger tax refund – is this not success? And what about the person who ignores his family commitments and mistreats his workers but gets on in business? These apparent successes are only temporary. They are bought at the expense of character. Cheaters grow more and more dishonest, and those who hurt others become callous and cruel. In the long run, evil behaviour does not lead to success; it leads only to more evil. Real success maintains personal integrity. If you are not a success by God's standards, you have not achieved true success. (See the chart in chapter 19.)

12:11 [g]Pr 28:19
12:13 [h]Pr 18:7 [i]Pr 21:23; 2Pe 2:9
12:14 [j]Pr 13:2; 15:23; 18:20 [k]Isa 3:10-11
12:15 [l]Pr 14:12; 16:2, 25; Lk 18:11
12:16 [m]Pr 29:11
12:17 [n]Pr 14:5, 25
12:18 [o]Ps 57:4 [p]Pr 15:4

but the kindest acts of the wicked are cruel.

11 He who works his land will have abundant food,
but he who chases fantasies lacks judgment.[g]

12 The wicked desire the plunder of evil men,
but the root of the righteous flourishes.

13 An evil man is trapped by his sinful talk,[h]
but a righteous man escapes trouble.[i]

14 From the fruit of his lips a man is filled with good things[j]
as surely as the work of his hands rewards him.[k]

15 The way of a fool seems right to him,[l]
but a wise man listens to advice.

16 A fool shows his annoyance at once,
but a prudent man overlooks an insult.[m]

17 A truthful witness gives honest testimony,
but a false witness tells lies.[n]

18 Reckless words pierce like a sword,[o]
but the tongue of the wise brings healing.[p]

19 Truthful lips endure for ever,
but a lying tongue lasts only a moment.

20 There is deceit in the hearts of those who plot evil,
but joy for those who promote peace.

TEACHING AND LEARNING

Good teaching comes from good learning—and Proverbs has more to say to students than to teachers. Proverbs is concerned with the learning of wisdom. The book makes it clear that there are no good alternatives to learning wisdom. We are either becoming wise learners or refusing to learn and becoming foolish failures. Proverbs encourages us to make the right choice.

Wise Learners	*Proverb(s)*	*Foolish Failures*
Quietly accept instruction and criticism	10:8; 23:12; 25:12	Ignore instruction
Love discipline	12:1	Hate correction
Listen to advice	12:15; 21:11; 24:6	Think they need no advice
Accept parents' discipline	13:1	Mock parents
Lead others to life	10:17	Lead others astray
Receive honour	13:18	End in poverty and shame
Profit from constructive rebuke	15:31, 32; 29:1	Self-destruct by refusing rebuke

Advice to Teachers:

Help people avoid traps (13:14).

Use pleasant words (16:21).

Speak at the right time (15:23; 18:20).

12:13 Sinful talk is twisting the facts to support your claims. Those who do this are likely to be trapped by their own lies. But for someone who always tells the truth, the facts—plain and unvarnished—give an unshakable defence. If you find that you always have to defend yourself to others, maybe your honesty is less than it should be. (See the chart in chapter 20.)

12:16 When someone annoys or insults you, it is natural to retaliate. But this solves nothing and only encourages trouble. Instead, answer slowly and quietly. Your positive response will achieve positive results. Proverbs 15:1 says, "A gentle answer turns away wrath."

12:19 Truth is always timely; it applies today and in the future. Because it is connected with God's changeless character, it is also changeless. Think for a moment about the centuries that have passed since these proverbs were written. Consider the countless hours that have been spent carefully studying every sentence of Scripture. The Bible has withstood the test of time. Because God is truth, you can trust his word to guide you.

21 No harm befalls the righteous,[q]
but the wicked have their fill of trouble.

22 The LORD detests lying lips,[r]
but he delights in men who are truthful.[s]

23 A prudent man keeps his knowledge to himself,[t]
but the heart of fools blurts out folly.

24 Diligent hands will rule,
but laziness ends in slave labour.[u]

25 An anxious heart weighs a man down,[v]
but a kind word cheers him up.

26 A righteous man is cautious in friendship,[a]
but the way of the wicked leads them astray.

27 The lazy man does not roast[b] his game,
but the diligent man prizes his possessions.

28 In the way of righteousness there is life;[w]
along that path is immortality.

13 A wise son heeds his father's instruction,
but a mocker does not listen to rebuke.[a]

2 From the fruit of his lips a man enjoys good things,[b]
but the unfaithful have a craving for violence.

3 He who guards his lips[c] guards his life,[d]
but he who speaks rashly will come to ruin.[e]

4 The sluggard craves and gets nothing,
but the desires of the diligent are fully satisfied.

5 The righteous hate what is false,
but the wicked bring shame and disgrace.

6 Righteousness guards the man of integrity,
but wickedness overthrows the sinner.[f]

7 One man pretends to be rich, yet has nothing;
another pretends to be poor, yet has great wealth.[g]

8 A man's riches may ransom his life,

a *26* Or *man is a guide to his neighbour* b *27* The meaning of the Hebrew for this word is uncertain.

12:21 [q]Ps 91:10
12:22 [r]Pr 6:17; Rev 22:15 [s]Pr 11:20
12:23 [t]Pr 10:14; 13:16
12:24 [u]Pr 10:4
12:25 [v]Pr 15:13; Isa 50:4
12:28 [w]Dt 30:15
13:1 [a]Pr 10:1
13:2 [b]Pr 12:14
13:3 [c]Jas 3:2 [d]Pr 21:23 [e]Pr 18:7, 20-21
13:6 [f]Pr 11:3, 5
13:7 [g]2Co 6:10

12:21 This is a general, but not universal, truth. Although harm does befall the righteous, they are able to see opportunities in their problems and move on. The wicked, without God's wisdom, are ill-equipped to handle their problems. (See the notes on 3:16, 17; 10:3; 11:8 for more about general truths that are not intended as universal statements.)

12:23 Prudent people have a quiet confidence. Insecure or uncertain people feel the need to prove themselves, but prudent people don't have to prove anything. They know they are capable, so they can get on with their work. Beware of showing off. If you are modest, people may not notice you at first, but they will respect you later.

12:27 The diligent make wise use of their possessions and resources; the lazy waste them. Waste has become a way of life for many who live in a land of plenty. Waste is poor stewardship. Make good use of everything God has given you, and prize it.

12:28 For many, death is a darkened door at the end of life, a passageway to an unknown and feared destiny. But for God's people, death is a bright pathway to a new and better life. So why do we fear death? Is it because of the pain we expect, the separation from loved ones, its surprise? God can help us deal with those fears. He has shown us that death is not final, but is just another step in the eternal life we received when we followed him.

13:3 You have not mastered self-control if you do not control what you say. Words can cut and destroy. James recognised this truth when he stated, "The tongue is a small part of the body, but it makes great boasts" (James 3:5). If you want to be self-controlled, begin with your tongue. Stop and think before you react or speak. If you can control this small but powerful member, you can control the rest of your body. (See the chart in chapter 27.)

13:6 Living in the right way is like posting a guard on your life. Every choice for good sets into motion other opportunities for good. Evil choices follow the same pattern, but in the opposite direction. Each decision you make to obey God's word will bring a greater sense of order to your life, while each decision to disobey will bring confusion and destruction. The right choices you make reflect your integrity. Obedience brings the greatest safety and security.

13:9
[h]Job 18:5; Pr 4:18-19; 24:20

but a poor man hears no threat.

9 The light of the righteous shines brightly,
but the lamp of the wicked is snuffed out.[h]

13:11
[i]Pr 10:2

10 Pride only breeds quarrels,
but wisdom is found in those who take advice.

11 Dishonest money dwindles away,[i]
but he who gathers money little by little makes it grow.

13:13
[j]Nu 15:31; 2Ch 36:16

12 Hope deferred makes the heart sick,
but a longing fulfilled is a tree of life.

13 He who scorns instruction will pay for it,[j]
but he who respects a command is rewarded.

13:14
[k]Pr 10:11
[l]Pr 14:27

14 The teaching of the wise is a fountain of life,[k]
turning a man from the snares of death.[l]

13:16
[m]Pr 12:23

15 Good understanding wins favour,
but the way of the unfaithful is hard.[a]

16 Every prudent man acts out of knowledge,
but a fool exposes his folly.[m]

13:17
[n]Pr 25:13

17 A wicked messenger falls into trouble,
but a trustworthy envoy brings healing.[n]

13:18
[o]Pr 15:5, 31-32

18 He who ignores discipline comes to poverty and shame,
but whoever heeds correction is honoured.[o]

19 A longing fulfilled is sweet to the soul,
but fools detest turning from evil.

13:20
[p]Pr 15:31

20 He who walks with the wise grows wise,
but a companion of fools suffers harm.[p]

13:21
[q]Ps 32:10

21 Misfortune pursues the sinner,
but prosperity is the reward of the righteous.[q]

13:22
[r]Job 27:17; Ecc 2:26

22 A good man leaves an inheritance for his children's children,
but a sinner's wealth is stored up for the righteous.[r]

a 15 Or *unfaithful does not endure*

13:10 "I was wrong" or "I need advice" are difficult phrases to utter because they require humility. Pride is an ingredient in every quarrel. It stirs up conflict and divides people. Humility, by contrast, heals. Guard against pride. If you find yourself constantly arguing, examine your life for pride. Be open to the advice of others, ask for help when you need it, and be willing to admit your mistakes.

13:13 God created us, knows us, and loves us. It only makes sense, then, to listen to his instructions and do what he says. The Bible is his unfailing word to us. It is like an owner's manual for a car. If you obey God's instructions, you will "run smoothly" and find his kind of power to live. If you ignore them, you will have breakdowns, accidents, and failures.

13:17 In Solomon's day, a king had to rely on messengers for information about his country. These messengers had to be trustworthy. Inaccurate information could even lead to bloodshed. Reliable communication is still vital. If the message received is different from the message sent, marriages, businesses, and diplomatic relations can all break down. It is important to choose your words well and to avoid reacting until you clearly understand what the other person means.

13:19 Whether a "longing fulfilled" is good or bad depends on the nature of the desire. It is "sweet to the soul" to achieve worthwhile goals, but not all goals are worth pursuing. When you set your heart on something, you may lose your ability to assess it objectively. With your desire blinding your judgment, you may proceed with an unwise relationship, a wasteful purchase, or a poorly conceived plan. Faithfulness is a virtue, but stubbornness is not.

13:20 The old saying "A rotten apple spoils the barrel" is often applied to friendships, and with good reason. Our friends and associates affect us, sometimes profoundly. Be careful whom you choose as your closest friends. Spend time with people you want to be like – because you and your friends will surely grow to resemble each other.

13:20 When most people need advice, they go to their friends first because friends accept them and usually agree with them. But that is why they may not be able to help them with difficult problems. Our friends are so much like us that they may not have any answers we haven't already heard. Instead, we should seek out older and wiser people to advise us. Wise people have experienced a lot of life – and have come through. They are not afraid to tell the truth. Who are the wise, godly people who can warn you of the pitfalls ahead?

23 A poor man's field may produce abundant food,
but injustice sweeps it away.

24 He who spares the rod hates his son,
but he who loves him is careful to discipline him.[s]

25 The righteous eat to their hearts' content,
but the stomach of the wicked goes hungry.[t]

14 The wise woman builds her house,[a]
but with her own hands the foolish one tears hers down.

2 He whose walk is upright fears the LORD,
but he whose ways are devious despises him.

3 A fool's talk brings a rod to his back,
but the lips of the wise protect them.[b]

4 Where there are no oxen, the manger is empty,
but from the strength of an ox comes an abundant harvest.

5 A truthful witness does not deceive,
but a false witness pours out lies.[c]

6 The mocker seeks wisdom and finds none,
but knowledge comes easily to the discerning.

7 Stay away from a foolish man,
for you will not find knowledge on his lips.

8 The wisdom of the prudent is to give thought to their ways,
but the folly of fools is deception.[d]

9 Fools mock at making amends for sin,
but goodwill is found among the upright.

10 Each heart knows its own bitterness,
and no-one else can share its joy.

11 The house of the wicked will be destroyed,
but the tent of the upright will flourish.[e]

12 There is a way that seems right to a man,[f]

13:24 [s]Pr 19:18; 22:15; 23:13-14; 29:15, 17; Heb 12:7

13:25 [t]Ps 34:10; Pr 10:3

14:1 [a]Pr 24:3

14:3 [b]Pr 12:6

14:5 [c]Pr 6:19; 12:17

14:8 [d]ver 24

14:11 [e]Pr 3:33; 12:7

14:12 [f]Pr 12:15

13:23 The poor are often victims of an unjust society. A poor man's soil may be good, but unjust laws may rob him of his own produce. This proverb does not take poverty lightly or wink at injustice; it simply describes what often occurs. We should do what we can to fight injustice of every sort. Our efforts may seem inadequate; but it is comforting to know that in the end God's justice will prevail.

13:24 It is not easy for a loving parent to discipline a child, but it is necessary. The greatest responsibility that God gives parents is the nurture and guidance of their children. Lack of discipline puts parents' love in question because it shows a lack of concern for the character development of their children. Disciplining children averts long-term disaster. Without correction, children grow up with no clear understanding of right and wrong and with little direction to their lives. Don't be afraid to discipline your children. It is an act of love. Remember, however, that your efforts cannot make your children wise; they can only encourage your children to seek God's wisdom above all else!

14:4 When a farmer has no oxen for ploughing, his food trough for the animals will be empty. The only way to keep your life free of people problems is to keep it free of other people. But if your life is empty of people, it is useless; and if you live only for yourself, your life loses its meaning. Instead of avoiding people, we should serve others, share the faith, and work for justice. Is your life clean, but empty? Or does it give evidence of your serving God wholeheartedly?

14:6 We all know mockers, people who scoff at every word of instruction or advice. They never find wisdom because they don't seek it seriously. Wisdom comes easily to those who pay attention to experienced people and to God. If the wisdom you need does not come easily to you, perhaps your attitude is the barrier.

14:9 How rarely we find goodwill around us today. Angry drivers scowl at each other in the streets. People fight to be first in line. Disgruntled employers and employees both demand their rights. But the common bond of God's people should be goodwill. Those with goodwill think the best of others and assume that others have good motives and intend to do what is right. When someone crosses you, and you feel your blood pressure rising, ask yourself, "How can I show goodwill to this person?"

14:12 The "way that seems right" may offer many options and require few sacrifices. Easy choices, however, should make us take a second look. Is this solution attractive because it allows me to be lazy? Because it doesn't ask me to change my life-style? Because it requires no moral restraints? The right choice often requires hard work and self-sacrifice. Don't be enticed by apparent shortcuts that seem right but end in death.

14:12 [g]Pr 16:25
14:13 [h]Ecc 2:2
14:14 [i]Pr 1:31 [j]Pr 12:14
14:16 [k]Pr 22:3
14:17 [l]ver 29
14:19 [m]Pr 11:29

but in the end it leads to death.[g]

13Even in laughter[h] the heart may ache,
and joy may end in grief.

14The faithless will be fully repaid for their ways,[i]
and the good man rewarded for his.[j]

15A simple man believes anything,
but a prudent man gives thought to his steps.

16A wise man fears the LORD and shuns evil,[k]
but a fool is hotheaded and reckless.

17A quick-tempered man does foolish things,[l]
and a crafty man is hated.

18The simple inherit folly,
but the prudent are crowned with knowledge.

19Evil men will bow down in the presence of the good,
and the wicked at the gates of the righteous.[m]

WISDOM AND FOOLISHNESS
The wise and the foolish are often contrasted in Proverbs. The characteristics, reputation, and results of each are worth knowing if wisdom is our goal.

	The Wise	*The Foolish*	
Characteristics	Help others with good advice	Lack judgment	10:21
	Enjoy wisdom	Enjoy foolishness	10:23
	Cautious with reason	Gullible	14:15
		Avoid the wise	15:12
	Seek knowledge	Feed on foolishness	15:14
	Value wisdom above riches		16:16
	Receive life	Receive punishment	16:22
	Respond to correction	Respond to punishment	17:10
	Pursue wisdom	Pursue illusive dreams	17:24
		Blame failure on God	19:3
	Profit from correction	An example to others	19:25
		Are proud and arrogant	21:24
		Scorn good advice	23:9
		Make truth useless	26:7
		Repeat their folly	26:11
	Trust in wisdom	Trust in themselves	28:26
	Control their anger	Unleash their anger	29:11
Reputation	Admired as counsellors	Beaten as servants	10:13
	Rewarded with knowledge	Inherit folly	14:18
		Cause strife and quarrels	22:10
		Receive no honour	26:1
	Keep peace	Stir up anger	29:8
Results	Stay on straight paths	Go the wrong way	15:21
		Lash out when discovered in folly	17:12
		Endangered by their words	18:6, 7
	Their wisdom conquers others' strength		21:22
	Avoid wicked paths	Walk a troublesome path	22:5
	Receive good advice		24:5
		Will never be chosen as counsellors	24:7
		Must be guided by hardship	26:3
		Persist in foolishness	27:22

20 The poor are shunned even by their neighbours,
but the rich have many friends.[n]

21 He who despises his neighbour sins,[o]
but blessed is he who is kind to the needy.[p]

22 Do not those who plot evil go astray?
But those who plan what is good find[a] love and faithfulness.

23 All hard work brings a profit,
but mere talk leads only to poverty.

24 The wealth of the wise is their crown,
but the folly of fools yields folly.

25 A truthful witness saves lives,
but a false witness is deceitful.[q]

26 He who fears the LORD has a secure fortress,[r]
and for his children it will be a refuge.

27 The fear of the LORD is a fountain of life,
turning a man from the snares of death.[s]

28 A large population is a king's glory,
but without subjects a prince is ruined.

29 A patient man has great understanding,
but a quick-tempered man displays folly.[t]

30 A heart at peace gives life to the body,
but envy rots the bones.[u]

31 He who oppresses the poor shows contempt for their Maker,[v]
but whoever is kind to the needy honours God.

32 When calamity comes, the wicked are brought down,[w]
but even in death the righteous have a refuge.[x]

33 Wisdom reposes in the heart of the discerning[y]
and even among fools she lets herself be known.[b]

34 Righteousness exalts a nation,[z]
but sin is a disgrace to any people.

35 A king delights in a wise servant,
but a shameful servant incurs his wrath.[a]

15 A gentle answer turns away wrath,[a]
but a harsh word stirs up anger.

2 The tongue of the wise commends knowledge,
but the mouth of the fool gushes folly.[b]

a *22 Or show* b *33* Hebrew; Septuagint and Syriac / *but in the heart of fools she is not known*

14:20 [n]Pr 19:4, 7
14:21 [o]Pr 11:12 [p]Ps 41:1; Pr 19:17
14:25 [q]ver 5
14:26 [r]Pr 18:10; 19:23; Isa 33:6
14:27 [s]Pr 13:14
14:29 [t]Ecc 7:8-9; Jas 1:19
14:30 [u]Pr 12:4
14:31 [v]Pr 17:5
14:32 [w]Pr 6:15 [x]Job 13:15; 2Ti 4:18
14:33 [y]Pr 2:6-10
14:34 [z]Pr 11:11
14:35 [a]Mt 24:45-51; 25:14-30
15:1 [a]Pr 25:15
15:2 [b]Pr 12:23

14:29 A quick temper can be like a fire out of control. It can burn us and everyone else in its path. Anger divides people. It pushes us into hasty decisions that only cause bitterness and guilt. Yet anger, in itself, is not wrong. Anger can be a legitimate reaction to injustice and sin. When you feel yourself getting angry, look for the cause. Are you reacting to an evil situation that you are going to set right? Or are you responding selfishly to a personal insult? Pray that God will help you control your quick temper, channelling your feelings into effective action and conquering selfish anger through humility and repentance.

14:31 God has a special concern for the poor. He insists that people who have material goods should be generous to those who are needy. Providing for the poor is not just a suggestion in the Bible; it is a command that may require a change of attitude (see Leviticus 23:22; Deuteronomy 15:7, 8; Psalms 113:5–9; 146:5–9; Isaiah 58:7; 2 Corinthians 9:9; James 2:1–9).

15:1 Have you ever tried to argue in a whisper? It is equally hard to argue with someone who insists on answering gently. On the other hand, a rising voice and harsh words almost always trigger an angry response. To turn away wrath and seek peace, choose gentle words.

15:3 [c]2Ch 16:9 [d]Job 31:4; Heb 4:13 [e]Job 34:21; Jer 16:17
15:5 [f]Pr 13:1
15:6 [g]Pr 8:21
15:8 [h]Pr 21:27; Isa 1:11; Jer 6:20 [i]ver 29
15:9 [j]Pr 21:21; 1Ti 6:11
15:10 [k]Pr 1:31-32; 5:12
15:11 [l]Job 26:6; Ps 139:8 [m]2Ch 6:30; Ps 44:21
15:12 [n]Am 5:10
15:13 [o]Pr 12:25; 17:22; 18:14
15:14 [p]Pr 18:15
15:15 [q]ver 13
15:16 [r]Ps 37:16-17; Pr 16:8; 1Ti 6:6
15:17 [s]Pr 17:1
15:18 [t]Pr 26:21 [u]Ge 13:8
15:19 [v]Pr 22:5

3 The eyes[c] of the LORD are everywhere,[d]
keeping watch on the wicked and the good.[e]

4 The tongue that brings healing is a tree of life,
but a deceitful tongue crushes the spirit.

5 A fool spurns his father's discipline,
but whoever heeds correction shows prudence.[f]

6 The house of the righteous contains great treasure,[g]
but the income of the wicked brings them trouble.

7 The lips of the wise spread knowledge;
not so the hearts of fools.

8 The LORD detests the sacrifice of the wicked,[h]
but the prayer of the upright pleases him.[i]

9 The LORD detests the way of the wicked
but he loves those who pursue righteousness.[j]

10 Stern discipline awaits him who leaves the path;
he who hates correction will die.[k]

11 Death and Destruction[a] lie open before the LORD[l]—
how much more the hearts of men![m]

12 A mocker resents correction;[n]
he will not consult the wise.

13 A happy heart makes the face cheerful,
but heartache crushes the spirit.[o]

14 The discerning heart seeks knowledge,[p]
but the mouth of a fool feeds on folly.

15 All the days of the oppressed are wretched,
but the cheerful heart has a continual feast.[q]

16 Better a little with the fear of the LORD
than great wealth with turmoil.[r]

17 Better a meal of vegetables where there is love
than a fattened calf with hatred.[s]

18 A hot-tempered man stirs up dissension,[t]
but a patient man calms a quarrel.[u]

19 The way of the sluggard is blocked with thorns,[v]
but the path of the upright is a highway.

a *11* Hebrew *Sheol and Abaddon*

15:3 At times it seems that God has let evil run rampant in the world, and we wonder if he even notices it. But God sees everything clearly – both the evil actions and the evil intentions lying behind them (15:11). He is not an indifferent observer. He cares and is active in our world. Right now, his work may be unseen and unfelt, but don't give up. One day he will wipe out evil and punish the evildoers, just as he will establish the good and reward those who do his will.

15:14 What we feed our minds is just as important as what we feed our bodies. The kinds of books we read, the people we talk to, the music we listen to, and the films we watch are all part of our mental diet. Be discerning because what you feed your mind influences your total health and well-being. Thus, a strong desire to discover knowledge is a mark of wisdom.

15:15 Our attitudes colour our whole personality. We cannot always choose what happens to us, but we can choose our attitude towards each situation. The secret to a cheerful heart is filling our minds with thoughts that are true, pure, and lovely, with thoughts that dwell on the good things in life (Philippians 4:8). This was Paul's secret as he faced imprisonment, and it can be ours as we face the struggles of daily living. Look at your attitudes and then examine what you allow to enter your mind and what you choose to dwell on. You may need to make some changes.

15:17–19 The "path of the upright" doesn't always seem easy (15:19), but look at the alternatives. Hatred (15:17), dissension (15:18), and laziness (15:19) cause problems that the upright person does not have to face. By comparison, his or her life is a smooth, level road because it is built on a solid foundation of love for God.

20 A wise son brings joy to his father,[w]
but a foolish man despises his mother.

21 Folly delights a man who lacks judgment,[x]
but a man of understanding keeps a straight course.

22 Plans fail for lack of counsel,
but with many advisers they succeed.[y]

23 A man finds joy in giving an apt reply[z]—
and how good is a timely word![a]

24 The path of life leads upward for the wise
to keep him from going down to the grave.[b]

25 The LORD tears down the proud man's house[b]
but he keeps the widow's boundaries intact.[c]

26 The LORD detests the thoughts of the wicked,[d]
but those of the pure are pleasing to him.

27 A greedy man brings trouble to his family,
but he who hates bribes will live.[e]

28 The heart of the righteous weighs its answers,[f]
but the mouth of the wicked gushes evil.

29 The LORD is far from the wicked
but he hears the prayer of the righteous.[g]

30 A cheerful look brings joy to the heart,
and good news gives health to the bones.

31 He who listens to a life-giving rebuke
will be at home among the wise.[h]

32 He who ignores discipline despises himself,[i]
but whoever heeds correction gains understanding.

33 The fear of the LORD[j] teaches a man wisdom,[c]
and humility comes before honour.[k]

16 To man belong the plans of the heart,
but from the LORD comes the reply of the tongue.[a]

2 All a man's ways seem innocent to him,
but motives are weighed by the LORD.[b]

3 Commit to the LORD whatever you do,

15:20 [w]Pr 10:1
15:21 [x]Pr 10:23
15:22 [y]Pr 11:14
15:23 [z]Pr 12:14 [a]Pr 25:11
15:25 [b]Pr 12:7 [c]Dt 19:14; Ps 68:5-6; Pr 23:10-11
15:26 [d]Pr 6:16
15:27 [e]Ex 23:8; Isa 33:15
15:28 [f]1Pe 3:15
15:29 [g]Ps 145:18-19
15:31 [h]ver 5
15:32 [i]Pr 1:7
15:33 [j]Pr 1:7 [k]Pr 18:12
16:1 [a]Pr 19:21
16:2 [b]Pr 21:2

[b] 24 Hebrew *Sheol* [c] 33 Or *Wisdom teaches the fear of the LORD*

15:22 People with tunnel vision, those who are locked into one way of thinking, are likely to miss the right road because they have closed their minds to any new options. We need the help of those who can enlarge our vision and broaden our perspective. Seek out the advice of those who know you and have a wealth of experience. Build a network of advisers. Then be open to new ideas and be willing to weigh their suggestions carefully. Your plans will be stronger and more likely to succeed.

15:28 The righteous weigh their answers; the wicked don't wait to speak because they don't care about the effects of their words. It is important to have something to say, but it is equally important to weigh it first. Do you carefully plan your words, or do you pour out your thoughts without concern for their impact?

16:1 "From the LORD comes the reply of the tongue" means that the final outcome of the plans we make is in God's hands. If this is so, why make plans? In doing God's will, there must be partnership between our efforts and God's control. He wants us to use our minds, to seek the advice of others, and to plan. Nevertheless, the results are up to him. Planning, then, helps us act God's way. As you live for him, ask for guidance as you plan, and then act on your plan as you trust in him.

16:2 "All a man's ways seem innocent to him." People can rationalise anything if they have no standards for judging right and wrong. We can always prove that we are right. Before putting any plan into action, ask yourself these three questions: (1) Is this plan in harmony with God's truth? (2) Will it work under real-life conditions? (3) Is my attitude pleasing to God?

16:3 There are different ways to fail to commit whatever we do to the Lord. Some people commit their work only superficially. They say the project is being done for the Lord, but in reality they are doing it for themselves. Others give God temporary control of their interests, only to take control back the moment things stop going

16:3
[c]Ps 37:5-6; Pr 3:5-6

16:4
[d]Isa 43:7
[e]Ro 9:22

16:5
[f]Pr 6:16
[g]Pr 11:20-21

16:6
[h]Pr 14:16

16:8
[i]Ps 37:16

16:9
[j]Jer 10:23

and your plans will succeed.[c]

4The LORD works out everything for his own ends[d]—
even the wicked for a day of disaster.[e]

5The LORD detests all the proud of heart.[f]
Be sure of this: They will not go unpunished.[g]

6Through love and faithfulness sin is atoned for;
through the fear of the LORD a man avoids evil.[h]

7When a man's ways are pleasing to the LORD,
he makes even his enemies live at peace with him.

8Better a little with righteousness
than much gain[i] with injustice.

9In his heart a man plans his course,
but the LORD determines his steps.[j]

10The lips of a king speak as an oracle,
and his mouth should not betray justice.

HOW GOD IS DESCRIBED IN PROVERBS

Proverbs is a book about wise living. It often focuses on a person's response and attitude towards God, who is the source of wisdom. And a number of proverbs point out aspects of God's character. Knowing God helps us on the way to wisdom.

God . . .	is aware of all that happens	15:3
	knows the heart of all people	15:11; 16:2; 21:2
	controls all things	16:33; 21:30
	is a place of safety	18:10
	rescues good people from danger	11:8, 21
	condemns the wicked	11:31
	delights in our prayers	15:8, 29
	loves those who obey him	15:9; 22:12
	cares for poor and needy	15:25; 22:22, 23
	purifies hearts	17:3
	hates evil	17:5; 21:27; 28:9
Our response should be . . .	to fear and reverence God	10:27; 14:26, 27; 15:16; 16:6; 19:23; 28:14
	to obey God's word	13:13; 19:16
	to please God	21:3
	to trust in God	22:17–19; 29:25

the way they expect. Still others commit a task fully to the Lord, but put forth no effort themselves, and then they wonder why they do not succeed. We must maintain a delicate balance: trusting God as if everything depended on him, while working as if everything depended on us. Think of a specific effort in which you are involved right now. Have you committed it to the Lord?

16:4 This verse doesn't mean that God created some people to be wicked, but rather that God uses even the activities of wicked people to fulfil his good purposes. God is infinite and we are finite. No matter how great our intellects, we will never be able to understand him completely. But we can accept by faith that he is all-powerful, all-loving, and perfectly good. We can believe that he is not the cause of evil (James 1:13, 17); and we can trust that there are no loose ends in his system of judgment. Evil is a temporary condition in the universe. One day God will destroy it. In the meantime, he uses even the evil intentions of people for his good purposes (see Genesis 50:20).

16:5 Pride is the inner voice that whispers, "My way is best." It is resisting God's leadership and believing that you are able to live without his help. Whenever you find yourself wanting to do it your way and looking down on other people, you are being pulled by pride. Only when you eliminate pride can God help you become all he meant you to be. (See the chart in chapter 19.)

16:7 We want other people to like us, and sometimes we will do almost anything to win their approval. But God tells us to put our energy into pleasing him instead. Our effort to be peacemakers will usually make us more attractive to those around us, even our enemies. But even if it doesn't, we haven't lost anything. We are still pleasing God, the only one who truly matters.

11 Honest scales and balances are from the LORD;
all the weights in the bag are of his making.[k]

12 Kings detest wrongdoing,
for a throne is established through righteousness.[l]

13 Kings take pleasure in honest lips;
they value a man who speaks the truth.[m]

14 A king's wrath is a messenger of death,[n]
but a wise man will appease it.

15 When a king's face brightens, it means life;[o]
his favour is like a rain cloud in spring.

16 How much better to get wisdom than gold,
to choose understanding rather than silver![p]

17 The highway of the upright avoids evil;
he who guards his way guards his life.

18 Pride goes before destruction,
a haughty spirit before a fall.[q]

19 Better to be lowly in spirit and among the oppressed
than to share plunder with the proud.

20 Whoever gives heed to instruction prospers,
and blessed is he who trusts in the LORD.[r]

21 The wise in heart are called discerning,
and pleasant words promote instruction.[a][s]

22 Understanding is a fountain of life to those who have it,[t]
but folly brings punishment to fools.

23 A wise man's heart guides his mouth,
and his lips promote instruction.[b]

24 Pleasant words are a honeycomb,
sweet to the soul and healing to the bones.[u]

25 There is a way that seems right to a man,[v]
but in the end it leads to death.[w]

26 The labourer's appetite works for him;
his hunger drives him on.

a *21* Or *words make a man persuasive* b *23* Or *mouth / and makes his lips persuasive*

16:11 [k]Pr 11:1
16:12 [l]Pr 25:5
16:13 [m]Pr 14:35
16:14 [n]Pr 19:12
16:15 [o]Job 29:24
16:16 [p]Pr 8:10, 19
16:18 [q]Pr 11:2; 18:12
16:20 [r]Ps 2:12; 34:8; Pr 19:8; Jer 17:7
16:21 [s]ver 23
16:22 [t]Pr 13:14
16:24 [u]Pr 24:13-14
16:25 [v]Pr 12:15 [w]Pr 14:12

16:11 Whether we buy or sell, make a product or offer a service, we know what is honest and what is dishonest. Sometimes we feel pressure to be dishonest in order to advance ourselves or gain more profit. But if we want to obey God, there is no middle ground: God demands honesty in every business transaction. No amount of rationalising can cover for a dishonest business practice. Honesty and fairness are not always easy, but they are what God demands. Ask him for discernment and courage to be consistently honest and fair.

16:18 Proud people take little account of their weaknesses and do not anticipate stumbling blocks. They think they are above the frailties of common people. In this state of mind they are easily tripped up. Ironically, proud people seldom realise that pride is their problem, although everyone around them is well aware of it. Ask someone you trust whether self-satisfaction has blinded you to warning signs. He or she may help you avoid a fall.

16:22 For centuries people sought a fountain of youth, a spring that promised to give eternal life and vitality. It was never found. But God's wisdom is a fountain of life that can make a person happy, healthy, and alive for ever. How? When we live by God's word, he washes away the deadly effects of sin (see Titus 3:4–8), and the hope of eternal life with him gives us a joyful perspective on our present life. The fountain of youth was only a dream, but the fountain of life is reality. The choice is yours. You can be enlightened by God's wisdom, or you can be dragged down by the weight of your own foolishness.

16:26 "The labourer's appetite works for him" means that no matter how much difficulty or drudgery we may find in our work, our appetite is an incentive to keep going. Hunger makes us work to satisfy that hunger.

27 A scoundrel plots evil,
and his speech is like a scorching fire.[x]

28 A perverse man stirs up dissension,[y]
and a gossip separates close friends.[z]

29 A violent man entices his neighbour
and leads him down a path that is not good.[a]

30 He who winks with his eye is plotting perversity;
he who purses his lips is bent on evil.

31 Grey hair is a crown of splendour;[b]
it is attained by a righteous life.

32 Better a patient man than a warrior,
a man who controls his temper than one who takes a city.

33 The lot is cast into the lap,
but its every decision is from the LORD.[c]

17

Better a dry crust with peace and quiet
than a house full of feasting,**a** with strife.[a]

2 A wise servant will rule over a disgraceful son,
and will share the inheritance as one of the brothers.

3 The crucible for silver and the furnace for gold,[b]
but the LORD tests the heart.[c]

4 A wicked man listens to evil lips;
a liar pays attention to a malicious tongue.

5 He who mocks the poor shows contempt for their Maker;[d]
whoever gloats over disaster[e] will not go unpunished.[f]

6 Children's children[g] are a crown to the aged,
and parents are the pride of their children.

7 Arrogant**b** lips are unsuited to a fool—
how much worse lying lips to a ruler!

8 A bribe is a charm to the one who gives it;
wherever he turns, he succeeds.

a *1* Hebrew *sacrifices* **b** *7* Or *Eloquent*

16:27 [x]Jas 3:6

16:28 [y]Pr 15:18 [z]Pr 17:9

16:29 [a]Pr 1:10; 12:26

16:31 [b]Pr 20:29

16:33 [c]Pr 18:18; 29:26

17:1 [a]Pr 15:16, 17

17:3 [b]Pr 27:21 [c]1Ch 29:17; Ps 26:2; Jer 17:10

17:5 [d]Pr 14:31 [e]Job 31:29 [f]Ob 1:12

17:6 [g]Pr 13:22

16:31 The Hebrews believed that a long life was a sign of God's blessing; therefore, grey hair and old age were good. While young people glory in their strength, old people can rejoice in their years of experience and practical wisdom. Grey hair is not a sign of disgrace to be covered over; it is a crown of splendour. As you deal with older people, treat them with respect.

16:32 Self-control is superior to conquest. Success in business, school, or home life can be ruined by a person who has lost control of his or her temper. So it is a great personal victory to control your temper. When you feel yourself ready to explode, remember that losing control may cause you to forfeit what you want the most.

16:33 The lot was almost always used in ceremonial settings and was the common method for determining God's will. Several important events occurred by lot, including the identification of Achan as the man who had sinned (Joshua 7:14), the division of the promised land among the tribes (Joshua 14:2), and the selection of the first king for the nation (1 Samuel 10:16–26).

17:3 It takes intense heat to purify gold and silver. Similarly, it often takes the heat of trials for the Christian to be purified. Through trials, God shows us what is in us and clears out anything that gets in the way of complete trust in him. Peter says, "These have come so that your faith—of greater worth than gold, which perishes even though refined by fire—may be proved genuine and may result in praise, glory and honour when Jesus Christ is revealed" (1 Peter 1:7). So when tough times come your way, realise that God wants to use them to refine your faith and purify your heart.

17:5 Few acts are as cruel as making fun of the less fortunate, but many people do this because it makes them feel good to be better off or more successful than someone else. Mocking the poor is mocking the God who made them. We also ridicule God when we mock the weak, those who are different, or anyone else. When you catch yourself putting down others just for fun, stop and think about who created them.

17:8 Solomon is not condoning bribery (see 17:15, 23), but he is making an observation about the way the world operates. Bribes may get people what they want, but the Bible clearly condemns using them (Exodus 23:8; Proverbs 17:23; Matthew 28:11–15).

9 He who covers over an offence promotes love,[h]
but whoever repeats the matter separates close friends.[i]

10 A rebuke impresses a man of discernment
more than a hundred lashes a fool.

11 An evil man is bent only on rebellion;
a merciless official will be sent against him.

12 Better to meet a bear robbed of her cubs
than a fool in his folly.

13 If a man pays back evil[j] for good,
evil will never leave his house.

14 Starting a quarrel is like breaching a dam;
so drop the matter before a dispute breaks out.[k]

15 Acquitting the guilty and condemning the innocent[l]—
the LORD detests them both.[m]

16 Of what use is money in the hand of a fool,
since he has no desire to get wisdom?[n]

17 A friend loves at all times,
and a brother is born for adversity.

18 A man lacking in judgment strikes hands in pledge
and puts up security for his neighbour.[o]

19 He who loves a quarrel loves sin;
he who builds a high gate invites destruction.

20 A man of perverse heart does not prosper;
he whose tongue is deceitful falls into trouble.

21 To have a fool for a son brings grief;
there is no joy for the father of a fool.[p]

22 A cheerful heart is good medicine,
but a crushed spirit dries up the bones.[q]

23 A wicked man accepts a bribe[r] in secret
to pervert the course of justice.

24 A discerning man keeps wisdom in view,
but a fool's eyes[s] wander to the ends of the earth.

25 A foolish son brings grief to his father
and bitterness to the one who bore him.[t]

17:9 [h]Pr 10:12 [i]Pr 16:28
17:13 [j]Ps 109:4-5; Jer 18:20
17:14 [k]Pr 20:3
17:15 [l]Pr 18:5 [m]Ex 23:6-7; Isa 5:23
17:16 [n]Pr 23:23
17:18 [o]Pr 6:1-5; 11:15; 22:26-27
17:21 [p]Pr 10:1
17:22 [q]Ps 22:15; Pr 15:13
17:23 [r]Ex 23:8
17:24 [s]Ecc 2:14
17:25 [t]Pr 10:1

17:9 This proverb is saying that we should be willing to forgive others' sins against us. Covering over offences is necessary to any relationship. It is tempting, especially in an argument, to bring up all the mistakes the other person has ever made. Love, however, keeps its mouth shut – difficult though that may be. Try never to bring anything into an argument that is unrelated to the topic being discussed. As we grow to be like Christ, we will acquire God's ability to forget the confessed sins of the past.

17:17 What kind of friend are you? There is a vast difference between knowing someone well and being a true friend. The greatest evidence of genuine friendship is loyalty (loving "at all times") (see 1 Corinthians 13:7) – being available to help in times of distress or personal struggles. Too many people are fair-weather friends. They stick around when the friendship helps them and leave when they're not getting anything out of the relationship. Think of your friends and assess your loyalty to them. Be the kind of true friend the Bible encourages.

17:22 To be cheerful is to be ready to greet others with a welcome, a word of encouragement, an enthusiasm for the task at hand, and a positive outlook on the future. Such people are as welcome as pain-relieving medicine.

17:24 While there is something to be said for having big dreams, this proverb points out the folly of chasing fantasies (having eyes that wander "to the ends of the earth", see 12:11). How much better to align your goals with God's, being the kind of person he wants you to be! Such goals (wisdom, honesty, patience, love) may not seem exciting, but they will determine your eternal future. Take time to think about your dreams and goals, and make sure they cover the really important areas of life.

17:26 [u]Pr 18:5

17:27 [v]Pr 14:29; Jas 1:19

17:28 [w]Job 13:5

18:2 [a]Pr 12:23

18:5 [b]Lev 19:15; Pr 24:23-25; 28:21 [c]Ps 82:2; Pr 17:15

18:7 [d]Ps 140:9 [e]Ps 64:8; Pr 10:14; 12:13; 13:3; Ecc 10:12

18:8 [f]Pr 26:22

18:9 [g]Pr 28:24

18:10 [h]2Sa 22:3; Ps 61:3

18:11 [i]Pr 10:15

26 It is not good to punish an innocent man,[u]
or to flog officials for their integrity.

27 A man of knowledge uses words with restraint,
and a man of understanding is even-tempered.[v]

28 Even a fool is thought wise if he keeps silent,
and discerning if he holds his tongue.[w]

18

An unfriendly man pursues selfish ends;
he defies all sound judgment.

2 A fool finds no pleasure in understanding
but delights in airing his own opinions.[a]

3 When wickedness comes, so does contempt,
and with shame comes disgrace.

4 The words of a man's mouth are deep waters,
but the fountain of wisdom is a bubbling brook.

5 It is not good to be partial to the wicked[b]
or to deprive the innocent of justice.[c]

6 A fool's lips bring him strife,
and his mouth invites a beating.

7 A fool's mouth is his undoing,
and his lips are a snare[d] to his soul.[e]

8 The words of a gossip are like choice morsels;
they go down to a man's inmost parts.[f]

9 One who is slack in his work
is brother to one who destroys.[g]

10 The name of the LORD is a strong tower;[h]
the righteous run to it and are safe.

11 The wealth of the rich is their fortified city;[i]
they imagine it an unscalable wall.

HUMILITY AND PRIDE
Proverbs is direct and forceful in rejecting pride. A proud attitude heads the list of seven things God hates (6:16, 17). The harmful results of pride are constantly contrasted with humility and its benefits.

Results of . . .	*Humility*	*Pride*	
	Leads to wisdom	Leads to disgrace	11:2
	Takes advice	Produces quarrels	13:10
	Leads to honour		15:33
		Leads to punishment	16:5
		Leads to destruction	16:18
	Ends in honour	Ends in downfall	18:12
	Brings one to honour	Brings one low	29:23

17:27, 28 This proverb highlights several benefits of keeping quiet: (1) it is the best policy if you have nothing worthwhile to say; (2) it allows you the opportunity to listen and learn; (3) it gives you something in common with those who are wiser. Make sure you pause to think and to listen so that when you do speak, you will have something important to say.

18:8 It is as hard to refuse to listen to gossip as it is to turn down a delicious dessert. Taking just one morsel of either one creates a taste for more. You can resist rumours the same way a determined dieter resists chocolates – never even open the box. If you don't nibble on the first bite of gossip, you can't take the second and the third.

18:11 In imagining that their wealth is their strongest defence, rich people are sadly mistaken. Money cannot provide safety – there are too many ways for it to lose its power. The government may cease to back it; thieves may steal it; inflation may rob it of all value. But God never loses his power. He is always dependable. Where do you look for security and safety – uncertain wealth or God who is always faithful?

12 Before his downfall a man's heart is proud,
but humility comes before honour.[j]

13 He who answers before listening—
that is his folly and his shame.[k]

14 A man's spirit sustains him in sickness,
but a crushed spirit who can bear?[l]

15 The heart of the discerning acquires knowledge;[m]
the ears of the wise seek it out.

16 A gift[n] opens the way for the giver
and ushers him into the presence of the great.

17 The first to present his case seems right,
till another comes forward and questions him.

18 Casting the lot settles disputes[o]
and keeps strong opponents apart.

19 An offended brother is more unyielding than a fortified city,
and disputes are like the barred gates of a citadel.

20 From the fruit of his mouth a man's stomach is filled;
with the harvest from his lips he is satisfied.[p]

21 The tongue has the power of life and death,
and those who love it will eat its fruit.[q]

22 He who finds a wife finds what is good[r]
and receives favour from the LORD.[s]

23 A poor man pleads for mercy,
but a rich man answers harshly.

24 A man of many companions may come to ruin,
but there is a friend who sticks closer than a brother.[t]

19 Better a poor man whose walk is blameless
than a fool whose lips are perverse.[a]

2 It is not good to have zeal without knowledge,
nor to be hasty and miss the way.[b]

18:12 [j]Pr 11:2; 15:33; 16:18
18:13 [k]Pr 20:25; Jn 7:51
18:14 [l]Pr 15:13; 17:22
18:15 [m]Pr 15:14
18:16 [n]Ge 32:20
18:18 [o]Pr 16:33
18:20 [p]Pr 12:14
18:21 [q]Pr 13:2-3; Mt 12:37
18:22 [r]Pr 12:4 [s]Pr 19:14; 31:10
18:24 [t]Pr 17:17; Jn 15:13-15
19:1 [a]Pr 28:6
19:2 [b]Pr 29:20

18:13, 15, 17 In these concise statements, there are three basic principles for making sound decisions: (1) get the facts before answering; (2) be open to new ideas; (3) make sure you hear both sides of the story before judging. All three principles centre around seeking additional information. This is difficult work, but the only alternative is prejudice—judging before getting the facts.

18:22 This verse states that it is good to be married. Today's emphasis on individual freedom is misguided. Strong individuals are important, but so are strong marriages. God created marriage for our enjoyment and he pronounced it good. This is one of many passages in the Bible that show marriage as a joyful and good creation of God (Genesis 2:21–25; Proverbs 5:15–19; John 2:1–11).

18:23 This verse does not condone insulting the poor; it is simply recording an unfortunate fact of life. It is wrong for rich people to treat the less fortunate with contempt and arrogance, and God will judge such actions severely (see 14:31).

18:24 Loneliness is everywhere—many people feel cut off and alienated from others. Being in a crowd just makes people more aware of their isolation. We all need friends who will stick close, listen, care, and offer help when it is needed—in good times and bad. It is better to have one such friend than dozens of superficial acquaintances. Instead of wishing you could find a true friend, seek to become one. There are people who need your friendship. Ask God to reveal them to you, and then take on the challenge of being a true friend.

19:1 A blameless life is far more valuable than wealth, but most people don't act as if they believe this. Afraid of not getting everything they want, they will pay any price to increase their wealth—cheating on their taxes, stealing from stores or employers, withholding tithes, refusing to give. But when we know and love God, we realise that a lower standard of living—or even poverty—is a small price to pay for personal integrity. Do your actions show that you sacrifice your integrity to increase your wealth? What changes do you need to make in order to get your priorities straight?

19:2 We often move hastily through life, rushing headlong into the unknown. Many people marry without knowing what to expect of their partner or of married life. Others try illicit sex or drugs without considering the consequences. Some plunge into jobs without evaluating whether they are suitable for that line of work. Don't rush into the unknown. Be sure you understand what you're getting into and where you want to go before you take the first step. And if it still seems unknown, be sure you are following God.

19:4
[c]Pr 14:20

19:5
[d]Ex 23:1
[e]Dt 19:19; Pr 21:28

19:6
[f]Pr 29:26
[g]Pr 17:8; 18:16

19:7
[h]ver 4; Ps 38:11

19:8
[i]Pr 16:20

19:9
[j]ver 5

19:10
[k]Pr 26:1
[l]Pr 30:21-23; Ecc 10:5-7

19:11
[m]Pr 16:32

19:12
[n]Ps 133:3
[o]Pr 16:14-15

19:13
[p]Pr 10:1
[q]Pr 21:9

19:14
[r]2Co 12:14
[s]Pr 18:22

19:15
[t]Pr 6:9; 10:4

3 A man's own folly ruins his life,
yet his heart rages against the LORD.

4 Wealth brings many friends,
but a poor man's friend deserts him.[c]

5 A false witness[d] will not go unpunished,
and he who pours out lies will not go free.[e]

6 Many curry favour with a ruler,[f]
and everyone is the friend of a man who gives gifts.[g]

7 A poor man is shunned by all his relatives—
how much more do his friends avoid him!
Though he pursues them with pleading,
they are nowhere to be found.[a][h]

8 He who gets wisdom loves his own soul;
he who cherishes understanding prospers.[i]

9 A false witness will not go unpunished,
and he who pours out lies will perish.[j]

10 It is not fitting for a fool[k] to live in luxury—
how much worse for a slave to rule over princes![l]

11 A man's wisdom gives him patience;[m]
it is to his glory to overlook an offence.

12 A king's rage is like the roar of a lion,
but his favour is like dew[n] on the grass.[o]

13 A foolish son is his father's ruin,[p]
and a quarrelsome wife is like a constant dripping.[q]

14 Houses and wealth are inherited from parents,[r]
but a prudent wife is from the LORD.[s]

15 Laziness brings on deep sleep,
and the shiftless man goes hungry.[t]

a 7 The meaning of the Hebrew for this sentence is uncertain.

HOW TO SUCCEED IN GOD'S EYES

Proverbs notes two significant by-products of wise living: success and good reputation. Several verses also point out what causes failure and poor reputation.

Qualities that promote success and a good reputation:	
Righteousness	10:7; 12:3; 28:12
Hating what is false	13:5
Committing all work to the Lord	16:3
Using words with restraint; being even-tempered	17:27, 28
Loving wisdom and understanding	19:8
Humility and fear of the Lord	22:4
Willingness to confess and renounce sin	28:13
Qualities that prevent success and cause a bad reputation:	
Wickedness	10:7; 12:3; 28:12
Seeking honour	25:27
Hatred	26:24–26
Praising oneself	27:2
Concealing sin	28:13

Other verses dealing with one's reputation are: 11:10, 16; 14:3; 19:10; 22:1; 23:17, 18; 24:13, 14

19:8 Is it good to love yourself? Yes, when your soul is at stake! This proverb does not condone the self-centred person who loves and protects his or her selfish interests and will do anything to serve them. Instead it encourages those who really care about themselves to seek wisdom.

16 He who obeys instructions guards his life,
but he who is contemptuous of his ways will die.[u]

17 He who is kind to the poor lends to the LORD,
and he will reward him for what he has done.[v]

18 Discipline your son, for in that there is hope;
do not be a willing party to his death.[w]

19 A hot-tempered man must pay the penalty;
if you rescue him, you will have to do it again.

20 Listen to advice and accept instruction,[x]
and in the end you will be wise.[y]

21 Many are the plans in a man's heart,
but it is the LORD's purpose that prevails.[z]

22 What a man desires is unfailing love;[b]
better to be poor than a liar.

23 The fear of the LORD leads to life:
Then one rests content, untouched by trouble.[a]

24 The sluggard buries his hand in the dish;
he will not even bring it back to his mouth![b]

25 Flog a mocker, and the simple will learn prudence;
rebuke a discerning man, and he will gain knowledge.[c]

26 He who robs his father and drives out his mother[d]
is a son who brings shame and disgrace.

27 Stop listening to instruction, my son,
and you will stray from the words of knowledge.

28 A corrupt witness mocks at justice,
and the mouth of the wicked gulps down evil.[e]

29 Penalties are prepared for mockers,
and beatings for the backs of fools.[f]

20 Wine is a mocker and beer a brawler;
whoever is led astray by them is not wise.[a]

2 A king's wrath is like the roar of a lion;[b]
he who angers him forfeits his life.[c]

3 It is to a man's honour to avoid strife,

19:16 [u]Pr 16:17; Lk 10:28
19:17 [v]Mt 10:42; 2Co 9:6-8
19:18 [w]Pr 13:24; 23:13-14
19:20 [x]Pr 4:1 [y]Pr 12:15
19:21 [z]Ps 33:11; Pr 16:9; Isa 14:24, 27
19:23 [a]Ps 25:13; Pr 12:21; 1Ti 4:8
19:24 [b]Pr 26:15
19:25 [c]Pr 9:9; 21:11
19:26 [d]Pr 28:24
19:28 [e]Job 15:16
19:29 [f]Pr 26:3
20:1 [a]Pr 31:4
20:2 [b]Pr 19:12 [c]Pr 8:36

b 22 *Or A man's greed is his shame*

19:16 The instructions we are told to obey are those found in God's word – both the Ten Commandments (Exodus 20) and other passages of instruction. To obey what God teaches in the Bible is self-preserving. To disobey is self-destructive.

19:17 Here God identifies with the poor as Jesus does in Matthew 25:31–46. As our Creator, God values all of us, whether we are poor or rich. When we help the poor, we honour both the Creator and his creation. God accepts our help as if we had offered it directly to him.

19:23 Those who fear the Lord are "untouched by trouble" because of their healthy habits, their beneficial life-style, and sometimes through God's direct intervention. Nevertheless, the fear of the Lord does not always protect us from trouble in this life: evil things still happen to people who love God. This verse is not a universal promise, but a general guideline. It describes what would happen if this world were sinless, and what will happen in the new earth, when faithful believers will be under God's protection for ever. (See the note on 3:16, 17 for more about this concept.)

19:24 "Buries his hand in the dish" refers to the custom of eating where a dish would be passed round and people would reach in and get food for themselves. This proverb is saying that some people are so lazy that they won't even feed themselves.

19:25 There is a great difference between the person who learns from criticism and the person who refuses to accept correction. How we respond to criticism determines whether or not we grow in wisdom. The next time someone criticises you, listen carefully to all that is said. You might learn something.

20:3 A person who is truly confident of his or her strength does not need to parade it. A truly brave person does not look for chances to prove it. A resourceful woman can find a way out of a fight. A man of endurance will avoid retaliating. Foolish people find it impossible to avoid strife. Men and women of character

20:3 [d]Pr 17:14

20:6 [e]Ps 12:1

20:7 [f]Ps 37:25-26; 112:2

20:8 [g]ver 26; Pr 25:4-5

20:9 [h]1Ki 8:46; Ecc 7:20; 1Jn 1:8

20:10 [i]ver 23; Pr 11:1

20:11 [j]Mt 7:16

but every fool is quick to quarrel.[d]

4 A sluggard does not plough in season;
so at harvest time he looks but finds nothing.

5 The purposes of a man's heart are deep waters,
but a man of understanding draws them out.

6 Many a man claims to have unfailing love,
but a faithful man who can find?[e]

7 The righteous man leads a blameless life;
blessed are his children after him.[f]

8 When a king sits on his throne to judge,
he winnows out all evil with his eyes.[g]

9 Who can say, "I have kept my heart pure;
I am clean and without sin"?[h]

10 Differing weights and differing measures—
the LORD detests them both.[i]

11 Even a child is known by his actions,
by whether his conduct is pure[j] and right.

12 Ears that hear and eyes that see—

HONESTY AND DISHONESTY
Proverbs tells us plainly that God despises all forms of dishonesty. Not only does God hate dishonesty, but we are told that it works against us—others no longer trust us, and we cannot even enjoy our dishonest gains. It is wiser to be honest because "a righteous man escapes trouble" (12:13).

Others' opinion	
Leaders value those who speak the truth.	16:13
Most people will appreciate truth more than flattery in the end.	28:23
Quality of life	
The righteous person's plans are just.	12:5
Truthful witnesses do not deceive; false witnesses pour out lies.	14:5
Truthful witnesses save lives.	14:25
The children of the righteous are blessed.	20:7
Short-term results	
Ill-gotten treasure is of no value.	10:2
The righteous are rescued from trouble.	11:8
The evil are trapped by sinful talk.	12:13
Fraudulent gain is sweet for a while.	20:17
Long-term results	
The upright are guided by integrity.	11:3
Truthful lips endure.	12:19
Riches gained quickly don't last.	20:21
Riches gained dishonestly don't last.	21:6
The blameless are kept safe.	28:18
God's opinion	
God delights in honesty.	11:1
God delights in those who are truthful.	12:22
God detests unjust measures.	20:10
God is pleased when we do what is right and just.	21:3

can. What kind of person are you?

20:4 You've heard similar warnings: if you don't study, you'll fail the exam; if you don't save, you won't have money when you need it. God wants us to anticipate future needs and prepare for them. We can't expect him to come to our rescue when we cause our own problems through lack of planning and action. He provides for us, but he also expects us to be responsible.

20:9 No-one is without sin. As soon as we confess our sin and repent, sinful thoughts and actions begin to creep back into our lives. We all need ongoing cleansing, moment by moment. Thank God he provides forgiveness by his mercy when we ask for it. Make confession and repentance a regular part of your talks with God. Rely on him moment by moment for the cleansing you need.

the LORD has made them both.[k]

13 Do not love sleep or you will grow poor;[l]
stay awake and you will have food to spare.

14 "It's no good, it's no good!" says the buyer;
then off he goes and boasts about his purchase.

15 Gold there is, and rubies in abundance,
but lips that speak knowledge are a rare jewel.

16 Take the garment of one who puts up security for a stranger;
hold it in pledge[m] if he does it for a wayward woman.[n]

17 Food gained by fraud tastes sweet to a man,[o]
but he ends up with a mouth full of gravel.

18 Make plans by seeking advice;
if you wage war, obtain guidance.[p]

19 A gossip betrays a confidence;[q]
so avoid a man who talks too much.

20 If a man curses his father or mother,[r]
his lamp will be snuffed out in pitch darkness.[s]

21 An inheritance quickly gained at the beginning
will not be blessed at the end.

22 Do not say, "I'll pay you back for this wrong!"[t]
Wait for the LORD, and he will deliver you.[u]

23 The LORD detests differing weights,
and dishonest scales do not please him.[v]

24 A man's steps are directed by the LORD.
How then can anyone understand his own way?[w]

25 It is a trap for a man to dedicate something rashly
and only later to consider his vows.[x]

26 A wise king winnows out the wicked;
he drives the threshing wheel over them.[y]

27 The lamp of the LORD searches the spirit of a man;[a]
it searches out his inmost being.

28 Love and faithfulness keep a king safe;
through love his throne is made secure.[z]

[a] 27 Or *The spirit of man is the LORD's lamp*

20:12 [k]Ps 94:9
20:13 [l]Pr 6:11; 19:15
20:16 [m]Ex 22:26 [n]Pr 27:13
20:17 [o]Pr 9:17
20:18 [p]Pr 11:14; 24:6
20:19 [q]Pr 11:13
20:20 [r]Pr 30:11 [s]Ex 21:17; Job 18:5
20:22 [t]Pr 24:29 [u]Ro 12:19
20:23 [v]ver 10
20:24 [w]Jer 10:23
20:25 [x]Ecc 5:2, 4-5
20:26 [y]ver 8
20:28 [z]Pr 29:14

20:23 "Differing weights" refers to the loaded scales a merchant might use in order to cheat the customers. Dishonesty is a difficult sin to avoid. It is easy to cheat if we think no-one else is looking. But dishonesty affects the very core of a person. It makes him untrustworthy and untrusting. It eventually makes him unable to know himself or relate to others. Don't take dishonesty lightly. Even the smallest portion of dishonesty contains enough of the poison of deceit to kill your spiritual life. If there is any dishonesty in your life, tell God about it now.

20:24 We are often confused by the events around us. Many things we will never understand; others will fall into place in years to come as we look back and see how God was working. This proverb counsels us not to worry if we don't understand everything as it happens. Instead, we should trust that God knows what he's doing, even if his timing or design is not clear to us. See Psalm 37:23 for a reassuring promise of God's direction in your life.

20:25 To dedicate something meant that you intended to give it as an offering to God. *Dedicated* means set apart for religious use. This proverb points out the evil of making a vow rashly and then reconsidering it. God takes vows seriously and requires that they be carried out (Deuteronomy 23:21–23). We often have good intentions when making a vow because we want to show God that we are determined to please him. Jesus, however, says it is better not to make promises to God because he knows how difficult they are to keep (Matthew 5:33–37). If you still feel it is important to make a vow, make sure that you weigh the consequences of breaking that vow. (In Judges 11, Jephthah made a rash promise to sacrifice the first thing he saw on his return home. As it happened, he saw his daughter first.) It is better not to make promises than to make them and then later want to change them. It is better still to count the cost beforehand and then to fulfil them. (For a list of other Bible people who made rash vows, see the chart in Judges 11.)

20:29
[a]Pr 16:31

20:30
[b]Pr 22:15

21:2
[a]Pr 16:2; 24:12; Lk 16:15

21:3
[b]1Sa 15:22; Pr 15:8; Isa 1:11; Hos 6:6; Mic 6:6-8

21:4
[c]Pr 6:17

21:5
[d]Pr 10:4; 28:22

21:6
[e]2Pe 2:3

21:8
[f]Pr 2:15

21:9
[g]Pr 25:24

21:11
[h]Pr 19:25

21:12
[i]Pr 14:11

21:13
[j]Mt 18:30-34; Jas 2:13

21:14
[k]Pr 18:16; 19:6

29 The glory of young men is their strength,
grey hair the splendour of the old.[a]

30 Blows and wounds cleanse[b] away evil,
and beatings purge the inmost being.

21

The king's heart is in the hand of the LORD;
he directs it like a watercourse wherever he pleases.

2 All a man's ways seem right to him,
but the LORD weighs the heart.[a]

3 To do what is right and just
is more acceptable to the LORD than sacrifice.[b]

4 Haughty eyes[c] and a proud heart,
the lamp of the wicked, are sin!

5 The plans of the diligent lead to profit[d]
as surely as haste leads to poverty.

6 A fortune made by a lying tongue
is a fleeting vapour and a deadly snare.[a][e]

7 The violence of the wicked will drag them away,
for they refuse to do what is right.

8 The way of the guilty is devious,[f]
but the conduct of the innocent is upright.

9 Better to live on a corner of the roof
than share a house with a quarrelsome wife.[g]

10 The wicked man craves evil;
his neighbour gets no mercy from him.

11 When a mocker is punished, the simple gain wisdom;
when a wise man is instructed, he gets knowledge.[h]

12 The Righteous One[b] takes note of the house of the wicked
and brings the wicked to ruin.[i]

13 If a man shuts his ears to the cry of the poor,
he too will cry out and not be answered.[j]

14 A gift given in secret soothes anger,
and a bribe concealed in the cloak pacifies great wrath.[k]

15 When justice is done, it brings joy to the righteous

[a] *6* Some Hebrew manuscripts, Septuagint and Vulgate; most Hebrew manuscripts *vapour for those who seek death* [b] *12* Or *The righteous man*

21:1 In Solomon's day, kings possessed absolute authority and were often considered to be like gods. This proverb shows that God, not earthly rulers, has ultimate authority over world politics. Although they may not have realised it, the earth's most powerful kings have always been under God's control. (See Isaiah 10:5–8 for an example of a king who was used for God's purposes.)

21:2 People can find an excuse for doing almost anything, but God looks behind the excuses to the motives of the heart. We often have to make choices in areas where the right action is difficult to discern. We can help ourselves make such decisions by trying to identify our motives first and then asking, "Would God be pleased with my real reasons for doing this?" God is not pleased when we do good deeds only to receive something in return.

21:3 Sacrifices and offerings are not bribes to make God overlook our character faults. If our personal and business dealings are not characterised by justice, no amount of generosity when the offering plate is passed will make up for it.

21:5 Faithful completion of mundane tasks is a great accomplishment. Such work is patiently carried out according to a plan. Diligence does not come naturally to most people; it is a result of strong character. Don't look for quick and easy answers. Be a diligent servant of God.

21:11, 12 It is usually better to learn from the mistakes of others than from our own. We can do this by listening to their advice. Take counsel from others instead of plunging ahead and learning the hard way.

21:13 We should work to meet the needs of the poor and protect their rights – we may be in need of such services ourselves someday.

but terror to evildoers.[l]

16 A man who strays from the path of understanding
comes to rest in the company of the dead.[m]

17 He who loves pleasure will become poor;
whoever loves wine and oil will never be rich.[n]

18 The wicked become a ransom[o] for the righteous,
and the unfaithful for the upright.

19 Better to live in a desert
than with a quarrelsome and ill-tempered wife.[p]

20 In the house of the wise are stores of choice food and oil,
but a foolish man devours all he has.

21 He who pursues righteousness and love
finds life, prosperity[c] and honour.[q]

22 A wise man attacks the city of the mighty[r]

c 21 Or *righteousness*

21:15 [l]Pr 10:29
21:16 [m]Ps 49:14
21:17 [n]Pr 23:20-21, 29-35
21:18 [o]Pr 11:8; Isa 43:3
21:19 [p]ver 9
21:21 [q]Mt 5:6
21:22 [r]Ecc 9:15-16

RIGHTEOUSNESS

Proverbs often compares the life-styles of the wicked and the righteous, and makes a strong case for living by God's pattern. The advantages of righteous living and the disadvantages of wicked living are pointed out. The kind of person we decide to be will affect every area of our lives.

	Righteous	*Wicked*	*References*
Outlook on life	Hopeful	Fearful	10:24
	Concerned about the welfare of God's creation	Even their kindness is cruel	12:10
	Understand justice	Don't understand justice	28:5
Response to life	Covered with blessings	Covered with violence	10:6
		Bent on evil	16:30
	Give thought to their ways	Put up a bold front	21:29
	Persevere against evil	Brought down by calamity	24:15, 16
		Hate those with integrity	29:10
How they are seen by others	Are appreciated	Do not endure	13:15
		Lead others into sin	16:29
	Conduct is upright	Conduct is devious	21:8
	Are not to desire the company of godless people	Plot violence	24:1, 2
	Others are glad when they triumph	Others hide when they rise to power	28:12
	Care for the poor	Unconcerned about the poor	29:7
	Detest the dishonest	Detest the upright	29:27
Quality of life	Stand firm	Swept away	10:25
	Delivered by righteousness	Trapped by evil desires	11:6

21:20 This proverb is about saving for the future. Easy credit has many people living on the edge of bankruptcy. The desire to keep up and to accumulate more pushes them to spend every penny they earn, and they stretch their credit to the limit. But anyone who spends all he has is spending more than he can afford. A wise person puts money aside for when he or she may have less. God approves of foresight and restraint. God's people need to examine their life-styles to see whether their spending is God-pleasing or merely self-pleasing.

21:23
[s]Jas 3:2
[t]Pr 12:13; 13:3

21:24
[u]Ps 1:1; Pr 1:22; Isa 16:6; Jer 48:29

21:25
[v]Pr 13:4

21:26
[w]Ps 37:26; Mt 5:42; Eph 4:28

21:27
[x]Isa 66:3; Jer 6:20; Am 5:22
[y]Pr 15:8

21:28
[z]Pr 19:5

and pulls down the stronghold in which they trust.

23 He who guards his mouth[s] and his tongue
keeps himself from calamity.[t]

24 The proud and arrogant[u] man—"Mocker" is his name;
he behaves with overweening pride.

25 The sluggard's craving will be the death of him,[v]
because his hands refuse to work.
26 All day long he craves for more,
but the righteous give without sparing.[w]

27 The sacrifice of the wicked is detestable[x]—
how much more so when brought with evil intent![y]

28 A false witness will perish,[z]
and whoever listens to him will be destroyed for ever.[d]

29 A wicked man puts up a bold front,

[d] 28 *Or / but the words of an obedient man will live on*

AND WICKEDNESS

	Righteous	*Wicked*	*References*
Quality of life (cont.)	No real harm befalls them	Constant trouble befalls them	12:21
	Income results in treasure	Income results in trouble	15:6
	Avoid evil		16:17
		Fall into constant trouble	17:20
	Are bold as lions	Are fearful constantly	28:1
	Will be safe	Will suddenly fall	28:18
Short-term results	Walk securely	Will be found out	10:9
	Rewarded with prosperity	Pursued by misfortune	13:21
Long-term results	God protects them	God destroys them	10:29
		Will be punished for rebellion	17:11
Eternal expectations	Never uprooted	Will not remain	10:30
	Earn a sure reward	Earn deceptive wages	11:18
	Attain life	Go to death	11:19
	End only in good	End only in wrath	11:23
	Will stand firm	Will be overthrown	12:7
	Have a refuge when they die	Will be brought down by calamity	14:32
God's opinion of them	Delights in the good	Detests the perverse	11:20
	Evil people will bow to them	They will bow to the righteous	14:19

21:27 The kind of worship ("sacrifice") described in this proverb is no better than a bribe. How do people try to bribe God? They may go to church, tithe, or volunteer, not because of their love and devotion to God, but because they hope God will bless them in return. But God has made it very clear that he desires obedience and love more than religious ritual (see 21:3; 1 Samuel 15:22). God does not want our sacrifices of time, energy, and money alone; he wants our hearts—our complete love and devotion. We may be able to bribe people (21:14), but we cannot bribe God.

but an upright man gives thought to his ways.

30 There is no wisdom,[a] no insight, no plan
that can succeed against the LORD.[b]

31 The horse is made ready for the day of battle,
but victory rests with the LORD.[c]

22

A good name is more desirable than great riches;
to be esteemed is better than silver or gold.[a]

2 Rich and poor have this in common:
The LORD is the Maker of them all.[b]

3 A prudent man sees danger and takes refuge,[c]
but the simple keep going and suffer for it.[d]

4 Humility and the fear of the LORD
bring wealth and honour and life.

5 In the paths of the wicked lie thorns and snares,[e]
but he who guards his soul stays far from them.

6 Train[a] a child in the way he should go,[f]
and when he is old he will not turn from it.

7 The rich rule over the poor,
and the borrower is servant to the lender.

8 He who sows wickedness reaps trouble,[g]
and the rod of his fury will be destroyed.[h]

9 A generous man will himself be blessed,[i]
for he shares his food with the poor.[j]

10 Drive out the mocker, and out goes strife;
quarrels and insults are ended.[k]

11 He who loves a pure heart and whose speech is gracious
will have the king for his friend.[l]

12 The eyes of the LORD keep watch over knowledge,
but he frustrates the words of the unfaithful.

a 6 Or *Start*

21:30 [a] Jer 9:23 [b] Isa 8:10; Ac 5:39

21:31 [c] Ps 3:8; 33:12-19; Isa 31:1

22:1 [a] Ecc 7:1

22:2 [b] Job 31:15

22:3 [c] Pr 14:16 [d] Pr 27:12

22:5 [e] Pr 15:19

22:6 [f] Eph 6:4

22:8 [g] Job 4:8 [h] Ps 125:3

22:9 [i] 2Co 9:6 [j] Pr 19:17

22:10 [k] Pr 18:6; 26:20

22:11 [l] Pr 16:13; Mt 5:8

21:31 This proverb refers to preparing for battle. All our preparation for any task is useless without God. But even with God's help we must still do our part and prepare. His control of the outcome does not negate our responsibilities. God may want you to produce a great book, but you must learn to write. God may want to use you in foreign missions, but you must learn the language. God will accomplish his purposes, and he will be able to use you if you have done your part by being well prepared.

22:4 This is a general observation that would have been especially applicable to an obedient Israelite living in Solomon's God-fearing kingdom. Nevertheless, some have been martyrs at a young age, and some have given away all their wealth for the sake of God's kingdom. The book of Proverbs describes life the way it should be. It does not dwell on the exceptions. (For more on this concept, see the note on 3:16, 17.)

22:6 "In the way he should go" is literally, "according to his [the child's] way". It is natural to want to bring up all our children alike or train them the same way. This verse implies that parents should discern the individuality and special strengths that God has given each one. While we should not condone or excuse self-will, each child has natural inclinations that parents can develop. By talking to teachers, other parents, and grandparents, we can better discern and develop the individual capabilities of each child.

22:6 Many parents want to make all the choices for their child, but this hurts him or her in the long run. When parents teach a child how to make decisions, they don't have to watch every step he or she takes. They know their children will remain on the right path because they have made the choice themselves. Train your children to choose the right way.

22:7 Does this mean we should never borrow? No, but it warns us never to take on a loan without carefully examining our ability to repay it. A loan we can handle is enabling; a loan we can't handle is enslaving. The borrower must realise that until the loan is repaid, he is a servant to the individual or institution that made it.

22:12 "Knowledge" refers to those who have knowledge, those who live right and speak the truth. It takes discipline, determination, and hard work to live God's way, but God protects and rewards those who make the commitment to follow him. The unfaithful may seem to have an easier time of it, but in the long run their plans fail and their lives amount to nothing. Don't resist God and expect lasting success.

22:13 [m]Pr 26:13
22:14 [n]Pr 2:16; 5:3-5; 7:5; 23:27 [o]Ecc 7:26
22:15 [p]Pr 13:24; 23:14
22:17 [q]Pr 5:1
22:21 [r]Lk 1:3-4; 1Pe 3:15
22:22 [s]Zec 7:10 [t]Ex 23:6; Mal 3:5
22:23 [u]Ps 12:5 [v]1Sa 25:39; Pr 23:10-11
22:25 [w]1Co 15:33
22:26 [x]Pr 11:15
22:27 [y]Pr 17:18
22:28 [z]Dt 19:14; Pr 23:10

13The sluggard says, "There is a lion outside!"[m]
or, "I will be murdered in the streets!"

14The mouth of an adulteress is a deep pit;[n]
he who is under the LORD's wrath will fall into it.[o]

15Folly is bound up in the heart of a child,
but the rod of discipline will drive it far from him.[p]

16He who oppresses the poor to increase his wealth
and he who gives gifts to the rich — both come to poverty.

Sayings of the Wise

17Pay attention and listen to the sayings of the wise;[q]
apply your heart to what I teach,
18for it is pleasing when you keep them in your heart
and have all of them ready on your lips.
19So that your trust may be in the LORD,
I teach you today, even you.
20Have I not written thirty[b] sayings for you,
sayings of counsel and knowledge,
21teaching you true and reliable words,[r]
so that you can give sound answers
to him who sent you?

22Do not exploit the poor[s] because they are poor
and do not crush the needy in court,[t]
23for the LORD will take up their case[u]
and will plunder those who plunder them.[v]

24Do not make friends with a hot-tempered man,
do not associate with one easily angered,
25or you may learn his ways
and get yourself ensnared.[w]

26Do not be a man who strikes hands in pledge[x]
or puts up security for debts;
27if you lack the means to pay,
your very bed will be snatched from under you.[y]

28Do not move an ancient boundary stone[z]
set up by your forefathers.

b 20 Or *not formerly written*; or *not written excellent*

22:13 This proverb refers to an excuse a lazy person might use to avoid going to work. The excuse sounds silly to us, but that's often how our excuses sound to others. Don't rationalise laziness. Take your responsibilities seriously and get to work.

22:15 Young children often do foolish and dangerous things simply because they don't understand the consequences. Wisdom and common sense are not transferred by just being a good example. The wisdom a child learns must be taught consciously. "The rod of discipline" stands for all forms of discipline or training. Just as God trains and corrects us to make us better, so parents must discipline their children to make them learn the difference between right and wrong. To see how God corrects us, read 3:11, 12.

22:22, 23 This proverb is a message of hope to people who must live and work under unjust authoritarian leaders. It is also a warning to those who enjoy ruling with an iron hand. Sometimes God intervenes and directly destroys tyrants. More often, he uses other rulers to overthrow them or their own oppressed people to rebel against them. If you are in a position of authority at church, work, or home, remember what happens to tyrants. Leadership through kindness is more effective and longer lasting than leadership by force.

22:24, 25 People tend to become like those with whom they spend a lot of time. Even the negative characteristics sometimes rub off. The Bible exhorts us to be cautious in our choice of companions. Choose people with characteristics you would like to develop in your own life.

22:26 This verse is saying that it is wise to be slow in accepting liability for another person's debt.

22:28 In Joshua 13 – 21, the land was divided and the boundaries marked out for each tribe. Moses had already warned the people that when they reached the promised land they shouldn't cheat their neighbours by moving one of the landmarks to give themselves more land and their neighbours less (Deuteronomy 19:14; 27:17). "Gerrymandering" — changing political boundaries so that one group of voters benefits and another loses — is a modern form of moving boundary markers.

29 Do you see a man skilled in his work?
He will serve[a] before kings;
he will not serve before obscure men.

22:29
[a]Ge 41:46

23

When you sit to dine with a ruler,
note well what[a] is before you,
2 and put a knife to your throat
if you are given to gluttony.
3 Do not crave his delicacies,[a]
for that food is deceptive.

4 Do not wear yourself out to get rich;
have the wisdom to show restraint.
5 Cast but a glance at riches, and they are gone,
for they will surely sprout wings
and fly off to the sky like an eagle.[b]

6 Do not eat the food of a stingy man,
do not crave his delicacies;[c]
7 for he is the kind of man
who is always thinking about the cost.[b]
"Eat and drink," he says to you,
but his heart is not with you.
8 You will vomit up the little you have eaten
and will have wasted your compliments.

9 Do not speak to a fool,
for he will scorn the wisdom of your words.[d]

10 Do not move an ancient boundary stone[e]
or encroach on the fields of the fatherless,
11 for their Defender[f] is strong;
he will take up their case against you.[g]

12 Apply your heart to instruction
and your ears to words of knowledge.

13 Do not withhold discipline from a child;
if you punish him with the rod, he will not die.
14 Punish him with the rod
and save his soul from death.[c]

15 My son, if your heart is wise,
then my heart will be glad;

a *1* Or *who* **b** *7* Or *for as he thinks within himself, / so he is*; or *for as he puts on a feast, / so he is*
c *14* Hebrew *Sheol*

23:3
[a]ver 6-8

23:5
[b]Pr 27:24

23:6
[c]Ps 141:4

23:9
[d]Pr 1:7; 9:7; Mt 7:6

23:10
[e]Dt 19:14; Pr 22:28

23:11
[f]Job 19:25
[g]Pr 22:22-23

23:1–3 The point of this proverb is to be careful when eating with an important or influential person because he or she may try to bribe you. No good will come from the meal.

23:4, 5 We have all heard of people who have won millions of pounds and then lost it all. Even the average person can spend an inheritance – or a pay cheque – with lightning speed and have little to show for it. Don't spend your time chasing fleeting earthly treasures. Instead store up treasures in heaven, for such treasures will never be lost. (See Luke 12:33, 34 for Jesus' teaching.)

23:6–8 In graphic language, the writer warns us not to envy the life-styles of those who have become rich by being stingy and miserly, and not to gain their favour by fawning over them. Their "friendship" is false – they will just use you for their own gain.

23:10, 11 The term *Defender* or *redeemer* refers to someone who bought back a family member who had fallen into slavery or who accepted the obligation to marry the widow of a family member (Ruth 4:3–10). God is also called a Redeemer (Exodus 6:6; Job 19:25). (For an explanation of ancient boundary stones, see the note on 22:28.)

23:12 The people most likely to gain knowledge are those who are willing to listen. It is a sign of strength, not weakness, to pay attention to what others have to say. People who are eager to listen continue to learn and grow throughout their lives. If we refuse to become set in our ways, we can always expand the limits of our knowledge.

23:13, 14 The stern tone of discipline here is offset by the affection expressed in verse 15. However, many parents are reluctant to discipline their children at all. Some fear they will forfeit their relationship, that their children will resent them, or that they will stifle their children's development. But correction won't kill children, and it may prevent them from foolish moves that will.

16my inmost being will rejoice
when your lips speak what is right.[h]

17Do not let your heart envy[i] sinners,
but always be zealous for the fear of the LORD.
18There is surely a future hope for you,
and your hope will not be cut off.[j]

19Listen, my son, and be wise,
and keep your heart on the right path.
20Do not join those who drink too much wine[k]
or gorge themselves on meat,
21for drunkards and gluttons become poor,[l]
and drowsiness clothes them in rags.

22Listen to your father, who gave you life,
and do not despise your mother when she is old.[m]
23Buy the truth and do not sell it;
get wisdom, discipline and understanding.[n]
24The father of a righteous man has great joy;
he who has a wise son delights in him.[o]
25May your father and mother be glad;
may she who gave you birth rejoice!

26My son,[p] give me your heart
and let your eyes keep to my ways,[q]
27for a prostitute is a deep pit[r]
and a wayward wife is a narrow well.
28Like a bandit she lies in wait,[s]
and multiplies the unfaithful among men.

29Who has woe? Who has sorrow?
Who has strife? Who has complaints?
Who has needless bruises? Who has bloodshot eyes?
30Those who linger over wine,[t]
who go to sample bowls of mixed wine.
31Do not gaze at wine when it is red,
when it sparkles in the cup,
when it goes down smoothly!
32In the end it bites like a snake
and poisons like a viper.
33Your eyes will see strange sights
and your mind imagine confusing things.
34You will be like one sleeping on the high seas,
lying on top of the rigging.
35"They hit me," you will say, "but I'm not hurt!
They beat me, but I don't feel it!
When will I wake up
so I can find another drink?"

23:16 [h]ver 24; Pr 27:11
23:17 [i]Ps 37:1; Pr 28:14
23:18 [j]Ps 9:18; Pr 24:14, 19-20
23:20 [k]Isa 5:11, 22; Ro 13:13; Eph 5:18
23:21 [l]Pr 21:17
23:22 [m]Lev 19:32; Pr 1:8; 30:17; Eph 6:1-2
23:23 [n]Pr 4:7
23:24 [o]ver 15-16; Pr 10:1; 15:20
23:26 [p]Pr 3:1; 5:1-6 [q]Ps 18:21; Pr 4:4
23:27 [r]Pr 22:14
23:28 [s]Pr 7:11-12; Ecc 7:26
23:30 [t]Ps 75:8; Isa 5:11; Eph 5:18

23:17, 18 How easy it is to envy those who succeed unhampered by Christian responsibility or God's laws. For a time they do seem to get on without paying any attention to what God wants. But to those who follow him, God promises a hope and a wonderful future even if we don't realise it in this life.

23:29, 30 The soothing comfort of alcohol is only temporary. Real relief comes from dealing with the cause of the anguish and sorrow and turning to God for peace. Don't lose yourself in alcohol; find yourself in God.

23:29–35 Israel was a wine-producing country. In the Old Testament, winepresses bursting with new wine were considered a sign of blessing (3:10). Wisdom is even said to have set her table with wine (9:2, 5). But the Old Testament writers were alert to the dangers of wine. It dulls the senses; it limits clear judgment (31:1–9); it lowers the capacity for control (4:17); it destroys a person's efficiency (21:17). To make wine an end in itself, a means of self-indulgence, or as an escape from life is to misuse it and invite the consequences of the drunkard.

24

Do not envy[a] wicked men,
do not desire their company;
2for their hearts plot violence,
and their lips talk about making trouble.[b]

3By wisdom a house is built,[c]
and through understanding it is established;
4through knowledge its rooms are filled
with rare and beautiful treasures.[d]

5A wise man has great power,
and a man of knowledge increases strength;
6for waging war you need guidance,
and for victory many advisers.[e]

7Wisdom is too high for a fool;
in the assembly at the gate he has nothing to say.

8He who plots evil
will be known as a schemer.
9The schemes of folly are sin,
and men detest a mocker.

10If you falter in times of trouble,
how small is your strength![f]

11Rescue those being led away to death;
hold back those staggering towards slaughter.[g]
12If you say, "But we knew nothing about this,"
does not he who weighs[h] the heart perceive it?
Does not he who guards your life know it?
Will he not repay each person according to what he has done?[i]

13Eat honey, my son, for it is good;
honey from the comb is sweet to your taste.
14Know also that wisdom is sweet to your soul;
if you find it, there is a future hope for you,
and your hope will not be cut off.[jk]

15Do not lie in wait like an outlaw against a righteous man's house,
do not raid his dwelling-place;
16for though a righteous man falls seven times, he rises again,
but the wicked are brought down by calamity.[l]

24:1 [a]Ps 37:1; 73:3; Pr 3:31-32; 23:17-18
24:2 [b]Ps 10:7
24:3 [c]Pr 14:1
24:4 [d]Pr 8:21
24:6 [e]Pr 11:14; 20:18; Lk 14:31
24:10 [f]Job 4:5; Jer 51:46; Heb 12:3
24:11 [g]Ps 82:4; Isa 58:6-7
24:12 [h]Pr 21:2 [i]Job 34:11; Ps 62:12; Ro 2:6*
24:14 [j]Ps 119:103; Pr 16:24 [k]Pr 23:18
24:16 [l]Job 5:19; Ps 34:19; Mic 7:8

24:5 The athlete who thinks – who assesses the situation and plans strategies – has an advantage over a physically stronger but unthinking opponent. And wisdom, not muscle, is certainly why God has put people in charge of the animal kingdom. We exercise regularly and eat well to build our strength, but do we take equal pains to develop wisdom? Because wisdom is a vital part of strength, it pays to attain it.

24:6 In any major decision we make concerning college, marriage, career, children, etc., it is not a sign of weakness to ask for advice. Instead, it is foolish not to ask for it. Find good advisers before making any big decision. They can help you expand your alternatives and evaluate your choices.

24:8 Plotting to do evil can be as wrong as doing it because what you think determines what you will do. Left unchecked, wrong desires will lead us to sin. God wants pure lives, free from sin, and planning evil spoils the purity even if the evil action has not yet been committed. Should you say, "Then I might as well go ahead and do it because I've already planned it"? No. You have sinned in your attitude, but you have not yet harmed other people. Stop in your tracks and ask God to forgive you and put you on a different path.

24:10 Times of trouble can be useful. They can show you who you really are, what kind of character you have developed. In addition, they can help you grow stronger. When Jeremiah questioned God because of the trouble he faced, God asked how he ever expected to face big challenges if the little ones tired him out (Jeremiah 12:5). Don't complain about your problems. The trouble you face today is training you to be strong for the more difficult situations you will face in the future.

24:17, 18 David, Solomon's father, refused to gloat over the death of his lifelong enemy Saul (see 2 Samuel 1). On the other hand, the nation of Edom rejoiced over Israel's defeat and was

24:17 [m]Ob 1:12 [n]Job 31:29
24:19 [o]Ps 37:1
24:20 [p]Job 18:5; Pr 13:9; 23:17-18
24:21 [q]Ro 13:1-5; 1Pe 2:17
24:23 [r]Pr 1:6 [s]Lev 19:15 [t]Pr 28:21
24:24 [u]Pr 17:15
24:28 [v]Ps 7:4; Pr 25:18; Eph 4:25
24:29 [w]Pr 20:22; Mt 5:38-41; Ro 12:17
24:30 [x]Pr 6:6-11; 26:13-16
24:33 [y]Pr 6:10
24:34 [z]Pr 10:4; Ecc 10:18

17 Do not gloat[m] when your enemy falls;
when he stumbles, do not let your heart rejoice,[n]
18 or the LORD will see and disapprove
and turn his wrath away from him.

19 Do not fret[o] because of evil men
or be envious of the wicked,
20 for the evil man has no future hope,
and the lamp of the wicked will be snuffed out.[p]

21 Fear the LORD and the king,[q] my son,
and do not join with the rebellious,
22 for those two will send sudden destruction upon them,
and who knows what calamities they can bring?

Further Sayings of the Wise

23 These also are sayings of the wise:[r]

To show partiality[s] in judging is not good:[t]
24 Whoever says to the guilty, "You are innocent"[u]—
peoples will curse him and nations denounce him.
25 But it will go well with those who convict the guilty,
and rich blessing will come upon them.

26 An honest answer
is like a kiss on the lips.

27 Finish your outdoor work
and get your fields ready;
after that, build your house.

28 Do not testify against your neighbour without cause,[v]
or use your lips to deceive.
29 Do not say, "I'll do to him as he has done to me;
I'll pay that man back for what he did."[w]

30 I went past the field of the sluggard,[x]
past the vineyard of the man who lacks judgment;
31 thorns had come up everywhere,
the ground was covered with weeds,
and the stone wall was in ruins.
32 I applied my heart to what I observed
and learned a lesson from what I saw:
33 A little sleep, a little slumber,
a little folding of the hands to rest[y]—
34 and poverty will come on you like a bandit
and scarcity like an armed man.[a][z]

[a] 34 Or *like a vagrant / and scarcity like a beggar*

punished by God for their attitude (Obadiah 1:12). To gloat over others' misfortune is to make yourself the avenger and to put yourself in the place of God, who alone is the real judge of all the earth (see Deuteronomy 32:35).

24:26 A kiss on the lips was a sign of true friendship. People often think that they should bend the truth to avoid hurting a friend. But one who gives an honest, straightforward answer is a true friend.

24:27 We should carry out our work in its proper order. If a farmer builds his house in the spring, he will miss the planting season and go a year without food. If a businessman invests his money in a house while his business is struggling to grow, he may lose both. It is possible to work hard and still lose everything if the timing is wrong or the resources to carry it out are not in place.

24:29 Here is a reverse version of the Golden Rule (see Luke 6:31). Revenge is the way the world operates, but it is not God's way.

C. WISDOM FOR THE LEADERS (25:1 – 31:31)

These proverbs were collected by Hezekiah's aides. The first section was written by Solomon, and the next two sections were written by others. While we can all learn from these proverbs, many were originally directed towards the king or those who dealt with the king. These are particularly helpful for those who are leaders or aspire to become leaders. The book ends with a description of a truly good wife, who is an example of godly wisdom.

More Proverbs of Solomon

25 These are more proverbs[a] of Solomon, copied by the men of Hezekiah king
of Judah:[b]

2 It is the glory of God to conceal a matter;
to search out a matter is the glory of kings.[c]
3 As the heavens are high and the earth is deep,
so the hearts of kings are unsearchable.

4 Remove the dross from the silver,
and out comes material for**a** the silversmith;
5 remove the wicked from the king's presence,[d]
and his throne will be established[e] through righteousness.[f]

6 Do not exalt yourself in the king's presence,
and do not claim a place among great men;
7 it is better for him to say to you, "Come up here,"[g]
than for him to humiliate you before a nobleman.

What you have seen with your eyes
8 do not bring**b** hastily to court,
for what will you do in the end
if your neighbour puts you to shame?[h]

9 If you argue your case with a neighbour,
do not betray another man's confidence,
10 or he who hears it may shame you
and you will never lose your bad reputation.

11 A word aptly spoken
is like apples of gold in settings of silver.[i]

12 Like an ear-ring of gold or an ornament of fine gold
is a wise man's rebuke to a listening ear.[j]

13 Like the coolness of snow at harvest time
is a trustworthy messenger to those who send him;
he refreshes the spirit of his masters.[k]

14 Like clouds and wind without rain

a *4* Or *comes a vessel from* **b** *7, 8* Or *nobleman / on whom you had set your eyes. / 8Do not go*

25:1 [a]1Ki 4:32 [b]Pr 1:1
25:2 [c]Pr 16:10-15
25:5 [d]Pr 20:8 [e]2Sa 7:13 [f]Pr 16:12; 29:14
25:7 [g]Lk 14:7-10
25:8 [h]Mt 5:25-26
25:11 [i]ver 12; Pr 15:23
25:12 [j]ver 11; Ps 141:5; Pr 13:18; 15:31
25:13 [k]Pr 10:26; 13:17

25:1 Hezekiah's story is told in 2 Kings 18 – 20; 2 Chronicles 29 – 32; and Isaiah 36 – 39. He was one of the few kings of Judah who honoured the Lord. By contrast, his father Ahaz actually nailed the temple door shut. Hezekiah restored the temple, destroyed idol worship centres, and earned the respect of surrounding nations, many of whom brought gifts to God because of him. It is not surprising that Hezekiah had these proverbs copied and read, for "in everything that he undertook in the service of God's temple and in obedience to the law and the commands, he sought his God and worked wholeheartedly. And so he prospered" (2 Chronicles 31:21).

25:6, 7 Jesus made this proverb into a parable (see Luke 14:7–11). We should not seek honour for ourselves. It is better to quietly and faithfully accomplish the work God has given us to do. As others notice the quality of our lives then they will draw attention to us.

25:13 It is often difficult to find people you can really trust. A faithful employee ("messenger") is punctual, responsible, honest, and hardworking. This person is invaluable as he or she helps take some of the pressure off his or her employer. Find out what your employer needs from you to make his or her job easier, and do it.

25:14 Most churches, missions organisations, and Christian groups depend on the gifts of people to keep their ministries going. But many who promise to give fail to do so. The Bible is very clear about the effect this has on those involved in the ministry. If you make a pledge, keep your promise.

25:15
[l]Ecc 10:4
[m]Pr 15:1

is a man who boasts of gifts he does not give.

15 Through patience a ruler can be persuaded,[l]
and a gentle tongue can break a bone.[m]

25:16
[n]ver 27

16 If you find honey, eat just enough —
too much of it, and you will vomit.[n]
17 Seldom set foot in your neighbour's house —
too much of you, and he will hate you.

25:18
[o]Ps 57:4;
Pr 12:18

18 Like a club or a sword or a sharp arrow
is the man who gives false testimony against his neighbour.[o]

19 Like a bad tooth or a lame foot
is reliance on the unfaithful in times of trouble.

25:22
[p]Ps 18:8
[q]2Sa 16:12;
2Ch 28:15;
Mt 5:44;
Ro 12:20*

20 Like one who takes away a garment on a cold day,
or like vinegar poured on soda,
is one who sings songs to a heavy heart.

21 If your enemy is hungry, give him food to eat;
if he is thirsty, give him water to drink.
22 In doing this, you will heap burning coals[p] on his head,
and the LORD will reward you.[q]

25:24
[r]Pr 21:9

23 As a north wind brings rain,
so a sly tongue brings angry looks.

25:25
[s]Pr 15:30

24 Better to live on a corner of the roof
than share a house with a quarrelsome wife.[r]

25 Like cold water to a weary soul
is good news from a distant land.[s]

25:27
[t]ver 16
[u]Pr 27:2;
Mt 23:12

26 Like a muddied spring or a polluted well
is a righteous man who gives way to the wicked.

27 It is not good to eat too much honey,[t]
nor is it honourable to seek one's own honour.[u]

26:1
[a]1Sa 12:17
[b]ver 8;
Pr 19:10

28 Like a city whose walls are broken down
is a man who lacks self-control.

26:2
[c]Nu 23:8;
Dt 23:5

26

Like snow in summer or rain[a] in harvest,
honour is not fitting for a fool.[b]

2 Like a fluttering sparrow or a darting swallow,
an undeserved curse does not come to rest.[c]

26:3
[d]Ps 32:9
[e]Pr 10:13

3 A whip for the horse, a halter for the donkey,[d]
and a rod for the backs of fools![e]

25:18 Lying ("false testimony") is vicious. Its effects can be as permanent as those of a stab wound. The next time you are tempted to pass on a bit of gossip, imagine yourself stabbing the victim of your remarks with a sword. This image may shock you into silence.

25:21, 22 God's form of retaliation is most effective and yet difficult to do. Paul quotes this proverb in Romans 12:19–21. In Matthew 5:44, Jesus encourages us to pray for those who hurt us. By returning good for evil, we are acknowledging God as the balancer of all accounts and trusting him to be the judge.

25:26 To "give way to the wicked" means setting aside your standards of right and wrong. No-one is helped by someone who compromises with the wicked.

25:27 Dwelling on the honours you deserve can only be harmful. It can make you bitter, discouraged, or angry, and it will not bring you the rewards that you think should be yours. Pining for what you should have received may make you miss the satisfaction of knowing you did your best.

25:28 Even though city walls restricted the inhabitants' movements, people were happy to have them. Without walls, they would have been vulnerable to attack by any passing group of marauders. Self-control limits us, to be sure, but it is necessary. An out-of-control life is open to all sorts of enemy attack. Think of self-control as a wall for defence and protection.

26:2 "An undeserved curse does not come to rest" means that it has no effect.

4 Do not answer a fool according to his folly,
or you will be like him yourself.[f]
5 Answer a fool according to his folly,
or he will be wise in his own eyes.[g]
6 Like cutting off one's feet or drinking violence
is the sending of a message by the hand of a fool.[h]
7 Like a lame man's legs that hang limp
is a proverb in the mouth of a fool.[i]
8 Like tying a stone in a sling
is the giving of honour to a fool.[j]
9 Like a thornbush in a drunkard's hand
is a proverb in the mouth of a fool.[k]
10 Like an archer who wounds at random
is he who hires a fool or any passer-by.
11 As a dog returns to its vomit,[l]
so a fool repeats his folly.[m]
12 Do you see a man wise in his own eyes?[n]
There is more hope for a fool than for him.[o]
13 The sluggard says,[p] "There is a lion in the road,
a fierce lion roaming the streets!"[q]
14 As a door turns on its hinges,
so a sluggard turns on his bed.[r]
15 The sluggard buries his hand in the dish;
he is too lazy to bring it back to his mouth.[s]
16 The sluggard is wiser in his own eyes
than seven men who answer discreetly.
17 Like one who seizes a dog by the ears
is a passer-by who meddles in a quarrel not his own.
18 Like a madman shooting

26:4 [f]ver 5; Isa 36:21
26:5 [g]ver 4; Pr 3:7
26:6 [h]Pr 10:26
26:7 [i]ver 9
26:8 [j]ver 1
26:9 [k]ver 7
26:11 [l]2Pe 2:22* [m]Ex 8:15; Ps 85:8
26:12 [n]Pr 3:7 [o]Pr 29:20
26:13 [p]Pr 6:6-11; 24:30-34 [q]Pr 22:13
26:14 [r]Pr 6:9
26:15 [s]Pr 19:24

26:4, 5 These two verses seem to be in contradiction. But the writer is saying that we shouldn't take a foolish person seriously and try to reason with his or her empty arguments. This will only make him or her proud and determined to win the argument. In some situations, you ought not even try to answer a fool, for there is no way you can penetrate his or her closed mind. You may, in fact, be stooping to that person's level if you do choose to answer. Such a fool will abuse you and you will be tempted to abuse him or her in return. There are other situations where your common sense tells you to answer in order to expose the fool's pride and folly.

26:7 In the mouth of a fool, a proverb becomes as useless as a paralysed leg. Some people are so blind that they won't get much wisdom from reading these proverbs. Only those who want to be wise have the receptive attitude needed to make the most of them. If we want to learn from God, he will respond and pour out his heart to us (1:23).

26:8 Sometimes when someone in a group causes discord or dissension, the leader tries to make him loyal and productive by giving him a place of privilege or responsibility. This usually doesn't work. In fact, it is like tying the stone to the sling – it won't go anywhere and will swing back and hurt you. The dissenter's new power may be just what he needs to manipulate the group.

26:9 Normally the first prick of a thorn alerts us, so we remove the thorn before it damages us. A drunk person, however, may not feel the thorn, and so it will work its way into his flesh. Similarly, a fool may not feel the sting of a proverb because he does not see where it touches his life. Instead of taking its point to heart, a fool will apply it to his church, his employer, his spouse, or whomever he is rebelling against. The next time you find yourself saying, "So-and-so should really pay attention to that," stop and ask yourself, "Is there a message in it for me?"

26:13–16 If a person is not willing to work, he or she can find endless excuses to avoid it. But laziness is more dangerous than a prowling lion. The less you do, the less you want to do, and the more useless you become. To overcome laziness, take a few small steps towards change. Set a concrete, realistic goal. Figure out the steps needed to reach it, and follow those steps. Pray for strength and persistence. To keep your excuses from making you useless, stop making useless excuses.

26:17 Seizing the ears of a stray dog is a good way to get bitten, and interfering in arguments is a good way to get hurt. Many times both arguers will turn on the person who interferes. It is best simply to keep out of arguments that are none of your business. If you must become involved, try to wait until the arguers have stopped fighting and cooled off a bit. Then maybe you can help them mend their differences and their relationship.

26:20
[t]Pr 22:10

26:21
[u]Pr 14:17; 15:18

26:22
[v]Pr 18:8

26:24
[w]Ps 31:18
[x]Ps 41:6; Pr 10:18; 12:20

26:25
[y]Ps 28:3
[z]Jer 9:4-8

26:27
[a]Ps 7:15
[b]Est 6:13
[c]Est 2:23; 7:9; Ps 35:8; 141:10; Pr 28:10; 29:6; Isa 50:11

26:28
[d]Ps 12:3; Pr 29:5

27:1
[a]1Ki 20:11
[b]Mt 6:34; Lk 12:19-20; Jas 4:13-16

27:2
[c]Pr 25:27

27:3
[d]Job 6:3

firebrands or deadly arrows
19 is a man who deceives his neighbour
and says, "I was only joking!"

20 Without wood a fire goes out;
without gossip a quarrel dies down.[t]

21 As charcoal to embers and as wood to fire,
so is a quarrelsome man for kindling strife.[u]

22 The words of a gossip are like choice morsels;
they go down to a man's inmost parts.[v]

23 Like a coating of glaze[a] over earthenware
are fervent lips with an evil heart.

24 A malicious man disguises himself with his lips,[w]
but in his heart he harbours deceit.[x]
25 Though his speech is charming,[y] do not believe him,
for seven abominations fill his heart.[z]
26 His malice may be concealed by deception,
but his wickedness will be exposed in the assembly.

27 If a man digs a pit,[a] he will fall into it;[b]
if a man rolls a stone, it will roll back on him.[c]

28 A lying tongue hates those it hurts,
and a flattering mouth[d] works ruin.

27 Do not boast[a] about tomorrow,
for you do not know what a day may bring forth.[b]

2 Let another praise you, and not your own mouth;
someone else, and not your own lips.[c]

3 Stone is heavy and sand[d] a burden,

a *23* With a different word division of the Hebrew; Masoretic Text *of silver dross*

THE FOUR TONGUES
What we say probably affects more people than any other action we take. It is not surprising, then, to find that Proverbs gives special attention to words and how they are used. Four common speech patterns are described in Proverbs. The first two should be copied, while the last two should be avoided.

The Controlled Tongue	Those with this speech pattern think before speaking, know when silence is best, and give wise advice.	10:19; 11:12, 13; 12:16; 13:3; 15:1, 4, 28; 16:23; 17:14, 27, 28; 21:23; 24:26
The Caring Tongue	Those with this speech pattern speak truthfully while seeking to encourage.	10:32; 12:18, 25; 15:23; 16:24; 25:15; 27:9
The Conniving Tongue	Those with this speech pattern are filled with wrong motives, gossip, slander, and a desire to twist truth.	6:12–14; 8:13; 16:28; 18:8; 25:18; 26:20–28
The Careless Tongue	Those with this speech pattern are filled with lies, curses, quick-tempered words—which can lead to rebellion and destruction.	10:18, 32; 11:9; 12:16, 18; 15:4; 17:9, 14, 19; 20:19; 25:23

Other verses about our speech include: 10:11, 20, 31; 12:6, 17–19; 13:2; 14:3; 19:5, 28; 25:11; 27:2, 5, 14, 17; 29:9

26:20 Talking about every little irritation or piece of gossip only keeps the fires of anger going. Refusing to discuss them cuts the fuel line and makes the fires die out. Does someone continually irritate you? Decide not to complain about the person, and see if your irritation dies from lack of fuel.

26:24–26 This proverb means that people with hate in their hearts may sound pleasant enough; don't believe what they say.

but provocation by a fool is heavier than both.

4Anger is cruel and fury overwhelming,
but who can stand before jealousy?[e]

5Better is open rebuke
than hidden love.

6Wounds from a friend can be trusted,
but an enemy multiplies kisses.[f]

7He who is full loathes honey,
but to the hungry even what is bitter tastes sweet.

8Like a bird that strays from its nest[g]
is a man who strays from his home.

9Perfume[h] and incense bring joy to the heart,
and the pleasantness of one's friend springs from his earnest counsel.

10Do not forsake your friend and the friend of your father,
and do not go to your brother's house when disaster[i] strikes you—
better a neighbour nearby than a brother far away.

11Be wise, my son, and bring joy to my heart;[j]
then I can answer anyone who treats me with contempt.[k]

12The prudent see danger and take refuge,
but the simple keep going and suffer for it.[l]

13Take the garment of one who puts up security for a stranger;
hold it in pledge if he does it for a wayward woman.[m]

14If a man loudly blesses his neighbour early in the morning,
it will be taken as a curse.

15A quarrelsome wife is like
a constant dripping[n] on a rainy day;
16restraining her is like restraining the wind
or grasping oil with the hand.

17As iron sharpens iron,
so one man sharpens another.

18He who tends a fig-tree will eat its fruit,[o]
and he who looks after his master will be honoured.[p]

27:4 [e]Nu 5:14
27:6 [f]Ps 141:5; Pr 28:23
27:8 [g]Isa 16:2
27:9 [h]Est 2:12; Ps 45:8
27:10 [i]Pr 17:17; 18:24
27:11 [j]Pr 10:1; 23:15-16 [k]Ge 24:60
27:12 [l]Pr 22:3
27:13 [m]Pr 20:16
27:15 [n]Est 1:18; Pr 19:13
27:18 [o]1Co 9:7 [p]Lk 19:12-27

27:6 Who would prefer a friend's wounds to an enemy's kisses? Anyone who considers the source. A friend who has your best interests at heart may have to give you unpleasant advice at times, but you know it is for your own good. An enemy, by contrast, may whisper sweet words and happily send you on your way to ruin. We tend to hear what we want to hear, even if an enemy is the only one who will say it. A friend's advice, no matter how painful, is much better.

27:15, 16 Quarrelsome nagging, a steady stream of unwanted advice, is a form of torture. People nag because they think they're not getting through, but nagging hinders communication more than it helps. When tempted to engage in this destructive habit, stop and examine your motives. Are you more concerned about yourself—getting your way, being right—than about the person you are pretending to help? If you are truly concerned about other people, think of a more effective way to get through to them. Surprise them with words of patience and love, and see what happens.

27:17 There is a mental sharpness that comes from being with good people. And a meeting of minds can help people see their ideas with new clarity, refine them, and shape them into brilliant insights. This requires discussion partners who can challenge each other and stimulate thought—people who focus on the idea without involving their egos in the discussion; people who know how to attack the thought and not the thinker. Two friends who bring their ideas together can help each other become sharper.

27:18 With all the problems and concerns a leader has, it can be easy to overlook the very people who most deserve attention—faithful employees or volunteers (those who tend the fig trees). The people who stand behind you, who work hard and help you get the job done, deserve to share in your success. Be sure that in all your worrying, planning, and organising, you don't forget the people who are helping you the most.

27:20 [q]Pr 30:15-16; Hab 2:5 [r]Ecc 1:8; 6:7

27:21 [s]Pr 17:3

27:23 [t]Pr 12:10

27:24 [u]Pr 23:5

28:1 [a]2Ki 7:7 [b]Lev 26:17; Ps 53:5 [c]Ps 138:3

28:6 [d]Pr 19:1

28:7 [e]Pr 23:19-21

28:8 [f]Ex 18:21 [g]Job 27:17; Pr 13:22 [h]Ps 112:9; Pr 14:31; Lk 14:12-14

19 As water reflects a face,
so a man's heart reflects the man.

20 Death and Destruction[a] are never satisfied,[q]
and neither are the eyes of man.[r]

21 The crucible for silver and the furnace for gold,[s]
but man is tested by the praise he receives.

22 Though you grind a fool in a mortar,
grinding him like grain with a pestle,
you will not remove his folly from him.

23 Be sure you know the condition of your flocks,[t]
give careful attention to your herds;
24 for riches do not endure for ever,[u]
and a crown is not secure for all generations.
25 When the hay is removed and new growth appears
and the grass from the hills is gathered in,
26 the lambs will provide you with clothing,
and the goats with the price of a field.
27 You will have plenty of goats' milk
to feed you and your family
and to nourish your servant girls.

28

The wicked man flees[a] though no-one pursues,[b]
but the righteous are as bold as a lion.[c]

2 When a country is rebellious, it has many rulers,
but a man of understanding and knowledge maintains order.

3 A ruler[a] who oppresses the poor
is like a driving rain that leaves no crops.

4 Those who forsake the law praise the wicked,
but those who keep the law resist them.

5 Evil men do not understand justice,
but those who seek the LORD understand it fully.

6 Better a poor man whose walk is blameless
than a rich man whose ways are perverse.[d]

7 He who keeps the law is a discerning son,
but a companion of gluttons disgraces his father.[e]

8 He who increases his wealth by exorbitant interest[f]
amasses it for another,[g] who will be kind to the poor.[h]

a 20 Hebrew *Sheol and Abaddon* a 3 Or *A poor man*

27:21 Praise tests a person, just as high temperatures test metal. How does praise affect you? Do you work to get it? Do you work harder after you've received it? Your attitude toward praise tells a lot about your character. People of high integrity are not swayed by praise. They are attuned to their inner convictions, and they do what they should whether or not they are praised for it.

27:23–27 Because life is short and our fortunes uncertain, we should be all the more diligent in what we do with our lives. We should act with foresight, giving responsible attention to our homes, our families, and our careers. We should be responsible stewards, like a farmer with his lands and herds. Thinking ahead is a duty, not an option, for God's people.

28:2 For a government or a society to endure, it needs wise, informed leaders—and these are hard to find. "It has many rulers" may mean that anarchy is prevailing. Each person's selfishness quickly affects others. A selfish employee who steals from his company ruins its productivity. A selfish driver who drinks before taking the wheel makes the roads unsafe. A selfish spouse who has an adulterous affair often breaks up several families. When enough people live for themselves with little concern for how their actions affect others, the resulting moral rot contaminates the entire nation. Are you part of the problem . . . or the solution?

28:5 Because justice is part of God's character, a person who follows God treats others justly. The beginning of justice is concern for what is happening to others. A Christian cannot be indifferent to human suffering because God isn't. And we certainly must not contribute to human suffering through selfish business practices or unfair government policies. Be sure you are more concerned for justice than for the bottom line.

9If anyone turns a deaf ear to the law,
even his prayers are detestable.[i]

10He who leads the upright along an evil path
will fall into his own trap,[j]
but the blameless will receive a good inheritance.

11A rich man may be wise in his own eyes,
but a poor man who has discernment sees through him.

12When the righteous triumph, there is great elation;[k]
but when the wicked rise to power, men go into hiding.[l]

13He who conceals his sins[m] does not prosper,
but whoever confesses and renounces them finds mercy.[n]

14Blessed is the man who always fears the LORD,
but he who hardens his heart falls into trouble.

15Like a roaring lion or a charging bear
is a wicked man ruling over a helpless people.

16A tyrannical ruler lacks judgment,
but he who hates ill-gotten gain will enjoy a long life.

17A man tormented by the guilt of murder
will be a fugitive[o] till death;
let no-one support him.

18He whose walk is blameless is kept safe,
but he whose ways are perverse will suddenly fall.[p]

19He who works his land will have abundant food,
but the one who chases fantasies will have his fill of
poverty.[q]

20A faithful man will be richly blessed,
but one eager to get rich will not go unpunished.[r]

21To show partiality is not good[s]—
yet a man will do wrong for a piece of bread.[t]

22A stingy man is eager to get rich
and is unaware that poverty awaits him.[u]

23He who rebukes a man will in the end gain more favour
than he who has a flattering tongue.[v]

24He who robs his father or mother[w]

28:9 [i]Ps 66:18; 109:7; Pr 15:8; Isa 1:13
28:10 [j]Pr 26:27
28:12 [k]2Ki 11:20 [l]Pr 11:10; 29:2
28:13 [m]Job 31:33 [n]Ps 32:1-5; 1Jn 1:9
28:17 [o]Ge 9:6
28:18 [p]Pr 10:9
28:19 [q]Pr 12:11
28:20 [r]ver 22; Pr 10:6; 1Ti 6:9
28:21 [s]Pr 18:5 [t]Eze 13:19
28:22 [u]ver 20; Pr 23:6
28:23 [v]Pr 27:5-6
28:24 [w]Pr 19:26

28:9 God does not listen to our prayers if we intend to go back to our sin as soon as we get off our knees. If we want to forsake our sin and follow him, however, he willingly listens—no matter how bad our sin has been. What closes his ears is not the depth of our sin, but our secret intention to do it again.

28:11 Rich people often think they are wonderful; depending on no-one, they take credit for all they do. But that's a hollow self-esteem. Through dependence on God in their struggles, the poor may develop a richness of spirit that no amount of wealth can provide. The rich man can lose all his material wealth, while no-one can take away the poor man's character. Don't be jealous of the rich; money may be all they will ever have.

28:13 It is human nature to hide our sins or overlook our mistakes. But it is hard to learn from a mistake you don't acknowledge making. And what good is a mistake if it doesn't teach you something? To learn from an error you need to admit it, confess it, analyse it, and make adjustments so that it doesn't happen again. Everybody makes mistakes, but only fools repeat them.

28:13 Something in each of us strongly resists admitting we are wrong. That is why we admire people who openly and graciously admit their mistakes and sins. These people have a strong self-image. They do not always have to be right to feel good about themselves. Be willing to reconsider—to admit you are wrong and to change your plans when necessary. And remember, the first step towards forgiveness is confession.

28:14 To fear the Lord means to revere and honour him.

28:17, 18 A sinner's conscience will drive him either into guilt resulting in repentance or to death itself because of a refusal to repent. It is no act of kindness to try to make him feel better; the more guilt he feels, the more likely he is to turn to God and repent. If we interfere with the natural consequences of his act, we may make it easier for him to continue in sin.

28:24
[x]Pr 18:9

and says, "It's not wrong"—
he is partner to him who destroys.[x]

28:25
[y]Pr 29:25

25 A greedy man stirs up dissension,
but he who trusts in the LORD[y] will prosper.

28:26
[z]Ps 4:5; Pr 3:5

26 He who trusts in himself is a fool,[z]
but he who walks in wisdom is kept safe.

28:27
[a]Dt 15:7; 24:19; Pr 19:17; 22:9

27 He who gives to the poor will lack nothing,[a]
but he who closes his eyes to them receives many curses.

28:28
[b]ver 12

28 When the wicked rise to power, people go into hiding;[b]
but when the wicked perish, the righteous thrive.

29:1
[a]2Ch 36:16; Pr 6:15

29 A man who remains stiff-necked after many rebukes
will suddenly be destroyed—without remedy.[a]

29:2
[b]Est 8:15
[c]Pr 28:12

2 When the righteous thrive, the people rejoice;[b]
when the wicked rule, the people groan.[c]

DILIGENCE AND LAZINESS
Proverbs makes it clear that diligence—being willing to work hard and do one's best at any job given to him or her—is a vital part of wise living. We work hard not to become rich, famous, or admired (although those may be by-products), but to serve God with our very best during our lives.

The Diligent	*The Lazy*	*References*
Become rich	Are soon poor	10:4
Gather crops early	Sleep during harvest	10:5
	Are an annoyance	10:26
Have abundant food	Chase fantasies	12:11
Hard work returns rewards		12:14
Will rule	Will become slaves	12:24
Prize their possessions	Waste good resources	12:27
Are fully satisfied	Want much but get little	13:4
Bring profit	Experience poverty	14:23
Have an easy path	Have trouble all through life	15:19
	Are like those who destroy	18:9
	Go hungry	19:15
	Won't feed themselves	19:24
	Won't plough in season	20:4
Stay awake and have food to spare	Love sleep and grow poor	20:13
Make careful plans	Make hasty speculations	21:5
	Love pleasure and become poor	21:17
Give without sparing	Desire things but refuse to work for them	21:25, 26
	Are full of excuses for not working	22:13
Will serve before kings		22:29
	Sleep too much, which leads to poverty	24:30–34
Reap abundance through hard work	Experience poverty because of laziness	28:19

28:26 For many people, the rugged individualist is a hero. We admire the bold, self-directed men and women who know what they want and fight for it. They are self-reliant, neither giving nor asking advice. What a contrast to God's way. A person can't know the future and can't predict the consequences of his or her choices with certainty. And so the totally self-reliant person is doomed to failure. The wise person depends on God.

28:27 God wants us to identify with the needy, not ignore them. The second part of this proverb could be restated positively: "those who open their eyes to poor people will be blessed". If we help others when they are in trouble, they will do whatever they can to return the favour (see 11:24, 25). Paul promises that God will supply all our needs (Philippians 4:19); he usually does this through other people. What can you do today to help God supply someone's need?

29:1 Making the same mistake over and over again is an invitation to disaster. Eventually people have to face the consequences of refusing to learn. If their mistake is refusing God's invitations or rejecting his commands, the consequences will be especially serious. In the end, God may have to turn them away. Make sure you are not stiff-necked.

3 A man who loves wisdom brings joy to his father,[d]
but a companion of prostitutes squanders his wealth.[e]

4 By justice a king gives a country stability,[f]
but one who is greedy for bribes tears it down.

5 Whoever flatters his neighbour
is spreading a net for his feet.

6 An evil man is snared by his own sin,[g]
but a righteous one can sing and be glad.

7 The righteous care about justice for the poor,[h]
but the wicked have no such concern.

8 Mockers stir up a city,
but wise men turn away anger.[i]

9 If a wise man goes to court with a fool,
the fool rages and scoffs, and there is no peace.

10 Bloodthirsty men hate a man of integrity
and seek to kill the upright.[j]

11 A fool gives full vent to his anger,
but a wise man keeps himself under control.[k]

12 If a ruler listens to lies,
all his officials become wicked.

13 The poor man and the oppressor have this in common:
The LORD gives sight to the eyes of both.[l]

14 If a king judges the poor with fairness,
his throne will always be secure.[m]

15 The rod of correction imparts wisdom,
but a child left to himself disgraces his mother.[n]

16 When the wicked thrive, so does sin,
but the righteous will see their downfall.[o]

17 Discipline your son, and he will give you peace;
he will bring delight to your soul.[p]

18 Where there is no revelation, the people cast off restraint;
but blessed is he who keeps the law.[q]

19 A servant cannot be corrected by mere words;
though he understands, he will not respond.

20 Do you see a man who speaks in haste?
There is more hope for a fool than for him.[r]

21 If a man pampers his servant from youth,

29:3 [d]Pr 10:1 [e]Pr 5:8-10; Lk 15:11-32
29:4 [f]Pr 8:15-16
29:6 [g]Ecc 9:12
29:7 [h]Job 29:16; Ps 41:1; Pr 31:8-9
29:8 [i]Pr 11:11; 16:14
29:10 [j]1Jn 3:12
29:11 [k]Pr 12:16; 19:11
29:13 [l]Pr 22:2; Mt 5:45
29:14 [m]Ps 72:1-5; Pr 16:12
29:15 [n]Pr 10:1; 13:24; 17:21, 25
29:16 [o]Ps 37:35-36; 58:10; 91:8; 92:11
29:17 [p]ver 15; Pr 10:1
29:18 [q]Ps 1:1-2; 119:1-2; Jn 13:17
29:20 [r]Pr 26:12; Jas 1:19

29:13 "The LORD gives sight to the eyes of both" means that everyone depends on God for sight. Both the oppressor and the poor have the gift of sight from the same God. God sees and judges both, and his judgment falls on those whose greed or power drives them to oppress the poor.

29:15 Parents of young children often tire of disciplining them. They feel as if all they do is nag, scold, and punish. When you're tempted to give up and let your children do what they want, or when you wonder if you've ruined every chance for a loving relationship with them, remember – kind, firm correction helps them learn, and learning makes them wise. Consistent, loving discipline will ultimately teach them to discipline themselves.

29:16 When the wicked are in leadership, sin prevails. In any organisation – whether a church, a business, a family, or a government – the climate comes from the top. The people become like their leaders. What kind of climate are you setting for the people you lead?

29:18 "Revelation" refers to words from God received by prophets. Where there is ignorance of God, crime and sin run wild. Public morality depends on the knowledge of God, but it also depends on keeping God's laws. In order for both nations and individuals to function well, people must know God's ways and keep his rules.

he will bring grief[a] in the end.

22 An angry man stirs up dissension,
and a hot-tempered one commits many sins.[s]

23 A man's pride brings him low,
but a man of lowly spirit gains honour.[t]

24 The accomplice of a thief is his own enemy;
he is put under oath and dare not testify.[u]

25 Fear of man will prove to be a snare,
but whoever trusts in the LORD[v] is kept safe.

26 Many seek an audience with a ruler,[w]
but it is from the LORD that man gets justice.

27 The righteous detest the dishonest;
the wicked detest the upright.[x]

Sayings of Agur

30 The sayings of Agur son of Jakeh—an oracle:[a]

This man declared to Ithiel,
to Ithiel and to Ucal:[b]

2 "I am the most ignorant of men;
I do not have a man's understanding.
3 I have not learned wisdom,
nor have I knowledge of the Holy One.[a]
4 Who has gone up[b] to heaven and come down?
Who has gathered up the wind in the hollow[c] of his hands?
Who has wrapped up the waters[d] in his cloak?[e]

29:22 [s]Pr 14:17; 15:18; 26:21
29:23 [t]Pr 11:2; 15:33; 16:18; Isa 66:2; Mt 23:12
29:24 [u]Lev 5:1
29:25 [v]Pr 28:25
29:26 [w]Pr 19:6
29:27 [x]ver 10
30:3 [a]Pr 9:10
30:4 [b]Ps 24:1-2; Jn 3:13; Eph 4:7-10 [c]Ps 104:3; Isa 40:12 [d]Job 26:8; 38:8-9 [e]Ge 1:2

a *21* The meaning of the Hebrew for this word is uncertain. a *1* Or *Jakeh of Massa* b *1* Masoretic Text; with a different word division of the Hebrew *declared, "I am weary, O God; / I am weary, O God, and faint.*

LEADERSHIP
Since many of the proverbs came from King Solomon, it is natural to expect some of his interest to be directed towards leadership.

Qualities of good leadership	*References*
Diligence	12:24
Trustworthy messengers	13:17
Don't penalise people for integrity	17:26
Listen before answering	18:13
Able to discern	18:15
Listen to both sides of the story	18:17
Able to stand up under adversity	24:10
Able to stand up under praise	27:21
What happens without good leadership	
Honouring the wrong people backfires	26:8
A wicked ruler is dangerous	28:15
People despair	29:2
A wicked ruler has wicked officials	29:12

Other verses to study: 24:27; 25:13; 27:18

29:24 This proverb is saying that a thief's accomplice won't tell the truth when under oath. Thus, by his perjury, he will hurt himself.

29:25 Fear of people can hamper everything you try to do. In extreme forms, it can make you afraid to leave your home. By contrast, fear of God—respect, reverence, and trust—is liberating.Why fear people who can do no eternal harm? Instead, fear God who can turn the harm intended by others into good for those who trust him.

30:1 The origin of these sayings is not clear. Nothing is known about Agur except that he was a wise teacher who may have come from Lemuel's kingdom (see the note on 31:1).

30:2–4 Because God is infinite, certain aspects of his nature will always remain a mystery. Compare these questions with the questions God asked Job (Job 38—41).

30:4 Some scholars feel that the son referred to is the Son of God, the preincarnate being of the Messiah who, before the

Who has established all the ends of the earth?
What is his name,[f] and the name of his son?
Tell me if you know!

5"Every word of God is flawless;[g]
he is a shield[h] to those who take refuge in him.
6Do not add[i] to his words,
or he will rebuke you and prove you a liar.

7"Two things I ask of you, O LORD;
do not refuse me before I die:
8Keep falsehood and lies far from me;
give me neither poverty nor riches,
but give me only my daily bread.[j]
9Otherwise, I may have too much and disown[k] you
and say, 'Who is the LORD?'[l]
Or I may become poor and steal,
and so dishonour the name of my God.[m]

10"Do not slander a servant to his master,
or he will curse you, and you will pay for it.

11"There are those who curse their fathers
and do not bless their mothers;[n]
12those who are pure in their own eyes[o]
and yet are not cleansed of their filth;[p]
13those whose eyes are ever so haughty,[q]
whose glances are so disdainful;
14those whose teeth[r] are swords
and whose jaws are set with knives[s]
to devour[t] the poor[u] from the earth,
the needy from among mankind.[v]

15"The leech has two daughters.
'Give! Give!' they cry.

"There are three things that are never satisfied,[w]
four that never say, 'Enough!':
16the grave,[c][x] the barren womb,
land, which is never satisfied with water,
and fire, which never says, 'Enough!'

17"The eye that mocks[y] a father,
that scorns obedience to a mother,
will be pecked out by the ravens of the valley,
will be eaten by the vultures.[z]

18"There are three things that are too amazing for me,
four that I do not understand:
19the way of an eagle in the sky,
the way of a snake on a rock,

c *16* Hebrew *Sheol*

30:4 [f]Rev 19:12
30:5 [g]Ps 12:6; 18:30 [h]Ge 15:1; Ps 84:11
30:6 [i]Dt 4:2; 12:32; Rev 22:18
30:8 [j]Mt 6:11
30:9 [k]Jos 24:27; Isa 1:4; 59:13 [l]Dt 6:12; 8:10-14; Hos 13:6 [m]Dt 8:12
30:11 [n]Pr 20:20
30:12 [o]Pr 16:2; Lk 18:11 [p]Jer 2:23, 35
30:13 [q]2Sa 22:28; Job 41:34; Ps 131:1; Pr 6:17
30:14 [r]Job 4:11; 29:17; Ps 3:7 [s]Ps 57:4 [t]Job 24:9; Ps 14:4 [u]Am 8:4; Mic 2:2 [v]Job 19:22
30:15 [w]Pr 27:20
30:16 [x]Pr 27:20; Isa 5:14; 14:9, 11; Hab 2:5
30:17 [y]Dt 21:18-21; Pr 23:22 [z]Job 15:23

foundation of the earth, participated in the creation. Colossians 1:16, 17 teaches that through Christ the world was created.

30:7–9 Having too much money can be dangerous, but so can having too little. Being poor can, in fact, be hazardous to spiritual as well as physical health. On the other hand, being rich is not the answer. As Jesus pointed out, rich people have trouble getting into God's kingdom (Matthew 19:23, 24). Like Paul, we can learn how to live whether we have little or plenty (Philippians 4:12), but our lives are more likely to be effective if we have "neither poverty nor riches".

30:13 This phrase refers to proud and haughty people who look down on others. Verses 11–14 contain a fourfold description of arrogance.

30:15ff "Three things . . . four" is a poetic way of saying the list is not complete. The writer of these proverbs is observing the world with delighted interest. Verses 15–30 are an invitation to look at nature from the perspective of a keen observer.

30:20 [a]Pr 5:6
30:22 [b]Pr 19:10; 29:2
30:25 [c]Pr 6:6-8
30:26 [d]Ps 104:18
30:27 [e]Ex 10:4
30:32 [f]Job 21:5; 29:9
31:1 [a]Pr 22:17
31:2 [b]Jdg 11:30; Isa 49:15
31:3 [c]Dt 17:17; 1Ki 11:3; Ne 13:26; Pr 5:1-14
31:4 [d]Pr 20:1; Ecc 10:16-17; Isa 5:22
31:5 [e]1Ki 16:9 [f]Pr 16:12; Hos 4:11

the way of a ship on the high seas,
and the way of a man with a maiden.

20"This is the way of an adulteress:
She eats and wipes her mouth
and says, 'I've done nothing wrong.'[a]

21"Under three things the earth trembles,
under four it cannot bear up:
22a servant who becomes king,[b]
a fool who is full of food,
23an unloved woman who is married,
and a maidservant who displaces her mistress.

24"Four things on earth are small,
yet they are extremely wise:
25Ants are creatures of little strength,
yet they store up their food in the summer;[c]
26conies[d][d] are creatures of little power,
yet they make their home in the crags;
27locusts[e] have no king,
yet they advance together in ranks;
28a lizard can be caught with the hand,
yet it is found in kings' palaces.

29"There are three things that are stately in their stride,
four that move with stately bearing:
30a lion, mighty among beasts,
who retreats before nothing;
31a strutting cock, a he-goat,
and a king with his army around him.[e]

32"If you have played the fool and exalted yourself,
or if you have planned evil,
clap your hand over your mouth![f]
33For as churning the milk produces butter,
and as twisting the nose produces blood,
so stirring up anger produces strife."

Sayings of King Lemuel

31 The sayings[a] of King Lemuel—an oracle[a] his mother taught him:

2"O my son, O son of my womb,
O son of my vows,[b][b]
3do not spend your strength on women,
your vigour on those who ruin kings.[c]

4"It is not for kings, O Lemuel—
not for kings to drink wine,[d]
not for rulers to crave beer,
5lest they drink[e] and forget what the law decrees,[f]
and deprive all the oppressed of their rights.

d *26* That is, the hyrax or rock badger **e** *31* Or *king secure against revolt.* **a** *1* Or *of Lemuel king of Massa, which* **b** *2* Or *I the answer to my prayers*

30:24–28 Ants can teach us about preparation; coneys (badgers) about wise building; locusts about co-operation and order; and lizards about fearlessness.

31:1 Little is known about Lemuel except that he was a king who received wise teachings from his mother. His name means "devoted to God". Some believe that Lemuel and Agur were both from the kingdom of Massa in northern Arabia.

31:4–7 Drunkenness might be understandable among dying people in great pain, but it is inexcusable for national leaders. Alcohol clouds the mind and can lead to injustice and poor decisions. Leaders have better things to do than anaesthetise themselves with alcohol.

6Give beer to those who are perishing,
wine[g] to those who are in anguish;
7let them drink[h] and forget their poverty
and remember their misery no more.

8"Speak[i] up for those who cannot speak for themselves,
for the rights of all who are destitute.
9Speak up and judge fairly;
defend the rights of the poor and needy."[j]

Epilogue: The Wife of Noble Character

10[c]A wife of noble character[k] who can find?[l]
She is worth far more than rubies.
11Her husband[m] has full confidence in her
and lacks nothing of value.[n]
12She brings him good, not harm,
all the days of her life.
13She selects wool and flax
and works with eager hands.[o]
14She is like the merchant ships,
bringing her food from afar.
15She gets up while it is still dark;
she provides food for her family
and portions for her servant girls.
16She considers a field and buys it;
out of her earnings she plants a vineyard.
17She sets about her work vigorously;
her arms are strong for her tasks.
18She sees that her trading is profitable,
and her lamp does not go out at night.
19In her hand she holds the distaff
and grasps the spindle with her fingers.
20She opens her arms to the poor
and extends her hands to the needy.[p]
21When it snows, she has no fear for her household;
for all of them are clothed in scarlet.
22She makes coverings for her bed;
she is clothed in fine linen and purple.
23Her husband is respected at the city gate,
where he takes his seat among the elders[q] of the land.
24She makes linen garments and sells them,
and supplies the merchants with sashes.
25She is clothed with strength and dignity;
she can laugh at the days to come.
26She speaks with wisdom,

c *10* Verses 10–31 are an acrostic, each verse beginning with a successive letter of the Hebrew alphabet.

31:6 [g]Ge 14:18
31:7 [h]Est 1:10
31:8 [i]1Sa 19:4; Job 29:12-17
31:9 [j]Lev 19:15; Dt 1:16; Pr 24:23; 29:7; Isa 1:17; Jer 22:16
31:10 [k]Ru 3:11; Pr 12:4; 18:22 [l]Pr 8:35; 19:14
31:11 [m]Ge 2:18 [n]Pr 12:4
31:13 [o]1Ti 2:9-10
31:20 [p]Dt 15:11; Eph 4:28; Heb 13:16
31:23 [q]Ex 3:16; Ru 4:1, 11; Pr 12:4

31:10–31 Proverbs has a lot to say about women. How fitting that the book ends with a picture of a woman of strong character, great wisdom, many skills, and great compassion.

Some people have the mistaken idea that the ideal woman in the Bible is retiring, servile, and entirely domestic. Not so! This woman is an excellent wife and mother. She is also a manufacturer, importer, manager, estate agent, farmer, seamstress, upholsterer, and merchant. Her strength and dignity do not come from her amazing achievements, however. They are a result of her reverence for God. In our society where physical appearance counts for so much, it may surprise us to realise that her appearance is never mentioned. Her attractiveness comes entirely from her character.

The woman described in this chapter has outstanding abilities. Her family's social position is high. In fact, she may not be one woman at all – she may be a composite portrait of ideal womanhood. Do not see her as a model to imitate in every detail; your days are not long enough to do everything she does! See her instead as an inspiration to be all you can be. We can't be just like her, but we can learn from her industry, integrity, and resourcefulness.

31:19 The distaff and spindle are two implements used in hand spinning.

31:26
[r]Pr 10:31

and faithful instruction is on her tongue.[r]
27 She watches over the affairs of her household
and does not eat the bread of idleness.
28 Her children arise and call her blessed;
her husband also, and he praises her:
29 "Many women do noble things,
but you surpass them all."
30 Charm is deceptive, and beauty is fleeting;
but a woman who fears the LORD is to be praised.
31 Give her the reward she has earned,
and let her works bring her praise[s] at the city gate.

31:31
[s]Pr 11:16

31:31 The book of Proverbs begins with the command to fear the Lord (1:7) and ends with the picture of a woman who fulfils this command. Her qualities are mentioned throughout the book: hard work, fear of God, respect for spouse, foresight, encouragement, care for others, concern for the poor, wisdom in handling money. These qualities, when coupled with the fear of God, lead to enjoyment, success, honour, and worth. Proverbs is very practical for our day because it shows us how to become wise, make good decisions, and live according to God's ideal.

ECCLESIASTES

VITAL STATISTICS

PURPOSE:
To spare future generations the bitterness of learning through their own experience that life is meaningless apart from God

AUTHOR:
Solomon

TO WHOM WRITTEN:
Solomon's subjects in particular, and all people in general

DATE WRITTEN:
Probably around 935 B.C., late in Solomon's life

SETTING:
Solomon was looking back on his life, much of which was lived apart from God

KEY VERSE:
"Now all has been heard; here is the conclusion of the matter: Fear God and keep his commandments, for this is the whole duty of man" (12:13).

THE MOULDED bunny lies in the basket, surrounded by green paper "grass". With Easter morning eyes wide with anticipation, the little boy carefully lifts the chocolate figure and bites into one of the long ears. But the sweet taste fades quickly, and the child looks again at the chocolate in his hand. It's hollow!

Empty, futile, hollow, nothing . . . the words ring of disappointment and disillusionment. Yet this is the life-experience of many. Grasping the sweet things—possessions, experience, power, and pleasure—they find nothing inside. Life is empty, meaningless . . . and they despair.

Almost 3,000 years ago, Solomon spoke of this human dilemma; but the insights and applications of his message are relevant in our time. Ecclesiastes, Solomon's written sermon, is an analysis of life's experiences and a critical essay about its meaning. In this profound book, Solomon takes us on a mental journey through his life, explaining how everything he tried, tested, or tasted was "meaningless"—useless, irrational, pointless, foolish, and empty—an exercise in futility. And remember, these words are from one who "had it all"—tremendous intellect, power, and wealth. After this biographical tour, Solomon made his triumphant conclusion: "Fear God and keep his commandments, for this is the whole duty of man. For God will bring every deed into judgment, including every hidden thing, whether it is good or evil" (12:13, 14).

When Solomon became king, he asked God for wisdom (2 Chronicles 1:7–12), and he became the wisest man in the world (1 Kings 4:29–34). He studied, taught, judged, and wrote. Kings and leaders from other nations came to Jerusalem to learn from him. But with all of his practical insight on life, Solomon failed to heed his own advice, and he began a downward spiral. Near the end of his life, Solomon looked back with an attitude of humility and repentance. He took stock of the world as he had experienced it, hoping to spare his readers the bitterness of learning through personal experience that everything apart from God is empty, hollow, and meaningless.

Although the tone of Ecclesiastes is negative and pessimistic, we must not conclude that the only chapter worth reading and applying is the last one, where he draws his conclusions. In reality, the entire book is filled with practical wisdom (how to accomplish things in the world and stay out of trouble) and spiritual wisdom (how to find and know eternal values). Solomon had a very honest approach to life. All of his remarks relating to the futility of life are there for a purpose—to lead people to seek true happiness in God alone. He was not trying to destroy all hope, but to direct our hopes to the only One who can truly fulfil them. Solomon affirms the value of knowledge, relationships, work, and pleasure, but only *in their proper place*. All of these temporal things in life must be seen in light of the eternal.

Read Ecclesiastes and learn about life. Hear the stern warnings and dire predictions, and commit yourself to remember your Creator now (12:1).

THE BLUEPRINT

1. Solomon's personal experience (1:1–2:26)
2. Solomon's general observations (3:1–5:20)
3. Solomon's practical counsel (6:1–8:17)
4. Solomon's final conclusion (9:1–12:14)

Ecclesiastes shows that certain paths in life lead to emptiness. This profound book also helps us to discover true purpose in life. Such wisdom can spare us from the emptiness that results from a life without God. Solomon teaches that people will not find meaning in life in knowledge, money, pleasure, work, or popularity. True satisfaction comes from knowing that what we are doing is part of God's purpose for our lives. This is a book that can help free us from our scramble for power, approval, and money, and draw us closer to God.

MEGATHEMES

THEME	EXPLANATION	IMPORTANCE
Searching	Solomon searched for satisfaction almost as though he were conducting a scientific experiment. Through this process, he discovered that life without God is a long and fruitless search for enjoyment, meaning, and fulfilment. True happiness is not in our power to accumulate or attain because we always want more than we can have. In addition, there are circumstances beyond our control that can snatch away our possessions or attainments.	People are still searching. Yet the more they try to get, the more they realise how little they really have. No pleasure or happiness is possible without God. Without him, satisfaction is a lost search. Above everything we should strive to know and love God. He gives wisdom, knowledge, and joy.
Emptiness	Solomon shows how empty it is to pursue the pleasures that this life has to offer rather than a relationship with an eternal God. The search for pleasure, wealth, and success is ultimately disappointing. Nothing in the world can fill the emptiness and satisfy the deep longings in our restless hearts.	The cure for emptiness is to centre on God. His love can also fill the emptiness of human experience. Fear God throughout your life and fill your life with serving God and others rather than with selfish pleasures.
Work	Solomon tried to shake people's confidence in their own efforts, abilities, and wisdom and to direct them to faith in God as the only sound basis for living. Without God, there is no lasting reward or benefit in hard work.	Work done with the wrong attitude will leave us empty. But work accepted as an assignment from God can be seen as a gift. Examine what you expect from your efforts. God gives you abilities and opportunities to work so that you can use your time well.
Death	The certainty of death makes all merely human achievements futile. God has a plan for human destiny that goes beyond life and death. The reality of aging and dying reminds each individual of the end to come when God will judge each person's life.	Because life is short, we need wisdom that is greater than this world can offer. We need the words of God. If we listen to him, his wisdom spares us the bitterness of futile human experience and gives us a hope that goes beyond death.
Wisdom	Human wisdom doesn't contain all the answers. Knowledge and education have their limits. To understand life, we need the wisdom that can be found only in God's word to us—the Bible.	When we realise that God will evaluate all that we do, we should learn to live wisely, remembering that he is present each day, and learn to obey his guidelines for living. But in order to have God's wisdom, we must first get to know and honour him.

1. Solomon's personal experience

Everything Is Meaningless

1 The words of the Teacher,[a] [a] son of David, king of Jerusalem:[b]

2"Meaningless! Meaningless!"
says the Teacher.
"Utterly meaningless!
Everything is meaningless."[c]

3What does man gain from all his labour
at which he toils under the sun?[d]
4Generations come and generations go,
but the earth remains for ever.[e]
5The sun rises and the sun sets,
and hurries back to where it rises.[f]
6The wind blows to the south
and turns to the north;
round and round it goes,
ever returning on its course.
7All streams flow into the sea,
yet the sea is never full.
To the place the streams come from,
there they return again.[g]
8All things are wearisome,
more than one can say.
The eye never has enough of seeing,[h]
nor the ear its fill of hearing.
9What has been will be again,
what has been done will be done again;[i]
there is nothing new under the sun.
10Is there anything of which one can say,
"Look! This is something new"?
It was here already, long ago;
it was here before our time.
11There is no remembrance of men of old,
and even those who are yet to come
will not be remembered
by those who follow.[j]

a *1* Or *leader of the assembly*; also in verses 2 and 12

1:1 [a] ver 12; Ecc 7:27; 12:10 [b] Pr 1:1
1:2 [c] Ps 39:5-6; 62:9; 144:4; Ecc 12:8; Ro 8:20-21
1:3 [d] Ecc 2:11, 22; 3:9; 5:15-16
1:4 [e] Ps 104:5; 119:90
1:5 [f] Ps 19:5-6
1:7 [g] Job 36:28
1:8 [h] Pr 27:20
1:9 [i] Ecc 2:12; 3:15
1:11 [j] Ecc 2:16

1:1 The author, Solomon (the "king over Israel in Jerusalem", see 1:12), referred to himself as the Teacher, or leader of the assembly. He was both assembling people to hear a message and gathering wise sayings (proverbs). Solomon, one person in the Bible who had everything (wisdom, power, riches, honour, reputation, God's favour), is the one who discussed the ultimate emptiness of all that this world has to offer. He tried to destroy people's confidence in their own efforts, abilities, and righteousness and direct them to commitment to God as the only reason for living.

1:1–11 Solomon had a reason for writing sceptically and pessimistically. Near the end of his life, he looked back over everything he had done, and most of it seemed meaningless. A common belief was that only good people prospered and that only the wicked suffered, but that hadn't proved true in his experience. Solomon wrote this book after he had tried everything and achieved much, only to find that nothing apart from God made him happy. He wanted his readers to avoid these same senseless pursuits. If we try to find meaning in our accomplishments rather than in God, we will never be satisfied, and everything we pursue will become wearisome.

1:2 Solomon's kingdom, Israel, was in its golden age, but Solomon wanted the people to understand that success and prosperity don't last long (Psalm 103:14–16; Isaiah 40:6–8; James 4:14). All human accomplishments will one day disappear, and we must keep this in mind in order to live wisely. If we don't, we will become either proud and self-sufficient when we succeed or sorely disappointed when we fail. Solomon's goal was to show that earthly possessions and accomplishments are ultimately meaningless. Only the pursuit of God brings real satisfaction. We should honour God in all we say, think, and do.

1:8–11 Many people feel restless and dissatisfied. They wonder: (1) If I am in God's will, why am I so tired and unfulfilled? (2) What is the meaning of life? (3) When I look back on it all, will I be happy with my accomplishments? (4) Why do I feel burned out, disillusioned, dry? (5) What is to become of me? Solomon tests our faith, challenging us to find true and lasting meaning in God alone. As you take a hard look at your life, as Solomon did his, you will see how important serving God is over all other options. Perhaps God is asking you to rethink your purpose and direction in life, just as Solomon did in Ecclesiastes.

Wisdom Is Meaningless

12 I, the Teacher,[k] was king over Israel in Jerusalem. 13 I devoted myself to study
and to explore by wisdom all that is done under heaven. What a heavy burden God
has laid on men![l] 14 I have seen all the things that are done under the sun; all of them
are meaningless, a chasing after the wind.[m]

> 15 What is twisted cannot be straightened;[n]
> what is lacking cannot be counted.

16 I thought to myself, "Look, I have grown and increased in wisdom more than
anyone who has ruled over Jerusalem before me;[o] I have experienced much of
wisdom and knowledge." 17 Then I applied myself to the understanding of wisdom,[p]
and also of madness and folly,[q] but I learned that this, too, is a chasing after the wind.

> 18 For with much wisdom comes much sorrow;
> the more knowledge, the more grief.[r]

Pleasures Are Meaningless

2 I thought in my heart, "Come now, I will test you with pleasure[a] to find out what
is good." But that also proved to be meaningless. 2 "Laughter,"[b] I said, "is
foolish. And what does pleasure accomplish?" 3 I tried cheering myself with wine,[c]
and embracing folly[d]—my mind still guiding me with wisdom. I wanted to see what
was worth while for men to do under heaven during the few days of their lives.
4 I undertook great projects: I built houses for myself[e] and planted vineyards.[f] 5 I
made gardens and parks and planted all kinds of fruit trees in them. 6 I made reservoirs
to water groves of flourishing trees. 7 I bought male and female slaves and had other
slaves who were born in my house. I also owned more herds and flocks than anyone
in Jerusalem before me. 8 I amassed silver and gold[g] for myself, and the treasure of
kings and provinces. I acquired men and women singers,[h] and a harem**[a]** as well—the
delights of the heart of man. 9 I became greater by far than anyone in Jerusalem before
me.[i] In all this my wisdom stayed with me.

> 10 I denied myself nothing my eyes desired;
> I refused my heart no pleasure.
> My heart took delight in all my work,
> and this was the reward for all my labour.

a *8* The meaning of the Hebrew for this phrase is uncertain.

1:12 [k]ver 1
1:13 [l]Ge 3:17; Ecc 3:10
1:14 [m]Ecc 2:11, 17
1:15 [n]Ecc 7:13
1:16 [o]1Ki 3:12; 4:30; Ecc 2:9
1:17 [p]Ecc 7:23 [q]Ecc 2:3, 12; 7:25
1:18 [r]Ecc 2:23; 12:12
2:1 [a]Ecc 7:4; 8:15; Lk 12:19
2:2 [b]Pr 14:13; Ecc 7:6
2:3 [c]ver 24-25; Ecc 3:12-13 [d]Ecc 1:17
2:4 [e]1Ki 7:1-12 [f]SS 8:11
2:8 [g]1Ki 9:28; 10:10, 14, 21 [h]2Sa 19:35
2:9 [i]1Ch 29:25; Ecc 1:16

1:12–15 "What is twisted cannot be straightened" refers to the ultimate perplexity and confusion that come to us because of all the unanswered questions in life. Solomon, writing about his own life, discovered that neither his accomplishments nor his wisdom could make him truly happy. True wisdom is found in God, and true happiness comes from pleasing him.

1:16–18 The more you understand, the more pain and difficulty you experience. For example, the more you know, the more imperfection you see around you; and the more you observe, the more evil becomes evident. As you set out with Solomon to find the meaning of life, you must be ready to feel more, think more, question more, hurt more, and do more. Are you ready to pay the price for wisdom?

1:16–18 Solomon highlights two kinds of wisdom in the book of Ecclesiastes: (1) human knowledge, reasoning, or philosophy, and (2) the wisdom that comes from God. In these verses Solomon is talking about human knowledge. When human knowledge ignores God, it only highlights our problems because it can't provide answers without God's eternal perspective and solution.

2:1ff Solomon conducted his search for life's meaning as an experiment. He first tried pursuing pleasure. He undertook great projects, bought slaves and herds and flocks, amassed wealth, acquired singers, added many women to his harem, and became the greatest person in Jerusalem. But none of these gave him satisfaction—"Yet when I surveyed all that my hands had done and what I had toiled to achieve, everything was meaningless, a chasing after the wind; nothing was gained under the sun" (2:11). Some of the pleasures Solomon sought were wrong and some were worthy, but even the worthy pursuits were futile when he pursued them as an end in themselves. We must look beyond our activities to the reasons we do them and the purpose they fulfil. Is your goal in life to search for meaning or to search for God who gives meaning?

2:4–6 Solomon had built houses, a temple, a kingdom, a family (see 1 Kings 3—11). In the course of history, they would all be ruined. In Psalm 127:1, Solomon wrote, "Unless the LORD builds the house, its builders labour in vain. Unless the LORD watches over the city, the watchmen stand guard in vain." This book is part of Solomon's testimony to what happens to a kingdom or family that forgets God. As you examine your projects or goals, what is your starting point, your motivation? Without God as your foundation, all you are living for is meaningless.

11 Yet when I surveyed all that my hands had done
and what I had toiled to achieve,
everything was meaningless, a chasing after the wind;[j]
nothing was gained under the sun.[k]

Wisdom and Folly Are Meaningless

12 Then I turned my thoughts to consider wisdom,
and also madness and folly.[l]
What more can the king's successor do
than what has already been done?[m]
13 I saw that wisdom[n] is better than folly,[o]
just as light is better than darkness.
14 The wise man has eyes in his head,
while the fool walks in the darkness;
but I came to realise
that the same fate overtakes them both.[p]

15 Then I thought in my heart,
"The fate of the fool will overtake me also.
What then do I gain by being wise?"[q]
I said in my heart,
"This too is meaningless."
16 For the wise man, like the fool, will not be long remembered;
in days to come both will be forgotten.[r]
Like the fool, the wise man too must die!

Toil Is Meaningless

17 So I hated life, because the work that is done under the sun was grievous to me.
All of it is meaningless, a chasing after the wind.[s] 18 I hated all the things I had toiled
for under the sun, because I must leave them to the one who comes after me.[t] 19 And
who knows whether he will be a wise man or a fool? Yet he will have control over
all the work into which I have poured my effort and skill under the sun. This too is
meaningless. 20 So my heart began to despair over all my toilsome labour under the
sun. 21 For a man may do his work with wisdom, knowledge and skill, and then he
must leave all he owns to someone who has not worked for it. This too is meaningless
and a great misfortune. 22 What does a man get for all the toil and anxious striving
with which he labours under the sun?[u] 23 All his days his work is pain and grief;[v]
even at night his mind does not rest. This too is meaningless.
24 A man can do nothing better than to eat and drink[w] and find satisfaction in his

2:11 [j]Ecc 1:14 [k]Ecc 1:3
2:12 [l]Ecc 1:17 [m]Ecc 1:9; 7:25
2:13 [n]Ecc 7:19; 9:18 [o]Ecc 7:11-12
2:14 [p]Ps 49:10; Pr 17:24; Ecc 3:19; 6:6; 7:2; 9:3, 11-12
2:15 [q]Ecc 6:8
2:16 [r]Ecc 1:11; 9:5
2:17 [s]Ecc 4:2
2:18 [t]Ps 39:6; 49:10
2:22 [u]Ecc 1:3; 3:9
2:23 [v]Job 5:7; 14:1; Ecc 1:18
2:24 [w]Ecc 8:15; 1Co 15:32

2:11 Solomon summarised all his attempts at finding life's meaning as "chasing after the wind". We feel the wind as it passes, but we can't catch hold of it or keep it. In all our accomplishments, even the big ones, our good feelings are only temporary. Security and self-worth are not found in these accomplishments, but far beyond them in the love of God. Think about what you consider worthwhile in your life – where you place your time, energy, and money. Will you one day look back and decide that these, too, were a "chasing after the wind"?

2:16 Solomon realised that wisdom alone cannot guarantee eternal life. Wisdom, riches, and personal achievement matter very little after death – and everyone must die. We must not build our lives on perishable pursuits, but on the solid foundation of God. Then even if everything we have is taken away, we will still have God, who is all we really need anyway. This is the point of the book of Job (see the introduction to Job).

2:16 Is death the ultimate equaliser of all people, no matter what they attained in life? While this appears to be true from an earthly perspective, God makes it clear (as Solomon later points out in 12:14) that what we do here has a great impact upon our eternal reward.

2:18–23 Solomon continues to show that hard work bears no lasting fruit for those who work solely to earn money and gain possessions. Not only will everything be left behind at death, but it may be left to those who have done nothing to earn it. In addition, it may not be well cared for, and all that was gained may be lost. In fact, Solomon's son, who inherited his throne, was often foolish – see 1 Kings 12. Hard work done with proper motives (caring for your family, serving God) is not wrong. We must work to survive, and, more important, we are responsible for the physical and spiritual well-being of those under our care. But the fruit of hard work done to glorify only ourselves will be passed on to those who may later lose or spoil it all. Such toil often leads to grief, while serving God leads to everlasting joy. Do you know the real reason you are working so hard?

2:24–26 Is Solomon recommending we make life a big, irresponsible party? No, he is encouraging us to take pleasure in what we're doing now and to enjoy life because it comes from God's hand. True enjoyment in life comes only as we follow God's guide-

2:24 [x]Ecc 3:22 [y]Ecc 3:12-13; 5:17-19; 9:7-10
2:26 [z]Job 27:17 [a]Pr 13:22
3:1 [a]ver 11, 17; Ecc 8:6
3:7 [b]Am 5:13
3:9 [c]Ecc 1:3
3:10 [d]Ecc 1:13
3:11 [e]ver 1 [f]Job 11:7; Ecc 8:17 [g]Job 28:23; Ro 11:33
3:13 [h]Ecc 2:3 [i]Ps 34:12 [j]Dt 12:7, 18; Ecc 2:24; 5:19
3:14 [k]Job 23:15; Ecc 5:7; 7:18; 8:12-13; Jas 1:17
3:15 [l]Ecc 6:10

work.[x] This too, I see, is from the hand of God,[y]
25 for without him, who can eat or find enjoyment?
26 To the man who pleases him, God gives wisdom, knowledge and happiness, but to the sinner he gives the task of gathering and storing up wealth[z] to hand it over to the one who pleases God.[a] This too is meaningless, a chasing after the wind.

2. Solomon's general observations

A Time for Everything

3 There is a time[a] for everything,
and a season for every activity under heaven:

2 a time to be born and a time to die,
a time to plant and a time to uproot,
3 a time to kill and a time to heal,
a time to tear down and a time to build,
4 a time to weep and a time to laugh,
a time to mourn and a time to dance,
5 a time to scatter stones and a time to gather them,
a time to embrace and a time to refrain,
6 a time to search and a time to give up,
a time to keep and a time to throw away,
7 a time to tear and a time to mend,
a time to be silent[b] and a time to speak,
8 a time to love and a time to hate,
a time for war and a time for peace.

9 What does the worker gain from his toil?[c]
10 I have seen the burden God has laid on men.[d]
11 He has made everything beautiful in its time.[e] He has also set eternity in the hearts of men; yet they cannot fathom[f] what God has done from beginning to end.[g]
12 I know that there is nothing better for men than to be happy and do good while they live.
13 That everyone may eat and drink,[h] and find satisfaction[i] in all his toil—this is the gift of God.[j]
14 I know that everything God does will endure for ever; nothing can be added to it and nothing taken from it. God does it so that men will revere him.[k]

15 Whatever is has already been,[l]

---

lines for living. Without him, satisfaction is a lost search. Those who really know how to enjoy life are the ones who take life each day as a gift from God, thanking him for it and serving him in it. Those without God will have no relief from toil and no direction to guide them through life's complications.

3:1–5:20 Solomon's point in this section is that God has a plan for all people. Thus he provides cycles of life, each with its work for us to do. Although we may face many problems that seem to contradict God's plan, these should not be barriers to believing in him, but rather opportunities to discover that, without God, life's problems have no lasting solutions!

3:1–8 Timing is important. All the experiences listed in these verses are appropriate at certain times. The secret to peace with God is to discover, accept, and appreciate God's perfect timing. The danger is to doubt or resent God's timing. This can lead to despair, rebellion, or moving ahead without his advice.

3:8 When is there a time for hating? We shouldn't hate evil people, but we should hate what they do. We should also hate it when people are mistreated, when children are starving, and when God is being dishonoured. In addition, we must hate sin in our lives—this is God's attitude (see Psalm 5:5).

3:9–13 Your ability to find satisfaction in your work depends to a large extent upon your attitude. You will become dissatisfied if you lose the sense of purpose God intended for your work. We can enjoy our work if we (1) remember that God has given us work to do (3:10), and (2) realise that the fruit of our labour is a gift from him (3:13). See your work as a way to serve God.

3:11 God has "set eternity in the hearts of men". This means that we can never be completely satisfied with earthly pleasures and pursuits. Because we are created in God's image, (1) we have a spiritual thirst, (2) we have eternal value, and (3) nothing but the eternal God can truly satisfy us. He has built in us a restless yearning for the kind of perfect world that can only be found in his perfect rule. He has given us a glimpse of the perfection of his creation. But it is only a glimpse; we cannot see into the future or comprehend everything. So we must trust him now and do his work on earth.

3:12 To be happy and do good while we live are worthy goals for life, but we can pursue them the wrong way. God wants us to enjoy life. When we have the proper view of God, we discover that real pleasure is found in enjoying whatever we have as gifts from God, not in what we accumulate.

3:14 What is the purpose of life? It is that we should revere the all-powerful God. To *revere* God means to respect and stand in awe of him because of who he is. Purpose in life starts with *whom* we know, not what we know or how good we are. It is impossible to fulfil your God-given purpose unless you revere God and give him first place in your life.

and what will be has been before;[m]
and God will call the past to account.[a]

16And I saw something else under the sun:

In the place of judgment—wickedness was there,
in the place of justice—wickedness was there.

17I thought in my heart,

"God will bring to judgment[n]
both the righteous and the wicked,
for there will be a time for every activity,
a time for every deed."[o]

18I also thought, "As for men, God tests them so that they may see that they are
like the animals.[p] 19Man's fate[q] is like that of the animals; the same fate awaits them
both: As one dies, so dies the other. All have the same breath;[b] man has no advantage
over the animal. Everything is meaningless. 20All go to the same place; all come from
dust, and to dust all return.[r] 21Who knows if the spirit of man rises upward[s] and
if the spirit of the animal[c] goes down into the earth?"

22So I saw that there is nothing better for a man than to enjoy his work,[t] because
that is his lot.[u] For who can bring him to see what will happen after him?

Oppression, Toil, Friendlessness

4 Again I looked and saw all the oppression[a] that was taking place under the sun:

I saw the tears of the oppressed—
and they have no comforter;
power was on the side of their oppressors—
and they have no comforter.[b]
2And I declared that the dead,[c]
who had already died,
are happier than the living,
who are still alive.[d]
3But better than both
is he who has not yet been,[e]
who has not seen the evil
that is done under the sun.[f]

4And I saw that all labour and all achievement spring from man's envy of his
neighbour. This too is meaningless, a chasing after the wind.[g]

a *15* Or *God calls back the past* **b** *19* Or *spirit* **c** *21* Or *Who knows the spirit of man, which rises upward, or the spirit of the animal, which*

3:15 [m]Ecc 1:9
3:17 [n]Job 19:29; Ecc 11:9; Mt 16:27; Ro 2:6-8; 2Th 1:6-7 [o]ver 1
3:18 [p]Ps 73:22
3:19 [q]Ecc 2:14
3:20 [r]Ge 2:7; 3:19; Job 34:15
3:21 [s]Ecc 12:7
3:22 [t]Ecc 2:24; 5:18 [u]Job 31:2
4:1 [a]Ps 12:5; Ecc 3:16 [b]La 1:16
4:2 [c]Jer 20:17-18; 22:10 [d]Job 3:17; 10:18
4:3 [e]Job 3:16; Ecc 6:3 [f]Job 3:22
4:4 [g]Ecc 1:14

3:16 There is wickedness in the place of justice. It even affects the legal system. Solomon asked how God's plan can be perfect when there is so much injustice and oppression in the world (4:1). He concluded that God does not ignore injustice, but will bring it to an end at his appointed time (12:13, 14).

3:16ff Solomon reflects on several apparent contradictions in God's control of the world: (1) there is wickedness where there should be justice (3:16, 17); (2) people created in God's image die just like the animals (3:18–21); (3) no-one comforts the oppressed (4:1–3); (4) many people are motivated by envy (4:4–6); (5) people are lonely (4:7–12); (6) recognition for accomplishments is temporary (4:13–16). It is easy to use such contradictions as excuses not to believe in God. But Solomon used them to show how we can honestly look at life's problems and still keep our faith. This life is not all there is, yet even in this life we should not pass judgment on God because we don't know everything. God's plan is for us to live for ever with him. So live with eternal values in view, realising that all contradictions will one day be cleared up by the Creator himself (12:14).

3:19–22 Our bodies can't live for ever in their present state. In that sense, humans and animals are alike. But Solomon acknowledged that God has given people the hope of eternity (see the note on 3:11), and that we will undergo judgment in the next life (3:17; 12:7, 14)—making us different from animals. Because man has eternity set in his heart, he has a unique purpose in God's overall plan. Yet we cannot discover God's purpose for our lives by our own efforts—only through building a relationship with him and seeking his guidance. Are you now living as God wants? Do you see life as a gift from him?

4:4–6 Some people are lazy while others are workaholics. The lazy person, seeing the futility of dashing about for success, folds his hands and hurts both himself and those who depend on him. The workaholic is often driven by envy, greed, and a constant desire to stay ahead of everyone else. Both extremes are foolish and irresponsible. The answer is to work hard but with moderation.

4:5
[h] Pr 6:10

5The fool folds his hands[h]
and ruins himself.
6Better one handful with tranquillity
than two handfuls with toil[i]
and chasing after the wind.

7Again I saw something meaningless under the sun:

8There was a man all alone;
he had neither son nor brother.
There was no end to his toil,
yet his eyes were not content[j] with his wealth.
"For whom am I toiling," he asked,
"and why am I depriving myself of enjoyment?"
This too is meaningless—
a miserable business!

4:6
[i] Pr 15:16-17; 16:8

9Two are better than one,
because they have a good return for their work:
10If one falls down,
his friend can help him up.
But pity the man who falls
and has no-one to help him up!
11Also, if two lie down together, they will keep warm.
But how can one keep warm alone?
12Though one may be overpowered,
two can defend themselves.
A cord of three strands is not quickly broken.

4:8
[j] Pr 27:20

Advancement Is Meaningless

13Better a poor but wise youth than an old but foolish king who no longer knows
how to take warning. 14The youth may have come from prison to the kingship, or he
may have been born in poverty within his kingdom. 15I saw that all who lived and
walked under the sun followed the youth, the king's successor. 16There was no end
to all the people who were before them. But those who came later were not pleased
with the successor. This too is meaningless, a chasing after the wind.

Stand in Awe of God

5 Guard your steps when you go to the house of God. Go near to listen rather than to offer the sacrifice of fools, who do not know that they do wrong.

5:2
[a] Jdg 11:35
[b] Job 6:24;
Pr 10:19; 20:25

2Do not be quick with your mouth,
do not be hasty in your heart
to utter anything before God.[a]
God is in heaven
and you are on earth,
so let your words be few.[b]
3As a dream[c] comes when there are many cares,
so the speech of a fool when there are many words.[d]

5:3
[c] Job 20:8
[d] Ecc 10:14

Take time to enjoy the other gifts God has given and realise that it is God who gives out the assignments and the rewards, not us.

4:9–12 There are advantages to co-operating with others. Life is designed for companionship, not isolation; for intimacy, not loneliness. Some people prefer isolation, thinking they cannot trust anyone. We are not here on earth to serve ourselves, however, but to serve God and others. Don't isolate yourself and try to go it alone. Seek companions; be a team member.

4:13–16 Advancement or getting to the top is meaningless. Position, popularity, and prestige are poor goals for a life's work. Although many seek them, they are shadows without substance. Many people seek recognition for their accomplishments; but people are fickle, changing quickly and easily. How much better to seek God's approval. His love never changes.

5:1 "Guard your steps" means "be careful". When we enter the house of God, we should have the attitude of being open and ready to listen to God, not to dictate to him what we think he should do.

4When you make a vow to God, do not delay in fulfilling it.[e] He has no pleasure
in fools; fulfil your vow.[f] 5It is better not to vow than to make a vow and not fulfil
it.[g] 6Do not let your mouth lead you into sin. And do not protest to the ⌞temple⌟
messenger, "My vow was a mistake." Why should God be angry at what you say and
destroy the work of your hands? 7Much dreaming and many words are meaningless.
Therefore stand in awe of God.[h]

5:4 [e]Dt 23:21; Jdg 11:35; Ps 119:60 [f]Nu 30:2; Ps 66:13-14; 76:11

Riches Are Meaningless

8If you see the poor oppressed[i] in a district, and justice and rights denied, do not
be surprised at such things; for one official is eyed by a higher one, and over them
both are others higher still. 9The increase from the land is taken by all; the king himself
profits from the fields.

5:5 [g]Nu 30:2-4; Pr 20:25; Jnh 2:9; Ac 5:4

10Whoever loves money never has money enough;
whoever loves wealth is never satisfied with his income.
This too is meaningless.

5:7 [h]Ecc 3:14; 12:13

11As goods increase,
so do those who consume them.
And what benefit are they to the owner
except to feast his eyes on them?

5:8 [i]Ps 12:5; Ecc 4:1

12The sleep of a labourer is sweet,
whether he eats little or much,
but the abundance of a rich man
permits him no sleep.[j]

5:12 [j]Job 20:20

13I have seen a grievous evil under the sun:[k]

wealth hoarded to the harm of its owner,
14 or wealth lost through some misfortune,
so that when he has a son
there is nothing left for him.
15Naked a man comes from his mother's womb,
and as he comes, so he departs.[l]
He takes nothing from his labour[m]
that he can carry in his hand.[n]

5:13 [k]Ecc 6:1-2

5:15 [l]Job 1:21 [m]Ps 49:17; 1Ti 6:7 [n]Ecc 1:3

16This too is a grievous evil:

As a man comes, so he departs,
and what does he gain,
since he toils for the wind?[o]
17All his days he eats in darkness,
with great frustration, affliction and anger.

5:16 [o]Pr 11:29; Ecc 1:3

18Then I realised that it is good and proper for a man to eat and drink,[p] and to find

5:18 [p]Ecc 2:3

5:4, 5 Solomon warns his readers about making foolish vows (promises) to God. In Israelite culture, making vows was a serious matter. Vows were voluntary but, once made, were unbreakable (Deuteronomy 23:21–23). It is foolish to make a vow you cannot keep or to play games with God by only partially fulfilling your vow (Proverbs 20:25). It's better not to vow than to make a vow to God and break it. It's better still to make a vow and keep it. (See the note on Matthew 5:33ff.)

5:10, 11 We always want more than we have. Solomon observed that those who love money and seek it obsessively never find the happiness it promises. Wealth also attracts scroungers and thieves, causes sleeplessness and fear, and ultimately ends in loss because it must be left behind (Mark 10:23–25; Luke 12:16–21). No matter how much you earn, if you try to create happiness by accumulating wealth, you will never have enough. Money in itself is not wrong, but loving money leads to all sorts of sin. Whatever financial situation you are in, don't depend on money to make you happy. Instead, use what you have for the Lord.

5:19, 20 God wants us to view what we have (whether it is much or little) with the right perspective – our possessions are a gift from God. Although they are not the source of joy, they are a reason to rejoice because every good thing comes from God. We should focus more on the Giver than the gift. We can be content with what

5:18 [q]Ecc 2:10, 24
5:19 [r]1Ch 29:12; 2Ch 1:12 [s]Ecc 6:2 [t]Job 31:2 [u]Ecc 2:24; 3:13
5:20 [v]Dt 12:7, 18
6:2 [a]Ps 17:14; Ecc 5:19 [b]Ecc 5:13
6:3 [c]Job 3:16; Ecc 4:3 [d]Job 3:3
6:7 [e]Pr 16:26; 27:20
6:8 [f]Ecc 2:15
6:9 [g]Ecc 1:14
6:12 [h]Job 10:20 [i]Job 14:2; Ps 39:6; Jas 4:14

satisfaction in his toilsome labour[q] under the sun during the few days of life God has
given him—for this is his lot. 19Moreover, when God gives any man wealth and
possessions,[r] and enables him to enjoy them,[s] to accept his lot[t] and be happy in
his work—this is a gift of God.[u] 20He seldom reflects on the days of his life, because
God keeps him occupied with gladness of heart.[v]

3. Solomon's practical counsel

6 I have seen another evil under the sun, and it weighs heavily on men: 2God gives
a man wealth, possessions and honour, so that he lacks nothing his heart desires,
but God does not enable him to enjoy them,[a] and a stranger enjoys them instead. This
is meaningless, a grievous evil.[b]

3A man may have a hundred children and live many years; yet no matter how long
he lives, if he cannot enjoy his prosperity and does not receive proper burial, I say
that a stillborn[c] child is better off than he.[d] 4It comes without meaning, it departs
in darkness, and in darkness its name is shrouded. 5Though it never saw the sun or
knew anything, it has more rest than does that man—6even if he lives a thousand years
twice over but fails to enjoy his prosperity. Do not all go to the same place?

7All man's efforts are for his mouth,
  yet his appetite is never satisfied.[e]
8What advantage has a wise man
  over a fool?[f]
What does a poor man gain
  by knowing how to conduct himself before others?
9Better what the eye sees
  than the roving of the appetite.
This too is meaningless,
  a chasing after the wind.[g]

10Whatever exists has already been named,
  and what man is has been known;
no man can contend
  with one who is stronger than he.
11The more the words,
  the less the meaning,
  and how does that profit anyone?

12For who knows what is good for a man in life, during the few and meaningless
days[h] he passes through like a shadow?[i] Who can tell him what will happen under
the sun after he is gone?

---

we have when we realise that with God we have everything we need.

6:1–8:15 In this section, Solomon shows that having the right attitude about God can help us deal with present injustices. Prosperity is not always good, and adversity is not always bad. But God is always good; if we live as he wants us to, we will be content.

6:1–6 "God does not enable him to enjoy them" probably means that the person has died. Even if he had lived a long life, it is ultimately meaningless in itself because all that he has accumulated is left behind. Everyone dies, and both rich and poor end up in the grave. Many people work hard to prolong life and improve their physical condition. Yet people don't spend nearly as much time or effort on their spiritual health. How shortsighted it is to work hard to extend this life and not take the steps God requires to gain eternal life.

6:6 "All go to the same place" means that everyone dies.

6:9 "The roving of the appetite" refers to wasting time dreaming and wishing for what one doesn't have.

6:10 God knows and directs everything that happens, and he is in complete control over our lives, even though at times it may not seem like it. How foolish it is for us to contend with our Creator, who knows us completely and can see the future. (See also Jeremiah 18:6; Romans 9:19–24.)

6:12 Solomon is stating the profound truth that we cannot predict what the future holds. The only one who knows what will happen after we're gone is God. No human knows the future, so each day must be lived for its own value. Solomon is arguing against the notion that human beings can take charge of their own destiny. In all our plans we should look up to God, not just ahead to the future.

Wisdom

7 A good name is better than fine perfume,[a]
and the day of death better than the day of birth.
2It is better to go to a house of mourning
than to go to a house of feasting,
for death[b] is the destiny[c] of every man;
the living should take this to heart.
3Sorrow is better than laughter,[d]
because a sad face is good for the heart.
4The heart of the wise is in the house of mourning,
but the heart of fools is in the house of pleasure.[e]
5It is better to heed a wise man's rebuke[f]
than to listen to the song of fools.
6Like the crackling of thorns[g] under the pot,
so is the laughter[h] of fools.
This too is meaningless.

7Extortion turns a wise man into a fool,
and a bribe[i] corrupts the heart.

8The end of a matter is better than its beginning,
and patience[j] is better than pride.
9Do not be quickly provoked[k] in your spirit,
for anger resides in the lap of fools.
10Do not say, "Why were the old days better than these?"
For it is not wise to ask such questions.

11Wisdom, like an inheritance, is a good thing[l]
and benefits those who see the sun.[m]
12Wisdom is a shelter
as money is a shelter,
but the advantage of knowledge is this:
that wisdom preserves the life of its possessor.

13Consider what God has done:[n]

Who can straighten
what he has made crooked?[o]

7:1 [a]Pr 22:1; SS 1:3
7:2 [b]Pr 11:19 [c]Ps 90:12
7:3 [d]Pr 14:13
7:4 [e]Ecc 2:1; Jer 16:8
7:5 [f]Ps 141:5; Pr 13:18; 15:31-32
7:6 [g]Ps 58:9; 118:12 [h]Ecc 2:2
7:7 [i]Ex 18:21; 23:8; Dt 16:19
7:8 [j]Pr 14:29; Gal 5:22; Eph 4:2
7:9 [k]Mt 5:22; Pr 14:17; Jas 1:19
7:11 [l]Pr 8:10-11; Ecc 2:13 [m]Ecc 11:7
7:13 [n]Ecc 2:24 [o]Ecc 1:15

7:1–4 This seems to contradict Solomon's previous advice to eat, drink, and find satisfaction in one's work – to enjoy what God has given. We are to enjoy what we have while we can, but realise that adversity also strikes. Adversity reminds us that life is short, teaches us to live wisely, and refines our character. Christianity and Judaism see value in suffering and sorrow. The Greeks and Romans despised it; Eastern religions seek to live above it; but Christians and Jews see it as a refining fire. Most would agree that we learn more about God from difficult times than from happy times. Do you try to avoid sorrow and suffering at all costs? See your struggles as great opportunities to learn from God.

7:2, 4 Many people avoid thinking about death, refuse to face it, and are reluctant to attend funerals. Solomon is not encouraging us to think morbidly, but he knows that it is helpful to think clearly about death. It reminds us that there is still time for change, time to examine the direction of our lives, and time to confess our sins and find forgiveness from God. Because everyone will eventually die, it makes sense to plan ahead to experience God's mercy rather than his justice.

7:7 Money talks, and it can confuse those who would otherwise judge fairly. We hear about bribes given to judges, police officers, and witnesses. Bribes are given to hurt those who tell the truth and help those who oppose it. The person who is involved in extortion or takes a bribe is indeed a fool, no matter how wise he thought he was beforehand. It is said that everyone has a price, but those who are truly wise cannot be bought at any price.

7:8 To finish what we start takes hard work, wise guidance, self-discipline, and patience. Anyone with vision can start a big project. But vision without wisdom often results in unfinished projects and goals.

7:14 God allows both good times and bad times to come to everyone. He blends them in our lives in such a way that we can't predict the future or count on human wisdom and power. We usually give ourselves the credit for the good times. Then in bad times, we tend to blame God without thanking him for the good that comes out of it. When life appears certain and controllable, don't let self-satisfaction or complacency make you too comfortable, or God may allow bad times to drive you back to him. When life seems uncertain and uncontrollable, don't despair – God is in control and will bring good results out of tough times.

14When times are good, be happy;
but when times are bad, consider:
God has made the one
as well as the other.
Therefore, a man cannot discover
anything about his future.

15In this meaningless life[p] of mine I have seen both of these:

a righteous man perishing in his righteousness,
and a wicked man living long in his wickedness.[q]
16Do not be over-righteous,
neither be overwise —
why destroy yourself?
17Do not be overwicked,
and do not be a fool —
why die before your time?[r]
18It is good to grasp the one
and not let go of the other.
The man who fears God[s] will avoid all ⌊extremes⌋.[a]

19Wisdom[t] makes one wise man more powerful[u]
than ten rulers in a city.

20There is not a righteous man[v] on earth
who does what is right and never sins.[w]

21Do not pay attention to every word people say,
or you[x] may hear your servant cursing you —
22for you know in your heart
that many times you yourself have cursed others.

23All this I tested by wisdom and I said,

"I am determined to be wise"[y] —
but this was beyond me.
24Whatever wisdom may be,
it is far off and most profound —
who can discover it?[z]
25So I turned my mind to understand,
to investigate and to search out wisdom and the scheme of things[a]
and to understand the stupidity of wickedness
and the madness of folly.[b]

26I find more bitter than death
the woman who is a snare,[c]
whose heart is a trap
and whose hands are chains.
The man who pleases God will escape her,
but the sinner she will ensnare.[d]

7:15 [p]Job 7:7 [q]Ecc 8:12-14; Jer 12:1
7:17 [r]Job 15:32; Ps 55:23
7:18 [s]Ecc 3:14
7:19 [t]Ecc 2:13 [u]Ecc 9:13-18
7:20 [v]Ps 14:3 [w]1Ki 8:46; 2Ch 6:36; Pr 20:9; Ro 3:23
7:21 [x]Pr 30:10
7:23 [y]Ecc 1:17; Ro 1:22
7:24 [z]Job 28:12
7:25 [a]Job 28:3 [b]Ecc 1:17
7:26 [c]Ex 10:7; Jdg 14:15 [d]Pr 2:16-19; 5:3-5; 7:23; 22:14

a *18* Or *will follow them both*

7:16–18 How can a person be too righteous or too wise? This is a warning against religious conceit – legalism or false righteousness. Solomon was saying that some people become too righteous or wise *in their own eyes* because they are deluded by their own religious acts. They are so rigid or narrow in their views that they lose their sensitivity to the true reason for being good – to honour God. Balance is important. God created us to be whole people who seek his righteousness and goodness. Thus we should avoid both extremes of legalism and immorality.

7:23–25 Solomon, the wisest man in the world, confessed how difficult it had been to act and think wisely. He emphasised that no matter how much we know, there are always mysteries we will never understand. So thinking you have enough wisdom is a sure sign that you don't.

27"Look," says the Teacher,[b][e] "this is what I have discovered:

"Adding one thing to another to discover the scheme of things—
28 while I was still searching
but not finding—
I found one ⌞upright⌟ man among a thousand,
but not one ⌞upright⌟ woman[f] among them all.
29This only have I found:
God made mankind upright,
but men have gone in search of many schemes."

8

Who is like the wise man?
Who knows the explanation of things?
Wisdom brightens a man's face
and changes its hard appearance.

Obey the King

2Obey the king's command, I say, because you took an oath before God. 3Do not
be in a hurry to leave the king's presence.[a] Do not stand up for a bad cause, for he
will do whatever he pleases. 4Since a king's word is supreme, who can say to him,
"What are you doing?[b]"

5Whoever obeys his command will come to no harm,
and the wise heart will know the proper time and procedure.
6For there is a proper time and procedure for every matter,[c]
though a man's misery weighs heavily upon him.

7Since no man knows the future,
who can tell him what is to come?
8No man has power over the wind to contain it;[a]
so no-one has power over the day of his death.
As no-one is discharged in time of war,
so wickedness will not release those who practise it.

9All this I saw, as I applied my mind to everything done under the sun. There is
a time when a man lords it over others to his own[b] hurt. 10Then too, I saw the wicked
buried[d]—those who used to come and go from the holy place and receive praise[c]
in the city where they did this. This too is meaningless.
11When the sentence for a crime is not quickly carried out, the hearts of the people
are filled with schemes to do wrong. 12Although a wicked man commits a hundred
crimes and still lives a long time, I know that it will go better[e] with God-fearing
men,[f] who are reverent before God.[g] 13Yet because the wicked do not fear God,[h]
it will not go well with them, and their days[i] will not lengthen like a shadow.

[b] 27 Or *leader of the assembly* [a] 8 Or *over his spirit to retain it* [b] 9 Or *to their* [c] 10 Some Hebrew manuscripts and Septuagint (Aquila); most Hebrew manuscripts *and are forgotten*

7:27 [e]Ecc 1:1
7:28 [f]1Ki 11:3
8:3 [a]Ecc 10:4
8:4 [b]Job 9:12; Est 1:19; Da 4:35
8:6 [c]Ecc 3:1
8:10 [d]Ecc 1:11
8:12 [e]Dt 12:28; Ps 37:11, 18-19; Pr 1:32-33; Isa 3:10-11 [f]Ex 1:20 [g]Ecc 3:14
8:13 [h]Ecc 3:14; Isa 3:11 [i]Dt 4:40; Job 5:26; Ps 34:12; Isa 65:20

7:27, 28 Did Solomon think women were not capable of being upright (wise and good)? No, because in the book of Proverbs he personified wisdom as a responsible woman. The point of Solomon's statement is not that women are unwise, but that hardly anyone, man or woman, is upright before God. In his search, Solomon found that goodness and wisdom were almost as scarce among men as among women, even though men were given religious education in his culture and women were not. In effect, the verse is saying, "I have found only one in a thousand people who is wise in God's eyes. No. I have found even fewer than that!"

7:29 God created human beings to live uprightly and do what is right. Instead, they have left God's path to follow their own downward road.

8:1 Wisdom is the ability to see life from God's perspective and then to know the best course of action to take. Most people would agree that wisdom is a valuable asset, but how can we acquire it? Proverbs 9:10 teaches that the fear of the Lord (respect and honour) is the beginning of wisdom. Wisdom comes from knowing and trusting God; it is not merely the way to find God. Knowing God will lead to understanding and then to sharing this knowledge with others.

8:10 This verse probably refers to how quickly we forget the evil done by some people after they have died. Returning from the cemetery, we praise them in the very city where they did their evil deeds.

8:11 If God doesn't punish us immediately, we must not assume that he doesn't care or that sin has no consequences, even though it is easy to sin when we don't feel the consequences right away. When a young child does something wrong, and the wrong is not discovered, it will be much easier for the child to repeat the act. But God knows every wrong we commit, and one day we will have to answer for all that we have done (12:14).

14 There is something else meaningless that occurs on earth: righteous men who get
what the wicked deserve, and wicked men who get what the righteous deserve.[j] This
too, I say, is meaningless.[k] 15 So I commend the enjoyment of life[l], because nothing
is better for a man under the sun than to eat and drink[m] and be glad.[n] Then joy will
accompany him in his work all the days of the life God has given him under the sun.
16 When I applied my mind to know wisdom[o] and to observe man's labour on
earth[p]—his eyes not seeing sleep day or night—17 then I saw all that God has done.[q]
No-one can comprehend what goes on under the sun. Despite all his efforts to search
it out, man cannot discover its meaning. Even if a wise man claims he knows, he
cannot really comprehend it.[r]

4. Solomon's final conclusion

A Common Destiny for All

9 So I reflected on all this and concluded that the righteous and the wise and what
they do are in God's hands, but no man knows whether love or hate awaits him.[a]
2 All share a common destiny—the righteous and the wicked, the good and the bad,**[a]**
the clean and the unclean, those who offer sacrifices and those who do not.

As it is with the good man,
so with the sinner;
as it is with those who take oaths,
so with those who are afraid to take them.[b]

3 This is the evil in everything that happens under the sun: The same destiny
overtakes all.[c] The hearts of men, moreover, are full of evil and there is madness
in their hearts while they live,[d] and afterwards they join the dead.[e] 4 Anyone who
is among the living has hope**[b]**—even a live dog is better off than a dead lion!

5 For the living know that they will die,
but the dead know nothing;[f]
they have no further reward,
and even the memory of them[g] is forgotten.[h]
6 Their love, their hate
and their jealousy have long since vanished;
never again will they have a part
in anything that happens under the sun.[i]

7 Go, eat your food with gladness, and drink your wine[j] with a joyful heart,[k] for
it is now that God favours what you do. 8 Always be clothed in white,[l] and always
anoint your head with oil. 9 Enjoy life with your wife,[m] whom you love, all the days
of this meaningless life that God has given you under the sun—all your meaningless

a *2* Septuagint (Aquila), Vulgate and Syriac; Hebrew does not have *and the bad.* **b** *4* Or *What then is to be chosen? With all who live, there is hope*

8:14 [j] Job 21:7; Ps 73:14; Mal 3:15 [k] Ecc 7:15
8:15 [l] Ps 42:8 [m] Ex 32:6; Ecc 2:3 [n] Ecc 2:24; 3:12-13; 5:18; 9:7
8:16 [o] Ecc 1:17 [p] Ecc 1:13
8:17 [q] Job 28:3 [r] Job 5:9; 28:23; Ecc 3:11; Ro 11:33
9:1 [a] Dt 33:3; Job 12:10; Ecc 10:14
9:2 [b] Job 9:22; Ecc 2:14; 6:6; 7:2
9:3 [c] Job 9:22; Ecc 2:14 [d] Jer 11:8; 13:10; 16:12; 17:9 [e] Job 21:26
9:5 [f] Job 14:21 [g] Ps 9:6 [h] Ecc 1:11; 2:16; Isa 26:14
9:6 [i] Job 21:21
9:7 [j] Nu 6:20 [k] Ecc 2:24; 8:15
9:8 [l] Ps 23:5; Rev 3:4
9:9 [m] Pr 5:18

8:15 Solomon recalls the remedy for life's unanswered questions. He recommends joy and contentment as encouragement for us along life's pilgrimage. We must accept each day with its daily measure of work, food, and pleasure. Let us learn to enjoy what God has given us to refresh and strengthen us to continue his work.

8:16, 17 Even if he had access to all the world's wisdom, the wisest man would know very little. No-one can fully comprehend God and all that he has done, and there are always more questions than answers. But the unknown should not cast a shadow over our joy, faith, or work because we know that someone greater is in control and that we can put our trust in him. Don't let what you don't know about the future destroy the joy God wants to give you today.

9:2 "All share a common destiny" means that all will die.

9:5, 10 When Solomon says the dead know nothing and that there is no work, planning, knowledge, or wisdom in death, he is not contrasting life with afterlife, but life with death. After you die, you can't change what you have done. Resurrection to a new life after death was a vague concept for Old Testament believers. It was only made clear after Jesus rose from the dead.

9:7–10 Considering the uncertainties of the future and the certainty of death, Solomon recommends enjoying life as God's gift. He may have been criticising those who put off all present pleasures in order to accumulate wealth, much like those who get caught up in today's rat race. Solomon asks, "What is your wealth really worth, anyway?" Because the future is so uncertain, we should enjoy God's gifts while we are able.

9:8 Wearing white clothes and having oil on the head were signs of happiness and celebration.

9:9 Solomon also wrote a proverb about marriage. "He who finds a wife finds what is good and receives favour from the LORD" (Proverbs 18:22). How sad it would be to be married and not appreciate the enjoyment and companionship God has given you.

days. For this is your lot[n] in life and in your toilsome labour under the sun.
10Whatever[o] your hand finds to do, do it with all your might,[p] for in the grave,[c][q]
where you are going, there is neither working nor planning nor knowledge nor
wisdom.[r]

11I have seen something else under the sun:

The race is not to the swift
or the battle to the strong,[s]
nor does food come to the wise[t]
or wealth to the brilliant
or favour to the learned;
but time and chance[u] happen to them all.[v]

12Moreover, no man knows when his hour will come:

As fish are caught in a cruel net,
or birds are taken in a snare,
so men are trapped by evil times[w]
that fall unexpectedly upon them.[x]

Wisdom Better Than Folly

13I also saw under the sun this example of wisdom[y] that greatly impressed me:
14There was once a small city with only a few people in it. And a powerful king came
against it, surrounded it and built huge siegeworks against it. 15Now there lived in
that city a man poor but wise, and he saved the city by his wisdom. But nobody
remembered that poor man.[z] 16So I said, "Wisdom is better than strength." But the
poor man's wisdom is despised, and his words are no longer heeded.[a]

17The quiet words of the wise are more to be heeded
than the shouts of a ruler of fools.
18Wisdom[b] is better than weapons of war,
but one sinner destroys much good.

10 As dead flies give perfume a bad smell,
so a little folly[a] outweighs wisdom and honour.
2The heart of the wise inclines to the right,
but the heart of the fool to the left.
3Even as he walks along the road,
the fool lacks sense
and shows everyone[b] how stupid he is.
4If a ruler's anger rises against you,
do not leave your post;[c]
calmness can lay great errors to rest.[d]

5There is an evil I have seen under the sun,

[c] *10* Hebrew *Sheol*

9:9 [n]Job 31:2
9:10 [o]1Sa 10:7 [p]Ecc 11:6; Ro 12:11; Col 3:23 [q]Nu 16:33 [r]Ecc 2:24
9:11 [s]Am 2:14-15 [t]Job 32:13; Isa 47:10; Jer 9:23 [u]Ecc 2:14 [v]Dt 8:18
9:12 [w]Pr 29:6 [x]Ps 73:22; Ecc 2:14; 8:7
9:13 [y]2Sa 20:22
9:15 [z]Ge 40:14; Ecc 1:11; 2:16; 4:13
9:16 [a]Pr 21:22; Ecc 7:19
9:18 [b]ver 16
10:1 [a]Pr 13:16; 18:2
10:3 [b]Pr 13:16; 18:2
10:4 [c]Ecc 8:3 [d]Pr 16:14; 25:15

9:10, 11 It isn't difficult to think of cases where the swiftest or the strongest don't win, the wise go hungry, and the intelligent are unrewarded with wealth or honour. Some people see such examples and call life unfair, and they are right. The world is finite, and sin has twisted life, making it what God did not intend. Solomon is trying to reduce our expectations. The book of Proverbs emphasises how life would go if everyone acted fairly; Ecclesiastes explains what usually happens in our sinful and imperfect world. We must keep our perspective. Don't let the inequities of life keep you from earnest, dedicated work. We serve God, not people (see Colossians 3:23).

9:13–18 Our society honours wealth, attractiveness, and success above wisdom. Yet wisdom is a greater asset than strength, although it is often unrecognised by the masses. Even though it is more effective, wisdom is not always heard, and wise people often go unheeded. From this parable we can learn to be receptive to wisdom, no matter who it comes from.

10:4 This proverb has implications for employer/employee relationships. Employees should ride out the temper tantrums of their employer. If we quietly do our work and don't get upset, the employer will probably get over his or her anger and calm down.

10:5–7 By describing these circumstances that aren't fair or don't make sense, Solomon is saying that wisdom alone can't bring justice. Solomon continues to build to his conclusion that everything we have (from wisdom to riches) is nothing without God. But when God uses what little we have, it becomes all we could ever want or need.

10:6 [e]Pr 29:2
10:7 [f]Pr 19:10
10:8 [g]Ps 7:15; 57:6; Pr 26:27 [h]Est 2:23; Ps 9:16; Am 5:19
10:9 [i]Pr 26:27
10:11 [j]Ps 58:5; Isa 3:3
10:12 [k]Pr 10:32 [l]Pr 10:14; 14:3; 15:2; 18:7
10:14 [m]Pr 15:2; Ecc 5:3; 6:12; 8:7 [n]Ecc 9:1
10:16 [o]Isa 3:4-5, 12
10:17 [p]Dt 14:26; 1Sa 25:36; Pr 31:4
10:18 [q]Pr 20:4; 24:30-34
10:19 [r]Ge 14:18; Jdg 9:13
10:20 [s]Ex 22:28

the sort of error that arises from a ruler:
6 Fools are put in many high positions,[e]
while the rich occupy the low ones.
7 I have seen slaves on horseback,
while princes go on foot like slaves.[f]

8 Whoever digs a pit may fall into it;[g]
whoever breaks through a wall may be bitten by a snake.[h]
9 Whoever quarries stones may be injured by them;
whoever splits logs may be endangered by them.[i]

10 If the axe is dull
and its edge unsharpened,
more strength is needed
but skill will bring success.

11 If a snake bites before it is charmed,
there is no profit for the charmer.[j]

12 Words from a wise man's mouth are gracious,[k]
but a fool is consumed by his own lips.[l]
13 At the beginning his words are folly;
at the end they are wicked madness—
14 and the fool multiplies words.[m]

No-one knows what is coming—
who can tell him what will happen after him?[n]

15 A fool's work wearies him;
he does not know the way to town.

16 Woe to you, O land whose king was a servant[a][o]
and whose princes feast in the morning.
17 Blessed are you, O land whose king is of noble birth
and whose princes eat at a proper time—
for strength and not for drunkenness.[p]

18 If a man is lazy, the rafters sag;
if his hands are idle, the house leaks.[q]

19 A feast is made for laughter,
and wine[r] makes life merry,
but money is the answer for everything.

20 Do not revile the king[s] even in your thoughts,
or curse the rich in your bedroom,
because a bird of the air may carry your words,
and a bird on the wing may report what you say.

[a] *16 Or king is a child*

10:10 Trying to do anything without the necessary skills or tools is like chopping wood with a dull axe. If your tool is dull, you should sharpen it to do a better job. Similarly, if you lack skills, you should sharpen them through training and practice. In each situation, sharpening the axe means recognising where a problem exists, acquiring or honing the skills (or tools) to do the job better, and then going out and doing it. Find the areas of your life where your "axe" is dull, and sharpen your skills so you can be more effective for God's work.

10:16–18 When the Israelites had immature and irresponsible leaders, their nation fell. The books of 1 and 2 Kings describe the decline of the kingdoms when the leaders were concerned only about themselves. These verses pinpoint the basic problems of these leaders—selfishness and laziness.

10:19 Government leaders, businesses, families, even churches get trapped into thinking money is the answer to every problem. We throw money at our problems. But just as the thrill of wine is only temporary, the soothing effect of the last purchase soon wears off and we have to buy more. Scripture recognises that money is necessary for survival, but it warns against the love of money (see Matthew 6:24; 1 Timothy 6:10; Hebrews 13:5). Money is dangerous because it deceives us into thinking that wealth is the easiest way to get everything we want. The love of money is sinful because we trust money rather than God to solve our problems. Those who pursue its empty promises will one day discover that they have nothing because they are spiritually bankrupt.

Bread Upon the Waters

11 Cast[a] your bread upon the waters,
for after many days you will find it again.[b]
2Give portions to seven, yes to eight,
for you do not know what disaster may come upon the land.

3If clouds are full of water,
they pour rain upon the earth.
Whether a tree falls to the south or to the north,
in the place where it falls, there will it lie.
4Whoever watches the wind will not plant;
whoever looks at the clouds will not reap.

5As you do not know the path of the wind,[c]
or how the body is formed[a] in a mother's womb,[d]
so you cannot understand the work of God,
the Maker of all things.

6Sow your seed in the morning,
and at evening let not your hands be idle,[e]
for you do not know which will succeed,
whether this or that,
or whether both will do equally well.

Remember Your Creator While Young

7Light is sweet,
and it pleases the eyes to see the sun.[f]
8However many years a man may live,
let him enjoy them all.
But let him remember[g] the days of darkness,
for they will be many.
Everything to come is meaningless.

9Be happy, young man, while you are young,
and let your heart give you joy in the days of your youth.
Follow the ways of your heart
and whatever your eyes see,
but know that for all these things
God will bring you to judgment.[h]
10So then, banish anxiety[i] from your heart
and cast off the troubles of your body,
for youth and vigour are meaningless.[j]

a 5 Or *know how life* (or *the spirit*) / *enters the body being formed*

11:1 [a]ver 6; Isa 32:20; Hos 10:12 [b]Dt 24:19; Pr 19:17; Mt 10:42

11:5 [c]Jn 3:8-10 [d]Ps 139:14-16

11:6 [e]Ecc 9:10

11:7 [f]Ecc 7:11

11:8 [g]Ecc 12:1

11:9 [h]Job 19:29; Ecc 2:24; 3:17; 12:14; Ro 10:10

11:10 [i]Ps 94:19 [j]Ecc 2:24

11:1–5 In these verses Solomon summarises that life involves both risk and opportunity. Because life has no guarantees, we must be prepared. "Cast your bread upon the waters" means that life has opportunities and we must seize them, not merely play it safe. Solomon does not support a despairing attitude. Just because life is uncertain does not mean we should do nothing. We need a spirit of trust and adventure, facing life's risks and opportunities with God-directed enthusiasm and faith.

11:4 Waiting for perfect conditions will mean inactivity. This practical insight is especially applicable to our spiritual life. If we wait for the perfect time and place for personal Bible reading, we will never begin. If we wait for a perfect church, we will never join. If we wait for the perfect ministry, we will never serve. Take steps now to grow spiritually. Don't wait for conditions that may never exist.

11:7, 8 Solomon is no dreary pessimist in 11:7 – 12:14. He encourages us to rejoice in every day but to remember that eternity is far longer than a person's life span. Psalm 90:12 says, "Teach us to number our days aright, that we may gain a heart of wisdom." The wise person does not just think about the moment and its impact; he or she takes the long-term view towards eternity. Approach your decisions from God's perspective – consider their impact ten years from now and into eternity. Live with the attitude that although our lives are short, we will live with God for ever.

11:9, 10 We often hear people say, "It doesn't matter." But many of your choices will be irreversible – they will stay with you for a lifetime. What you do when you're young *does* matter. Enjoy life now, but don't do anything physically, morally, or spiritually that will prevent you from enjoying life when you are old.

12:1
[a]Ecc 11:8
[b]2Sa 19:35

12:4
[c]Jer 25:10

12:5
[d]Job 17:13; 10:21
[e]Jer 9:17; Am 5:16

12:7
[f]Ge 3:19; Job 34:15; Ps 146:4
[g]Ecc 3:21
[h]Job 20:8; Zec 12:1

12:8
[i]Ecc 1:2

12:9
[j]1Ki 4:32

12:10
[k]Pr 22:20-21

12:11
[l]Ezr 9:8

12

Remember[a] your Creator
in the days of your youth,
before the days of trouble[b] come
and the years approach when you will say,
"I find no pleasure in them"—
2before the sun and the light
and the moon and the stars grow dark,
and the clouds return after the rain;
3when the keepers of the house tremble,
and the strong men stoop,
when the grinders cease because they are few,
and those looking through the windows grow dim;
4when the doors to the street are closed
and the sound of grinding fades;
when men rise up at the sound of birds,
but all their songs grow faint;[c]
5when men are afraid of heights
and of dangers in the streets;
when the almond tree blossoms
and the grasshopper drags himself along
and desire no longer is stirred.
Then man goes to his eternal home[d]
and mourners[e] go about the streets.

6Remember him—before the silver cord is severed,
or the golden bowl is broken;
before the pitcher is shattered at the spring,
or the wheel broken at the well,
7and the dust returns[f] to the ground it came from,
and the spirit returns to God[g] who gave it.[h]

8"Meaningless! Meaningless!" says the Teacher.[a]
"Everything is meaningless!"[i]

The Conclusion of the Matter

9Not only was the Teacher wise, but also he imparted knowledge to the people. He
pondered and searched out and set in order many proverbs.[j] 10The Teacher searched
to find just the right words, and what he wrote was upright and true.[k]

11The words of the wise are like goads, their collected sayings like firmly embedded
nails[l]—given by one Shepherd. 12Be warned, my son, of anything in addition to
them.

a *8* Or *the leader of the assembly*; also in verses 9 and 10

12:1 A life without God can produce a bitter, lonely, and hopeless old age. A life centred around God is fulfilling; it will make the "days of trouble"—when disabilities, sickness, and handicaps cause barriers to enjoying life—satisfying because of the hope of eternal life. Being young is exciting. But the excitement of youth can become a barrier to closeness with God if it makes young people focus on passing pleasures instead of eternal values. Make your strength available to God when it is still yours—during your youthful years. Don't waste it on evil or meaningless activities that become bad habits and make you callous. Seek God now.

12:6–8 The silver cord, golden bowl, pitcher, and wheel symbolise life's fragility. How easily death comes to us; how swiftly and unexpectedly we can return to the dust from which we came. Therefore, we should recognise life as a precious resource to be used wisely and not squandered frivolously.

12:7, 8 Stripped of God's Spirit, our bodies return to dust. Stripped of God's purpose, our work is in vain. Stripped of God's love, our service is futile. We must put God first over all we do and in all we do because without him we have nothing. Knowing that life is futile without God motivates the wise person to seek God first.

12:11 A goad (also called an oxgoad) was a sharp metal tip attached to a handle and used to keep oxen or cattle moving. Like a goad, a wise word or important truth might be unpleasant when first applied, but it will keep us moving in God's direction.

12:12 There are endless opinions about life and philosophies about how we should live that could be read and studied for ever. It is not wrong to study these opinions, but we should spend the majority of our time feeding on the truth of God's word. Wisdom should lead to action. Wise students of the Bible will understand and do what they are taught. Because our time on earth is so short, we should use it to learn important truths—they affect this life and eternity.

Of making many books there is no end, and much study wearies the body.[m]

13Now all has been heard;
here is the conclusion of the matter:
Fear God and keep his commandments,[n]
for this is the whole ⌞duty⌟ of man.[o]
14For God will bring every deed into judgment,[p]
including every hidden thing,[q]
whether it is good or evil.

12:12 [m]Ecc 1:18

12:13 [n]Dt 4:2; 10:12 [o]Mic 6:8

12:14 [p]Ecc 3:17 [q]Mt 10:26; 1Co 4:5

12:13, 14 In his conclusion, Solomon presents his antidotes for the two main ailments presented in this book. Those who lack purpose and direction in life should fear God and keep his commandments. Those who think life is unfair should remember that God will review every person's life to determine how he or she has responded to him, and he will bring every deed into judgment. Have you committed your life to God, both present and future? Does your life measure up to his standards?

12:13, 14 The book of Ecclesiastes cannot be interpreted correctly without reading these final verses. No matter what the mysteries and apparent contradictions of life are, we must work towards the single purpose of knowing God.

In Ecclesiastes, Solomon shows us that we should enjoy life, but this does not exempt us from obeying God's commandments. We should search for purpose and meaning in life, but they cannot be found in human endeavours. We should acknowledge the evil, foolishness, and injustice in life, yet maintain a positive attitude and strong faith in God.

All people will have to stand before God and be judged for what they did in this life. We will not be able to use life's inconsistencies as an excuse for failing to live properly. To live properly, we need to (1) recognise that human effort apart from God is futile; (2) put God first – now; (3) receive everything good as a gift from God; (4) realise that God will judge both evil and good; (5) know that God will judge the quality of every person's life. How strange that people spend their lives striving for the very enjoyment that God gives freely, as a gift.

SONG OF SONGS

SATURATED with stories of sexual escapades, secret rendezvous, and extramarital affairs, today's media preach that immorality means freedom, perversion is natural, and commitment is old-fashioned. Sex, created by God and pronounced good in Eden, has been twisted, exploited, and turned into an urgent, illicit, casual, and self-gratifying activity. Love has turned into lust, giving into getting, and lasting commitment into "no strings attached".

In reality, sexual intercourse, the physical and emotional union of male and female, should be a holy means of celebrating love, producing children, and experiencing pleasure, protected by the commitment of marriage.

God thinks sex is important, and Scripture contains numerous guidelines for its use and warnings about its misuse. And sex is always mentioned in the context of a loving relationship between husband and wife. Perhaps the highlight of this is Song of Songs, the intimate story of a man and a woman, their love, courtship, and marriage. Solomon probably wrote this "song" in his youth, before being overtaken by his own obsession with women, sex, and pleasure.

A moving story, drama, and poem, Song of Songs features the love dialogue between a simple Jewish maiden (the Shulammite woman) and her lover (Solomon, the king). They describe in intimate detail their feelings for each other and their longings to be together. Throughout the dialogue, sex and marriage are put in their proper, God-given perspective.

There has been much debate over the meaning of this song. Some say it is an allegory of God's love for Israel and/or for the church. Others say it is a literal story about married love. But in reality, it is both—an historical story with two layers of meaning. On one level we learn about love, marriage, and sex; and on the other level we see God's overwhelming love for his people. As you read Song of Songs, remember that you are loved by God, and commit yourself to seeing life, sex, and marriage from his point of view.

VITAL STATISTICS

PURPOSE:
To tell of the love between a bridegroom (King Solomon) and his bride, to affirm the sanctity of marriage, and to picture God's love for his people

AUTHOR:
Solomon

DATE WRITTEN:
Probably early in Solomon's reign

SETTING:
Israel—the Shulammite woman's garden and the king's palace

KEY VERSE:
"I am my lover's and my lover is mine; he browses among the lilies" (6:3).

KEY PEOPLE:
King Solomon, the Shulammite woman, and friends

THE BLUEPRINT

1. The wedding day (1:1—2:7)
2. Memories of courtship (2:8—3:5)
3. Memories of engagement (3:6—5:1)
4. A troubling dream (5:2—6:3)
5. Praising the bride's beauty (6:4—7:9a)
6. The bride's tender appeal (7:9b—8:4)
7. The power of love (8:5–14)

Song of Songs is a wedding song honouring marriage. The most explicit statements on sex in the Bible can be found in this book. It has often been criticised through the centuries because of its sensuous language. The purity and sacredness of love represented here, however, are greatly needed in our day where distorted attitudes about love and marriage are commonplace. God created sex and intimacy, and they are holy and good when enjoyed within the bounds of marriage. A husband and wife honour God when they love and enjoy each other.

MEGATHEMES

THEME	EXPLANATION	IMPORTANCE
Sex	Sex is God's gift to his creatures. He endorses sex, but restricts its expression to those committed to each other in marriage.	God wants sex to be motivated by love and commitment, not lust. It is for mutual pleasure, not selfish enjoyment.
Love	As the relationship developed, the beauty and wonder of a romance unfolded between Solomon and his bride. The intense power of love affected the hearts, minds, and bodies of the two lovers.	Because love is such a powerful expression of feeling and commitment between two people, it is not to be regarded casually. We are not to manipulate others into loving us, and love should not be prematurely encouraged in a relationship.
Commitment	The power of love requires more than the language of feeling to protect it. Sexual expression is such an integral part of our selfhood that we need the boundary of marriage to safeguard our love. Marriage is the celebration of daily commitment to each other.	While romance keeps a marriage interesting, commitment keeps romance from dwindling away. The decision to commit yourself to your spouse alone *begins* at the marriage altar. It must be maintained day by day.
Beauty	The two lovers praise the beauty they see in each other. The language they use shows the spontaneity and mystery of love. Our praise should not be limited to physical beauty; beautiful personality and moral purity should also be praised.	Our love for our spouse makes him or her appear beautiful. It is the inner qualities that keep love alive. Don't just look for physical attractiveness in a spouse. Look for the qualities that don't fade with time—spiritual commitment, integrity, sensitivity, and sincerity.
Problems	Over time, feelings of loneliness, indifference, and isolation came between Solomon and his bride. During those times, love grew cold and barriers were raised.	Through careful communication, lovers can be reconciled, commitment can be renewed, and romance refreshed. Don't let walls come between you and your partner. Take care of problems while they are still small.

1. The wedding day

1 Solomon's Song of Songs.[a]

1:1
a 1Ki 4:32

Beloved[a]

2 Let him kiss me with the kisses of his mouth—
for your love[b] is more delightful than wine.

a *2* Primarily on the basis of the gender of the Hebrew pronouns used, male and female speakers are indicated in the margins by the captions *Lover* and *Beloved* respectively. The words of others are marked *Friends.* In some instances the divisions and their captions are debatable.

1:2
b SS 4:10

1:1 Solomon, a son of King David, became king and was chosen by God to build the temple in Jerusalem. God gave him extraordinary wisdom. Much of his reign was characterised by wisdom and reverence for God, although towards the end of his life he became

1:3 [c]SS 4:10 [d]Ecc 7:1 [e]Ps 45:14

3 Pleasing is the fragrance of your perfumes;[c]
your name[d] is like perfume poured out.
No wonder the maidens[e] love you!
4 Take me away with you—let us hurry!
Let the king bring me into his chambers.[f]

1:4 [f]Ps 45:15

Friends

We rejoice and delight in you;[b]
we will praise your love more than wine.

Beloved

How right they are to adore you!

1:5 [g]SS 2:14; 4:3 [h]SS 2:7; 5:8; 5:16

5 Dark am I, yet lovely,[g]
O daughters of Jerusalem,[h]
dark like the tents of Kedar,
like the tent curtains of Solomon.[c]
6 Do not stare at me because I am dark,
because I am darkened by the sun.
My mother's sons were angry with me
and made me take care of the vineyards;[i]
my own vineyard I have neglected.

1:6 [i]Ps 69:8; SS 8:12

7 Tell me, you whom I love, where you graze your flock
and where you rest your sheep[j] at midday.
Why should I be like a veiled woman
beside the flocks of your friends?

1:7 [j]SS 3:1-4; Isa 13:20

Friends

8 If you do not know, most beautiful of women,[k]
follow the tracks of the sheep
and graze your young goats
by the tents of the shepherds.

1:8 [k]SS 5:9; 6:1

b 4 The Hebrew is masculine singular. c 5 Or *Salma*

---

proud and turned from God. Read about Solomon in 1 Kings 1–11 and 1 Chronicles 28–2 Chronicles 9. Solomon wrote more than 3,000 proverbs (see the book of Proverbs) and over 1,000 songs, one of which is this book, Song of Songs. His Profile is found in 1 Kings 3.

1:1ff Solomon frequently visited the various parts of his kingdom. One day, as he visited some royal vineyards in the north, his royal entourage came by surprise upon a beautiful peasant woman tending the vines. Embarrassed, she ran from them. But Solomon could not forget her. Later, disguised as a shepherd, he returned to the vineyards and won her love. Then, he revealed his true identity and asked her to return to Jerusalem with him. Solomon and his beloved are being married in the palace as this book begins.

The Song of Songs is a series of seven poems, not necessarily in chronological order. It reflects upon the first meeting of Solomon and the peasant woman, their engagement, their wedding, their wedding night, and the growth of their marriage after the wedding.

1:1ff There are three characters or groups of characters in this book: the girl (the "beloved"), Solomon (the "lover"), and "friends". The girl who caught Solomon's attention may have been from Shunem, a farming community about 60 miles north of Jerusalem. Her tanned skin indicates that she probably worked outside in the vineyards (1:6)—thus she may not have been from the upper class. The friends include either members of Solomon's harem or workers in the palace, as well as the girl's brothers (as in 8:8, 9).

1:1-4 This vivid description of a love relationship begins with a picture of love itself. Love is "more delightful than wine"; it makes the lovers rejoice. Acts 10:9–16 teaches that what God has created and cleansed we should not misuse or call common. We can enjoy love. God created it as a gift to us and a delight for all our senses.

1:5 Kedar was a nomadic community in northern Arabia. It was known for its tents that were woven from black goat hair.

1:6 The vineyard mentioned here was apparently owned by Solomon (because he came to visit it) and leased to the girl's stepbrothers (her "mother's sons"), who made her take care of the vineyards in the hot sun. Thus she could not take care of her own skin ("my own vineyard I have neglected"). When she was brought to Jerusalem, the young girl was embarrassed about her tanned complexion because the girls in the city had the fair, delicate skin that was considered much more beautiful. But Solomon loved her dark skin.

1:7 The girl felt insecure at being different from the women of Jerusalem (1:6) and at being alone while her lover was away (1:7). She longed for the security of his presence. The basis of true love is commitment; so in a relationship where there is genuine love, there is never any fear of deceit, manipulation, or exploitation.

Lover

9 I liken you, my darling, to a mare
harnessed to one of the chariots[l] of Pharaoh.
10 Your cheeks[m] are beautiful with ear-rings,
your neck with strings of jewels.[n]
11 We will make you ear-rings of gold,
studded with silver.

Beloved

12 While the king was at his table,
my perfume spread its fragrance.[o]
13 My lover is to me a sachet of myrrh
resting between my breasts.
14 My lover is to me a cluster of henna[p] blossoms
from the vineyards of En Gedi.[q]

Lover

15 How beautiful[r] you are, my darling!
Oh, how beautiful!
Your eyes are doves.[s]

Beloved

16 How handsome you are, my lover!
Oh, how charming!
And our bed is verdant.

Lover

17 The beams of our house are cedars;[t]
our rafters are firs.

Beloved[a]

2 I am a rose[b][a] of Sharon,[b]
a lily[c] of the valleys.

Lover

2 Like a lily among thorns
is my darling among the maidens.

Beloved

3 Like an apple tree among the trees of the forest
is my lover[d] among the young men.
I delight[e] to sit in his shade,
and his fruit is sweet to my taste.[f]
4 He has taken me to the banquet hall,[g]
and his banner[h] over me is love.
5 Strengthen me with raisins,
refresh me with apples,[i]

1:9 [l] 2Ch 1:17
1:10 [m] SS 5:13 [n] Isa 61:10
1:12 [o] SS 4:11-14
1:14 [p] SS 4:13 [q] 1Sa 23:29
1:15 [r] SS 4:7 [s] SS 2:14; 4:1; 5:2, 12; 6:9
1:17 [t] 1Ki 6:9
2:1 [a] Isa 35:1 [b] 1Ch 27:29 [c] SS 5:13; Hos 14:5
2:3 [d] SS 1:14 [e] SS 1:4 [f] SS 4:16
2:4 [g] Est 1:11 [h] Nu 1:52
2:5 [i] SS 7:8

[a] *1* Or *Lover* [b] *1* Possibly a member of the crocus family

1:14 En Gedi was an oasis hidden at the base of rugged limestone cliffs west of the Dead Sea. It was known for its fruitful palm trees and fragrant balsam oil. The terrain surrounding En Gedi was some of the most desolate in Palestine, and it had an extremely hot desert climate. The henna blossoms in En Gedi would have appeared all the more beautiful because of their stark surroundings; thus Solomon was complimenting his beloved's beauty and comparing her favourably with the women she feared.

1:16, 17 The lover and his beloved describe their woodland surroundings as a wedding bedroom.

2:1 The rose of Sharon and lily of the valleys were flowers commonly found in Israel. Perhaps the girl was saying, "I'm not so special; I'm just an ordinary flower," to which Solomon replied, "Oh, no, you are extraordinary—a lily among thorns." Solomon used the language of love. There is nothing more vital than encouraging and appreciating the person you love. Be sure to tell your spouse "I love you" every day, and show that love by your actions.

for I am faint with love.[j]
6His left arm is under my head,
and his right arm embraces me.[k]
7Daughters of Jerusalem, I charge you[l]
by the gazelles and by the does of the field:
Do not arouse or awaken love
until it so desires.[m]

2. Memories of courtship

8Listen! My lover!
Look! Here he comes,
leaping across the mountains,
bounding over the hills.[n]
9My lover is like a gazelle[o] or a young stag.[p]
Look! There he stands behind our wall,
gazing through the windows,
peering through the lattice.
10My lover spoke and said to me,
"Arise, my darling,
my beautiful one, and come with me.
11See! The winter is past;
the rains are over and gone.
12Flowers appear on the earth;
the season of singing has come,
the cooing of doves
is heard in our land.
13The fig-tree forms its early fruit;[q]
the blossoming[r] vines spread their fragrance.
Arise, come, my darling;
my beautiful one, come with me."

Lover

14My dove[s] in the clefts of the rock,
in the hiding-places on the mountainside,
show me your face,
let me hear your voice;
for your voice is sweet,
and your face is lovely.[t]
15Catch for us the foxes,[u]
the little foxes
that ruin the vineyards,[v]
our vineyards that are in bloom.[w]

Beloved

16My lover is mine and I am his;[x]
he browses among the lilies.[y]
17Until the day breaks

2:5 [j]SS 5:8
2:6 [k]SS 8:3
2:7 [l]SS 5:8 [m]SS 3:5; 8:4
2:8 [n]ver 17; SS 8:14
2:9 [o]2Sa 2:18 [p]ver 17; SS 8:14
2:13 [q]Isa 28:4; Jer 24:2; Hos 9:10; Mic 7:1; Na 3:12 [r]SS 7:12
2:14 [s]Ge 8:8; SS 1:15 [t]SS 1:5; 8:13
2:15 [u]Jdg 15:4 [v]SS 1:6 [w]SS 7:12
2:16 [x]SS 7:10 [y]SS 4:5; 6:3

2:7 Feelings of love can create intimacy that overpowers reason. Young people are too often in a hurry to develop an intimate relationship based on their strong feelings. But feelings aren't enough to support a lasting relationship. This verse encourages us not to force romance lest the feelings of love grow faster than the commitment needed to make love last. Patiently wait for feelings of love and commitment to develop together.

2:8—3:5 In this section Solomon's beloved reflects on her courtship with Solomon, remembering the first day they met and recalling one of her dreams about their being together.

2:12, 13 The lovers celebrated their joy in the creation and in their love. God created the world, the beauty we see, the joy of love and sex, and gave us senses to enjoy them. Never let problems, conflicts, or the ravages of time ruin your ability to enjoy God's gifts. Take time to enjoy the world God has created.

2:15 "The little foxes" are an example of the kinds of problems that can disturb or destroy a relationship. The lovers wanted anything that could potentially cause problems between them to be removed. It is often the "little foxes" that cause the biggest problems in marriage. These irritations must not be minimised or ignored, but identified so that, together, the couple can deal with them.

and the shadows flee,[z]
turn, my lover,[a]
and be like a gazelle
or like a young stag[b]
on the rugged hills.[c c]

3 All night long on my bed
I looked[a] for the one my heart loves;
I looked for him but did not find him.
2 I will get up now and go about the city,
through its streets and squares;
I will search for the one my heart loves.
So I looked for him but did not find him.
3 The watchmen found me
as they made their rounds in the city.[b]
"Have you seen the one my heart loves?"
4 Scarcely had I passed them
when I found the one my heart loves.
I held him and would not let him go
till I had brought him to my mother's house,[c]
to the room of the one who conceived me.[d]
5 Daughters of Jerusalem, I charge you[e]
by the gazelles and by the does of the field:
Do not arouse or awaken love
until it so desires.[f]

3. Memories of engagement

6 Who is this coming up from the desert[g]
like a column of smoke,
perfumed with myrrh[h] and incense
made from all the spices[i] of the merchant?
7 Look! It is Solomon's carriage,
escorted by sixty warriors,[j]
the noblest of Israel,
8 all of them wearing the sword,
all experienced in battle,
each with his sword at his side,
prepared for the terrors of the night.[k]
9 King Solomon made for himself the carriage;
he made it of wood from Lebanon.
10 Its posts he made of silver,
its base of gold.
Its seat was upholstered with purple,
its interior lovingly inlaid
by[a] the daughters of Jerusalem.

2:17 [z] SS 4:6 [a] SS 1:14 [b] ver 9 [c] ver 8

3:1 [a] SS 5:6; Isa 26:9

3:3 [b] SS 5:7

3:4 [c] SS 8:2 [d] SS 6:9

3:5 [e] SS 2:7 [f] SS 8:4

3:6 [g] SS 8:5 [h] SS 1:13; 4:6, 14 [i] Ex 30:34

3:7 [j] 1Sa 8:11

3:8 [k] Job 15:22; Ps 91:5

[c] 17 Or *the hills of Bether* [a] 10 Or *its inlaid interior a gift of love / from*

3:1–4 Many scholars agree that in these verses the girl was recalling a dream that caused her to become so concerned about her lover's whereabouts that she arose in the middle of the night to search for him. When you love someone, you will do all you can to ensure the safety of that person and care for his or her needs, even at a cost to your personal comfort. This shows up most often in small actions – walking downstairs to get your spouse a glass of water, leaving work early to attend some function your child is involved in, or sacrificing your personal comfort to tend to the needs of a friend.

3:6–5:1 Here the scene changes. Some believe that the wedding procession is described in 3:6–11, the wedding night in 4:1–5:1, and the consummation of the marriage in 4:16–5:1. Another possible explanation is that the period of Solomon's engagement to the girl is being remembered. In the previous section (2:8–3:5), Solomon and the girl fell in love. In this section, Solomon returns to the girl in all his royal splendour (3:6–11), expresses his great love for her (4:1–5), and then proposes (4:7–15). The girl accepts (4:16), and Solomon responds to her acceptance (5:1).

3:7, 9 Solomon's carriage was probably a covered and curtained couch used for carrying a single passenger on the shoulders of men.

11 Come out, you daughters of Zion,[l]
and look at King Solomon wearing the crown,
the crown with which his mother crowned him
on the day of his wedding,
the day his heart rejoiced.[m]

Lover

4 How beautiful you are, my darling!
Oh, how beautiful!
Your eyes behind your veil are doves.[a]
Your hair is like a flock of goats
descending from Mount Gilead.[b]
2 Your teeth are like a flock of sheep just shorn,
coming up from the washing.
Each has its twin;
not one of them is alone.[c]
3 Your lips are like a scarlet ribbon;
your mouth[d] is lovely.
Your temples behind your veil
are like the halves of a pomegranate.[e]
4 Your neck is like the tower[f] of David,
built with elegance;**a**
on it hang a thousand shields,[g]
all of them shields of warriors.
5 Your two breasts[h] are like two fawns,
like twin fawns of a gazelle[i]
that browse among the lilies.[j]
6 Until the day breaks
and the shadows flee,[k]
I will go to the mountain of myrrh[l]
and to the hill of incense.
7 All beautiful[m] you are, my darling;
there is no flaw in you.

8 Come with me from Lebanon, my bride,[n]
come with me from Lebanon.
Descend from the crest of Amana,
from the top of Senir,[o] the summit of Hermon,[p]
from the lions' dens
and the mountain haunts of the leopards.
9 You have stolen my heart, my sister, my bride;
you have stolen my heart
with one glance of your eyes,
with one jewel of your necklace.[q]
10 How delightful[r] is your love[s], my sister, my bride!
How much more pleasing is your love than wine,
and the fragrance of your perfume than any spice!
11 Your lips drop sweetness as the honeycomb, my bride;
milk and honey are under your tongue.[t]
The fragrance of your garments is like that of Lebanon.[u]

3:11 [l] Isa 4:4 [m] Isa 62:5
4:1 [a] SS 1:15; 5:12 [b] SS 6:5; Mic 7:14
4:2 [c] SS 6:6
4:3 [d] SS 5:16 [e] SS 6:7
4:4 [f] SS 7:4 [g] Eze 27:10
4:5 [h] SS 7:3 [i] Pr 5:19 [j] SS 2:16; 6:2-3
4:6 [k] SS 2:17 [l] ver 14
4:7 [m] SS 1:15
4:8 [n] SS 5:1 [o] Dt 3:9 [p] 1Ch 5:23
4:9 [q] Ge 41:42
4:10 [r] SS 7:6 [s] SS 1:2
4:11 [t] Ps 19:10; SS 5:1 [u] Hos 14:6

a *4* The meaning of the Hebrew for this word is uncertain.

4:1–7 We feel like awkward onlookers when we read this intensely private and intimate exchange. In the ecstasy of their love, the lovers praised each other using beautiful imagery. Their words may seem strange to readers from a different culture, but their intense feelings of love and admiration are universal. Communicating love and expressing admiration in both words and actions can enhance every marriage.

12 You are a garden locked up, my sister, my bride;
you are a spring enclosed, a sealed fountain.[v]
13 Your plants are an orchard of pomegranates[w]
with choice fruits,
with henna[x] and nard,
14 nard and saffron,
calamus and cinnamon,[y]
with every kind of incense tree,
with myrrh[z] and aloes
and all the finest spices.[a]
15 You are[b] a garden fountain,
a well of flowing water
streaming down from Lebanon.

Beloved

16 Awake, north wind,
and come, south wind!
Blow on my garden,
that its fragrance may spread abroad.
Let my lover come into his garden
and taste its choice fruits.[b]

Lover

5 I have come into my garden, my sister, my bride;[a]
I have gathered my myrrh with my spice.
I have eaten my honeycomb and my honey;
I have drunk my wine and my milk.[b]

Friends

Eat, O friends, and drink;
drink your fill, O lovers.

4. A troubling dream

Beloved

2 I slept but my heart was awake.
Listen! My lover is knocking:
"Open to me, my sister, my darling,
my dove, my flawless[c] one.[d]

b *15* Or *I am* (spoken by the *Beloved*)

4:12 [v]Pr 5:15-18
4:13 [w]SS 6:11; 7:12 [x]SS 1:14
4:14 [y]Ex 30:23 [z]SS 3:6 [a]SS 1:12
4:16 [b]SS 2:3; 5:1
5:1 [a]SS 4:8 [b]SS 4:11; Isa 55:1
5:2 [c]SS 4:7 [d]SS 6:9

4:12 In comparing his bride to a locked garden, Solomon was praising her virginity. Virginity, considered old-fashioned by many in today's culture, has always been God's plan for unmarried people – and with good reason. Sex without marriage is cheap. It cannot compare with the joy of giving yourself completely to the one who is totally committed to you.

4:15 Solomon's bride was as refreshing to him as a fountain. Could your spouse say the same about you? Sometimes the familiarity that comes with marriage causes us to forget the overwhelming feelings of love and refreshment we shared at the beginning. Many marriages could benefit from a course in "refreshing". Do you refresh your spouse, or are you a burden of complaints, sorrows, and problems? Partners in marriage should continually work at refreshing each other by an encouraging word, an unexpected gift, a change of pace, a surprise call or note, or even a withholding of a discussion of some problem until the proper time. Your spouse needs you to be a haven of refreshment because the rest of the world usually isn't.

5:2ff This new section tells how the couple's marriage grew and matured in spite of problems. Some time had passed since the wedding, and the girl felt as though some indifference had developed in their relationship. She had become cool to her husband's advances, and by the time she changed her mind and responded to him, he had left. Her self-centredness and impatience, though brief, caused separation. But she quickly moved to correct the problem by searching for her husband (5:6–8).

5:2–8 It is inevitable that, with the passing of time and the growth of familiarity, a marriage will start to lose its initial sparkle. Glances and touches no longer produce the same emotional response. Conflicts and pressures may creep in, causing you to lose your tenderness towards your spouse. The world is not a haven for lovers; in fact, external stress often works against the marriage relationship. But spouses can learn to be havens for each other. If intimacy and passion decline, remember that they can be renewed and regenerated. Take time to remember those first thrills, the excitement of sex, your spouse's strengths, and the commitment you made. When you focus on the positives, reconciliation and renewal can result.

My head is drenched with dew,
my hair with the dampness of the night."
3 I have taken off my robe —
must I put it on again?
I have washed my feet —
must I soil them again?
4 My lover thrust his hand through the latch-opening;
my heart began to pound for him.
5 I arose to open for my lover,
and my hands dripped with myrrh,[e]
my fingers with flowing myrrh,
on the handles of the lock.
6 I opened for my lover,[f]
but my lover had left; he was gone.[g]
My heart sank at his departure.[a]
I looked[h] for him but did not find him.
I called him but he did not answer.
7 The watchmen found me
as they made their rounds in the city.[i]
They beat me, they bruised me;
they took away my cloak,
those watchmen of the walls!
8 O daughters of Jerusalem, I charge you[j] —
if you find my lover,
what will you tell him?
Tell him I am faint with love.[k]

Friends

9 How is your beloved better than others,
most beautiful of women?[l]
How is your beloved better than others,
that you charge us so?

Beloved

10 My lover is radiant and ruddy,
outstanding among ten thousand.[m]
11 His head is purest gold;
his hair is wavy
and black as a raven.
12 His eyes are like doves[n]
by the water streams,
washed in milk,[o]
mounted like jewels.
13 His cheeks[p] are like beds of spice[q]
yielding perfume.
His lips are like lilies[r]
dripping with myrrh.
14 His arms are rods of gold
set with chrysolite.
His body is like polished ivory
decorated with sapphires.[b][s]
15 His legs are pillars of marble
set on bases of pure gold.

5:5 [e] ver 13
5:6 [f] SS 6:1 [g] SS 6:2 [h] SS 3:1
5:7 [i] SS 3:3
5:8 [j] SS 2:7; 3:5 [k] SS 2:5
5:9 [l] SS 1:8; 6:1
5:10 [m] Ps 45:2
5:12 [n] SS 1:15; 4:1 [o] Ge 49:12
5:13 [p] SS 1:10 [q] SS 6:2 [r] SS 2:1
5:14 [s] Job 28:6

[a] 6 Or *heart had gone out to him when he spoke* [b] 14 Or *lapis lazuli*

5:7 The girl was alone outside during the night. In Old Testament times, she would have been looked upon as a criminal or a prostitute and treated as such. This image symbolises the pain she felt at being separated from her lover.

His appearance is like Lebanon,[t]
choice as its cedars.
16His mouth[u] is sweetness itself;
he is altogether lovely.
This is my lover,[v] this my friend,
O daughters of Jerusalem.[w]

Friends

6 Where has your lover[a] gone,
most beautiful of women?[b]
Which way did your lover turn,
that we may look for him with you?

Beloved

2My lover has gone[c] down to his garden,[d]
to the beds of spices,[e]
to browse in the gardens
and to gather lilies.
3I am my lover's and my lover is mine;[f]
he browses among the lilies.[g]

5. Praising the bride's beauty

Lover

4You are beautiful, my darling, as Tirzah,[h]
lovely as Jerusalem,[i]
majestic as troops with banners.[j]
5Turn your eyes from me;
they overwhelm me.
Your hair is like a flock of goats
descending from Gilead.[k]
6Your teeth are like a flock of sheep
coming up from the washing.
Each has its twin,
not one of them is alone.[l]
7Your temples behind your veil[m]
are like the halves of a pomegranate.[n]
8Sixty queens[o] there may be,
and eighty concubines,[p]
and virgins beyond number;
9but my dove,[q] my perfect one,[r] is unique,
the only daughter of her mother,
the favourite of the one who bore her.[s]
The maidens saw her and called her blessed;
the queens and concubines praised her.

5:15 [t]1Ki 4:33; SS 7:4
5:16 [u]SS 4:3 [v]SS 7:9 [w]SS 1:5
6:1 [a]SS 5:6 [b]SS 1:8
6:2 [c]SS 5:6 [d]SS 4:12 [e]SS 5:13
6:3 [f]SS 7:10 [g]SS 2:16
6:4 [h]Jos 12:24 [i]Ps 48:2; 50:2 [j]ver 10
6:5 [k]SS 4:1
6:6 [l]SS 4:2
6:7 [m]Ge 24:65 [n]SS 4:3
6:8 [o]Ps 45:9 [p]Ge 22:24
6:9 [q]SS 1:15 [r]SS 5:2 [s]SS 3:4

5:16 The girl calls Solomon her "friend". In a healthy marriage, lovers are also good friends. Too often people are driven into marriage by the exciting feelings of love and passion before they take the time to develop a deep friendship. This involves listening, sharing, and showing understanding for the other's likes and dislikes. Friendship takes time, but it makes a love relationship much deeper and far more satisfying.

6:3 The girl said that she and her lover belonged to each other—they had given themselves to each other unreservedly. No matter how close we may be to our parents or our best friends, it is only in marriage that we realise complete union of mind, heart, and body.

6:4 Tirzah was a city about 35 miles northeast of Jerusalem. Its name means "pleasure" or "beauty". Jeroboam made Tirzah the first capital of the divided northern kingdom (1 Kings 14:17). "Majestic as troops with banners" means that the beloved must have had awe-inspiring beauty, like a mighty army readying for battle.

6:8, 9 Solomon did indeed have many queens (wives) and concubines (1 Kings 11:3). Polygamy, though not condoned, was common in Old Testament days. Solomon says that his love for this woman has not diminished since their wedding night, even though many other women are available to him.

6:11
[t]SS 7:12

6:13
[u]Ex 15:20

7:1
[a]Ps 45:13

7:3
[b]SS 4:5

7:4
[c]Ps 144:12; SS 4:4
[d]Nu 21:26
[e]SS 5:15

7:5
[f]Isa 35:2

7:6
[g]SS 1:15
[h]SS 4:10

7:7
[i]SS 4:5

7:8
[j]SS 2:5

Friends

10 Who is this that appears like the dawn,
fair as the moon, bright as the sun,
majestic as the stars in procession?

Lover

11 I went down to the grove of nut trees
to look at the new growth in the valley,
to see if the vines had budded
or the pomegranates were in bloom.[t]
12 Before I realised it,
my desire set me among the royal chariots of my people.[a]

Friends

13 Come back, come back, O Shulammite;
come back, come back, that we may gaze on you!

Lover

Why would you gaze on the Shulammite
as on the dance[u] of Mahanaim?

7

How beautiful your sandalled feet,
O prince's[a] daughter!
Your graceful legs are like jewels,
the work of a craftsman's hands.
2 Your navel is a rounded goblet
that never lacks blended wine.
Your waist is a mound of wheat
encircled by lilies.
3 Your breasts[b] are like two fawns,
twins of a gazelle.
4 Your neck is like an ivory tower.[c]
Your eyes are the pools of Heshbon[d]
by the gate of Bath Rabbim.
Your nose is like the tower of Lebanon[e]
looking towards Damascus.
5 Your head crowns you like Mount Carmel.[f]
Your hair is like royal tapestry;
the king is held captive by its tresses.
6 How beautiful[g] you are and how pleasing,
O love, with your delights![h]
7 Your stature is like that of the palm,
and your breasts[i] like clusters of fruit.
8 I said, "I will climb the palm tree;
I will take hold of its fruit."
May your breasts be like the clusters of the vine,
the fragrance of your breath like apples,[j]
9 and your mouth like the best wine.

a *12* Or *among the chariots of Amminadab*; or *among the chariots of the people of the prince*

7:1 *Graceful* can mean "curvaceous".

7:4, 5 The phrase "your eyes are the pools of Heshbon" suggests sparkling eyes. Heshbon was the ancient capital of the Amorites. Bath Rabbim may have been a gate of Heshbon. The "tower of Lebanon" may have been a watchtower (evidently a prominent one and seen as very beautiful). Some suggest that this refers to the Lebanon mountain range. Mount Carmel overlooks the Mediterranean Sea and Palestine.

6. The bride's tender appeal

Beloved

May the wine go straight to my lover,[k]
flowing gently over lips and teeth.[a]
10 I belong to my lover,
and his desire[l] is for me.[m]
11 Come, my lover, let us go to the countryside,
let us spend the night in the villages.[b]
12 Let us go early to the vineyards[n]
to see if the vines have budded,[o]
if their blossoms[p] have opened,
and if the pomegranates[q] are in bloom[r]—
there I will give you my love.
13 The mandrakes[s] send out their fragrance,
and at our door is every delicacy,
both new and old,
that I have stored up for you, my lover.[t]

8 If only you were to me like a brother,
who was nursed at my mother's breasts!
Then, if I found you outside,
I would kiss you,
and no-one would despise me.
2 I would lead you
and bring you to my mother's house[a]—
she who has taught me.
I would give you spiced wine to drink,
the nectar of my pomegranates.
3 His left arm is under my head
and his right arm embraces me.[b]
4 Daughters of Jerusalem, I charge you:
Do not arouse or awaken love
until it so desires.[c]

7. The power of love

Friends

5 Who is this coming up from the desert[d]
leaning on her lover?

Beloved

Under the apple tree I roused you;
there your mother conceived[e] you,
there she who was in labour gave you birth.
6 Place me like a seal over your heart,

7:9 [k]SS 5:16
7:10 [l]Ps 45:11 [m]SS 2:16; 6:3
7:12 [n]SS 1:6 [o]SS 2:15 [p]SS 2:13 [q]SS 4:13 [r]SS 6:11
7:13 [s]Ge 30:14 [t]SS 4:16
8:2 [a]SS 3:4
8:3 [b]SS 2:6
8:4 [c]SS 2:7; 3:5
8:5 [d]SS 3:6 [e]SS 3:4

[a] *9* Septuagint, Aquila, Vulgate and Syriac; Hebrew *lips of sleepers* [b] *11* Or *henna bushes*

7:10–13 As a marriage matures, there should be more love and freedom between marriage partners. Here the girl takes the initiative in lovemaking. Many cultures have stereotypes of the roles men and women play in lovemaking, but the security of true love gives both marriage partners the freedom to initiate acts of love and express their true feelings.

7:13 Mandrakes were a somewhat rare plant often thought to increase fertility. Mandrakes are also mentioned in Genesis 30:14–17.

8:1 In the ancient Near East, it was improper to show public affection except between family members. The girl is wishing that she could freely show affection to her lover, even in public.

8:6, 7 In this final description of their love, the girl includes some of its significant characteristics (see also 1 Corinthians 13). Love is

like a seal on your arm;
for love[f] is as strong as death,
its jealousy[a][g] unyielding as the grave.[b]
It burns like blazing fire,
like a mighty flame.[c]
7 Many waters cannot quench love;
rivers cannot wash it away.
If one were to give
all the wealth of his house for love,
it[d] would be utterly scorned.[h]

Friends

8 We have a young sister,
and her breasts are not yet grown.
What shall we do for our sister
for the day she is spoken for?
9 If she is a wall,
we will build towers of silver on her.
If she is a door,
we will enclose her with panels of cedar.

Beloved

10 I am a wall,
and my breasts are like towers.
Thus I have become in his eyes
like one bringing contentment.
11 Solomon had a vineyard[i] in Baal Hamon;
he let out his vineyard to tenants.
Each was to bring for its fruit
a thousand shekels[e][j] of silver.
12 But my own vineyard[k] is mine to give;
the thousand shekels are for you, O Solomon,
and two hundred[f] are for those who tend its fruit.

Lover

13 You who dwell in the gardens
with friends in attendance,
let me hear your voice!

8:6 [f]SS 1:2 [g]Nu 5:14
8:7 [h]Pr 6:35
8:11 [i]Ecc 2:4 [j]Isa 7:23
8:12 [k]SS 1:6

[a] 6 Or *ardour* [b] 6 Hebrew *Sheol* [c] 6 Or */ like the very flame of the LORD* [d] 7 Or *he* [e] 11 That is, about 25 pounds (about 11.5 kilograms); also in verse 12 [f] 12 That is, about 5 pounds (about 2.3 kilograms)

---

as strong as death; it cannot be killed by time or disaster; and it cannot be bought for any price because it is freely given. Love is priceless, and even the richest king cannot buy it. Love must be accepted as a gift from God and then shared within the guidelines God provides. Accept the love of your spouse as God's gift, and strive to make your love a reflection of the perfect love that comes from God himself.

8:8, 9 The girl was reflecting on the days when she was younger and under the care of her brothers, who wondered how to help her prepare for marriage. They decided that if she was like a wall, standing firm against sexual temptation, they would praise her. But if she was like a door, open to immorality, they would take steps to guard her from doing something foolish. In 8:10, she testifies that she has been persistent in her morality and thus has found favour in Solomon's eyes.

8:11, 12 Solomon could demand rent from the tenants for his vineyard, but the girl had her own vineyard and it was her right to assign it. But she willingly gave Solomon its fruit. In a good marriage, there is no private property, for everything is shared between the partners. Note: Baal Hamon is mentioned only here in the Bible, and its location is unknown.

Beloved

14Come away, my lover,
and be like a gazelle[l]
or like a young stag[m]
on the spice-laden mountains.[n]

8:14
[l]Pr 5:19
[m]SS 2:9
[n]SS 2:8, 17

8:14 The love between Solomon and his bride did not diminish in intensity after their wedding night. The lovers relied on each other and kept no secrets from each other. Devotion and commitment were the keys to their relationship, just as they are in our relationships to our spouses and to God. The faithfulness of our marital love should reflect God's perfect faithfulness to us.

Paul shows how marriage represents Christ's relationship to his church (Ephesians 5:22–33), and John pictures the second coming as a great marriage feast for Christ and his bride, his faithful followers (Revelation 19:7, 8; 21:1, 2). Many theologians have thought that Song of Songs is an allegory showing Christ's love for his church. It makes even better sense to say that it is a love poem about a real human love relationship, and that all loving, committed marriages reflect God's love.

ISAIAH

Amos becomes a prophet	Hosea becomes a prophet	Micah becomes a prophet	Isaiah becomes a prophet	Ahaz becomes king of Judah	Hoshea becomes king of Israel	Israel falls to the Assyrians	Hezekiah becomes king of Judah	Sennacherib surrounds Jerusalem	Manasseh becomes king of Judah	Isaiah's ministry ends	Josiah becomes king of Judah
760 B.C.	753	742	740	735	732	722	715	701	697	681	640

SLOWLY he rose, and the crowd fell silent. Those at the back leaned forward, straining to hear. The atmosphere was electric. He spoke, and his carefully chosen words flew like swift arrows and found their mark. The great man, a spokesman for God, was warning . . . and condemning. The crowd became restless—shifting positions, clenching fists, and murmuring. Some agreed with his message, nodding their heads and weeping softly. But most were angry, and they began to shout back insults and threats.

Such was the life of a prophet.

The "office" of prophet was instituted during the days of Samuel, the last of the judges. Prophets stood with the priests as God's special representatives. The prophet's role was to speak for God, confronting the people and their leaders with God's commands and promises. Because of this confrontational stance and the continuing tendency of people to disobey God, true prophets were not usually very popular. But though their message often went unheeded, they faithfully and forcefully proclaimed the truth.

The book of Isaiah is the first of the writings of the Prophets in the Bible; and Isaiah, the author, is generally considered to be the greatest prophet. He was probably brought up in an aristocratic home and was married to a prophetess. In the beginning of his ministry he was well-liked. But, like most prophets, he soon became unpopular because his messages were so difficult to hear. He called the people to turn from their lives of sin and warned them of God's judgment and punishment. Isaiah had an active ministry for 60 years before he was executed during Manasseh's reign (according to tradition). As God's special messenger to Judah, Isaiah prophesied during the reigns of several of its rulers. Many of those messages are recorded in his book: Uzziah and Jotham, chapters 1—6; Ahaz, chapters 7—14; and Hezekiah, chapters 15—39.

The first half of the book of Isaiah (chapters 1—39) contains scathing denunciations and pronouncements as he calls Judah, Israel, and the surrounding nations to repent of their sins. However, the last 27 chapters (40—66) are filled with consolation and hope as Isaiah unfolds God's promise of future blessings through his Messiah.

As you read Isaiah, imagine this strong and courageous man of God, fearlessly proclaiming God's word, and listen to his message in relation to your own life—*return, repent, and be renewed*. Then trust in God's *redemption* through Christ and *rejoice*. Your Saviour has come, and he's coming again!

VITAL STATISTICS

PURPOSE:
To call the nation of Judah back to God and to tell of God's salvation through the Messiah

AUTHOR:
The prophet Isaiah son of Amoz

DATE WRITTEN:
The events of chapters 1—39 occurred during Isaiah's ministry, so they were probably written about 700 B.C. Chapters 40—66, however, may have been written near the end of his life, about 681 B.C.

SETTING:
Isaiah is speaking and writing mainly in Jerusalem

KEY VERSE:
"But he was pierced for our transgressions, he was crushed for our iniquities; the punishment that brought us peace was upon him, and by his wounds we are healed" (53:5).

KEY PEOPLE:
Isaiah, his two sons Shear-Jashub and Maher-Shalal-Hash-Baz

SPECIAL FEATURES:
The book of Isaiah contains both prose and poetry and uses personification (attributing personal qualities to divine beings or inanimate objects). Also, many of the prophecies in Isaiah contain predictions that foretell a soon-to-occur event and a distant future event at the same time.

THE BLUEPRINT

A. WORDS OF JUDGMENT (1:1—39:8) 1. The sins of Israel and Judah 2. Judgment against pagan nations 3. God's purpose in judgment 4. Jerusalem's true and false hopes 5. Events during the reign of Hezekiah	The 39 chapters in the first half of Isaiah generally carry the message of judgment for sin. Isaiah brings the message of judgment to Judah, Israel, and the surrounding pagan nations. Judah had a form of godliness, but in their hearts they were corrupt. Isaiah's warnings were intended to purify the people by helping them to understand God's true nature and message. However, they ignored the repeated warnings that Isaiah brought. We need not repeat their error; rather, we should heed the prophetic voice.
B. WORDS OF COMFORT (40:1—66:24) 1. Israel's release from captivity 2. The future Redeemer 3. The future kingdom	The 27 chapters in the second half of Isaiah generally bring a message of forgiveness, comfort, and hope. This message of hope looks forward to the coming of the Messiah. Isaiah speaks more about the Messiah than does any other Old Testament prophet. He describes the Messiah as both a suffering servant and a sovereign Lord. The fact that the Messiah was to be both a suffering servant and a sovereign Lord could not be understood clearly until New Testament times. Based on what Jesus Christ has done, God freely offers forgiveness to all who turn to him in faith. This is God's message of comfort to us because those who heed it find eternal peace and fellowship with him.

MEGATHEMES

THEME	EXPLANATION	IMPORTANCE
Holiness	God is highly exalted above all his creatures. His moral perfection stands in contrast to evil people and nations. God is perfect and sinless in all his motives and actions, so he is in perfect control of his power, judgment, love, and mercy. His holy nature is our yardstick for morality.	Because God is without sin, he alone can help us with our sin. It is only right that we regard him as supreme in power and moral perfection. We must never treat God as common or ordinary. He alone deserves our devotion and praise. He is always truthful, fair, and just.
Punishment	Because God is holy, he requires his people to treat others justly. He promised to punish Israel, Judah, and other nations for faithless immorality and idolatry. True faith had degenerated into national pride and empty religious rituals.	We must trust in God alone and fulfil his commands. We cannot forsake justice nor give in to selfishness. If we harden our hearts against his message, punishment will surely come to us.
Salvation	Because God's judgment is coming, we need a Saviour. No man or nation can be saved without God's help. Christ's perfect sacrifice for our sins is foretold and portrayed in Isaiah. All who trust God can be freed from their sin and restored to him.	Christ died to save us from our sin. We cannot save ourselves. He is willing to save all those who turn from their sin and come to him. Salvation is from God alone. No amount of good works can earn it.
Messiah	God will send the Messiah to save his people. He will set up his own kingdom as the faithful Prince of Peace who rules with righteousness. He will come as sovereign Lord, but he will do so as a servant who will die to take away sins.	Our trust must be in the Messiah, not in ourselves or in any nation or power. There is no hope unless we believe in him. Trust Christ fully and let him rule in your life as your sovereign Lord.
Hope	God promises comfort, deliverance, and restoration in his future kingdom. The Messiah will rule over his faithful followers in the age to come. Hope is possible because Christ is coming.	We can be refreshed because there is compassion for those who repent. No matter how bleak our situation or how evil the world is, we must continue to be God's faithful people who hope for his return.

A. WORDS OF JUDGMENT (1:1–39:8)

Isaiah begins by bringing a message of divine judgment for both Israel and Judah. Although the advance of the Assyrians poses a problem for Judah, God foretells the destruction of Assyria and other evil surrounding nations through the prophet Isaiah. This section ends with the Assyrian invasion being held off, demonstrating the clear unfolding of God's plan and promises for the nation at this time.

1. The sins of Israel and Judah

1:1 [a]Nu 12:6 [b]Isa 40:9 [c]Isa 2:1 [d]2Ch 26:22 [e]2Ki 16:1

1 The vision[a] concerning Judah and Jerusalem[b] that Isaiah son of Amoz saw[c]
during the reigns of Uzziah,[d] Jotham, Ahaz[e] and Hezekiah, kings of Judah.

A Rebellious Nation

2Hear, O heavens! Listen, O earth!
For the LORD has spoken:[f]
"I reared children and brought them up,
but they have rebelled[g] against me.
3The ox knows his master,
the donkey his owner's manger,
but Israel does not know,[h]
my people do not understand."

1:2 [f]Mic 1:2 [g]Isa 30:1, 9; 65:2

1:3 [h]Jer 8:7; 9:3, 6

4Ah, sinful nation,
a people loaded with guilt,
a brood of evildoers,[i]
children given to corruption!
They have forsaken the LORD;
they have spurned the Holy One[j] of Israel
and turned their backs on him.

1:4 [i]Isa 14:20 [j]Isa 5:19, 24

5Why should you be beaten any more?
Why do you persist in rebellion?[k]
Your whole head is injured,
your whole heart afflicted.[l]
6From the sole of your foot to the top of your head
there is no soundness[m]—
only wounds and bruises

1:5 [k]Isa 31:6 [l]Isa 33:6, 24

1:6 [m]Ps 38:3

ISAIAH served as a prophet to Judah from 740–681 B.C.

Climate of the times	Society was in great upheaval. Under King Ahaz and King Manasseh the people reverted to idolatry, and there was even child sacrifice.
Main message	Although judgment from other nations was inevitable, the people could still have a special relationship with God.
Importance of message	Sometimes we must suffer judgment and discipline before we are restored to God.
Contemporary prophets	Hosea (753–715) Micah (742–687)

1:1 Isaiah was a prophet during the time when the original nation of Israel had been divided into two kingdoms—Israel in the north, and Judah in the south. The northern kingdom had sinned greatly against God, and the southern kingdom was headed in the same direction—perverting justice, oppressing the poor, turning from God to idols, and looking for military aid from pagan nations rather than from God. Isaiah came primarily as a prophet to Judah, but his message was also for the northern kingdom. Sometimes "Israel" refers to both kingdoms. Isaiah lived to see the destruction and captivity of the northern kingdom in 722 B.C.; thus, his ministry began with warning the northern kingdom.

1:2–4 Here "Israel" means the southern kingdom, Judah. The people of Judah were sinning greatly and refused to know and understand God. God brought charges against them through Isaiah because they had rebelled and had forsaken the Lord. By these acts, they had broken their moral and spiritual covenant with God (see Deuteronomy 28). By breaking their agreement, they were bringing God's punishment upon themselves. First God gave them prosperity, but they didn't serve him. Then God sent them warnings, but they refused to listen. Finally, he would bring the fire of his judgment (see 1:7).

1:4–9 As long as the people of Judah continued to sin, they cut themselves off from God's help and isolated themselves. When you feel lonely and separated from God, remember that God does not abandon you. Our sins cut us off from him. The only sure cure for this kind of loneliness is to restore a meaningful relationship with God by confessing your sin, obeying his instructions, and communicating regularly with him (see Psalm 140:13; Isaiah 1:16–19; 1 John 1:9).

and open sores,
not cleansed or bandaged[n]
or soothed with oil.[o]

7 Your country is desolate,[p]
your cities burned with fire;
your fields are being stripped by foreigners
right before you,
laid waste as when overthrown by strangers.
8 The Daughter of Zion is left
like a shelter in a vineyard,
like a hut[q] in a field of melons,
like a city under siege.
9 Unless the LORD Almighty
had left us some survivors,[r]
we would have become like Sodom,
we would have been like Gomorrah.[s]

10 Hear the word of the LORD,[t]
you rulers of Sodom;[u]
listen to the law[v] of our God,
you people of Gomorrah!
11 "The multitude of your sacrifices—
what are they to me?" says the LORD.
"I have more than enough of burnt offerings,
of rams and the fat of fattened animals;[w]
I have no pleasure
in the blood of bulls[x] and lambs and goats.[y]
12 When you come to appear before me,
who has asked this of you,[z]
this trampling of my courts?
13 Stop bringing meaningless offerings![a]
Your incense[b] is detestable to me.
New Moons, Sabbaths and convocations[c]—
I cannot bear your evil assemblies.
14 Your New Moon festivals and your appointed feasts[d]
my soul hates.
They have become a burden to me;
I am weary[e] of bearing them.

1:6 [n]Isa 30:26; Jer 8:22 [o]Lk 10:34
1:7 [p]Lev 26:34
1:8 [q]Job 27:18
1:9 [r]Isa 10:20-22; 37:4, 31-32 [s]Ge 19:24; Ro 9:29*
1:10 [t]Isa 28:14 [u]Isa 3:9; Eze 16:49; Ro 9:29; Rev 11:8 [v]Isa 8:20
1:11 [w]Ps 50:8 [x]Jer 6:20 [y]1Sa 15:22; Mal 1:10
1:12 [z]Ex 23:17
1:13 [a]Isa 66:3 [b]Jer 7:9 [c]1Ch 23:31
1:14 [d]Lev 23:1-44; Nu 28:11-29:39; Isa 29:1 [e]Isa 7:13; 43:22, 24

1:7 Was this destruction taking place at that time? Judah was attacked many times during Isaiah's lifetime. To be stripped (devastated) by foreigners was the worst kind of judgment. This verse could be a picture of the results of these invasions or a prediction of the coming invasion of Israel by Assyria. But most likely it pointed to Babylon's future invasion of Judah and the fall of Jerusalem in 586 B.C. as well.

1:9 Sodom and Gomorrah were two cities that God completely destroyed for their great wickedness (Genesis 19:1–25). They are mentioned elsewhere in the Bible as examples of God's judgment against sin (Jeremiah 50:40; Ezekiel 16:46–63; Matthew 11:23, 24; Jude 1:7). "Some survivors" from Judah were spared by God because they were faithful.

1:10 Isaiah compared the rulers and people of Judah to the rulers and people of Sodom and Gomorrah. To hear what God wanted to say, the people had to listen and be willing to obey. When we can't hear God's message, perhaps we are not listening carefully or we are not truly willing to do what he says.

1:10–14 God was unhappy with their sacrifices, but he was not revoking the system of sacrifices he had initiated with Moses. Instead, God was calling for sincere faith and devotion. The leaders were carefully making the traditional sacrifices and offerings at holy celebrations, but they were still unfaithful to God in their hearts. Sacrifices were to be an outward sign of their inward faith in God, but the outward signs became empty because no inward faith existed. Why, then, did they continue to offer sacrifices? Like many people today, they had come to place more faith in the rituals of their religion than in the God they worshipped. Examine your own religious practices: do they spring from your faith in the living God? God does not take pleasure in our outward expressions if our inward faith is missing (see Deuteronomy 10:12–16; 1 Samuel 15:22, 23; Psalm 51:16–19; Hosea 6:6).

1:13 "New Moons" and "Sabbaths" refer to monthly offerings (Numbers 28:11–14) and weekly and special annual Sabbaths on the Day of Atonement and Feast of Tabernacles (Leviticus 16:31, 23–34, 39). For all the feasts, see the chart in Leviticus 23. Although the people did not feel sorry for their sins, they continued to offer sacrifices for forgiveness. Gifts and sacrifices mean nothing to God when they come from someone with a corrupt heart. God wants us to love him, trust him, and turn from our sin; after that, he will be pleased with our "sacrifices" of time, money, or service.

1:15
[f] Isa 8:17; 59:2; Mic 3:4
[g] Isa 59:3

1:16
[h] Isa 52:11
[i] Isa 55:7; Jer 25:5

1:17
[j] Zep 2:3
[k] Ps 82:3

1:18
[l] Isa 41:1; 43:9, 26
[m] Ps 51:7; Rev 7:14

1:19
[n] Dt 30:15-16; Isa 55:2

1:20
[o] Isa 3:25; 65:12
[p] Isa 34:16; 40:5; 58:14; Mic 4:4

1:21
[q] Isa 57:3-9; Jer 2:20

1:23
[r] Ex 23:8
[s] Isa 10:2; Jer 5:28; Eze 22:6-7; Zec 7:10

1:24
[t] Isa 35:4; 59:17; 61:2; 63:4

15 When you spread out your hands in prayer,
I will hide[f] my eyes from you;
even if you offer many prayers,
I will not listen.
Your hands are full of blood;[g]
16 wash and make yourselves clean.
Take your evil deeds
out of my sight![h]
Stop doing wrong,[i]
17 learn to do right!
Seek justice,[j]
encourage the oppressed.[a]
Defend the cause of the fatherless,[k]
plead the case of the widow.

18 "Come now, let us reason together,"[l]
says the LORD.
"Though your sins are like scarlet,
they shall be as white as snow;[m]
though they are red as crimson,
they shall be like wool.
19 If you are willing and obedient,
you will eat the best from the land;[n]
20 but if you resist and rebel,
you will be devoured by the sword."[o]
For the mouth of the LORD has spoken.[p]

21 See how the faithful city
has become a harlot![q]
She once was full of justice;
righteousness used to dwell in her—
but now murderers!
22 Your silver has become dross,
your choice wine is diluted with water.
23 Your rulers are rebels,
companions of thieves;
they all love bribes[r]
and chase after gifts.
They do not defend the cause of the fatherless;
the widow's case does not come before them.[s]
24 Therefore the Lord, the LORD Almighty,
the Mighty One of Israel, declares:
"Ah, I will get relief from my foes
and avenge[t] myself on my enemies.
25 I will turn my hand against you;

[a] *17* Or */ rebuke the oppressor*

1:18 Scarlet, or crimson, was the colour of a deep-red permanent dye, and its deep stain was virtually impossible to remove from clothing. The bloodstained hands of the murderers are probably in view here (see 1:15, 21). The stain of sin seems equally permanent, but God can remove sin's stain from our lives as he promised to do for the Israelites. We don't have to go through life permanently soiled. God's word assures us that if we are willing and obedient, Christ will forgive and remove our most indelible stains (Psalm 51:1–7).

1:21, 22 "The faithful city" refers to Jerusalem, representing all of Judah. God compares the actions of his people to a harlot. The people had turned from the worship of the true God to worshipping idols. Their faith was defective, impure, and diluted. Idolatry, outward or inward, is spiritual adultery, breaking our commitment to God in order to love something else. Jesus described the people of his day as adulterous, even though they were religiously strict. As the church, we are the "bride" of Christ (Revelation 19:7), and, by faith, we can be clothed in his righteousness. Has your faith become impure? Ask God to restore you. Keep your devotion to him strong and pure.

1:25 God promised to refine his people similar to the way that metal is purged with lye in a smelting pot. This process involves melting the metal and skimming off the impure dross until the worker can see his own image in the liquid metal. We must be willing to submit to God, allowing him to remove our sin so that we might reflect his image.

I will thoroughly purge away your dross
and remove all your impurities.[u]
26I will restore your judges as in days of old,[v]
your counsellors as at the beginning.
Afterwards you will be called
the City of Righteousness,[w]
the Faithful City."[x]

27Zion will be redeemed with justice,
her penitent ones with righteousness.[y]
28But rebels and sinners will both be broken,
and those who forsake the LORD will perish.[z]

29"You will be ashamed because of the sacred oaks[a]
in which you have delighted;
you will be disgraced because of the gardens[b]
that you have chosen.
30You will be like an oak with fading leaves,
like a garden without water.
31The mighty man will become tinder
and his work a spark;
both will burn together,
with no-one to quench the fire.[c]"

The Mountain of the LORD

2 This is what Isaiah son of Amoz saw concerning Judah and Jerusalem:[a]

2In the last days

the mountain[b] of the LORD's temple will be established
as chief among the mountains;
it will be raised above the hills,
and all nations will stream to it.

3Many peoples will come and say,

"Come, let us go up to the mountain of the LORD,
to the house of the God of Jacob.
He will teach us his ways,
so that we may walk in his paths."
The law[c] will go out from Zion,
the word of the LORD from Jerusalem.[d]
4He will judge between the nations
and will settle disputes for many peoples.

1:25 [u]Eze 22:22; Mal 3:3

1:26 [v]Jer 33:7, 11 [w]Isa 33:5; 62:1; Zec 8:3 [x]Isa 60:14; 62:2

1:27 [y]Isa 35:10; 62:12; 63:4

1:28 [z]Ps 9:5; Isa 24:20; 66:24; 2Th 1:8-9

1:29 [a]Isa 57:5 [b]Isa 65:3; 66:17

1:31 [c]Isa 5:24; 9:18-19; 26:11; 33:14; 66:15-16, 24

2:1 [a]Isa 1:1

2:2 [b]Isa 27:13; 56:7; 66:20; Mic 4:7

2:3 [c]Isa 51:4, 7 [d]Lk 24:47

1:29, 30 Throughout history, the oak tree has been a symbol of strength, but the people were worshipping "sacred oaks". Ezekiel mentions that groves of oak trees were used as places for idol worship (Ezekiel 6:13). Are you devoted to symbols of strength and power that rival God's place in your life? Do you have interests and commitments where your love for them borders on worship? Make God your first loyalty; everything else will fade in time and burn away under his scrutiny.

1:31 A spark set to tinder ignites a quick, devouring fire. God compares mighty people whose evil deeds devour them to a roaring fire. Our lives can be destroyed quickly by a small but deadly spark of evil. What potential "fire hazards" do you need to remove?

2:2 The temple was built on the mountain of the Lord, Mount Moriah, highly visible to all the people of Jerusalem. For more on the significance of the temple, see the note on 2 Chronicles 5:1ff. In the last days the temple will attract the nations, not because of its architecture and prominence, but because of God's presence and influence.

2:2–4 God gave Isaiah the gift of seeing the future. At this time, God showed Isaiah what would eventually happen to Jerusalem. Revelation 21 depicts the glorious fulfilment of this prophecy in the new Jerusalem, where only those whose names are written in the Lamb's book of life will be allowed to enter. God made a covenant (promise) with his people and will never break it. God's faithfulness gives us hope for the future.

2:4, 5 This describes a wonderful future of peace when instruments of war will be converted to instruments of farming, when we will be taught God's laws and will obey them. Although we know that eventually God will remove all sin and thus the causes of war, conflicts, and other problems, we should not wait for him to act before we begin to obey him. Just as Judah was told in 2:5, we should walk in his light now. Though our eternal reward awaits us, we already can enjoy many benefits of obedience now as we apply God's word to our lives.

2:4
[e]Joel 3:10
[f]Ps 46:9; Isa 9:5; 11:6-9; 32:18; Hos 2:18; Zec 9:10

They will beat their swords into ploughshares
and their spears into pruning hooks.[e]
Nation will not take up sword against nation,[f]
nor will they train for war any more.

2:5
[g]Isa 58:1
[h]Isa 60:1, 19-20; 1Jn 1:5, 7

5 Come, O house of Jacob,[g]
let us walk in the light[h] of the LORD.

The Day of the LORD

2:6
[i]Dt 31:17
[j]2Ki 1:2
[k]Pr 6:1
[l]2Ki 16:7

6 You have abandoned[i] your people,
the house of Jacob.
They are full of superstitions from the East;
they practise divination like the Philistines[j]
and clasp hands[k] with pagans.[l]

2:7
[m]Dt 17:16
[n]Isa 31:1; Mic 5:10

7 Their land is full of silver and gold;
there is no end to their treasures.
Their land is full of horses;[m]
there is no end to the chariots.[n]

2:8
[o]Isa 10:9-11
[p]Isa 17:8

8 Their land is full of idols;[o]
they bow down to the work of their hands,
to what their fingers[p] have made.

2:9
[q]Ps 62:9
[r]Isa 5:15
[s]Ne 4:5

9 So man will be brought low[q]
and mankind humbled[r]—
do not forgive them.[a] [s]

2:10
[t]2Th 1:9; Rev 6:15-16

10 Go into the rocks,
hide in the ground
from dread of the LORD
and the splendour of his majesty![t]

2:11
[u]Isa 5:15; 37:23

11 The eyes of the arrogant man will be humbled
and the pride[u] of men brought low;
the LORD alone will be exalted in that day.

2:12
[v]Isa 24:4, 21; Mal 4:1
[w]Job 40:11

12 The LORD Almighty has a day in store
for all the proud and lofty,
for all that is exalted[v]
(and they will be humbled),[w]

2:13
[x]Zec 11:2

13 for all the cedars of Lebanon, tall and lofty,
and all the oaks of Bashan,[x]

2:14
[y]Isa 30:25; 40:4

14 for all the towering mountains
and all the high hills,[y]

2:15
[z]Isa 25:2, 12

15 for every lofty tower
and every fortified wall,[z]

[a] 9 Or *not raise them up*

2:6 The people were following practices of the Assyrian empire. "Divination like the Philistines" meant claiming to know and control the future by the power of demons or by interpreting omens. These practices were forbidden by God (see Leviticus 19:26; Deuteronomy 18:10, 14). The Philistines worshipped Dagon, Ashtoreth, and Baal-Zebub. During the more sinful periods of their history, the people of Israel worshipped these pagan gods along with Yahweh, and even gave them Hebrew names.

2:8, 9 Under the reign of evil kings, idol worship flourished in both Israel and Judah. A few good kings in Judah stopped it during their reigns. Though very few people worship carved or moulded images today, worshipping objects that symbolise power continues. We pay homage to cars, homes, sports stars, celebrities, money, etc. Idol worship is evil because (1) it insults God when we worship something he created rather than worshipping him; (2) it keeps us from knowing and serving God when we put our confidence in anything other than him; (3) it causes us to rely on our own efforts rather than on God. (See also Deuteronomy 27:15.)

2:12 The "day" of the Lord Almighty is the day of judgment, the time when God will judge both evil and good. That day will come, and we will want a proper relationship with God when it does. God alone must be exalted (2:11, 17) as the first step towards developing that relationship with him.

2:15–17 Lofty towers were part of a city or nation's defences. This phrase refers to security based on military fortresses. "Every trading ship" pictures economic prosperity; and a "stately vessel" is a pleasure vessel. Nothing can compare with or rival the place God must have in our hearts and minds. To place our hope elsewhere is nothing but false pride. Place your confidence in God alone.

16 for every trading ship[b] [a]
and every stately vessel.
17 The arrogance of man will be brought low
and the pride of men humbled;
the LORD alone will be exalted in that day, [b]
18 and the idols will totally disappear. [c]

19 Men will flee to caves in the rocks
and to holes in the ground
from the dread of the LORD
and the splendour of his majesty,
when he rises to shake the earth. [d]
20 In that day men will throw away
to the rodents and bats [e]
their idols of silver and idols of gold,
which they made to worship.
21 They will flee to caverns in the rocks
and to the overhanging crags
from dread of the LORD
and the splendour of his majesty,
when he rises to shake the earth. [f]

22 Stop trusting in man, [g]
who has but a breath in his nostrils.
Of what account is he? [h]

Judgment on Jerusalem and Judah

3 See now, the Lord,
the LORD Almighty,
is about to take from Jerusalem and Judah
both supply and support:
all supplies of food [a] and all supplies of water, [b]
2 the hero and warrior, [c]
the judge and prophet,
the soothsayer and elder, [d]
3 the captain of fifty and man of rank,
the counsellor, skilled craftsman and clever enchanter.

4 I will make boys their officials;
mere children will govern them. [e]
5 People will oppress each other —
man against man, neighbour against neighbour. [f]
The young will rise up against the old,
the base against the honourable.

6 A man will seize one of his brothers
at his father's home, and say,
"You have a cloak, you be our leader;

2:16 [a] 1Ki 10:22
2:17 [b] ver 11
2:18 [c] Isa 21:9
2:19 [d] Heb 12:26
2:20 [e] Lev 11:19
2:21 [f] ver 19
2:22 [g] Ps 146:3; Jer 17:5 [h] Ps 8:4; 144:3; Isa 40:15; Jas 4:14
3:1 [a] Lev 26:26 [b] Isa 5:13; Eze 4:16
3:2 [c] Eze 17:13 [d] 2Ki 24:14; Isa 9:14-15
3:4 [e] Ecc 10:16 *fn*
3:5 [f] Isa 9:19; Jer 9:8; Mic 7:2, 6

b *16* Hebrew *every ship of Tarshish*

2:19 See Revelation 6:15–17 for a description of the dread in God's enemies on the day of his wrath.

2:22 "But a breath in his nostrils" refers to mankind's mortality. People are very limited when compared to God. They can be unreliable, selfish, and shortsighted. Yet we trust our lives and futures more readily to mortal human beings than to the all-knowing God. Beware of people who want you to trust them instead of God. Remember that only God is completely reliable. He is perfect and he loves us with an enduring love (Psalm 100:5).

3:1–3 Jerusalem besieged, her leaders destroyed – this unhappy picture would soon become a reality. Disobedience would bring serious affliction and great destruction, as God had warned (Deuteronomy 28).

3:2 Isaiah was not condoning the use of soothsayers (diviners) by including them on this list. He was showing how far the nation had sunk. See the note on 2:6.

3:4–9 This section describes what happens when a nation loses its leadership.

take charge of this heap of ruins!"
7 But in that day he will cry out,
"I have no remedy.[g]
I have no food or clothing in my house;
do not make me the leader of the people."

8 Jerusalem staggers,
Judah is falling;[h]
their words[i] and deeds are against the LORD,
defying[j] his glorious presence.
9 The look on their faces testifies against them;
they parade their sin like Sodom;[k]
they do not hide it.
Woe to them!
They have brought disaster[l] upon themselves.

10 Tell the righteous it will be well[m] with them,
for they will enjoy the fruit of their deeds.[n]
11 Woe to the wicked! Disaster[o] is upon them!
They will be paid back for what their hands have done.

12 Youths[p] oppress my people,
women rule over them.
O my people, your guides lead you astray;[q]
they turn you from the path.

13 The LORD takes his place in court;
he rises to judge[r] the people.
14 The LORD enters into judgment[s]
against the elders and leaders of his people:
"It is you who have ruined my vineyard;
the plunder[t] from the poor is in your houses.
15 What do you mean by crushing my people[u]
and grinding the faces of the poor?"
declares the Lord, the LORD Almighty.

16 The LORD says,
"The women of Zion[v] are haughty,
walking along with outstretched necks,
flirting with their eyes,

3:7 [g]Eze 34:4; Hos 5:13
3:8 [h]Isa 1:7 [i]Isa 9:15, 17 [j]Ps 73:9, 11
3:9 [k]Ge 13:13 [l]Pr 8:36; Ro 6:23
3:10 [m]Dt 28:1-14 [n]Ps 128:2
3:11 [o]Dt 28:15-68
3:12 [p]ver 4 [q]Isa 9:16
3:13 [r]Mic 6:2
3:14 [s]Job 22:4 [t]Job 24:9; Jas 2:6
3:15 [u]Ps 94:5
3:16 [v]SS 3:11

3:9–11 The people would be proud of their sins, parading them out in the open. But sin is self-destructive. In today's world, sinful living often appears glamorous, exciting, and clever. But sin is wrong regardless of how society perceives it, and, in the long run, sin will make us miserable and destroy us. God tries to protect us by warning us about the harm we will cause ourselves by sinning. Those who are proud of their sins will receive the punishment from God they deserve. Having rejected God's path to life (see Psalm 1), the only alternative is the path to destruction.

3:10, 11 In the middle of this gloomy message, God gives hope – eventually the righteous will receive God's reward and the wicked will receive their punishment. It is disheartening to see the wicked prosper while we struggle to obey God and follow his plan. Yet we keep holding on to God's truth and take heart! God will bring about justice in the end, and he will reward those who have been faithful.

3:14 The elders and leaders were responsible for helping people, but instead they stole from the poor. Because they were unjust, Isaiah said the leaders would be the first to receive God's judgment. Leaders will be held accountable for how they lead. If you are in a position of leadership, you must lead according to God's just commands. Corruption will bring God's wrath, especially if others follow your example.

3:14 Why is justice so important in the Bible? (1) Justice is part of God's nature; it is the way he runs the universe. (2) It is a natural desire in every person. Even as sinners, we all want justice for ourselves. (3) When government and church leaders are unjust, the poor and powerless suffer. Thus they are hindered from worshipping God. (4) God holds the poor in high regard. They are the ones most likely to turn to him for help and comfort. Injustice, then, attacks God's children. When we do nothing to help the oppressed, we are in fact joining with the oppressor. Because we follow a just God, we must uphold justice.

3:16–26 The women of Judah had placed their emphasis on clothing and jewellery rather than on God. They dressed to be noticed, to gain approval, and to be fashionable. Yet they ignored the real purpose for their lives. Instead of being concerned about the oppression around them (3:14, 15), they were self-serving and self-centred. People who abuse their possessions will end up with nothing. These verses are not an indictment against clothing and jewellery, but a judgment on those who use them lavishly while remaining blind to the needs of others. When God blesses you with money or position, don't flaunt it. Use what you have to help others, not impress them.

tripping along with mincing steps,
with ornaments jingling on their ankles.
17 Therefore the Lord will bring sores on the heads of the women of Zion;
the LORD will make their scalps bald."

18 In that day the Lord will snatch away their finery: the bangles and headbands and
crescent necklaces,[w] 19 the ear-rings and bracelets and veils, 20 the head-dresses[x] and
ankle chains and sashes, the perfume bottles and charms, 21 the signet rings and nose
rings, 22 the fine robes and the capes and cloaks, the purses 23 and mirrors, and the linen
garments and tiaras and shawls.

24 Instead of fragrance[y] there will be a stench;
instead of a sash,[z] a rope;
instead of well-dressed hair, baldness;[a]
instead of fine clothing, sackcloth;[b]
instead of beauty,[c] branding.
25 Your men will fall by the sword,[d]
your warriors in battle.
26 The gates of Zion will lament and mourn;[e]
destitute, she will sit on the ground.[f]

4 In that day seven women
will take hold of one man[a]
and say, "We will eat our own food[b]
and provide our own clothes;
only let us be called by your name.
Take away our disgrace!"[c]

The Branch of the LORD

2 In that day the Branch of the LORD[d] will be beautiful and glorious, and the fruit[e]
of the land will be the pride and glory of the survivors in Israel. 3 Those who are left
in Zion, who remain[f] in Jerusalem, will be called holy,[g] all who are recorded[h]
among the living in Jerusalem. 4 The Lord will wash away the filth[i] of the women
of Zion; he will cleanse the bloodstains[j] from Jerusalem by a spirit[a] of judgment[k]
and a spirit[a] of fire.[l] 5 Then the LORD will create over all of Mount Zion and over
those who assemble there a cloud of smoke by day and a glow of flaming fire by
night;[m] over all the glory[n] will be a canopy. 6 It will be a shelter[o] and shade from
the heat of the day, and a refuge[p] and hiding-place from the storm and rain.

The Song of the Vineyard

5 I will sing for the one I love
a song about his vineyard:[a]
My loved one had a vineyard
on a fertile hillside.
2 He dug it up and cleared it of stones
and planted it with the choicest vines.[b]

a 4 Or *the Spirit*

3:18 [w] Jdg 8:21
3:20 [x] Ex 39:28
3:24 [y] Est 2:12 [z] Pr 31:24 [a] Isa 22:12 [b] La 2:10; Eze 27:30-31 [c] 1Pe 3:3
3:25 [d] Isa 1:20
3:26 [e] Jer 14:2 [f] La 2:10
4:1 [a] Isa 13:12 [b] 2Th 3:12 [c] Ge 30:23
4:2 [d] Isa 11:1-5; 53:2; Jer 23:5-6; Zec 3:8; 6:12 [e] Ps 72:16
4:3 [f] Ro 11:5 [g] Isa 52:1; 60:21 [h] Lk 10:20
4:4 [i] Isa 3:24 [j] Isa 1:15 [k] Isa 28:6 [l] Isa 1:31; Mt 3:11
4:5 [m] Ex 13:21 [n] Isa 60:1
4:6 [o] Ps 27:5 [p] Isa 25:4
5:1 [a] Ps 80:8-9
5:2 [b] Jer 2:21

4:2–4 The "Branch of the LORD" probably refers to the Messiah, although some believe it refers to Judah. The point is that during the distress predicted by Isaiah, some people will be protected by God's loving grace. Those protected will be set apart to God when Messiah rules the earth (Jeremiah 23:5, 6; Zechariah 6:12, 13). Their distinctive mark will be their holiness, not wealth or prestige. This holiness comes from a sincere desire to obey God and from wholehearted devotion to him. Evil will not always continue as it does now. The time will come when God will put an end to all evil, and his faithful followers will share in his glorious reign.

5:1–7 The lesson of the song of the vineyard shows that God's chosen nation was to bear fruit – to carry out his work, to uphold justice. It did bear fruit, but the fruit was bad. This passage uses plays on words: the Hebrew words for *justice* and *bloodshed* sound very much alike, as do those for *righteousness* and *distress*. Jesus said, "By their fruit you will recognise them" (Matthew 7:20). Have you examined your own "fruit" lately? Is it good or bad – useful or wild?

5:2 [c]Mt 21:19; Mk 11:13; Lk 13:6

He built a watchtower in it
and cut out a winepress as well.
Then he looked for a crop of good grapes,
but it yielded only bad fruit.[c]

5:3 [d]Mt 21:40

3"Now you dwellers in Jerusalem and men of Judah,
judge between me and my vineyard.[d]
4What more could have been done for my vineyard
than I have done for it?[e]

5:4 [e]2Ch 36:15; Jer 2:5-7; Mic 6:3-4; Mt 23:37

When I looked for good grapes,
why did it yield only bad?
5Now I will tell you
what I am going to do to my vineyard:
I will take away its hedge,
and it will be destroyed;

5:5 [f]Ps 80:12 [g]Isa 28:3, 18; La 1:15; Lk 21:24

I will break down its wall,[f]
and it will be trampled.[g]
6I will make it a wasteland,
neither pruned nor cultivated,
and briers and thorns[h] will grow there.
I will command the clouds
not to rain on it."

5:6 [h]Isa 7:23, 24; Heb 6:8

7The vineyard[i] of the LORD Almighty
is the house of Israel,
and the men of Judah
are the garden of his delight.

5:7 [i]Ps 80:8 [j]Isa 59:15

And he looked for justice,[j] but saw bloodshed;
for righteousness, but heard cries of distress.

Woes and Judgments

5:8 [k]Jer 22:13 [l]Mic 2:2; Hab 2:9-12

8Woe[k] to you who add house to house
and join field to field[l]
till no space is left
and you live alone in the land.

9The LORD Almighty has declared in my hearing:[m]

5:9 [m]Isa 22:14 [n]Isa 6:11-12; Mt 23:38

"Surely the great houses will become desolate,[n]
the fine mansions left without occupants.
10A ten-acre**a** vineyard will produce only a bath**b** of wine,
a homer**c** of seed only an ephah**d** of grain."[o]

5:10 [o]Lev 26:26

11Woe to those who rise early in the morning
to run after their drinks,
who stay up late at night
till they are inflamed with wine.[p]

5:11 [p]Pr 23:29-30

12They have harps and lyres at their banquets,
tambourines and flutes and wine,
but they have no regard[q] for the deeds of the LORD,

5:12 [q]Job 34:27

a *10* Hebrew *ten-yoke,* that is, the land ploughed by 10 yoke of oxen in one day **b** *10* That is, probably about 5 gallons (about 22 litres) **c** *10* That is, probably about 6 bushels (about 220 litres) **d** *10* That is, probably about ⅗ bushel (about 22 litres)

5:8–25 In this section, God condemns six sins: (1) exploiting others (5:8–10); (2) drunkenness (5:11, 12); (3) taking sarcastic pride in sin (5:18, 19); (4) confusing moral standards (5:20); (5) being conceited (5:21); (6) perverting justice (5:22–24). Because of these sins, God punished Israel with destruction by Assyria (5:25–30). A similar fate was awaiting Judah if they didn't turn from these sins.

5:11–13 These people spent many hours drinking and partying, but Isaiah predicted that eventually many would die of hunger and thirst. Ironically, our pleasures – if they do not have God's blessing – may destroy us. Leaving God out of our lives allows sin to come into them. God wants us to enjoy life (1 Timothy 6:17) but to avoid those activities that could lead us away from him.

no respect for the work of his hands.[r]
13Therefore my people will go into exile
for lack of understanding;[s]
their men of rank will die of hunger
and their masses will be parched with thirst.
14Therefore the grave[e][t] enlarges its appetite
and opens its mouth[u] without limit;
into it will descend their nobles and masses
with all their brawlers and revellers.
15So man will be brought low[v]
and mankind humbled,[w]
the eyes of the arrogant[x] humbled.
16But the LORD Almighty will be exalted by his justice,[y]
and the holy God will show himself holy[z] by his
righteousness.
17Then sheep will graze as in their own pasture;[a]
lambs will feed[f] among the ruins of the rich.

18Woe to those who draw sin along with cords of deceit,
and wickedness[b] as with cart ropes,
19to those who say, "Let God hurry,
let him hasten his work
so that we may see it.
Let it approach,
let the plan of the Holy One of Israel come,
so that we may know it."[c]

20Woe to those who call evil good
and good evil,
who put darkness for light
and light for darkness,[d]
who put bitter for sweet
and sweet for bitter.[e]

21Woe to those who are wise in their own eyes[f]
and clever in their own sight.

22Woe to those who are heroes at drinking wine[g]
and champions at mixing drinks,
23who acquit the guilty for a bribe,[h]
but deny justice[i] to the innocent.[j]
24Therefore, as tongues of fire lick up straw
and as dry grass sinks down in the flames,
so their roots will decay[k]
and their flowers blow away like dust;
for they have rejected the law of the LORD Almighty

5:12 [r]Ps 28:5; Am 6:5-6
5:13 [s]Isa 1:3; Hos 4:6
5:14 [t]Pr 30:16 [u]Nu 16:30
5:15 [v]Isa 10:33 [w]Isa 2:9 [x]Isa 2:11
5:16 [y]Isa 28:17; 30:18; 33:5; 61:8 [z]Isa 29:23
5:17 [a]Isa 7:25; Zep 2:6, 14
5:18 [b]Isa 59:4-8; Jer 23:14
5:19 [c]Jer 17:15; Eze 12:22; 2Pe 3:4
5:20 [d]Mt 6:22-23; Lk 11:34-35 [e]Am 5:7
5:21 [f]Pr 3:7; Ro 12:16; 1Co 3:18-20
5:22 [g]Pr 23:20
5:23 [h]Ex 23:8 [i]Isa 10:2 [j]Ps 94:21; Jas 5:6
5:24 [k]Job 18:16

e *14* Hebrew *Sheol* f *17* Septuagint; Hebrew / *strangers will eat*

5:13 The nation's heroes – the "men of rank" – would suffer the same humiliation as the common people. Why? Because they lived by their own values rather than God's. Many of today's media and sports heroes are idolised because of their ability to live as they please. Are your heroes those who defy God, or those who defy the world in order to serve God?

5:18, 19 Some people drag their sins around with them. Some do so arrogantly, but for others, their sins have become a burden that wears them out. Are you dragging around a cartload of sins that you refuse to give up? Before you find yourself worn out and useless, turn to the One who promises to take away your burden of sin and replace it with a purpose for living that is a joy to fulfil (see Matthew 11:28–30).

5:20 When people do not carefully observe the distinction between good and evil, destruction soon follows. It is easy for people to say, "No-one can decide for anyone else what is really right or wrong." They may think getting drunk can't hurt them, extramarital sex isn't really wrong, or money doesn't control them. But when we make excuses for our actions, we break down the distinction between right and wrong. If we do not take God's word, the Bible, as our standard, soon all moral choices will become blurred. Without God, we are headed for a breakdown and much suffering.

5:24 The people suffered because they rejected God's law. It is sad to see so many people today searching for meaning in life while spurning God's word. We can avoid the error of Israel and Judah by making reading the Bible a high priority in our lives.

and spurned the word[l] of the Holy One of Israel.
25Therefore the LORD's anger[m] burns against his people;
his hand is raised and he strikes them down.
The mountains shake,
and the dead bodies are like refuse[n] in the streets.

Yet for all this, his anger is not turned away,[o]
his hand is still upraised.[p]

26He lifts up a banner for the distant nations,
he whistles[q] for those at the ends of the earth.[r]
Here they come,
swiftly and speedily!
27Not one of them grows tired or stumbles,
not one slumbers or sleeps;
not a belt is loosened at the waist,[s]
not a sandal thong is broken.[t]
28Their arrows are sharp,[u]
all their bows[v] are strung;
their horses' hoofs seem like flint,
their chariot wheels like a whirlwind.
29Their roar is like that of the lion,[w]
they roar like young lions;
they growl as they seize[x] their prey
and carry it off with no-one to rescue.[y]
30In that day they will roar over it
like the roaring of the sea.[z]
And if one looks at the land,
he will see darkness and distress;[a]
even the light will be darkened[b] by the clouds.

Isaiah's Commission

6 In the year that King Uzziah[a] died,[b] I saw the Lord[c] seated on a throne,[d] high
and exalted, and the train of his robe filled the temple. 2Above him were
seraphs,[e] each with six wings: With two wings they covered their faces, with two
they covered their feet,[f] and with two they were flying. 3And they were calling to
one another:

"Holy, holy, holy is the LORD Almighty;
the whole earth is full of his glory."[g]

5:24 [l]Isa 8:6; 30:9, 12
5:25 [m]2Ki 22:13 [n]2Ki 9:37 [o]Jer 4:8; Da 9:16 [p]Isa 9:12, 17, 21; 10:4
5:26 [q]Isa 7:18; Zec 10:8 [r]Dt 28:49; Isa 13:5; 18:3
5:27 [s]Job 12:18 [t]Joel 2:7-8
5:28 [u]Ps 45:5 [v]Ps 7:12
5:29 [w]Jer 51:38; Zep 3:3; Zec 11:3 [x]Isa 10:6; 49:24-25 [y]Isa 42:22; Mic 5:8
5:30 [z]Lk 21:25 [a]Isa 8:22; Jer 4:23-28 [b]Joel 2:10
6:1 [a]2Ch 26:22, 23 [b]2Ki 15:7 [c]Jn 12:41 [d]Rev 4:2
6:2 [e]Rev 4:8 [f]Eze 1:11
6:3 [g]Ps 72:19; Rev 4:8

5:26–30 This passage describes what God would do if the people disobeyed him (Deuteronomy 28). Assyria began to torment Israel during the reign of Ahaz (735 – 715 B.C.). This powerful aggressor destroyed the northern kingdom in 722 B.C. and scattered the people throughout its own empire. Sin has consequences. Although this judgment was not immediate, eventually Israel was punished.

6:1 The year that King Uzziah died was approximately 740 B.C. He remained leprous until he died because he tried to take over the high priest's duties (2 Chronicles 26:18–21). Although Uzziah was generally a good king with a long and prosperous reign, many of his people turned away from God.

6:1ff Isaiah's vision was his commission to be God's messenger to his people. Isaiah was given a difficult mission. He had to tell people who believed they were blessed by God that instead God was going to destroy them because of their disobedience.

6:1ff Isaiah's lofty view of God in 6:1–4 gives us a sense of God's greatness, mystery, and power. Isaiah's example of recognising his sinfulness before God encourages us to confess our sin. His picture of forgiveness reminds us that we, too, are forgiven. When we recognise how great our God is, how sinful we are, and the extent of God's forgiveness, we receive power to do his work. How does your concept of the greatness of God measure up to Isaiah's?

6:1–3 The throne, the attending seraphs or angels, and the threefold *holy* all stressed God's holiness. Seraphs were a type of angel whose name is derived from the word for "burn", perhaps indicating their purity as God's ministers. In a time when moral and spiritual decay had peaked, it was important for Isaiah to see God in his holiness. Holiness means morally perfect, pure, and set apart from all sin. We also need to discover God's holiness. Our daily frustrations, society's pressures, and our shortcomings reduce and narrow our view of God. We need the Bible's view of God as high and lifted up to empower us to deal with our problems and concerns. God's moral perfection, properly seen, will purify us from sin, cleanse our minds from our problems, and enable us to worship and to serve.

4At the sound of their voices the doorposts and thresholds shook and the temple was
filled with smoke.
5"Woe to me!" I cried. "I am ruined! For I am a man of unclean lips, and I live
among a people of unclean lips,[h] and my eyes have seen the King,[i] the LORD
Almighty."
6Then one of the seraphs flew to me with a live coal in his hand, which he had taken
with tongs from the altar. 7With it he touched my mouth and said, "See, this has
touched your lips;[j] your guilt is taken away and your sin atoned for.[k]"
8Then I heard the voice[l] of the Lord saying, "Whom shall I send? And who will
go for us?"
And I said, "Here am I. Send me!"
9He said, "Go[m] and tell this people:

" 'Be ever hearing, but never understanding;
be ever seeing, but never perceiving.'[n]
10Make the heart of this people calloused;[o]
make their ears dull
and close their eyes.[a]
Otherwise they might see with their eyes,
hear with their ears,[p]
understand with their hearts,
and turn and be healed."[q]

11Then I said, "For how long, O Lord?"[r]
And he answered:

"Until the cities lie ruined[s]
and without inhabitant,
until the houses are left deserted
and the fields ruined and ravaged,
12until the LORD has sent everyone far away[t]
and the land is utterly forsaken.[u]
13And though a tenth remains[v] in the land,
it will again be laid waste.
But as the terebinth and oak
leave stumps when they are cut down,
so the holy seed will be the stump in the land."[w]

[a] 9, 10 Hebrew; Septuagint *'You will be ever hearing, but never understanding; / you will be ever seeing, but never perceiving.' / 10 This people's heart has become calloused; / they hardly hear with their ears, / and they have closed their eyes*

6:5 [h] Jer 9:3-8 [i] Jer 51:57
6:7 [j] Jer 1:9 [k] 1Jn 1:7
6:8 [l] Ac 9:4
6:9 [m] Eze 3:11 [n] Mt 13:15*; Lk 8:10*
6:10 [o] Dt 32:15; Ps 119:70 [p] Jer 5:21 [q] Mt 13:13-15; Mk 4:12*; Ac 28:26-27*
6:11 [r] Ps 79:5 [s] Lev 26:31
6:12 [t] Dt 28:64 [u] Jer 4:29
6:13 [v] Isa 1:9 [w] Job 14:7

6:5–8 Seeing the Lord and listening to the praise of the angels, Isaiah realised that he was unclean before God, with no hope of measuring up to God's standard of holiness. When Isaiah's lips were touched with a live burning coal, however, he was told that his sins were forgiven. It wasn't the coal that cleansed him, but God. In response Isaiah submitted himself entirely to God's service. No matter how difficult his task would be, he said, "Here am I. Send me!" The painful cleansing process was necessary before Isaiah could fulfil the task to which God was calling him. Before we accept God's call to speak for him to those around us, we must be cleansed as Isaiah was, confessing our sins and submitting to God's control. Letting God purify us may be painful, but we must be purified so that we can truly represent God, who is pure and holy.

6:8 The more clearly Isaiah saw God (6:5), the more aware Isaiah became of his own powerlessness and inadequacy to do anything of lasting value without God. But he was willing to be God's spokesman. When God calls, will you also say, "Here am I. Send me!"?

6:9–13 God told Isaiah that the people would listen but not learn from his message because their hearts had become calloused (hardened) beyond repentance. God's patience with their chronic rebellion was finally exhausted. His judgment was to abandon them to their rebellion and hardness of heart. Why did God send Isaiah if he knew the people wouldn't listen? Although the nation itself would not repent and would reap judgment, some individuals would listen. In 6:13 God explains his plan for a remnant (holy seed) of faithful followers. God is merciful even when he judges. We can gain encouragement from God's promise to preserve his people. If we are faithful to him we can be sure of his mercy.

6:11–13 When would the people listen? Only after they had come to the end and had nowhere to turn but to God. This would happen when the land was destroyed by invading armies and the people taken into captivity. The "tenth" refers either to those who remained in the land after the captivity, or those who returned from Babylon to rebuild the land. Each group was about a tenth of the total population. When will we listen to God? Must we, like Judah, go through calamities before we will listen to God's words? Consider what God may be telling you, and obey him before time runs out.

7:1
[a]2Ki 15:37
[b]2Ch 28:5
[c]2Ki 15:25

7:2
[d]ver 13;
Isa 22:22
[e]Isa 9:9

The Sign of Immanuel

7 When Ahaz son of Jotham, the son of Uzziah, was king of Judah, King Rezin[a]
of Aram[b] and Pekah[c] son of Remaliah king of Israel marched up to fight against
Jerusalem, but they could not overpower it.
2 Now the house of David[d] was told, "Aram has allied itself with[a] Ephraim[e]";
so the hearts of Ahaz and his people were shaken, as the trees of the forest are shaken
by the wind.

[a] 2 Or *has set up camp in*

ISAIAH

Trees and prophets share at least one important characteristic—both are planted for the future. Yet seedlings are often overlooked and prophets often ignored. Isaiah is one of the best examples of this. The people of his time could have been rescued by his words. Instead, they refused to believe him. With the passing of centuries, however, Isaiah's words have cast a shadow on all of history.

Isaiah was active as a prophet during the reigns of five kings, but he did not set out to be a prophet. By the time King Uzziah died, Isaiah may have been established as a scribe in the royal palace in Jerusalem. It was a respectable career, but God had other plans for his servant. Isaiah's account of God's call leaves little doubt about what motivated the prophet for the next half century. His vision of God was unforgettable.

The encounter with God permanently affected Isaiah's character. He reflected the God he represented. Isaiah's messages—some comforting, some confronting—are so distinct that some have guessed they came from different authors. Isaiah's testimony is that the messages came from the only One capable of being perfect in justice as well as in mercy—God himself.

When he called Isaiah as a prophet, God did not encourage him with predictions of great success. God told Isaiah that the people would not listen. But he was to speak and write his messages anyway because eventually some *would* listen. God compared his people to a tree that would have to be cut down so that a new tree could grow from the old stump (Isaiah 6:13).

We who are part of that future can see that many of the promises God gave through Isaiah have been fulfilled in Jesus Christ. We also gain the hope of knowing that God is active in all of history, including our own.

Strengths and accomplishments:
- Considered the greatest Old Testament prophet
- Quoted at least 50 times in the New Testament
- Had powerful messages of both judgment and hope
- Carried out a consistent ministry even though there was little positive response from his listeners
- His ministry spanned the reigns of five kings of Judah

Lessons from his life:
- God's help is needed in order to confront sin effectively while comforting people
- One result of experiencing forgiveness is the desire to share that forgiveness with others
- God is purely and perfectly holy, just, and loving

Vital statistics:
- Where: Jerusalem
- Occupations: Scribe, prophet
- Relatives: Father: Amoz. Sons: Shear-Jashub, Maher-Shalal-Hash-Baz
- Contemporaries: Uzziah, Jotham, Ahaz, Hezekiah, Manasseh, Micah

Key verse:
"Then I heard the voice of the Lord saying, 'Whom shall I send? And who will go for us?' And I said, 'Here am I. Send me!' " (Isaiah 6:8).

Isaiah's story is told in 2 Kings 19:2—20:19. He is also mentioned in 2 Chronicles 26:22; 32:20, 32; Matthew 3:3; 8:17; 12:17–21; John 12:38–41; Romans 10:16, 20, 21.

7:1 The year was 734 B.C. Ahaz, king of Judah in Jerusalem, was about to be attacked by an alliance of the northern kingdom of Israel and Aram. He was frightened by the possible end of his reign and by the invading armies who killed many people or took them as captives (2 Chronicles 28:5–21). But, as Isaiah predicted, the kingdom of Judah did not come to an end at this time. The sign of Immanuel would be a sign of deliverance.

7:2 "The house of David" refers to Judah, the southern kingdom. "Ephraim", the dominant tribe in the north, is a reference to Israel, the northern kingdom.

3 Then the LORD said to Isaiah, "Go out, you and your son Shear-Jashub,[b] to meet
Ahaz at the end of the aqueduct of the Upper Pool, on the road to the Washerman's
Field.[f] 4 Say to him, 'Be careful, keep calm[g] and don't be afraid.[h] Do not lose
heart[i] because of these two smouldering stubs[j] of firewood—because of the fierce
anger[k] of Rezin and Aram and of the son of Remaliah. 5 Aram, Ephraim and Remaliah's son have plotted your ruin, saying, 6 "Let us invade Judah; let us tear it apart
and divide it among ourselves, and make the son of Tabeel king over it." 7 Yet this
is what the Sovereign LORD says:

> " 'It will not take place,
> it will not happen,[l]
> 8 for the head of Aram is Damascus,[m]
> and the head of Damascus is only Rezin.
> Within sixty-five years
> Ephraim will be too shattered[n] to be a people.
> 9 The head of Ephraim is Samaria,
> and the head of Samaria is only Remaliah's son.
> If you do not stand firm in your faith,[o]
> you will not stand at all.' "[p]

10 Again the LORD spoke to Ahaz, 11 "Ask the LORD your God for a sign, whether
in the deepest depths or in the highest heights."
12 But Ahaz said, "I will not ask; I will not put the LORD to the test."
13 Then Isaiah said, "Hear now, you house of David! Is it not enough to try the
patience of men? Will you try the patience of my God[q] also? 14 Therefore the Lord
himself will give you[c] a sign: The virgin will be with child and will give birth to a
son,[r] and[d] will call him Immanuel.[e][s] 15 He will eat curds and honey[t] when he
knows enough to reject the wrong and choose the right. 16 But before the boy knows[u]
enough to reject the wrong and choose the right, the land of the two kings you dread
will be laid waste.[v] 17 The LORD will bring on you and on your people and on the
house of your father a time unlike any since Ephraim broke away[w] from Judah—he
will bring the king of Assyria.[x]"
18 In that day the LORD will whistle[y] for flies from the distant streams of Egypt and

7:3 [f] 2Ki 18:17; Isa 36:2
7:4 [g] Isa 30:15 [h] Isa 35:4 [i] Dt 20:3 [j] Zec 3:2 [k] Isa 10:24
7:7 [l] Isa 8:10; Ac 4:25
7:8 [m] Ge 14:15 [n] Isa 17:1-3
7:9 [o] 2Ch 20:20 [p] Isa 8:6-8; 30:12-14
7:13 [q] Isa 25:1
7:14 [r] Lk 1:31 [s] Isa 8:8, 10; Mt 1:23*
7:15 [t] ver 22
7:16 [u] Isa 8:4 [v] Isa 17:3; Hos 5:9, 13; Am 1:3-5
7:17 [w] 1Ki 12:16 [x] 2Ch 28:20
7:18 [y] Isa 5:26

b 3 *Shear-Jashub* means *a remnant will return.* c 14 The Hebrew is plural. d 14 Masoretic Text; Dead Sea Scrolls *and he* or *and they* e 14 *Immanuel* means *God with us.*

7:3 *Shear-Jashub* means "a remnant will return". God told Isaiah to give his son this name as a reminder of his plan for mercy. From the beginning of God's judgment he planned to restore a remnant of his people. Shear-Jashub was a reminder to the people of God's faithfulness to them.

7:3 The "aqueduct of the Upper Pool" may have been the site of the Gihon spring, located east of Jerusalem. The Gihon spring was the main source of water for the holy city, and was also the spring that emptied into Hezekiah's famous water tunnel (2 Chronicles 32:30). The Washerman's Field was a well-known place where clothing or newly woven cloth was laid in the sun to dry and whiten (see 36:2).

7:4–8:15 Isaiah predicted the breakup of Israel's alliance with Aram (7:4–9). Because of this alliance, Israel would be destroyed; Assyria would be the instrument God would use to destroy them (7:8–25) and to punish Judah. But God would not let Assyria destroy Judah (8:1–15). They would be spared because God's gracious plans cannot be thwarted.

7:8 Ahaz, one of Judah's worst kings, refused God's help and instead, he tried to buy aid from the Assyrians with silver and gold from the temple (2 Kings 16:8). When the Assyrians came, they brought further trouble instead of help. In 722 B.C., Samaria, the capital of Ephraim (another name for Israel, the northern kingdom), fell to the Assyrian armies, thus ending the northern kingdom.

7:12 Ahaz appeared righteous by saying he would not test God with a sign ("I will not ask; I will not put the LORD to the test"). In fact, God had told him to ask, but Ahaz didn't really want to know what God would say. Often we use some excuse, such as not wanting to bother God, to keep us from communicating with him. Don't let anything keep you from hearing and obeying God.

7:14–16 *Virgin* is translated from a Hebrew word used for an unmarried woman old enough to be married, one who is sexually mature (see Genesis 24:43; Exodus 2:8; Psalm 68:25; Proverbs 30:19; Song of Songs 1:3; 6:8). Some have compared this young woman to Isaiah's young wife and newborn son (8:1–4). This is not likely because she had a child, Shear-Jashub, and her second child was not named Immanuel. Some believe that Isaiah's first wife may have died, and so this is his second wife. It is more likely that this prophecy had a double fulfilment. (1) A young woman from the house of Ahaz who was not married would marry and have a son. Before three years passed (one year for pregnancy and two for the child to be old enough to talk), the two invading kings would be destroyed. (2) Matthew 1:23 quotes Isaiah 7:14 to show a further fulfilment of this prophecy in that a virgin named Mary conceived and bore a son, Immanuel, the Christ.

7:18 Flies and bees are symbols of God's judgment (see Exodus 23:28). Egypt and Assyria did not at this time devastate Judah. Hezekiah followed Ahaz as king, and he honoured God; therefore God held back his hand of judgment. Two more evil kings reigned before Josiah, of whom it was said that no other king turned so completely to the Lord (2 Kings 23:25). However, Judah's doom had been sealed by the extreme evil of Josiah's father, Amon. During Josiah's reign, Egypt marched against the Assyrians. Josiah

for bees from the land of Assyria.[z] 19They will all come and settle in the steep ravines
and in the crevices[a] in the rocks, on all the thornbushes and at all the water holes.
20In that day the Lord will use[b] a razor hired from beyond the River[f]—the king of
Assyria[c]—to shave your head and the hair of your legs, and to take off your beards
also. 21In that day, a man will keep alive a young cow and two goats. 22And because
of the abundance of the milk they give, he will have curds to eat. All who remain
in the land will eat curds and honey. 23In that day, in every place where there were
a thousand vines worth a thousand silver shekels,[g] there will be only briers and
thorns.[d] 24Men will go there with bow and arrow, for the land will be covered with
briers and thorns. 25As for all the hills once cultivated by the hoe, you will no longer
go there for fear of the briers and thorns; they will become places where cattle are
turned loose and where sheep run.[e]

Assyria, the LORD's Instrument

8 The LORD said to me, "Take a large scroll[a] and write on it with an ordinary pen:
Maher-Shalal-Hash-Baz.[a][b] 2And I will call in Uriah[c] the priest and Zechariah
son of Jeberekiah as reliable witnesses for me."

3Then I went to the prophetess, and she conceived and gave birth to a son. And
the LORD said to me, "Name him Maher-Shalal-Hash-Baz. 4Before the boy knows[d]
how to say 'My father' or 'My mother', the wealth of Damascus and the plunder of
Samaria will be carried off by the king of Assyria.[e]"

5The LORD spoke to me again:

6"Because this people has rejected[f]
the gently flowing waters of Shiloah[g]
and rejoices over Rezin
and the son of Remaliah,[h]
7therefore the Lord is about to bring against them
the mighty floodwaters[i] of the River[b]—
the king of Assyria[j] with all his pomp.
It will overflow all its channels,
run over all its banks
8and sweep on into Judah, swirling over it,
passing through it and reaching up to the neck.
Its outspread wings will cover the breadth of your land,
O Immanuel!"[c][k]

9Raise the war cry,[d][l] you nations, and be shattered!
Listen, all you distant lands.
Prepare[m] for battle, and be shattered!

7:18 [z]Isa 13:5
7:19 [a]Isa 2:19
7:20 [b]Isa 10:15 [c]Isa 8:7; 10:5
7:23 [d]Isa 5:6
7:25 [e]Isa 5:17
8:1 [a]Isa 30:8 [b]ver 3; Hab 2:2
8:2 [c]2Ki 16:10
8:4 [d]Isa 7:16 [e]Isa 7:8
8:6 [f]Isa 5:24 [g]Jn 9:7 [h]Isa 7:1
8:7 [i]Isa 17:12-13 [j]Isa 7:20
8:8 [k]Isa 7:14
8:9 [l]Isa 17:12-13 [m]Joel 3:9

f *20* That is, the Euphrates **g** *23* That is, about 25 pounds (about 11.5 kilograms) **a** *1* *Maher-Shalal-Hash-Baz* means *quick to the plunder, swift to the spoil*; also in verse 3. **b** *7* That is, the Euphrates **c** *8* *Immanuel* means *God with us.* **d** *9* Or *Do your worst*

---

then declared war on Egypt, though God told him not to. After Josiah was killed (2 Chronicles 35:20–27), only weak kings reigned in Judah. The Egyptians carried off Josiah's son, Jehoahaz, after three months. The next king, Jehoiakim, was taken by Nebuchadnezzar to Babylon. Egypt and Assyria had dealt death blows to Judah.

7:20 Hiring Assyria to save them would be Judah's downfall (2 Kings 16:7, 8). To "shave" Judah's hair was symbolic of total humiliation. Numbers 6:9 explains that after being defiled, a person who had been set apart for the Lord had to shave his head as part of the cleansing process. Shaving bodily hair was an embarrassment—an exposure of nakedness. For a Hebrew man, having his beard shaved was humiliating (2 Samuel 10:4, 5).

7:21–25 Judah's rich farmland would be trampled until it became pastureland fit only for grazing. No longer would it be a place of agricultural abundance, a land "flowing with milk and honey" (Exodus 3:8), but a land with only curds, briers, and thorns.

8:1–4 These verses predict the fall of Israel and Aram. Aram fell to Assyria in 732 B.C., and Israel followed in 722 B.C. Isaiah put his message on a large scroll in a public place. God was warning all his people.

8:6–8 "The gently flowing waters of Shiloah" refers to God's gentle and sustaining care. Because Judah rejected God's kindness, choosing instead to seek help from other nations, God would punish them. We see two distinct attributes of God—his love and his wrath. To ignore his love and guidance results in sin and invites his wrath. We must recognise the consequences of our choices. God wants to protect us from bad choices, but he still gives us the freedom to make them.

8:7, 8 The heart of the Assyrian empire was located between the Tigris and Euphrates Rivers. This flood is a poetic way of describing the overwhelming force of the Assyrian army.

8:9 To "be shattered" means to lose courage by the pressure of sudden fear.

Prepare for battle, and be shattered!
10Devise your strategy, but it will be thwarted;[n]
propose your plan, but it will not stand,[o]
for God is with us.[e][p]

Fear God

11The LORD spoke to me with his strong hand upon me,[q] warning me not to
follow[r] the way of this people. He said:

12"Do not call conspiracy[s]
everything that these people call conspiracy;[f]
do not fear what they fear,
and do not dread it.[t]
13The LORD Almighty is the one you are to regard as holy,[u]
he is the one you are to fear,
he is the one you are to dread,[v]
14and he will be a sanctuary;[w]
but for both houses of Israel he will be
a stone that causes men to stumble
and a rock that makes them fall.[x]
And for the people of Jerusalem he will be
a trap and a snare.[y]
15Many of them will stumble;[z]
they will fall and be broken,
they will be snared and captured."

16Bind up the testimony
and seal[a] up the law among my disciples.
17I will wait[b] for the LORD,
who is hiding[c] his face from the house of Jacob.
I will put my trust in him.

18Here am I, and the children the LORD has given me.[d] We are signs[e] and symbols
in Israel from the LORD Almighty, who dwells on Mount Zion.[f]
19When men tell you to consult[g] mediums and spiritists, who whisper and mutter,[h] should not a people enquire of their God? Why consult the dead on behalf of
the living? 20To the law[i] and to the testimony! If they do not speak according to this
word, they have no light[j] of dawn. 21Distressed and hungry, they will roam through
the land; when they are famished, they will become enraged and, looking upward,
will curse[k] their king and their God. 22Then they will look towards the earth and see
only distress and darkness and fearful gloom, and they will be thrust into utter
darkness.[l]

[e] 10 Hebrew *Immanuel* [f] 12 Or *Do not call for a treaty / every time these people call for a treaty*

8:10 [n] Job 5:12 [o] Isa 7:7 [p] Isa 7:14; Ro 8:31
8:11 [q] Eze 3:14 [r] Eze 2:8
8:12 [s] Isa 7:2; 30:1 [t] 1Pe 3:14*
8:13 [u] Nu 20:12 [v] Isa 29:23
8:14 [w] Isa 4:6; Eze 11:16 [x] Lk 2:34; Ro 9:33*; 1Pe 2:8* [y] Isa 24:17-18
8:15 [z] Isa 28:13; 59:10; Lk 20:18; Ro 9:32
8:16 [a] Isa 29:11-12
8:17 [b] Hab 2:3 [c] Dt 31:17; Isa 54:8
8:18 [d] Heb 2:13* [e] Lk 2:34 [f] Ps 9:11
8:19 [g] 1Sa 28:8 [h] Isa 29:4
8:20 [i] Isa 1:10; Lk 16:29 [j] Mic 3:6
8:21 [k] Rev 16:11
8:22 [l] ver 20; Isa 5:30

8:11–15 Isaiah, along with most of the prophets, was viewed as a traitor because he did not support Judah's national policies. He called the people to commit themselves first to God, and then to the king. He even predicted the overthrow of the government.

8:16 "Bind up the testimony" and "seal up the law" mean that the words would be written down and preserved for future generations. Because some people faithfully passed on these words from generation to generation, we have the book of Isaiah today. Each of us needs to accept the responsibility to pass on God's word to our children and grandchildren, encouraging them to love the Bible, read it, and learn from it. Then they will faithfully pass it on to their children and grandchildren.

8:17 Isaiah decided to wait for the Lord, though God was "hiding his face from the house of Jacob". Many of the prophecies God gave through the prophets would not come true for 700 years; others still haven't been fulfilled. Are you willing to accept the Lord's timing, not yours?

8:19 The people would consult mediums and spiritists to seek answers from dead people instead of consulting the living God. God alone knows the future, and only he is eternal. We can trust God to guide us.

8:21 After rejecting God's plan for them, the people of Judah would blame God for their trials. People continually blame God for their self-induced problems. How do you respond to the unpleasant results of your own choices? Where do you fix the blame? Instead of blaming God, look for ways to grow through your failures.

9:1
[a] 2Ki 15:29

9:2
[b] Eph 5:8
[c] Lk 1:79
[d] Mt 4:15-16*

9:4
[e] Jdg 7:25
[f] Isa 14:25
[g] Isa 10:27
[h] Isa 14:4; 49:26; 51:13; 54:14

9:5
[i] Isa 2:4

9:6
[j] Isa 53:2; Lk 2:11
[k] Jn 3:16
[l] Mt 28:18
[m] Isa 28:29
[n] Isa 10:21; 11:2
[o] Isa 26:3, 12; 66:12

9:7
[p] Da 2:44; Lk 1:33
[q] Isa 11:4; 16:5; 32:1, 16

To Us a Child Is Born

9 Nevertheless, there will be no more gloom for those who were in distress. In the
past he humbled the land of Zebulun and the land of Naphtali,[a] but in the future
he will honour Galilee of the Gentiles, by the way of the sea, along the Jordan—

2The people walking in darkness
have seen a great light;[b]
on those living in the land of the shadow of death[a][c]
a light has dawned.[d]
3You have enlarged the nation
and increased their joy;
they rejoice before you
as people rejoice at the harvest,
as men rejoice
when dividing the plunder.
4For as in the day of Midian's defeat,[e]
you have shattered
the yoke[f] that burdens them,
the bar across their shoulders,[g]
the rod of their oppressor.[h]
5Every warrior's boot used in battle
and every garment rolled in blood
will be destined for burning,[i]
will be fuel for the fire.
6For to us a child is born,[j]
to us a son is given,[k]
and the government[l] will be on his shoulders.
And he will be called
Wonderful Counsellor,[b][m] Mighty God,[n]
Everlasting Father, Prince of Peace.[o]
7Of the increase of his government and peace
there will be no end.[p]
He will reign on David's throne
and over his kingdom,
establishing and upholding it
with justice[q] and righteousness
from that time on and for ever.

[a] *2* Or *land of darkness* [b] *6* Or *Wonderful, Counsellor*

NAMES FOR MESSIAH
Isaiah uses four names to describe the Messiah. These names have special meaning to us.

Wonderful Counsellor	• He is exceptional, distinguished, and without peer, the one who gives the right advice.
Mighty God	• He is God himself.
Everlasting Father	• He is timeless; he is God our Father.
Prince of Peace	• His government is one of justice and peace.

9:1 In our gloom and despair, we fear that our sorrows and troubles will never end. But we can take comfort in this certainty: although the Lord may not always take us around our troubles, if we follow him wholeheartedly, he will lead us safely through them.

9:1–7 This child who would become their deliverer is the Messiah, Jesus. Matthew quotes these verses in describing Christ's ministry (Matthew 4:15, 16). The territories of Zebulun and Naphtali represent the northern kingdom as a whole. These were also the territories where Jesus grew up and often ministered; this is why they would see "a great light".

9:2 The apostle John also referred to Jesus as the "light" (John 1:9). Jesus referred to himself as "the light of the world" (John 8:12).

9:2–6 In a time of great darkness, God promised to send a light who would shine on everyone living in the shadow of death. He is both 'Wonderful Counsellor" and "Mighty God". This message of hope was fulfilled in the birth of Christ and the establishment of his eternal kingdom. He came to deliver all people from their slavery to sin.

The zeal[r] of the LORD Almighty
will accomplish this.

The LORD's Anger Against Israel

8 The Lord has sent a message against Jacob;
it will fall on Israel.
9 All the people will know it—
Ephraim and the inhabitants of Samaria[s]—
who say with pride
and arrogance[t] of heart,
10 "The bricks have fallen down,
but we will rebuild with dressed stone;
the fig-trees have been felled,
but we will replace them with cedars."
11 But the LORD has strengthened Rezin's[u] foes against them
and has spurred their enemies on.
12 Arameans[v] from the east and Philistines[w] from the west
have devoured[x] Israel with open mouth.

Yet for all this, his anger is not turned away,
his hand is still upraised.[y]

13 But the people have not returned to him who struck[z] them,
nor have they sought[a] the LORD Almighty.
14 So the LORD will cut off from Israel both head and tail,
both palm branch and reed[b] in a single day;[c]
15 the elders[d] and prominent men are the head,
the prophets who teach lies are the tail.
16 Those who guide[e] this people mislead them,
and those who are guided are led astray.[f]
17 Therefore the Lord will take no pleasure in the young men,[g]
nor will he pity[h] the fatherless and widows,
for everyone is ungodly[i] and wicked,[j]
every mouth speaks vileness.[k]

Yet for all this, his anger is not turned away,
his hand is still upraised.[l]

18 Surely wickedness burns like a fire;[m]
it consumes briers and thorns,
it sets the forest thickets ablaze,[n]
so that it rolls upward in a column of smoke.
19 By the wrath[o] of the LORD Almighty
the land will be scorched
and the people will be fuel for the fire;[p]
no-one will spare his brother.[q]
20 On the right they will devour,
but still be hungry;[r]
on the left they will eat,[s]
but not be satisfied.
Each will feed on the flesh of his own offspring:[c]
21 Manasseh will feed on Ephraim, and Ephraim on Manasseh;

[c] 20 Or *arm*

9:7 [r] Isa 37:32; 59:17
9:9 [s] Isa 7:9 [t] Isa 46:12
9:11 [u] Isa 7:8
9:12 [v] 2Ki 16:6 [w] 2Ch 28:18 [x] Ps 79:7 [y] Isa 5:25
9:13 [z] Jer 5:3 [a] Isa 31:1; Hos 7:7, 10
9:14 [b] Isa 19:15 [c] Rev 18:8
9:15 [d] Isa 3:2-3
9:16 [e] Mt 15:14; 23:16, 24 [f] Isa 3:12
9:17 [g] Jer 18:21 [h] Isa 27:11 [i] Isa 10:6 [j] Isa 1:4 [k] Mt 12:34 [l] Isa 5:25
9:18 [m] Mal 4:1 [n] Ps 83:14
9:19 [o] Isa 13:9, 13 [p] Isa 1:31 [q] Mic 7:2, 6
9:20 [r] Lev 26:26 [s] Isa 49:26

9:8–10 Pride made Israel think it would recover and rebuild in its own strength. Even though God made Israel a nation and gave them the land they occupied, the people put their trust in themselves rather than in him. Too often we take pride in our accomplishments, forgetting that it is God who has given us our every resource and ability. We may even become proud of our unique status as Christians. God is not pleased with *any* pride or trust in ourselves because it cuts off our contact with him.

9:21 Ephraim and Manasseh were tribes in the northern kingdom descended from Joseph's two sons. They fought a civil war be-

9:21 [t]2Ch 28:6 [u]Isa 5:25
10:1 [a]Ps 58:2
10:2 [b]Isa 3:14 [c]Isa 5:23
10:3 [d]Job 31:14; Hos 9:7 [e]Lk 19:44 [f]Isa 20:6
10:4 [g]Isa 24:22 [h]Isa 22:2; 34:3; 66:16 [i]Isa 5:25
10:5 [j]Isa 14:25; Zep 2:13 [k]Jer 51:20 [l]Isa 13:3, 5, 13; 30:30; 66:14
10:6 [m]Isa 9:17 [n]Isa 9:19 [o]Isa 5:29
10:7 [p]Ge 50:20; Ac 4:23-28
10:8 [q]2Ki 18:24
10:9 [r]Ge 10:10 [s]2Ch 35:20 [t]2Ki 17:6 [u]2Ki 16:9
10:10 [v]2Ki 19:18
10:12 [w]Isa 28:21-22; 65:7 [x]2Ki 19:31

together they will turn against Judah.[t]

Yet for all this, his anger is not turned away,
his hand is still upraised.[u]

10 Woe to those who make unjust laws,
to those who issue oppressive decrees,[a]
2 to deprive[b] the poor of their rights
and withhold justice from the oppressed of my people,[c]
making widows their prey
and robbing the fatherless.
3 What will you do on the day of reckoning,[d]
when disaster[e] comes from afar?
To whom will you run for help?[f]
Where will you leave your riches?
4 Nothing will remain but to cringe among the captives[g]
or fall among the slain.[h]

Yet for all this, his anger is not turned away,[i]
his hand is still upraised.

God's Judgment on Assyria

5 "Woe to the Assyrian,[j] the rod of my anger,
in whose hand is the club[k] of my wrath![l]
6 I send him against a godless[m] nation,
I dispatch him against a people who anger me,[n]
to seize loot and snatch plunder,[o]
and to trample them down like mud in the streets.
7 But this is not what he intends,[p]
this is not what he has in mind;
his purpose is to destroy,
to put an end to many nations.
8 'Are not my commanders[q] all kings?' he says.
9 'Has not Calno[r] fared like Carchemish?[s]
Is not Hamath like Arpad,
and Samaria[t] like Damascus?[u]
10 As my hand seized the kingdoms of the idols,[v]
kingdoms whose images excelled those of Jerusalem and
Samaria—
11 shall I not deal with Jerusalem and her images
as I dealt with Samaria and her idols?' "

12 When the Lord has finished all his work[w] against Mount Zion[x] and Jerusalem,

---

cause of their selfishness and wickedness (see Judges 12:4).

10:1 God will judge crooked judges and those who make unjust laws. Those who oppress others will be oppressed themselves. It is not enough to live in a land founded on justice; each individual must deal justly with the poor and the powerless. Don't pass your responsibility off to your nation or even your church. You are accountable to God for what you do.

10:7 Although Assyria did not know it was part of God's plan, God used this nation to judge his people. God accomplishes his plans in history despite people or nations who reject him. He did not merely set the world in motion and let it go! Because our all-powerful, sovereign God is still in control today, we have security even in a rapidly changing world.

10:9 Calno, Carchemish, Hamath, Arpad, Samaria, and Damascus were cities conquered by Assyria. Assured of great victories that would enlarge their empire, the king of Assyria gave an arrogant speech. Already Assyria had conquered several cities and thought Judah would be defeated along with the others. Little did they know that they were under the mightier hand of God.

10:10 Samaria and Jerusalem were filled with idols that were powerless against the Assyrian military machine. Only the God of the universe could and would overthrow Assyria, but not until he had used the Assyrians for his purposes.

10:12 The predicted punishment of the Assyrians soon took place. In 701 B.C., 185,000 Assyrian soldiers were slain by the angel of the Lord (37:36, 37). Later, the Assyrian empire fell to Babylon, never to rise again as a world power.

10:12 The Assyrians were haughty. Proud of the victories God permitted, they thought they had accomplished everything in their own power. Our perspective can become distorted by our accomplishments if we fail to recognise God working his purposes through us. When we think we are strong enough for anything, we are bound to fail because pride has blinded us to the reality that God is ultimately in control.

he will say, "I will punish the king of Assyria[y] for the wilful pride of his heart and
the haughty look in his eyes. 13For he says:

" 'By the strength of my hand I have done this,[z]
and by my wisdom, because I have understanding.
I removed the boundaries of nations,
I plundered their treasures;[a]
like a mighty one I subdued[a] their kings.
14As one reaches into a nest,[b]
so my hand reached for the wealth[c] of the nations;
as men gather abandoned eggs,
so I gathered all the countries;
not one flapped a wing,
or opened its mouth to chirp.' "
15Does the axe raise itself above him who swings it,
or the saw boast against him who uses it?[d]
As if a rod were to wield him who lifts it up,
or a club[e] brandish him who is not wood!
16Therefore, the Lord, the LORD Almighty,
will send a wasting disease[f] upon his sturdy warriors;
under his pomp[g] a fire will be kindled
like a blazing flame.
17The Light of Israel will become a fire,[h]
their Holy One[i] a flame;
in a single day it will burn and consume
his thorns[j] and his briers.[k]
18The splendour of his forests[l] and fertile fields
it will completely destroy,
as when a sick man wastes away.
19And the remaining trees of his forests will be so few[m]
that a child could write them down.

The Remnant of Israel

20In that day[n] the remnant of Israel,
the survivors of the house of Jacob,
will no longer rely[o] on him
who struck them down[p]
but will truly rely[q] on the LORD,
the Holy One of Israel.
21A remnant[r] will return,[b] a remnant of Jacob
will return to the Mighty God.[s]
22Though your people, O Israel, be like the sand by the sea,
only a remnant will return.[t]
Destruction has been decreed,[u]
overwhelming and righteous.

10:12 [y]Jer 50:18
10:13 [z]Isa 37:24; Da 4:30 [a]Eze 28:4
10:14 [b]Jer 49:16; Ob 1:4 [c]Job 31:25
10:15 [d]Isa 45:9; Ro 9:20-21 [e]ver 5
10:16 [f]ver 18; Isa 17:4 [g]Isa 8:7
10:17 [h]Isa 31:9 [i]Isa 37:23 [j]Nu 11:1-3 [k]Isa 9:18
10:18 [l]2Ki 19:23
10:19 [m]Isa 21:17
10:20 [n]Isa 11:10, 11 [o]2Ki 16:7 [p]2Ch 28:20 [q]Isa 17:7
10:21 [r]Isa 6:13 [s]Isa 9:6
10:22 [t]Ro 9:27-28 [u]Isa 28:22; Da 9:27

[a] *13* Or *I subdued the mighty,* [b] *21* Hebrew *shear-jashub*; also in verse 22

10:15 No instrument or tool accomplishes its purposes without a greater power. The Assyrians were a tool in God's hands, but they failed to recognise it. When a tool boasts of greater power than the one who uses it, it is in danger of being discarded. We are useful only to the extent that we allow God to use us.

10:17 Assyria's downfall came in 612 B.C. when Nineveh, the capital city, was destroyed. Assyria had been God's instrument of judgment against Israel, but it too would be judged for its wickedness. No-one escapes God's judgment against sin, not even the most powerful of nations (Psalm 2).

10:20, 21 Once Assyria's army was destroyed, a small group of God's people would stop relying on Assyria and start trusting God. This remnant would be but a fraction of Israel's former population: see Ezra 2:64, 65 for the small number who returned to Judah (see also 11:10–16).

10:20, 21 Those who remained faithful to God despite the horrors of the invasion are called the remnant. The key to being a part of the remnant was *faith.* Being a descendant of Abraham, living in the promised land, having trusted God at one time – none of these was good enough. Are you relying on your Christian heritage, the rituals of worship, or past experience to put you in a right relationship with God? The key to being set apart by God is faith in him.

23The Lord, the LORD Almighty, will carry out
the destruction decreed upon the whole land.[v]

24Therefore, this is what the Lord, the LORD Almighty, says:

"O my people who live in Zion,[w]
do not be afraid of the Assyrians,
who beat[x] you with a rod
and lift up a club against you, as Egypt did.
25Very soon[y] my anger against you will end
and my wrath[z] will be directed to their destruction."

26The LORD Almighty will lash[a] them with a whip,
as when he struck down Midian[b] at the rock of Oreb;
and he will raise his staff over the waters,[c]
as he did in Egypt.
27In that day their burden will be lifted from your shoulders,
their yoke[d] from your neck;[e]
the yoke will be broken
because you have grown so fat.[c]

28They enter Aiath;
they pass through Migron;[f]
they store supplies at Michmash.[g]
29They go over the pass, and say,
"We will camp overnight at Geba."
Ramah[h] trembles;
Gibeah of Saul flees.
30Cry out, O Daughter of Gallim![i]
Listen, O Laishah!
Poor Anathoth![j]
31Madmenah is in flight;
the people of Gebim take cover.
32This day they will halt at Nob;[k]
they will shake their fist
at the mount of the Daughter of Zion,[l]
at the hill of Jerusalem.

33See, the Lord, the LORD Almighty,
will lop off the boughs with great power.
The lofty trees will be felled,
the tall[m] ones will be brought low.
34He will cut down the forest thickets with an axe;
Lebanon will fall before the Mighty One.

The Branch From Jesse

11 A shoot will come up from the stump of Jesse;[a]
from his roots a Branch[b] will bear fruit.
2The Spirit[c] of the LORD will rest on him —
the Spirit of wisdom[d] and of understanding,
the Spirit of counsel and of power,[e]
the Spirit of knowledge and of the fear of the LORD —

10:23 [v]Isa 28:22; Ro 9:27-28*
10:24 [w]Ps 87:5-6 [x]Ex 5:14
10:25 [y]Isa 17:14 [z]ver 5; Da 11:36
10:26 [a]Isa 37:36-38 [b]Isa 9:4 [c]Ex 14:16
10:27 [d]Isa 9:4 [e]Isa 14:25
10:28 [f]1Sa 14:2 [g]1Sa 13:2
10:29 [h]Jos 18:25
10:30 [i]1Sa 25:44 [j]Ne 11:32
10:32 [k]1Sa 21:1 [l]Jer 6:23
10:33 [m]Am 2:9
11:1 [a]ver 10; Isa 9:7; Rev 5:5 [b]Isa 4:2
11:2 [c]Isa 42:1; 48:16; 61:1; Mt 3:16; Jn 1:32-33 [d]Eph 1:17 [e]2Ti 1:7

c *27* Hebrew; Septuagint *broken / from your shoulders*

10:28–34 The way these cities are listed approximates the route the Assyrians would take in their invasion of Judah in 701 B.C. They would go from Aiath (probably Ai) at the northern border to Nob (only two miles from Jerusalem).

11:1–9 Assyria would be like a tree cut down at the height of its power (10:33, 34), never to rise again. Judah (the royal line of David) would be like a tree chopped down to a stump. But from that stump a new shoot would grow – the Messiah. He would be greater than the original tree and would bear much fruit. The Messiah is the fulfilment of God's promise that a descendant of David would rule for ever (2 Samuel 7:16).

3 and he will delight in the fear of the LORD.

He will not judge by what he sees with his eyes,[f]
or decide by what he hears with his ears;[g]
4 but with righteousness[h] he will judge the needy,
with justice[i] he will give decisions for the poor[j] of the earth.
He will strike[k] the earth with the rod of his mouth;
with the breath[l] of his lips he will slay the wicked.
5 Righteousness will be his belt
and faithfulness[m] the sash round his waist.[n]

6 The wolf will live with the lamb,[o]
the leopard will lie down with the goat,
the calf and the lion and the yearling[a] together;
and a little child will lead them.
7 The cow will feed with the bear,
their young will lie down together,
and the lion will eat straw like the ox.
8 The infant will play near the hole of the cobra,
and the young child put his hand into the viper's nest.
9 They will neither harm nor destroy[p]
on all my holy mountain,
for the earth[q] will be full of the knowledge[r] of the LORD
as the waters cover the sea.

10 In that day the Root of Jesse will stand as a banner[s] for the peoples; the nations[t]
will rally to him,[u] and his place of rest[v] will be glorious. 11 In that day[w] the Lord
will reach out his hand a second time to reclaim the remnant that is left of his people
from Assyria,[x] from Lower Egypt, from Upper Egypt,[b] from Cush,[c] from Elam,[y]
from Babylonia,[d] from Hamath and from the islands[z] of the sea.

12 He will raise a banner for the nations
and gather the exiles of Israel;
he will assemble the scattered people[a] of Judah
from the four quarters of the earth.
13 Ephraim's jealousy will vanish,
and Judah's enemies[e] will be cut off;
Ephraim will not be jealous of Judah,
nor Judah hostile towards Ephraim.[b]
14 They will swoop down on the slopes of Philistia to the west;

11:3 [f] Jn 7:24 [g] Jn 2:25
11:4 [h] Ps 72:2 [i] Isa 9:7 [j] Isa 3:14 [k] Mal 4:6 [l] Job 4:9; 2Th 2:8
11:5 [m] Isa 25:1 [n] Eph 6:14
11:6 [o] Isa 65:25
11:9 [p] Job 5:23 [q] Ps 98:2-3; Isa 52:10 [r] Isa 45:6, 14; Hab 2:14
11:10 [s] Jn 12:32 [t] Isa 49:23; Lk 2:32 [u] Ro 15:12* [v] Isa 14:3; 28:12; 32:17-18
11:11 [w] Isa 10:20 [x] Isa 19:24; Hos 11:11; Mic 7:12; Zec 10:10 [y] Ge 10:22 [z] Isa 42:4, 10, 12; 66:19
11:12 [a] Zep 3:10
11:13 [b] Jer 3:18; Eze 37:16-17, 22; Hos 1:11

a 6 Hebrew; Septuagint *lion will feed* **b** 11 Hebrew *from Pathros* **c** 11 That is, the upper Nile region
d 11 Hebrew *Shinar* **e** 13 Or *hostility*

11:3–5 God will judge with righteousness and justice. How we long for fair treatment from others, but do we give it? We hate those who base their judgments on appearance, false evidence, or hearsay, but are we quick to judge others using those standards? Only Christ can be the perfectly fair judge. Only as he governs our hearts can we learn to be as fair in our treatment of others as we expect others to be towards us.

11:4, 5 Judah had become corrupt and was surrounded by hostile, foreign powers. The nation desperately needed a revival of righteousness, justice, and faithfulness. They needed to turn from selfishness and show justice to the poor and the oppressed. The righteousness that God values is more than refraining from sin. It is actively turning towards others and offering them the help they need.

11:6–10 A golden age is yet to come, a time of peace when children could play with formerly dangerous animals. Not all of this was fulfilled at Christ's first coming. For example, nature has not returned to its intended balance and harmony (see Romans 8:9–22). Such perfect tranquillity is possible only when Christ reigns over the earth.

11:11 When will this remnant of God's people be returned to their land? Old Testament prophecy is often applied both to the near future and the distant future. Judah would soon be exiled to Babylon, and a remnant would return to Jerusalem in 537 B.C. at Cyrus' decree. In the ages to come, however, God's people would be dispersed throughout the world. These cities represent the four corners of the known world – Hamath in the north, Egypt in the south, Assyria and Babylonia in the east, the islands of the sea in the west. Ultimately God's people will be regathered when Christ comes to reign over the earth.

11:13 Ephraim, the dominant tribe of the north, is used as another name for Israel, the northern kingdom.

11:14 Edom, Moab, and Ammon were three countries bordering Judah (along with Philistia). They were the nations who, when Judah was defeated, rejoiced and took their land.

together they will plunder the people to the east.
They will lay hands on Edom[c] and Moab,[d]
and the Ammonites will be subject to them.
15The LORD will dry up
the gulf of the Egyptian sea;
with a scorching wind he will sweep his hand[e]
over the Euphrates River.[f][f]
He will break it up into seven streams
so that men can cross over in sandals.
16There will be a highway[g] for the remnant of his people
that is left from Assyria,
as there was for Israel
when they came up from Egypt.[h]

Songs of Praise

12 In that day you will say:

"I will praise[a] you, O LORD.
Although you were angry with me,
your anger has turned away
and you have comforted me.
2Surely God is my salvation;
I will trust[b] and not be afraid.
The LORD, the LORD, is my strength and my song;
he has become my salvation.[c]"
3With joy you will draw water[d]
from the wells of salvation.

4In that day you will say:

"Give thanks to the LORD, call on his name;[e]
make known among the nations what he has done,
and proclaim that his name is exalted.
5Sing[f] to the LORD, for he has done glorious things;[g]
let this be known to all the world.
6Shout aloud and sing for joy, people of Zion,
for great is the Holy One of Israel[h] among you.[i]"

2. Judgment against heathen nations

A Prophecy Against Babylon

13 An oracle concerning Babylon that Isaiah son of Amoz saw:

2Raise a banner[a] on a bare hilltop,
shout to them;
beckon to them

11:14 [c]Da 11:41; Joel 3:19 [d]Isa 16:14; 25:10
11:15 [e]Isa 19:16 [f]Isa 7:20
11:16 [g]Isa 19:23; 62:10 [h]Ex 14:26-31
12:1 [a]Isa 25:1
12:2 [b]Isa 26:3 [c]Ex 15:2; Ps 118:14
12:3 [d]Jn 4:10, 14
12:4 [e]Ps 105:1; Isa 24:15
12:5 [f]Ex 15:1 [g]Ps 98:1
12:6 [h]Isa 49:26 [i]Zep 3:14-17
13:2 [a]Jer 50:2; 51:27

f *15* Hebrew *the River*

11:15, 16 Isaiah is talking about a new or second exodus when God will bring his scattered people back to Judah and the Messiah will come to rule the world. The Lord dried up the Red Sea so the Israelites could walk through it on their way to the promised land (Exodus 14). He dried up the Jordan River so the nation could cross into the land (Joshua 3). God will again provide the way of return for his people.

12:1ff This chapter is a hymn of praise—another graphic description of the people's joy when Jesus Christ comes to reign over the earth. Even now we need to express our gratitude to God—thanking him, praising him, and telling others about him. From the depths of our gratitude, we must praise him. And we should share the Good News with others.

13:1ff Chapters 1–12 speak of judgment against the southern kingdom and, to a lesser extent, against the northern kingdom. Chapters 13–23 are about the judgment on other nations. Chapter 13 is an oracle or message from God concerning Babylon. Long before Babylon became a world power and threatened Judah, Isaiah spoke of its destruction. Babylon was the rallying point of rebellion against God after the flood (Genesis 11). Revelation 17 and 18 use Babylon as a symbol of God's enemies. At the time of this oracle, Babylon was still part of the Assyrian empire. Isaiah communicated a message of challenge and hope to God's people, telling them not to rely on other nations but to rely on God alone. And he let them know that their greatest enemies would receive from God the punishment they deserve.

to enter the gates of the nobles.
3I have commanded my holy ones;
I have summoned my warriors[b] to carry out my wrath—
those who rejoice[c] in my triumph.

4Listen, a noise on the mountains,
like that of a great multitude![d]
Listen, an uproar among the kingdoms,
like nations massing together!
The LORD Almighty is mustering
an army for war.
5They come from faraway lands,
from the ends of the heavens[e]—
the LORD and the weapons of his wrath—
to destroy[f] the whole country.

6Wail,[g] for the day[h] of the LORD is near;
it will come like destruction from the Almighty.[a]
7Because of this, all hands will go limp,
every man's heart will melt.[i]
8Terror[j] will seize them,
pain and anguish will grip them;
they will writhe like a woman in labour.
They will look aghast at each other,
their faces aflame.[k]

9See, the day of the LORD is coming
—a cruel day, with wrath and fierce anger—
to make the land desolate
and destroy the sinners within it.
10The stars of heaven and their constellations
will not show their light.
The rising sun[l] will be darkened[m]
and the moon will not give its light.[n]
11I will punish[o] the world for its evil,
the wicked for their sins.
I will put an end to the arrogance of the haughty
and will humble the pride of the ruthless.
12I will make man[p] scarcer than pure gold,
more rare than the gold of Ophir.
13Therefore I will make the heavens tremble;[q]
and the earth will shake from its place
at the wrath of the LORD Almighty,
in the day of his burning anger.

14Like a hunted gazelle,
like sheep without a shepherd,[r]
each will return to his own people,
each will flee to his native land.[s]
15Whoever is captured will be thrust through;
all who are caught will fall[t] by the sword.[u]
16Their infants[v] will be dashed to pieces before their eyes;
their houses will be looted and their wives ravished.

17See, I will stir up[w] against them the Medes,
who do not care for silver

13:3 [b]Joel 3:11 [c]Ps 149:2
13:4 [d]Joel 3:14
13:5 [e]Isa 5:26 [f]Isa 24:1
13:6 [g]Eze 30:2 [h]Isa 2:12; Joel 1:15
13:7 [i]Eze 21:7
13:8 [j]Isa 21:4 [k]Na 2:10
13:10 [l]Isa 24:23 [m]Isa 5:30; Rev 8:12 [n]Eze 32:7; Mt 24:29*; Mk 13:24*
13:11 [o]Isa 3:11; 11:4; 26:21
13:12 [p]Isa 4:1
13:13 [q]Isa 34:4; 51:6; Hag 2:6
13:14 [r]1Ki 22:17 [s]Jer 50:16
13:15 [t]Jer 51:4 [u]Isa 14:19; Jer 50:25
13:16 [v]Ps 137:9
13:17 [w]Jer 51:1

[a] 6 Hebrew *Shaddai*

13:12 Ophir was known for its rare and valuable gold. It is thought to have been located on the southwestern coast of Arabia.

13:17
[x]Pr 6:34-35

13:19
[y]Da 4:30
[z]Rev 14:8
[a]Ge 19:24

13:20
[b]Isa 14:23; 34:10-15
[c]2Ch 17:11

13:21
[d]Rev 18:2

13:22
[e]Isa 25:2
[f]Isa 34:13
[g]Jer 51:33

14:1
[a]Ps 102:13; Isa 49:10, 13; 54:7-8, 10
[b]Isa 41:8; 44:1; 49:7; Zec 1:17; 2:12
[c] Eph 2:12-19

14:2
[d]Isa 60:9
[e]Isa 49:7, 23
[f]Isa 60:14; 61:5

14:3
[g]Isa 11:10

14:4
[h]Hab 2:6
[i]Isa 9:4

14:5
[j]Ps 125:3

14:6
[k]Isa 10:14
[l]Isa 47:6

14:7
[m]Ps 98:1; 126:1-3

and have no delight in gold.[x]
18 Their bows will strike down the young men;
they will have no mercy on infants
nor will they look with compassion on children.
19 Babylon, the jewel of kingdoms,
the glory[y] of the Babylonians'[b] pride,
will be overthrown[z] by God
like Sodom and Gomorrah.[a]
20 She will never be inhabited[b]
or lived in through all generations;
no Arab[c] will pitch his tent there,
no shepherd will rest his flocks there.
21 But desert creatures[d] will lie there,
jackals will fill her houses;
there the owls will dwell,
and there the wild goats will leap about.
22 Hyenas will howl in her strongholds,[e]
jackals[f] in her luxurious palaces.
Her time is at hand,[g]
and her days will not be prolonged.

14

The LORD will have compassion[a] on Jacob;
once again he will choose[b] Israel
and will settle them in their own land.
Aliens[c] will join them
and unite with the house of Jacob.
2 Nations will take them
and bring[d] them to their own place.
And the house of Israel will possess the nations[e]
as menservants and maidservants in the LORD's land.
They will make captives of their captors
and rule over their oppressors.[f]

3 On the day the LORD gives you relief[g] from suffering and turmoil and cruel
bondage, 4 you will take up this taunt[h] against the king of Babylon:

How the oppressor[i] has come to an end!
How his fury[a] has ended!
5 The LORD has broken the rod of the wicked,[j]
the sceptre of the rulers,
6 which in anger struck down peoples[k]
with unceasing blows,
and in fury subdued nations
with relentless aggression.[l]
7 All the lands are at rest and at peace;
they break into singing.[m]

[b] *19* Or *Chaldeans'* [a] *4* Dead Sea Scrolls, Septuagint and Syriac; the meaning of the word in the Masoretic Text is uncertain.

13:20 Even before Babylon became a world power, Isaiah prophesied that, though it would shine for a while, Babylon's destruction would be so complete that the land would never again be inhabited. Babylon, in present-day Iraq, still lies in utter ruin, burned under mounds of dirt and sand.

14:1 A prominent theme in Isaiah is that aliens (non-Israelites) would join the returning Israelites (56:6, 7; 60:10; 61:5). God's intention was that through his faithful people all the world would be blessed (Genesis 12:3). Through the family of David, the whole world could be saved by Christ. We must not limit God's love to our own people. God loves the whole world.

14:4–11 These verses could have both present and future significance in reference to Babylon. The historical city and empire would be permanently destroyed. Babylon has also been used as a picture of all those who oppose God. Thus, in the end times, all who oppose God will be destroyed and all evil will be removed from the earth for ever.

14:5, 6 Power fades quickly. God permitted Babylon to have temporary power for a purpose – to punish his wayward people. When the purpose ended, so did the power. Beware of placing confidence in human power because one day it will fade, no matter how strong it appears now.

8 Even the pine trees[n] and the cedars of Lebanon
exult over you and say,
"Now that you have been laid low,
no woodsman comes to cut us down."
9 The grave[b][o] below is all astir
to meet you at your coming;
it rouses the spirits of the departed to greet you—
all those who were leaders in the world;
it makes them rise from their thrones—
all those who were kings over the nations.
10 They will all respond,
they will say to you,
"You also have become weak, as we are;
you have become like us."[p]
11 All your pomp has been brought down to the grave,
along with the noise of your harps;
maggots are spread out beneath you
and worms[q] cover you.
12 How you have fallen[r] from heaven,
O morning star,[s] son of the dawn!
You have been cast down to the earth,
you who once laid low the nations!
13 You said in your heart,
"I will ascend[t] to heaven;
I will raise my throne[u]
above the stars of God;
I will sit enthroned on the mount of assembly,
on the utmost heights of the sacred mountain.[c]
14 I will ascend above the tops of the clouds;
I will make myself like the Most High."[v]
15 But you are brought down to the grave,
to the depths[w] of the pit.
16 Those who see you stare at you,
they ponder your fate:[x]
"Is this the man who shook the earth
and made kingdoms tremble,
17 the man who made the world a desert,[y]
who overthrew its cities
and would not let his captives go home?"
18 All the kings of the nations lie in state,
each in his own tomb.
19 But you are cast out[z] of your tomb
like a rejected branch;
you are covered with the slain,
with those pierced by the sword,
those who descend to the stones of the pit.[a]

14:8 [n]Eze 31:16
14:9 [o]Eze 32:21
14:10 [p]Eze 32:21
14:11 [q]Isa 51:8
14:12 [r]Isa 34:4; Lk 10:18 [s]2Pe 1:19; Rev 2:28; 8:10; 9:1
14:13 [t]Da 5:23; 8:10; Mt 11:23 [u]Eze 28:2; 2Th 2:4
14:14 [v]Isa 47:8; 2Th 2:4
14:15 [w]Mt 11:23; Lk 10:15
14:16 [x]Jer 50:23
14:17 [y]Joel 2:3
14:19 [z]Isa 22:16-18 [a]Jer 41:7-9

[b] *9* Hebrew *Sheol*; also in verses 11 and 15 [c] *13* Or *the north*; Hebrew *Zaphon*

14:12 "Morning star, son of the dawn" could be names used to worship the kings of Assyria and Babylon. More likely, it means that they will fade like the morning star when the sun rises.

14:12–14 There are several interpretations for the fallen one in these verses. (1) He is Satan, because the person here is too powerful to be any human king. Although Satan may fit verses 12–14, he does not fit well with the rest of the chapter. (2) This could be Sennacherib or Nebuchadnezzar, kings with supreme power. Their people looked upon them as gods. These kings wanted to rule the world. (3) This could refer to both Satan and a great human king, possibly Nebuchadnezzar, because Babylon is pictured as the seat of evil in Revelation 17, 18. Pride was Satan's sin as well as Babylon's. Common to all three viewpoints is the truth that pride wilfully opposes God and will result in judgment. Israel made the mistake of being too proud to depend on God, and we are vulnerable to that same mistake.

14:20
[b]Job 18:19
[c]Isa 1:4
[d]Ps 21:10

14:21
[e]Ex 20:5; Lev 26:39

14:22
[f]1Ki 14:10; Job 18:19

14:23
[g]Isa 34:11-15; Zep 2:14

14:24
[h]Isa 45:23
[i]Ac 4:28

14:25
[j]Isa 10:5, 12
[k]Isa 9:4
[l]Isa 10:27

14:26
[m]Isa 23:9
[n]Ex 15:12

14:27
[o]2Ch 20:6; Isa 43:13; Da 4:35

14:28
[p]Isa 13:1
[q]2Ki 16:20

14:29
[r]2Ch 26:6
[s]Isa 11:8

14:30
[t]Isa 3:15
[u]Isa 7:21-22
[v]Isa 8:21; 9:20; 51:19
[w]Jer 25:16

14:31
[x]Isa 3:26
[y]Jer 1:14

Like a corpse trampled underfoot,
20 you will not join them in burial,
for you have destroyed your land
and killed your people.

The offspring[b] of the wicked[c]
will never be mentioned[d] again.
21 Prepare a place to slaughter his sons
for the sins of their forefathers;[e]
they are not to rise to inherit the land
and cover the earth with their cities.

22 "I will rise up against them,"
declares the LORD Almighty.
"I will cut off from Babylon her name and survivors,
her offspring and descendants,[f]"
declares the LORD.

23 "I will turn her into a place for owls[g]
and into swampland;
I will sweep her with the broom of destruction,"
declares the LORD Almighty.

A Prophecy Against Assyria

24 The LORD Almighty has sworn,[h]

"Surely, as I have planned, so it will be,
and as I have purposed, so it will stand.[i]
25 I will crush the Assyrian[j] in my land;
on my mountains I will trample him down.
His yoke[k] will be taken from my people,
and his burden removed from their shoulders.[l]"

26 This is the plan[m] determined for the whole world;
this is the hand[n] stretched out over all nations.
27 For the LORD Almighty has purposed, and who can thwart him?
His hand is stretched out, and who can turn it back?[o]

A Prophecy Against the Philistines

28 This oracle[p] came in the year King Ahaz[q] died:

29 Do not rejoice, all you Philistines,[r]
that the rod that struck you is broken;
from the root of that snake will spring up a viper,[s]
its fruit will be a darting, venomous serpent.
30 The poorest of the poor will find pasture,
and the needy[t] will lie down in safety.[u]
But your root I will destroy by famine;[v]
it will slay[w] your survivors.

31 Wail, O gate![x] Howl, O city!
Melt away, all you Philistines!
A cloud of smoke comes from the north,[y]
and there is not a straggler in its ranks.
32 What answer shall be given

14:24–27 This prophecy came true as Isaiah predicted (see 2 Kings 19 and Isaiah 37:21–38).

14:28–31 Isaiah received this message from the Lord in 715 B.C., the year that King Ahaz of Judah died. "The rod that struck you" (14:29) was not Ahaz but Shalmaneser V or Sargon of Assyria. The "cloud of smoke" from the north (14:31) refers to the soldiers of Sargon of Assyria.

to the envoys[z] of that nation?
"The LORD has established Zion,[a]
and in her his afflicted people will find refuge.[b]"

14:32 [z]Isa 37:9 [a]Ps 87:2, 5; Isa 44:28; 54:11 [b]Isa 4:6; Jas 2:5

A Prophecy Against Moab

15 An oracle concerning Moab:[a]

Ar in Moab is ruined,[b]
destroyed in a night!
Kir in Moab is ruined,
destroyed in a night!
2 Dibon goes up to its temple,
to its high places[c] to weep;
Moab wails over Nebo and Medeba.
Every head is shaved[d]
and every beard cut off.
3 In the streets they wear sackcloth;
on the roofs and in the public squares[e]
they all wail,
prostrate with weeping.[f]
4 Heshbon and Elealeh[g] cry out,
their voices are heard all the way to Jahaz.
Therefore the armed men of Moab cry out,
and their hearts are faint.

5 My heart cries out over Moab;[h]
her fugitives flee as far as Zoar,
as far as Eglath Shelishiyah.
They go up the way to Luhith,
weeping as they go;
on the road to Horonaim[i]
they lament their destruction.[j]
6 The waters of Nimrim are dried up[k]
and the grass is withered;[l]
the vegetation is gone
and nothing green is left.
7 So the wealth they have acquired[m] and stored up
they carry away over the Ravine of the Poplars.
8 Their outcry echoes along the border of Moab;
their wailing reaches as far as Eglaim,
their lamentation as far as Beer Elim.
9 Dimon's[a] waters are full of blood,
but I will bring still more upon Dimon[a]—
a lion[n] upon the fugitives of Moab
and upon those who remain in the land.

15:1 [a]Isa 11:14 [b]Jer 48:24, 41
15:2 [c]Jer 48:35 [d]Lev 21:5
15:3 [e]Jer 48:38 [f]Isa 22:4
15:4 [g]Nu 32:3
15:5 [h]Jer 48:31 [i]Jer 48:3, 34 [j]Jer 4:20; 48:5
15:6 [k]Isa 19:5-7; Jer 48:34 [l]Joel 1:12
15:7 [m]Isa 30:6; Jer 48:36
15:9 [n]2Ki 17:25

16 Send lambs[a] as tribute
to the ruler of the land,
from Sela,[b] across the desert,

16:1 [a]2Ki 3:4 [b]2Ki 14:7

[a] 9 Masoretic Text; Dead Sea Scrolls, some Septuagint manuscripts and Vulgate *Dibon*

15:1 Moab was east of the Dead Sea. The Moabites were descendants of Lot through his incestuous relationship with his older daughter (Genesis 19:31–38). Moab had always been Israel's enemy. They oppressed Israel and invaded their land (Judges 3:12–14), fought against Saul (1 Samuel 14:47) and against David (2 Samuel 8:2, 11, 12). Moab would be punished for treating Israel harshly.

16:1ff Attacked by the Assyrians, Moabite refugees would flee to Sela, which lay in the country of Edom to the south. Desperate Moabites would send a tribute of lambs to Jerusalem asking for Judah's protection. Jerusalem would be a safe refuge for a while.

16:1
[c]Isa 10:32

to the mount of the Daughter of Zion.[c]
2Like fluttering birds
pushed from the nest,[d]
so are the women of Moab
at the fords of the Arnon.[e]

16:2
[d]Pr 27:8
[e]Nu 21:13-14;
Jer 48:20

3"Give us counsel,
render a decision.
Make your shadow like night—
at high noon.
Hide the fugitives,[f]
do not betray the refugees.
4Let the Moabite fugitives stay with you;
be their shelter from the destroyer."

16:3
[f]1Ki 18:4

The oppressor[g] will come to an end,
and destruction will cease;
the aggressor will vanish from the land.
5In love a throne[h] will be established;
in faithfulness a man will sit on it—
one from the house[a] of David[i]—
one who in judging seeks justice[j]
and speeds the cause of righteousness.

16:4
[g]Isa 9:4

16:5
[h]Da 7:14;
Mic 4:7
[i]Lk 1:32
[j]Isa 9:7

6We have heard of Moab's[k] pride[l]—
her overweening pride and conceit,
her pride and her insolence—
but her boasts are empty.
7Therefore the Moabites wail,[m]
they wail together for Moab.
Lament and grieve
for the men[b][n] of Kir Hareseth.[o]
8The fields of Heshbon wither,
the vines of Sibmah also.
The rulers of the nations
have trampled down the choicest vines,
which once reached Jazer
and spread towards the desert.
Their shoots spread out
and went as far as the sea.
9So I weep,[p] as Jazer weeps,
for the vines of Sibmah.
O Heshbon, O Elealeh,
I drench you with tears!
The shouts of joy over your ripened fruit
and over your harvests[q] have been stilled.
10Joy and gladness are taken away from the orchards;[r]
no-one sings or shouts in the vineyards;
no-one treads[s] out wine at the presses,[t]
for I have put an end to the shouting.
11My heart laments for Moab[u] like a harp,
my inmost being[v] for Kir Hareseth.

16:6
[k]Am 2:1;
Zep 2:8
[l]Ob 1:3;
Zep 2:10

16:7
[m]Jer 48:20
[n]1Ch 16:3
[o]2Ki 3:25

16:9
[p]Isa 15:3
[q]Jer 40:12

16:10
[r]Isa 24:7-8
[s]Jdg 9:27
[t]Job 24:11

16:11
[u]Isa 15:5
[v]Isa 63:15;
Hos 11:8;
Php 2:1

a *5* Hebrew *tent* **b** *7* Or *"raisin cakes,"* a word play

Isaiah advised Judah to accept these refugees as a sign of compassion during the enemy's time of devastation.

16:10 The treading of grapes (squeezing the juice from grapes by mashing them with bare feet) was the climax of the harvest season, a time of great joy in the vineyards. But the joy of harvest would soon be ended because the people in their pride ignored God and rebelled against him.

[12]When Moab appears at her high place,[w]
she only wears herself out;
when she goes to her shrine[w] to pray,
it is to no avail.[x]

[13]This is the word the LORD has already spoken concerning Moab. [14]But now the
LORD says: "Within three years, as a servant bound by contract would count them,
Moab's splendour and all her many people will be despised,[y] and her survivors will
be very few and feeble."[z]

An Oracle Against Damascus

17 An oracle concerning Damascus:[a]

"See, Damascus will no longer be a city
but will become a heap of ruins.[b]
[2]The cities of Aroer will be deserted
and left to flocks,[c] which will lie down,
with no-one to make them afraid.[d]
[3]The fortified city will disappear from Ephraim,
and royal power from Damascus;
the remnant of Aram will be
like the glory[e] of the Israelites,"[f]
declares the LORD Almighty.

[4]"In that day the glory of Jacob will fade;
the fat of his body will waste[g] away.
[5]It will be as when a reaper gathers the standing corn
and harvests[h] the corn with his arm—
as when a man gleans ears of corn
in the Valley of Rephaim.
[6]Yet some gleanings will remain,[i]
as when an olive tree is beaten,[j]
leaving two or three olives on the topmost branches,
four or five on the fruitful boughs,"
declares the LORD, the God of Israel.

[7]In that day men will look[k] to their Maker
and turn their eyes to the Holy One[l] of Israel.
[8]They will not look to the altars,
the work of their hands,[m]

16:12 [w]Isa 15:2 [x]1Ki 18:29
16:14 [y]Isa 25:10; Jer 48:42 [z]Isa 21:17
17:1 [a]Ge 14:15; Jer 49:23; Ac 9:2 [b]Isa 25:2; Am 1:3; Zec 9:1
17:2 [c]Isa 7:21; Eze 25:5 [d]Jer 7:33; Mic 4:4
17:3 [e]ver 4; Hos 9:11 [f]Isa 7:8, 16; 8:4
17:4 [g]Isa 10:16
17:5 [h]ver 11; Jer 51:33; Joel 3:13; Mt 13:30
17:6 [i]Dt 4:27; Isa 24:13 [j]Isa 27:12
17:7 [k]Isa 10:20 [l]Mic 7:7
17:8 [m]Isa 2:18, 20; 30:22

16:12 When the people of Moab experienced God's wrath, they sought their own idols and gods. Nothing happened, however, because there was no-one there to save them. When we seek our own ways of escape in order to get through our daily troubles, the effect is the same: no pleasure, pastime, or man-made religious idea will come to save us. Our hope lies in God, the only One who can hear and help.

16:13, 14 Tiglath-Pileser III invaded Moab in 732 B.C.; Sennacherib invaded Moab the same year that he invaded Judah, 701 B.C. The earlier event occurred three years after Isaiah's prediction, marking Isaiah as a true prophet. In these events, the people of Israel saw prophecy fulfilled before their very eyes.

17:1ff The northern kingdom and Aram made an alliance to fight against Assyria. But Tiglath-Pileser III captured Damascus, the capital of Aram, in 732 B.C. and annexed the northern kingdom to the Assyrian empire. Ahaz, king of Judah, paid tribute to Tiglath-Pileser III (2 Kings 16:1–14).

17:7–11 God's message to Damascus is that it will be completely destroyed. The Arameans had turned from the God who could save them, depending instead on their idols and their own strength. No matter how successful they were, God's judgment was sure. Often we depend on the trappings of success (expensive cars, pastimes, clothes, homes) to give us fulfilment. But God says we will reap grief and pain if we have depended on temporal things to give us eternal security. If we don't want the same treatment Damascus received, we must turn from these false allurements and trust in God.

17:8 The Asherah poles were images of Asherah, a Canaanite goddess who was the female consort of Baal. Queen Jezebel may have brought the worship of Asherah into the northern kingdom. The cult encouraged immoral sexual practices and attracted many people. The Bible warns against worshipping Asherah poles (Exodus 34:13; Deuteronomy 12:3; 16:21), and Manasseh was condemned for putting up an Asherah pole in the temple (2 Kings 21:7). Unlike pagan gods, our God does not try to attract the greatest number of people but instead seeks the greatest good for all people.

17:10 [n]Isa 51:13 [o]Ps 68:19; Isa 12:2

and they will have no regard for the Asherah poles[a]
and the incense altars their fingers have made.

9In that day their strong cities, which they left because of the Israelites, will be like
places abandoned to thickets and undergrowth. And all will be desolation.

10You have forgotten[n] God your Saviour;[o]
you have not remembered the Rock, your fortress.
Therefore, though you set out the finest plants
and plant imported vines,

17:11 [p]Ps 90:6 [q]Hos 8:7 [r]Job 4:8

11though on the day you set them out, you make them grow,
and on the morning[p] when you plant them, you bring them to bud,
yet the harvest will be as nothing[q]
in the day of disease and incurable pain.[r]

17:12 [s]Ps 18:4; Jer 6:23; Lk 21:25

12Oh, the raging of many nations—
they rage like the raging sea![s]
Oh, the uproar of the peoples—
they roar like the roaring of great waters!

17:13 [t]Ps 9:5 [u]Isa 13:14 [v]Isa 41:2, 15-16 [w]Job 21:18

13Although the peoples roar like the roar of surging waters,
when he rebukes[t] them they flee[u] far away,
driven before the wind like chaff[v] on the hills,
like tumble-weed before a gale.[w]

17:14 [x]2Ki 19:35

14In the evening, sudden terror!
Before the morning, they are gone![x]
This is the portion of those who loot us,
the lot of those who plunder us.

A Prophecy Against Cush

18:1 [a]Isa 20:3-5; Eze 30:4-5, 9; Zep 2:12; 3:10

18 Woe to the land of whirring wings[a]
along the rivers of Cush,[b][a]
2which sends envoys by sea
in papyrus[b] boats over the water.

18:2 [b]Ex 2:3 [c]Ge 10:8-9; 2Ch 12:3 [d]ver 7

Go, swift messengers,
to a people tall and smooth-skinned,
to a people feared far and wide,
an aggressive[c] nation of strange speech,
whose land is divided by rivers.[d]

18:3 [e]Isa 5:26

3All you people of the world,
you who live on the earth,
when a banner[e] is raised on the mountains,
you will see it,
and when a trumpet sounds,
you will hear it.

18:4 [f]Isa 26:21; Hos 5:15 [g]Isa 26:19; Hos 14:5

4This is what the LORD says to me:
"I will remain quiet and will look on from my dwelling-place,[f]
like shimmering heat in the sunshine,
like a cloud of dew[g] in the heat of harvest."

a *8* That is, symbols of the goddess Asherah a *1* Or *of locusts* b *1* That is, the upper Nile region

18:1ff This prophecy was probably given in the days of Hezekiah (2 Kings 19; 20). The "land of whirring wings" refers to locusts, and probably pictures the armies of Cush. The king of Cush had heard that Assyria's great army was marching south towards them. He sent messengers up the Nile asking the surrounding nations to form an alliance. Judah was also asked, but Isaiah told the messengers to return home because Judah needed only God's help to repel the Assyrians. Isaiah prophesied that Assyria would be destroyed at the proper time (37:21–38).

18:3 This is a signal of the doom of Cush and Assyria's victory over Cush (see 20:1–6).

5For, before the harvest, when the blossom is gone
and the flower becomes a ripening grape,
he will cut off the shoots with pruning knives,
and cut down and take away the spreading branches.[h]
6They will all be left to the mountain birds of prey
and to the wild animals;[i]
the birds will feed on them all summer,
the wild animals all winter.

7At that time gifts will be brought to the LORD Almighty

from a people tall and smooth-skinned,
from a people feared far and wide,
an aggressive nation of strange speech,
whose land is divided by rivers —

the gifts will be brought to Mount Zion, the place of the Name of the LORD Almighty.[j]

A Prophecy About Egypt

19 An oracle[a] concerning Egypt:[bc]

See, the LORD rides on a swift cloud[d]
and is coming to Egypt.
The idols of Egypt tremble before him,
and the hearts of the Egyptians melt[e] within them.

2"I will stir up Egyptian against Egyptian —
brother will fight against brother,[f]
neighbour against neighbour,
city against city,
kingdom against kingdom.[g]
3The Egyptians will lose heart,
and I will bring their plans to nothing;
they will consult the idols and the spirits of the dead,
the mediums and the spiritists.[h]
4I will hand the Egyptians over
to the power of a cruel master,
and a fierce king[i] will rule over them,"
declares the Lord, the LORD Almighty.

5The waters of the river will dry up,[j]
and the river bed will be parched and dry.
6The canals will stink;[k]
the streams of Egypt will dwindle and dry up.[l]
The reeds and rushes will wither,[m]
7 also the plants along the Nile,
at the mouth of the river.
Every sown field[n] along the Nile
will become parched, will blow away and be no more.
8The fishermen[o] will groan and lament,
all who cast hooks[p] into the Nile;
those who throw nets on the water
will pine away.
9Those who work with combed flax will despair,

18:5
[h]Isa 17:10-11; Eze 17:6

18:6
[i]Isa 56:9; Jer 7:33; Eze 32:4; 39:17

18:7
[j]Ps 68:31

19:1
[a]Isa 13:1; Jer 43:12
[b]Joel 3:19
[c]Ex 12:12
[d]Ps 18:10; 104:3; Rev 1:7
[e]Jos 2:11

19:2
[f]Jdg 7:22; Mt 10:21, 36
[g]2Ch 20:23

19:3
[h]Isa 8:19; 47:13; Da 2:2, 10

19:4
[i]Isa 20:4; Jer 46:26; Eze 29:19

19:5
[j]Jer 51:36

19:6
[k]Ex 7:18
[l]Isa 37:25; Eze 30:12
[m]Isa 15:6

19:7
[n]Isa 23:3

19:8
[o]Eze 47:10
[p]Hab 1:15

19:1 Egypt, the nation where God's people were enslaved for 400 years (Exodus 1), was hated by the people of Israel. Yet Judah was considering an alliance with Egypt against Assyria (2 Kings 18:17ff). But Isaiah warned against this alliance because God would destroy Assyria in his time.

19:9 [q]Pr 7:16; Eze 27:7
19:11 [r]Nu 13:22 [s]1Ki 4:30; Ac 7:22
19:12 [t]1Co 1:20 [u]Isa 14:24; Ro 9:17
19:13 [v]Jer 2:16; Eze 30:13, 16
19:14 [w]Mt 17:17
19:15 [x]Isa 9:14
19:16 [y]Jer 51:30; Na 3:13 [z]Heb 10:31 [a]Isa 11:15
19:17 [b]Isa 14:24
19:18 [c]Zep 3:9
19:19 [d]Jos 22:10

the weavers of fine linen[q] will lose hope.
10The workers in cloth will be dejected,
and all the wage earners will be sick at heart.

11The officials of Zoan[r] are nothing but fools;
the wise counsellors of Pharaoh give senseless advice.
How can you say to Pharaoh,
"I am one of the wise men,[s]
a disciple of the ancient kings"?

12Where are your wise men[t] now?
Let them show you and make known
what the LORD Almighty
has planned[u] against Egypt.
13The officials of Zoan have become fools,
the leaders of Memphis[a][v] are deceived;
the cornerstones of her peoples
have led Egypt astray.
14The LORD has poured into them
a spirit of dizziness;[w]
they make Egypt stagger in all that she does,
as a drunkard staggers around in his vomit.
15There is nothing Egypt can do—
head or tail, palm branch or reed.[x]

16In that day the Egyptians will be like women.[y] They will shudder with fear[z]
at the uplifted hand[a] that the LORD Almighty raises against them. 17And the land of
Judah will bring terror to the Egyptians; everyone to whom Judah is mentioned will
be terrified, because of what the LORD Almighty is planning[b] against them.
18In that day five cities in Egypt will speak the language of Canaan and swear
allegiance[c] to the LORD Almighty. One of them will be called the City of Destruction.[b]
19In that day there will be an altar[d] to the LORD in the heart of Egypt, and a

[a] *13* Hebrew *Noph* [b] *18* Most manuscripts of the Masoretic Text; some manuscripts of the Masoretic Text, Dead Sea Scrolls and Vulgate *City of the Sun* (that is, Heliopolis)

ALLIANCES TODAY

Government	We rely on government legislation to protect the moral decisions we want made, but legislation cannot change people's hearts.
Science	We enjoy the benefits of science and technology. We look to scientific predictions and analysis before we look to the Bible.
Education	We act as though education and qualifications can guarantee our future and success without considering what God plans for our future.
Medical care	We regard medicine as the way to prolong life and preserve its quality—quite apart from faith and moral living.
Financial systems	We place our faith in financial "security"—making as much money as we can for ourselves—forgetting that, while being wise with our money, we must trust God for our needs.

Isaiah warned Judah not to ally with Egypt (20:5; 30:1, 2; 31:1). He knew that trust in any nation or any military might was futile. Their only hope was to trust in God. Although we don't consciously put our hope for deliverance in political alliances in quite the same way, we often put our hope in other forces.

19:11–15 Egypt was noted for its wisdom, but here its wise men and officials were deceived and foolish. True wisdom can come only from God. We must ask him for wisdom to guide our decisions, or we will also be uncertain and misdirected. Are you confused about something in your life now? Ask God for wisdom to deal with it.

19:19, 23 After Egypt's chastening, it would turn from idols and worship the one true God. Even more amazing is Isaiah's prophecy that the two chief oppressors of Israel, Egypt and Assyria, would unite in worship. This prophecy will come true "in that day", the future day of Christ's reign.

monument[e] to the LORD at its border. 20 It will be a sign and witness to the LORD
Almighty in the land of Egypt. When they cry out to the LORD because of their
oppressors, he will send them a saviour and defender, and he will rescue[f] them. 21 So
the LORD will make himself known to the Egyptians, and in that day they will
acknowledge[g] the LORD. They will worship[h] with sacrifices and grain offerings; they
will make vows to the LORD and keep them. 22 The LORD will strike[i] Egypt with a
plague; he will strike them and heal them. They will turn[j] to the LORD, and he will
respond to their pleas and heal[k] them.
23 In that day there will be a highway[l] from Egypt to Assyria. The Assyrians will
go to Egypt and the Egyptians to Assyria. The Egyptians and Assyrians will worship[m]
together. 24 In that day Israel will be the third, along with Egypt and Assyria, a blessing
on the earth. 25 The LORD Almighty will bless them, saying, "Blessed be Egypt my
people,[n] Assyria my handiwork,[o] and Israel my inheritance.[p]"

A Prophecy Against Egypt and Cush

20 In the year that the supreme commander,[a] sent by Sargon king of Assyria,
came to Ashdod and attacked and captured it— 2 at that time the LORD spoke
through Isaiah son of Amoz.[b] He said to him, "Take off the sackcloth[c] from your
body and the sandals[d] from your feet." And he did so, going around stripped[e] and
barefoot.[f]
3 Then the LORD said, "Just as my servant Isaiah has gone stripped and barefoot for
three years, as a sign[g] and portent against Egypt and Cush,[a][h] 4 so the king[i] of
Assyria will lead away stripped and barefoot the Egyptian captives and Cushite exiles,
young and old, with buttocks bared—to Egypt's shame.[j] 5 Those who trusted in Cush
and boasted in Egypt[k] will be afraid and put to shame. 6 In that day the people who
live on this coast will say, 'See what has happened to those we relied on, those we
fled to for help[l] and deliverance from the king of Assyria! How then can we
escape?[m]' "

A Prophecy Against Babylon

21 An oracle concerning the Desert[a] by the Sea:

Like whirlwinds sweeping through the southland,[b]
an invader comes from the desert,
from a land of terror.

2 A dire[c] vision has been shown to me:
The traitor betrays,[d] the looter takes loot.
Elam,[e] attack! Media, lay siege!
I will bring to an end all the groaning she caused.

3 At this my body is racked with pain,

a *3* That is, the upper Nile region; also in verse 5

19:19 [e]Ge 28:18
19:20 [f]Isa 49:24-26
19:21 [g]Isa 11:9 [h]Isa 56:7; Mal 1:11
19:22 [i]Heb 12:11 [j]Isa 45:14; Hos 14:1 [k]Dt 32:39
19:23 [l]Isa 11:16 [m]Isa 27:13
19:25 [n]Ps 100:3 [o]Isa 29:23; 45:11; 60:21; 64:8; Eph 2:10 [p]Hos 2:23
20:1 [a]2Ki 18:17
20:2 [b]Isa 13:1 [c]Zec 13:4; Mt 3:4 [d]Eze 24:17, 23 [e]1Sa 19:24 [f]Mic 1:8
20:3 [g]Isa 8:18 [h]Isa 37:9; 43:3
20:4 [i]Isa 19:4 [j]Isa 47:3; Jer 13:22, 26
20:5 [k]2Ki 18:21; Isa 30:5
20:6 [l]Isa 10:3 [m]Jer 30:15-17; Mt 23:33; 1Th 5:3; Heb 2:3
21:1 [a]Isa 13:21; Jer 51:43 [b]Zec 9:14
21:2 [c]Ps 60:3 [d]Isa 33:1 [e]Isa 22:6; Jer 49:34

19:20 When Egypt calls to God for help, he will send a saviour to deliver them. Our Saviour, Jesus Christ, is available to all who call upon him. We too can pray and receive his saving power (John 1:12).

19:22 Egypt is but one Gentile nation who will bow before the Lord. Philippians 2:10, 11 says *every* knee will bow, every tongue confess that Jesus Christ is Lord. So we shouldn't be surprised that Egyptians and Assyrians are part of the "every". Each of us is part of that "every" too. We may bow now in devotion, or later in submission.

19:23–25 In Jesus Christ, former enemies may unite in love. In Christ, people and nations that are poles apart politically will bow at his feet as brothers and sisters. Christ breaks down every barrier that threatens relationships (see Ephesians 2:13–19).

20:1ff Sargon II was king of Assyria from 722–705 B.C., and this event happened in 711 B.C. Isaiah graphically reminds Judah that they should not count on foreign alliances to protect them.

20:2 God's command to Isaiah was to walk about naked for three years, a humiliating experience. God was using Isaiah to demonstrate the humiliation that Egypt and Cush would experience at the hands of Assyria. But the message was really for Judah: Don't put your trust in foreign governments, or you will experience this kind of shame and humiliation from your captors.

20:2 God asked Isaiah to do something that seemed shameful and illogical. At times, God may ask us to do things we don't understand. We must obey God in complete faith, for he will never ask us to do something wrong.

21:1ff "The Desert by the Sea" is Babylon by the Persian Gulf. Some scholars say this prophecy was fulfilled at Babylon's fall in 539 B.C. (see Daniel 5). But others say this was a prophecy of Babylon's revolt against Assyria around 700 B.C.

pangs seize me, like those of a woman in labour;[f]
I am staggered by what I hear,
I am bewildered by what I see.
4My heart falters,
fear makes me tremble;
the twilight I longed for
has become a horror to me.

5They set the tables,
they spread the rugs,
they eat, they drink![g]
Get up, you officers,
oil the shields!

6This is what the Lord says to me:

"Go, post a lookout
and have him report what he sees.
7When he sees chariots[h]
with teams of horses,
riders on donkeys
or riders on camels,
let him be alert,
fully alert."

8And the lookout[a][i] shouted,

"Day after day, my lord, I stand on the watchtower;
every night I stay at my post.
9Look, here comes a man in a chariot
with a team of horses.
And he gives back the answer:
'Babylon[j] has fallen,[k] has fallen!
All the images of its gods[l]
lie shattered on the ground!' "

10O my people, crushed on the threshing-floor,[m]
I tell you what I have heard
from the LORD Almighty,
from the God of Israel.

A Prophecy Against Edom

11An oracle concerning Dumah:[b][n]

Someone calls to me from Seir,[o]

21:3 [f]Ps 48:6; Isa 26:17
21:5 [g]Jer 51:39, 57; Da 5:2
21:7 [h]ver 9
21:8 [i]Hab 2:1
21:9 [j]Rev 14:8 [k]Jer 51:8; Rev 18:2 [l]Isa 46:1; Jer 50:2; 51:44
21:10 [m]Jer 51:33
21:11 [n]Ge 25:14 [o]Ge 32:3

[a] *8* Dead Sea Scrolls and Syriac; Masoretic Text *A lion* [b] *11* *Dumah* means *silence* or *stillness*, a word play on *Edom*.

21:5 If the prophecy refers to the fall of Babylon in 539 B.C., this may picture the feast in Daniel 5.

21:6, 7 Lookouts (watchmen on the city walls) often appear in prophetic visions of destruction. They are the first to see trouble coming. The prophet Habakkuk was a watchman (Habakkuk 2:1). The vision of the riders could represent the Medes and Persians attacking Babylon in 539 B.C.

21:8, 9 Babylon was not only a great and powerful city, it was also filled with horrible sin (idolatry, witchcraft, and temple prostitution). Babylon was, and remains, a symbol of all that stands against God. Despite all its glory and power, Babylon would be destroyed, along with all its idols. They would give no help in time of trouble.

21:10 Threshing and winnowing were two steps in ancient Israel's farming process. The heads of wheat (often used to symbolise Israel) were first trampled to break open the seeds and expose the valued grain inside (threshing). The seeds were then thrown into the air, and the worthless chaff blew away while the grain fell back to the ground (winnowing). Israel would experience this same kind of process – the worthless, sinful, rebellious people would be taken away, but God would keep the good "grain" to replenish Israel.

21:11 Dumah, or Edom, had been a constant enemy of God's people. They rejoiced when Israel fell to the Assyrians, and this sealed Edom's doom (34:8ff; 63:4). Seir was another name for Edom because the hill country of Seir was given to Esau and his descendants (see Joshua 24:4). Obadiah foretells, in great detail, the destruction of Edom.

"Watchman, what is left of the night?
Watchman, what is left of the night?"
12The watchman replies,
"Morning is coming, but also the night.
If you would ask, then ask;
and come back yet again."

A Prophecy Against Arabia

13An oracle[p] concerning Arabia:

You caravans of Dedanites,
who camp in the thickets of Arabia,
14 bring water for the thirsty;
you who live in Tema,[q]
bring food for the fugitives.
15They flee[r] from the sword,
from the drawn sword,
from the bent bow
and from the heat of battle.

16This is what the Lord says to me: "Within one year, as a servant bound by
contract[s] would count it, all the pomp[t] of Kedar[u] will come to an end. 17The
survivors of the bowmen, the warriors of Kedar, will be few.[v]" The LORD, the God
of Israel, has spoken.

A Prophecy About Jerusalem

22 An oracle[a] concerning the Valley[b] of Vision:

What troubles you now,
that you have all gone up on the roofs,
2O town full of commotion,
O city of tumult and revelry?[c]
Your slain were not killed by the sword,
nor did they die in battle.
3All your leaders have fled together;
they have been captured without using the bow.
All you who were caught were taken prisoner together,
having fled while the enemy was still far away.
4Therefore I said, "Turn away from me;
let me weep[d] bitterly.
Do not try to console me
over the destruction of my people."[e]

5The Lord, the LORD Almighty, has a day
of tumult and trampling and terror[f]
in the Valley of Vision,
a day of battering down walls
and of crying out to the mountains.
6Elam[g] takes up the quiver,[h]

21:13 [p]Isa 13:1
21:14 [q]Ge 25:15
21:15 [r]Isa 13:14
21:16 [s]Isa 16:14 [t]Isa 17:3 [u]Ps 120:5; Isa 60:7
21:17 [v]Isa 10:19
22:1 [a]Isa 13:1 [b]Ps 125:2; Jer 21:13; Joel 3:2, 12, 14
22:2 [c]Isa 32:13
22:4 [d]Isa 15:3; Lk 19:41 [e]Jer 9:1
22:5 [f]La 1:5
22:6 [g]Isa 21:2 [h]Jer 49:35

21:13ff The places listed here are all in Arabia. They are border cities that controlled the trade routes through the land. This is Isaiah's prediction of disaster.

22:1–13 "The Valley of Vision" refers to the city of Jerusalem, where God revealed himself. Jerusalem would be attacked unless God's people returned to him. Instead they used every means of protection possible except asking God for help. They wanted to trust in their ingenuity, their weapons, and even their pagan neighbours (see 2 Chronicles 32 for the description of a siege of Jerusalem).

22:4 Isaiah had warned his people, but they did not repent; thus they would experience God's judgment. Because of his care for them, Isaiah was hurt by their punishment and mourned deeply for them. Sometimes people we care for ignore our attempts to help, so they suffer the very grief we wanted to spare them. At times like that we grieve because of our concern. God expects us to be involved with others, and this may sometimes require us to suffer with them.

22:6, 7 Elam and Kir were under Assyrian rule. The entire Assyrian army, including its vassals, joined in the attack against Jerusalem.

22:6 [i]2Ki 16:9

with her charioteers and horses;
Kir[i] uncovers the shield.
7 Your choicest valleys are full of chariots,
and horsemen are posted at the city gates;[j]
8 the defences of Judah are stripped away.

22:7 [j]2Ch 32:1-2

And you looked in that day
to the weapons[k] in the Palace of the Forest;[l]
9 you saw that the City of David
had many breaches in its defences;
you stored up water
in the Lower Pool.[m]
10 You counted the buildings in Jerusalem
and tore down houses to strengthen the wall.
11 You built a reservoir between the two walls[n]
for the water of the Old Pool,[o]
but you did not look to the One who made it,
or have regard for the One who planned it long ago.

22:8 [k]2Ch 32:5 [l]1Ki 7:2

22:9 [m]2Ch 32:4

22:11 [n]2Ki 25:4; Jer 39:4 [o]2Ch 32:4

12 The Lord, the LORD Almighty,
called you on that day
to weep[p] and to wail,
to tear out your hair[q] and put on sackcloth.[r]
13 But see, there is joy and revelry,
slaughtering of cattle and killing of sheep,
eating of meat and drinking of wine![s]
"Let us eat and drink," you say,
"for tomorrow we die!"[t]

22:12 [p]Joel 2:17 [q]Mic 1:16 [r]Joel 1:13

22:13 [s]Isa 5:22; 28:7-8; 56:12; Lk 17:26-29 [t]1Co 15:32*

14 The LORD Almighty has revealed this in my hearing:[u] "Till your dying day this sin will not be atoned[v] for," says the Lord, the LORD Almighty.

15 This is what the Lord, the LORD Almighty, says:

"Go, say to this steward,
to Shebna,[w] who is in charge of the palace:
16 What are you doing here and who gave you permission
to cut out a grave[x] for yourself here,
hewing your grave on the height
and chiselling your resting place in the rock?

22:14 [u]Isa 5:9 [v]Isa 13:11; 26:21; 30:13-14; Eze 24:13

22:15 [w]2Ki 18:18; Isa 36:3

17 "Beware, the LORD is about to take firm hold of you
and hurl you away, O you mighty man.
18 He will roll you up tightly like a ball
and throw[y] you into a large country.
There you will die
and there your splendid chariots will remain—
you disgrace to your master's house!

22:16 [x]Mt 27:60

22:18 [y]Isa 17:13

22:8–11 The leaders did what they could to prepare for war: they got weapons, inspected the walls, and stored up water in a reservoir. But all their work was pointless because they never asked God for help. Too often we take steps that, though good in themselves, really won't give us the help we need. We must get the weapons and inspect the walls, but God must guide the work.

22:13, 14 The people said, "Let us eat and drink," because they had given up hope. Attacked on every side (22:7), they should have repented (22:12), but they chose to feast instead. The root problem was that Judah did not trust God's power or his promises (see 56:12; 1 Corinthians 15:32). When you face difficulties, turn to God. Today we still see people giving up hope. There are two common responses to hopelessness: despair and self-indulgence. But this life is not all there is, so we are not to act as if we had no hope. Our proper response should be to trust God and his promise to include us in the perfect and just new world that he will create.

22:15–25 Shebna, a high court steward or official, was just as materialistic as the rest of the people in Jerusalem (22:13). He may have been in the group favouring an alliance with foreigners, thus ignoring Isaiah's advice. The Lord revealed that Shebna would lose his position and be replaced by Eliakim (22:21). Eliakim would be the "peg" driven into "a firm place" (22:23). Unfortunately, Eliakim too would fall (22:25).

[19]I will depose you from your office,
and you will be ousted from your position.

[20]"In that day I will summon my servant, Eliakim[z] son of Hilkiah. [21]I will clothe
him with your robe and fasten your sash around him and hand your authority over to
him. He will be a father to those who live in Jerusalem and to the house of Judah.
[22]I will place on his shoulder the key[a] to the house of David;[b] what he opens no-one
can shut, and what he shuts no-one can open.[c] [23]I will drive him like a peg[d] into
a firm place;[e] he will be a seat**a** of honour[f] for the house of his father. [24]All the
glory of his family will hang on him: its offspring and offshoots—all its lesser vessels,
from the bowls to all the jars.

[25]"In that day," declares the LORD Almighty, "the peg[g] driven into the firm place
will give way; it will be sheared off and will fall, and the load hanging on it will be
cut down." The LORD has spoken.[h]

A Prophecy About Tyre

23 An oracle concerning Tyre:[a]

Wail, O ships[b] of Tarshish![c]
For Tyre is destroyed
and left without house or harbour.
From the land of Cyprus**a**
word has come to them.

[2]Be silent, you people of the island
and you merchants of Sidon,
whom the seafarers have enriched.
[3]On the great waters
came the grain of the Shihor;
the harvest of the Nile**b**[d] was the revenue of Tyre,[e]
and she became the market-place of the nations.

[4]Be ashamed, O Sidon,[f] and you, O fortress of the sea,
for the sea has spoken:
"I have neither been in labour nor given birth;
I have neither reared sons nor brought up daughters."
[5]When word comes to Egypt,
they will be in anguish at the report from Tyre.

[6]Cross over to Tarshish;
wail, you people of the island.
[7]Is this your city of revelry,[g]
the old, old city,
whose feet have taken her
to settle in far-off lands?
[8]Who planned this against Tyre,
the bestower of crowns,
whose merchants are princes,
whose traders are renowned in the earth?
[9]The LORD Almighty planned it,

a *23* Or *throne* **a** *1* Hebrew *Kittim* **b** *2, 3* Masoretic Text; one Dead Sea Scroll *Sidon, / who cross over the sea; / your envoys* [3]*are on the great waters. / The grain of the Shihor, / the harvest of the Nile,*

22:20 [z]2Ki 18:18; Isa 36:3
22:22 [a]Rev 3:7 [b]Isa 7:2 [c]Job 12:14
22:23 [d]Zec 10:4 [e]Ezr 9:8 [f]1Sa 2:7-8; Job 36:7
22:25 [g]ver 23 [h]Isa 46:11; Mic 4:4
23:1 [a]Jos 19:29; 1Ki 5:1; Jer 47:4; Eze 26, 27, 28; Joel 3:4-8; Am 1:9-10; Zec 9:2-4 [b]1Ki 10:22 [c]Ge 10:4; Isa 2:16 *fn*
23:3 [d]Isa 19:7 [e]Eze 27:3
23:4 [f]Ge 10:15, 19
23:7 [g]Isa 22:2; 32:13

23:1ff Isaiah's prophecies against other nations began in the east with Babylon (chapter 13) and ended in the west with Tyre in Phoenicia. Tyre was one of the most famous cities of the ancient world. A major trading centre with a large seaport, Tyre was very wealthy and very evil. Tyre was rebuked by Jeremiah (Jeremiah 25:22, 27; 47:4), Ezekiel (Ezekiel 26–28), Joel (Joel 3:4–8), Amos (Amos 1:9, 10), and Zechariah (Zechariah 9:3, 4). This is another warning against political alliances with unstable neighbours.

23:5 Why would Egypt be "in anguish" when Tyre fell? Egypt depended on Tyre's shipping expertise to promote and carry their products around the world. Egypt would lose an important trading partner with the fall of Tyre.

23:9
[h] Job 40:11
[i] Isa 13:11
[j] Isa 5:13; 9:15

23:11
[k] Ex 14:21
[l] Isa 25:2; Zec 9:3-4

23:12
[m] Rev 18:22
[n] Isa 47:1

23:13
[o] Isa 10:5
[p] Isa 10:7

23:14
[q] Isa 2:16 *fn*

23:15
[r] Jer 25:22

23:17
[s] Eze 16:26; Na 3:4; Rev 17:1

23:18
[t] Ex 28:36; Ps 72:10
[u] Isa 60:5-9; Mic 4:13

24:1
[a] ver 20; Isa 2:19-21; 33:9

to bring low[h] the pride of all glory
and to humble[i] all who are renowned[j] on the earth.

10 Till[c] your land as along the Nile,
O Daughter of Tarshish,
for you no longer have a harbour.
11 The LORD has stretched out his hand[k] over the sea
and made its kingdoms tremble.
He has given an order concerning Phoenicia[d]
that her fortresses be destroyed.[l]
12 He said, "No more of your revelling,[m]
O Virgin Daughter[n] of Sidon, now crushed!

"Up, cross over to Cyprus;[e]
even there you will find no rest."
13 Look at the land of the Babylonians,[f]
this people that is now of no account!
The Assyrians[o] have made it
a place for desert creatures;
they raised up their siege towers,
they stripped its fortresses bare
and turned it into a ruin.[p]

14 Wail, you ships of Tarshish;[q]
your fortress is destroyed!

15 At that time Tyre[r] will be forgotten for seventy years, the span of a king's life. But at the end of these seventy years, it will happen to Tyre as in the song of the prostitute:

16 "Take up a harp, walk through the city,
O prostitute forgotten;
play the harp well, sing many a song,
so that you will be remembered."

17 At the end of seventy years, the LORD will deal with Tyre. She will return to her hire as a prostitute[s] and will ply her trade with all the kingdoms on the face of the earth. 18 Yet her profit and her earnings will be set apart for the LORD;[t] they will not be stored up or hoarded. Her profits will go to those who live before the LORD,[u] for abundant food and fine clothes.

3. God's purpose in judgment

The LORD's Devastation of the Earth

24 See, the LORD is going to lay waste the earth[a]
and devastate it;
he will ruin its face
and scatter its inhabitants—
2 it will be the same

[c] *10* Dead Sea Scrolls and some Septuagint manuscripts; Masoretic Text *Go through* [d] *11* Hebrew *Canaan*
[e] *12* Hebrew *Kittim* [f] *13* Or *Chaldeans*

23:9 God would destroy Tyre because he hated its people's pride. Pride separates people from God, and he will not tolerate it. We must examine our lives and remember that all true accomplishment comes from our Creator. We have no reason for pride in ourselves.

23:15, 16 Some scholars believe this is a literal 70 years; some say it is symbolic of a long period of time. If it is literal, this may have occurred between 700 – 630 B.C. during the Assyrian captivity of Israel, or it may have been during the 70-year captivity of the Jews in Babylon (605 – 536 B.C.). During the 70 years, the Jews would forget about Tyre. But when they returned from captivity, they would once again trade with Tyre.

24 – 27 These four chapters are often called "Isaiah's Apocalypse". They discuss God's judgment on the entire world for its sin. Isaiah's prophecies were first directed to Judah, then to Israel, then to the surrounding nations, and finally to the whole world. These chapters describe the last days when God will judge the whole world. At that time he will finally and permanently remove evil.

for priest as for people,[b]
for master as for servant,
for mistress as for maid,
for seller as for buyer,[c]
for borrower as for lender,
for debtor as for creditor.[d]
3The earth will be completely laid waste
and totally plundered.[e]
The LORD has spoken this word.

4The earth dries up and withers,
the world languishes and withers,
the exalted[f] of the earth languish.
5The earth is defiled[g] by its people;
they have disobeyed[h] the laws,
violated the statutes
and broken the everlasting covenant.
6Therefore a curse consumes the earth;
its people must bear their guilt.
Therefore earth's inhabitants are burned up,[i]
and very few are left.
7The new wine dries up and the vine withers;[j]
all the merrymakers groan.[k]
8The gaiety of the tambourines[l] is stilled,
the noise[m] of the revellers has stopped,
the joyful harp[n] is silent.[o]
9No longer do they drink wine[p] with a song;
the beer is bitter[q] to its drinkers.
10The ruined city lies desolate;
the entrance to every house is barred.
11In the streets they cry out for wine;
all joy turns to gloom,[r]
all gaiety is banished from the earth.
12The city is left in ruins,
its gate is battered to pieces.
13So will it be on the earth
and among the nations,
as when an olive tree is beaten,[s]
or as when gleanings are left after the grape harvest.

14They raise their voices, they shout for joy;[t]
from the west they acclaim the LORD's majesty.
15Therefore in the east give glory[u] to the LORD;
exalt[v] the name of the LORD, the God of Israel,
in the islands of the sea.
16From the ends of the earth we hear singing:
"Glory[w] to the Righteous One."

But I said, "I waste away, I waste away!

24:2 [b]Hos 4:9 [c]Eze 7:12 [d]Lev 25:35-37; Dt 23:19-20
24:3 [e]Isa 6:11-12
24:4 [f]Isa 2:12
24:5 [g]Ge 3:17; Nu 35:33 [h]Isa 10:6; 59:12
24:6 [i]Isa 1:31
24:7 [j]Joel 1:10-12 [k]Isa 16:8-10
24:8 [l]Isa 5:12 [m]Jer 7:34; 16:9; 25:10; Hos 2:11 [n]Rev 18:22 [o]Eze 26:13
24:9 [p]Isa 5:11, 22 [q]Isa 5:20
24:11 [r]Isa 16:10; 32:13; Jer 14:3
24:13 [s]Isa 17:6
24:14 [t]Isa 12:6
24:15 [u]Isa 66:19 [v]Isa 25:3; Mal 1:11
24:16 [w]Isa 28:5

24:4, 5 Not only the people suffered from their sins; even the land suffered the effects of evil and lawbreaking. Today we see the results of sin in our own land—pollution, crime, addiction, poverty. Sin affects every aspect of society so extensively that even those faithful to God suffer. We cannot blame God for these conditions because human sin has brought them about. The more we who are believers renounce sin, speak against immoral practices, and share God's word with others, the more we slow our society's deterioration. We must not give up: sin is rampant, but we can make a difference.

24:14–16 The believers who are left behind after God judges Judah will sing to the glory of God's righteousness. Isaiah grieved because of his world's condition. We too can become depressed by the evil all around us. At those times we need to hold on to God's promises for the future and look forward to singing praises to him when he restores heaven and earth.

24:16 [x]Isa 21:2; Jer 5:11
24:17 [y]Jer 48:43
24:18 [z]Ge 7:11 [a]Ps 18:7
24:19 [b]Dt 11:6
24:20 [c]Isa 19:14 [d]Isa 1:2, 28; 43:27
24:21 [e]Isa 10:12
24:22 [f]Isa 10:4 [g]Isa 42:7, 22 [h]Eze 38:8
24:23 [i]Isa 13:10 [j]Rev 22:5 [k]Heb 12:22 [l]Isa 60:19
25:1 [a]Ps 98:1 [b]Nu 23:19
25:2 [c]Isa 17:1 [d]Isa 17:3 [e]Isa 13:22
25:3 [f]Isa 13:11
25:4 [g]Isa 4:6; 17:10; 27:5; 33:16 [h]Isa 29:5; 49:25

Woe to me!
The treacherous betray!
With treachery the treacherous betray![x]"
17 Terror and pit and snare[y] await you,
O people of the earth.
18 Whoever flees at the sound of terror
will fall into a pit;
whoever climbs out of the pit
will be caught in a snare.

The floodgates of the heavens[z] are opened,
the foundations of the earth shake.[a]
19 The earth is broken up,
the earth is split asunder,[b]
the earth is thoroughly shaken.
20 The earth reels like a drunkard,[c]
it sways like a hut in the wind;
so heavy upon it is the guilt of its rebellion[d]
that it falls—never to rise again.

21 In that day the LORD will punish[e]
the powers in the heavens above
and the kings on the earth below.
22 They will be herded together
like prisoners[f] bound in a dungeon;[g]
they will be shut up in prison
and be punished[a] after many days.[h]
23 The moon will be abashed, the sun[i] ashamed;
for the LORD Almighty will reign[j]
on Mount Zion[k] and in Jerusalem,
and before its elders, gloriously.[l]

Praise to the LORD

25 O LORD, you are my God;
I will exalt you and praise your name,
for in perfect faithfulness
you have done marvellous things,[a]
things planned[b] long ago.
2 You have made the city a heap of rubble,[c]
the fortified[d] town a ruin,
the foreigners' stronghold[e] a city no more;
it will never be rebuilt.
3 Therefore strong peoples will honour you;
cities of ruthless[f] nations will revere you.
4 You have been a refuge[g] for the poor,
a refuge for the needy in his distress,
a shelter from the storm
and a shade from the heat.
For the breath of the ruthless[h]
is like a storm driving against a wall

[a] *22* Or *released*

24:21 "The powers in the heavens above" refer to spiritual forces opposed to God. Nobody, not even the fallen angels, will escape due punishment.

25:1 Isaiah exalted and praised God because he realised that God completes his plans as promised. God also fulfils his promises to you. Think of the prayers he has answered, and praise him for his goodness and faithfulness.

25:4 The poor suffered because ruthless people oppressed them. But God is concerned for the poor and is a refuge for them. When we are disadvantaged or oppressed, we can turn to God for comfort and help. Jesus states that the kingdom of God belongs to the poor (Luke 6:20).

5 and like the heat of the desert.
You silence[i] the uproar of foreigners;
as heat is reduced by the shadow of a cloud,
so the song of the ruthless is stilled.

6On this mountain[j] the LORD Almighty will prepare
a feast[k] of rich food for all peoples,
a banquet of aged wine —
the best of meats and the finest of wines.[l]
7On this mountain he will destroy
the shroud[m] that enfolds all peoples,
the sheet that covers all nations;
8 he will swallow up death[n] for ever.
The Sovereign LORD will wipe away the tears[o]
from all faces;
he will remove the disgrace[p] of his people
from all the earth.
The LORD has spoken.

9In that day they will say,

"Surely this is our God;[q]
we trusted in him, and he saved[r] us.
This is the LORD, we trusted in him;
let us rejoice[s] and be glad in his salvation."

10The hand of the LORD will rest on this mountain;
but Moab[t] will be trampled under him
as straw is trampled down in the manure.
11They will spread out their hands in it,
as a swimmer spreads out his hands to swim.
God will bring down[u] their pride[v]
despite the cleverness**a** of their hands.
12He will bring down your high fortified walls
and lay them low;[w]
he will bring them down to the ground,
to the very dust.

A Song of Praise

26 In that day this song will be sung in the land of Judah:

We have a strong city;[a]
God makes salvation
its walls[b] and ramparts.
2Open the gates

a *11* The meaning of the Hebrew for this word is uncertain.

25:5 [i]Jer 51:55
25:6 [j]Isa 2:2 [k]Isa 1:19; Mt 8:11; 22:4 [l]Pr 9:2
25:7 [m]2Co 3:15-16; Eph 4:18
25:8 [n]Hos 13:14; 1Co 15:54-55* [o]Isa 30:19; 35:10; 51:11; 65:19; Rev 7:17; 21:4 [p]Mt 5:11; 1Pe 4:14
25:9 [q]Isa 40:9 [r]Ps 20:5; Isa 33:22; 35:4; 49:25; 60:16 [s]Isa 35:2, 10
25:10 [t]Am 2:1-3
25:11 [u]Isa 5:25; 14:26; 16:14 [v]Job 40:12
25:12 [w]Isa 15:1
26:1 [a]Isa 14:32 [b]Isa 60:18

25:6 Here is a marvellous prophecy of "all peoples" – Gentiles and Jews together – at God's Messianic feast, celebrating the overthrow of evil and the joy of eternity with God. It shows that God intended his saving message to go out to the whole world, not just to the Jews. During the feast, God will end death for ever (25:7, 8). The people who participate in this great feast will be those who have been living by faith. That is why they say, "Surely this is our God; we trusted in him, and he saved us" (25:9). See also chapter 55 for another presentation of this great banquet.

25:8 When the Lord speaks, he does what he says. It is comforting to know that God's plans and activities are closely tied to his word. When we pray according to God's will (as expressed in the Bible) and claim his promises (as recorded in the Bible), he hears us and answers our requests.

25:8 Part of this verse is quoted in 1 Corinthians 15:54 to describe Christ's victory over death. God's ultimate victory is seen when death, our ultimate enemy, is defeated (see also Hosea 13:14). Another part of this verse is quoted in Revelation 21:4, which describes the glorious scene of God's presence with his people.

25:10 Moab was a symbol of all who oppose God and are rebellious to the end. Moab was Israel's enemy for years (see the note on 15:1).

26:1ff People will praise God on the day of the Lord when Christ establishes his kingdom (see chapter 12). Chapter 26 is a psalm of trust, praise, and meditation. Once more, God revealed the future to Isaiah.

that the righteous[c] nation may enter,
the nation that keeps faith.
3 You will keep in perfect peace
him whose mind is steadfast,
because he trusts in you.
4 Trust[d] in the LORD for ever,
for the LORD, the LORD, is the Rock eternal.
5 He humbles those who dwell on high,
he lays the lofty city low;
he levels it to the ground[e]
and casts it down to the dust.
6 Feet trample it down—
the feet of the oppressed,
the footsteps of the poor.[f]

7 The path of the righteous is level;
O upright One, you make the way of the righteous smooth.[g]
8 Yes, LORD, walking in the way of your laws,[a][h]
we wait for you;
your name[i] and renown
are the desire of our hearts.
9 My soul yearns for you in the night;
in the morning my spirit longs[j] for you.
When your judgments come upon the earth,
the people of the world learn righteousness.[k]
10 Though grace is shown to the wicked,
they do not learn righteousness;
even in a land of uprightness they go on doing evil[l]
and regard[m] not the majesty of the LORD.
11 O LORD, your hand is lifted high,
but they do not see[n] it.
Let them see your zeal for your people and be put to shame;
let the fire[o] reserved for your enemies consume them.

12 LORD, you establish peace for us;
all that we have accomplished you have done for us.
13 O LORD, our God, other lords[p] besides you have ruled over us,
but your name alone do we honour.[q]
14 They are now dead,[r] they live no more;
those departed spirits do not rise.
You punished them and brought them to ruin;[s]
you wiped out all memory of them.
15 You have enlarged the nation, O LORD;
you have enlarged the nation.
You have gained glory for yourself;
you have extended all the borders[t] of the land.

[a] 8 Or *judgments*

26:2 [c] Isa 54:14; 58:8; 62:2
26:4 [d] Isa 12:2; 50:10
26:5 [e] Isa 25:12
26:6 [f] Isa 3:15
26:7 [g] Isa 42:16
26:8 [h] Isa 56:1 [i] Isa 12:4
26:9 [j] Ps 63:1; 78:34; Isa 55:6 [k] Mt 6:33
26:10 [l] Isa 32:6 [m] Isa 22:12-13; Hos 11:7; Jn 5:37-38; Ro 2:4
26:11 [n] Isa 44:9, 18 [o] Heb 10:27
26:13 [p] Isa 2:8; 10:5, 11 [q] Isa 63:7
26:14 [r] Dt 4:28 [s] Isa 10:3
26:15 [t] Isa 33:17

26:3 We can never avoid strife in the world around us, but with God we can know perfect peace even in turmoil. When we are devoted to him, our whole attitude is steady and stable. Supported by God's unchanging love and mighty power, we are not shaken by the surrounding chaos (see Philippians 4:7). Do you want peace? Keep your thoughts on and your trust in God.

26:7, 8 At times the "path of the righteous" doesn't seem smooth and it isn't easy to do God's will, but we are never alone when we face tough times. God is there to help us through difficulties, to comfort us, and to lead us. God does this by giving us a purpose (keeping our mind centred on him, 26:3) and giving us provisions as we travel. God provides us with relationships of family, friends, and mentors. God gives us wisdom to make decisions and faith to trust him. Don't despair; stay on God's path.

26:10 Even wicked people receive God's benefits, but that doesn't teach them to do what is right. Sometimes God's judgment teaches us more than God's good gifts. If you have been enriched by God's goodness and grace, respond to him with your grateful devotion.

16 LORD, they came to you in their distress;[u]
when you disciplined them,
they could barely whisper a prayer.[b]
17 As a woman with child and about to give birth[v]
writhes and cries out in her pain,
so were we in your presence, O LORD.
18 We were with child, we writhed in pain,
but we gave birth[w] to wind.
We have not brought salvation[x] to the earth;
we have not given birth to people of the world.

19 But your dead[y] will live;
their bodies will rise.
You who dwell in the dust,
wake up and shout for joy.
Your dew is like the dew of the morning;
the earth will give birth to her dead.[z]

20 Go, my people, enter your rooms
and shut the doors[a] behind you;
hide[b] yourselves for a little while
until his wrath has passed by.[c]
21 See, the LORD is coming[d] out of his dwelling[e]
to punish[f] the people of the earth for their sins.
The earth will disclose the blood[g] shed upon her;
she will conceal her slain no longer.

Deliverance of Israel

27 In that day,

the LORD will punish with his sword,[a]
his fierce, great and powerful sword,
Leviathan[b] the gliding serpent,
Leviathan the coiling serpent;
he will slay the monster[c] of the sea.

2 In that day—

"Sing about a fruitful vineyard:[d]
3 I, the LORD, watch over it;

b *16* The meaning of the Hebrew for this clause is uncertain.

26:16 [u]Hos 5:15
26:17 [v]Jn 16:21
26:18 [w]Isa 33:11; 59:4 [x]Ps 17:14
26:19 [y]Isa 25:8; Eph 5:14 [z]Eze 37:1-14; Da 12:2
26:20 [a]Ex 12:23 [b]Ps 91:1, 4 [c]Ps 30:5; Isa 54:7-8
26:21 [d]Jude 1:14 [e]Mic 1:3 [f]Isa 13:9, 11; 30:12-14 [g]Job 16:18; Lk 11:50-51
27:1 [a]Isa 34:6; 66:16 [b]Job 3:8 [c]Ps 74:13
27:2 [d]Jer 2:21

26:16–19 The people realised the pain of being away from God's presence, and yet they are assured that they will live again. God turned his back on his people when they disobeyed, but a small number never lost hope and continued to seek him. No matter how difficult times may be, we have hope when we keep our trust in him. Can you wait patiently for God to act?

26:19 Some people say there is no life after death. Others believe that there is, but it is not physical life. But Isaiah tells us that our bodies shall rise again. According to 1 Corinthians 15:50–53, all the dead believers will arise with new imperishable bodies—bodies like the one Jesus had when he was resurrected (see Philippians 3:21). Isaiah 26:19 is not the only Old Testament verse to speak about the resurrection; see also Job 19:26; Psalm 16:10; Daniel 12:2, 13.

26:20, 21 When God comes to judge the earth, the guilty will find no place to hide. Jesus said that the hidden will be made known because his truth, like a light shining in a dark corner, will reveal it (Matthew 10:26). Instead of trying to hide your shameful thoughts and actions from God, confess them to him and receive his forgiveness.

27:1 "That day" is a reference to the end of the evil world as we know it. In ancient Aramean (Ugaritic) literature, Leviathan was a seven-headed monster, the enemy of God's created order. Thus Isaiah is comparing God's slaughter of the wicked to the conquering of a great enemy. Although evil is a powerful foe, God will crush it and abolish it from the earth for ever.

27:2–6 The trampled vineyard of chapter 5 will be restored in God's new earth. God will protect and care for the vineyard, his people. It will no longer produce worthless fruit but will produce enough good fruit for the whole world. Gentiles will come to know God through Israel.

I water[e] it continually.
I guard it day and night
so that no-one may harm it.
4 I am not angry.
If only there were briers and thorns confronting me!
I would march against them in battle;
I would set them all on fire.[f]
5Or else let them come to me for refuge;[g]
let them make peace[h] with me,
yes, let them make peace with me."

6In days to come Jacob will take root,
Israel will bud and blossom[i]
and fill all the world with fruit.[j]

7Has ⌊the LORD⌋ struck her
as he struck[k] down those who struck her?
Has she been killed
as those were killed who killed her?
8By warfare[a] and exile[l] you contend with her—
with his fierce blast he drives her out,
as on a day the east wind blows.
9By this, then, will Jacob's guilt be atoned for,
and this will be the full fruitage of the removal of his sin:[m]
When he makes all the altar stones
to be like chalk stones crushed to pieces,
no Asherah poles[b][n] or incense altars
will be left standing.
10The fortified city stands desolate,[o]
an abandoned settlement, forsaken like the desert;
there the calves graze,
there they lie down;[p]
they strip its branches bare.
11When its twigs are dry, they are broken off
and women come and make fires with them.
For this is a people without understanding;[q]
so their Maker has no compassion on them,
and their Creator[r] shows them no favour.[s]

12In that day the LORD will thresh from the flowing Euphrates[c] to the Wadi
of Egypt,[t] and you, O Israelites, will be gathered[u] up one by one. 13And in that
day a great trumpet[v] will sound. Those who were perishing in Assyria and those who
were exiled in Egypt[w] will come and worship the LORD on the holy mountain in
Jerusalem.

[a] 8 See Septuagint; the meaning of the Hebrew for this word is uncertain. [b] 9 That is, symbols of the goddess Asherah [c] 12 Hebrew *River*

27:3 [e]Isa 58:11
27:4 [f]Isa 10:17; Mt 3:12; Heb 6:8
27:5 [g]Isa 25:4 [h]Job 22:21; Ro 5:1; 2Co 5:20
27:6 [i]Hos 14:5-6 [j]Isa 37:31
27:7 [k]Isa 37:36-38
27:8 [l]Isa 50:1; 54:7
27:9 [m]Ro 11:27* [n]Ex 34:13
27:10 [o]Isa 32:14; Jer 26:6 [p]Isa 17:2
27:11 [q]Dt 32:28; Isa 1:3; Jer 8:7 [r]Dt 32:18; Isa 43:1, 7, 15; 44:1-2, 21, 24 [s]Isa 9:17
27:12 [t]Ge 15:18 [u]Dt 30:4; Isa 11:12; 17:6
27:13 [v]Lev 25:9; Mt 24:31 [w]Isa 19:21, 25

27:9 Only God can take away sin, but to be driven out of the land was considered the penalty that would purify God's people. Deuteronomy 28:49–52, 64 explains God's warning about these consequences.

27:11 Isaiah compares the state of Israel's spiritual life with dry twigs that are broken off and used to make fires. Trees in Scripture often represent spiritual life. The trunk is the channel of strength from God; the branches are the people who serve him. Tree branches sometimes waver and blow in the wind. Like Israel, they may dry up from internal rottenness and become useless for anything except building a fire. What kind of branch are you? If you are withering spiritually, check to see if you are firmly attached to God.

27:12 To "thresh" means to "judge". God's purpose in judging the earth is not vengeance, but purging. He wants to correct us and bring us back to him. God does not punish us for our sin just to make us suffer, but to make those who are faithful better equipped for fruitful service.

27:12 A wadi is a stream or dry riverbed.

4. Jerusalem's true and false hopes

Woe to Ephraim

28 Woe to that wreath, the pride of Ephraim's[a] drunkards,
to the fading flower, his glorious beauty,
set on the head of a fertile valley[b]—
to that city, the pride of those laid low by wine![c]
2 See, the Lord has one who is powerful[d] and strong.
Like a hailstorm[e] and a destructive wind,[f]
like a driving rain and a flooding[g] downpour,
he will throw it forcefully to the ground.
3 That wreath, the pride of Ephraim's[h] drunkards,
will be trampled underfoot.
4 That fading flower, his glorious beauty,
set on the head of a fertile valley,[i]
will be like a fig[j] ripe before harvest—
as soon as someone sees it and takes it in his hand,
he swallows it.

5 In that day the LORD Almighty
will be a glorious crown,[k]
a beautiful wreath
for the remnant of his people.
6 He will be a spirit of justice[l]
to him who sits in judgment,[m]
a source of strength
to those who turn back the battle[n] at the gate.

7 And these also stagger from wine[o]
and reel[p] from beer:
Priests[q] and prophets[r] stagger from beer
and are befuddled with wine;
they reel from beer,
they stagger when seeing visions,[s]
they stumble when rendering decisions.
8 All the tables are covered with vomit[t]
and there is not a spot without filth.

9 "Who is it he is trying to teach?[u]
To whom is he explaining his message?
To children weaned[v] from their milk,[w]
to those just taken from the breast?
10 For it is:
Do and do, do and do,
rule on rule, rule on rule;[a]
a little here, a little there."

11 Very well then, with foreign lips and strange tongues[x]
God will speak to this people,[y]
12 to whom he said,

a *10* Hebrew */ sav lasav sav lasav / kav lakav kav lakav* (possibly meaningless sounds; perhaps a mimicking of the prophet's words); also in verse 13

28:1 [a] ver 3; Isa 9:9 [b] ver 4 [c] Hos 7:5
28:2 [d] Isa 40:10 [e] Isa 30:30; Eze 13:11 [f] Isa 29:6 [g] Isa 8:7
28:3 [h] ver 1
28:4 [i] ver 1 [j] Hos 9:10; Na 3:12
28:5 [k] Isa 62:3
28:6 [l] Isa 11:2-4; 32:1, 16 [m] Jn 5:30 [n] 2Ch 32:8
28:7 [o] Isa 22:13 [p] Isa 56:10-12 [q] Isa 24:2 [r] Isa 9:15 [s] Isa 29:11; Hos 4:11
28:8 [t] Jer 48:26
28:9 [u] ver 26; Isa 30:20; 48:17; 50:4; 54:13 [v] Ps 131:2 [w] Heb 5:12-13
28:11 [x] Isa 33:19 [y] 1Co 14:21*

28:1 Ephraim represents the northern kingdom of Israel, ruled by a line of evil kings. When Israel split into two kingdoms after Solomon's reign, Jerusalem ended up in the southern kingdom. Leaders in the northern kingdom, wishing to stay entirely separate from their relatives to the south, set up idols to keep the people from going to the temple in Jerusalem to worship (see 1 Kings 12). Thus the people in the northern kingdom were led into idolatry. Isaiah gave this message to Israel to warn them, as well as to Judah to encourage them to repent before being punished as the northern kingdom would be only a few years later.

28:9–14 These verses characterise the people's reaction to Isaiah. In effect, they were saying, "He's speaking to us like a school teacher speaks to small children. We don't need to be taught. We'll make up our own minds." For this attitude, Isaiah prophesied that the Assyrians would teach them in a way they would like even less.

"This is the resting-place, let the weary rest";[z]
and, "This is the place of repose"—
but they would not listen.
13So then, the word of the LORD to them will become:
Do and do, do and do,
rule on rule, rule on rule;
a little here, a little there—
so that they will go and fall backwards,
be injured[a] and snared and captured.[b]

14Therefore hear the word of the LORD,[c] you scoffers
who rule this people in Jerusalem.
15You boast, "We have entered into a covenant with death,
with the grave**b** we have made an agreement.
When an overwhelming scourge sweeps by,[d]
it cannot touch us,
for we have made a lie[e] our refuge
and falsehood**c** our hiding-place.[f]"

16So this is what the Sovereign LORD says:

"See, I lay a stone in Zion,
a tested stone,[g]
a precious cornerstone for a sure foundation;
the one who trusts will never be dismayed.[h]
17I will make justice[i] the measuring line
and righteousness the plumb-line;[j]
hail will sweep away your refuge, the lie,
and water will overflow your hiding-place.
18Your covenant with death will be annulled;
your agreement with the grave will not stand.[k]
When the overwhelming scourge sweeps by,[l]
you will be beaten down[m] by it.
19As often as it comes it will carry you away;[n]
morning after morning, by day and by night,
it will sweep through."

The understanding of this message
will bring sheer terror.[o]
20The bed is too short to stretch out on,
the blanket too narrow to wrap around you.[p]
21The LORD will rise up as he did at Mount Perazim,[q]
he will rouse himself as in the Valley of Gibeon[r]—
to do his work,[s] his strange work,
and perform his task, his alien task.
22Now stop your mocking,
or your chains will become heavier;
the Lord, the LORD Almighty, has told me

b *15* Hebrew *Sheol*; also in verse 18 **c** *15* Or *false gods*

28:12 [z]Isa 11:10; Mt 11:28-29
28:13 [a]Mt 21:44 [b]Isa 8:15
28:14 [c]Isa 1:10
28:15 [d]ver 2, 18; Isa 8:7-8; 30:28; Da 11:22 [e]Isa 9:15 [f]Isa 29:15
28:16 [g]Ps 118:22; Isa 8:14-15; Mt 21:42; Ac 4:11; Eph 2:20 [h]Ro 9:33*; 10:11*; 1Pe 2:6*
28:17 [i]Isa 5:16 [j]2Ki 21:13
28:18 [k]Isa 7:7 [l]ver 15 [m]Da 8:13
28:19 [n]2Ki 24:2 [o]Job 18:11
28:20 [p]Isa 59:6
28:21 [q]1Ch 14:11 [r]Jos 10:10, 12; 1Ch 14:16 [s]Isa 10:12; Lk 19:41-44

28:15 Judah was afraid of the Assyrians, the "overwhelming scourge". Instead of trusting God, the Judeans turned to other sources for security. God accused them of making a covenant with death. It is used to mean the grave or state of being dead. This passage may refer to Hezekiah's alliance with Pharaoh Tirhakah against Assyria (2 Kings 19:9; Isaiah 37:9). God would cancel this agreement—Egypt would be of no help when Assyria attacked. Is it worth compromising what you believe in for temporary protection against an enemy? If you want lasting protection, turn to the only one able to deliver you from *eternal* death—God.

28:16 If you're building anything, you need a firm base. Isaiah speaks of a foundation stone, a *cornerstone,* that will be laid in Zion. This cornerstone is the Messiah, the foundation on whom we build our lives. Is your life built on the flimsy base of your own successes or dreams? Or is it set on a firm foundation (see Psalm 118:22; 1 Peter 2:8)?

28:21 God fought on Joshua's side at the Valley of Gibeon (Joshua 10:1–14) and on David's side at Mount Perazim (2 Samuel 5:20). But here he would fight *against* Israel, his own people, in these same places.

of the destruction decreed[t] against the whole land.[u]

23Listen and hear my voice;
pay attention and hear what I say.
24When a farmer ploughs for planting, does he plough continually?
Does he keep on breaking up and harrowing the soil?
25When he has levelled the surface,
does he not sow caraway and scatter cummin?[v]
Does he not plant wheat in its place,[d]
barley in its plot,[d]
and spelt[w] in its field?
26His God instructs him
and teaches him the right way.

27Caraway is not threshed with a sledge,
nor is a cartwheel rolled over cummin;
caraway is beaten out with a rod,
and cummin with a stick.
28Grain must be ground to make bread;
so one does not go on threshing it for ever.
Though he drives the wheels of his threshing-cart over it,
his horses do not grind it.
29All this also comes from the LORD Almighty,
wonderful in counsel[x] and magnificent in wisdom.[y]

Woe to David's City

29 Woe[a] to you, Ariel, Ariel,[b]
the city where David settled!
Add year to year
and let your cycle of festivals[c] go on.
2Yet I will besiege Ariel;
she will mourn and lament,[d]
she will be to me like an altar hearth.[a]
3I will encamp against you all around;
I will encircle[e] you with towers
and set up my siege works against you.
4Brought low, you will speak from the ground;
your speech will mumble[f] out of the dust.
Your voice will come ghostlike from the earth;
out of the dust your speech will whisper.

5But your many enemies will become like fine dust,
the ruthless hordes like blown chaff.[g]
Suddenly,[h] in an instant,
6 the LORD Almighty will come
with thunder and earthquake[i] and great noise,
with windstorm and tempest and flames of a devouring fire.
7Then the hordes of all the nations[j] that fight against Ariel,
that attack her and her fortress and besiege her,
will be as it is with a dream,[k]

d *25* The meaning of the Hebrew for this word is uncertain. a *2* The Hebrew for *altar hearth* sounds like the Hebrew for *Ariel*.

28:22 [t]Isa 10:22 [u]Isa 10:23
28:25 [v]Mt 23:23 [w]Ex 9:32
28:29 [x]Isa 9:6 [y]Ro 11:33
29:1 [a]Isa 22:12-13 [b]2Sa 5:9 [c]Isa 1:14
29:2 [d]Isa 3:26; La 2:5
29:3 [e]Lk 19:43-44
29:4 [f]Isa 8:19
29:5 [g]Isa 17:13 [h]Isa 17:14; 1Th 5:3
29:6 [i]Mt 24:7; Mk 13:8; Lk 21:11; Rev 11:19
29:7 [j]Mic 4:11-12; Zec 12:9 [k]Job 20:8

28:23–29 The farmer uses special tools to plant and harvest tender herbs so he will not destroy them. He takes into account how fragile they are. In the same way God takes all our individual circumstances and weaknesses into account. He deals with each of us sensitively. We should follow his example when we deal with others. Different people require different treatment. Be sensitive to the needs of those around you and the special treatment they may need.

29:1 *Ariel* is a special name for Jerusalem, David's city. It may mean "lion of God" (Jerusalem is as strong as a lion) or "altar hearth" (Jerusalem is the place of the altar in the temple. See 29:2; Ezekiel 43:15, 16).

with a vision in the night—
8as when a hungry man dreams that he is eating,
but he awakens,[l] and his hunger remains;
as when a thirsty man dreams that he is drinking,
but he awakens faint, with his thirst unquenched.
So will it be with the hordes of all the nations
that fight against Mount Zion.

9Be stunned and amazed,
blind yourselves and be sightless;
be drunk,[m] but not from wine,[n]
stagger, but not from beer.
10The LORD has brought over you a deep sleep:
He has sealed your eyes[o] (the prophets);[p]
he has covered your heads (the seers).[q]

11For you this whole vision is nothing but words sealed[r] in a scroll. And if you
give the scroll to someone who can read, and say to him, "Read this, please," he will
answer, "I can't; it is sealed." 12Or if you give the scroll to someone who cannot read,
and say, "Read this, please," he will answer, "I don't know how to read."

13The Lord says:

"These people come near to me with their mouth
and honour me with their lips,
but their hearts are far from me.[s]
Their worship of me
is made up only of rules taught by men.[b][t]
14Therefore once more I will astound these people
with wonder upon wonder;[u]
the wisdom of the wise[v] will perish,
the intelligence of the intelligent will vanish.[w]"
15Woe to those who go to great depths
to hide their plans from the LORD,
who do their work in darkness and think,
"Who sees us?[x] Who will know?"[y]
16You turn things upside down,
as if the potter were thought to be like the clay!
Shall what is formed say to him who formed it,
"He did not make me"?
Can the pot say of the potter,[z]
"He knows nothing"?

17In a very short time, will not Lebanon be turned into a fertile
field[a]
and the fertile field seem like a forest?[b]
18In that day the deaf[c] will hear the words of the scroll,
and out of gloom and darkness

29:8 [l]Ps 73:20
29:9 [m]Isa 51:17 [n]Isa 51:21-22
29:10 [o]Ps 69:23; Isa 6:9-10; Ro 11:8* [p]Mic 3:6 [q]1Sa 9:9
29:11 [r]Isa 8:16; Mt 13:11; Rev 5:1-2
29:13 [s]Eze 33:31 [t]Mt 15:8-9*; Mk 7:6-7*; Col 2:22
29:14 [u]Hab 1:5 [v]Jer 8:9; 49:7 [w]Isa 6:9-10; 1Co 1:19*
29:15 [x]Ps 10:11-13; 94:7; Isa 57:12 [y]Job 22:13
29:16 [z]Isa 45:9; 64:8; Ro 9:20-21*
29:17 [a]Ps 84:6 [b]Isa 32:15
29:18 [c]Mk 7:37

b 13 Hebrew; Septuagint *They worship me in vain; / their teachings are but rules taught by men*

29:13, 14 The people claimed to be close to God, but they were disobedient and merely went through the motions; therefore, God would bring judgment upon them. Religion had become routine instead of real. Jesus quoted Isaiah's condemnation of Israel's hypocrisy when he spoke to the Pharisees, the religious leaders of his day (Matthew 15:7–9; Mark 7:6, 7). We are all capable of hypocrisy. Often we slip into routine patterns when we worship and we neglect to give God our love and devotion. If we want to be called God's people, we must be obedient and worship him honestly and sincerely.

29:15 Thinking God couldn't see them and didn't know what was happening, the people of Jerusalem tried to hide their plans from him. How strange that so many people think they can hide from God. In Psalm 139 we learn that God has examined us and knows everything about us. Would you be embarrassed if your best friends knew your personal thoughts? Remember that God knows all of them.

29:17–24 The world described here, under Christ's rule, will be far different from the one we live in today. There will be no more violence or gloom. This new world will be characterised by joy, understanding, justice, and praise to God.

the eyes of the blind will see.[d]
19Once more the humble[e] will rejoice in the LORD;
the needy[f] will rejoice in the Holy One of Israel.
20The ruthless will vanish,
the mockers[g] will disappear,
and all who have an eye for evil[h] will be cut down—
21those who with a word make a man out to be guilty,
who ensnare the defender in court[i]
and with false testimony deprive the innocent of justice.[j]

22Therefore this is what the LORD, who redeemed Abraham,[k] says to the house of Jacob:

"No longer will Jacob be ashamed;[l]
no longer will their faces grow pale.
23When they see among them their children,[m]
the work of my hands,[n]
they will keep my name holy;
they will acknowledge the holiness of the Holy One of Jacob,
and will stand in awe of the God of Israel.
24Those who are wayward[o] in spirit will gain understanding;[p]
those who complain will accept instruction."[q]

Woe to the Obstinate Nation

30 "Woe[a] to the obstinate children,"[b]
declares the LORD,
"to those who carry out plans that are not mine,
forming an alliance,[c] but not by my Spirit,
heaping sin upon sin;
2who go down to Egypt[d]
without consulting[e] me;
who look for help to Pharaoh's protection,[f]
to Egypt's shade for refuge.
3But Pharaoh's protection will be to your shame,
Egypt's shade will bring you disgrace.[g]
4Though they have officials in Zoan[h]
and their envoys have arrived in Hanes,
5everyone will be put to shame
because of a people[i] useless to them,
who bring neither help nor advantage,
but only shame and disgrace."

6An oracle concerning the animals of the Negev:

Through a land of hardship and distress,[j]
of lions and lionesses,
of adders and darting snakes,[k]
the envoys carry their riches on donkeys' backs,
their treasures[l] on the humps of camels,
to that unprofitable nation,

29:18 [d]Isa 32:3; 35:5; Mt 11:5
29:19 [e]Isa 61:1; Mt 5:5; 11:29 [f]Isa 14:30; Mt 11:5; Jas 1:9; 2:5
29:20 [g]Isa 28:22 [h]Isa 59:4; Mic 2:1
29:21 [i]Am 5:10, 15 [j]Isa 32:7
29:22 [k]Isa 41:8; 63:16 [l]Isa 49:23
29:23 [m]Isa 49:20-26 [n]Isa 19:25
29:24 [o]Isa 28:7; Heb 5:2 [p]Isa 41:20; 60:16 [q]Isa 30:21
30:1 [a]Isa 29:15 [b]Isa 1:2 [c]Isa 8:12
30:2 [d]Isa 31:1 [e]Nu 27:21 [f]Isa 36:9
30:3 [g]Isa 20:4-5; 36:6
30:4 [h]Isa 19:11
30:5 [i]ver 7
30:6 [j]Ex 5:10, 21; Isa 8:22; Jer 11:4 [k]Dt 8:15 [l]Isa 15:7

30:1 The obstinate children are the people of Judah (see 1:2), those who have rebelled against God. The negotiations for an alliance were underway, and Isaiah condemned their twisted plans. The people of Judah sought advice from everyone but God. When we are driven by fear, we tend to search everywhere for comfort, advice, and relief, hoping to find an easy way out of our troubles. Instead, we should consult God. Although he gives emergency help in a crisis, he prefers to be our Guide throughout our lives. By reading his word and actively seeking to do his will, we can maintain our bond with him who provides stability no matter what the crisis.

30:2ff Hezekiah had been seeking a defensive alliance with Egypt against Sennacherib of Assyria (see 2 Kings 18:21).

30:6 This oracle is titled "concerning the animals of the Negev", but is directed to those who carried bribes to Egypt through the desert in the Negev region.

30:8
[m] Isa 8:1; Hab 2:2

30:9
[n] Isa 28:15; 59:3-4
[o] Isa 1:10

30:10
[p] Jer 11:21; Am 7:13
[q] 1Ki 22:8
[r] Eze 13:7; Ro 16:18

30:11
[s] Job 21:14

30:12
[t] Isa 5:24
[u] Isa 5:7

30:13
[v] Ps 62:3
[w] 1Ki 20:30
[x] Isa 29:5

30:14
[y] Ps 2:9; Jer 19:10-11

30:15
[z] Isa 32:17

30:16
[a] Isa 31:1, 3

30:17
[b] Lev 26:8; Jos 23:10
[c] Lev 26:36; Dt 28:25

7 to Egypt, whose help is utterly useless.
Therefore I call her
Rahab the Do-Nothing.

8 Go now, write it on a tablet for them,
inscribe it on a scroll,[m]
that for the days to come
it may be an everlasting witness.
9 These are rebellious people, deceitful[n] children,
children unwilling to listen to the LORD's instruction.[o]
10 They say to the seers,
"See no more visions[p]!"
and to the prophets,
"Give us no more visions of what is right!
Tell us pleasant things,[q]
prophesy illusions.[r]
11 Leave this way,
get off this path,
and stop confronting[s] us
with the Holy One of Israel!"

12 Therefore, this is what the Holy One of Israel says:

"Because you have rejected this message,[t]
relied on oppression[u]
and depended on deceit,
13 this sin will become for you
like a high wall,[v] cracked and bulging,
that collapses[w] suddenly,[x] in an instant.
14 It will break in pieces like pottery,[y]
shattered so mercilessly
that among its pieces not a fragment will be found
for taking coals from a hearth
or scooping water out of a cistern."

15 This is what the Sovereign LORD, the Holy One of Israel, says:

"In repentance and rest is your salvation,
in quietness and trust[z] is your strength,
but you would have none of it.
16 You said, 'No, we will flee on horses.'[a]
Therefore you will flee!
You said, 'We will ride off on swift horses.'
Therefore your pursuers will be swift!
17 A thousand will flee
at the threat of one;
at the threat of five[b]
you will all flee[c] away,
till you are left
like a flagstaff on a mountaintop,

30:7 Rahab was a mythological female sea monster associated with Leviathan (see the note on 27:1; also Job 9:13; 26:12). It was a name associated with Egypt, where hippopotamuses, perhaps a likeness to Rahab, sat on the Nile River and did nothing.

30:10, 11 Some people in Judah may have sought refuge in Egypt. In their desire to find security, they wanted to hear only good news. They did not welcome the truth from God's prophets. Often the truth makes us uncomfortable. We prefer lies and illusions when they make us feel more secure. It is much better to face reality than to live a lie. Don't settle for something that makes you feel comfortable but is not true.

30:15 God warned Judah that turning to Egypt and other nations for military might could not save them. Only God could do that. They must wait for him in "quietness and trust". No amount of fast talking or hasty activity could speed up God's grand design. We have nothing to say to God but thank you. Salvation comes from God alone. Because he has saved us, we can trust him and be peacefully confident that he will give us strength to face our difficulties. We should lay aside our busy care and endless effort and allow him to act.

like a banner on a hill."

18Yet the LORD longs[d] to be gracious to you;
he rises to show you compassion.
For the LORD is a God of justice.[e]
Blessed are all who wait for him![f]

19O people of Zion, who live in Jerusalem, you will weep no more.[g] How gracious
he will be when you cry for help! As soon as he hears, he will answer[h] you.
20Although the Lord gives you the bread[i] of adversity and the water of affliction,
your teachers will be hidden[j] no more; with your own eyes you will see them.
21Whether you turn to the right or to the left, your ears will hear a voice[k] behind you,
saying, "This is the way; walk in it." 22Then you will defile your idols[l] overlaid with
silver and your images covered with gold; you will throw them away like a menstrual
cloth and say to them, "Away with you!"

23He will also send you rain[m] for the seed you sow in the ground, and the food
that comes from the land will be rich and plentiful. In that day your cattle will graze
in broad meadows.[n] 24The oxen and donkeys that work the soil will eat fodder and
mash, spread out with fork[o] and shovel. 25In the day of great slaughter, when the
towers[p] fall, streams of water will flow[q] on every high mountain and every lofty
hill. 26The moon will shine like the sun,[r] and the sunlight will be seven times
brighter, like the light of seven full days, when the LORD binds up the bruises of his
people and heals[s] the wounds he inflicted.

27See, the Name[t] of the LORD comes from afar,
with burning anger[u] and dense clouds of smoke;
his lips are full of wrath,[v]
and his tongue is a consuming fire.
28His breath[w] is like a rushing torrent,
rising up to the neck.[x]
He shakes the nations in the sieve[y] of destruction;
he places in the jaws of the peoples
a bit[z] that leads them astray.
29And you will sing
as on the night you celebrate a holy festival;
your hearts will rejoice
as when people go up with flutes
to the mountain[a] of the LORD,
to the Rock of Israel.
30The LORD will cause men to hear his majestic voice
and will make them see his arm coming down
with raging anger and consuming fire,
with cloudburst, thunderstorm and hail.
31The voice of the LORD will shatter Assyria;[b]
with his sceptre he will strike[c] them down.
32Every stroke the LORD lays on them
with his punishing rod
will be to the music of tambourines and harps,
as he fights them in battle with the blows of his arm.[d]
33Topheth[e] has long been prepared;
it has been made ready for the king.

30:18 [d]Isa 42:14; 2Pe 3:9, 15 [e]Isa 5:16 [f]Isa 25:9
30:19 [g]Isa 60:20; 61:3 [h]Ps 50:15; Isa 58:9; 65:24; Mt 7:7-11
30:20 [i]1Ki 22:27 [j]Ps 74:9; Am 8:11
30:21 [k]Isa 29:24
30:22 [l]Ex 32:4
30:23 [m]Isa 65:21-22 [n]Ps 65:13
30:24 [o]Mt 3:12; Lk 3:17
30:25 [p]Isa 2:15 [q]Isa 41:18
30:26 [r]Isa 24:23; 60:19-20; Rev 21:23; 22:5 [s]Dt 32:39; Isa 1:5
30:27 [t]Isa 59:19 [u]Isa 66:14 [v]Isa 10:5
30:28 [w]Isa 11:4 [x]Isa 8:8 [y]Am 9:9 [z]2Ki 19:28; Isa 37:29
30:29 [a]Ps 42:4
30:31 [b]Isa 10:5, 12 [c]Isa 11:4
30:32 [d]Isa 11:15; Eze 32:10
30:33 [e]2Ki 23:10

30:20 The Lord gave his people the bread of adversity and the water of affliction, but he promised to be with them, teach them, and guide them during hard times. God expects a lot from us, and following him can often be painful; but he always acts out of his love for us. Next time you go through a difficult time, try to appreciate the experience and grow from it, learning what God wants to teach you. God may be showing you his love by patiently walking with you through adversity.

30:21 When the people of Jerusalem left God's path, he would correct them. He will do the same for us. But when we hear his voice of correction, we must be willing to follow it!

30:33
[f]Ge 19:24

Its fire pit has been made deep and wide,
with an abundance of fire and wood;
the breath of the LORD,
like a stream of burning sulphur,[f]
sets it ablaze.

31:1
[a]Dt 17:16; Isa 30:2, 5
[b]Isa 2:7
[c]Ps 20:7; Da 9:13

Woe to Those Who Rely on Egypt

31 Woe to those who go down to Egypt[a] for help,
who rely on horses,
who trust in the multitude of their chariots[b]
and in the great strength of their horsemen,
but do not look to the Holy One of Israel,
or seek help from the LORD.[c]

31:2
[d]Ro 16:27
[e]Isa 45:7
[f]Nu 23:19
[g]Isa 32:6

2 Yet he too is wise[d] and can bring disaster;[e]
he does not take back his words.[f]
He will rise up against the house of the wicked,[g]
against those who help evildoers.

31:3
[h]Isa 36:9
[i]Eze 28:9; 2Th 2:4
[j]Isa 9:17, 21
[k]Isa 30:5-7

3 But the Egyptians[h] are men and not God;[i]
their horses are flesh and not spirit.
When the LORD stretches out his hand,[j]
he who helps will stumble,
he who is helped[k] will fall;
both will perish together.

31:4
[l]Nu 24:9; Hos 11:10; Am 3:8
[m]Isa 42:13

4 This is what the LORD says to me:

"As a lion[l] growls,
a great lion over his prey—
and though a whole band of shepherds
is called together against him,
he is not frightened by their shouts
or disturbed by their clamour—
so the LORD Almighty will come down[m]
to do battle on Mount Zion and on its heights.

31:5
[n]Ps 91:4
[o]Isa 37:35; 38:6

5 Like birds hovering overhead,
the LORD Almighty will shield[n] Jerusalem;
he will shield it and deliver[o] it,
he will 'pass over' it and will rescue it."

31:7
[p]Isa 2:20; 30:22

6 Return to him you have so greatly revolted against, O Israelites. 7 For in that day
every one of you will reject the idols of silver and gold[p] your sinful hands have made.

31:8
[q]Isa 10:12
[r]Isa 14:25; 37:7
[s]Ge 49:15

8 "Assyria[q] will fall by a sword that is not of man;
a sword, not of mortals, will devour[r] them.
They will flee before the sword
and their young men will be put to forced labour.[s]

31:9
[t]Dt 32:31, 37

9 Their stronghold[t] will fall because of terror;
at sight of the battle standard their commanders will panic,"
declares the LORD,

31:1 It was wrong for Judah to look to other nations for military help. (1) They were trusting in human beings instead of God. Judah sought protection from those who had far less power than God. Both Egypt and Judah would fall as a result of their arrogance. (2) They were serving their own interests instead of God's, and thus they did not even consult him. They violated God's stipulation in Deuteronomy 17:16. (3) They did not want to pay the price of looking to God and repenting of their sinful ways. When we have problems, it is good to seek help, but we must never bypass God or his previous directions to us.

31:7 Someday these people would throw their idols away, recognising that they are nothing but man-made objects. Idols such as money, fame, or success are seductive. Instead of contributing to our spiritual development, they rob us of our time, energy, and devotion that ought to be directed towards God. At first our idols seem exciting and promise to take us places, but in the end we will find that we have become their slaves. We need to recognise their worthlessness now, before they rob us of our freedom.

whose fire[u] is in Zion,
whose furnace is in Jerusalem.

The Kingdom of Righteousness

32 See, a king[a] will reign in righteousness
and rulers will rule with justice.[b]
2Each man will be like a shelter[c] from the wind
and a refuge from the storm,
like streams of water in the desert
and the shadow of a great rock in a thirsty land.

3Then the eyes of those who see will no longer be closed,[d]
and the ears of those who hear will listen.
4The mind of the rash will know and understand,[e]
and the stammering tongue will be fluent and clear.
5No longer will the fool[f] be called noble
nor the scoundrel be highly respected.
6For the fool speaks folly,[g]
his mind is busy with evil:
He practises ungodliness[h]
and spreads error[i] concerning the LORD;
the hungry he leaves empty[j]
and from the thirsty he withholds water.
7The scoundrel's methods are wicked,[k]
he makes up evil schemes[l]
to destroy the poor with lies,
even when the plea of the needy[m] is just.
8But the noble man makes noble plans,
and by noble deeds[n] he stands.

The Women of Jerusalem

9You women who are so complacent,
rise up and listen[o] to me;
you daughters who feel secure,[p]
hear what I have to say!
10In little more than a year
you who feel secure will tremble;
the grape harvest will fail,[q]
and the harvest of fruit will not come.
11Tremble, you complacent women;
shudder, you daughters who feel secure!
Strip off your clothes,[r]
put sackcloth round your waists.
12Beat your breasts[s] for the pleasant fields,
for the fruitful vines
13and for the land of my people,

31:9 [u]Isa 10:17
32:1 [a]Eze 37:24 [b]Ps 72:1-4; Isa 9:7
32:2 [c]Isa 4:6
32:3 [d]Isa 29:18
32:4 [e]Isa 29:24
32:5 [f]1Sa 25:25
32:6 [g]Pr 19:3 [h]Isa 9:17 [i]Isa 9:16 [j]Isa 3:15
32:7 [k]Jer 5:26-28 [l]Mic 7:3 [m]Isa 61:1
32:8 [n]Pr 11:25
32:9 [o]Isa 28:23 [p]Isa 47:8; Am 6:1; Zep 2:15
32:10 [q]Isa 5:5-6; 24:7
32:11 [r]Isa 47:2
32:12 [s]Na 2:7

32:1 Having suffered much injustice from evil rulers, many in Judah were hungry for a strong king who would rule with justice. This desire will be fulfilled when Christ reigns. Evil will be banished, and the King will reign in righteousness and rule with justice. In the immediate future, Judah would be destroyed and taken into captivity. But one day, God's Son, the King unlike any other king, will reign in righteousness.

32:5, 6 When the righteous King comes, people's motives will become transparent. Fools will not be regarded as noble. Those who have opposed God's standards of living will be unable to maintain their deception. In the blazing light of the holy Saviour, sin cannot disguise itself and appear good. Christ's revealing light shines into the darkest corners of our hearts, showing sin clearly for what it is. When King Jesus reigns in your heart, there is no place for sin, no matter how well hidden you may think it is.

32:9–13 The people turned their backs on God and concentrated on their own pleasures. This warning is not just to the women of Jerusalem (see 3:16–4:1), but to all who sit back in their thoughtless complacency, enjoying crops, clothes, land, and cities while an enemy approaches. Wealth and luxury bring false security, lulling us into thinking all is well when disaster is around the corner. By abandoning God's purpose for our lives, we also abandon his help.

32:13
[t]Isa 5:6
[u]Isa 22:2

32:14
[v]Isa 13:22
[w]Isa 6:11; 27:10
[x]Isa 34:13
[y]Ps 104:11

32:15
[z]Isa 11:2; Joel 2:28
[a]Ps 107:35; Isa 35:1-2
[b]Isa 29:17

32:17
[c]Ps 119:165; Ro 14:17; Jas 3:18
[d]Isa 30:15

32:18
[e]Hos 2:18-23

32:19
[f]Isa 28:17; 30:30
[g]Isa 10:19; Zec 11:2
[h]Isa 24:10; 27:10

32:20
[i]Ecc 11:1
[j]Isa 30:24

33:1
[a]Hab 2:8; Mt 7:2
[b]Isa 21:2

33:2
[c]Isa 40:10; 51:9; 59:16
[d]Isa 25:9

33:3
[e]Isa 59:16-18

33:5
[f]Ps 97:9
[g]Isa 28:6
[h]Isa 1:26

33:6
[i]Isa 51:6

a land overgrown with thorns and briers[t]—
yes, mourn for all houses of merriment
and for this city of revelry.[u]
14The fortress[v] will be abandoned,
the noisy city deserted;[w]
citadel and watchtower[x] will become a wasteland for ever,
the delight of donkeys,[y] a pasture for flocks,
15till the Spirit[z] is poured upon us from on high,
and the desert becomes a fertile field,[a]
and the fertile field seems like a forest.[b]
16Justice will dwell in the desert
and righteousness live in the fertile field.
17The fruit of righteousness will be peace;[c]
the effect of righteousness will be quietness and confidence[d]
for ever.
18My people will live in peaceful dwelling-places,
in secure homes,
in undisturbed places of rest.[e]
19Though hail[f] flattens the forest[g]
and the city is levelled[h] completely,
20how blessed you will be,
sowing[i] your seed by every stream,
and letting your cattle and donkeys range free.[j]

Distress and Help

33 Woe to you, O destroyer,
you who have not been destroyed!
Woe to you, O traitor,
you who have not been betrayed!
When you stop destroying,
you will be destroyed;[a]
when you stop betraying,
you will be betrayed.[b]

2O LORD, be gracious to us;
we long for you.
Be our strength[c] every morning,
our salvation[d] in time of distress.
3At the thunder of your voice, the peoples flee;
when you rise up,[e] the nations scatter.
4Your plunder, O nations, is harvested as by young locusts;
like a swarm of locusts men pounce on it.

5The LORD is exalted,[f] for he dwells on high;
he will fill Zion with justice[g] and righteousness.[h]
6He will be the sure foundation for your times,
a rich store of salvation[i] and wisdom and knowledge;

32:15–17 God acts from above to change man's condition here on earth. Only when God's Spirit is among us can we achieve true peace and fruitfulness (Ezekiel 36:22–38; Galatians 5:22, 23). This will happen in the end times. We can also have God's Spirit with us now, for he is available to all believers through Christ (John 15:26). But the outpouring mentioned here happens when the worldwide kingdom of God is established for all eternity (see Joel 2:28, 29).

33:1 The "destroyer" is Assyria. Assyria continually broke its promises, but demanded that others keep theirs. It is easy to put ourselves in the same selfish position, demanding our rights while ignoring the rights of others. Broken promises shatter trust and destroy relationships. Determine to keep your promises; at the same time, ask forgiveness for past promises you have broken. Treat others with the same fairness that you demand for yourself.

33:2 These are the words of the righteous remnant who were waiting for God to deliver them from their oppression.

33:4 See 2 Kings 19:20–37 and Isaiah 37:21–38 for a description of the victory over Assyria described here.

33:5 When Christ's kingdom is established, Zion—Jerusalem—will be the home of justice and righteousness because the Messiah will reign there. As a light to the world, the new Jerusalem will be the Holy City (Revelation 21:2).

the fear[j] of the LORD is the key to this treasure.[a]

7Look, their brave men cry aloud in the streets;
the envoys[k] of peace weep bitterly.
8The highways are deserted,
no travellers are on the roads.[l]
The treaty is broken,
its witnesses[b] are despised,
no-one is respected.
9The land mourns[c][m] and wastes away,
Lebanon[n] is ashamed and withers;[o]
Sharon is like the Arabah,
and Bashan and Carmel drop their leaves.

10"Now will I arise,[p]" says the LORD.
"Now will I be exalted;
now will I be lifted up.
11You conceive[q] chaff,
you give birth[r] to straw;
your breath is a fire[s] that consumes you.
12The peoples will be burned as if to lime;
like cut thornbushes they will be set ablaze.[t]"

13You who are far away,[u] hear[v] what I have done;
you who are near, acknowledge my power!
14The sinners in Zion are terrified;
trembling[w] grips the godless:
"Who of us can dwell with the consuming fire?[x]
Who of us can dwell with everlasting burning?"
15He who walks righteously[y]
and speaks what is right,[z]
who rejects gain from extortion
and keeps his hand from accepting bribes,
who stops his ears against plots of murder
and shuts his eyes[a] against contemplating evil—
16this is the man who will dwell on the heights,
whose refuge[b] will be the mountain fortress.[c]
His bread will be supplied,
and water will not fail[d] him.

17Your eyes will see the king[e] in his beauty
and view a land that stretches afar.[f]
18In your thoughts you will ponder the former terror:[g]
"Where is that chief officer?
Where is the one who took the revenue?
Where is the officer in charge of the towers?"
19You will see those arrogant people no more,
those people of an obscure speech,
with their strange, incomprehensible tongue.[h]

20Look upon Zion, the city of our festivals;

[a] 6 Or *is a treasure from him* [b] 8 Dead Sea Scrolls; Masoretic Text / *the cities* [c] 9 Or *dries up*

33:6 [j] Isa 11:2-3; Mt 6:33
33:7 [k] 2Ki 18:37
33:8 [l] Jdg 5:6; Isa 35:8
33:9 [m] Isa 3:26 [n] Isa 2:13; 35:2 [o] Isa 24:4
33:10 [p] Ps 12:5; Isa 2:21
33:11 [q] Ps 7:14; Isa 59:4; Jas 1:15 [r] Isa 26:18 [s] Isa 1:31
33:12 [t] Isa 10:17
33:13 [u] Ps 48:10; 49:1 [v] Isa 49:1
33:14 [w] Isa 32:11 [x] Isa 30:30; Heb 12:29
33:15 [y] Isa 58:8 [z] Ps 15:2; 24:4 [a] Ps 119:37
33:16 [b] Isa 25:4 [c] Isa 26:1 [d] Isa 49:10
33:17 [e] Isa 6:5 [f] Isa 26:15
33:18 [g] Isa 17:14
33:19 [h] Isa 28:11; Jer 5:15

33:8 The Assyrians broke their peace treaty (2 Kings 18:14–17).

33:9 These fruitful, productive areas would become deserts. Lebanon was known for its huge cedars. Sharon was very fertile. Bashan was very productive in grain and cattle. Carmel was thickly forested.

33:14–16 These sinners realised that they could not live in the presence of the holy God, for he is like a fire that consumes evil. Only those who walk righteously and speak what is right can live with God. Isaiah gives examples of how to demonstrate our righteousness and uprightness: we can reject gain from extortion and bribes, refuse to listen to plots of wrong actions, and shut our eyes to evil. If we are fair and honest in our relationships, we will dwell with God, and he will supply our needs.

33:20
[i] Isa 32:18
[j] Ps 46:5; 125:1-2

33:21
[k] Isa 41:18; 48:18; 66:12

33:22
[l] Isa 11:4
[m] Isa 2:3; Jas 4:12
[n] Ps 89:18
[o] Isa 25:9

33:23
[p] 2Ki 7:8
[q] 2Ki 7:16

33:24
[r] Isa 30:26
[s] Jer 50:20; 1Jn 1:7-9

34:1
[a] Isa 41:1; 43:9
[b] Ps 49:1
[c] Dt 32:1

34:2
[d] Isa 13:5
[e] Isa 30:25

34:3
[f] Joel 2:20; Am 4:10
[g] ver 7; Eze 14:19; 35:6; 38:22

34:4
[h] Isa 13:13; 2Pe 3:10
[i] Eze 32:7-8
[j] Joel 2:31; Mt 24:29*; Rev 6:13

34:5
[k] Dt 32:41-42; Jer 46:10; Eze 21:5
[l] Am 1:11-12
[m] Isa 24:6; Mal 1:4

34:7
[n] Ps 68:30

your eyes will see Jerusalem,
a peaceful abode,[i] a tent that will not be moved;[j]
its stakes will never be pulled up,
nor any of its ropes broken.
21 There the LORD will be our Mighty One.
It will be like a place of broad rivers and streams.[k]
No galley with oars will ride them,
no mighty ship will sail them.
22 For the LORD is our judge,[l]
the LORD is our lawgiver,[m]
the LORD is our king;[n]
it is he who will save[o] us.

23 Your rigging hangs loose:
The mast is not held secure,
the sail is not spread.
Then an abundance of spoils will be divided
and even the lame[p] will carry off plunder.[q]
24 No-one living in Zion will say, "I am ill";[r]
and the sins of those who dwell there will be forgiven.[s]

Judgment Against the Nations

34 Come near, you nations, and listen;
pay attention, you peoples![a]
Let the earth[b] hear, and all that is in it,
the world, and all that comes out of it![c]
2 The LORD is angry with all nations;
his wrath is upon all their armies.
He will totally destroy[a][d] them,
he will give them over to slaughter.[e]
3 Their slain will be thrown out,
their dead bodies will send up a stench;[f]
the mountains will be soaked with their blood.[g]
4 All the stars of the heavens will be dissolved[h]
and the sky rolled up[i] like a scroll;
all the starry host will fall[j]
like withered leaves from the vine,
like shrivelled figs from the fig-tree.

5 My sword[k] has drunk its fill in the heavens;
see, it descends in judgment on Edom,[l]
the people I have totally destroyed.[m]
6 The sword of the LORD is bathed in blood,
it is covered with fat—
the blood of lambs and goats,
fat from the kidneys of rams.
For the LORD has a sacrifice in Bozrah
and a great slaughter in Edom.
7 And the wild oxen will fall with them,
the bull calves and the great bulls.[n]
Their land will be drenched with blood,
and the dust will be soaked with fat.

a *2* The Hebrew term refers to the irrevocable giving over of things or persons to the LORD, often by totally destroying them; also in verse 5.

34:5 The Edomites shared a common ancestry with Israel. The Israelites were descended from Jacob; the Edomites from Jacob's twin brother, Esau. Edom was always Israel's bitter enemy. The destruction of Edom mentioned here is a picture of the ultimate end of all who oppose God and his people.

8For the LORD has a day of vengeance,[o]
a year of retribution, to uphold Zion's cause.
9Edom's streams will be turned into pitch,
her dust into burning sulphur;
her land will become blazing pitch!
10It will not be quenched night and day;
its smoke will rise for ever.[p]
From generation to generation it will lie desolate;[q]
no-one will ever pass through it again.
11The desert owl[b][r] and screech owl[b] will possess it;
the great owl[b] and the raven will nest there.
God will stretch out over Edom
the measuring line of chaos
and the plumb-line[s] of desolation.
12Her nobles will have nothing there to be called a kingdom,
all her princes[t] will vanish[u] away.
13Thorns will overrun her citadels,
nettles and brambles her strongholds.[v]
She will become a haunt for jackals,[w]
a home for owls.
14Desert creatures will meet with hyenas,[x]
and wild goats will bleat to each other;
there the night creatures will also repose
and find for themselves places of rest.
15The owl will nest there and lay eggs,
she will hatch them, and care for her young under the shadow of her wings;
there also the falcons[y] will gather,
each with its mate.

16Look in the scroll[z] of the LORD and read:

None of these will be missing,
not one will lack her mate.
For it is his mouth[a] that has given the order,
and his Spirit will gather them together.
17He allots their portions;[b]
his hand distributes them by measure.
They will possess it for ever
and dwell there from generation to generation.[c]

Joy of the Redeemed

35 The desert[a] and the parched land will be glad;
the wilderness will rejoice and blossom.[b]
Like the crocus, 2it will burst into bloom;

b *11* The precise identification of these birds is uncertain.

34:8 [o]Isa 63:4
34:10 [p]Rev 14:10-11; 19:3 [q]Isa 13:20; 24:1; Eze 29:12; Mal 1:3
34:11 [r]Zep 2:14; Rev 18:2 [s]2Ki 21:13; La 2:8
34:12 [t]Jer 27:20; 39:6 [u]Isa 41:11-12
34:13 [v]Isa 13:22; 32:13 [w]Ps 44:19; Jer 9:11; 10:22
34:14 [x]Isa 13:22
34:15 [y]Dt 14:13
34:16 [z]Isa 30:8 [a]Isa 1:20; 58:14
34:17 [b]Isa 17:14; Jer 13:25 [c]ver 10
35:1 [a]Isa 27:10; 41:18-19 [b]Isa 51:3

34:16 Isaiah referred to the prophecies that God commanded him to write down as the "scroll of the LORD". Whoever lived to see the time of Edom's destruction would have only to look to these prophecies to find agreement between what happened and what was predicted. Prophecy predicts and history reveals what has been in God's mind for all time.

35:1ff In chapters 1–34, Isaiah has delivered a message of judgment on all nations, including Israel and Judah, for rejecting God. Although there have been glimpses of relief and restoration for the remnant of faithful believers, the climate of wrath, fury, judgment, and destruction has prevailed. Now Isaiah breaks through with a vision of beauty and encouragement. God is just as thorough in his mercy as he is severe in his judgment. God's complete moral perfection is revealed by his hatred of all sin, and this leads to judgment. This same moral perfection is revealed in his love for all he has created. This leads to mercy for those who have sinned but who have sincerely loved Jesus and put their trust in him.

35:1ff This chapter is a beautiful picture of the final kingdom in which God will establish his justice and destroy all evil. This is the world the redeemed can anticipate after the judgment when creation itself will rejoice in God. Chapter 34 spoke of great distress when God will judge all people for their actions. Chapter 35 pictures the days when life will be peaceful at last and everything will be made right. Carmel and Sharon were regions of thick vegetation and fertile soil. They were symbols of productivity and plenty.

it will rejoice greatly and shout for joy.[c]
The glory of Lebanon[d] will be given to it,
the splendour of Carmel[e] and Sharon;
they will see the glory of the LORD,
the splendour of our God.[f]

3 Strengthen the feeble hands,
steady the knees[g] that give way;
4 say to those with fearful hearts,
"Be strong, do not fear;
your God will come,
he will come with vengeance;[h]
with divine retribution
he will come to save you."

5 Then will the eyes of the blind be opened[i]
and the ears of the deaf[j] unstopped.
6 Then will the lame[k] leap like a deer,
and the mute tongue[l] shout for joy.
Water will gush forth in the wilderness
and streams[m] in the desert.
7 The burning sand will become a pool,
the thirsty ground bubbling springs.[n]
In the haunts where jackals[o] once lay,
grass and reeds and papyrus will grow.

8 And a highway[p] will be there;
it will be called the Way of Holiness.[q]
The unclean[r] will not journey on it;
it will be for those who walk in that Way;
wicked fools will not go about on it.[a]
9 No lion[s] will be there,
nor will any ferocious beast[t] get up on it;
they will not be found there.
But only the redeemed[u] will walk there,
10 and the ransomed of the LORD will return.
They will enter Zion with singing;
everlasting joy[v] will crown their heads.
Gladness and joy will overtake them,
and sorrow and sighing will flee away.[w]

5. Events during the reign of Hezekiah

Sennacherib Threatens Jerusalem

36 In the fourteenth year of King Hezekiah's reign, Sennacherib[a] king of Assyria
attacked all the fortified cities of Judah and captured them. 2 Then the king of
Assyria sent his field commander with a large army from Lachish to King Hezekiah
at Jerusalem. When the commander stopped at the aqueduct of the Upper Pool, on
the road to the Washerman's Field,[b] 3 Eliakim[c] son of Hilkiah the palace administrator, Shebna[d] the secretary, and Joah son of Asaph the recorder went out to him.
4 The field commander said to them, "Tell Hezekiah,

a 8 Or / *the simple will not stray from it*

35:2 [c] Isa 25:9; 55:12 [d] Isa 32:15 [e] SS 7:5 [f] Isa 25:9
35:3 [g] Job 4:4; Heb 12:12
35:4 [h] Isa 1:24; 34:8
35:5 [i] Mt 11:5; Jn 9:6-7 [j] Isa 29:18; 50:4
35:6 [k] Mt 15:30; Jn 5:8-9; Ac 3:8 [l] Isa 32:4; Mt 9:32-33; 12:22; Lk 11:14 [m] Isa 41:18; Jn 7:38
35:7 [n] Isa 49:10 [o] Isa 13:22
35:8 [p] Isa 11:16; 33:8; Mt 7:13-14 [q] Isa 4:3; 1Pe 1:15 [r] Isa 52:1
35:9 [s] Isa 30:6 [t] Isa 34:14 [u] Isa 51:11; 62:12; 63:4
35:10 [v] Isa 25:9 [w] Isa 30:19; 51:11; Rev 7:17; 21:4
36:1 [a] 2Ch 32:1
36:2 [b] Isa 7:3
36:3 [c] Isa 22:20-21 [d] 2Ki 18:18

35:8–10 This highway, the "Way of Holiness", is the way that righteous pilgrims will take from the desert of suffering to Zion (Jerusalem). It is found only by following God. Only the redeemed will travel God's highway; they will be protected from wicked travellers and harmful animals. God is preparing a way for his people to travel to his home, and he will walk with us. God never stops at simply pointing the way; he is always beside us as we go.

36:4–6 Chapter 19 describes Isaiah's prophecy of judgment upon Egypt, while chapters 30 and 31 pronounce woe on those from Judah who would ally themselves with Egypt in the face of Assyria's impending attack. Sennacherib of Assyria was taunting Judah for trusting in Egypt. Even the Assyrians knew that Egypt could not help Judah.

" 'This is what the great king, the king of Assyria, says: On what are you
basing this confidence of yours? 5You say you have strategy and military
strength—but you speak only empty words. On whom are you depending, that
you rebel[e] against me? 6Look now, you are depending on Egypt,[f] that splintered reed[g] of a staff, which pierces a man's hand and wounds him if he leans
on it! Such is Pharaoh king of Egypt to all who depend on him. 7And if you say
to me, "We are depending on the LORD our God"—isn't he the one whose high
places and altars Hezekiah removed,[h] saying to Judah and Jerusalem, "You must
worship before this altar"?[i]
8" 'Come now, make a bargain with my master, the king of Assyria: I will give
you two thousand horses—if you can put riders on them! 9How then can you
repulse one officer of the least of my master's officials, even though you are
depending on Egypt[j] for chariots and horsemen?[k] 10Furthermore, have I come
to attack and destroy this land without the LORD? The LORD himself told[l] me
to march against this country and destroy it.' "

11Then Eliakim, Shebna and Joah said to the field commander, "Please speak to
your servants in Aramaic,[m] since we understand it. Don't speak to us in Hebrew in
the hearing of the people on the wall."
12But the commander replied, "Was it only to your master and you that my master
sent me to say these things, and not to the men sitting on the wall—who, like you,
will have to eat their own filth and drink their own urine?"
13Then the commander stood and called out in Hebrew,[n] "Hear the words of the
great king, the king of Assyria! 14This is what the king says: Do not let Hezekiah
deceive you. He cannot deliver you! 15Do not let Hezekiah persuade you to trust in
the LORD when he says, 'The LORD will surely deliver us; this city will not be given
into the hand of the king of Assyria.'[o]
16"Do not listen to Hezekiah. This is what the king of Assyria says: Make peace
with me and come out to me. Then every one of you will eat from his own vine and
fig-tree[p] and drink water from his own cistern,[q] 17until I come and take you to a
land like your own—a land of corn and new wine, a land of bread and vineyards.
18"Do not let Hezekiah mislead you when he says, 'The LORD will deliver us.' Has
the god of any nation ever delivered his land from the hand of the king of Assyria?
19Where are the gods of Hamath and Arpad? Where are the gods of Sepharvaim? Have
they rescued Samaria from my hand? 20Who of all the gods[r] of these countries has
been able to save his land from me? How then can the LORD deliver Jerusalem from
my hand?"

36:5 [e] 2Ki 18:7
36:6 [f] Isa 30:2, 5 [g] Eze 29:6-7
36:7 [h] 2Ki 18:4 [i] Dt 12:2-5
36:9 [j] Isa 31:3 [k] Isa 30:2-5
36:10 [l] 1Ki 13:18
36:11 [m] Ezr 4:7
36:13 [n] 2Ch 32:18
36:15 [o] Isa 37:10
36:16 [p] 1Ki 4:25; Zec 3:10 [q] Pr 5:15
36:20 [r] 1Ki 20:23

36:5 Hezekiah put great trust in Pharaoh's promise to help Israel against the Assyrians, but promises are only as good as the credibility of the person making them. It was Pharaoh's word against God's. How quickly we organise our lives around human advice while we neglect God's eternal promises. When choosing between God's word and someone else's, whose will you believe?

36:7 The field commander from Assyria claimed that Hezekiah had insulted God by tearing down his altars and making the people worship only in Jerusalem. But Hezekiah's reform sought to eliminate idol worship (which occurred mainly on high hills) so that the people worshipped only the true God. Either the Assyrians didn't know about the religion of the true God, or they wanted to deceive the people into thinking they had angered a powerful god.

In the same way, Satan tries to confuse or deceive us. People don't necessarily need to be sinful to be ineffective for God; they need only be confused about what God wants. To avoid Satan's deceit, study God's word carefully and regularly. When you know what God says, you will not fall for Satan's lies.

36:10 Sennacherib continued his demoralisation campaign by sending the field commander to try to convince the people of Judah that God had turned against them. The Assyrians hoped to convince the people of Judah to surrender without fighting. But Isaiah had already said that the Assyrians *would not* destroy Jerusalem, so the people did not need to be afraid of them (10:24–27; 29:5–8).

36:11 Aramaic was an international language at this time. See also 22:15–25 for Isaiah's prophecies concerning Eliakim and Shebna.

36:17 Sennacherib's commander tried yet another ploy to demoralise the people. He appealed to the starving city under siege by offering to take them to a land with plenty of food if they surrendered. The Assyrian policy for dealing with conquered nations was to resettle the inhabitants and then to move other conquered peoples into the recently conquered area. This provided manpower for their armies and prevented revolts in conquered territories.

36:19, 20 The field commander said that the gods of the other cities he had conquered had not been able to save their people, so how could the God of Jerusalem save them? The Lord was supposedly the God of Samaria (the northern kingdom), and it fell. But the Lord was the God of Samaria in name only because the people were not worshipping him. That is why prophets foretold the fall of Samaria. But for the Lord's own sake and for the sake of David, the Lord would rescue them from the Assyrian army (37:35).

36:21 [s]Pr 9:7-8; 26:4

37:2 [a]Isa 1:1

37:3 [b]Isa 26:18; 66:9; Hos 13:13

37:4 [c]Isa 36:13, 18-20 [d]Isa 1:9

37:6 [e]Isa 7:4

37:7 [f]ver 9

37:8 [g]Nu 33:20

21 But the people remained silent and said nothing in reply, because the king had
commanded, "Do not answer him."[s]
22 Then Eliakim son of Hilkiah the palace administrator, Shebna the secretary, and
Joah son of Asaph the recorder went to Hezekiah, with their clothes torn, and told
him what the field commander had said.

Jerusalem's Deliverance Foretold

37 When King Hezekiah heard this, he tore his clothes and put on sackcloth and
went into the temple of the LORD. 2 He sent Eliakim the palace administrator,
Shebna the secretary, and the leading priests, all wearing sackcloth, to the prophet
Isaiah son of Amoz.[a] 3 They told him, "This is what Hezekiah says: This day is a
day of distress and rebuke and disgrace, as when children come to the point of birth[b]
and there is no strength to deliver them. 4 It may be that the LORD your God will hear
the words of the field commander, whom his master, the king of Assyria, has sent
to ridicule the living God, and that he will rebuke him for the words the LORD your
God has heard.[c] Therefore pray for the remnant[d] that still survives."
5 When King Hezekiah's officials came to Isaiah, 6 Isaiah said to them, "Tell your
master, 'This is what the LORD says: Do not be afraid[e] of what you have heard—those
words with which the underlings of the king of Assyria have blasphemed me. 7 Listen!
I am going to put a spirit in him so that when he hears a certain report,[f] he will return
to his own country, and there I will have him cut down with the sword.' "
8 When the field commander heard that the king of Assyria had left Lachish, he
withdrew and found the king fighting against Libnah.[g]

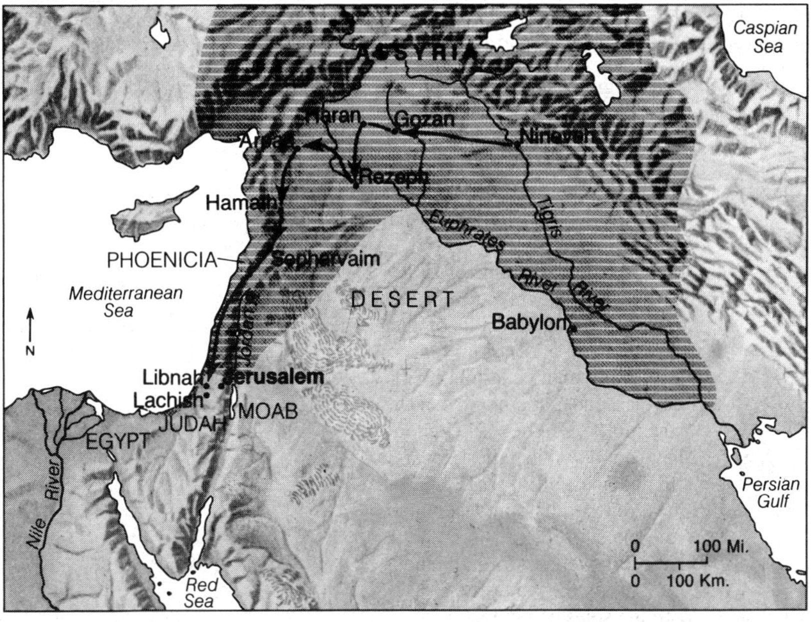

ASSYRIA ADVANCES As Sennacherib beautified his capital city, Nineveh, Hezekiah withheld tribute and prepared for battle. The Assyrians advanced towards their rebellious western border, attacking swiftly down the Mediterranean coast. From Lachish, Sennacherib threatened to take Jerusalem, but Isaiah knew his threats would die with him on his return to Nineveh.

37:3 Judah is compared to a woman who is trying to give birth to a child but is too weak to deliver. When the situation seemed hopeless, Hezekiah didn't give up. Instead, he asked the prophet Isaiah to pray that God would help his people. No matter how bad your circumstances seem, don't despair. Turn to God.

37:4 Hezekiah did exactly what Isaiah had been calling the people to do (chapters 1–35). He turned to God and watched him come to Judah's aid. Turning to God means believing that God is there and that he is able to help us.

37:8–10 Although the answer to Hezekiah's prayer was already in motion because Tirhakah was poised to attack, Hezekiah did not know it. He persisted in prayer and faith even though he could not see the answer coming. When we pray, we must have faith that God has already prepared the best answer. Our task is to ask in faith and wait in humility.

9Now Sennacherib received a report[h] that Tirhakah, the Cushite[a] king ⌞of Egypt⌟,
was marching out to fight against him. When he heard it, he sent messengers to
Hezekiah with this word: 10"Say to Hezekiah king of Judah: Do not let the god you
depend on deceive you when he says, 'Jerusalem will not be handed over to the king
of Assyria.'[i] 11Surely you have heard what the kings of Assyria have done to all the
countries, destroying them completely. And will you be delivered?[j] 12Did the gods
of the nations that were destroyed by my forefathers[k] deliver them—the gods of
Gozan, Haran,[l] Rezeph and the people of Eden who were in Tel Assar? 13Where
is the king of Hamath, the king of Arpad, the king of the city of Sepharvaim, or of
Hena or Ivvah?"

Hezekiah's Prayer

14Hezekiah received the letter from the messengers and read it. Then he went up
to the temple of the LORD and spread it out before the LORD. 15And Hezekiah prayed
to the LORD: 16"O LORD Almighty, God of Israel, enthroned between the cherubim,
you alone are God[m] over all the kingdoms of the earth. You have made heaven and
earth. 17Give ear, O LORD, and hear;[n] open your eyes, O LORD, and see;[o] listen to
all the words Sennacherib has sent to insult the living God.

18"It is true, O LORD, that the Assyrian kings have laid waste all these peoples and
their lands.[p] 19They have thrown their gods into the fire and destroyed them,[q] for
they were not gods[r] but only wood and stone, fashioned by human hands. 20Now,
O LORD our God, deliver us from his hand, so that all kingdoms on earth may know
that you alone, O LORD, are God."[b][s]

Sennacherib's Fall

21Then Isaiah son of Amoz[t] sent a message to Hezekiah: "This is what the LORD,
the God of Israel, says: Because you have prayed to me concerning Sennacherib king
of Assyria, 22this is the word the LORD has spoken against him:

"The Virgin Daughter of Zion
    despises and mocks you.
The Daughter of Jerusalem
    tosses her head[u] as you flee.
23Who is it you have insulted and blasphemed?[v]
    Against whom have you raised your voice
and lifted your eyes in pride?[w]
    Against the Holy One of Israel!
24By your messengers
    you have heaped insults on the Lord.
And you have said,
    'With my many chariots
I have ascended the heights of the mountains,
    the utmost heights of Lebanon.[x]
I have cut down its tallest cedars,
    the choicest of its pines.
I have reached its remotest heights,
    the finest of its forests.
25I have dug wells in foreign lands[c]
    and drunk the water there.
With the soles of my feet
    I have dried up all the streams of Egypt.[y]'

26"Have you not heard?

[a] *9* That is, from the upper Nile region [b] *20* Dead Sea Scrolls (see also 2 Kings 19:19); Masoretic Text *alone are the LORD* [c] *25* Dead Sea Scrolls (see also 2 Kings 19:24); Masoretic Text does not have *in foreign lands.*

37:9 [h]ver 7
37:10 [i]Isa 36:15
37:11 [j]Isa 36:18-20
37:12 [k]2Ki 18:11 [l]Ge 11:31; 12:1-4; Ac 7:2
37:16 [m]Dt 10:17; Ps 86:10; 136:2-3
37:17 [n]2Ch 6:40 [o]Da 9:18
37:18 [p]2Ki 15:29; Na 2:11-12
37:19 [q]Isa 26:14 [r]Isa 41:24, 29
37:20 [s]Ps 46:10
37:21 [t]ver 2
37:22 [u]Job 16:4
37:23 [v]ver 4 [w]Isa 2:11
37:24 [x]Isa 14:8
37:25 [y]Dt 11:10

37:16 Cherubim are mighty angels. God is "enthroned between the cherubim" refers to the atonement cover on the ark of the covenant in the Jerusalem temple. This is a description of God's holiness, power, and sovereignty.

37:26 [z]Ac 2:23; 4:27-28; 1Pe 2:8 [a]Isa 10:6; 25:1 [b]Isa 25:2

Long ago I ordained[z] it.
In days of old I planned[a] it;
now I have brought it to pass,
that you have turned fortified cities
into piles of stone.[b]

37:27 [c]Ps 129:6

27Their people, drained of power,
are dismayed and put to shame.
They are like plants in the field,
like tender green shoots,
like grass sprouting on the roof,[c]
scorched[d] before it grows up.

37:28 [d]Ps 139:1-3 [e]Ps 2:1

28"But I know where you stay
and when you come and go[d]
and how you rage[e] against me.
29Because you rage against me
and because your insolence[f] has reached my ears,

37:29 [f]Isa 10:12 [g]Isa 30:28; Eze 38:4 [h]ver 34

I will put my hook in your nose[g]
and my bit in your mouth,
and I will make you return
by the way you came.[h]

30"This will be the sign for you, O Hezekiah:

37:31 [i]Isa 27:6

"This year you will eat what grows by itself,
and the second year what springs from that.
But in the third year sow and reap,
plant vineyards and eat their fruit.
31Once more a remnant of the house of Judah
will take root below and bear fruit[i] above.

37:32 [j]Isa 9:7

32For out of Jerusalem will come a remnant,
and out of Mount Zion a band of survivors.
The zeal[j] of the LORD Almighty
will accomplish this.

37:34 [k]ver 29

33"Therefore this is what the LORD says concerning the king of Assyria:

"He will not enter this city
or shoot an arrow here.
He will not come before it with shield
or build a siege ramp against it.

37:35 [l]Isa 31:5; 38:6 [m]Isa 43:25; 48:9, 11 [n]2Ki 20:6

34By the way that he came he will return;[k]
he will not enter this city,"
declares the LORD.
35"I will defend[l] this city and save it,
for my sake[m] and for the sake of David[n] my servant!"

37:36 [o]Isa 10:12

36Then the angel of the LORD went out and put to death a hundred and eighty-five
thousand men in the Assyrian[o] camp. When the people got up the next morning—there were all the dead bodies! 37So Sennacherib king of Assyria broke camp
and withdrew. He returned to Nineveh[p] and stayed there.
38One day, while he was worshipping in the temple of his god Nisroch, his sons

37:37 [p]Ge 10:11

[d] *27* Some manuscripts of the Masoretic Text, Dead Sea Scrolls and some Septuagint manuscripts (see also 2 Kings 19:26); most manuscripts of the Masoretic Text *roof / and terraced fields*

37:29 This was a common torture the Assyrians used on their captives. They were often led away with hooks in their noses or bits in their mouths as signs of humiliation.

37:35 God would defend Jerusalem for the sake of his honour and for David's sake in remembrance of his promise to David. Assyria had insulted God. They would not be his instrument to punish Jerusalem. What Jerusalem could not possibly do, God would do for them. God is prepared to do the impossible if we trust him enough to ask.

37:38 The death of Sennacherib was prophesied by Isaiah in 10:12, 33, 34 and in 37:7. His death is also recorded in 2 Kings 19.

Adrammelech and Sharezer cut him down with the sword, and they escaped to the
land of Ararat.[q] And Esarhaddon his son succeeded him as king.

Hezekiah's Illness

38 In those days Hezekiah became ill and was at the point of death. The prophet
Isaiah son of Amoz[a] went to him and said, "This is what the LORD says: Put
your house in order,[b] because you are going to die; you will not recover."
2Hezekiah turned his face to the wall and prayed to the LORD, 3"Remember,
O LORD, how I have walked[c] before you faithfully and with wholehearted devotion[d]
and have done what is good in your eyes.[e]" And Hezekiah wept[f] bitterly.
4Then the word of the LORD came to Isaiah: 5"Go and tell Hezekiah, 'This is what
the LORD, the God of your father David, says: I have heard your prayer and seen your
tears; I will add fifteen years[g] to your life. 6And I will deliver you and this city from
the hand of the king of Assyria. I will defend[h] this city.
7" 'This is the LORD's sign[i] to you that the LORD will do what he has promised:
8I will make the shadow cast by the sun go back the ten steps it has gone down on
the stairway of Ahaz.' " So the sunlight went back the ten steps it had gone down.[j]

9A writing of Hezekiah king of Judah after his illness and recovery:

10I said, "In the prime of my life[k]
must I go through the gates of death[a][l]
and be robbed of the rest of my years?[m]"
11I said, "I will not again see the LORD,
the LORD, in the land of the living;[n]
no longer will I look on mankind,
or be with those who now dwell in this world.[b]
12Like a shepherd's tent[o] my house
has been pulled down[p] and taken from me.
Like a weaver I have rolled[q] up my life,
and he has cut me off from the loom;[r]
day and night[s] you made an end of me.
13I waited patiently till dawn,
but like a lion he broke[t] all my bones;[u]
day and night you made an end of me.
14I cried like a swift or thrush,
I moaned like a mourning dove.[v]
My eyes grew weak as I looked to the heavens.
I am troubled; O Lord, come to my aid!"[w]

15But what can I say?
He has spoken to me, and he himself has done this.[x]
I will walk humbly[y] all my years
because of this anguish of my soul.[z]
16Lord, by such things men live;
and my spirit finds life in them too.
You restored me to health

[a] 10 Hebrew *Sheol* [b] 11 A few Hebrew manuscripts; most Hebrew manuscripts *in the place of cessation*

37:38 [q]Ge 8:4; Jer 51:27
38:1 [a]Isa 37:2 [b]2Sa 17:23
38:3 [c]Ne 13:14; Ps 26:3 [d]1Ch 29:19 [e]Dt 6:18 [f]Ps 6:8
38:5 [g]2Ki 18:2
38:6 [h]Isa 31:5; 37:35
38:7 [i]Isa 7:11, 14
38:8 [j]Jos 10:13
38:10 [k]Ps 102:24 [l]Ps 107:18; 2Co 1:9 [m]Job 17:11
38:11 [n]Ps 27:13; 116:9
38:12 [o]2Co 5:1, 4; 2Pe 1:13-14 [p]Job 4:21 [q]Heb 1:12 [r]Job 7:6 [s]Ps 73:14
38:13 [t]Ps 51:8 [u]Job 10:16; Da 6:24
38:14 [v]Isa 59:11 [w]Job 17:3
38:15 [x]Ps 39:9 [y]1Ki 21:27 [z]Job 7:11

38:1ff The events of chapters 38 and 39 happened before those of chapters 36 and 37.

38:1–5 When Isaiah went to Hezekiah, who was extremely ill, and told him of his impending death, Hezekiah immediately turned to God. God responded to his prayer, allowing Hezekiah to live another 15 years. In response to fervent prayer, God may change the course of our lives too. Never hesitate to ask God for radical changes if you will honour him with those changes.

38:1–6 According to 2 Chronicles 32:24–26, Hezekiah had a problem with pride even after this double miracle of healing and deliverance. Eventually he and his subjects humbled themselves, so God's judgment was put off for several more generations.

38:16–18 Hezekiah realised that his prayer brought deliverance and forgiveness. His words "the grave cannot praise you" may reveal that he was unaware of the blessedness of the future life for those who trust in God (57:1, 2), or he may have meant that dead bodies cannot praise God. In either case, Hezekiah knew that God had spared his life, so in his poem Hezekiah praises God. Hezekiah recognised the good that came from his bitter experience. The next time you have difficult struggles, pray for God's help to gain something beneficial from them.

38:16
[a]Ps 119:25

38:17
[b]Ps 30:3
[c]Jer 31:34
[d]Isa 43:25; Mic 7:19

38:18
[e]Ecc 9:10
[f]Ps 6:5; 88:10-11; 115:17
[g]Ps 30:9

38:19
[h]Dt 6:7; Ps 118:17; 119:175
[i]Dt 11:19

38:20
[j]Ps 68:25
[k]Ps 33:2
[l]Ps 116:2
[m]Ps 116:17-19

39:1
[a]2Ch 32:31

39:2
[b]2Ch 32:31
[c]2Ki 18:15

39:3
[d]Dt 28:49

39:6
[e]2Ki 24:13; Jer 20:5

39:7
[f]2Ki 24:15; Da 1:1-7

and let me live.[a]
17 Surely it was for my benefit
that I suffered such anguish.
In your love you kept me
from the pit[b] of destruction;
you have put all my sins[c]
behind your back.[d]
18 For the grave[c][e] cannot praise you,
death cannot sing your praise;[f]
those who go down to the pit[g]
cannot hope for your faithfulness.
19 The living, the living—they praise[h] you,
as I am doing today;
fathers tell their children[i]
about your faithfulness.

20 The LORD will save me,
and we will sing[j] with stringed instruments[k]
all the days of our lives[l]
in the temple[m] of the LORD.

21 Isaiah had said, "Prepare a poultice of figs and apply it to the boil, and he will recover."

22 Hezekiah had asked, "What will be the sign that I will go up to the temple of the LORD?"

Envoys From Babylon

39 At that time Merodach-Baladan son of Baladan king of Babylon[a] sent Hezekiah letters and a gift, because he had heard of his illness and recovery.
2 Hezekiah received the envoys[b] gladly and showed them what was in his storehouses—the silver, the gold,[c] the spices, the fine oil, his entire armoury and everything found among his treasures. There was nothing in his palace or in all his kingdom that Hezekiah did not show them.
3 Then Isaiah the prophet went to King Hezekiah and asked, "What did those men say, and where did they come from?"

"From a distant land,[d]" Hezekiah replied. "They came to me from Babylon."
4 The prophet asked, "What did they see in your palace?"

"They saw everything in my palace," Hezekiah said. "There is nothing among my treasures that I did not show them."
5 Then Isaiah said to Hezekiah, "Hear the word of the LORD Almighty:
6 The time will surely come when everything in your palace, and all that your fathers have stored up until this day, will be carried off to Babylon.[e] Nothing will be left, says the LORD.
7 And some of your descendants, your own flesh and blood who will be born to you, will be taken away, and they will become eunuchs in the palace of the king of Babylon.[f]"

[c] 18 Hebrew *Sheol*

38:19 Hezekiah spoke of the significance of passing the joy of the Lord from father to child, from generation to generation. The heritage of our faith has come to us because of faithful men and women who have carried God's message to us across the centuries. Do you share with your children or other young people the excitement of your relationship with God?

39:1ff Merodach-Baladan, a Babylonian prince, was planning a revolt against Assyria and was forming an alliance. He probably hoped to convince Hezekiah to join this alliance against Assyria. Hezekiah, feeling honoured by this attention and perhaps feeling some sympathy for their proposal, showed the Babylonian envoys his treasures. But Isaiah warned the king not to trust Babylon. Someday they would turn on Judah and devour Jerusalem's wealth.

39:4–7 What was so wrong about showing these Babylonians around? Hezekiah failed to see that the Babylonians would become his next threat, and that they, not the Assyrians, would conquer his city. When Isaiah told him that Babylon would someday carry it all away, this was an amazing prophecy because Babylon was struggling for independence under Assyria. Hezekiah's self-satisfied display of his earthly treasures brought its own consequences (2 Kings 25; Daniel 1:1, 2). His response (39:8) may seem a bit shortsighted, but he was simply expressing gratitude for the blessing from God that peace would reign during his lifetime and that God's judgment would not be more severe.

8“The word of the LORD you have spoken is good,” Hezekiah replied. For he thought, “There will be peace and security in my lifetime.[g]”

39:8 [g] 2Ch 32:26

B. WORDS OF COMFORT (40:1–66:24)

Isaiah now speaks of events that will occur after the captivity. This includes the decree by Cyrus to release the remnant captives and allow them to return to Jerusalem after he conquered Babylon. But Isaiah also foretells the coming of the suffering Servant, Jesus Christ, and describes his life and death with incredible detail. Isaiah also speaks about the coming of the new heavens and earth, when God's people will be completely restored. Because all believers will participate in this new world to come, we can have confident hope in the future.

1. Israel's release from captivity

Comfort for God's People

40 Comfort, comfort[a] my people,
says your God.
2Speak tenderly[b] to Jerusalem,
and proclaim to her
that her hard service has been completed,[c]
that her sin has been paid for,
that she has received from the LORD's hand
double[d] for all her sins.

3A voice of one calling:
“In the desert prepare
the way[e] for the LORD;[a]
make straight in the wilderness
a highway for our God.[b][f]
4Every valley shall be raised up,
every mountain and hill made low;
the rough ground shall become level,[g]
the rugged places a plain.
5And the glory of the LORD will be revealed,
and all mankind together will see it.[h]
For the mouth of the LORD has spoken.”[i]

6A voice says, “Cry out.”
And I said, “What shall I cry?”

a 3 Or *A voice of one calling in the desert: / “Prepare the way for the LORD* b 3 Hebrew; Septuagint *make straight the paths of our God*

40:1 [a] Isa 12:1; 49:13; 51:3, 12; 52:9; 61:2; 66:13; Jer 31:13; Zep 3:14-17; 2Co 1:3

40:2 [b] Isa 35:4 [c] Isa 41:11-13; 49:25 [d] Isa 61:7; Jer 16:18; Zec 9:12; Rev 18:6

40:3 [e] Mal 3:1 [f] Mt 3:3*; Mk 1:3*; Jn 1:23*

40:4 [g] Isa 45:2, 13

40:5 [h] Isa 52:10; Lk 3:4-6* [i] Isa 1:20; 58:14

39:8 Hezekiah, one of Judah's most faithful kings, worked hard throughout his reign to stamp out idol worship and to purify the worship of the true God at the Jerusalem temple. Nevertheless, he knew his kingdom was not pure. Powerful undercurrents of evil invited destruction, and only God's miraculous interventions preserved Judah from its enemies. Here Hezekiah was grateful that God would preserve peace during his reign. As soon as Hezekiah died, the nation rushed back to its sinful ways under the leadership of Manasseh, Hezekiah's son. He actually rebuilt the centres of idolatry his father had destroyed.

40:1ff The book of Isaiah makes a dramatic shift at this point. The following chapters discuss the majesty of God, who is coming to rule the earth and judge all people. God will reunite Israel and Judah and restore them to glory. Instead of warning the people of impending judgment, Isaiah here comforts them. Chapter 40 refers to the restoration after the exile. Cyrus is the instrument of their deliverance from Babylon. Secondly, it looks to the end of time when “Babylon”—the future evil world system—will be destroyed and the persecution of God's people will end.

40:1, 2 Judah still had 100 years of trouble before Jerusalem would fall, then 70 years of exile. So God tells Isaiah to speak tenderly and to comfort Jerusalem.

The seeds of comfort may take root in the soil of adversity. When your life seems to be falling apart, ask God to comfort you. You may not escape adversity, but you may find God's comfort as you face it. Sometimes, however, the only comfort we have is in the knowledge that someday we will be with God. Appreciate the comfort and encouragement found in his word, his presence, and his people.

40:3–5 Preparing a straight highway means removing obstacles and rolling out the red carpet for the coming of the Lord. The desert is a picture of life's trials and sufferings. We are not immune to these, but our faith need not be hindered by them. Isaiah told people to prepare to see God work. John the Baptist used these words as he challenged the people to prepare for the coming Messiah (Matthew 3:3).

40:6–8 People are compared here to grass and flowers that wither away. We are mortal, but God's word is eternal and unfailing. Public opinion changes and is unreliable, but God's word is constant. Only in God's eternal word will we find lasting solutions to our problems and needs.

40:6 [j]Job 14:2
40:7 [k]Job 41:21
40:8 [l]Isa 55:11; 59:21 [m]Mt 5:18; 1Pe 1:24-25*
40:9 [n]Isa 52:7-10; 61:1; Ro 10:15 [o]Isa 25:9
40:10 [p]Rev 22:7 [q]Isa 59:16 [r]Isa 9:6-7 [s]Isa 62:11; Rev 22:12
40:11 [t]Eze 34:23; Mic 5:4; Jn 10:11
40:12 [u]Job 38:10 [v]Pr 30:4 [w]Heb 1:10-12
40:13 [x]Ro 11:34*; 1Co 2:16*
40:14 [y]Job 21:22; Col 2:3
40:16 [z]Ps 50:9-11; Mic 6:7; Heb 10:5-9
40:17 [a]Isa 30:28 [b]Isa 29:7 [c]Da 4:35
40:18 [d]Ex 8:10; 1Sa 2:2; Isa 46:5 [e]Ac 17:29
40:19 [f]Ps 115:4

"All men are like grass,[j]
and all their glory is like the flowers of the field.
7The grass withers and the flowers fall,
because the breath[k] of the LORD blows on them.
Surely the people are grass.
8The grass withers and the flowers fall,
but the word[l] of our God stands for ever.[m]"

9You who bring good tidings[n] to Zion,
go up on a high mountain.
You who bring good tidings to Jerusalem,[c]
lift up your voice with a shout,
lift it up, do not be afraid;
say to the towns of Judah,
"Here is your God!"[o]
10See, the Sovereign LORD comes[p] with power,
and his arm[q] rules[r] for him.
See, his reward[s] is with him,
and his recompense accompanies him.
11He tends his flock like a shepherd:[t]
He gathers the lambs in his arms
and carries them close to his heart;
he gently leads those that have young.

12Who has measured the waters[u] in the hollow of his hand,[v]
or with the breadth of his hand marked off the heavens?[w]
Who has held the dust of the earth in a basket,
or weighed the mountains on the scales
and the hills in a balance?
13Who has understood the mind[d] of the LORD,
or instructed him as his counsellor?[x]
14Whom did the LORD consult to enlighten him,
and who taught him the right way?
Who was it that taught him knowledge[y]
or showed him the path of understanding?

15Surely the nations are like a drop in a bucket;
they are regarded as dust on the scales;
he weighs the islands as though they were fine dust.
16Lebanon is not sufficient for altar fires,
nor its animals[z] enough for burnt offerings.
17Before him all the nations[a] are as nothing;[b]
they are regarded by him as worthless
and less than nothing.[c]

18To whom, then, will you compare God?[d]
What image[e] will you compare him to?
19As for an idol,[f] a craftsman casts it,

c *9* Or *O Zion, bringer of good tidings, / go up on a high mountain. / O Jerusalem, bringer of good tidings*
d *13* Or *Spirit*; or *spirit*

40:11 God is often pictured as a shepherd, gently caring for and guiding his flock. He is powerful (40:10), yet careful and gentle. He is called a shepherd (Psalm 23); the Good Shepherd (John 10:11, 14); the Great Shepherd (Hebrews 13:20); and the Chief Shepherd (1 Peter 5:4). Note that the shepherd is caring for the most defenceless members of his society: children and those caring for them. This reinforces the prophetic theme that the truly powerful nation is not the one with a strong military presence , but rather the one that relies on God's caring strength.

40:12–31 Isaiah describes God's power to create, his provision to sustain, and his presence to help. God is almighty and all-powerful; but even so, he cares for each of us personally. No person or thing can be compared to God (40:25). We describe God as best we can with our limited knowledge and language, but we only limit our understanding of him and his power when we compare him to what we experience on earth. What is your concept of God, especially as revealed in his Son, Jesus Christ? Don't limit his work in your life by underestimating him.

and a goldsmith[g] overlays it with gold[h]
and fashions silver chains for it.
20 A man too poor to present such an offering
selects wood that will not rot.
He looks for a skilled craftsman
to set up an idol that will not topple.[i]

21 Do you not know?
Have you not heard?
Has it not been told[j] you from the beginning?
Have you not understood[k] since the earth was founded?[l]
22 He sits enthroned above the circle of the earth,
and its people are like grasshoppers.[m]
He stretches out the heavens like a canopy,[n]
and spreads them out like a tent[o] to live in.
23 He brings princes[p] to naught
and reduces the rulers of this world to nothing.[q]
24 No sooner are they planted,
no sooner are they sown,
no sooner do they take root in the ground,
than he blows[r] on them and they wither,
and a whirlwind sweeps them away like chaff.

25 "To whom will you compare me?[s]
Or who is my equal?" says the Holy One.
26 Lift your eyes and look to the heavens:[t]
Who created[u] all these?
He who brings out the starry host[v] one by one,
and calls them each by name.
Because of his great power and mighty strength,
not one of them is missing.[w]

27 Why do you say, O Jacob,
and complain, O Israel,
"My way is hidden from the LORD;
my cause is disregarded by my God"?[x]
28 Do you not know?
Have you not heard?[y]
The LORD is the everlasting[z] God,
the Creator of the ends of the earth.
He will not grow tired or weary,
and his understanding no-one can fathom.[a]
29 He gives strength to the weary[b]
and increases the power of the weak.
30 Even youths grow tired and weary,
and young men[c] stumble and fall;
31 but those who hope[d] in the LORD
will renew their strength.[e]
They will soar on wings like eagles;[f]
they will run and not grow weary,
they will walk and not be faint.[g]

40:19 [g]Isa 41:7; Jer 10:3 [h]Isa 2:20
40:20 [i]1Sa 5:3
40:21 [j]Ps 19:1; 50:6; Ac 14:17 [k]Ro 1:19 [l]Isa 48:13; 51:13
40:22 [m]Nu 13:33; Ps 104:2; Isa 42:5 [n]Job 22:14 [o]Job 36:29
40:23 [p]Isa 34:12 [q]Job 12:21; Ps 107:40
40:24 [r]Isa 41:16
40:25 [s]ver 18
40:26 [t]Isa 51:6 [u]Ps 89:11-13; Isa 42:5 [v]Ps 147:4 [w]Isa 34:16
40:27 [x]Job 27:2; Lk 18:7-8
40:28 [y]ver 21 [z]Ps 90:2 [a]Ps 147:5; Ro 11:33
40:29 [b]Isa 50:4; Jer 31:25
40:30 [c]Isa 9:17; Jer 6:11; 9:21
40:31 [d]Lk 18:1 [e]2Co 4:16 [f]Ex 19:4; Ps 103:5 [g]2Co 4:1; Heb 12:1-3

40:29–31 Even the strongest people get tired at times, but God's power and strength never diminish. He is never too tired or too busy to help and listen. His strength is our source of strength. When you feel all of life crushing you and cannot go another step, remember that you can call upon God to renew your strength.

40:31 Hoping in the Lord is expecting that his promise of strength will help us to rise above life's distractions and difficulties. It also means trusting in God. Trusting helps us to be prepared when he speaks to us. Then we will be patient when he asks us to wait and expect him to fulfil the promises found in his word.

41:1
[a]Hab 2:20; Zec 2:13
[b]Isa 11:11
[c]Isa 48:16
[d]Isa 1:18; 34:1; 50:8

41:2
[e]Ezr 1:2
[f]ver 25; Isa 45:1, 13
[g]2Sa 22:43
[h]Isa 40:24

41:4
[i]ver 26; Isa 46:10
[j]Isa 44:6; 48:12; Rev 1:8, 17; 22:13

41:5
[k]Eze 26:17-18

41:7
[l]Isa 40:19

41:8
[m]Isa 29:22; 51:2; 63:16
[n]2Ch 20:7; Jas 2:23

41:9
[o]Isa 11:12
[p]Dt 7:6

41:10
[q]Jos 1:9; Isa 43:2, 5; Ro 8:31
[r]ver 13-14; Isa 44:2; 49:8

41:11
[s]Isa 17:12
[t]Isa 45:24
[u]Ex 23:22
[v]Isa 29:8

The Helper of Israel

41 "Be silent[a] before me, you islands![b]
Let the nations renew their strength!
Let them come forward[c] and speak;
let us meet together[d] at the place of judgment.

2"Who has stirred[e] up one from the east,[f]
calling him in righteousness to his service?[a]
He hands nations over to him
and subdues kings before him.
He turns them to dust[g] with his sword,
to wind-blown chaff[h] with his bow.
3He pursues them and moves on unscathed,
by a path his feet have not travelled before.
4Who has done this and carried it through,
calling forth the generations from the beginning?[i]
I, the LORD—with the first of them
and with the last[j]—I am he."

5The islands[k] have seen it and fear;
the ends of the earth tremble.
They approach and come forward;
6 each helps the other
and says to his brother, "Be strong!"
7The craftsman encourages the goldsmith,[l]
and he who smooths with the hammer
spurs on him who strikes the anvil.
He says of the welding, "It is good."
He nails down the idol so that it will not topple.

8"But you, O Israel, my servant,
Jacob, whom I have chosen,
you descendants of Abraham[m] my friend,[n]
9I took you from the ends of the earth,[o]
from its farthest corners I called you.
I said, 'You are my servant';
I have chosen[p] you and have not rejected you.
10So do not fear, for I am with you;[q]
do not be dismayed, for I am your God.
I will strengthen you and help[r] you;
I will uphold you with my righteous right hand.

11"All who rage[s] against you
will surely be ashamed and disgraced;[t]
those who oppose[u] you
will be as nothing and perish.[v]

[a] 2 Or *whom victory meets at every step*

41:1ff The "one from the east" is Cyrus II of Persia, who would be king within a century and a half (he is also mentioned by name in 44:28). He conquered Babylon in 539 B.C. and was responsible for the decree releasing the exiled Jews to return to Jerusalem. God could even use a pagan ruler to protect and care for Israel, because God is in control of all world empires and politics.

41:4 Each generation gets caught up in its own problems, but God's plan embraces all generations. When your great-grandparents lived, God worked personally in the lives of his people. When your great-grandchildren live, God will still work personally in the lives of his people. He is the only one who sees 100 years from now as clearly as 100 years ago. When you are concerned about the future, talk with God, who knows the generations of the future as well as he knows the generations of the past.

41:8–10 God chose Israel through Abraham because he wanted to, not because the people deserved it (Deuteronomy 7:6–8; 9:4–6). Although God chose the Israelites to represent him to the world, they failed to do this; so God punished them and sent them into captivity. Now all believers are God's chosen people, and all share the responsibility of representing him to the world. One day God will bring all his faithful people together. We need not fear because (1) God is with us ("I am with you"), (2) God has established a relationship with us ("I am your God"), and (3) God gives us assurance of his strength, help, and victory over sin and death. Have you realised all the ways God has helped you?

12Though you search for your enemies,
you will not find them.[w]
Those who wage war against you
will be as nothing[x] at all.
13For I am the LORD, your God,
who takes hold of your right hand[y]
and says to you, Do not fear;
I will help[z] you.
14Do not be afraid, O worm Jacob,
O little Israel,
for I myself will help you," declares the LORD,
your Redeemer, the Holy One of Israel.
15"See, I will make you into a threshing-sledge,[a]
new and sharp, with many teeth.
You will thresh the mountains and crush them,
and reduce the hills to chaff.
16You will winnow[b] them, the wind will pick them up,
and a gale will blow them away.
But you will rejoice in the LORD
and glory[c] in the Holy One of Israel.

17"The poor and needy search for water,[d]
but there is none;
their tongues are parched with thirst.
But I the LORD will answer[e] them;
I, the God of Israel, will not forsake them.
18I will make rivers flow[f] on barren heights,
and springs within the valleys.
I will turn the desert[g] into pools of water,
and the parched ground into springs.[h]
19I will put in the desert
the cedar and the acacia, the myrtle and the olive.
I will set pines in the wasteland,
the fir and the cypress together,[i]
20so that people may see and know,
may consider and understand,
that the hand of the LORD has done this,
that the Holy One of Israel has created[j] it.

21"Present your case," says the LORD.
"Set forth your arguments," says Jacob's King.[k]
22"Bring in ⌞your idols⌟ to tell us
what is going to happen.[l]
Tell us what the former things were,
so that we may consider them
and know their final outcome.
Or declare to us the things to come,[m]
23 tell us what the future holds,
so that we may know[n] you are gods.
Do something, whether good or bad,[o]
so that we will be dismayed and filled with fear.
24But you are less than nothing[p]

41:12 [w]Ps 37:35-36 [x]Isa 17:14
41:13 [y]Isa 42:6; 45:1 [z]ver 10
41:15 [a]Mic 4:13
41:16 [b]Jer 51:2 [c]Isa 45:25
41:17 [d]Isa 43:20 [e]Isa 30:19
41:18 [f]Isa 30:25 [g]Isa 43:19 [h]Isa 35:7
41:19 [i]Isa 60:13
41:20 [j]Job 12:9
41:21 [k]Isa 43:15
41:22 [l]Isa 43:9; 45:21 [m]Isa 46:10
41:23 [n]Isa 42:9; 44:7-8; 45:3 [o]Jer 10:5
41:24 [p]Isa 37:19; 44:9; 1Co 8:4

41:21–24 Israel was surrounded by many nations whose gods supposedly had special powers, such as raising crops and providing victories in war. These gods, however, failed to deliver. A god with limited or no power at all is not really a god. When we are tempted to put our trust in something other than the living God—money, career, family, or even military power—we should stop and ask some serious questions. Will it come through? Will it unfailingly provide what I am looking for? God delivers. When he makes a promise, he keeps it. He is the only completely trustworthy God.

41:24 [q]Ps 115:8
41:25 [r]ver 2 [s]2Sa 22:43
41:26 [t]Hab 2:18-19
41:27 [u]Isa 48:3, 16 [v]Isa 40:9
41:28 [w]Isa 50:2; 59:16; 63:5 [x]Isa 40:13-14
41:29 [y]ver 24 [z]Jer 5:13
42:1 [a]Isa 43:10; Lk 9:35; 1Pe 2:4, 6 [b]Isa 11:2; Mt 3:16-17; Jn 3:34
42:3 [c]Ps 72:2
42:4 [d]Ge 49:10; Mt 12:18-21*

and your works are utterly worthless;
he who chooses you is detestable.[q]

25 "I have stirred up one from the north,[r] and he comes—
one from the rising sun who calls on my name.
He treads[s] on rulers as if they were mortar,
as if he were a potter treading the clay.
26 Who told of this from the beginning, so that we could know,
or beforehand, so that we could say, 'He was right'?
No-one told of this,
no-one foretold it,
no-one heard any words[t] from you.
27 I was the first to tell[u] Zion, 'Look, here they are!'
I gave to Jerusalem a messenger of good tidings.[v]
28 I look but there is no-one[w]—
no-one among them to give counsel,[x]
no-one to give answer when I ask them.
29 See, they are all false!
Their deeds amount to nothing;[y]
their images are but wind[z] and confusion.

The Servant of the LORD

42 "Here is my servant, whom I uphold,
my chosen one[a] in whom I delight;
I will put my Spirit[b] on him
and he will bring justice to the nations.
2 He will not shout or cry out,
or raise his voice in the streets.
3 A bruised reed he will not break,
and a smouldering wick he will not snuff out.
In faithfulness he will bring forth justice;[c]
4 he will not falter or be discouraged
till he establishes justice on earth.
In his law the islands will put their hope."[d]

5 This is what God the LORD says—
he who created the heavens and stretched them out,

THE SERVANT IN ISAIAH

The nation Israel is called the servant:	41:8 42:19 43:10 44:1, 2, 21 45:4 48:20
The Messiah is called the Servant:	42:1–17 49:3, 5–7 50:10 52:13 53:11

The nation was given a mission to serve God, to be custodian of his word, and to be a light to the Gentile nations. Because of sin and rebellion, they failed. God sent his Son, Christ, as Messiah to fulfil his mission on earth.

42:1–4 These verses are quoted in Matthew 12:18–21 with reference to Christ. The chosen servant reveals a character of gentleness, encouragement, justice, and truth. When you feel broken and bruised or burned out in your spiritual life, God won't step on you or toss you aside as useless, but will gently pick you up. God's loving attributes are desperately needed in the world today. Through God's Spirit, we can show such sensitivity to people around us, reflecting God's goodness and honesty to them.

42:1–9 Sometimes called the Servant Song, these verses are about the Servant-Messiah, not the servant Cyrus (described in chapter 41). Israel and the Messiah are both often called *servant.* Israel, as God's servant, was to help bring the world to a knowledge of God. The Messiah, Jesus, would fulfil this task and show God himself to the world.

who spread out the earth and all that comes out of it,[e]
who gives breath[f] to its people,
and life to those who walk on it:
6"I, the LORD, have called[g] you in righteousness;[h]
I will take hold of your hand.
I will keep[i] you and will make you
to be a covenant[j] for the people
and a light for the Gentiles,[k]
7to open eyes that are blind,[l]
to free[m] captives from prison[n]
and to release from the dungeon those who sit in darkness.

8"I am the LORD; that is my name![o]
I will not give my glory to another[p]
or my praise to idols.
9See, the former things have taken place,
and new things I declare;
before they spring into being
I announce them to you."

Song of Praise to the LORD

10Sing to the LORD a new song,[q]
his praise from the ends of the earth,[r]
you who go down to the sea, and all that is in it,[s]
you islands, and all who live in them.
11Let the desert[t] and its towns raise their voices;
let the settlements where Kedar[u] lives rejoice.
Let the people of Sela sing for joy;
let them shout from the mountaintops.[v]
12Let them give glory[w] to the LORD
and proclaim his praise in the islands.
13The LORD will march out like a mighty[x] man,
like a warrior he will stir up his zeal;[y]
with a shout[z] he will raise the battle cry
and will triumph over his enemies.[a]

14"For a long time I have kept silent,
I have been quiet and held myself back.
But now, like a woman in childbirth,
I cry out, I gasp and pant.
15I will lay waste[b] the mountains and hills
and dry up all their vegetation;
I will turn rivers into islands
and dry up[c] the pools.
16I will lead[d] the blind[e] by ways they have not known,
along unfamiliar paths I will guide them;
I will turn the darkness into light before them
and make the rough places smooth.[f]
These are the things I will do;
I will not forsake[g] them.

42:5 [e]Ps 24:2 [f]Ac 17:25
42:6 [g]Isa 43:1 [h]Jer 23:6 [i]Isa 26:3 [j]Isa 49:8 [k]Lk 2:32; Ac 13:47
42:7 [l]Isa 35:5 [m]Isa 49:9; 61:1 [n]Lk 4:19; 2Ti 2:26; Heb 2:14-15
42:8 [o]Ex 3:15 [p]Isa 48:11
42:10 [q]Ps 33:3; 40:3; 98:1 [r]Isa 49:6 [s]1Ch 16:32; Ps 96:11
42:11 [t]Isa 32:16 [u]Isa 60:7 [v]Isa 52:7; Na 1:15
42:12 [w]Isa 24:15
42:13 [x]Isa 9:6 [y]Isa 26:11 [z]Hos 11:10 [a]Isa 66:14
42:15 [b]Eze 38:20 [c]Isa 50:2; Na 1:4-6
42:16 [d]Lk 1:78-79 [e]Isa 32:3 [f]Lk 3:5 [g]Heb 13:5

42:6, 7 Part of Christ's mission on earth was to demonstrate God's righteousness and to be a light for the Gentiles (to all nations). Through Christ, all people have the opportunity to share in his mission. God calls us to be servants of his Son, demonstrating God's righteousness and bringing his light. What a rare privilege it is to help the Messiah fulfil his mission! But we must seek his righteousness (Matthew 6:33) before we demonstrate it to others, and let his light shine in us before we can be lights ourselves (Matthew 5:16; 2 Corinthians 4:6).

42:10 Look at all the Lord will do for us and through us (42:6–9)! Majestic works prompt majestic responses. Do you really appreciate the good that God does for you and through you? If so, let your praise to him reflect how you really feel.

42:17
[h]Ps 97:7; Isa 1:29; 44:11; 45:16

17 But those who trust in idols,
who say to images, 'You are our gods,'
will be turned back in utter shame.[h]

Israel Blind and Deaf

42:18
[i]Isa 35:5

18 "Hear, you deaf;[i]
look, you blind, and see!
19 Who is blind[j] but my servant,[k]
and deaf like the messenger[l] I send?
Who is blind like the one committed[m] to me,
blind like the servant of the LORD?

42:19
[j]Isa 43:8; Eze 12:2
[k]Isa 41:8-9
[l]Isa 44:26
[m]Isa 26:3

20 You have seen many things, but have paid no attention;
your ears are open, but you hear nothing."[n]

42:20
[n]Jer 6:10

21 It pleased the LORD
for the sake of his righteousness
to make his law[o] great and glorious.

42:21
[o]ver 4

22 But this is a people plundered and looted,
all of them trapped in pits[p]
or hidden away in prisons.[q]
They have become plunder,
with no-one to rescue them;
they have been made loot,
with no-one to say, "Send them back."

42:22
[p]Isa 24:18
[q]Isa 24:22

23 Which of you will listen to this
or pay close attention[r] in time to come?

42:23
[r]Isa 48:18

24 Who handed Jacob over to become loot,
and Israel to the plunderers?
Was it not the LORD,
against whom we have sinned?
For they would not follow[s] his ways;
they did not obey his law.

42:24
[s]Isa 30:15

25 So he poured out on them his burning anger,
the violence of war.
It enveloped them in flames,[t] yet they did not understand;
it consumed them, but they did not take it to heart.[u]

42:25
[t]2Ki 25:9
[u]Isa 29:13; 47:7; 57:1, 11; Hos 7:9

Israel's Only Saviour

43 But now, this is what the LORD says—
he who created you, O Jacob,
he who formed[a] you, O Israel:[b]
"Fear not, for I have redeemed[c] you;
I have summoned you by name;[d] you are mine.

43:1
[a]ver 7
[b]Ge 32:28; Isa 44:21
[c]Isa 44:2, 6
[d]Isa 42:6; 45:3-4

2 When you pass through the waters,[e]

43:2
[e]Isa 8:7

42:19, 20 How could Israel and Judah be God's servants and yet be so blind? How could they be so close to God and see so little? Jesus condemned the religious leaders of his day for the same disregard of God (John 9:39–41). Yet do we not fail in the same way? Sometimes partial blindness—seeing but not understanding, or knowing what is right but not doing it—can be worse than not seeing at all.

42:23 We may condemn our predecessors for their failures, but we are twice as guilty if we repeat the same mistakes that we recognise as failures. Often we are so ready to direct God's message at others that we can't see how it touches our own lives. Make sure you are willing to take your own advice as you teach or lead.

43:1ff Chapter 42 ends with God's sorrow over the spiritual decay of his people. In chapter 43, God says that despite the people's spiritual failure, he will show them mercy, bring them back from captivity, and restore them. He would give them an outpouring of love, not wrath. Then the world would know that God alone had done this.

43:1–4 God created Israel and made it special to him. God redeemed Israel and summoned them by name to be those who belong to him. God protected Israel in times of trouble. We are important to God, and he also summons us by name and gives us his name (43:7)! When we bear God's wonderful name, we must never do anything that would bring shame to it.

43:2 Going through rivers of difficulty will either cause you to drown or force you to grow stronger. If you go in your own strength, you are more likely to drown. If you invite the Lord to go with you, he will protect you.

I will be with you;[f]
and when you pass through the rivers,
they will not sweep over you.
When you walk through the fire,[g]
you will not be burned;
the flames will not set you ablaze.[h]
3For I am the LORD, your God,[i]
the Holy One of Israel, your Saviour;
I give Egypt for your ransom,
Cush[a][j] and Seba in your stead.[k]
4Since you are precious and honoured in my sight,
and because I love[l] you,
I will give men in exchange for you,
and people in exchange for your life.
5Do not be afraid,[m] for I am with you;[n]
I will bring your children[o] from the east
and gather you from the west.
6I will say to the north, 'Give them up!'
and to the south,[p] 'Do not hold them back.'
Bring my sons from afar
and my daughters[q] from the ends of the earth—
7everyone who is called by my name,[r]
whom I created for my glory,
whom I formed and made.[s]"

8Lead out those who have eyes but are blind,[t]
who have ears but are deaf.[u]
9All the nations gather together[v]
and the peoples assemble.
Which of them foretold[w] this
and proclaimed to us the former things?
Let them bring in their witnesses to prove they were right,
so that others may hear and say, "It is true."
10"You are my witnesses," declares the LORD,
"and my servant[x] whom I have chosen,
so that you may know and believe me
and understand that I am he.
Before me no god[y] was formed,
nor will there be one after me.
11I, even I, am the LORD,
and apart from me there is no saviour.[z]
12I have revealed and saved and proclaimed—
I, and not some foreign god[a] among you.
You are my witnesses,[b]" declares the LORD, "that I am God.
13 Yes, and from ancient days[c] I am he.
No-one can deliver out of my hand.
When I act, who can reverse it?"[d]

[a] *3* That is, the upper Nile region

43:2
[f]Dt 31:6, 8
[g]Isa 29:6; 30:27
[h]Ps 66:12; Da 3:25-27

43:3
[i]Ex 20:2
[j]Isa 20:3
[k]Pr 21:18

43:4
[l]Isa 63:9

43:5
[m]Isa 44:2
[n]Jer 30:10-11
[o]Isa 41:8

43:6
[p]Ps 107:3
[q]2Co 6:18

43:7
[r]Isa 56:5; 63:19; Jas 2:7
[s]ver 1, 21; Ps 100:3; Eph 2:10

43:8
[t]Isa 6:9-10
[u]Isa 42:20; Eze 12:2

43:9
[v]Isa 41:1
[w]Isa 41:26

43:10
[x]Isa 41:8-9
[y]Isa 44:6, 8

43:11
[z]Isa 45:21

43:12
[a]Dt 32:12; Ps 81:9
[b]Isa 44:8

43:13
[c]Ps 90:2
[d]Job 9:12; Isa 14:27

43:3 God gave other nations to Persia in exchange for returning the Jews to their homeland. Egypt, Cush, and parts of Arabia (Seba) had attacked Persia, and the Persians defeated them.

43:5, 6 Isaiah was speaking primarily of Israel's return from Babylon. But there is a broader meaning: all God's people will be regathered when Christ comes to rule in peace over the earth.

43:10, 11 Israel's task was to be a witness (44:8), telling the world who God is and what he has done. Believers today share the responsibility of being God's witnesses. Do people know what God is like through your words and example? They cannot see God directly, but they can see him reflected in you.

43:14
[e]Isa 13:14-15
[f]Isa 23:13

43:16
[g]Ps 77:19;
Isa 11:15; 51:10

43:17
[h]Ps 118:12;
Isa 1:31
[i]Ex 14:9

43:19
[j]2Co 5:17;
Rev 21:5
[k]Ex 17:6;
Nu 20:11

43:20
[l]Isa 13:22
[m]Isa 48:21

43:21
[n]Ps 102:18;
1Pe 2:9

43:22
[o]Isa 30:11

43:23
[p]Zec 7:5-6;
Mal 1:6-8
[q]Am 5:25
[r]Jer 7:22
[s]Ex 30:35;
Lev 2:1

43:24
[t]Ex 30:23
[u]Isa 1:14; 7:13
[v]Mal 2:17

43:25
[w]Ac 3:19
[x]Isa 37:35;
Eze 36:22
[y]Isa 38:17;
Jer 31:34

43:26
[z]Isa 1:18
[a]Isa 41:1; 50:8

God's Mercy and Israel's Unfaithfulness

14This is what the LORD says—
your Redeemer, the Holy One of Israel:
"For your sake I will send to Babylon
and bring down as fugitives[e] all the Babylonians,[b][f]
in the ships in which they took pride.
15I am the LORD, your Holy One,
Israel's Creator, your King."

16This is what the LORD says—
he who made a way through the sea,
a path through the mighty waters,[g]
17who drew out[h] the chariots and horses,
the army and reinforcements together,[i]
and they lay there, never to rise again,
extinguished, snuffed out like a wick:
18"Forget the former things;
do not dwell on the past.
19See, I am doing a new thing![j]
Now it springs up; do you not perceive it?
I am making a way in the desert[k]
and streams in the wasteland.
20The wild animals honour me,
the jackals[l] and the owls,
because I provide water[m] in the desert
and streams in the wasteland,
to give drink to my people, my chosen,
21 the people I formed for myself
that they may proclaim my praise.[n]

22"Yet you have not called upon me, O Jacob,
you have not wearied yourselves for me, O Israel.[o]
23You have not brought me sheep for burnt offerings,
nor honoured[p] me with your sacrifices.[q]
I have not burdened you with grain offerings
nor wearied you with demands[r] for incense.[s]
24You have not bought any fragrant calamus[t] for me,
or lavished on me the fat of your sacrifices.
But you have burdened me with your sins
and wearied[u] me with your offences.[v]

25"I, even I, am he who blots out
your transgressions,[w] for my own sake,[x]
and remembers your sins no more.[y]
26Review the past for me,
let us argue the matter together;[z]
state the case[a] for your innocence.
27Your first father sinned;

[b] *14* Or *Chaldeans*

43:15–21 This section pictures a new exodus for a people once again oppressed, as the Israelites had been as slaves in Egypt before the exodus. They would cry to God, and again he would hear and deliver them. A new exodus would take place through a new desert. The past miracles were nothing compared to what God would do for his people in the future.

43:22–24 Calamus may have been an ingredient in the incense used in worship. A sacrifice required both giving up a valuable animal and pleading with God for forgiveness. But the people presented God with sins instead of sacrifices. Can you imagine bringing the best of your sins to God's altar? This ironic picture shows the depths to which Israel had sunk. What do you present to God—your sins, or a plea for his forgiveness?

43:25 How tempting it is to remind someone of a past offence! But when God forgives our sins he totally forgets them. We never have to fear that he will remind us of them later. Because God forgives our sin, we need to forgive others.

your spokesmen[b] rebelled against me.
28So I will disgrace the dignitaries of your temple,
and I will consign Jacob to destruction[c]
and Israel to scorn.[c]

Israel the Chosen

44 "But now listen, O Jacob, my servant,[a]
Israel, whom I have chosen.
2This is what the LORD says—
he who made you, who formed you in the womb,
and who will help[b] you:
Do not be afraid, O Jacob, my servant,
Jeshurun,[c] whom I have chosen.
3For I will pour water[d] on the thirsty land,
and streams on the dry ground;
I will pour out my Spirit[e] on your offspring,
and my blessing on your descendants.[f]
4They will spring up like grass in a meadow,
like poplar trees[g] by flowing streams.[h]
5One will say, 'I belong to the LORD';
another will call himself by the name of Jacob;
still another will write on his hand,[i] 'The LORD's',[j]
and will take the name Israel.

The LORD, Not Idols

6"This is what the LORD says—
Israel's King[k] and Redeemer,[l] the LORD Almighty:
I am the first and I am the last;[m]
apart from me there is no God.
7Who then is like me? Let him proclaim it.
Let him declare and lay out before me
what has happened since I established my ancient people,
and what is yet to come—
yes, let him foretell[n] what will come.
8Do not tremble, do not be afraid.
Did I not proclaim this and foretell it long ago?
You are my witnesses. Is there any God[o] besides me?
No, there is no other Rock;[p] I know not one."

9All who make idols are nothing,
and the things they treasure are worthless.[q]
Those who would speak up for them are blind;
they are ignorant, to their own shame.
10Who shapes a god and casts an idol,
which can profit him nothing?[r]
11He and his kind will be put to shame;[s]
craftsmen are nothing but men.
Let them all come together and take their stand;
they will be brought down to terror and infamy.[t]

c *28* The Hebrew term refers to the irrevocable giving over of things or persons to the LORD, often by totally destroying them.

43:27 [b]Isa 9:15; 28:7; Jer 5:31
43:28 [c]Jer 24:9; Eze 5:15
44:1 [a]ver 21; Jer 30:10; 46:27-28
44:2 [b]Isa 41:10 [c]Dt 32:15
44:3 [d]Joel 3:18 [e]Joel 2:28; Ac 2:17 [f]Isa 61:9; 65:23
44:4 [g]Lev 23:40 [h]Job 40:22
44:5 [i]Ex 13:9 [j]Zec 8:20-22
44:6 [k]Isa 41:21 [l]Isa 43:1 [m]Isa 41:4; Rev 1:8, 17; 22:13
44:7 [n]Isa 41:22, 26
44:8 [o]Isa 43:10 [p]Dt 4:35; 1Sa 2:2
44:9 [q]Isa 41:24
44:10 [r]Isa 41:29; Jer 10:5; Ac 19:26
44:11 [s]Isa 1:29 [t]Isa 42:17

44:2 Jeshurun ("the upright one") is a poetic name for Israel (Deuteronomy 32:15; 33:5, 26).

44:5 The time will come when Israel will be proud of belonging to God. If we are truly God's, we should be unashamed and delighted to let everyone know about our relationship with him (44:8).

44:9–20 Here Isaiah describes how people make their own gods. How absurd to make a god from the same tree that gives firewood. Do we make our own gods—money, fame, or power? If we make a god of our own choosing, we deceive ourselves. We cannot expect it to empower our lives.

44:12 [u]Isa 40:19; 41:6-7 [v]Jer 10:3-5; Ac 17:29

44:13 [w]Isa 41:7 [x]Ps 115:4-7 [y]Jdg 17:4-5

44:15 [z]ver 19 [a]2Ch 25:14

44:17 [b]1Ki 18:26 [c]Isa 45:20

44:18 [d]Isa 1:3 [e]Isa 6:9-10

44:19 [f]Isa 5:13; 27:11; 45:20 [g]Dt 27:15

44:20 [h]Ps 102:9 [i]Job 15:31; Ro 1:21-23, 28; 2Th 2:11; 2Ti 3:13 [j]Isa 59:3, 4, 13; Ro 1:25

12 The blacksmith[u] takes a tool
and works with it in the coals;
he shapes an idol with hammers,
he forges it with the might of his arm.[v]
He gets hungry and loses his strength;
he drinks no water and grows faint.
13 The carpenter[w] measures with a line
and makes an outline with a marker;
he roughs it out with chisels
and marks it with compasses.
He shapes it in the form of man,[x]
of man in all his glory,
that it may dwell in a shrine.[y]
14 He cut down cedars,
or perhaps took a cypress or oak.
He let it grow among the trees of the forest,
or planted a pine, and the rain made it grow.
15 It is man's fuel[z] for burning;
some of it he takes and warms himself,
he kindles a fire and bakes bread.
But he also fashions a god and worships it;
he makes an idol and bows[a] down to it.
16 Half of the wood he burns in the fire;
over it he prepares his meal,
he roasts his meat and eats his fill.
He also warms himself and says,
"Ah! I am warm; I see the fire."
17 From the rest he makes a god, his idol;
he bows down to it and worships.
He prays[b] to it and says,
"Save[c] me; you are my god."
18 They know nothing, they understand[d] nothing;
their eyes[e] are plastered over so that they cannot see,
and their minds closed so that they cannot understand.
19 No-one stops to think,
no-one has the knowledge or understanding[f] to say,
"Half of it I used for fuel;
I even baked bread over its coals,
I roasted meat and I ate.
Shall I make a detestable[g] thing from what is left?
Shall I bow down to a block of wood?"
20 He feeds on ashes,[h] a deluded[i] heart misleads him;
he cannot save himself, or say,
"Is not this thing in my right hand a lie?[j]"

TODAY'S IDOLATRY

Isaiah tells us, "Who shapes a god and casts an idol, which can profit him nothing?" We think of idols as statues of wood or stone, but in reality an idol is anything natural that is given sacred value and power. If your answer to any of the following questions is anything or anyone other than God, you may need to consider who or what you are worshipping.

- Who created me?
- Whom do I ultimately trust?
- Whom do I look to for ultimate truth?
- Whom do I look to for security and happiness?
- Who is in charge of my future?

21"Remember[k] these things, O Jacob,
for you are my servant, O Israel.
I have made you, you are my servant;[l]
O Israel, I will not forget you.[m]
22I have swept away[n] your offences like a cloud,
your sins like the morning mist.
Return[o] to me,
for I have redeemed[p] you."

23Sing for joy,[q] O heavens, for the LORD has done this;
shout aloud, O earth[r] beneath.
Burst into song, you mountains,[s]
you forests and all your trees,
for the LORD has redeemed Jacob,
he displays his glory[t] in Israel.

Jerusalem to Be Inhabited

24"This is what the LORD says—
your Redeemer,[u] who formed you in the womb:

I am the LORD,
who has made all things,
who alone stretched out the heavens,[v]
who spread out the earth by myself,

25who foils[w] the signs of false prophets
and makes fools of diviners,[x]
who overthrows the learning of the wise[y]
and turns it into nonsense,[z]
26who carries out the words[a] of his servants
and fulfils[b] the predictions of his messengers,

who says of Jerusalem, 'It shall be inhabited,'
of the towns of Judah, 'They shall be built,'
and of their ruins, 'I will restore them,'[c]
27who says to the watery deep, 'Be dry,
and I will dry up your streams,'
28who says of Cyrus,[d] 'He is my shepherd
and will accomplish all that I please;
he will say of Jerusalem,[e] "Let it be rebuilt,"
and of the temple,[f] "Let its foundations be laid." '

45 "This is what the LORD says to his anointed,
to Cyrus, whose right hand I take hold[a] of
to subdue nations[b] before him

44:21 [k]Isa 46:8; Zec 10:9 [l]ver 1-2 [m]Isa 49:15
44:22 [n]Isa 43:25; Ac 3:19 [o]Isa 55:7 [p]1Co 6:20
44:23 [q]Isa 42:10 [r]Ps 148:7 [s]Ps 98:8 [t]Isa 61:3
44:24 [u]Isa 43:14 [v]Isa 42:5
44:25 [w]Ps 33:10 [x]Isa 47:13 [y]1Co 1:27 [z]2Sa 15:31; 1Co 1:19-20
44:26 [a]Zec 1:6 [b]Isa 55:11; Mt 5:18 [c]Isa 49:8-21
44:28 [d]2Ch 36:22 [e]Isa 14:32 [f]Ezr 1:2-4
45:1 [a]Ps 73:23; Isa 41:13; 42:6 [b]Jer 50:35

44:21 God said that we should serve our Creator (17:7; 40:28; 43:15; 45:9). Idolaters do the opposite—serving or worshipping what they have made rather than the One who made them. Our Creator paid the price to set us free from our sins against him. By contrast, no idol ever created anybody, and no idol can redeem us from our sins.

44:25, 26 False prophets were people who claimed to bring messages from the gods. Diviners were people who would fake omens for their own benefit. Because God is truth, he is the standard for all teachings. We can always trust his word as absolute truth. His word is completely accurate, and against it we can measure all other teachings. If you are unsure about a teaching, test it against God's word. God condemned the false prophets because they gave advice opposite to his.

44:28 Isaiah, who prophesied from about 740–681 B.C., called Cyrus by name almost 150 years before he ruled (559–530 B.C.)! Later historians said that Cyrus read this prophecy and was so moved that he carried it out. Isaiah also predicted that Jerusalem would fall more than 100 years before it happened (586 B.C.) and that the temple would be rebuilt about 200 years before it happened. It is clear these prophecies came from a God who knows the future.

45:1-8 This is the only place in the Bible where a Gentile ruler is said to be "anointed". God is the power over all powers, and he anoints whom he chooses for his special tasks. Cyrus' kingdom spread across 2,000 miles (the largest of any empire then known), including the territories of both the Assyrian and the Babylonian empires. Why did God anoint Cyrus? Because God had a special task for him to do for Israel. Cyrus would allow God's city, Jerusalem, to be rebuilt, and he would set the exiles free without ex-

and to strip kings of their armour,
to open doors before him
so that gates will not be shut:
2 I will go before you
and will level[c] the mountains;[a]
I will break down gates of bronze
and cut through bars of iron.[d]
3 I will give you the treasures[e] of darkness,
riches stored in secret places,[f]
so that you may know[g] that I am the LORD,
the God of Israel, who summons you by name.[h]
4 For the sake of Jacob my servant,[i]
of Israel my chosen,
I summon you by name
and bestow on you a title of honour,
though you do not acknowledge[j] me.
5 I am the LORD, and there is no other;[k]
apart from me there is no God.[l]
I will strengthen you,[m]
though you have not acknowledged me,
6 so that from the rising of the sun
to the place of its setting[n]
men may know there is none besides me.[o]
I am the LORD, and there is no other.
7 I form the light and create darkness,
I bring prosperity and create disaster;[p]
I, the LORD, do all these things.

8 "You heavens above, rain[q] down righteousness;[r]
let the clouds shower it down.
Let the earth open wide,
let salvation[s] spring up,
let righteousness grow with it;
I, the LORD, have created it.

9 "Woe to him who quarrels[t] with his Maker,
to him who is but a potsherd among the potsherds on the ground.
Does the clay say to the potter,[u]
'What are you making?'
Does your work say,
'He has no hands'?
10 Woe to him who says to his father,
'What have you begotten?'
or to his mother,
'What have you brought to birth?'

11 "This is what the LORD says—
the Holy One of Israel, and its Maker:
Concerning things to come,
do you question me about my children,

45:2 [c]Isa 40:4 [d]Ps 107:16; Jer 51:30
45:3 [e]Jer 50:37 [f]Jer 41:8 [g]Isa 41:23 [h]Ex 33:12; Isa 43:1
45:4 [i]Isa 41:8-9 [j]Ac 17:23
45:5 [k]Isa 44:8 [l]Ps 18:31 [m]Ps 18:39
45:6 [n]Isa 43:5; Mal 1:11 [o]ver 5, 18
45:7 [p]Isa 31:2; Am 3:6
45:8 [q]Ps 72:6; Joel 3:18 [r]Ps 85:11; Isa 60:21; 61:10, 11; Hos 10:12 [s]Isa 12:3
45:9 [t]Job 15:25 [u]Isa 29:16; Ro 9:20-21*

[a] *2* Dead Sea Scrolls and Septuagint; the meaning of the word in the Masoretic Text is uncertain.

---

pecting anything in return. Few kings of Israel or Judah had done as much for God's people as Cyrus would.

45:7 God is ruler over light and darkness, over prosperity and disaster. Our lives are sprinkled with both types of experiences, and both are needed for us to grow spiritually. When good times come, thank God and use your prosperity for him. When bad times come, don't resent them, but ask what you can learn from this refining experience to make you a better servant of God.

45:9 A potsherd is a broken piece of pottery, essentially worthless.

or give me orders about the work of my hands?[v]
12It is I who made the earth
and created mankind upon it.
My own hands stretched out the heavens;[w]
I marshalled their starry hosts.[x]
13I will raise up Cyrus[b][y] in my righteousness:
I will make all his ways straight.
He will rebuild my city
and set my exiles free,
but not for a price or reward,[z]
says the LORD Almighty."

14This is what the LORD says:

"The products of Egypt and the merchandise of Cush,[c]
and those tall Sabeans—
they will come over to you
and will be yours;
they will trudge behind you,
coming over to you in chains.[a]
They will bow down before you
and plead[b] with you, saying,
'Surely God is with you,[c] and there is no other;
there is no other god.' "

15Truly you are a God who hides[d] himself,
O God and Saviour of Israel.
16All the makers of idols will be put to shame and disgraced;[e]
they will go off into disgrace together.
17But Israel will be saved[f] by the LORD
with an everlasting salvation;[g]
you will never be put to shame or disgraced,
to ages everlasting.

18For this is what the LORD says—
he who created the heavens,
he is God;
he who fashioned and made the earth,
he founded it;
he did not create it to be empty,[h]
but formed it to be inhabited[i]—
he says:
"I am the LORD,
and there is no other.[j]
19I have not spoken in secret,[k]
from somewhere in a land of darkness;
I have not said to Jacob's descendants,[l]
'Seek me in vain.'
I, the LORD, speak the truth;
I declare what is right.[m]

20"Gather together[n] and come;
assemble, you fugitives from the nations.

45:11 [v]Isa 19:25
45:12 [w]Ge 2:1; Isa 42:5 [x]Ne 9:6
45:13 [y]2Ch 36:22; Isa 41:2 [z]Isa 52:3
45:14 [a]Isa 14:1-2 [b]Jer 16:19; Zec 8:20-23 [c]1Co 14:25
45:15 [d]Ps 44:24
45:16 [e]Isa 44:9, 11
45:17 [f]Ro 11:26 [g]Isa 26:4
45:18 [h]Ge 1:2 [i]Ge 1:26; Isa 42:5 [j]ver 5
45:19 [k]Isa 48:16 [l]Isa 41:8 [m]Dt 30:11
45:20 [n]Isa 43:9

b *13* Hebrew *him* c *14* That is, the upper Nile region

45:14 The Sabeans were people from Seba in southern Arabia.

45:17 Until this time, Israel had anticipated temporal salvation—God would save them from their enemies. Here Isaiah tells of everlasting salvation with God.

45:18, 19 God's promises are public, and their fulfilment is sure. So why do we ever doubt him? We never have to be uncertain when we have a God of truth and righteousness.

45:20 [o] Isa 44:19 [p] Isa 46:1; Jer 10:5 [q] Isa 44:17; 46:6-7
45:21 [r] Isa 41:22 [s] ver 5
45:22 [t] Zec 12:10 [u] Nu 21:8-9; 2Ch 20:12 [v] Isa 49:6, 12
45:23 [w] Ge 22:16 [x] Heb 6:13 [y] Isa 55:11 [z] Ps 63:11; Isa 19:18; Ro 14:11*; Php 2:10-11
45:24 [a] Jer 33:16 [b] Isa 41:11
45:25 [c] Isa 41:16
46:1 [a] Isa 21:9; Jer 50:2; 51:44 [b] Isa 45:20

Ignorant[o] are those who carry[p] about idols of wood,
who pray to gods that cannot save.[q]
21 Declare what is to be, present it—
let them take counsel together.
Who foretold[r] this long ago,
who declared it from the distant past?
Was it not I, the LORD?
And there is no God apart from me,[s]
a righteous God and a Saviour;
there is none but me.

22 "Turn[t] to me and be saved,[u]
all you ends of the earth;[v]
for I am God, and there is no other.
23 By myself I have sworn,[w]
my mouth has uttered in all integrity[x]
a word that will not be revoked:[y]
Before me every knee will bow;
by me every tongue will swear.[z]
24 They will say of me, 'In the LORD alone
are righteousness[a] and strength.' "
All who have raged against him
will come to him and be put to shame.[b]
25 But in the LORD all the descendants of Israel
will be found righteous and will exult.[c]

Gods of Babylon

46 Bel[a] bows down, Nebo stoops low;
their idols are borne by beasts of burden.[a]
The images that are carried[b] about are burdensome,
a burden for the weary.

a *1* Or *are but beasts and cattle*

MAJOR IDOLS MENTIONED IN THE BIBLE

Name	*Where they were worshipped*	*What they stood for*	*What the worship included*
Bel (Marduk)	Babylon	Weather, war, sun god	Prostitution, child sacrifice
Nebo (Son of Marduk)	Babylon	Learning, astronomy, science	
Ashtoreth (Asherah)	Canaan	Goddess of love, childbirth, and fertility	Prostitution
Chemosh	Moab		Child sacrifice
Molech	Ammon	National god	Child sacrifice
Baal	Canaan	Rain, harvest, symbolised strength and fertility	Prostitution
Dagon	Philistia	Harvest, grain, success in farming	Child sacrifice

45:22 Salvation is for all nations, not just the Israelites. Many times it seems as though Israel had an inside track on salvation. But God makes it clear that his people include *all* those who follow him. Israel was to be the means through which the whole world would come to know God. Jesus, the Messiah, fulfilled Israel's role and gave all people the opportunity to follow God. (See also Romans 11:11; Galatians 3:28; Ephesians 3:6; Philippians 2:10.)

46:1–4 Cyrus would carry out God's judgment against Babylon. Bel was the chief deity of the Babylonians; Nebo was the god of science and learning. These "gods", however, needed animals and people to carry them around and could not even save themselves from being taken into captivity. They had no power at all. In contrast to gods who must be hauled around by people, our God created us and cares for us. His love is so enduring that he will care for us throughout our lifetime and even through death.

2They stoop and bow down together;
unable to rescue the burden,
they themselves go off into captivity.[c]

3"Listen[d] to me, O house of Jacob,
all you who remain of the house of Israel,
you whom I have upheld since you were conceived,
and have carried since your birth.
4Even to your old age and grey hairs[e]
I am he,[f] I am he who will sustain you.
I have made you and I will carry you;
I will sustain you and I will rescue you.

5"To whom will you compare me or count me equal?
To whom will you liken me that we may be compared?[g]
6Some pour out gold from their bags
and weigh out silver on the scales;
they hire a goldsmith[h] to make it into a god,
and they bow down and worship it.[i]
7They lift it to their shoulders and carry[j] it;
they set it up in its place, and there it stands.
From that spot it cannot move.
Though one cries out to it, it does not answer;
it cannot save[k] him from his troubles.

8"Remember[l] this, fix it in mind,
take it to heart, you rebels.
9Remember the former things, those of long ago;[m]
I am God, and there is no other;
I am God, and there is none like me.[n]
10I make known the end from the beginning,
from ancient times,[o] what is still to come.
I say: My purpose will stand,[p]
and I will do all that I please.
11From the east I summon a bird of prey;
from a far-off land, a man to fulfil my purpose.
What I have said, that will I bring about;
what I have planned, that will I do.
12Listen[q] to me, you stubborn-hearted,
you who are far from righteousness.[r]
13I am bringing my righteousness near,
it is not far away;
and my salvation will not be delayed.
I will grant salvation to Zion,
my splendour[s] to Israel.

The Fall of Babylon

47 "Go down, sit in the dust,
Virgin Daughter[a] of Babylon;
sit on the ground without a throne,

46:2 [c]Jdg 18:17-18; 2Sa 5:21
46:3 [d]ver 12
46:4 [e]Ps 71:18 [f]Isa 43:13
46:5 [g]Isa 40:18, 25
46:6 [h]Isa 40:19 [i]Isa 44:17
46:7 [j]ver 1 [k]Isa 44:17; Isa 45:20
46:8 [l]Isa 44:21
46:9 [m]Dt 32:7 [n]Isa 45:5, 21
46:10 [o]Isa 45:21 [p]Pr 19:21; Ac 5:39
46:12 [q]ver 3 [r]Ps 119:150; Isa 48:1; Jer 2:5
46:13 [s]Isa 44:23
47:1 [a]Isa 23:12

46:8–11 Israel was tempted to waver between the Lord God and pagan gods. Isaiah affirms the sole lordship of God. God is unique in his knowledge and in his control of the future. His consistent purpose is to carry out what he has planned. When we are tempted to pursue anything that promises pleasure, comfort, peace, or security apart from God, we must remember our commitment to God.

46:13 Much of the book of Isaiah speaks of a future deliverance when we will all live with God in perfect peace. God offers not only this future hope but also help for our present needs. His righteousness is near us, and we do not have to wait for his salvation.

47:1ff Here Isaiah predicted the fall of Babylon more than 150 years before it happened. At this time, Babylon had not yet emerged as the mightiest force on earth, the proud empire that would destroy Judah and Jerusalem. But the Babylonians, Judah's captors, would become captives themselves in 539 B.C. God, not Babylon, has the ultimate power. He used Babylon to punish his

Daughter of the Babylonians.[a][b]
No more will you be called
tender or delicate.[c]
2 Take millstones[d] and grind[e] flour;
take off your veil.[f]
Lift up your skirts,[g] bare your legs,
and wade through the streams.
3 Your nakedness[h] will be exposed
and your shame[i] uncovered.
I will take vengeance;[j]
I will spare no-one."

4 Our Redeemer—the LORD Almighty is his name[k]—
is the Holy One of Israel.

5 "Sit in silence, go into darkness,[l]
Daughter of the Babylonians;
no more will you be called
queen of kingdoms.[m]
6 I was angry[n] with my people
and desecrated my inheritance;
I gave them into your hand,[o]
and you showed them no mercy.
Even on the aged
you laid a very heavy yoke.
7 You said, 'I will continue for ever—
the eternal queen!'[p]
But you did not consider these things
or reflect[q] on what might happen.[r]

8 "Now then, listen, you wanton creature,
lounging in your security[s]
and saying to yourself,
'I am, and there is none besides me.[t]
I will never be a widow[u]
or suffer the loss of children.'
9 Both of these will overtake you
in a moment,[v] on a single day:
loss of children[w] and widowhood.
They will come upon you in full measure,
in spite of your many sorceries[x]
and all your potent spells.[y]
10 You have trusted[z] in your wickedness
and have said, 'No-one sees me.'[a]
Your wisdom[b] and knowledge mislead[c] you
when you say to yourself,
'I am, and there is none besides me.'
11 Disaster will come upon you,
and you will not know how to conjure it away.
A calamity will fall upon you
that you cannot ward off with a ransom;

47:1 [b]Ps 137:8; Jer 50:42; 51:33; Zec 2:7 [c]Dt 28:56
47:2 [d]Ex 11:5; Mt 24:41 [e]Jdg 16:21 [f]Ge 24:65 [g]Isa 32:11
47:3 [h]Eze 16:37; Na 3:5 [i]Isa 20:4 [j]Isa 34:8
47:4 [k]Jer 50:34
47:5 [l]Isa 13:10 [m]Isa 13:19
47:6 [n]2Ch 28:9 [o]Isa 10:13
47:7 [p]ver 5; Rev 18:7 [q]Isa 42:23, 25 [r]Dt 32:29
47:8 [s]Isa 32:9 [t]Isa 45:6; Zep 2:15 [u]Rev 18:7
47:9 [v]Ps 73:19; 1Th 5:3; Rev 18:8-10 [w]Isa 13:18 [x]Na 3:4 [y]Rev 18:23
47:10 [z]Ps 52:7; 62:10 [a]Isa 29:15 [b]Isa 5:21 [c]Isa 44:20

a *1* Or *Chaldeans*; also in verse 5

sinful people; he would use Medo-Persia to destroy Babylon and free his people.

47:8, 9 Caught up in the pursuit of power and pleasure, Babylon believed in its own greatness and claimed to be the *only* power on earth. Babylon felt completely secure, and Nebuchadnezzar, its king, exalted himself as a "god". But the true God taught Nebuchadnezzar a powerful lesson by taking everything away from him (Daniel 4:28–37). Our society is addicted to pleasure and power, but these can quickly pass away. Look at your own life and ask yourself how you can be more responsible with the talents and possessions God has given you. How can you use your life for God's honour rather than your own?

a catastrophe you cannot foresee
will suddenly[d] come upon you.

12"Keep on, then, with your magic spells
and with your many sorceries,[e]
which you have laboured at since childhood.
Perhaps you will succeed,
perhaps you will cause terror.
13All the counsel you have received has only worn you out![f]
Let your astrologers[g] come forward,
those stargazers who make predictions month by month,
let them save[h] you from what is coming upon you.
14Surely they are like stubble;[i]
the fire will burn them up.
They cannot even save themselves
from the power of the flame.[j]
Here are no coals to warm anyone;
here is no fire to sit by.
15That is all they can do for you—
these you have laboured with
and trafficked[k] with since childhood.
Each of them goes on in his error;
there is not one that can save you.

Stubborn Israel

48 "Listen to this, O house of Jacob,
you who are called by the name of Israel
and come from the line of Judah,
you who take oaths in the name of the LORD
and invoke[a] the God of Israel—
but not in truth[b] or righteousness—
2you who call yourselves citizens of the holy city[c]
and rely[d] on the God of Israel—
the LORD Almighty is his name:
3I foretold the former things[e] long ago,
my mouth announced[f] them and I made them known;
then suddenly I acted, and they came to pass.
4For I knew how stubborn[g] you were;
the sinews of your neck[h] were iron,
your forehead[i] was bronze.
5Therefore I told you these things long ago;
before they happened I announced them to you
so that you could not say,
'My idols did them;[j]
my wooden image and metal god ordained them.'
6You have heard these things; look at them all.
Will you not admit them?

"From now on I will tell you of new things,
of hidden things unknown to you.
7They are created now, and not long ago;

47:11 [d]1Th 5:3
47:12 [e]ver 9
47:13 [f]Isa 57:10; Jer 51:58 [g]Isa 44:25 [h]ver 15
47:14 [i]Isa 5:24; Na 1:10 [j]Isa 10:17; Jer 51:30, 32, 58
47:15 [k]Rev 18:11
48:1 [a]Isa 58:2 [b]Jer 4:2
48:2 [c]Isa 52:1 [d]Isa 10:20; Mic 3:11; Ro 2:17
48:3 [e]Isa 41:22 [f]Isa 45:21
48:4 [g]Dt 31:27 [h]Ex 32:9; Ac 7:51 [i]Eze 3:9
48:5 [j]Jer 44:15-18

47:12–15 The people of Babylon sought advice and help from astrologers and stargazers. But like the idols of wood or gold, astrologers could not even deliver themselves from what was to come from the hand of God. Why rely on those who are powerless? The helpless cannot help us. Alternatives to God are destined to fail. If you want help, find it in God, who has proved his power in creation and in history.

48:1 The people of Judah felt confident because they lived in Jerusalem, the city with God's temple. They depended on their heritage, their city, and their temple—but this was false security because they did not depend on God. Do you feel secure because you go to church or live in a Christian country? Heritage, buildings, or nations cannot give us a relationship with God; we must truly depend on him personally, with all our hearts and minds.

you have not heard of them before today.
So you cannot say,
'Yes, I knew of them.'
8You have neither heard nor understood;
from of old your ear has not been open.
Well do I know how treacherous you are;
you were called a rebel[k] from birth.
9For my own name's sake I delay my wrath;[l]
for the sake of my praise I hold it back from you,
so as not to cut you off.[m]
10See, I have refined you, though not as silver;
I have tested you in the furnace[n] of affliction.
11For my own sake,[o] for my own sake, I do this.
How can I let myself be defamed?[p]
I will not yield my glory to another.[q]

Israel Freed

12"Listen[r] to me, O Jacob,
Israel, whom I have called:
I am he;
I am the first and I am the last.[s]
13My own hand laid the foundations of the earth,[t]
and my right hand spread out the heavens;[u]
when I summon them,
they all stand up together.[v]

14"Come together,[w] all of you, and listen:
Which of ⌊the idols⌋ has foretold these things?
The LORD's chosen ally
will carry out his purpose[x] against Babylon;
his arm will be against the Babylonians.[a]
15I, even I, have spoken;
yes, I have called[y] him.
I will bring him,
and he will succeed in his mission.

16"Come near[z] me and listen to this:

"From the first announcement I have not spoken in secret;[a]
at the time it happens, I am there."

And now the Sovereign LORD has sent[b] me,
with his Spirit.

17This is what the LORD says—

a *14* Or *Chaldeans*; also in verse 20

48:8
[k]Dt 9:7, 24; Ps 58:3

48:9
[l]Ps 78:38; Isa 30:18
[m]Ne 9:31

48:10
[n]1Ki 8:51

48:11
[o]1Sa 12:22; Isa 37:35
[p]Dt 32:27; Jer 14:7, 21; Eze 20:9, 14, 22, 44
[q]Isa 42:8

48:12
[r]Isa 46:3
[s]Isa 41:4; Rev 1:17; 22:13

48:13
[t]Heb 1:10-12
[u]Ex 20:11
[v]Isa 40:26

48:14
[w]Isa 43:9
[x]Isa 46:10-11

48:15
[y]Isa 45:1

48:16
[z]Isa 41:1
[a]Isa 45:19
[b]Zec 2:9, 11

48:9–11 There was nothing in Israel's actions, attitudes, or accomplishments to compel God to love and to save them. But for his own sake, to show who he is and what he can do, he saved them. God does not save us because we are good but because he loves us and because of his forgiving nature.

48:10 Do you find it easy to complain when your life becomes complicated or difficult? Why would a loving God allow all kinds of unpleasant experiences to come to his children? This verse shows us plainly that God tests us in the "furnace of affliction". Rather than complain, our response should be to turn to God in faith for the strength to endure, and rejoice in our sufferings (see Romans 5:3; James 1:2–4). For without the testing, we would never know what we are capable of doing, nor would we grow. And without the refining, we will not become more pure and more like Christ. What kinds of adversity are you currently facing?

48:14, 15 "The LORD's chosen ally" refers to Cyrus—and this must have shocked his audience. How could the Lord choose a pagan king, an enemy? But it was Cyrus whom God would use to free his people from their captivity in Babylon. Cyrus' mission was to set Israel free by conquering Babylon, then to decree that all Jews could return to their homeland. Who but a prophet of God could tell such an inconceivable but true story almost 200 years before it happened?

48:17, 18 Like a loving parent, God teaches and directs us. We should listen to him because peace and righteousness come to us as we obey his word. Refusing to pay attention to God's commands invites punishment and threatens that peace and righteousness.

your Redeemer,[c] the Holy One[d] of Israel:
"I am the LORD your God,
who teaches you what is best for you,
who directs[e] you in the way[f] you should go.
18If only you had paid attention[g] to my commands,
your peace[h] would have been like a river,
your righteousness[i] like the waves of the sea.
19Your descendants would have been like the sand,
your children like its numberless grains;[j]
their name would never be cut off[k]
nor destroyed from before me."

20Leave Babylon,
flee[l] from the Babylonians!
Announce this with shouts of joy[m]
and proclaim it.
Send it out to the ends of the earth;
say, "The LORD has redeemed[n] his servant Jacob."
21They did not thirst[o] when he led them through the deserts;
he made water flow[p] for them from the rock;
he split the rock
and water gushed out.[q]

22"There is no peace," says the LORD, "for the wicked."[r]

2. The future Redeemer

The Servant of the LORD

49 Listen to me, you islands;
hear this, you distant nations:
Before I was born[a] the LORD called[b] me;
from my birth he has made mention of my name.
2He made my mouth like a sharpened sword,[c]
in the shadow of his hand he hid me;
he made me into a polished arrow
and concealed me in his quiver.
3He said to me, "You are my servant,[d]
Israel, in whom I will display my splendour.[e]"
4But I said, "I have laboured to no purpose;
I have spent my strength in vain[f] and for nothing.
Yet what is due to me is in the LORD's hand,
and my reward[g] is with my God."

5And now the LORD says—
he who formed me in the womb to be his servant
to bring Jacob back to him
and gather Israel[h] to himself,
for I am honoured[i] in the eyes of the LORD
and my God has been my strength—
6he says:

48:17
[c]Isa 49:7
[d]Isa 43:14
[e]Isa 49:10
[f]Ps 32:8

48:18
[g]Dt 32:29
[h]Ps 119:165;
Isa 66:12
[i]Isa 45:8

48:19
[j]Ge 22:17
[k]Isa 56:5; 66:22

48:20
[l]Jer 50:8; 51:6, 45;
Zec 2:6-7;
Rev 18:4
[m]Isa 49:13
[n]Isa 52:9; 63:9

48:21
[o]Isa 41:17
[p]Isa 30:25
[q]Ex 17:6;
Nu 20:11;
Ps 105:41;
Isa 35:6

48:22
[r]Isa 57:21

49:1
[a]Isa 44:24; 46:3;
Mt 1:20
[b]Isa 7:14; 9:6; 44:2;
Jer 1:5;
Gal 1:15

49:2
[c]Isa 11:4;
Rev 1:16

49:3
[d]Zec 3:8
[e]Isa 44:23

49:4
[f]Isa 65:23
[g]Isa 35:4

49:5
[h]Isa 11:12
[i]Isa 43:4

48:20 Do you see the captives leaving Babylon many years later? No wonder they are shouting with joy, as their ancestors shouted joyfully after they crossed the Red Sea, free from slavery at last! What is holding you captive? Be free! The Lord has redeemed his servants from the slavery of sin. When you let him free you from your captivity, you will feel like shouting with joy.

48:22 Many people cry out for comfort, security, and relief, but they haven't taken the first steps to turn away from sin and open the channels to God. They have not repented and trusted in him. If you want true peace, seek God first. Then he will give you his peace.

49:1–7 Before the servant, the Messiah, was born, God had chosen him to bring the light of the gospel (the message of salvation) to the world (see Acts 13:47). Christ offered salvation to all nations, and his apostles began the missionary movement to take this gospel to the ends of the earth. Missionary work today continues Jesus' Great Commission (Matthew 28:18–20), taking the light of the gospel to all nations.

49:6 [j]Lk 2:32 [k]Ac 13:47*
49:7 [l]Isa 48:17 [m]Ps 22:6; 69:7-9 [n]Isa 52:15
49:8 [o]Ps 69:13 [p]2Co 6:2* [q]Isa 26:3 [r]Isa 42:6 [s]Isa 44:26
49:9 [t]Isa 42:7; 61:1; Lk 4:19 [u]Isa 41:18
49:10 [v]Isa 33:16 [w]Ps 121:6; Rev 7:16 [x]Isa 14:1 [y]Isa 35:7
49:11 [z]Isa 11:16 [a]Isa 40:4
49:12 [b]Isa 43:5-6
49:13 [c]Isa 44:23 [d]Isa 40:1
49:15 [e]Isa 44:21
49:16 [f]SS 8:6 [g]Ps 48:12-13; Isa 62:6

"It is too small a thing for you to be my servant
to restore the tribes of Jacob
and bring back those of Israel I have kept.
I will also make you a light for the Gentiles,[j]
that you may bring my salvation to the ends of the earth."[k]

7This is what the LORD says—
the Redeemer and Holy One of Israel[l]—
to him who was despised[m] and abhorred by the nation,
to the servant of rulers:
"Kings[n] will see you and rise up,
princes will see and bow down,
because of the LORD, who is faithful,
the Holy One of Israel, who has chosen you."

Restoration of Israel

8This is what the LORD says:

"In the time of my favour[o] I will answer you,
and in the day of salvation I will help you;[p]
I will keep[q] you and will make you
to be a covenant for the people,[r]
to restore the land[s]
and to reassign its desolate inheritances,
9to say to the captives,[t] 'Come out,'
and to those in darkness, 'Be free!'

"They will feed beside the roads
and find pasture on every barren hill.[u]
10They will neither hunger nor thirst,[v]
nor will the desert heat or the sun beat upon them.[w]
He who has compassion[x] on them will guide them
and lead them beside springs[y] of water.
11I will turn all my mountains into roads,
and my highways[z] will be raised up.[a]
12See, they will come from afar[b]—
some from the north, some from the west,
some from the region of Aswan."[a]

13Shout for joy, O heavens;
rejoice, O earth;
burst into song, O mountains![c]
For the LORD comforts[d] his people
and will have compassion on his afflicted ones.

14But Zion said, "The LORD has forsaken me,
the Lord has forgotten me."

15"Can a mother forget the baby at her breast
and have no compassion on the child she has borne?
Though she may forget,
I will not forget you![e]
16See, I have engraved[f] you on the palms of my hands;
your walls[g] are ever before me.

a *12* Dead Sea Scrolls; Masoretic Text *Sinim*

49:12 The region of Aswan is in southern Egypt (see Ezekiel 29:10).

49:14, 15 The people of Israel felt that God had forsaken them in Babylon; but Isaiah pointed out that God would never forget them, as a loving mother would not forget her little child. When we feel that God has forsaken us, we must ask if we have forsaken and forgotten God (see Deuteronomy 31:6).

17Your sons hasten back,
and those who laid you waste[h] depart from you.
18Lift up your eyes and look around;
all your sons gather[i] and come to you.
As surely as I live,[j]" declares the LORD,
"you will wear[k] them all as ornaments;
you will put them on, like a bride.

19"Though you were ruined and made desolate[l]
and your land laid waste,[m]
now you will be too small for your people,[n]
and those who devoured you will be far away.
20The children born during your bereavement
will yet say in your hearing,
'This place is too small for us;
give us more space to live in.'[o]
21Then you will say in your heart,
'Who bore me these?
I was bereaved and barren;
I was exiled and rejected.[p]
Who brought these up?
I was left[q] all alone,
but these — where have they come from?' "

22This is what the Sovereign LORD says:

"See, I will beckon to the Gentiles,
I will lift up my banner[r] to the peoples;
they will bring your sons in their arms
and carry your daughters on their shoulders.[s]
23Kings[t] will be your foster fathers,
and their queens your nursing mothers.[u]
They will bow down before you with their faces to the ground;
they will lick the dust[v] at your feet.
Then you will know that I am the LORD;[w]
those who hope in me will not be disappointed."

24Can plunder be taken from warriors,[x]
or captives rescued from the fierce?**b**

25But this is what the LORD says:

"Yes, captives[y] will be taken from warriors,[z]
and plunder retrieved from the fierce;
I will contend with those who contend with you,
and your children I will save.[a]
26I will make your oppressors[b] eat[c] their own flesh;
they will be drunk on their own blood,[d] as with wine.
Then all mankind will know[e]
that I, the LORD, am your Saviour,
your Redeemer, the Mighty One of Jacob."

49:17 [h]Isa 10:6
49:18 [i]Isa 43:5; 54:7; Isa 60:4 [j]Isa 45:23 [k]Isa 52:1
49:19 [l]Isa 54:1, 3 [m]Isa 5:6 [n]Zec 10:10
49:20 [o]Isa 54:1-3
49:21 [p]Isa 5:13 [q]Isa 1:8
49:22 [r]Isa 11:10 [s]Isa 60:4
49:23 [t]Isa 60:3, 10-11 [u]Isa 60:16 [v]Ps 72:9 [w]Mic 7:17
49:24 [x]Mt 12:29; Lk 11:21
49:25 [y]Isa 14:2 [z]Jer 50:33-34 [a]Isa 25:9; 35:4
49:26 [b]Isa 9:4 [c]Isa 9:20 [d]Rev 16:6 [e]Eze 39:7

b *24* Dead Sea Scrolls, Vulgate and Syriac (see also Septuagint and verse 25); Masoretic Text *righteous*

49:24, 25 God would prove to the world that he is God by doing the impossible – causing warriors to set their captives free; and these warriors would even return the plunder they had taken from the captives! God had done this before at the exodus and would do it again when the exiles returned to Israel. Never should we doubt that God will fulfil his promises. He will even do the impossible to make them come true.

50:1 [a]Dt 24:1; Jer 3:8; Hos 2:2 [b]Ne 5:5; Mt 18:25 [c]Dt 32:30; Isa 52:3
50:2 [d]Isa 41:28 [e]Nu 11:23; Isa 59:1 [f]Ge 18:14 [g]Ex 14:22; Jos 3:16
50:3 [h]Rev 6:12
50:4 [i]Ex 4:12 [j]Mt 11:28 [k]Ps 5:3; 119:147; 143:8
50:5 [l]Isa 35:5 [m]Mt 26:39; Jn 8:29; 14:31; 15:10; Ac 26:19; Heb 5:8
50:6 [n]Isa 53:5; Mt 27:30; Mk 14:65; 15:19; Lk 22:63 [o]La 3:30; Mt 26:67
50:7 [p]Isa 42:1 [q]Eze 3:8-9
50:8 [r]Isa 43:26; Ro 8:32-34 [s]Isa 41:1
50:9 [t]Isa 41:10 [u]Job 13:28; Isa 51:8
50:10 [v]Isa 49:3 [w]Isa 26:4
50:11 [x]Pr 26:18

Israel's Sin and the Servant's Obedience

50 This is what the LORD says:

"Where is your mother's certificate of divorce[a]
with which I sent her away?
Or to which of my creditors
did I sell[b] you?
Because of your sins you were sold;[c]
because of your transgressions your mother was sent away.
2 When I came, why was there no-one?
When I called, why was there no-one to answer?[d]
Was my arm too short[e] to ransom you?
Do I lack the strength[f] to rescue you?
By a mere rebuke I dry up the sea,[g]
I turn rivers into a desert;
their fish rot for lack of water
and die of thirst.
3 I clothe the sky with darkness
and make sackcloth[h] its covering."

4 The Sovereign LORD has given me an instructed tongue,[i]
to know the word that sustains the weary.[j]
He wakens me morning by morning,[k]
wakens my ear to listen like one being taught.
5 The Sovereign LORD has opened my ears,[l]
and I have not been rebellious;[m]
I have not drawn back.
6 I offered my back to those who beat[n] me,
my cheeks to those who pulled out my beard;
I did not hide my face
from mocking and spitting.[o]
7 Because the Sovereign LORD helps[p] me,
I will not be disgraced.
Therefore have I set my face like flint,[q]
and I know I will not be put to shame.
8 He who vindicates me is near.
Who then will bring charges against me?[r]
Let us face each other![s]
Who is my accuser?
Let him confront me!
9 It is the Sovereign LORD who helps[t] me.
Who is he who will condemn me?
They will all wear out like a garment;
the moths[u] will eat them up.

10 Who among you fears the LORD
and obeys the word of his servant?[v]
Let him who walks in the dark,
who has no light,
trust[w] in the name of the LORD
and rely on his God.
11 But now, all you who light fires
and provide yourselves with flaming torches,[x]

50:1, 2 God promised to fight for Israel, but Israel sold itself into sin. Israel had caused its own problems. "Was my arm too short?" means "Am I powerless to help?" The people of Israel forgot God and trusted in other countries to help them. God did not reject Israel, but Israel rejected God.

50:10, 11 If we walk by our own light and reject God's, we become self-sufficient, and the result of self-sufficiency is torment. When we place confidence in our own intelligence, appearance, or accomplishments instead of in God, we risk torment later when these strengths fade.

go, walk in the light of your fires[y]
and of the torches you have set ablaze.
This is what you shall receive from my hand:
You will lie down in torment.[z]

Everlasting Salvation for Zion

51 "Listen[a] to me, you who pursue righteousness[b]
and who seek the LORD:
Look to the rock from which you were cut
and to the quarry from which you were hewn;
2look to Abraham,[c] your father,
and to Sarah, who gave you birth.
When I called him he was but one,
and I blessed him and made him many.[d]
3The LORD will surely comfort[e] Zion
and will look with compassion on all her ruins;[f]
he will make her deserts like Eden,[g]
her wastelands like the garden of the LORD.
Joy and gladness[h] will be found in her,
thanksgiving and the sound of singing.

4"Listen to me, my people;[i]
hear me, my nation:
The law will go out from me;
my justice[j] will become a light to the nations.[k]
5My righteousness draws near speedily,
my salvation is on the way,[l]
and my arm[m] will bring justice to the nations.
The islands will look to me
and wait in hope for my arm.
6Lift up your eyes to the heavens,
look at the earth beneath;
the heavens will vanish like smoke,[n]
the earth will wear out like a garment[o]
and its inhabitants die like flies.
But my salvation will last for ever,
my righteousness will never fail.

7"Hear me, you who know what is right,[p]
you people who have my law in your hearts:[q]
Do not fear the reproach of men
or be terrified by their insults.[r]
8For the moth will eat them up like a garment;[s]
the worm will devour them like wool.
But my righteousness will last for ever,[t]
my salvation through all generations."

9Awake, awake! Clothe yourself with strength,[u]
O arm of the LORD;

50:11 [y]Jas 3:6 [z]Isa 65:13-15
51:1 [a]Isa 46:3 [b]ver 7; Ps 94:15; Ro 9:30-31
51:2 [c]Isa 29:22; Ro 4:16; Heb 11:11 [d]Ge 12:2
51:3 [e]Isa 40:1 [f]Isa 52:9 [g]Ge 2:8 [h]Isa 25:9; 66:10
51:4 [i]Ps 50:7 [j]Isa 2:4 [k]Isa 42:4, 6
51:5 [l]Isa 46:13 [m]Isa 40:10; 63:1, 5
51:6 [n]Mt 24:35; 2Pe 3:10 [o]Ps 102:25-26
51:7 [p]ver 1 [q]Ps 37:31 [r]Mt 5:11; Ac 5:41
51:8 [s]Isa 50:9 [t]ver 6
51:9 [u]Isa 52:1

51:1, 2 The faithful remnant may have felt alone because they were few. But God reminded them of their ancestors, the source of their spiritual heritage—Abraham and Sarah. Abraham was only one person, but much came from his faithfulness. If the faithful few would remain faithful, even more could come from them. If we Christians, even a faithful few, remain faithful, think what God can do through us!

51:7 Isaiah encouraged those who follow God's laws. He gave them hope when they faced people's reproach or insults because of their faith. We need not fear when people insult us for our faith because God is with us and truth will prevail. If people make fun of you or dislike you because you believe in God, remember that they are not against you personally but against God. God will deal with them; you should concentrate on loving and obeying him.

51:9, 10 "Rahab" was a derogatory term used for Egypt (see the note on 30:7). God had performed many powerful miracles in founding Israel, perhaps none more exciting than the drying up of the sea (the Red Sea, see Exodus 14). Our God is the same God who made a road in the depths of the sea. His methods may change, but his love and care do not.

awake, as in days gone by,
as in generations of old.[v]
Was it not you who cut Rahab to pieces,
who pierced that monster[w] through?
10 Was it not you who dried up the sea,[x]
the waters of the great deep,
who made a road in the depths of the sea
so that the redeemed might cross over?
11 The ransomed[y] of the LORD will return.
They will enter Zion with singing;
everlasting joy will crown their heads.
Gladness and joy[z] will overtake them,
and sorrow and sighing will flee away.[a]

12 "I, even I, am he who comforts[b] you.
Who are you that you fear mortal men,[c]
the sons of men, who are but grass,[d]
13 that you forget[e] the LORD your Maker,[f]
who stretched out the heavens[g]
and laid the foundations of the earth,
that you live in constant terror[h] every day
because of the wrath of the oppressor,
who is bent on destruction?
For where is the wrath of the oppressor?
14 The cowering prisoners will soon be set free;
they will not die in their dungeon,
nor will they lack bread.[i]
15 For I am the LORD your God,
who churns up the sea[j] so that its waves roar—
the LORD Almighty is his name.
16 I have put my words in your mouth[k]
and covered you with the shadow of my hand[l]—
I who set the heavens in place,
who laid the foundations of the earth,
and who say to Zion, 'You are my people.' "

The Cup of the LORD's Wrath

17 Awake, awake![m]
Rise up, O Jerusalem,
you who have drunk from the hand of the LORD
the cup of his wrath,[n]
you who have drained to its dregs
the goblet that makes men stagger.[o]
18 Of all the sons[p] she bore
there was none to guide her;[q]
of all the sons she brought up
there was none to take her by the hand.
19 These double calamities[r] have come upon you—
who can comfort you?—
ruin and destruction, famine[s] and sword—

51:9 [v]Dt 4:34 [w]Ps 74:13
51:10 [x]Ex 14:22
51:11 [y]Isa 35:9 [z]Jer 33:11 [a]Rev 7:17
51:12 [b]2Co 1:4 [c]Ps 118:6; Isa 2:22 [d]Isa 40:6-7; 1Pe 1:24
51:13 [e]Isa 17:10 [f]Isa 45:11 [g]Ps 104:2; Isa 48:13 [h]Isa 7:4
51:14 [i]Isa 49:10
51:15 [j]Jer 31:35
51:16 [k]Dt 18:18; Isa 59:21 [l]Ex 33:22
51:17 [m]Isa 52:1 [n]Job 21:20; Rev 14:10; 16:19 [o]Ps 60:3
51:18 [p]Ps 88:18 [q]Isa 49:21
51:19 [r]Isa 47:9 [s]Isa 14:30

51:12–16 God's people feared Babylon, but not God. They had reason to fear Babylon for the harm it wanted to do, but they should also have realised that God's power is much greater than Babylon's. Babylon was interested in making the people captives; God was interested in setting them free. The people had misplaced their fear and their love. Jerusalem should have feared God's power and loved his mercy.

51:17–52:10 Jerusalem was God's holy city, the city with God's temple. But the people of Judah experienced ruin instead of prosperity, destruction instead of liberty. Because of their sins, the people suffered. But God promised to restore Jerusalem as a holy city where sinners cannot enter. "Lay bare his holy arm" (52:10) means that God has revealed his holy power and justice. God reigns. He is in control.

who can[a] console you?
20 Your sons have fainted;
they lie at the head of every street,[t]
like antelope caught in a net.
They are filled with the wrath of the LORD
and the rebuke of your God.

21 Therefore hear this, you afflicted one,
made drunk,[u] but not with wine.
22 This is what your Sovereign LORD says,
your God, who defends[v] his people:
"See, I have taken out of your hand
the cup[w] that made you stagger;
from that cup, the goblet of my wrath,
you will never drink again.
23 I will put it into the hands of your tormentors,[x]
who said to you,
'Fall prostrate[y] that we may walk[z] over you.'
And you made your back like the ground,
like a street to be walked over."

52

Awake, awake,[a] O Zion,
clothe yourself with strength.[b]
Put on your garments of splendour,[c]
O Jerusalem, the holy city.[d]
The uncircumcised and defiled
will not enter you again.[e]
2 Shake off your dust;[f]
rise up, sit enthroned, O Jerusalem.
Free yourself from the chains on your neck,
O captive Daughter of Zion.

3 For this is what the LORD says:

"You were sold for nothing,[g]
and without money[h] you will be redeemed."

4 For this is what the Sovereign LORD says:

"At first my people went down to Egypt[i] to live;
lately, Assyria has oppressed them.

5 "And now what do I have here?" declares the LORD.

"For my people have been taken away for nothing,
and those who rule them mock,"[a]
declares the LORD.

"And all day long
my name is constantly blasphemed.[j]
6 Therefore my people will know[k] my name;
therefore in that day they will know
that it is I who foretold it.
Yes, it is I."

7 How beautiful on the mountains
are the feet of those who bring good news,[l]

a *19* Dead Sea Scrolls, Septuagint, Vulgate and Syriac; Masoretic Text / *how can I* a *5* Dead Sea Scrolls and Vulgate; Masoretic Text *wail*

51:20 [t] Isa 5:25; Jer 14:16
51:21 [u] ver 17; Isa 29:9
51:22 [v] Isa 49:25 [w] ver 17
51:23 [x] Isa 49:26; Jer 25:15-17, 26, 28; 49:12 [y] Zec 12:2 [z] Jos 10:24
52:1 [a] Isa 51:17 [b] Isa 51:9 [c] Ex 28:2, 40; Ps 110:3; Zec 3:4 [d] Ne 11:1; Mt 4:5; Rev 21:2 [e] Na 1:15; Rev 21:27
52:2 [f] Isa 29:4
52:3 [g] Ps 44:12 [h] Isa 45:13
52:4 [i] Ge 46:6
52:5 [j] Eze 36:20; Ro 2:24*
52:6 [k] Isa 49:23
52:7 [l] Isa 40:9; Ro 10:15*

52:7 God says that the feet of those who bring good news are "beautiful". It is a wonderful privilege to be able to share God's Good News with others, his news of redemption, salvation, and peace. To whom do you need to give the Good News?

52:7 [m]Na 1:15; Eph 6:15 [n]Ps 93:1
52:8 [o]Isa 62:6
52:9 [p]Ps 98:4 [q]Isa 51:3 [r]Isa 48:20
52:10 [s]Isa 66:18 [t]Ps 98:2-3; Lk 3:6
52:11 [u]Isa 48:20 [v]Isa 1:16; 2Co 6:17* [w]2Ti 2:19
52:12 [x]Ex 12:11 [y]Mic 2:13 [z]Ex 14:19
52:13 [a]Isa 42:1 [b]Isa 57:15; Php 2:9
52:15 [c]Ro 15:21*; Eph 3:4-5
53:1 [a]Ro 10:16* [b]Jn 12:38*
53:2 [c]Isa 52:14

who proclaim peace,[m]
who bring good tidings,
who proclaim salvation,
who say to Zion,
"Your God reigns!"[n]
8 Listen! Your watchmen[o] lift up their voices;
together they shout for joy.
When the LORD returns to Zion,
they will see it with their own eyes.
9 Burst into songs of joy[p] together,
you ruins[q] of Jerusalem,
for the LORD has comforted his people,
he has redeemed Jerusalem.[r]
10 The LORD will lay bare his holy arm
in the sight of all the nations,[s]
and all the ends of the earth will see
the salvation[t] of our God.

11 Depart,[u] depart, go out from there!
Touch no unclean thing![v]
Come out from it and be pure,[w]
you who carry the vessels of the LORD.
12 But you will not leave in haste[x]
or go in flight;
for the LORD will go before you,[y]
the God of Israel will be your rear guard.[z]

The Suffering and Glory of the Servant

13 See, my servant[a] will act wisely;[b]
he will be raised and lifted up and highly exalted.[b]
14 Just as there were many who were appalled at him[c]—
his appearance was so disfigured beyond that of any man
and his form marred beyond human likeness—
15 so will he sprinkle many nations,[d]
and kings will shut their mouths because of him.
For what they were not told, they will see,
and what they have not heard, they will understand.[c]

53 Who has believed our message[a]
and to whom has the arm of the LORD been revealed?[b]
2 He grew up before him like a tender shoot,
and like a root out of dry ground.
He had no beauty or majesty to attract us to him,
nothing in his appearance[c] that we should desire him.

b 13 Or *will prosper* c 14 Hebrew *you* d 15 Hebrew; Septuagint *so will many nations marvel at him*

52:12 The people did not have to leave in fearful haste because Cyrus, God's anointed (45:1), decreed that the Jewish exiles could return safely to Jerusalem (Ezra 1:1–4). They had the king's approval, his guaranteed protection. More important, the Lord would go ahead to point the way and be behind to protect them.

52:13 The "servant", as the term is used here, is the Messiah, our Lord Jesus. He would be highly exalted because of his sacrifice, described in chapter 53.

52:14, 15 This servant, Christ, would be "marred beyond human likeness"; but through his suffering, he would cleanse the nations (Hebrews 10:14; 1 Peter 1:2).

53:1ff This chapter continues to speak of the Messiah, Jesus, who would suffer for the sins of all people. Such a prophecy is astounding! Who would believe that God would choose to save the world through a humble, suffering servant rather than a glorious king? The idea is contrary to human pride and worldly ways. But God often works in ways we don't expect. The Messiah's strength is shown by humility, suffering, and mercy.

53:2 There was nothing beautiful or majestic in the physical appearance of this servant. Israel would miscalculate the servant's importance—they would consider him an ordinary man. But even though Jesus would not attract a large following based on his physical appearance, he would bring salvation and healing. Many people miscalculate the importance of Jesus' life and work, and they need faithful Christians to point out his extraordinary nature.

3He was despised and rejected by men,
a man of sorrows, and familiar with suffering.[d]
Like one from whom men hide their faces
he was despised,[e] and we esteemed him not.

53:3 [d]ver 4, 10; Lk 18:31-33 [e]Ps 22:6; Jn 1:10-11

4Surely he took up our infirmities
and carried our sorrows,[f]
yet we considered him stricken by God,[g]
smitten by him, and afflicted.
5But he was pierced for our transgressions,[h]
he was crushed for our iniquities;
the punishment that brought us peace was upon him,
and by his wounds we are healed.[i]
6We all, like sheep, have gone astray,
each of us has turned to his own way;
and the LORD has laid on him
the iniquity of us all.

53:4 [f]Mt 8:17* [g]Jn 19:7

53:5 [h]Ro 4:25; 1Co 15:3; Heb 9:28 [i]1Pe 2:24-25

7He was oppressed and afflicted,
yet he did not open his mouth;[j]
he was led like a lamb to the slaughter,
and as a sheep before her shearers is silent,
so he did not open his mouth.
8By oppression[a] and judgment he was taken away.
And who can speak of his descendants?
For he was cut off from the land of the living;[k]
for the transgression[l] of my people he was stricken.[b]
9He was assigned a grave with the wicked,
and with the rich[m] in his death,
though he had done no violence,[n]
nor was any deceit in his mouth.[o]

53:7 [j]Mk 14:61

53:8 [k]Da 9:26; Ac 8:32-33* [l]ver 12

53:9 [m]Mt 27:57-60 [n]Isa 42:1-3 [o]1Pe 2:22*

10Yet it was the LORD's will[p] to crush[q] him and cause him to
suffer,[r]
and though the LORD makes[c] his life a guilt offering,
he will see his offspring[s] and prolong his days,
and the will of the LORD will prosper in his hand.
11After the suffering[t] of his soul,
he will see the light ⌞of life⌟[d] and be satisfied;[e]

53:10 [p]Isa 46:10 [q]ver 5 [r]ver 3 [s]Ps 22:30

53:11 [t]Jn 10:14-18

[a] 8 Or *From arrest* [b] 8 Or *away. / Yet who of his generation considered / that he was cut off from the land of the living / for the transgression of my people, / to whom the blow was due?* [c] 10 Hebrew *though you make* [d] 11 Dead Sea Scrolls (see also Septuagint); Masoretic Text does not have *the light ⌞of life⌟*. [e] 11 Or (with Masoretic Text) 11 *He will see the result of the suffering of his soul / and be satisfied*

53:3 This man of sorrows was despised and rejected by those around him, and he is still despised and rejected by many today. Some reject Christ by standing against him. Others despise Christ and his great gift of forgiveness. Do you despise him, reject him, or accept him?

53:4, 5 How could an Old Testament person understand the idea of Christ dying for our sins (our transgressions and iniquities)—actually bearing the punishment that we deserved? The sacrifices suggested this idea, but it is one thing to kill a lamb, and something quite different to think of God's chosen servant as that Lamb. But God was pulling aside the curtain of time to let the people of Isaiah's day look ahead to the suffering of the future Messiah and the resulting forgiveness made available to all mankind.

53:6 Isaiah speaks of Israel straying from God and compares them to wandering sheep. Yet God would send the Messiah to bring them back into the fold. We have the hindsight to see and know the identity of the promised Messiah who has come and died for our sins. But if we can see all that Jesus did and still reject him, our sin is much greater than that of the ancient Israelites who could not see what we have seen. Have you given your life to Jesus Christ, the "Good Shepherd" (John 10:11–16), or are you still like a wandering sheep?

53:7–12 In the Old Testament, people offered animals as sacrifices for their sins. Here, the sinless servant of the Lord offers himself for our sins. He is the Lamb (53:7) offered for the sins of all people (John 1:29; Revelation 5:6–14). The Messiah suffered for our sakes, bearing our sins to make us acceptable to God. What can we say to such love? How will we respond to him?

53:11 "My righteous servant will justify many" tells of the enormous family of believers who will become righteous, not by their own works, but by the Messiah's great work on the cross. They are justified because they have claimed Christ, the righteous servant, as their Saviour and Lord (see Romans 10:9; 2 Corinthians 5:21). Their life of sin is stripped away, and they are clothed with Christ's goodness (Ephesians 4:22–24).

by his knowledge[f] my righteous servant will justify[u] many,
and he will bear their iniquities.
12 Therefore I will give him a portion among the great,[g][v]
and he will divide the spoils with the strong,[h]
because he poured out his life unto death,[w]
and was numbered with the transgressors.[x]
For he bore the sin of many,
and made intercession for the transgressors.

The Future Glory of Zion

54 "Sing, O barren woman,
you who never bore a child;
burst into song, shout for joy,
you who were never in labour;
because more are the children[a] of the desolate woman
than of her who has a husband,[b]"
says the LORD.

2 "Enlarge the place of your tent,[c]
stretch your tent curtains wide,
do not hold back;
lengthen your cords,
strengthen your stakes.[d]
3 For you will spread out to the right and to the left;
your descendants will dispossess nations
and settle in their desolate[e] cities.

4 "Do not be afraid; you will not suffer shame.
Do not fear disgrace; you will not be humiliated.
You will forget the shame of your youth
and remember no more the reproach[f] of your widowhood.
5 For your Maker is your husband[g] —
the LORD Almighty is his name —
the Holy One of Israel is your Redeemer;[h]
he is called the God of all the earth.[i]
6 The LORD will call you back[j]
as if you were a wife deserted[k] and distressed in spirit —
a wife who married young,
only to be rejected," says your God.
7 "For a brief moment[l] I abandoned you,
but with deep compassion I will bring you back.[m]
8 In a surge of anger[n]
I hid my face from you for a moment,
but with everlasting kindness[o]
I will have compassion on you,"
says the LORD your Redeemer.

9 "To me this is like the days of Noah,

[f] 11 Or *by knowledge of him* [g] 12 Or *many* [h] 12 Or *numerous*

53:11 [u] Ro 5:18-19
53:12 [v] Php 2:9 [w] Mt 26:28, 38, 39, 42 [x] Mk 15:27*; Lk 22:37*; 23:32
54:1 [a] Isa 49:20 [b] 1Sa 2:5; Gal 4:27*
54:2 [c] Isa 49:19-20 [d] Ex 35:18; 39:40
54:3 [e] Isa 49:19
54:4 [f] Isa 51:7
54:5 [g] Jer 3:14 [h] Isa 48:17 [i] Isa 6:3
54:6 [j] Isa 49:14-21 [k] Isa 50:1-2; 62:4, 12
54:7 [l] Isa 26:20 [m] Isa 49:18
54:8 [n] Isa 60:10 [o] ver 10

54:1 To be childless ("barren") at that time was a woman's great shame, a disgrace. Families depended on children for survival, especially when the parents became elderly. Israel (Zion) was unfruitful, like a childless woman, but God would permit her to have many children and would change her mourning into singing.

54:6–8 God said that he had abandoned Israel for a brief moment, so the nation was like a young wife rejected by her husband. But God still called Israel his own. The God we serve is holy, and he cannot tolerate sin. When his people blatantly sinned, God in his anger chose to punish them. Sin separates us from God and brings us pain and suffering. But if we confess our sin and repent, then God will forgive us. Have you ever been separated from a loved one and then experienced joy when that person returned? That is like the joy God experiences when you repent and return to him.

54:9–13 God made a covenant with Noah that he has never broken (Genesis 9:8–17). Likewise, God made a covenant of peace with the people of Israel that the time would come when he would stop rebuking them, would restore their wealth, and would personally teach their children.

when I swore that the waters of Noah would never again cover
the earth.[p]
So now I have sworn not to be angry[q] with you,
never to rebuke you again.
10Though the mountains be shaken[r]
and the hills be removed,
yet my unfailing love for you will not be shaken[s]
nor my covenant[t] of peace be removed,"
says the LORD, who has compassion[u] on you.

11"O afflicted[v] city, lashed by storms[w] and not comforted,[x]
I will build you with stones of turquoise,[a][y]
your foundations[z] with sapphires.[b]
12I will make your battlements of rubies,
your gates of sparkling jewels,
and all your walls of precious stones.
13All your sons will be taught by the LORD,[a]
and great will be your children's peace.[b]
14In righteousness you will be established:
Tyranny[c] will be far from you;
you will have nothing to fear.
Terror will be far removed;
it will not come near you.
15If anyone does attack you, it will not be my doing;
whoever attacks you will surrender[d] to you.

16"See, it is I who created the blacksmith
who fans the coals into flame
and forges a weapon fit for its work.
And it is I who have created the destroyer to work havoc;
17 no weapon forged against you will prevail,[e]
and you will refute[f] every tongue that accuses you.
This is the heritage of the servants of the LORD,
and this is their vindication from me,"
declares the LORD.

Invitation to the Thirsty

55

"Come, all you who are thirsty,[a]
come to the waters;
and you who have no money,
come, buy[b] and eat!
Come, buy wine and milk[c]
without money and without cost.[d]
2Why spend money on what is not bread,
and your labour on what does not satisfy?[e]
Listen, listen to me, and eat what is good,[f]
and your soul will delight in the richest of fare.
3Give ear and come to me;
hear me, that your soul may live.[g]
I will make an everlasting covenant[h] with you,

54:9 [p]Ge 8:21 [q]Isa 12:1
54:10 [r]Ps 46:2 [s]Isa 51:6 [t]Ps 89:34 [u]ver 8
54:11 [v]Isa 14:32 [w]Isa 28:2; 29:6 [x]Isa 51:19 [y]1Ch 29:2; Rev 21:18 [z]Isa 28:16; Rev 21:19-20
54:13 [a]Jn 6:45* [b]Isa 48:18
54:14 [c]Isa 9:4
54:15 [d]Isa 41:11-16
54:17 [e]Isa 29:8 [f]Isa 45:24-25
55:1 [a]Jn 4:14; 7:37 [b]La 5:4; Mt 13:44; Rev 3:18 [c]SS 5:1 [d]Hos 14:4; Mt 10:8; Rev 21:6
55:2 [e]Ps 22:26; Ecc 6:2; Hos 8:7 [f]Isa 1:19
55:3 [g]Lev 18:5; Ro 10:5 [h]Isa 61:8

a *11* The meaning of the Hebrew for this word is uncertain. **b** *11* Or *lapis lazuli*

55:1–6 Food costs money, lasts only a short time, and meets only physical needs. But God offers us *free* nourishment that feeds our soul. How do we get it? We come (55:1), listen (55:2), seek, and call on God (55:6). God's salvation is freely offered, but to nourish our souls we must eagerly receive it. We will starve spiritually without this food as surely as we will starve physically without our daily bread.

55:3 God's covenant with David promised a permanent homeland for the Israelites, no threat from pagan nations, and no wars (2 Samuel 7:10, 11). But Israel did not fulfil its part of the covenant by obeying God and staying away from idols. Even so, God was ready to renew his covenant again. He is a forgiving God!

55:3
[i]Isa 54:8
[j]Ac 13:34*

55:4
[k]Jer 30:9; Eze 34:23-24

55:5
[l]Isa 49:6
[m]Isa 60:9

55:6
[n]Ps 32:6; Isa 49:8; 2Co 6:1-2
[o]Isa 65:24

55:7
[p]Isa 32:7; 59:7
[q]Isa 44:22
[r]Isa 54:10
[s]Isa 1:18; 40:2

55:8
[t]Isa 53:6

55:9
[u]Ps 103:11

55:10
[v]Isa 30:23
[w]2Co 9:10

55:11
[x]Isa 45:23
[y]Isa 44:26

55:12
[z]Isa 54:10, 13
[a]1Ch 16:33
[b]Ps 98:8

55:13
[c]Isa 5:6
[d]Isa 41:19
[e]Isa 63:12

56:1
[a]Isa 1:17
[b]Ps 85:9

my faithful love[i] promised to David.[j]
4 See, I have made him a witness to the peoples,
a leader and commander[k] of the peoples.
5 Surely you will summon nations[l] you know not,
and nations that do not know you will hasten to you,
because of the LORD your God,
the Holy One of Israel,
for he has endowed you with splendour."[m]

6 Seek the LORD while he may be found;[n]
call[o] on him while he is near.
7 Let the wicked forsake his way
and the evil man his thoughts.[p]
Let him turn[q] to the LORD, and he will have mercy[r] on him,
and to our God, for he will freely pardon.[s]

8 "For my thoughts are not your thoughts,
neither are your ways my ways,"[t]
declares the LORD.
9 "As the heavens are higher than the earth,[u]
so are my ways higher than your ways
and my thoughts than your thoughts.
10 As the rain[v] and the snow
come down from heaven,
and do not return to it
without watering the earth
and making it bud and flourish,
so that it yields seed for the sower and bread for the eater,[w]
11 so is my word that goes out from my mouth:
It will not return to me empty,[x]
but will accomplish what I desire
and achieve the purpose[y] for which I sent it.
12 You will go out in joy
and be led forth in peace;[z]
the mountains and hills
will burst into song before you,
and all the trees[a] of the field
will clap their hands.[b]
13 Instead of the thornbush will grow the pine tree,
and instead of briers[c] the myrtle[d] will grow.
This will be for the LORD's renown,[e]
for an everlasting sign,
which will not be destroyed."

Salvation for Others

56 This is what the LORD says:

"Maintain justice[a]
and do what is right,
for my salvation[b] is close at hand
and my righteousness will soon be revealed.

55:6 Isaiah tells us to call on the Lord while he is near. God is not planning to move away from us, but we often move far from him or erect a barrier between ourselves and him. Don't wait until you have drifted far away from God to seek him. Later in life turning to him may be far more difficult. Or God may come to judge the earth before you decide to turn to him. Seek God now, while you can, before it is too late.

55:8, 9 The people of Israel were foolish to act as if they knew what God was thinking and planning. His knowledge and wisdom are far greater than man's. We are foolish to try to fit God into our mould—to make his plans and purposes conform to ours. Instead, we must strive to fit into *his* plans.

2Blessed[c] is the man who does this,
the man who holds it fast,
who keeps the Sabbath[d] without desecrating it,
and keeps his hand from doing any evil."
3Let no foreigner who has bound himself to the LORD say,
"The LORD will surely exclude me from his people."
And let not any eunuch[e] complain,
"I am only a dry tree."
4For this is what the LORD says:

"To the eunuchs who keep my Sabbaths,
who choose what pleases me
and hold fast to my covenant—
5to them I will give within my temple and its walls[f]
a memorial and a name
better than sons and daughters;
I will give them an everlasting name
that will not be cut off.[g]
6And foreigners who bind themselves to the LORD
to serve[h] him,
to love the name of the LORD,
and to worship him,
all who keep the Sabbath[i] without desecrating it
and who hold fast to my covenant—
7these I will bring to my holy mountain[j]
and give them joy in my house of prayer.
Their burnt offerings and sacrifices[k]
will be accepted on my altar;
for my house will be called
a house of prayer for all nations.[l]"[m]
8The Sovereign LORD declares—
he who gathers the exiles of Israel:
"I will gather[n] still others to them
besides those already gathered."

God's Accusation Against the Wicked

9Come, all you beasts of the field,[o]
come and devour, all you beasts of the forest!
10Israel's watchmen[p] are blind,
they all lack knowledge;
they are all mute dogs,
they cannot bark;
they lie around and dream,
they love to sleep.[q]

56:2 [c]Ps 119:2 [d]Ex 20:8, 10; Isa 58:13
56:3 [e]Jer 38:7 *fn*; Ac 8:27
56:5 [f]Isa 26:1; 60:18 [g]Isa 48:19; 55:13
56:6 [h]Isa 60:7, 10; 61:5 [i]ver 2, 4
56:7 [j]Isa 2:2 [k]Ro 12:1; Heb 13:15 [l]Mt 21:13*; Lk 19:46* [m]Mk 11:17*
56:8 [n]Isa 11:12; 60:3-11; Jn 10:16
56:9 [o]Isa 18:6; Jer 12:9
56:10 [p]Eze 3:17 [q]Na 3:18

56:2 God commanded his people to rest and honour him on the Sabbath (Exodus 20:8–11). He wants us to serve him every day, but he wants us to make one day special when we rest and focus our thoughts on him. For the Israelites, this special day was the Sabbath (Saturday). Some Christians set Saturday aside as this special day, but many accept Sunday (the day of the week that Jesus rose from the dead) as the "Lord's Day", a day of rest and honour to God.

56:3 Isaiah clearly proclaims the radical message that God's blessings are for *all* people, even foreigners and eunuchs, who were often excluded from worship and not even considered citizens in Israel. Whatever your race, social position, work, or financial situation, God's blessings are as much for you as for anyone else. No-one must exclude in any way those God chooses to include.

56:7 Jesus quoted from this verse when he threw the money changers out of the temple (Mark 11:17). See the note on Mark 11:15–17.

56:9–11 The "watchmen" were the nation's leaders. The leaders of Israel were blind to every danger. Apathetic about their people's needs, they were more concerned about satisfying their own greed. Leadership's special privileges can cause leaders either to sacrifice for the good of their people or to sacrifice their people for their own greed. If you are in a leadership position, use it for the good of your people.

56:11
[r]Eze 34:2
[s]Isa 1:3
[t]Isa 57:17; Eze 13:19; Mic 3:11

11They are dogs with mighty appetites;
they never have enough.
They are shepherds[r] who lack understanding;[s]
they all turn to their own way,
each seeks his own gain.[t]
12"Come," each one cries, "let me get wine!
Let us drink our fill of beer!
And tomorrow will be like today,
or even far better."[u]

56:12
[u]Ps 10:6; Lk 12:18-19

57

57:1
[a]Ps 12:1
[b]Isa 42:25
[c]2Ki 22:20

The righteous perish,[a]
and no-one ponders it in his heart;[b]
devout men are taken away,
and no-one understands
that the righteous are taken away
to be spared from evil.[c]
2Those who walk uprightly[d]
enter into peace;
they find rest as they lie in death.

57:2
[d]Isa 26:7

3"But you—come here, you sons of a sorceress,
you offspring of adulterers[e] and prostitutes![f]
4Whom are you mocking?
At whom do you sneer
and stick out your tongue?
Are you not a brood of rebels,
the offspring of liars?
5You burn with lust among the oaks
and under every spreading tree;[g]
you sacrifice your children[h] in the ravines
and under the overhanging crags.
6⌊The idols⌋[i] among the smooth stones of the ravines are your portion;
they, they are your lot.
Yes, to them you have poured out drink offerings[j]
and offered grain offerings.
In the light of these things, should I relent?[k]
7You have made your bed on a high and lofty hill;[l]
there you went up to offer your sacrifices.
8Behind your doors and your doorposts
you have put your pagan symbols.
Forsaking me, you uncovered your bed,
you climbed into it and opened it wide;
you made a pact with those whose beds you love,[m]
and you looked on their nakedness.[n]
9You went to Molech[a] with olive oil
and increased your perfumes.
You sent your ambassadors[b][o] far away;
you descended to the grave[c] itself!
10You were wearied by all your ways,
but you would not say, 'It is hopeless.'[p]

57:3
[e]Mt 16:4
[f]Isa 1:21

57:5
[g]2Ki 16:4
[h]Lev 18:21; Ps 106:37-38; Eze 16:20

57:6
[i]Jer 3:9
[j]Jer 7:18
[k]Jer 5:9, 29; 9:9

57:7
[l]Jer 3:6; Eze 16:16

57:8
[m]Eze 16:26; 23:7
[n]Eze 23:18

57:9
[o]Eze 23:16, 40

57:10
[p]Jer 2:25; 18:12

[a]9 Or *to the king* [b]9 Or *idols* [c]9 Hebrew *Sheol*

57:7, 8 Marriage is an exclusive relationship where a man and a woman become one. Adultery breaks this beautiful bond of unity. When the people turned from God and gave their love to idols, God said they were committing adultery—breaking their exclusive commitment to God. How could people give their love to worthless wood and stone instead of to the God who made them and loved them so very much?

57:9 Molech was an Ammonite god whose worship included child sacrifice.

You found renewal of your strength,
and so you did not faint.

11 "Whom have you so dreaded and feared[q]
that you have been false to me,
and have neither remembered[r] me
nor pondered this in your hearts?
Is it not because I have long been silent[s]
that you do not fear me?
12 I will expose your righteousness and your works,[t]
and they will not benefit you.
13 When you cry out[u] for help,
let your collection ⌞of idols⌟ save you!
The wind will carry all of them off,
a mere breath will blow them away.
But the man who makes me his refuge
will inherit the land[v]
and possess my holy mountain."[w]

Comfort for the Contrite

14 And it will be said:

"Build up, build up, prepare the road!
Remove the obstacles out of the way of my people."[x]
15 For this is what the high and lofty[y] One says—
he who lives for ever,[z] whose name is holy:
"I live in a high and holy place,
but also with him who is contrite[a] and lowly in spirit,[b]
to revive the spirit of the lowly
and to revive the heart of the contrite.[c]
16 I will not accuse for ever,
nor will I always be angry,[d]
for then the spirit of man would grow faint before me—
the breath of man that I have created.
17 I was enraged by his sinful greed;[e]
I punished him, and hid my face in anger,
yet he kept on in his wilful ways.[f]
18 I have seen his ways, but I will heal[g] him;
I will guide him and restore comfort[h] to him,
19 creating praise on the lips[i] of the mourners in Israel.
Peace, peace,[j] to those far and near,"[k]
says the LORD. "And I will heal them."
20 But the wicked[l] are like the tossing sea,
which cannot rest,
whose waves cast up mire and mud.
21 "There is no peace," [m] says my God, "for the wicked."[n]

57:11 [q]Pr 29:25 [r]Jer 2:32; 3:21 [s]Ps 50:21

57:12 [t]Isa 29:15; Mic 3:2-4, 8

57:13 [u]Jer 22:20; 30:15 [v]Ps 37:9 [w]Isa 65:9-11

57:14 [x]Isa 62:10; Jer 18:15

57:15 [y]Isa 52:13 [z]Dt 33:27 [a]Ps 147:3 [b]Ps 34:18; 51:17; Isa 66:2 [c]Isa 61:1

57:16 [d]Ps 85:5; 103:9; Mic 7:18

57:17 [e]Isa 56:11 [f]Isa 1:4

57:18 [g]Isa 30:26 [h]Isa 61:1-3

57:19 [i]Isa 6:7; Heb 13:15 [j]Eph 2:17 [k]Ac 2:39

57:20 [l]Job 18:5-21

57:21 [m]Isa 59:8 [n]Isa 48:22

57:12 God says that he will expose their righteousness and works for what they really were—mere pretentions of doing good. Isaiah warned these people that their righteousness and works would not save them any more than their weak, worthless idols. We cannot gain our salvation through good deeds because our best deeds are not good enough to outweigh our sins. Salvation is a gift from God, received only through faith in Christ, not good deeds (Ephesians 2:8, 9).

57:14–21 Verses 1–13 speak of pride and lust; verses 14–21 tell how God relates to those who are humble and repentant ("contrite"). The high and holy God came down to our level to save us because it is impossible for us go up to his level to save ourselves (see 2 Chronicles 6:18; Psalm 51:1–7; Philippians 2).

True Fasting

58
"Shout it aloud,[a] do not hold back.
Raise your voice like a trumpet.
Declare to my people their rebellion[b]
and to the house of Jacob their sins.
2For day after day they seek[c] me out;
they seem eager to know my ways,
as if they were a nation that does what is right
and has not forsaken the commands of its God.
They ask me for just decisions
and seem eager for God to come near[d] them.
3'Why have we fasted,'[e] they say,
'and you have not seen it?
Why have we humbled ourselves,
and you have not noticed?'[f]

"Yet on the day of your fasting, you do as you please[g]
and exploit all your workers.
4Your fasting ends in quarrelling and strife,[h]
and in striking each other with wicked fists.
You cannot fast as you do today
and expect your voice to be heard[i] on high.
5Is this the kind of fast[j] I have chosen,
only a day for a man to humble[k] himself?
Is it only for bowing one's head like a reed
and for lying on sackcloth and ashes?[l]
Is that what you call a fast,
a day acceptable to the LORD?

6"Is not this the kind of fasting I have chosen:
to loose the chains of injustice[m]
and untie the cords of the yoke,
to set the oppressed[n] free
and break every yoke?
7Is it not to share your food with the hungry[o]
and to provide the poor wanderer with shelter[p]—
when you see the naked, to clothe[q] him,
and not to turn away from your own flesh and blood?[r]
8Then your light will break forth like the dawn,[s]
and your healing[t] will quickly appear;
then your righteousness[a] will go before you,
and the glory of the LORD will be your rear guard.[u]
9Then you will call,[v] and the LORD will answer;
you will cry for help, and he will say: Here am I.

"If you do away with the yoke of oppression,
with the pointing finger[w] and malicious talk,[x]
10and if you spend yourselves on behalf of the hungry
and satisfy the needs of the oppressed,[y]
then your light[z] will rise in the darkness,

a 8 Or *your righteous One*

58:1
a Isa 40:6
b Isa 48:8

58:2
c Isa 48:1; Tit 1:16; Jas 4:8
d Isa 29:13

58:3
e Lev 16:29
f Mal 3:14
g Isa 22:13; Zec 7:5-6

58:4
h 1Ki 21:9-13; Isa 59:6
i Isa 59:2

58:5
j Zec 7:5
k 1Ki 21:27
l Job 2:8

58:6
m Ne 5:10-11
n Jer 34:9

58:7
o Eze 18:16; Lk 3:11
p Isa 16:4; Heb 13:2
q Job 31:19-20; Mt 25:36
r Ge 29:14; Lk 10:31-32

58:8
s Job 11:17
t Isa 30:26
u Ex 14:19

58:9
v Ps 50:15
w Pr 6:13
x Ps 12:2; Isa 59:13

58:10
y Dt 15:7-8
z Isa 42:16

58:1ff True worship was more than religious ritual, going to the temple every day, fasting, and listening to Scripture readings. These people missed the point of a living, vital relationship with God. He doesn't want us acting piously when we have unforgiven sin in our hearts and perform sinful practices with our hands. More important even than correct worship and doctrine is genuine compassion for the poor, the helpless, and the oppressed.

58:6–12 We cannot be saved by deeds of service without faith in Christ, but our faith lacks sincerity if it doesn't reach out to others. Fasting can be beneficial spiritually and physically, but at its best fasting helps only the person doing it. God says he wants our service to go beyond our own personal growth to acts of kindness, charity, justice, and generosity. True fasting is more than what we don't eat; it is pleasing God by applying his word to our society.

and your night will become like the noonday.[a]
11The LORD will guide you always;
he will satisfy your needs[b] in a sun-scorched land
and will strengthen your frame.
You will be like a well-watered garden,[c]
like a spring[d] whose waters never fail.
12Your people will rebuild the ancient ruins[e]
and will raise up the age-old foundations;[f]
you will be called Repairer of Broken Walls,
Restorer of Streets with Dwellings.

13"If you keep your feet from breaking the Sabbath[g]
and from doing as you please on my holy day,
if you call the Sabbath a delight[h]
and the LORD's holy day honourable,
and if you honour it by not going your own way
and not doing as you please or speaking idle words,
14then you will find your joy[i] in the LORD,
and I will cause you to ride on the heights[j] of the land
and to feast on the inheritance of your father Jacob."
The mouth of the LORD has spoken.[k]

58:10 [a]Job 11:17
58:11 [b]Ps 107:9 [c]SS 4:15 [d]Jn 4:14
58:12 [e]Isa 49:8 [f]Isa 44:28
58:13 [g]Isa 56:2 [h]Ps 84:2, 10
58:14 [i]Job 22:26 [j]Dt 32:13 [k]Isa 1:20

Sin, Confession and Redemption

59

Surely the arm of the LORD is not too short[a] to save,
nor his ear too dull to hear.[b]
2But your iniquities have separated
you from your God;
your sins have hidden his face from you,
so that he will not hear.[c]
3For your hands are stained with blood,[d]
your fingers with guilt.
Your lips have spoken lies,
and your tongue mutters wicked things.
4No-one calls for justice;
no-one pleads his case with integrity.
They rely on empty arguments and speak lies;
they conceive trouble and give birth to evil.[e]
5They hatch the eggs of vipers
and spin a spider's web.[f]
Whoever eats their eggs will die,
and when one is broken, an adder is hatched.
6Their cobwebs are useless for clothing;
they cannot cover themselves with what they make.[g]
Their deeds are evil deeds,
and acts of violence[h] are in their hands.
7Their feet rush into sin;
they are swift to shed innocent blood.[i]
Their thoughts are evil thoughts;[j]

59:1 [a]Nu 11:23; Isa 50:2 [b]Isa 58:9; 65:24
59:2 [c]Isa 1:15; 58:4
59:3 [d]Isa 1:15
59:4 [e]Job 15:35; Ps 7:14
59:5 [f]Job 8:14
59:6 [g]Isa 28:20 [h]Isa 58:4
59:7 [i]Pr 6:17 [j]Mk 7:21-22

58:13, 14 The day of rest should also be honoured not only because Sabbath-keeping is a commandment but also because it is best for us and because it honours God. Keeping the Sabbath honours God, our Creator, who also rested on the seventh day (Genesis 2:3). It also unifies our family and sets priorities for them. Our day of rest refreshes us spiritually and physically – providing time when we can gather together for worship and when we can reflect on God without the stress of our everyday activities.

59:1–14 Sin offends our holy God and separates us from him. Because God is holy, he cannot ignore, excuse, or tolerate sin as though it didn't matter. Sin cuts people off from him, forming a wall to isolate God from the people he loves. No wonder this long list of wretched sins makes God angry and forces him to look the other way. People who die with their life of sin unforgiven separate themselves eternally from God. God wants them to live with him for ever, but he cannot take them into his holy presence unless their sin is removed. Have you confessed your sin to God, allowing him to remove it? The Lord can save you if you turn to him.

ruin and destruction mark their ways.[k]
8The way of peace they do not know;
there is no justice in their paths.
They have turned them into crooked roads;
no-one who walks in them will know peace.[l]

9So justice is far from us,
and righteousness does not reach us.
We look for light, but all is darkness;[m]
for brightness, but we walk in deep shadows.
10Like the blind[n] we grope along the wall,
feeling our way like men without eyes.
At midday we stumble[o] as if it were twilight;
among the strong, we are like the dead.[p]
11We all growl like bears;
we moan mournfully like doves.[q]
We look for justice, but find none;
for deliverance, but it is far away.

12For our offences[r] are many in your sight,
and our sins testify[s] against us.
Our offences are ever with us,
and we acknowledge our iniquities:
13rebellion and treachery against the LORD,
turning our backs[t] on our God,
fomenting oppression[u] and revolt,
uttering lies[v] our hearts have conceived.
14So justice is driven back,
and righteousness[w] stands at a distance;
truth[x] has stumbled in the streets,
honesty cannot enter.
15Truth is nowhere to be found,
and whoever shuns evil becomes a prey.

The LORD looked and was displeased
that there was no justice.
16He saw that there was no-one,[y]
he was appalled that there was no-one to intervene;
so his own arm worked salvation[z] for him,
and his own righteousness sustained him.
17He put on righteousness as his breastplate,[a]
and the helmet[b] of salvation on his head;
he put on the garments[c] of vengeance
and wrapped himself in zeal[d] as in a cloak.
18According to what they have done,
so will he repay
wrath to his enemies
and retribution to his foes;
he will repay the islands their due.
19From the west,[e] men will fear the name of the LORD,
and from the rising of the sun,[f] they will revere his glory.
For he will come like a pent-up flood

59:7 [k]Ro 3:15-17*
59:8 [l]Isa 57:21; Lk 1:79
59:9 [m]Isa 5:30; 8:20
59:10 [n]Dt 28:29 [o]Isa 8:15 [p]La 3:6
59:11 [q]Isa 38:14; Eze 7:16
59:12 [r]Ezr 9:6 [s]Isa 3:9
59:13 [t]Pr 30:9; Mt 10:33; Tit 1:16 [u]Isa 5:7 [v]Mk 7:21-22
59:14 [w]Isa 1:21 [x]Isa 48:1
59:16 [y]Isa 41:28 [z]Ps 98:1; Isa 63:5
59:17 [a]Eph 6:14 [b]Eph 6:17; 1Th 5:8 [c]Isa 63:3 [d]Isa 9:7
59:19 [e]Isa 49:12 [f]Ps 113:3

59:15 Because of Israel's wilful, persistent rebellion (chapters 56 – 59), the nation became unable to take action against its sins. Sin fills the vacuum left when God's truth no longer fills our lives. Only God can defeat sin.

59:16, 17 God would, in fact, act to rescue the nation from enemy armies (Assyria and Babylon) and to punish wicked Israelites as well. He would also rescue his people from sin. Because this is an impossible task for any human, God himself, as the Messiah, would personally step in to help (Romans 11:26, 27). Whether we sin once or many times, out of rebellion or out of ignorance, our sin separates us from God and will continue to separate us until God forgives us and removes it.

that the breath of the LORD drives along.[a]

20"The Redeemer will come to Zion,
to those in Jacob who repent of their sins,"[g]
declares the LORD.

21"As for me, this is my covenant with them," says the LORD. "My Spirit,[h] who
is on you, and my words that I have put in your mouth will not depart from your mouth,
or from the mouths of your children, or from the mouths of their descendants from
this time on and for ever," says the LORD.

3. The future kingdom

The Glory of Zion

60 "Arise,[a] shine, for your light[b] has come,
and the glory of the LORD rises upon you.
2See, darkness covers the earth
and thick darkness[c] is over the peoples,
but the LORD rises upon you
and his glory appears over you.
3Nations[d] will come to your light,
and kings[e] to the brightness of your dawn.

4"Lift up your eyes and look about you:
All assemble[f] and come to you;
your sons come from afar,
and your daughters[g] are carried on the arm.[h]
5Then you will look and be radiant,
your heart will throb and swell with joy;
the wealth on the seas will be brought to you,
to you the riches of the nations will come.
6Herds of camels will cover your land,
young camels of Midian[i] and Ephah.[j]
And all from Sheba[k] will come,
bearing gold and incense[l]
and proclaiming the praise[m] of the LORD.
7All Kedar's[n] flocks will be gathered to you,
the rams of Nebaioth will serve you;
they will be accepted as offerings on my altar,
and I will adorn my glorious temple.[o]

8"Who are these[p] that fly along like clouds,
like doves to their nests?
9Surely the islands[q] look to me;
in the lead are the ships of Tarshish,[a][r]
bringing[s] your sons from afar,

a *19 Or When the enemy comes in like a flood, / the Spirit of the LORD will put him to flight* a *9 Or the trading ships*

59:20 g Ac 2:38-39; Ro 11:26-27*
59:21 h Isa 11:2; 44:3
60:1 a Isa 52:2 b Eph 5:14
60:2 c Jer 13:16; Col 1:13
60:3 d Isa 45:14; Rev 21:24 e Isa 49:23
60:4 f Isa 11:12 g Isa 43:6 h Isa 49:20-22
60:6 i Ge 25:2 j Ge 25:4 k Ps 72:10 l Isa 43:23; Mt 2:11 m Isa 42:10
60:7 n Ge 25:13 o ver 13; Hag 2:3, 7, 9
60:8 p Isa 49:21
60:9 q Isa 11:11 r Isa 2:16 *fn* s Isa 14:2; 43:6

59:21 When the Holy Spirit dwells within his people, they change. Their former desires no longer entice them; now their chief aim is to please God. We who are Christians today are the heirs of this prophecy; we are able to respond to God's will and distinguish between good and evil because the Holy Spirit dwells within us (John 14:26; Philippians 2:13; Hebrews 5:14).

60:1ff As we read these promises, we long for their fulfilment. But we must patiently wait for God's timing. He is in control of history, and he weaves together all our lives into his plan.

60:6, 7 The places mentioned belonged to obscure tribes in the Arabian desert hundreds of miles from Israel. All people would come to Jerusalem because God would be living there and they would be attracted to his light. Don't be discouraged when you look around and see so few people turning to God; one day people throughout the earth will recognise him as the one true God.

60:19, 20 See Revelation 21:23, 24 and 22:5, where this beautiful reality is also promised.

with their silver and gold,
to the honour of the LORD your God,
the Holy One of Israel,
for he has endowed you with splendour.[t]
10"Foreigners[u] will rebuild your walls,
and their kings[v] will serve you.
Though in anger I struck you,
in favour I will show you compassion.[w]
11Your gates[x] will always stand open,
they will never be shut, day or night,
so that men may bring you the wealth of the nations[y]—
their kings[z] led in triumphal procession.
12For the nation or kingdom that will not serve[a] you will perish;
it will be utterly ruined.

13"The glory of Lebanon[b] will come to you,
the pine, the fir and the cypress together,[c]
to adorn the place of my sanctuary;
and I will glorify the place of my feet.[d]
14The sons of your oppressors[e] will come bowing before you;
all who despise you will bow down[f] at your feet
and will call you the City of the LORD,
Zion[g] of the Holy One of Israel.

15"Although you have been forsaken[h] and hated,
with no-one travelling[i] through,
I will make you the everlasting pride[j]
and the joy[k] of all generations.
16You will drink the milk of nations
and be nursed[l] at royal breasts.
Then you will know that I, the LORD, am your Saviour,
your Redeemer,[m] the Mighty One of Jacob.
17Instead of bronze I will bring you gold,
and silver in place of iron.
Instead of wood I will bring you bronze,
and iron in place of stones.
I will make peace your governor
and righteousness your ruler.
18No longer will violence be heard in your land,
nor ruin or destruction within your borders,
but you will call your walls Salvation[n]
and your gates Praise.
19The sun will no more be your light by day,
nor will the brightness of the moon shine on you,
for the LORD will be your everlasting light,[o]
and your God will be your glory.[p]
20Your sun[q] will never set again,
and your moon will wane no more;
the LORD will be your everlasting light,
and your days of sorrow[r] will end.
21Then will all your people be righteous[s]
and they will possess[t] the land for ever.
They are the shoot I have planted,[u]
the work of my hands,[v]
for the display of my splendour.[w]
22The least of you will become a thousand,
the smallest a mighty nation.
I am the LORD;
in its time I will do this swiftly."

60:9
[t]Isa 55:5

60:10
[u]Isa 14:1-2
[v]Isa 49:23; Rev 21:24
[w]Isa 54:8

60:11
[x]ver 18; Isa 62:10; Rev 21:25
[y]ver 5; Rev 21:26
[z]Ps 149:8

60:12
[a]Isa 14:2

60:13
[b]Isa 35:2
[c]Isa 41:19
[d]1Ch 28:2; Ps 132:7

60:14
[e]Isa 14:2
[f]Isa 49:23; Rev 3:9
[g]Heb 12:22

60:15
[h]Isa 1:7-9; 6:12
[i]Isa 33:8
[j]Isa 4:2
[k]Isa 65:18

60:16
[l]Isa 49:23; 66:11, 12
[m]Isa 59:20

60:18
[n]Isa 26:1

60:19
[o]Rev 22:5
[p]Zec 2:5; Rev 21:23

60:20
[q]Isa 30:26
[r]Isa 35:10

60:21
[s]Rev 21:27
[t]Ps 37:11, 22; Isa 57:13; 61:7
[u]Mt 15:13
[v]Isa 19:25; 29:23; Eph 2:10
[w]Isa 52:1

The Year of the LORD's Favour

61 The Spirit[a] of the Sovereign LORD is on me,
because the LORD has anointed[b] me
to preach good news to the poor.[c]
He has sent me to bind up[d] the broken-hearted,
to proclaim freedom for the captives[e]
and release from darkness for the prisoners,[a]
2 to proclaim the year of the LORD's favour[f]
and the day of vengeance[g] of our God,
to comfort[h] all who mourn,
3 and provide for those who grieve in Zion—
to bestow on them a crown of beauty
instead of ashes,
the oil of gladness
instead of mourning,
and a garment of praise
instead of a spirit of despair.
They will be called oaks of righteousness,
a planting of the LORD
for the display of his splendour.[i]

4 They will rebuild the ancient ruins[j]
and restore the places long devastated;
they will renew the ruined cities
that have been devastated for generations.
5 Aliens[k] will shepherd your flocks;
foreigners will work your fields and vineyards.
6 And you will be called priests[l] of the LORD,
you will be named ministers of our God.
You will feed on the wealth[m] of nations,
and in their riches you will boast.

7 Instead of their shame
my people will receive a double[n] portion,
and instead of disgrace
they will rejoice in their inheritance;
and so they will inherit a double portion in their land,
and everlasting joy will be theirs.

8 "For I, the LORD, love justice;[o]
I hate robbery and iniquity.
In my faithfulness I will reward them
and make an everlasting covenant[p] with them.
9 Their descendants will be known among the nations
and their offspring among the peoples.
All who see them will acknowledge
that they are a people the LORD has blessed."

a *1* Hebrew; Septuagint *the blind*

61:1 [a] Isa 11:2 [b] Ps 45:7 [c] Mt 11:5; Lk 7:22 [d] Isa 57:15 [e] Isa 42:7; 49:9
61:2 [f] Isa 49:8; Lk 4:18-19* [g] Isa 34:8 [h] Isa 57:18; Mt 5:4
61:3 [i] Isa 60:20-21
61:4 [j] Isa 49:8; Eze 36:33; Am 9:14
61:5 [k] Isa 14:1-2
61:6 [l] Ex 19:6; 1Pe 2:5 [m] Isa 60:11
61:7 [n] Isa 40:2; Zec 9:12
61:8 [o] Ps 11:7; Isa 5:16 [p] Isa 55:3

61:1, 2 Jesus quoted these words in Luke 4:18, 19. As he read to the people in the synagogue, he stopped in the middle of 61:2 after the words, "to proclaim the year of the LORD's favour". Rolling up the scroll, he said, "Today this scripture is fulfilled in your hearing" (Luke 4:21). The next phrase in 61:2, "and the day of vengeance of our God", will come true when Jesus returns to earth again. We are now under God's favour; his wrath is yet to come.

61:6 Under the old covenant, God ordained the priests of Israel to stand between him and his people. They brought God's word to the people and the people's needs and sins to God. Under the new covenant, all believers are priests of the Lord, reading God's word and seeking to understand it, confessing their sins directly to God, and ministering to others.

61:8 We suffer for many reasons—our own mistakes, someone else's mistakes, injustice. When we suffer for our own mistakes, we get what we deserve. When we suffer because of others or because of injustice, God is angry. God in his mercy says that his people have suffered enough. God will reward those who suffer because of injustice. He will settle all accounts.

10 I delight greatly in the LORD;
my soul rejoices[q] in my God.
For he has clothed me with garments of salvation
and arrayed me in a robe of righteousness,[r]
as a bridegroom adorns his head like a priest,
and as a bride[s] adorns herself with her jewels.
11 For as the soil makes the young plant come up
and a garden causes seeds to grow,
so the Sovereign LORD will make righteousness[t] and praise
spring up before all nations.

Zion's New Name

62 For Zion's sake I will not keep silent,
for Jerusalem's sake I will not remain quiet,
till her righteousness[a] shines out like the dawn,
her salvation like a blazing torch.
2 The nations[b] will see your righteousness,
and all kings your glory;
you will be called by a new name[c]
that the mouth of the LORD will bestow.
3 You will be a crown[d] of splendour in the LORD's hand,
a royal diadem in the hand of your God.
4 No longer will they call you Deserted,[e]
or name your land Desolate.
But you will be called Hephzibah,[a]
and your land Beulah;[b]
for the LORD will take delight[f] in you,
and your land will be married.[g]
5 As a young man marries a maiden,
so will your sons[c] marry you;
as a bridegroom rejoices over his bride,
so will your God rejoice[h] over you.

6 I have posted watchmen[i] on your walls, O Jerusalem;
they will never be silent day or night.
You who call on the LORD,
give yourselves no rest,
7 and give him no rest[j] till he establishes Jerusalem
and makes her the praise of the earth.

8 The LORD has sworn by his right hand
and by his mighty arm:
"Never again will I give your grain[k]
as food for your enemies,
and never again will foreigners drink the new wine
for which you have toiled;
9 but those who harvest it will eat it
and praise the LORD,
and those who gather the grapes will drink it
in the courts of my sanctuary."

a 4 *Hephzibah* means *my delight is in her.* b 4 *Beulah* means *married.* c 5 Or *Builder*

61:10 [q] Isa 25:9; Hab 3:18 [r] Ps 132:9; Isa 52:1 [s] Isa 49:18; Rev 21:2
61:11 [t] Ps 85:11
62:1 [a] Isa 1:26
62:2 [b] Isa 52:10; 60:3 [c] ver 4, 12
62:3 [d] Isa 28:5; Zec 9:16; 1Th 2:19
62:4 [e] Isa 54:6 [f] Jer 32:41; Zep 3:17 [g] Jer 3:14; Hos 2:19
62:5 [h] Isa 65:19
62:6 [i] Isa 52:8; Eze 3:17
62:7 [j] Mt 15:21-28; Lk 18:1-8
62:8 [k] Dt 28:30-33; Isa 1:7; Jer 5:17

61:10 "Me" could refer to the Messiah, the person anointed with the Spirit of the Lord (61:1), or to Zion (62:1), which symbolises God's people. The imagery of the bridegroom is often used in Scripture to depict the Messiah (see Matthew 9:15), while the imagery of the bride is used to depict God's people (see Revelation 19:6–8). We too can be clothed with the righteousness of Christ when we believe in him (2 Corinthians 5:21).

62:1–7 Many commentators believe Isaiah is speaking in verse 1. If so, Isaiah's zeal for his people and his desire to see the work of salvation completed caused him to pray without resting, hoping that Israel would be saved. We should have Isaiah's zeal to see God's will done. This is what we mean when we pray, "Your kingdom come, your will be done on earth as it is in heaven." It is good to keep praying persistently for others.

10Pass through, pass through the gates![l]
Prepare the way for the people.
Build up, build up the highway![mn]
Remove the stones.
Raise a banner[o] for the nations.

11The LORD has made proclamation
to the ends of the earth:
"Say to the Daughter of Zion,[p]
'See, your Saviour comes![q]
See, his reward is with him,
and his recompense accompanies him.' "[r]
12They will be called[s] the Holy People,[t]
the Redeemed[u] of the LORD;
and you will be called Sought After,
the City No Longer Deserted.[v]

62:10 [l]Isa 60:11 [m]Isa 57:14 [n]Isa 11:16 [o]Isa 11:10

62:11 [p]Zec 9:9; Mt 21:5 [q]Rev 22:12 [r]Isa 40:10

62:12 [s]ver 4 [t]1Pe 2:9 [u]Isa 35:9 [v]Isa 42:16

God's Day of Vengeance and Redemption

63 Who is this coming from Edom,
from Bozrah,[a] with his garments stained crimson?
Who is this, robed in splendour,
striding forward in the greatness of his strength?

"It is I, speaking in righteousness,
mighty to save."[b]

2Why are your garments red,
like those of one treading the winepress?

3"I have trodden the winepress[c] alone;
from the nations no-one was with me.
I trampled them in my anger
and trod them down in my wrath;[d]
their blood spattered my garments,[e]
and I stained all my clothing.
4For the day of vengeance was in my heart,
and the year of my redemption has come.
5I looked, but there was no-one[f] to help,
I was appalled that no-one gave support;
so my own arm[g] worked salvation for me,
and my own wrath sustained me.[h]
6I trampled the nations in my anger;
in my wrath I made them drunk[i]
and poured their blood[j] on the ground."

63:1 [a]Am 1:12 [b]Zep 3:17

63:3 [c]Rev 14:20; 19:15 [d]Isa 22:5 [e]Rev 19:13

63:5 [f]Isa 41:28 [g]Ps 44:3; 98:1 [h]Isa 59:16

63:6 [i]Isa 29:9 [j]Isa 34:3

Praise and Prayer

7I will tell of the kindnesses[k] of the LORD,
the deeds for which he is to be praised,
according to all the LORD has done for us—
yes, the many good things he has done
for the house of Israel,
according to his compassion[l] and many kindnesses.

63:7 [k]Isa 54:8 [l]Ps 51:1; Eph 2:4

62:12 The people of Jerusalem (Zion) will have new names—"the Holy People" and "the Redeemed of the LORD". Believers today also have new names—Christians. In 1 Peter 2:5, we are called "a holy priesthood".

63:1–4 Edom was a constant enemy of Israel despite its common ancestry in Isaac (Genesis 25:23). Edom rejoiced at any trouble Israel faced. The imagery in this passage is of a watchman on the wall of Jerusalem, seeing Edom approaching and fearing that the Edomite king in his crimson garment is leading an attack. But it turns out to be the Lord, in bloodstained clothes, who has trampled and destroyed Edom. Bozrah is a city in Edom. (For other prophecies against Edom, see Amos 1:11, 12; Obadiah 1:10, 11; Malachi 1:2–4.)

8He said, "Surely they are my people,[m]
sons who will not be false to me";
and so he became their Saviour.
9In all their distress he too was distressed,
and the angel of his presence[n] saved them.
In his love and mercy he redeemed[o] them;
he lifted them up and carried[p] them
all the days of old.
10Yet they rebelled[q]
and grieved his Holy Spirit.[r]
So he turned and became their enemy[s]
and he himself fought against them.

11Then his people recalled[a] the days of old,
the days of Moses and his people —
where is he who brought them through the sea,[t]
with the shepherd of his flock?
Where is he who set
his Holy Spirit[u] among them,
12who sent his glorious arm of power
to be at Moses' right hand,
who divided the waters[v] before them,
to gain for himself everlasting renown,
13who led[w] them through the depths?
Like a horse in open country,
they did not stumble;[x]
14like cattle that go down to the plain,
they were given rest by the Spirit of the LORD.
This is how you guided your people
to make for yourself a glorious name.

15Look down from heaven[y] and see
from your lofty throne,[z] holy and glorious.
Where are your zeal[a] and your might?
Your tenderness and compassion[b] are withheld from us.
16But you are our Father,
though Abraham does not know us

63:8 [m]Isa 51:4
63:9 [n]Ex 33:14 [o]Dt 7:7-8 [p]Dt 1:31
63:10 [q]Ps 78:40 [r]Ps 51:11; Ac 7:51; Eph 4:30 [s]Ps 106:40
63:11 [t]Ex 14:22, 30 [u]Nu 11:17
63:12 [v]Ex 14:21-22; Isa 11:15
63:13 [w]Dt 32:12 [x]Jer 31:9
63:15 [y]Dt 26:15; Ps 80:14 [z]Ps 123:1 [a]Isa 9:7; 26:11 [b]Jer 31:20; Hos 11:8

[a] *11* Or *But may he recall*

THE SPIRIT IN ISAIAH

Reference	*Main Teaching*
11:2	The Spirit of the Lord brings wisdom, understanding, knowledge, and the fear of the Lord.
32:15	The Spirit of the Lord brings abundance.
34:16	The Spirit of the Lord carries out God's word.
40:13	The Spirit of the Lord is the Master Counsellor.
42:1	The Messiah, God's Servant, will be given the Spirit.
44:3–5	Through the Spirit, God's true children will thrive.
48:16	The Spirit of the Lord sent Isaiah to prophesy.
61:1	God's servants (Isaiah and then Jesus) were anointed by the Spirit to proclaim the good news.
63:10, 11	The Spirit of the Lord was grieved because of God's people.
63:14	The Spirit of the Lord gives rest.

63:10 Grieving the Holy Spirit is wilfully thwarting his leading by disobedience or rebellion. Isaiah mentions the work of the Holy Spirit more than any other Old Testament writer. See the note on Ephesians 4:28–32 for more on grieving the Holy Spirit.

63:15 – 64:7 On behalf of the faithful remnant, Isaiah asks God for two favours: to show tenderness and compassion to them and to punish their enemies. Before making these requests, Isaiah recited the Lord's past favours, reminding him of his compassion in former days (63:7–14).

or Israel acknowledge[c] us;
you, O LORD, are our Father,
our Redeemer[d] from of old is your name.
17 Why, O LORD, do you make us wander from your ways
and harden our hearts so we do not revere[e] you?
Return[f] for the sake of your servants,
the tribes that are your inheritance.
18 For a little while your people possessed your holy place,
but now our enemies have trampled down your sanctuary.[g]
19 We are yours from of old;
but you have not ruled over them,
they have not been called by your name.[b]

64

Oh, that you would rend the heavens[a] and come down,[b]
that the mountains[c] would tremble before you!
2 As when fire sets twigs ablaze
and causes water to boil,
come down to make your name known to your enemies
and cause the nations to quake[d] before you!
3 For when you did awesome[e] things that we did not expect,
you came down, and the mountains trembled before you.
4 Since ancient times no-one has heard,
no ear has perceived,
no eye has seen any God besides you,
who acts on behalf of those who wait for him.[f]
5 You come to the help of those who gladly do right,[g]
who remember your ways.
But when we continued to sin against them,
you were angry.
How then can we be saved?
6 All of us have become like one who is unclean,
and all our righteous[h] acts are like filthy rags;
we all shrivel up like a leaf,[i]
and like the wind our sins sweep us away.
7 No-one[j] calls on your name
or strives to lay hold of you;
for you have hidden[k] your face from us
and made us waste away[l] because of our sins.

8 Yet, O LORD, you are our Father.[m]
We are the clay, you are the potter;[n]
we are all the work of your hand.
9 Do not be angry[o] beyond measure, O LORD;
do not remember our sins[p] for ever.
Oh, look upon us we pray,
for we are all your people.
10 Your sacred cities have become a desert;

63:16 [c]Job 14:21 [d]Isa 41:14; 44:6
63:17 [e]Isa 29:13 [f]Nu 10:36
63:18 [g]Ps 74:3-8
64:1 [a]Ps 18:9; 144:5 [b]Mic 1:3 [c]Ex 19:18
64:2 [d]Ps 99:1; Jer 5:22; 33:9
64:3 [e]Ps 65:5
64:4 [f]Isa 30:18; 1Co 2:9*
64:5 [g]Isa 26:8
64:6 [h]Isa 46:12; 48:1 [i]Ps 90:5-6
64:7 [j]Isa 59:4 [k]Dt 31:18; Isa 1:15; 54:8 [l]Isa 9:18
64:8 [m]Isa 63:16 [n]Isa 29:16
64:9 [o]Isa 57:17; 60:10 [p]Isa 43:25

b *19* Or *We are like those you have never ruled, / like those never called by your name*

64:1–6 God's appearance is so intense that it is like a consuming fire that burns everything in its path. If we are so impure, how can we be saved? Only by God's mercy. The Israelites had experienced God's appearance at Mount Sinai (Exodus 19:16–19). When God met with Moses there was a thunderstorm, smoke, and an earthquake. If God were to meet us today, his glory would overwhelm us, especially when we look at our "filthy rags" (64:6).

64:6 Sin makes us unclean so that we cannot approach God (6:5; Romans 3:23) any more than a beggar in rotten rags could dine at a king's table. Our best efforts are still infected with sin. Our only hope, therefore, is faith in Jesus Christ, who can cleanse us and bring us into God's presence (read Romans 3).

This passage can easily be misunderstood. It doesn't mean that God will reject us if we come to him in faith, nor that he despises our efforts to please him. It means that if we come to him demanding acceptance on the basis of our "good" conduct, God will point out that our righteousness is nothing compared to his infinite righteousness. This message is primarily for the unrepentant person, not the true follower of God.

64:11
[q]Ps 74:3-7
[r]La 1:7, 10

64:12
[s]Ps 74:10-11; Isa 42:14
[t]Ps 83:1

65:1
[a]Hos 1:10; Ro 9:24-26; 10:20*
[b]Eph 2:12

65:2
[c]Isa 1:2, 23; Ro 10:21*
[d]Ps 81:11-12; Isa 66:18

65:3
[e]Job 1:11
[f]Isa 1:29

65:4
[g]Lev 11:7

65:5
[h]Mt 9:11; Lk 7:39; 18:9-12

65:6
[i]Ps 50:3
[j]Jer 16:18
[k]Ps 79:12

65:7
[l]Isa 22:14
[m]Ex 20:5
[n]Isa 57:7

65:9
[o]Isa 45:19
[p]Am 9:11-15

even Zion is a desert, Jerusalem a desolation.
11 Our holy and glorious temple,[q] where our fathers praised you,
has been burned with fire,
and all that we treasured[r] lies in ruins.
12 After all this, O LORD, will you hold yourself back?[s]
Will you keep silent[t] and punish us beyond measure?

Judgment and Salvation

65 "I revealed myself to those who did not ask for me;
I was found by those who did not seek me.[a]
To a nation[b] that did not call on my name,
I said, 'Here am I, here am I.'
2 All day long I have held out my hands
to an obstinate people,[c]
who walk in ways not good,
pursuing their own imaginations[d]—
3 a people who continually provoke me
to my very face,[e]
offering sacrifices in gardens[f]
and burning incense on altars of brick;
4 who sit among the graves
and spend their nights keeping secret vigil;
who eat the flesh of pigs,[g]
and whose pots hold broth of unclean meat;
5 who say, 'Keep away; don't come near me,
for I am too sacred[h] for you!'
Such people are smoke in my nostrils,
a fire that keeps burning all day.

6 "See, it stands written before me;
I will not keep silent[i] but will pay back[j] in full;
I will pay it back into their laps[k]—
7 both your sins[l] and the sins of your fathers,"[m]
says the LORD.
"Because they burned sacrifices on the mountains
and defied me on the hills,[n]
I will measure into their laps
the full payment for their former deeds."

8 This is what the LORD says:

"As when juice is still found in a cluster of grapes
and men say, 'Don't destroy it,
there is yet some good in it,'
so will I do on behalf of my servants;
I will not destroy them all.
9 I will bring forth descendants[o] from Jacob,
and from Judah those who will possess[p] my mountains;

65:1 Israel considered itself to be the only people of God, but the time would come when other nations would seek him. Paul mentions Isaiah's statement in Romans 10:20 and points out that these other nations were the Gentiles. God's people today are those who accept Jesus as Saviour and Lord, whether they are Jews or Gentiles. The gospel is for every person. Do not ignore or reject anyone when you share the gospel. You may be surprised at how many are sincerely searching for God.

65:3–5 God said these people directly disobeyed his laws when they worshipped and sacrificed to idols (Exodus 20:1–6), consulted the dead and evil spirits (Leviticus 19:31), and ate forbidden foods (Leviticus 11). But they were so perverse that they still thought they were more sacred than others. Jesus called such people hypocrites (Matthew 23:13–36).

65:6 God said he would pay back the people for their sins. Judgment is not our job but his because he alone is just. Who else knows our hearts and minds? Who else knows what is a completely fair reward or punishment?

65:8, 9 God will always preserve a faithful remnant of his people. No matter how bad the world is, there are always a few who remain loyal to him. Jesus made this point in Matthew 13:36–43.

my chosen people will inherit them,
  and there will my servants live.[q]
10 Sharon[r] will become a pasture for flocks,
  and the Valley of Achor[s] a resting place for herds,
  for my people who seek[t] me.

11 "But as for you who forsake[u] the LORD
  and forget my holy mountain,
who spread a table for Fortune
  and fill bowls of mixed wine for Destiny,
12 I will destine you for the sword,[v]
  and you will all bend down for the slaughter;
for I called but you did not answer,[w]
  I spoke but you did not listen.[x]
You did evil in my sight
  and chose what displeases me."

13 Therefore this is what the Sovereign LORD says:

"My servants will eat,[y]
  but you will go hungry;
my servants will drink,
  but you will go thirsty;[z]
my servants will rejoice,
  but you will be put to shame.[a]
14 My servants will sing
  out of the joy of their hearts,
but you will cry out[b]
  from anguish of heart
  and wail in brokenness of spirit.
15 You will leave your name
  to my chosen ones as a curse;[c]
the Sovereign LORD will put you to death,
  but to his servants he will give another name.
16 Whoever invokes a blessing in the land
  will do so by the God of truth;[d]
he who takes an oath in the land
  will swear[e] by the God of truth.
For the past troubles will be forgotten
  and hidden from my eyes.

New Heavens and a New Earth

17 "Behold, I will create
  new heavens and a new earth.[f]
The former things will not be remembered,[g]
  nor will they come to mind.
18 But be glad and rejoice[h] for ever
  in what I will create,
for I will create Jerusalem to be a delight
  and its people a joy.
19 I will rejoice[i] over Jerusalem
  and take delight in my people;

65:9 [q] Isa 32:18
65:10 [r] Isa 35:2 [s] Jos 7:26 [t] Isa 51:1
65:11 [u] Dt 29:24-25; Isa 1:28
65:12 [v] Isa 27:1 [w] Pr 1:24-25; Isa 41:28; 66:4 [x] 2Ch 36:15-16; Jer 7:13
65:13 [y] Isa 1:19 [z] Isa 41:17 [a] Isa 44:9
65:14 [b] Mt 8:12; Lk 13:28
65:15 [c] Zec 8:13
65:16 [d] Ps 31:5 [e] Isa 19:18
65:17 [f] Isa 66:22; 2Pe 3:13 [g] Isa 43:18; Jer 3:16
65:18 [h] Ps 98:1-9; Isa 25:9
65:19 [i] Isa 35:10; 62:5

65:10 Sharon is a plain in the western part of Israel. The Valley of Achor is in the east, near Jericho. The Valley of Achor was also called the Valley of Trouble because Achan was executed there for hiding the devoted goods of battle (Joshua 7:10–26). Even in this valley there will be peace: the coming restoration will be complete.

65:17–25 In 65:17–19 we have a pictorial description of the new heavens and the new earth. They are eternal, and in them safety, peace, and plenty will be available to all (see also 66:22, 23; 2 Peter 3:13; Revelation 21:1). Verses 20–25 may refer to the reign of Christ on earth because sin and death have not yet been finally destroyed.

65:19 [j]Isa 25:8; Rev 7:17

the sound of weeping and of crying[j]
will be heard in it no more.

20"Never again will there be in it
an infant who lives but a few days,
or an old man who does not live out his years;[k]
he who dies at a hundred
will be thought a mere youth;
he who fails to reach[a] a hundred
will be considered accursed.
21They will build houses[l] and dwell in them;
they will plant vineyards and eat their fruit.[m]
22No longer will they build houses and others live in them,
or plant and others eat.
For as the days of a tree,[n]
so will be the days[o] of my people;
my chosen ones will long enjoy
the works of their hands.
23They will not toil in vain
or bear children doomed to misfortune;
for they will be a people blessed[p] by the LORD,
they and their descendants[q] with them.
24Before they call[r] I will answer;
while they are still speaking[s] I will hear.
25The wolf and the lamb[t] will feed together,
and the lion will eat straw like the ox,
but dust will be the serpent's[u] food.
They will neither harm nor destroy
on all my holy mountain,"
says the LORD.

65:20 [k]Ecc 8:13
65:21 [l]Isa 32:18 [m]Isa 37:30; Am 9:14
65:22 [n]Ps 92:12-14 [o]Ps 21:4; 91:16
65:23 [p]Dt 28:3-12; Isa 61:9 [q]Ac 2:39
65:24 [r]Isa 55:6 [s]Da 9:20-23; 10:12
65:25 [t]Isa 11:6 [u]Ge 3:14; Mic 7:17

Judgment and Hope

66 This is what the LORD says:

"Heaven is my throne,[a]
and the earth is my footstool.[b]
Where is the house[c] you will build for me?
Where will my resting place be?
2Has not my hand made all these things,[d]
and so they came into being?"
declares the LORD.

"This is the one I esteem:
he who is humble and contrite in spirit,[e]
and trembles at my word.[f]
3But whoever sacrifices a bull[g]
is like one who kills a man,
and whoever offers a lamb,

66:1 [a]Mt 23:22 [b]1Ki 8:27; Mt 5:34-35 [c]2Sa 7:7; Jn 4:20-21; Ac 7:49*; 17:24
66:2 [d]Isa 40:26; Ac 7:50* [e]Isa 57:15; Mt 5:3-4; Lk 18:13-14 [f]Ezr 9:4
66:3 [g]Isa 1:11

a *20* Or / *the sinner who reaches*

66:1 Even the beautiful temple in Jerusalem was woefully inadequate for a God who is present everywhere. God cannot be confined to any human structure (see 2 Chronicles 6:18; Acts 7:49, 50). This chapter is a fitting climax to the book. God will lift up the humble, judge all people, destroy the wicked, bring all believers together, and establish the new heavens and the new earth. Let this hope encourage you each day.

66:2, 3 These key verses summarise Isaiah's message. He contrasted two ways of living: that of humble persons who have a profound reverence for God's messages and their application to life, and that of those who choose their own way. The sacrifices of the arrogant were only external compliance. In their hearts they were murderers, perverts, and idolaters. God shows mercy to the humble, but he curses the proud and self-sufficient (see Luke 1:51–53). Our society urges us to be assertive and to affirm ourselves. Don't let your freedom and right to choose lead you away from God's pathway to eternal life.

like one who breaks a dog's neck;
whoever makes a grain offering
is like one who presents pig's blood,
and whoever burns memorial incense,[h]
like one who worships an idol.
They have chosen their own ways,[i]
and their souls delight in their abominations;
4so I also will choose harsh treatment for them
and will bring upon them what they dread.[j]
For when I called, no-one answered,[k]
when I spoke, no-one listened.
They did evil[l] in my sight
and chose what displeases me."[m]

5Hear the word of the LORD,
you who tremble at his word;
"Your brothers who hate[n] you,
and exclude you because of my name, have said,
'Let the LORD be glorified,
that we may see your joy!'
Yet they will be put to shame.[o]
6Hear that uproar from the city,
hear that noise from the temple!
It is the sound of the LORD
repaying[p] his enemies all they deserve.

7"Before she goes into labour,[q]
she gives birth;
before the pains come upon her,
she delivers a son.[r]
8Who has ever heard of such a thing?
Who has ever seen[s] such things?
Can a country be born in a day
or a nation be brought forth in a moment?
Yet no sooner is Zion in labour
than she gives birth to her children.
9Do I bring to the moment of birth[t]
and not give delivery?" says the LORD.
"Do I close up the womb
when I bring to delivery?" says your God.
10"Rejoice[u] with Jerusalem and be glad for her,
all you who love[v] her;
rejoice greatly with her,
all you who mourn over her.
11For you will nurse[w] and be satisfied
at her comforting breasts;
you will drink deeply
and delight in her overflowing abundance."

12For this is what the LORD says:

"I will extend peace to her like a river,[x]
and the wealth[y] of nations like a flooding stream;
you will nurse and be carried[z] on her arm
and dandled on her knees.
13As a mother comforts her child,

66:3 [h]Lev 2:2 [i]Isa 57:17
66:4 [j]Pr 10:24 [k]Pr 1:24; Jer 7:13 [l]2Ki 21:2, 4, 6 [m]Isa 65:12
66:5 [n]Ps 38:20; Isa 60:15 [o]Lk 13:17
66:6 [p]Isa 65:6; Joel 3:7
66:7 [q]Isa 54:1 [r]Rev 12:5
66:8 [s]Isa 64:4
66:9 [t]Isa 37:3
66:10 [u]Dt 32:43; Ro 15:10 [v]Ps 26:8
66:11 [w]Isa 60:16
66:12 [x]Isa 48:18 [y]Ps 72:3; Isa 60:5; 61:6 [z]Isa 60:4

66:7–9 God will not leave his work of national restoration unfinished. In this image of birth, God shows that he will accomplish what he has promised. It is as unstoppable as the birth of a baby. When all the pain is over, the joy begins.

66:13
[a] Isa 40:1; 2Co 1:4

66:14
[b] Isa 10:5

66:15
[c] Ps 68:17
[d] Ps 9:5

66:16
[e] Isa 30:30
[f] Isa 27:1

66:17
[g] Isa 1:29
[h] Lev 11:7
[i] Ps 37:20; Isa 1:28

66:19
[j] Isa 11:10; 49:22
[k] Isa 2:16
[l] Eze 27:10
[m] Ge 10:2
[n] Isa 11:11
[o] 1Ch 16:24; Isa 24:15

66:20
[p] Isa 52:11

66:21
[q] Ex 19:6; Isa 61:6; 1Pe 2:5, 9

66:22
[r] Isa 65:17; Heb 12:26-27; 2Pe 3:13; Rev 21:1
[s] Jn 10:27-29; 1Pe 1:4-5

66:23
[t] Eze 46:1-3
[u] Isa 19:21

66:24
[v] Isa 14:11
[w] Isa 1:31; Mk 9:48*

so will I comfort[a] you;
and you will be comforted over Jerusalem."

14 When you see this, your heart will rejoice
and you will flourish like grass;
the hand of the LORD will be made known to his servants,
but his fury[b] will be shown to his foes.
15 See, the LORD is coming with fire,
and his chariots[c] are like a whirlwind;
he will bring down his anger with fury,
and his rebuke[d] with flames of fire.
16 For with fire[e] and with his sword[f]
the LORD will execute judgment upon all men,
and many will be those slain by the LORD.

17 "Those who consecrate and purify themselves to go into the gardens,[g] following
the one in the midst of[a] those who eat the flesh of pigs[h] and rats and other abominable
things—they will meet their end[i] together," declares the LORD.
18 "And I, because of their actions and their imaginations, am about to come[b] and
gather all nations and tongues, and they will come and see my glory.
19 "I will set a sign[j] among them, and I will send some of those who survive to
the nations—to Tarshish,[k] to the Libyans[c] and Lydians[l] (famous as archers), to
Tubal[m] and Greece, and to the distant islands[n] that have not heard of my fame or
seen my glory.[o] They will proclaim my glory among the nations. 20 And they will
bring all your brothers, from all the nations, to my holy mountain in Jerusalem as an
offering to the LORD—on horses, in chariots and wagons, and on mules and camels,"
says the LORD. "They will bring them, as the Israelites bring their grain offerings, to
the temple of the LORD in ceremonially clean vessels.[p] 21 And I will select some of
them also to be priests[q] and Levites," says the LORD.

22 "As the new heavens and the new earth[r] that I make will endure before me,"
declares the LORD, "so will your name and descendants endure.[s] 23 From one New
Moon to another and from one Sabbath[t] to another, all mankind will come and bow
down[u] before me," says the LORD. 24 "And they will go out and look upon the dead
bodies of those who rebelled against me; their worm[v] will not die, nor will their fire
be quenched,[w] and they will be loathsome to all mankind."

a *17* Or *gardens behind one of your temples, and* **b** *18* The meaning of the Hebrew for this clause is uncertain.
c *19* Some Septuagint manuscripts *Put* (Libyans); Hebrew *Pul*

66:15–17 This is a vivid picture of the great judgment that will occur at Christ's second coming (2 Thessalonians 1:7–9).

66:19 God's people will go out as missionaries to all parts of the earth—to Tarshish (Spain), to the Libyans in northern Africa, to the Lydians in western Asia Minor, to northeastern Asia Minor (Tubal), and to Greece.

66:22–24 Isaiah brings his book to a close with great drama. For the faithless there is a sobering portrayal of judgment. For the faithful, there is a glorious picture of rich reward—"so will your name and descendants endure". The contrast is so striking that it would seem that everyone would want to be God's follower. But we are often just as rebellious, foolish, and reluctant to change as the Israelites. We are just as negligent in feeding the hungry, working for justice, and obeying God's word. Make sure you are among those who will be richly blessed.

JEREMIAH

Zephaniah becomes a prophet 640 B.C.	*Jeremiah becomes a prophet 627*	*King Josiah killed in battle 609*	*Daniel taken captive 605*	*Ezekiel begins to prophesy in Babylonia 593*	*Judah falls: Jerusalem destroyed; Jeremiah's ministry ends 586*	*First exiles return to Juda 538*

VITAL STATISTICS

PURPOSE:
To urge God's people to turn from their sins and back to God

AUTHOR:
Jeremiah

TO WHOM WRITTEN:
Judah (the southern kingdom) and its capital city, Jerusalem

DATE WRITTEN:
During Jeremiah's ministry, approximately 627–586 B.C.

SETTING:
Jeremiah ministered under Judah's last five kings—Josiah, Jehoahaz, Jehoiakim, Jehoiachin, and Zedekiah. The nation was sliding quickly towards destruction and was eventually conquered by Babylon in 586 B.C. (see 2 Kings 21—25). The prophet Zephaniah preceded Jeremiah, and Habakkuk was Jeremiah's contemporary.

KEY VERSE:
"'Your wickedness will punish you; your backsliding will rebuke you. Consider then and realise how evil and bitter it is for you when you forsake the LORD your God and have no awe of me,' declares the Lord, the LORD Almighty" (2:19).

KEY PEOPLE:
Judah's kings (listed above), Baruch, Ebed-Melech, King Nebuchadnezzar, the Recabites

KEY PLACES:
Anathoth, Jerusalem, Ramah, Egypt

SPECIAL FEATURES:
This book is a combination of history, poetry, and biography. Jeremiah often used symbolism to communicate his message.

WHAT is success? Most definitions include references to achieving goals and acquiring wealth, prestige, favour, and power. "Successful" people enjoy the good life—being financially and emotionally secure, being surrounded by admirers, and enjoying the fruits of their labours. They are leaders, opinion makers, and trendsetters. Their example is emulated; their accomplishments are noticed. They know who they are and where they are going, and they stride confidently to meet their goals.

By these standards, Jeremiah was a miserable failure. For 40 years he served as God's spokesman to Judah; but when Jeremiah spoke, nobody listened. Consistently and passionately he urged them to act, but nobody moved. And he certainly did not attain material success. He was poor and underwent severe deprivation to deliver his prophecies. He was thrown into prison (chapter 37) and into a cistern (chapter 38), and he was taken to Egypt against his will (chapter 43). He was rejected by his neighbours (11:19–21), his family (12:6), the false priests and prophets (20:1, 2; 28:1–17), his friends (20:10), his audience (26:8), and the kings (36:23). Throughout his life, Jeremiah stood alone, declaring God's messages of doom, announcing the new covenant, and weeping over the fate of his beloved country. In the eyes of the world, Jeremiah was not a success.

But in God's eyes, Jeremiah was one of the most successful people in all of history. Success, as measured by God, involves obedience and faithfulness. Regardless of opposition and personal cost, Jeremiah courageously and faithfully proclaimed the word of God. He was obedient to his calling. Jeremiah's book begins with his call to be a prophet. The next 38 chapters are prophecies about Israel (the nation united) and Judah (the southern kingdom). Chapters 2—20 are general and undated, and chapters 21—39 are particular and dated. The basic theme of Jeremiah's message is simple: "Repent and turn to God, or he will punish." But then, because the people rejected this warning, Jeremiah moved to predicting specifically the destruction of Jerusalem. This terrible event is described in chapter 39. Chapters 40—45 describe events following Jerusalem's fall. The book concludes with prophecies concerning a variety of nations (chapters 46—52).

As you read Jeremiah, feel with him as he agonises over the message he must deliver, pray with him for those who refuse to respond to the truth, and watch his example of faith and courage. Then commit yourself to being successful in God's eyes.

THE BLUEPRINT

A. GOD'S JUDGMENT ON JUDAH (1:1—45:5) 1. The call of Jeremiah 2. Jeremiah condemns Judah for her sins 3. Jeremiah prophesies destruction 4. Jeremiah accuses Judah's leaders 5. Restoration is promised 6. God's promised judgment arrives	Jeremiah confronts many people with their sins: kings, false prophets, those at the temple, and those at the gates. A lack of response made Jeremiah wonder if he was doing any good at all. He often felt discouraged and sometimes bitter. To bring such gloomy messages to these people was a hard task. We too have a responsibility to bring this news to a fallen world: those who continue in their sinful ways are eternally doomed. Although we may feel discouraged at the lack of response, we must press on to tell others about the consequences of sin and the hope that God offers. Those who tell people only what they want to hear are being unfaithful to God's message.
B. GOD'S JUDGMENT ON THE NATIONS (46:1—52:34) 1. Prophecies about foreign nations 2. The fall of Jerusalem	Jeremiah lived to see many of his prophecies come true—most notably the fall of Jerusalem. The fulfilment of this and other prophecies against the foreign nations came as a result of sin. Those who refuse to confess their sin bring judgment upon themselves.

MEGATHEMES

THEME	EXPLANATION	IMPORTANCE
Sin	King Josiah's reformation failed because the people's repentance was shallow. They continued in their selfishness and worship of idols. All the leaders rejected God's law and will for the people. Jeremiah lists all their sins, predicts God's judgment, and begs for repentance.	Judah's deterioration and disaster came from their callous disregard and disobedience of God. When we ignore sin and refuse to listen to God's warning, we invite disaster. Don't settle for half measures in removing sin.
Punishment	Because of sin, Jerusalem was destroyed, the temple was ruined, and the people were captured and carried off to Babylon. The people were responsible for their destruction and captivity because they refused to listen to God's message.	Unconfessed sin brings God's full punishment. It is useless to blame anyone else for our sin—we are accountable to God before anyone else. We must answer to him for how we live.
God is Lord of all	God is the righteous Creator. He is accountable to no one but himself. He wisely and lovingly directs all creation to fulfil his plans, and he brings events to pass according to his timetable. He is Lord over all the world.	Because of God's majestic power and love, our only duty is to submit to his authority. By following his plans, not our own, we can have a loving relationship with him and serve him with our whole hearts.
New Hearts	Jeremiah predicted that after the destruction of the nation, God would send a new shepherd, the Messiah. He would lead them into a new future, a new covenant, and a new day of hope. He would accomplish this by changing their sinful hearts into hearts of love for God.	God still restores his people by renewing their hearts. His love can transform the problems created by sin. We can have assurance of a new heart by loving God, trusting Christ to save us, and repenting of our sin.
Faithful Service	Jeremiah served God faithfully for 40 years. During that time the people ignored, rejected, and persecuted him. Jeremiah's preaching was unsuccessful by human standards, yet he did not fail in his task. He remained faithful to God.	People's acceptance or rejection of us is not the measure of our success. God's approval alone should be our standard for service. We must bring God's message to others even when we are rejected. We must do God's work even if it means suffering for it.

A. GOD'S JUDGMENT ON JUDAH (1:1–45:5)

Jeremiah was called by God to be a prophet to Judah (the southern kingdom). He faithfully confronted the leaders and the people with their sin, prophesied both their 70-year captivity in Babylon and their eventual return from exile. After surviving the fall of Jerusalem, Jeremiah was forcibly taken to Egypt. Yet Jeremiah remained faithful in spite of Jerusalem's destruction. Years of obedience had made him strong and courageous. May we be able to stand through difficult times as did Jeremiah.

1. The call of Jeremiah

1 The words of Jeremiah son of Hilkiah, one of the priests at Anathoth[a] in the
territory of Benjamin. 2 The word of the LORD came to him in the thirteenth year
of the reign of Josiah son of Amon king of Judah, 3 and through the reign of Jehoiakim[b] son of Josiah king of Judah, down to the fifth month of the eleventh year of
Zedekiah[c] son of Josiah king of Judah, when the people of Jerusalem went into
exile.[d]

4 The word of the LORD came to me, saying,

> 5 "Before I formed you in the womb I knew[a][e] you,
> before you were born[f] I set you apart;
> I appointed you as a prophet to the nations.[g]"

6 "Ah, Sovereign LORD," I said, "I do not know how to speak;[h] I am only a child."[i]
7 But the LORD said to me, "Do not say, 'I am only a child.' You must go to everyone
I send you to and say whatever I command you. 8 Do not be afraid[j] of them, for I
am with you[k] and will rescue you," declares the LORD.
9 Then the LORD reached out his hand and touched[l] my mouth and said to me,
"Now, I have put my words in your mouth.[m] 10 See, today I appoint you over nations
and kingdoms to uproot and tear down, to destroy and overthrow, to build and to
plant."[n]
11 The word of the LORD came to me: "What do you see, Jeremiah?"[o]
"I see the branch of an almond tree," I replied.
12 The LORD said to me, "You have seen correctly, for I am watching[b] to see that
my word is fulfilled."

a 5 Or *chose* **b** 12 The Hebrew for *watching* sounds like the Hebrew for *almond tree.*

1:1 [a] Jos 21:18; 1Ch 6:60; Jer 32:7-9
1:3 [b] 2Ki 23:34 [c] 2Ki 24:17; Jer 39:2 [d] Jer 52:15
1:5 [e] Ps 139:16 [f] Isa 49:1 [g] ver 10; Jer 25:15-26
1:6 [h] Ex 4:10; 6:12 [i] 1Ki 3:7
1:8 [j] Eze 2:6 [k] Jos 1:5; Jer 15:20
1:9 [l] Isa 6:7 [m] Ex 4:12
1:10 [n] Jer 18:7-10; 24:6; 31:4, 28
1:11 [o] Jer 24:3; Am 7:8

1:1, 2 After King Solomon's death, the united kingdom of Israel had split into rival northern and southern kingdoms. The northern kingdom was called Israel; the southern, Judah. Jeremiah was from Anathoth, four miles north of Jerusalem in the southern kingdom. He lived and prophesied during the reigns of the last five kings of Judah. This was a chaotic time politically, morally, and spiritually. As Babylon, Egypt, and Assyria battled for world supremacy, Judah found itself caught in the middle of the triangle. Although Jeremiah prophesied for 40 years, he never saw his people heed his words and turn from their sins.

1:5 God knew you, as he knew Jeremiah, long before you were born or even conceived. He thought about you and planned for you. When you feel discouraged or inadequate, remember that God has always thought of you as valuable and that he has a purpose in mind for you.

1:5 Jeremiah was "appointed" by God "as a prophet to the nations". God has a purpose for each Christian, but some people are appointed by God for specific kinds of work. Samson (Judges 13:3–5), David (1 Samuel 16:12, 13), John the Baptist (Luke 1:13–17), and Paul (Galatians 1:15, 16) were also called to do particular jobs for God. Whatever work you do should be done for the glory of God (Philippians 1:11). If God gives you a specific task, accept it cheerfully and do it with diligence. If God has not given you a specific call or assignment, then seek to fulfil the mission common to all believers – to love, obey, and serve God – until his guidance becomes more clear.

1:6–8 Often people struggle with new challenges because they lack self-confidence, feeling that they have inadequate ability, training, or experience. Jeremiah thought he was "only a child" – too young and inexperienced to be God's spokesman to the world. But God promised to be with him. We should not allow feelings of inadequacy to keep us from obeying God's call. He will *always* be with us. When you find yourself avoiding something you know you should do, be careful not to use lack of self-confidence as an excuse. If God gives you a job to do, he will provide all you need to do it.

1:8 God promised to "rescue" Jeremiah from trouble, not to keep trouble from coming. God did not insulate him from being jailed, deported, or insulted. God does not keep us from encountering life's storms, but he will see us through them. In fact, God walks through these storms with us and rescues us.

1:10 God appointed Jeremiah to bring his word to "nations and kingdoms". Jeremiah's work was to warn not only the Jews but all the nations of the world about God's judgment on sin. Don't forget in reading the Old Testament that, while God was consistently working through the people of Judah and Israel, his plan was to communicate to every nation and person. We are included in Jeremiah's message of judgment and hope, and as believers we are to share God's desire to reach the whole world for him.

1:11–14 The vision of the branch of an almond tree revealed the beginning of God's judgment because the almond tree is among the first to blossom in the spring. God saw the sins of Judah and the nations, and he would carry out swift and certain judgment. The boiling pot tilting away from the north and spilling over Judah pictured Babylon delivering God's scalding judgment against Jeremiah's people.

1:13
[p]Zec 4:2

1:15
[q]Jer 4:16; 9:11

1:16
[r]Dt 28:20
[s]Jer 17:13
[t]Jer 7:9; 19:4

1:17
[u]Eze 2:6

1:18
[v]Isa 50:7

1:19
[w]Jer 20:11
[x]ver 8

2:2
[a]Eze 16:8-14, 60; Hos 2:15
[b]Dt 2:7

13The word of the LORD came to me again: "What do you see?"[p]
"I see a boiling pot, tilting away from the north," I answered.
14The LORD said to me, "From the north disaster will be poured out on all who live
in the land. 15I am about to summon all the peoples of the northern kingdoms,"
declares the LORD.

"Their kings will come and set up their thrones
in the entrance of the gates of Jerusalem;
they will come against all her surrounding walls
and against all the towns of Judah.[q]
16I will pronounce my judgments on my people
because of their wickedness[r] in forsaking me,[s]
in burning incense to other gods[t]
and in worshipping what their hands have made.

17"Get yourself ready! Stand up and say to them whatever I command you. Do not
be terrified[u] by them, or I will terrify you before them. 18Today I have made you[v]
a fortified city, an iron pillar and a bronze wall to stand against the whole
land—against the kings of Judah, its officials, its priests and the people of the land.
19They will fight against you but will not overcome you, for I am with you[w] and will
rescue[x] you," declares the LORD.

2. Jeremiah condemns Judah for her sins

Israel Forsakes God

2 The word of the LORD came to me: 2"Go and proclaim in the hearing of Jerusalem:

" 'I remember the devotion of your youth,[a]
how as a bride you loved me
and followed me through the desert,[b]
through a land not sown.

JEREMIAH served as a prophet to Judah from 627 B.C. until the exile in 586 B.C.

Climate of the times	• Society was deteriorating economically, politically, spiritually. • Wars and captivity. • God's word was deemed offensive.
Main message	Repentance from sin would postpone Judah's coming judgment at the hands of Babylon.
Importance of message	Repentance is one of the greatest needs in our immoral world. God's promises to the faithful shine brightly by bringing hope for tomorrow and strength for today.
Contemporary prophets	Habakkuk (612–588) Zephaniah (640–621)

1:14–19 The problems we face may not seem as ominous as Jeremiah's, but they are critical to us and may overwhelm us! God's promise to Jeremiah and to us is that nothing will defeat us completely; he will help us through the most agonising problems. Face each day with the assurance that God will be with you and see you through.

1:16 The people of Judah sinned greatly by continuing to burn incense to and worship other gods. God had commanded them specifically against this (Exodus 20:3–6) because idolatry places trust in created things rather than the Creator. Although these people belonged to God, they chose to follow false gods. Many "gods" entice us to turn away from God. Material possessions, dreams for the future, approval of others, and vocational goals compete for our total commitment. Striving after these at the expense of our commitment to God puts our heart where Judah's was—and God severely punished Judah.

2:1–3:5 In this section, the marriage analogy sharply contrasts God's love for his people with their love for other gods and reveals Judah's faithlessness. Jeremiah condemned Judah (he sometimes called Judah "Jerusalem", the name of its capital city) for seeking security in worthless, changeable things rather than the unchangeable God. We may be tempted to seek security from possessions, people, or our own abilities, but these will fail us. There is no lasting security apart from the eternal God.

2:2 We appreciate a friend who remains true to his or her commitment, and we are disappointed with someone who fails to keep a promise. God was pleased when his people obeyed initially, but he became angry with them when they refused to keep their commitment. Temptations distract us from God. Think about your original commitment to obey God, and ask yourself if you are remaining truly devoted.

3Israel was holy[c] to the LORD,[d]
the firstfruits[e] of his harvest;
all who devoured[f] her were held guilty,[g]
and disaster overtook them,' "
declares the LORD.

4Hear the word of the LORD, O house of Jacob,
all you clans of the house of Israel.

5This is what the LORD says:

"What fault did your fathers find in me,
that they strayed so far from me?
They followed worthless idols
and became worthless[h] themselves.
6They did not ask, 'Where is the LORD,
who brought us up out of Egypt[i]
and led us through the barren wilderness,
through a land of deserts[j] and rifts,[k]
a land of drought and darkness,[a]
a land where no-one travels and no-one lives?'
7I brought you into a fertile land
to eat its fruit and rich produce.[l]
But you came and defiled my land
and made my inheritance detestable.[m]
8The priests did not ask,
'Where is the LORD?'
Those who deal with the law did not know me;[n]
the leaders rebelled against me.
The prophets prophesied by Baal,[o]
following worthless idols.[p]

9"Therefore I bring charges[q] against you again,"
declares the LORD.
"And I will bring charges against your children's children.
10Cross over to the coasts of Kittim[b] and look,
send to Kedar[c] and observe closely;
see if there has ever been anything like this:
11Has a nation ever changed its gods?
(Yet they are not gods[r] at all.)
But my people have exchanged their[d] Glory[s]
for worthless idols.
12Be appalled at this, O heavens,

2:3 [c]Dt 7:6 [d]Ex 19:6 [e]Jas 1:18; Rev 14:4 [f]Isa 41:11; Jer 30:16 [g]Jer 50:7
2:5 [h]2Ki 17:15
2:6 [i]Hos 13:4 [j]Dt 8:15 [k]Dt 32:10
2:7 [l]Nu 13:27; Dt 8:7-9; 11:10-12 [m]Ps 106:34-39; Jer 16:18
2:8 [n]Jer 4:22 [o]Jer 23:13 [p]Jer 16:19
2:9 [q]Eze 20:35-36; Mic 6:2
2:11 [r]Isa 37:19; Jer 16:20 [s]Ps 106:20; Ro 1:23

[a] *6* Or *and the shadow of death* [b] *10* That is, Cyprus and western coastlands [c] *10* The home of Bedouin tribes in the Syro-Arabian desert [d] *11* Masoretic Text; an ancient Hebrew scribal tradition *my*

2:3 The firstfruits, or the first part, of the harvest were set aside for God (Deuteronomy 26:1–11). That's how Israel was dedicated to him in years gone by. Israel had been as eager to please God as if she were his young bride, a holy, devoted people. This contrasted greatly with the situation in Jeremiah's time.

2:4–8 The united nation of Israel included both the "house of Israel" and the "house of Jacob" (Judah). Jeremiah knew Israel's history well. The prophets recited history to the people for several reasons: (1) to remind them of God's faithfulness; (2) to make sure the people wouldn't forget (they didn't have Bibles to read); (3) to emphasise God's love for them; (4) to remind the people that there was a time when they *were* close to God. We should learn from history so we can build on the successes and avoid repeating the failures of others.

2:8 Baal was the chief male god of the Canaanite religion. "Baals" (2:23) refers to the fact that Baal was worshipped in many centres in Canaanite practice. Baal was the god of fertility. Worship of Baal included animal sacrifice and sacred prostitution (male and female) in the high places. Jezebel, the wife of King Ahab, introduced Baal worship into the northern kingdom, and eventually it spread to Judah. The sexual orientation of this worship was a constant temptation to the Israelites, who were called to be holy.

2:10 God was saying that even pagan nations like Kittim (Cyprus, in the west) and Kedar (the home of Arab tribes living in the desert east of Palestine) remained loyal to their national gods. But Israel had abandoned the one and only God for a completely worthless object of worship.

2:13 Who would set aside a sparkling spring of water for a cistern, a pit that collected rainwater? God told the Israelites they

2:13 [t]Ps 36:9; Jn 4:14
2:14 [u]Ex 4:22
2:15 [v]Jer 4:7; 50:17

and shudder with great horror,"
declares the LORD.

13"My people have committed two sins:
They have forsaken me,
the spring of living water,[t]
and have dug their own cisterns,
broken cisterns that cannot hold water.
14Is Israel a servant, a slave[u] by birth?
Why then has he become plunder?
15Lions[v] have roared;
they have growled at him.

JEREMIAH

Endurance is not a common quality. Many people lack the long-term commitment, caring, and willingness that are vital to sticking with a task against all odds. But Jeremiah was a prophet who endured.

Jeremiah's call by God teaches how intimately God knows us. He valued us before anyone else knew we would exist. He cared for us while we were in our mother's womb. He planned our lives while our bodies were still being formed. He values us more highly than we value ourselves.

Jeremiah had to depend on God's love as he developed endurance. His audiences were usually antagonistic or apathetic to his messages. He was ignored; his life was often threatened. He saw both the excitement of a spiritual awakening and the sorrow of a national return to idolatry. With the exception of the good King Josiah, Jeremiah watched king after king ignore his warnings and lead the people away from God. He saw fellow prophets murdered. He himself was severely persecuted. Finally, he watched Judah's defeat at the hands of the Babylonians.

Jeremiah responded to all this with God's message and human tears. He felt first hand God's love for his people and the people's rejection of that love. But even when he was angry with God and tempted to give up, Jeremiah knew he had to keep going. God had called him to endure. He expressed intense feelings, but he also saw beyond the feelings to the God who was soon to execute justice, but who afterwards would administer mercy.

It may be easy for us to identify with Jeremiah's frustrations and discouragement, but we need to realise that this prophet's life is also an encouragement to faithfulness.

Strengths and accomplishments:
- Wrote two Old Testament books, Jeremiah and Lamentations
- Ministered during the reigns of the last five kings of Judah
- Was a catalyst for the great spiritual reformation under King Josiah
- Acted as God's faithful messenger in spite of many attempts on his life
- Was so deeply sorrowful for the fallen condition of Judah that he earned the title "weeping prophet"

Lessons from his life:
- The majority opinion is not necessarily God's will
- Although punishment for sin is severe, there is hope in God's mercy
- God will not accept empty or insincere worship
- Serving God does not guarantee earthly security

Vital statistics:
- Where: Anathoth
- Occupation: Prophet
- Relative: Father: Hilkiah
- Contemporaries: Josiah, Jehoahaz, Jehoiakim, Jehoiachin, Zedekiah, Baruch

Key verses:
" 'Ah, Sovereign LORD,' I said, 'I do not know how to speak; I am only a child.' But the LORD said to me, 'Do not say, "I am only a child." You must go to everyone I send you to and say whatever I command you. Do not be afraid of them, for I am with you and will rescue you,' declares the LORD" (Jeremiah 1:6–8).

Jeremiah's story is told in the book of Jeremiah. He is also mentioned in Ezra 1:1; Daniel 9:2; Matthew 2:17; 16:14; 27:9. See also 2 Chronicles 34, 35 for the story of the spiritual revival under Josiah.

were doing that very thing when they turned from him, the spring of living water, to the worship of idols. Not only that, but the cisterns they chose were broken and empty. The people had built religious systems in which to store truth, but those systems were worthless. Why should we cling to the broken promises of unstable "cisterns" (money, power, religious systems, or whatever transitory thing we are putting in place of God) when God promises to constantly refresh us with himself, the living water (John 4:10)?

They have laid waste[w] his land;
his towns are burned and deserted.
16 Also, the men of Memphis[e][x] and Tahpanhes[y]
have shaved the crown of your head.[f]
17 Have you not brought this on yourselves[z]
by forsaking the LORD your God
when he led you in the way?
18 Now why go to Egypt[a]
to drink water from the Shihor?[g][b]
And why go to Assyria
to drink water from the River?[h]
19 Your wickedness will punish you;
your backsliding[c] will rebuke[d] you.
Consider then and realise
how evil and bitter[e] it is for you
when you forsake the LORD your God
and have no awe[f] of me,"
declares the Lord, the LORD Almighty.

20 "Long ago you broke off your yoke[g]
and tore off your bonds;
you said, 'I will not serve you!'
Indeed, on every high hill[h]
and under every spreading tree[i]
you lay down as a prostitute.
21 I had planted[j] you like a choice vine[k]
of sound and reliable stock.
How then did you turn against me
into a corrupt,[l] wild vine?
22 Although you wash yourself with soda
and use an abundance of soap,
the stain of your guilt is still before me,"
declares the Sovereign LORD.
23 "How can you say, 'I am not defiled;[m]
I have not run after the Baals'?[n]
See how you behaved in the valley;[o]
consider what you have done.
You are a swift she-camel
running[p] here and there,
24 a wild donkey[q] accustomed to the desert,
sniffing the wind in her craving —
in her heat who can restrain her?
Any males that pursue her need not tire themselves;

2:15 [w]Isa 1:7
2:16 [x]Isa 19:13 [y]Jer 43:7-9
2:17 [z]Jer 4:18
2:18 [a]Isa 30:2 [b]Jos 13:3
2:19 [c]Jer 3:11, 22 [d]Isa 3:9; Hos 5:5 [e]Job 20:14; Am 8:10 [f]Ps 36:1
2:20 [g]Lev 26:13 [h]Isa 57:7; Jer 17:2 [i]Dt 12:2
2:21 [j]Ex 15:17 [k]Ps 80:8 [l]Isa 5:4
2:23 [m]Pr 30:12 [n]Jer 9:14 [o]Jer 7:31 [p]ver 33; Jer 31:22
2:24 [q]Jer 14:6

[e] *16* Hebrew *Noph* [f] *16* Or *have cracked your skull* [g] *18* That is, a branch of the Nile [h] *18* That is, the Euphrates

2:16, 17 Memphis was near modern Cairo's present location in lower Egypt, and Tahpanhes was in northeastern Egypt. Jeremiah could be speaking of Pharaoh Shishak's previous invasion of Judah in 926 B.C. (1 Kings 14:25), or he may have been predicting Pharaoh Neco's invasion in 609 B.C. when King Josiah of Judah would be killed (2 Kings 23:29, 30). Jeremiah's point is that the people brought this on themselves by rebelling against God.

2:22 The stain of sin is more than skin-deep. Israel had stains that could not be washed out, even with the strongest cleansers. Spiritual cleansing must reach deep into the heart – and this is a job that God alone can do. We cannot ignore the effects of sin and hope they will go away. Your sin has caused a deep stain that God can and will remove if you are willing to let him cleanse you (Isaiah 1:18; Ezekiel 36:25).

2:23–27 The people are compared to animals who search for mates in mating season. Unrestrained, they rush for power, money, alliances with foreign powers, and other gods. The idols did not seek the people; the people sought the idols and then ran wildly after them. Then they became so comfortable in their sin that they could not think of giving it up. Their only shame was in getting caught. If we desire something so much that we'll do anything to get it, this is a sign that we are addicted to it and out of tune with God.

2:25
[r] Dt 32:16; Jer 3:13; 14:10

2:26
[s] Jer 48:27

2:27
[t] Jer 3:9
[u] Jer 18:17; 32:33
[v] Jdg 10:10; Isa 26:16

2:28
[w] Isa 45:20
[x] Dt 32:37
[y] 2Ki 17:29; Jer 11:13

2:29
[z] Jer 5:1; 6:13; Da 9:11

2:30
[a] Ne 9:26; Ac 7:52; 1Th 2:15

2:31
[b] Isa 45:19

at mating time they will find her.
25 Do not run until your feet are bare
and your throat is dry.
But you said, 'It's no use!
I love foreign gods,[r]
and I must go after them.'

26 "As a thief is disgraced[s] when he is caught,
so the house of Israel is disgraced—
they, their kings and their officials,
their priests and their prophets.
27 They say to wood, 'You are my father,'
and to stone,[t] 'You gave me birth.'
They have turned their backs to me
and not their faces;[u]
yet when they are in trouble,[v] they say,
'Come and save us!'
28 Where then are the gods[w] you made for yourselves?
Let them come if they can save you
when you are in trouble![x]
For you have as many gods
as you have towns,[y] O Judah.

29 "Why do you bring charges against me?
You have all[z] rebelled against me,"
declares the LORD.

30 "In vain I punished your people;
they did not respond to correction.
Your sword has devoured your prophets[a]
like a ravening lion.

31 "You of this generation, consider the word of the LORD:

"Have I been a desert to Israel
or a land of great darkness?[b]
Why do my people say, 'We are free to roam;
we will come to you no more'?
32 Does a maiden forget her jewellery,

THE KINGS OF JEREMIAH'S LIFETIME

King	*Story of his reign*	*Dates of his reign*	*Character of reign*	*Jeremiah's message to the king*
Josiah	2 Kings 22:1–23:30	640–609 B.C.	Mostly good	3:6–25
Jehoahaz	2 Kings 23:31–33	609 B.C.	Evil	22:11–17
Jehoiakim	2 Kings 23:34–24:7	609–598 B.C.	Evil	22:18–23; 25:1–38; 26:1–24; 27:1–11; 35:1–19; 36:1–32
Jehoiachin	2 Kings 24:8–17	598–597 B.C.	Evil	13:18–27 22:24–30
Zedekiah	2 Kings 24:18–25:26	597–586 B.C.	Evil	21:1–14; 24:8–10; 27:12–22; 32:1–5; 34:1–22; 37:1–21; 38:1–28; 51:59–64

2:30 Being a prophet in Jeremiah's day was a risky business. Prophets had to criticise the policies of evil kings, and this made them appear to be traitors. The kings hated the prophets for standing against their policies, and the people often hated the prophets for preaching against their idolatrous life-styles. (See Acts 7:52.)

2:31, 32 Forgetting can be dangerous, whether it is intentional or an oversight. Israel forgot God by focusing its affections on the allurements of the world. The more we focus on the pleasures of the world, the easier it becomes to forget God's care, his love, his dependability, his guidance, and most of all, God himself. What pleases you most? Have you been forgetting God lately?

a bride her wedding ornaments?
Yet my people have forgotten me,
days without number.
33 How skilled you are at pursuing love!
Even the worst of women can learn from your ways.
34 On your clothes men find
the lifeblood[c] of the innocent poor,
though you did not catch them breaking in.[d]
Yet in spite of all this
35 you say, 'I am innocent;
he is not angry with me.'
But I will pass judgment[e] on you
because you say, 'I have not sinned.'[f]
36 Why do you go about so much,
changing[g] your ways?
You will be disappointed by Egypt[h]
as you were by Assyria.
37 You will also leave that place
with your hands on your head,[i]
for the LORD has rejected those you trust;
you will not be helped[j] by them.

3 "If a man divorces[a] his wife
and she leaves him and marries another man,
should he return to her again?
Would not the land be completely defiled?
But you have lived as a prostitute with many lovers[b]—
would you now return to me?"
declares the LORD.

2 "Look up to the barren heights and see.
Is there any place where you have not been ravished?
By the roadside[c] you sat waiting for lovers,
sat like a nomad[a] in the desert.
You have defiled the land[d]
with your prostitution and wickedness.
3 Therefore the showers have been withheld,[e]
and no spring rains[f] have fallen.
Yet you have the brazen look of a prostitute;
you refuse to blush with shame.[g]
4 Have you not just called to me:
'My Father,[h] my friend from my youth,[i]
5 will you always be angry?[j]
Will your wrath continue for ever?'

a 2 *Or an Arab*

2:34 [c] 2Ki 21:16 [d] Ex 22:2
2:35 [e] Jer 25:31 [f] 1Jn 1:8, 10
2:36 [g] Jer 31:22 [h] Isa 30:2, 3, 7
2:37 [i] 2Sa 13:19 [j] Jer 37:7
3:1 [a] Dt 24:1-4 [b] Jer 2:20, 25; Eze 16:26, 29
3:2 [c] Ge 38:14; Eze 16:25 [d] Jer 2:7
3:3 [e] Lev 26:19 [f] Jer 14:4 [g] Jer 6:15; 8:12; Zep 3:5
3:4 [h] ver 19 [i] Jer 2:2
3:5 [j] Ps 103:9; Isa 57:16

2:36 God is not against alliances or working partnerships, but he is against people trusting others for the help that should come from him. This was the problem in Jeremiah's time. After the days of David and Solomon, Israel fell apart because the leaders turned to other nations and gods instead of the true God. They played power politics, thinking that their strong neighbours could protect them. But Judah would soon learn that its alliance with Egypt would be just as disappointing as its former alliance with Assyria (2 Kings 16:8, 9; Isaiah 7:13–25).

3:1 This law, found in Deuteronomy 24:1–4, says that a divorced woman who remarries can never be reunited with her first husband. Judah "divorced" God and "married" other gods. God had every right to permanently disown his wayward people, but in his mercy he was willing to take them back again.

3:2 "Like a nomad in the desert" means, as an Arab thief might hide and wait to plunder a passing caravan, Judah ran to idolatry. It was a national preoccupation.

3:4, 5 In spite of their great sin, the people of Israel continued to talk as if they were God's children. The only way they could do this was to minimise their sin. When we know we've done something wrong, we want to downplay the error and relieve some of the guilt we feel. As we minimise our sinfulness, we naturally shy away from making changes, and so we keep on sinning. But if we view every wrong attitude and action as a serious offence against God, we will begin to understand what living for God is all about. Is there any sin in your life that you've written off as too small to worry about? God says that we must confess and turn away from *every* sin.

3:6 [k]Jer 17:2 [l]Jer 2:20
3:7 [m]Eze 16:46
3:8 [n]Eze 16:47; 23:11
3:9 [o]ver 2 [p]Isa 57:6 [q]Jer 2:27
3:10 [r]Jer 12:2
3:11 [s]Eze 16:52; 23:11 [t]ver 7
3:12 [u]2Ki 17:3-6 [v]ver 14; Jer 31:21, 22; Eze 33:11 [w]Ps 86:15
3:13 [x]Dt 30:1-3; Jer 14:20; 1Jn 1:9 [y]Jer 2:25 [z]Dt 12:2 [a]ver 25
3:14 [b]Hos 2:19
3:15 [c]Ac 20:28
3:16 [d]Isa 65:17
3:17 [e]Jer 17:12; Eze 43:7 [f]Isa 60:9 [g]Jer 11:8

This is how you talk,
but you do all the evil you can."

Unfaithful Israel

6 During the reign of King Josiah, the LORD said to me, "Have you seen what
faithless Israel has done? She has gone up on every high hill and under every spreading
tree[k] and has committed adultery[l] there. 7 I thought that after she had done all this
she would return to me but she did not, and her unfaithful sister[m] Judah saw it. 8 I
gave faithless Israel her certificate of divorce and sent her away because of all her
adulteries. Yet I saw that her unfaithful sister Judah had no fear;[n] she also went out
and committed adultery. 9 Because Israel's immorality mattered so little to her, she
defiled the land[o] and committed adultery with stone[p] and wood.[q] 10 In spite of all
this, her unfaithful sister Judah did not return to me with all her heart, but only in
pretence,[r]" declares the LORD.
11 The LORD said to me, "Faithless Israel is more righteous[s] than unfaithful[t]
Judah. 12 Go, proclaim this message towards the north:[u]

" 'Return,[v] faithless Israel,' declares the LORD,
'I will frown on you no longer,
for I am merciful,' declares the LORD,
'I will not be angry[w] for ever.
13 Only acknowledge[x] your guilt—
you have rebelled against the LORD your God,
you have scattered your favours to foreign gods[y]
under every spreading tree,[z]
and have not obeyed[a] me,' "
declares the LORD.

14 "Return,[b] faithless people," declares the LORD, "for I am your husband. I will
choose you—one from a town and two from a clan—and bring you to Zion. 15 Then
I will give you shepherds[c] after my own heart, who will lead you with knowledge
and understanding. 16 In those days, when your numbers have increased greatly in the
land," declares the LORD, "men will no longer say, 'The ark of the covenant of the
LORD.' It will never enter their minds or be remembered;[d] it will not be missed, nor
will another one be made. 17 At that time they will call Jerusalem The Throne[e] of the
LORD, and all nations will gather in Jerusalem to honour[f] the name of the LORD. No
longer will they follow the stubbornness of their evil hearts.[g] 18 In those days the

3:6–6:30 The northern kingdom, Israel, had fallen to Assyria, and its people had been taken into captivity. The tragic lesson of their fall should have caused the southern kingdom, Judah, to return to God, but Judah paid no attention. Jeremiah urged Judah to return to God to avoid certain disaster. This message came between 627 and 621 B.C., during Josiah's reign. Although Josiah obeyed God's commands, his example apparently did not penetrate the hearts of the people. If the people refused to repent, God said he would destroy the nation because of the evils of Josiah's grandfather, King Manasseh (2 Kings 23:25–27).

3:11–13 Israel was not even trying to look as if it were obeying God, but Judah maintained the appearance of right faith without a true heart. Believing the right doctrines without heartfelt commitment is like offering sacrifices without true repentance. Judah's false repentance brought Jeremiah's words of condemnation. To live without faith is hopeless; to express sorrow without change is treacherous and unfaithful. Being sorry for sin is not enough. Repentance demands a change of mind and heart that results in changed behaviour.

3:12–18 The northern kingdom, Israel, was in captivity, being punished for its sins. The people of Judah undoubtedly looked down on these northern neighbours for their blatant heresy and degraded morals. Even so, Jeremiah promised the remnant of Israel God's blessings if they would turn to him. Judah, still secure in its own mind, should have turned to God after seeing the destruction of Israel. But the people of Judah refused, so Jeremiah startled them by telling about God's promise to Israel's remnant if they would repent.

3:15 God promised to give his people leaders ("shepherds" after his own heart) who would follow him, filled with knowledge (wisdom) and understanding. God saw Israel's lack of direction, so he promised to provide the right kind of leadership. We look to and trust our leaders for guidance and direction. But if they do not follow God, they will lead us astray. Pray for God-honouring leaders in our nations, communities, and churches—those who will be good examples and bring us God's wisdom.

3:16, 17 In the days of David and Solomon's reign over a united Israel, the people had a beautiful temple where they worshipped God. The temple housed the ark of the covenant, the symbol of God's presence with the people. The ark held the tablets of the Ten Commandments (see Exodus 25:10–22). Those days with the ark wouldn't be missed in the future kingdom because God's presence by the Holy Spirit would be there personally among his people.

house of Judah will join the house of Israel,[h] and together[i] they will come from a northern[j] land to the land[k] I gave your forefathers as an inheritance.
19"I myself said,

" 'How gladly would I treat you like sons
and give you a desirable land,
the most beautiful inheritance of any nation.'
I thought you would call me 'Father'[l]
and not turn away from following me.
20But like a woman unfaithful to her husband,
so you have been unfaithful to me, O house of Israel,"
declares the LORD.

21A cry is heard on the barren heights,[m]
the weeping and pleading of the people of Israel,
because they have perverted their ways
and have forgotten the LORD their God.

22"Return,[n] faithless people;
I will cure[o] you of backsliding."

"Yes, we will come to you,
for you are the LORD our God.
23Surely the ⌊idolatrous⌋ commotion on the hills
and mountains is a deception;
surely in the LORD our God
is the salvation[p] of Israel.
24From our youth shameful[q] gods have consumed
the fruits of our fathers' labour—
their flocks and herds,
their sons and daughters.
25Let us lie down in our shame,[r]
and let our disgrace cover us.
We have sinned against the LORD our God,
both we and our fathers;
from our youth[s] till this day
we have not obeyed the LORD our God."

4

"If you will return[a], O Israel,
return to me,"
declares the LORD.

"If you put your detestable idols[b] out of my sight
and no longer go astray,
2and if in a truthful, just and righteous way
you swear,[c] 'As surely as the LORD lives,'[d]
then the nations will be blessed[e] by him
and in him they will glory."

3This is what the LORD says to the men of Judah and to Jerusalem:

"Break up your unploughed ground[f]

3:18 [h]Hos 1:11 [i]Isa 11:13; Jer 50:4 [j]Jer 16:15; 31:8 [k]Am 9:15
3:19 [l]ver 4; Isa 63:16
3:21 [m]ver 2
3:22 [n]Hos 14:4 [o]Jer 33:6; Hos 6:1
3:23 [p]Ps 3:8; Jer 17:14
3:24 [q]Hos 9:10
3:25 [r]Ezr 9:6 [s]Jer 22:21
4:1 [a]Jer 3:1, 22; Joel 2:12 [b]Jer 35:15
4:2 [c]Dt 10:20; Isa 65:16 [d]Jer 12:16 [e]Ge 22:18; Gal 3:8
4:3 [f]Hos 10:12

3:22–25 Jeremiah predicted a day when the nation would be reunited, true worship would be reinstated, and sin would be seen for what it is. Our world glorifies the thrill that comes from wealth, competition, and sexual pleasure, and it ignores the sin that is so often associated with these thrills. It is sad that so few see sin as it really is—a deception. Most people can't see this until they are destroyed by the sin they pursue. The advantage of believing God's word is that we don't have to learn by hard experience the destructive results of sin.

4:3 Jeremiah told the people to break up the hardness of their hearts as a plough breaks up unploughed ground—soil that has not been tilled for a season. Good kings like Josiah had tried to turn the people back to God, but the people had continued to worship their idols in secret. Their hearts had become hardened to God's will. Jeremiah said the people needed to remove the sin that hardened their hearts before the good seed of God's commands could take root. Likewise we must remove our heart-hardening sin if we expect God's word to take root and grow in our lives.

and do not sow among thorns.[g]
4 Circumcise yourselves to the LORD,
circumcise your hearts,[h]
you men of Judah and people of Jerusalem,
or my wrath[i] will break out and burn like fire
because of the evil you have done—
burn with no-one to quench[j] it.

Disaster From the North

5 "Announce in Judah and proclaim in Jerusalem and say:
'Sound the trumpet throughout the land!'
Cry aloud and say:
'Gather together!
Let us flee to the fortified cities!'[k]
6 Raise the signal to go to Zion!
Flee for safety without delay!
For I am bringing disaster from the north,[l]
even terrible destruction."

7 A lion[m] has come out of his lair;
a destroyer of nations has set out.
He has left his place
to lay waste[n] your land.
Your towns will lie in ruins[o]
without inhabitant.
8 So put on sackcloth,[p]
lament and wail,
for the fierce anger[q] of the LORD
has not turned away from us.

9 "In that day," declares the LORD,
"the king and the officials will lose heart,
the priests will be horrified,
and the prophets will be appalled."[r]

10 Then I said, "Ah, Sovereign LORD, how completely you have deceived[s] this
people and Jerusalem by saying, 'You will have peace,'[t] when the sword is at our
throats."
11 At that time this people and Jerusalem will be told, "A scorching wind[u] from
the barren heights in the desert blows towards my people, but not to winnow or
cleanse; 12 a wind too strong for that comes from me.[a] Now I pronounce my judgments[v] against them."

13 Look! He advances like the clouds,[w]
his chariots[x] come like a whirlwind,[y]
his horses are swifter than eagles.[z]
Woe to us! We are ruined!
14 O Jerusalem, wash[a] the evil from your heart and be saved.
How long will you harbour wicked thoughts?
15 A voice is announcing from Dan,[b]

a *12* Or *comes at my command*

4:3 [g]Mk 4:18
4:4 [h]Dt 10:16; Jer 9:26; Ro 2:28-29 [i]Zep 2:2 [j]Am 5:6
4:5 [k]Jos 10:20; Jer 8:14
4:6 [l]Jer 1:13-15; 50:3
4:7 [m]2Ki 24:1; Jer 2:15 [n]Isa 1:7 [o]Jer 25:9
4:8 [p]Isa 22:12; Jer 6:26 [q]Jer 30:24
4:9 [r]Isa 29:9
4:10 [s]2Th 2:11 [t]Jer 14:13
4:11 [u]Eze 17:10; Hos 13:15
4:12 [v]Jer 1:16
4:13 [w]Isa 19:1 [x]Isa 66:15 [y]Isa 5:28 [z]Dt 28:49; Hab 1:8
4:14 [a]Jas 4:8
4:15 [b]Jer 8:16

4:6, 7 The disaster from the north would come from Babylon when Nabopolassar and Nebuchadnezzar II would attack (see 2 Chronicles 36).

4:10 Jeremiah, deeply moved by God's words, expressed his sorrow and confusion to God. Jeremiah was intercessor for the people. These people had false expectations because of the past promises of blessings, their blindness to their own sin, and the false prophets who kept telling them that all was well.

4:15 Disaster was announced first from Dan and then on to the hills of Ephraim because Dan was located at the northern border of Israel. Thus the Danites would be the first to see the approaching armies as they invaded from the north. No-one would be able to stop the armies because they would be coming as punishment for the people's sin.

proclaiming disaster from the hills of Ephraim.
16"Tell this to the nations,
proclaim it to Jerusalem:
'A besieging army is coming from a distant land,
raising a war cry[c] against the cities of Judah.
17They surround[d] her like men guarding a field,
because she has rebelled[e] against me,' "
declares the LORD.

18"Your own conduct and actions[f]
have brought this upon you.[g]
This is your punishment.
How bitter[h] it is!
How it pierces to the heart!"

19Oh, my anguish, my anguish![i]
I writhe in pain.
Oh, the agony of my heart!
My heart pounds within me,
I cannot keep silent.[j]
For I have heard the sound of the trumpet;
I have heard the battle cry.[k]
20Disaster follows disaster;[l]
the whole land lies in ruins.
In an instant my tents[m] are destroyed,
my shelter in a moment.
21How long must I see the battle standard
and hear the sound of the trumpet?

22"My people are fools;[n]
they do not know me.[o]
They are senseless children;
they have no understanding.
They are skilled in doing evil;[p]
they know not how to do good."[q]

23I looked at the earth,
and it was formless and empty;[r]
and at the heavens,
and their light was gone.
24I looked at the mountains,
and they were quaking;[s]
all the hills were swaying.
25I looked, and there were no people;
every bird in the sky had flown away.[t]
26I looked, and the fruitful land was a desert;
all its towns lay in ruins
before the LORD, before his fierce anger.

27This is what the LORD says:

"The whole land will be ruined,
though I will not destroy[u] it completely.

4:16 [c]Eze 21:22
4:17 [d]2Ki 25:1, 4 [e]Jer 5:23
4:18 [f]Ps 107:17; Isa 50:1 [g]Jer 2:17 [h]Jer 2:19
4:19 [i]Isa 16:11; 22:4; Jer 9:10 [j]Jer 20:9 [k]Nu 10:9
4:20 [l]Ps 42:7; Eze 7:26 [m]Jer 10:20
4:22 [n]Jer 10:8 [o]Jer 2:8 [p]Jer 13:23; 1Co 14:20 [q]Ro 16:19
4:23 [r]Ge 1:2
4:24 [s]Isa 5:25; Eze 38:20
4:25 [t]Jer 9:10; 12:4; Zep 1:3
4:27 [u]Jer 5:10, 18; 12:12; 30:11; 46:28

4:19–31 Jeremiah was anguished by the sure devastation of the coming judgment. This judgment would continue until the people turned from their sin and listened to God. Although this prophecy refers to the future destruction by Babylon, it could also describe the judgment of all sinners at the end of the world.

4:22 Judah was skilled in doing evil and did not know how to do good. Right living is more than simply avoiding sin. It requires decision and discipline. We must develop skills in right living because our behaviour attracts attention to our God. We should pursue excellence in Christian living with as much effort as we pursue excellence at work.

4:27 God warned that destruction was certain, but he promised that the faithful remnant would be spared. God is committed to preserving those who are faithful to him.

4:28 [v]Jer 12:4, 11; 14:2; Hos 4:3 [w]Isa 5:30; 50:3 [x]Nu 23:19 [y]Jer 23:20; 30:24

4:29 [z]Jer 6:23 [a]2Ki 25:4 [b]ver 7

4:30 [c]Isa 10:3-4 [d]Eze 23:40 [e]2Ki 9:30 [f]La 1:2; Eze 23:9, 22

4:31 [g]Jer 13:21 [h]Isa 42:14 [i]Isa 1:15; La 1:17

5:1 [a]2Ch 16:9; Eze 22:30 [b]Ge 18:32 [c]Ge 18:24

5:2 [d]Jer 4:2

5:3 [e]2Ch 16:9 [f]Isa 9:13 [g]Jer 2:30; Zep 3:2 [h]Jer 7:26; 19:15; Eze 3:8-9

5:4 [i]Jer 8:7

5:5 [j]Mic 3:1, 9

28 Therefore the earth will mourn[v]
and the heavens above grow dark,[w]
because I have spoken and will not relent,[x]
I have decided and will not turn back.[y]"

29 At the sound of horsemen and archers[z]
every town takes to flight.[a]
Some go into the thickets;
some climb up among the rocks.
All the towns are deserted;[b]
no-one lives in them.

30 What are you doing,[c] O devastated one?
Why dress yourself in scarlet
and put on jewels[d] of gold?
Why shade your eyes with paint?[e]
You adorn yourself in vain.
Your lovers[f] despise you;
they seek your life.

31 I hear a cry as of a woman in labour,[g]
a groan as of one bearing her first child—
the cry of the Daughter of Zion gasping for breath,[h]
stretching out her hands[i] and saying,
"Alas! I am fainting;
my life is given over to murderers."

Not One Is Upright

5 "Go up and down[a] the streets of Jerusalem,
look around and consider,
search through her squares.
If you can find but one person[b]
who deals honestly and seeks the truth,
I will forgive[c] this city.
2 Although they say, 'As surely as the LORD lives,'[d]
still they are swearing falsely."

3 O LORD, do not your eyes[e] look for truth?
You struck[f] them, but they felt no pain;
you crushed them but they refused correction.[g]
They made their faces harder than stone[h]
and refused to repent.
4 I thought, "These are only the poor;
they are foolish,
for they do not know[i] the way of the LORD,
the requirements of their God.
5 So I will go to the leaders[j]
and speak to them;
surely they know the way of the LORD,

5:1 Jerusalem was the capital city and centre of worship for Judah, but God challenged anyone to find *one* honest and truthful person in the entire city. God was willing to spare the city if one upright person could be found (he made a similar statement about Sodom; see Genesis 18:32). Think how significant your testimony may be in your city or community. You may represent the only witness for God to many people. Are you faithful to that opportunity?

5:3 Nothing but truth is acceptable to God. When we pray, sing, speak, or serve, nothing closes the door of God's acceptance more than hypocrisy, lying, or pretence. God sees through us and refuses to listen. To be close to God, be honest with him.

5:4, 5 Even the leaders who knew God's laws and understood his words of judgment had rejected him. They were supposed to teach and guide the people, but instead they led them into sin. Jeremiah observed the poor and foolish (ignorant)—those who were uninformed of God's ways—and realised they were not learning God's laws from their leaders. Thus God's search in Jerusalem was complete. There were no true followers in any level of society.

the requirements of their God."
But with one accord they too had broken off the yoke
and torn off the bonds.[k]
6 Therefore a lion from the forest will attack them,
a wolf from the desert will ravage them,
a leopard[l] will lie in wait near their towns
to tear to pieces any who venture out,
for their rebellion is great
and their backslidings many.[m]

7 "Why should I forgive you?
Your children have forsaken me
and sworn[n] by gods that are not gods.[o]
I supplied all their needs,
yet they committed adultery[p]
and thronged to the houses of prostitutes.
8 They are well-fed, lusty stallions,
each neighing for another man's wife.[q]
9 Should I not punish them for this?"[r]
declares the LORD.
"Should I not avenge myself
on such a nation as this?

10 "Go through her vineyards and ravage them,
but do not destroy them completely.[s]
Strip off her branches,
for these people do not belong to the LORD.
11 The house of Israel and the house of Judah
have been utterly unfaithful[t] to me,"
declares the LORD.

12 They have lied about the LORD;
they said, "He will do nothing!
No harm will come to us;[u]
we will never see sword or famine.[v]
13 The prophets[w] are but wind
and the word is not in them;
so let what they say be done to them."

14 Therefore this is what the LORD God Almighty says:

"Because the people have spoken these words,
I will make my words in your mouth[x] a fire[y]
and these people the wood it consumes.
15 O house of Israel," declares the LORD,
"I am bringing a distant nation[z] against you—
an ancient and enduring nation,
a people whose language[a] you do not know,
whose speech you do not understand.
16 Their quivers are like an open grave;
all of them are mighty warriors.
17 They will devour[bc] your harvests and food,
devour[de] your sons and daughters;
they will devour[f] your flocks and herds,

5:5 [k]Ps 2:3; Jer 2:20
5:6 [l]Hos 13:7 [m]Jer 30:14
5:7 [n]Jos 23:7; Zep 1:5 [o]Dt 32:21; Jer 2:11; Gal 4:8 [p]Nu 25:1
5:8 [q]Jer 29:23; Eze 22:11
5:9 [r]ver 29; Jer 9:9
5:10 [s]Jer 4:27
5:11 [t]Jer 3:20
5:12 [u]Jer 23:17 [v]2Ch 36:16; Jer 14:13
5:13 [w]Jer 14:15
5:14 [x]Jer 1:9; Hos 6:5 [y]Jer 23:29
5:15 [z]Dt 28:49; Isa 5:26; Jer 4:16 [a]Isa 28:11
5:17 [b]Jer 8:16 [c]Lev 26:16 [d]Jer 50:7, 17 [e]Dt 28:32 [f]Dt 28:31

5:7 God held these people responsible for the sins of their children because the children had followed their parents' example. The sin of leading others, especially our children, astray by our example is one for which God will hold us accountable.

5:15 Babylon was indeed an ancient nation. The old Babylonian empire had lasted from about 1900 B.C. to 1550 B.C., and earlier kingdoms had been on her soil as early as 3000 B.C. Babylon in Jeremiah's day would shortly rebel against Assyrian domination, form its own army, conquer Assyria, and become the next dominant world power.

devour your vines and fig-trees.
With the sword they will destroy
the fortified cities in which you trust.[g]

18“Yet even in those days,” declares the LORD, “I will not destroy[h] you completely.
19And when the people ask,[i] ‘Why has the LORD our God done all this to us?’ you
will tell them, ‘As you have forsaken me and served foreign gods[j] in your own land,
so now you will serve foreigners[k] in a land not your own.’

20“Announce this to the house of Jacob
and proclaim it in Judah:
21Hear this, you foolish and senseless people,
who have eyes[l] but do not see,
who have ears but do not hear:[m]
22Should you not fear[n] me?” declares the LORD.
“Should you not tremble in my presence?
I made the sand a boundary for the sea,
an everlasting barrier it cannot cross.
The waves may roll, but they cannot prevail;
they may roar, but they cannot cross it.
23But these people have stubborn and rebellious[o] hearts;
they have turned aside and gone away.
24They do not say to themselves,
‘Let us fear the LORD our God,
who gives autumn and spring rains[p] in season,
who assures us of the regular weeks of harvest.’[q]
25Your wrongdoings have kept these away;
your sins have deprived you of good.

26“Among my people are wicked men
who lie in wait[r] like men who snare birds
and like those who set traps to catch men.
27Like cages full of birds,
their houses are full of deceit;[s]
they have become rich[t] and powerful
28 and have grown fat[u] and sleek.
Their evil deeds have no limit;
they do not plead the case of the fatherless[v] to win it,
they do not defend the rights of the poor.[w]
29Should I not punish them for this?”
declares the LORD.
“Should I not avenge myself
on such a nation as this?

30“A horrible[x] and shocking thing
has happened in the land:
31The prophets prophesy lies,[y]
the priests rule by their own authority,

5:17 [g]Dt 28:33
5:18 [h]Jer 4:27
5:19 [i]Dt 29:24-26; 1Ki 9:9 [j]Jer 16:13 [k]Dt 28:48
5:21 [l]Isa 6:10; Eze 12:2 [m]Mt 13:15; Mk 8:18
5:22 [n]Dt 28:58
5:23 [o]Dt 21:18
5:24 [p]Ps 147:8; Joel 2:23 [q]Ge 8:22; Ac 14:17
5:26 [r]Ps 10:8; Pr 1:11
5:27 [s]Jer 9:6 [t]Jer 12:1
5:28 [u]Dt 32:15 [v]Zec 7:10 [w]Isa 1:23; Jer 7:6
5:30 [x]Jer 23:14; Hos 6:10
5:31 [y]Eze 13:6; Mic 2:11

5:21 Have you spoken to someone, only to realise that the person hasn't heard a word you were saying? Jeremiah told the people that their eyes and ears did them no good because they refused to see or hear God's message. The people of Judah and Israel were foolishly deaf when God promised blessings for obedience and destruction for disobedience. When God speaks through his word or his messengers, we harm ourselves if we fail to listen. God's message will never change us unless we listen to it.

5:22–24 What is your attitude when you come into God's presence? We should come with fear and trembling (that is, awe and respect) because God sets the boundaries of the roaring seas and establishes the rains and harvests. God had to strip away all the benefits that Judah and Israel had grown to respect more than him, with the hope that the people would turn back to God. Don't wait until God removes your cherished resources before committing yourself to him as you should.

5:28, 29 People and nations who please God treat the fatherless (orphans) justly and care for the poor. Wicked men in Israel treated the defenceless unjustly, which displeased God greatly. Some defenceless people – orphans, the poor, the homeless, and the lonely – are within your reach. What action can you take to help at least one of them?

and my people love it this way.
But what will you do in the end?

Jerusalem Under Siege

6 "Flee for safety, people of Benjamin!
Flee from Jerusalem!
Sound the trumpet in Tekoa![a]
Raise the signal over Beth Hakkerem![b]
For disaster looms out of the north,[c]
even terrible destruction.
2 I will destroy the Daughter of Zion,
so beautiful and delicate.
3 Shepherds[d] with their flocks will come against her;
they will pitch their tents round[e] her,
each tending his own portion."

4 "Prepare for battle against her!
Arise, let us attack at noon![f]
But, alas, the daylight is fading,
and the shadows of evening grow long.
5 So arise, let us attack at night
and destroy her fortresses!"

6 This is what the LORD Almighty says:

"Cut down the trees[g]
and build siege ramps[h] against Jerusalem.
This city must be punished;
it is filled with oppression.
7 As a well pours out its water,
so she pours out her wickedness.
Violence[i] and destruction[j] resound in her;
her sickness and wounds are ever before me.
8 Take warning, O Jerusalem,
or I will turn away[k] from you
and make your land desolate
so that no-one can live in it."

9 This is what the LORD Almighty says:

"Let them glean the remnant of Israel
as thoroughly as a vine;
pass your hand over the branches again,
like one gathering grapes."

10 To whom can I speak and give warning?
Who will listen to me?
Their ears are closed[a][l]

a 10 Hebrew *uncircumcised*

6:1 [a] 2Ch 11:6 [b] Ne 3:14 [c] Jer 4:6
6:3 [d] Jer 12:10 [e] 2Ki 25:4; Lk 19:43
6:4 [f] Jer 15:8
6:6 [g] Dt 20:19-20 [h] Jer 32:24
6:7 [i] Ps 55:9; Eze 7:11, 23 [j] Jer 20:8
6:8 [k] Eze 23:18; Hos 9:12
6:10 [l] Ac 7:51

6:1 The Lord warned Jeremiah's own tribe of Benjamin to flee, not to the security of the great walled city of Jerusalem because it would be under siege, but towards Tekoa, a town about 12 miles south of Jerusalem. The warning smoke signal was lit at Beth Hakkerem, halfway between Jerusalem and Bethlehem.

6:3 The shepherds were the leaders of Babylon's armies, and their flocks were their troops.

6:9 The remnant mentioned here is not to be confused with the righteous remnant. This remnant is those left after the first wave of destruction. Like a grape-gatherer, Babylon wouldn't be satisfied until every person was taken. Babylonians invaded Judah three times until they destroyed the nation and its temple completely (2 Kings 24; 25).

6:10 The people became angry and closed their ears. They wanted no part of God's commands because living for God did not appear very exciting. As in Jeremiah's day, people today dislike God's demand for disciplined living. As unsettling as people's responses might be, we must continue to share God's word. Our responsibility is to present God's word; their responsibility is to accept it. We must not let what people want to hear determine what we say.

so that they cannot hear.
The word[m] of the LORD is offensive to them;
they find no pleasure in it.
11 But I am full of the wrath[n] of the LORD,
and I cannot hold it in.[o]

"Pour it out on the children in the street
and on the young men[p] gathered together;
both husband and wife will be caught in it,
and the old, those weighed down with years.
12 Their houses will be turned over to others,[q]
together with their fields and their wives,[r]
when I stretch out my hand[s]
against those who live in the land,"
declares the LORD.

13 "From the least to the greatest,
all are greedy for gain;[t]
prophets and priests alike,
all practise deceit.[u]
14 They dress the wound of my people
as though it were not serious.
'Peace, peace,' they say,
when there is no peace.[v]
15 Are they ashamed of their loathsome conduct?
No, they have no shame at all;
they do not even know how to blush.[w]
So they will fall among the fallen;
they will be brought down when I punish them,"
says the LORD.

16 This is what the LORD says:

"Stand at the crossroads and look;
ask for the ancient paths,[x]
ask where the good way[y] is, and walk in it,
and you will find rest[z] for your souls.
But you said, 'We will not walk in it.'
17 I appointed watchmen[a] over you and said,
'Listen to the sound of the trumpet!'
But you said, 'We will not listen.'[b]
18 Therefore hear, O nations;
observe, O witnesses,
what will happen to them.
19 Hear, O earth:[c]
I am bringing disaster on this people,
the fruit of their schemes,[d]
because they have not listened to my words
and have rejected my law.[e]
20 What do I care about incense from Sheba
or sweet calamus[f] from a distant land?

6:10 [m] Jer 20:8
6:11 [n] Jer 7:20 [o] Job 32:20; Jer 20:9 [p] Jer 9:21
6:12 [q] Dt 28:30 [r] Jer 8:10; 38:22 [s] Isa 5:25
6:13 [t] Isa 56:11 [u] Jer 8:10
6:14 [v] Jer 4:10; 8:11; Eze 13:10
6:15 [w] Jer 3:3; 8:10-12
6:16 [x] Jer 18:15 [y] Ps 119:3 [z] Mt 11:29
6:17 [a] Eze 3:17 [b] Jer 11:7-8; 25:4
6:19 [c] Isa 1:2; Jer 22:29 [d] Pr 1:31 [e] Jer 8:9
6:20 [f] Ex 30:23

6:14 "Ignore it and maybe it will go away!" Sound familiar? This was Israel's response to Jeremiah's warnings. They kept listening to predictions of peace because they did not like Jeremiah's condemnation of their sin. But denying the truth never changes it; what God says always happens. Sin is never removed by denying its existence. We must confess to God that we have sinned and ask him to forgive us.

6:16 The right path for living is ancient and has been marked out by God. But the people refused to take God's path, going their own way instead. We face the same decision today, going God's old but true way, or following a new path of our own choosing. Don't be misled. The only way to find peace and "rest for your souls" is to walk on God's path.

6:20 Sheba, located in southwest Arabia, was a centre of trade in incense and spices used in pagan religious rituals.

Your burnt offerings are not acceptable;[g]
your sacrifices[h] do not please me."[i]

21 Therefore this is what the LORD says:

"I will put obstacles before this people.
Fathers and sons alike will stumble[j] over them;
neighbours and friends will perish."

22 This is what the LORD says:

"Look, an army is coming
from the land of the north;[k]
a great nation is being stirred up
from the ends of the earth.
23 They are armed with bow and spear;
they are cruel and show no mercy.[l]
They sound like the roaring sea
as they ride on their horses;[m]
they come like men in battle formation
to attack you, O Daughter of Zion."

24 We have heard reports about them,
and our hands hang limp.
Anguish[n] has gripped us,
pain like that of a woman in labour.[o]
25 Do not go out to the fields
or walk on the roads,
for the enemy has a sword,
and there is terror on every side.[p]
26 O my people, put on sackcloth[q]
and roll in ashes;[r]
mourn with bitter wailing
as for an only son,[s]
for suddenly the destroyer
will come upon us.

27 "I have made you a tester[t] of metals
and my people the ore,
that you may observe
and test their ways.
28 They are all hardened rebels,[u]
going about to slander.[v]
They are bronze and iron;[w]
they all act corruptly.
29 The bellows blow fiercely
to burn away the lead with fire,
but the refining goes on in vain;
the wicked are not purged out.
30 They are called rejected silver,
because the LORD has rejected them."[x]

6:20 [g]Am 5:22 [h]Ps 50:8-10; Jer 7:21; Mic 6:7-8 [i]Isa 1:11
6:21 [j]Isa 8:14
6:22 [k]Jer 1:15; 10:22
6:23 [l]Isa 13:18 [m]Jer 4:29
6:24 [n]Jer 4:19 [o]Jer 4:31; 50:41-43
6:25 [p]Jer 49:29
6:26 [q]Jer 4:8 [r]Jer 25:34; Mic 1:10 [s]Zec 12:10
6:27 [t]Jer 9:7
6:28 [u]Jer 5:23 [v]Jer 9:4 [w]Eze 22:18
6:30 [x]Ps 119:119; Jer 7:29; Hos 9:17

6:29, 30 Metal is purified by fire. As it is heated, impurities are burned away and only the pure metal remains. As God tested the people of Judah, however, he could find no purity in their lives. They continued in their sinful ways. Do you see impurities in your life that should be burned away? Confess these to God and allow him to purify you as he sees fit. Take time right now to reflect on the areas of your life that he has already refined; then thank him for what he is doing.

False Religion Worthless

7 This is the word that came to Jeremiah from the LORD: 2"Stand[a] at the gate of
the LORD's house and there proclaim this message:
" 'Hear the word of the LORD, all you people of Judah who come through these gates
to worship the LORD. 3This is what the LORD Almighty, the God of Israel, says:
Reform your ways[b] and your actions, and I will let you live in this place. 4Do not
trust in deceptive[c] words and say, "This is the temple of the LORD, the temple of the
LORD, the temple of the LORD!" 5If you really change your ways and your actions and
deal with each other justly,[d] 6if you do not oppress the alien, the fatherless or the
widow and do not shed innocent blood[e] in this place, and if you do not follow other
gods[f] to your own harm, 7then I will let you live in this place, in the land[g] I gave
to your forefathers for ever and ever. 8But look, you are trusting in deceptive[h] words
that are worthless.
9" 'Will you steal and murder, commit adultery and perjury,[a] burn incense to
Baal[i] and follow other gods[j] you have not known, 10and then come and stand before
me in this house,[k] which bears my Name, and say, "We are safe"—safe to do all
these detestable things? 11Has this house,[l] which bears my Name, become a den of
robbers[m] to you? But I have been watching![n] declares the LORD.
12" 'Go now to the place in Shiloh[o] where I first made a dwelling for my Name,
and see what I did[p] to it because of the wickedness of my people Israel. 13While you
were doing all these things, declares the LORD, I spoke to you again and again,[q] but
you did not listen;[r] I called[s] you, but you did not answer.[t] 14Therefore, what I did
to Shiloh I will now do to the house that bears my Name,[u] the temple[v] you trust in,
the place I gave to you and your fathers. 15I will thrust you from my presence, just
as I did all your brothers, the people of Ephraim.'[w]
16"So do not pray for this people nor offer any plea[x] or petition for them; do not
plead with me, for I will not listen to you. 17Do you not see what they are doing in
the towns of Judah and in the streets of Jerusalem? 18The children gather wood, the
fathers light the fire, and the women knead the dough and make cakes of bread for
the Queen of Heaven.[y] They pour out drink offerings[z] to other gods to provoke[a]
me to anger. 19But am I the one they are provoking?[b] declares the LORD. Are they not
rather harming themselves, to their own shame?[c]
20" 'Therefore this is what the Sovereign LORD says: My anger[d] and my wrath will

7:2 [a]Jer 17:19
7:3 [b]Jer 18:11; 26:13
7:4 [c]Mic 3:11
7:5 [d]Jer 22:3
7:6 [e]Jer 2:34; 19:4 [f]Dt 8:19
7:7 [g]Dt 4:40
7:8 [h]ver 4
7:9 [i]Jer 11:13, 17 [j]Ex 20:3
7:10 [k]Jer 32:34; Eze 23:38-39
7:11 [l]Isa 56:7 [m]Mt 21:13*; Mk 11:17*; Lk 19:46* [n]Jer 29:23
7:12 [o]Jos 18:1 [p]1Sa 4:10-11, 22; Ps 78:60-64
7:13 [q]2Ch 36:15 [r]Isa 65:12 [s]Pr 1:24 [t]Jer 35:17
7:14 [u]1Ki 9:7 [v]ver 4
7:15 [w]Ps 78:67
7:16 [x]Ex 32:10; Dt 9:14; Jer 15:1
7:18 [y]Jer 44:17-19 [z]Jer 19:13 [a]1Ki 14:9
7:19 [b]Dt 32:21 [c]Jer 9:19
7:20 [d]Jer 42:18; La 2:3-5

[a] 9 Or *and swear by false gods*

7:1–10:25 As this section opens, God sends Jeremiah to the temple gates to confront the false belief that God will not let harm come to the temple and those who live near it. Jeremiah rebukes the people for their false and worthless religion, their idolatry, and the shameless behaviour of the people and their leaders. Judah, he says, is ripe for judgment and exile. This happened during the reign of Jehoiakim, a puppet of Egypt. The nation, in shock over the death of Josiah, was going through a spiritual reversal that removed much of the good Josiah had done. The themes of this section are false religion, idolatry, and hypocrisy. Jeremiah was almost put to death for this sermon, but he was saved by the officials of Judah (see chapter 26).

7:2, 3 The people followed a worship ritual but maintained a sinful life-style. It was religion without personal commitment to God. We can easily do the same. Attending church, taking communion, teaching in Sunday school, singing in the choir—all are empty exercises unless we are truly doing them for God. It is good to do these activities, not because we ought to do them for the church, but because we want to do them for God.

7:9–11 There are several parallels between how the people of Judah viewed their temple and how many today view their churches. (1) *They didn't make the temple part of their daily living.* We go to beautiful churches well-prepared for worship, but often we don't take the presence of God with us through the week. (2) *The image of the temple became more important than the substance of faith.* The image of going to church and belonging to a group can become more important than a life changed for God. (3) *The people used their temple as a sanctuary.* Many use religious affiliation as a hiding place, thinking it will protect them from evil and problems.

7:11, 12 Jesus used these words from 7:11 in clearing the temple (Mark 11:17; Luke 19:46). This passage applied to the evil in the temple in Jesus' day as well as in Jeremiah's. God's tabernacle had been at Shiloh, but Shiloh had been abandoned (Psalm 78:60; Jeremiah 26:6). If God did not preserve Shiloh because the tabernacle was there, why would he preserve Jerusalem because of the temple?

7:15 Ephraim is another name for Israel, the northern kingdom, which had been taken into captivity by Assyria in 722 B.C.

7:18 The Queen of Heaven was a name for Ishtar, the Mesopotamian goddess of love and fertility. After the fall of Jerusalem, the refugees from Judah who fled to Egypt continued to worship her (44:17). A papyrus dating from the 5th century B.C., found at Hermopolis in Egypt, mentions the Queen of Heaven among the gods honoured by the Jewish community living there.

7:19 This verse answers the question, "Who gets hurt when we turn away from God?" We do! Separating ourselves from God is like keeping a green plant away from sunlight or water. God is our only source of spiritual strength. Cut yourself off from him, and you cut off life itself.

be poured[e] out on this place, on man and beast, on the trees of the field and on the
fruit of the ground, and it will burn and not be quenched.[f]
21" 'This is what the LORD Almighty, the God of Israel, says: Go ahead, add your
burnt offerings to your other sacrifices[g] and eat[h] the meat yourselves! 22For when
I brought your forefathers out of Egypt and spoke to them, I did not just give them
commands about burnt offerings and sacrifices,[i] 23but I gave them this command:
Obey[j] me, and I will be your God and you will be my people.[k] Walk in all the ways
I command you, that it may go well[l] with you. 24But they did not listen or pay
attention;[m] instead, they followed the stubborn inclinations of their evil hearts. They
went backward and not forward. 25From the time your forefathers left Egypt until now,
day after day, again and again[n] I sent you my servants the prophets.[o] 26But they did
not listen to me or pay attention. They were stiff-necked and did more evil than their
forefathers.'[p]
27"When you tell[q] them all this, they will not listen[r] to you; when you call to them,
they will not answer. 28Therefore say to them, 'This is the nation that has not obeyed
the LORD its God or responded to correction. Truth has perished; it has vanished from
their lips. 29Cut off[s] your hair and throw it away; take up a lament on the barren
heights, for the LORD has rejected and abandoned[t] this generation that is under his
wrath.

The Valley of Slaughter

30" 'The people of Judah have done evil in my eyes, declares the LORD. They have
set up their detestable idols[u] in the house that bears my Name and have defiled[v] it.
31They have built the high places of Topheth[w] in the Valley of Ben Hinnom to burn
their sons and daughters[x] in the fire—something I did not command, nor did it enter
my mind.[y] 32So beware, the days are coming, declares the LORD, when people will
no longer call it Topheth or the Valley of Ben Hinnom, but the Valley of Slaughter,[z]
for they will bury[a] the dead in Topheth until there is no more room. 33Then the
carcasses of this people will become food[b] for the birds of the air and the beasts of
the earth, and there will be no-one to frighten them away. 34I will bring an end to
the sounds[c] of joy and gladness and to the voices of bride and bridegroom[d] in the
towns of Judah and the streets of Jerusalem, for the land will become desolate.[e]
8 " 'At that time, declares the LORD, the bones of the kings and officials of Judah,
the bones of the priests and prophets, and the bones of the people of Jerusalem
will be removed from their graves. 2They will be exposed to the sun and the moon
and all the stars of the heavens, which they have loved and served[a] and which they
have followed and consulted and worshipped. They will not be gathered up or buried,
but will be like refuse lying on the ground. 3Wherever I banish them, all the survivors
of this evil nation will prefer death to life,[b] declares the LORD Almighty.'

Sin and Punishment

4"Say to them, 'This is what the LORD says:

" 'When men fall down, do they not get up?[c]

7:20 [e]Jer 6:11-12; [f]Jer 11:16
7:21 [g]Isa 1:11; Am 5:21-22 [h]Hos 8:13
7:22 [i]1Sa 15:22; Ps 51:16; Hos 6:6
7:23 [j]Ex 19:5 [k]Lev 26:12 [l]Ex 15:26
7:24 [m]Ps 81:11-12; Jer 11:8
7:25 [n]2 Ch 36:15 [o]Jer 25:4
7:26 [p]Jer 16:12
7:27 [q]Eze 2:7 [r]Eze 3:7
7:29 [s]Job 1:20; Isa 15:2; Mic 1:16 [t]Jer 6:30
7:30 [u]Eze 7:20-22 [v]Jer 32:34
7:31 [w]2Ki 23:10 [x]Ps 106:38 [y]Jer 19:5
7:32 [z]Jer 19:6 [a]Jer 19:11
7:33 [b]Dt 28:26
7:34 [c]Isa 24:8; Eze 26:13 [d]Rev 18:23 [e]Lev 26:34
8:2 [a]2Ki 23:5; Ac 7:42
8:3 [b]Job 3:22; Rev 9:6
8:4 [c]Pr 24:16

7:21–23 God had set up a system of sacrifices to encourage the people to obey him joyfully (see the book of Leviticus). He required the people to make these sacrifices, not because the sacrifices themselves pleased him, but because they caused the people to recognise their sin and refocus on living for God. They faithfully made the sacrifices but forgot the reason they were offering them, and thus they disobeyed God. Jeremiah reminded the people that acting out religious rituals was meaningless unless they were prepared to obey God in all areas of life. (See the chart in Hosea 6.)

7:25 From the time of Moses to the end of the Old Testament period, God sent many prophets to Israel and Judah. No matter how bad the circumstances were, God always raised up a prophet to speak against their stubborn spiritual attitudes.

7:31, 32 The high places (or altars) of Topheth (meaning "fire-place") were set up in the Valley of Ben Hinnom, where debris and rubbish from the city were thrown away. This altar was used to worship Molech—a god who required child sacrifice (2 Kings 23:10). Their valley of sacrifice would become their valley of slaughter by the Babylonians. At the place where the people had killed their children in sinful idol worship, they themselves would be slaughtered.

8:1, 2 The threat that the graves of Judah's people would be opened was horrible to a people who highly honoured the dead and believed that it was the utmost desecration to open graves. This would be an ironic punishment for idol worshippers—their bones would be laid out before the sun, moon, and stars—the gods they thought could save them.

8:4–6 When people fall down or realise that they are headed in

When a man turns away, does he not return?
5 Why then have these people turned away?
Why does Jerusalem always turn away?
They cling to deceit;[d]
they refuse to return.[e]
6 I have listened attentively,
but they do not say what is right.
No-one repents[f] of his wickedness,
saying, "What have I done?"
Each pursues his own course[g]
like a horse charging into battle.
7 Even the stork in the sky
knows her appointed seasons,
and the dove, the swift and the thrush
observe the time of their migration.
But my people do not know[h]
the requirements of the LORD.

8 " 'How can you say, "We are wise,
for we have the law[i] of the LORD,"
when actually the lying pen of the scribes
has handled it falsely?
9 The wise[j] will be put to shame;
they will be dismayed and trapped.
Since they have rejected the word[k] of the LORD,
what kind of wisdom do they have?
10 Therefore I will give their wives to other men
and their fields to new owners.[l]
From the least to the greatest,
all are greedy for gain;[m]
prophets and priests alike,
all practise deceit.
11 They dress the wound of my people
as though it were not serious.
"Peace, peace," they say,
when there is no peace.[n]
12 Are they ashamed of their loathsome conduct?
No, they have no shame[o] at all;
they do not even know how to blush.
So they will fall among the fallen;
they will be brought down when they are punished,[p]
says the LORD.[q]

13 " 'I will take away their harvest,
declares the LORD.
There will be no grapes on the vine.[r]
There will be no figs[s] on the tree,
and their leaves will wither.[t]
What I have given them
will be taken[u] from them.' "[a]

14 "Why are we sitting here?

8:5 [d] Jer 5:27 [e] Jer 7:24; 9:6
8:6 [f] Rev 9:20 [g] Ps 14:1-3
8:7 [h] Isa 1:3; Jer 5:4-5
8:8 [i] Ro 2:17
8:9 [j] Jer 6:15 [k] Jer 6:19
8:10 [l] Jer 6:12 [m] Isa 56:11
8:11 [n] Jer 6:14
8:12 [o] Jer 3:3 [p] Ps 52:5-7; Isa 3:9 [q] Jer 6:15
8:13 [r] Joel 1:7 [s] Lk 13:6 [t] Mt 21:19 [u] Jer 5:17

a *13* The meaning of the Hebrew for this sentence is uncertain.

the wrong direction, it only makes sense for them to get up or change direction. But as God watched the nation, he saw people living sinful lives by choice, deceiving themselves that there would be no consequences. They had lost their perspective concerning God's will for their lives and were trying to minimize their sin. Are there some indicators that you have fallen down or are heading the wrong way? What are you doing to get back on the right path?

Gather together!
Let us flee to the fortified cities[v]
and perish there!
For the LORD our God has doomed us to perish
and given us poisoned water[w] to drink,
because we have sinned[x] against him.
15 We hoped for peace[y]
but no good has come,
for a time of healing
but there was only terror.[z]
16 The snorting of the enemy's horses
is heard from Dan;[a]
at the neighing of their stallions
the whole land trembles.
They have come to devour
the land and everything in it,
the city and all who live there."

17 "See, I will send venomous snakes[b] among you,
vipers that cannot be charmed,[c]
and they will bite you,"
declares the LORD.

18 O my Comforter[b] in sorrow,
my heart is faint[d] within me.
19 Listen to the cry of my people
from a land far away:[e]
"Is the LORD not in Zion?
Is her King no longer there?"

"Why have they provoked me to anger with their images,
with their worthless foreign idols?"[f]

20 "The harvest is past,
the summer has ended,
and we are not saved."

21 Since my people are crushed, I am crushed;
I mourn,[g] and horror grips me.
22 Is there no balm in Gilead?[h]
Is there no physician there?
Why then is there no healing[i]
for the wound of my people?

9 1 Oh, that my head were a spring of water
and my eyes a fountain of tears!
I would weep[a] day and night
for the slain of my people.[b]

b *18* The meaning of the Hebrew for this word is uncertain.

8:14 [v] Jer 4:5; Jer 35:11 [w] Dt 29:18; Jer 9:15; 23:15 [x] Jer 14:7, 20
8:15 [y] ver 11 [z] Jer 14:19
8:16 [a] Jer 4:15
8:17 [b] Nu 21:6; Dt 32:24 [c] Ps 58:5
8:18 [d] La 5:17
8:19 [e] Jer 9:16 [f] Dt 32:21
8:21 [g] Jer 14:17
8:22 [h] Ge 37:25 [i] Jer 30:12
9:1 [a] Jer 13:17; La 2:11, 18 [b] Isa 22:4

8:16 Dan was the northernmost tribe in Israel.

8:18 Jeremiah was pleading with God to save his people.

8:20–22 These words vividly portray Jeremiah's emotion as he watched his people reject God. He responded with anguish to a world dying in sin. We watch that same world still dying in sin, still rejecting God. But how often is our heart broken for our lost friends and neighbours, our lost world? Only when we have Jeremiah's kind of passionate concern will we be moved to help. We must begin by asking God to break our hearts for the world he loves.

8:22 Gilead was famous for its healing balm (medicine). This is a rhetorical question. The obvious answer is, "Yes – God," but Israel was not applying the "balm"; they were not obeying the Lord. Although the people's spiritual sickness was still very deep, it could be healed. But the people refused the medicine. God could heal their self-inflicted wounds, but he would not force his healing on them.

9:1–6 Jeremiah felt conflicting emotions concerning his people. Lying, deceit, treachery, adultery, and idolatry had become common sins. He was angered by their sin, but he had compassion too. He was set apart from them by his mission for God, but he was also one of them. Jesus had similar feelings when he stood before Jerusalem, the city that would reject him (Matthew 23:37).

2Oh, that I had in the desert
a lodging place for travellers,
so that I might leave my people
and go away from them;
for they are all adulterers,[c]
a crowd of unfaithful people.

3"They make ready their tongue
like a bow, to shoot lies;[d]
it is not by truth
that they triumph[a] in the land.
They go from one sin to another;
they do not acknowledge me,"
declares the LORD.

4"Beware of your friends;
do not trust your brothers.[e]
For every brother is a deceiver,[b][f]
and every friend a slanderer.
5Friend deceives friend,
and no-one speaks the truth.
They have taught their tongues to lie;
they weary themselves with sinning.
6You[c] live in the midst of deception;[g]
in their deceit they refuse to acknowledge me,"
declares the LORD.

7Therefore this is what the LORD Almighty says:

"See, I will refine[h] and test[i] them,
for what else can I do
because of the sin of my people?
8Their tongue[j] is a deadly arrow;
it speaks with deceit.
With his mouth each speaks cordially to his neighbour,
but in his heart he sets a trap[k] for him.
9Should I not punish them for this?"
declares the LORD.
"Should I not avenge[l] myself
on such a nation as this?"

10I will weep and wail for the mountains
and take up a lament concerning the desert pastures.
They are desolate and untravelled,
and the lowing of cattle is not heard.
The birds of the air[m] have fled
and the animals are gone.

11"I will make Jerusalem a heap of ruins,
a haunt of jackals;[n]
and I will lay waste the towns of Judah
so that no-one can live there."[o]

12What man is wise[p] enough to understand this? Who has been instructed by the
LORD and can explain it? Why has the land been ruined and laid waste like a desert
that no-one can cross?
13The LORD said, "It is because they have forsaken my law, which I set before them;
they have not obeyed me or followed my law.[q] 14Instead, they have followed[r] the
stubbornness of their hearts;[s] they have followed the Baals, as their fathers taught
them." 15Therefore, this is what the LORD Almighty, the God of Israel, says: "See,

[a] 3 Or *lies; / they are not valiant for truth* [b] 4 Or *a deceiving Jacob* [c] 6 That is, Jeremiah (the Hebrew is singular)

9:2 [c]Jer 5:7-8; 23:10; Hos 4:2
9:3 [d]Ps 64:3
9:4 [e]Mic 7:5-6 [f]Ge 27:35
9:6 [g]Jer 5:27
9:7 [h]Isa 1:25 [i]Jer 6:27
9:8 [j]ver 3 [k]Jer 5:26
9:9 [l]Jer 5:9, 29
9:10 [m]Jer 4:25; 12:4; Hos 4:3
9:11 [n]Isa 34:13 [o]Isa 25:2; Jer 26:9
9:12 [p]Ps 107:43; Hos 14:9
9:13 [q]2Ch 7:19; Ps 89:30-32
9:14 [r]Jer 2:8, 23 [s]Jer 7:24

I will make this people eat bitter food[t] and drink poisoned water.[u] 16I will scatter
them among nations[v] that neither they nor their fathers have known,[w] and I will
pursue them with the sword[x] until I have destroyed them."[y]

17This is what the LORD Almighty says:

"Consider now! Call for the wailing women[z] to come;
send for the most skilful of them.
18Let them come quickly
and wail over us
till our eyes overflow with tears
and water streams from our eyelids.[a]
19The sound of wailing is heard from Zion:
'How ruined[b] we are!
How great is our shame!
We must leave our land
because our houses are in ruins.' "

20Now, O women, hear the word of the LORD;
open your ears to the words of his mouth.
Teach your daughters how to wail;
teach one another a lament.[c]
21Death has climbed in through our windows
and has entered our fortresses;
it has cut off the children from the streets
and the young men[d] from the public squares.

22Say, "This is what the LORD declares:

" 'The dead bodies of men will lie
like refuse[e] on the open field,
like cut corn behind the reaper,
with no-one to gather them.' "

23This is what the LORD says:

"Let not the wise man boast of his wisdom[f]
or the strong man boast of his strength[g]
or the rich man boast of his riches,[h]
24but let him who boasts boast[i] about this:
that he understands and knows me,
that I am the LORD,[j] who exercises kindness,[k]
justice and righteousness[l] on earth,
for in these I delight,"
declares the LORD.

25"The days are coming," declares the LORD, "when I will punish all who are
circumcised only in the flesh[m]—26Egypt, Judah, Edom, Ammon, Moab and all who
live in the desert in distant places.[d][n] For all these nations are really uncircumcised,
and even the whole house of Israel is uncircumcised in heart.[o]"

d 26 *Or desert and who clip the hair by their foreheads*

9:15 [t]La 3:15 [u]Jer 8:14
9:16 [v]Lev 26:33 [w]Dt 28:64 [x]Eze 5:2 [y]Jer 44:27; Eze 5:12
9:17 [z]2Ch 35:25; Ecc 12:5; Am 5:16
9:18 [a]Jer 14:17
9:19 [b]Jer 4:13
9:20 [c]Isa 32:9-13
9:21 [d]2Ch 36:17
9:22 [e]Jer 8:2
9:23 [f]Ecc 9:11 [g]1Ki 20:11 [h]Eze 28:4-5
9:24 [i]1Co 1:31*; Gal 6:14 [j]2Co 10:17* [k]Ps 51:1; Mic 7:18 [l]Ps 36:6
9:25 [m]Ro 2:8-9
9:26 [n]Jer 25:23 [o]Lev 26:41; Ac 7:51; Ro 2:28

9:23, 24 People tend to admire four qualities in others: human wisdom, power (strength), kindness, and riches. But God puts a higher priority on knowing him personally and living a life that reflects his justice and righteousness. What do you want people to admire most about you?

9:25, 26 Circumcision went back to the time of Abraham. For the people of Israel it was a symbol of their covenant relationship to God (Genesis 17:9–14). Circumcision was also practised by pagan nations, but not as the sign of a covenant with God. By Jeremiah's time, the Israelites had forgotten the spiritual significance of circumcision even though they continued to perform the physical ritual.

10:2
[a]Lev 20:23

10:3
[b]Isa 40:19

10:4
[c]Isa 41:7

10:5
[d]1Co 12:2
[e]Ps 115:5, 7
[f]Isa 41:24; 46:7

10:6
[g]Ps 48:1

10:7
[h]Ps 22:28; Rev 15:4

10:8
[i]Isa 40:19; Jer 4:22

10:9
[j]Ps 115:4; Isa 40:19

10:10
[k]Ps 76:7

10:11
[l]Ps 96:5; Isa 2:18

God and Idols

10 Hear what the LORD says to you, O house of Israel. 2This is what the LORD
says:

"Do not learn the ways of the nations[a]
or be terrified by signs in the sky,
though the nations are terrified by them.
3For the customs of the peoples are worthless;
they cut a tree out of the forest,
and a craftsman[b] shapes it with his chisel.
4They adorn it with silver and gold;
they fasten it with hammer and nails
so that it will not totter.[c]
5Like a scarecrow in a melon patch,
their idols cannot speak;[d]
they must be carried
because they cannot walk.[e]
Do not fear them;
they can do no harm
nor can they do any good."[f]

6No-one is like you, O LORD;
you are great,[g]
and your name is mighty in power.
7Who should not revere you,
O King of the nations?[h]
This is your due.
Among all the wise men of the nations
and in all their kingdoms,
there is no-one like you.
8They are all senseless and foolish;[i]
they are taught by worthless wooden idols.
9Hammered silver is brought from Tarshish
and gold from Uphaz.
What the craftsman and goldsmith have made[j]
is then dressed in blue and purple—
all made by skilled workers.
10But the LORD is the true God;
he is the living God, the eternal King.
When he is angry, the earth trembles;
the nations cannot endure his wrath.[k]

11"Tell them this: 'These gods, who did not make the heavens and the earth, will
perish[l] from the earth and from under the heavens.' "[a]

12But God made the earth by his power;

a *11* The text of this verse is in Aramaic.

10:2, 3 Most people would like to know the future. Decisions would be easier, certain failures avoided, and some successes assured. The people of Judah wanted to know the future too, and they tried to discern it through reading the signs in the sky. Jeremiah's response applies today: God made the earth and the heavens, including the stars that people consult and worship (10:12). No-one will discover the future in made-up charts of God's stars. But God, who promises to guide you, knows your future and will be with you all the way. He may not reveal your future to you, but he will walk with you as the future unfolds. Don't trust the stars; trust the One who made the stars.

10:8 Those who put their trust in a chunk of wood, even though it is carved well and clothed beautifully, are foolish. The simplest person who worships God is wiser than the wisest person who worships a worthless substitute, because this person has discerned who God really is. In what or whom do you place your trust?

10:9 Tarshish was located at the westward limit of the ancient world, perhaps in what is now Spain (see Jonah 1:3). It was a source of silver, tin, lead, and iron for Tyre (Ezekiel 27:12). The location of Uphaz is unknown. Instead, it may be a metallurgical term for "refined gold". No matter how well made or how beautiful idols are, they can never have the power and life of the true and living God.

he founded the world by his wisdom
and stretched out the heavens[m] by his understanding.
13 When he thunders,[n] the waters in the heavens roar;
he makes clouds rise from the ends of the earth.
He sends lightning with the rain[o]
and brings out the wind from his storehouses.

14 Everyone is senseless and without knowledge;
every goldsmith is shamed by his idols.
His images are a fraud;
they have no breath in them.
15 They are worthless,[p] the objects of mockery;
when their judgment comes, they will perish.
16 He who is the Portion[q] of Jacob is not like these,
for he is the Maker of all things,[r]
including Israel, the tribe of his inheritance[s]—
the LORD Almighty is his name.[t]

Coming Destruction

17 Gather up your belongings[u] to leave the land,
you who live under siege.
18 For this is what the LORD says:
"At this time I will hurl[v] out
those who live in this land;
I will bring distress on them
so that they may be captured."

19 Woe to me because of my injury!
My wound[w] is incurable!
Yet I said to myself,
"This is my sickness, and I must endure[x] it."
20 My tent[y] is destroyed;
all its ropes are snapped.
My sons are gone from me and are no more;[z]
no-one is left now to pitch my tent
or to set up my shelter.
21 The shepherds are senseless
and do not enquire of the LORD;
so they do not prosper
and all their flock is scattered.[a]
22 Listen! The report is coming—
a great commotion from the land of the north!
It will make the towns of Judah desolate,
a haunt of jackals.[b]

Jeremiah's Prayer

23 I know, O LORD, that a man's life is not his own;
it is not for man to direct his steps.[c]
24 Correct me, LORD, but only with justice—
not in your anger,[d]
lest you reduce me to nothing.[e]
25 Pour out your wrath on the nations[f]

10:12 [m]Ge 1:1, 8; Job 9:8; Isa 40:22
10:13 [n]Job 36:29 [o]Ps 135:7
10:15 [p]Isa 41:24; Jer 14:22
10:16 [q]Dt 32:9; Ps 119:57 [r]ver 12 [s]Ps 74:2 [t]Jer 31:35; 32:18
10:17 [u]Eze 12:3-12
10:18 [v]1Sa 25:29
10:19 [w]Jer 14:17 [x]Mic 7:9
10:20 [y]Jer 4:20 [z]Jer 31:15; La 1:5
10:21 [a]Jer 23:2
10:22 [b]Jer 9:11
10:23 [c]Pr 20:24
10:24 [d]Ps 6:1; 38:1 [e]Jer 30:11
10:25 [f]Zep 3:8

10:19–21 In this section, Jeremiah uses the picture of nomads wandering in the desert trying to pitch their tents. The shepherds of the nation are the evil leaders responsible for the distress. The flock is the people of Judah. Instead of guiding the people to God, the leaders were leading them astray.

10:23, 24 God's ability to direct our lives well is infinitely beyond our ability. Sometimes we are afraid of God's power and God's plans because we know his power would easily crush us if he used it against us. Don't be afraid to let God correct your plans. He will give you wisdom if you are willing.

that do not acknowledge you,
on the peoples who do not call on your name.[g]
For they have devoured[h] Jacob;
they have devoured him completely
and destroyed his homeland.[i]

3. Jeremiah prophesies destruction

The Covenant Is Broken

11 This is the word that came to Jeremiah from the LORD: 2"Listen to the terms of this covenant and tell them to the people of Judah and to those who live in Jerusalem. 3Tell them that this is what the LORD, the God of Israel, says: 'Cursed[a] is the man who does not obey the terms of this covenant—4the terms I commanded your forefathers when I brought them out of Egypt, out of the iron-smelting furnace.[b]' I said, 'Obey[c] me and do everything I command you, and you will be my people,[d] and I will be your God. 5Then I will fulfil the oath I swore[e] to your forefathers, to give them a land flowing with milk and honey'—the land you possess today."

I answered, "Amen, LORD."

6The LORD said to me, "Proclaim all these words in the towns of Judah and in the streets of Jerusalem: 'Listen to the terms of this covenant and follow[f] them. 7From the time I brought your forefathers up from Egypt until today, I warned them again and again,[g] saying, "Obey me." 8But they did not listen or pay attention;[h] instead, they followed the stubbornness of their evil hearts. So I brought on them all the curses[i] of the covenant I had commanded them to follow but that they did not keep.' "

9Then the LORD said to me, "There is a conspiracy[j] among the people of Judah and those who live in Jerusalem. 10They have returned to the sins of their forefathers,[k] who refused to listen to my words. They have followed other gods[l] to serve them. Both the house of Israel and the house of Judah have broken the covenant I made with their forefathers. 11Therefore this is what the LORD says: 'I will bring on them a disaster[m] they cannot escape. Although they cry[n] out to me, I will not listen[o] to them. 12The towns of Judah and the people of Jerusalem will go and cry out to the gods to whom they burn incense,[p] but they will not help them at all when disaster[q] strikes. 13You have as many gods as you have towns, O Judah; and the altars you have set up to burn incense[r] to that shameful[s] god Baal are as many as the streets of Jerusalem.'

14"Do not pray[t] for this people nor offer any plea or petition for them, because I will not listen[u] when they call to me in the time of their distress.

15"What is my beloved doing in my temple
as she works out her evil schemes with many?
Can consecrated meat avert ⌊your punishment⌋?
When you engage in your wickedness,
then you rejoice."[a]

16The LORD called you a thriving olive tree
with fruit beautiful in form.
But with the roar of a mighty storm
he will set it on fire,[v]
and its branches will be broken.[w]

10:25 [g]Job 18:21; Ps 14:4 [h]Ps 79:7; Jer 8:16 [i]Ps 79:6-7
11:3 [a]Dt 27:26; Gal 3:10
11:4 [b]Dt 4:20; 1Ki 8:51 [c]Ex 24:8 [d]Jer 7:23; 31:33
11:5 [e]Ex 13:5; Dt 7:12; Ps 105:8-11
11:6 [f]Dt 15:5; Ro 2:13; Jas 1:22
11:7 [g]2Ch 36:15
11:8 [h]Jer 7:26 [i]Lev 26:14-43
11:9 [j]Eze 22:25
11:10 [k]Dt 9:7 [l]Jdg 2:12-13
11:11 [m]2Ki 22:16 [n]Jer 14:12; Eze 8:18 [o]ver 14; Pr 1:28; Isa 1:15; Zec 7:13
11:12 [p]Jer 44:17 [q]Dt 32:37
11:13 [r]Jer 7:9 [s]Jer 3:24
11:14 [t]Ex 32:10 [u]ver 11
11:16 [v]Jer 21:14 [w]Isa 27:11; Ro 11:17-24

a *15* Or *Could consecrated meat avert your punishment? / Then you would rejoice*

11:1–13:27 This section concerns the broken covenant, and a rebuke for those who returned to idols after Josiah's reform. Jeremiah's rebuke prompted a threat against his life by his own countrymen. As Jeremiah suffered, he pondered the prosperity of the wicked. As he brought these words to a close, he used a ruined linen belt and filled wineskins as object lessons of God's coming judgment (see the note on 13:1–11).

11:14 At first glance this command is shocking—God tells Jeremiah not to pray, and says he won't listen to the people if they pray. A time comes when God must dispense justice. Sin brings its own bitter reward. If the people were unrepentant and continued in their sin, neither their prayers nor Jeremiah's would prevent God's judgment. Their only hope was repentance—sorrow for sin, turning from it, and turning to God. How can we keep praying for God's help if we haven't committed our lives to him? God's blessings come when we are committed to him, not when we selfishly hang on to our sinful ways.

[17]The LORD Almighty, who planted[x] you, has decreed disaster for you, because the house of Israel and the house of Judah have done evil and provoked me to anger by burning incense to Baal.[y]

Plot Against Jeremiah

[18]Because the LORD revealed their plot to me, I knew it, for at that time he showed
me what they were doing. [19]I had been like a gentle lamb led to the slaughter; I did
not realise that they had plotted[z] against me, saying,

"Let us destroy the tree and its fruit;
let us cut him off from the land of the living,[a]
that his name be remembered[b] no more."
[20]But, O LORD Almighty, you who judge righteously
and test the heart and mind,[c]
let me see your vengeance upon them,
for to you I have committed my cause.

[21]"Therefore this is what the LORD says about the men of Anathoth who are seeking
your life[d] and saying, 'Do not prophesy in the name of the LORD or you will die[e]
by our hands' — [22]therefore this is what the LORD Almighty says: 'I will punish them.
Their young men[f] will die by the sword, their sons and daughters by famine. [23]Not
even a remnant[g] will be left to them, because I will bring disaster on the men of
Anathoth in the year of their punishment.[h]' "

Jeremiah's Complaint

12 You are always righteous,[a] O LORD,
when I bring a case before you.
Yet I would speak with you about your justice:
Why does the way of the wicked prosper?[b]
Why do all the faithless live at ease?
[2]You have planted[c] them, and they have taken root;
they grow and bear fruit.
You are always on their lips
but far from their hearts.[d]
[3]Yet you know me, O LORD;
you see me and test[e] my thoughts about you.
Drag them off like sheep to be butchered!
Set them apart for the day of slaughter![f]
[4]How long will the land lie parched[a][g]
and the grass in every field be withered?[h]
Because those who live in it are wicked,
the animals and birds have perished.[i]
Moreover, the people are saying,
"He will not see what happens to us."

[a] 4 Or *land mourn*

11:17 [x]Isa 5:2; Jer 12:2 [y]Jer 7:9
11:19 [z]Jer 18:18; 20:10 [a]Job 28:13; Isa 53:8 [b]Ps 83:4
11:20 [c]Ps 7:9
11:21 [d]Jer 12:6 [e]Jer 26:8, 11; 38:4
11:22 [f]Jer 18:21
11:23 [g]Jer 6:9 [h]Jer 23:12
12:1 [a]Ezr 9:15 [b]Jer 5:27-28
12:2 [c]Jer 11:17 [d]Isa 29:13; Jer 3:10; Mt 15:8; Tit 1:16
12:3 [e]Ps 7:9; 11:5; 139:1-4; Jer 11:20 [f]Jer 17:18
12:4 [g]Jer 4:28 [h]Joel 1:10-12 [i]Jer 4:25; 9:10

11:18–23 To Jeremiah's surprise, the people of Anathoth, his home town, were plotting to kill him. They wanted to silence Jeremiah's message for several reasons: (1) economic – his condemnation of idol worship would hurt the business of the idol-makers; (2) religious – the message of doom and gloom made the people feel depressed and guilty; (3) political – he openly rebuked their hypocritical politics; and (4) personal – the people hated him for showing them that they were wrong. Jeremiah had two options: run and hide, or call on God. Jeremiah called, and God answered. Like Jeremiah, we can either run and hide when we face threats because of our faithfulness to God, or we can call on God for help. Hiding compromises our message; calling on God lets him reinforce it.

12:1–6 Many people have asked, "Why does the way of the wicked prosper?" (See, for example, Job 21:4–21 and Habakkuk 1:1–4.) Jeremiah knew that God's justice would ultimately come, but he was impatient because he wanted justice to come quickly. God didn't give a doctrinal answer; instead he gave a challenge – if Jeremiah couldn't handle this, how would he handle the injustices ahead? It is natural for us to demand fair play and cry for justice against those who take advantage of others. But when we call for justice, we must realise that we ourselves would be in big trouble if God gave each of us what we truly deserve.

12:5 [j]Jer 49:19; 50:44
12:6 [k]Pr 26:24-25; Jer 9:4 [l]Ps 12:2
12:7 [m]Jer 7:29
12:8 [n]Hos 9:15; Am 6:8
12:9 [o]Isa 56:9; Jer 15:3; Eze 23:25
12:10 [p]Jer 23:1 [q]Isa 5:1-7
12:11 [r]ver 4; Isa 42:25; Jer 23:10
12:12 [s]Jer 47:6 [t]Jer 3:2
12:13 [u]Lev 26:20; Dt 28:38; Mic 6:15; Hag 1:6 [v]Jer 4:26
12:14 [w]Zec 2:7-9
12:15 [x]Am 9:14-15
12:16 [y]Jer 4:2 [z]Jos 23:7 [a]Isa 49:6; Jer 3:17
12:17 [b]Isa 60:12

God's Answer

5"If you have raced with men on foot
and they have worn you out,
how can you compete with horses?
If you stumble in safe country,[b]
how will you manage in the thickets[j] by[c] the Jordan?
6Your brothers, your own family—
even they have betrayed you;
they have raised a loud cry against you.[k]
Do not trust them,
though they speak well of you.[l]

7"I will forsake my house,
abandon[m] my inheritance;
I will give the one I love
into the hands of her enemies.
8My inheritance has become to me
like a lion in the forest.
She roars at me;
therefore I hate her.[n]
9Has not my inheritance become to me
like a speckled bird of prey
that other birds of prey surround and attack?
Go and gather all the wild beasts;
bring them to devour.[o]
10Many shepherds[p] will ruin my vineyard
and trample down my field;
they will turn my pleasant field
into a desolate wasteland.[q]
11It will be made a wasteland,
parched and desolate before me;[r]
the whole land will be laid waste
because there is no-one who cares.
12Over all the barren heights in the desert
destroyers will swarm,
for the sword of the LORD[s] will devour
from one end of the land to the other;[t]
no-one will be safe.
13They will sow wheat but reap thorns;
they will wear themselves out but gain nothing.[u]
So bear the shame of your harvest
because of the LORD's fierce anger."[v]

14This is what the LORD says: "As for all my wicked neighbours who seize the inheritance I gave to my people Israel, I will uproot[w] them from their lands and I will uproot the house of Judah from among them. 15But after I uproot them, I will again have compassion and will bring[x] each of them back to his own inheritance and his own country. 16And if they learn well the ways of my people and swear by my name, saying, 'As surely as the LORD lives'[y]—even as they once taught my people to swear by Baal[z]—then they will be established among my people.[a] 17But if any nation does not listen, I will completely uproot and destroy[b] it," declares the LORD.

b *5* Or *If you put your trust in a land of safety* **c** *5* Or *the flooding of*

12:5, 6 Life was extremely difficult for Jeremiah despite his love for and obedience to God. When he called to God for relief, God's reply in effect was, "If you think this is bad, how are you going to cope when it gets really tough?" Not all of God's answers to prayer are nice or easy to handle. Any Christian who has experienced war, bereavement, or a serious illness knows this. But we are to be committed to God even when the going gets tough and when his answers to our prayers don't bring immediate relief.

A Linen Belt

13 This is what the LORD said to me: "Go and buy a linen belt and put it round
your waist, but do not let it touch water." 2So I bought a belt, as the LORD
directed, and put it round my waist.
3Then the word of the LORD came to me a second time: 4"Take the belt you bought
and are wearing round your waist, and go now to Perath[a] and hide it there in a crevice
in the rocks." 5So I went and hid it at Perath, as the LORD told me.[a]
6Many days later the LORD said to me, "Go now to Perath and get the belt I told
you to hide there." 7So I went to Perath and dug up the belt and took it from the place
where I had hidden it, but now it was ruined and completely useless.
8Then the word of the LORD came to me: 9"This is what the LORD says: 'In the same
way I will ruin the pride of Judah and the great pride[b] of Jerusalem. 10These wicked
people, who refuse to listen to my words, who follow the stubbornness of their hearts[c]
and go after other gods[d] to serve and worship them, will be like this belt—completely
useless! 11For as a belt is bound round a man's waist, so I bound the whole house
of Israel and the whole house of Judah to me,' declares the LORD, 'to be my people
for my renown[e] and praise and honour.[f] But they have not listened.'[g]

Wineskins

12"Say to them: 'This is what the LORD, the God of Israel, says: Every wineskin
should be filled with wine.' And if they say to you, 'Don't we know that every
wineskin should be filled with wine?' 13then tell them, 'This is what the LORD says:
I am going to fill with drunkenness[h] all who live in this land, including the kings
who sit on David's throne, the priests, the prophets and all those living in Jerusalem.
14I will smash them one against the other, fathers and sons alike, declares the LORD.
I will allow no pity or mercy or compassion[i] to keep me from destroying[j] them.' "

Threat of Captivity

15Hear and pay attention,
  do not be arrogant,
  for the LORD has spoken.
16Give glory[k] to the LORD your God
  before he brings the darkness,
 before your feet stumble[l]
  on the darkening hills.
 You hope for light,
  but he will turn it to thick darkness
  and change it to deep gloom.[m]
17But if you do not listen,[n]
  I will weep in secret
  because of your pride;
 my eyes will weep bitterly,
  overflowing with tears,[o]
  because the LORD's flock[p] will be taken captive.[q]

13:5 [a]Ex 40:16
13:9 [b]Lev 26:19
13:10 [c]Jer 11:8; 16:12 [d]Jer 9:14
13:11 [e]Jer 32:20; 33:9 [f]Ex 19:5-6 [g]Jer 7:26
13:13 [h]Ps 60:3; 75:8; Isa 51:17; 63:6; Jer 51:57
13:14 [i]Jer 16:5 [j]Dt 29:20; Eze 5:10
13:16 [k]Jos 7:19 [l]Jer 23:12 [m]Isa 59:9
13:17 [n]Mal 2:2 [o]Jer 9:1 [p]Ps 80:1; Jer 23:1 [q]Jer 14:18

a 4 Or possibly *the Euphrates*; also in verses 5–7

13:1 A linen belt was one of the more intimate pieces of clothing, clinging close to the body. It was like underwear. Jeremiah's action showed how God would ruin Judah just as Jeremiah had ruined the linen belt.

13:1–11 Actions speak louder than words. Jeremiah often used vivid object lessons to arouse the people's curiosity and get his point across. This lesson of the linen belt illustrated Judah's destiny. Although the people had once been close to God, their pride had made them useless. Proud people may look important, but God says their pride makes them good for nothing, completely useless. Pride rots our hearts until we lose our usefulness to God.

13:15 While it is good to respect our country and our church, our loyalties always carry a hidden danger—arrogance. When is pride harmful? When it causes us to (1) look down on others; (2) be selfish with our resources; (3) force our solutions on others' problems; (4) think God is blessing us because of our own merits; (5) be content with our plans rather than seeking God's plans.

13:18 The king was Jehoiachin, and the queen mother was Nehushta. The king's father, Jehoiakim, had surrendered to Nebuchadnezzar but later rebelled. During Jehoiachin's reign, Nebuchadnezzar's armies besieged Jerusalem, and both Jehoiachin and Nehushta surrendered. Jehoiachin was sent to Babylon

13:19
[r]Jer 20:4; 52:30

13:20
[s]Jer 6:22; Hab 1:6
[t]Jer 23:2

13:21
[u]Jer 38:22
[v]Jer 4:31

13:22
[w]Jer 9:2-6; 16:10-12
[x]Eze 16:37; Na 3:5-6

13:24
[y]Ps 1:4
[z]Lev 26:33

13:25
[a]Job 20:29; Mt 24:51

13:26
[b]La 1:8; Eze 16:37; Hos 2:10

13:27
[c]Jer 2:20
[d]Eze 6:13
[e]Hos 8:5

18 Say to the king and to the queen mother,
"Come down from your thrones,
for your glorious crowns
will fall from your heads."
19 The cities in the Negev will be shut up,
and there will be no-one to open them.
All Judah[r] will be carried into exile,
carried completely away.

20 Lift up your eyes and see
those who are coming from the north.[s]
Where is the flock[t] that was entrusted to you,
the sheep of which you boasted?
21 What will you say when ⌞the LORD⌟ sets over you
those you cultivated as your special allies?[u]
Will not pain grip you
like that of a woman in labour?[v]
22 And if you ask yourself,
"Why has this happened to me?"—
it is because of your many sins[w]
that your skirts have been torn off
and your body ill-treated.[x]
23 Can the Ethiopian[b] change his skin
or the leopard its spots?
Neither can you do good
who are accustomed to doing evil.

24 "I will scatter you like chaff[y]
driven by the desert wind.[z]
25 This is your lot,
the portion[a] I have decreed for you,"
declares the LORD,
"because you have forgotten me
and trusted in false gods.
26 I will pull up your skirts over your face
that your shame may be seen[b]—
27 your adulteries and lustful neighings,
your shameless prostitution![c]
I have seen your detestable acts
on the hills and in the fields.[d]
Woe to you, O Jerusalem!
How long will you be unclean?"[e]

b *23* Hebrew *Cushite* (probably a person from the upper Nile region)

and imprisoned (2 Kings 24:1–12). Jeremiah's prophecy came true.

13:19 The Negev region is the dry wasteland stretching south from Beersheba. The towns in this area would be closed to any refugees fleeing the invading army.

13:23 Not even the threat of captivity could move the people to repent. The people had become so accustomed to doing evil that they had lost their ability to change. God never rejects those who sincerely turn to him. God is warning them to repent before it becomes impossible to change. We must never put off until tomorrow those changes God wants us to make. Our attitudes and patterns for living can become so set that we will lose all desire to change and will no longer fear the consequences.

Drought, Famine, Sword

14 This is the word of the LORD to Jeremiah concerning the drought:

2"Judah mourns,[a]
her cities languish;
they wail for the land,
and a cry goes up from Jerusalem.
3The nobles send their servants for water;
they go to the cisterns
but find no water.[b]
They return with their jars unfilled;
dismayed and despairing,
they cover their heads.[c]
4The ground is cracked
because there is no rain in the land;[d]
the farmers are dismayed
and cover their heads.
5Even the doe in the field
deserts her newborn fawn
because there is no grass.[e]
6Wild donkeys stand on the barren heights[f]
and pant like jackals;
their eyesight fails
for lack of pasture."

7Although our sins testify[g] against us,
O LORD, do something for the sake of your name.
For our backsliding[h] is great;
we have sinned[i] against you.
8O Hope[j] of Israel,
its Saviour in times of distress,
why are you like a stranger in the land,
like a traveller who stays only a night?
9Why are you like a man taken by surprise,
like a warrior powerless to save?[k]
You are among[l] us, O LORD,
and we bear your name;[m]
do not forsake us!

10This is what the LORD says about this people:

"They greatly love to wander;
they do not restrain their feet.[n]
So the LORD does not accept[o] them;
he will now remember[p] their wickedness
and punish them for their sins."[q]

11Then the LORD said to me, "Do not pray[r] for the well-being of this people.
12Although they fast, I will not listen to their cry;[s] though they offer burnt offerings[t]
and grain offerings, I will not accept[u] them. Instead, I will destroy them with the
sword, famine and plague."
13But I said, "Ah, Sovereign LORD, the prophets keep telling them, 'You will not
see the sword or suffer famine.[v] Indeed, I will give you lasting peace in this place.' "
14Then the LORD said to me, "The prophets are prophesying lies[w] in my name. I

14:2 [a]Isa 3:26; Jer 8:21
14:3 [b]2Ki 18:31; Job 6:19-20 [c]2Sa 15:30
14:4 [d]Jer 3:3
14:5 [e]Isa 15:6
14:6 [f]Job 39:5-6; Jer 2:24
14:7 [g]Hos 5:5 [h]Jer 5:6 [i]Jer 8:14
14:8 [j]Jer 17:13
14:9 [k]Isa 50:2 [l]Jer 8:19 [m]Isa 63:19; Jer 15:16
14:10 [n]Ps 119:101; Jer 2:25 [o]Jer 6:20; Am 5:22 [p]Hos 9:9 [q]Jer 44:21-23; Hos 8:13
14:11 [r]Ex 32:10
14:12 [s]Isa 1:15; Jer 11:11 [t]Jer 7:21 [u]Jer 6:20
14:13 [v]Jer 5:12
14:14 [w]Jer 27:14

14:1–15:21 This section opens with God sending a drought on Judah and refusing to answer their prayers for rain. It continues with Jeremiah's description of judgment to come.

14:1ff Drought was a judgment with devastating consequences. As usual, when their backs were to the wall, the people cried out to God. But God rejected their plea because they did not repent; they merely wanted his rescue. Not even Jeremiah's prayers would help. Their only hope was to turn to God.

have not sent[x] them or appointed them or spoken to them. They are prophesying to
you false visions,[y] divinations,[z] idolatries[a] and the delusions of their own minds.
15Therefore, this is what the LORD says about the prophets who are prophesying in
my name: I did not send them, yet they are saying, 'No sword or famine will touch
this land.' Those same prophets will perish[a] by sword and famine.[b] 16And the people
they are prophesying to will be thrown out into the streets of Jerusalem because of
the famine and sword. There will be no-one to bury[c] them or their wives, their sons
or their daughters.[d] I will pour out on them the calamity they deserve.[e]

17"Speak this word to them:

" 'Let my eyes overflow with tears[f]
night and day without ceasing;
for my virgin daughter — my people —
has suffered a grievous wound,
a crushing blow.[g]
18If I go into the country,
I see those slain by the sword;
if I go into the city,
I see the ravages of famine.[h]
Both prophet and priest
have gone to a land they know not.' "

19Have you rejected Judah completely?[i]
Do you despise Zion?
Why have you afflicted us
so that we cannot be healed?[j]
We hoped for peace
but no good has come,
for a time of healing
but there is only terror.[k]
20O LORD, we acknowledge our wickedness
and the guilt of our fathers;
we have indeed sinned[l] against you.
21For the sake of your name[m] do not despise us;
do not dishonour your glorious throne.[n]
Remember your covenant with us
and do not break it.
22Do any of the worthless idols of the nations bring rain?[o]
Do the skies themselves send down showers?
No, it is you, O LORD our God.
Therefore our hope is in you,
for you are the one who does all this.

15 Then the LORD said to me: "Even if Moses[a] and Samuel[b] were to stand before
me, my heart would not go out to this people.[c] Send them away from my
presence![d] Let them go! 2And if they ask you, 'Where shall we go?' tell them, 'This
is what the LORD says:

14:14 [x]Jer 23:21, 32 [y]Jer 23:16 [z]Eze 12:24
14:15 [a]Eze 14:9 [b]Jer 5:12-13
14:16 [c]Ps 79:3 [d]Jer 7:33 [e]Pr 1:31
14:17 [f]Jer 9:1 [g]Jer 8:21
14:18 [h]Eze 7:15
14:19 [i]Jer 7:29 [j]Jer 30:12-13 [k]Jer 8:15
14:20 [l]Da 9:7-8
14:21 [m]ver 7 [n]Jer 3:17
14:22 [o]Ps 135:7
15:1 [a]Ex 32:11; Nu 14:13-20 [b]1Sa 7:9 [c]Jer 7:16; Eze 14:14, 20 [d]2Ki 17:20

a *14* Or *visions, worthless divinations*

14:14 What made the people listen to and support the false prophets? These "prophets" said what the people wanted to hear. False teachers earn fame and money by telling people what they want to hear, but they lead people away from God. If we encourage false teachers, we are as guilty as they are.

14:19–22 Interceding for the people, Jeremiah asked God if Judah's repentance would bring his help. But God refused to come to their aid (15:1) because the people were insincere, wicked, and stubborn. They knew he wanted to bless them, and they knew what they needed to do to receive that blessing. They wanted God to do his part, but they did not want to do theirs. It's easy to express sorrow for wrong actions, especially when we want something, but we must be willing to stop doing what is wrong. God will forgive those who are truly repentant, but hypocrites will be severely punished.

15:1 Moses and Samuel were two of God's greatest prophets. Like Jeremiah, both interceded between God and the people (Exodus 32:11; Numbers 14:11–20; 1 Samuel 7:9; 12:17; Psalm 99:6). Intercession is often effective. In this case, however, the people were so wicked and stubborn that God knew they would not turn to him.

" 'Those destined for death, to death;
those for the sword, to the sword;[e]
those for starvation, to starvation;[f]
those for captivity, to captivity.'[g]

3"I will send four kinds of destroyers[h] against them," declares the LORD, "the
sword to kill and the dogs to drag away and the birds[i] of the air and the beasts of
the earth to devour and destroy.[j] 4I will make them abhorrent[k] to all the kingdoms
of the earth[l] because of what Manasseh[m] son of Hezekiah king of Judah did in
Jerusalem.

5"Who will have pity[n] on you, O Jerusalem?
Who will mourn for you?
Who will stop to ask how you are?
6You have rejected[o] me," declares the LORD.
"You keep on backsliding.
So I will lay hands[p] on you and destroy you;
I can no longer show compassion.
7I will winnow them with a winnowing fork
at the city gates of the land.
I will bring bereavement and destruction on my people,[q]
for they have not changed their ways.
8I will make their widows more numerous
than the sand of the sea.
At midday I will bring a destroyer[r]
against the mothers of their young men;
suddenly I will bring down on them
anguish and terror.
9The mother of seven will grow faint[s]
and breathe her last.
Her sun will set while it is still day;
she will be disgraced and humiliated.
I will put the survivors to the sword[t]
before their enemies,"
declares the LORD.

10Alas, my mother, that you gave me birth,[u]
a man with whom the whole land strives and contends![v]
I have neither lent[w] nor borrowed,
yet everyone curses me.

11The LORD said,

"Surely I will deliver you[x] for a good purpose;
surely I will make your enemies plead[y] with you
in times of disaster and times of distress.

12"Can a man break iron—
iron from the north[z]—or bronze?
13Your wealth and your treasures
I will give as plunder, without charge,[a]
because of all your sins
throughout your country.[b]
14I will enslave you to your enemies

15:2 [e]Jer 43:11 [f]Jer 14:12 [g]Rev 13:10
15:3 [h]Lev 26:16 [i]Dt 28:26 [j]Lev 26:22; Eze 14:21
15:4 [k]Jer 24:9; 29:18 [l]Dt 28:25 [m]2Ki 21:2; 23:26-27
15:5 [n]Isa 51:19; Jer 13:14; 21:7; Na 3:7
15:6 [o]Jer 6:19; 7:24 [p]Zep 1:4
15:7 [q]Jer 18:21
15:8 [r]Jer 6:4
15:9 [s]1Sa 2:5 [t]Jer 21:7
15:10 [u]Job 3:1 [v]Jer 1:19 [w]Lev 25:36
15:11 [x]Jer 40:4 [y]Jer 21:1-2; 37:3; 42:1-3
15:12 [z]Jer 28:14
15:13 [a]Ps 44:12 [b]Jer 17:3

15:3, 4 The goal of these destroyers was to destroy the living and devour the dead. This would happen because of Manasseh's evil reign and the people's sin (2 Kings 21:1–16; 23:26; 24:3), and the destruction would be complete. The people may have argued that they should not be responsible for Manasseh's sins, but they continued what Manasseh began. If we follow corrupt leaders knowingly, we can't excuse ourselves by blaming their bad example.

in[a] a land you do not know,[c]
for my anger will kindle a fire[d]
that will burn against you."

15You understand, O LORD;
remember me and care for me.
Avenge me on my persecutors.[e]
You are long-suffering—do not take me away;
think of how I suffer reproach for your sake.[f]
16When your words came, I ate[g] them;
they were my joy and my heart's delight,[h]
for I bear your name,[i]
O LORD God Almighty.
17I never sat[j] in the company of revellers,
never made merry with them;
I sat alone because your hand was on me
and you had filled me with indignation.
18Why is my pain unending
and my wound grievous and incurable?[k]
Will you be to me like a deceptive brook,
like a spring that fails?[l]

19Therefore this is what the LORD says:

"If you repent, I will restore you
that you may serve[m] me;
if you utter worthy, not worthless, words,
you will be my spokesman.
Let this people turn to you,
but you must not turn to them.
20I will make you a wall to this people,
a fortified wall of bronze;
they will fight against you
but will not overcome you,
for I am with you
to rescue and save you,"[n]
declares the LORD.
21"I will save you from the hands of the wicked
and redeem[o] you from the grasp of the cruel."[p]

Day of Disaster

16 Then the word of the LORD came to me: 2"You must not marry[a] and have sons or daughters in this place." 3For this is what the LORD says about the sons and daughters born in this land and about the women who are their mothers and the men who are their fathers:[b] 4"They will die of deadly diseases. They will not be mourned or buried[c] but will be like refuse lying on the ground.[d] They will perish by sword and famine, and their dead bodies will become food for the birds of the air and the beasts of the earth."[e]

15:14 [c]Dt 28:36; Jer 16:13 [d]Dt 32:22; Ps 21:9
15:15 [e]Jer 12:3 [f]Ps 69:7-9
15:16 [g]Eze 3:3; Rev 10:10 [h]Ps 119:72, 103 [i]Jer 14:9
15:17 [j]Ps 1:1; 26:4-5; Jer 16:8
15:18 [k]Jer 30:15; Mic 1:9 [l]Job 6:15
15:19 [m]Zec 3:7
15:20 [n]Jer 20:11; Eze 3:8
15:21 [o]Jer 50:34 [p]Ge 48:16
16:2 [a]1Co 7:26-27
16:3 [b]Jer 6:21
16:4 [c]Jer 25:33 [d]Ps 83:10; Jer 9:22 [e]Ps 79:1-3; Jer 15:3; 34:20

a *14* Some Hebrew manuscripts, Septuagint and Syriac (see also Jer. 17:4); most Hebrew manuscripts *I will cause your enemies to bring you / into*

15:17–21 Jeremiah accused God of not helping him when he really needed it. Jeremiah had taken his eyes off God's purposes and was feeling sorry for himself. He was angry, hurt, and afraid. In response, God didn't get angry with Jeremiah; he answered by rearranging Jeremiah's priorities. As God's mouthpiece, he was to influence the people, not let them influence him. There are three important lessons in this passage: (1) in prayer we can reveal our deepest thoughts to God; (2) God expects us to trust him, no matter what; (3) we are here to influence others for God.

16:1–17:18 This section portrays the coming day of disaster. It begins by showing Jeremiah's loneliness. He is a social outcast because of his harsh messages and his celibate life-style. He must not marry, have children, or take part in funerals or festivals. The section concludes with another appeal to avoid judgment by turning to God. The people did not heed Jeremiah's words, however, and the first wave of destruction came almost immediately, in 605 B.C. (2 Kings 24:8–12). The second wave came in 597 B.C., and Judah was completely destroyed in 586 B.C.

5For this is what the LORD says: "Do not enter a house where there is a funeral meal;
do not go to mourn or show sympathy, because I have withdrawn my blessing, my
love and my pity from this people," declares the LORD. 6"Both high and low will die
in this land.[f] They will not be buried or mourned, and no-one will cut[g] himself or
shave[h] his head for them. 7No-one will offer food to comfort those who mourn[i] for
the dead—not even for a father or a mother—nor will anyone give them a drink to
console them.
8"And do not enter a house where there is feasting and sit down to eat and drink.[j]
9For this is what the LORD Almighty, the God of Israel, says: Before your eyes and
in your days I will bring an end to the sounds[k] of joy and gladness and to the voices
of bride and bridegroom in this place.[l]
10"When you tell these people all this and they ask you, 'Why has the LORD decreed
such a great disaster against us? What wrong have we done? What sin have we
committed against the LORD our God?'[m] 11then say to them, 'It is because your fathers
forsook me,' declares the LORD, 'and followed other gods and served and worshipped
them. They forsook me and did not keep my law.[n] 12But you have behaved more
wickedly than your fathers.[o] See how each of you is following the stubbornness of
his evil heart[p] instead of obeying me. 13So I will throw you out of this land into a
land neither you nor your fathers have known,[q] and there you will serve other gods[r]
day and night, for I will show you no favour.'[s]
14"However, the days are coming," declares the LORD, "when men will no longer
say, 'As surely as the LORD lives, who brought the Israelites up out of Egypt,'[t] 15but
they will say, 'As surely as the LORD lives, who brought the Israelites up out of the
land of the north and out of all the countries where he had banished them.'[u] For I
will restore[v] them to the land I gave to their forefathers.
16"But now I will send for many fishermen," declares the LORD, "and they will catch
them.[w] After that I will send for many hunters,[x] them down on
every mountain and hill and from the crevices of the rocks.[y] 17My eyes are on all
their ways; they are not hidden[z] from me, nor is their sin concealed from my eyes.[a]
18I will repay them double[b] for their wickedness and their sin, because they have
defiled my land[c] with the lifeless forms of their vile images and have filled my
inheritance with their detestable idols."

19O LORD, my strength and my fortress,
my refuge in time of distress,
to you the nations will come[d]
from the ends of the earth and say,
"Our fathers possessed nothing but false gods,[e]
worthless idols that did them no good.
20Do men make their own gods?
Yes, but they are not gods!"[f]

21"Therefore I will teach them—

16:6 [f]Eze 9:5-6 [g]Lev 19:28 [h]Jer 41:5; 47:5
16:7 [i]Eze 24:17; Hos 9:4
16:8 [j]Ecc 7:2-4; Jer 15:17
16:9 [k]Isa 24:8; Eze 26:13; Hos 2:11 [l]Rev 18:23
16:10 [m]Dt 29:24; Jer 5:19
16:11 [n]Dt 29:25-26; 1Ki 9:9; Ps 106:35-43; Jer 22:9
16:12 [o]Jer 7:26 [p]Ecc 9:3; Jer 13:10
16:13 [q]Dt 28:36; Jer 5:19 [r]Dt 4:28 [s]Jer 15:5
16:14 [t]Dt 15:15; Jer 23:7-8
16:15 [u]Isa 11:11; Jer 23:8 [v]Jer 24:6
16:16 [w]Am 4:2; Hab 1:14-15 [x]Am 9:3; Mic 7:2 [y]1Sa 26:20
16:17 [z]1Co 4:5; Heb 4:13 [a]Pr 15:3
16:18 [b]Isa 40:2; Rev 18:6 [c]Nu 35:34; Jer 2:7
16:19 [d]Isa 2:2; Jer 3:17 [e]Ps 4:2
16:20 [f]Ps 115:4-7; Isa 37:19; Jer 2:11

16:5–7 In Jeremiah's culture, it was unthinkable not to show grief publicly. The absence of mourning showed the people how complete their devastation would be. So many people would die that it would be impossible to carry out mourning rituals for all of them.

16:8–13 Jeremiah was also told not to participate in parties or other joyful events to show how seriously God took the nation's sins. In both cases (no public grief or joy), Jeremiah's life was to be an attention-seeker and an illustration of God's truth. Sometimes we think that the only way to communicate is through speaking or teaching, but God can use a wide variety of means to bring his message. Use your creativity.

16:14, 15 The book of Exodus records God's miraculous rescue of his people from Egyptian slavery (Exodus 1—15). The people's return from exile would be so momentous that it would overshadow even the exodus from Egypt. Even though his people had been so stubborn, God would once again show his great mercy.

16:17 Small children think that if they can't see you, then you can't see them. The people of Israel may have wished that hiding from God were as simple as closing their eyes. Although they closed their eyes to their sinful ways, their sins certainly weren't hidden from God. He who sees everything cannot be deceived. Do you have a sinful attitude or action that you hope God won't notice? He knows about it. The first step of repentance is to acknowledge that God knows about your sins.

16:19 In this prayer, Jeremiah approached God with three descriptive names: strength, fortress, and refuge. Each name gives a slightly different glimpse of how Jeremiah experienced God's presence, and each is a picture of security and protection. Let God be your strength when you feel weak, your fortress when enemies come against you, and your refuge when you need to retreat from life's pressures.

this time I will teach them
my power and might.
Then they will know
that my name is the LORD.

17
"Judah's sin is engraved with an iron tool,[a]
inscribed with a flint point,
on the tablets of their hearts[b]
and on the horns of their altars.
2Even their children remember
their altars and Asherah poles[a][c]
beside the spreading trees
and on the high hills.[d]
3My mountain in the land
and your[b] wealth and all your treasures
I will give away as plunder,[e]
together with your high places,[f]
because of sin throughout your country.[g]
4Through your own fault you will lose
the inheritance[h] I gave you.
I will enslave you to your enemies[i]
in a land[j] you do not know,
for you have kindled my anger,
and it will burn[k] for ever."

5This is what the LORD says:

"Cursed is the one who trusts in man,[l]
who depends on flesh for his strength
and whose heart turns away from the LORD.
6He will be like a bush in the wastelands;
he will not see prosperity when it comes.
He will dwell in the parched places of the desert,
in a salt[m] land where no-one lives.

7"But blessed is the man who trusts[n] in the LORD,
whose confidence is in him.
8He will be like a tree planted by the water
that sends out its roots by the stream.
It does not fear when heat comes;
its leaves are always green.
It has no worries in a year of drought[o]
and never fails to bear fruit."[p]

9The heart[q] is deceitful above all things

17:1 [a]Job 19:24 [b]Pr 3:3; 2Co 3:3
17:2 [c]2Ch 24:18 [d]Jer 2:20
17:3 [e]2Ki 24:13 [f]Jer 26:18; Mic 3:12 [g]Jer 15:13
17:4 [h]La 5:2 [i]Dt 28:48; Jer 12:7 [j]Jer 16:13 [k]Jer 7:20; 15:14
17:5 [l]Isa 2:22; 30:1-3
17:6 [m]Dt 29:23; Job 39:6
17:7 [n]Ps 34:8; 40:4; Pr 16:20
17:8 [o]Jer 14:1-6 [p]Ps 1:3; 92:12-14
17:9 [q]Ecc 9:3; Mt 13:15; Mk 7:21-22

a *2* That is, symbols of the goddess Asherah **b** *2, 3* Or *hills / 3and the mountains of the land. / Your*

17:1 God's people continued to sin even though they had the law, the prophets of God, and history filled with God's miracles. How could they do that? Why do we continue to cherish sin even though we understand the eternal consequences? Jeremiah says the heart is deceitful (17:9), and "Judah's sin is engraved . . . on the tablets of their hearts". The Hebrews symbolised the various aspects of a person by locating them in certain physical organs. The heart was the organ of reason, intelligence, and will. So deep is our tendency to sin that only God's redemption can deliver us.

17:5–8 Two kinds of people are contrasted here: those who trust in human beings and those who trust in the Lord. The people of Judah were trusting in false gods and military alliances instead of God, and thus they were barren and unfruitful. In contrast, those who trust in the Lord flourish like trees planted by water (see Psalm 1). In times of trouble, those who trust in human beings will be impoverished and spiritually weak, so they will have no strength to draw on. But those who trust in the Lord will have abundant strength, not only for their own needs, but even for the needs of others. Are you satisfied with being unfruitful, or do you, like a well-watered tree, have strength for the time of crisis and even some to share as you bear fruit for the Lord?

17:9, 10 God makes it clear why we sin – it's a matter of the heart. Our hearts have been inclined towards sin from the time we were born. It is easy to fall into the routine of forgetting and forsaking God. But we can still choose whether or not to continue in sin. We can yield to a specific temptation, or we can ask God to help us resist temptation when it comes.

and beyond cure.
Who can understand it?

10"I the LORD search the heart[r]
and examine the mind,[s]
to reward[t] a man according to his conduct,
according to what his deeds deserve."[u]

11Like a partridge that hatches eggs it did not lay
is the man who gains riches by unjust means.
When his life is half gone, they will desert him,
and in the end he will prove to be a fool.[v]

12A glorious throne,[w] exalted from the beginning,
is the place of our sanctuary.
13O LORD, the hope[x] of Israel,
all who forsake[y] you will be put to shame.
Those who turn away from you will be written in the dust
because they have forsaken the LORD,
the spring of living water.

14Heal me, O LORD, and I shall be healed;
save me and I shall be saved,
for you are the one I praise.[z]
15They keep saying to me,
"Where is the word of the LORD?
Let it now be fulfilled!"[a]
16I have not run away from being your shepherd;
you know I have not desired the day of despair.
What passes my lips is open before you.
17Do not be a terror[b] to me;
you are my refuge[c] in the day of disaster.
18Let my persecutors be put to shame,
but keep me from shame;
let them be terrified,
but keep me from terror.
Bring on them the day of disaster;
destroy them with double destruction.[d]

Keeping the Sabbath Holy

19This is what the LORD said to me: "Go and stand at the gate of the people, through
which the kings of Judah go in and out; stand also at all the other gates of Jerusalem.[e]
20Say to them, 'Hear the word of the LORD, O kings of Judah and all people of Judah
and everyone living in Jerusalem[f] who come through these gates.[g] 21This is what
the LORD says: Be careful not to carry a load on the Sabbath[h] day or bring it through
the gates of Jerusalem. 22Do not bring a load out of your houses or do any work on
the Sabbath, but keep the Sabbath day holy, as I commanded your forefathers.[i] 23Yet
they did not listen or pay attention;[j] they were stiff-necked[k] and would not listen
or respond to discipline.[l] 24But if you are careful to obey me, declares the LORD,
and bring no load through the gates of this city on the Sabbath, but keep the Sabbath
day holy by not doing any work on it, 25then kings who sit on David's throne[m] will
come through the gates of this city with their officials. They and their officials will

17:10 [r]1Sa 16:7; Rev 2:23 [s]Ps 17:3; 139:23; Jer 11:20; 20:12; Ro 8:27 [t]Ps 62:12; Jer 32:19 [u]Ro 2:6
17:11 [v]Lk 12:20
17:12 [w]Jer 3:17
17:13 [x]Jer 14:8 [y]Isa 1:28; Jer 2:17
17:14 [z]Ps 109:1
17:15 [a]Isa 5:19; 2Pe 3:4
17:17 [b]Ps 88:15-16 [c]Jer 16:19; Na 1:7
17:18 [d]Ps 35:1-8
17:19 [e]Jer 7:2; 26:2
17:20 [f]Jer 19:3 [g]Jer 22:2
17:21 [h]Nu 15:32-36; Ne 13:15-21; Jn 5:10
17:22 [i]Ex 20:8; 31:13; Isa 56:2-6; Eze 20:12
17:23 [j]Jer 7:26 [k]Jer 19:15 [l]Jer 7:28
17:25 [m]2Sa 7:13; Isa 9:7; Jer 22:2, 4; Lk 1:32

17:11 There is a right way and a wrong way to do any task. Jeremiah says that the man who becomes rich by unjust means will end up foolish and poor. Whether at work, school, or play, we should strive to be honest in all our dealings. Getting a promotion, passing an exam, or gaining prestige unjustly will never bring God's blessing or lasting happiness.

17:19–27 The people were working on the Sabbath, their day of rest (Exodus 20:8–11). They considered making money more important than keeping God's law. If they would repent and put God first in their lives, God promised them honour among the nations. Over a century later, when Nehemiah led the exiles on their return to Jerusalem, one of his most important reforms was to reinstitute Sabbath observance (Nehemiah 13:15–22).

17:26
[n] Jer 32:44; 33:13; Zec 7:7

17:27
[o] Jer 22:5
[p] Jer 7:20
[q] 2Ki 25:9; Am 2:5

18:6
[a] Isa 45:9; Ro 9:20-21

18:7
[b] Jer 1:10

18:8
[c] Jer 26:13; Jnh 3:8-10
[d] Eze 18:21; Hos 11:8-9

18:9
[e] Jer 1:10; 31:28

18:10
[f] Eze 33:18
[g] 1Sa 2:29-30

come riding in chariots and on horses, accompanied by the men of Judah and those
living in Jerusalem, and this city will be inhabited for ever. 26 People will come from
the towns of Judah and the villages around Jerusalem, from the territory of Benjamin
and the western foothills, from the hill country and the Negev,[n] bringing burnt
offerings and sacrifices, grain offerings, incense and thank-offerings to the house of
the LORD. 27 But if you do not obey[o] me to keep the Sabbath day holy by not carrying
any load as you come through the gates of Jerusalem on the Sabbath day, then I will
kindle an unquenchable fire[p] in the gates of Jerusalem that will consume her fortresses.' "[q]

At the Potter's House

18 This is the word that came to Jeremiah from the LORD: 2 "Go down to the potter's
house, and there I will give you my message." 3 So I went down to the potter's
house, and I saw him working at the wheel. 4 But the pot he was shaping from the
clay was marred in his hands; so the potter formed it into another pot, shaping it as
seemed best to him.
5 Then the word of the LORD came to me: 6 "O house of Israel, can I not do with
you as this potter does?" declares the LORD. "Like clay[a] in the hand of the potter,
so are you in my hand, O house of Israel. 7 If at any time I announce that a nation
or kingdom is to be uprooted,[b] torn down and destroyed, 8 and if that nation I warned
repents of its evil, then I will relent[c] and not inflict on it the disaster[d] I had planned.
9 And if at another time I announce that a nation or kingdom is to be built[e] up and
planted, 10 and if it does evil[f] in my sight and does not obey me, then I will
reconsider[g] the good I had intended to do for it.

GOD'S OBJECT LESSONS IN JEREMIAH

Reference	*Object Lesson*	*Significance*
1:11, 12	Branch of an almond tree	God will carry out his threats of punishment.
1:13	Boiling pot, tilting away from the north	God will punish Judah.
13:1–11	A ruined linen belt	Because the people refused to listen to God, they had become useless, good for nothing, like a ruined linen belt.
18:1–17	Potter's clay	God could destroy his sinful people if he so desired. This is a warning to them to repent before he is forced to bring judgment.
19:1–12	Broken clay jars	God would smash Judah just as Jeremiah smashed the clay jars.
24:1–10	Two baskets of figs	Good figs represent God's remnant. Poor figs are the people left behind.
27:2–11	Yoke	Any nation who refused to submit to Babylon's yoke of control would be punished.
43:8–13	Large stones	The stones marked the place where Nebuchadnezzar would set his throne when God allowed him to conquer Egypt.
51:59–64	Scroll sunk in the river	Babylon would sink to rise no more.

17:26 The Negev is the southern part of Judah.

18:1 – 19:15 The parables in these chapters, probably written during the early years of Jehoiakim's reign, illustrate God's sovereignty over the nation. God has power over the clay (Judah), and he continues to work with it to make it a useful vessel. But Judah must soon repent, or the clay will harden the wrong way. Then it will be worth nothing and will be broken and destroyed.

18:6 As the potter moulded or shaped a clay pot on the potter's wheel, defects often appeared. The potter had power over the clay, to permit the defects to remain or to reshape the pot. Likewise, God had power to reshape the nation to conform to his purposes. Our strategy should not be to become mindless and passive – one aspect of clay – but to be willing and receptive to God's impact on us. As we yield to God, he begins reshaping us into valuable vessels.

11"Now therefore say to the people of Judah and those living in Jerusalem, 'This
is what the LORD says: Look! I am preparing a disaster[h] for you and devising a plan
against you. So turn[i] from your evil ways,[j] each one of you, and reform your ways
and your actions.' 12But they will reply, 'It's no use.[k] We will continue with our own
plans; each of us will follow the stubbornness of his evil heart.' "

13Therefore this is what the LORD says:

"Enquire among the nations:
Who has ever heard anything like this?[l]
A most horrible[m] thing has been done
by Virgin Israel.
14Does the snow of Lebanon
ever vanish from its rocky slopes?
Do its cool waters from distant sources
ever cease to flow?[a]
15Yet my people have forgotten me;
they burn incense to worthless idols,[n]
which made them stumble in their ways
and in the ancient paths.[o]
They made them walk in bypaths
and on roads not built up.[p]
16Their land will be laid waste,[q]
an object of lasting scorn;[r]
all who pass by will be appalled
and will shake their heads.[s]
17Like a wind[t] from the east,
I will scatter them before their enemies;
I will show them my back and not my face[u]
in the day of their disaster."

18They said, "Come, let's make plans[v] against Jeremiah; for the teaching of the
law by the priest[w] will not be lost, nor will counsel from the wise, nor the word from
the prophets.[x] So come, let's attack him with our tongues[y] and pay no attention to
anything he says."

19Listen to me, O LORD;
hear what my accusers are saying!
20Should good be repaid with evil?
Yet they have dug a pit[z] for me.
Remember that I stood before you
and spoke on their behalf[a]
to turn your wrath away from them.
21So give their children over to famine;[b]
hand them over to the power of the sword.
Let their wives be made childless and widows;[c]
let their men be put to death,
their young men slain by the sword in battle.
22Let a cry[d] be heard from their houses
when you suddenly bring invaders against them,
for they have dug a pit to capture me

18:11 [h]Jer 4:6 [i]2Ki 17:13; Isa 1:16-19 [j]Jer 7:3

18:12 [k]Isa 57:10; Jer 2:25

18:13 [l]Isa 66:8; Jer 2:10 [m]Jer 5:30

18:15 [n]Jer 10:15 [o]Jer 6:16 [p]Isa 57:14; 62:10

18:16 [q]Jer 25:9 [r]Jer 19:8 [s]Ps 22:7

18:17 [t]Jer 13:24 [u]Jer 2:27

18:18 [v]Jer 11:19 [w]Mal 2:7 [x]Jer 5:13 [y]Ps 52:2

18:20 [z]Ps 35:7; 57:6 [a]Ps 106:23

18:21 [b]Jer 11:22 [c]Ps 109:9

18:22 [d]Jer 6:26

a *14* The meaning of the Hebrew for this sentence is uncertain.

18:12 Our society admires assertiveness, independence, and defiance of authority. In a relationship with God these qualities become stubbornness, self-importance, and refusal to listen or change. Left unchecked, stubbornness becomes a way of life hostile to God.

18:18 Jeremiah's words and actions challenged the people's social and moral behaviour. He had openly spoken against the king, the officials, the priests and prophets, the scribes, and the wise (4:9; 8:8, 9). He wasn't afraid to give unpopular criticism. The people could either obey him or silence him. They chose the latter. They did not think they needed Jeremiah; their false prophets told them what they wanted to hear. How do you respond to criticism? Listen carefully – God may be trying to tell you something.

18:22
[e]Ps 140:5

18:23
[f]Jer 11:21
[g]Ps 109:14

19:1
[a]Jer 18:2
[b]Nu 11:17

19:2
[c]Jos 15:8

19:3
[d]Jer 17:20
[e]Jer 6:19
[f]1Sa 3:11

19:4
[g]Dt 28:20;
Isa 65:11
[h]Lev 18:21
[i]2Ki 21:16;
Jer 2:34

19:5
[j]Lev 18:21;
Ps 106:37-38
[k]Jer 7:31; 32:35

19:6
[l]Jos 15:8
[m]Jer 7:32

19:7
[n]Lev 26:17;
Dt 28:25
[o]Jer 16:4; 34:20
[p]Ps 79:2

19:8
[q]Jer 18:16

19:9
[r]Lev 26:29;
Dt 28:49-57;
La 4:10
[s]Isa 9:20

19:10
[t]ver 1

19:11
[u]Ps 2:9;
Isa 30:14
[v]Jer 7:32

19:13
[w]Jer 32:29; 52:13
[x]Dt 4:19;
Ac 7:42
[y]Jer 7:18;
Eze 20:28

19:14
[z]2Ch 20:5;
Jer 26:2

19:15
[a]Ne 9:16;
Jer 7:26; 17:23

and have hidden snares[e] for my feet.
23But you know, O LORD,
all their plots to kill[f] me.
Do not forgive[g] their crimes
or blot out their sins from your sight.
Let them be overthrown before you;
deal with them in the time of your anger.

19 This is what the LORD says: "Go and buy a clay jar from a potter.[a] Take along
some of the elders[b] of the people and of the priests 2and go out to the Valley
of Ben Hinnom,[c] near the entrance of the Potsherd Gate. There proclaim the words
I tell you, 3and say, 'Hear the word of the LORD, O kings[d] of Judah and people of
Jerusalem. This is what the LORD Almighty, the God of Israel, says: Listen! I am going
to bring a disaster[e] on this place that will make the ears of everyone who hears of
it tingle.[f] 4For they have forsaken[g] me and made this a place of foreign gods; they
have burned sacrifices[h] in it to gods that neither they nor their fathers nor the kings
of Judah ever knew, and they have filled this place with the blood of the innocent.[i]
5They have built the high places of Baal to burn their sons[j] in the fire as offerings
to Baal—something I did not command or mention, nor did it enter my mind.[k] 6So
beware, the days are coming, declares the LORD, when people will no longer call this
place Topheth or the Valley of Ben Hinnom,[l] but the Valley of Slaughter.[m]
7" 'In this place I will ruin**a** the plans of Judah and Jerusalem. I will make them
fall by the sword before their enemies,[n] at the hands of those who seek their lives,
and I will give their carcasses[o] as food[p] to the birds of the air and the beasts of the
earth. 8I will devastate this city and make it an object of scorn;[q] all who pass by will
be appalled and will scoff because of all its wounds. 9I will make them eat[r] the flesh
of their sons and daughters, and they will eat one another's flesh during the stress of
the siege imposed on them by the enemies[s] who seek their lives.'
10"Then break the jar[t] while those who go with you are watching, 11and say to
them, 'This is what the LORD Almighty says: I will smash[u] this nation and this city
just as this potter's jar is smashed and cannot be repaired. They will bury[v] the dead
in Topheth until there is no more room. 12This is what I will do to this place and to
those who live here, declares the LORD. I will make this city like Topheth. 13The
houses[w] in Jerusalem and those of the kings of Judah will be defiled like this place,
Topheth—all the houses where they burned incense on the roofs to all the starry
hosts[x] and poured out drink offerings[y] to other gods.' "
14Jeremiah then returned from Topheth, where the LORD had sent him to prophesy,
and stood in the court[z] of the LORD's temple and said to all the people, 15"This is
what the LORD Almighty, the God of Israel, says: 'Listen! I am going to bring on this
city and the villages around it every disaster I pronounced against them, because they
were stiff-necked[a] and would not listen to my words.' "

a *7* The Hebrew for *ruin* sounds like the Hebrew for *jar* (see verses 1 and 10).

19:6 The Valley of Ben Hinnom was the rubbish dump of Jerusalem and the place where children were sacrificed to the god Molech. It is also mentioned in 7:31, 32. Topheth was located in the valley and means "fireplace" and was probably where children were burned as sacrifices.

19:7–13 The horrible carnage that Jeremiah predicted happened twice, in 586 B.C. during the Babylonian invasion under Nebuchadnezzar, and in A.D. 70 when Titus destroyed Jerusalem. During the Babylonian siege, food became so scarce that people became cannibals, even eating their own children. (See Leviticus 26:29 and Deuteronomy 28:53–57 for prophecies concerning this; and see 2 Kings 6:28, 29; Lamentations 2:20; 4:10 for accounts of actual occurrences.)

Jeremiah and Pashhur

20 When the priest Pashhur son of Immer,[a] the chief officer[b] in the temple of
the LORD, heard Jeremiah prophesying these things, 2he had Jeremiah the
prophet beaten[c] and put in the stocks[d] at the Upper Gate of Benjamin[e] at the LORD's
temple. 3The next day, when Pashhur released him from the stocks, Jeremiah said to
him, "The LORD's name for you is not Pashhur, but Magor-Missabib.[a][f] 4For this
is what the LORD says: 'I will make you a terror to yourself and to all your friends;
with your own eyes[g] you will see them fall by the sword of their enemies. I will
hand[h] all Judah over to the king of Babylon, who will carry[i] them away to Babylon
or put them to the sword. 5I will hand over to their enemies all the wealth[j] of this
city—all its products, all its valuables and all the treasures of the kings of Judah. They
will take it away[k] as plunder and carry it off to Babylon. 6And you, Pashhur, and
all who live in your house will go into exile to Babylon. There you will die and be
buried, you and all your friends to whom you have prophesied[l] lies.' "

Jeremiah's Complaint

7O LORD, you deceived[b] me, and I was deceived;[b]
you overpowered me and prevailed.
I am ridiculed all day long;
everyone mocks me.
8Whenever I speak, I cry out
proclaiming violence and destruction.[m]
So the word of the LORD has brought me
insult and reproach[n] all day long.
9But if I say, "I will not mention him
or speak any more in his name,"
his word is in my heart like a fire,[o]
a fire shut up in my bones.
I am weary of holding it in;[p]
indeed, I cannot.
10I hear many whispering,
"Terror[q] on every side!
Report[r] him! Let's report him!"
All my friends[s]
are waiting for me to slip,[t] saying,
"Perhaps he will be deceived;
then we will prevail[u] over him
and take our revenge on him."

11But the LORD[v] is with me like a mighty warrior;
so my persecutors[w] will stumble and not prevail.[x]
They will fail and be thoroughly disgraced;[y]
their dishonour will never be forgotten.

[a] *3 Magor-Missabib* means *terror on every side.* [b] *7* Or *persuaded*

20:1 [a] 1Ch 24:14 [b] 2Ki 25:18
20:2 [c] Jer 1:19 [d] Job 13:27 [e] Jer 37:13; 38:7; Zec 14:10
20:3 [f] ver 10
20:4 [g] Jer 29:21 [h] Jer 21:10 [i] Jer 52:27
20:5 [j] Jer 17:3 [k] 2Ki 20:17
20:6 [l] Jer 14:15; La 2:14
20:8 [m] Jer 6:7 [n] 2Ch 36:16; Jer 6:10
20:9 [o] Ps 39:3 [p] Job 32:18-20; Ac 4:20
20:10 [q] Ps 31:13; Jer 6:25 [r] Isa 29:21 [s] Ps 41:9 [t] Lk 11:53-54 [u] 1Ki 19:2
20:11 [v] Jer 1:8; Ro 8:31 [w] Jer 17:18 [x] Jer 15:20 [y] Jer 23:40

20:1ff This event took place during the reign of Jehoiakim of Judah. Jeremiah preached at the Valley of Ben Hinnom, the centre of idolatry in the city. He also preached in the temple, which should have been the centre of true worship. Both places attracted many people; both were places of false worship.

20:1–3 Pashhur was the official in charge of maintaining order in the temple (see 29:26 for a description of the responsibility). He was also a priest and had pretended to be a prophet. After hearing Jeremiah's words, Pashhur had him beaten and put in the stocks (locked up) instead of taking his message to heart and acting on it. The truth sometimes stings, but our reaction to the truth shows what we are made of. We can deny the charges and destroy evidence of our misdeeds, or we can take the truth humbly to heart and let it change us. Pashhur may have thought he was a strong leader, but he was really a coward.

20:4–6 This prophecy of destruction came true in three waves of invasion by Babylon. The first wave happened within the year (605 B.C.). Pashhur was probably exiled to Babylon during the second wave in 597 B.C. when Jehoiachin was taken captive. The third invasion occurred in 586 B.C.

20:7–18 Jeremiah cried out in despair mixed with praise, unburdening his heart to God. He had faithfully proclaimed God's word and had received nothing in return but persecution and sorrow. Yet when he withheld God's word for a while, it became fire in his bones until he could hold it back no longer. When God's living message of forgiveness becomes fire in your bones, you too will feel compelled to share it with others, regardless of the results.

20:12 [z]Jer 17:10 [a]Ps 54:7; 59:10 [b]Ps 62:8; Jer 11:20
20:13 [c]Ps 35:10
20:14 [d]Job 3:3; Jer 15:10
20:16 [e]Ge 19:25
20:17 [f]Job 10:18-19
20:18 [g]Ps 90:9
21:1 [a]2Ki 24:18; Jer 52:1 [b]Jer 38:1 [c]2Ki 25:18; Jer 29:25; 37:3
21:2 [d]Jer 37:3, 7 [e]2Ki 25:1 [f]Ps 44:1-4; Jer 32:17
21:4 [g]Jer 32:5 [h]Jer 37:8-10
21:5 [i]Jer 6:12
21:6 [j]Jer 14:12
21:7 [k]2Ki 25:7; Jer 52:9 [l]Jer 37:17; 39:5 [m]2Ch 36:17; Eze 7:9; Hab 1:6

12 O LORD Almighty, you who examine the righteous
 and probe the heart and mind,[z]
let me see your vengeance[a] upon them,
 for to you I have committed[b] my cause.

13 Sing to the LORD!
 Give praise to the LORD!
He rescues[c] the life of the needy
 from the hands of the wicked.

14 Cursed be the day I was born![d]
 May the day my mother bore me not be blessed!
15 Cursed be the man who brought my father the news,
 who made him very glad, saying,
 "A child is born to you—a son!"
16 May that man be like the towns[e]
 the LORD overthrew without pity.
May he hear wailing in the morning,
 a battle cry at noon.
17 For he did not kill me in the womb,[f]
 with my mother as my grave,
 her womb enlarged for ever.
18 Why did I ever come out of the womb
 to see trouble and sorrow
 and to end my days in shame?[g]

4. Jeremiah accuses Judah's leaders

God Rejects Zedekiah's Request

21 The word came to Jeremiah from the LORD when King Zedekiah[a] sent to him
Pashhur[b] son of Malkijah and the priest Zephaniah[c] son of Maaseiah. They
said: 2 "Enquire[d] now of the LORD for us because Nebuchadnezzar[a][e] king of
Babylon is attacking us. Perhaps the LORD will perform wonders[f] for us as in times
past so that he will withdraw from us."
3 But Jeremiah answered them, "Tell Zedekiah, 4 'This is what the LORD, the God
of Israel, says: I am about to turn[g] against you the weapons of war that are in your
hands, which you are using to fight the king of Babylon and the Babylonians[b] who
are outside the wall besieging[h] you. And I will gather them inside this city. 5 I myself
will fight against you with an outstretched hand[i] and a mighty arm in anger and fury
and great wrath. 6 I will strike down those who live in this city—both men and
animals—and they will die of a terrible plague.[j] 7 After that, declares the LORD, I
will hand over Zedekiah[k] king of Judah, his officials and the people in this city who
survive the plague, sword and famine, to Nebuchadnezzar king of Babylon[l] and to
their enemies who seek their lives. He will put them to the sword; he will show them
no mercy or pity or compassion.'[m]

[a] *2* Hebrew *Nebuchadrezzar*, of which *Nebuchadnezzar* is a variant; here and often in Jeremiah and Ezekiel
[b] *4* Or *Chaldeans*; also in verse 9

21:1 Chapters 21–28 are Jeremiah's messages concerning Nebuchadnezzar's attacks on Jerusalem between 588 and 586 B.C. (see also 2 Kings 25). King Zedekiah decided to rebel against Nebuchadnezzar (2 Kings 24:20), and the nobles advised allying with Egypt. Jeremiah pronounced judgment on the kings (21:1–23:8) and false prophets (23:9–40) for leading the people astray.

21:1, 2 King Zedekiah was probably referring to God's deliverance of Jerusalem from Sennacherib, king of Assyria, in the days of Hezekiah (Isaiah 36; 37). But Zedekiah's hopes were dashed. He was Judah's last ruler during the time of the exile of 586 B.C.

21:1, 2 Pashhur came to the prophet for help. (This is not the same Pashhur as in 20:1.) God still had work for Jeremiah to do. In living out our faith, we may find that rejection, disappointment, or hard work has brought us to the point of despondency. But we are still needed. God has important work for us as well.

21:1–14 Jeremiah had foretold Jerusalem's destruction. The city's leaders had denied his word and mocked his announcements. In desperation, King Zedekiah turned to God for help, but without acknowledging God's warnings or admitting his sin. Too often we expect God to help us in our time of trouble even though we have ignored him in our time of prosperity. But God wants a lasting relationship. Are you trying to build a lasting friendship with God, or are you merely using him occasionally to escape trouble? What would you think of your family or friends if they thought of you only as a temporary resource?

8"Furthermore, tell the people, 'This is what the LORD says: See, I am setting before
you the way of life and the way of death. 9Whoever stays in this city will die by the
sword, famine or plague.[n] But whoever goes out and surrenders to the Babylonians
who are besieging you will live; he will escape with his life.[o] 10I have determined
to do this city harm[p] and not good, declares the LORD. It will be given into the hands[q]
of the king of Babylon, and he will destroy it with fire.'[r]
11"Moreover, say to the royal house[s] of Judah, 'Hear the word of the LORD; 12O
house of David, this is what the LORD says:

" 'Administer justice[t] every morning;
rescue from the hand of his oppressor
the one who has been robbed,
or my wrath will break out and burn like fire
because of the evil you have done—
burn with no-one to quench[u] it.
13I am against[v] you, ⌊Jerusalem,⌋
you who live above this valley[w]
on the rocky plateau,
declares the LORD—
you who say, "Who can come against us?
Who can enter our refuge?"[x]
14I will punish you as your deeds[y] deserve,
declares the LORD.
I will kindle a fire[z] in your forests[a]
that will consume everything around you.' "

Judgment Against Evil Kings

22 This is what the LORD says: "Go down to the palace of the king of Judah and
proclaim this message there: 2'Hear the word of the LORD, O king of Judah,
you who sit on David's throne[a]—you, your officials and your people who come
through these gates.[b] 3This is what the LORD says: Do what is just[c] and right. Rescue
from the hand of his oppressor[d] the one who has been robbed. Do no wrong or
violence to the alien, the fatherless or the widow,[e] and do not shed innocent blood
in this place. 4For if you are careful to carry out these commands, then kings[f] who
sit on David's throne will come through the gates of this palace, riding in chariots and
on horses, accompanied by their officials and their people. 5But if you do not obey[g]
these commands, declares the LORD, I swear[h] by myself that this palace will become
a ruin.' "
6For this is what the LORD says about the palace of the king of Judah:

"Though you are like Gilead to me,
like the summit of Lebanon,
I will surely make you like a desert,[i]
like towns not inhabited.
7I will send destroyers[j] against you,
each man with his weapons,
and they will cut[k] up your fine cedar beams
and throw them into the fire.

8"People from many nations will pass by this city and will ask one another, 'Why
has the LORD done such a thing to this great city?'[l] 9And the answer will be: 'Because

21:9 [n]Jer 14:12 [o]Jer 38:2, 17; 39:18; 45:5
21:10 [p]Jer 44:11, 27; Am 9:4 [q]Jer 32:28; 38:2-3 [r]Jer 52:13
21:11 [s]Jer 13:18
21:12 [t]Jer 22:3 [u]Isa 1:31
21:13 [v]Eze 13:8 [w]Ps 125:2 [x]Jer 49:4; Ob 1:3-4
21:14 [y]Isa 3:10-11 [z]2Ch 36:19; Jer 52:13 [a]Eze 20:47
22:2 [a]Jer 17:25; Lk 1:32 [b]Jer 17:20
22:3 [c]Mic 6:8; Zec 7:9 [d]Ps 72:4; Jer 21:12 [e]Ex 22:22
22:4 [f]Jer 17:25
22:5 [g]Jer 17:27 [h]Heb 6:13
22:6 [i]Mic 3:12
22:7 [j]Jer 4:7 [k]Isa 10:34
22:8 [l]Dt 29:25-26; 1Ki 9:8-9; Jer 16:10-11

21:13 Jerusalem was built on a plateau with valleys on three sides. Because of its strategic location, the inhabitants thought they were safe.

22:1ff Chapters 22–25 may not be in chronological order. In 21:8–10 God implied that it was too late for repentance. In 22:4, however, God said that there was still time to change. The events to which this chapter refer occurred before those of chapter 21.

22:3 God gave the king the basis for rebuilding the nation—turn from evil and do right. Doing what is right is more than simply believing all the right doctrines about God. It means living in obedience to God. Good deeds do not save us, but they display our faith (James 2:17–26).

they have forsaken the covenant of the LORD their God and have worshipped and served other gods.[m]' "

10Do not weep for the dead[n] ⌞king⌟ or mourn[o] his loss;
rather, weep bitterly for him who is exiled,
because he will never return
nor see his native land again.

11For this is what the LORD says about Shallum[a][p] son of Josiah, who succeeded his
father as king of Judah but has gone from this place: "He will never return. 12He will
die[q] in the place where they have led him captive; he will not see this land again."

13"Woe to him who builds[r] his palace by unrighteousness,
his upper rooms by injustice,
making his countrymen work for nothing,
not paying[s] them for their labour.
14He says, 'I will build myself a great palace[t]
with spacious upper rooms.'
So he makes large windows in it,
panels it with cedar[u]
and decorates it in red.

15"Does it make you a king
to have more and more cedar?
Did not your father have food and drink?
He did what was right and just,[v]
so all went well[w] with him.
16He defended the cause of the poor and needy,[x]
and so all went well.
Is that not what it means to know me?"
declares the LORD.
17"But your eyes and your heart
are set only on dishonest gain,
on shedding innocent blood[y]
and on oppression and extortion."

18Therefore this is what the LORD says about Jehoiakim son of Josiah king of Judah:

"They will not mourn for him:
'Alas, my brother! Alas, my sister!'
They will not mourn for him:
'Alas, my master! Alas, his splendour!'
19He will have the burial of a donkey—
dragged away and thrown[z]
outside the gates of Jerusalem."

20"Go up to Lebanon and cry out,
let your voice be heard in Bashan,
cry out from Abarim,[a]
for all your allies are crushed.

a *11* Also called *Jehoahaz*

22:9 [m]2Ki 22:17; 2Ch 34:25
22:10 [n]Ecc 4:2 [o]ver 18
22:11 [p]2Ki 23:31
22:12 [q]2Ki 23:34
22:13 [r]Mic 3:10; Hab 2:9 [s]Lev 19:13; Jas 5:4
22:14 [t]Isa 5:8-9 [u]2Sa 7:2
22:15 [v]2Ki 23:25 [w]Ps 128:2; Isa 3:10
22:16 [x]Ps 72:1-4, 12-13
22:17 [y]2Ki 24:4
22:19 [z]Jer 36:30
22:20 [a]Nu 27:12

22:10–12 Good King Josiah had died at the battle of Megiddo (2 Kings 23:29); his son Shallum (Jehoahaz) reigned for only three months in 609 B.C. before being taken away to Egypt by Pharaoh Neco. He would be the first ruler to die in exile. The people were told not to waste their tears on the death of Josiah, but to cry for the king who was taken into exile and would never return.

22:15, 16 God passed judgment on King Jehoiakim. His father, Josiah, had been one of Judah's great kings, but Jehoiakim was evil. Josiah had been faithful to his responsibility to be a model of right living, but Jehoiakim had been unfaithful to his responsibility to imitate his father. God's judgment was on unfaithful Jehoiakim. He could not claim his father's blessings when he had not followed his father's God. We may inherit our parents' money, but we cannot inherit their faith. A great heritage, a good education, or a beautiful home doesn't guarantee strong character. We must have our own relationship with God.

21I warned you when you felt secure,
but you said, 'I will not listen!'
This has been your way from your youth;[b]
you have not obeyed[c] me.
22The wind will drive all your shepherds away,
and your allies will go into exile.
Then you will be ashamed and disgraced
because of all your wickedness.
23You who live in 'Lebanon',[b]
who are nestled in cedar buildings,
how you will groan when pangs come upon you,
pain[d] like that of a woman in labour!

24"As surely as I live," declares the LORD, "even if you, Jehoiachin[c][e] son of
Jehoiakim king of Judah, were a signet ring on my right hand, I would still pull you
off. 25I will hand you over[f] to those who seek your life, those you fear—to Nebuchadnezzar king of Babylon and to the Babylonians.[d] 26I will hurl[g] you and the
mother who gave you birth into another country, where neither of you was born, and
there you both will die. 27You will never come back to the land you long to return
to."

28Is this man Jehoiachin a despised, broken pot,[h]
an object no-one wants?
Why will he and his children be hurled[i] out,
cast into a land[j] they do not know?
29O land,[k] land, land,
hear the word of the LORD!
30This is what the LORD says:
"Record this man as if childless,[l]
a man who will not prosper[m] in his lifetime,
for none of his offspring will prosper,
none will sit on the throne[n] of David
or rule any more in Judah."

The Righteous Branch

23 "Woe to the shepherds[a] who are destroying and scattering[b] the sheep of my
pasture!"[c] declares the LORD. 2Therefore this is what the LORD, the God of
Israel, says to the shepherds who tend my people: "Because you have scattered my
flock and driven them away and have not bestowed care on them, I will bestow
punishment on you for the evil[d] you have done," declares the LORD. 3"I myself will
gather the remnant[e] of my flock out of all the countries where I have driven them
and will bring them back to their pasture, where they will be fruitful and increase in
number. 4I will place shepherds[f] over them who will tend them, and they will no
longer be afraid[g] or terrified, nor will any be missing,[h]" declares the LORD.

5"The days are coming," declares the LORD,

[b] *23* That is, the palace in Jerusalem (see 1 Kings 7:2) [c] *24* Hebrew *Coniah*, a variant of *Jehoiachin*; also in verse 28 [d] *25* Or *Chaldeans*

22:21 [b]Jer 3:25; 32:30 [c]Jer 7:23-28
22:23 [d]Jer 4:31
22:24 [e]2Ki 24:6, 8; Jer 37:1
22:25 [f]2Ki 24:16; Jer 34:20
22:26 [g]2Ki 24:8; 2Ch 36:10
22:28 [h]Ps 31:12; Jer 48:38; Hos 8:8 [i]Jer 15:1 [j]Jer 17:4
22:29 [k]Jer 6:19; Mic 1:2
22:30 [l]1Ch 3:18; Mt 1:12 [m]Jer 10:21 [n]Ps 94:20
23:1 [a]Jer 10:21; Eze 34:1-10; Zec 11:15-17 [b]Isa 56:11 [c]Eze 34:31
23:2 [d]Jer 21:12
23:3 [e]Isa 11:10-12; Jer 32:37; Eze 34:11-16
23:4 [f]Jer 3:15; 31:10; Eze 34:23 [g]Jer 30:10; 46:27-28 [h]Jn 6:39

22:21 Jehoiakim had been hardheaded and hardhearted since childhood. God warned him, but he refused to listen. His prosperity always took a higher priority than his relationship with God. If you ever find yourself so comfortable that you don't have time for God, stop and ask which is more important—the comforts of this life or a close relationship with God.

22:24, 25 A signet ring was extremely valuable because a king used it to authenticate important documents. Jehoiachin's sins spoiled his usefulness to God. Even if he were God's own signet ring, God would depose him because of his sins (see 24:1).

22:30 Zedekiah reigned after Jehoiachin but died before him (52:10, 11). Jehoiachin was the last king of David's line to sit on the throne in Judah (1 Chronicles 3:15–20). He had seven sons, but not one served as king. Jehoiachin's grandson Zerubbabel ruled after the return from exile (Ezra 2:2). He was only a governor, not a king.

23:1–4 Those responsible to lead Israel in God's path were the very ones responsible for Israel's present plight, and so God had decreed harsh judgment against them. Leaders are held responsible for those entrusted to their care. Whom has God placed in your care? Remember that you are accountable to God for those you influence and lead.

23:5 [i]Isa 4:2 [j]Isa 9:7 [k]Isa 11:1; Zec 6:12
23:6 [l]Jer 33:16; Mt 1:21-23 [m]Ro 3:21-22; 1Co 1:30
23:7 [n]Jer 16:14
23:8 [o]Isa 43:5-6; Am 9:14-15
23:9 [p]Jer 20:8-9
23:10 [q]Jer 9:2 [r]Ps 107:34; Jer 9:10 [s]Hos 4:2-3
23:11 [t]Jer 6:13; 8:10; Zep 3:4 [u]Jer 7:10
23:12 [v]Ps 35:6; Jer 13:16 [w]Jer 11:23
23:13 [x]Jer 2:8
23:14 [y]Jer 5:30 [z]Jer 29:23 [a]Eze 13:22

"when I will raise up to David[a] a righteous Branch,[i]
a King who will reign[j] wisely
and do what is just and right[k] in the land.
6 In his days Judah will be saved
and Israel will live in safety.
This is the name[l] by which he will be called:
The LORD Our Righteousness.[m]

7 "So then, the days are coming," declares the LORD, "when people will no longer say,
'As surely as the LORD lives, who brought the Israelites up out of Egypt,'[n] 8 but they
will say, 'As surely as the LORD lives, who brought the descendants of Israel up out
of the land of the north and out of all the countries where he had banished them.' Then
they will live in their own land."[o]

Lying Prophets

9 Concerning the prophets:

My heart is broken within me;
all my bones tremble.
I am like a drunken man,
like a man overcome by wine,
because of the LORD
and his holy words.[p]
10 The land is full of adulterers;[q]
because of the curse[b] the land lies parched[c]
and the pastures[r] in the desert are withered.[s]
The ⌊prophets⌋ follow an evil course
and use their power unjustly.

11 "Both prophet and priest are godless;[t]
even in my temple[u] I find their wickedness,"
declares the LORD.
12 "Therefore their path will become slippery;[v]
they will be banished to darkness
and there they will fall.
I will bring disaster on them
in the year they are punished,[w]"
declares the LORD.

13 "Among the prophets of Samaria
I saw this repulsive thing:
They prophesied by Baal[x]
and led my people Israel astray.
14 And among the prophets of Jerusalem
I have seen something horrible:[y]
They commit adultery and live a lie.[z]
They strengthen the hands of evildoers,[a]

a 5 Or *up from David's line* b 10 Or *because of these things* c 10 Or *land mourns*

23:5, 6 Jeremiah contrasted the present corrupt leaders with the coming Messiah, the perfect King who would come from David's line to reign over Israel. The King is called a righteous Branch because he will sprout up from the stump of David's fallen dynasty (Isaiah 11:1). This new growth will have God's own characteristics. Like the Creator, the Branch will be righteous.

23:9–14 How did the nation become so corrupt? A major factor was false prophecy. The false prophets had a large, enthusiastic audience and were very popular because they made the people believe that all was well. By contrast, Jeremiah's message from God was unpopular because it showed the people how bad they were.

There are four warning signs of false prophets – characteristics we need to watch for even today. (1) They may appear to speak God's message, but they do not live according to his principles. (2) They water down God's message in order to make it more palatable. (3) They encourage their listeners, often subtly, to disobey God. (4) They tend to be arrogant and self-serving, appealing to the desires of their audience instead of being true to God's word.

23:14 Sodom and Gomorrah were sinful cities destroyed by God (Genesis 19:23, 24). In the Bible they typify the ultimate in degrading, sinful behaviour and rebellion against God.

so that no-one turns from his wickedness.
They are all like Sodom[b] to me;
the people of Jerusalem are like Gomorrah."[c]

15Therefore, this is what the LORD Almighty says concerning the prophets:

"I will make them eat bitter food
and drink poisoned water,[d]
because from the prophets of Jerusalem
ungodliness has spread throughout the land."

16This is what the LORD Almighty says:

"Do not listen[e] to what the prophets are prophesying to you;
they fill you with false hopes.
They speak visions[f] from their own minds,
not from the mouth[g] of the LORD.
17They keep saying to those who despise me,
'The LORD says: You will have peace.'[h]
And to all who follow the stubbornness[i] of their hearts
they say, 'No harm[j] will come to you.'
18But which of them has stood in the council of the LORD
to see or to hear his word?
Who has listened and heard his word?
19See, the storm[k] of the LORD
will burst out in wrath,
a whirlwind swirling down
on the heads of the wicked.
20The anger[l] of the LORD will not turn back[m]
until he fully accomplishes
the purposes of his heart.
In days to come
you will understand it clearly.
21I did not send[n] these prophets,
yet they have run with their message;
I did not speak to them,
yet they have prophesied.
22But if they had stood in my council,
they would have proclaimed my words to my people
and would have turned[o] them from their evil ways
and from their evil deeds.

23"Am I only a God nearby,[p]"
declares the LORD,
"and not a God far away?
24Can anyone hide[q] in secret places
so that I cannot see him?"
declares the LORD.
"Do not I fill heaven and earth?"[r]
declares the LORD.

25"I have heard what the prophets say who prophesy lies[s] in my name. They say,
'I had a dream![t] I had a dream!' 26How long will this continue in the hearts of these
lying prophets, who prophesy the delusions[u] of their own minds? 27They think the
dreams they tell one another will make my people forget[v] my name, just as their
fathers forgot[w] my name through Baal worship. 28Let the prophet who has a dream

23:14 [b]Ge 18:20 [c]Isa 1:9-10; Jer 20:16
23:15 [d]Jer 8:14; 9:15
23:16 [e]Jer 27:9-10, 14; Mt 7:15 [f]Jer 14:14 [g]Jer 9:20
23:17 [h]Jer 8:11 [i]Jer 13:10 [j]Jer 5:12; Am 9:10; Mic 3:11
23:19 [k]Jer 25:32; 30:23
23:20 [l]2Ki 23:26 [m]Jer 30:24
23:21 [n]Jer 14:14; 27:15
23:22 [o]Jer 25:5; Zec 1:4
23:23 [p]Ps 139:1-10
23:24 [q]Job 22:12-14 [r]1Ki 8:27
23:25 [s]Jer 14:14 [t]ver 28, 32; Jer 29:8
23:26 [u]1Ti 4:1-2
23:27 [v]Dt 13:1-3; Jer 29:8 [w]Jdg 3:7; 8:33-34

23:20 "In days to come you will understand it clearly" means that the people would see the truth of this prophecy when Jerusalem fell.

23:28 True prophets and false prophets are as different as straw and grain. Straw is useless for food and cannot compare to nourishing grain. To share the gospel is a great responsibility because

23:29 [x]Jer 5:14
23:30 [y]Ps 34:16 [z]Dt 18:20; Jer 14:15
23:31 [a]ver 17
23:32 [b]ver 25 [c]Jer 7:8; La 2:14
23:33 [d]Mal 1:1 [e]ver 39
23:34 [f]La 2:14 [g]Zec 13:3
23:35 [h]Jer 33:3; 42:4
23:36 [i]Gal 1:7-8; 2Pe 3:16
23:39 [j]Jer 7:15
23:40 [k]Jer 20:11; Eze 5:14-15
24:1 [a]2Ki 24:16; 2Ch 36:9; Jer 29:2 [b]Am 8:1-2
24:2 [c]Isa 5:4
24:3 [d]Jer 1:11; Am 8:2

tell his dream, but let the one who has my word speak it faithfully. For what has straw
to do with grain?" declares the LORD. 29"Is not my word like fire,"[x] declares the
LORD, "and like a hammer that breaks a rock in pieces?
30"Therefore," declares the LORD, "I am against[y] the prophets[z] who steal from
one another words supposedly from me. 31Yes," declares the LORD, "I am against the
prophets who wag their own tongues and yet declare, 'The LORD declares.'[a] 32In-
deed, I am against those who prophesy false dreams,[b]" declares the LORD. "They tell
them and lead my people astray with their reckless lies, yet I did not send or appoint
them. They do not benefit[c] these people in the least," declares the LORD.

False Oracles and False Prophets

33"When these people, or a prophet or a priest, ask you, 'What is the oracle[d][d]
of the LORD?' say to them, 'What oracle?[e] I will forsake[e] you, declares the LORD.'
34If a prophet or a priest or anyone else claims, 'This is the oracle[f] of the LORD,'
I will punish[g] that man and his household. 35This is what each of you keeps on saying
to his friend or relative: 'What is the LORD's answer?'[h] or 'What has the LORD
spoken?' 36But you must not mention 'the oracle of the LORD' again, because every
man's own word becomes his oracle and so you distort[i] the words of the living God,
the LORD Almighty, our God. 37This is what you keep saying to a prophet: 'What is
the LORD's answer to you?' or 'What has the LORD spoken?' 38Although you claim,
'This is the oracle of the LORD,' this is what the LORD says: You used the words, 'This
is the oracle of the LORD,' even though I told you that you must not claim, 'This is
the oracle of the LORD.' 39Therefore, I will surely forget you and cast[j] you out of
my presence along with the city I gave to you and your fathers. 40I will bring upon
you everlasting disgrace[k]—everlasting shame that will not be forgotten."

Two Baskets of Figs

24 After Jehoiachin[a][a] son of Jehoiakim king of Judah and the officials, the
craftsmen and the artisans of Judah were carried into exile from Jerusalem to
Babylon by Nebuchadnezzar king of Babylon, the LORD showed me two baskets of
figs[b] placed in front of the temple of the LORD. 2One basket had very good figs, like
those that ripen early; the other basket had very poor[c] figs, so bad that they could
not be eaten.
3Then the LORD asked me, "What do you see,[d] Jeremiah?"
"Figs," I answered. "The good ones are very good, but the poor ones are so bad
that they cannot be eaten."
4Then the word of the LORD came to me: 5"This is what the LORD, the God of Israel,
says: 'Like these good figs, I regard as good the exiles from Judah, whom I sent away

[d] 33 Or *burden* (see Septuagint and Vulgate) [e] 33 Hebrew; Septuagint and Vulgate *'You are the burden'*; the Hebrew for *oracle* and *burden* is the same. [a] 1 Hebrew *Jeconiah*, a variant of *Jehoiachin*

---

the way we present it and live it will encourage people either to accept it or reject it. Whether we speak from a pulpit, teach in a class, or share with friends, we are entrusted with accurately communicating and living out God's word. As you share God's word with friends and neighbours, they will look for its effectiveness in your life. Unless it has changed you, why should they let it change them? If you preach it, make sure you live it!

23:33–40 People mocked Jeremiah by saying sarcastically, "What is the oracle of the LORD?" (*oracle* meaning "utterance" or "burden"). The people mocked Jeremiah and God because it seemed that Jeremiah brought nothing but God's sad news of condemnation. But this sad news was the truth. If they had accepted it, they would have had to repent and turn to God. Because they did not want to do this, they rejected Jeremiah's message. Have you ever rejected a message or made fun of it because it would require you to change your ways? Before dismissing someone who brings sad news, look carefully at your motives.

24:1 This happened in 597 B.C. Jehoiachin was taken to Babylon, and Zedekiah became king. Often royal officials were exiled to keep them from exerting power and starting a rebellion. Skilled craftsmen and artisans were taken because they were valuable for Babylon's building programme. Jeremiah foretold this event in 22:24–28.

24:2–10 The good figs represented the exiles to Babylon – not because they themselves were good, but because their hearts would respond to God. He would preserve them and bring them back to the land. The poor figs represented those who remained in Judah or ran away to Egypt. Those people may have arrogantly believed they would be blessed if they remained in the land or escaped to Egypt, but the opposite was true because God would use the captivity to refine the exiles. We may assume we are blessed when life goes well and cursed when it does not. But trouble is a blessing when it makes us stronger, and prosperity is a curse if it entices us away from God. If you are facing trouble, ask God to help you grow stronger for him. If things are going your way, ask God to help you use your prosperity for him.

from this place to the land of the Babylonians.[b] 6My eyes will watch over them for
their good, and I will bring them back[e] to this land. I will build[f] them up and not
tear them down; I will plant them and not uproot them. 7I will give them a heart to
know me, that I am the LORD. They will be my people,[g] and I will be their God,
for they will return[h] to me with all their heart.[i]
8" 'But like the poor[j] figs, which are so bad that they cannot be eaten,' says the
LORD, 'so will I deal with Zedekiah king of Judah, his officials[k] and the survivors[l]
from Jerusalem, whether they remain in this land or live in Egypt.[m] 9I will make them
abhorrent[n] and an offence to all the kingdoms of the earth, a reproach and a byword,[o]
an object of ridicule and cursing,[p] wherever I banish[q] them. 10I will send the
sword,[r] famine and plague[s] against them until they are destroyed from the land I
gave to them and their fathers.' "

Seventy Years of Captivity

25 The word came to Jeremiah concerning all the people of Judah in the fourth
year of Jehoiakim[a] son of Josiah king of Judah, which was the first year of
Nebuchadnezzar[b] king of Babylon. 2So Jeremiah the prophet said to all the people
of Judah[c] and to all those living in Jerusalem: 3For twenty-three years—from the
thirteenth year of Josiah[d] son of Amon king of Judah until this very day—the word
of the LORD has come to me and I have spoken to you again and again,[e] but you have
not listened.[f]
4And though the LORD has sent all his servants the prophets[g] to you again and
again, you have not listened or paid any attention. 5They said, "Turn now, each of
you, from your evil ways and your evil practices, and you can stay in the land the
LORD gave to you and your fathers for ever and ever. 6Do not follow other gods[h]
to serve and worship them; do not provoke me to anger with what your hands have
made. Then I will not harm you."
7"But you did not listen to me," declares the LORD, "and you have provoked me
with what your hands have made,[i] and you have brought harm[j] to yourselves."
8Therefore the LORD Almighty says this: "Because you have not listened to my
words, 9I will summon[k] all the peoples of the north[l] and my servant[m] Nebuchadnezzar king of Babylon," declares the LORD, "and I will bring them against this land and
its inhabitants and against all the surrounding nations. I will completely destroy[a] them
and make them an object of horror and scorn,[n] and an everlasting ruin. 10I will banish
from them the sounds[o] of joy and gladness, the voices of bride and bridegroom,[p]
the sound of millstones[q] and the light of the lamp.[r] 11This whole country will
become a desolate wasteland,[s] and these nations will serve the king of Babylon for
seventy years.[t]
12"But when the seventy years[u] are fulfilled, I will punish the king of Babylon and
his nation, the land of the Babylonians,[b] for their guilt," declares the LORD, "and
will make it desolate[v] for ever. 13I will bring upon that land all the things I have
spoken against it, all that are written in this book and prophesied by Jeremiah against
all the nations. 14They themselves will be enslaved[w] by many nations[x] and great
kings; I will repay[y] them according to their deeds and the work of their hands."

b 5 Or *Chaldeans* a 9 The Hebrew term refers to the irrevocable giving over of things or persons to the LORD, often by totally destroying them. b 12 Or *Chaldeans*

24:6 [e]Jer 29:10; Eze 11:17 [f]Jer 33:7; 42:10
24:7 [g]Isa 51:16; Jer 31:33; Heb 8:10 [h]Jer 32:40 [i]Eze 11:19
24:8 [j]Jer 29:17 [k]Jer 39:6 [l]Jer 39:9 [m]Jer 44:1, 26
24:9 [n]Jer 15:4; 34:17 [o]Dt 28:25; 1Ki 9:7 [p]Jer 29:18 [q]Dt 28:37
24:10 [r]Isa 51:19 [s]Jer 27:8
25:1 [a]2Ki 24:2; Jer 36:1 [b]2Ki 24:1
25:2 [c]Jer 18:11
25:3 [d]Jer 1:2 [e]Jer 11:7; 26:5 [f]Jer 7:26
25:4 [g]Jer 7:25
25:6 [h]Dt 8:19
25:7 [i]Dt 32:21 [j]2Ki 21:15
25:9 [k]Isa 13:3-5 [l]Jer 1:15 [m]Jer 27:6 [n]Jer 18:16
25:10 [o]Isa 24:8; Eze 26:13 [p]Jer 7:34 [q]Ecc 12:3-4 [r]Rev 18:22-23
25:11 [s]Jer 4:26-27; 12:11-12 [t]2Ch 36:21
25:12 [u]Jer 29:10 [v]Isa 13:19-22; 14:22-23
25:14 [w]Jer 27:7 [x]Jer 50:9; 51:27-28 [y]Jer 51:6

24:6 The exiles in Babylon were cared for by the Lord. Although they were moved to a foreign land, their captivity was not enslavement. The people could function in business and own homes. Some, like Daniel, even held high positions in the government (see Daniel 2:48).

25:1ff Jeremiah gave this message in 605 B.C., the year Nebuchadnezzar came to power. From verse 3 we learn that the beginning of Jeremiah's ministry was in 627 B.C. He predicted the 70 years of captivity a full 20 years before it began.

25:2–6 Imagine preaching the same message for 23 years and continually being rejected! Jeremiah faced this; but because he had committed his life to God, he continued to proclaim the message—"Turn now, each of you, from your evil ways and your evil practices." Regardless of the people's response, Jeremiah did not give up. God never stops loving us, even when we reject him. We can thank God that he won't give up on us, and, like Jeremiah, we can commit ourselves to never forsaking him. No matter how people respond when you tell them about God, remain faithful to God's high call and continue to witness for him.

25:12 This event is further described in Daniel 5. The troops of Cyrus the Great entered Babylon in 539 B.C. and killed Belshazzar, the last Babylonian ruler.

The Cup of God's Wrath

15This is what the LORD, the God of Israel, said to me: "Take from my hand this
cup[z] filled with the wine of my wrath and make all the nations to whom I send you
drink it. 16When they drink it, they will stagger[a] and go mad[b] because of the sword
I will send among them."

17So I took the cup from the LORD's hand and made all the nations to whom he
sent[c] me drink it: 18Jerusalem and the towns of Judah, its kings and officials, to make
them a ruin and an object of horror and scorn and cursing,[d] as they are today;[e]
19Pharaoh king of Egypt, his attendants, his officials and all his people, 20and all the
foreign people there; all the kings of Uz;[f] all the kings of the Philistines (those of
Ashkelon,[g] Gaza, Ekron, and the people left at Ashdod); 21Edom, Moab and Ammon;[h] 22all the kings of Tyre and Sidon;[i] the kings of the coastlands[j] across the
sea; 23Dedan, Tema, Buz and all who are in distant places;**c**[k] 24all the kings of
Arabia[l] and all the kings of the foreign people who live in the desert; 25all the kings
of Zimri, Elam[m] and Media; 26and all the kings of the north,[n] near and far, one after
the other—all the kingdoms on the face of the earth. And after all of them, the king
of Sheshach**d**[o] will drink it too.

27"Then tell them, 'This is what the LORD Almighty, the God of Israel, says: Drink,
get drunk[p] and vomit, and fall to rise no more because of the sword[q] I will send
among you.' 28But if they refuse to take the cup from your hand and drink, tell them,
'This is what the LORD Almighty says: You must drink it! 29See, I am beginning to
bring disaster[r] on the city that bears my Name,[s] and will you indeed go unpunished?[t] You will not go unpunished, for I am calling down a sword upon all[u] who
live on the earth, declares the LORD Almighty.'

30"Now prophesy all these words against them and say to them:

" 'The LORD will roar[v] from on high;
  he will thunder[w] from his holy dwelling
  and roar mightily against his land.
He will shout like those who tread the grapes,
  shout against all who live on the earth.
31The tumult will resound to the ends of the earth,
  for the LORD will bring charges[x] against the nations;
he will bring judgment on all mankind
  and put the wicked to the sword,' "

declares the LORD.

32This is what the LORD Almighty says:

"Look! Disaster is spreading
  from nation to nation;[y]
a mighty storm[z] is rising
  from the ends of the earth."

33At that time those slain[a] by the LORD will be everywhere—from one end of the
earth to the other. They will not be mourned or gathered[b] up or buried,[c] but will
be like refuse lying on the ground.

34Weep and wail, you shepherds;
  roll[d] in the dust, you leaders of the flock.
For your time to be slaughtered[e] has come;
  you will fall and be shattered like fine pottery.
35The shepherds will have nowhere to flee,
  the leaders of the flock no place to escape.[f]

c *23* Or *who clip the hair by their foreheads* **d** *26* *Sheshach* is a cryptogram for Babylon.

25:15 [z]Isa 51:17; Ps 75:8; Rev 14:10
25:16 [a]Na 3:11 [b]Jer 51:7
25:17 [c]Jer 1:10
25:18 [d]Jer 24:9 [e]Jer 44:22
25:20 [f]Job 1:1 [g]Jer 47:5
25:21 [h]Jer 49:1
25:22 [i]Jer 47:4 [j]Jer 31:10
25:23 [k]Jer 9:26; 49:32
25:24 [l]2Ch 9:14
25:25 [m]Ge 10:22
25:26 [n]Jer 50:3, 9 [o]Jer 51:41
25:27 [p]ver 16, 28; Hab 2:16 [q]Eze 21:4
25:29 [r]Jer 13:12-14 [s]1Pe 4:17 [t]Pr 11:31 [u]ver 30-31
25:30 [v]Isa 16:10; 42:13 [w]Joel 3:16; Am 1:2
25:31 [x]Hos 4:1; Joel 3:2; Mic 6:2
25:32 [y]Isa 34:2 [z]Jer 23:19
25:33 [a]Isa 66:16; Eze 39:17-20 [b]Jer 16:4 [c]Ps 79:3
25:34 [d]Jer 6:26 [e]Isa 34:6; Jer 50:27
25:35 [f]Job 11:20

25:15–38 Judah would not be the only nation to drink the cup of God's wrath. Here Jeremiah listed other wicked nations who would experience God's wrath at the hand of Babylon. Finally, Babylon itself (called Sheshach in 25:26) would be destroyed because of its sin.

36 Hear the cry of the shepherds,
the wailing of the leaders of the flock,
for the LORD is destroying their pasture.
37 The peaceful meadows will be laid waste
because of the fierce anger of the LORD.
38 Like a lion[g] he will leave his lair,
and their land will become desolate
because of the sword[e] of the oppressor
and because of the LORD's fierce anger.

Jeremiah Threatened With Death

26 Early in the reign of Jehoiakim[a] son of Josiah king of Judah, this word came
from the LORD: 2 "This is what the LORD says: Stand in the courtyard[b] of the
LORD's house and speak to all the people of the towns of Judah who come to worship
in the house of the LORD. Tell[c] them everything I command you; do not omit[d] a
word. 3 Perhaps they will listen and each will turn[e] from his evil way. Then I will
relent[f] and not bring on them the disaster I was planning because of the evil they
have done. 4 Say to them, 'This is what the LORD says: If you do not listen[g] to me
and follow my law,[h] which I have set before you, 5 and if you do not listen to the
words of my servants the prophets, whom I have sent to you again and again (though
you have not listened[i]), 6 then I will make this house like Shiloh[j] and this city an
object of cursing[k] among all the nations of the earth.' "
7 The priests, the prophets and all the people heard Jeremiah speak these words in
the house of the LORD. 8 But as soon as Jeremiah finished telling all the people
everything the LORD had commanded him to say, the priests, the prophets and all the
people seized him and said, "You must die! 9 Why do you prophesy in the LORD's name
that this house will be like Shiloh and this city will be desolate and deserted?"[l] And
all the people crowded around Jeremiah in the house of the LORD.
10 When the officials of Judah heard about these things, they went up from the royal
palace to the house of the LORD and took their places at the entrance of the New Gate
of the LORD's house. 11 Then the priests and the prophets said to the officials and all
the people, "This man should be sentenced to death[m] because he has prophesied
against this city. You have heard it with your own ears!"
12 Then Jeremiah said to all the officials[n] and all the people: "The LORD sent me
to prophesy[o] against this house and this city all the things you have heard.[p] 13 Now
reform[q] your ways and your actions and obey the LORD your God. Then the LORD
will relent and not bring the disaster he has pronounced against you. 14 As for me, I
am in your hands;[r] do with me whatever you think is good and right. 15 Be assured,
however, that if you put me to death, you will bring the guilt of innocent blood on
yourselves and on this city and on those who live in it, for in truth the LORD has sent
me to you to speak all these words in your hearing."

[e] *38* Some Hebrew manuscripts and Septuagint (see also Jer. 46:16 and 50:16); most Hebrew *manuscripts anger*

25:38 [g] Jer 4:7
26:1 [a] 2Ki 23:36
26:2 [b] Jer 19:14 [c] Jer 1:17; Mt 28:20; Ac 20:27 [d] Dt 4:2
26:3 [e] Jer 36:7 [f] Jer 18:8
26:4 [g] Lev 26:14 [h] 1Ki 9:6
26:5 [i] Jer 25:4
26:6 [j] Jos 18:1 [k] 2Ki 22:19
26:9 [l] Jer 9:11
26:11 [m] Dt 18:20; Jer 18:23; 38:4; Mt 26:66; Ac 6:11
26:12 [n] Jer 1:18 [o] Am 7:15; Ac 4:18-20; 5:29 [p] ver 2, 15
26:13 [q] Jer 7:5; Joel 2:12-14
26:14 [r] Jer 38:5

26:1ff The events described in this chapter took place in 609–608 B.C., before the events described in chapter 25. Jehoiakim was a materialistic and self-centred king who persecuted and murdered innocent people (36:22–32; 2 Kings 23:36–24:6). Chapter 26 describes how and why Jeremiah was on trial for his life.

26:2 God reminded Jeremiah that he wanted his entire message given – "Do not omit a word." Jeremiah may have been tempted to leave out the parts that would turn his audience against him, would sound too harsh, or would make him sound like a traitor. But by God's command, he was not to delete parts of God's message to suit himself, his audience, or the circumstances in which he found himself. Like Jeremiah, we must never ignore or repress important parts of God's word to please anyone.

26:2–9 Shiloh was where the tabernacle had been set up after the conquest of Canaan (Joshua 18:1). It was destroyed in 1050 B.C. by the Philistines. "I will make this house like Shiloh" means that Jerusalem and the temple would be destroyed. When Jeremiah said that Jerusalem, the city of God, would become an object of cursing and the temple would be destroyed (26:6), the priests and false prophets were infuriated. The temple was important to them because the people's reverence for it brought them power. By saying that the temple would be destroyed, Jeremiah undermined their authority. Jesus also infuriated the religious leaders of his time by foretelling the destruction of Jerusalem and the temple (Matthew 24:2).

26:11 Jeremiah was branded a traitor because he prophesied the destruction of the city and the temple. But the "courageous" people advocated a foreign alliance to fight Babylon and retain their independence.

16Then the officials[s] and all the people said to the priests and the prophets, "This man should not be sentenced to death![t] He has spoken to us in the name of the LORD our God."

17Some of the elders of the land stepped forward and said to the entire assembly of people, 18"Micah[u] of Moresheth prophesied in the days of Hezekiah king of Judah. He told all the people of Judah, 'This is what the LORD Almighty says:

" 'Zion[v] will be ploughed like a field,
Jerusalem will become a heap of rubble,[w]
the temple hill[x] a mound overgrown with thickets.'[a][y]

19"Did Hezekiah king of Judah or anyone else in Judah put him to death? Did not Hezekiah[z] fear the LORD and seek his favour? And did not the LORD relent,[a] so that he did not bring the disaster[b] he pronounced against them? We are about to bring a terrible disaster[c] on ourselves!"

20(Now Uriah son of Shemaiah from Kiriath Jearim[d] was another man who prophesied in the name of the LORD; he prophesied the same things against this city and this land as Jeremiah did. 21When King Jehoiakim[e] and all his officers and officials heard his words, the king sought to put him to death. But Uriah heard of it and fled[f] in fear to Egypt. 22King Jehoiakim, however, sent Elnathan[g] son of Acbor to Egypt, along with some other men. 23They brought Uriah out of Egypt and took him to King Jehoiakim, who had him struck down with a sword and his body thrown into the burial place of the common people.)

24Furthermore, Ahikam[h] son of Shaphan supported Jeremiah, and so he was not handed over to the people to be put to death.

Judah to Serve Nebuchadnezzar

27 Early in the reign of Zedekiah[a][a] son of Josiah king of Judah, this word came to Jeremiah from the LORD: 2This is what the LORD said to me: "Make a yoke[b] out of straps and crossbars and put it on your neck. 3Then send word to the kings of Edom, Moab, Ammon,[c] Tyre and Sidon through the envoys who have come to Jerusalem to Zedekiah king of Judah. 4Give them a message for their masters and say, 'This is what the LORD Almighty, the God of Israel, says: "Tell this to your masters: 5With my great power and outstretched arm[d] I made the earth and its people and the animals that are on it, and I give[e] it to anyone I please. 6Now I will hand all your countries over to my servant[f] Nebuchadnezzar[g] king of Babylon; I will make even the wild animals subject to him.[h] 7All nations will serve[i] him and his son and his grandson until the time[j] for his land comes; then many nations and great kings will subjugate[k] him.

8" ' "If, however, any nation or kingdom will not serve Nebuchadnezzar king of Babylon or bow its neck under his yoke, I will punish that nation with the sword, famine and plague, declares the LORD, until I destroy it by his hand. 9So do not listen to your prophets, your diviners, your interpreters of dreams, your mediums[l] or your sorcerers who tell you, 'You will not serve the king of Babylon.' 10They prophesy

26:16 [s]Ac 23:9 [t]Ac 5:34-39; 23:29
26:18 [u]Mic 1:1 [v]Isa 2:3 [w]Ne 4:2; Jer 9:11 [x]Mic 4:1; Zec 8:3 [y]Jer 17:3
26:19 [z]2Ch 32:24-26; Isa 37:14-20 [a]Ex 32:14; 2Sa 24:16 [b]Jer 44:7 [c]Hab 2:10
26:20 [d]Jos 9:17
26:21 [e]1Ki 19:2 [f]Mt 10:23
26:22 [g]Jer 36:12, 25
26:24 [h]2Ki 22:12
27:1 [a]2Ch 36:11
27:2 [b]Jer 28:10, 13
27:3 [c]Jer 25:21
27:5 [d]Dt 9:29 [e]Ps 115:16
27:6 [f]Jer 25:9 [g]Jer 21:7; Eze 29:18-20 [h]Jer 28:14; Da 2:37-38
27:7 [i]2Ch 36:20 [j]Jer 25:12 [k]Jer 25:14; Da 5:28
27:9 [l]Dt 18:11

a *18* Micah 3:12 a *1* A few Hebrew manuscripts and Syriac (see also Jer. 27:3, 12 and 28:1); most Hebrew manuscripts *Jehoiakim* (most Septuagint manuscripts do not have this verse.)

26:17–19 The elders remembered the words of the prophet Micah (Micah 3:12), which were similar to the words Jeremiah spoke. When Micah called the people to repent, they turned from their wickedness. Although these people did not kill Jeremiah, they missed the main point – that the application of the story was for them. They spared Jeremiah, but they did not spare themselves by repenting of their sins. As you recall a great story of the Bible, ask how it can be applied to *your* life.

26:20–23 Uriah is an otherwise unknown prophet who was executed for faithfully proclaiming God's words. This shows us that God has had other prophets whose words are not included in the Bible.

27:1ff The year was 593 B.C., and Nebuchadnezzar had already invaded Judah once and had taken many captives. Jeremiah wore a yoke (a wooden frame used to fasten a team of animals to a plough) as a symbol of bondage. This was an object lesson, telling the people they must put themselves under Babylon's yoke or be destroyed.

27:5, 6 God punished the people of Judah in an unusual way, by appointing a foreign ruler to be his "servant". Nebuchadnezzar was not employed to proclaim God's message, but to fulfil God's promise of judgment on sin. Because God is in control of all events, he uses whomever he wants. God may use unlikely people or circumstances to correct you. Be ready to accept God's improvement, even if it comes from unexpected sources.

lies[m] to you that will only serve to remove you far from your lands; I will banish you
and you will perish. 11 But if any nation will bow its neck under the yoke[n] of the king
of Babylon and serve him, I will let that nation remain in its own land to till it and
to live there, declares the LORD." ' "
12 I gave the same message to Zedekiah king of Judah. I said, "Bow your neck under
the yoke of the king of Babylon; serve him and his people, and you will live. 13 Why
will you and your people die[o] by the sword, famine and plague with which the LORD
has threatened any nation that will not serve the king of Babylon? 14 Do not listen to
the words of the prophets who say to you, 'You will not serve the king of Babylon,'
for they are prophesying lies[p] to you. 15 'I have not sent[q] them,' declares the LORD.
'They are prophesying lies in my name.[r] Therefore, I will banish you and you will
perish,[s] both you and the prophets who prophesy to you.' "
16 Then I said to the priests and all these people, "This is what the LORD says: Do
not listen to the prophets who say, 'Very soon now the articles[t] from the LORD's
house will be brought back from Babylon.' They are prophesying lies to you. 17 Do
not listen to them. Serve the king of Babylon, and you will live. Why should this city
become a ruin? 18 If they are prophets and have the word of the LORD, let them plead[u]
with the LORD Almighty that the furnishings remaining in the house of the LORD and
in the palace of the king of Judah and in Jerusalem not be taken to Babylon. 19 For
this is what the LORD Almighty says about the pillars, the Sea,[v] the movable stands
and the other furnishings[w] that are left in this city, 20 which Nebuchadnezzar king of
Babylon did not take away when he carried[x] Jehoiachin[b][y] son of Jehoiakim king
of Judah into exile from Jerusalem to Babylon, along with all the nobles of Judah and
Jerusalem—21 yes, this is what the LORD Almighty, the God of Israel, says about the
things that are left in the house of the LORD and in the palace of the king of Judah
and in Jerusalem: 22 'They will be taken[z] to Babylon and there they will remain until
the day[a] I come for them,' declares the LORD. 'Then I will bring[b] them back and
restore them to this place.' "

The False Prophet Hananiah

28 In the fifth month of that same year, the fourth year, early in the reign of
Zedekiah[a] king of Judah, the prophet Hananiah son of Azzur, who was from
Gibeon,[b] said to me in the house of the LORD in the presence of the priests and all
the people: 2 "This is what the LORD Almighty, the God of Israel, says: 'I will break
the yoke[c] of the king of Babylon. 3 Within two years I will bring back to this place
all the articles[d] of the LORD's house that Nebuchadnezzar king of Babylon removed
from here and took to Babylon. 4 I will also bring back to this place Jehoiachin[e] son
of Jehoiakim king of Judah and all the other exiles from Judah who went to Babylon,'
declares the LORD, 'for I will break the yoke of the king of Babylon.' "
5 Then the prophet Jeremiah replied to the prophet Hananiah before the priests and
all the people who were standing in the house of the LORD. 6 He said, "Amen! May
the LORD do so! May the LORD fulfil the words you have prophesied by bringing the
articles of the LORD's house and all the exiles back to this place from Babylon.
7 Nevertheless, listen to what I have to say in your hearing and in the hearing of all
the people: 8 From early times the prophets who preceded you and me have prophesied

b *20* Hebrew *Jeconiah*, a variant of *Jehoiachin*; also in 28:4 and 29:2

27:10 [m] Jer 23:25
27:11 [n] Jer 21:9
27:13 [o] Eze 18:31
27:14 [p] Jer 14:14
27:15 [q] Jer 23:21 [r] Jer 29:9 [s] Jer 6:15
27:16 [t] 2Ki 24:13; 2Ch 36:7, 10; Jer 28:3; Da 1:2
27:18 [u] 1Sa 7:8
27:19 [v] 2Ki 25:13 [w] Jer 52:17-23
27:20 [x] 2Ch 36:10; Jer 24:1 [y] Jer 22:24
27:22 [z] 2Ki 25:13 [a] 2Ch 36:21 [b] Ezr 1:7; 7:19
28:1 [a] Jer 27:1, 3 [b] Jos 9:3
28:2 [c] Jer 27:12
28:3 [d] 2Ki 24:13
28:4 [e] Jer 22:24-27

27:12–18 Zedekiah was in a difficult situation. Jeremiah called on him to surrender to Nebuchadnezzar at a time when many of the other leaders wanted him to form an alliance and fight. It would be disgraceful for a king to surrender, and he would look like a coward. This was a great opportunity for the false prophets, who kept saying that the Babylonians would not defeat the great city of Jerusalem and that God would never allow the magnificent, holy temple to be destroyed.

27:19–22 When Nebuchadnezzar invaded Judah, first in 605 and then in 597 B.C., he took away many important people living in Jerusalem – including Daniel and Ezekiel. Although these men were captives, they had a profound impact on the exiles and leaders in Babylon. Jeremiah predicted that more people and even the precious objects in the temple would be taken. This happened in 586 B.C. during Babylon's third and last invasion.

28:8–17 Jeremiah spoke the truth, but it was unpopular; Hananiah spoke lies, but his deceitful words brought false hope and comfort to the people. God had already outlined the marks of a true prophet (Deuteronomy 13; 18:20–22): a true prophet's predictions always come true and his words never contradict previous revelation. Jeremiah's predictions were already coming true, from Hananiah's death to the Babylonian invasions. But the people still

war, disaster and plague[f] against many countries and great kingdoms. 9But the
prophet who prophesies peace will be recognised as one truly sent by the LORD only
if his prediction comes true.[g]"
10Then the prophet Hananiah took the yoke[h] off the neck of the prophet Jeremiah
and broke it, 11and he said[i] before all the people, "This is what the LORD says: 'In
the same way will I break the yoke of Nebuchadnezzar king of Babylon off the neck
of all the nations within two years.' " At this, the prophet Jeremiah went on his way.
12Shortly after the prophet Hananiah had broken the yoke off the neck of the prophet
Jeremiah, the word of the LORD came to Jeremiah: 13"Go and tell Hananiah, 'This
is what the LORD says: You have broken a wooden yoke, but in its place you will get
a yoke of iron. 14This is what the LORD Almighty, the God of Israel, says: I will put
an iron yoke[j] on the necks of all these nations to make them serve[k] Nebuchadnezzar
king of Babylon, and they will serve him. I will even give him control over the wild
animals.[l]' "
15Then the prophet Jeremiah said to Hananiah the prophet, "Listen, Hananiah! The
LORD has not sent[m] you, yet you have persuaded this nation to trust in lies.[n]
16Therefore, this is what the LORD says: 'I am about to remove you from the face of
the earth.[o] This very year you are going to die, because you have preached rebellion[p]
against the LORD.' "
17In the seventh month of that same year, Hananiah the prophet died.

A Letter to the Exiles

29 This is the text of the letter that the prophet Jeremiah sent from Jerusalem to
the surviving elders among the exiles and to the priests, the prophets and all
the other people Nebuchadnezzar had carried into exile from Jerusalem to Babylon.[a]
2(This was after King Jehoiachin[b] and the queen mother, the court officials and the
leaders of Judah and Jerusalem, the craftsmen and the artisans had gone into exile from
Jerusalem.) 3He entrusted the letter to Elasah son of Shaphan and to Gemariah son
of Hilkiah, whom Zedekiah king of Judah sent to King Nebuchadnezzar in Babylon.
It said:

4This is what the LORD Almighty, the God of Israel, says to all those I carried[c]
into exile from Jerusalem to Babylon: 5"Build[d] houses and settle down; plant
gardens and eat what they produce. 6Marry and have sons and daughters; find
wives for your sons and give your daughters in marriage, so that they too may
have sons and daughters. Increase in number there; do not decrease. 7Also, seek
the peace and prosperity of the city to which I have carried you into exile. Pray[e]
to the LORD for it, because if it prospers, you too will prosper." 8Yes, this is what
the LORD Almighty, the God of Israel, says: "Do not let the prophets and diviners
among you deceive[f] you. Do not listen to the dreams you encourage them to
have.[g] 9They are prophesying lies[h] to you in my name. I have not sent them,"
declares the LORD.
10This is what the LORD says: "When seventy years[i] are completed for
Babylon, I will come to you and fulfil my gracious promise to bring you back[j]

28:8 [f]Lev 26:14-17; Isa 5:5-7
28:9 [g]Dt 18:22
28:10 [h]Jer 27:2
28:11 [i]Jer 14:14; 27:10
28:14 [j]Dt 28:48 [k]Jer 25:11 [l]Jer 27:6
28:15 [m]Jer 29:31 [n]Jer 20:6; 29:21; La 2:14; Eze 13:6
28:16 [o]Ge 7:4 [p]Dt 13:5; Jer 29:32
29:1 [a]2Ch 36:10
29:2 [b]2Ki 24:12; Jer 22:24-28
29:4 [c]Jer 24:5
29:5 [d]ver 28
29:7 [e]Ezr 6:10; 1Ti 2:1-2
29:8 [f]Jer 37:9 [g]Jer 23:27
29:9 [h]Jer 14:14; 27:15
29:10 [i]2Ch 36:21; Jer 25:12; Da 9:2 [j]Jer 21:22

---

preferred to listen to comforting lies rather than painful truth.

29:4–7 Jeremiah wrote to the captives in Babylon (29:4–23 is the letter) instructing them to go on with their lives and to pray for the pagan nation that enslaved them. Life cannot grind to a halt during troubled times. In an unpleasant or distressing situation, we must adjust and keep moving. You may find it difficult to pray for those in authority if they are evil, but that is when your prayers are most needed (1 Timothy 2:1, 2). When you enter times of trouble or sudden change, pray diligently and move ahead, doing whatever you can rather than giving up because of fear and uncertainty.

29:10 Scholars differ on the exact dates of this 70-year period in Babylon. Some say it refers to the years 605 – 538 B.C., from the first deportation to Babylon to the arrival of the first exiles back in Jerusalem after Cyrus' freedom decree. Others point to the years 586 – 516 B.C., from the last deportation to Babylon and the destruction of the temple until its rebuilding. A third possibility is that 70 years is an approximate number meaning a lifetime. All agree that God sent his people to Babylon for a long time, not the short captivity predicted by the false prophets.

to this place. 11 For I know the plans[k] I have for you," declares the LORD, "plans to prosper you and not to harm you, plans to give you hope and a future. 12 Then you will call upon me and come and pray to me, and I will listen[l] to you. 13 You will seek[m] me and find me when you seek me with all your heart.[n] 14 I will be found by you," declares the LORD, "and will bring you back[o] from captivity.[a] I will gather you from all the nations and places where I have banished you," declares the LORD, "and will bring you back to the place from which I carried you into exile."[p]

15 You may say, "The LORD has raised up prophets for us in Babylon," 16 but this is what the LORD says about the king who sits on David's throne and all the people who remain in this city, your countrymen who did not go with you into exile— 17 yes, this is what the LORD Almighty says: "I will send the sword, famine and plague[q] against them and I will make them like poor figs[r] that are so bad they cannot be eaten. 18 I will pursue them with the sword, famine and plague and will make them abhorrent[s] to all the kingdoms of the earth and an object of cursing and horror,[t] of scorn and reproach, among all the nations where I drive them. 19 For they have not listened to my words,"[u] declares the LORD, "words that I sent to them again and again by my servants the prophets.[v] And you exiles have not listened either," declares the LORD.

20 Therefore, hear the word of the LORD, all you exiles whom I have sent[w] away from Jerusalem to Babylon. 21 This is what the LORD Almighty, the God of Israel, says about Ahab son of Kolaiah and Zedekiah son of Maaseiah, who are prophesying lies[x] to you in my name: "I will hand them over to Nebuchadnezzar king of Babylon, and he will put them to death before your very eyes. 22 Because of them, all the exiles from Judah who are in Babylon will use this curse: 'The LORD treat you like Zedekiah and Ahab, whom the king of Babylon burned[y] in the fire.' 23 For they have done outrageous things in Israel; they have committed adultery[z] with their neighbours' wives and in my name have spoken lies, which I did not tell them to do. I know[a] it and am a witness to it," declares the LORD.

Message to Shemaiah

24 Tell Shemaiah the Nehelamite, 25 "This is what the LORD Almighty, the God of Israel, says: You sent letters in your own name to all the people in Jerusalem, to Zephaniah[b] son of Maaseiah the priest, and to all the other priests. You said to Zephaniah, 26 'The LORD has appointed you priest in place of Jehoiada to be in charge of the house of the LORD; you should put any madman[c] who acts like a prophet into the stocks[d] and neck-irons. 27 So why have you not reprimanded Jeremiah from Anathoth, who poses as a prophet among you? 28 He has sent this message[e] to us in

a *14* Or *will restore your fortunes*

29:11 [k] Ps 40:5
29:12 [l] Ps 145:19
29:13 [m] Mt 7:7 [n] Dt 4:29; Jer 24:7
29:14 [o] Dt 30:3; Jer 30:3 [p] Jer 23:3-4
29:17 [q] Jer 27:8 [r] Jer 24:8-10
29:18 [s] Jer 15:4 [t] Dt 28:25; Jer 42:18
29:19 [u] Jer 6:19 [v] Jer 25:4
29:20 [w] Jer 24:5
29:21 [x] ver 9; Jer 14:14
29:22 [y] Da 3:6
29:23 [z] Jer 23:14 [a] Heb 4:13
29:25 [b] 2Ki 25:18; Jer 21:1
29:26 [c] 2Ki 9:11; Hos 9:7; Jn 10:20 [d] Jer 20:2
29:28 [e] ver 1

29:11 We're all encouraged by a leader who stirs us to move ahead; someone who believes we can do the task he has given and who will be with us all the way. God is that kind of leader. He knows the future, and his plans for us are good and full of hope. As long as God, who knows the future, provides our agenda and goes with us as we fulfil his mission, we can have boundless hope. This does not mean that we will be spared pain, suffering, or hardship, but that God will see us through to a glorious conclusion.

29:12–14 God did not forget his people, even though they were captive in Babylon. He planned to give them a new beginning with a new purpose—to turn them into new people. In times of deep trouble, it may appear as though God has forgotten you. But God may be preparing you, as he did the people of Judah, for a new beginning with him at the centre.

29:13 According to God's wise plan, his people were to have hope and a future; consequently they could call upon him in confidence. Although the exiles were in a difficult place and time, they should not despair because they had God's presence, the privilege of prayer, and God's grace. God can be found when we seek him wholeheartedly. Neither strange lands, sorrows, frustration, nor physical problems can break that communion.

29:21 These false prophets, Ahab and Zedekiah, should not be confused with the kings who had the same names. Their family connections clearly identify them.

29:24–28 These verses describe the reaction of Shemaiah, a false prophet exiled in 597 B.C. who had protested about Jeremiah's letter. To discredit Jeremiah, Shemaiah accused him of false prophecy. Although Jeremiah's message was true and his words were from God, the people hated him because he told them to make the most of the exile. But Jeremiah's truth from God offered temporary correction and long-term benefit, while the false teachers' lies offered only temporary comfort and long-term punishment.

Babylon: It will be a long time.[f] Therefore build[g] houses and settle down; plant
gardens and eat what they produce.' "
29Zephaniah the priest, however, read the letter to Jeremiah the prophet. 30Then
the word of the LORD came to Jeremiah: 31"Send this message to all the exiles: 'This
is what the LORD says about Shemaiah[h] the Nehelamite: Because Shemaiah has
prophesied to you, even though I did not send[i] him, and has led you to believe a
lie, 32this is what the LORD says: I will surely punish Shemaiah the Nehelamite and
his descendants.[j] He will have no-one left among this people, nor will he see the
good[k] things I will do for my people, declares the LORD, because he has preached
rebellion[l] against me.' "

5. Restoration is promised

Restoration of Israel

30 This is the word that came to Jeremiah from the LORD: 2"This is what the LORD,
the God of Israel, says: 'Write[a] in a book all the words I have spoken to you.
3The days are coming,' declares the LORD, 'when I will bring[b] my people Israel and
Judah back from captivity[a] and restore[c] them to the land I gave to their forefathers
to possess,' says the LORD."
4These are the words the LORD spoke concerning Israel and Judah: 5"This is what
the LORD says:

" 'Cries of fear[d] are heard—
terror, not peace.
6Ask and see:
Can a man bear children?
Then why do I see every strong man
with his hands on his stomach like a woman in labour,[e]
every face turned deathly pale?
7How awful that day[f] will be!
None will be like it.
It will be a time of trouble[g] for Jacob,
but he will be saved[h] out of it.

8" 'In that day,' declares the LORD Almighty,
'I will break the yoke[i] off their necks
and will tear off their bonds;
no longer will foreigners enslave them.[j]
9Instead, they will serve the LORD their God
and David[k] their king,[l]
whom I will raise up for them.

10" 'So do not fear,[m] O Jacob my servant;[n]
do not be dismayed, O Israel,'
declares the LORD.
'I will surely save[o] you out of a distant place,
your descendants from the land of their exile.
Jacob will again have peace and security,[p]
and no-one will make him afraid.
11I am with you and will save you,'
declares the LORD.

a 3 Or *will restore the fortunes of my people Israel and Judah*

29:28 [f]ver 10 [g]ver 5
29:31 [h]ver 24 [i]Jer 14:14; 28:15
29:32 [j]1Sa 2:30-33 [k]ver 10 [l]Jer 28:16
30:2 [a]Isa 30:8
30:3 [b]Jer 29:14 [c]Jer 16:15
30:5 [d]Jer 6:25
30:6 [e]Jer 4:31
30:7 [f]Isa 2:12; Joel 2:11 [g]Zep 1:15 [h]ver 10
30:8 [i]Isa 9:4 [j]Eze 34:27
30:9 [k]Isa 55:3-4; Lk 1:69; Ac 2:30; 13:23 [l]Eze 34:23-24; 37:24; Hos 3:5
30:10 [m]Isa 43:5; Jer 46:27-28 [n]Isa 44:2 [o]Jer 29:14 [p]Isa 35:9

30:1ff Chapters 30 and 31 show that Jeremiah spoke of hope and consolation as well as trouble and gloom. The people would one day be restored to their land, and God would make a new covenant with them to replace the one they broke. Where once they sinned and disobeyed, eventually they would repent and obey.

30:8, 9 Like Isaiah, Jeremiah associated events of the near future and those of the distant future. Reading these prophecies is like looking at several mountain peaks in a range. From a distance they look as though they are next to each other, when actually they are miles apart. Jeremiah presents near and distant events as if they will all happen soon. He sees the exile, but he also sees the future day when Christ will reign for ever. The reference to David is not to King David, but to his famous descendant, the Messiah (Luke 1:69).

'Though I completely destroy all the nations
among which I scatter you,
I will not completely destroy[q] you.
I will discipline[r] you but only with justice;
I will not let you go entirely unpunished.'[s]

12"This is what the LORD says:

" 'Your wound is incurable,
your injury beyond healing.[t]
13There is no-one to plead your cause,
no remedy for your sore,
no healing[u] for you.
14All your allies[v] have forgotten you;
they care nothing for you.
I have struck you as an enemy[w] would
and punished you as would the cruel,[x]
because your guilt is so great
and your sins[y] so many.
15Why do you cry out over your wound,
your pain that has no cure?
Because of your great guilt and many sins
I have done these things to you.

16" 'But all who devour[z] you will be devoured;
all your enemies will go into exile.[a]
Those who plunder[b] you will be plundered;
all who make spoil of you I will despoil.
17But I will restore you to health
and heal your wounds,'

declares the LORD,

'because you are called an outcast,[c]
Zion for whom no-one cares.'

18"This is what the LORD says:

" 'I will restore the fortunes[d] of Jacob's tents
and have compassion[e] on his dwellings;
the city will be rebuilt[f] on her ruins,
and the palace will stand in its proper place.
19From them will come songs[g] of thanksgiving[h]
and the sound of rejoicing.[i]
I will add to their numbers,[j]
and they will not be decreased;
I will bring them honour,[k]
and they will not be disdained.
20Their children[l] will be as in days of old,
and their community will be established[m] before me;
I will punish all who oppress them.
21Their leader[n] will be one of their own;

30:11 [q]Jer 4:27; 46:28 [r]Jer 10:24 [s]Am 9:8
30:12 [t]Jer 15:18
30:13 [u]Jer 8:22; 14:19; 46:11
30:14 [v]Jer 22:20; La 1:2 [w]Job 13:24 [x]Job 30:21 [y]Jer 5:6
30:16 [z]Isa 33:1; Jer 2:3; 10:25 [a]Isa 14:2; Joel 3:4-8 [b]Jer 50:10
30:17 [c]Jer 33:24
30:18 [d]ver 3; Jer 31:23 [e]Ps 102:13 [f]Jer 31:4, 24, 38
30:19 [g]Isa 35:10; 51:11 [h]Isa 51:3 [i]Ps 126:1-2; Jer 31:4 [j]Jer 33:22 [k]Isa 60:9
30:20 [l]Isa 54:13; Jer 31:17 [m]Isa 54:14
30:21 [n]ver 9

30:12, 13, 17 The medical language here conveys the idea that sin is terminal. Sinful people cannot be cured by being good or being religious. Beware of putting your confidence in useless cures while your sin spreads and causes you pain. God alone can cure the disease of sin, but you must be willing to let him do it.

30:15 Judah protested against their punishment, even though the sin that caused the pain was scandalous. But punishment is an opportunity for growth because it makes us aware of sin's consequences. The people should have asked how they could profit from their mistakes. Remember this the next time you are corrected.

30:18 This prophecy that Jerusalem would be rebuilt was not completely fulfilled by the work of Ezra, Nehemiah, and Zerubbabel. The city was indeed rebuilt after the captivity, but the final restoration will occur when all believers are gathered in Christ's kingdom. This restoration will include buildings (30:18), people (30:19), and rulers (30:21).

30:21 This verse refers to the restoration after the Babylonian captivity, as well as to the final restoration under Christ.

30:21 [o]Nu 16:5
30:23 [p]Jer 23:19
30:24 [q]Jer 4:8 [r]Jer 4:28 [s]Jer 23:19-20
31:1 [a]Jer 30:22
31:2 [b]Nu 14:20 [c]Ex 33:14
31:3 [d]Dt 4:37 [e]Hos 11:4
31:4 [f]Jer 30:19
31:5 [g]Jer 50:19 [h]Isa 65:21; Am 9:14
31:6 [i]Isa 2:3; Jer 50:4-5; Mic 4:2
31:7 [j]Dt 28:13; Isa 61:9 [k]Ps 14:7; 28:9 [l]Isa 37:31
31:8 [m]Jer 3:18; 23:8 [n]Dt 30:4; Eze 34:12-14

their ruler will arise from among them.
I will bring him near[o] and he will come close to me,
for who is he who will devote himself
to be close to me?'

declares the LORD.

22" 'So you will be my people,
and I will be your God.' "

23See, the storm[p] of the LORD
will burst out in wrath,
a driving wind swirling down
on the heads of the wicked.
24The fierce anger[q] of the LORD will not turn back[r]
until he fully accomplishes
the purposes of his heart.
In days to come
you will understand[s] this.

31 "At that time," declares the LORD, "I will be the God[a] of all the clans of Israel,
and they will be my people."
2This is what the LORD says:

"The people who survive the sword
will find favour[b] in the desert;
I will come to give rest[c] to Israel."

3The LORD appeared to us in the past,[a] saying:

"I have loved[d] you with an everlasting love;
I have drawn[e] you with loving-kindness.
4I will build you up again
and you will be rebuilt, O Virgin Israel.
Again you will take up your tambourines
and go out to dance with the joyful.[f]
5Again you will plant vineyards
on the hills of Samaria;[g]
the farmers will plant them
and enjoy their fruit.[h]
6There will be a day when watchmen cry out
on the hills of Ephraim,
'Come, let us go up to Zion,
to the LORD our God.' "[i]

7This is what the LORD says:

"Sing with joy for Jacob;
shout for the foremost[j] of the nations.
Make your praises heard, and say,
'O LORD, save[k] your people,
the remnant[l] of Israel.'
8See, I will bring them from the land of the north[m]
and gather[n] them from the ends of the earth.

a *3* Or *LORD has appeared to us from afar*

31:1 This promise is to all the clans (tribes) of Israel, not only to the tribe of Judah. The restoration will include all people who trust God.

31:3 God reaches towards his people with kindness motivated by deep and everlasting love. He is eager to do the best for them if they will only let him. After many words of warning about sin, this reminder of God's magnificent love is a breath of fresh air. Rather than thinking of God with dread, look carefully and see him lovingly drawing us towards himself.

Among them will be the blind[o] and the lame,[p]
expectant mothers and women in labour;
a great throng will return.
9They will come with weeping;[q]
they will pray as I bring them back.
I will lead[r] them beside streams of water
on a level[s] path where they will not stumble,
because I am Israel's father,[t]
and Ephraim is my firstborn son.

10"Hear the word of the LORD, O nations;
proclaim it in distant coastlands:[u]
'He who scattered Israel will gather[v] them
and will watch over his flock like a shepherd.'[w]
11For the LORD will ransom Jacob
and redeem[x] them from the hand of those stronger[y] than they.
12They will come and shout for joy on the heights[z] of Zion;
they will rejoice in the bounty[a] of the LORD—
the grain, the new wine and the oil,[b]
the young of the flocks and herds.
They will be like a well-watered garden,[c]
and they will sorrow[d] no more.
13Then maidens will dance and be glad,
young men and old as well.
I will turn their mourning[e] into gladness;
I will give them comfort and joy[f] instead of sorrow.
14I will satisfy[g] the priests with abundance,
and my people will be filled with my bounty,"
declares the LORD.

15This is what the LORD says:

"A voice is heard in Ramah,[h]
mourning and great weeping,
Rachel weeping for her children
and refusing to be comforted,[i]
because her children are no more."[j]

16This is what the LORD says:

"Restrain your voice from weeping
and your eyes from tears,[k]
for your work will be rewarded,[l]"
declares the LORD.
"They will return[m] from the land of the enemy.
17So there is hope for your future,"
declares the LORD.
"Your children will return to their own land.

18"I have surely heard Ephraim's moaning:
'You disciplined[n] me like an unruly calf,[o]

31:8 [o]Isa 42:16 [p]Eze 34:16; Mic 4:6
31:9 [q]Ps 126:5 [r]Isa 63:13 [s]Isa 49:11 [t]Ex 4:22; Jer 3:4
31:10 [u]Isa 66:19; Jer 25:22 [v]Jer 50:19 [w]Isa 40:11; Eze 34:12
31:11 [x]Isa 44:23; 48:20 [y]Ps 142:6
31:12 [z]Eze 17:23; Mic 4:1 [a]Joel 3:18 [b]Hos 2:21-22 [c]Isa 58:11 [d]Isa 65:19; Jn 16:22; Rev 7:17
31:13 [e]Isa 61:3 [f]Ps 30:11; Isa 51:11
31:14 [g]ver 25
31:15 [h]Jos 18:25 [i]Ge 37:35 [j]Jer 10:20; Mt 2:17-18*
31:16 [k]Isa 25:8; 30:19 [l]Ru 2:12 [m]Jer 30:3; Eze 11:17
31:18 [n]Job 5:17 [o]Hos 4:16

31:14 This means that many sacrifices will be made at the temple so that the priests will have a feast with their portion. It is also a symbol of life and prosperity (Psalm 36:8; 63:5; Isaiah 55:2).

31:15 Rachel, Jacob's favourite wife, was the symbolic mother of the northern tribes, who were taken away by the Assyrians as slaves. Rachel is pictured crying for the exiles at Ramah, a staging point of deportation. This verse is quoted in Matthew 2:18 to describe the sadness of the mothers of Bethlehem as the male children were killed. The weeping was great in both cases.

31:18–20 "I beat my breast" was an expression picturing grief and mourning. Ephraim was one of the major tribes of the northern kingdom. Although the northern kingdom had sunk into the most degrading sins, God still loved the people. A remnant would turn to God, repenting of their sins, and God would forgive. God still loves you, despite anything you may have done. He will forgive you if you turn back to him.

and I have been disciplined.
Restore[p] me, and I will return,
because you are the LORD my God.
19 After I strayed,[q]
I repented;
after I came to understand,
I beat[r] my breast.
I was ashamed and humiliated
because I bore the disgrace of my youth.'
20 Is not Ephraim my dear son,
the child in whom I delight?
Though I often speak against him,
I still remember[s] him.
Therefore my heart yearns for him;
I have great compassion[t] for him,"
declares the LORD.

21 "Set up road signs;
put up guideposts.
Take note of the highway,[u]
the road that you take.
Return,[v] O Virgin[w] Israel,
return to your towns.
22 How long will you wander,[x]
O unfaithful[y] daughter?
The LORD will create a new thing on earth—
a woman will surround[b] a man."

23 This is what the LORD Almighty, the God of Israel, says: "When I bring them
back from captivity,[c][z] the people in the land of Judah and in its towns will once
again use these words: 'The LORD bless you, O righteous dwelling,[a] O sacred
mountain.'[b] 24 People will live[c] together in Judah and all its towns—farmers and
those who move about with their flocks. 25 I will refresh the weary and satisfy the
faint."[d]
26 At this I awoke[e] and looked around. My sleep had been pleasant to me.
27 "The days are coming," declares the LORD, "when I will plant[f] the house of Israel
and the house of Judah with the offspring of men and of animals. 28 Just as I watched
over them to uproot and tear down, and to overthrow, destroy and bring disaster,[g]
so I will watch over them to build and to plant,"[h] declares the LORD. 29 "In those days
people will no longer say,

'The fathers[i] have eaten sour grapes,
and the children's teeth are set on edge.'[j]

30 Instead, everyone will die for his own sin;[k] whoever eats sour grapes—his own
teeth will be set on edge.

31 "The time is coming," declares the LORD,
"when I will make a new covenant[l]
with the house of Israel
and with the house of Judah.
32 It will not be like the covenant[m]
I made with their forefathers[n]
when I took them by the hand

31:18 [p] Ps 80:3
31:19 [q] Eze 36:31 [r] Eze 21:12; Lk 18:13
31:20 [s] Hos 4:4; 11:8 [t] Isa 55:7; 63:15; Mic 7:18
31:21 [u] Jer 50:5 [v] Isa 52:11 [w] ver 4
31:22 [x] Jer 2:23 [y] Jer 3:6
31:23 [z] Jer 30:18 [a] Isa 1:26 [b] Ps 48:1; Zec 8:3
31:24 [c] Zec 8:4-8
31:25 [d] Jn 4:14
31:26 [e] Zec 4:1
31:27 [f] Eze 36:9-11; Hos 2:23
31:28 [g] Jer 18:8; 44:27 [h] Jer 1:10
31:29 [i] La 5:7 [j] Eze 18:2
31:30 [k] Isa 3:11; Gal 6:7
31:31 [l] Jer 32:40; Eze 37:26; Lk 22:20; Heb 8:8-12*; 10:16-17
31:32 [m] Ex 24:8 [n] Dt 5:3

b 22 Or *will go about ⌞seeking⌟*; or *will protect* **c** 23 Or *I restore their fortunes*

31:29, 30 The people tried to blame God's judgment on the sins of their fathers. One person's sin does indeed affect other people, but all people are still held personally accountable for the sin in their own lives (Deuteronomy 24:16; Ezekiel 18:2). What excuses do you use for your sins?

to lead them out of Egypt,
because they broke my covenant,
though I was a husband to[d] them,"[e]
declares the LORD.
33"This is the covenant that I will make with the house of Israel
after that time," declares the LORD.
"I will put my law in their minds
and write it on their hearts.[o]
I will be their God,
and they will be my people.[p]
34No longer will a man teach[q] his neighbour,
or a man his brother, saying, 'Know the LORD,'
because they will all know[r] me,
from the least of them to the greatest,"
declares the LORD.
"For I will forgive[s] their wickedness
and will remember their sins[t] no more."

35This is what the LORD says,

he who appoints[u] the sun
to shine by day,
who decrees the moon and stars
to shine by night,[v]
who stirs up the sea
so that its waves roar—
the LORD Almighty is his name:[w]
36"Only if these decrees[x] vanish from my sight,"
declares the LORD,
"will the descendants[y] of Israel ever cease
to be a nation before me."

37This is what the LORD says:

"Only if the heavens above can be measured[z]
and the foundations of the earth below be searched out
will I reject[a] all the descendants of Israel
because of all they have done,"
declares the LORD.

38"The days are coming," declares the LORD, "when this city will be rebuilt[b] for
me from the Tower of Hananel[c] to the Corner Gate.[d] 39The measuring line will
stretch from there straight to the hill of Gareb and then turn to Goah. 40The whole
valley[e] where dead bodies[f] and ashes are thrown, and all the terraces out to the
Kidron Valley[g] on the east as far as the corner of the Horse Gate,[h] will be holy[i]
to the LORD. The city will never again be uprooted or demolished."

d *32* Hebrew; Septuagint and Syriac *covenant, / and I turned away from* **e** *32* Or *was their master*

31:33 [o]2Co 3:3 [p]Jer 24:7; Heb 10:16
31:34 [q]1Jn 2:27 [r]Jn 6:45 [s]Isa 54:13; Jer 33:8; 50:20 [t]Ro 11:27; Mic 7:19; Heb 10:17*
31:35 [u]Ps 136:7-9 [v]Ge 1:16 [w]Jer 10:16
31:36 [x]Isa 54:9-10; Jer 33:20-26 [y]Ps 89:36-37
31:37 [z]Jer 33:22 [a]Jer 33:24-26; Ro 11:1-5
31:38 [b]Jer 30:18 [c]Ne 3:1 [d]2Ki 14:13; Zec 14:10
31:40 [e]Jer 7:31-32 [f]Jer 8:2 [g]2Sa 15:23; Jn 18:1 [h]2Ki 11:16 [i]Joel 3:17; Zec 14:21

31:33 God would write his law on their hearts rather than on tablets of stone, as he did the Ten Commandments. In 17:1 their sin was engraved on their hearts so that they wanted above all to disobey. This change seems to describe an experience very much like the new birth, with God taking the initiative. When we turn our lives over to God, he, by his Holy Spirit, builds into us the desire to obey him.

31:33 The old covenant, broken by the people, would be replaced by a new covenant. The foundation of this new covenant is Christ (Hebrews 8:6). It is revolutionary, involving not only Israel and Judah, but even the Gentiles. It offers a unique personal relationship with God himself, with his laws written on individuals' hearts instead of on stone. Jeremiah looked forward to the day when Jesus would come to establish this covenant. But for us today, this covenant is here. We have the wonderful opportunity to make a fresh start and establish a permanent, personal relationship with God (see 29:11; 32:38–40).

31:35–37 God has the power to do away with the decrees of nature or even to do away with his people. But he will do neither. This is not a prediction; it is a promise. This is God's way of saying that he will not reject Israel any more than he will do away with nature's laws. Neither will happen!

31:38–40 These points mark the boundaries of restored Jerusalem in the days of Nehemiah. Gareb and Goah are unknown. The valley of the dead bodies and ashes is probably the Valley of Ben Hinnom where children were sacrificed in pagan worship.

Jeremiah Buys a Field

32 This is the word that came to Jeremiah from the LORD in the tenth[a] year of
Zedekiah king of Judah, which was the eighteenth[b] year of Nebuchadnezzar.
2The army of the king of Babylon was then besieging Jerusalem, and Jeremiah the
prophet was confined in the courtyard of the guard[c] in the royal palace of Judah.
3Now Zedekiah king of Judah had imprisoned him there, saying, "Why do you
prophesy[d] as you do? You say, 'This is what the LORD says: I am about to hand this
city over to the king of Babylon, and he will capture[e] it. 4Zedekiah king of Judah
will not escape[f] out of the hands of the Babylonians**a** but will certainly be handed
over to the king of Babylon, and will speak with him face to face and see him with
his own eyes. 5He will take[g] Zedekiah to Babylon, where he will remain until I deal
with him, declares the LORD. If you fight against the Babylonians, you will not
succeed.' "[h]
6Jeremiah said, "The word of the LORD came to me: 7Hanamel son of Shallum your
uncle is going to come to you and say, 'Buy my field at Anathoth, because as nearest
relative it is your right and duty[i] to buy it.'
8"Then, just as the LORD had said, my cousin Hanamel came to me in the courtyard
of the guard and said, 'Buy my field at Anathoth in the territory of Benjamin. Since
it is your right to redeem it and possess it, buy it for yourself.'
"I knew that this was the word of the LORD; 9so I bought the field at Anathoth from
my cousin Hanamel and weighed out for him seventeen shekels**b** of silver.[j] 10I
signed and sealed the deed, had it witnessed,[k] and weighed out the silver on the
scales. 11I took the deed of purchase—the sealed copy containing the terms and
conditions, as well as the unsealed copy—12and I gave this deed to Baruch[l] son of
Neriah,[m] the son of Mahseiah, in the presence of my cousin Hanamel and of the
witnesses who had signed the deed and of all the Jews sitting in the courtyard of the
guard.
13"In their presence I gave Baruch these instructions: 14'This is what the LORD
Almighty, the God of Israel, says: Take these documents, both the sealed and unsealed
copies of the deed of purchase, and put them in a clay jar so that they will last a long
time. 15For this is what the LORD Almighty, the God of Israel, says: Houses, fields
and vineyards will again be bought in this land.'[n]
16"After I had given the deed of purchase to Baruch son of Neriah, I prayed to the
LORD:

17"Ah, Sovereign LORD,[o] you have made the heavens and the earth by your great
power and outstretched arm.[p] Nothing is too hard[q] for you. 18You show love[r]
to thousands but bring the punishment for the fathers' sins into the laps of their
children[s] after them. O great and powerful God, whose name is the LORD
Almighty,[t] 19great are your purposes and mighty are your deeds.[u] Your eyes
are open to all the ways of men;[v] you reward everyone according to his conduct
and as his deeds deserve.[w] 20You performed miraculous signs and wonders in
Egypt[x] and have continued them to this day, both in Israel and among all
mankind, and have gained the renown that is still yours. 21You brought your
people Israel out of Egypt with signs and wonders, by a mighty hand[y] and an

a *4* Or *Chaldeans*; also in verses 5, 24, 25, 28, 29 and 43 **b** *9* That is, about 7 ounces (about 200 grams)

32:1 [a]2Ki 25:1 [b]Jer 25:1; 39:1
32:2 [c]Ne 3:25; Jer 37:21
32:3 [d]Jer 26:8-9 [e]ver 28; Jer 34:2-3
32:4 [f]Jer 38:18, 23; 39:5-7; 52:9
32:5 [g]Jer 39:7; Eze 12:13 [h]Jer 21:4
32:7 [i]Lev 25:24-25; Ru 4:3-4; Mt 27:10*
32:9 [j]Ge 23:16
32:10 [k]Ru 4:9
32:12 [l]ver 16; Jer 36:4; 43:3, 6; 45:1 [m]Jer 51:59
32:15 [n]ver 43-44; Jer 30:18; Am 9:14-15
32:17 [o]Jer 1:6 [p]2Ki 19:15; Ps 102:25 [q]Mt 19:26
32:18 [r]Dt 5:10 [s]Ex 20:5 [t]Jer 10:16
32:19 [u]Isa 28:29 [v]Pr 5:21; Jer 16:17 [w]Jer 17:10; Mt 16:27
32:20 [x]Ex 9:16
32:21 [y]Ex 6:6; 1Ch 17:21; Da 9:15

32:1–12 God told Jeremiah to buy a field outside Jerusalem. The city had been under siege for a year, and Jeremiah bought land that the soldiers occupied—certainly a poor investment. In addition, Jeremiah was a prisoner in the palace. But Jeremiah was demonstrating his faith in God's promises to bring his people back and to rebuild Jerusalem.

32:6–17 Trust doesn't come easy. It wasn't easy for Jeremiah to publicly buy land already captured by the enemy. But he trusted God. It wasn't easy for David to believe that he would become king, even after he was anointed. But he trusted God (1 Samuel 16–31). It wasn't easy for Moses to believe that he and his people would escape Egypt, even after God spoke to him from a burning bush. But he trusted God (Exodus 3:1–4:20). It isn't easy for us to believe that God can fulfil his "impossible" promises either, but we must trust him. God, who worked in the lives of biblical heroes, will work in our lives too, if we will let him.

32:17–25 After Jeremiah bought the field, he began to wonder if such a move was wise. He sought relief in prayer from his nagging doubts. In this prayer, Jeremiah affirmed that God is Creator (32:17), the wise Judge of all the ways of people (32:19), and Redeemer (32:21). God loves us and sees our situation. Whenever we doubt God's wisdom or wonder if it is practical to obey him, we can review what we already know about him. Such thoughts and prayers will quiet our doubts and calm our fears.

outstretched arm and with great terror.[z] 22You gave them this land you had
sworn to give to their forefathers, a land flowing with milk and honey.[a] 23They
came in and took possession[b] of it, but they did not obey you or follow your
law;[c] they did not do what you commanded them to do. So you brought all this
disaster[d] upon them.
24"See how the siege ramps are built up to take the city. Because of the sword,
famine and plague,[e] the city will be handed over to the Babylonians who are
attacking it. What you said[f] has happened, as you now see. 25And though the
city will be handed over to the Babylonians, you, O Sovereign LORD, say to me,
'Buy the field with silver and have the transaction witnessed.' "

26Then the word of the LORD came to Jeremiah: 27"I am the LORD, the God of all
mankind.[g] Is anything too hard for me? 28Therefore, this is what the LORD says: I
am about to hand this city over to the Babylonians and to Nebuchadnezzar[h] king of
Babylon, who will capture it.[i] 29The Babylonians who are attacking this city will
come in and set it on fire; they will burn it down,[j] along with the houses[k] where
the people provoked me to anger by burning incense on the roofs to Baal and by
pouring out drink offerings[l] to other gods.
30"The people of Israel and Judah have done nothing but evil in my sight from their
youth;[m] indeed, the people of Israel have done nothing but provoke[n] me with what
their hands have made,[o] declares the LORD. 31From the day it was built until now,
this city has so aroused my anger and wrath that I must remove[p] it from my sight.
32The people of Israel and Judah have provoked me by all the evil[q] they have
done—they, their kings and officials, their priests and prophets, the men of Judah and
the people of Jerusalem. 33They turned their backs[r] to me and not their faces; though
I taught[s] them again and again, they would not listen or respond to discipline. 34They
set up their abominable idols in the house that bears my Name and defiled[t] it. 35They
built high places for Baal in the Valley of Ben Hinnom to sacrifice their sons and
daughters**[c]** to Molech,[u] though I never commanded, nor did it enter my mind,[v] that
they should do such a detestable thing and so make Judah sin.
36"You are saying about this city, 'By the sword, famine and plague[w] it will be
handed over to the king of Babylon'; but this is what the LORD, the God of Israel,
says: 37I will surely gather[x] them from all the lands where I banish them in my furious
anger and great wrath; I will bring them back to this place and let them live in safety.[y]
38They will be my people,[z] and I will be their God. 39I will give them singleness[a]
of heart and action, so that they will always fear me for their own good and the good
of their children after them. 40I will make an everlasting covenant[b] with them: I will
never stop doing good to them, and I will inspire them to fear me, so that they will
never turn away from me.[c] 41I will rejoice in doing them good[d] and will assuredly
plant[e] them in this land with all my heart and soul.
42"This is what the LORD says: As I have brought all this great calamity on this
people, so I will give them all the prosperity I have promised[f] them. 43Once more
fields will be bought[g] in this land of which you say, 'It is a desolate waste, without
men or animals, for it has been handed over to the Babylonians.' 44Fields will be
bought for silver, and deeds[h] will be signed, sealed and witnessed in the territory of
Benjamin, in the villages around Jerusalem, in the towns of Judah and in the towns
of the hill country, of the western foothills and of the Negev,[i] because I will restore[j]
their fortunes,**[d]** declares the LORD."

c *35 Or to make their sons and daughters pass through the fire,* **d** *44 Or will bring them back from captivity*

32:21 [z]Dt 26:8
32:22 [a]Ex 3:8; Jer 11:5
32:23 [b]Ps 44:2; 78:54-55 [c]Ne 9:26; Jer 11:8 [d]Da 9:14
32:24 [e]Jer 14:12 [f]Dt 4:25-26; Jos 23:15-16
32:27 [g]Nu 16:22
32:28 [h]2Ch 36:17 [i]ver 3
32:29 [j]2Ch 36:19; Jer 21:10; 37:8, 10; 52:13 [k]Jer 19:13 [l]Jer 44:18
32:30 [m]Jer 22:21 [n]Jer 8:19 [o]Jer 25:7
32:31 [p]2Ki 23:27; 24:3
32:32 [q]Isa 1:4-6; Da 9:8
32:33 [r]Jer 2:27; Eze 8:16 [s]Jer 7:13
32:34 [t]Jer 7:30
32:35 [u]Lev 18:21 [v]Jer 7:31; 19:5
32:36 [w]ver 24
32:37 [x]Jer 23:3, 6 [y]Dt 30:3; Eze 34:28
32:38 [z]Jer 24:7; 2Co 6:16*
32:39 [a]Eze 11:19
32:40 [b]Isa 55:3 [c]Jer 24:7
32:41 [d]Dt 30:9 [e]Jer 24:6; 31:28; Am 9:15
32:42 [f]Jer 31:28
32:43 [g]ver 15
32:44 [h]ver 10 [i]Jer 17:26 [j]Jer 33:7, 11, 26

32:35 These high places were where the most important and grotesque part of Molech worship took place. Children were offered in sacrifice to this pagan god.

32:36–42 God uses his power to accomplish *his* purposes through *his* people. God doesn't give you power to be all you want to be, but he gives you power to be all *he* wants you to be. The people of Israel had to learn that trusting God meant radically realigning their purposes and desires towards him. God gave them "singleness of heart" towards him (32:39). We must develop that singleness of heart and action to love God above anything else.

32:44 The hill country is in western Palestine. The Negev is the southern part of Judah.

33:1 [a]Jer 32:2-3; 37:21; 38:28
33:2 [b]Jer 10:16 [c]Ex 3:15; 15:3
33:3 [d]Isa 55:6; Jer 29:12
33:4 [e]Eze 4:2 [f]Jer 32:24; Hab 1:10
33:5 [g]Jer 21:4-7 [h]Isa 8:17
33:7 [i]Jer 32:44 [j]Jer 30:3; Am 9:14 [k]Isa 1:26
33:8 [l]Heb 9:13-14 [m]Jer 31:34; Mic 7:18; Zec 13:1
33:9 [n]Jer 13:11 [o]Isa 62:7; Jer 3:17
33:10 [p]Jer 32:43
33:11 [q]Isa 51:3 [r]Lev 7:12 [s]1Ch 16:8; Ps 136:1 [t]1Ch 16:34; 2Ch 5:13; Ps 100:4-5
33:12 [u]Jer 32:43 [v]Isa 65:10; Eze 34:11-15
33:13 [w]Jer 17:26 [x]Lev 27:32
33:14 [y]Jer 29:10
33:15 [z]Ps 72:2 [a]Isa 4:2; 11:1; Jer 23:5
33:16 [b]Isa 45:17 [c]1Co 1:30
33:17 [d]2Sa 7:13; 1Ki 2:4; Ps 89:29-37; Lk 1:33

Promise of Restoration

33 While Jeremiah was still confined in the courtyard[a] of the guard, the word of
the LORD came to him a second time:
2“This is what the LORD says, he who
made the earth,[b] the LORD who formed it and established it—the LORD is his name:[c]
3‘Call[d] to me and I will answer you and tell you great and unsearchable things you
do not know.’
4For this is what the LORD, the God of Israel, says about the houses
in this city and the royal palaces of Judah that have been torn down to be used against
the siege[e] ramps[f] and the sword
5in the fight with the Babylonians:**a** ‘They will
be filled with the dead bodies of the men I will slay in my anger and wrath.[g] I will
hide my face[h] from this city because of all its wickedness.

6“ ‘Nevertheless, I will bring health and healing to it; I will heal my people and
will let them enjoy abundant peace and security.
7I will bring Judah[i] and Israel back
from captivity**b**[j] and will rebuild them as they were before.[k]
8I will cleanse[l] them
from all the sin they have committed against me and will forgive[m] all their sins of
rebellion against me.
9Then this city will bring me renown, joy, praise[n] and honour[o]
before all nations on earth that hear of all the good things I do for it; and they will
be in awe and will tremble at the abundant prosperity and peace I provide for it.’

10“This is what the LORD says: ‘You say about this place, “It is a desolate waste,
without men or animals.”[p] Yet in the towns of Judah and the streets of Jerusalem
that are deserted, inhabited by neither men nor animals, there will be heard once more
11the sounds of joy and gladness,[q] the voices of bride and bridegroom, and the voices
of those who bring thank-offerings[r] to the house of the LORD, saying,

> “Give thanks to the LORD Almighty,
> for the LORD is good;[s]
> his love endures for ever.”[t]

For I will restore the fortunes of the land as they were before,’ says the LORD.

12“This is what the LORD Almighty says: ‘In this place, desolate[u] and without men
or animals—in all its towns there will again be pastures for shepherds to rest their
flocks.[v]
13In the towns of the hill country, of the western foothills and of the Negev,[w]
in the territory of Benjamin, in the villages around Jerusalem and in the towns of
Judah, flocks will again pass under the hand[x] of the one who counts them,’ says the
LORD.

14“ ‘The days are coming,’ declares the LORD, ‘when I will fulfil the gracious
promise[y] I made to the house of Israel and to the house of Judah.

> 15“ ‘In those days and at that time
> I will make a righteous[z] Branch[a] sprout from David’s line;
> he will do what is just and right in the land.
> 16In those days Judah will be saved[b]
> and Jerusalem will live in safety.
> This is the name by which it**c** will be called:
> The LORD Our Righteousness.’[c]

17For this is what the LORD says: ‘David will never fail[d] to have a man to sit on the

a 5 Or *Chaldeans* **b** 7 Or *will restore the fortunes of Judah and Israel* **c** 16 Or *he*

33:1ff God would restore Jerusalem, not because the people cried, but because it was part of his ultimate plan. The Babylonian disaster did not change God’s purposes for his people. Although Jerusalem would be destroyed, it would be restored (after the 70-year captivity and in the end times when the Messiah will rule). God’s justice is always tempered by his mercy.

33:3 God assured Jeremiah that he had only to call to God and God would answer (see also Psalm 145:18; Isaiah 58:9; Matthew 7:7). God is ready to answer our prayers, but we must ask for his assistance. Surely God could take care of our needs without our asking. But when we ask, we are acknowledging that he alone is God and that we cannot accomplish in our own strength all that is his domain to do. When we ask, we must humble ourselves, lay aside our willfulness and worry, and determine to obey him.

33:15, 16 These verses refer to both the first and second comings of Christ. At his first coming he would set up his reign in the hearts of believers; at his second coming he would execute justice and righteousness throughout the whole earth. Christ is the “righteous Branch” sprouting from David, the man after God’s own heart.

throne of the house of Israel, 18 nor will the priests, who are Levites,[e] ever fail to
have a man to stand before me continually to offer burnt offerings, to burn grain
offerings and to present sacrifices.[f]"
19 The word of the LORD came to Jeremiah: 20 "This is what the LORD says: 'If you
can break my covenant with the day[g] and my covenant with the night, so that day
and night no longer come at their appointed time, 21 then my covenant[h] with David
my servant—and my covenant with the Levites who are priests ministering before
me—can be broken and David will no longer have a descendant to reign on his
throne.[i] 22 I will make the descendants of David my servant and the Levites who
minister before me as countless[j] as the stars of the sky and as measureless as the sand
on the seashore.'"
23 The word of the LORD came to Jeremiah: 24 "Have you not noticed that these
people are saying, 'The LORD has rejected the two kingdoms[d][k] he chose'? So they
despise[l] my people and no longer regard them as a nation.[m] 25 This is what the LORD
says: 'If I have not established my covenant with day and night[n] and the fixed laws
of heaven and earth,[o] 26 then I will reject[p] the descendants of Jacob[q] and David my
servant and will not choose one of his sons to rule over the descendants of Abraham,
Isaac and Jacob. For I will restore their fortunes[e][r] and have compassion on them.'"

6. God's promised judgment arrives

Warning to Zedekiah

34 While Nebuchadnezzar king of Babylon and all his army and all the kingdoms
and peoples[a] in the empire he ruled were fighting against Jerusalem[b] and all
its surrounding towns, this word came to Jeremiah from the LORD: 2 "This is what the
LORD, the God of Israel, says: Go to Zedekiah[c] king of Judah and tell him, 'This
is what the LORD says: I am about to hand this city over to the king of Babylon, and
he will burn it down.[d] 3 You will not escape from his grasp but will surely be captured
and handed over[e] to him. You will see the king of Babylon with your own eyes, and
he will speak with you face to face. And you will go to Babylon.
4 " 'Yet hear the promise of the LORD, O Zedekiah king of Judah. This is what the
LORD says concerning you: You will not die by the sword; 5 you will die peacefully.
As people made a funeral fire[f] in honour of your fathers, the former kings who
preceded you, so they will make a fire in your honour and lament, "Alas,[g] O master!"
I myself make this promise, declares the LORD.'"
6 Then Jeremiah the prophet told all this to Zedekiah king of Judah, in Jerusalem,

[d] 24 Or *families* [e] 26 Or *will bring them back from captivity*

33:18 [e] Dt 18:1 [f] Heb 13:15
33:20 [g] Ps 89:36
33:21 [h] Ps 89:34 [i] 2Ch 7:18
33:22 [j] Ge 15:5
33:24 [k] Eze 37:22 [l] Ne 4:4 [m] Jer 30:17
33:25 [n] Jer 31:35-36 [o] Ps 74:16-17
33:26 [p] Jer 31:37 [q] Isa 14:1 [r] ver 7
34:1 [a] Jer 27:7 [b] 2Ki 25:1; Jer 39:1
34:2 [c] 2Ch 36:11 [d] ver 22; Jer 32:29; 37:8
34:3 [e] 2Ki 25:7; Jer 21:7; 32:4
34:5 [f] 2Ch 16:14; 21:19 [g] Jer 22:18

33:18 As Christ fulfils the role of King, he also fulfils the role of Priest, maintaining constant fellowship with God and mediating for the people (see the note on 22:30). This verse does not mean that actual priests will perform sacrifices, for sacrifices will no longer be necessary (Hebrews 7:24, 25). Now that Christ is our High Priest, all believers are priests of God, and we can come before him personally.

34:1ff This chapter describes the fulfilment of many of Jeremiah's predictions. In the book of Jeremiah, many prophecies were both given and quickly fulfilled.

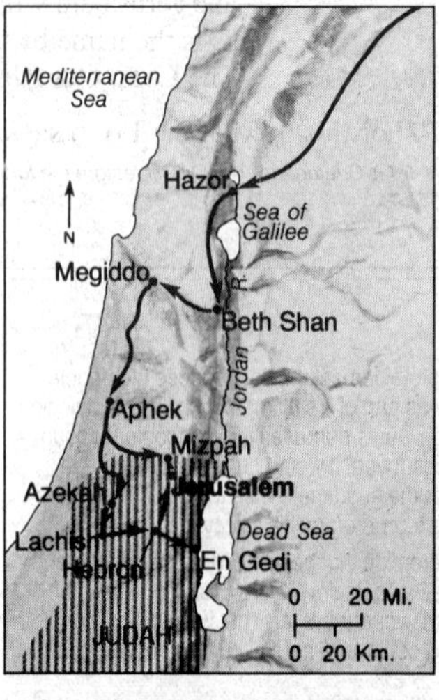

BABYLON ATTACKS JUDAH
Zedekiah incurred Babylon's wrath in allying with Egypt (37:5) and not surrendering as God told him through Jeremiah (38:17). Nebuchadnezzar attacked Judah for the third and final time, moving systematically until all its cities fell. Jerusalem withstood siege for several months but was burned, as Jeremiah predicted (chapter 39).

7while the army of the king of Babylon was fighting against Jerusalem and the other
cities of Judah that were still holding out—Lachish[h] and Azekah.[i] These were the
only fortified cities left in Judah.

Freedom for Slaves

8The word came to Jeremiah from the LORD after King Zedekiah had made a
covenant with all the people[j] in Jerusalem to proclaim freedom[k] for the slaves.
9Everyone was to free his Hebrew slaves, both male and female; no-one was to hold
a fellow Jew in bondage.[l] 10So all the officials and people who entered into this
covenant agreed that they would free their male and female slaves and no longer hold
them in bondage. They agreed, and set them free. 11But afterwards they changed their
minds and took back the slaves they had freed and enslaved them again.
12Then the word of the LORD came to Jeremiah: 13"This is what the LORD, the God
of Israel, says: I made a covenant with your forefathers[m] when I brought them out
of Egypt, out of the land of slavery. I said, 14'Every seventh year each of you must
free any fellow Hebrew who has sold himself to you. After he has served you for six
years, you must let him go free.'[a][n] Your fathers, however, did not listen to me or
pay attention[o] to me. 15Recently you repented and did what is right in my sight: Each
of you proclaimed freedom to his countrymen.[p] You even made a covenant before
me in the house that bears my Name.[q] 16But now you have turned round[r] and
profaned[s] my name; each of you has taken back the male and female slaves you had
set free to go where they wished. You have forced them to become your slaves again.
17"Therefore, this is what the LORD says: You have not obeyed me; you have not
proclaimed freedom for your fellow countrymen. So I now proclaim 'freedom' for
you,[t] declares the LORD—'freedom' to fall by the sword, plague and famine. I will
make you abhorrent to all the kingdoms of the earth.[u] 18The men who have violated
my covenant and have not fulfilled the terms of the covenant they made before me,
I will treat like the calf they cut in two and then walked between its pieces.[v] 19The
leaders of Judah and Jerusalem, the court officials,[w] the priests and all the people of
the land who walked between the pieces of the calf, 20I will hand over[x] to their
enemies who seek their lives.[y] Their dead bodies will become food for the birds of
the air and the beasts of the earth.[z]
21"I will hand Zedekiah[a] king of Judah and his officials[b] over to their enemies
who seek their lives, to the army of the king of Babylon, which has withdrawn[c] from
you. 22I am going to give the order, declares the LORD, and I will bring them back
to this city. They will fight against it, take[d] it and burn[e] it down. And I will lay
waste the towns of Judah so that no-one can live there."

The Recabites

35 This is the word that came to Jeremiah from the LORD during the reign of
Jehoiakim[a] son of Josiah king of Judah: 2"Go to the Recabite[b] family and
invite them to come to one of the side rooms[c] of the house of the LORD and give them
wine to drink."

a *14* Deut. 15:12

34:7 [h]Jos 10:3 [i]Jos 10:10; 2Ch 11:9
34:8 [j]2Ki 11:17 [k]Ex 21:2; Lev 25:10, 39-41; Ne 5:5-8
34:9 [l]Lev 25:39-46
34:13 [m]Ex 24:8
34:14 [n]Ex 21:2 [o]Dt 15:12; 2Ki 17:14
34:15 [p]ver 8 [q]Jer 7:10-11; 32:34
34:16 [r]Eze 3:20; 18:24 [s]Ex 20:7; Lev 19:12
34:17 [t]Mt 7:2; Gal 6:7 [u]Dt 28:25, 64; Jer 29:18
34:18 [v]Ge 15:10
34:19 [w]Zep 3:3-4
34:20 [x]Jer 21:7 [y]Jer 11:21 [z]Dt 28:26; Jer 7:33; 19:7
34:21 [a]Jer 32:4 [b]Jer 39:6; 52:24-27 [c]Jer 37:5
34:22 [d]Jer 39:1-2 [e]Jer 39:8
35:1 [a]2Ch 36:5
35:2 [b]2Ki 10:15; 1Ch 2:55 [c]1Ki 6:5

34:8, 9 Babylon had laid siege to Jerusalem, and the city was about to fall. Zedekiah finally decided to listen to Jeremiah and try to appease God—so he freed the slaves. He thought he could win God's favour with a kind act, but what he needed was a change of heart. The people had been disobeying God's law from the beginning (Exodus 21:2–11; Leviticus 25:39–55; Deuteronomy 15:12–18). When the siege was temporarily lifted, the people became bold and returned to their sins (34:11–17; 37:5, 11).

34:15, 16 The people of Israel had a hard time keeping their promises to God. In the temple, they would solemnly promise to obey God, but back in their homes and at work they wouldn't do it. God expressed his great displeasure. If you want to please God, make sure you keep your promises. God wants promises lived out, not just piously made.

34:18–20 Cutting a calf in two and walking between the halves was a customary way to ratify a contract (Genesis 15:9, 10). This action symbolised the judgment on anyone who broke the contract. God was saying, "You have broken the contract you made with me, so you know the judgment awaiting you!"

35:1ff The Recabites' code of conduct resembled that of the Nazirites, who took a special vow of dedication to God (Numbers 6). For 200 years, they had obeyed their ancestors' vow to abstain from wine. While the rest of the nation was breaking its covenant with God, these people were steadfast in their commitment. God wanted the rest of his people to remain as committed to their covenant with him as the Recabites were to their vow. God had Jeremiah tempt the Recabites with wine to demonstrate their commitment and dedication. God knew they wouldn't break their vow.

3 So I went to get Jaazaniah son of Jeremiah, the son of Habazziniah, and his
brothers and all his sons—the whole family of the Recabites. 4 I brought them into
the house of the LORD, into the room of the sons of Hanan son of Igdaliah the man
of God.[d] It was next to the room of the officials, which was over that of Maaseiah
son of Shallum[e] the door-keeper.[f] 5 Then I set bowls full of wine and some cups
before the men of the Recabite family and said to them, "Drink some wine."
6 But they replied, "We do not drink wine, because our forefather Jonadab[g] son
of Recab gave us this command: 'Neither you nor your descendants must ever drink
wine.[h] 7 Also you must never build houses, sow seed or plant vineyards; you must
never have any of these things, but must always live in tents.[i] Then you will live
a long time in the land[j] where you are nomads.' 8 We have obeyed everything our
forefather[k] Jonadab son of Recab commanded us. Neither we nor our wives nor our
sons and daughters have ever drunk wine 9 or built houses to live in or had vineyards,
fields or crops.[l] 10 We have lived in tents and have fully obeyed everything our
forefather Jonadab commanded us. 11 But when Nebuchadnezzar king of Babylon
invaded[m] this land, we said, 'Come, we must go to Jerusalem[n] to escape the
Babylonian[a] and Aramean armies.' So we have remained in Jerusalem."
12 Then the word of the LORD came to Jeremiah, saying: 13 "This is what the LORD
Almighty, the God of Israel, says: Go and tell the men of Judah and the people of
Jerusalem, 'Will you not learn a lesson[o] and obey my words?' declares the LORD.
14 'Jonadab son of Recab ordered his sons not to drink wine and this command has
been kept. To this day they do not drink wine, because they obey their forefather's
command. But I have spoken to you again and again,[p] yet you have not obeyed[q]
me. 15 Again and again I sent all my servants the prophets[r] to you. They said, "Each
of you must turn[s] from your wicked ways and reform[t] your actions; do not follow
other gods to serve them. Then you shall live in the land[u] I have given to you and
your fathers." But you have not paid attention or listened[v] to me. 16 The descendants
of Jonadab son of Recab have carried out the command their forefather[w] gave them,
but these people have not obeyed me.'
17 "Therefore, this is what the LORD God Almighty, the God of Israel, says: 'Listen!
I am going to bring on Judah and on everyone living in Jerusalem every disaster[x]
I pronounced against them. I spoke to them, but they did not listen;[y] I called to them,
but they did not answer.' "[z]
18 Then Jeremiah said to the family of the Recabites, "This is what the LORD
Almighty, the God of Israel, says: 'You have obeyed the command of your forefather
Jonadab and have followed all his instructions and have done everything he ordered.'
19 Therefore, this is what the LORD Almighty, the God of Israel, says: 'Jonadab son
of Recab shall never fail[a] to have a man to serve[b] me.' "

Jehoiakim Burns Jeremiah's Scroll

36 In the fourth year of Jehoiakim[a] son of Josiah king of Judah, this word came
to Jeremiah from the LORD: 2 "Take a scroll[b] and write on it all the words I
have spoken to you concerning Israel, Judah and all the other nations from the time

a *11* Or *Chaldean*

35:4 [d] Dt 33:1 [e] 1Ch 9:19 [f] 2Ki 12:9
35:6 [g] 2Ki 10:15 [h] Lev 10:9; Nu 6:2-4; Lk 1:15
35:7 [i] Heb 11:9 [j] Ex 20:12; Eph 6:2-3
35:8 [k] Pr 1:8; Col 3:20
35:9 [l] 1Ti 6:6
35:11 [m] 2Ki 24:1 [n] Jer 8:14
35:13 [o] Jer 6:10; 32:33
35:14 [p] Jer 7:13; 25:3 [q] Isa 30:9
35:15 [r] Jer 7:25 [s] Jer 26:3 [t] Isa 1:16-17; Jer 4:1; 18:11; Eze 18:30 [u] Jer 25:5 [v] Jer 7:26
35:16 [w] Mal 1:6
35:17 [x] Jos 23:15; Jer 21:4-7 [y] Pr 1:24; Ro 10:21 [z] Isa 65:12; 66:4; Jer 7:13
35:19 [a] Jer 33:17 [b] Jer 15:19
36:1 [a] 2Ch 36:5
36:2 [b] Ex 17:14; Jer 30:2; Hab 2:2

35:6 Jonadab son of Recab had joined Jehu in purging the northern kingdom of Baal worship (2 Kings 10:15–28).

35:13–17 There is a vivid contrast between the Recabites and the other Israelites. (1) The Recabites kept their vows to a fallible human leader; the people of Israel broke their covenant with their infallible divine Leader. (2) Jonadab once told his family not to drink, and they obeyed; God constantly commanded Israel to turn from sin, and they refused. (3) The Recabites obeyed laws that dealt with temporal issues; Israel refused to obey God's laws that dealt with eternal issues. (4) The Recabites had obeyed for hundreds of years; Israel had disobeyed for hundreds of years. (5) The Recabites would be rewarded; Israel would be punished. We are often willing to observe customs merely for the sake of tradition; how much more should we obey God's word because it is eternal.

36:1ff This happened in the summer of 605 B.C., shortly after Nebuchadnezzar's victory over the Egyptian army at Carchemish, before the events recorded in chapters 34 and 35.

36:2–4 Most people in ancient times could neither read nor write, so those who could were extremely valuable. These scribes held positions of great importance and were very respected for their knowledge. Baruch was Jeremiah's scribe. Writing was often done on vellum or papyrus sheets that were sewn or glued together and stored in long rolls called scrolls. After the exile, scribes became teachers of the law. In New Testament times, the scribes formed a powerful political party.

I began speaking to you in the reign of Josiah[c] till now. 3Perhaps[d] when the people of Judah hear[e] about every disaster I plan to inflict on them, each of them will turn[f] from his wicked way; then I will forgive[g] their wickedness and their sin."

4So Jeremiah called Baruch[h] son of Neriah, and while Jeremiah dictated[i] all the words the LORD had spoken to him, Baruch wrote them on the scroll.[j] 5Then Jeremiah told Baruch, "I am restricted; I cannot go to the LORD's temple. 6So you go to the house of the LORD on a day of fasting[k] and read to the people from the scroll the words of the LORD that you wrote as I dictated. Read them to all the people of Judah who come in from their towns. 7Perhaps they will bring their petition before the LORD, and each will turn[l] from his wicked ways, for the anger[m] and wrath pronounced against this people by the LORD are great."

8Baruch son of Neriah did everything Jeremiah the prophet told him to do; at the LORD's temple he read the words of the LORD from the scroll. 9In the ninth month[n] of the fifth year of Jehoiakim son of Josiah king of Judah, a time of fasting[o] before the LORD was proclaimed for all the people in Jerusalem and those who had come from the towns of Judah. 10From the room of Gemariah son of Shaphan the secretary,[p] which was in the upper courtyard at the entrance of the New Gate[q] of the temple, Baruch read to all the people at the LORD's temple the words of Jeremiah from the scroll.

11When Micaiah son of Gemariah, the son of Shaphan, heard all the words of the LORD from the scroll, 12he went down to the secretary's room in the royal palace, where all the officials were sitting: Elishama the secretary, Delaiah son of Shemaiah, Elnathan[r] son of Acbor, Gemariah son of Shaphan, Zedekiah son of Hananiah, and all the other officials. 13After Micaiah told them everything he had heard Baruch read to the people from the scroll, 14all the officials sent Jehudi[s] son of Nethaniah, the son of Shelemiah, the son of Cushi, to say to Baruch, "Bring the scroll from which you have read to the people and come." So Baruch son of Neriah went to them with the scroll in his hand. 15They said to him, "Sit down, please, and read it to us."

So Baruch read it to them. 16When they heard all these words, they looked at each other in fear and said to Baruch, "We must report all these words to the king." 17Then they asked Baruch, "Tell us, how did you come to write all this? Did Jeremiah dictate it?"

18"Yes," Baruch replied, "he dictated[t] all these words to me, and I wrote them in ink on the scroll."

19Then the officials said to Baruch, "You and Jeremiah, go and hide.[u] Don't let anyone know where you are."

20After they put the scroll in the room of Elishama the secretary, they went to the king in the courtyard and reported everything to him. 21The king sent Jehudi[v] to get the scroll, and Jehudi brought it from the room of Elishama the secretary and read it to the king[w] and all the officials standing beside him. 22It was the ninth month and the king was sitting in the winter apartment,[x] with a fire burning in the brazier in front of him. 23Whenever Jehudi had read three or four columns of the scroll, the king cut them off with a scribe's knife and threw them into the brazier, until the entire scroll was burned in the fire.[y] 24The king and all his attendants who heard all these words showed no fear,[z] nor did they tear their clothes.[a] 25Even though Elnathan, Delaiah and Gemariah urged the king not to burn the scroll, he would not listen to them.

36:2 c Jer 1:2; 25:3
36:3 d ver 7; Eze 12:3 e Mk 4:12 f Jer 26:3; Jnh 3:8; Ac 3:19 g Jer 18:8
36:4 h Jer 32:12 i ver 18 j Eze 2:9
36:6 k ver 9
36:7 l Jer 26:3 m Dt 31:17
36:9 n ver 22 o 2Ch 20:3
36:10 p Jer 52:25 q Jer 26:10
36:12 r Jer 26:22
36:14 s ver 21
36:18 t ver 4
36:19 u 1Ki 17:3
36:21 v ver 14 w 2Ki 22:10
36:22 x Am 3:15
36:23 y 1Ki 22:8
36:24 z Ps 36:1 a Ge 37:29; 2Ki 22:11; Isa 37:1

36:9 A time of fasting (when people abstained from eating food to show their humility and repentance) was often called during times of national emergency. Babylon was destroying city after city and closing in on Jerusalem. As the people came to the temple, Baruch told them how to avert the coming tragedy. But they refused to listen.

36:10–32 God told Jeremiah to write his words on a scroll. Because he was not allowed to go to the temple, Jeremiah asked his scribe, Baruch, to whom he had dictated the scroll to read it to the people gathered there. Baruch then read it to the officials, and finally Jehudi read it to the king himself. Although the king burned the scroll, he could not destroy the word of God. Today many people try to put God's word aside or say that it contains errors and therefore cannot be trusted. People may reject God's word, but they cannot destroy it. God's word will stand for ever (Psalm 119:89).

36:22 A brazier is a pan for holding burning coals, used to heat a room.

36:25 Only three leaders protested this evil act of burning the scroll containing God's word. This shows how complacent and insensitive to God the people had become.

26 Instead, the king commanded Jerahmeel, a son of the king, Seraiah son of Azriel
and Shelemiah son of Abdeel to arrest[b] Baruch the scribe and Jeremiah the prophet.
But the LORD had hidden[c] them.
27 After the king burned the scroll containing the words that Baruch had written at
Jeremiah's dictation,[d] the word of the LORD came to Jeremiah: 28 "Take another scroll
and write on it all the words that were on the first scroll, which Jehoiakim king of
Judah burned up. 29 Also tell Jehoiakim king of Judah, 'This is what the LORD says:
You burned that scroll and said, "Why did you write on it that the king of Babylon
would certainly come and destroy this land and cut off both men and animals from
it?"[e] 30 Therefore, this is what the LORD says about Jehoiakim king of Judah: He will
have no-one to sit on the throne of David; his body will be thrown out[f] and exposed
to the heat by day and the frost by night. 31 I will punish him and his children and his
attendants for their wickedness; I will bring on them and those living in Jerusalem and
the people of Judah every disaster[g] I pronounced against them, because they have
not listened.' "
32 So Jeremiah took another scroll and gave it to the scribe Baruch son of Neriah,
and as Jeremiah dictated,[h] Baruch wrote[i] on it all the words of the scroll that
Jehoiakim king of Judah had burned[j] in the fire. And many similar words were added
to them.

Jeremiah in Prison

37 Zedekiah[a] son of Josiah was made king[b] of Judah by Nebuchadnezzar king
of Babylon; he reigned in place of Jehoiachin**a**[c] son of Jehoiakim. 2 Neither
he nor his attendants nor the people of the land paid any attention[d] to the words the
LORD had spoken through Jeremiah the prophet.
3 King Zedekiah, however, sent Jehucal son of Shelemiah with the priest Zephaniah[e] son of Maaseiah to Jeremiah the prophet with this message: "Please pray[f] to
the LORD our God for us."
4 Now Jeremiah was free to come and go among the people, for he had not yet been
put in prison.[g] 5 Pharaoh's army had marched out of Egypt,[h] and when the Babylonians**b** who were besieging Jerusalem heard the report about them, they withdrew[i]
from Jerusalem.[j]
6 Then the word of the LORD came to Jeremiah the prophet: 7 "This is what the LORD,
the God of Israel, says: Tell the king of Judah, who sent you to enquire[k] of me,
'Pharaoh's army, which has marched out to support you, will go back to its own land,
to Egypt.[l] 8 Then the Babylonians will return and attack this city; they will capture
it and burn[m] it down.'
9 "This is what the LORD says: Do not deceive[n] yourselves, thinking, 'The Babylonians will surely leave us.' They will not! 10 Even if you were to defeat the entire
Babylonian**c** army that is attacking you and only wounded men were left in their tents,
they would come out and burn this city down."
11 After the Babylonian army had withdrawn[o] from Jerusalem because of Pharaoh's
army, 12 Jeremiah started to leave the city to go to the territory of Benjamin to get his

a *1* Hebrew *Coniah*, a variant of *Jehoiachin* **b** *5* Or *Chaldeans*; also in verses 8, 9, 13 and 14 **c** *10* Or *Chaldean*; also in verse 11

36:26 [b]Mt 23:34 [c]Jer 15:21
36:27 [d]ver 4
36:29 [e]Isa 30:10
36:30 [f]Jer 22:19
36:31 [g]Pr 29:1
36:32 [h]ver 4 [i]Ex 34:1 [j]ver 23
37:1 [a]2Ki 24:17 [b]Eze 17:13 [c]2Ki 24:8, 12; 2Ch 36:10; Jer 22:24
37:2 [d]2Ki 24:19; 2Ch 36:12, 14
37:3 [e]Jer 29:25; 52:24 [f]1Ki 13:6; Jer 21:1-2; 42:2
37:4 [g]ver 15; Jer 32:2
37:5 [h]Eze 17:15 [i]Jer 34:21 [j]2Ki 24:7
37:7 [k]2Ki 22:18 [l]Jer 2:36; La 4:17
37:8 [m]Jer 34:22; 39:8
37:9 [n]Jer 29:8
37:11 [o]ver 5

36:30 Jehoiakim's son, Jehoiachin, was king for three months before he was taken into captivity, but this did not qualify as sitting "on the throne of David" – an expression that implied permanence. Jehoiakim did not secure a dynasty. Zedekiah, the next ruler, was Jehoiachin's uncle. Thus the line of mortal human kings descended from David's son Solomon was finished, but in less than 600 years the eternal King would come through the descendants of Solomon's brother Nathan (see also the note on 22:30).

37:1ff King Jehoiakim died on the way to Babylon (2 Chronicles 36:6), and his son Jehoiachin was appointed king, but Jehoiachin was taken captive to Babylon three months later. Nebuchadnezzar then appointed Zedekiah as his vassal in Judah.

37:2, 3 King Zedekiah and his officials did not want to listen to Jeremiah's words, but they wanted the blessings of his prayers. They wanted a superficial religion that wouldn't cost anything. But God is not pleased with those who come to him only for what they can get rather than seeking to establish or deepen a relationship with him. We would not accept that kind of relationship with someone else, and we shouldn't expect God to accept it from us.

37:5 When Nebuchadnezzar besieged Jerusalem in 589 B.C., Pharaoh Hophra marched against him at Zedekiah's invitation. Jerusalem looked to Egypt for help in spite of Jeremiah's warnings. But the Egyptians were no help, for as soon as the Babylonians turned on them, they retreated. Jeremiah's warnings had been correct.

share of the property[p] among the people there. 13But when he reached the Benjamin
Gate, the captain of the guard, whose name was Irijah son of Shelemiah, the son of
Hananiah, arrested him and said, "You are deserting to the Babylonians!"
14"That's not true!" Jeremiah said. "I am not deserting to the Babylonians." But
Irijah would not listen to him; instead, he arrested[q] Jeremiah and brought him to the
officials. 15They were angry with Jeremiah and had him beaten[r] and imprisoned in
the house[s] of Jonathan the secretary, which they had made into a prison.
16Jeremiah was put into a vaulted cell in a dungeon, where he remained a long time.
17Then King Zedekiah sent for him and had him brought to the palace, where he
asked[t] him privately,[u] "Is there any word from the LORD?"
"Yes," Jeremiah replied, "you will be handed over[v] to the king of Babylon."
18Then Jeremiah said to King Zedekiah, "What crime[w] have I committed against
you or your officials or this people, that you have put me in prison? 19Where are your
prophets who prophesied to you, 'The king of Babylon will not attack you or this
land'? 20But now, my lord the king, please listen. Let me bring my petition before
you: Do not send me back to the house of Jonathan the secretary, or I shall die there."
21King Zedekiah then gave orders for Jeremiah to be placed in the courtyard of the
guard and given bread from the street of the bakers each day until all the bread[x] in
the city was gone.[y] So Jeremiah remained in the courtyard of the guard.[z]

Jeremiah Thrown Into a Cistern

38 Shephatiah son of Mattan, Gedaliah son of Pashhur, Jehucal[a][a] son of Shelemiah, and Pashhur son of Malkijah heard what Jeremiah was telling all the people
when he said, 2"This is what the LORD says: 'Whoever stays in this city will die by
the sword, famine or plague,[b] but whoever goes over to the Babylonians[b] will live.
He will escape with his life; he will live.'[c] 3And this is what the LORD says: 'This
city will certainly be handed over to the army of the king of Babylon, who will capture
it.' "[d]
4Then the officials[e] said to the king, "This man should be put to death.[f] He is
discouraging the soldiers who are left in this city, as well as all the people, by the
things he is saying to them. This man is not seeking the good of these people but their
ruin."
5"He is in your hands," King Zedekiah answered. "The king can do nothing to
oppose you."
6So they took Jeremiah and put him into the cistern of Malkijah, the king's son,
which was in the courtyard of the guard.[g] They lowered Jeremiah by ropes into the
cistern; it had no water in it, only mud, and Jeremiah sank down into the mud.
7But Ebed-Melech,[h] a Cushite,[c] an official[d][i] in the royal palace, heard that they
had put Jeremiah into the cistern. While the king was sitting in the Benjamin Gate,[j]

a *1* Hebrew *Jucal,* a variant of *Jehucal* b *2* Or *Chaldeans*; also in verses 18, 19 and 23 c *7* Probably from the upper Nile region d *7* Or *a eunuch*

37:12 [p]Jer 32:9
37:14 [q]Jer 40:4
37:15 [r]Jer 20:2 [s]Jer 38:26
37:17 [t]Jer 15:11 [u]Jer 38:16 [v]Jer 21:7
37:18 [w]1Sa 26:18; Jn 10:32; Ac 25:8
37:21 [x]Isa 33:16; Jer 38:9 [y]2Ki 25:3; Jer 52:6 [z]Jer 32:2; 38:6, 13, 28
38:1 [a]Jer 37:3
38:2 [b]Jer 34:17 [c]Jer 21:9; 39:18; 45:5
38:3 [d]Jer 21:4, 10; 32:3
38:4 [e]Jer 36:12 [f]Jer 26:11
38:6 [g]Jer 37:21
38:7 [h]Jer 39:16 [i]Ac 8:27 [j]Job 29:7

37:17 Zedekiah wavered between surrender and resistance. Too frightened and weak to exercise authority, he asked Jeremiah to come secretly to the palace, perhaps hoping for some better news from God. Zedekiah was desperate; he wanted to hear a word from the Lord, but he feared the political ramifications of being caught talking to Jeremiah.

38:4, 5 No wonder Judah was in turmoil: the king agreed with everybody. He listened to Jeremiah (37:21); then he agreed Jeremiah should be killed (38:5); and finally he rescued Jeremiah (38:10). Jeremiah was not popular; his words undermined the morale of the army and the people. Zedekiah couldn't decide between public opinion and God's will. What is most influential in your life—what others say and think or what God wants?

38:6 Officials put Jeremiah in a cistern to kill him. A cistern was a large hole in the ground lined with rocks to collect rainwater. The bottom would have been dark, damp, and, in this case, full of mud. Jeremiah could drown, die of exposure, or starve to death in the cistern.

38:6 Judah's leaders persecuted Jeremiah repeatedly for faithfully proclaiming God's messages. For 40 years of faithful ministry, he received no acclaim, no love, no popular following. He was beaten, jailed, threatened, and even forced to leave his homeland. Only the pagan Babylonians showed him any respect (39:11, 12). God does not guarantee that his servants will escape persecution, even when they are faithful. But God does promise that he will be with them and will give them strength to endure (2 Corinthians 1:3–7). As you minister to others, recognise that your service is for God and not just for human approval. God rewards our faithfulness, but not always during our stay on earth.

38:7, 8 The Benjamin Gate was one of Jerusalem's city gates where legal matters were handled. A palace official, Ebed-Melech, had access to the king. When Ebed-Melech heard of Jeremiah's plight, he went immediately to deal with the injustice.

8Ebed-Melech went out of the palace and said to him, 9"My lord the king, these men
have acted wickedly in all they have done to Jeremiah the prophet. They have thrown
him into a cistern, where he will starve to death when there is no longer any bread[k]
in the city."
10Then the king commanded Ebed-Melech the Cushite, "Take thirty men from here
with you and lift Jeremiah the prophet out of the cistern before he dies."
11So Ebed-Melech took the men with him and went to a room under the treasury
in the palace. He took some old rags and worn-out clothes from there and let them
down with ropes to Jeremiah in the cistern. 12Ebed-Melech the Cushite said to
Jeremiah, "Put these old rags and worn-out clothes under your arms to pad the ropes."
Jeremiah did so, 13and they pulled him up with the ropes and lifted him out of the
cistern. And Jeremiah remained in the courtyard of the guard.[l]

Zedekiah Questions Jeremiah Again

14Then King Zedekiah sent for Jeremiah the prophet and had him brought to the
third entrance to the temple of the LORD. "I am going to ask you something," the king
said to Jeremiah. "Do not hide[m] anything from me."
15Jeremiah said to Zedekiah, "If I give you an answer, will you not kill me? Even
if I did give you counsel, you would not listen to me."
16But King Zedekiah swore this oath secretly[n] to Jeremiah: "As surely as the LORD
lives, who has given us breath,[o] I will neither kill you nor hand you over to those
who are seeking your life."[p]
17Then Jeremiah said to Zedekiah, "This is what the LORD God Almighty, the God
of Israel, says: 'If you surrender to the officers of the king of Babylon, your life will
be spared and this city will not be burned down; you and your family will live.[q] 18But
if you will not surrender to the officers of the king of Babylon, this city will be handed
over[r] to the Babylonians and they will burn[s] it down; you yourself will not escape[t]
from their hands.' "
19King Zedekiah said to Jeremiah, "I am afraid[u] of the Jews who have gone over[v]
to the Babylonians, for the Babylonians may hand me over to them and they will
ill-treat me."
20"They will not hand you over," Jeremiah replied. "Obey[w] the LORD by doing
what I tell you. Then it will go well with you, and your life[x] will be spared. 21But
if you refuse to surrender, this is what the LORD has revealed to me: 22All the women[y]
left in the palace of the king of Judah will be brought out to the officials of the king
of Babylon. Those women will say to you:

" 'They misled you and overcame you—
those trusted friends of yours.
Your feet are sunk in the mud;
your friends have deserted you.'

23"All your wives and children[z] will be brought out to the Babylonians. You
yourself will not escape from their hands but will be captured[a] by the king of Babylon;
and this city will[e] be burned down."
24Then Zedekiah said to Jeremiah, "Do not let anyone know about this conversation, or you may die. 25If the officials hear that I talked with you, and they come to
you and say, 'Tell us what you said to the king and what the king said to you; do not
hide it from us or we will kill you,' 26then tell them, 'I was pleading with the king
not to send me back to Jonathan's house[b] to die there.' "
27All the officials did come to Jeremiah and question him, and he told them

e 23 Or *and you will cause this city to*

38:9 [k]Jer 37:21
38:13 [l]Jer 37:21
38:14 [m]1Sa 3:17
38:16 [n]Jer 37:17 [o]Isa 42:5; 57:16 [p]ver 4
38:17 [q]2Ki 24:12; Jer 21:9
38:18 [r]ver 3; Jer 34:3 [s]Jer 37:8 [t]Jer 24:8; 32:4
38:19 [u]Isa 51:12; Jn 12:42 [v]Jer 39:9
38:20 [w]Jer 11:4 [x]Isa 55:3
38:22 [y]Jer 6:12
38:23 [z]2Ki 25:6 [a]Jer 41:10
38:26 [b]Jer 37:15

38:9–13 Ebed-Melech feared God more than man. He alone among the palace officials stood up against the murder plot. His obedience could have cost him his life. Because he obeyed, however, he was spared when Jerusalem fell (39:15–18). You can either go along with the crowd or speak up for God. When someone is treated unkindly or unjustly, for example, reach out to that person with God's love. You may be the only one who does. And, when you are being treated unkindly yourself, be sure to thank God when he sends an "Ebed-Melech" your way.

38:27 The officials wanted accurate information, but not God's

everything the king had ordered him to say. So they said no more to him, for no-one
had heard his conversation with the king.
28 And Jeremiah remained in the courtyard of the guard[c] until the day Jerusalem
was captured.

The Fall of Jerusalem

39 This is how Jerusalem was taken: 1 In the ninth year of Zedekiah king of Judah,
in the tenth month, Nebuchadnezzar king of Babylon marched against Jerusalem with his whole army and laid siege[a] to it. 2 And on the ninth day of the fourth
month of Zedekiah's eleventh year, the city wall was broken through. 3 Then all the
officials[b] of the king of Babylon came and took seats in the Middle Gate: Nergal-
Sharezer of Samgar, Nebo-Sarsekim[a] a chief officer, Nergal-Sharezer a high official
and all the other officials of the king of Babylon. 4 When Zedekiah king of Judah and
all the soldiers saw them, they fled; they left the city at night by way of the king's
garden, through the gate between the two walls, and headed towards the Arabah.[b]
5 But the Babylonian[c] army pursued them and overtook Zedekiah[c] in the plains
of Jericho. They captured him and took him to Nebuchadnezzar king of Babylon at
Riblah[d] in the land of Hamath, where he pronounced sentence on him. 6 There at
Riblah the king of Babylon slaughtered the sons of Zedekiah before his eyes and also
killed all the nobles of Judah. 7 Then he put out Zedekiah's eyes[e] and bound him with
bronze shackles to take him to Babylon.[f]
8 The Babylonians[d] set fire[g] to the royal palace and the houses of the people and
broke down the walls[h] of Jerusalem. 9 Nebuzaradan commander of the imperial guard
carried into exile to Babylon the people who remained in the city, along with those
who had gone over to him, and the rest of the people.[i] 10 But Nebuzaradan the
commander of the guard left behind in the land of Judah some of the poor people,
who owned nothing; and at that time he gave them vineyards and fields.
11 Now Nebuchadnezzar king of Babylon had given these orders about Jeremiah
through Nebuzaradan commander of the imperial guard: 12 "Take him and look after
him; don't harm[j] him but do for him whatever he asks." 13 So Nebuzaradan the
commander of the guard, Nebushazban a chief officer, Nergal-Sharezer a high official
and all the other officers of the king of Babylon 14 sent and had Jeremiah taken out
of the courtyard of the guard.[k] They handed him over to Gedaliah son of Ahikam,[l]
the son of Shaphan, to take him back to his home. So he remained among his own
people.[m]
15 While Jeremiah had been confined in the courtyard of the guard, the word of the
LORD came to him: 16 "Go and tell Ebed-Melech[n] the Cushite, 'This is what the LORD
Almighty, the God of Israel, says: I am about to fulfil my words against this city
through disaster,[o] not prosperity. At that time they will be fulfilled before your eyes.

a 3 Or *Nergal-Sharezer, Samgar-Nebo, Sarsekim* b 4 Or *the Jordan Valley* c 5 Or *Chaldean* d 8 Or *Chaldeans*

38:28 c Jer 37:21; 39:14
39:1 a 2Ki 25:1; Jer 52:4; Eze 24:2
39:3 b Jer 21:4
39:5 c Jer 32:4 d 2Ki 23:33
39:7 e Eze 12:13 f Jer 32:5
39:8 g Jer 38:18 h Ne 1:3
39:9 i Jer 40:1
39:12 j Pr 16:7; 1Pe 3:13
39:14 k Jer 38:28 l 2Ki 22:12 m Jer 40:5
39:16 n Jer 38:7 o Jer 21:10; Da 9:12

---

truth. They wanted to use this information against God, his prophet, and the king. But Jeremiah told the officials only what the king ordered him to say. We must not withhold God's truth from others, but we should withhold information that will be used to bring evil to God's people.

39:1ff Zedekiah, son of Josiah and last king of Judah, ruled for 11 years, from 597 to 586 B.C. Zedekiah's two older brothers, Jehoahaz and Jehoiakim, and his nephew Jehoiachin ruled before him. When Jehoiachin was exiled to Babylon, Nebuchadnezzar made 21-year-old Mattaniah the king, changing his name to Zedekiah. Zedekiah rebelled against Nebuchadnezzar, who captured him, killed his sons in front of him, and then blinded him and took him back to Babylon where he later died (see 2 Kings 24; 25; 2 Chronicles 36; and Jeremiah 52).

39:5 Riblah was 200 miles north of Jerusalem. This was the Babylonian headquarters for ruling the region.

39:10 Babylon had a shrewd foreign policy towards conquered lands. They deported the rich and powerful, leaving only the very poor in charge, thus making them grateful to their conquerors. This policy assured that conquered populations would be too loyal and too weak to revolt.

39:11, 12 God had promised to rescue Jeremiah from his trouble (1:8). The superstitious Babylonians, who highly respected magicians and fortune-tellers, treated Jeremiah as a seer. Because he had been imprisoned by his own people, they assumed he was a traitor and on their side. They undoubtedly knew he had counselled co-operation with Babylon and predicted a Babylonian victory. So the Babylonians freed Jeremiah and protected him.

39:13, 14 What a difference there is between Jeremiah's fate and Zedekiah's! Jeremiah was freed; Zedekiah was imprisoned. Jeremiah was saved because of his faith; Zedekiah was destroyed because of his fear. Jeremiah was treated with respect; Zedekiah was treated with contempt. Jeremiah was concerned for the people; Zedekiah was concerned for himself.

17But I will rescue[p] you on that day, declares the LORD; you will not be handed over
to those you fear. 18I will save you; you will not fall by the sword[q] but will escape
with your life,[r] because you trust[s] in me, declares the LORD.' "

Jeremiah Freed

40 The word came to Jeremiah from the LORD after Nebuzaradan commander of
the imperial guard had released him at Ramah. He had found Jeremiah bound
in chains among all the captives from Jerusalem and Judah who were being carried
into exile to Babylon. 2When the commander of the guard found Jeremiah, he said
to him, "The LORD your God decreed this disaster for this place.[a] 3And now the LORD
has brought it about; he has done just as he said he would. All this happened because
you people sinned[b] against the LORD and did not obey[c] him. 4But today I am freeing
you from the chains on your wrists. Come with me to Babylon, if you like, and I will
look after you; but if you do not want to, then don't come. Look, the whole country
lies before you; go wherever you please."[d] 5However, before Jeremiah turned to
go,[a] Nebuzaradan added, "Go back to Gedaliah[e] son of Ahikam, the son of Shaphan, whom the king of Babylon has appointed over the towns of Judah, and live with
him among the people, or go anywhere else you please."[f]
Then the commander gave him provisions and a present and let him go. 6So
Jeremiah went to Gedaliah son of Ahikam at Mizpah[g] and stayed with him among
the people who were left behind in the land.

Gedaliah Assassinated

7When all the army officers and their men who were still in the open country heard
that the king of Babylon had appointed Gedaliah son of Ahikam as governor over the
land and had put him in charge of the men, women and children who were the
poorest[h] in the land and who had not been carried into exile to Babylon, 8they came
to Gedaliah at Mizpah[i]—Ishmael[j] son of Nethaniah, Johanan and Jonathan the sons
of Kareah, Seraiah son of Tanhumeth, the sons of Ephai the Netophathite,[k] and
Jaazaniah[b] the son of the Maacathite,[l] and their men. 9Gedaliah son of Ahikam,
the son of Shaphan, took an oath to reassure them and their men. "Do not be afraid
to serve[m] the Babylonians,"[c] he said. "Settle down in the land and serve the king
of Babylon, and it will go well with you.[n] 10I myself will stay in Mizpah[o] to
represent you before the Babylonians who come to us, but you are to harvest the wine,
summer fruit and oil, and put them in your storage jars, and live in the towns you
have taken over."[p]
11When all the Jews in Moab,[q] Ammon, Edom and all the other countries heard
that the king of Babylon had left a remnant in Judah and had appointed Gedaliah son
of Ahikam, the son of Shaphan, as governor over them, 12they all came back to the
land of Judah, to Gedaliah at Mizpah, from all the countries where they had been
scattered.[r] And they harvested an abundance of wine and summer fruit.
13Johanan son of Kareah and all the army officers still in the open country came
to Gedaliah at Mizpah[s] 14and said to him, "Don't you know that Baalis king of the

39:17 [p]Ps 41:1-2
39:18 [q]Jer 45:5 [r]Jer 21:9; 38:2 [s]Jer 17:7
40:2 [a]Jer 50:7
40:3 [b]Da 9:11 [c]Dt 29:24-28; Ro 2:5-9
40:4 [d]Ge 13:9; Jer 39:11-12
40:5 [e]2Ki 25:22 [f]Jer 39:14
40:6 [g]Jdg 20:1; 1Sa 7:5-17
40:7 [h]Jer 39:10
40:8 [i]ver 13 [j]ver 14; Jer 41:1, 2 [k]2Sa 23:28 [l]Dt 3:14
40:9 [m]Jer 27:11 [n]Jer 38:20
40:10 [o]ver 6 [p]Dt 1:39
40:11 [q]Nu 25:1
40:12 [r]Jer 43:5
40:13 [s]ver 8

[a] 5 Or *Jeremiah answered* [b] 8 Hebrew *Jezaniah,* a variant of *Jaazaniah* [c] 9 Or *Chaldeans*; also in verse 10

39:17, 18 Ebed-Melech had risked his life to save God's prophet Jeremiah (38:7–13). When Babylon conquered Jerusalem, God protected Ebed-Melech from the Babylonians. God has special rewards for his faithful people, but not everyone will receive them in this life (see the note on 38:6).

40–45 These six chapters cover events following Jerusalem's fall to Babylon.

40:2, 3 The Babylonian commander, who did not know God, acknowledged that God had given the Babylonians victory. It is strange when people recognise that God exists and does miracles, but they still do not personally accept him. Knowing God is more than knowing about him. Be sure you know him personally.

40:4 Jeremiah was free to go anywhere. In Babylon he would have had great comfort and power. In Judah he would continue to face hardship. In Babylon Jeremiah would have been favoured by the Babylonians, but hated by the Judean exiles. In Judah he would remain poor and unwanted, but the Judean remnant would know he was not a traitor. Jeremiah returned to Judah.

40:6 Mizpah was a few miles north of Jerusalem. Not thoroughly destroyed by the Babylonians, Mizpah served as a refuge after the destruction of Jerusalem.

40:13–41:3 Gedaliah, appointed governor of Judah, foolishly ignored the warnings of assassination. Ishmael, in the line of David, may have been angry that he had been passed over for leadership. This is similar to the chaotic political situation that Ezra and Nehemiah faced when they returned to rebuild the temple and the city.

Ammonites[t] has sent Ishmael son of Nethaniah to take your life?" But Gedaliah son
of Ahikam did not believe them.
[15]Then Johanan son of Kareah said privately to Gedaliah in Mizpah, "Let me go
and kill Ishmael son of Nethaniah, and no-one will know it. Why should he take your
life and cause all the Jews who are gathered around you to be scattered and the remnant
of Judah to perish?"
[16]But Gedaliah son of Ahikam said to Johanan son of Kareah, "Don't do such a
thing! What you are saying about Ishmael is not true."

41 In the seventh month Ishmael[a] son of Nethaniah, the son of Elishama, who
was of royal blood and had been one of the king's officers, came with ten men
to Gedaliah son of Ahikam at Mizpah. While they were eating together there, [2]Ish-
mael[b] son of Nethaniah and the ten men who were with him got up and struck down
Gedaliah son of Ahikam, the son of Shaphan, with the sword, killing the one whom
the king of Babylon had appointed[c] as governor over the land.[d] [3]Ishmael also killed
all the Jews who were with Gedaliah at Mizpah, as well as the Babylonian[a] soldiers
who were there.
[4]The day after Gedaliah's assassination, before anyone knew about it, [5]eighty men
who had shaved off their beards,[e] torn their clothes and cut themselves came from
Shechem,[f] Shiloh[g] and Samaria,[h] bringing grain offerings and incense with them
to the house of the LORD.[i] [6]Ishmael son of Nethaniah went out from Mizpah to meet
them, weeping[j] as he went. When he met them, he said, "Come to Gedaliah son of
Ahikam." [7]When they went into the city, Ishmael son of Nethaniah and the men who
were with him slaughtered them and threw them into a cistern. [8]But ten of them said
to Ishmael, "Don't kill us! We have wheat and barley, oil and honey, hidden in a
field."[k] So he let them alone and did not kill them with the others. [9]Now the cistern
where he threw all the bodies of the men he had killed along with Gedaliah was the
one King Asa[l] had made as part of his defence[m] against Baasha[n] king of Israel.
Ishmael son of Nethaniah filled it with the dead.
[10]Ishmael made captives of all the rest of the people[o] who were in Mizpah—the
king's daughters along with all the others who were left there, over whom Nebuzaradan commander of the imperial guard had appointed Gedaliah son of Ahikam. Ishmael
son of Nethaniah took them captive and set out to cross over to the Ammonites.[p]
[11]When Johanan[q] son of Kareah and all the army officers who were with him heard
about all the crimes Ishmael son of Nethaniah had committed, [12]they took all their
men and went to fight Ishmael son of Nethaniah. They caught up with him near the
great pool[r] in Gibeon. [13]When all the people[s] Ishmael had with him saw Johanan
son of Kareah and the army officers who were with him, they were glad. [14]All the
people Ishmael had taken captive at Mizpah turned and went over to Johanan son of
Kareah. [15]But Ishmael son of Nethaniah and eight of his men escaped[t] from Johanan
and fled to the Ammonites.

Flight to Egypt

[16]Then Johanan son of Kareah and all the army officers who were with him led away
all the survivors[u] from Mizpah whom he had recovered from Ishmael son of Nethaniah after he had assassinated Gedaliah son of Ahikam: the soldiers, women, children
and court officials he had brought from Gibeon. [17]And they went on, stopping at
Geruth Kimham[v] near Bethlehem on their way to Egypt[w] [18]to escape the Babylonians.[b] They were afraid[x] of them because Ishmael son of Nethaniah had killed
Gedaliah[y] son of Ahikam, whom the king of Babylon had appointed as governor over
the land.

a *3* Or *Chaldean* **b** *18* Or *Chaldeans*

40:14 [t]2Sa 10:1-19; Jer 25:21; 41:10
41:1 [a]Jer 40:8
41:2 [b]Ps 41:9; 109:5 [c]Jer 40:5 [d]2Sa 3:27; 20:9-10
41:5 [e]Lev 19:27 [f]Ge 33:18; Jdg 9:1-57; 1Ki 12:1 [g]Jos 18:1 [h]1Ki 16:24 [i]2Ki 25:9
41:6 [j]2Sa 3:16
41:8 [k]Isa 45:3
41:9 [l]1Ki 15:22; 2Ch 16:6 [m]Jdg 6:2 [n]2Ch 16:1
41:10 [o]Jer 40:7, 12 [p]Jer 40:14
41:11 [q]Jer 40:8
41:12 [r]2Sa 2:13
41:13 [s]ver 10
41:15 [t]Job 21:30; Pr 28:17
41:16 [u]Jer 43:4
41:17 [v]2Sa 19:37 [w]Jer 42:14
41:18 [x]Isa 51:12; Jer 42:16; Lk 12:4-5 [y]Jer 40:5

41:4–9 The 80 men came from three cities of the northern kingdom to worship in Jerusalem. Ishmael probably killed them for the money and food they were carrying. Without a king, with no law and no loyalty to God, Judah was subjected to complete anarchy.

41:16, 17 Johanan and his group were already on their way to Egypt, headed south from Gibeon, stopping first at Geruth Kimham, near Bethlehem. Their visit to Jeremiah (42:1–6) was hypocritical, as Jeremiah later told them (42:20).

42 Then all the army officers, including Johanan[a] son of Kareah and Jezaniah[a]
son of Hoshaiah, and all the people from the least to the greatest[b] approached
2 Jeremiah the prophet and said to him, "Please hear our petition and pray[c] to the LORD
your God for this entire remnant.[d] For as you now see, though we were once many,
now only a few[e] are left. 3 Pray that the LORD your God will tell us where we should
go and what we should do."[f]
4 "I have heard you," replied Jeremiah the prophet. "I will certainly pray[g] to the
LORD your God as you have requested; I will tell you everything the LORD says and
will keep nothing back from you."[h]
5 Then they said to Jeremiah, "May the LORD be a true and faithful witness[i] against
us if we do not act in accordance with everything the LORD your God sends you to
tell us. 6 Whether it is favourable or unfavourable, we will obey the LORD our God,
to whom we are sending you, so that it will go well[j] with us, for we will obey[k] the
LORD our God."
7 Ten days later the word of the LORD came to Jeremiah. 8 So he called together
Johanan son of Kareah and all the army officers[l] who were with him and all the
people from the least to the greatest. 9 He said to them, "This is what the LORD, the
God of Israel, to whom you sent me to present your petition, says:[m] 10 'If you stay
in this land, I will build[n] you up and not tear you down; I will plant[o] you and not
uproot you,[p] for I am grieved over the disaster I have inflicted on you.[q] 11 Do not
be afraid of the king of Babylon,[r] whom you now fear.[s] Do not be afraid of him,
declares the LORD, for I am with you and will save[t] you and deliver you from his
hands.[u] 12 I will show you compassion so that he will have compassion on you and
restore you to your land.'[v]
13 "However, if you say, 'We will not stay in this land,' and so disobey[w] the LORD
your God, 14 and if you say, 'No, we will go and live in Egypt,[x] where we will not
see war or hear the trumpet or be hungry for bread,' 15 then hear the word of the LORD,
O remnant of Judah. This is what the LORD Almighty, the God of Israel, says: 'If you
are determined to go to Egypt and you do go to settle there, 16 then the sword[y] you
fear will overtake you there, and the famine you dread will follow you into Egypt,
and there you will die. 17 Indeed, all who are determined to go to Egypt to settle there
will die by the sword, famine and plague;[z] not one of them will survive or escape
the disaster I will bring on them.' 18 This is what the LORD Almighty, the God of Israel,
says: 'As my anger and wrath[a] have been poured out on those who lived in Jerusalem,[b] so will my wrath be poured out on you when you go to Egypt. You will be
an object of cursing and horror,[c] of condemnation and reproach; you will never see
this place again.'[d]
19 "O remnant of Judah, the LORD has told you, 'Do not go to Egypt.'[e] Be sure
of this: I warn you today 20 that you made a fatal mistake[b] when you sent me to the
LORD your God and said, 'Pray to the LORD our God for us; tell us everything he says
and we will do it.'[f] 21 I have told you today, but you still have not obeyed the LORD
your God in all he sent me to tell you.[g] 22 So now, be sure of this: You will die by
the sword, famine and plague[h] in the place where you want to go to settle."[i]
43 When Jeremiah finished telling the people all the words of the LORD their
God—everything the LORD had sent him to tell them[a]— 2 Azariah son of
Hoshaiah and Johanan[b] son of Kareah and all the arrogant men said to Jeremiah, "You
are lying! The LORD our God has not sent you to say, 'You must not go to Egypt to
settle there.' 3 But Baruch son of Neriah is inciting you against us to hand us over to
the Babylonians,[a] so that they may kill us or carry us into exile to Babylon."[c]
4 So Johanan son of Kareah and all the army officers and all the people disobeyed

[a] 1 Hebrew; Septuagint (see also 43:2) *Azariah* [b] 20 Or *you erred in your hearts* [a] 3 Or *Chaldeans*

42:1 [a] Jer 40:13; 41:11 [b] Jer 6:13; 44:12
42:2 [c] Jer 36:7; Ac 8:24; Jas 5:16 [d] Isa 1:9 [e] Lev 26:22; La 1:1
42:3 [f] Ps 86:11; Pr 3:6
42:4 [g] Ex 8:29; 1Sa 12:23 [h] 1Ki 22:14; 1Sa 3:17
42:5 [i] Ge 31:50
42:6 [j] Dt 5:29; 6:3; Jer 7:23 [k] Ex 24:7; Jos 24:24
42:8 [l] ver 1
42:9 [m] 2Ki 22:15
42:10 [n] Jer 24:6 [o] Jer 31:28 [p] Eze 36:36 [q] Jer 18:8
42:11 [r] Jer 27:11 [s] Nu 14:9 [t] Isa 43:5 [u] Jer 1:8; Ro 8:31
42:12 [v] Ps 106:44-46
42:13 [w] Jer 44:16
42:14 [x] Nu 11:4-5
42:16 [y] Eze 11:8
42:17 [z] ver 22; Jer 44:13
42:18 [a] Dt 29:18-20; Jer 7:20 [b] 2Ch 36:19; Jer 39:1-9 [c] Jer 29:18 [d] Jer 22:10
42:19 [e] Dt 17:16; Isa 30:7
42:20 [f] ver 2
42:21 [g] Eze 2:7; Zec 7:11-12
42:22 [h] ver 17; Eze 6:11 [i] Hos 9:6
43:1 [a] Jer 26:8; 42:9-22
43:2 [b] Jer 42:1
43:3 [c] Jer 38:4

42:5, 6 Johanan and his associates spoke their own curse; Jeremiah merely elaborated on it. It was a tragic mistake to ask for God's guidance with no intention of following it. Be sure never to ask God for something that you know in your heart you really do not want. It is better not to pray than to pray hypocritically. God cannot be deceived.

43:1–3 Johanan and his tiny band had come to Jeremiah for God's approval of their plan, not for God's direction. This is a recurring problem for most of us—seeking God's approval of our desires rather than asking him for guidance. It's not good to make

the LORD's command[d] to stay in the land of Judah.[e] 5Instead, Johanan son of Kareah
and all the army officers led away all the remnant of Judah who had come back to
live in the land of Judah from all the nations where they had been scattered.[f] 6They
also led away all the men, women and children and the king's daughters whom
Nebuzaradan commander of the imperial guard had left with Gedaliah son of Ahikam,
the son of Shaphan, and Jeremiah the prophet and Baruch son of Neriah. 7So they
entered Egypt in disobedience to the LORD and went as far as Tahpanhes.[g]
8In Tahpanhes[h] the word of the LORD came to Jeremiah: 9"While the Jews are
watching, take some large stones with you and bury them in clay in the brick pavement
at the entrance to Pharaoh's palace in Tahpanhes. 10Then say to them, 'This is what
the LORD Almighty, the God of Israel, says: I will send for my servant[i] Nebuchadnezzar king of Babylon, and I will set his throne over these stones I have buried here;
he will spread his royal canopy above them. 11He will come and attack Egypt,[j]
bringing death to those destined for death, captivity to those destined for captivity,
and the sword to those destined for the sword.[k] 12He[b] will set fire to the temples
of the gods[l] of Egypt; he will burn their temples and take their gods captive. As a
shepherd wraps[m] his garment round him, so will he wrap Egypt round himself and
depart from there unscathed. 13There in the temple of the sun[c] in Egypt he will
demolish the sacred pillars and will burn down the temples of the gods of Egypt.' "

Disaster Because of Idolatry

44 This word came to Jeremiah concerning all the Jews living in Lower Egypt — in
Migdol,[a] Tahpanhes[b] and Memphis[a][c] — and in Upper Egypt:[b][d] 2"This is
what the LORD Almighty, the God of Israel, says: You saw the great disaster I brought
on Jerusalem and on all the towns of Judah. Today they lie deserted and in ruins[e]
3because of the evil they have done. They provoked me to anger by burning incense
and by worshipping other gods[f] that neither they nor you nor your fathers[g] ever
knew. 4Again and again[h] I sent my servants the prophets,[i] who said, 'Do not do
this detestable thing that I hate!' 5But they did not listen or pay attention; they did
not turn from their wickedness or stop burning incense to other gods.[j] 6Therefore,
my fierce anger was poured out; it raged against the towns of Judah and the streets
of Jerusalem and made them the desolate ruins they are today.
7"Now this is what the LORD God Almighty, the God of Israel, says: Why bring
such great disaster[k] on yourselves by cutting off from Judah the men and women,[l]
the children and infants, and so leave yourselves without a remnant? 8Why provoke

43:4 [d]Jer 42:5-6 [e]Jer 42:10
43:5 [f]Jer 40:12
43:7 [g]Jer 2:16; 44:1
43:8 [h]Jer 2:16
43:10 [i]Isa 44:28; Jer 25:9; 27:6
43:11 [j]Jer 46:13-26; Eze 29:19-20 [k]Jer 15:2; 44:13; Zec 11:9
43:12 [l]Jer 46:25; Eze 30:13 [m]Ps 104:2; 109:18-19
44:1 [a]Ex 14:2 [b]Jer 43:7, 8 [c]Isa 19:13 [d]Isa 11:11; Jer 46:14
44:2 [e]Isa 6:11; Jer 9:11; 34:22
44:3 [f]ver 8; Dt 13:6-11; 29:26 [g]Dt 32:17; Jer 19:4
44:4 [h]Jer 7:13 [i]Jer 7:25; 25:4; 26:5
44:5 [j]Jer 11:8-10
44:7 [k]Jer 26:19 [l]Jer 51:22

b *12* Or *I* **c** *13* Or *in Heliopolis* **a** *1* Hebrew *Noph* **b** *1* Hebrew *in Pathros*

---

plans unless we are willing for God to change them, and it is not good to pray unless we are willing to accept God's answer.

43:4–7 Afraid to obey the Lord, the people headed for Egypt, even forcing Jeremiah to go with them. (They thought that perhaps God would spare them if Jeremiah was with them.) Jeremiah had served as a prophet for 40 years. Many of his words had already come true, and he had turned down an offer to live comfortably in Babylon, returning instead to his beloved people. But the people still rejected Jeremiah's advice. The response of our audience is not necessarily a measure of our success. Jeremiah was doing all God asked, but he had been called to minister to a very stubborn group of people.

43:10–13 Nebuchadnezzar invaded Egypt in 568 – 567 B.C. Like Judah, Egypt rebelled against him and was quickly crushed. So much for the great empire on which Judah had constantly placed its hopes!

44:1ff This message, given in 580 B.C. while Jeremiah was in Egypt against his will, reminded the people that their following other gods had brought destruction on their land. Jeremiah told them that they would never return to Judah because the escape to Egypt had been against God's advice (42:9ff). But the people refused to learn any lessons from all the destruction their sins had caused.

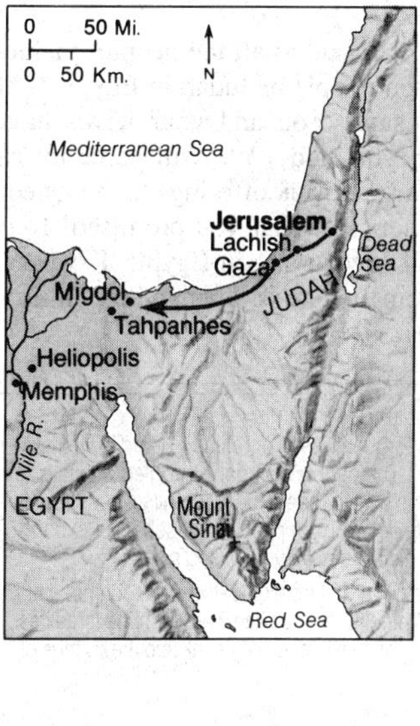

ESCAPE TO EGYPT
With Judah in turmoil after the murder of Gedaliah, the people turned to Jeremiah for guidance. Jeremiah had God's answer, "Stay in this land". But the leaders disobeyed and went to Egypt, taking Jeremiah with them. In Egypt, Jeremiah told them they were in grave danger.

me to anger with what your hands have made,[m] burning incense to other gods in
Egypt, where you have come to live?[n] You will destroy yourselves and make
yourselves an object of cursing and reproach[o] among all the nations on earth. 9Have
you forgotten the wickedness committed by your fathers and by the kings and queens
of Judah and the wickedness committed by you and your wives in the land of Judah
and the streets of Jerusalem?[p] 10To this day they have not humbled themselves or
shown reverence, nor have they followed my law[q] and the decrees I set before you
and your fathers.[r]

11"Therefore, this is what the LORD Almighty, the God of Israel, says: I am
determined to bring disaster[s] on you and to destroy all Judah. 12I will take away the
remnant[t] of Judah who were determined to go to Egypt to settle there. They will all
perish in Egypt; they will fall by the sword or die from famine. From the least to the
greatest, they will die by sword or famine.[u] They will become an object of cursing
and horror, of condemnation and reproach.[v] 13I will punish those who live in Egypt
with the sword, famine and plague,[w] as I punished Jerusalem. 14None of the remnant
of Judah who have gone to live in Egypt will escape or survive to return to the land
of Judah, to which they long to return and live; none will return except a few
fugitives."[x]

15Then all the men who knew that their wives were burning incense to other gods,
along with all the women who were present—a large assembly—and all the people
living in Lower and Upper Egypt,[c] said to Jeremiah, 16"We will not listen[y] to the
message you have spoken to us in the name of the LORD! 17We will certainly do
everything we said we would:[z] We will burn incense to the Queen of Heaven[a] and
will pour out drink offerings to her just as we and our fathers, our kings and our
officials did in the towns of Judah and in the streets of Jerusalem. At that time we
had plenty of food and were well off and suffered no harm.[b] 18But ever since we
stopped burning incense to the Queen of Heaven and pouring out drink offerings to
her, we have had nothing and have been perishing by sword and famine.[c]"

19The women added, "When we burned incense to the Queen of Heaven[d] and
poured out drink offerings to her, did not our husbands know that we were making
cakes like her image and pouring out drink offerings to her?"

20Then Jeremiah said to all the people, both men and women, who were answering
him, 21"Did not the LORD remember[e] and think about the incense[f] burned in the
towns of Judah and the streets of Jerusalem[g] by you and your fathers,[h] your kings
and your officials and the people of the land? 22When the LORD could no longer endure
your wicked actions and the detestable things you did, your land became an object
of cursing[i] and a desolate waste without inhabitants, as it is today.[j] 23Because you
have burned incense and have sinned against the LORD and have not obeyed him or
followed his law or his decrees or his stipulations, this disaster[k] has come upon you,
as you now see."[l]

24Then Jeremiah said to all the people, including the women,[m] "Hear the word of
the LORD, all you people of Judah in Egypt.[n] 25This is what the LORD Almighty, the
God of Israel, says: You and your wives have shown by your actions what you
promised when you said, 'We will certainly carry out the vows we made to burn
incense and pour out drink offerings to the Queen of Heaven.'[o]

"Go ahead then, do what you promised! Keep your vows![p] 26But hear the word
of the LORD, all Jews living in Egypt: 'I swear[q] by my great name,' says the LORD,
'that no-one from Judah living anywhere in Egypt shall ever again invoke my name

c 15 Hebrew *in Egypt and Pathros*

44:8 [m]Jer 25:6-7 [n]1Co 10:22 [o]Jer 42:18
44:9 [p]ver 17, 21
44:10 [q]Jos 1:7 [r]1Ki 9:6-9
44:11 [s]Jer 21:10; Am 9:4
44:12 [t]ver 7 [u]Isa 1:28 [v]Jer 29:18; 42:15-18
44:13 [w]Jer 42:17
44:14 [x]ver 28; Jer 22:24-27; Ro 9:27
44:16 [y]Jer 11:8-10
44:17 [z]Dt 23:23 [a]ver 25; Jer 7:18 [b]Hos 2:5-13
44:18 [c]Mal 3:13-15
44:19 [d]Jer 7:18
44:21 [e]Isa 64:9; Jer 14:10 [f]Jer 11:13 [g]ver 9 [h]Ps 79:8
44:22 [i]Jer 25:18 [j]Ge 19:13; Ps 107:33-34
44:23 [k]Jer 40:2 [l]1Ki 9:9; Jer 7:13-15; Da 9:11-12
44:24 [m]ver 15 [n]Jer 43:7
44:25 [o]ver 17 [p]Eze 20:39
44:26 [q]Ge 22:16; Isa 48:1; Heb 6:13-17

44:9, 10 When we forget a lesson or refuse to learn it, we risk repeating our mistakes. The people of Judah struggled with this; to forget their former sins was to repeat them. To fail to learn from failure is to ensure future failure. Your past is your school of experience. Let your past mistakes point you to God's way.

44:15–18 The further we drift from God, the more confused our thinking becomes. Whatever spiritual life was left in the Israelites when they went to Egypt was lost as they sank into the depths of idolatry. (For more information on the "Queen of Heaven", see the note on 7:18.) The escape to Egypt had brought a change in their pagan worship habits, and they blamed their troubles on their neglect of their idols. But idol worship had started all their problems in the first place. The people refused to recognise the true source of their problems—departure from God's leading. When calamity forces you to examine your life, take a close look at God's instructions for you.

or swear, "As surely as the Sovereign LORD lives."[r] 27For I am watching over them
for harm,[s] not for good; the Jews in Egypt will perish by sword and famine until they
are all destroyed. 28Those who escape the sword and return to the land of Judah from
Egypt will be very few.[t] Then the whole remnant of Judah who came to live in Egypt
will know whose word will stand — mine or theirs.[u]
29" 'This will be the sign to you that I will punish you in this place,' declares the
LORD, 'so that you will know that my threats of harm against you will surely stand.'[v]
30This is what the LORD says: 'I am going to hand Pharaoh[w] Hophra king of Egypt
over to his enemies who seek his life, just as I handed Zedekiah[x] king of Judah over
to Nebuchadnezzar king of Babylon, the enemy who was seeking his life.' "[y]

A Message to Baruch

45 This is what Jeremiah the prophet told Baruch[a] son of Neriah in the fourth
year of Jehoiakim[b] son of Josiah king of Judah, after Baruch had written on
a scroll the words Jeremiah was then dictating: 2"This is what the LORD, the God of
Israel, says to you, Baruch: 3You said, 'Woe to me! The LORD has added sorrow to
my pain; I am worn out with groaning[c] and find no rest.' "
4⌞The LORD said,⌟ "Say this to him: 'This is what the LORD says: I will overthrow
what I have built and uproot what I have planted,[d] throughout the land.[e] 5Should
you then seek great things for yourself? Seek them not.[f] For I will bring disaster on
all people, declares the LORD, but wherever you go I will let you escape with your
life.' "[g]

B. GOD'S JUDGMENT ON THE NATIONS (46:1 — 52:34)

All of Jeremiah's prophecies against foreign nations have been grouped together. Many of the people in these nations assumed that they were free from judgment and punishment for their sin. Following these prophecies is a historical appendix recounting the fall of Jerusalem. Just as Jerusalem received its punishment, these nations were certain to receive theirs as well. Those today who think that judgment will never touch them are forewarned.

1. Prophecies about foreign nations

A Message About Egypt

46 This is the word of the LORD that came to Jeremiah the prophet concerning the
nations:[a]

2Concerning Egypt:

This is the message against the army of Pharaoh Neco[b] king of Egypt, which was
defeated at Carchemish[c] on the Euphrates River by Nebuchadnezzar king of Babylon
in the fourth year of Jehoiakim[d] son of Josiah king of Judah:

3"Prepare your shields,[e] both large and small,

44:26 [r]Dt 32:40; Ps 50:16
44:27 [s]Jer 31:28
44:28 [t]ver 13-14; Isa 10:19 [u]ver 17, 25-26
44:29 [v]Pr 19:21
44:30 [w]Jer 46:26; Eze 30:21 [x]2Ki 25:1-7 [y]Jer 39:5
45:1 [a]Jer 32:12; 36:4, 18, 32 [b]2Ch 36:5
45:3 [c]Ps 69:3
45:4 [d]Jer 11:17 [e]Isa 5:5-7; Jer 18:7-10
45:5 [f]Mt 6:25-27, 33 [g]Jer 21:9; 38:2; 39:18
46:1 [a]Jer 1:10; 25:15-38
46:2 [b]2Ki 23:29 [c]2Ch 35:20 [d]Jer 45:1
46:3 [e]Isa 21:5; Jer 51:11-12

44:28 After Jeremiah's forced move to Egypt, there is no word in the Bible about the events in the rest of his life.

44:30 Pharaoh Hophra ruled Egypt from 588 to 569 B.C. and was killed by Ahmose, one of his generals, who was then crowned in his place.

45:1ff The event relating to this chapter is recorded in 36:1–8. The chapter was written in 605 – 604 B.C. Baruch was the scribe who recorded Jeremiah's words on a scroll.

45:5 Baruch had long been serving this unpopular prophet, writing his book of struggles and judgments, and now he was upset. God told Baruch to take his eyes off himself and whatever rewards he thought he deserved. If Baruch did this, God would protect him. It is easy to lose the joy of serving our God when we take our eyes off him. The more we look away from God's purposes towards our own sacrifices, the more frustrated we will become. As you serve God, beware of focusing on what you are giving up. When this happens, ask God's forgiveness; then look at him rather than at yourself.

46:1ff In this chapter, we gain several insights about God and his plan for this world: (1) Although God chose Israel for a special purpose, he loves all people and wants all to come to him. (2) God is holy and will not tolerate sin. (3) God's judgments are not based on prejudice and a desire for revenge, but on fairness and justice. (4) God does not delight in judgment, but in salvation. (5) God is impartial — he judges everyone by the same standard.

46:2 At the battle of Carchemish in 605 B.C., Babylon and Egypt, the two major world powers after Assyria's fall, clashed. The Babylonians entered Carchemish by surprise and defeated Egypt. This battle, which passed world leadership to Babylon, was Nebuchadnezzar's first victory, establishing him in his new position as king of the Babylonian empire. With Egypt's power declining, it was both poor strategy and disobedience to God for Judah to form an alliance with Egypt.

and march out for battle!
4Harness the horses,
mount the steeds!
Take your positions
with helmets on!
Polish[f] your spears,
put on your armour![g]
5What do I see?
They are terrified,
they are retreating,
their warriors are defeated.
They flee[h] in haste
without looking back,
and there is terror[i] on every side,"
declares the LORD.
6"The swift cannot flee[j]
nor the strong escape.
In the north by the River Euphrates
they stumble and fall.[k]
7"Who is this that rises like the Nile,
like rivers of surging waters?[l]
8Egypt rises like the Nile,
like rivers of surging waters.
She says, 'I will rise and cover the earth;
I will destroy cities and their people.'
9Charge, O horses!
Drive furiously, O charioteers![m]
March on, O warriors—
men of Cush[a] and Put who carry shields,
men of Lydia[n] who draw the bow.
10But that day[o] belongs to the Lord, the LORD Almighty—
a day of vengeance, for vengeance on his foes.
The sword will devour[p] till it is satisfied,
till it has quenched its thirst with blood.
For the Lord, the LORD Almighty, will offer sacrifice[q]
in the land of the north by the River Euphrates.
11"Go up to Gilead and get balm,[r]
O Virgin[s] Daughter of Egypt.
But you multiply remedies in vain;
there is no healing[t] for you.
12The nations will hear of your shame;
your cries will fill the earth.
One warrior will stumble over another;
both will fall[u] down together."

13This is the message the LORD spoke to Jeremiah the prophet about the coming of Nebuchadnezzar king of Babylon to attack Egypt:[v]

14"Announce this in Egypt, and proclaim it in Migdol;
proclaim it also in Memphis[b] and Tahpanhes:[w]
'Take your positions and get ready,
for the sword devours those around you.'
15Why will your warriors be laid low?

46:4 [f]Eze 21:9-11 [g]1Sa 17:5, 38; 2Ch 26:14; Ne 4:16
46:5 [h]ver 21 [i]Jer 49:29
46:6 [j]Isa 30:16 [k]ver 12, 16; Da 11:19
46:7 [l]Jer 47:2
46:9 [m]Jer 47:3 [n]Isa 66:19
46:10 [o]Joel 1:15 [p]Dt 32:42 [q]Zep 1:7
46:11 [r]Jer 8:22 [s]Isa 47:1 [t]Jer 30:13; Mic 1:9
46:12 [u]Isa 19:4; Na 3:8-10
46:13 [v]Isa 19:1
46:14 [w]Jer 43:8

[a] *9* That is, the upper Nile region [b] *14* Hebrew *Noph*; also in verse 19

46:9 The soldiers from Cush and Put were from eastern and northern Africa. The men of Lydia may have been from Greece.

They cannot stand, for the LORD will push them down.[x]
16They will stumble[y] repeatedly;
they will fall[z] over each other.
They will say, 'Get up, let us go back
to our own people and our native lands,
away from the sword of the oppressor.'
17There they will exclaim,
'Pharaoh king of Egypt is only a loud noise;
he has missed his opportunity.[a]'

18"As surely as I live," declares the King,[b]
whose name is the LORD Almighty,
"one will come who is like Tabor[c] among the mountains,
like Carmel[d] by the sea.
19Pack your belongings for exile,[e]
you who live in Egypt,
for Memphis will be laid waste
and lie in ruins without inhabitant.

20"Egypt is a beautiful heifer,
but a gadfly is coming
against her from the north.[f]
21The mercenaries[g] in her ranks
are like fattened calves.
They too will turn and flee[h] together,
they will not stand their ground,
for the day[i] of disaster is coming upon them,
the time for them to be punished.
22Egypt will hiss like a fleeing serpent
as the enemy advances in force;
they will come against her with axes,
like men who cut down trees.
23They will chop down her forest,"
declares the LORD,
"dense though it be.
They are more numerous than locusts,[j]
they cannot be counted.
24The Daughter of Egypt will be put to shame,
handed over to the people of the north.[k]"

25The LORD Almighty, the God of Israel, says: "I am about to bring punishment
on Amon god of Thebes,[c][l] on Pharaoh, on Egypt and her gods[m] and her kings, and
on those who rely[n] on Pharaoh. 26I will hand them over[o] to those who seek their
lives, to Nebuchadnezzar king[p] of Babylon and his officers. Later, however, Egypt
will be inhabited[q] as in times past," declares the LORD.

27"Do not fear,[r] O Jacob my servant;
do not be dismayed, O Israel.
I will surely save you out of a distant place,
and your descendants from the land of their exile.[s]
Jacob will again have peace and security,
and no-one will make him afraid.

c 25 Hebrew *No*

46:15 [x]Isa 66:15-16
46:16 [y]Lev 26:37 [z]ver 6
46:17 [a]Isa 19:11-16
46:18 [b]Jer 48:15 [c]Jos 19:22 [d]1Ki 18:42
46:19 [e]Isa 20:4
46:20 [f]ver 24; Jer 47:2
46:21 [g]2Ki 7:6 [h]ver 5 [i]Ps 37:13
46:23 [j]Jdg 7:12
46:24 [k]Jer 1:15
46:25 [l]Eze 30:14; Na 3:8 [m]Jer 43:12 [n]Isa 20:6
46:26 [o]Jer 44:30 [p]Eze 32:11 [q]Eze 29:11-16
46:27 [r]Isa 41:13; 43:5 [s]Isa 11:11; Jer 50:19

46:17 In 589 B.C. when Nebuchadnezzar besieged Jerusalem, Pharaoh Hophra marched against him at Zedekiah's invitation. But when the Babylonians stood up to the Egyptians, Pharaoh Hophra and his troops retreated. Jeremiah had prophesied that Pharaoh Hophra would be killed by his enemies (44:30). This was fulfilled nearly 20 years later when his co-regent Ahmose led a revolt.

28 Do not fear, O Jacob my servant,
for I am with you,"[t] declares the LORD.
"Though I completely destroy[u] all the nations
among which I scatter you,
I will not completely destroy you.
I will discipline you but only with justice;
I will not let you go entirely unpunished."

46:28 [t] Isa 8:9-10 [u] Jer 4:27

A Message About the Philistines

47 This is the word of the LORD that came to Jeremiah the prophet concerning the Philistines before Pharaoh attacked Gaza:[a]

47:1 [a] Ge 10:19; Am 1:6; Zec 9:5-7

2 This is what the LORD says:

"See how the waters are rising in the north;[b]
they will become an overflowing torrent.
They will overflow the land and everything in it,
the towns and those who live in them.
The people will cry out;
all who dwell in the land will wail
3 at the sound of the hoofs of galloping steeds,
at the noise of enemy chariots
and the rumble of their wheels.
Fathers will not turn to help their children;
their hands will hang limp.
4 For the day has come
to destroy all the Philistines
and to cut off all survivors
who could help Tyre[c] and Sidon.[d]
The LORD is about to destroy the Philistines,[e]
the remnant from the coasts of Caphtor.[a][f]
5 Gaza will shave[g] her head in mourning;
Ashkelon[h] will be silenced.
O remnant on the plain,
how long will you cut yourselves?

47:2 [b] Isa 8:7; 14:31

47:4 [c] Am 1:9-10; Zec 9:2-4 [d] Jer 25:22 [e] Ge 10:14; Joel 3:4 [f] Dt 2:23

47:5 [g] Jer 41:5; Mic 1:16 [h] Jer 25:20

6 " 'Ah, sword[i] of the LORD,' ⌞you cry,⌟
'how long till you rest?
Return to your scabbard;
cease and be still.'
7 But how can it rest
when the LORD has commanded it,
when he has ordered it
to attack Ashkelon and the coast?"

47:6 [i] Jer 12:12

A Message About Moab

48 Concerning Moab:

This is what the LORD Almighty, the God of Israel, says:

"Woe to Nebo,[a] for it will be ruined.

48:1 [a] Nu 32:38

[a] *4* That is, Crete

46:28 God punished his people in order to bring them back to himself, and he punishes us to correct and purify us. No-one welcomes punishment, but we should all welcome its results: correction and purity.

47:1 Located on the coastal plain next to Judah, Philistia had always been a thorn in Israel's side. The two nations battled constantly. Other prophets who spoke against Philistia include Isaiah (14:28–32), Ezekiel (25:15–17), Amos (1:6–8), and Zephaniah (2:4–7).

48:1 The Moabites were descendants of Lot through an incestuous relationship with one of his daughters (Genesis 19:30–37). They led the Israelites into idolatry (Numbers 25:1–3) and joined

Kiriathaim[b] will be disgraced and captured;
the stronghold[a] will be disgraced and shattered.
2 Moab will be praised[c] no more;
in Heshbon[b][d] men will plot her downfall:
'Come, let us put an end to that nation.'
You too, O Madmen,[c] will be silenced;
the sword will pursue you.
3 Listen to the cries from Horonaim,[e]
cries of great havoc and destruction.
4 Moab will be broken;
her little ones will cry out.[d]
5 They go up the way to Luhith,[f]
weeping bitterly as they go;
on the road down to Horonaim
anguished cries over the destruction are heard.
6 Flee! Run for your lives;
become like a bush[e] in the desert.[g]
7 Since you trust in your deeds and riches,
you too will be taken captive,
and Chemosh[h] will go into exile,[i]
together with his priests and officials.
8 The destroyer will come against every town,
and not a town will escape.
The valley will be ruined
and the plateau destroyed,
because the LORD has spoken.
9 Put salt on Moab,
for she will be laid waste;[f]
her towns will become desolate,
with no-one to live in them.

10 "A curse on him who is lax in doing the LORD's work!
A curse on him who keeps his sword[j] from bloodshed![k]

11 "Moab has been at rest[l] from youth,
like wine left on its dregs,[m]
not poured from one jar to another—
she has not gone into exile.
So she tastes as she did,
and her aroma is unchanged.
12 But days are coming,"
declares the LORD,
"when I will send men who pour from jars,
and they will pour her out;
they will empty her jars
and smash her jugs.

48:1 [b] Nu 32:37
48:2 [c] Isa 16:14 [d] Nu 21:25
48:3 [e] Isa 15:5
48:5 [f] Isa 15:5
48:6 [g] Jer 17:6
48:7 [h] Nu 21:29 [i] Isa 46:1-2; Jer 49:3
48:10 [j] Jer 47:6 [k] 1Ki 20:42; 2Ki 13:15-19
48:11 [l] Zec 1:15 [m] Zep 1:12

[a] *1* Or */ Misgab* [b] *2* The Hebrew for *Heshbon* sounds like the Hebrew for *plot.* [c] *2* The name of the Moabite town Madmen sounds like the Hebrew for *be silenced.* [d] *4* Hebrew; Septuagint */ proclaim it to Zoar* [e] *6* Or *like Aroer* [f] *9* Or *Give wings to Moab, / for she will fly away*

the bands of raiders Nebuchadnezzar sent into Judah in 602 B.C. They were later conquered by Babylon and disappeared as a nation.

48:7 Chemosh was the main god of the nation of Moab (Numbers 21:29), and child sacrifice was an important part of his worship (2 Kings 3:26, 27).

48:9 Putting salt on a city was a symbolic act to show that it was totally destroyed (see Judges 9:45). Salt in the fields would make them unfit for crops.

48:11, 12 When making wine, the grapes were crushed. After 40 days, the wine was poured off from the dregs in the bottom of the jar. If this was not done, the wine would be inferior. The prophet was saying that because of Moab's complacency and refusal to do God's work, Moab would be totally destroyed.

13 Then Moab will be ashamed[n] of Chemosh,
as the house of Israel was ashamed
when they trusted in Bethel.

14 "How can you say, 'We are warriors,[o]
men valiant in battle'?
15 Moab will be destroyed and her towns invaded;
her finest young men will go down in the slaughter,[p]"
declares the King,[q] whose name is the LORD Almighty.[r]
16 "The fall of Moab is at hand;[s]
her calamity will come quickly.
17 Mourn for her, all who live around her,
all who know her fame;
say, 'How broken is the mighty sceptre,
how broken the glorious staff!'
18 "Come down from your glory
and sit on the parched ground,[t]
O inhabitants of the Daughter of Dibon,[u]
for he who destroys Moab
will come up against you
and ruin your fortified cities.[v]
19 Stand by the road and watch,
you who live in Aroer.[w]
Ask the man fleeing and the woman escaping,
ask them, 'What has happened?'
20 Moab is disgraced, for she is shattered.
Wail[x] and cry out!
Announce by the Arnon[y]
that Moab is destroyed.
21 Judgment has come to the plateau—
to Holon, Jahzah[z] and Mephaath,[a]
22 to Dibon,[b] Nebo and Beth Diblathaim,
23 to Kiriathaim, Beth Gamul and Beth Meon,[c]
24 to Kerioth[d] and Bozrah—
to all the towns of Moab, far and near.
25 Moab's horn[g][e] is cut off;
her arm[f] is broken,"
declares the LORD.

26 "Make her drunk,[g]
for she has defied the LORD.
Let Moab wallow in her vomit;
let her be an object of ridicule.
27 Was not Israel the object of your ridicule?[h]
Was she caught among thieves,
that you shake your head[i] in scorn[j]
whenever you speak of her?
28 Abandon your towns and dwell among the rocks,
you who live in Moab.
Be like a dove[k] that makes its nest
at the mouth of a cave.[l]

29 "We have heard of Moab's pride[m]—

48:13 [n] Hos 10:6
48:14 [o] Ps 33:16
48:15 [p] Jer 50:27 [q] Jer 46:18 [r] Jer 51:57
48:16 [s] Isa 13:22
48:18 [t] Isa 47:1 [u] Nu 21:30; Jos 13:9 [v] ver 8
48:19 [w] Dt 2:36
48:20 [x] Isa 16:7 [y] Nu 21:13
48:21 [z] Nu 21:23; Isa 15:4 [a] Jos 13:18
48:22 [b] Jos 13:9, 17
48:23 [c] Jos 13:17
48:24 [d] Am 2:2
48:25 [e] Ps 75:10 [f] Ps 10:15; Eze 30:21
48:26 [g] Jer 25:16, 27
48:27 [h] Jer 2:26 [i] Job 16:4; Jer 18:16 [j] Mic 7:8-10
48:28 [k] Ps 55:6-7 [l] Jdg 6:2
48:29 [m] Job 40:12; Isa 16:6

g *25 Horn* here symbolises strength.

48:13 After Israel divided into northern and southern kingdoms, the northern kingdom set up golden calf-idols in Bethel and Dan to keep people from going to worship in Jerusalem, capital of the southern kingdom (1 Kings 12:25–29).

48:29 Moab was condemned for its pride. God cannot tolerate pride because pride is taking personal credit for what God has

her overweening pride and conceit,
her pride and arrogance
and the haughtiness of her heart.
30 I know her insolence but it is futile,"
declares the LORD,
"and her boasts accomplish nothing.
31 Therefore I wail[n] over Moab,
for all Moab I cry out,
I moan for the men of Kir Hareseth.[o]
32 I weep for you, as Jazer weeps,
O vines of Sibmah.[p]
Your branches spread as far as the sea;
they reached as far as the sea of Jazer.
The destroyer has fallen
on your ripened fruit and grapes.
33 Joy and gladness are gone
from the orchards and fields of Moab.
I have stopped the flow of wine[q] from the presses;
no-one treads them with shouts of joy.[r]
Although there are shouts,
they are not shouts of joy.

34 "The sound of their cry rises
from Heshbon to Elealeh[s] and Jahaz,[t]
from Zoar[u] as far as Horonaim[v] and Eglath Shelishiyah,
for even the waters of Nimrim are dried up.[w]
35 In Moab I will put an end
to those who make offerings on the high places[x]
and burn incense[y] to their gods,"
declares the LORD.

36 "So my heart laments[z] for Moab like a flute;
it laments like a flute for the men of Kir Hareseth.
The wealth they acquired[a] is gone.
37 Every head is shaved[b]
and every beard cut off;
every hand is slashed
and every waist is covered with sackcloth.[c]
38 On all the roofs in Moab
and in the public squares
there is nothing but mourning,
for I have broken Moab
like a jar[d] that no-one wants,"
declares the LORD.

39 "How shattered she is! How they wail!
How Moab turns her back in shame!
Moab has become an object of ridicule,
an object of horror to all those around her."

40 This is what the LORD says:

"Look! An eagle is swooping[e] down,
spreading its wings[f] over Moab.
41 Kerioth[h] will be captured

48:31 [n] Isa 15:5-8 [o] 2Ki 3:25
48:32 [p] Isa 16:8-9
48:33 [q] Isa 16:10 [r] Joel 1:12
48:34 [s] Nu 32:3 [t] Isa 15:4 [u] Ge 13:10 [v] Isa 15:5 [w] Isa 15:6
48:35 [x] Isa 15:2; 16:12 [y] Jer 11:13
48:36 [z] Isa 16:11 [a] Isa 15:7
48:37 [b] Isa 15:2; Jer 41:5 [c] Ge 37:34
48:38 [d] Jer 22:28
48:40 [e] Dt 28:49; Hab 1:8 [f] Isa 8:8

h *41* Or *The cities*

done or looking down on others. God does not condemn our taking satisfaction in what we do (Ecclesiastes 3:22), but he stands against overestimating our own importance. Romans 12:3 teaches us to have an honest estimate of ourselves.

48:31 Kir Hareseth was a stronghold city in Moab. God's compassion reaches to all creation, even to his enemies.

and the strongholds taken.
In that day the hearts of Moab's warriors
will be like the heart of a woman in labour.[g]
42Moab will be destroyed[h] as a nation[i]
because she defied[j] the LORD.
43Terror and pit and snare[k] await you,
O people of Moab,"
declares the LORD.

44"Whoever flees[l] from the terror
will fall into a pit,
whoever climbs out of the pit
will be caught in a snare;
for I will bring upon Moab
the year[m] of her punishment,"
declares the LORD.

45"In the shadow of Heshbon
the fugitives stand helpless,
for a fire has gone out from Heshbon,
a blaze from the midst of Sihon;[n]
it burns the foreheads of Moab,
the skulls[o] of the noisy boasters.
46Woe to you, O Moab![p]
The people of Chemosh are destroyed;
your sons are taken into exile
and your daughters into captivity.

47"Yet I will restore[q] the fortunes of Moab
in days to come,"
declares the LORD.

Here ends the judgment on Moab.

A Message About Ammon

49 Concerning the Ammonites:[a]

This is what the LORD says:

"Has Israel no sons?
Has she no heirs?
Why then has Molech[a] taken possession of Gad?
Why do his people live in its towns?
2But the days are coming,"
declares the LORD,
"when I will sound the battle cry[b]
against Rabbah[c] of the Ammonites;
it will become a mound of ruins,
and its surrounding villages will be set on fire.
Then Israel will drive out
those who drove her out,[d]"
says the LORD.

3"Wail, O Heshbon, for Ai[e] is destroyed!
Cry out, O inhabitants of Rabbah!
Put on sackcloth and mourn;

a *1* Or *their king*; Hebrew *malcam*; also in verse 3

48:41 [g]Isa 21:3
48:42 [h]Ps 83:4; Isa 16:14 [i]ver 2 [j]ver 26
48:43 [k]Isa 24:17
48:44 [l]1Ki 19:17; Isa 24:18 [m]Jer 11:23
48:45 [n]Nu 21:21, 26-28 [o]Nu 24:17
48:46 [p]Nu 21:29
48:47 [q]Jer 12:15; 49:6, 39
49:1 [a]Am 1:13; Zep 2:8-9
49:2 [b]Jer 4:19 [c]Dt 3:11 [d]Isa 14:2; Eze 21:28-32; 25:2-11
49:3 [e]Jos 8:28

49:1 The Ammonites were descendants of Lot through an incestuous relationship with one of his daughters (as were the Moabites; see Genesis 19:30–38). They were condemned for stealing land from God's people and for worshipping the idol Molech, to whom they made child sacrifices.

49:3 [f]Jer 48:7

rush here and there inside the walls,
for Molech will go into exile,[f]
together with his priests and officials.
4Why do you boast of your valleys,
boast of your valleys so fruitful?

49:4 [g]Jer 9:23; 1Ti 6:17 [h]Jer 21:13

O unfaithful daughter,
you trust in your riches[g] and say,
'Who will attack me?'[h]
5I will bring terror on you
from all those around you,"
declares the Lord, the LORD Almighty.
"Every one of you will be driven away,
and no-one will gather the fugitives.

49:6 [i]ver 39; Jer 48:47

6"Yet afterwards, I will restore[i] the fortunes of the Ammonites,"
declares the LORD.

A Message About Edom

49:7 [j]Ge 25:30; Eze 25:12 [k]Ge 36:11, 15, 34

7Concerning Edom:[j]

This is what the LORD Almighty says:

"Is there no longer wisdom in Teman?[k]
Has counsel perished from the prudent?
Has their wisdom decayed?

49:8 [l]Jer 25:23

8Turn and flee, hide in deep caves,
you who live in Dedan,[l]
for I will bring disaster on Esau
at the time I punish him.
9If grape-pickers came to you,
would they not leave a few grapes?

49:10 [m]Mal 1:2-5

If thieves came during the night,
would they not steal only as much as they wanted?
10But I will strip Esau bare;
I will uncover his hiding-places,
so that he cannot conceal himself.

49:11 [n]Hos 14:3

His children, relatives and neighbours will perish,
and he will be no more.[m]
11Leave your orphans;[n] I will protect their lives.
Your widows too can trust in me."

49:12 [o]Jer 25:15 [p]Jer 25:28-29

12This is what the LORD says: "If those who do not deserve to drink the cup[o] must
drink it, why should you go unpunished?[p] You will not go unpunished, but must drink
it. 13I swear[q] by myself," declares the LORD, "that Bozrah[r] will become a ruin and
an object of horror, of reproach and of cursing; and all its towns will be in ruins for
ever."

49:13 [q]Ge 22:16 [r]Ge 36:33; Isa 34:6

14I have heard a message from the LORD:
An envoy was sent to the nations to say,
"Assemble yourselves to attack it!
Rise up for battle!"

49:7 Because the Israelites descended from Jacob and the Edomites from his twin brother, Esau, both nations descended from their father, Isaac. There was constant conflict between these nations, and Edom rejoiced at the fall of Jerusalem (see the book of Obadiah). Teman, a town in the northern part of Edom, was known for its wisdom and was the home town of Eliphaz, one of Job's friends (Job 2:11). But even the wisdom of Teman could not save Edom from God's wrath.

49:8 Dedan was a flourishing city that supported caravan travel. God told its inhabitants to flee to the caves or they too would be destroyed. Teman and Dedan were at opposite ends of the country, so this shows the completeness of God's destruction of Edom. Bozrah (49:13) is a town in northern Edom.

15"Now I will make you small among the nations,
despised among men.
16The terror you inspire
and the pride of your heart have deceived you,
you who live in the clefts of the rocks,
who occupy the heights of the hill.
Though you build your nest[s] as high as the eagle's,
from there I will bring you down,"
declares the LORD.

17"Edom will become an object of horror;[t]
all who pass by will be appalled and will scoff
because of all its wounds.[u]
18As Sodom and Gomorrah[v] were overthrown,
along with their neighbouring towns,"
says the LORD,
"so no-one will live there;
no man will dwell[w] in it.

19"Like a lion coming up from Jordan's thickets[x]
to a rich pasture-land,
I will chase Edom from its land in an instant.
Who is the chosen one I will appoint for this?
Who is like me and who can challenge me?[y]
And what shepherd can stand against me?"
20Therefore, hear what the LORD has planned against Edom,
what he has purposed[z] against those who live in Teman:
The young of the flock[a] will be dragged away;
he will completely destroy[b] their pasture because of them.
21At the sound of their fall the earth will tremble;[c]
their cry[d] will resound to the Red Sea.[b]
22Look! An eagle will soar and swoop[e] down,
spreading its wings over Bozrah.
In that day the hearts of Edom's warriors
will be like the heart of a woman in labour.[f]

A Message About Damascus

23Concerning Damascus:[g]

"Hamath[h] and Arpad[i] are dismayed,
for they have heard bad news.
They are disheartened,
troubled like[c] the restless sea.[j]
24Damascus has become feeble,
she has turned to flee
and panic has gripped her;
anguish and pain have seized her,
pain like that of a woman in labour.
25Why has the city of renown not been abandoned,
the town in which I delight?

49:16 [s]Job 39:27; Am 9:2
49:17 [t]ver 13 [u]Jer 50:13; Eze 35:7
49:18 [v]Ge 19:24; Dt 29:23 [w]ver 33
49:19 [x]Jer 12:5 [y]Jer 50:44
49:20 [z]Isa 14:27 [a]Jer 50:45 [b]Mal 1:3-4
49:21 [c]Eze 26:15 [d]Jer 50:46; Eze 26:18
49:22 [e]Hos 8:1 [f]Isa 13:8; Jer 48:40-41
49:23 [g]Ge 14:15; 2Ch 16:2; Ac 9:2 [h]Isa 10:9; Am 6:2; Zec 9:2 [i]2Ki 18:34 [j]Ge 49:4; Isa 57:20

b *21* Hebrew *Yam Suph*; that is, Sea of Reeds **c** *23* Hebrew *on* or *by*

49:16 Edom was located in a rock fortress that is known today as Petra, in southern Jordan. Edom thought it was invincible because of its location. Edom was destroyed because of her pride. Pride destroys individuals as well as nations. It makes us think we can take care of ourselves without God's help. Even serving God and others can lead us into pride. Take stock of your life and service for God; ask God to point out and remove any pride you may be harbouring.

49:23–26 Damascus was the capital of Aram, north of Israel. This city was defeated by both Assyria and Babylon. Nebuchadnezzar attacked and defeated Damascus in 605 B.C. (Amos 1:4, 5). It is difficult to attribute the defeat of the army to a particular event, but God utterly destroyed Aram.

49:26 [k]Jer 50:30

26 Surely, her young men will fall in the streets;
all her soldiers will be silenced[k] in that day,"
declares the LORD Almighty.
27 "I will set fire[l] to the walls of Damascus;
it will consume the fortresses of Ben-Hadad.[m]"

49:27 [l]Jer 43:12; Am 1:4 [m]1Ki 15:18

A Message About Kedar and Hazor

28 Concerning Kedar[n] and the kingdoms of Hazor, which Nebuchadnezzar king of Babylon attacked:

This is what the LORD says:

"Arise, and attack Kedar
and destroy the people of the East.[o]
29 Their tents and their flocks will be taken;
their shelters will be carried off
with all their goods and camels.
Men will shout to them,
'Terror[p] on every side!'

49:28 [n]Ge 25:13 [o]Jdg 6:3

49:29 [p]Jer 6:25; 46:5

30 "Flee quickly away!
Stay in deep caves, you who live in Hazor,"
declares the LORD.
"Nebuchadnezzar king of Babylon has plotted against you;
he has devised a plan against you.

49:31 [q]Eze 38:11

31 "Arise and attack a nation at ease,
which lives in confidence,"
declares the LORD,
"a nation that has neither gates nor bars;[q]
its people live alone.
32 Their camels will become plunder,
and their large herds will be booty.
I will scatter to the winds those who are in distant places[d][r]
and will bring disaster on them from every side,"
declares the LORD.

49:32 [r]Jer 9:26

33 "Hazor will become a haunt of jackals,
a desolate[s] place for ever.
No-one will live there;
no man will dwell[t] in it."

49:33 [s]Jer 10:22 [t]ver 18; Jer 51:37

A Message About Elam

34 This is the word of the LORD that came to Jeremiah the prophet concerning Elam,[u] early in the reign of Zedekiah[v] king of Judah:

49:34 [u]Ge 10:22 [v]2Ki 24:18

35 This is what the LORD Almighty says:

"See, I will break the bow[w] of Elam,
the mainstay of their might.
36 I will bring against Elam the four winds[x]
from the four quarters of the heavens;
I will scatter them to the four winds,
and there will not be a nation
where Elam's exiles do not go.
37 I will shatter Elam before their foes,

49:35 [w]Isa 22:6

49:36 [x]ver 32

d *32* Or *who clip the hair by their foreheads*

49:28 Kedar and Hazor were nomadic tribes east of Israel and south of Aram, in the desert. In 599 B.C. Nebuchadnezzar destroyed them.

49:34 Elam lay east of Babylon and was attacked by Nebuchadnezzar in 597 B.C. Later Elam became the nucleus of the Persian empire (Daniel 8:2) and the residence of Darius.

before those who seek their lives;
I will bring disaster upon them,
even my fierce anger,"[y]
declares the LORD.
"I will pursue them with the sword[z]
until I have made an end of them.
38 I will set my throne in Elam
and destroy her king and officials,"
declares the LORD.

39 "Yet I will restore[a] the fortunes of Elam
in days to come,"
declares the LORD.

A Message About Babylon

50 This is the word the LORD spoke through Jeremiah the prophet concerning Babylon[a] and the land of the Babylonians:**a**

2 "Announce and proclaim[b] among the nations,
lift up a banner and proclaim it;
keep nothing back, but say,
'Babylon will be captured;[c]
Bel[d] will be put to shame,
Marduk[e] filled with terror.
Her images will be put to shame
and her idols filled with terror.'
3 A nation from the north will attack her
and lay waste her land.
No-one will live[f] in it;
both men and animals[g] will flee away.

4 "In those days, at that time,"
declares the LORD,
"the people of Israel and the people of Judah together[h]
will go in tears[i] to seek[j] the LORD their God.
5 They will ask the way to Zion
and turn their faces towards it.
They will come[k] and bind themselves to the LORD
in an everlasting covenant[l]
that will not be forgotten.

6 "My people have been lost sheep;[m]
their shepherds have led them astray
and caused them to roam on the mountains.
They wandered over mountain and hill[n]
and forgot their own resting place.[o]
7 Whoever found them devoured them;
their enemies said, 'We are not guilty,[p]
for they sinned against the LORD, their true pasture,
the LORD, the hope[q] of their fathers.'

a *1* Or *Chaldeans*; also in verses 8, 25, 35 and 45

49:37 [y]Jer 30:24 [z]Jer 9:16
49:39 [a]Jer 48:47
50:1 [a]Ge 10:10; Isa 13:1
50:2 [b]Jer 4:16 [c]Jer 51:31 [d]Isa 46:1 [e]Jer 51:47
50:3 [f]ver 13; Isa 14:22-23 [g]Zep 1:3
50:4 [h]Jer 3:18; Hos 1:11 [i]Ezr 3:12; Jer 31:9 [j]Hos 3:5
50:5 [k]Jer 33:7 [l]Isa 55:3; Jer 32:40; Heb 8:6-10
50:6 [m]Isa 53:6; Mt 9:36; 10:6 [n]Jer 3:6; Eze 34:6 [o]ver 19
50:7 [p]Jer 2:3 [q]Jer 14:8

49:38 The throne represents God's judgment and sovereignty. God would preside over Elam's destruction. He is the King over all kings, including Elam's.

50:1ff At the height of its power, the Babylonian empire seemed immovable. But when Babylon had finished serving God's purpose of punishing Judah for her sins, it would be punished and crushed for its own. Babylon was destroyed in 539 B.C. by the Medo-Persians (Daniel 5:30, 31). Babylon is also used in Scripture as a symbol of all evil. This message can thus apply to the end times when God wipes out all evil, once and for all.

50:3 The nation from the north was Medo-Persia, an alliance of Media and Persia that would become the next world power. Cyrus took the city of Babylon by surprise and brought the nation to its knees in 539 B.C. (Daniel 5:30, 31). The complete destruction of the city was accomplished by later Persian kings.

8“Flee[r] out of Babylon;
leave the land of the Babylonians,
and be like the goats that lead the flock.
9For I will stir up and bring against Babylon
an alliance of great nations from the land of the north.
They will take up their positions against her,
and from the north she will be captured.
Their arrows will be like skilled warriors
who do not return empty-handed.
10So Babylonia[b] will be plundered;
all who plunder her will have their fill,”
declares the LORD.

11“Because you rejoice and are glad,
you who pillage my inheritance,[s]
because you frolic like a heifer threshing corn
and neigh like stallions,
12your mother will be greatly ashamed;
she who gave you birth will be disgraced.
She will be the least of the nations—
a wilderness, a dry land, a desert.
13Because of the LORD’s anger she will not be inhabited
but will be completely desolate.
All who pass Babylon will be horrified and scoff[t]
because of all her wounds.[u]

14“Take up your positions round Babylon,
all you who draw the bow.[v]
Shoot at her! Spare no arrows,
for she has sinned against the LORD.
15Shout[w] against her on every side!
She surrenders, her towers fall,
her walls[x] are torn down.
Since this is the vengeance[y] of the LORD,
take vengeance on her;
do to her[z] as she has done to others.
16Cut off from Babylon the sower,
and the reaper with his sickle at harvest.
Because of the sword[a] of the oppressor
let everyone return to his own people,[b]
let everyone flee to his own land.[c]

17“Israel is a scattered flock
that lions[d] have chased away.
The first to devour him
was the king[e] of Assyria;
the last to crush his bones
was Nebuchadnezzar[f] king[g] of Babylon.”

18Therefore this is what the LORD Almighty, the God of Israel, says:

“I will punish the king of Babylon and his land
as I punished the king[h] of Assyria.[i]

50:8 [r]Isa 48:20; Jer 51:6; Rev 18:4
50:11 [s]Isa 47:6
50:13 [t]Jer 18:16 [u]Jer 49:17
50:14 [v]ver 29, 42
50:15 [w]Jer 51:14 [x]Jer 51:44, 58 [y]Jer 51:6 [z]Ps 137:8; Rev 18:6
50:16 [a]Jer 25:38 [b]Isa 13:14 [c]Jer 51:9
50:17 [d]Jer 2:15 [e]2Ki 17:6 [f]2Ki 24:10, 14 [g]2Ki 25:7
50:18 [h]Isa 10:12 [i]Eze 31:3

b *10* Or *Chaldea*

50:17–20 God would punish wicked Babylon as he punished Assyria for what they had done to Israel. Assyria was crushed by Babylon, over which it had once ruled. Babylon in turn would be crushed by Medo-Persia, formerly under its authority. These verses also look to the time when the Messiah will rule and Israel will be fully restored. No sin will then be found in Israel because those who sought God will be forgiven.

19 But I will bring[j] Israel back to his own pasture
and he will graze on Carmel and Bashan;
his appetite will be satisfied
on the hills[k] of Ephraim and Gilead.
20 In those days, at that time,"
declares the LORD,
"search will be made for Israel's guilt,
but there will be none,
and for the sins[l] of Judah,
but none will be found,
for I will forgive[m] the remnant[n] I spare.

21 "Attack the land of Merathaim
and those who live in Pekod.[o]
Pursue, kill and completely destroy[c] them,"
declares the LORD.
"Do everything I have commanded you.
22 The noise[p] of battle is in the land,
the noise of great destruction!
23 How broken and shattered
is the hammer of the whole earth!
How desolate[q] is Babylon
among the nations!
24 I set a trap[r] for you, O Babylon,
and you were caught before you knew it;
you were found and captured[s]
because you opposed[t] the LORD.
25 The LORD has opened his arsenal
and brought out the weapons[u] of his wrath,
for the Sovereign LORD Almighty has work to do
in the land of the Babylonians.[v]
26 Come against her from afar.
Break open her granaries;
pile her up like heaps of grain.
Completely destroy[w] her
and leave her no remnant.
27 Kill all her young bulls;
let them go down to the slaughter!
Woe to them! For their day has come,
the time for them to be punished.
28 Listen to the fugitives and refugees from Babylon
declaring in Zion[x]
how the LORD our God has taken vengeance,[y]
vengeance for his temple.

29 "Summon archers against Babylon,
all those who draw the bow.[z]
Encamp all round her;
let no-one escape.
Repay[a] her for her deeds;[b]
do to her as she has done.
For she defied[c] the LORD,
the Holy One of Israel.

c 21 The Hebrew term refers to the irrevocable giving over of things or persons to the LORD, often by totally destroying them; also in verse 26.

50:19 [j] Jer 31:10; Eze 34:13 [k] Jer 31:5; 33:12
50:20 [l] Mic 7:18, 19 [m] Jer 31:34 [n] Isa 1:9
50:21 [o] Eze 23:23
50:22 [p] Jer 4:19-21; 51:54
50:23 [q] Isa 14:16
50:24 [r] Da 5:30-31 [s] Jer 51:31 [t] Job 9:4
50:25 [u] Isa 13:5 [v] Jer 51:25, 55
50:26 [w] Isa 14:22-23
50:28 [x] Isa 48:20; Jer 51:10 [y] ver 15
50:29 [z] ver 14 [a] Rev 18:6 [b] Jer 51:56 [c] Isa 47:10

50:21 Merathaim was located in southern Babylonia; Pekod was in eastern Babylonia.

50:32 Pride (arrogance) was Babylon's characteristic sin. Pride comes from feeling self-sufficient or believing that we don't need

30Therefore, her young men[d] will fall in the streets;
all her soldiers will be silenced in that day,"
declares the LORD.

31"See, I am against[e] you, O arrogant one,"
declares the Lord, the LORD Almighty,
"for your day has come,
the time for you to be punished.
32The arrogant one will stumble and fall
and no-one will help her up;
I will kindle a fire[f] in her towns
that will consume all who are around her."

33This is what the LORD Almighty says:

"The people of Israel are oppressed,[g]
and the people of Judah as well.
All their captors hold them fast,
refusing to let them go.[h]
34Yet their Redeemer is strong;
the LORD Almighty[i] is his name.
He will vigorously defend their cause[j]
so that he may bring rest[k] to their land,
but unrest to those who live in Babylon.

35"A sword[l] against the Babylonians!"
declares the LORD—
"against those who live in Babylon
and against her officials and wise[m] men!
36A sword against her false prophets!
They will become fools.
A sword against her warriors![n]
They will be filled with terror.
37A sword against her horses and chariots[o]
and all the foreigners in her ranks!
They will become women.[p]
A sword against her treasures!
They will be plundered.
38A drought on**d** her waters!
They will dry[q] up.
For it is a land of idols,[r]
idols that will go mad with terror.

39"So desert creatures and hyenas will live there,
and there the owl will dwell.
It will never again be inhabited
or lived in from generation to generation.[s]
40As God overthrew Sodom and Gomorrah[t]
along with their neighbouring towns,"
declares the LORD,
"so no-one will live there;
no man will dwell in it.

41"Look! An army is coming from the north;[u]

50:30 [d]Isa 13:18; Jer 49:26
50:31 [e]Jer 21:13
50:32 [f]Jer 21:14; 49:27
50:33 [g]Isa 58:6 [h]Isa 14:17
50:34 [i]Jer 51:19 [j]Jer 15:21; 51:36 [k]Isa 14:7
50:35 [l]Jer 47:6 [m]Da 5:7
50:36 [n]Jer 49:22
50:37 [o]Jer 51:21 [p]Jer 51:30; Na 3:13
50:38 [q]Jer 51:36 [r]ver 2
50:39 [s]Isa 13:19-22; 34:13-15; Jer 51:37; Rev 18:2
50:40 [t]Ge 19:24
50:41 [u]Jer 6:22

d *38* Or *A sword against*

God. Proud nations or people, however, will eventually fail because they refuse to recognise God as the ultimate power. Getting rid of pride is not easy, but we can admit that it often rules us and ask God to forgive us and help us overcome it. The best antidote to pride is to focus our attention on the greatness and goodness of God.

50:39 Babylon remains a wasteland to this day. See also Isaiah 13:19–22.

a great nation and many kings
are being stirred up from the ends of the earth.[v]
42 They are armed with bows[w] and spears;
they are cruel and without mercy.[x]
They sound like the roaring sea[y]
as they ride on their horses;
they come like men in battle formation
to attack you, O Daughter of Babylon.[z]
43 The king of Babylon has heard reports about them,
and his hands hang limp.
Anguish has gripped him,
pain like that of a woman in labour.
44 Like a lion coming up from Jordan's thickets
to a rich pasture-land,
I will chase Babylon from its land in an instant.
Who is the chosen[a] one I will appoint for this?
Who is like me and who can challenge me?[b]
And what shepherd can stand against me?"
45 Therefore, hear what the LORD has planned against Babylon,
what he has purposed[c] against the land of the Babylonians:
The young of the flock will be dragged away;
he will completely destroy their pasture because of them.
46 At the sound of Babylon's capture the earth will tremble;
its cry[d] will resound among the nations.

51

This is what the LORD says:

"See, I will stir up the spirit of a destroyer
against Babylon and the people of Leb Kamai.**[a]**
2 I will send foreigners to Babylon
to winnow[a] her and to devastate her land;
they will oppose her on every side
in the day of her disaster.
3 Let not the archer string his bow,[b]
nor let him put on his armour.[c]
Do not spare her young men;
completely destroy**[b]** her army.
4 They will fall[d] down slain in Babylon,**[c]**
fatally wounded in her streets.[e]
5 For Israel and Judah have not been forsaken[f]
by their God, the LORD Almighty,
though their land**[d]** is full of guilt[g]
before the Holy One of Israel.

6 "Flee[h] from Babylon!
Run for your lives!
Do not be destroyed because of her sins.[i]
It is time for the LORD's vengeance;[j]
he will pay[k] her what she deserves.

a *1 Leb Kamai* is a cryptogram for Chaldea, that is, Babylonia. **b** *3* The Hebrew term refers to the irrevocable giving over of things or persons to the LORD, often by totally destroying them. **c** *4* Or *Chaldea* **d** *5* Or / *and the land of the Babylonians*,

50:41 [v]Isa 13:4; Jer 51:22-28
50:42 [w]ver 14 [x]Isa 13:18 [y]Isa 5:30 [z]Jer 6:23
50:44 [a]Nu 16:5 [b]Job 41:10; Isa 46:9; Jer 49:19
50:45 [c]Ps 33:11; Isa 14:24; Jer 51:11
50:46 [d]Rev 18:9-10
51:2 [a]Isa 41:16; Jer 15:7; Mt 3:12
51:3 [b]Jer 50:29 [c]Jer 46:4
51:4 [d]Isa 13:15 [e]Jer 49:26; 50:30
51:5 [f]Isa 54:6-8 [g]Hos 4:1
51:6 [h]Jer 50:8 [i]Nu 16:26; Rev 18:4 [j]Jer 50:15 [k]Jer 25:14

50:44–46 This invader was Cyrus, who attacked Babylon by surprise and overthrew it. The world was shocked that its greatest empire was overthrown so quickly. No earthly power, no matter how great, can last for ever.

51:2 Winnowers worked to separate the wheat from the chaff. When they threw the mixture into the air, the wind blew away the worthless chaff while the wheat settled to the floor. Babylon would be blown away like chaff in the wind. (See also Matthew 3:12 where John the Baptist says Jesus will separate the wheat from the chaff.)

51:7
[l]Jer 25:15-16; Rev 14:8-10; 17:4

51:8
[m]Isa 21:9; Rev 14:8
[n]Jer 46:11

51:9
[o]Isa 13:14; Jer 50:16
[p]Rev 18:4-5

51:10
[q]Mic 7:9
[r]Jer 50:28

51:11
[s]Jer 50:9
[t]Jer 46:4
[u]ver 28
[v]Jer 50:45
[w]Jer 50:28

51:13
[x]Rev 17:1, 15
[y]Isa 45:3; Hab 2:9

51:14
[z]Am 6:8
[a]ver 27; Na 3:15
[b]Jer 50:15

51:15
[c]Ge 1:1; Job 9:8; Ps 104:2

51:16
[d]Ps 18:11-13
[e]Ps 135:7; Jnh 1:4

51:17
[f]Isa 44:20; Hab 2:18-19

51:18
[g]Jer 18:15

7 Babylon was a gold cup[l] in the LORD's hand;
she made the whole earth drunk.
The nations drank her wine;
therefore they have now gone mad.
8 Babylon will suddenly fall[m] and be broken.
Wail over her!
Get balm[n] for her pain;
perhaps she can be healed.

9 " 'We would have healed Babylon,
but she cannot be healed;
let us leave[o] her and each go to his own land,
for her judgment[p] reaches to the skies,
it rises as high as the clouds.'

10 " 'The LORD has vindicated[q] us;
come, let us tell in Zion
what the LORD our God has done.'[r]

11 "Sharpen the arrows,[s]
take up the shields![t]
The LORD has stirred up the kings of the Medes,[u]
because his purpose[v] is to destroy Babylon.
The LORD will take vengeance,
vengeance for his temple.[w]
12 Lift up a banner against the walls of Babylon!
Reinforce the guard,
station the watchmen,
prepare an ambush!
The LORD will carry out his purpose,
his decree against the people of Babylon.
13 You who live by many waters[x]
and are rich in treasures,[y]
your end has come,
the time for you to be cut off.
14 The LORD Almighty has sworn by himself:[z]
I will surely fill you with men, as with a swarm of locusts,[a]
and they will shout[b] in triumph over you.

15 "He made the earth by his power;
he founded the world by his wisdom
and stretched[c] out the heavens by his understanding.
16 When he thunders,[d] the waters in the heavens roar;
he makes clouds rise from the ends of the earth.
He sends lightning with the rain
and brings out the wind from his storehouses.[e]

17 "Every man is senseless and without knowledge;
every goldsmith is shamed by his idols.
His images are a fraud;[f]
they have no breath in them.
18 They are worthless,[g] the objects of mockery;
when their judgment comes, they will perish.
19 He who is the Portion of Jacob is not like these,

51:11 Cyrus, king of Persia, had allied with Babylon to defeat Nineveh (capital of the Assyrian empire) in 612 B.C. Then the Medes joined Persia to defeat Babylon (539 B.C.).

51:17–19 It is foolish to trust in man-made images rather than in God. It is easy to think that the things we see and touch will bring us more security than God. But things rust, rot, and decay. God is eternal. Why put your trust in something that will disappear within a few years?

for he is the Maker of all things,
including the tribe of his inheritance—
the LORD Almighty is his name.

20 "You are my war club,[h]
my weapon for battle—
with you I shatter[i] nations,
with you I destroy kingdoms,
21 with you I shatter horse and rider,[j]
with you I shatter chariot and driver,
22 with you I shatter man and woman,
with you I shatter old man and youth,
with you I shatter young man and maiden,[k]
23 with you I shatter shepherd and flock,
with you I shatter farmer and oxen,
with you I shatter governors and officials.[l]

24 "Before your eyes I will repay[m] Babylon and all who live in Babylonia[e] for all
the wrong they have done in Zion," declares the LORD.

25 "I am against you, O destroying mountain,
you who destroy the whole earth,"
declares the LORD.
"I will stretch out my hand against you,
roll you off the cliffs,
and make you a burnt-out mountain.[n]
26 No rock will be taken from you for a cornerstone,
nor any stone for a foundation,
for you will be desolate[o] for ever,"
declares the LORD.

27 "Lift up a banner[p] in the land!
Blow the trumpet among the nations!
Prepare the nations for battle against her;
summon against her these kingdoms:[q]
Ararat,[r] Minni and Ashkenaz.[s]
Appoint a commander against her;
send up horses like a swarm of locusts.
28 Prepare the nations for battle against her—
the kings of the Medes,[t]
their governors and all their officials,
and all the countries they rule.
29 The land trembles and writhes,
for the LORD's purposes against Babylon stand—
to lay waste the land of Babylon
so that no-one will live there.[u]
30 Babylon's warriors[v] have stopped fighting;
they remain in their strongholds.
Their strength is exhausted;
they have become like women.[w]
Her dwellings are set on fire;
the bars[x] of her gates are broken.
31 One courier[y] follows another
and messenger follows messenger
to announce to the king of Babylon
that his entire city is captured,
32 the river crossings seized,
the marshes set on fire,
and the soldiers terrified.[z]"

[e] 24 Or *Chaldea*; also in verse 35

51:20 [h] Isa 10:5 [i] Mic 4:13
51:21 [j] Ex 15:1
51:22 [k] 2Ch 36:17; Isa 13:17-18
51:23 [l] ver 57
51:24 [m] Jer 50:15
51:25 [n] Zec 4:7
51:26 [o] ver 29; Isa 13:19-22; Jer 50:12
51:27 [p] Isa 13:2; Jer 50:2 [q] Jer 25:14 [r] Ge 8:4 [s] Ge 10:3
51:28 [t] ver 11
51:29 [u] ver 43; Isa 13:20
51:30 [v] Jer 50:36 [w] Isa 19:16 [x] Isa 45:2; La 2:9; Na 3:13
51:31 [y] 2Sa 18:19-31
51:32 [z] Jer 50:36

51:33 [a] Isa 21:10 [b] Isa 17:5; Hos 6:11
51:34 [c] Jer 50:17
51:35 [d] ver 24; Ps 137:8
51:36 [e] Ps 140:12; Jer 50:34; La 3:58 [f] ver 6; Ro 12:19 [g] Jer 50:38
51:37 [h] Isa 13:22; Rev 18:2 [i] Jer 50:13, 39
51:39 [j] ver 57
51:41 [k] Jer 25:26 [l] Isa 13:19
51:42 [m] Isa 8:7
51:43 [n] ver 29, 62; Isa 13:20; Jer 2:6

33 This is what the LORD Almighty, the God of Israel, says:
"The Daughter of Babylon is like a threshing-floor[a]
at the time it is trampled;
the time to harvest[b] her will soon come."

34 "Nebuchadnezzar[c] king of Babylon has devoured us,
he has thrown us into confusion,
he has made us an empty jar.
Like a serpent he has swallowed us
and filled his stomach with our delicacies,
and then has spewed us out.
35 May the violence done to our flesh[f] be upon Babylon,"
say the inhabitants of Zion.
"May our blood be on those who live in Babylonia,"
says Jerusalem.[d]

36 Therefore, this is what the LORD says:

"See, I will defend your cause[e]
and avenge[f] you;
I will dry up[g] her sea
and make her springs dry.
37 Babylon will be a heap of ruins,
a haunt[h] of jackals,
an object of horror and scorn,
a place where no-one lives.[i]
38 Her people all roar like young lions,
they growl like lion cubs.
39 But while they are aroused,
I will set out a feast for them
and make them drunk,
so that they shout with laughter—
then sleep for ever and not awake,"
declares the LORD.[j]

40 "I will bring them down
like lambs to the slaughter,
like rams and goats.

41 "How Sheshach[g][k] will be captured,[l]
the boast of the whole earth seized!
What a horror Babylon will be
among the nations!
42 The sea will rise over Babylon;
its roaring waves[m] will cover her.
43 Her towns will be desolate,
a dry and desert land,
a land where no-one lives,
through which no man travels.[n]

[f] 35 Or *done to us and to our children* [g] 41 *Sheshach* is a cryptogram for Babylon.

51:33 Grain was threshed on a threshing floor, where sheaves were brought from the field. The stalks of grain were distributed on the floor, a large level section of hard ground. There the grain was crushed to separate the kernels from the stalk; then the kernels were beaten with a wooden tool. Sometimes a wooden sledge was pulled over the grain by animals to break the kernels loose. Babylon would soon be "threshed" as God judged it for its sins.

51:36 This verse may refer to an event accomplished by Cyrus, who took Babylon by surprise by diverting the river that ran through the city far upstream and walking in on the dry river bed. More likely it is saying that Babylon will be deprived of life-giving water. Unlike Jerusalem, Babylon will not be restored.

44 I will punish Bel[o] in Babylon
and make him spew out[p] what he has swallowed.
The nations will no longer stream to him.
And the wall[q] of Babylon will fall.

45 "Come out[r] of her, my people!
Run[s] for your lives!
Run from the fierce anger of the LORD.
46 Do not lose heart or be afraid[t]
when rumours[u] are heard in the land;
one rumour comes this year, another the next,
rumours of violence in the land
and of ruler against ruler.
47 For the time will surely come
when I will punish the idols[v] of Babylon;
her whole land will be disgraced[w]
and her slain will all lie fallen within her.
48 Then heaven and earth and all that is in them
will shout[x] for joy over Babylon,
for out of the north[y]
destroyers will attack her,"
declares the LORD.

49 "Babylon must fall because of Israel's slain,
just as the slain in all the earth
have fallen because of Babylon.[z]
50 You who have escaped the sword,
leave[a] and do not linger!
Remember[b] the LORD in a distant land,
and think on Jerusalem."

51 "We are disgraced,[c]
for we have been insulted
and shame covers our faces,
because foreigners have entered
the holy places of the LORD's house."[d]

52 "But days are coming," declares the LORD,
"when I will punish her idols,[e]
and throughout her land
the wounded will groan.
53 Even if Babylon reaches the sky[f]
and fortifies her lofty stronghold,
I will send destroyers[g] against her,"
declares the LORD.

54 "The sound of a cry comes from Babylon,
the sound of great destruction[h]
from the land of the Babylonians.[h]
55 The LORD will destroy Babylon;
he will silence her noisy din.
Waves[i] ⌊of enemies⌋ will rage like great waters;
the roar of their voices will resound.
56 A destroyer[j] will come against Babylon;

51:44 [o] Isa 46:1 [p] ver 34 [q] ver 58; Jer 50:15
51:45 [r] Rev 18:4 [s] ver 6; Isa 48:20; Jer 50:8
51:46 [t] Jer 46:27 [u] 2Ki 19:7
51:47 [v] ver 52; Isa 46:1-2; Jer 50:2 [w] Jer 50:12
51:48 [x] Isa 44:23; Rev 18:20 [y] ver 11
51:49 [z] Ps 137:8; Jer 50:29
51:50 [a] ver 45 [b] Ps 137:6
51:51 [c] Ps 44:13-16; 79:4 [d] La 1:10
51:52 [e] ver 47
51:53 [f] Ge 11:4; Isa 14:13-14 [g] Jer 49:16
51:54 [h] Jer 50:22
51:55 [i] Ps 18:4
51:56 [j] ver 48

h 54 Or *Chaldeans*

51:44 Bel is one of the names of Marduk, the chief god of the city of Babylon.

51:51 The people were paralysed with guilt over their past. The Babylonian armies had desecrated the temple, and the people were ashamed to return to Jerusalem. But God told them to return to the city because he would destroy Babylon for its sins.

51:56
[k]Ps 46:9
[l]ver 6;
Ps 94:1-2;
Hab 2:8

51:57
[m]Ps 76:5;
Jer 25:27
[n]Jer 46:18; 48:15

51:58
[o]ver 44
[p]ver 64
[q]Hab 2:13

51:59
[r]Jer 36:4
[s]Jer 52:1
[t]Jer 28:1

51:60
[u]Jer 30:2; 36:2

51:62
[v]Isa 13:20;
Jer 50:13, 39

51:64
[w]ver 58
[x]Job 31:40

52:1
[a]2Ki 24:17
[b]Jos 10:29;
2Ki 8:22

52:2
[c]Jer 36:30

52:3
[d]Isa 3:1
[e]Eze 17:12-16

52:4
[f]Zec 8:19
[g]2Ki 25:1-7;
Jer 39:1
[h]Eze 24:1-2

52:6
[i]Isa 3:1

52:9
[j]Jer 32:4
[k]Nu 34:11
[l]Nu 13:21

her warriors will be captured,
and their bows will be broken.[k]
For the LORD is a God of retribution;
he will repay[l] in full.
57I will make her officials and wise men drunk,
her governors, officers and warriors as well;
they will sleep[m] for ever and not awake,"
declares the King,[n] whose name is the LORD Almighty.

58This is what the LORD Almighty says:

"Babylon's thick wall[o] will be levelled
and her high gates set on fire;
the peoples[p] exhaust themselves for nothing,
the nations' labour is only fuel for the flames."[q]

59This is the message Jeremiah gave to the staff officer Seraiah son of Neriah,[r]
the son of Mahseiah, when he went to Babylon with Zedekiah[s] king of Judah in the
fourth[t] year of his reign. 60Jeremiah had written on a scroll[u] about all the disasters
that would come upon Babylon – all that had been recorded concerning Babylon. 61He
said to Seraiah, "When you get to Babylon, see that you read all these words aloud.
62Then say, 'O LORD, you have said you will destroy this place, so that neither man
nor animal will live in it; it will be desolate[v] for ever.' 63When you finish reading
this scroll, tie a stone to it and throw it into the Euphrates. 64Then say, 'So will
Babylon sink to rise no more because of the disaster I will bring upon her. And her
people[w] will fall.' "

The words of Jeremiah end[x] here.

2. The fall of Jerusalem

52 Zedekiah[a] was twenty-one years old when he became king, and he reigned
in Jerusalem for eleven years. His mother's name was Hamutal daughter of
Jeremiah; she was from Libnah.[b] 2He did evil in the eyes of the LORD, just as
Jehoiakim[c] had done. 3It was because of the LORD's anger that all this happened to
Jerusalem and Judah,[d] and in the end he thrust them from his presence.

Now Zedekiah rebelled[e] against the king of Babylon.

4So in the ninth year of Zedekiah's reign, on the tenth[f] day of the tenth month,
Nebuchadnezzar king of Babylon marched against Jerusalem[g] with his whole army.
They camped outside the city and built siege works all around it.[h] 5The city was kept
under siege until the eleventh year of King Zedekiah.

6By the ninth day of the fourth month the famine in the city had become so severe
that there was no food for the people to eat.[i] 7Then the city wall was broken through,
and the whole army fled. They left the city at night through the gate between the two
walls near the king's garden, though the Babylonians**[a]** were surrounding the city.
They fled towards the Arabah,**[b]** 8but the Babylonian**[c]** army pursued King Zedekiah
and overtook him in the plains of Jericho. All his soldiers were separated from him
and scattered, 9and he was captured.[j]

He was taken to the king of Babylon at Riblah[k] in the land of Hamath,[l] where

a *7* Or *Chaldeans*; also in verse 17 **b** *7* Or *the Jordan Valley* **c** *8* Or *Chaldean*; also in verse 14

51:59 Jeremiah could not visit Babylon, so he sent the message with Seraiah, the officer who cared for the comforts of the army. Seriah was probably Baruch's brother (32:12).

51:60–64 In this last of Jeremiah's messages, we find again the twin themes of God's sovereignty and his judgment. Babylon had been allowed to oppress the people of Israel, but Babylon itself would be judged. Although God brings good out of evil, he does not allow evil to remain unpunished. The wicked may succeed for a while, but resist the temptation to follow them or you may share in their judgment.

52:1ff This chapter provides more detail about the destruction of Jerusalem recorded in chapter 39 (similar material is found in 2 Kings 24:18 – 25:21). This appendix shows that Jeremiah's prophecies concerning the destruction of Jerusalem and the Babylonian captivity happened just as he predicted. For more information on Zedekiah, see the note on 39:1.

52:8, 9 Riblah was 200 miles north of Jerusalem. This was the Babylonian headquarters for ruling the region. Hamath was the district of Aram containing the nation's capital.

he pronounced sentence on him. 10 There at Riblah the king of Babylon slaughtered
the sons[m] of Zedekiah before his eyes; he also killed all the officials of Judah. 11 Then
he put out Zedekiah's eyes, bound him with bronze shackles and took him to Babylon,
where he put him in prison till the day of his death.[n]
12 On the tenth day of the fifth[o] month, in the nineteenth year of Nebuchadnezzar
king of Babylon, Nebuzaradan[p] commander of the imperial guard, who served the
king of Babylon, came to Jerusalem. 13 He set fire[q] to the temple[r] of the LORD, the
royal palace and all the houses of Jerusalem. Every important building he burned
down. 14 The whole Babylonian army under the commander of the imperial guard
broke down all the walls[s] around Jerusalem. 15 Nebuzaradan the commander of the
guard carried into exile some of the poorest people and those who remained in the
city, along with the rest of the craftsmen[d] and those who had gone over to the king
of Babylon. 16 But Nebuzaradan left behind[t] the rest of the poorest people of the land
to work the vineyards and fields.
17 The Babylonians broke up the bronze pillars,[u] the movable stands[v] and the
bronze Sea[w] that were at the temple of the LORD and they carried all the bronze to
Babylon.[x] 18 They also took away the pots, shovels, wick trimmers, sprinkling bowls,
dishes and all the bronze articles used in the temple service.[y] 19 The commander of
the imperial guard took away the basins, censers,[z] sprinkling bowls, pots, lampstands, dishes and bowls used for drink offerings—all that were made of pure gold
or silver.
20 The bronze from the two pillars, the Sea and the twelve bronze bulls under it,
and the movable stands, which King Solomon had made for the temple of the LORD,
was more than could be weighed.[a] 21 Each of the pillars was eighteen cubits high and
twelve cubits in circumference;[e] each was four fingers thick, and hollow.[b] 22 The
bronze capital[c] on the top of the one pillar was five cubits[f] high and was decorated
with a network and pomegranates of bronze all around. The other pillar, with its
pomegranates, was similar. 23 There were ninety-six pomegranates on the sides; the
total number of pomegranates[d] above the surrounding network was a hundred.
24 The commander of the guard took as prisoners Seraiah[e] the chief priest, Zephaniah[f] the priest next in rank and the three doorkeepers. 25 Of those still in the city,
he took the officer in charge of the fighting men, and seven royal advisers. He also
took the secretary who was chief officer in charge of conscripting the people of the
land and sixty of his men who were found in the city. 26 Nebuzaradan[g] the commander
took them all and brought them to the king of Babylon at Riblah. 27 There at Riblah,
in the land of Hamath, the king had them executed.
So Judah went into captivity, away[h] from her land. 28 This is the number of the
people Nebuchadnezzar carried into exile:[i]

in the seventh year, 3,023 Jews;
29 in Nebuchadnezzar's eighteenth year,
832 people from Jerusalem;
30 in his twenty-third year,
745 Jews taken into exile by Nebuzaradan the commander of
the imperial guard.
There were 4,600 people in all.

Jehoiachin Released

31 In the thirty-seventh year of the exile of Jehoiachin king of Judah, in the year
Evil-Merodach[g] became king of Babylon, he released Jehoiachin king of Judah and
freed him from prison on the twenty-fifth day of the twelfth month. 32 He spoke kindly

d *15* Or *populace* **e** *21* That is, about 27 feet (about 8.1 metres) high and 18 feet (about 5.5 metres) in circumference **f** *22* That is, about 7 ½ feet (about 2.3 metres) **g** *31* Also called *Amel-Marduk*

52:10 [m] Jer 22:30
52:11 [n] Eze 12:13
52:12 [o] Zec 7:5; 8:19 [p] Jer 39:9
52:13 [q] 2Ch 36:19; Ps 74:8; La 2:6 [r] Ps 79:1; Mic 3:12
52:14 [s] Ne 1:3
52:16 [t] Jer 40:6
52:17 [u] 1Ki 7:15 [v] 1Ki 7:27-37 [w] 1Ki 7:23 [x] Jer 27:19-22
52:18 [y] Ex 27:3; 1Ki 7:45
52:19 [z] 1Ki 7:50
52:20 [a] 1Ki 7:47
52:21 [b] 1Ki 7:15
52:22 [c] 1Ki 7:16
52:23 [d] 1Ki 7:20
52:24 [e] 2Ki 25:18 [f] Jer 21:1; 37:3
52:26 [g] ver 12
52:27 [h] Jer 20:4
52:28 [i] 2Ki 24:14-16; 2Ch 36:20

52:21 A cubit was a standard of measure about 17 to 20 inches long.

52:31 Babylon's king showed kindness to Jehoiachin. In 561 B.C. Jehoiachin was released from prison and allowed to eat with the king. God continued to show kindness to the descendants of King David, even in exile.

52:33 [j]2Sa 9:7
52:34 [k]2Sa 9:10

to him and gave him a seat of honour higher than those of the other kings who were
with him in Babylon. 33 So Jehoiachin put aside his prison clothes and for the rest of
his life ate regularly at the king's table.[j] 34 Day by day the king of Babylon gave
Jehoiachin a regular allowance[k] as long as he lived, till the day of his death.

52:34 In the world's eyes, Jeremiah looked totally unsuccessful. He had no money, family, or friends. He prophesied the destruction of the nation, the capital city, and the temple, but the political and religious leaders would not accept or follow his advice. No group of people liked him or listened to him. Yet as we look back, we see that he successfully completed the work God gave him to do. Success must never be measured by popularity, fame, or fortune, for these are temporal measures. King Zedekiah, for example, lost everything by pursuing selfish goals. God measures our success with the yardsticks of obedience, faithfulness, and righteousness. If you are faithfully doing the work God gives you, you are successful in his eyes.

LAMENTATIONS

VITAL STATISTICS

PURPOSE:
To teach people that to disobey God is to invite disaster, and to show that God suffers when his people suffer

AUTHOR:
Jeremiah

DATE WRITTEN:
Soon after the fall of Jerusalem in 586 B.C.

SETTING:
Jerusalem had been destroyed by Babylon and her people killed, tortured, or taken captive.

KEY VERSE:
"My eyes fail from weeping, I am in torment within, my heart is poured out on the ground because my people are destroyed, because children and infants faint in the streets of the city" (2:11).

KEY PEOPLE:
Jeremiah, the people of Jerusalem

KEY PLACE:
Jerusalem

SPECIAL FEATURES:
Three strands of Hebrew thought meet in Lamentations—prophecy, ritual, and wisdom. Lamentations is written in the rhythm and style of ancient Jewish funeral songs or chants. It contains five poems corresponding to the five chapters (see the note on 3:1ff).

TEARS are defined simply as "drops of salty fluid flowing from the eyes". They can be caused by irritation or laughter but are usually associated with weeping, sorrow, and grief. When we cry, friends wonder what's wrong and try to console us. Babies cry for food, and children cry at the loss of a pet; adults cry when confronted with trauma and death.

Jeremiah's grief ran deep. Called the "weeping prophet", his tears flowed from a broken heart. As God's spokesman, he knew what lay ahead for Judah, his country, and for Jerusalem, the capital and "the city of God". God's judgment would fall and destruction would come. And Jeremiah wept. His tears were not self-centred, mourning over personal suffering or loss. He wept because the people had rejected their God—the God who had made them, loved them, and sought repeatedly to bless them. Jeremiah's heart was broken because he knew that the selfishness and sinfulness of the people would bring them much suffering and an extended exile. Jeremiah's tears were tears of empathy and sympathy. His heart was broken with those things that break God's heart.

Jeremiah's two books focus on one event—the destruction of Jerusalem. The book of Jeremiah predicts it, and Lamentations looks back on it. Known as the book of tears, Lamentations is a dirge, a funeral song written for the fallen city of Jerusalem.

What makes a person cry says a lot about that person—whether he or she is self-centred or God-centred. The book of Lamentations allows us to see what made Jeremiah sorrowful. As one of God's choice servants, he stands alone in the depth of his emotions, his care for the people, his love for the nation, and his devotion to God.

What causes your tears? Do you weep because your selfish pride has been wounded, or because the people around you sin against and reject the God who loves them dearly? Do you weep because you have lost something that gives you pleasure, or because people all around you will suffer for their sinfulness? Our world is filled with injustice, poverty, war, and rebellion against God, all of which should move us to tears and to action. Read Lamentations and learn what it means to grieve with God.

THE BLUEPRINT

1. Jeremiah mourns for Jerusalem (1:1–22)
2. God's anger at sin (2:1–22)
3. Hope in the midst of affliction (3:1–66)
4. God's anger is satisfied (4:1–22)
5. Jeremiah pleads for restoration (5:1–22)

Jeremiah grieves deeply because of the destruction of Jerusalem and the devastation of his nation. But in the middle of the book, in the depths of his grief, there shines a ray of hope. God's compassion is ever-present. His faithfulness is great. Jeremiah realises that it is only the Lord's mercy that has prevented total annihilation. This book shows us the serious consequences of human sin and how we can still have hope in the midst of tragedy because God is able to turn it around for good. We see the timeless importance of prayer and confession of sin. We will all face tragedy in our lives. But in the midst of our afflictions, there is hope in God.

MEGATHEMES

THEME	EXPLANATION	IMPORTANCE
Destruction of Jerusalem	Lamentations is a sad funeral song for the great capital city of the Jews. The temple has been destroyed, the king is gone, and the people are in exile. God had warned that he would destroy them if they abandoned him. Now, afterwards, the people realise their condition and confess their sin.	God's warnings are justified. He does what he says he will do. His punishment for sin is certain. Only by confessing and renouncing our sin can we turn to him for deliverance. How much better to do so before his warnings are fulfilled.
God's Mercy	God's compassion was at work even when the Israelites were experiencing the affliction of their Babylonian conquerors. Although the people had been unfaithful, God's faithfulness was great. He used this affliction to bring his people back to him.	God will always be faithful to his people. His merciful, refining work is evident even in affliction. At those times, we must pray for forgiveness and then turn to him for deliverance.
Sin's Consequences	God was angry at the prolonged rebellion by his people. Sin is the cause of their misery, and destruction is the result of their sin. The destruction of the nation shows the vanity of human glory and pride.	To continue in rebellion against God is to invite disaster. We must never trust our own leadership, resources, intelligence, or power more than God. If we do, we will experience consequences similar to Jerusalem's.
Hope	God's mercy in sparing some of the people offers hope for better days. One day, the people will be restored to a true and fervent relationship with God.	Only God can deliver us from sin. Without him there is no comfort or hope for the future. Because of Christ's death for us and his promise to return, we have a bright hope for tomorrow.

1. Jeremiah mourns for Jerusalem

1[a] How deserted lies the city,
once so full of people!
How like a widow[a] is she,
who once was great[b] among the nations!
She who was queen among the provinces
has now become a slave.[c]

2 Bitterly she weeps[d] at night,
tears are upon her cheeks.
Among all her lovers[e]
there is none to comfort her.
All her friends have betrayed[f] her;
they have become her enemies.[g]

3 After affliction and harsh labour,

1:1 [a] Isa 47:8 [b] 1Ki 4:21 [c] Isa 3:26; Jer 40:9

1:2 [d] Ps 6:6 [e] Jer 3:1 [f] Jer 4:30; Mic 7:5 [g] ver 16

a This chapter is an acrostic poem, the verses of which begin with the successive letters of the Hebrew alphabet.

1:1 This is the prophet Jeremiah's song of sorrow for Jerusalem's destruction. The nation of Judah had been utterly defeated, the temple destroyed, and captives taken away to Babylon. Jeremiah's tears were for the suffering and humiliation of the people, but those tears penetrated even deeper into his heart. He wept because God had rejected the people for their rebellious ways. Each year this book was read aloud to remind all the Jews that their great city fell because of their stubborn sinfulness.

1:2 The term *lovers* refers to nations such as Egypt, to whom Judah kept turning for help. As the Babylonians closed in on Jerusalem, the nation of Judah turned away from God and sought help and protection from other nations instead.

Judah has gone into exile.[h]
She dwells among the nations;
she finds no resting place.[i]
All who pursue her have overtaken her
in the midst of her distress.

4The roads to Zion mourn,
for no-one comes to her appointed feasts.
All her gateways are desolate,[j]
her priests groan,
her maidens grieve,
and she is in bitter anguish.[k]
5Her foes have become her masters;
her enemies are at ease.
The LORD has brought her grief[l]
because of her many sins.
Her children have gone into exile,[m]
captive before the foe.
6All the splendour has departed
from the Daughter of Zion.[n]
Her princes are like deer
that find no pasture;
in weakness they have fled
before the pursuer.
7In the days of her affliction and wandering
Jerusalem remembers all the treasures
that were hers in days of old.
When her people fell into enemy hands,
there was no-one to help her.[o]
Her enemies looked at her
and laughed at her destruction.

8Jerusalem has sinned[p] greatly
and so has become unclean.
All who honoured her despise her,
for they have seen her nakedness;[q]
she herself groans[r]
and turns away.

9Her filthiness clung to her skirts;
she did not consider her future.[s]
Her fall[t] was astounding;
there was none to comfort[u] her.
"Look, O LORD, on my affliction,[v]
for the enemy has triumphed."

10The enemy laid hands
on all her treasures;[w]
she saw pagan nations
enter her sanctuary[x]—
those you had forbidden[y]
to enter your assembly.

1:3 [h]Jer 13:19 [i]Dt 28:65
1:4 [j]Jer 9:11 [k]Joel 1:8-13
1:5 [l]Jer 30:15 [m]Jer 39:9; 52:28-30
1:6 [n]Jer 13:18
1:7 [o]Jer 37:7; La 4:17
1:8 [p]ver 20; Isa 59:2-13 [q]Jer 13:22, 26 [r]ver 21, 22
1:9 [s]Dt 32:28-29; Isa 47:7; Eze 24:13 [t]Jer 13:18 [u]Ecc 4:1; Jer 16:7 [v]Ps 25:18
1:10 [w]Isa 64:11 [x]Ps 74:7-8; Jer 51:51 [y]Dt 23:3

1:9 The warning was loud and clear: If Judah played with fire, its people would get burned. Jerusalem foolishly took a chance and lost, refusing to believe that immoral living brings God's punishment. The ultimate consequence of sin is punishment (Romans 6:23). We can choose to ignore God's warnings, but as surely as judgment came upon Jerusalem, so will it come upon those who defy God. Are you listening to God's word? Are you obeying it? Obedience is a sure sign of your love for God.

1:11 [z]Ps 38:8 [a]Jer 52:6

11 All her people groan[z]
as they search for bread;[a]
they barter their treasures for food
to keep themselves alive.
"Look, O LORD, and consider,
for I am despised."

1:12 [b]Jer 18:16 [c]ver 18 [d]Isa 13:13; Jer 30:24

12 "Is it nothing to you, all you who pass by?[b]
Look around and see.
Is any suffering like my suffering[c]
that was inflicted on me,
that the LORD brought on me
in the day of his fierce anger?[d]

1:13 [e]Job 30:30 [f]Jer 44:6 [g]Hab 3:16

13 "From on high he sent fire,
sent it down into my bones.[e]
He spread a net for my feet
and turned me back.
He made me desolate,[f]
faint[g] all the day long.

1:14 [h]Dt 28:48; Isa 47:6 [i]Jer 32:5

14 "My sins have been bound into a yoke;**[b]**[h]
by his hands they were woven together.
They have come upon my neck
and the Lord has sapped my strength.
He has handed me over[i]
to those I cannot withstand.

1:15 [j]Jer 37:10 [k]Isa 41:2 [l]Isa 28:18; Jer 18:21

15 "The Lord has rejected
all the warriors in my midst;[j]
he has summoned an army[k] against me
to**[c]** crush my young men.[l]
In his winepress the Lord has trampled
the Virgin Daughter of Judah.

1:16 [m]La 2:11, 18; 3:48-49 [n]Ps 69:20; Ecc 4:1 [o]ver 2; Jer 13:17; 14:17

16 "This is why I weep
and my eyes overflow with tears.[m]
No-one is near to comfort[n] me,
no-one to restore my spirit.
My children are destitute
because the enemy has prevailed."[o]

1:17 [p]Jer 4:31

17 Zion stretches out her hands,[p]
but there is no-one to comfort her.
The LORD has decreed for Jacob
that his neighbours become his foes;
Jerusalem has become
an unclean thing among them.

1:18 [q]1Sa 12:14 [r]ver 12

18 "The LORD is righteous,
yet I rebelled[q] against his command.
Listen, all you peoples;
look upon my suffering.[r]

b *14* Most Hebrew manuscripts; Septuagint *He kept watch over my sins* **c** *15* Or *has set a time for me / when he will*

1:14 At first, sin seems to offer freedom. But the liberty to do anything we want gradually becomes a desire to do everything. Then we become captive to sin, bound by its "yoke". Freedom from sin's captivity comes only from God. He gives us freedom, not to do anything we want, but to do what he knows is best for us. Strange as it may seem, true freedom comes in obeying God – following his guidance so that we can receive his best.

1:16 God is the comforter, but because of the people's sins, he had to turn away from them and become their judge.

My young men and maidens
have gone into exile.[s]

19“I called to my allies
but they betrayed me.
My priests and my elders
perished[t] in the city
while they searched for food
to keep themselves alive.

20“See, O LORD, how distressed[u] I am!
I am in torment[v] within,
and in my heart I am disturbed,
for I have been most rebellious.
Outside, the sword bereaves;
inside, there is only death.[w]

21“People have heard my groaning,[x]
but there is no-one to comfort me.[y]
All my enemies have heard of my distress;
they rejoice[z] at what you have done.
May you bring the day[a] you have announced
so that they may become like me.

22“Let all their wickedness come before you;
deal with them
as you have dealt with me
because of all my sins.[b]
My groans are many
and my heart is faint.”

2. God’s anger at sin

2[a] How the Lord has covered the Daughter of Zion
with the cloud of his anger![b][a]
He has hurled down the splendour of Israel
from heaven to earth;
he has not remembered his footstool[b]
in the day of his anger.

2Without pity[c] the Lord has swallowed[d] up
all the dwellings of Jacob;
in his wrath he has torn down
the strongholds[e] of the Daughter of Judah.
He has brought her kingdom and its princes
down to the ground[f] in dishonour.

3In fierce anger he has cut off
every horn[c][g] of Israel.
He has withdrawn his right hand[h]
at the approach of the enemy.
He has burned in Jacob like a flaming fire

a This chapter is an acrostic poem, the verses of which begin with the successive letters of the Hebrew alphabet.
b 1 Or *How the LORD in his anger / has treated the Daughter of Zion with contempt!* c 3 Or */ all the strength*; or *every king; horn* here symbolises strength.

1:18 [s]Dt 28:32, 41
1:19 [t]Jer 14:15; La 2:20
1:20 [u]Jer 4:19 [v]La 2:11 [w]Dt 32:25; Eze 7:15
1:21 [x]ver 8 [y]ver 4 [z]La 2:15 [a]Isa 47:11; Jer 30:16
1:22 [b]Ne 4:5
2:1 [a]La 3:44 [b]Ps 99:5; 132:7
2:2 [c]La 3:43 [d]Ps 21:9 [e]Ps 89:39-40; Mic 5:11 [f]Isa 25:12
2:3 [g]Ps 75:5, 10 [h]Ps 74:11

1:19 Jerusalem’s allies could not come to help because, like Jerusalem, they failed to seek God. Though these allies appeared strong, they were actually weak because God was not with them. Dependable assistance can come only from an ally whose power is from God. When you seek wise counsel, go to Christians who get their wisdom from the all-knowing God.

1:22 Babylon, although sinful, was God’s instrument for punishing Judah and its capital, Jerusalem. The people of Jerusalem were pleading for God to punish sinful Babylon as he had punished them (“deal with them as you have dealt with me”). God would do this, for he had already passed judgment on Babylon (see Jeremiah 50:1–27).

2:3
[i]Isa 42:25; Jer 21:4-5, 14

2:4
[j]Job 16:13; La 3:12-13
[k]Eze 24:16, 25
[l]Isa 42:25; Jer 7:20

2:5
[m]Jer 30:14
[n]ver 2
[o]Jer 9:17-20

2:6
[p]Jer 52:13
[q]La 1:4; Zep 3:18
[r]La 4:16

2:7
[s]Ps 74:7-8; Isa 64:11; Jer 33:4-5
[t]Jer 52:13

2:8
[u]2Ki 21:13; Isa 34:11
[v]Isa 3:26

2:9
[w]Ne 1:3
[x]Dt 28:36; 2Ki 24:15
[y]2Ch 15:3
[z]Jer 14:14

2:10
[a]Job 2:12
[b]Isa 15:3

that consumes everything around it.[i]

4 Like an enemy he has strung his bow;[j]
his right hand is ready.
Like a foe he has slain
all who were pleasing to the eye;[k]
he has poured out his wrath like fire[l]
on the tent of the Daughter of Zion.

5 The Lord is like an enemy;[m]
he has swallowed up Israel.
He has swallowed up all her palaces
and destroyed her strongholds.[n]
He has multiplied mourning and lamentation
for the Daughter of Judah.[o]

6 He has laid waste his dwelling like a garden;
he has destroyed his place of meeting.[p]
The LORD has made Zion forget
her appointed feasts and her Sabbaths;[q]
in his fierce anger he has spurned
both king and priest.[r]

7 The Lord has rejected his altar
and abandoned his sanctuary.
He has handed over to the enemy
the walls of her palaces;[s]
they have raised a shout in the house of the LORD
as on the day of an appointed feast.[t]

8 The LORD determined to tear down
the wall around the Daughter of Zion.
He stretched out a measuring line[u]
and did not withhold his hand from destroying.
He made ramparts and walls lament;
together they wasted away.[v]

9 Her gates[w] have sunk into the ground;
their bars he has broken and destroyed.
Her king and her princes are exiled[x] among the nations,
the law[y] is no more,
and her prophets no longer find
visions[z] from the LORD.

10 The elders of the Daughter of Zion
sit on the ground in silence;
they have sprinkled dust on their heads[a]
and put on sackcloth.[b]
The young women of Jerusalem

2:6 King Solomon's temple (here called God's "dwelling" and "place of meeting") in Jerusalem represented God's presence with the people (1 Kings 8:1–11). The temple was the central place of worship. Its destruction symbolised God's rejection of his people—that he no longer lived among them.

2:7 Our place of worship is not as important to God as our pattern of worship. A church building may be beautiful, but if its people don't sincerely follow God, the church will decay from within. The people of Judah, despite their beautiful temple, had rejected in their daily lives what they proclaimed in their worship rituals. Thus their worship had turned into a mocking lie. When you worship, are you saying words you don't really mean? Do you pray for help you don't really believe will come? Do you express love for God you don't really have? Earnestly seek God and catch a fresh vision of his love and care. Then worship him wholeheartedly.

2:9 Four powerful symbols and sources of security were lost: the protection of the *gates,* the leadership of the *king and princes,* the guidance of the *law,* and the vision of the *prophets.* With those four factors present, the people were lulled into a false sense of security and felt comfortable with their sins. But after each was removed, the people were confronted with the choice of repenting and returning to God or continuing on this path of suffering. Don't substitute symbols, even good ones, for the reality of a living, personal relationship with God himself.

have bowed their heads to the ground.[c]

11My eyes fail from weeping,[d]
I am in torment within,[e]
my heart is poured out[f] on the ground
because my people are destroyed,
because children and infants faint[g]
in the streets of the city.

12They say to their mothers,
"Where is bread and wine?"
as they faint like wounded men
in the streets of the city,
as their lives ebb away
in their mothers' arms.[h]

13What can I say for you?
With what can I compare you,
O Daughter of Jerusalem?
To what can I liken you,
that I may comfort you,
O Virgin Daughter of Zion?[i]
Your wound is as deep as the sea.[j]
Who can heal you?

14The visions of your prophets
were false and worthless;
they did not expose your sin
to ward off your captivity.[k]
The oracles they gave you
were false and misleading.[l]

15All who pass your way
clap their hands at you;[m]
they scoff[n] and shake their heads
at the Daughter of Jerusalem:
"Is this the city that was called
the perfection of beauty,[o]
the joy of the whole earth?"[p]

16All your enemies open their mouths
wide against you;[q]
they scoff and gnash their teeth[r]
and say, "We have swallowed her up.[s]
This is the day we have waited for;
we have lived to see it."

17The LORD has done what he planned;

2:10 [c]Job 2:13; Isa 3:26
2:11 [d]La 1:16; 3:48-51 [e]La 1:20 [f]ver 19; Ps 22:14 [g]La 4:4
2:12 [h]La 4:4
2:13 [i]Isa 37:22 [j]Jer 14:17; La 1:12
2:14 [k]Isa 58:1 [l]Jer 2:8; 23:25-32, 33-40; 29:9; Eze 13:3; 22:28
2:15 [m]Eze 25:6 [n]Jer 19:8 [o]Ps 50:2 [p]Ps 48:2
2:16 [q]Ps 56:2; La 3:46 [r]Job 16:9 [s]Ps 35:25

2:11 Jeremiah's tears were sincere and full of compassion. Sorrow does not mean that we lack faith or strength. There is nothing wrong with crying—Jesus himself felt sorrow and even wept (John 11:35). How do we react to the tearing down of our society and to moral degradation? This may not be as obvious as an invading enemy army, but the destruction is just as certain. We too should be deeply moved when we see the moral decay that surrounds us.

2:14 False prophets were everywhere in Jeremiah's day. They gave false and misleading "oracles" (messages to people from God). While Jeremiah warned the people of coming destruction and lengthy captivity, the false prophets said that all was well and so the people need not fear. All of Jeremiah's words came true because he was a true prophet of God (Jeremiah 14:14–16).

2:15 Clapping hands, scoffing, and shaking heads were all signs of derision and mockery. They were contemptuous gestures.

he has fulfilled his word,
which he decreed long ago.[t]
He has overthrown you without pity,[u]
he has let the enemy gloat over you,
he has exalted the horn[d] of your foes.[v]

18 The hearts of the people
cry out to the Lord.[w]
O wall of the Daughter of Zion,
let your tears[x] flow like a river
day and night;[y]
give yourself no relief,
your eyes no rest.[z]

19 Arise, cry out in the night,
as the watches of the night begin;
pour out your heart[a] like water
in the presence of the Lord.[b]
Lift up your hands to him
for the lives of your children,
who faint[c] from hunger
at the head of every street.

20 "Look, O LORD, and consider:
Whom have you ever treated like this?
Should women eat their offspring,[d]
the children they have cared for?[e]
Should priest and prophet be killed[f]
in the sanctuary of the Lord?

21 "Young and old lie together
in the dust of the streets;
my young men and maidens
have fallen by the sword.[g]
You have slain them in the day of your anger;
you have slaughtered them without pity.[h]

22 "As you summon to a feast day,
so you summoned against me terrors[i] on every side.
In the day of the LORD's anger
no-one escaped or survived;
those I cared for and reared,[j]
my enemy has destroyed."

2:17 [t]Dt 28:15-45 [u]ver 2; Eze 5:11 [v]Ps 89:42
2:18 [w]Ps 119:145 [x]La 1:16 [y]Jer 9:1 [z]La 3:49
2:19 [a]1Sa 1:15; Ps 62:8 [b]Isa 26:9 [c]Isa 51:20
2:20 [d]Dt 28:53; Jer 19:9 [e]La 4:10 [f]Ps 78:64; Jer 14:15
2:21 [g]2Ch 36:17; Ps 78:62-63; Jer 6:11 [h]Jer 13:14; La 3:43; Zec 11:6
2:22 [i]Ps 31:13; Jer 6:25 [j]Hos 9:13

d *17* *Horn* here symbolises strength.

2:19 Chapter 1 describes Jerusalem's desolation and calls for God's revenge on his enemies. Chapter 2 includes a call for God's people to pour out their hearts in the Lord's presence. The people must turn from their sins; they must sincerely mourn over their wrongs against God (3:40–42). The people had much to cry about. Because of their stubborn rebellion against God, they had brought great suffering to all, especially to the innocent. Was this suffering God's fault? No, it was the fault of the wayward people. Sinful people brought destruction on themselves, but tragically, sin's consequences affected everyone – good and evil alike.

2:19 The people's suffering and sin should have brought them to the Lord, weeping for forgiveness. Only when sin breaks our hearts can God come to our rescue. Just feeling sorry about experiencing sin's consequences does not bring forgiveness. But if we cry out to God, he will forgive us.

2:21, 22 This horrible scene could have been avoided. Jeremiah had warned the people for years that this day of destruction would come, and it broke his heart to see it fulfilled. We are always shocked when we hear of tragedy striking the innocent. But often innocent bystanders are victims of judgment on a nation. Sin has a way of causing great sorrow and devastation to many.

3. Hope in the midst of affliction

3[a] I am the man who has seen affliction
by the rod of his wrath.[a]
2He has driven me away and made me walk
in darkness[b] rather than light;
3indeed, he has turned his hand against me[c]
again and again, all day long.

4He has made my skin and my flesh grow old
and has broken my bones.[d]
5He has besieged me and surrounded me
with bitterness[e] and hardship.[f]
6He has made me dwell in darkness
like those long dead.[g]

7He has walled me in so that I cannot escape;[h]
he has weighed me down with chains.[i]
8Even when I call out or cry for help,
he shuts out my prayer.[j]
9He has barred my way with blocks of stone;
he has made my paths crooked.[k]

10Like a bear lying in wait,
like a lion in hiding,
11he dragged me from the path and mangled[l] me
and left me without help.
12He drew his bow[m]
and made me the target[n] for his arrows.[o]

13He pierced my heart
with arrows from his quiver.[p]
14I became the laughing-stock[q] of all my people;
they mock me in song[r] all day long.
15He has filled me with bitter herbs
and sated me with gall.[s]

16He has broken my teeth with gravel;[t]
he has trampled me in the dust.
17I have been deprived of peace;
I have forgotten what prosperity is.
18So I say, "My splendour is gone
and all that I had hoped from the LORD."[u]

19I remember my affliction and my wandering,
the bitterness and the gall.
20I well remember them,
and my soul is downcast[v] within me.[w]
21Yet this I call to mind

[a] This chapter is an acrostic poem; the verses of each stanza begin with the successive letters of the Hebrew alphabet, and the verses within each stanza begin with the same letter.

3:1 [a]Job 19:21; Ps 88:7
3:2 [b]Jer 4:23
3:3 [c]Isa 5:25
3:4 [d]Ps 51:8; Isa 38:13; Jer 50:17
3:5 [e]ver 19 [f]Jer 23:15
3:6 [g]Ps 88:5-6
3:7 [h]Job 3:23 [i]Jer 40:4
3:8 [j]Job 30:20; Ps 22:2
3:9 [k]Isa 63:17; Hos 2:6
3:11 [l]Hos 6:1
3:12 [m]La 2:4 [n]Job 7:20 [o]Ps 7:12-13; 38:2
3:13 [p]Job 6:4
3:14 [q]Jer 20:7 [r]Job 30:9
3:15 [s]Jer 9:15
3:16 [t]Pr 20:17
3:18 [u]Job 17:15
3:20 [v]Ps 42:5 [w]Ps 42:11

3:1ff In Jeremiah's darkest moment, his hope was strengthened with this assurance: God had been faithful and would continue to be faithful. Jeremiah saw both God's judgment and God's steadfast love. In the time of judgment, Jeremiah could still cling to God's love just as in times of prosperity he had warned of God's judgment.

3:1ff In the original Hebrew, the first four chapters in Lamentations are acrostic poems. Each verse in each chapter begins with a successive letter of the Hebrew alphabet. Chapter 3 has 66 verses rather than 22 because it is a triple acrostic: the first three verses begin with the equivalent of *A*, the next three with *B*, and so on (see the NIV text note). This was a typical form of Hebrew poetry. Other examples of acrostics are Psalms 37, 119, and 145, and Proverbs 31:10–31.

3:21, 22 Jeremiah saw one ray of hope in all the sin and sorrow surrounding him: "Because of the LORD's great love we are not consumed, for his compassions never fail." God willingly responds with help when we ask. Perhaps there is some sin in your life that you thought God would not forgive. God's steadfast love and mercy are greater than any sin, and he promises forgiveness.

3:22 [x]Ps 78:38; Mal 3:6
3:23 [y]Zep 3:5
3:24 [z]Ps 16:5
3:25 [a]Isa 25:9; 30:18
3:26 [b]Ps 37:7; 40:1
3:28 [c]Jer 15:17
3:29 [d]Jer 31:17
3:30 [e]Job 16:10; Isa 50:6
3:31 [f]Ps 94:14; Isa 54:7
3:32 [g]Ps 78:38; Hos 11:8
3:33 [h]Eze 33:11
3:36 [i]Jer 22:3; Hab 1:13
3:37 [j]Ps 33:9-11
3:38 [k]Job 2:10; Isa 45:7; Jer 32:42
3:39 [l]Jer 30:15; Mic 7:9
3:40 [m]2Co 13:5 [n]Ps 119:59; 139:23-24
3:41 [o]Ps 25:1; 28:2

and therefore I have hope:

22 Because of the LORD's great love we are not consumed,
for his compassions never fail.[x]
23 They are new every morning;
great is your faithfulness.[y]
24 I say to myself, "The LORD is my portion;[z]
therefore I will wait for him."

25 The LORD is good to those whose hope is in him,
to the one who seeks him;[a]
26 it is good to wait quietly
for the salvation of the LORD.[b]
27 It is good for a man to bear the yoke
while he is young.

28 Let him sit alone in silence,[c]
for the LORD has laid it on him.
29 Let him bury his face in the dust—
there may yet be hope.[d]
30 Let him offer his cheek to one who would strike him,[e]
and let him be filled with disgrace.

31 For men are not cast off
by the Lord for ever.[f]
32 Though he brings grief, he will show compassion,
so great is his unfailing love.[g]
33 For he does not willingly bring affliction
or grief to the children of men.[h]

34 To crush underfoot
all prisoners in the land,
35 to deny a man his rights
before the Most High,
36 to deprive a man of justice—
would not the Lord see such things?[i]

37 Who can speak and have it happen
if the Lord has not decreed it?[j]
38 Is it not from the mouth of the Most High
that both calamities and good things come?[k]
39 Why should any living man complain
when punished for his sins?[l]

40 Let us examine our ways and test them,[m]
and let us return to the LORD.[n]
41 Let us lift up our hearts and our hands
to God in heaven,[o] and say:

3:23 Jeremiah knew from personal experience about God's faithfulness. God had promised that punishment would follow disobedience, and it did. But God also had promised future restoration and blessing, and Jeremiah knew that God would keep that promise also. Trusting in God's faithfulness day by day makes us confident in his great promises for the future.

3:27–33 To "bear the yoke" means willingly to come under God's discipline and learn what he wants to teach. This involves several important factors: (1) silent reflection on what God wants, (2) repentant humility, (3) self-control in the face of adversity, and (4) confident patience, depending on the divine Teacher to bring about loving lessons in our lives. God has several long-term and short-term lessons for you right now. Are you doing your homework?

3:30 To "offer his cheek to one who would strike him" means to submit to physical abuse without defending yourself or fighting back. Jesus taught his followers to turn the other cheek (Matthew 5:39), and he exemplified this at the highest level just before his crucifixion (Matthew 27:27–31; Luke 22:64; John 18:22; 19:3).

3:39–42 Parents discipline children to produce right behaviour. God disciplined Judah to produce right living and genuine worship. We must not complain about discipline but learn from it, trusting God and being willing to change. We must allow God's correction to bring about the kind of behaviour in our lives that pleases him.

42“We have sinned and rebelled[p]
and you have not forgiven.[q]

43“You have covered yourself with anger and pursued us;
you have slain without pity.[r]
44You have covered yourself with a cloud[s]
so that no prayer[t] can get through.
45You have made us scum[u] and refuse
among the nations.

46“All our enemies have opened their mouths
wide against us.[v]
47We have suffered terror and pitfalls,[w]
ruin and destruction.[x]”
48Streams of tears flow from my eyes[y]
because my people are destroyed.[z]

49My eyes will flow unceasingly,
without relief,[a]
50until the LORD looks down
from heaven and sees.[b]
51What I see brings grief to my soul
because of all the women of my city.

52Those who were my enemies without cause
hunted me like a bird.[c]
53They tried to end my life in a pit[d]
and threw stones at me;
54the waters closed over my head,[e]
and I thought I was about to be cut off.

55I called on your name, O LORD,
from the depths of the pit.[f]
56You heard my plea:[g] “Do not close your ears
to my cry for relief.”
57You came near when I called you,
and you said, “Do not fear.”[h]

58O Lord, you took up my case;[i]
you redeemed my life.[j]
59You have seen, O LORD, the wrong done to me.[k]
Uphold my cause!
60You have seen the depth of their vengeance,
all their plots against me.[l]

61O LORD, you have heard their insults,
all their plots against me—
62what my enemies whisper and mutter
against me all day long.[m]
63Look at them! Sitting or standing,
they mock me in their songs.

64Pay them back what they deserve, O LORD,
for what their hands have done.[n]
65Put a veil over their hearts,[o]
and may your curse be on them!

3:42 [p]Da 9:5 [q]Jer 5:7-9
3:43 [r]La 2:2, 17, 21
3:44 [s]Ps 97:2 [t]ver 8
3:45 [u]1Co 4:13
3:46 [v]La 2:16
3:47 [w]Jer 48:43 [x]Isa 24:17-18; 51:19
3:48 [y]La 1:16 [z]La 2:11
3:49 [a]Jer 14:17
3:50 [b]Isa 63:15
3:52 [c]Ps 35:7
3:53 [d]Jer 37:16
3:54 [e]Ps 69:2; Jnh 2:3-5
3:55 [f]Ps 130:1; Jnh 2:2
3:56 [g]Ps 55:1
3:57 [h]Isa 41:10
3:58 [i]Jer 51:36 [j]Ps 34:22; Jer 50:34
3:59 [k]Jer 18:19-20
3:60 [l]Jer 11:20; 18:18
3:62 [m]Eze 36:3
3:64 [n]Ps 28:4
3:65 [o]Isa 6:10

3:52–57 At one point in his ministry, Jeremiah was thrown into an empty cistern, and he was left to die in the mire at the bottom (Jeremiah 38:6–13). But God rescued him. Jeremiah used this experience as a picture of the nation sinking into sin. If they turned to God, he would rescue them.

4:1
[a] Eze 7:19

66 Pursue them in anger and destroy them
from under the heavens of the LORD.

4. God's anger is satisfied

4 [a] How the gold has lost its lustre,
the fine gold become dull!
The sacred gems are scattered
at the head of every street. [a]

4:3
[b] Job 39:16

2 How the precious sons of Zion,
once worth their weight in gold,
are now considered as pots of clay,
the work of a potter's hands!

3 Even jackals offer their breasts
to nurse their young,
but my people have become heartless
like ostriches in the desert. [b]

4:4
[c] Ps 22:15
[d] La 2:11, 12

4 Because of thirst the infant's tongue
sticks to the roof of its mouth; [c]
the children beg for bread,
but no-one gives it to them. [d]

4:5
[e] Jer 6:2
[f] Am 6:3-7

5 Those who once ate delicacies
are destitute in the streets.
Those nurtured in purple [e]
now lie on ash heaps. [f]

6 The punishment of my people
is greater than that of Sodom, [g]
which was overthrown in a moment
without a hand turned to help her.

4:6
[g] Ge 19:25

7 Their princes were brighter than snow
and whiter than milk,
their bodies more ruddy than rubies,
their appearance like sapphires. [b]

8 But now they are blacker [h] than soot;
they are not recognised in the streets.
Their skin has shrivelled on their bones; [i]
it has become as dry as a stick.

4:8
[h] Job 30:28
[i] Ps 102:3-5

9 Those killed by the sword are better off
than those who die of famine;
racked with hunger, they waste away
for lack of food from the field. [j]

10 With their own hands compassionate women

4:9
[j] Jer 15:2; 16:4

[a] This chapter is an acrostic poem, the verses of which begin with the successive letters of the Hebrew alphabet.
[b] *7* Or *lapis lazuli*

4:1ff This chapter contrasts the situation before the siege of Jerusalem with the situation after the siege. The sights and sounds of prosperity were gone because of the people's sin. This chapter warns us not to assume that when life is going well, it will always stay that way. We must be careful not to glory in our prosperity and fall into spiritual bankruptcy.

4:1–10 When a city was under siege, the city wall – built for protection – sealed the people inside. They could not get out to the fields to get food and water because the enemy was camped around the city. As food in the city ran out, the people watched their enemies harvest and eat the food in the fields. The siege was a test of wills to see which army could outlast the other. Jerusalem was under siege for two years. Life became so harsh that people even ate their own children, and dead bodies were left to rot in the streets. All hope was gone.

4:6 Sodom, destroyed by burning sulphur from heaven because of its wickedness (Genesis 18:20 – 19:29), became a symbol of God's ultimate judgment. Yet the sin of Jerusalem was even greater than the sin of Sodom!

have cooked their own children,[k]
who became their food
when my people were destroyed.

11The LORD has given full vent to his wrath;
he has poured out his fierce anger.
He kindled a fire[l] in Zion
that consumed her foundations.[m]

12The kings of the earth did not believe,
nor did any of the world's people,
that enemies and foes could enter
the gates of Jerusalem.[n]

13But it happened because of the sins of her prophets
and the iniquities of her priests,[o]
who shed within her
the blood of the righteous.

14Now they grope through the streets
like men who are blind.[p]
They are so defiled with blood[q]
that no-one dares to touch their garments.

15"Go away! You are unclean!" men cry to them.
"Away! Away! Don't touch us!"
When they flee and wander about,
people among the nations say,
"They can stay here no longer."[r]

16The LORD himself has scattered them;
he no longer watches over them.[s]
The priests are shown no honour,
the elders[t] no favour.

17Moreover, our eyes failed,
looking in vain[u] for help;[v]
from our towers we watched
for a nation[w] that could not save us.

18Men stalked us at every step,
so we could not walk in our streets.
Our end was near, our days were numbered,
for our end had come.[x]

19Our pursuers were swifter
than eagles[y] in the sky;
they chased us[z] over the mountains
and lay in wait for us in the desert.

20The LORD's anointed,[a] our very life breath,

4:10 [k]Lev 26:29; Dt 28:53-57; Jer 19:9; La 2:20; Eze 5:10
4:11 [l]Jer 17:27 [m]Dt 32:22; Jer 7:20; Eze 22:31
4:12 [n]1Ki 9:9; Jer 21:13
4:13 [o]Jer 5:31; 6:13; Eze 22:28; Mic 3:11
4:14 [p]Isa 59:10 [q]Jer 2:34; 19:4
4:15 [r]Lev 13:46
4:16 [s]Isa 9:14-16 [t]La 5:12
4:17 [u]Isa 20:5; Eze 29:16 [v]La 1:7 [w]Jer 37:7
4:18 [x]Eze 7:2-12; Am 8:2
4:19 [y]Dt 28:49 [z]Isa 5:26-28
4:20 [a]2Sa 19:21

4:13–15 To be defiled or unclean meant to be unfit to enter the temple or to worship before God. The priests and prophets should have been the most careful to maintain ceremonial purity so that they could continue to perform their duties before God. But many priests and prophets did evil and were defiled. As the nation's leaders, their example led the people into sin and caused the ultimate downfall of the nation and its capital city, Jerusalem.

4:17 Judah asked Egypt to help them fight the Babylonian army. Egypt gave Judah false hope – they started to help, but then retreated (Jeremiah 37:5–7). Jeremiah warned Judah not to ally itself with Egypt. He told the leaders to rely on God, but they refused to listen.

4:20 King Zedekiah, although called "the LORD's anointed", had little spiritual depth and leadership power. Instead of putting his faith in God and listening to God's true prophet, Jeremiah, he listened to the false prophets. To make matters worse, the people chose to follow and trust in their king (2 Chronicles 36:11–23). They chose the path of false confidence and complacency, wanting to feel secure rather than to follow the directives God was giving his people through Jeremiah. But the object of their confidence – King Zedekiah – was captured.

was caught in their traps.[b]
We thought that under his shadow
we would live among the nations.

21 Rejoice and be glad, O Daughter of Edom,
you who live in the land of Uz.
But to you also the cup[c] will be passed;
you will be drunk and stripped naked.[d]

22 O Daughter of Zion, your punishment will end;[e]
he will not prolong your exile.
But, O Daughter of Edom, he will punish your sin
and expose your wickedness.[f]

5. Jeremiah pleads for restoration

5 Remember, O LORD, what has happened to us;
look, and see our disgrace.[a]
2 Our inheritance[b] has been turned over to aliens,
our homes[c] to foreigners.
3 We have become orphans and fatherless,
our mothers like widows.[d]
4 We must buy the water we drink;
our wood can be had only at a price.[e]
5 Those who pursue us are at our heels;
we are weary[f] and find no rest.
6 We submitted to Egypt and Assyria[g]
to get enough bread.
7 Our fathers sinned and are no more,
and we bear their punishment.[h]
8 Slaves[i] rule over us,
and there is none to free us from their hands.[j]
9 We get our bread at the risk of our lives
because of the sword in the desert.
10 Our skin is hot as an oven,
feverish from hunger.[k]
11 Women have been ravished[l] in Zion,
and virgins in the towns of Judah.
12 Princes have been hung up by their hands;
elders are shown no respect.[m]
13 Young men toil at the millstones;
boys stagger under loads of wood.
14 The elders are gone from the city gate;
the young men have stopped their music.[n]
15 Joy is gone from our hearts;
our dancing has turned to mourning.[o]
16 The crown[p] has fallen from our head.
Woe to us, for we have sinned![q]
17 Because of this our hearts[r] are faint;
because of these things our eyes[s] grow dim

4:20 [b] Jer 39:5; Eze 12:12-13; 19:4, 8
4:21 [c] Jer 25:15 [d] Isa 34:6-10; Am 1:11-12; Ob 1:16
4:22 [e] Isa 40:2; Jer 33:8 [f] Ps 137:7; Mal 1:4
5:1 [a] Ps 44:13-16; 89:50
5:2 [b] Ps 79:1 [c] Zep 1:13
5:3 [d] Jer 15:8; 18:21
5:4 [e] Isa 3:1
5:5 [f] Ne 9:37
5:6 [g] Hos 9:3
5:7 [h] Jer 14:20; 16:12
5:8 [i] Ne 5:15 [j] Zec 11:6
5:10 [k] La 4:8-9
5:11 [l] Zec 14:2
5:12 [m] La 4:16
5:14 [n] Isa 24:8; Jer 7:34
5:15 [o] Jer 25:10
5:16 [p] Ps 89:39 [q] Isa 3:11
5:17 [r] Isa 1:5 [s] Ps 6:7

4:21, 22 Edom was Judah's arch-enemy, even though they had a common ancestor, Isaac (see Genesis 25:19–26; 36:1). Edom had actively aided Babylon in the siege of Jerusalem. As a reward, Nebuchadnezzar gave the outlying lands of Judah to Edom. Jeremiah said that Edom would be judged for her treachery against her brothers. (See also Jeremiah 49:7–22; Ezekiel 25:12–14; Amos 9:12; Obadiah 1–21.)

5:1ff After expressing the full extent of his or her grief, the true believer should turn to God in prayer. Here Jeremiah prayed for mercy for his people. At the end of his prayer he wondered if God was "angry with us beyond measure". But God would not stay angry with them for ever – as it says in Micah 7:18, "You do not stay angry for ever but delight to show mercy."

5:14 During peace and prosperity, the leaders and elders of the city would sit at the city gate and talk over politics, theology, and philosophy, and conduct business.

18 for Mount Zion, which lies desolate,[t]
with jackals prowling over it.

19 You, O LORD, reign for ever;
your throne endures[u] from generation to generation.
20 Why do you always forget us?[v]
Why do you forsake us so long?
21 Restore[w] us to yourself, O LORD, that we may return;
renew our days as of old
22 unless you have utterly rejected us
and are angry with us beyond measure.[x]

5:18 [t]Mic 3:12
5:19 [u]Ps 45:6; 102:12, 24-27
5:20 [v]Ps 13:1; 44:24
5:21 [w]Ps 80:3
5:22 [x]Isa 64:9

5:22 A high calling flouted by low living results in deep suffering. Lamentations gives us a portrait of the bitter suffering the people of Jerusalem experienced when sin caught up with them and God turned his back on them. Every material goal they had lived for collapsed. But although God turned away from them because of their sin, he did not abandon them – that was their great hope. Despite their sinful past, God would restore them if they returned to him. Hope is found only in the Lord. Thus our grief should turn us towards him, not away from him.

EZEKIEL

Jeremiah becomes a prophet to Judah 627 B.C.	Daniel taken captive to Babylon 605	Ezekiel taken captive to Babylon 597	Ezekiel becomes a prophet to exiles 593	Judah falls; Jerusalem destroyed 586	Ezekiel's ministry ends 571	Babylon overthrown by Cyrus 539	First exiles return to Judah 538

A computer can be programmed to respond to your command. And by conditioning a dog with rewards and punishments, you can teach it to obey. But as every parent knows, children are not so easily taught. People have wills and must choose to submit, to follow the instructions of their parents and leaders. Surely discipline is part of the process—boys and girls should know the consequences of disobedience—but there is a choice to be made. They are not machines or animals.

God's children must learn to obey their heavenly Father. Created in his image, they have a choice, and God allows them to choose.

Ezekiel was a man who chose to obey God. Although he was a priest (1:3), he served as a Jewish "street preacher" in Babylon for 22 years, telling everyone about God's judgment and salvation, and calling them to repent and obey. And Ezekiel *lived* what he preached. During his ministry God told him to illustrate his messages with dramatic object lessons. Some of these acts included (1) lying on his side for 390 days during which he could eat only one eight-ounce meal a day cooked over manure, (2) shaving his head and beard, and (3) showing no sorrow when his wife died. He obeyed and faithfully proclaimed God's word.

God may not ask you to do anything quite so dramatic or difficult; but if he did, would you do it?

The book of Ezekiel chronicles the prophet's life and ministry. Beginning with his call as a prophet and commissioning as a "watchman for the house of Israel" (chapters 1—3), Ezekiel immediately began to preach and demonstrate God's truth, as he predicted the approaching siege and destruction of Jerusalem (chapters 4—24). This devastation would be God's judgment for the people's idolatry. Ezekiel challenged them to turn from their wicked ways. In the next section, he spoke to the surrounding nations, prophesying that God would judge them for their sins as well (chapters 25—32). The book concludes with a message of hope, as Ezekiel proclaimed the faithfulness of God and foretold the future blessings for God's people (chapters 33—48).

As you read this exciting record, watch Ezekiel fearlessly preach the word of God to the exiled Jews in the streets of Babylon and hear the timeless truth of God's love and power. Think about each person's responsibility to trust God, and about the inevitability of God's judgment against idolatry, rebellion, and indifference. Then commit yourself to obeying God, whatever, wherever, and whenever he asks.

VITAL STATISTICS

PURPOSE:
To announce God's judgment on Israel and other nations and to foretell the eventual salvation of God's people

AUTHOR:
Ezekiel—the son of Buzi, a Zadokite priest

TO WHOM WRITTEN:
The Jews in captivity in Babylonia, and God's people everywhere

DATE WRITTEN:
Approximately 571 B.C.

SETTING:
Ezekiel was a younger contemporary of Jeremiah. While Jeremiah ministered to the people still in Judah, Ezekiel prophesied to those already exiled in Babylonia after the defeat of Jehoiachin. He was taken there in 597 B.C.

KEY VERSES:
"For I will take you out of the nations; I will gather you from all the countries and bring you back into your own land. I will sprinkle clean water on you, and you will be clean; I will cleanse you from all your impurities and from all your idols. I will give you a new heart and put a new spirit in you; I will remove from you your heart of stone and give you a heart of flesh" (36:24–26).

KEY PEOPLE:
Ezekiel, Israel's leaders, Ezekiel's wife, Nebuchadnezzar, "the prince"

KEY PLACES:
Jerusalem, Babylon, and Egypt

THE BLUEPRINT

A. MESSAGES OF DOOM (1:1—24:27)
1. Ezekiel's call and commission
2. Visions of sin and judgment
3. Punishment is certain

While Jeremiah was prophesying in Jerusalem that the city would soon fall to the Babylonians, Ezekiel was giving the same message to the captives who were already in Babylon. Like those in Jerusalem, the captives stubbornly believed that Jerusalem would not fall and that they would soon return to their land. Ezekiel warned them that punishment was certain because of their sins and that God was purifying his people. God will always punish sin, whether we believe it or not.

B. MESSAGES AGAINST FOREIGN NATIONS (25:1—32:32)	Ezekiel condemns the sinful actions of seven nations. The people in these nations were saying that God was obviously too weak to defend his people and the city of Jerusalem. But God was allowing his people to be defeated in order to punish them for their sins. These pagan nations, however, would face a similar fate, and then they would know that God is all-powerful. Those who dare to mock God today will also face a terrible fate.
C. MESSAGES OF HOPE (33:1—48:35) 1. Restoring the people of God 2. Restoring the worship of God	After the fall of Jerusalem, Ezekiel delivered messages of future restoration and hope to the people. God is holy, but Jerusalem and the temple had become defiled. The nation had to be cleansed through 70 years of captivity. Ezekiel gives a vivid picture of the unchangeable holiness of God. We too must gain a vision of the glory of God, a fresh sense of his greatness, as we face the struggles of daily life.

MEGATHEMES

THEME	EXPLANATION	IMPORTANCE
God's Holiness	Ezekiel saw a vision that revealed God's absolute moral perfection. God was spiritually and morally superior to members of Israel's corrupt and compromising society. Ezekiel wrote to let the people know that God was also present in Babylon, not just in Jerusalem.	Because God is morally perfect, he can help us live above our tendency to compromise with this world. When we focus on his greatness, he gives us the power to overcome sin and to reflect his holiness.
Sin	Israel had sinned, and God's punishment came. The fall of Jerusalem and the Babylonian exile were used by God to correct the rebels and draw them back from their sinful way of life. Ezekiel warned them that not only was the nation responsible for sin, but each individual was also accountable to God.	We cannot excuse ourselves from our responsibilities before God. We are accountable to God for our choices. Rather than neglect him, we must recognise sin for what it is—rebellion against God—and choose to follow him instead.
Restoration	Ezekiel consoles the people by telling them that the day will come when God will restore those who turn from sin. God will be their King and Shepherd. He will give his people a new heart to worship him, and he will establish a new government and a new temple.	The certainty of future restoration encourages believers in times of trial. But we must be faithful to God because we love him, not merely for what he can do for us. Is our faith in *him* or merely in our future benefits?
Leaders	Ezekiel condemned the shepherds (unfaithful priests and leaders) who led the people astray. By contrast, he served as a caring shepherd and a faithful watchman to warn the people about their sin. One day God's perfect Shepherd, the Messiah, will lead his people.	Jesus is our perfect leader. If we truly want him to lead us, our devotion must be more than talk. If we are given the responsibility of leading others, we must take care of them even if it means sacrificing personal pleasure, happiness, time, or money. We are responsible for those we lead.
Worship	An angel gave Ezekiel a vision of the temple in great detail. God's holy presence had departed from Israel and the temple because of sin. The building of a future temple portrays the return of God's glory and presence. God will cleanse his people and restore true worship.	All of God's promises will be fulfilled under the rule of the Messiah. The faithful followers will be restored to perfect fellowship with God and with one another. To be prepared for this time, we must focus on God. We do this through regular worship. Through worship we learn about God's holiness and the changes we must make in how we live.

1:1
[a]Eze 11:24-25
[b]Mt 3:16;
Ac 7:56
[c]Ex 24:10

1:2
[d]2Ki 24:15

1:3
[e]2Ki 3:15;
Eze 3:14, 22

1:4
[f]Jer 1:14

A. MESSAGES OF DOOM (1:1–24:27)

Ezekiel prophesied to the exiles in Babylon. He had to dispel the false hope that Israel's captivity would be short, explain the reasons for the severe judgments on their nation, and bring a message of future hope. Although the people did not respond positively, they heard the messages and knew the truth. God's people were not without explanation and direction, and neither are we.

1. Ezekiel's call and commission

The Living Creatures and the Glory of the LORD

1 In the[a] thirtieth year, in the fourth month on the fifth day, while I was among
the exiles[a] by the Kebar River, the heavens were opened[b] and I saw visions[c]
of God.
2On the fifth of the month—it was the fifth year of the exile of King Jehoiachin[d]—3the word of the LORD came to Ezekiel the priest, the son of Buzi,[b] by the
Kebar River in the land of the Babylonians.[c] There the hand of the LORD was upon
him.[e]
4I looked, and I saw a windstorm coming out of the north[f]—an immense cloud
with flashing lightning and surrounded by brilliant light. The centre of the fire looked

[a] 1 Or ˌmy˛ [b] 3 Or *Ezekiel son of Buzi the priest* [c] 3 Or *Chaldeans*

EZEKIEL served as a prophet to the exiles in Babylon from 593–571 B.C.

Climate of the times	• Ezekiel and his people are taken to Babylon as captives. • The Jews become foreigners in a strange land ruled by an authoritarian government.
Main message	Because of the people's sins, God allowed the nation of Judah to be destroyed. But there was still hope—God promised to restore the land to those who remained faithful to him.
Importance of message	God never forgets those who faithfully seek to obey him. They have a glorious future ahead.
Contemporary prophets	Daniel (605–536) Habakkuk (612–588) Jeremiah (627–586)

1:1 Ezekiel, born and raised in the land of Judah, was preparing to become a priest in God's temple when the Babylonians attacked in 597 B.C. and carried him away along with 10,000 other captives (2 Kings 24:10–14). The nation was on the brink of complete destruction. Five years later, when Ezekiel was 30 (the normal age for becoming a priest), God called him to be a prophet. During the first six years when Ezekiel ministered in Babylonia (1:3), Jeremiah was preaching to the Jews still in Judah, and Daniel was serving in Nebuchadnezzar's court. The Kebar River connected to the Euphrates in Babylonia and was the location of a Jewish settlement of exiles.

1:1 Why did the Jewish exiles in Babylonia need a prophet? God wanted Ezekiel to (1) help the exiles understand why they had been taken captive, (2) dispel the false hope that the captivity was going to be short, (3) bring a new message of hope, and (4) call the people to a new awareness of their dependence upon God.

1:1 God communicated to Ezekiel in visions. A vision is a miraculous revelation of God's truth. These visions seem strange to us because they are *apocalyptic*. This means that Ezekiel saw symbolic pictures that vividly conveyed an idea. Daniel and John were two other Bible writers who used apocalyptic imagery. The people in exile had lost their perspective of God's purpose and presence, and Ezekiel came to them with a vision from God to show God's awesome glory and holiness and to warn the exiles of sin's consequences before it was too late.

1:1ff Ezekiel's latest dated message from God (29:17) was given in 571 B.C. He was taken captive during the second Babylonian invasion of Judah in 597 B.C. The Babylonians invaded Judah a third and final time in 586 B.C., completely destroying Jerusalem, burning the temple, and deporting the rest of the people (see 2 Kings 25). Ezekiel dates all his messages from the year he was taken captive (597). His first prophecy to the exiles occurred four years after he arrived in the land of Babylon (593 B.C.).

1:3 The name *Ezekiel* means "God is strong" or "God strengthens". In a very real sense, this sums up the basic message of the book—that in spite of the captivity, God's sovereign strength prevails, and he will judge his enemies and restore his true people.

1:4ff In this first vision, God called Ezekiel to be a prophet (see 2:5). Nothing in Ezekiel's previous experience had prepared him for such a display of God's glorious presence and power. The immense cloud flashed with lightning and was surrounded by a brilliant light. From the fire in the cloud came four living creatures. They showed Ezekiel that Jerusalem's coming destruction was God's punishment of Judah for its sins. (These living creatures are also seen in Revelation 4:6, 7.)

When Ezekiel received this vision, he was far away from the temple in Jerusalem, the physical symbol of God's presence. Through this vision, he learned that God is present everywhere and that God's activities in heaven are shaping the events on earth.

like glowing metal,[g] 5and in the fire was what looked like four living creatures.[h]
In appearance their form was that of a man,[i] 6but each of them had four faces[j] and
four wings. 7Their legs were straight; their feet were like those of a calf and gleamed
like burnished bronze.[k] 8Under their wings on their four sides they had the hands of
a man.[l] All four of them had faces and wings, 9and their wings touched one another.
Each one went straight ahead; they did not turn as they moved.[m]
10Their faces looked like this: Each of the four had the face of a man, and on the
right side each had the face of a lion, and on the left the face of an ox; each also had
the face of an eagle.[n] 11Such were their faces. Their wings[o] were spread out
upwards; each had two wings, one touching the wing of another creature on either
side, and two wings covering its body. 12Each one went straight ahead. Wherever the
spirit would go, they would go, without turning as they went. 13The appearance of
the living creatures was like burning coals of fire or like torches. Fire moved back
and forth among the creatures; it was bright, and lightning[p] flashed out of it. 14The
creatures sped back and forth like flashes of lightning.[q]
15As I looked at the living creatures, I saw a wheel on the ground beside each
creature with its four faces. 16This was the appearance and structure of the wheels:
They sparkled like chrysolite,[r] and all four looked alike. Each appeared to be made
like a wheel intersecting a wheel. 17As they moved, they would go in any one of the
four directions the creatures faced; the wheels did not turn[s] about[d] as the creatures
went. 18Their rims were high and awesome, and all four rims were full of eyes[t] all
around.
19When the living creatures moved, the wheels beside them moved; and when the
living creatures rose from the ground, the wheels also rose. 20Wherever the spirit
would go, they would go,[u] and the wheels would rise along with them, because the
spirit of the living creatures was in the wheels. 21When the creatures moved, they also
moved; when the creatures stood still, they also stood still; and when the creatures
rose from the ground, the wheels rose along with them, because the spirit of the living
creatures was in the wheels.[v]
22Spread out above the heads of the living creatures was what looked like an
expanse,[w] sparkling like ice, and awesome. 23Under the expanse their wings were
stretched out one towards the other, and each had two wings covering its body.
24When the creatures moved, I heard the sound of their wings, like the roar of rushing
waters, like the voice[x] of the Almighty,[e] like the tumult of an army.[y] When they
stood still, they lowered their wings.
25Then there came a voice from above the expanse over their heads as they stood

d *17* Or *aside* **e** *24* Hebrew *Shaddai*

1:4 [g]Eze 8:2
1:5 [h]Rev 4:6 [i]ver 26
1:6 [j]Eze 10:14
1:7 [k]Da 10:6; Rev 1:15
1:8 [l]Eze 10:8
1:9 [m]Eze 10:22
1:10 [n]Eze 10:14; Rev 4:7
1:11 [o]Isa 6:2
1:13 [p]Rev 4:5
1:14 [q]Ps 29:7
1:16 [r]Eze 10:9-11; Da 10:6
1:17 [s]ver 9
1:18 [t]Eze 10:12; Rev 4:6
1:20 [u]ver 12
1:21 [v]Eze 10:17
1:22 [w]Eze 10:1
1:24 [x]Eze 10:5; 43:2; Da 10:6; Rev 1:15; 19:6 [y]2Ki 7:6

1:5 Each of the four living creatures had four faces, symbolising God's perfect nature. Some believe that the lion represented strength; the ox, diligent service; the man, intelligence; and the eagle, divinity. Others see these as the most majestic of God's creatures and say that they therefore represent God's whole creation. The early church fathers saw a connection between these beings and the four Gospels: the lion with Matthew, presenting Christ as the Lion of Judah; the ox with Mark, portraying Christ as the Servant; the human with Luke, portraying Christ as the perfect human; the eagle with John, portraying Christ as the Son of God, exalted and divine. The vision of John in Revelation 4 parallels Ezekiel's vision.

1:16–18 The "wheel intersecting a wheel" was probably two wheels at right angles to each other, one on a north-south and the other on an east-west axis. Able to move anywhere, these wheels show that God is present everywhere and is able to see all things (1:18). God is not restricted to Jerusalem, but rules all of life and history. Though the exiles had experienced great change, God was still in control.

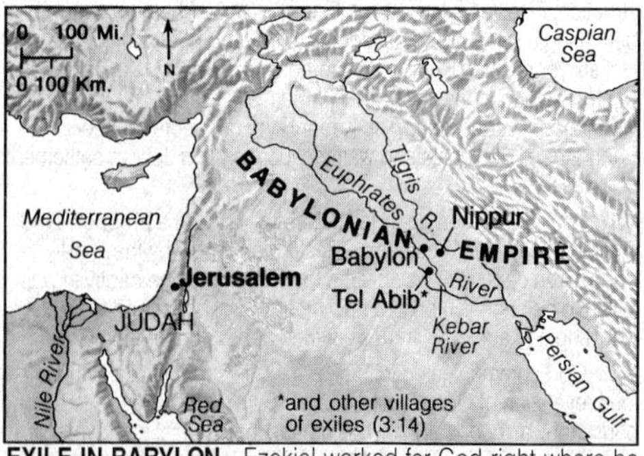

EXILE IN BABYLON Ezekiel worked for God right where he was—among the exiles in various colonies near the Kebar River in Babylonia. Jerusalem and its temple lay over 500 miles away, but Ezekiel helped the people to understand that although they were far from home, they did not need to be far from God.

with lowered wings. 26 Above the expanse over their heads was what looked like a
throne of sapphire,[f][z] and high above on the throne was a figure like that of a man.[a]
27 I saw that from what appeared to be his waist up he looked like glowing metal, as
if full of fire, and that from there down he looked like fire; and brilliant light
surrounded him.[b] 28 Like the appearance of a rainbow[c] in the clouds on a rainy day,
so was the radiance around him.[d]

This was the appearance of the likeness of the glory[e] of the LORD. When I saw
it, I fell face down,[f] and I heard the voice of one speaking.

Ezekiel's Call

2 He said to me, "Son of man, stand[a] up on your feet and I will speak to you."
2 As he spoke, the Spirit came into me and raised me[b] to my feet, and I heard
him speaking to me.

3 He said: "Son of man, I am sending you to the Israelites, to a rebellious nation
that has rebelled against me; they and their fathers have been in revolt against me to
this very day.[c] 4 The people to whom I am sending you are obstinate and stubborn.[d]
Say to them, 'This is what the Sovereign LORD says.' 5 And whether they listen or
fail to listen[e]—for they are a rebellious house[f]—they will know that a prophet has
been among them.[g] 6 And you, son of man, do not be afraid[h] of them or their words.
Do not be afraid, though briers and thorns[i] are all around you and you live among
scorpions. Do not be afraid of what they say or terrified by them, though they are a
rebellious house.[j] 7 You must speak my words to them, whether they listen or fail
to listen, for they are rebellious.[k] 8 But you, son of man, listen to what I say to you.
Do not rebel like that rebellious house;[l] open your mouth and eat[m] what I give you."

9 Then I looked, and I saw a hand[n] stretched out to me. In it was a scroll, 10 which

f 26 Or *lapis lazuli*

1:26 [z] Ex 24:10; Eze 10:1 [a] Rev 1:13
1:27 [b] Eze 8:2
1:28 [c] Ge 9:13; Rev 10:1 [d] Rev 4:2 [e] Eze 8:4 [f] Eze 3:23; Da 8:17; Rev 1:17
2:1 [a] Da 10:11
2:2 [b] Eze 3:24; Da 8:18
2:3 [c] Jer 3:25; Eze 20:8-24
2:4 [d] Eze 3:7
2:5 [e] Eze 3:11 [f] Eze 3:27 [g] Eze 33:33
2:6 [h] Jer 1:8, 17 [i] Isa 9:18; Mic 7:4 [j] Eze 3:9
2:7 [k] Jer 1:7; Eze 3:10-11
2:8 [l] Isa 50:5 [m] Jer 15:16; Rev 10:9
2:9 [n] Eze 8:3

1:26 This "figure like that of a man" revealed God's holiness and prepared Ezekiel for what God was about to tell him. The figure represented God himself on the throne. In a similar way, Christ revealed God in human form and prepared us for his message of salvation. Christ came into history in a real, human body.

1:27, 28 The glory of the Lord appeared like fire and brilliant light to Ezekiel. Ezekiel fell face down, overwhelmed by the contrast between God's holiness and his own sinfulness and insignificance. Eventually every person will fall before God, either out of reverence and awe for his mercy or out of fear of his judgment. Based on the way you are living today, how will you respond to God's holiness?

1:27, 28 The four living creatures and the four wheels are powerful pictures of judgment, yet the rainbow over the throne symbolises God's never-ending faithfulness to his people. Just as God sent a rainbow to Noah to symbolise his promise never again to destroy the earth by a flood (Genesis 9:8–17), so this rainbow symbolises God's promise to preserve those who remain faithful to him. The purpose of God's judgment is to correct us and, ultimately, to allow perfect peace and righteousness to reign on the earth for ever.

2:1 The immortal God addressed Ezekiel by calling him *son of man,* emphasising the distance between them. It is amazing that God chooses to work his divine will on earth through finite, imperfect beings. We are made from the dust of the ground, yet God chooses to place within us his life and breath and to ask us to serve him.

2:2 We can only imagine what it was like for Ezekiel to experience this vision. Certainly there was much he did not understand, but Ezekiel knew that each part had significance because it came from God. When God saw Ezekiel's open and obedient attitude, he filled him with his Spirit and gave him power for the job ahead. God doesn't expect us to understand everything about him, but to be willing and obedient servants, faithful to what we know is true and right.

2:3–5 The world of business defines success in terms of giving customers what they want. Ezekiel, however, was called to give God's message to the people, whether they would listen or not. The measure of Ezekiel's success would not be how well the people responded, but how well he obeyed God and thus fulfilled God's purpose for him. Isaiah and Jeremiah also prophesied with little positive response (see Isaiah 6:9–12; Jeremiah 1:17–19). God's truth does not depend on how people respond. God will not judge us for how well others respond to our faith, but for how faithful we have been. God always gives us the strength to accomplish what he asks us to do.

2:4, 5 God called the people "obstinate and stubborn" because they refused to admit their sin. Rebelliousness was the nation's primary characteristic at this time. Even when God pointed out their wrongdoing, the people ignored the truth. Is God pointing at some sin in your life? Don't be stubborn – confess your sin and begin to live for God. By obeying him now you will be ready for God's final review of your life (Matthew 25:31–46).

2:6–8 God gave Ezekiel the difficult responsibility of presenting his message to ungrateful and abusive people. Sometimes we must be an example to or share our faith with unkind people. The Lord told Ezekiel not to be afraid and rebel, but to speak his words, whether or not the people would listen. He also wants us to tell the Good News, whether it's convenient or not (2 Timothy 4:2).

2:6–10 Three times God told Ezekiel not to be afraid. When God's Spirit is within us, we can lay aside our fears of rejection or ridicule. God's strength is powerful enough to help us live for him even under the heaviest criticism.

2:9, 10 Ancient books were usually scrolls, each one page (up to 30 feet long) rolled up simultaneously from both ends. Normally, scrolls had writing on only one side. But in this case, the warnings overflowed to the scroll's other side, showing the full measure of judgment about to descend on Judah.

he unrolled before me. On both sides of it were written words of lament and mourning
and woe.[o]
3 And he said to me, "Son of man, eat what is before you, eat this scroll; then go
and speak to the house of Israel." 2So I opened my mouth, and he gave me the
scroll to eat.
3Then he said to me, "Son of man, eat this scroll I am giving you and fill your
stomach with it." So I ate[a] it, and it tasted as sweet as honey[b] in my mouth.
4He then said to me: "Son of man, go now to the house of Israel and speak my words
to them. 5You are not being sent to a people of obscure speech and difficult language,[c] but to the house of Israel—6not to many peoples of obscure speech and
difficult language, whose words you cannot understand. Surely if I had sent you to
them, they would have listened to you.[d] 7But the house of Israel is not willing to
listen to you because they are not willing to listen to me, for the whole house of Israel
is hardened and obstinate.[e] 8But I will make you as unyielding and hardened as they
are.[f] 9I will make your forehead like the hardest stone, harder than flint. Do not be
afraid of them or terrified by them, though they are a rebellious house.[g]"
10And he said to me, "Son of man, listen carefully and take to heart all the words
I speak to you. 11Go now to your countrymen in exile and speak to them. Say to them,
'This is what the Sovereign LORD says,' whether they listen or fail to listen.[h]"
12Then the Spirit lifted me up,[i] and I heard behind me a loud rumbling
sound—May the glory of the LORD be praised in his dwelling-place!—13the sound
of the wings of the living creatures brushing against each other and the sound of the
wheels beside them, a loud rumbling sound.[j] 14The Spirit then lifted me up and took
me away, and I went in bitterness and in the anger of my spirit, with the strong hand
of the LORD upon me. 15I came to the exiles who lived at Tel Abib near the Kebar
River.[k] And there, where they were living, I sat among them for seven
days[l]—overwhelmed.

Warning to Israel

16At the end of seven days the word of the LORD came to me:[m] 17"Son of man,
I have made you a watchman[n] for the house of Israel; so hear the word I speak and
give them warning from me. 18When I say to a wicked man, 'You will surely die,'
and you do not warn him or speak out to dissuade him from his evil ways in order

2:10 [o]Rev 8:13
3:3 [a]Jer 15:16 [b]Ps 19:10; Ps 119:103; Rev 10:9-10
3:5 [c]Isa 28:11; Jnh 1:2
3:6 [d]Mt 11:21-23
3:7 [e]Eze 2:4; Jn 15:20-23
3:8 [f]Jer 1:18
3:9 [g]Isa 50:7; Eze 2:6; Mic 3:8
3:11 [h]Eze 2:4-5, 7
3:12 [i]Eze 8:3; Ac 8:39
3:13 [j]Eze 1:24; 10:5, 16-17
3:15 [k]Ps 137:1 [l]Job 2:13
3:16 [m]Jer 42:7
3:17 [n]Isa 52:8; Jer 6:17; Eze 33:7-9

3:1–3 In his vision, Ezekiel ate God's message and found this spiritual food not only good for him, but also as sweet as honey (see Revelation 10:8–10 for a similar use of this image). If you "digest" God's word, you will find that not only does it make you stronger in your faith, but its wisdom also sweetens your life. You need to feed yourself spiritually just as you do physically. This means doing more than simply giving God's message a casual glance. You must make digesting God's word a regular part of your life.

3:10, 11 Ezekiel needed to take God's words to heart before preaching them to others. God's message must sink deep into your heart and show in your actions before you can effectively help others understand and apply the gospel.

3:14, 15 Ezekiel was bitter and angry, not at God, but at the sins and attitudes of the people. Ezekiel's extraordinary vision had ended, and he had to begin the tedious job of prophesying among his people, who cared little about God's messages. Before the exile, the people had heard Jeremiah, but they would not listen. Here Ezekiel had to give a similar message, and he expected to be rejected as well. But Ezekiel had the vision of the living creatures and the rumbling wheels on his side. He had nothing to fear because God was with him. Despite knowing the probable outcome, Ezekiel obeyed God.

As we grow, we will have times of great joy when we feel close to God, and times when sins, struggles, or everyday tasks overwhelm us. Like Ezekiel, we should obey God even when we don't feel like it. Don't let feelings hinder your obedience.

3:15 Ezekiel sat quietly among the people for seven days. This was the customary period of mourning for the dead (Genesis 50:10; 1 Samuel 31:13; Job 2:13). Ezekiel was mourning for those who were spiritually dead. Tel Abib was the location of the settlement of Jews who were exiled from Jerusalem.

3:17, 18 A watchman's job was to stand on the city wall and warn the people of approaching danger. Ezekiel's role was to be a spiritual watchman, warning the people of the judgment to come. Some think that "accountable for his blood" means that just as a watchman on the wall would pay with his life if he failed to warn the city of approaching enemies, Ezekiel would have been held accountable if he had refused to warn the people of coming judgment. Others believe this phrase simply means that God would hold Ezekiel responsible.

3:18–21 In these verses, God is not talking about loss of salvation but rather about physical death. If the people back in Judah continued in their sins, they and their land and cities would be destroyed by Nebuchadnezzar's armies. If, on the other hand, the people would turn to God, God would spare them. God would hold Ezekiel responsible for his fellow Jews if he failed to warn them of the consequences of their sins. All people are individually responsible to God, but believers have a special responsibility to warn unbelievers of the consequences of rejecting God. If we fail to do this, God will hold us responsible for what happens to them. This should motivate us to begin sharing our faith with others—by both word and deed—and to avoid becoming callous or unconcerned in our attitude.

3:18 [o]ver 20; Eze 33:6
3:19 [p]2Ki 17:13; Eze 14:14, 20; Ac 18:6; 20:26; 1Ti 4:14-16
3:20 [q]Ps 125:5; Eze 18:24; 33:12, 18
3:21 [r]Ac 20:31
3:22 [s]Eze 1:3 [t]Ac 9:6

to save his life, that wicked man will die for[a] his sin, and I will hold you accountable
for his blood.[o] 19But if you do warn the wicked man and he does not turn from his
wickedness or from his evil ways, he will die for his sin; but you will have saved
yourself.[p]
20"Again, when a righteous man turns from his righteousness and does evil, and
I put a stumbling-block before him, he will die. Since you did not warn him, he will
die for his sin. The righteous things he did will not be remembered, and I will hold
you accountable for his blood.[q] 21But if you do warn the righteous man not to sin
and he does not sin, he will surely live because he took warning, and you will have
saved yourself.[r]"
22The hand of the LORD[s] was upon me there, and he said to me, "Get up and go[t]

a *18* Or *in*; also in verses 19 and 20

EZEKIEL

Although Ezekiel's visions and prophecies were clear and vivid, very little is known about the prophet's personal life. He was among the thousands of young men deported from Judah to Babylon when King Jehoiakim surrendered. Until those tragic days, Ezekiel was being trained for the priesthood. But during the exile in Babylon, God called Ezekiel to be his prophet during one of Israel's darkest times.

Ezekiel experienced the same kind of shocking encounter with God that Isaiah had reported 150 years earlier. Like Isaiah, Ezekiel was never the same after his personal encounter with God. Although God's messages through both these prophets had many points in common, the conditions in which they lived were very different. Isaiah warned of the coming storm; Ezekiel spoke in the midst of the storm of national defeat that devastated his people. He announced that even Jerusalem would not escape destruction. In addition, during this time Ezekiel had to endure the pain of his wife's death.

God's description of Ezekiel as a watchman on the walls of the city captures the personal nature of his ministry. A watchman's job was dangerous. If he failed at his post, he and the entire city might be destroyed. His own safety depended on the quality of his work. The importance of each person's accountability before God was a central part of Ezekiel's message. He taught the exiles that God expected personal obedience and worship from each of them.

As in Ezekiel's day, it is easy for us today to forget that God has a personal interest in each one of us. We may feel insignificant or out of control when we look at world events. But knowing that God is ultimately in control, that he cares, and that he is willing to be known by us can bring a new sense of purpose to our lives. How do you measure your worth? Are you valuable because of your achievements and potential, or because God, your Creator and Designer, declares you valuable?

Strengths and accomplishments:
- Was a priest by training, a prophet by God's call
- Received vivid visions and delivered powerful messages
- Served as God's messenger during Israel's captivity in Babylon
- God shaped his character to fit his mission—a tough and courageous man to reach a hard and stubborn people (Ezekiel 3:8)

Lessons from his life:
- Even the repeated failures of his people will not prevent God's plan for the world from being fulfilled
- Each person's response to God determines his or her eternal destiny
- In seemingly hopeless situations God still has people through whom he can work

Vital statistics:
- Where: Babylon
- Occupation: Prophet to the captives in Babylon
- Relatives: Father: Buzi. Wife: Unknown
- Contemporaries: Jehoiachin, Jeremiah, Jehoiakim, Nebuchadnezzar

Key verses:
"And he said to me, 'Son of man, listen carefully and take to heart all the words I speak to you. Go now to your countrymen in exile and speak to them. Say to them, "This is what the Sovereign LORD says," whether they listen or fail to listen'" (Ezekiel 3:10, 11).

Ezekiel's story is told in the book of Ezekiel and 2 Kings 24:10–17.

out to the plain,[u] and there I will speak to you." 23So I got up and went out to the
plain. And the glory of the LORD was standing there, like the glory I had seen by the
Kebar River,[v] and I fell face down.[w]
24Then the Spirit came into me and raised me[x] to my feet. He spoke to me and
said: "Go, shut yourself inside your house. 25And you, son of man, they will tie with
ropes; you will be bound so that you cannot go out among the people.[y] 26I will make
your tongue stick to the roof of your mouth so that you will be silent and unable to
rebuke them, though they are a rebellious house.[z] 27But when I speak to you, I will
open your mouth and you shall say to them, 'This is what the Sovereign LORD says.'[a]
Whoever will listen let him listen, and whoever will refuse let him refuse; for they
are a rebellious house.[b]

2. Visions of sin and judgment

Siege of Jerusalem Symbolised

4 "Now, son of man, take a clay tablet, put it in front of you and draw the city of
Jerusalem on it. 2Then lay siege to it: Erect siege works against it, build a ramp[a]
up to it, set up camps against it and put battering-rams around it.[b] 3Then take an iron
pan, place it as an iron wall between you and the city and turn your face towards it.
It will be under siege, and you shall besiege it. This will be a sign[c] to the house of
Israel.[d]
4"Then lie on your left side and put the sin of the house of Israel upon yourself.**[a]**
You are to bear their sin for the number of days you lie on your side. 5I have assigned
you the same number of days as the years of their sin. So for 390 days you will bear
the sin of the house of Israel.
6"After you have finished this, lie down again, this time on your right side, and
bear the sin of the house of Judah. I have assigned you 40 days, a day for each year.[e]
7Turn your face towards the siege of Jerusalem and with bared arm prophesy against
her. 8I will tie you up with ropes so that you cannot turn from one side to the other
until you have finished the days of your siege.[f]
9"Take wheat and barley, beans and lentils, millet and spelt;[g] put them in a storage
jar and use them to make bread for yourself. You are to eat it during the 390 days
you lie on your side. 10Weigh out twenty shekels**[b]** of food to eat each day and eat
it at set times. 11Also measure out a sixth of a hin**[c]** of water and drink it at set times.
12Eat the food as you would a barley cake; bake it in the sight of the people, using
human excrement[h] for fuel." 13The LORD said, "In this way the people of Israel will
eat defiled food among the nations where I will drive them."[i]
14Then I said, "Not so, Sovereign LORD![j] I have never defiled myself. From my

a *4* Or *your side* **b** *10* That is, about 8 ounces (about 0.2 kilogram) **c** *11* That is, about 1 pint (about 0.6 litre)

3:22 [u]Eze 8:4
3:23 [v]Eze 1:1 [w]Eze 1:28
3:24 [x]Eze 2:2
3:25 [y]Eze 4:8
3:26 [z]Eze 2:5; 24:27; 33:22
3:27 [a]ver 11 [b]Eze 12:3; 24:27; 33:22
4:2 [a]Jer 6:6 [b]Eze 21:22
4:3 [c]Isa 8:18; 20:3; Eze 12:3-6; 24:24, 27 [d]Jer 39:1
4:6 [e]Nu 14:34; Da 9:24-26; 12:11-12
4:8 [f]Eze 3:25
4:9 [g]Isa 28:25
4:12 [h]Isa 36:12
4:13 [i]Hos 9:3
4:14 [j]Jer 1:6; Eze 9:8; 20:49

3:23 Ezekiel recognised his helplessness before God and fell face down in his presence. Sometimes our prosperity, popularity, or physical strength blinds us to our spiritual helplessness. But nothing we do on our own can accomplish much for God. Only when God is in control of our wills can we accomplish great tasks for him. The first step to being God's person is to admit that you need his help; then you can begin to see what God can really do in your life.

3:24–27 Ezekiel was allowed to speak only when God had a message for the people. Thus the people knew that whatever Ezekiel said was God's message. They did not have to wonder whether Ezekiel was speaking by God's authority or his own.

4:1ff Ezekiel acted out the coming siege and fall of Jerusalem before it actually happened. God gave Ezekiel specific instructions about what to do and say and how to do and say it. Each detail had a specific meaning. Often we ignore or disregard the smaller details of God's word, thinking God probably doesn't care. Like Ezekiel, we should want to obey God completely, even in the details.

4:4–17 Ezekiel's unusual actions symbolically portrayed the fate of Jerusalem. He lay on his left side for 390 days to show that Israel would be punished for 390 years; then he lay on his right side for 40 days to show that Judah would be punished for 40 years. Ezekiel was not allowed to move, symbolising the fact that the people of Jerusalem would be imprisoned within the walls of the city. We know that Ezekiel did not have to lie on his side all day because these verses tell of other tasks God asked him to do during this time. The small amount of food he was allowed to eat represented the normal ration provided to those living in a city under siege by enemy armies. The food that was to be cooked over human excrement was a symbol of Judah's spiritual uncleanness.

Certainly many people saw these spectacles and, in the process, heard Ezekiel's occasional speeches (3:27). How many of us would be willing to so dramatically portray the sins of our nation? We need to pray for greater boldness in our witness.

4:12–14 Ezekiel asked God not to make him use human excrement for fuel because it violated the laws for purity (Leviticus 21, 22; Deuteronomy 23:12–14). As a priest, Ezekiel would have been careful to keep all these laws. To use human excrement for fuel would paint a dramatic picture of ruin. If nothing was left in the city that could be burned, it would be impossible to continue to follow God's laws for sacrifices.

4:14 [k]Lev 11:39 [l]Ex 22:31; Dt 14:3; Ac 10:14
4:16 [m]Ps 105:16; Eze 5:16 [n]ver 10-11; Lev 26:26; Isa 3:1; Eze 12:19
4:17 [o]Lev 26:39; Eze 24:23; 33:10
5:1 [a]Isa 7:20 [b]Eze 44:20 [c]Lev 21:5
5:2 [d]ver 12; Lev 26:33
5:3 [e]Jer 39:10
5:6 [f]Jer 11:10; Eze 16:47-51; Zec 7:11
5:7 [g]2Ch 33:9; Jer 2:10-11; Eze 16:47
5:8 [h]Eze 15:7
5:9 [i]Da 9:12; Mt 24:21
5:10 [j]Lev 26:29; La 2:20

youth until now I have never eaten anything found dead[k] or torn by wild animals.
No unclean meat has ever entered my mouth.[l]"
15"Very well," he said, "I will let you bake your bread over cow manure instead
of human excrement."
16He then said to me: "Son of man, I will cut off[m] the supply of food in Jerusalem.
The people will eat rationed food in anxiety and drink rationed water in despair,[n] 17for
food and water will be scarce. They will be appalled at the sight of each other and
will waste away because of[d] their sin.[o]

5 "Now, son of man, take a sharp sword and use it as a barber's razor[a] to shave[b]
your head and your beard.[c] Then take a set of scales and divide up the hair.
2When the days of your siege come to an end, burn a third of the hair with fire inside
the city. Take a third and strike it with the sword all around the city. And scatter a
third to the wind. For I will pursue them with drawn sword.[d] 3But take a few strands
of hair and tuck them away in the folds of your garment.[e] 4Again, take a few of these
and throw them into the fire and burn them up. A fire will spread from there to the
whole house of Israel.
5"This is what the Sovereign LORD says: This is Jerusalem, which I have set in the
centre of the nations, with countries all around her. 6Yet in her wickedness she has
rebelled against my laws and decrees more than the nations and countries around her.
She has rejected my laws and has not followed my decrees.[f]
7"Therefore this is what the Sovereign LORD says: You have been more unruly than
the nations around you and have not followed my decrees or kept my laws. You have
not even[a] conformed to the standards of the nations around you.[g]
8"Therefore this is what the Sovereign LORD says: I myself am against you,
Jerusalem, and I will inflict punishment on you in the sight of the nations.[h] 9Because
of all your detestable idols, I will do to you what I have never done before and will
never do again.[i] 10Therefore in your midst fathers will eat their children, and children
will eat their fathers.[j] I will inflict punishment on you and will scatter all your

d *17* Or *away in* **a** *7* Most Hebrew manuscripts; some Hebrew manuscripts and Syriac *You have*

EZEKIEL'S ACTS OF OBEDIENCE

2:1	Stood and received God's message
3:24–27	Shut himself inside his house
3:27	Faithfully proclaimed God's message
4:1ff	Drew the city of Jerusalem on a clay tablet
4:4, 5	Lay on his left side for 390 days
4:6	Lay on his right side for 40 days
4:9–17	Followed specific cooking instructions
5:1–4	Shaved his head and beard
12:3–7	Left home to demonstrate exile
13:1ff	Spoke against false prophets
19:1ff	Sang a lament concerning the leaders
21:2	Prophesied against Israel and the temple
21:19–23	Marked out two roads for Babylon's king
24:16, 17	Did not mourn his wife's death

5:1–10 Shaving one's head and beard signified mourning, humiliation, and repentance. God told Ezekiel to shave his head and beard and then to divide the hair into three parts, symbolising what was going to happen to the people in Jerusalem (see 5:12). Along with verbal prophecies, God asked Ezekiel to use dramatic visual images to command the people's attention and to burn an indelible impression on their minds. Just as God gave Ezekiel creative ways to communicate his message to the exiles, we can creatively communicate the Good News about God to a lost generation.

5:3, 4 The few strands of hair Ezekiel put in his garment symbolised the small remnant of faithful people whom God would preserve. But even some from this remnant would be judged and destroyed because their faith was not genuine. Where will you stand in the coming judgment? Matthew 7:22, 23 warns that many who believe they are safe are not. Make sure your commitment is vital and heartfelt.

5:7 The people's wickedness was so great that they couldn't even keep the laws of the pagan nations around them, not to mention God's laws.

survivors to the winds.[k] 11Therefore as surely as I live, declares the Sovereign LORD,
because you have defiled my sanctuary with all your vile images[l] and detestable
practices,[m] I myself will withdraw my favour; I will not look on you with pity or spare
you.[n] 12A third of your people will die of the plague or perish by famine inside you;
a third will fall by the sword outside your walls; and a third I will scatter to the winds
and pursue with drawn sword.[o]
13"Then my anger will cease and my wrath[p] against them will subside, and I will
be avenged.[q] And when I have spent my wrath upon them, they will know that I the
LORD have spoken in my zeal.
14"I will make you a ruin and a reproach among the nations around you, in the sight
of all who pass by.[r] 15You will be a reproach and a taunt, a warning and an object
of horror to the nations around you when I inflict punishment on you in anger and
in wrath and with stinging rebuke.[s] I the LORD have spoken.[t] 16When I shoot at
you with my deadly and destructive arrows of famine, I will shoot to destroy you.
I will bring more and more famine upon you and cut off your supply of food.[u] 17I
will send famine and wild beasts against you, and they will leave you childless. Plague
and bloodshed[v] will sweep through you, and I will bring the sword against you. I
the LORD have spoken.[w]"

A Prophecy Against the Mountains of Israel

6 The word of the LORD came to me: 2"Son of man, set your face against the
mountains[a] of Israel; prophesy against them 3and say: 'O mountains of Israel,
hear the word of the Sovereign LORD. This is what the Sovereign LORD says to the
mountains and hills, to the ravines and valleys:[b] I am about to bring a sword against
you, and I will destroy your high places.[c] 4Your altars will be demolished and your
incense altars[d] will be smashed; and I will slay your people in front of your idols.
5I will lay the dead bodies of the Israelites in front of their idols, and I will scatter
your bones[e] around your altars. 6Wherever you live, the towns will be laid waste and
the high places demolished, so that your altars will be laid waste and devastated, your
idols[f] smashed and ruined, your incense altars[g] broken down, and what you have
made wiped out.[h] 7Your people will fall slain among you, and you will know that
I am the LORD.
8" 'But I will spare some, for some of you will escape[i] the sword when you are
scattered among the lands and nations.[j] 9Then in the nations where they have been
carried captive, those who escape will remember me—how I have been grieved[k] by
their adulterous hearts, which have turned away from me, and by their eyes, which
have lusted after their idols.[l] They will loathe themselves for the evil they have done
and for all their detestable practices.[m] 10And they will know that I am the LORD; I
did not threaten in vain to bring this calamity on them.
11" 'This is what the Sovereign LORD says: Strike your hands together and stamp

5:10 [k]Lev 26:33; Ps 44:11; Eze 12:14; Zec 2:6
5:11 [l]Eze 7:20 [m]2Ch 36:14; Eze 8:6 [n]Eze 7:4, 9
5:12 [o]ver 2, 17; Jer 15:2; 21:9; Eze 6:11-12; 12:14
5:13 [p]Eze 21:17; 36:6 [q]Isa 1:24
5:14 [r]Lev 26:32; Ne 2:17; Ps 74:3-10; 79:1-4
5:15 [s]1Ki 9:7; Jer 22:8-9; 24:9 [t]Eze 25:17
5:16 [u]Dt 32:24
5:17 [v]Eze 38:22 [w]Eze 14:21
6:2 [a]Eze 36:1
6:3 [b]Eze 36:4 [c]Lev 26:30
6:4 [d]2Ch 14:5
6:5 [e]Jer 8:1-2
6:6 [f]Mic 1:7; Zec 13:2 [g]Lev 26:30 [h]Isa 6:11; Eze 5:14
6:8 [i]Jer 44:28 [j]Isa 6:13; Jer 44:14; Eze 12:16; 14:22
6:9 [k]Ps 78:40; Isa 7:13 [l]Eze 20:7, 24 [m]Eze 20:43; 36:31

5:11 It was a serious sin to defile the temple, God's sanctuary, by worshipping idols and practising evil within its very walls. In the New Testament, we learn that God now makes his home *within* those who are his. Our bodies are God's temple (see 1 Corinthians 6:19). We defile God's temple today by allowing gossiping, bitterness, love of money, lying, or any other wrong actions or attitudes to be part of our lives. By asking the Holy Spirit's help, we can keep from defiling his temple, our bodies.

5:13 Have you ever seen someone try to discipline a child by saying, "If you do that one more time . . ."? If the parent doesn't follow through, the child learns not to listen. Empty threats backfire. God was going to punish the Israelites for their blatant sins, and he wanted them to know that he would do what he said. The people learned the hard way that God always follows through on his word. Too many people ignore God's warnings, treating them as empty threats. But what God threatens, he does. Don't make the mistake of thinking God doesn't really mean what he says.

6:1ff This is the beginning of a two-part message. Remember that Ezekiel could speak only when giving messages from God. The message in chapter 6 is that Judah's idolatry will surely call down God's judgment. The message in chapter 7 describes the nature of that judgment—utter destruction of the nation. Nevertheless, God in his mercy saved a remnant. Ezekiel prophesies against the mountains of Israel because mountains were sites of the "high places" used to worship idols.

6:8–10 A ray of light appears in this prophecy of darkness—God would spare a remnant of people, but only after they had learned some hard lessons. God sometimes has to break a person in order to bring him or her to true repentance. The people needed new attitudes, but they wouldn't change until God broke their hearts with humiliation, pain, suffering, and defeat. Does your heart long for God enough to change those areas displeasing him? Or will God have to break your heart?

6:11 Prophets often used this threefold description of judgment upon Jerusalem—sword, famine, and plague—as a way of saying that the destruction would be complete. The sword meant death in battle; famine came when enemies besieged a city; plague was always a danger during famine. Don't make the mistake of undere-

your feet and cry out "Alas!" because of all the wicked and detestable practices of the house of Israel, for they will fall by the sword, famine and plague.[n] 12He that is far away will die of the plague, and he that is near will fall by the sword, and he that survives and is spared will die of famine. So will I spend my wrath upon them.[o] 13And they will know that I am the LORD, when their people lie slain among their idols around their altars, on every high hill and on all the mountaintops, under every spreading tree and every leafy oak[p]—places where they offered fragrant incense to all their idols.[q] 14And I will stretch out my hand[r] against them and make the land a desolate waste from the desert to Diblah[a]—wherever they live. Then they will know that I am the LORD.[s]' "

The End Has Come

7 The word of the LORD came to me: 2"Son of man, this is what the Sovereign LORD says to the land of Israel: The end![a] The end has come upon the four corners[b] of the land. 3The end is now upon you and I will unleash my anger against you. I will judge you according to your conduct and repay you for all your detestable practices. 4I will not look on you with pity[c] or spare you; I will surely repay you for your conduct and the detestable practices among you. Then you will know that I am the LORD.

5"This is what the Sovereign LORD says: Disaster![d] An unheard-of[a] disaster is coming. 6The end has come! The end has come! It has roused itself against you. It has come! 7Doom has come upon you—you who dwell in the land. The time has come, the day is near;[e] there is panic, not joy, upon the mountains. 8I am about to pour out my wrath[f] on you and spend my anger against you; I will judge you according to your conduct and repay you for all your detestable practices.[g] 9I will not look on you with pity or spare you; I will repay you in accordance with your conduct and the detestable practices among you. Then you will know that it is I the LORD who strikes the blow.

10"The day is here! It has come! Doom has burst forth, the rod[h] has budded, arrogance has blossomed! 11Violence has grown into[b] a rod to punish wickedness; none of the people will be left, none of that crowd—no wealth, nothing of value.[i] 12The time has come, the day has arrived. Let not the buyer rejoice nor the seller grieve, for wrath is upon the whole crowd.[j] 13The seller will not recover the land he has sold as long as both of them live, for the vision concerning the whole crowd will not be reversed. Because of their sins, not one of them will preserve his life.[k] 14Though they blow the trumpet and get everything ready, no-one will go into battle, for my wrath is upon the whole crowd.

15"Outside is the sword, inside are plague and famine; those in the country will die by the sword, and those in the city will be devoured by famine and plague.[l] 16All who survive and escape will be in the mountains, moaning like doves[m] of the valleys, each because of his sins.[n] 17Every hand will go limp,[o] and every knee will become as weak as water. 18They will put on sackcloth and be clothed with terror.[p] Their

a *14* Most Hebrew manuscripts; a few Hebrew manuscripts *Riblah* **a** *5* Most Hebrew manuscripts; some Hebrew manuscripts and Syriac *Disaster after* **b** *11* Or *The violent one has become*

6:11 [n]Eze 5:12; 21:14, 17; 25:6
6:12 [o]Eze 5:12
6:13 [p]Isa 57:5 [q]1Ki 14:23; Jer 2:20; Eze 20:28; Hos 4:13
6:14 [r]Isa 5:25 [s]Eze 14:13
7:2 [a]Am 8:2, 10 [b]Rev 7:1; 20:8
7:4 [c]Eze 5:11
7:5 [d]2Ki 21:12
7:7 [e]Eze 12:23; Zep 1:14
7:8 [f]Isa 42:25; Eze 9:8; 14:19; Na 1:6 [g]Eze 20:8, 21; 36:19
7:10 [h]Ps 89:32; Isa 10:5
7:11 [i]Jer 16:6; Zep 1:18
7:12 [j]ver 7; Isa 5:13-14; Eze 30:3
7:13 [k]Lev 25:24-28
7:15 [l]Dt 32:25; Jer 14:18; La 1:20; Eze 5:12
7:16 [m]Isa 59:11 [n]Ezr 9:15; Eze 6:8
7:17 [o]Isa 13:7; Eze 21:7; 22:14
7:18 [p]Ps 55:5

---

stimating the extent of God's judgment. If you ignore the biblical warnings and turn away from God, God's punishment awaits you.

6:14 The phrase, "Then they will know that I am the LORD" (or a variation on this phrase) occurs 65 times in the book of Ezekiel. The purpose of all God's punishment was not to take revenge, but to impress upon the people the truth that the Lord is the only true and living God. People in Ezekiel's day were worshipping man-made idols and calling them gods. Today money, sex, and power have become idols for many. Punishment will come upon all who put other things ahead of God. It is easy to forget that the Lord alone is God, the supreme authority and the only source of eternal love and life. Remember that God may use the difficulties of your life to teach you that he alone is God.

7:10, 11 In chapter 7, Ezekiel predicts the complete destruction of Judah. The wicked and proud will finally get what they deserve. If it seems as though God ignores the evil and proud people of our day, be assured that a day of judgment will come, just as it came for the people of Judah. God is waiting patiently for sinners to repent (see 2 Peter 3:9), but when his judgment comes, "none of the people will be left". What you decide about God now will determine your fate then.

7:12, 13 The nation of Judah trusted in its prosperity and possessions instead of in God. So God planned to destroy the basis of its prosperity. Whenever we begin to trust in jobs, the economy, a political system, or military might for our security, we put God in the back seat.

faces will be covered with shame and their heads will be shaved.[q] 19They will throw
their silver into the streets, and their gold will be an unclean thing. Their silver and
gold will not be able to save them in the day of the LORD's wrath.[r] They will not
satisfy their hunger or fill their stomachs with it, for it has made them stumble[s] into
sin.[t] 20They were proud of their beautiful jewellery and used it to make their
detestable idols and vile images.[u] Therefore I will turn these into an unclean thing
for them. 21I will hand it all over as plunder to foreigners and as loot to the wicked
of the earth, and they will defile it.[v] 22I will turn my face[w] away from them, and
they will desecrate my treasured place; robbers will enter it and desecrate it.
23"Prepare chains, because the land is full of bloodshed[x] and the city is full of
violence. 24I will bring the most wicked of the nations to take possession of their
houses; I will put an end to the pride of the mighty, and their sanctuaries[y] will be
desecrated.[z] 25When terror comes, they will seek peace, but there will be none.[a]
26Calamity upon calamity[b] will come, and rumour upon rumour. They will try to get
a vision from the prophet; the teaching of the law by the priest will be lost, as will
the counsel of the elders.[c] 27The king will mourn, the prince will be clothed with
despair,[d] and the hands of the people of the land will tremble. I will deal with them
according to their conduct,[e] and by their own standards I will judge them. Then they
will know that I am the LORD.[f]"

Idolatry in the Temple

8 In the sixth year, in the sixth month on the fifth day, while I was sitting in my
house and the elders[a] of Judah were sitting before[b] me, the hand of the Sovereign LORD came upon me there.[c] 2I looked, and I saw a figure like that of a man.[a]
From what appeared to be his waist down he was like fire, and from there up his
appearance was as bright as glowing metal.[d] 3He stretched out what looked like a
hand and took me by the hair of my head. The Spirit lifted me up[e] between earth
and heaven and in visions of God he took me to Jerusalem, to the entrance to the north
gate of the inner court, where the idol that provokes to jealousy[f] stood. 4And there
before me was the glory[g] of the God of Israel, as in the vision I had seen in the plain.[h]
5Then he said to me, "Son of man, look towards the north." So I looked, and in
the entrance north of the gate of the altar I saw this idol[i] of jealousy.
6And he said to me, "Son of man, do you see what they are doing—the utterly
detestable[j] things the house of Israel is doing here, things that will drive me far from
my sanctuary? But you will see things that are even more detestable."
7Then he brought me to the entrance to the court. I looked, and I saw a hole in the

[a] 2 Or *saw a fiery figure*

7:18 [q] Isa 15:2-3; Eze 27:31; Am 8:10
7:19 [r] Eze 13:5; Zep 1:7, 18 [s] Eze 14:3 [t] Pr 11:4
7:20 [u] Jer 7:30
7:21 [v] 2Ki 24:13
7:22 [w] Eze 39:23-24
7:23 [x] 2Ki 21:16
7:24 [y] Eze 24:21 [z] 2Ch 7:20; Eze 28:7
7:25 [a] Eze 13:10, 16
7:26 [b] Jer 4:20 [c] Isa 47:11; Eze 20:1-3; Mic 3:6
7:27 [d] Ps 109:19; Eze 26:16 [e] Eze 18:20 [f] ver 4
8:1 [a] Eze 14:1 [b] Eze 33:31 [c] Eze 1:1-3
8:2 [d] Eze 1:4, 26-27
8:3 [e] Eze 3:12; 11:1 [f] Ex 20:5; Dt 32:16
8:4 [g] Eze 1:28 [h] Eze 3:22
8:5 [i] Ps 78:58; Jer 32:34
8:6 [j] Eze 5:11

7:19 God's people had allowed their love of money to lead them into sin. And for this, God would destroy them. Money has a strange power to lead people into sin. Paul said that "the love of money is a root of all kinds of evil" (1 Timothy 6:10). It is ironic that we use money—a gift of God—to buy things that separate us from him. It is tragic that we spend so much money seeking to satisfy ourselves, and so little time seeking God, the true source of satisfaction.

7:20 God gave the people silver and gold, but they used that silver and gold to make idols. The resources God gives us should be used to do his work and carry out his will, but too often we use them to satisfy our own desires. When we abuse God's gifts or use resources selfishly, we miss the real purpose God had in mind. This is as shortsighted as idolatry.

7:24 The people of Jerusalem took great pride in their buildings. The temple itself was a source of pride (see 24:20, 21). This pride would be crushed when the evil and godless Babylonians destroyed Jerusalem's houses and holy places. If you are going through a humiliating experience, God may be using that experience to weed out pride in your life.

8:1ff This prophecy's date corresponds to 592 B.C. The message of chapters 8—11 is directed specifically towards Jerusalem and its leaders. Chapter 8 records Ezekiel being taken in a vision from Babylon to the temple in Jerusalem to see the great wickedness being practised there. The people and their religious leaders were thoroughly corrupt. While Ezekiel's first vision (chapters 1—3) showed that judgment was from God, this vision showed that their sin was the reason for judgment.

8:2 This person could have been an angel or a manifestation of God himself. In Ezekiel's previous vision, a man with a similar appearance was pictured as God on his throne (1:26–28).

8:3–5 This "idol that provokes to jealousy" could be an image of Asherah, the Canaanite goddess of fertility, whose character encouraged sexual immorality and self-gratification. King Manasseh had placed such an idol in the temple (2 Kings 21:7). King Josiah had burned the Asherah pole (2 Kings 23:6), but there were certainly many other idols around.

8:6ff In scene after scene, God revealed to Ezekiel the extent to which the people had embraced idolatry and wickedness. God's Spirit works within us in a similar way, revealing sin that lurks in our lives. How comfortable would you feel if God revealed secrets in your life today?

8:10 [k]Ex 20:4
8:11 [l]Nu 16:17 [m]Nu 16:35
8:12 [n]Ps 10:11; Isa 29:15; Eze 9:9
8:16 [o]Joel 2:17 [p]Dt 4:19; 17:3; Job 31:28; Jer 2:27; Eze 11:1, 12
8:17 [q]Eze 9:9 [r]Eze 16:26
8:18 [s]Eze 9:10; 24:14 [t]Isa 1:15; Jer 11:11; Mic 3:4; Zec 7:13
9:2 [a]Lev 16:4; Eze 10:2; Rev 15:6
9:3 [b]Eze 10:4 [c]Eze 11:22

wall. 8 He said to me, "Son of man, now dig into the wall." So I dug into the wall
and saw a doorway there.
9 And he said to me, "Go in and see the wicked and detestable things they are doing
here." 10 So I went in and looked, and I saw portrayed all over the walls all kinds of
crawling things and detestable animals and all the idols of the house of Israel.[k] 11 In
front of them stood seventy elders of the house of Israel, and Jaazaniah son of Shaphan
was standing among them. Each had a censer[l] in his hand, and a fragrant cloud of
incense[m] was rising.
12 He said to me, "Son of man, have you seen what the elders of the house of Israel
are doing in the darkness, each at the shrine of his own idol? They say, 'The LORD
does not see[n] us; the LORD has forsaken the land.' " 13 Again, he said, "You will see
them doing things that are even more detestable."
14 Then he brought me to the entrance to the north gate of the house of the LORD,
and I saw women sitting there, mourning for Tammuz. 15 He said to me, "Do you see
this, son of man? You will see things that are even more detestable than this."
16 He then brought me into the inner court of the house of the LORD, and there at
the entrance to the temple, between the portico and the altar,[o] were about twenty-five
men. With their backs towards the temple of the LORD and their faces towards the east,
they were bowing down to the sun in the east.[p]
17 He said to me, "Have you seen this, son of man? Is it a trivial matter for the house
of Judah to do the detestable things they are doing here? Must they also fill the land
with violence[q] and continually provoke me to anger?[r] Look at them putting the
branch to their nose! 18 Therefore I will deal with them in anger; I will not look on
them with pity[s] or spare them. Although they shout in my ears, I will not listen[t]
to them."

Idolaters Killed

9 Then I heard him call out in a loud voice, "Bring the guards of the city here, each
with a weapon in his hand." 2 And I saw six men coming from the direction of
the upper gate, which faces north, each with a deadly weapon in his hand. With them
was a man clothed in linen[a] who had a writing kit at his side. They came in and stood
beside the bronze altar.
3 Now the glory[b] of the God of Israel went up from above the cherubim,[c] where
it had been, and moved to the threshold of the temple. Then the LORD called to the

---

8:14 Tammuz was the Babylonian god of spring. He was the husband or lover of the goddess Ishtar. The followers of this cult believed that the green vegetation shrivelled and died in the hot summer because Tammuz had died and descended into the underworld. Thus, the worshippers wept and mourned his death. In the springtime, when the new vegetation appeared, they rejoiced, believing that Tammuz had come back to life. God was showing Ezekiel that many people were no longer worshipping the *true* God of life and vegetation. We must also be careful not to spend so much time thinking about the benefits of creation that we lose sight of the Creator.

8:17 The branch to the nose could refer either to a cultic worship practice, or to the fact that Judah's sins had become a stench to God.

9:1ff This chapter presents a picture of coming judgment. After Ezekiel had seen how corrupt Jerusalem had become, God called one man to spare the small minority who had been faithful. Then he called six men to slaughter the wicked people in the city. This judgment was ordered by God himself (9:5–7).

9:2 The writing kit was a common object in Ezekiel's day. It included a long narrow board with a groove to hold the reed brush that was used to write on parchment, papyrus, or dried clay. The board had hollowed out areas for holding cakes of black and red ink that had to be moistened before use.

9:3 What is God's glory? It is the manifestation of God's character—his ultimate power, transcendence, and moral perfection. God is completely above man and his limitations. Yet God reveals himself to us so that we can worship and follow him.

9:3 Cherubim ("cherub" is singular) are an order of powerful angelic beings created to glorify God. They are associated with God's absolute holiness and moral perfection. God placed cherubim at the entrance of Eden to keep Adam and Eve out after they sinned (Genesis 3:24). Representations of cherubim were used to decorate the tabernacle and temple. The lid of the ark of the covenant, called the atonement cover, was adorned with two gold cherubim (Exodus 37:6–9). It was a symbol of the very presence of God. The cherubim seen by Ezekiel left the temple along with the glory of God (chapter 10). Ezekiel then recognised them as the living creatures he had seen in his first vision (see chapter 1).

man clothed in linen who had the writing kit at his side 4and said to him, “Go
throughout the city of Jerusalem and put a mark[d] on the foreheads of those who grieve
and lament[e] over all the detestable things that are done in it.[f]”
5As I listened, he said to the others, “Follow him through the city and kill, without
showing pity[g] or compassion. 6Slaughter old men, young men and maidens, women
and children, but do not touch anyone who has the mark. Begin at my sanctuary.”
So they began with the elders[h] who were in front of the temple.[i]
7Then he said to them, “Defile the temple and fill the courts with the slain. Go!”
So they went out and began killing throughout the city. 8While they were killing and
I was left alone, I fell face down,[j] crying out, “Ah, Sovereign LORD! Are you going
to destroy the entire remnant of Israel in this outpouring of your wrath on Jerusalem?[k]”
9He answered me, “The sin of the house of Israel and Judah is exceedingly great;
the land is full of bloodshed and the city is full of injustice.[l] They say, ‘The LORD
has forsaken the land; the LORD does not see.’[m] 10So I will not look on them with
pity[n] or spare them, but I will bring down on their own heads what they have done.[o]”
11Then the man in linen with the writing kit at his side brought back word, saying,
“I have done as you commanded.”

The Glory Departs From the Temple

10 I looked, and I saw the likeness of a throne[a] of sapphire[a][b] above the
expanse[c] that was over the heads of the cherubim. 2The LORD said to the man
clothed in linen,[d] “Go in among the wheels[e] beneath the cherubim. Fill[f] your hands
with burning coals from among the cherubim and scatter them over the city.” And
as I watched, he went in.
3Now the cherubim were standing on the south side of the temple when the man
went in, and a cloud filled the inner court. 4Then the glory of the LORD[g] rose from
above the cherubim and moved to the threshold of the temple. The cloud filled the
temple, and the court was full of the radiance of the glory of the LORD. 5The sound
of the wings of the cherubim could be heard as far away as the outer court, like the
voice[h] of God Almighty[b] when he speaks.
6When the LORD commanded the man in linen, “Take fire from among the wheels,
from among the cherubim,” the man went in and stood beside a wheel. 7Then one
of the cherubim reached out his hand to the fire that was among them. He took up
some of it and put it into the hands of the man in linen, who took it and went out.
8(Under the wings of the cherubim could be seen what looked like the hands of a
man.)[i]
9I looked, and I saw beside the cherubim four wheels, one beside each of the

a *1* Or *lapis lazuli* b *5* Hebrew *El-Shaddai*

9:4 [d]Ex 12:7; 2Co 1:22; Rev 7:3; 9:4 [e]Ps 119:136; Jer 13:17; Eze 21:6 [f]Ps 119:53
9:5 [g]Eze 5:11
9:6 [h]Eze 8:11-13, 16 [i]2Ch 36:17; Jer 25:29; 1Pe 4:17
9:8 [j]Jos 7:6 [k]Eze 11:13; Am 7:1-6
9:9 [l]Eze 22:29 [m]Job 22:13; Eze 8:12
9:10 [n]Eze 7:4; 8:18 [o]Isa 65:6; Eze 11:21
10:1 [a]Rev 4:2 [b]Ex 24:10 [c]Eze 1:22
10:2 [d]Eze 9:2 [e]Eze 1:15 [f]Rev 8:5
10:4 [g]Eze 1:28; 9:3
10:5 [h]Job 40:9; Eze 1:24
10:8 [i]Eze 1:8

9:4, 5 God told the man with the writing kit to put a mark on those who were faithful to God. Their faithfulness was determined by their sensitivity to and sorrow over their nation's sin. Those with the mark were spared when the six men began to destroy the wicked people. During the exodus, the Israelites put a mark of blood on their door-frames to save them from death. In the final days, God will mark the foreheads of those destined for salvation (Revelation 7:3), and Satan will mark his followers (Revelation 13:16, 17), who, like him, are destined for destruction. When God punishes sin, he won't forget his promise to preserve his people.

9:6 The spiritual leaders (“elders”) of Israel blatantly promoted their idolatrous beliefs, and the people abandoned God and followed them. Spiritual leaders are especially accountable to God because they are entrusted with the task of teaching the truth (see James 3:1). When they pervert the truth, they can lead countless people away from God and even cause a nation to fall. It is not surprising, then, that when God began to judge the nation, he started at the temple and worked outward (see 1 Peter 4:17). How sad it is that in the temple, the one place where they should have been teaching God's truth, they were teaching lies.

9:9, 10 The people said that the Lord had forsaken the land and wouldn't see their sin. People have many convenient explanations to make it easier to sin: “It doesn't matter”, “Everybody's doing it”, or “Nobody will ever know”. Do you find yourself making excuses for sin? Rationalising sin makes it easier to commit, but rationalisation does not convince God or cancel the punishment.

10:1ff Chapters 8 – 11 depict God's glory departing from the temple. In 8:3, 4, his glory was over the northern gate. It then moved to the door (the “threshold”, 9:3), the south side of the temple (10:3, 4), the eastern gate (10:18, 19; 11:1), and finally the mountain east of the temple (11:23), probably the Mount of Olives. Because of the nation's sins, God's glory had departed.

10:2 God's perfect holiness demands judgment for sin. The cherubim are mighty angels. The burning coals scattered over the city represent the purging of sin. For Jerusalem, this meant the destruction of all the people who blatantly sinned and refused to repent. Shortly after this prophecy, the Babylonians destroyed Jerusalem by fire (2 Kings 25:9; 2 Chronicles 36:19).

10:9 [j]Eze 1:15-16; Rev 21:20
10:12 [k]Rev 4:6-8 [l]Eze 1:15-21
10:14 [m]1Ki 7:36 [n]Eze 1:6 [o]Eze 1:10; Rev 4:7
10:15 [p]Eze 1:3, 5
10:17 [q]Eze 1:20-21
10:18 [r]Ps 18:10
10:19 [s]Eze 11:1, 22
10:20 [t]Eze 1:1
10:21 [u]Eze 41:18 [v]Eze 1:6
11:1 [a]Eze 8:16; 10:19; 43:4-5
11:3 [b]Jer 1:13; Eze 24:3 [c]ver 7, 11
11:4 [d]Eze 3:4, 17
11:5 [e]Jer 17:10
11:6 [f]Eze 7:23; 22:6
11:7 [g]Eze 24:3-13; Mic 3:2-3
11:8 [h]Pr 10:24
11:9 [i]Ps 106:41 [j]Dt 28:36; Eze 5:8

cherubim; the wheels sparkled like chrysolite.[j] 10 As for their appearance, the four of them looked alike; each was like a wheel intersecting a wheel. 11 As they moved, they would go in any one of the four directions the cherubim faced; the wheels did not turn about[c] as the cherubim went. The cherubim went in whatever direction the head faced, without turning as they went. 12 Their entire bodies, including their backs, their hands and their wings, were completely full of eyes,[k] as were their four wheels.[l] 13 I heard the wheels being called "the whirling wheels". 14 Each of the cherubim[m] had four faces:[n] One face was that of a cherub, the second the face of a man, the third the face of a lion, and the fourth the face of an eagle.[o]

15 Then the cherubim rose upwards. These were the living creatures[p] I had seen by the Kebar River. 16 When the cherubim moved, the wheels beside them moved; and when the cherubim spread their wings to rise from the ground, the wheels did not leave their side. 17 When the cherubim stood still, they also stood still; and when the cherubim rose, they rose with them, because the spirit of the living creatures was in them.[q]

18 Then the glory of the LORD departed from over the threshold of the temple and stopped above the cherubim.[r] 19 While I watched, the cherubim spread their wings and rose from the ground, and as they went, the wheels went with them.[s] They stopped at the entrance to the east gate of the LORD's house, and the glory of the God of Israel was above them.

20 These were the living creatures I had seen beneath the God of Israel by the Kebar River,[t] and I realised that they were cherubim. 21 Each had four faces[u] and four wings,[v] and under their wings was what looked like the hands of a man. 22 Their faces had the same appearance as those I had seen by the Kebar River. Each one went straight ahead.

Judgment on Israel's Leaders

11 Then the Spirit lifted me up and brought me to the gate of the house of the LORD that faces east. There at the entrance to the gate were twenty-five men, and I saw among them Jaazaniah son of Azzur and Pelatiah son of Benaiah, leaders of the people.[a] 2 The LORD said to me, "Son of man, these are the men who are plotting evil and giving wicked advice in this city. 3 They say, 'Will it not soon be time to build houses?[a] This city is a cooking pot,[b] and we are the meat.'[c] 4 Therefore prophesy[d] against them; prophesy, son of man."

5 Then the Spirit of the LORD came upon me, and he told me to say: "This is what the LORD says: That is what you are saying, O house of Israel, but I know what is going through your mind.[e] 6 You have killed many people in this city and filled its streets with the dead.[f]

7 "Therefore this is what the Sovereign LORD says: The bodies you have thrown there are the meat and this city is the pot, but I will drive you out of it.[g] 8 You fear the sword, and the sword is what I will bring against you, declares the Sovereign LORD.[h] 9 I will drive you out of the city and hand you over[i] to foreigners and inflict punishment on you.[j] 10 You will fall by the sword, and I will execute judgment on

c *11* Or *aside* **a** *3* Or *This is not the time to build houses.*

10:18 God's glory departed from the temple and was never completely present again until Christ himself visited it in New Testament times. God's holiness required that he leave the temple because the people had so defiled it. God had to completely destroy what people had perverted in order for true worship to be revived. We must commit ourselves, our families, our churches, and our nation to follow God faithfully so that we never have to experience God's abandoning us.

11:1–4 God had abandoned his altar and temple (chapters 9—11); here his judgment was complete as his glory stopped above the mountain east of the city (11:23). The city gate was where merchants and politicians conducted business, so the 25 men may have represented the nation's rulers. Because of their leadership positions, they were responsible for leading the people astray. They had wrongly said that they were secure from another attack by the Babylonians. "This city is a cooking pot, and we are the meat" means they believed that they were the elite, the influential, the ones who would be protected from all harm. Without God our situation is always precarious.

11:5 God knew everything about the Israelites, even their thoughts. He also knows everything about us, even the sins we try to hide. Instead of worrying about people noticing how we look or what we do, we should care about what God thinks, for he sees everything. Trying to hide our thoughts and actions from God is futile. "Secret" sins are never secret from God. The only effective way to deal with sin is to confess it and ask God to help us overcome it.

you at the borders of Israel.[k] Then you will know that I am the LORD. 11This city
will not be a pot[l] for you, nor will you be the meat in it; I will execute judgment
on you at the borders of Israel. 12And you will know that I am the LORD, for you have
not followed my decrees[m] or kept my laws but have conformed to the standards of
the nations around you.[n]"
13Now as I was prophesying, Pelatiah[o] son of Benaiah died. Then I fell face down
and cried out in a loud voice, "Ah, Sovereign LORD! Will you completely destroy the
remnant of Israel?[p]"
14The word of the LORD came to me: 15"Son of man, your brothers — your brothers
who are your blood-relatives[b] and the whole house of Israel — are those of whom the
people of Jerusalem have said, 'They are[c] far away from the LORD; this land was
given to us as our possession.'[q]

Promised Return of Israel

16"Therefore say: 'This is what the Sovereign LORD says: Although I sent them far
away among the nations and scattered them among the countries, yet for a little while
I have been a sanctuary[r] for them in the countries where they have gone.'
17"Therefore say: 'This is what the Sovereign LORD says: I will gather you from
the nations and bring you back from the countries where you have been scattered, and
I will give you back the land of Israel again.'[s]
18"They will return to it and remove all its vile images[t] and detestable idols.[u] 19I
will give them an undivided heart[v] and put a new spirit in them; I will remove from
them their heart of stone[w] and give them a heart of flesh.[x] 20Then they will follow
my decrees and be careful to keep my laws.[y] They will be my people, and I will be
their God.[z] 21But as for those whose hearts are devoted to their vile images and
detestable idols, I will bring down on their own heads what they have done, declares
the Sovereign LORD.[a]"
22Then the cherubim, with the wheels beside them, spread their wings, and the glory
of the God of Israel was above them.[b] 23The glory[c] of the LORD went up from within
the city and stopped above the mountain[d] east of it. 24The Spirit[e] lifted me up and
brought me to the exiles in Babylonia[d] in the vision[f] given by the Spirit of God.
Then the vision I had seen went up from me, 25and I told the exiles everything the
LORD had shown me.[g]

[b] 15 *Or are in exile with you* (see Septuagint and Syriac) [c] 15 Or *those to whom the people of Jerusalem have said, 'Stay* [d] 24 Or *Chaldea*

11:10 [k] 2Ki 14:25
11:11 [l] ver 3
11:12 [m] Lev 18:4; Eze 18:9 [n] Eze 8:10
11:13 [o] ver 1 [p] Eze 9:8
11:15 [q] Eze 33:24
11:16 [r] Ps 90:1; 91:9; Isa 8:14
11:17 [s] Jer 3:18; 24:5-6; Eze 28:25; 34:13
11:18 [t] Eze 5:11 [u] Eze 37:23
11:19 [v] Jer 32:39 [w] Zec 7:12 [x] Eze 18:31; 36:26; 2Co 3:3
11:20 [y] Ps 105:45 [z] Eze 14:11; 36:26-28
11:21 [a] Eze 9:10; 16:43
11:22 [b] Eze 10:19
11:23 [c] Eze 8:4; 10:4 [d] Zec 14:4
11:24 [e] Eze 8:3 [f] 2Co 12:2-4
11:25 [g] Eze 3:4, 11

11:12 From the time they entered the promised land, the Israelites were warned not to copy the customs and religious practices of other nations. Disobeying this command and following pagan customs instead of God's laws always got them into trouble. Today, believers are still tempted to conform to the ways of the world. But we must get our standards of right and wrong from God, not from the popular trends of society.

11:14ff God promised the exiles in Babylonia that he would continue to be with them even though they were not in Jerusalem. This was a major concern to the Jews because they believed that God was present primarily in the temple. But God assured them that he would continue to be their God regardless of where they were. In the midst of Ezekiel's burning message of judgment stands a cool oasis – God's promise to restore the faithful few to their homeland. God's arms are now open to receive those who will repent of their sins.

11:15–21 God's messages through Ezekiel are full of irony. Here God says that the Jews in captivity are the faithful ones, and those in Jerusalem are the sinful and wicked ones. This was the opposite of the people's perception. Appearances can be deceiving. God will evaluate your life by your faith and obedience, not by your apparent earthly success. Furthermore, we should not judge others by outward appearances.

11:16 God was a sanctuary for the righteous remnant. Idolatrous people, even though they worshipped in the Jerusalem temple (11:15), would find no true sanctuary; but the faithful exiles, even though they were far from home, would be protected by God. Likewise, our external circumstances do not truly indicate our standing with God. Those who appear safe and secure may be far from him, while those going through difficult times may be safely under God's spiritual protection. We can depend on God to keep us safe if we pledge ourselves to his care.

11:18, 19 "Undivided heart" indicates a unanimous singleness of purpose. No longer will God's people seek many gods; they will be content with God. The hard, deaf, immovable heart of stone will be radically transplanted with a tender, receptive, and responsive heart of flesh (see Jeremiah 32:39; Ezekiel 18:31; 36:26). This new life can only be the work of the Holy Spirit. It is God's work, but we must recognise and turn from our sin. When we do, God will give us new motives, new guidelines, and new purpose. Have you received your new heart?

11:23 God's glory left Jerusalem and stood above a mountain on the east side of the city – almost certainly the Mount of Olives. Ezekiel 43:1–4 implies that God will return the same way he left, when he comes back to earth to set up his perfect kingdom.

12:2 [a]Isa 6:10; Eze 2:6-8; Mt 13:15
12:3 [b]Jer 36:3 [c]Jer 26:3 [d]2Ti 2:25-26
12:4 [e]ver 12; Jer 39:4
12:6 [f]ver 12; Isa 8:18; 20:3; Eze 4:3; 24:24
12:7 [g]Eze 24:18; 37:10
12:9 [h]Eze 17:12; 20:49; 24:19
12:11 [i]2Ki 25:7; Jer 15:2; 52:15
12:12 [j]Jer 39:4 [k]Jer 52:7
12:13 [l]Eze 17:20; 19:8; Hos 7:12 [m]Isa 24:17-18 [n]Jer 39:7 [o]Jer 52:11; Eze 17:16
12:14 [p]2Ki 25:5; Eze 5:10, 12
12:16 [q]Jer 22:8-9; Eze 6:8-10; 14:22
12:18 [r]La 5:9; Eze 4:16
12:19 [s]Eze 6:6-14; Mic 7:13; Zec 7:14 [t]Eze 4:16; 23:33
12:20 [u]Isa 7:23-24; Jer 4:7
12:22 [v]Eze 11:3; Am 6:3; 2Pe 3:4
12:23 [w]Ps 37:13; Joel 2:1; Zep 1:14

3. Punishment is certain

The Exile Symbolised

12 The word of the LORD came to me: 2"Son of man, you are living among a
rebellious people. They have eyes to see but do not see and ears to hear but
do not hear, for they are a rebellious people.[a]
3"Therefore, son of man, pack your belongings for exile and in the daytime, as they
watch, set out and go from where you are to another place. Perhaps[b] they will
understand,[c] though they are a rebellious house.[d] 4During the daytime, while they
watch, bring out your belongings packed for exile. Then in the evening, while they
are watching, go out like those who go into exile.[e] 5While they watch, dig through
the wall and take your belongings out through it. 6Put them on your shoulder as they
are watching and carry them out at dusk. Cover your face so that you cannot see the
land, for I have made you a sign[f] to the house of Israel."
7So I did as I was commanded.[g] During the day I brought out my things packed
for exile. Then in the evening I dug through the wall with my hands. I took my
belongings out at dusk, carrying them on my shoulders while they watched.
8In the morning the word of the LORD came to me: 9"Son of man, did not that
rebellious house of Israel ask you, 'What are you doing?'[h]
10"Say to them, 'This is what the Sovereign LORD says: This oracle concerns the
prince in Jerusalem and the whole house of Israel who are there.' 11Say to them, 'I
am a sign to you.'
"As I have done, so it will be done to them. They will go into exile as captives.[i]
12"The prince among them will put his things on his shoulder at dusk[j] and leave,
and a hole will be dug in the wall for him to go through. He will cover his face so
that he cannot see the land.[k] 13I will spread my net[l] for him, and he will be caught
in my snare;[m] I will bring him to Babylonia, the land of the Chaldeans, but he will
not see[n] it, and there he will die.[o] 14I will scatter to the winds all those around
him—his staff and all his troops—and I will pursue them with drawn sword.[p]
15"They will know that I am the LORD, when I disperse them among the nations
and scatter them through the countries. 16But I will spare a few of them from the
sword, famine and plague, so that in the nations where they go they may acknowledge
all their detestable practices. Then they will know that I am the LORD.[q]"
17The word of the LORD came to me: 18"Son of man, tremble as you eat your food,[r]
and shudder in fear as you drink your water. 19Say to the people of the land: 'This
is what the Sovereign LORD says about those living in Jerusalem and in the land of
Israel: They will eat their food in anxiety and drink their water in despair, for their
land will be stripped of everything[s] in it because of the violence of all who live
there.[t] 20The inhabited towns will be laid waste and the land will be desolate. Then
you will know that I am the LORD.[u]' "
21The word of the LORD came to me: 22"Son of man, what is this proverb you have
in the land of Israel: 'The days go by and every vision comes to nothing'?[v] 23Say
to them, 'This is what the Sovereign LORD says: I am going to put an end to this
proverb, and they will no longer quote it in Israel.' Say to them, 'The days are near
when every vision will be fulfilled.[w] 24For there will be no more false visions or

12:1ff Ezekiel played the role of a captive being led away to exile, portraying what was about to happen to King Zedekiah and the people remaining in Jerusalem. The exiles knew exactly what Ezekiel was doing because only six years earlier they had made similar preparations as they left Jerusalem for Babylonia. This was to show the people that they should not trust the king or the capital city to save them from the Babylonian army—only God could do that. And the exiles who hoped for an early return from exile would be disappointed. Ezekiel's graphic demonstration was proven correct to the last detail. But when he warned them, many refused to listen.

12:10–12 Zedekiah, Judah's last king (597–586 B.C.), was reigning in Jerusalem when Ezekiel gave these oracles or messages from God. Ezekiel showed the people what would happen to Zedekiah. Jerusalem would be attacked again, and Zedekiah would join the exiles already in Babylon. Zedekiah would be unable to see because Nebuchadnezzar would have his eyes gouged out (2 Kings 25:3–7; Jeremiah 52:10, 11).

12:21–28 These two short messages were warnings that God's words would come true—*soon!* Less than six years later, Jerusalem would be destroyed. Yet the people were sceptical. Unbelief and false security led them to believe it would never happen. The apostle Peter dealt with this problem in the church (2 Peter 3:9). It is dangerous to say Christ will never return or to regard his coming as so far in the future as to be irrelevant today. All that God says is sure to happen. Don't dare assume that you have plenty of time to get right with God.

flattering divinations[x] among the people of Israel. 25But I the LORD will speak what
I will, and it shall be fulfilled without delay. For in your days, you rebellious house,
I will fulfil whatever I say, declares the Sovereign LORD.[y] "
26The word of the LORD came to me: 27"Son of man, the house of Israel is saying,
'The vision he sees is for many years from now, and he prophesies about the distant
future.'[z]
28"Therefore say to them, 'This is what the Sovereign LORD says: None of my words
will be delayed any longer; whatever I say will be fulfilled, declares the Sovereign
LORD.' "

False Prophets Condemned

13 The word of the LORD came to me: 2"Son of man, prophesy against the prophets
of Israel who are now prophesying. Say to those who prophesy out of their own
imagination: 'Hear the word of the LORD![a] 3This is what the Sovereign LORD says:
Woe to the foolish**a** prophets[b] who follow their own spirit and have seen nothing![c]
4Your prophets, O Israel, are like jackals among ruins. 5You have not gone up to the
breaks in the wall to repair[d] it for the house of Israel so that it will stand firm in the
battle on the day of the LORD.[e] 6Their visions are false and their divinations a lie.
They say, "The LORD declares", when the LORD has not sent them; yet they expect
their words to be fulfilled.[f] 7Have you not seen false visions and uttered lying
divinations when you say, "The LORD declares", though I have not spoken?
8" 'Therefore this is what the Sovereign LORD says: Because of your false words
and lying visions, I am against you, declares the Sovereign LORD. 9My hand will be
against the prophets who see false visions and utter lying divinations. They will not
belong to the council of my people or be listed in the records[g] of the house of Israel,
nor will they enter the land of Israel. Then you will know that I am the Sovereign
LORD.[h]
10" 'Because they lead my people astray,[i] saying, "Peace", when there is no peace,
and because, when a flimsy wall is built, they cover it with whitewash,[j] 11therefore
tell those who cover it with whitewash that it is going to fall. Rain will come in
torrents, and I will send hailstones hurtling down, and violent winds will burst forth.[k]
12When the wall collapses, will people not ask you, "Where is the whitewash you
covered it with?"
13" 'Therefore this is what the Sovereign LORD says: In my wrath I will unleash a
violent wind, and in my anger hailstones[l] and torrents of rain will fall with destructive
fury.[m] 14I will tear down the wall you have covered with whitewash and will level
it to the ground so that its foundation[n] will be laid bare. When it**b** falls,[o] you will
be destroyed in it; and you will know that I am the LORD. 15So I will spend my wrath
against the wall and against those who covered it with whitewash. I will say to you,
"The wall is gone and so are those who whitewashed it, 16those prophets of Israel who
prophesied to Jerusalem and saw visions of peace for her when there was no peace,
declares the Sovereign LORD.[p]" '
17"Now, son of man, set your face against the daughters[q] of your people who
prophesy out of their own imagination. Prophesy against them[r] 18and say, 'This is
what the Sovereign LORD says: Woe to the women who sew magic charms on all their
wrists and make veils of various lengths for their heads in order to ensnare people.
Will you ensnare the lives of my people but preserve your own? 19You have profaned[s]

a 3 Or *wicked* **b** 14 Or *the city*

12:24 [x]Jer 14:14; Eze 13:23; Zec 13:2-4
12:25 [y]Isa 14:24; Hab 1:5
12:27 [z]Da 10:14
13:2 [a]ver 17; Jer 23:16; 37:19
13:3 [b]La 2:14 [c]Jer 23:25-32
13:5 [d]Isa 58:12; Eze 22:30 [e]Eze 7:19
13:6 [f]Jer 28:15; Eze 22:28
13:9 [g]Jer 17:13 [h]Eze 20:38
13:10 [i]Jer 50:6 [j]Eze 7:25; 22:28
13:11 [k]Eze 38:22
13:13 [l]Rev 11:19; 16:21 [m]Ex 9:25; Isa 30:30
13:14 [n]Mic 1:6 [o]Jer 6:15
13:16 [p]Isa 57:21; Jer 6:14
13:17 [q]Rev 2:20 [r]ver 2
13:19 [s]Eze 20:39; 22:26

13:1ff This warning was directed against false prophets whose messages were not from God, but were lies intended to win popularity by saying whatever made the people happy. False prophets did not care about the truth as Ezekiel did. They lulled people into a false sense of security, making Ezekiel's job even more difficult. Beware of people who bend the truth in their quest for popularity and power.

13:10–12 These false prophets covered their lies (a "flimsy wall") with "whitewash" – a pleasing front. Such superficiality can't hold up under God's scrutiny.

13:17 In the Bible, the gift of prophecy was given to women as well as men. Miriam (Exodus 15:20), Deborah (Judges 4:4), and Huldah (2 Kings 22:14) were prophetesses. But the women mentioned here are more like the witch of 1 Samuel 28:7, and they are condemned for disheartening the righteous (13:22).

13:18 These magic charms and veils were used in witchcraft practices. They were advertised as good luck charms, but were used to ensnare the people in idolatry.

me among my people for a few handfuls of barley and scraps of bread. By lying to
my people, who listen to lies, you have killed those who should not have died and
have spared those who should not live.[t]
20" 'Therefore this is what the Sovereign LORD says: I am against your magic
charms with which you ensnare people like birds and I will tear them from your arms;
I will set free the people that you ensnare like birds. 21 I will tear off your veils and
save my people from your hands, and they will no longer fall prey to your power.
Then you will know that I am the LORD.[u] 22 Because you disheartened the righteous
with your lies, when I had brought them no grief, and because you encouraged the
wicked not to turn from their evil ways and so save their lives,[v] 23 therefore you will
no longer see false visions or practise divination.[w] I will save my people from your
hands. And then you will know that I am the LORD.[x]' "

Idolaters Condemned

14 Some of the elders of Israel came to me and sat down in front of me.[a] 2 Then
the word of the LORD came to me: 3 "Son of man, these men have set up idols
in their hearts and put wicked stumbling-blocks[b] before their faces. Should I let them
enquire of me at all?[c] 4 Therefore speak to them and tell them, 'This is what the
Sovereign LORD says: When any Israelite sets up idols in his heart and puts a wicked
stumbling-block before his face and then goes to a prophet, I the LORD will answer
him myself in keeping with his great idolatry. 5 I will do this to recapture the hearts
of the people of Israel, who have all deserted[d] me for their idols.'[e]
6 "Therefore say to the house of Israel, 'This is what the Sovereign LORD says:
Repent! Turn from your idols and renounce all your detestable practices![f]
7 " 'When any Israelite or any alien[g] living in Israel separates himself from me and
sets up idols in his heart and puts a wicked stumbling-block before his face and then
goes to a prophet to enquire of me, I the LORD will answer him myself. 8 I will set
my face against[h] that man and make him an example and a byword.[i] I will cut him
off from my people. Then you will know that I am the LORD.
9 " 'And if the prophet[j] is enticed[k] to utter a prophecy, I the LORD have enticed
that prophet, and I will stretch out my hand against him and destroy him from among
my people Israel.[l] 10 They will bear their guilt—the prophet will be as guilty as the
one who consults him. 11 Then the people of Israel will no longer stray[m] from me,
nor will they defile themselves any more with all their sins. They will be my people,
and I will be their God, declares the Sovereign LORD.[n]' "

Judgment Inescapable

12 The word of the LORD came to me: 13 "Son of man, if a country sins against me
by being unfaithful and I stretch out my hand against it to cut off its food supply[o]
and send famine upon it and kill its men and their animals,[p] 14 even if these three

13:19 [t]Pr 28:21
13:21 [u]Ps 91:3
13:22 [v]Jer 23:14; Eze 33:14-16
13:23 [w]ver 6; Eze 12:24 [x]Mic 3:6
14:1 [a]Eze 8:1; 20:1
14:3 [b]ver 7; Eze 7:19 [c]Isa 1:15; Eze 20:31
14:5 [d]Zec 11:8 [e]Jer 2:11
14:6 [f]Isa 2:20; 30:22
14:7 [g]Ex 12:48; 20:10
14:8 [h]Eze 15:7 [i]Eze 5:15
14:9 [j]Jer 14:15 [k]Jer 4:10 [l]1Ki 22:23
14:11 [m]Eze 48:11 [n]Eze 11:19-20; 37:23
14:13 [o]Lev 26:26 [p]Eze 5:16; 6:14; 15:8

14:3 God condemned the elders for worshipping idols in their hearts and then daring to come to God's prophet for advice. On the outside, they appeared to worship God, making regular visits to the temple to offer sacrifices. But they were not sincere. It is easy for us to criticise the Israelites for worshipping idols when they so clearly needed God instead. But we have idols in our hearts when we pursue reputation, acceptance, wealth, or sensual pleasure with the intensity and commitment that should be reserved for serving God.

14:3–5 For Hebrew writers, important functions of life were assigned to different physical organs. The heart was considered the core of a person's intellectual and spiritual function. Because all people have someone or something as the object of their heart's devotion, they have the potential for idolatry within them. God wants to recapture the hearts of his people. We must never let anything captivate our allegiance or imagination in such a way that it replaces or weakens our devotion to God.

14:6–11 The people of Judah, though eager to accept the messages of false prophets, considered the presence of a few God-fearing men in the nation an insurance policy against disaster. At a pinch, they could always ask God's prophets for advice. But merely having God's people around doesn't help. We must remember that the relationship our pastor, family, or friends have with God will not protect us from the consequences of our own sins. Each person is responsible for his or her own relationship with God. Is your faith personal and real, or are you resting in what others have done?

14:14 Noah, Daniel, and Job were great men in Israel's history, renowned for their relationships with God and for their wisdom (see Genesis 6:8, 9; Daniel 2:47, 48; Job 1:1). Daniel had been taken into captivity during Babylon's first invasion of Judah in 605 B.C., eight years before Ezekiel was taken captive. At the time of Ezekiel's message, Daniel occupied a high government position in Babylon. But even these great men of God could not have saved the people of Judah because God had already passed judgment on the nation's pervasive evil.

men—Noah,[q] Daniel[a][r] and Job[s]—were in it, they could save only themselves by
their righteousness,[t] declares the Sovereign LORD.
15"Or if I send wild beasts[u] through that country and they leave it childless and
it becomes desolate so that no-one can pass through it because of the beasts,[v] 16as
surely as I live, declares the Sovereign LORD, even if these three men were in it, they
could not save their own sons or daughters. They alone would be saved, but the land
would be desolate.[w]
17"Or if I bring a sword[x] against that country and say, 'Let the sword pass
throughout the land,' and I kill its men and their animals,[y] 18as surely as I live,
declares the Sovereign LORD, even if these three men were in it, they could not save
their own sons or daughters. They alone would be saved.
19"Or if I send a plague into that land and pour out my wrath[z] upon it through
bloodshed, killing its men and their animals,[a] 20as surely as I live, declares the
Sovereign LORD, even if Noah, Daniel and Job were in it, they could save neither son
nor daughter. They would save only themselves by their righteousness.[b]
21"For this is what the Sovereign LORD says: How much worse will it be when I
send against Jerusalem my four dreadful judgments—sword and famine and wild
beasts and plague—to kill its men and their animals![c] 22Yet there will be some
survivors—sons and daughters who will be brought out of it.[d] They will come to you,
and when you see their conduct[e] and their actions, you will be consoled regarding
the disaster I have brought upon Jerusalem—every disaster I have brought upon it.
23You will be consoled when you see their conduct and their actions, for you will know
that I have done nothing in it without cause, declares the Sovereign LORD.[f]"

Jerusalem, A Useless Vine

15 The word of the LORD came to me: 2"Son of man, how is the wood of a vine[a]
better than that of a branch on any of the trees in the forest? 3Is wood ever taken
from it to make anything useful? Do they make pegs from it to hang things on? 4And
after it is thrown on the fire as fuel and the fire burns both ends and chars the middle,
is it then useful for anything?[b] 5If it was not useful for anything when it was whole,
how much less can it be made into something useful when the fire has burned it and
it is charred?
6"Therefore this is what the Sovereign LORD says: As I have given the wood of the
vine among the trees of the forest as fuel for the fire, so will I treat the people living
in Jerusalem. 7I will set my face against[c] them. Although they have come out of the
fire, the fire will yet consume them. And when I set my face against them, you will
know that I am the LORD.[d] 8I will make the land desolate[e] because they have been
unfaithful,[f] declares the Sovereign LORD."

An Allegory of Unfaithful Jerusalem

16 The word of the LORD came to me: 2"Son of man, confront Jerusalem with her
detestable practices[a] 3and say, 'This is what the Sovereign LORD says to
Jerusalem: Your ancestry[b] and birth were in the land of the Canaanites; your father
was an Amorite and your mother a Hittite.[c] 4On the day you were born[d] your cord
was not cut, nor were you washed with water to make you clean, nor were you rubbed

a *14* Or *Danel*; the Hebrew spelling may suggest a person other than the prophet Daniel; also in verse 20.

14:14 [q]Ge 6:8 [r]ver 20; Eze 28:3; Da 1:6; 6:13 [s]Job 1:1 [t]Job 42:9; Jer 15:1; Eze 18:20
14:15 [u]Eze 5:17 [v]Lev 26:22
14:16 [w]Eze 18:20
14:17 [x]Lev 26:25; Eze 5:12; 21:3-4 [y]Eze 25:13; Zep 1:3
14:19 [z]Eze 7:8 [a]Eze 38:22
14:20 [b]ver 14
14:21 [c]Jer 15:3; Eze 5:17; 33:27; Am 4:6-10; Rev 6:8
14:22 [d]Eze 12:16 [e]Eze 20:43
14:23 [f]Jer 22:8-9
15:2 [a]Isa 5:1-7; Jer 2:21; Hos 10:1
15:4 [b]Eze 19:14; Jn 15:6
15:7 [c]Ps 34:16; Eze 14:8 [d]Isa 24:18; Am 9:1-4
15:8 [e]Eze 14:13 [f]Eze 17:20
16:2 [a]Eze 20:4; 22:2
16:3 [b]Eze 21:30 [c]ver 45
16:4 [d]Hos 2:3

15:1ff The messages given to Ezekiel in chapters 15—17 provided further evidence that God was going to destroy Jerusalem. The first message was about a vine, useless at first and even more useless after being burned. The people of Jerusalem were useless to God because of their idol worship, and so they would be destroyed and their cities burned. Isaiah also compared the nation of Israel to a vineyard (see Isaiah 5:1–8). Have you also become dormant and unfruitful to God? How can you begin fulfilling his plan for you?

16:1ff This message reminded Jerusalem of its former despised status among the Canaanite nations. Using the imagery of a young baby growing to mature womanhood, God reminded Jerusalem that he raised her from a lowly state to great glory as his bride. However, she betrayed God's trust and prostituted herself by seeking alliances with pagan nations and adopting their customs. If we push God aside for anything, even education, family, career, or pleasure, we are abandoning him in the same way.

16:3 *Canaan* was the ancient name of the territory taken over by the children of Israel. The Bible often uses this name to refer to all the corrupt pagan nations of the region. The Amorites and Hittites, two Canaanite peoples, were known for their wickedness. But here God implies that his people are no better than the Canaanites.

with salt or wrapped in cloths. 5 No-one looked on you with pity or had compassion
enough to do any of these things for you. Rather, you were thrown out into the open
field, for on the day you were born you were despised.
6 “ ‘Then I passed by and saw you kicking about in your blood, and as you lay there
in your blood I said to you, “Live!”[a][e] 7 I made you grow[f] like a plant of the field.
You grew up and developed and became the most beautiful of jewels.[b] Your breasts
were formed and your hair grew, you who were naked and bare.[g]
8 “ ‘Later I passed by, and when I looked at you and saw that you were old enough
for love, I spread the corner of my garment[h] over you and covered your nakedness.
I gave you my solemn oath and entered into a covenant with you, declares the
Sovereign LORD, and you became mine.[i]
9 “ ‘I bathed[c] you with water and washed[j] the blood from you and put ointments
on you. 10 I clothed you with an embroidered[k] dress and put leather sandals on you.
I dressed you in fine linen[l] and covered you with costly garments.[m] 11 I adorned you
with jewellery:[n] I put bracelets[o] on your arms and a necklace[p] around your neck,
12 and I put a ring on your nose,[q] ear-rings on your ears and a beautiful crown[r] on
your head. 13 So you were adorned with gold and silver; your clothes were of fine linen
and costly fabric and embroidered cloth. Your food was fine flour, honey and olive
oil.[s] You became very beautiful and rose to be a queen.[t] 14 And your fame[u] spread
among the nations on account of your beauty,[v] because the splendour I had given
you made your beauty perfect, declares the Sovereign LORD.
15 “ ‘But you trusted in your beauty and used your fame to become a prostitute. You
lavished your favours on anyone who passed by[w] and your beauty became his.[d][x]
16 You took some of your garments to make gaudy high places, where you carried on
your prostitution.[y] Such things should not happen, nor should they ever occur. 17 You
also took the fine jewellery I gave you, the jewellery made of my gold and silver, and
you made for yourself male idols and engaged in prostitution with them.[z] 18 And you
took your embroidered clothes to put on them, and you offered my oil and incense
before them. 19 Also the food I provided for you—the fine flour, olive oil and honey
I gave you to eat—you offered as fragrant incense before them. That is what happened, declares the Sovereign LORD.[a]
20 “ ‘And you took your sons and daughters[b] whom you bore to me[c] and sacrificed
them as food to the idols. Was your prostitution not enough?[d] 21 You slaughtered my
children and sacrificed them[e] to the idols.[e] 22 In all your detestable practices and your
prostitution you did not remember the days of your youth,[f] when you were naked
and bare, kicking about in your blood.[g]
23 “ ‘Woe! Woe to you, declares the Sovereign LORD. In addition to all your other
wickedness, 24 you built a mound for yourself and made a lofty shrine[h] in every public
square.[i] 25 At the head of every street you built your lofty shrines and degraded your
beauty, offering your body with increasing promiscuity to anyone who passed by.[j]
26 You engaged in prostitution with the Egyptians, your lustful neighbours, and provoked[k] me to anger with your increasing promiscuity.[l] 27 So I stretched out my
hand[m] against you and reduced your territory; I gave you over to the greed of your
enemies, the daughters of the Philistines,[n] who were shocked by your lewd conduct.
28 You engaged in prostitution with the Assyrians[o] too, because you were insatiable;

[a] 6 A few Hebrew manuscripts, Septuagint and Syriac; most Hebrew manuscripts *“Live!” And as you lay there in your blood I said to you, “Live!”* [b] 7 Or *became mature* [c] 9 Or *I had bathed* [d] 15 Most Hebrew manuscripts; one Hebrew manuscript (see some Septuagint manuscripts) *by. Such a thing should not happen* [e] 21 Or *and made them pass through ˌthe fireˌ*

16:6 [e]Ex 19:4
16:7 [f]Dt 1:10 [g]Ex 1:7
16:8 [h]Ru 3:9 [i]Jer 2:2; Hos 2:7, 19-20
16:9 [j]Ru 3:3
16:10 [k]Ex 26:36 [l]Eze 27:16 [m]ver 18
16:11 [n]Eze 23:40 [o]Isa 3:19; Eze 23:42 [p]Ge 41:42
16:12 [q]Isa 3:21 [r]Isa 28:5; Jer 13:18
16:13 [s]1Sa 10:1 [t]Dt 32:13-14; 1Ki 4:21
16:14 [u]1Ki 10:24 [v]La 2:15
16:15 [w]ver 25 [x]Isa 57:8; Jer 2:20; Eze 23:3; 27:3
16:16 [y]2Ki 23:7
16:17 [z]Eze 7:20
16:19 [a]Hos 2:8
16:20 [b]Jer 7:31 [c]Ex 13:2 [d]Ps 106:37-38; Isa 57:5; Eze 23:37
16:21 [e]2Ki 17:17; Jer 19:5
16:22 [f]Jer 2:2; Hos 11:1 [g]ver 6
16:24 [h]ver 31; Isa 57:7 [i]Ps 78:58; Jer 2:20; 3:2; Eze 20:28
16:25 [j]ver 15; Pr 9:14
16:26 [k]Eze 8:17 [l]Eze 20:8; 23:19-21
16:27 [m]Eze 20:33 [n]2Ch 28:18
16:28 [o]2Ki 16:7

16:15 God cared for and loved Judah, only to have it turn away to other nations and their false gods. The nation had grown to maturity and became famous, but it forgot who had given it its life (16:22). This is a picture of spiritual adultery (called apostasy—turning from the one true God). As you become wise and more mature, don't turn away from the One who truly loves you.

16:20, 21 Child sacrifice had been practised by the Canaanites long before Israel invaded their land. But it was strictly forbidden by God (Leviticus 20:1–3). By Ezekiel's time, however, the people were openly sacrificing their own children (2 Kings 16:3; 21:6). Jeremiah confirmed that this was a common practice (Jeremiah 7:31; 32:35). Because of such vile acts among the people and priesthood, the temple became unfit for God to inhabit. When God left the temple, he was no longer Judah's guide and protector.

16:27 The conduct of the Jews was so lewd that even those who worshipped other gods, including their great enemy the Philistines, would have been ashamed to behave that way. The Jews outdid them in doing evil.

and even after that, you still were not satisfied. 29 Then you increased your promiscuity
to include Babylonia,[f][p] a land of merchants, but even with this you were not
satisfied.
30" 'How weak-willed you are, declares the Sovereign LORD, when you do all these
things, acting like a brazen prostitute![q] 31 When you built your mounds at the head
of every street and made your lofty shrines[r] in every public square, you were unlike
a prostitute, because you scorned payment.
32" 'You adulterous wife! You prefer strangers to your own husband! 33 Every
prostitute receives a fee, but you give gifts[s] to all your lovers, bribing them to come
to you from everywhere for your illicit favours.[t] 34 So in your prostitution you are
the opposite of others; no-one runs after you for your favours. You are the very
opposite, for you give payment and none is given to you.
35" 'Therefore, you prostitute, hear the word of the LORD! 36 This is what the
Sovereign LORD says: Because you poured out your wealth[g] and exposed your
nakedness in your promiscuity with your lovers, and because of all your detestable
idols, and because you gave them your children's blood,[u] 37 therefore I am going to
gather all your lovers, with whom you found pleasure, those you loved as well as those
you hated. I will gather them against you from all around and will strip you in front
of them, and they will see all your nakedness.[v] 38 I will sentence you to the punishment of women who commit adultery and who shed blood;[w] I will bring upon you
the blood vengeance of my wrath and jealous anger.[x] 39 Then I will hand you over
to your lovers, and they will tear down your mounds and destroy your lofty shrines.
They will strip you of your clothes and take your fine jewellery and leave you naked
and bare.[y] 40 They will bring a mob against you, who will stone[z] you and hack you
to pieces with their swords. 41 They will burn down[a] your houses and inflict punishment on you in the sight of many women.[b] I will put a stop[c] to your prostitution,
and you will no longer pay your lovers. 42 Then my wrath against you will subside
and my jealous anger will turn away from you; I will be calm and no longer angry.[d]
43" 'Because you did not remember[e] the days of your youth but enraged me with
all these things, I will surely bring down[f] on your head what you have done, declares
the Sovereign LORD. Did you not add lewdness to all your other detestable practices?[g]
44" 'Everyone who quotes proverbs will quote this proverb about you: "Like
mother, like daughter." 45 You are a true daughter of your mother, who despised her
husband and her children; and you are a true sister of your sisters, who despised their
husbands and their children. Your mother was a Hittite and your father an Amorite.[h]
46 Your older sister was Samaria, who lived to the north of you with her daughters;
and your younger sister, who lived to the south of you with her daughters, was
Sodom.[i] 47 You not only walked in their ways and copied their detestable practices,
but in all your ways you soon became more depraved than they.[j] 48 As surely as I
live, declares the Sovereign LORD, your sister Sodom and her daughters never did what
you and your daughters have done.[k]
49" 'Now this was the sin of your sister Sodom:[l] She and her daughters were
arrogant,[m] overfed and unconcerned; they did not help the poor and needy.[n] 50 They
were haughty and did detestable things before me. Therefore I did away with them
as you have seen.[o] 51 Samaria did not commit half the sins you did. You have done

[f] 29 Or *Chaldea* [g] 36 Or *lust*

16:29 [p] Eze 23:14-17
16:30 [q] Jer 3:3
16:31 [r] ver 24
16:33 [s] Isa 30:6; 57:9 [t] Hos 8:9-10
16:36 [u] Jer 19:5; Eze 23:10
16:37 [v] Jer 13:22
16:38 [w] Eze 23:45 [x] Lev 20:10; Eze 23:25
16:39 [y] Eze 23:26; Hos 2:3
16:40 [z] Jn 8:5, 7
16:41 [a] Dt 13:16 [b] Eze 23:10 [c] Eze 23:27, 48
16:42 [d] Isa 54:9; Eze 5:13; 39:29
16:43 [e] Ps 78:42 [f] Eze 22:31 [g] ver 22; Eze 11:21
16:45 [h] Eze 23:2
16:46 [i] Ge 13:10-13; Eze 23:4
16:47 [j] 2Ki 21:9; Eze 5:7
16:48 [k] Mt 10:15; 11:23-24
16:49 [l] Ge 13:13 [m] Ps 138:6 [n] Eze 18:7, 12, 16; Lk 12:16-20
16:50 [o] Ge 18:20-21; 19:5

16:44–52 The city of Sodom, a symbol of total corruption, was completely destroyed by God for its wickedness (Genesis 19:24, 25). Samaria, the capital of what had been the northern kingdom (Israel), was despised and rejected by the Jews in Judah. To be called a sister of Samaria and Sodom was bad enough, but to be called *more depraved* than that meant that Judah's sins were an unspeakable abomination and that its doom was inevitable. The reason it was considered worse was not necessarily that Judah's sins were worse, but that Judah knew better. In that light, we who live in an age when God's message is made clear to us through the Bible are worse than Judah if we continue in sin! (See also Matthew 11:20–24.)

16:49 It is easy to judge and condemn Sodom, especially for its terrible sexual sins. Ezekiel reminded Judah, however, that Sodom was destroyed because its people were arrogant, overfed, and unconcerned about the needy people within their reach. It is easy to be selective in what we consider gross sin. If we do not commit such horrible sins as adultery, homosexuality, stealing, and murder, we may think we are living good enough lives. But what about sins like arrogance, gluttony, and indifference to the needy? These sins may not be as shocking to you as the others, but they are also forbidden by God.

more detestable things than they, and have made your sisters seem righteous by all these things you have done.[p] 52Bear your disgrace, for you have furnished some justification for your sisters. Because your sins were more vile than theirs, they appear more righteous than you. So then, be ashamed and bear your disgrace, for you have made your sisters appear righteous.

53" 'However, I will restore[q] the fortunes of Sodom and her daughters and of Samaria and her daughters, and your fortunes along with them, 54so that you may bear your disgrace[r] and be ashamed of all you have done in giving them comfort. 55And your sisters, Sodom with her daughters and Samaria with her daughters, will return to what they were before; and you and your daughters will return to what you were before.[s] 56You would not even mention your sister Sodom in the day of your pride, 57before your wickedness was uncovered. Even so, you are now scorned by the daughters of Edom[h][t] and all her neighbours and the daughters of the Philistines—all those around you who despise you. 58You will bear the consequences of your lewdness and your detestable practices, declares the LORD.[u]

59" 'This is what the Sovereign LORD says: I will deal with you as you deserve, because you have despised my oath by breaking the covenant.[v] 60Yet I will remember the covenant I made with you in the days of your youth, and I will establish an everlasting covenant[w] with you. 61Then you will remember your ways and be ashamed[x] when you receive your sisters, both those who are older than you and those who are younger. I will give them to you as daughters, but not on the basis of my covenant with you. 62So I will establish my covenant with you, and you will know that I am the LORD.[y] 63Then, when I make atonement[z] for you for all you have done, you will remember and be ashamed and never again open your mouth[a] because of your humiliation, declares the Sovereign LORD.[b]' "

Two Eagles and a Vine

17 The word of the LORD came to me: 2"Son of man, set forth an allegory and tell the house of Israel a parable.[a] 3Say to them, 'This is what the Sovereign LORD says: A great eagle[b] with powerful wings, long feathers and full plumage of varied colours came to Lebanon.[c] Taking hold of the top of a cedar, 4he broke off its topmost shoot and carried it away to a land of merchants, where he planted it in a city of traders.

5" 'He took some of the seed of your land and put it in fertile soil. He planted it like a willow by abundant water,[d] 6and it sprouted and became a low, spreading vine. Its branches turned towards him, but its roots remained under it. So it became a vine and produced branches and put out leafy boughs.

7" 'But there was another great eagle with powerful wings and full plumage. The vine now sent out its roots towards him from the plot where it was planted and stretched out its branches to him for water.[e] 8It had been planted in good soil by abundant water so that it would produce branches, bear fruit and become a splendid vine.'

9"Say to them, 'This is what the Sovereign LORD says: Will it thrive? Will it not be uprooted and stripped of its fruit so that it withers? All its new growth will wither.

16:51 [p]Jer 3:8-11
16:53 [q]Isa 19:24-25
16:54 [r]Jer 2:26; Eze 14:22
16:55 [s]Mal 3:4
16:57 [t]2Ki 16:6
16:58 [u]Eze 23:49
16:59 [v]Eze 17:19
16:60 [w]Jer 32:40; Eze 37:26
16:61 [x]Eze 20:43
16:62 [y]Jer 24:7; Eze 20:37, 43-44; Hos 2:19-20
16:63 [z]Ps 65:3; 79:9 [a]Ro 3:19 [b]Ps 39:9; Da 9:7-8
17:2 [a]Eze 20:49
17:3 [b]Hos 8:1 [c]Jer 22:23
17:5 [d]Dt 8:7-9; Isa 44:4
17:7 [e]Eze 31:4

h *57* Many Hebrew manuscripts and Syriac; most Hebrew manuscripts, Septuagint and Vulgate *Aram*

16:59–63 Although the people had broken their promises and did not deserve anything but punishment, God would not break his promises. If the people turned back to him, he would again forgive them and renew his covenant. This covenant was put into effect when Jesus paid for the sins of all mankind by his death on the cross (Hebrews 10:8–10). No-one is beyond the reach of God's forgiveness. Although we don't deserve anything but punishment for our sins, God's arms are still outstretched. He will not break his promise to give us salvation and forgiveness if we repent and turn to him.

17:1ff The first eagle in this chapter represents King Nebuchadnezzar of Babylon (see 17:12), who appointed or "planted" Zedekiah as king in Jerusalem. Zedekiah rebelled against this arrangement and tried to ally with Egypt, the second eagle, to battle against Babylon. This took place while Ezekiel, miles away in Babylon, was describing these events. Jeremiah, a prophet in Judah, was also warning Zedekiah not to form this alliance (Jeremiah 2:36, 37). Although many miles apart, the prophets had the same message because both spoke for God. God still directs his chosen spokesmen to speak his truth all around the world.

It will not take a strong arm or many people to pull it up by the roots. 10 Even if it[f]
is transplanted, will it thrive? Will it not wither completely when the east wind strikes
it—wither away in the plot where it grew?' "
11 Then the word of the LORD came to me: 12 "Say to this rebellious house, 'Do you
not know what these things mean?[g]' Say to them: 'The king of Babylon went to
Jerusalem and carried off her king and her nobles,[h] bringing them back with him to
Babylon.[i] 13 Then he took a member of the royal family and made a treaty with him,
putting him under oath.[j] He also carried away the leading men of the land, 14 so that
the kingdom would be brought low,[k] unable to rise again, surviving only by keeping
his treaty. 15 But the king rebelled[l] against him by sending his envoys to Egypt to
get horses and a large army.[m] Will he succeed? Will he who does such things escape?
Will he break the treaty and yet escape?[n]
16 " 'As surely as I live, declares the Sovereign LORD, he shall die[o] in Babylon,
in the land of the king who put him on the throne, whose oath he despised and whose
treaty he broke.[p] 17 Pharaoh[q] with his mighty army and great horde will be of no
help to him in war, when ramps[r] are built and siege works erected to destroy many
lives.[s] 18 He despised the oath by breaking the covenant. Because he had given his
hand in pledge[t] and yet did all these things, he shall not escape.
19 " 'Therefore this is what the Sovereign LORD says: As surely as I live, I will bring
down on his head my oath that he despised and my covenant that he broke.[u] 20 I will
spread my net[v] for him, and he will be caught in my snare. I will bring him to Babylon
and execute judgment[w] upon him there because he was unfaithful to me. 21 All his
fleeing troops will fall by the sword,[x] and the survivors[y] will be scattered to the
winds.[z] Then you will know that I the LORD have spoken.
22 " 'This is what the Sovereign LORD says: I myself will take a shoot from the very
top of a cedar and plant it; I will break off a tender sprig from its topmost shoots and
plant it on a high and lofty mountain.[a] 23 On the mountain heights of Israel I will plant
it; it will produce branches and bear fruit and become a splendid cedar. Birds of every
kind will nest in it; they will find shelter in the shade of its branches.[b] 24 All the trees
of the field[c] will know that I the LORD bring down the tall tree and make the low
tree grow tall. I dry up the green tree and make the dry tree flourish.
" 'I the LORD have spoken, and I will do it.[d]' "

The Soul Who Sins Will Die

18 The word of the LORD came to me: 2 "What do you people mean by quoting
this proverb about the land of Israel:

> " 'The fathers eat sour grapes,
> and the children's teeth are set on edge'?[a]

3 "As surely as I live, declares the Sovereign LORD, you will no longer quote this
proverb in Israel. 4 For every living soul belongs to me, the father as well as the
son—both alike belong to me. The soul who sins is the one who will die.[b]

> 5 "Suppose there is a righteous man

17:10 [f]Hos 13:15
17:12 [g]Eze 12:9 [h]2Ki 24:15 [i]Eze 24:19
17:13 [j]2Ch 36:13
17:14 [k]Eze 29:14
17:15 [l]Jer 52:3 [m]Dt 17:16 [n]Jer 34:3; 38:18
17:16 [o]Jer 52:11; Eze 12:13 [p]2Ki 24:17
17:17 [q]Jer 37:7 [r]Eze 4:2 [s]Isa 36:6; Jer 37:5; Eze 29:6-7
17:18 [t]1Ch 29:24
17:19 [u]Eze 16:59
17:20 [v]Eze 12:13; 32:3 [w]Jer 2:35; Eze 20:36
17:21 [x]Eze 12:14 [y]2Ki 25:11 [z]2Ki 25:5
17:22 [a]Jer 23:5; Eze 20:40; 36:1, 36; 37:22
17:23 [b]Ps 92:12; Isa 2:2; Eze 31:6; Da 4:12; Hos 14:5-7; Mt 13:32
17:24 [c]Ps 96:12 [d]Eze 19:12; 21:26; 22:14; Am 9:11
18:2 [a]Isa 3:15; Jer 31:29; La 5:7
18:4 [b]ver 20; Isa 42:5; Ro 6:23

17:10 This east wind was the hot, dry wind blowing off the desert, a wind that could wither a flourishing crop. The hot wind of Nebuchadnezzar's armies was about to overcome the nation of Judah.

17:22, 23 Ezekiel's prophecy of judgment ends in hope. When the people put their hope in foreign alliances, they were disappointed. Only God could give them true hope. God said he would plant a tender sprig, the Messiah, whose kingdom would grow and become a shelter for all who come to him (see Isaiah 11:1–5). This prophecy was fulfilled at the coming of Jesus Christ.

18:1ff The people of Judah believed they were being punished for the sins of their ancestors, not their own. They thought this way because this was the teaching of the Ten Commandments (Exodus 20:5). Ezekiel taught that the destruction of Jerusalem was due to the spiritual decay in previous generations. But this belief in the corporate life of Israel led to fatalism and irresponsibility. So Ezekiel gave God's new policy for this new land because the people had misconstrued the old one. God judges each person individually. Although we often suffer from the effects of sins committed by those who came before us, God does not punish us for someone else's sins, and we can't use their mistakes as an excuse for our sins. Each person is accountable to God for his or her actions.

In addition, some people of Judah used the corporate umbrella of God's blessing as an excuse for disobeying God. They thought that because of their righteous ancestors (18:5–9) they would live. God told them that they would not; they were the evil sons of righteous parents and, as such, would die (18:10–13). If, however, anyone returned to God, he or she would live (18:14–18).

who does what is just and right.
6He does not eat at the mountain[c] shrines
or look to the idols[d] of the house of Israel.
He does not defile his neighbour's wife
or lie with a woman during her period.
7He does not oppress[e] anyone,
but returns what he took in pledge[f] for a loan.
He does not commit robbery,
but gives his food to the hungry
and provides clothing for the naked.[g]
8He does not lend at usury
or take excessive interest.[a][h]
He withholds his hand from doing wrong
and judges fairly[i] between man and man.
9He follows my decrees
and faithfully keeps my laws.
That man is righteous;[j]
he will surely live,[k]
declares the Sovereign LORD.

10"Suppose he has a violent son, who sheds blood[l] or does any of these other
things[b] 11(though the father has done none of them):

"He eats at the mountain shrines.
He defiles his neighbour's wife.
12He oppresses the poor[m] and needy.
He commits robbery.
He does not return what he took in pledge.
He looks to the idols.
He does detestable things.[n]
13He lends at usury and takes excessive interest.[o]

Will such a man live? He will not! Because he has done all these detestable things, he will surely be put to death and his blood will be on his own head.[p]

14"But suppose this son has a son who sees all the sins his father commits, and
though he sees them, he does not do such things:[q]

15"He does not eat at the mountain shrines
or look to the idols of the house of Israel.
He does not defile his neighbour's wife.
16He does not oppress anyone
or require a pledge for a loan.
He does not commit robbery,
but gives his food to the hungry
and provides clothing for the naked.[r]
17He withholds his hand from sin[c]
and takes no usury or excessive interest.
He keeps my laws and follows my decrees.

He will not die for his father's sin; he will surely live. 18But his father will die for
his own sin, because he practised extortion, robbed his brother and did what was wrong among his people.

19"Yet you ask, 'Why does the son not share the guilt of his father?' Since the son

18:6 [c]Eze 22:9 [d]Dt 4:19; Eze 6:13; 20:24
18:7 [e]Ex 22:21 [f]Ex 22:26; Dt 24:12 [g]Dt 15:11; Mt 25:36
18:8 [h]Ex 22:25; Lev 25:35-37; Dt 23:19-20 [i]Zec 8:16
18:9 [j]Hab 2:4 [k]Lev 18:5; Eze 20:11; Am 5:4
18:10 [l]Ex 21:12
18:12 [m]Am 4:1 [n]2Ki 21:11; Isa 59:6-7; Jer 22:17; Eze 8:6, 17
18:13 [o]Ex 22:25 [p]Eze 33:4-5
18:14 [q]2Ch 34:21; Pr 23:24
18:16 [r]Ps 41:1; Isa 58:10

a *8* Or *take interest*; similarly in verses 13 and 17 b *10* Or *things to a brother* c *17* Septuagint (see also verse 8); Hebrew *from the poor*

18:8 The law of Moses had rules about charging interest (Exodus 22:25; Leviticus 25:36; Deuteronomy 23:19, 20) to prevent God's people from taking advantage of the poor or of fellow Israelites.

18:12 Returning what one took in pledge referred to the lender letting the debtor use the cloak each night that he has placed as security on his loan. Without the cloak, the debtor would be cold at night. (See Exodus 22:26 and Deuteronomy 24:10–13 for the giving of this law.)

has done what is just and right and has been careful to keep all my decrees, he will
surely live.[s] 20The soul who sins is the one who will die. The son will not share the
guilt of the father, nor will the father share the guilt of the son. The righteousness of
the righteous man will be credited to him, and the wickedness of the wicked will be
charged against him.[t]
21"But if a wicked man turns away from all the sins he has committed and keeps
all my decrees and does what is just and right, he will surely live; he will not die.[u]
22None of the offences he has committed will be remembered against him. Because
of the righteous things he has done, he will live.[v] 23Do I take any pleasure in the
death of the wicked? declares the Sovereign LORD. Rather, am I not pleased[w] when
they turn from their ways and live?[x]
24"But if a righteous man turns from his righteousness and commits sin and does
the same detestable things the wicked man does, will he live? None of the righteous
things he has done will be remembered. Because of the unfaithfulness he is guilty of
and because of the sins he has committed, he will die.[y]
25"Yet you say, 'The way of the Lord is not just.' Hear, O house of Israel: Is my
way unjust?[z] Is it not your ways that are unjust? 26If a righteous man turns from his
righteousness and commits sin, he will die for it; because of the sin he has committed
he will die. 27But if a wicked man turns away from the wickedness he has committed
and does what is just and right, he will save his life.[a] 28Because he considers all the
offences he has committed and turns away from them, he will surely live; he will not
die. 29Yet the house of Israel says, 'The way of the Lord is not just.' Are my ways
unjust, O house of Israel? Is it not your ways that are unjust?
30"Therefore, O house of Israel, I will judge you, each one according to his ways,
declares the Sovereign LORD. Repent![b] Turn away from all your offences; then sin
will not be your downfall.[c] 31Rid yourselves of all the offences you have committed,
and get a new heart[d] and a new spirit. Why will you die, O house of Israel?[e] 32For
I take no pleasure in the death of anyone, declares the Sovereign LORD. Repent and
live![f]

A Lament for Israel's Princes

19 "Take up a lament[a] concerning the princes[b] of Israel 2and say:

" 'What a lioness was your mother
among the lions!
She lay down among the young lions
and reared her cubs.
3She brought up one of her cubs,
and he became a strong lion.
He learned to tear the prey
and he devoured men.
4The nations heard about him,
and he was trapped in their pit.

18:19 [s]Ex 20:5; Dt 5:9; Jer 15:4; Zec 1:3-6
18:20 [t]Dt 24:16; 1Ki 8:32; 2Ki 14:6; Isa 3:11; Mt 16:27; Ro 2:9
18:21 [u]Eze 33:12, 19
18:22 [v]Ps 18:20-24; Isa 43:25; Mic 7:19
18:23 [w]Ps 147:11 [x]Eze 33:11; 1Ti 2:4
18:24 [y]1Sa 15:11; 2Ch 24:17-20; Eze 3:20; 20:27; 2Pe 2:20-22
18:25 [z]Ge 18:25; Jer 12:1; Eze 33:17; Zep 3:5; Mal 2:17; 3:13-15
18:27 [a]Isa 1:18
18:30 [b]Mt 3:2 [c]Eze 7:3; 33:20; Hos 12:6
18:31 [d]Ps 51:10 [e]Isa 1:16-17; Eze 11:19; 36:26
18:32 [f]Eze 33:11
19:1 [a]Eze 26:17; 27:2, 32 [b]2Ki 24:6

18:23 God is a God of love, but he is also a God of perfect justice. His perfect love causes him to be merciful to those who recognise their sin and turn back to him, but he cannot wink at those who wilfully sin. Wicked people die both physically and spiritually. God takes no joy in their deaths; he would prefer that they turn to him and have eternal life. Likewise, we should not rejoice in the misfortunes of non-believers. Instead, we should do all in our power to bring them to faith.

18:25 A typical childish response to punishment is to say, "That isn't fair"! In reality, God is fair, but *we* have broken the rules. It is not God who must live up to our ideas of fairness; instead, we must live up to his. Don't spend your time looking for the loopholes in God's law. Instead, live up to God's standards.

18:30–32 Ezekiel's solution to the problem of inherited guilt is for each person to have a changed life. This is God's work in us and not something we can do for ourselves. The Holy Spirit does it (Psalm 51:10–12). If we renounce our life's direction of sin and rebellion and turn to God, he will give us a new direction, a new love, and a new power to change. You can begin by faith, trusting in God's power to change your heart and mind. Then determine to live each day with him in control (Ephesians 4:22–24).

19:1ff Ezekiel used illustrations to communicate many of his messages. With the picture of the lioness and her cubs, he raised the curiosity of his listeners. The lioness symbolised the nation of Judah, and the two cubs were two of its kings. The first cub was King Jehoahaz, who was taken captive to Egypt in 609 B.C. by Pharaoh Neco (2 Kings 23:31–33). The second cub was either King Jehoiachin, who had already been taken into captivity in Babylon (2 Kings 24:8ff), or King Zedekiah, who soon would be (2 Kings 25:7). This illustration showed that for Judah, there was no hope for a quick return from exile, and no escape from the approaching Babylonian armies.

19:4 [c]2Ki 23:33-34; 2Ch 36:4
19:5 [d]2Ki 23:34
19:6 [e]2Ki 24:9; 2Ch 36:9
19:7 [f]Eze 30:12
19:8 [g]2Ki 24:2 [h]2Ki 24:11
19:9 [i]2Ch 36:6 [j]2Ki 24:15
19:10 [k]Ps 80:8-11
19:11 [l]Eze 31:3; Da 4:11
19:12 [m]Eze 17:10 [n]Isa 27:11; Eze 28:17; Hos 13:15
19:13 [o]Eze 20:35 [p]Hos 2:3
19:14 [q]Eze 20:47 [r]Eze 15:4

They led him with hooks
to the land of Egypt.[c]

5" 'When she saw her hope unfulfilled,
her expectation gone,
she took another of her cubs
and made him a strong lion.[d]
6He prowled among the lions,
for he was now a strong lion.
He learned to tear the prey
and he devoured men.[e]
7He broke down[a] their strongholds
and devastated[f] their towns.
The land and all who were in it
were terrified by his roaring.
8Then the nations[g] came against him,
those from regions round about.
They spread their net for him,
and he was trapped in their pit.[h]
9With hooks they pulled him into a cage
and brought him to the king of Babylon.[i]
They put him in prison,
so his roar was heard no longer
on the mountains of Israel.[j]

10" 'Your mother was like a vine in your vineyard[b]
planted by the water;
it was fruitful and full of branches
because of abundant water.[k]
11Its branches were strong,
fit for a ruler's sceptre.
It towered high
above the thick foliage,
conspicuous for its height
and for its many branches.[l]
12But it was uprooted[m] in fury
and thrown to the ground.
The east wind made it shrivel,
it was stripped of its fruit;
its strong branches withered
and fire consumed them.[n]
13Now it is planted in the desert,[o]
in a dry and thirsty land.[p]
14Fire spread from one of its main[c] branches
and consumed[q] its fruit.
No strong branch is left on it
fit for a ruler's sceptre.'[r]

This is a lament and is to be used as a lament."

a *7* Targum (see Septuagint); Hebrew *He knew* **b** *10* Two Hebrew manuscripts; most Hebrew manuscripts *your blood* **c** *14* Or *from under its*

19:11, 12 Not even the political and military might of Judah's kings could save the nation. Like branches of a vine, they would be cut off and uprooted by "the east wind" – the powerful Babylonian army.

Rebellious Israel

20 In the seventh year, in the fifth month on the tenth day, some of the elders of
Israel came to enquire of the LORD, and they sat down in front of me.[a]
2 Then the word of the LORD came to me: 3 "Son of man, speak to the elders of Israel
and say to them, 'This is what the Sovereign LORD says: Have you come to enquire[b]
of me? As surely as I live, I will not let you enquire of me, declares the Sovereign
LORD.[c]'
4 "Will you judge them? Will you judge them, son of man? Then confront them with
the detestable practices of their fathers[d] 5 and say to them: 'This is what the Sovereign
LORD says: On the day I chose[e] Israel, I swore with uplifted hand to the descendants
of the house of Jacob and revealed myself to them in Egypt. With uplifted hand I said
to them, "I am the LORD your God.[f]" 6 On that day I swore to them that I would bring
them out of Egypt into a land I had searched out for them, a land flowing with milk
and honey,[g] the most beautiful of all lands.[h] 7 And I said to them, "Each of you,
get rid of the vile images[i] you have set your eyes on, and do not defile yourselves
with the idols of Egypt. I am the LORD your God.[j]"
8 " 'But they rebelled against me and would not listen to me; they did not get rid
of the vile images they had set their eyes on, nor did they forsake the idols of Egypt.[k]
So I said I would pour out my wrath on them and spend my anger against them in
Egypt.[l] 9 But for the sake of my name I did what would keep it from being profaned
in the eyes of the nations they lived among and in whose sight I had revealed myself
to the Israelites by bringing them out of Egypt.[m] 10 Therefore I led them out of Egypt
and brought them into the desert.[n] 11 I gave them my decrees and made known to them
my laws, for the man who obeys them will live by them.[o] 12 Also I gave them my
Sabbaths as a sign[p] between us, so they would know that I the LORD made them holy.
13 " 'Yet the people of Israel rebelled[q] against me in the desert. They did not follow
my decrees but rejected my laws—although the man who obeys them will live by
them—and they utterly desecrated my Sabbaths. So I said I would pour out my wrath[r]
on them and destroy them in the desert.[s] 14 But for the sake of my name I did what
would keep it from being profaned in the eyes of the nations in whose sight I had
brought them out.[t] 15 Also with uplifted hand I swore to them in the desert that I would
not bring them into the land I had given them—a land flowing with milk and honey,
most beautiful of all lands[u]— 16 because they rejected my laws and did not follow my
decrees and desecrated my Sabbaths. For their hearts[v] were devoted to their idols.[w]
17 Yet I looked on them with pity and did not destroy them or put an end to them in
the desert. 18 I said to their children in the desert, "Do not follow the statutes of your
fathers[x] or keep their laws or defile yourselves with their idols. 19 I am the LORD your
God;[y] follow my decrees and be careful to keep my laws.[z] 20 Keep my Sabbaths holy,
that they may be a sign between us. Then you will know that I am the LORD your
God.[a]"
21 " 'But the children rebelled against me: They did not follow my decrees, they were
not careful to keep my laws—although the man who obeys them will live by
them—and they desecrated my Sabbaths. So I said I would pour out my wrath on them
and spend my anger against them in the desert. 22 But I withheld[b] my hand, and for
the sake of my name I did what would keep it from being profaned in the eyes of the
nations in whose sight I had brought them out. 23 Also with uplifted hand I swore to

20:1 [a]Eze 8:1
20:3 [b]Eze 14:3 [c]Mic 3:7
20:4 [d]Eze 16:2; 22:2; Mt 23:32
20:5 [e]Dt 7:6 [f]Ex 6:7
20:6 [g]Ex 3:8; Jer 32:22 [h]Dt 8:7; Ps 48:2; Da 8:9
20:7 [i]Ex 20:4 [j]Ex 20:2; Lev 18:3; Dt 29:18
20:8 [k]Eze 7:8 [l]Isa 63:10
20:9 [m]Eze 36:22; 39:7
20:10 [n]Ex 13:18
20:11 [o]Lev 18:5; Dt 4:7-8; Ro 10:5
20:12 [p]Ex 31:13
20:13 [q]Ps 78:40 [r]Dt 9:8 [s]Nu 14:29; Ps 95:8-10; Isa 56:6
20:14 [t]Eze 36:23
20:15 [u]Ps 95:11; 106:26
20:16 [v]Nu 15:39 [w]Am 5:26
20:18 [x]Zec 1:4
20:19 [y]Ex 20:2 [z]Dt 5:32-33; 6:1-2; 8:1; 11:1; 12:1
20:20 [a]Jer 17:22
20:22 [b]Ps 78:38

20:1ff Here Ezekiel gives a panoramic view of Israel's history of rebellion. The emphasis is on God's attempts to bring the nation back to himself and on God's mercy for his constantly rebellious and disobedient people. Ezekiel gives the message that the people alone are responsible for the troubles and judgments they have experienced. Those who persist in rebellion God will "purge" (20:38), while he will bring the faithful "into the land of Israel, the land I had sworn with uplifted hand to give to your fathers". The reason: that "you will know that I am the LORD" (20:42).

20:12, 13 The Sabbath, instituted by God at creation, was entrusted to Israel as a sign that God had created and redeemed them (Exodus 20:8–11; Deuteronomy 5:12–15). This day of rest was a gift from a loving God, not a difficult obligation. But the people repeatedly desecrated the Sabbath and ignored their God (see also 20:20, 21). It was meant to be a memory device but they ignored it. Today, many Christians celebrate the Lord's Day, Sunday, as their Sabbath. Whatever the day, we must be careful to fulfil God's purpose for the Sabbath. He wants us to rest, to refocus, and to remember him.

20:23, 24 At the very beginning of Israel's history, God clearly warned the people about the consequences of disobedience (Deuteronomy 28:15ff). When the people disobeyed, God let them

them in the desert that I would disperse them among the nations and scatter[c] them
through the countries, 24 because they had not obeyed my laws but had rejected my
decrees and desecrated my Sabbaths,[d] and their eyes ⌞lusted⌟ after[e] their fathers'
idols.[f] 25 I also gave them over[g] to statutes that were not good and laws they could
not live by;[h] 26 I let them become defiled through their gifts—the sacrifice of every
firstborn[a]—that I might fill them with horror so that they would know that I am the
LORD.[i]

27 "Therefore, son of man, speak to the people of Israel and say to them, 'This is
what the Sovereign LORD says: In this also your fathers blasphemed[j] me by forsaking
me:[k] 28 When I brought them into the land[l] I had sworn to give them and they saw
any high hill or any leafy tree, there they offered their sacrifices, made offerings that
provoked me to anger, presented their fragrant incense and poured out their drink
offerings.[m] 29 Then I said to them: What is this high place you go to?' " (It is called
Bamah[b] to this day.)

Judgment and Restoration

30 "Therefore say to the house of Israel: 'This is what the Sovereign LORD says: Will
you defile yourselves[n] the way your fathers did and lust after their vile images?[o]
31 When you offer your gifts—the sacrifice of your sons[p] in[c] the fire—you continue
to defile yourselves with all your idols to this day. Am I to let you enquire of me,
O house of Israel? As surely as I live, declares the Sovereign LORD, I will not let you
enquire of me.[q]

32 " 'You say, "We want to be like the nations, like the peoples of the world, who
serve wood and stone." But what you have in mind will never happen. 33 As surely
as I live, declares the Sovereign LORD, I will rule over you with a mighty hand and
an outstretched arm and with outpoured wrath.[r] 34 I will bring you from the nations[s]
and gather you from the countries where you have been scattered—with a mighty hand
and an outstretched arm and with outpoured wrath.[t] 35 I will bring you into the desert
of the nations and there, face to face, I will execute judgment[u] upon you. 36 As I
judged your fathers in the desert of the land of Egypt, so I will judge you, declares
the Sovereign LORD.[v] 37 I will take note of you as you pass under my rod,[w] and I
will bring you into the bond of the covenant.[x] 38 I will purge[y] you of those who revolt
and rebel against me. Although I will bring them out of the land where they are living,
yet they will not enter the land of Israel. Then you will know that I am the LORD.[z]

39 " 'As for you, O house of Israel, this is what the Sovereign LORD says: Go and
serve your idols,[a] every one of you! But afterwards you will surely listen to me and
no longer profane my holy name with your gifts and idols.[b] 40 For on my holy
mountain, the high mountain of Israel, declares the Sovereign LORD, there in the land
the entire house of Israel will serve me, and there I will accept them. There I will

a *26* Or—*making every firstborn pass through ⌞the fire⌟* **b** *29* *Bamah* means *high place.* **c** *31* Or—*making your sons pass through*

20:23 [c]Lev 26:33; Dt 28:64
20:24 [d]ver 13 [e]Eze 6:9 [f]ver 16
20:25 [g]Ps 81:12 [h]2Th 2:11
20:26 [i]2Ki 17:17
20:27 [j]Ro 2:24 [k]Eze 18:24
20:28 [l]Ps 78:55, 58 [m]Eze 6:13
20:30 [n]ver 43 [o]Jer 16:12
20:31 [p]Eze 16:20 [q]Ps 106:37-39; Jer 7:31
20:33 [r]Jer 21:5
20:34 [s]2Co 6:17* [t]Isa 27:12-13; Jer 44:6; La 2:4
20:35 [u]Jer 2:35
20:36 [v]Nu 11:1-35; 1Co 10:5-10
20:37 [w]Lev 27:32; Jer 33:13 [x]Eze 16:62
20:38 [y]Eze 34:17-22; Am 9:9-10 [z]Ps 95:11; Jer 44:14; Eze 13:9; Mal 3:3; Heb 4:3
20:39 [a]Jer 44:25 [b]Isa 1:13; Eze 43:7; Am 4:4

---

experience those devastating consequences to remind them of the seriousness of their sins. If you choose to live for yourself, apart from God, you may experience similar destructive consequences. However, even through such consequences, God may be drawing you to himself. Let your misfortunes bring you to your senses and to the merciful God before it is too late.

20:25 Why would God give them laws that weren't good? This isn't talking about any aspect of the Mosaic Law—Ezekiel reinforces that law (20:11, 13, 21). Evidently the Jews had taken Exodus 13:12 and 22:29, the dedication of firstborn animals and children, as a justification for child sacrifice to the Canaanite god Molech. God was giving them over to this delusion to get them to acknowledge him, to jar their consciences, and to revitalise their faith (20:26).

20:35, 36 When the Israelites disobeyed God by refusing to enter the promised land the first time, God chose to purify his people by forcing them to wander in the desert until that entire generation died (Numbers 14:26–35). Here he promised to purge the nation of its rebellious people again as they crossed the vast desert from their captivity in Babylon. Only those who faithfully followed God would be able to return to their land. The purpose of this desert judgment would be to purge all those who worship idols and to restore all those faithful to God.

20:39 The Israelites were worshipping idols and giving gifts to God at the same time! They did not believe in their God as the one true God; instead, they worshipped him along with the other gods of the land. Perhaps they enjoyed the immoral pleasures of idol worship; or perhaps they didn't want to miss out on the benefits the idols might give them. Often people believe in God and give him gifts of church attendance or service, while still holding on to their idols of money, power, or pleasure. They don't want to miss out on any possible benefits. But God wants all of our lives and all of our devotion; he will not share it because devotion to anything else is idol worship. Beware of trying to keep God pleased while you also pursue the pleasures of sin. You must choose one or the other.

require your offerings[c] and your choice gifts,[d] along with all your holy sacrifices.[d]
41 I will accept you as fragrant incense when I bring you out from the nations and gather
you from the countries where you have been scattered, and I will show myself holy[e]
among you in the sight of the nations.[f] 42 Then you will know that I am the LORD,[g]
when I bring you into the land of Israel,[h] the land I had sworn with uplifted hand
to give to your fathers. 43 There you will remember your conduct and all the actions
by which you have defiled yourselves, and you will loathe yourselves for all the evil
you have done.[i] 44 You will know that I am the LORD, when I deal with you for my
name's sake[j] and not according to your evil ways and your corrupt practices, O house
of Israel, declares the Sovereign LORD.[k]' "

Prophecy Against the South

45 The word of the LORD came to me: 46 "Son of man, set your face towards the south;
preach against the south and prophesy against[l] the forest of the southland.[m] 47 Say
to the southern forest: 'Hear the word of the LORD. This is what the Sovereign LORD
says: I am about to set fire to you, and it will consume all your trees, both green and
dry. The blazing flame will not be quenched, and every face from south to north will
be scorched by it.[n] 48 Everyone will see that I the LORD have kindled it; it will not
be quenched.[o]' "

49 Then I said, "Ah, Sovereign LORD! They are saying of me, 'Isn't he just telling
parables?[p]' "

Babylon, God's Sword of Judgment

21 The word of the LORD came to me: 2 "Son of man, set your face against
Jerusalem and preach against the sanctuary. Prophesy against[a] the land of
Israel 3 and say to her: 'This is what the LORD says: I am against you.[b] I will draw
my sword from its scabbard and cut off from you both the righteous and the wicked.[c]
4 Because I am going to cut off the righteous and the wicked, my sword will be
unsheathed against everyone from south to north.[d] 5 Then all people will know that
I the LORD have drawn my sword from its scabbard; it will not return[e] again.'[f]

6 "Therefore groan, son of man! Groan before them with broken heart and bitter
grief.[g] 7 And when they ask you, 'Why are you groaning?' you shall say, 'Because
of the news that is coming. Every heart will melt and every hand go limp;[h] every
spirit will become faint and every knee become as weak as water.' It is coming! It
will surely take place, declares the Sovereign LORD."

8 The word of the LORD came to me: 9 "Son of man, prophesy and say, 'This is what
the Lord says:

" 'A sword, a sword,
sharpened and polished—
10 sharpened for the slaughter,[i]
polished to flash like lightning!

" 'Shall we rejoice in the sceptre of my son ⌊Judah⌋? The sword despises every such
stick.

11 " 'The sword is appointed to be polished,[j]

[d] 40 Or *and the gifts of your firstfruits*

20:40 [c] Isa 60:7 [d] Isa 56:7; Mal 3:4
20:41 [e] Eze 28:25; 36:23 [f] Eze 11:17
20:42 [g] Eze 38:23 [h] Eze 34:13; 36:24
20:43 [i] Eze 6:9; 16:61; Hos 5:15
20:44 [j] Eze 36:22 [k] Eze 24:24
20:46 [l] Eze 21:2; Am 7:16 [m] Isa 30:6; Jer 13:19
20:47 [n] Isa 9:18-19; 13:8; Jer 21:14
20:48 [o] Jer 7:20
20:49 [p] Mt 13:13; Jn 16:25
21:2 [a] Eze 20:46
21:3 [b] Jer 21:13 [c] ver 9-11; Job 9:22
21:4 [d] Eze 20:47
21:5 [e] ver 30 [f] Na 1:9
21:6 [g] Isa 22:4
21:7 [h] Eze 22:14; 7:17
21:10 [i] Ps 110:5-6; Isa 34:5-6
21:11 [j] Jer 46:4

20:45–47 "Towards the south" refers to Jerusalem and Judah. "The southland" is the region of the Negev, which is compared to a forest about to be destroyed by fire.

20:49 Ezekiel was exasperated and discouraged. Many Israelites were complaining that he spoke only in riddles ("parables"), so they refused to listen. No matter how important our work or how significant our ministry, we will have moments of discouragement. Apparently God did not answer Ezekiel's plea; instead, he gave Ezekiel another message to proclaim. What has been discouraging you? Have you felt like giving up? Instead, continue doing what God has told you to do. He promises to reward the faithful (Mark 13:13). God's cure for discouragement may be another assignment. In serving others, we may find the renewal we need.

21:1ff The short message in 20:45–48 introduces the first of three messages about the judgments that would come upon Jerusalem: (1) the sword of the Lord (21:1–7); (2) the sharpened sword (21:8–17); (3) the sword of Nebuchadnezzar (21:18–22). The city would be destroyed because it was defiled. According to Jewish law, defiled objects were to be passed through fire in order to purify them (see Numbers 31:22, 23; Psalm 66:10–12; Proverbs 17:3). God's judgment is designed to purify; destruction is often a necessary part of that process.

to be grasped with the hand;
it is sharpened and polished,
made ready for the hand of the slayer.
12 Cry out and wail, son of man,
for it is against my people;
it is against all the princes of Israel.
They are thrown to the sword
along with my people.
Therefore beat your breast.[k]

13 " 'Testing will surely come. And what if the sceptre ⌊of Judah⌋, which the sword despises, does not continue? declares the Sovereign LORD.'

14 "So then, son of man, prophesy
and strike your hands[l] together.
Let the sword strike twice,
even three times.
It is a sword for slaughter—
a sword for great slaughter,
closing in on them from every side.[m]
15 So that hearts may melt[n]
and the fallen be many,
I have stationed the sword for slaughter[a]
at all their gates.
Oh! It is made to flash like lightning,
it is grasped for slaughter.[o]
16 O sword, slash to the right,
then to the left,
wherever your blade is turned.
17 I too will strike my hands[p] together,
and my wrath[q] will subside.
I the LORD have spoken."

18 The word of the LORD came to me: 19 "Son of man, mark out two roads for the
sword of the king of Babylon to take, both starting from the same country. Make a
signpost where the road branches off to the city. 20 Mark out one road for the sword
to come against Rabbah of the Ammonites[r] and another against Judah and fortified
Jerusalem. 21 For the king of Babylon will stop at the fork in the road, at the junction
of the two roads, to seek an omen: He will cast lots[s] with arrows, he will consult
his idols, he will examine the liver.[t] 22 Into his right hand will come the lot for
Jerusalem, where he is to set up battering-rams, to give the command to slaughter,
to sound the battle cry, to set battering-rams against the gates, to build a ramp and
to erect siege works.[u] 23 It will seem like a false omen to those who have sworn
allegiance to him, but he will remind[v] them of their guilt and take them captive.
24 "Therefore this is what the Sovereign LORD says: 'Because you people have
brought to mind your guilt by your open rebellion, revealing your sins in all that you
do—because you have done this, you will be taken captive.

[a] *15* Septuagint; the meaning of the Hebrew for this word is uncertain.

21:12 [k] Jer 31:19
21:14 [l] Nu 24:10 [m] Eze 6:11; 30:24
21:15 [n] 2Sa 17:10 [o] Ps 22:14
21:17 [p] ver 14; Eze 22:13 [q] Eze 5:13
21:20 [r] Dt 3:11; Jer 49:2; Am 1:14
21:21 [s] Pr 16:33 [t] Nu 22:7; 23:23
21:22 [u] Eze 4:2; 26:9
21:23 [v] Nu 5:15

21:12 Beating the breast was a gesture of grief.

21:18–23 Ammon evidently rebelled against Babylon about the same time as King Zedekiah of Judah. In 589 B.C. the nations of Judah and Ammon were among those who conspired against Babylon (Jeremiah 27:3). Ezekiel gave this message to the exiles who had heard the news and were again filled with hope of returning to their homeland. Ezekiel said that Babylon's king would march his armies into the region to stop the rebellion. Travelling from the north, he would stop at a fork in the road, one leading to Rabbah, the capital of Ammon, and the other leading to Jerusalem, the capital of Judah. He had to decide which city to destroy. Just as Ezekiel predicted, King Nebuchadnezzar went to Jerusalem and besieged it.

21:21 Nebuchadnezzar had three ways to get advice on the future. One was shaking the arrows, much like drawing straws, to see which course of action was right; the second was consulting an idol to see if some spirit might direct him; the third was having priests inspect the liver of a sacrificed animal to see if its shape and size would indicate a decision.

25“ ‘O profane and wicked prince of Israel, whose day has come, whose time of
punishment has reached its climax,[w] 26this is what the Sovereign LORD says: Take
off the turban, remove the crown.[x] It will not be as it was: The lowly will be exalted
and the exalted will be brought low.[y] 27A ruin! A ruin! I will make it a ruin! It will
not be restored until he comes to whom it rightfully belongs; to him I will give it.’[z]
28“And you, son of man, prophesy and say, ‘This is what the Sovereign LORD says
about the Ammonites[a] and their insults:

“ ‘A sword,[b] a sword,
drawn for the slaughter,
polished to consume
and to flash like lightning!
29Despite false visions concerning you
and lying divinations about you,
it will be laid on the necks
of the wicked who are to be slain,
whose day has come,
whose time of punishment has reached its climax.[c]
30Return the sword to its scabbard.[d]
In the place where you were created,
in the land of your ancestry,[e]
I will judge you.
31I will pour out my wrath upon you
and breathe out my fiery anger[f] against you;
I will hand you over to brutal men,
men skilled in destruction.[g]
32You will be fuel for the fire,[h]
your blood will be shed in your land,
you will be remembered[i] no more;
for I the LORD have spoken.’ ”

Jerusalem's Sins

22 The word of the LORD came to me: 2“Son of man, will you judge her? Will
you judge this city of bloodshed?[a] Then confront her with all her detestable
practices[b] 3and say: ‘This is what the Sovereign LORD says: O city that brings on
herself doom by shedding blood[c] in her midst and defiles herself by making idols,
4you have become guilty because of the blood you have shed[d] and have become
defiled by the idols you have made. You have brought your days to a close, and the
end of your years has come.[e] Therefore I will make you an object of scorn to the
nations and a laughing-stock to all the countries.[f] 5Those who are near and those who
are far away will mock you, O infamous city, full of turmoil.
6“ ‘See how each of the princes of Israel who are in you uses his power to shed
blood.[g] 7In you they have treated father and mother with contempt;[h] in you they have
oppressed the alien and ill-treated the fatherless and the widow.[i] 8You have despised
my holy things and desecrated my Sabbaths.[j] 9In you are slanderous men[k] bent on
shedding blood; in you are those who eat at the mountain shrines[l] and commit lewd
acts.[m] 10In you are those who dishonour their fathers' bed; in you are those who
violate women during their period, when they are ceremonially unclean.[n] 11In you

21:25 [w]Eze 35:5
21:26 [x]Jer 13:18 [y]Ps 75:7; Eze 17:24
21:27 [z]Ps 2:6; Jer 23:5-6; Eze 37:24; Hag 2:21-22
21:28 [a]Zep 2:8 [b]Jer 12:12
21:29 [c]ver 25; Eze 22:28; 35:5
21:30 [d]Jer 47:6 [e]Eze 16:3
21:31 [f]Eze 22:20-21 [g]Jer 51:20-23
21:32 [h]Mal 4:1 [i]Eze 25:10
22:2 [a]Eze 24:6, 9; Na 3:1 [b]Eze 16:2
22:3 [c]ver 6, 13, 27; Eze 23:37, 45
22:4 [d]2Ki 21:16 [e]Eze 21:25 [f]Eze 5:14
22:6 [g]Isa 1:23
22:7 [h]Dt 5:16; 27:16 [i]Ex 22:21-22
22:8 [j]Eze 23:38-39
22:9 [k]Lev 19:16 [l]Eze 18:11 [m]Hos 4:10, 14
22:10 [n]Lev 18:8, 19

21:28 The Ammonites and Israelites were usually fighting with each other. God told the Israelites not to ally with foreign nations, but Judah and Ammon united against Babylon in 589 B.C. (Jeremiah 27:3). God first judged Judah when Nebuchadnezzar first went to Jerusalem (21:22); but Ammon will also be judged, not for allying with Judah, but for watching Jerusalem's destruction with insulting delight.

22:1ff Chapter 22 explains why Jerusalem's judgment would come (22:2–16), how it would come (22:17–22), and who would be judged by it (22:23–31).

22:6–13 The leaders were especially responsible for the moral climate of the nation because God chose them to lead. The same is true today (see James 3:1). Unfortunately, many of the sins mentioned here have been committed in recent years by Christian leaders. We are living in a time of unprecedented attacks by Satan. We must uphold our leaders in prayer, and leaders must seek accountability to help them keep their moral and spiritual integrity.

one man commits a detestable offence with his neighbour's wife, another shamefully
defiles his daughter-in-law,[o] and another violates his sister,[p] his own father's
daughter. 12 In you men accept bribes[q] to shed blood; you take usury and excessive
interest[a] and make unjust gain from your neighbours[r] by extortion. And you have
forgotten me, declares the Sovereign LORD.

13 " 'I will surely strike my hands[s] together at the unjust gain[t] you have made and
at the blood[u] you have shed in your midst. 14 Will your courage endure or your hands
be strong in the day I deal with you? I the LORD have spoken,[v] and I will do it.[w]
15 I will disperse you among the nations and scatter[x] you through the countries; and
I will put an end to your uncleanness.[y] 16 When you have been defiled[b] in the eyes
of the nations, you will know that I am the LORD.' "

17 Then the word of the LORD came to me: 18 "Son of man, the house of Israel has
become dross[z] to me; all of them are the copper, tin, iron and lead left inside a
furnace. They are but the dross of silver.[a] 19 Therefore this is what the Sovereign
LORD says: 'Because you have all become dross, I will gather you into Jerusalem. 20 As
men gather silver, copper, iron, lead and tin into a furnace to melt it with a fiery blast,
so will I gather you in my anger and my wrath and put you inside the city and melt
you.[b] 21 I will gather you and I will blow on you with my fiery wrath, and you will
be melted inside her. 22 As silver is melted[c] in a furnace, so you will be melted inside
her, and you will know that I the LORD have poured out my wrath upon you.' "[d]

23 Again the word of the LORD came to me: 24 "Son of man, say to the land, 'You
are a land that has had no rain or showers[c] in the day of wrath.'[e] 25 There is a
conspiracy[f] of her princes[d] within her like a roaring lion tearing its prey; they devour
people,[g] take treasures and precious things and make many widows[h] within her.
26 Her priests do violence to my law[i] and profane my holy things; they do not
distinguish between the holy and the common;[j] they teach that there is no difference
between the unclean and the clean;[k] and they shut their eyes to the keeping of my
Sabbaths, so that I am profaned among them.[l] 27 Her officials within her are like
wolves tearing their prey; they shed blood and kill people to make unjust gain.[m] 28 Her
prophets whitewash[n] these deeds for them by false visions and lying divinations.
They say, 'This is what the Sovereign LORD says'—when the LORD has not spoken.[o]
29 The people of the land practise extortion and commit robbery; they oppress the poor
and needy and ill-treat the alien,[p] denying them justice.[q]

30 "I looked for a man among them who would build up the wall[r] and stand before
me in the gap on behalf of the land so that I would not have to destroy it, but I found
none.[s] 31 So I will pour out my wrath on them and consume them with my fiery anger,
bringing down[t] on their own heads all they have done, declares the Sovereign
LORD.[u]"

22:11 [o]Lev 18:15 [p]Lev 18:9; 2Sa 13:14
22:12 [q]Dt 27:25; Mic 7:3 [r]Lev 19:13
22:13 [s]Eze 21:17 [t]Isa 33:15 [u]ver 3
22:14 [v]Eze 24:14 [w]Eze 17:24; 21:7
22:15 [x]Dt 4:27; Zec 7:14 [y]Eze 23:27
22:18 [z]Ps 119:119; Isa 1:22 [a]Jer 6:28-30
22:20 [b]Mal 3:2
22:22 [c]Isa 1:25 [d]Eze 20:8, 33
22:24 [e]Eze 24:13
22:25 [f]Jer 11:9 [g]Hos 6:9 [h]Jer 15:8
22:26 [i]Mal 2:7-8 [j]Eze 44:23 [k]Lev 10:10 [l]1Sa 2:12-17; Jer 2:8, 26; Hag 2:11-14
22:27 [m]Isa 1:23
22:28 [n]Eze 13:10 [o]Eze 13:2, 6-7
22:29 [p]Ex 22:21; 23:9 [q]Isa 5:7
22:30 [r]Eze 13:5 [s]Ps 106:23; Jer 5:1
22:31 [t]Eze 16:43 [u]Eze 7:8-9; 9:10; Ro 2:8

a *12* Or *usury and interest* **b** *16* Or *When I have allotted you your inheritance* **c** *24* Septuagint; Hebrew *has not been cleansed or rained on* **d** *25* Septuagint; Hebrew *prophets*

22:17-22 Precious metals are refined with intense heat to remove the impurities. When heated, the dross (impurities) rises to the top of the molten metal and is skimmed off and thrown away. The purpose of the invasion of Jerusalem was to refine the people, but the refining process showed that the people, like worthless dross, had nothing good in them.

22:26 The priests were supposed to keep God's worship pure and teach the people right living. But the worship of God had become commonplace to them; they ignored the Sabbath, and they refused to teach the people. They no longer carried out their God-given duties (Leviticus 10:10, 11; Ezekiel 44:23). When doing God's work becomes no more important than any mundane task, we are no longer giving God the reverence he deserves. Instead of bringing God down to our level, we should live up to his level.

22:30 The wall spoken of here is not made of stones, but of faithful people united in their efforts to resist evil. This wall was in disrepair because there was no-one who could lead the people back to God. The feeble attempts to repair the gap—through religious rituals or messages based on opinion rather than God's will—were as worthless as whitewash, only covering over the real problems. What the people really needed was total spiritual reconstruction! When we give the appearance of loving God without living his way, we are covering up sins that could eventually damage us beyond repair. Don't use religion as a whitewash; repair your life by applying the principles of God's word. Then you can join with others to stand "in the gap" and make a difference for God in the world.

Two Adulterous Sisters

23 The word of the LORD came to me: 2"Son of man, there were two women,
daughters of the same mother.[a] 3They became prostitutes in Egypt,[b] engaging in prostitution[c] from their youth. In that land their breasts were fondled and their
virgin bosoms caressed. 4The older was named Oholah, and her sister was Oholibah.
They were mine and gave birth to sons and daughters. Oholah is Samaria, and
Oholibah is Jerusalem.
5"Oholah engaged in prostitution while she was still mine; and she lusted after her
lovers, the Assyrians[d]—warriors[e] 6clothed in blue, governors and commanders, all
of them handsome young men, and mounted horsemen. 7She gave herself as a
prostitute to all the elite of the Assyrians and defiled herself with all the idols of
everyone she lusted after.[f] 8She did not give up the prostitution she began in Egypt,[g]
when during her youth men slept with her, caressed her virgin bosom and poured out
their lust upon her.[h]
9"Therefore I handed her over[i] to her lovers, the Assyrians, for whom she lusted.[j]
10They stripped[k] her naked, took away her sons and daughters and killed her with
the sword. She became a byword among women,[l] and punishment was inflicted on
her.[m]
11"Her sister Oholibah saw this, yet in her lust and prostitution she was more
depraved than her sister.[n] 12She too lusted after the Assyrians—governors and
commanders, warriors in full dress, mounted horsemen, all handsome young men.[o]
13I saw that she too defiled herself; both of them went the same way.
14"But she carried her prostitution still further. She saw men portrayed on a wall,[p]
figures of Chaldeans**a** portrayed in red,[q] 15with belts round their waists and flowing
turbans on their heads; all of them looked like Babylonian chariot officers, natives of
Chaldea.**b** 16As soon as she saw them, she lusted after them and sent messengers to
them in Chaldea. 17Then the Babylonians came to her, to the bed of love, and in their
lust they defiled her. After she had been defiled by them, she turned away from them
in disgust. 18When she carried on her prostitution openly and exposed her nakedness,
I turned away[r] from her in disgust, just as I had turned away from her sister.[s] 19Yet
she became more and more promiscuous as she recalled the days of her youth, when
she was a prostitute in Egypt. 20There she lusted after her lovers, whose genitals were
like those of donkeys and whose emission was like that of horses. 21So you longed
for the lewdness of your youth, when in Egypt your bosom was caressed and your
young breasts fondled.**c**[t]
22"Therefore, Oholibah, this is what the Sovereign LORD says: I will stir up your

a *14* Or *Babylonians* **b** *15* Or *Babylonia*; also in verse 16 **c** *21* Syriac (see also verse 3); Hebrew *caressed because of your young breasts*

23:2 [a]Jer 3:7; Eze 16:45
23:3 [b]Jos 24:14 [c]Lev 17:7
23:5 [d]2Ki 16:7; Hos 5:13 [e]Hos 8:9
23:7 [f]Hos 5:3; 6:10
23:8 [g]Ex 32:4 [h]Eze 16:15
23:9 [i]2Ki 18:11 [j]Hos 11:5
23:10 [k]Hos 2:10 [l]Eze 16:41 [m]Eze 16:36
23:11 [n]Jer 3:8-11; Eze 16:51
23:12 [o]2Ki 16:7-15; 2Ch 28:16
23:14 [p]Eze 8:10 [q]Jer 22:14
23:18 [r]Ps 78:59; 106:40; Jer 6:8 [s]Jer 12:8; Am 5:21
23:21 [t]Eze 16:26

23:1ff Ezekiel continued his discussion of the reasons for God's judgment by telling a further allegory. He compared the northern and southern kingdoms to two sisters who became prostitutes. The proud citizens of Jerusalem had long scorned their sister city of Samaria, thinking that they of Jerusalem were superior. But God called both of these cities prostitutes—a shock to the people of Jerusalem who thought that they were righteous. Just as the imagery of this message was shocking and distasteful to the people, so our sins are repugnant to God.

23:4–6 Oholah (meaning, "her tent"), the northern kingdom of Israel, was lured away from God by the dashing Assyrians—their fashionable clothes and powerful positions. The people coveted youth, strength, power, wealth, and pleasure—the same qualities people think will bring happiness today. But the charming Assyrians drew Israel away from God.

23:11ff Oholibah (meaning, "my tent is in her") was shown to be worse because she did not learn from the judgment upon her sister, but continued in her lust for the Assyrians and Babylonians. Therefore, her judgment was equally certain. Just as Oholibah was privileged and should have known better, so we are privileged because we know about Christ. We need to be doubly sure that we follow him.

23:12 "She too lusted after the Assyrians" may mean excessively trying to please and probably refers to Ahaz paying protection money to Tiglath-Pileser III (2 Kings 16:7, 8).

23:16 An invitation to Chaldea (Babylon) was given by Hezekiah to the envoys from Babylon (2 Kings 20:12ff; Isaiah 38; 39).

23:17 At first, Judah made an alliance with Babylonia (Chaldea), but then changed its mind. During the reigns of the last two Judean kings, Jehoiakim and Zedekiah, Judah looked to Egypt for help. Judah's unfaithfulness (its alliances with godless nations) cost it the only real protection it ever had—God.

23:21 "Lewdness" is promiscuity (see also 23:27, 49)—giving sexual favours instead of being faithful to a spouse or to God. We don't think of ourselves as being spiritually promiscuous, but we often spend more time seeking advice from magazines, television adverts, and non-Christian experts than we do from God and his word.

23:22–26 This predicts the last attack on Jerusalem that would destroy the city and bring to Babylonia the third wave of captives in 586 B.C. (2 Kings 25; Jeremiah 52). The first attack came in

lovers against you, those you turned away from in disgust, and I will bring them against you from every side[u]— 23 the Babylonians[v] and all the Chaldeans, the men of Pekod[w] and Shoa and Koa, and all the Assyrians with them, handsome young men, all of them governors and commanders, chariot officers and men of high rank, all mounted on horses.[x] 24 They will come against you with weapons,[d] chariots and wagons[y] and with a throng of people; they will take up positions against you on every side with large and small shields and with helmets. I will turn you over to them for punishment,[z] and they will punish you according to their standards. 25 I will direct my jealous anger against you, and they will deal with you in fury. They will cut off your noses and your ears, and those of you who are left will fall by the sword. They will take away your sons and daughters,[a] and those of you who are left will be consumed by fire.[b] 26 They will also strip[c] you of your clothes and take your fine jewellery.[d] 27 So I will put a stop[e] to the lewdness and prostitution you began in Egypt. You will not look on these things with longing or remember Egypt any more.

28 "For this is what the Sovereign LORD says: I am about to hand you over[f] to those you hate, to those you turned away from in disgust. 29 They will deal with you in hatred and take away everything you have worked for. They will leave you naked and bare, and the shame of your prostitution will be exposed. Your lewdness and promiscuity[g] 30 have brought this upon you, because you lusted after the nations and defiled yourself with their idols.[h] 31 You have gone the way of your sister; so I will put her cup[i] into your hand.[j]

32 "This is what the Sovereign LORD says:

> "You will drink your sister's cup,
>   a cup large and deep;
> it will bring scorn and derision,
>   for it holds so much.[k]
> 33 You will be filled with drunkenness and sorrow,
>   the cup of ruin and desolation,
>   the cup of your sister Samaria.[l]
> 34 You will drink it[m] and drain it dry;
>   you will dash it to pieces
>   and tear your breasts.

I have spoken, declares the Sovereign LORD.

35 "Therefore this is what the Sovereign LORD says: Since you have forgotten[n] me and thrust me behind your back,[o] you must bear the consequences of your lewdness and prostitution."

36 The LORD said to me: "Son of man, will you judge Oholah and Oholibah? Then confront[p] them with their detestable practices,[q] 37 for they have committed adultery and blood is on their hands. They committed adultery with their idols; they even sacrificed their children, whom they bore to me,[e] as food for them.[r] 38 They have also done this to me: At that same time they defiled my sanctuary and desecrated my Sabbaths. 39 On the very day they sacrificed their children to their idols, they entered my sanctuary and desecrated[s] it. That is what they did in my house.[t]

40 "They even sent messengers for men who came from far away,[u] and when they arrived you bathed yourself for them, painted your eyes[v] and put on your jewellery.[w] 41 You sat on an elegant couch,[x] with a table[y] spread before it on which you had placed the incense and oil that belonged to me.

42 "The noise of a carefree crowd was around her; Sabeans[f] were brought from the desert along with men from the rabble, and they put bracelets[z] on the arms of the

d *24* The meaning of the Hebrew for this word is uncertain. **e** *37* Or *even made the children they bore to me pass through* ⌞the fire⌟ **f** *42* Or *drunkards*

23:22 [u]Eze 16:37
23:23 [v]2Ki 20:14-18 [w]Jer 50:21 [x]2Ki 24:2
23:24 [y]Jer 47:3; Eze 26:7, 10; Na 2:4 [z]Jer 39:5-6
23:25 [a]ver 47 [b]Eze 20:47-48
23:26 [c]Jer 13:22 [d]Isa 3:18-23; Eze 16:39
23:27 [e]Eze 16:41
23:28 [f]Jer 34:20
23:29 [g]Dt 28:48
23:30 [h]Eze 6:9
23:31 [i]Jer 25:15 [j]2Ki 21:13
23:32 [k]Ps 60:3; Isa 51:17; Jer 25:15
23:33 [l]Jer 25:15-16
23:34 [m]Ps 75:8; Isa 51:17
23:35 [n]Isa 17:10; Jer 3:21 [o]1Ki 14:9
23:36 [p]Eze 16:2 [q]Isa 58:1; Eze 22:2; Mic 3:8
23:37 [r]Eze 16:36
23:39 [s]2Ki 21:4 [t]Jer 7:10
23:40 [u]Isa 57:9 [v]2Ki 9:30 [w]Jer 4:30; Eze 16:13-19
23:41 [x]Est 1:6; Pr 7:17; Am 6:4 [y]Isa 65:11; Eze 44:16
23:42 [z]Ge 24:30

---

605 B.C., the second in 597 B.C. Pekod, Shoa, and Koa were Babylonian allies.

23:39 The Israelites went so far as to sacrifice their own children to idols and then to sacrifice to the Lord the same day. This made a mockery of worship. We cannot praise God and wilfully sin at the same time. That would be like celebrating one's wedding anniversary and then going to bed with a neighbour.

woman and her sister and beautiful crowns on their heads.[a] 43Then I said about the
one worn out by adultery, 'Now let them use her as a prostitute,[b] for that is all she
is.' 44And they slept with her. As men sleep with a prostitute, so they slept with those
lewd women, Oholah and Oholibah. 45But righteous men will sentence them to the
punishment of women who commit adultery and shed blood, because they are adulterous and blood is on their hands.[c]

46"This is what the Sovereign LORD says: Bring a mob[d] against them and give them
over to terror and plunder. 47The mob will stone them and cut them down with their
swords; they will kill their sons and daughters and burn[e] down their houses.[f]

48"So I will put an end to lewdness in the land, that all women may take warning
and not imitate you.[g] 49You will suffer the penalty for your lewdness and bear the
consequences of your sins of idolatry. Then you will know that I am the Sovereign
LORD.[h]"

The Cooking Pot

24 In the ninth year, in the tenth month on the tenth day, the word of the LORD
came to me:[a] 2"Son of man, record this date, this very date, because the king
of Babylon has laid siege to Jerusalem this very day.[b] 3Tell this rebellious house[c]
a parable[d] and say to them: 'This is what the Sovereign LORD says:

" 'Put on the cooking pot;[e] put it on
and pour water into it.
4Put into it the pieces of meat,
all the choice pieces—the leg and the shoulder.
Fill it with the best of these bones;
5 take the pick of the flock.[f]
Pile wood beneath it for the bones;
bring it to the boil
and cook the bones in it.[g]

6" 'For this is what the Sovereign LORD says:

" 'Woe to the city of bloodshed,[h]
to the pot now encrusted,
whose deposit will not go away!
Empty it piece by piece
without casting lots[i] for them.

7" 'For the blood she shed is in her midst:
She poured it on the bare rock;
she did not pour it on the ground,
where the dust would cover it.[j]
8To stir up wrath and take revenge
I put her blood on the bare rock,
so that it would not be covered.

9" 'Therefore this is what the Sovereign LORD says:

" 'Woe to the city of bloodshed!
I, too, will pile the wood high.

23:42 [a] Eze 16:11-12
23:43 [b] ver 3
23:45 [c] Lev 20:10; Eze 16:38; Hos 6:5
23:46 [d] Eze 16:40
23:47 [e] 2Ch 36:19 [f] 2Ch 36:17; Eze 16:40-41
23:48 [g] 2Pe 2:6
23:49 [h] Eze 7:4; 9:10; 20:38
24:1 [a] Eze 8:1
24:2 [b] 2Ki 25:1; Jer 39:1; 52:4
24:3 [c] Isa 1:2; Eze 2:3, 6 [d] Eze 17:2; 20:49 [e] Jer 1:13; Eze 11:3
24:5 [f] Jer 52:10 [g] Jer 52:24-27
24:6 [h] Eze 22:2 [i] Ob 1:11; Na 3:10
24:7 [j] Lev 17:13

24:1–14 Ezekiel gave this illustration in 588 B.C., three years after the first of the previous messages (see 20:1, 2). The people in Judah thought they were the choice meat because they hadn't been taken into captivity in 597 when the Babylonians last invaded the land. Ezekiel used this illustration before (chapter 11) to show that though the people thought they were safe and secure inside the cooking pot, this pot would actually be the place of their destruction. This message was given to the exiles in Babylonia the very day that the Babylonians attacked Jerusalem (24:2), beginning a siege that lasted over two years and resulted in the city's destruction. When God's punishment comes, it is relentless.

24:6–13 The city of Jerusalem was like a pot so encrusted with sin that it would not come clean. God wanted to cleanse the lives of those who lived in Jerusalem, and he wants to cleanse our lives today. Sometimes he tries to purify us through difficulties and troublesome circumstances. When you face tough times, allow the sin to be burned from your life. Look at your problems as opportunities for your faith to grow. When these times come, unnecessary priorities and diversions are purged away. We can re-examine our lives so that we will do what really counts.

10So heap on the wood
and kindle the fire.
Cook the meat well,
mixing in the spices;
and let the bones be charred.
11Then set the empty pot on the coals
till it becomes hot and its copper glows
so its impurities may be melted
and its deposit burned away.[k]
12It has frustrated all efforts;
its heavy deposit has not been removed,
not even by fire.

13" 'Now your impurity is lewdness. Because I tried to cleanse you but you would
not be cleansed from your impurity, you will not be clean again until my wrath against
you has subsided.[l]

14" 'I the LORD have spoken. The time has come for me to act. I will not hold back;
I will not have pity, nor will I relent. You will be judged according to your conduct
and your actions,[m] declares the Sovereign LORD.[n]' "

Ezekiel's Wife Dies

15The word of the LORD came to me: 16"Son of man, with one blow I am about
to take away from you the delight of your eyes. Yet do not lament or weep or shed
any tears.[o] 17Groan quietly; do not mourn for the dead. Keep your turban fastened
and your sandals on your feet; do not cover the lower part of your face or eat the
customary food ⌊of mourners⌋.[p]"
18So I spoke to the people in the morning, and in the evening my wife died. The
next morning I did as I had been commanded.
19Then the people asked me, "Won't you tell us what these things have to do with
us?[q]"
20So I said to them, "The word of the LORD came to me: 21Say to the house of Israel,
'This is what the Sovereign LORD says: I am about to desecrate my sanctuary—the
stronghold in which you take pride, the delight of your eyes,[r] the object of your
affection. The sons and daughters[s] you left behind will fall by the sword.[t] 22And
you will do as I have done. You will not cover the lower part of your face or eat the
customary food ⌊of mourners⌋.[u] 23You will keep your turbans on your heads and your
sandals on your feet. You will not mourn[v] or weep but will waste away because of[a]
your sins and groan among yourselves.[w] 24Ezekiel will be a sign[x] to you; you will
do just as he has done. When this happens, you will know that I am the Sovereign
LORD.'
25"And you, son of man, on the day I take away their stronghold, their joy and
glory, the delight of their eyes, their heart's desire, and their sons and daughters[y]
as well—26on that day a fugitive will come to tell you[z] the news. 27At that time your
mouth will be opened; you will speak with him and will no longer be silent. So you
will be a sign to them, and they will know that I am the LORD.[a]"

[a] 23 Or *away in*

24:11 [k]Jer 21:10; Eze 22:15
24:13 [l]Jer 6:28-30; Eze 16:42; 22:24
24:14 [m]Eze 36:19 [n]Eze 18:30
24:16 [o]Jer 13:17; 16:5; 22:10
24:17 [p]Jer 16:7
24:19 [q]Eze 12:9; 37:18
24:21 [r]Ps 27:4 [s]Eze 23:25 [t]Jer 7:14, 15; Eze 23:47
24:22 [u]Jer 16:7
24:23 [v]Job 27:15 [w]Ps 78:64
24:24 [x]Isa 20:3; Eze 4:3; 12:11
24:25 [y]Jer 11:22
24:26 [z]1Sa 4:12; Job 1:15-19
24:27 [a]Eze 3:26; 33:22

24:15–18 God told Ezekiel that his wife would die and that he should not grieve for her. Ezekiel obeyed God fully, even as Hosea did when he was told to marry an unfaithful woman (Hosea 1:2, 3). In both cases, these unusual events were intended as symbolic acts t o give pictures of God's relationship with his people. Obeying God can carry a high cost. The only grief more excruciating than losing your spouse and not being allowed to grieve would be to lose eternal life because you did not obey God. Ezekiel always obeyed God wholeheartedly. We should be wholehearted in our obedience. We can begin by doing all that God commands us to do, even when we don't feel like it. Are you willing to serve God as completely as Ezekiel did?

24:20–24 Ezekiel was not allowed to mourn for his dead wife in order to show his fellow exiles that they were not to mourn over Jerusalem when it was destroyed. Any personal sorrow felt would soon be eclipsed by national sorrow over the horror of the city's total destruction. The individuals would waste away because of their sins, which caused the city's destruction.

24:27 For some time Ezekiel had not been allowed to speak except when God gave him a message to deliver to the people (3:25–27). This restriction would soon end when Jerusalem was destroyed and all Ezekiel's prophecies about Judah and Jerusalem had come true (33:21, 22).

B. MESSAGES AGAINST FOREIGN NATIONS (25:1 – 32:32)

These messages were given concerning seven nations which surrounded Judah. The Ammonites were judged because of their joy over the desecration of the temple, the Moabites because they scorned Judah as special people, the Edomites because of their special hatred of the Jews, and the Philistines because of their vengeance. All these nations would soon realise that God is supreme. Nations today are also under limits imposed by God.

A Prophecy Against Ammon

25 The word of the LORD came to me: 2“Son of man, set your face against the
Ammonites[a] and prophesy against them.[b] 3Say to them, ‘Hear the word of
the Sovereign LORD. This is what the Sovereign LORD says: Because you said
“Aha![c]” over my sanctuary when it was desecrated and over the land of Israel when
it was laid waste and over the people of Judah when they went into exile,[d] 4therefore
I am going to give you to the people of the East[e] as a possession. They will set up
their camps and pitch their tents among you; they will eat your fruit and drink your
milk.[f] 5I will turn Rabbah[g] into a pasture for camels and Ammon into a resting place
for sheep.[h] Then you will know that I am the LORD. 6For this is what the Sovereign
LORD says: Because you have clapped your hands and stamped your feet, rejoicing
with all the malice of your heart against the land of Israel,[i] 7therefore I will stretch
out my hand[j] against you and give you as plunder to the nations. I will cut you off
from the nations and exterminate you from the countries. I will destroy[k] you, and
you will know that I am the LORD.[l]’ ”

A Prophecy Against Moab

8“This is what the Sovereign LORD says: ‘Because Moab[m] and Seir said, “Look,
the house of Judah has become like all the other nations,” 9therefore I will expose
the flank of Moab, beginning at its frontier towns—Beth Jeshimoth[n], Baal Meon[o]
and Kiriathaim[p]—the glory of that land. 10I will give Moab along with the Ammonites to the people of the East as a possession, so that the Ammonites will not be
remembered[q] among the nations; 11and I will inflict punishment on Moab. Then they
will know that I am the LORD.’ ”

A Prophecy Against Edom

12“This is what the Sovereign LORD says: ‘Because Edom[r] took revenge on the
house of Judah and became very guilty by doing so, 13therefore this is what the
Sovereign LORD says: I will stretch out my hand against Edom and kill its men and

25:2 [a]Eze 21:28; Zep 2:8-9 [b]Jer 49:1-6
25:3 [c]Eze 26:2; 36:2 [d]Pr 17:5
25:4 [e]Jdg 6:3 [f]Dt 28:33, 51; Jdg 6:33
25:5 [g]Dt 3:11; Eze 21:20 [h]Isa 17:2
25:6 [i]Ob 1:12; Zep 2:8
25:7 [j]Zep 1:4 [k]Eze 21:31 [l]Am 1:14-15
25:8 [m]Jer 48:1; Am 2:1
25:9 [n]Nu 33:49 [o]Nu 32:3; Jos 13:17 [p]Nu 32:37; Jos 13:19
25:10 [q]Eze 21:32
25:12 [r]2Ch 28:17

25:1ff Chapters 25 – 32 are God's word concerning the seven nations surrounding Judah. The judgments in these chapters are not simply the vengeful statements of Jews against their enemies; they are God's judgments on nations that failed to acknowledge the one true God and fulfil the good purposes God intended for them. The Ammonites were judged because of their joy over the desecration of the temple (25:1–7), the Moabites because they found pleasure in Judah's wickedness (25:8–11), the Edomites because of their racial hatred for the Jews (25:12–14), and the Philistines because they sought revenge against Judah for defeating them in battle (25:15–17).

25:5 Rabbah was the capital city of the Ammonites.

25:9 These towns were on the northern border of Moab.

25:13, 14 The Edomites were blood brothers of the Jews, both nations having descended from Isaac (Genesis 25:19–26). Edom shared its northern border with Israel, and the two nations were always in conflict. The Edomites hated Israel so much that they rejoiced when Jerusalem, Israel's capital, was destroyed. Teman was in the northern part of Edom; Dedan was in the southern part. Thus, Ezekiel was saying that the entire country would be destroyed.

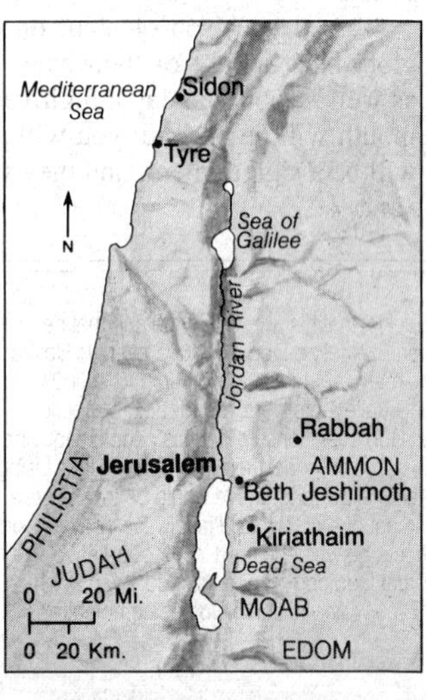

JUDAH'S ENEMIES
Ammon, Moab, Edom, and Philistia, although once united with Judah against Babylon, had abandoned Judah and rejoiced to see its ruin. But these nations were as sinful as Judah and would also feel the sting of God's judgment.

their animals.[s] I will lay it waste, and from Teman to Dedan[t] they will fall by the sword. 14I will take vengeance on Edom by the hand of my people Israel, and they will deal with Edom in accordance with my anger[u] and my wrath; they will know my vengeance, declares the Sovereign LORD.' "

A Prophecy Against Philistia

15"This is what the Sovereign LORD says: 'Because the Philistines[v] acted in vengeance and took revenge with malice in their hearts, and with ancient hostility sought to destroy Judah, 16therefore this is what the Sovereign LORD says: I am about to stretch out my hand against the Philistines,[w] and I will cut off the Kerethites[x] and destroy those remaining along the coast. 17I will carry out great vengeance on them and punish them in my wrath. Then they will know that I am the LORD, when I take vengeance on them.' "

A Prophecy Against Tyre

26 In the eleventh year, on the first day of the month, the word of the LORD came to me: 2"Son of man, because Tyre[a] has said of Jerusalem, 'Aha![b] The gate to the nations is broken, and its doors have swung open to me; now that she lies in ruins I will prosper,' 3therefore this is what the Sovereign LORD says: I am against you, O Tyre, and I will bring many nations against you, like the sea[c] casting up its waves. 4They will destroy[d] the walls of Tyre[e] and pull down her towers; I will scrape away her rubble and make her a bare rock. 5Out in the sea[f] she will become a place to spread fishing nets, for I have spoken, declares the Sovereign LORD. She will become plunder[g] for the nations, 6and her settlements on the mainland will be ravaged by the sword. Then they will know that I am the LORD.

7"For this is what the Sovereign LORD says: From the north I am going to bring against Tyre Nebuchadnezzar[a][h] king of Babylon, king of kings,[i] with horses and chariots,[j] with horsemen and a great army. 8He will ravage your settlements on the mainland with the sword; he will set up siege works[k] against you, build a ramp[l] up to your walls and raise his shields against you. 9He will direct the blows of his battering-rams against your walls and demolish your towers with his weapons. 10His horses will be so many that they will cover you with dust. Your walls will tremble at the noise of the war horses, wagons and chariots[m] when he enters your gates as men enter a city whose walls have been broken through. 11The hoofs[n] of his horses will trample all your streets; he will kill your people with the sword, and your strong pillars[o] will fall to the ground.[p] 12They will plunder your wealth and loot your merchandise; they will break down your walls and demolish your fine houses and throw your stones, timber and rubble into the sea.[q] 13I will put an end[r] to your noisy songs, and the music of your harps[s] will be heard no more.[t] 14I will make you a bare rock, and you will become a place to spread fishing nets. You will never be rebuilt,[u] for I the LORD have spoken, declares the Sovereign LORD.

15"This is what the Sovereign LORD says to Tyre: Will not the coastlands[v] tremble[w] at the sound of your fall, when the wounded groan and the slaughter takes place

[a] 7 Hebrew *Nebuchadrezzar*, of which *Nebuchadnezzar* is a variant; here and often in Ezekiel and Jeremiah

25:13 [s]Eze 29:8 [t]Jer 25:23
25:14 [u]Eze 35:11
25:15 [v]2Ch 28:18
25:16 [w]Jer 47:1-7 [x]1Sa 30:14; Zep 2:4-5
26:2 [a]2Sa 5:11; Isa 23 [b]Eze 25:3
26:3 [c]Isa 5:30; Jer 50:42; 51:42
26:4 [d]Isa 23:1, 11 [e]Am 1:10
26:5 [f]Eze 27:32 [g]Eze 29:19
26:7 [h]Jer 27:6 [i]Ezr 7:12; Da 2:37 [j]Eze 23:24; Na 2:3-4
26:8 [k]Jer 6:6 [l]Eze 21:22
26:10 [m]Jer 4:13
26:11 [n]Isa 5:28 [o]Jer 43:13 [p]Isa 26:5
26:12 [q]Isa 23:8; Eze 27:3-27; 28:8
26:13 [r]Jer 7:34 [s]Isa 14:11 [t]Jer 25:10; Rev 18:22
26:14 [u]Job 12:14; Mal 1:4
26:15 [v]Eze 27:35 [w]Jer 49:21

25:16 The Kerethites originated in Crete, from which they take their name. They were either a clan of the Philistines, or possibly a separate people who migrated from the Aegean to Palestine about the same time. The Kerethites and Philistines were closely intermixed once they were in Palestine and are often mentioned together.

26:1ff This message came to Ezekiel in 586 B.C. Chapters 26 and 27 are a prophecy against Tyre, the capital of Phoenicia just north of Israel. Part of the city was on the coastline, and part was on a beautiful island. Tyre rejoiced when Jerusalem fell, because Tyre and Judah always competed for the lucrative trade that came through their lands from Egypt in the south and Mesopotamia to the north. Tyre dominated the sea trading routes while Judah dominated the land caravan routes. After Judah was defeated, Tyre thought it had all the trade routes to itself. But this gloating didn't last long. In 586 B.C., Nebuchadnezzar attacked the city. It took him 15 years to capture Tyre (586–571) because the city's back side lay on the sea so fresh supplies could be shipped in daily.

26:14 After a 15-year siege, Nebuchadnezzar could not conquer the part of Tyre located on the island; thus certain aspects of the description in 26:12, 14 exceed the actual damage done to Tyre by Nebuchadnezzar. But the prophecy predicted what would happen to the island settlement later during the conquests of Alexander the Great. Alexander threw the rubble of the mainland city into the sea until it made a bridge to the island. Then he marched across the bridge and destroyed the island (332 B.C.). Today the island city is still a pile of rubble, a testimony to God's judgment.

in you? 16Then all the princes of the coast will step down from their thrones and lay
aside their robes and take off their embroidered garments. Clothed[x] with terror, they
will sit on the ground, trembling[y] every moment, appalled[z] at you. 17Then they will
take up a lament[a] concerning you and say to you:

" 'How you are destroyed, O city of renown,
peopled by men of the sea!
You were a power on the seas,
you and your citizens;
you put your terror
on all who lived there.[b]
18Now the coastlands tremble
on the day of your fall;
the islands in the sea
are terrified at your collapse.'[c]

19"This is what the Sovereign LORD says: When I make you a desolate city, like
cities no longer inhabited, and when I bring the ocean depths over you and its vast
waters cover you,[d] 20then I will bring you down with those who go down to the pit,[e]
to the people of long ago. I will make you dwell in the earth below, as in ancient ruins,
with those who go down to the pit, and you will not return or take your place**b** in
the land of the living.[f] 21I will bring you to a horrible end and you will be no more.
You will be sought, but you will never again be found, declares the Sovereign
LORD."[g]

A Lament for Tyre

27 The word of the LORD came to me: 2"Son of man, take up a lament concerning
Tyre. 3Say to Tyre, situated at the gateway to the sea,[a] merchant of peoples
on many coasts, 'This is what the Sovereign LORD says:

" 'You say, O Tyre,
"I am perfect in beauty.[b]"
4Your domain was on the high seas;
your builders brought your beauty to perfection.
5They made all your timbers
of pine trees from Senir;**a**[c]
they took a cedar from Lebanon
to make a mast for you.
6Of oaks[d] from Bashan
they made your oars;
of cypress wood**b** from the coasts of Cyprus**c**[e]
they made your deck, inlaid with ivory.
7Fine embroidered linen from Egypt was your sail
and served as your banner;
your awnings were of blue and purple[f]
from the coasts of Elishah.
8Men of Sidon and Arvad[g] were your oarsmen;
your skilled men, O Tyre, were aboard as your seamen.[h]
9Veteran craftsmen of Gebal**d**[i] were on board
as shipwrights to caulk your seams.

26:16 [x]Job 8:22 [y]Hos 11:10 [z]Eze 32:10
26:17 [a]Eze 19:1; 27:32 [b]Isa 14:12
26:18 [c]Isa 23:5; 41:5; Eze 27:35
26:19 [d]Isa 8:7-8
26:20 [e]Eze 32:18; Am 9:2; Jnh 2:2, 6 [f]Eze 32:24, 30
26:21 [g]Eze 27:36; 28:19; Rev 18:21
27:3 [a]ver 33 [b]Eze 28:2
27:5 [c]Dt 3:9
27:6 [d]Nu 21:33; Jer 22:20; Zec 11:2 [e]Ge 10:4; Isa 23:12
27:7 [f]Ex 25:4; Jer 10:9
27:8 [g]Ge 10:18 [h]1Ki 9:27
27:9 [i]Jos 13:5; 1Ki 5:18

b *20* Septuagint; Hebrew *return, and I will give glory* **a** *5* That is, Hermon **b** *6* Targum; the Masoretic Text has a different division of the consonants. **c** *6* Hebrew *Kittim* **d** *9* That is, Byblos

27:1ff Chapter 27 is a funeral lament over Tyre's fall. It compares the city to a ship (27:1–9), mentions many of its trading partners (27:10–25), and then describes how the ship sank (27:26–36). Jesus spoke of Tyre in Matthew 11:22 as a city worthy of God's judgment.

27:3, 4 The beauty of Tyre was the source of its pride, and Tyre's pride guaranteed its judgment. Unwarranted conceit or pride in our own accomplishments should be a danger signal to us (see James 4:13–17). God is not against our finding pleasure or satisfaction in what we do; he is against arrogant, inflated self-esteem that looks down on others. We must acknowledge God as the basis and source of our lives.

All the ships of the sea and their sailors
came alongside to trade for your wares.

10" 'Men of Persia,[j] Lydia and Put[k]
served as soldiers in your army.
They hung their shields and helmets on your walls,
bringing you splendour.
11 Men of Arvad and Helech
manned your walls on every side;
men of Gammad
were in your towers.
They hung their shields around your walls;
they brought your beauty to perfection.

12" 'Tarshish[l] did business with you because of your great wealth of goods;[m] they
exchanged silver, iron, tin and lead for your merchandise.
13" 'Greece, Tubal and Meshech[n] traded with you; they exchanged slaves[o] and
articles of bronze for your wares.
14" 'Men of Beth Togarmah[p] exchanged work horses, war horses and mules for
your merchandise.
15" 'The men of Rhodes[e][q] traded with you, and many coastlands[r] were your
customers; they paid you with ivory[s] tusks and ebony.
16" 'Aram[f][t] did business with you because of your many products; they exchanged turquoise,[u] purple fabric, embroidered work, fine linen, coral and rubies for
your merchandise.
17" 'Judah and Israel traded with you; they exchanged wheat from Minnith[v] and
confections,[g] honey, oil and balm for your wares.
18" 'Damascus,[w] because of your many products and great wealth of goods, did
business with you in wine from Helbon and wool from Zahar.
19" 'Danites and Greeks from Uzal bought your merchandise; they exchanged
wrought iron, cassia and calamus for your wares.
20" 'Dedan traded in saddle blankets with you.
21" 'Arabia and all the princes of Kedar[x] were your customers; they did business
with you in lambs, rams and goats.
22" 'The merchants of Sheba[y] and Raamah traded with you; for your merchandise
they exchanged the finest of all kinds of spices[z] and precious stones, and gold.
23" 'Haran,[a] Canneh and Eden[b] and merchants of Sheba, Asshur and Kilmad
traded with you. 24 In your market-place they traded with you beautiful garments, blue
fabric, embroidered work and multicoloured rugs with cords twisted and tightly
knotted.

25" 'The ships of Tarshish[c] serve
as carriers for your wares.
You are filled with heavy cargo
in the heart of the sea.
26 Your oarsmen take you
out to the high seas.
But the east wind[d] will break you to pieces
in the heart of the sea.
27 Your wealth,[e] merchandise and wares,
your mariners, seamen and shipwrights,
your merchants and all your soldiers,
and everyone else on board
will sink into the heart of the sea
on the day of your shipwreck.
28 The shorelands will quake[f]
when your seamen cry out.

27:10 [j]Eze 38:5 [k]Eze 30:5
27:12 [l]Ge 10:4 [m]ver 18, 33
27:13 [n]Ge 10:2; Isa 66:19; Eze 38:2 [o]Rev 18:13
27:14 [p]Ge 10:3; Eze 38:6
27:15 [q]Ge 10:7 [r]Jer 25:22 [s]1Ki 10:22; Rev 18:12
27:16 [t]Jdg 10:6; Isa 7:1-8 [u]Eze 28:13
27:17 [v]Jdg 11:33
27:18 [w]Ge 14:15; Eze 47:16-18
27:21 [x]Ge 25:13; Isa 60:7
27:22 [y]Ge 10:7, 28; 1Ki 10:1-2; Isa 60:6 [z]Ge 43:11
27:23 [a]2Ki 19:12 [b]Isa 37:12
27:25 [c]Isa 2:16 *fn*
27:26 [d]Ps 48:7; Jer 18:17
27:27 [e]Pr 11:4
27:28 [f]Eze 26:15

e *15* Septuagint; Hebrew *Dedan* **f** *16* Most Hebrew manuscripts; some Hebrew manuscripts and Syriac *Edom*
g *17* The meaning of the Hebrew for this word is uncertain.

29 All who handle the oars
will abandon their ships;
the mariners and all the seamen
will stand on the shore.
30 They will raise their voice
and cry bitterly over you;
they will sprinkle dust[g] on their heads
and roll[h] in ashes.[i]
31 They will shave their heads because of you
and will put on sackcloth.
They will weep[j] over you with anguish of soul
and with bitter mourning.[k]
32 As they wail and mourn over you,
they will take up a lament[l] concerning you:
"Who was ever silenced like Tyre,
surrounded by the sea?"
33 When your merchandise went out on the seas,
you satisfied many nations;
with your great wealth[m] and your wares
you enriched the kings of the earth.
34 Now you are shattered by the sea
in the depths of the waters;
your wares and all your company
have gone down with you.[n]
35 All who live in the coastlands[o]
are appalled at you;
their kings shudder with horror
and their faces are distorted with fear.
36 The merchants among the nations hiss at you;[p]
you have come to a horrible end
and will be no more.[q]' "

A Prophecy Against the King of Tyre

28 The word of the LORD came to me: 2 "Son of man, say to the ruler of Tyre, 'This is what the Sovereign LORD says:

" 'In the pride of your heart
you say, "I am a god;
I sit on the throne[a] of a god
in the heart of the seas."
But you are a man and not a god,
though you think you are as wise as a god.[b]
3 Are you wiser than Daniel?[a][c]
Is no secret hidden from you?
4 By your wisdom and understanding
you have gained wealth for yourself
and amassed gold and silver
in your treasuries.[d]
5 By your great skill in trading
you have increased your wealth,

a 3 Or *Danel*; the Hebrew spelling may suggest a person other than the prophet Daniel.

27:30 [g] 2Sa 1:2 [h] Jer 6:26 [i] Rev 18:18-19
27:31 [j] Isa 16:9 [k] Isa 22:12; Eze 7:18
27:32 [l] Eze 26:17
27:33 [m] ver 12; Eze 28:4-5
27:34 [n] Zec 9:4
27:35 [o] Eze 26:15
27:36 [p] Jer 18:16; 19:8; 49:17; 50:13; Zep 2:15 [q] Ps 37:10, 36; Eze 26:21
28:2 [a] Isa 14:13 [b] Ps 9:20; 82:6-7; Isa 31:3; 2Th 2:4
28:3 [c] Da 1:20; 5:11-12
28:4 [d] Zec 9:3

28:1ff Previously Ezekiel had prophesied against the city of Tyre (chapters 26; 27). Here he focused his prophecy on Tyre's leader. The chief sin of Tyre's king was pride – believing himself to be a god. But Ezekiel also may have made a broader spiritual application, speaking about the spiritual king of Tyre, Satan, whom the people were really following (see the note on 28:12–19).

28:2, 3 Daniel, an important official in Nebuchadnezzar's kingdom (14:14), was already renowned for his wisdom. Daniel proclaimed that all his wisdom came from God (Daniel 2:20–23). By contrast, the king of Tyre thought that he himself *was* a god. When truly wise people get closer to God, they recognise their need to depend on him for guidance.

28:5
[e]Job 31:25; Ps 52:7; 62:10; Hos 12:8; 13:6

and because of your wealth
your heart has grown proud.[e]

6" 'Therefore this is what the Sovereign LORD says:

" 'Because you think you are wise,
as wise as a god,

28:7
[f]Eze 30:11; 31:12; 32:12; Hab 1:6

7I am going to bring foreigners against you,
the most ruthless of nations;[f]
they will draw their swords against your beauty and wisdom
and pierce your shining splendour.
8They will bring you down to the pit,[g]
and you will die a violent death
in the heart of the seas.[h]

28:8
[g]Eze 32:30
[h]Eze 27:27

9Will you then say, "I am a god,"
in the presence of those who kill you?
You will be but a man, not a god,
in the hands of those who slay you.
10You will die the death of the uncircumcised[i]
at the hands of foreigners.

28:10
[i]Eze 31:18; 32:19, 24

I have spoken, declares the Sovereign LORD.' "

11The word of the LORD came to me: 12"Son of man, take up a lament[j] concerning
the king of Tyre and say to him: 'This is what the Sovereign LORD says:

" 'You were the model of perfection,
full of wisdom and perfect in beauty.[k]

28:12
[j]Eze 19:1
[k]Eze 27:2-4

13You were in Eden,[l]
the garden of God;[m]
every precious stone adorned you:
ruby, topaz and emerald,
chrysolite, onyx and jasper,
sapphire,[b] turquoise[n] and beryl.[c]

28:13
[l]Ge 2:8
[m]Eze 31:8-9
[n]Eze 27:16

Your settings and mountings[d] were made of gold;
on the day you were created they were prepared.
14You were anointed[o] as a guardian cherub,[p]
for so I ordained you.
You were on the holy mount of God;
you walked among the fiery stones.

28:14
[o]Ex 30:26; 40:9
[p]Ex 25:17-20

15You were blameless in your ways
from the day you were created
till wickedness was found in you.
16Through your widespread trade
you were filled with violence,[q]
and you sinned.

28:16
[q]Hab 2:17
[r]Ge 3:24

So I drove you in disgrace from the mount of God,
and I expelled you, O guardian cherub,[r]
from among the fiery stones.
17Your heart became proud[s]
on account of your beauty,

28:17
[s]Eze 31:10

b *13* Or *lapis lazuli* c *13* The precise identification of some of these precious stones is uncertain.
d *13* The meaning of the Hebrew for this phrase is uncertain.

28:6–10 The enemy army ("foreigners") that attacked Tyre was the Babylonian army under Nebuchadnezzar. This attack occurred in 573/572 B.C.

28:12–19 Some of the phrases in this passage describing the human king of Tyre may describe Satan. Great care must be taken to interpret these verses with discernment. It is clear that, at times, Ezekiel describes this king in terms that could not apply to a mere man. This king had been in the Garden of Eden (28:13), had been "anointed as a guardian cherub" (28:14), and had access to the holy mountain of God (28:14), but was driven from there (28:16, 17). Ezekiel, therefore, may have been condemning not only the king of Tyre, but Satan, who had motivated the king to sin.

and you corrupted your wisdom
because of your splendour.
So I threw you to the earth;
I made a spectacle of you before kings.
18 By your many sins and dishonest trade
you have desecrated your sanctuaries.
So I made a fire come out from you,
and it consumed you,
and I reduced you to ashes[t] on the ground
in the sight of all who were watching.
19 All the nations who knew you
are appalled at you;
you have come to a horrible end
and will be no more.[u]' "

A Prophecy Against Sidon

20 The word of the LORD came to me: 21 "Son of man, set your face against[v] Sidon;[w]
prophesy against her 22 and say: 'This is what the Sovereign LORD says:

" 'I am against you, O Sidon,
and I will gain glory[x] within you.
They will know that I am the LORD,
when I inflict punishment[y] on her
and show myself holy within her.
23 I will send a plague upon her
and make blood flow in her streets.
The slain will fall within her,
with the sword against her on every side.
Then they will know that I am the LORD.[z]

24 " 'No longer will the people of Israel have malicious neighbours who are painful
briers and sharp thorns.[a] Then they will know that I am the Sovereign LORD.
25 " 'This is what the Sovereign LORD says: When I gather[b] the people of Israel from
the nations where they have been scattered,[c] I will show myself holy[d] among them
in the sight of the nations. Then they will live in their own land, which I gave to my
servant Jacob.[e] 26 They will live there in safety[f] and will build houses and plant
vineyards; they will live in safety when I inflict punishment on all their neighbours
who maligned them. Then they will know that I am the LORD their God.[g]' "

A Prophecy Against Egypt

29 In the tenth year, in the tenth month on the twelfth day, the word of the LORD
came to me:[a] 2 "Son of man, set your face against Pharaoh king of Egypt[b]
and prophesy against him and against all Egypt.[c] 3 Speak to him and say: 'This is
what the Sovereign LORD says:

28:18 [t]Mal 4:3
28:19 [u]Jer 51:64; Eze 26:21; 27:36
28:21 [v]Eze 6:2 [w]Ge 10:15; Jer 25:22
28:22 [x]Eze 39:13 [y]Eze 30:19
28:23 [z]Eze 38:22
28:24 [a]Nu 33:55; Jos 23:13; Eze 2:6
28:25 [b]Ps 106:47; Jer 32:37 [c]Isa 11:12 [d]Eze 20:41 [e]Jer 23:8; Eze 11:17; 34:27; 37:25
28:26 [f]Jer 23:6 [g]Isa 65:21; Jer 32:15; Eze 38:8; Am 9:14-15
29:1 [a]ver 17; Eze 26:1
29:2 [b]Jer 25:19 [c]Isa 19:1-17; Jer 46:2; Eze 30:1-26; 31:1-18; 32:1-32

28:20, 21 Sidon was another famous seaport, located about 25 miles north of Tyre. God charged this city with contempt for his people. Sidon's economy was bound to Tyre's, so when Tyre fell to Nebuchadnezzar, Sidon was doomed to follow.

28:24–26 This promise that God's people will live in complete safety has yet to be fulfilled. While many were allowed to return from exile under Zerubbabel, Ezra, and Nehemiah, and although the political nation is restored today, the inhabitants do not yet live in complete safety (28:26). Therefore, this promise will have its ultimate fulfilment when Christ sets up his eternal kingdom. Then all people who have been faithful to God will dwell together in harmony and complete safety.

29:1ff There are seven prophecies in chapters 29 – 32, all dealing with judgment on Egypt. This is probably the first prophecy that was given by Ezekiel in 587 B.C. Hezekiah, Jehoiakim, and Zedekiah (kings of Judah) had all sought help from Egypt despite God's warnings.

There are three key reasons for this prophecy: (1) Egypt was an ancient enemy of the Jews, having once enslaved them for 400 years; (2) Egypt worshipped many gods; (3) Egypt's wealth and power made it seem like a good ally. Egypt offered to help Judah only because of the benefits it hoped to receive from such an alliance. When the Egyptians didn't get what they hoped for, they bailed out of their agreement without regard to any promises they had made.

29:2ff Egypt had great artistic treasures, a flourishing civilisation, and world-renowned military power. Unfortunately, it was also evil, egotistical, idolatrous, and treated slaves cruelly. For those sins God condemned Egypt. At the battle of Carchemish in 605 B.C.,

" 'I am against you, Pharaoh[d] king of Egypt,
you great monster[e] lying among your streams.
You say, "The Nile is mine;
I made it for myself."
4But I will put hooks[f] in your jaws
and make the fish of your streams stick to your scales.
I will pull you out from among your streams,
with all the fish sticking to your scales.[g]
5I will leave you in the desert,
you and all the fish of your streams.
You will fall on the open field
and not be gathered or picked up.
I will give you as food
to the beasts of the earth and the birds of the air.[h]

6Then all who live in Egypt will know that I am the LORD.

" 'You have been a staff of reed[i] for the house of Israel. 7When they grasped you
with their hands, you splintered[j] and you tore open their shoulders; when they leaned
on you, you broke and their backs were wrenched.[a][k]
8" 'Therefore this is what the Sovereign LORD says: I will bring a sword against
you and kill your men and their animals.[l] 9Egypt will become a desolate wasteland.
Then they will know that I am the LORD.
" 'Because you said, "The Nile is mine; I made it,[m]" 10therefore I am against you
and against your streams, and I will make the land of Egypt a ruin and a desolate waste
from Migdol to Aswan,[n] as far as the border of Cush.[b] 11No foot of man or animal
will pass through it; no-one will live there for forty years.[o] 12I will make the land
of Egypt desolate among devastated lands, and her cities will lie desolate for forty
years among ruined cities. And I will disperse the Egyptians among the nations and
scatter them through the countries.[p]
13" 'Yet this is what the Sovereign LORD says: At the end of forty years I will gather
the Egyptians from the nations where they were scattered. 14I will bring them back
from captivity and return them to Upper Egypt,[c][q] the land of their ancestry. There
they will be a lowly[r] kingdom. 15It will be the lowliest of kingdoms and will never
again exalt itself above the other nations.[s] I will make it so weak that it will never
again rule over the nations. 16Egypt will no longer be a source of confidence[t] for
the people of Israel but will be a reminder of their sin in turning to her for help. Then
they will know that I am the Sovereign LORD.[u]' "

17In the twenty-seventh year, in the first month on the first day, the word of the

[a] *7* Syriac (see also Septuagint and Vulgate); Hebrew *and you caused their backs to stand* [b] *10* That is, the upper Nile region [c] *14* Hebrew *to Pathros*

29:3 [d]Jer 44:30 [e]Ps 74:13; Isa 27:1; Eze 32:2
29:4 [f]2Ki 19:28 [g]Eze 38:4
29:5 [h]Jer 7:33; 34:20; Eze 32:4-6; 39:4
29:6 [i]2Ki 18:21; Isa 36:6
29:7 [j]Isa 36:6 [k]Eze 17:15-17
29:8 [l]Eze 14:17; 32:11-13
29:9 [m]Eze 30:7-8, 13-19
29:10 [n]Eze 30:6
29:11 [o]Eze 32:13
29:12 [p]Jer 46:19; Eze 30:7, 23, 26
29:14 [q]Eze 30:14 [r]Eze 17:14
29:15 [s]Zec 10:11
29:16 [t]Isa 36:4, 6 [u]Isa 30:2; Hos 8:13

Babylon crushed Egypt along with Assyria, its rivals for the position of world ruler.

29:9, 10 The Nile was Egypt's pride and joy, a life-giving river cutting through the middle of the desert. Rather than thanking God, however, Egypt declared, "The Nile is mine; I made it". We do the same when we say "This house is mine; I built it", or "I have brought myself to the place where I am today", or "I have built this church, business, or reputation, from the ground up". These statements reveal our pride. Sometimes we take for granted what God has given us, thinking we have made it ourselves. Of course, we have put forth a lot of hard effort, but God supplied the resources, gave us the abilities, and provided us with the opportunities to make it happen. Instead of claiming our own greatness, as the Egyptians did, we should proclaim God's greatness and give him the credit. (Migdol is in the north of Egypt, and Aswan in the south. Thus, this meant all of Egypt.)

29:13–16 This 40-year period of desolation in Egypt is hard to pinpoint. Nebuchadnezzar attacked Egypt around 572 B.C. and carried many people off to Babylon, while others fled for safety to surrounding nations. Approximately 33 years later, Cyrus, king of the Persian empire, conquered Babylon and allowed the nations which Babylon had conquered to return to their homelands. Adding a possible seven-year regrouping and travel period, this could then make up that 40-year time period. Since that time, Egypt has never returned to its previous dominance as a world power. Upper Egypt was the region south of the Nile delta.

29:17, 18 This prophecy was given in 571 B.C. and is actually the latest prophecy in Ezekiel. Nebuchadnezzar had finally conquered Tyre after a long and costly 15-year siege (586–571 B.C.). He had not counted on such an expense, so he went south and conquered Egypt to make up for all he had lost in taking Tyre. Ezekiel placed this prophecy here to describe *who* would bring this punishment to Egypt. God was using Nebuchadnezzar, an evil man, as an instrument of his judgment on Tyre, Judah, and Egypt—evil nations themselves. When Babylon didn't recognise God's favour, he judged it too.

LORD came to me:[v] 18“Son of man, Nebuchadnezzar[w] king of Babylon drove his
army in a hard campaign against Tyre; every head was rubbed bare[x] and every
shoulder made raw. Yet he and his army got no reward from the campaign he led
against Tyre. 19Therefore this is what the Sovereign LORD says: I am going to give
Egypt to Nebuchadnezzar king of Babylon, and he will carry off its wealth. He will
loot and plunder the land as pay for his army.[y] 20I have given him Egypt as a reward
for his efforts because he and his army did it for me, declares the Sovereign LORD.[z]
21“On that day I will make a horn[d][a] grow for the house of Israel, and I will open
your mouth[b] among them. Then they will know that I am the LORD.[c]”

A Lament for Egypt

30 The word of the LORD came to me: 2“Son of man, prophesy and say: ‘This is
what the Sovereign LORD says:

“ ‘Wail[a] and say,
“Alas for that day!”
3For the day is near,[b]
the day of the LORD[c] is near —
a day of clouds,
a time of doom for the nations.
4A sword will come against Egypt,
and anguish will come upon Cush.[a]
When the slain fall in Egypt,
her wealth will be carried away
and her foundations torn down.[d]

5Cush and Put,[e] Lydia and all Arabia, Libya[b] and the people[f] of the covenant land
will fall by the sword along with Egypt.
6“ ‘This is what the LORD says:

“ ‘The allies of Egypt will fall
and her proud strength will fail.
From Migdol to Aswan[g]
they will fall by the sword within her,
declares the Sovereign LORD.
7“ ‘They will be desolate
among desolate lands,
and their cities will lie
among ruined cities.[h]
8Then they will know that I am the LORD,
when I set fire to Egypt
and all her helpers are crushed.

9“ ‘On that day messengers will go out from me in ships to frighten Cush[i] out of
her complacency. Anguish[j] will take hold of them on the day of Egypt’s doom, for
it is sure to come.[k]

10“ ‘This is what the Sovereign LORD says:

“ ‘I will put an end to the hordes of Egypt
by the hand of Nebuchadnezzar king of Babylon.[l]
11He and his army — the most ruthless of nations[m] —
will be brought in to destroy the land.
They will draw their swords against Egypt
and fill the land with the slain.
12I will dry up[n] the streams of the Nile[o]

d *21* *Horn* here symbolises strength. **a** *4* That is, the upper Nile region; also in verses 5 and 9 **b** *5* Hebrew *Cub*

29:17 [v]Eze 24:1
29:18 [w]Jer 27:6; Eze 26:7-8 [x]Jer 48:37
29:19 [y]Jer 43:10-13; Eze 30:4, 10, 24-25
29:20 [z]Isa 10:6-7; 45:1; Jer 25:9
29:21 [a]Ps 132:17 [b]Eze 33:22 [c]Eze 24:27
30:2 [a]Isa 13:6
30:3 [b]Eze 7:7; Joel 2:1, 11; Ob 1:15 [c]ver 18; Eze 7:12, 19
30:4 [d]Eze 29:19
30:5 [e]Eze 27:10 [f]Jer 25:20
30:6 [g]Eze 29:10
30:7 [h]Eze 29:12
30:9 [i]Isa 18:1-2 [j]Isa 23:5 [k]Eze 32:9-10
30:10 [l]Eze 29:19
30:11 [m]Eze 28:7
30:12 [n]Isa 19:6 [o]Eze 29:9

30:1–19 This is a lament for Egypt and its allies. Because of the Egyptians’ pride and idolatry, they would be brought down.

30:12 Egypt’s pharaohs claimed that they had made the Nile — the river on which the entire nation depended. If God dried up the

30:13
[p]Jer 43:12
[q]Isa 19:13
[r]Zec 10:11

30:14
[s]Eze 29:14
[t]Ps 78:12, 43
[u]Jer 46:25

30:17
[v]Ge 41:45

30:18
[w]Lev 26:13
[x]ver 3

30:20
[y]Eze 26:1; 29:17; 31:1

30:21
[z]Jer 48:25
[a]Jer 30:13; 46:11

30:22
[b]Jer 46:25
[c]Ps 37:17

30:23
[d]Eze 29:12

30:24
[e]Zec 10:6, 12
[f]Eze 21:14; Zep 2:12

and sell the land to evil men;
by the hand of foreigners
I will lay waste the land and everything in it.

I the LORD have spoken.

13" 'This is what the Sovereign LORD says:

" 'I will destroy the idols[p]
and put an end to the images in Memphis.[c][q]
No longer will there be a prince in Egypt,[r]
and I will spread fear throughout the land.
14I will lay[s] waste Upper Egypt,[d]
set fire to Zoan[t]
and inflict punishment on Thebes.[e][u]
15I will pour out my wrath on Pelusium,[f]
the stronghold of Egypt,
and cut off the hordes of Thebes.
16I will set fire to Egypt;
Pelusium will writhe in agony.
Thebes will be taken by storm;
Memphis will be in constant distress.
17The young men of Heliopolis[g][v] and Bubastis[h]
will fall by the sword,
and the cities themselves will go into captivity.
18Dark will be the day at Tahpanhes
when I break the yoke of Egypt;[w]
there her proud strength will come to an end.
She will be covered with clouds,
and her villages will go into captivity.[x]
19So I will inflict punishment on Egypt,
and they will know that I am the LORD.' "

20In the eleventh year, in the first month on the seventh day, the word of the LORD
came to me:[y] 21"Son of man, I have broken the arm[z] of Pharaoh king of Egypt. It
has not been bound up for healing[a] or put in a splint so as to become strong enough
to hold a sword. 22Therefore this is what the Sovereign LORD says: I am against
Pharaoh king of Egypt.[b] I will break both his arms, the good arm as well as the broken
one, and make the sword fall from his hand.[c] 23I will disperse the Egyptians among
the nations and scatter them through the countries.[d] 24I will strengthen[e] the arms
of the king of Babylon and put my sword[f] in his hand, but I will break the arms of
Pharaoh, and he will groan before him like a mortally wounded man. 25I will
strengthen the arms of the king of Babylon, but the arms of Pharaoh will fall limp.
Then they will know that I am the LORD, when I put my sword into the hand of the
king of Babylon and he brandishes it against Egypt. 26I will disperse the Egyptians

[c] *13* Hebrew *Noph*; also in verse 16 [d] *14* Hebrew *waste Pathros* [e] *14* Hebrew *No*; also in verses 15 and 16
[f] *15* Hebrew *Sin*; also in verse 16 [g] *17* Hebrew *Awen* (or *On*) [h] *17* Hebrew *Pi Beseth*

Nile, the nation would be doomed.

30:13–19 The list of cities to be destroyed shows the breadth of the destruction; the drying up of the Nile (30:12) shows its depth. Egypt would be completely incapacitated. This was a clear message to Judah not to trust Egypt for help against the Babylonians.

30:20, 21 This message came in 587 B.C. while Jerusalem was under attack from Babylon. Judah had rebelled against Babylon and made an alliance with Egypt in spite of God's warnings (Jeremiah 2:36, 37). Pharaoh Hophra made a half-hearted attempt to help Jerusalem, but when Nebuchadnezzar's army turned on him, he fled back to Egypt (Jeremiah 37:5–7). This defeat is what Ezekiel meant when he said that God had broken the arm of Pharaoh.

30:21–26 This prophecy was given to Ezekiel in 587 B.C. God destroyed Egypt's military superiority and gave it to Babylon. God allows nations to rise to power to accomplish a particular purpose, often beyond our immediate understanding. When you read about armies and wars, don't despair. Remember that God is sovereign and in charge of everything, even military might. As well as praying for your military and government leaders, pray that God's greater purposes would be carried out and that his will would be done "on earth as it is in heaven" (see Matthew 6:10).

among the nations and scatter them through the countries. Then they will know that I am the LORD.[g]"

30:26 [g]Eze 29:12

A Cedar in Lebanon

31 In the eleventh year,[a] in the third month on the first day, the word of the LORD
came to me:[b] 2"Son of man, say to Pharaoh king of Egypt and to his hordes:

" 'Who can be compared with you in majesty?
3Consider Assyria, once a cedar in Lebanon,
with beautiful branches overshadowing the forest;
it towered on high,
its top above the thick foliage.[c]
4The waters nourished it,
deep springs made it grow tall;
their streams flowed
all around its base
and sent their channels
to all the trees of the field.
5So it towered higher
than all the trees of the field;
its boughs increased
and its branches grew long,
spreading because of abundant waters.[d]
6All the birds of the air
nested in its boughs,
all the beasts of the field
gave birth under its branches;
all the great nations
lived in its shade.[e]
7It was majestic in beauty,
with its spreading boughs,
for its roots went down
to abundant waters.
8The cedars[f] in the garden of God
could not rival it,
nor could the pine trees
equal its boughs,
nor could the plane trees
compare with its branches—
no tree in the garden of God
could match its beauty.[g]
9I made it beautiful
with abundant branches,
the envy of all the trees of Eden[h]
in the garden of God.[i]

10" 'Therefore this is what the Sovereign LORD says: Because it towered on high,
lifting its top above the thick foliage, and because it was proud[j] of its height, 11I
handed it over to the ruler of the nations, for him to deal with according to its
wickedness. I cast it aside,[k] 12and the most ruthless of foreign nations[l] cut it down

31:1 [a]Jer 52:5 [b]Eze 30:20
31:3 [c]Isa 10:34
31:5 [d]Eze 17:5
31:6 [e]Eze 17:23; Mt 13:32
31:8 [f]Ps 80:10 [g]Ge 2:8-9
31:9 [h]Ge 2:8 [i]Ge 13:10; Eze 28:13
31:10 [j]Isa 14:13-14; Eze 28:17
31:11 [k]Da 5:20
31:12 [l]Eze 28:7

31:1ff This message was given in 587 B.C. Ezekiel compared Egypt to Assyria, calling Assyria a great cedar tree. The Egyptians were to look at the fall of the mighty nation of Assyria (whose demise they had seen) as an example of what would happen to them. Just like Assyria, Egypt took pride in its strength and beauty; this would be its downfall. She would crash like a mighty tree and be sent to the place of the dead. There is no permanence apart from God, even for a great society with magnificent culture and military power.

31:9 "All the trees of Eden" may refer to all the other nations of the world who were jealous of Assyria's power and grandeur.

31:11 The "ruler of the nations" may be Nebuchadnezzar (see Daniel 2:37, 38).

and left it. Its boughs fell on the mountains and in all the valleys;[m] its branches lay
broken in all the ravines of the land. All the nations of the earth came out from under
its shade and left it.[n] 13All the birds of the air settled on the fallen tree, and all
the beasts of the field were among its branches.[o] 14Therefore no other trees by the
waters are ever to tower proudly on high, lifting their tops above the thick foliage.
No other trees so well-watered are ever to reach such a height; they are all destined
for death,[p] for the earth below, among mortal men, with those who go down to
the pit.[q]

15" 'This is what the Sovereign LORD says: On the day it was brought down to the
grave[a] I covered the deep springs with mourning for it; I held back its streams, and
its abundant waters were restrained. Because of it I clothed Lebanon with gloom, and
all the trees of the field withered away. 16I made the nations tremble[r] at the sound
of its fall when I brought it down to the grave with those who go down to the pit.
Then all the trees[s] of Eden, the choicest and best of Lebanon, all the trees that were
well-watered, were consoled[t] in the earth below.[u] 17Those who lived in its shade,
its allies among the nations, had also gone down to the grave with it, joining those
killed by the sword.[v]

18" 'Which of the trees of Eden can be compared with you in splendour and majesty?
Yet you, too, will be brought down with the trees of Eden to the earth below; you
will lie among the uncircumcised,[w] with those killed by the sword.

" 'This is Pharaoh and all his hordes, declares the Sovereign LORD.' "

A Lament for Pharaoh

32 In the twelfth year, in the twelfth month on the first day, the word of the LORD
came to me:[a] 2"Son of man, take up a lament[b] concerning Pharaoh king of
Egypt and say to him:

" 'You are like a lion[c] among the nations;
you are like a monster in the seas
thrashing about in your streams,
churning the water with your feet
and muddying the streams.[d]

3" 'This is what the Sovereign LORD says:

" 'With a great throng of people
I will cast my net over you,
and they will haul you up in my net.[e]
4I will throw you on the land
and hurl you on the open field.
I will let all the birds of the air settle on you
and all the beasts of the earth gorge themselves on you.[f]
5I will spread your flesh on the mountains
and fill the valleys[g] with your remains.
6I will drench the land with your flowing blood[h]
all the way to the mountains,
and the ravines will be filled with your flesh.

a *15* Hebrew *Sheol*; also in verses 16 and 17

31:12 [m]Eze 32:5; 35:8 [n]Eze 32:11-12; Da 4:14
31:13 [o]Isa 18:6; Eze 29:5; 32:4
31:14 [p]Ps 82:7 [q]Ps 63:9; Eze 26:20; 32:24
31:16 [r]Eze 26:15 [s]Isa 14:8 [t]Eze 14:22; 32:31 [u]Isa 14:15; Eze 32:18
31:17 [v]Ps 9:17
31:18 [w]Jer 9:26; Eze 32:19, 21
32:1 [a]Eze 31:1; 33:21
32:2 [b]Eze 19:1; 27:2 [c]Eze 19:3, 6; Na 2:11-13 [d]Eze 29:3; 34:18
32:3 [e]Eze 12:13
32:4 [f]Isa 18:6; Eze 31:12-13
32:5 [g]Eze 31:12
32:6 [h]Isa 34:3

32:1ff This prophecy was given in 585 B.C., two months after the news of Jerusalem's fall had reached the exiles in Babylon. Ezekiel prophesied numerous judgments upon many wicked nations. These judgments served a positive purpose: they showed that evil forces are continually being overcome and that one day God will overthrow all evil, making the world the perfect place he intended. They also serve as warnings that God alone is sovereign. Even the mightiest rulers, like Pharaoh, will fall before God. All are accountable to him.

32:2 Although Pharaoh thought of himself as a strong lion, in God's eyes he was nothing but a crocodile ("monster") muddying the water. God's judgment would reduce Pharaoh to his true size. Anyone who defies God will face his judgment.

7When I snuff you out, I will cover the heavens
and darken their stars;
I will cover the sun with a cloud,
and the moon will not give its light.[i]
8All the shining lights in the heavens
I will darken over you;
I will bring darkness over your land,
declares the Sovereign LORD.

9I will trouble the hearts of many peoples
when I bring about your destruction among the nations,
among[a] lands you have not known.
10I will cause many peoples to be appalled at you,
and their kings will shudder with horror because of you
when I brandish my sword before them.
On the day[j] of your downfall
each of them will tremble
every moment for his life.[k]

11" 'For this is what the Sovereign LORD says:

" 'The sword of the king of Babylon[l]
will come against you.
12I will cause your hordes to fall
by the swords of mighty men—
the most ruthless of all nations.[m]
They will shatter the pride of Egypt,
and all her hordes will be overthrown.[n]
13I will destroy all her cattle
from beside abundant waters
no longer to be stirred by the foot of man
or muddied by the hoofs of cattle.[o]
14Then I will let her waters settle
and make her streams flow like oil,
declares the Sovereign LORD.
15When I make Egypt desolate
and strip the land of everything in it,
when I strike down all who live there,
then they will know that I am the LORD.[p]'

16"This is the lament[q] they will chant for her. The daughters of the nations will chant it; for Egypt and all her hordes they will chant it, declares the Sovereign LORD."

a 9 Hebrew; Septuagint *bring you into captivity among the nations, / to*

32:7 [i]Isa 13:10; 34:4; Eze 30:3; Joel 2:2, 31; 3:15; Mt 24:29; Rev 8:12
32:10 [j]Jer 46:10 [k]Eze 26:16; 27:35
32:11 [l]Jer 46:26
32:12 [m]Eze 28:7 [n]Eze 31:11-12
32:13 [o]Eze 29:8, 11
32:15 [p]Ex 7:5; 14:4, 18; Ps 107:33-34; Eze 6:7
32:16 [q]2Sa 1:17; 2Ch 35:25; Eze 26:17

32:18 The Hebrews believed in an afterlife for all people, good and bad. Ezekiel's message assumed that the evil nations had already been sent there (to the "pit") and that Egypt would share their fate. The words here are more poetic than doctrinal (see Job 24:19; Psalm 16:10; Isaiah 38:10, and the note on Matthew 25:46). The Egyptians had a preoccupation with the afterlife (the pyramids were built solely to ensure the pharaohs' comfort in the next life). This message should remind us that any attempt to control our afterlife and ignore God is foolish. God alone controls the future and life after death.

32:21–32 In these verses, Ezekiel conducts a guided tour of the grave, the region of the afterlife. In the grave, all of God's enemies are condemned in judgment; many of them experience the fate they so quickly imposed on others. Though Babylon is not mentioned, Ezekiel's readers would have concluded that if all the other nations would be judged for their rebellion against God, Babylon would be judged as well. These words would comfort the captives.

17 In the twelfth year, on the fifteenth day of the month, the word of the LORD came
to me:[r] 18 "Son of man, wail for the hordes of Egypt and consign[s] to the earth below
both her and the daughters of mighty nations, with those who go down to the pit.[t]
19 Say to them, 'Are you more favoured than others? Go down and be laid among the
uncircumcised.'[u] 20 They will fall among those killed by the sword. The sword is
drawn; let her be dragged[v] off with all her hordes. 21 From within the grave[b][w] the
mighty leaders will say of Egypt and her allies, 'They have come down and they lie
with the uncircumcised, with those killed by the sword.'

22 "Assyria is there with her whole army; she is surrounded by the graves of all her
slain, all who have fallen by the sword. 23 Their graves are in the depths of the pit[x]
and her army lies around her grave. All who had spread terror in the land of the living
are slain, fallen by the sword.

24 "Elam[y] is there, with all her hordes around her grave. All of them are slain, fallen
by the sword.[z] All who had spread terror in the land of the living[a] went down
uncircumcised to the earth below. They bear their shame with those who go down to
the pit.[b] 25 A bed is made for her among the slain, with all her hordes around her
grave. All of them are uncircumcised, killed by the sword. Because their terror had
spread in the land of the living, they bear their shame with those who go down to the
pit; they are laid among the slain.

26 "Meshech and Tubal[c] are there, with all their hordes around their graves. All
of them are uncircumcised, killed by the sword because they spread their terror in the
land of the living. 27 Do they not lie with the other uncircumcised warriors who have
fallen, who went down to the grave with their weapons of war, whose swords were
placed under their heads? The punishment for their sins rested on their bones, though
the terror of these warriors had stalked through the land of the living.

28 "You too, O Pharaoh, will be broken and will lie among the uncircumcised, with
those killed by the sword.

29 "Edom[d] is there, her kings and all her princes; despite their power, they are laid
with those killed by the sword. They lie with the uncircumcised, with those who go
down to the pit.[e]

30 "All the princes of the north[f] and all the Sidonians[g] are there; they went down
with the slain in disgrace despite the terror caused by their power. They lie uncircumcised with those killed by the sword and bear their shame with those who go down
to the pit.

31 "Pharaoh — he and all his army — will see them and he will be consoled[h] for all
his hordes that were killed by the sword, declares the Sovereign LORD. 32 Although
I had him spread terror in the land of the living, Pharaoh and all his hordes will be
laid among the uncircumcised, with those killed by the sword, declares the Sovereign
LORD."

[b] *21* Hebrew *Sheol*; also in verse 27

32:17 [r] ver 1
32:18 [s] Jer 1:10 [t] Eze 31:14, 16; Mic 1:8
32:19 [u] ver 29-30; Eze 28:10; 31:18
32:20 [v] Ps 28:3
32:21 [w] Isa 14:9
32:23 [x] Isa 14:15
32:24 [y] Ge 10:22 [z] Jer 49:37 [a] Job 28:13 [b] Eze 26:20
32:26 [c] Ge 10:2; Eze 27:13
32:29 [d] Isa 34:5-15; Jer 49:7; Eze 35:15; Ob 1:1 [e] Eze 25:12-14
32:30 [f] Jer 25:26; Eze 38:6; 39:2 [g] Jer 25:22; Eze 28:21
32:31 [h] Eze 14:22; 31:16

32:24–26 Elam was a nation of fierce warriors from the region east of Assyria. They were conquered by Nebuchadnezzar (Jeremiah 49:34–39) and eventually rebuilt themselves and became part of Persia. Meshech and Tubal were territories located in the eastern region of Asia Minor, now eastern and central Turkey. In chapters 38 and 39 they are described as allies of Gog, the chief prince of an alliance. They are included with the evil nations that will be judged for fighting against God's people.

32:30 The princes of the north were probably the princes of the Phoenician city-states.

32:32 After reading Ezekiel's prophecies against all these foreign nations, we may wonder if he was blindly loyal to his own nation. But Ezekiel spoke only when God gave him a message (3:27). Besides, God's prophets pronounced judgment on God's sinful people just as much as on God's enemies. But if Babylon was God's enemy, why isn't it mentioned in Ezekiel's judgments? Perhaps because (1) God wanted to foster a spirit of co-operation between the exiles and Babylon in order to preserve his people; (2) God was still using Babylon to refine his own people; (3) God wanted to use Daniel, a powerful official in Babylon, to draw the Babylonians to him.

C. MESSAGES OF HOPE (33:1 — 48:35)

This section begins a new direction in Ezekiel's prophecies. Ezekiel is reminded that he is the nation's watchman. Before Jerusalem's fall, he told the people of their punishment and dispersion. Now he is to proclaim the hope of restoration, but even this message does not improve the people's response. They listen to him with curiosity and then live as they please. Today we have the good news of forgiveness, but how easy it is to ignore the message and continue to live sinful lives.

1. Restoring the people of God

Ezekiel a Watchman

33 The word of the LORD came to me: 2"Son of man, speak to your countrymen
and say to them: 'When I bring the sword[a] against a land, and the people of
the land choose one of their men and make him their watchman,[b] 3and he sees the
sword coming against the land and blows the trumpet[c] to warn the people, 4then if
anyone hears the trumpet but does not take warning[d] and the sword comes and takes
his life, his blood will be on his own head.[e] 5Since he heard the sound of the trumpet
but did not take warning, his blood will be on his own head. If he had taken warning,
he would have saved himself. 6But if the watchman sees the sword coming and does
not blow the trumpet to warn the people and the sword comes and takes the life of
one of them, that man will be taken away because of his sin, but I will hold the
watchman accountable for his blood.'[f]
7"Son of man, I have made you a watchman for the house of Israel; so hear the
word I speak and give them warning from me.[g] 8When I say to the wicked, 'O wicked
man, you will surely die,[h]' and you do not speak out to dissuade him from his ways,
that wicked man will die for[a] his sin, and I will hold you accountable for his blood.[i]
9But if you do warn the wicked man to turn from his ways and he does not do so,
he will die for his sin, but you will be saved yourself.[j]
10"Son of man, say to the house of Israel, 'This is what you are saying: "Our
offences and sins weigh us down, and we are wasting away[k] because of[b] them. How
then can we live?"' 11Say to them, 'As surely as I live, declares the Sovereign LORD,
I take no pleasure in the death of the wicked, but rather that they turn from their ways
and live.[m] Turn! Turn from your evil ways! Why will you die, O house of Israel?'[n]
12"Therefore, son of man, say to your countrymen, 'The righteousness of the
righteous man will not save him when he disobeys, and the wickedness of the wicked
man will not cause him to fall when he turns from it. The righteous man, if he sins,
will not be allowed to live because of his former righteousness.'[o] 13If I tell the
righteous man that he will surely live, but then he trusts in his righteousness and does
evil, none of the righteous things he has done will be remembered; he will die for the
evil he has done.[p] 14And if I say to the wicked man, 'You will surely die,' but he
then turns away from his sin and does what is just[q] and right — 15if he gives back
what he took in pledge for a loan, returns what he has stolen,[r] follows the decrees
that give life, and does no evil, he will surely live; he will not die.[s] 16None of the

a 8 Or *in*; also in verse 9 b 10 Or *away in*

33:2 [a] Jer 12:12 [b] Eze 3:11
33:3 [c] Hos 8:1
33:4 [d] 2Ch 25:16 [e] Jer 6:17; Eze 18:13; Zec 1:4; Ac 18:6
33:6 [f] Eze 3:18
33:7 [g] Jer 26:2; Eze 3:17
33:8 [h] ver 14 [i] Eze 18:4
33:9 [j] Eze 3:17-19
33:10 [k] Eze 24:23 [l] Lev 26:39; Eze 4:17
33:11 [m] Eze 18:32; 2Pe 3:9 [n] Eze 18:23
33:12 [o] 2Ch 7:14; Eze 3:20
33:13 [p] Eze 18:24; Heb 10:38; 2Pe 2:20-21
33:14 [q] Eze 18:27
33:15 [r] Ex 22:1-4; Lev 6:2-5 [s] Eze 20:11; Lk 19:8

33:1ff This chapter sets forth a new direction for Ezekiel's prophecies. Up to this point, Ezekiel has pronounced judgment upon Judah (chapters 1 — 24) and the surrounding evil nations (chapters 25 — 32) for their sins. After Jerusalem fell, he turned from messages of doom and judgment to messages of comfort, hope, and future restoration for God's people (chapters 33 — 48). God previously appointed Ezekiel to be a watchman warning the nation of coming judgment (see 3:17–21). Here God appointed him to be a watchman again, but this time to preach a message of hope. There are still sections full of warnings (33:23 — 34:10; 36:1–7), but these are part of the larger picture of hope. God will remember to bless those who are faithful to him. We must pay attention to both aspects of Ezekiel's message: warning and promise. Those who persist in rebelling against God should take warning. Those faithful to God should find encouragement and hope.

33:10–12 The exiles were discouraged by their past sins. This is an important turning point in this book — elsewhere in Ezekiel the people had refused to face their sins. Here, they felt heavy guilt for rebelling against God for so many years. Therefore, God assured them of forgiveness if they repented. God *wants* everyone to turn to him. He looks at what we are and will become, not what we have been. God gives you the opportunity to turn to him, if you will take it. Sincerely follow God, and ask him to forgive you when you fail.

33:13 Past good deeds will not save a person who decides to turn to a life of sin. Some people think they have done enough good deeds to overshadow the sins they don't want to give up. But it's useless to try to be good in some areas so you can be deliberately bad in others. God wants wholehearted love and obedience.

33:15 While good deeds will not save us, our salvation must lead to righteous actions (see Ephesians 2:10; James 2:14–17). This includes restitution for past sins (as exemplified in the story of Zacchaeus, see Luke 19:1–10). God expects us to make restitution, whenever necessary, for the wrongs we have committed.

sins he has committed will be remembered against him. He has done what is just and
right; he will surely live.[t]
17"Yet your countrymen say, 'The way of the Lord is not just.' But it is their way
that is not just. 18If a righteous man turns from his righteousness and does evil, he
will die for it.[u] 19And if a wicked man turns away from his wickedness and does what
is just and right, he will live by doing so. 20Yet, O house of Israel, you say, 'The
way of the Lord is not just.' But I will judge each of you according to his own ways."

Jerusalem's Fall Explained

21In the twelfth year of our exile, in the tenth month on the fifth day, a man who
had escaped[v] from Jerusalem came to me and said, "The city has fallen![w]" 22Now
the evening before the man arrived, the hand of the LORD was upon me,[x] and he
opened my mouth[y] before the man came to me in the morning. So my mouth was
opened and I was no longer silent.[z]
23Then the word of the LORD came to me: 24"Son of man, the people living in those
ruins[a] in the land of Israel are saying, 'Abraham was only one man, yet he possessed
the land. But we are many; surely the land has been given to us as our possession.'[b]
25Therefore say to them, 'This is what the Sovereign LORD says: Since you eat meat
with the blood[c] still in it and look to your idols and shed blood, should you then
possess the land?[d] 26You rely on your sword, you do detestable things, and each of
you defiles his neighbour's wife.[e] Should you then possess the land?'
27"Say this to them: 'This is what the Sovereign LORD says: As surely as I live,
those who are left in the ruins will fall by the sword, those out in the country I will
give to the wild animals to be devoured, and those in strongholds and caves will die
of a plague.[f] 28I will make the land a desolate waste, and her proud strength will
come to an end, and the mountains of Israel will become desolate so that no-one will
cross them. 29Then they will know that I am the LORD, when I have made the land
a desolate waste because of all the detestable things they have done.'
30"As for you, son of man, your countrymen are talking together about you by the
walls and at the doors of the houses, saying to each other, 'Come and hear the message
that has come from the LORD.' 31My people come to you, as they usually do, and sit
before[g] you to listen to your words, but they do not put them into practice. With their
mouths they express devotion, but their hearts are greedy for unjust gain.[h] 32Indeed,
to them you are nothing more than one who sings love songs with a beautiful voice
and plays an instrument well, for they hear your words but do not put them into
practice.[i]
33"When all this comes true — and it surely will — then they will know that a prophet
has been among them.[j]"

33:16 [t]Isa 43:25; Eze 18:22
33:18 [u]Eze 3:20; Eze 18:26
33:21 [v]Eze 24:26 [w]2Ki 25:4, 10; Jer 39:1-2; Eze 32:1
33:22 [x]Eze 1:3 [y]Lk 1:64 [z]Eze 3:26-27; 24:27
33:24 [a]Eze 36:4 [b]Isa 51:2; Jer 40:7; Eze 11:15; Ac 7:5
33:25 [c]Ge 9:4; Dt 12:16 [d]Jer 7:9-10; Eze 22:6, 27
33:26 [e]Eze 22:11
33:27 [f]1Sa 13:6; Isa 2:19; Jer 42:22; Eze 39:4
33:31 [g]Eze 8:1 [h]Ps 78:36-37; Isa 29:13; Eze 22:27; Mt 13:22; 1Jn 3:18
33:32 [i]Mk 6:20
33:33 [j]1Sa 3:20; Jer 28:9; Eze 2:5

33:21, 22 Near the beginning of his ministry, Ezekiel was unable to speak except to give specific messages from God (3:26, 27). After Ezekiel's prophecies came true and the false prophets were exposed, Ezekiel was again able to talk freely. No longer needing to prove himself, he was free to offer God's message of restoration and hope.

33:30–32 The people refused to act upon Ezekiel's message. When people mock your witness for Christ or fail to act upon your advice, don't give up. You are not witnessing for them alone, but out of faithfulness to God. You cannot make them accept your message; you can only be faithful in delivering it.

33:31 In your heart, do you really love God? These people gave the appearance of following God, but they loved their money more. Many today also give the outward impression of being religious while remaining inwardly greedy. Jesus warned that we cannot love God and Money at the same time (Matthew 6:24). It's easy to say "I surrender all" when we don't have much. It's when we start gaining some money that it becomes difficult to avoid loving it.

33:32 The people were coming to listen to Ezekiel in order to be entertained. They weren't interested in hearing a message from the Lord and then putting it into practice. Many people see church as entertainment. They enjoy the music, the people, and the activities, but they don't take the messages to heart. They don't seek to be challenged or to serve. Have you reduced church services to the level of entertainment, or does your worship truly have an impact on your life? Listen to God's words and then obey — apply his words and put them into practice in your life.

Shepherds and Sheep

34 The word of the LORD came to me: 2"Son of man, prophesy against the
shepherds of Israel; prophesy and say to them: 'This is what the Sovereign
LORD says: Woe to the shepherds of Israel who only take care of themselves! Should
not shepherds take care of the flock?[a] 3You eat the curds, clothe yourselves with the
wool and slaughter the choice animals, but you do not take care of the flock.[b] 4You
have not strengthened the weak or healed the sick or bound up the injured. You have
not brought back the strays or searched for the lost. You have ruled them harshly and
brutally.[c] 5So they were scattered because there was no shepherd,[d] and when they
were scattered they became food for all the wild animals.[e] 6My sheep wandered over
all the mountains and on every high hill. They were scattered over the whole earth,
and no-one searched or looked for them.[f]
7" 'Therefore, you shepherds, hear the word of the LORD: 8As surely as I live,
declares the Sovereign LORD, because my flock lacks a shepherd and so has been
plundered and has become food for all the wild animals, and because my shepherds
did not search for my flock but cared for themselves rather than for my flock,
9therefore, O shepherds, hear the word of the LORD: 10This is what the Sovereign
LORD says: I am against[g] the shepherds and will hold them accountable for my flock.
I will remove them from tending the flock so that the shepherds can no longer feed
themselves. I will rescue[h] my flock from their mouths, and it will no longer be food
for them.[i]
11" 'For this is what the Sovereign LORD says: I myself will search for my sheep
and look after them. 12As a shepherd[j] looks after his scattered flock when he is with
them, so will I look after my sheep. I will rescue them from all the places where they
were scattered on a day of clouds and darkness.[k] 13I will bring them out from the
nations and gather them from the countries, and I will bring them into their own land.
I will pasture them on the mountains of Israel, in the ravines and in all the settlements
in the land.[l] 14I will tend them in a good pasture, and the mountain heights of Israel[m]
will be their grazing land. There they will lie down in good grazing land, and there
they will feed in a rich pasture[n] on the mountains of Israel.[o] 15I myself will tend
my sheep and make them lie down, declares the Sovereign LORD.[p] 16I will search
for the lost and bring back the strays. I will bind up the injured and strengthen the
weak,[q] but the sleek and the strong I will destroy. I will shepherd the flock with
justice.[r]
17" 'As for you, my flock, this is what the Sovereign LORD says: I will judge
between one sheep and another, and between rams and goats.[s] 18Is it not enough for
you to feed on the good pasture? Must you also trample the rest of your pasture with
your feet? Is it not enough for you to drink clear water? Must you also muddy the
rest with your feet? 19Must my flock feed on what you have trampled and drink what
you have muddied with your feet?
20" 'Therefore this is what the Sovereign LORD says to them: See, I myself will
judge between the fat sheep and the lean sheep. 21Because you shove with flank and

34:2 [a]Ps 78:70-72; Isa 40:11; Jer 3:15; 23:1; Mic 3:11; Jn 10:11; 21:15-17
34:3 [b]Isa 56:11; Eze 22:27; Zec 11:16
34:4 [c]Zec 11:15-17
34:5 [d]Nu 27:17 [e]ver 28; Isa 56:9
34:6 [f]Ps 142:4; 1Pe 2:25
34:10 [g]Jer 21:13 [h]Ps 72:14 [i]1Sa 2:29-30; Zec 10:3
34:12 [j]Isa 40:11; Jer 31:10; Lk 19:10 [k]Eze 30:3
34:13 [l]Jer 23:3
34:14 [m]Eze 20:40 [n]Ps 23:2 [o]Eze 36:29-30
34:15 [p]Ps 23:1-2
34:16 [q]Mic 4:6 [r]Isa 10:16; Lk 5:32
34:17 [s]Mt 25:32-33

34:1ff Ezekiel called the exiles "Israel", referring to all Jews in captivity from both the northern and southern kingdoms. Ezekiel criticised Israel's leaders for taking care of themselves rather than taking care of their people. He outlined their sins (34:1–6) and pronounced judgment upon them (34:7–10). Then he promised that a true shepherd (the Messiah) would come who would take care of the people as the other leaders were supposed to do (34:11–31). This beautiful message portrays the fate of the present shepherds, the work of the new shepherd, and the future of the sheep.

34:4–6 God would judge the religious leaders because they were selfishly caught up in their own concerns and were neglecting their service to others. Spiritual leaders must be careful not to pursue self-development at the expense of broken, scattered people. When we give too much attention to our own needs and ideas, we may push God aside and abandon those who depend on us.

34:9, 10 Those shepherds who failed their flock would be removed from office and held responsible for what happened to the people they were supposed to lead. Christian leaders must heed this warning and care for their flock, or total failure and judgment will be the result (see 1 Corinthians 9:24–27). True leadership focuses on helping others, not just on getting ahead.

34:11–16 God promises to take over as shepherd of his scattered flock. When our leaders fail us, we must not despair but remember that God is in control and that he promises to return and care for his flock. Thus we know that we can turn to God for help. He is still in control and can transform any tragic situation to produce good for his kingdom (see Genesis 50:20; Romans 8:28).

34:18–20 A bad shepherd is not only selfish but destructive. A minister who muddies the waters for others by raising unnecessary doubts, teaching false ideas, and acting sinfully is destroying his flock's spiritual nourishment.

shoulder, butting all the weak sheep with your horns[t] until you have driven them
away, 22 I will save my flock, and they will no longer be plundered. I will judge
between one sheep and another.[u] 23 I will place over them one shepherd, my servant
David, and he will tend[v] them; he will tend them and be their shepherd. 24 I the LORD
will be their God,[w] and my servant David will be prince among them. I the LORD
have spoken.[x]
25 " 'I will make a covenant of peace with them and rid the land of wild beasts[y]
so that they may live in the desert and sleep in the forests in safety.[z] 26 I will bless[a]
them and the places surrounding my hill.[a] I will send down showers in season;[b] there
will be showers of blessing.[c] 27 The trees of the field will yield their fruit and the
ground will yield its crops; the people will be secure in their land. They will know
that I am the LORD, when I break the bars of their yoke[d] and rescue them from the
hands of those who enslaved them.[e] 28 They will no longer be plundered by the
nations, nor will wild animals devour them. They will live in safety, and no-one will
make them afraid.[f] 29 I will provide for them a land renowned[g] for its crops, and
they will no longer be victims of famine[h] in the land or bear the scorn[i] of the
nations.[j] 30 Then they will know that I, the LORD their God, am with them and that
they, the house of Israel, are my people, declares the Sovereign LORD.[k] 31 You my
sheep, the sheep of my pasture,[l] are people, and I am your God, declares the
Sovereign LORD.' "

A Prophecy Against Edom

35 The word of the LORD came to me: 2 "Son of man, set your face against Mount
Seir; prophesy against it 3 and say: 'This is what the Sovereign LORD says: I
am against you, Mount Seir, and I will stretch out my hand[a] against you and make
you a desolate waste.[b] 4 I will turn your towns into ruins and you will be desolate.
Then you will know that I am the LORD.[c]
5 " 'Because you harboured an ancient hostility and delivered the Israelites over to
the sword at the time of their calamity, the time their punishment reached its climax,[d]
6 therefore as surely as I live, declares the Sovereign LORD, I will give you over to
bloodshed and it will pursue you.[e] Since you did not hate bloodshed, bloodshed will
pursue you. 7 I will make Mount Seir a desolate waste and cut off from it all who come
and go. 8 I will fill your mountains with the slain; those killed by the sword will fall
on your hills and in your valleys and in all your ravines.[f] 9 I will make you desolate
for ever; your towns will not be inhabited. Then you will know that I am the LORD.[g]
10 " 'Because you have said, "These two nations and countries will be ours and we

a 26 Or *I will make them and the places surrounding my hill a blessing*

34:21 [t]Dt 33:17
34:22 [u]Ps 72:12-14; Jer 23:2-3
34:23 [v]Isa 40:11
34:24 [w]Eze 36:28 [x]Jer 30:9
34:25 [y]Lev 26:6 [z]Isa 11:6-9; Hos 2:18
34:26 [a]Ge 12:2 [b]Ps 68:9 [c]Dt 11:13-15; Isa 44:3
34:27 [d]Lev 26:13 [e]Jer 30:8
34:28 [f]Jer 30:10; Eze 39:26
34:29 [g]Isa 4:2 [h]Eze 36:29 [i]Eze 36:6 [j]Eze 36:15
34:30 [k]Eze 14:11; 37:27
34:31 [l]Ps 100:3; Jer 23:1
35:3 [a]Jer 6:12 [b]Eze 25:12-14
35:4 [c]ver 9
35:5 [d]Ps 137:7; Eze 21:29
35:6 [e]Isa 63:2-6
35:8 [f]Eze 31:12
35:9 [g]Jer 49:13

BAD SHEPHERDS VERSUS GOOD SHEPHERDS

Bad Shepherds	*Good Shepherds*
Take care of themselves	Take care of their flock
Worry about their own health	Strengthen the weak and sick, search for the lost
Rule harshly and brutally	Rule lovingly and gently
Abandon and scatter the sheep	Gather and protect the sheep
Keep the best for themselves	Give their best to the sheep

34:23–25 In contrast to the present evil shepherds (leaders) of God's people (34:1–6), God will send a perfect shepherd, the Messiah ("my servant David"), who will take care of every need his people have and set up a kingdom of perfect peace and justice (see Psalm 23; Jeremiah 23:5, 6; John 10:11; Hebrews 13:20, 21; Revelation 21). "Peace" here means more than the absence of conflict. It is contentment, fulfilment, and security.

35:1ff Ezekiel gave another prophecy against Edom (also called Seir); his first prophecy against Edom is found in 25:12–14. In this prophecy, Ezekiel is probably using Edom to represent *all* the nations opposed to God's people. Chapter 36 says that Israel will be restored, while this chapter says that Edom (God's enemies) will be made "a desolate waste".

35:2 Edom offered to help destroy Jerusalem and rejoiced when the city fell. Edom's long-standing hostility against God's people resulted in God's judgment.

35:6–8 Ezekiel prophesied not only against the people of Edom, but also against their mountains and land. Their home territory was Mount Seir. Mountains, symbols of strength and power, represented the pride of these people who thought they could get away with evil. Edom's desire for revenge turned against them. Edom received the punishment they were so hasty to give out. God has a way of turning our treatment of others into a boomerang. So we must be careful in our judgment of others (Matthew 7:1, 2).

will take possession[h] of them," even though I the LORD was there, 11therefore as
surely as I live, declares the Sovereign LORD, I will treat you in accordance with the
anger[i] and jealousy you showed in your hatred of them and I will make myself known
among them when I judge you.[j] 12Then you will know that I the LORD have heard
all the contemptible things you have said against the mountains of Israel. You said,
"They have been laid waste and have been given over to us to devour.[k]" 13You
boasted against me and spoke against me without restraint, and I heard it.[l] 14This
is what the Sovereign LORD says: While the whole earth rejoices, I will make you
desolate.[m] 15Because you rejoiced[n] when the inheritance of the house of Israel
became desolate, that is how I will treat you. You will be desolate, O Mount Seir,[o]
you and all of Edom.[p] Then they will know that I am the LORD.' "

A Prophecy to the Mountains of Israel

36 "Son of man, prophesy to the mountains of Israel and say, 'O mountains of
Israel, hear the word of the LORD. 2This is what the Sovereign LORD says: The
enemy said of you, "Aha![a] The ancient heights[b] have become our possession.[c]" '
3Therefore prophesy and say, 'This is what the Sovereign LORD says: Because they
ravaged and hounded you from every side so that you became the possession of the
rest of the nations and the object of people's malicious talk and slander,[d] 4therefore,
O mountains of Israel, hear the word of the Sovereign LORD: This is what the
Sovereign LORD says to the mountains and hills, to the ravines and valleys,[e] to the
desolate ruins and the deserted towns that have been plundered and ridiculed by the
rest of the nations around you[f]— 5this is what the Sovereign LORD says: In my
burning zeal I have spoken against the rest of the nations, and against Edom, for with
glee and with malice in their hearts they made my land their own possession so that
they might plunder its pasture-land.'[g] 6Therefore prophesy concerning the land of
Israel and say to the mountains and hills, to the ravines and valleys: 'This is what the
Sovereign LORD says: I speak in my jealous wrath because you have suffered the scorn
of the nations.[h] 7Therefore this is what the Sovereign LORD says: I swear with uplifted
hand that the nations around you will also suffer scorn.

8" 'But you, O mountains of Israel, will produce branches and fruit[i] for my people
Israel, for they will soon come home. 9I am concerned for you and will look on you
with favour; you will be ploughed and sown, 10and I will multiply the number of
people upon you, even the whole house of Israel. The towns will be inhabited and
the ruins rebuilt.[j] 11I will increase the number of men and animals upon you, and
they will be fruitful and become numerous. I will settle people on you as in the past[k]
and will make you prosper more than before.[l] Then you will know that I am the
LORD. 12I will cause people, my people Israel, to walk upon you. They will possess
you, and you will be their inheritance;[m] you will never again deprive them of their
children.

13" 'This is what the Sovereign LORD says: Because people say to you, "You devour
men[n] and deprive your nation of its children," 14therefore you will no longer devour
men or make your nation childless, declares the Sovereign LORD. 15No longer will
I make you hear the taunts of the nations, and no longer will you suffer the scorn of
the peoples or cause your nation to fall, declares the Sovereign LORD.[o]' "

16Again the word of the LORD came to me: 17"Son of man, when the people of Israel
were living in their own land, they defiled it by their conduct and their actions. Their
conduct was like a woman's monthly uncleanness in my sight.[p] 18So I poured out[q]
my wrath on them because they had shed blood in the land and because they had
defiled it with their idols. 19I dispersed them among the nations, and they were
scattered[r] through the countries; I judged them according to their conduct and their

35:10 [h]Ps 83:12; Eze 36:2, 5
35:11 [i]Eze 25:14 [j]Ps 9:16; Mt 7:2
35:12 [k]Jer 50:7
35:13 [l]Da 11:36
35:14 [m]Jer 51:48
35:15 [n]Ob 1:12 [o]ver 3 [p]Isa 34:5-6, 11; Jer 50:11-13; La 4:21
36:2 [a]Eze 25:3 [b]Dt 32:13 [c]Eze 35:10
36:3 [d]Ps 44:13-14
36:4 [e]Eze 6:3 [f]Dt 11:11; Ps 79:4; Eze 34:28
36:5 [g]Jer 50:11; Eze 25:12-14; 35:10, 15
36:6 [h]Ps 123:3-4; Eze 34:29
36:8 [i]Isa 27:6
36:10 [j]ver 33; Isa 49:17-23
36:11 [k]Mic 7:14 [l]Jer 31:28; Eze 16:55
36:12 [m]Eze 47:14, 22
36:13 [n]Nu 13:32
36:15 [o]Ps 89:50-51; Eze 34:29
36:17 [p]Jer 2:7
36:18 [q]2Ch 34:21
36:19 [r]Dt 28:64

36:1ff In this prophecy, Ezekiel said that Israel would be restored as a nation and would return to its own land. The mountains were symbolic of Israel's strength (see the note on 35:6–8). To the exiles in Babylon, this seemed impossible. This message again emphasises God's sovereignty and trustworthiness. He would first judge the nations used to punish Israel (36:1–7) and then restore his people (36:8–15).

36:2 "The ancient heights" refers to the promised land—the land of Israel. Israel's enemies challenged not only their boundaries but also God's promises to Israel.

actions.[s] 20And wherever they went among the nations they profaned[t] my holy
name, for it was said of them, 'These are the LORD's people, and yet they had to leave
his land.'[u] 21I had concern for my holy name, which the house of Israel profaned
among the nations where they had gone.[v]

22"Therefore say to the house of Israel, 'This is what the Sovereign LORD says: It
is not for your sake, O house of Israel, that I am going to do these things, but for the
sake of my holy name, which you have profaned[w] among the nations where you have
gone.[x] 23I will show the holiness of my great name, which has been profaned among
the nations, the name you have profaned among them. Then the nations will know
that I am the LORD, declares the Sovereign LORD, when I show myself holy[y] through
you before their eyes.[z]

24" 'For I will take you out of the nations; I will gather you from all the countries
and bring you back into your own land.[a] 25I will sprinkle[b] clean water on you, and
you will be clean; I will cleanse[c] you from all your impurities and from all your
idols.[d] 26I will give you a new heart[e] and put a new spirit in you; I will remove from
you your heart of stone and give you a heart of flesh.[f] 27And I will put my Spirit[g]
in you and move you to follow my decrees and be careful to keep my laws. 28You
will live in the land I gave your forefathers; you will be my people,[h] and I will be
your God.[i] 29I will save you from all your uncleanness. I will call for the corn and
make it plentiful and will not bring famine[j] upon you. 30I will increase the fruit of
the trees and the crops of the field, so that you will no longer suffer disgrace among
the nations because of famine.[k] 31Then you will remember your evil ways and wicked
deeds, and you will loathe yourselves for your sins and detestable practices.[l] 32I want
you to know that I am not doing this for your sake, declares the Sovereign LORD. Be
ashamed and disgraced for your conduct, O house of Israel![m]

33" 'This is what the Sovereign LORD says: On the day I cleanse you from all your
sins, I will resettle your towns, and the ruins will be rebuilt. 34The desolate land will
be cultivated instead of lying desolate in the sight of all who pass through it. 35They
will say, "This land that was laid waste has become like the garden of Eden;[n] the
cities that were lying in ruins, desolate and destroyed, are now fortified and inhabited.[o]" 36Then the nations around you that remain will know that I the LORD have
rebuilt what was destroyed and have replanted what was desolate. I the LORD have
spoken, and I will do it.'[p]

37"This is what the Sovereign LORD says: Once again I will yield to the plea of the

36:19 [s]Eze 39:24
36:20 [t]Ro 2:24 [u]Isa 52:5; Jer 33:24; Eze 12:16
36:21 [v]Ps 74:18; Isa 48:9
36:22 [w]Ro 2:24* [x]Ps 106:8
36:23 [y]Eze 20:41 [z]Ps 126:2; Isa 5:16
36:24 [a]Eze 34:13; 37:21
36:25 [b]Heb 9:13; 10:22 [c]Ps 51:2, 7 [d]Zec 13:2
36:26 [e]Jer 24:7 [f]Ps 51:10; Eze 11:19
36:27 [g]Eze 37:14
36:28 [h]Jer 30:22 [i]Eze 14:11; 37:14, 27
36:29 [j]Eze 34:29
36:30 [k]Lev 26:4-5; Eze 34:27; Hos 2:21-22
36:31 [l]Eze 6:9; 20:43
36:32 [m]Dt 9:5
36:35 [n]Joel 2:3 [o]Isa 51:3
36:36 [p]Eze 17:22; 22:14; 37:14; 39:27-28

OLD AND NEW COVENANTS

	Old Covenant	*New Covenant*
	Placed upon stone	Placed upon people's hearts
	Based on the law	Based on desire to love and serve God
	Must be taught	Known by all
	Legal relationship with God	Personal relationship with God

36:21–23 Why did God want to protect his holy name—his reputation—among the nations of the world? God was concerned about the salvation not only of his people, but also of the whole world. To allow his people to remain in sin and be permanently destroyed by their enemies would lead other nations to conclude that their pagan gods were more powerful than Israel's God (Isaiah 48:11). Thus, to protect his holy name, God would return a remnant of his people to their land. God will not share his glory with false gods—he alone is the one true God. The people had the responsibility to represent God properly to the rest of the world. Believers today have that same responsibility. How do you represent God to the world?

36:25–27 God promised to restore Israel not only physically, but spiritually. To accomplish this, God would give them a new heart for following him and put his Spirit within them (see 11:19, 20; Psalm 51:7–11) to transform them and empower them to do his will. Again the new covenant was promised (16:61–63; 34:23–25), ultimately to be fulfilled in Christ. No matter how impure your life is right now, God offers you a fresh start. You can have your sins washed away, receive a new heart for God, and have his Spirit within you—if you accept God's promise. Why try to patch up your old life when you can have a new one?

36:32 God said his people should be ashamed of their sins. The people had become so callous that they had lost all sensitivity to sin. First they had to "remember" (36:31) their sins, then despise them, and finally repent of them (see James 4:8, 9). As we examine our lives, we may find that we too have lost our sensitivity to certain sins. But if we measure ourselves against God's standards of right living, we will be ashamed. To regain sensitivity we must recognise our sin for what it is, feel sorry for displeasing God, and ask his forgiveness. The Holy Spirit will guide us, making us responsive and receptive to God's truth (John 14:26; 16:8, 13).

36:37, 38 God said that if the people asked, he would come to their aid. We cannot expect his mercy, however, until we have sought new hearts from him (36:26). We can be thankful that his invitation is open to all.

house of Israel and do this for them: I will make their people as numerous as sheep,
38as numerous as the flocks for offerings[q] at Jerusalem during her appointed feasts.
So will the ruined cities be filled with flocks of people. Then they will know that I
am the LORD."

The Valley of Dry Bones

37 The hand of the LORD was upon me,[a] and he brought me out by the Spirit[b]
of the LORD and set me in the middle of a valley;[c] it was full of bones.[d] 2He
led me to and fro among them, and I saw a great many bones on the floor of the valley,
bones that were very dry. 3He asked me, "Son of man, can these bones live?"
I said, "O Sovereign LORD, you alone know.[e]"
4Then he said to me, "Prophesy to these bones and say to them, 'Dry bones, hear
the word of the LORD![f] 5This is what the Sovereign LORD says to these bones: I will
make breath[a] enter you, and you will come to life.[g] 6I will attach tendons to you
and make flesh come upon you and cover you with skin; I will put breath in you, and
you will come to life. Then you will know that I am the LORD.[h]' "
7So I prophesied as I was commanded. And as I was prophesying, there was a noise,
a rattling sound, and the bones came together, bone to bone. 8I looked, and tendons
and flesh appeared on them and skin covered them, but there was no breath in them.
9Then he said to me, "Prophesy to the breath;[i] prophesy, son of man, and say to
it, 'This is what the Sovereign LORD says: Come from the four winds, O breath, and
breathe into these slain, that they may live.' " 10So I prophesied as he commanded
me, and breath entered them; they came to life and stood up on their feet—a vast
army.[j]
11Then he said to me: "Son of man, these bones are the whole house of Israel. They
say, 'Our bones are dried up and our hope is gone; we are cut off.'[k] 12Therefore
prophesy and say to them: 'This is what the Sovereign LORD says: O my people, I
am going to open your graves and bring you up from them; I will bring you back to
the land of Israel.[l] 13Then you, my people, will know that I am the LORD, when I
open your graves and bring you up from them. 14I will put my Spirit[m] in you and
you will live, and I will settle you in your own land. Then you will know that I the
LORD have spoken, and I have done it, declares the LORD.[n]' "

One Nation Under One King

15The word of the LORD came to me: 16"Son of man, take a stick of wood and write
on it, 'Belonging to Judah and the Israelites[o] associated with him.[p]' Then take
another stick of wood, and write on it, 'Ephraim's stick, belonging to Joseph and all
the house of Israel associated with him.' 17Join them together into one stick so that
they will become one in your hand.[q]
18"When your countrymen ask you, 'Won't you tell us what you mean by this?'[r]
19say to them, 'This is what the Sovereign LORD says: I am going to take the stick
of Joseph—which is in Ephraim's hand—and of the Israelite tribes associated with
him, and join it to Judah's stick, making them a single stick of wood, and they will

[a] 5 The Hebrew for this word can also mean *wind* or *spirit* (see verses 6–14).

36:38 [q] 1Ki 8:63; 2Ch 35:7-9
37:1 [a] Eze 1:3; 8:3 [b] Eze 11:24; Lk 4:1; Ac 8:39 [c] Jer 7:32 [d] Jer 8:2; Eze 40:1
37:3 [e] Dt 32:39; 1Sa 2:6; Isa 26:19
37:4 [f] Jer 22:29
37:5 [g] Ge 2:7; Ps 104:29-30
37:6 [h] Eze 38:23; Joel 2:27; 3:17
37:9 [i] Ps 104:30
37:10 [j] Rev 11:11
37:11 [k] La 3:54
37:12 [l] Dt 32:39; 1Sa 2:6; Isa 26:19; Hos 13:14; Am 9:14-15
37:14 [m] Joel 2:28-29 [n] Eze 36:27-28, 36
37:16 [o] 1Ki 12:20; 2Ch 10:17-19 [p] Nu 17:2-3; 2Ch 15:9
37:17 [q] ver 24; Isa 11:13; Jer 50:4; Hos 1:11
37:18 [r] Eze 24:19

37:1ff This vision illustrates the promise of chapter 36—new life and a nation restored, both physically and spiritually. The dry bones are a picture of the Jews in captivity—scattered and dead. The two sticks (37:15–17) represent the reunion of the entire nation of Israel that had divided into northern and southern kingdoms after Solomon. The scattered exiles of both Israel and Judah would be released from the "graves" of captivity and one day regathered in their homeland, with the Messiah as their leader. This vision has yet to be fulfilled. Ezekiel felt he was speaking to the dead as he preached to the exiles because they rarely responded to his message. But these bones responded! And just as God brought life to the dead bones, he would bring life again to his spiritually dead people.

37:4, 5 The dry bones represented the people's spiritually dead condition. Your church may seem like a heap of dry bones to you, spiritually dead with no hope of vitality. But just as God promised to restore his nation, he can restore any church, no matter how dry or dead it may be. Rather than give up, pray for renewal, for God can restore it to life. The hope and prayer of every church should be that God will put his Spirit into it (37:14). In fact, God is at work calling his people back to himself, bringing new life into dead churches.

37:16 The first stick was for Judah, being the leading tribe in the southern kingdom. The other was for Joseph, because he was the father of Ephraim, the leading tribe in the northern kingdom.

become one in my hand.'[s] 20Hold before their eyes the sticks you have written on
21and say to them, 'This is what the Sovereign LORD says: I will take the Israelites
out of the nations where they have gone. I will gather them from all around and bring
them back into their own land.[t] 22I will make them one nation in the land, on the
mountains of Israel. There will be one king over all of them and they will never again
be two nations or be divided into two kingdoms.[u] 23They will no longer defile[v]
themselves with their idols and vile images or with any of their offences, for I will
save them from all their sinful backsliding,[b] and I will cleanse them. They will be
my people, and I will be their God.[w]
24" 'My servant David[x] will be king over them, and they will all have one
shepherd.[y] They will follow my laws and be careful to keep my decrees.[z] 25They
will live in the land I gave to my servant Jacob, the land where your fathers lived.[a]
They and their children and their children's children will live there for ever,[b] and
David my servant will be their prince for ever.[c] 26I will make a covenant of peace[d]
with them; it will be an everlasting covenant. I will establish them and increase their
numbers,[e] and I will put my sanctuary among them for ever.[f] 27My dwelling-place[g]
will be with them; I will be their God, and they will be my people.[h] 28Then the nations
will know that I the LORD make Israel holy,[i] when my sanctuary is among them for
ever.' "

A Prophecy Against Gog

38 The word of the LORD came to me: 2"Son of man, set your face against Gog,
of the land of Magog,[a] the chief prince of[a] Meshech and Tubal;[b] prophesy
against him 3and say: 'This is what the Sovereign LORD says: I am against you,
O Gog, chief prince of[b] Meshech and Tubal.[c] 4I will turn you around, put hooks[d] in
your jaws and bring you out with your whole army — your horses, your horsemen fully
armed, and a great horde with large and small shields, all of them brandishing their
swords.[e] 5Persia, Cush[c][f] and Put[g] will be with them, all with shields and helmets,
6also Gomer[h] with all its troops, and Beth Togarmah[i] from the far north with all
its troops — the many nations with you.
7" 'Get ready; be prepared,[j] you and all the hordes gathered about you, and take
command of them. 8After many days[k] you will be called to arms. In future years you
will invade a land that has recovered from war, whose people were gathered from
many nations[l] to the mountains of Israel, which had long been desolate. They had
been brought out from the nations, and now all of them live in safety.[m] 9You and
all your troops and the many nations with you will go up, advancing like a storm;[n]
you will be like a cloud[o] covering the land.
10" 'This is what the Sovereign LORD says: On that day thoughts will come into your
mind and you will devise an evil scheme.[p] 11You will say, "I will invade a land of
unwalled villages; I will attack a peaceful and unsuspecting people — all of them living
without walls and without gates and bars.[q] 12I will plunder and loot and turn my hand
against the resettled ruins and the people gathered from the nations, rich in livestock

37:19 [s]Zec 10:6
37:21 [t]Isa 43:5-6; Eze 36:24; 39:27
37:22 [u]Isa 11:13; Jer 3:18; Hos 1:11
37:23 [v]Eze 36:25; 43:7 [w]Eze 11:18; 36:28
37:24 [x]Hos 3:5 [y]Isa 40:11; Eze 34:23 [z]Ps 78:70-71
37:25 [a]Eze 28:25 [b]Am 9:15 [c]Isa 11:1
37:26 [d]Isa 55:3 [e]Jer 30:19 [f]Eze 16:62
37:27 [g]Lev 26:11; Jn 1:14 [h]2Co 6:16*
37:28 [i]Ex 31:13; Eze 20:12
38:2 [a]Ge 10:2 [b]Rev 20:8
38:3 [c]Eze 39:1
38:4 [d]2Ki 19:28 [e]Eze 29:4; Da 11:40
38:5 [f]Ge 10:6 [g]Eze 27:10
38:6 [h]Ge 10:2 [i]Eze 27:14
38:7 [j]Isa 8:9
38:8 [k]Isa 24:22 [l]Isa 11:11 [m]Jer 23:6
38:9 [n]Isa 28:2 [o]Jer 4:13; Joel 2:2
38:10 [p]Ps 36:4; Mic 2:1
38:11 [q]Jer 49:31; Zec 2:4

[b] *23* Many Hebrew manuscripts (see also Septuagint); most Hebrew manuscripts *all their dwelling-places where they sinned* [a] *2* Or *the prince of Rosh,* [b] *3* Or *Gog, prince of Rosh,* [c] *5* That is, the upper Nile region

37:24, 25 The Messiah was often called David because he is David's descendant. David was a good king, but the Messiah would be the perfect King (Revelation 17:14; 19:16; 21:1ff).

37:26, 27 God's promise here goes beyond the physical and geographical restoration of Israel. He promises to breathe new spiritual life into his people so that their hearts and attitudes will be right with him and united with one another. This same process is described throughout God's word as the cleansing and renewing of our hearts by God's Spirit (Titus 3:4–6).

38:1ff In chapter 37, Ezekiel revealed how Israel (God's people) would be restored to their land from many parts of the world. Once Israel became strong, an alliance of nations from the north would attack, led by Gog (see also Revelation 20:8). Their purpose would be to destroy God's people. Gog's allies would come from the mountainous area south-east of the Black Sea and south-west of the Caspian Sea (central Turkey), as well as from the area that is present-day Iran, Ethiopia, Libya, and possibly the Soviet Union. Gog could be a person (he sometimes is identified with Gyges, king of Lydia in 660 B.C.), or Gog could also be a symbol of all the evil in the world. Whether symbolic or literal, Gog represents the combined military might of all the forces opposed to God.

Many say that the battle Ezekiel described will occur at the end of human history, but there are many differences between the events described here and those in Revelation 20. Regardless of when this battle will occur, the message is clear: God will deliver his people — no enemy can stand before his mighty power.

and goods, living at the centre of the land." 13 Sheba[r] and Dedan and the merchants
of Tarshish and all her villages[d] will say to you, "Have you come to plunder? Have
you gathered your hordes to loot, to carry off silver and gold, to take away livestock
and goods and to seize much plunder?[s]" '
14 "Therefore, son of man, prophesy and say to Gog: 'This is what the Sovereign
LORD says: In that day, when my people Israel are living in safety,[t] will you not take
notice of it? 15 You will come from your place in the far north, you and many nations
with you, all of them riding on horses, a great horde, a mighty army.[u] 16 You will
advance against my people Israel like a cloud[v] that covers the land. In days to come,
O Gog, I will bring you against my land, so that the nations may know me when I
show myself holy through you before their eyes.[w]
17 " 'This is what the Sovereign LORD says: Are you not the one I spoke of in former
days by my servants the prophets of Israel? At that time they prophesied for years that
I would bring you against them. 18 This is what will happen in that day: When Gog
attacks the land of Israel, my hot anger will be aroused, declares the Sovereign LORD.
19 In my zeal and fiery wrath I declare that at that time there shall be a great earthquake
in the land of Israel.[x] 20 The fish of the sea, the birds of the air, the beasts of the field,
every creature that moves along the ground, and all the people on the face of the earth
will tremble at my presence. The mountains will be overturned, the cliffs will crumble
and every wall will fall to the ground.[y] 21 I will summon a sword[z] against Gog on
all my mountains, declares the Sovereign LORD. Every man's sword will be against
his brother.[a] 22 I will execute judgment[b] upon him with plague and bloodshed; I will
pour down torrents of rain, hailstones[c] and burning sulphur on him and on his troops
and on the many nations with him. 23 And so I will show my greatness and my holiness,
and I will make myself known in the sight of many nations. Then they will know that
I am the LORD.[d]'

39 "Son of man, prophesy against Gog and say: 'This is what the Sovereign LORD
says: I am against you, O Gog, chief prince of[a] Meshech and Tubal.[a] 2 I will
turn you around and drag you along. I will bring you from the far north and send you
against the mountains of Israel. 3 Then I will strike your bow[b] from your left hand
and make your arrows[c] drop from your right hand. 4 On the mountains of Israel you
will fall, you and all your troops and the nations with you. I will give you as food
to all kinds of carrion birds and to the wild animals.[d] 5 You will fall in the open field,
for I have spoken, declares the Sovereign LORD. 6 I will send fire[e] on Magog and
on those who live in safety in the coastlands,[f] and they will know that I am the
LORD.
7 " 'I will make known my holy name among my people Israel. I will no longer let
my holy name be profaned,[g] and the nations will know that I the LORD am the Holy
One in Israel.[h] 8 It is coming! It will surely take place, declares the Sovereign LORD.
This is the day I have spoken of.
9 " 'Then those who live in the towns of Israel will go out and use the weapons for
fuel and burn them up—the small and large shields, the bows and arrows, the war

d *13* Or *her strong lions* **a** *1* Or *Gog, prince of Rosh,*

38:13 [r]Eze 27:22 [s]Isa 10:6; Jer 15:13
38:14 [t]ver 8; Zec 2:5
38:15 [u]Eze 39:2
38:16 [v]ver 9 [w]Isa 29:23; Eze 39:21
38:19 [x]Ps 18:7; Eze 5:13; Hag 2:6, 21
38:20 [y]Hos 4:3; Na 1:5
38:21 [z]Eze 14:17 [a]1Sa 14:20; 2Ch 20:23; Hag 2:22
38:22 [b]Isa 66:16; Jer 25:31 [c]Ps 18:12; Rev 16:21
38:23 [d]Eze 36:23
39:1 [a]Eze 38:2, 3
39:3 [b]Hos 1:5 [c]Ps 76:3
39:4 [d]ver 17-20; Eze 29:5; 33:27
39:6 [e]Eze 30:8; Am 1:4 [f]Jer 25:22
39:7 [g]Ex 20:7 [h]Isa 12:6; Eze 36:16, 23

38:13 Sheba and Dedan, great trading centres in Arabia, would in effect say to Gog, "Who are you to usurp our position as the world's trade leaders?" Sheba and Dedan would then join this alliance. Tarshish was the leading trade centre in the west; many believe it was in Spain.

38:21 God will directly intervene in the defence of Israel, unleashing severe natural disasters on the invaders from the north. In the end, the stricken pagan nations will turn on themselves in confusion and panic. All those who set themselves against God will be destroyed.

39:1ff The story of the battle continues. The defeat of the evil forces will be final and complete; they will be destroyed by divine intervention. Because of this victory, God's name will be known throughout the world. His glory will be evident, and the nations will understand that he alone is in charge of human history. God will clearly show his love for his people by restoring them to their homeland.

clubs and spears. For seven years they will use them for fuel.[i] 10They will not need
to gather wood from the fields or cut it from the forests, because they will use the
weapons for fuel. And they will plunder those who plundered them and loot those who
looted them, declares the Sovereign LORD.[j]
11" 'On that day I will give Gog a burial place in Israel, in the valley of those who
travel east towards[b] the Sea.[c] It will block the way of travellers, because Gog and
all his hordes will be buried there. So it will be called the Valley of Hamon
Gog.[d][k]
12" 'For seven months the house of Israel will be burying them in order to cleanse
the land.[l] 13All the people of the land will bury them, and the day I am glorified[m]
will be a memorable day for them, declares the Sovereign LORD.
14" 'Men will be regularly employed to cleanse the land. Some will go throughout
the land and, in addition to them, others will bury those that remain on the ground.
At the end of the seven months they will begin their search. 15As they go through the
land and one of them sees a human bone, he will set up a marker beside it until the
gravediggers have buried it in the Valley of Hamon Gog. 16(Also a town called
Hamonah[e] will be there.) And so they will cleanse the land.'
17"Son of man, this is what the Sovereign LORD says: Call out to every kind of bird[n]
and all the wild animals: 'Assemble and come together from all around to the sacrifice
I am preparing for you, the great sacrifice on the mountains of Israel. There you will
eat flesh and drink blood. 18You will eat the flesh of mighty men and drink the blood
of the princes of the earth as if they were rams and lambs, goats and bulls—all of
them fattened animals from Bashan.[o] 19At the sacrifice I am preparing for you, you
will eat fat till you are glutted and drink blood till you are drunk. 20At my table you
will eat your fill of horses and riders, mighty men and soldiers of every kind,' declares
the Sovereign LORD.[p]
21"I will display my glory among the nations, and all the nations will see the
punishment I inflict and the hand I lay upon them.[q] 22From that day forward the house
of Israel will know that I am the LORD their God. 23And the nations will know that
the people of Israel went into exile for their sin, because they were unfaithful to me.
So I hid my face from them and handed them over to their enemies, and they all fell
by the sword.[r] 24I dealt with them according to their uncleanness and their offences,
and I hid my face from them.[s]
25"Therefore this is what the Sovereign LORD says: I will now bring Jacob back from
captivity[f][t] and will have compassion[u] on all the people of Israel, and I will be
zealous for my holy name.[v] 26They will forget their shame and all the unfaithfulness
they showed towards me when they lived in safety[w] in their land with no-one to make
them afraid.[x] 27When I have brought them back from the nations and have gathered
them from the countries of their enemies, I will show myself holy through them in
the sight of many nations.[y] 28Then they will know that I am the LORD their God,
for though I sent them into exile among the nations, I will gather them to their own
land, not leaving any behind. 29I will no longer hide my face from them, for I will
pour out my Spirit[z] on the house of Israel, declares the Sovereign LORD."

[b] *11* Or *of* [c] *11* That is, the Dead Sea [d] *11* *Hamon Gog* means *hordes of Gog.* [e] *16* *Hamonah* means *horde.* [f] *25* Or *now restore the fortunes of Jacob*

39:9 [i]Ps 46:9
39:10 [j]Isa 14:2; 33:1; Hab 2:8
39:11 [k]Eze 38:2
39:12 [l]Dt 21:23
39:13 [m]Eze 28:22
39:17 [n]Rev 19:17
39:18 [o]Ps 22:12; Jer 51:40
39:20 [p]Rev 19:17-18
39:21 [q]Ex 9:16; Isa 37:20; Eze 38:16
39:23 [r]Isa 1:15; 59:2; Jer 22:8-9; 44:23
39:24 [s]Jer 2:17, 19; 4:18; Eze 36:19
39:25 [t]Jer 33:7; Eze 34:13 [u]Jer 30:18 [v]Isa 27:12-13
39:26 [w]1Ki 4:25 [x]Isa 17:2; Eze 34:28; Mic 4:4
39:27 [y]Eze 36:23-24; 37:21; 38:16
39:29 [z]Joel 2:28; Ac 2:17

39:12–16 Two themes are intertwined: God's total victory over his enemies, and the need to cleanse the land to make it holy. After the final battle, teams will be used to give proper burial to the bodies of the dead enemies in order for the land to be cleansed. The land would have been defiled by unburied corpses. Those who would come in contact with the corpses out in the open would become ceremonially unclean (according to Numbers 19:14–16). Yet there will be so many that all kinds of birds will be called in order to help dispose of the corpses (39:17–20). The message for us is an exciting one: with God on our side, we are assured of ultimate victory over his foes because God will fight on our behalf (see also Zephaniah 3:14–17; Romans 8:38, 39).

39:29 Both in this prophecy and in Joel 2:28, 29, God promises to pour out his Spirit on mankind. The early church believed this began to be fulfilled at Pentecost, when God's Holy Spirit came to live in all believers (Acts 2:1–18).

2. Restoring the worship of God

The New Temple Area

40 In the twenty-fifth year of our exile, at the beginning of the year, on the tenth
of the month, in the fourteenth year after the fall of the city[a]—on that very
day the hand of the LORD was upon me[b] and he took me there. 2In visions[c] of God
he took me to the land of Israel and set me on a very high mountain,[d] on whose south
side were some buildings that looked like a city. 3He took me there, and I saw a man
whose appearance was like bronze;[e] he was standing in the gateway with a linen cord
and a measuring rod[f] in his hand. 4The man said to me, "Son of man, look with your
eyes and hear with your ears and pay attention to everything I am going to show you,
for that is why you have been brought here. Tell[g] the house of Israel everything you
see.[h]"

The East Gate to the Outer Court

5I saw a wall completely surrounding the temple area. The length of the measuring
rod in the man's hand was six long cubits, each of which was a cubit**[a]** and a
handbreadth.**[b]** He measured[i] the wall; it was one measuring rod thick and one rod
high.
6Then he went to the gate facing east.[j] He climbed its steps and measured the
threshold of the gate; it was one rod deep.**[c]** 7The alcoves[k] for the guards were one
rod long and one rod wide, and the projecting walls between the alcoves were five
cubits thick. And the threshold of the gate next to the portico facing the temple was
one rod deep.
8Then he measured the portico of the gateway; 9it**[d]** was eight cubits deep and its
jambs were two cubits thick. The portico of the gateway faced the temple.
10Inside the east gate were three alcoves on each side; the three had the same

a *5* The common cubit was about 1 ½ feet (about 0.5 metre). **b** *5* That is, about 3 inches (about 8 centimetres)
c *6* Septuagint; Hebrew *deep, the first threshold, one rod deep* **d** *8, 9* Many Hebrew manuscripts, Septuagint, Vulgate and Syriac; most Hebrew manuscripts *gateway facing the temple; it was one rod deep. 9Then he measured the portico of the gateway; it*

40:1 [a]2Ki 25:7; Jer 39:1-10; 52:4-11; Eze 33:21 [b]Eze 1:3
40:2 [c]Da 7:1, 7 [d]Eze 17:22; Rev 21:10
40:3 [e]Eze 1:7; Da 10:6; Rev 1:15 [f]Eze 47:3; Zec 2:1-2; Rev 11:1; 21:15
40:4 [g]Jer 26:2 [h]Eze 44:5
40:5 [i]Eze 42:20
40:6 [j]Eze 8:16
40:7 [k]ver 36

40:1ff The building of the temple envisioned a time of complete restoration to the exiles, a time when God would return to his people. The temple was built in 520–515 B.C. (see Ezra 5, 6), but fell short of Ezekiel's plan (Haggai 2:3; Zechariah 4:10). This vision of the temple has been interpreted in four main ways: (1) This is the temple Zerubbabel should have built in 520–515 B.C. and is the actual blueprint Ezekiel intended. But due to disobedience (43:2–10), it was never followed. (2) This is a literal temple to be rebuilt during the millennial reign of Christ. (3) This temple is symbolic of the true worship of God by the Christian church right now. (4) This temple is symbolic of the future and eternal reign of God when his presence and blessing fill the earth.

Whether the temple is literal or symbolic, it seems clear that this is a vision of God's final perfect kingdom. This gave hope to the people of Ezekiel's time who had just seen their nation and its temple destroyed with no hope of rebuilding it in the near future. The details given in this vision gave the people even more hope that what Ezekiel saw had come from God and would surely happen in the future.

40:1ff One argument against the view that Ezekiel's temple is a literal building of the future is that sacrifices are mentioned (40:38–43). If the sacrifices were to be reinstituted in the last days, then Christ's final sacrifice would not have been final. The New Testament makes it clear that Christ died once and for all (Romans 6:10; Hebrews 9:12; 10:10, 18). Our sins have been removed; no further sacrifice is needed.

In Ezekiel's day, however, the only kind of worship the people knew was the kind that revolved around the sacrifices and ceremonies described in Exodus through Deuteronomy. Ezekiel had to explain the new order of worship in terms the people would understand. The next nine chapters tell how the temple is the focal point of everything, showing that the ideal relationship with God is when all of life centres on him.

40:1ff Ezekiel explained God's dwelling place in words and images the people could understand. God wanted them to see the great splendour he had planned for those who lived faithfully. This kind of temple was never built, but it was a vision intended to typify God's perfect plan for his people—the centrality of worship, the presence of the Lord, the blessings flowing from it, and the orderliness of worship and worship duties. Don't let the details obscure the point of this vision—one day all those who have been faithful to God will enjoy eternal life with him. Let the majesty of this vision lift you and teach you about the God you worship and serve.

40:1—43:27 This vision came to Ezekiel in 573 B.C. Chapters 40—43 give the temple's measurements and then describe how it would be filled with God's glory. Because Ezekiel was a priest, he would have been familiar with the furnishings and ceremonies of Solomon's temple. As in Revelation 11:1, 2, the command to "measure" defines the areas God has marked out for special use. As you read all these details, remember that God is sovereign over all our worship and over the timetable for restoring the faithful to himself.

40:3, 4 Who was this man? He was obviously not a human being, so he may have been the angel in 9:1–11 or one like him. Some say he may have been Christ himself because he speaks as God had been speaking to Ezekiel, calling him "Son of man".

40:5 The long cubit was about 21 inches (53 cm), compared with the ordinary cubit of about 18 inches (46 cm).

measurements, and the faces of the projecting walls on each side had the same measurements. 11 Then he measured the width of the entrance to the gateway; it was ten cubits and its length was thirteen cubits. 12 In front of each alcove was a wall one cubit high, and the alcoves were six cubits square. 13 Then he measured the gateway from the top of the rear wall of one alcove to the top of the opposite one; the distance was twenty-five cubits from one parapet opening to the opposite one. 14 He measured along the faces of the projecting walls all around the inside of the gateway—sixty cubits. The measurement was up to the portico[e] facing the courtyard.[f] [l] 15 The distance from the entrance of the gateway to the far end of its portico was fifty cubits. 16 The alcoves and the projecting walls inside the gateway were surmounted by narrow parapet openings all round, as was the portico; the openings all round faced inward. The faces of the projecting walls were decorated with palm trees.[m]

The Outer Court

17 Then he brought me into the outer court.[n] There I saw some rooms and a pavement that had been constructed all round the court; there were thirty rooms[o] along the pavement.[p] 18 It abutted the sides of the gateways and was as wide as they were long; this was the lower pavement. 19 Then he measured the distance from the inside of the lower gateway to the outside of the inner court;[q] it was a hundred cubits[r] on the east side as well as on the north.

The North Gate

20 Then he measured the length and width of the gate facing north, leading into the outer court. 21 Its alcoves[s]—three on each side—its projecting walls and its portico had the same measurements as those of the first gateway. It was fifty cubits long and twenty-five cubits wide. 22 Its openings, its portico[t] and its palm tree decorations had the same measurements as those of the gate facing east. Seven steps led up to it, with its portico opposite them. 23 There was a gate to the inner court facing the north gate, just as there was on the east. He measured from one gate to the opposite one; it was a hundred cubits.[u]

The South Gate

24 Then he led me to the south side and I saw a gate facing south. He measured its jambs and its portico, and they had the same measurements as the others. 25 The gateway and its portico had narrow openings all round, like the openings of the others. It was fifty cubits long and twenty-five cubits wide.[v] 26 Seven steps led up to it, with its portico opposite them; it had palm tree decorations on the faces of the projecting walls on each side.[w] 27 The inner court[x] also had a gate facing south, and he measured from this gate to the outer gate on the south side; it was a hundred cubits.

Gates to the Inner Court

28 Then he brought me into the inner court through the south gate, and he measured the south gate; it had the same measurements[y] as the others. 29 Its alcoves, its projecting walls and its portico had the same measurements as the others. The gateway and its portico had openings all round. It was fifty cubits long and twenty-five cubits wide. 30 (The porticoes[z] of the gateways around the inner court were twenty-five cubits wide and five cubits deep.) 31 Its portico[a] faced the outer court; palm trees decorated its jambs, and eight steps led up to it.

32 Then he brought me to the inner court on the east side, and he measured the gateway; it had the same measurements as the others. 33 Its alcoves, its projecting walls and its portico had the same measurements as the others. The gateway and its portico had openings all round. It was fifty cubits long and twenty-five cubits wide. 34 Its portico[b] faced the outer court; palm trees decorated the jambs on either side, and eight steps led up to it.

35 Then he brought me to the north gate[c] and measured it. It had the same measurements as the others, 36 as did its alcoves,[d] its projecting walls and its portico, and it had openings all round. It was fifty cubits long and twenty-five cubits wide. 37 Its

e *14* Septuagint; Hebrew *projecting wall* **f** *14* The meaning of the Hebrew for this verse is uncertain.

40:14 [l] Ex 27:9
40:16 [m] ver 21-22; 2Ch 3:5; Eze 41:26
40:17 [n] Rev 11:2 [o] Eze 41:6 [p] Eze 42:1
40:19 [q] Eze 46:1 [r] ver 23, 27
40:21 [s] ver 7
40:22 [t] ver 49
40:23 [u] ver 19
40:25 [v] ver 33
40:26 [w] ver 22
40:27 [x] ver 32
40:28 [y] ver 35
40:30 [z] ver 21
40:31 [a] ver 22
40:34 [b] ver 22
40:35 [c] Eze 44:4; 47:2
40:36 [d] ver 7

portico[g] faced the outer court; palm trees decorated the jambs on either side, and eight
steps led up to it.

The Rooms for Preparing Sacrifices

[38]A room with a doorway was by the portico in each of the inner gateways, where
the burnt offerings[e] were washed. [39]In the portico of the gateway were two tables
on each side, on which the burnt offerings,[f] sin offerings[g] and guilt offerings[h] were
slaughtered. [40]By the outside wall of the portico of the gateway, near the steps at the
entrance to the north gateway were two tables, and on the other side of the steps were
two tables. [41]So there were four tables on one side of the gateway and four on the
other—eight tables in all—on which the sacrifices were slaughtered. [42]There were
also four tables of dressed stone[i] for the burnt offerings, each a cubit and a half long,
a cubit and a half wide and a cubit high. On them were placed the utensils for
slaughtering the burnt offerings and the other sacrifices.[j] [43]And double-pronged
hooks, each a handbreadth long, were attached to the wall all around. The tables were
for the flesh of the offerings.

Rooms for the Priests

[44]Outside the inner gate, within the inner court, were two rooms, one[h] at the side
of the north gate and facing south, and another at the side of the south[i] gate and facing
north. [45]He said to me, "The room facing south is for the priests who have charge
of the temple,[k] [46]and the room facing north[l] is for the priests who have charge of
the altar.[m] These are the sons of Zadok,[n] who are the only Levites who may draw
near to the LORD to minister before him.[o]"
[47]Then he measured the court: It was square—a hundred cubits long and a hundred
cubits wide. And the altar was in front of the temple.

The Temple

[48]He brought me to the portico of the temple[p] and measured the jambs of the
portico; they were five cubits wide on either side. The width of the entrance was
fourteen cubits and its projecting walls were[j] three cubits wide on either side. [49]The
portico[q] was twenty cubits wide, and twelve[k] cubits from front to back. It was
reached by a flight of stairs,[l] and there were pillars[r] on each side of the jambs.

41 Then the man brought me to the outer sanctuary[a] and measured the jambs; the
width of the jambs was six cubits[a] on each side.[b] [2]The entrance was ten cubits
wide, and the projecting walls on each side of it were five cubits wide. He also
measured the outer sanctuary; it was forty cubits long and twenty cubits wide.[b]
[3]Then he went into the inner sanctuary and measured the jambs of the entrance; each
was two cubits wide. The entrance was six cubits wide, and the projecting walls on
each side of it were seven cubits wide. [4]And he measured the length of the inner
sanctuary; it was twenty cubits, and its width was twenty cubits across the end of the
outer sanctuary.[c] He said to me, "This is the Most Holy Place.[d]"
[5]Then he measured the wall of the temple; it was six cubits thick, and each side
room round the temple was four cubits wide. [6]The side rooms were on three levels,
one above another, thirty[e] on each level. There were ledges all round the wall of the
temple to serve as supports for the side rooms, so that the supports were not inserted
into the wall of the temple.[f] [7]The side rooms all round the temple were wider at each
successive level. The structure surrounding the temple was built in ascending stages,

40:38 [e]2Ch 4:6; Eze 42:13
40:39 [f]Eze 46:2 [g]Lev 4:3, 28 [h]Lev 7:1
40:42 [i]Ex 20:25 [j]ver 39
40:45 [k]1Ch 9:23
40:46 [l]Eze 42:13 [m]Nu 18:5 [n]1Ki 2:35 [o]Nu 16:5; Eze 43:19; 44:15; 45:4; 48:11
40:48 [p]1Ki 6:2
40:49 [q]ver 22; 1Ki 6:3 [r]1Ki 7:15
41:1 [a]ver 23
41:2 [b]2Ch 3:3
41:4 [c]1Ki 6:20 [d]Ex 26:33; Heb 9:3-8
41:6 [e]Eze 40:17 [f]1Ki 6:5

[g] *37* Septuagint (see also verses 31 and 34); Hebrew *jambs* [h] *44* Septuagint; Hebrew *were rooms for singers, which were* [i] *44* Septuagint; Hebrew *east* [j] *48* Septuagint; Hebrew *entrance was* [k] *49* Septuagint; Hebrew *eleven* [l] *49* Hebrew; Septuagint *Ten steps led up to it* [a] *1* The common cubit was about 1½ feet (about 0.5 metre). [b] *1* One Hebrew manuscript and Septuagint; most Hebrew manuscripts *side, the width of the tent*

40:38, 39 The washing of the sacrifices was done according to the standards of preparation established in Leviticus 1:6–9. This washing was part of the process of presenting an acceptable sacrifice to God.

41:4 God's holiness is a central theme throughout both the Old and New Testaments. The Most Holy Place was the innermost room in the temple (Exodus 26:33, 34). This was where the ark of the covenant was kept and where God's glory was said to dwell. This room was entered only once a year by the high priest, who performed a ceremony to atone for the nation's sins.

so that the rooms widened as one went upward. A stairway[g] went up from the lowest floor to the top floor through the middle floor.

8 I saw that the temple had a raised base all round it, forming the foundation of the side rooms. It was the length of the rod, six long cubits. 9 The outer wall of the side rooms was five cubits thick. The open area between the side rooms of the temple 10 and the ⌞priests'⌟ rooms was twenty cubits wide all round the temple. 11 There were entrances to the side rooms from the open area, one on the north and another on the south; and the base adjoining the open area was five cubits wide all round.

12 The building facing the temple courtyard on the west side was seventy cubits wide. The wall of the building was five cubits thick all round, and its length was ninety cubits.

13 Then he measured the temple; it was a hundred cubits long, and the temple courtyard and the building with its walls were also a hundred cubits long. 14 The width of the temple courtyard on the east, including the front of the temple, was a hundred cubits.[h]

15 Then he measured the length of the building facing the courtyard at the rear of the temple, including its galleries[i] on each side; it was a hundred cubits.

The outer sanctuary, the inner sanctuary and the portico facing the court, 16 as well as the thresholds and the narrow windows[j] and galleries round the three of them—everything beyond and including the threshold was covered with wood. The floor, the wall up to the windows, and the windows were covered.[k] 17 In the space above the outside of the entrance to the inner sanctuary and on the walls at regular intervals all round the inner and outer sanctuary 18 were carved[l] cherubim[m] and palm trees.[n] Palm trees alternated with cherubim. Each cherub had two faces:[o] 19 the face of a man towards the palm tree on one side and the face of a lion towards the palm tree on the other. They were carved all round the whole temple.[p] 20 From the floor to the area above the entrance, cherubim and palm trees were carved on the wall of the outer sanctuary.

21 The outer sanctuary[q] had a rectangular door-frame, and the one at the front of the Most Holy Place was similar. 22 There was a wooden altar[r] three cubits high and two cubits square;**c** its corners, its base**d** and its sides were of wood. The man said to me, "This is the table[s] that is before the LORD." 23 Both the outer sanctuary[t] and the Most Holy Place had double doors.[u] 24 Each door had two leaves—two hinged leaves[v] for each door. 25 And on the doors of the outer sanctuary were carved cherubim and palm trees like those carved on the walls, and there was a wooden overhang on the front of the portico. 26 On the side walls of the portico were narrow windows with palm trees carved on each side. The side rooms of the temple also had overhangs.[w]

Rooms for the Priests

42 Then the man led me northward into the outer court and brought me to the rooms[a] opposite the temple courtyard[b] and opposite the outer wall on the north side.[c] 2 The building whose door faced north was a hundred cubits**a** long and fifty cubits wide. 3 Both in the section twenty cubits from the inner court and in the section opposite the pavement of the outer court, gallery[d] faced gallery at the three levels.[e] 4 In front of the rooms was an inner passageway ten cubits wide and a hundred cubits**b** long. Their doors were on the north.[f] 5 Now the upper rooms were narrower, for the galleries took more space from them than from the rooms on the lower and middle floors of the building. 6 The rooms on the third floor had no pillars, as the courts had; so they were smaller in floor space than those on the lower and middle floors. 7 There was an outer wall parallel to the rooms and the outer court; it extended in front of the rooms for fifty cubits. 8 While the row of rooms on the side next to the outer

41:7 [g] 1Ki 6:8
41:14 [h] Eze 40:47
41:15 [i] Eze 42:3
41:16 [j] 1Ki 6:4 [k] ver 25-26; 1Ki 6:15; Eze 42:3
41:18 [l] 1Ki 6:18 [m] Ex 37:7; 2Ch 3:7 [n] 1Ki 6:29; 7:36 [o] Eze 10:21
41:19 [p] Eze 10:14
41:21 [q] ver 1
41:22 [r] Ex 30:1 [s] Ex 25:23; Eze 23:41; 44:16; Mal 1:7, 12
41:23 [t] ver 1 [u] 1Ki 6:32
41:24 [v] 1Ki 6:34
41:26 [w] ver 15-16; Eze 40:16
42:1 [a] ver 13 [b] Eze 41:12-14 [c] Eze 40:17
42:3 [d] Eze 41:15 [e] Eze 41:16
42:4 [f] Eze 46:19

c *22* Septuagint; Hebrew *long* **d** *22* Septuagint; Hebrew *length* **a** *2* The common cubit was about 1½ feet (about 0.5 metre). **b** *4* Septuagint and Syriac; Hebrew *and one cubit*

41:18 Cherubim are mighty angels.

41:22 The dimensions given would fit either the table of the bread of the Presence (Exodus 25:30) or the altar of incense (Exodus 30:1–3).

court was fifty cubits long, the row on the side nearest the sanctuary was a hundred
cubits long. 9The lower rooms had an entrance[g] on the east side as one enters them
from the outer court.
10On the south side[c] along the length of the wall of the outer court, adjoining the
temple courtyard and opposite the outer wall, were rooms[h] 11with a passageway in
front of them. These were like the rooms on the north; they had the same length and
width, with similar exits and dimensions. Similar to the doorways on the north 12were
the doorways of the rooms on the south. There was a doorway at the beginning of
the passageway that was parallel to the corresponding wall extending eastward, by
which one enters the rooms.
13Then he said to me, "The north[i] and south rooms facing the temple courtyard
are the priests' rooms, where the priests who approach the LORD will eat the most holy
offerings. There they will put the most holy offerings—the grain offerings, the sin
offerings[j] and the guilt offerings[k]—for the place is holy.[l] 14Once the priests enter
the holy precincts, they are not to go into the outer court until they leave behind the
garments[m] in which they minister, for these are holy. They are to put on other clothes
before they go near the places that are for the people.[n]"
15When he had finished measuring what was inside the temple area, he led me out
by the east gate[o] and measured the area all around: 16He measured the east side with
the measuring rod; it was five hundred cubits.[d] 17He measured the north side; it was
five hundred cubits[e] by the measuring rod. 18He measured the south side; it was five
hundred cubits by the measuring rod. 19Then he turned to the west side and measured;
it was five hundred cubits by the measuring rod. 20So he measured[p] the area on all
four sides. It had a wall round it,[q] five hundred cubits long and five hundred cubits
wide,[r] to separate the holy from the common.[s]

The Glory Returns to the Temple

43 Then the man brought me to the gate facing east,[a] 2and I saw the glory of the
God of Israel coming from the east. His voice was like the roar of rushing
waters,[b] and the land was radiant with his glory.[c] 3The vision I saw was like the
vision I had seen when he[a] came to destroy the city and like the visions I had seen
by the Kebar River, and I fell face down. 4The glory[d] of the LORD entered the temple
through the gate facing east.[e] 5Then the Spirit[f] lifted me up[g] and brought me into
the inner court, and the glory of the LORD filled the temple.
6While the man was standing beside me, I heard someone speaking to me from
inside the temple. 7He said: "Son of man, this is the place of my throne and the place
for the soles of my feet. This is where I will live among the Israelites for ever. The
house of Israel will never again defile my holy name—neither they nor their
kings—by their prostitution[b] and the lifeless idols[c] of their kings at their high
places.[h] 8When they placed their threshold next to my threshold and their doorposts
beside my doorposts, with only a wall between me and them, they defiled my holy
name by their detestable practices. So I destroyed them in my anger. 9Now let them

c 10 Septuagint; Hebrew *Eastward* d 16 See Septuagint of verse 17; Hebrew *rods*; also in verses 18 and 19.
e 17 Septuagint; Hebrew *rods* a 3 Some Hebrew manuscripts and Vulgate; most Hebrew manuscripts *I*
b 7 Or *their spiritual adultery*; also in verse 9 c 7 Or *the corpses*; also in verse 9

42:9 g Eze 44:5; 46:19
42:10 h ver 1
42:13 i Eze 40:46; j Lev 10:17; 6:25; k Lev 14:13; l Ex 29:31; Lev 6:29; 7:6; 10:12-13; Nu 18:9-10
42:14 m Eze 44:19; n Ex 29:9; Lev 8:7-9
42:15 o Eze 43:1
42:20 p Eze 40:5; q Zec 2:5; r Eze 45:2; Rev 21:16; s Eze 22:26
43:1 a Eze 10:19; 42:15; 44:1; 46:1
43:2 b Rev 1:15; c Isa 6:3; Eze 11:23; Rev 18:1
43:4 d Eze 1:28; e Eze 10:19
43:5 f Eze 11:24; g Eze 3:12; 8:3
43:7 h Lev 26:30

42:14 Approaching our holy God must not be taken lightly. The holy garments the priests were required to wear may symbolise the importance of having a holy heart when approaching God. The priests had to wear these special clothes in order to minister in the inner rooms of the temple. Because the garments were holy, the priests had to change their clothes before going back out to the public.

42:16–20 The perfect symmetry of Ezekiel's temple may represent the order and harmony in God's future kingdom.

43:1ff This is the culmination of chapters 40–42 because God's glory returns to the temple. It reverses the negative cast of the book and serves as a fitting end for all the passages dealing with the blessings reserved for the restored remnant. All true believers should long for that moment when God's name will finally be glorified and he will live among his people for ever.

43:2 In 11:23, God's glory stopped over the Mount of Olives, to the east of Jerusalem, before leaving the city. This prophecy states that his glory would also return from the east.

43:2–4 Just as it was completely devastating when God's glory departed (11:23) from his temple, so it was overwhelming awe and joy beyond expression when Ezekiel saw God's glory return.

43:3 The Kebar River connected with the Euphrates River and was the location of a Jewish settlement of exiles in Babylonia.

43:9–11 God's departure from the city had been a signal for the destruction of the city and the temple. Now for God to return, his conditions had to be met: idolatry had to be removed. Some com-

43:9 [i]Eze 37:26-28
43:10 [j]Eze 16:61
43:11 [k]Eze 44:5
43:12 [l]Eze 40:2
43:13 [m]2Ch 4:1
43:15 [n]Ex 27:2
43:17 [o]Ex 20:26
43:18 [p]Ex 40:29 [q]Lev 1:5, 11; Heb 9:21-22
43:19 [r]Lev 4:3; Eze 45:18-19 [s]Eze 44:15 [t]Nu 16:40; Eze 40:46
43:20 [u]ver 17 [v]Lev 16:19
43:21 [w]Ex 29:14; Heb 13:11
43:23 [x]Ex 29:1
43:24 [y]Lev 2:13; Mk 9:49-50
43:25 [z]Lev 8:33 [a]Ex 29:37
43:27 [b]Lev 9:1 [c]Lev 17:5

put away from me their prostitution and the lifeless idols of their kings, and I will live
among them for ever.[i]
10"Son of man, describe the temple to the people of Israel, that they may be
ashamed[j] of their sins. Let them consider the plan, 11and if they are ashamed of all
they have done, make known to them the design of the temple—its arrangement, its
exits and entrances—its whole design and all its regulations[d] and laws. Write these
down before them so that they may be faithful to its design and follow all its
regulations.[k]
12"This is the law of the temple: All the surrounding area[l] on top of the mountain
will be most holy. Such is the law of the temple.

The Altar

13"These are the measurements of the altar[m] in long cubits, that cubit being a cubit[e]
and a handbreadth:[f] Its gutter is a cubit deep and a cubit wide, with a rim of one
span[g] around the edge. And this is the height of the altar: 14From the gutter on the
ground up to the lower ledge it is two cubits high and a cubit wide, and from the smaller
ledge up to the larger ledge it is four cubits high and a cubit wide. 15The altar hearth
is four cubits high, and four horns[n] project upward from the hearth. 16The altar hearth
is square, twelve cubits long and twelve cubits wide. 17The upper ledge also is square,
fourteen cubits long and fourteen cubits wide, with a rim of half a cubit and a gutter
of a cubit all round. The steps[o] of the altar face east."
18Then he said to me, "Son of man, this is what the Sovereign LORD says: These
will be the regulations for sacrificing burnt offerings[p] and sprinkling blood[q] upon
the altar when it is built: 19You are to give a young bull[r] as a sin offering to the priests,
who are Levites, of the family of Zadok,[s] who come near[t] to minister before me,
declares the Sovereign LORD. 20You are to take some of its blood and put it on the
four horns of the altar and on the four corners of the upper ledge[u] and all round the
rim, and so purify the altar[v] and make atonement for it. 21You are to take the bull
for the sin offering and burn it in the designated part of the temple area outside the
sanctuary.[w]
22"On the second day you are to offer a male goat without defect for a sin offering,
and the altar is to be purified as it was purified with the bull. 23When you have finished
purifying it, you are to offer a young bull and a ram from the flock, both without
defect.[x] 24You are to offer them before the LORD, and the priests are to sprinkle salt[y]
on them and sacrifice them as a burnt offering to the LORD.
25"For seven days[z] you are to provide a male goat daily for a sin offering; you
are also to provide a young bull and a ram from the flock, both without defect.[a] 26For
seven days they are to make atonement for the altar and cleanse it; thus they will
dedicate it. 27At the end of these days, from the eighth day[b] on, the priests are to
present your burnt offerings and fellowship offerings[h][c] on the altar. Then I will
accept you, declares the Sovereign LORD."

d *11* Some Hebrew manuscripts and Septuagint; most Hebrew manuscripts *regulations and its whole design*
e *13* The common cubit was about 1½ feet (about 0.5 metre). **f** *13* That is, about 3 inches (about 8 centimetres)
g *13* That is, about 9 inches (about 23 centimetres) **h** *27* Traditionally *peace offerings*

---

mentators feel these verses indicate that Ezekiel was commanding the people of his day to build this temple according to the designs and regulations that the angelic architect had given. But the people never repented, the conditions were not met, so the fulfilment was postponed.

43:12 The basic law of God's temple was holiness. In all he does, God is holy, perfect, and blameless. There is no trace of evil or sin in him. Just as God is holy, so we are to be holy (Leviticus 19:1; 1 Peter 1:15, 16). People are holy when they are devoted to God and separated from sin. If we do not understand the basic concept of holiness, we will never progress very far in our Christian growth.

43:18–27 This vision was simultaneously flashing back to Mount Sinai and forward to Mount Calvary. When the people returned from exile, they would seek forgiveness through the sacrificial system instituted in Moses' day. Today, Christ's death has made the forgiveness of our sins possible, making us acceptable to God (Hebrews 9:9–15). God stands ready to forgive those who come to him in faith.

The Prince, the Levites, the Priests

44 Then the man brought me back to the outer gate of the sanctuary, the one facing
east,[a] and it was shut. 2The LORD said to me, "This gate is to remain shut.
It must not be opened; no-one may enter through it.[b] It is to remain shut because the
LORD, the God of Israel, has entered through it. 3The prince himself is the only one
who may sit inside the gateway to eat in the presence[c] of the LORD. He is to enter
by way of the portico of the gateway and go out the same way.[d]"
4Then the man brought me by way of the north gate to the front of the temple. I
looked and saw the glory of the LORD filling the temple[e] of the LORD, and I fell face
down.[f]
5The LORD said to me, "Son of man, look carefully, listen closely and give attention
to everything I tell you concerning all the regulations regarding the temple of the
LORD. Give attention to the entrance of the temple and all the exits of the sanctuary.[g]
6Say to the rebellious house[h] of Israel, 'This is what the Sovereign LORD says:
Enough of your detestable practices, O house of Israel! 7In addition to all your other
detestable practices, you brought foreigners uncircumcised in heart[i] and flesh into
my sanctuary, desecrating my temple while you offered me food, fat and blood, and
you broke my covenant.[j] 8Instead of carrying out your duty in regard to my holy
things, you put others in charge of my sanctuary.[k] 9This is what the Sovereign LORD
says: No foreigner uncircumcised in heart and flesh is to enter my sanctuary, not even
the foreigners who live among the Israelites.[l]
10" 'The Levites who went far from me when Israel went astray[m] and who wandered
from me after their idols must bear the consequences of their sin.[n] 11They may serve
in my sanctuary, having charge of the gates of the temple and serving in it; they may
slaughter the burnt offerings[o] and sacrifices for the people and stand before the people
and serve them.[p] 12But because they served them in the presence of their idols and
made the house of Israel fall into sin, therefore I have sworn with uplifted hand[q] that
they must bear the consequences of their sin, declares the Sovereign LORD.[r] 13They
are not to come near to serve me as priests or come near any of my holy things or
my most holy offerings; they must bear the shame[s] of their detestable practices.[t]
14Yet I will put them in charge of the duties of the temple and all the work that is
to be done in it.[u]
15" 'But the priests, who are Levites and descendants of Zadok and who faithfully
carried out the duties of my sanctuary when the Israelites went astray from me, are
to come near to minister before me; they are to stand before me to offer sacrifices of
fat and blood, declares the Sovereign LORD.[v] 16They alone are to enter my sanctuary;
they alone are to come near my table[w] to minister before me and perform my
service.[x]
17" 'When they enter the gates of the inner court, they are to wear linen clothes;[y]
they must not wear any woollen garment while ministering at the gates of the inner
court or inside the temple. 18They are to wear linen turbans[z] on their heads and linen
undergarments[a] round their waists. They must not wear anything that makes them
perspire.[b] 19When they go out into the outer court where the people are, they are to
take off the clothes they have been ministering in and leave them in the sacred rooms,

44:1 [a]Eze 43:1
44:2 [b]Eze 43:4-5
44:3 [c]Ex 24:9-11 [d]Eze 46:2, 8
44:4 [e]Isa 6:4; Rev 15:8 [f]Eze 1:28; 3:23
44:5 [g]Eze 40:4; 43:10-11
44:6 [h]Eze 3:9
44:7 [i]Lev 26:41 [j]Ge 17:14; Ex 12:48; Lev 22:25
44:8 [k]Lev 22:2; Nu 18:7
44:9 [l]Joel 3:17; Zec 14:21
44:10 [m]2Ki 23:8 [n]Nu 18:23
44:11 [o]2Ch 29:34 [p]Nu 3:5-37; 16:9; 1Ch 26:12-19
44:12 [q]Ps 106:26 [r]2Ki 16:10-16
44:13 [s]Eze 16:61 [t]Nu 18:3
44:14 [u]Nu 18:4; 1Ch 23:28-32
44:15 [v]Jer 33:18; Eze 40:46; Zec 3:7
44:16 [w]Eze 41:22 [x]Nu 18:5
44:17 [y]Ex 39:27-28; Rev 19:8
44:18 [z]Ex 28:39; Isa 3:20 [a]Ex 28:42 [b]Lev 16:4

44:2 Why was this east gate to remain closed? Several reasons have been suggested: (1) This was the gate through which God entered the temple, and no-one else could walk where God had (43:2); (2) the closed gate indicated that God would never again leave the temple (10:19; 11:23); (3) it would prevent people from worshipping the sun as it rises in the east from within the temple grounds (8:16).

44:3 Although Christ is called a prince (37:25), this prince is probably not Christ because he offers a sacrifice to God (46:4) and he can enter only by the "portico of the gateway". He is a princely ruler of the city, but he is distinguished from other princes because he will be just and fair (see 45:8). Another view is that this picture anticipates Christ offering a sacrifice of his own life to God.

44:9 Unbelievers would not be allowed to enter the temple. Ezekiel's vision was for a restored, purified worship where only those who prepared themselves physically and spiritually could participate. In 47:22, 23, we find that people from other nations are allowed to join in worship by accepting the standards of faith and practice declared in the law (see Leviticus 24:22; Numbers 15:29).

44:15 Zadok's descendants are mentioned because many of the priests in Zadok's line had remained faithful to God, while others had become corrupt. Zadok supported God's choice of Solomon to succeed David, and was therefore appointed high priest during his reign (1 Kings 1:32–35; 2:27, 35). Zadok's descendants were considered the true priestly line throughout the time between the Old and New Testaments.

and put on other clothes, so that they do not consecrate[c] the people by means of their garments.[d]

20" 'They must not shave their heads or let their hair grow long, but they are to keep the hair of their heads trimmed.[e] 21 No priest is to drink wine when he enters the inner court.[f] 22 They must not marry widows or divorced women; they may marry only virgins of Israelite descent or widows of priests.[g] 23 They are to teach my people the difference between the holy and the common[h] and show them how to distinguish between the unclean and the clean.[i]

24" 'In any dispute, the priests are to serve as judges[j] and decide it according to my ordinances. They are to keep my laws and my decrees for all my appointed feasts, and they are to keep my Sabbaths holy.[k]

25" 'A priest must not defile himself by going near a dead person; however, if the dead person was his father or mother, son or daughter, brother or unmarried sister, then he may defile himself.[l] 26 After he is cleansed, he must wait seven days.[m] 27 On the day he goes into the inner court of the sanctuary to minister in the sanctuary, he is to offer a sin offering for himself, declares the Sovereign LORD.

28" 'I am to be the only inheritance[n] the priests have. You are to give them no possession in Israel; I will be their possession. 29 They will eat the grain offerings, the sin offerings and the guilt offerings; and everything in Israel devoted[a] to the LORD[o] will belong to them.[p] 30 The best of all the firstfruits[q] and of all your special gifts will belong to the priests. You are to give them the first portion of your ground meal[r] so that a blessing[s] may rest on your household.[t] 31 The priests must not eat anything, bird or animal, found dead or torn by wild animals.[u]

Division of the Land

45 " 'When you allot the land as an inheritance,[a] you are to present to the LORD a portion of the land as a sacred district, 25,000 cubits long and 20,000[a] cubits wide; the entire area will be holy.[b] 2 Of this, a section 500 cubits square[c] is to be for the sanctuary, with 50 cubits around it for open land. 3 In the sacred district, measure off a section 25,000 cubits[b] long and 10,000 cubits[c] wide. In it will be the sanctuary, the Most Holy Place. 4 It will be the sacred portion of the land for the priests,[d] who minister in the sanctuary and who draw near to minister before the LORD. It will be a place for their houses as well as a holy place for the sanctuary.[e] 5 An area 25,000 cubits long and 10,000 cubits wide will belong to the Levites, who serve in the temple, as their possession for towns to live in.[d][f]

6" 'You are to give the city as its property an area 5,000 cubits wide and 25,000 cubits long, adjoining the sacred portion; it will belong to the whole house of Israel.[g]

7" 'The prince will have the land bordering each side of the area formed by the sacred district and the property of the city. It will extend westward from the west side and eastward from the east side, running lengthwise from the western to the eastern border parallel to one of the tribal portions.[h] 8 This land will be his possession in Israel. And my princes will no longer oppress my people but will allow the house of Israel to possess the land according to their tribes.[i]

9" 'This is what the Sovereign LORD says: You have gone far enough, O princes of Israel! Give up your violence and oppression and do what is just and right.[j] Stop

a *29* The Hebrew term refers to the irrevocable giving over of things or persons to the LORD. a *1* Septuagint (see also verses 3 and 5 and 48:9); Hebrew *10,000* b *3* That is, about 7 miles (about 11 kilometres) c *3* That is, about 3 miles (about 5 kilometres) d *5* Septuagint; Hebrew *temple; they will have as their possession 20 rooms*

44:19 [c]Lev 6:27; Eze 46:20 [d]Lev 6:10-11; Eze 42:14
44:20 [e]Lev 21:5; Nu 6:5
44:21 [f]Lev 10:9
44:22 [g]Lev 21:7
44:23 [h]Eze 22:26 [i]Mal 2:7
44:24 [j]Dt 17:8-9; 1Ch 23:4 [k]2Ch 19:8
44:25 [l]Lev 21:1-4
44:26 [m]Nu 19:14
44:28 [n]Nu 18:20; Dt 10:9; 18:1-2; Jos 13:33
44:29 [o]Lev 27:21 [p]Nu 18:9, 14
44:30 [q]Nu 18:12-13 [r]Nu 15:18-21 [s]Mal 3:10 [t]Ne 10:35-37
44:31 [u]Ex 22:31; Lev 22:8
45:1 [a]Eze 47:21-22 [b]Eze 48:8-9, 29
45:2 [c]Eze 42:20
45:4 [d]Eze 40:46 [e]Eze 48:10-11
45:5 [f]Eze 48:13
45:6 [g]Eze 48:15-18
45:7 [h]Eze 48:21
45:8 [i]Nu 26:53; Eze 46:18
45:9 [j]Jer 22:3; Zec 7:9-10; 8:16

44:20–31 These laws were originally given to God's people in the desert. They are recorded in the books of Exodus and Leviticus. They reveal the importance of approaching God respectfully, and they give guidelines for the priests to live above reproach so they could carry out their responsibility to teach the people "to distinguish between the unclean and the clean" (44:23).

45:1–7 The land allotted to the temple was in the centre of the nation. God is central to life. He must be our first priority.

45:8–12 Greed and extortion were two of the major social sins of the nation during this time (see Amos 5:10–13). In the new economy there would be plenty of land for the "princes" (45:7, 8) and no longer any basis for greed. Therefore, God commanded the princes and the people to be just and right, especially in their business dealings. Consider the ways that you measure goods, money, or services. If you are paid for an hour of work, be sure you work for a full hour. If you sell a bushel of apples, make sure it is a full bushel. God is completely trustworthy, and his followers should be too.

dispossessing my people, declares the Sovereign LORD. 10You are to use accurate
scales,[k] an accurate ephah[e][l] and an accurate bath.[f] 11The ephah[m] and the bath
are to be the same size, the bath containing a tenth of a homer[g] and the ephah a tenth
of a homer; the homer is to be the standard measure for both. 12The shekel[h] is to
consist of twenty gerahs.[n] Twenty shekels plus twenty-five shekels plus fifteen
shekels equal one mina.[i]

Offerings and Holy Days

13" 'This is the special gift you are to offer: a sixth of an ephah from each homer
of wheat and a sixth of an ephah from each homer of barley. 14The prescribed portion
of oil, measured by the bath, is a tenth of a bath from each cor (which consists of
ten baths or one homer, for ten baths are equivalent to a homer). 15Also one sheep
is to be taken from every flock of two hundred from the well-watered pastures of Israel.
These will be used for the grain offerings, burnt offerings[o] and fellowship offerings[j]
to make atonement[p] for the people, declares the Sovereign LORD. 16All the people
of the land will participate in this special gift for the use of the prince in Israel. 17It
will be the duty of the prince to provide the burnt offerings, grain offerings and drink
offerings at the festivals, the New Moons and the Sabbaths[q]—at all the appointed
feasts of the house of Israel. He will provide the sin offerings, grain offerings, burnt
offerings and fellowship offerings to make atonement for the house of Israel.[r]
18" 'This is what the Sovereign LORD says: In the first month[s] on the first day you
are to take a young bull without defect[t] and purify the sanctuary.[u] 19The priest is
to take some of the blood of the sin offering and put it on the doorposts of the temple,
on the four corners of the upper ledge[v] of the altar[w] and on the gateposts of the inner
court. 20You are to do the same on the seventh day of the month for anyone who sins
unintentionally[x] or through ignorance; so you are to make atonement for the temple.
21" 'In the first month on the fourteenth day you are to observe the Passover,[y] a
feast lasting seven days, during which you shall eat bread made without yeast. 22On
that day the prince is to provide a bull as a sin offering for himself and for all the people
of the land.[z] 23Every day during the seven days of the Feast he is to provide seven
bulls and seven rams[a] without defect as a burnt offering to the LORD, and a male goat
for a sin offering.[b] 24He is to provide as a grain offering[c] an ephah for each bull
and an ephah for each ram, along with a hin[k] of oil for each ephah.[d]
25" 'During the seven days of the Feast,[e] which begins in the seventh month on
the fifteenth day, he is to make the same provision for sin offerings, burnt offerings,
grain offerings and oil.[f]

46 " 'This is what the Sovereign LORD says: The gate of the inner court[a] facing
east[b] is to be shut on the six working days, but on the Sabbath day and on
the day of the New Moon[c] it is to be opened. 2The prince is to enter from the outside
through the portico[d] of the gateway and stand by the gatepost. The priests are to
sacrifice his burnt offering and his fellowship offerings.[a] He is to worship at the
threshold of the gateway and then go out, but the gate will not be shut until evening.[e]
3On the Sabbaths and New Moons the people of the land are to worship in the presence
of the LORD at the entrance to that gateway.[f] 4The burnt offering the prince brings
to the LORD on the Sabbath day is to be six male lambs and a ram, all without defect.

e *10* An ephah was a dry measure. **f** *10* A bath was a liquid measure. **g** *11* A homer was a dry measure.
h *12* A shekel weighed about 2/5 ounce (about 11.5 grams). **i** *12* That is, 60 shekels; the common mina was 50 shekels. **j** *15* Traditionally *peace offerings*; also in verse 17 **k** *24* That is, probably about 6 pints (about 4 litres) **a** *2* Traditionally *peace offerings*; also in verse 12

45:10 [k]Dt 25:15; Pr 11:1; Am 8:4-6; Mic 6:10-11 [l]Lev 19:36
45:11 [m]Isa 5:10
45:12 [n]Ex 30:13; Lev 27:25; Nu 3:47
45:15 [o]Lev 1:4 [p]Lev 6:30
45:17 [q]Lev 23:38; Isa 66:23 [r]1Ki 8:62; 2Ch 31:3; Eze 46:4-12
45:18 [s]Ex 12:2 [t]Lev 22:20; Heb 9:14 [u]Lev 16:16, 33
45:19 [v]Eze 43:17 [w]Lev 16:18-19; Eze 43:20
45:20 [x]Lev 4:27
45:21 [y]Ex 12:11; Lev 23:5-6
45:22 [z]Lev 4:14
45:23 [a]Job 42:8 [b]Nu 28:16-25
45:24 [c]Nu 28:12-13 [d]Eze 46:5-7
45:25 [e]Dt 16:13 [f]Lev 23:34-43; Nu 29:12-38
46:1 [a]Eze 40:19 [b]1Ch 9:18 [c]ver 6; Isa 66:23
46:2 [d]ver 8 [e]ver 12; Eze 44:3
46:3 [f]Lk 1:10

45:17 The conditions and regulations for these offerings are described in detail in Leviticus 1–7.

45:21 The Passover was an annual seven-day feast instituted by God so that his people would remember when he brought them out of slavery in Egypt. On that first Passover night, the destroyer passed over the homes marked by lamb's blood; he struck only the unmarked homes (see Exodus 11; 12).

45:25 This annual feast celebrated in October is called the Feast of Tabernacles. It commemorates God's protection of his people as they travelled through the desert from Egypt to the promised land (see Leviticus 23:33–43; Deuteronomy 16:13–17).

46:1–15 Ezekiel continued to describe various aspects of daily worship. While allowing for diversity in worship, God prescribed order and continuity. This continuity gave a healthy rhythm to the spiritual life of his people.

5 The grain offering given with the ram is to be an ephah,[b] and the grain offering with
the lambs is to be as much as he pleases, along with a hin[c] of oil for each ephah.[g]
6 On the day of the New Moon[h] he is to offer a young bull, six lambs and a ram,
all without defect. 7 He is to provide as a grain offering one ephah with the bull, one
ephah with the ram, and with the lambs as much as he wants to give, along with a
hin of oil with each ephah.[i] 8 When the prince enters, he is to go in through the
portico[j] of the gateway, and he is to come out the same way.[k]
9 " 'When the people of the land come before the LORD at the appointed feasts,[l]
whoever enters by the north gate to worship is to go out by the south gate; and whoever
enters by the south gate is to go out by the north gate. No-one is to return through
the gate by which he entered, but each is to go out by the opposite gate. 10 The prince
is to be among them, going in when they go in and going out when they go out.[m]
11 " 'At the festivals and the appointed feasts, the grain offering is to be an ephah
with a bull, an ephah with a ram, and with the lambs as much as one pleases, along
with a hin of oil for each ephah.[n] 12 When the prince provides[o] a freewill offering[p]
to the LORD—whether a burnt offering or fellowship offerings—the gate facing east
is to be opened for him. He shall offer his burnt offering or his fellowship offerings
as he does on the Sabbath day. Then he shall go out, and after he has gone out, the
gate will be shut.[q]
13 " 'Every day you are to provide a year-old lamb without defect for a burnt offering
to the LORD; morning by morning you shall provide it.[r] 14 You are also to provide
with it morning by morning a grain offering, consisting of a sixth of an ephah with
a third of a hin of oil to moisten the flour. The presenting of this grain offering to
the LORD is a lasting ordinance.[s] 15 So the lamb and the grain offering and the oil
shall be provided morning by morning for a regular[t] burnt offering.[u]
16 " 'This is what the Sovereign LORD says: If the prince makes a gift from his
inheritance to one of his sons, it will also belong to his descendants; it is to be their
property by inheritance.[v] 17 If, however, he makes a gift from his inheritance to one
of his servants, the servant may keep it until the year of freedom;[w] then it will revert
to the prince. His inheritance belongs to his sons only; it is theirs. 18 The prince must
not take any of the inheritance[x] of the people, driving them off their property. He
is to give his sons their inheritance out of his own property, so that none of my people
will be separated from his property.' "
19 Then the man brought me through the entrance[y] at the side of the gate to the
sacred rooms facing north, which belonged to the priests, and showed me a place at
the western end. 20 He said to me, "This is the place where the priests will cook the
guilt offering and the sin offering and bake the grain offering, to avoid bringing them
into the outer court and consecrating[z] the people."[a]
21 He then brought me to the outer court and led me round to its four corners, and
I saw in each corner another court. 22 In the four corners of the outer court were
enclosed[d] courts, forty cubits long and thirty cubits wide; each of the courts in the
four corners was the same size. 23 Around the inside of each of the four courts was
a ledge of stone, with places for fire built all round under the ledge. 24 He said to me,
"These are the kitchens where those who minister at the temple will cook the sacrifices
of the people."

The River From the Temple

47 The man brought me back to the entrance of the temple, and I saw water[a]
coming out from under the threshold of the temple towards the east (for the
temple faced east). The water was coming down from under the south side of the
temple, south of the altar.[b] 2 He then brought me out through the north gate and led

46:5 [g] ver 11; Eze 45:24
46:6 [h] ver 1; Nu 10:10
46:7 [i] Eze 45:24
46:8 [j] ver 2 [k] Eze 44:3
46:9 [l] Ex 23:14; 34:20
46:10 [m] 2Sa 6:14-15; Ps 42:4
46:11 [n] ver 5
46:12 [o] Eze 45:17 [p] Lev 7:16 [q] ver 2
46:13 [r] Ex 29:38; Nu 28:3
46:14 [s] Da 8:11
46:15 [t] Ex 29:42 [u] Ex 29:38; Nu 28:5-6
46:16 [v] 2Ch 21:3
46:17 [w] Lev 25:10
46:18 [x] Lev 25:23; Eze 45:8; Mic 2:1-2
46:19 [y] Eze 42:9
46:20 [z] Lev 6:27 [a] Zec 14:20
47:1 [a] Isa 55:1 [b] Ps 46:4; Joel 3:18; Rev 22:1

[b] *5* That is, probably about 3/5 bushel (about 22 litres) [c] *5* That is, probably about 6 pints (about 4 litres)
[d] *22* The meaning of the Hebrew for this word is uncertain.

47:1-12 This river is similar to the river mentioned in Revelation 22:1, 2. Both rivers are associated with the river in the Garden of Eden (see Genesis 2:10). The river symbolises life from God and the blessings that flow from his throne. It is a gentle, safe, deep river, expanding as it flows.

me round the outside to the outer gate facing east, and the water was flowing from
the south side.
3As the man went eastward with a measuring line[c] in his hand, he measured off
a thousand cubits[a] and then led me through water that was ankle-deep. 4He measured
off another thousand cubits and led me through water that was knee-deep. He measured off another thousand and led me through water that was up to the waist. 5He
measured off another thousand, but now it was a river that I could not cross, because
the water had risen and was deep enough to swim in—a river that no-one could
cross.[d] 6He asked me, "Son of man, do you see this?"
Then he led me back to the bank of the river. 7When I arrived there, I saw a great
number of trees on each side of the river.[e] 8He said to me, "This water flows towards
the eastern region and goes down into the Arabah,[b][f] where it enters the Sea.[c] When
it empties into the Sea,[c] the water there becomes fresh.[g] 9Swarms of living creatures
will live wherever the river flows. There will be large numbers of fish, because this
water flows there and makes the salt water fresh; so where the river flows everything
will live.[h] 10Fishermen[i] will stand along the shore; from En Gedi[j] to En Eglaim
there will be places for spreading nets.[k] The fish will be of many kinds[l]—like the
fish of the Great Sea.[d][m] 11But the swamps and marshes will not become fresh; they
will be left for salt.[n] 12Fruit trees of all kinds will grow on both banks of the river.[o]
Their leaves will not wither, nor will their fruit[p] fail. Every month they will bear,
because the water from the sanctuary flows to them. Their fruit will serve for food
and their leaves for healing.[q]"

The Boundaries of the Land

13This is what the Sovereign LORD says: "These are the boundaries[r] by which you
are to divide the land for an inheritance among the twelve tribes of Israel, with two
portions for Joseph.[s] 14You are to divide it equally among them. Because I swore
with uplifted hand to give it to your forefathers, this land will become your inheritance.[t]

15"This is to be the boundary of the land:

"On the north side it will run from the Great Sea by the Hethlon road[u] past Lebo[e]
Hamath to Zedad, 16Berothah[f][v] and Sibraim (which lies on the border between
Damascus and Hamath),[w] as far as Hazer Hatticon, which is on the border of
Hauran. 17The boundary will extend from the sea to Hazar Enan,[g] along the
northern border of Damascus, with the border of Hamath to the north. This will
be the north boundary.[x]
18"On the east side the boundary will run between Hauran and Damascus, along the
Jordan between Gilead and the land of Israel, to the eastern sea and as far as
Tamar.[h] This will be the east boundary.
19"On the south side it will run from Tamar as far as the waters of Meribah Kadesh,[y]
then along the Wadi ⌞of Egypt⌟[z] to the Great Sea.[a] This will be the south
boundary.
20"On the west side, the Great Sea will be the boundary to a point opposite Lebo[i]
Hamath.[b] This will be the west boundary.[c]

21"You are to distribute this land among yourselves according to the tribes of Israel.

a *3* That is, about 1,500 feet (about 460 metres) b *8* Or *the Jordan Valley* c *8* That is, the Dead Sea
d *10* That is, the Mediterranean; also in verses 15, 19 and 20 e *15* Or *past the entrance to* f *15, 16* See
Septuagint and Ezekiel 48:1; Hebrew *road to go into Zedad, 16Hamath, Berothah* g *17* Hebrew *Enon,* a variant
of *Enan* h *18* Septuagint and Syriac; Hebrew *Israel. You will measure to the eastern sea* i *20* Or *opposite the
entrance to*

47:3 c Eze 40:3
47:5 d Isa 11:9; Hab 2:14
47:7 e ver 12; Rev 22:2
47:8 f Dt 3:17; Jos 3:16 g Isa 41:18
47:9 h Isa 12:3; 55:1; Jn 4:14; 7:37-38
47:10 i Mt 4:19 j Jos 15:62 k Eze 26:5 l Ps 104:25; Mt 13:47 m Nu 34:6
47:11 n Dt 29:23
47:12 o ver 7; Rev 22:2 p Ps 1:3 q Ge 2:9; Jer 17:8
47:13 r Nu 34:2-12 s Ge 48:5
47:14 t Ge 12:7; Dt 1:8; Eze 20:5-6
47:15 u Eze 48:1
47:16 v 2Sa 8:8 w Nu 13:21; Eze 48:1
47:17 x Eze 48:1
47:19 y Dt 32:51 z Isa 27:12 a Eze 48:28
47:20 b Eze 48:1 c Nu 34:6

47:8, 9 The Arabah is the geological depression in which the Dead Sea lies. The sea that will become fresh refers to the Dead Sea, a body of water so salty that nothing can live in it. The river will freshen the Dead Sea's water so it can support life. This is another picture of the life-giving nature of the water that flows from God's temple. God's power can transform us no matter how lifeless or corrupt we may be. Even when we feel messed up and beyond hope, his power can heal us.

47:10 En Gedi and En Eglaim were on the western shore of the Dead Sea.

47:19 A wadi is a seasonal stream or river-bed that is dry much of the year.

47:22
[d]Isa 14:1
[e]Nu 26:55-56; Isa 56:6-7; Ro 10:12; Eph 2:12-16; 3:6; Col 3:11

48:1
[a]Ge 30:6
[b]Eze 47:15-17
[c]Eze 47:20

48:2
[d]Jos 19:24-31

48:3
[e]Jos 19:32-39

48:4
[f]Jos 17:1-11

48:5
[g]Jos 16:5-9
[h]Jos 17:7-10
[i]Jos 17:17

48:6
[j]Jos 13:15-21

48:7
[k]Jos 15:1-63

48:8
[l]ver 21

48:9
[m]Eze 45:1

48:10
[n]ver 21; Eze 45:3-4

48:11
[o]2Sa 8:17
[p]Lev 8:35
[q]Eze 14:11; 44:15

48:13
[r]Eze 45:5

48:14
[s]Lev 25:34; 27:10, 28

48:16
[t]Rev 21:16

48:18
[u]Eze 45:6

22 You are to allot it as an inheritance for yourselves and for the aliens[d] who have settled among you and who have children. You are to consider them as native-born Israelites; along with you they are to be allotted an inheritance among the tribes of Israel.[e] 23 In whatever tribe the alien settles, there you are to give him his inheritance," declares the Sovereign LORD.

The Division of the Land

48 "These are the tribes, listed by name: At the northern frontier, Dan[a] will have one portion; it will follow the Hethlon road[b] to Lebo[a] Hamath;[c] Hazar Enan and the northern border of Damascus next to Hamath will be part of its border from the east side to the west side.

2 "Asher[d] will have one portion; it will border the territory of Dan from east to west.

3 "Naphtali[e] will have one portion; it will border the territory of Asher from east to west.

4 "Manasseh[f] will have one portion; it will border the territory of Naphtali from east to west.

5 "Ephraim[g] will have one portion; it will border the territory of Manasseh[h] from east to west.[i]

6 "Reuben[j] will have one portion; it will border the territory of Ephraim from east to west.

7 "Judah[k] will have one portion; it will border the territory of Reuben from east to west.

8 "Bordering the territory of Judah from east to west will be the portion you are to present as a special gift. It will be 25,000 cubits[b] wide, and its length from east to west will equal one of the tribal portions; the sanctuary will be in the centre of it.[l]

9 "The special portion you are to offer to the LORD will be 25,000 cubits long and 10,000 cubits[c] wide.[m] 10 This will be the sacred portion for the priests. It will be 25,000 cubits long on the north side, 10,000 cubits wide on the west side, 10,000 cubits wide on the east side and 25,000 cubits long on the south side. In the centre of it will be the sanctuary of the LORD.[n] 11 This will be for the consecrated priests, the Zadokites,[o] who were faithful in serving me[p] and did not go astray as the Levites did when the Israelites went astray.[q] 12 It will be a special gift to them from the sacred portion of the land, a most holy portion, bordering the territory of the Levites.

13 "Alongside the territory of the priests, the Levites will have an allotment 25,000 cubits long and 10,000 cubits wide. Its total length will be 25,000 cubits and its width 10,000 cubits.[r] 14 They must not sell or exchange any of it. This is the best of the land and must not pass into other hands, because it is holy to the LORD.[s]

15 "The remaining area, 5,000 cubits wide and 25,000 cubits long, will be for the common use of the city, for houses and for pasture-land. The city will be in the centre of it 16 and will have these measurements: the north side 4,500 cubits, the south side 4,500 cubits, the east side 4,500 cubits, and the west side 4,500 cubits.[t] 17 The pasture-land for the city will be 250 cubits on the north, 250 cubits on the south, 250 cubits on the east, and 250 cubits on the west. 18 What remains of the area, bordering on the sacred portion and running the length of it, will be 10,000 cubits on the east side and 10,000 cubits on the west side. Its produce will supply food for the workers of the city.[u] 19 The workers from the city who farm it will come from all the tribes of Israel. 20 The entire portion will be a square, 25,000 cubits on each side. As a special gift you will set aside the sacred portion, along with the property of the city.

21 "What remains on both sides of the area formed by the sacred portion and the city

a *1* Or *to the entrance to* **b** *8* That is, about 7 miles (about 11 kilometres) **c** *9* That is, about 3 miles (about 5 kilometres)

47:22, 23 In the restoration there will be room for foreigners ("aliens"). The regulations of Leviticus 24:22 and Numbers 15:29 provided for this. Isaiah also taught it (Isaiah 56:3–8). The children of foreigners will even inherit property like Israelites. Anyone who accepts the standards and is willing to obey may enjoy the blessings of God's rule.

48:1ff The land would be divided into 13 parallel portions (one for each tribe plus a sacred district) that would stretch from the Jordan River or Dead Sea to the Mediterranean Sea. The division of the land shows that in God's kingdom there is a place for all who believe in and obey the one true God (see John 14:1–6).

property will belong to the prince. It will extend eastward from the 25,000 cubits of
the sacred portion to the eastern border, and westward from the 25,000 cubits to the
western border. Both these areas running the length of the tribal portions will belong
to the prince, and the sacred portion with the temple sanctuary will be in the centre
of them.[v] 22So the property of the Levites and the property of the city will lie in the
centre of the area that belongs to the prince. The area belonging to the prince will lie
between the border of Judah and the border of Benjamin.
23"As for the rest of the tribes: Benjamin[w] will have one portion; it will extend from
the east side to the west side.
24"Simeon[x] will have one portion; it will border the territory of Benjamin from
east to west.
25"Issachar[y] will have one portion; it will border the territory of Simeon from east
to west.
26"Zebulun[z] will have one portion; it will border the territory of Issachar from east
to west.
27"Gad[a] will have one portion; it will border the territory of Zebulun from east to
west.
28"The southern boundary of Gad will run south from Tamar[b] to the waters of
Meribah Kadesh, then along the Wadi ⌞of Egypt⌟ to the Great Sea.[d][c]
29"This is the land you are to allot as an inheritance to the tribes of Israel, and these
will be their portions," declares the Sovereign LORD.

The Gates of the City

30"These will be the exits of the city: Beginning on the north side, which is 4,500
cubits long, 31the gates of the city will be named after the tribes of Israel. The three
gates on the north side will be the gate of Reuben, the gate of Judah and the gate of
Levi.
32"On the east side, which is 4,500 cubits long, will be three gates: the gate of
Joseph, the gate of Benjamin and the gate of Dan.
33"On the south side, which measures 4,500 cubits, will be three gates: the gate
of Simeon, the gate of Issachar and the gate of Zebulun.
34"On the west side, which is 4,500 cubits long, will be three gates: the gate of
Gad, the gate of Asher and the gate of Naphtali.
35"The distance all around will be 18,000 cubits.
"And the name of the city from that time on will be:

THE LORD IS THERE.[d]"

d *28* That is, the Mediterranean

48:21 [v]ver 8, 10; Eze 45:7
48:23 [w]Jos 18:11-28
48:24 [x]Ge 29:33; Jos 19:1-9
48:25 [y]Jos 19:17-23
48:26 [z]Jos 19:10-16
48:27 [a]Jos 13:24-28
48:28 [b]Ge 14:7 [c]Eze 47:19
48:35 [d]Isa 12:6; 24:23; Jer 3:17; 14:9; Jer 33:16; Joel 3:21; Zec 2:10; Rev 21:3

48:28 The Great Sea is the Mediterranean.

48:35 The book of Ezekiel begins by describing the holiness of God that Israel had despised and ignored. As a result, God's presence departed from the temple, the city, and the people. The book ends with a detailed vision of the new temple, the new city, and the new people – all demonstrating God's holiness. The pressures of everyday life may persuade us to focus on the here and now and thus forget God. That is why worship is so important; it takes our eyes off our current worries, gives us a glimpse of God's holiness, and allows us to look towards his future kingdom. God's presence makes everything glorious, and worship brings us into his presence.

D A N I E L

Daniel taken captive to Babylon 605	*Ezekiel becomes a prophet to exiles 593*	*Judah falls; Jerusalem is destroyed; Jeremiah's ministry ends 586*	*Daniel's first vision 553*	*Babylon overthrown; Daniel thrown to lions 539*	*First exiles return to Judah 538*	*Daniel's ministry ends 536*

AN EARTHQUAKE shakes the foundation of our security; a tornado blows away a lifetime of treasures; an assassin's bullet changes national history; a drunk driver claims an innocent victim; a divorce shatters a home. International and personal tragedies make our world seem a fearful place, overflowing with evil and seemingly out of control. And the litany of bombings, coups, murders, and natural disasters could cause us to think that God is absent or impotent. "Where is God?" we cry, engulfed by sorrow and despair.

Twenty-five centuries ago, Daniel could have despaired. He and thousands of his countrymen had been deported to a foreign land after Judah was conquered. Daniel found himself facing an egocentric despot and surrounded by idolaters. Instead of giving in or giving up, this courageous young man held fast to his faith in his God. Daniel knew that despite the circumstances, God was sovereign and was working out his plan for nations and individuals. The book of Daniel centres around this profound truth—the sovereignty of God.

After a brief account of Nebuchadnezzar's siege and defeat of Jerusalem, the scene quickly shifts to Daniel and his three friends, Hananiah, Misha-el, and Azariah (Shadrach, Meshach, and Abednego). These men held prominent positions within the Babylonian government. Daniel, in particular, held such a position because of his ability to interpret the king's dreams that tell of God's unfolding plan (chapters 2 and 4). Sandwiched between the dreams is the fascinating account of Daniel's three friends and the furnace (chapter 3). Because they refused to bow down to an image of gold, they were condemned to a fiery death. But God intervened and spared their lives.

Belshazzar ruled Babylon after Nebuchadnezzar, and chapter 5 tells of his encounter with God's message written on a wall. Daniel, who was summoned to interpret the message, predicted Babylon's fall to the Medes and Persians. This prediction came true that very night, and Darius the Mede conquered the Babylonian kingdom.

Daniel became one of Darius' most trusted advisers. His privileged position angered other administrators, who plotted his death by persuading the king to outlaw prayer. In spite of the law, Daniel continued to pray to his sovereign Lord. As a result, he was condemned to die in a den of hungry lions. Again, God intervened and saved him, shutting the mouths of the lions (chapter 6).

The book concludes with a series of visions that Daniel had during the reigns of Belshazzar (chapters 7; 8), Darius (chapter 9), and Cyrus (chapters 10—12). These dreams dramatically outline God's future plans, beginning with Babylon and continuing to the end of the age. They give a preview of God's redemption and have been called the key to all biblical prophecy.

God is sovereign. He was in control in Babylon, and he has been moving in history, controlling the destinies of people ever since. And he is here now! Despite news reports or personal stress, we can be confident that God is in control. As you read Daniel, watch God work and find your security in his sovereignty.

VITAL STATISTICS

PURPOSE:
To give an historical account of the faithful Jews who lived in captivity and to show how God is in control of heaven and earth, directing the forces of nature, the destiny of nations, and the care of his people

AUTHOR:
Daniel

TO WHOM WRITTEN:
The other captives in Babylon and God's people everywhere

DATE WRITTEN:
Approximately 535 B.C., recording events that occurred from about 605–535 B.C.

SETTING:
Daniel had been taken captive and deported to Babylon by Nebuchadnezzar in 605 B.C. There he served in the government for about 60 years during the reigns of Nebuchadnezzar, Belshazzar, Darius, and Cyrus.

KEY VERSE:
"He [God] reveals deep and hidden things; he knows what lies in darkness, and light dwells with him" (2:22).

KEY PEOPLE:
Daniel, Nebuchadnezzar, Shadrach, Meshach, Abednego, Belshazzar, Darius

KEY PLACES:
Nebuchadnezzar's palace, the fiery furnace, Belshazzar's banquet, the den of lions

SPECIAL FEATURES:
Daniel's apocalyptic visions (chapters 8—12) give a glimpse of God's plan for the ages, including a direct prediction of the Messiah.

THE BLUEPRINT

A. DANIEL'S LIFE (1:1—6:28)	Daniel and his three friends chose not to eat the king's food. They did not bow down to the king's image, even under penalty of death. Daniel continued to pray even though he knew he might be noticed and sentenced to death. These men are inspiring examples to us of living a faithful life in a sinful world. When we face trials, we can expect God to remain present with us through our trials. May God grant us the same courage to remain faithful under pressure.
B. DANIEL'S VISIONS (7:1—12:13)	These visions gave the captives added confidence that God is in control of history. They were to wait patiently and in faith and not to worship the gods of Babylon or accept their way of life. God still rules over human activities. Evil will be overcome, so we should wait patiently and not give in to the temptations and pressures of the sinful way of life around us.

MEGATHEMES

THEME	EXPLANATION	IMPORTANCE
God is in Control	God is all-knowing, and he is in charge of world events. God overrules and removes rebellious leaders who defy him. God will overcome evil; no-one is exempt. But he will deliver the faithful who follow him.	Although nations vie for world control now, one day Christ's kingdom will replace and surpass the kingdoms of this world. Our faith is sure because our future is secure in Christ. We must have courage and put our faith in God who controls everything.
Purpose in Life	Daniel and his three friends are examples of dedication and commitment. They determined to serve God regardless of the consequences. They did not give in to pressures from an ungodly society because they had a clear purpose in life.	It is wise to make trusting and obeying God alone our true purpose in life. This will give us direction and peace in spite of the circumstances or consequences. We should disobey anyone who asks us to disobey God. Our first allegiance must be to God.
Perseverance	Daniel served for 70 years in a foreign land that was hostile to God, yet he did not compromise his faith in God. He was truthful, persistent in prayer, and disinterested in power for personal glory.	In order to fulfil your life's purpose, you need staying power. Don't let your Christian distinctives become blurred. Be relentless in your prayers, stay firm in your integrity, and be content to serve God wherever he puts you.
God's Faithfulness	God was faithful in Daniel's life. He delivered him from prison, from a den of lions, and from enemies who hated him. God cares for his people and deals patiently with them.	We can trust God to be with us through any trial because he promises to be there. Because he has been faithful to us, we should remain faithful to him.

A. DANIEL'S LIFE (1:1—6:28)

While Ezekiel was ministering to the captives in Babylon, Daniel was drafted as a counsellor to King Nebuchadnezzar. With God's help, Daniel interpreted two of the king's dreams, Daniel's three friends were rescued from certain death in the fiery furnace, and Daniel was rescued from a lions' den. Daniel's life is a picture of the triumph of faith. May God grant us this type of faith so that we may also live courageously each day.

Daniel's Training in Babylon

1 In the third year of the reign of Jehoiakim king of Judah, Nebuchadnezzar[a] king
of Babylon came to Jerusalem and besieged it.[b] 2 And the Lord delivered Jehoiakim king of Judah into his hand, along with some of the articles from the temple of

1:1 [a]2Ki 24:1 [b]2Ch 36:6

1:1, 2 Born during the middle of Josiah's reign (2 Kings 22; 23), Daniel grew up during the king's reforms. During this time, Daniel probably heard Jeremiah, a prophet he quoted in 9:2. In 609 B.C., Josiah was killed in a battle against Egypt, and within four years, the southern kingdom of Judah had returned to its evil ways.

In 605 B.C. Nebuchadnezzar became king of Babylonia. In

1:2
[c]2Ch 36:7; Jer 27:19-20; Zec 5:5-11

1:3
[d]2Ki 20:18; 24:15; Isa 39:7

1:5
[e]ver 8, 10
[f]ver 19

1:6
[g]Eze 14:14

1:7
[h]Da 4:8; 5:12
[i]Da 2:49; 3:12

God. These he carried off to the temple of his god in Babylonia[a] and put in the
treasure-house of his god.[c]
3Then the king ordered Ashpenaz, chief of his court officials, to bring in some of
the Israelites from the royal family and the nobility[d]—4young men without any
physical defect, handsome, showing aptitude for every kind of learning, well informed, quick to understand, and qualified to serve in the king's palace. He was to
teach them the language and literature of the Babylonians.[b] 5The king assigned them
a daily amount of food and wine[e] from the king's table. They were to be trained for
three years, and after that they were to enter the king's service.[f]
6Among these were some from Judah: Daniel,[g] Hananiah, Mishael and Azariah.
7The chief official gave them new names: to Daniel, the name Belteshazzar;[h] to
Hananiah, Shadrach; to Mishael, Meshach; and to Azariah, Abednego.[i]

[a]2 Hebrew *Shinar* [b]4 Or *Chaldeans*

DANIEL served as a prophet to the exiles in Babylon from 605–536 B.C.

Climate of the times	The people of Judah were captives in a strange land, feeling hopeless.
Main message	God is sovereign over all of human history, past, present, and future.
Importance of message	We should spend less time wondering when future events will happen and more time learning how we should live now.
Contemporary prophets	Jeremiah (627–586) Habakkuk (612–588) Ezekiel (593–571)

September of that year, he swept into Palestine and surrounded Jerusalem, making Judah his vassal state. To demonstrate his dominance, Nebuchadnezzar took many of Jerusalem's wisest men and most beautiful women to Babylon as captives. Daniel was among this group.

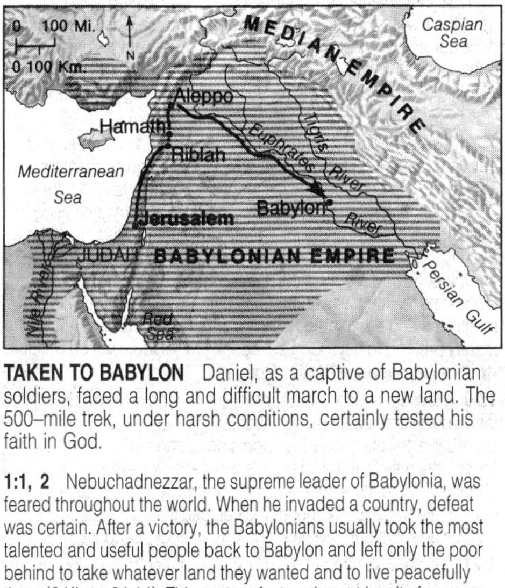

TAKEN TO BABYLON Daniel, as a captive of Babylonian soldiers, faced a long and difficult march to a new land. The 500–mile trek, under harsh conditions, certainly tested his faith in God.

1:1, 2 Nebuchadnezzar, the supreme leader of Babylonia, was feared throughout the world. When he invaded a country, defeat was certain. After a victory, the Babylonians usually took the most talented and useful people back to Babylon and left only the poor behind to take whatever land they wanted and to live peacefully there (2 Kings 24:14). This system fostered great loyalty from conquered lands and ensured a steady supply of wise and talented people for civil service.

1:2 At certain times God allows his work to suffer. In this instance, the Babylonians raided the temple of God, and took the worship articles to the temple of a god in Babylon. This god may have been Bel, also called Marduk, the chief god of the Babylonians. Those who loved the Lord must have felt disheartened and discouraged. We feel greatly disappointed when our churches suffer physical damage, split, close down for financial reasons, or are wracked by scandals. We do not know why God allows his church to experience these calamities. But like the people who witnessed the plundering of the temple by the Babylonians, we must trust that God is in control and that he is watching over all who trust in him.

1:4 The common language of Babylonia was Aramaic, while the language of scholarship included the ancient and complicated Babylonian language. The academic programme would have included mathematics, astronomy, history, science, and magic. These young men demonstrated not only aptitude, but also discipline. This character trait, combined with integrity, served them well in their new culture.

1:7 Nebuchadnezzar changed the names of Daniel and his friends because he wanted to make them Babylonian – in their own eyes and in the eyes of the Babylonian people. New names would help them assimilate into the culture. Daniel means "God is my Judge" in Hebrew; his name was changed to Belteshazzar meaning "Bel, protect his life"! (Bel, also called Marduk, was the chief Babylonian god.) Hananiah means "the Lord shows grace"; his new name, Shadrach, probably means "under the command of Aku" (the moon god). Mishael means "who is like God?;" his new name, Meshach, probably means "who is like Aku?" Azariah means "the Lord helps"; his new name, Abednego, means "servant of Nego/Nebo" (or Nabu, the god of learning and writing). This was how the king attempted to change the religious loyalty of these young men from Judah's God to Babylonia's gods.

8But Daniel resolved not to defile[j] himself with the royal food and wine, and he
asked the chief official for permission not to defile himself in this way. 9Now God
had caused the official to show favour[k] and sympathy[l] to Daniel, 10but the official
told Daniel, "I am afraid of my lord the king, who has assigned your[c] food and drink.
Why should he see you looking worse than the other young men of your age? The
king would then have my head because of you."
11Daniel then said to the guard whom the chief official had appointed over Daniel,
Hananiah, Mishael and Azariah, 12"Please test your servants for ten days: Give us
nothing but vegetables to eat and water to drink. 13Then compare our appearance with
that of the young men who eat the royal food, and treat your servants in accordance
with what you see." 14So he agreed to this and tested them for ten days.
15At the end of the ten days they looked healthier and better nourished than any
of the young men who ate the royal food.[m] 16So the guard took away their choice
food and the wine they were to drink and gave them vegetables instead.[n]
17To these four young men God gave knowledge and understanding[o] of all kinds
of literature and learning.[p] And Daniel could understand visions and dreams of all
kinds.[q]
18At the end of the time[r] set by the king to bring them in, the chief official
presented them to Nebuchadnezzar. 19The king talked with them, and he found none
equal to Daniel, Hananiah, Mishael and Azariah; so they entered the king's service.[s]
20In every matter of wisdom and understanding about which the king questioned them,
he found them ten times better than all the magicians and enchanters in his whole
kingdom.[t]
21And Daniel remained there until the first year of King Cyrus.[u]

c *10* The Hebrew for *your* and *you* in this verse is plural.

1:8 [j]Eze 4:13-14
1:9 [k]Ge 39:21; Pr 16:7 [l]1Ki 8:50; Ps 106:46
1:15 [m]Ex 23:25
1:16 [n]ver 12-13
1:17 [o]1Ki 3:12 [p]Da 2:23; Jas 1:5 [q]Da 2:19, 30; 7:1; 8:1
1:18 [r]ver 5
1:19 [s]Ge 41:46
1:20 [t]1Ki 4:30; Da 2:13, 28
1:21 [u]Da 6:28; 10:1

1:8 Daniel resolved not to eat this food, either because the meat was some food forbidden by Jewish law, like pork (see Leviticus 11), or because accepting the king's food and drink was the first step towards depending on his gifts and favours. Although Daniel was in a culture that did not honour God, he still obeyed God's laws.

1:8 *Resolve* is a strong word that means to be devoted to principle and to be committed to a course of action. When Daniel resolved not to defile himself, he was being true to a lifelong determination to do what was right and not to give in to the pressures around him. We too are often assaulted by pressures to compromise our standards and live more like the world around us. Merely wanting or preferring God's will and way is not enough to stand against the onslaught of temptation. Like Daniel, we must resolve to obey God.

1:8 It is easier to resist temptation if you have thought through your convictions well before the temptation arrives. Daniel and his friends made their decision to be faithful to the laws of God before they were faced with the king's delicacies, so they did not hesitate to stick with their convictions. We will get into trouble if we have not previously decided where to draw the line. Before such situations arise, decide on your commitments. Then when temptation comes, you will be ready to say no.

1:9 God moved with an unseen hand to change the heart of this Babylonian official. The strong moral conviction of these four young men made an impact. God promises to be with his people in times of trial and temptation (Psalm 106:46; Isaiah 43:2–5; 1 Corinthians 10:13). His active intervention often comes when we take a stand for him. Stand for God and trust him to protect you in ways you may not be able to see.

1:10 Anything short of complete obedience meant execution for the officials who served Nebuchadnezzar. Even in such a small matter as this, the official feared for his life.

1:12 The Babylonians were trying to change the *thinking* of these Jews by giving them a Babylonian education, their *loyalty* by changing their names, and their *lifestyle* by changing their diet. Without compromising, Daniel found a way to live by God's standards in a culture that did not honour God. Wisely choosing to negotiate rather than to rebel, Daniel suggested an experimental ten-day diet of vegetables and water, instead of the royal foods and wine the king offered. Without compromising, Daniel quickly thought of a practical, creative solution that saved his life and the lives of his companions. As God's people, we may adjust to our culture as long as we do not compromise God's laws.

1:17 Daniel and his friends learned all they could about their new culture so they could do their work with excellence. But while they learned, they maintained steadfast allegiance to God, and God gave them skill and wisdom. Culture need not be God's enemy. If it does not violate his commands, it can aid in accomplishing his purpose. We who follow God are free to be competent leaders in our culture, but we are required to pledge our allegiance to God first.

1:20 Nebuchadnezzar put Daniel and his friends on his staff of advisers. This staff included many "magicians and enchanters". These were astrologers who claimed to be able to tell the future through occult practices. They were masters at communicating their message so that it sounded authoritative – as though it came directly from their gods. In addition to knowledge, Daniel and his three friends had wisdom and understanding, given to them by God. Thus the king was far more pleased with them than with his magicians and enchanters. As we serve others, we must not merely pretend to have God's wisdom. Our wisdom will be genuine when we are rightly related to God.

1:20 How did the captives survive in a foreign culture? They learned about the culture, achieved excellence in their work, served the people, prayed for God's help, and maintained their integrity. We may feel like foreigners whenever we experience change. Alien cultures come in many forms: a new job, a new school, a new neighbourhood. We can use the same principles to help us adapt to our new surroundings without abandoning God.

1:21 Daniel was one of the first captives taken to Babylon, and he lived to see the first exiles return to Jerusalem in 538 B.C. Throughout this time Daniel honoured God, and God honoured him. While serving as an adviser to the kings of Babylon, Daniel was God's

2:1 [a]Job 33:15, 18; Da 4:5 [b]Ge 41:8 [c]Est 6:1; Da 6:18
2:2 [d]Ge 41:8 [e]Ex 7:11 [f]ver 10; Da 5:7 [g]Da 4:6
2:3 [h]Da 4:5
2:4 [i]Ezr 4:7 [j]Da 3:9; 5:10
2:5 [k]ver 12 [l]Ezr 6:11; Da 3:29
2:6 [m]ver 48; Da 5:7, 16
2:9 [n]Est 4:11 [o]Isa 41:22-24

Nebuchadnezzar's Dream

2 In the second year of his reign, Nebuchadnezzar had dreams;[a] his mind was
troubled[b] and he could not sleep.[c] 2So the king summoned the magicians,[d]
enchanters, sorcerers[e] and astrologers[a][f] to tell him what he had dreamed.[g] When
they came in and stood before the king, 3he said to them, "I have had a dream that
troubles[h] me and I want to know what it means."[b]
4Then the astrologers answered the king in Aramaic,[c][i] "O king, live for ever![j]
Tell your servants the dream, and we will interpret it."
5The king replied to the astrologers, "This is what I have firmly decided: If you
do not tell me what my dream was and interpret it, I will have you cut into pieces[k]
and your houses turned into piles of rubble.[l] 6But if you tell me the dream and explain
it, you will receive from me gifts and rewards and great honour.[m] So tell me the dream
and interpret it for me."
7Once more they replied, "Let the king tell his servants the dream, and we will
interpret it."
8Then the king answered, "I am certain that you are trying to gain time, because
you realise that this is what I have firmly decided: 9If you do not tell me the dream,
there is just one penalty[n] for you. You have conspired to tell me misleading and
wicked things, hoping the situation will change. So then, tell me the dream, and I will
know that you can interpret it for me."[o]
10The astrologers answered the king, "There is not a man on earth who can do what
the king asks! No king, however great and mighty, has ever asked such a thing of any

a 2 Or *Chaldeans*; also in verses 4, 5 and 10 b 3 Or *was* c 4 The text from here through chapter 7 is in Aramaic.

THE FULFILMENT OF DANIEL'S INTERPRETATION

The large statue in Nebuchadnezzar's dream (2:24–45) represented the four kingdoms that would dominate as world powers. We recognise these as the Babylonian empire, the Medo-Persian empire, the Grecian empire, and the Roman empire. All of these will be crushed and brought to an end by the kingdom of God, which will continue for ever.

Part	*Material*	*Empire*	*Period of Domination*
Head	Gold	Babylonian	606 B.C.—539 B.C.
Chest and Arms	Silver	Medo-Persian	539 B.C.—331 B.C.
Belly and Thighs	Bronze	Grecian	331 B.C.—146 B.C.
Legs and Feet	Iron and Clay	Roman	146 B.C.—A.D. 476

spokesman to the Babylonian empire. Babylon was a wicked nation, but it would have been much worse without Daniel's influence.

2:1–11 Dreams were considered to be messages from the gods, and the wise men were expected to interpret them. Usually the wise men could give some sort of interpretation as long as they knew what the dream was about. This time, however, Nebuchadnezzar demanded to be told the dream also. God sent a series of dreams to Nebuchadnezzar with prophetic messages that could be revealed and understood only by a servant of God. People from other time periods who received dreams from God include Jacob (Genesis 28:10–15), Joseph (Genesis 37:5–11), Pharaoh's cupbearer and his baker (Genesis 40), Pharaoh (Genesis 41), Solomon (1 Kings 3:5–15), and Joseph (Matthew 1:20–24).

2:10, 11 The astrologers told the king that "not a man on earth" could know the dreams of another person. What the king asked was humanly impossible. But Daniel could tell what the king had dreamed, and he could also give the interpretation because God was working through him. In daily life, we face many apparently impossible situations that would be hopeless if we had to handle them with our limited strength. But God specialises in working through us to achieve the impossible.

2:10, 11 The astrologers were unable to persuade the king with any amount of logic or rational argument. The king asked for something impossible and didn't want anyone to change his mind. When power goes to a leader's head, whether at work, at home, or in the church, that leader can sometimes begin demanding the impossible from subordinates. At times, this may be the challenge needed to motivate workers to achieve more than they thought they could. At other times, it may be the rantings and ravings of someone deluded with power. Just as Daniel dealt wisely in the situation, we can ask God to give us wisdom to know how to deal with unreasonable bosses.

magician or enchanter or astrologer.[p] 11 What the king asks is too difficult. No-one
can reveal it to the king except the gods,[q] and they do not live among men."
12 This made the king so angry and furious[r] that he ordered the execution[s] of all
the wise men of Babylon. 13 So the decree was issued to put the wise men to death,
and men were sent to look for Daniel and his friends to put them to death.[t]
14 When Arioch, the commander of the king's guard, had gone out to put to death
the wise men of Babylon, Daniel spoke to him with wisdom and tact. 15 He asked the
king's officer, "Why did the king issue such a harsh decree?" Arioch then explained
the matter to Daniel. 16 At this, Daniel went in to the king and asked for time, so that
he might interpret the dream for him.
17 Then Daniel returned to his house and explained the matter to his friends Hananiah, Mishael and Azariah.[u] 18 He urged them to plead for mercy[v] from the God of
heaven concerning this mystery,[w] so that he and his friends might not be executed
with the rest of the wise men of Babylon. 19 During the night the mystery[x] was
revealed to Daniel in a vision.[y] Then Daniel praised the God of heaven 20 and said:

"Praise be to the name of God for ever and ever;[z]
  wisdom and power[a] are his.
21 He changes times and seasons;[b]
  he sets up kings and deposes[c] them.
He gives wisdom[d] to the wise
  and knowledge to the discerning.
22 He reveals deep and hidden things;[e]
  he knows what lies in darkness,[f]
  and light[g] dwells with him.
23 I thank and praise you, O God of my fathers:[h]
  You have given me wisdom[i] and power,
you have made known to me what we asked of you,
  you have made known to us the dream of the king."

Daniel Interprets the Dream

24 Then Daniel went to Arioch,[j] whom the king had appointed to execute the wise

2:10 [p] ver 27
2:11 [q] Da 5:11
2:12 [r] Da 3:13, 19 [s] ver 5
2:13 [t] Da 1:20
2:17 [u] Da 1:6
2:18 [v] Isa 37:4 [w] Jer 33:3
2:19 [x] ver 28 [y] Job 33:15; Da 1:17
2:20 [z] Ps 113:2; 145:1-2 [a] Jer 32:19
2:21 [b] Da 7:25 [c] Job 12:19; Ps 75:6-7 [d] Jas 1:5
2:22 [e] Job 12:22; Ps 25:14; Da 5:11 [f] Ps 139:11-12; Jer 23:24; Heb 4:13 [g] Isa 45:7; Jas 1:17
2:23 [h] Ex 3:15 [i] Da 1:17
2:24 [j] ver 14

2:11 The astrologers said that the gods "do not live among men". Of course their gods didn't – they didn't even exist! This exposed the limitations of the astrologers. They could invent interpretations of dreams but could not tell Nebuchadnezzar *what* he had dreamed. Although his request was unreasonable, Nebuchadnezzar was furious when his advisers couldn't fulfil it. It was not unusual in these times for astrologers to be in conflict with the king. They sometimes used their craft to gain political power.

2:11 By answering that the gods "do not live among men", the astrologers betrayed their concept of the gods. Theirs was a hollow religion, a religion of convenience. They believed in the gods, but that belief made no difference in their conduct. Today, many people profess to believe in God, but it is also a hollow belief. In essence, they are practical atheists because they don't listen to him or do what he says. Do you believe in God? He *does* live among people, and he wants to change your life.

2:16–18 Daniel was at a crisis point. Imagine going to see the powerful, temperamental king who had just angrily ordered your death! Daniel did not shrink back in fear, however, but confidently believed God would tell him all the king wanted to know. When the king gave Daniel time to find the answer, Daniel found his three friends and they prayed. When you find yourself in a tight spot, share your needs with trusted friends who also believe in God's power. Prayer is more effective than panic. Panic confirms your hopelessness; prayer confirms your hope in God. Daniel's trust in God saved himself, his three friends, and all the other wise men of Babylon.

2:19–23 After Daniel asked God to reveal Nebuchadnezzar's dream to him, he saw a vision of the dream. Daniel's prayer was answered. Before rushing to Arioch with the news, Daniel took time to give God credit for all wisdom and power, thanking God for answering his request. How do you feel when your prayers are answered? Excited, surprised, relieved? There are times when we seek God in prayer and, after having been answered, dash off in our excitement, forgetting to give God credit for the answer. Match your persistence in prayer with gratitude when your requests are answered.

2:21 If you ever think that you have much to learn in life, and if you ever wish that you knew more about how to handle people, then look to God for wisdom. While educational institutions provide degrees at great expense, God gives wisdom freely to all who ask. (See James 1:5 for more on asking God for wisdom.)

2:21 When we see evil leaders who live long and good leaders who die young, we may wonder if God controls world events. Daniel saw evil rulers with almost limitless power, but Daniel knew and proclaimed that God "sets up kings and deposes them", that he controls everything that happens. God governs the world according to his purposes. You may be dismayed when you see evil people prosper, but God is in control. Let this knowledge give you confidence and peace no matter what happens.

2:24 Daniel did not use his success to promote his own self-interest. He thought of others. When striving to succeed or survive, remember the needs of others.

2:25 [k]Da 1:6; 5:13; 6:13
2:26 [l]Da 1:7
2:27 [m]ver 10
2:28 [n]Ge 40:8; Am 4:13 [o]Ge 49:1; Da 10:14 [p]Da 4:5
2:30 [q]Isa 45:3; Da 1:17; Am 4:13

men of Babylon, and said to him, "Do not execute the wise men of Babylon. Take
me to the king, and I will interpret his dream for him."
25 Arioch took Daniel to the king at once and said, "I have found a man among the
exiles from Judah[k] who can tell the king what his dream means."
26 The king asked Daniel (also called Belteshazzar),[l] "Are you able to tell me what
I saw in my dream and interpret it?"
27 Daniel replied, "No wise man, enchanter, magician or diviner can explain to the
king the mystery he has asked about,[m] 28 but there is a God in heaven who reveals
mysteries.[n] He has shown King Nebuchadnezzar what will happen in days to come.[o]
Your dream and the visions that passed through your mind[p] as you lay on your bed
are these:
29 "As you were lying there, O king, your mind turned to things to come, and the
revealer of mysteries showed you what is going to happen. 30 As for me, this mystery
has been revealed[q] to me, not because I have greater wisdom than other living men,
but so that you, O king, may know the interpretation and that you may understand
what went through your mind.

DANIEL

Daniel's early life demonstrates that there is more to being young than making mistakes. No characteristic wins the hearts of adults more quickly than wisdom in the words and actions of a young person. Daniel and his friends had been taken from their homes in Judah and exiled. Their futures were in doubt, but they all had personal traits that qualified them for jobs as servants in the king's palace. They took advantage of the opportunity without letting the opportunity take advantage of them.

Our first hint of Daniel's greatness comes in his quiet refusal to give up his convictions. He had applied God's will to his own life, and he resisted changing the good habits he had formed. Both his physical and spiritual diets were an important part of his relationship with God. He ate carefully and lived prayerfully. One of the benefits of being in training for royal service was eating food from the king's table. Daniel tactfully chose a simpler menu and proved it was a healthy choice. As with Daniel, mealtimes are obvious and regular tests of our efforts to control our appetites.

While Daniel limited his food intake, he indulged in prayer. He was able to communicate with God because he made it a habit. He put into practice his convictions, even when that meant being thrown into a den of hungry lions. His life proved he made the right choice.

Do you hold so strongly to your faith in God that whatever happens you will do what God says? Such conviction keeps you a step ahead of temptation; such conviction gives you wisdom and stability in changing circumstances. Prayerfully live out your convictions in everyday life and trust God for the results.

Strengths and accomplishments:
- Although young when deported, remained true to his faith
- Served as an adviser to two Babylonian kings and two Medo-Persian kings
- Was a man of prayer and a statesman with the gift of prophecy
- Survived the lions' den

Lessons from his life:
- Quiet convictions often earn long-term respect
- Don't wait until you are in a tough situation to learn about prayer
- God can use people wherever they are

Vital statistics:
- Where: Judah and the courts of both Babylon and Persia
- Occupation: A captive from Israel who became an adviser of kings
- Contemporaries: Hananiah, Mishael, Azariah, Nebuchadnezzar, Belshazzar, Darius, Cyrus

Key verse:
"This man Daniel, whom the king called Belteshazzar, was found to have a keen mind and knowledge and understanding, and also the ability to interpret dreams, explain riddles and solve difficult problems. Call for Daniel, and he will tell you what the writing means" (5:12).

Daniel's story is told in the book of Daniel. He is also mentioned in Matthew 24:15.

2:27–30 Before Daniel told the king anything else, he gave credit to God, explaining that he did not know the dream through his own wisdom but only because God revealed it. How easily we take credit for what God does through us! This robs God of the honour that he alone deserves. Instead we should be like Daniel and point people to God so that we give him the glory.

31 "You looked, O king, and there before you stood a large statue — an enormous,
dazzling statue,[r] awesome in appearance. 32 The head of the statue was made of pure
gold, its chest and arms of silver, its belly and thighs of bronze, 33 its legs of iron,
its feet partly of iron and partly of baked clay. 34 While you were watching, a rock
was cut out, but not by human hands.[s] It struck the statue on its feet of iron and clay
and smashed them.[t] 35 Then the iron, the clay, the bronze, the silver and the gold
were broken to pieces at the same time and became like chaff on a threshing-floor in
the summer. The wind swept them away[u] without leaving a trace. But the rock that
struck the statue became a huge mountain[v] and filled the whole earth.
36 "This was the dream, and now we will interpret it to the king. 37 You, O king,
are the king of kings.[w] The God of heaven has given you dominion[x] and power and
might and glory; 38 in your hands he has placed mankind and the beasts of the field
and the birds of the air. Wherever they live, he has made you ruler over them all.[y]
You are that head of gold.
39 "After you, another kingdom will rise, inferior to yours. Next, a third kingdom,
one of bronze, will rule over the whole earth. 40 Finally, there will be a fourth
kingdom, strong as iron — for iron breaks and smashes everything — and as iron breaks
things to pieces, so it will crush and break all the others.[z] 41 Just as you saw that the
feet and toes were partly of baked clay and partly of iron, so this will be a divided
kingdom; yet it will have some of the strength of iron in it, even as you saw iron mixed
with clay. 42 As the toes were partly iron and partly clay, so this kingdom will be partly
strong and partly brittle. 43 And just as you saw the iron mixed with baked clay, so
the people will be a mixture and will not remain united, any more than iron mixes
with clay.
44 "In the time of those kings, the God of heaven will set up a kingdom that will
never be destroyed, nor will it be left to another people. It will crush[a] all those
kingdoms[b] and bring them to an end, but it will itself endure for ever.[c] 45 This is
the meaning of the vision of the rock[d] cut out of a mountain, but not by human
hands[e] — a rock that broke the iron, the bronze, the clay, the silver and the gold to
pieces.
"The great God has shown the king what will take place in the future. The dream
is true and the interpretation is trustworthy."
46 Then King Nebuchadnezzar fell prostrate[f] before Daniel and paid him honour
and ordered that an offering[g] and incense be presented to him. 47 The king said to
Daniel, "Surely your God is the God of gods[h] and the Lord of kings[i] and a revealer
of mysteries,[j] for you were able to reveal this mystery."
48 Then the king placed Daniel in a high position and lavished many gifts on him.

2:31 [r] Hab 1:7
2:34 [s] Zec 4:6 [t] ver 44-45; Ps 2:9; Isa 60:12; Da 8:25
2:35 [u] Ps 1:4; 37:10; Isa 17:13 [v] Isa 2:3; Mic 4:1
2:37 [w] Eze 26:7 [x] Jer 27:7
2:38 [y] Jer 27:6; Da 4:21-22
2:40 [z] Da 7:7, 23
2:44 [a] Ps 2:9; 1Co 15:24 [b] Isa 60:12 [c] Ps 145:13; Isa 9:7; Da 4:34; 6:26; 7:14, 27; Mic 4:7, 13; Lk 1:33
2:45 [d] Isa 28:16 [e] Da 8:25
2:46 [f] Da 8:17; Ac 10:25 [g] Ac 14:13
2:47 [h] Da 11:36 [i] Da 4:25 [j] ver 22, 28

2:31ff The head of gold on the statue in the dream represented Nebuchadnezzar, ruler of the Babylonian empire. The silver chest and two arms represented the Medo-Persian empire, which conquered Babylon in 539 B.C. The belly and thighs of bronze were Greece and Macedonia under Alexander the Great, who conquered the Medo-Persian empire in 334–330 B.C. The legs of iron represented Rome, which conquered the Greeks in 63 B.C. The feet of clay and iron represented the break-up of the Roman empire, when the territory Rome ruled divided into a mixture of strong and weak nations. The type of metal in each part depicted the strength of the political power it represented. The rock cut out of the mountain depicted God's kingdom, which would be ruled eternally by the Messiah, the King of kings. The dream revealed Daniel's God as the power behind all earthly kingdoms.

2:36 When Daniel says "we", he is referring to himself and his three friends. Just as Daniel involved them in praying for God's help, he gave them credit when he presented the interpretation. Because they helped Daniel in the prayer, he was careful to share the credit with them.

2:44 God's kingdom will never be destroyed. If you are upset by threats of war and the prosperity of evil leaders, remember that God, not world leaders, decides the outcome of history. Under God's protection, God's kingdom is indestructible. Those who believe in God are members of his kingdom and are secure in him.

2:47 Nebuchadnezzar honoured Daniel and Daniel's God. If Daniel had taken the credit himself, the king would have honoured only Daniel. Because Daniel gave God the credit, the king honoured both of them. Part of our mission in this world is to show unbelievers what God is like. We can do that by giving God credit for what he does in our lives. Our acts of love and compassion may impress people, and if we give God credit for our actions, they will want to know more about him. Give thanks to God for what he is doing in and through you.

2:49 After being named ruler over the whole province of Babylon and placed in charge of the wise men, Daniel requested that his companions, Shadrach, Meshach, and Abednego, be appointed as his assistants. Daniel knew that he could not handle such an

He made him ruler over the entire province of Babylon and placed him in charge of
all its wise men.[k] 49Moreover, at Daniel's request the king appointed Shadrach,
Meshach and Abednego administrators over the province of Babylon,[l] while Daniel
himself remained at the royal court.

The Image of Gold and the Fiery Furnace

3 King Nebuchadnezzar made an image[a] of gold, ninety feet high and nine feet[a]
wide, and set it up on the plain of Dura in the province of Babylon. 2He then
summoned the satraps, prefects, governors, advisers, treasurers, judges, magistrates
and all the other provincial officials[b] to come to the dedication of the image he had
set up. 3So the satraps, prefects, governors, advisers, treasurers, judges, magistrates
and all the other provincial officials assembled for the dedication of the image that
King Nebuchadnezzar had set up, and they stood before it.
4Then the herald loudly proclaimed, "This is what you are commanded to do,
O peoples, nations and men of every language:[c] 5As soon as you hear the sound of the
horn, flute, zither, lyre, harp, pipes and all kinds of music, you must fall down and
worship the image of gold that King Nebuchadnezzar has set up.[d] 6Whoever does
not fall down and worship will immediately be thrown into a blazing furnace."[e]
7Therefore, as soon as they heard the sound of the horn, flute, zither, lyre, harp
and all kinds of music, all the peoples, nations and men of every language fell down
and worshipped the image of gold that King Nebuchadnezzar had set up.[f]
8At this time some astrologers[b][g] came forward and denounced the Jews. 9They
said to King Nebuchadnezzar, "O king, live for ever![h] 10You have issued a decree,[i]
O king, that everyone who hears the sound of the horn, flute, zither, lyre, harp, pipes
and all kinds of music must fall down and worship the image of gold,[j] 11and that
whoever does not fall down and worship will be thrown into a blazing furnace. 12But
there are some Jews whom you have set over the affairs of the province of Babylon—Shadrach, Meshach and Abednego[k]—who pay no attention[l] to you, O king.
They neither serve your gods nor worship the image of gold you have set up."[m]
13Furious[n] with rage, Nebuchadnezzar summoned Shadrach, Meshach and Abednego. So these men were brought before the king, 14and Nebuchadnezzar said to them,
"Is it true, Shadrach, Meshach and Abednego, that you do not serve my gods[o] or

a *1* Aramaic *sixty cubits high and six cubits wide* (about 27 metres high and 2.7 metres wide) **b** *8* Or *Chaldeans*

2:48 [k]ver 6; Da 4:9; 5:11
2:49 [l]Da 1:7
3:1 [a]Isa 46:6; Jer 16:20; Hab 2:19
3:2 [b]ver 27; Da 6:7
3:4 [c]Da 4:1; 6:25
3:5 [d]ver 10, 15
3:6 [e]ver 11, 15, 21; Jer 29:22; Da 6:7; Mt 13:42, 50; Rev 13:15
3:7 [f]ver 5
3:8 [g]Da 2:10
3:9 [h]Ne 2:3; Da 5:10; 6:6
3:10 [i]Da 6:12 [j]ver 4-6
3:12 [k]Da 2:49 [l]Da 6:13 [m]Est 3:3
3:13 [n]Da 2:12
3:14 [o]Isa 46:1; Jer 50:2

---

enormous responsibility without capable assistants, so he chose the best men he knew—his three Hebrew companions. A competent leader never does all the work alone; he or she knows how to delegate and supervise. Moses, Israel's greatest leader, shared the burden of administration with dozens of assistants. (This story is in Exodus 18:13–27.)

3:1 In Babylon's religious culture, statues were frequently worshipped. Nebuchadnezzar hoped to use this huge image (ninety feet high by nine feet wide) as a strategy to unite the nation and solidify his power by centralising worship. This gold image may have been inspired by his dream. Instead of having only a head of gold, however, it was gold from head to toe. Nebuchadnezzar wanted his kingdom to last for ever. When he made the statue, Nebuchadnezzar showed that his devotion to Daniel's God was short-lived. He neither feared nor obeyed the God who was behind the dream.

3:2 Satraps were governors over major divisions of the empire, serving as the chief representatives of the king. Prefects were the governors over conquered cities. Governors were civil administrators over provinces.

3:6 This blazing furnace was not a small oven for cooking dinner or heating a house; it was a huge industrial furnace that could have been used for baking bricks or smelting metals. The temperatures were hot enough to assure that no-one could survive. The roaring flames could be seen leaping from its top opening, and a fiery blast killed the soldiers who went up to the large opening (3:22).

3:12 We don't know if other Jews refused to fall down and worship the image, but these three were singled out as public examples. Why didn't the three men just bow to the image and tell God that they didn't mean it? They had determined never to worship another god, and they courageously took their stand. As a result, they were condemned and led away to be executed. The men did not know whether they would be delivered from the fire; all they knew was that they would not fall down and worship an idol. Are you ready to take a stand for God no matter what? When you stand for God, you will stand out. It may be painful, and it may not always have a happy ending. Be prepared to say, "If he rescues me, or if he doesn't, I will serve only God."

3:13 Nebuchadnezzar had lost control. How could anyone dare to disobey his commands? As the supreme ruler of Babylonia, he expected absolute obedience. But his pride had caused him to go beyond his own authority. His demands were unjust and his reactions extreme. If you find yourself angered when people don't follow your directions, ask yourself, "Why am I reacting?" Your ego may be overly involved with your authority.

worship the image[p] of gold I have set up? 15Now when you hear the sound of the
horn, flute, zither, lyre, harp, pipes and all kinds of music, if you are ready to fall
down and worship the image I made, very good. But if you do not worship it, you
will be thrown immediately into a blazing furnace. Then what god[q] will be able to
rescue[r] you from my hand?"
16Shadrach, Meshach and Abednego[s] replied to the king, "O Nebuchadnezzar, we
do not need to defend ourselves before you in this matter. 17If we are thrown into the
blazing furnace, the God we serve is able to save[t] us from it, and he will rescue[u]
us from your hand, O king. 18But even if he does not, we want you to know, O king,
that we will not serve your gods or worship the image of gold you have set up.[v]"
19Then Nebuchadnezzar was furious with Shadrach, Meshach and Abednego, and
his attitude towards them changed. He ordered the furnace to be heated seven[w] times
hotter than usual 20and commanded some of the strongest soldiers in his army to tie
up Shadrach, Meshach and Abednego and throw them into the blazing furnace. 21So
these men, wearing their robes, trousers, turbans and other clothes, were bound and
thrown into the blazing furnace. 22The king's command was so urgent and the furnace
so hot that the flames of the fire killed the soldiers who took up Shadrach, Meshach
and Abednego,[x] 23and these three men, firmly tied, fell into the blazing furnace.
24Then King Nebuchadnezzar leaped to his feet in amazement and asked his
advisers, "Weren't there three men that we tied up and threw into the fire?"
They replied, "Certainly, O king."
25He said, "Look! I see four men walking around in the fire, unbound and unharmed, and the fourth looks like a son of the gods."
26Nebuchadnezzar then approached the opening of the blazing furnace and shouted,
"Shadrach, Meshach and Abednego, servants of the Most High God,[y] come out!
Come here!"
So Shadrach, Meshach and Abednego came out of the fire, 27and the satraps,
prefects, governors and royal advisers[z] crowded around them.[a] They saw that the
fire[b] had not harmed their bodies, nor was a hair of their heads singed; their robes
were not scorched, and there was no smell of fire on them.

3:14 [p]ver 1
3:15 [q]Isa 36:18-20 [r]Ex 5:2; 2Ch 32:15
3:16 [s]Da 1:7
3:17 [t]Ps 27:1-2 [u]Job 5:19; Jer 1:8
3:18 [v]ver 28; Jos 24:15
3:19 [w]Lev 26:18-28
3:22 [x]Da 1:7
3:26 [y]Da 4:2, 34
3:27 [z]ver 2 [a]Isa 43:2; Heb 11:32-34 [b]Da 6:23

3:15 The three men were given one more chance. Here are eight excuses they could have used to bow to the image and save their lives: (1) We will fall down but not actually *worship* the idol. (2) We won't become idol worshippers, but will worship it this one time, and then ask God for forgiveness. (3) The king has absolute power, and we must obey him. God will understand. (4) The king appointed us – we owe this to him. (5) This is a foreign land, so God will excuse us for following the customs of the land. (6) Our ancestors set up idols in God's temple! This isn't half as bad! (7) We're not hurting anybody. (8) If we get ourselves killed and some pagans take our high positions, they won't help our people in exile!

Although all these excuses sound sensible at first, they are dangerous rationalisations. To fall down and worship the image would violate God's command in Exodus 20:3, "You shall have no other gods before me." It would also destroy their testimony for God for ever. Never again could they talk about the power of their God above all other gods. What excuses do you use for not standing up for him?

3:16–18 Shadrach, Meshach, and Abednego were pressured to deny God, but they chose to be faithful to him no matter what happened! They trusted God to deliver them, but they were determined to be faithful regardless of the consequences. If God always rescued those who were true to him, Christians would not need faith. Their religion would be a great insurance policy, and there would be lines of selfish people ready to sign up. We should be faithful to serve God whether he intervenes on our behalf or not. Our eternal reward is worth any suffering we may have to endure first.

3:19 "His attitude toward them changed." When we do something that offends non-Christians, their attitude toward us often changes because they are basically selfish. Christians should be different; they should still love those who offend them.

3:25 It was obvious to those watching that this fourth person was supernatural. We cannot be certain who the fourth man was. It could have been an angel or a pre-incarnate appearance of Christ. In either case, God sent a heavenly visitor to accompany these faithful men during their time of great trial.

3:25–30 God's deliverance of Shadrach, Meshach, and Abednego was a great victory of faith for the Jews in captivity. They were protected from harm, they were comforted in trial, God was glorified, and they were rewarded. Let us resolve to be true to God no matter how difficult the pressure or punishment. God's protection transcends anything we could imagine.

3:27 These young men had been completely untouched by the fire and heat. Only the rope that bound them had been burned. No human can bind us if God wants us to be free. The power available to us is the same that delivered Shadrach, Meshach, and Abednego and raised Christ from the dead (Ephesians 1:18–20). Trust God in every situation. There are eternal reasons for temporary trials; so be thankful that your destiny is in God's hands, not in human hands.

3:28, 29 Nebuchadnezzar was not making a commitment here to serve the Hebrews' God alone. Instead, he was acknowledging that God is powerful, and he commanded his people not to speak against God. Nebuchadnezzar didn't tell the people to throw away all the other gods, but to add this one to the list.

3:28
[c] Ps 34:7; Da 6:22; Ac 5:19
[d] Job 13:15; Ps 26:1; 84:12; Jer 17:7
[e] ver 18
3:29
[f] Da 6:26
[g] Ezr 6:11
[h] Da 6:27
3:30
[i] Da 2:49

28 Then Nebuchadnezzar said, "Praise be to the God of Shadrach, Meshach and
Abednego, who has sent his angel[c] and rescued his servants! They trusted[d] in him
and defied the king's command and were willing to give up their lives rather than serve
or worship any god except their own God.[e] 29 Therefore I decree[f] that the people
of any nation or language who say anything against the God of Shadrach, Meshach
and Abednego be cut into pieces and their houses be turned into piles of rubble,[g] for
no other god can save[h] in this way."
30 Then the king promoted Shadrach, Meshach and Abednego in the province of
Babylon.[i]

Shadrach/Meshach/Abednego

Friendships make life enjoyable and difficult times bearable. Friendships are tested and strengthened by hardships. Such was the relationship between three young Jewish men deported to Babylon along with Daniel. Shadrach, Meshach, and Abednego help us think about the real meaning of friendship. As much as these friends meant to each other, they never allowed their friendship to usurp God's place in their lives—not even in the face of death.

Together they silently defied King Nebuchadnezzar's order to fall down and worship the image of gold. They shared a courageous act, while others, eager to get rid of them, told the king that the three Jews were being disloyal. While this was not true, Nebuchadnezzar could not spare them without shaming himself.

This was the moment of truth. Death was about to end their friendship. A small compromise would have allowed them to live and go on enjoying each other, serving God, and serving their people while in this foreign land. But they were wise enough to see that compromise would have poisoned the very conviction that bound them so closely—each had a higher allegiance to God. So they did not hesitate to place their lives in the hands of God. The rest was victory!

When we leave God out of our most important relationships, we tend to expect those relationships to meet needs in us that only God can meet. Friends are helpful, but they cannot meet our deepest spiritual needs. Leaving God out of our relationships indicates how unimportant he really is in our own lives. Our relationship with God should be important enough to touch our other relationships—especially our closest friendships.

Strengths and accomplishments:
- Stood with Daniel against eating food from the king's table
- Shared a friendship that stood the tests of hardship, success, wealth, and possible death
- Unwilling to compromise their convictions even in the face of death
- Survived the fiery furnace

Lessons from their lives:
- There is great strength in real friendship
- It is important to stand with others with whom we share convictions
- God can be trusted even when we can't predict the outcome

Vital statistics:
- Where: Babylon
- Occupations: King's servants and advisers
- Contemporaries: Daniel, Nebuchadnezzar

Key verses:
"Shadrach, Meshach and Abednego replied to the king, 'O Nebuchadnezzar, we do not need to defend ourselves before you in this matter. If we are thrown into the blazing furnace, the God we serve is able to save us from it, and he will rescue us from your hand, O king. But even if he does not, we want you to know, O king, that we will not serve your gods or worship the image of gold you have set up' " (3:16–18).

The story of Shadrach (Hananiah), Meshach (Mishael), and Abednego (Azariah) is told in the book of Daniel.

3:30 Where was Daniel in this story? The Bible doesn't say, but there are several possibilities. (1) He may have been on official business in another part of the kingdom. (2) He may have been present, but because he was a ruler, the officials didn't accuse him of not falling down and worshipping the image. (3) He may have been in the capital city handling the administration while Nebuchadnezzar was away. (4) He may have been considered exempt from bowing down to the image because of his reputation for interpreting dreams through his God. Whether Daniel was there or not, we can be sure that he would not have worshipped the image.

Nebuchadnezzar's Dream of a Tree

4 King Nebuchadnezzar,

To the peoples, nations and men of every language,[a] who live in all the world:

May you prosper greatly![b]

2It is my pleasure to tell you about the miraculous signs[c] and wonders that
the Most High God[d] has performed for me.

3How great are his signs,
how mighty his wonders![e]
His kingdom is an eternal kingdom;
his dominion endures[f] from generation to generation.

4I, Nebuchadnezzar, was at home in my palace, contented[g] and prosperous.
5I had a dream[h] that made me afraid. As I was lying in my bed, the images and
visions that passed through my mind[i] terrified me. 6So I commanded that all
the wise men of Babylon be brought before me to interpret[j] the dream for me.
7When the magicians,[k] enchanters, astrologers**a** and diviners[l] came, I told
them the dream, but they could not interpret it for me.[m] 8Finally, Daniel came
into my presence and I told him the dream. (He is called Belteshazzar,[n] after
the name of my god, and the spirit of the holy gods[o] is in him.)
9I said, "Belteshazzar, chief[p] of the magicians, I know that the spirit of the
holy gods[q] is in you, and no mystery is too difficult for you. Here is my dream;
interpret it for me. 10These are the visions I saw while lying in my bed:[r] I looked,
and there before me stood a tree in the middle of the land. Its height was
enormous.[s] 11The tree grew large and strong and its top touched the sky; it was
visible to the ends of the earth. 12Its leaves were beautiful, its fruit abundant,
and on it was food for all. Under it the beasts of the field found shelter, and the
birds of the air lived in its branches;[t] from it every creature was fed.
13"In the visions I saw while lying in my bed,[u] I looked, and there before me
was a messenger,**b** a holy one,[v] coming down from heaven. 14He called in a
loud voice: 'Cut down the tree and trim off its branches; strip off its leaves and
scatter its fruit. Let the animals flee from under it and the birds from its
branches.[w] 15But let the stump and its roots, bound with iron and bronze, remain
in the ground, in the grass of the field.
" 'Let him be drenched with the dew of heaven, and let him live with the
animals among the plants of the earth. 16Let his mind be changed from that of
a man and let him be given the mind of an animal, till seven times**c** pass by for
him.[x]
17" 'The decision is announced by messengers, the holy ones declare the
verdict, so that the living may know that the Most High[y] is sovereign[z] over
the kingdoms of men and gives them to anyone he wishes and sets over them
the lowliest[a] of men.'
18"This is the dream that I, King Nebuchadnezzar, had. Now, Belteshazzar,
tell me what it means, for none of the wise men in my kingdom can interpret
it for me.[b] But you can,[c] because the spirit of the holy gods is in you."[d]

a *7* Or *Chaldeans* **b** *13* Or *watchman*; also in verses 17 and 23 **c** *16* Or *years*; also in verses 23, 25 and 32

4:1 [a]Da 3:4 [b]Da 6:25
4:2 [c]Ps 74:9 [d]Da 3:26
4:3 [e]Ps 105:27; Da 6:27 [f]Da 2:44
4:4 [g]Ps 30:6
4:5 [h]Da 2:1 [i]Da 2:28
4:6 [j]Da 2:2
4:7 [k]Ge 41:8 [l]Isa 44:25; Da 2:2 [m]Da 2:10
4:8 [n]Da 1:7 [o]Da 5:11, 14
4:9 [p]Da 2:48 [q]Da 5:11-12
4:10 [r]ver 5 [s]Eze 31:3-4
4:12 [t]Eze 17:23; Mt 13:32
4:13 [u]Da 7:1 [v]ver 23; Dt 33:2; Da 8:13
4:14 [w]Eze 31:12; Mt 3:10
4:16 [x]ver 23, 32
4:17 [y]ver 2, 25; Ps 83:18 [z]Jer 27:5-7; Da 2:21; 5:18-21 [a]Da 11:21
4:18 [b]Ge 41:8; Da 5:8, 15 [c]Ge 41:15 [d]ver 7-9

4:2, 3 Although Nebuchadnezzar praised Daniel's God, he still did not believe in him completely or submit to him alone (4:8). Many people attend church and use spiritual language, but they really don't believe in God or obey him. Profession doesn't always mean possession. How do your beliefs match with your obedience?

4:17 One of the most difficult lessons to learn is that God is sovereign. He is above all of those who are above us. He limits the power and authority of all the government, business, and religious leaders in the world. Those who live in freedom and have a relatively high degree of independence find this difficult to understand. While we may feel as though we are free to do what we please, God is sovereign over all of our plans and desires.

4:19
[e]Da 7:15, 28; 8:27; 10:16-17

Daniel Interprets the Dream

19Then Daniel (also called Belteshazzar) was greatly perplexed for a time, and
his thoughts terrified[e] him. So the king said, "Belteshazzar, do not let the dream
or its meaning alarm you."
Belteshazzar answered, "My lord, if only the dream applied to your enemies
and its meaning to your adversaries! 20The tree you saw, which grew large and
strong, with its top touching the sky, visible to the whole earth, 21with beautiful

NEBUCHADNEZZAR

Nebuchadnezzar was one world leader who decided he could get more co-operation from the people he conquered by letting them keep their gods. Their lands he took, their riches he robbed, their lives he controlled, but their idols he allowed them to worship, sometimes even worshipping them himself. Nebuchadnezzar's plan worked well, with one glaring exception. When he conquered the little nation of Judah, he met a God who demanded *exclusive* worship—not just his share among many gods. In a sense, Nebuchadnezzar had always been able to rule the gods. This new God was different; this God dared to claim that he had made Nebuchadnezzar all that he was. One of the great conquerors in history was himself conquered by his Creator.

The Bible allows us to note the ways in which God worked on Nebuchadnezzar. God allowed him victories, but he was accomplishing God's purposes. God allowed him to deport the best young Jewish leaders as his palace servants, while placing close to him a young man named Daniel, who would change the king's life. God allowed Nebuchadnezzar to attempt to kill three of his servants to teach the king that he did not really have power over life and death. God warned him of the dangers of his pride, and then allowed Nebuchadnezzar to live through seven years of insanity before restoring him to the throne. God showed the king who was really in control!

These lessons are clear to us today because of our place in history. When our attention shifts to our own lives, we find ourselves unable to see how God is working. But we do have the advantage of God's word as our guide for today's challenges. We are commanded to obey God; we are also commanded to trust him. Trusting him covers those times when we are not sure about the outcome. God has entrusted us with this day; have we trusted him with our lives?

Strengths and accomplishments:
- Greatest of the Babylonian kings
- Known as a builder of cities
- Described in the Bible as one of the foreign rulers God used for his purposes

Weaknesses and mistakes:
- Thought of himself as a god and was persuaded to build an image of gold that all were to worship
- Became extremely proud, which led to a bout of insanity
- Tended to forget the demonstrations of God's power he had witnessed

Lessons from his life:
- History records the actions of God's willing servants and those who were his unwitting tools
- A leader's greatness is affected by the quality of his advisers
- Uncontrolled pride is self-destructive

Vital statistics:
- Where: Babylon
- Occupation: King
- Relatives: Father: Nabopolassar. Son: Evil-Merodach. Grandson: Belshazzar
- Contemporaries: Jeremiah, Ezekiel, Daniel, Jehoiakim, Jehoiachin

Key verse:
"Now I, Nebuchadnezzar, praise and exalt and glorify the King of heaven, because everything he does is right and all his ways are just. And those who walk in pride he is able to humble" (4:37).

Nebuchadnezzar's story is told in 2 Kings 24; 25; 2 Chronicles 36; Jeremiah 21—52; Daniel 1—4.

4:19 When Daniel understood Nebuchadnezzar's dream, he was stunned, and he wondered how to break the news. He told the king he wished what the dream foreshadowed would happen to the king's enemies and not to Nebuchadnezzar. How could Daniel be so deeply grieved at the fate of Nebuchadnezzar—the king who was responsible for the destruction of Daniel's home and nation? Daniel had forgiven Nebuchadnezzar, and so God was able to use Daniel. Very often when we have been wronged by someone, we find it difficult to forget the past. We may even be glad when that person suffers. Forgiveness means putting the past behind us. Can you love someone who has hurt you? Can you serve someone who mistreated you? Ask God to help you forgive, forget, and love. God may use you in an extraordinary way in that person's life!

leaves and abundant fruit, providing food for all, giving shelter to the beasts of
the field, and having nesting places in its branches for the birds of the air—22you,
O king, are that tree![f] You have become great and strong; your greatness has
grown until it reaches the sky, and your dominion extends to distant parts of the
earth.[g]
23“You, O king, saw a messenger, a holy one,[h] coming down from heaven
and saying, ‘Cut down the tree and destroy it, but leave the stump, bound with
iron and bronze, in the grass of the field, while its roots remain in the ground.
Let him be drenched with the dew of heaven; let him live like the wild animals,
until seven times pass by for him.’[i]
24“This is the interpretation, O king, and this is the decree[j] the Most High
has issued against my lord the king: 25You will be driven away from people and
will live with the wild animals; you will eat grass like cattle and be drenched with
the dew of heaven. Seven times will pass by for you until you acknowledge that
the Most High[k] is sovereign over the kingdoms of men and gives them to anyone
he wishes.[l] 26The command to leave the stump of the tree with its roots[m] means
that your kingdom will be restored to you when you acknowledge that Heaven
rules.[n] 27Therefore, O king, be pleased to accept my advice: Renounce your sins
by doing what is right, and your wickedness by being kind to the oppressed.[o]
It may be that then your prosperity will continue.[p]”

The Dream Is Fulfilled

28All this happened[q] to King Nebuchadnezzar. 29Twelve months later, as the
king was walking on the roof of the royal palace of Babylon, 30he said, “Is not
this the great Babylon I have built as the royal residence, by my mighty power
and for the glory of my majesty?”[r]
31The words were still on his lips when a voice came from heaven, “This is
what is decreed for you, King Nebuchadnezzar: Your royal authority has been
taken from you. 32You will be driven away from people and will live with the
wild animals; you will eat grass like cattle. Seven times will pass by for you until
you acknowledge that the Most High is sovereign over the kingdoms of men and
gives them to anyone he wishes.”
33Immediately what had been said about Nebuchadnezzar was fulfilled. He
was driven away from people and ate grass like cattle. His body was drenched
with the dew of heaven until his hair grew like the feathers of an eagle and his
nails like the claws of a bird.[s]

34At the end of that time, I, Nebuchadnezzar, raised my eyes towards heaven,
and my sanity was restored. Then I praised the Most High; I honoured and
glorified him who lives for ever.[t]

His dominion is an eternal dominion;
his kingdom endures from generation to generation.[u]
35All the peoples of the earth
are regarded as nothing.[v]
He does as he pleases[w]
with the powers of heaven
and the peoples of the earth.
No-one can hold back his hand
or say to him: “What have you done?”[x]

4:22 [f] 2Sa 12:7 [g] Jer 27:7; Da 2:37-38; 5:18-19
4:23 [h] ver 13 [i] Da 5:21
4:24 [j] Job 40:12; Ps 107:40
4:25 [k] ver 17; Ps 83:18 [l] Jer 27:5; Da 5:21
4:26 [m] ver 15 [n] Da 2:37
4:27 [o] Isa 55:6-7 [p] 1Ki 21:29; Ps 41:3; Eze 18:22
4:28 [q] Nu 23:19
4:30 [r] Isa 37:24-25; Da 5:20; Hab 2:4
4:33 [s] Da 5:20-21
4:34 [t] Da 12:7; Rev 4:10 [u] Ps 145:13; Da 2:44; 5:21; 6:26; Lk 1:33
4:35 [v] Isa 40:17 [w] Ps 115:3; 135:6 [x] Isa 45:9; Ro 9:20

4:23ff Although much of the world thought that Nebuchadnezzar was a mighty (even divine) king, God demonstrated that Nebuchadnezzar was an ordinary man. The king would go insane and become like an animal for a set period of time ("seven times"). God humiliated Nebuchadnezzar to show that Almighty God, not Nebuchadnezzar, was Lord of the nations. No matter how powerful a person may become, self-centred pride will push God from his or her life. Pride may be one of the most dangerous temptations you will face. Don't let your accomplishments cause you to forget God.

4:27–33 Daniel pleaded with Nebuchadnezzar to change his ways, and God gave Nebuchadnezzar 12 months to do it. Unfortunately, there was no repentance in the heart of this proud king, and so the dream was fulfilled.

4:34 Ancient kings tried to avoid mentioning their weaknesses or defeats in their monuments and official records. From Nebuchadnezzar's records, however, we can infer that for a time during his

36 At the same time that my sanity was restored, my honour and splendour were
returned to me for the glory of my kingdom.[y] My advisers and nobles sought
me out, and I was restored to my throne and became even greater than before.
37 Now I, Nebuchadnezzar, praise and exalt and glorify the King of heaven,
because everything he does is right and all his ways are just.[z] And those who
walk in pride he is able to humble.[a]

The Writing on the Wall

5 King Belshazzar gave a great banquet[a] for a thousand of his nobles and drank
wine with them. 2 While Belshazzar was drinking his wine, he gave orders to bring
in the gold and silver goblets[b] that Nebuchadnezzar his father[a] had taken from the
temple in Jerusalem, so that the king and his nobles, his wives and his concubines
might drink from them.[c] 3 So they brought in the gold goblets that had been taken
from the temple of God in Jerusalem, and the king and his nobles, his wives and his
concubines drank from them. 4 As they drank the wine, they praised the gods of gold
and silver, of bronze, iron, wood and stone.[d]
5 Suddenly the fingers of a human hand appeared and wrote on the plaster of the
wall, near the lampstand in the royal palace. The king watched the hand as it wrote.
6 His face turned pale and he was so frightened[e] that his knees knocked together and
his legs gave way.[f]
7 The king called out for the enchanters, astrologers[b] and diviners[g] to be brought
and said to these wise[h] men of Babylon, "Whoever reads this writing and tells me
what it means will be clothed in purple and have a gold chain placed around his neck,[i]
and he will be made the third highest ruler in the kingdom."[j]
8 Then all the king's wise men came in, but they could not read the writing or tell
the king what it meant.[k] 9 So King Belshazzar became even more terrified[l] and his
face grew more pale. His nobles were baffled.
10 The queen,[c] hearing the voices of the king and his nobles, came into the banquet
hall. "O king, live for ever!"[m] she said. "Don't be alarmed! Don't look so pale!
11 There is a man in your kingdom who has the spirit of the holy gods[n] in him. In
the time of your father he was found to have insight and intelligence and wisdom[o]
like that of the gods. King Nebuchadnezzar your father—your father the king, I
say—appointed him chief of the magicians, enchanters, astrologers and diviners.[p]
12 This man Daniel, whom the king called Belteshazzar,[q] was found to have a keen
mind and knowledge and understanding, and also the ability to interpret dreams,

[a] *2* Or *ancestor*; or *predecessor*; also in verses 11, 13 and 18 [b] *7* Or *Chaldeans*; also in verse 11
[c] *10* Or *queen mother*

4:36 [y]Pr 22:4
4:37 [z]Dt 32:4; Ps 33:4-5 [a]Ex 18:11; Job 40:11-12; Da 5:20, 23
5:1 [a]Est 1:3
5:2 [b]2Ki 24:13; Jer 52:19 [c]Est 1:7; Da 1:2
5:4 [d]Ps 135:15-18; Hab 2:19; Rev 9:20
5:6 [e]Da 4:5 [f]Eze 7:17
5:7 [g]Isa 44:25 [h]Da 4:6-7 [i]Ge 41:42 [j]Da 2:5-6, 48; 6:2-3
5:8 [k]Da 2:10, 27
5:9 [l]Isa 21:4
5:10 [m]Da 3:9
5:11 [n]Da 4:8-9, 19 [o]ver 14; Da 1:17 [p]Da 2:47-48
5:12 [q]Da 1:7

43-year reign he did not rule. The Bible, however, explains Nebuchadnezzar's pride and punishment.

4:36 Nebuchadnezzar's pilgrimage with God is one of the themes of this book. In 2:47, he acknowledged that God revealed mysteries to Daniel. In 3:28, 29 he praised the God who rescued the three Hebrews. Despite Nebuchadnezzar's recognition that God exists and works great miracles, in 4:30 we see that he still did not acknowledge God as his Lord. We may recognise that God exists and does wonderful miracles, but God is not going to change us until we acknowledge him as Lord.

5:1 Sixty-six years have elapsed since chapter 1, which tells of Nebuchadnezzar's strike against Jerusalem in 605 B.C. Nebuchadnezzar died in 562 B.C. after a reign of 43 years. His son, Evil-Merodach, ruled from 562–560 B.C.; his brother-in-law Neriglissar reigned four years from 560–556 B.C. After a two-month reign by Labashi-Marduk in 556 B.C., the Babylonian empire continued from 556–539 B.C. under the command of Nabonidus. Belshazzar was the son of Nabonidus. He co-reigned with his father from 553–539 B.C. Nebuchadnezzar is called Belshazzar's "father". The term could also mean "ancestor".

5:1 Archaeologists have recently discovered Belshazzar's name on several documents. He ruled with his father, Nabonidus, staying home to administer the affairs of the kingdom while his father tried to reopen trade routes taken over by Cyrus and the Persians. Belshazzar was in charge of the city of Babylon when it was captured.

5:7 Belshazzar served as co-regent with his father Nabonidus. Thus, Nabonidus was the first ruler and his son Belshazzar, the second. The person who could read the writing would be given third place, which was the highest position and honour that Belshazzar could offer.

5:8 Although the writing on the wall contained only three words in Aramaic, a language understood by Babylonians (see 2:4), the people could not determine its prophetic significance. God gave Daniel alone the ability to interpret the message of doom to Babylon. The wise men of the kingdom were ignorant of God's wisdom, no matter how great the reward. Daniel did not rush into the banquet hall with the others. His loyalty was to God, not money.

5:10 This queen was either Nabonidus' wife or the wife of one of his predecessors, possibly even of Nebuchadnezzar. She was not Belshazzar's wife, because his wives were with him in the banquet hall.

explain riddles and solve difficult problems.[r] Call for Daniel, and he will tell you
what the writing means."
13So Daniel was brought before the king, and the king said to him, "Are you Daniel,
one of the exiles my father the king brought from Judah?[s] 14I have heard that the
spirit of the gods is in you and that you have insight, intelligence and outstanding
wisdom. 15The wise men and enchanters were brought before me to read this writing
and tell me what it means, but they could not explain it. 16Now I have heard that you
are able to give interpretations and to solve difficult problems. If you can read this
writing and tell me what it means, you will be clothed in purple and have a gold chain
placed around your neck, and you will be made the third highest ruler in the kingdom."
17Then Daniel answered the king, "You may keep your gifts for yourself and give
your rewards to someone else.[t] Nevertheless, I will read the writing for the king and
tell him what it means.
18"O king, the Most High God gave your father Nebuchadnezzar sovereignty and
greatness and glory and splendour.[u] 19Because of the high position he gave him, all
the peoples and nations and men of every language dreaded and feared him. Those
the king wanted to put to death, he put to death;[v] those he wanted to spare, he spared;
those he wanted to promote, he promoted; and those he wanted to humble, he
humbled. 20But when his heart became arrogant and hardened with pride,[w] he was
deposed from his royal throne and stripped[x] of his glory.[y] 21He was driven away
from people and given the mind of an animal; he lived with the wild donkeys and ate
grass like cattle; and his body was drenched with the dew of heaven, until he
acknowledged that the Most High God is sovereign[z] over the kingdoms of men and
sets over them anyone he wishes.[a]
22"But you his son,[d] O Belshazzar, have not humbled[b] yourself, though you knew
all this. 23Instead, you have set yourself up against[c] the Lord of heaven. You had
the goblets from his temple brought to you, and you and your nobles, your wives and
your concubines drank wine from them. You praised the gods of silver and gold, of
bronze, iron, wood and stone, which cannot see or hear or understand.[d] But you did
not honour the God who holds in his hand your life[e] and all your ways.[f] 24Therefore
he sent the hand that wrote the inscription.
25"This is the inscription that was written:

MENE, MENE, TEKEL, PARSIN[e]

26"This is what these words mean:

Mene[f]: God has numbered the days[g] of your reign and brought it to an end.[h]

27*Tekel*[g]: You have been weighed on the scales and found wanting.[i]

[d] 22 Or *descendant*; or *successor* [e] 25 Aramaic *UPARSIN* (that is, *AND PARSIN*) [f] 26 *Mene* can mean *numbered* or *mina* (a unit of money). [g] 27 *Tekel* can mean *weighed* or *shekel*.

5:12 [r] ver 14-16; Da 6:3
5:13 [s] Da 6:13
5:17 [t] 2Ki 5:16
5:18 [u] Jer 27:7; Da 2:37-38
5:19 [v] Da 2:12-13; 3:6
5:20 [w] Da 4:30 [x] Jer 13:18 [y] Job 40:12; Isa 14:13-15
5:21 [z] Eze 17:24 [a] Da 4:16-17, 35
5:22 [b] Ex 10:3; 2Ch 33:23
5:23 [c] Jer 50:29 [d] Ps 115:4-8; Hab 2:19 [e] Job 12:10 [f] Job 31:4; Jer 10:23
5:26 [g] Jer 27:7 [h] Isa 13:6
5:27 [i] Ps 62:9

5:17 The king offered Daniel beautiful gifts and great power if he would explain the writing, but Daniel turned him down. Daniel was not motivated by material rewards. His entire life had been characterised by doing right. Daniel was not showing disrespect in refusing the gifts, but he was growing older himself and knew the gifts would do him little good. Daniel wanted to show that he was giving an unbiased interpretation to the king. Doing right should be our first priority, not gaining power or rewards. Do you love God enough to do what is right, even if it means giving up personal rewards?

5:21–23 Belshazzar knew Babylonian history, and so he knew how God had humbled Nebuchadnezzar. Nevertheless, Belshazzar's banquet was a rebellious challenge to God's authority as he took the sacred goblets from God's temple and drank from them. No one who understands that God is the Creator of the universe should be foolish enough to challenge him.

5:22 Often kings would kill the bearer of bad news. But Daniel was not afraid to tell the truth to the king even though it was not what he wanted to hear. We should be just as courageous in telling the truth under pressure.

5:24 Belshazzar used the goblets from the temple for his party, and God condemned him for this act. We must not use for sinful purposes that which has been dedicated to God. Today this would include church buildings, financial donations, and anything else that has been set apart for serving God. Be careful how you use what is God's.

5:27 The writing on the wall was a message for all those who defy God. Although Belshazzar had power and wealth, his kingdom was totally corrupt, and he could not withstand the judgment of God. God's time of judgment comes for all people. If you have forgotten God and slipped into a sinful way of life, turn away from your sin now before he removes any opportunities to repent. Ask God to forgive you, and begin to live by his standards of justice.

28 *Peres*[h]: Your kingdom is divided and given to the Medes[j] and Persians."[k]

29 Then at Belshazzar's command, Daniel was clothed in purple, a gold chain was
placed around his neck, and he was proclaimed the third highest ruler in the kingdom.
30 That very night Belshazzar,[l] king of the Babylonians,[i] was slain,[m] 31 and
Darius[n] the Mede took over the kingdom, at the age of sixty-two.

Daniel in the Den of Lions

6 It pleased Darius[a] to appoint 120 satraps[b] to rule throughout the kingdom, 2 with
three administrators over them, one of whom was Daniel.[c] The satraps were
made accountable[d] to them so that the king might not suffer loss. 3 Now Daniel so
distinguished himself among the administrators and the satraps by his exceptional
qualities that the king planned to set him over the whole kingdom.[e] 4 At this, the
administrators and the satraps tried to find grounds for charges against Daniel in his
conduct of government affairs, but they were unable to do so. They could find no
corruption in him, because he was trustworthy and neither corrupt nor negligent.
5 Finally these men said, "We will never find any basis for charges against this man
Daniel unless it has something to do with the law of his God."[f]
6 So the administrators and the satraps went as a group to the king and said: "O King
Darius, live for ever![g] 7 The royal administrators, prefects, satraps, advisers and
governors[h] have all agreed that the king should issue an edict and enforce the decree
that anyone who prays to any god or man during the next thirty days, except to you,
O king, shall be thrown into the lions' den.[i] 8 Now, O king, issue the decree and put

[h] 28 *Peres* (the singular of *Parsin*) can mean *divided* or *Persia* or *a half mina* or *a half shekel.*
[i] 30 Or *Chaldeans*

5:28 [j] Isa 13:17 [k] Da 6:28
5:30 [l] ver 1 [m] Isa 21:9; Jer 51:31
5:31 [n] Da 6:1; 9:1
6:1 [a] Da 5:31 [b] Est 1:1
6:2 [c] Da 2:48-49 [d] Ezr 4:22
6:3 [e] Ge 41:41; Est 10:3; Da 5:12-14
6:5 [f] Ac 24:13-16
6:6 [g] Ne 2:3; Da 2:4
6:7 [h] Da 3:2 [i] Ps 59:3; 64:2-6; Da 3:6

KINGS DANIEL SERVED

Name	*Empire*	*Story told in*	*Memorable event*
Nebuchadnezzar	Babylonia	chapters 1–4	Shadrach, Meshach, and Abednego thrown into fiery furnace; Nebuchadnezzar went mad for 7 years
Belshazzar	Babylonia	chapters 5, 7, 8	Daniel read the writing on the wall, which signalled the end of the Babylonian empire
Darius	Medo-Persia	chapters 6, 9	Daniel thrown into a lions' den
Cyrus	Medo-Persia	chapters 10–12	The exiles return to their homeland in Judah and their capital city, Jerusalem

5:28 The Medes and Persians joined forces to overthrow Babylon. This event was predicted in the second phase of Nebuchadnezzar's dream in chapter 2 – the silver chest and arms.

5:31 Darius and his soldiers entered Babylon by diverting the river that ran through the city, then walking in on the dry river-bed.

5:31 This Darius is not to be confused with Darius I, mentioned in Ezra, Haggai, and Zechariah, or Darius II (the Persian), mentioned in Nehemiah. Darius the Mede is named only in the book of Daniel. Other records name no king between Belshazzar and Cyrus. Thus, Darius may have been (1) appointed by Cyrus to rule over Babylon as a province of Persia, (2) another name for Cyrus himself or for his son, Cambyses, or (3) a descendant of Xerxes I.

6:1–3 At this time, Daniel was over 80 years old and one of Darius's top three administrators. Daniel was working with those who did not believe in his God, but he worked more efficiently and capably than all the rest. Thus, he attracted the attention of the pagan king and earned a place of respect. One of the best ways to influence non-Christian employers is to work diligently and responsibly. How well do you represent God to your employer?

6:3, 4 Daniel made enemies at work by doing a good job. Perhaps you have had a similar experience. When you begin to excel, you will find that co-workers may look for ways to hold you back and tear you down. How should you deal with those who would cheer at your downfall and even try to hasten it? Conduct your whole life above reproach. Then you will have nothing to hide, and your enemies will have a difficult time finding legitimate charges against you. Of course, this will not always save you from attacks, and, like Daniel, you will have to rely on God for protection.

6:4, 5 The jealous officials couldn't find anything about Daniel's life to criticise, so they attacked his religion. If you face jealous critics because of your faith, be glad they're criticising that part of your life – perhaps they had to focus on your religion as a last resort! Respond by continuing to believe and live as you should. Then remember that God is in control, fighting this battle for you.

6:8, 9 In Babylon, the king's word *was* the law. In the Medo-Persian empire, however, when a law was made, even the king couldn't change it. Darius was an effective government administrator, but he had a fatal flaw – pride. By appealing to his vanity, the men talked Darius into signing a law effectively making himself a god for 30 days. This law could not be broken – not even by an important official like Daniel. Another example of the irrevocable nature of the laws of the Medes and Persians appears in Esther 8:8.

it in writing so that it cannot be altered—in accordance with the laws of the Medes
and Persians, which cannot be repealed."[j] 9 So King Darius put the decree in writing.
10 Now when Daniel learned that the decree had been published, he went home to
his upstairs room where the windows opened towards[k] Jerusalem. Three times a day
he got down on his knees[l] and prayed, giving thanks to his God, just as he had done
before.[m] 11 Then these men went as a group and found Daniel praying and asking God
for help. 12 So they went to the king and spoke to him about his royal decree: "Did
you not publish a decree that during the next thirty days anyone who prays to any god
or man except to you, O king, would be thrown into the lions' den?"
The king answered, "The decree stands—in accordance with the laws of the Medes
and Persians, which cannot be repealed."[n]
13 Then they said to the king, "Daniel, who is one of the exiles from Judah,[o] pays
no attention[p] to you, O king, or to the decree you put in writing. He still prays three
times a day." 14 When the king heard this, he was greatly distressed;[q] he was
determined to rescue Daniel and made every effort until sundown to save him.
15 Then the men went as a group to the king and said to him, "Remember, O king,
that according to the law of the Medes and Persians no decree or edict that the king
issues can be changed."[r]
16 So the king gave the order, and they brought Daniel and threw him into the lions'
den.[s] The king said to Daniel, "May your God, whom you serve continually, rescue[t]
you!"
17 A stone was brought and placed over the mouth of the den, and the king sealed[u]
it with his own signet ring and with the rings of his nobles, so that Daniel's situation
might not be changed. 18 Then the king returned to his palace and spent the night
without eating[v] and without any entertainment being brought to him. And he could
not sleep.[w]
19 At the first light of dawn, the king got up and hurried to the lions' den. 20 When
he came near the den, he called to Daniel in an anguished voice, "Daniel, servant of
the living God, has your God, whom you serve continually, been able to rescue you
from the lions?"[x]
21 Daniel answered, "O king, live for ever![y] 22 My God sent his angel,[z] and he
shut the mouths of the lions.[a] They have not hurt me, because I was found innocent
in his sight.[b] Nor have I ever done any wrong before you, O king."
23 The king was overjoyed and gave orders to lift Daniel out of the den. And when
Daniel was lifted from the den, no wound[c] was found on him, because he had
trusted[d] in his God.
24 At the king's command, the men who had falsely accused Daniel were brought
in and thrown into the lions' den,[e] along with their wives and children.[f] And before

6:8 [j]Est 1:19
6:10 [k]1Ki 8:48-49 [l]Ps 95:6 [m]Ac 5:29
6:12 [n]Est 1:19; Da 3:8-12
6:13 [o]Da 2:25; 5:13 [p]Est 3:8; Da 3:12
6:14 [q]Mk 6:26
6:15 [r]Est 8:8
6:16 [s]ver 7 [t]Job 5:19; Ps 37:39-40
6:17 [u]Mt 27:66
6:18 [v]2Sa 12:17 [w]Est 6:1; Da 2:1
6:20 [x]Da 3:17
6:21 [y]Da 2:4
6:22 [z]Da 3:28 [a]Ps 91:11-13; Heb 11:33 [b]Ac 12:11; 2Ti 4:17
6:23 [c]Da 3:27 [d]1Ch 5:20
6:24 [e]Dt 19:18-19; Est 7:9-10; Ps 54:5 [f]Dt 24:16; 2Ki 14:6

6:10 Daniel stood alone. Although he knew about the law against praying to anyone except the king, he continued to pray three times a day as he always had. Daniel had a disciplined prayer life. Our prayers are usually interrupted not by threats, but simply by the pressure of our schedules. Don't let threats or pressures cut into your prayer time. Pray regularly, no matter what, for prayer is your lifeline to God.

6:10 Daniel made no attempt to hide his daily prayer routine from his enemies in government, even though he knew he would be disobeying the new law. Hiding his daily prayers would have been futile because surely the conspirators would have caught him at something else during the month. Also, hiding would have demonstrated that he was afraid of the other government officials. Daniel continued to pray because he could not look to the king for the guidance and strength that he needed during this difficult time. Only God could provide what he really needed.

6:16 Lions roamed the countryside and forests in Mesopotamia, and the people feared them and greatly respected their power. Some kings hunted lions for sport. The Persians captured lions, keeping them in large parks where they were fed and attended. Lions were also used for executing people. But God has ways of delivering his people (6:22) that none of us can imagine. It is always premature to give up and give in to the pressure of unbelievers, because God has power they know nothing about. God can even shut the lions' mouths.

6:16 Even unbelievers attested to Daniel's consistency. By his continual service, Daniel had demonstrated his faithful devotion to God. What can unbelievers determine about your life?

6:21–23 The man or woman who trusts in God and obeys his will is untouchable until God takes him or her. To trust God is to have immeasurable peace. God, who delivered Daniel, will deliver you. Do you trust him with your life?

6:24 In accordance with Persian custom, this cruel punishment was transferred to those who had conspired against the king by provoking him into an unjust action (see also Esther 7:9, 10). The king's great anger resulted in the execution of the evil officials and their families. Evil deeds often backfire on those who plan cruelty.

6:24 [g]Isa 38:13
6:25 [h]Da 4:1
6:26 [i]Ps 99:1-3; Da 3:29 [j]Da 2:44; 4:34
6:27 [k]Da 4:3 [l]ver 22
6:28 [m]2Ch 36:22; Da 1:21
7:1 [a]Da 5:1 [b]Da 1:17 [c]Jer 36:4
7:2 [d]Rev 7:1
7:3 [e]Rev 13:1
7:4 [f]Jer 4:7 [g]Eze 17:3

they reached the floor of the den, the lions overpowered them and crushed all their bones.[g]

25 Then King Darius wrote to all the peoples, nations and men of every language throughout the land:

"May you prosper greatly![h]

26 "I issue a decree that in every part of my kingdom people must fear and reverence the God of Daniel.[i]

"For he is the living God
and he endures for ever;
his kingdom will not be destroyed,
his dominion will never end.[j]
27 He rescues and he saves;
he performs signs and wonders[k]
in the heavens and on the earth.
He has rescued Daniel
from the power of the lions."[l]

28 So Daniel prospered during the reign of Darius and the reign of Cyrus[a][m] the Persian.

B. DANIEL'S VISIONS (7:1 – 12:13)

Daniel had many dreams and visions he did not understand. He dreamed of four beasts, which represented four kingdoms of the world, and of a ram and goat, which depicted two of those kingdoms in greater detail. Daniel's visions reveal that the Messiah will be the ruler of a spiritual kingdom that will overpower and overshadow all other earthly kingdoms. These visions help us see that we should interpret all of history in the light of God's eternal kingdom.

Daniel's Dream of Four Beasts

7 In the first year of Belshazzar[a] king of Babylon, Daniel had a dream, and visions passed through his mind[b] as he was lying on his bed. He wrote[c] down the substance of his dream.

2 Daniel said: "In my vision at night I looked, and there before me were the four winds of heaven[d] churning up the great sea. 3 Four great beasts,[e] each different from the others, came up out of the sea.

4 "The first was like a lion,[f] and it had the wings of an eagle.[g] I watched until its wings were torn off and it was lifted from the ground so that it stood on two feet like a man, and the heart of a man was given to it.

5 "And there before me was a second beast, which looked like a bear. It was raised

[a] *28 Or Darius, that is, the reign of Cyrus*

6:25–27 Nebuchadnezzar had come to believe that Israel's God was real because of the faithfulness of Daniel and his friends. Here Darius was also convinced of God's power because Daniel was faithful and God rescued him. Although Daniel was captive in a strange land, his devotion to God was a testimony to powerful rulers. If you find yourself in new surroundings, take the opportunity to testify about God's power in your life. Be faithful to God so he can use you to make an impact on others.

7:1 Chronologically, this chapter takes place before chapter 5. At this time, Belshazzar had just been given a position of authority (553 B.C.), and Daniel was probably in his late sixties. The first six chapters of Daniel present history; the last six chapters are visions relating mainly to the future.

7:1ff Daniel had a vision of four great beasts, each representing a world empire. This was similar to Nebuchadnezzar's dream in chapter 2. Nebuchadnezzar's dream covered the political aspects of the empires; Daniel's dream depicted their moral characteristics. These nations, which would reign over Israel, were evil and cruel; but Daniel also saw God's everlasting, indestructible kingdom arrive and conquer them all.

7:4–8 The lion with an eagle's wings represents Babylon with her swift conquests (statues of winged lions have been recovered from Babylon's ruins). The bear that ravaged the lion is Medo-Persia. The three ribs in its mouth represent the conquests of three major enemies. The leopard is Greece. Its wings show the swiftness of Alexander the Great's campaign as he conquered much of the civilised world in four years (334–330 B.C.). The leopard's four heads are the four divisions of the Greek empire after Alexander's death.

The fourth beast points to both Rome and the end times. Many Bible scholars believe that the horns correspond to ten kings who will reign shortly before God sets up his everlasting kingdom. These ten kings had still not come to power at the time of John's vision recorded in the book of Revelation (Revelation 17:12). The little horn is a future human ruler or the antichrist (see also 2 Thessalonians 2:3, 4). God is illustrating the final end of all worldly kingdoms in contrast to his eternal kingdom.

up on one of its sides, and it had three ribs in its mouth between its teeth. It was told,
'Get up and eat your fill of flesh!'[h]
6 “After that, I looked, and there before me was another beast, one that looked like
a leopard.[i] And on its back it had four wings like those of a bird. This beast had
four heads, and it was given authority to rule.
7 “After that, in my vision at night I looked, and there before me was a fourth
beast—terrifying and frightening and very powerful. It had large iron[j] teeth; it
crushed and devoured its victims and trampled underfoot whatever was left. It was
different from all the former beasts, and it had ten horns.[k]
8 “While I was thinking about the horns, there before me was another horn, a little[l]
one, which came up among them; and three of the first horns were uprooted before
it. This horn had eyes like the eyes of a man[m] and a mouth that spoke boastfully.[n]
9 “As I looked,

> “thrones were set in place,
>   and the Ancient of Days took his seat.
> His clothing was as white as snow;
>   the hair of his head was white like wool.[o]
> His throne was flaming with fire,
>   and its wheels[p] were all ablaze.
> 10 A river of fire[q] was flowing,
>   coming out from before him.[r]
> Thousands upon thousands attended him;
>   ten thousand times ten thousand stood before him.
> The court was seated,
>   and the books[s] were opened.

11 “Then I continued to watch because of the boastful words the horn was speaking.
I kept looking until the beast was slain and its body destroyed and thrown into the
blazing fire.[t] 12 (The other beasts had been stripped of their authority, but were
allowed to live for a period of time.)
13 “In my vision at night I looked, and there before me was one like a son of man,[u]
coming with the clouds of heaven.[v] He approached the Ancient of Days and was led
into his presence. 14 He was given authority,[w] glory and sovereign power; all peoples,
nations and men of every language worshipped him.[x] His dominion is an everlasting
dominion that will not pass away, and his kingdom is one that will never be destroyed.[y]

The Interpretation of the Dream

15 “I, Daniel, was troubled in spirit, and the visions that passed through my mind
disturbed me.[z] 16 I approached one of those standing there and asked him the true
meaning of all this.
“So he told me and gave me the interpretation[a] of these things: 17 ‘The four great
beasts are four kingdoms that will rise from the earth. 18 But the saints of the Most

7:5 [h]Da 2:39
7:6 [i]Rev 13:2
7:7 [j]Da 2:40 [k]Rev 12:3
7:8 [l]Da 8:9 [m]Rev 9:7 [n]Ps 12:3; Rev 13:5-6
7:9 [o]Rev 1:14 [p]Eze 1:15; 10:6
7:10 [q]Ps 50:3; 97:3; Isa 30:27 [r]Dt 33:2; Ps 68:17; Rev 5:11 [s]Rev 20:11-15
7:11 [t]Rev 19:20
7:13 [u]Mt 8:20*; Rev 1:13* [v]Mt 24:30; Rev 1:7
7:14 [w]Mt 28:18 [x]Ps 72:11; 102:22; 1Co 15:27; Eph 1:22 [y]Da 2:44; Heb 12:28; Rev 11:15
7:15 [z]Da 4:19
7:16 [a]Da 8:16; 9:22; Zec 1:9

7:9 Here the prophecy shifts to the end times. This judgment scene is similar to one that was seen by the apostle John (Revelation 1:14, 15). The Ancient of Days is Almighty God, who assigns power to kingdoms and who will himself judge those kingdoms in the end.

7:10 Daniel saw God judging millions of people as they stood before him. We all must stand before Almighty God and give an account of our lives. If your life were judged by God today, what would he say about it? How would he measure it against his will for us? We should live each day with the full awareness that we must appear before God to give account for how we used our lives. How will your life measure up?

7:11, 12 The slaying of the beast represents the fall of Rome. While this beast was destroyed, the other beasts were allowed to live for a period of time. The kingdoms (or their cultures) continued to be recognizable in some form; history did not end when God intervened with his judgment.

7:13, 14 This “one like a son of man” is the Messiah. Jesus used this verse to refer to himself (Matthew 26:64; Luke 21:27; John 1:51). The clouds of heaven portray the Son of Man as divine; throughout the Bible clouds represent his majesty and awesome presence. God’s glory appeared in a cloud in Exodus 16:10 and 19:9 at the giving of the law at Sinai.

7:18 The “saints of the Most High” are the true Israel, the people ruled by the Messiah. Jesus Christ gave the kingdom to the new Israel, his church, made up of all faithful believers. His coming ushered in the kingdom of God, and all believers are its citizens (see also 7:22, 27). Although God may allow persecution to continue for a while, the destiny of his followers is to possess the kingdom and be with him for ever.

High will receive the kingdom and will possess it for ever—yes, for ever and ever.’[b]
19 “Then I wanted to know the true meaning of the fourth beast, which was different
from all the others and most terrifying, with its iron teeth and bronze claws—the beast
that crushed and devoured its victims and trampled underfoot whatever was left. 20 I
also wanted to know about the ten horns on its head and about the other horn that came
up, before which three of them fell—the horn that looked more imposing than the
others and that had eyes and a mouth that spoke boastfully. 21 As I watched, this horn
was waging war against the saints and defeating them,[c] 22 until the Ancient of Days
came and pronounced judgment in favour of the saints of the Most High, and the time
came when they possessed the kingdom.
23 “He gave me this explanation: ‘The fourth beast is a fourth kingdom that will
appear on earth. It will be different from all the other kingdoms and will devour the
whole earth, trampling it down and crushing it.[d] 24 The ten horns[e] are ten kings who
will come from this kingdom. After them another king will arise, different from the
earlier ones; he will subdue three kings. 25 He will speak against the Most High[f] and
oppress his saints and try to change the set times[g] and the laws. The saints will be
handed over to him for a time, times and half a time.[a][h]
26 “ ‘But the court will sit, and his power will be taken away and completely
destroyed for ever. 27 Then the sovereignty, power and greatness of the kingdoms
under the whole heaven will be handed over to the saints, the people of the Most High.
His kingdom will be an everlasting[i] kingdom, and all rulers will worship[j] and obey
him.’
28 “This is the end of the matter. I, Daniel, was deeply troubled[k] by my thoughts,
and my face turned pale, but I kept the matter to myself.”

Daniel’s Vision of a Ram and a Goat

8 In the third year of King Belshazzar’s reign, I, Daniel, had a vision, after the one
that had already appeared to me. 2 In my vision I saw myself in the citadel of
Susa[a] in the province of Elam;[b] in the vision I was beside the Ulai Canal. 3 I looked
up,[c] and there before me was a ram with two horns, standing beside the canal, and
the horns were long. One of the horns was longer than the other but grew up later.
4 I watched the ram as he charged towards the west and the north and the south. No
animal could stand against him, and none could rescue from his power. He did as he
pleased[d] and became great.
5 As I was thinking about this, suddenly a goat with a prominent horn between his
eyes came from the west, crossing the whole earth without touching the ground. 6 He
came towards the two-horned ram I had seen standing beside the canal and charged
at him in great rage. 7 I saw him attack the ram furiously, striking the ram and
shattering his two horns. The ram was powerless to stand against him; the goat

a 25 Or *for a year, two years and half a year*

7:18 [b] Isa 60:12-14; Rev 2:26; 20:4
7:21 [c] Rev 13:7
7:23 [d] Da 2:40
7:24 [e] Rev 17:12
7:25 [f] Isa 37:23; Da 11:36 [g] Da 2:21 [h] Da 8:24; 12:7; Rev 12:14
7:27 [i] Da 2:44; 4:34; Lk 1:33; Rev 11:15; 22:5 [j] Ps 22:27; 72:11; 86:9
7:28 [k] Da 4:19
8:2 [a] Est 1:2 [b] Ge 10:22
8:3 [c] Da 10:5
8:4 [d] Da 11:3, 16

7:24 The ten horns, or ten kings, are also mentioned in Revelation 17:12. There were also ten toes in Nebuchadnezzar’s vision (2:41, 42). While all do not agree concerning the identity of these ten kings, we are reminded in Revelation 17:12–14 that these kings will make war against Christ, but, as the King of kings, he will conquer them. The other king mentioned here in verse 24 is the future antichrist of 2 Thessalonians 2:3, 4.

7:25 While the exact meaning of this “time, times and half a time” is debated, we do know that God told Daniel that persecution would continue only a relatively short time. God has promised to give his kingdom to his saints.

8:1 As with chapter 7, this chapter precedes chapter 5 chronologically; the dream probably occurred in 551 B.C. when Daniel was about 70 years old. Chapters 7 and 8 correspond to the first and third years of Belshazzar and belong chronologically between chapters 4 and 5. Chapter 9 took place at approximately the same time as chapter 6. It gives us more details about the Medo-Persian and Greek empires, the two world powers that ruled after Babylonia.

8:2 Susa was one of the capitals of the Babylonian empire. Located in what is now Iran, Susa was a well-developed city. It was the winter capital of the Persian empire and a mighty fortress (citadel). In his vision, Daniel saw himself in this important location. The earliest known code of law, the Code of Hammurapi, was found there. Susa rivalled Babylon itself in cultural sophistication.

8:3 The two horns were the kings of Media and Persia (8:20). The longer horn represented the growing dominance of Persia in the Medo-Persian empire.

8:5–7 The goat represented Greece, and its large horn, Alexander the Great (8:21). This is an amazing prediction because Greece was not yet considered a world power when this prophecy was given. Alexander the Great conquered the world with great speed and military strategy, indicated by the goat’s rapid movement. Shattering both horns symbolised Alexander breaking both parts of the Medo-Persian empire.

knocked him to the ground and trampled on him,[e] and none could rescue the ram
from his power. 8The goat became very great, but at the height of his power his large
horn was broken off,[f] and in its place four prominent horns grew up towards the four
winds of heaven.[g]
9Out of one of them came another horn, which started small but grew in power to
the south and to the east and towards the Beautiful Land.[h] 10It grew until it reached[i]
the host of the heavens, and it threw some of the starry host down to the earth[j] and
trampled[k] on them. 11It set itself up to be as great as the Prince of the host;[l] it took
away the daily sacrifice[m] from him, and the place of his sanctuary was brought low.[n]
12Because of rebellion, the host ⌞of the saints⌟[a] and the daily sacrifice were given over
to it. It prospered in everything it did, and truth was thrown to the ground.
13Then I heard a holy one[o] speaking, and another holy one said to him, "How long
will it take for the vision to be fulfilled[p]—the vision concerning the daily sacrifice,
the rebellion that causes desolation, and the surrender of the sanctuary and of the host
that will be trampled[q] underfoot?"
14He said to me, "It will take 2,300 evenings and mornings; then the sanctuary will
be reconsecrated."[r]

The Interpretation of the Vision

15While I, Daniel, was watching the vision[s] and trying to understand it, there
before me stood one who looked like a man.[t] 16And I heard a man's voice from the
Ulai calling, "Gabriel,[u] tell this man the meaning of the vision."
17As he came near the place where I was standing, I was terrified and fell prostrate.[v] "Son of man," he said to me, "understand that the vision concerns the time
of the end."[w]
18While he was speaking to me, I was in a deep sleep, with my face to the ground.[x]
Then he touched me and raised me to my feet.[y]
19He said: "I am going to tell you what will happen later in the time of wrath,
because the vision concerns the appointed time of the end.[b][z] 20The two-horned ram
that you saw represents the kings of Media and Persia. 21The shaggy goat is the king
of Greece,[a] and the large horn between his eyes is the first king.[b] 22The four horns
that replaced the one that was broken off represent four kingdoms that will emerge
from his nation but will not have the same power.
23"In the latter part of their reign, when rebels have become completely wicked,
a stern-faced king, a master of intrigue, will arise. 24He will become very strong, but
not by his own power. He will cause astounding devastation and will succeed in
whatever he does. He will destroy the mighty men and the holy people.[c] 25He will
cause deceit to prosper, and he will consider himself superior. When they feel secure,

a 12 Or *rebellion, the armies* b 19 Or *because the end will be at the appointed time*

8:7 [e]Da 7:7
8:8 [f]2Ch 26:16-21; Da 5:20 [g]Da 7:2; Rev 7:1
8:9 [h]Da 11:16
8:10 [i]Isa 14:13 [j]Rev 12:4 [k]Da 7:7
8:11 [l]Da 11:36-37 [m]Eze 46:13-14 [n]Da 11:31; 12:11
8:13 [o]Da 4:23 [p]Da 12:6 [q]Lk 21:24; Rev 11:2
8:14 [r]Da 12:11-12
8:15 [s]ver 1 [t]Da 10:16-18
8:16 [u]Da 9:21; Lk 1:19
8:17 [v]Eze 1:28; Da 2:46; Rev 1:17 [w]Hab 2:3
8:18 [x]Da 10:9 [y]Eze 2:2; Da 10:16-18
8:19 [z]Hab 2:3
8:21 [a]Da 10:20 [b]Da 11:3
8:24 [c]Da 7:25; 11:36

8:8 Alexander the Great died in his thirties at the height of his power. His kingdom was split into four parts under four generals: Ptolemy I of Egypt and Palestine; Seleucus of Babylonia and Syria; Lysimachus of Asia Minor; and Antipater of Macedon and Greece.

8:9 Israel ("the Beautiful Land") was attacked by Antiochus IV Epiphanes (the small horn) in the second century B.C. He was the eighth ruler of the Seleucid empire (Babylonia and Syria). He overthrew the high priest, looted the temple, and replaced worship of God with a Greek form of worship. A further fulfilment of this prophecy of a powerful horn will occur in the future with the coming of the antichrist (see 8:17, 19, 23; 11:36; 2 Thessalonians 2:4).

8:11 The "Prince of the host" here refers to a heavenly authority, perhaps an angel or even God himself. (See also Joshua 5:13–15.)

8:14 The phrase "evenings and mornings" means evening and morning sacrifices, and refers to the time from the desecration of the altar in the temple by Antiochus IV Epiphanes to the restoration of temple worship under Judas Maccabeus in 165 B.C.

8:16 Gabriel is an angel, the heavenly messenger God used to explain Daniel's visions (9:21). He also announced the birth of John the Baptist (Luke 1:11) and the Messiah (Luke 1:26).

8:17 The "time of the end", in this case, refers to the whole period from the end of the exile until the second coming of Christ. Many of the events that would happen under Antiochus IV Epiphanes will be repeated on a broader scale just before Christ's second coming. During these times, God deals with Israel in a radically different way, with divine discipline coming through Gentile nations. This period is sometimes referred to as the "times of the Gentiles" (Luke 21:24).

8:23 This stern-faced king describes both Antiochus IV Epiphanes and the antichrist at the end of human history.

8:25 This Prince of princes is God himself. No human power could defeat the king whom Daniel saw in his vision, but God would bring him down. Antiochus IV Epiphanes reportedly went insane and died in Persia in 164 B.C. God's power and justice will prevail, so we should never give up our faith or lose hope, no matter how powerful God's enemies may seem.

he will destroy many and take his stand against the Prince of princes.[d] Yet he will be destroyed, but not by human power.[e]

26 “The vision of the evenings and mornings that has been given you is true,[f] but seal[g] up the vision, for it concerns the distant future.”[h]

27 I, Daniel, was exhausted and lay ill for several days. Then I got up and went about the king’s business.[i] I was appalled[j] by the vision; it was beyond understanding.

Daniel’s Prayer

9 In the first year of Darius[a] son of Xerxes[a] (a Mede by descent), who was made ruler over the Babylonian[b] kingdom— 2 in the first year of his reign, I, Daniel, understood from the Scriptures, according to the word of the LORD given to Jeremiah the prophet, that the desolation of Jerusalem would last seventy[b] years. 3 So I turned to the Lord God and pleaded with him in prayer and petition, in fasting, and in sackcloth and ashes.[c]

4 I prayed to the LORD my God and confessed:

“O Lord, the great and awesome God,[d] who keeps his covenant of love[e] with all who love him and obey his commands, 5 we have sinned and done wrong.[f] We have been wicked and have rebelled; we have turned away[g] from your commands and laws.[h] 6 We have not listened to your servants the prophets,[i] who spoke in your name to our kings, our princes and our fathers, and to all the people of the land.

7 “Lord, you are righteous, but this day we are covered with shame[j]— the men of Judah and people of Jerusalem and all Israel, both near and far, in all the countries where you have scattered[k] us because of our unfaithfulness to you.[l] 8 O LORD, we and our kings, our princes and our fathers are covered with shame because we have sinned against you. 9 The Lord our God is merciful and forgiving,[m] even though we have rebelled against him;[n] 10 we have not obeyed the LORD our God or kept the laws he gave us through his servants the prophets.[o] 11 All Israel has transgressed your law and turned away, refusing to obey you.

“Therefore the curses and sworn judgments written in the Law of Moses, the servant of God, have been poured out on us, because we have sinned[p] against you. 12 You have fulfilled[q] the words spoken against us and against our rulers by bringing upon us great disaster. Under the whole heaven nothing has ever been done like what has been done to Jerusalem.[r] 13 Just as it is written in the Law of Moses, all this disaster has come upon us, yet we have not sought the favour

a *1* Hebrew *Ahasuerus* **b** *1* Or *Chaldean*

8:25 [d] Da 11:36 [e] Da 2:34; 11:21
8:26 [f] Da 10:1 [g] Rev 22:10 [h] Da 10:14
8:27 [i] Da 2:48 [j] Da 7:28
9:1 [a] Da 5:31
9:2 [b] 2Ch 36:21; Jer 29:10; Zec 7:5
9:3 [c] Ne 1:4; Jer 29:12
9:4 [d] Dt 7:21 [e] Dt 7:9
9:5 [f] Ps 106:6 [g] Isa 53:6 [h] ver 11; La 1:20
9:6 [i] 2Ch 36:16; Jer 44:5
9:7 [j] Ps 44:15 [k] Dt 4:27; Am 9:9 [l] Jer 3:25
9:9 [m] Ps 130:4 [n] Ne 9:17; Jer 14:7
9:10 [o] 2Ki 17:13-15; 18:12
9:11 [p] Isa 1:4-6; Jer 8:5-10
9:12 [q] Isa 44:26; Zec 1:6 [r] Jer 44:2-6; Eze 5:9

9:1 The vision in chapter 9 was given to Daniel during the same time period of chapter 6. This Darius is the person mentioned in chapter 6. The Xerxes (or Ahasuerus) mentioned here is not Esther’s husband. The events described in the book of Esther happened about 50 years later.

9:2, 3 Daniel pleaded with God to bring about the promised return of his people to their land. The prophet Jeremiah had written that God would not allow the captives to return to their land for 70 years (Jeremiah 25:11, 12; 29:10). Daniel knew of this prophecy and realised that this 70-year period was coming to an end.

9:3ff In Daniel’s prayer for the nation he confessed his own sin, using the pronoun “we” throughout. In times of adversity, it’s easy to blame others and excuse our own actions. If any Israelite was righteous, it was Daniel; and yet he confessed his sinfulness and need for God’s forgiveness. Instead of looking for others to blame, first look inside and confess your own sins to God.

9:3–19 Daniel knew how to pray. As he prayed, he fasted, confessed his sins, and pleaded that God would reveal his will. He prayed with complete surrender to God and with complete openness to what God was saying to him. When you pray, do you speak openly to God? Examine your attitude. Talk to God with openness, vulnerability, and honesty.

9:4–6 The captives from Judah had rebelled against God. Their sins had led to their captivity. But God is merciful even to rebels, if they confess their sins and return to him. Don’t let your past disobedience keep you from returning to God. He is waiting for you and wants you to return to him.

9:6 God had sent many prophets to speak to his people through the years, but their messages had been ignored. The truth was too painful to hear. God still speaks clearly and accurately through the Bible, and he also speaks through preachers, teachers, and concerned friends. Sometimes the truth hurts, and we would rather hear words that soothe, even if they are false. If you are unwilling to accept God’s message, maybe you are trying to avoid making a painful change. Don’t settle for a soothing lie that will bring harsh judgment. Accepting the truth, even if it is painful, can only help you.

9:11–13 Daniel mentioned the curses outlined in Deuteronomy 28. God had given the people of Israel a choice: obey me and receive blessings, or disobey me and face curses. The affliction was meant to turn the people to God. When we face difficult circumstances, we should ask ourselves if God has reason to send judgment. If we think so, we must urgently seek his forgiveness. Then we can ask him to help us through our troubles.

of the LORD our God by turning from our sins and giving attention to your truth.[s]
14The LORD did not hesitate to bring the disaster[t] upon us, for the LORD our God
is righteous in everything he does; yet we have not obeyed him.[u]
15"Now, O Lord our God, who brought your people out of Egypt with a mighty
hand[v] and who made for yourself a name[w] that endures to this day, we have
sinned, we have done wrong. 16O Lord, in keeping with all your righteous acts,[x]
turn away your anger and your wrath from Jerusalem,[y] your city, your holy
hill.[z] Our sins and the iniquities of our fathers have made Jerusalem and your
people an object of scorn[a] to all those around us.
17"Now, our God, hear the prayers and petitions of your servant. For your
sake, O Lord, look with favour[b] on your desolate sanctuary. 18Give ear, O God,
and hear; open your eyes and see[c] the desolation of the city that bears your
Name.[d] We do not make requests of you because we are righteous, but because
of your great mercy. 19O Lord, listen! O Lord, forgive![e] O Lord, hear and act!
For your sake, O my God, do not delay, because your city and your people bear
your Name."

The Seventy "Sevens"

20While I was speaking and praying, confessing my sin and the sin of my people
Israel and making my request to the LORD my God for his holy hill[f]—21while I was
still in prayer, Gabriel,[g] the man I had seen in the earlier vision, came to me in swift
flight about the time of the evening sacrifice.[h] 22He instructed me and said to me,
"Daniel, I have now come to give you insight and understanding. 23As soon as you
began to pray, an answer was given, which I have come to tell you, for you are highly
esteemed.[i] Therefore, consider the message and understand the vision:[j]
24"Seventy 'sevens'[c] are decreed for your people and your holy city to finish[d]
transgression, to put an end to sin, to atone[k] for wickedness, to bring in everlasting
righteousness,[l] to seal up vision and prophecy and to anoint the most holy.[e]
25"Know and understand this: From the issuing of the decree[f] to restore and
rebuild[m] Jerusalem until the Anointed One,[g][n] the ruler, comes, there will be seven
'sevens', and sixty-two 'sevens'. It will be rebuilt with streets and a trench, but in
times of trouble. 26After the sixty-two 'sevens', the Anointed One will be cut off[o]
and will have nothing.[h] The people of the ruler who will come will destroy the city
and the sanctuary. The end will come like a flood:[p] War will continue until the end,

c *24* Or *'weeks'*; also in verses 25 and 26 d *24* Or *restrain* e *24* Or *Most Holy Place*; or *most holy One*
f *25* Or *word* g *25* Or *an anointed one*; also in verse 26 h *26* Or *off and will have no-one*; or *off, but not for himself*

9:13 [s]Isa 9:13; Jer 2:30
9:14 [t]Jer 44:27 [u]Ne 9:33
9:15 [v]Jer 32:21 [w]Ne 9:10
9:16 [x]Ps 31:1 [y]Jer 32:32 [z]Zec 8:3 [a]Eze 5:14
9:17 [b]Nu 6:24-26; Ps 80:19
9:18 [c]Ps 80:14 [d]Isa 37:17; Jer 7:10-12; 25:29
9:19 [e]Ps 44:23
9:20 [f]ver 3; Ps 145:18; Isa 58:9
9:21 [g]Da 8:16; Lk 1:19 [h]Ex 29:39
9:23 [i]Da 10:19; Lk 1:28 [j]Da 10:11-12; Mt 24:15
9:24 [k]Isa 53:10 [l]Isa 56:1
9:25 [m]Ezr 4:24 [n]Jn 4:25
9:26 [o]Isa 53:8 [p]Na 1:8

9:14 Daniel spoke about how God continually tried to bring Israel back to himself. Yet even after disaster struck them, they refused to obey him. God still uses circumstances, other people, and most importantly his word to bring his people back to him. What would it take for God to get your attention?

9:17–19 It would be a mistake to read the Bible as dry history and miss the deep personal feelings. In this section, Daniel was crying out to the Lord. He had a deep concern for his nation and his people. So often our prayers are without passion and true compassion for others. Are you willing to pray by pouring out your deep feelings to God?

9:18 Daniel begged for mercy, not for help, because he knew that his people deserved God's wrath and punishment. God sends his help, not because we deserve it, but because he wants to show great mercy. If God would refuse to help us because of our sin, how could we complain? But when he sends mercy when we deserve punishment, how can we withhold our praise and thanksgiving?

9:23 Just as God answered Daniel's prayer, so we can have confidence that God hears and answers our prayers.

9:24, 25 Each day of these 70 weeks ("seventy 'sevens' ") may represent one year. The Bible often uses round numbers to make a point, not to give an exact count. For example, Jesus said we are to forgive others "seventy-seven" times (Matthew 18:22). He did not mean a literal 77 times only, but that we should be abundantly forgiving. Similarly, some scholars see this figure of 70 weeks as a figurative time period. Others, however, interpret this time period as a literal 70 weeks or 490 years, observing that Christ's death came at the end of the 69 weeks (i.e., 483 years later). One interpretation places the 70th week as the seven years of the great tribulation, still in the future. Consequently the number would symbolise both the first and second comings of Christ.

9:25 A "trench" can mean a moat or a conduit for water. This shows that Jerusalem will be rebuilt as a complete, fully functioning city.

9:26 The Messiah, the Anointed One, will be rejected and killed by his own people. His perfect eternal kingdom will come later.

9:26, 27 There has been much discussion on the numbers, times, and events in these verses, and there are three basic views: (1) the prophecy was fulfilled in the past at the desecration of the temple by Antiochus IV Epiphanes in 168–167 B.C. (see 11:31); (2) it was fulfilled in the past at the destruction of the temple by the Roman general Titus in A.D. 70 when one million Jews were killed; or (3) it is still to be fulfilled in the future under the antichrist (see Matthew 24:15).

9:27
[q] Isa 10:22
10:1
[a] Da 1:21
[b] Da 1:7
[c] Da 8:26
10:2
[d] Ezr 9:4
10:4
[e] Ge 2:14
10:5
[f] Eze 9:2; Rev 15:6
[g] Jer 10:9
10:6
[h] Mt 17:2
[i] Rev 19:12
[j] Rev 1:15
10:7
[k] 2Ki 6:17-20; Ac 9:7
10:8
[l] Ge 32:24
[m] Da 8:27
[n] Hab 3:16
10:9
[o] Da 8:18
10:10
[p] Jer 1:9
[q] Rev 1:17
10:11
[r] Da 9:23
[s] Eze 2:1
10:12
[t] Da 9:3
[u] Da 9:20
10:13
[v] ver 21; Da 12:1; Jude 1:9
10:14
[w] Da 9:22
[x] Da 2:28; 8:26; Hab 2:3
10:15
[y] Eze 24:27; Lk 1:20
10:16
[z] Isa 6:7; Jer 1:9; Da 8:15-18
[a] Isa 21:3
10:17
[b] Da 4:19

and desolations have been decreed. 27 He will confirm a covenant with many for one
'seven'.[i] In the middle of the 'seven'[i] he will put an end to sacrifice and offering.
And on a wing ⌊of the temple⌋ he will set up an abomination that causes desolation,
until the end that is decreed[q] is poured out on him.[j]"[k]

Daniel's Vision of a Man

10 In the third year of Cyrus[a] king of Persia, a revelation was given to Daniel
(who was called Belteshazzar).[b] Its message was true[c] and it concerned a
great war.[a] The understanding of the message came to him in a vision.
2 At that time I, Daniel, mourned[d] for three weeks. 3 I ate no choice food; no meat
or wine touched my lips; and I used no lotions at all until the three weeks were over.
4 On the twenty-fourth day of the first month, as I was standing on the bank of the
great river, the Tigris,[e] 5 I looked up and there before me was a man dressed in linen,[f]
with a belt of the finest gold[g] round his waist. 6 His body was like chrysolite, his face
like lightning,[h] his eyes like flaming torches,[i] his arms and legs like the gleam of
burnished bronze,[j] and his voice like the sound of a multitude.
7 I, Daniel, was the only one who saw the vision; the men with me did not see it,[k]
but such terror overwhelmed them that they fled and hid themselves. 8 So I was left
alone,[l] gazing at this great vision; I had no strength left,[m] my face turned deathly
pale and I was helpless.[n] 9 Then I heard him speaking, and as I listened to him, I fell
into a deep sleep, my face to the ground.[o]
10 A hand touched me[p] and set me trembling on my hands and knees.[q] 11 He said,
"Daniel, you who are highly esteemed,[r] consider carefully the words I am about to
speak to you, and stand up,[s] for I have now been sent to you." And when he said
this to me, I stood up trembling.
12 Then he continued, "Do not be afraid, Daniel. Since the first day that you set your
mind to gain understanding and to humble[t] yourself before your God, your words
were heard, and I have come in response to them.[u] 13 But the prince of the Persian
kingdom resisted me twenty-one days. Then Michael,[v] one of the chief princes, came
to help me, because I was detained there with the king of Persia. 14 Now I have come
to explain[w] to you what will happen to your people in the future, for the vision
concerns a time yet to come.[x]"
15 While he was saying this to me, I bowed with my face towards the ground and
was speechless.[y] 16 Then one who looked like a man[b] touched my lips, and I opened
my mouth and began to speak.[z] I said to the one standing before me, "I am overcome
with anguish[a] because of the vision, my lord, and I am helpless. 17 How can I, your
servant, talk with you, my lord? My strength is gone and I can hardly breathe."[b]

[i] *27* Or *'week'* [j] *27* Or *it* [k] *27* Or *And one who causes desolation will come upon the pinnacle of the abominable ⌊temple⌋, until the end that is decreed is poured out on the desolated ⌊city⌋* [a] *1* Or *true and burdensome*
[b] *16* Most manuscripts of the Masoretic Text; one manuscript of the Masoretic Text, Dead Sea Scrolls and Septuagint *Then something that looked like a man's hand*

10:1ff This is Daniel's final vision (536 B.C.). In it, he was given further insight into the great spiritual battle between God's people and those who want to destroy them. There is also more detailed information on the future, specifically the struggles between the Ptolemies (kings of the South) and the Seleucids (kings of the North).

10:1ff Prior to this vision, Cyrus allowed the Jews to return to Jerusalem, but Daniel stayed in Babylonia. Why didn't Daniel return to Jerusalem? He may have been too old to make the long, hazardous journey (he was over 80); his government duties could have prevented him; or God may have told him to stay behind to complete the work he was called to do.

10:3 Daniel refrained from eating choice foods and using lotions because these were signs of feasting and rejoicing.

10:5, 6 The man seen by Daniel was a heavenly being. Some commentators believe that this was an appearance of Christ (see Revelation 1:13–15), while others think it was an angel (because he required Michael's help – 10:13). In either case, Daniel caught a glimpse of the battle between good and evil supernatural powers.

10:6 Chrysolite is a translucent, semi-precious stone.

10:10–18 Daniel was frightened by this vision, but the messenger reassured him. Daniel lost his speech, but the messenger's touch restored it. Daniel felt weak and helpless, but the messenger's words strengthened him. God can bring us healing when we are hurt, peace when we are troubled, and strength when we are weak. Trust God to minister to you as he did to Daniel.

10:12, 13 Although God sent a messenger to Daniel, a powerful spiritual being ("prince of the Persian kingdom") detained the messenger for three weeks. Daniel faithfully continued praying and fasting, and God's messenger eventually arrived, assisted by Michael, the archangel. Answers to our prayers may be hindered by unseen obstacles. Don't expect God's answers to come too easily or too quickly. Prayer may be challenged by evil forces, so pray fervently and pray earnestly. Then expect God to answer at the right time.

18 Again the one who looked like a man touched[c] me and gave me strength. 19 "Do
not be afraid, O man highly esteemed," he said. "Peace![d] Be strong now; be
strong."[e]
When he spoke to me, I was strengthened and said, "Speak, my lord, since you
have given me strength."[f]
20 So he said, "Do you know why I have come to you? Soon I will return to fight
against the prince of Persia, and when I go, the prince of Greece[g] will come; 21 but
first I will tell you what is written in the Book of Truth.[h] (No-one supports me against
11 them except Michael,[i] your prince. 1 And in the first year of Darius[a] the
Mede, I took my stand to support and protect him.)

The Kings of the South and the North

2 "Now then, I tell you the truth:[b] Three more kings will appear in Persia, and then
a fourth, who will be far richer than all the others. When he has gained power by his
wealth, he will stir up everyone against the kingdom of Greece.[c] 3 Then a mighty king
will appear, who will rule with great power and do as he pleases.[d] 4 After he has
appeared, his empire will be broken up and parcelled out towards the four winds of
heaven.[e] It will not go to his descendants, nor will it have the power he exercised,
because his empire will be uprooted and given to others.
5 "The king of the South will become strong, but one of his commanders will become
even stronger than he and will rule his own kingdom with great power. 6 After some
years, they will become allies. The daughter of the king of the South will go to the
king of the North to make an alliance, but she will not retain her power, and he and
his power**a** will not last. In those days she will be handed over, together with her royal
escort and her father**b** and the one who supported her.
7 "One from her family line will arise to take her place. He will attack the forces
of the king of the North[f] and enter his fortress; he will fight against them and be
victorious. 8 He will also seize their gods,[g] their metal images and their valuable
articles of silver and gold and carry them off to Egypt.[h] For some years he will leave
the king of the North alone. 9 Then the king of the North will invade the realm of the
king of the South but will retreat to his own country. 10 His sons will prepare for war
and assemble a great army, which will sweep on like an irresistible flood[i] and carry
the battle as far as his fortress.
11 "Then the king of the South will march out in a rage and fight against the king
of the North, who will raise a large army, but it will be defeated.[j] 12 When the army
is carried off, the king of the South will be filled with pride and will slaughter many

a6 Or *offspring* **b**6 Or *child* (see Vulgate and Syriac)

10:18 [c]ver 16
10:19 [d]Jdg 6:23; Isa 35:4 [e]Jos 1:9 [f]Isa 6:1-8
10:20 [g]Da 8:21; 11:2
10:21 [h]Da 11:2
10:21 [i]ver 13; Jude 1:9
11:1 [a]Da 5:31
11:2 [b]Da 10:21 [c]Da 10:20
11:3 [d]Da 8:4, 21
11:4 [e]Da 7:2; 8:22
11:7 [f]ver 6
11:8 [g]Isa 37:19; 46:1-2 [h]Jer 43:12
11:10 [i]Isa 8:8; Jer 46:8; Da 9:26
11:11 [j]Da 8:7-8

10:20, 21 The heavenly warfare was to be directed against Persia, and then Greece. Each of these nations was to have power over God's people. Both Persia and Greece were represented by evil angelic "princes", or demons. But God is in control of the past, present, and future, and he has all events recorded in his "Book of Truth".

11:2 The angelic messenger was revealing Israel's future (see 10:20, 21). Only God can reveal future events so clearly. God's work not only deals with the sweeping panorama of history, but also focuses on the intricate details of people's lives. And his plans—whether for nations or individuals—are unshakable.

11:2 The fourth Persian king may have been Xerxes I (486–465 B.C.), who launched an all-out effort against Greece in 480 (Esther 1:1).

11:2ff Babylonia was defeated by Medo-Persia. Medo-Persia was defeated by Greece under Alexander the Great, who conquered most of the Mediterranean and Middle Eastern lands. After Alexander's death, the empire was divided into four parts. The Ptolemies gained control of the southern section of Palestine, and the Seleucids took the northern part. Verses 1–20 show the conflict between the Ptolemies and Seleucids over control of Palestine in 300–200 B.C. Verses 21–35 describe the persecution of Israel under Antiochus IV Epiphanes. In verses 36–45 the prophecy shifts to the end times. Antiochus IV fades from view and the antichrist of the last days becomes the centre of attention.

11:3 This mighty king of Greece was Alexander the Great, who conquered Medo-Persia and built a huge empire in only four years.

11:4, 5 Eventually Alexander the Great's empire was divided into four nations. These four weaker nations were comprised of the following regions: (1) Egypt, (2) Babylonia and Syria, (3) Asia Minor, and (4) Macedon and Greece. The king of Egypt ("the king of the South") was Ptolemy I or perhaps a reference to the Ptolemaic dynasty in general.

11:6, 7 These prophecies seem to have been fulfilled many years later in the Seleucid wars between Egypt and Syria. In 252 B.C., Ptolemy II of Egypt ("the South") gave his daughter Berenice in marriage to Antiochus II of Syria ("the North") to finalise a peace treaty between their two lands. But Berenice was murdered in Antioch by Antiochus II's former wife, Laodice. Berenice's brother, Ptolemy III, ascended the Egyptian throne and declared war against the Seleucids to avenge his sister's murder.

11:9–11 The king of Syria ("the North") was Seleucus II, and the king of Egypt ("the South") was Ptolemy IV.

thousands, yet he will not remain triumphant. 13For the king of the North will muster another army, larger than the first; and after several years, he will advance with a huge army fully equipped.

14"In those times many will rise against the king of the South. The violent men among your own people will rebel in fulfilment of the vision, but without success. 15Then the king of the North will come and build up siege ramps[k] and will capture a fortified city. The forces of the South will be powerless to resist; even their best troops will not have the strength to stand. 16The invader will do as he pleases;[l] no-one will be able to stand against him.[m] He will establish himself in the Beautiful Land and will have the power to destroy it.[n] 17He will determine to come with the might of his entire kingdom and will make an alliance with the king of the South. And he will give him a daughter in marriage in order to overthrow the kingdom, but his plans[c] will not succeed[o] or help him. 18Then he will turn his attention to the coastlands[p] and will take many of them, but a commander will put an end to his insolence and will turn his insolence back upon him.[q] 19After this, he will turn back towards the fortresses of his own country but will stumble and fall,[r] to be seen no more.[s]

20"His successor will send out a tax collector to maintain the royal splendour.[t] In a few years, however, he will be destroyed, yet not in anger or in battle.

21"He will be succeeded by a contemptible[u] person who has not been given the honour of royalty.[v] He will invade the kingdom when its people feel secure, and he will seize it through intrigue. 22Then an overwhelming army will be swept away before him; both it and a prince of the covenant will be destroyed.[w] 23After coming to an agreement with him, he will act deceitfully,[x] and with only a few people he will rise to power. 24When the richest provinces feel secure, he will invade them and will achieve what neither his fathers nor his forefathers did. He will distribute plunder, loot and wealth among his followers.[y] He will plot the overthrow of fortresses—but only for a time.

25"With a large army he will stir up his strength and courage against the king of the South. The king of the South will wage war with a large and very powerful army, but he will not be able to stand because of the plots devised against him. 26Those who eat from the king's provisions will try to destroy him; his army will be swept away, and many will fall in battle. 27The two kings, with their hearts bent on evil,[z] will sit at the same table and lie[a] to each other, but to no avail, because an end will still come at the appointed time.[b] 28The king of the North will return to his own country with great wealth, but his heart will be set against the holy covenant. He will take action against it and then return to his own country.

29"At the appointed time he will invade the South again, but this time the outcome will be different from what it was before. 30Ships of the western coastlands[d][c] will oppose him, and he will lose heart. Then he will turn back and vent his fury against the holy covenant. He will return and show favour to those who forsake the holy covenant.

c *17* Or *but she* **d** *30* Hebrew *of Kittim*

11:15 [k]Eze 4:2
11:16 [l]Da 8:4 [m]Jos 1:5; Da 8:7 [n]Da 8:9
11:17 [o]Ps 20:4
11:18 [p]Isa 66:19; Jer 25:22 [q]Hos 12:14
11:19 [r]Ps 27:2 [s]Ps 37:36; Eze 26:21
11:20 [t]Isa 60:17
11:21 [u]Da 4:17 [v]Da 8:25
11:22 [w]Da 8:10-11
11:23 [x]Da 8:25
11:24 [y]Ne 9:25
11:27 [z]Ps 64:6 [a]Ps 12:2; Jer 9:5 [b]Hab 2:3
11:30 [c]Ge 10:4

11:13 This king of the North may have been Antiochus III (the Great). He defeated many Egyptian cities (11:15) and established himself in Israel ("the Beautiful Land", 11:16). He was later defeated by the Romans at Magnesia (11:18).

11:17 The invader, Antiochus III, tried to bring peace between Egypt and Syria by having his daughter marry Ptolemy V Epiphanes of Egypt, but the plan failed.

11:20 The successor to Antiochus III was Seleucus IV. He sent Heliodorus to collect money from the temple treasury in Jerusalem.

11:21 Seleucus IV was succeeded by his brother, Antiochus IV Epiphanes, who found favour with the Romans.

11:22 The "overwhelming army" refers to the way all opposition against Antiochus IV will be broken. The prince of the covenant may be the high priest Onias III, who was assassinated by Menelaus in 170 B.C.

11:27 These two treacherous kings were probably Antiochus IV of Syria and Ptolemy VI of Egypt. Treachery and deceit are a power broker's way to position himself over someone else. When two power brokers try to gain the upper hand, it is a mutually weakening and self-destructive process. It is also futile because God ultimately holds all power in his hands.

11:29–31 Antiochus IV would again invade "the South", but enemy ships would cause him to retreat. On his way back, he plundered Jerusalem, desecrated the temple, and stopped the Jews' daily sacrifices. The temple was desecrated when he sacrificed pigs on an altar erected in honour of Zeus. According to Jewish law, pigs were unclean and were not to be touched or eaten. To sacrifice a pig in the temple was the worst kind of insult an enemy could level against the Jews. This happened in 168–167 B.C.

31"His armed forces will rise up to desecrate the temple fortress and will abolish
the daily sacrifice. Then they will set up the abomination that causes desolation.[d]
32With flattery he will corrupt those who have violated the covenant, but the people
who know their God will firmly resist[e] him.
33"Those who are wise will instruct[f] many, though for a time they will fall by the
sword or be burned or captured or plundered.[g] 34When they fall, they will receive
a little help, and many who are not sincere[h] will join them. 35Some of the wise will
stumble, so that they may be refined,[i] purified and made spotless until the time of
the end, for it will still come at the appointed time.

The King Who Exalts Himself

36"The king will do as he pleases. He will exalt and magnify himself above every
god and will say unheard-of things[j] against the God of gods.[k] He will be successful
until the time of wrath[l] is completed, for what has been determined must take place.
37He will show no regard for the gods of his fathers or for the one desired by women,
nor will he regard any god, but will exalt himself above them all. 38Instead of them,
he will honour a god of fortresses; a god unknown to his fathers he will honour with
gold and silver, with precious stones and costly gifts. 39He will attack the mightiest
fortresses with the help of a foreign god and will greatly honour those who acknowledge him. He will make them rulers over many people and will distribute the land
at a price.[e]
40"At the time of the end the king of the South[m] will engage him in battle, and
the king of the North will storm[n] out against him with chariots and cavalry and a great
fleet of ships. He will invade many countries and sweep through them like a flood.[o]
41He will also invade the Beautiful Land. Many countries will fall, but Edom,[p]
Moab[q] and the leaders of Ammon will be delivered from his hand. 42He will extend
his power over many countries; Egypt will not escape. 43He will gain control of the
treasures of gold and silver and all the riches of Egypt,[r] with the Libyans[s] and
Nubians in submission. 44But reports from the east and the north will alarm him, and
he will set out in a great rage to destroy and annihilate many. 45He will pitch his royal
tents between the seas at[f] the beautiful holy mountain. Yet he will come to his end,
and no-one will help him.

The End Times

12 "At that time Michael,[a] the great prince who protects your people, will arise.
There will be a time of distress[b] such as has not happened from the beginning
of nations until then. But at that time your people—everyone whose name is found

e 39 Or *land for a reward* f 45 Or *the sea and*

11:31 [d]Da 8:11-13; 9:27; Mt 24:15*; Mk 13:14*
11:32 [e]Mic 5:7-9
11:33 [f]Mal 2:7 [g]Mt 24:9; Jn 16:2; Heb 11:32-38
11:34 [h]Mt 7:15; Ro 16:18
11:35 [i]Ps 78:38; Da 12:10; Zec 13:9; Jn 15:2
11:36 [j]Rev 13:5-6 [k]Dt 10:17; Isa 14:13-14; Da 7:25; 8:11-12, 25; 2Th 2:4 [l]Isa 10:25; 26:20
11:40 [m]Isa 21:1 [n]Isa 5:28 [o]Eze 38:4
11:41 [p]Isa 11:14 [q]Jer 48:47
11:43 [r]Eze 30:4 [s]2Ch 12:3; Na 3:9
12:1 [a]Da 10:13 [b]Da 9:12; Mt 24:21; Mk 13:19; Rev 16:18

11:32 This reference to those who have violated the covenant may include Menelaus, the high priest, who was won over by Antiochus and who conspired with him against the Jews who were loyal to God. The "people who know their God" may refer to the Maccabees and their sympathisers, but a further fulfilment may lie in the future.

11:33, 34 Those who are wise will teach many, but they will also face great persecution. Difficult times remind us of our weaknesses and our inability to cope. We want answers, leadership, and clear direction. During these times, God's word begins to interest even those who would never look at it. We should be ready to use our opportunities to share God's word in needy times. We must also be prepared to face persecution and rejection as we teach and preach.

11:35 God's messenger described a time of trial when even wise believers may stumble. This could mean (1) falling into sin, (2) being fearful and losing faith, (3) mistakenly following wrong teaching, or (4) experiencing severe suffering and martyrdom. If we persevere in our faith, any such experience will only refine us and make us stronger. Are you facing trials? Recognise them as opportunities to strengthen your faith. If we remain steadfast in these experiences, we will be stronger in our faith and closer to God.

11:36–39 These verses could refer to Antiochus IV Epiphanes, Titus (the Roman general), or the antichrist. Some of these events may have been fulfilled in the past, and some have yet to be fulfilled.

11:37 The "one desired by women" may refer to Tammuz, a Babylonian fertility god. Tammuz is also mentioned in Ezekiel 8:14. In other words, this person won't recognise any deity or religions at all, not even pagan ones. Instead, he will proclaim himself to be divine and the ultimate power.

11:38 The "god of fortresses" is believed by some to be Jupiter or Zeus. The implication is that this king will make *war* his god. More than all his predecessors, he will wage war and glorify its horrors.

11:40 The antichrist of the last days becomes the centre of attention from this point through the rest of the book of Daniel.

written in the book[c]—will be delivered.[d] 2 Multitudes who sleep in the dust of the
earth will awake: some to everlasting life, others to shame and everlasting contempt.[e]
3 Those who are wise[a][f] will shine[g] like the brightness of the heavens, and those who
lead many to righteousness, like the stars for ever and ever.[h] 4 But you, Daniel, close
up and seal[i] the words of the scroll until the time of the end.[j] Many will go here
and there to increase knowledge."

5 Then I, Daniel, looked, and there before me stood two others, one on this bank
of the river and one on the opposite bank.[k] 6 One of them said to the man clothed
in linen,[l] who was above the waters of the river, "How long will it be before these
astonishing things are fulfilled?"[m]

7 The man clothed in linen, who was above the waters of the river, lifted his right
hand and his left hand towards heaven, and I heard him swear by him who lives for
ever,[n] saying, "It will be for a time, times and half a time.[b][o] When the power of
the holy people[p] has been finally broken, all these things will be completed.[q]"

8 I heard, but I did not understand. So I asked, "My lord, what will the outcome
of all this be?"

9 He replied, "Go your way, Daniel, because the words are closed up and sealed
until the time of the end.[r] 10 Many will be purified, made spotless and refined,[s] but
the wicked will continue to be wicked.[t] None of the wicked will understand, but those
who are wise will understand.[u]

11 "From the time that the daily sacrifice is abolished and the abomination that causes
desolation[v] is set up, there will be 1,290 days. 12 Blessed is the one who waits[w] for
and reaches the end of the 1,335 days.[x]

[a] 3 Or *who impart wisdom* [b] 7 Or *a year, two years and half a year*

12:1 [c] Ex 32:32; Ps 56:8 [d] Jer 30:7
12:2 [e] Isa 26:19; Mt 25:46; Jn 5:28-29
12:3 [f] Da 11:33 [g] Mt 13:43; Jn 5:35 [h] 1Co 15:42
12:4 [i] Isa 8:16 [j] ver 9, 13; Rev 22:10
12:5 [k] Da 10:4
12:6 [l] Eze 9:2 [m] Da 8:13
12:7 [n] Rev 10:5-6 [o] Da 7:25 [p] Da 8:24 [q] Lk 21:24; Rev 10:7
12:9 [r] ver 4
12:10 [s] Da 11:35 [t] Isa 32:7; Rev 22:11 [u] Hos 14:9
12:11 [v] Da 8:11; 9:27; Mt 24:15*; Mk 13:14*
12:12 [w] Isa 30:18 [x] Da 8:14

11:45 "The beautiful holy mountain" is Mount Zion or the city of Jerusalem.

12:1 Great suffering is in store for God's people throughout the years ahead. This way of describing the future is also used by Jeremiah (Jeremiah 30:7) and Jesus (Matthew 24:21ff). Yet the great suffering is tempered by a great promise of hope for true believers.

12:2 This is a clear reference to the resurrection of both the righteous and the wicked, although the eternal fates of each will be quite different. Up to this point in time, teaching about the resurrection was not common, although every Israelite believed that one day he or she would be included in the restoration of the new kingdom. This reference to a bodily resurrection of both the saved and the lost was a sharp departure from common belief. (See also Job 19:25, 26; Psalm 16:10; and Isaiah 26:19 for other Old Testament references to the resurrection.)

12:3 Many people try to be stars in the world of entertainment, only to find their stardom temporary. God tells us how we can be eternal "stars"—by being wise and leading many to God's righteousness. If we share our Lord with others, we can be true stars—radiantly beautiful in God's sight!

12:4 Closing up and sealing the words of the scroll meant that it was to be kept safe and preserved. This was to be done so that believers of all times could look back on God's work in history and find hope. Daniel did not understand the exact meaning of the times and events in his vision. We can see events as they unfold, for we are in the end times. The whole book will not be understood until the climax of earth's history.

12:7 "Time, times and half a time" may add up to 3 1/2 years (see the NIV text note), and may be taken as either literal or figurative.

12:7 "The power of the holy people" seems to be crushed again and again throughout history. God's recurring purpose in this is to break the pride and self-sufficiency of his rebellious people and to bring them to accept him as their Lord.

12:10 Trials and persecutions make very little sense to us when we experience them. But they can purify us if we are willing to learn from them. After you survive a difficult time, seek to learn from it so that it can help you in the future. See Romans 5:3–5 for more on God's purpose in our sufferings.

12:11 "The abomination" set up in the temple refers to the altar of Zeus, where Antiochus IV Epiphanes sacrificed a pig. Some think it will have another fulfilment in the antichrist and one of his horrible acts of evil (Matthew 24:15). However, this and the predictions at the early part of the chapter may refer specifically to Antiochus IV Epiphanes, and the rest of the prophecy may refer to the end times.

12:11, 12 Either these are further calculations relating to the persecution of the Jews under Antiochus IV Epiphanes, or they refer to the end times. The abolishing of the daily sacrifices means the removal of worship of the true God, as well as oppression of believers. There is much speculation about these numbers in verses 11 and 12. The point is that this time of persecution has an end; God is in control of it, and he will be victorious over evil.

13 "As for you, go your way till the end. You will rest,[y] and then at the end of the days you will rise to receive your allotted inheritance.[z]"

12:13
[y] Isa 57:2
[z] Rev 14:13

12:13 The promise of resurrection was reaffirmed to Daniel. He would one day see the fulfilment of his words, but he was not to spend the rest of his life wondering what his visions might mean. Instead, he was to rest in the comfort of God's sovereignty and look forward to the time when he would rise to receive and share eternal life with God. God does not reveal everything to us in this life. We must be content with the partial picture until he wants us to see more. He will tell us all we need to know.

12:13 Daniel stands tall in the gallery of God's remarkable servants. Born of royal heritage, yet taken into captivity when only a teenager, Daniel determined to remain faithful to God in the land of his captivity. Even at great personal cost, Daniel spent his entire lifetime advising his captors with unusual wisdom. God chose him as his servant to record some of the events of the captivity and some significant events concerning the future. As an old man, having been faithful to God throughout his years, Daniel was assured by God that he would rise from the dead and receive his portion in God's eternal kingdom. Faithfulness to God has a rich reward, not necessarily in this life, but most certainly in the life to come.

HOSEA

Jeroboam II becomes king of Israel 793 B.C.	*Amos becomes a prophet 760*	*Hosea becomes a prophet; King Zechariah of Israel is killed 753*	*King Shallum of Israel is killed 752*	*Tiglath-Pileser III invades Israel 743*	*Micah becomes a prophet to Judah 742*	*Isaiah becomes a prophet to Judah 740*	*Israel (northern kingdom) falls 722*	*Hosea's ministry ends 715*

THE BRIDEGROOM stands to attention as the music swells and the bride begins her long walk down the aisle, arm in arm with her father. The smiling but nervous husband-to-be follows every step, his eyes brimming with love. Then happy tears are shed, vows stated, and families merged. A wedding is a joyous celebration of love. It is the holy mystery of two becoming one, of beginning life together, and of commitment. Marriage is ordained by God and illustrates his relationship with his people. Thus, there is perhaps no greater tragedy than the violation of those sacred vows.

God told Hosea to find a wife, and told him beforehand that she would be unfaithful to him. Although she would bear many children, some of these offspring would be fathered by others. In obedience to God, Hosea married Gomer. His relationship with her, her adultery, and their children became living, prophetic examples to Israel.

The book of Hosea is a love story—real, tragic, and true. Transcending the tale of young man and wife, it tells of God's love for his people and the response of his "bride". A covenant had been made and God had been faithful. His love was steadfast and his commitment unbroken. But Israel, like Gomer, was adulterous and unfaithful, spurning God's love and turning instead to false gods. Then, after warning of judgment, God reaffirmed his love and offered reconciliation. His love and mercy were overflowing, but justice would be served.

The book begins with God's marriage instructions to Hosea. After Hosea's marriage, children were born, and each given a name signifying a divine message (chapter 1). Then, as predicted, Gomer left Hosea to pursue her lusts (chapter 2). But Hosea (whose name means "salvation") found her, redeemed her, and brought her home again, fully reconciled (chapter 3). Images of God's love, judgment, grace, and mercy were woven into their relationship. Next, God outlined his case against the people of Israel—their sins would ultimately cause their destruction (chapters 4; 6; 7; 12) and would rouse his anger, resulting in punishment (chapters 5; 8—10, 12; 13). But even in the midst of Israel's immorality, God was merciful and offered hope, expressing his infinite love for his people (chapter 11) and the fact that their repentance would bring about blessing (chapter 14).

The book of Hosea dramatically portrays our God's constant and persistent love. As you read this book, watch the prophet submit himself willingly to his Lord's direction; grieve with him over the unfaithfulness of his wife and his people; and hear the clear warning of judgment. Then reaffirm your commitment to being God's person, faithful in your love and true to your vows.

VITAL STATISTICS

PURPOSE:
To illustrate God's love for his sinful people

AUTHOR:
Hosea son of Beeri ("Hosea" means "salvation")

TO WHOM WRITTEN:
Israel (the northern kingdom) and God's people everywhere

DATE WRITTEN:
Approximately 715 B.C., recording events from about 753–715 B.C.

SETTING:
Hosea began his ministry during the end of the prosperous but morally declining reign of Jeroboam II of Israel (the upper classes were doing well, but they were oppressing the poor). He prophesied until shortly after the fall of Samaria in 722 B.C.

KEY VERSE:
"The LORD said to me, 'Go, show your love to your wife again, though she is loved by another and is an adulteress. Love her as the LORD loves the Israelites, though they turn to other gods and love the sacred raisin cakes'" (3:1).

KEY PEOPLE:
Hosea, Gomer, their children

KEY PLACES:
The northern kingdom (Israel), Samaria, Ephraim

SPECIAL FEATURES:
Hosea employs many images from daily life—God is depicted as husband, father, lion, leopard, bear, dew, rain, moth, and others; Israel is pictured as wife, sick person, vine, grapes, early fruit, olive tree, woman in childbirth, oven, morning mist, chaff, and smoke, to name a few.

THE BLUEPRINT

A. HOSEA'S WAYWARD WIFE (1:1–3:5)	Hosea was commanded by God to marry a woman who was unfaithful in marriage and would cause him many heartaches. Just as Gomer lost interest in Hosea and ran after other lovers, we too can easily lose appreciation for our special relationship with God and pursue dreams and goals that do not include him. When we compromise our Christian life-styles and adopt the ways of the world, we are being unfaithful.
B. GOD'S WAYWARD PEOPLE (4:1–14:9) 1. Israel's sinfulness 2. Israel's punishment 3. God's love for Israel	God wanted the people in the northern kingdom to turn from their sin and return to worshipping him alone, but they persisted in their wickedness. Throughout the book, Israel is described as ignorant of God, with no desire to please him. Israel did not understand God at all, just as Gomer did not understand Hosea. Like a loving husband or patient father, God wants people to know him and to turn to him daily.

MEGATHEMES

THEME	EXPLANATION	IMPORTANCE
The Nation's Sin	Just as Hosea's wife, Gomer, was unfaithful to him, so the nation of Israel had been unfaithful to God. Israel's idolatry was like adultery. They sought illicit relationships with Assyria and Egypt in pursuit of military might, and they mixed Baal worship with the worship of God.	Like Gomer, we can chase after other loves—love of power, pleasure, money, or recognition. The temptations in this world can be very seductive. Are we loyal to God, remaining completely faithful, or have other loves taken his rightful place?
God's Judgment	Hosea solemnly warned Judah against following Israel's example. Because Judah broke the covenant, turned away from God, and forgot her Maker, she experienced a devastating invasion and exile. Sin has terrible consequences.	Disaster surely follows ingratitude towards God and rebellion. The Lord is our only true refuge. If we harden our hearts against him, there is no safety or security anywhere else. We cannot escape God's judgment.
God's Love	Just as Hosea went after his unfaithful wife to bring her back, so the Lord pursues us with his love. His love is tender, loyal, unchanging, and undying. No matter what, God still loves us.	Have you forgotten God and become disloyal to him? Don't let prosperity diminish your love for him or let success blind you to your need for his love.
Restoration	Although God will discipline his people for sin, he encourages and restores those who have repented. True repentance opens the way to a new beginning. God forgives and restores.	There is still hope for those who turn back to God. No loyalty, achievement, or honour can be compared to loving him. Turn to the Lord while the offer still stands. No matter how far you have strayed, God is willing to bring you back.

A. HOSEA'S WAYWARD WIFE (1:1–3:5)

Hosea highlights the parallels between his relationship with Gomer and God's relationship with the nation of Israel. Although Israel made a covenant with the one true God, she went after other false gods. In the same way, Hosea married Gomer, knowing in advance that she would leave him. Hosea dealt with his wife tenderly in spite of her sin. And God was merciful towards the people of Israel despite their sins. God has not changed; he is still merciful and forgiving.

1 The word of the LORD that came to Hosea son of Beeri during the reigns of Uzziah,
Jotham, Ahaz and Hezekiah, kings of Judah,[a] and during the reign of Jeroboam[b]
son of Joash king of Israel:[c]

1:1 [a]Isa 1:1; Mic 1:1 [b]2Ki 13:13 [c]Am 1:1

1:1 Hosea was a prophet to the northern kingdom of Israel. He served from 753 to 715 B.C. Under the reign of Jeroboam II, the northern kingdom had prospered materially but had decayed spiritually. The people were greedy and had adopted the moral behaviour and idolatrous religion of the surrounding Canaanites.

Hosea's role was to show how the northern kingdom had been unfaithful to God, their "husband" and provider, and had married themselves to Baal and the gods of Canaan. He warned that unless they repented of their sin and turned back to God, they were headed for destruction. Hosea spoke of God's characteristics—his

1:2
[d]Jer 3:1; Hos 2:2, 5; 3:1
[e]Dt 31:16; Jer 3:14; Eze 23:3-21; Hos 5:3

1:4
[f]2Ki 10:1-14; Hos 2:22

1:5
[g]2Ki 15:29

1:6
[h]ver 3
[i]Hos 2:4

1:7
[j]Ps 44:6
[k]Zec 4:6

Hosea's Wife and Children

2When the LORD began to speak through Hosea, the LORD said to him, "Go, take
to yourself an adulterous[d] wife and children of unfaithfulness, because the land is
guilty of the vilest adultery[e] in departing from the LORD." 3So he married Gomer
daughter of Diblaim, and she conceived and bore him a son.
4Then the LORD said to Hosea, "Call him Jezreel,[f] because I will soon punish the
house of Jehu for the massacre at Jezreel, and I will put an end to the kingdom of
Israel. 5In that day I will break Israel's bow in the Valley of Jezreel.[g]"
6Gomer[h] conceived again and gave birth to a daughter. Then the LORD said to
Hosea, "Call her Lo-Ruhamah,[a] for I will no longer show love to the house of
Israel,[i] that I should at all forgive them. 7Yet I will show love to the house of Judah;
and I will save them—not by bow,[j] sword or battle, or by horses and horsemen, but
by the LORD their God.[k]"

a 6 *Lo-Ruhamah* means *not loved.*

HOSEA served as a prophet to Israel (the northern kingdom) from 753–715 B.C.

Climate of the times	Israel's last six kings were especially wicked; they promoted heavy taxes, oppression of the poor, idol worship, and total disregard for God. Israel was subjected to Assyria and was forced to pay tribute, which depleted its few remaining resources.
Main message	The people of Israel had sinned against God, as an adulterous woman sins against her husband. Judgment was sure to come for living in total disregard for God and fellow humans. Israel fell to Assyria in 722 B.C.
Importance of message	When we sin, we sever our relationship with God, breaking our commitment to him. While all must answer to God for their sins, those who seek God's forgiveness are spared eternal judgment.
Contemporary prophets	Jonah (793–753) Amos (760–750) Micah (742–687) Isaiah (740–681)

---

powerful love and fierce justice—and how their practical experience of these should affect their lives and make them return to God. Unfortunately, the people had broken their covenant with God, and they would receive the punishments God had promised (Deuteronomy 27; 28).

1:2, 3 Did God really order his prophet to marry a woman who would commit adultery? Some who find it difficult to believe God could make such a request view this story as an illustration, not an historical event. Many, however, think the story is historical and give one of these explanations: (1) According to God's law, a priest could not marry a prostitute or a divorced woman (Leviticus 21:7). However, Hosea was not a priest. (2) It is possible that Gomer was not an adulterous woman when Hosea married her, and that God was letting Hosea know that Gomer would later turn to adultery and prostitution. In any case, Hosea knew ahead of time that his wife would be unfaithful and that their married life would become a living object lesson to the adulterous northern kingdom. Hosea's marriage to an unfaithful woman would illustrate God's relationship to the unfaithful nation of Israel.

1:2, 3 It is difficult to imagine Hosea's feelings when God told him to marry a woman who would be unfaithful to him. He may not have wanted to do it, but he obeyed. God often required extraordinary obedience from his prophets who were facing extraordinary times. God may ask you to do something difficult and extraordinary, too. If he does, how will you respond? Will you obey him, trusting that he who knows everything has a special purpose for his request? Will you be able to accept the fact that the pain involved in obedience may benefit those you serve, and not you personally?

1:4, 5 Elijah had predicted that the family of Israel's King Ahab would be destroyed because of their wickedness (1 Kings 21:20–22), but Jehu went too far in carrying out God's command (2 Kings 10:1–11). Therefore, Jehu's dynasty would also be punished—in the Valley of Jezreel, the very place where he carried out the massacre of Ahab's family. God's promise to put an end to Israel as an independent kingdom ("break Israel's bow") came true 25 years later when the Assyrians conquered the northern kingdom and carried the people into captivity.

1:6, 8 In 1:3, we read that Gomer "bore him [Hosea] a son". In 1:6 and 1:8, we learn that Gomer gave birth to two more children, but there is no indication that Hosea was their natural father, and some translations imply that he was not. Whether or not the children were Hosea's, the key to this part of the story is found in the names God chose for the children, showing his reaction to Israel's unfaithfulness. God's reaction to unfaithfulness is no different today. He wants our complete devotion.

1:7 God said he would personally rescue the people of Judah from their enemies with no help from their armies or weapons. Although God asks us to do our part, we should remember that he is not limited to human effort. God often chooses to work through people, but only because it is good for *them.* He can accomplish all his purposes without any help from us if he so chooses. You are very important to God, but on your own you have neither the ability to fulfil nor the power to disrupt God's plans.

8 After she had weaned Lo-Ruhamah, Gomer had another son. 9 Then the LORD said,
"Call him Lo-Ammi,[b] for you are not my people, and I am not your God.
10 "Yet the Israelites will be like the sand on the seashore, which cannot be measured
or counted.[l] In the place where it was said to them, 'You are not my people', they
will be called 'sons of the living God'.[m] 11 The people of Judah and the people of Israel
will be reunited,[n] and they will appoint one leader[o] and will come up out of the
land,[p] for great will be the day of Jezreel.

2 "Say of your brothers, 'My people', and of your sisters, 'My loved one'.[a]

Israel Punished and Restored

2 "Rebuke your mother,[b] rebuke her,
for she is not my wife,
and I am not her husband.
Let her remove the adulterous[c] look from her face
and the unfaithfulness from between her breasts.
3 Otherwise I will strip her naked
and make her as bare as on the day she was born;[d]
I will make her like a desert,[e]
turn her into a parched land,
and slay her with thirst.
4 I will not show my love to her children,[f]
because they are the children of adultery.
5 Their mother has been unfaithful
and has conceived them in disgrace.
She said, 'I will go after my lovers,[g]
who give me my food and my water,
my wool and my linen, my oil and my drink.'[h]
6 Therefore I will block her path with thornbushes;
I will wall her in so that she cannot find her way.[i]
7 She will chase after her lovers but not catch them;
she will look for them but not find them.[j]
Then she will say,

[b] 9 *Lo-Ammi* means *not my people.*

1:10 [l] Ge 22:17; Jer 33:22 [m] ver 9; Ro 9:26*
1:11 [n] Isa 11:12, 13 [o] Jer 23:5-8 [p] Eze 37:15-28
2:1 [a] ver 23
2:2 [b] ver 5; Isa 50:1; Hos 1:2 [c] Eze 23:45
2:3 [d] Eze 16:4, 22 [e] Isa 32:13-14
2:4 [f] Eze 8:18
2:5 [g] Jer 3:6 [h] Jer 44:17-18
2:6 [i] Job 3:23; 19:8; La 3:9
2:7 [j] Hos 5:13

1:9 Here God was in essence dissolving the covenant (Jeremiah 7:23). The name of the third child conveys the finality of God's judgment. God's warnings recorded in Deuteronomy 28:15–68 were beginning to come true: Israel was abandoning God, and in turn, he was leaving them alone and without his blessings.

1:10 The Old Testament prophetic books sometimes use the word "Israelites" to refer to the people of the united kingdom (north and south) and sometimes just to the northern kingdom. In talking about past events, Hosea usually thought of Israel as the northern kingdom with its capital in Samaria. But when Hosea spoke about future events relating to God's promises of restoration, it is difficult to understand his words as applying only to the northern kingdom because the exiled northerners would become hopelessly intermingled with their conquerors. Thus most scholars see the promises of return as either: (1) conditional – the Israelites chose not to return to God, and therefore they were not entitled to the blessings included in the promises of restoration, or (2) unconditional – God's promises of restoration have been fulfilled in Jesus Christ, and therefore the church (the new Israel) receives his blessings (Romans 9:25, 26; 1 Peter 2:10).

1:10, 11 Although Israel was unfaithful, God's commitment remained unchanged. This promise of a future reuniting reiterated the covenant made with Moses (Deuteronomy 30:1–10) and foreshadowed the prophecies of Jeremiah (Jeremiah 29:11–14; 31:31–40) and Ezekiel (Ezekiel 11:16–21). It was a prediction of the day when all the people of God will be united under Christ. Today all believers everywhere are God's chosen people, a royal priesthood (see 1 Peter 2:9).

1:11 Just as the other children's names carried significance, so did Jezreel. In verse 4, the name depicts divine judgment; here it represents the scattering. The name means "God scatters". Here it represents the scattering a farmer does when he plants seeds. This was a sign of a new day and a new relationship between God and Israel.

2:2ff Israel's punishment and restoration are the themes of this chapter. As in a court case, the adulteress is brought to trial and found guilty. But after her punishment, she is joyfully and tenderly restored to God.

2:5–7 The Israelites were thanking false gods (specifically Baal, the god whom they believed controlled weather and thus farming) for their food, shelter, and clothing, instead of the true God who gave those blessings. Therefore, God would block Israel's "path with thornbushes" and "wall her in" by making the rewards of idol worship so disappointing that the people would be persuaded to turn back to God. Despite Israel's unfaithfulness, God was still faithful and merciful. He would continue to hold his arms out to his people, even to the point of placing obstacles in their wayward path to turn them back to him.

2:7 Just as Gomer would return to her husband if she thought she would be better off with him, so people often return to God when they find life's struggle too difficult to handle. Returning to God out of desperation is better than rebelling against him, but it is better yet to turn to God out of gratitude for his care.

2:7 [k]Jer 2:2; 3:1 [l]Eze 16:8
2:8 [m]Isa 1:3 [n]Eze 16:15-19; Hos 8:4
2:9 [o]Hos 8:7 [p]Hos 9:2
2:10 [q]Eze 16:37
2:11 [r]Jer 7:34 [s]Isa 1:14; Jer 16:9; Hos 3:4; Am 8:10
2:12 [t]Isa 7:23; Jer 8:13 [u]Isa 5:6 [v]Hos 13:8
2:13 [w]Hos 11:2 [x]Eze 16:17 [y]Hos 4:13 [z]Hos 4:6; 8:14; 13:6

'I will go back to my husband as at first,[k]
for then I was better off[l] than now.'
8She has not acknowledged[m] that I was the one
who gave her the grain, the new wine and oil,
who lavished on her the silver and gold—
which they used for Baal.[n]

9"Therefore I will take away my grain[o] when it ripens,
and my new wine[p] when it is ready.
I will take back my wool and my linen,
intended to cover her nakedness.
10So now I will expose her lewdness
before the eyes of her lovers;
no-one will take her out of my hands.[q]
11I will stop[r] all her celebrations:
her yearly festivals, her New Moons,
her Sabbath days—all her appointed feasts.[s]
12I will ruin her vines[t] and her fig-trees,
which she said were her pay from her lovers;
I will make them a thicket,[u]
and wild animals will devour them.[v]
13I will punish her for the days
she burned incense to the Baals;[w]
she decked herself with rings and jewellery,[x]
and went after her lovers,[y]
but me she forgot,[z]"

declares the LORD.

SPIRITUAL UNFAITHFULNESS

Spiritual adultery and physical adultery are alike in many ways, and both are dangerous. God was disappointed with his people because they had committed spiritual adultery against him, as Gomer had committed physical adultery against Hosea.

Parallels	*The danger*
Both spiritual and physical adultery are against God's law.	When we break God's law in full awareness of what we're doing, our hearts become hardened to the sin and our relationship with God is broken.
Both spiritual and physical adultery begin with disappointment and dissatisfaction—either real or imagined—with an already existing relationship.	The feeling that God disappoints can lead you away from him. Feelings of disappointment and dissatisfaction are normal and, when endured, will pass.
Both spiritual and physical adultery begin with diverting affection from one object of devotion to another.	The diverting of our affection is the first step in the blinding process that leads into sin.
Both spiritual and physical adultery involve a process of deterioration; it is not usually an impulsive decision.	The process is dangerous because you don't always realise it is happening until it is too late.
Both spiritual and physical adultery involve the creation of a fantasy about what a new object of love can do for you.	Such fantasy creates unrealistic expectations of what a new relationship can do and only leads to disappointment in all existing and future relationships.

2:8 Material possessions are success symbols in most societies. Israel was a wealthy nation at this time, and Gomer may have accumulated silver and gold. But Gomer didn't realise that Hosea had given her all she owned, just as Israel did not recognise God as the Giver of blessings. Both Gomer and Israel used their possessions irresponsibly as they ran after other lovers and other gods. How do you use your possessions? Use what God has given you to honour him.

2:12 The Israelites were so immersed in idolatry that they actually believed pagan gods gave them their vineyards and orchards ("her vines and her fig-trees"). They had forgotten that the entire land was a gift from God (Deuteronomy 32:49). Today many people give credit to everything and everyone but God for their prosperity—luck, hard work, quick thinking, the right contacts. When *you* succeed, who gets the credit?

2:13 Baal was the most important of the Canaanite gods, and his name came to be used to describe all the local deities worshipped throughout the land occupied by Israel. Unfortunately, Israel did not get rid of the idols and pagan worship centres as they had been commanded. Instead, they tolerated and frequently joined Baal worshippers, often through the influence of corrupt kings. One Israelite king especially noted for his Baal worship was Ahab. The prophet Elijah, in a dramatic showdown with Ahab's hired prophets, proved God's power far superior to Baal's (1 Kings 18).

14"Therefore I am now going to allure her;
I will lead her into the desert
and speak tenderly to her.
15There I will give her back her vineyards,
and will make the Valley of Achor[a][a] a door of hope.
There she will sing[b][b] as in the days of her youth,[c]
as in the day she came up out of Egypt.[d]

16"In that day," declares the LORD,
"you will call me 'my husband';
you will no longer call me 'my master'.[c]
17I will remove the names of the Baals from her lips;[e]
no longer will their names be invoked.[f]
18In that day I will make a covenant for them
with the beasts of the field and the birds of the air
and the creatures that move along the ground.[g]
Bow and sword and battle
I will abolish[h] from the land,
so that all may lie down in safety.[i]
19I will betroth[j] you to me for ever;
I will betroth you in[d] righteousness and justice,[k]
in[e] love and compassion.
20I will betroth you in faithfulness,
and you will acknowledge[l] the LORD.

21"In that day I will respond,"
declares the LORD—
"I will respond[m] to the skies,
and they will respond to the earth;
22and the earth will respond to the grain,
the new wine and oil,[n]
and they will respond to Jezreel.[f]
23I will plant[o] her for myself in the land;
I will show my love to the one I called 'Not my loved one'.[g][p]
I will say to those called 'Not my people',[h] 'You are my people';[q]
and they will say, 'You are my God.[r]'"

2:15 [a]Jos 7:24, 26 [b]Ex 15:1-18 [c]Jer 2:2 [d]Hos 12:9

2:17 [e]Ex 23:13; Ps 16:4 [f]Jos 23:7

2:18 [g]Job 5:22 [h]Isa 2:4 [i]Jer 23:6; Eze 34:25

2:19 [j]Isa 62:4 [k]Isa 1:27

2:20 [l]Jer 31:34; Hos 6:6; 13:4

2:21 [m]Isa 55:10; Zec 8:12

2:22 [n]Jer 31:12; Joel 2:19

2:23 [o]Jer 31:27 [p]Hos 1:6 [q]Hos 1:10 [r]Ro 9:25*; 1Pe 2:10

[a] *15 Achor* means *trouble.* [b] *15* Or *respond* [c] *16* Hebrew *baal* [d] *19* Or *with*; also in verse 20 [e] *19* Or *with*
[f] *22 Jezreel* means *God plants.* [g] *23* Hebrew *Lo-Ruhamah* [h] *23* Hebrew *Lo-Ammi*

2:14, 15 God was promising (1) to bring the people to the desert, a place free from distractions, so he could clearly communicate with them, and (2) to change what had been a time of difficulty into a day of hope. The Valley of Achor ("trouble") is the site where Achan had sinned by keeping forbidden war plunder (see Joshua 7). He had brought great disaster to Joshua's troops when they were attempting to conquer the land. God uses even our negative experiences to create opportunities to turn back to him. As you face problems and trials, remember that God speaks to you in the desert, and not just in times of prosperity.

2:16 Not until Judah's exile would the entire nation begin to come to its senses, give up its idols, and turn back to God; and not until that day when God rules through Jesus the Messiah will the relationship between God and his people be restored. In that day, God will no longer be like a master to them; he will be like a husband (Isaiah 54:4–8). The relationship will be deep and personal, the kind of relationship we can know, though imperfectly, in marriage.

2:19, 20 The time will come when unfaithfulness will be impossible—God will bind us to himself in his perfect righteousness, justice, love, compassion, and faithfulness. Betrothal in Hosea's time was more than a simple agreement to marry. It was a binding engagement, a deep commitment between two families for a future, permanent relationship. God was promising a fresh new beginning, not just a temporary rewriting of a tired old agreement. (See Jeremiah 31:31–34.)

2:19, 20 God's wedding gift to his people, both in Hosea's day and in our own, is his compassion. Through no merit of our own, God forgives us and makes us right with him. There is no way for us by our own efforts to reach God's high standard for moral and spiritual life, but he graciously accepts us, forgives us, and draws us into a relationship with himself. In that relationship we have personal and intimate communion with him.

3:1 [a]Hos 1:2 [b]2Sa 6:19
3:4 [c]Hos 13:11 [d]Da 11:31; Hos 2:11 [e]Jdg 17:5-6; Zec 10:2
3:5 [f]Eze 34:23-24 [g]Jer 50:4-5
4:1 [a]Jer 7:28
4:2 [b]Hos 7:3; 10:4 [c]Hos 6:9 [d]Hos 7:1
4:3 [e]Jer 4:28

Hosea's Reconciliation With His Wife

3 The LORD said to me, "Go, show your love to your wife again, though she is loved
by another and is an adulteress.[a] Love her as the LORD loves the Israelites,
though they turn to other gods and love the sacred raisin cakes.[b]"
2 So I bought her for fifteen shekels[a] of silver and about a homer and a lethek[b]
of barley. 3 Then I told her, "You are to live with[c] me for many days; you must not
be a prostitute or be intimate with any man, and I will live with[c] you."
4 For the Israelites will live for many days without king or prince,[c] without
sacrifice[d] or sacred stones, without ephod or idol.[e] 5 Afterwards the Israelites will
return and seek the LORD their God and David their king.[f] They will come trembling
to the LORD and to his blessings in the last days.[g]

B. GOD'S WAYWARD PEOPLE (4:1 – 14:9)

The rest of the book deals with Israel's sin and her impending judgment. Hosea points out the moral and spiritual decay of the nation. He describes the punishment awaiting the people and pleads with them to return to God. Although judgment and condemnation of sin are prevalent in the book, a strand of love and restoration runs throughout. Even in the midst of judgment, God is merciful and will restore those who repent and turn to him.

1. Israel's sinfulness

The Charge Against Israel

4 Hear the word of the LORD, you Israelites,
because the LORD has a charge to bring
against you who live in the land:
"There is no faithfulness, no love,
no acknowledgment[a] of God in the land.
2 There is only cursing,[a] lying[b] and murder,[c]
stealing[d] and adultery;
they break all bounds,
and bloodshed follows bloodshed.
3 Because of this the land mourns,[b][e]

[a] *2* That is, about 6 ounces (about 170 grams) [b] *2* That is, probably about 9 bushels (about 330 litres)
[c] *3* Or *wait for* [a] *2* That is, to pronounce a curse upon [b] *3* Or *dries up*

3:1 This short chapter pictures the nation's exile and return. Israel would experience a time of purification in a foreign land, but God would still love the people and would be willing to accept them back. God commanded Hosea to show the same forgiving spirit to Gomer. Although Hosea had good reason to divorce Gomer, he was told to buy her back and love her.

3:2 Apparently Gomer was on her own for a while. Needing to support herself, she must have either sold herself into slavery or become the mistress of another man. In either case, Hosea had to pay to get her back – although the required amount was pitifully small. Gomer was no longer worth much to anyone except Hosea, but he loved her just as God loved Israel. No matter how low we sink, God is willing to buy us back – to redeem us – and to lift us up again.

3:3 After this, Gomer is no longer mentioned by Hosea. This is explained in 3:4. Gomer's isolation showed how God would deal with the northern kingdom (5:6, 15). It is dangerous to rebel against God. If he were ever to withdraw his love and mercy, we would be without hope.

3:4 God would separate the Israelites from their treasured idolatrous practices. Sacrifices and sacred stones were elements of idol worship. Here the ephod is not the official vest of the priest, but an image used in idol worship; the idols were household gods, which were strictly forbidden for God's people.

3:4, 5 The northern kingdom had rebelled against David's dynasty and had taken Jeroboam as their king (1 Kings 12; 13). Their rebellion was both political and religious. At that time, they reverted back to the worship of golden idols. "David their king" refers to the time of Messiah's rule when all people will bow before him in humility and submission. Those who won't accept Christ's blessings now will face his power and judgment later. How much better it is to love and follow Christ now than face his angry judgment later.

4:1ff In this chapter, God brings a charge of disobedience against Israel. The religious leaders had failed to turn the people to God, and ritual prostitution had replaced right worship. The nation had declined spiritually and morally, breaking the laws that God had given them. The people found it easy to condemn Hosea's wife for her adultery. They were not so quick to see that *they* had been unfaithful to God.

4:1–3 God explained the reasons for Israel's suffering. Their lawless behaviour had brought the twin judgments of increased violence and ecological crisis. There is not always a direct cause-and-effect relationship between our actions and the problems we face. Nevertheless, when we are surrounded with difficulties, we should seriously ask, "Have I done anything sinful or irresponsible that has caused my suffering?" If we discover that we are at fault, even partially, we must change our ways before God will help us.

4:2 This verse may allude to the assassinations of kings during Hosea's lifetime. Shallum killed Zechariah (the king, not the prophet) and took the throne. Then Menahem killed Shallum and destroyed an entire city because it refused to accept him as king (2 Kings 15:8–16). God pointed out that even murder was being taken casually in Israel.

and all who live in it waste away;[f]
the beasts of the field and the birds of the air
and the fish of the sea are dying.[g]

4 "But let no man bring a charge,
let no man accuse another,
for your people are like those
who bring charges against a priest.[h]
5 You stumble[i] day and night,
and the prophets stumble with you.
So I will destroy your mother[j]—
6 my people are destroyed from lack of knowledge.[k]

"Because you have rejected knowledge,
I also reject you as my priests;
because you have ignored the law[l] of your God,
I also will ignore your children.
7 The more the priests increased,
the more they sinned against me;
they exchanged[c] their[d] Glory[m] for something disgraceful.[n]
8 They feed on the sins of my people
and relish their wickedness.[o]
9 And it will be: Like people, like priests.[p]
I will punish both of them for their ways
and repay them for their deeds.[q]

10 "They will eat but not have enough;[r]
they will engage in prostitution but not increase,
because they have deserted[s] the LORD
to give themselves 11 to prostitution,[t]
to old wine and new,
which take away the understanding[u] 12 of my people.
They consult a wooden idol[v]
and are answered by a stick of wood.[w]
A spirit of prostitution leads them astray;[x]
they are unfaithful to their God.
13 They sacrifice on the mountaintops
and burn offerings on the hills,

4:3 [f]Isa 33:9 [g]Jer 4:25; Zep 1:3
4:4 [h]Dt 17:12; Eze 3:26
4:5 [i]Eze 14:7 [j]Hos 2:2
4:6 [k]Hos 2:13; Mal 2:7-8 [l]Hos 8:1, 12
4:7 [m]Hab 2:16 [n]Hos 10:1, 6; 13:6
4:8 [o]Isa 56:11; Mic 3:11
4:9 [p]Isa 24:2 [q]Jer 5:31; Hos 8:13; 9:9, 15
4:10 [r]Lev 26:26; Mic 6:14 [s]Hos 7:14; 9:17
4:11 [t]Hos 5:4 [u]Pr 20:1
4:12 [v]Jer 2:27 [w]Hab 2:19 [x]Isa 44:20

c 7 Syriac and an ancient Hebrew scribal tradition; Masoretic Text *I will exchange* d 7 Masoretic Text; an ancient Hebrew scribal tradition *my*

4:4–9 Hosea levelled his charges against the religious leaders. Who were these religious leaders? When Jeroboam I rebelled against Solomon's son Rehoboam and set up a rival kingdom in the north, he also set up his own religious system (see 1 Kings 12:25–33). In violation of God's law, he made two golden calves and told the people to worship them. He also appointed his own priests, who were not descendants of Aaron. At first the residents of the northern kingdom continued to worship God, even though they were doing it in the wrong way, but very soon they also began to worship Canaanite gods. Before long they had substituted Baal for God and no longer worshipped God at all. It is not surprising that Jeroboam's false priests were unable to preserve the true worship of God.

4:6–9 God accused the religious leaders of keeping the people from knowing him ("destroyed from lack of knowledge"). They were supposed to be spiritual leaders, but they had become leaders in wrongdoing. The people may have said to one another, "It must be all right if the priests do it." Spiritual leadership is a heavy responsibility. Whether you teach a school class, pastor a oongregation, or lead a Bible study, don't take your leadership responsibilities lightly. Be a leader who leads others to God.

4:8 The priests relished the people's sins. Every time a person brought a sin offering, the priest received a portion of it. The more the people sinned, the more the priests received. Because they couldn't eat all of the offerings themselves, they sold some and gave some to their relatives. The priests profited from the continuation of sin; it gave them power and position in the community. So instead of trying to lead the people out of sin, they encouraged sin to increase their profits.

4:10–12 The chief Canaanite gods, Baal and Asherah, represented the power of fertility and sexual reproduction. Not surprisingly, their worship included rituals with vile sexual practices. Male worshippers had sex with female temple prostitutes, or priestesses, and young women wishing to bear children had sex with male priests. But God said their efforts to increase fertility would not succeed.

4:12 The "stick of wood", or divining rod, was a way of attempting to tell the future. By divorcing themselves from God's authoritative religion centred in Jerusalem, inhabitants of the northern kingdom had effectively cut themselves off from God's word and from his way of forgiveness. The drive to be free from all restrictions can move us completely out of God's will.

4:13
[y] Isa 1:29
[z] Jer 3:6; Hos 11:2
[a] Jer 2:20; Am 7:17
[b] Hos 2:13

under oak,[y] poplar and terebinth,
where the shade is pleasant.[z]
Therefore your daughters turn to prostitution[a]
and your daughters-in-law to adultery.[b]

4:14
[c] ver 11

14 "I will not punish your daughters
when they turn to prostitution,
nor your daughters-in-law
when they commit adultery,
because the men themselves consort with harlots[c]
and sacrifice with shrine-prostitutes—
a people without understanding will come to ruin!

4:15
[d] Hos 9:15; 12:11; Am 4:4

15 "Though you commit adultery, O Israel,
let not Judah become guilty.

"Do not go to Gilgal;[d]
do not go up to Beth Aven.[e]
And do not swear, 'As surely as the LORD lives!'
16 The Israelites are stubborn,
like a stubborn heifer.
How then can the LORD pasture them
like lambs[e] in a meadow?

4:16
[e] Isa 5:17; 7:25

17 Ephraim is joined to idols;
leave him alone!
18 Even when their drinks are gone,
they continue their prostitution;
their rulers dearly love shameful ways.
19 A whirlwind[f] will sweep them away,
and their sacrifices will bring them shame.[g]

4:19
[f] Hos 12:1; 13:15
[g] Isa 1:29

Judgment Against Israel

5:1
[a] Hos 6:9; 9:8

5 "Hear this, you priests!
Pay attention, you Israelites!
Listen, O royal house!
This judgment is against you:
You have been a snare[a] at Mizpah,
a net spread out on Tabor.
2 The rebels are deep in slaughter.[b]
I will discipline all of them.[c]
3 I know all about Ephraim;
Israel is not hidden from me.
Ephraim, you have now turned to prostitution;
Israel is corrupt.[d]

5:2
[b] Hos 4:2
[c] Hos 9:15

5:3
[d] Hos 6:10

[e] *15 Beth Aven* means *house of wickedness* (a name for Bethel, which means *house of God*).

4:15 God sent a warning to the southern kingdom of Judah that its priests should not become like those in Israel. Israel's priests who remained in the north had forgotten their spiritual heritage and had sold out to Baal. They were promoting idol worship and ritual prostitution. Israel would not escape punishment, but Judah could if it refused to follow Israel's example.

4:17 Ephraim is another name for Israel, the northern kingdom, because Ephraim was the most powerful of the ten tribes in the north. In the same way, the southern kingdom was called Judah after its most powerful tribe.

4:19 The whirlwind that would sweep Israel away referred to the Assyrian invasion that would destroy the nation about 20 years later.

5:1, 2 Mizpah and Tabor may have been sites prominent in the false worship of Baal. The leaders probably even encouraged the people to sin at these places. With both their civil and religious leaders hopelessly corrupt, the people of Israel did not have much of a chance. They looked to their leaders for guidance, and they should have found it. Today we can often choose our own leaders, but we still need to be aware of whether they are taking us towards or away from God. God held the people responsible for what they did. Similarly, God holds us responsible for our actions and choices.

4"Their deeds do not permit them
to return to their God.
A spirit of prostitution[e] is in their heart;
they do not acknowledge[f] the LORD.
5Israel's arrogance testifies[g] against them;
the Israelites, even Ephraim, stumble in their sin;
Judah also stumbles with them.
6When they go with their flocks and herds
to seek the LORD,[h]
they will not find him;
he has withdrawn[i] himself from them.
7They are unfaithful[j] to the LORD;
they give birth to illegitimate[k] children.
Now their New Moon festivals
will devour[l] them and their fields.

8"Sound the trumpet in Gibeah,[m]
the horn in Ramah.[n]
Raise the battle cry in Beth Aven;[a][o]
lead on, O Benjamin.
9Ephraim will be laid waste
on the day of reckoning.[p]
Among the tribes of Israel
I proclaim what is certain.[q]
10Judah's leaders are like those
who move boundary stones.[r]
I will pour out my wrath[s] on them
like a flood of water.
11Ephraim is oppressed,
trampled in judgment,
intent on pursuing idols.[b][t]
12I am like a moth[u] to Ephraim,
like rot to the people of Judah.

13"When Ephraim saw his sickness,
and Judah his sores,
then Ephraim turned to Assyria,[v]
and sent to the great king for help.[w]
But he is not able to cure[x] you,
not able to heal your sores.[y]
14For I will be like a lion[z] to Ephraim,
like a great lion to Judah.
I will tear them to pieces and go away;
I will carry them off, with no-one to rescue them.[a]
15Then I will go back to my place
until they admit their guilt.

5:4 [e]Hos 4:11 [f]Hos 4:6
5:5 [g]Hos 7:10
5:6 [h]Mic 6:6-7 [i]Pr 1:28; Isa 1:15; Eze 8:6
5:7 [j]Hos 6:7 [k]Hos 2:4 [l]Hos 2:11-12
5:8 [m]Hos 9:9; 10:9 [n]Isa 10:29 [o]Hos 4:15
5:9 [p]Isa 37:3; Hos 9:11-17 [q]Isa 46:10; Zec 1:6
5:10 [r]Dt 19:14 [s]Eze 7:8
5:11 [t]Hos 9:16; Mic 6:16
5:12 [u]Isa 51:8
5:13 [v]Hos 7:11; 8:9 [w]Hos 10:6 [x]Hos 14:3 [y]Jer 30:12
5:14 [z]Am 3:4 [a]Mic 5:8

a *8 Beth Aven* means *house of wickedness* (a name for Bethel, which means *house of God*). **b** *11* The meaning of the Hebrew for this word is uncertain.

5:4 Persistent sin hardens a person's heart, making it difficult to repent. Deliberately choosing to disobey God can sear the conscience; each sin makes the next one easier to commit. Don't allow sin to groove a hard path deep within you. Steer as far away from sinful practices as possible.

5:8 Gibeah and Ramah were Israelite cities near Jerusalem. Hosea prophesied that these cities would sound the alarm of the coming judgment.

5:10 Those who "move boundary stones" are guilty of a serious crime (Deuteronomy 27:17). Hosea was saying that the leaders of Judah were like those who cheat people by moving the boundary stones on their land (see Deuteronomy 19:14).

5:13 During the reigns of Menahem and Hoshea, Israel turned to Assyria for help (2 Kings 15:19, 20; 17:3, 4). But even the great world powers of that time could not help Israel, for God himself had determined to judge the nation. If we neglect God's call to repentance, how can we escape? (See Hebrews 2:3.)

5:15
[b]Hos 3:5
[c]Jer 2:27
[d]Isa 64:9

And they will seek my face;[b]
in their misery[c] they will earnestly seek me.[d]"

2. Israel's punishment

Israel Unrepentant

6:1
[a]Hos 5:14
[b]Dt 32:39; Jer 30:17; Hos 14:4

6:2
[c]Ps 30:5

6:3
[d]Joel 2:23
[e]Ps 72:6

6:4
[f]Hos 11:8
[g]Hos 7:1; 13:3

6:5
[h]Jer 1:9-10; 23:29
[i]Heb 4:12

6:6
[j]Isa 1:11; Mt 9:13*; 12:7*
[k]Hos 2:20

6 "Come, let us return to the LORD.
He has torn us to pieces[a]
but he will heal us;
he has injured us
but he will bind up our wounds.[b]
2 After two days he will revive us;[c]
on the third day he will restore us,
that we may live in his presence.
3 Let us acknowledge the LORD;
let us press on to acknowledge him.
As surely as the sun rises,
he will appear;
he will come to us like the winter rains,[d]
like the spring rains that water the earth.[e]"

4 "What can I do with you, Ephraim?[f]
What can I do with you, Judah?
Your love is like the morning mist,
like the early dew that disappears.[g]
5 Therefore I cut you in pieces with my prophets,
I killed you with the words of my mouth;[h]
my judgments flashed like lightning upon you.[i]
6 For I desire mercy, not sacrifice,[j]
and acknowledgment[k] of God rather than burnt offerings.

OBEDIENCE VERSUS SACRIFICES
God says many times that he doesn't want our gifts and sacrifices when we give them out of ritual or hypocrisy. God wants us first to love and obey him.

1 Samuel 15:22, 23	Obedience is far better than sacrifice.
Psalm 40:6–8	God doesn't want burnt offerings; he wants our lifelong service.
Psalm 51:16–19	God isn't interested in penance; he wants a broken and contrite heart.
Jeremiah 7:21–23	It isn't sacrifices God wants; he desires our obedience and promises that he will be our God and we will be his people.
Hosea 6:6	God doesn't want sacrifices; he wants our loving loyalty. He doesn't want offerings; he wants us to acknowledge him.
Amos 5:21–24	God hates pretence and hypocrisy; he wants to see justice flow like a river.
Micah 6:6–8	God is not satisfied with offerings; he wants us to be fair and just and merciful, and to walk humbly with him.
Matthew 9:13	God doesn't want sacrifices; he wants us to be merciful.

6:1–3 This is presumption, not genuine repentance. The people did not understand the depth of their sins. They did not turn from idols, regret their sins, or pledge to make changes. They thought that God's wrath would last only a few days; little did they know that their nation would soon be taken into exile. Israel was interested in God only for the material benefits he provided; they did not value the eternal benefits that come from worshipping him. Before judging Israel, however, consider your attitude. What do you hope to gain from your religion? Do you "repent" easily, without seriously considering what changes need to take place in your life?

6:4 God answered his people, pointing out that their profession of loyalty, like mist and dew, evaporated easily and had no substance. Many find it easy and comfortable to maintain the appearance of being committed without deep and sincere loyalty. If you profess loyalty to God, back it up with your actions.

6:6 Religious rituals can help people understand God and nourish their relationship with him. That is why God instituted circumcision and the sacrificial system in the Old Testament and baptism and the Lord's Supper in the New Testament. But a religious ritual is helpful only if it is carried out with an attitude of love for and obedience to God. If a person's heart is far from God, ritual will become empty mockery. God didn't want the Israelites' rituals; he wanted their hearts. Why do you worship? What is the motive behind your "offerings" and "sacrifices"?

[7]Like Adam,[a] they have broken the covenant[l]—
they were unfaithful[m] to me there.
[8]Gilead is a city of wicked men,
stained with footprints of blood.
[9]As marauders lie in ambush for a man,
so do bands of priests;
they murder on the road to Shechem,
committing shameful crimes.[n]
[10]I have seen a horrible[o] thing
in the house of Israel.
There Ephraim is given to prostitution
and Israel is defiled.[p]

[11]"Also for you, Judah,
a harvest[q] is appointed.

"Whenever I would restore the fortunes of my people,

7

[1]whenever I would heal Israel,
the sins of Ephraim are exposed
and the crimes of Samaria revealed.[a]
They practise deceit,[b]
thieves break into houses,[c]
bandits rob in the streets;
[2]but they do not realise
that I remember[d] all their evil deeds.
Their sins engulf them;[e]
they are always before me.

[3]"They delight the king with their wickedness,
the princes with their lies.[f]
[4]They are all adulterers,[g]
burning like an oven
whose fire the baker need not stir
from the kneading of the dough till it rises.
[5]On the day of the festival of our king
the princes become inflamed with wine,[h]
and he joins hands with the mockers.
[6]Their hearts are like an oven;[i]
they approach him with intrigue.
Their passion smoulders all night;
in the morning it blazes like a flaming fire.
[7]All of them are hot as an oven;

6:7 [l]Hos 8:1 [m]Hos 5:7
6:9 [n]Jer 7:9-10; Eze 22:9; Hos 7:1
6:10 [o]Jer 5:30 [p]Hos 5:3
6:11 [q]Jer 51:33; Joel 3:13
7:1 [a]Hos 6:4 [b]ver 13 [c]Hos 4:2
7:2 [d]Jer 14:10; Hos 8:13 [e]Jer 2:19
7:3 [f]Hos 4:2; Mic 7:3
7:4 [g]Jer 9:2
7:5 [h]Isa 28:1, 7
7:6 [i]Ps 21:9

[a] *7* Or *As at Adam*; or *Like men*

6:7 One of Hosea's key themes is that Israel had broken the covenant God had made with them at Mount Sinai (Exodus 19; 20). God wanted to make Israel a blessing and a light to all the nations (Genesis 12:2, 3; Isaiah 49:6); and if God's chosen people obeyed him and proclaimed him to the world, he would give them special blessings. If they broke the covenant, however, they would suffer severe penalties, as they should have known (see Deuteronomy 28:15–68). Sadly, the people broke the agreement and proved themselves unfaithful to God. How about you? Have you also broken faith with God? What about your forgotten promises to serve him?

6:8, 9 Gilead was once a sacred place, but here it was corrupt. Shechem was once a city of refuge designated by Joshua (Joshua 20:1, 2, 7, 8); Gilead was a region that included Ramoth, also a city of refuge. At this time these areas were associated with murder and crime, with bands of evil priests lying in wait to murder travellers passing through the territory.

6:11 So that Judah would not become proud as they saw the northern kingdom's destruction, Hosea interjected a solemn warning about God's "harvest". God's temple was in Judah (Jerusalem), and the people thought that what happened in Israel could never happen to them. But when they had become utterly corrupt, they too were led off into captivity (see 2 Kings 25).

7:1, 2 God sees and knows everything. Like Israel, we often forget this. Thoughts like "No-one will ever know", or "No-one is watching" may tempt us to try to get away with sin. If you are facing difficult temptations, you will be less likely to give in if you remind yourself that God is watching. When faced with the opportunity to sin, remember that God sees everything.

7:7 "Hot as an oven" refers to the lust for power and intrigue that was burning in these leaders' hearts. Three Israelite kings were assassinated during Hosea's lifetime—Zechariah, Shallum, and Pekahiah (2 Kings 15:8–26). The kings' foreign relations and

they devour their rulers.
All their kings fall,
and none of them calls[j] on me.

8 "Ephraim mixes[k] with the nations;
Ephraim is a flat cake not turned over.
9 Foreigners sap his strength,[l]
but he does not realise it.
His hair is sprinkled with grey,
but he does not notice.
10 Israel's arrogance testifies against him,[m]
but despite all this
he does not return to the LORD his God
or search[n] for him.

11 "Ephraim is like a dove,[o]
easily deceived and senseless—
now calling to Egypt,
now turning to Assyria.[p]
12 When they go, I will throw my net[q] over them;
I will pull them down like birds of the air.
When I hear them flocking together,
I will catch them.
13 Woe[r] to them,
because they have strayed[s] from me!
Destruction to them,
because they have rebelled against me!
I long to redeem them
but they speak lies against me.[t]
14 They do not cry out to me from their hearts[u]
but wail upon their beds.
They gather together[a] for grain and new wine[v]
but turn away from me.[w]
15 I trained them and strengthened them,
but they plot evil[x] against me.
16 They do not turn to the Most High;
they are like a faulty bow.[y]
Their leaders will fall by the sword
because of their insolent words.
For this they will be ridiculed[z]
in the land of Egypt.[a]

7:7 [j]ver 16
7:8 [k]ver 11; Ps 106:35; Hos 5:13
7:9 [l]Isa 1:7; Hos 8:7
7:10 [m]Hos 5:5 [n]Isa 9:13
7:11 [o]Hos 11:11 [p]Hos 5:13; 12:1
7:12 [q]Eze 12:13
7:13 [r]Hos 9:12 [s]Jer 14:10; Eze 34:4-6; Hos 9:17 [t]ver 1; Mt 23:37
7:14 [u]Jer 3:10 [v]Am 2:8 [w]Hos 13:16
7:15 [x]Na 1:9, 11
7:16 [y]Ps 78:9, 57 [z]Eze 23:32 [a]Hos 9:3

a *14* Most Hebrew manuscripts; some Hebrew manuscripts and Septuagint *They slash themselves*

---

domestic lives were ruined because they ignored God and his word.

7:8 The people of Israel had intermarried with foreign people and had picked up their evil ways. When we spend a lot of time with people, we can easily pick up their attitudes and begin to imitate their actions. When you work, live, or play with unbelievers, beware of the influence they may have on you. Instead of drifting into bad habits, see if you can have a positive influence and point these people to God.

7:10 Arrogance (pride) keeps a person from returning to God because arrogance acknowledges no need of help from anyone, human or divine. Pride intensifies all our other sins because we cannot repent of any of them without first giving up our pride.

7:11 Israel's King Menahem had paid Assyria to support him in power (2 Kings 15:19, 20); King Hoshea turned against Assyria and went to Egypt for help (2 Kings 17:4). Israel's kings went back and forth, allying themselves with different nations when they should have allied themselves with God.

7:16 A faulty bow is unreliable. Its arrows miss the target, and its owner would be quite vulnerable in battle. Life without God is as unreliable as a faulty bow. Without God's direction, our thoughts are filled with lust, cheating, selfishness, and deceit. As long as we are warped by sin, we will never reach our true potential.

7:16 People look everywhere except to God for happiness and fulfilment, pursuing possessions, activities, and relationships. In reality, only God can truly satisfy the deep longings of the soul. Look first to heaven, to the Most High God. He will meet your *spiritual* needs, not all your materialistic wants.

Israel to Reap the Whirlwind

8 "Put the trumpet to your lips!
An eagle[a] is over the house of the LORD
because the people have broken my covenant
and rebelled against my law.[b]
2 Israel cries out to me,
'O our God, we acknowledge you!'
3 But Israel has rejected what is good;
an enemy will pursue him.
4 They set up kings without my consent;
they choose princes without my approval.[c]
With their silver and gold
they make idols[d] for themselves
to their own destruction.
5 Throw out your calf-idol, O Samaria![e]
My anger burns against them.
How long will they be incapable of purity?[f]
6 They are from Israel!
This calf—a craftsman has made it;
it is not God.
It will be broken in pieces,
that calf of Samaria.

7 "They sow the wind
and reap the whirlwind.[g]
The stalk has no head;
it will produce no flour.
Were it to yield grain,
foreigners would swallow it up.[h]
8 Israel is swallowed up;[i]
now she is among the nations
like a worthless[j] thing.
9 For they have gone up to Assyria
like a wild donkey wandering alone.
Ephraim has sold herself to lovers.
10 Although they have sold themselves among the nations,
I will now gather them together.[k]
They will begin to waste away[l]
under the oppression of the mighty king.

11 "Though Ephraim built many altars for sin offerings,
these have become altars for sinning.[m]
12 I wrote for them the many things of my law,

8:1 [a]Dt 28:49; Jer 4:13 [b]Hos 4:6; 6:7
8:4 [c]Hos 13:10 [d]Hos 2:8
8:5 [e]Hos 10:5 [f]Jer 13:27
8:7 [g]Pr 22:8; Isa 66:15; Hos 10:12-13; Na 1:3 [h]Hos 2:9
8:8 [i]Jer 51:34 [j]Jer 22:28
8:10 [k]Eze 16:37; 22:20 [l]Jer 42:2
8:11 [m]Hos 10:1; 12:11

8:1–4 "An eagle is over the house of the LORD" referred to Assyria coming to attack Israel and take the people into captivity (2 Kings 15:28, 29). The people would call to God, but it would be too late because they had stubbornly refused to give up their idols. We, like Israel, often call on God to ease our pain without wanting him to change our behaviour. And we, like Israel, may repent after it is too late to avoid the painful consequences of sin.

8:5 Samaria was the capital of the northern kingdom, and sometimes it stands for the whole kingdom of Israel. Jeroboam I had set up worship of calf-idols at Bethel and Dan and had encouraged the people to worship them (1 Kings 12:25–33). Thus the people were worshipping the image of a created animal rather than the Creator.

8:7 Crop yield is the result of good seed planted in good soil and given the proper proportions of sunlight, moisture, and fertiliser. A single seed can produce multiple fruit in good conditions. Israel, however, had sown its spiritual seed to the wind—it had invested itself in activities without substance. Like the wind that comes and goes, its idolatry and foreign alliances offered no protection. In seeking self-preservation apart from God, it had brought about its own destruction. Like a forceful whirlwind, God's judgment would come upon Israel by means of the Assyrians. When we seek security in anything except God, we expose ourselves to great danger. Without God there is no lasting security.

8:11 The altars that were supposed to remove sin were actually increasing sin through their misuse in worshipping Baal.

8:12 Though the laws were written for *them,* Israel considered them "alien". It is easy to listen to a sermon and think of all the people we know who should be listening, or to read the Bible and think of those who should do what the passage teaches. The Israelites did this constantly, applying God's laws to others but not to themselves. This is just another way to deflect God's will and avoid

but they regarded them as something alien.
13They offer sacrifices given to me
and they eat[n] the meat,
but the LORD is not pleased with them.
Now he will remember[o] their wickedness
and punish their sins:[p]
They will return to Egypt.[q]
14Israel has forgotten[r] his Maker
and built palaces;
Judah has fortified many towns.
But I will send fire upon their cities
that will consume their fortresses."[s]

Punishment for Israel

9 Do not rejoice, O Israel;
do not be jubilant[a] like the other nations.
For you have been unfaithful[b] to your God;
you love the wages of a prostitute
at every threshing-floor.
2Threshing-floors and winepresses will not feed the people;
the new wine[c] will fail them.
3They will not remain[d] in the LORD's land;
Ephraim will return to Egypt[e]
and eat unclean[a] food in Assyria.[f]
4They will not pour out wine offerings to the LORD,
nor will their sacrifices please[g] him.
Such sacrifices will be to them like the bread of mourners;
all who eat them will be unclean.[h]
This food will be for themselves;
it will not come into the temple of the LORD.

5What will you do[i] on the day of your appointed feasts,[j]
on the festival days of the LORD?
6Even if they escape from destruction,
Egypt will gather them,
and Memphis[k] will bury them.
Their treasures of silver will be taken over by briers,
and thorns[l] will overrun their tents.

8:13 [n]Jer 7:21 [o]Hos 7:2 [p]Hos 4:9 [q]Hos 9:3, 6
8:14 [r]Dt 32:18; Hos 2:13 [s]Jer 17:27
9:1 [a]Isa 22:12-13 [b]Hos 10:5
9:2 [c]Hos 2:9
9:3 [d]Lev 25:23 [e]Hos 8:13 [f]Eze 4:13; Hos 7:11
9:4 [g]Jer 6:20; Hos 8:13 [h]Hag 2:13-14
9:5 [i]Isa 10:3; Jer 5:31 [j]Hos 2:11
9:6 [k]Isa 19:13 [l]Isa 5:6; Hos 10:8

[a] *3* That is, ceremonially unclean

---

making needed changes. As you think of others who need to apply what you are hearing or reading, check to see if the same application could fit you. Apply the lessons to your own life first because often our own faults are the very first ones we see in others.

8:13 The people's sacrifices had become mere ritual, and God refused to accept them. We have rituals too – attending church, observing a regular quiet time, celebrating Christian holidays, praying before meals. Rituals give us security in a changing world. Because they are repeated often, they can drive God's lessons deep within us. But rituals can be abused. Beware if you find yourself observing a religious ritual for any of the following reasons: (1) to gain community approval, (2) to avoid the risks of doing something different, (3) to make thought unnecessary, (4) to substitute for personal relationships, (5) to make up for bad behaviour, (6) to earn God's favour. We should not reject the rituals of our worship, but we must be careful with them. Think about why you do them. Focus on God, and perform every act with sincere devotion.

8:13 In Egypt, the Israelites had been slaves (Exodus 1:11). The people would not literally return to Egypt, but they would return to slavery – this time scattered throughout the Assyrian empire.

8:14 Israel had placed its confidence in military strength, strong defences, and economic stability, just as nations do today. But because of the people's inner moral decay, their apparent sources of strength were inadequate. There is a tendency in many nations towards removing all traces of God from daily life. But if a nation forgets its Maker, its strengths may prove worthless when put to the test.

9:1 A threshing floor was a flat area, often built on a hilltop, where harvesters beat the wheat and separated it from the chaff. Often men would stay overnight at the threshing floor to protect their grain, so prostitutes would visit there. Because of the location of threshing floors in the hilltops, they began to be used as places to sacrifice to false gods.

9:6 Israel's leaders vacillated between alliances with Egypt and alliances with Assyria. Hosea was saying that both were wrong. Breaking an alliance with untrustworthy Assyria and fleeing for help to the equally untrustworthy Egypt would not forestall Israel's destruction. Their only hope was to return to God.

[7]The days of punishment[m] are coming,
the days of reckoning are at hand.
Let Israel know this.
Because your sins[n] are so many
and your hostility so great,
the prophet is considered a fool,[o]
the inspired man a maniac.
[8]The prophet, along with my God,
is the watchman over Ephraim,[b]
yet snares[p] await him on all his paths,
and hostility in the house of his God.
[9]They have sunk deep into corruption,
as in the days of Gibeah.[q]
God will remember[r] their wickedness
and punish them for their sins.

[10]"When I found Israel,
it was like finding grapes in the desert;
when I saw your fathers,
it was like seeing the early fruit on the fig-tree.
But when they came to Baal Peor,[s]
they consecrated themselves to that shameful idol[t]
and became as vile as the thing they loved.
[11]Ephraim's glory will fly away like a bird[u]—
no birth, no pregnancy, no conception.[v]
[12]Even if they bring up children,
I will bereave them of every one.
Woe[w] to them
when I turn away from them![x]
[13]I have seen Ephraim, like Tyre,
planted in a pleasant place.[y]
But Ephraim will bring out
their children to the slayer."

[14]Give them, O LORD—
what will you give them?
Give them wombs that miscarry
and breasts that are dry.[z]

[15]"Because of all their wickedness in Gilgal,[a]

b *8* Or *The prophet is the watchman over Ephraim, / the people of my God*

9:7 [m]Isa 34:8; Jer 10:15; Mic 7:4 [n]Jer 16:18 [o]Isa 44:25; La 2:14; Eze 14:9-10
9:8 [p]Hos 5:1
9:9 [q]Jdg 19:16-30; Hos 5:8; 10:9 [r]Hos 8:13
9:10 [s]Nu 25:1-5; Ps 106:28-29 [t]Jer 11:13; Hos 4:14
9:11 [u]Hos 4:7; 10:5 [v]ver 14
9:12 [w]Hos 7:13 [x]Dt 31:17
9:13 [y]Eze 27:3
9:14 [z]ver 11; Lk 23:29
9:15 [a]Hos 4:15

9:7 By the time Israel began to experience the consequences of its sins, it was no longer listening to God's messengers. Refusing to hear the truth from prophets who spoke out so clearly about its sins, the nation did not hear God's warnings about what was soon to happen. We all listen and read selectively—focusing on what seems to support our present lifestyle, ignoring what demands a radical reordering of our priorities. In doing this, we are likely to miss the warnings we need most. Listen to people who think your approach is all wrong. Read articles that present viewpoints you would be unlikely to take. Ask yourself, "Is God speaking to me through these speakers and writers? Is there something I need to change?"

9:9 A couple had stopped to stay overnight in Gibeah when some wicked men gathered around the house and demanded that the man come out so they could have sex with him. Instead, the traveller gave them his concubine. They raped and abused her all night and then left her dead on the doorstep (Judges 19:14–30). That horrible act revealed the depths to which the people had sunk. Gibeah was destroyed for its evil (Judges 20:8–48), but Hosea said that the whole nation was now as evil as that city. Just as the city didn't escape punishment, neither would the nation.

9:10 Baal Peor was the god of Peor, a mountain in Moab. In Numbers 22, Balaam, a prophet, was hired by King Balak of Moab to curse the Israelites as they were coming through his land. The Moabites enticed the Israelites into sexual sin and Baal worship. Before long, the Israelites became as corrupt as the gods they worshipped. People can take on the characteristics of what or whom they love. What do you worship? Are you becoming more like God, or are you becoming more like someone or something else?

9:14 Hosea prayed this prayer when he foresaw the destruction that Israel's sins would bring (2 Kings 17:7–23). This vision of Israel's terrible fate moved him to pray that women would not get pregnant and that children would die as infants so they would not have to experience the tremendous suffering and pain that lay ahead.

9:15 At Gilgal, both the political and the religious failure of the nation began. Here idols and kings were substituted for God. Saul,

9:15 [b] Hos 7:2 [c] Isa 1:23; Hos 4:9; 5:2
9:16 [d] Hos 5:11 [e] Hos 8:7 [f] ver 12
9:17 [g] Hos 4:10 [h] Dt 28:65; Hos 7:13
10:1 [a] Eze 15:2 [b] 1Ki 14:23 [c] Hos 8:11; 12:11
10:2 [d] 1Ki 18:21 [e] Hos 13:16 [f] ver 8 [g] Mic 5:13
10:4 [h] Hos 4:2 [i] Eze 17:19; Am 5:7
10:5 [j] Hos 5:8 [k] 2Ki 23:5 [l] Hos 8:5; 9:1, 3, 11
10:6 [m] Hos 11:5 [n] Hos 5:13 [o] Isa 30:3; Hos 4:7
10:7 [p] Hos 13:11

I hated them there.
Because of their sinful deeds,[b]
I will drive them out of my house.
I will no longer love them;
all their leaders are rebellious.[c]
16 Ephraim[d] is blighted,
their root is withered,
they yield no fruit.[e]
Even if they bear children,
I will slay[f] their cherished offspring."

17 My God will reject them
because they have not obeyed[g] him;
they will be wanderers among the nations.[h]

10 Israel was a spreading vine;[a]
he brought forth fruit for himself.
As his fruit increased,
he built more altars;[b]
as his land prospered,
he adorned his sacred stones.[c]
2 Their heart is deceitful,[d]
and now they must bear their guilt.[e]
The LORD will demolish their altars[f]
and destroy their sacred stones.[g]

3 Then they will say, "We have no king
because we did not revere the LORD.
But even if we had a king,
what could he do for us?"
4 They make many promises,
take false oaths[h]
and make agreements;[i]
therefore lawsuits spring up
like poisonous weeds in a ploughed field.
5 The people who live in Samaria fear
for the calf-idol of Beth Aven.**a**[j]
Its people will mourn over it,
and so will its idolatrous priests,[k]
those who had rejoiced over its splendour,
because it is taken from them into exile.[l]
6 It will be carried to Assyria[m]
as tribute for the great king.[n]
Ephraim will be disgraced;[o]
Israel will be ashamed of its wooden idols.**b**
7 Samaria and its king will float away[p]

a *5 Beth Aven* means *house of wickedness* (a name for Bethel, which means *house of God*). **b** *6 Or its counsel*

the united nation's first king, was crowned at Gilgal (1 Samuel 11:15), but by Hosea's time, Baal worship flourished there (4:15; 12:11).

10:1 Israel prospered under Jeroboam II, gaining military and economic strength. But the more prosperous the nation became, the more love it lavished on idols. It seems as though the more God gives, the more we spend. We want bigger houses, better cars, and finer clothes. But the finest things the world offers line the pathway to destruction. As you prosper, consider where your money is going. Is it being used for God's purposes, or are you spending it all on yourself?

10:4 God was angry with the people of Israel for their insincere promises. Because the people did not keep their word, there were many lawsuits. People break their promises, but God always keeps his. Are you remaining true to your promises, both to other people and to God? If not, ask God for forgiveness and help to get back on track. Then be careful about the promises you make. Never make a promise unless you are sure you can keep it.

10:5 Beth Aven means "house of wickedness", and it refers to Bethel ("house of God") where false worship took place. If the Israelites' idols were really gods, they should have been able to protect the people. How ironic that the people were fearing for their gods' safety! For more information on this calf-idol, see the notes on 3:4, 5 and 8:5.

like a twig on the surface of the waters.
8The high places of wickedness[c][q] will be destroyed—
it is the sin of Israel.
Thorns[r] and thistles will grow up
and cover their altars.[s]
Then they will say to the mountains, "Cover us!"
and to the hills, "Fall on us!"[t]

9"Since the days of Gibeah,[u] you have sinned, O Israel,
and there you have remained.[d]
Did not war overtake
the evildoers in Gibeah?
10When I please, I will punish[v] them;
nations will be gathered against them
to put them in bonds for their double sin.
11Ephraim is a trained heifer
that loves to thresh;
so I will put a yoke
on her fair neck.
I will drive Ephraim,
Judah must plough,
and Jacob must break up the ground.
12Sow for yourselves righteousness,[w]
reap the fruit of unfailing love,
and break up your unploughed ground;[x]
for it is time to seek[y] the LORD,
until he comes
and showers righteousness[z] on you.
13But you have planted wickedness,
you have reaped evil,[a]
you have eaten the fruit of deception.
Because you have depended on your own strength
and on your many warriors,[b]
14the roar of battle will rise against your people,
so that all your fortresses will be devastated[c]—
as Shalman devastated Beth Arbel on the day of battle,
when mothers were dashed to the ground with their children.[d]
15Thus will it happen to you, O Bethel,
because your wickedness is great.
When that day dawns,
the king of Israel will be completely destroyed.[e]

10:8 [q]1Ki 12:28-30; Hos 4:13 [r]Hos 9:6 [s]ver 2; Isa 32:13 [t]Lk 23:30*; Rev 6:16
10:9 [u]Hos 5:8
10:10 [v]Eze 5:13; Hos 4:9
10:12 [w]Pr 11:18 [x]Jer 4:3 [y]Hos 12:6 [z]Isa 45:8
10:13 [a]Job 4:8; Hos 7:3; 11:12; Gal 6:7-8 [b]Ps 33:16
10:14 [c]Isa 17:3 [d]Hos 13:16
10:15 [e]ver 7

c *8* Hebrew *aven*, a reference to Beth Aven (a derogatory name for Bethel) d *9* Or *there a stand was taken*

10:9, 10 For information on "the days of Gibeah", see the note on 9:9 or read Judges 19 and 20. Gibeah stands for cruelty and sensuality as in Judges, and for rebellion as in Saul's day (Gibeah was Saul's home town, see 1 Samuel 11:4; 10:5).

10:12 Hosea repeatedly uses illustrations about fields and crops. Here he envisions a ploughed field, earth that is ready to receive seeds. It is no longer stony and hard; it has been carefully prepared, and it is available. Is your life ready for God to work in it? You can break up the unploughed ground of your heart by acknowledging your sins and receiving God's forgiveness and guidance.

10:13 The Israelites trusted in the lie that military power could keep them safe. Believers today are also capable of falling for lies. Those who want to lead others astray often follow these rules for effective lying: make it big; keep it simple; repeat it often. Believers can avoid falling for lies by asking: (1) Am I believing this because there is personal gain in it for me? (2) Am I discounting important facts? (3) Does this conflict with a direct command of Scripture? (4) Are there any biblical parallels to the situation I'm facing that would help me know what to believe?

10:14 Some say Shalman was Shalmaneser, king of Assyria; others say Shalman was Salmanu, a Moabite king mentioned in the inscriptions of Tiglath-Pileser. Shalman had invaded Gilead around 740 B.C. and destroyed the city of Beth Arbel, killing many people, including women and children. This kind of cruelty was not uncommon in ancient warfare. Hosea was saying that such would be Israel's fate.

10:15 Because Israel had put its confidence in military might rather than in God, it would be destroyed by military power. Israel's king, who had led the people into idol worship, would be the first to fall. Divine judgment is *sometimes* swift, but it is *always* sure.

3. God's love for Israel

11 "When Israel was a child, I loved him,
and out of Egypt I called my son.[a]
2 But the more I[a] called Israel,
the further they went from me.[b]
They sacrificed to the Baals[b]
and they burned incense to images.[c]
3 It was I who taught Ephraim to walk,
taking them by the arms;[d]
but they did not realise
it was I who healed[e] them.
4 I led them with cords of human kindness,
with ties of love;[f]
I lifted the yoke[g] from their neck
and bent down to feed[h] them.

5 "Will they not return to Egypt[i]
and will not Assyria[j] rule over them
because they refuse to repent?
6 Swords[k] will flash in their cities,
will destroy the bars of their gates
and put an end to their plans.
7 My people are determined to turn from me.[l]
Even if they call to the Most High,
he will by no means exalt them.

8 "How can I give you up, Ephraim?[m]
How can I hand you over, Israel?
How can I treat you like Admah?
How can I make you like Zeboiim?[n]
My heart is changed within me;
all my compassion is aroused.
9 I will not carry out my fierce anger,[o]
nor will I turn and devastate[p] Ephraim.
For I am God, and not man[q]—
the Holy One among you.

11:1 [a] Ex 4:22; Hos 12:9, 13; 13:4; Mt 2:15*
11:2 [b] Hos 2:13 [c] 2Ki 17:15; Isa 65:7; Jer 18:15
11:3 [d] Dt 1:31; Hos 7:15 [e] Jer 30:17
11:4 [f] Jer 31:2-3 [g] Lev 26:13 [h] Ex 16:32; Ps 78:25
11:5 [i] Hos 7:16 [j] Hos 10:6
11:6 [k] Hos 13:16
11:7 [l] Jer 3:6-7; 8:5
11:8 [m] Hos 6:4 [n] Ge 14:8
11:9 [o] Dt 13:17; Jer 30:11 [p] Mal 3:6 [q] Nu 23:19

[a] *2* Some Septuagint manuscripts; Hebrew *they* [b] *2* Septuagint; Hebrew *them*

11:1ff In the final four chapters, Hosea shifts to the theme of God's intense love for Israel. God had always loved Israel as a parent loves a stubborn child, and that is why he would not release Israel from the consequences of its behaviour. The Israelites were sinful, and they would be punished like a rebellious son brought by his parents before the elders (Deuteronomy 21:18–21). All through Israel's sad history, God repeatedly offered to restore the nation if it would only turn to him. By stubbornly refusing God's invitation, the northern kingdom had sealed its doom. It would be destroyed, never to rise again. Even so, Israel as a nation was not finished. A remnant of faithful Israelites would return to Jerusalem, where one day the Messiah would come, offering pardon and reconciliation to all who would faithfully follow him.

11:3 God had consistently provided for his people, but they refused to see what he had done, and they showed no interest in thanking him. Ungratefulness is a common human fault. For example, when was the last time you thanked your parents for caring for you? Your pastor for the service he gives your church? Your child's teacher for the care taken with each day's activities? Your heavenly Father for his guidance? Many of the benefits and privileges we enjoy are the result of loving actions done long ago. Look for hidden acts of nurturing, and thank those who make the world better through their love. But begin by thanking God for all his blessings.

11:4 God's discipline requires times of leading and times of feeding. Sometimes the rope is taut; sometimes it is slack. God's discipline is always loving, and its object is always the well-being of the beloved. When you are called to discipline others—children, students, employees, or church members—do not be rigid. Vary your approach according to the goals you are seeking to accomplish. In each case, ask yourself, "Does this person need guidance, or does he or she need to be nurtured?"

11:5 The northern kingdom survived for only two centuries after its break with Jerusalem. Its spiritual and political leaders did not help the people learn the way to God, so as a nation they would never repent. Hosea prophesied its downfall, which happened when Shalmaneser of Assyria conquered Israel in 722 B.C. Judah also would go into captivity, but a remnant would return to their homeland.

11:8 Admah and Zeboiim were cities of the plain that perished with Sodom and Gomorrah (Genesis 14:8; Deuteronomy 29:23).

11:9 "I am God, and not man. . ." It is easy for us to define God in terms of our own expectations and behaviour. In so doing, we make him just slightly larger than ourselves. In reality, God is infinitely greater than we are. We should seek to become like him rather than attempting to remake him in our image.

I will not come in wrath.[c]
10They will follow the LORD;
he will roar like a lion.
When he roars,
his children will come trembling from the west.[r]
11They will come trembling
like birds from Egypt,
like doves from Assyria.[s]
I will settle them in their homes,"[t]
declares the LORD.

Israel's Sin

12Ephraim has surrounded me with lies,[u]
the house of Israel with deceit.
And Judah is unruly against God,
even against the faithful Holy One.

12

1Ephraim feeds on the wind;[a]
he pursues the east wind all day
and multiplies lies and violence.
He makes a treaty with Assyria
and sends olive oil to Egypt.[b]
2The LORD has a charge[c] to bring against Judah;
he will punish Jacob[a] according to his ways
and repay him according to his deeds.[d]
3In the womb he grasped his brother's heel;[e]
as a man he struggled[f] with God.
4He struggled with the angel and overcame him;
he wept and begged for his favour.
He found him at Bethel[g]
and talked with him there—
5the LORD God Almighty,
the LORD is his name[h] of renown!
6But you must return to your God;
maintain love and justice,[i]
and wait for your God always.[j]

7The merchant uses dishonest scales;[k]
he loves to defraud.

c 9 Or *come against any city* a 2 *Jacob* means *he grasps the heel* (figuratively, *he deceives*).

11:10 [r]Hos 6:1-3
11:11 [s]Isa 11:11 [t]Eze 28:26
11:12 [u]Hos 4:2
12:1 [a]Eze 17:10 [b]2Ki 17:4
12:2 [c]Mic 6:2 [d]Hos 4:9
12:3 [e]Ge 25:26 [f]Ge 32:24-29
12:4 [g]Ge 28:12-15; 35:15
12:5 [h]Ex 3:15
12:6 [i]Mic 6:8 [j]Hos 6:1-3; 10:12; Mic 7:7
12:7 [k]Am 8:5

11:12 Unlike Israel, Judah had some fairly good kings—Asa, Jehoshaphat, Joash, Amaziah, Azariah (Uzziah), Jotham, and especially Hezekiah and Josiah. Under some of these kings, God's law was dusted off and taught to the people. The priests continued to serve in God's appointed temple in Jerusalem, and the festivals were celebrated at least some of the time. Unfortunately, the political or religious leaders were unable to completely wipe out idol worship and pagan rites (although Hezekiah and Josiah came close), which continued to fester until they eventually erupted and infected the whole country. Still, the influence of the good kings enabled Judah to survive more than 150 years longer than Israel, and that memory of their positive influence fortified a small group—a remnant—of faithful people who would one day return and restore their land and temple.

12:2–5 Jacob, whose name was later changed to Israel, was the common ancestor of all 12 tribes of Israel (both northern and southern kingdoms). Like the nations that descended from him, Jacob practised deceit. Unlike Israel and Judah, however, he constantly searched for God. Jacob wrestled with the angel in order to be blessed, but his descendants thought their blessings came from their own successes. Jacob purged his house of idols (Genesis 35:2), but his descendants could not stop their idol worship.

12:6 The two principles that Hosea called his nation to live by, love and justice, are at the very foundation of God's character. They are essential to his followers, but they are not easy to keep in balance. Some people are loving to the point that they excuse wrong-doing. Others are just to the extent that they forget love. Love without justice, because it is not aiming at a higher standard, leaves people in their sins. Justice without love, because it has no heart, drives people away from God. To specialise in one at the expense of the other is to distort our witness. Today's church, just like Hosea's nation, must live by both principles.

12:7, 8 In Israel, dishonesty had become an accepted means of attaining wealth. Israelites who were financially successful could not imagine that God would consider them sinful. They thought that their wealth was a sign of God's approval, and they didn't bother to consider how they had received it. But God said that Israel's riches would not make up for its sin. Remember that God's measure of success is different from ours. He calls us to faithfulness, not to affluence. Character is more important to him than our wallets.

8Ephraim boasts,
"I am very rich; I have become wealthy.[l]
With all my wealth they will not find in me
any iniquity or sin."

9"I am the LORD your God,
⌊who brought you⌋ out of[b] Egypt;[m]
I will make you live in tents[n] again,
as in the days of your appointed feasts.
10I spoke to the prophets,
gave them many visions
and told parables[o] through them."[p]

11Is Gilead wicked?[q]
Its people are worthless!
Do they sacrifice bulls in Gilgal?[r]
Their altars will be like piles of stones
on a ploughed field.[s]
12Jacob fled to the country of Aram;[c][t]
Israel served to get a wife,
and to pay for her he tended sheep.[u]
13The LORD used a prophet to bring Israel up from Egypt,
by a prophet he cared for him.[v]
14But Ephraim has bitterly provoked him to anger;
his Lord will leave upon him the guilt of his bloodshed[w]
and will repay him for his contempt.[x]

The LORD's Anger Against Israel

13 When Ephraim spoke, men trembled;[a]
he was exalted[b] in Israel.
But he became guilty of Baal worship[c] and died.
2Now they sin more and more;
they make idols for themselves from their silver,[d]
cleverly fashioned images,
all of them the work of craftsmen.
It is said of these people,
"They offer human sacrifice
and kiss[a] the calf-idols.[e]"

12:8 [l]Ps 62:10; Rev 3:17
12:9 [m]Lev 23:43; Hos 11:1 [n]Ne 8:17
12:10 [o]Eze 20:49 [p]2Ki 17:13; Jer 7:25
12:11 [q]Hos 6:8 [r]Hos 4:15 [s]Hos 8:11
12:12 [t]Ge 28:5 [u]Ge 29:18
12:13 [v]Ex 13:3; Isa 63:11-14
12:14 [w]Eze 18:13 [x]Da 11:18
13:1 [a]Jdg 12:1 [b]Jdg 8:1 [c]Hos 11:2
13:2 [d]Isa 46:6; Jer 10:4 [e]Isa 44:17-20

[b] *9* Or *God / ever since you were in* [c] *12* That is, North-west Mesopotamia [a] *2* Or *"Men who sacrifice / kiss*

CYCLES OF JUDGMENT/ SALVATION IN HOSEA

Judgment	1:2–9; 2:2–13; 4:1—5:14; 6:4—11:7; 11:12—13:16
Salvation	1:10—2:1; 2:14—3:5; 5:15—6:3; 11:8–11; 14:1–9

God promises to judge, but he also promises mercy. Here you can see the cycles of judgment and salvation in Hosea. Prophecies of judgment are consistently followed by prophecies of forgiveness.

12:8 Rich people and nations often claim that their material success is due to their own hard work, initiative, and intelligence. Because they have every possession they want, they don't feel the need for God. They believe that their riches are their own, and they think that they have the right to use them any way they please. If you find yourself feeling proud of your accomplishments, remember that all your opportunities, abilities, and resources come from God, and that you hold them in sacred trust for him.

12:9 Once a year the Israelites spent a week living in tents during the Feast of Tabernacles, which commemorated God's protection as they wandered in the desert for 40 years (see Deuteronomy 1:19—2:1). Here, because of their sin, God would cause them to live in tents again—this time not as part of a festival, but in actual bondage.

12:12 Hosea was using this reference to Jacob to say, "Don't forget your humble beginnings. What you have is not a result of your own efforts, but it is yours because God has been gracious to you."

12:13 The prophet who brought Israel up from Egypt was Moses (Exodus 13:17–19).

13:1 Israel, represented here by the northern tribe of Ephraim, had been great, but by Hosea's time the people had rebelled against God and had lost their authority among the nations. Greatness in the past is no guarantee of greatness in the future. It is good to remember what God has done for you and through you, but it is equally important to keep your relationship with him vital and up to date. Commit yourself to God moment by moment.

3Therefore they will be like the morning mist,
like the early dew that disappears,[f]
like chaff[g] swirling from a threshing-floor,[h]
like smoke[i] escaping through a window.

4"But I am the LORD your God,
⌞who brought you⌟ out of[b] Egypt.[j]
You shall acknowledge no God but me,[k]
no Saviour[l] except me.
5I cared for you in the desert,
in the land of burning heat.
6When I fed them, they were satisfied;
when they were satisfied, they became proud;
then they forgot me.[m]
7So I will come upon them like a lion,
like a leopard I will lurk by the path.
8Like a bear robbed of her cubs,[n]
I will attack them and rip them open.
Like a lion I will devour them;
a wild animal will tear them apart.[o]

9"You are destroyed, O Israel,
because you are against me,[p] against your helper.[q]
10Where is your king,[r] that he may save you?
Where are your rulers in all your towns,
of whom you said,
'Give me a king and princes'?[s]
11So in my anger I gave you a king,
and in my wrath I took him away.[t]
12The guilt of Ephraim is stored up,
his sins are kept on record.[u]
13Pains as of a woman in childbirth[v] come to him,
but he is a child without wisdom;
when the time arrives,
he does not come to the opening of the womb.[w]

14"I will ransom them from the power of the grave;[c][x]
I will redeem them from death.
Where, O death, are your plagues?
Where, O grave,[c] is your destruction?[y]

"I will have no compassion,
15 even though he thrives[z] among his brothers.
An east wind[a] from the LORD will come,
blowing in from the desert;
his spring will fail

b 4 Or *God / ever since you were in* c 14 Hebrew *Sheol*

13:3 [f]Hos 6:4 [g]Isa 17:13 [h]Da 2:35 [i]Ps 68:2
13:4 [j]Hos 12:9 [k]Ex 20:3 [l]Isa 43:11; 45:21-22
13:6 [m]Dt 32:12-15; Hos 2:13
13:8 [n]2Sa 17:8 [o]Ps 50:22
13:9 [p]Jer 2:17-19 [q]Dt 33:29
13:10 [r]2Ki 17:4 [s]1Sa 8:6; Hos 8:4
13:11 [t]1Ki 14:10; Hos 10:7
13:12 [u]Dt 32:34
13:13 [v]Isa 13:8; Mic 4:9-10 [w]Isa 66:9
13:14 [x]Ps 49:15; Eze 37:12-13 [y]1Co 15:55*
13:15 [z]Hos 10:1 [a]Eze 19:12

13:4–6 When abundant possessions made Israel feel self-sufficient, it turned its back on God and forgot him. Self-sufficiency is as destructive today as it was in Hosea's time. Do you see your constant need of God's presence and help? Learn to rely on God both in good times and bad. If you are travelling along a smooth and easy path right now, beware of forgetting who gave you your good fortune. Don't depend on your gifts; depend on the Giver. See Deuteronomy 6:10–12 and 8:7–20 for God's warning.

13:11 God had warned Israel that kings would cause more problems than they would solve, and he reluctantly gave them Saul as their first king (1 Samuel 8:4–22). The second king, David, was a good king, and Solomon, David's son, had his strengths. But after the nation divided in two, the northern kingdom never had another good ruler. Evil kings led the nations deeper into idolatry and unwise political alliances. Eventually the evil kings destroyed the nation; with Hoshea, the northern kingdom's kings were cut off (2 Kings 17:1–6).

13:12 Ephraim's (Israel's) sins were recorded for later punishment. All our sins are known and will be revealed at the day of judgment (2 Corinthians 5:10; Revelation 20:11–15).

13:14 The apostle Paul used this passage to teach the resurrection of our bodies from death (1 Corinthians 15:55). For those who have trusted in Christ for deliverance from sin, death holds no threat of annihilation.

13:15
[b] Jer 51:36
[c] Jer 20:5

13:16
[d] Hos 10:2
[e] Hos 7:14
[f] Hos 11:6
[g] 2Ki 8:12; Hos 10:14
[h] 2Ki 15:16; Isa 13:16

and his well dry up.[b]
His storehouse will be plundered[c]
of all its treasures.
16 The people of Samaria must bear their guilt,[d]
because they have rebelled[e] against their God.
They will fall by the sword;[f]
their little ones will be dashed[g] to the ground,
their pregnant women[h] ripped open."

Repentance to Bring Blessing

14:1
[a] Hos 5:5

14:2
[b] Mic 7:18-19
[c] Heb 13:15

14:3
[d] Ps 33:17; Isa 31:1
[e] Hos 8:6
[f] Ps 10:14; 68:5

14:4
[g] Hos 6:1
[h] Zep 3:17

14:5
[i] SS 2:1
[j] Isa 35:2
[k] Job 29:19

14:6
[l] Ps 52:8; Jer 11:16
[m] SS 4:11

14:7
[n] Ps 91:1-4
[o] Hos 2:22
[p] Eze 17:23

14:8
[q] ver 3

14 Return, O Israel, to the LORD your God.
Your sins have been your downfall![a]
2 Take words with you
and return to the LORD.
Say to him:
"Forgive all our sins
and receive us graciously,[b]
that we may offer the fruit of our lips.[a] [c]
3 Assyria cannot save us;
we will not mount war-horses.[d]
We will never again say 'Our gods'[e]
to what our own hands have made,
for in you the fatherless[f] find compassion."

4 "I will heal[g] their waywardness
and love them freely,[h]
for my anger has turned away from them.
5 I will be like the dew to Israel;
he will blossom like a lily.[i]
Like a cedar of Lebanon[j]
he will send down his roots;[k]
6 his young shoots will grow.
His splendour will be like an olive tree,[l]
his fragrance like a cedar of Lebanon.[m]
7 Men will dwell again in his shade.[n]
He will flourish like the corn.
He will blossom like a vine,
and his fame will be like the wine[o] from Lebanon.[p]
8 O Ephraim, what more have I[b] to do with idols?[q]
I will answer him and care for him.
I am like a green pine tree;
your fruitfulness comes from me."

a *2* Or *offer our lips as sacrifices of bulls* **b** *8* Or *What more has Ephraim*

14:1ff Verses 1–3 are Hosea's call to repent. Verses 4–8 are God's promise of restoration. God had to punish Israel for its gross and repeated violations of his law, but he would do so with a heavy heart. What God really wanted to do was restore the nation and make it prosper.

14:1, 2 The people could return to God by asking him to forgive their sins. The same is true for us: we can pray Hosea's prayer and know our sins are forgiven because Christ died for them on the cross (John 3:16).

Forgiveness begins when we see the destructiveness of sin and the futility of life without God. Then we must admit we cannot save ourselves; our only hope is in God's mercy. When we request forgiveness, we must recognise that we do not deserve it and therefore cannot demand it. Our appeal must be for God's love and mercy, not for his justice. Although we cannot demand forgiveness, we can be confident that we have received it because God is gracious and loving and wants to restore us to himself, just as he wanted to restore Israel.

14:2 "The fruit of our lips" refers to thank offerings to God. God desired real, heartfelt repentance, not merely annual sacrifices.

14:3–8 When our will is weak, when our thinking is confused, and when our conscience is burdened with a load of guilt, we must remember that God cares for us continually; his compassion never fails. When friends and family desert us, when co-workers don't understand us, and when we are tired of being good, God's compassion never fails. When we can't see the way or seem to hear God's voice, and when we lack courage to go on, God's compassion never fails. When our shortcomings and our awareness of our sins overcome us, God's compassion never fails.

9 Who is wise?[r] He will realise these things.
Who is discerning? He will understand them.[s]
The ways of the LORD are right;[t]
the righteous walk[u] in them,
but the rebellious stumble in them.

14:9
[r]Ps 107:43
[s]Pr 10:29; Isa 1:28
[t]Ps 111:7-8; Zep 3:5; Ac 13:10
[u]Isa 26:7

14:9 Hosea closes with an appeal to listen, learn, and benefit from God's word. To those receiving the Lord's message through Hosea, this meant the difference between life and death. For you, the reader of the book of Hosea, the choice is similar: either listen to the book's message and follow God's ways, or refuse to walk along the Lord's path. But people who insist on following their own direction without God's guidance are "like deep darkness; they do not know what makes them stumble" (Proverbs 4:19). If you are lost, you can find the way by turning from your sin and following God.

14:9 God's concern for *justice* that requires faithfulness and *love* that offers forgiveness can be seen in his dealings with Hosea. We can err by forgetting God's love and feeling that our sins are hopeless, but we can also err by forgetting his wrath against our sins and thinking he will continue to accept us no matter how we act. *Forgiveness* is a key word: when God forgives us, he judges the sin but shows mercy to the sinner. We should never be afraid to come to God for a clean slate and a renewed life.

JOEL

King Ahab dies in battle 853 B.C. | Elisha becomes a prophet 848 | Jehu becomes king of Israel; Athaliah seizes Judah's throne 841 | Joel becomes a prophet? Joash becomes king of Judah 835 | Jehoahaz becomes king of Israel 814 | Jehoash becomes king of Israel 798 | Joel's ministry ends 796?

A single bomb devastates a city, and the world is ushered into the nuclear age. A split atom . . . power and force such as we have never seen.

At a launch site, rockets roar and a payload is thrust into space. Discoveries dreamed of for centuries are ours as we begin to explore the edge of the universe.

Volcanoes, earthquakes, tidal waves, hurricanes, and tornadoes unleash uncontrollable and unstoppable force. And we can only avoid them and then pick up the pieces.

Power, strength, might—we stand in awe at the natural and man-made display. But these forces cannot touch the power of our omnipotent God. Creator of galaxies, atoms, and natural laws, the sovereign Lord rules all there is and ever will be. How silly to live without him; how foolish to run and hide from him; how ridiculous to disobey him. But we do. Since Eden, we have sought independence from his control, as though we were gods and could control our destiny. And he has allowed our rebellion. But soon *the day of the Lord* will come.

It is about this day that the prophet Joel speaks, and it is the theme of his book. On this day God will judge all unrighteousness and disobedience—all accounts will be settled and the crooked made straight.

We know very little about Joel—only that he was a prophet and the son of Pethuel. He may have lived in Jerusalem because his audience was Judah, the southern kingdom. Whoever he was, Joel speaks forthrightly and forcefully in this short and powerful book. His message is one of foreboding and warning, but it is also filled with hope. Joel states that our Creator, the omnipotent Judge, is also merciful, and he wants to bless all those who trust him.

Joel begins by describing a terrible plague of locusts that covers the land and devours the crops. The devastation wrought by these creatures is but a foretaste of the coming judgment of God, the "day of the LORD". Joel therefore urges the people to turn from their sin and turn back to God. Woven into this message of judgment and the need for repentance is an affirmation of God's kindness and the blessings he promises for all who follow him. In fact, "everyone who calls on the name of the LORD will be saved" (2:32).

As you read Joel, catch his vision of the power and might of God and of God's ultimate judgment of sin. Choose to follow, obey, and worship God alone as your sovereign Lord.

VITAL STATISTICS

PURPOSE:
To warn Judah of God's impending judgment because of their sins, and to urge them to turn back to God

AUTHOR:
Joel son of Pethuel

TO WHOM WRITTEN:
The people of Judah, the southern kingdom, and God's people everywhere

DATE WRITTEN:
Probably during the time Joel may have prophesied, from about 835 to 796 B.C.

SETTING:
The people of Judah had become prosperous and complacent. Taking God for granted, they had turned to self-centredness, idolatry, and sin. Joel warned them that this kind of lifestyle would inevitably bring down God's judgment.

KEY VERSES:
"'Even now,' declares the LORD, 'return to me with all your heart, with fasting and weeping and mourning.' Rend your heart and not your garments. Return to the LORD your God, for he is gracious and compassionate, slow to anger and abounding in love, and he relents from sending calamity" (2:12, 13).

KEY PEOPLE:
Joel, the people of Judah

KEY PLACE:
Jerusalem

THE BLUEPRINT

1. The day of the locusts (1:1—2:27)
2. The day of the Lord (2:28—3:21)

The locust plague was only a foretaste of the judgment to come in the day of the Lord. This is a timeless call to repentance with the promise of blessing. Just as the people faced the tragedy of their crops being destroyed, we too will face tragic judgment if we live in sin. But God's grace is available to us both now and in that coming day.

MEGATHEMES

THEME	EXPLANATION	IMPORTANCE
Punishment	Like a destroying army of locusts, God's punishment for sin is overwhelming, dreadful, and unavoidable. When it comes, there will be no food, no water, no protection, and no escape. The day for settling accounts with God for how we have lived is fast approaching.	God is the one with whom we must all reckon—not nature, the economy, or a foreign invader. We can't ignore or offend God for ever. We must pay attention to his message now, or we will face his anger later.
Forgiveness	God stood ready to forgive and restore all those who would come to him and turn away from sin. God wanted to shower his people with his love and restore them to a proper relationship with him.	Forgiveness comes by turning from sin and turning towards God. It is not too late to receive God's forgiveness. God's greatest desire is for you to come to him.
Promise of the Holy Spirit	Joel predicts the time when God will pour out his Holy Spirit on all people. It will be the beginning of new and fresh worship of God by those who believe in him, but also the beginning of judgment on all who reject him.	God is in control. Justice and restoration are in his hands. The Holy Spirit confirms God's love for us just as he did for the first Christians (Acts 2). We must be faithful to God and place our lives under the guidance and power of his Holy Spirit.

1. The day of the locusts

1 The word of the LORD that came[a] to Joel[b] son of Pethuel.

An Invasion of Locusts

2 Hear this,[c] you elders;
listen, all who live in the land.[d]
Has anything like this ever happened in your days
or in the days of your forefathers?[e]
3 Tell it to your children,[f]
and let your children tell it to their children,
and their children to the next generation.
4 What the locust swarm has left
the great locusts have eaten;
what the great locusts have left
the young locusts have eaten;
what the young locusts have left

1:1
[a] Jer 1:2
[b] Ac 2:16

1:2
[c] Hos 5:1
[d] Hos 4:1
[e] Joel 2:2

1:3
[f] Ex 10:2; Ps 78:4

1:1 Joel was a prophet to the nation of Judah, also known as the southern kingdom. The book does not mention when Joel lived, but many believe that he prophesied during the reign of King Joash (835–796 B.C.). But the date of Joel's book is not nearly so important as its timeless message: sin brings God's judgment; yet with God's justice there is also great mercy.

1:3 God urged parents to pass their history down to their children, telling over and over the important lessons they learned. One of the greatest gifts you can give younger people is your life's story to help them repeat your successes and avoid your mistakes.

1:4 A locust plague can be as devastating as an invading army. Locusts gather in swarms too great to number (1:6) and fly several feet above the ground, seeming to darken the sun as they pass by (2:2). When they land, they devour almost every piece of vegetation (1:7–12), covering and entering everything in their path (2:9).

1:4 Joel's detailed description has caused many to believe that he was referring to an actual locust plague that had come or was about to come upon the land. Another view is that the locusts symbolise an invading enemy army. Both may be foreseen. The locusts represent devastation, and Joel's point was that God would punish the people because of their sin. Joel calls this judgment the "day of the LORD" (see the note on 1:15).

1:4 [g]Dt 28:39; Na 3:15

other locusts[a] have eaten.[g]

5Wake up, you drunkards, and weep!
Wail, all you drinkers of wine;[h]
wail because of the new wine,
for it has been snatched from your lips.
6A nation has invaded my land,
powerful and without number;[i]
it has the teeth[j] of a lion,
the fangs of a lioness.
7It has laid waste[k] my vines
and ruined my fig-trees.[l]
It has stripped off their bark
and thrown it away,
leaving their branches white.

8Mourn like a virgin[b] in sackcloth[m]
grieving for the husband[c] of her youth.
9Grain offerings and drink offerings[n]
are cut off from the house of the LORD.
The priests are in mourning,
those who minister before the LORD.
10The fields are ruined,
the ground is dried up;[d][o]
the grain is destroyed,
the new wine[p] is dried up,
the oil fails.
11Despair, you farmers,[q]
wail, you vine growers;
grieve for the wheat and the barley,
because the harvest of the field is destroyed.[r]
12The vine is dried up
and the fig-tree is withered;
the pomegranate, the palm and the apple tree—
all the trees of the field—are dried up.[s]
Surely the joy of mankind
is withered away.

1:5 [h]Joel 3:3

1:6 [i]Joel 2:2, 11, 25 [j]Rev 9:8

1:7 [k]Isa 5:6 [l]Am 4:9

1:8 [m]ver 13; Isa 22:12; Am 8:10

1:9 [n]Hos 9:4; Joel 2:14, 17

1:10 [o]Isa 24:4 [p]Hos 9:2

1:11 [q]Jer 14:3-4; Am 5:16 [r]Isa 17:11

1:12 [s]Hag 2:19

[a] *4* The precise meaning of the four Hebrew words used here for locusts is uncertain. [b] *8* Or *young woman* [c] *8* Or *betrothed* [d] *10* Or *ground mourns*

JOEL served as a prophet to Judah, possibly from 835–796 B.C.	*Climate of the times*	Wicked Queen Athaliah seized power in a bloody coup, but was overthrown after a few years. Joash was crowned king, but he was only seven years old and in great need of spiritual guidance. Joash followed God in his early years, but then turned away from him.
	Main message	A plague of locusts had come to discipline the nation. Joel called the people to turn back to God before an even greater judgment occurred.
	Importance of message	God judges all people for their sins, but he is merciful to those who turn to him and offers them eternal salvation.
	Contemporary prophets	Elisha (848–797) Jonah (793–753)

1:5 The people's physical and moral senses were dulled, making them oblivious to sin. Joel called them to awaken from their complacency and admit their sins before it was too late. Otherwise, everything would be destroyed, even the grapes that caused their drunkenness. Our times of peace and prosperity can lull us to sleep. We must never let material abundance hinder our spiritual readiness.

1:9 Because of the devastation, there was no fine flour or wine for the grain or drink offerings (see Leviticus 1 and 2 for a detailed explanation of these offerings).

A Call to Repentance

13 Put on sackcloth,[t] O priests, and mourn;
wail, you who minister[u] before the altar.
Come, spend the night in sackcloth,
you who minister before my God;
for the grain offerings and drink offerings[v]
are withheld from the house of your God.
14 Declare a holy fast;[w]
call a sacred assembly.
Summon the elders
and all who live in the land
to the house of the LORD your God,
and cry out[x] to the LORD.

15 Alas for that[y] day!
For the day of the LORD[z] is near;
it will come like destruction from the Almighty.[e]

16 Has not the food been cut off[a]
before our very eyes—
joy and gladness
from the house of our God?[b]
17 The seeds are shrivelled
beneath the clods.[f][c]
The storehouses are in ruins,
the granaries have been broken down,
for the grain has dried up.
18 How the cattle moan!
The herds mill about
because they have no pasture;
even the flocks of sheep are suffering.

19 To you, O LORD, I call,[d]
for fire[e] has devoured the open pastures[f]
and flames have burned up all the trees of the field.
20 Even the wild animals pant for you;[g]
the streams of water have dried up[h]
and fire has devoured the open pastures.

An Army of Locusts

2 Blow the trumpet[a] in Zion;[b]
sound the alarm on my holy hill.
Let all who live in the land tremble,

1:13 [t] Jer 4:8 [u] Joel 2:17 [v] ver 9
1:14 [w] 2Ch 20:3 [x] Jnh 3:8
1:15 [y] Jer 30:7 [z] Isa 13:6, 9; Joel 2:1, 11, 31
1:16 [a] Isa 3:7 [b] Dt 12:7
1:17 [c] Isa 17:10-11
1:19 [d] Ps 50:15 [e] Am 7:4 [f] Jer 9:10
1:20 [g] Ps 104:21 [h] 1Ki 17:7
2:1 [a] Jer 4:5 [b] ver 15

e *15* Hebrew *Shaddai* f *17* The meaning of the Hebrew for this word is uncertain.

1:13 Sackcloth is the clothing put on by mourners at a funeral. Used here, it would be a sign of repentance.

1:14 A fast was a period of time when no food was eaten and people approached God with humility, sorrow for sin, and urgent prayer. In the Old Testament, people would often fast during times of calamity in order to focus their attention on God and to demonstrate their change of heart and their true devotion (see, for example, Judges 20:26; 1 Kings 21:27; Ezra 8:21; Jonah 3:5). The sacred assembly was a public religious gathering called so that everyone could repent and pray to God for mercy.

1:15 The "day of the LORD" is a common phrase in the Old Testament and in the book of Joel (see 2:1, 11, 31; 3:14). It always refers to some extraordinary happening, whether a present event (like a locust plague), an event in the near future (like the destruction of Jerusalem or the defeat of enemy nations), or the final period of history when God will defeat all the forces of evil.

Even when the day of the Lord refers to a present event, it also foreshadows the *final* day of the Lord. This final event of history has two aspects to it: (1) the last judgment on all evil and sin, and (2) the final reward for faithful believers. Righteousness and truth will prevail, but not before much suffering (Zechariah 14:1–3). If you trust the Lord, looking towards this final day should give you hope, because then all who are faithful will be united for ever with God.

1:15–19 Without God, destruction is sure. Those who have not personally accepted God's love and forgiveness will stand before him with no appeal. Be sure to call on God's love and mercy while you have the opportunity (2:32).

2:1ff Joel was still describing the devastating effects of the locust plague (see 2:25). The alarm showed that the crisis was at hand.

for the day of the LORD[c] is coming.
It is close at hand[d]—
2 a day of darkness[e] and gloom,[f]
a day of clouds and blackness.
Like dawn spreading across the mountains
a large and mighty army[g] comes,
such as never was of old[h]
nor ever will be in ages to come.

3 Before them fire devours,
behind them a flame blazes.
Before them the land is like the garden of Eden,[i]
behind them, a desert waste[j]—
nothing escapes them.
4 They have the appearance of horses;[k]
they gallop along like cavalry.
5 With a noise like that of chariots[l]
they leap over the mountaintops,
like a crackling fire[m] consuming stubble,
like a mighty army drawn up for battle.

6 At the sight of them, nations are in anguish;[n]
every face turns pale.[o]
7 They charge like warriors;
they scale walls like soldiers.
They all march in line,
not swerving[p] from their course.
8 They do not jostle each other;
each marches straight ahead.
They plunge through defences
without breaking ranks.
9 They rush upon the city;
they run along the wall.
They climb into the houses;
like thieves they enter through the windows.[q]

10 Before them the earth shakes,[r]
the sky trembles,
the sun and moon are darkened,[s]
and the stars no longer shine.[t]
11 The LORD[u] thunders
at the head of his army;
his forces are beyond number,
and mighty are those who obey his command.
The day of the LORD is great;[v]
it is dreadful.
Who can endure it?[w]

Rend Your Heart

12 "Even now," declares the LORD,
"return[x] to me with all your heart,
with fasting and weeping and mourning."

2:1 [c] Joel 1:15; Zep 1:14-16 [d] Ob 1:15
2:2 [e] Am 5:18 [f] Da 9:12 [g] Joel 1:6 [h] Joel 1:2
2:3 [i] Ge 2:8 [j] Ps 105:34-35
2:4 [k] Rev 9:7
2:5 [l] Rev 9:9 [m] Isa 5:24; 30:30
2:6 [n] Isa 13:8 [o] Na 2:10
2:7 [p] Isa 5:27
2:9 [q] Jer 9:21
2:10 [r] Ps 18:7 [s] Mt 24:29 [t] Isa 13:10; Eze 32:8
2:11 [u] Joel 1:15 [v] Zep 1:14; Rev 18:8 [w] Eze 22:14
2:12 [x] Jer 4:1; Hos 12:6

However, Joel implied that the locust plague would be only the forerunner of an even greater crisis if the people didn't turn from their sins.

2:3 The Garden of Eden was Adam and Eve's first home (Genesis 2:8). Known for its beauty, here it is used to describe the beauty of the land prior to the devastation.

2:12, 13 God told the people to turn to him while there was still time. Destruction would soon be upon them. Time is also running out for us. Because we don't know when our lives will end, we should trust and obey God now, while we can. Don't let anything hold you back from turning to him.

13Rend your heart[y]
and not your garments.[z]
Return to the LORD your God,
for he is gracious and compassionate,
slow to anger and abounding in love,[a]
and he relents from sending calamity.[b]
14Who knows? He may turn[c] and have pity
and leave behind a blessing[d]—
grain offerings and drink offerings[e]
for the LORD your God.

15Blow the trumpet[f] in Zion,
declare a holy fast,[g]
call a sacred assembly.[h]
16Gather the people,
consecrate[i] the assembly;
bring together the elders,
gather the children,
those nursing at the breast.
Let the bridegroom[j] leave his room
and the bride her chamber.
17Let the priests, who minister before the LORD,
weep between the temple porch and the altar.[k]
Let them say, "Spare your people, O LORD.
Do not make your inheritance an object of scorn,[l]
a byword among the nations.
Why should they say among the peoples,
'Where is their God?[m]' "

The LORD's Answer

18Then the LORD will be jealous[n] for his land
and take pity on his people.

19The LORD will reply**[a]** to them:

"I am sending you grain, new wine and oil,[o]
enough to satisfy you fully;
never again will I make you
an object of scorn[p] to the nations.

20"I will drive the northern army[q] far from you,
pushing it into a parched and barren land,
with its front columns going into the eastern[r] sea**[b]**
and those in the rear into the western sea.**[c]**
And its stench[s] will go up;
its smell will rise."

Surely he has done great things.**[d]**
21 Be not afraid,[t] O land;

a *18, 19* Or LORD *was jealous . . . / and took pity . . . / 19 The* LORD *replied* **b** *20* That is, the Dead Sea **c** *20* That is, the Mediterranean **d** *20* Or *rise. / Surely it has done great things."*

2:13 [y]Ps 34:18; Isa 57:15 [z]Job 1:20 [a]Ex 34:6 [b]Jer 18:8
2:14 [c]Jer 26:3 [d]Hag 2:19 [e]Joel 1:13
2:15 [f]Nu 10:2 [g]Jer 36:9 [h]Joel 1:14
2:16 [i]Ex 19:10, 22 [j]Ps 19:5
2:17 [k]Eze 8:16; Mt 23:35 [l]Dt 9:26-29; Ps 44:13 [m]Ps 42:3
2:18 [n]Zec 1:14
2:19 [o]Jer 31:12 [p]Eze 34:29
2:20 [q]Jer 1:14-15 [r]Zec 14:8 [s]Isa 34:3
2:21 [t]Isa 54:4; Zep 3:16-17

2:13 Deep remorse was often shown by tearing (rending) one's clothes. But God didn't want an outward display of penitence without true inward repentance (1 Samuel 16:7; Matthew 23:1–36). Be sure your attitude towards God is correct, not just your outward actions.

2:18 Joel reached a turning point in his prophecy, moving from prophesying about an outpouring of God's judgment to prophesying about an outpouring of God's forgiveness and blessing. But this would come only if the people began to live as God wanted them to, giving up their sins. Where there is repentance, there is hope. This section of the book feeds that hope. Without it, Joel's prophecy could bring only despair. This promise of forgiveness should have encouraged the people to repent.

2:20 Joel foresaw the invasion from the north by the armies of Assyria and Babylon, typified by the locusts.

2:21 Joel contrasts the fear of God's judgment (2:1) with the joy

be glad and rejoice.
Surely the LORD has done great things. [u]
22 Be not afraid, O wild animals,
for the open pastures are becoming green. [v]
The trees are bearing their fruit;
the fig-tree and the vine yield their riches. [w]
23 Be glad, O people of Zion,
rejoice [x] in the LORD your God,
for he has given you
the autumn rains in righteousness. [e]
He sends you abundant showers,
both autumn and spring rains, [y] as before.
24 The threshing-floors will be filled with grain;
the vats will overflow [z] with new wine [a] and oil.

25 "I will repay you for the years the locusts have eaten—
the great locust and the young locust,
the other locusts and the locust swarm [f]—
my great army that I sent among you.
26 You will have plenty to eat, until you are full, [b]
and you will praise [c] the name of the LORD your God,
who has worked wonders [d] for you;
never again will my people be shamed.
27 Then you will know that I am in Israel,
that I am the LORD [e] your God,
and that there is no other;
never again will my people be shamed.

2. The day of the LORD

28 "And afterwards,
I will pour out my Spirit [f] on all people.
Your sons and daughters will prophesy,
your old men will dream dreams,
your young men will see visions.
29 Even on my servants, [g] both men and women,
I will pour out my Spirit in those days.
30 I will show wonders in the heavens [h]
and on the earth, [i]
blood and fire and billows of smoke.

2:21 [u] Ps 126:3
2:22 [v] Ps 65:12 [w] Joel 1:18-20
2:23 [x] Ps 149:2; Isa 12:6; 41:16; Hab 3:18; Zec 10:7 [y] Lev 26:4
2:24 [z] Lev 26:10; Mal 3:10 [a] Am 9:13
2:26 [b] Lev 26:5 [c] Isa 62:9 [d] Ps 126:3; Isa 25:1
2:27 [e] Joel 3:17
2:28 [f] Eze 39:29
2:29 [g] 1Co 12:13; Gal 3:28
2:30 [h] Lk 21:11 [i] Mk 13:24-25

e *23* Or / *the teacher for righteousness:* f *25* The precise meaning of the four Hebrew words used here for locusts is uncertain.

---

of God's intervention (2:21). On the day of the Lord, sin will bring judgment, and only God's forgiveness will bring rejoicing. Unless you repent, your sin will result in punishment. Let God intervene in your life. Then you will be able to rejoice in that day because you will have nothing to fear. Before, there were fasting, plagues, and funeral dirges; then, there will be feasting, harvesting, and songs of praise. When God rules, his restoration will be complete. In the meantime, we must remember that God does not promise that all his followers will be prosperous now. When God pardons, he restores our relationship with him, but this does not guarantee individual wealth. Instead, God promises to meet the deepest needs of those who love him—by loving us, forgiving us, giving us purpose in life, and giving us a caring Christian community.

2:26, 27 If the Jews would never again experience a disaster like this locust plague ("never again will my people be shamed"), how do we explain the captivity in Babylon, the Jews' slavery under the Greeks and Romans, and their persecution under Hitler? It is important not to take these verses out of context. This is still part of the "blessings" section of Joel's prophecy. Only if the people truly repented would they avoid a disaster like the one Joel had described. God's blessings are promised only to those who sincerely and consistently follow him. God does promise that after the final day of judgment, his people will never again experience this kind of disaster (Zechariah 14:9–11; Revelation 21).

2:28–32 Peter quoted this passage (see Acts 2:16–21)—the outpouring of the Spirit predicted by Joel occurred on Pentecost. While in the past, God's Spirit seemed available to kings, prophets, and judges, Joel envisioned a time when the Spirit would be available to every believer. Ezekiel also spoke of an outpouring of the Spirit (Ezekiel 39:28, 29). God's Spirit is available now to anyone who calls on the Lord (2:32).

2:30 These "wonders" would give a hint or a picture of a coming event.

31 The sun will be turned to darkness[j]
and the moon to blood
before the coming of the great and dreadful day of the
LORD.[k]
32 And everyone who calls
on the name of the LORD will be saved;[l]
for on Mount Zion[m] and in Jerusalem
there will be deliverance,[n]
as the LORD has said,
among the survivors[o]
whom the LORD calls.

The Nations Judged

3

"In those days and at that time,
when I restore the fortunes[a] of Judah and Jerusalem,
2 I will gather all nations
and bring them down to the Valley of Jehoshaphat.**a**
There I will enter into judgment[b] against them
concerning my inheritance, my people Israel,
for they scattered my people among the nations
and divided up my land.
3 They cast lots for my people
and traded boys for prostitutes;
they sold girls for wine[c]
that they might drink.

4 "Now what have you against me, O Tyre and Sidon[d] and all you regions of
Philistia? Are you repaying me for something I have done? If you are paying me back,
I will swiftly and speedily return on your own heads what you have done.[e] 5 For you
took my silver and my gold and carried off my finest treasures to your temples.[f] 6 You
sold the people of Judah and Jerusalem to the Greeks, that you might send them far
from their homeland.
7 "See, I am going to rouse them out of the places to which you sold them,[g] and
I will return on your own heads what you have done. 8 I will sell your sons[h] and
daughters to the people of Judah,[i] and they will sell them to the Sabeans, a nation
far away." The LORD has spoken.

a *2 Jehoshaphat* means *the LORD judges*; also in verse 12.

2:31 [j]Mt 24:29 [k]Isa 13:9-10; Mal 4:1, 5
2:32 [l]Ac 2:17-21*; Ro 10:13* [m]Isa 46:13 [n]Ob 1:17 [o]Isa 11:11; Mic 4:7; Ro 9:27
3:1 [a]Jer 16:15
3:2 [b]Eze 36:5
3:3 [c]Am 2:6
3:4 [d]Mt 11:21 [e]Isa 34:8
3:5 [f]2Ch 21:16-17
3:7 [g]Isa 43:5-6; Jer 23:8
3:8 [h]Isa 60:14 [i]Isa 14:2

2:31, 32 The "day of the LORD" is used here as God's appointed time to judge the nations (see the note on 1:15). Judgment and mercy go hand in hand. Joel had said that if the people repented, the Lord would save them from judgment (2:12–14). In this day of judgment and catastrophe, therefore, some will be saved. God's intention is not to destroy but to heal and to save. However, we must accept his salvation or we will certainly perish with the unrepentant.

3:1, 2 The phrase "at that time" refers to the time when those who call on the Lord will be saved (2:32). God will not only bless believers with everything they need; he will also bless them by destroying all evil and ending the pain and suffering on earth. This prophecy had three fulfilments: immediate, ongoing, and final. Its immediate interpretation could apply to King Jehoshaphat's recent battle against several enemy nations, including Moab and Ammon (2 Chronicles 20). Its ongoing fulfilment could be the partial restoration of the people to their land after the exile to Babylon. The final fulfilment will come in the great battle that precedes the Messiah's reign over the earth (Revelation 20:7–9).

3:2 The geographic location of the Valley of Jehoshaphat is not known, and some suggest it is being used as a symbol for the place where the Lord is to judge. Some think it may be a future valley created by the splitting of the Mount of Olives when the Messiah returns (Zechariah 14:4). The most important fact for us is that the name means "the LORD judges".

3:4 Tyre and Sidon were major cities in Phoenicia to the north-west of Israel; Philistia was the nation south-west of Judah. Phoenicia and Philistia were small countries who rejoiced at the fall of Judah and Israel because they would benefit from the increased trade. God would judge them for their wrong attitude.

3:6 Jews were sold to Greeks, a pagan and unclean people. Some think this verse and 3:1 indicate that Joel lived after the captivity in Babylon (586 B.C.), when the Greek culture began to flourish. But archaeological studies have shown that the Greeks were trading with Phoenicia as early as 800 B.C. Also 3:4 mentions Tyre, Sidon, and Philistia. These places were contemporary with Judah before their captivity.

3:8 The Sabeans came from Sheba, a nation in south-western Arabia. One of Sheba's queens had visited Solomon over a century earlier (1 Kings 10:1–13). The Sabeans controlled the eastern trade routes.

3:9 [j]Isa 8:9 [k]Jer 46:4

3:10 [l]Isa 2:4; Mic 4:3 [m]Zec 12:8

3:11 [n]Eze 38:15-16; Zep 3:8 [o]Isa 13:3

3:12 [p]Isa 2:4

3:13 [q]Hos 6:11; Mt 13:39; Rev 14:15-19 [r]Rev 14:20

3:14 [s]Isa 34:2-8; Joel 1:15

3:16 [t]Am 1:2 [u]Eze 38:19 [v]Jer 16:19

3:17 [w]Joel 2:27 [x]Isa 4:3

3:18 [y]Ex 3:8 [z]Isa 30:25; 35:6 [a]Rev 22:1-2 [b]Eze 47:1; Am 9:13

9 Proclaim this among the nations:
Prepare for war![j]
Rouse the warriors![k]
Let all the fighting men draw near and attack.
10 Beat your ploughshares into swords
and your pruning hooks[l] into spears.
Let the weakling[m] say,
"I am strong!"
11 Come quickly, all you nations from every side,
and assemble[n] there.

Bring down your warriors,[o] O LORD!

12 "Let the nations be roused;
let them advance into the Valley of Jehoshaphat,
for there I will sit
to judge[p] all the nations on every side.
13 Swing the sickle,
for the harvest[q] is ripe.
Come, trample the grapes,
for the winepress[r] is full
and the vats overflow—
so great is their wickedness!"

14 Multitudes, multitudes
in the valley of decision!
For the day of the LORD[s] is near
in the valley of decision.
15 The sun and moon will be darkened,
and the stars no longer shine.
16 The LORD will roar from Zion
and thunder from Jerusalem;[t]
the earth and the sky will tremble.[u]
But the LORD will be a refuge for his people,
a stronghold[v] for the people of Israel.

Blessings for God's People

17 "Then you will know that I, the LORD your God,[w]
dwell in Zion,[x] my holy hill.
Jerusalem will be holy;
never again will foreigners invade her.

18 "In that day the mountains will drip new wine,
and the hills will flow with milk;[y]
all the ravines of Judah will run with water.[z]
A fountain will flow out of the LORD's house[a]
and will water the valley of acacias.[b] [b]

b *18* Or *Valley of Shittim*

3:14 Joel described multitudes waiting in the "valley of decision" (the valley of judgment of verses 2 and 12). Billions of people have lived on earth, and every one of them—dead, living, and yet to be born—will face judgment. Look around you. See your friends, those with whom you work and live. Have they received God's forgiveness? Have they been warned about sin's consequences? If we understand the severity of God's final judgment, we will want to take God's offer of hope to those we know.

3:17 The last word will be God's; his ultimate sovereignty will be revealed in the end. We cannot predict when that end will come, but we can have confidence in his control over the world's events. The world's history, as well as our own pilgrimage, is in God's hands. We can be secure in his love and trust him to guide our decisions.

3:18 The picture of this restored land is one of perfect beauty, similar to the Garden of Eden. The life-giving fountain flowing from the Lord's house illustrates the blessings that come from God. Those who attach themselves to him will be for ever fruitful. (See also Ezekiel 47:1–12; Revelation 22:1, 2.)

19 But Egypt will be desolate,
Edom a desert waste,
because of violence[c] done to the people of Judah,
in whose land they shed innocent blood.
20 Judah will be inhabited for ever[d]
and Jerusalem through all generations.
21 Their bloodguilt, which I have not pardoned,
I will pardon.[e]"

The LORD dwells in Zion!

3:19 [c]Ob 1:10
3:20 [d]Am 9:15
3:21 [e]Eze 36:25

3:19 Egypt and Edom were two of Israel's most persistent enemies. They represent all the nations hostile to God's people. God's promise that they would be destroyed is also a promise that all evil in the world will one day be destroyed.

3:20, 21 The word *Judah* is used here to refer to all God's people—anyone who has called on the name of the Lord. There is full assurance of victory and peace for those who trust in God (2:32).

3:21 Joel began with a prophecy about the destruction of the land and ended with a prophecy about its restoration. He began by stressing the need for repentance and ended with the promise of forgiveness that repentance brings. Joel was trying to convince the people to wake up (1:5), get rid of their complacency, and realise the danger of living apart from God. His message to us is that there is still time; anyone who calls on God's name can be saved (2:12–14, 32). Those who turn to God will enjoy the blessings mentioned in Joel's prophecy; those who refuse will face destruction.

AMOS

Jeroboam II becomes king of Israel 793 B.C.	Amos becomes a prophet to Israel 760	Hosea becomes a prophet to Israel 753	King Shallum of Israel is assassinated 752	Amos' ministry ends 750	Isaiah becomes a prophet to Judah 740

WHEN we hear, "He's a man of God", the images that most often come to mind are of some famous evangelist, a vicar, a missionary, or a chaplain—professionals, Christian workers, those who preach and teach the word as a vocation.

Surely Amos was a man of God—a person whose life was devoted to serving the Lord and whose lifestyle reflected this devotion—but he was a layperson. Herding sheep and tending sycamore-fig trees in the Judean countryside, Amos was not the son of a prophet; he was not the son of a priest. As a humble shepherd, he could have stayed in Tekoa, doing his job, providing for his family, and worshipping his God. But God gave Amos a vision of the future (1:2), and told him to take his message to Israel, the northern kingdom (7:15). Amos obeyed, and thus proved he was a man of God.

Amos' message has had an impact on God's people throughout the centuries, and it needs to be heard today, by individuals and nations. Although they were divided from their southern brothers and sisters in Judah, the northern Israelites were still God's people. But they were living beneath a pious veneer of religion, worshipping idols, and oppressing the poor. Amos, a fiery, fearless, and honest shepherd from the south, confronted them with their sin and warned them of the impending judgment.

The book of Amos opens with this humble shepherd watching his sheep. God then gave him a vision of what was about to happen to the nation of Israel. God condemned all the nations who have sinned against him and harmed his people. Beginning with Aram, he moved quickly through Philistia, Tyre, Edom, Ammon, and Moab. All were condemned, and we can almost hear the Israelites shouting, "Amen!" And then, even Judah, Amos' homeland, was included in God's scathing denunciation (2:4, 5). How Amos' listeners must have enjoyed hearing those words! Suddenly, however, Amos turned to the people of Israel and pronounced God's judgment on *them*. The next four chapters enumerate and describe their sins. It is no wonder that Amaziah the priest intervened and tried to stop the preaching (7:10–13). Fearlessly, Amos continued to relate the visions of future judgment that God had given to him (chapters 8; 9). After all the chapters on judgment, the book concludes with a message of hope. Eventually God will restore his people and make them great again (9:8–15).

As you read Amos' book, put yourself in the place of those Israelites and listen to God's message. Have you grown complacent? Have other concerns taken God's place in your life? Do you ignore those in need or oppress the poor? Picture yourself as Amos, faithfully doing what God calls you to do. You, too, can be God's person. Listen for his clear call and do what he says, wherever it leads.

VITAL STATISTICS

PURPOSE:
To pronounce God's judgment upon Israel, the northern kingdom, for their complacency, idolatry, and oppression of the poor

AUTHOR:
Amos

TO WHOM WRITTEN:
Israel, the northern kingdom, and God's people everywhere

DATE WRITTEN:
Probably during the reigns of Jeroboam II of Israel and Uzziah (Azariah) of Judah (about 760–750 B.C.)

SETTING:
The wealthy people of Israel were enjoying peace and prosperity. They were quite complacent and were oppressing the poor, even selling them into slavery. Soon, however, Israel would be conquered by Assyria, and the rich would themselves become slaves.

KEY VERSE:
"But let justice roll on like a river, righteousness like a never-failing stream!" (5:24).

KEY PEOPLE:
Amos, Amaziah, Jeroboam II

KEY PLACES:
Bethel, Samaria

SPECIAL FEATURES:
Amos uses striking metaphors from his shepherding and farming experience—a loaded cart (2:13), a roaring lion (3:8), a mutilated sheep (3:12), pampered cows (4:1), and a basket of fruit (8:1, 2).

THE BLUEPRINT

1. Announcement of judgment (1:1–2:16)
2. Reasons for judgment (3:1–6:14)
3. Visions of judgment (7:1–9:15)

Amos speaks with brutal frankness in denouncing sin. He collided with the false religious leaders of his day and was not intimidated by priest or king. He continued to speak his message boldly. God requires truth and goodness, justice and righteousness, from all people and nations today as well. Many of the conditions in Israel during Amos' time are evident in today's societies. We need Amos' courage to ignore danger and stand against sin.

MEGATHEMES

THEME	EXPLANATION	IMPORTANCE
Everyone Answers to God	Amos pronounced judgment from God on all the surrounding nations. Then he included Judah and Israel. God is in supreme control of all the nations. Everyone is accountable to him.	All people will have to account for their sin. When those who reject God seem to do well, don't envy their prosperity or feel sorry for yourself. Remember that we must all answer to God for how we live.
Complacency	Everyone was optimistic, business was booming, and people were happy (except for the poor and oppressed). With all the comfort and luxury came self-sufficiency and a false sense of security. But prosperity brought corruption and destruction.	A complacent present leads to a disastrous future. Don't congratulate yourself for the blessings and benefits you now enjoy. They are from God. If you are more satisfied with yourself than with God, remember that everything is meaningless without him. A self-sufficient attitude may be your downfall.
Oppressing the Poor	The wealthy and powerful people of Samaria, the capital of Israel, had become prosperous, greedy, and unjust. Illegal and immoral slavery came as the result of over-taxation and land-grabbing. There was also cruelty and indifference towards the poor. God is weary of greed and will not tolerate injustice.	God made all people; therefore, to ignore the poor is to ignore those whom God loves and whom Christ came to save. We must go beyond feeling sorry for the poor and oppressed. We must act compassionately to stop injustice and to help care for those in need.
Superficial Religion	Although many people had abandoned real faith in God, they still pretended to be religious. They were carrying on nominal religious performances instead of having spiritual integrity and practising heartfelt obedience towards God.	Merely participating in ceremony or ritual falls short of true religion. God wants simple trust in him, not showy external actions. Don't settle for impressing others with external rituals when God wants heartfelt obedience and commitment.

1. Announcement of judgment

1 The words of Amos, one of the shepherds of Tekoa[a]—what he saw concerning
Israel two years before the earthquake,[b] when Uzziah[c] was king of Judah and
Jeroboam[d] son of Jehoash**[a]** was king of Israel.[e]

a *1* Hebrew *Joash*, a variant of *Jehoash*

1:1
[a] 2Sa 14:2
[b] Zec 14:5
[c] 2Ch 26:23
[d] 2Ki 14:23
[e] Hos 1:1

1:1 Amos was a shepherd and fig grower from the southern kingdom (Judah), but he prophesied to the northern kingdom (Israel). Israel was politically at the height of its power with a prosperous economy, but the nation was spiritually corrupt. Idols were worshipped throughout the land, and especially at Bethel, which was supposed to be the nation's religious centre. Like Hosea, Amos was sent by God to denounce this social and religious corruption. About 30 or 40 years after Amos prophesied, Assyria destroyed the capital city, Samaria, and conquered Israel (722 B.C.). Uzziah reigned in Judah from 792–740; Jeroboam II reigned in Israel from 793–753.

1:1 Tekoa, Amos's home town, was located in the rugged sheep country of Judah, about ten miles south of Jerusalem. Long before Amos was born, a woman of Tekoa had helped reconcile David and his rebellious son, Absalom (2 Samuel 14:1–23).

1:1 Amos raised sheep—not a particularly "spiritual" job—yet he became a channel of God's message to others. Your job may not cause you to feel spiritual or successful, but it is a vital work if you are in the place God wants you to be. God can work through you to do extraordinary things, no matter how ordinary your occupation.

1:1 The prophet Zechariah and other historical records from this period mention an earthquake that occurred at this time (Zechariah 14:5).

1:2 [f]Isa 42:13 [g]Joel 3:16 [h]Am 9:3 [i]Jer 12:4

2 He said:

"The LORD roars[f] from Zion
and thunders from Jerusalem;[g]
the pastures of the shepherds dry up,[b]
and the top of Carmel[h] withers."[i]

1:3 [j]Isa 8:4; 17:1-3 [k]Am 2:6

Judgment on Israel's Neighbours

3 This is what the LORD says:

"For three sins of Damascus,[j]
even for four, I will not turn back ⌞my wrath⌟.[k]
Because she threshed Gilead
with sledges having iron teeth,

1:4 [l]Jer 49:27 [m]Jer 17:27 [n]1Ki 20:1; 2Ki 6:24

4 I will send fire[l] upon the house of Hazael
that will consume the fortresses[m] of Ben-Hadad.[n]
5 I will break down the gate[o] of Damascus;
I will destroy the king who is in[c] the Valley of Aven[d]
and the one who holds the sceptre in Beth Eden.
The people of Aram will go into exile to Kir,[p]"
says the LORD.

1:5 [o]Jer 51:30 [p]2Ki 16:9

6 This is what the LORD says:

"For three sins of Gaza,[q]
even for four, I will not turn back ⌞my wrath⌟.
Because she took captive whole communities
and sold them to Edom,[r]

1:6 [q]1Sa 6:17; Zep 2:4 [r]Ob 1:11

[b]2 Or *shepherds mourn* [c]5 Or *the inhabitants of* [d]5 *Aven* means *wickedness.*

AMOS served as a prophet to Israel (the northern kingdom) from 760–750 B.C.

Climate of the times	Israel was enjoying peace and economic prosperity. But this blessing had caused her to become a selfish, materialistic society. Those who were well-off ignored the needs of those less fortunate. The people were self-centred and indifferent towards God.
Main message	Amos spoke against those who exploited or ignored the needy.
Importance of message	Believing in God is more than a matter of individual faith. God calls all believers to work against injustices in society and to aid those less fortunate.
Contemporary prophets	Jonah (793–753) Hosea (753–715)

1:2 In the Bible, God is often pictured as a shepherd and his people as sheep. As a shepherd, God leads and protects his flock. But here God is depicted as a ferocious lion ready to devour those who are evil or unfaithful. (See also Hosea 11:10.)

1:2 Carmel means "fertile field". It was a very fertile area. A drought capable of drying up this area would have to be quite severe.

1:3 Damascus was the capital of Aram. In the past, Aram had been one of Israel's most formidable enemies. After the defeat of Aram by Assyria in 732 B.C. (2 Kings 16:9), Damascus was no longer a real threat.

1:3–2:6 Amos pronounced God's judgment on nation after nation around Israel's borders – even Judah. Perhaps the people of Israel cheered when they heard the rebukes levelled against those nations. But then Amos proclaimed God's judgment on Israel. They could not excuse their own sin just because the sins of their neighbours seemed worse. God is no respecter of persons. He judges all people fairly and impartially.

1:3–2:6 The accusation "For three sins . . . even for four" means that these nations had sinned again and again. This phrase echoes through these verses as God evaluates nation after nation. Each nation had persistently refused to follow God's commands. A sinful practice can become a way of life. Ignoring or denying the problem will not help us. We must begin the process of correction by confessing our sins to God and asking him to forgive us. Otherwise, we have no hope but to continue our pattern of sin.

1:4 The "house of Hazael" refers to the king of Aram. Ben-Hadad was Hazael's son (2 Kings 13:24).

1:5 The Arameans had been slaves in Kir, but here they were free (9:7). Decreeing that the Arameans should go back to Kir was like saying the Israelites should go back to Egypt as slaves (Exodus 1).

7I will send fire upon the walls of Gaza
that will consume her fortresses.
8I will destroy the king[e] of Ashdod[s]
and the one who holds the sceptre in Ashkelon.
I will turn my hand[t] against Ekron,
till the last of the Philistines[u] is dead,"
says the Sovereign LORD.[v]

9This is what the LORD says:

"For three sins of Tyre,[w]
even for four, I will not turn back ⌊my wrath⌋.
Because she sold whole communities of captives to Edom,
disregarding a treaty of brotherhood,
10I will send fire upon the walls of Tyre
that will consume her fortresses.[x]"

11This is what the LORD says:

"For three sins of Edom,[y]
even for four, I will not turn back ⌊my wrath⌋.
Because he pursued his brother with a sword,
stifling all compassion,[f]
because his anger raged continually
and his fury flamed unchecked,[z]
12I will send fire upon Teman[a]
that will consume the fortresses of Bozrah."

13This is what the LORD says:

"For three sins of Ammon,[b]
even for four, I will not turn back ⌊my wrath⌋.
Because he ripped open the pregnant women[c] of Gilead
in order to extend his borders,
14I will set fire to the walls of Rabbah[d]
that will consume her fortresses
amid war cries[e] on the day of battle,
amid violent winds on a stormy day.
15Her king[g] will go into exile,
he and his officials together,"
says the LORD.

2 This is what the LORD says:

"For three sins of Moab,
even for four, I will not turn back ⌊my wrath⌋.

e *8* Or *inhabitants* f *11* Or *sword / and destroyed his allies* g *15* Or / *Molech*; Hebrew *malcam*

1:8 s2Ch 26:6 tPs 81:14 uEze 25:16 vIsa 14:28-32; Zep 2:4-7
1:9 w1Ki 5:1; 9:11-14; Isa 23:1-18; Jer 25:22; Joel 3:4; Mt 11:21
1:10 xZec 9:1-4
1:11 yNu 20:14-21; 2Ch 28:17; Jer 49:7-22 zEze 25:12-14
1:12 aOb 1:9-10
1:13 bJer 49:1-6; Eze 21:28; 25:2-7 cHos 13:16
1:14 dDt 3:11 eAm 2:2

1:7, 8 Gaza, Ashdod, Ashkelon, and Ekron were four of the five major cities of Philistia, an enemy who often threatened Israel. The fifth city, Gath, had probably already been destroyed. Therefore, Amos was saying that the entire nation of Philistia would be destroyed for its sins.

1:9 Tyre was one of two major cities in Phoenicia. Several treaties had been made with this city, which supplied the cedar used to build David's palace and God's temple (2 Samuel 5:11; 1 Kings 5).

1:11, 12 Both Edom and Israel had descended from Isaac: Edom from Isaac's son Esau, and Israel from Esau's twin brother, Jacob (Genesis 25:19–28; 27). But these two nations, like the two brothers, were always fighting. Edom had rejoiced at Israel's misfortunes. As a result, God promised to destroy Edom completely, from Teman in the south to Bozrah in the north.

1:13–15 The Ammonites had descended from an incestuous relationship between Lot and his younger daughter (Genesis 19:30–38). The Ammonites were hostile to Israel; and although Israel began to worship their idols, the Ammonites still attacked (Judges 10:6–8). After Saul had been anointed Israel's king, his first victory in battle was against the Ammonites (1 Samuel 11). Rabbah was Ammon's capital city. Amos's prophecy of Ammon's destruction was fulfilled through the Assyrian invasion.

2:1–3 The Moabites had descended from an incestuous relationship between Lot and his older daughter (Genesis 19:30–38). Balak, king of Moab, had tried to hire the prophet Balaam to curse the Israelites so they could be defeated (Numbers 22–24). Balaam spoke instead the Lord's word of blessing, but some of the Moabites had succeeded in getting Israel to worship Baal (Numbers

2:3 [a]Ps 2:10 [b]Isa 40:23
2:4 [c]2Ki 17:19; Hos 12:2 [d]Jer 6:19 [e]Eze 20:24 [f]Isa 9:16 [g]Isa 28:15 [h]2Ki 22:13; Jer 16:12
2:5 [i]Jer 17:27; Hos 8:14
2:6 [j]Joel 3:3; Am 8:6
2:7 [k]Am 5:11-12; 8:4
2:8 [l]Ex 22:26 [m]Am 4:1; 6:6
2:9 [n]Nu 21:23-26; Jos 10:12

Because he burned, as if to lime,
the bones of Edom's king,
2 I will send fire upon Moab
that will consume the fortresses of Kerioth.[a]
Moab will go down in great tumult
amid war cries and the blast of the trumpet.
3 I will destroy her ruler[a]
and kill all her officials with him,"[b]
says the LORD.

4 This is what the LORD says:

"For three sins of Judah,[c]
even for four, I will not turn back ⌊my wrath⌋.
Because they have rejected the law[d] of the LORD
and have not kept his decrees,[e]
because they have been led astray[f] by false gods,[b][g]
the gods[c] their ancestors followed,[h]
5 I will send fire upon Judah
that will consume the fortresses of Jerusalem.[i]"

Judgment on Israel

6 This is what the LORD says:

"For three sins of Israel,
even for four, I will not turn back ⌊my wrath⌋.
They sell the righteous for silver,
and the needy for a pair of sandals.[j]
7 They trample on the heads of the poor
as upon the dust of the ground
and deny justice to the oppressed.
Father and son use the same girl
and so profane my holy name.[k]
8 They lie down beside every altar
on garments taken in pledge.[l]
In the house of their god
they drink wine[m] taken as fines.

9 "I destroyed the Amorite[n] before them,
though he was tall as the cedars

[a] 2 Or *of her cities* [b] 4 Or *by lies* [c] 4 Or *lies*

25:1–3). The Moabites were known for their atrocities (2 Kings 3:26, 27). An archaeological artefact, the Moabite Stone, reveals that Moab was always ready to profit from the downfall of others.

2:4–6 After Solomon died, the kingdom divided, and the tribes of Judah and Benjamin became the southern kingdom (Judah) under Solomon's son, Rehoboam. The other ten tribes became the northern kingdom (Israel) and followed Jeroboam, who had rebelled against Rehoboam.

God had punished other nations harshly for their evil actions and atrocities. But God also promised to judge both Israel and Judah because they ignored the revealed law of God. The other nations were ignorant, but Judah and Israel, God's people, knew what God wanted. Still they ignored him and joined pagan nations in worshipping idols. If we know God's word and refuse to obey it, like Israel we will carry a greater guilt.

2:4–6 Amos must have won over his audience as he proclaimed God's judgment against the evil nations surrounding Israel. But then he even spoke against his own nation, Judah, before focusing on God's indictment of Israel.

2:6ff God condemned Israel for five specific sins: (1) selling the poor as slaves (see Deuteronomy 15:7–11; Amos 8:6), (2) exploiting the poor (see Exodus 23:6; Deuteronomy 16:19), (3) engaging in perverse sexual sins (see Leviticus 20:11, 12), (4) taking illegal collateral for loans (see Exodus 22:26, 27; Deuteronomy 24:6, 12, 13), and (5) worshipping false gods (see Exodus 20:3–5).

2:6, 7 Amos was speaking to the upper class. There was no middle class in the country—only the very rich and the very poor. The rich kept religious rituals. They gave extra tithes, went to places of worship, and offered sacrifices. But they were greedy and unjust, and they took advantage of the helpless. Be sure that you do not neglect the needs of the poor while you faithfully attend church and fulfil religious rituals. God expects us to live out our faith—this means responding to those in need.

2:9–11 The prophets were constantly challenging people to remember what God had done! When we read a list like this one, we are amazed at Israel's forgetfulness. But what would the prophets say about us? God's past faithfulness should have reminded the Israelites to obey him; likewise, what he has done for us should remind us to live for him.

and strong as the oaks.
I destroyed his fruit above
and his roots[o] below.

10"I brought you up out of Egypt,[p]
and I led you for forty years in the desert[q]
to give you the land of the Amorites.[r]
11I also raised up prophets[s] from among your sons
and Nazirites[t] from among your young men.
Is this not true, people of Israel?"
declares the LORD.

12"But you made the Nazirites drink wine
and commanded the prophets not to prophesy.[u]

13"Now then, I will crush you
as a cart crushes when loaded with grain.
14The swift will not escape,
the strong[v] will not muster their strength,
and the warrior will not save his life.[w]
15The archer[x] will not stand his ground,
the fleet-footed soldier will not get away,
and the horseman will not save his life.
16Even the bravest warriors[y]
will flee naked on that day,"
declares the LORD.

2. Reasons for judgment

Witnesses Summoned Against Israel

3 Hear this word the LORD has spoken against you, O people of Israel—against the whole family I brought up out of Egypt:[a]

2"You only have I chosen[b]
of all the families of the earth;
therefore I will punish you
for all your sins.[c]"

3Do two walk together
unless they have agreed to do so?
4Does a lion roar in the thicket
when he has no prey?[d]
Does he growl in his den
when he has caught nothing?
5Does a bird fall into a trap on the ground
where no snare has been set?
Does a trap spring up from the earth

2:9 [o]Eze 17:9; Mal 4:1
2:10 [p]Ex 20:2; Am 3:1 [q]Dt 2:7 [r]Ex 3:8; Am 9:7
2:11 [s]Dt 18:18; Jer 7:25 [t]Nu 6:2-3; Jdg 13:5
2:12 [u]Isa 30:10; Jer 11:21; Am 7:12-13; Mic 2:6
2:14 [v]Jer 9:23 [w]Ps 33:16; Isa 30:16-17
2:15 [x]Eze 39:3
2:16 [y]Jer 48:41
3:1 [a]Am 2:10
3:2 [b]Dt 7:6; Lk 12:47 [c]Jer 14:10
3:4 [d]Ps 104:21; Hos 5:14

2:11 The Nazirites took a vow of service to God. The vow included abstaining from wine and never cutting their hair. But instead of being respected for their disciplined and temperate lives, they were being urged to break their vows. If the Nazirites were corrupted, there would remain little influence for good among the Israelites.

2:16 "That day" refers to when Assyria would attack Israel, destroy Samaria, and take the people captive (722 B.C.). This military defeat came only a few decades after this pronouncement.

2:16 Television and films are filled with images of people who seem to have no fear. Many today have modelled their lives after these images—they want to be tough. But God is not impressed with bravado. He says that even the toughest people will run in fear when God's judgment comes. Do you know people who think they can make it through life without God? Don't be swayed by their self-assured rhetoric. Recognise that God fears no-one, and one day all people will fear him.

3:2 God chose Israel to be the people through whom all other nations of the world could know him. He made this promise to Abraham, father of the Israelites (Genesis 12:1–3). Israel didn't have to do anything to be chosen; God had given them this special privilege because he wanted to, not because they deserved special treatment (Deuteronomy 9:4–6). Pride in their privileged position, however, ruined Israel's sensitivity to the will of God and to the plight of others.

3:3–6 With a series of seven rhetorical questions, Amos shows how two events can be linked together. Once one event takes place, the second will surely follow. Amos was showing that God's revelation to him was the sure sign that judgment would follow.

when there is nothing to catch?
6 When a trumpet sounds in a city,
do not the people tremble?
When disaster comes to a city,
has not the LORD caused it?[e]

7 Surely the Sovereign LORD does nothing
without revealing his plan[f]
to his servants the prophets.[g]

8 The lion has roared —
who will not fear?
The Sovereign LORD has spoken —
who can but prophesy?[h]

9 Proclaim to the fortresses of Ashdod
and to the fortresses of Egypt:
"Assemble yourselves on the mountains of Samaria;[i]
see the great unrest within her
and the oppression among her people."

10 "They do not know how to do right,[j]" declares the LORD,
"who hoard plunder[k] and loot in their fortresses."[l]

11 Therefore this is what the Sovereign LORD says:

"An enemy will overrun the land;
he will pull down your strongholds
and plunder your fortresses.[m]"

12 This is what the LORD says:

"As a shepherd saves from the lion's[n] mouth
only two leg bones or a piece of an ear,
so will the Israelites be saved,
those who sit in Samaria
on the edge of their beds
and in Damascus on their couches."[a][o]

13 "Hear this and testify[p] against the house of Jacob," declares the Lord, the LORD God Almighty.

14 "On the day I punish Israel for her sins,
I will destroy the altars of Bethel;[q]
the horns of the altar will be cut off

3:6 [e] Isa 14:24-27; 45:7
3:7 [f] Ge 18:17; Da 9:22; Jn 15:15; Rev 10:7 [g] Jer 23:22
3:8 [h] Jer 20:9; Jnh 1:1-3; 3:1-3; Ac 4:20
3:9 [i] Am 4:1; 6:1
3:10 [j] Jer 4:22; Am 5:7; 6:12 [k] Hab 2:8 [l] Zep 1:9
3:11 [m] Am 2:5; 6:14
3:12 [n] 1Sa 17:34 [o] Am 6:4
3:13 [p] Eze 2:7
3:14 [q] Am 5:5-6

[a] *12* The meaning of the Hebrew for this line is uncertain.

3:6 This verse means that God himself would be sending disaster to Israel.

3:7 Even in anger, God is merciful: he always warned his people through prophets before punishing them. Warnings about sin and judgment apply to people today just as they did to Israel. Because we have been warned about our sin, we have no excuse when punishment comes. God had warned his people through his prophets, so they could not rationalise or complain when God punished them for refusing to repent. Do not take lightly the warnings in God's word about judgment. His warnings are a way of showing mercy to you.

3:9 Ashdod was a Philistine city and the site of the temple of Dagon, a pagan god. Amos pictured Philistia and Egypt summoned to witness Israel's great sins. Even Israel's most wicked and idolatrous neighbours would see God judge Israel.

3:10 Israel no longer knew how to do what was right. The more they sinned, the harder it was to remember what God wanted. The same is true for us. The longer we wait to deal with sin, the greater it holds onto us. Finally, we forget what it means to do right. Are you on the verge of forgetting?

3:11, 12 The enemy mentioned here was Assyria, who conquered Israel and did just as Amos predicted. The people were scattered to foreign lands, and foreigners were placed in the land to keep the peace. Israel's leaders had robbed their defenceless countrymen, and here they would be rendered defenceless by the Assyrians. Amos added that even if the Israelites tried to repent, it would be too late. The destruction would be so complete that nothing of value would be left.

3:14 God's judgment against Israel's altars shows that he was rejecting Israel's entire religious system because it was so polluted. The horns of the altar stood for protection (1 Kings 1:49–53), and the false altars would soon be gone. Then the people would have no sanctuary, protection, or refuge (see 4:4) when judgment came.

and fall to the ground.
15I will tear down the winter house[r]
along with the summer house;[s]
the houses adorned with ivory[t] will be destroyed
and the mansions will be demolished,"
declares the LORD.

3:15
[r]Jer 36:22
[s]Jdg 3:20
[t]1Ki 22:39

Israel Has Not Returned to God

4 Hear this word, you cows of Bashan[a] on Mount Samaria,[b]
you women who oppress the poor and crush the needy
and say to your husbands, "Bring us some drinks![c]"
2The Sovereign LORD has sworn by his holiness:
"The time will surely come
when you will be taken away[d] with hooks,
the last of you with fish-hooks.
3You will each go straight out
through breaks in the wall,[e]
and you will be cast out towards Harmon,"[a]
declares the LORD.

4"Go to Bethel and sin;
go to Gilgal[f] and sin yet more.
Bring your sacrifices every morning,[g]
your tithes[h] every three years.[b][i]
5Burn leavened bread[j] as a thank-offering
and brag about your freewill offerings[k]—
boast about them, you Israelites,
for this is what you love to do,"
declares the Sovereign LORD.

6"I gave you empty stomachs[c] in every city
and lack of bread in every town,
yet you have not returned to me,"
declares the LORD.[l]

7"I also withheld rain from you
when the harvest was still three months away.
I sent rain on one town,
but withheld it from another.[m]
One field had rain;
another had none and dried up.
8People staggered from town to town for water[n]
but did not get enough to drink,
yet you have not returned[o] to me,"

4:1
[a]Ps 22:12;
Eze 39:18
[b]Am 3:9
[c]Am 2:8; 5:11; 8:6

4:2
[d]Am 6:8

4:3
[e]Eze 12:5

4:4
[f]Hos 4:15
[g]Nu 28:3
[h]Dt 14:28
[i]Eze 20:39;
Am 5:21-22

4:5
[j]Lev 7:13
[k]Lev 22:18-21

4:6
[l]Isa 3:1;
Jer 5:3;
Hag 2:17

4:7
[m]Ex 9:4, 26;
Dt 11:17;
2Ch 7:13

4:8
[n]Eze 4:16-17
[o]Jer 3:7

[a] 3 Masoretic Text; with a different word division of the Hebrew (see Septuagint) *out, O mountain of oppression*
[b] 4 Or *tithes on the third day* [c] 6 Hebrew *you cleanness of teeth*

4:1 Israel's wealthy women were called "cows of Bashan"—pampered, sleek, and well-fed (see Psalm 22:12). These women selfishly pushed their husbands to oppress the helpless in order to support their lavish life-styles. Be careful not to desire material possessions so much that you are willing to oppress others and displease God to get them.

4:4 Amos sarcastically invited the people to sin in Bethel and Gilgal where they worshipped idols instead of God. Bethel was where God had renewed his covenant to Abraham with Jacob (Genesis 28:10–22). At this time, Bethel was the religious centre of the northern kingdom, and Jeroboam had placed an idol there to discourage the people from travelling to Jerusalem in the southern kingdom to worship (1 Kings 12:26–29). Gilgal was Israel's first camp site after entering the promised land (Joshua 4:19). Here Joshua had renewed the covenant and the rite of circumcision, and the people had celebrated the Passover (Joshua 5:2–11). Saul was crowned Israel's first king in Gilgal (1 Samuel 11:15).

4:6–13 No matter how God warned the people—through famine, drought, blight, locusts, plagues, or war—they still ignored him. Because the Israelites didn't get the message, they would have to meet God face to face in judgment. No longer would they ignore God; they would have to face the One they had rejected, the One they had refused to obey when he commanded them to care for the poor. One day each of us will meet God face to face to account for what we have done or refused to do. Are you prepared to meet him?

4:8
[p]Jer 14:4

4:9
[q]Dt 28:22
[r]Joel 1:7
[s]Jer 3:10; Hag 2:17

4:10
[t]Ex 9:3; Dt 28:27
[u]Isa 9:13

4:11
[v]Ge 19:24; Jer 23:14

4:13
[w]Ps 65:6
[x]Da 2:28
[y]Mic 1:3
[z]Isa 47:4; Am 5:8, 27; 9:6

5:1
[a]Eze 19:1

5:2
[b]Jer 14:17
[c]Jer 50:32; Am 8:14

5:3
[d]Isa 6:13; Am 6:9

5:4
[e]Isa 55:3; Jer 29:13

5:5
[f]1Sa 11:14; Am 4:4
[g]Am 8:14
[h]1Sa 7:16

declares the LORD.[p]

9"Many times I struck your gardens and vineyards,
I struck them with blight and mildew.[q]
Locusts devoured your fig and olive trees,[r]
yet you have not returned[s] to me,"
declares the LORD.

10"I sent plagues[t] among you
as I did to Egypt.
I killed your young men with the sword,
along with your captured horses.
I filled your nostrils with the stench of your camps,
yet you have not returned to me,"
declares the LORD.[u]

11"I overthrew some of you
as I[d] overthrew Sodom and Gomorrah.[v]
You were like a burning stick snatched from the fire,
yet you have not returned to me,"
declares the LORD.

12"Therefore this is what I will do to you, Israel,
and because I will do this to you,
prepare to meet your God, O Israel."

13He who forms the mountains,[w]
creates the wind,
and reveals his thoughts[x] to man,
he who turns dawn to darkness,
and treads the high places of the earth[y]—
the LORD God Almighty is his name.[z]

A Lament and Call to Repentance

5 Hear this word, O house of Israel, this lament[a] I take up concerning you:

2"Fallen is Virgin[b] Israel,
never to rise again,
deserted in her own land,
with no-one to lift her up.[c]"

3This is what the Sovereign LORD says:

"The city that marches out a thousand strong for Israel
will have only a hundred left;
the town that marches out a hundred strong
will have only ten left.[d]"

4This is what the LORD says to the house of Israel:

"Seek me and live;[e]
5 do not seek Bethel,
do not go to Gilgal,[f]
do not journey to Beersheba.[g]
For Gilgal will surely go into exile,
and Bethel will be reduced to nothing."[a][h]

d *11* Hebrew *God* **a** *5* Or *grief*; or *wickedness*; Hebrew *aven*, a reference to Beth Aven (a derogatory name for Bethel)

5:1 Amos shocked his listeners by singing a lament or song of grief for them as though they had already been destroyed. The Israelites believed that their wealth and religious ritual made them secure, but Amos lamented their sure destruction.

6Seek[i] the LORD and live,[j]
or he will sweep through the house of Joseph like a fire;[k]
it will devour,
and Bethel[l] will have no-one to quench it.

7You who turn justice into bitterness[m]
and cast righteousness to the ground
8(he who made the Pleiades and Orion,[n]
who turns blackness into dawn[o]
and darkens day into night,[p]
who calls for the waters of the sea
and pours them out over the face of the land—
the LORD is his name[q]—
9he flashes destruction on the stronghold
and brings the fortified city to ruin),[r]
10you hate the one who reproves in court[s]
and despise him who tells the truth.[t]

11You trample on the poor[u]
and force him to give you grain.
Therefore, though you have built stone mansions,[v]
you will not live in them;
though you have planted lush vineyards,
you will not drink their wine.[w]
12For I know how many are your offences
and how great your sins.

You oppress the righteous and take bribes
and you deprive the poor of justice in the courts.[x]
13Therefore the prudent man keeps quiet in such times,
for the times are evil.

14Seek good, not evil,
that you may live.
Then the LORD God Almighty will be with you,
just as you say he is.
15Hate evil,[y] love good;
maintain justice in the courts.
Perhaps the LORD God Almighty will have mercy[z]

5:6 [i]Isa 55:6 [j]ver 14 [k]Dt 4:24 [l]Am 3:14
5:7 [m]Am 6:12
5:8 [n]Job 9:9 [o]Isa 42:16 [p]Ps 104:20; Am 8:9 [q]Ps 104:6-9; Am 4:13
5:9 [r]Mic 5:11
5:10 [s]Isa 29:21 [t]1Ki 22:8
5:11 [u]Am 8:6 [v]Am 3:15 [w]Mic 6:15
5:12 [x]Isa 5:23; Am 2:6-7
5:15 [y]Ps 97:10; Ro 12:9 [z]Joel 2:14

5:6 There is one sure remedy for a world that is sick and dying in sin—"seek the LORD and live". Sin seeks to destroy, but hope is found in seeking God. In times of difficulty, seek God. In personal discomfort and struggle, seek God. When others are struggling, encourage them to seek God too.

5:7 The law courts should have been places of justice where the poor and oppressed could find relief. Instead, they had become places of greed and injustice.

5:8 Pleiades and Orion are star constellations. For thousands of years, navigators have staked lives and fortunes on the reliability of the stars. The constancy and orderliness of the heavens challenge us to look beyond them to their Creator.

5:10–12 "One who reproves in court" refers to an honest judge, a champion of justice. A society is in trouble when those who try to do right are hated for their commitment to justice. Any society that exploits the poor and defenceless or hates the truth is bent on destroying itself.

5:12 Why does God put so much emphasis on the way we treat the poor and needy? How we treat the rich, or those of equal standing, often reflects what we hope to get from them. But because the poor can give us nothing, how we treat them reflects our true character. Do we, like Christ, give without thought of gain? We should treat the poor as we would like God to treat us.

5:12 Here are eight common excuses for not helping the poor and needy: (1) They don't deserve help. They got themselves into poverty; let them get themselves out. (2) God's call to help the poor applies to another time. (3) We don't know any people like this. (4) I have my own needs. (5) Any money I give will be wasted, stolen, or spent. The poor will never see it. (6) I may become a victim myself. (7) I don't know where to start, and I don't have time. (8) My little bit won't make any difference.

Instead of making lame excuses, ask what can be done to help. Does your church have schemes to help the needy? Could you volunteer to work with a community group that fights poverty? As one individual, you may not be able to accomplish much, but join up with similarly motivated people and watch mountains begin to move.

5:15 If Israel were to sweep away the corrupt system of false accusations, bribery, and corruption, and were to insist that only just decisions be given, this would show their change of heart. We dare not read this passage lightly or write it off simply as encouragement to be good. It is a command to reform our own legal and social system.

on the remnant[a] of Joseph.

16Therefore this is what the Lord, the LORD God Almighty, says:

"There will be wailing[b] in all the streets
and cries of anguish in every public square.
The farmers[c] will be summoned to weep
and the mourners to wail.
17There will be wailing in all the vineyards,
for I will pass through[d] your midst,"
says the LORD.[e]

The Day of the LORD

18Woe to you who long
for the day of the LORD![f]
Why do you long for the day of the LORD?
That day will be darkness,[g] not light.[h]
19It will be as though a man fled from a lion
only to meet a bear,
as though he entered his house
and rested his hand on the wall
only to have a snake bite him.[i]
20Will not the day of the LORD be darkness, not light—
pitch-dark, without a ray of brightness?[j]

21"I hate, I despise your religious feasts;[k]
I cannot stand your assemblies.[l]
22Even though you bring me burnt offerings and grain offerings,
I will not accept them.
Though you bring choice fellowship offerings,**b**
I will have no regard for them.[mn]
23Away with the noise of your songs!
I will not listen to the music of your harps.[o]
24But let justice[p] roll on like a river,
righteousness like a never-failing stream![q]

25"Did you bring me sacrifices[r] and offerings
for forty years[s] in the desert, O house of Israel?
26You have lifted up the shrine of your king,
the pedestal of your idols,
the star of your god—**c**
which you made for yourselves.

5:15 aMic 5:7, 8
5:16 bJer 9:17 cJoel 1:11
5:17 dEx 12:12 eIsa 16:10; Jer 48:33
5:18 fJoel 1:15 gJoel 2:2 hIsa 5:19, 30; Jer 30:7
5:19 iJob 20:24; Isa 24:17-18; Jer 15:2-3; 48:44
5:20 jIsa 13:10; Zep 1:15
5:21 kLev 26:31 lIsa 1:11-16
5:22 mAm 4:4; Mic 6:6-7 nIsa 66:3
5:23 oAm 6:5
5:24 pJer 22:3 qMic 6:8
5:25 rIsa 43:23 sDt 32:17

b *22* Traditionally *peace offerings* **c** *26* Or *lifted up Sakkuth your king / and Kaiwan your idols, / your star-gods*; Septuagint *lifted up the shrine of Molech / and the star of your god Rephan, / their idols*

5:16 Failure to honour the dead was considered horrible in Israel, so loud weeping was common at funerals. Paid mourners, usually women, cried and mourned loudly with dirges and eulogies. Amos said there would be so many funerals that there would be a shortage of professional mourners, so farmers would be called from the fields to help. (See also Jeremiah 9:17–20.)

5:18 Here "the day of the LORD" means the imminent destruction by the Assyrian army, as well as the future day of God's judgment. For the faithful, "the day of the LORD" will be glorious, but for the unfaithful it will be a day of darkness and doom. (See Joel 1:15 for more discussion of the day of the Lord.)

5:18–24 These people were calling for the day of the Lord, thinking it would bring an end to their troubles. But God said, "You don't know what you are asking for." This "day of the LORD" would bring justice, and justice would bring the punishment the people deserved for their sins.

5:21–23 God hates false worship ("religious feasts" and "assemblies") by people who go through the motions out of pretence or for show. If we are living sinful lives and using religious ritual and traditions to make ourselves look good, God will despise our worship and will not accept what we offer. He wants sincere hearts, not the songs of hypocrites. When you worship at church, are you more concerned about your image or your attitude toward God?

5:26 In days past, Israel had turned to worshipping stars and planets, preferring nature over nature's God (2 Kings 23:4, 5). Pagan religion allowed them to indulge in sexual immorality and to become wealthy through any means possible. Because they refused to worship and obey the one true God, they would cause their own destruction.

27Therefore I will send you into exile beyond Damascus,"
says the LORD, whose name is God Almighty.[t]

Woe to the Complacent

6 Woe to you[a] who are complacent in Zion,
and to you who feel secure on Mount Samaria,
you notable men of the foremost nation,
to whom the people of Israel come![b]
2Go to Calneh[c] and look at it;
go from there to great Hamath,[d]
and then go down to Gath[e] in Philistia.
Are they better off than[f] your two kingdoms?
Is their land larger than yours?
3You put off the evil day
and bring near a reign of terror.[g]
4You lie on beds inlaid with ivory
and lounge on your couches.
You dine on choice lambs
and fattened calves.[h]
5You strum away on your harps[i] like David
and improvise on musical instruments.[j]
6You drink wine[k] by the bowlful
and use the finest lotions,
but you do not grieve[l] over the ruin of Joseph.
7Therefore you will be among the first to go into exile;
your feasting and lounging will end.

The LORD Abhors the Pride of Israel

8The Sovereign LORD has sworn by himself[m]—the LORD God Almighty declares:

"I abhor[n] the pride of Jacob[o]
and detest his fortresses;
I will deliver up[p] the city
and everything in it.[q]"

9If ten[r] men are left in one house, they too will die. 10And if a relative who is
to burn the bodies[s] comes to carry them out of the house and asks anyone still hiding
there, "Is anyone with you?" and he says, "No," then he will say, "Hush![t] We must
not mention the name of the LORD."

11For the LORD has given the command,
and he will smash the great house[u] into pieces
and the small house into bits.[v]

12Do horses run on the rocky crags?
Does one plough there with oxen?

5:27 [t]Am 4:13; Ac 7:42-43*
6:1 [a]Lk 6:24 [b]Isa 32:9-11
6:2 [c]Ge 10:10 [d]2Ki 18:34 [e]2Ch 26:6 [f]Na 3:8
6:3 [g]Isa 56:12; Am 9:10
6:4 [h]Eze 34:2-3; Am 3:12
6:5 [i]Isa 5:12; Am 5:23 [j]1Ch 15:16
6:6 [k]Am 2:8 [l]Eze 9:4
6:8 [m]Ge 22:16; Heb 6:13 [n]Lev 26:30 [o]Ps 47:4 [p]Am 4:2 [q]Dt 32:19
6:9 [r]Am 5:3
6:10 [s]1Sa 31:12 [t]Am 8:3
6:11 [u]Am 3:15 [v]Isa 55:11

5:27 Israel's captivity was indeed beyond Damascus—the people were taken to Assyria. God's punishment was more than defeat; it was complete exile from their homeland.

6:1–6 Amos levelled his attack at those living in complacency and luxury in both Israel and Judah. Great wealth and comfortable life-styles may make people think they are secure, but God is not pleased if we isolate ourselves from others' needs. God wants us to care for others as he cares for us. His kingdom has no place for selfishness or indifference. We must learn to put the needs of others before our wants. Using our wealth to help others is one way to guard against pride and complacency.

6:2 Great cities to the east, north, and west had been destroyed because of their pride. What happened to them would happen to Israel because Israel's sin was just as great as theirs.

6:4 Ivory was an imported luxury, rare and extremely expensive. Even a small amount of ivory symbolised wealth. Something as extravagant as a bed inlaid with ivory shows the gross waste of resources that should have been used to help the poor.

6:8–11 The people had built luxurious homes to flaunt their achievements. While it is not wrong to live in comfortable houses, we must not let them become sources of inflated pride and self-glorification. God gave our homes to us, and they are to be used for service, not just for show.

6:10 Amos gives us a picture of God's fearful judgment: the people hesitate to speak God's name, even during a time of grief, for fear that they will attract his attention and be judged also.

6:12
[w]Hos 10:4
[x]Am 5:7

6:13
[y]Job 8:15;
Isa 28:14-15

6:14
[z]Jer 5:15
[a]1Ki 8:65
[b]Am 3:11

7:1
[a]Am 8:1
[b]Joel 1:4

7:2
[c]Ex 10:15
[d]Isa 37:4
[e]Eze 11:13

7:3
[f]Dt 32:36;
Jer 26:19;
Jnh 3:10
[g]Hos 11:8

7:4
[h]Isa 66:16
[i]Dt 32:22

7:5
[j]ver 1-2;
Joel 2:17

7:6
[k]Jnh 3:10

7:8
[l]Jer 1:11, 13
[m]Isa 28:17;
La 2:8;
Am 8:2
[n]2Ki 21:13
[o]Jer 15:6;
Eze 7:2-9

But you have turned justice into poison[w]
and the fruit of righteousness into bitterness[x]—
13 you who rejoice in the conquest of Lo Debar[a]
and say, "Did we not take Karnaim[b] by our own strength?[y]"
14 For the LORD God Almighty declares,
"I will stir up a nation[z] against you, O house of Israel,
that will oppress you all the way
from Lebo[c] Hamath[a] to the valley of the Arabah.[b]"

3. Visions of judgment

Locusts, Fire and a Plumb Line

7 This is what the Sovereign LORD showed me:[a] He was preparing swarms of
locusts[b] after the king's share had been harvested and just as the second crop
was coming up. 2 When they had stripped the land clean,[c] I cried out, "Sovereign
LORD, forgive! How can Jacob survive?[d] He is so small![e]"
3 So the LORD relented.[f]
"This will not happen," the LORD said.[g]
4 This is what the Sovereign LORD showed me: The Sovereign LORD was calling for
judgment by fire;[h] it dried up the great deep and devoured[i] the land. 5 Then I cried
out, "Sovereign LORD, I beg you, stop! How can Jacob survive? He is so small![j]"
6 So the LORD relented.[k]
"This will not happen either," the Sovereign LORD said.

7 This is what he showed me: the Lord was standing by a wall that had been built
true to plumb, with a plumb-line in his hand. 8 And the LORD asked me, "What do
you see,[l] Amos?[m]"
"A plumb-line,[n]" I replied.
Then the Lord said, "Look, I am setting a plumb-line among my people Israel; I
will spare them no longer.[o]

9 "The high places of Isaac will be destroyed

a 13 *Lo Debar* means *nothing.* b 13 *Karnaim* means *horns*; *horn* here symbolises strength. c 14 Or *from the entrance to*

AMOS' VISIONS

Vision	*Reference*	*Significance*
Swarm of locusts	7:1–3	God was preparing punishment, which he delayed only because of Amos' intervention.
Fire	7:4–6	God was preparing to devour the land, but Amos intervened on behalf of the people.
Wall and plumb-line	7:7–9	God would see if the people were crooked, and, if they were, he would punish them.
Basket of ripe fruit	8:1ff	The people were ripe for punishment; though once beautiful, they were now rotten.
God standing by the altar	9:1ff	Punishment was executed.

Amos had a series of visions concerning God's judgment on Israel. God was planning to judge Israel by sending a swarm of locusts or by sending fire. In spite of Amos' intercession on Israel's behalf, God would still carry out his judgment because Israel persisted in her disobedience.

6:13, 14 Karnaim was a city north-east of Israel, an insignificant border town compared to the nation they were about to face, Assyria. Lebo Hamath was to the north, and the valley of the Arabah to the south. The entire nation would be destroyed by Assyria (2 Kings 17).

7:1ff The following series of visions conveyed God's message to the people using images that were familiar to them – locusts, fire, and a plumb-line.

7:1–6 Twice Amos was shown a vision of Israel's impending punishment, and his immediate response was to pray that God would spare Israel. Prayer is a powerful privilege. Amos' prayers should remind us to pray for our nation.

7:7–9 A plumb-line is a device used to ensure the straightness of a wall. A wall that is not straight will eventually collapse. God wants people to be right with him; he wants the sin that makes us crooked removed immediately. God's word is the plumb-line that helps us be aware of our sin. How do you measure up to God's plumb-line?

and the sanctuaries[p] of Israel will be ruined;
with my sword I will rise against the house of Jeroboam.[q]"

Amos and Amaziah

10Then Amaziah the priest of Bethel[r] sent a message to Jeroboam[s] king of Israel:
"Amos is raising a conspiracy[t] against you in the very heart of Israel. The land cannot
bear all his words.[u] 11For this is what Amos is saying:

" 'Jeroboam will die by the sword,
and Israel will surely go into exile,
away from their native land.' "

12Then Amaziah said to Amos, "Get out, you seer! Go back to the land of Judah.
Earn your bread there and do your prophesying there.[v] 13Don't prophesy any more
at Bethel, because this is the king's sanctuary and the temple of the kingdom.[w]"
14Amos answered Amaziah, "I was neither a prophet[x] nor a prophet's son, but I
was a shepherd, and I also took care of sycamore-fig trees. 15But the LORD took me
from tending the flock[y] and said to me, 'Go, prophesy to my people Israel.'[z] 16Now
then, hear the word of the LORD. You say,

" 'Do not prophesy against[a] Israel,
and stop preaching against the house of Isaac.'

17"Therefore this is what the LORD says:

" 'Your wife will become a prostitute[b] in the city,
and your sons and daughters will fall by the sword.
Your land will be measured and divided up,
and you yourself will die in a pagan[a] country.
And Israel will certainly go into exile,
away from their native land.[c]' "

A Basket of Ripe Fruit

8 This is what the Sovereign LORD showed me: a basket of ripe fruit. 2"What do
you see,[a] Amos?[b]" he asked.
"A basket of ripe fruit," I answered.
Then the LORD said to me, "The time is ripe for my people Israel; I will spare them
no longer.[c]
3"In that day," declares the Sovereign LORD, "the songs in the temple will turn to
wailing.[a][d] Many, many bodies—flung everywhere! Silence![e]"

4Hear this, you who trample the needy
and do away with the poor[f] of the land,[g]

7:9 [p]Lev 26:31 [q]2Ki 15:9; Isa 63:18; Hos 10:8
7:10 [r]1Ki 12:32 [s]2Ki 14:23 [t]Jer 38:4 [u]Jer 26:8-11
7:12 [v]Mt 8:34
7:13 [w]Am 2:12; Ac 4:18
7:14 [x]2Ki 2:5; 4:38
7:15 [y]2Sa 7:8 [z]Jer 7:1-2; Eze 2:3-4
7:16 [a]Eze 20:46; Mic 2:6
7:17 [b]Hos 4:13 [c]2Ki 17:6; Eze 4:13; Hos 9:3
8:2 [a]Jer 24:3 [b]Am 7:8 [c]Eze 7:2-9
8:3 [d]Am 5:16 [e]Am 5:23; 6:10
8:4 [f]Pr 30:14 [g]Ps 14:4; Am 2:7

[a] *17* Hebrew *an unclean* [a] *3* Or *"the temple singers will wail*

7:10 Prophets like Amos were often seen as traitors and conspirators because they spoke out against the king and his advisers, questioning their authority and exposing their sin. The kings often saw the prophets as enemies rather than as God's spokesmen who were really trying to help them and the nation.

7:10ff Amaziah was the chief priest in Bethel, representing Israel's official religion. He was not concerned about hearing God's message; he was only worried about his own position. Maintaining his position was more important than listening to the truth. Don't let your desire for prestige, authority, or money keep you tied to a job or position you should leave. Don't let anything come between you and obeying God.

7:14, 15 Without any special preparation, education, or upbringing, Amos obeyed God's call to "Go, prophesy to my people Israel." Obedience is the test of a faithful servant of God. Are you obeying God's call to you?

8:5, 6 These merchants were keeping the religious festivals, but not in spirit. They couldn't wait for the holy days and Sabbaths to be over so they could go back to making money. Their real interest was in enriching themselves, even if that meant cheating (short-changing the quantity while boosting the price, or even selling chaff as wheat). Do you take a day to rest and worship God at least once a week, or is making money more important to you than anything else? When you give time to God, is your heart in your worship? Or is your religion only a front for unethical practices?

8:5
[h] 2Ki 4:23; Ne 13:15-16; Hos 12:7; Mic 6:10-11

8:6
[i] Am 2:6

8:7
[j] Am 6:8
[k] Hos 8:13

8:8
[l] Hos 4:3
[m] Ps 18:7; Jer 46:8; Am 9:5

8:9
[n] Job 5:14; Isa 59:9-10; Jer 15:9; Am 5:8; Mic 3:6

8:10
[o] Jer 48:37
[p] Jer 6:26; Zec 12:10
[q] Eze 7:18

8:11
[r] 1Sa 3:1; 2Ch 15:3; Eze 7:26

8:12
[s] Eze 20:3, 31

8:13
[t] Isa 41:17; Hos 2:3

8:14
[u] 1Ki 12:29
[v] Am 5:5
[w] Am 5:2

5saying,
"When will the New Moon be over
that we may sell grain,
and the Sabbath be ended
that we may market wheat?"—
skimping the measure,
boosting the price
and cheating with dishonest scales,[h]
6buying the poor with silver
and the needy for a pair of sandals,
selling even the sweepings with the wheat.[i]

7The LORD has sworn by the Pride of Jacob:[j] "I will never forget[k] anything they have done.

8"Will not the land tremble[l] for this,
and all who live in it mourn?
The whole land will rise like the Nile;
it will be stirred up and then sink
like the river of Egypt.[m]

9"In that day," declares the Sovereign LORD,

"I will make the sun go down at noon
and darken the earth in broad daylight.[n]
10I will turn your religious feasts into mourning
and all your singing into weeping.
I will make all of you wear sackcloth[o]
and shave your heads.
I will make that time like mourning for an only son[p]
and the end of it like a bitter day.[q]

11"The days are coming," declares the Sovereign LORD,
"when I will send a famine through the land—
not a famine of food or a thirst for water,
but a famine of hearing the words of the LORD.[r]
12Men will stagger from sea to sea
and wander from north to east,
searching for the word of the LORD,
but they will not find it.[s]

13"In that day

"the lovely young women and strong young men
will faint because of thirst.[t]
14They who swear by the shame[b] of Samaria,
or say, 'As surely as your god lives, O Dan',[u]
or, 'As surely as the god[c] of Beersheba[v] lives'—
they will fall,
never to rise again.[w]"

b *14* Or *by Ashima*; or *by the idol* **c** *14* Or *power*

8:11–13 The people had no appetite for God's word when prophets like Amos brought it. Because of their apathy, God said he would take away even the opportunity to hear his word. We have God's word, the Bible. But many still look everywhere for answers to life's problems *except* in Scripture. You can help them by directing them to the Bible, showing them the parts that speak to their special needs and questions. God's word is available to us. Let us help people know it before a time comes when they cannot find it.

Israel to Be Destroyed

9 I saw the Lord standing by the altar, and he said:
"Strike the tops of the pillars
so that the thresholds shake.
Bring them down on the heads[a] of all the people;
those who are left I will kill with the sword.
Not one will get away,
none will escape.
2Though they dig down to the depths of the grave,[a][b]
from there my hand will take them.
Though they climb up to the heavens,[c]
from there I will bring them down.[d]
3Though they hide themselves on the top of Carmel,[e]
there I will hunt them down and seize them.[f]
Though they hide from me at the bottom of the sea,
there I will command the serpent to bite them.[g]
4Though they are driven into exile by their enemies,
there I will command the sword[h] to slay them.
I will fix my eyes upon them
for evil[i] and not for good.[j]"[k]

5The Lord, the LORD Almighty,
he who touches the earth and it melts,[l]
and all who live in it mourn—
the whole land rises like the Nile,
then sinks like the river of Egypt[m]—
6he who builds his lofty palace[b] in the heavens
and sets its foundation[c] on the earth,
who calls for the waters of the sea
and pours them out over the face of the land—
the LORD is his name.[n]

7"Are not you Israelites
the same to me as the Cushites?"[d][o]
declares the LORD.
"Did I not bring Israel up from Egypt,
the Philistines from Caphtor[e][p]
and the Arameans from Kir?[q]

8"Surely the eyes of the Sovereign LORD

[a] 2 Hebrew *to Sheol* [b] 6 The meaning of the Hebrew for this phrase is uncertain. [c] 6 The meaning of the Hebrew for this word is uncertain. [d] 7 That is, people from the upper Nile region [e] 7 That is, Crete

9:1 [a]Ps 68:21
9:2 [b]Ps 139:8 [c]Jer 51:53 [d]Ob 1:4
9:3 [e]Am 1:2 [f]Ps 139:8-10 [g]Jer 16:16-17
9:4 [h]Lev 26:33; Eze 5:12 [i]Jer 21:10 [j]Jer 39:16 [k]Jer 44:11
9:5 [l]Ps 46:2; Mic 1:4 [m]Am 8:8
9:6 [n]Ps 104:1-3, 5-6, 13; Am 5:8
9:7 [o]Isa 20:4; 43:3 [p]Dt 2:23; Jer 47:4 [q]2Ki 16:9; Isa 22:6; Am 1:5; 2:10

9:1 Judgment would begin at the altar, the centre of the nation's life, the place where the people expected protection and blessing. This judgment would cover all 12 tribes. Commentators disagree concerning this altar—some think it was the altar at Bethel; more likely it was the altar in the temple in Jerusalem. God would destroy their base of security in order to bring them to himself. But in 9:11 he promises to restore his renewed people and their broken world.

9:2–4 The grave was the place of the dead, and Carmel is a mountain. Both were symbols of inaccessibility. No one can escape God's judgment. This was good news for the faithful but bad news for the unfaithful. Whether we go to the mountain tops or the bottom of the sea, God will find us and judge us for our deeds. Amos pictured the judgment of the wicked as a monster of the sea, relentlessly pursuing the condemned. For God's faithful followers, however, the judgment brings a new earth of peace and prosperity. Does God's judgment sound like good news or bad news to you?

9:7 Cush, south of Egypt, was a remote and exotic land to the Israelites. Caphtor is the island of Crete, where the Philistines lived as they migrated to Palestine. God would judge Israel no differently than he judges foreign nations. He is not the God of Israel only; he is God of the universe, and he controls all nations.

9:8 Amos assured the Israelites that God would not "totally destroy" Israel—in other words, the punishment would not be permanent or total. God wants to redeem, not punish. But when punishment is necessary, he doesn't withhold it. Like a loving father, God disciplines those he loves in order to correct them. If God disciplines you, accept it as a sign of his love.

9:8, 9 Although Assyria would destroy Israel and take the people into exile, some would be preserved. This exile had been predicted hundreds of years earlier (Deuteronomy 28:63–68). Although the nation would be purified through this invasion and captivity, not one true believer would be eternally lost. Our system of justice is not always perfect, but God is. Sinners will not get away, and the faithful will not be forgotten. True believers will not be lost.

9:8 [r]Jer 44:27
9:9 [s]Lk 22:31 [t]Isa 30:28
9:10 [u]Am 6:3
9:11 [v]Ps 80:12
9:12 [w]Nu 24:18 [x]Isa 43:7 [y]Ac 15:16-17*
9:13 [z]Lev 26:5 [a]Joel 3:18
9:14 [b]Isa 61:4 [c]Jer 30:18; 31:28; Eze 28:25-26
9:15 [d]Isa 60:21 [e]Jer 24:6; Eze 34:25-28; 37:12, 25

are on the sinful kingdom.
I will destroy it
from the face of the earth –
yet I will not totally destroy
the house of Jacob,"
declares the LORD.[r]

9"For I will give the command,
and I will shake the house of Israel
among all the nations
as grain[s] is shaken in a sieve,[t]
and not a pebble will reach the ground.
10All the sinners among my people
will die by the sword,
all those who say,
'Disaster will not overtake or meet us.'[u]

Israel's Restoration

11"In that day I will restore
David's fallen tent.
I will repair its broken places,
restore its ruins,
and build it as it used to be,[v]
12so that they may possess the remnant of Edom[w]
and all the nations that bear my name,"[f][x]
declares the LORD, who will do these things.[y]

13"The days are coming," declares the LORD,

"when the reaper will be overtaken by the ploughman[z]
and the planter by the one treading grapes.
New wine will drip from the mountains
and flow from all the hills.[a]
14I will bring back my exiled[g] people Israel;
they will rebuild the ruined cities[b] and live in them.
They will plant vineyards and drink their wine;
they will make gardens and eat their fruit.[c]
15I will plant[d] Israel in their own land,
never again to be uprooted
from the land I have given them,"
says the LORD your God.[e]

f 12 Hebrew; Septuagint *so that the remnant of men / and all the nations that bear my name may seek* ⌞*the Lord*⌟
g 14 Or *will restore the fortunes of my*

9:11, 12 In the punishment, the house of David was reduced to a "fallen tent". God's covenant with David stated that one of David's descendants would always sit on his throne (2 Samuel 7:12–16). The exile made this promise seem impossible. But "in that day" God would raise up and restore the kingdom to its promised glory. This was a promise to both Israel and Judah, not to be fulfilled by an earthly, political ruler, but by the Messiah, who would renew the spiritual kingdom and rule for ever.

James quoted these verses (Acts 15:16, 17), finding the promise fulfilled in Christ's resurrection and in the presence of both Jews and Gentiles in the church. "Possess the remnant of Edom" envisions the Messianic kingdom, which will be universal and include Gentiles. When God brings in the Gentiles, he is restoring the ruins. After the Gentiles are called together, God will renew and restore the fortunes of the new Israel. All the land that was once under David's rule will again be part of God's nation.

9:13 This verse describes a time of such an abundance of crops that the people won't be able to harvest them all.

9:13–15 The Jews of Amos's day had lost sight of God's care and love for them. The rich were carefree and comfortable, refusing to help others in need. They observed their religious rituals in hopes of appeasing God, but they did not truly love him. Amos announced God's warnings of destruction for their evil ways.

We must not assume that going to church and being good is enough. God expects our belief in him to penetrate all areas of our conduct and to extend to all people and circumstances. We should let Amos' words inspire us to live faithfully according to God's desires.

OBADIAH

VITAL STATISTICS

PURPOSE:
To show that God judges those who have harmed his people

AUTHOR:
Obadiah. Very little is known about this man, whose name means "servant (or worshipper) of the LORD"

TO WHOM WRITTEN:
The Edomites, the Jews in Judah, and God's people everywhere

DATE WRITTEN:
Possibly during the reign of Jehoram in Judah, 853–841 B.C., or possibly during Jeremiah's ministry, 627-586 B.C.

SETTING:
Historically, Edom had constantly harassed the Jews. Prior to the time this book was written, they had participated in attacks against Judah. Given the dates above, this prophecy came after the division of Israel into the northern and southern kingdoms and before the conquering of Judah by Nebuchadnezzar in 586 B.C.

KEY VERSE:
"The day of the LORD is near for all nations. As you have done, it will be done to you; your deeds will return upon your own head" (verse 15).

KEY PEOPLE:
The Edomites

KEY PLACES:
Edom, Jerusalem

SPECIAL FEATURES:
The book of Obadiah uses vigorous poetic language and is written in the form of a dirge of doom.

WRINKLED face, tiny hands with fingernail chips, rolls of new skin, and miniature eyes, nose, and mouth—she's a newborn. After months of formation, she burst forth into the world and into her family. "She has her mother's eyes", "I can certainly tell who her parents are", "Now that's your nose" . . . relatives and friends gaze into the little face and see her mum and dad. Mother and Father rejoice in their daughter, a miracle, a new member of the family. As loving parents, they will protect, nurture, feed, guide, and discipline her. This is their duty and joy.

God too has children—men and women whom he has chosen as his very own. There have always been individuals marked as his, but with Abraham he promised to build a nation. Israel was to be God's country, and her people, the Jews, his very own sons and daughters. Through the following centuries, there was discipline and punishment, but always love and mercy. God, the eternal Father, protected and cared for his children.

Obadiah, the shortest book in the Old Testament, is a dramatic example of God's response to anyone who would harm his children. Edom was a mountainous nation, occupying the region southeast of the Dead Sea including Petra, the spectacular city discovered by archaeologists a few decades ago. As descendants of Esau (Genesis 25:19—27:45), the Edomites were blood relatives of Israel and, like their father, they were rugged, fierce, and proud warriors with a seemingly invincible mountain home. Of all people, they should have rushed to the aid of their northern brothers. Instead, however, they gloated over Israel's problems, captured and delivered fugitives to the enemy, and even looted Israel's countryside.

Obadiah gave God's message to Edom. Because of their indifference to and defiance of God, their cowardice and pride, and their treachery towards their brothers in Judah, they stood condemned and would be destroyed. The book begins with the announcement that disaster was coming to Edom (verses 1–9). Despite their "impregnable" cliffs and mountains, they would not be able to escape God's judgment. Obadiah then gave the reasons for their destruction (verses 10–14)—their blatant arrogance towards God and their persecution of God's children. This concise prophecy ends with a description of the "day of the LORD", when judgment will fall on all who have harmed God's people (verses 15–21).

Today, God's holy nation is his church—all who have trusted Christ for their salvation and have given their lives to him. These men and women are God's born again and adopted children. As you read Obadiah, catch a glimpse of what it means to be God's child, under his love and protection. See how the heavenly Father responds to all who would attack those whom he loves.

THE BLUEPRINT

1. Edom's destruction (1–16)
2. Israel's restoration (17–21)

The book of Obadiah shows the outcome of the ancient feud between Edom and Israel. Edom was proud of her high position, but God would bring her down. Those who are high and powerful today should not be overconfident in themselves, whether they are a nation, a corporation, a church, or a family. Just as Edom was destroyed for her pride, so will anyone who lives in defiance of God.

MEGATHEMES

THEME	EXPLANATION	IMPORTANCE
Justice	Obadiah predicted that God would destroy Edom as punishment for standing by when Babylon invaded Judah. Because of their treachery, Edom's land would be given to Judah in the day when God rights the wrongs against his people.	God will judge and fiercely punish all who harm his people. We can be confident in God's final victory. He is our champion, and we can trust him to bring about true justice.
Pride	Because of their seemingly invincible rock fortress, the Edomites were proud and self-confident. But God humbled them and their nation disappeared from the face of the earth.	All those who defy God will meet their doom as Edom did. Any nation who trusts in its power, wealth, technology, or wisdom more than in God will be brought low. All who are proud will one day be shocked to discover that no-one is exempt from God's justice.

1:1
[a] Isa 63:1-6; Jer 49:7-22; Eze 25:12-14; Am 1:11-12
[b] Isa 18:2
[c] Jer 6:4-5

1. Edom's destruction

1 The vision of Obadiah.

This is what the Sovereign LORD says about Edom[a] —

We have heard a message from the LORD:
An envoy[b] was sent to the nations to say,
"Rise, and let us go against her for battle"[c] —

2 "See, I will make you small among the nations;
you will be utterly despised.

1 Obadiah was a prophet from Judah who told of God's judgment against the nation of Edom. Two commonly accepted dates for this prophecy are (1) between 853 and 841 B.C., when King Jehoram and Jerusalem were attacked by a Philistine/Arab coalition (2 Chronicles 21:16ff), or (2) 586 B.C., when Jerusalem was completely destroyed by the Babylonians (2 Kings 25; 2 Chronicles 36). Edom had rejoiced over the misfortunes of both Israel and Judah, and yet the Edomites and Jews descended from two brothers – Esau and Jacob (Genesis 25:19–26). But just as these two brothers were constantly fighting, so were Israel and Edom. God pronounced judgment on Edom for their callous and malicious actions towards his people.

3The pride[d] of your heart has deceived you,
you who live in the clefts of the rocks[a]
and make your home on the heights,
you who say to yourself,
'Who can bring me down to the ground?'[e]
4Though you soar like the eagle
and make your nest[f] among the stars,
from there I will bring you down,"[g]
declares the LORD.[h]

5"If thieves came to you,
if robbers in the night—
Oh, what a disaster awaits you—
would they not steal only as much as they wanted?
If grape pickers came to you,
would they not leave a few grapes?[i]
6But how Esau will be ransacked,
his hidden treasures pillaged!
7All your allies[j] will force you to the border;
your friends will deceive and overpower you;
those who eat your bread[k] will set a trap for you,[b]
but you will not detect it.

8"In that day," declares the LORD,
"will I not destroy[l] the wise men of Edom,

1:3 [d]Isa 16:6 [e]Isa 14:13-15; Rev 18:7
1:4 [f]Hab 2:9 [g]Isa 14:13 [h]Job 20:6
1:5 [i]Dt 24:21
1:7 [j]Jer 30:14 [k]Ps 41:9
1:8 [l]Job 5:12; Isa 29:14

[a] *3* Or *of Sela* [b] *7* The meaning of the Hebrew for this clause is uncertain.

HISTORY OF THE CONFLICT BETWEEN ISRAEL AND EDOM

The nation of Israel descended from Jacob; the nation of Edom descended from Esau	Genesis 25:23
Jacob and Esau struggled in their mother's womb	Genesis 25:19–26
Esau sold his birthright and blessing to Jacob	Genesis 25:29–34
Edom refused to let the Israelites pass through its land	Numbers 20:14–22
Israel's kings had constant conflict with Edom	
• Saul	1 Samuel 14:47
• David	2 Samuel 8:13, 14
• Solomon	1 Kings 11:14–22
• Jehoram	2 Kings 8:20–22; 2 Chronicles 21:8ff
• Ahaz	2 Chronicles 28:16
Edom urged Babylon to destroy Jerusalem	Psalm 137:7

3 Edom was Judah's southern neighbour, sharing a common boundary. But neighbours are not always friends, and Edom liked nothing about Judah. Edom's capital at this time was Sela (perhaps the later city of Petra), a city considered impregnable because it was cut into rock cliffs and set in a canyon that could be entered only through a narrow gap. What Edom perceived as its strengths would be its downfall: (1) safety in their city (vv. 3, 4)—God would send them plummeting from the heights; (2) pride in their self-sufficiency (v. 4)—God would humble them; (3) wealth (vv. 5, 6)—thieves would steal all they had; (4) allies (v. 7)—God would cause them to turn against Edom; (5) wisdom (vv. 8, 9)—the wise would be destroyed.

3 The Edomites felt secure, and they were proud of their self-sufficiency. But they were fooling themselves because there is no lasting security apart from God. Is your security in objects or people? Ask yourself how much lasting security they really offer. Possessions and people can disappear in a moment, but God does not change. Only he can supply true security.

4 The Edomites were proud of their city carved right into the rock. Today Sela, or Petra, is considered one of the marvels of the ancient world, but only as a tourist attraction. The Bible warns that pride is the surest route to self-destruction (Proverbs 16:18). Just as Petra and Edom fell, so will proud people fall. A humble person is more secure than a proud person because humility gives a more accurate perspective of oneself and the world.

4–9 Esau was named here (v. 6) because he was the father of the nation of Edom. God did not pronounce these harsh judgments against Edom out of vengeance but in order to bring about justice. God is morally perfect and demands complete justice and fairness. The Edomites were simply getting what they deserved. Because they murdered, they would be murdered. Because they robbed, they would be robbed. Because they took advantage of others, they would be used. Don't talk yourself into sin, thinking that "nobody will know" or "I won't get caught". God knows all our sins, and he will be just.

8 Edom was noted for its wise men. There is a difference, however, between human wisdom and God's wisdom. The Edomites may have been wise in the ways of the world, but they were foolish because they ignored and even mocked God.

1:9
[m]Ge 36:11, 34

1:10
[n]Joel 3:19
[o]Ps 137:7; Am 1:11-12
[p]Eze 35:9

1:11
[q]Na 3:10

1:12
[r]Eze 35:15
[s]Pr 17:5
[t]Mic 4:11

1:13
[u]Eze 35:5

1:15
[v]Eze 30:3
[w]Jer 50:29; Hab 2:8

1:16
[x]Jer 25:15; 49:12

men of understanding in the mountains of Esau?
9 Your warriors, O Teman,[m] will be terrified,
and everyone in Esau's mountains
will be cut down in the slaughter.
10 Because of the violence[n] against your brother Jacob,[o]
you will be covered with shame;
you will be destroyed for ever.[p]
11 On the day you stood aloof
while strangers carried off his wealth
and foreigners entered his gates
and cast lots[q] for Jerusalem,
you were like one of them.
12 You should not look down on your brother
in the day of his misfortune,
nor rejoice[r] over the people of Judah
in the day of their destruction,[s]
nor boast so much
in the day of their trouble.[t]
13 You should not march through the gates of my people
in the day of their disaster,
nor look down on them in their calamity[u]
in the day of their disaster,
nor seize their wealth
in the day of their disaster.
14 You should not wait at the crossroads
to cut down their fugitives,
nor hand over their survivors
in the day of their trouble.

15 "The day of the LORD is near[v]
for all nations.
As you have done, it will be done to you;
your deeds[w] will return upon your own head.
16 Just as you drank on my holy hill,
so all the nations will drink[x] continually;
they will drink and drink
and be as if they had never been.

---

9 Eliphaz, one of Job's three friends (Job 2:11), was from Teman, about five miles east of Petra. Teman was named after Esau's grandson (Genesis 36:11).

10, 11 The Israelites had descended from Jacob, and the Edomites, from his brother, Esau (Genesis 25:19–26). Instead of helping Israel and Judah when they were in need, Edom allowed them to be destroyed and even plundered what was left behind. Edom, therefore, acted like a stranger, and it would be punished. Anyone who does not help God's people is God's enemy. If you have withheld your help from someone in a time of need, this is sin (James 4:17). Sin includes not only what we do, but also what we refuse to do. Don't ignore or refuse to help those in need.

12 Edom was glad to see Judah in trouble. Their hatred made them want the nation destroyed. For their wrong attitudes and actions, God wiped out Edom. How often do you find yourself rejoicing at the misfortunes of others? Because God alone is the judge, we must never be happy about others' misfortunes, even if we think they deserve them (see Proverbs 24:17).

12–14 Of all Israel and Judah's neighbours, Edom was the only one not promised any mercy from God. This was because they looted Jerusalem and rejoiced at the misfortunes of Israel and Judah. They betrayed their blood brothers in times of crisis and aided their brothers' enemies. (See also Psalm 137:7; Jeremiah 49:7–22; Ezekiel 25:12–14; Amos 1:11, 12.)

15 Why will God's judgment fall on all the nations? Edom was not the only nation to rejoice at Judah's fall. All nations and individuals will be judged for the way they have treated God's people. Some nations today treat God's people favourably, while others are hostile toward them. God will judge all people according to the way they treat others, especially believers (Revelation 20:12, 13). Jesus talked about this in Matthew 25:31–46.

2. Israel's restoration

17 But on Mount Zion will be deliverance;[y]
it will be holy,[z]
and the house of Jacob
will possess its inheritance.
18 The house of Jacob will be a fire
and the house of Joseph a flame;
the house of Esau will be stubble,
and they will set it on fire and consume[a] it.
There will be no survivors
from the house of Esau."
The LORD has spoken.

19 People from the Negev will occupy
the mountains of Esau,
and people from the foothills will possess
the land of the Philistines.[b]
They will occupy the fields of Ephraim and Samaria,[c]
and Benjamin will possess Gilead.
20 This company of Israelite exiles who are in Canaan
will possess ⌞the land⌟ as far as Zarephath;[d]
the exiles from Jerusalem who are in Sepharad
will possess the towns of the Negev.[e]
21 Deliverers will go up on[c] Mount Zion
to govern the mountains of Esau.
And the kingdom will be the LORD's.[f]

c 21 Or *from*

1:17 [y]Am 9:11-15 [z]Isa 4:3
1:18 [a]Zec 12:6
1:19 [b]Isa 11:14 [c]Jer 31:5
1:20 [d]1Ki 17:9-10 [e]Jer 33:13
1:21 [f]Ps 22:28; Zec 14:9, 16; Rev 11:15

Climate of the times	Edom was a constant thorn in Judah's side. The Edomites often participated in attacks initiated by other enemies.
Main message	God will judge Edom for its evil actions towards God's people.
Importance of message	Just as Edom was destroyed and disappeared as a nation, so God will destroy proud and wicked people.
Contemporary prophets	Elijah (875–848) Micaiah (865–853) Jehu (855–840?)

OBADIAH served as a prophet to Judah possibly around 853 B.C.

17–21 The Edomites were routed by Judas Maccabeus in 164 B.C. The nation no longer existed by the first century A.D. At the time of Obadiah's prophecy, Edom may have seemed more likely to survive than Judah. Yet Edom has vanished, and Judah still exists. This demonstrates the absolute certainty of God's word and of the punishment awaiting all who have mistreated God's people.

19 The Negev was the southern part of Judah, a dry, hot region. The foothills were in the western part of Judah.

20 The boundaries of the kingdom would be extended to include the Canaanites (Phoenicians) as far south as Zarephath, located between Tyre and Sidon on the Mediterranean coast. Sepharad was most likely the city of Sardis.

21 Obadiah brought God's message of judgment on Edom. God was displeased with both their inward and their outward rebellion. People today are much the same as people in Obadiah's time, filled with arrogance, envy, and dishonesty. We may wonder where it will all end. Regardless of sin's effects, however, God is in control. Don't despair or give up hope. Know that when all is said and done, the Lord will still be King, and the confidence you place in him will not be in vain.

21 Edom is an example to all the nations that are hostile to God. Nothing can break God's promise to protect his people from complete destruction. In the book of Obadiah we see four aspects of God's message of judgment: (1) evil will certainly be punished; (2) those faithful to God have hope for a new future; (3) God is sovereign in human history; (4) God's ultimate purpose is to establish his eternal kingdom. The Edomites had been cruel to God's people. They were arrogant and proud, and they took advantage of others' misfortunes. Any nation that mistreats people who obey God will be punished, regardless of how invincible they appear. Similarly we, as individuals, cannot allow ourselves to feel so comfortable with our wealth or security that we fail to help God's people. This is sin. And because God is just, sin will be punished.

JONAH

Jeroboam II becomes king; Jonah becomes a prophet 793 B.C.	*Uzziah (Azariah) becomes king of Judah 792*	*Jonah preaches to Nineveh 785?*	*Shalmaneser IV becomes king of Assyria 783*	*Ashur-dan III becomes king of Assyria 772*	*Amos becomes a prophet 760*	*Ashur-Nirari V becomes king of Assyria 754*	*Jonah's ministry ends 753*	*Israel falls to Assyria 722*

SIN runs rampant in society—daily headlines and overflowing prisons bear dramatic witness to that fact. With child abuse, pornography, serial killings, terrorism, anarchy, and ruthless dictatorships, the world seems to be filled to overflowing with violence, hatred, and corruption. Reading, hearing, and perhaps even experiencing these tragedies, we begin to understand the necessity of God's judgment. We may even find ourselves wishing for vengeance by any means upon the violent perpetrators. Surely they are beyond redemption! But suppose that in the midst of such thoughts, God told you to take the gospel to the worst of the offenders—how would you respond?

Jonah was given such a task. Assyria—a great but evil empire—was Israel's most dreaded enemy. The Assyrians flaunted their power before God and the world through numerous acts of heartless cruelty. So when Jonah heard God tell him to go to Assyria and call the people to repentance, he ran in the opposite direction.

The book of Jonah tells the story of this prophet's flight and how God stopped him and turned him around. But it is much more than a story of a man and a great fish—Jonah's story is a profound illustration of God's mercy and grace. No-one deserved God's favour less than the people of Nineveh, Assyria's capital. Jonah knew this. But he knew that God would forgive and bless them if they would turn from their sin and worship him. Jonah also knew the power of God's message, that even through his own weak preaching, they would respond and be spared God's judgment. But Jonah hated the Assyrians, and he wanted vengeance, not mercy. So he ran. Eventually, Jonah obeyed and preached in the streets of Nineveh, and the people repented and were delivered from judgment. Then Jonah sulked and complained to God, "I knew that you are a gracious and compassionate God, slow to anger and abounding in love, a God who relents from sending calamity" (4:2). In the end, God confronted Jonah about his self-centred values and lack of compassion, saying, "But Nineveh has more than a hundred and twenty thousand people who cannot tell their right hand from their left, and many cattle as well. Should I not be concerned about that great city?" (4:11).

As you read Jonah, see the full picture of God's love and compassion and realise that no-one is beyond redemption. The gospel is for all who will repent and believe. Begin to pray for those who seem to be furthest from the kingdom, and look for ways to tell them about God. Learn from the story of this reluctant prophet and determine to obey God, doing whatever he asks and going wherever he leads.

VITAL STATISTICS

PURPOSE:
To show the extent of God's grace—the message of salvation is for *all* people

AUTHOR:
Jonah son of Amittai

TO WHOM WRITTEN:
Israel and God's people everywhere

DATE WRITTEN:
Approximately 785–760 B.C.

SETTING:
Jonah preceded Amos and ministered under Jeroboam II, Israel's most powerful king (793–753 B.C.; see 2 Kings 14:23–25). Assyria was Israel's great enemy, and Israel was conquered by them in 722 B.C. Nineveh's repentance must have been short-lived, for it was destroyed in 612 B.C.

KEY VERSE:
"But Nineveh has more than a hundred and twenty thousand people who cannot tell their right hand from their left, and many cattle as well. Should I not be concerned about that great city?" (4:11).

KEY PEOPLE:
Jonah, the ship's captain and crew

KEY PLACES:
Joppa, Nineveh

SPECIAL FEATURES:
This book is different from the other prophetic books because it tells the story of the prophet and does not centre on his prophecies. In fact, only one verse summarises his message to the people of Nineveh (3:4). Jonah is an historical narrative. It is also mentioned by Jesus as a picture of his death and resurrection (Matthew 12:38–42).

THE BLUEPRINT

1. Jonah forsakes his mission (1:1—2:10)
2. Jonah fulfils his mission (3:1—4:11)

Jonah was a reluctant prophet given a mission he found distasteful. He chose to run away from God rather than obey him. Like Jonah, we may have to do things in life that we don't want to do. Sometimes we find ourselves wanting to turn and run. But it is better to obey God than to defy him or run away. Often, in spite of our defiance, God in his mercy will give us another chance to serve him when we return to him.

MEGATHEMES

THEME	EXPLANATION	IMPORTANCE
God's Sovereignty	Although the prophet Jonah tried to run away from God, God was in control. By controlling the stormy seas and a great fish, God displayed his absolute, yet loving guidance.	Rather than running from God, trust him with your past, present, and future. Saying no to God quickly leads to disaster. Saying yes brings new understanding of God and his purpose in the world.
God's Message to all the World	God had given Jonah a purpose—to preach to the great Assyrian city of Nineveh. Jonah hated Nineveh, and so he responded with anger and indifference. Jonah had yet to learn that God loves all people. Through Jonah, God reminded Israel of their missionary purpose.	We must not limit our focus to our own people. God wants his people to proclaim his love in words and actions to the whole world. He wants us to be his missionaries wherever we are, wherever he sends us.
Repentance	When the reluctant preacher went to Nineveh, there was a great response. The people repented and turned to God. This was a powerful rebuke to Israel, who thought themselves better and yet refused to respond to God's message. God will forgive all those who turn from their sin.	God doesn't honour sham or pretence. He wants the sincere devotion of each person. It is not enough to share the privileges of Christianity; we must ask God to forgive us and to remove our sin. Refusing to repent is the same as loving our sin.
God's Compassion	God's message of love and forgiveness was not for the Jews alone. God loves all the people of the world. The Assyrians didn't deserve it, but God spared them when they repented. In his mercy, God did not reject Jonah for aborting his mission. God has great love, patience, and forgiveness.	God loves each of us, even when we fail him. But he also loves other people, including those not of our group, background, race, or denomination. When we accept his love, we must also learn to accept all those whom he loves. We will find it much easier to love others when we love God.

1. Jonah forsakes his mission

Jonah Flees From the LORD

1 The word of the LORD came to Jonah[a] son of Amittai:[b] 2"Go to the great city
of Nineveh[c] and preach against it, because its wickedness has come up before
me."

1:1
[a]Mt 12:39-41
[b]2Ki 14:25

1:2
[c]Ge 10:11

1:1, 2 Jonah is mentioned in 2 Kings 14:25. He prophesied during the reign of Jeroboam II, the king of Israel from 793–753 B.C. He may have been a member of the company of prophets mentioned in connection with Elisha's ministry (2 Kings 2:3).

God told Jonah to preach to Nineveh, the most important city in Assyria, the rising world power of Jonah's day. Within 50 years, Nineveh would become the capital of the vast Assyrian empire. Jonah doesn't say much about Nineveh's wickedness, but the prophet Nahum gives us more insight. Nahum says that Nineveh was guilty of (1) evil plots against God (Nahum 1:9), (2) exploitation of the helpless (Nahum 2:12), (3) cruelty in war (Nahum 2:12, 13), (4) idolatry, prostitution, and witchcraft (Nahum 3:4). God told

1:3
d Ps 139:7
e Jos 19:46; Ac 9:36, 43

3But Jonah ran[d] away from the LORD and headed for Tarshish. He went down to
Joppa,[e] where he found a ship bound for that port. After paying the fare, he went
aboard and sailed for Tarshish to flee from the LORD.
4Then the LORD sent a great wind on the sea, and such a violent storm arose that

JONAH served as a prophet to Israel and Assyria from 793–753 B.C.

Climate of the times	Nineveh was the most important city in Assyria and would soon become the capital of the huge Assyrian empire. But Nineveh was also a very wicked city.
Main message	Jonah, who hated the powerful and wicked Assyrians, was called by God to warn the Assyrians that they would receive judgment if they did not repent.
Importance of message	Jonah didn't want to go to Nineveh, so he tried to run from God. But God has ways of teaching us to obey and follow him. When Jonah preached, the city repented and God withheld his judgment. Even the most wicked will be saved if they truly repent of their sins and turn to God.
Contemporary prophets	Joel (853–796?) Amos (760–750)

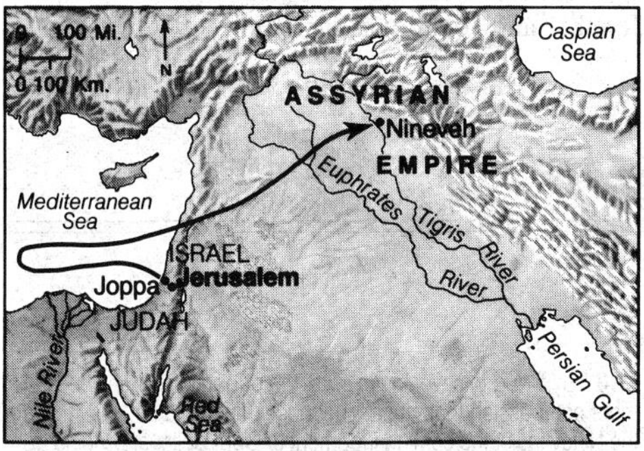

JONAH'S ROUNDABOUT JOURNEY God told Jonah to go to Nineveh, the capital of the Assyrian empire. Many of Jonah's countrymen had experienced the atrocities of these fierce people. The last place Jonah wanted to go on a missionary trip was to Nineveh! So he went in the opposite direction. He boarded a ship in Joppa that was headed for Tarshish. But Jonah could not run from God.

Jonah to go to Nineveh, about 500 miles north-east of Israel, to warn of judgment and to declare that the people could receive mercy and forgiveness if they repented.

1:3 Nineveh was a powerful and wicked city. Jonah had grown up hating the Assyrians and fearing their atrocities. His hatred was so strong that he didn't want them to receive God's mercy. Jonah was actually afraid the people would repent (4:2, 3). Jonah's attitude is representative of Israel's reluctance to share God's love and mercy with others, even though this was their God-given mission (Genesis 12:3). They, like Jonah, did not want non-Jews (Gentiles) to obtain God's favour.

1:3 Jonah knew that God had a specific job for him, but he didn't want to do it. Tarshish could be one of any number of Phoenicia's western ports. Nineveh was toward the east. Jonah decided to go as far west as he could. When God gives us directions through his word, sometimes we run in fear or in stubbornness, claiming that God is asking too much. It may have been fear, or anger at the wideness of God's mercy, that made Jonah run. But running got him into worse trouble. In the end, Jonah understood that it is best to do what God asks in the first place. But by then he had paid a costly price for running. It is far better to obey from the start.

1:4 Before settling in the promised land, the Israelites had been nomads, wandering from place to place, seeking good pastureland for their flocks. Although they were not a seafaring people, their location along the Mediterranean Sea and near the neighbouring maritime powers of Phoenicia and Philistia allowed much contact with ships and sailors. The ship Jonah sailed on was probably a large trading vessel with a deck.

1:4 Jonah's disobedience to God endangered the lives of the ship's crew. We have a great responsibility to obey God's word because our sin and disobedience can hurt others around us.

1:4, 5 While the storm raged, Jonah was sound asleep below deck. Even as he ran from God, Jonah's actions apparently didn't bother his conscience. But the absence of guilt isn't always a barometer of whether we are doing right. Because we can deny reality, we cannot measure obedience by our feelings. Instead, we must compare what we do with God's standards for living.

the ship threatened to break up.[f] 5All the sailors were afraid and each cried out to
his own god. And they threw the cargo into the sea to lighten the ship.[g]
But Jonah had gone below deck, where he lay down and fell into a deep sleep. 6The
captain went to him and said, "How can you sleep? Get up and call[h] on your god!
Maybe he will take notice of us, and we will not perish."[i]
7Then the sailors said to each other, "Come, let us cast lots to find out who is
responsible for this calamity."[j] They cast lots and the lot fell on Jonah.
8So they asked him, "Tell us, who is responsible for making all this trouble for us?
What do you do? Where do you come from? What is your country? From what people
are you?"
9He answered, "I am a Hebrew and I worship the LORD, the God of heaven,[k] who
made the sea and the land.[l]"
10This terrified them and they asked, "What have you done?" (They knew he was
running away from the LORD, because he had already told them so.)
11The sea was getting rougher and rougher. So they asked him, "What should we
do to you to make the sea calm down for us?"
12"Pick me up and throw me into the sea," he replied, "and it will become calm.
I know that it is my fault that this great storm has come upon you."[m]
13Instead, the men did their best to row back to land. But they could not, for the
sea grew even wilder than before.[n] 14Then they cried to the LORD, "O LORD, please
do not let us die for taking this man's life. Do not hold us accountable for killing an
innocent man,[o] for you, O LORD, have done as you pleased."[p] 15Then they took
Jonah and threw him overboard, and the raging sea grew calm.[q] 16At this the men
greatly feared[r] the LORD, and they offered a sacrifice to the LORD and made vows
to him.
17But the LORD provided a great fish to swallow Jonah,[s] and Jonah was inside the
fish three days and three nights.

1:4 [f]Ps 107:23-26
1:5 [g]Ac 27:18-19
1:6 [h]Jnh 3:8 [i]Ps 107:28
1:7 [j]Jos 7:10-18; 1Sa 14:42
1:9 [k]Ac 17:24 [l]Ps 146:6
1:12 [m]2Sa 24:17; 1Ch 21:17
1:13 [n]Pr 21:30
1:14 [o]Dt 21:8 [p]Ps 115:3
1:15 [q]Ps 107:29; Lk 8:24
1:16 [r]Mk 4:41
1:17 [s]Mt 12:40; 16:4; Lk 11:30

1:7 The crew cast lots to find the guilty person, relying on their superstition to give them the answer. Their system worked, but only because God intervened to let Jonah know that he couldn't run away.

1:9–12 You cannot seek God's love and run from him at the same time. Jonah soon realised that no matter where he went, he couldn't get away from God. But before Jonah could return to God, he first had to stop going in the opposite direction. What has God told you to do? If you want more of God's love and power, you must be willing to carry out the responsibilities he gives you. You cannot say that you truly believe in God if you don't do what he says (1 John 2:3–6).

1:12 Jonah knew that he had disobeyed and that the storm was his fault, but he didn't say anything until the crew cast lots and the lot fell on him (1:7). Then Jonah was willing to give his life to save the sailors, although he had refused to do the same for the people of Nineveh. Jonah's hatred for the Assyrians had affected his perspective.

1:13 By trying to save Jonah's life, the pagan sailors showed more compassion than Jonah, because Jonah did not want to warn the Ninevites of the coming judgment of God. Believers should be ashamed when unbelievers show more concern and compassion than they do. God wants us to be concerned for all of his people, lost and saved.

1:14–16 Jonah had disobeyed God. While he was running away, he stopped and submitted to God. Then the ship's crew began to worship God because they saw the storm quieten down. God is able to use even our mistakes to help others come to know him. It may be painful, but admitting our sins can be a powerful example to those who don't know God. Ironically, the pagan sailors did what the entire nation of Israel would not do – prayed to God and vowed to serve him.

1:17 Many have tried to dismiss this miraculous event as fiction, but the Bible does not describe it as a dream or a legend. We should not explain away this miracle as if we could pick and choose which of the miracles in the Bible we believe and which ones we don't. That kind of attitude would allow us to question any part of the Bible and cause us to lose our trust in the Bible as God's true and reliable word. Jonah's experience was used by Christ himself as an illustration of Christ's death and resurrection (Matthew 12:39, 40).

2:1ff This is a prayer of thanksgiving, not a prayer for deliverance. Jonah was simply thankful that he had not drowned. He was delivered in a most spectacular way and was overwhelmed that he had escaped certain death. Even from inside the fish, Jonah's prayer was heard by God. We can pray anywhere and at any time,

2:2
[a]Ps 18:6; 120:1

Jonah's Prayer

2 From inside the fish Jonah prayed to the LORD his God. 2He said:

"In my distress I called to the LORD,[a]
and he answered me.
From the depths of the grave[a] I called for help,
and you listened to my cry.

2:3
[b]Ps 88:6
[c]Ps 42:7

3You hurled me into the deep,[b]
into the very heart of the seas,
and the currents swirled about me;
all your waves and breakers
swept over me.[c]

2:4
[d]Ps 31:22

4I said, 'I have been banished
from your sight;[d]
yet I will look again
towards your holy temple.'

2:5
[e]Ps 69:1-2

5The engulfing waters threatened me,[b]
the deep surrounded me;
seaweed was wrapped around my head.[e]
6To the roots of the mountains I sank down;
the earth beneath barred me in for ever.
But you brought my life up from the pit,
O LORD my God.

2:7
[f]Ps 77:11-12
[g]2Ch 30:27
[h]Ps 11:4; 18:6

7"When my life was ebbing away,
I remembered[f] you, LORD,
and my prayer[g] rose to you,
to your holy temple.[h]

2:8
[i]2Ki 17:15; Jer 10:8

8"Those who cling to worthless idols[i]
forfeit the grace that could be theirs.
9But I, with a song of thanksgiving,
will sacrifice[j] to you.
What I have vowed[k] I will make good.
Salvation[l] comes from the LORD."

2:9
[j]Ps 50:14, 23; Hos 14:2
[k]Ecc 5:4-5
[l]Ps 3:8

10And the LORD commanded the fish, and it vomited Jonah onto dry land.

[a] 2 Hebrew *Sheol* [b] 5 Or *waters were at my throat*

---

and God will hear us. Your sin is never too great, your predicament never too difficult, for God.

2:1–7 Jonah said, "When my life was ebbing away, I remembered you, LORD" (2:7). Often we act the same way. When life is going well, we tend to take God for granted; but when we lose hope, we cry out to him. This kind of relationship with God can result only in an inconsistent, up-and-down spiritual life. A consistent, daily commitment to God promotes a solid relationship with him. Look to God during both the good and bad times, and you will have a stronger spiritual life.

2:2 Jonah pictured his predicament in the belly of the fish as though he had been buried alive.

2:8 Those who worship worthless idols forfeit God's grace and abandon any hope for mercy from the Lord. Any object of our devotion that replaces God is a lying vanity. We deceive ourselves with something that is ultimately empty and foolish. Make sure that nothing takes God's rightful place in your life.

2:9 Obviously Jonah was not in a position to bargain with God. Instead, he simply thanked God for saving his life. Our troubles should cause us to cling tightly to God, not attempt to bargain our way out of the pain. We can thank and praise God for what he has already done for us, and for his love and mercy.

2:9 It took a miracle of deliverance to get Jonah to do as God had commanded. As a prophet, Jonah was obligated to obey God's word, but he had tried to escape his responsibilities. At this time, he pledged to keep his vows. Jonah's story began with a tragedy, but a greater tragedy would have happened if God had allowed him to keep running. When you know God wants you to do something, don't run. God may not stop you as he did Jonah.

2. Jonah fulfils his mission

Jonah Goes to Nineveh

3 Then the word of the LORD came to Jonah[a] a second time: 2"Go to the great city
of Nineveh and proclaim to it the message I give you."
3Jonah obeyed the word of the LORD and went to Nineveh. Now Nineveh was a
very important city—a visit required three days. 4On the first day, Jonah started into
the city. He proclaimed: "Forty more days and Nineveh will be overturned." 5The
Ninevites believed God. They declared a fast, and all of them, from the greatest to
the least, put on sackcloth.[b]
6When the news reached the king of Nineveh, he rose from his throne, took off
his royal robes, covered himself with sackcloth and sat down in the dust.[c] 7Then he
issued a proclamation in Nineveh:

"By the decree of the king and his nobles:

Do not let any man or beast, herd or flock, taste anything; do not let them eat
or drink.[d] 8But let man and beast be covered with sackcloth. Let everyone call[e]
urgently on God. Let them give up their evil ways and their violence. 9Who
knows?[f] God may yet relent and with compassion turn[g] from his fierce anger
so that we will not perish."

10When God saw what they did and how they turned from their evil ways, he had
compassion[h] and did not bring upon them the destruction[i] he had threatened.[j]

Jonah's Anger at the LORD's Compassion

4 But Jonah was greatly displeased and became angry.[a] 2He prayed to the LORD,
"O LORD, is this not what I said when I was still at home? That is why I was so
quick to flee to Tarshish. I knew[b] that you are a gracious and compassionate God,
slow to anger and abounding in love,[c] a God who relents from sending calamity.[d]
3Now, O LORD, take away my life,[e] for it is better for me to die[f] than to live."

3:1 [a] Jnh 1:1
3:5 [b] Da 9:3; Lk 11:32
3:6 [c] Job 2:8, 13; Eze 27:30-31
3:7 [d] 2Ch 20:3
3:8 [e] Ps 130:1; Jnh 1:6
3:9 [f] 2Sa 12:22 [g] Joel 2:14
3:10 [h] Am 7:6 [i] Jer 18:8 [j] Ex 32:14
4:1 [a] ver 4; Lk 15:28
4:2 [b] Jer 20:7-8 [c] Ex 34:6; Ps 86:5, 15 [d] Joel 2:13
4:3 [e] 1Ki 19:4 [f] Job 7:15

3:1, 2 Jonah had run away from God, but was given a second chance to participate in God's work. You may feel as though you are disqualified from serving God because of past mistakes. But serving God is not an earned position—no-one qualifies for God's service. But God still asks us to carry out his work. You may yet have another chance.

3:1, 2 Jonah was to preach only what God told him—a message of doom to one of the most powerful cities in the world. This was not the most desirable assignment, but those who bring God's word to others should not let social pressures or fear of people dictate their words. They are called to preach God's message and his truth, no matter how unpopular it may be.

3:3 The Hebrew text makes no distinction between the city proper (the walls of which were only about eight miles in circumference, accommodating a population of about 175,000 persons) and the administrative district of Nineveh that was about 30 to 60 miles across. A "very important city", Nineveh took three days just to visit.

3:4–9 God's word is for everyone. Despite the wickedness of the Ninevite people, they were open to God's message and repented immediately. If we simply proclaim what we know about God, we may be surprised at how many people will listen.

3:10 The pagan people of Nineveh believed Jonah's message and repented. What a miraculous effect God's words had on those evil people! Their repentance stood in stark contrast to Israel's stubbornness. The people of Israel had heard many messages from the prophets, but they had refused to repent. The people of Nineveh only needed to hear God's message once. Jesus said that at the judgment, the men of Nineveh will stand up to condemn the Israelites for their failure to repent (Matthew 12:39–41). It is not our hearing God's word that pleases him, but our responding obediently to it.

3:10 God responded in mercy by cancelling his threatened punishment. God had said that any nation on which he had pronounced judgment would be saved if they repented (Jeremiah 18:7, 8). God forgave Nineveh, just as he had forgiven Jonah. The purpose of God's judgment is correction, not revenge. He is always ready to show compassion to anyone willing to seek him.

4:1 Why did Jonah become angry when God spared Nineveh? The Jews did not want to share God's message with Gentile nations in Jonah's day, just as they resisted that role in Paul's day (1 Thessalonians 2:14–16). They had forgotten their original purpose as a nation—to be a blessing to the rest of the world by sharing God's message with other nations (Genesis 22:18). Jonah thought that God should not freely give his salvation to a wicked pagan nation. Yet this is exactly what God does for all who come to him today in faith.

4:1, 2 Jonah revealed the reason for his reluctance to go to Nineveh (1:3). He didn't want the Ninevites forgiven; he wanted them destroyed. Jonah did not understand that the God of Israel was also the God of the whole world. Are you surprised when some unlikely person turns to God? Is it possible that your view is as narrow as Jonah's? We must not forget that, in reality, *we* do not deserve to be forgiven by God.

4:3 Jonah had run from the job of delivering God's message of destruction to Nineveh (1:2, 3); then he wanted to die because the destruction wouldn't happen. How quickly Jonah had forgotten God's mercy for him when he was in the fish (2:9, 10). Jonah was happy when God saved him, but angry when Nineveh was saved. But Jonah was learning a valuable lesson about God's mercy and

4:4
[g] Mt 20:11-15

4 But the LORD replied, "Have you any right to be angry?"[g]
5 Jonah went out and sat down at a place east of the city. There he made himself
a shelter, sat in its shade and waited to see what would happen to the city. 6 Then the
LORD God provided a vine and made it grow up over Jonah to give shade for his head
to ease his discomfort, and Jonah was very happy about the vine. 7 But at dawn the
next day God provided a worm, which chewed the vine so that it withered.[h] 8 When
the sun rose, God provided a scorching east wind, and the sun blazed on Jonah's head
so that he grew faint. He wanted to die, and said, "It would be better for me to die
than to live."

4:7
[h] Joel 1:12

9 But God said to Jonah, "Do you have a right to be angry about the vine?"
"I do," he said. "I am angry enough to die."
10 But the LORD said, "You have been concerned about this vine, though you did
not tend it or make it grow. It sprang up overnight and died overnight. 11 But Nineveh[i]
has more than a hundred and twenty thousand people who cannot tell their right hand
from their left, and many cattle as well. Should I not be concerned[j] about that great
city?"

4:11
[i] Jnh 1:2; 3:2
[j] Jnh 3:10

MIRACLES IN THE BOOK OF JONAH

God sent a violent storm	1:4
God provided a great fish to swallow Jonah	1:17
God ordered the fish to vomit Jonah	2:10
God made a vine to shade Jonah	4:6
God provided a worm to eat the vine	4:7
God provided a scorching wind to blow on Jonah	4:8

forgiveness. God's forgiveness was not only for Jonah or for Israel alone; it extends to all who repent and believe.

4:3 Jonah may have been more concerned about his own reputation than God's. He knew that if the people repented, none of his warnings to Nineveh would come true. This would embarrass him, although it would give glory to God. Are you more interested in getting glory for God or for yourself?

4:5–11 God ministered tenderly to Jonah just as he had done to Nineveh and to Israel, and just as he does to us. God could have destroyed Jonah for his defiant anger, but instead he gently taught him a lesson. If we will obey God's will, he will lead us. His harsh judgment is reserved for those who persist in rebellion.

4:9 Jonah was angry at the withering of the vine, but not over what could have happened to Nineveh. Most of us have cried at the death of a pet or when an object with sentimental value is broken, but have we cried over the fact that a friend does not know God? How easy it is to be more sensitive to our own interests than to the spiritual needs of people around us.

4:10, 11 Sometimes people wish that judgment and destruction would come upon sinful people whose wickedness seems to demand immediate punishment. But God is more merciful than we can imagine. God feels compassion for the sinners we want judged, and he devises plans to bring them to himself. What is your attitude towards those who are especially wicked? Do you want them destroyed? Or do you wish that they could experience God's mercy and forgiveness?

4:11 God spared the sailors when they pleaded for mercy. God saved Jonah when he prayed from inside the fish. God saved the people of Nineveh when they responded to Jonah's preaching. God answers the prayers of those who call upon him. God will always work his will, and he desires that all should come to him, trust in him, and be saved. We can be saved if we heed God's warnings to us through his Word. If we respond in obedience, God will be gracious, and we will receive his mercy, not his punishment.

MICAH

Hosea becomes a prophet 753 B.C. | *Jotham becomes king of Judah 750* | *Tiglath-Pileser III invades Israel 743* | *Micah becomes a prophet; Pekahiah becomes king 742* | *Isaiah becomes a prophet 740* | *Ahaz becomes king of Judah 735*

VITAL STATISTICS

PURPOSE:
To warn God's people that judgment is coming and to offer pardon to all who repent

AUTHOR:
Micah, a native of Moresheth, near Gath, about 20 miles southwest of Jerusalem

TO WHOM WRITTEN:
The people of Israel (the northern kingdom) and of Judah (the southern kingdom)

DATE WRITTEN:
Possibly during the reigns of Jotham, Ahaz, and Hezekiah (742–687 B.C.)

SETTING:
The political situation is described in 2 Kings 15—20 and 2 Chronicles 26—30. Micah was a contemporary of Isaiah and Hosea.

KEY VERSE:
"He has showed you, O man, what is good. And what does the LORD require of you? To act justly and to love mercy and to walk humbly with your God" (6:8).

KEY PEOPLE:
The people of Samaria and Jerusalem

KEY PLACES:
Samaria, Jerusalem, Bethlehem

SPECIAL FEATURES:
This is a beautiful example of classical Hebrew poetry. There are three parts, each beginning with "Hear" or "Listen" (1:2; 3:1; 6:1) and closing with a promise.

"I HATE YOU!" she screams, and runs from the room. Words from a child, thrown as emotional darts. Perhaps she learned the phrase from Mum and Dad, or maybe it just burst forth from that inner well of "sinful nature". Whatever the case, "hate" and "love" have become society's by-words, almost tired clichés, tossed carelessly at objects, situations, and even people.

The casual use of such words as "love" and "hate" has emptied them of their meaning. We no longer understand statements that describe a loving God who hates sin. So we picture God as gentle and kind—a cosmic "pushover"; and our concept of what he hates is tempered by our misconceptions and wishful thinking.

The words of the prophets stand in stark contrast to such misconceptions. God's hatred is real—burning, consuming, and destroying. He hates sin, and he stands as the righteous judge, ready to mete out just punishment to all who defy his rule. God's love is also real. So real that he sent his Son, the Messiah, to save and accept judgment in the sinner's place. Love and hate are together—both unending, irresistible, and unfathomable.

In seven short chapters, Micah presents this true picture of God—the almighty Lord who hates sin and loves the sinner. Much of the book is devoted to describing God's judgment on Israel (the northern kingdom), on Judah (the southern kingdom), and on all the earth. This judgment will come "because of Jacob's transgression, because of the sins of the house of Israel" (1:5). And the prophet lists their despicable sins, including fraud (2:2), theft (2:8), greed (2:9), debauchery (2:11), oppression (3:3), hypocrisy (3:4), heresy (3:5), injustice (3:9), extortion and lying (6:12), murder (7:2), and other offences. God's judgment will come.

In the midst of this overwhelming prediction of destruction, Micah gives hope and consolation because he also describes God's love. The truth is that judgment comes only after countless opportunities to repent, to turn back to true worship and obedience—"to act justly and to love mercy and to walk humbly with your God" (6:8). But even in the midst of judgment, God promises to deliver the small minority who have continued to follow him. He states, "Their king will pass through before them, the LORD at their head" (2:13). The king, of course, is Jesus; and we read in 5:2 that he will be born as a baby in Bethlehem, an obscure Judean village.

As you read Micah, catch a glimpse of God's anger in action as he judges and punishes sin. See God's love in action as he offers eternal life to all who repent and believe. And then determine to join the faithful remnant of God's people who live according to his will.

Israel (the northern kingdom) falls 722	*Hosea's ministry ends; Hezekiah becomes king of Judah 715*	*Sennacherib surrounds Jerusalem 701*	*Micah's ministry ends 687*

THE BLUEPRINT

1. The trial of the capitals (1:1—2:13)
2. The trial of the leaders (3:1—5:15)
3. The trial of the people (6:1—7:20)

Micah emphasised the need for justice and peace. Like a lawyer, he set forth God's case against Israel and Judah, their leaders, and their people. Throughout the book are prophecies about Jesus, the Messiah, who will gather the people into one nation. He will be their king and ruler, acting mercifully towards them. Micah makes it clear that God hates unkindness, idolatry, injustice, and empty ritual—and he still hates these today. But God is very willing to pardon the sins of any who repent.

MEGATHEMES

THEME	EXPLANATION	IMPORTANCE
Perverting Faith	God will judge the false prophets, dishonest leaders, and selfish priests in Israel and Judah. While they publicly carried out religious ceremonies, they were privately seeking to gain money and influence. To mix selfish motives with an empty display of religion is to pervert faith.	Don't try to mix your own selfish desires with true faith in God. One day God will reveal how foolish it is to substitute anything for loyalty to him. Coming up with your own private blend of religion will pervert your faith.
Oppression	Micah predicted ruin for all nations and leaders who were oppressive towards others. The upper classes oppressed and exploited the poor. Yet no-one was speaking against them or doing anything to stop them. God will not put up with such injustice.	We dare not ask God to help us while we ignore those who are needy and oppressed, or while we silently condone the actions of those who oppress them.
The Messiah—King of Peace	God promised to provide a new King to bring strength and peace to his people. Hundreds of years before Christ's birth, God promised that the eternal King would be born in Bethlehem. It was God's great plan to restore his people through the Messiah.	Christ our King leads us just as God promised. But until his final judgment, his leadership is only visible among those who welcome his authority. We can have God's peace now by giving up our sins and welcoming him as King.
Pleasing God	Micah preached that God's greatest desire was not the offering of sacrifices at the temple. God delights in faith that produces justice, love for others, and obedience to him.	True faith in God generates kindness, compassion, justice, and humility. We can please God by seeking these results in our work, our family, our church, and our neighbourhood.

1:1
[a] Jer 26:18
[b] 1Ch 3:12
[c] 1Ch 3:13
[d] Hos 1:1
[e] Isa 1:1

1. The trial of the capitals

1 The word of the LORD that came to Micah of Moresheth[a] during the reigns of
Jotham,[b] Ahaz[c] and Hezekiah, kings of Judah[d]—the vision[e] he saw concerning Samaria and Jerusalem.

1:1 Micah and Isaiah lived at the same time, about 750–680 B.C., and undoubtedly knew of each other. Micah directed his message mainly to Judah, the southern kingdom, but he also had some words for Israel, the northern kingdom. Judah was enjoying great prosperity at this time. Of the three kings mentioned, Jotham (750–732) and Hezekiah (715–686) had tried to follow God (2 Kings 15:32–38; 18—20), but Ahaz (735–715) was one of the most evil kings ever to reign in Judah (2 Kings 16). Moresheth was a Judean village, near Gath on the border with Philistia.

2Hear, O peoples, all of you,[f]
listen, O earth[g] and all who are in it,
that the Sovereign LORD may witness[h] against you,
the Lord from his holy temple.[i]

Judgment Against Samaria and Jerusalem

3Look! The LORD is coming from his dwelling-place;[j]
he comes down and treads the high places of the earth.[k]
4The mountains melt[l] beneath him
and the valleys split apart,[m]
like wax before the fire,
like water rushing down a slope.
5All this is because of Jacob's transgression,
because of the sins of the house of Israel.
What is Jacob's transgression?
Is it not Samaria?[n]
What is Judah's high place?
Is it not Jerusalem?

6"Therefore I will make Samaria a heap of rubble,
a place for planting vineyards.
I will pour her stones[o] into the valley
and lay bare her foundations.[p]
7All her idols[q] will be broken to pieces;
all her temple gifts will be burned with fire;
I will destroy all her images.[r]
Since she gathered her gifts from the wages of prostitutes,[s]
as the wages of prostitutes they will again be used."

Weeping and Mourning

8Because of this I will weep[t] and wail;
I will go about barefoot and naked.
I will howl like a jackal
and moan like an owl.
9For her wound[u] is incurable;
it has come to Judah.[v]
It[a] has reached the very gate[w] of my people,
even to Jerusalem itself.
10Tell it not in Gath;[b]
weep not at all.[c]
In Beth Ophrah[d]
roll in the dust.
11Pass on in nakedness[x] and shame,

1:2 [f]Ps 50:7 [g]Jer 6:19 [h]Ge 31:50; Dt 4:26; Isa 1:2 [i]Ps 11:4
1:3 [j]Isa 18:4 [k]Am 4:13
1:4 [l]Ps 46:2, 6 [m]Nu 16:31; Na 1:5
1:5 [n]Am 8:14
1:6 [o]Am 5:11 [p]Eze 13:14
1:7 [q]Eze 6:6 [r]Dt 9:21 [s]Dt 23:17-18
1:8 [t]Isa 15:3
1:9 [u]Jer 46:11 [v]2Ki 18:13 [w]Isa 3:26
1:11 [x]Eze 23:29

a *9* Or *He* **b** *10* *Gath* sounds like the Hebrew for *tell.* **c** *10* Hebrew; Septuagint may suggest *not in Acco.* The Hebrew for *in Acco* sounds like the Hebrew for *weep.* **d** *10* *Beth Ophrah* means *house of dust.*

1:3 "High places" could simply mean "mountain tops" or may refer to the altars dedicated to various idols, usually placed in such elevated areas (see also 1:5).

1:3–7 Jerusalem was the capital city of Judah (the southern kingdom); Samaria was the capital city of Israel (the northern kingdom). The destruction of Samaria was literally fulfilled during Micah's lifetime, in 722 B.C. (2 Kings 17:1–18), just as he had predicted.

1:5 There are two sins identified in Micah's message—the perversion of worship (1:7; 3:5–7, 11; 5:12, 13) and injustice toward others (2:1, 2, 8, 9; 3:2, 3, 9–11; 7:2–6). Rampant in the capital cities, these sins infiltrated and infected the entire country.

1:9 Samaria's sins were incurable, and God's judgment on the city had already begun. This sin was not like a gash in the skin, but more like a stab wound in a vital organ, causing an injury that would soon prove fatal (Samaria was, in fact, destroyed early in Micah's ministry). Tragically, Samaria's sin had influenced Jerusalem, and judgment would come to its very gates. This probably refers to Sennacherib's siege in 701 B.C. (see 2 Kings 18, 19).

1:10–16 Micah declared God's judgment on city after city because of the people's sins. There is a clever word-play in the Hebrew of 1:10–13 (see the NIV text notes). Micah bitterly denounced each town by using puns. *Shaphir* sounds like the Hebrew word for "pleasant"; *Zaanan* sounds like the verb meaning "come out"; and *Maroth* sounds like a word for "bitter". Read 1:11 aloud, substituting the meaning for each city's name, and you will realise the effect of Micah's word choice. Not all these cities can be identified now, but Lachish was on the border with Philistia and took the brunt of the Assyrian invasion.

you who live in Shaphir.[e]
Those who live in Zaanan[f]
will not come out.
Beth Ezel is in mourning;
its protection is taken from you.
12 Those who live in Maroth[g] writhe in pain,
waiting for relief,[y]
because disaster has come from the LORD,
even to the gate of Jerusalem.
13 You who live in Lachish,[h][z]
harness the team to the chariot.
You were the beginning of sin
to the Daughter of Zion,
for the transgressions of Israel
were found in you.
14 Therefore you will give parting gifts[a]
to Moresheth Gath.
The town of Aczib[i][b] will prove deceptive[c]
to the kings of Israel.
15 I will bring a conqueror against you
who live in Mareshah.[j][d]
He who is the glory of Israel
will come to Adullam.[e]
16 Shave[f] your heads in mourning
for the children in whom you delight;
make yourselves as bald as the vulture,
for they will go from you into exile.

1:12 [y]Jer 14:19
1:13 [z]Jos 10:3
1:14 [a]2Ki 16:8 [b]Jos 15:44 [c]Jer 15:18
1:15 [d]Jos 15:44 [e]Jos 12:15
1:16 [f]Job 1:20

[e] *11 Shaphir* means *pleasant.* [f] *11 Zaanan* sounds like the Hebrew for *come out.* [g] *12 Maroth* sounds like the Hebrew for *bitter.* [h] *13 Lachish* sounds like the Hebrew for *team.* [i] *14 Aczib* means *deception.* [j] *15 Mareshah* sounds like the Hebrew for *conqueror.*

MICAH served as a prophet to Judah from 742–687 B.C.

Climate of the times	King Ahaz set up pagan idols in the temple and finally nailed the temple door shut. Four different nations harassed Judah. When Hezekiah became king, the nation began a slow road to recovery and economic strength. Hezekiah probably heeded much of Micah's advice.
Main message	Prediction of the fall of both the northern kingdom of Israel and the southern kingdom of Judah. This was God's discipline upon the people, actually showing how much he cared for them. Hezekiah's good reign helped postpone Judah's punishment.
Importance of message	Choosing to live a life apart from God is making a commitment to sin. Sin leads to judgment and death. God alone shows us the way to eternal peace. His discipline often keeps us on the right path.
Contemporary prophets	Hosea (753–715) Isaiah (740–681)

1:13 The people of Lachish had influenced many to follow their evil example. They were "the beginning of sin". We often do the same when we sin. Regardless of whether you consider yourself a leader, your daily actions and words are observed by others who may choose to follow your example, whether you know it or not.

1:14 Moresheth Gath was Micah's home town (1:1).

1:15 The terrain surrounding Adullam had numerous caves. Micah was warning that when the enemy approached, Judah's proud princes would be forced to flee and hide in these caves.

1:16 Micah pictured the devastating sorrow of parents seeing their children taken away to be slaves in a distant land. This happened frequently in both Israel and Judah, most horribly when each nation was completely conquered – Israel in 722 B.C. and Judah in 586 B.C.

Man's Plans and God's

2 Woe to those who plan iniquity,
to those who plot evil on their beds![a]
At morning's light they carry it out
because it is in their power to do it.
2They covet fields[b] and seize them,
and houses, and take them.
They defraud[c] a man of his home,
a fellow-man of his inheritance.

3Therefore, the LORD says:

"I am planning disaster[d] against this people,
from which you cannot save yourselves.
You will no longer walk proudly,[e]
for it will be a time of calamity.
4In that day men will ridicule you;
they will taunt you with this mournful song:
'We are utterly ruined;[f]
my people's possession is divided up.
He takes it from me!
He assigns our fields to traitors.' "
5Therefore you will have no-one in the assembly of the LORD
to divide the land[g] by lot.

False Prophets

6"Do not prophesy," their prophets say.
"Do not prophesy about these things;
disgrace[h] will not overtake us.[i]"
7Should it be said, O house of Jacob:
"Is the Spirit of the LORD angry?
Does he do such things?"

"Do not my words do good[j]
to him whose ways are upright?[k]
8Lately my people have risen up
like an enemy.
You strip off the rich robe
from those who pass by without a care,
like men returning from battle.
9You drive the women of my people
from their pleasant homes.[l]
You take away my blessing
from their children for ever.
10Get up, go away!
For this is not your resting place,[m]
because it is defiled,[n]
it is ruined, beyond all remedy.
11If a liar and deceiver[o] comes and says,

2:1 [a]Ps 36:4
2:2 [b]Isa 5:8 [c]Jer 22:17
2:3 [d]Jer 18:11; Am 3:1-2 [e]Isa 2:12
2:4 [f]Jer 4:13
2:5 [g]Jos 18:4
2:6 [h]Mic 6:16 [i]Am 2:12
2:7 [j]Ps 119:65 [k]Ps 15:2; 84:11
2:9 [l]Jer 10:20
2:10 [m]Dt 12:9 [n]Lev 18:25-29; Ps 106:38-39
2:11 [o]Jer 5:31

2:1, 2 Micah spoke out against those who planned evil deeds at night and rose at dawn to do them. A person's thoughts and plans reflect his or her character. What do you think about as you lie down to sleep? Do your desires involve greed or stepping on others to achieve your goals? Evil thoughts lead to evil deeds.

2:5 Those who have been oppressing others will find the tables turned. They will end up not having any share in the decisions to divide the land because they won't have any surviving relatives.

2:6, 7 If these messages seem harsh, remember that God did not want to take revenge on Israel; he wanted to get them back on the right path. The people had rejected what was true and right, and they needed stern discipline. Children may think discipline is harsh, but it helps to keep them going in the right direction. If we only want God's comforting messages, we may miss what he has for us. Listen whenever God speaks, even when the message is hard to take.

2:11 [p]Isa 30:10

'I will prophesy for you plenty of wine and beer,'
he would be just the prophet for this people![p]

Deliverance Promised

2:12 [q]Mic 4:7; 5:7; 7:18

12"I will surely gather all of you, O Jacob;
I will surely bring together the remnant[q] of Israel.
I will bring them together like sheep in a pen,
like a flock in its pasture;
the place will throng with people.

2:13 [r]Isa 52:12

13One who breaks open the way will go up before[r] them;
they will break through the gate and go out.
Their king will pass through before them,
the LORD at their head."

2. The trial of the leaders

Leaders and Prophets Rebuked

3:1 [a]Jer 5:5

3

Then I said,

"Listen, you leaders[a] of Jacob,
you rulers of the house of Israel.
Should you not know justice,

3:2 [b]Ps 53:4; Eze 22:27

2 you who hate good and love evil;
who tear the skin from my people
and the flesh from their bones;[b]

3:3 [c]Ps 14:4 [d]Zep 3:3 [e]Eze 11:7

3who eat my people's flesh,[c]
strip off their skin
and break their bones in pieces;[d]
who chop them up like meat for the pan,
like flesh for the pot.[e]"

3:4 [f]Ps 18:41; Isa 1:15 [g]Dt 31:17

4Then they will cry out to the LORD,
but he will not answer them.[f]
At that time he will hide his face[g] from them
because of the evil they have done.

MICAH'S CHARGES OF INJUSTICE
Micah charged the people with injustice of many kinds.

Plotting evil	2:1
Fraud, coveting, violence	2:2
Stealing, dishonesty	2:8
Driving widows from their homes	2:9
Hating good, loving evil	3:1, 2
Despising justice, distorting what is right	3:9
Murder	3:10
Taking bribes	3:11

2:11 The people liked the false prophets who told them only what they wanted to hear. Micah spoke against prophets who encouraged the people to feel comfortable in their sin. Preachers are popular when they don't ask too much of us and when they tell us our greed or lust might even be good for us. But a true teacher of God speaks the truth, regardless of what the listeners want to hear.

2:12, 13 Micah's prophecy telescopes two great events—Judah's return from captivity in Babylon, and the great gathering of all believers when the Messiah returns. God gave his prophets visions of various future events, but not necessarily the ability to discern when these events would happen. For example, they could not see the long period of time between the Babylonian captivity and the coming of the Messiah, but they could clearly see that the Messiah was coming. The purpose of this prophecy was not to predict exactly *how* this would occur, but *that* it would. This gave the people hope and helped them turn from sin.

3:1ff Micah denounced the sins of the leaders, priests, and prophets ("leaders of Jacob" and "rulers")—those responsible for teaching the people right from wrong. The leaders, who should have known the law and taught it to the people, had set the law aside and had become the worst of sinners. They were taking advantage of the very people they were supposed to serve. All sin is bad, but the sin that leads others astray is the worst of all.

3:2-4 The leaders had no compassion or respect for those they were supposed to serve. They were treating the people miserably in order to satisfy their own desires, and then they had the gall to ask for God's help when they found themselves in trouble. We, like the leaders, should not treat God like a light switch to be turned on only as needed. Instead, we should always rely on him.

5This is what the LORD says:

"As for the prophets
who lead my people astray,[h]
if one feeds them,
they proclaim 'peace';
if he does not,
they prepare to wage war against him.
6Therefore night will come over you, without visions,
and darkness, without divination.[i]
The sun will set for the prophets,[j]
and the day will go dark for them.
7The seers will be ashamed[k]
and the diviners disgraced.[l]
They will all cover their faces
because there is no answer from God."

8But as for me, I am filled with power,
with the Spirit of the LORD,
and with justice and might,
to declare to Jacob his transgression,
to Israel his sin.[m]
9Hear this, you leaders of the house of Jacob,
you rulers of the house of Israel,
who despise justice
and distort all that is right;[n]
10who build[o] Zion with bloodshed,[p]
and Jerusalem with wickedness.[q]
11Her leaders judge for a bribe,
her priests teach for a price,
and her prophets tell fortunes for money.[r]
Yet they lean upon the LORD and say,
"Is not the LORD among us?
No disaster will come upon us."[s]
12Therefore because of you,
Zion will be ploughed like a field,
Jerusalem will become a heap of rubble,[t]
the temple hill a mound overgrown with thickets.

The Mountain of the LORD

4 In the last days

the mountain[a] of the LORD's temple will be established
as chief among the mountains;

3:5 [h]Isa 3:12; 9:16
3:6 [i]Isa 8:19-22 [j]Isa 29:10
3:7 [k]Mic 7:16 [l]Isa 44:25
3:8 [m]Isa 58:1
3:9 [n]Ps 58:1-2; Isa 1:23
3:10 [o]Jer 22:13 [p]Hab 2:12 [q]Eze 22:27
3:11 [r]Isa 1:23; Jer 6:13; Hos 4:8, 18 [s]Jer 7:4
3:12 [t]Jer 26:18
4:1 [a]Zec 8:3

3:5–7 Micah remained true to his calling and proclaimed God's words. In contrast, the false prophets' messages were geared to the favours they received. Not all those who claim to have messages from God really do. Micah prophesied that one day the false prophets would be shamed by their actions.

3:8 Micah attributed the power of his ministry to the Spirit of the Lord. Our power comes from the same source. Jesus told his followers they would receive power to witness about him when the Holy Spirit came on them (Acts 1:8). You can't witness effectively by relying on your own strength, because fear will keep you from speaking out for God. Only by relying on the power of the Holy Spirit can you live and witness for him.

3:11 Micah warned the leaders, priests, and prophets of his day to avoid bribes. Pastors today accept bribes when they allow those who contribute much to control the church. When fear of losing money or members influences pastors to remain silent when they should speak up for what is right, their churches are in danger. We should remember that Judah was finally destroyed because of the behaviour of its religious leaders. A similar warning must be directed at those who have money—*never* use your resources to influence or manipulate God's ministers—that is bribery.

3:12 Jerusalem would be destroyed just as Samaria was (1:6). This happened in 586 B.C. when Nebuchadnezzar and the Babylonian army attacked the city (2 Kings 25). Although Micah blamed the corrupt leaders, the people were not without fault. They allowed the corruption to continue without turning to God or calling for justice.

4:1ff The phrase "in the last days" describes the days when God will reign over his perfect kingdom (see 4:1–8). The "mountain of the LORD" is Mount Zion. This will be an era of peace and blessing,

it will be raised above the hills,[b]
and peoples will stream to it.[c]

2Many nations will come and say,

"Come, let us go up to the mountain of the LORD,[d]
to the house of the God of Jacob.[e]
He will teach us his ways,[f]
so that we may walk in his paths."
The law will go out from Zion,
the word of the LORD from Jerusalem.
3He will judge between many peoples
and will settle disputes for strong nations far and wide.[g]
They will beat their swords into ploughshares
and their spears into pruning hooks.[h]
Nation will not take up sword against nation,
nor will they train for war any more.[i]
4Every man will sit under his own vine
and under his own fig-tree,[j]
and no-one will make them afraid,[k]
for the LORD Almighty has spoken.[l]
5All the nations may walk
in the name of their gods;[m]
we will walk in the name of the LORD
our God for ever and ever.[n]

The LORD's Plan

6"In that day," declares the LORD,

"I will gather the lame;
I will assemble the exiles[o]
and those I have brought to grief.[p]
7I will make the lame a remnant,[q]
those driven away a strong nation.
The LORD will rule over them in Mount Zion
from that day and for ever.[r]
8As for you, O watchtower of the flock,
O stronghold[a] of the Daughter of Zion,
the former dominion will be restored[s] to you;
kingship will come to the Daughter of Jerusalem."

9Why do you now cry aloud—
have you no king?[t]
Has your counsellor perished,
that pain seizes you like that of a woman in labour?[u]
10Writhe in agony, O Daughter of Zion,
like a woman in labour,
for now you must leave the city
to camp in the open field.

4:1 [b]Eze 17:22 [c]Ps 22:27; 86:9; Jer 3:17
4:2 [d]Jer 31:6 [e]Zec 2:11; 14:16 [f]Ps 25:8-9; Isa 54:13
4:3 [g]Isa 11:4 [h]Joel 3:10 [i]Isa 2:4
4:4 [j]1Ki 4:25 [k]Lev 26:6 [l]Isa 1:20; Zec 3:10
4:5 [m]2Ki 17:29 [n]Jos 24:14-15; Isa 26:8; Zec 10:12
4:6 [o]Ps 147:2 [p]Eze 34:13, 16; 37:21; Zep 3:19
4:7 [q]Mic 2:12 [r]Da 7:14; Lk 1:33; Rev 11:15
4:8 [s]Isa 1:26
4:9 [t]Jer 8:19 [u]Jer 30:6

a 8 Or *hill*

---

a time when war will be for ever ended. We cannot pinpoint its date, but God has promised that it *will* arrive (see also Isaiah 2:2; Jeremiah 16:15; Joel 3:1ff; Zechariah 14:9–11; Malachi 3:17, 18; Revelation 19–22).

Verses 9–13 predicted the Babylonian captivity in 586 B.C., even before Babylon became a powerful empire. Just as God promises a time of peace and prosperity, he also promises judgment and punishment for all who refuse to follow him. Both results are certain.

4:9–13 Micah predicted the end of the kings. This was a drastic statement to the people of Judah, who thought that their kingdom would last for ever. Micah also said that Babylon would destroy the land of Judah and carry away its king, but that after a while God would help his people return to their land. This all happened just as Micah prophesied, and these events are recorded in 2 Chronicles 36:9–23 and Ezra 1; 2.

You will go to Babylon;[v]
there you will be rescued.
There the LORD will redeem[w] you
out of the hand of your enemies.

11 But now many nations
are gathered against you.
They say, "Let her be defiled,
let our eyes gloat[x] over Zion!"
12 But they do not know
the thoughts of the LORD;
they do not understand his plan,[y]
he who gathers them like sheaves to the threshing-floor.

13 "Rise and thresh, O Daughter of Zion,
for I will give you horns of iron;
I will give you hoofs of bronze
and you will break to pieces many nations."[z]

You will devote their ill-gotten gains to the LORD,
their wealth to the Lord of all the earth.

A Promised Ruler From Bethlehem

5 Marshal your troops, O city of troops,[a]
for a siege is laid against us.
They will strike Israel's ruler
on the cheek[a] with a rod.

2 "But you, Bethlehem[b] Ephrathah,[c]
though you are small among the clans[b] of Judah,
out of you will come for me
one who will be ruler over Israel,
whose origins[c] are from of old,[d]
from ancient times."[d][e]

3 Therefore Israel will be abandoned
until the time when she who is in labour gives birth
and the rest of his brothers return
to join the Israelites.

4 He will stand and shepherd his flock[f]
in the strength of the LORD,
in the majesty of the name of the LORD his God.
And they will live securely, for then his greatness[g]
will reach to the ends of the earth.
5 And he will be their peace.[h]

a *1* Or *Strengthen your walls, O walled city* **b** *2* Or *rulers* **c** *2* Hebrew *goings out* **d** *2* Or *from days of eternity*

4:10 [v]2Ki 20:18; Isa 43:14 [w]Isa 48:20
4:11 [x]La 2:16; Ob 1:12
4:12 [y]Isa 55:8; Ro 11:33-34
4:13 [z]Da 2:44
5:1 [a]La 3:30
5:2 [b]Jn 7:42 [c]Ge 48:7 [d]Ps 102:25 [e]Mt 2:6*
5:4 [f]Isa 40:11; 49:9; Eze 34:11-15, 23; Mic 7:14 [g]Isa 52:13; Lk 1:32
5:5 [h]Isa 9:6; Lk 2:14; Col 1:19-20

4:12 When God reveals the future, his purpose goes beyond satisfying our curiosity. He wants us to change our present behaviour because of what we know about the future. For ever begins now; and a glimpse of God's plan for his followers should motivate us to serve him, no matter what the rest of the world may do.

5:1 This ruler was probably King Zedekiah, who was reigning in Jerusalem when Nebuchadnezzar conquered the city (2 Kings 25:1, 2). Zedekiah was the last of the kings in David's line to sit on the throne in Jerusalem. Micah said that the next king in David's line would be the Messiah, who would establish a kingdom that would never end.

5:1ff Jerusalem's leaders were obsessed with wealth and position, but Micah prophesied that mighty Jerusalem, with all its wealth and power, would be besieged and destroyed. Its king could not save it. In contrast, Bethlehem, a tiny town, would be the birthplace of the only king who could save his people. This deliverer, the Messiah, would be born as a baby in Bethlehem (Luke 2:4–7), and eventually would reign as the eternal King (Revelation 19–22).

5:2 Ephrathah was the district in which Bethlehem was located.

5:2 This ruler is Jesus, the Messiah. Micah accurately predicted Christ's birthplace hundreds of years before Jesus was born. The promised eternal King in David's line, who would come to live as a man, had been alive for ever – "from of old, from ancient times".

5:5 [i]Isa 8:7 [j]Isa 10:24-27
5:6 [k]Ge 10:8 [l]Zep 2:13 [m]Na 2:11-13
5:7 [n]Mic 2:12 [o]Isa 44:4
5:8 [p]Ge 49:9 [q]Mic 4:13; Zec 10:5 [r]Ps 50:22; Hos 5:14
5:9 [s]Ps 10:12
5:10 [t]Hos 14:3; Zec 9:10
5:11 [u]Isa 6:11 [v]Hos 10:14; Am 5:9
5:12 [w]Dt 18:10-12; Isa 2:6; 8:19
5:13 [x]Eze 6:9; Zec 13:2
5:14 [y]Ex 34:13
5:15 [z]Isa 65:12

Deliverance and Destruction

When the Assyrian invades[i] our land
 and marches through our fortresses,
we will raise against him seven shepherds,
 even eight leaders of men.[j]
6They will rule[e] the land of Assyria with the sword,
 the land of Nimrod[k] with drawn sword.[f][l]
He will deliver us from the Assyrian
 when he invades our land
 and marches into our borders.[m]

7The remnant[n] of Jacob will be
 in the midst of many peoples
like dew from the LORD,
 like showers on the grass,[o]
which do not wait for man
 or linger for mankind.
8The remnant of Jacob will be among the nations,
 in the midst of many peoples,
like a lion among the beasts of the forest,[p]
 like a young lion among flocks of sheep,
which mauls and mangles[q] as it goes,
 and no-one can rescue.[r]
9Your hand will be lifted up[s] in triumph over your enemies,
 and all your foes will be destroyed.

10"In that day," declares the LORD,

"I will destroy your horses from among you
 and demolish your chariots.[t]
11I will destroy the cities[u] of your land
 and tear down all your strongholds.[v]
12I will destroy your witchcraft
 and you will no longer cast spells.[w]
13I will destroy your carved images
 and your sacred stones from among you;
you will no longer bow down
 to the work of your hands.[x]
14I will uproot from among you your Asherah poles[g][y]
 and demolish your cities.
15I will take vengeance[z] in anger and wrath
 upon the nations that have not obeyed me."

[e] *6* Or *crush* [f] *6* Or *Nimrod in its gates* [g] *14* That is, symbols of the goddess Asherah

---

Although eternal, Christ entered human history as the man, Jesus of Nazareth.

5:5 This chapter provides one of the clearest Old Testament prophecies of Christ's coming. The key descriptive phrase is "and he will be their peace". In one of Christ's final talks he said, "Peace I leave with you; my peace I give you. I do not give to you as the world gives. Do not let your hearts be troubled and do not be afraid" (John 14:27). Because of Christ's first coming, we have the opportunity to experience peace with God with no more fear of judgment and no more conflict and guilt. Christ's peace gives us assurance even though wars continue. At Christ's second coming, all wars and weapons will be destroyed (4:3–5).

5:5 Micah's prophecy of seven shepherds and eight leaders is a figurative way of saying that the Messiah will raise up many good leaders when he returns to reign. This contrasts with Micah's words in chapter three about Judah's corrupt leaders. "The Assyrian" symbolically refers to all nations in every age that oppose God's people. These good leaders will help Christ defeat all evil in the world.

5:6 The land of Nimrod is another name for Assyria, which, in this case, is a symbol of all the evil nations in the world.

5:10 When God rules in his eternal kingdom, our strength and deliverance will not be found in military might but in God's almighty power. God will destroy all the weapons that people use for security. There will be no need for armies because God will rule in the heart of every person. Instead of being overwhelmed by fear of invasion or nuclear attack, we should have confidence in God.

5:12–14 Carved images, sacred stones, and Asherah poles were all part of pagan worship.

3. The trial of the people

The LORD's Case Against Israel

6 Listen to what the LORD says:

"Stand up, plead your case before the mountains;[a]
let the hills hear what you have to say.
2Hear,[b] O mountains, the LORD's accusation;[c]
listen, you everlasting foundations of the earth.
For the LORD has a case against his people;
he is lodging a charge[d] against Israel.

3"My people, what have I done to you?
How have I burdened[e] you? Answer me.
4I brought you up out of Egypt
and redeemed you from the land of slavery.[f]
I sent Moses[g] to lead you,
also Aaron[h] and Miriam.[i]
5My people, remember
what Balak[j] king of Moab counselled
and what Balaam son of Beor answered.
Remember ⌊your journey⌋ from Shittim[k] to Gilgal,[l]
that you may know the righteous acts[m] of the LORD."

6With what shall I come before the LORD
and bow down before the exalted God?
Shall I come before him with burnt offerings,
with calves a year old?[n]
7Will the LORD be pleased with thousands of rams,[o]
with ten thousand rivers of oil?[p]
Shall I offer my firstborn[q] for my transgression,
the fruit of my body for the sin of my soul?[r]
8He has showed you, O man, what is good.
And what does the LORD require of you?
To act justly[s] and to love mercy
and to walk humbly[t] with your God.[u]

Israel's Guilt and Punishment

9Listen! The LORD is calling to the city—
and to fear your name is wisdom—

6:1 [a]Ps 50:1; Eze 6:2
6:2 [b]Dt 32:1 [c]Hos 12:2 [d]Ps 50:7
6:3 [e]Jer 2:5
6:4 [f]Dt 7:8 [g]Ex 4:16 [h]Ps 77:20 [i]Ex 15:20
6:5 [j]Nu 22:5-6 [k]Nu 25:1 [l]Jos 5:9-10 [m]Jdg 5:11; 1Sa 12:7
6:6 [n]Ps 40:6-8; 51:16-17
6:7 [o]Isa 40:16 [p]Ps 50:8-10 [q]Lev 18:21 [r]2Ki 16:3
6:8 [s]Isa 1:17; Jer 22:3 [t]Isa 57:15 [u]Dt 10:12-13; 1Sa 15:22; Hos 6:6

6:1ff Here Micah pictures a courtroom. God, the judge, tells his people what he requires of them and recites all the ways they have wronged both him and others. Chapters 4 and 5 are full of hope; chapters 6 and 7 proclaim judgment and appeal to the people to repent.

6:1, 2 God called to the mountains to confirm the people's guilt. The mountains would serve as excellent witnesses, for it was in the high places that the people had built pagan altars and had sacrificed to false gods (1 Kings 14:23; Jeremiah 17:2, 3; Ezekiel 20:28).

6:3 The people would never be able to answer this question because God had done nothing wrong. In fact, God had been exceedingly patient with them, had always lovingly guided them, and had given them every opportunity to return to him. If God asked you, "What have I done to you?" how would you reply?

6:5 The story of Balak and Balaam is found in Numbers 22–24. Shittim was the Israelites' campsite east of the Jordan River just before they entered the promised land (Joshua 2:1). There the people received many of God's instructions about how to live. Gilgal, their first campsite after crossing the Jordan (Joshua 4:19), was where the people renewed their covenant with God (Joshua 5:3–9). These two places represent God's loving care for his people: his willingness both to protect them and to warn them about potential troubles. In Micah's day, the people had forgotten this covenant and its benefits and had turned away from God.

6:5 God continued to be kind to his forgetful people, but their short memory and lack of thankfulness condemned them. When people refuse to see how fortunate they are and begin to take God's gifts for granted, they become self-centred. Regularly remember God's goodness and thank him. Remembering God's past protection will help you see his present provision.

6:8 People have tried all kinds of ways to please God (6:6, 7), but God has made his wishes clear: he wants his people to be just, merciful, and to walk humbly with him. In your efforts to please God, examine these areas on a regular basis. Are you fair in your dealings with people? Do you show mercy to those who wrong you? Are you learning humility?

6:10
[v]Eze 45:9-10;
Am 3:10; 8:4-6

6:11
[w]Lev 19:36;
Hos 12:7

6:12
[x]Isa 1:23
[y]Isa 3:8
[z]Jer 9:3

6:13
[a]Isa 1:7; 6:11

6:14
[b]Isa 9:20
[c]Isa 30:6

6:15
[d]Dt 28:38;
Jer 12:13
[e]Am 5:11;
Zep 1:13

6:16
[f]1Ki 16:25
[g]1Ki 16:29-33
[h]Jer 7:24
[i]Jer 25:9
[j]Jer 51:51

7:2
[a]Ps 12:1
[b]Mic 3:10
[c]Jer 5:26

7:3
[d]Pr 4:16

7:4
[e]Eze 2:6
[f]Isa 22:5;
Hos 9:7

"Heed the rod and the One who appointed it.[a]
10 Am I still to forget, O wicked house,
your ill-gotten treasures
and the short ephah,[b] which is accursed?[v]
11 Shall I acquit a man with dishonest scales,[w]
with a bag of false weights?
12 Her rich men are violent;[x]
her people are liars[y]
and their tongues speak deceitfully.[z]
13 Therefore, I have begun to destroy[a] you,
to ruin you because of your sins.
14 You will eat but not be satisfied;[b]
your stomach will still be empty.[c]
You will store up but save nothing,[c]
because what you save I will give to the sword.
15 You will plant but not harvest;[d]
you will press olives but not use the oil on yourselves,
you will crush grapes but not drink the wine.[e]
16 You have observed the statutes of Omri[f]
and all the practices of Ahab's[g] house,
and you have followed their traditions.[h]
Therefore I will give you over to ruin[i]
and your people to derision;
you will bear the scorn[j] of the nations."[d]

Israel's Misery

7 What misery is mine!
I am like one who gathers summer fruit
at the gleaning of the vineyard;
there is no cluster of grapes to eat,
none of the early figs that I crave.
2 The godly have been swept from the land;[a]
not one upright man remains.
All men lie in wait to shed blood;[b]
each hunts his brother with a net.[c]
3 Both hands are skilled in doing evil;[d]
the ruler demands gifts,
the judge accepts bribes,
the powerful dictate what they desire—
they all conspire together.
4 The best of them is like a brier,[e]
the most upright worse than a thorn hedge.
The day of your watchmen has come,
the day God visits you.
Now is the time of their confusion.[f]

[a] *9* The meaning of the Hebrew for this line is uncertain. [b] *10* An ephah was a dry measure. [c] *14* The meaning of the Hebrew for this word is uncertain. [d] *16* Septuagint; Hebrew *scorn due to my people*

6:16 Omri reigned over Israel and led the people into idol worship (1 Kings 16:21–26). Ahab, his son, was Israel's most wicked king (1 Kings 16:29–33). If the people were following the commands and practices of these kings, they were in bad shape. Such pervasive evil was ripe for punishment.

7:1ff This chapter begins in gloom (7:1–6) and ends in hope (7:8–20). Micah watched as society rotted around him. Rulers demanded gifts; judges accepted bribes; corruption was universal. But God promised to lead the people out of the darkness of sin and into his light. Then the people would praise him for his faithfulness. God alone is perfectly faithful.

7:1–4 Micah could not find an upright person anywhere in the land. Even today, uprightness (honesty, integrity) is difficult to find. Society rationalises sin, and even Christians sometimes compromise Christian principles in order to do what they want. It is easy to justify our actions to ourselves, especially when "everyone else is doing it". But the standards for honesty come from God, not society. We are honest because God is truth, and we are to be like him.

5Do not trust a neighbour;
put no confidence in a friend.[g]
Even with her who lies in your embrace
be careful of your words.
6For a son dishonours his father,
a daughter rises up against her mother,[h]
a daughter-in-law against her mother-in-law—
a man's enemies are the members of his own household.[i]

7But as for me, I watch in hope[j] for the LORD,
I wait for God my Saviour;
my God will hear[k] me.

Israel Will Rise

8Do not gloat over me,[l] my enemy!
Though I have fallen, I will rise.[m]
Though I sit in darkness,
the LORD will be my light.[n]
9Because I have sinned against him,
I will bear the LORD's wrath,[o]
until he pleads my case
and establishes my right.
He will bring me out into the light;
I will see his righteousness.[p]
10Then my enemy will see it
and will be covered with shame,[q]
she who said to me,
"Where is the LORD your God?"
My eyes will see her downfall;[r]
even now she will be trampled[s] underfoot
like mire in the streets.

11The day for building your walls[t] will come,
the day for extending your boundaries.
12In that day people will come to you
from Assyria and the cities of Egypt,
even from Egypt to the Euphrates
and from sea to sea
and from mountain to mountain.[u]
13The earth will become desolate because of its inhabitants,
as the result of their deeds.[v]

Prayer and Praise

14Shepherd[w] your people with your staff,[x]
the flock of your inheritance,
which lives by itself in a forest,
in fertile pasture-lands.[a]
Let them feed in Bashan and Gilead[y]

7:5 [g]Jer 9:4
7:6 [h]Eze 22:7 [i]Mt 10:35-36*
7:7 [j]Ps 130:5; Isa 25:9 [k]Ps 4:3
7:8 [l]Pr 24:17 [m]Ps 37:24; Am 9:11 [n]Isa 9:2
7:9 [o]La 3:39-40 [p]Isa 46:13
7:10 [q]Ps 35:26 [r]Isa 51:23 [s]Zec 10:5
7:11 [t]Isa 54:11
7:12 [u]Isa 19:23-25
7:13 [v]Isa 3:10-11
7:14 [w]Mic 5:4 [x]Ps 23:4 [y]Jer 50:19

a 14 Or *in the middle of Carmel*

7:5, 6 Sin had affected the government leaders and society in general. Deceit and dishonesty had even ruined the family, the core of society. As a result, the only way left to purify the people was God's judgment. This would draw the nation back to God and restore them from the inside out.

7:7–10 Micah showed great faith in God both personally (7:7) and on Israel's behalf (7:8–10) as he proclaimed that (1) he would wait upon God, because God hears and saves when help is needed, (2) God would bring his people through when times were tough, (3) Israel must be patient in punishment because God would bring them out of the darkness, and (4) their enemies would be punished. We too can have a relationship with God that can allow us to have confidence like Micah's. It doesn't take unusual talent; it simply takes faith in God and a willingness to act on that faith.

7:14 Bashan and Gilead were fertile areas east of the Jordan, previously the territory of Reuben, Gad, and the half tribe of Manasseh.

7:15 [z]Ex 3:20; Ps 78:12

7:16 [a]Isa 26:11

7:17 [b]Isa 25:3; 49:23; 59:19

7:18 [c]Isa 43:25; Jer 50:20 [d]Ps 103:8-13 [e]Mic 2:12 [f]Ex 34:9 [g]Ps 103:9 [h]Jer 32:41

7:19 [i]Isa 43:25 [j]Jer 31:34

7:20 [k]Dt 7:8; Lk 1:72

as in days long ago.

15"As in the days when you came out of Egypt,
I will show them my wonders.[z]"

16Nations will see and be ashamed,[a]
deprived of all their power.
They will lay their hands on their mouths
and their ears will become deaf.
17They will lick dust like a snake,
like creatures that crawl on the ground.
They will come trembling out of their dens;
they will turn in fear[b] to the LORD our God
and will be afraid of you.
18Who is a God like you,
who pardons sin[c] and forgives[d] the transgression
of the remnant[e] of his inheritance?[f]
You do not stay angry[g] for ever
but delight to show mercy.[h]
19You will again have compassion on us;
you will tread our sins underfoot
and hurl all our iniquities[i] into the depths of the sea.[j]
20You will be true to Jacob,
and show mercy to Abraham,
as you pledged on oath to our fathers[k]
in days long ago.

7:18 God delights to show mercy! He does not forgive grudgingly, but is glad when we repent and offers forgiveness to all who come back to him. Today you can confess your sins and receive his loving forgiveness. Don't be too proud to accept God's free offer.

7:20 In an age when religion was making little difference in people's lives, Micah said that God expected his people to be just, merciful, and humble (6:8). He requires the same of Christians today. In a world that is unjust, we must act justly. In a world of tough breaks, we must be merciful. In a world of pride and self-sufficiency, we must walk humbly with God. Only when we live according to God's way will we begin to affect our homes, our society, and our world.

NAHUM

Manasseh becomes king of Judah 697 B.C.

Ashurbanipal becomes king of Assyria 669

The fall of Thebes; Nahum becomes a prophet 663

VITAL STATISTICS

PURPOSE:
To pronounce God's judgment on Assyria and to comfort Judah with this truth

AUTHOR:
Nahum

TO WHOM WRITTEN:
The people of Nineveh and Judah

DATE WRITTEN:
Some time during Nahum's prophetic ministry (probably between 663 and 612 B.C.)

SETTING:
This particular prophecy took place after the fall of Thebes in 663 B.C. (see 3:8–10)

KEY VERSES:
"The LORD is good, a refuge in times of trouble. He cares for those who trust in him, but with an overwhelming flood he will make an end of Nineveh; he will pursue his foes into darkness. Whatever they plot against the LORD he will bring to an end; trouble will not come a second time" (1:7–9).

KEY PLACE:
Nineveh

THE SHRILL whistle pierces the air, and all action on the field abruptly stops. Pointing to the offending player, the referee shouts, "Foul!"

Rules, fouls, and penalties are part of any game and are regulated and enforced rigorously by referees, umpires, judges, and other officials. Every participant knows that boundaries must be set and behaviour monitored, or the game will degenerate into chaos.

There are laws in the world as well—boundaries and rules for living established by God. But men and women regularly flaunt these regulations, hiding their infractions or overpowering others and declaring that might makes right. God calls this sin—wilful disobedience, rebellion against his control, or apathy. And at times it seems as though the violators succeed—no whistles blow, no fouls are called, and individual dictators rule. The truth is, however, that ultimately justice will be served in the world. God will settle all accounts.

Assyria was the most powerful nation on earth. Proud in their self-sufficiency and military might, they plundered, oppressed, and slaughtered their victims. One hundred years earlier, Jonah had preached in the streets of the great city Nineveh; the people had heard God's message and had turned from their evil. But generations later, evil was again reigning, and the prophet Nahum pronounced judgment on this wicked nation. Nineveh is called a "city of blood" (3:1), a city of cruelty (3:19), and the Assyrians are judged for their arrogance (1:11), idolatry (1:14), murder, lies, treachery, and social injustice (3:1–19). Because of their sins, Nahum predicted that this proud and powerful nation would be utterly destroyed. The end came within 50 years.

In this judgment of Assyria and its capital city, Nineveh, God is judging a sinful world. And the message is clear—disobedience, rebellion, and injustice will not prevail but will be punished severely by a righteous and holy God who rules over all the earth.

As you read Nahum, sense God's wrath as he avenges sin and brings about justice. Then decide to live under his guidance and within his rules, commands, and guidelines for life.

THE BLUEPRINT

1. Nineveh's judge (1:1–15)
2. Nineveh's judgment (2:1—3:19)

Nineveh, the capital of the Assyrian empire, is the subject of Nahum's prophecy. The news of its coming destruction was a relief for Judah, which was subject to Assyrian domination. No longer would Judah be forced to pay tribute as insurance against invasions. Judah was comforted to know that God was still in control. Nineveh is an example to all rulers and nations of the world today. God is sovereign over even those who are seemingly invincible. We can be confident that God's power and justice will one day conquer all evil.

Josiah becomes king of Judah; Zephaniah becomes a prophet 640	Jeremiah becomes a prophet 627	Nineveh falls 612	Assyria completely conquered 609	Babylonians win battle of Carchemish 605	Judah falls to Babylon 586

MEGATHEMES

THEME	EXPLANATION	IMPORTANCE
God Judges	God would judge the city of Nineveh for its idolatry, arrogance, and oppression. Although Assyria was the leading military power in the world, God would completely destroy this "invincible" nation. God allows no person or power to usurp or scoff at his authority.	Anyone who remains arrogant and resists God's authority will face his anger. No ruler or nation will get away with rejecting him. No individual will be able to hide from his judgment. Yet those who keep trusting God will be kept safe for ever.
God Rules	God rules over all the earth, even over those who don't acknowledge him. God is all-powerful, and no-one can thwart his plans. God will overcome any who attempt to defy him. Human power is futile against God.	If you are impressed by or afraid of any weapons, armies, or powerful people, remember that God alone can truly rescue you from fear or oppression. We must place our confidence in God because he alone rules all of history, all the earth, and our lives.

1:1
[a] Isa 13:1; 19:1; Jer 23:33-34
[b] Jnh 1:2; Na 2:8; Zep 2:13

1. Nineveh's judge

1 An oracle[a] concerning Nineveh.[b] The book of the vision of Nahum the Elkoshite.

The LORD's Anger Against Nineveh

1:2
[c] Ex 20:5
[d] Dt 32:41; Ps 94:1

2 The LORD is a jealous[c] and avenging God;
the LORD takes vengeance[d] and is filled with wrath.
The LORD takes vengeance on his foes
and maintains his wrath against his enemies.

NAHUM served as a prophet to Judah and Assyria from 663–612 B.C.

Climate of the times	Manasseh, one of Judah's most wicked kings, ruled the land. He openly defied God and persecuted God's people. Assyria, the world power at that time, made Judah one of its vassal states. The people of Judah wanted to be like the Assyrians, who seemed to have all the power and possessions they wanted.
Main message	The mighty empire of Assyria that oppressed God's people would soon tumble.
Importance of message	Those who do evil and oppress others will one day meet a bitter end.
Contemporary prophet	Zephaniah (640–621)

1:1 Nahum, like Jonah, was a prophet to Nineveh, the capital of the Assyrian empire, and he prophesied between 663 and 612 B.C. Jonah had seen Nineveh repent a century earlier (see the book of Jonah), but the city had fallen back into wickedness. Assyria, the world power controlling the Fertile Crescent, seemed unstoppable. Its ruthless and savage warriors had already conquered Israel, the northern kingdom, and were causing great suffering in Judah. So Nahum proclaimed God's anger against Assyria's evil. Within a few decades, the mighty Assyrian empire would be toppled by Babylon.

1:1 An oracle is a message from God. Elkosh was a village thought by some to be in south-west Judah.

1:2 God alone has the right to be jealous and to carry out vengeance. Jealousy and vengeance may be surprising terms to associate with God. When humans are jealous and take vengeance, they are usually acting in a spirit of selfishness. But it is appropriate for God to insist on our complete allegiance, and it is just for him to punish unrepentant evildoers. His jealousy and vengeance are unmixed with selfishness. Their purpose is to remove sin and restore peace to the world (Deuteronomy 4:24; 5:9).

3The LORD is slow to anger[e] and great in power;
the LORD will not leave the guilty unpunished.[f]
His way is in the whirlwind and the storm,
and clouds[g] are the dust of his feet.
4He rebukes the sea and dries it up;
he makes all the rivers run dry.
Bashan and Carmel[h] wither
and the blossoms of Lebanon fade.
5The mountains quake[i] before him
and the hills melt away.[j]
The earth trembles at his presence,
the world and all who live in it.
6Who can withstand his indignation?
Who can endure[k] his fierce anger?
His wrath is poured out like fire;[l]
the rocks are shattered[m] before him.

7The LORD is good,[n]
a refuge in times of trouble.
He cares for[o] those who trust in him,
8 but with an overwhelming flood
he will make an end of ⌊Nineveh⌋;
he will pursue his foes into darkness.

9Whatever they plot against the LORD
he[a] will bring to an end;
trouble will not come a second time.
10They will be entangled among thorns[p]
and drunk from their wine;
they will be consumed like dry stubble.[b][q]
11From you, ⌊O Nineveh,⌋ has one come forth
who plots evil against the LORD
and counsels wickedness.

12This is what the LORD says:

"Although they have allies and are numerous,
they will be cut off[r] and pass away.
Although I have afflicted you, ⌊O Judah,⌋
I will afflict you no more.[s]

1:3 [e]Ne 9:17 [f]Ex 34:7 [g]Ps 104:3
1:4 [h]Isa 33:9
1:5 [i]Ex 19:18 [j]Mic 1:4
1:6 [k]Mal 3:2 [l]Jer 10:10 [m]1Ki 19:11
1:7 [n]Jer 33:11 [o]Ps 1:6
1:10 [p]2Sa 23:6 [q]Isa 5:24; Mal 4:1
1:12 [r]Isa 10:34 [s]Isa 54:6-8; La 3:31-32

a *9* Or *What do you foes plot against the LORD? / He* b *10* The meaning of the Hebrew for this verse is uncertain.

1:3 God is slow to get angry, but when he is ready to punish, even the earth trembles. Often people avoid God because they see evildoers in the world and hypocrites in the church. They don't realise that because God is slow to anger, he gives his true followers time to share his love and truth with evildoers. But judgment *will* come; God will not allow sin to go unchecked for ever. When people wonder why God doesn't punish evil immediately, help them remember that if he did, none of us would be here. We can all be thankful that God gives people time to turn to him.

1:4 Bashan and Carmel were very fertile areas.

1:6 No person on earth can safely defy God, the Almighty, the Creator of all the universe. God, who controls the sun, the galaxies, and the vast stretches beyond, also controls the rise and fall of nations. How could a small temporal kingdom like Assyria, no matter how powerful, challenge God's awesome power? If only Assyria could have looked ahead to see the desolate mound of rubble that it would become – and yet God would still be alive and well! Don't defy God; he will be here for ever with greater power than that of all armies and nations combined.

1:6–8 To people who refuse to believe, God's punishment is like an angry fire. To those who love him, his mercy is a refuge, supplying all their needs without diminishing his supply. But to God's enemies he is an overwhelming flood that will sweep them away. The relationship we have with God is up to us. What kind of relationship will you choose?

1:11 The one "who plots evil against the LORD and counsels wickedness" could have been (1) Ashurbanipal (669–627 B.C.), king of Assyria during much of Nahum's life and the one who brought Assyria to the zenith of its power; (2) Sennacherib (705–681), who openly defied God (2 Kings 18:13–35), epitomising rebellion against God; (3) no one king in particular, but the entire evil monarchy. The point is that Nineveh would be destroyed for rebelling against God.

1:12–15 The good news for Judah, whom Assyria afflicted, was that its conquerors and tormentors would be destroyed and would never rise to torment it again. Nineveh was so completely wiped out that its ruins were not identified until 1845.

1:13
[t]Isa 9:4

13Now I will break their yoke[t] from your neck
and tear your shackles away."

1:14
[u]Isa 14:22
[v]Mic 5:13
[w]Eze 32:22-23

14The LORD has given a command concerning you, ⌞Nineveh⌟:
"You will have no descendants to bear your name.[u]
I will destroy the carved images[v] and cast idols
that are in the temple of your gods.
I will prepare your grave,[w]
for you are vile."

1:15
[x]Isa 40:9;
Ro 10:15
[y]Isa 52:7
[z]Lev 23:2-4
[a]Isa 52:1

15Look, there on the mountains,
the feet of one who brings good news,[x]
who proclaims peace![y]
Celebrate your festivals,[z] O Judah,
and fulfil your vows.
No more will the wicked invade you;[a]
they will be completely destroyed.

2. Nineveh's judgment

Nineveh to Fall

2:1
[a]Jer 51:20

2 An attacker[a] advances against you, ⌞Nineveh⌟.
Guard the fortress,
watch the road,
brace yourselves,
marshal all your strength!

2:2
[b]Eze 37:23
[c]Isa 60:15

2The LORD will restore[b] the splendour[c] of Jacob
like the splendour of Israel,
though destroyers have laid them waste
and have ruined their vines.

2:3
[d]Eze 23:14-15

3The shields of his soldiers are red;
the warriors are clad in scarlet.[d]
The metal on the chariots flashes
on the day they are made ready;
the spears of pine are brandished.[a]

2:4
[e]Jer 4:13

4The chariots[e] storm through the streets,
rushing back and forth through the squares.
They look like flaming torches;
they dart about like lightning.

2:5
[f]Jer 46:12

5He summons his picked troops,
yet they stumble[f] on their way.
They dash to the city wall;
the protective shield is put in place.

2:6
[g]Na 3:13

6The river gates[g] are thrown open
and the palace collapses.

2:7
[h]Isa 59:11

7It is decreed[b] that ⌞the city⌟
be exiled and carried away.
Its slave girls moan[h] like doves

a *3* Hebrew; Septuagint and Syriac / *the horsemen rush to and fro* b *7* The meaning of the Hebrew for this word is uncertain.

2:1ff This chapter predicts the events of 612 B.C., when the combined armies of the Babylonians and the Medes sacked the seemingly impregnable Nineveh.

2:2 Assyria had plundered and crushed the northern kingdom (Israel) and had deported its people in 722 B.C. (2 Kings 17:3–6; 18:9–11). Assyria had also attacked the southern kingdom (here called Jacob) and had forced it to pay tribute.

2:6 This reference to the opening of river gates could refer either to the enemy flowing into Nineveh like a flood (1:8) or to an actual flood of water. Some scholars suggest that dam gates, which were found in archaeological excavations, were closed to dam up the river. When an enormous amount of water had been accumulated, the gates were opened, allowing the water to flood Nineveh.

and beat upon their breasts.[i]
8Nineveh is like a pool,
and its water is draining away.
"Stop! Stop!" they cry,
but no-one turns back.
9Plunder the silver!
Plunder the gold!
The supply is endless,
the wealth from all its treasures!
10She is pillaged, plundered, stripped!
Hearts melt, knees give way,
bodies tremble, every face grows pale.[j]

11Where now is the lions' den,[k]
the place where they fed their young,
where the lion and lioness went,
and the cubs, with nothing to fear?
12The lion killed[l] enough for his cubs
and strangled the prey for his mate,
filling his lairs with the kill
and his dens with the prey.

13"I am against[m] you,"
declares the LORD Almighty.
"I will burn up your chariots in smoke,[n]
and the sword will devour your young lions.
I will leave you no prey on the earth.
The voices of your messengers
will no longer be heard."

2:7 [i]Isa 32:12
2:10 [j]Isa 29:22
2:11 [k]Isa 5:29
2:12 [l]Jer 51:34
2:13 [m]Jer 21:13; Na 3:5 [n]Ps 46:9

Woe to Nineveh

3 Woe to the city of blood,[a]
full of lies,
full of plunder,
never without victims!
2The crack of whips,
the clatter of wheels,
galloping horses
and jolting chariots!
3Charging cavalry,
flashing swords
and glittering spears!
Many casualties,
piles of dead,
bodies without number,
people stumbling over the corpses[b]—
4all because of the wanton lust of a harlot,

3:1 [a]Eze 22:2; Mic 3:10
3:3 [b]2Ki 19:35; Isa 34:3

2:12–3:1 The major source of wealth for the Assyrian economy was the plunder taken from other nations. The Assyrians had taken the food of innocent people to maintain their luxurious standard of living, depriving others to supply their excesses. Depriving innocent people to support the luxury of a few is a sin that angers God. As Christians we must stand firm against this common but evil practice.

2:13 God had given the people of Nineveh a chance to repent, which they did after hearing Jonah (see the book of Jonah). But they had returned to their sin, and its consequences were destroying them. There is a point for people, cities, and nations after which there is no turning back; Assyria had passed that point. We must warn others to repent while there is still time.

3:4 Nineveh had used its beauty, prestige, and power to seduce other nations. Like a harlot, she had enticed them into false friendships. Then when the other nations relaxed, thinking Assyria was a friend, Assyria destroyed and plundered them. Beautiful and impressive on the outside, Nineveh was vicious and deceitful on the inside. Beneath beautiful façades sometimes lie seduction and death. Don't let an attractive institution, company, movement, or person seduce you into lowering your standards or compromising your moral principles.

alluring, the mistress of sorceries,[c]
who enslaved nations by her prostitution[d]
and peoples by her witchcraft.

5"I am against[e] you," declares the LORD Almighty.
"I will lift your skirts[f] over your face.
I will show the nations your nakedness[g]
and the kingdoms your shame.
6I will pelt you with filth,[h]
I will treat you with contempt[i]
and make you a spectacle.[j]
7All who see you will flee from you and say,
'Nineveh[k] is in ruins — who will mourn for her?'[l]
Where can I find anyone to comfort[m] you?"

8Are you better than[n] Thebes,[a][o]
situated on the Nile,[p]
with water around her?
The river was her defence,
the waters her wall.
9Cush[b][q] and Egypt were her boundless strength;
Put[r] and Libya[s] were among her allies.
10Yet she was taken captive[t]
and went into exile.
Her infants were dashed[u] to pieces
at the head of every street.
Lots were cast for her nobles,
and all her great men were put in chains.
11You too will become drunk;[v]
you will go into hiding[w]
and seek refuge from the enemy.

12All your fortresses are like fig-trees
with their first ripe fruit;
when they are shaken,
the figs[x] fall into the mouth of the eater.
13Look at your troops —
they are all women![y]
The gates[z] of your land
are wide open to your enemies;
fire has consumed their bars.[a]

14Draw water for the siege,[b]
strengthen your defences![c]
Work the clay,
tread the mortar,
repair the brickwork!
15There the fire will devour you;
the sword will cut you down
and, like grasshoppers, consume you.
Multiply like grasshoppers,

3:4 [c]Isa 47:9 [d]Isa 23:17; Eze 16:25-29
3:5 [e]Na 2:13 [f]Jer 13:22 [g]Isa 47:3
3:6 [h]Job 9:31 [i]1Sa 2:30; Jer 51:37 [j]Isa 14:16
3:7 [k]Na 1:1 [l]Jer 15:5 [m]Isa 51:19
3:8 [n]Am 6:2 [o]Jer 46:25 [p]Isa 19:6-9
3:9 [q]2Ch 12:3 [r]Eze 27:10 [s]Eze 30:5
3:10 [t]Isa 20:4 [u]Isa 13:16; Hos 13:16
3:11 [v]Isa 49:26 [w]Isa 2:10
3:12 [x]Isa 28:4
3:13 [y]Isa 19:16; Jer 50:37 [z]Na 2:6 [a]Isa 45:2
3:14 [b]2Ch 32:4 [c]Na 2:1

[a] *8* Hebrew *No Amon* [b] *9* That is, the upper Nile region

3:8–10 Thebes was a city in Egypt, the previous world power, which stood in the path of Assyria's expansion in the south. The Assyrians conquered Thebes 51 years before this prophecy was given. To Judah, surrounded to the north and south by Assyria, the situation appeared hopeless. But God said that the same atrocities done in Thebes would happen in Nineveh.

3:8–10 No power on earth can protect us from God's judgment or be a suitable substitute for his power in our lives. Thebes and Assyria put their trust in alliances and military power, but history would show that these were inadequate. Don't insist on learning through personal experience; instead, learn the lessons history has already taught. Put your trust in God above all else.

multiply like locusts![d]
16 You have increased the number of your merchants
till they are more than the stars of the sky,
but like locusts they strip the land
and then fly away.
17 Your guards are like locusts,[e]
your officials like swarms of locusts
that settle in the walls on a cold day—
but when the sun appears they fly away,
and no-one knows where.

18 O king of Assyria, your shepherds[c] slumber;[f]
your nobles lie down to rest.[g]
Your people are scattered[h] on the mountains
with no-one to gather them.
19 Nothing can heal your wound;[i]
your injury is fatal.
Everyone who hears the news about you
claps his hands[j] at your fall,
for who has not felt
your endless cruelty?

c 18 Or *rulers*

3:15 [d] Joel 1:4
3:17 [e] Jer 51:27
3:18 [f] Ps 76:5-6 [g] Isa 56:10 [h] 1Ki 22:17
3:19 [i] Jer 30:13; Mic 1:9 [j] Job 27:23; La 2:15; Zep 2:15

3:19 All the nations hated to be ruled by the merciless Assyrians, but the nations wanted to be like Assyria—powerful, wealthy, prestigious—and they courted Assyria's friendship. In the same way, we don't like the idea of being ruled harshly, so we do what we can to stay on good terms with a powerful leader. And deep down, we would like to have that kind of power. The thought of being on top can be captivating. But power is seductive, so we should not scheme to get it or hold on to it. Those who lust after power will be powerfully destroyed, as was the mighty Assyrian empire.

HABAKKUK

Jeremiah becomes a prophet 627 B.C.	Habakkuk becomes a prophet 612	King Josiah dies in battle 609	Daniel taken captive to Babylon 605	Ezekiel a captive in Babylon; Zedekiah becomes king 597	Habakkuk's ministry ends 588	Fall of Judah; Jerusalem destroyed 586

FROM innocent childhood queries to complex university discussions, life is filled with questions. Asking how and why and when, we probe beneath the surface to find satisfying answers. But not all questions have answers wrapped and neatly tied. These unanswered problems create more questions and nagging, spirit-destroying doubt. Some choose to live with their doubts, ignoring them and moving on with life. Others become cynical and hardened. But there are those who reject those options and continue to ask, looking for answers.

Habakkuk was a man who sought answers. Troubled by what he observed, he asked difficult questions. These questions were not merely intellectual exercises or bitter complaints. Habakkuk saw a dying world, and it broke his heart. Why is there evil in the world? Why do the wicked seem to be winning? He boldly and confidently took his complaints directly to God. And God answered . . . with an avalanche of proof and prediction.

The prophet's questions and God's answers are recorded in this book. As we turn the pages, we are immediately confronted with his urgent cries, "How long, O LORD, must I call for help, but you do not listen? Or cry out to you, 'Violence!' but you do not save?" (1:2). In fact, most of the first chapter is devoted to his questions. As chapter two begins, Habakkuk declares that he will wait to hear God's answers to his complaints. Then God begins to speak, telling the prophet to write his answer plainly so that all will see and understand. It may seem, God says, as though the wicked triumph, but eventually they will be judged, and righteousness will prevail. Judgment may not come quickly, but it *will* come. God's answers fill chapter two. Then Habakkuk concludes his book with a prayer of triumph. With questions answered and a new understanding of God's power and love, Habakkuk rejoices in who God is and in what he will do. "Yet I will rejoice in the LORD, I will be joyful in God my Saviour. The Sovereign LORD is my strength; he makes my feet like the feet of a deer, he enables me to go on the heights" (3:18, 19).

Listen to the profound questions that Habakkuk boldly brings to God, and realise that you can also bring your complaints and enquiries to him. Listen to God's answers and rejoice that he is at work in the world and in your life.

VITAL STATISTICS

PURPOSE:
To show that God is still in control of the world despite the apparent triumph of evil

AUTHOR:
Habakkuk

TO WHOM WRITTEN:
Judah (the southern kingdom), and God's people everywhere

DATE WRITTEN:
Between 612 and 588 B.C.

SETTING:
Babylon was becoming the dominant world power and Judah would soon feel Babylon's destructive force

KEY VERSE:
"LORD, I have heard of your fame; I stand in awe of your deeds, O LORD. Renew them in our day, in our time make them known; in wrath remember mercy" (3:2).

KEY PEOPLE:
Habakkuk, the Babylonians

KEY PLACE:
Judah

THE BLUEPRINT

1. Habakkuk's complaints (1:1—2:20)
2. Habakkuk's prayer (3:1–19)

When Habakkuk was troubled he brought his concerns directly to God. After receiving God's answers, he responded with a prayer of faith. Habakkuk's example is one that should encourage us as we struggle to move from doubt to faith. We don't have to be afraid to ask questions of God. The problem is not with God and his ways, but with our limited understanding of him.

MEGATHEMES

THEME	EXPLANATION	IMPORTANCE
Struggle and Doubt	Habakkuk asked God why the wicked in Judah were not being punished for their sin. He couldn't understand why a just God would allow such evil to exist. God promised to use the Babylonians to punish Judah. When Habakkuk cried out for answers in his time of struggle, God answered him with words of hope.	God wants us to come to him with our struggles and doubts. But his answers may not be what we expect. God sustains us by revealing himself to us. Trusting him leads to quiet hope, not bitter resignation.
God's Sovereignty	Habakkuk asked God why he would use the wicked Babylonians to punish his people. God said that he would also punish the Babylonians after they had fulfilled his purpose.	God is still in control of this world in spite of the apparent triumph of evil. God doesn't overlook sin. One day he will rule the whole earth with perfect justice.
Hope	God is the Creator; he is all-powerful. He has a plan, and he will carry it out. He will punish sin. He is our strength and our place of safety. We can have confidence that he will love us and guard our relationship with him for ever.	Hope means going beyond our unpleasant daily experiences to the joy of knowing God. We live by trusting in him, not in the benefits, happiness, or success we may experience in this life. Our hope comes from God.

1. Habakkuk's complaints

1 The oracle[a] that Habakkuk the prophet received.

2How long, O LORD, must I call for help,
but you do not listen?[b]
Or cry out to you, "Violence!"
but you do not save?[c]
3Why do you make me look at injustice?
Why do you tolerate[d] wrong?
Destruction and violence[e] are before me;
there is strife,[f] and conflict abounds.
4Therefore the law[g] is paralysed,
and justice never prevails.
The wicked hem in the righteous,
so that justice is perverted.[h]

The LORD's Answer

5"Look at the nations and watch—
and be utterly amazed.[i]
For I am going to do something in your days

1:1 [a]Na 1:1
1:2 [b]Ps 13:1-2; 22:1-2 [c]Jer 14:9
1:3 [d]ver 13 [e]Jer 20:8 [f]Ps 55:9
1:4 [g]Ps 119:126 [h]Job 19:7; Isa 1:23; 5:20; Eze 9:9
1:5 [i]Isa 29:9

1:1 Habakkuk lived in Judah during the reign of Jehoiakim (2 Kings 23:36–24:5). He prophesied between the fall of Nineveh (the capital of Assyria) in 612 B.C. and the Babylonian invasion of Judah in 588 B.C. With Assyria in disarray, Babylon was becoming the dominant world power. This book records the prophet's dialogue with God concerning the questions, "Why does God often seem indifferent in the face of evil?" "Why do evil people seem to go unpunished?" While other prophetic books brought God's word to people, this brought people's questions to God. An "oracle" is a message from God.

1:2–4 Saddened by the violence and corruption he saw around him, Habakkuk poured out his heart to God. Today injustice is still rampant, but don't let your concern cause you to doubt God or rebel against him. Instead, consider the message that God gave Habakkuk and recognise God's long-range plans and purposes. Realise that God is doing right, even when you do not understand why he works as he does.

1:5 God responded to Habakkuk's questions and concerns by stating that he would do amazing acts that would astound Habakkuk. When circumstances around us become almost unbearable, we wonder if God has forgotten us. But remember, he is in control. God has a plan and will judge evildoers in his time. If we are truly humble, we will be willing to accept God's answers and await his timing.

1:5ff God told the inhabitants of Jerusalem that they would be utterly amazed at what he was about to do. The people would, in fact, see a series of unbelievable events: (1) their own independent and prosperous kingdom, Judah, would suddenly become a vassal nation; (2) Egypt, a world power for centuries, would be crushed almost overnight; (3) Nineveh, the capital of the Assyrian empire, would be so completely ransacked that people would forget where it had been; and (4) the Babylonians would rise to power. Though these words were indeed amazing, the people saw them fulfilled during their lifetime.

1:5 [j]Ac 13:41*
1:6 [k]2Ki 24:2 [l]Jer 13:20
1:7 [m]Isa 18:7; Jer 39:5-9
1:8 [n]Jer 4:13
1:9 [o]Hab 2:5
1:10 [p]2Ch 36:6
1:11 [q]Jer 4:11-12 [r]Da 4:30
1:12 [s]Isa 31:1 [t]Isa 10:6

that you would not believe,
even if you were told.[j]
6 I am raising up the Babylonians,[a][k]
that ruthless and impetuous people,
who sweep across the whole earth
to seize dwelling-places not their own.[l]
7 They are a feared and dreaded people;[m]
they are a law to themselves
and promote their own honour.
8 Their horses are swifter[n] than leopards,
fiercer than wolves at dusk.
Their cavalry gallops headlong;
their horsemen come from afar.
They fly like a vulture swooping to devour;
9 they all come bent on violence.
Their hordes[b] advance like a desert wind
and gather prisoners[o] like sand.
10 They deride kings
and scoff at rulers.[p]
They laugh at all fortified cities;
they build earthen ramps and capture them.
11 Then they sweep past like the wind[q] and go on—
guilty men, whose own strength is their god."[r]

Habakkuk's Second Complaint

12 O LORD, are you not from everlasting?
My God, my Holy One,[s] we will not die.
O LORD, you have appointed[t] them to execute judgment;
O Rock, you have ordained them to punish.

[a] *6* Or *Chaldeans* [b] *9* The meaning of the Hebrew for this word is uncertain.

HABAKKUK served as a prophet to Judah from 612–588 B.C.

Climate of the times	Judah's last four kings were wicked men who rejected God and oppressed their own people. Babylon invaded Judah twice before finally destroying it in 586. It was a time of fear, oppression, persecution, lawlessness, and immorality.
Main message	Habakkuk couldn't understand why God seemed to do nothing about the wickedness in society. Then he realised that faith in God alone would supply the answers to his questions.
Importance of message	Instead of questioning the ways of God, we should realise that he is totally just, and we should have faith that he is in control and that one day evil will be utterly destroyed.
Contemporary prophets	Jeremiah (627–586) Daniel (605–536) Ezekiel (593–571)

1:6 The Babylonians, who lived north-west of the Persian Gulf, made a rapid rise to power around 630 B.C. They began to assert themselves against the Assyrian empire, and by 605 B.C. had conquered Assyria and Egypt to become the strongest world power. But they were as wicked as the Assyrians, for they loved to collect prisoners (1:9), were proud of their warfare tactics (1:10), and trusted in their military strength (1:11).

1:10 Armies were able to take fortified (walled) cities by building earthen ramps—heaping mounds of earth against the walls.

1:11 Babylon was proud of its military might, strategies, armies, and weapons. With no regard for humanity, the armies brought home riches, plunder, prisoners, and tribute from the nations they conquered. Such is the essence of idolatry—asking the gods we make to help us get all we want. The essence of Christianity is asking the God *who made us* to help us give all we can in service to him. The goal of idolatry is self-glory; the aim of Christianity is God's glory.

13 Your eyes are too pure to look on evil;
you cannot tolerate wrong.[u]
Why then do you tolerate the treacherous?
Why are you silent while the wicked
swallow up those more righteous than themselves?
14 You have made men like fish in the sea,
like sea creatures that have no ruler.
15 The wicked foe pulls all of them up with hooks,[v]
he catches them in his net,[w]
he gathers them up in his drag-net;
and so he rejoices and is glad.
16 Therefore he sacrifices to his net
and burns incense[x] to his drag-net,
for by his net he lives in luxury
and enjoys the choicest food.
17 Is he to keep on emptying his net,
destroying nations without mercy?[y]

2 I will stand at my watch[a]
and station myself on the ramparts;[b]
I will look to see what he will say[c] to me,
and what answer I am to give to this complaint.[a][d]

The LORD's Answer

2 Then the LORD replied:

"Write[e] down the revelation
and make it plain on tablets
so that a herald[b] may run with it.
3 For the revelation awaits an appointed time;
it speaks of the end[f]
and will not prove false.
Though it linger, wait[g] for it;
it[c] will certainly come and will not delay.[h]

4 "See, he is puffed up;
his desires are not upright—

a 1 Or *and what to answer when I am rebuked* b 2 Or *so that whoever reads it* c 3 Or *Though he linger, wait for him; / he*

1:13 [u] La 3:34-36
1:15 [v] Isa 19:8 [w] Jer 16:16
1:16 [x] Jer 44:8
1:17 [y] Isa 14:6; 19:8
2:1 [a] Isa 21:8 [b] Ps 48:13 [c] Ps 85:8 [d] Ps 5:3
2:2 [e] Rev 1:19
2:3 [f] Da 8:17; 10:14 [g] Ps 27:14 [h] Eze 12:25; Heb 10:37-38

1:13 Judah's forthcoming punishment would be at the hands of the Babylonians. Habakkuk was appalled that God would use a nation more wicked than Judah to punish Judah. But the Babylonians did not know they were being used by God to help Judah return to him, and Babylon's pride in its victories would be its downfall. Evil is self-destructive, and it is never beyond God's control. God may use whatever unusual instrument he chooses to correct or punish us. When we deserve punishment or correction, how can we complain about the kind of "rod" God uses on us?

2:1 The watchman and watchtower, often used by the prophets to show an attitude of expectation (Isaiah 21:8, 11; Jeremiah 6:17; Ezekiel 3:17), are pictures of Habakkuk's attitude of patient waiting and watching for God's response. Stone watchtowers were built on city walls or ramparts so that watchmen could see people (enemies or messengers) approaching their city while still at a distance. Watchtowers were also erected in vineyards to help guard the ripening grapes (Isaiah 5:2). Habakkuk wanted to be in the best position to receive God's message.

2:2ff This chapter records God's answers to Habakkuk's questions: (1) How long would evil prevail (1:2, 3)? (2) Why was Babylon chosen to punish Judah (1:13)? God said that the judgment, though slow to come, was certain. Although God used Babylon against Judah, he knew Babylon's sins and would punish it in due time.

2:3 Evil and injustice seem to have the upper hand in the world. Like Habakkuk, Christians often feel angry and discouraged as they see what goes on. Habakkuk complained vigorously to God about the situation. God's answer to Habakkuk is the same answer he would give us, "Be patient! I will work out my plans in my perfect timing." It isn't easy to be patient, but it helps to remember that God hates sin even more than we do. Punishment of sin will certainly come. As God told Habakkuk, "Wait for it." To trust God fully means to trust him even when we don't understand why events occur as they do.

2:4 The wicked Babylonians trusted in themselves and would fall; but the righteous live by their faith and trust in God. This verse has inspired countless Christians. Paul quotes it in Romans 1:17 and Galatians 3:11. The writer of Hebrews quotes it in 10:38, just before the famous chapter on faith. And it is helpful to all Christians who must live through difficult times without seeing signs of hope. Christians must trust that God is directing all things according to his purposes.

2:4 [i]Ro 1:17*; Gal 3:11*; Heb 10:37-38*
2:5 [j]Pr 20:1 [k]Pr 27:20; 30:15-16
2:6 [l]Isa 14:4 [m]Am 2:8
2:7 [n]Pr 29:1
2:8 [o]Isa 33:1; Zec 2:8-9 [p]ver 17
2:9 [q]Jer 22:13
2:10 [r]Jer 26:19 [s]ver 16
2:11 [t]Jos 24:27; Lk 19:40
2:12 [u]Mic 3:10
2:13 [v]Isa 50:11 [w]Isa 47:13
2:14 [x]Nu 14:21 [y]Isa 11:9
2:16 [z]ver 10 [a]La 4:21 [b]Isa 51:22
2:17 [c]Jer 51:35 [d]Jer 50:15 [e]ver 8
2:18 [f]Jer 5:21

but the righteous will live by his faith[d] [i]—
5 indeed, wine[j] betrays him;
he is arrogant and never at rest.
Because he is as greedy as the grave[e]
and like death is never satisfied,[k]
he gathers to himself all the nations
and takes captive all the peoples.

6 "Will not all of them taunt[l] him with ridicule and scorn, saying,

" 'Woe to him who piles up stolen goods
and makes himself wealthy by extortion![m]
How long must this go on?'
7 Will not your debtors[f] suddenly arise?
Will they not wake up and make you tremble?
Then you will become their victim.[n]
8 Because you have plundered many nations,
the peoples who are left will plunder you.[o]
For you have shed man's blood;[p]
you have destroyed lands and cities and everyone in them.

9 "Woe to him who builds[q] his realm by unjust gain
to set his nest on high,
to escape the clutches of ruin!
10 You have plotted the ruin[r] of many peoples,
shaming[s] your own house and forfeiting your life.
11 The stones[t] of the wall will cry out,
and the beams of the woodwork will echo it.

12 "Woe to him who builds a city with bloodshed[u]
and establishes a town by crime!
13 Has not the LORD Almighty determined
that the people's labour is only fuel for the fire,[v]
that the nations exhaust themselves for nothing?[w]
14 For the earth will be filled with the knowledge of the glory[x] of the LORD,
as the waters cover the sea.[y]

15 "Woe to him who gives drink to his neighbours,
pouring it from the wineskin till they are drunk,
so that he can gaze on their naked bodies.
16 You will be filled with shame[z] instead of glory.
Now it is your turn! Drink and be exposed![g] [a]
The cup[b] from the LORD's right hand is coming round to you,
and disgrace will cover your glory.
17 The violence[c] you have done to Lebanon will overwhelm you,
and your destruction of animals will terrify you.[d]
For you have shed man's blood;[e]
you have destroyed lands and cities and everyone in them.

18 "Of what value is an idol,[f] since a man has carved it?

d *4* Or *faithfulness* **e** *5* Hebrew *Sheol* **f** *7* Or *creditors* **g** *16* Masoretic Text; Dead Sea Scrolls, Aquila, Vulgate and Syriac (see also Septuagint) *and stagger*

2:9–13 Babylon's riches had come from the misfortunes of others, but these riches would only be fuel for the fire. The victims and their cities would cry out against Babylon. Money is not evil, but God condemns the love of riches and the evil means of acquiring it (1 Timothy 6:10). Be careful not to hunger for wealth so much that you lose your appetite for God. Do not allow money to take the place of family, friends, or God.

2:18 Idolatry may seem like a sin that modern people need not fear. But idolatry is not just bowing down to idols; it is trusting in what one has made, and therefore, in one's own power as creator and sustainer. If we say we worship God but put our trust in bank accounts, homes, businesses, and organisations, then we are idolaters. Do you trust God more than you trust what your hands have made?

Or an image that teaches lies?
For he who makes it trusts in his own creation;
he makes idols that cannot speak.[g]
19 Woe to him who says to wood, 'Come to life!'
Or to lifeless stone, 'Wake up!'[h]
Can it give guidance?
It is covered with gold and silver;[i]
there is no breath in it.
20 But the LORD is in his holy temple;[j]
let all the earth be silent[k] before him."

2. Habakkuk's prayer

3 A prayer of Habakkuk the prophet. On *shigionoth.*[a]

2 LORD, I have heard[a] of your fame;
I stand in awe[b] of your deeds, O LORD.
Renew[c] them in our day,
in our time make them known;
in wrath remember mercy.[d]

3 God came from Teman,
the Holy One from Mount Paran. *Selah*[b]
His glory covered the heavens
and his praise filled the earth.[e]
4 His splendour was like the sunrise;
rays flashed from his hand,
where his power was hidden.
5 Plague went before him;
pestilence followed his steps.
6 He stood, and shook the earth;
he looked, and made the nations tremble.
The ancient mountains crumbled
and the age-old hills collapsed.[f]
His ways are eternal.
7 I saw the tents of Cushan in distress,
the dwellings of Midian[g] in anguish.[h]

8 Were you angry with the rivers,[i] O LORD?
Was your wrath against the streams?
Did you rage against the sea
when you rode with your horses
and your victorious chariots?[j]
9 You uncovered your bow,

2:18 [g]Ps 115:4-5; Jer 10:14
2:19 [h]1Ki 18:27 [i]Jer 10:4
2:20 [j]Ps 11:4 [k]Isa 41:1
3:2 [a]Ps 44:1 [b]Ps 119:120 [c]Ps 85:6 [d]Isa 54:8
3:3 [e]Ps 48:10
3:6 [f]Ps 114:1-6
3:7 [g]Jdg 7:24-25 [h]Ex 15:14
3:8 [i]Ex 7:20 [j]Ps 68:17

a *1* Probably a literary or musical term b *3* A word of uncertain meaning; possibly a musical term; also in verses 9 and 13

2:20 Idols have no life, no personhood, no power; they are empty chunks of wood or stone. Temples built to idols are equally empty; no-one lives there. But the Lord *is* in his temple. He is real, alive, and powerful. He is truly and fully God. Idolaters command their idols to save them, but we who worship the living God come to him in silent awe, great respect, and reverence. We acknowledge that God is in control and knows what he is doing. Idols remain silent, because they cannot answer. The living God, by contrast, speaks through his word. Approach God reverently and wait silently to hear what he has to say.

3:1ff Habakkuk praised God for answering his questions. Evil will not triumph for ever; God is in control, and he can be completely trusted to vindicate those who are faithful to him. We must patiently wait for him to act (3:16).

3:2 Habakkuk knew that God was going to discipline the people of Judah and that it wasn't going to be a pleasant experience. But Habakkuk accepted God's will, asking for help and mercy. Habakkuk did not ask to escape the discipline, but he accepted the truth that Judah needed to learn a lesson. God still disciplines in love to bring his children back to him (Hebrews 12:5, 6). Accept God's discipline gladly, and ask him to help you change.

3:3 The word "Selah" occurs 71 times in Psalms and three times in Habakkuk. Although its precise meaning is unknown, it most likely was a musical term. It could be a signal to lift up the hands or voice in worship, or it could be an exclamation like "Amen!" or "Hallelujah!" affirming the truth of the passage.

you called for many arrows.[k] *Selah*
You split the earth with rivers;
10 the mountains saw you and writhed.
Torrents of water swept by;
the deep roared[l]
and lifted its waves[m] on high.

11 Sun and moon stood still[n] in the heavens
at the glint of your flying arrows,[o]
at the lightning of your flashing spear.
12 In wrath you strode through the earth
and in anger you threshed[p] the nations.
13 You came out to deliver[q] your people,
to save your anointed one.
You crushed[r] the leader of the land of wickedness,
you stripped him from head to foot. *Selah*
14 With his own spear you pierced his head
when his warriors stormed out to scatter us,[s]
gloating as though about to devour
the wretched[t] who were in hiding.
15 You trampled the sea with your horses,
churning the great waters.[u]

16 I heard and my heart pounded,
my lips quivered at the sound;
decay crept into my bones,
and my legs trembled.
Yet I will wait patiently for the day of calamity
to come on the nation invading us.
17 Though the fig-tree does not bud
and there are no grapes on the vines,
though the olive crop fails
and the fields produce no food,[v]
though there are no sheep in the pen
and no cattle in the stalls,[w]
18 yet I will rejoice in the LORD,[x]
I will be joyful in God my Saviour.

19 The Sovereign LORD is my strength;[y]
he makes my feet like the feet of a deer,
he enables me to go on the heights.[z]

For the director of music. On my stringed instruments.

3:9 [k]Ps 7:12-13
3:10 [l]Ps 98:7 [m]Ps 93:3
3:11 [n]Jos 10:13 [o]Ps 18:14
3:12 [p]Isa 41:15
3:13 [q]Ps 20:6; 28:8 [r]Ps 68:21; 110:6
3:14 [s]Jdg 7:22 [t]Ps 64:2-5
3:15 [u]Ex 15:8; Ps 77:19
3:17 [v]Joel 1:10-12, 18 [w]Jer 5:17
3:18 [x]Isa 61:10; Php 4:4
3:19 [y]Dt 33:29; Ps 46:1-5 [z]Dt 32:13; 2Sa 22:34; Ps 18:33

3:17–19 Crop failure and the death of animals would devastate Judah. But Habakkuk affirmed that even in the times of starvation and loss, he would still rejoice in the Lord. Habakkuk's feelings were not controlled by the events around him but by faith in God's ability to give him strength. When nothing makes sense, and when troubles seem more than you can bear, remember that God gives strength. Take your eyes off your difficulties and look to God.

3:19 God will give his followers surefooted confidence through difficult times. They will run like deer across rough and dangerous terrain. At the proper time, God will bring about his justice and completely rid the world of evil. In the meantime, God's people need to live in the strength of his Spirit, confident in his ultimate victory over evil.

3:19 The note to the director of music was to be used when this passage was sung as a psalm in temple worship.

3:19 Habakkuk had asked God why evil people prosper while the righteous suffer. God's answer: they don't, not in the long run. Habakkuk saw his own limitations in contrast to God's unlimited control of all the world's events. God is alive and in control of the world and its events. We cannot see all that God is doing, and we cannot see all that God will do. But we can be assured that he is God and will do what is right. Knowing this can give us confidence and hope in a confusing world.

ZEPHANIAH

Zephaniah becomes a prophet; Josiah becomes king of Judah 640 B.C.	*Jeremiah becomes a prophet 627*	*Book of the Law found in the temple 622*	*Zephaniah's ministry ends 621*	*Habakkuk becomes a prophet 612*

VITAL STATISTICS

PURPOSE:
To shake the people of Judah out of their complacency and urge them to return to God

AUTHOR:
Zephaniah

TO WHOM WRITTEN:
Judah and all nations

DATE WRITTEN:
Probably near the end of Zephaniah's ministry (640–621 B.C.), when King Josiah's great reforms began

SETTING:
King Josiah of Judah was attempting to reverse the evil trends set by the two previous kings of Judah—Manasseh and Amon. Josiah was able to extend his influence because there wasn't a strong superpower dominating the world at that time (Assyria was declining rapidly). Zephaniah's prophecy may have been the motivating factor in Josiah's reform. Zephaniah was a contemporary of Jeremiah.

KEY VERSE:
"Seek the LORD, all you humble of the land, you who do what he commands. Seek righteousness, seek humility; perhaps you will be sheltered on the day of the LORD's anger" (2:3).

KEY PLACE:
Jerusalem

OVERWHELMING grief, prolonged distress, incessant abuse, continual persecution, and imminent punishment breed hopelessness and despair. "If only", we cry as we search our minds for a way out and look to the skies for rescue. With just a glimmer of hope we would take courage and carry on, enduring until the end.

Hope is the silver shaft of sun breaking through the storm-darkened sky, words of comfort in the intensive care unit, a letter from overseas, the first spring bird perched on a snow-covered twig, and the finish line in sight. It is a rainbow, a song, a loving touch. Hope is knowing God and resting in his love.

As God's prophet, Zephaniah was bound to speak the truth—this he did clearly, thundering certain judgment and horrible punishment for all who would defy the Lord. God's awful wrath would sweep away everything in the land and destroy it. "'I will sweep away both men and animals; I will sweep away the birds of the air and the fish of the sea. The wicked will have only heaps of rubble when I cut off man from the face of the earth,' declares the LORD" (1:3). No living thing in the land would escape. And that terrible day was coming soon: "The great day of the LORD is near—near and coming quickly. Listen! The cry on the day of the LORD will be bitter, the shouting of the warrior there. That day will be a day of wrath, a day of distress and anguish, a day of trouble and ruin, a day of darkness and gloom, a day of clouds and blackness" (1:14, 15). We can sense the oppression and depression his listeners must have felt. They were judged guilty, and they were doomed.

But in the midst of this terrible pronouncement, there is hope. The first chapter of Zephaniah's prophecy is filled with terror. In chapter two, however, a whispered promise appears. "Seek the LORD, all you humble of the land, you who do what he commands. Seek righteousness, seek humility; perhaps you will be sheltered on the day of the LORD's anger" (2:3). And a few verses later we read of a "remnant of the house of Judah" (2:7) who will be restored.

Finally in chapter three, the quiet refrain grows to a crescendo as God's salvation and deliverance for those who are faithful to him are declared. "Sing, O Daughter of Zion; shout aloud, O Israel! Be glad and rejoice with all your heart, O Daughter of Jerusalem! The LORD has taken away your punishment, he has turned back your enemy. The LORD, the King of Israel, is with you; never again will you fear any harm" (3:14, 15). This is true hope, grounded in the knowledge of God's justice and in his love for his people.

As you read Zephaniah, listen carefully to the words of judgment. God does not take sin lightly, and it will be punished. But be encouraged by the words of hope—our God reigns, and he will rescue his own. Decide to be part of that faithful remnant of souls who humbly worship and obey the living Lord.

Josiah dies in battle 609	*First captives taken to Babylon 605*	*Babylon's second attack on Judah 597*	*Judah (the southern kingdom) falls 586*

THE BLUEPRINT

1. The day of wrath (1:1—3:8)
2. The day of hope (3:9–20)

Zephaniah warned the people of Judah that if they refused to repent, the entire nation, including the beloved city of Jerusalem, would be lost. The people knew that God would eventually bless them, but Zephaniah made it clear that there would be judgment first, then blessing. This judgment would not be merely punishment for sin, but also a process of purifying the people. Though we live in a fallen world surrounded by evil, we can hope in the perfect kingdom of God to come and we can allow any punishment that touches us now to purify us from sin.

MEGATHEMES

THEME	EXPLANATION	IMPORTANCE
Day of Judgment	Destruction was coming because Judah had forsaken the Lord. The people worshipped Baal, Molech, and the starry hosts. Even the priests mixed pagan practices with faith in God. God's punishment for sin was on the way.	To escape God's judgment we must listen to him, accept his correction, trust him, and seek his guidance. If we accept him as our Lord, we can escape his condemnation.
Indifference to God	Although there had been occasional attempts at renewal, Judah had no sorrow for her sins. The people were prosperous, and they no longer cared about God. God's demands for righteous living seemed irrelevant to Judah, whose security and wealth made her complacent.	Don't let material comfort be a barrier to your commitment to God. Prosperity can produce an attitude of proud self-sufficiency. The only antidote is to admit that money won't save us and that we cannot save ourselves. Only God can save us and cure our indifference to spiritual matters.
Day of Cheer	The day of judgment will also be a day of cheer. God will judge all those who mistreat his people. He will purify his people, purging away all sin and evil. God will restore his people and give them hope.	When people are purged of sin, there is great relief and hope. No matter how difficult our experience now, we can look forward to the day of celebration when God will completely restore us. It will truly be our day of cheer.

1:1
[a] 2Ki 22:1; 2Ch 34:1-35:25

1. The day of wrath

1 The word of the LORD that came to Zephaniah son of Cushi, the son of Gedaliah, the son of Amariah, the son of Hezekiah, during the reign of Josiah[a] son of Amon king of Judah:

1:1 Zephaniah prophesied in the days of Josiah king of Judah (640–609 B.C.). Josiah followed God, and during his reign the Book of the Law was discovered in the temple. After reading it, Josiah began a great religious revival in Judah (2 Kings 22:1 – 23:25). Zephaniah helped fan the revival by warning the people that judgment would come if they did not turn from their sins. Although this great revival turned the nation back to God, it did not fully eliminate idolatry and lasted only a short time. Twelve years after Josiah's death, Judah was invaded by Babylon, and a number of people were sent into exile.

Warning of Coming Destruction

2"I will sweep away everything
from the face of the earth,"[b]
declares the LORD.

3"I will sweep away both men and animals;
I will sweep away the birds of the air[c]
and the fish of the sea.
The wicked will have only heaps of rubble[a]
when I cut off man from the face of the earth,"[d]
declares the LORD.

Against Judah

4"I will stretch out my hand[e] against Judah
and against all who live in Jerusalem.
I will cut off from this place every remnant of Baal,[f]
the names of the pagan and the idolatrous priests[g]—
5those who bow down on the roofs
to worship the starry host,
those who bow down and swear by the LORD
and who also swear by Molech,[b][h]
6those who turn back from following[i] the LORD
and neither seek[j] the LORD nor enquire[k] of him.
7Be silent[l] before the Sovereign LORD,
for the day of the LORD[m] is near.
The LORD has prepared a sacrifice;[n]
he has consecrated those he has invited.
8On the day of the LORD's sacrifice
I will punish[o] the princes
and the king's sons[p]
and all those clad
in foreign clothes.
9On that day I will punish
all who avoid stepping on the threshold,[c]
who fill the temple of their gods

a *3* The meaning of the Hebrew for this line is uncertain. **b** *5* Hebrew *Malcam,* that is, Milcom **c** *9* See 1 Samuel 5:5.

1:2 [b]Ge 6:7
1:3 [c]Jer 4:25 [d]Hos 4:3
1:4 [e]Jer 6:12 [f]Mic 5:13 [g]Hos 10:5
1:5 [h]Jer 5:7
1:6 [i]Isa 1:4; Jer 2:13 [j]Isa 9:13 [k]Hos 7:7
1:7 [l]Hab 2:20; Zec 2:13 [m]ver 14; Isa 13:6 [n]Isa 34:6; Jer 46:10
1:8 [o]Isa 24:21 [p]Jer 39:6

1:2ff The people of Judah were clearly warned by the highest authority of all—God. They refused to listen, either because they doubted God's prophet and thus did not believe that the message was from God, or because they doubted God himself and thus did not believe that he would do what he said. If we refuse to listen to God's word, the Bible, we are as shortsighted as the people of Judah, and like them, we will be punished.

1:4 When the Israelites arrived in the promised land, God had commanded that they completely rid the land of its pagan inhabitants, who worshipped idols. But the Israelites failed to do so, and gradually they began to worship the Canaanites' gods. The Canaanites believed in many gods that represented many aspects of life, and the chief god was Baal, symbolising strength and fertility. God was extremely angry when his people turned from him to Baal.

1:4–6 The terrain of history is littered with idols and their worship. More than just a stone statue, an idol can be anything reverenced more than God. Thus idol worship is prevalent even today as people trust in themselves, money, or power and not in God. But ultimately all idols will prove worthless, and the true God will prevail. Seek God first (Matthew 6:33), and have no other gods before him (Exodus 20:3).

1:5 The people had become polytheistic, worshipping the Lord *and* all the other gods of the land. They added the "best" of pagan worship to true faith in God. But God commands that he alone be worshipped (Exodus 20:1–5); thus the people committed a horrible sin. One of these other gods was Molech, the national god of the Ammonites. Molech worship included child sacrifice, an abominable sin. From the time of Moses, the Israelites had been warned about worshipping this false god (Leviticus 18:21; 20:5), but they refused to take heed. Because of their sins, God would destroy them.

1:7 A day of judgment and great slaughter occurred during the lifetime of these people when Babylon invaded the land. The prophet saw these prophecies as future events, but he could not see when or in what order these events would take place. Many think that these prophecies have a double fulfilment—one for the near future (soon after the prophecy was made) and another for the distant future (possibly during the end times). Some scholars believe that these prophecies of judgment refer to events entirely in the future.

1:8, 9 Wearing "foreign" (pagan) clothes showed a desire for foreign gods and foreign ways. Leaders who should have been good examples to the people were adopting foreign practices and thus showing their contempt for the Lord by ignoring his commands against adopting pagan culture. To "avoid stepping on the threshold" was a pagan observance (see 1 Samuel 5:5).

with violence and deceit.[q]

10“On that day,” declares the LORD,
“a cry will go up from the Fish Gate,[r]
wailing from the New Quarter,
and a loud crash from the hills.
11Wail,[s] you who live in the market district;[d]
all your merchants will be wiped out,
all who trade with[e] silver will be ruined.[t]
12At that time I will search Jerusalem with lamps
and punish those who are complacent,[u]
who are like wine left on its dregs,[v]
who think, ‘The LORD will do nothing,[w]
either good or bad.’
13Their wealth will be plundered,[x]
their houses demolished.
They will build houses
but not live in them;
they will plant vineyards
but not drink the wine.[y]

The Great Day of the LORD

14“The great day of the LORD[z] is near[a]—
near and coming quickly.
Listen! The cry on the day of the LORD will be bitter,
the shouting of the warrior there.
15That day will be a day of wrath,
a day of distress and anguish,
a day of trouble and ruin,
a day of darkness and gloom,
a day of clouds and blackness,[b]
16a day of trumpet and battle cry[c]
against the fortified cities
and against the corner towers.[d]

1:9 [q]Am 3:10
1:10 [r]2Ch 33:14
1:11 [s]Jas 5:1 [t]Hos 9:6
1:12 [u]Am 6:1 [v]Jer 48:11 [w]Eze 8:12
1:13 [x]Jer 15:13 [y]Dt 28:30, 39; Am 5:11; Mic 6:15
1:14 [z]ver 7; Joel 1:15 [a]Eze 7:7
1:15 [b]Isa 22:5; Joel 2:2
1:16 [c]Jer 4:19 [d]Isa 2:15

d *11* Or *the Mortar* **e** *11* Or *in*

ZEPHANIAH served as a prophet to Judah from 640–621 B.C.

Climate of the times	Josiah was the last good king in Judah. His bold attempts to reform the nation and turn it back to God were probably influenced by Zephaniah.
Main message	A day will come when God, as Judge, will severely punish all nations. But after judgment, he will show mercy to all who have been faithful to him.
Importance of message	We will all be judged for our disobedience to God; but if we remain faithful to him, he will show us mercy.
Contemporary prophet	Jeremiah (627–586)

1:12 God would search the city with lamps and punish those who deserve punishment. Because they did not search their own hearts, and because they were content with the moral chaos around them (“like wine left on its dregs”) and indifferent to God, God would use the Babylonians to judge them. Within 20 years, the Babylonians would enter Jerusalem, drag people out of hiding, and take them captive or kill them. No-one would escape God’s judgment; there would be no place to hide.

1:12–14 Some people think of God as an indulgent heavenly grandfather, nice to have around, but not a real force in shaping modern life. They don’t believe in his power or his coming judgment. But God is holy, and therefore he will actively judge and justly punish everyone who is content to live in sin, indifferent to him, or unconcerned about justice. When people are indifferent to God, they tend to think that he is indifferent to them and their sin. They will be surprised to find that “the great day of the LORD is near”.

1:14–18 The great day of the Lord was near; the Babylonians would soon come and destroy Jerusalem. The day of the Lord is also near for us. God promises a final judgment, a day of worldwide destruction (Revelation 20:12–15). The Babylonian conquest occurred just as surely and horribly as Zephaniah had predicted. And God’s final day of judgment is also sure—but so is his ability to save. To be spared from judgment, recognise that you have sinned, that your sin will bring judgment, that you cannot save yourself, and that God alone can save you.

17 I will bring distress on the people
and they will walk like blind[e] men,
because they have sinned against the LORD.
Their blood will be poured out[f] like dust
and their entrails like filth.[g]
18 Neither their silver nor their gold
will be able to save them
on the day of the LORD's wrath.[h]
In the fire of his jealousy
the whole world will be consumed,[i]
for he will make a sudden end
of all who live in the earth.[j]"

2 Gather together,[a] gather together,
O shameful[b] nation,
2 before the appointed time arrives
and that day sweeps on like chaff,[c]
before the fierce anger[d] of the LORD comes upon you,
before the day of the LORD's wrath comes upon you.
3 Seek[e] the LORD, all you humble of the land,
you who do what he commands.
Seek righteousness, seek humility;[f]
perhaps you will be sheltered[g]
on the day of the LORD's anger.

Against Philistia

4 Gaza[h] will be abandoned
and Ashkelon left in ruins.
At midday Ashdod will be emptied
and Ekron uprooted.
5 Woe to you who live by the sea,
O Kerethite[i] people;
the word of the LORD is against you,[j]
O Canaan, land of the Philistines.

"I will destroy you,
and none will be left."[k]

6 The land by the sea, where the Kerethites[a] dwell,
will be a place for shepherds and sheep pens.[l]
7 It will belong to the remnant of the house of Judah;
there they will find pasture.

1:17 [e] Isa 59:10 [f] Ps 79:3 [g] Jer 9:22
1:18 [h] Eze 7:19 [i] ver 2-3; Zep 3:8 [j] Ge 6:7
2:1 [a] 2Ch 20:4; Joel 1:14 [b] Jer 3:3; 6:15
2:2 [c] Isa 17:13; Hos 13:3 [d] La 4:11
2:3 [e] Am 5:6 [f] Ps 45:4; Am 5:14-15 [g] Ps 57:1
2:4 [h] Am 1:6, 7-8; Zec 9:5-7
2:5 [i] Eze 25:16 [j] Am 3:1 [k] Isa 14:30
2:6 [l] Isa 5:17

a *6* The meaning of the Hebrew for this word is uncertain.

1:18 Money is not evil in itself, but it is useless to save us. In this life, money can warp our perspective, giving us feelings of security and power. Just as the Israelites' wealth could not save them from the Babylonian invasion, so at the final judgment, our riches will be worthless. Only Christ's redemptive work on our behalf matters for eternity. Christ alone will ransom us if we believe in him. Don't trust money; trust Christ.

2:1–3 There was still time for the people to avert God's judgment. They simply had to turn from their sins, humble themselves, and obey God. The Old Testament prophets announced news of destruction, but they also offered the only means of escape and protection – turning from sin and walking with God (see also Micah 6:8).

2:4 The four cities mentioned here are in Philistia, the nation south-west of Judah on the coast of the Mediterranean Sea. Age-old enemies of Israel from the days of Joshua, the Philistines were known for their cruelty. God judged these cities for their idolatry and their constant taunting of Israel. These four cities were four of the five capitals. The fifth (Gath) had probably already been destroyed.

2:5 The Kerethites were a clan of the Philistines located near southern Judah. They migrated to Palestine along with other Philistine people. Their name may have been derived from "Crete", the island where they lived before they moved to Palestine.

2:7 All the prophets, even while prophesying doom and destruction, speak of a "remnant" – a small group of God's people who remain faithful to him and whom God will restore to the land. Although God said he would destroy Judah, he also promised to save a remnant, thus keeping his original covenant to preserve Abraham's descendants (Genesis 17:4–8). Because God is holy, he cannot allow sin to continue. But God is also faithful to his promises. He cannot stay angry for ever with Israel, or with you, if you are his child, because he loves his children and always seeks their good.

2:7
[m]Ps 126:4; Jer 32:44

In the evening they will lie down
in the houses of Ashkelon.
The LORD their God will care for them;
he will restore their fortunes.[b][m]

2:8
[n]Jer 48:27
[o]Eze 25:3

Against Moab and Ammon

8"I have heard the insults[n] of Moab
and the taunts of the Ammonites,
who insulted[o] my people
and made threats against their land.

2:9
[p]Isa 15:1-16:14; Jer 48:1-47
[q]Dt 29:23
[r]Jer 49:1-6; Eze 25:1-7
[s]Isa 11:14
[t]Am 2:1-3

9Therefore, as surely as I live,"
declares the LORD Almighty, the God of Israel,
"surely Moab[p] will become like Sodom,[q]
the Ammonites[r] like Gomorrah—
a place of weeds and salt pits,
a wasteland for ever.
The remnant of my people will plunder[s] them;
the survivors of my nation will inherit their land.[t]"

2:10
[u]Isa 16:6
[v]Jer 48:27

10This is what they will get in return for their pride,[u]
for insulting[v] and mocking the people of the LORD Almighty.
11The LORD will be awesome[w] to them
when he destroys all the gods[x] of the land.
The nations on every shore will worship him,[y]
every one in its own land.

2:11
[w]Joel 2:11
[x]Zep 1:4
[y]Zep 3:9

Against Cush

12"You too, O Cushites,[c][z]
will be slain by my sword.[a]"

2:12
[z]Isa 18:1; 20:4
[a]Jer 46:10

Against Assyria

13He will stretch out his hand against the north
and destroy Assyria,
leaving Nineveh[b] utterly desolate
and dry as the desert.[c]

2:13
[b]Na 1:1
[c]Mic 5:6

14Flocks and herds will lie down there,

[b] *7* Or *will bring back their captives* [c] *12* That is, people from the upper Nile region

---

2:8 The Moabites and Ammonites lived to the east of Judah, and they often ridiculed and attacked Judah. These nations worshipped Chemosh and Molech (1 Kings 11:7). Moab's king once sacrificed his son on the city wall to stop an invasion (2 Kings 3:26, 27). God would judge these nations for their wickedness and for their treatment of his people.

2:8–11 Judah had been taunted and mocked by the neighbouring nations, Moab and Ammon, but God reminded them that he had "heard the insults . . . and the taunts" (2:8), and that the taunters would be punished for their pride (2:10). At times the whole world seems to mock God and those who have faith in him. When you are ridiculed, remember that God hears and will answer. Eventually, in God's timing, justice will be carried out.

2:9 The nations of Moab and Ammon trace their roots to Lot's incest with his daughters after escaping the destruction of evil Sodom and Gomorrah (Genesis 19). Ironically, Moab and Ammon would be the same kind of perpetual wasteland that God had made those evil cities. Sodom and Gomorrah were so completely destroyed that their exact location is still unknown.

2:12 Cush, at the southern end of the Red Sea, controlled Egypt at this time. No-one can escape deserved judgment. The Cushites were "slain by [God's] sword" when the Babylonians invaded Egypt in 605 B.C. (See Isaiah 18 and Ezekiel 30:9 for other prophecies concerning Cush.)

2:13 Zephaniah mentioned the large nation to the south and then moved to the nation that invaded from the north, Assyria. Though declining, Assyria was still the strongest military power of the day, dominating the world for three centuries and destroying anyone in its path. Nineveh, the large capital city, was considered impregnable. However, just as Zephaniah predicted, Nineveh was wiped out in 612 B.C. by the Babylonians, who would become the next world power.

2:13–15 To predict the destruction of Nineveh ten years before it happened would be equivalent to predicting the destruction of Tokyo, Moscow, or New York. Nineveh was the ancient Near Eastern centre for culture, technology, and beauty. It had great libraries, buildings, and a vast irrigation system that created lush gardens in the city. The city wall was 60 miles long, 100 feet high, and over 30 feet wide and was fortified with 1,500 towers. Yet the entire city was destroyed so completely that its very existence was questioned until it was discovered, with great difficulty, by 19th century archaeologists. Nineveh had indeed become as desolate and dry as the desert.

creatures of every kind.
The desert owl[d] and the screech owl
will roost on her columns.
Their calls will echo through the windows,
rubble will be in the doorways,
the beams of cedar will be exposed.
15This is the carefree[e] city
that lived in safety.[f]
She said to herself,
"I am, and there is none besides me."[g]
What a ruin she has become,
a lair for wild beasts!
All who pass by her scoff[h]
and shake their fists.

The Future of Jerusalem

3 Woe to the city of oppressors,[a]
rebellious and defiled![b]
2She obeys[c] no-one,
she accepts no correction.[d]
She does not trust in the LORD,
she does not draw near[e] to her God.
3Her officials are roaring lions,
her rulers are evening wolves,[f]
who leave nothing for the morning.
4Her prophets are arrogant;
they are treacherous[g] men.
Her priests profane the sanctuary
and do violence to the law.[h]
5The LORD within her is righteous;
he does no wrong.[i]
Morning by morning he dispenses his justice,
and every new day he does not fail,
yet the unrighteous know no shame.

6"I have cut off nations;
their strongholds are demolished.
I have left their streets deserted,
with no-one passing through.
Their cities are destroyed;[j]
no-one will be left—no-one at all.
7I said to the city,

2:14 [d]Isa 14:23
2:15 [e]Isa 32:9 [f]Isa 47:8 [g]Eze 28:2 [h]Na 3:19
3:1 [a]Jer 6:6 [b]Eze 23:30
3:2 [c]Jer 22:21 [d]Jer 7:28 [e]Ps 73:28; Jer 5:3
3:3 [f]Eze 22:27
3:4 [g]Jer 9:4 [h]Eze 22:26
3:5 [i]Dt 32:4
3:6 [j]Lev 26:31

3:1ff After predicting the destruction of the surrounding nations, Zephaniah returned to the problem at hand—sin in Jerusalem. The city of God, and God's people themselves, had become "defiled"—as sinful as their pagan neighbours. The people pretended to worship and serve God, but in their hearts they had rejected him and continued to be complacent about their sins. They no longer cared about the consequences of turning away from God.

3:2 Do you know people who refuse to listen when someone disagrees with their opinions? Their root problem is pride—inflated self-esteem. God's people had become so proud that they would not hear or accept God's correction. Do you find it difficult to listen to the spiritual counsel of others or God's words from the Bible? Don't let pride make you unable or unwilling to let God work in your life. You will be more willing to listen when you consider how weak and sinful you really are compared to God.

3:3, 4 Leading God's people is a privilege and a responsibility. Through Zephaniah, God rebuked all types of leadership in Jerusalem—officials, rulers, prophets, and priests—because of their callous disobedience, irresponsibility, and sin. If you are a leader in the church, consider yourself in a privileged position, but be careful. God holds you responsible for the purity of your actions, the quality of your example, and the truth of your words.

3:5 Jerusalem's citizens, of all people, had no excuse for their sins. Jerusalem, where the temple was located, was the religious centre of the nation. But even though the people didn't follow God, God was "within" the city, present in the midst of corruption, persecution, and unbelief. No matter how spiritually desolate the world seems, God is here, and he is at work. Ask yourself, "What is he doing now, and how can I be part of his work?"

3:7 We may wonder how the Israelites could have had such clear warnings and still not turn to God. The problem was that they had

3:7
[k]Hos 9:9

3:8
[l]Ps 27:14
[m]Joel 3:2
[n]Zep 1:18

3:9
[o]Zep 2:11
[p]Isa 19:18

3:10
[q]Ps 68:31
[r]Isa 60:7

3:11
[s]Joel 2:26-27

3:12
[t]Isa 14:32
[u]Na 1:7

3:13
[v]Isa 10:21; Mic 4:7
[w]Ps 119:3
[x]Rev 14:5
[y]Eze 34:15; Zep 2:7
[z]Eze 34:25-28

3:14
[a]Zec 2:10
[b]Isa 12:6

'Surely you will fear me
and accept correction!'
Then her dwelling would not be cut off,
nor all my punishments come upon her.
But they were still eager
to act corruptly[k] in all they did.

2. The day of hope

8Therefore wait[l] for me," declares the LORD,
"for the day I will stand up to testify.[a]
I have decided to assemble the nations,[m]
to gather the kingdoms
and to pour out my wrath on them —
all my fierce anger.
The whole world will be consumed[n]
by the fire of my jealous anger.

9"Then will I purify the lips of the peoples,
that all of them may call[o] on the name of the LORD
and serve[p] him shoulder to shoulder.
10From beyond the rivers of Cush[b][q]
my worshippers, my scattered people,
will bring me offerings.[r]
11On that day you will not be put to shame[s]
for all the wrongs you have done to me,
because I will remove from this city
those who rejoice in their pride.
Never again will you be haughty
on my holy hill.
12But I will leave within you
the meek[t] and humble,
who trust[u] in the name of the LORD.
13The remnant[v] of Israel will do no wrong;[w]
they will speak no lies,[x]
nor will deceit be found in their mouths.
They will eat and lie down[y]
and no-one will make them afraid.[z]"

14Sing, O Daughter of Zion;[a]
shout aloud,[b] O Israel!
Be glad and rejoice with all your heart,

a *8* Septuagint and Syriac; Hebrew *will rise up to plunder* **b** *10* That is, the upper Nile region

allowed sin to so harden them that they no longer cared to follow God. They refused to heed God's warnings and they refused to repent. The more God punished them, the more they sinned. In fact, they "were eager" to sin. If you disobey God now, your heart may grow hard, and you may lose your desire for God.

3:8 In the last days, God will judge all people according to what they have done (Revelation 20:12). Justice will prevail; evildoers will be punished; and the obedient will be blessed. Don't try to avenge yourself. Be patient, and God's justice will come.

3:9 God will purify lips and unify language so that all his people from all nations will be able to worship him in unison. In the new earth, all believers will speak the same language; the confusion of languages at the tower of Babel will be reversed (Genesis 11). God will purify our hearts, so that the words coming from our lips will be pure as well.

3:10 The "scattered people" refers to Jews dispersed beyond the rivers of Cush. It symbolises that all Jews, no matter how far they have been scattered, will return to worship God.

3:11, 12 God will remove the proud people and leave the meek and humble. God is opposed to the proud and haughty of every generation. But those who are meek and humble, both physically and spiritually, will be rewarded because they trust in God. Self-reliance and arrogance have no place among God's people or in his kingdom.

3:14–18 The Lord himself will remove his hand of judgment, disperse Israel's enemies, and come to live among his people. He will give them gladness. We sin when we pursue happiness by cutting ourselves off from fellowship with God — the only person who can make us truly happy. Zephaniah points out that gladness results when we allow God to be with us. We do that by faithfully following him and obeying his commands. Then God rejoices over us with singing. If you want to be happy, draw close to the source of happiness by obeying God.

O Daughter of Jerusalem!
15The LORD has taken away your punishment,
he has turned back your enemy.
The LORD, the King of Israel, is with you;[c]
never again will you fear[d] any harm.
16On that day they will say to Jerusalem,
"Do not fear, O Zion;
do not let your hands hang limp.[e]
17The LORD your God is with you,
he is mighty to save.[f]
He will take great delight[g] in you,
he will quiet you with his love,
he will rejoice over you with singing."

18"The sorrows for the appointed feasts
I will remove from you;
they are a burden and a reproach to you.[c]
19At that time I will deal
with all who oppressed you;
I will rescue the lame
and gather those who have been scattered.[h]
I will give them praise[i] and honour
in every land where they were put to shame.
20At that time I will gather you;
at that time I will bring[j] you home.
I will give you honour[k] and praise
among all the peoples of the earth
when I restore your fortunes[d][l]
before your very eyes,"
says the LORD.

c 18 Or *"I will gather you who mourn for the appointed feasts; / your reproach is a burden to you* d 20 Or *I bring back your captives*

3:15
[c]Eze 37:26-28
[d]Isa 54:14

3:16
[e]Job 4:3; Isa 35:3-4; Heb 12:12

3:17
[f]Isa 63:1
[g]Isa 62:4

3:19
[h]Eze 34:16; Mic 4:6
[i]Isa 60:18

3:20
[j]Jer 29:14; Eze 37:12
[k]Isa 56:5; 66:22
[l]Joel 3:1

3:20 "Before your very eyes" does not necessarily mean that this promise would be fulfilled during Zephaniah's generation. Rather, it means that the restoration will be an obvious work of the Lord.

3:20 The message of doom in the beginning of the book becomes a message of hope by the end. There will be a new day when God will bless his people. If the leaders in the church today were to hear a message from a prophet of God, the message would probably resemble the book of Zephaniah. Under Josiah's religious reforms, the people did return to God *outwardly,* but their hearts were far from him. Zephaniah encouraged the nation to gather together and pray for salvation. We must also ask ourselves: Is our reform merely an outward show, or is it changing our hearts and lives? We need to gather together and pray, to walk humbly with God, to do what is right, and to hear the message of hope regarding the new world to come.

HAGGAI

Babylon overthrown by Cyrus 539	*Cyrus' decree allowing the exiles to return 538*	*Temple construction begins 536*	*Temple work halted 530*	*Haggai, Zechariah become prophets; temple work resumed 520*	*Temple completed 516*	*Ezra comes to Jerusalem 458*	*Nehemiah comes to Jerusalem 445*

PRESSURES, demands, expectations, and tasks push in from all sides and assault our schedules. Do this! Be there! Finish that! Call them! It seems as though everyone wants something from us—family, friends, employer, school, church, clubs. Soon there is little left to give, as we run out of energy and time. We find ourselves rushing through life, attending to the necessary, the immediate, and the urgent. The important is all too often left in the dust. Our problem is not the volume of demands or lack of organisation, but values—what is *truly* important to us.

Our values and priorities are reflected in how we use our resources—time, money, strength, and talent. Often our actions belie our words. We say God is number one, but then we relegate him to a lesser number on our "to do" lists.

Twenty-five centuries ago, a voice was heard, calling men and women to the right priorities. Haggai knew what was important and what had to be done, and he challenged God's people to respond.

In 586 B.C., the armies of Babylon had destroyed the temple in Jerusalem—God's house, the symbol of his presence with them. In 538 B.C. King Cyrus decreed that Jews could return to their beloved city and rebuild the temple. So they travelled to Jerusalem and began the work. But then they forgot their purpose and lost their priorities, as opposition and apathy brought the work to a standstill (Ezra 4:4, 5). Then Haggai spoke, calling them back to God's values. "Is it a time for you yourselves to be living in your panelled houses, while this house remains a ruin?" (1:4). The people were more concerned with their own needs than with doing God's will, and, as a result, they suffered. Then Haggai called them to action: "This is what the LORD Almighty says: 'Give careful thought to your ways. Go up into the mountains and bring down timber and build the house, so that I may take pleasure in it and be honoured,' says the LORD" (1:7, 8). And God's message through his servant Haggai became the catalyst for finishing the work.

Although Haggai is a small book, it is filled with challenge and promise, reminding us of God's claim on our lives and our priorities. As you read Haggai, imagine him walking the streets and alleys of Jerusalem, urging the people to get back to doing God's work. And listen to Haggai speaking to you, urging you to reorder your priorities in accordance with God's will. What has God told you to do? Put all else aside and obey him.

VITAL STATISTICS

PURPOSE:
To call the people to complete the rebuilding of the temple

AUTHOR:
Haggai

TO WHOM WRITTEN:
The people living in Jerusalem and those who had returned from exile

DATE WRITTEN:
520 B.C.

SETTING:
The temple in Jerusalem had been destroyed in 586 B.C. Cyrus allowed the Jews to return to their homeland and rebuild their temple in 538 B.C. They began the work but were unable to complete it. Through the ministry of Haggai and Zechariah, the temple was completed (520–515 B.C.).

KEY VERSE:
"Is it a time for you yourselves to be living in your panelled houses, while this house remains a ruin?" (1:4).

KEY PEOPLE:
Haggai, Zerubbabel, Joshua

KEY PLACE:
Jerusalem

SPECIAL FEATURES:
Haggai was the first of the post-exilic prophets. The other two were Zechariah and Malachi. The literary style of this book is simple and direct.

THE BLUEPRINT

1. The call to rebuild the temple (1:1–15)
2. Encouragement to complete the temple (2:1–23)

When the exiles first returned from Babylon, they set about rebuilding the temple right away. Although they began with the right attitudes, they slipped back into wrong behaviour, and the work came to a standstill. In the same way, we need to be on guard to keep our priorities straight. Remain active in your service to God and continue to put first things first.

MEGATHEMES

THEME	EXPLANATION	IMPORTANCE
Right Priorities	God had given the Jews the assignment to finish the temple in Jerusalem when they returned from captivity. After 15 years, they still had not completed it. They were more concerned about building their own homes than finishing God's work. Haggai told them to get their priorities straight.	It is easy to make other priorities more important than doing God's work. But God wants us to follow through and build up his kingdom. Don't stop and don't make excuses. Set your heart on what is right and do it. Get your priorities straight.
God's Encouragement	Haggai encouraged the people as they worked. He assured them of the divine presence of the Holy Spirit and of final victory, and instilled in them the hope that the Messiah would reign.	If God gives you a task, don't be afraid to get started. His resources are infinite. God will help you to complete it by giving you encouragement from others along the way.

1. The call to rebuild the temple

1 In the second year of King Darius,[a] on the first day of the sixth month, the word
of the LORD came through the prophet Haggai[b] to Zerubbabel[c] son of Shealtiel,
governor[d] of Judah, and to Joshua[a][e] son of Jehozadak,[f] the high priest:
2This is what the LORD Almighty says: "These people say, 'The time has not yet
come for the LORD's house to be built.' "
3Then the word of the LORD came through the prophet Haggai:[g] 4"Is it a time for
you yourselves to be living in your panelled houses,[h] while this house remains a
ruin?[i]"
5Now this is what the LORD Almighty says: "Give careful thought[j] to your ways.
6You have planted much, but have harvested little.[k] You eat, but never have enough.
You drink, but never have your fill. You put on clothes, but are not warm. You earn
wages,[l] only to put them in a purse with holes in it."
7This is what the LORD Almighty says: "Give careful thought to your ways. 8Go
up into the mountains and bring down timber and build the house, so that I may take

1:1 [a]Ezr 4:24 [b]Ezr 5:1 [c]Mt 1:12-13 [d]Ezr 5:3 [e]Ezr 2:2 [f]1Ch 6:15; Ezr 3:2
1:3 [g]Ezr 5:1
1:4 [h]2Sa 7:2 [i]ver 9; Jer 33:12
1:5 [j]La 3:40
1:6 [k]Dt 28:38 [l]Hag 2:16; Zec 8:10

a *1* A variant of *Jeshua*; here and elsewhere in Haggai

1:1 Zerubbabel, governor of Judah, and Joshua, the high priest, were key leaders in rebuilding the temple. They had already re-established the altar, but work on the temple had slowed. Haggai gave a message to these outstanding leaders and to the exiles who had returned from Babylon, encouraging them to complete the rebuilding of the temple in Jerusalem.

1:1ff The Jews who had returned from Babylon in 538 B.C. to rebuild the temple in Jerusalem were not able to finish their work because they were hindered by their enemies. After opposition put a halt to progress, no further work had been done on the temple for over 15 years. In August, 520 B.C., Haggai delivered a message to encourage the people to rebuild the temple! Haggai was probably born in captivity in Babylon and returned to Jerusalem with Zerubbabel in 538 B.C. (Ezra 1; 2). Haggai and Zechariah, two prophets who encouraged the temple rebuilding, are mentioned in Ezra 5:1.

1:2–15 Haggai encouraged the people to finish rebuilding the temple. Opposition from hostile neighbours had caused them to feel discouraged and to neglect the temple, and thus neglect God. But Haggai's message turned them around and motivated them to pick up their tools and continue the work they had begun.

1:3–6 God asked his people how they could live in luxury when his house was lying in ruins. The temple was the focal point of Judah's relationship with God, but it was still demolished. Instead of rebuilding the temple, the people put their energies into beautifying their own homes. However, the harder the people worked for themselves, the less they had, because they ignored their spiritual lives. The same happens to us. If we put God first, he will provide for our deepest needs. If we put him in any other place, all our efforts will be futile. Caring only for your physical needs while ignoring your relationship with God will lead to ruin.

1:6 Because the people had not given God first place in their lives, their work was not fruitful or productive, and their material possessions did not satisfy. While they concentrated on building and beautifying their own homes, God's blessing was withheld because they no longer put him in first place. Moses had predicted that this would be the result if the people neglected God (Deuteronomy 28:38–45).

1:8 [m]Ps 132:13-14
1:9 [n]ver 4
1:10 [o]Lev 26:19; Dt 28:23
1:11 [p]Dt 28:22; 1Ki 17:1 [q]Hag 2:17
1:12 [r]ver 1 [s]ver 14; Isa 1:9; Hag 2:2 [t]Isa 50:10 [u]Dt 31:12
1:13 [v]Mt 28:20; Ro 8:31
1:14 [w]Ezr 5:2 [x]ver 12
1:15 [y]ver 1
2:3 [a]Ezr 3:12 [b]Zec 4:10
2:4 [c]1Ch 28:20; Zec 8:9; Eph 6:10 [d]2Sa 5:10; Ac 7:9

pleasure[m] in it and be honoured," says the LORD. 9"You expected much, but see, it
turned out to be little. What you brought home, I blew away. Why?" declares the LORD
Almighty. "Because of my house, which remains a ruin,[n] while each of you is busy
with his own house. 10Therefore, because of you the heavens have withheld their dew
and the earth its crops.[o] 11I called for a drought[p] on the fields and the mountains,
on the grain, the new wine, the oil and whatever the ground produces, on men and
cattle, and on the labour of your hands.[q]"

12Then Zerubbabel[r] son of Shealtiel, Joshua son of Jehozadak, the high priest, and
the whole remnant[s] of the people obeyed[t] the voice of the LORD their God and the
message of the prophet Haggai, because the LORD their God had sent him. And the
people feared[u] the LORD.
13Then Haggai, the LORD's messenger, gave this message of the LORD to the people:
"I am with[v] you," declares the LORD. 14So the LORD stirred up the spirit of Zerubbabel[w] son of Shealtiel, governor of Judah, and the spirit of Joshua son of Jehozadak,
the high priest, and the spirit of the whole remnant[x] of the people. They came and
began work on the house of the LORD Almighty, their God, 15on the twenty-fourth
day of the sixth month[y] in the second year of King Darius.

2. Encouragement to complete the temple

The Promised Glory of the New House

2 On the twenty-first day of the seventh month, the word of the LORD came through
the prophet Haggai: 2"Speak to Zerubbabel son of Shealtiel, governor of Judah,
to Joshua son of Jehozadak, the high priest, and to the remnant of the people. Ask
them, 3'Who of you is left who saw this house[a] in its former glory? How does it look
to you now? Does it not seem to you like nothing?[b] 4But now be strong, O Zerubbabel,' declares the LORD. 'Be strong,[c] O Joshua son of Jehozadak, the high priest.
Be strong, all you people of the land,' declares the LORD, 'and work. For I am with[d]

HAGGAI served as a prophet to Judah about 520 B.C., after the return from exile.

Climate of the times	The people of Judah had been exiled to Babylon in 586 B.C., and Jerusalem and the temple had been destroyed. Under Cyrus, King of Persia, the Jews were allowed to return to Judah and rebuild their temple.
Main message	The people returned to Jerusalem to begin rebuilding the temple, but they hadn't finished. Haggai's message encouraged the people to finish rebuilding God's temple.
Importance of message	The temple lay half-finished while the people lived in beautiful homes. Haggai warned them against putting their possessions and jobs ahead of God. We must put God first in our lives.
Contemporary prophet	Zechariah (520–480)

1:9 Judah's problem was confused priorities. Like Judah, our priorities involving occupation, family, and God's work are often confused. Jobs, homes, holidays, and leisure activities may rank higher on our list of importance than God. What is most important to you? Where is God on your list of priorities?

1:11 Grain, grapes for wine, and olives for oil were Israel's major crops. The people depended on these for security while neglecting the worship of God. As a result, God would send a drought to destroy their livelihood and call them back to himself.

1:14, 15 The people began rebuilding the temple just 23 days after Haggai's first message. Rarely did a prophet's message produce such a quick response. How often we hear a sermon and respond, "That was an excellent point – I ought to do that", only to leave church and forget to act. These people put their words into action. When you hear a good sermon or lesson, ask what you should *do* about it, and then make plans to put it into practice.

2:1–9 This is Haggai's second message. It was given during the Feast of Tabernacles in October, 520 B.C. The older people could remember the incredible beauty of Solomon's temple, destroyed 66 years earlier. Many were discouraged because the rebuilt temple was inferior to Solomon's. But Haggai encouraged them with God's message that the glory of this temple would surpass that of its predecessor. The most important part of the temple is God's presence. Some 500 years later, Jesus Christ would walk in the temple courts.

2:4 "Be strong . . . and work. For I am with you." Judah's people had returned to worshipping God, and God had promised to bless their efforts. But it was time for them to *work.* We must be people of prayer, Bible study, and worship – but eventually we must get out and *do* what God has in mind for us. He wants to change the world through us. God has given you a job to do in the church, at your place of employment, and at home. The time has come to be strong and work because God is with you!

you,' declares the LORD Almighty. 5'This is what I covenanted with you when you
came out of Egypt.[e] And my Spirit[f] remains among you. Do not fear.'
6"This is what the LORD Almighty says: 'In a little while[g] I will once more shake
the heavens and the earth,[h] the sea and the dry land. 7I will shake all nations, and
the desired of all nations will come, and I will fill this house[i] with glory,' says the
LORD Almighty. 8'The silver is mine and the gold is mine,' declares the LORD
Almighty. 9'The glory[j] of this present house will be greater than the glory of the
former house,' says the LORD Almighty. 'And in this place I will grant peace,' declares
the LORD Almighty."

Blessings for a Defiled People

10On the twenty-fourth day of the ninth month,[k] in the second year of Darius, the
word of the LORD came to the prophet Haggai: 11"This is what the LORD Almighty
says: 'Ask the priests[l] what the law says: 12If a person carries consecrated meat in
the fold of his garment, and that fold touches some bread or stew, some wine, oil or
other food, does it become consecrated?[m]' "
The priests answered, "No."
13Then Haggai said, "If a person defiled by contact with a dead body touches one
of these things, does it become defiled?"
"Yes," the priests replied, "it becomes defiled.[n]"
14Then Haggai said, " 'So it is with this people and this nation in my sight,' declares
the LORD. 'Whatever they do and whatever they offer[o] there is defiled.
15" 'Now give careful thought[p] to this from this day on[a]—consider how things
were before one stone was laid[q] on another in the LORD's temple.[r] 16When anyone
came to a heap of twenty measures, there were only ten. When anyone went to a wine
vat to draw fifty measures, there were only twenty.[s] 17I struck all the work of your
hands[t] with blight,[u] mildew and hail, yet you did not turn to me,' declares the
LORD.[v] 18'From this day on, from this twenty-fourth day of the ninth month, give
careful thought to the day when the foundation[w] of the LORD's temple was laid. Give
careful thought: 19Is there yet any seed left in the barn? Until now, the vine and the
fig-tree, the pomegranate and the olive tree have not borne fruit.
" 'From this day on I will bless you.' "

a 15 Or *to the days past*

2:5 [e]Ex 29:46 [f]Ne 9:20; Isa 63:11
2:6 [g]Isa 10:25 [h]Heb 12:26*
2:7 [i]Isa 60:7
2:9 [j]Ps 85:9
2:10 [k]ver 1
2:11 [l]Lev 10:10-11; Dt 17:8-11; Mal 2:7
2:12 [m]Lev 6:27; Mt 23:19
2:13 [n]Lev 22:4-6
2:14 [o]Isa 1:13
2:15 [p]Hag 1:5 [q]Ezr 3:10 [r]Ezr 4:24
2:16 [s]Hag 1:6
2:17 [t]Hag 1:11 [u]Dt 28:22; 1Ki 8:37; Am 4:9 [v]Am 4:6
2:18 [w]Zec 8:9

2:5 The Israelites had been led from captivity in Egypt to their promised land. They were God's chosen people, guided and cared for by his Holy Spirit. Although God had punished them for their sins, he kept his promise and never left them (Exodus 29:45, 46). No matter what difficulties we face or how frustrating our work may be, God's Spirit is with us.

2:6–9 The focus shifts from the local temple being rebuilt in Jerusalem to the worldwide reign of the Messiah on earth. The words "in a little while" are not limited to the immediate historical context; they refer to God's control of history—he can act any time he chooses. God will act *in his time* (see also Hebrews 12:26, 27).

2:7 When God promised to shake all the nations with his judgment, he was speaking of both his present judgment on evil nations and future judgment during the last days.

2:7–9 The "desired of all nations" has two possible meanings: (1) It could refer to the Messiah, Jesus, who, some 500 years later, would enter the temple and fill it with his glory and his peace (Luke 2:27, 32). (2) It could also refer to the riches that would flow into the temple, given as offerings to God's people.

2:8, 9 God wanted the temple to be rebuilt, and he had the gold and silver to do it, but he needed willing hands. God has chosen to do his work through people. He provides the resources, but willing hands must do the work. Are your hands available for God's work in the world?

2:10–19 The example given in this message (delivered in December, 520 B.C.) makes it clear that holiness will not rub off on others, but contamination will. ("Consecrated meat" is meat made holy for the sacrifice.) As the people began to obey God, God promised to encourage and prosper them. But they needed to understand that activities in the temple would not clean up their sin; only repentance and obedience could do that. If we insist on harbouring wrong attitudes and sins or on maintaining close relationships with sinful people, we will be defiled. Holy living will come only when we are empowered by God's Holy Spirit.

2:14 When a child eats spaghetti with sauce, very soon his or her face, hands, and clothes become red. Sin and selfish attitudes produce the same result: they stain everything they touch. Even good deeds done for God can be tainted by sinful attitudes. The only remedy is God's cleansing.

2:16 A "heap" refers to a stack of grain at the harvest. For many years, the grain had only given 50 per cent of the expected yield, and wine had done even worse.

2:18, 19 The people relaid the temple foundation, and immediately God blessed them. He did not wait for the project to be completed. God often sends his encouragement and approval with our first few obedient steps. He is eager to bless us!

2:21
[x] Ezr 5:2

2:22
[y] Da 2:44
[z] Mic 5:10
[a] Jdg 7:22

2:23
[b] Isa 43:10

Zerubbabel the LORD's Signet Ring

20 The word of the LORD came to Haggai a second time on the twenty-fourth day
of the month: 21 "Tell Zerubbabel[x] governor of Judah that I will shake the heavens
and the earth. 22 I will overturn royal thrones and shatter the power of the foreign
kingdoms.[y] I will overthrow chariots[z] and their drivers; horses and their riders will
fall, each by the sword of his brother.[a]
23 " 'On that day,' declares the LORD Almighty, 'I will take you, my servant[b]
Zerubbabel son of Shealtiel,' declares the LORD, 'and I will make you like my signet
ring, for I have chosen you,' declares the LORD Almighty."

2:20–23 Haggai's final message acknowledged that he was merely the messenger who brings the word of the Lord. It is addressed to Zerubbabel, the governor of Judah.

2:23 A signet ring was used to guarantee the authority and authenticity of a letter. It served as a signature when pressed in soft wax on a written document. God was reaffirming and guaranteeing his promise of a Messiah through David's line (Matthew 1:12).

2:23 God closed his message to Zerubbabel with this tremendous affirmation: "I have chosen you." Such a proclamation is ours as well—each of us has been chosen by God (Ephesians 1:4). This truth should make us see our value in God's eyes and motivate us to work for him. When you feel down, remind yourself, "God has chosen me!"

2:23 Haggai's message to the people sought to get their priorities straight, help them stop worrying, and motivate them to rebuild the temple. Like them, we often place a higher priority on our personal comfort than on God's work and true worship. But God is pleased and promises strength and guidance when we give him first place in our lives.

ZECHARIAH

Daniel taken to Babylon 605 B.C. | Ezekiel taken to Babylon 597 | Jerusalem falls 586 | Babylon overthrown by Cyrus 539 | Cyrus' decree allowing the exiles to return 538

VITAL STATISTICS

PURPOSE:
To give hope to God's people by revealing God's future deliverance through the Messiah

AUTHOR:
Zechariah

TO WHOM WRITTEN:
The Jews in Jerusalem who had returned from their captivity in Babylon and to God's people everywhere

DATE WRITTEN:
Chapters 1—8 were written about 520-518 B.C. Chapters 9—14 were written around 480 B.C.

SETTING:
The exiles had returned from Babylon to rebuild the temple, but the work had been thwarted and stalled. Haggai and Zechariah confronted the people with their task and encouraged them to complete it.

KEY VERSES:
"Rejoice greatly, O Daughter of Zion! Shout, Daughter of Jerusalem! See, your king comes to you, righteous and having salvation, gentle and riding on a donkey, on a colt, the foal of a donkey. . . . He will proclaim peace to the nations. His rule will extend from sea to sea and from the River to the ends of the earth" (9:9, 10).

KEY PEOPLE:
Zerubbabel, Joshua

KEY PLACE:
Jerusalem

SPECIAL FEATURES:
This book is the most apocalyptic and messianic of all the minor prophets.

THE FUTURE—that vast uncharted sea of the unknown, holding joy or terror, comfort or pain, love or loneliness. Some people fear the days to come, wondering what evils lurk in the shadows; others consult seers and future-telling charlatans, trying desperately to discover its secrets. But tomorrow's story is known only to God and to those special messengers, called prophets, to whom God has revealed a chapter or two.

A prophet's primary task was to proclaim the word of the Lord, pointing out sin, explaining its consequences, and calling men and women to repentance and obedience. Elijah, Elisha, Isaiah, Jeremiah, Ezekiel, Hosea, and Amos stand with scores of others who faithfully delivered God's message despite rejection, ridicule, and persecution. And at times they were given prophetic visions foretelling coming events.

Nestled near the end of the Old Testament, among what are known as "minor prophets", is the book of Zechariah. As one of three post-exilic prophets, along with Haggai and Malachi, Zechariah ministered to the small remnant of Jews who had returned to Judah to rebuild the temple and their nation. Like Haggai, he encouraged the people to finish rebuilding the temple, but his message went far beyond those physical walls and contemporary issues. With spectacular apocalyptic imagery and graphic detail, Zechariah told of the Messiah, the One whom God would send to rescue his people and to reign over all the earth. Zechariah is one of our most important prophetic books, giving detailed messianic references that were clearly fulfilled in the life of Jesus Christ. The rebuilding of the temple, he says, was just the first act in the drama of the end and the ushering in of the messianic age. Zechariah proclaimed a stirring message of hope to these ex-captives and exiles—their King was coming!

Jesus is Messiah, the promised "great deliverer" of Israel. Unlike Zechariah's listeners, we can look back at Christ's ministry and mission. As you study Zechariah's prophecy, you will see details of Christ's life that were written 500 years before their fulfilment. Read and stand in awe of our God who keeps his promises. But there is also a future message that has not yet been fulfilled—the return of Christ at the end of the age. As you read Zechariah, therefore, think through the implications of this promised event. *Your King is coming,* and he will reign for ever and ever.

God knows and controls the future. We may never see more than a moment ahead, but we can be secure if we trust in him. Read Zechariah and strengthen your faith in God—he alone is your hope and security.

Temple construction begins 536	Temple work halted 530	Haggai, Zechariah become prophets; temple work resumed 520	Temple completed 516	Ezra comes to Jerusalem 458	Nehemiah comes to Jerusalem 445

THE BLUEPRINT

A. MESSAGES WHILE REBUILDING THE TEMPLE (1:1—8:23) 1. Zechariah's night visions 2. Zechariah's words of encouragement	Zechariah encouraged the people to put away the sin in their lives and to continue rebuilding the temple. His visions described the judgment of Israel's enemies, the blessings to Jerusalem, and the need for God's people to remain pure—avoiding hypocrisy, superficiality, and sin. Zechariah's visions provided hope for the people. We also need to follow carefully the instruction to remain pure until Christ returns again.
B. MESSAGES AFTER COMPLETING THE TEMPLE (9:1—14:21)	Besides encouragement and hope, Zechariah's messages were also a warning that God's messianic kingdom would not begin as soon as the temple was complete. Israel's enemies would be judged and the King would come, but God's people would themselves face many difficult circumstances before experiencing the blessing of the messianic kingdom. We too may face much sorrow, disappointment, and distress before coming into Christ's eternal kingdom.

MEGATHEMES

THEME	EXPLANATION	IMPORTANCE
God's Jealousy	God was angry at his people for ignoring his prophets through the years, and he was concerned that they not follow the careless and false leaders who exploited them. Disobedience was the root of their problems and the cause of their misery. God was jealous for their devotion to him.	God is jealous for our devotion. To avoid Israel's ruin, don't walk in their steps. Don't reject God, follow false teachers, or lead others astray. Turn to God, faithfully obey his commands, and make sure you are leading others correctly.
Rebuild the Temple	The Jews were discouraged. They were free from exile, yet the temple was not completed. Zechariah encouraged them to rebuild it. God would both protect his workmen and empower them by his Holy Spirit to carry out his work.	More than the rebuilding of the temple was at stake—the people were staging the first act in God's wonderful drama of the end times. Those of us who believe in God must complete his work. To do so we must have the Holy Spirit's help. God will empower us with his Spirit.
The King is Coming	The Messiah will come both to rescue people from sin and to reign as king. He will establish his kingdom, conquer all his enemies, and rule over all the earth. Everything will one day be under his loving and powerful control.	The Messiah came as a servant to die for us. He will return as a victorious King. At that time, he will usher in peace throughout the world. Submit to his leadership now to be ready for the King's triumphant return.
God's Protection	There was opposition to God's plan in Zechariah's day, and he prophesied future times of trouble. But God's word endures. God remembers the agreements he makes with his people. He cares for his people and will deliver them from all the world powers that oppress them.	Although evil is still present, God's infinite love and personal care have been demonstrated through the centuries. God keeps his promises. Although our bodies may be destroyed, we need never fear our ultimate destiny if we love and obey him.

A. MESSAGES WHILE REBUILDING THE TEMPLE (1:1—8:23)

Zechariah begins by describing eight visions that came to him at night. Then he gives a collection of messages about the crowning of Joshua, answers to questions of feasting and fasting, and encouragment to continue rebuilding the temple. We, too, can be inspired to continue following God in faithfulness throughout our lives.

1. Zechariah's night visions

A Call to Return to the LORD

1 In the eighth month of the second year of Darius,[a] the word of the LORD came
to the prophet Zechariah[b] son of Berekiah,[c] the son of Iddo:[d]
2"The LORD was very angry[e] with your forefathers. 3Therefore tell the people: This
is what the LORD Almighty says: 'Return to me,' declares the LORD Almighty, 'and
I will return to you,'[f] says the LORD Almighty. 4Do not be like your forefathers,[g]
to whom the earlier prophets proclaimed: This is what the LORD Almighty says: 'Turn
from your evil ways[h] and your evil practices.' But they would not listen or pay
attention to me,[i] declares the LORD. 5Where are your forefathers now? And the
prophets, do they live for ever? 6But did not my words and my decrees, which I
commanded my servants the prophets, overtake your forefathers?
"Then they repented and said, 'The LORD Almighty has done to us what our ways
and practices deserve,[j] just as he determined to do.' "

The Man Among the Myrtle Trees

7On the twenty-fourth day of the eleventh month, the month of Shebat, in the second
year of Darius, the word of the LORD came to the prophet Zechariah son of Berekiah,
the son of Iddo.
8During the night I had a vision—and there before me was a man riding a red[k]
horse! He was standing among the myrtle trees in a ravine. Behind him were red,
brown and white horses.[l]
9I asked, "What are these, my lord?"
The angel[m] who was talking with me answered, "I will show you what they are."
10Then the man standing among the myrtle trees explained, "They are the ones the
LORD has sent to go throughout the earth."[n]
11And they reported to the angel of the LORD, who was standing among the myrtle
trees, "We have gone throughout the earth and found the whole world at rest and in
peace."[o]
12Then the angel of the LORD said, "LORD Almighty, how long will you withhold
mercy from Jerusalem and from the towns of Judah, which you have been angry with
these seventy[p] years?" 13So the LORD spoke kind and comforting words to the angel
who talked with me.[q]

1:1 [a]Ezr 4:24; 6:15 [b]Ezr 5:1 [c]Mt 23:35; Lk 11:51 [d]ver 7; Ne 12:4
1:2 [e]2Ch 36:16
1:3 [f]Mal 3:7; Jas 4:8
1:4 [g]2Ch 36:15 [h]Ps 106:6 [i]2Ch 24:19; Ps 78:8; Jer 6:17
1:6 [j]Jer 12:14-17; La 2:17
1:8 [k]Rev 6:4 [l]Zec 6:2-7
1:9 [m]Zec 4:1, 4-5
1:10 [n]Zec 6:5-8
1:11 [o]Isa 14:7
1:12 [p]Da 9:2
1:13 [q]Zec 4:1

1:1 Born in Babylon during the exile, Zechariah was a fairly young man when he returned to Jerusalem in 538 B.C. King Cyrus of Persia had defeated Babylon in 539 and had decreed that captives in exile could return to their homelands. Zechariah and Haggai were among the first to leave. Zechariah, a prophet and a priest, began ministering at the same time as the prophet Haggai (520–518 B.C.). His first prophecy was delivered two months after Haggai's first prophecy.

Like Haggai, Zechariah encouraged the people to continue rebuilding the temple, whose reconstruction had been halted for nearly 15 years. Zechariah combated the people's spiritual apathy, despair over pressures from their enemies, and discouragement about the smaller scale of the new temple foundation. Neglect of our spiritual priorities can be just as devastating today to fulfilling God's purpose.

1:2–6 The familiar phrase "Like father, like son" implies that children turn out like their parents. But here, God warned Israel *not* to be like their forefathers, who disobeyed him and reaped the consequences—his punishment. We are responsible before God for our actions. We aren't trapped by our heredity or environment, and we can't use these as excuses for our sins. We are free to choose, and individually we must return to God and follow him.

1:5, 6 The words God had spoken through his prophets a century earlier, before the captivity, also applied to Zechariah's generation, and they are still relevant for us. Because God's word endures, we must read, study, and apply what is preserved for us in Scripture. Learn the lessons of God's word so you will not have to repeat the mistakes of others.

1:7–17 The man among the myrtle trees was the angel of the Lord (1:11). The horses and their colours were symbols of God's involvement in world governments. The full meaning of the colours is unknown, although the red horse is often associated with war and the white horse with final victory.

1:11 The angel of the Lord saw that all the nations were secure and at peace while Israel was still oppressed and despised. But God was planning a change. He had released his people, and he would allow them to return and rebuild his temple.

1:12 Seventy years was the time that God had decreed for Israel to remain in captivity (Jeremiah 25:11; 29:10). This time was over, and the angel asked God to act swiftly to complete the promised return of his people to Jerusalem.

1:13 God's people had lived under his judgment for 70 years

14Then the angel who was speaking to me said, "Proclaim this word: This is what
the LORD Almighty says: 'I am very jealous[r] for Jerusalem and Zion, 15but I am very
angry with the nations that feel secure.[s] I was only a little angry, but they added to
the calamity.'[t]
16"Therefore, this is what the LORD says: 'I will return[u] to Jerusalem with mercy,
and there my house will be rebuilt. And the measuring line[v] will be stretched out over
Jerusalem,' declares the LORD Almighty.
17"Proclaim further: This is what the LORD Almighty says: 'My towns will again
overflow with prosperity, and the LORD will again comfort[w] Zion and choose[x]
Jerusalem.' "[y]

Four Horns and Four Craftsmen

18Then I looked up—and there before me were four horns! 19I asked the angel who
was speaking to me, "What are these?"
He answered me, "These are the horns[z] that scattered Judah, Israel and Jerusalem."
20Then the LORD showed me four craftsmen. 21I asked, "What are these coming
to do?"
He answered, "These are the horns that scattered Judah so that no-one could raise
his head, but the craftsmen have come to terrify them and throw down these horns
of the nations who lifted up their horns[a] against the land of Judah to scatter its
people."[b]

A Man With a Measuring Line

2 Then I looked up—and there before me was a man with a measuring line in his
hand! 2I asked, "Where are you going?"
He answered me, "To measure Jerusalem, to find out how wide and how long it
is."[a]
3Then the angel who was speaking to me left, and another angel came to meet him
4and said to him: "Run, tell that young man, 'Jerusalem will be a city without walls[b]
because of the great number[c] of men and livestock in it. 5And I myself will be a wall[d]
of fire around it,' declares the LORD, 'and I will be its glory[e] within.'
6"Come! Come! Flee from the land of the north," declares the LORD, "for I have
scattered you to the four winds of heaven,"[f] declares the LORD.

1:14 [r]Joel 2:18; Zec 8:2
1:15 [s]Jer 48:11 [t]Ps 123:3-4; Am 1:11
1:16 [u]Zec 8:3 [v]Zec 2:1-2
1:17 [w]Isa 51:3 [x]Isa 14:1 [y]Zec 2:12
1:19 [z]Am 6:13
1:21 [a]Ps 75:4 [b]Ps 75:10
2:2 [a]Eze 40:3; Rev 21:15
2:4 [b]Eze 38:11 [c]Isa 49:20; Jer 30:19; 33:22
2:5 [d]Isa 26:1 [e]Rev 21:23
2:6 [f]Eze 17:21

ZECHARIAH served as a prophet to Judah about 520 B.C., after the return from exile.

Climate of the times	The exiles had returned from captivity to rebuild their temple. But work on the temple had stalled and the people were ignoring their service to God.
Main message	Zechariah, like Haggai, encouraged the people to finish rebuilding the temple. His visions gave the people hope. He told the people of a future King who would one day establish an eternal kingdom.
Importance of message	Even in times of discouragement and despair, God is working out his plan. God protects and guides us; we must trust and follow him.
Contemporary prophet	Haggai (about 520 B.C.)

during their captivity in Babylon. But here God spoke words of comfort and assurance. God promises that when we return to him, he will heal us (Hosea 6:1). If you feel wounded and torn by the events of your life, turn to God so he can heal and comfort you.

1:15 Although the pagan nations afflicted God's people beyond his intentions, God was not powerless to stop them. God used these nations to punish his sinful people. When the nations went beyond his plans by trying to destroy Israel as a nation, he intervened.

1:18–21 The horns were the four world powers that oppressed Israel—Egypt, Assyria, Babylon, and Medo-Persia. The four craftsmen (1:20) were the nations used to overthrow Israel's enemies. God raised them up to judge the oppressors of his people.

2:1 The man with the measuring line symbolises the hope of a rebuilt Jerusalem and a restored people. The man would be measuring to mark out the boundaries for a foundation (see 1:16; and Jeremiah 31:38–40).

2:6, 7 Many of the captive Israelites did not return to Jerusalem because they preferred to stay with the security and wealth they had experienced in Babylon. But Zechariah instructed them to leave Babylon quickly. This was an urgent request because Babylon would be destroyed and because its decadent culture would cause God's people to forget their spiritual priorities. A vast majority of the Israelites rejected these warnings and remained in Babylon.

[7]"Come, O Zion! Escape, you who live in the Daughter of Babylon!"[g] [8]For this
is what the LORD Almighty says: "After he has honoured me and has sent me against
the nations that have plundered you—for whoever touches you touches the apple of
his eye[h]—[9]I will surely raise my hand against them so that their slaves will plunder
them.[a][i] Then you will know that the LORD Almighty has sent me.[j]
[10]"Shout and be glad, O Daughter of Zion.[k] For I am coming,[l] and I will live
among you,"[m] declares the LORD. [11]"Many nations will be joined with the LORD in
that day and will become my people. I will live among you and you will know that
the LORD Almighty has sent me to you. [12]The LORD will inherit[n] Judah as his portion
in the holy land and will again choose[o] Jerusalem. [13]Be still[p] before the LORD, all
mankind, because he has roused himself from his holy dwelling."

Clean Garments for the High Priest

3 Then he showed me Joshua[a][a] the high priest standing before the angel of the
LORD, and Satan[b][b] standing at his right side to accuse him. [2]The LORD said to
Satan, "The LORD rebuke you,[c] Satan! The LORD, who has chosen[d] Jerusalem,
rebuke you! Is not this man a burning stick snatched from the fire?"[e]
[3]Now Joshua was dressed in filthy clothes as he stood before the angel. [4]The angel
said to those who were standing before him, "Take off his filthy clothes."
Then he said to Joshua, "See, I have taken away your sin,[f] and I will put rich
garments[g] on you."
[5]Then I said, "Put a clean turban[h] on his head." So they put a clean turban on his
head and clothed him, while the angel of the LORD stood by.
[6]The angel of the LORD gave this charge to Joshua: [7]"This is what the LORD
Almighty says: 'If you will walk in my ways and keep my requirements, then you
will govern my house[i] and have charge of my courts, and I will give you a place
among these standing here.
[8]" 'Listen, O high priest Joshua and your associates seated before you, who are men

a *8, 9* Or *says after . . . eye:* [9]*"I . . . plunder them."* **a** *1* A variant of *Jeshua*; here and elsewhere in Zechariah
b *1* *Satan* means *accuser.*

2:7 [g]Isa 48:20
2:8 [h]Dt 32:10
2:9 [i]Isa 14:2; [j]Zec 4:9
2:10 [k]Zep 3:14; [l]Zec 9:9; [m]Lev 26:12; Zec 8:3
2:12 [n]Dt 32:9; Ps 33:12; Jer 10:16; [o]Zec 1:17
2:13 [p]Hab 2:20
3:1 [a]Hag 1:1; Zec 6:11; [b]Ps 109:6
3:2 [c]Jude 1:9; [d]Isa 14:1; [e]Am 4:11; Jude 1:23
3:4 [f]Eze 36:25; Mic 7:18; [g]Isa 52:1; Rev 19:8
3:5 [h]Ex 29:6
3:7 [i]Dt 17:8-11; Eze 44:15-16

2:8 Believers are precious to God (Psalm 116:15); they are his very own children (Psalm 103:13). Treating any believer unkindly is the same as treating God that way. As Jesus told his disciples, when we help others we are helping him; when we neglect or abuse them, we are neglecting or abusing him (Matthew 25:34–46). Be careful, therefore, how you treat fellow believers—that is the way you are treating God.

2:9–12 *Me* (2:9) may refer to the Messiah who, in the end, will judge all who have oppressed God's people. God promises to live among his people, and he says that many nations will come to know him (John 1:14; Revelation 21:3).

2:11, 12 God did not forget his words to Abraham, "All peoples on earth will be blessed through you" (Genesis 12:3). Abraham, the father of the nation of Israel, was promised that his descendants would bless the whole world. Since the coming of Jesus, the Messiah, this promise is being fulfilled—people from all nations are coming to God through him.

3:1 Joshua was Israel's high priest when the remnant returned to Jerusalem and began rebuilding the walls (Haggai 1:1, 12; 2:4).

3:1–3 Satan accused Joshua, who here represents the nation of Israel. The accusations were accurate—Joshua stood in "filthy clothes" (sins). Yet God revealed his mercy, stating that he chose to save his people in spite of their sin. Satan is always accusing people of their sins before God (Job 1:6). But he greatly misunderstands the breadth of God's mercy and forgiveness towards those who believe in him. Satan the accuser will ultimately be destroyed (Revelation 12:10), while everyone who is a believer will be saved (John 3:16). To be prepared, we can ask God to remove our clothing of sin and dress us with his goodness.

3:2 God punished Judah through the fire of great trials, but he rescued the nation before it was completely destroyed, like "a burning stick snatched from the fire".

3:2–4 Zechariah's vision graphically portrays how we receive God's mercy. We do nothing ourselves. God removes our filthy clothes (sins), then provides us with new, clean, rich garments (the righteousness and holiness of God—2 Corinthians 5:21; Ephesians 4:24; Revelation 19:8). All we need to do is repent and ask God to forgive us. When Satan tries to make you feel dirty and unworthy, remember that the clean clothes of Christ's righteousness make you worthy to draw near to God.

3:5–7 The Greek name for Joshua is Jesus, meaning "the LORD saves". This Joshua should not be confused with the warrior of the book of Joshua. Both the warrior Joshua and the high priest Joshua, however, have been seen as symbols of Jesus, the Messiah.

3:7–10 There was no priesthood during the exile, so it had to be reinstated upon the return to the land. In this vision, Joshua is installed as high priest. One of the high priest's duties was to offer a sacrifice on the Day of Atonement to make amends for all the sins of the people. The priest was the mediator between God and the nation. Thus, he represented the coming Messiah (Isaiah 11:1), who would change the entire order of God's dealing with people's sin (Hebrews 10:8–14 explains this in detail). Jesus, the Messiah, was the High Priest who offered, once for all, the sacrifice of himself to take away our sins. In the new order, every Christian is a priest offering a holy, cleansed life to God (1 Peter 2:9; Revelation 5:10).

3:8, 9 The "Branch" refers to the Messiah. The meaning of the stone with seven eyes is unclear. It could mean (1) the Branch himself as the foundation stone of the temple, (2) the rock struck by Moses that produced water for the Israelites (Numbers 20:7–11), or (3) the renewed spiritual priesthood of the church (1 Peter 2:5).

ZECHARIAH'S VISIONS

Vision	*Reference*	*Significance*
Zechariah sees messengers reporting to God that the surrounding nations that have oppressed Judah are living in careless and sinful ease.	1:7–17	Israel was asking, "Why isn't God punishing the wicked?" Wicked nations may prosper, but not for ever. God will bring upon them the judgment they deserve.
Zechariah sees four horns, representing the four world powers that oppressed and scattered the people of Judah and Israel. Then he sees four craftsmen who will throw down the horns.	1:18–21	God will do what he promised. After the evil nations have carried out his will in punishing his people, God will destroy those nations for their sin.
Zechariah sees a man measuring the city of Jerusalem. The city will one day be full of people, and God himself will be a wall around the city.	2:1–13	The city will be restored in God's future kingdom. God will keep his promise to protect his people.
Zechariah sees Joshua the high priest standing before God. Joshua's filthy clothes are exchanged for clean garments; Satan's accusations against him are rejected by God.	3:1–10	The story of Joshua the high priest pictures how the filthy clothes of sin are replaced with the pure linen of God's righteousness. Christ has taken our clothes of sin and replaced them with God's righteousness. (See Ephesians 4:24; 1 John 1:9.)
Zechariah sees a lampstand that is continually kept burning by an unlimited reservoir of oil. This picture reminds the people that it is only through God's Spirit that they will succeed, not by their own might and resources.	4:1–14	The Spirit of God is given without measure. Human effort does not make a difference. The work of God is not accomplished in human strength.
Zechariah sees a flying scroll, which represents God's curse.	5:1–4	By God's word and Spirit every person will be judged. The individual's sin is the focus here, not the sins of the nation. Each person is responsible for his or her deeds; no-one has an excuse. God's curse is a symbol of destruction; all sin will be judged and removed.
Zechariah sees a vision of a woman in a basket. She represents the wickedness of the nations. The angel packed the woman back into the basket and sent her back to Babylon.	5:5–11	Sins of the individual were judged in the last vision (5:1–4); now sin is being removed from society. Sin has to be eradicated in order to clean up the nation and the individual.
Zechariah sees a vision of four horses and chariots. The horses represent God's judgment on the world—one is sent north, the direction from which most of Judah's enemies came. The other horses are patrolling the world, ready to execute judgment at God's command.	6:1–8	Judgment will come upon those who oppress God's people—it will come in God's time and at his command.

These verses were fulfilled hundreds of years later by Jesus Christ. God said, "I will remove the sin of this land in a single day", and this was fulfilled in Christ who "died for sins once for all, the righteous for the unrighteous, to bring you to God" (1 Peter 3:18). You cannot remove your sins by your own effort. You must allow God to remove them through Christ.

symbolic[j] of things to come: I am going to bring my servant, the Branch.[k] 9See,
the stone I have set in front of Joshua! There are seven eyes[c] on that one stone,[l]
and I will engrave an inscription on it,' says the LORD Almighty, 'and I will remove
the sin[m] of this land in a single day.
10" 'In that day each of you will invite his neighbour to sit under his vine and
fig-tree,[n]' declares the LORD Almighty."

The Gold Lampstand and the Two Olive Trees

4 Then the angel who talked with me returned and wakened[a] me, as a man is
wakened from his sleep.[b] 2He asked me, "What do you see?"[c]
I answered, "I see a solid gold lampstand[d] with a bowl at the top and seven lights[e]
on it, with seven channels to the lights. 3Also there are two olive trees[f] by it, one
on the right of the bowl and the other on its left."
4I asked the angel who talked with me, "What are these, my lord?"
5He answered, "Do you not know what these are?"
"No, my lord," I replied.[g]
6So he said to me, "This is the word of the LORD to Zerubbabel:[h] 'Not by might
nor by power, but by my Spirit,'[i] says the LORD Almighty.
7"What[a] are you, O mighty mountain? Before Zerubbabel you will become level
ground.[j] Then he will bring out the capstone[k] to shouts of 'God bless it! God bless
it!' "
8Then the word of the LORD came to me: 9"The hands of Zerubbabel have laid the
foundation[l] of this temple; his hands will also complete it.[m] Then you will know
that the LORD Almighty has sent me[n] to you.
10"Who despises the day of small things?[o] Men will rejoice when they see the
plumb-line in the hand of Zerubbabel.
"(These seven are the eyes[p] of the LORD, which range throughout the earth.)"
11Then I asked the angel, "What are these two olive trees[q] on the right and the
left of the lampstand?"
12Again I asked him, "What are these two olive branches beside the two gold pipes
that pour out golden oil?"
13He replied, "Do you not know what these are?"
"No, my lord," I said.
14So he said, "These are the two who are anointed[r] to[b] serve the Lord of all the
earth."

c *9 Or facets* **a** *7 Or Who* **b** *14 Or two who bring oil and*

3:8 [j]Eze 12:11 [k]Isa 4:2
3:9 [l]Isa 28:16 [m]Jer 50:20
3:10 [n]1Ki 4:25; Mic 4:4
4:1 [a]Da 8:18 [b]Jer 31:26
4:2 [c]Jer 1:13 [d]Ex 25:31; Rev 1:12 [e]Rev 4:5
4:3 [f]ver 11; Rev 11:4
4:5 [g]Zec 1:9
4:6 [h]Ezr 5:2 [i]Isa 11:2-4; Hos 1:7
4:7 [j]Jer 51:25 [k]Ps 118:22
4:9 [l]Ezr 3:11 [m]Ezr 3:8; 6:15; Zec 6:12 [n]Zec 2:9
4:10 [o]Hag 2:3 [p]Zec 3:9; Rev 5:6
4:11 [q]ver 3; Rev 11:4
4:14 [r]Ex 29:7; 40:15; Da 9:24-26; Zec 3:1-7

3:10 God promises that each person will have his or her own place of security during Christ's reign (see also Micah 4:4). Sitting under the vine and fig tree was a symbol of peace and prosperity.

4:1 The gold lampstand with a bowl and seven lights on it represents a steady supply of oil, signifying that God's power would be reflected in the light. Oil was obtained from crushed olives and used in bowls with wicks to produce light. The two olive trees stood for the priestly and royal offices.

4:6 Zerubbabel was given the responsibility of rebuilding the temple in Jerusalem (Ezra 3:2, 8; Haggai 1:1; 2:23). While the prophets Haggai and Zechariah gave the moral and spiritual encouragement to resume work on the temple, Zerubbabel saw that the task was carried out. As the work was being completed, the prophets encouraged Zerubbabel and told him of a time when spiritual apathy and foreign oppression would for ever be abolished.

4:6 Many people believe that to survive in this world a person must be tough, strong, unbending, and harsh. But God says, "Not by might nor by power, but by my Spirit". The key words are "by my Spirit". It is *only* through God's Spirit that anything of lasting value is accomplished. The returned exiles were indeed weak – harassed by their enemies, tired, discouraged, and poor. But actually they had God on their side! As you live for God, determine not to trust in your own strength or abilities. Instead, depend on God and work in the power of his Spirit! (See also Hosea 1:7.)

4:9 The temple was completed in 516 B.C. (Ezra 6:14, 15).

4:10 Many of the older Jews were disheartened when they realised this new temple would not match the size and splendour of the previous temple built during King Solomon's reign. But bigger and more beautiful is not always better. What you do for God may seem small and insignificant at the time, but God rejoices in what is right, not necessarily in what is big. Be faithful in the small opportunities. Begin where you are and do what you can, and leave the results to God.

4:14 The two anointed ones may be Joshua and Zerubbabel, dedicated for this special task. Also note that in Revelation 11:3, two witnesses arise to prophesy to the nations during the time of tribulation. These witnesses will be killed but will rise again.

The Flying Scroll

5 I looked again — and there before me was a flying scroll![a]
2He asked me, "What do you see?"
I answered, "I see a flying scroll, thirty feet long and fifteen feet wide."[a]
3And he said to me, "This is the curse[b] that is going out over the whole land; for
according to what it says on one side, every thief[c] will be banished, and according
to what it says on the other, everyone who swears falsely[d] will be banished. 4The
LORD Almighty declares, 'I will send it out, and it will enter the house of the thief
and the house of him who swears falsely by my name. It will remain in his house and
destroy it, both its timbers and its stones.[e]' "

The Woman in a Basket

5Then the angel who was speaking to me came forward and said to me, "Look up
and see what this is that is appearing."
6I asked, "What is it?"
He replied, "It is a measuring basket."[b] And he added, "This is the iniquity[c] of
the people throughout the land."
7Then the cover of lead was raised, and there in the basket sat a woman! 8He said,
"This is wickedness," and he pushed her back into the basket and pushed the lead cover
down over its mouth.[f]
9Then I looked up — and there before me were two women, with the wind in their
wings! They had wings like those of a stork,[g] and they lifted up the basket between
heaven and earth.
10"Where are they taking the basket?" I asked the angel who was speaking to me.
11He replied, "To the country of Babylonia[d][h] to build a house[i] for it. When it
is ready, the basket will be set there in its place."[j]

Four Chariots

6 I looked up again — and there before me were four chariots[a] coming out from
between two mountains — mountains of bronze! 2The first chariot had red horses,
the second black,[b] 3the third white,[c] and the fourth dappled — all of them powerful.
4I asked the angel who was speaking to me, "What are these, my lord?"
5The angel answered me, "These are the four spirits[a][d] of heaven, going out from
standing in the presence of the Lord of the whole world. 6The one with the black horses
is going towards the north country, the one with the white horses towards the west,[b]
and the one with the dappled horses towards the south."
7When the powerful horses went out, they were straining to go throughout the
earth.[e] And he said, "Go throughout the earth!" So they went throughout the earth.
8Then he called to me, "Look, those going towards the north country have given
my Spirit[c] rest[f] in the land of the north."

5:1 [a]Eze 2:9; Rev 5:1
5:3 [b]Isa 24:6; 43:28; Mal 3:9; 4:6 [c]Ex 20:15; Mal 3:8 [d]Isa 48:1
5:4 [e]Lev 14:34-45; Hab 2:9-11; Mal 3:5
5:8 [f]Mic 6:11
5:9 [g]Lev 11:19
5:11 [h]Ge 10:10 [i]Jer 29:5, 28 [j]Da 1:2
6:1 [a]ver 5
6:2 [b]Rev 6:5
6:3 [c]Rev 6:2
6:5 [d]Eze 37:9; Mt 24:31; Rev 7:1
6:7 [e]Zec 1:10
6:8 [f]Eze 5:13; 24:13

a *2* Hebrew *twenty cubits long and ten cubits wide* (about 9 metres long and 4.5 metres wide) **b** *6* Hebrew *an ephah*; also in verses 7–11 **c** *6* Or *appearance* **d** *11* Hebrew *Shinar* **a** *5* Or *winds* **b** *6* Or *horses after them* **c** *8* Or *spirit*

5:1–9 The judgment of the flying scroll was levelled against those who violated God's law, specifically by stealing and lying (5:1–4). The woman in a basket personified wickedness, and so this vision showed that wickedness would be not only severely punished (the vision of the flying scroll), but also banished (the vision of the woman in a basket, 5:6–9).

5:9–11 The woman in a basket was carried away "to the country of Babylonia", which had become a symbol for the centre of world idolatry and wickedness. This woman was a picture to Zechariah that wickedness and sin would be taken away from Israel, and one day sin would be removed from the entire earth. When Christ died, he removed sin's power and penalty. When we trust Christ to forgive us, he removes the penalty of sin and gives us the power to overcome sin in our lives. When Christ returns, he will remove all sin from the earth, allowing people to live in eternal safety and security.

6:1–8 The four chariots were similar to the four horsemen in the first vision. These chariots represent the four angels of God's judgment on the earth.

6:8 The black horse that went north executed God's judgment in the north country. God is angry with sin and with the wicked (Psalm 7:11), and his anger is expressed in judgment. As much as we like to concentrate on God's love and mercy, anger and judgment are also part of his righteous character. If you have unconfessed or habitual sin in your life, confess it and turn away from it. Confession releases God's mercy, but refusing to repent invites his judgment.

2. Zechariah's words of encouragement

A Crown for Joshua

9The word of the LORD came to me: 10"Take ⌞silver and gold⌟ from the exiles Heldai,
Tobijah and Jedaiah, who have arrived from Babylon.[g] Go the same day to the house
of Josiah son of Zephaniah. 11Take the silver and gold and make a crown,[h] and set
it on the head of the high priest, Joshua[i] son of Jehozadak.[j] 12Tell him this is what
the LORD Almighty says: 'Here is the man whose name is the Branch,[k] and he will
branch out from his place and build the temple of the LORD.[l] 13It is he who will build
the temple of the LORD, and he will be clothed with majesty and will sit and rule on
his throne. And he will be a priest[m] on his throne. And there will be harmony between
the two.' 14The crown will be given to Heldai,[d] Tobijah, Jedaiah and Hen[e] son of
Zephaniah as a memorial in the temple of the LORD. 15Those who are far away will
come and help to build the temple of the LORD,[n] and you will know that the LORD
Almighty has sent me to you.[o] This will happen if you diligently obey[p] the LORD
your God."

Justice and Mercy, Not Fasting

7 In the fourth year of King Darius, the word of the LORD came to Zechariah on
the fourth day of the ninth month, the month of Kislev.[a] 2The people of Bethel
had sent Sharezer and Regem-Melech, together with their men, to entreat[b] the LORD
3by asking the priests of the house of the LORD Almighty and the prophets, "Should
I mourn[c] and fast in the fifth[d] month, as I have done for so many years?"
4Then the word of the LORD Almighty came to me: 5"Ask all the people of the land
and the priests, 'When you fasted[e] and mourned in the fifth and seventh months for
the past seventy years, was it really for me that you fasted? 6And when you were eating
and drinking, were you not just feasting for yourselves? 7Are these not the words the
LORD proclaimed through the earlier prophets[f] when Jerusalem and its surrounding
towns were at rest[g] and prosperous, and the Negev and the western foothills[h] were
settled?' "
8And the word of the LORD came again to Zechariah: 9"This is what the LORD
Almighty says: 'Administer true justice;[i] show mercy and compassion to one another. 10Do not oppress the widow or the fatherless, the alien[j] or the poor. In your
hearts do not think evil of each other.'[k]
11"But they refused to pay attention; stubbornly they turned their backs and stopped
up their ears.[l] 12They made their hearts as hard as flint[m] and would not listen to the
law or to the words that the LORD Almighty had sent by his Spirit through the earlier
prophets.[n] So the LORD Almighty was very angry.[o]

d 14 Syriac; Hebrew *Helem* **e** 14 Or *and the gracious one, the*

6:10 [g]Ezr 7:14-16; Jer 28:6
6:11 [h]Ps 21:3 [i]Zec 3:1 [j]Ezr 3:2
6:12 [k]Isa 4:2; Zec 3:8 [l]Ezr 3:8-10; Zec 4:6-9
6:13 [m]Ps 110:4
6:15 [n]Isa 60:10 [o]Zec 2:9-11 [p]Isa 58:12; Jer 7:23; Zec 3:7
7:1 [a]Ne 1:1
7:2 [b]Jer 26:19; Zec 8:21
7:3 [c]Zec 12:12-14 [d]Jer 52:12-14; Zec 8:19
7:5 [e]Isa 58:5
7:7 [f]Zec 1:4 [g]Jer 22:21 [h]Jer 17:26
7:9 [i]Zec 8:16
7:10 [j]Ex 22:21 [k]Ex 22:22; Isa 1:17
7:11 [l]Jer 8:5; 11:10; 17:23
7:12 [m]Jer 17:1; Eze 11:19 [n]Ne 9:29 [o]Da 9:12

6:9–15 This vision is about the Messiah, the King-Priest. In the days of the kings and after the exile, Judah's government was to be ruled by two distinct persons—the king, ruling the nation's political life, and the high priest, ruling its religious life. Kings and priests had often been corrupt. God was telling Zechariah that someone worthy of the crown would come to rule as both king ("rule on his throne") and priest ("a priest on his throne"). This was an unlikely combination for that day.

6:15 Some of God's promises are conditional—we must obey him to receive them. The rebuilding of the temple required careful obedience. God would protect the people as long as they obeyed. Casual or occasional obedience, the result of a half-hearted or divided commitment, would not lead to blessing. Many of God's blessings come to us as a result of diligent obedience. Inconsistent obedience can't produce consistent blessing.

7:1ff The fourth year of King Darius' reign was 518 B.C. For the previous 70 years, the people had been holding a fast in August to remember the destruction of Jerusalem. Because Jerusalem was being rebuilt, they came to the temple to ask if they had to continue this annual fast. God did not answer their question directly. Instead, he told them that their acts of justice and mercy were more important than their fasting. What he wanted from his people was true justice in their dealings and mercy and compassion for the weak.

7:5–7 The Israelites had lost their sincere desire for a loving relationship with God. Zechariah told them that they had been fasting without a proper attitude of repentance or worship. They fasted and mourned during their exile with no thought of God or their sins that had caused the exile in the first place. When you go to church, pray, or have fellowship with other believers, are you doing these from habit or for what you get out of it? God says that an attitude of worship without a sincere desire to know and love him will lead to ruin.

7:7 The Negev was the southern part of Judah.

7:11, 12 Zechariah explained to the people that their ancestors brought God's great wrath on themselves by hardening their hearts. Any sin seems more natural the second time—as we become hardened, each repetition is easier. Ignoring or refusing God's warning hardens you each time you do wrong. Read God's word and apply it to your life. Sensitivity and submission to God's word can soften your heart and allow you to live as you should.

13" 'When I called, they did not listen;[p] so when they called, I would not listen,'[q]
says the LORD Almighty.[r] 14'I scattered[s] them with a whirlwind[t] among all the
nations, where they were strangers. The land was left so desolate behind them that
no-one could come or go. This is how they made the pleasant land desolate.[u]' "

The LORD Promises to Bless Jerusalem

8 Again the word of the LORD Almighty came to me. 2This is what the LORD
Almighty says: "I am very jealous for Zion; I am burning with jealousy for her."
3This is what the LORD says: "I will return[a] to Zion and dwell in Jerusalem.[b] Then
Jerusalem will be called the City of Truth, and the mountain of the LORD Almighty
will be called the Holy Mountain."
4This is what the LORD Almighty says: "Once again men and women of ripe old
age will sit in the streets of Jerusalem,[c] each with cane in hand because of his age.
5The city streets will be filled with boys and girls playing there.[d]"
6This is what the LORD Almighty says: "It may seem marvellous to the remnant of
this people at that time,[e] but will it seem marvellous to me?[f]" declares the LORD
Almighty.
7This is what the LORD Almighty says: "I will save my people from the countries
of the east and the west.[g] 8I will bring them back[h] to live in Jerusalem; they will
be my people,[i] and I will be faithful and righteous to them as their God."
9This is what the LORD Almighty says: "You who now hear these words spoken
by the prophets[j] who were there when the foundation was laid for the house of the
LORD Almighty, let your hands be strong[k] so that the temple may be built. 10Before
that time there were no wages[l] for man or beast. No-one could go about his business
safely because of his enemy, for I had turned every man against his neighbour. 11But
now I will not deal with the remnant of this people as I did in the past,"[m] declares
the LORD Almighty.
12"The seed will grow well, the vine will yield its fruit,[n] the ground will produce
its crops,[o] and the heavens will drop their dew.[p] I will give all these things as an
inheritance[q] to the remnant of this people. 13As you have been an object of cursing[r]
among the nations, O Judah and Israel, so will I save you, and you will be a blessing.[s]
Do not be afraid, but let your hands be strong."
14This is what the LORD Almighty says: "Just as I had determined to bring disaster[t]
upon you and showed no pity when your fathers angered me," says the LORD
Almighty, 15"so now I have determined to do good[u] again to Jerusalem and Judah.
Do not be afraid. 16These are the things you are to do: Speak the truth[v] to each other,
and render true and sound judgment in your courts;[w] 17do not plot evil[x] against your

7:13 [p] Pr 1:24 [q] Isa 1:15; Jer 11:11; 14:12; Mic 3:4 [r] Pr 1:28
7:14 [s] Dt 4:27; 28:64-67 [t] Jer 23:19 [u] Jer 44:6
8:3 [a] Zec 1:16 [b] Zec 2:10
8:4 [c] Isa 65:20
8:5 [d] Jer 30:20; 31:13
8:6 [e] Ps 118:23; 126:1-3 [f] Jer 32:17, 27
8:7 [g] Ps 107:3; Isa 11:11; 43:5
8:8 [h] Zec 10:10 [i] Eze 11:19-20; 36:28; Zec 2:11
8:9 [j] Ezr 5:1 [k] Hag 2:4
8:10 [l] Hag 1:6
8:11 [m] Isa 12:1
8:12 [n] Joel 2:22 [o] Ps 67:6 [p] Ge 27:28 [q] Ob 1:17
8:13 [r] Jer 42:18 [s] Ge 12:2
8:14 [t] Jer 31:28; Eze 24:14
8:15 [u] ver 13; Jer 29:11; Mic 7:18-20
8:16 [v] Ps 15:2; Eph 4:25 [w] Zec 7:9
8:17 [x] Pr 3:29

8:3 One day Christ will reign in his kingdom on earth. There all his people will live with him. This truth should encourage us to look forward to the Messiah's reign.

8:4, 5 In troubled times, the very old and very young are the first to suffer and die. But both groups are plentiful in this vision, filling the streets with their normal everyday activities. This is a sign of the complete peace and prosperity of God's new earth.

8:6 The remnant was the small group of exiles who had returned from Babylon to rebuild Jerusalem and the temple. Struggling to survive in the land, they became discouraged over the opposition they often faced from hostile neighbours. It was hard to believe that one day God himself would reign from this city and that their land would enjoy great peace and prosperity. Our God is all-powerful; he can do anything! When confronting seemingly impossible tasks or situations, remember that "with God all things are possible" (Matthew 19:26).

8:8 The covenant relationship will be renewed, and the whole community will be filled with the presence of God. This promise of forgiveness and restoration extends to all God's people wherever they may be found. (For other references to this promise, see Exodus 6:6, 7; 19:5, 6; 29:45; Leviticus 26:12; Deuteronomy 7:6; Jeremiah 31:1, 33.)

8:9 God had to give the temple workers a little push to get them moving. They had heard the prophets' words of encouragement; at this time they needed to stop just listening and get to work. We need to listen to what God says, but after he has made our course of action plain, we need to "be strong" and do what he wants.

8:13–15 For more than 15 years, God and his prophets had been urging the people to finish building the temple. Here again, God encouraged them with visions of the future. We may be tempted to slow down for many reasons: people aren't responding; we feel physically or emotionally drained; the workers are uncooperative; the work is distasteful, too difficult, or not worth the effort. God's promises about the future should encourage us *now.* He knows what the results of our labours will be, and thus he can give us a perspective that will help us continue in our work for him.

8:14–17 God promised to give his people rich rewards, reassuring them that despite the punishments they had endured, he would not change his mind to bless them. But he also said they had a job to do – "These are the things you are to do". God will be faithful, but we also have responsibilities: to tell the truth, exercise justice, and live peacefully. If you expect God to do his part, be sure to do yours.

neighbour, and do not love to swear falsely.[y] I hate all this," declares the LORD.
18 Again the word of the LORD Almighty came to me. 19 This is what the LORD
Almighty says: "The fasts of the fourth,[z] fifth,[a] seventh[b] and tenth[c] months will
become joyful[d] and glad occasions and happy festivals for Judah. Therefore love
truth[e] and peace."
20 This is what the LORD Almighty says: "Many peoples and the inhabitants of many
cities will yet come, 21 and the inhabitants of one city will go to another and say, 'Let
us go at once to entreat[f] the LORD and seek the LORD Almighty. I myself am going.'
22 And many peoples and powerful nations will come to Jerusalem to seek the LORD
Almighty and to entreat him."[g]
23 This is what the LORD Almighty says: "In those days ten men from all languages
and nations will take firm hold of one Jew by the hem of his robe and say, 'Let us
go with you, because we have heard that God is with you.' "[h]

B. MESSAGES AFTER COMPLETING THE TEMPLE (9:1–14:21)

After the temple was completed, Zechariah gave several prophecies about Israel's future, which describe the first and second comings of Jesus Christ. This book contains more about the person, work, and glory of Christ than the other minor prophets combined. Israel's King would come, but he would be rejected by his people. They would later repent and be restored to God. The King who is coming is our King. May we be found faithful and pure in his sight when we meet him face to face.

Judgment on Israel's Enemies

An Oracle

9 The word of the LORD is against the land of Hadrach
  and will rest upon Damascus[a] —
for the eyes of men and all the tribes of Israel
  are on the LORD — [a]
2 and upon Hamath[b] too, which borders on it,
  and upon Tyre[c] and Sidon, though they are very skilful.
3 Tyre has built herself a stronghold;
  she has heaped up silver like dust,
  and gold like the dirt of the streets.[d]
4 But the Lord will take away her possessions
  and destroy her power on the sea,
  and she will be consumed by fire.[e]
5 Ashkelon will see it and fear;
  Gaza will writhe in agony,
  and Ekron too, for her hope will wither.
Gaza will lose her king
  and Ashkelon will be deserted.
6 Foreigners will occupy Ashdod,
  and I will cut off the pride of the Philistines.

a 1 Or *Damascus. / For the eye of the LORD is on all mankind, / as well as on the tribes of Israel.*

8:17 [y] Pr 6:16-19
8:19 [z] Jer 39:2 [a] Jer 52:12 [b] 2Ki 25:25 [c] Jer 52:4 [d] Ps 30:11 [e] ver 16
8:21 [f] Zec 7:2
8:22 [g] Ps 117:1; Isa 60:3; Zec 2:11
8:23 [h] Isa 45:14; 1Co 14:25
9:1 [a] Isa 17:1
9:2 [b] Jer 49:23 [c] Eze 28:1-19
9:3 [d] Job 27:16; Eze 28:4
9:4 [e] Isa 23:1; Eze 26:3-5; 28:18

8:19–22 There will come a time when fasting for sins will be replaced by feasting and joy. People from all nations will "seek the LORD Almighty". This was also promised in 2:11.

8:23 In the past, Jerusalem had often borne the brunt of cruel jokes from other nations (8:13). The city was not respected; its citizens had sinned so much that God let them be kicked around by their enemies. But eventually, says Zechariah, Jerusalem will be a holy place – respected highly throughout the world because its people will have a change of heart toward God. People from other nations will see how God has rewarded his people for their faithfulness and will want to be included in their great blessings.

9:1–17 An oracle is a message from God. Hadrach was probably a city in northern Aram. The last six chapters of the book are two messages delivered late in Zechariah's life. These messages point to the Messiah and his second coming. Some of these prophecies were fulfilled before the Messiah came, perhaps by Alexander the Great; others were fulfilled during the Messiah's time on earth; and others will be fulfilled when he returns. Those who oppressed Jerusalem – Aram, Philistia, Phoenicia – would be crushed. Zion's promised King would come – first as a servant on a donkey's colt, later as a powerful ruler and judge.

9:5–7 Zechariah mentions four key cities in Philistia: Ashkelon, Gaza, and Ekron would be destroyed, and Ashdod would be overtaken by foreigners. This would happen because of their great evil and idolatry. But those left in the land would be adopted into Israel as a new clan, as the Jebusites were (when David conquered Jerusalem, he did not wipe out the Jebusites, but absorbed them into Judah).

7I will take the blood from their mouths,
the forbidden food from between their teeth.
Those who are left will belong to our God
and become leaders in Judah,
and Ekron will be like the Jebusites.
8But I will defend my house
against marauding forces.
Never again will an oppressor overrun my people,
for now I am keeping watch.[f]

The Coming of Zion's King

9Rejoice greatly, O Daughter of Zion!
Shout, Daughter of Jerusalem!
See, your king[b] comes to you,
righteous and having salvation,[g]
gentle and riding on a donkey,
on a colt, the foal of a donkey.[h]
10I will take away the chariots from Ephraim
and the war-horses from Jerusalem,
and the battle-bow will be broken.[i]
He will proclaim peace to the nations.
His rule will extend from sea to sea
and from the River[c] to the ends of the earth.[d][j]
11As for you, because of the blood of my covenant[k] with you,
I will free your prisoners[l] from the waterless pit.
12Return to your fortress,[m] O prisoners of hope;
even now I announce that I will restore twice as much to you.
13I will bend Judah as I bend my bow
and fill it with Ephraim.[n]
I will rouse your sons, O Zion,
against your sons, O Greece,[o]
and make you like a warrior's sword.[p]

The LORD Will Appear

14Then the LORD will appear over them;[q]
his arrow will flash like lightning.[r]
The Sovereign LORD will sound the trumpet;
he will march in the storms[s] of the south,
15 and the LORD Almighty will shield[t] them.

b 9 Or *King* c 10 That is, the Euphrates d 10 Or *the end of the land*

9:8 f Isa 52:1; 54:14
9:9 g Isa 9:6-7; 43:3-11; Jer 23:5-6; Zep 3:14-15; Zec 2:10 h Mt 21:5*; Jn 12:15*
9:10 i Hos 1:7; 2:18; Mic 4:3; 5:10; Zec 10:4 j Ps 72:8
9:11 k Ex 24:8 l Isa 42:7
9:12 m Joel 3:16
9:13 n Isa 49:2 o Joel 3:6 p Jer 51:20
9:14 q Isa 31:5 r Ps 18:14; Hab 3:11 s Isa 21:1; 66:15
9:15 t Isa 37:35; Zec 12:8

9:8 Several centuries after Zechariah's day, Antiochus IV Epiphanes would invade Israel; and in A.D. 70, Titus, a Roman general, would completely destroy the temple. This promise, therefore, may have been conditional upon the people's obedience. The day will come, however, when God's people will never again have to worry about invading enemies (Joel 3:17).

9:9 The Triumphal Entry of Jesus riding into Jerusalem (Matthew 21:1–11) was predicted here more than 500 years before it happened. Just as this prophecy was fulfilled when Jesus came to earth, so the prophecies of his second coming are just as certain to come true. We are to be ready for his return, for he is coming!

9:10 Ephraim is another name for the northern kingdom of Israel. When we view two distant mountains, they appear to be close together, perhaps even to touch each other. But as we approach them, we can see that they are in fact far apart, even separated by a huge valley. This is the situation with many Old Testament prophecies. Verse 9 was clearly fulfilled in Christ's first coming, but verse 10 can now be seen to refer to his second coming. At that time all nations will be subject to Christ, and his rule will extend over the whole earth. In Philippians 2:9, 10, we are told that at that time every knee will bow to Christ and every tongue will confess him as Lord.

9:11 Covenants in Old Testament times were sealed or confirmed with blood, much as we would sign our name to a contract. The old covenant was sealed by the blood of sacrifices, pointing ahead to the blood Christ would shed at Calvary, his "signature" that confirmed God's new covenant with his people. Because God had made a covenant with these people, he delivered them from the "waterless pit", the cistern-like prison of exile.

9:14–17 After Solomon's reign, the kingdom was divided into the northern kingdom (called Israel or Ephraim) and the southern kingdom (called Judah). This prophecy says that all Israel, north and south, will someday be reunited. The first part of this chapter tells how God will help his people avoid war; here God explains that he will appear to help his people when war is inevitable. Verses 14–16 explain how the Jews will win over the Greeks, but it is also a figurative picture of the ultimate future victory over evil by God's people.

They will destroy
and overcome with slingstones.
They will drink and roar as with wine;
they will be full like a bowl
used for sprinkling[e] the corners[u] of the altar.
16The LORD their God will save them on that day
as the flock of his people.
They will sparkle in his land
like jewels in a crown.[v]
17How attractive and beautiful they will be!
Grain will make the young men thrive,
and new wine the young women.

The LORD Will Care for Judah

10 Ask the LORD for rain in the springtime;
it is the LORD who makes the storm clouds.
He gives showers of rain to men,
and plants of the field to everyone.
2The idols[a] speak deceit,
diviners see visions that lie;
they tell dreams that are false,
they give comfort in vain.
Therefore the people wander like sheep
oppressed for lack of a shepherd.[b]

3"My anger burns against the shepherds,
and I will punish the leaders;[c]
for the LORD Almighty will care
for his flock, the house of Judah,
and make them like a proud horse in battle.
4From Judah will come the cornerstone,
from him the tent peg,[d]
from him the battle-bow,[e]
from him every ruler.
5Together they[a] will be like mighty men
trampling the muddy streets in battle.[f]
Because the LORD is with them,
they will fight and overthrow the horsemen.[g]

6"I will strengthen the house of Judah
and save the house of Joseph.
I will restore them
because I have compassion on them.[h]
They will be as though
I had not rejected them,

9:15 [u]Ex 27:2
9:16 [v]Isa 62:3; Jer 31:11
10:2 [a]Eze 21:21 [b]Eze 34:5; Hos 3:4; Mt 9:36
10:3 [c]Jer 25:34
10:4 [d]Isa 22:23 [e]Zec 9:10
10:5 [f]2Sa 22:43 [g]Am 2:15; Hag 2:22
10:6 [h]Zec 8:7-8

[e] *15 Or bowl, / like* [a] *4, 5 Or ruler, all of them together. / 5They*

10:2 We often create idols of money, power, fame, or success, and then we expect them to give us happiness and security. But these idols can't supply what we need any more than a stone image can make it rain. How foolish it is to trust in idols. Instead, trust God's promises for your future.

10:4 Zechariah's prophecy, more than 500 years before Christ's first coming, called Christ a "cornerstone" (see also Isaiah 28:16), a "tent peg" (Isaiah 22:23), a "bow" that wins the battle, and a "ruler" who was a man of action (see also Genesis 49:10; Micah 5:2). This Messiah would be strong, stable, victorious, and trustworthy—all in all, the answer to Israel's problems. Only in the Messiah will all the promises to God's people be fulfilled.

10:6 The "house of Judah" refers to the southern kingdom, and the "house of Joseph" refers to the northern kingdom. Ephraim, the leading tribe of the northern kingdom, was the son of Joseph. One day God will unite all his people. This verse tells about God's reuniting of the Jews (see also Jeremiah 31:10). This was a startling idea: the people of the northern kingdom of Israel were so completely absorbed into other cultures after their captivity in 722 B.C. that a regathering could not be done by human means, but only by God.

10:6, 12 God promises to strengthen his people. When we stay closely connected to God, his Spirit will enable us to do his will, despite the obstacles. When we stray away from God, we will be cut off from our power source.

10:6 [i]Zec 13:9
10:7 [j]Zec 9:15
10:8 [k]Isa 5:26 [l]Jer 33:22; Eze 36:11
10:9 [m]Eze 6:9
10:10 [n]Isa 11:11 [o]Jer 50:19 [p]Isa 49:19
10:11 [q]Isa 19:5-7; 51:10 [r]Zep 2:13 [s]Eze 30:13
10:12 [t]Mic 4:5
11:1 [a]Eze 31:3
11:2 [b]Isa 32:19
11:3 [c]Jer 2:15; 50:44
11:5 [d]Jer 50:7; Eze 34:2-3
11:6 [e]Zec 14:13 [f]Isa 9:19-21; Jer 13:14; Mic 5:8; 7:2-6

for I am the LORD their God
and I will answer[i] them.
7The Ephraimites will become like mighty men,
and their hearts will be glad as with wine.[j]
Their children will see it and be joyful;
their hearts will rejoice in the LORD.
8I will signal[k] for them
and gather them in.
Surely I will redeem them;
they will be as numerous[l] as before.
9Though I scatter them among the peoples,
yet in distant lands they will remember me.[m]
They and their children will survive,
and they will return.
10I will bring them back from Egypt
and gather them from Assyria.[n]
I will bring them to Gilead[o] and Lebanon,
and there will not be room[p] enough for them.
11They will pass through the sea of trouble;
the surging sea will be subdued
and all the depths of the Nile will dry up.[q]
Assyria's pride[r] will be brought down
and Egypt's sceptre[s] will pass away.
12I will strengthen them in the LORD
and in his name they will walk,[t]"
declares the LORD.

11 Open your doors, O Lebanon,[a]
so that fire may devour your cedars!
2Wail, O pine tree, for the cedar has fallen;
the stately trees are ruined!
Wail, oaks of Bashan;
the dense forest[b] has been cut down!
3Listen to the wail of the shepherds:
their rich pastures are destroyed!
Listen to the roar of the lions;
the lush thicket of the Jordan is ruined![c]

Two Shepherds

4This is what the LORD my God says: "Pasture the flock marked for slaughter.
5Their buyers slaughter them and go unpunished. Those who sell them say, 'Praise
the LORD, I am rich!' Their own shepherds do not spare them.[d] 6For I will no longer
have pity on the people of the land," declares the LORD. "I will hand everyone over
to his neighbour[e] and his king. They will oppress the land, and I will not rescue them
from their hands."[f]

10:10 This pictured return from Egypt and Assyria was a symbolic way of saying that the people would be returned from all the countries where they had been dispersed. Egypt and Assyria evoked memories of slavery and separation.

10:11 The "sea of trouble" refers to the Red Sea, through which the Israelites were miraculously delivered from Egypt. Just as the Israelites returned once again from Egypt and other lands, they would be protected by God's miraculous power.

11:4–17 In this message, God told Zechariah to act out the roles of two different kinds of shepherds. The first type of shepherd demonstrated how God would reject his people (the sheep) because they rejected him (11:4–14). The second type of shepherd demonstrated how God would give over his people to evil shepherds (11:15–17). (See Ezekiel 34 for a detailed portrayal of the evil shepherds of Israel.)

11:4 God told Zechariah to take a job as shepherd of a flock of sheep being fattened for slaughter. The Messiah would shepherd God's people during a time of spiritual and political confusion. The flock represented the people feeding on their own greed and evil desires until they were ripe for God's judgment.

[7]So I pastured the flock marked for slaughter, particularly the oppressed of the
flock. Then I took two staffs and called one Favour and the other Union, and I pastured
the flock. [8]In one month I got rid of the three shepherds.

The flock detested me, and I grew weary of them [9]and said, "I will not be your
shepherd. Let the dying die, and the perishing perish.[g] Let those who are left eat one
another's flesh."

[10]Then I took my staff called Favour[h] and broke it, revoking[i] the covenant I had
made with all the nations. [11]It was revoked on that day, and so the afflicted of the
flock who were watching me knew it was the word of the LORD.

[12]I told them, "If you think it best, give me my pay; but if not, keep it." So they
paid me thirty pieces of silver.[j]

[13]And the LORD said to me, "Throw it to the potter"—the handsome price at which
they priced me! So I took the thirty pieces of silver and threw them into the house
of the LORD to the potter.[k]

[14]Then I broke my second staff called Union, breaking the brotherhood between
Judah and Israel.

[15]Then the LORD said to me, "Take again the equipment of a foolish shepherd. [16]For
I am going to raise up a shepherd over the land who will not care for the lost, or seek
the young, or heal the injured, or feed the healthy, but will eat the meat of the choice
sheep, tearing off their hoofs.

> [17]"Woe to the worthless shepherd,[l]
> who deserts the flock!
> May the sword strike his arm[m] and his right eye!
> May his arm be completely withered,
> his right eye totally blinded!"[n]

11:9 [g]Jer 15:2; 43:11
11:10 [h]ver 7 [i]Ps 89:39; Jer 14:21
11:12 [j]Ex 21:32; Mt 26:15
11:13 [k]Mt 27:9-10*; Ac 1:18-19
11:17 [l]Jer 23:1 [m]Eze 30:21-22 [n]Jer 23:1

Jerusalem's Enemies to Be Destroyed

An Oracle

12 This is the word of the LORD concerning Israel. The LORD, who stretches out
the heavens,[a] who lays the foundation of the earth,[b] and who forms the spirit
of man[c] within him, declares: [2]"I am going to make Jerusalem a cup[d] that sends
all the surrounding peoples reeling.[e] Judah[f] will be besieged as well as Jerusalem.
[3]On that day, when all the nations[g] of the earth are gathered against her, I will make
Jerusalem an immovable rock[h] for all the nations. All who try to move it will injure[i]
themselves. [4]On that day I will strike every horse with panic and its rider with
madness," declares the LORD. "I will keep a watchful eye over the house of Judah,

12:1 [a]Isa 42:5; Jer 51:15 [b]Ps 102:25; Heb 1:10 [c]Isa 57:16
12:2 [d]Ps 75:8 [e]Isa 51:23 [f]Zec 14:14
12:3 [g]Zec 14:2 [h]Da 2:34-35 [i]Mt 21:44

11:7 Zechariah took two shepherds' staffs and named them "Favour" and "Union". He broke the first one ("Favour") to show that God's gracious covenant with his people was broken. He broke the second one ("Union") to show that "the brotherhood between Judah and Israel" was broken (11:14).

11:8 The identity of the three evil shepherds is not known. But God knew they were unfit to shepherd his people, and so he removed them.

11:12 To pay this shepherd 30 pieces of silver was an insult—this was the price paid to an owner for a slave gored by an ox (Exodus 21:32). This is also the amount Judas received for betraying Jesus (Matthew 27:3–10). The priceless Messiah was sold for the price of a slave.

11:13 Potters were in the lowest social class. The "handsome price" (a sarcastic comment) was so little that it could be thrown to the potter. It is significant that the 30 pieces of silver paid to Judas for betraying Jesus were returned to the temple and used to buy a potter's field (Matthew 27:3–10).

11:14 Because the people had rejected the Messiah, God would reject them—symbolised by Zechariah breaking the staff called "Union". Not long after Zechariah's time, the Jews began to divide into numerous factions—Pharisees, Sadducees, Essenes, Herodians, and Zealots. The discord among these groups was a key factor leading to the destruction of Jerusalem in A.D. 70.

11:15–17 Israel would not only reject the true shepherd; it would accept instead a worthless shepherd. This shepherd would serve his own concerns rather than the concerns of his flock and would destroy rather than defend them. Condemnation is his rightful fate because he trusted his arm (military might) and his eye (intellect). God would destroy both areas.

11:17 It is a great tragedy for God's people when their leaders fail to care for them adequately. God holds leaders particularly accountable for the condition of his people. The New Testament tells church leaders, "Not many of you should presume to be teachers . . . because you know that we who teach will be judged more strictly" (James 3:1). If God puts you in a position of leadership, remember that it is also a place of great responsibility.

12:1–14 This chapter pictures the final siege against the people of Jerusalem.

12:3, 4 This speaks of a great future battle against Jerusalem. Some say it is Armageddon, the last great battle on earth. Those who oppose God's people will not prevail for ever. Eventually, evil, pain, and oppression will be abolished once and for all.

12:4 jPs 76:6
12:6 kIsa 10:17-18; Zec 11:1 lOb 1:18
12:7 mJer 30:18; Am 9:11
12:8 nJoel 3:16; Zec 9:15 oPs 82:6 pMic 7:8
12:9 qZec 14:2-3
12:10 rIsa 44:3; Eze 39:29; Joel 2:28-29 sJn 19:34, 37*; Rev 1:7
12:11 t2Ki 23:29
12:12 uMt 24:30; Rev 1:7
13:1 aJer 17:13 bPs 51:2; Heb 9:14
13:2 cEx 23:13; Eze 36:25; Hos 2:17 d1Ki 22:22; Jer 23:14-15
13:3 eDt 13:6-11; 18:20; Jer 23:34; Eze 14:9
13:4 fJer 6:15; Mic 3:6-7 gMt 3:4 h2Ki 1:8; Isa 20:2
13:5 iAm 7:14

but I will blind all the horses of the nations.[j] 5 Then the leaders of Judah will say
in their hearts, 'The people of Jerusalem are strong, because the LORD Almighty is
their God.'
6 "On that day I will make the leaders of Judah like a brazier[k] in a woodpile, like
a flaming torch among sheaves. They will consume[l] right and left all the surrounding
peoples, but Jerusalem will remain intact in her place.
7 "The LORD will save the dwellings of Judah first, so that the honour of the house
of David and of Jerusalem's inhabitants may not be greater than that of Judah.[m] 8 On
that day the LORD will shield[n] those who live in Jerusalem, so that the feeblest among
them will be like David, and the house of David will be like God,[o] like the Angel
of the LORD going before[p] them. 9 On that day I will set out to destroy all the nations
that attack Jerusalem.[q]

Mourning for the One They Pierced

10 "And I will pour out on the house of David and the inhabitants of Jerusalem a
spirit**[a]** of grace and supplication.[r] They will look on**[b]** me, the one they have
pierced,[s] and they will mourn for him as one mourns for an only child, and grieve
bitterly for him as one grieves for a firstborn son. 11 On that day the weeping in
Jerusalem will be great, like the weeping of Hadad Rimmon in the plain of Megiddo.[t]
12 The land will mourn,[u] each clan by itself, with their wives by themselves: the clan
of the house of David and their wives, the clan of the house of Nathan and their wives,
13 the clan of the house of Levi and their wives, the clan of Shimei and their wives,
14 and all the rest of the clans and their wives.

Cleansing From Sin

13 "On that day a fountain[a] will be opened to the house of David and the
inhabitants of Jerusalem, to cleanse[b] them from sin and impurity.
2 "On that day, I will banish the names of the idols[c] from the land, and they will
be remembered no more," declares the LORD Almighty. "I will remove both the
prophets[d] and the spirit of impurity from the land. 3 And if anyone still prophesies,
his father and mother, to whom he was born, will say to him, 'You must die, because
you have told lies in the LORD's name.' When he prophesies, his own parents will
stab him.[e]
4 "On that day every prophet will be ashamed[f] of his prophetic vision. He will not
put on a prophet's garment[g] of hair[h] in order to deceive. 5 He will say, 'I am not
a prophet. I am a farmer; the land has been my livelihood since my youth.'**[a]**[i] 6 If

a *10* Or *the Spirit* **b** *10* Or *to* **a** *5* Or *farmer; a man sold me in my youth*

12:7 As water flows downhill, so a city's influence usually flows to its surrounding countryside. But this time, the countryside of Judah (the "dwellings") would have priority over Jerusalem so that the people of Jerusalem would not become proud. Don't think you have to witness first to the "important" people – famous athletes, film stars, and prominent businessmen. Christ came to seek and save the lost (Luke 19:10), even the "down-and-out" lost. We must be careful to avoid spiritual pride or we, like Jerusalem, may be the last to know what God is doing.

12:10 The Holy Spirit was poured out at Pentecost, 50 days after Christ's resurrection (see Acts 2). Zechariah calls the Spirit "a spirit of grace and supplication". It is this Spirit who convicts us of sin, reveals to us God's righteousness and judgment, and helps us as we pray. "In the same way, the Spirit helps us in our weakness. We do not know what we ought to pray for, but the Spirit himself intercedes for us with groans that words cannot express" (Romans 8:26). Ask God to fill you with his Spirit.

12:10–14 Eventually *all* people will realise that Jesus, the man who was pierced and killed, is indeed the Messiah. There will be an awakening, with sorrow for sin and genuine revival. The crucified Messiah will be clearly revealed (Philippians 2:10; Revelation 5:13).

12:11 Hadad Rimmon could refer to the place near the plain of Megiddo where King Josiah was killed. Josiah's death was greatly mourned by his people (see 2 Chronicles 35:22–25).

12:12–14 These verses are saying that all Israel will mourn – king, prophet, priest, and people. Each family will go into private mourning, husbands and wives by themselves, to face their sorrow.

13:1ff There will be a never-ending supply of God's mercy, forgiveness, and cleansing power. This picture of a fountain is similar to the never-ending stream flowing out from the temple (Ezekiel 47:1). The fountain is used in Scripture to symbolise God's forgiveness. In John 4, Jesus tells of his "living water" that satisfies completely. Are you spiritually thirsty? Do you need to experience God's forgiveness? Drink from the fountain – ask Jesus to forgive you and give you his salvation.

13:2–6 This chapter pictures the final days of the earth as we know it. For God's new era to begin, there must be a cleansing – all evil must be abolished. Therefore, idols will be banished, and false prophets will be ashamed of themselves and will no longer try to deceive God's people.

someone asks him, ‘What are these wounds on your body?’[b] he will answer, ‘The
wounds I was given at the house of my friends.’

The Shepherd Struck, the Sheep Scattered

7 “Awake, O sword,[j] against my shepherd,[k]
against the man who is close to me!”
declares the LORD Almighty.
“Strike the shepherd,
and the sheep will be scattered,[l]
and I will turn my hand against the little ones.
8 In the whole land,” declares the LORD,
“two-thirds will be struck down and perish;
yet one-third will be left in it.[m]
9 This third I will bring into the fire;[n]
I will refine them like silver[o]
and test them like gold.
They will call[p] on my name
and I will answer[q] them;
I will say, ‘They are my people,’[r]
and they will say, ‘The LORD is our God.[s]’ ”

The LORD Comes and Reigns

14 A day of the LORD[a] is coming when your plunder will be divided among you.
2 I will gather all the nations to Jerusalem to fight against it; the city will be
captured, the houses ransacked, and the women raped. Half of the city will go into
exile, but the rest of the people will not be taken from the city.[b]
3 Then the LORD will go out and fight[c] against those nations, as he fights in the
day of battle. 4 On that day his feet will stand on the Mount of Olives,[d] east of
Jerusalem, and the Mount of Olives will be split in two from east to west, forming
a great valley, with half of the mountain moving north and half moving south. 5 You
will flee by my mountain valley, for it will extend to Azel. You will flee as you fled
from the earthquake[a][e] in the days of Uzziah king of Judah. Then the LORD my God
will come,[f] and all the holy ones with him.[g]
6 On that day there will be no light,[h] no cold or frost. 7 It will be a unique[i] day,
without daytime or night-time[j]—a day known to the LORD. When evening comes,
there will be light.[k]
8 On that day living water[l] will flow out from Jerusalem, half to the eastern[m] sea[b]
and half to the western sea,[c] in summer and in winter.

13:7 [j]Jer 47:6 [k]Isa 40:11; 53:4; Eze 37:24 [l]Mt 26:31*; Mk 14:27*
13:8 [m]Eze 5:2-4, 12
13:9 [n]Mal 3:2 [o]Isa 48:10; 1Pe 1:6-7 [p]Ps 50:15 [q]Zec 10:6 [r]Jer 30:22 [s]Jer 29:12
14:1 [a]Isa 13:9; Mal 4:1
14:2 [b]Isa 13:6; Zec 13:8
14:3 [c]Zec 9:14-15
14:4 [d]Eze 11:23
14:5 [e]Am 1:1 [f]Isa 29:6; 66:15-16 [g]Mt 16:27; 25:31
14:6 [h]Isa 13:10; Jer 4:23
14:7 [i]Jer 30:7 [j]Rev 21:23-25; 22:5 [k]Isa 30:26
14:8 [l]Eze 47:1-12; Jn 7:38; Rev 22:1-2 [m]Joel 2:20

b *6* Or *wounds between your hands* **a** *5* Or *5 My mountain valley will be blocked and will extend to Azel. It will be blocked as it was blocked because of the earthquake* **b** *8* That is, the Dead Sea **c** *8* That is, the Mediterranean

13:7 Just before his arrest, Jesus quoted from this verse, referring to himself and his disciples (Matthew 26:31, 32). He knew beforehand that his disciples would scatter when he was arrested. The Roman “sword” was the military power that put Christ to death.

13:9 This “third” was a remnant, a small part of the whole. Throughout the history of Israel, whenever the whole nation seemed to turn against God, God said that a righteous remnant still trusted and followed him. These believers were refined like silver and gold through the fire of their difficult circumstances. Determine to be part of God's remnant, that small part of the whole that is obedient to him. Obey God no matter what the rest of the world does. This may mean trials and troubles at times; but as fire purifies gold and silver, you will be purified and made more like Christ.

14:1 Many times in the Bible we are encouraged to watch for the day of the Lord. What if you knew exactly when this would happen? Would you live differently? Christ could return at any moment. Be ready for him by studying the Scriptures carefully and by making sure that you live as he intends—in obedience and spiritual readiness.

14:1–21 This chapter portrays the eventual triumph of the Messiah over all the earth and his reign over God's people. But the chronological order of these future events is not clear. They show that God has various ways of dealing with his people. Now we are to watch as the events unfold and God provides an escape for his people.

14:4 On the Mount of Olives, Jesus spoke with his disciples about the end times (Matthew 24). Near this mountain, an angel promised that Jesus would return in the same manner as he had left (Acts 1:11; see also Ezekiel 11:23).

14:5 Only God's people will escape God's punishment (Matthew 24:16–20). In this time of confusion, God will clearly know who his people are. (See the note on Amos 1:1 concerning the earthquake in King Uzziah's day.)

14:8 The eastern sea and the western sea refer to the Dead Sea and the Mediterranean Sea respectively.

9 The LORD will be king over the whole earth.[n] On that day there will be one LORD,
and his name the only name.[o]
10 The whole land, from Geba[p] to Rimmon, south of Jerusalem, will become like
the Arabah. But Jerusalem will be raised up[q] and remain in its place,[r] from the
Benjamin Gate to the site of the First Gate, to the Corner Gate, and from the Tower
of Hananel to the royal winepresses. 11 It will be inhabited; never again will it be
destroyed. Jerusalem will be secure.[s]
12 This is the plague with which the LORD will strike all the nations that fought
against Jerusalem: Their flesh will rot while they are still standing on their feet, their
eyes will rot in their sockets, and their tongues will rot in their mouths.[t] 13 On that
day men will be stricken by the LORD with great panic. Each man will seize the hand
of another, and they will attack each other.[u] 14 Judah[v] too will fight at Jerusalem.
The wealth of all the surrounding nations will be collected[w]—great quantities of gold
and silver and clothing. 15 A similar plague[x] will strike the horses and mules, the
camels and donkeys, and all the animals in those camps.
16 Then the survivors from all the nations that have attacked Jerusalem will go up
year after year to worship the King, the LORD Almighty, and to celebrate the Feast
of Tabernacles.[y] 17 If any of the peoples of the earth do not go up to Jerusalem to
worship the King, the LORD Almighty, they will have no rain.[z] 18 If the Egyptian
people do not go up and take part, they will have no rain. The LORD[d] will bring on
them the plague he inflicts on the nations that do not go up to celebrate the Feast of
Tabernacles.[a] 19 This will be the punishment of Egypt and the punishment of all the
nations that do not go up to celebrate the Feast of Tabernacles.
20 On that day HOLY TO THE LORD will be inscribed on the bells of the horses, and
the cooking pots[b] in the LORD's house will be like the sacred bowls[c] in front of the
altar. 21 Every pot in Jerusalem and Judah will be holy[d] to the LORD Almighty, and
all who come to sacrifice will take some of the pots and cook in them. And on that
day[e] there will no longer be a Canaanite[e][f] in the house of the LORD Almighty.[g]

d 18 Or *part, then the LORD* **e** 21 Or *merchant*

14:9 [n]Dt 6:4; Isa 45:24; Rev 11:15 [o]Eph 4:5-6
14:10 [p]1Ki 15:22 [q]Jer 30:18; Am 9:11 [r]Zec 12:6
14:11 [s]Eze 34:25-28
14:12 [t]Lev 26:16; Dt 28:22
14:13 [u]Zec 11:6
14:14 [v]Zec 12:2 [w]Isa 23:18
14:15 [x]ver 12
14:16 [y]Isa 60:6-9
14:17 [z]Jer 14:4; Am 4:7
14:18 [a]ver 12
14:20 [b]Eze 46:20 [c]Zec 9:15
14:21 [d]Ro 14:6-7 [e]Ne 8:10 [f]Zec 9:8 [g]Eze 44:9

14:10 Jerusalem is honoured as the city of God and the focal point of all the world's worship. Jerusalem's elevation is a dramatic way of showing God's supremacy.

14:16 This Feast of Tabernacles is the only feast still appropriate during the Messiah's reign. The Passover was fulfilled in Christ's death; the Day of Atonement, in acceptance of Christ's salvation; the Feast of Firstfruits, in his resurrection; and Pentecost, with the arrival of the Holy Spirit. But the Feast of Tabernacles, a festival of thanksgiving, celebrates the harvest of human souls for the Lord. Jesus may have alluded to it in John 4:35.

14:20, 21 In the future, even such common objects as horses' bells and cooking pots will be holy. This vision of a restored, holy Jerusalem stands in contrast to its broken walls and unpleasant living conditions. One day God would fulfil the people's dreams for Jerusalem beyond what they could imagine. God still wants to do much more for us than we can imagine (Ephesians 3:20). When we walk with him, we will discover this more deeply each day.

14:21 Zechariah was speaking to a people who were enduring hardships—they were being harassed by neighbours; they were discouraged over their small numbers and seemingly inadequate temple; and their worship was apathetic. But God said, "I am very jealous for Jerusalem" (1:14). He promised to restore their land, their city, and their temple. Like other prophets, Zechariah blended prophecies of the present, near future, and final days into one sweeping panorama. Through his message we learn that our hope is found in God and his Messiah, who are in complete control of the world.

MALACHI

First exiles return to Jerusalem 538	Temple reconstruction begins 536	Haggai, Zechariah become prophets 520	Temp comp 516

VITAL STATISTICS

PURPOSE:
To confront the people with their sins and to restore their relationship with God

AUTHOR:
Malachi

TO WHOM WRITTEN:
The Jews in Jerusalem and God's people everywhere

DATE WRITTEN:
About 430 B.C.

SETTING:
Malachi, Haggai, and Zechariah were post-exilic prophets to Judah (the southern kingdom). Haggai and Zechariah rebuked the people for their failure to rebuild the temple. Malachi confronted them with their neglect of the temple and their false and profane worship.

KEY VERSES:
"Surely the day is coming; it will burn like a furnace. . . . But for you who revere my name, the sun of righteousness will rise with healing in its wings. And you will go out and leap like calves released from the stall" (4:1, 2).

KEY PEOPLE:
Malachi, the priests

KEY PLACES:
Jerusalem, the temple

SPECIAL FEATURES:
Malachi's literary style employs a dramatic use of questions asked by God and his people (for example, see 3:7, 8).

A VASE shatters, brushed by a careless elbow; a toy breaks, pushed beyond its limit by young fingers; and fabric rips, pulled by strong and angry hands. Spills and rips take time to clean up or repair and money to replace, but far more costly are shattered relationships. Unfaithfulness, untruths, hateful words, and forsaken vows tear delicate personal bonds and inflict wounds not easily healed. Most tragic, however, are broken relationships with God.

God loves perfectly and completely. And his love is a love of action—giving, guiding, and guarding. He is altogether faithful, true to his promises to his chosen people. But consistently they spurn their loving God, breaking the covenant, following other gods, and living for themselves. So the relationship is shattered.

But the breach is not irreparable; all hope is not lost. God can heal and mend and reweave the fabric. Forgiveness is available. And that is grace.

This is the message of Malachi, God's prophet in Jerusalem. His words reminded the Jews, God's chosen nation, of their wilful disobedience, beginning with the priests (1:1—2:9) and then including every person (2:10—3:15). They had shown contempt for God's name (1:6), offered false worship (1:7–14), led others into sin (2:7–9), broken God's laws (2:11–16), called evil "good" (2:17), kept God's tithes and offerings for themselves (3:8–12), and become arrogant (3:13–15). The relationship was broken, and judgment and punishment would be theirs. In the midst of this wickedness, however, there were a faithful few—the remnant—who loved and honoured God. God would shower his blessings upon these men and women (3:16–18).

Malachi paints a stunning picture of Israel's unfaithfulness that clearly shows them to be worthy of punishment, but woven throughout this message is hope—the possibility of forgiveness. This is beautifully expressed in 4:2—"But for you who revere my name, the sun of righteousness will rise with healing in its wings. And you will go out and leap like calves released from the stall."

Malachi concludes with a promise of the coming of "the prophet Elijah", who will offer God's forgiveness to all people through repentance and faith (4:5, 6).

The book of Malachi forms a bridge between the Old Testament and the New Testament. As you read Malachi, see yourself as the recipient of this word of God to his people. Evaluate the depth of your commitment, the sincerity of your worship, and the direction of your life. Then allow God to restore your relationship with him through his love and forgiveness.

Ezra comes to Jerusalem 458	Nehemiah comes to Jerusalem 445	Malachi becomes a prophet 430

THE BLUEPRINT

1. The sinful priests (1:1—2:9)
2. The sinful people (2:10—3:15)
3. The faithful few (3:16—4:6)

Malachi rebuked the people and the priests for neglecting the worship of God and failing to live according to God's will. If the priests were unfaithful, how could they lead the people? They had become stumbling blocks instead of spiritual leaders. If the people were divorcing their wives and marrying pagan women, how could they lead their children? Their relationship to God had become inconsequential. When our relationship with God becomes less important than it should be, we can strengthen it by setting aside our sinful habits, thinking often of our Lord, and giving God our best each day.

MEGATHEMES

THEME	EXPLANATION	IMPORTANCE
God's Love	God loves his people even when they ignore or disobey him. He has great blessings to bestow on those who are faithful to him. His love never ends.	Because God loves us so much, he hates hypocrisy and careless living. This kind of living denies him the relationship he wants to have with us. What we give and how we live reflects the sincerity of our love for God.
The Sin of the Priests	Malachi singled out the priests for condemnation. They knew what God required, yet their sacrifices were unworthy and their service was insincere; they were lazy, arrogant, and insensitive. They had a casual attitude towards the worship of God and observance of God's standards.	If religious leaders go wrong, how will the people be led? We are all leaders in some capacity. Don't neglect your responsibilities or be ruled by what is convenient. Neglect and insensitivity are acts of disobedience. God wants leaders who are faithful and sincere.
The Sin of the People	The people had not learned the lesson of the exile, nor had they listened to the prophets. Men were callously divorcing their faithful wives to marry younger pagan women. This was against God's law because it disobeyed his commands about marriage and threatened the religious training of the children. But pride had hardened the hearts of the people.	God deserves our very best honour, respect, and faithfulness. But sin hardens our hearts to our true condition. Pride is unwarranted self-esteem; it is setting your own judgment above God's and looking down on others. Don't let pride keep you from giving God your devotion, money, marriage, and family.
The Lord's Coming	God's love for his faithful people is demonstrated by the Messiah's coming. The Messiah will lead the people to the realisation of all their fondest hopes. The day of the Lord's coming will be a day of comfort and healing for a faithful few, and a day of judgment for those who reject him.	Christ's first coming refined and purified all those who believe in him. His return will expose and condemn those who are proud, insensitive, or unprepared. Yet God can heal and mend. Forgiveness is available to all who come to him.

1. The sinful priests

1 An oracle:[a] The word[b] of the LORD to Israel through Malachi.[a]

Jacob Loved, Esau Hated

2 "I have loved[c] you," says the LORD.
"But you ask, 'How have you loved us?'
"Was not Esau Jacob's brother?" the LORD says. "Yet I have loved Jacob,[d] 3 but
Esau I have hated, and I have turned his mountains into a wasteland[e] and left his
inheritance to the desert jackals.[f]"
4 Edom may say, "Though we have been crushed, we will rebuild[g] the ruins."
But this is what the LORD Almighty says: "They may build, but I will demolish.
They will be called the Wicked Land, a people always under the wrath of the LORD.[h]
5 You will see it with your own eyes and say, 'Great[i] is the LORD—even beyond the
borders of Israel!'[j]

Blemished Sacrifices

6 "A son honours his father, and a servant his master. If I am a father, where is the
honour due to me? If I am a master, where is the respect[k] due to me?" says the LORD
Almighty.[l] "It is you, O priests, who show contempt for my name.
"But you ask, 'How have we shown contempt for your name?'
7 "You place defiled food[m] on my altar.
"But you ask, 'How have we defiled you?'
"By saying that the LORD's table is contemptible. 8 When you bring blind animals
for sacrifice, is that not wrong? When you sacrifice crippled or diseased animals,[n]
is that not wrong? Try offering them to your governor! Would he be pleased with you?
Would he accept you?" says the LORD Almighty.[o]
9 "Now implore God to be gracious to us. With such offerings[p] from your hands,
will he accept you?"—says the LORD Almighty.
10 "Oh, that one of you would shut the temple doors, so that you would not light

1:1 [a]Na 1:1 [b]1Pe 4:11
1:2 [c]Dt 4:37 [d]Ro 9:13*
1:3 [e]Isa 34:10 [f]Eze 35:3-9
1:4 [g]Isa 9:10 [h]Eze 25:12-14
1:5 [i]Ps 35:27; Mic 5:4 [j]Am 1:11-12
1:6 [k]Isa 1:2 [l]Job 5:17
1:7 [m]ver 12; Lev 21:6
1:8 [n]Lev 22:22; Dt 15:21 [o]Isa 43:23
1:9 [p]Lev 23:33-44

a *1 Malachi means my messenger.*

1:1 An oracle is a message from God. Malachi, the last Old Testament prophet, preached after Haggai, Zechariah, and Nehemiah—about 430 B.C. The temple had been rebuilt for almost a century, and the people were losing their enthusiasm for worship. Apathy and disillusionment had set in because the exciting Messianic prophecies of Isaiah, Jeremiah, and Micah had not been fulfilled. Many of the sins that had brought the downfall of Jerusalem in 586 B.C. were still being practised in Judah. Malachi confronted the hypocrites with their sin by portraying a graphic dialogue between a righteous God and his hardened people.

1:2 God's first message through Malachi was "I have loved you". Although this message applied specifically to Israel, it is a message of hope for all people in all times. Unfortunately, many people are cynical about God's love, using political and economic progress as a measure of success. Because the government was corrupt and the economy poor, the Israelites assumed that God didn't love them. They were wrong. God loves all people because he made them; however, his *eternal* rewards go only to those who are faithful to him.

1:2–5 The phrase "Esau I have hated" does not refer to Esau's eternal destiny. It simply means that God chose Jacob, not his brother Esau, to be the one through whom the nation of Israel and the Messiah would come (see Romans 9:10–13). God allowed Esau to father a nation, but this nation, Edom, later became one of Israel's chief enemies. The story of Jacob and Esau is found in Genesis 25:19–26. Because God chose Jacob and his descendants as the nation through whom the world would be blessed, God cared for them in a special way. Ironically, they rejected God after he chose them.

1:6ff God charged the priests with failing to honour him (to the point of showing contempt for his name) and failing to be good spiritual examples to the people. The temple had been rebuilt in 516 B.C., and worship was being conducted there, but the priests did not worship God properly—they were not following his laws for the sacrifices. Ezra, the priest, had sparked a great revival around 458 B.C. However, by Malachi's time, the nation's leaders had once again fallen away from God, and the people right along with them. The worship of God was no longer from heartfelt adoration; instead it was simply a burdensome job for the priests.

1:6–8 God's law required that only perfect animals be offered to God (see for example Leviticus 1:3). But these priests were allowing the people to offer blind, crippled, and diseased animals to God. God accused them of dishonouring him by offering imperfect sacrifices, and he was greatly displeased. The New Testament says that our lives should be living sacrifices to God (Romans 12:1). If we give God only our leftover time, money, and energy, we repeat the same sin as these worshippers who didn't want to bring anything valuable to God. What we give God reflects our true attitude toward him.

1:7, 8 The people sacrificed to God wrongly through (1) expedience—being as cheap as possible, (2) neglect—not caring how they offered the sacrifice, and (3) outright disobedience—sacrificing their own way and not as God had commanded. Their methods of giving showed their real attitudes towards God. How about your attitude? Do expedience, neglect, or disobedience characterise your giving?

1:10 As intermediaries between God and the people, priests were responsible for reflecting God's attitudes and character. By accepting imperfect sacrifices, they were leading the people to believe that God accepted those sacrifices as well. But God says, "I am not pleased with you". As Christians, we are often in the same position as these priests because we reflect God to our friends and

1:10 [q]Hos 5:6 [r]Isa 1:11-14; Jer 14:12
1:11 [s]Isa 60:6-7; Rev 8:3
1:12 [t]ver 7
1:13 [u]Isa 43:22-24
1:14 [v]Lev 22:18-21 [w]1Ti 6:15
2:1 [a]ver 7
2:2 [b]Dt 28:20
2:3 [c]Ex 29:14 [d]1Ki 14:10
2:4 [e]Nu 3:12
2:5 [f]Dt 33:9 [g]Nu 25:12

useless fires on my altar! I am not pleased[q] with you," says the LORD Almighty, "and
I will accept no offering[r] from your hands. 11 My name will be great among the
nations, from the rising to the setting of the sun. In every place incense[s] and pure
offerings will be brought to my name, because my name will be great among the
nations," says the LORD Almighty.
12 "But you profane it by saying of the Lord's table, 'It is defiled', and of its food,[t]
'It is contemptible.' 13 And you say, 'What a burden!'[u] and you sniff at it contemptu-
ously," says the LORD Almighty.
"When you bring injured, crippled or diseased animals and offer them as sacrifices,
should I accept them from your hands?" says the LORD. 14 "Cursed is the cheat who
has an acceptable male in his flock and vows to give it, but then sacrifices a blemished
animal[v] to the Lord. For I am a great king,[w]" says the LORD Almighty, "and my
name is to be feared among the nations.

Admonition for the Priests

2 "And now this admonition is for you, O priests.[a] 2 If you do not listen, and if
you do not set your heart to honour my name," says the LORD Almighty, "I will
send a curse[b] upon you, and I will curse your blessings. Yes, I have already cursed
them, because you have not set your heart to honour me.
3 "Because of you I will rebuke**a** your descendants;**b** I will spread on your faces
the offal[c] from your festival sacrifices, and you will be carried off with it.[d] 4 And
you will know that I have sent you this admonition so that my covenant with Levi[e]
may continue," says the LORD Almighty. 5 "My covenant was with him, a covenant[f]
of life and peace,[g] and I gave them to him; this called for reverence and he revered

a *3* Or *cut off* (see Septuagint) **b** *3* Or *will blight your corn*

MALACHI served as a prophet to Judah about 430 B.C. He was the last of the Old Testament prophets.

Climate of the times	The city of Jerusalem and the temple had been rebuilt for almost a century, but the people had become complacent in their worship of God.
Main message	The people's relationship with God was broken because of their sin, and they would soon be punished. But the few who repented would receive God's blessing, highlighted in his promise to send a Messiah.
Importance of message	Hypocrisy, neglecting God, and careless living have devastating consequences. Serving and worshipping God must be the primary focus of our lives, both now and in eternity.
Contemporary prophets	None

---

family. What image of God's character and attitudes do they see in you? If you casually accept sin, you are like these priests in Malachi's day, and God will not be pleased with you.

1:11 A theme that can be heard throughout the Old Testament is affirmed in this book – "my name will be great among the nations". God had a chosen people, the Jews, through whom he planned to save and bless the entire world. Today God still wants to save and bless the world through all who believe in him – Jews and Gentiles. Christians are now his chosen people, and our pure offering to the Lord is our new life in Christ. Are you available to God to be used in making his name great to the nations? This mission begins in our homes and in our neighbourhoods, but it doesn't stop there. We must work and pray for God's worldwide mission.

1:13 Worship was a "burden" to these priests. Too many think that following God is supposed to make life easy and more comfortable. They are looking for a God of convenience. The truth is that it often takes hard work to live by God's high standards. He may call us to face poverty or suffering. But if serving God is more important to us than anything else, what we must give up is of little importance compared to what we gain – eternal life with God.

2:1, 2 God warned the priests that if they did not honour his name, he would punish them. Like these priests, we too are called to honour God's name – to worship him. This means acknowledging God for who he is – the almighty Creator of the universe who alone is perfect and who reaches down to sinful mankind with perfect love. According to this definition, are you honouring God's name?

2:1, 2 The priests didn't take seriously (set their hearts to) God's priority, even though he had reminded them through his word many times. How do you find out what is most important to God? Begin by loving him with all your heart, soul, and strength (Deuteronomy 6:5). This means listening to what God says in his word and then setting your heart, mind, and will on doing what he says. When we love God, his word becomes a shining light that guides our daily activities. The priests in Malachi's day had stopped loving God, and thus they did not know nor care what he wanted.

2:4–6 Levi "walked with [God] . . . and turned many from sin" (2:6). Levi was the ancestor of the tribe of Levites, the tribe set apart for service to God (Numbers 1:47–54). The Levites became God's ministers, first in the tabernacle, then in the temple. In these verses, God was addressing the priests who were from this tribe, saying that they should listen to the laws he gave their ancestor Levi, and follow his example.

me and stood in awe of my name. 6 True instruction[h] was in his mouth and nothing
false was found on his lips. He walked with me in peace and uprightness, and turned
many from sin.[i]
7 "For the lips of a priest[j] ought to preserve knowledge, and from his mouth men
should seek instruction[k]—because he is the messenger[l] of the LORD Almighty. 8 But
you have turned from the way and by your teaching have caused many to stumble;[m]
you have violated the covenant with Levi," says the LORD Almighty. 9 "So I have
caused you to be despised[n] and humiliated before all the people, because you have
not followed my ways but have shown partiality in matters of the law."

2. The sinful people

Judah Unfaithful

10 Have we not all one Father?[c][o] Did not one God create us? Why do we profane
the covenant[p] of our fathers by breaking faith with one another?
11 Judah has broken faith. A detestable thing has been committed in Israel and in
Jerusalem: Judah has desecrated the sanctuary the LORD loves, by marrying[q] the
daughter of a foreign god.[r] 12 As for the man who does this, whoever he may be,
may the LORD cut him off[s] from the tents of Jacob[d]—even though he brings
offerings[t] to the LORD Almighty.
13 Another thing you do: You flood the LORD's altar with tears. You weep and wail
because he no longer pays attention[u] to your offerings or accepts them with pleasure
from your hands. 14 You ask, "Why?" It is because the LORD is acting as the witness
between you and the wife of your youth,[v] because you have broken faith with her,
though she is your partner, the wife of your marriage covenant.
15 Has not ⌞the LORD⌟ made them one?[w] In flesh and spirit they are his. And why
one? Because he was seeking godly offspring.[e][x] So guard yourself in your spirit,
and do not break faith with the wife of your youth.
16 "I hate divorce,[y]" says the LORD God of Israel, "and I hate a man's covering
himself[f] with violence as well as with his garment," says the LORD Almighty.
So guard yourself in your spirit, and do not break faith.

[c] 10 *Or father* [d] 12 Or 12 *May the LORD cut off from the tents of Jacob anyone who gives testimony on behalf of the man who does this* [e] 15 Or 15 *But the one ⌞who is our father⌟ did not do this, not as long as life remained in him. And what was he seeking? An offspring from God* [f] 16 Or *his wife*

2:6 [h] Dt 33:10 [i] Jer 23:22; Jas 5:19-20
2:7 [j] Jer 18:18 [k] Lev 10:11 [l] Nu 27:21
2:8 [m] Jer 18:15
2:9 [n] 1Sa 2:30
2:10 [o] 1Co 8:6 [p] Ex 19:5
2:11 [q] Ne 13:23 [r] Ezr 9:1; Jer 3:7-9
2:12 [s] Eze 24:21 [t] Mal 1:10
2:13 [u] Jer 14:12
2:14 [v] Pr 5:18
2:15 [w] Ge 2:24; Mt 19:4-6 [x] 1Co 7:14
2:16 [y] Dt 24:1; Mt 5:31-32; 19:4-9

2:7, 8 Malachi was angry at the priests because, though they were to be God's messengers, they did not know God's will. And this lack of knowledge caused them to lead God's people astray. Their ignorance was wilful and inexcusable. Pastors and leaders of God's people *must* know God's word—what it says, what it means, and how it applies to daily life. How much time do you spend in God's word?

2:9 The priests had allowed influential and favoured people to break the law. The priests were so dependent on these people for support that they could not afford to confront them when they did wrong. In your church, are certain people allowed to do wrong without criticism? There should be no double standard based on wealth or position. Let your standards be those presented in God's word. Playing favourites is contemptible in God's sight (see James 2:1–9).

2:10–16 The people were being unfaithful. Though not openly saying they rejected God, they were living as if he did not exist. Men were marrying pagan women who worshipped idols. Divorce was common, occurring for no reason other than a desire for change. People acted as if they could do anything without being punished. And they wondered why God refused to accept their offerings and bless them (2:13)! We cannot successfully separate our dealings with God from the rest of our lives. He must be Lord of all.

2:11, 12 After the temple had been rebuilt and the walls completed, the people were excited to see past prophecies coming true. But as time passed, the prophecies about the destruction of God's enemies and a coming Messiah were not immediately fulfilled. The people became discouraged, and they grew complacent about obeying all of God's laws. This complacency gradually led to blatant sin, such as marriage to those who worshipped idols. Ezra and Nehemiah had also confronted this problem years earlier (Ezra 9, 10; Nehemiah 13:23–31).

2:14 The people were complaining about their adverse circumstances when they had only themselves to blame. People often try to avoid guilt feelings by shifting the blame. But this doesn't solve the problem. When you face problems, look first at yourself. If you changed your attitude or behaviour, would the problem be solved?

2:14, 15 Divorce in these times was practised exclusively by men. They broke faith with their wives and ignored the bonding between a husband and a wife that God instills (the two become one person), as well as his purpose for them (raising children who love the Lord, "godly offspring"). Not only were men breaking faith with their wives, they were also ignoring the bonding relationship and spiritual purpose of being united with God.

2:15, 16 "Guard yourself in your spirit, and do not break faith" means to have the same commitment to marriage that God has to his promises with his people. We need passion in the marriage relationship to keep the commitment and intimacy satisfying, but this passion should be focused exclusively on our spouse.

2:17
[z]Isa 43:24

3:1
[a]Isa 40:3; Mt 11:10*; Mk 1:2*; Lk 7:27*

3:2
[b]Eze 22:14; Rev 6:17
[c]Zec 13:9; Mt 3:10-12

3:3
[d]Da 12:10
[e]Isa 1:25

3:4
[f]2Ch 7:12; Ps 51:19; Mal 1:11
[g]2Ch 7:3

3:5
[h]Jer 7:9
[i]Lev 19:13; Jas 5:4
[j]Ex 22:22

3:6
[k]Nu 23:19; Jas 1:17

3:7
[l]Jer 7:26; Ac 7:51
[m]Zec 1:3

3:8
[n]Ne 13:10-12

3:10
[o]Ne 13:12
[p]2Ki 7:2

3:12
[q]Isa 61:9
[r]Isa 62:4

The Day of Judgment

17 You have wearied[z] the LORD with your words.
"How have we wearied him?" you ask.
By saying, "All who do evil are good in the eyes of the LORD, and he is pleased
with them" or "Where is the God of justice?"
3 "See, I will send my messenger, who will prepare the way before me.[a] Then
suddenly the Lord you are seeking will come to his temple; the messenger of the
covenant, whom you desire, will come," says the LORD Almighty.
2 But who can endure[b] the day of his coming? Who can stand when he appears?
For he will be like a refiner's fire[c] or a launderer's soap.
3 He will sit as a refiner
and purifier of silver;[d] he will purify[e] the Levites and refine them like gold and
silver. Then the LORD will have men who will bring offerings in righteousness,
4 and
the offerings[f] of Judah and Jerusalem will be acceptable to the LORD, as in days gone
by, as in former years.[g]
5 "So I will come near to you for judgment. I will be quick to testify against
sorcerers, adulterers and perjurers,[h] against those who defraud labourers of their
wages,[i] who oppress the widows[j] and the fatherless, and deprive aliens of justice,
but do not fear me," says the LORD Almighty.

Robbing God

6 "I the LORD do not change.[k] So you, O descendants of Jacob, are not destroyed.
7 Ever since the time of your forefathers you have turned away[l] from my decrees and
have not kept them. Return to me, and I will return to you,"[m] says the LORD Almighty.
"But you ask, 'How are we to return?'
8 "Will a man rob God? Yet you rob me.
"But you ask, 'How do we rob you?'
"In tithes[n] and offerings.
9 You are under a curse—the whole nation of
you—because you are robbing me.
10 Bring the whole tithe into the storehouse,[o] that
there may be food in my house. Test me in this," says the LORD Almighty, "and see
if I will not throw open the floodgates[p] of heaven and pour out so much blessing that
you will not have room enough for it.
11 I will prevent pests from devouring your crops,
and the vines in your fields will not cast their fruit," says the LORD Almighty.
12 "Then
all the nations will call you blessed,[q] for yours will be a delightful land,"[r] says the
LORD Almighty.

2:17—3:6 God was tired of the way the people had cynically twisted his truths. He would punish those who insisted that because God was silent, he approved of their actions or at least would never punish them. God would also punish those who professed a counterfeit faith while acting sinfully (see 3:5).

3:1 There are two messengers in this verse. The first is usually understood to be John the Baptist (Matthew 11:10; Luke 7:27). The second messenger is Jesus, the Messiah, for whom both Malachi and John the Baptist prepared the way.

3:2, 3 In the process of refining metals, the raw metal is heated with fire until it melts. The impurities separate from it and rise to the surface. They are skimmed off, leaving the pure metal. Without this heating and melting, there could be no purifying. As the impurities are skimmed off the top, the reflection of the worker appears in the smooth, pure surface. As we are purified by God, his reflection in our lives will become more and more clear to those around us. God says that leaders (here the Levites) should be especially open to his purification process in their lives. Launderer's soap was alkali used to whiten cloth. It is also used here as a symbol of the purifying process.

3:7 God's patience seems endless! Throughout history, his people have disobeyed, even scorned, his laws, but he has always been willing to accept them back. Here, however, the people have the nerve to imply that they never disobeyed ("How are we to return?")! Many people have turned their backs on forgiveness and restoration because they have refused to admit their sin. Don't follow their example. God is ready to return to us if we are willing to return to him.

3:8–12 Malachi urged the people to stop holding back their tithes, to stop keeping from God what he deserved. The tithing system began during the time of Moses (Leviticus 27:30–34; Deuteronomy 14:22). The Levites received some of the tithe because they could not possess land of their own (Numbers 18:20, 21). During Malachi's day, the people were not giving tithes, so the Levites went to work to earn a living, thereby neglecting their God-given responsibilities to care for the temple and for the service of worship. Everything we have is from God; so when we refuse to return to him a part of what he has given, we rob him. Do you selfishly want to keep 100 per cent of what God gives, or are you willing to return at least 10 per cent for helping to advance God's kingdom?

3:8–12 The people of Malachi's day ignored God's command to give a tithe of their income to his temple. They may have feared losing what they had worked so hard to get, but in this they misjudged God. "Give, and it will be given to you" he says (Luke 6:38). When we give, we must remember that the blessings God promises are not always material and may not be experienced completely here on earth, but we will certainly receive them in our future life with him.

3:10 The "storehouse" was a place in the temple for storing grain and other food given as tithes. The priests lived off these gifts.

13“You have said harsh things[s] against me,” says the LORD.
“Yet you ask, ‘What have we said against you?’
14“You have said, ‘It is futile[t] to serve God. What did we gain by carrying out
his requirements and going about like mourners[u] before the LORD Almighty? 15But
now we call the arrogant blessed. Certainly the evildoers[v] prosper, and even those
who challenge God escape.’ ”

3. The faithful few

16Then those who feared the LORD talked with each other, and the LORD listened
and heard.[w] A scroll[x] of remembrance was written in his presence concerning those
who feared the LORD and honoured his name.
17“They will be mine,” says the LORD Almighty, “in the day when I make up my
treasured possession.[a][y] I will spare[z] them, just as in compassion a man spares his
son who serves him. 18And you will again see the distinction between the righteous[a]
and the wicked, between those who serve God and those who do not.

The Day of the LORD

4 “Surely the day is coming;[a] it will burn like a furnace. All the arrogant and every
evildoer will be stubble,[b] and that day that is coming will set them on fire,” says
the LORD Almighty. “Not a root or a branch will be left to them. 2But for you who
revere my name, the sun of righteousness[c] will rise with healing[d] in its wings. And
you will go out and leap[e] like calves released from the stall. 3Then you will trample[f]
down the wicked; they will be ashes[g] under the soles of your feet on the day when
I do these things,” says the LORD Almighty.
4“Remember the law[h] of my servant Moses, the decrees and laws I gave him at
Horeb for all Israel.
5“See, I will send you the prophet Elijah[i] before that great and dreadful day of
the LORD comes.[j] 6He will turn the hearts of the fathers to their children,[k] and the
hearts of the children to their fathers; or else I will come and strike[l] the land with
a curse.”[m]

a 17 Or *Almighty, “my treasured possession, in the day when I act*

3:13 [s]Mal 2:17
3:14 [t]Ps 73:13 [u]Isa 58:3
3:15 [v]Jer 7:10
3:16 [w]Ps 34:15 [x]Ps 56:8
3:17 [y]Dt 7:6 [z]Ps 103:13; Isa 26:20
3:18 [a]Ge 18:25
4:1 [a]Joel 2:31 [b]Isa 5:24; Ob 1:18
4:2 [c]Lk 1:78; Eph 5:14 [d]Isa 30:26 [e]Isa 35:6
4:3 [f]Job 40:12 [g]Eze 28:18
4:4 [h]Ps 147:19
4:5 [i]Mt 11:14 [j]Joel 2:31
4:6 [k]Lk 1:17 [l]Isa 11:4; Rev 19:15 [m]Zec 5:3

3:13–15 These verses describe the people’s arrogant attitude towards God. When we ask, “What good does it do to serve God?” we are really asking, “What good does it do for *me?*” Our focus is selfish. Our real question should be, “What good does it do for God?” We must serve God just because he is God and deserves to be served.

3:16 The “scroll of remembrance” may or may not be an actual book. The point is that God will remember those who remain faithful to him, and who love, fear, honour, and respect him.

3:17 God’s treasured possession are those faithful to him. This fulfils the promise he made in the covenant to his people (Exodus 19:5). According to 1 Peter 2:9, believers are God’s treasured possession. Have you committed your life to God for safe-keeping?

4:2 In the day of the Lord, God’s wrath towards the wicked will burn like a furnace (4:1). But he will be like the healing warmth of the sun to those who love and obey him. John the Baptist prophesied that with the coming of Jesus, the dawn was about to break with light for those in sin’s darkness (Luke 1:76–79). In Isaiah 60:20 and Revelation 21:23, 24 we learn that no light will be needed in God’s holy city, because God himself will be the light.

4:2ff These last verses of the Old Testament are filled with hope. Regardless of how life looks now, God controls the future, and everything will be made right. We who have loved and served God look forward to a joyful celebration. This hope for the future becomes ours when we trust God with our lives.

4:4 These laws, given to Moses at Horeb (Mount Sinai), were the foundation of the nation’s civil, moral, and ceremonial life (Exodus 20; Deuteronomy 4:5, 6). We still must obey these moral laws because they apply to all generations.

4:5, 6 Elijah was one of the greatest prophets who ever lived (his story is recorded in 1 Kings 17 – 2 Kings 2). With Malachi’s death, the voice of God’s prophets would be silent for 400 years. Then a prophet would come, like Elijah, to herald Christ’s coming (Matthew 17:10–13; Luke 1:17). This prophet was John the Baptist. John prepared people’s hearts for Jesus by urging people to repent of their sins. Christ’s coming would bring unity and peace, but also judgment on those who refused to turn from their sins.

4:6 Malachi gives us practical guidelines about commitment to God. God deserves the best we have to offer (1:7–10). We must be willing to change our wrong ways of living (2:1, 2). We should make family a life-long priority (2:13–16). We should welcome God’s refining process in our lives (3:3). We should tithe our income (3:8–12). There is no room for pride (3:13–15).

Malachi closes his messages by pointing to that great final day of judgment. For those who are committed to God, judgment day will be a day of joy because it will usher in eternity in God’s presence. Those who have ignored God will be “stubble”, to be burned up (4:1). To help the people prepare for that day of judgment, God would send a prophet like Elijah (John the Baptist), who would prepare the way for Jesus, the Messiah. The New Testament begins with this prophet calling the people to turn from their sins and to turn towards God. Such a commitment to God demands great sacrifice on our part, but we can be sure it will be worth it all in the end.

The New Testament

MATTHEW

Herod the Great begins to rule 37 B.C.

Jesus is born 6/5 B.C.

Escape to Egypt 5/4 B.C.

Herod the Great dies 4 B.C.

Return to Nazareth 4/3 B.C.

Judea becomes a Roman province A.D. 6

Jesus visits temple as a bo 6/7

VITAL STATISTICS

PURPOSE:
To prove that Jesus is the Messiah, the eternal King

AUTHOR:
Matthew (Levi)

TO WHOM WRITTEN:
Matthew wrote especially to the Jews

DATE WRITTEN:
Probably between A.D. 60–65

SETTING:
Matthew was a Jewish tax collector who became one of Jesus' disciples. This Gospel forms the connecting link between the Old and New Testaments because of its emphasis on the fulfilment of prophecy.

KEY VERSE:
"Do not think that I have come to abolish the Law or the Prophets; I have not come to abolish them but to fulfil them" (5:17).

KEY PEOPLE:
Jesus, Mary, Joseph, John the Baptist, the disciples, the religious leaders, Caiaphas, Pilate, Mary Magdalene

KEY PLACES:
Bethlehem, Jerusalem, Capernaum, Galilee, Judea

SPECIAL FEATURES:
Matthew is filled with messianic language ("Son of David" is used throughout) and Old Testament references (53 quotes and 76 other references). This Gospel was not written as a chronological account; its purpose was to present the clear evidence that Jesus is the Messiah, the Saviour.

AS the procession slowly winds through the city, thousands pack the pavements hoping to catch a glimpse. Marching bands with great fanfare announce the arrival, and bodyguards scan the crowd and run alongside the limousine. Pomp, ceremony, protocol—modern symbols of position and evidences of importance—herald the arrival of royalty. We honour and respect them.

The Jews waited for a leader who had been promised centuries before by prophets. They believed that this leader—the Messiah ("anointed one")—would rescue them from their Roman oppressors and establish a new kingdom. As their king, he would rule the world with justice. However, many Jews overlooked prophecies that also spoke of this king as a suffering servant who would be rejected and killed. It is no wonder, then, that few recognised Jesus as the Messiah. How could this humble carpenter's son from Nazareth be their king? But Jesus was and is the King of all the earth!

Matthew (Levi) was one of Jesus' 12 disciples. Once he was a despised tax collector, but his life was changed by this man from Galilee. Matthew wrote this Gospel to his fellow Jews to prove that Jesus is the Messiah and to explain God's kingdom.

Matthew begins his account by giving Jesus' genealogy. He then tells of Jesus' birth and early years, including the family's escape to Egypt from the murderous Herod and their return to Nazareth. Following Jesus' baptism by John (3:17) and his defeat of Satan in the desert, Jesus begins his public ministry by calling his first disciples and giving the Sermon on the Mount (chapters 5—7). Matthew shows Christ's authority by reporting his miracles of healing the sick and the demon-possessed, and even raising the dead.

Despite opposition from the Pharisees and others in the religious establishment (chapters 12—15), Jesus continued to teach concerning the kingdom of heaven (chapters 16—20). During this time, Jesus spoke with his disciples about his imminent death and resurrection (16:21), and revealed his true identity to Peter, James, and John (17:1–5). Near the end of his ministry, Jesus entered Jerusalem in a triumphant procession (21:1–11). But soon opposition mounted and Jesus knew that his death was near. So he taught his disciples about the future—what they could expect before his return (chapter 24) and how to live until then (chapter 25).

In Matthew's finale (chapters 26—28), he focuses on Jesus' final days on earth—the Last Supper, his prayer in Gethsemane, the betrayal by Judas, the flight of the disciples, Peter's denial, the trials before Caiaphas and Pilate, Jesus' final words on the cross, and his burial in a borrowed tomb. But the story does not end there, for the Messiah rose from the dead—conquering death and then telling his followers to continue his work by making disciples in all nations.

As you read this Gospel, listen to Matthew's clear message: Jesus is the Christ, the King of kings and Lord of lords. Celebrate his victory over evil and death, and make Jesus the Lord of your life.

Tiberius Caesar becomes emperor 14	Pontius Pilate appointed governor 26	Jesus begins his ministry 26/27	Jesus chooses twelve disciples 28	Jesus feeds 5,000 29	Jesus is crucified, rises again, and ascends 30

THE BLUEPRINT

A. BIRTH AND PREPARATION OF JESUS, THE KING (1:1—4:11)

The people of Israel were waiting for the Messiah, their king. Matthew begins his book by showing how Jesus Christ was a descendant of David. But Matthew goes on to show that God did not send Jesus to be an earthly king, but a heavenly king. His kingdom would be much greater than David's because it would never end. Even at Jesus' birth, many recognised him as a king. Herod, the ruler, as well as Satan, was afraid of Jesus' kingship and tried to stop him, but others worshipped him and brought royal gifts. We must be willing to recognise Jesus for who he really is and worship him as king of our lives.

B. MESSAGE AND MINISTRY OF JESUS, THE KING (4:12—25:46)

1. Jesus begins his ministry
2. Jesus gives the Sermon on the Mount
3. Jesus performs many miracles
4. Jesus teaches about the kingdom
5. Jesus encounters differing reactions to his ministry
6. Jesus faces conflict with the religious leaders
7. Jesus teaches on the Mount of Olives

Jesus gave the Sermon on the Mount, directions for living in his kingdom. He also told many parables about the difference between his kingdom and the kingdoms of earth. Forgiveness, peace, and putting others first are some of the characteristics that make one great in the future kingdom of God. And to be great in God's kingdom, we must live by God's standards right now. Jesus came to show us how to live as faithful subjects in his kingdom.

C. DEATH AND RESURRECTION OF JESUS, THE KING (26:1—28:20)

Jesus was formally presented to the nation of Israel, but rejected. How strange for the king to be accused, arrested, and crucified. But Jesus demonstrated his power even over death through his resurrection, and gained access for us into his kingdom. With all this evidence that Jesus is God's Son, we too should accept him as our Lord.

MEGATHEMES

THEME	EXPLANATION	IMPORTANCE
Jesus Christ, the King	Jesus is revealed as the King of kings. His miraculous birth, his life and teaching, his miracles, and his triumph over death show his true identity.	Jesus cannot be equated with any person or power. He is the supreme ruler of time and eternity, heaven and earth, humans and angels. We should give him his rightful place as king of our lives.
The Messiah	Jesus was the Messiah, the One for whom the Jews had waited to deliver them from Roman oppression. Yet tragically, they didn't recognise him when he came because his kingship was not what they expected. The true purpose of God's anointed deliverer was to die for all people to free them from sin's oppression.	Because Jesus was sent by God, we can trust him with our lives. It is worth everything we have to acknowledge him and give ourselves to him, because he came to be our Messiah, our Saviour.
Kingdom of God	Jesus came to earth to begin his kingdom. His full kingdom will be realised at his return and will be made up of anyone who has faithfully followed him.	The way to enter God's kingdom is by faith—believing in Christ to save us from sin and change our lives. We must do the work of his kingdom now to be prepared for his return.
Teachings	Jesus taught the people through sermons, illustrations, and parables. Through his teachings, he showed the true ingredients of faith and how to guard against a fruitless and hypocritical life.	Jesus' teachings show us how to prepare for life in his eternal kingdom by living properly right now. He lived what he taught, and we too must practise what we preach.

Resurrection	When Jesus rose from the dead, he rose in power as the true king. In his victory over death, he established his credentials as king and his power and authority over evil.	The resurrection shows Jesus' all-powerful life for us—not even death could stop his plan of offering eternal life. Those who believe in Jesus can hope for a resurrection like his. Our role is to tell his story to all the earth so that everyone may share in his victory.

KEY PLACES IN MATTHEW

Jesus' earthly story begins in the town of Bethlehem in the Roman province of Judea (2:1). A threat to kill the infant king led Joseph to take his family to Egypt (2:14). When they returned, God led them to settle in Nazareth in Galilee (2:22, 23). At about the age of 30, Jesus was baptised in the Jordan River and was tempted by Satan in the Judean desert (3:13; 4:1). Jesus set up his base of operations in Capernaum (4:12, 13) and from there ministered throughout Israel, telling parables, teaching about the kingdom, and healing the sick. He travelled to the region of the Gadarenes and healed two demon-possessed men (8:28ff); fed over 5,000 people with five loaves and two fish on the shores of Galilee near Bethsaida (14:15ff); healed the sick in Gennesaret (14:34ff); ministered to the Gentiles in Tyre and Sidon (15:21ff); visited Caesarea Philippi, where Peter declared him as the Messiah (16:13ff); and taught in Perea, across the Jordan (19:1). As he set out on his last visit to Jerusalem, he told the disciples what would happen to him there (20:17ff). He spent some time in Jericho (20:29) and then stayed in Bethany at night as he went back and forth into Jerusalem during his last week (21:17ff). In Jerusalem he would be crucified, but he would rise again.

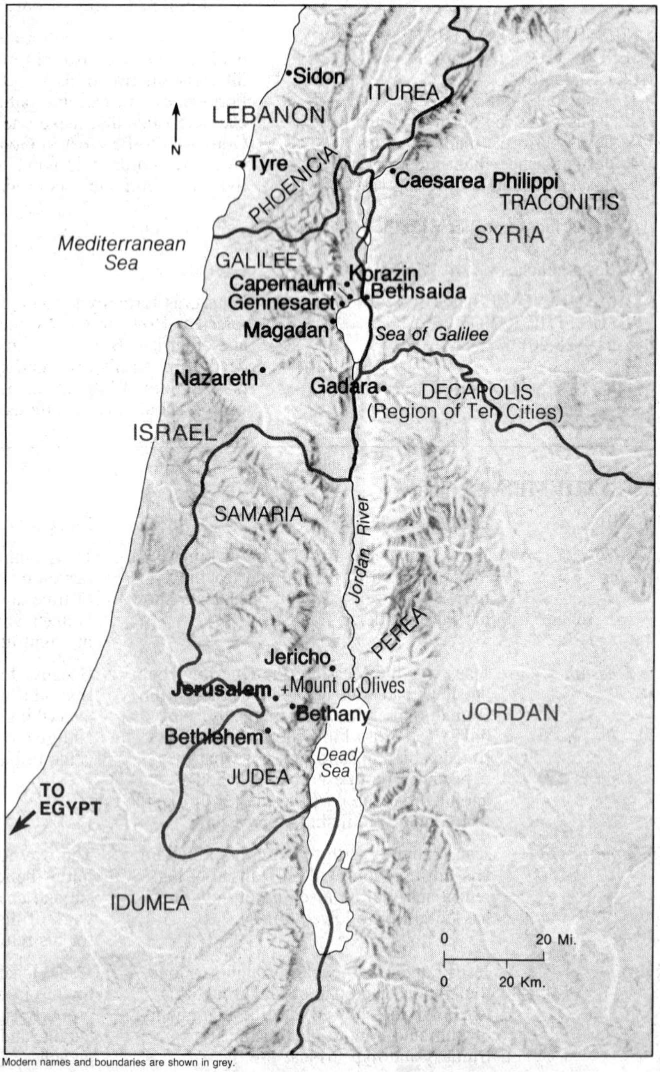

Modern names and boundaries are shown in grey.

A. BIRTH AND PREPARATION OF JESUS, THE KING (1:1–4:11)

Matthew opens his Gospel with a genealogy to prove that Jesus is the descendant of both King David and Abraham, just as the Old Testament had predicted. Jesus' birth didn't go unnoticed, for both shepherds and Magi came to worship him. The Jewish people were waiting for the Messiah to appear. Finally, he was born, but the Jews didn't recognise him because they were looking for a different kind of king.

The Ancestors of Jesus

(3/Luke 3:23–38)

1 A record of the genealogy of Jesus Christ the son of David,[a] the son of Abraham:[b]

2 Abraham was the father of Isaac,[c]
Isaac the father of Jacob,[d]
Jacob the father of Judah and his brothers,[e]
3 Judah the father of Perez and Zerah, whose mother was Tamar,[f]
Perez the father of Hezron,
Hezron the father of Ram,
4 Ram the father of Amminadab,
Amminadab the father of Nahshon,
Nahshon the father of Salmon,
5 Salmon the father of Boaz, whose mother was Rahab,
Boaz the father of Obed, whose mother was Ruth,
Obed the father of Jesse,
6 and Jesse the father of King David.[g]

David was the father of Solomon, whose mother had been Uriah's wife,[h]
7 Solomon the father of Rehoboam,
Rehoboam the father of Abijah,
Abijah the father of Asa,
8 Asa the father of Jehoshaphat,
Jehoshaphat the father of Jehoram,
Jehoram the father of Uzziah,
9 Uzziah the father of Jotham,
Jotham the father of Ahaz,
Ahaz the father of Hezekiah,
10 Hezekiah the father of Manasseh,[i]
Manasseh the father of Amon,
Amon the father of Josiah,
11 and Josiah the father of Jeconiah[a] and his brothers at the time of the exile to Babylon.[j]

a *11* That is, Jehoiachin; also in verse 12

1:1 [a] 2Sa 7:12-16; Isa 9:6, 7; 11:1; Jer 23:5, 6; Mt 9:27; Lk 1:32, 69; Ro 1:3; Rev 22:16 [b] Ge 22:18; Gal 3:16

1:2 [c] Ge 21:3, 12 [d] Ge 25:26 [e] Ge 29:35

1:3 [f] Ge 38:27-30

1:6 [g] 1Sa 16:1; 17:12 [h] 2Sa 12:24

1:10 [i] 2Ki 20:21

1:11 [j] 2Ki 24:14-16; Jer 27:20; Da 1:1, 2

1:1 Presenting this genealogy was one of the most interesting ways that Matthew could begin a book for a Jewish audience. Because a person's family line proved his or her standing as one of God's chosen people, Matthew began by showing that Jesus was a descendant of Abraham, the father of all Jews, and a direct descendant of David, fulfilling Old Testament prophecies about the Messiah's line. The facts of this ancestry were carefully preserved. This is the first of many proofs recorded by Matthew to show that Jesus is the true Messiah.

1:1ff More than 400 years had passed since the last Old Testament prophecies, and faithful Jews all over the world were still waiting for the Messiah (Luke 3:15). Matthew wrote this book to Jews to present Jesus as King and Messiah, the promised descendant of David who would reign for ever (Isaiah 11:1–5). The Gospel of Matthew links the Old and New Testaments and contains many references that show how Jesus fulfilled Old Testament prophecy.

1:1ff Jesus entered human history when the land of Palestine was controlled by Rome and considered an insignificant outpost of the vast and mighty Roman empire. The presence of Roman soldiers in Israel gave the Jews military peace, but at the price of oppression, slavery, injustice, and immorality. Into this kind of world came the promised Messiah.

1:1–17 In the first 17 verses we meet 46 people whose lifetimes span 2,000 years. All were ancestors of Jesus, but they varied considerably in personality, spirituality, and experience. Some were heroes of faith – like Abraham, Isaac, Ruth, and David. Some had shady reputations – like Rahab and Tamar. Many were very ordinary – like Hezron, Ram, Nahshon, and Akim. And others were evil – like Manasseh and Abijah. God's work in history is not limited by human failures or sins, and he works through ordinary people. Just as God used all kinds of people to bring his Son into the world, he uses all kinds today to accomplish his will. And God wants to use you.

1:11 The exile occurred in 586 B.C. when Nebuchadnezzar, king of Babylonia, conquered Judah, destroyed Jerusalem, and took thousands of captives to Babylonia.

12After the exile to Babylon:
Jeconiah was the father of Shealtiel,[k]
Shealtiel the father of Zerubbabel,[l]
13Zerubbabel the father of Abiud,
Abiud the father of Eliakim,
Eliakim the father of Azor,
14Azor the father of Zadok,
Zadok the father of Akim,
Akim the father of Eliud,
15Eliud the father of Eleazar,
Eleazar the father of Matthan,
Matthan the father of Jacob,
16and Jacob the father of Joseph, the husband of Mary,[m] of whom was born
Jesus, who is called Christ.[n]

17Thus there were fourteen generations in all from Abraham to David, fourteen from David to the exile to Babylon, and fourteen from the exile to the Christ.[b]

An Angel Appears to Joseph
(8)

18This is how the birth of Jesus Christ came about: His mother Mary was pledged to be married to Joseph, but before they came together, she was found to be with child through the Holy Spirit.[o] 19Because Joseph her husband was a righteous man and did not want to expose her to public disgrace, he had in mind to divorce[p] her quietly.
20But after he had considered this, an angel of the Lord appeared to him in a dream

[b] *17 Or Messiah.* "The Christ" (Greek) and "the Messiah" (Hebrew) both mean "the Anointed One".

1:12 [k]1Ch 3:17 [l]1Ch 3:19; Ezr 3:2
1:16 [m]Lk 1:27 [n]Mt 27:17
1:18 [o]Lk 1:35
1:19 [p]Dt 24:1

1:16 Because Mary was a virgin when she became pregnant, Matthew lists Joseph only as the husband of Mary, not the father of Jesus. Matthew's genealogy gives Jesus' legal (or royal) lineage through Joseph. Mary's ancestral line is recorded in Luke 3:23–38. Both Mary and Joseph were direct descendants of David.

Matthew traced the genealogy back to Abraham, while Luke traced it back to Adam. Matthew wrote to the Jews, so Jesus was shown as a descendant of their father, Abraham. Luke wrote to the Gentiles, so he emphasised Jesus as the Saviour of all people.

1:17 Matthew breaks Israel's history into three sets of 14 generations, but there were probably more generations than those listed here. Genealogies often compressed history, meaning that not every generation of ancestors was specifically listed. Thus the phrase *the father of* can also be translated "the ancestor of".

1:18 There were three steps in a Jewish marriage. First, the two families agreed to the union. Second, a public announcement was made. At this point, the couple were "pledged". This was similar to engagement today except that their relationship could be broken only through death or divorce (even though sexual relations were not yet permitted). Third, the couple were married and began living together. Because Mary and Joseph were engaged, Mary's apparent unfaithfulness carried a severe social stigma. According to Jewish civil law, Joseph had a right to divorce her, and the Jewish authorities could have had her stoned to death (Deuteronomy 22:23, 24).

1:18 Why is the virgin birth important to the Christian faith? Jesus Christ, God's Son, had to be free from the sinful nature passed on to all other human beings by Adam. Because Jesus was born of a woman, he was a human being; but as the Son of God, Jesus was born without any trace of human sin. Jesus is both fully human and fully divine.

Because Jesus lived as a man, we know that he fully understands our experiences and struggles (Hebrews 4:15, 16). Because he is God, he has the power and authority to deliver us from sin (Colossians 2:13–15). We can tell Jesus all our thoughts, feelings, and needs. He has been where we are now, and he has the ability to help.

1:18–25 Joseph was faced with a difficult choice after discovering that Mary was pregnant. Although he knew that taking Mary as his wife could be humiliating, Joseph chose to obey the angel's command to marry her. His action revealed four admirable qualities: (1) righteousness (1:19), (2) discretion and sensitivity (1:19), (3) responsiveness to God (1:24), and (4) self-discipline (1:25).

1:19 Perhaps Joseph thought he had only two options: divorce Mary quietly, or have her stoned. But God had a third option—marry her (1:20–23). In view of the circumstances, this had not occurred to Joseph. But God often shows us that there are more options available than we think. Although Joseph seemed to be doing the right thing by breaking the engagement, only God's guidance helped him make the best decision. When our decisions affect the lives of others, we must always seek God's wisdom.

1:20 The conception and birth of Jesus Christ are supernatural events beyond human logic or reasoning. Because of this, God sent angels to help certain people understand the significance of what was happening (see 2:13, 19; Luke 1:11, 26; 2:9).

Angels are spiritual beings created by God who help carry out his work on earth. They bring God's messages to people (Luke 1:26), protect God's people (Daniel 6:22), offer encouragement (Genesis 16:7ff), give guidance (Exodus 14:19), carry out punishment (2 Samuel 24:16), patrol the earth (Zechariah 1:9–14), and fight the forces of evil (2 Kings 6:16–18; Revelation 20:1, 2). There are both good and bad angels (Revelation 12:7), but because bad angels are allied with the devil, or Satan, they have considerably less power and authority than good angels. Eventually the main role of angels will be to offer continuous praise to God (Revelation 7:11, 12).

1:20–23 The angel declared to Joseph that Mary's child was conceived by the Holy Spirit and would be a son. This reveals an important truth about Jesus—he is both God and human. The infinite, unlimited God took on the limitations of humanity so he could live and die for the salvation of all who would believe in him.

1:21
[q]Lk 1:31
[r]Lk 2:11;
Ac 5:31; 13:23, 28

and said, "Joseph son of David, do not be afraid to take Mary home as your wife,
because what is conceived in her is from the Holy Spirit. 21 She will give birth to a
son, and you are to give him the name Jesus,[c][q] because he will save his people from
their sins."[r]
22 All this took place to fulfil what the Lord had said through the prophet: 23 "The

c 21 *Jesus* is the Greek form of *Joshua*, which means *the* L*ORD* *saves.*

JOSEPH

The strength of what we believe is measured by how much we are willing to suffer for those beliefs. Joseph was a man with strong beliefs. He was prepared to do what was right, despite the pain he knew it would cause. But Joseph had another trait—he not only tried to do what was right, he also tried to do it in the right way.

When Mary told Joseph about her pregnancy, Joseph knew the child was not his. His respect for Mary's character and the explanation she gave him, as well as her attitude towards the expected child, must have made it hard to think his fiancée had done something wrong. Still, someone else was the child's father—and it was mind-boggling to accept that the "someone else" was God.

Joseph decided he had to break off the engagement, but he was determined to do it in a way that would not cause public shame to Mary. He intended to act with justice and love.

At this point, God sent a messenger to Joseph to confirm Mary's story and open another way of obedience for Joseph—to take Mary as his wife. Joseph obeyed God, married Mary, and honoured her virginity until the baby was born.

We do not know how long Joseph lived in his role as Jesus' earthly father—he is last mentioned when Jesus was 12 years old. But Joseph trained his son in the trade of carpentry, made sure he had good spiritual training in Nazareth, and took the whole family on the yearly trip to Jerusalem for the Passover, which Jesus continued to observe during his adult years.

Joseph knew Jesus was someone special from the moment he heard the angel's words. His strong belief in that fact, and his willingness to follow God's leading, empowered him to be Jesus' chosen earthly father.

Strengths and accomplishments:
- A man of integrity
- A descendant of King David
- Jesus' legal and earthly father
- A person sensitive to God's guidance and willing to do God's will no matter what the consequence

Lessons from his life:
- God honours integrity
- Social position is of little importance when God chooses to use us
- Being obedient to the guidance we have from God leads to more guidance from him
- Feelings are not accurate measures of the rightness or wrongness of an action

Vital statistics:
- Where: Nazareth, Bethlehem
- Occupation: Carpenter
- Relatives: Wife: Mary. Children: Jesus, James, Joses, Judas, Simon, and daughters
- Contemporaries: Herod the Great, John the Baptist, Simeon, Anna

Key verses:
"Because Joseph her husband was a righteous man and did not want to expose her to public disgrace, he had in mind to divorce her quietly. But after he had considered this, an angel of the Lord appeared to him in a dream and said, 'Joseph son of David, do not be afraid to take Mary home as your wife, because what is conceived in her is from the Holy Spirit' " (Matthew 1:19, 20).

Joseph's story is told in Matthew 1:16—2:23; Luke 1:26—2:52.

1:21 *Jesus* means "the LORD saves". Jesus came to earth to save us because we can't save ourselves from sin and its consequences. No matter how good we are, we can't eliminate the sinful nature present in all of us. Only Jesus can do that. Jesus didn't come to help people save themselves; he came to be their Saviour from the power and penalty of sin. Thank Christ for his death on the cross for your sin, and then ask him to take control of your life. Your new life begins at that moment.

1:23 Jesus was to be called *Immanuel* ("God with us"), as predicted by Isaiah the prophet (Isaiah 7:14). Jesus was God in the flesh; thus God was literally among us, "with us". Through the Holy Spirit, Christ is present today in the life of every believer. Perhaps not even Isaiah understood how far-reaching the meaning of "Immanuel" would be.

virgin will be with child and will give birth to a son, and they will call him Immanuel"[d][s]—which means, "God with us."
24When Joseph woke up, he did what the angel of the Lord had commanded him
and took Mary home as his wife. 25But he had no union with her until she gave birth
to a son. And he gave him the name Jesus.[t]

1:23 [s]Isa 7:14; 8:8, 10
1:25 [t]ver 21

Visitors Arrive from Eastern Lands
(12)

2 After Jesus was born in Bethlehem in Judea,[a] during the time of King Herod,[b]
Magi[a] from the east came to Jerusalem 2and asked, "Where is the one who has
been born king of the Jews?[c] We saw his star[d] in the east[b] and have come to worship
him."
3When King Herod heard this he was disturbed, and all Jerusalem with him. 4When
he had called together all the people's chief priests and teachers of the law, he asked

2:1 [a]Lk 2:4-7 [b]Lk 1:5
2:2 [c]Jer 23:5; Mt 27:11; Mk 15:2; Jn 1:49; 18:33-37 [d]Nu 24:17

[d] *23* Isaiah 7:14 [a] *1* Traditionally *Wise Men* [b] *2* Or *star when it rose*

1:24 Joseph changed his plans quickly after learning that Mary had not been unfaithful to him (1:19). He obeyed God and proceeded with the marriage plans. Although others may have disapproved of his decision, Joseph went ahead with what he knew was right. Sometimes we avoid doing what is right because of what others might think. Like Joseph, we must choose to obey God rather than seek the approval of others.

2:1 Bethlehem is a small town five miles south of Jerusalem. It sits on a high ridge over 2,000 feet above sea level. It is mentioned in more detail in the Gospel of Luke. Luke also explains why Joseph and Mary were in Bethlehem when Jesus was born, rather than in Nazareth, their home town.

2:1 The land of Israel was divided into four political districts and several lesser territories. Judea was to the south, Samaria in the middle, Galilee to the north, and Idumea to the southeast. Bethlehem of Judea (also called Judah, 2:6) had been prophesied as the Messiah's birthplace (Micah 5:2). Jerusalem was also in Judea and was the seat of government for Herod the Great, king over all four political districts. After Herod's death, the districts were divided among three separate rulers (see the note on 2:19–22). Although he was a ruthless, evil man who murdered many in his own family, Herod the Great supervised the renovation of the temple, making it much larger and more beautiful. This made him popular with many Jews. Jesus would visit Jerusalem many times because the great Jewish festivals were held there.

2:1, 2 Not much is known about these Magi (traditionally called wise men). We don't know where they came from or how many there were. Tradition says they were men of high position from Parthia, near the site of ancient Babylon. How did they know that the star represented the Messiah? (1) They could have been Jews who remained in Babylon after the exile and knew the Old Testament predictions of the Messiah's coming. (2) They may have been eastern astrologers who studied ancient manuscripts from around the world. Because of the Jewish exile centuries earlier, they would have had copies of the Old Testament in their land. (3) They may have had a special message from God directing them to the Messiah. Some scholars say these Magi were each from a different land, representing the entire world bowing before Jesus. These men from faraway lands recognised Jesus as the Messiah when most of God's chosen people in Israel did not. Matthew pictures Jesus as King over the whole world, not just Judea.

2:1, 2 The Magi travelled thousands of miles to see the king of the Jews. When they finally found him, they responded with joy, worship, and gifts. This is so different from the approach people often take today. We expect God to come looking for us, to explain himself, prove who he is, and give *us* gifts. But those who are wise still seek and worship Jesus today, not for what they can get, but for who he is.

2:2 The Magi said they saw Jesus' star. Balaam referred to a coming "star . . . out of Jacob" (Numbers 24:17). Some say this star may have been a conjunction of Jupiter, Saturn, and Mars in 6 B.C., and others offer other explanations. But couldn't God, who created the heavens, have created a special star to signal the arrival of his Son? Whatever the nature of the star, these Magi travelled thousands of miles searching for a king, and they found him.

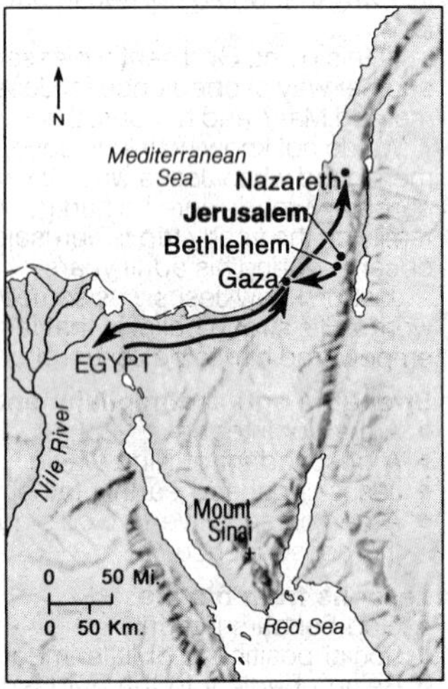

THE FLIGHT TO EGYPT
Herod planned to kill the baby Jesus, whom he perceived to be a future threat to his position. Warned of this treachery in a dream, Joseph took his family to Egypt until Herod's death, which occurred a year or two later. They then planned to return to Judea, but God led them instead to Nazareth in Galilee.

2:3 Herod the Great was quite disturbed when the Magi asked about a newborn king of the Jews because: (1) Herod was not the rightful heir to the throne of David; therefore many Jews hated him as a usurper. If Jesus really was an heir, trouble would arise. (2) Herod was ruthless and, because of his many enemies, he was suspicious that someone would try to overthrow him. (3) Herod didn't want the Jews, a religious people, to unite around a religious figure. (4) If these Magi were of Jewish descent and from Parthia (the most powerful region next to Rome), they would have welcomed a Jewish king who could swing the balance of power away from Rome. The land of Israel, far from Rome, would have been easy prey for a nation trying to gain more control.

2:4 The chief priests and teachers of the law were aware of Micah 5:2 and other prophecies about the Messiah. The Magi's news troubled Herod because he knew that the Jewish people expected the Messiah to come soon (Luke 3:15). Most Jews expected the Messiah to be a great military and political deliverer, like Alexander the Great. Herod's counsellors would have told Herod this. No wonder this ruthless man took no chances and ordered all the baby boys in Bethlehem to be killed (2:16)!

2:5
[e]Jn 7:42

them where the Christ[c] was to be born. 5"In Bethlehem[e] in Judea," they replied,
"for this is what the prophet has written:

6" 'But you, Bethlehem, in the land of Judah,
are by no means least among the rulers of Judah;
for out of you will come a ruler
who will be the shepherd of my people Israel.'[d]"[f]

2:6
[f]Mic 5:2; 2Sa 5:2

7Then Herod called the Magi secretly and found out from them the exact time the
star had appeared. 8He sent them to Bethlehem and said, "Go and make a careful
search for the child. As soon as you find him, report to me, so that I too may go and
worship him."
9After they had heard the king, they went on their way, and the star they had seen
in the east[e] went ahead of them until it stopped over the place where the child was.
10When they saw the star, they were overjoyed. 11On coming to the house, they saw
the child with his mother Mary, and they bowed down and worshipped him.[g] Then
they opened their treasures and presented him with gifts[h] of gold and of incense and
of myrrh. 12And having been warned[i] in a dream[j] not to go back to Herod, they
returned to their country by another route.

2:11
[g]Isa 60:3
[h]Ps 72:10

2:12
[i]Heb 11:7
[j]ver 13, 19, 22; Mt 27:19

c *4* Or *Messiah* d *6* Micah 5:2 e *9* Or *seen when it rose*

GOSPEL ACCOUNTS FOUND ONLY IN MATTHEW

Passage	*Subject*
1:20–24	Joseph's dream*
2:1–12	The visit of the Magi
2:13–15	Escape to Egypt*
2:16–18	Slaughter of the children*
27:3–10	The death of Judas*
27:19	The dream of Pilate's wife
27:52	The other resurrections
28:11–15	The bribery of the guards
28:19, 20	The baptism emphasis in the Great Commission*

Matthew records nine special events that are not mentioned in any of the other Gospels. In each case, the most apparent reason for Matthew's choice has to do with his purpose in communicating the gospel to Jewish people. Five cases are fulfilments of Old Testament prophecies (marked with asterisks above). The other four would have been of particular interest to the Jews of Matthew's day.

2:5, 6 Matthew often quoted Old Testament prophets. This prophecy, paraphrasing Micah 5:2, had been delivered seven centuries earlier.

2:6 Most religious leaders believed in a literal fulfilment of all Old Testament prophecy; therefore, they believed the Messiah would be born in Bethlehem. Ironically, when Jesus was born, these same religious leaders became his greatest enemies. When the Messiah for whom they had been waiting finally came, they didn't recognise him.

2:8 Herod did not want to worship Christ—he was lying. This was a trick to get the Magi to return to him and reveal the whereabouts of the newborn king. Herod's plan was to kill Jesus.

2:11 Jesus was probably one or two years old when the Magi found him. By this time, Mary and Joseph were married, living in a house, and intending to stay in Bethlehem for a while. For more on why Joseph and Mary stayed, see the note on Luke 2:39.

2:11 The Magi gave these expensive gifts because they were worthy presents for a future king. Bible students have seen in the gifts symbols of Christ's identity and what he would accomplish. Gold was a gift for a king; incense, a gift for deity; myrrh, a spice for a person who was going to die. These gifts may have provided the financial resources for the trip to Egypt and back.

2:11 The Magi brought gifts and worshipped Jesus for who he was. This is the essence of true worship—honouring Christ for who he is and being willing to give him what is valuable to you. Worship God because he is the perfect, just, and almighty Creator of the universe, worthy of the best you have to give.

2:12 After finding Jesus and worshipping him, the Magi were warned by God not to return through Jerusalem as they had intended. Finding Jesus may mean that your life must take a different direction, one that is responsive and obedient to God's word. Are you willing to be led a different way?

The Escape to Egypt
(13)

13When they had gone, an angel[k] of the Lord appeared to Joseph in a dream.[l]
"Get up," he said, "take the child and his mother and escape to Egypt. Stay there until
I tell you, for Herod is going to search for the child to kill him."
14So he got up, took the child and his mother during the night and left for Egypt,
15where he stayed until the death of Herod. And so was fulfilled what the Lord had
said through the prophet: "Out of Egypt I called my son."[f][m]
16When Herod realised that he had been outwitted by the Magi, he was furious,
and he gave orders to kill all the boys in Bethlehem and its vicinity who were two
years old and under, in accordance with the time he had learned from the Magi. 17Then
what was said through the prophet Jeremiah was fulfilled:

18"A voice is heard in Ramah,
weeping and great mourning,
Rachel weeping for her children
and refusing to be comforted,
because they are no more."[g][n]

The Return to Nazareth
(14)

19After Herod died, an angel of the Lord appeared in a dream[o] to Joseph in Egypt
20and said, "Get up, take the child and his mother and go to the land of Israel, for
those who were trying to take the child's life are dead."
21So he got up, took the child and his mother and went to the land of Israel. 22But
when he heard that Archelaus was reigning in Judea in place of his father Herod, he
was afraid to go there. Having been warned in a dream,[p] he withdrew to the district
of Galilee,[q] 23and he went and lived in a town called Nazareth.[r] So was fulfilled[s]
what was said through the prophets: "He will be called a Nazarene."[t]

2:13 [k]Ac 5:19 [l]ver 12, 19, 22
2:15 [m]Hos 11:1; Ex 4:22, 23
2:18 [n]Jer 31:15
2:19 [o]ver 12, 13, 22
2:22 [p]ver 12, 13, 19; Mt 27:19 [q]Lk 2:39
2:23 [r]Lk 1:26; Jn 1:45, 46 [s]Mt 1:22 [t]Mk 1:24

f *15* Hosea 11:1 **g** *18* Jer. 31:15

2:13 This was the second dream or vision that Joseph received from God. Joseph's first dream revealed that Mary's child would be the Messiah (1:20, 21). His second dream told him how to protect the child's life. Although Joseph was not Jesus' natural father, he was Jesus' legal father and was responsible for his safety and well-being. Divine guidance comes only to prepared hearts. Joseph remained receptive to God's guidance.

2:14, 15 Going to Egypt was not unusual because there were colonies of Jews in several major Egyptian cities. These colonies had developed during the time of the great captivity (see Jeremiah 43; 44). There is an interesting parallel between this flight to Egypt and Israel's history. As an infant nation, Israel went to Egypt, just as Jesus did as a child. God led Israel out (Hosea 11:1); God brought Jesus back. Both events show God working to save his people.

2:16 Herod, the king of the Jews, killed all the boys under two years of age in an obsessive attempt to kill Jesus, the newborn King. He stained his hands with blood, but he did not harm Jesus. Herod was king by a human appointment; Jesus was King by a divine appointment. No-one can thwart God's plans.

2:16 Herod was afraid that this newborn king would one day take his throne. He completely misunderstood the reason for Christ's coming. Jesus didn't want Herod's throne; he wanted to be king of Herod's life. Jesus wanted to give Herod eternal life, not take away his present life. Today people are often afraid that Christ wants to take things away when, in reality, he wants to give them real freedom, peace, and joy. Don't fear Christ – give him the throne of your life.

2:17, 18 Rachel was the wife of Jacob, one of the great men of God in the Old Testament. From Jacob's 12 sons had come the 12 tribes of Israel. Rachel was buried near Bethlehem (Genesis 35:19). For more about the significance of this verse, see the note on Jeremiah 31:15, from which this verse was quoted.

2:19–22 Herod the Great died in 4 B.C. of an incurable disease. Rome trusted him but didn't trust his sons. Herod knew that Rome wouldn't give his successor as much power, so he divided his kingdom into three parts, one for each son. Archelaus received Judea, Samaria, and Idumea; Herod Antipas received Galilee and Perea; Herod Philip II received Traconitis. Archelaus, a violent man, began his reign by slaughtering 3,000 influential people. Nine years later, he was banished. God didn't want Joseph's family to go into the region of this evil ruler.

2:23 Nazareth sat in the hilly area of southern Galilee near the crossroads of great caravan trade routes. The town itself was rather small. The Roman garrison in charge of Galilee was housed there. The people of Nazareth had constant contact with people from all over the world, so world news reached them quickly. The people of Nazareth had an attitude of independence that many of the Jews despised. This may have been why Nathanael commented, "Nazareth! Can anything good come from there?" (see John 1:46).

2:23 The Old Testament does not record this specific statement, "He will be called a Nazarene." Many scholars believe, however, that Matthew is referring to Isaiah 11:1 where the Hebrew word for "branch" is similar to the word for Nazarene. Or he may be referring to a prophecy unrecorded in the Bible. In any case, Matthew paints the picture of Jesus as the true Messiah announced by God through the prophets; and he makes the point that Jesus, the Messiah, had unexpectedly humble beginnings, just as the Old Testament had predicted (see Micah 5:2).

3:1
[a]Lk 1:13, 57-66; 3:2-19
3:2
[b]Da 2:44; Mt 4:17; 6:10; Lk 11:20; 21:31; Ac 1:3, 6

John the Baptist Prepares the Way for Jesus
(16/Mark 1:1–8; Luke 3:1–18)

3 In those days John the Baptist[a] came, preaching in the Desert of Judea 2and
saying, "Repent, for the kingdom of heaven[b] is near." 3This is he who was
spoken of through the prophet Isaiah:

HEROD

The Bible records history. It has proved itself an accurate and reliable record of people, events, and places. Independent historical accounts verify the Bible's descriptions and details of many famous lives. One of these was the father of the Herodian family, Herod the Great.

Herod is remembered as a builder of cities and the lavish rebuilder of the temple in Jerusalem. But he also destroyed people. He showed little greatness in either his personal actions or his character. He was ruthless in ruling his territory. His suspicions and jealousy led to the murder of several of his children and the death of his wife Mariamne.

Herod's title, king of the Jews, was granted by Rome but never accepted by the Jewish people. He was not part of the Davidic family line, and he was only partly Jewish. Although Israel benefited from Herod's lavish efforts to repair the temple in Jerusalem, he won little admiration because he also rebuilt various pagan temples. Herod's costly attempt to gain the loyalty of the people failed because it was superficial. His only loyalty was to himself.

Because his royal title was not genuine, Herod was constantly worried about losing his position. His actions when hearing from the Magi about their search for the new king are consistent with all that we know about Herod. He planned to locate and kill the child before he could become a threat. The murder of innocent children that followed is a tragic lesson in what can happen when actions are motivated by selfishness. Herod's suspicions did not spare even his own family. His life was self-destructive.

Strengths and accomplishments:
- Was given the title king of the Jews by the Romans
- Held on to his power for more than 30 years
- Was an effective, though ruthless, ruler
- Sponsored a great variety of large building projects

Weaknesses and mistakes:
- Tended to treat those around him with fear, suspicion, and jealousy
- Had several of his own children and at least one wife killed
- Ordered the killing of the infants in Bethlehem
- Although claiming to be a God-worshipper, he was still involved in many forms of pagan religion

Lessons from his life:
- Great power brings neither peace nor security
- No-one can prevent God's plans from being carried out
- Superficial loyalty does not impress people or God

Vital statistics:
- Occupation: King of Judea from 37 to 4 B.C.
- Relatives: Father: Antipater. Sons: Archelaus, Antipater, Antipas, Philip, and others. Wives: Doris, Mariamne, and others
- Contemporaries: Zechariah, Elizabeth, Mary, Joseph, Mark Antony, Augustus

Notes about Herod the Great are found in Matthew 2:1–22 and Luke 1:5.

3:1, 2 Almost 30 years had passed since the events of chapter 2. Here John the Baptist burst onto the scene. His theme was "Repent"! Repentance means doing an about-face – a 180-degree turn – from the kind of self-centredness that leads to wrong actions such as lying, cheating, stealing, gossiping, taking revenge, abusing, and indulging in sexual immorality. A person who repents stops rebelling and begins following God's way of living prescribed in his word. The first step in turning to God is to admit your sin, as John urged. Then God will receive you and help you live the way he wants. Remember that only God can get rid of sin. He doesn't expect us to clean up our lives *before* we come to him.

3:1, 2 John the Baptist's Profile is found in John 1.

3:2 The kingdom of heaven began when God himself entered human history as a man. Today Jesus Christ reigns in the hearts of believers, but the kingdom of heaven will not be fully realised until all evil in the world is judged and removed. Christ came to earth first as a suffering servant; he will come again as King and Judge to rule victoriously over all the earth.

3:3 The prophet quoted is Isaiah (40:3), one of the greatest prophets of the Old Testament and one of the most quoted in the New. Like Isaiah, John was a prophet who urged the people to confess their sins and live for God. Both prophets taught that the message of repentance is good news to those who listen and seek the healing forgiveness of God's love, but terrible news to those who refuse to listen and thus cut off their only hope.

3:3 John the Baptist *prepared* the way for Jesus. People who do not know Jesus need to be prepared to meet him. We can prepare them by explaining their need for forgiveness, demonstrating Christ's teachings by our conduct, and telling them how Christ can give their lives meaning. We can "make straight paths for him" by correcting misconceptions that might be hindering people from approaching Christ. Someone you know may be open to a relationship with Christ. What can you do to prepare the way for this person?

"A voice of one calling in the desert,
'Prepare the way for the Lord,
make straight paths for him.' "[a][c]

4John's clothes were made of camel's hair, and he had a leather belt round his
waist.[d] His food was locusts[e] and wild honey. 5People went out to him from
Jerusalem and all Judea and the whole region of the Jordan. 6Confessing their sins,
they were baptised by him in the Jordan River.
7But when he saw many of the Pharisees and Sadducees coming to where he was
baptising, he said to them: "You brood of vipers![f] Who warned you to flee from the
coming wrath?[g] 8Produce fruit in keeping with repentance.[h] 9And do not think you

[a] 3 Isaiah 40:3

3:3 [c]Isa 40:3; Mal 3:1; Lk 1:76; Jn 1:23
3:4 [d]2Ki 1:8 [e]Lev 11:22
3:7 [f]Mt 12:34; 23:33 [g]Ro 1:18; 1Th 1:10
3:8 [h]Ac 26:20

3:4 John was markedly different from other religious leaders of his day. While many were greedy, selfish, and preoccupied with winning the praise of the people, John was concerned only with the praise of God. Having separated himself from the evil and hypocrisy of his day, John lived differently from other people to show that his message was new. John not only preached God's law, he *lived* it. Do you practise what you preach? Could people discover what you believe by observing the way you live?

3:4–6 John must have presented a strange image! Many people came to hear this preacher who wore odd clothes and ate unusual food. Some probably came simply out of curiosity and ended up repenting of their sins as they listened to his powerful message. People may be curious about your Christian life-style and values. You can use their simple curiosity as an opener to share how Christ makes a difference in you.

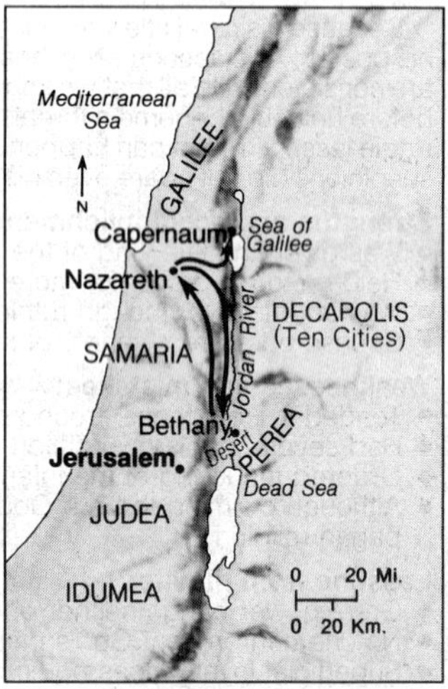

JESUS BEGINS HIS MINISTRY
From his childhood home, Nazareth, Jesus set out to begin his earthly ministry. He was baptised by John the Baptist in the Jordan River, tempted by Satan in the desert, and then returned to Galilee. Between the temptation and his move to Capernaum (4:12, 13), he ministered in Judea, Samaria, and Galilee (see John 1–4).

3:5 Why did John attract so many people? He was the first true prophet in 400 years. He denounced both Herod and the religious leaders, daring acts that fascinated the common people. But John also had strong words for his audience—they too were sinners and needed to repent. His message was powerful and true. The people were expecting a prophet like Elijah (Malachi 4:5; Luke 1:17), and John seemed to be the one!

3:6 When you wash dirty hands, the results are immediately visible. But repentance happens inside with a cleansing that isn't seen right away. So John used a symbolic action that people could see: baptism. The Jews used baptism to initiate converts, so John's audience was familiar with the rite. Here, baptism was used as a sign of repentance and forgiveness. *Repent* means "to turn", implying a change in behaviour. It is turning from sin towards God. Have you repented of sin in your life? Can others see the difference it makes in you? A changed life with new and different behaviour makes your repentance real and visible.

3:6 The Jordan River is about 70 miles long, its main section stretching between the Sea of Galilee and the Dead Sea. Jerusalem lies about 20 miles west of the Jordan. This river was Israel's eastern border, and many significant events in the nation's history took place there. It was by the Jordan River that the Israelites renewed their covenant with God before entering the promised land (Joshua 1; 2). Here John the Baptist calls them to renew their covenant with God again, this time through baptism.

can say to yourselves, 'We have Abraham as our father.' I tell you that out of these
stones God can raise up children for Abraham. 10The axe is already at the root of the

THE PHARISEES AND SADDUCEES

The Pharisees and Sadducees were the two major religious groups in Israel at the time of Christ. The Pharisees were more religiously minded, while the Sadducees were more politically minded. Although the groups disliked and distrusted each other, they became allies in their common hatred for Jesus.

Name	*Positive Characteristics*	*Negative Characteristics*
PHARISEES	• Were committed to obeying all of God's commands • Were admired by the common people for their apparent piety • Believed in a bodily resurrection and eternal life • Believed in angels and demons	• Behaved as though their own religious rules were just as important as God's rules for living • Their piety was often hypocritical and their efforts often forced others to try to live up to standards they themselves could not live up to • Believed that salvation came from perfect obedience to the law and was not based on forgiveness of sins • Became so obsessed with obeying their legal interpretations in every detail that they completely ignored God's message of mercy and grace • Were more concerned with appearing to be good than obeying God
SADDUCEES	• Believed strongly in the Mosaic law and in Levitical purity • Were more practically minded than the Pharisees	• Relied on logic while placing little importance on faith • Did not believe all the Old Testament was God's word • Did not believe in a bodily resurrection or eternal life • Did not believe in angels or demons • Were often willing to compromise their values with the Romans and others in order to maintain their status and influential positions

3:7 The Jewish religious leaders were divided into several groups. Two of the most prominent groups were the Pharisees and the Sadducees. The Pharisees separated themselves from anything non-Jewish and carefully followed both the Old Testament laws and the oral traditions handed down through the centuries. The Sadducees believed the Pentateuch alone (Genesis—Deuteronomy) to be God's word. They were descended mainly from priestly nobility, while the Pharisees came from all classes of people. The two groups disliked each other greatly, and both opposed Jesus. John the Baptist criticised the Pharisees for being legalistic and hypocritical, following the letter of the law while ignoring its true intent. He criticised the Sadducees for using religion to advance their political position. For more information on these two groups, see the chart in Mark 2.

3:8 John the Baptist called people to more than words or ritual; he told them to change their behaviour. "Produce fruit in keeping with repentance" means that God looks beyond our words and religious activities to see if our conduct backs up what we say, and he judges our words by the actions that accompany them. Do your actions match your words?

3:9, 10 Just as a fruit tree is expected to bear fruit, God's people should produce a crop of good deeds. God has no use for people who call themselves Christians but do nothing about it. Like many people in John's day who were God's people in name only, we are of no value if we are Christians in name only. If others can't see our faith in the way we treat them, we may not be God's people at all.

3:10 God's message hasn't changed since the Old Testament—people will be judged for their unproductive lives. God calls us to be *active* in our obedience. John compared people who claim they believe God but don't live for God to unproductive trees that will be cut down. To be productive for God, we must obey his teachings, resist temptation, actively serve and help others, and share our faith. How productive are you for God?

trees, and every tree that does not produce good fruit will be cut down and thrown
into the fire.[i]
11 "I baptise you with[b] water for repentance. But after me will come one who is
more powerful than I, whose sandals I am not fit to carry. He will baptise you with
the Holy Spirit[j] and with fire.[k] 12 His winnowing fork is in his hand, and he will
clear his threshing-floor, gathering his wheat into the barn and burning up the chaff
with unquenchable fire."[l]

John Baptises Jesus
(17/Mark 1:9–11; Luke 3:21, 22)

13 Then Jesus came from Galilee to the Jordan to be baptised by John.[m] 14 But John
tried to deter him, saying, "I need to be baptised by you, and do you come to me?"
15 Jesus replied, "Let it be so now; it is proper for us to do this to fulfil all
righteousness." Then John consented.
16 As soon as Jesus was baptised, he went up out of the water. At that moment
heaven was opened, and he saw the Spirit of God[n] descending like a dove and lighting
on him. 17 And a voice from heaven[o] said, "This is my Son,[p] whom I love; with
him I am well pleased."[q]

Satan Tempts Jesus in the Desert
(18/Mark 1:12, 13; Luke 4:1–13)

4 Then Jesus was led by the Spirit into the desert to be tempted by the devil. 2 After
fasting for forty days and forty nights,[a] he was hungry. 3 The tempter[b] came
to him and said, "If you are the Son of God,[c] tell these stones to become bread."

[b] *11* Or *in*

3:10 [i] Mt 7:19; Lk 13:6-9; Jn 15:2, 6
3:11 [j] Mk 1:8 [k] Isa 4:4; Ac 2:3, 4
3:12 [l] Mt 13:30
3:13 [m] Mk 1:4
3:16 [n] Isa 11:2; 42:1
3:17 [o] Mt 17:5; Jn 12:28 [p] Ps 2:7; 2Pe 1:17, 18 [q] Isa 42:1; Mt 12:18; 17:5; Mk 1:11; 9:7; Lk 9:35
4:2 [a] Ex 34:28; 1Ki 19:8
4:3 [b] 1Th 3:5 [c] Mt 3:17; Jn 5:25; Ac 9:20

3:11 John baptised people as a sign that they had asked God to forgive their sins and had decided to live as he wanted them to live. Baptism was an *outward* sign of commitment. To be effective, it had to be accompanied by an *inward* change of attitude leading to a changed life – the work of the Holy Spirit. John said that Jesus would baptise with the Holy Spirit and fire. This looked ahead to Pentecost (Acts 2), when the Holy Spirit would be sent by Jesus in the form of tongues of fire, empowering his followers to preach the gospel. John's statement also symbolises the work of the Holy Spirit in bringing God's judgment on those who refuse to repent. Everyone will one day be baptised – either now by God's Holy Spirit, or later by the fire of his judgment.

3:12 A winnowing fork is a pitchfork used to toss wheat in the air to separate wheat from chaff. The wheat is the part of the plant that is useful; chaff is the worthless outer shell. Because it is useless, chaff is burned; wheat, however, is gathered. "Winnowing" is often used as a picture of God's judgment. Unrepentant people will be judged and discarded because they are worthless in doing God's work; those who repent and believe will be saved and used by God.

3:13–15 John had been explaining that Jesus' baptism would be much greater than his, when suddenly Jesus came to him and asked to be baptised! John felt unqualified. He wanted Jesus to baptise him. Why did Jesus ask to be baptised? It was not for repentance for sin because Jesus never sinned. "To fulfil all righteousness" means to accomplish God's mission. Jesus saw his baptism as advancing God's work. Jesus was baptised because (1) he was confessing sin on behalf of the nation, as Nehemiah, Ezra, Moses, and Daniel had done; (2) he was showing support for what John was doing; (3) he was inaugurating his public ministry; (4) he was identifying with the penitent people of God, not with the critical Pharisees who were only watching. Jesus, the perfect man, didn't need baptism for sin, but he accepted baptism in obedient service to the Father, and God showed his approval.

3:15 Put yourself in John's shoes. Your work is going well, people are taking notice, everything is growing. But you know that the purpose of your work is to prepare the people for Jesus (John 1:35–37). Then Jesus arrives, and his coming tests your integrity. Will you be able to turn your followers over to him? John passed the test by publicly baptising Jesus. Soon he would say, "He must become greater; I must become less" (John 3:30). Can we, like John, put our egos and profitable work aside in order to point others to Jesus? Are we willing to lose some of our status so that everyone will benefit?

3:16, 17 The doctrine of the Trinity means that God is three persons and yet one in essence. In this passage, all three persons of the Trinity are present and active. God the Father speaks; God the Son is baptised; God the Holy Spirit descends on Jesus. God is one, yet in three persons at the same time. This is one of God's incomprehensible mysteries. Other Bible references that speak of the Father, Son, and Holy Spirit are Matthew 28:19; John 15:26; 1 Corinthians 12:4–13; 2 Corinthians 13:14; Ephesians 2:18; 1 Thessalonians 1:2–5; and 1 Peter 1:2.

4:1 This time of testing showed that Jesus really was the Son of God, able to overcome the devil and his temptations. A person has not shown true obedience if he or she has never had an opportunity to disobey. We read in Deuteronomy 8:2 that God led Israel into the desert to humble and test them. God wanted to see whether or not his people would really obey him. We too will be tested. Because we know that testing will come, we should be alert and ready for it. Remember, your convictions are only strong if they hold up under pressure!

4:1 The devil, also called Satan, tempted Eve in the Garden of Eden, and here he tempted Jesus in the desert. Satan is a fallen angel. He is *real,* not symbolic, and is constantly fighting against those who follow and obey God. Satan's temptations are real, and he is always trying to get us to live his way or our way rather than God's way. Jesus will one day reign over all creation, but Satan tried to force his hand and get him to declare his kingship prematurely. If Jesus had given in, his mission on earth – to die for our sins and give us the opportunity to have eternal life – would have been lost. When temptations seem especially strong, or when you think you can rationalise giving in, consider whether Satan may be

4:4 [d]Dt 8:3
4:5 [e]Ne 11:1; Da 9:24; Mt 27:53

4Jesus answered, "It is written: 'Man does not live on bread alone, but on every
word that comes from the mouth of God.'[a]"[d]
5Then the devil took him to the holy city[e] and had him stand on the highest point

a *4* Deut. 8:3

THE TEMPTATIONS

Temptation	*Real needs used as basis for temptation*	*Possible doubts that made the temptations real*	*Potential weaknesses Satan sought to exploit*	*Jesus' answer*
Make bread	Physical need: Hunger	Would God provide food?	Hunger, impatience, need to "prove his Sonship"	Deuteronomy 8:3 "Depend on God" Focus: God's purpose
Dare God to rescue you (based on misapplied Scripture, Psalm 91:11, 12)	Emotional need: Security	Would God protect?	Pride, insecurity, need to test God	Deuteronomy 6:16 "Don't test God" Focus: God's plan
Worship me! (Satan)	Psychological need: Significance, power, achievement	Would God rule?	Desire for quick power, easy solutions, need to prove equality with God	Deuteronomy 6:13 "No compromise with evil" Focus: God's person

As if going through a final test of preparation, Jesus was tempted by Satan in the desert. Three specific parts of the temptation are listed by Matthew. They are familiar because we face the same kinds of temptations. As the chart shows, temptation is often the combination of a real need and a possible doubt that creates an inappropriate desire. Jesus demonstrates both the importance and effectiveness of knowing and applying Scripture to combat temptation.

trying to block God's purposes for your life or for someone else's life.

4:1ff This temptation by the devil shows us that Jesus was human, and it gave Jesus the opportunity to reaffirm God's plan for his ministry. It also gives us an example to follow when we are tempted. Jesus' temptation was an important demonstration of his sinlessness. He would face temptation and not give in.

4:1ff Jesus was tempted by the devil, but he never sinned! Although we may feel dirty after being tempted, we should remember that temptation itself is not sin. We sin when we give in and disobey God. Remembering this will help us turn away from the temptation.

4:1ff Jesus wasn't tempted inside the temple or at his baptism but in the desert where he was tired, alone, and hungry, and thus most vulnerable. The devil often tempts us when we are vulnerable—when we are under physical or emotional stress (for example, lonely, tired, weighing big decisions, or faced with uncertainty). But he also likes to tempt us through our strengths, where we are most susceptible to pride (see the note on Luke 4:3ff). We must guard at all times against his attacks.

4:1–10 The devil's temptations focused on three crucial areas: (1) physical needs and desires, (2) possessions and power, and (3) pride (see 1 John 2:15, 16 for a similar list). But Jesus did not give in. Hebrews 4:15 says that Jesus "has been tempted in every way, just as we are—yet was without sin". He knows firsthand what we are experiencing, and he is willing and able to help us in our struggles. When you are tempted, turn to him for strength.

4:3, 4 Jesus was hungry and weak after fasting for 40 days, but he chose not to use his divine power to satisfy his natural desire for food. Food, hunger, and eating are good, but the timing was wrong. Jesus was in the desert to fast, not to eat. And because Jesus had given up the unlimited, independent use of his divine power in order to experience humanity fully, he wouldn't use his power to change the stones to bread. We too may be tempted to satisfy a perfectly normal desire in a wrong way or at the wrong time. If we indulge in sex before marriage or if we steal to get food, we are trying to satisfy God-given desires in wrong ways. Remember, many of your desires are normal and good, but God wants you to satisfy them in the right way and at the right time.

4:3, 4 Jesus was able to resist all of the devil's temptations because he not only knew Scripture, but he also obeyed it. Ephesians 6:17 says that God's word is a sword to use in spiritual combat. Knowing Bible verses is an important step in helping us resist the devil's attacks, but we must also obey the Bible. Note that Satan had memorised Scripture, but he failed to obey it. Knowing and obeying the Bible helps us follow God's desires rather than the devil's.

4:5 The temple was the religious centre of the Jewish nation and the place where the people expected the Messiah to arrive (Malachi 3:1). Herod the Great had renovated the temple in hopes of gaining the Jews' confidence. The temple was the tallest building in the area, and this "highest point" was probably the corner wall that jutted out of the hillside, overlooking the valley below. From this spot, Jesus could see all of Jerusalem behind him and the country for miles in front of him.

4:5–7 God is not our magician in the sky ready to perform on request. In response to Satan's temptations, Jesus said not to put God to the test (Deuteronomy 6:16). You may want to ask God to do something to prove his existence or his love for you. Jesus once taught through a parable that people who don't believe what is written in the Bible won't believe even if someone were to come back from the dead to warn them (Luke 16:31)! God wants us to live by faith, not by magic. Don't try to manipulate God by asking for signs.

of the temple. [6]"If you are the Son of God," he said, "throw yourself down. For it
is written:

" 'He will command his angels concerning you,
and they will lift you up in their hands,
so that you will not strike your foot against a stone.'[b]"[f]

[7]Jesus answered him, "It is also written: 'Do not put the Lord your God to the
test.'[c]"[g]
[8]Again, the devil took him to a very high mountain and showed him all the
kingdoms of the world and their splendour. [9]"All this I will give you," he said, "if
you will bow down and worship me."
[10]Jesus said to him, "Away from me, Satan![h] For it is written: 'Worship the Lord
your God, and serve him only.'[d]"[i]
[11]Then the devil left him, and angels came and attended him.[j]

B. MESSAGE AND MINISTRY OF JESUS, THE KING (4:12—25:46)

Matthew features Jesus' sermons. The record of Jesus' actions is woven around great passages of his teaching. This section of Matthew, then, is topical rather than chronological. Matthew records for us the Sermon on the Mount, the parables of the kingdom, Jesus' teachings on forgiveness, and parables about the end of the age.

1. Jesus begins his ministry

Jesus Preaches in Galilee

(30/Mark 1:14, 15; Luke 4:14, 15; John 4:43–45)

[12]When Jesus heard that John had been put in prison,[k] he returned to Galilee.[l]
[13]Leaving Nazareth, he went and lived in Capernaum,[m] which was by the lake in the
area of Zebulun and Naphtali—[14]to fulfil what was said through the prophet Isaiah:

[15]"Land of Zebulun and land of Naphtali,
the way to the sea, along the Jordan,
Galilee of the Gentiles—
[16]the people living in darkness
have seen a great light;
on those living in the land of the shadow of death
a light has dawned."[e][n]

[b] *6* Psalm 91:11,12 [c] *7* Deut. 6:16 [d] *10* Deut. 6:13 [e] *16* Isaiah 9:1,2

4:6 [f]Ps 91:11, 12
4:7 [g]Dt 6:16
4:10 [h]1Ch 21:1 [i]Dt 6:13
4:11 [j]Mt 26:53; Lk 22:43; Heb 1:14
4:12 [k]Mt 14:3 [l]Mk 1:14
4:13 [m]Mk 1:21; Lk 4:23, 31; Jn 2:12; 4:46, 47
4:16 [n]Isa 9:1, 2; Lk 2:32

4:6 The devil used Scripture to try to convince Jesus to sin! Sometimes friends or colleagues will present attractive and convincing reasons why you should try something you know is wrong. They may even find Bible verses that *seem* to support their viewpoint. Study the Bible carefully, especially the broader contexts of specific verses, so that you understand God's principles for living and what he wants for your life. Only if you really understand what the *whole* Bible says will you be able to recognise errors of interpretation when people take verses out of context and twist them to say what they want them to say.

4:8, 9 Did the devil have the power to give Jesus the kingdoms of the world? Didn't God, the Creator of the world, have control over these kingdoms? The devil may have been lying about his implied power, or he may have based his offer on his temporary control and free rein over the earth because of humanity's sinfulness. Jesus' temptation was to take the world as a political ruler right then, without carrying out his plan to save the world from sin. Satan was trying to distort Jesus' perspective by making him focus on worldly power and not on God's plans.

4:8–10 The devil offered the whole world to Jesus if Jesus would only bow down and worship him. Today the devil offers us the world by trying to entice us with materialism and power. We can resist temptations the same way Jesus did. If you find yourself craving something that the world offers, quote Jesus' words to the devil: "Worship the Lord your God, and serve him only."

4:11 Angels, like these who waited on Jesus, have a significant role as God's messengers. These spiritual beings were involved in Jesus' life on earth by (1) announcing Jesus' birth to Mary, (2) reassuring Joseph, (3) naming Jesus, (4) announcing Jesus' birth to the shepherds, (5) protecting Jesus by sending his family to Egypt, (6) ministering to Jesus in Gethsemane. For more on angels, see the note on 1:20.

4:12, 13 Jesus moved from Nazareth, his home town, to Capernaum, about 20 miles further north. Capernaum became Jesus' home base during his ministry in Galilee. Jesus probably moved (1) to get away from intense opposition in Nazareth, (2) to have an impact on the greatest number of people (Capernaum was a busy city and Jesus' message could reach more people and spread more quickly), and (3) to utilise extra resources and support for his ministry.

Jesus' move fulfilled the prophecy of Isaiah 9:1, 2, which states that the Messiah will be a light to the land of Zebulun and Naphtali, the region of Galilee where Capernaum was located. Zebulun and Naphtali were two of the original 12 tribes of Israel.

4:14–16 By quoting from the book of Isaiah, Matthew continues to tie Jesus' ministry to the Old Testament. This was helpful for his Jewish readers, who were familiar with these Scriptures. In addition, it shows the unity of God's purposes as he works with his people throughout all ages.

4:17
[o]Mt 3:2

4:18
[p]Mt 15:29; Mk 7:31; Jn 6:1
[q]Mt 16:17, 18

4:19
[r]Mk 10:21, 28, 52

4:21
[s]Mt 20:20

4:23
[t]Mk 1:39; Lk 4:15, 44
[u]Mt 9:35; 13:54; Mk 1:21; Lk 4:15; Jn 6:59
[v]Mk 1:14
[w]Mt 3:2; Ac 20:25
[x]Mt 8:16; 15:30; Ac 10:38

4:24
[y]Lk 2:2
[z]Mt 8:16, 28; 9:32; 15:22; Mk 1:32; 5:15, 16, 18
[a]Mt 17:15
[b]Mt 8:6; 9:2; Mk 2:3

4:25
[c]Mk 3:7, 8; Lk 6:17

17 From that time on Jesus began to preach, "Repent, for the kingdom of heaven[o]
is near."

Four Fishermen Follow Jesus
(33/Mark 1:16–20)

18 As Jesus was walking beside the Sea of Galilee,[p] he saw two brothers, Simon
called Peter[q] and his brother Andrew. They were casting a net into the lake, for they
were fishermen. 19 "Come, follow me,"[r] Jesus said, "and I will make you fishers of
men." 20 At once they left their nets and followed him.
21 Going on from there, he saw two other brothers, James son of Zebedee and his
brother John.[s] They were in a boat with their father Zebedee, preparing their nets.
Jesus called them, 22 and immediately they left the boat and their father and followed
him.

Jesus Preaches throughout Galilee
(36/Mark 1:35–39; Luke 4:42–44)

23 Jesus went throughout Galilee,[t] teaching in their synagogues,[u] preaching the
good news[v] of the kingdom,[w] and healing every disease and sickness among the
people.[x] 24 News about him spread all over Syria,[y] and people brought to him all
who were ill with various diseases, those suffering severe pain, the demon-
possessed,[z] those having seizures,[a] and the paralysed,[b] and he healed them.
25 Large crowds from Galilee, the Decapolis,[f] Jerusalem, Judea and the region across
the Jordan followed him.[c]

[f] *25* That is, the Ten Cities

4:17 The "kingdom of heaven" has the same meaning as the "kingdom of God" in Mark and Luke. Matthew uses this phrase because the Jews, out of their intense reverence and respect, did not pronounce God's name. The kingdom of heaven is still near because it has arrived in our hearts. See the note on 3:2 for more on the kingdom of heaven.

4:17 Jesus started his ministry with the very word people had heard John the Baptist say: "Repent". The message is the same today as when Jesus and John gave it. Becoming a follower of Christ means turning away from our self-centredness and "self" control and turning our lives over to Christ's direction and control.

4:18 The Sea of Galilee is really a large lake. About 30 fishing towns surrounded it during Jesus' day, and Capernaum was the largest.

4:18–20 Jesus told Peter and Andrew to leave their fishing business and become "fishers of men", to help others find God. Jesus was calling them away from their productive trades to be productive spiritually. We all need to fish for souls. If we practise Christ's teachings and share the gospel with others, we will be able to draw those around us to Christ like a fisherman who pulls fish into his boat with nets.

4:19, 20 These men already knew Jesus. He had talked to Peter and Andrew previously (John 1:35–42) and had been preaching in the area. When Jesus called them, they knew what kind of man he was and were willing to follow him. They were not in a hypnotic trance when they followed but had been thoroughly convinced that following him would change their lives for ever.

4:21, 22 James and his brother, John, along with Peter and Andrew, were the first disciples that Jesus called to work with him. Jesus' call motivated these men to get up and leave their jobs immediately. They didn't make excuses about why it wasn't a good time. They left at once and followed. Jesus calls each of us to follow him. When Jesus asks us to serve him, we must be like the disciples and do it at once.

4:23 Jesus was teaching, preaching, and healing. These were the three main aspects of his ministry. *Teaching* shows Jesus' concern for understanding; *preaching* shows his concern for commitment; and *healing* shows his concern for wholeness. His miracles of healing authenticated his teaching and preaching, proving that he truly was from God.

4:23 Jesus soon developed a powerful preaching ministry and often spoke in the synagogues. Most towns that had ten or more Jewish families had a synagogue. The building served as a religious gathering place on the Sabbath and as a school during the week. The leader of the synagogue was not a preacher as much as an administrator. His job was to find and invite rabbis to teach and preach. It was customary to invite visiting rabbis like Jesus to speak.

4:23, 24 Jesus preached the gospel – the Good News – to everyone who wanted to hear it. The gospel is that the kingdom of heaven has come, that God is with us, and that he cares for us. Christ can heal us, not just of physical sickness, but of spiritual sickness as well. There's no sin or problem too great or too small for him to handle. Jesus' words were good news because they offered freedom, hope, peace of heart, and eternal life with God.

4:25 Decapolis was a group of ten Gentile cities east of the Sea of Galilee, joined together for better trade and mutual defence. The word about Jesus was out, and Jews and Gentiles were coming long distances to hear him.

2. Jesus gives the Sermon on the Mount

Jesus Gives the Beatitudes
(49/Luke 6:17–26)

5 Now when he saw the crowds, he went up on a mountainside and sat down. His
disciples came to him, 2and he began to teach them, saying:

3"Blessed are the poor in spirit,
for theirs is the kingdom of heaven.[a]
4Blessed are those who mourn,
for they will be comforted.[b]
5Blessed are the meek,
for they will inherit the earth.[c]
6Blessed are those who hunger and thirst for righteousness,
for they will be filled.[d]
7Blessed are the merciful,
for they will be shown mercy.
8Blessed are the pure in heart,[e]
for they will see God.[f]
9Blessed are the peacemakers,
for they will be called sons of God.[g]
10Blessed are those who are persecuted because of righteousness,[h]
for theirs is the kingdom of heaven.

11"Blessed are you when people insult you,[i] persecute you and falsely say all kinds
of evil against you because of me. 12Rejoice and be glad,[j] because great is your
reward in heaven, for in the same way they persecuted the prophets who were before
you.[k]

5:3 [a]ver 10, 19; Mt 25:34
5:4 [b]Isa 61:2, 3; Rev 7:17
5:5 [c]Ps 37:11; Ro 4:13
5:6 [d]Isa 55:1, 2
5:8 [e]Ps 24:3, 4 [f]Heb 12:14; Rev 22:4
5:9 [g]ver 44, 45; Ro 8:14
5:10 [h]1Pe 3:14
5:11 [i]1Pe 4:14
5:12 [j]Ac 5:41; 1Pe 4:13, 16 [k]Mt 23:31, 37; Ac 7:52; 1Th 2:15

5:1ff Matthew 5–7 is called the Sermon on the Mount because Jesus gave it on a hillside near Capernaum. This "sermon" probably covered several days of preaching. In it, Jesus proclaimed his attitude towards the law. Position, authority, and money are not important in his kingdom – what matters is faithful obedience from the heart. The Sermon on the Mount challenged the proud and legalistic religious leaders of the day. It called them back to the messages of the Old Testament prophets who, like Jesus, taught that heartfelt obedience is more important than legalistic observance.

5:1, 2 Enormous crowds were following Jesus – he was the talk of the town, and everyone wanted to see him. The disciples, who were the closest associates of this popular man, were certainly tempted to feel important, proud, and possessive. Being with Jesus gave them not only prestige, but also opportunity for receiving money and power.

The crowds were gathering once again. But before speaking to them, Jesus pulled his disciples aside and warned them about the temptations they would face as his followers. Don't expect fame and fortune, Jesus was saying, but mourning, hunger, and persecution. Nevertheless, Jesus assured his disciples, they would be rewarded – but perhaps not in this life. There may be times when following Jesus will bring us great popularity. If we don't live by Jesus' words in this sermon, we will find ourselves using God's message only to promote our personal interests.

5:3–5 Jesus began his sermon with words that seem to contradict each other. But God's way of living usually contradicts the world's. If you want to live for God you must be ready to say and do what seems strange to the world. You must be willing to give when others take, to love when others hate, to help when others abuse. By giving up your own rights in order to serve others, you will one day receive everything God has in store for you.

5:3–12 There are at least four ways to understand the Beatitudes. (1) They are a code of ethics for the disciples and a standard of conduct for all believers. (2) They contrast kingdom values (what is eternal) with worldly values (what is temporary). (3) They contrast the superficial "faith" of the Pharisees with the real faith Christ wants. (4) They show how the Old Testament expectations will be fulfilled in the new kingdom. These beatitudes are not multiple choice – pick what you like and leave the rest. They must be taken as a whole. They describe what we should be like as Christ's followers.

5:3–12 Each beatitude tells how to be *blessed.* "Blessed" means more than happiness. It implies the fortunate or enviable state of those who are in God's kingdom. The Beatitudes don't promise laughter, pleasure, or earthly prosperity. To Jesus, "blessed" means the experience of hope and joy, independent of outward circumstances. To find hope and joy, the deepest form of happiness, follow Jesus no matter what the cost.

5:3–12 With Jesus' announcement that the kingdom was near (4:17), people were naturally asking, "How do I qualify to be in God's kingdom?" Jesus said that God's kingdom is organised differently from worldly kingdoms. In the kingdom of heaven, wealth and power and authority are unimportant. Kingdom people seek different blessings and benefits, and they have different attitudes. Are your attitudes a carbon copy of the world's selfishness, pride, and lust for power, or do they reflect the humility and self-sacrifice of Jesus, your King?

5:11, 12 Jesus said to rejoice when we're persecuted. Persecution can be good because (1) it takes our eyes off earthly rewards, (2) it strips away superficial belief, (3) it strengthens the faith of those who endure, and (4) our attitude through it serves as an example to others who follow. We can be comforted to know that God's greatest prophets were persecuted (Elijah, Jeremiah, Daniel). The fact that we are being persecuted proves that we have been faithful; faithless people would be unnoticed. In the future God will reward the faithful by receiving them into his eternal kingdom where there is no more persecution.

5:13 [l]Mk 9:50; Lk 14:34, 35

5:14 [m]Jn 8:12

5:15 [n]Mk 4:21; Lk 8:16

5:16 [o]Mt 9:8

Jesus Teaches about Salt and Light
(50)

13"You are the salt of the earth. But if the salt loses its saltiness, how can it be made
salty again? It is no longer good for anything, except to be thrown out and trampled
by men.[l]
14"You are the light of the world.[m] A city on a hill cannot be hidden. 15Neither
do people light a lamp and put it under a bowl. Instead they put it on its stand, and
it gives light to everyone in the house.[n] 16In the same way, let your light shine before
men, that they may see your good deeds and praise[o] your Father in heaven.

KEY LESSONS FROM THE SERMON ON THE MOUNT

Beatitude	*Old Testament anticipation*	*Clashing worldly values*	*God's reward*	*How to develop this attitude*
Poor in spirit (5:3)	Isaiah 57:15	Pride and personal independence	Kingdom of heaven	James 4:7–10
Mourning (5:4)	Isaiah 61:1, 2	Happiness at any cost	Comfort (2 Corinthians 1:4)	Psalm 51 James 4:7–10
Meekness (5:5)	Psalm 37:5–11	Power	Inherit the earth	Matthew 11:27–30
Righteousness (5:6)	Isaiah 11:4, 5; 42:1–4	Pursuing personal needs	Filled (satisfied)	John 16:5–11 Philippians 3:7–11
Mercy (5:7)	Psalm 41:1	Strength without feeling	Be shown mercy	Ephesians 5:1, 2
Pure in heart (5:8)	Psalm 24:3, 4; 51:10	Deception is acceptable	See God	1 John 3:1–3
Peacemaker (5:9)	Isaiah 57:18, 19; 60:17	Personal peace is pursued without concern for the world's chaos	Be called sons of God	Romans 12:9–21 Hebrews 12:10, 11
Persecuted (5:10)	Isaiah 52:13; 53:12	Weak commitments	Inherit the kingdom of heaven	2 Timothy 3:12

In his longest recorded sermon, Jesus began by describing the traits he was looking for in his followers. He called those who developed those traits blessed because God had something special in store for them. Each beatitude is an almost direct contradiction of society's typical way of life. In the last beatitude, Jesus even points out that a serious effort to develop these traits is bound to create opposition. The best example of each trait is found in Jesus himself. If our goal is to become like him, the Beatitudes will challenge the way we live each day.

5:13 If a seasoning has no flavour, it has no value. If Christians make no effort to affect the world around them, they are of little value to God. If we are too much like the world, we are worthless. Christians should not blend in with everyone else. Instead, we should affect others positively, just as seasoning brings out the best flavour in food.

5:14–16 Can you hide a city that is sitting on top of a hill? Its light at night can be seen for miles. If we live for Christ, we will glow like lights, showing others what Christ is like. We hide our light by (1) being quiet when we should speak, (2) going along with the crowd, (3) denying the light, (4) letting sin dim our light, (5) not explaining our light to others, or (6) ignoring the needs of others. Be a beacon of truth – don't shut your light off from the rest of the world.

Jesus Teaches about the Law
(51)

17 "Do not think that I have come to abolish the Law or the Prophets; I have not
come to abolish them but to fulfil them.[p] 18 I tell you the truth, until heaven and earth
disappear, not the smallest letter, not the least stroke of a pen, will by any means
disappear from the Law until everything is accomplished.[q] 19 Anyone who breaks one
of the least of these commandments[r] and teaches others to do the same will be called
least in the kingdom of heaven, but whoever practises and teaches these commands
will be called great in the kingdom of heaven. 20 For I tell you that unless your
righteousness surpasses that of the Pharisees and the teachers of the law, you will
certainly not enter the kingdom of heaven.

Jesus Teaches about Anger
(52)

21 "You have heard that it was said to the people long ago, 'Do not murder,[a][s] and
anyone who murders will be subject to judgment.' 22 But I tell you that anyone who
is angry with his brother[b] will be subject to judgment.[t] Again, anyone who says
to his brother, 'Raca,'[c] is answerable to the Sanhedrin.[u] But anyone who says, 'You
fool!' will be in danger of the fire of hell.[v]
23 "Therefore, if you are offering your gift at the altar and there remember that your

[a] 21 Exodus 20:13 [b] 22 Some manuscripts *brother without cause* [c] 22 An Aramaic term of contempt

5:17 [p] Ro 3:31
5:18 [q] Lk 16:17
5:19 [r] Jas 2:10
5:21 [s] Ex 20:13; Dt 5:17
5:22 [t] 1Jn 3:15 [u] Mt 26:59 [v] Jas 3:6

5:17 God's moral and ceremonial laws were given to help people love God with all their hearts and minds. Throughout Israel's history, however, these laws had often been misquoted and misapplied. By Jesus' time, religious leaders had turned the laws into a confusing mass of rules. When Jesus talked about a new way to understand God's law, he was actually trying to bring people back to its *original* purpose. Jesus did not speak against the law itself, but against the abuses and excesses to which it had been subjected. (See John 1:17.)

5:17–20 If Jesus did not come to abolish the law, does that mean all the Old Testament laws still apply to us today? In the Old Testament, there were three categories of law: ceremonial, civil, and moral.

(1) The *ceremonial law* related specifically to Israel's worship (see Leviticus 1:2, 3, for example). Its primary purpose was to point forward to Jesus Christ; these laws, therefore, were no longer necessary after Jesus' death and resurrection. While we are no longer bound by ceremonial laws, the principles behind them – to worship and love a holy God – still apply. Jesus was often accused by the Pharisees of violating ceremonial law.

(2) The *civil law* applied to daily living in Israel (see Deuteronomy 24:10, 11, for example). Because modern society and culture are so radically different from that time and setting, these guidelines cannot all be followed specifically. But the principles behind the commands are timeless and should guide our conduct. Jesus demonstrated these principles by example.

(3) The *moral law* (such as the Ten Commandments) is the direct command of God, and it requires strict obedience (see Exodus 20:13, for example). The moral law reveals the nature and will of God, and it still applies today. Jesus obeyed the moral law completely.

5:19 Some of those in the crowd were experts at telling others what to do, but they missed the central point of God's laws themselves. Jesus made it clear, however, that obeying God's law is more important than explaining it. It's much easier to study God's laws and tell others to obey them than to put them into practice. How are you doing at obeying God *yourself?*

5:20 The Pharisees were exacting and scrupulous in their attempts to follow their laws. So how could Jesus reasonably call us to a greater righteousness than theirs? The Pharisees' weakness was that they were content to obey the laws outwardly without allowing God to change their hearts (or attitudes). Jesus was saying, therefore, that the *quality* of our goodness should be greater than that of the Pharisees. They looked pious, but they were far from the kingdom of God. God judges our hearts as well as our deeds, for it is in the heart that our real allegiance lies. Be just as concerned about your attitudes that people don't see as about your actions that are seen by all.

5:20 Jesus was saying that his listeners needed a different kind of righteousness altogether (love and obedience), not just a more intense version of the Pharisees' righteousness (legal compliance). Our righteousness must (1) come from what God does in us, not what we can do by ourselves, (2) be God-centred, not self-centred, (3) be based on reverence for God, not approval from people, and (4) go beyond keeping the law to living by the principles behind the law.

5:21, 22 When Jesus said, "But I tell you," he was not doing away with the law or adding his own beliefs. Rather, he was giving a fuller understanding of why God made that law in the first place. For example, Moses said, "You shall not murder" (Exodus 20:13); Jesus taught that we should not even become angry enough to murder, for then we have already committed murder in our heart. The Pharisees read this law and, not having literally murdered anyone, felt righteous. Yet they were angry enough with Jesus that they would soon plot his death, though they would not do the dirty work themselves. We miss the intent of God's word when we read his rules for living without trying to understand why he made them. When do you keep God's rules but close your eyes to his intent?

5:21, 22 Killing is a terrible sin, but *anger* is a great sin too because it also violates God's command to love. Anger in this case refers to a seething, brooding bitterness against someone. It is a dangerous emotion that always threatens to leap out of control, leading to violence, emotional hurt, increased mental stress, and spiritual damage. Anger keeps us from developing a spirit pleasing to God. Have you ever been proud that you didn't strike out and say what was really on your mind? Self-control is good, but Christ wants us to practise thought-control as well. Jesus said that we will be held accountable even for our attitudes.

5:23, 24 Broken relationships can hinder our relationship with God. If we have a problem or grievance with a friend, we should resolve the problem as soon as possible. We are hypocrites if we claim to love God while we hate others. Our attitudes towards others reflect our relationship with God (1 John 4:20).

5:27 [w]Ex 20:14; Dt 5:18
5:28 [x]Pr 6:25
5:29 [y]Mt 18:6, 8, 9; Mk 9:42-47

brother has something against you, [24]leave your gift there in front of the altar. First
go and be reconciled to your brother; then come and offer your gift.
[25]"Settle matters quickly with your adversary who is taking you to court. Do it while
you are still with him on the way, or he may hand you over to the judge, and the judge
may hand you over to the officer, and you may be thrown into prison. [26]I tell you
the truth, you will not get out until you have paid the last penny.[d]

Jesus Teaches about Lust
(53)

[27]"You have heard that it was said, 'Do not commit adultery.'[e][w] [28]But I tell you
that anyone who looks at a woman lustfully has already committed adultery with her
in his heart.[x] [29]If your right eye causes you to sin,[y] gouge it out and throw it away.
It is better for you to lose one part of your body than for your whole body to be thrown
into hell. [30]And if your right hand causes you to sin, cut it off and throw it away.
It is better for you to lose one part of your body than for your whole body to go into
hell.

[d] *26* Greek *kodrantes* [e] *27* Exodus 20:14

SIX WAYS TO THINK LIKE CHRIST

Reference	*Example*	*It's not enough to:*	*We must also:*
5:21, 22	Murder	Avoid killing	Avoid anger and hatred
5:23–26	Offerings	Offer regular gifts	Have right relationships with God and others
5:27–30	Adultery	Avoid adultery	Keep our hearts from lusting and be faithful
5:31, 32	Divorce	Be legally married	Live out our marriage commitments
5:33–37	Oaths	Make an oath	Avoid casual and irresponsible commitments to God
5:38–47	Revenge	Seek justice for ourselves	Show mercy and love to others

We are, more often than not, guilty of avoiding the extreme sins while regularly committing the types of sins with which Jesus was most concerned. In these six examples, our real struggle with sin is exposed. Jesus pointed out what kind of lives would be required of his followers. Are you living as Jesus taught?

5:25, 26 In Jesus' day, someone who couldn't pay a debt was thrown into prison until the debt was paid. Unless someone came to pay the debt for the prisoner, he or she would probably die there. It is practical advice to resolve our differences with our enemies before their anger causes more trouble (Proverbs 25:8–10). You may not get into a disagreement that takes you to court, but even small conflicts mend more easily if you try to make peace right away. In a broader sense, these verses advise us to get things right with our brothers and sisters before we have to stand before God.

5:27, 28 The Old Testament law said that it is wrong for a person to have sex with someone other than his or her spouse (Exodus 20:14). But Jesus said that the *desire* to have sex with someone other than your spouse is mental adultery and thus sin. Jesus emphasised that if the *act* is wrong, then so is the *intention.* To be faithful to your spouse with your body but not your mind is to break the trust so vital to a strong marriage. Jesus is not condemning natural interest in the opposite sex or even healthy sexual desire, but the deliberate and repeated filling of one's mind with fantasies that would be evil if acted out.

5:27, 28 Some think that if lustful thoughts are sin, why shouldn't a person go ahead and do the lustful actions too? Acting out sinful desires is harmful in several ways: (1) it causes people to excuse sin rather than to stop sinning; (2) it destroys marriages; (3) it is deliberate rebellion against God's word; (4) it always hurts someone else in addition to the sinner. Sinful action is more dangerous than sinful desire, and that is why desires should not be acted out. Nevertheless, sinful desire is just as damaging to righteousness. Left unchecked, wrong desires will result in wrong actions and turn people away from God.

5:29, 30 When Jesus said to get rid of your hand or your eye, he was speaking figuratively. He didn't mean literally to gouge out your eye, because even a blind person can lust. But if that were the only choice, it would be better to go into heaven with one eye or hand than to go to hell with two. We sometimes tolerate sins in our lives that, left unchecked, could eventually destroy us. It is better to experience the pain of removal (getting rid of a bad habit or something we treasure, for instance) than to allow the sin to bring judgment and condemnation. Examine your life for anything that causes you to sin, and take every necessary action to remove it.

Jesus Teaches about Divorce
(54)

31 "It has been said, 'Anyone who divorces his wife must give her a certificate of
divorce.'[f][z] 32 But I tell you that anyone who divorces his wife, except for marital
unfaithfulness, causes her to become an adulteress, and anyone who marries the
divorced woman commits adultery.[a]

Jesus Teaches about Vows
(55)

33 "Again, you have heard that it was said to the people long ago, 'Do not break
your oath,[b] but keep the oaths you have made to the Lord.'[c] 34 But I tell you, Do
not swear at all:[d] either by heaven, for it is God's throne;[e] 35 or by the earth, for
it is his footstool; or by Jerusalem, for it is the city of the Great King.[f] 36 And do
not swear by your head, for you cannot make even one hair white or black. 37 Simply
let your 'Yes' be 'Yes', and your 'No', 'No';[g] anything beyond this comes from the
evil one.[h]

Jesus Teaches about Retaliation
(56)

38 "You have heard that it was said, 'Eye for eye, and tooth for tooth.'[g][i] 39 But
I tell you, Do not resist an evil person. If someone strikes you on the right cheek,
turn to him the other also.[j] 40 And if someone wants to sue you and take your tunic,
let him have your cloak as well. 41 If someone forces you to go one mile, go with him
two miles. 42 Give to the one who asks you, and do not turn away from the one who
wants to borrow from you.[k]

Jesus Teaches about Loving Enemies
(57/Luke 6:27–36)

43 "You have heard that it was said, 'Love your neighbour[h][l] and hate your
enemy.'[m] 44 But I tell you: Love your enemies[i] and pray for those who persecute

[f] *31* Deut. 24:1 [g] *38* Exodus 21:24; Lev. 24:20 and Deut. 19:21 [h] *43* Lev. 19:18 [i] *44* Some late manuscripts *enemies, bless those who curse you, do good to those who hate you*

5:31 [z]Dt 24:1-4
5:32 [a]Lk 16:18
5:33 [b]Lev 19:12 [c]Nu 30:2; Dt 23:21; Mt 23:16-22
5:34 [d]Jas 5:12 [e]Isa 66:1; Mt 23:22
5:35 [f]Ps 48:2
5:37 [g]Jas 5:12 [h]Mt 6:13; 13:19, 38; Jn 17:15; 2Th 3:3; 1Jn 2:13, 14; 3:12; 5:18, 19
5:38 [i]Ex 21:24; Lev 24:20; Dt 19:21
5:39 [j]Lk 6:29; Ro 12:17, 19; 1Co 6:7; 1Pe 3:9
5:42 [k]Dt 15:8; Lk 6:30
5:43 [l]Lev 19:18 [m]Dt 23:6

5:31, 32 Divorce is as hurtful and destructive today as in Jesus' day. God intends marriage to be a lifetime commitment (Genesis 2:24). When entering into marriage, people should never consider divorce an option for solving problems or a way out of a relationship that seems dead. In these verses, Jesus is also attacking those who purposefully abuse the marriage contract, using divorce to satisfy their lustful desire to marry someone else. Are your actions today helping your marriage grow stronger, or are you tearing it apart?

5:32 Jesus said that divorce is not permissible except for unfaithfulness. This does not mean that divorce should automatically occur when a spouse commits adultery. The word translated "unfaithfulness" implies a sexually immoral life-style, not a confessed and repented act of adultery. Those who discover that their partner has been unfaithful should first make every effort to forgive, reconcile, and restore their relationship. We are always to look for reasons to restore the marriage relationship rather than for excuses to leave it.

5:33ff Here, Jesus was emphasising the importance of telling the truth. People were breaking promises and using sacred language casually and carelessly. Keeping oaths and promises is important; it builds trust and makes committed human relationships possible. The Bible condemns making vows or taking oaths casually, giving your word while knowing that you won't keep it, or swearing falsely in God's name (Exodus 20:7; Leviticus 19:12; Numbers 30:1, 2; Deuteronomy 19:16–20). Oaths are needed in certain situations only because we live in a sinful society that breeds distrust.

5:33–37 Oaths, or vows, were common, but Jesus told his followers not to use them – their word alone should be enough (see James 5:12). Are you known as a person of your word? Truthfulness seems so rare that we feel we must end our statements with "I promise". If we tell the truth all the time, we will have less pressure to back up our words with an oath or promise.

5:38 God's purpose behind this law was an expression of mercy. The law was given to judges and said, in effect, "Make the punishment fit the crime." It was not a guide for personal revenge (Exodus 21:23–25; Leviticus 24:19, 20; Deuteronomy 19:21). These laws were given to *limit* vengeance and help the court administer punishment that was neither too strict nor too lenient. Some people, however, were using this phrase to justify their vendettas against others. People still try to excuse their acts of revenge by saying, "I was just doing to him what he did to me."

5:38–42 When we are wronged, often our first reaction is to get even. Instead Jesus said we should do *good* to those who wrong us! Our desire should not be to keep score, but to love and forgive. This is not natural – it is supernatural. Only God can give us the strength to love as he does. Instead of planning vengeance, pray for those who hurt you.

5:39–44 To many Jews of Jesus' day, these statements were offensive. Any Messiah who would turn the other cheek was not the military leader they wanted to lead a revolt against Rome. Since they were under Roman oppression, they wanted retaliation against their enemies, whom they hated. But Jesus suggested a new, radical response to injustice: instead of demanding rights, give them up freely! According to Jesus, it is more important to *give* justice and mercy than to receive it.

5:43, 44 By telling us not to retaliate, Jesus keeps us from taking the law into our own hands. By loving and praying for our

you,[n] 45that you may be sons[o] of your Father in heaven. He causes his sun to rise
on the evil and the good, and sends rain on the righteous and the unrighteous.[p] 46If
you love those who love you, what reward will you get?[q] Are not even the tax
collectors doing that? 47And if you greet only your brothers, what are you doing more
than others? Do not even pagans do that? 48Be perfect, therefore, as your heavenly
Father is perfect.[r]

Jesus Teaches about Giving to the Needy
(58)

6 "Be careful not to do your 'acts of righteousness' before men, to be seen by
them.[a] If you do, you will have no reward from your Father in heaven.
2"So when you give to the needy, do not announce it with trumpets, as the
hypocrites do in the synagogues and on the streets, to be honoured by men. I tell you
the truth, they have received their reward in full. 3But when you give to the needy,
do not let your left hand know what your right hand is doing, 4so that your giving
may be in secret. Then your Father, who sees what is done in secret, will reward you.[b]

5:44 [n]Lk 6:27, 28; 23:34; Ac 7:60; Ro 12:14; 1Co 4:12; 1Pe 2:23

5:45 [o]ver 9 [p]Job 25:3

5:46 [q]Lk 6:32

5:48 [r]Lev 19:2; 1Pe 1:16

6:1 [a]Mt 23:5

6:4 [b]ver 6, 18; Col 3:23, 24

JESUS AND THE OLD TESTAMENT LAW

Reference	*Examples of Old Testament mercy in justice:*
Leviticus 19:18	"Do not seek revenge or bear a grudge against one of your people, but love your neighbour as yourself. I am the LORD."
Proverbs 24:28, 29	"Do not testify against your neighbour without cause, or use your lips to deceive. Do not say, 'I'll do to him as he has done to me; I'll pay that man back for what he did.' "
Proverbs 25:21, 22	"If your enemy is hungry, give him food to eat; if he is thirsty, give him water to drink. In doing this, you will heap burning coals on his head, and the LORD will reward you."
Lamentations 3:27-31	"It is good for a man to . . . offer his cheek to one who would strike him, and let him be filled with disgrace. For men are not cast off by the Lord for ever."

What seems to be a case of Jesus contradicting the laws of the Old Testament deserves a careful look. It is too easy to overlook how much mercy was written into the Old Testament laws. Above are several examples. What God designed as a system of justice with mercy had been distorted over the years into a licence for revenge. It was this misapplication of the law that Jesus attacked.

---

enemies, we can overcome evil with good.

The Pharisees interpreted Leviticus 19:18 as teaching that they should love only those who love in return, and Psalm 139:19–22 and 140:9–11 as meaning that they should hate their enemies. But Jesus says we are to love our enemies. If you love your enemies and treat them well, you will truly show that Jesus is Lord of your life. This is possible only for those who give themselves fully to God, because only he can deliver people from natural selfishness. We must trust the Holy Spirit to help us *show* love to those for whom we may not *feel* love.

5:48 How can we be perfect? (1) *In character.* In this life we cannot be flawless, but we can aspire to be as much like Christ as possible. (2) *In holiness.* Like the Pharisees, we are to separate ourselves from the world's sinful values. But unlike the Pharisees, we are to be devoted to God's desires rather than our own, and carry his love and mercy into the world. (3) *In maturity.* We can't achieve Christlike character and holy living all at once, but we must grow towards maturity and wholeness. Just as we expect different behaviour from a baby, a child, a teenager, and an adult, so God expects different behaviour from us, depending on our stage of spiritual development. (4) *In love.* We can seek to love others as completely as God loves us.

We can be perfect if our behaviour is appropriate for our maturity level—perfect, yet with much room to grow. Our tendency to sin must never deter us from striving to be more like Christ. Christ calls all of his disciples to excel, to rise above mediocrity, and to mature in every area, becoming like him. Those who strive to become perfect will one day be perfect, even as Christ is perfect (1 John 3:2, 3).

6:2 The term *hypocrites,* as used here, describes people who do good acts for appearances only—not out of compassion or other good motives. Their actions may be good, but their motives are hollow. These empty acts are their only reward, but God will reward those who are sincere in their faith.

6:3 When Jesus says not to let your left hand know what your right hand is doing, he is teaching that our motives for giving to God and to others must be pure. It is easy to give with mixed motives, to do something for someone if it will benefit us in return. But believers should avoid all scheming and give for the pleasure of giving and as a response to God's love. Why do *you* give?

6:3, 4 It's easier to do what's right when we gain recognition and praise. To be sure our motives are not selfish, we should do our good deeds quietly or in secret, with no thought of reward. Jesus says we should check our motives in three areas: generosity (6:4), prayer (6:6), and fasting (6:18). Those acts should not be self-centred, but God-centred, done not to make us look good but to make God look good. The reward God promises is not material, and it is never given to those who seek it. Doing something only for ourselves is not a loving sacrifice. With your next good deed, ask, "Would I still do this if no-one would ever know I did it?"

Jesus Teaches about Prayer
(59)

5“And when you pray, do not be like the hypocrites, for they love to pray standing[c]
in the synagogues and on the street corners to be seen by men. I tell you the truth,
they have received their reward in full. 6But when you pray, go into your room, close
the door and pray to your Father,[d] who is unseen. Then your Father, who sees what
is done in secret, will reward you. 7And when you pray, do not keep on babbling[e]
like pagans, for they think they will be heard because of their many words.[f] 8Do not
be like them, for your Father knows what you need[g] before you ask him.
9“This, then, is how you should pray:

“ ‘Our Father in heaven,
hallowed be your name,
10your kingdom[h] come,
your will be done[i]
on earth as it is in heaven.
11Give us today our daily bread.[j]
12Forgive us our debts,
as we also have forgiven our debtors.[k]
13And lead us not into temptation,[l]
but deliver us from the evil one.’[a] [m]

14For if you forgive men when they sin against you, your heavenly Father will also
forgive you.[n] 15But if you do not forgive men their sins, your Father will not forgive
your sins.[o]

Jesus Teaches about Fasting
(60)

16“When you fast, do not look sombre[p] as the hypocrites do, for they disfigure
their faces to show men they are fasting. I tell you the truth, they have received their

6:5 [c]Mk 11:25; Lk 18:10-14
6:6 [d]2Ki 4:33
6:7 [e]Ecc 5:2 [f]1Ki 18:26-29
6:8 [g]ver 32
6:10 [h]Mt 3:2 [i]Mt 26:39
6:11 [j]Pr 30:8
6:12 [k]Mt 18:21-35
6:13 [l]Jas 1:13 [m]Mt 5:37
6:14 [n]Mt 18:21-35; Mk 11:25, 26; Eph 4:32; Col 3:13
6:15 [o]Mt 18:35
6:16 [p]Isa 58:5

a *13* Or *from evil*; some late manuscripts *one, / for yours is the kingdom and the power and the glory for ever. Amen.*

6:5, 6 Some people, especially the religious leaders, wanted to be seen as “holy”, and public prayer was one way to get attention. Jesus saw through their self-righteous acts, however, and taught that the essence of prayer is not public style but private communication with God. There is a place for public prayer, but to pray only where others will notice you indicates that your real audience is not God.

6:7, 8 Repeating the same words over and over like a magic incantation is no way to ensure that God will hear your prayer. It’s not wrong to come to God many times with the same requests – Jesus encourages *persistent* prayer. But he condemns the shallow repetition of words that are not offered with a sincere heart. We can never pray too much if our prayers are honest and sincere. Before you start to pray, make sure you mean what you say.

6:9 This is often called the Lord’s Prayer because Jesus gave it to the disciples. It can be a pattern for our prayers. We should praise God, pray for his work in the world, pray for our daily needs, and pray for help in our daily struggles.

6:9 The phrase “Our Father in heaven” indicates that God is not only majestic and holy, but also personal and loving. The first line of this model prayer is a statement of praise and a commitment to hallow, or honour, God’s holy name. We can honour God’s name by being careful to use it respectfully. If we use God’s name lightly, we’re not remembering God’s holiness.

6:10 The phrase “Your kingdom come” is a reference to God’s spiritual reign, not Israel’s freedom from Rome. God’s kingdom was announced in the covenant with Abraham (8:11; Luke 13:28), is present in Christ’s reign in believers’ hearts (Luke 17:21), and will be complete when all evil is destroyed and God establishes the new heaven and earth (Revelation 21:1).

6:10 When we pray “Your will be done”, we are not resigning ourselves to fate, but praying that God’s perfect purpose will be accomplished in this world as well as in the next.

6:11 When we pray “Give us today our daily bread”, we are acknowledging that God is our sustainer and provider. It is a misconception to think that we provide for our needs ourselves. We must trust God *daily* to provide what he knows we need.

6:13 God doesn’t lead us into temptations, but sometimes he allows us to be tested by them. As disciples, we should pray to be delivered from these trying times and for deliverance from Satan (“the evil one”) and his deceit. All Christians struggle with temptation. Sometimes it is so subtle that we don’t even realise what is happening to us. God has promised that he won’t allow us to be tempted beyond what we can bear (1 Corinthians 10:13). Ask God to help you recognise temptation and to give you strength to overcome it and choose God’s way instead. For more on temptation, see the notes on 4:1.

6:14, 15 Jesus gives a startling warning about forgiveness: if we refuse to forgive others, God will also refuse to forgive us. Why? Because when we don’t forgive others, we are denying our common ground as sinners in need of God’s forgiveness. God’s forgiveness of sin is not the direct result of our forgiving others, but it is based on our realising what forgiveness means (see Ephesians 4:32). It is easy to ask God for forgiveness, but difficult to grant it to others. Whenever we ask God to forgive us for sin, we should ask ourselves, “Have I forgiven the people who have wronged me?”

6:16 Fasting – going without food in order to spend time in prayer – is noble *and* difficult. It gives us time to pray, teaches self-discipline, reminds us that we can live with a lot less, and helps us appreciate God’s gifts. Jesus was not condemning fasting, but

reward in full. 17But when you fast, put oil on your head and wash your face, 18so
that it will not be obvious to men that you are fasting, but only to your Father, who
is unseen; and your Father, who sees what is done in secret, will reward you.[q]

Jesus Teaches about Money
(61)

19"Do not store up for yourselves treasures on earth,[r] where moth and rust
destroy,[s] and where thieves break in and steal. 20But store up for yourselves treasures
in heaven,[t] where moth and rust do not destroy, and where thieves do not break in
and steal.[u] 21For where your treasure is, there your heart will be also.[v]
22"The eye is the lamp of the body. If your eyes are good, your whole body will
be full of light. 23But if your eyes are bad, your whole body will be full of darkness.
If then the light within you is darkness, how great is that darkness!
24"No-one can serve two masters. Either he will hate the one and love the other,
or he will be devoted to the one and despise the other. You cannot serve both God
and Money.[w]

Jesus Teaches about Worry
(62)

25"Therefore I tell you, do not worry[x] about your life, what you will eat or drink;
or about your body, what you will wear. Is not life more important than food, and
the body more important than clothes? 26Look at the birds of the air; they do not sow
or reap or store away in barns, and yet your heavenly Father feeds them.[y] Are you

6:18 [q]ver 4, 6
6:19 [r]Pr 23:4; Heb 13:5 [s]Jas 5:2, 3
6:20 [t]Mt 19:21; Lk 12:33; 18:22; 1Ti 6:19 [u]Lk 12:33
6:21 [v]Lk 12:34
6:24 [w]Lk 16:13
6:25 [x]ver 27, 28, 31, 34; Lk 10:41; 12:11, 22; Php 4:6; 1Pe 5:7
6:26 [y]Job 38:41; Ps 147:9

SEVEN REASONS FOR NOT WORRYING

6:25	The same God who created life in you can be trusted with the details of your life.
6:26	Worrying about the future hampers your efforts for today.
6:27	Worrying is more harmful than helpful.
6:28–30	God does not ignore those who depend on him.
6:31, 32	Worry shows a lack of faith in and understanding of God.
6:33	There are real challenges God wants us to pursue, and worrying keeps us from them.
6:34	Living one day at a time keeps us from being consumed with worry.

hypocrisy – fasting in order to gain public approval. Fasting was mandatory for the Jewish people once a year, on the Day of Atonement (Leviticus 23:32). The Pharisees voluntarily fasted twice a week to impress the people with their "holiness". Jesus commended acts of self-sacrifice done quietly and sincerely. He wanted people to adopt spiritual disciplines for the right reasons, not from a selfish desire for praise.

6:17 Olive oil was used as a common cosmetic like a lotion. Jesus was saying, "Go about your normal daily routine when you fast. Don't make a show of it."

6:20 Storing up treasures in heaven is not limited to tithing but is accomplished by all acts of obedience to God. There is a sense in which giving our money to God's work is like investing in heaven. But our intention should be to seek the fulfilment of God's purposes in all we do, not merely what we do with our money.

6:22, 23 Spiritual vision is our capacity to see clearly what God wants us to do and to see the world from his point of view. But this spiritual insight can be easily clouded. Self-serving desires, interests, and goals block that vision. Serving God is the best way to restore it. A "good" eye is one that is fixed on God.

6:24 Jesus says we can have only one master. We live in a materialistic society where many people serve money. They spend all their lives collecting and storing it, only to die and leave it behind. Their desire for money and what it can buy far outweighs their commitment to God and spiritual matters. Whatever you store up, you will spend much of your time and energy thinking about. Don't fall into the materialistic trap, because "the love of money is a root of all kinds of evil" (1 Timothy 6:10). Can you honestly say that God, and not money, is your master? One test is to ask which one occupies more of your thoughts, time, and efforts.

6:24 Jesus contrasted heavenly values with earthly values when he explained that our first loyalty should be to those things that do not fade, cannot be stolen or used up, and never wear out. We should not be fascinated with our possessions, lest *they* possess *us*. This means we may have to do some cutting back if our possessions are becoming too important to us. Jesus is calling for a decision that allows us to live contentedly with whatever we have because we have chosen what is eternal and lasting.

6:25 Because of the ill effects of worry, Jesus tells us not to worry about those needs that God promises to supply. Worry may (1) damage your health, (2) cause the object of your worry to consume your thoughts, (3) disrupt your productivity, (4) negatively affect the way you treat others, and (5) reduce your ability to trust in God. How many ill effects of worry are you experiencing? Here is the difference between worry and genuine concern – worry immobilises, but concern moves you to action.

not much more valuable than they?[z] 27Who of you by worrying can add a single hour
to his life?[b][a]
28"And why do you worry about clothes? See how the lilies of the field grow. They
do not labour or spin. 29Yet I tell you that not even Solomon in all his splendour[b]
was dressed like one of these. 30If that is how God clothes the grass of the field, which
is here today and tomorrow is thrown into the fire, will he not much more clothe you,
O you of little faith?[c] 31So do not worry, saying, 'What shall we eat?' or 'What shall
we drink?' or 'What shall we wear?' 32For the pagans run after all these things, and
your heavenly Father knows that you need them.[d] 33But seek first his kingdom and
his righteousness, and all these things will be given to you as well.[e] 34Therefore do
not worry about tomorrow, for tomorrow will worry about itself. Each day has enough
trouble of its own.

Jesus Teaches about Criticising Others
(63/Luke 6:37–42)

7 "Do not judge, or you too will be judged.[a] 2For in the same way as you judge
others, you will be judged, and with the measure you use, it will be measured
to you.[b]
3"Why do you look at the speck of sawdust in your brother's eye and pay no
attention to the plank in your own eye? 4How can you say to your brother, 'Let me
take the speck out of your eye,' when all the time there is a plank in your own eye?
5You hypocrite, first take the plank out of your own eye, and then you will see clearly
to remove the speck from your brother's eye.
6"Do not give dogs what is sacred; do not throw your pearls to pigs. If you do, they
may trample them under their feet, and then turn and tear you to pieces.

Jesus Teaches about Asking, Seeking, Knocking
(64)

7"Ask and it will be given to you;[c] seek and you will find; knock and the door
will be opened to you. 8For everyone who asks receives; he who seeks finds;[d] and
to him who knocks, the door will be opened.
9"Which of you, if his son asks for bread, will give him a stone? 10Or if he asks
for a fish, will give him a snake? 11If you, then, though you are evil, know how to

b *27* Or *single cubit to his height*

6:26 [z]Mt 10:29-31
6:27 [a]Ps 39:5
6:29 [b]1Ki 10:4-7
6:30 [c]Mt 8:26; 14:31; 16:8
6:32 [d]ver 8
6:33 [e]Mt 19:29; Mk 10:29-30
7:1 [a]Lk 6:37; Ro 14:4, 10, 13; 1Co 4:5; Jas 4:11, 12
7:2 [b]Mk 4:24; Lk 6:38
7:7 [c]Mt 21:22; Mk 11:24; Jn 14:13, 14; 15:7, 16; 16:23, 24; Jas 1:5-8; 4:2, 3; 1Jn 3:22; 5:14, 15
7:8 [d]Pr 8:17; Jer 29:12, 13

6:33 To "seek first his kingdom and his righteousness" means to turn to God first for help, to fill your thoughts with his desires, to take his character for your pattern, and to serve and obey him in everything. What is really important to you? People, objects, goals, and other desires all compete for priority. Any of these can quickly push God out of first place if you don't actively choose to give him first place in *every* area of your life.

6:34 Planning for tomorrow is time well spent; worrying about tomorrow is time wasted. Sometimes it's difficult to tell the difference. Careful planning is thinking ahead about goals, steps, and schedules, and trusting in God's guidance. When done well, planning can help alleviate worry. Worriers, by contrast, are consumed by fear and find it difficult to trust God. They let their plans interfere with their relationship with God. Don't let worries about tomorrow affect your relationship with God today.

7:1, 2 Jesus tells us to examine our own motives and conduct instead of judging others. The traits that bother us in others are often the habits we dislike in ourselves. Our untamed bad habits and behaviour patterns are the very ones that we most want to change in others. Do you find it easy to magnify others' faults while excusing your own? If you are ready to criticise someone, check to see if you deserve the same criticism. Judge yourself first, and then lovingly forgive and help your neighbour.

7:1–5 Jesus' statement, "Do not judge", is against the kind of hypocritical, judgmental attitude that tears others down in order to build oneself up. It is not a blanket statement against all critical thinking, but a call to be *discerning* rather than negative. Jesus said to expose false teachers (7:15–23), and Paul taught that we should exercise church discipline (1 Corinthians 5:1, 2) and trust God to be the final Judge (1 Corinthians 4:3–5).

7:6 Pigs were unclean animals according to God's law (Deuteronomy 14:8). Anyone who touched an unclean animal became "ceremonially unclean" and could not go to the temple to worship until the uncleanness was removed. Jesus says that we should not entrust holy teachings to unholy or unclean people. It is futile to try to teach holy concepts to people who don't want to listen and will only tear apart what we say. We should not stop giving God's word to unbelievers, but we should be wise and discerning in what we teach to whom, so that we will not be wasting our time.

7:7, 8 Jesus tells us to persist in pursuing God. People often give up after a few half-hearted efforts and conclude that God cannot be found. But knowing God takes faith, focus, and follow-up, and Jesus assures us that we will be rewarded. Don't give up in your efforts to seek God. Continue to ask him for more knowledge, patience, wisdom, love, and understanding. He will give them to you.

7:9, 10 The child in Jesus' example asked his father for bread and fish—good and necessary items. If the child had asked for a poisonous snake, would the wise father have granted his request? Sometimes God knows we are praying for "snakes" and does not give us what we ask for, even though we persist in our prayers. As we learn to know God better as a loving Father, we learn to ask for what is good for us, and then he grants it.

7:12 [e]Lk 6:31 [f]Ro 13:8-10; Gal 5:14

7:13 [g]Lk 13:24

7:15 [h]Jer 23:16; Mt 24:24; Mk 13:22; Lk 6:26; 2Pe 2:1; 1Jn 4:1; Rev 16:13 [i]Ac 20:29

7:16 [j]Mt 12:33; Lk 6:44 [k]Jas 3:12

7:19 [l]Mt 3:10

7:21 [m]Hos 8:2; Mt 25:11 [n]Ro 2:13; Jas 1:22

7:22 [o]Mt 10:15 [p]1Co 13:1-3

7:23 [q]Ps 6:8; Mt 25:12, 41; Lk 13:25-27

7:24 [r]Jas 1:22-25

give good gifts to your children, how much more will your Father in heaven give good
gifts to those who ask him! 12So in everything, do to others what you would have them
do to you,[e] for this sums up the Law and the Prophets.[f]

Jesus Teaches about the Way to Heaven
(65)

13"Enter through the narrow gate.[g] For wide is the gate and broad is the road that
leads to destruction, and many enter through it. 14But small is the gate and narrow
the road that leads to life, and only a few find it.

Jesus Teaches about Fruit in People's Lives
(66/Luke 6:43–45)

15"Watch out for false prophets.[h] They come to you in sheep's clothing, but
inwardly they are ferocious wolves.[i] 16By their fruit you will recognise them.[j] Do
people pick grapes from thornbushes, or figs from thistles?[k] 17Likewise every good
tree bears good fruit, but a bad tree bears bad fruit. 18A good tree cannot bear bad
fruit, and a bad tree cannot bear good fruit. 19Every tree that does not bear good fruit
is cut down and thrown into the fire.[l] 20Thus, by their fruit you will recognise them.

Jesus Teaches about Those Who Build Houses on Rock and Sand
(67/Luke 6:46–49)

21"Not everyone who says to me, 'Lord, Lord,'[m] will enter the kingdom of heaven,
but only he who does the will of my Father who is in heaven.[n] 22Many will say to
me on that day,[o] 'Lord, Lord, did we not prophesy in your name, and in your name
drive out demons and perform many miracles?'[p] 23Then I will tell them plainly, 'I
never knew you. Away from me, you evildoers!'[q]
24"Therefore everyone who hears these words of mine and puts them into practice[r]
is like a wise man who built his house on the rock. 25The rain came down, the streams
rose, and the winds blew and beat against that house; yet it did not fall, because it

---

7:11 Christ is showing us the heart of God the Father. God is not selfish, begrudging, or stingy, and we don't have to beg or grovel as we come with our requests. He is a loving Father who understands, cares, and comforts. If humans can be kind, imagine how kind God, the Creator of kindness, can be.

7:11 Jesus used the expression "If you, then, though you are evil" to contrast sinful and fallible human beings with the holy and perfect God.

7:12 This is commonly known as the Golden Rule. In many religions it is stated negatively: "Don't do to others what you don't want done to you." By stating it positively, Jesus made it more significant. It is not very hard to refrain from harming others; it is much more difficult to take the initiative in doing something good for them. The Golden Rule as Jesus formulated it is the foundation of active goodness and mercy – the kind of love God shows to us every day. Think of a good and merciful action you can take today.

7:13, 14 The gate that leads to eternal life (John 10:7–9) is called "narrow". This does not mean that it is difficult to become a Christian, but that there is only *one* way to live eternally with God and only a few that decide to walk that road. Believing in Jesus is the only way to heaven, because he alone died for our sins and made us right before God. Living his way may not be popular, but it is true and right. Thank God there is one way!

7:15 False prophets were common in Old Testament times. They prophesied only what the king and the people wanted to hear, claiming it was God's message. False teachers are just as common today. Jesus says to beware of those whose words sound religious but who are motivated by money, fame, or power. You can tell who they are because in their teaching they minimise Christ and glorify themselves.

7:20 We should evaluate teachers' words by examining their lives. Just as trees are consistent in the kind of fruit they produce, good teachers consistently exhibit good behaviour and high moral character as they attempt to live out the truths of Scripture. This does not mean we should have witch hunts, throwing out Sunday school teachers, pastors, and others who are less than perfect. Every one of us is subject to sin, and we must show the same mercy to others that we need for ourselves. When Jesus talks about bad trees, he means teachers who deliberately teach false doctrine. We must examine the teachers' motives, the direction they are taking, and the results they are seeking.

7:21 Some self-professed athletes can "talk" a great game, but that tells you nothing about their athletic skills. And not everyone who talks about heaven belongs to God's kingdom. Jesus is more concerned about our *walk* than our *talk*. He wants us to *do* right, not just *say* the right words. Your house (which represents your life, 7:24) will withstand the storms of life only if you do what is right instead of just talking about it. What you do cannot be separated from what you believe.

7:21–23 Jesus exposed those people who sounded religious but had no personal relationship with him. On "that day" (the day of judgment), only our relationship with Christ – our acceptance of him as Saviour and our obedience to him – will matter. Many people think that if they are "good" people and say religious things, they will be rewarded with eternal life. In reality, faith in Christ is what will count at the judgment.

7:22 "That day" is the final day of reckoning when God will settle all accounts, judging sin and rewarding faith.

7:24 To build "on the rock" means to be a hearing, responding disciple, not a false, superficial one. Practising obedience becomes the solid foundation to weather the storms of life. See James 1:22–27 for more on putting into practice what we hear.

had its foundation on the rock. 26But everyone who hears these words of mine and
does not put them into practice is like a foolish man who built his house on sand. 27The
rain came down, the streams rose, and the winds blew and beat against that house,
and it fell with a great crash."

28When Jesus had finished saying these things,[s] the crowds were amazed at his
teaching,[t] 29because he taught as one who had authority, and not as their teachers
of the law.

3. Jesus performs many miracles

Jesus Heals a Man with Leprosy
(38/Mark 1:40–45; Luke 5:12–16)

8 When he came down from the mountainside, large crowds followed him. 2A man
with leprosy[a][a] came and knelt before him[b] and said, "Lord, if you are willing,
you can make me clean."
3Jesus reached out his hand and touched the man. "I am willing," he said. "Be
clean!" Immediately he was cured[b] of his leprosy. 4Then Jesus said to him, "See that
you don't tell anyone.[c] But go, show yourself to the priest and offer the gift Moses
commanded,[d] as a testimony to them."

A Roman Centurion Demonstrates Faith
(68/Luke 7:1–10)

5When Jesus had entered Capernaum, a centurion came to him, asking for help.
6"Lord," he said, "my servant lies at home paralysed and in terrible suffering."
7Jesus said to him, "I will go and heal him."
8The centurion replied, "Lord, I do not deserve to have you come under my roof.
But just say the word, and my servant will be healed.[e] 9For I myself am a man under

[a] *2* The Greek word was used for various diseases affecting the skin—not necessarily leprosy. [b] *3* Greek *made clean*

7:28
[s]Mt 11:1; 13:53; 19:1; 26:1
[t]Mt 13:54; Mk 1:22; 6:2; Lk 4:32; Jn 7:46

8:2
[a]Lk 5:12
[b]Mt 9:18; 15:25; 18:26; 20:20

8:4
[c]Mt 9:30; Mk 5:43; 7:36; 8:30
[d]Lev 14:2-32

8:8
[e]Ps 107:20

7:26 Like a house of cards, the fool's life crumbles. Most people do not deliberately seek to build on a false or inferior foundation; instead, they just don't think about their life's purpose. Many people are headed for destruction, not out of stubbornness but out of thoughtlessness. Part of our responsibility as believers is to help others stop and think about where their lives are headed and to point out the consequences of ignoring Christ's message.

7:29 The teachers of the law (religious scholars) often cited traditions and quoted authorities to support their arguments and interpretations. But Jesus spoke with a new authority—his own. He didn't need to quote anyone because he was the original Word (John 1:1).

8:2, 3 Leprosy, like AIDS today, was a terrifying disease because there was no known cure. In Jesus' day, the Greek word for *leprosy* was used for a variety of similar diseases, and some forms were contagious. If a person contracted the contagious type, a priest declared him a leper and banished him from his home and city. The leper was sent to live in a community with other lepers until he either got better or died. Yet when the leper begged Jesus to heal him, Jesus reached out and touched him, even though his skin was covered with the dreaded disease.

Sin is also an incurable disease—and we all have it. Only Christ's healing touch can miraculously take away our sins and restore us to real living. But first, just like the leper, we must realise our inability to cure ourselves and ask for Christ's saving help.

8:4 The law required a healed leper to be examined by the priest (Leviticus 14). Jesus wanted this man to give his story firsthand to the priest to prove that his leprosy was completely gone so that he could be restored to his community.

8:5, 6 The centurion could have let many obstacles stand between him and Jesus—pride, doubt, money, language, distance, time, self-sufficiency, power, race. But he didn't. If he did not let these barriers block his approach to Jesus, we don't need to either. What keeps you from Christ?

8:8–12 A centurion was a career military officer in the Roman army with control over 100 soldiers. Roman soldiers, of all people, were hated by the Jews for their oppression, control, and ridicule. Yet this man's genuine faith amazed Jesus! This hated Gentile's faith put to shame the stagnant piety of many of the Jewish religious leaders.

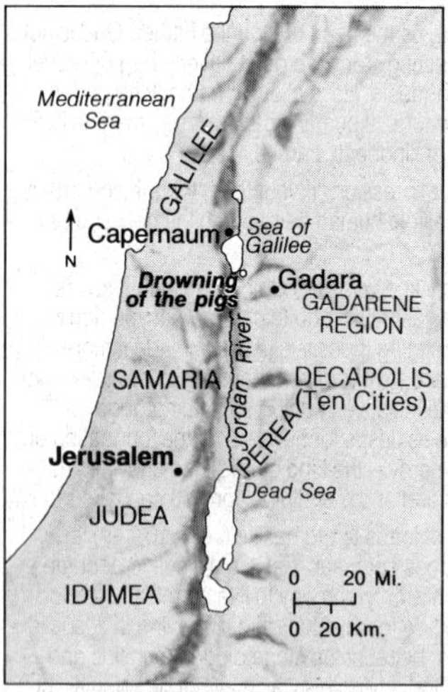

JESUS' MIRACULOUS POWER DISPLAYED
Jesus finished the sermon he had given on a hillside near Galilee and returned to Capernaum. As he and his disciples crossed the Sea of Galilee, Jesus calmed a fierce storm. Then, in the Gentile Gadarene region, Jesus commanded demons to come out of two men.

8:10 [f]Mt 15:28

8:11 [g]Ps 107:3; Isa 49:12; 59:19; Mal 1:11 [h]Lk 13:29

8:12 [i]Mt 13:38 [j]Mt 13:42, 50; 22:13; 24:51; 25:30; Lk 13:28

8:13 [k]Mt 9:22

authority, with soldiers under me. I tell this one, 'Go,' and he goes; and that one,
'Come,' and he comes. I say to my servant, 'Do this,' and he does it."
10 When Jesus heard this, he was astonished and said to those following him, "I tell
you the truth, I have not found anyone in Israel with such great faith.[f] 11 I say to you
that many will come from the east and the west,[g] and will take their places at the
feast with Abraham, Isaac and Jacob in the kingdom of heaven.[h] 12 But the subjects
of the kingdom[i] will be thrown outside, into the darkness, where there will be
weeping and gnashing of teeth."[j]
13 Then Jesus said to the centurion, "Go! It will be done just as you believed it
would."[k] And his servant was healed at that very hour.

Jesus Heals Peter's Mother-in-Law and Many Others
(35/Mark 1:29–34; Luke 4:38–41)

8:16 [l]Mt 4:23, 24

8:17 [m]Mt 1:22 [n]Isa 53:4

14 When Jesus came into Peter's house, he saw Peter's mother-in-law lying in bed
with a fever. 15 He touched her hand and the fever left her, and she got up and began
to wait on him.
16 When evening came, many who were demon-possessed were brought to him, and
he drove out the spirits with a word and healed all the sick.[l] 17 This was to fulfil[m]
what was spoken through the prophet Isaiah:

> "He took up our infirmities
> and carried our diseases."[c][n]

Jesus Teaches about the Cost of Following Him
(122/Luke 9:51–62)

8:18 [o]Mk 4:35

8:20 [p]Da 7:13; Mt 12:8, 32, 40; 16:13, 27, 28; 17:9; 19:28; Mk 2:10; 8:31

18 When Jesus saw the crowd around him, he gave orders to cross to the other side
of the lake.[o] 19 Then a teacher of the law came to him and said, "Teacher, I will follow
you wherever you go."
20 Jesus replied, "Foxes have holes and birds of the air have nests, but the Son of
Man[p] has nowhere to lay his head."

c *17* Isaiah 53:4

8:10–12 Jesus told the crowd that many religious Jews who should be in the kingdom would be excluded because of their lack of faith. Entrenched in their religious traditions, they could not accept Christ and his new message. We must be careful not to become so set in our religious habits that we expect God to work only in specified ways. Don't limit God by your mind-set and lack of faith.

8:11, 12 "The east and the west" stands for the four corners of the earth. All the faithful people of God will be gathered to feast with the Messiah (Isaiah 6; 55). The Jews should have known that when the Messiah came, his blessings would be for Gentiles too (see Isaiah 66:12, 19). But this message came as a shock because they were too wrapped up in their own affairs and destiny. In claiming God's promises, we must not apply them so personally that we forget to see what God wants to do to reach *all* the people he loves.

8:11, 12 Matthew emphasises this universal theme – Jesus' message is for everyone. The Old Testament prophets knew this (see Isaiah 56:3, 6–8; 66:12, 19; Malachi 1:11), but many New Testament Jewish leaders chose to ignore it. Each individual has to choose to accept or reject the gospel, and no-one can become part of God's kingdom on the basis of heritage or connections. Having a Christian family is a wonderful blessing, but it won't guarantee you eternal life. *You* must believe in and follow Christ.

8:14 Peter was one of Jesus' 12 disciples. His Profile is found in chapter 27.

8:14, 15 Peter's mother-in-law gives us a beautiful example to follow. Her response to Jesus' touch was to wait on Jesus and his disciples – immediately. Has God ever helped you through a dangerous or difficult situation? If so, you should ask, "How can I express my gratitude to him?" Because God has promised us all the rewards of his kingdom, we should look for ways to serve him and his followers now.

8:16, 17 Matthew continues to show Jesus' kingly nature. Through a single touch, Jesus healed (8:3, 15); when he spoke a single word, evil spirits fled his presence (8:16). Jesus has authority over all evil powers and all earthly disease. He also has power and authority to conquer sin. Sickness and evil are consequences of living in a fallen world. But in the future, when God removes all sin, there will be no more sickness and death. Jesus' healing miracles were a taste of what the whole world will one day experience in God's kingdom.

8:19, 20 Following Jesus is not always easy or comfortable. Often it means great cost and sacrifice, with no earthly rewards or security. Jesus didn't have a place to call home. You may find that following Christ costs you popularity, friendships, leisure time, or treasured habits. But while the cost of following Christ is high, the value of being Christ's disciple is even higher. Discipleship is an investment that lasts for eternity and yields incredible rewards.

21 Another disciple said to him, "Lord, first let me go and bury my father."
22 But Jesus told him, "Follow me,[q] and let the dead bury their own dead."

Jesus Calms the Storm
(87/Mark 4:35–41; Luke 8:22–25)

23 Then he got into the boat and his disciples followed him. 24 Without warning, a
furious storm came up on the lake, so that the waves swept over the boat. But Jesus
was sleeping. 25 The disciples went and woke him, saying, "Lord, save us! We're
going to drown!"
26 He replied, "You of little faith,[r] why are you so afraid?" Then he got up and
rebuked the winds and the waves, and it was completely calm.[s]
27 The men were amazed and asked, "What kind of man is this? Even the winds and
the waves obey him!"

Jesus Sends the Demons into a Herd of Pigs
(88/Mark 5:1–20; Luke 8:26–39)

28 When he arrived at the other side in the region of the Gadarenes,[d] two demon-
possessed[t] men coming from the tombs met him. They were so violent that no-one
could pass that way. 29 "What do you want with us,[u] Son of God?" they shouted.
"Have you come here to torture us before the appointed time?"[v]
30 Some distance from them a large herd of pigs was feeding. 31 The demons begged
Jesus, "If you drive us out, send us into the herd of pigs."
32 He said to them, "Go!" So they came out and went into the pigs, and the whole

8:22 [q]Mt 4:19
8:26 [r]Mt 6:30 [s]Ps 65:7; 89:9; 107:29
8:28 [t]Mt 4:24
8:29 [u]Jdg 11:12; 2Sa 16:10; 1Ki 17:18; Mk 1:24; Lk 4:34; Jn 2:4 [v]2Pe 2:4

d *28* Some manuscripts *Gergesenes*; others *Gerasenes*

8:21, 22 It is possible that this disciple was not asking permission to go to his father's funeral, but rather to put off following Jesus until his elderly father died. Perhaps he was the firstborn son and wanted to be sure to claim his inheritance. Perhaps he didn't want to face his father's wrath if he left the family business to follow an itinerant preacher. Whether his concern was financial security, family approval, or something else, he did not want to commit himself to Jesus just yet. Jesus, however, would not accept his excuse.

8:21, 22 Jesus was always direct with those who wanted to follow him. He made sure they counted the cost and set aside any conditions they might have for following him. As God's Son, Jesus did not hesitate to demand complete loyalty. Even family loyalty was not to take priority over the demands of obedience. His direct challenge forces us to ask ourselves about our own priorities in following him. The decision to follow Jesus should not be put off, even though other loyalties compete for our attention. Nothing should be placed above a total commitment to living for him.

8:23 This would have been a fishing boat because many of Jesus' disciples were fishermen. Josephus, an ancient historian, wrote that there were usually more than 300 fishing boats on the Sea of Galilee at one time. This boat was large enough to hold Jesus and his 12 disciples and was powered both by oars and sails. During a storm, however, the sails were taken down to keep them from ripping and to make the boat easier to control.

8:24 The Sea of Galilee is an unusual stretch of water. It is relatively small (13 miles long, 7 miles wide), but it is 150 feet deep, and the shoreline is 680 feet below sea level. Sudden storms can appear over the surrounding mountains with little warning, stirring the water into violent 20-foot waves. The disciples had not foolishly set out in a storm. They had been caught without warning, and their danger was great.

8:25 Although the disciples had witnessed many miracles, they panicked in this storm. As experienced sailors, they knew its danger; what they did not know was that Christ could control the forces of nature. There is often a stormy area of our human nature where we feel God can't or won't work. When we truly understand who God is, however, we will realise that he controls both the storms of nature and the storms of the troubled heart. Jesus' power that calmed this storm can also help us deal with the problems we face. Jesus is willing to help if we only ask him. We should never discount his power even in terrible trials.

8:28 The region of the Gadarenes is located southeast of the Sea of Galilee, near the town of Gadara, one of the most important cities of the region (see map). Gadara was a member of the Decapolis (see the note on Mark 5:20). These ten cities with independent governments were largely inhabited by Gentiles, which explains the herd of pigs (8:30). The Jews did not keep pigs because pigs were considered unclean and thus unfit to eat.

8:28 Demon-possessed people are under the control of one or more demons. Demons are fallen angels who joined Satan in his rebellion against God and are now evil spirits under Satan's control. They help Satan tempt people to sin and have great destructive powers. But whenever they are confronted by Jesus, they lose their power. These demons recognised Jesus as God's Son (8:29), but they didn't think they had to obey him. Just believing is not enough (see James 2:19 for a discussion of belief and devils). Faith is more than belief. By faith, you accept what Jesus has done for you, receive him as the only one who can save you from sin, and live out your faith by obeying his commands.

8:28 Matthew says there were two demon-possessed men, while Mark and Luke refer to only one. Apparently Mark and Luke mention only the man who did the talking.

8:28 According to Jewish ceremonial laws, the men Jesus encountered were unclean in three ways: they were Gentiles (non-Jews), they were demon-possessed, and they lived in a graveyard. Jesus helped them anyway. We should not turn our backs on people who are "unclean" or repulsive to us, or who violate our moral standards and religious beliefs. Instead, we must realise that every human individual is a unique creation of God, needing to be touched by his love.

8:29 The Bible tells us that at the end of the world the devil and his angels will be thrown into the lake of burning sulphur (Revelation 20:10). When the demons asked if Jesus had come to torment them "before the appointed time", they showed they knew their ultimate fate.

8:34 [w]Lk 5:8; Ac 16:39
9:1 [a]Mt 4:13
9:2 [b]Mt 4:24 [c]ver 22 [d]Jn 16:33 [e]Lk 7:48
9:3 [f]Mt 26:65; Jn 10:33
9:4 [g]Ps 94:11; Mt 12:25; Lk 6:8; 9:47; 11:17
9:6 [h]Mt 8:20
9:8 [i]Mt 5:16; 15:31; Lk 7:16; 13:13; 17:15; 23:47; Jn 15:8; Ac 4:21; 11:18; 21:20

herd rushed down the steep bank into the lake and died in the water. 33 Those tending
the pigs ran off, went into the town and reported all this, including what had happened
to the demon-possessed men. 34 Then the whole town went out to meet Jesus. And
when they saw him, they pleaded with him to leave their region.[w]

Jesus Heals a Paralysed Man
(39/Mark 2:1–12; Luke 5:17–26)

9 Jesus stepped into a boat, crossed over and came to his own town.[a] 2 Some men
brought to him a paralytic,[b] lying on a mat. When Jesus saw their faith,[c] he
said to the paralytic, "Take heart,[d] son; your sins are forgiven."[e]
3 At this, some of the teachers of the law said to themselves, "This fellow is
blaspheming!"[f]
4 Knowing their thoughts,[g] Jesus said, "Why do you entertain evil thoughts in your
hearts? 5 Which is easier: to say, 'Your sins are forgiven,' or to say, 'Get up and walk'?
6 But so that you may know that the Son of Man[h] has authority on earth to forgive
sins. . . ." Then he said to the paralytic, "Get up, take your mat and go home." 7 And
the man got up and went home. 8 When the crowd saw this, they were filled with awe;
and they praised God,[i] who had given such authority to men.

Jesus Eats with Sinners at Matthew's House
(40/Mark 2:13–17; Luke 5:27–32)

9 As Jesus went on from there, he saw a man named Matthew sitting at the tax
collector's booth. "Follow me," he told him, and Matthew got up and followed him.
10 While Jesus was having dinner at Matthew's house, many tax collectors and
"sinners" came and ate with him and his disciples. 11 When the Pharisees saw this,

---

8:32 When the demons entered the pigs, they drove the animals into the sea. The demons' action proves their destructive intent – if they could not destroy the men, they would destroy the pigs. Jesus' action, by contrast, shows the value he places on each human life.

8:34 Why did the people ask Jesus to leave? Unlike their own pagan gods, Jesus could not be contained, controlled, or appeased. They feared Jesus' supernatural power, a power that they had never before witnessed. And they were upset about losing a herd of pigs more than they were glad about the deliverance of the demon-possessed men. Are you more concerned about property than people? Human beings are created in God's image and have eternal value. How foolish and yet how easy it is to value possessions, investments, and even animals above human life. Would you rather have Jesus leave you than finish his work in you?

9:1 "His own town" was Capernaum, a good choice for Jesus' base of operations. It was a wealthy city due to fishing and trade. Situated on the Sea of Galilee in a densely populated area, Capernaum housed the Roman garrison that kept peace in the region. The city was a cultural melting pot, greatly influenced by Greek and Roman manners, dress, architecture, and politics.

9:2 Among the first words Jesus said to the paralysed man were "Your sins are forgiven." Then he healed the man. We must be careful not to concentrate on God's power to heal physical sickness more than on his power to forgive spiritual sickness in the form of sin. Jesus saw that even more than physical health, this man needed spiritual health. Spiritual health comes only from Jesus' healing touch.

9:2 Both the man's body and his spirit were paralysed – he could not walk, and he did not know Jesus. But the man's spiritual state was Jesus' first concern. If God does not heal us or someone we love, we need to remember that physical healing is not Christ's only concern. We will all be completely healed in Christ's coming kingdom; but first we have to come to know Jesus.

9:3 Blaspheming is claiming to be God and applying his characteristics to yourself. The religious leaders rightly saw that Jesus was claiming to be God. What they did not understand was that he *is* God and thus has the authority to heal and to forgive sins.

9:5, 6 It's easy to tell someone his sins are forgiven; it's a lot more difficult to reverse a case of paralysis! Jesus backed up his words by healing the man's legs. Jesus' action showed that his words were true; he had the power to forgive as well as to heal. Talk is cheap, but our words lack meaning if our actions do not back them up. We can say we love God or others, but if we are not taking practical steps to demonstrate that love, our words are empty and meaningless. How well do your actions back up what you say?

9:9 Matthew was a Jew who was appointed by the Romans to be the area's tax collector. He collected taxes from the citizens as well as from merchants passing through the town. Tax collectors were expected to take a commission on the taxes they collected, but most of them overcharged and kept the profits. Thus, tax collectors were hated by the Jews because of their reputation for cheating and because of their support of Rome.

9:9 When Jesus called Matthew to be one of his disciples, Matthew got up and followed, leaving a lucrative career. When God calls you to follow or obey him, do you do it with as much abandon as Matthew? Sometimes the decision to follow Christ requires difficult or painful choices. Like Matthew, we must decide to leave behind those things that would keep us from following Christ.

9:10–13 When he visited Matthew, Jesus hurt his own reputation. Matthew was cheating the people, but Jesus found and changed him. We should not be afraid to reach out to people who are living in sin – God's message can change anyone.

9:11, 12 The Pharisees constantly tried to trap Jesus, and they thought his association with these "baddies" was the perfect opportunity. They were more concerned with their own appearance of holiness than with helping people, with criticism than encouragement, with outward respectability than practical help. But God is concerned for all people, including the sinful and hurting ones. The Christian life is not a popularity contest! Following Jesus' example, we should share the gospel with the poor, immoral, lonely, and outcast, not just the rich, moral, popular, and powerful.

they asked his disciples, "Why does your teacher eat with tax collectors and 'sinners'?"[j]
12On hearing this, Jesus said, "It is not the healthy who need a doctor, but the sick.
13But go and learn what this means: 'I desire mercy, not sacrifice.'[a][k] For I have not
come to call the righteous, but sinners."[l]

9:11 [j]Mt 11:19; Lk 5:30; 15:2; Gal 2:15
9:13 [k]Hos 6:6; Mic 6:6-8; Mt 12:7 [l]1Ti 1:15

Religious Leaders Ask Jesus about Fasting
(41/Mark 2:18–22; Luke 5:33–39)

14Then John's disciples came and asked him, "How is it that we and the Pharisees
fast,[m] but your disciples do not fast?"
15Jesus answered, "How can the guests of the bridegroom mourn while he is with
them?[n] The time will come when the bridegroom will be taken from them; then they
will fast.[o]
16"No-one sews a patch of unshrunk cloth on an old garment, for the patch will pull
away from the garment, making the tear worse. 17Neither do men pour new wine into
old wineskins. If they do, the skins will burst, the wine will run out and the wineskins
will be ruined. No, they pour new wine into new wineskins, and both are preserved."

9:14 [m]Lk 18:12
9:15 [n]Jn 3:29 [o]Ac 13:2, 3; 14:23

Jesus Heals a Bleeding Woman and Restores a Girl to Life
(89/Mark 5:21–43; Luke 8:40–56)

18While he was saying this, a ruler came and knelt before him[p] and said, "My
daughter has just died. But come and put your hand on her,[q] and she will live."
19Jesus got up and went with him, and so did his disciples.
20Just then a woman who had been subject to bleeding for twelve years came up
behind him and touched the edge of his cloak.[r] 21She said to herself, "If I only touch
his cloak, I will be healed."
22Jesus turned and saw her. "Take heart, daughter," he said, "your faith has healed
you."[s] And the woman was healed from that moment.[t]
23When Jesus entered the ruler's house and saw the flute players and the noisy

9:18 [p]Mt 8:2 [q]Mk 5:23
9:20 [r]Mt 14:36; Mk 3:10
9:22 [s]Mk 10:52; Lk 7:50; 17:19; 18:42 [t]Mt 15:28

[a] 13 Hosea 6:6

9:13 Those who are sure that they are righteous can't be saved because the first step in following Jesus is acknowledging our need and admitting that we don't have all the answers. For more on "I desire mercy, not sacrifice", see the chart in Hosea 6.

9:14 John's disciples fasted (went without food) as a sign of mourning for sin and to prepare for the Messiah's coming. Jesus' disciples did not need to fast because he is the Messiah and was with them! Jesus did not condemn fasting – he himself fasted (4:2). He emphasised that fasting must be done for the right reasons.

9:14 John the Baptist's message was harsh, and it focused on law. When people look at God's law and compare themselves to it, they realise how far they fall short and how badly they need to repent. Jesus' message focused on life, the result of turning from sin and turning to him. John's disciples had the right start, but they needed to take the next step and trust in Jesus. Where is your focus – on law or on Christ?

9:15 The arrival of the kingdom of heaven was like a wedding feast with Jesus as the bridegroom. His disciples, therefore, were filled with joy. It would not be right to mourn or fast when the bridegroom was present.

9:17 In Bible times, wine was not kept in glass bottles but in goatskins sewn around the edges to form watertight bags. New wine expanded as it fermented, stretching its wineskin. After the wine had aged, the stretched skin would burst if more new wine was poured into it. New wine, therefore, was always put into new wineskins.

9:17 Jesus did not come to patch up the old religious system of Judaism with its rules and traditions. If he had, his message would have damaged it. His purpose was to bring in something new, though it had been prophesied for centuries. This new message, the gospel, said that Jesus Christ, God's Son, came to earth to offer all people forgiveness of sins and reconciliation with God. The gospel did not fit into the old rigid legalistic system of religion. It needed a fresh start. The message will always remain "new" because it must be accepted and applied in every generation. When we follow Christ, we must be prepared for new ways to live, new ways to look at people, and new ways to serve.

9:18 Mark and Luke say this man's name was Jairus (Mark 5:22; Luke 8:41). As ruler of the synagogue, Jairus was responsible for administration – looking after the building, supervising worship, running the school on weekdays, and finding rabbis to teach on the Sabbath. For more information on synagogues, read the first note on Mark 1:21.

9:20–22 This woman had suffered for 12 years with bleeding (perhaps a menstrual disorder). In our times of desperation, we don't have to worry about the correct way to reach out to God. Like this woman, we can simply reach out in faith. He will respond.

9:22 God changed a situation that had been a problem for years. Like the leper and the demon-possessed men (see the note on 8:3 and the second note on 8:28), this diseased woman was considered unclean. For 12 years, she too had been one of the "untouchables" and had not been able to lead a normal life. But Jesus changed that and restored her. Sometimes we are tempted to give up on people or situations that have not changed for many years. God can change what seems unchangeable, giving new purpose and hope.

9:23–26 The synagogue ruler didn't come to Jesus until his daughter was dead – it was too late for anyone else to help. But Jesus simply went to the girl and raised her! In our lives, Christ can make a difference when it seems too late for anyone else to help.

9:23 [u]2Ch 35:25; Jer 9:17, 18
9:24 [v]Ac 20:10 [w]Jn 11:11-14
9:26 [x]Mt 4:24
9:27 [y]Mt 15:22; Mk 10:47; Lk 18:38-39

crowd,[u] 24he said, "Go away. The girl is not dead[v] but asleep."[w] But they laughed
at him. 25After the crowd had been put outside, he went in and took the girl by the
hand, and she got up. 26News of this spread through all that region.[x]

Jesus Heals the Blind and Mute
(90)

27As Jesus went on from there, two blind men followed him, calling out, "Have
mercy on us, Son of David!"[y]

MATTHEW

More than any other disciple, Matthew had a clear idea of how much it would cost to follow Jesus, yet he did not hesitate for a moment. When he left his tax-collecting booth, he guaranteed himself unemployment. For several of the other disciples, there was always fishing to return to, but for Matthew, there was no turning back.

Two changes happened to Matthew when he decided to follow Jesus. First, Jesus gave him a new life. He not only belonged to a new group; he belonged to the Son of God. He was not just accepting a different way of life; he was now an accepted person. For a despised tax collector, that change must have been wonderful! Secondly, Jesus gave Matthew a new purpose for his skills. When he followed Jesus, the only tool from his past job that he carried with him was his pen. From the beginning, God had made him a record-keeper. Jesus' call eventually allowed him to put his skills to their finest work. Matthew was a keen observer, and he undoubtedly recorded what he saw going on around him. The Gospel that bears his name came as a result.

Matthew's experience points out that each of us, from the beginning, is one of God's works in progress. Much of what God has for us he gives long before we are able to consciously respond to him. He trusts us with skills and abilities ahead of schedule. He has made us each capable of being his servant. When we trust him with what he has given us, we begin a life of real adventure. Matthew couldn't have known that God would use the very skills he had sharpened as a tax collector to record the greatest story ever lived. And God has no less meaningful a purpose for each one of us. Have you recognised Jesus saying to you, "Follow me"? What has been your response?

Strengths and accomplishments:
- Was one of Jesus' 12 disciples
- Responded immediately to Jesus' call
- Invited many friends to his home to meet Jesus
- Compiled the Gospel of Matthew
- Clarified for his Jewish audience Jesus' fulfilment of Old Testament prophecies

Lessons from his life:
- Jesus consistently accepted people from every level of society
- Matthew was given a new life, and his God-given skills of record-keeping and attention to detail were given new purpose
- Having been accepted by Jesus, Matthew immediately tried to bring others into contact with Jesus

Vital statistics:
- Where: Capernaum
- Occupations: Tax collector, disciple of Jesus
- Relative: Father: Alphaeus
- Contemporaries: Jesus, Pilate, Herod, other disciples

Key verse:
"As he walked along, he saw Levi son of Alphaeus sitting at the tax collector's booth. 'Follow me,' Jesus told him, and Levi got up and followed him" (Mark 2:14).

Matthew's story is told in the Gospels. He is also mentioned in Acts 1:13.

He can bring healing to broken relationships, release from addiction, and forgiveness and healing to emotional scars. If your situation looks hopeless, remember that Christ can do the impossible.

9:27 "Son of David" was a popular way of addressing Jesus as the Messiah because it was known that the Messiah would be a descendant of David (Isaiah 9:7). This is the first time the title is used in Matthew. Jesus' ability to give sight to the blind was prophesied in Isaiah 29:18; 35:5; 42:7.

9:27–30 Jesus didn't respond immediately to the blind men's pleas. He waited to see if they had faith. Not everyone who says he wants help really believes God can help him. Jesus may have waited and questioned these men to emphasise and increase their faith. When you think that God is too slow in answering your prayers, consider that he might be testing you as he did the blind men. Do you believe that God can help you? Do you *really* want his help?

28 When he had gone indoors, the blind men came to him, and he asked them, "Do
you believe that I am able to do this?"
"Yes, Lord," they replied.
29 Then he touched their eyes and said, "According to your faith will it be done to
you";[z] 30 and their sight was restored. Jesus warned them sternly, "See that no-one
knows about this."[a] 31 But they went out and spread the news about him all over that
region.[b]
32 While they were going out, a man who was demon-possessed[c] and could not
talk[d] was brought to Jesus. 33 And when the demon was driven out, the man who had
been mute spoke. The crowd was amazed and said, "Nothing like this has ever been
seen in Israel."[e]
34 But the Pharisees said, "It is by the prince of demons that he drives out demons."[f]

Jesus Urges the Disciples to Pray for Workers
(92)

35 Jesus went through all the towns and villages, teaching in their synagogues,
preaching the good news of the kingdom and healing every disease and sickness.[g]
36 When he saw the crowds, he had compassion on them,[h] because they were harassed
and helpless, like sheep without a shepherd.[i] 37 Then he said to his disciples, "The
harvest[j] is plentiful but the workers are few.[k] 38 Ask the Lord of the harvest,
therefore, to send out workers into his harvest field."

Jesus Sends Out the Twelve Disciples
(93/Mark 6:7–13; Luke 9:1–6)

10 He called his twelve disciples to him and gave them authority to drive out evil[a]
spirits[a] and to heal every disease and sickness.
2 These are the names of the twelve apostles: first, Simon (who is called Peter) and
his brother Andrew; James son of Zebedee, and his brother John; 3 Philip and Bartholo-

a 1 Greek *unclean*

9:29 [z] ver 22
9:30 [a] Mt 8:4
9:31 [b] ver 26; Mk 7:36
9:32 [c] Mt 4:24 [d] Mt 12:22-24
9:33 [e] Mk 2:12
9:34 [f] Mt 12:24; Lk 11:15
9:35 [g] Mt 4:23
9:36 [h] Mt 14:14 [i] Nu 27:17; Eze 34:5, 6; Zec 10:2; Mk 6:34
9:37 [j] Jn 4:35 [k] Lk 10:2
10:1 [a] Mk 3:13-15; Lk 9:1

9:28 These blind men were persistent. They went right into the house where Jesus was staying. They knew Jesus could heal them, and they would let nothing stop them from finding him. That's real faith in action. If you believe Jesus is the answer to your every need, don't let anything or anyone stop you from reaching him.

9:30 Jesus told the people to keep quiet about his healings because he did not want to be known only as a miracle worker. He healed because he had compassion on people, but he also wanted to bring *spiritual* healing to a sin-sick world.

9:32 While Jesus was on earth, demonic forces seemed especially active. Although we cannot always be sure why or how demon-possession occurs, it causes both physical and mental problems. In this case, the demon made the man unable to talk. For more on demons and demon-possession, read the notes on 8:28 and Mark 1:23.

9:34 In chapter 9, the Pharisees accuse Jesus of four different sins: blasphemy, befriending outcasts, impiety, and serving Satan. Matthew shows how Jesus was maligned by those who should have received him most gladly. Why did the Pharisees do this? (1) Jesus bypassed their religious authority. (2) He weakened their control over the people. (3) He challenged their cherished beliefs. (4) He exposed their insincere motives.

9:34 While the Pharisees questioned, debated, and dissected Jesus, people were being healed and lives changed right in front of them. Their scepticism was based not on insufficient evidence but on jealousy of Jesus' popularity.

9:35 The good news of the kingdom was that the promised and long-awaited Messiah had finally come. His healing miracles were a sign that his teaching was true.

9:35–38 Jesus needs workers who know how to deal with people's problems. We can comfort others and show them the way to live because we have been helped with our problems by God and his labourers (2 Corinthians 1:3–7).

9:36 Ezekiel also compared Israel to sheep without a shepherd (Ezekiel 34:5, 6). Jesus came to be the Shepherd, the One who could show people how to avoid life's pitfalls (see John 10:14).

9:37, 38 Jesus looked at the crowds following him and referred to them as a field ripe for harvest. Many people are ready to give their lives to Christ if someone would show them how. Jesus commands us to pray that people will respond to this need for workers. Often, when we pray for something, God answers our prayers by using *us*. Be prepared for God to use you to show another person the way to him.

10:1 Jesus *called* his 12 disciples. He didn't draft them, force them, or ask them to volunteer; he chose them to serve him in a special way. Christ calls us today. He doesn't twist our arms and make us do something we don't want to do. We can choose to join him or remain behind. When Christ calls you to follow him, how do you respond?

10:2–4 The list of Jesus' 12 disciples doesn't give us many details – probably because there weren't many impressive details to tell. Jesus called people from all walks of life – fishermen, political activists, tax collectors. He called common people and uncommon leaders; rich and poor; educated and uneducated. Today, many people think only certain people are fit to follow Christ, but this was not the attitude of the Master himself. God can use anyone, no matter how insignificant he or she appears. When you feel small and useless, remember that God uses ordinary people to do his extraordinary work.

10:3 Bartholomew is probably another name for Nathanael, whom we meet in John 1:45–51. Thaddaeus is also known as Judas son of James. The disciples are also listed in Mark 3:16–19; Luke 6:14–16; and Acts 1:13.

mew; Thomas and Matthew the tax collector; James son of Alphaeus, and Thaddaeus;
4 Simon the Zealot and Judas Iscariot, who betrayed him.[b]
5 These twelve Jesus sent out with the following instructions: "Do not go among the
Gentiles or enter any town of the Samaritans.[c] 6 Go rather to the lost sheep of Israel.[d]
7 As you go, preach this message: 'The kingdom of heaven[e] is near.' 8 Heal the sick,
raise the dead, cleanse those who have leprosy,[b] drive out demons. Freely you have
received, freely give. 9 Do not take along any gold or silver or copper in your belts;[f]
10 take no bag for the journey, or extra tunic, or sandals or a staff; for the worker is
worth his keep.[g]
11 "Whatever town or village you enter, search for some worthy person there and
stay at his house until you leave. 12 As you enter the home, give it your greeting.[h]
13 If the home is deserving, let your peace rest on it; if it is not, let your peace return
to you. 14 If anyone will not welcome you or listen to your words, shake the dust off
your feet[i] when you leave that home or town. 15 I tell you the truth, it will be more
bearable for Sodom and Gomorrah[j] on the day of judgment[k] than for that town.[l]
16 I am sending you out like sheep among wolves.[m] Therefore be as shrewd as snakes
and as innocent as doves.[n]

Jesus Prepares the Disciples for Persecution
(94)

17 "Be on your guard against men; they will hand you over to the local councils[o]
and flog you in their synagogues.[p] 18 On my account you will be brought before
governors and kings[q] as witnesses to them and to the Gentiles. 19 But when they arrest

10:4 [b]Mt 26:14-16, 25, 47; Jn 13:2, 26, 27
10:5 [c]2Ki 17:24; Lk 9:52; Jn 4:4-26, 39, 40; Ac 8:5, 25
10:6 [d]Jer 50:6; Mt 15:24
10:7 [e]Mt 3:2
10:9 [f]Lk 22:35
10:10 [g]1Ti 5:18
10:12 [h]1Sa 25:6
10:14 [i]Ne 5:13; Lk 10:11; Ac 13:51
10:15 [j]2Pe 2:6; [k]Mt 12:36; 2Pe 2:9; 1Jn 4:17; [l]Mt 11:22, 24
10:16 [m]Lk 10:3; [n]Ro 16:19
10:17 [o]Mt 5:22; [p]Mt 23:34; Mk 13:9; Ac 5:40; 26:11
10:18 [q]Ac 25:24-26

b *8* The Greek word was used for various diseases affecting the skin—not necessarily leprosy.

10:4 Simon the Zealot may have been a member of the Zealots, a radical political party working for the violent overthrow of Roman rule in Israel.

10:5, 6 Why didn't Jesus send the disciples to the Gentiles or the Samaritans? A Gentile is anyone who is not a Jew. The Samaritans were a race that resulted from intermarriage between Jews and Gentiles after the Old Testament captivities (see 2 Kings 17:24). Jesus asked his disciples to go only to the Jews because he came *first* to the Jews (Romans 1:16). God chose them to tell the rest of the world about him. Jewish disciples and apostles preached the gospel of the risen Christ all around the Roman empire, and soon Gentiles were pouring into the church. The Bible clearly teaches that God's message of salvation is for *all* people, regardless of race, sex, or national origin (Genesis 12:3; Isaiah 25:6; 56:3–7; Malachi 1:11; Acts 10:34, 35; Romans 3:29, 30; Galatians 3:28).

10:7 The Jews were waiting for the Messiah to usher in his kingdom. They hoped for a political and military kingdom that would free them from Roman rule and bring back the days of glory under David and Solomon. But Jesus was talking about a spiritual kingdom. The gospel today is that the kingdom is still *near.* Jesus, the Messiah, has already begun his kingdom on earth in the hearts of his followers. One day the kingdom will be fully realised. Then evil will be destroyed and all people will live in peace with one another.

10:8 Jesus gave the disciples a principle to guide their actions as they ministered to others: "Freely you have received, freely give." Because God has showered us with his blessings, we should give generously to others of our time, love, and possessions.

10:10 Jesus said that those who minister are to be cared for. The disciples could expect food and shelter in return for the spiritual service they provided. Who ministers to you? Make sure you take care of the pastors, missionaries, and teachers who serve God by serving you (see 1 Corinthians 9:9, 10; 1 Timothy 5:17).

10:10 Mark's account (6:8) says to take a staff (walking stick), and Matthew and Luke (9:3) say not to. Jesus may have meant that they were not to take an *extra* pair of sandals, staff, and bag. In any case, the principle was that they were to go out ready for duty and travel, unencumbered by excess material goods.

10:14 Why did Jesus tell his disciples to shake the dust off their feet if a city or home didn't welcome them? When leaving Gentile cities, pious Jews often shook the dust from their feet to show their separation from Gentile practices. If the disciples shook the dust of a *Jewish* town from their feet, it would show their separation from Jews who rejected their Messiah. This gesture was to show the people that they were making a wrong choice—that the opportunity to choose Christ might not present itself again. Are you receptive to teaching from God? If you ignore the Spirit's prompting, you may not get another chance.

10:15 The cities of Sodom and Gomorrah were destroyed by fire from heaven because of their wickedness (Genesis 19:24, 25). Those who reject the gospel when they hear it will be worse off than the wicked people of these destroyed cities, who never heard the gospel at all.

10:16 The opposition of the Pharisees would be like ravaging wolves. The disciples' only hope would be to look to their Shepherd for protection. We may face similar hostility. Like the disciples, we are not to be sheeplike in our attitude but sensible and prudent. We are not to be gullible pawns but neither are we to be deceitful connivers. We must find a balance between wisdom and vulnerability to accomplish God's work.

10:17, 18 Later the disciples experienced these hardships (Acts 5:40; 12:1–3), not only from without (governments, courts), but also from within (friends, family; 10:21). Living for God often brings persecution, but with it comes the opportunity to tell the good news of salvation. In times of persecution, we can be confident because Jesus has "overcome the world" (John 16:33). And those who stand firm to the end will be saved (10:22).

10:19, 20 Jesus told the disciples that when arrested for preaching the gospel, they should not worry about what to say in their defence—God's Spirit would speak through them. This promise was fulfilled in Acts 4:8–14 and elsewhere. Some mistakenly think this means we don't have to prepare to present the gospel because God will take care of everything. Scripture teaches, however, that we are to make carefully prepared, thoughtful statements (Colossians 4:6). Jesus is not telling us to stop preparing but to stop worrying.

you, do not worry about what to say or how to say it.[r] At that time you will be given
what to say, 20 for it will not be you speaking, but the Spirit of your Father[s] speaking
through you.
21 "Brother will betray brother to death, and a father his child; children will rebel
against their parents[t] and have them put to death. 22 All men will hate you because
of me, but he who stands firm to the end will be saved.[u] 23 When you are persecuted
in one place, flee to another. I tell you the truth, you will not finish going through
the cities of Israel before the Son of Man comes.
24 "A student is not above his teacher, nor a servant above his master.[v] 25 It is
enough for the student to be like his teacher, and the servant like his master. If the
head of the house has been called Beelzebub,[c][w] how much more the members of
his household!
26 "So do not be afraid of them. There is nothing concealed that will not be disclosed,
or hidden that will not be made known.[x] 27 What I tell you in the dark, speak in the
daylight; what is whispered in your ear, proclaim from the roofs. 28 Do not be afraid
of those who kill the body but cannot kill the soul. Rather, be afraid of the One[y] who
can destroy both soul and body in hell. 29 Are not two sparrows sold for a penny?[d]
Yet not one of them will fall to the ground apart from the will of your Father. 30 And
even the very hairs of your head are all numbered.[z] 31 So don't be afraid; you are
worth more than many sparrows.[a]
32 "Whoever acknowledges me before men,[b] I will also acknowledge him before
my Father in heaven. 33 But whoever disowns me before men, I will disown him before
my Father in heaven.[c]
34 "Do not suppose that I have come to bring peace to the earth. I did not come to
bring peace, but a sword. 35 For I have come to turn

" 'a man against his father,
a daughter against her mother,
a daughter-in-law against her mother-in-law[d]—
36 a man's enemies will be the members of his own
household.'[e][e]

37 "Anyone who loves his father or mother more than me is not worthy of me; anyone
who loves his son or daughter more than me is not worthy of me;[f] 38 and anyone who

c 25 Greek *Beezeboul* or *Beelzeboul* d 29 Greek *an assarion* e 36 Micah 7:6

10:19 [r]Ex 4:12
10:20 [s]Ac 4:8
10:21 [t]ver 35, 36; Mic 7:6
10:22 [u]Mt 24:13; Mk 13:13
10:24 [v]Lk 6:40; Jn 13:16; 15:20
10:25 [w]Mk 3:22
10:26 [x]Mk 4:22; Lk 8:17
10:28 [y]Isa 8:12, 13; Heb 10:31
10:30 [z]1Sa 14:45; 2Sa 14:11; Lk 21:18; Ac 27:34
10:31 [a]Mt 12:12
10:32 [b]Ro 10:9
10:33 [c]Mk 8:38; 2Ti 2:12
10:35 [d]ver 21
10:36 [e]Mic 7:6
10:37 [f]Lk 14:26

10:22 Standing firm to the end is not a way to be saved but the evidence that a person is really committed to Jesus. Persistence is not a means to earn salvation; it is the by-product of a truly devoted life.

10:23 Christ warned the disciples against premature martyrdom. They were to leave before the persecution got too great. We have plenty of work to do and many people to reach. Our work won't be finished until Christ returns. And only after he returns will the whole world realise his true identity (see 24:14; Romans 14:9–12).

10:25 Beelzebub was also known as the lord of flies and the prince of demons. The Pharisees accused Jesus of using Beelzebub's power to drive out demons (see 12:24). Good is sometimes labelled evil. If Jesus, who is perfect, was called evil, his followers should expect that similar accusations will be directed at them. But those who stand firm will be vindicated (10:22).

10:29–31 Jesus said that God is aware of everything that happens even to sparrows, and you are far more valuable to him than they are. You are so valuable that God sent his only Son to die for you (John 3:16). Because God places such value on you, you need never fear personal threats or difficult trials. These can't shake God's love or dislodge his Spirit from within you.

But this doesn't mean that God will take away all your troubles (see 10:16). The real test of value is how well something holds up under the wear, tear, and abuse of everyday life. Those who stand up for Christ in spite of their troubles truly have lasting value and will receive great rewards (see 5:11, 12).

10:34 Jesus did not come to bring the kind of peace that glosses over deep differences just for the sake of superficial harmony. Conflict and disagreement will arise between those who choose to follow Christ and those who don't. Yet we can look forward to the day when all conflict will be resolved. For more on Jesus as peacemaker, see Isaiah 9:6; Matthew 5:9; John 14:27.

10:34–39 Christian commitment may separate friends and loved ones. In saying this, Jesus was not encouraging disobedience to parents or conflict at home. Rather, he was showing that his presence demands a decision. Because some will follow Christ and some won't, conflict will inevitably arise. As we take our cross and follow him, our different values, morals, goals, and purposes will set us apart from others. Don't neglect your family, but remember that your commitment to God is even more important than they are. God should be your first priority.

10:37 Christ calls us to a higher mission than to find comfort and tranquillity in this life. Love of family is a law of God, but even this love can be self-serving and used as an excuse not to serve God or do his work.

10:38 To take our cross and follow Jesus means to be willing to identify with him publicly, to experience almost certain opposition, and to be committed to facing even suffering and death for his sake.

10:38 [g]Mt 16:24; Lk 14:27
10:39 [h]Lk 17:33; Jn 12:25
10:40 [i]Mt 18:5; Gal 4:14 [j]Lk 9:48; Jn 12:44; 13:20
10:42 [k]Mt 25:40; Mk 9:41; Heb 6:10
11:1 [a]Mt 7:28
11:2 [b]Mt 14:3
11:3 [c]Ps 118:26; Jn 11:27; Heb 10:37
11:5 [d]Isa 35:4-6; 61:1; Lk 4:18, 19
11:6 [e]Mt 13:21
11:7 [f]Mt 3:1
11:9 [g]Mt 21:26; Lk 1:76

does not take his cross and follow me is not worthy of me.[g] 39Whoever finds his life
will lose it, and whoever loses his life for my sake will find it.[h]
40"He who receives you receives me,[i] and he who receives me receives the one
who sent me.[j] 41Anyone who receives a prophet because he is a prophet will receive
a prophet's reward, and anyone who receives a righteous man because he is a righteous
man will receive a righteous man's reward. 42And if anyone gives even a cup of cold
water to one of these little ones because he is my disciple, I tell you the truth, he will
certainly not lose his reward."[k]

4. Jesus teaches about the kingdom

Jesus Eases John's Doubt

(70/Luke 7:18–35)

11 After Jesus had finished instructing his twelve disciples,[a] he went on from
there to teach and preach in the towns of Galilee.**[a]**
2When John heard in prison[b] what Christ was doing, he sent his disciples 3to ask
him, "Are you the one who was to come,[c] or should we expect someone else?"
4Jesus replied, "Go back and report to John what you hear and see: 5The blind
receive sight, the lame walk, those who have leprosy**[b]** are cured, the deaf hear, the
dead are raised, and the good news is preached to the poor.[d] 6Blessed is the man who
does not fall away on account of me."[e]
7As John's[f] disciples were leaving, Jesus began to speak to the crowd about John:
"What did you go out into the desert to see? A reed swayed by the wind? 8If not, what
did you go out to see? A man dressed in fine clothes? No, those who wear fine clothes
are in kings' palaces. 9Then what did you go out to see? A prophet?[g] Yes, I tell you,
and more than a prophet. 10This is the one about whom it is written:

a *1* Greek *in their towns* **b** *5* The Greek word was used for various diseases affecting the skin—not necessarily leprosy.

COUNTING THE COST OF FOLLOWING CHRIST
Jesus helped his disciples to prepare for the rejection many of them would experience by being Christians. Being God's person will usually create reactions from others who are resisting him.

Who may oppose us?	*Natural response*	*Possible pressures*		*Needed truth*
GOVERNMENT 10:18–19	Fear and worry	Threats 10:26	→	The truth will be revealed (10:26)
		Physical harm 10:28	→	Our soul cannot be harmed (10:28)
RELIGIOUS PEOPLE 10:17		Public ridicule 10:22	→	God himself will acknowledge us if we acknowledge him (10:32)
FAMILY 10:21		Rejection by loved ones 10:34–37	→	God's love can sustain us (10:31)

10:39 This verse is a positive and negative statement of the same truth: clinging to this life may cause us to forfeit the best from Christ in this world *and* in the next. The more we love this life's rewards (leisure, power, popularity, financial security), the more we will discover how empty they really are. The best way to enjoy life, therefore, is to loosen our greedy grasp on earthly rewards so that we can be free to follow Christ. In doing so, we will inherit eternal life and begin at once to experience the benefits of following Christ.

10:42 How much we love God can be measured by how well we treat others. Jesus' example of giving a cup of cold water to a thirsty child is a good model of unselfish service. A child usually can't or won't return a favour. God notices every good deed we do or don't do as if he were the one receiving it. Is there something unselfish you can do for someone else today? Although no-one else may see you, God will notice.

11:2, 3 John had been put in prison by Herod. Herod had married his own sister-in-law, and John publicly rebuked Herod's flagrant sin (14:3–5). John's Profile is found in John 1. Herod's Profile is found in Mark 6.

11:4–6 As John sat in prison, he began to have some doubts about whether Jesus really was the Messiah. If John's purpose was to prepare people for the coming Messiah (3:3), and if Jesus really was that Messiah, then why was John in prison when he could have been preaching to the crowds, preparing their hearts?

Jesus answered John's doubts by pointing to Jesus' acts of healing the blind, lame, and deaf, curing the lepers, raising the dead, and preaching the good news to the poor. With so much evidence, Jesus' identity was obvious. If you sometimes doubt your salvation, the forgiveness of your sins, or God's work in your life, look at the evidence in Scripture and the changes in your life. When you doubt, don't turn away from Christ; turn *to* him.

"'I will send my messenger ahead of you,
who will prepare your way before you.'[c][h]

11I tell you the truth: Among those born of women there has not risen anyone greater
than John the Baptist; yet he who is least in the kingdom of heaven is greater than
he. 12From the days of John the Baptist until now, the kingdom of heaven has been
forcefully advancing, and forceful men lay hold of it. 13For all the Prophets and the
Law prophesied until John. 14And if you are willing to accept it, he is the Elijah who
was to come.[i] 15He who has ears, let him hear.[j]
16"To what can I compare this generation? They are like children sitting in the
market-places and calling out to others:

17" 'We played the flute for you,
and you did not dance;
we sang a dirge,
and you did not mourn.'

18For John came neither eating[k] nor drinking,[l] and they say, 'He has a demon.'
19The Son of Man came eating and drinking, and they say, 'Here is a glutton and a
drunkard, a friend of tax collectors and "sinners".'[m] But wisdom is proved right by
her actions."

Jesus Promises Rest for the Soul
(71)

20Then Jesus began to denounce the cities in which most of his miracles had been
performed, because they did not repent. 21"Woe to you, Korazin! Woe to you,
Bethsaida![n] If the miracles that were performed in you had been performed in Tyre
and Sidon,[o] they would have repented long ago in sackcloth and ashes.[p] 22But I tell
you, it will be more bearable for Tyre and Sidon on the day of judgment than for you.[q]
23And you, Capernaum,[r] will you be lifted up to the skies? No, you will go down
to the depths.[d][s] If the miracles that were performed in you had been performed in
Sodom, it would have remained to this day. 24But I tell you that it will be more
bearable for Sodom on the day of judgment than for you."[t]
25At that time Jesus said, "I praise you, Father,[u] Lord of heaven and earth, because
you have hidden these things from the wise and learned, and revealed them to little
children.[v] 26Yes, Father, for this was your good pleasure.

[c] *10* Mal. 3:1 [d] *23* Greek *Hades*

11:10 [h]Mal 3:1; Mk 1:2
11:14 [i]Mal 4:5; Mt 17:10-13; Mk 9:11-13; Lk 1:17; Jn 1:21
11:15 [j]Mt 13:9, 43; Mk 4:23; Lk 14:35; Rev 2:7
11:18 [k]Mt 3:4 [l]Lk 1:15
11:19 [m]Mt 9:11
11:21 [n]Mk 6:45; Lk 9:10; Jn 12:21 [o]Mt 15:21; Lk 6:17; Ac 12:20 [p]Jnh 3:5-9
11:22 [q]ver 24; Mt 10:15
11:23 [r]Mt 4:13 [s]Isa 14:13-15
11:24 [t]Mt 10:15
11:25 [u]Lk 22:42; Jn 11:41 [v]1Co 1:26-29

11:11 No man ever fulfilled his God-given purpose better than John. Yet in God's coming kingdom all members will have a greater spiritual heritage than John because they will have seen and known Christ and his finished work on the cross.

11:12 There are three common views about the meaning of this verse. (1) Jesus may have been referring to a vast movement towards God, the momentum that began with John's preaching. (2) He may have been reflecting the Jewish activists' expectation that God's kingdom would come through a violent overthrow of Rome. (3) Or he may have meant that entering God's kingdom takes courage, unwavering faith, determination, and endurance because of the growing opposition levelled at Jesus' followers.

11:14 John was not a resurrected Elijah, but he took on Elijah's prophetic role – boldly confronting sin and pointing people to God (Malachi 3:1). See Elijah's Profile in 1 Kings 18.

11:16–19 Jesus condemned the attitude of his generation. No matter what he said or did, they took the opposite view. They were cynical and sceptical because he challenged their comfortable, secure, and self-centred lives. Too often we justify our inconsistencies because listening to God may require us to change the way we live.

11:21–24 Tyre, Sidon, and Sodom were ancient cities with a long-standing reputation for wickedness (Genesis 18; 19; Ezekiel 27; 28). Each was destroyed by God for its evil. The people of Bethsaida, Korazin, and Capernaum saw Jesus firsthand, and yet they stubbornly refused to repent of their sins and believe in him. Jesus said that if some of the wickedest cities in the world had seen him, they would have repented. Because Bethsaida, Korazin, and Capernaum saw Jesus and didn't believe, they would suffer even greater punishment than that of the wicked cities who didn't see Jesus. Similarly, nations and cities with churches on every corner and Bibles in every home will have no excuse on judgment day if they do not repent and believe.

11:25 Jesus mentioned two kinds of people in his prayer: the "wise" – arrogant in their own knowledge – and the "little children" – humbly open to receiving the truth of God's word. Are you wise in your own eyes, or do you seek the truth in childlike faith, realising that only God holds all the answers?

11:27 In the Old Testament, "know" means more than knowledge. It implies an intimate relationship. The communion between God the Father and God the Son is the core of their relationship. For anyone else to know God, God must reveal himself to that person, by the Son's choice. How fortunate we are that Jesus has clearly revealed to us God, his truth, and how we can know him.

11:27
[w]Mt 28:18
[x]Jn 3:35; 13:3; 17:2
[y]Jn 10:15
11:28
[z]Jn 7:37
11:29
[a]Jn 13:15; Php 2:5; 1Pe 2:21; 1Jn 2:6
[b]Jer 6:16
11:30
[c]1Jn 5:3
12:1
[a]Dt 23:25
12:2
[b]ver 10; Lk 13:14; 14:3; Jn 5:10; 7:23; 9:16
12:3
[c]1Sa 21:6
12:4
[d]Lev 24:5, 9
12:5
[e]Nu 28:9, 10; Jn 7:22, 23
12:6
[f]ver 41, 42
12:7
[g]Hos 6:6; Mic 6:6-8; Mt 9:13
12:8
[h]Mt 8:20

27"All things have been committed to me[w] by my Father.[x] No-one knows the Son
except the Father, and no-one knows the Father except the Son and those to whom
the Son chooses to reveal him.[y]
28"Come to me,[z] all you who are weary and burdened, and I will give you rest.
29Take my yoke upon you and learn from me,[a] for I am gentle and humble in heart,
and you will find rest for your souls.[b] 30For my yoke is easy and my burden is
light."[c]

The Disciples Pick Wheat on the Sabbath
(45/Mark 2:23–28; Luke 6:1–5)

12 At that time Jesus went through the cornfields on the Sabbath. His disciples
were hungry and began to pick some ears of corn[a] and eat them. 2When the
Pharisees saw this, they said to him, "Look! Your disciples are doing what is unlawful
on the Sabbath."[b]
3He answered, "Haven't you read what David did when he and his companions were
hungry?[c] 4He entered the house of God, and he and his companions ate the consecrated bread—which was not lawful for them to do, but only for the priests.[d] 5Or
haven't you read in the Law that on the Sabbath the priests in the temple desecrate
the day[e] and yet are innocent? 6I tell you that one**[a]** greater than the temple is here.[f]
7If you had known what these words mean, 'I desire mercy, not sacrifice,'**[b]**[g] you
would not have condemned the innocent. 8For the Son of Man[h] is Lord of the
Sabbath."

a *6* Or *something*; also in verses 41 and 42 **b** *7* Hosea 6:6

11:28–30 A yoke is a heavy wooden harness that fits over the shoulders of an ox or oxen. It is attached to a piece of equipment the oxen are to pull. A person may be carrying heavy burdens of (1) sin, (2) excessive demands of religious leaders (23:4; Acts 15:10), (3) oppression and persecution, or (4) weariness in the search for God.

Jesus frees people from all these burdens. The rest that Jesus promises is love, healing, and peace with God, not the end of all labour. A relationship with God changes meaningless, wearisome toil into spiritual productivity and purpose.

12:1, 2 The Pharisees had established 39 categories of actions forbidden on the Sabbath, based on interpretations of God's law and on Jewish custom. Harvesting was one of those forbidden actions. By picking wheat and rubbing it in their hands, the disciples were technically harvesting, according to the religious leaders. Jesus and the disciples were picking grain because they were hungry, not because they wanted to harvest the grain for a profit. They were not working on the Sabbath. The Pharisees, however, could not (and did not want to) see beyond their law's technicalities. They had no room for compassion, and they were determined to accuse Jesus of wrongdoing.

12:4 This story is recorded in 1 Samuel 21:1–6. The bread of the Presence was replaced every week, and the old loaves were eaten by the priests. The loaves given to David were the old loaves that had just been replaced with fresh ones. Although the priests were the only ones allowed to eat this bread, God did not punish David because his need for food was more important than the priestly regulations. Jesus was saying, "If you condemn me, you must also condemn David," something the religious leaders could never do without causing a great uproar among the people. Jesus was not condoning disobedience to God's laws. Instead he was emphasising discernment and compassion in enforcing the laws.

12:5 The Ten Commandments prohibit work on the Sabbath (Exodus 20:8–11). That was the *letter* of the law. But because the *purpose* of the Sabbath is to rest and to worship God, the priests were allowed to work by performing sacrifices and conducting worship services. This "Sabbath work" was serving and worshipping God. Jesus always emphasised the intent of the law, the meaning behind the letter. The Pharisees had lost the spirit of the law and were rigidly demanding that the letter (and their interpretation of it) be obeyed.

12:6 The Pharisees were so concerned about religious rituals that they missed the whole purpose of the temple—to bring people to God. And because Jesus Christ is even greater than the temple, how much better can he bring people to God. God is far more important than the created instruments of worship. If we become more concerned with the means of worship than with the One we worship, we will miss God even as we think we are worshipping him.

12:7 Jesus repeated to the Pharisees words the Jewish people had heard time and again throughout their history (1 Samuel 15:22, 23; Psalm 40:6–8; Isaiah 1:11–17; Jeremiah 7:21–23; Hosea 6:6). Our heart attitude towards God comes first. Only then can we properly obey and observe religious regulations and rituals.

12:8 When Jesus said he was Lord of the Sabbath, he claimed to be greater than the law and above the law. To the Pharisees, this was heresy. They did not realise that Jesus, the divine Son of God, had created the Sabbath. The Creator is always greater than the creation; thus Jesus had the authority to overrule their traditions and regulations.

Jesus Heals a Man's Hand on the Sabbath
(46/Mark 3:1–6; Luke 6:6–11)

9Going on from that place, he went into their synagogue, 10and a man with a
shrivelled hand was there. Looking for a reason to accuse Jesus, they asked him, "Is
it lawful to heal on the Sabbath?"[i]
11He said to them, "If any of you has a sheep and it falls into a pit on the Sabbath,
will you not take hold of it and lift it out?[j] 12How much more valuable is a man than
a sheep![k] Therefore it is lawful to do good on the Sabbath."
13Then he said to the man, "Stretch out your hand." So he stretched it out and it
was completely restored, just as sound as the other. 14But the Pharisees went out and
plotted how they might kill Jesus.[l]

Large Crowds Follow Jesus
(47/Mark 3:7–12)

15Aware of this, Jesus withdrew from that place. Many followed him, and he healed
all their sick,[m] 16warning them not to tell who he was.[n] 17This was to fulfil what
was spoken through the prophet Isaiah:

> 18"Here is my servant whom I have chosen,
> the one I love, in whom I delight;[o]
> I will put my Spirit on him,
> and he will proclaim justice to the nations.
> 19He will not quarrel or cry out;
> no-one will hear his voice in the streets.
> 20A bruised reed he will not break,
> and a smouldering wick he will not snuff out,
> till he leads justice to victory.
> 21 In his name the nations will put their hope."[c][p]

Religious Leaders Accuse Jesus of Being under Satan's Power
(74/Mark 3:20–30)

22Then they brought him a demon-possessed man who was blind and mute, and
Jesus healed him, so that he could both talk and see.[q] 23All the people were astonished
and said, "Could this be the Son of David?"[r]
24But when the Pharisees heard this, they said, "It is only by Beelzebub,[d][s] the
prince of demons, that this fellow drives out demons."[t]

c *21* Isaiah 42:1–4 d *24* Greek *Beezeboul* or *Beelzeboul*; also in verse 27

12:10 [i]ver 2; Lk 13:14; 14:3; Jn 9:16
12:11 [j]Lk 14:5
12:12 [k]Mt 10:31
12:14 [l]Mt 26:4; 27:1; Mk 3:6; Lk 6:11; Jn 5:18; 11:53
12:15 [m]Mt 4:23
12:16 [n]Mt 8:4
12:18 [o]Mt 3:17
12:21 [p]Isa 42:1-4
12:22 [q]Mt 4:24; 9:32-33
12:23 [r]Mt 9:27
12:24 [s]Mk 3:22 [t]Mt 9:34

12:9 For more information on synagogues, read the notes on Mark 1:21 and 5:22.

12:10 As they pointed to the man with the shrivelled hand, the Pharisees tried to trick Jesus by asking him if it was legal to heal on the Sabbath. Their Sabbath rules said that people could be helped on the Sabbath only if their lives were in danger. Jesus healed on the Sabbath several times, and none of those healings was in response to emergencies. If Jesus had waited until another day, he would have been submitting to the Pharisees' authority, showing that their petty rules were equal to God's law. If he healed the man on the Sabbath, the Pharisees could claim that because Jesus broke their rules, his power was not from God. But Jesus made it clear how ridiculous and petty their rules were. God is a God of people, not rules. The best time to reach out to someone is when he or she needs help.

12:10-12 The Pharisees placed their laws above human need. They were so concerned about Jesus breaking one of their rules that they did not care about the man's shrivelled hand. What is your attitude towards others? If your convictions don't allow you to help certain people, your convictions may not be in tune with God's word. Don't allow dogma to blind you to human need.

12:14 The Pharisees plotted Jesus' death because they were outraged. Jesus had overruled their authority (Luke 6:11) and had exposed their evil attitudes in front of the entire crowd in the synagogue. Jesus had showed that the Pharisees were more loyal to their religious system than to God.

12:15 Up to this point, Jesus had been aggressively confronting the Pharisees' hypocrisy. Here he decided to withdraw from the synagogue before a major confrontation developed because it was not time for him to die. Jesus had many lessons still to teach his disciples and the people.

12:16 Jesus did not want those he healed to tell others about his miracles because he didn't want the people coming to him for the wrong reasons. That would hinder his teaching ministry and arouse false hopes about an earthly kingdom. But the news of Jesus' miracles spread, and many came to see for themselves (see Mark 3:7, 8).

12:17-21 The people expected the Messiah to be a king. This quotation from Isaiah's prophecy (Isaiah 42:1–4) showed that the Messiah was indeed a king, but it illustrated what *kind* of king – a quiet, gentle ruler who brings justice to the nations. Like the crowd in Jesus' day, we may want Christ to rule as a king and bring great and visible victories in our lives. But often Christ's work is quiet, and it happens according to *his* perfect timing, not ours.

12:25
[u] Mt 9:4

12:26
[v] Mt 4:10

12:27
[w] Ac 19:13

12:30
[x] Mk 9:40; Lk 11:23

12:31
[y] Mk 3:28, 29; Lk 12:10

12:32
[z] Tit 2:12
[a] Mk 10:30; Lk 20:34, 35; Eph 1:21; Heb 6:5

12:33
[b] Mt 7:16, 17; Lk 6:43, 44

12:34
[c] Mt 3:7; 23:33
[d] Mt 15:18; Lk 6:45

12:38
[e] Mt 16:1; Mk 8:11, 12; Lk 11:16; Jn 2:18; 6:30; 1Co 1:22

12:39
[f] Mt 16:4; Lk 11:29

25 Jesus knew their thoughts[u] and said to them, "Every kingdom divided against
itself will be ruined, and every city or household divided against itself will not stand.
26 If Satan[v] drives out Satan, he is divided against himself. How then can his kingdom
stand? 27 And if I drive out demons by Beelzebub, by whom do your people[w] drive
them out? So then, they will be your judges. 28 But if I drive out demons by the Spirit
of God, then the kingdom of God has come upon you.

29 "Or again, how can anyone enter a strong man's house and carry off his possessions unless he first ties up the strong man? Then he can rob his house.

30 "He who is not with me is against me, and he who does not gather with me
scatters.[x] 31 And so I tell you, every sin and blasphemy will be forgiven men, but
the blasphemy against the Spirit will not be forgiven.[y] 32 Anyone who speaks a word
against the Son of Man will be forgiven, but anyone who speaks against the Holy Spirit
will not be forgiven, either in this age[z] or in the age to come.[a]

33 "Make a tree good and its fruit will be good, or make a tree bad and its fruit will
be bad, for a tree is recognised by its fruit.[b] 34 You brood of vipers,[c] how can you
who are evil say anything good? For out of the overflow of the heart the mouth
speaks.[d] 35 The good man brings good things out of the good stored up in him, and
the evil man brings evil things out of the evil stored up in him. 36 But I tell you that
men will have to give account on the day of judgment for every careless word they
have spoken. 37 For by your words you will be acquitted, and by your words you will
be condemned."

Religious Leaders Ask Jesus for a Miracle
(75)

38 Then some of the Pharisees and teachers of the law said to him, "Teacher, we
want to see a miraculous sign from you."[e]

39 He answered, "A wicked and adulterous generation asks for a miraculous sign!
But none will be given it except the sign of the prophet Jonah.[f] 40 For as Jonah was

---

12:24 The Pharisees had already accused Jesus of being in league with the prince of demons (9:34). They were trying to discredit him by using an emotional argument. Refusing to believe that Jesus came from God, they said he was in league with Satan. Jesus easily exposed the foolishness of their argument.

12:25 In the incarnation, Jesus gave up the complete and unlimited use of his supernatural abilities. But he still had profound insight into human nature. His discernment stopped the religious leaders' attempts to trick him. The resurrected Christ knows all our thoughts. This can be comforting because he knows what we really mean when we speak to him. It can be threatening because we cannot hide from him, and he knows our selfish motives.

12:29 At Jesus' birth, Satan's power and control were disrupted. In the desert Jesus overcame the devil's temptations, and at the resurrection he defeated Satan's ultimate weapon, death. Eventually Satan will be constrained for ever (Revelation 20:10), and evil will no longer pervade the earth. Jesus has complete power and authority over Satan and all his forces.

12:30 It is impossible to be neutral about Christ. Anyone who is not actively following him has chosen to reject him. Any person who tries to remain neutral in the struggle of good against evil is choosing to be separated from God, who alone is good. To refuse to follow Christ is to choose to be on Satan's side.

12:31, 32 The Pharisees had blasphemed against the Spirit by attributing the power by which Christ did miracles to Satan (12:24) instead of the Holy Spirit. The unpardonable sin is the deliberate refusal to acknowledge God's power in Christ. It indicates a deliberate and irreversible hardness of heart. Sometimes believers worry that they have accidently committed this unforgivable sin. But only those who have turned their backs on God and rejected all faith have any need to worry. Jesus said they can't be forgiven – not because their sin is worse than any other, but because they will never ask for forgiveness. Whoever rejects the prompting of the Holy Spirit removes himself or herself from the only force that can lead him or her to repentance and restoration to God.

12:34–36 Jesus reminds us that what we say reveals what is in our hearts. What kinds of words come from your mouth? That is an indication of what your heart is really like. You can't solve your heart problem, however, just by cleaning up your speech. You must allow the Holy Spirit to fill you with new attitudes and motives; then your speech will be cleansed at its source.

12:38–40 The Pharisees were asking for another miraculous sign, but they were not sincerely seeking to know Jesus. Jesus knew they had already seen enough miraculous proof to convince them that he was the Messiah if they would just open their hearts. But they had already decided not to believe in him, and more miracles would not change that.

Many people have said, "If I could just see a real miracle, then I could really believe in God." But Jesus' response to the Pharisees applies to us. We have plenty of evidence – Jesus' birth, death, resurrection, and ascension, and centuries of his work in believers around the world. Instead of looking for additional evidence or miracles, accept what God has already given and move forward. He may use your life as evidence to reach another person.

12:39–41 Jonah was a prophet sent to the Assyrian city of Nineveh (see the book of Jonah). Because Assyria was such a cruel and warlike nation, Jonah tried to run from his assignment and ended up spending three days in the belly of a huge fish. When Jonah got out, he grudgingly went to Nineveh, preached God's message, and saw the city repent. By contrast, when Jesus came to his people, they refused to repent. Here Jesus is clearly saying that his resurrection will prove he is the Messiah. Three days after his death Jesus will come back to life, just as Jonah was given a new chance at life after three days in the fish.

three days and three nights in the belly of a huge fish,[g] so the Son of Man[h] will be
three days and three nights in the heart of the earth.[i] 41 The men of Nineveh[j] will
stand up at the judgment with this generation and condemn it; for they repented at the
preaching of Jonah,[k] and now one[e] greater than Jonah is here. 42 The Queen of the
South will rise at the judgment with this generation and condemn it; for she came[l]
from the ends of the earth to listen to Solomon's wisdom, and now one greater than
Solomon is here.

43 "When an evil[f] spirit comes out of a man, it goes through arid places seeking
rest and does not find it. 44 Then it says, 'I will return to the house I left.' When it
arrives, it finds the house unoccupied, swept clean and put in order. 45 Then it goes
and takes with it seven other spirits more wicked than itself, and they go in and live
there. And the final condition of that man is worse than the first.[m] That is how it will
be with this wicked generation."

Jesus Describes His True Family
(76/Mark 3:31–35; Luke 8:19–21)

46 While Jesus was still talking to the crowd, his mother[n] and brothers[o] stood
outside, wanting to speak to him. 47 Someone told him, "Your mother and brothers
are standing outside, wanting to speak to you."[g]

48 He replied to him, "Who is my mother, and who are my brothers?" 49 Pointing
to his disciples, he said, "Here are my mother and my brothers. 50 For whoever does
the will of my Father in heaven[p] is my brother and sister and mother."

Jesus Tells the Parable of the Four Soils
(77/Mark 4:1–9; Luke 8:4–8)

13 That same day Jesus went out of the house[a] and sat by the lake. 2 Such large
crowds gathered round him that he got into a boat[b] and sat in it, while all the
people stood on the shore. 3 Then he told them many things in parables, saying: "A
farmer went out to sow his seed. 4 As he was scattering the seed, some fell along the
path, and the birds came and ate it up. 5 Some fell on rocky places, where it did not
have much soil. It sprang up quickly, because the soil was shallow. 6 But when the
sun came up, the plants were scorched, and they withered because they had no root.
7 Other seed fell among thorns, which grew up and choked the plants. 8 Still other seed
fell on good soil, where it produced a crop—a hundred,[c] sixty or thirty times what
was sown. 9 He who has ears, let him hear."[d]

[e] *41* Or *something*; also in verse 42 [f] *43* Greek *unclean* [g] *47* Some manuscripts do not have verse 47.

12:40 [g] Jnh 1:17 [h] Mt 8:20 [i] Mt 16:21
12:41 [j] Jnh 1:2 [k] Jnh 3:5
12:42 [l] 1Ki 10:1; 2Ch 9:1
12:45 [m] 2Pe 2:20
12:46 [n] Mt 1:18; 2:11, 13, 14, 20; Lk 1:43; 2:33, 34, 48, 51; Jn 2:1, 5; 19:25, 26 [o] Mt 13:55; Jn 2:12; 7:3, 5; Ac 1:14; 1Co 9:5; Gal 1:19
12:50 [p] Jn 15:14
13:1 [a] ver 36; Mt 9:28
13:2 [b] Lk 5:3
13:8 [c] Ge 26:12
13:9 [d] Mt 11:15

12:41, 42 In Jonah's day, Nineveh was the capital of the Assyrian empire, and it was as powerful as it was evil (Jonah 1:2). But the entire city repented at Jonah's preaching. The Queen of the South travelled far to see Solomon, king of Israel, and learn about his great wisdom (1 Kings 10:1–10; also see the note on Luke 11:31, 32 for more on the Queen of Sheba). These Gentiles recognised the truth about God when it was presented to them, unlike the religious leaders who ignored the truth even though it stared them in the face. How have you responded to the evidence and truth that you have?

12:43–45 Jesus was describing the attitude of the nation of Israel and the religious leaders in particular. Just cleaning up one's life without filling it with God leaves plenty of room for Satan to enter. The book of Ezra records how the people rid themselves of idolatry, but failed to replace it with love for God and obedience to him. Ridding our lives of sin is the first step. We must also take the second step: filling our lives with God's word and the Holy Spirit. Unfilled and complacent people are easy targets for Satan.

12:46–50 Jesus was not denying his responsibility to his earthly family. On the contrary, he criticised the religious leaders for not following the Old Testament command to honour their parents (15:1–9). He provided for his mother's security as he hung on the cross (John 19:25–27). His mother and brothers were present in the upper room at Pentecost (Acts 1:14). Instead Jesus was pointing out that spiritual relationships are as binding as physical ones, and he was paving the way for a new community of believers (the universal church), our spiritual family.

13:2, 3 Jesus used many illustrations, or *parables,* when speaking to the crowds. A parable compares something familiar to something unfamiliar. It helps us understand spiritual truth by using everyday objects and relationships. Parables compel listeners to discover truth, while at the same time concealing the truth from those too lazy or too stubborn to see it. To those who are honestly searching, the truth becomes clear. We must be careful not to read too much into parables, forcing them to say what they don't mean. All parables have one meaning unless otherwise specified by Jesus.

13:8 This parable should encourage spiritual "sowers"—those who teach, preach, and lead others. The farmer sowed good seed, but not all the seed sprouted, and even the plants that grew had varying yields. Don't be discouraged if you do not always see results as you faithfully teach the word. Belief cannot be forced to follow a mathematical formula (i.e., a 4:1 ratio of seeds planted to seeds sprouted). Rather, it is a miracle of God's Holy Spirit as he uses your words to lead others to him.

13:9 Human ears hear many sounds, but there is a deeper kind

Jesus Explains the Parable of the Four Soils
(78/Mark 4:10–25; Luke 8:9–18)

10 The disciples came to him and asked, "Why do you speak to the people in
parables?"
11 He replied, "The knowledge of the secrets of the kingdom of heaven has been
given to you,[e] but not to them. 12 Whoever has will be given more, and he will have
an abundance. Whoever does not have, even what he has will be taken from him.[f]
13 This is why I speak to them in parables:

"Though seeing, they do not see;
though hearing, they do not hear or understand.[g]

14 In them is fulfilled the prophecy of Isaiah:

" 'You will be ever hearing but never understanding;
you will be ever seeing but never perceiving.
15 For this people's heart has become calloused;
they hardly hear with their ears,
and they have closed their eyes.
Otherwise they might see with their eyes,
hear with their ears,
understand with their hearts
and turn, and I would heal them.'[a][h]

16 But blessed are your eyes because they see, and your ears because they hear.[i] 17 For
I tell you the truth, many prophets and righteous men longed to see what you see[j]
but did not see it, and to hear what you hear but did not hear it.
18 "Listen then to what the parable of the sower means: 19 When anyone hears the
message about the kingdom[k] and does not understand it, the evil one[l] comes and
snatches away what was sown in his heart. This is the seed sown along the path. 20 The
one who received the seed that fell on rocky places is the man who hears the word
and at once receives it with joy. 21 But since he has no root, he lasts only a short time.
When trouble or persecution comes because of the word, he quickly falls away.[m]
22 The one who received the seed that fell among the thorns is the man who hears the
word, but the worries of this life and the deceitfulness of wealth[n] choke it, making
it unfruitful. 23 But the one who received the seed that fell on good soil is the man
who hears the word and understands it. He produces a crop, yielding a hundred, sixty
or thirty times what was sown."[o]

Jesus Tells the Parable of the Weeds
(80)

24 Jesus told them another parable: "The kingdom of heaven is like[p] a man who
sowed good seed in his field. 25 But while everyone was sleeping, his enemy came

a *15* Isaiah 6:9,10

13:11 [e]Mt 11:25; 16:17; 19:11; Jn 6:65; 1Co 2:10, 14; Col 1:27; 1Jn 2:20, 27
13:12 [f]Mt 25:29; Lk 19:26
13:13 [g]Dt 29:4; Jer 5:21; Eze 12:2
13:15 [h]Isa 6:9, 10; Jn 12:40; Ac 28:26, 27; Ro 11:8
13:16 [i]Mt 16:17
13:17 [j]Jn 8:56; Heb 11:13; 1Pe 1:10-12
13:19 [k]Mt 4:23 [l]Mt 5:37
13:21 [m]Mt 11:6
13:22 [n]Mt 19:23; 1Ti 6:9, 10, 17
13:23 [o]ver 8
13:24 [p]ver 31, 33, 45, 47; Mt 18:23; 20:1; 22:2; 25:1; Mk 4:26, 30

---

of listening that results in spiritual understanding. If you honestly seek God's will, you have spiritual hearing, and these parables will give you new perspectives.

13:10 When speaking in parables, Jesus was not hiding truth from sincere seekers, because those who were receptive to spiritual truth understood the illustrations. To others they were only stories without meaning. This allowed Jesus to give spiritual food to those who hu .gered for it while preventing his enemies from trapping him sooner than they might otherwise have done.

13:12 This phrase means that we are responsible to use well what we have. When people reject Jesus, their hardness of heart drives away or renders useless even the little understanding they had.

13:22 How easy it is to agree with Christ with no intention of obeying. It is easy to denounce worries of this life and the deceitfulness of wealth, and still do nothing to change our ways. In light of eternal life with God, are your present worries justified? If you had everything you could want but forfeited eternal life with God, would those things be so desirable?

13:23 The four types of soil represent different responses to God's message. People respond differently because they are in different states of readiness. Some are hardened, others are shallow, others are contaminated by distracting worries, and some are receptive. How has God's word taken root in your life? What kind of soil are you?

13:24ff Jesus gives the meaning of this parable in verses 36–43. All the parables in this chapter teach us about God and his kingdom. They explain what the kingdom is really like as opposed to our expectations of it. The kingdom of heaven is not a geographic location, but a spiritual realm where God rules and where we share in his eternal life. We join that kingdom when we trust in Christ as Saviour.

and sowed weeds among the wheat, and went away. 26When the wheat sprouted and
formed ears, then the weeds also appeared.
27"The owner's servants came to him and said, 'Sir, didn't you sow good seed in
your field? Where then did the weeds come from?'
28" 'An enemy did this,' he replied.
"The servants asked him, 'Do you want us to go and pull them up?'
29" 'No,' he answered, 'because while you are pulling the weeds, you may root up
the wheat with them. 30Let both grow together until the harvest. At that time I will
tell the harvesters: First collect the weeds and tie them in bundles to be burned; then
gather the wheat and bring it into my barn.' "[q]

Jesus Tells the Parable of the Mustard Seed
(81/Mark 4:30–34)

31He told them another parable: "The kingdom of heaven is like[r] a mustard seed,[s]
which a man took and planted in his field. 32Though it is the smallest of all your seeds,
yet when it grows, it is the largest of garden plants and becomes a tree, so that the
birds of the air come and perch in its branches."[t]

Jesus Tells the Parable of the Yeast
(82)

33He told them still another parable: "The kingdom of heaven is like[u] yeast that
a woman took and mixed into a large amount**[b]** of flour[v] until it worked all through
the dough."[w]
34Jesus spoke all these things to the crowd in parables; he did not say anything to
them without using a parable.[x] 35So was fulfilled what was spoken through the
prophet:

> "I will open my mouth in parables,
> I will utter things hidden since the creation of the world."**[c]**[y]

Jesus Explains the Parable of the Weeds
(83)

36Then he left the crowd and went into the house. His disciples came to him and
said, "Explain to us the parable[z] of the weeds in the field."
37He answered, "The one who sowed the good seed is the Son of Man.[a] 38The
field is the world, and the good seed stands for the sons of the kingdom. The weeds
are the sons of the evil one,[b] 39and the enemy who sows them is the devil. The
harvest[c] is the end of the age,[d] and the harvesters are angels.[e]
40"As the weeds are pulled up and burned in the fire, so it will be at the end of
the age. 41The Son of Man[f] will send out his angels,[g] and they will weed out of
his kingdom everything that causes sin and all who do evil. 42They will throw them
into the fiery furnace, where there will be weeping and gnashing of teeth.[h] 43Then

b *33* Greek *three satas* (probably about 3/5 bushel or 22 litres) **c** *35* Psalm 78:2

13:30 [q]Mt 3:12
13:31 [r]ver 24 [s]Mt 17:20; Lk 17:6
13:32 [t]Ps 104:12; Eze 17:23; 31:6; Da 4:12
13:33 [u]ver 24 [v]Ge 18:6 [w]Gal 5:9
13:34 [x]Mk 4:33; Jn 16:25
13:35 [y]Ps 78:2; Ro 16:25, 26; 1Co 2:7; Eph 3:9; Col 1:26
13:36 [z]Mt 15:15
13:37 [a]Mt 8:20
13:38 [b]Jn 8:44, 45; 1Jn 3:10
13:39 [c]Joel 3:13 [d]Mt 24:3; 28:20 [e]Rev 14:15
13:41 [f]Mt 8:20 [g]Mt 24:31
13:42 [h]ver 50; Mt 8:12

13:30 The young weeds and the young blades of wheat look the same and can't be distinguished until they are grown and ready for harvest. Weeds (unbelievers) and wheat (believers) must live side by side in this world. God allows unbelievers to remain for a while, just as a farmer allows weeds to remain in his field so the surrounding wheat isn't uprooted with them. At the harvest, however, the weeds will be uprooted and thrown away. God's harvest (judgment) of all people is coming. We are to make ourselves ready by making sure that our faith is sincere.

13:31, 32 The mustard seed was the smallest seed a farmer used. Jesus used this parable to show that the kingdom has small beginnings but will grow and produce great results.

13:33 In other Bible passages, yeast is used as a symbol of evil or uncleanness. Here it is a positive symbol of growth. Although yeast looks like a minor ingredient, it permeates the whole loaf. Although the kingdom began small and was nearly invisible, it would soon grow and have a great impact on the world.

13:40–43 At the end of the world, angels will separate the evil from the good. There are true and false believers in churches today, but we should be cautious in our judgments because only Christ is qualified to make the final separation. If you start judging, you may damage some of the good "plants". It's more important to judge our own response to God than to analyse others' responses.

13:42 Jesus often uses these terms to refer to the coming judgment. The weeping indicates sorrow or remorse, and gnashing of teeth shows extreme anxiety or pain. Those who say they don't care what happens to them after they die don't realise what they are saying. They will be punished for living in selfishness and indifference to God.

13:43 Those who receive God's favour stand in bright contrast to

13:43 [i]Da 12:3 [j]Mt 11:15

the righteous will shine like the sun[i] in the kingdom of their Father. He who has ears,
let him hear.[j]

Jesus Tells the Parable of Hidden Treasure
(84)

13:44 [k]ver 24 [l]Isa 55:1; Php 3:7, 8

44"The kingdom of heaven is like[k] treasure hidden in a field. When a man found
it, he hid it again, and then in his joy went and sold all he had and bought that field.[l]

Jesus Tells the Parable of the Pearl Merchant
(85)

13:45 [m]ver 24

45"Again, the kingdom of heaven is like[m] a merchant looking for fine pearls.
46When he found one of great value, he went away and sold everything he had and
bought it.

Jesus Tells the Parable of the Fishing Net
(86)

13:47 [n]ver 24 [o]Mt 22:10

47"Once again, the kingdom of heaven is like[n] a net that was let down into the
lake and caught all kinds[o] of fish. 48When it was full, the fishermen pulled it up on
the shore. Then they sat down and collected the good fish in baskets, but threw the
bad away. 49This is how it will be at the end of the age. The angels will come and
separate the wicked from the righteous[p] 50and throw them into the fiery furnace,
where there will be weeping and gnashing of teeth.[q]

13:49 [p]Mt 25:32

13:50 [q]Mt 8:12

51"Have you understood all these things?" Jesus asked.
"Yes," they replied.
52He said to them, "Therefore every teacher of the law who has been instructed
about the kingdom of heaven is like the owner of a house who brings out of his
storeroom new treasures as well as old."

13:53 [r]Mt 7:28

5. Jesus encounters differing reactions to his ministry

The People of Nazareth Refuse to Believe
(91/Mark 6:1–6)

13:54 [s]Mt 4:23 [t]Mt 7:28

53When Jesus had finished these parables,[r] he moved on from there. 54Coming
to his home town, he began teaching the people in their synagogue,[s] and they were
amazed.[t] "Where did this man get this wisdom and these miraculous powers?" they

---

those who receive his judgment. A similiar illustration is used in Daniel 12:3.

13:44–46 The kingdom of heaven is more valuable than anything else we can have, and a person must be willing to give up everything to obtain it. The man who discovered the treasure in the field stumbled upon it by accident but knew its value when he found it. The merchant was earnestly searching for the pearl of great value, and, when he found it, he sold everything he had to purchase it.

13:47–49 The parable of the fishing net has the same meaning as the parable of the wheat and weeds. We are to obey God and tell others about his grace and goodness, but we cannot dictate who is part of the kingdom of heaven and who is not. This sorting will be done at the last judgment by those infinitely more qualified than we.

13:52 Anyone who understands God's real purpose in the law as revealed in the Old Testament has a real treasure. The Old Testament points the way to Jesus, the Messiah. Jesus always upheld its authority and relevance. But there is a double benefit to those who understand Jesus' teaching about the kingdom of heaven. This was a new treasure that Jesus was revealing. Both the old and new teaching give practical guidelines for faith and for living in the world. The religious leaders, however, were trapped in the old and blind to the new. They were looking for a future kingdom *preceded* by judgment. Jesus, however, taught that the kingdom was *now* and the judgment was future. The religious leaders were looking for a physical and temporal kingdom (via military rebellion and physical rule), but they were blind to the spiritual significance of the kingdom that Christ brought.

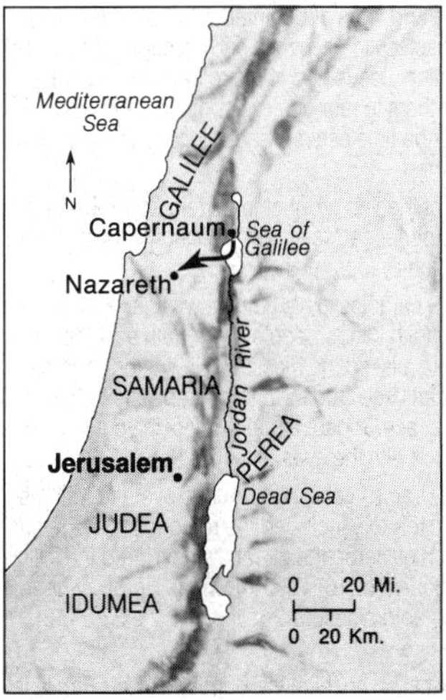

NAZARETH REJECTS JESUS
Chronologically, this return to Nazareth occurred after Jesus was in the Gadarene region and healed the demon-possessed men (8:28–34), then recrossed the sea to Capernaum. From there he travelled to Nazareth, where he had grown up, only to discover that the people refused to believe he was the Christ.

asked. 55"Isn't this the carpenter's son?[u] Isn't his mother's[v] name Mary, and aren't
his brothers James, Joseph, Simon and Judas? 56Aren't all his sisters with us? Where
then did this man get all these things?" 57And they took offence[w] at him.
But Jesus said to them, "Only in his home town and in his own house is a prophet
without honour."[x]
58And he did not do many miracles there because of their lack of faith.

Herod Kills John the Baptist
(95/Mark 6:14–29; Luke 9:7–9)

14 At that time Herod[a] the tetrarch heard the reports about Jesus,[b] 2and he said
to his attendants, "This is John the Baptist;[c] he has risen from the dead! That
is why miraculous powers are at work in him."
3Now Herod had arrested John and bound him and put him in prison[d] because of
Herodias, his brother Philip's wife,[e] 4for John had been saying to him: "It is not
lawful for you to have her."[f] 5Herod wanted to kill John, but he was afraid of the
people, because they considered him a prophet.[g]
6On Herod's birthday the daughter of Herodias danced for them and pleased Herod
so much 7that he promised with an oath to give her whatever she asked. 8Prompted
by her mother, she said, "Give me here on a platter the head of John the Baptist."
9The king was distressed, but because of his oaths and his dinner guests, he ordered
that her request be granted 10and had John beheaded[h] in the prison. 11His head was
brought in on a platter and given to the girl, who carried it to her mother. 12John's
disciples came and took his body and buried it.[i] Then they went and told Jesus.

Jesus Feeds Five Thousand
(96/Mark 6:30–44; Luke 9:10–17; John 6:1–15)

13When Jesus heard what had happened, he withdrew by boat privately to a solitary
place. Hearing of this, the crowds followed him on foot from the towns. 14When Jesus
landed and saw a large crowd, he had compassion on them[j] and healed their sick.[k]
15As evening approached, the disciples came to him and said, "This is a remote
place, and it's already getting late. Send the crowds away, so that they can go to the
villages and buy themselves some food."
16Jesus replied, "They do not need to go away. You give them something to eat."
17"We have here only five loaves[l] of bread and two fish," they answered.
18"Bring them here to me," he said. 19And he directed the people to sit down on

13:55 [u]Lk 3:23; Jn 6:42 [v]Mt 12:46
13:57 [w]Jn 6:61 [x]Lk 4:24; Jn 4:44
14:1 [a]Mk 8:15; Lk 3:1, 19; 13:31; 23:7, 8; Ac 4:27; 12:1 [b]Lk 9:7-9
14:2 [c]Mt 3:1
14:3 [d]Mt 4:12; 11:2 [e]Lk 3:19, 20
14:4 [f]Lev 18:16; 20:21
14:5 [g]Mt 11:9
14:10 [h]Mt 17:12
14:12 [i]Ac 8:2
14:14 [j]Mt 9:36 [k]Mt 4:23
14:17 [l]Mt 16:9

13:55 The residents of Jesus' home town had known Jesus since he was a young child and were acquainted with his family; they could not bring themselves to believe in his message. They were too close to the situation. Jesus had come to them as a prophet, one who challenged them to respond to unpopular spiritual truth. They did not listen to the timeless message because they could not see beyond the man.

13:57 Jesus was not the first prophet to be rejected in his own country. Jeremiah experienced rejection in his home town, even by members of his own family (Jeremiah 12:5, 6).

13:58 Jesus did few miracles in his home town "because of their lack of faith". Lack of faith blinds people to the truth and robs them of hope. These people missed the Messiah. How does your faith measure up? If you can't see God's work, perhaps it is because of your unbelief. Believe, ask God for a mighty work in your life, and expect him to act. Look with the eyes of faith.

14:1 Herod was a tetrarch – one of four rulers over the four districts of Palestine. His territory included the regions of Galilee and Perea. He was the son of Herod the Great, who ordered the killing of the babies in Bethlehem (2:16). Also known as Herod Antipas, he heard Jesus' case before Jesus' crucifixion (Luke 23:6–12). His Profile is found in Mark 6.

14:2 For more information on John the Baptist, see his Profile in John 1.

14:3 Philip, Herod's half brother, was another of Palestine's four rulers. His territories were Iturea and Traconitis, northeast of the Sea of Galilee (Luke 3:1). Philip's wife, Herodias, left Philip to live with Herod Antipas. John the Baptist condemned the two for living immorally (see Mark 6:17, 18).

14:9 Herod did not want to kill John the Baptist, but he gave the order so that he wouldn't be embarrassed in front of his guests. How easy it is to give in to the crowd and to let ourselves be pressured into doing wrong. Don't get into a situation where it will be too embarrassing to do what is right. Determine to do what is right, no matter how embarrassing or painful it may be.

14:13, 14 Jesus sought solitude after the news of John's death. Sometimes we may need to deal with our grief alone. Jesus did not dwell on his grief, but returned to the ministry he came to do.

14:14 Jesus performed some miracles as signs of his identity. He used other miracles to teach important truths. But here we read that he healed people because he "had compassion on them". Jesus was, and is, a loving, caring, and feeling person. When you are suffering, remember that Jesus hurts with you. He has compassion on you.

14:19–21 Jesus multiplied five loaves and two fish to feed over 5,000 people. What he was originally given seemed insufficient, but in his hands it became more than enough. We often feel that our contribution to Jesus is meagre, but he can use and multiply

14:19
[m]1Sa 9:13;
Mt 26:26;
Mk 8:6;
Lk 24:30;
Ac 2:42; 27:35;
1Ti 4:4

14:23
[n]Lk 3:21

14:26
[o]Lk 24:37

14:27
[p]Mt 9:2;
Ac 23:11
[q]Da 10:12;
Mt 17:7; 28:10;
Lk 1:13, 30; 2:10;
Ac 18:9; 23:11;
Rev 1:17

14:31
[r]Mt 6:30

14:33
[s]Ps 2:7;
Mt 4:3

the grass. Taking the five loaves and the two fish and looking up to heaven, he gave
thanks and broke the loaves.[m] Then he gave them to the disciples, and the disciples
gave them to the people. 20 They all ate and were satisfied, and the disciples picked
up twelve basketfuls of broken pieces that were left over. 21 The number of those who
ate was about five thousand men, besides women and children.

Jesus Walks on Water
(97/Mark 6:45–52; John 6:16–21)

22 Immediately Jesus made the disciples get into the boat and go on ahead of him
to the other side, while he dismissed the crowd. 23 After he had dismissed them, he
went up on a mountainside by himself to pray.[n] When evening came, he was there
alone, 24 but the boat was already a considerable distance[a] from land, buffeted by the
waves because the wind was against it.
25 During the fourth watch of the night Jesus went out to them, walking on the lake.
26 When the disciples saw him walking on the lake, they were terrified. "It's a ghost,"[o]
they said, and cried out in fear.
27 But Jesus immediately said to them: "Take courage![p] It is I. Don't be afraid."[q]
28 "Lord, if it's you," Peter replied, "tell me to come to you on the water."
29 "Come," he said.
Then Peter got down out of the boat, walked on the water and came towards Jesus.
30 But when he saw the wind, he was afraid and, beginning to sink, cried out, "Lord,
save me!"
31 Immediately Jesus reached out his hand and caught him. "You of little faith,"[r]
he said, "why did you doubt?"
32 And when they climbed into the boat, the wind died down. 33 Then those who were
in the boat worshipped him, saying, "Truly you are the Son of God."[s]

[a] *24* Greek *many stadia*

---

whatever we give him, whether it is talent, time, or treasure. It is when we give them to Jesus that our resources are multiplied.

14:21 The text states that there were 5,000 men present, *besides* women and children. Therefore, the total number of people Jesus fed could have been 10 to 15 thousand. The number of men is listed separately because in the Jewish culture of the day, men and women usually ate separately when in public. The children ate with the women.

14:23 Seeking solitude was an important priority for Jesus (see also 14:13). He made room in his busy schedule to be alone with the Father. Spending time with God in prayer nurtures a vital relationship and equips us to meet life's challenges and struggles. Develop the discipline of spending time alone with God – it will help you grow spiritually and become more and more like Christ.

14:28 Peter was not putting Jesus to the test, something we are told not to do (4:7). Instead he was the only one in the boat to react in faith. His impulsive request led him to experience a rather unusual demonstration of God's power. Peter started to sink because he took his eyes off Jesus and focused on the high waves around him. His faith wavered when he realised what he was doing. We may not walk on water, but we do walk through tough situations. If we focus on the waves of difficult circumstances around us without looking to Jesus for help, we too may despair and sink. To maintain your faith when situations are difficult, keep your eyes on Jesus' power rather than on your inadequacies.

14:30, 31 Although we start out with good intentions, sometimes our faith falters. This doesn't necessarily mean we have failed. When Peter's faith faltered, he reached out to Christ, the only one who could help. He was afraid, but he still looked to Christ. When you are apprehensive about the troubles around you and doubt Christ's presence or ability to help, you must remember that he is the *only* one who can really help.

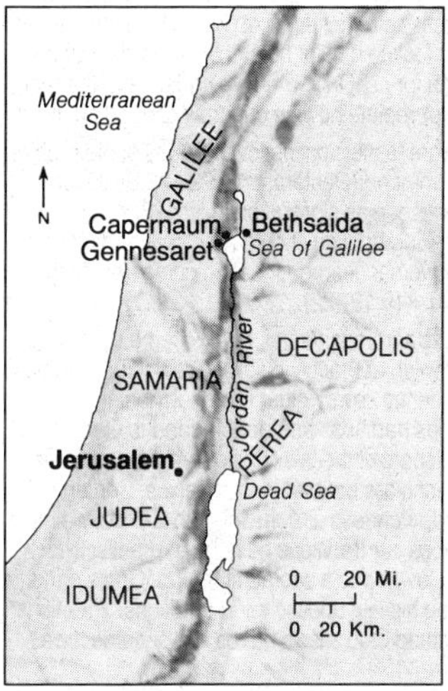

JESUS WALKS ON THE SEA
The miraculous feeding of the 5,000 occurred on the shores of the Sea of Galilee near Bethsaida. Jesus then sent his disciples across the lake. Several hours later they encountered a storm, and Jesus came to them– walking on the water. The boat then landed at Gennesaret.

Jesus Heals All Who Touch Him
(98/Mark 6:53–56)

34When they had crossed over, they landed at Gennesaret. 35And when the men
of that place recognised Jesus, they sent word to all the surrounding country. People
brought all their sick to him 36and begged him to let the sick just touch the edge of
his cloak,[t] and all who touched him were healed.

14:36
[t]Mt 9:20

Jesus Teaches about Inner Purity
(102/Mark 7:1–23)

15 Then some Pharisees and teachers of the law came to Jesus from Jerusalem and
asked, 2"Why do your disciples break the tradition of the elders? They don't
wash their hands before they eat!"[a]

15:2
[a]Lk 11:38

3Jesus replied, "And why do you break the command of God for the sake of your
tradition? 4For God said, 'Honour your father and mother'[a][b] and 'Anyone who
curses his father or mother must be put to death.'[b][c] 5But you say that if a man says
to his father or mother, 'Whatever help you might otherwise have received from me
is a gift devoted to God,' 6he is not to 'honour his father'[c] with it. Thus you nullify
the word of God for the sake of your tradition. 7You hypocrites! Isaiah was right when
he prophesied about you:

15:4
[b]Ex 20:12; Dt 5:16; Eph 6:2
[c]Ex 21:17; Lev 20:9

> 8" 'These people honour me with their lips,
> but their hearts are far from me.
> 9They worship me in vain;
> their teachings are but rules taught by men.'[d] [d][e]"

15:9
[d]Col 2:20-22
[e]Isa 29:13; Mal 2:2

[a] *4* Exodus 20:12; Deut. 5:16 [b] *4* Exodus 21:17; Lev. 20:9 [c] *6* Some manuscripts *father or his mother*
[d] *9* Isaiah 29:13

14:34 Gennesaret was located on the west side of the Sea of Galilee in a fertile, well-watered area.

14:35, 36 The people recognised Jesus as a great healer, but how many understood who he truly was? They came to Jesus for physical healing, but did they come for spiritual healing? They came to prolong their lives on earth, but did they come to secure their eternal lives? People may seek Jesus to learn valuable lessons from his life or in the hope of finding relief from pain. But we miss Jesus' whole message if we seek him only to heal our bodies but not our souls; if we look to him for help only in this life, rather than for his eternal plan for us. Only when we understand the real Jesus Christ can we appreciate how he can truly change our lives.

14:36 Jewish men wore tassels on the lower edges of their robes according to God's command (Deuteronomy 22:12). By Jesus' day, these tassels were seen as signs of holiness (23:5). It was natural that people seeking healing should reach out and touch these. But as one sick woman learned, healing came from faith and not from Jesus' cloak (9:19–22).

15:1, 2 The Pharisees and teachers of the law came from Jerusalem, the centre of Jewish authority, to scrutinise Jesus' activities. Over the centuries since the Jews' return from Babylonian captivity, hundreds of religious traditions had been added to God's laws. The Pharisees and teachers of the law considered them all equally important. Many traditions are not bad in themselves. Certain religious traditions can add richness and meaning to life. But we must not assume that because our traditions have been practised for years they should be elevated to a sacred standing. God's principles never change, and his law doesn't need additions. Traditions should help us understand God's laws better, not become laws themselves.

15:5, 6 This was the practice of *Corban* (literally, "offering"; see Mark 7:11). Anyone who made a Corban vow was required to dedicate money to God's temple that otherwise would have gone to support his parents. Corban had become a religiously acceptable way to neglect parents, circumventing the child's responsibility to them. Although the action – giving money to God – seemed worthy

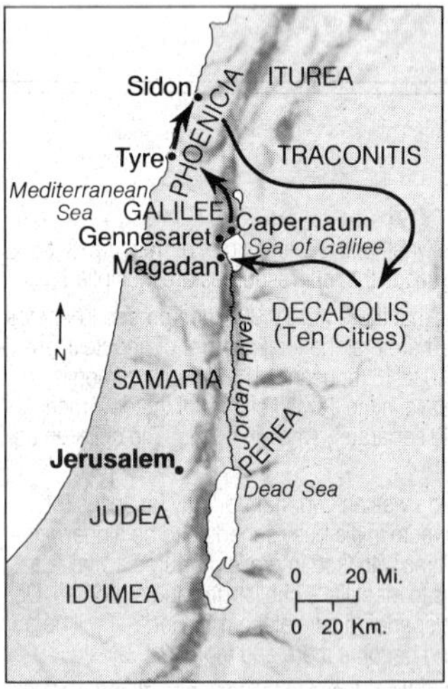

MINISTRY IN PHOENICIA
After preaching again in Capernaum, Jesus left Galilee for Phoenicia, where he preached in Tyre and Sidon. On his return, he travelled through the region of the Decapolis (Ten Cities), fed the 4,000 beside the sea, then crossed to Magadan.

and no doubt conferred prestige on the giver, many people who took the Corban vow were disregarding God's command to care for needy parents. These religious leaders were ignoring God's clear command to honour their parents.

15:8, 9 The prophet Isaiah also criticised hypocrites (Isaiah 29:13), and Jesus applied Isaiah's words to these religious leaders. When we claim to honour God while our hearts are far from him, our worship means nothing. It is not enough to act religiously. Our actions and our attitudes must be sincere. If they are not, Isaiah's words also describe us.

15:9 The Pharisees knew a lot about God, but they didn't know God. It is not enough to study religion or even to study the Bible. We must respond to God himself.

15:11 [f]Ac 10:14, 15 [g]ver 18
15:13 [h]Isa 60:21; 61:3; Jn 15:2
15:14 [i]Mt 23:16, 24; Ro 2:19 [j]Lk 6:39
15:15 [k]Mt 13:36
15:16 [l]Mt 16:9
15:18 [m]Mt 12:34; Lk 6:45; Jas 3:6
15:19 [n]Gal 5:19-21
15:20 [o]Ro 14:14
15:21 [p]Mt 11:21
15:22 [q]Mt 9:27 [r]Mt 4:24
15:24 [s]Mt 10:6, 23; Ro 15:8
15:25 [t]Mt 8:2

10 Jesus called the crowd to him and said, "Listen and understand. 11 What goes into
a man's mouth does not make him 'unclean',[f] but what comes out of his mouth, that
is what makes him 'unclean'."[g]
12 Then the disciples came to him and asked, "Do you know that the Pharisees were
offended when they heard this?"
13 He replied, "Every plant that my heavenly Father has not planted[h] will be pulled
up by the roots. 14 Leave them; they are blind guides.[e][i] If a blind man leads a blind
man, both will fall into a pit."[j]
15 Peter said, "Explain the parable to us."[k]
16 "Are you still so dull?"[l] Jesus asked them. 17 "Don't you see that whatever enters
the mouth goes into the stomach and then out of the body? 18 But the things that come
out of the mouth come from the heart,[m] and these make a man 'unclean'. 19 For out
of the heart come evil thoughts, murder, adultery, sexual immorality, theft, false
testimony, slander.[n] 20 These are what make a man 'unclean';[o] but eating with
unwashed hands does not make him 'unclean'."

Jesus Sends a Demon Out of a Girl
(103/Mark 7:24–30)

21 Leaving that place, Jesus withdrew to the region of Tyre and Sidon.[p] 22 A
Canaanite woman from that vicinity came to him, crying out, "Lord, Son of David,[q]
have mercy on me! My daughter is suffering terribly from demon-possession."[r]
23 Jesus did not answer a word. So his disciples came to him and urged him, "Send
her away, for she keeps crying out after us."
24 He answered, "I was sent only to the lost sheep of Israel."[s]
25 The woman came and knelt before him.[t] "Lord, help me!" she said.
26 He replied, "It is not right to take the children's bread and toss it to their dogs."
27 "Yes, Lord," she said, "but even the dogs eat the crumbs that fall from their
masters' table."

e *14* Some manuscripts *guides of the blind*

15:11 Jesus was referring to the Jewish regulations concerning food and drink. This verse could be paraphrased: "You're not made unclean by eating non-kosher food! It is what you *say* and *think* that makes you unclean!" This statement offended the Pharisees who were very concerned about what people ate and drank.

15:13, 14 Jesus told his disciples to leave the Pharisees alone because the Pharisees were blind to God's truth. Anyone who listened to their teaching would risk spiritual blindness as well. Not all religious leaders clearly see God's truth. Make sure that those you listen to and learn from are those with good spiritual eyesight—they teach and follow the principles of Scripture.

15:15 Later Peter would be faced with the issue of clean and unclean food (see the notes on 15:11 and Acts 10:12). Then he would learn that nothing should be a barrier to proclaiming the gospel to the Gentiles (non-Jews).

15:16–20 We work hard to keep our outward appearance attractive, but what is in our hearts is even more important. The way we are deep down (where others can't see) matters much to God. What are you like inside? When people become Christians, God makes them different on the inside. He will continue the process of change inside them if they only ask. God wants us to seek healthy thoughts and motives, not just healthy food and exercise.

15:22 This woman is called a "Greek, born in Syrian Phoenicia" in Mark's Gospel (7:26), indicating that she was from the territory northwest of Galilee where the cities of Tyre and Sidon were located. Matthew calls her a Canaanite, naming her ancient ancestors who were enemies of Israel. Matthew's Jewish audience would have immediately understood the significance of Jesus helping this woman.

15:23 The disciples asked Jesus to get rid of the woman because she was bothering them with her nagging persistence. They showed no compassion for her or sensitivity to her needs. It is possible to become so occupied with spiritual matters that we miss real needs around us. This is especially likely if we are prejudiced against needy people or if they cause us inconvenience. Instead of being bothered, be aware of the opportunities that surround you. Be open to the beauty of God's message for *all* people, and make an effort not to shut out those who are different from you.

15:24 Jesus' words do not contradict the truth that God's message is for all people (Psalm 22:27; Isaiah 56:7; Matthew 28:19; Romans 15:9–12). After all, when Jesus said these words, he was in Gentile territory on a mission to Gentile people. He ministered to Gentiles on many other occasions too. Jesus was simply telling the woman that Jews were to have the first opportunity to accept him as the Messiah because God wanted them to present the message of salvation to the rest of the world (see Genesis 12:3). Jesus was not rejecting the Canaanite woman. He may have wanted to test her faith, or he may have wanted to use the situation as another opportunity to teach that faith is available to all people.

15:26–28 *Dog* was a term the Jews commonly applied to Gentiles because the Jews considered these pagan people no more likely than dogs to receive God's blessing. Jesus was not degrading the woman by using this term, he was reflecting the Jews' attitude so as to contrast it with his own. The woman did not argue. Instead, using Jesus' choice of words, she agreed to be considered a dog as long as she could receive God's blessing for her daughter. Ironically, many Jews would lose God's blessing and salvation because they rejected Jesus, and many Gentiles would find salvation because they recognised and accepted him.

28Then Jesus answered, "Woman, you have great faith! *u* Your request is granted." And her daughter was healed from that very hour.

15:28
uMt 9:22

The Crowd Marvels at Jesus' Healings
(104/Mark 7:31–37)

29Jesus left there and went along the Sea of Galilee. Then he went up on a mountainside and sat down. 30Great crowds came to him, bringing the lame, the blind, the crippled, the mute and many others, and laid them at his feet; and he healed them. *v* 31The people were amazed when they saw the mute speaking, the crippled made well, the lame walking and the blind seeing. And they praised the God of Israel. *w*

15:30
vMt 4:23

15:31
wMt 9:8

Jesus Feeds Four Thousand
(105/Mark 8:1–10)

32Jesus called his disciples to him and said, "I have compassion for these people; *x* they have already been with me three days and have nothing to eat. I do not want to send them away hungry, or they may collapse on the way."

15:32
xMt 9:36

33His disciples answered, "Where could we get enough bread in this remote place to feed such a crowd?"

34"How many loaves do you have?" Jesus asked.

"Seven," they replied, "and a few small fish."

35He told the crowd to sit down on the ground. 36Then he took the seven loaves and the fish, and when he had given thanks, he broke them *y* and gave them to the disciples, and they in turn to the people. 37They all ate and were satisfied. Afterwards the disciples picked up seven basketfuls of broken pieces that were left over. *z* 38The number of those who ate was four thousand, besides women and children. 39After Jesus had sent the crowd away, he got into the boat and went to the vicinity of Magadan.

15:36
yMt 14:19

15:37
zMt 16:10

Religious Leaders Ask for a Sign in the Sky
(106/Mark 8:11–13)

16 The Pharisees and Sadducees *a* came to Jesus and tested him by asking him to show them a sign from heaven. *b*

2He replied, *a* "When evening comes, you say, 'It will be fair weather, for the sky is red,' 3and in the morning, 'Today it will be stormy, for the sky is red and overcast.' You know how to interpret the appearance of the sky, but you cannot interpret the signs of the times. *c* 4A wicked and adulterous generation looks for a miraculous sign,

a 2 Some early manuscripts do not have the rest of verse 2 and all of verse 3.

16:1
aAc 4:1
bMt 12:38

16:3
cLk 12:54-56

15:29-31 A great crowd was brought to Jesus to be healed, and he healed them all. Jesus is still able to heal broken lives, and we can be the ones who bring suffering people to him. Who do you know that needs Christ's healing touch? You can bring them to Jesus through prayer or through explaining to them the reason for the hope that you have (1 Peter 3:15). Then let Christ do the healing.

15:32ff This feeding of 4,000 is a separate event from the feeding of the 5,000 (14:13–21), confirmed by Mark 8:19, 20. This was the beginning of Jesus' expanded ministry to the Gentiles.

15:33 Jesus had already fed more than 5,000 people with five loaves and two fish. Here, in a similar situation, the disciples were again perplexed. How easily we throw up our hands in despair when faced with difficult situations. Like the disciples, we often forget that if God has cared for us in the past, he will do the same now. When facing a difficult situation, remember how God cared for you and trust him to work faithfully again.

15:39 Magadan was located on the west shore of the Sea of Galilee. Also known as Dalmanutha (Mark 8:10), this was Mary Magdalene's home town.

16:1 The Pharisees and Sadducees were Jewish religious leaders of two different parties, and their views were diametrically op-

posed on many issues. The Pharisees carefully followed their religious rules and traditions, believing that this was the way to God. They also believed in the authority of all Scripture and in the resurrection of the dead. The Sadducees accepted only the books of Moses as Scripture and did not believe in life after death. In Jesus, however, these two groups had a common enemy, and they joined forces to try to kill him. For more information on the Pharisees and Sadducees, see the charts in chapter 3 and Mark 2.

16:1 The Pharisees and Sadducees demanded a sign *from heaven.* They tried to explain away Jesus' other miracles as sleight of hand, coincidence, or use of evil power, but they believed that only God could do a sign in the sky. This, they were sure, would be a feat beyond Jesus' power. Although Jesus could have easily impressed them, he refused. He knew that even a miracle in the sky would not convince them he was the Messiah because they had already decided not to believe in him.

16:4 By using the sign of Jonah, who was inside a great fish for three days, Jesus was predicting his death and resurrection (see also 12:38–42).

16:4 Many people, like these Jewish leaders, say they want to see a miracle so that they can believe. But Jesus knew that miracles never convince the sceptical. Jesus had been healing, raising

16:4 [d]Mt 12:39
16:6 [e]Lk 12:1
16:8 [f]Mt 6:30
16:9 [g]Mt 14:17-21
16:10 [h]Mt 15:34-38
16:12 [i]Ac 4:1
16:14 [j]Mt 3:1; 14:2 [k]Mk 6:15; Jn 1:21
16:16 [l]Mt 4:3; Ps 42:2; Jn 11:27; Ac 14:15; 2Co 6:16; 1Th 1:9; 1Ti 3:15; Heb 10:31; 12:22

but none will be given it except the sign of Jonah."[d] Jesus then left them and went
away.

Jesus Warns against Wrong Teaching
(107/Mark 8:14–21)

5 When they went across the lake, the disciples forgot to take bread. 6 "Be careful,"
Jesus said to them. "Be on your guard against the yeast of the Pharisees and Sadducees."[e]
7 They discussed this among themselves and said, "It is because we didn't bring any
bread."
8 Aware of their discussion, Jesus asked, "You of little faith,[f] why are you talking
among yourselves about having no bread? 9 Do you still not understand? Don't you
remember the five loaves for the five thousand, and how many basketfuls you
gathered?[g] 10 Or the seven loaves for the four thousand, and how many basketfuls
you gathered?[h] 11 How is it you don't understand that I was not talking to you about
bread? But be on your guard against the yeast of the Pharisees and Sadducees." 12 Then
they understood that he was not telling them to guard against the yeast used in bread,
but against the teaching of the Pharisees and Sadducees.[i]

Peter Says Jesus Is the Messiah
(109/Mark 8:27–30; Luke 9:18–20)

13 When Jesus came to the region of Caesarea Philippi, he asked his disciples, "Who
do people say the Son of Man is?"
14 They replied, "Some say John the Baptist;[j] others say Elijah; and still others,
Jeremiah or one of the prophets."[k]
15 "But what about you?" he asked. "Who do you say I am?"
16 Simon Peter answered, "You are the Christ,[b] the Son of the living God."[l]
17 Jesus replied, "Blessed are you, Simon son of Jonah, for this was not revealed

b 16 Or *Messiah*; also in verse 20

---

people from the dead, and feeding thousands, and still people wanted him to prove himself. Do you doubt Christ because you haven't *seen* a miracle? Do you expect God to prove himself to you personally before you believe? Jesus says, "Blessed are those who have not seen and yet have believed" (John 20:29). We have all the miracles recorded in the Old and New Testaments, 2,000 years of church history, and the witness of thousands. With all this evidence, those who won't believe are either too proud or too stubborn. If you simply step forward in faith and believe, then you will begin to see the miracles that God can do with your life!

16:12 Yeast is put into bread to make it rise, and it takes only a little to affect a whole batch of dough. Jesus used yeast as an example of how a small amount of evil can affect a large group of people. The wrong teachings of the Pharisees and Sadducees were leading many people astray. Beware of the tendency to say, "How can this little wrong possibly affect anyone?"

16:13 Caesarea Philippi was located several miles north of the Sea of Galilee, in the territory ruled by Philip. The influence of Greek and Roman culture was everywhere, and pagan temples and idols abounded. When Philip became ruler, he rebuilt and renamed the city after the emperor (Caesar) and himself. The city was originally called Caesarea, the same name as the capital city of Philip's brother Herod's territory.

16:13–17 The disciples answered Jesus' question with the common view—that Jesus was one of the great prophets come back to life. This belief may have stemmed from Deuteronomy 18:18, where God said he would raise up a prophet from among the people. (John the Baptist's Profile is in John 1; Elijah's Profile is in

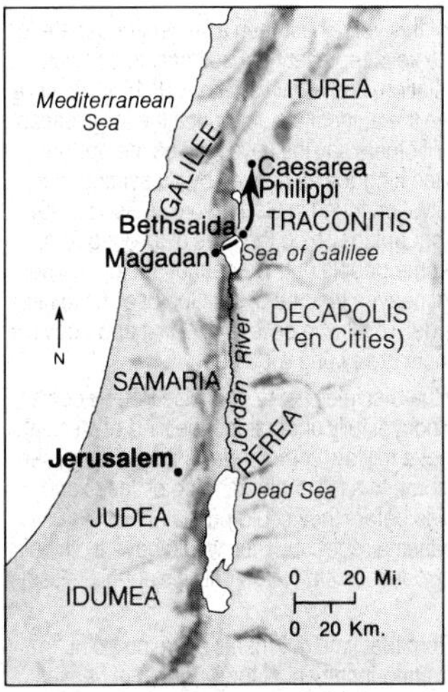

JOURNEY TO CAESAREA PHILIPPI
Jesus left Magadan, crossed the lake, and landed in Bethsaida. There he healed a man who had been born blind. From there, he and his disciples went to Caesarea Philippi, where Peter confessed Jesus as the Messiah and Son of God.

1 Kings 18; and Jeremiah's Profile is in Jeremiah 2.) Peter, however, confessed Jesus as divine and as the promised and long-awaited Messiah. If Jesus were to ask you this question, how would you answer? Is he your Lord and Messiah?

to you by man,[m] but by my Father in heaven. 18 And I tell you that you are Peter,[c][n]
and on this rock I will build my church,[o] and the gates of Hades[d] will not overcome
it.[e] 19 I will give you the keys[p] of the kingdom of heaven; whatever you bind on earth
will be[f] bound in heaven, and whatever you loose on earth will be[f] loosed in
heaven."[q] 20 Then he warned his disciples not to tell anyone[r] that he was the Christ.

Jesus Predicts His Death the First Time
(110/Mark 8:31–9:1; Luke 9:21–27)

21 From that time on Jesus began to explain to his disciples that he must go to
Jerusalem and suffer many things[s] at the hands of the elders, chief priests and teachers
of the law, and that he must be killed and on the third day[t] be raised to life.[u]
22 Peter took him aside and began to rebuke him. "Never, Lord!" he said. "This shall
never happen to you!"
23 Jesus turned and said to Peter, "Get behind me, Satan![v] You are a stumbling-
block to me; you do not have in mind the things of God, but the things of men."
24 Then Jesus said to his disciples, "If anyone would come after me, he must deny
himself and take up his cross and follow me.[w] 25 For whoever wants to save his life[g]
will lose it, but whoever loses his life for me will find it.[x] 26 What good will it be
for a man if he gains the whole world, yet forfeits his soul? Or what can a man give

[c] *18 Peter* means *rock.* [d] *18* Or *hell* [e] *18* Or *not prove stronger than it* [f] *19* Or *have been* [g] *25* The Greek word means either *life* or *soul*; also in verse 26.

16:17 [m] 1Co 15:50; Gal 1:16; Eph 6:12; Heb 2:14
16:18 [n] Jn 1:42 [o] Eph 2:20
16:19 [p] Isa 22:22; Rev 3:7 [q] Mt 18:18; Jn 20:23
16:20 [r] Mk 8:30
16:21 [s] Mk 10:34; Lk 17:25 [t] Jn 2:19 [u] Mt 17:22, 23; Mk 9:31; Lk 9:22; 18:31-33; 24:6, 7
16:23 [v] Mt 4:10
16:24 [w] Mt 10:38; Lk 14:27
16:25 [x] Jn 12:25

16:18 The rock on which Jesus would build his church has been identified as: (1) Jesus himself (his work of salvation by dying for us on the cross); (2) Peter (the first great leader in the church at Jerusalem); (3) the confession of faith that Peter gave and that all subsequent true believers would give. It seems most likely that the rock refers to Peter as the leader of the church (for his function, not necessarily his character). Just as Peter had revealed the true identity of Christ, so Jesus revealed Peter's identity and role.

Later, Peter reminds Christians that they are the church built on the foundation of the apostles and prophets, with Jesus Christ as the cornerstone (1 Peter 2:4–6). All believers are joined into this church by faith in Jesus Christ as Saviour, the same faith that Peter expressed here (see also Ephesians 2:20, 21). Jesus praised Peter for his confession of faith. It is faith like Peter's that is the foundation of Christ's kingdom.

16:19 The meaning of this verse has been a subject of debate for centuries. Some say the keys represent the authority to carry out church discipline, legislation, and administration (18:15–18); while others say the keys give the authority to announce the forgiveness of sins (John 20:23). Still others say the keys may be the opportunity to bring people to the kingdom of heaven by presenting them with the message of salvation found in God's word (Acts 15:7–9). The religious leaders thought they held the keys of the kingdom, and they tried to shut some people out. We cannot decide to open or close the kingdom of heaven for others, but God uses us to help others find the way inside. To all who believe in Christ and obey his words, the kingdom doors are swung wide open.

16:20 Jesus warned the disciples not to publicise Peter's confession because they did not yet fully understand the kind of Messiah he had come to be – not a military commander but a suffering servant. They needed to come to a full understanding of Jesus and their mission as disciples before they could proclaim it to others in a way that would not cause a rebellion. They would have a difficult time understanding what Jesus came to do until his earthly mission was complete.

16:21 The phrase "From that time on" marks a turning point. In 4:17 it signalled Jesus' announcement of the kingdom of heaven. Here it points to his new emphasis on his death and resurrection. The disciples still didn't grasp Jesus' true purpose because of their preconceived notions about what the Messiah should be. This is the first of three times that Jesus predicted his death (see 17:22, 23; 20:18 for others).

16:21–28 This passage corresponds to Daniel's prophecies: the Messiah would be cut off (Daniel 9:26); there would be a period of trouble (9:27); and the king would come in glory (7:13, 14). The disciples would endure the same suffering as their King and, like him, would be rewarded in the end.

16:22 Peter, Jesus' friend and devoted follower who had just eloquently proclaimed Jesus' true identity, sought to protect him from the suffering he prophesied. But if Jesus hadn't suffered and died, Peter (and we) would have died in his sins. Great temptations can come from those who love us and seek to protect us. Be cautious of advice from a friend who says, "Surely God doesn't want you to face this." Often our most difficult temptations come from those who are only trying to protect us from discomfort.

16:23 In his desert temptations, Jesus heard the message that he could achieve greatness without dying (4:6). Here he heard the same message from Peter. Peter had just recognised Jesus as Messiah; here, however, he forsook God's perspective and evaluated the situation from a human one. Satan is always trying to get us to leave God out of the picture. Jesus rebuked Peter for this attitude.

16:24 When Jesus used this picture of his followers taking up their crosses to follow him, the disciples knew what he meant. Crucifixion was a common Roman method of execution, and condemned criminals had to carry their crosses through the streets to the execution site. Following Jesus, therefore, meant a true commitment, the risk of death, and no turning back (see 10:39).

16:25 The possibility of losing their lives was very real for the disciples as well as for Jesus. Real discipleship implies real commitment – pledging our whole existence to his service. If we try to save our physical life from death, pain, or discomfort, we may risk losing our true eternal life. If we protect ourselves from pain, we begin to die spiritually and emotionally. Our lives turn inward, and we lose our intended purpose. When we give our lives in service to Christ, however, we discover the real purpose of living.

16:26 When we don't know Christ, we make choices as though this life is all we have. In reality, this life is just the introduction to eternity. How we live this brief span, however, determines our eternal state. What we accumulate on earth has no value in purchasing eternal life. Even the highest social or civic honours cannot earn us entrance into heaven. Evaluate all that happens from an eternal perspective, and you will find your values and decisions changing.

in exchange for his soul? 27 For the Son of Man[y] is going to come[z] in his Father's
glory with his angels, and then he will reward each person according to what he has
done.[a] 28 I tell you the truth, some who are standing here will not taste death before
they see the Son of Man coming in his kingdom."

Jesus Is Transfigured on the Mountain
(111/Mark 9:2–13; Luke 9:28–36)

17 After six days Jesus took with him Peter, James and John the brother of James,
and led them up a high mountain by themselves. 2 There he was transfigured
before them. His face shone like the sun, and his clothes became as white as the light.
3 Just then there appeared before them Moses and Elijah, talking with Jesus.
4 Peter said to Jesus, "Lord, it is good for us to be here. If you wish, I will put up
three shelters—one for you, one for Moses and one for Elijah."
5 While he was still speaking, a bright cloud enveloped them, and a voice from the
cloud said, "This is my Son, whom I love; with him I am well pleased.[a] Listen to
him!"[b]
6 When the disciples heard this, they fell face down to the ground, terrified. 7 But
Jesus came and touched them. "Get up," he said. "Don't be afraid."[c] 8 When they
looked up, they saw no-one except Jesus.
9 As they were coming down the mountain, Jesus instructed them, "Don't tell
anyone[d] what you have seen, until the Son of Man[e] has been raised from the dead."[f]
10 The disciples asked him, "Why then do the teachers of the law say that Elijah
must come first?"
11 Jesus replied, "To be sure, Elijah comes and will restore all things.[g] 12 But I tell
you, Elijah has already come,[h] and they did not recognise him, but have done to him
everything they wished.[i] In the same way the Son of Man is going to suffer[j] at their
hands." 13 Then the disciples understood that he was talking to them about John the
Baptist.

16:27 [y]Mt 8:20 [z]Ac 1:11 [a]Job 34:11; Ps 62:12; Jer 17:10; Ro 2:6; 2Co 5:10; Rev 22:12
17:5 [a]Mt 3:17; 2Pe 1:17 [b]Ac 3:22, 23
17:7 [c]Mt 14:27
17:9 [d]Mk 8:30 [e]Mt 8:20 [f]Mt 16:21
17:11 [g]Mal 4:6; Lk 1:16, 17
17:12 [h]Mt 11:14 [i]Mt 14:3, 10 [j]Mt 16:21

16:27 Jesus Christ has been given the authority to judge all the earth (Romans 14:9–11; Philippians 2:9–11). Although his judgment is already working in our lives, there is a future, final judgment when Christ returns (25:31–46) and everyone's life is reviewed and evaluated. This will not be confined to unbelievers; Christians too will face a judgment. Their eternal destiny is secure, but Jesus will look at how they handled gifts, opportunities, and responsibilities in order to determine their heavenly rewards. At the time of judgment, God will deliver the righteous and condemn the wicked. We should not judge others' salvation; that is God's work.

16:28 Because all the disciples died *before* Christ's return, many believe that Jesus' words were fulfilled at the transfiguration when Peter, James, and John saw his glory (17:1–3). Others say this statement refers to Pentecost (Acts 2) and the beginning of Christ's church. In either case, certain disciples were eyewitnesses to the power and glory of Christ's kingdom.

17:1ff The transfiguration was a vision, a brief glimpse of the true glory of the King (16:27, 28). This was a special revelation of Jesus' divinity to three of the disciples, and it was God's divine affirmation of everything Jesus had done and was about to do.

17:3–5 Moses and Elijah were the two greatest prophets in the Old Testament. Moses represents the law, or the old covenant. He wrote the Pentateuch, and he predicted the coming of a great prophet (Deuteronomy 18:15–19). Elijah represents the prophets who foretold the coming of the Messiah (Malachi 4:5, 6). Moses' and Elijah's presence with Jesus confirmed Jesus' Messianic mission—to fulfil God's law and the words of God's prophets. Just as God's voice in the cloud over Mount Sinai gave authority to his law (Exodus 19:9), God's voice at the transfiguration gave authority to Jesus' words.

17:4 Peter wanted to build three shelters for these three great men to stay to show how the Feast of Tabernacles was fulfilled in the coming of God's kingdom. Peter had the right idea about Christ, but his timing was wrong. Peter wanted to act, but this was a time for worship and adoration. He wanted to capture the moment, but he was supposed to learn and move on.

17:5 Jesus is more than just a great leader, a good example, a good influence, or a great prophet. He is the Son of God. When you understand this profound truth, the only adequate response is worship. When you have a correct understanding of Christ, you will obey him.

17:9 Jesus told Peter, James, and John not to tell anyone what they had seen until after his resurrection because Jesus knew that they didn't fully understand it and could not explain what they didn't understand. Their question (17:10ff) revealed their misunderstandings. They knew that Jesus was the Messiah, but they had much more to learn about the significance of his death and resurrection.

17:10–12 Based on Malachi 4:5, 6, the teachers of the Old Testament law believed that Elijah must appear before the Messiah would appear. Jesus referred to John the Baptist, not to the Old Testament prophet Elijah. John the Baptist took on Elijah's prophetic role—boldly confronting sin and pointing people to God. Malachi had prophesied that a prophet like Elijah would come (Malachi 4:5).

Jesus Heals a Demon-Possessed Boy
(112/Mark 9:14–29; Luke 9:37–43)

14 When they came to the crowd, a man approached Jesus and knelt before him.
15 "Lord, have mercy on my son," he said. "He has seizures[k] and is suffering greatly.
He often falls into the fire or into the water. 16 I brought him to your disciples, but
they could not heal him."
17 "O unbelieving and perverse generation," Jesus replied, "how long shall I stay
with you? How long shall I put up with you? Bring the boy here to me." 18 Jesus
rebuked the demon, and it came out of the boy, and he was healed from that moment.
19 Then the disciples came to Jesus in private and asked, "Why couldn't we drive
it out?"
20 He replied, "Because you have so little faith. I tell you the truth, if you have
faith[l] as small as a mustard seed,[m] you can say to this mountain, 'Move from here
to there' and it will move.[n] Nothing will be impossible for you."[a]

Jesus Predicts His Death the Second Time
(113/Mark 9:30–32; Luke 9:44, 45)

22 When they came together in Galilee, he said to them, "The Son of Man[o] is going
to be betrayed into the hands of men. 23 They will kill him,[p] and on the third day[q]
he will be raised to life."[r] And the disciples were filled with grief.

Peter Finds the Coin in the Fish's Mouth
(114)

24 After Jesus and his disciples arrived in Capernaum, the collectors of the two-
drachma tax[s] came to Peter and asked, "Doesn't your teacher pay the temple tax?"[b]
25 "Yes, he does," he replied.
When Peter came into the house, Jesus was the first to speak. "What do you think,

[a] 20 Some manuscripts *you.* 21 *But this kind does not go out except by prayer and fasting.* [b] 24 Greek *the two drachmas*

17:15 [k]Mt 4:24
17:20 [l]Mt 21:21 [m]Mt 13:31; Mk 11:23; Lk 17:6 [n]1Co 13:2
17:22 [o]Mt 8:20
17:23 [p]Ac 2:23; 3:13 [q]Mt 16:21 [r]Mt 16:21
17:24 [s]Ex 30:13

17:17 The disciples had been given the authority to do the healing, but they had not yet learned how to appropriate the power of God. Jesus' frustration is with the unbelieving and unresponsive generation. His disciples were merely a reflection of that attitude in this instance. Jesus' purpose was not to criticise the disciples, but to encourage them to greater faith.

17:17–20 The disciples were unable to drive out this demon, and they asked Jesus why. He pointed to their lack of faith. It is the power of God, not our faith, that moves mountains, but faith must be present to do so. The mustard seed was the smallest particle imaginable. Even small or undeveloped faith would have been sufficient. Perhaps the disciples had tried to drive out the demon with their own ability rather than God's. There is great power in even a little faith when God is with us. If we feel weak or powerless as Christians, we should examine our faith, making sure we are trusting not in our own abilities to produce results, but in God's.

17:20 Jesus wasn't condemning the disciples for substandard faith; he was trying to show how important faith would be in their future ministry. If you are facing a problem that seems as big and immovable as a mountain, turn your eyes from the mountain and look to Christ for more faith. Only then will your work for him become useful and vibrant.

17:22, 23 Once again Jesus predicted his death (see also 16:21); but more important, he told of his resurrection. Unfortunately, the disciples heard only the first part of Jesus' words and became discouraged. They couldn't understand why Jesus wanted to go back to Jerusalem where he would walk right into trouble.

The disciples didn't fully comprehend the purpose of Jesus' death and resurrection until Pentecost (Acts 2). We shouldn't be upset with ourselves for being slow to understand everything about Jesus. After all, the disciples were with him, saw his miracles, heard his words, and still had difficulty understanding. Despite their questions and doubts, however, they believed. We should do no less.

17:22, 23 The disciples didn't understand why Jesus kept talking about his death because they expected him to set up a political kingdom. His death, they thought, would dash their hopes. They didn't know that Jesus' death and resurrection would make his kingdom possible.

17:24 All Jewish males had to pay a temple tax to support temple upkeep (Exodus 30:11–16). Tax collectors set up booths to collect these taxes. Only Matthew records this incident—perhaps because he had been a tax collector himself.

17:24–27 As usual, Peter answered a question without really knowing the answer, putting Jesus and the disciples in an awkward position. Jesus used this situation, however, to emphasise his kingly role. Just as kings pay no taxes and collect none from their family, Jesus, the King, owed no taxes. But Jesus supplied the tax payment for both himself and Peter rather than offend those who didn't understand his kingship. Although Jesus supplied the tax money, Peter had to go and get it. Ultimately all that we have comes to us from God's supply, but he may want us to be active in the process.

17:24–27 As God's people, we are foreigners on earth because our loyalty is always to our real King—Jesus. Still we have to co-operate with the authorities and be responsible citizens. An ambassador to another country keeps the local laws in order to represent well the one who sent him. We are Christ's ambassadors (2 Corinthians 5:20). Are you being a good foreign ambassador for him to this world?

17:25 [t]Mt 22:17-21; Ro 13:7
17:27 [u]Jn 6:61
18:3 [a]Mt 19:14; 1Pe 2:2 [b]Mt 3:2
18:4 [c]Mk 9:35
18:5 [d]Mt 10:40
18:6 [e]Mt 5:29 [f]Mk 9:42; Lk 17:2
18:7 [g]Lk 17:1
18:8 [h]Mt 5:29; Mk 9:43, 45
18:9 [i]Mt 5:29 [j]Mt 5:22
18:10 [k]Ge 48:16; Ps 34:7; Ac 12:11, 15; Heb 1:14

Simon?" he asked. "From whom do the kings of the earth collect duty and
taxes[t]—from their own sons or from others?"
26"From others," Peter answered.
"Then the sons are exempt," Jesus said to him. 27"But so that we may not offend[u]
them, go to the lake and throw out your line. Take the first fish you catch; open its
mouth and you will find a four-drachma coin. Take it and give it to them for my tax
and yours."

The Disciples Argue about Who Would Be the Greatest
(115/Mark 9:33–37; Luke 9:46–48)

18 At that time the disciples came to Jesus and asked, "Who is the greatest in the
kingdom of heaven?"
2He called a little child and had him stand among them. 3And he said: "I tell you
the truth, unless you change and become like little children,[a] you will never enter
the kingdom of heaven.[b] 4Therefore, whoever humbles himself like this child is the
greatest in the kingdom of heaven.[c]
5"And whoever welcomes a little child like this in my name welcomes me.[d] 6But
if anyone causes one of these little ones who believe in me to sin,[e] it would be better
for him to have a large millstone hung around his neck and to be drowned in the depths
of the sea.[f]

Jesus Warns against Temptation
(117/Mark 9:42–50)

7"Woe to the world because of the things that cause people to sin! Such things must
come, but woe to the man through whom they come![g] 8If your hand or your foot
causes you to sin,[h] cut it off and throw it away. It is better for you to enter life maimed
or crippled than to have two hands or two feet and be thrown into eternal fire. 9And
if your eye causes you to sin,[i] gouge it out and throw it away. It is better for you
to enter life with one eye than to have two eyes and be thrown into the fire of hell.[j]

Jesus Warns against Looking Down on Others
(118)

10"See that you do not look down on one of these little ones. For I tell you that
their angels[k] in heaven always see the face of my Father in heaven.**[a]**
12"What do you think? If a man owns a hundred sheep, and one of them wanders
away, will he not leave the ninety-nine on the hills and go to look for the one that
wandered off? 13And if he finds it, I tell you the truth, he is happier about that one

a *10* Some manuscripts *heaven.* 11 *The Son of Man came to save what was lost.*

18:1 From Mark's Gospel we learn that Jesus precipitated this conversation by asking the disciples what they had been discussing among themselves earlier (Mark 9:33, 34).

18:1–4 Jesus used a child to help his self-centred disciples get the point. We are not to be *childish* (like the disciples, arguing over petty issues), but rather *childlike,* with humble and sincere hearts. Are you being childlike or childish?

18:3, 4 The disciples had become so preoccupied with the organisation of Jesus' earthly kingdom that they had lost sight of its divine purpose. Instead of seeking a place of service, they sought positions of advantage. It is easy to lose our eternal perspective and compete for promotions or status in the church. It is difficult to identify with "children"—weak and dependent people with no status or influence.

18:6 Children are trusting by nature. They trust adults, and through that trust their capacity to trust God grows. God holds parents and other adults who influence young children accountable for how they affect these little ones' ability to trust. Jesus warned that anyone who turns little children away from faith will receive severe punishment.

18:7ff Jesus warned the disciples about two ways to cause "little ones" to sin: tempting them (18:7–9) and neglecting or demeaning them (18:10–14). As leaders, we are to help young people or new believers avoid anything or anyone that could cause them to stumble in their faith and lead them to sin. We must never take lightly the spiritual education and protection of the young in age and in the faith.

18:8, 9 We must remove stumbling blocks that cause us to sin. This does not mean to cut off a part of the body; it means that any person, project, or teaching in the church that threatens the spiritual growth of the body must be removed. For the individual, any relationship, practice, or activity that leads to sin should be stopped. Jesus says it would be better to go to heaven with one hand than to hell with both. Sin, of course, affects more than our hands; it affects our minds and hearts.

18:10 Our concern for children must match God's treatment of them. Certain angels are assigned to watch over children, and they have direct access to God. These words ring out sharply in cultures where children are taken lightly, ignored, or aborted. If their angels have constant access to God, the least we can do is to allow children to approach us easily in spite of our far too busy schedules.

sheep than about the ninety-nine that did not wander off. 14In the same way your
Father in heaven is not willing that any of these little ones should be lost.

Jesus Teaches How to Treat a Believer Who Sins
(119)

15"If your brother sins against you,[b] go and show him his fault,[l] just between the
two of you. If he listens to you, you have won your brother over. 16But if he will not
listen, take one or two others along, so that 'every matter may be established by the
testimony of two or three witnesses.'[c][m] 17If he refuses to listen to them, tell it to
the church;[n] and if he refuses to listen even to the church, treat him as you would
a pagan or a tax collector.[o]

18"I tell you the truth, whatever you bind on earth will be[d] bound in heaven, and
whatever you loose on earth will be[d] loosed in heaven.[p]

19"Again, I tell you that if two of you on earth agree about anything you ask for,
it will be done for you[q] by my Father in heaven. 20For where two or three come
together in my name, there am I with them."

Jesus Tells the Parable of the Unforgiving Debtor
(120)

21Then Peter came to Jesus and asked, "Lord, how many times shall I forgive my
brother when he sins against me?[r] Up to seven times?"[s]

22Jesus answered, "I tell you, not seven times, but seventy-seven times.[e][t]

23"Therefore, the kingdom of heaven is like[u] a king who wanted to settle accounts[v] with his servants. 24As he began the settlement, a man who owed him ten
thousand talents[f] was brought to him. 25Since he was not able to pay,[w] the master
ordered that he and his wife and his children and all that he had be sold[x] to repay
the debt.

26"The servant fell on his knees before him.[y] 'Be patient with me,' he begged,
'and I will pay back everything.' 27The servant's master took pity on him, cancelled
the debt and let him go.

28"But when that servant went out, he found one of his fellow-servants who owed
him a hundred denarii.[g] He grabbed him and began to choke him. 'Pay back what
you owe me!' he demanded.

29"His fellow-servant fell to his knees and begged him, 'Be patient with me, and
I will pay you back.'

30"But he refused. Instead, he went off and had the man thrown into prison until

[b] *15* Some manuscripts do not have *against you.* [c] *16* Deut. 19:15 [d] *18* Or *have been* [e] *22* Or *seventy times seven* [f] *24* That is, millions of pounds [g] *28* That is, a few pounds

18:15 [l]Lev 19:17; Lk 17:3; Gal 6:1; Jas 5:19, 20
18:16 [m]Nu 35:30; Dt 17:6; 19:15; Jn 8:17; 2Co 13:1; 1Ti 5:19; Heb 10:28
18:17 [n]1Co 6:1-6 [o]Ro 16:17; 2Th 3:6, 14
18:18 [p]Mt 16:19; Jn 20:23
18:19 [q]Mt 7:7
18:21 [r]Mt 6:14 [s]Lk 17:4
18:22 [t]Ge 4:24
18:23 [u]Mt 13:24 [v]Mt 25:19
18:25 [w]Lk 7:42 [x]Lev 25:39; 2Ki 4:1; Ne 5:5, 8
18:26 [y]Mt 8:2

18:14 Just as a shepherd is concerned enough about one lost sheep to go and search in the hills for it, so God is concerned about every human being he has created (he is "not wanting anyone to perish", 2 Peter 3:9). You come in contact with children who need Christ at home, at school, in church, and in the neighbourhood. Steer them towards Christ by your example, your words, and your acts of kindness.

18:15–17 These are Jesus' guidelines for dealing with those who sin against us. They were meant for (1) Christians, not unbelievers, (2) sins committed against *you* and not others, and (3) conflict resolution in the context of the church, not the community at large. Jesus' words are not a licence for a frontal attack on every person who hurts or slights us. They are not a licence to start a destructive gossip campaign or to call for a church trial. They are designed to reconcile those who disagree so that all Christians can live in harmony.

When someone wrongs us, we often do the opposite of what Jesus recommends. We turn away in hatred or resentment, seek revenge, or engage in gossip. By contrast, we should go to that person *first,* as difficult as that may be. Then we should forgive that person as often as he or she needs it (18:21, 22). This will create a much better chance of restoring the relationship.

18:18 This *binding* and *loosing* refers to the decisions of the church in conflicts. Among believers, there is no court of appeals beyond the church. Ideally, the church's decisions should be God-guided and based on discernment of his word. Believers have the responsibility, therefore, to bring their problems to the church, and the church has the responsibility to use God's guidance in seeking to resolve conflicts. Handling problems God's way will have an impact now and for eternity.

18:19, 20 Jesus looked ahead to a new day when he would be present with his followers not in body, but through his Holy Spirit. In the body of believers (the church), the sincere agreement of two people is more powerful than the superficial agreement of thousands, because Christ's Holy Spirit is with them. Two or more believers, *filled with the Holy Spirit,* will pray according to God's will, not their own; thus their requests will be granted.

18:22 The rabbis taught that people should forgive those who offend them – but only three times. Peter, trying to be especially generous, asked Jesus if seven (the "perfect" number) was enough times to forgive someone. But Jesus answered, "Seventy-seven times," meaning that we shouldn't even keep track of how many times we forgive someone. We should always forgive those who are truly repentant, no matter how many times they ask.

18:35 [z]Mt 6:14; Jas 2:13
19:1 [a]Mt 7:28
19:2 [b]Mt 4:23
19:3 [c]Mt 5:31
19:4 [d]Ge 1:27; 5:2
19:5 [e]Ge 2:24; 1Co 6:16; Eph 5:31

he could pay the debt. 31When the other servants saw what had happened, they were
greatly distressed and went and told their master everything that had happened.
32"Then the master called the servant in. 'You wicked servant,' he said, 'I cancelled
all that debt of yours because you begged me to. 33Shouldn't you have had mercy on
your fellow-servant just as I had on you?' 34In anger his master turned him over to
the jailers to be tortured, until he should pay back all he owed.
35"This is how my heavenly Father will treat each of you unless you forgive your
brother from your heart."[z]

6. Jesus faces conflict with the religious leaders

Jesus Teaches about Marriage and Divorce

(173/Mark 10:1–12)

19 When Jesus had finished saying these things,[a] he left Galilee and went into
the region of Judea to the other side of the Jordan. 2Large crowds followed him,
and he healed them[b] there.
3Some Pharisees came to him to test him. They asked, "Is it lawful for a man to
divorce his wife[c] for any and every reason?"
4"Haven't you read," he replied, "that at the beginning the Creator 'made them male
and female',[a][d] 5and said, 'For this reason a man will leave his father and mother
and be united to his wife, and the two will become one flesh'[b]?[e] 6So they are no
longer two, but one. Therefore what God has joined together, let man not separate."

[a] *4* Gen. 1:27 [b] *5* Gen. 2:24

JESUS AND FORGIVENESS

Jesus forgave	*Reference*
the paralytic lowered on a mat through the roof.	Matthew 9:2–8
the woman caught in adultery.	John 8:3–11
the woman who anointed his feet with oil.	Luke 7:47–50
Peter, for denying he knew Jesus.	John 18:15–18, 25–27; 21:15–19
the criminal on the cross.	Luke 23:39–43
the people who crucified him.	Luke 23:34

Jesus not only taught frequently about forgiveness, he also demonstrated his own willingness to forgive. Here are several examples that should be an encouragement to recognise his willingness to forgive us also.

18:30 In Bible times, serious consequences awaited those who could not pay their debts. A person lending money could seize the borrower who couldn't pay and force him or his family to work until the debt was paid. The debtor could also be thrown into prison, or his family could be sold into slavery to help pay off the debt. It was hoped that the debtor, while in prison, would sell off his land or that relatives would pay the debt. If not, the debtor could remain in prison for life.

18:35 Because God has forgiven all our sins, we should not withhold forgiveness from others. Realising how completely Christ has forgiven us should produce a free and generous attitude of forgiveness towards others. When we don't forgive others, we are setting ourselves outside and above Christ's law of love.

19:3–12 John was put in prison and killed, at least in part, for his public opinions on marriage and divorce, so the Pharisees hoped to trap Jesus too. They were trying to trick Jesus by having him choose sides in a theological controversy. Two schools of thought represented two opposing views of divorce. One group supported divorce for almost any reason. The other believed that divorce could be allowed only for marital unfaithfulness. This conflict hinged on how each group interpreted Deuteronomy 24:1–4. In his answer, however, Jesus focused on marriage rather than divorce. He pointed out that God intended marriage to be permanent and gave four reasons for the importance of marriage (19:4–6).

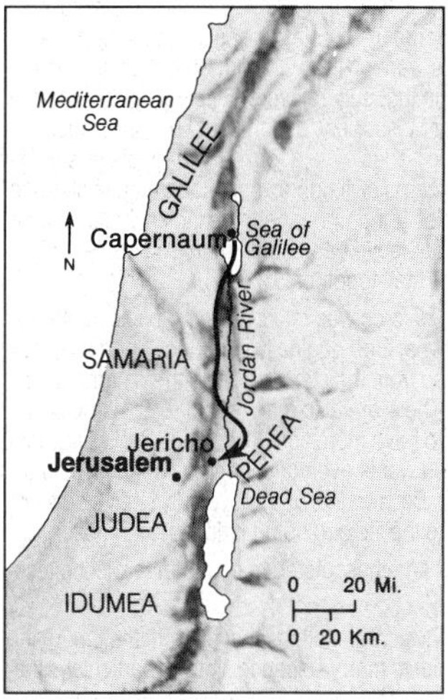

JESUS TRAVELS TOWARDS JERUSALEM
Jesus left Galilee for the last time—heading towards his death in Jerusalem. He again crossed the Jordan, spending some time in Perea before going on to Jericho.

7"Why then," they asked, "did Moses command that a man give his wife a certificate of divorce and send her away?"[f]
8Jesus replied, "Moses permitted you to divorce your wives because your hearts
were hard. But it was not this way from the beginning. 9I tell you that anyone who
divorces his wife, except for marital unfaithfulness, and marries another woman
commits adultery."[g]
10The disciples said to him, "If this is the situation between a husband and wife,
it is better not to marry."
11Jesus replied, "Not everyone can accept this word, but only those to whom it has
been given.[h] 12For some are eunuchs because they were born that way; others were
made that way by men; and others have renounced marriage[c] because of the kingdom
of heaven. The one who can accept this should accept it."

Jesus Blesses Little Children
(174/Mark 10:13–16; Luke 18:15–17)

13Then little children were brought to Jesus for him to place his hands on them[i]
and pray for them. But the disciples rebuked those who brought them.
14Jesus said, "Let the little children come to me, and do not hinder them, for the
kingdom of heaven belongs[j] to such as these."[k] 15When he had placed his hands
on them, he went on from there.

Jesus Speaks to the Rich Young Man
(175/Mark 10:17–31; Luke 18:18–30)

16Now a man came up to Jesus and asked, "Teacher, what good thing must I do
to get eternal life[l]?"[m]
17"Why do you ask me about what is good?" Jesus replied. "There is only One who
is good. If you want to enter life, obey the commandments."[n]
18"Which ones?" the man enquired.
Jesus replied, " 'Do not murder, do not commit adultery,[o] do not steal, do not give
false testimony, 19honour your father and mother,'[d][p] and 'love your neighbour as
yourself.'[e]"[q]

19:7 [f]Dt 24:1-4; Mt 5:31
19:9 [g]Mt 5:32; Lk 16:18
19:11 [h]Mt 13:11; 1Co 7:7-9, 17
19:13 [i]Mk 5:23
19:14 [j]Mt 25:34 [k]Mt 18:3; 1Pe 2:2
19:16 [l]Mt 25:46 [m]Lk 10:25
19:17 [n]Lev 18:5
19:18 [o]Jas 2:11
19:19 [p]Ex 20:12-16; Dt 5:16-20 [q]Lev 19:18; Mt 5:43

c *12 Or have made themselves eunuchs* d *19* Exodus 20:12–16; Deut. 5:16–20 e *19* Lev. 19:18

19:7, 8 This law is found in Deuteronomy 24:1–4. In Moses' day, as well as in Jesus' day, the practice of marriage fell far short of God's intention. The same is true today. Jesus said that Moses gave this law only because of the people's hard hearts—permanent marriage was God's intention. But because sinful human nature made divorce inevitable, Moses instituted some laws to help its victims. These were civil laws designed especially to protect the women who, in that culture, were quite vulnerable when living alone. Because of Moses' law, a man could no longer just throw his wife out—he had to write a formal letter of dismissal. This was a radical step towards civil rights, for it made men think twice about divorce. God designed marriage to be indissoluble. Instead of looking for reasons to leave each other, married couples should concentrate on how to stay together (19:3–9).

19:10–12 Although divorce was relatively easy in Old Testament times (19:7), it is not what God originally intended. Couples should decide against divorce from the start and build their marriage on mutual commitment. There are also many good reasons for not marrying, one being to have more time to work for God's kingdom. Don't assume that God wants everyone to marry. For many it may be better if they don't. Be sure that you prayerfully seek God's will before you plunge into the lifelong commitment of marriage.

19:12 A "eunuch" is an emasculated male—a man with no testicles.

19:12 Some have physical limitations that prevent their marrying, while others choose not to marry because, in their particular situation, they can serve God better as single people. Jesus was not teaching us to avoid marriage because it is inconvenient or takes away our freedom. That would be selfishness. A good reason to remain single is to use the time and freedom to serve God. Paul elaborates on this in 1 Corinthians 7.

19:13–15 The disciples must have forgotten what Jesus had said about children (18:4–6). Jesus wanted little children to come because he loves them and because they have the kind of attitude needed to approach God. He didn't mean that heaven is only for children, but that people need childlike attitudes of trust in God. The receptiveness of little children was a great contrast to the stubbornness of the religious leaders who let their education and sophistication stand in the way of the simple faith needed to believe in Jesus.

19:16 To this man seeking assurance of eternal life, Jesus pointed out that salvation does not come from good deeds unaccompanied by love for God. The man needed a whole new starting point. Instead of adding another commandment to keep or good deed to perform, the young man needed to submit humbly to the lordship of Christ.

19:17 In response to the young man's question about how to have eternal life, Jesus told him to keep God's Ten Commandments. Jesus then listed six of them, all referring to relationships with others. When the young man replied that he had kept the commandments, Jesus told him that he must do something more—sell everything and give the money to the poor. Jesus' statement exposed the man's weakness. In reality, his wealth was his god, his idol, and he would not give it up. Thus he violated the first and greatest commandment (Exodus 20:3; Matthew 22:36–40).

19:21 [r]Mt 5:48 [s]Lk 12:33; Ac 2:45; 4:34-35 [t]Mt 6:20

19:23 [u]Mt 13:22; 1Ti 6:9, 10

19:26 [v]Ge 18:14; Job 42:2; Jer 32:17; Zec 8:6; Lk 1:37; 18:27; Ro 4:21

19:27 [w]Mt 4:19

19:28 [x]Mt 20:21; 25:31 [y]Lk 22:28-30; Rev 3:21; 4:4; 20:4

19:29 [z]Mt 6:33; 25:46

19:30 [a]Mt 20:16; Mk 10:31; Lk 13:30

20:1 [a]Mt 13:24 [b]Mt 21:28, 33

20“All these I have kept,” the young man said. “What do I still lack?”
21Jesus answered, “If you want to be perfect,[r] go, sell your possessions and give
to the poor,[s] and you will have treasure in heaven.[t] Then come, follow me.”
22When the young man heard this, he went away sad, because he had great wealth.
23Then Jesus said to his disciples, “I tell you the truth, it is hard for a rich man[u]
to enter the kingdom of heaven. 24Again I tell you, it is easier for a camel to go through
the eye of a needle than for a rich man to enter the kingdom of God.”
25When the disciples heard this, they were greatly astonished and asked, “Who then
can be saved?”
26Jesus looked at them and said, “With man this is impossible, but with God all
things are possible.”[v]
27Peter answered him, “We have left everything to follow you![w] What then will
there be for us?”
28Jesus said to them, “I tell you the truth, at the renewal of all things, when the
Son of Man sits on his glorious throne,[x] you who have followed me will also sit on
twelve thrones, judging the twelve tribes of Israel.[y] 29And everyone who has left
houses or brothers or sisters or father or mother[f] or children or fields for my sake
will receive a hundred times as much and will inherit eternal life.[z] 30But many who
are first will be last, and many who are last will be first.[a]

Jesus Tells the Parable of the Workers Paid Equally (176)

20 “For the kingdom of heaven is like[a] a landowner who went out early in the
morning to hire men to work in his vineyard.[b] 2He agreed to pay them a
denarius for the day and sent them into his vineyard.
3“About the third hour he went out and saw others standing in the market-place
doing nothing. 4He told them, ‘You also go and work in my vineyard, and I will pay
you whatever is right.’ 5So they went.
“He went out again about the sixth hour and the ninth hour and did the same thing.
6About the eleventh hour he went out and found still others standing around. He asked
them, ‘Why have you been standing here all day long doing nothing?’
7“ ‘Because no-one has hired us,’ they answered.

[f] *29* Some manuscripts *mother or wife*

19:21 When Jesus told this young man that he would “be perfect” if he gave everything he had to the poor, Jesus wasn’t speaking in the temporal, human sense. He was explaining how to be justified and made whole or complete in God’s sight.

19:21 Should all believers sell everything they own? No. We are responsible to care for our own needs and the needs of our families so as not to be a burden on others. We should, however, be willing to give up anything if God asks us to do so. This kind of attitude allows nothing to come between us and God and keeps us from using our God-given wealth selfishly. If you are comforted by the fact that Christ did not tell all his followers to sell all their possessions, then you may be too attached to what you have.

19:22 We cannot love God with all our hearts and yet keep our money to ourselves. Loving him totally means using our money in ways that please him.

19:24 Because it is impossible for a camel to go through the eye of a needle, it appears impossible for a rich person to get into the kingdom of God. Jesus explained, however, that “with God all things are possible” (19:26). Even rich people can enter the kingdom if God brings them in. Faith in Christ, not in self or riches, is what counts. On what are you counting for salvation?

19:25, 26 The disciples were astonished. They thought that if anyone could be saved, it would be the rich, whom their culture considered especially blessed by God.

19:27 In the Bible, God gives rewards to his people according to his justice. In the Old Testament, obedience often brought reward in this life (Deuteronomy 28), but obedience and immediate reward are not always linked. If they were, good people would always be rich, and suffering would always be a sign of sin. As believers, our true reward is God’s presence and power through the Holy Spirit. Later, in eternity, we will be rewarded for our faith and service. If material rewards in this life came to us for every faithful deed, we would be tempted to boast about our achievements and act out of wrong motivations.

19:29 Jesus assured the disciples that anyone who gives up something valuable for his sake will be repaid many times over in this life, although not necessarily in the same form. For example, a person may be rejected by his or her family for accepting Christ, but he or she will gain the larger family of believers.

19:30 Jesus turned the world’s values upside down. Consider the most powerful or well-known people in our world – how many got where they are by being humble, self-effacing, and gentle? Not many! But in the life to come, the last will be first – if they are in last place because of choosing to follow Jesus. Don’t forfeit eternal rewards for temporary benefits. Be willing to make sacrifices now for greater rewards later. Be willing to accept human disapproval, while knowing that you have God’s approval.

20:1ff Jesus further clarified the membership rules of the kingdom of heaven – entrance is by God’s grace alone. In this parable, God is the landowner, and believers are the workers. This parable speaks especially to those who feel superior because of heritage or favoured position, to those who feel superior because they have spent so much time with Christ, and to new believers as reassurance of God’s grace.

“He said to them, ‘You also go and work in my vineyard.’
8“When evening came,[c] the owner of the vineyard said to his foreman, ‘Call the
workers and pay them their wages, beginning with the last ones hired and going on
to the first.’
9“The workers who were hired about the eleventh hour came and each received a
denarius. 10So when those came who were hired first, they expected to receive more.
But each one of them also received a denarius. 11When they received it, they began
to grumble[d] against the landowner. 12‘These men who were hired last worked only
one hour,’ they said, ‘and you have made them equal to us who have borne the burden
of the work and the heat[e] of the day.’
13“But he answered one of them, ‘Friend,[f] I am not being unfair to you. Didn’t
you agree to work for a denarius? 14Take your pay and go. I want to give the man
who was hired last the same as I gave you. 15Don’t I have the right to do what I want
with my own money? Or are you envious because I am generous?’[g]
16“So the last will be first, and the first will be last.”[h]

Jesus Predicts His Death the Third Time
(177/Mark 10:32–34; Luke 18:31–34)

17Now as Jesus was going up to Jerusalem, he took the twelve disciples aside and
said to them, 18“We are going up to Jerusalem,[i] and the Son of Man[j] will be
betrayed to the chief priests and the teachers of the law.[k] They will condemn him
to death 19and will turn him over to the Gentiles to be mocked and flogged[l] and
crucified.[m] On the third day[n] he will be raised to life!”[o]

Jesus Teaches about Serving Others
(178/Mark 10:35–45)

20Then the mother of Zebedee’s sons[p] came to Jesus with her sons and, kneeling
down,[q] asked a favour of him.
21“What is it you want?” he asked.
She said, “Grant that one of these two sons of mine may sit at your right and the
other at your left in your kingdom.”[r]
22“You don’t know what you are asking,” Jesus said to them. “Can you drink the
cup[s] I am going to drink?”
“We can,” they answered.
23Jesus said to them, “You will indeed drink from my cup,[t] but to sit at my right

20:8 [c]Lev 19:13; Dt 24:15
20:11 [d]Jnh 4:1
20:12 [e]Jnh 4:8; Lk 12:55; Jas 1:11
20:13 [f]Mt 22:12; 26:50
20:15 [g]Dt 15:9; Mk 7:22
20:16 [h]Mt 19:30
20:18 [i]Lk 9:51 [j]Mt 8:20 [k]Mt 16:21; 27:1, 2
20:19 [l]Mt 16:21 [m]Ac 2:23 [n]Mt 16:21 [o]Mt 16:21
20:20 [p]Mt 4:21 [q]Mt 8:2
20:21 [r]Mt 19:28
20:22 [s]Isa 51:17, 22; Jer 49:12; Mt 26:39, 42; Mk 14:36; Lk 22:42; Jn 18:11
20:23 [t]Ac 12:2; Rev 1:9

20:15 This parable is not about rewards but about salvation. It is a strong teaching about *grace,* God’s generosity. We shouldn’t begrudge those who turn to God in the last moments of life, because, in reality, *no-one* deserves eternal life.

Many people we don’t expect to see in the kingdom will be there. The criminal who repented as he was dying (Luke 23:40–43) will be there along with people who have believed and served God for many years. Do you resent God’s gracious acceptance of the despised, the outcast, and the sinners who have turned to him for forgiveness? Are you ever jealous of what God has given to another person? Instead, focus on God’s gracious benefits to you, and be thankful for what you have.

20:17–19 Jesus predicted his death and resurrection for the third time (see 16:21 and 17:22, 23 for the first two times). But the disciples still didn’t understand what he meant. They continued to argue greedily over their positions in Christ’s kingdom (20:20–28).

20:20 The mother of James and John came to Jesus and “kneeling down, asked a favour of him”. She gave Jesus worship, but her real motive was to get something from him. Too often this happens in our churches and in our lives. We play religious games, expecting God to give us something in return. True worship, however, adores and praises Christ for who he is and for what he has done.

20:20 The mother of James and John asked Jesus to give her sons special positions in his kingdom. Parents naturally want to see their children promoted and honoured, but this desire is dangerous if it causes them to lose sight of God’s specific will for their children. God may have different work in mind – not as glamorous, but just as important. Thus parents’ desires for their children’s advancement must be held in check as they pray that God’s will be done in their children’s lives.

20:20 According to 27:56, the mother of James and John was at the cross when Jesus was crucified. Some have suggested that she was the sister of Mary, the mother of Jesus. A close family relationship could have prompted her to make this request for her sons.

20:22 James, John, and their mother failed to grasp Jesus’ previous teachings on rewards (19:16–30) and eternal life (20:1–16). They failed to understand the suffering they must face before living in the glory of God’s kingdom. The “cup” was the suffering and crucifixion that Christ faced. Both James and John would also face great suffering. James would be put to death for his faith, and John would be exiled.

20:23 Jesus was showing that he was under the authority of the Father, who alone makes the decisions about leadership in heaven. Such rewards are not granted as favours. They are for those who have maintained their commitment to Jesus in spite of severe trials.

20:24 The other disciples were upset with James and John for trying to grab the top positions. *All* the disciples wanted to be the

20:24 [u]Lk 22:24, 25

or left is not for me to grant. These places belong to those for whom they have been
prepared by my Father."
24 When the ten heard about this, they were indignant[u] with the two brothers.
25 Jesus called them together and said, "You know that the rulers of the Gentiles lord
it over them, and their high officials exercise authority over them. 26 Not so with you.
Instead, whoever wants to become great among you must be your servant,[v] 27 and
whoever wants to be first must be your slave — 28 just as the Son of Man[w] did not come
to be served, but to serve,[x] and to give his life as a ransom[y] for many."

20:26 [v]Mt 23:11; Mk 9:35

Jesus Heals a Blind Beggar
(179/Mark 10:46–52; Luke 18:35–43)

20:28 [w]Mt 8:20 [x]Lk 22:27; Jn 13:13-16; 2Co 8:9; Php 2:7 [y]Isa 53:10; Mt 26:28; 1Ti 2:6; Tit 2:14; Heb 9:28; 1Pe 1:18, 19

29 As Jesus and his disciples were leaving Jericho, a large crowd followed him.
30 Two blind men were sitting by the roadside, and when they heard that Jesus was
going by, they shouted, "Lord, Son of David,[z] have mercy on us!"
31 The crowd rebuked them and told them to be quiet, but they shouted all the louder,
"Lord, Son of David, have mercy on us!"
32 Jesus stopped and called them. "What do you want me to do for you?" he asked.
33 "Lord," they answered, "we want our sight."
34 Jesus had compassion on them and touched their eyes. Immediately they received
their sight and followed him.

20:30 [z]Mt 9:27

Jesus Rides into Jerusalem on a Donkey
(183/Mark 11:1–11; Luke 19:28–44; John 12:12–19)

21 As they approached Jerusalem and came to Bethphage on the Mount of
Olives,[a] Jesus sent two disciples, 2 saying to them, "Go to the village ahead
of you, and at once you will find a donkey tied there, with her colt by her. Untie them
and bring them to me. 3 If anyone says anything to you, tell him that the Lord needs
them, and he will send them right away."
4 This took place to fulfil what was spoken through the prophet:

21:1 [a]Mt 24:3; 26:30; Mk 14:26; Lk 19:37; 21:37; 22:39; Jn 8:1; Ac 1:12

---

greatest (18:1), but Jesus taught them that the greatest person in God's kingdom is the servant of all. Authority is given not for self-importance, ambition, or respect, but for useful service to God and his creation.

20:27 Jesus described leadership from a new perspective. Instead of using people, we are to serve them. Jesus' mission was to serve others and to give his life away. A real leader has a servant's heart. Servant leaders appreciate others' worth and realise that they're not above any job. If you see something that needs to be done, don't wait to be asked. Take the initiative and do it like a faithful servant.

20:28 A ransom was the price paid to release a slave from bondage. Jesus often told his disciples that he must die, but here he told them why – to redeem all people from the bondage of sin and death. The disciples thought that as long as Jesus was alive, he could save them. But Jesus revealed that only his death would save them and the world.

20:29–34 Matthew records that there were two blind men, while Mark and Luke mention only one. This is probably the same event, but Mark and Luke singled out the more vocal of the two men.

20:30 The blind men called Jesus "Son of David" because the Jews knew that the Messiah would be a descendant of David (see Isaiah 9:6, 7; 11:1; Jeremiah 23:5, 6). These blind beggars could *see* that Jesus was the long-awaited Messiah, while the religious leaders who witnessed Jesus' miracles were blind to his identity, refusing to open their eyes to the truth. Seeing with your eyes doesn't guarantee seeing with your heart.

20:32, 33 Although Jesus was concerned about the coming events in Jerusalem, he demonstrated what he had just told the disciples about service (20:28) by stopping to care for the blind men.

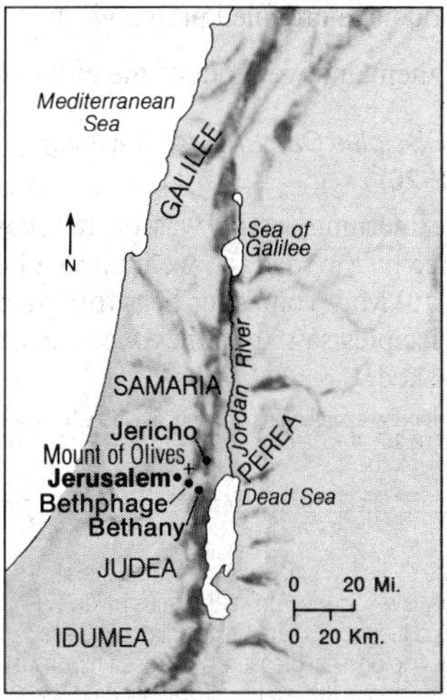

PREPARATION FOR THE TRIUMPHAL ENTRY
On their way from Jericho, Jesus and the disciples neared Bethphage, on the slope of the Mount of Olives just outside Jerusalem. Two disciples went into the village, as Jesus told them, to bring back a donkey and its colt. Jesus rode into Jerusalem on the donkey, an unmistakable sign of his kingship.

21:2–5 Matthew mentions a donkey and a colt, while the other Gospels mention only the colt. This was the same event, but Matthew focuses on the prophecy in Zechariah 9:9, where a donkey and a colt are mentioned. He shows how Jesus' actions fulfilled the prophet's words, thus giving another indication that Jesus was indeed the Messiah. When Jesus entered Jerusalem on a donkey's colt, he affirmed his Messianic royalty as well as his humility.

> 5“Say to the Daughter of Zion,
> ‘See, your king comes to you,
> gentle and riding on a donkey,
> on a colt, the foal of a donkey.’ ”[a][b]

6The disciples went and did as Jesus had instructed them. 7They brought the donkey
and the colt, placed their cloaks on them, and Jesus sat on them. 8A very large crowd
spread their cloaks[c] on the road, while others cut branches from the trees and spread
them on the road. 9The crowds that went ahead of him and those that followed shouted,

> “Hosanna[b] to the Son of David!”[d]
>
> “Blessed is he who comes in the name of the Lord!”[c][e]
>
> “Hosanna[b] in the highest!”[f]

10When Jesus entered Jerusalem, the whole city was stirred and asked, “Who is
this?”
11The crowds answered, “This is Jesus, the prophet[g] from Nazareth in Galilee.”

Jesus Clears the Temple Again
(184/Mark 11:12–19; Luke 19:45–48)

12Jesus entered the temple area and drove out all who were buying[h] and selling
there. He overturned the tables of the money-changers[i] and the benches of those
selling doves.[j] 13“It is written,” he said to them, “ ‘My house will be called a house
of prayer,’[d][k] but you are making it a ‘den of robbers’.[e]”[l]
14The blind and the lame came to him at the temple, and he healed them.[m] 15But
when the chief priests and the teachers of the law saw the wonderful things he did
and the children shouting in the temple area, “Hosanna to the Son of David,”[n] they
were indignant.[o]
16“Do you hear what these children are saying?” they asked him.
“Yes,” replied Jesus, “have you never read,

> “ ‘From the lips of children and infants
> you have ordained praise’[f]?”[p]

17And he left them and went out of the city to Bethany,[q] where he spent the night.

Jesus Says the Disciples Can Pray for Anything
(188/Mark 11:20–26)

18Early in the morning, as he was on his way back to the city, he was hungry.
19Seeing a fig-tree by the road, he went up to it but found nothing on it except leaves.
Then he said to it, “May you never bear fruit again!” Immediately the tree withered.[r]
20When the disciples saw this, they were amazed. “How did the fig-tree wither so
quickly?” they asked.

21:5 [b]Zec 9:9; Isa 62:11
21:8 [c]2Ki 9:13
21:9 [d]ver 15; Mt 9:27 [e]Ps 118:26; Mt 23:39 [f]Lk 2:14
21:11 [g]Lk 7:16, 39; 24:19; Jn 1:21, 25; 6:14; 7:40
21:12 [h]Dt 14:26 [i]Ex 30:13 [j]Lev 1:14
21:13 [k]Isa 56:7 [l]Jer 7:11
21:14 [m]Mt 4:23
21:15 [n]ver 9; Mt 9:27 [o]Lk 19:39
21:16 [p]Ps 8:2
21:17 [q]Mt 26:6; Mk 11:1; Lk 24:50; Jn 11:1, 18; 12:1
21:19 [r]Isa 34:4; Jer 8:13

[a] *5* Zech. 9:9 [b] *9* A Hebrew expression meaning “Save!” which became an exclamation of praise; also in verse 15 [c] *9* Psalm 118:26 [d] *13* Isaiah 56:7 [e] *13* Jer. 7:11 [f] *16* Psalm 8:2

21:8 This verse is one of the few places where the Gospels record that Jesus’ glory is recognised on earth. Jesus boldly declared himself King, and the crowd gladly joined him. But these same people would bow to political pressure and desert him in just a few days. Today we celebrate this event on Palm Sunday. That day should remind us to guard against superficial acclaim for Christ.

21:12 This is the second time Jesus cleared the temple (see John 2:13–17). Merchants and money changers set up their booths in the court of the Gentiles in the temple, crowding out the Gentiles who had come from all over the civilised world to worship God. The merchants sold sacrificial animals at high prices, taking advantage of those who had come long distances. The money changers exchanged all international currency for the special temple coins – the only money the merchants would accept. They often deceived foreigners who didn’t know the exchange rates. Their commercialism in God’s house frustrated people’s attempts to worship. This, of course, greatly angered Jesus. Any practice that interferes with worshipping God should be stopped.

21:19 Why did Jesus curse the fig tree? This was not a thoughtless, angry act, but an acted-out parable. Jesus was showing his anger at religion without substance. Just as the fig tree looked good from a distance but was fruitless on close examination, so the temple looked impressive at first glance, but its sacrifices and other activities were hollow because they were not done to worship God sincerely (see 21:43). If you only appear to have faith without putting it to work in your life, you are like the fig tree that withered and died because it bore no fruit. Genuine faith means bearing fruit for God’s kingdom. For more information about the fig tree, see the note on Mark 11:13–26.

21:21 [s]Mt 17:20; Lk 17:6; 1Co 13:2; Jas 1:6

21Jesus replied, "I tell you the truth, if you have faith and do not doubt,[s] not only
can you do what was done to the fig-tree, but also you can say to this mountain, 'Go,
throw yourself into the sea,' and it will be done. 22If you believe, you will receive
whatever you ask for[t] in prayer."

21:22 [t]Mt 7:7

Religious Leaders Challenge Jesus' Authority
(189/Mark 11:27–33; Luke 20:1–8)

23Jesus entered the temple courts, and, while he was teaching, the chief priests and
the elders of the people came to him. "By what authority[u] are you doing these things?"
they asked. "And who gave you this authority?"

21:23 [u]Ac 4:7; 7:27

24Jesus replied, "I will also ask you one question. If you answer me, I will tell you
by what authority I am doing these things. 25John's baptism—where did it come from?
Was it from heaven, or from men?"

They discussed it among themselves and said, "If we say, 'From heaven', he will
ask, 'Then why didn't you believe him?' 26But if we say, 'From men'—we are afraid
of the people, for they all hold that John was a prophet."[v]

21:26 [v]Mt 11:9; Mk 6:20

27So they answered Jesus, "We don't know."

Then he said, "Neither will I tell you by what authority I am doing these
things.

21:28 [w]ver 33; Mt 20:1

Jesus Tells the Parable of the Two Sons
(190)

28"What do you think? There was a man who had two sons. He went to the first
and said, 'Son, go and work today in the vineyard.'[w]

29" 'I will not,' he answered, but later he changed his mind and went.

30"Then the father went to the other son and said the same thing. He answered, 'I
will, sir,' but he did not go.

21:31 [x]Lk 7:29 [y]Lk 7:50

31"Which of the two did what his father wanted?"

"The first," they answered.

Jesus said to them, "I tell you the truth, the tax collectors[x] and the prostitutes[y]
are entering the kingdom of God ahead of you. 32For John came to you to show you
the way of righteousness,[z] and you did not believe him, but the tax collectors[a] and
the prostitutes[b] did. And even after you saw this, you did not repent[c] and believe
him.

21:32 [z]Mt 3:1-12 [a]Lk 3:12, 13; 7:29 [b]Lk 7:36-50 [c]Lk 7:30

21:21 Many have wondered about Jesus' statement that if we have faith and don't doubt, we can move mountains. Jesus, of course, was not suggesting that his followers use prayer as "magic" and perform capricious "mountain-moving" acts. Instead, he was making a strong point about the disciples' (and our) lack of faith. What kinds of mountains do you face? Have you talked to God about them? How strong is your faith?

21:22 This verse is not a guarantee that we can get *anything* we want simply by asking Jesus and believing. God does not grant requests that would hurt us or others or that would violate his own nature or will. Jesus' statement is not a blank cheque. To be fulfilled, our requests must be in harmony with the principles of God's kingdom. The stronger our belief, the more likely our prayers will be in line with God's will, and then God will be happy to grant them.

21:23–25 In Jesus' world, as in ours, people looked for the outward sign of authority—education, title, position, connections. But Jesus' authority came from who he was, not from any outward and superficial trappings. As followers of Christ, God has given us authority—we can confidently speak and act on his behalf because he has authorised us. Are you exercising your authority?

21:23–27 The Pharisees demanded to know where Jesus got his authority. If Jesus said his authority came from God, they would accuse him of blasphemy. If he said that he was acting on his own authority, the crowds would be convinced that the Pharisees had the greater authority. But Jesus answered them with a seemingly unrelated question that exposed their real motives. They didn't really want an answer to their question; they only wanted to trap him. Jesus showed that the Pharisees wanted the truth only if it supported their own views and causes.

21:25 For more information on John the Baptist, see Matthew 3 and his Profile in John 1.

21:30 The son who said he would obey and then didn't represented the nation of Israel in Jesus' day. They said they wanted to do God's will, but they constantly disobeyed. They were insincere, just going through the motions. It is dangerous to pretend to obey God when our hearts are far from him because God knows our true intentions. Our actions must match our words.

Jesus Tells the Parable of the Wicked Tenants
(191/Mark 12:1–12; Luke 20:9–19)

33"Listen to another parable: There was a landowner who planted[d] a vineyard. He
put a wall around it, dug a winepress in it and built a watchtower.[e] Then he rented
the vineyard to some farmers and went away on a journey.[f] 34When the harvest time
approached, he sent his servants[g] to the tenants to collect his fruit.
35"The tenants seized his servants; they beat one, killed another, and stoned a
third.[h] 36Then he sent other servants[i] to them, more than the first time, and the
tenants treated them in the same way. 37Last of all, he sent his son to them. 'They
will respect my son,' he said.
38"But when the tenants saw the son, they said to each other, 'This is the heir.[j]
Come, let's kill him[k] and take his inheritance.'[l] 39So they took him and threw him
out of the vineyard and killed him.
40"Therefore, when the owner of the vineyard comes, what will he do to those
tenants?"
41"He will bring those wretches to a wretched end,"[m] they replied, "and he will
rent the vineyard to other tenants,[n] who will give him his share of the crop at harvest
time."
42Jesus said to them, "Have you never read in the Scriptures:

" 'The stone the builders rejected
has become the capstone;[g]
the Lord has done this,
and it is marvellous in our eyes'[h]?[o]

43"Therefore I tell you that the kingdom of God will be taken away from you[p] and
given to a people who will produce its fruit. 44He who falls on this stone will be broken
to pieces, but he on whom it falls will be crushed."[i][q]
45When the chief priests and the Pharisees heard Jesus' parables, they knew he was
talking about them. 46They looked for a way to arrest him, but they were afraid of
the crowd because the people held that he was a prophet.[r]

Jesus Tells the Parable of the Wedding Feast
(192)

22 Jesus spoke to them again in parables, saying: 2"The kingdom of heaven is
like[a] a king who prepared a wedding banquet for his son. 3He sent his
servants[b] to those who had been invited to the banquet to tell them to come, but they
refused to come.
4"Then he sent some more servants[c] and said, 'Tell those who have been invited
that I have prepared my dinner: My oxen and fattened cattle have been slaughtered,
and everything is ready. Come to the wedding banquet.'
5"But they paid no attention and went off—one to his field, another to his business.

[g] *42* Or *cornerstone* [h] *42* Psalm 118:22,23 [i] *44* Some manuscripts do not have verse 44.

21:33 [d]Ps 80:8 [e]Isa 5:1-7 [f]Mt 25:14, 15
21:34 [g]Mt 22:3
21:35 [h]2Ch 24:21; Mt 23:34, 37; Heb 11:36, 37
21:36 [i]Mt 22:4
21:38 [j]Heb 1:2 [k]Mt 12:14 [l]Ps 2:8
21:41 [m]Mt 8:11, 12 [n]Ac 13:46; 18:6; 28:28
21:42 [o]Ps 118:22, 23; Ac 4:11; 1Pe 2:7
21:43 [p]Mt 8:12
21:44 [q]Lk 2:34
21:46 [r]ver 11, 26
22:2 [a]Mt 13:24
22:3 [b]Mt 21:34
22:4 [c]Mt 21:36

21:33ff The main elements in this parable are (1) the landowner—God, (2) the vineyard—Israel, (3) the tenants—the Jewish religious leaders, (4) the landowner's servants—the prophets and priests who remained faithful to God and preached to Israel, (5) the son—Jesus (21:38), and (6) the other tenants—the Gentiles. Jesus was exposing the religious leaders' murderous plot (21:45).

21:37 In trying to reach us with his love, God finally sent his own Son. Jesus' perfect life, his words of truth, and his sacrifice of love are meant to cause us to listen to him and to follow him as Lord. If we ignore God's gracious gift of his Son, we reject God himself.

21:42 Jesus refers to himself as "the stone the builders rejected". Although Jesus was rejected by many of his people, he will become the capstone, or cornerstone, of his new building, the church (see Acts 4:11; 1 Peter 2:7).

21:44 Jesus used this metaphor to show that one stone can affect people in different ways, depending on how they relate to it (see Isaiah 8:14, 15; 28:16; Daniel 2:34, 44, 45). Ideally they will build on it; many, however, will trip over it. And at the last judgment God's enemies will be crushed by it. In the end, Christ, the "building block", will become the "crushing stone". He offers mercy and forgiveness *now* and promises judgment later. We should choose him now!

22:1–14 In this culture, two invitations were expected when banquets were given. The first asked the guests to attend; the second announced that all was ready. In this story the king invited his guests three times—and each time they rejected his invitation. God wants us to join him at his banquet, which will last for eternity. That's why he sends us invitations again and again. Have you accepted his invitation?

22:7 [d] Lk 19:27
22:9 [e] Eze 21:21
22:10 [f] Mt 13:47, 48
22:12 [g] Mt 20:13; 26:50
22:13 [h] Mt 8:12
22:14 [i] Rev 17:14
22:16 [j] Mk 3:6
22:17 [k] Mt 17:25
22:21 [l] Ro 13:7
22:22 [m] Mk 12:12
22:23 [n] Ac 4:1 [o] Ac 23:8; 1Co 15:12
22:24 [p] Dt 25:5, 6

6 The rest seized his servants, ill-treated them and killed them. 7 The king was enraged.
He sent his army and destroyed those murderers[d] and burned their city.
8 "Then he said to his servants, 'The wedding banquet is ready, but those I invited
did not deserve to come. 9 Go to the street corners[e] and invite to the banquet anyone
you find.' 10 So the servants went out into the streets and gathered all the people they
could find, both good and bad,[f] and the wedding hall was filled with guests.
11 "But when the king came in to see the guests, he noticed a man there who was
not wearing wedding clothes. 12 'Friend,'[g] he asked, 'how did you get in here without
wedding clothes?' The man was speechless.
13 "Then the king told the attendants, 'Tie him hand and foot, and throw him outside,
into the darkness, where there will be weeping and gnashing of teeth.'[h]
14 "For many are invited, but few are chosen."[i]

Religious Leaders Question Jesus about Paying Taxes
(193/Mark 12:13–17; Luke 20:20–26)

15 Then the Pharisees went out and laid plans to trap him in his words. 16 They sent
their disciples to him along with the Herodians.[j] "Teacher," they said, "we know
you are a man of integrity and that you teach the way of God in accordance with the
truth. You aren't swayed by men, because you pay no attention to who they are. 17 Tell
us then, what is your opinion? Is it right to pay taxes[k] to Caesar or not?"
18 But Jesus, knowing their evil intent, said, "You hypocrites, why are you trying
to trap me? 19 Show me the coin used for paying the tax." They brought him a denarius,
20 and he asked them, "Whose portrait is this? And whose inscription?"
21 "Caesar's," they replied.
Then he said to them, "Give to Caesar what is Caesar's,[l] and to God what is
God's."
22 When they heard this, they were amazed. So they left him and went away.[m]

Religious Leaders Question Jesus about the Resurrection
(194/Mark 12:18–27; Luke 20:27–40)

23 That same day the Sadducees,[n] who say there is no resurrection,[o] came to him
with a question. 24 "Teacher," they said, "Moses told us that if a man dies without
having children, his brother must marry the widow and have children for him.[p]

22:11, 12 It was customary for wedding guests to be given garments to wear to the banquet. It was unthinkable to refuse to wear these garments. That would insult the host, who could only assume that the guest was arrogant and thought he didn't need these garments, or that he did not want to take part in the wedding celebration. The wedding clothes picture the righteousness needed to enter God's kingdom – the total acceptance in God's eyes that Christ gives every believer. Christ has provided this garment of righteousness for everyone, but each person must choose to put it on in order to enter the King's banquet (eternal life). There is an open invitation, but we must be ready. For more on the imagery of clothes of righteousness and salvation, see Psalm 132:16; Isaiah 61:10; Zechariah 3:3–5; Revelation 3:4, 5; 19:7, 8.

22:15–17 The Pharisees, a religious group, opposed the Roman occupation of Palestine. The Herodians, a political party, supported Herod Antipas and the policies instituted by Rome. Normally these two groups were bitter enemies, but here they united against Jesus. Thinking they had a foolproof plan to corner him, together their representatives asked Jesus about paying Roman taxes. If Jesus agreed that it was right to pay taxes to Caesar, the Pharisees would say he was opposed to God, the only King they recognised. If Jesus said the taxes should not be paid, the Herodians would hand him over to Herod on the charge of rebellion. In this case the Pharisees were not motivated by love for God's laws, and the Herodians were not motivated by love for Roman justice. Jesus' answer exposed their evil motives and embarrassed them both.

22:17 The Jews were required to pay taxes to support the Roman government. They hated this taxation because the money went directly into Caesar's treasury, where some of it went to support the pagan temples and decadent life-style of the Roman aristocracy. Caesar's image on the coins was a constant reminder of Israel's subjection to Rome.

22:19 The denarius was the usual day's wage for a labourer.

22:21 Jesus avoided this trap by showing that we have dual citizenship (1 Peter 2:17). Our citizenship in the nation requires that we pay money for the services and benefits we receive. Our citizenship in the kingdom of heaven requires that we pledge to God our primary obedience and commitment.

22:23ff After the Pharisees and Herodians had failed to trap Jesus, the Sadducees smugly stepped in to try. They did not believe in the resurrection because the Pentateuch (Genesis – Deuteronomy) has no direct teaching on it. The Pharisees had never been able to come up with a convincing argument from the Pentateuch for the resurrection, and the Sadducees thought they had trapped Jesus for sure. But Jesus was about to show them otherwise (see 22:31, 32 for Jesus' answer).

22:24 For more information on Moses, see his Profile in Exodus 14.

22:24 The law said that when a woman's husband died without having a son, the man's brother had a responsibility to marry and care for the widow (Deuteronomy 25:5, 6). This law protected women who were left alone, because in that culture they usually had no other means to support themselves.

25Now there were seven brothers among us. The first one married and died, and since
he had no children, he left his wife to his brother. 26The same thing happened to the
second and third brother, right on down to the seventh. 27Finally, the woman died.
28Now then, at the resurrection, whose wife will she be of the seven, since all of them
were married to her?"
29Jesus replied, "You are in error because you do not know the Scriptures[q] or the
power of God. 30At the resurrection people will neither marry nor be given in
marriage;[r] they will be like the angels in heaven. 31But about the resurrection of the
dead—have you not read what God said to you, 32'I am the God of Abraham, the
God of Isaac, and the God of Jacob'[a]?[s] He is not the God of the dead but of the
living."
33When the crowds heard this, they were astonished at his teaching.[t]

Religious Leaders Question Jesus about the Greatest Commandment
(195/Mark 12:28–34)

34Hearing that Jesus had silenced the Sadducees,[u] the Pharisees got together.
35One of them, an expert in the law,[v] tested him with this question: 36"Teacher,
which is the greatest commandment in the Law?"
37Jesus replied: " 'Love the Lord your God with all your heart and with all your
soul and with all your mind.'[b][w] 38This is the first and greatest commandment. 39And
the second is like it: 'Love your neighbour as yourself.'[c][x] 40All the Law and the
Prophets hang on these two commandments."[y]

Religious Leaders Cannot Answer Jesus' Question
(196/Mark 12:35–37; Luke 20:41–44)

41While the Pharisees were gathered together, Jesus asked them, 42"What do you
think about the Christ?[d] Whose son is he?"
"The son of David,"[z] they replied.
43He said to them, "How is it then that David, speaking by the Spirit, calls him
'Lord'? For he says,

44" 'The Lord said to my Lord:
"Sit at my right hand
until I put your enemies
under your feet." '[e][a]

[a] *32* Exodus 3:6 [b] *37* Deut. 6:5 [c] *39* Lev. 19:18 [d] *42* Or *Messiah* [e] *44* Psalm 110:1

22:29 [q]Jn 20:9
22:30 [r]Mt 24:38
22:32 [s]Ex 3:6; Ac 7:32
22:33 [t]Mt 7:28
22:34 [u]Ac 4:1
22:35 [v]Lk 7:30; 10:25; 11:45; 14:3
22:37 [w]Dt 6:5
22:39 [x]Lev 19:18; Mt 5:43; 19:19; Gal 5:14
22:40 [y]Mt 7:12
22:42 [z]Mt 9:27
22:44 [a]Ps 110:1; Ac 2:34, 35; 1Co 15:25; Heb 1:13; 10:13

22:29, 30 The Sadducees asked Jesus what marriage would be like in heaven. Jesus said it was more important to understand God's power than know what heaven will be like. In every generation and culture, ideas of eternal life tend to be based on images and experiences of present life. Jesus answered that these faulty ideas are caused by ignorance of God's word. We must not make up our own ideas about eternity and heaven by thinking of it and God in human terms. We should concentrate more on our relationship with God than on what heaven will look like. Eventually we will find out, and it will be far beyond our greatest expectations.

22:31, 32 Because the Sadducees accepted only the Pentateuch as God's divine word, Jesus answered them from the book of Exodus (3:6). God would not have said, "I am the God of Abraham, the God of Isaac, and the God of Jacob" if God thought of Abraham, Isaac, and Jacob as dead. From God's perspective, they are alive. Jesus' use of the present tense pointed to the resurrection and the eternal life that all believers enjoy in him.

22:34 We might think the Pharisees would have been glad to see the Sadducees silenced. The question that the Sadducees had always used to trap them was finally answered by Jesus. But the Pharisees were too proud to be impressed. Jesus' answer gave them a theological victory over the Sadducees, but they were more interested in defeating Jesus than in learning the truth.

22:35–40 The Pharisees, who had classified over 600 laws, often tried to distinguish the more important from the less important. So one of them, an "expert in the law", asked Jesus to identify the most important law. Jesus quoted from Deuteronomy 6:5 and Leviticus 19:18. By fulfilling these two commands, a person keeps all the others. They summarise the Ten Commandments and the other Old Testament moral laws.

22:37–40 Jesus says that if we truly love God and our neighbour, we will naturally keep the commandments. This is looking at God's law positively. Rather than worrying about all we should *not* do, we should concentrate on all we *can* do to show our love for God and others.

22:41–45 The Pharisees, Herodians, and Sadducees had asked their questions. Then Jesus turned the tables and asked them a penetrating question—who they thought the Messiah was. The Pharisees knew that the Messiah would be a descendant of David, but they did not understand that he would be God himself. Jesus quoted from Psalm 110:1 to show that the Messiah would be greater than David. (Hebrews 1:13 uses the same text as proof of Christ's deity.) The most important question we will ever answer is what we believe about Christ. Other theological questions are irrelevant until we believe that Jesus is who he said he is.

45If then David calls him 'Lord', how can he be his son?" 46No-one could say a word
in reply, and from that day on no-one dared to ask him any more questions.[b]

Jesus Warns against the Religious Leaders
(197/Mark 12:38–40; Luke 20:45–47)

23 Then Jesus said to the crowds and to his disciples: 2"The teachers of the law[a]
and the Pharisees sit in Moses' seat. 3So you must obey them and do everything
they tell you. But do not do what they do, for they do not practise what they preach.
4They tie up heavy loads and put them on men's shoulders, but they themselves are
not willing to lift a finger to move them.[b]
5"Everything they do is done for men to see:[c] They make their phylacteries[a][d]
wide and the tassels on their garments[e] long; 6they love the place of honour at
banquets and the most important seats in the synagogues;[f] 7they love to be greeted
in the market-places and to have men call them 'Rabbi'.[g]
8"But you are not to be called 'Rabbi', for you have only one Master and you are
all brothers. 9And do not call anyone on earth 'father', for you have one Father,[h]
and he is in heaven. 10Nor are you to be called 'teacher', for you have one Teacher,
the Christ.[b] 11The greatest among you will be your servant.[i] 12For whoever exalts
himself will be humbled, and whoever humbles himself will be exalted.[j]

Jesus Condemns the Religious Leaders
(198)

13"Woe to you, teachers of the law and Pharisees, you hypocrites![k] You shut the
kingdom of heaven in men's faces. You yourselves do not enter, nor will you let those
enter who are trying to.[c][l]
15"Woe to you, teachers of the law and Pharisees, you hypocrites! You travel over
land and sea to win a single convert,[m] and when he becomes one, you make him twice
as much a son of hell[n] as you are.
16"Woe to you, blind guides![o] You say, 'If anyone swears by the temple, it means
nothing; but if anyone swears by the gold of the temple, he is bound by his oath.'[p]
17You blind fools! Which is greater: the gold, or the temple that makes the gold
sacred?[q] 18You also say, 'If anyone swears by the altar, it means nothing; but if

a *5* That is, boxes containing Scripture verses, worn on forehead and arm **b** *10* Or *Messiah* **c** *13* Some manuscripts *to.* 14*Woe to you, teachers of the law and Pharisees, you hypocrites! You devour widows' houses and for a show make lengthy prayers. Therefore you will be punished more severely.*

22:46 [b]Mk 12:34; Lk 20:40
23:2 [a]Ezr 7:6, 25; Ne 8:4
23:4 [b]Lk 11:46; Ac 15:10; Gal 6:13
23:5 [c]Mt 6:1, 2, 5, 16 [d]Ex 13:9; Dt 6:8 [e]Nu 15:38; Dt 22:12
23:6 [f]Lk 11:43; 14:7; 20:46
23:7 [g]ver 8; Mk 9:5; 10:51; Jn 1:38, 49
23:9 [h]Mal 1:6; Mt 7:11
23:11 [i]Mt 20:26; Mk 9:35
23:12 [j]Lk 14:11
23:13 [k]ver 15, 23, 25, 27, 29 [l]Lk 11:52
23:15 [m]Ac 2:11; 6:5; 13:43 [n]Mt 5:22
23:16 [o]ver 24; Mt 15:14 [p]Mt 5:33-35
23:17 [q]Ex 30:29

23:2, 3 The Pharisees' traditions and their interpretations and applications of the laws had become as important to them as God's law itself. Their laws were not all bad – some were beneficial. The problem arose when the religious leaders (1) took man-made rules as seriously as God's laws, (2) told the people to obey these rules but did not do so themselves, or (3) obeyed the rules not to honour God but to make themselves look good. Usually Jesus did not condemn what the Pharisees taught, but what they *were* – hypocrites.

23:5 Phylacteries were little leather boxes containing Scripture verses. Very religious people wore these boxes on their forehead and arms in order to obey Deuteronomy 6:8 and Exodus 13:9, 16. But the phylacteries had become more important for the status they gave than for the truth they contained.

23:5–7 Jesus again exposed the hypocritical attitudes of the religious leaders. They knew the Scriptures but did not live by them. They didn't care about *being* holy – just *looking* holy in order to receive the people's admiration and praise. Today, like the Pharisees, many people who know the Bible do not let it change their lives. They say they follow Jesus, but they don't live by his standards of love. People who live this way are hypocrites. We must make sure that our actions match our beliefs.

23:5–7 People desire positions of leadership not only in business but also in the church. It is dangerous when love for the position grows stronger than loyalty to God. This is what happened to the Pharisees and teachers of the law. Jesus is not against all leadership – we need Christian leaders – but against leadership that serves itself rather than others.

23:11, 12 Jesus challenged society's norms. To him, greatness comes from serving – giving of yourself to help God and others. Service keeps us aware of others' needs, and it stops us from focusing only on ourselves. Jesus came as a servant. What kind of greatness do you seek?

23:13, 14 Being a religious leader in Jerusalem was very different from being a pastor in a secular society today. Israel's history, culture, and daily life centred around its relationship with God. The religious leaders were the best known, most powerful, and most respected of all leaders. Jesus made these stinging accusations because the leaders' hunger for more power, money, and status had made them lose sight of God, and their blindness was spreading to the whole nation.

23:15 The Pharisees' converts were attracted to Pharisaism, not to God. By getting caught up in the details of their additional laws and regulations, they completely missed God, to whom the laws pointed. A religion of deeds puts pressure on people to surpass others in what they know and do. Thus, a hypocritical teacher was likely to have students who were even more hypocritical. We must make sure we are not creating Pharisees by emphasising outward obedience at the expense of inner renewal.

anyone swears by the gift on it, he is bound by his oath.' 19You blind men! Which
is greater: the gift, or the altar that makes the gift sacred?[r] 20Therefore, he who swears
by the altar swears by it and by everything on it. 21And he who swears by the temple
swears by it and by the one who dwells[s] in it. 22And he who swears by heaven swears
by God's throne and by the one who sits on it.[t]
23"Woe to you, teachers of the law and Pharisees, you hypocrites! You give a
tenth[u] of your spices—mint, dill and cummin. But you have neglected the more
important matters of the law—justice, mercy and faithfulness.[v] You should have
practised the latter, without neglecting the former. 24You blind guides![w] You strain
out a gnat but swallow a camel.
25"Woe to you, teachers of the law and Pharisees, you hypocrites! You clean the
outside of the cup and dish,[x] but inside they are full of greed and self-indulgence.[y]
26Blind Pharisee! First clean the inside of the cup and dish, and then the outside also
will be clean.
27"Woe to you, teachers of the law and Pharisees, you hypocrites! You are like
whitewashed tombs,[z] which look beautiful on the outside but on the inside are full
of dead men's bones and everything unclean. 28In the same way, on the outside you
appear to people as righteous but on the inside you are full of hypocrisy and wickedness.
29"Woe to you, teachers of the law and Pharisees, you hypocrites! You build tombs
for the prophets[a] and decorate the graves of the righteous. 30And you say, 'If we had
lived in the days of our forefathers, we would not have taken part with them in
shedding the blood of the prophets.' 31So you testify against yourselves that you are
the descendants of those who murdered the prophets.[b] 32Fill up, then, the measure[c]
of the sin of your forefathers!
33"You snakes! You brood of vipers![d] How will you escape being condemned to
hell?[e] 34Therefore I am sending you prophets and wise men and teachers. Some of
them you will kill and crucify;[f] others you will flog in your synagogues[g] and pursue
from town to town.[h] 35And so upon you will come all the righteous blood that has
been shed on earth, from the blood of righteous Abel[i] to the blood of Zechariah son
of Barakiah,[j] whom you murdered between the temple and the altar.[k] 36I tell you
the truth, all this will come upon this generation.[l]

Jesus Grieves over Jerusalem Again
(199)

37"O Jerusalem, Jerusalem, you who kill the prophets and stone those sent to you,[m]
how often I have longed to gather your children together, as a hen gathers her chicks

23:19 [r]Ex 29:37
23:21 [s]1Ki 8:13; Ps 26:8
23:22 [t]Ps 11:4; Mt 5:34
23:23 [u]Lev 27:30 [v]Mic 6:8; Lk 11:42
23:24 [w]ver 16
23:25 [x]Mk 7:4 [y]Lk 11:39
23:27 [z]Lk 11:44; Ac 23:3
23:29 [a]Lk 11:47, 48
23:31 [b]Ac 7:51-52
23:32 [c]1Th 2:16
23:33 [d]Mt 3:7; 12:34 [e]Mt 5:22
23:34 [f]2Ch 36:15, 16; Lk 11:49 [g]Mt 10:17 [h]Mt 10:23
23:35 [i]Ge 4:8; Heb 11:4 [j]Zec 1:1 [k]2Ch 24:21
23:36 [l]Mt 10:23; 24:34
23:37 [m]2Ch 24:21; Mt 5:12

23:23, 24 It's possible to obey the details of the laws but still be disobedient in our general behaviour. For example, we could be very precise and faithful about giving 10 per cent of our money to God, but refuse to give one minute of our time in helping others. Tithing is important, but giving a tithe does not exempt us from fulfilling God's other directives.

23:24 The Pharisees strained their water so they wouldn't accidentally swallow a gnat—an unclean insect according to the law. Meticulous about the details of ceremonial cleanliness, they had nevertheless lost their perspective on inner purity.
Ceremonially clean on the outside, they had corrupt hearts.

23:25–28 Jesus condemned the Pharisees and religious leaders for outwardly appearing saintly and holy but inwardly remaining full of corruption and greed. Living our Christianity merely as a show for others is like washing a cup on the outside only. When we are clean on the inside, our cleanliness on the outside won't be a sham.

23:34–36 These prophets, wise men, and teachers were probably leaders in the early church who were persecuted, scourged, and killed, as Jesus predicted. The people of Jesus' generation said they would not act as their fathers did in killing the prophets whom God had sent to them (23:30), but they were about to kill the Messiah himself and his faithful followers. Thus they would become guilty of all the righteous blood shed through the centuries.

23:35 Jesus was giving a brief history of Old Testament martyrdom. Abel was the first martyr (Genesis 4); Zechariah was the last mentioned in the Hebrew Bible, which ended with 2 Chronicles. Zechariah is a classic example of a man of God who was killed by those who claimed to be God's people (see 2 Chronicles 24:20, 21).

23:37 Jesus wanted to gather his people together as a hen protects her chicks under her wings, but they wouldn't let him. Jesus also wants to protect us if we will just come to him. Many times we hurt and don't know where to turn. We reject Christ's help because we don't think he can give us what we need. But who knows our needs better than our Creator? Those who turn to Jesus will find that he helps and comforts as no-one else can.

23:37 Jerusalem was the capital city of God's chosen people, the ancestral home of David, Israel's greatest king, and the location of the temple, the earthly dwelling place of God. It was intended to be the centre of worship of the true God and a symbol of justice to all people. But Jerusalem had become blind to God and insensitive to human need. Here we see the depth of Jesus' feelings for lost people and for his beloved city, which would soon be destroyed.

under her wings, but you were not willing. 38 Look, your house is left to you desolate.[n] 39 For I tell you, you will not see me again until you say, 'Blessed is he who
comes in the name of the Lord.'[d]"[o]

7. Jesus teaches on the Mount of Olives

Jesus Tells about the Future

(201/Mark 13:1–23; Luke 21:5–24)

24 Jesus left the temple and was walking away when his disciples came up to him
to call his attention to its buildings. 2 "Do you see all these things?" he asked.
"I tell you the truth, not one stone here will be left on another;[a] every one will be
thrown down."
3 As Jesus was sitting on the Mount of Olives,[b] the disciples came to him privately.
"Tell us," they said, "when will this happen, and what will be the sign of your coming
and of the end of the age?"
4 Jesus answered: "Watch out that no-one deceives you. 5 For many will come in
my name, claiming, 'I am the Christ,'[a] and will deceive many.[c] 6 You will hear of
wars and rumours of wars, but see to it that you are not alarmed. Such things must
happen, but the end is still to come. 7 Nation will rise against nation, and kingdom
against kingdom.[d] There will be famines[e] and earthquakes in various places. 8 All
these are the beginning of birth-pains.
9 "Then you will be handed over to be persecuted[f] and put to death,[g] and you will
be hated by all nations because of me. 10 At that time many will turn away from the

23:38 [n] 1Ki 9:7, 8; Jer 22:5
23:39 [o] Ps 118:26; Mt 21:9
24:2 [a] Lk 19:44
24:3 [b] Mt 21:1
24:5 [c] ver 11, 23, 24; 1Jn 2:18
24:7 [d] Isa 19:2 [e] Ac 11:28
24:9 [f] Mt 10:17 [g] Jn 16:2

d *39* Psalm 118:26 **a** *5* Or *Messiah*; also in verse 23

THE SEVEN WOES

23:14	Not letting others enter the kingdom of heaven and not entering yourselves
23:15	Converting people away from God to be like yourselves
23:16–22	Blindly leading God's people to follow man-made traditions instead of God's word
23:23, 24	Involving yourself in every last detail and ignoring what is really important: justice, mercy, and faith
23:25, 26	Keeping up appearances while your private world is corrupt
23:27, 28	Acting spiritual to cover up sin
23:29–36	Pretending to have learned from past history, but your present behaviour shows you have learned nothing

Jesus mentioned seven ways to guarantee God's anger, often called the "seven woes". These seven statements about the religious leaders must have been spoken with a mixed tone of judgment and sorrow. They were strong and unforgettable. They are still applicable whenever we become so involved in perfecting the practice of religion that we forget that God is also concerned with mercy, real love, and forgiveness.

24:1, 2 Although no-one knows exactly what this temple looked like, it must have been beautiful. Herod had helped the Jews remodel and beautify it, no doubt to stay on friendly terms with his subjects. Next to the inner temple, where the sacred objects were kept and the sacrifices offered, there was a large area called the court of the Gentiles (this was where the money changers and merchants had their booths). Outside these courts were long porches. Solomon's porch was 1,562 feet long; the royal portico was decorated with 160 columns stretching along its 921-foot length. Gazing at this glorious and massive structure, the disciples found Jesus' words about its destruction difficult to believe. But the temple was indeed destroyed only 40 years later when the Romans sacked Jerusalem in A.D. 70.

24:3ff Jesus was sitting on the Mount of Olives, the very place where the prophet Zechariah had predicted that the Messiah would stand when he came to establish his kingdom (Zechariah 14:4). It was a fitting place for the disciples to ask Jesus when he would come in power and what they could expect then. Jesus' reply emphasised the events that would take place before the end of the age. He pointed out that his disciples should be less concerned with knowing the exact date and more concerned with being prepared—living God's way consistently so that no matter when Jesus came in glory, he would claim them as his own.

24:4 The disciples asked Jesus for the sign of his coming and of the end of the age. Jesus' first response was "Watch out that no-one deceives you." The fact is that whenever we look for signs, we become very susceptible to being deceived. There are many "false prophets" (24:11, 24) around with counterfeit signs of spiritual power and authority. The only sure way to keep from being deceived is to focus on Christ and his words. Don't look for special signs, and don't spend time looking at other people. Look at Christ.

24:9–13 You may not be facing intense persecution now, but Christians in other parts of the world are. As you hear about Christians suffering for their faith, remember that they are your brothers and sisters in Christ. Pray for them. Ask God what you can do to help them in their troubles. When one part suffers, the *whole* body suffers. But when all the parts join together to ease the suffering, the whole body benefits (1 Corinthians 12:26).

faith and will betray and hate each other, 11 and many false prophets[h] will appear and
deceive many people. 12 Because of the increase of wickedness, the love of most will
grow cold, 13 but he who stands firm to the end will be saved.[i] 14 And this gospel
of the kingdom[j] will be preached in the whole world[k] as a testimony to all nations,
and then the end will come.
15 "So when you see standing in the holy place[l] 'the abomination that causes
desolation',[b][m] spoken of through the prophet Daniel—let the reader understand—16 then let those who are in Judea flee to the mountains. 17 Let no-one on the
roof of his house[n] go down to take anything out of the house. 18 Let no-one in the
field go back to get his cloak. 19 How dreadful it will be in those days for pregnant
women and nursing mothers![o] 20 Pray that your flight will not take place in winter
or on the Sabbath. 21 For then there will be great distress, unequalled from the
beginning of the world until now—and never to be equalled again.[p] 22 If those days
had not been cut short, no-one would survive, but for the sake of the elect[q] those
days will be shortened. 23 At that time if anyone says to you, 'Look, here is the Christ!'
or, 'There he is!' do not believe it.[r] 24 For false Christs and false prophets will appear
and perform great signs and miracles[s] to deceive even the elect—if that were
possible. 25 See, I have told you ahead of time.

Jesus Tells about His Return
(202/Mark 13:24–31; Luke 21:25–33)

26 "So if anyone tells you, 'There he is, out in the desert,' do not go out; or, 'Here
he is, in the inner rooms,' do not believe it. 27 For as lightning[t] that comes from the
east is visible even in the west, so will be the coming of the Son of Man.[u] 28 Wherever
there is a carcass, there the vultures will gather.[v]
29 "Immediately after the distress of those days

" 'the sun will be darkened,
  and the moon will not give its light;
the stars will fall from the sky,
  and the heavenly bodies will be shaken.'[c][w]

[b] *15* Daniel 9:27; 11:31; 12:11 [c] *29* Isaiah 13:10; 34:4

24:11 [h] Mt 7:15
24:13 [i] Mt 10:22
24:14 [j] Mt 4:23; [k] Ro 10:18; Col 1:6, 23; Lk 2:1; 4:5; Ac 11:28; 17:6; Rev 3:10; 16:14
24:15 [l] Ac 6:13; [m] Da 9:27; 11:31; 12:11
24:17 [n] 1Sa 9:25; Mt 10:27; Lk 12:3; Ac 10:9
24:19 [o] Lk 23:29
24:21 [p] Da 12:1; Joel 2:2
24:22 [q] ver 24, 31
24:23 [r] Lk 17:23; 21:8
24:24 [s] 2Th 2:9-11; Rev 13:13
24:27 [t] Lk 17:24; [u] Mt 8:20
24:28 [v] Lk 17:37
24:29 [w] Isa 13:10; 34:4; Eze 32:7; Joel 2:10, 31; Zep 1:15; Rev 6:12, 13; 8:12

24:11 The Old Testament frequently mentions false prophets (see 2 Kings 3:13; Isaiah 44:25; Jeremiah 23:16; Ezekiel 13:2, 3; Micah 3:5; Zechariah 13:2). False prophets claimed to receive messages from God, but they preached a "health and wealth" message. They said what the people wanted to hear, even when the nation was not following God as it should. There were false prophets in Jesus' day, and we have them today. They are the popular leaders who tell people what they want to hear—such as "God wants you to be rich", "Do whatever your desires tell you", or "There is no such thing as sin or hell". Jesus said false teachers would come, and he warned his disciples, as he warns us, not to listen to their dangerous words.

24:12 With false teaching and loose morals comes a particularly destructive disease—the loss of true love for God and others. Sin cools your love for God and others by turning your focus on yourself. You cannot truly love if you think only of yourself.

24:13 Jesus predicted that his followers would be severely persecuted by those who hated what he stood for. In the midst of terrible persecutions, however, they could have hope, knowing that salvation was theirs. Times of trial serve to sift true Christians from false or fair-weather Christians. When you are pressured to give up and turn your back on Christ, don't do it. Remember the benefits of standing firm, and continue to live for Christ.

24:14 Jesus said that before he returns, the gospel of the kingdom (the message of salvation) would be preached throughout the world. This was the disciples' mission—and it is ours today. Jesus talked about the end times and final judgment to show his followers the urgency of spreading the good news of salvation to everyone.

24:15, 16 What was this "abomination that causes desolation" mentioned by both Daniel and Jesus? Rather than one specific object, event, or person, it could be seen as any deliberate attempt to mock and deny the reality of God's presence. Daniel's prediction came true in 168 B.C. when Antiochus Epiphanes sacrificed a pig to Zeus on the sacred temple altar (Daniel 9:27; 11:30, 31). Jesus' words were remembered in A.D. 70 when Titus placed an idol on the site of the burned temple after destroying Jerusalem. In the end times the antichrist will set up an image of himself and order everyone to worship it (2 Thessalonians 2:4; Revelation 13:14, 15). These are all "abominations" that mock God.

24:21, 22 Jesus, talking about the end times, telescoped near future and far future events, as did the Old Testament prophets. Many of these persecutions have already occurred; more are yet to come. But God is in control of even the length of persecutions. He will not forget his people. This is all we need to know about the future to motivate us to live the right way now.

24:23, 24 Jesus' warnings about false teachers still hold true. Upon close examination it becomes clear that many nice-sounding messages don't agree with God's message in the Bible. Only a solid foundation in God's word can equip us to perceive the errors and distortions in false teaching.

24:24–28 In times of persecution even strong believers will find it difficult to be loyal. To keep from being deceived by false messiahs, we must understand that Jesus' return will be unmistakable (Mark 13:26); no-one will doubt that it is he. If you have to be told that the Messiah has come, then he hasn't (24:27). Christ's coming will be obvious to everyone.

24:30 [x]Da 7:13; Rev 1:7
24:31 [y]Mt 13:41 [z]Isa 27:13; Zec 9:14; 1Co 15:52; 1Th 4:16; Rev 8:2; 10:7; 11:15
24:33 [a]Jas 5:9
24:34 [b]Mt 16:28; 23:36
24:35 [c]Mt 5:18
24:36 [d]Ac 1:7
24:37 [e]Ge 6:5; 7:6-23
24:38 [f]Mt 22:30
24:40 [g]Lk 17:34
24:41 [h]Lk 17:35
24:42 [i]Mt 25:13; Lk 12:40
24:43 [j]Lk 12:39
24:44 [k]1Th 5:6
24:45 [l]Mt 25:21, 23
24:46 [m]Rev 16:15
24:47 [n]Mt 25:21, 23
24:49 [o]Lk 21:34
24:51 [p]Mt 8:12

30 "At that time the sign of the Son of Man will appear in the sky, and all the nations
of the earth will mourn. They will see the Son of Man coming on the clouds of the
sky,[x] with power and great glory. 31 And he will send his angels[y] with a loud trumpet
call,[z] and they will gather his elect from the four winds, from one end of the heavens
to the other.
32 "Now learn this lesson from the fig-tree: As soon as its twigs get tender and its
leaves come out, you know that summer is near. 33 Even so, when you see all these
things, you know that it**[d]** is near, right at the door.[a] 34 I tell you the truth, this
generation**[e]** will certainly not pass away until all these things have happened.[b]
35 Heaven and earth will pass away, but my words will never pass away.[c]

Jesus Tells about Remaining Watchful
(203/Mark 13:32–37; Luke 21:34–38)

36 "No-one knows about that day or hour, not even the angels in heaven, nor the
Son,**[f]** but only the Father.[d] 37 As it was in the days of Noah,[e] so it will be at the
coming of the Son of Man. 38 For in the days before the flood, people were eating and
drinking, marrying and giving in marriage,[f] up to the day Noah entered the ark; 39 and
they knew nothing about what would happen until the flood came and took them all
away. That is how it will be at the coming of the Son of Man. 40 Two men will be
in the field; one will be taken and the other left.[g] 41 Two women will be grinding with
a hand mill; one will be taken and the other left.[h]
42 "Therefore keep watch, because you do not know on what day your Lord will
come.[i] 43 But understand this: If the owner of the house had known at what time of
night the thief was coming,[j] he would have kept watch and would not have let his
house be broken into. 44 So you also must be ready,[k] because the Son of Man will
come at an hour when you do not expect him.
45 "Who then is the faithful and wise servant,[l] whom the master has put in charge
of the servants in his household to give them their food at the proper time? 46 It will
be good for that servant whose master finds him doing so when he returns.[m] 47 I tell
you the truth, he will put him in charge of all his possessions.[n] 48 But suppose that
servant is wicked and says to himself, 'My master is staying away a long time,' 49 and
he then begins to beat his fellow-servants and to eat and drink with drunkards.[o] 50 The
master of that servant will come on a day when he does not expect him and at an hour
he is not aware of. 51 He will cut him to pieces and assign him a place with the
hypocrites, where there will be weeping and gnashing of teeth.[p]

d *33* Or *he* **e** *34* Or *race* **f** *36* Some manuscripts do not have *nor the Son.*

24:30 The nations of the earth will mourn because unbelievers will suddenly realise they have chosen the wrong side. Everything they have scoffed about will be happening, and it will be too late for them.

24:36 It is good that we don't know exactly when Christ will return. If we knew the precise date, we might be tempted to be lazy in our work for Christ. Worse still, we might plan to keep sinning and then turn to God right at the end. Heaven is not our only goal; we have work to do here. And we must keep on doing it until death or until we see the unmistakable return of our Saviour.

24:40–42 Christ's second coming will be swift and sudden. There will be no opportunity for last-minute repentance or bargaining. The choice we have already made will determine our eternal destiny.

24:44 Jesus' purpose in telling about his return is not to stimulate predictions and calculations about the date, but to warn us to be prepared. Will you be ready? The only safe choice is to obey him *today* (24:46).

24:45–47 Jesus asks us to spend the time of waiting taking care of his people and doing his work here on earth, both within the church and outside it. This is the best way to prepare for Christ's return.

24:50 Knowing that Christ's return will be sudden and unexpected should motivate us always to be prepared. We are not to live irresponsibly – sitting and waiting, doing nothing; seeking self-serving pleasure; using his tarrying as an excuse not to do God's work of building his kingdom; developing a false security based on precise calculations of events; or letting our curiosity about the end times divert us from doing God's work.

24:51 "Weeping and gnashing of teeth" is a phrase used to describe despair. God's coming judgment is as certain as Jesus' return to earth.

Jesus Tells the Parable of the Ten Bridesmaids
(204)

25 "At that time the kingdom of heaven will be like[a] ten virgins who took their
lamps[b] and went out to meet the bridegroom.[c] 2Five of them were foolish
and five were wise.[d] 3The foolish ones took their lamps but did not take any oil with
them. 4The wise, however, took oil in jars along with their lamps. 5The bridegroom
was a long time in coming, and they all became drowsy and fell asleep.[e]
6"At midnight the cry rang out: 'Here's the bridegroom! Come out to meet him!'
7"Then all the virgins woke up and trimmed their lamps. 8The foolish ones said
to the wise, 'Give us some of your oil; our lamps are going out.'[f]
9" 'No,' they replied, 'there may not be enough for both us and you. Instead, go
to those who sell oil and buy some for yourselves.'
10"But while they were on their way to buy the oil, the bridegroom arrived. The
virgins who were ready went in with him to the wedding banquet.[g] And the door was
shut.
11"Later the others also came. 'Sir! Sir!' they said. 'Open the door for us!'
12"But he replied, 'I tell you the truth, I don't know you.'
13"Therefore keep watch, because you do not know the day or the hour.[h]

Jesus Tells the Parable of the Loaned Money
(205)

14"Again, it will be like a man going on a journey,[i] who called his servants and
entrusted his property to them. 15To one he gave five talents[a] of money, to another
two talents, and to another one talent, each according to his ability.[j] Then he went
on his journey. 16The man who had received the five talents went at once and put his
money to work and gained five more. 17So also, the one with the two talents gained
two more. 18But the man who had received the one talent went off, dug a hole in the
ground and hid his master's money.
19"After a long time the master of those servants returned and settled accounts with
them.[k] 20The man who had received the five talents brought the other five. 'Master,'
he said, 'you entrusted me with five talents. See, I have gained five more.'
21"His master replied, 'Well done, good and faithful servant! You have been
faithful with a few things; I will put you in charge of many things.[l] Come and share
your master's happiness!'
22"The man with the two talents also came. 'Master,' he said, 'you entrusted me
with two talents; see, I have gained two more.'
23"His master replied, 'Well done, good and faithful servant! You have been
faithful with a few things; I will put you in charge of many things.[m] Come and share
your master's happiness!'

a *15* A talent was worth several hundred pounds.

25:1 [a]Mt 13:24 [b]Lk 12:35-38; Ac 20:8; Rev 4:5 [c]Rev 19:7; 21:2
25:2 [d]Mt 24:45
25:5 [e]1Th 5:6
25:8 [f]Lk 12:35
25:10 [g]Rev 19:9
25:13 [h]Mt 24:42, 44; Mk 13:35; Lk 12:40
25:14 [i]Mt 21:33; Lk 19:12
25:15 [j]Mt 18:24, 25
25:19 [k]Mt 18:23
25:21 [l]ver 23; Mt 24:45, 47; Lk 16:10
25:23 [m]ver 21

25:1ff Jesus told the following parables to clarify further what it means to be ready for his return and how to live until he comes. In the story of the ten virgins (25:1–13), we are taught that every person is responsible for his or her own spiritual condition. The story of the talents (25:14–30) shows the necessity of using well what God has entrusted to us. The parable of the sheep and goats (25:31–46) stresses the importance of serving others in need. No parable by itself *completely* describes our preparation. Instead, each paints one part of the whole picture.

25:1ff This parable is about a wedding. On the wedding day the bridegroom went to the bride's house for the ceremony; then the bride and groom, along with a great procession, returned to the groom's house where a feast took place, often lasting a full week.

These ten virgins were waiting to join the procession, and they hoped to take part in the wedding banquet. But when the groom didn't come at the expected time, five of them ran out of lamp oil. By the time they had purchased extra oil, it was too late to join the feast.

When Jesus returns to take his people to heaven, we must be ready. Spiritual preparation cannot be bought or borrowed at the last minute. Our relationship with God must be our own.

25:15 The master divided the money (talents) among his servants according to their abilities. No-one received more or less than he could handle. If he failed in his assignment, his excuse could not be that he was overwhelmed. Failure could come only from laziness or hatred towards the master. The talents represent any kind of resource we are given. God gives us time, gifts, and other resources according to our abilities, and he expects us to invest them wisely until he returns. We are responsible to use well what God has given us. The issue is not how much we have, but how well we use what we have.

25:21 Jesus is coming back—we know this is true. Does this mean we must leave our jobs in order to serve God? No, it means we are to use our time, talents, and treasures diligently in order to serve God completely in whatever we do. For a few people, this may mean changing professions. For most of us, it means doing our daily work out of love for God.

24 “Then the man who had received the one talent came. ‘Master,’ he said, ‘I knew
that you are a hard man, harvesting where you have not sown and gathering where
you have not scattered seed. 25 So I was afraid and went out and hid your talent in
the ground. See, here is what belongs to you.’
26 “His master replied, ‘You wicked, lazy servant! So you knew that I harvest where
I have not sown and gather where I have not scattered seed? 27 Well then, you should
have put my money on deposit with the bankers, so that when I returned I would have
received it back with interest.
28 “ ‘Take the talent from him and give it to the one who has the ten talents. 29 For
everyone who has will be given more, and he will have an abundance. Whoever does
not have, even what he has will be taken from him.[n] 30 And throw that worthless
servant outside, into the darkness, where there will be weeping and gnashing of
teeth.’[o]

Jesus Tells about the Final Judgment
(206)

31 “When the Son of Man comes[p] in his glory, and all the angels with him, he will
sit on his throne[q] in heavenly glory. 32 All the nations will be gathered before him,
and he will separate[r] the people one from another as a shepherd separates the sheep
from the goats.[s] 33 He will put the sheep on his right and the goats on his left.
34 “Then the King will say to those on his right, ‘Come, you who are blessed by
my Father; take your inheritance, the kingdom[t] prepared for you since the creation
of the world.[u] 35 For I was hungry and you gave me something to eat, I was thirsty
and you gave me something to drink, I was a stranger and you invited me in,[v] 36 I
needed clothes and you clothed me,[w] I was sick and you looked after me,[x] I was
in prison and you came to visit me.’[y]
37 “Then the righteous will answer him, ‘Lord, when did we see you hungry and
feed you, or thirsty and give you something to drink? 38 When did we see you a stranger
and invite you in, or needing clothes and clothe you? 39 When did we see you sick
or in prison and go to visit you?’
40 “The King will reply, ‘I tell you the truth, whatever you did for one of the least
of these brothers of mine, you did for me.’[z]
41 “Then he will say to those on his left, ‘Depart from me,[a] you who are cursed,
into the eternal fire[b] prepared for the devil and his angels.[c] 42 For I was hungry and
you gave me nothing to eat, I was thirsty and you gave me nothing to drink, 43 I was
a stranger and you did not invite me in, I needed clothes and you did not clothe me,
I was sick and in prison and you did not look after me.’

25:29 [n]Mt 13:12; Mk 4:25; Lk 8:18; 19:26

25:30 [o]Mt 8:12

25:31 [p]Mt 16:27; Lk 17:30 [q]Mt 19:28

25:32 [r]Mal 3:18 [s]Eze 34:17, 20

25:34 [t]Mt 3:2; 5:3, 10, 19; 19:14; Ac 20:32; 1Co 15:50; Gal 5:21; Jas 2:5 [u]Heb 4:3; 9:26; Rev 13:8; 17:8

25:35 [v]Job 31:32; Isa 58:7; Eze 18:7; Heb 13:2

25:36 [w]Isa 58:7; Eze 18:7; Jas 2:15, 16 [x]Jas 1:27 [y]2Ti 1:16

25:40 [z]Pr 19:17; Mt 10:40, 42; Heb 6:10; 13:2

25:41 [a]Mt 7:23 [b]Isa 66:24; Mt 3:12; 5:22; Mk 9:43, 48; Lk 3:17; Jude 7 [c]2Pe 2:4

25:24–30 This last man was thinking only of himself. He hoped to play it safe and protect himself from his hard master, but he was judged for his self-centredness. We must not make excuses to avoid doing what God calls us to do. If God truly is our Master, we must obey willingly. Our time, abilities, and money aren't ours in the first place – we are caretakers, not owners. When we ignore, squander, or abuse what we are given, we are rebellious and deserve to be punished.

25:29, 30 This parable describes the consequences of two attitudes to Christ's return. The person who diligently prepares for it by investing his or her time and talent to serve God will be rewarded. The person who has no heart for the work of the kingdom will be punished. God rewards faithfulness. Those who bear no fruit for God's kingdom cannot expect to be treated the same as those who are faithful.

25:31–46 God will separate his obedient followers from pretenders and unbelievers. The real evidence of our belief is the way we act. To treat all those we encounter as if they are Jesus is no easy task. What we do for others demonstrates what we really think about Jesus' words to us – feed the hungry, give the homeless a place to stay, look after the sick. How well do your actions separate you from pretenders and unbelievers?

25:32 Jesus used sheep and goats to picture the division between believers and unbelievers. Sheep and goats often grazed together but were separated when the time came to shear the sheep. Ezekiel 34:17–24 also refers to the separation of sheep and goats.

25:34–40 This parable describes acts of mercy we can all do every day. These acts do not depend on wealth, ability, or intelligence; they are simple acts freely given and freely received. We have no excuse to neglect those who have deep needs, and we cannot hand over this responsibility to the church or government. Jesus demands our personal involvement in caring for others' needs (Isaiah 58:7).

25:40 There has been much discussion about the identity of the "brothers". Some have said they are the Jews; others say they are all Christians; still others say they are suffering people everywhere. Such a debate is much like the lawyer's earlier question to Jesus, "Who is my neighbour?" (Luke 10:29). The point of this parable is not the *who,* but the *what* – the importance of serving where service is needed. The focus of this parable is that we should love every person and serve anyone we can. Such love for others glorifies God by reflecting our love for him.

44"They also will answer, 'Lord, when did we see you hungry or thirsty or a stranger
or needing clothes or sick or in prison, and did not help you?'
45"He will reply, 'I tell you the truth, whatever you did not do for one of the least
of these, you did not do for me.'[d]
46"Then they will go away to eternal punishment, but the righteous to eternal
life.[e]"[f]

C. DEATH AND RESURRECTION OF JESUS, THE KING (26:1 – 28:20)

After facing much opposition for his teaching, Jesus is betrayed by Judas, disowned by the disciples, crucified, and buried. Three days later he rises from the dead and appears to the disciples, confirming that he is indeed King over life and death. The long-awaited King has brought in his kingdom, but it is different than expected, for he reigns in our hearts until the day he comes again to establish a new and perfect world.

Religious Leaders Plot to Kill Jesus
(207/Mark 14:1, 2; Luke 22:1, 2)

26 When Jesus had finished saying all these things,[a] he said to his disciples, 2"As
you know, the Passover[b] is two days away—and the Son of Man will be
handed over to be crucified."
3Then the chief priests and the elders of the people assembled[c] in the palace of
the high priest, whose name was Caiaphas,[d] 4and they plotted to arrest Jesus in some
sly way and kill him.[e] 5"But not during the Feast," they said, "or there may be a
riot[f] among the people."

A Woman Anoints Jesus with Perfume
(182/Mark 14:3–9; John 12:1–11)

6While Jesus was in Bethany[g] in the home of a man known as Simon the Leper,
7a woman came to him with an alabaster jar of very expensive perfume, which she
poured on his head as he was reclining at the table.

25:45 [d]Pr 14:31; 17:5
25:46 [e]Mt 19:29; Jn 3:15, 16, 36; 17:2, 3; Ro 2:7; Gal 6:8; 5:11, 13, 20 [f]Da 12:2; Jn 5:29; Ac 24:15; Ro 2:7, 8; Gal 6:8
26:1 [a]Mt 7:28
26:2 [b]Jn 11:55; 13:1
26:3 [c]Ps 2:2 [d]ver 57; Jn 11:47-53; 18:13, 14, 24, 28
26:4 [e]Mt 12:14
26:5 [f]Mt 27:24
26:6 [g]Mt 21:17

25:46 Eternal punishment takes place in hell (the lake of fire, or Gehenna), the place of punishment after death for all those who refuse to repent. In the Bible, three words are used in connection with eternal punishment.

(1) *Sheol*, or "the grave", is used in the Old Testament to mean the place of the dead, generally thought to be under the earth. (See Job 24:19; Psalm 16:10; Isaiah 38:10.)

(2) *Hades* is the Greek word for the underworld, the realm of the dead. It is the word used in the New Testament for Sheol. (See Matthew 16:18; Revelation 1:18; 20:13, 14.)

(3) *Gehenna*, or hell, was named after the Valley of Hinnom near Jerusalem where children were sacrificed by fire to the pagan gods (see 2 Kings 23:10; 2 Chronicles 28:3). This is the place of eternal fire (Matthew 5:22; 10:28; Mark 9:43; Luke 12:5; James 3:6; Revelation 19:20) prepared for the devil, his angels, and all those who do not believe in God (25:46; Revelation 20:9, 10). This is the final and eternal state of the wicked after the resurrection and the last judgment.

When Jesus warns against unbelief, he is trying to save us from agonising punishment.

26:3 Caiaphas was the ruling high priest during Jesus' ministry. He was the son-in-law of Annas, the previous high priest. The Roman government had taken over the process of appointing all political and religious leaders. Caiaphas served for 18 years, longer than most high priests, suggesting that he was gifted at co-operating with the Romans. He was the first to recommend Jesus' death in order to "save" the nation (John 11:49, 50).

26:3–5 This was a deliberate plot to kill Jesus. Without this plot, there would have been no groundswell of popular opinion against him. In fact, because of Jesus' popularity, the religious leaders were afraid to arrest him during the Passover. They did not want their actions to incite a riot.

26:6–13 Matthew and Mark put this event just before the Last Supper, while John has it just before the Triumphal Entry. Of the three, John places this event in the most likely chronological order. We must remember that the main purpose of the Gospel writers was to give an accurate record of Jesus' message, not to present an exact chronological account of his life. Matthew and Mark may have chosen to place this event here to contrast the complete devotion of Mary with the betrayal of Judas, the next event they record in their Gospels.

26:7 This woman was Mary, the sister of Martha and Lazarus, who lived in Bethany (John 12:1–3). Alabaster jars were carved

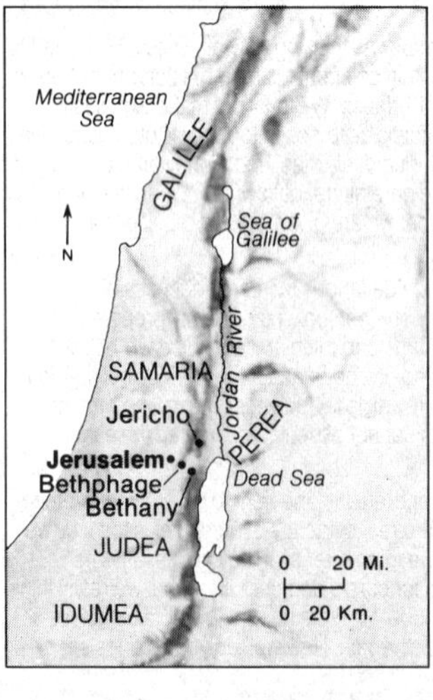

VISIT IN BETHANY
Chronologically, the events of Matthew 26:6–13 precede the events of 21:1ff. In 20:29, Jesus left Jericho, heading towards Jerusalem. Then he arrived in Bethany, where a woman anointed him. From there he went towards Bethphage, where two of his disciples got the donkey that he would ride into Jerusalem.

26:11 [h]Dt 15:11

26:12 [i]Jn 19:40

8When the disciples saw this, they were indignant. "Why this waste?" they asked.
9"This perfume could have been sold at a high price and the money given to the poor."
10Aware of this, Jesus said to them, "Why are you bothering this woman? She has
done a beautiful thing to me. 11The poor you will always have with you,[h] but you
will not always have me. 12When she poured this perfume on my body, she did it to
prepare me for burial.[i] 13I tell you the truth, wherever this gospel is preached
throughout the world, what she has done will also be told, in memory of her."

MARY
LAZARUS' SISTER

Hospitality is an art. Making sure a guest is welcomed, warmed, and well-fed requires creativity, organisation, and teamwork. Their ability to accomplish these goals makes Mary and her sister Martha one of the best hospitality teams in the Bible. Their frequent guest was Jesus Christ.

For Mary, hospitality meant giving more attention to the guest himself than to the needs he might have. She would rather talk than cook. She was more interested in her guest's words than in the cleanliness of her home or the timeliness of her meals. She let her older sister Martha take care of those details. Mary's approach to events shows her to be mainly a "responder". She did little preparation—her role was participation. Unlike her sister, who had to learn to stop and listen, Mary needed to learn that action is often appropriate and necessary.

We first meet Mary during a visit Jesus paid to her home. She simply sat at his feet and listened. When Martha became irritated at her sister's lack of help, Jesus stated that Mary's choice to enjoy his company was the most appropriate response at the time. Our last glimpse of Mary shows her to have become a woman of thoughtful and worshipful action. Again she was at Jesus' feet, washing them with perfume and wiping them with her hair. She seemed to understand, better even than the disciples, why Jesus was going to die. Jesus said her act of worship would be told everywhere, along with the gospel, as an example of costly service.

What kind of hospitality does Jesus receive in your life? Are you so busy planning and running your life that you neglect precious time with him? Or do you respond to him by listening to his word, then finding ways to worship him with your life? It is that kind of hospitality he longs for from each of us.

Strengths and accomplishments:
- Perhaps the only person who understood and accepted Jesus' coming death, taking time to anoint his body while he was still living
- Learned when to listen and when to act

Lessons from her life:
- The busyness of serving God can become a barrier to knowing him personally
- Small acts of obedience and service have widespread effects

Vital statistics:
- Where: Bethany
- Relatives: Sister: Martha. Brother: Lazarus

Key verses:
"When she poured this perfume on my body, she did it to prepare me for burial. I tell you the truth, wherever this gospel is preached throughout the world, what she has done will also be told, in memory of her" (Matthew 26:12, 13).

Mary's story is told in Matthew 26:6–13; Mark 14:3–9; Luke 10:38–42; John 11:17–45; 12:1–11.

from a translucent gypsum. These jars were used to hold perfumed oil.

26:8 All the disciples were indignant, but John's Gospel singles out Judas Iscariot as especially so (John 12:4).

26:11 Here Jesus brought back to mind Deuteronomy 15:11: "There will always be poor people in the land." This statement does not justify ignoring the needs of the poor. Scripture continually calls us to care for the needy. The passage in Deuteronomy continues: "Therefore I command you to be open-handed towards your brothers and towards the poor and needy in your land." Rather, by saying this, Jesus highlighted the special sacrifice Mary made for him.

Judas Agrees to Betray Jesus
(208/Mark 14:10, 11; Luke 22:3–6)

14 Then one of the Twelve—the one called Judas Iscariot[j]—went to the chief
priests 15 and asked, "What are you willing to give me if I hand him over to you?"
So they counted out for him thirty silver coins.[k] 16 From then on Judas watched for
an opportunity to hand him over.

Disciples Prepare for the Passover
(209/Mark 14:12–16; Luke 22:7–13)

17 On the first day of the Feast of Unleavened Bread,[l] the disciples came to Jesus
and asked, "Where do you want us to make preparations for you to eat the Passover?"
18 He replied, "Go into the city to a certain man and tell him, 'The Teacher says:
My appointed time[m] is near. I am going to celebrate the Passover with my disciples
at your house.' " 19 So the disciples did as Jesus had directed them and prepared the
Passover.

Jesus and the Disciples Have the Last Supper
(211/Mark 14:17–26; Luke 22:14–30; John 13:21–30)

20 When evening came, Jesus was reclining at the table with the Twelve. 21 And
while they were eating, he said, "I tell you the truth, one of you will betray me."[n]
22 They were very sad and began to say to him one after the other, "Surely not I,
Lord?"
23 Jesus replied, "The one who has dipped his hand into the bowl with me will betray
me.[o] 24 The Son of Man will go just as it is written about him.[p] But woe to that man
who betrays the Son of Man! It would be better for him if he had not been born."

26:14 [j] ver 25, 47; Mt 10:4
26:15 [k] Ex 21:32; Zec 11:12
26:17 [l] Ex 12:18-20
26:18 [m] Jn 7:6, 8, 30; 12:23; 13:1; 17:1
26:21 [n] Lk 22:21-23; Jn 13:21
26:23 [o] Ps 41:9; Jn 13:18
26:24 [p] Isa 53; Da 9:26; Mk 9:12; Lk 24:25-27, 46; Ac 17:2, 3; 26:22, 23

26:14, 15 Why would Judas want to betray Jesus? Judas, like the other disciples, expected Jesus to start a political rebellion and overthrow Rome. As treasurer, Judas certainly assumed (as did the other disciples—see Mark 10:35–37) that he would be given an important position in Jesus' new government. But when Jesus praised Mary for pouring out perfume worth a year's salary, Judas may have realised that Jesus' kingdom was not physical or political, but spiritual. Judas' greedy desire for money and status could not be realised if he followed Jesus, so he betrayed Jesus in exchange for money and favour from the religious leaders.

26:15 Matthew alone records the exact amount of money Judas accepted to betray Jesus—30 silver coins, the price of a slave (Exodus 21:32). The religious leaders had planned to wait until after the Passover to take Jesus, but with Judas' unexpected offer, they accelerated their plans.

26:17 The Passover took place on one night and at one meal, but the Feast of Unleavened Bread, which was celebrated with it, continued for a week. The people removed all yeast from their homes in commemoration of their ancestors' exodus from Egypt, when they did not have time to let the bread dough rise. Thousands of people poured into Jerusalem from all over the Roman empire for this feast. For more information on how the Passover was celebrated, see the notes on Mark 14:1 and in Exodus 12.

26:23 In Jesus' time, some food was eaten from a common bowl into which everyone dipped their hand.

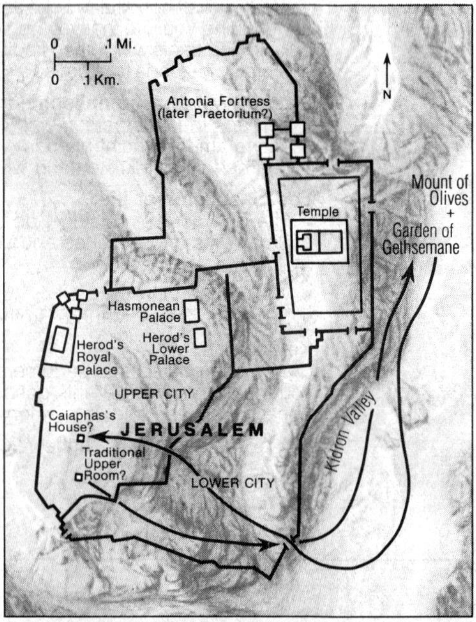

THE PASSOVER MEAL AND GETHSEMANE Jesus, who would soon be the final Passover Lamb, ate the traditional Passover meal with his disciples in the upper room of a house in Jerusalem. During the meal they partook of the wine and bread, which would be the elements of future communion celebrations, and then went out to the Garden of Gethsemane on the Mount of Olives.

26:25 [q]Mt 23:7
26:26 [r]Mt 14:19; 1Co 10:16
26:28 [s]Ex 24:6-8; Heb 9:20 [t]Mt 20:28; Mk 1:4
26:29 [u]Ac 10:41
26:30 [v]Mt 21:1; Mk 14:26
26:31 [w]Mt 11:6 [x]Zec 13:7; Jn 16:32
26:32 [y]Mt 28:7, 10, 16
26:34 [z]ver 75; Jn 13:38
26:35 [a]Jn 13:37
26:37 [b]Mt 4:21
26:38 [c]Jn 12:27 [d]ver 40, 41

25 Then Judas, the one who would betray him, said, "Surely not I, Rabbi?"[q]
Jesus answered, "Yes, it is you."[a]
26 While they were eating, Jesus took bread, gave thanks and broke it,[r] and gave
it to his disciples, saying, "Take and eat; this is my body."
27 Then he took the cup, gave thanks and offered it to them, saying, "Drink from
it, all of you. 28 This is my blood of the[b] covenant,[s] which is poured out for many
for the forgiveness of sins.[t] 29 I tell you, I will not drink of this fruit of the vine from
now on until that day when I drink it anew with you[u] in my Father's kingdom."
30 When they had sung a hymn, they went out to the Mount of Olives.[v]

Jesus Again Predicts Peter's Denial
(222/Mark 14:27–31)

31 Then Jesus told them, "This very night you will all fall away on account of me,[w]
for it is written:

> " 'I will strike the shepherd,
> and the sheep of the flock will be scattered.'[c][x]

32 But after I have risen, I will go ahead of you into Galilee."[y]
33 Peter replied, "Even if all fall away on account of you, I never will."
34 "I tell you the truth," Jesus answered, "this very night, before the cock crows,
you will disown me three times."[z]
35 But Peter declared, "Even if I have to die with you,[a] I will never disown you."
And all the other disciples said the same.

Jesus Agonizes in the Garden
(223/Mark 14:32–42; Luke 22:39–46)

36 Then Jesus went with his disciples to a place called Gethsemane, and he said to
them, "Sit here while I go over there and pray." 37 He took Peter and the two sons
of Zebedee[b] along with him, and he began to be sorrowful and troubled. 38 Then he
said to them, "My soul is overwhelmed with sorrow[c] to the point of death. Stay here
and keep watch with me."[d]

a *25* Or *"You yourself have said it"* b *28* Some manuscripts *the new* c *31* Zech. 13:7

26:26 Each name we use for this sacrament brings out a different dimension to it. It is the *Lord's Supper* because it commemorates the Passover meal Jesus ate with his disciples; it is the *Eucharist* (thanksgiving) because in it we thank God for Christ's work for us; it is *Communion* because through it we commune with God and with other believers. As we eat the bread and drink the wine, we should be quietly reflective as we recall Jesus' death and his promise to come again, grateful for God's wonderful gift to us, and joyful as we meet with Christ and the body of believers.

26:28 How does Jesus' blood relate to the new covenant? People under the old covenant (those who lived before Jesus) could approach God only through a priest and an animal sacrifice. Now all people can come directly to God through faith because Jesus' death has made us acceptable in God's eyes (Romans 3:21–24).

The old covenant was a shadow of the new (Jeremiah 31:31; Hebrews 8:1ff), pointing forward to the day when Jesus himself would be the final and ultimate sacrifice for sin. Rather than an unblemished lamb slain on the altar, the perfect Lamb of God was slain on the cross, a sinless sacrifice so that our sins could be forgiven once and for all. All those who believe in Christ receive that forgiveness.

26:29 Again Jesus assured his disciples of victory over death and of their future with him. The next few hours would bring apparent defeat, but soon they would experience the power of the Holy Spirit and witness the great spread of the gospel message. And one day, they would all be together again in God's new kingdom.

26:30 It is possible that the hymn the disciples sang was from Psalms 115–118, the traditional psalms sung as part of the Passover meal.

26:35 All the disciples declared that they would die before disowning Jesus. A few hours later, however, they all scattered. Talk is cheap. It is easy to say we are devoted to Christ, but our claims are meaningful only when they are tested in the crucible of persecution. How strong is your faith? Is it strong enough to stand up under intense trial?

26:37, 38 Jesus was in great anguish over his approaching physical pain, separation from the Father, and death for the sins of the world. The divine course was set, but he, in his human nature, still struggled (Hebrews 5:7–9). Because of the anguish Jesus experienced, he can relate to our suffering. Jesus' strength to obey came from his relationship with God the Father, who is also the source of our strength (John 17:11, 15, 16, 21, 26).

39Going a little farther, he fell with his face to the ground and prayed, "My Father,
if it is possible, may this cup[e] be taken from me. Yet not as I will, but as you will."[f]
40Then he returned to his disciples and found them sleeping. "Could you men not
keep watch with me[g] for one hour?" he asked Peter. 41"Watch and pray so that you
will not fall into temptation.[h] The spirit is willing, but the body is weak."
42He went away a second time and prayed, "My Father, if it is not possible for this
cup to be taken away unless I drink it, may your will be done."
43When he came back, he again found them sleeping, because their eyes were
heavy. 44So he left them and went away once more and prayed the third time, saying
the same thing.
45Then he returned to the disciples and said to them, "Are you still sleeping and
resting? Look, the hour[i] is near, and the Son of Man is betrayed into the hands of
sinners. 46Rise, let us go! Here comes my betrayer!"

Jesus Is Betrayed and Arrested
(224/Mark 14:43–52; Luke 22:47–53; John 18:1–11)

47While he was still speaking, Judas, one of the Twelve, arrived. With him was
a large crowd armed with swords and clubs, sent from the chief priests and the elders
of the people. 48Now the betrayer had arranged a signal with them: "The one I kiss
is the man; arrest him." 49Going at once to Jesus, Judas said, "Greetings, Rabbi!"[j]
and kissed him.
50Jesus replied, "Friend,[k] do what you came for."[d]
Then the men stepped forward, seized Jesus and arrested him. 51With that, one of
Jesus' companions reached for his sword,[l] drew it out and struck the servant of the
high priest, cutting off his ear.[m]
52"Put your sword back in its place," Jesus said to him, "for all who draw the sword
will die by the sword.[n] 53Do you think I cannot call on my Father, and he will at
once put at my disposal more than twelve legions of angels?[o] 54But how then would
the Scriptures be fulfilled[p] that say it must happen in this way?"
55At that time Jesus said to the crowd, "Am I leading a rebellion, that you have
come out with swords and clubs to capture me? Every day I sat in the temple courts
teaching,[q] and you did not arrest me. 56But this has all taken place that the writings
of the prophets might be fulfilled."[r] Then all the disciples deserted him and fled.

d *50 Or "Friend, why have you come?"*

26:39 [e]Mt 20:22 [f]ver 42; Ps 40:6-8; Isa 50:5; Jn 5:30; 6:38
26:40 [g]ver 38
26:41 [h]Mt 6:13
26:45 [i]ver 18
26:49 [j]ver 25
26:50 [k]Mt 20:13; 22:12
26:51 [l]Lk 22:36, 38 [m]Jn 18:10
26:52 [n]Ge 9:6; Rev 13:10
26:53 [o]2Ki 6:17; Da 7:10; Mt 4:11
26:54 [p]ver 24
26:55 [q]Mk 12:35; Lk 21:37; Jn 7:14, 28; 18:20
26:56 [r]ver 24

26:39 Jesus was not rebelling against his Father's will when he asked that the cup of suffering and separation be taken away. In fact, he reaffirmed his desire to do God's will by saying, "Yet not as I will, but as you will." His prayer reveals to us his terrible suffering. His agony was worse than death because he paid for *all* sin by being separated from God. The sinless Son of God took our sins upon himself to save us from suffering and separation.

26:39 In times of suffering people sometimes wish they knew the future, or they wish they could understand the reason for their anguish. Jesus knew what lay ahead of him, and he knew the reason. Even so, his struggle was intense – more wrenching than any struggle we will ever have to face. What does it take to be able to say "as you will"? It takes firm trust in God's plans; it takes prayer and obedience each step of the way.

26:40, 41 Jesus used Peter's drowsiness to warn him about the kinds of temptation he would soon face. The way to overcome temptation is to keep watch and pray. Watching means being aware of the possibilities of temptation, sensitive to the subtleties, and spiritually equipped to fight it. Because temptation strikes where we are most vulnerable, we can't resist it alone. Prayer is essential because God's strength can shore up our defences and defeat Satan's power.

26:48 Judas had told the crowd to arrest the man he kissed. This was not an arrest by Roman soldiers under Roman law, but an arrest by the religious leaders. Judas pointed Jesus out not because Jesus was hard to recognise, but because Judas had agreed to be the formal accuser in case a trial was called. Judas was able to lead the group to one of Jesus' retreats where no onlookers would interfere with the arrest.

26:51–53 The man who cut off the servant's ear was Peter (John 18:10). Peter was trying to prevent what he saw as *defeat.* He didn't realise that Jesus had to die in order to gain *victory.* But Jesus demonstrated perfect commitment to his Father's will. His kingdom would not be advanced with swords, but with faith and obedience.

26:55 Although the religious leaders could have arrested Jesus at any time, they came at night because they were afraid of the crowds that followed him each day (see 26:5).

26:56 A few hours earlier, this band of men had said they would rather die than desert their Lord (see the note on 26:35).

Caiaphas Questions Jesus
(226/Mark 14:53–65)

57Those who had arrested Jesus took him to Caiaphas,[s] the high priest, where the
teachers of the law and the elders had assembled. 58But Peter followed him at a
distance, right up to the courtyard of the high priest.[t] He entered and sat down with
the guards[u] to see the outcome.
59The chief priests and the whole Sanhedrin[v] were looking for false evidence
against Jesus so that they could put him to death. 60But they did not find any, though
many false witnesses[w] came forward.
Finally two[x] came forward 61and declared, "This fellow said, 'I am able to destroy
the temple of God and rebuild it in three days.' "[y]
62Then the high priest stood up and said to Jesus, "Are you not going to answer?
What is this testimony that these men are bringing against you?" 63But Jesus remained
silent.[z]

26:57 [s]ver 3
26:58 [t]Jn 18:15 [u]Jn 7:32, 45, 46
26:59 [v]Mt 5:22
26:60 [w]Ps 27:12; 35:11; Ac 6:13 [x]Dt 19:15
26:61 [y]Jn 2:19
26:63 [z]Mt 27:12, 14

BETRAYED!

Delilah betrayed Samson to the Philistines.	Judges 16:16–21
Absalom betrayed David, his father.	2 Samuel 15:10–17
Jehu betrayed Joram and killed him.	2 Kings 9:14–27
Officials betrayed Joash and killed him.	2 Kings 12:20, 21
Judas betrayed Jesus.	Matthew 26:46–56

Scripture records a number of occasions in which a person or group was betrayed. The tragedies caused by these violations of trust are a strong lesson about the importance of keeping our commitments.

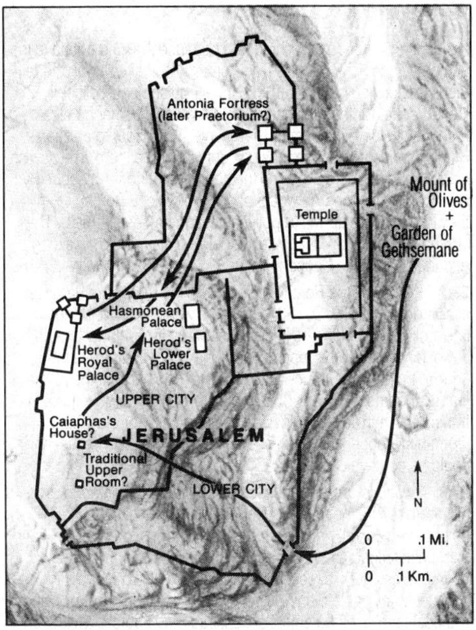

JESUS' TRIAL After Judas singled Jesus out for arrest, the mob took Jesus first to Caiaphas, the high priest. This trial, a mockery of justice, ended at daybreak with their decision to kill him—but the Jews needed Rome's permission for the death sentence. Jesus was taken to Pilate (who was probably in the Praetorium), then to Herod (Luke 23:5–12), and back to Pilate, who sentenced him to die.

26:57 Earlier in the evening, Jesus had been questioned by Annas (the former high priest and father-in-law of Caiaphas). Annas then sent Jesus to Caiaphas' home to be questioned (John 18:12–24). Because of their haste to complete the trial and see Jesus die before the Sabbath, less than 24 hours away, the religious leaders met in Caiaphas' home at night instead of waiting for daylight and meeting in the temple.

26:59 The Sanhedrin was the most powerful religious and political body of the Jewish people. Although the Romans controlled Israel's government, they gave the people power to handle religious disputes and some civil disputes, so the Sanhedrin made many of the local decisions affecting daily life. But a death sentence had to be approved by the Romans (John 18:31).

26:60, 61 The Sanhedrin tried to find witnesses who would distort some of Jesus' teachings. Finally they found two witnesses who distorted Jesus' words about the temple (see John 2:19). They claimed that Jesus had said he could destroy the temple—a blasphemous boast. Actually Jesus had said, "Destroy this temple, and I will raise it again in three days." Jesus, of course, was talking about his body, not the building. Ironically, the religious leaders were about to destroy Jesus' body just as he had said, and three days later he would rise from the dead.

The high priest said to him, "I charge you under oath[a] by the living God:[b] Tell
us if you are the Christ,[e] the Son of God."
64"Yes, it is as you say," Jesus replied. "But I say to all of you: In the future you
will see the Son of Man sitting at the right hand of the Mighty One[c] and coming on
the clouds of heaven."[d]
65Then the high priest tore his clothes[e] and said, "He has spoken blasphemy! Why
do we need any more witnesses? Look, now you have heard the blasphemy. 66What
do you think?"
"He is worthy of death,"[f] they answered.
67Then they spat in his face and struck him with their fists.[g] Others slapped him
68and said, "Prophesy to us, Christ. Who hit you?"[h]

Peter Denies Knowing Jesus

(227/Mark 14:66–72; Luke 22:54–65; John 18:25–27)

69Now Peter was sitting out in the courtyard, and a servant girl came to him. "You
also were with Jesus of Galilee," she said.
70But he denied it before them all. "I don't know what you're talking about," he
said.
71Then he went out to the gateway, where another girl saw him and said to the
people there, "This fellow was with Jesus of Nazareth."
72He denied it again, with an oath: "I don't know the man!"
73After a little while, those standing there went up to Peter and said, "Surely you
are one of them, for your accent gives you away."

[e] *63* Or *Messiah*; also in verse 68

26:63 [a]Lev 5:1 [b]Mt 16:16

26:64 [c]Ps 110:1 [d]Da 7:13; Rev 1:7

26:65 [e]Mk 14:63

26:66 [f]Lev 24:16; Jn 19:7

26:67 [g]Mt 16:21; 27:30

26:68 [h]Lk 22:63-65

26:64 Jesus declared his royalty in no uncertain terms. In saying he was the Son of Man, Jesus was claiming to be the Messiah, as his listeners well knew. He knew this declaration would be his undoing, but he did not panic. He was calm, courageous, and determined.

26:65, 66 The high priest accused Jesus of blasphemy—calling himself God. To the Jews, this was a great crime, punishable by death (Leviticus 24:16). The religious leaders refused even to consider that Jesus' words might be true. They had decided against Jesus, and in so doing, they sealed their own fate as well as his. Like the members of the Sanhedrin, you must decide whether Jesus' words are blasphemy or truth. Your decision has eternal implications.

26:69ff There were three stages to Peter's denial. First he acted confused and tried to divert attention from himself by changing the subject. Second, using an oath he denied that he knew Jesus. Third, he began to curse and swear. Believers who deny Christ often begin doing so subtly by pretending not to know him. When opportunities to discuss religious issues come up, they walk away or pretend they don't know the answers. With only a little more pressure, they can be induced to deny flatly their relationship with Christ. If you find yourself subtly diverting conversation so you don't have to talk about Christ, watch out. You may be on the road to disowning him.

26:72–74 That Peter denied knowing Jesus, using an oath and calling down curses, does not mean he used foul language. This was the kind of swearing that a person does in a court of law. Peter was swearing that he did not know Jesus and was invoking a curse on himself if his words were untrue. In effect he was saying, "May God strike me dead if I am lying."

27:1, 2 The religious leaders had to persuade the Roman government to sentence Jesus to death because they did not have the authority to do it themselves. The Romans had taken away the religious leaders' authority to inflict capital punishment. Politically, it looked better for the religious leaders anyway if someone else was responsible for killing Jesus. They wanted the death to appear Roman-sponsored so the crowds couldn't blame them. The Jewish leaders had arrested Jesus on theological grounds—blasphemy; but because this charge would be thrown out of a Roman court, they had to come up with a political reason for Jesus' death. Their strategy was to show Jesus as a rebel who claimed to be a king and thus a threat to Caesar.

27:2 Pilate was the Roman governor for the regions of Samaria and Judea from A.D. 26–36. Jerusalem was located in Judea. Pilate took special pleasure in demonstrating his authority over the Jews; for example, he impounded money from the temple treasuries to build an aqueduct. Pilate was not popular, but the religious leaders had no other way to get rid of Jesus than to go to him. Ironically, when Jesus, a Jew, came before him for trial, Pilate found him innocent. He could not find a single fault in Jesus, nor could he contrive one.

27:3, 4 Jesus' formal accuser (see 26:48 note) wanted to drop his charges, but the religious leaders refused to halt the trial. When he betrayed Jesus, perhaps Judas was trying to force Jesus' hand to get him to lead a revolt against Rome. This did not work, of course. Whatever his reason, Judas changed his mind, but it was too late. Many of the plans we set into motion cannot be reversed. It is best to think of the potential consequences before we launch into an action we may later regret.

27:4 The priests' job was to teach people about God and act as intercessors for them, helping administer the sacrifices to cover their sins. Judas returned to the priests, exclaiming that he had sinned. Rather than helping him find forgiveness, however, the priests said, "That's your responsibility." Not only had they rejected the Messiah, they had rejected their role as priests.

26:75 [i]ver 34; Jn 13:38

74 Then he began to call down curses on himself and he swore to them, "I don't know
the man!"
Immediately a cock crowed. 75 Then Peter remembered the word Jesus had spoken:
"Before the cock crows, you will disown me three times."[i] And he went outside and
wept bitterly.

27:1 [a]Mt 12:14; Mk 15:1; Lk 22:66

The Council of Religious Leaders Condemns Jesus
(228/Mark 15:1; Luke 22:66–71)

27:2 [b]Mt 20:19 [c]Mk 15:1; Lk 13:1; Ac 3:13; 1Ti 6:13

27 Early in the morning, all the chief priests and the elders of the people came
to the decision to put Jesus to death.[a] 2 They bound him, led him away and
handed him over[b] to Pilate, the governor.[c]

Judas Kills Himself
(229)

27:3 [d]Mt 10:4 [e]Mt 26:14, 15

3 When Judas, who had betrayed him,[d] saw that Jesus was condemned, he was
seized with remorse and returned the thirty silver coins[e] to the chief priests and the
elders. 4 "I have sinned," he said, "for I have betrayed innocent blood."

PETER

Jesus' first words to Simon Peter were "Come, follow me" (Mark 1:17). His last words to him were "You must follow me" (John 21:22). Every step of the way between those two challenges, Peter never failed to follow—even though he often stumbled.

When Jesus entered Peter's life, this plain fisherman became a new person with new goals and new priorities. He did not become a perfect person, however, and he never stopped being Simon Peter. We may wonder what Jesus saw in Simon that made him greet this potential disciple with a new name, Peter—the "rock". Impulsive Peter certainly didn't act like a rock much of the time. But when Jesus chose his followers, he wasn't looking for models; he was looking for real people. He chose people who could be changed by his love, and then he sent them out to communicate that his acceptance was available to anyone—even to those who often fail.

We may wonder what Jesus sees in us when he calls us to follow him. But we know Jesus accepted Peter, and, in spite of his failures, Peter went on to do great things for God. Are you willing to keep following Jesus, even when you fail?

Strengths and accomplishments:
- Became the recognised leader among Jesus' disciples—one of the inner group of three
- Was the first great voice of the gospel during and after Pentecost
- Probably knew Mark and gave him information for the Gospel of Mark
- Wrote 1 and 2 Peter

Weaknesses and mistakes:
- Often spoke without thinking; was brash and impulsive
- During Jesus' trial, denied three times that he even knew Jesus
- Later found it hard to treat Gentile Christians as equals

Lessons from his life:
- Enthusiasm has to be backed up by faith and understanding, or it fails
- God's faithfulness can compensate for our greatest unfaithfulness
- It is better to be a follower who fails than one who fails to follow

Vital statistics:
- Occupations: Fisherman, disciple
- Relatives: Father: John. Brother: Andrew
- Contemporaries: Jesus, Pilate, Herod

Key verse:
"And I tell you that you are Peter, and on this rock I will build my church, and the gates of Hades will not overcome it" (Matthew 16:18).

Peter's story is told in the Gospels and the book of Acts. He is mentioned in Galatians 1:18 and 2:7–14; and he wrote the books of 1 and 2 Peter.

"What is that to us?" they replied. "That's your responsibility."[f]
5So Judas threw the money into the temple[g] and left. Then he went away and
hanged himself.[h]
6The chief priests picked up the coins and said, "It is against the law to put this
into the treasury, since it is blood money." 7So they decided to use the money to buy
the potter's field as a burial place for foreigners. 8That is why it has been called the
Field of Blood[i] to this day. 9Then what was spoken by Jeremiah the prophet was
fulfilled:[j] "They took the thirty silver coins, the price set on him by the people
of Israel, 10and they used them to buy the potter's field, as the Lord commanded
me."[a][k]

Jesus Stands Trial before Pilate
(230/Mark 15:2–5; Luke 23:1–5; John 18:28–37)

11Meanwhile Jesus stood before the governor, and the governor asked him, "Are
you the king of the Jews?"[l]
"Yes, it is as you say," Jesus replied.
12When he was accused by the chief priests and the elders, he gave no answer.[m]
13Then Pilate asked him, "Don't you hear the testimony they are bringing against
you?"[n] 14But Jesus made no reply,[o] not even to a single charge—to the great
amazement of the governor.

Pilate Hands Jesus Over to Be Crucified
(232/Mark 15:6–15; Luke 23:13–25; John 18:39—19:16)

15Now it was the governor's custom at the Feast to release a prisoner[p] chosen by
the crowd. 16At that time they had a notorious prisoner, called Barabbas. 17So when
the crowd had gathered, Pilate asked them, "Which one do you want me to release
to you: Barabbas, or Jesus who is called Christ?"[q] 18For he knew it was out of envy
that they had handed Jesus over to him.
19While Pilate was sitting on the judge's seat,[r] his wife sent him this message:
"Don't have anything to do with that innocent[s] man, for I have suffered a great deal
today in a dream[t] because of him."
20But the chief priests and the elders persuaded the crowd to ask for Barabbas and
to have Jesus executed.[u]

[a] *10* See Zech. 11:12,13; Jer. 19:1–13; 32:6–9.

27:4 [f]ver 24
27:5 [g]Lk 1:9, 21 [h]Ac 1:18
27:8 [i]Ac 1:19
27:9 [j]Mt 1:22
27:10 [k]Zec 11:12, 13; Jer 32:6-9
27:11 [l]Mt 2:2
27:12 [m]Mt 26:63; Mk 14:61; Jn 19:9
27:13 [n]Mt 26:62
27:14 [o]Mk 14:61
27:15 [p]Jn 18:39
27:17 [q]ver 22; Mt 1:16
27:19 [r]Jn 19:13
27:19 [s]ver 24 [t]Ge 20:6; Nu 12:6; 1Ki 3:5; Job 33:14-16; Mt 1:20; 2:12, 13, 19, 22
27:20 [u]Ac 3:14

27:5 According to Matthew, Judas hanged himself. Acts 1:18, however, says that he fell and burst open. The best explanation is that the limb from which he was hanging broke, and the resulting fall split open his body.

27:6 These chief priests felt no guilt in giving Judas money to betray an innocent man, but when Judas returned the money, the priests couldn't accept it because it was wrong to accept blood money—payment for murder! Their hatred for Jesus had caused them to lose all sense of justice.

27:9, 10 This prophecy is found specifically in Zechariah 11:12, 13, but may also have been taken from Jeremiah 17:2, 3; 18:1–4; 19:1–11; or 32:6–15. In Old Testament times, Jeremiah was considered the collector of some of the prophets' writings, so perhaps his name is cited rather than Zechariah.

27:12 Standing before Pilate, the religious leaders accused Jesus of a different crime than the ones for which they had arrested him. They arrested him for blasphemy (claiming to be God), but that charge would mean nothing to the Romans. So the religious leaders had to accuse Jesus of crimes that would have concerned the Roman government, such as encouraging the people not to pay taxes, claiming to be a king, and causing riots. These accusations were not true, but the religious leaders were determined to kill Jesus, and they broke several commandments in order to do so.

27:14 Jesus' silence fulfilled the words of the prophet (Isaiah 53:7). Pilate was amazed that Jesus didn't try to defend himself. He recognised the obvious plot against Jesus and wanted to let him go, but Pilate was already under pressure from Rome to keep peace in his territory. The last thing he needed was a rebellion over this quiet and seemingly insignificant man.

27:15, 16 Barabbas had taken part in a rebellion against the Roman government (Mark 15:7). Although an enemy to Rome, he may have been a hero to the Jews. Ironically, Barabbas was guilty of the crime for which Jesus was accused. *Barabbas* means "son of the father", which was actually Jesus' position with God.

27:19 For a leader who was supposed to administer justice, Pilate proved to be more concerned about political expediency than about doing what was right. He had several opportunities to make the right decision. His conscience told him Jesus was innocent; Roman law said an innocent man should not be put to death; and

27:22 [v]Mt 1:16
27:24 [w]Mt 26:5 [x]Ps 26:6 [y]Dt 21:6-8 [z]ver 4
27:25 [a]Jos 2:19; Ac 5:28
27:26 [b]Isa 53:5; Jn 19:1
27:27 [c]Jn 18:28, 33; 19:9
27:28 [d]Jn 19:2
27:29 [e]Isa 53:3; Jn 19:2, 3
27:30 [f]Mt 16:21; 26:67
27:31 [g]Isa 53:7
27:32 [h]Heb 13:12 [i]Ac 2:10; 6:9; 11:20; 13:1 [j]Mk 15:21; Lk 23:26
27:33 [k]Jn 19:17
27:34 [l]ver 48; Ps 69:21

21 "Which of the two do you want me to release to you?" asked the governor.
"Barabbas," they answered.
22 "What shall I do, then, with Jesus who is called Christ?"[v] Pilate asked.
They all answered, "Crucify him!"
23 "Why? What crime has he committed?" asked Pilate.
But they shouted all the louder, "Crucify him!"
24 When Pilate saw that he was getting nowhere, but that instead an uproar[w] was
starting, he took water and washed his hands[x] in front of the crowd. "I am innocent
of this man's blood,"[y] he said. "It is your responsibility!"[z]
25 All the people answered, "Let his blood be on us and on our children!"[a]
26 Then he released Barabbas to them. But he had Jesus flogged,[b] and handed him
over to be crucified.

Roman Soldiers Mock Jesus
(233/Mark 15:16–20)

27 Then the governor's soldiers took Jesus into the Praetorium[c] and gathered the
whole company of soldiers round him. 28 They stripped him and put a scarlet robe on
him,[d] 29 and then twisted together a crown of thorns and set it on his head. They put
a staff in his right hand and knelt in front of him and mocked him. "Hail, king of the
Jews!" they said.[e] 30 They spat on him, and took the staff and struck him on the head
again and again.[f] 31 After they had mocked him, they took off the robe and put his
own clothes on him. Then they led him away to crucify him.[g]

Jesus Is Led Away to Be Crucified
(234/Mark 15:21–24; Luke 23:26–31; John 19:17)
Jesus Is Placed on the Cross
(235/Mark 15:25–32; Luke 23:32–43; John 19:18–27)

32 As they were going out,[h] they met a man from Cyrene,[i] named Simon, and they
forced him to carry the cross.[j] 33 They came to a place called Golgotha (which means
The Place of the Skull).[k] 34 There they offered Jesus wine to drink, mixed with gall;[l]

---

his wife had a troubling dream. Pilate had no good excuse to condemn Jesus, but he was afraid of the crowd.

27:21 Crowds are fickle. They loved Jesus on Sunday because they thought he was going to inaugurate his kingdom. Then they hated him on Friday when his power appeared broken. In the face of the mass uprising against Jesus, his friends were afraid to speak up.

27:21 Faced with a clear choice, the people chose Barabbas, a revolutionary and murderer, over the Son of God. Faced with the same choice today, people are still choosing "Barabbas". They would rather have the tangible force of human power than the salvation offered by the Son of God.

27:24 At first Pilate hesitated to give the religious leaders permission to crucify Jesus. He thought they were simply jealous of a teacher who was more popular with the people than they were. But when the Jews threatened to report Pilate to Caesar (John 19:12), Pilate became afraid. Historical records indicate that the Jews had already threatened to lodge a formal complaint against Pilate for his stubborn flouting of their traditions – and such a complaint would most likely have led to his recall by Rome. His job was in jeopardy. The Roman government could not afford to put large numbers of troops in all the regions under their control, so one of Pilate's main duties was to do whatever was necessary to maintain peace.

27:24 In making no decision, Pilate made the decision to let the crowds crucify Jesus. Although he washed his hands, the guilt remained. Washing your hands of a tough situation doesn't cancel your guilt. It merely gives you a false sense of peace. Don't make excuses – take responsibility for the decisions you make.

27:27 A company of soldiers was a division of the Roman legion, containing about 200 men.

27:29 People often make fun of Christians for their faith, but believers can take courage from the fact that Jesus himself was mocked as greatly as anyone. Taunting may hurt our feelings, but we should never let it change our faith (see 5:11, 12).

27:32 Condemned prisoners had to carry their own crosses to the execution site. Jesus, weakened from the beatings he had received, was physically unable to carry his cross any further. Thus a bystander, Simon, was forced to do so. Simon was from Cyrene, in northern Africa, and was probably one of the thousands of Jews visiting Jerusalem for the Passover.

27:33 Some scholars say Golgotha ("skull") derives its name from its appearance. Golgotha may have been a regular place of execution in a prominent public place outside the city. Executions held there would serve as a deterrent to criminals.

27:34 Wine mixed with gall was offered to Jesus to help reduce his pain, but Jesus refused to drink it. Gall is generally understood to be a narcotic that was used to deaden pain. Jesus would suffer fully conscious and with a clear mind.

but after tasting it, he refused to drink it. 35 When they had crucified him, they divided
up his clothes by casting lots.[b][m] 36 And sitting down, they kept watch[n] over him
there. 37 Above his head they placed the written charge against him: THIS IS JESUS, THE
KING OF THE JEWS. 38 Two robbers were crucified with him,[o] one on his right and
one on his left. 39 Those who passed by hurled insults at him, shaking their heads[p]
40 and saying, "You who are going to destroy the temple and build it in three days,[q]
save yourself![r] Come down from the cross, if you are the Son of God!"[s]
41 In the same way the chief priests, the teachers of the law and the elders mocked
him. 42 "He saved others," they said, "but he can't save himself! He's the King of
Israel![t] Let him come down now from the cross, and we will believe[u] in him. 43 He
trusts in God. Let God rescue him[v] now if he wants him, for he said, 'I am the Son
of God.' " 44 In the same way the robbers who were crucified with him also heaped
insults on him.

Jesus Dies on the Cross

(236/Mark 15:33–41; Luke 23:44–49; John 19:28–37)

45 From the sixth hour until the ninth hour darkness[w] came over all the land.
46 About the ninth hour Jesus cried out in a loud voice, "*Eloi, Eloi,*[c] *lama sabach-
thani?*"—which means, "My God, my God, why have you forsaken me?"[d][x]
47 When some of those standing there heard this, they said, "He's calling Elijah."
48 Immediately one of them ran and got a sponge. He filled it with wine vinegar,[y]
put it on a stick, and offered it to Jesus to drink. 49 The rest said, "Now leave him
alone. Let's see if Elijah comes to save him."
50 And when Jesus had cried out again in a loud voice, he gave up his spirit.[z]

b *35* A few late manuscripts *lots that the word spoken by the prophet might be fulfilled: "They divided my garments among themselves and cast lots for my clothing."* (Psalm 22:18) c *46* Some manuscripts *Eli, Eli*
d *46* Psalm 22:1

27:35 [m]Ps 22:18
27:36 [n]ver 54
27:38 [o]Isa 53:12
27:39 [p]Ps 22:7; 109:25; La 2:15
27:40 [q]Mt 26:61; Jn 2:19 [r]ver 42 [s]Mt 4:3, 6
27:42 [t]Jn 1:49; 12:13 [u]Jn 3:15
27:43 [v]Ps 22:8
27:45 [w]Am 8:9
27:46 [x]Ps 22:1
27:48 [y]ver 34; Ps 69:21
27:50 [z]Jn 19:30

27:35 The soldiers customarily took the clothing of those they crucified. These soldiers cast lots and divided Jesus' clothing among themselves, fulfilling the prophecy made by David. Much of Psalm 22 parallels Jesus' crucifixion.

27:40 This accusation was used against Jesus in his trial by the Sanhedrin (26:61). It is ironic that Jesus was in the very process of fulfilling his own prophecy. Because Jesus is the Son of God, who always obeys the will of the Father, he did not come down from the cross.

27:44 Later one of these robbers repented. Jesus promised that the repentant robber would join him in paradise (Luke 23:39–43).

27:45 We do not know how this darkness occurred, but it is clear that God caused it. Nature testified to the gravity of Jesus' death, while Jesus' friends and enemies alike fell silent in the encircling gloom. The darkness on that Friday afternoon was both physical and spiritual.

27:46 Jesus was not questioning God; he was quoting the first line of Psalm 22—a deep expression of the anguish he felt when he took on the sins of the world, which caused him to be separated from his Father. *This* was what Jesus dreaded as he prayed to God in the garden to take the cup from him (26:39). The physical agony was horrible, but even worse was the period of spiritual separation from God. Jesus suffered this double death so that we would never have to experience eternal separation from God.

27:47 The bystanders misinterpreted Jesus' words and thought he was calling for Elijah. Because Elijah ascended into heaven without dying (2 Kings 2:11), they thought he would return again to rescue them from great trouble (Malachi 4:5). At their annual Passover feast, each family set an extra place for Elijah in expectation of his return.

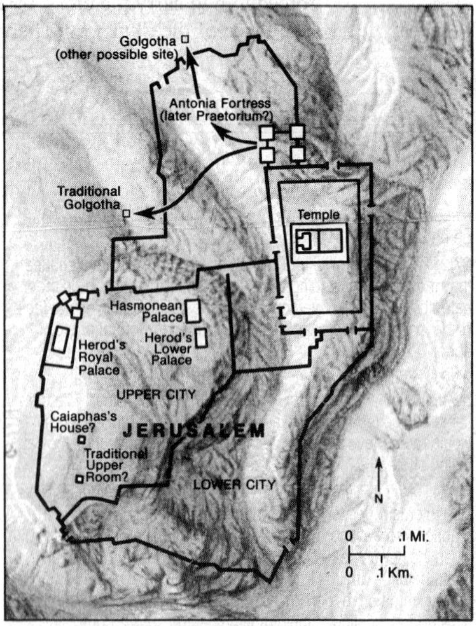

THE WAY OF THE CROSS The Roman soldiers took Jesus into the Praetorium and mocked him, dressing him in a scarlet robe and a crown of thorns. They then led him to the crucifixion site outside the city. He was so weakened by his beatings that he could not carry his cross, and a man from Cyrene was forced to carry it to Golgotha.

51 At that moment the curtain of the temple[a] was torn in two from top to bottom.
The earth shook and the rocks split.[b] 52 The tombs broke open and the bodies of many
holy people who had died were raised to life. 53 They came out of the tombs, and after
Jesus' resurrection they went into the holy city[c] and appeared to many people.
54 When the centurion and those with him who were guarding[d] Jesus saw the
earthquake and all that had happened, they were terrified, and exclaimed, "Surely he
was the Son[e] of God!"[e]
55 Many women were there, watching from a distance. They had followed Jesus
from Galilee to care for his needs.[f] 56 Among them were Mary Magdalene, Mary the
mother of James and Joses, and the mother of Zebedee's sons.[g]

Jesus Is Laid in the Tomb
(237/Mark 15:42–47; Luke 23:50–56; John 19:38–42)

57 As evening approached, there came a rich man from Arimathea, named Joseph,
who had himself become a disciple of Jesus. 58 Going to Pilate, he asked for Jesus'
body, and Pilate ordered that it be given to him. 59 Joseph took the body, wrapped it
in a clean linen cloth, 60 and placed it in his own new tomb[h] that he had cut out of
the rock. He rolled a big stone in front of the entrance to the tomb and went away.
61 Mary Magdalene and the other Mary were sitting there opposite the tomb.

Guards Are Posted at the Tomb
(238)

62 The next day, the one after Preparation Day, the chief priests and the Pharisees
went to Pilate. 63 "Sir," they said, "we remember that while he was still alive that
deceiver said, 'After three days I will rise again.'[i] 64 So give the order for the tomb
to be made secure until the third day. Otherwise, his disciples may come and steal

27:51 [a] Ex 26:31-33; Heb 9:3, 8 [b] ver 54
27:53 [c] Mt 4:5
27:54 [d] ver 36 [e] Mt 4:3; 17:5
27:55 [f] Lk 8:2, 3
27:56 [g] Mk 15:47; Lk 24:10; Jn 19:25
27:60 [h] Mt 27:66; 28:2; Mk 16:4
27:63 [i] Mt 16:21

[e] *54 Or a son*

THE SEVEN LAST WORDS OF JESUS ON THE CROSS

"Father, forgive them, for they do not know what they are doing."	Luke 23:34
"I tell you the truth, today you will be with me in paradise."	Luke 23:43
Speaking to John and Mary, "Dear woman, here is your son. . . . Here is your mother."	John 19:26, 27
"My God, my God, why have you forsaken me?"	Matthew 27:46; Mark 15:34
"I am thirsty."	John 19:28
"It is finished."	John 19:30
"Father, into your hands I commit my spirit."	Luke 23:46

The statements that Jesus made from the cross have been treasured by all who have followed him as Lord. They demonstrate both his humanity and his divinity. They also capture the last moments of all that Jesus went through to gain our forgiveness.

27:51 The temple had three main parts – the courts, the Holy Place (where only the priests could enter), and the Most Holy Place (where only the high priest could enter, and only once a year, to atone for the sins of the nation – Leviticus 16:1–35). The curtain separating the Holy Place from the Most Holy Place was torn in two at Christ's death, symbolising that the barrier between God and humanity was removed. Now all people are free to approach God because of Christ's sacrifice for our sins (see Hebrews 9:1–14; 10:19–22).

27:52, 53 Christ's death was accompanied by at least four miraculous events: darkness, the tearing in two of the curtain in the temple, an earthquake, and dead people rising from their tombs. Jesus' death, therefore, could not have gone unnoticed. Everyone knew something significant had happened.

27:57, 58 Joseph of Arimathea was a secret disciple of Jesus. He was a religious leader, an honoured member of the Sanhedrin (Mark 15:43). In the past, Joseph had been afraid to speak against the religious leaders who opposed Jesus; now he was bold, courageously asking to take Jesus' body from the cross and to bury it. The disciples who publicly followed Jesus had fled, but this Jewish leader, who followed Jesus in secret, came forward and did what was right.

27:60 The tomb where Jesus was laid was probably a man-made cave cut out of one of the many limestone hills in the area. These caves were often large enough to walk into.

27:64 The religious leaders took Jesus' resurrection claims more seriously than the disciples did. The disciples didn't remember Jesus' teaching about his resurrection (20:17–19); but the religious leaders did. Because of his claims, they were almost as afraid of Jesus after his death as when he was alive. They tried to take every precaution that his body would remain in the tomb.

the body and tell the people that he has been raised from the dead. This last deception
will be worse than the first."
65 "Take a guard,"[j] Pilate answered. "Go, make the tomb as secure as you know
how." 66 So they went and made the tomb secure by putting a seal[k] on the stone[l]
and posting the guard.[m]

Jesus Rises from the Dead

(239/Mark 16:1–8; Luke 24:1–12; John 20:1–9)

28 After the Sabbath, at dawn on the first day of the week, Mary Magdalene and
the other Mary[a] went to look at the tomb.
2 There was a violent earthquake,[b] for an angel[c] of the Lord came down from
heaven and, going to the tomb, rolled back the stone and sat on it. 3 His appearance
was like lightning, and his clothes were white as snow.[d] 4 The guards were so afraid
of him that they shook and became like dead men.
5 The angel said to the women, "Do not be afraid,[e] for I know that you are looking
for Jesus, who was crucified. 6 He is not here; he has risen, just as he said.[f] Come
and see the place where he lay. 7 Then go quickly and tell his disciples: 'He has risen
from the dead and is going ahead of you into Galilee.[g] There you will see him.' Now
I have told you."

Jesus Appears to the Women

(241)

8 So the women hurried away from the tomb, afraid yet filled with joy, and ran to
tell his disciples. 9 Suddenly Jesus met them.[h] "Greetings," he said. They came to

27:65 [j] ver 66; Mt 28:11
27:66 [k] Da 6:17 [l] ver 60; Mt 28:2 [m] Mt 28:11
28:1 [a] Mt 27:56
28:2 [b] Mt 27:51 [c] Jn 20:12
28:3 [d] Da 10:6; Mk 9:3; Jn 20:12
28:5 [e] ver 10; Mt 14:27
28:6 [f] Mt 16:21
28:7 [g] ver 10, 16; Mt 26:32
28:9 [h] Jn 20:14-18

HOW JESUS' TRIAL WAS ILLEGAL

1. Even before the trial began, it had been determined that Jesus must die (John 11:50; Mark 14:1). There was no "innocent until proved guilty" approach.
2. False witnesses were sought to testify against Jesus (Matthew 26:59). Usually the religious leaders went through an elaborate system of screening witnesses to ensure justice.
3. No defence for Jesus was sought or allowed (Luke 22:67–71).
4. The trial was conducted at night (Mark 14:53–65; 15:1), which was illegal according to the religious leaders' own laws.
5. The high priest put Jesus under oath, but then incriminated him for what he said (Matthew 26:63–66).
6. Cases involving such serious charges were to be tried only in the Sanhedrin's regular meeting place, not in the high priest's palace (Mark 14:53–65).

The religious leaders were not interested in giving Jesus a fair trial. In their minds, Jesus had to die. This blind obsession led them to pervert the justice they were appointed to protect. Here are many examples of the actions taken by the religious leaders that were illegal according to their own laws.

27:66 The Pharisees were so afraid of Jesus' predictions about his resurrection that they made sure the tomb was thoroughly sealed and guarded. Because the tomb was hewn out of rock in the side of a hill, there was only one entrance. The tomb was sealed by stringing a cord across the stone that was rolled over the entrance. The cord was sealed at each end with clay. But the religious leaders took a further precaution, asking that guards be placed at the tomb's entrance. With such precautions, the only way the tomb could be empty would be for Jesus to rise from the dead. The Pharisees failed to understand that no rock, seal, guard, or army could prevent the Son of God from rising again.

28:1 The other Mary was not Jesus' mother. She could have been the wife of Clopas (John 19:25). Or, if she was the mother of James and John (Matthew 27:56), she may have been Jesus' aunt.

28:2 The stone was not rolled back so Jesus could get out, but so others could get in and see that Jesus had indeed risen from the dead, just as he had promised.

28:5–7 The angel who announced the good news of the resurrection to the women gave them four messages: (1) *Do not be afraid.* The reality of the resurrection brings joy, not fear. When you are afraid, remember the empty tomb. (2) *He is not here.* Jesus is not dead and is not to be looked for among the dead. He is alive, with his people. (3) *Come and see.* The women could check the evidence themselves. The tomb was empty then, and it is empty today. The resurrection is a historical fact. (4) *Go quickly and tell.* They were to spread the joy of the resurrection. We too are to spread the great news about Jesus' resurrection.

28:6 Jesus' resurrection is the key to the Christian faith. Why? (1) Just as he promised, Jesus rose from the dead. We can be confident, therefore, that he will accomplish all he has promised. (2) Jesus' bodily resurrection shows us that the living Christ is ruler

28:10
[i]Jn 20:17; Ro 8:29; Heb 2:11-13, 17

28:11
[j]Mt 27:65, 66

28:14
[k]Mt 27:2

28:16
[l]ver 7, 10; Mt 26:32

28:18
[m]Da 7:13, 14; Lk 10:22; Jn 3:35; 17:2; 1Co 15:27; Eph 1:20-22; Php 2:9, 10

28:19
[n]Mk 16:15, 16; Lk 24:47; Ac 1:8; 14:21
[o]Ac 2:38; 8:16; Ro 6:3, 4

28:20
[p]Ac 2:42
[q]Mt 18:20; Ac 18:10
[r]Mt 13:39

him, clasped his feet and worshipped him. 10Then Jesus said to them, "Do not be
afraid. Go and tell my brothers[i] to go to Galilee; there they will see me."

Religious Leaders Bribe the Guards
(242)

11While the women were on their way, some of the guards[j] went into the city and
reported to the chief priests everything that had happened. 12When the chief priests
had met with the elders and devised a plan, they gave the soldiers a large sum of
money, 13telling them, "You are to say, 'His disciples came during the night and stole
him away while we were asleep.' 14If this report gets to the governor,[k] we will satisfy
him and keep you out of trouble." 15So the soldiers took the money and did as they
were instructed. And this story has been widely circulated among the Jews to this very
day.

Jesus Gives the Great Commission
(248/Mark 16:15–18)

16Then the eleven disciples went to Galilee, to the mountain where Jesus had told
them to go.[l] 17When they saw him, they worshipped him; but some doubted. 18Then
Jesus came to them and said, "All authority in heaven and on earth has been given
to me.[m] 19Therefore go and make disciples of all nations,[n] baptising them in[a] the
name of the Father and of the Son and of the Holy Spirit,[o] 20and teaching[p] them
to obey everything I have commanded you. And surely I am with you[q] always, to
the very end of the age."[r]

a *19* Or *into*; see Acts 8:16; 19:5; Rom. 6:3; 1 Cor. 1:13; 10:2 and Gal. 3:27.

---

of God's eternal kingdom, not a false prophet or imposter. (3) We can be certain of our resurrection because he was resurrected. Death is not the end – there is future life. (4) The power that brought Jesus back to life is available to us to bring our spiritually dead selves back to life. (5) The resurrection is the basis for the church's witness to the world. Jesus is more than just a human leader; he is the Son of God.

28:10 By "brothers", Jesus probably meant his disciples. This showed that he had forgiven them, even after they had disowned and deserted him. Their relationship would now be even stronger than before.

28:10 Jesus told the women to pass a message on to the disciples – that he would meet them in Galilee, as he had previously told them (Mark 14:28). But the disciples, afraid of the religious leaders, stayed hidden behind locked doors in Jerusalem (John 20:19). So Jesus met them there first (Luke 24:36) and then later in Galilee (John 21).

28:11–15 Jesus' resurrection was already causing a great stir in Jerusalem. A group of women were moving quickly through the streets, looking for the disciples to tell them the amazing news that Jesus was alive. At the same time, a group of religious leaders were plotting how to cover up the resurrection.

Today there is still a great stir over the resurrection, and there are still only two choices – to believe that Jesus rose from the dead, or to be closed to the truth – denying it, ignoring it, or trying to explain it away.

28:18 God gave Jesus authority over heaven and earth. On the basis of that authority, Jesus told his disciples to make more disciples as they preached, baptised, and taught. With this same authority, Jesus still commands us to tell others the Good News and make them disciples for the kingdom.

28:18–20 When someone is dying or leaving us, his or her last words are very important. Jesus left the disciples with these last words of instruction: they were under his authority; they were to make more disciples; they were to baptise and teach these new disciples to obey Christ; Christ would be with them always. Whereas in previous missions Jesus had sent his disciples only to the Jews (10:5, 6), their mission from now on would be worldwide. Jesus is Lord of the earth, and he died for the sins of people from all nations.

We are to go – whether it is next door or to another country – and make disciples. It is not an option, but a command to all who call Jesus "Lord". We are not all evangelists in the formal sense, but we have all received gifts that we can use to help fulfil the Great Commission. As we obey, we have comfort in the knowledge that Jesus is always with us.

28:19 Jesus' words affirm the reality of the Trinity. Some people accuse theologians of making up the concept of the Trinity and reading it into Scripture. As we see here, the concept comes directly from Jesus himself. He did not say baptise them into the *names,* but into the *name* of the Father, Son, and Holy Spirit. The word *Trinity* does not occur in Scripture, but it well describes the three-in-one nature of the Father, Son, and Holy Spirit.

28:19 The disciples were to baptise people because baptism unites a believer with Jesus Christ in his or her death to sin and resurrection to new life. Baptism symbolises submission to Christ, a willingness to live God's way, and identification with God's covenant people.

28:20 How is Jesus *with* us? Jesus was with the disciples physically until he ascended into heaven, and then spiritually through the Holy Spirit (Acts 1:4). The Holy Spirit would be Jesus' presence that would never leave them (John 14:26). Jesus continues to be with us today through his Spirit.

28:20 The Old Testament prophecies and genealogies in the book of Matthew present Jesus' credentials for being King of the world – not a military or political leader, as the disciples had originally hoped, but a spiritual King who can overcome all evil and rule in the heart of every person. If we refuse to serve the King faithfully, we are disloyal subjects, fit only to be banished from the kingdom. We must make Jesus King of our lives and worship him as our Saviour, King, and Lord.

MARK

Herod the Great begins to rule 37 B.C.	Jesus is born 6/5 B.C.	Escape to Egypt 5/4 B.C.	Herod the Great dies 4 B.C.	Return to Nazareth 4/3 B.C.	Jesus visits temple as a boy A.D. 6/7

VITAL STATISTICS

PURPOSE:
To present the person, work, and teachings of Jesus

AUTHOR:
John Mark. He was not one of the 12 disciples but he accompanied Paul on his first missionary journey (Acts 13:13).

TO WHOM WRITTEN:
The Christians in Rome, where he wrote the Gospel

DATE WRITTEN:
Between A.D. 55 and 65

SETTING:
The Roman empire under Tiberius Caesar. The empire, with its common language and excellent transportation and communication systems, was ripe to hear Jesus' message, which spread quickly from nation to nation.

KEY VERSE:
"For even the Son of Man did not come to be served, but to serve, and to give his life as a ransom for many" (10:45).

KEY PEOPLE:
Jesus, the 12 disciples, Pilate, the Jewish religious leaders

KEY PLACES:
Capernaum, Nazareth, Caesarea Philippi, Jericho, Bethany, Mount of Olives, Jerusalem, Golgotha

SPECIAL FEATURES:
Mark was probably the first Gospel written. The other Gospels quote all but 31 verses of Mark. Mark records more miracles than does any other Gospel.

WE'RE number one! . . . The greatest, strongest, prettiest . . . champions! Daily those proclamations boldly assert claims of supremacy. Everyone wants to be and be with a winner. Losers are those who finish less than first. In direct contrast are the words of Jesus, "And whoever wants to be first must be slave of all. For even the Son of Man did not come to be served, but to serve, and to give his life as a ransom for many" (10:44, 45). Jesus *is* the greatest—God incarnate, our Messiah—but he entered history as a servant.

This is the message of Mark. Written to encourage Roman Christians and to prove beyond a doubt that Jesus is the Messiah, Mark presents a rapid succession of vivid pictures of Jesus in action—his true identity revealed by what he does, not necessarily by what he says. It is Jesus on the move.

Omitting the birth of Jesus, Mark begins with John the Baptist's preaching. Then, moving quickly past Jesus' baptism, temptation in the desert, and call of the disciples, Mark takes us directly into Jesus' public ministry. We see Jesus confronting a demon, healing a leper, and forgiving and healing the paralytic lowered into Jesus' presence by friends.

Next, Jesus called Matthew (Levi) and had dinner with him and his questionable associates. This initiated the conflict with the Pharisees and other religious leaders who condemned Jesus for eating with sinners and breaking the Sabbath.

In chapter 4, Mark pauses to give a sample of Jesus' teaching—the parable of the sower and the illustration of the mustard seed—and then plunges back into the action. Jesus calmed the waves, drove out demons, and healed Jairus' daughter.

After returning to Nazareth for a few days and experiencing rejection in his home town, Jesus commissioned the disciples to spread the good news everywhere. Opposition from Herod and the Pharisees increased and John the Baptist was beheaded. But Jesus continued to move, feeding 5,000, reaching out to the Syrophoenician woman, healing the deaf man, and feeding 4,000.

Finally it was time to reveal his true identity to the disciples. Did they really know who Jesus was? Peter proclaimed him Messiah, but then promptly showed that he did not understand Jesus' mission. After the transfiguration, Jesus continued to teach and heal, confronting the Pharisees about divorce and the rich young man about eternal life. Blind Bartimaeus was healed.

Events moved rapidly towards a climax. The Last Supper, the betrayal, the crucifixion, and the resurrection are dramatically portrayed, along with more examples of Jesus' teachings. Mark shows us Jesus—moving, serving, sacrificing, and saving! As you read Mark, be ready for action, be open for God's move into your life, and be challenged to move into your world to serve.

Tiberius Caesar becomes emperor 14	John's ministry begins 26	Jesus begins his ministry 26/27	Jesus chooses twelve disciples 28	Jesus feeds 5,000 29	Jesus is crucified, rises again, and ascends 30

THE BLUEPRINT

A. BIRTH AND PREPARATION OF JESUS, THE SERVANT (1:1–13)	Jesus did not arrive unannounced or unexpected. The Old Testament prophets had clearly predicted the coming of a great One, sent by God himself, who would offer salvation and eternal peace to Israel and the entire world. Then came John the Baptist, who announced that the long-awaited Messiah had finally come and would soon be among the people. In God's work in the world today, Jesus does not come unannounced or unexpected. Yet many still reject him. We have the witness of the Bible, but some choose to ignore it, just as many ignored John the Baptist in his day.
B. MESSAGE AND MINISTRY OF JESUS, THE SERVANT (1:14—13:37) 1. Jesus' ministry in Galilee 2. Jesus' ministry beyond Galilee 3. Jesus' ministry in Jerusalem	Jesus had all the power of almighty God—he raised the dead, gave sight to the blind, restored deformed bodies, and quieted stormy seas. But with all this power, Jesus came to mankind as a servant. We can use his life as a pattern for how to live today. As Jesus served God and others, so should we.
C. DEATH AND RESURRECTION OF JESUS, THE SERVANT (14:1—16:20)	Jesus came as a servant, so many did not recognise or acknowledge him as the Messiah. We, too, must be careful we don't reject God or his will because he doesn't quite fit our image of what God should be.

MEGATHEMES

THEME	EXPLANATION	IMPORTANCE
Jesus Christ	Jesus Christ alone is the Son of God. In Mark, Jesus demonstrates his divinity by overcoming disease, demons, and death. Although he had the power to be king of the earth, Jesus chose to obey the Father and die for us.	When Jesus rose from the dead, he proved that he was God, that he could forgive sin, and that he has the power to change our lives. By trusting in him for forgiveness, we can begin a new life with him as our guide.
Servant	As the Messiah, Jesus fulfilled the prophecies of the Old Testament by coming to earth. He did not come as a conquering king; he came as a servant. He helped mankind by telling them about God and healing them. Even more, by giving his life as a sacrifice for sin, he did the ultimate act of service.	Because of Jesus' example, we should be willing to serve God and others. Real greatness in Christ's kingdom is shown by service and sacrifice. Ambition or love of power or position should not be our motive; instead, we should do God's work because we love him.
Miracles	Mark records more of Jesus' miracles than sermons. Jesus is clearly a man of power and action, not just words. Jesus did miracles to convince the people who he was and to teach the disciples his true identity as God.	The more convinced we become that Jesus is God, the more we will see his power and his love. His mighty works show us he is able to save anyone regardless of his or her past. His miracles of forgiveness bring healing, wholeness, and changed lives to those who trust him.
Spreading the Gospel	Jesus directed his public ministry to the Jews first. When the Jewish leaders opposed him, Jesus also went to the non-Jewish world, healing and preaching. Roman soldiers, Syrians, and other Gentiles heard the good news. Many believed and followed him. Jesus' final message to his disciples challenged them to go into all the world and preach the gospel of salvation.	Jesus crossed national, racial, and economic barriers to spread his good news. Jesus' message of faith and forgiveness is for the whole world—not just our church, neighbourhood, or nation. We must reach out beyond our own people and needs to fulfil the worldwide vision of Jesus Christ that people everywhere might hear this great message and be saved from sin and death.

KEY PLACES IN MARK

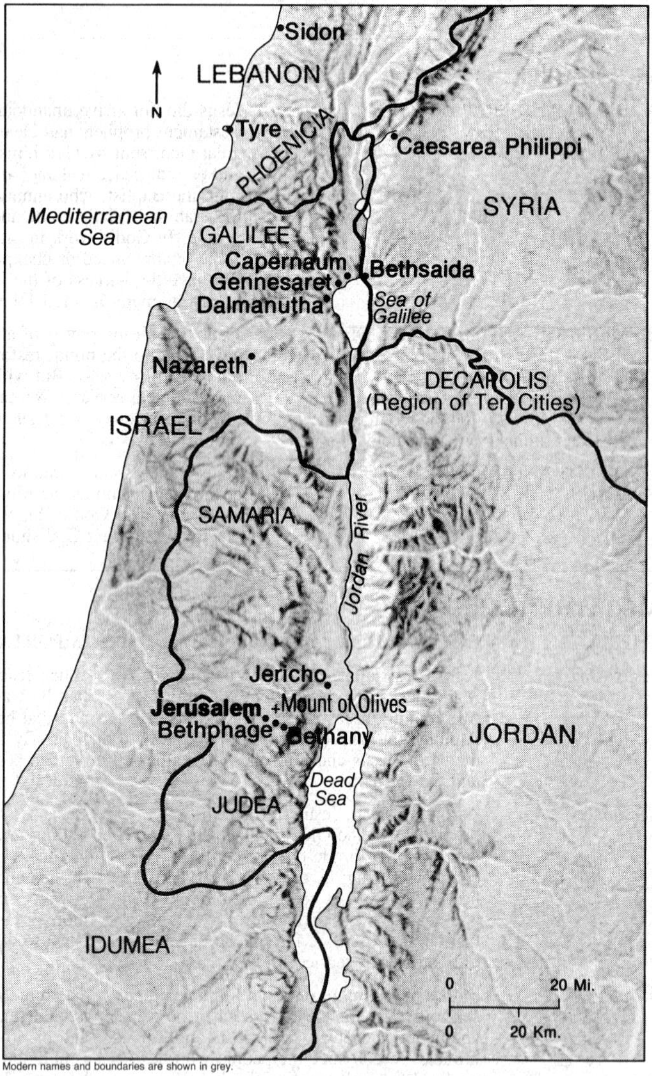

Modern names and boundaries are shown in grey.

Of the four Gospels, Mark's narrative is the most chronological—that is, most of the stories are positioned in the order they actually occurred. Though the shortest of the four, the Gospel of Mark contains the most events; it is action-packed. Most of this action centres in Galilee, where Jesus began his ministry. Capernaum served as his base of operation (1:21; 2:1; 9:33), from which he would go out to cities like Bethsaida—where he healed a blind man (8:22ff); Gennesaret—where he performed many healings (6:53ff); Tyre and Sidon (to the far north)—where he healed many, drove out demons, and met the Syrophoenician woman (3:8; 7:24ff); and Caesarea Philippi—where Peter declared him to be the Messiah (8:27ff). After his ministry in Galilee and the surrounding regions, Jesus headed for Jerusalem (10:1). Before going there, Jesus told his disciples three times that he would be crucified there and then come back to life (8:31; 9:31; 10:33, 34).

A. BIRTH AND PREPARATION OF JESUS, THE SERVANT (1:1–13)

Mark, the shortest of the four Gospels, opens with Jesus' baptism and temptation. Moving right into action, Mark quickly prepares us for Christ's ministry. The Gospel of Mark is concise, straightforward, and chronological.

John the Baptist Prepares the Way for Jesus

(16/Matthew 3:1–12; Luke 3:1–18)

1:1 [a]Mt 4:3

1 The beginning of the gospel about Jesus Christ, the Son of God.[a] [a]

2 It is written in Isaiah the prophet:

1:2 [b]Mal 3:1; Mt 11:10; Lk 7:27

"I will send my messenger ahead of you,
who will prepare your way"[b] [b]—
3 "a voice of one calling in the desert,
'Prepare the way for the Lord,
make straight paths for him.' "[c] [c]

1:3 [c]Isa 40:3; Jn 1:23

1:4 [d]Mt 3:1 [e]Ac 13:24 [f]Lk 1:77

4 And so John[d] came, baptising in the desert region and preaching a baptism of
repentance[e] for the forgiveness of sins.[f] 5 The whole Judean countryside and all the
people of Jerusalem went out to him. Confessing their sins, they were baptised by him
in the Jordan River. 6 John wore clothing made of camel's hair, with a leather belt

a *1* Some manuscripts do not have *the Son of God.* **b** *2* Mal. 3:1 **c** *3* Isaiah 40:3

1:1 When you experience the excitement of a big event, you naturally want to tell someone. Telling the story can bring back that original thrill as you relive the experience. Reading Mark's first words, you can sense his excitement. Picture yourself in the crowd as Jesus heals and teaches. Imagine yourself as one of the disciples. Respond to his words of love and encouragement. And remember that Jesus came for us who live today as well as for those who lived 2,000 years ago.

1:1 Mark was not one of the 12 disciples of Jesus, but he probably knew Jesus personally. Mark wrote his Gospel in the form of a fast-paced story, like a popular novel. The book portrays Jesus as a man who backed up his words with action that constantly proved who he is—the Son of God. Because Mark wrote the Gospel for Christians in Rome, where many gods were worshipped, he wanted his readers to know that Jesus is *the one true* Son of God.

1:2 Jesus came at a time in history when the entire civilised world was relatively peaceful under Roman rule, travel was easy, and there was a common language. The news about Jesus' life, death, and resurrection could spread quickly throughout the vast Roman empire.

In Israel, common men and women were ready for Jesus too. There had been no God-sent prophets for 400 years, since the days of Malachi (who wrote the last book of the Old Testament). There was growing anticipation that a great prophet, or the Messiah mentioned in the Old Testament, would soon come (see Luke 3:15).

1:2, 3 Isaiah was one of the greatest prophets of the Old Testament. The second half of the book of Isaiah is devoted to the promise of salvation. Isaiah wrote about the coming of the Messiah, Jesus Christ, and the man who would announce his coming, John the Baptist. John's call to "make straight paths for him" meant that people should give up their selfish way of living, renounce their sins, seek God's forgiveness, and establish a relationship with the almighty God by believing and obeying his words as found in Scripture (Isaiah 1:18–20; 57:15).

1:2, 3 Mark 1:2, 3 is a composite quotation, taken first from Malachi 3:1 and then from Isaiah 40:3.

1:2, 3 Hundreds of years earlier, the prophet Isaiah had predicted that John the Baptist and Jesus would come. How did he know? God promised Isaiah that a Redeemer would come to Israel, and that a messenger calling in the desert would prepare the way for him. Isaiah's words comforted many people as they looked forward to the Messiah, and knowing that God keeps his promises can comfort you too. As you read the book of Mark, realise that it is more than just a story; it is part of God's word. In it God is revealing to you his plans for human history.

1:4 Why does the Gospel of Mark begin with the story of John the Baptist and not mention the story of Jesus' birth? Important Roman officials of this day were always preceded by an announcer or herald. When the herald arrived in town, the people knew that someone of prominence would soon arrive. Because Mark's audience was primarily Roman Christians, he began his book with John the Baptist, whose mission it was to announce the coming of Jesus, the most important man who ever lived. Roman Christians would have been less interested in Jesus' birth than in this messenger who prepared the way.

1:4 John chose to live in the desert (1) to get away from distractions so he could hear God's instructions; (2) to capture the undivided attention of the people; (3) to symbolise a sharp break with the hypocrisy of the religious leaders who preferred their luxurious homes and positions of authority to doing God's work; (4) to fulfil Old Testament prophecies that said John would be "a voice of one calling: in the desert prepare the way for the LORD" (Isaiah 40:3).

1:4 In John's ministry, baptism was a visible sign that a person had decided to change his or her life, giving up a sinful and selfish way of living and turning to God. John took a known custom and gave it new meaning. The Jews often baptised non-Jews who had converted to Judaism. But to baptise a Jew as a sign of repentance was a radical departure from Jewish custom. The early church took baptism a step further, associating it with Jesus' death and resurrection (see, for example, Romans 6:3, 4; 1 Peter 3:21).

1:5 The purpose of John's preaching was to prepare people to accept Jesus as God's Son. When John challenged the people to confess sin individually, he signalled the start of a new way to relate to God.

Is change needed in your life before you can hear and understand Jesus' message? You have to admit that you need forgiveness before you can accept it. To prepare to receive Christ, repent. Denounce the world's dead-end attractions, sinful temptations, and harmful attitudes.

1:6 John's clothes were not the latest style of his day. He dressed much like the prophet Elijah (2 Kings 1:8) in order to distinguish himself from the religious leaders, whose flowing robes reflected their great pride in their position (12:38). John's striking appearance reinforced his striking message.

round his waist, and he ate locusts[g] and wild honey. 7And this was his message:
"After me will come one more powerful than I, the thongs of whose sandals I am not
worthy to stoop down and untie.[h] 8I baptise you with[d] water, but he will baptise
you with the Holy Spirit."[i]

John Baptises Jesus
(17/Matthew 3:13–17; Luke 3:21, 22)

9At that time Jesus came from Nazareth[j] in Galilee and was baptised by John in
the Jordan. 10As Jesus was coming up out of the water, he saw heaven being torn open
and the Spirit descending on him like a dove.[k] 11And a voice came from heaven: "You
are my Son,[l] whom I love; with you I am well pleased."

Satan Tempts Jesus in the Desert
(18/Matthew 4:1–11; Luke 4:1–13)

12At once the Spirit sent him out into the desert, 13and he was in the desert for forty
days, being tempted by Satan.[m] He was with the wild animals, and angels attended
him.

[d] 8 Or *in*

1:6 [g] Lev 11:22
1:7 [h] Ac 13:25
1:8 [i] Isa 44:3; Joel 2:28; Ac 1:5; 2:4; 11:16; 19:4-6
1:9 [j] Mt 2:23
1:10 [k] Jn 1:32
1:11 [l] Mt 3:17
1:13 [m] Mt 4:10

1:7, 8 Although John was the first genuine prophet in 400 years, Jesus the Messiah would be infinitely greater than he. John was pointing out how insignificant he was compared to the one who was coming. John was not even worthy of doing the most menial tasks for him, like untying his sandals. What John began, Jesus finished. What John prepared, Jesus fulfilled.

1:8 John said Jesus would baptise them with the Holy Spirit, sending the Holy Spirit to live within each believer. John's baptism with water prepared a person to receive Christ's message. This baptism demonstrated repentance, humility, and willingness to turn from sin. This was the *beginning* of the spiritual process.

When Jesus baptises with the Holy Spirit, however, the entire person is transformed by the Spirit's power. Jesus offers to us both forgiveness of sin and the power to live for him.

1:9 If John's baptism was for repentance from sin, why was Jesus baptised? While even the greatest prophets (Isaiah, Jeremiah, Ezekiel) had to confess their sinfulness and need for repentance, Jesus didn't need to admit sin – he was sinless. Although Jesus didn't need forgiveness, he was baptised for the following reasons: (1) to begin his mission to bring the message of salvation to all people; (2) to show support for John's ministry; (3) to identify with our humanness and sin; (4) to give us an example to follow. We know that John's baptism was different from Christian baptism in the church because Paul had John's followers baptised again (see Acts 19:2–5).

1:9 Jesus grew up in Nazareth, where he had lived since he was a young boy (Matthew 2:22, 23). Nazareth was a small town in Galilee, located about halfway between the Sea of Galilee and the Mediterranean Sea. The city was despised and avoided by many Jews because it had a reputation for independence. Nazareth was a crossroads for trade routes and had contact with other cultures. (See also John 1:46.)

1:10, 11 The Spirit descended like a dove on Jesus, and the voice from heaven proclaimed the Father's approval of Jesus as his divine Son. That Jesus is God's divine Son is the foundation for all we read about Jesus in the Gospels. Here we see all three members of the Trinity together – God the Father, God the Son, and God the Holy Spirit.

1:12, 13 Jesus left the crowds and went into the desert where he was tempted by Satan. Temptation is bad for us only when we give in. We should not hate or resent times of inner testing, because through them God can strengthen our character and teach us valuable lessons. When you face Satan and must deal with his temptations and the turmoil he brings, remember Jesus. He used God's word against Satan and won. You can do the same.

1:12, 13 Satan is an angel who rebelled against God. He is real, not symbolic, and is constantly working against God and those who obey him. Satan tempted Eve in the garden and persuaded her to sin; he tempted Jesus in the desert and did not persuade him to fall. To be tempted is not a sin. Tempting others or giving in to temptation *is* sin. For a more detailed account of Jesus' temptation, read Matthew 4:1–11.

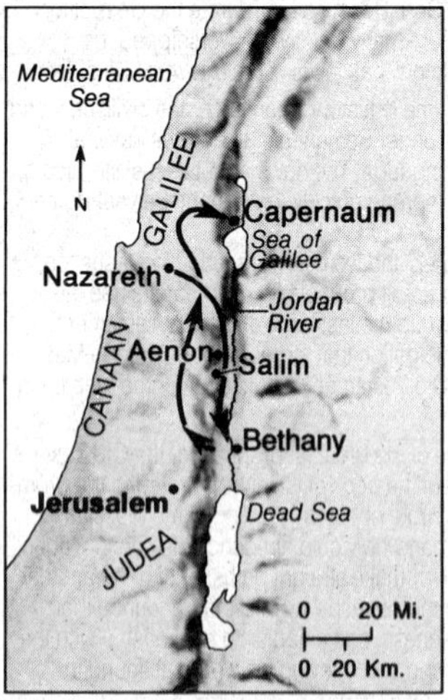

JESUS BEGINS HIS MINISTRY
When Jesus came from his home in Nazareth to begin his ministry, he first took two steps in preparation – baptism by John in the Jordan River, and temptation by Satan in the rough Judean desert. After the temptations, Jesus returned to Galilee and later set up his home base in Capernaum.

1:12, 13 To identify fully with human beings, Jesus had to endure Satan's temptations. Although Jesus is God, he is also man. And as fully human, he was not exempt from Satan's attacks. Because Jesus faced temptations and overcame them, he can assist us in two important ways: (1) as an example of how to face temptation without sinning, and (2) as a helper who knows just what we need because he went through the same experience. (See Hebrews 4:16 for more on Jesus and temptation.)

B. MESSAGE AND MINISTRY OF JESUS, THE SERVANT (1:14–13:37)

Mark tells us dramatic, action-packed stories. He gives us the most vivid account of Christ's activities. He features facts and actions rather than teachings. The way Jesus lived his life is the perfect example of how we should live our lives today.

1. Jesus' ministry in Galilee

Jesus Preaches in Galilee

(30/Matthew 4:12–17; Luke 4:14, 15; John 4:43–45)

14 After John was put in prison, Jesus went into Galilee,[n] proclaiming the good
news of God.[o] 15 "The time has come,"[p] he said. "The kingdom of God is near.
Repent and believe the good news!"[q]

Four Fishermen Follow Jesus

(33/Matthew 4:18–22)

16 As Jesus walked beside the Sea of Galilee, he saw Simon and his brother Andrew
casting a net into the lake, for they were fishermen. 17 "Come, follow me," Jesus said,
"and I will make you fishers of men." 18 At once they left their nets and followed him.
19 When he had gone a little farther, he saw James son of Zebedee and his brother
John in a boat, preparing their nets. 20 Without delay he called them, and they left their
father Zebedee in the boat with the hired men and followed him.

Jesus Teaches with Great Authority

(34/Luke 4:31–37)

21 They went to Capernaum, and when the Sabbath came, Jesus went into the
synagogue and began to teach.[r] 22 The people were amazed at his teaching, because
he taught them as one who had authority, not as the teachers of the law.[s] 23 Just then
a man in their synagogue who was possessed by an evil[e] spirit cried out, 24 "What
do you want with us,[t] Jesus of Nazareth?[u] Have you come to destroy us? I know
who you are — the Holy One of God!"[v]

1:14 [n] Mt 4:12 [o] Mt 4:23
1:15 [p] Gal 4:4; Eph 1:10 [q] Ac 20:21
1:21 [r] Mt 4:23; Mk 10:1
1:22 [s] Mt 7:28, 29
1:24 [t] Mt 8:29 [u] Mt 2:23; Lk 24:19; Ac 24:5 [v] Lk 1:35; Jn 6:69; Ac 3:14

[e] 23 Greek *unclean*; also in verses 26 and 27

1:14, 15 What is the good news of God? These first words spoken by Jesus in Mark give the core of his teaching: that the long-awaited Messiah has come to break the power of sin and begin God's personal reign on earth. Most of the people who heard this message were oppressed, poor, and without hope. Jesus' words were good news because they offered freedom, justice, and hope.

1:16 Fishing was a major industry around the Sea of Galilee. Fishing with nets was the most common method. Capernaum, the largest of the more than 30 fishing towns around the lake at that time, became Jesus' new home (Matthew 4:12, 13).

1:16–20 We often assume that Jesus' disciples were great men of faith from the first time they met Jesus. But they had to grow in their faith just as all believers do (14:48–50, 66–72; John 14:1–9; 20:26–29). This is apparently not the only time Jesus called Peter (Simon), James, and John to follow him (see Luke 5:1–11 and John 1:35–42 for two other times). Although it took time for Jesus' call and his message to get through, the disciples *followed.* In the same way, we may question and falter, but we must never stop following Jesus.

1:21 Because the temple in Jerusalem was too far for many Jews to travel to regularly for worship, many towns had synagogues serving both as places of worship and as schools. Beginning in the days of Ezra, about 450 B.C., a group of ten Jewish families could start a synagogue. There, during the week, Jewish boys were taught the Old Testament law and Jewish religion. Girls could not attend. Each Saturday, the Sabbath, the Jewish men would gather to listen to a rabbi teach from the Scriptures. Because there was no permanent rabbi or teacher, it was customary for the synagogue leader to ask visiting teachers to speak. This is why Jesus often spoke in the synagogues in the towns he visited.

1:21 Jesus had recently moved to Capernaum from Nazareth (Matthew 4:12, 13). Capernaum was a thriving town with great wealth as well as great sin and decadence. Because it was the headquarters for many Roman troops, pagan influences from all over the Roman empire were pervasive. This was an ideal place for Jesus to challenge both Jews and non-Jews with the gospel of God's kingdom.

1:22 The Jewish teachers often quoted from well-known rabbis to give their words more authority. But Jesus didn't have that need. Because Jesus is God, he knew exactly what the Scriptures said and meant. He was the ultimate authority.

1:23 Evil spirits, or demons, are ruled by Satan. They work to tempt people to sin. They were not created by Satan — because God is the Creator of all. Rather they are fallen angels who joined Satan in his rebellion. Though not all disease comes from Satan, demons can cause a person to become mute, deaf, blind, or insane. But in every case where demons confronted Jesus, they lost their power. Thus God limits what evil spirits can do; they can do nothing without his permission. During Jesus' life on earth, demons were allowed to be very active to demonstrate once and for all Christ's power and authority over them.

1:23ff Many psychologists dismiss all accounts of demon-possession as a primitive way to describe mental illness. Although throughout history mental illness has often been wrongly diagnosed as demon-possession, clearly a hostile outside force controlled the man described here. Mark emphasised Jesus' conflict with evil powers to show his superiority over them, so he recorded many stories about Jesus driving out evil spirits. Jesus didn't have to conduct an elaborate exorcism ritual. His word was enough to send out the demons.

1:23, 24 The evil spirit knew at once that Jesus was the Holy One of God. By including this event in his Gospel, Mark was establishing Jesus' credentials, showing that even the spiritual underworld recognised Jesus as the Messiah.

25 “Be quiet!” said Jesus sternly. “Come out of him!”[w] 26 The evil spirit shook the
man violently and came out of him with a shriek.[x]
27 The people were all so amazed[y] that they asked each other, “What is this? A new
teaching—and with authority! He even gives orders to evil spirits and they obey him.”
28 News about him spread quickly over the whole region[z] of Galilee.

Jesus Heals Peter's Mother-in-Law and Many Others
(35/Matthew 8:14–17; Luke 4:38–41)

29 As soon as they left the synagogue,[a] they went with James and John to the home
of Simon and Andrew. 30 Simon's mother-in-law was in bed with a fever, and they
told Jesus about her. 31 So he went to her, took her hand and helped her up.[b] The
fever left her and she began to wait on them.
32 That evening after sunset the people brought to Jesus all the sick and demon-
possessed.[c] 33 The whole town gathered at the door, 34 and Jesus healed many who
had various diseases.[d] He also drove out many demons, but he would not let the
demons speak because they knew who he was.[e]

Jesus Preaches throughout Galilee
(36/Matthew 4:23–25; Luke 4:42–44)

35 Very early in the morning, while it was still dark, Jesus got up, left the house
and went off to a solitary place, where he prayed.[f] 36 Simon and his companions went
to look for him, 37 and when they found him, they exclaimed: “Everyone is looking
for you!”
38 Jesus replied, “Let us go somewhere else—to the nearby villages—so that I can
preach there also. That is why I have come.”[g] 39 So he travelled throughout Galilee,
preaching in their synagogues[h] and driving out demons.[i]

Jesus Heals a Man with Leprosy
(38/Matthew 8:1–4; Luke 5:12–16)

40 A man with leprosy[f] came to him and begged him on his knees,[j] “If you are
willing, you can make me clean.”
41 Filled with compassion, Jesus reached out his hand and touched the man. “I am
willing,” he said. “Be clean!” 42 Immediately the leprosy left him and he was cured.
43 Jesus sent him away at once with a strong warning: 44 “See that you don't tell this

[f] *40* The Greek word was used for various diseases affecting the skin—not necessarily leprosy.

1:25 [w] ver 34
1:26 [x] Mk 9:20
1:27 [y] Mk 10:24, 32
1:28 [z] Mt 9:26
1:29 [a] ver 21, 23
1:31 [b] Lk 7:14
1:32 [c] Mt 4:24
1:34 [d] Mt 4:23 [e] Mk 3:12; Ac 16:17, 18
1:35 [f] Lk 3:21
1:38 [g] Isa 61:1
1:39 [h] Mt 4:23 [i] Mt 4:24
1:40 [j] Mk 10:17

1:29–31 Each Gospel writer had a slightly different perspective as he wrote; thus the comparable stories in the Gospels often highlight different details. In Matthew, Jesus touched the woman's hand. In Mark, he helped her up. In Luke, he spoke to the fever, and it left her. The accounts do not conflict. Each writer chose to emphasise different details of the story in order to emphasise a certain characteristic of Jesus.

1:32, 33 The people came to Jesus in the evening after sunset. This was the Sabbath (1:21), their day of rest, lasting from sunset Friday to sunset Saturday. The Jewish leaders had proclaimed that it was against the law to be healed on the Sabbath (Matthew 12:10; Luke 13:14). The people didn't want to break this law or the Jewish law that prohibited travelling on the Sabbath, so they waited until sunset. After the sun went down, the crowds were free to find Jesus so he could heal them.

1:34 Why didn't Jesus want the demons to reveal who he was? (1) By commanding the demons to remain silent, Jesus proved his authority and power over them. (2) Jesus wanted the people to believe he was the Messiah because of what he said and did, not because of the demons' words. (3) Jesus wanted to reveal his identity as the Messiah according to his timetable, not according to Satan's timetable. Satan wanted the people to follow Jesus around for what they could get out of him, not because he was the Son of God who could truly set them free from sin's guilt and power.

1:35 Jesus took time to pray. Finding time to pray is not easy, but prayer is the vital link between us and God. Like Jesus, we must break away from others to talk with God, even if we have to get up very early in the morning to do it!

1:39 The Romans divided the land of Israel into three separate regions: Galilee, Samaria, and Judea. Galilee was the northernmost region, an area about 60 miles long and 30 miles wide. Jesus did much of his ministry in this area, an ideal place for him to teach because there were over 250 towns concentrated there, with many synagogues.

1:40, 41 In keeping with the law in Leviticus 13 and 14, Jewish leaders declared people with leprosy unclean. This meant that lepers were unfit to participate in any religious or social activity. Because the law said that contact with any unclean person made a person unclean too, some people even threw rocks at lepers to keep them at a safe distance. Even the mention of the name of this disabling disease terrified people. But Jesus touched this man who had leprosy.

The real value of a person is inside, not outside. Although a person's body may be diseased or deformed, the person inside is no less valuable to God. No person is too disgusting for God's touch. In a sense, we are all people with leprosy because we have all been deformed by the ugliness of sin. But God, by sending his Son Jesus, has touched us, giving us the opportunity to be healed. When you feel repulsed by someone, stop and remember how God feels about that person—and about you.

1:44 [k]Mt 8:4 [l]Lev 13:49 [m]Lev 14:1-32
1:45 [n]Lk 5:15, 16 [o]Mk 2:13; Lk 5:17; Jn 6:2
2:2 [a]ver 13; Mk 1:45
2:3 [b]Mt 4:24
2:5 [c]Lk 7:48
2:7 [d]Isa 43:25
2:10 [e]Mt 8:20
2:12 [f]Mt 9:8 [g]Mt 9:33
2:13 [h]Mk 1:45; Lk 5:15; Jn 6:2

to anyone.[k] But go, show yourself to the priest[l] and offer the sacrifices that Moses commanded for your cleansing,[m] as a testimony to them." 45 Instead he went out and began to talk freely, spreading the news. As a result, Jesus could no longer enter a town openly but stayed outside in lonely places.[n] Yet the people still came to him from everywhere.[o]

Jesus Heals a Paralysed Man
(39/Matthew 9:1–8; Luke 5:17–26)

2 A few days later, when Jesus again entered Capernaum, the people heard that he had come home. 2 So many[a] gathered that there was no room left, not even outside the door, and he preached the word to them. 3 Some men came, bringing to him a paralytic,[b] carried by four of them. 4 Since they could not get him to Jesus because of the crowd, they made an opening in the roof above Jesus and, after digging through it, lowered the mat the paralysed man was lying on. 5 When Jesus saw their faith, he said to the paralytic, "Son, your sins are forgiven."[c]

6 Now some teachers of the law were sitting there, thinking to themselves, 7 "Why does this fellow talk like that? He's blaspheming! Who can forgive sins but God alone?"[d]

8 Immediately Jesus knew in his spirit that this was what they were thinking in their hearts, and he said to them, "Why are you thinking these things? 9 Which is easier: to say to the paralytic, 'Your sins are forgiven,' or to say, 'Get up, take your mat and walk'? 10 But that you may know that the Son of Man[e] has authority on earth to forgive sins . . . ." He said to the paralytic, 11 "I tell you, get up, take your mat and go home." 12 He got up, took his mat and walked out in full view of them all. This amazed everyone and they praised God,[f] saying, "We have never seen anything like this!"[g]

Jesus Eats with Sinners at Matthew's House
(40/Matthew 9:9–13; Luke 5:27–32)

13 Once again Jesus went out beside the lake. A large crowd came to him,[h] and he began to teach them. 14 As he walked along, he saw Levi son of Alphaeus sitting

---

1:43, 44 Although leprosy was incurable, many different types of skin diseases were classified together as "leprosy". According to the Old Testament laws about leprosy (Leviticus 13; 14), when a leper was cured, he or she had to go to a priest to be examined. Then the leper was to give a thank offering at the temple. Jesus adhered to these laws by sending the man to the priest, demonstrating Jesus' complete regard for God's law. Sending a healed leper to a priest was also a way of verifying Jesus' great miracle to the community.

2:3 The paralytic's need moved his friends to action, and they brought him to Jesus. When you recognise someone's need, do you act? Many people have physical and spiritual needs you can meet, either by yourself or with others who are also concerned. Human need moved these four men; let it also move you to compassionate action.

2:4 Houses in Bible times were built of stone. They had flat roofs made of mud mixed with straw. Outside stairways led to the roofs. These friends may have carried the lame man up the outside stairs to the roof. They then could easily have taken apart the mud and straw mixture to make a hole through which to lower their friend to Jesus.

2:5–7 Before saying to the paralytic, "Get up," Jesus said, "Son, your sins are forgiven." To the Jewish leaders this statement was blasphemous, claiming to do something only God could do. According to the law, the punishment for this sin was death (Leviticus 24:15, 16).

The religious leaders understood correctly that Jesus was claiming divine prerogatives, but their judgment of him was wrong. Jesus was not blaspheming because his claim was true. Jesus is God, and he proved his claim by healing the paralytic (2:9–12).

2:10 This is the first time in Mark that Jesus is referred to as the "Son of Man". The title *Son of Man* emphasises that Jesus is fully human, while *Son of God* (see, for example, John 20:31) emphasises that he is fully God. As God's Son, Jesus has the authority to forgive sin. As a man, he can identify with our deepest needs and sufferings and help us overcome sin (see the note on 8:29–31).

2:14 Levi is another name for Matthew, the disciple who wrote the Gospel of Matthew. See Matthew's Profile in Matthew 9 for more information.

2:14 Capernaum was a key military centre for Roman troops, as well as a thriving business community. Several major routes intersected in Capernaum, with merchants passing through from as far away as Egypt to the south and Mesopotamia to the north.

Levi (Matthew), a Jew, was appointed by the Romans to be the area's tax collector. He collected taxes from citizens as well as from merchants passing through town. Tax collectors were expected to take a commission on the taxes they collected. Most of them overcharged and vastly benefited themselves. Tax collectors were despised by the Jews because of their reputation for cheating and their support of Rome. The Jews must also have hated to think that some of the money collected went to support pagan religions and temples.

2:14, 15 The day that Levi met Jesus, Levi held a meeting at his house to introduce others to Jesus. Levi didn't waste any time in starting to witness! Some people feel that new believers should wait for maturity or training before they begin to tell others about Christ. But like Levi, new believers can share their faith right away with whatever knowledge, skill, or experience they already have.

at the tax collector's booth. "Follow me,"[i] Jesus told him, and Levi got up and 2:14 [i]Mt 4:19
followed him.
15While Jesus was having dinner at Levi's house, many tax collectors and "sinners"
were eating with him and his disciples, for there were many who followed him.
16When the teachers of the law who were Pharisees[j] saw him eating with the 2:16 [j]Ac 23:9
"sinners" and tax collectors, they asked his disciples: "Why does he eat with tax [k]Mt 9:11
collectors and 'sinners'?"[k]
17On hearing this, Jesus said to them, "It is not the healthy who need a doctor, but
the sick. I have not come to call the righteous, but sinners."[l]

2:17 [l]Lk 19:10; 1Ti 1:15

Religious Leaders Ask Jesus about Fasting
(41/Matthew 9:14–17; Luke 5:33–39)

18Now John's disciples and the Pharisees were fasting.[m] Some people came and
asked Jesus, "How is it that John's disciples and the disciples of the Pharisees are
fasting, but yours are not?" 2:18 [m]Mt 6:16-18; Ac 13:2
19Jesus answered, "How can the guests of the bridegroom fast while he is with
them? They cannot, so long as they have him with them. 20But the time will come
when the bridegroom will be taken from them,[n] and on that day they will fast.
21"No-one sews a patch of unshrunk cloth on an old garment. If he does, the new
piece will pull away from the old, making the tear worse. 22And no-one pours new 2:20 [n]Lk 17:22
wine into old wineskins. If he does, the wine will burst the skins, and both the wine
and the wineskins will be ruined. No, he pours new wine into new wineskins."

The Disciples Pick Wheat on the Sabbath
(45/Matthew 12:1–8; Luke 6:1–5) 2:23 [o]Dt 23:25

23One Sabbath Jesus was going through the cornfields, and as his disciples walked
along, they began to pick some ears of corn.[o] 24The Pharisees said to him, "Look,
why are they doing what is unlawful on the Sabbath?"[p]
25He answered, "Have you never read what David did when he and his companions 2:24 [p]Mt 12:2

2:16, 17 The self-righteous Pharisees were indignant that Jesus would eat a meal with such sinners. But Jesus gladly associated with sinners because he loved them and because he knew that they needed to hear what he had to say. Jesus spent time with whoever needed or wanted to hear his message – poor, rich, bad, good. We, too, must befriend those who need Christ, even if they do not seem to be ideal companions. Are there people you have been neglecting because of their reputation? They may be the ones who most need to see and hear the message of Christ's love in and from you.

2:18ff John had two goals: to lead people to repent of their sin, and to prepare them for Christ's coming. John's message was sobering, so he and his followers fasted. Fasting is both an outward sign of humility and regret for sin, and an inner discipline that clears the mind and keeps the spirit alert. Fasting empties the body of food; repentance empties the life of sin. Jesus' disciples did not need to fast to prepare for his coming because he was with them. Jesus did not condemn fasting, however. He himself fasted for 40 days (Matthew 4:2). Nevertheless, Jesus emphasised fasting with the right motives. The Pharisees fasted twice a week to show others how holy they were. Jesus explained that if people fast only to impress others, they will be twisting the purpose of fasting.

2:19 Jesus compared himself to a bridegroom. In the Bible, the image of a bride is often used for God's people, and the image of a bridegroom for the God who loves them (Isaiah 62:5; Matthew 25:1–14; Revelation 21:2).

2:22 A wineskin was a goatskin sewed together at the edges to form a watertight bag. New wine, expanding as it aged, stretched the wineskin. New wine, therefore, could not be put into a wineskin that had already been stretched, or the taut skin would burst.

The Pharisees had become rigid like old wineskins. They could not accept faith in Jesus that would not be contained or limited by man-made ideas or rules. Your heart, like a wineskin, can become rigid and prevent you from accepting the new life that Christ offers. Keep your heart pliable and open to accepting the life-changing truths of Christ.

2:23 Jesus and his disciples were not stealing when they picked the grain. Leviticus 19:9, 10 and Deuteronomy 23:25 say that farmers were to leave the edges of their fields unharvested so that some of their crops could be picked by travellers and by the poor. Just as walking on a pavement is not trespassing on private property, picking heads of grain at the edge of a field was not stealing.

2:24 God's law said that crops should not be harvested on the Sabbath (Exodus 34:21). This law prevented farmers from becoming greedy and ignoring God on the Sabbath. It also protected labourers from being overworked.

The Pharisees interpreted the action of Jesus and his disciples – picking the grain and eating it as they walked through the fields – as harvesting; and so they judged Jesus a lawbreaker. But Jesus and the disciples clearly were not harvesting the grain for personal gain; they were simply looking for something to eat. The Pharisees were so focused on the words of the rule that they missed its intent.

2:24 Many of the Pharisees were so caught up in their man-made laws and traditions that they lost sight of what was good and right. Jesus implied in Mark 3:4 that the Sabbath is a day to do good. God provided the Sabbath as a day of rest and worship, but he didn't mean that concern for rest should keep us from lifting a finger to help others. Don't allow your Sabbath to become a time of selfish indulgence.

2:25–28 Jesus used the example of David to point out how ridiculous the Pharisees' accusations were (this incident occurred in 1 Samuel 21:1–6). God created the Sabbath for our benefit, not his own. God derives no benefit from having us rest on the Sab-

2:26
q2Sa 8:17
rLev 24:5-9
s1Sa 21:1-6
2:27
tEx 23:12
uCol 2:16
2:28
vMt 8:20

were hungry and in need? 26In the days of Abiathar the high priest,[q] he entered the
house of God and ate the consecrated bread, which is lawful only for priests to eat.[r]
And he also gave some to his companions."[s]
27Then he said to them, "The Sabbath was made for man,[t] not man for the
Sabbath.[u] 28So the Son of Man[v] is Lord even of the Sabbath."

PROMINENT JEWISH RELIGIOUS AND POLITICAL GROUPS

Name and Selected References	*Description*	*Agreement with Jesus*	*Disagreement with Jesus*
PHARISEES Matthew 5:20 Matthew 23:1–36 Luke 6:2 Luke 7:36–47	Strict group of religious Jews who advocated minute obedience to the Jewish law and traditions. Very influential in the synagogues.	Respect for the law, belief in the resurrection of the dead, committed to obeying God's will.	Rejected Jesus' claim to be Messiah because he did not follow all their traditions and associated with notoriously wicked people.
SADDUCEES Matthew 3:7 Matthew 16:11, 12 Mark 12:18	Wealthy, upper class, Jewish priestly party. Rejected the authority of the Bible beyond the five books of Moses. Profited from business in the temple. They, along with the Pharisees, were one of the two major parties of the Jewish council.	Showed great respect for the five books of Moses, as well as the sanctity of the temple.	Denied the resurrection of the dead. Thought the temple could also be used as a place to transact business.
TEACHERS OF THE LAW Matthew 7:29 Mark 2:6 Mark 2:16	Professional interpreters of the law—who especially emphasised the traditions. Many teachers of the law were Pharisees.	Respect for the law. Committed to obeying God.	Denied Jesus' authority to reinterpret the law. Rejected Jesus as Messiah because he did not obey all of their traditions.
HERODIANS Matthew 22:16 Mark 3:6 Mark 12:13	A Jewish political party of King Herod's supporters.	Unknown. In the Gospels they tried to trap Jesus with questions and plotted to kill him.	Afraid of Jesus causing political instability. They saw Jesus as a threat to their political future at a time when they were trying to regain from Rome some of their lost political power.
ZEALOTS Luke 6:15 Acts 1:14	A fiercely dedicated group of Jewish patriots determined to end Roman rule in Israel.	Concerned about the future of Israel. Believed in the Messiah but did not recognise Jesus as the One sent by God.	Believed that the Messiah must be a political leader who would deliver Israel from Roman occupation.
ESSENES none	Jewish monastic group practising ritual purity and personal holiness.	Emphasised justice, honesty, commitment.	Believed ceremonial rituals made them righteous.

bath, but we are restored both physically and spiritually when we take time to rest and to focus on God. For the Pharisees, Sabbath laws had become more important than Sabbath rest. Both David and Jesus understood that the intent of God's law is to promote love for God and others. When we apply a law to other people, we should make sure that we understand its purpose and intent so we don't make harmful or inappropriate judgments.

2:26 The "consecrated bread" was the bread set before God in the tabernacle. Every Sabbath, 12 baked loaves of bread were placed on the table in the Holy Place. Then the priests ate the old ones. See Exodus 25:30 and Leviticus 24:5–9 for more about the consecrated bread, also called the bread of the Presence.

Jesus Heals a Man's Hand on the Sabbath
(46/Matthew 12:9–14; Luke 6:6–11)

3 Another time he went into the synagogue,[a] and a man with a shrivelled hand was
there. 2 Some of them were looking for a reason to accuse Jesus, so they watched
him closely[b] to see if he would heal him on the Sabbath.[c] 3 Jesus said to the man
with the shrivelled hand, "Stand up in front of everyone."
4 Then Jesus asked them, "Which is lawful on the Sabbath: to do good or to do evil,
to save life or to kill?" But they remained silent.
5 He looked round at them in anger and, deeply distressed at their stubborn hearts,
said to the man, "Stretch out your hand." He stretched it out, and his hand was
completely restored. 6 Then the Pharisees went out and began to plot with the Herodians[d] how they might kill Jesus.[e]

Large Crowds Follow Jesus
(47/Matthew 12:15–21)

7 Jesus withdrew with his disciples to the lake, and a large crowd from Galilee
followed.[f] 8 When they heard all he was doing, many people came to him from Judea,
Jerusalem, Idumea, and the regions across the Jordan and around Tyre and Sidon.[g]
9 Because of the crowd he told his disciples to have a small boat ready for him, to keep
the people from crowding him. 10 For he had healed many,[h] so that those with diseases
were pushing forward to touch him.[i] 11 Whenever the evil**[a]** spirits saw him, they fell
down before him and cried out, "You are the Son of God."[j] 12 But he gave them strict
orders not to tell who he was.[k]

Jesus Selects the Twelve Disciples
(48/Luke 6:12–16)

13 Jesus went up on a mountainside and called to him those he wanted, and they came
to him.[l] 14 He appointed twelve—designating them apostles**[b]**[m]—that they might be

a *11* Greek *unclean*; also in verse 30 **b** *14* Some manuscripts do not have *designating them apostles.*

3:1 [a]Mt 4:23; Mk 1:21
3:2 [b]Mt 12:10 [c]Lk 14:1
3:6 [d]Mt 22:16; Mk 12:13 [e]Mt 12:14
3:7 [f]Mt 4:25
3:8 [g]Mt 11:21
3:10 [h]Mt 4:23 [i]Mt 9:20
3:11 [j]Mt 4:3; Mk 1:23, 24
3:12 [k]Mt 8:4; Mk 1:24, 25, 34; Ac 16:17, 18
3:13 [l]Mt 5:1
3:14 [m]Mk 6:30

3:2 Already the Pharisees had turned against Jesus. They were jealous of his popularity, his miracles, and the authority in his teaching and actions. They valued their status in the community and their opportunity for personal gain so much that they lost sight of their goal as religious leaders—to point people towards God. Of all people, the Pharisees should have recognised the Messiah, but they refused to acknowledge him because they were not willing to give up their treasured position and power. When Jesus exposed their attitudes, he became their enemy instead of their Messiah, and they began looking for ways to turn the people against him.

3:5 Jesus was angry about the Pharisees' uncaring attitudes. Anger itself is not wrong. It depends on what makes us angry and what we do with our anger. Too often we express our anger in selfish and harmful ways. By contrast, Jesus expressed his anger by correcting a problem—healing the man's hand. Use your anger to find constructive solutions rather than to tear people down.

3:6 The Pharisees were a Jewish religious group that zealously followed the Old Testament laws, as well as their own religious traditions. They were highly respected in the community, but they hated Jesus because he challenged their proud attitudes and dishonourable motives.

The Herodians were a Jewish political party that hoped to restore Herod the Great's line to the throne. Jesus was a threat to them as well because he challenged their political ambitions. The Pharisees and Herodians, normally enemies, joined forces against Jesus because he exposed them for what they were.

3:6 The Pharisees accused Jesus of breaking their law that said medical attention could be given to no-one on the Sabbath except in matters of life and death. Ironically, the Pharisees themselves were breaking God's law by plotting murder.

3:7, 8 While Jesus was drawing fire from the religious leaders, he was gaining great popularity among the people. Some were curious, some sought healing, some wanted evidence to use against him, and others wanted to know if Jesus truly was the Messiah. Most of them could only dimly guess at the real meaning of what was happening among them. Today crowds still follow Jesus, and they come for the same variety of reasons. What is your primary reason for following Jesus?

3:11 The evil spirits knew that Jesus was the Son of God, but they refused to turn from their evil purposes. Knowing about Jesus, or even believing that he is God's Son, does not guarantee salvation. You must also want to follow and obey him (see also James 2:17).

3:12 Jesus warned the evil spirits not to reveal his identity because he did not want them to reinforce a popular misconception. The huge crowds were looking for a political and military leader who would free them from Rome's control, and they thought that the Messiah predicted by the Old Testament prophets would be this kind of man. Jesus wanted to teach the people about the kind of Messiah he really was—one who was far different from their expectations. Christ's kingdom is spiritual. It begins not with the overthrow of governments, but with the overthrow of sin in people's hearts.

3:14 From the hundreds of people who followed him from place to place, Jesus chose 12 to be his *apostles. Apostle* means messenger or authorised representative. He did not choose these 12 to be his associates and companions because of their faith; their faith often faltered. He didn't choose them because of their talent and ability; no-one stood out with unusual ability. The disciples represented a wide range of backgrounds and life experiences, but apparently they had no more leadership potential than those who were not chosen. The one characteristic they all shared was their willingness to obey Jesus. After Jesus' ascension, they were filled with the Holy Spirit and empowered to carry out special roles in the

with him and that he might send them out to preach 15 and to have authority to drive
out demons.[n] 16 These are the twelve he appointed: Simon (to whom he gave the name
Peter);[o] 17 James son of Zebedee and his brother John (to them he gave the name
Boanerges, which means Sons of Thunder); 18 Andrew, Philip, Bartholomew, Mat-
thew, Thomas, James son of Alphaeus, Thaddaeus, Simon the Zealot 19 and Judas
Iscariot, who betrayed him.

Religious Leaders Accuse Jesus of Being under Satan's Power
(74/Matthew 12:22–37)

20 Then Jesus entered a house, and again a crowd gathered,[p] so that he and his
disciples were not even able to eat.[q] 21 When his family heard about this, they went
to take charge of him, for they said, "He is out of his mind."[r]
22 And the teachers of the law who came down from Jerusalem[s] said, "He is
possessed by Beelzebub![c][t] By the prince of demons he is driving out demons."[u]
23 So Jesus called them and spoke to them in parables:[v] "How can Satan[w] drive
out Satan? 24 If a kingdom is divided against itself, that kingdom cannot stand. 25 If
a house is divided against itself, that house cannot stand. 26 And if Satan opposes
himself and is divided, he cannot stand; his end has come. 27 In fact, no-one can enter
a strong man's house and carry off his possessions unless he first ties up the strong
man. Then he can rob his house.[x] 28 I tell you the truth, all the sins and blasphemies
of men will be forgiven them. 29 But whoever blasphemes against the Holy Spirit will
never be forgiven; he is guilty of an eternal sin."[y]
30 He said this because they were saying, "He has an evil spirit."

Jesus Describes His True Family
(76/Matthew 12:46–50; Luke 8:19–21)

31 Then Jesus' mother and brothers arrived.[z] Standing outside, they sent someone
in to call him. 32 A crowd was sitting around him, and they told him, "Your mother
and brothers are outside looking for you."

c *22* Greek *Beezeboul* or *Beelzeboul*

3:15 [n] Mt 10:1
3:16 [o] Jn 1:42
3:20 [p] ver 7 [q] Mk 6:31
3:21 [r] Jn 10:20; Ac 26:24
3:22 [s] Mt 15:1 [t] Mt 10:25; 11:18; 12:24; Jn 7:20; 8:48, 52; 10:20 [u] Mt 9:34
3:23 [v] Mk 4:2 [w] Mt 4:10
3:27 [x] Isa 49:24, 25
3:29 [y] Mt 12:31, 32; Lk 12:10
3:31 [z] ver 21

growth of the early church. We should not disqualify ourselves from service to Christ because we do not have the expected credentials. Being a good disciple is simply a matter of following Jesus with a willing heart.

3:14, 15 Why did Jesus choose 12 men? The number 12 corresponds to the 12 tribes of Israel (Matthew 19:28), showing the continuity between the old religious system and the new one based on Jesus' message. Many people followed Jesus, but these 12 received the most intense training. We see the impact of these men throughout the rest of the New Testament.

3:18 The Zealots were Jewish nationalists who opposed the Roman occupation of Palestine.

3:21 With the crowds pressing in on him, Jesus didn't even take time to eat. Because of this, his friends and family came to take charge of him (3:31, 32), thinking he had gone "over the top" as a religious fanatic. They were concerned for him, but they missed the point of his ministry. Even those who were closest to Jesus were slow to understand who he was and what he had come to do.

3:22–27 The Pharisees and the teachers of the law could not deny the reality of Jesus' miracles and supernatural power. They refused to believe that his power was from God, however, because then they would have had to accept him as the Messiah. Their pride would not let them do that. So in an attempt to destroy Jesus' popularity among the people, the teachers of the law accused him of having power from Satan. Jesus' reply showed that their argument didn't make sense. (*Beelzebub* refers to Satan.)

3:27 Although God permits Satan to work in our world, God is still in control. Jesus, because he is God, has power over Satan; Jesus is able to drive out demons and end their terrible work in people's lives. One day Satan will be bound for ever (Revelation 20:10).

3:28, 29 Christians sometimes wonder if they have committed this sin of blasphemy against the Holy Spirit. Christians need not worry about this sin because this sin is attributing to the devil what is the work of the Holy Spirit. It reveals a heart-attitude of unbelief and unrepentance. Deliberate, ongoing rejection of the work of the Holy Spirit is blasphemy because it is rejecting God himself. The religious leaders accused Jesus of blasphemy, but ironically they were the guilty ones when they looked Jesus in the face and accused him of being possessed by Satan.

3:31–35 Jesus' mother was Mary (Luke 1:30, 31), and his brothers were probably the other children Mary and Joseph had after Jesus (see also 6:3). Some Christians believe the ancient tradition that Jesus was Mary's only child. If this is true, the "brothers" were possibly cousins (cousins were often called brothers in those days). Some have offered yet another suggestion: when Joseph married Mary, he was a widower, and these were his children by his first marriage. Most likely, these were Jesus' half brothers (see Mark 6:3, 4).

Jesus' family did not yet fully understand his ministry, as can be seen in verse 21. Jesus explained that in our spiritual family, the relationships are ultimately more important and longer lasting than those formed in our physical families.

THE TWELVE

Name	*Occupation*	*Outstanding Characteristics*	*Major Events in His Life*
SIMON PETER (son of John)	Fisherman	Impulsive; later—bold in preaching about Jesus	One of three in core group of disciples; recognised Jesus as the Messiah; disowned Christ and repented; preached Pentecost sermon; a leader of the Jerusalem church; baptised Gentiles; wrote 1 and 2 Peter.
JAMES (son of Zebedee), he and his brother John were called the "Sons of Thunder"	Fisherman	Ambitious, short-tempered, judgmental, deeply committed to Jesus	Also in core group; he and his brother John asked Jesus for places of honour in his kingdom; wanted to call fire down to destroy a Samaritan village; first disciple to be martyred.
JOHN (son of Zebedee), James' brother, and "the disciple whom Jesus loved"	Fisherman	Ambitious, judgmental, later—very loving	Third disciple in core group; asked Jesus for a place of honour in his kingdom; wanted to call down fire on a Samaritan village; a leader of the Jerusalem church; wrote the Gospel of John and 1, 2, 3 John and Revelation.
ANDREW (Peter's brother)	Fisherman	Eager to bring others to Jesus	Accepted John the Baptist's testimony about Jesus; told Peter about Jesus; he and Philip told Jesus that Greeks wanted to see him.
PHILIP	Fisherman	Questioning attitude	Told Nathanael about Jesus; wondered how Jesus could feed the 5,000; asked Jesus to show his followers God the Father; he and Andrew told Jesus that Greeks wanted to see him.
BARTHOLOMEW (Nathanael)	Unknown	Honesty and straightforwardness	Initially rejected Jesus because Jesus was from Nazareth but acknowledged him as the "Son of God" and "King of Israel" when they met.
MATTHEW (Levi)	Tax collector	Despised outcast because of his dishonest career	Abandoned his corrupt (and financially profitable) way of life to follow Jesus; invited Jesus to a party with his notorious friends; wrote the Gospel of Matthew.
THOMAS (the Twin)	Unknown	Courage and doubt	Suggested the disciples go with Jesus to Bethany—even if it meant death; asked Jesus about where he was going; refused to believe Jesus was risen until he could see Jesus alive and touch his wounds.
JAMES (son of Alphaeus)	Unknown	Unknown	Became one of Jesus' disciples.
THADDAEUS (Judas son of James)	Unknown	Unknown	Asked Jesus why he would reveal himself to his followers and not to the world.
SIMON THE ZEALOT	Unknown	Fierce patriotism	Became a disciple of Jesus.
JUDAS ISCARIOT	Unknown	Treacherous and greedy	Became one of Jesus' disciples; betrayed Jesus; killed himself.

Jesus' faithful disciples were ordinary men who became extraordinary because of Jesus Christ. Despite their confusion and lack of understanding during his lifetime, they became powerful witnesses to his resurrection. Their lives were transformed by God's power. The story of Jesus' disciples does not end with the Gospels. It continues in the book of Acts and many of the letters.

DISCIPLES

What Jesus Said about Him	A Key Lesson from His Life	Selected References
Named him Peter, "rock"; called him "Satan" when he urged Jesus to reject the cross; said he would become a fisher of men; he received revelation from God; he would disown Jesus; he would later be crucified for his faith.	Christians falter at times, but when they return to Jesus, he forgives them and strengthens their faith.	Matthew 4:18–20 Mark 8:29–33 Luke 22:31–34 John 21:15–19 Acts 2:14–41 Acts 10:1–11:18
Called James and John "Sons of Thunder"; said he would be a fisher of men; would drink the cup Jesus drank.	Christians must be willing to die for Jesus.	Mark 3:17 Mark 10:35–40 Luke 9:52–56 Acts 12:1, 2
Called James and John "Sons of Thunder"; said he would be a fisher of men; would drink the cup Jesus drank; would take care of Jesus' mother after Jesus' death.	The transforming power of the love of Christ is available to all.	Mark 1:19 Mark 10:35–40 Luke 9:52–56 John 19:26, 27 John 21:20–24
Said he would become a fisher of men.	Christians are to tell other people about Jesus.	Matthew 4:18–20 John 1:35–42; 6:8, 9 John 12:20–22
Asked if Philip realised that to know and see him was to know and see the Father.	God uses our questions to teach us.	Matthew 10:3 John 1:43–46; 6:2–7 John 12:20–22 John 14:8–11
Called him "a true Israelite" and a man "in whom there is nothing false".	Jesus respects honesty in people—even if they challenge him because of it.	Mark 3:18 John 1:45–51 John 21:1–13
Called him to be a disciple.	Christianity is not for people who think they're already good; it is for people who know they've failed and want help.	Matthew 9:9–13 Mark 2:15–17 Luke 5:27–32
Said Thomas believed because he actually saw Jesus after the resurrection.	Even when Christians experience serious doubts, Jesus reaches out to them to restore their faith.	Matthew 10:3 John 14:5; 20:24–29 John 21:1–13
Unknown	Unknown	Matthew 10:3 Mark 3:18 Luke 6:15
Unknown	Christians follow Jesus because they believe in him; they do not always understand the details of God's plan.	Matthew 10:3 Mark 3:18 John 14:22
Unknown	If we are willing to give up our plans for the future, we can participate in Jesus' plans.	Matthew 10:4 Mark 3:18 Luke 6:15
Called him "a devil"; said Judas would betray Jesus.	It is not enough to be familiar with Jesus' teachings. Jesus' true followers love and obey him.	Matthew 26:20–25 Luke 22:47, 48 John 12:4–8

33“Who are my mother and my brothers?” he asked.
34Then he looked at those seated in a circle around him and said, “Here are my
mother and my brothers! 35Whoever does God’s will is my brother and sister and
mother.”

Jesus Tells the Parable of the Four Soils
(77/Matthew 13:1–9; Luke 8:4–8)

4 Again Jesus began to teach by the lake.[a] The crowd that gathered round him was
so large that he got into a boat and sat in it out on the lake, while all the people
were along the shore at the water’s edge. 2He taught them many things by parables,[b]
and in his teaching said: 3“Listen! A farmer went out to sow his seed.[c] 4As he was
scattering the seed, some fell along the path, and the birds came and ate it up. 5Some
fell on rocky places, where it did not have much soil. It sprang up quickly, because
the soil was shallow. 6But when the sun came up, the plants were scorched, and they
withered because they had no root. 7Other seed fell among thorns, which grew up and
choked the plants, so that they did not bear grain. 8Still other seed fell on good soil.
It came up, grew and produced a crop, multiplying thirty, sixty, or even a hundred
times.”[d]
9Then Jesus said, “He who has ears to hear, let him hear.”[e]

Jesus Explains the Parable of the Four Soils
(78/Matthew 13:10–23; Luke 8:9–18)

10When he was alone, the Twelve and the others around him asked him about the
parables. 11He told them, “The secret of the kingdom of God[f] has been given to you.
But to those on the outside[g] everything is said in parables 12so that,

> “ ‘they may be ever seeing but never perceiving,
> and ever hearing but never understanding;
> otherwise they might turn and be forgiven!’ [a]”[h]

13Then Jesus said to them, “Don’t you understand this parable? How then will you
understand any parable? 14The farmer sows the word.[i] 15Some people are like seed
along the path, where the word is sown. As soon as they hear it, Satan[j] comes and
takes away the word that was sown in them. 16Others, like seed sown on rocky places,
hear the word and at once receive it with joy. 17But since they have no root, they last
only a short time. When trouble or persecution comes because of the word, they

a *12* Isaiah 6:9,10

4:1 [a]Mk 2:13; 3:7
4:2 [b]ver 11; Mk 3:23
4:3 [c]ver 26
4:8 [d]Jn 15:5; Col 1:6
4:9 [e]ver 23; Mt 11:15
4:11 [f]Mt 3:2 [g]1Co 5:12, 13; Col 4:5; 1Th 4:12; 1Ti 3:7
4:12 [h]Isa 6:9, 10; Mt 13:13-15
4:14 [i]Mk 16:20; Lk 1:2; Ac 4:31; 8:4; 16:6; 17:11; Php 1:14
4:15 [j]Mt 4:10

3:33–35 God’s family is accepting and doesn’t exclude anyone. Although Jesus cared for his mother and brothers, he also cared for all those who loved him. Jesus did not show partiality; he allowed everyone the privilege of obeying God and becoming part of his family. In our increasingly computerised, impersonal world, warm relationships among members of God’s family take on major importance. The church can give the loving, personalised care that many people find nowhere else.

4:2 Jesus taught the people by telling parables, short stories using familiar scenes to explain spiritual truth. This method of teaching compels the listener to think. It conceals the truth from those who are too stubborn or prejudiced to hear what is being taught. Most parables have one main point, so we must be careful not to go beyond what Jesus intended to teach.

4:3 Seed was sown by hand. As the farmer walked across the field, he threw handfuls of seed onto the ground from a large bag slung across his shoulders. The plants did not grow in neat rows as accomplished by today’s machine planting. No matter how skilful, no farmer could keep some of his seed from falling by the wayside, from being scattered among rocks and thorns, or from being carried off by the wind. So the farmer would throw the seed liberally, and enough would fall on good ground to ensure the harvest.

4:9 We hear with our ears, but there is a deeper kind of listening with the mind and heart that is necessary in order to gain spiritual understanding from Jesus’ words. Some people in the crowd were looking for evidence to use against Jesus; others truly wanted to learn and grow. Jesus’ words were for the honest seekers.

4:11, 12 Some people do not understand God’s truth because they are not ready for it. God reveals truth to people who will act on it, who will make it visible in their lives. When you talk to people about God, be aware that they will not understand if they are not yet ready. Be patient, taking every chance to tell them more of the truth about God, and praying that the Holy Spirit will open their minds and hearts to receive the truth and act on it.

4:14–20 The four soils represent four different ways people respond to God’s message. Usually we think that Jesus was talking about four different kinds of people. But he may also have been talking about (1) different times or phases in a person’s life, or (2) how we willingly receive God’s message in some areas of our lives and resist it in others. For example, you may be open to God about your future, but closed concerning how you spend your money. You may respond like good soil to God’s demand for worship, but like rocky soil to his demand to give to people in need. We must strive to be like good soil in every area of our lives at all times.

quickly fall away. 18 Still others, like seed sown among thorns, hear the word; 19 but
the worries of this life, the deceitfulness of wealth[k] and the desires for other things
come in and choke the word, making it unfruitful. 20 Others, like seed sown on good
soil, hear the word, accept it, and produce a crop—thirty, sixty or even a hundred
times what was sown."

21 He said to them, "Do you bring in a lamp to put it under a bowl or a bed? Instead,
don't you put it on its stand?[l] 22 For whatever is hidden is meant to be disclosed, and
whatever is concealed is meant to be brought out into the open.[m] 23 If anyone has ears
to hear, let him hear."[n]

24 "Consider carefully what you hear," he continued. "With the measure you use,
it will be measured to you—and even more.[o] 25 Whoever has will be given more;
whoever does not have, even what he has will be taken from him."[p]

Jesus Tells the Parable of the Growing Seed
(79)

26 He also said, "This is what the kingdom of God is like.[q] A man scatters seed
on the ground. 27 Night and day, whether he sleeps or gets up, the seed sprouts and
grows, though he does not know how. 28 All by itself the soil produces corn—first
the stalk, then the ear, then the full grain in the ear. 29 As soon as the grain is ripe,
he puts the sickle to it, because the harvest has come."[r]

Jesus Tells the Parable of the Mustard Seed
(81/Matthew 13:31, 32)

30 Again he said, "What shall we say the kingdom of God is like,[s] or what parable
shall we use to describe it? 31 It is like a mustard seed, which is the smallest seed you
plant in the ground. 32 Yet when planted, it grows and becomes the largest of all garden
plants, with such big branches that the birds of the air can perch in its shade."

33 With many similar parables Jesus spoke the word to them, as much as they could
understand.[t] 34 He did not say anything to them without using a parable.[u] But when
he was alone with his own disciples, he explained everything.

Jesus Calms the Storm
(87/Matthew 8:23–27; Luke 8:22–25)

35 That day when evening came, he said to his disciples, "Let us go over to the other
side." 36 Leaving the crowd behind, they took him along, just as he was, in the boat.[v]
There were also other boats with him. 37 A furious squall came up, and the waves broke

4:19 [k]Mt 19:23; 1Ti 6:9, 10, 17; 1Jn 2:15-17

4:21 [l]Mt 5:15

4:22 [m]Jer 16:17; Mt 10:26; Lk 8:17; 12:2

4:23 [n]ver 9; Mt 11:15

4:24 [o]Mt 7:2; Lk 6:38

4:25 [p]Mt 13:12; 25:29

4:26 [q]Mt 13:24

4:29 [r]Rev 14:15

4:30 [s]Mt 13:24

4:33 [t]Jn 16:12

4:34 [u]Jn 16:25

4:36 [v]ver 1; Mk 3:9; 5:2, 21; 6:32, 45

4:19 Worldly worries, the false sense of security brought about by prosperity, and the desire for things plagued first-century disciples as they do us today. How easy it is for our daily routines to become overcrowded. A life packed with materialistic pursuits deafens us to God's word. Stay free so you can hear God when he speaks.

4:21 If a lamp doesn't help people see, it is useless. Does your life show other people how to find God and how to live for him? If not, ask what "bowls" have extinguished your light. Complacency, resentment, stubbornness of heart, or disobedience could keep God's light from shining through you to others.

4:24, 25 The light of Jesus' truth is revealed to us, not hidden. But we may not be able to see or to use all of that truth right now. Only as we put God's teachings into practice will we understand and see more of the truth. The truth is clear, but our ability to understand is imperfect. As we obey, we will sharpen our vision and increase our understanding (see James 1:22–25).

4:25 This verse simply means that we are responsible to use well what we have. How much we have is not nearly as important as what we do with it.

4:26–29 This parable about the kingdom of God, recorded only by Mark, reveals that spiritual growth is a continual, gradual process that is finally consummated in a harvest of spiritual maturity. We can understand the process of spiritual growth by comparing it to the slow but certain growth of a plant.

4:30–32 Jesus used this parable to explain that although Christianity had very small beginnings, it would grow into a worldwide community of believers. When you feel alone in your stand for Christ, realise that God is building a worldwide kingdom. He has faithful followers in every part of the world, and your faith, no matter how small, can join with that of others to accomplish great things.

4:33, 34 Jesus adapted his methods to his audience's ability and desire to understand. He didn't speak in parables to confuse people, but to challenge sincere seekers to discover the meaning of his words. Much of Jesus' teaching was against hypocrisy and impure motives—characteristics of the religious leaders. Had Jesus spoken against the leaders directly, his public ministry would have been hampered. Those who listened carefully to Jesus knew what he was talking about.

4:37, 38 The Sea of Galilee is 680 feet below sea level and is surrounded by hills. Winds blowing across the land intensify close to the sea, often causing violent and unexpected storms. The disciples were seasoned fishermen who had spent their lives fishing on this huge lake, but during this squall they panicked.

over the boat, so that it was nearly swamped. 38 Jesus was in the stern, sleeping on
a cushion. The disciples woke him and said to him, "Teacher, don't you care if we
drown?"
39 He got up, rebuked the wind and said to the waves, "Quiet! Be still!" Then the
wind died down and it was completely calm.
40 He said to his disciples, "Why are you so afraid? Do you still have no faith?"[w]
41 They were terrified and asked each other, "Who is this? Even the wind and the
waves obey him!"

Jesus Sends the Demons into a Herd of Pigs
(88/Matthew 8:28–34; Luke 8:26–39)

5 They went across the lake to the region of the Gerasenes.[a] 2 When Jesus got out
of the boat,[a] a man with an evil[b] spirit[b] came from the tombs to meet him.
3 This man lived in the tombs, and no-one could bind him any more, not even with
a chain. 4 For he had often been chained hand and foot, but he tore the chains apart
and broke the irons on his feet. No-one was strong enough to subdue him. 5 Night and
day among the tombs and in the hills he would cry out and cut himself with stones.
6 When he saw Jesus from a distance, he ran and fell on his knees in front of him.
7 He shouted at the top of his voice, "What do you want with me,[c] Jesus, Son of the
Most High God?[d] Swear to God that you won't torture me!" 8 For Jesus had said to
him, "Come out of this man, you evil spirit!"
9 Then Jesus asked him, "What is your name?"
"My name is Legion,"[e] he replied, "for we are many." 10 And he begged Jesus
again and again not to send them out of the area.
11 A large herd of pigs was feeding on the nearby hillside. 12 The demons begged
Jesus, "Send us among the pigs; allow us to go into them." 13 He gave them permis-

[a] 1 Some manuscripts *Gadarenes*; other manuscripts *Gergesenes* [b] 2 Greek *unclean*; also in verses 8 and 13

4:40 [w]Mt 14:31; Mk 16:14
5:2 [a]Mk 4:1 [b]Mk 1:23
5:7 [c]Mt 8:29 [d]Mt 4:3; Lk 1:32; 6:35; Ac 16:17; Heb 7:1
5:9 [e]ver 15

4:38–40 The disciples panicked because the storm threatened to destroy them all, and Jesus seemed unaware and unconcerned. Theirs was a physical storm, but storms come in other forms. Think about the storms in your life – the situations that cause you great anxiety. Whatever your difficulty, you have two options: You can worry and assume that Jesus no longer cares, or you can resist fear, putting your trust in him. When you feel like panicking, confess your need for God and then trust him to care for you.

4:41 The disciples lived with Jesus, but they underestimated him. They did not see that his power applied to their very own situation. Jesus has been with his people for 20 centuries, and yet we, like the disciples, underestimate his power to handle crises in our lives. The disciples did not yet know enough about Jesus. We cannot make the same excuse.

5:1, 2 Although we cannot be sure why demon-possession occurs, we know that evil spirits can use the human body to distort and destroy man's relationship with God and likeness to him. Even today, demons are dangerous, powerful, and destructive. While it is important to recognise their evil activity so that we can stay away from demons, we should avoid any curiosity about or involvement with demonic forces or the occult (Deuteronomy 18:10–12). If we resist the devil and his influences, he will flee from us (James 4:7).

5:9 The evil spirit said its name was Legion. A legion was the largest unit of the Roman army, consisting of 3,000 to 6,000 soldiers. Obviously this man was possessed by many demons.

5:10 Mark often highlights the supernatural struggle between Jesus and Satan. The demons' goal was to control the humans they inhabited; Jesus' goal was to give people freedom from sin and Satan's control. The demons knew they had no power over Jesus; so when they saw Jesus, they begged not to be sent out of the area ("into the Abyss" in Luke 8:31). Jesus granted their request to enter into the herd of pigs (5:13) but ended their destructive work in people. Perhaps Jesus let the demons destroy the pigs to demonstrate his own superiority over a very powerful yet destructive force. He could have sent them to hell, but he did not, because the time for judgment had not yet come. In the end, the devil and all his angels will be sent into eternal fire (Matthew 25:41).

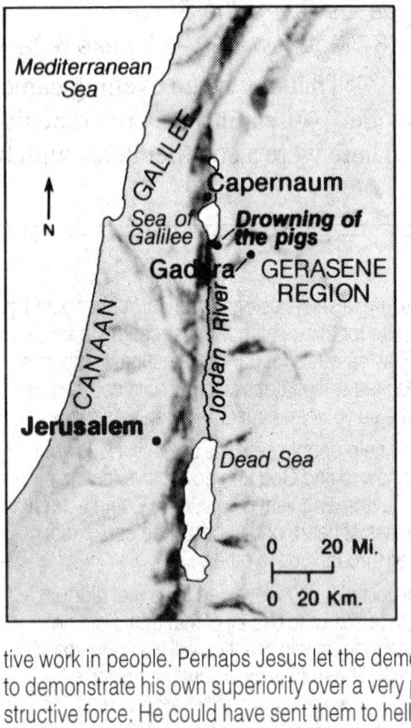

HEALING A DEMON-POSSESSED MAN
From Capernaum, Jesus and his disciples crossed the Sea of Galilee. A storm blew up unexpectedly, but Jesus calmed it. Landing in the region of the Gerasenes, Jesus sent demons out of a man and into a herd of pigs that plunged over the steep bank into the lake.

5:11 According to Old Testament law (Leviticus 11:7), pigs were "unclean" animals. This meant that they could not be eaten or even touched by a Jew. This incident took place southeast of the Sea of Galilee in the region of the Gerasenes, a Gentile region, which explains how a herd of pigs could be involved.

5:15 [f] ver 9 [g] ver 16, 18; Mt 4:24

sion, and the evil spirits came out and went into the pigs. The herd, about two thousand
in number, rushed down the steep bank into the lake and were drowned.
14 Those tending the pigs ran off and reported this in the town and countryside, and
the people went out to see what had happened. 15 When they came to Jesus, they saw
the man who had been possessed by the legion[f] of demons,[g] sitting there, dressed
and in his right mind; and they were afraid. 16 Those who had seen it told the people
what had happened to the demon-possessed man—and told about the pigs as well.
17 Then the people began to plead with Jesus to leave their region.
18 As Jesus was getting into the boat, the man who had been demon-possessed
begged to go with him. 19 Jesus did not let him, but said, "Go home to your family
and tell them[h] how much the Lord has done for you, and how he has had mercy on
you." 20 So the man went away and began to tell in the Decapolis[c][i] how much Jesus
had done for him. And all the people were amazed.

5:19 [h] Mt 8:4

5:20 [i] Mt 4:25; Mk 7:31

c *20* That is, the Ten Cities

THE TOUCH OF JESUS
What kind of people did Jesus associate with? Whom did he consider important enough to touch? Here we see many of the people Jesus came to know. Some reached out to him; he reached out to them all. Regardless of how great or unknown, rich or poor, young or old, sinner or saint—Jesus cares equally for all. No person is beyond the loving touch of Jesus.

Jesus Talked with . . .	*Reference*
A despised tax collector	Matthew 9:9
An insane hermit	Mark 5:1–15
The Roman governor	Mark 15:1–15
A young boy	Mark 9:17–27
A prominent religious leader	John 3:1–21
A housewife	Luke 10:38–42
An expert in the law	Matthew 22:35
A criminal	Luke 23:40–43
A synagogue ruler	Mark 5:22
Fishermen	Matthew 4:18–20
A king	Luke 23:7–11
A poor widow	Luke 7:11–17; 21:1–4
A Roman centurion	Luke 7:1–10
A group of children	Mark 10:13–16
A prophet	Matthew 3
An adulterous woman	John 8:1–11
The Jewish council	Luke 22:66–71
A sick woman	Mark 5:25–34
A rich man	Mark 10:17–23
A blind beggar	Mark 10:46
Jewish political leaders	Mark 12:13
A group of women	Luke 8:2, 3
The high priest	Matthew 26:62–68
An outcast with leprosy	Luke 17:11–19
A royal official	John 4:46–53
A young girl	Mark 5:41, 42
A traitor	John 13:1–3, 27
A helpless and paralysed man	Mark 2:1–12
An angry mob of soldiers and police	John 18:3–9
A woman from a foreign land	Mark 7:25–30
A doubting follower	John 20:24–29
An enemy who hated him	Acts 9:1–9
A Samaritan woman	John 4:1–26

5:17 After such a wonderful miracle of saving a man's life, why did the people want Jesus to leave? They were undoubtedly afraid of his supernatural power. They may have also feared that Jesus would continue destroying their pigs. They would rather give up Jesus than lose their source of income and security.

5:19 Jesus told this man to tell his friends about the miraculous healing. Most of the time, Jesus urged those he healed to keep quiet. Why the difference? Here are possible answers: (1) The demon-possessed man had been alone and unable to speak. Telling others what Jesus did for him would prove that he was healed. (2) This was mainly a Gentile and pagan area, so Jesus was not expecting great crowds to follow him or religious leaders to hinder him. (3) By sending the man away with this good news, Jesus was expanding his ministry to people who were not Jews.

5:19, 20 This man had been demon-possessed but became a living example of Jesus' power. He wanted to go with Jesus, but Jesus told him to go home and share his story with his friends. If you have experienced Jesus' power, you too are a living example. Are you, like this man, enthusiastic about sharing the Good News with those around you? Just as we would tell others about a doctor who cured a physical disease, we should tell about Christ who cures our sin.

5:20 Decapolis, or the Ten Cities, was located southeast of the Sea of Galilee. Ten cities, each with its own independent government, formed an alliance for protection and for increased trade opportunities. These cities had been settled several centuries earlier by Greek traders and immigrants. Although Jews also lived in the area, they were not in the majority. Many people from the Decapolis followed Jesus (Matthew 4:25).

Jesus Heals a Bleeding Woman and Restores a Girl to Life
(89/Matthew 9:18–26; Luke 8:40–56)

21 When Jesus had again crossed over by boat to the other side of the lake,[j] a large
crowd gathered round him while he was by the lake.[k] 22 Then one of the synagogue
rulers,[l] named Jairus, came there. Seeing Jesus, he fell at his feet 23 and pleaded
earnestly with him, "My little daughter is dying. Please come and put your hands on[m]
her so that she will be healed and live." 24 So Jesus went with him.
A large crowd followed and pressed around him. 25 And a woman was there who
had been subject to bleeding[n] for twelve years. 26 She had suffered a great deal under
the care of many doctors and had spent all she had, yet instead of getting better she
grew worse. 27 When she heard about Jesus, she came up behind him in the crowd
and touched his cloak, 28 because she thought, "If I just touch his clothes,[o] I will be
healed." 29 Immediately her bleeding stopped and she felt in her body that she was
freed from her suffering.[p]
30 At once Jesus realised that power[q] had gone out from him. He turned around
in the crowd and asked, "Who touched my clothes?"
31 "You see the people crowding against you," his disciples answered, "and yet you
can ask, 'Who touched me?' "
32 But Jesus kept looking around to see who had done it. 33 Then the woman,
knowing what had happened to her, came and fell at his feet and, trembling with fear,
told him the whole truth. 34 He said to her, "Daughter, your faith has healed you.[r]
Go in peace[s] and be freed from your suffering."
35 While Jesus was still speaking, some men came from the house of Jairus, the
synagogue ruler.[t] "Your daughter is dead," they said. "Why bother the teacher any
more?"
36 Ignoring what they said, Jesus told the synagogue ruler, "Don't be afraid; just
believe."
37 He did not let anyone follow him except Peter, James and John the brother of
James.[u] 38 When they came to the home of the synagogue ruler,[v] Jesus saw a
commotion, with people crying and wailing loudly. 39 He went in and said to them,
"Why all this commotion and wailing? The child is not dead but asleep."[w] 40 But they
laughed at him.
After he put them all out, he took the child's father and mother and the disciples
who were with him, and went in where the child was. 41 He took her by the hand[x]

5:21 [j]Mt 9:1 [k]Mk 4:1
5:22 [l]ver 35, 36, 38; Lk 13:14; Ac 13:15; 18:8, 17
5:23 [m]Mt 19:13; Mk 6:5; 7:32; 8:23; 16:18; Lk 4:40; 13:13; Ac 6:6
5:25 [n]Lev 15:25-30
5:28 [o]Mt 9:20
5:29 [p]ver 34
5:30 [q]Lk 5:17; 6:19
5:34 [r]Mt 9:22 [s]Ac 15:33
5:35 [t]ver 22
5:37 [u]Mt 4:21
5:38 [v]ver 22
5:39 [w]Mt 9:24
5:41 [x]Mk 1:31

5:22 Jesus crossed back over the Sea of Galilee, probably landing at Capernaum. Jairus was the elected ruler of the local synagogue. He was responsible for supervising worship, running the weekly school, and caring for the building. Many synagogue rulers had close ties with the Pharisees. It is likely, therefore, that some synagogue rulers had been pressured not to support Jesus. For Jairus to bow before Jesus was a significant and perhaps daring act of respect and worship.

5:25–34 This woman had a seemingly incurable condition causing her to bleed constantly. This may have been a menstrual or uterine disorder that would have made her ritually unclean (Leviticus 15:25–27) and would have excluded her from most social contact. She desperately wanted Jesus to heal her, but she knew that her bleeding would cause Jesus to be unclean under Jewish law if she touched him. Still, the woman reached out by faith and was healed. Sometimes we feel that our problems will keep us from God. But he is always ready to help. We should never allow our fear to keep us from approaching him.

5:32–34 Jesus was not angry with this woman for touching him. He knew she had touched him, but he stopped and asked who did it in order to teach her something about faith. Although the woman was healed when she touched him, Jesus said her faith caused the cure. Genuine faith involves action. Faith that isn't put into action is not faith at all.

5:35, 36 Jairus' crisis made him feel confused, afraid, and without hope. Jesus' words to Jairus in the midst of crisis speak to us as well: "Don't be afraid; just believe." In Jesus' mind, there was both hope and promise. The next time you feel hopeless and afraid, look at your problem from Jesus' point of view. He is the source of all hope and promise.

5:38 Loud weeping and wailing was customary at a person's death. Lack of it was the ultimate disgrace and disrespect. There were some people, usually women, who made mourning a profession and were paid by the dead person's family to weep over the body. On the day of death, the body was carried through the streets, followed by mourners, family members, and friends.

5:39, 40 The mourners began to laugh at Jesus when he said, "The child is not dead but asleep." The girl was dead, but Jesus used the image of sleep to indicate that her condition was temporary and that she would be restored.

Jesus tolerated the crowd's abuse in order to teach an important lesson about maintaining hope and trust in him. Today, most of the world laughs at Christ's claims, which seem ridiculous to them. When you are belittled for expressing faith in Jesus and hope for eternal life, remember that unbelievers don't see from God's perspective. For a clear statement about life after death, see 1 Thessalonians 4:13, 14.

5:41 *Talitha koum* is Aramaic, one of the original languages of Palestine. Jesus' disciples spoke not only Aramaic, but probably Greek and Hebrew also.

5:41, 42 Jesus not only demonstrated great power; he also showed tremendous compassion. Jesus' power over nature, evil

and said to her, *"Talitha koum!"* (which means, "Little girl, I say to you, get up!").[y]
42Immediately the girl stood up and walked around (she was twelve years old). At
this they were completely astonished. 43He gave strict orders not to let anyone know
about this,[z] and told them to give her something to eat.

The People of Nazareth Refuse to Believe
(91/Matthew 13:53–58)

6 Jesus left there and went to his home town,[a] accompanied by his disciples.
2When the Sabbath came,[b] he began to teach in the synagogue,[c] and many who
heard him were amazed.[d]
"Where did this man get these things?" they asked. "What's this wisdom that has
been given him, that he even does miracles! 3Isn't this the carpenter? Isn't this Mary's
son and the brother of James, Joseph,[a] Judas and Simon?[e] Aren't his sisters here
with us?" And they took offence at him.[f]
4Jesus said to them, "Only in his home town, among his relatives and in his own
house is a prophet without honour."[g] 5He could not do any miracles there, except
lay his hands on[h] a few sick people and heal them. 6And he was amazed at their lack
of faith.

Jesus Sends Out the Twelve Disciples
(93/Matthew 10:1–16; Luke 9:1–6)

Then Jesus went round teaching from village to village.[i] 7Calling the Twelve to
him,[j] he sent them out two by two[k] and gave them authority over evil[b] spirits.[l]
8These were his instructions: "Take nothing for the journey except a staff—no
bread, no bag, no money in your belts. 9Wear sandals but not an extra tunic.

a *3* Greek *Joses,* a variant of *Joseph* **b** *7* Greek *unclean*

5:41 [y]Lk 7:14; Ac 9:40
5:43 [z]Mt 8:4
6:1 [a]Mt 2:23
6:2 [b]Mk 1:21 [c]Mt 4:23 [d]Mt 7:28
6:3 [e]Mt 12:46 [f]Mt 11:6; Jn 6:61
6:4 [g]Lk 4:24; Jn 4:44
6:5 [h]Mk 5:23
6:6 [i]Mt 9:35; Mk 1:39; Lk 13:22
6:7 [j]Mk 3:13 [k]Dt 17:6; Lk 10:1 [l]Mt 10:1

---

spirits, and death was motivated by compassion—for a demon-possessed man who lived among tombs, for a diseased woman, and for the family of a dead girl. The rabbis of the day considered such people unclean. Polite society avoided them. But Jesus reached out and helped anyone in need.

5:43 Jesus told the girl's parents not to spread the news of the miracle. He wanted the facts to speak for themselves, and the time was not yet right for a major confrontation with the religious leaders. Jesus still had much to accomplish, and he didn't want people following him just to see his miracles.

6:2, 3 Jesus was teaching effectively and wisely, but the people of his home town saw him as only a carpenter. "He's no better than we are—he's just a common labourer," they said. They were offended that others could be impressed by Jesus and follow him. They rejected his authority because he was one of their peers. They thought they knew him, but their preconceived notions about who he was made it impossible for them to accept his message. Don't let prejudice blind you to truth. As you learn more about Jesus, try to see him for who he really is.

6:4 Jesus said that a prophet (in other words, a worker for God) is never honoured in his home town. But that doesn't make his work any less important. A person doesn't need to be respected or honoured to be useful to God. If friends, neighbours, or family don't respect your Christian work, don't let their rejection keep you from serving God.

6:5 Jesus could have done greater miracles in Nazareth, but he chose not to because of the people's pride and unbelief. The miracles he did had little effect on the people because they did not accept his message or believe that he was from God. Therefore, Jesus looked elsewhere, seeking those who would respond to his miracles and message.

6:7 The disciples were sent out in pairs. Individually they could have reached more areas of the country, but this was not Christ's plan. One advantage of going out in twos was that they could strengthen and encourage each other, especially when they faced

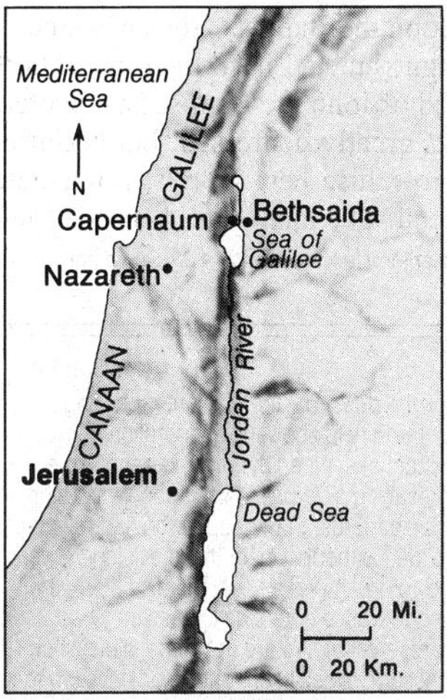

PREACHING IN GALILEE
After returning to his home town, Nazareth, from Capernaum, Jesus preached in the villages of Galilee and sent his disciples out to preach as well. After meeting back in Capernaum, they left by boat to rest, only to be met by the crowds who followed the boat along the shore.

rejection. Our strength comes from God, but he meets many of our needs through our teamwork with others. As you serve Christ, don't try to go it alone.

6:8, 9 Mark records that the disciples were instructed to take nothing with them *except* staffs, while in the Matthew and Luke accounts Jesus told them *not* to take staffs. One explanation is that Matthew and Luke were referring to a club used for protection, whereas Mark was talking about a shepherd's crook. In any case, the point in all three accounts is the same—the disciples were to leave at once, without extensive preparation, trusting in God's care rather than in their own resources.

10 Whenever you enter a house, stay there until you leave that town. 11 And if any place
will not welcome you or listen to you, shake the dust off your feet[m] when you leave,
as a testimony against them."
12 They went out and preached that people should repent.[n] 13 They drove out many
demons and anointed many sick people with oil[o] and healed them.

Herod Kills John the Baptist
(95/Matthew 14:1–12; Luke 9:7–9)

14 King Herod heard about this, for Jesus' name had become well known. Some
were saying,[c] "John the Baptist[p] has been raised from the dead, and that is why
miraculous powers are at work in him."
15 Others said, "He is Elijah."[q]
And still others claimed, "He is a prophet,[r] like one of the prophets of long ago."[s]
16 But when Herod heard this, he said, "John, the man I beheaded, has been raised
from the dead!"
17 For Herod himself had given orders to have John arrested, and he had him bound
and put in prison.[t] He did this because of Herodias, his brother Philip's wife, whom
he had married. 18 For John had been saying to Herod, "It is not lawful for you to have
your brother's wife."[u] 19 So Herodias nursed a grudge against John and wanted to kill
him. But she was not able to, 20 because Herod feared John and protected him,
knowing him to be a righteous and holy man.[v] When Herod heard John, he was
greatly puzzled;[d] yet he liked to listen to him.
21 Finally the opportune time came. On his birthday Herod gave a banquet[w] for his
high officials and military commanders and the leading men of Galilee.[x] 22 When the
daughter of Herodias came in and danced, she pleased Herod and his dinner guests.
The king said to the girl, "Ask me for anything you want, and I'll give it to you."
23 And he promised her with an oath, "Whatever you ask I will give you, up to half
my kingdom."[y]
24 She went out and said to her mother, "What shall I ask for?"
"The head of John the Baptist," she answered.
25 At once the girl hurried in to the king with the request: "I want you to give me
right now the head of John the Baptist on a platter."
26 The king was greatly distressed, but because of his oaths and his dinner guests,
he did not want to refuse her. 27 So he immediately sent an executioner with orders
to bring John's head. The man went, beheaded John in the prison, 28 and brought back

[c] *14* Some early manuscripts *He was saying* [d] *20* Some early manuscripts *he did many things*

6:11 [m] Mt 10:14
6:12 [n] Lk 9:6
6:13 [o] Jas 5:14
6:14 [p] Mt 3:1
6:15 [q] Mal 4:5 [r] Mt 21:11 [s] Mt 16:14; Mk 8:28
6:17 [t] Mt 4:12; 11:2; Lk 3:19, 20
6:18 [u] Lev 18:16; 20:21
6:20 [v] Mt 11:9; 21:26
6:21 [w] Est 1:3; 2:18 [x] Lk 3:1
6:23 [y] Est 5:3, 6; 7:2

6:11 Pious Jews shook the dust from their feet after passing through Gentile cities or territory to show their separation from Gentile influences and practices. When the disciples shook the dust from their feet after leaving a *Jewish* town, it was a vivid sign that they wished to remain separate from people who had rejected Jesus and his message. Jesus made it clear that the listeners were responsible for what they did with the gospel. The disciples were not to blame if the message was rejected, as long as they had faithfully and carefully presented it. We are not responsible when others reject Christ's message of salvation, but we do have the responsibility to share the gospel clearly and faithfully.

6:14, 15 Herod, along with many others, wondered who Jesus really was. Unable to accept Jesus' claim to be God's Son, many people made up their own explanations for his power and authority. Herod thought that Jesus was John the Baptist come back to life, while those who were familiar with the Old Testament thought he was Elijah (Malachi 4:5). Still others believed that Jesus was a teaching prophet in the tradition of Moses, Isaiah, or Jeremiah. Today people still have to make up their minds about Jesus. Some think that if they can name what he is – prophet, teacher, good man – they can weaken the power of his claim on their lives. But what they *think* does not change who Jesus *is.*

6:17–19 Palestine was divided into four territories, each with a different ruler. Herod Antipas, called Herod in the Gospels, was ruler over Galilee; his brother Philip ruled over Traconitis and Idumea. Philip's wife was Herodias, but she left him to marry Herod Antipas. When John confronted the two for committing adultery, Herodias formulated a plot to kill him. Instead of trying to get rid of her sin, Herodias tried to get rid of the one who brought it to public attention. This is exactly what the religious leaders were trying to do to Jesus.

6:20 Herod arrested John the Baptist under pressure from his wife and advisers. Though Herod respected John's integrity, in the end Herod had John killed because of pressure from his peers and family. What you do under pressure often shows what you are really like.

6:22, 23 As a ruler under Roman authority, Herod had no kingdom to give. The offer of half his kingdom was Herod's way of saying that he would give Herodias' daughter almost anything she wanted. When Herodias asked for John's head, Herod would have been greatly embarrassed in front of his guests if he had denied her request. Words are powerful. Because they can lead to great sin, we should use them with great care.

6:30 Mark uses the word *apostles* here and in 3:14. *Apostle* means "one sent" as messenger, authorised agent, or missionary.

6:30 [z]Mt 10:2; Lk 9:10; 17:5; 22:14; 24:10; Ac 1:2, 26 [a]Lk 9:10

his head on a platter. He presented it to the girl, and she gave it to her mother. 29On
hearing of this, John's disciples came and took his body and laid it in a tomb.

Jesus Feeds Five Thousand

(96/Matthew 14:13–21; Luke 9:10–17; John 6:1–15)

30The apostles[z] gathered round Jesus and reported to him all they had done and
taught.[a] 31Then, because so many people were coming and going that they did not
even have a chance to eat,[b] he said to them, "Come with me by yourselves to a quiet
place and get some rest."

6:31 [b]Mk 3:20

HEROD ANTIPAS

Most people dislike having their sins pointed out, especially in public. The shame of being exposed is often stronger than the guilt brought on by the wrongdoing. Herod Antipas was a man experiencing both guilt and shame.

Herod's ruthless ambition was public knowledge, as was his illegal marriage to his brother's wife, Herodias. One man made Herod's sin a public issue. That man was John the Baptist. John had been preaching in the desert, and thousands flocked to hear him. Apparently it was no secret that John had rebuked Herod for his adulterous marriage. Herodias was particularly anxious to have John silenced. As a solution, Herod imprisoned John.

Herod liked John. John was probably one of the few people he met who spoke only the truth to him. But the truth about his sin was a bitter pill to swallow, and Herod wavered at the point of conflict: he couldn't afford to have John constantly reminding the people of their leader's sinfulness, but he was afraid to have John killed. He put off the choice. Eventually Herodias forced his hand, and John was executed. Of course, this only served to increase Herod's guilt.

Upon hearing about Jesus, Herod immediately identified him with John. He couldn't decide what to do about Jesus. He didn't want to repeat the mistake he had made with John, so he tried to threaten Jesus just before Jesus' final journey to Jerusalem. When the two met briefly during Jesus' trial, Jesus would not speak to Herod. Herod had proved himself a poor listener to John, and Jesus had nothing to add to John's words. Herod responded with spite and mocking. Having rejected the messenger, he found it easy to reject the Messiah.

For each person, God chooses the best possible ways to reveal himself. He uses his word, various circumstances, our minds, or other people to get our attention. He is persuasive and persistent, but never forces himself on us. To miss or resist God's message, as did Herod, is tragedy. How aware are you of God's attempts to enter your life? Have you welcomed him?

Strengths and accomplishments:
- Built the city of Tiberias and oversaw other architectural projects
- Ruled the region of Galilee for the Romans

Weaknesses and mistakes:
- Consumed with his quest for power
- Put off decisions or made wrong ones under pressure
- Divorced his wife to marry the wife of his half brother, Philip
- Imprisoned John the Baptist and later ordered his execution
- Had a minor part in the execution of Jesus

Lessons from his life:
- A life motivated by ambition is usually characterised by self-destruction
- Opportunities to do good usually come to us in the form of choices to be made

Vital statistics:
- Where: Jerusalem
- Occupation: Roman tetrarch of the region of Galilee and Perea
- Relatives: Father: Herod the Great. Mother: Malthace. First wife: daughter of Aretas IV. Second wife: Herodias
- Contemporaries: John the Baptist, Jesus, Pilate

Key verse:
"When Herod heard John, he was greatly puzzled; yet he liked to listen to him" (Mark 6:20).

Herod Antipas' story is told in the Gospels. He is also mentioned in Acts 4:27; 13:1.

The word became an official title for Jesus' 12 disciples after his death and resurrection (Acts 1:25, 26; Ephesians 2:20).

6:31 When the disciples had returned from their mission, Jesus took them away to rest. Doing God's work is very important, but Jesus recognised that to do it effectively we need periodic rest and renewal. Jesus and his disciples, however, did not always find it easy to get the rest they needed!

32 So they went away by themselves in a boat[c] to a solitary place. 33 But many who
saw them leaving recognised them and ran on foot from all the towns and got there
ahead of them. 34 When Jesus landed and saw a large crowd, he had compassion on
them, because they were like sheep without a shepherd.[d] So he began teaching them
many things.
35 By this time it was late in the day, so his disciples came to him. "This is a remote
place," they said, "and it's already very late. 36 Send the people away so that they can
go to the surrounding countryside and villages and buy themselves something to eat."
37 But he answered, "You give them something to eat."[e]
They said to him, "That would take eight months of a man's wages![e] Are we to
go and spend that much on bread and give it to them to eat?"
38 "How many loaves do you have?" he asked. "Go and see."
When they found out, they said, "Five — and two fish."[f]
39 Then Jesus directed them to have all the people sit down in groups on the green
grass. 40 So they sat down in groups of hundreds and fifties. 41 Taking the five loaves
and the two fish and looking up to heaven, he gave thanks and broke the loaves.[g]
Then he gave them to his disciples to set before the people. He also divided the two
fish among them all. 42 They all ate and were satisfied, 43 and the disciples picked up
twelve basketfuls of broken pieces of bread and fish. 44 The number of the men who
had eaten was five thousand.

Jesus Walks on Water
(97/Matthew 14:22–33; John 6:16–21)

45 Immediately Jesus made his disciples get into the boat[h] and go on ahead of him
to Bethsaida,[i] while he dismissed the crowd. 46 After leaving them, he went up on
a mountainside to pray.[j]
47 When evening came, the boat was in the middle of the lake, and he was alone
on land. 48 He saw the disciples straining at the oars, because the wind was against
them. About the fourth watch of the night he went out to them, walking on the lake.
He was about to pass by them, 49 but when they saw him walking on the lake, they

e 37 Greek *take two hundred denarii*

6:32 [c] ver 45; Mk 4:36
6:34 [d] Mt 9:36
6:37 [e] 2Ki 4:42-44
6:38 [f] Mt 15:34; Mk 8:5
6:41 [g] Mt 14:19
6:45 [h] ver 32 [i] Mt 11:21
6:46 [j] Lk 3:21

6:34 This crowd was as pitiful as a flock of sheep without a shepherd. Sheep are easily scattered; without a shepherd they are in grave danger. Jesus was the Shepherd who could teach them what they needed to know and keep them from straying from God. See Psalm 23; Isaiah 40:11; and Ezekiel 34:5ff for descriptions of the Good Shepherd.

6:37 In this chapter different people have examined Jesus' life and ministry: his neighbours and family, Herod the king, and the disciples. Yet none of these appreciated Jesus for who he was. The disciples were still pondering, still confused, still unbelieving. They did not realise that Jesus could provide for them. They were so preoccupied with the immensity of the task that they could not see what was possible with God. Do you let what seems impossible about Christianity keep you from believing?

6:37–42 When Jesus asked the disciples to provide food for over 5,000 people, they asked in astonishment if they should go and spend eight months' wages on bread. How do you react when you are given an impossible task? A situation that seems impossible with human resources is simply an opportunity for God. The disciples did everything they could by gathering the available food and organising the people into groups. Then, in answer to prayer, God did the impossible. When facing a seemingly impossible task, do what you can and ask God to do the rest. He may see fit to make the impossible happen.

6:49 The disciples were surprised to see Jesus walking beside them on the water. But they should have realised that Jesus would help them when they were in trouble. Though they had lost sight of Jesus, he had not lost sight of them. His concern for them overcame their lack of faith. The next time you are in "deep water", remember that Christ knows your struggle and cares for you.

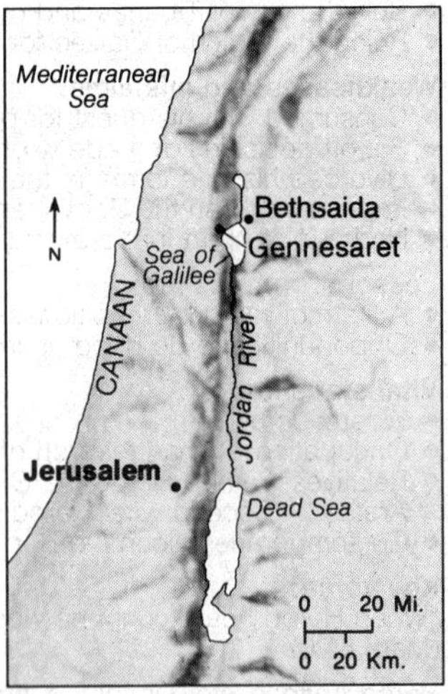

JESUS WALKS ON THE WATER
After feeding the people who had followed to hear him at Bethsaida, Jesus sent the people home, sent his disciples by boat towards Bethsaida, and went to pray. The disciples encountered a storm and Jesus walked to them on the water. They landed at Gennesaret.

6:49, 50 The disciples were afraid, but Jesus' presence calmed their fears. We all experience fear. Do we try to deal with it ourselves, or do we let Jesus deal with it? In times of fear and uncertainty, it is calming to know that Christ is always with us (Matthew 28:20). To recognise Christ's presence is the antidote to fear.

6:49 [k]Lk 24:37
6:50 [l]Mt 14:27
6:51 [m]ver 32 [n]Mk 4:39
6:52 [o]Mk 8:17-21
6:53 [p]Jn 6:24, 25
6:56 [q]Mt 9:20
7:2 [a]Ac 10:14, 28; 11:8; Ro 14:14
7:3 [b]ver 5, 8, 9, 13; Lk 11:38
7:4 [c]Mt 23:25; Lk 11:39
7:5 [d]ver 3; Gal 1:14; Col 2:8

thought he was a ghost.[k] They cried out, 50because they all saw him and were
terrified.
Immediately he spoke to them and said, "Take courage! It is I. Don't be afraid."[l]
51Then he climbed into the boat[m] with them, and the wind died down.[n] They were
completely amazed, 52for they had not understood about the loaves; their hearts were
hardened.[o]

Jesus Heals All Who Touch Him
(98/Matthew 14:34–36)

53When they had crossed over, they landed at Gennesaret and anchored there.[p]
54As soon as they got out of the boat, people recognised Jesus. 55They ran throughout
that whole region and carried the sick on mats to wherever they heard he was. 56And
wherever he went—into villages, towns or countryside—they placed the sick in the
market-places. They begged him to let them touch even the edge of his cloak,[q] and
all who touched him were healed.

Jesus Teaches about Inner Purity
(102/Matthew 15:1–20)

7 The Pharisees and some of the teachers of the law who had come from Jerusalem
gathered round Jesus and 2saw some of his disciples eating food with hands that
were "unclean",[a] that is, unwashed. 3(The Pharisees and all the Jews do not eat unless
they give their hands a ceremonial washing, holding to the tradition of the elders.[b]
4When they come from the market-place they do not eat unless they wash. And they
observe many other traditions, such as the washing of cups, pitchers and kettles.**a)**[c]
5So the Pharisees and teachers of the law asked Jesus, "Why don't your disciples
live according to the tradition of the elders[d] instead of eating their food with 'unclean'
hands?"
6He replied, "Isaiah was right when he prophesied about you hypocrites; as it is
written:

a *4* Some early manuscripts *pitchers, kettles and dining couches*

REAL LEADERSHIP
Mark gives us some of the best insights into Jesus' character.

Herod as a leader	*Jesus as a leader*
Selfish	Compassionate
Murderer	Healer
Immoral	Just and good
Political opportunist	Servant
King over small territory	King over all creation

6:52 The disciples didn't want to believe, perhaps because (1) they couldn't accept the fact that this human named Jesus was really the Son of God; (2) they dared not believe that the Messiah would choose them as his followers—it was too good to be true; (3) they still did not understand the real purpose of Jesus' coming to earth. Their disbelief took the form of misunderstanding.

Even after watching Jesus miraculously feed 5,000 people, they still could not take the final step of faith and believe that he was God's Son. If they had, they would not have been amazed that Jesus could walk on water. The disciples did not transfer the truth they already knew about Jesus to their own lives. We read that Jesus walked on the water, and yet we often marvel that he is able to work in our lives. We must not only believe that these miracles really occurred; we must also transfer the truth to our own life situations.

6:53 Gennesaret was a small fertile plain located on the west side of the Sea of Galilee. Capernaum, Jesus' home, sat at the northern edge of this plain.

7:1ff The religious leaders sent some investigators from their headquarters in Jerusalem to check up on Jesus. The delegation didn't like what they found, however, because Jesus scolded them for keeping the law and the traditions in order to look holy instead of to honour God. The prophet Isaiah accused the religious leaders of his day of doing the same thing (Isaiah 29:13). Jesus used Isaiah's words to accuse these men.

7:3, 4 Mark explained these Jewish rituals because he was writing to a non-Jewish audience. Before each meal, devout Jews performed a short ceremony, washing their hands and arms in a specific way. The disciples did not have dirty hands; they were simply not carrying out this traditional cleansing. The Pharisees thought this ceremony cleansed them from any contact they might have had with anything considered unclean. Jesus said they were wrong in thinking they were acceptable to God just because they were clean on the outside.

7:6, 7 Hypocrisy is pretending to be something you are not and have no intention of being. Jesus called the Pharisees hypocrites because they worshipped God for the wrong reasons. Their worship was not motivated by love, but by a desire to attain profit, to appear holy, and to increase their status. We become hypocrites when we (1) pay more attention to reputation than to character, (2) carefully follow certain religious practices while allowing our hearts to remain distant from God, and (3) emphasise our virtues but others' sins.

" 'These people honour me with their lips,
but their hearts are far from me.
7They worship me in vain;
their teachings are but rules taught by men.'[b][e]
8You have let go of the commands of God and are holding on to the traditions of
men."[f]
9And he said to them: "You have a fine way of setting aside the commands of God
in order to observe[c] your own traditions![g] 10For Moses said, 'Honour your father
and your mother,'[d][h] and, 'Anyone who curses his father or mother must be put to
death.'[e][i] 11But you say[j] that if a man says to his father or mother: 'Whatever help
you might otherwise have received from me is Corban' (that is, a gift devoted to God),
12then you no longer let him do anything for his father or mother. 13Thus you nullify
the word of God[k] by your tradition[l] that you have handed down. And you do many
things like that."
14Again Jesus called the crowd to him and said, "Listen to me, everyone, and
understand this. 15Nothing outside a man can make him 'unclean' by going into him.
Rather, it is what comes out of a man that makes him 'unclean'."[f]
17After he had left the crowd and entered the house, his disciples asked him[m] about
this parable. 18"Are you so dull?" he asked. "Don't you see that nothing that enters
a man from the outside can make him 'unclean'? 19For it doesn't go into his heart
but into his stomach, and then out of his body." (In saying this, Jesus declared all
foods[n] "clean".)[o]
20He went on: "What comes out of a man is what makes him 'unclean'. 21For from
within, out of men's hearts, come evil thoughts, sexual immorality, theft, murder,
adultery, 22greed,[p] malice, deceit, lewdness, envy, slander, arrogance and folly.
23All these evils come from inside and make a man 'unclean'."

2. Jesus' ministry beyond Galilee

Jesus Sends a Demon Out of a Girl
(103/Matthew 15:21–28)

24Jesus left that place and went to the vicinity of Tyre.[g][q] He entered a house and
did not want anyone to know it; yet he could not keep his presence secret. 25In fact,
as soon as she heard about him, a woman whose little daughter was possessed by an

[b] *6,7* Isaiah 29:13 [c] *9* Some manuscripts *set up* [d] *10* Exodus 20:12; Deut. 5:16 [e] *10* Exodus 21:17; Lev. 20:9
[f] *15* Some early manuscripts *'unclean'. 16If anyone has ears to hear, let him hear."* [g] *24* Many early manuscripts *Tyre and Sidon*

7:7 [e]Isa 29:13
7:8 [f]ver 3
7:9 [g]ver 3
7:10 [h]Ex 20:12; Dt 5:16 [i]Ex 21:17; Lev 20:9
7:11 [j]Mt 23:16, 18
7:13 [k]Heb 4:12 [l]ver 3
7:17 [m]Mk 9:28
7:19 [n]Ro 14:1-12; Col 2:16; 1Ti 4:3-5 [o]Ac 10:15
7:22 [p]Mt 20:15
7:24 [q]Mt 11:21

7:8, 9 The Pharisees added hundreds of their own petty rules and regulations to God's holy laws, and then they tried to force people to follow these rules. These men claimed to know God's will in every detail of life. There are still religious leaders today who add rules and regulations to God's word, causing much confusion among believers. It is idolatry to claim that your interpretation of God's word is as important as God's word itself. It is especially dangerous to set up unbiblical standards for *others* to follow. Instead, look to Christ for guidance about your own behaviour, and let him lead others in the details of their lives.

7:10, 11 The Pharisees used God as an excuse to avoid helping their families. They thought it was more important to put money in the temple treasury than to help their needy parents, although God's law specifically says to honour fathers and mothers (Exodus 20:12) and to care for those in need (Leviticus 25:35–43). (For an explanation of *Corban,* see the note on Matthew 15:5, 6.) We should give money and time to God, but we must never use God as an excuse to neglect our responsibilities. Helping those in need is one of the most important ways to honour God.

7:18, 19 Do we worry more about what is in our diets than what is in our hearts and minds? As they interpreted the dietary laws (Leviticus 11), the Jews believed they could be clean before God because of what they refused to eat. But Jesus pointed out that sin actually begins in the attitudes and intentions of the inner person. Jesus did not degrade the law, but he paved the way for the change made clear in Acts 10:9–29 when God removed the cultural restrictions regarding food. We are not pure because of outward acts – we become pure on the inside as Christ renews our minds and transforms us into his image.

7:20–23 An evil action begins with a single thought. Allowing our minds to dwell on lust, envy, hatred, or revenge will lead to sin. Don't defile yourself by focusing on evil. Instead, follow Paul's advice in Philippians 4:8 and think about what is true, noble, right, pure, lovely, and admirable.

7:24 Jesus travelled about 30 miles to Tyre and then went to Sidon. These were port cities on the Mediterranean Sea north of Israel. Both cities had flourishing trade and were very wealthy. They were proud, historic Canaanite cities.

In David's day, Tyre was on friendly terms with Israel (2 Samuel 5:11), but soon afterwards the city became known for its wickedness. Its king even claimed to be God (Ezekiel 28:1ff). Tyre rejoiced when Jerusalem was destroyed in 586 B.C., because without Israel's competition, Tyre's trade and profits would increase. It was into this evil and materialistic culture that Jesus brought his message. It is interesting that Jesus stressed the importance of inner purity just before visiting Tyre.

7:25 [r]Mt 4:24
7:31 [s]ver 24; Mt 11:21 [t]Mt 4:18 [u]Mt 4:25; Mk 5:20
7:32 [v]Mt 9:32; Lk 11:14 [w]Mk 5:23
7:33 [x]Mk 8:23
7:34 [y]Mk 6:41; Jn 11:41 [z]Mk 8:12
7:35 [a]Isa 35:5, 6
7:36 [b]Mt 8:4

evil[h] spirit[r] came and fell at his feet. 26The woman was a Greek, born in Syrian
Phoenicia. She begged Jesus to drive the demon out of her daughter.
27"First let the children eat all they want," he told her, "for it is not right to take
the children's bread and toss it to their dogs."
28"Yes, Lord," she replied, "but even the dogs under the table eat the children's
crumbs."
29Then he told her, "For such a reply, you may go; the demon has left your
daughter."
30She went home and found her child lying on the bed, and the demon gone.

The Crowd Marvels at Jesus' Healings
(104/Matthew 15:29–31)

31Then Jesus left the vicinity of Tyre[s] and went through Sidon, down to the Sea
of Galilee[t] and into the region of the Decapolis.[i][u] 32There some people brought
to him a man who was deaf and could hardly talk,[v] and they begged him to place
his hand on[w] the man.
33After he took him aside, away from the crowd, Jesus put his fingers into the man's
ears. Then he spat[x] and touched the man's tongue. 34He looked up to heaven[y] and
with a deep sigh[z] said to him, "*Ephphatha!*" (which means, "Be opened!"). 35At this,
the man's ears were opened, his tongue was loosened and he began to speak plainly.[a]
36Jesus commanded them not to tell anyone.[b] But the more he did so, the more
they kept talking about it. 37People were overwhelmed with amazement. "He has done
everything well," they said. "He even makes the deaf hear and the mute speak."

[h] *25* Greek *unclean* [i] *31* That is, the Ten Cities

GOSPEL ACCOUNTS FOUND ONLY IN MARK

Section	*Topic*	*Significance*
4:26–29	Story of the growing seed	We must share the good news of Jesus with other people, but only God makes it grow in their lives.
7:31–37	Jesus heals a deaf man who could hardly talk	Jesus cares about our physical as well as spiritual needs.
8:22–26	Jesus heals the blind man at Bethsaida	Jesus is considerate because he makes sure this man's sight is fully restored.

7:26 This woman is called a Greek, born in Syrian Phoenicia, in Mark and a Canaanite in Matthew. Mark's designation refers to her political background. His Roman audience would easily identify her by the part of the empire that was her home. Matthew's description was designed for his Jewish audience, who remembered the Canaanites as bitter enemies when Israel was settling in the promised land.

7:27, 28 *Dog* refers to little dogs or house pets, not outdoor scavengers. Jesus was saying that his first priority was to provide food for the children (teach his disciples), not to allow pets to interrupt the family meal.

The woman did not try to argue. Using Jesus' choice of imagery, she pointed out that she was willing to be considered an interruption as long as she could receive God's healing for her daughter. Ironically, many Jews would lose God's spiritual healing because they rejected Jesus, while many Gentiles, whom the Jews rejected, would find salvation because they recognised Jesus.

7:29 This miracle shows that Jesus' power over demons is so great that he doesn't need to be present physically in order to free someone. His power transcends any distance.

7:36 Jesus asked the people not to talk about this healing, because he didn't want to be seen simply as a miracle worker. He didn't want the people to miss his real message. We must not be so concerned about what Jesus can do for us that we forget to listen to his message.

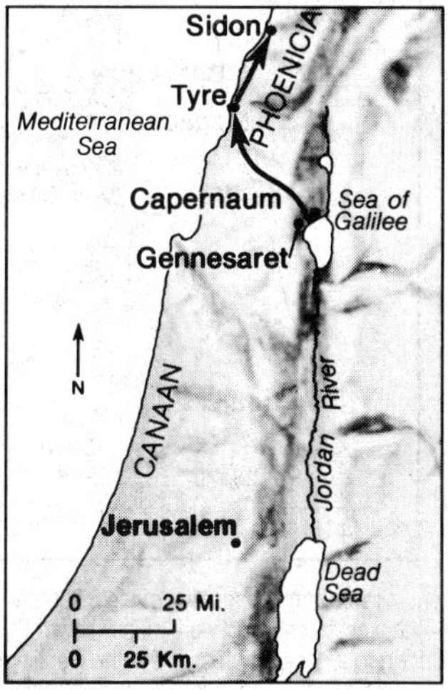

MINISTRY IN PHOENICIA
Jesus' ministry was to all people—first to Jews but also to Gentiles. Jesus took his disciples from Galilee to Tyre and Sidon, large cities in Phoenicia, where he healed a Gentile woman's daughter.

Jesus Feeds Four Thousand
(105/Matthew 15:32–39)

8:2 [a]Mt 9:36

8 During those days another large crowd gathered. Since they had nothing to eat,
Jesus called his disciples to him and said, 2"I have compassion for these people;[a]
they have already been with me three days and have nothing to eat. 3If I send them
home hungry, they will collapse on the way, because some of them have come a long
distance."

8:7 [b]Mt 14:19

4His disciples answered, "But where in this remote place can anyone get enough
bread to feed them?"
5"How many loaves do you have?" Jesus asked.
"Seven," they replied.
6He told the crowd to sit down on the ground. When he had taken the seven loaves
and given thanks, he broke them and gave them to his disciples to set before the
people, and they did so. 7They had a few small fish as well; he gave thanks for them
also and told the disciples to distribute them.[b] 8The people ate and were satisfied.
Afterwards the disciples picked up seven basketfuls of broken pieces that were left
over.[c] 9About four thousand men were present. And having sent them away, 10he
got into the boat with his disciples and went to the region of Dalmanutha.

8:8 [c]ver 20

8:11 [d]Mt 12:38

Religious Leaders Ask for a Sign in the Sky
(106/Matthew 16:1–4)

11The Pharisees came and began to question Jesus. To test him, they asked him for
a sign from heaven.[d] 12He sighed deeply[e] and said, "Why does this generation ask
for a miraculous sign? I tell you the truth, no sign will be given to it." 13Then he left
them, got back into the boat and crossed to the other side.

8:12 [e]Mk 7:34

Jesus Warns against Wrong Teaching
(107/Matthew 16:5–12)

14The disciples had forgotten to bring bread, except for one loaf they had with them
in the boat. 15"Be careful," Jesus warned them. "Watch out for the yeast[f] of the
Pharisees[g] and that of Herod."[h]

8:15 [f]1Co 5:6-8 [g]Lk 12:1 [h]Mt 14:1; Mk 12:13

CONTINUED MINISTRY
After taking a roundabout way back to Galilee through Decapolis (the Ten Cities), Jesus returned to Dalmanutha where Jewish leaders questioned his authority. From there he went to Bethsaida and on to Caesarea Philippi. Here he talked with his disciples about his authority and coming events.

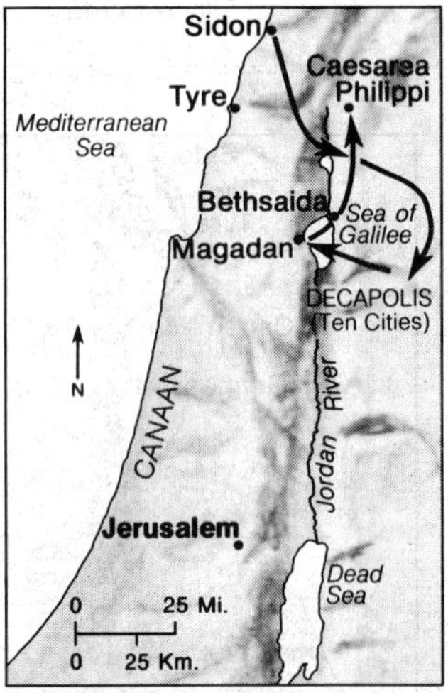

8:1ff This is a different miracle from the feeding of the 5,000 described in chapter 6. At that time, those fed were mostly Jews. This time Jesus was ministering to a non-Jewish crowd in the Gentile region of the Decapolis. Jesus' actions and message were beginning to have an impact on large numbers of Gentiles. That Jesus would compassionately minister to non-Jews was very reassuring to Mark's primarily Roman audience.

8:1–3 Do you ever feel that God is so busy with important concerns that he can't possibly be aware of your needs? Just as Jesus was concerned about these people's need for food, he is concerned about our daily needs. At another time Jesus said, "So do not worry, saying, 'What shall we eat?' or 'What shall we drink?' or 'What shall we wear?' . . . your heavenly Father knows that you need them" (Matthew 6:31, 32). Do you have concerns that you think would not interest God? There is nothing too large for him to handle and no need too small to escape his interest.

8:11 The Pharisees had tried to explain away Jesus' previous miracles by claiming they were done by luck, coincidence, or evil power. Here they demanded a sign from heaven—something only God could do. Jesus refused their demand because he knew that even this kind of miracle would not convince them. They had already decided not to believe. Hearts can become so hard that even the most convincing facts and demonstrations will not change them.

8:15 Mark mentions the yeast of the Pharisees and Herod, while Matthew talks about the yeast of the Pharisees and Sadducees. Mark's audience, mostly non-Jews, would have known about Herod, but not necessarily about the Jewish religious sect of the Sadducees. Thus Mark quoted the part of Jesus' statement that his readers would understand. This reference to Herod may mean the Herodians, a group of Jews who supported the king. Many Herodians were also Sadducees.

8:15ff Yeast in this passage symbolises evil. Just as only a small amount of yeast is needed to make a batch of bread rise, so the

16 They discussed this with one another and said, "It is because we have no bread."
17 Aware of their discussion, Jesus asked them: "Why are you talking about having
no bread? Do you still not see or understand? Are your hearts hardened?[i] 18 Do you
have eyes but fail to see, and ears but fail to hear? And don't you remember? 19 When
I broke the five loaves for the five thousand, how many basketfuls of pieces did you
pick up?"
"Twelve,"[j] they replied.
20 "And when I broke the seven loaves for the four thousand, how many basketfuls
of pieces did you pick up?"
They answered, "Seven."[k]
21 He said to them, "Do you still not understand?"[l]

Jesus Restores Sight to a Blind Man
(108)

22 They came to Bethsaida,[m] and some people brought a blind man[n] and begged
Jesus to touch him. 23 He took the blind man by the hand and led him outside the
village. When he had spat[o] on the man's eyes and put his hands on[p] him, Jesus
asked, "Do you see anything?"
24 He looked up and said, "I see people; they look like trees walking around."
25 Once more Jesus put his hands on the man's eyes. Then his eyes were opened,
his sight was restored, and he saw everything clearly. 26 Jesus sent him home, saying,
"Don't go into the village."[a]

Peter Says Jesus Is the Messiah
(109/Matthew 16:13–20; Luke 9:18–20)

27 Jesus and his disciples went on to the villages around Caesarea Philippi. On the
way he asked them, "Who do people say I am?"
28 They replied, "Some say John the Baptist;[q] others say Elijah;[r] and still others,
one of the prophets."
29 "But what about you?" he asked. "Who do you say I am?"
Peter answered, "You are the Christ."[b] [s]
30 Jesus warned them not to tell anyone about him.[t]

8:17 [i] Isa 6:9, 10; Mk 6:52
8:19 [j] Mt 14:20; Mk 6:41-44; Lk 9:17; Jn 6:13
8:20 [k] ver 6-9; Mt 15:37
8:21 [l] Mk 6:52
8:22 [m] Mt 11:21 [n] Mk 10:46; Jn 9:1
8:23 [o] Mk 7:33 [p] Mk 5:23
8:28 [q] Mt 3:1 [r] Mal 4:5
8:29 [s] Jn 6:69; 11:27
8:30 [t] Mt 8:4; 16:20; 17:9; Mk 9:9; Lk 9:21

[a] *26* Some manuscripts *Don't go and tell anyone in the village* [b] *29* Or *Messiah.* "The Christ" (Greek) and "the Messiah" (Hebrew) both mean "the Anointed One".

---

hardheartedness of the religious and political leaders could permeate and contaminate the entire society and make it rise up against Jesus.

8:17, 18 How could the disciples experience so many of Jesus' miracles and yet be so slow to comprehend who he was? They had already seen Jesus feed over 5,000 people with five loaves and two fish (6:35–44), yet here they doubted whether he could feed another large group.

Sometimes we are also slow to catch on. Although Christ has brought us through trials and temptations in the past, we don't believe that he will do it in the future. Is your heart too closed to take in all that God can do for you? Don't be like the disciples. Remember what Christ has done, and have faith that he will do it again.

8:25 Why did Jesus touch the man a second time before he could see? This miracle was not too difficult for Jesus, but he chose to do it in stages, possibly to show the disciples that some healing would be gradual rather than instantaneous or to demonstrate that spiritual truth is not always perceived clearly at first. Before Jesus left, however, the man was healed completely.

8:27 Caesarea Philippi was an especially pagan city known for its worship of Greek gods and its temples devoted to the ancient god Pan. The ruler Philip, referred to in Mark 6:17, changed the city's name from Caesarea to Caesarea Philippi so that it would not be confused with the coastal city of Caesarea (Acts 8:40), the capital of the territory ruled by his brother Herod Antipas. This pagan city where many gods were recognised was a fitting place for Jesus to ask the disciples to recognise him as the Son of God.

8:28 For the story of John the Baptist, see Mark 1:1–11 and 6:14–29. For the story of Elijah, see 1 Kings 17 – 20 and 2 Kings 1:2.

8:29 Jesus asked the disciples who other people thought he was; then he asked them the same question. It is not enough to know what others say about Jesus: you must know, understand, and accept for yourself that he is the Messiah. You must move from curiosity to commitment, from admiration to adoration.

8:29–31 The name for Jesus, *Son of Man,* is Jesus' most common title for himself. It comes from Daniel 7:13, where the Son of Man is a heavenly figure who, in the end times, has authority and power. The name refers to Jesus as the Messiah, the representative man, the human agent of God who is vindicated by God. In this passage, *Son of Man* is linked closely with Peter's confession of Jesus as the Christ and confirms its Messianic significance.

From this point on, Jesus spoke plainly and directly to his disciples about his death and resurrection. He began to prepare them for what was going to happen to him by telling them three times that he would soon die (8:31; 9:31; 10:33, 34).

8:30 Why did Jesus warn his own disciples not to tell anyone the truth about him? Jesus knew they needed more instruction about the work he would accomplish through his death and resurrection. Without more teaching, the disciples would have only half the picture. When they confessed Jesus as the Christ, they still didn't know all that it meant.

Jesus Predicts His Death the First Time
(110/Matthew 16:21–28; Luke 9:21–27)

31 He then began to teach them that the Son of Man[u] must suffer many things[v]
and be rejected by the elders, chief priests and teachers of the law,[w] and that he must
be killed[x] and after three days[y] rise again.[z] 32 He spoke plainly[a] about this, and
Peter took him aside and began to rebuke him.
33 But when Jesus turned and looked at his disciples, he rebuked Peter. "Get behind
me, Satan!"[b] he said. "You do not have in mind the things of God, but the things
of men."
34 Then he called the crowd to him along with his disciples and said: "If anyone
would come after me, he must deny himself and take up his cross and follow me.[c]
35 For whoever wants to save his life[c] will lose it, but whoever loses his life for me
and for the gospel will save it.[d] 36 What good is it for a man to gain the whole world,
yet forfeit his soul? 37 Or what can a man give in exchange for his soul? 38 If anyone
is ashamed of me and my words in this adulterous and sinful generation, the Son of
Man[e] will be ashamed of him[f] when he comes[g] in his Father's glory with the holy
angels."
9 And he said to them, "I tell you the truth, some who are standing here will not
taste death before they see the kingdom of God come[a] with power."[b]

Jesus Is Transfigured on the Mountain
(111/Matthew 17:1–13; Luke 9:28–36)

2 After six days Jesus took Peter, James and John[c] with him and led them up a high
mountain, where they were all alone. There he was transfigured before them. 3 His

c 35 The Greek word means either *life* or *soul*; also in verse 36.

8:31 [u]Mt 8:20 [v]Mt 16:21 [w]Mt 27:1, 2 [x]Ac 2:23; 3:13 [y]Mt 16:21 [z]Mt 16:21
8:32 [a]Jn 18:20
8:33 [b]Mt 4:10
8:34 [c]Mt 10:38; Lk 14:27
8:35 [d]Jn 12:25
8:38 [e]Mt 8:20 [f]Mt 10:33; Lk 12:9 [g]1Th 2:19
9:1 [a]Mk 13:30; Lk 22:18 [b]Mt 24:30; 25:31
9:2 [c]Mt 4:21

8:32, 33 In this moment, Peter was not considering God's purposes, but only his own natural human desires and feelings. Peter wanted Christ to be king, but not the suffering servant prophesied in Isaiah 53. He was ready to receive the glory of following the Messiah, but not the persecution.

The Christian life is not a paved road to wealth and ease. It often involves hard work, persecution, deprivation, and deep suffering. Peter saw only part of the picture. Don't repeat his mistake. Instead, focus on the good that God can bring out of apparent evil, and the resurrection that follows crucifixion.

8:33 Peter was often the spokesman for all the disciples. In singling him out, Jesus may have been addressing all of them indirectly. Unknowingly, the disciples were trying to prevent Jesus from going to the cross and thus fulfilling his mission on earth. Satan also tempted Jesus to avoid the way of the cross (Matthew 4). Whereas Satan's motives were evil, the disciples were motivated by love and admiration for Jesus. Nevertheless, the disciples' job was not to guide and protect Jesus, but to follow him. Only after Jesus' death and resurrection would they fully understand why he had to die.

8:34 The Romans, Mark's original audience, knew what taking up the cross meant. Death on a cross was a form of execution used by Rome for dangerous criminals. A prisoner carried his own cross to the place of execution, signifying submission to Rome's power.

Jesus used the image of carrying a cross to illustrate the ultimate submission required of his followers. He is not against pleasure, nor was he saying that we should seek pain needlessly. Jesus was talking about the heroic effort needed to follow him moment by moment, to do his will even when the work is difficult and the future looks bleak.

8:35 We should be willing to lose our lives for the sake of the gospel, not because our lives are useless but because nothing – not even life itself – can compare to what we gain with Christ. Jesus wants us to *choose* to follow him rather than to lead a life of sin and self-satisfaction. He wants us to stop trying to control our own destiny and to let him direct us. This makes good sense because, as the Creator, Christ knows better than we do what real life is about. He asks for submission, not self-hatred; he asks us only to lose our self-centred determination to be in charge.

8:36, 37 Many people spend all their energy seeking pleasure. Jesus said, however, that a world of pleasure centred on possessions, position, or power is ultimately worthless. Whatever you have on earth is only temporary; it cannot be exchanged for your soul. If you work hard at getting what you want, you might eventually have a "pleasurable" life, but in the end you will find it hollow and empty. Are you willing to make the pursuit of God more important than the selfish pursuit of pleasure? Follow Jesus, and you will know what it means to live abundantly now and to have eternal life as well.

8:38 Jesus constantly turns the world's perspective upside down with talk of first and last, saving and losing. Here he gives us a choice. We can reject Jesus now and be rejected by him at his second coming, or we can accept him now and be accepted by him then. Rejecting Christ may help us escape shame for the time being, but it will guarantee an eternity of shame later.

9:1 What did Jesus mean when he said that some of the disciples would see the kingdom of God come with power? There are several possibilities. He could have been foretelling his transfiguration, resurrection and ascension, the coming of the Holy Spirit at Pentecost, or his second coming. The transfiguration is a strong possibility because Mark immediately tells that story. In the transfiguration (9:2–8), Peter, James, and John saw Jesus' glory, identity, and power as the Son of God (2 Peter 1:16).

9:2 We don't know why Jesus singled out Peter, James, and John for this special revelation of his glory and purity. Perhaps they were the ones most ready to understand and accept this great truth. These three disciples were the inner circle of the group of 12. They were among the first to hear Jesus' call (1:16–19). They headed the Gospel lists of disciples (3:16). And they were present at certain healings where others were excluded (Luke 8:51).

9:2 Jesus took the disciples to either Mount Hermon or Mount Tabor. A mountain was often associated with closeness to God and readiness to receive his words. God had appeared to both Moses (Exodus 24:12–18) and Elijah (1 Kings 19:8–18) on mountains.

clothes became dazzling white,[d] whiter than anyone in the world could bleach them.
4 And there appeared before them Elijah and Moses, who were talking with Jesus.
5 Peter said to Jesus, "Rabbi,[e] it is good for us to be here. Let us put up three
shelters—one for you, one for Moses and one for Elijah." 6 (He did not know what
to say, they were so frightened.)
7 Then a cloud appeared and enveloped them, and a voice came from the cloud:[f]
"This is my Son, whom I love. Listen to him!"[g]
8 Suddenly, when they looked round, they no longer saw anyone with them except
Jesus.
9 As they were coming down the mountain, Jesus gave them orders not to tell
anyone[h] what they had seen until the Son of Man[i] had risen from the dead. 10 They
kept the matter to themselves, discussing what "rising from the dead" meant.
11 And they asked him, "Why do the teachers of the law say that Elijah must come
first?"
12 Jesus replied, "To be sure, Elijah does come first, and restores all things. Why
then is it written that the Son of Man[j] must suffer much[k] and be rejected?[l] 13 But
I tell you, Elijah has come,[m] and they have done to him everything they wished, just
as it is written about him."

Jesus Heals a Demon-Possessed Boy
(112/Matthew 17:14–21; Luke 9:37–43)

14 When they came to the other disciples, they saw a large crowd around them and
the teachers of the law arguing with them. 15 As soon as all the people saw Jesus, they
were overwhelmed with wonder and ran to greet him.
16 "What are you arguing with them about?" he asked.
17 A man in the crowd answered, "Teacher, I brought you my son, who is possessed
by a spirit that has robbed him of speech. 18 Whenever it seizes him, it throws him
to the ground. He foams at the mouth, gnashes his teeth and becomes rigid. I asked
your disciples to drive out the spirit, but they could not."
19 "O unbelieving generation," Jesus replied, "how long shall I stay with you? How
long shall I put up with you? Bring the boy to me."
20 So they brought him. When the spirit saw Jesus, it immediately threw the boy
into a convulsion. He fell to the ground and rolled around, foaming at the mouth.[n]
21 Jesus asked the boy's father, "How long has he been like this?"
"From childhood," he answered. 22 "It has often thrown him into fire or water to
kill him. But if you can do anything, take pity on us and help us."

9:3 [d]Mt 28:3
9:5 [e]Mt 23:7
9:7 [f]Ex 24:16 [g]Mt 3:17
9:9 [h]Mk 8:30 [i]Mt 8:20
9:12 [j]Mt 8:20 [k]Mt 16:21 [l]Lk 23:11
9:13 [m]Mt 11:14
9:20 [n]Mk 1:26

9:3ff The transfiguration revealed Christ's divine nature. God's voice exalted Jesus above Moses and Elijah as the long-awaited Messiah with full divine authority. Moses represented the law, and Elijah, the prophets. Their appearance showed Jesus as the fulfilment of both the Old Testament law and the prophetic promises.

Jesus was not a reincarnation of Elijah or Moses. He was not merely one of the prophets. As God's only Son, he far surpasses them in authority and power. Many voices try to tell us how to live and how to know God personally. Some of these are helpful; many are not. We must first listen to the Bible, and then evaluate all other authorities in light of God's revelation.

9:9, 10 Jesus told Peter, James, and John not to speak about what they had seen because they would not fully understand it until Jesus had risen from the dead. Then they would realise that only through dying could Jesus show his power over death and his authority to be King of all. The disciples could not be powerful witnesses for God until they had grasped this truth.

It was natural for the disciples to be confused about Jesus' death and resurrection because they could not see into the future. We, on the other hand, have God's revealed word, the Bible, to give us the full meaning of Jesus' death and resurrection. We have no excuse for our unbelief.

9:11–13 When Jesus said that Elijah had indeed come, he was speaking of John the Baptist (Matthew 17:11–13), who had fulfilled the role prophesied for Elijah.

9:12, 13 It was difficult for the disciples to grasp the idea that their Messiah would have to suffer. The Jews who studied the Old Testament prophecies expected the Messiah to be a great king like David, who would overthrow the enemy, Rome. Their vision was limited to their own time and experience.

They could not understand that the values of God's eternal kingdom were different from the values of the world. They wanted relief from their present problems. But deliverance from sin is far more important than deliverance from physical suffering or political oppression. Our understanding of and appreciation for Jesus must go beyond what he can do for us here and now.

9:18 Why couldn't the disciples drive out the evil spirit? In 6:13 we read that they drove out demons while on their mission to the villages. Perhaps they had special authority only for that trip, or perhaps their faith was faltering. Mark tells this story to show that the battle with Satan is a difficult, ongoing struggle. Victory over sin and temptation comes through faith in Jesus Christ, not through our own efforts.

23“ ‘If you can’?” said Jesus. “Everything is possible for him who believes.”[o]
24Immediately the boy’s father exclaimed, “I do believe; help me overcome my
unbelief!”
25When Jesus saw that a crowd was running to the scene,[p] he rebuked the evil[a]
spirit. “You deaf and mute spirit,” he said, “I command you, come out of him and
never enter him again.”
26The spirit shrieked, convulsed him violently and came out. The boy looked so
much like a corpse that many said, “He’s dead.” 27But Jesus took him by the hand
and lifted him to his feet, and he stood up.
28After Jesus had gone indoors, his disciples asked him privately,[q] “Why couldn’t
we drive it out?”
29He replied, “This kind can come out only by prayer.”[b]

Jesus Predicts His Death the Second Time
(113/Matthew 17:22, 23; Luke 9:44, 45)

30They left that place and passed through Galilee. Jesus did not want anyone to
know where they were, 31because he was teaching his disciples. He said to them, “The
Son of Man[r] is going to be betrayed into the hands of men. They will kill him,[s]
and after three days[t] he will rise.”[u] 32But they did not understand what he meant[v]
and were afraid to ask him about it.

The Disciples Argue about Who Would Be the Greatest
(115/Matthew 18:1–6; Luke 9:46–48)

33They came to Capernaum.[w] When he was in the house,[x] he asked them, “What
were you arguing about on the road?” 34But they kept quiet because on the way they
had argued about who was the greatest.[y]
35Sitting down, Jesus called the Twelve and said, “If anyone wants to be first, he
must be the very last, and the servant of all.”[z]
36He took a little child and had him stand among them. Taking him in his arms,[a]
he said to them, 37“Whoever welcomes one of these little children in my name
welcomes me; and whoever welcomes me does not welcome me but the one who sent
me.”[b]

a *25* Greek *unclean* b *29* Some manuscripts *prayer and fasting*

9:23 [o]Mt 21:21; Mk 11:23; Jn 11:40
9:25 [p]ver 15
9:28 [q]Mk 7:17
9:31 [r]Mt 8:20 [s]ver 12; Ac 2:23; 3:13 [t]Mt 16:21 [u]Mt 16:21
9:32 [v]Lk 2:50; 9:45; 18:34; Jn 12:16
9:33 [w]Mt 4:13 [x]Mk 1:29
9:34 [y]Lk 22:24
9:35 [z]Mt 18:4; 20:26; Mk 10:43; Lk 22:26
9:36 [a]Mk 10:16
9:37 [b]Mt 10:40

9:23 Jesus’ words do not mean that we can automatically obtain anything we want if we just think positively. Jesus meant that anything is *possible* if we believe, because nothing is too difficult for God. We cannot have everything we pray for as if by magic; but with faith, we can have everything we need to serve him.

9:24 The attitude of trust and confidence that the Bible calls *belief* or *faith* (Hebrews 11:1, 6) is not something we can obtain without help. Faith is a gift from God (Ephesians 2:8, 9). No matter how much faith we have, we never reach the point of being self-sufficient. Faith is not stored away like money in the bank. Growing in faith is a constant process of daily renewing our trust in Jesus.

9:29 The disciples would often face difficult situations that could be resolved only through prayer. Prayer is the key that unlocks faith in our lives. Effective prayer needs both an attitude—complete dependence—and an action—asking. Prayer demonstrates our reliance on God as we humbly invite him to fill us with faith and power. There is no substitute for prayer, especially in circumstances that seem impossible.

9:30, 31 At times, Jesus limited his public ministry in order to train his disciples in depth. He knew the importance of equipping them to carry on when he returned to heaven. It takes time to learn. Deep spiritual growth isn’t instant, regardless of the quality of experience or teaching. If even the disciples needed to lay aside their work periodically in order to learn from the Master, how much more do we need to alternate working and learning.

9:30, 31 Leaving Caesarea Philippi, Jesus began his last tour through the region of Galilee.

9:32 Why were the disciples afraid to ask Jesus about his prediction of his death? Perhaps it was because the last time they reacted to Jesus’ sobering words they were scolded (8:32, 33). In their minds, Jesus seemed morbidly preoccupied with death. Actually it was the disciples who were wrongly preoccupied—constantly thinking about the kingdom they hoped Jesus would bring and their positions in it. If Jesus died, the kingdom as they imagined it could not come. Consequently they preferred not to ask him about his predictions.

9:34 The disciples, caught up in their constant struggle for personal success, were embarrassed to answer Jesus’ question. It is always painful to compare our motives with Christ’s. It is not wrong for believers to be industrious or ambitious. But when ambition pushes obedience and service to one side, it becomes sin. Pride or insecurity can cause us to overvalue position and prestige. In God’s kingdom, such motives are destructive. The only safe ambition is directed towards Christ’s kingdom, not our own advancement.

9:36, 37 Jesus taught the disciples to welcome children. This was a new approach in a society where children were usually treated as second-class citizens. It is important not only to treat children well, but also to teach them about Jesus. Children’s ministries should never be regarded as less important than those of adults.

9:38
[c]Nu 11:27-29

9:40
[d]Mt 12:30; Lk 11:23

9:41
[e]Mt 10:42

9:42
[f]Mt 5:29
[g]Mt 18:6; Lk 17:2

9:43
[h]Mt 5:29
[i]Mt 5:30; 18:8
[j]Mt 25:41

9:45
[k]Mt 5:29
[l]Mt 18:8

9:47
[m]Mt 5:29
[n]Mt 5:29; 18:9

9:48
[o]Isa 66:24; Mt 25:41

9:49
[p]Lev 2:13

9:50
[q]Mt 5:13; Lk 14:34, 35
[r]Col 4:6
[s]Ro 12:18; 2Co 13:11; 1Th 5:13

The Disciples Forbid Another to Use Jesus' Name
(116/Luke 9:49, 50)

38 “Teacher,” said John, “we saw a man driving out demons in your name and we
told him to stop, because he was not one of us.”[c]
39 “Do not stop him,” Jesus said. “No-one who does a miracle in my name can in
the next moment say anything bad about me,
40 for whoever is not against us is for
us.[d]
41 I tell you the truth, anyone who gives you a cup of water in my name because
you belong to Christ will certainly not lose his reward.[e]

Jesus Warns against Temptation
(117/Matthew 18:7–9)

42 “And if anyone causes one of these little ones who believe in me to sin,[f] it would
be better for him to be thrown into the sea with a large millstone tied around his neck.[g]
43 If your hand causes you to sin,[h] cut it off. It is better for you to enter life maimed
than with two hands to go into hell,[i] where the fire never goes out.[c][j]
45 And if your
foot causes you to sin,[k] cut it off. It is better for you to enter life crippled than to
have two feet and be thrown into hell.[d][l]
47 And if your eye causes you to sin,[m] pluck
it out. It is better for you to enter the kingdom of God with one eye than to have two
eyes and be thrown into hell,[n]
48 where

> “ ‘their worm does not die,
> and the fire is not quenched.’[e][o]

49 Everyone will be salted[p] with fire.
50 “Salt is good, but if it loses its saltiness, how can you make it salty again?[q] Have
salt in yourselves,[r] and be at peace with each other.”[s]

c *43* Some manuscripts *out,* [44]*where / “ ‘their worm does not die, / and the fire is not quenched.’* **d** *45* Some manuscripts *hell,* [46]*where / “ ‘their worm does not die, / and the fire is not quenched.’* **e** *48* Isaiah 66:24

9:38 The disciples were jealous of a man who healed in Jesus' name because they were more concerned about their own group's position than in helping to free those troubled by demons. We do the same today when we refuse to participate in worthy causes because (1) other people or groups are not affiliated with our denomination, (2) these projects do not involve the kind of people with whom we feel most comfortable, (3) others don't do things the way we are used to doing things, (4) our efforts won't receive enough recognition. Correct theology is important but should never be an excuse to avoid helping people in need.

9:40 Jesus was not saying that being indifferent or neutral towards him is as good as being committed. As he explained in Matthew 12:30, “He who is not with me is against me.” In both cases, Jesus was pointing out that neutrality towards him is not possible. Nevertheless, his followers will not all resemble each other or belong to the same groups. People who are on Jesus' side have the same goal of building up the kingdom of God, and they should not let their differences interfere with this goal. Those who share a common faith in Christ should co-operate. People don't have to be just like us to be following Jesus with us.

9:41, 42 Luke 9:48 states, “He who is least among you all—he is the greatest.” In Jesus' eyes, whoever welcomes a child welcomes Jesus; giving a cup of cold water to a person in need is the same as giving an offering to God. By contrast, harming others or failing to care for them is a sin, even if they are unimportant people in the world's eyes. It is possible for thoughtless, selfish people to gain a measure of worldly greatness, but lasting greatness is measured by God's standards. What do you use as your measure—personal achievement or unselfish service?

9:42 This caution against harming little ones in the faith applies both to what we do individually as teachers and examples and to what we allow to fester in our Christian fellowship. Our thoughts and actions must be motivated by love (1 Corinthians 13), and we must be careful about judging others (Matthew 7:1–5; Romans 14:1—15:4). However, we also have a responsibility to confront flagrant sin within the church (1 Corinthians 5:12, 13).

9:43ff Jesus used startling language to stress the importance of cutting sin out of our lives. Painful discipline is required of his true followers. Giving up a relationship, job, or habit that is against God's will may seem just as painful as cutting off a hand. Our high goal, however, is worth any sacrifice; Christ is worth any possible loss. Nothing should stand in the way of faith. We must be ruthless in removing sins from our lives now in order to avoid being stuck with them for eternity. Make your choices from an eternal perspective.

9:48, 49 With these strange words, Jesus pictured the serious and eternal consequences of sin. To the Jews, worms and fire represented both internal and external pain. What could be worse?

9:50 Jesus used salt to illustrate three qualities that should be found in his people: (1) *We should remember God's faithfulness,* just as salt when used with a sacrifice recalled God's covenant with his people (Leviticus 2:13). (2) *We should make a difference in the “flavour” of the world we live in,* just as salt changes meat's flavour (see Matthew 5:13). (3) *We should counteract the moral decay in society,* just as salt preserves food from decay. When we lose this desire to “salt” the earth with the love and message of God, we become useless to him.

Jesus Teaches about Marriage and Divorce
(173/Matthew 19:1–12)

10 Jesus then left that place and went into the region of Judea and across the
Jordan.[a] Again crowds of people came to him, and as was his custom, he
taught them.[b]
2Some Pharisees[c] came and tested him by asking, "Is it lawful for a man to divorce
his wife?"
3"What did Moses command you?" he replied.
4They said, "Moses permitted a man to write a certificate of divorce and send her
away."[d]
5"It was because your hearts were hard[e] that Moses wrote you this law," Jesus
replied. 6"But at the beginning of creation God 'made them male and female'.[a][f]
7'For this reason a man will leave his father and mother and be united to his wife,[b]
8and the two will become one flesh.'[c][g] So they are no longer two, but one.
9Therefore what God has joined together, let man not separate."
10When they were in the house again, the disciples asked Jesus about this. 11He
answered, "Anyone who divorces his wife and marries another woman commits
adultery against her.[h] 12And if she divorces her husband and marries another man,
she commits adultery."[i]

Jesus Blesses Little Children
(174/Matthew 19:13–15; Luke 18:15–17)

13People were bringing little children to Jesus to have him touch them, but the
disciples rebuked them. 14When Jesus saw this, he was indignant. He said to them,

10:1 [a]Mk 1:5; Jn 10:40; 11:7 [b]Mt 4:23; Mk 2:13; 4:2; 6:6, 34
10:2 [c]Mk 2:16
10:4 [d]Dt 24:1-4; Mt 5:31
10:5 [e]Ps 95:8; Heb 3:15
10:6 [f]Ge 1:27; 5:2
10:8 [g]Ge 2:24; 1Co 6:16
10:11 [h]Mt 5:32; Lk 16:18
10:12 [i]Ro 7:3; 1Co 7:10, 11

[a] 6 Gen. 1:27 [b] 7 Some early manuscripts do not have *and be united to his wife.* [c] 8 Gen. 2:24

FINAL TRIP TO JUDEA
Jesus quietly left Capernaum, heading towards the borders of Judea before crossing the Jordan River. He preached there before going to Jericho. This trip from Galilee was his last; he would not return before his death.

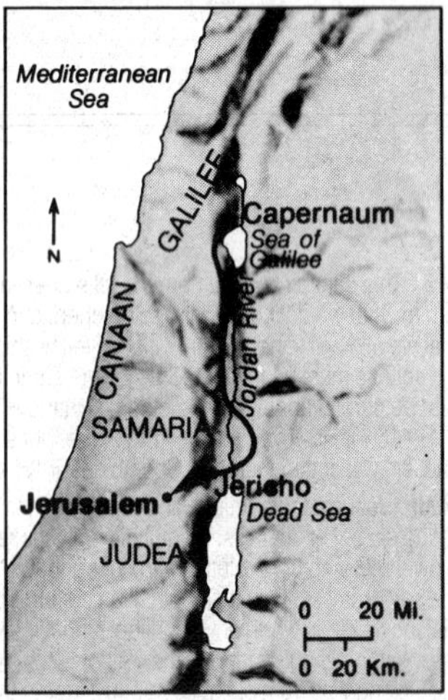

10:2 The Pharisees were trying to trap Jesus with their question. If he supported divorce, he would be upholding the Pharisees' procedures, and they doubted that he would do that. If Jesus spoke against divorce, however, some members of the crowd would dislike his position – some may have used the law to their advantage to divorce their wives. More important, he might incur the wrath of Herod, who had already killed John the Baptist for speaking out against divorce and adultery (6:17–28). This is what the Pharisees wanted.

The Pharisees saw divorce as a legal issue rather than a spiritual one. Jesus used this test as an opportunity to review God's intended purpose for marriage and to expose the Pharisees' selfish motives. They were not thinking about what God intended for marriage, but had settled for marriages of convenience. In addition, they were quoting Moses unfairly and out of context. Jesus showed these legal experts how superficial their knowledge really was.

10:5–9 God allowed divorce as a concession to people's sinfulness. Divorce was not approved, but it was instituted to protect the injured party in a bad situation. Unfortunately, the Pharisees used Deuteronomy 24:1 as a proof text for divorce. Jesus explained that this was not God's intent; instead, God wants married people to consider their marriage permanent. Don't enter marriage with the option of getting out. Your marriage is more likely to be happy if from the outset you are committed to permanence. Don't be hard-hearted like these Pharisees, but be hardheaded in your determination, with God's help, to stay together.

10:6–9 Women were often treated as property. Marriage and divorce were regarded as transactions similar to buying and selling land. But Jesus condemned this attitude, clarifying God's original intention – that marriage bring oneness (Genesis 2:24). Jesus held up God's ideal for marriage and told his followers to live by that ideal.

10:13–16 Jesus was often criticised for spending too much time with the wrong people – children, tax collectors, and sinners (Matthew 9:11; Luke 15:1, 2; 19:7). Some, including the disciples, thought Jesus should be spending more time with important leaders and the devout, because this was the way to improve his position and avoid criticism. But Jesus didn't need to improve his position. He was God, and he wanted to speak to those who needed him most.

10:14 Adults are not as trusting as little children. To feel secure, all children need is a loving look and gentle touch from someone who cares. Complete intellectual understanding is not one of their requirements. They believe us if they trust us. Jesus said that people should believe in him with this kind of childlike faith. We should not have to understand all the mysteries of the universe; it should be enough to know that God loves us and provides forgiveness for our sin. This doesn't mean that we should be childish or immature, but we should trust God with a child's simplicity and receptivity.

10:17–23 This young man wanted to be sure he would get eter-

"Let the little children come to me, and do not hinder them, for the kingdom of God
belongs to such as these.[j] 15 I tell you the truth, anyone who will not receive the
kingdom of God like a little child will never enter it."[k] 16 And he took the children
in his arms,[l] put his hands on them and blessed them.

Jesus Speaks to the Rich Young Man
(175/Matthew 19:16–30; Luke 18:18–30)

17 As Jesus started on his way, a man ran up to him and fell on his knees[m] before
him. "Good teacher," he asked, "what must I do to inherit eternal life?"[n]
18 "Why do you call me good?" Jesus answered. "No-one is good—except God
alone. 19 You know the commandments: 'Do not murder, do not commit adultery, do
not steal, do not give false testimony, do not defraud, honour your father and
mother.'[d]"[o]
20 "Teacher," he declared, "all these I have kept since I was a boy."
21 Jesus looked at him and loved him. "One thing you lack," he said. "Go, sell
everything you have and give to the poor,[p] and you will have treasure in heaven.[q]
Then come, follow me."[r]
22 At this the man's face fell. He went away sad, because he had great wealth.
23 Jesus looked around and said to his disciples, "How hard it is for the rich[s] to
enter the kingdom of God!"
24 The disciples were amazed at his words. But Jesus said again, "Children, how
hard it is[e] to enter the kingdom of God![t] 25 It is easier for a camel to go through
the eye of a needle than for a rich man to enter the kingdom of God."[u]
26 The disciples were even more amazed, and said to each other, "Who then can
be saved?"
27 Jesus looked at them and said, "With man this is impossible, but not with God;
all things are possible with God."[v]
28 Peter said to him, "We have left everything to follow you!"[w]
29 "I tell you the truth," Jesus replied, "no-one who has left home or brothers or
sisters or mother or father or children or fields for me and the gospel 30 will fail to
receive a hundred times as much[x] in this present age (homes, brothers, sisters,

10:14 [j]Mt 25:34
10:15 [k]Mt 18:3
10:16 [l]Mk 9:36
10:17 [m]Mk 1:40 [n]Lk 10:25; Ac 20:32
10:19 [o]Ex 20:12-16; Dt 5:16-20
10:21 [p]Ac 2:45 [q]Mt 6:20; Lk 12:33 [r]Mt 4:19
10:23 [s]Ps 52:7; 62:10; 1Ti 6:9, 10, 17
10:24 [t]Mt 7:13, 14
10:25 [u]Lk 12:16-20
10:27 [v]Mt 19:26
10:28 [w]Mt 4:19
10:30 [x]Mt 6:33

d *19* Exodus 20:12–16; Deut. 5:16–20 e *24* Some manuscripts *is for those who trust in riches*

---

nal life, so he asked what he could *do.* He said he'd never once broken any of the laws Jesus mentioned (10:19), and perhaps he had even kept the Pharisees' loophole-filled version of them. But Jesus lovingly broke through the young man's pride with a challenge that brought out his true motives: "Go, sell everything you have and give to the poor." This challenge exposed the barrier that could keep this young man out of the kingdom: his love of money. Money represented his pride of accomplishment and self-effort. Ironically, his attitude made him unable to keep the first commandment, to let nothing be more important than God (Exodus 20:3). He could not meet the one requirement Jesus gave—to turn his whole heart and life over to God. The man came to Jesus wondering what he could do; he left seeing what he was unable to do. What barriers are keeping you from turning your life over to Christ?

10:18 When Jesus asked this question, he was saying, "Do you really know the One to whom you are talking?" Because only God is truly good, the man was calling Jesus "God", whether or not he realised it.

10:21 What does your money mean to you? Although Jesus wanted this man to sell everything and give his money to the poor, this does not mean that all believers should sell all their possessions. Most of his followers did not sell everything, although they used their possessions to serve others. Instead, this story shows us that we must not let anything we have or desire keep us from following Jesus. We must remove all barriers to serving him fully. If Jesus asked, could you give up your house? your car? your level of income? your position on the ladder of promotion? Your reaction may show your attitude towards money—whether it is your servant or your master.

10:21 Jesus showed genuine love for this man, even though he knew that the man might not follow him. Love is able to give tough advice; it doesn't hedge around the truth. Christ loved us enough to die for us, and he also loves us enough to talk straight to us. If his love were superficial, he would give us only his approval; but because his love is complete, he gives us life-changing challenges.

10:23 Jesus said it was very difficult for the rich to enter the kingdom of God. This is true because the rich, with most of their basic physical needs met, often become self-reliant. When they feel empty, they can buy something new to dull the pain that was meant to drive them towards God. Their abundance and self-sufficiency become their deficiency. The person who has everything on earth can still lack what is most important—eternal life.

10:26 The disciples were amazed. Was not wealth a blessing from God, a reward for being good? This misconception is still common today. Although many believers enjoy material prosperity, many others live in hardship. Wealth is not a sign of faith or of partiality on God's part.

10:29, 30 Jesus assured the disciples that anyone who gives up something valuable for his sake will be repaid a hundred times over in this life, although not necessarily in the same form. For example, someone may be rejected by his family for accepting Christ, but he or she will gain the larger family of believers. Along with these rewards, however, we experience persecution because the world hates God. Jesus emphasised persecution to make sure that we do not selfishly follow him only for the rewards.

mothers, children and fields—and with them, persecutions) and in the age to come,[y]
eternal life.[z] 31But many who are first will be last, and the last first."[a]

Jesus Predicts His Death the Third Time
(177/Matthew 20:17–19; Luke 18:31–34)

32They were on their way up to Jerusalem, with Jesus leading the way, and the
disciples were astonished, while those who followed were afraid. Again he took the
Twelve[b] aside and told them what was going to happen to him. 33"We are going up
to Jerusalem,"[c] he said, "and the Son of Man[d] will be betrayed to the chief priests
and teachers of the law.[e] They will condemn him to death and will hand him over
to the Gentiles, 34who will mock him and spit on him, flog him[f] and kill him.[g] Three
days later[h] he will rise."[i]

Jesus Teaches about Serving Others
(178/Matthew 20:20–28)

35Then James and John, the sons of Zebedee, came to him. "Teacher," they said,
"we want you to do for us whatever we ask."
36"What do you want me to do for you?" he asked.
37They replied, "Let one of us sit at your right and the other at your left in your
glory."[j]
38"You don't know what you are asking,"[k] Jesus said. "Can you drink the cup[l]
I drink or be baptised with the baptism I am baptised with?"[m]
39"We can," they answered.
Jesus said to them, "You will drink the cup I drink and be baptised with the baptism
I am baptised with,[n] 40but to sit at my right or left is not for me to grant. These places
belong to those for whom they have been prepared."
41When the ten heard about this, they became indignant with James and John.
42Jesus called them together and said, "You know that those who are regarded as rulers
of the Gentiles lord it over them, and their high officials exercise authority over them.
43Not so with you. Instead, whoever wants to become great among you must be your
servant,[o] 44and whoever wants to be first must be slave of all. 45For even the Son

10:30 [y]Mt 12:32 [z]Mt 25:46
10:31 [a]Mt 19:30
10:32 [b]Mk 3:16-19
10:33 [c]Lk 9:51 [d]Mt 8:20 [e]Mt 27:1, 2
10:34 [f]Mt 16:21 [g]Ac 2:23; 3:13 [h]Mt 16:21 [i]Mt 16:21
10:37 [j]Mt 19:28
10:38 [k]Job 38:2 [l]Mt 20:22 [m]Lk 12:50
10:39 [n]Ac 12:2; Rev 1:9
10:43 [o]Mk 9:35

10:31 Jesus explained that in the world to come, the values of this world will be reversed. Those who seek status and importance here will have none in heaven. Those who are humble here will be great in heaven. The corrupt condition of our society encourages confusion in values. We are bombarded by messages that tell us how to be important and how to feel good, and Jesus' teaching about service to others seems alien. But those who have humbly served others are most qualified to be great in heaven.

10:32 Because Jesus had just spoken to them about facing persecution, the disciples were astonished as they thought about what awaited them in Jerusalem.

10:33, 34 Jesus' death and resurrection should have come as no surprise to the disciples. Here he clearly explained to them what would happen to him. Unfortunately, they didn't really hear what he was saying. Jesus said he was the Messiah, but they thought the Messiah would be a conquering king. He spoke to them of resurrection, but they heard only his words about death. Because Jesus often spoke in parables, the disciples may have thought that his words on death and resurrection were another parable they weren't astute enough to understand. The Gospels include Jesus' predictions of his death and resurrection to show that these events were God's plan from the beginning and not accidents.

10:35 Mark records that John and James went to Jesus with their request; in Matthew, their mother also made the request. There is no contradiction in the accounts—mother and sons were in agreement in requesting honoured places in Christ's kingdom.

10:37 The disciples, like most Jews of that day, had the wrong idea of the Messiah's kingdom as predicted by the Old Testament prophets. They thought Jesus would establish an earthly kingdom that would free Israel from Rome's oppression, and James and John wanted honoured places in it. But Jesus' kingdom is not of this world; it is not centred in palaces and thrones, but in the hearts and lives of his followers. The disciples did not understand this until after Jesus' resurrection.

10:38, 39 James and John said they were willing to face any trial for Christ. Both did suffer: James died as a martyr (Acts 12:2), and John was forced to live in exile (Revelation 1:9). It is easy to say we will endure anything for Christ, and yet most of us complain over the most minor problems. If we say we are willing to suffer on a large scale for Christ, we must also be willing to suffer the irritations that come with serving others.

10:38–40 Jesus didn't ridicule James and John for asking, but he denied their request. We can feel free to ask God for anything, but our request may be denied. God wants to give us what is best for us, not merely what we want. He denies some requests for our own good.

10:42–45 James and John wanted the highest positions in Jesus' kingdom. But Jesus told them that true greatness comes in serving others. Peter, one of the disciples who had heard this message, expands the thought in 1 Peter 5:1–4.

Most businesses, organisations, and institutions measure greatness by high personal achievement. In Christ's kingdom, however, service is the way to get on. The desire to be on top will hinder, not help. Rather than seeking to have your needs met, look for ways that you can minister to the needs of others.

10:45 This verse reveals not only the motive for Jesus' ministry, but also the basis for our salvation. A ransom was the price paid to release a slave. Jesus paid a ransom for us because we could not

10:45 [p]Mt 20:28 [q]Mt 20:28

of Man did not come to be served, but to serve,[p] and to give his life as a ransom
for many."[q]

Jesus Heals a Blind Beggar
(179/Matthew 20:29–34; Luke 18:35–43)

10:47 [r]Mk 1:24 [s]Mt 9:27

46Then they came to Jericho. As Jesus and his disciples, together with a large
crowd, were leaving the city, a blind man, Bartimaeus (that is, the Son of Timaeus),
was sitting by the roadside begging. 47When he heard that it was Jesus of Nazareth,[r]
he began to shout, "Jesus, Son of David,[s] have mercy on me!"
48Many rebuked him and told him to be quiet, but he shouted all the more, "Son
of David, have mercy on me!"

10:51 [t]Mt 23:7

49Jesus stopped and said, "Call him."
So they called to the blind man, "Cheer up! On your feet! He's calling you."
50Throwing his cloak aside, he jumped to his feet and came to Jesus.

10:52 [u]Mt 9:22 [v]Mt 4:19

51"What do you want me to do for you?" Jesus asked him.
The blind man said, "Rabbi,[t] I want to see."
52"Go," said Jesus, "your faith has healed you."[u] Immediately he received his sight
and followed[v] Jesus along the road.

11:1 [a]Mt 21:17 [b]Mt 21:1

3. Jesus' ministry in Jerusalem

Jesus Rides into Jerusalem on a Donkey
(183/Matthew 21:1–11; Luke 19:28–44; John 12:12–19)

11:2 [c]Nu 19:2; Dt 21:3; 1Sa 6:7

11:4 [d]Mk 14:16

11 As they approached Jerusalem and came to Bethphage and Bethany[a] at the
Mount of Olives,[b] Jesus sent two of his disciples, 2saying to them, "Go to the
village ahead of you, and just as you enter it, you will find a colt tied there, which
no-one has ever ridden.[c] Untie it and bring it here. 3If anyone asks you, 'Why are
you doing this?' tell him, 'The Lord needs it and will send it back here shortly.' "
4They went and found a colt outside in the street, tied at a doorway.[d] As they untied
it, 5some people standing there asked, "What are you doing, untying that colt?" 6They
answered as Jesus had told them to, and the people let them go. 7When they brought
the colt to Jesus and threw their cloaks over it, he sat on it. 8Many people spread their

---

pay it ourselves. His death released all of us from our slavery to sin. The disciples thought Jesus' life and power would save them from Rome; Jesus said his *death* would save them from sin, an even greater slavery than Rome's. More about the ransom Jesus paid for us is found in 1 Peter 1:18, 19.

10:46 Jericho was a popular resort city rebuilt by Herod the Great in the Judean desert, not far from the Jordan River crossing. Jesus was on his way to Jerusalem (10:32), and, after crossing over from Perea, he would naturally enter Jericho.

10:46 Beggars were a common sight in most towns. Because most occupations of that day required physical labour, anyone with a crippling disease or disability was at a severe disadvantage and was usually forced to beg, even though God's laws commanded care for such needy people (Leviticus 25:35–38). Blindness was considered a curse from God for sin (John 9:2), but Jesus refuted this idea when he reached out to heal the blind.

10:47 "Son of David" was a popular way of addressing Jesus as the Messiah, because it was known that the Messiah would be a descendant of King David (Isaiah 9:7). The fact that Bartimaeus called Jesus the Son of David shows that he recognised Jesus as the Messiah. His faith in Jesus as the Messiah brought about his healing.

11:1, 2 This was Sunday of the week that Jesus would be crucified, and the great Passover festival was about to begin. Jews came to Jerusalem from all over the Roman world during this week-long celebration to remember the great exodus from Egypt (see Exodus 12:37–51). Many in the crowds had heard of or seen Jesus and were hoping he would come to the temple (John 11:55–57).

Jesus did come, not as a warring king on a horse or in a chariot, but as a gentle and peaceable king on a donkey's colt, just as Zechariah 9:9 had predicted. Jesus knew that those who would hear him teach at the temple would return to their homes throughout the world and announce the coming of the Messiah.

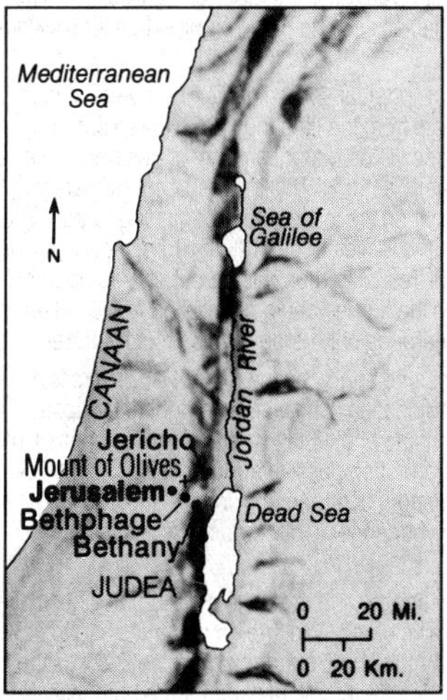

JESUS NEARS JERUSALEM
Leaving Jericho, Jesus headed towards acclaim, then crucifixion, in Jerusalem. During his last week, he stayed outside the city in Bethany, a village on the Mount of Olives, entering Jerusalem to teach, eat the Passover, and finally be crucified.

cloaks on the road, while others spread branches they had cut in the fields. 9 Those 11:9 [e]Ps 118:25, 26;
who went ahead and those who followed shouted, Mt 23:39

> "Hosanna!"[a]
>
> "Blessed is he who comes in the name of the Lord!"[b e]
>
> 10 "Blessed is the coming kingdom of our father David!"
>
> "Hosanna in the highest!"[f]

11:10 [f]Lk 2:14

11 Jesus entered Jerusalem and went to the temple. He looked around at everything,
but since it was already late, he went out to Bethany with the Twelve.[g]

Jesus Clears the Temple Again
(184/Matthew 21:12–17; Luke 19:45–48)

12 The next day as they were leaving Bethany, Jesus was hungry. 13 Seeing in the
distance a fig-tree in leaf, he went to find out if it had any fruit. When he reached 11:11 [g]Mt 21:12, 17
it, he found nothing but leaves, because it was not the season for figs.[h] 14 Then he
said to the tree, "May no-one ever eat fruit from you again." And his disciples heard
him say it.
15 On reaching Jerusalem, Jesus entered the temple area and began driving out those
who were buying and selling there. He overturned the tables of the money-changers
and the benches of those selling doves, 16 and would not allow anyone to carry

[a] *9* A Hebrew expression meaning "Save!" which became an exclamation of praise; also in verse 10. [b] *9* Psalm 118:25,26

11:13 [h]Lk 13:6-9

11:9, 10 The people exclaimed "Hosanna" (meaning, "Save!"), because they recognised that Jesus was fulfilling the prophecy in Zechariah 9:9. (See also Psalm 24:7–10; 118:26.) They spoke of David's kingdom because of God's words to David in 2 Samuel 7:12–14. The crowd correctly saw Jesus as the fulfilment of these prophecies, but they did not understand where Jesus' kingship would lead him. This same crowd cried out "Crucify him!" when Jesus stood on trial only a few days later.

11:11–21 In this passage, two unusual incidents are related: the cursing of the fig tree and the clearing of the temple. The cursing of the fig tree was an acted-out parable related to the clearing of the temple. The temple was supposed to be a place of worship, but true worship had disappeared. The fig tree showed promise of fruit, but it produced none. Jesus was showing his anger at religious life without substance. If you claim to have faith without putting it to work in your life, you are like the barren fig tree. Genuine faith has great potential; ask God to help you bear fruit for his kingdom.

11:13–26 Fig trees, a popular source of inexpensive food in Israel, require three years from the time they are planted until they can bear fruit. Each tree yields a great amount of fruit twice a year, in late spring and in early autumn. This incident occurred early in the spring fig season when the leaves were beginning to bud. The figs normally grow as the leaves fill out, but this tree, though full of leaves, had none. The tree looked promising but offered no fruit. Jesus' harsh words to the fig tree could be applied to the nation of Israel. Fruitful in appearance only, Israel was spiritually barren.

11:15–17 Jesus became angry, but he did not sin. There is a place for righteous indignation. Christians are right to be upset about sin and injustice and should take a stand against them. Unfortunately, believers are often passive about these important issues and instead get angry over personal insults and petty irritations. Make sure your anger is directed towards the right issues.

11:15–17 Money changers and merchants did big business during Passover. Those who came from foreign countries had to have their money changed into temple currency because this was the only money accepted for the temple tax and for the purchase of sacrificial animals. Often the inflated exchange rate benefited the money changers, and the exorbitant prices of animals made the merchants wealthy. Their stalls were set up in the temple's court of the Gentiles, frustrating the intentions of non-Jews who had come to worship God (Isaiah 56:6, 7). Jesus became angry because God's house of worship had become a place of extortion and a barrier to Gentiles who wanted to worship.

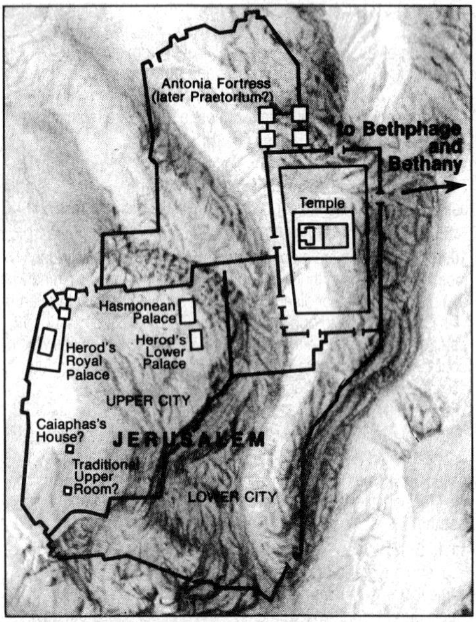

CLEARING THE TEMPLE On Monday morning of his last week, Jesus left Bethany, entered Jerusalem, and cleared the temple of money changers and merchants.

11:17
[i] Isa 56:7
[j] Jer 7:11

11:18
[k] Mt 21:46; Mk 12:12; Lk 20:19
[l] Mt 7:28

11:19
[m] Lk 21:37

11:21
[n] Mt 23:7

11:23
[o] Mt 21:21

11:24
[p] Mt 7:7

11:25
[q] Mt 6:14

merchandise through the temple courts. 17 And as he taught them, he said, "Is it not
written:

" 'My house will be called
a house of prayer for all nations'[c]?[i]

But you have made it 'a den of robbers'.[d]"[j]
18 The chief priests and the teachers of the law heard this and began looking for a
way to kill him, for they feared him,[k] because the whole crowd was amazed at his
teaching.[l]
19 When evening came, they[e] went out of the city.[m]

Jesus Says the Disciples Can Pray for Anything
(188/Matthew 21:18–22)

20 In the morning, as they went along, they saw the fig-tree withered from the roots.
21 Peter remembered and said to Jesus, "Rabbi,[n] look! The fig-tree you cursed has
withered!"
22 "Have[f] faith in God," Jesus answered. 23 "I tell you the truth, if anyone says to
this mountain, 'Go, throw yourself into the sea,' and does not doubt in his heart but
believes that what he says will happen, it will be done for him.[o] 24 Therefore I tell
you, whatever you ask for in prayer, believe that you have received it, and it will be
yours.[p] 25 And when you stand praying, if you hold anything against anyone, forgive
him, so that your Father in heaven may forgive you your sins."[g][q]

[c] *17* Isaiah 56:7 [d] *17* Jer. 7:11 [e] *19* Some early manuscripts *he* [f] *22* Some early manuscripts *If you have* [g] *25* Some manuscripts *sins.* 26 *But if you do not forgive, neither will your Father who is in heaven forgive your sins.*

KEY CHARACTERISTICS OF CHRIST IN THE GOSPELS

Characteristic	*References*
Jesus is the Son of God	Matthew 16:15, 16; Mark 1:1 Luke 22:70, 71; John 8:24
Jesus is God who became human	John 1:1, 2, 14; 20:28
Jesus is the Christ, the Messiah	Matthew 26:63, 64; Mark 14:61, 62 Luke 9:20; John 4:25, 26
Jesus came to help sinners	Luke 5:32; Matthew 9:13
Jesus has power to forgive sins	Mark 2:9–12; Luke 24:47
Jesus has authority over death	Mark 5:22–24, 35–42 John 11:1–44; Luke 24:5, 6 Matthew 28:5, 6
Jesus has power to give eternal life	John 10:28; 17:2
Jesus healed the sick	Matthew 8:5–13; Mark 1:32–34 Luke 5:12–15; John 9:1–7
Jesus taught with authority	Mark 1:21, 22; Matthew 7:29
Jesus was compassionate	Mark 1:41; Mark 8:2; Matthew 9:36
Jesus experienced sorrow	Matthew 26:38; John 11:35
Jesus never disobeyed God	Matthew 3:15; John 8:46

11:22, 23 The kind of prayer that moves mountains is prayer for the fruitfulness of God's kingdom. It would seem impossible to move a mountain into the sea, so Jesus used that picture to say that God can do anything. God will answer your prayers, but not as a result of your positive mental attitude. Other conditions must be met: (1) you must be a believer; (2) you must not hold a grudge against another person; (3) you must not pray with selfish motives; (4) your request must be for the good of God's kingdom. To pray effectively, you need faith in God, not faith in the object of your request. If you focus only on your request, you will be left with nothing if your request is refused.

11:24 Jesus, our example for prayer, prayed, "Everything is possible for you . . . Yet not what I will, but what you will" (14:36). Our prayers are often motivated by our own interests and desires. We like to hear that we can have anything. But Jesus prayed with *God's* interests in mind. When we pray, we should express our desires, but want his will above ours. Check yourself to see if your prayers focus on your interests or God's.

Religious Leaders Challenge Jesus' Authority
(189/Matthew 21:23–27; Luke 20:1–8)

27They arrived again in Jerusalem, and while Jesus was walking in the temple
courts, the chief priests, the teachers of the law and the elders came to him. 28"By
what authority are you doing these things?" they asked. "And who gave you authority
to do this?"
29Jesus replied, "I will ask you one question. Answer me, and I will tell you by
what authority I am doing these things. 30John's baptism—was it from heaven, or
from men? Tell me!"
31They discussed it among themselves and said, "If we say, 'From heaven', he will
ask, 'Then why didn't you believe him?' 32But if we say, 'From men' . . . ." (They
feared the people, for everyone held that John really was a prophet.)[r]
33So they answered Jesus, "We don't know."
Jesus said, "Neither will I tell you by what authority I am doing these things."

Jesus Tells the Parable of the Wicked Tenants
(191/Matthew 21:33–46; Luke 20:9–19)

12 He then began to speak to them in parables: "A man planted a vineyard.[a] He
put a wall around it, dug a pit for the winepress and built a watchtower. Then
he rented the vineyard to some farmers and went away on a journey. 2At harvest time
he sent a servant to the tenants to collect from them some of the fruit of the vineyard.
3But they seized him, beat him and sent him away empty-handed. 4Then he sent
another servant to them; they struck this man on the head and treated him shamefully.
5He sent still another, and that one they killed. He sent many others; some of them
they beat, others they killed.
6"He had one left to send, a son, whom he loved. He sent him last of all,[b] saying,
'They will respect my son.'
7"But the tenants said to one another, 'This is the heir. Come, let's kill him, and
the inheritance will be ours.' 8So they took him and killed him, and threw him out
of the vineyard.
9"What then will the owner of the vineyard do? He will come and kill those tenants
and give the vineyard to others. 10Haven't you read this scripture:

> " 'The stone the builders rejected
> has become the capstone;[a][c]
> 11the Lord has done this,
> and it is marvellous in our eyes'[b]?"[d]

12Then they looked for a way to arrest him because they knew he had spoken the
parable against them. But they were afraid of the crowd;[e] so they left him and went
away.[f]

a *10* Or *cornerstone* b *11* Psalm 118:22,23

11:32 [r]Mt 11:9
12:1 [a]Isa 5:1-7
12:6 [b]Heb 1:1-3
12:10 [c]Ac 4:11
12:11 [d]Ps 118:22, 23
12:12 [e]Mk 11:18 [f]Mt 22:22

11:27ff The religious leaders asked Jesus who gave him the authority to chase away the merchants and money changers. Their question was a trap. If Jesus said his authority was from God, they would accuse him of blasphemy; if he said his authority was his own, they would dismiss him as a fanatic. To expose their real motives, Jesus countered their question with a question about John the Baptist. The leaders' silence proved that they were not interested in the truth. They simply wanted to get rid of Jesus because he was undermining their authority.

11:30 For more information, see John the Baptist's Profile in John 1.

12:1 Parables are story illustrations that use something familiar to help us understand something new. This method of teaching compels listeners to discover truth for themselves. The message gets through only to those who are willing to listen and learn.

12:1 Israel, pictured as a vineyard, was the nation that God had cultivated to bring salvation to the world. The religious leaders not only frustrated their nation's purpose; they also killed those who were trying to fulfil it. They were so jealous and possessive that they ignored the welfare of the very people they were supposed to be bringing to God.

12:1ff In this parable, the man who planted the vineyard is God; the vineyard is the nation Israel; the tenants are Israel's religious leaders; the servants are the prophets and priests who remained faithful to God; the son is Jesus; and the others are the Gentiles. By telling this story, Jesus exposed the religious leaders' plot to kill him and warned that their sins would be punished.

12:10, 11 Jesus referred to himself as the stone rejected by the builders. Although he would be rejected by most of the Jewish leaders, he would become the cornerstone of a new "building", the church (Acts 4:11, 12). The cornerstone was used as a base to make sure the other stones of the building were straight and level. Likewise, Jesus' life and teaching would be the church's foundation.

12:13
[g]Mt 22:16; Mk 3:6
[h]Mt 12:10

Religious Leaders Question Jesus about Paying Taxes
(193/Matthew 22:15–22; Luke 20:20–26)

13 Later they sent some of the Pharisees and Herodians[g] to Jesus to catch him[h] in
his words. 14 They came to him and said, "Teacher, we know you are a man of
integrity. You aren't swayed by men, because you pay no attention to who they are;
but you teach the way of God in accordance with the truth. Is it right to pay taxes
to Caesar or not? 15 Should we pay or shouldn't we?"

12:17
[i]Ro 13:7

But Jesus knew their hypocrisy. "Why are you trying to trap me?" he asked. "Bring
me a denarius and let me look at it." 16 They brought the coin, and he asked them,
"Whose portrait is this? And whose inscription?"

"Caesar's," they replied.

17 Then Jesus said to them, "Give to Caesar what is Caesar's and to God what is
God's."[i]

And they were amazed at him.

12:18
[j]Ac 4:1
[k]Ac 23:8; 1Co 15:12

Religious Leaders Question Jesus about the Resurrection
(194/Matthew 22:23–33; Luke 20:27–40)

18 Then the Sadducees,[j] who say there is no resurrection,[k] came to him with a
question. 19 "Teacher," they said, "Moses wrote for us that if a man's brother dies and
leaves a wife but no children, the man must marry the widow and have children for
his brother.[l] 20 Now there were seven brothers. The first one married and died without
leaving any children. 21 The second one married the widow, but he also died, leaving
no child. It was the same with the third. 22 In fact, none of the seven left any children.
Last of all, the woman died too. 23 At the resurrection[c] whose wife will she be, since
the seven were married to her?"

12:19
[l]Dt 25:5

24 Jesus replied, "Are you not in error because you do not know the Scriptures[m]
or the power of God? 25 When the dead rise, they will neither marry nor be given in

12:24
[m]2Ti 3:15-17

[c] *23* Some manuscripts *resurrection, when men rise from the dead,*

12:13 The Pharisees were primarily a religious group concerned for ritual purity; the Herodians were a Jewish political group that approved of Herod's compromises with Rome. Normally the two groups had nothing to do with each other.

The Pharisees did not like Jesus because he exposed their hypocrisy. The Herodians also saw Jesus as a threat. Supporters of the dynasty of Herod the Great, they had lost political control when, as a result of reported unrest, Rome deposed Archelaus (Herod's son with authority over Judea), and replaced him with a Roman governor. The Herodians feared that Jesus would cause still more instability in Judea, and that Rome might react by never allowing the Roman leaders to step down and be replaced by a descendant of Herod.

12:14 Anyone who avoided paying taxes faced harsh penalties. The Jews hated to pay taxes to Rome because the money supported their oppressors and symbolised their subjection. Much of the tax money also went to maintain the pagan temples and luxurious life-styles of Rome's upper class. The Pharisees and Herodians hoped to trap Jesus with this tax question. Either a yes or a no could lead him into trouble. A yes would mean he supported Rome, which would turn the people against him. A no would bring accusations of treason and rebellion against Rome and could lead to civil penalties.

12:15 A denarius was the usual day's wage for a labourer.

12:17 The Pharisees and Herodians thought they had the perfect question to trap Jesus. But Jesus answered wisely, once again exposing their self-interest and wrong motives. Jesus said that the coin bearing the emperor's image should be given to the emperor. But our lives, which bear God's image, belong to God. Are you giving God all that is rightfully his? Give your life to God – you bear his image.

12:18–23 After the Pharisees and Herodians failed to trap Jesus with their tax question, the Sadducees stepped in with a question they were sure would stump him. This was a question that they had successfully used against the Pharisees, who could not come up with an answer. The Sadducees did not believe in life after death because the Pentateuch (Genesis – Deuteronomy) had no direct teaching about it, and the writings of Moses were the only Scriptures they followed. But Jesus was about to point out that Moses' books support the idea of eternal life (12:26).

12:19 According to Old Testament law, when a man died without a son, his brother had to marry the widow and produce children to care for her and allow the family line to continue. The first son of this marriage was considered the heir of the dead man (Deuteronomy 25:5, 6).

12:24 What life will be like after the resurrection is far beyond our ability to understand or imagine (Isaiah 64:4; 1 Corinthians 2:9). We need not be afraid of eternal life because of the unknowns, however. Instead of wondering what God's coming kingdom will be like, we should concentrate on our relationship with Christ right now because in the new kingdom, we will be with him. If we learn to love and trust Christ *now,* we will not be afraid of what he has in store for us then.

12:25–27 Jesus' statement does not mean that people won't recognise their partners in the coming kingdom. It simply means that God's new order will not be an extension of this life and that the same physical and natural rules won't apply. Jesus' comment in verse 25 was not intended to be the final word on marriage in heaven. Instead, this response was Jesus' refusal to answer the Sadducees' riddle and fall into their trap. Sidestepping their question about the much-married woman, he gave a definitive answer to their question about the resurrection.

marriage; they will be like the angels in heaven.[n] 26 Now about the dead rising — have
you not read in the book of Moses, in the account of the bush, how God said to him,
'I am the God of Abraham, the God of Isaac, and the God of Jacob'[d]?[o] 27 He is not
the God of the dead, but of the living. You are badly mistaken!"

Religious Leaders Question Jesus about the Greatest Commandment
(195/Matthew 22:34–40)

28 One of the teachers of the law[p] came and heard them debating. Noticing that
Jesus had given them a good answer, he asked him, "Of all the commandments, which
is the most important?"
29 "The most important one," answered Jesus, "is this: 'Hear, O Israel, the Lord our
God, the Lord is one.[e] 30 Love the Lord your God with all your heart and with all
your soul and with all your mind and with all your strength.'[f][q] 31 The second is this:
'Love your neighbour as yourself.'[g][r] There is no commandment greater than these."
32 "Well said, teacher," the man replied. "You are right in saying that God is one
and there is no other but him.[s] 33 To love him with all your heart, with all your
understanding and with all your strength, and to love your neighbour as yourself is
more important than all burnt offerings and sacrifices."[t]
34 When Jesus saw that he had answered wisely, he said to him, "You are not far
from the kingdom of God."[u] And from then on no-one dared ask him any more
questions.[v]

Religious Leaders Cannot Answer Jesus' Question
(196/Matthew 22:41–46; Luke 20:41–44)

35 While Jesus was teaching in the temple courts,[w] he asked, "How is it that the
teachers of the law say that the Christ[h] is the son of David?[x] 36 David himself,
speaking by the Holy Spirit,[y] declared:

" 'The Lord said to my Lord:
"Sit at my right hand
until I put your enemies
under your feet." '[i][z]

37 David himself calls him 'Lord'. How then can he be his son?"
The large crowd[a] listened to him with delight.

Jesus Warns against the Religious Leaders
(197/Matthew 23:1–12; Luke 20:45–47)

38 As he taught, Jesus said, "Watch out for the teachers of the law. They like to walk
around in flowing robes and be greeted in the market-places, 39 and have the most

[d] *26* Exodus 3:6 [e] *29* Or *the Lord our God is one Lord* [f] *30* Deut. 6:4,5 [g] *31* Lev. 19:18 [h] *35* Or *Messiah*
[i] *36* Psalm 110:1

12:25 [n] 1Co 15:42, 49, 52
12:26 [o] Ex 3:6
12:28 [p] Lk 10:25-28; 20:39
12:30 [q] Dt 6:4, 5
12:31 [r] Lev 19:18; Mt 5:43
12:32 [s] Dt 4:35, 39; Isa 45:6, 14; 46:9
12:33 [t] 1Sa 15:22; Hos 6:6; Mic 6:6-8; Heb 10:8
12:34 [u] Mt 3:2 [v] Mt 22:46; Lk 20:40
12:35 [w] Mt 26:55 [x] Mt 9:27
12:36 [y] 2Sa 23:2 [z] Ps 110:1; Mt 22:44
12:37 [a] Jn 12:9

12:26 The Sadducees' real question was not about marriage but about the doctrine of resurrection. Because the Sadducees believed only in the Pentateuch (Genesis to Deuteronomy), Jesus quoted from Exodus 3:6 to prove that there is life after death. The Pharisees had overlooked this verse in their debates with the Sadducees. God spoke of Abraham, Isaac, and Jacob years after their deaths as if they *still lived.* God's covenant with all people exists beyond death.

12:28 By Jesus' time, the Jews had accumulated hundreds of laws – 613 by one historian's count. Some religious leaders tried to distinguish between major and minor laws, and some taught that all laws were equally binding and that it was dangerous to make any distinctions. This teacher's question could have provoked controversy among these groups, but Jesus' answer summarised all of God's laws.

12:29–31 God's laws are not burdensome. They can be reduced to two simple principles: love God and love others. These commands are from the Old Testament (Deuteronomy 6:5; Leviticus 19:18). When you love God completely and care for others as you care for yourself, then you have fulfilled the intent of the Ten Commandments and the other Old Testament laws. According to Jesus, these two commandments summarise all God's laws. Let them rule your thoughts, decisions, and actions. When you are uncertain about what to do, ask yourself which course of action best demonstrates love for God and love for others.

12:32–34 This man had caught the intent of God's law as it is so often stressed in the Old Testament – that true obedience comes from the heart. Because all the Old Testament commands lead to Christ, his next step was faith in Jesus himself. This, however, was the most difficult step to take.

12:35–37 Jesus quoted Psalm 110:1 to show that David considered the Messiah to be his Lord, not just his son. The religious leaders did not understand that the Messiah would be far more than a human descendant of David; he would be God himself in human form.

12:38–40 Jesus again exposed the religious leaders' impure mo-

12:39 [b]Lk 11:43

important seats in the synagogues and the places of honour at banquets.[b] 40They devour widows' houses and for a show make lengthy prayers. Such men will be punished most severely."

A Poor Widow Gives All She Has
(200/Luke 21:1–4)

12:41 [c]2Ki 12:9; Jn 8:20

41Jesus sat down opposite the place where the offerings were put[c] and watched the crowd putting their money into the temple treasury. Many rich people threw in large amounts. 42But a poor widow came and put in two very small copper coins,[j] worth only a fraction of a penny.[k]

43Calling his disciples to him, Jesus said, "I tell you the truth, this poor widow has put more into the treasury than all the others. 44They all gave out of their wealth; but she, out of her poverty, put in everything—all she had to live on."[d]

12:44 [d]2Co 8:12

[j] *42* Greek *two lepta* [k] *42* Greek *kodrantes*

WHAT JESUS SAID ABOUT LOVE
In Mark 12:28 a teacher of the law asked Jesus which of all the commandments was the most important to follow. Jesus mentioned two commandments, one from Deuteronomy 6:5, the other from Leviticus 19:18. Both had to do with love. Why is love so important? Jesus said that all of the commandments were given for two simple reasons—to help us love God and love others as we should.

What else did Jesus say about love?	*Reference*
God loves us.	John 3:16
We are to love God.	Matthew 22:37
Because God loves us, he cares for us.	Matthew 6:25–34
God wants everyone to know how much he loves them.	John 17:23
God loves even those who hate him; we are to do the same.	Matthew 5:43–47; Luke 6:35
God seeks out even those most alienated from him.	Luke 15
God must be your first love.	Matthew 6:24; 10:37
You love God when you obey him.	John 14:21; 15:10
God loves Jesus his Son.	John 5:20; 10:17
Jesus loves God.	John 14:31
Those who refuse Jesus don't have God's love.	John 5:41–44
Jesus loves us just as God loves Jesus.	John 15:9
Jesus proved his love for us by dying on the cross so that we could live eternally with him.	John 3:14, 15; 15:13, 14
The love between God and Jesus is the perfect example of how we are to love others.	John 17:21–26
We are to love one another (John 13:34, 35) and demonstrate that love.	Matthew 5:40–42; 10:42
We are *not* to love the praise of men (John 12:43), selfish recognition (Matthew 23:6), earthly belongings (Luke 16:19–31), or anything more than God.	Luke 16:13
Jesus' love extends to each individual.	John 10:11–15; Mark 10:21
Jesus wants us to love him through the good and through the difficult times.	Matthew 26:31–35
Jesus wants our love to be genuine.	John 21:15–17

tives. The teachers of the law received no pay, so they depended on the hospitality extended by devout Jews. Some of them used this custom to exploit people, cheating the poor out of everything they had and taking advantage of the rich. Through their pious actions they hoped to gain status, recognition, and respect.

12:38–40 Jesus warned against trying to make a good impression. These teachers of the law were religious hypocrites who had no love for God. True followers of Christ are not distinguished by showy spirituality. Reading the Bible, praying in public, or following church rituals can be empty if the motive for doing them is to be noticed or honoured. Let your actions be consistent with your beliefs. Live for Christ, even when no-one is looking.

12:40 The punishment for these teachers of the law would be especially severe because as teachers they were responsible for shaping the faith of the people. But they saddled people with petty rules while they lived greedily and deceitfully. Their behaviour oppressed and misled the very people they were supposed to lead.

12:41 There were several boxes in the temple where money could be placed. Some were for collecting the temple tax from Jewish males; the others were for freewill offerings. These particular collection boxes were probably in the court of the women.

12:41–44 In the Lord's eyes, this poor widow gave more than all the others put together, though her gift was by far the smallest. The value of a gift is not determined by its amount, but by the spirit in which it is given. A gift given grudgingly or for recognition loses its value. When you give, remember—gifts of any size are pleasing to God when they are given out of gratitude and a spirit of generosity.

Jesus Tells about the Future
(201/Matthew 24:1–25; Luke 21:5–24)

13 As he was leaving the temple, one of his disciples said to him, "Look, Teacher!
What massive stones! What magnificent buildings!"
2 "Do you see all these great buildings?" replied Jesus. "Not one stone here will be
left on another; every one will be thrown down."[a]
3 As Jesus was sitting on the Mount of Olives[b] opposite the temple, Peter, James,
John[c] and Andrew asked him privately, 4 "Tell us, when will these things happen?
And what will be the sign that they are all about to be fulfilled?"
5 Jesus said to them: "Watch out that no-one deceives you.[d] 6 Many will come in
my name, claiming, 'I am he,' and will deceive many. 7 When you hear of wars and
rumours of wars, do not be alarmed. Such things must happen, but the end is still to
come. 8 Nation will rise against nation, and kingdom against kingdom. There will be
earthquakes in various places, and famines. These are the beginning of birth-pains.
9 "You must be on your guard. You will be handed over to the local councils and
flogged in the synagogues.[e] On account of me you will stand before governors and
kings as witnesses to them. 10 And the gospel must first be preached to all nations.
11 Whenever you are arrested and brought to trial, do not worry beforehand about what
to say. Just say whatever is given you at the time, for it is not you speaking, but the
Holy Spirit.[f]
12 "Brother will betray brother to death, and a father his child. Children will rebel
against their parents and have them put to death.[g] 13 All men will hate you because
of me,[h] but he who stands firm to the end will be saved.[i]
14 "When you see 'the abomination that causes desolation'**[a]**[j] standing where it**[b]**

a *14* Daniel 9:27; 11:31; 12:11 **b** *14* Or *he*; also in verse 29

13:2 [a]Lk 19:44
13:3 [b]Mt 21:1 [c]Mt 4:21
13:5 [d]ver 22; Jer 29:8; Eph 5:6; 2Th 2:3, 10-12; 1Ti 4:1; 2Ti 3:13; 1Jn 4:6
13:9 [e]Mt 10:17
13:11 [f]Mt 10:19, 20; Lk 12:11, 12
13:12 [g]Mic 7:6; Mt 10:21; Lk 12:51-53
13:13 [h]Jn 15:21 [i]Mt 10:22
13:14 [j]Da 9:27; 11:31; 12:11

13:1, 2 About 15 years before Jesus was born (20 B.C.), Herod the Great began to remodel and rebuild the temple, which had stood for nearly 500 years since the days of Ezra (Ezra 6:14, 15). Herod made the temple one of the most beautiful buildings in Jerusalem – not to honour God, but to appease the Jews whom he ruled. The magnificent building project was not completely finished until A.D. 64. Jesus' prophecy that not one stone would be left on another was fulfilled in A.D. 70, when the Romans completely destroyed the temple and the entire city of Jerusalem.

13:3ff The disciples wanted to know when the temple would be destroyed. Jesus gave them a prophetic picture of that time, including events leading up to it. He also talked about future events connected with his return to earth to judge all people. Jesus predicted both near and distant events without putting them in chronological order. Some of the disciples lived to see the destruction of Jerusalem in A.D. 70. This event would assure them that everything else Jesus predicted would also happen.

Jesus warned his followers about the future so that they could learn how to live in the present. Many predictions Jesus made in this passage have not yet been fulfilled. He did not make them so that we would guess when they might be fulfilled, but to help us remain spiritually alert and prepared at all times as we wait for his return.

13:3, 4 The Mount of Olives rises above Jerusalem to the east. From its slopes a person can look down into the city and see the temple. Zechariah 14:1–4 predicts that the Messiah will stand on this very mountain when he returns to set up his eternal kingdom.

13:5–7 What are the signs of the end times? There have been people in every generation since Christ's resurrection claiming to know exactly when Jesus would return. No-one has been right yet, however, because Christ will return on God's timetable, not ours. Jesus predicted that before his return, many believers would be misled by false teachers claiming to have revelations from God.

According to Scripture, the one clear sign of Christ's return will be his unmistakable appearance in the clouds, which will be seen by all people (13:26; Revelation 1:7). In other words, you do not have to wonder whether a certain person is the Messiah or whether these are the "end times". When Jesus returns, *you will know* beyond a doubt, because it will be evident to all true believers. Beware of groups who claim special knowledge of the last days, because no-one knows when that time will be (13:32). Be cautious about saying, "This is it!" but be bold in your total commitment to have your heart and life ready for Christ's return.

13:9, 10 As the early church began to grow, most of the disciples experienced the kind of persecution Jesus was talking about. Since the time of Christ, Christians have been persecuted in their own lands and on foreign mission fields. Though you may be safe from persecution now, your vision of God's kingdom must not be limited by what happens only to you. A glance at a newspaper will reveal that many Christians in other parts of the world daily face hardships and persecution. Persecutions are an opportunity for Christians to witness for Christ to those opposed to him. These persecutions serve God's desire that the gospel be proclaimed to everyone.

13:11 Jesus did not imply that studying the Bible and gaining knowledge is useless or wrong. Before and after his resurrection Jesus himself taught his disciples what to say and how to say it. But Jesus was teaching the kind of attitude we should have when we must take a stand for the gospel. We don't have to be fearful or defensive about our faith because the Holy Spirit will be present to give us the right words to say.

13:13 To believe in Jesus and stand "firm to the end" will take perseverance because our faith will be challenged and opposed. Severe trials will sift true Christians from fair-weather believers. Enduring to the end does not earn salvation for us, but marks us as already saved. The assurance of our salvation will keep us going through the times of persecution.

13:14 The "abomination that causes desolation" is the desecration of the temple by God's enemies. This happened repeatedly in Israel's history: in 597 B.C. when Nebuchadnezzar looted the temple and took Judean captives to Babylon (2 Chronicles 36); in 168 B.C. when Antiochus Epiphanes sacrificed a pig to Zeus on the sacred temple altar (Daniel 9:27; 11:30, 31); in A.D. 70 when the Roman general Titus placed an idol on the site of the burned-out

does not belong — let the reader understand — then let those who are in Judea flee to the mountains. 15Let no-one on the roof of his house go down or enter the house to take anything out. 16Let no-one in the field go back to get his cloak. 17How dreadful it will be in those days for pregnant women and nursing mothers![k] 18Pray that this will not take place in winter, 19because those will be days of distress unequalled from the beginning, when God created the world,[l] until now — and never to be equalled again.[m] 20If the Lord had not cut short those days, no-one would survive. But for the sake of the elect, whom he has chosen, he has shortened them. 21At that time if anyone says to you, 'Look, here is the Christ!'[c] or, 'Look, there he is!' do not believe it.[n] 22For false Christs and false prophets[o] will appear and perform signs and miracles[p] to deceive the elect — if that were possible. 23So be on your guard;[q] I have told you everything ahead of time.

Jesus Tells about His Return
(202/Matthew 24:26–35; Luke 21:25–33)

24"But in those days, following that distress,

" 'the sun will be darkened,
and the moon will not give its light;
25the stars will fall from the sky,
and the heavenly bodies will be shaken.'[d][r]

26"At that time men will see the Son of Man coming in clouds[s] with great power and glory. 27And he will send his angels and gather his elect from the four winds, from the ends of the earth to the ends of the heavens.[t]

28"Now learn this lesson from the fig-tree: As soon as its twigs get tender and its leaves come out, you know that summer is near. 29Even so, when you see these things happening, you know that it is near, right at the door. 30I tell you the truth, this generation[e][u] will certainly not pass away until all these things have happened.[v] 31Heaven and earth will pass away, but my words will never pass away.[w]

13:17 [k]Lk 23:29
13:19 [l]Mk 10:6 [m]Da 9:26; 12:1; Joel 2:2
13:21 [n]Lk 17:23; 21:8
13:22 [o]Mt 7:15 [p]Jn 4:48; 2Th 2:9, 10
13:23 [q]2Pe 3:17
13:25 [r]Isa 13:10; 34:4; Mt 24:29
13:26 [s]Da 7:13; Mt 16:27; Rev 1:7
13:27 [t]Zec 2:6
13:30 [u]Mk 9:1 [v]Lk 17:25
13:31 [w]Mt 5:18

[c] *21* Or *Messiah* [d] *25* Isaiah 13:10; 34:4 [e] *30* Or *race*

JESUS' PROPHECIES IN THE OLIVET DISCOURSE

Type of Prophecy	*Old Testament References*	*Other New Testament References*
The Last Days Mark 13:1–23 Matthew 24:1–28 Luke 21:5–24	Daniel 9:26, 27 Daniel 11:31 Joel 2:2	John 15:21 Revelation 11:2 1 Timothy 4:1, 2
The Second Coming of Christ Mark 13:24–27 Luke 21:25–28 Matthew 24:29–31	Isaiah 13:6–10 Ezekiel 32:7 Daniel 7:13, 14	Revelation 6:12 Mark 14:62 1 Thessalonians 4:16

In Mark 13, often called the Olivet Discourse, Jesus talked a lot about two things: the end times and his second coming. Jesus was not trying to encourage his disciples to speculate about exactly when he would return by sharing these prophecies with them. Instead, he urges all his followers to be watchful and prepared for his coming. If we serve Jesus faithfully now, we will be ready when he returns.

temple after the destruction of Jerusalem. Just a few years after Jesus gave this warning, in A.D. 38, the emperor Caligula made plans to put his own statue in the temple, but he died before this could be carried out.

13:20 The *elect* are God's chosen people, those who are saved. See Romans 8:29, 30 and Ephesians 1:4, 5 for more on God's choice.

13:22, 23 Is it possible for Christians to be deceived? Yes. So convincing will be the arguments and proofs from deceivers in the end times that it will be difficult *not* to fall away from Christ. If we are prepared, Jesus says, we can remain faithful. But if we are not prepared, we will turn away. To penetrate the disguises of false teachers we can ask: (1) Have their predictions come true, or do they have to revise them to fit what's already happened? (2) Does any teaching utilise a small section of the Bible to the neglect of the whole? (3) Does the teaching contradict what the Bible says about God? (4) Are the practices meant to glorify the teacher or Christ? (5) Do the teachings promote hostility towards other Christians?

13:31 In Jesus' day the world seemed concrete, dependable, and permanent. These days many people fear its destruction by nuclear war. Jesus tells us, however, that even if the earth passes away, the truth of his words will never be changed or abolished. God and his word provide the only stability in our unstable world. How shortsighted people are who spend their time learning about this temporary world and accumulating its possessions, while neglecting the Bible and its eternal truths!

Jesus Tells about Remaining Watchful
(203/Matthew 24:36–51; Luke 21:34–38)

32"No-one knows about that day or hour, not even the angels in heaven, nor the
Son, but only the Father.[x] 33Be on guard! Be alert![f][y] You do not know when that
time will come. 34It's like a man going away: He leaves his house and puts his
servants[z] in charge, each with his assigned task, and tells the one at the door to keep
watch.
35"Therefore keep watch because you do not know when the owner of the house
will come back—whether in the evening, or at midnight, or when the cock crows,
or at dawn. 36If he comes suddenly, do not let him find you sleeping. 37What I say
to you, I say to everyone: 'Watch!' "[a]

C. DEATH AND RESURRECTION OF JESUS, THE SERVANT (14:1—16:20)

Mark tells us about Jesus' ultimate deed of servanthood—dying for us on the cross. Jesus died for our sin so that we wouldn't have to. Now we can have eternal fellowship with God instead of eternal suffering and death. When first written in Rome, this Gospel was encouraging to Roman Christians during times of persecution. Christ's victory through suffering can encourage us during difficult times too.

Religious Leaders Plot to Kill Jesus
(207/Matthew 26:1–5; Luke 22:1, 2)

14 Now the Passover[a] and the Feast of Unleavened Bread were only two days
away, and the chief priests and the teachers of the law were looking for some
sly way to arrest Jesus and kill him.[b] 2"But not during the Feast," they said, "or the
people may riot."

A Woman Anoints Jesus with Perfume
(182/Matthew 26:6–13; John 12:1–11)

3While he was in Bethany,[c] reclining at the table in the home of a man known
as Simon the Leper, a woman came with an alabaster jar of very expensive perfume,
made of pure nard. She broke the jar and poured the perfume on his head.[d]

f 33 Some manuscripts *alert and pray*

13:32 [x]Ac 1:7; 1Th 5:1, 2
13:33 [y]1Th 5:6
13:34 [z]Mt 25:14
13:37 [a]Lk 12:35-40
14:1 [a]Jn 11:55; 13:1 [b]Mt 12:14
14:3 [c]Mt 21:17 [d]Lk 7:37-39

13:32 When Jesus said that even he did not know the time of the end, he was affirming his humanity. Of course God the Father knows the time, and Jesus and the Father are one. But when Jesus became a man, he voluntarily gave up the unlimited use of his divine attributes.

The emphasis of this verse is not on Jesus' lack of knowledge, but rather on the fact that no-one knows. It is God the Father's secret to be revealed when he wills. No-one can predict by Scripture or science the exact day of Jesus' return. Jesus is teaching that preparation, not calculation, is needed.

13:33, 34 Months of planning go into a wedding, the birth of a baby, a career change, a speaking engagement, the purchase of a home. Do you place the same importance on preparing for Christ's return, the most important event in your life? Its results will last for eternity. You dare not postpone your preparations because you do not know when his return will occur. The way to prepare is to study God's word and live by its instructions each day. Only then will you be ready.

13:35–37 The entire thirteenth chapter of Mark tells us how to live while we wait for Christ's return: (1) We are not to be misled by confusing claims or speculative interpretations of what will happen (13:5, 6). (2) We should not be afraid to tell people about Christ, despite what they might say or do to us (13:9–11). (3) We must stand firm by faith and not be surprised by persecutions (13:13). (4) We must be morally alert, obedient to the commands for living found in God's word. This chapter was not given to promote discussions on prophetic timetables, but to stimulate right living for God in a world where he is largely ignored.

14:1 The Passover commemorated the night the Israelites were freed from Egypt (Exodus 12), when God "passed over" homes marked by the blood of a lamb while killing firstborn sons in unmarked homes. The day of Passover was followed by a seven-day festival called the Feast of Unleavened Bread. This, too, recalled the Israelites' quick escape from Egypt when they didn't have time to let their bread rise, so they baked it without yeast. This holiday found people gathering for a special meal that included lamb, wine, bitter herbs, and unleavened bread. Eventually the whole week came to be called Passover.

14:1 The Jewish leaders plotted secretly to kill Jesus—his murder was carefully planned. The murder plot was not being planned because popular opinion had turned against Jesus. In fact, the leaders were afraid of Jesus' popularity.

14:3 Bethany is located on the eastern slope of the Mount of Olives (Jerusalem is on the western side). This town was the home of Jesus' friends Lazarus, Mary, and Martha, who were also present at this dinner (John 11:2). The woman who anointed Jesus' feet was Mary, Lazarus' and Martha's sister (John 12:1–3). An alabaster jar was a beautiful and expensive carved vase. Nard was expensive perfume.

JUDAS ISCARIOT

It is easy to overlook the fact that Jesus chose Judas to be his disciple. We may also forget that while Judas betrayed Jesus, *all* the disciples abandoned him. With the other disciples, Judas shared a persistent misunderstanding of Jesus' mission. They all expected Jesus to make the right political moves. When he kept talking about dying, they all felt varying degrees of anger, fear, and disappointment. They didn't understand why they had been chosen if Jesus' mission was doomed to fail.

We do not know the exact motivation behind Judas' betrayal. What is clear is that Judas allowed his desires to place him in a position where Satan could manipulate him. Judas accepted payment to set Jesus up for the religious leaders. He identified Jesus for the guards in the dimly lit Garden of Gethsemane. It is possible that he was trying to force Jesus' hand—would Jesus or would Jesus not rebel against Rome and set up a new political government?

Whatever his plan, though, at some point Judas realised he didn't like the way things were turning out. He tried to undo the evil he had done by returning the money to the priests, but it was too late. The wheels of God's sovereign plan had been set in motion. How sad that Judas ended his life in despair without ever experiencing the gift of reconciliation God could give even to him through Jesus Christ.

Human feelings towards Judas have always been mixed. Some have fervently hated him for his betrayal. Others have pitied him for not realising what he was doing. A few have tried to make him a hero for his part in ending Jesus' earthly mission. Some have questioned God's fairness in allowing one man to bear such guilt. While there are many feelings about Judas, there are some facts to consider as well. He, by his own choice, betrayed God's Son into the hands of soldiers (Luke 22:48). He was a thief (John 12:6). Jesus knew that Judas' life of evil would not change (John 6:70). Judas' betrayal of Jesus was part of God's sovereign plan (Psalm 41:9; Zechariah 11:12, 13; Matthew 20:18; 26:20–25; Acts 1:16, 20).

In betraying Jesus, Judas made the greatest mistake in history. But the fact that Jesus knew Judas would betray him doesn't mean that Judas was a puppet of God's will. Judas made the choice. God knew what that choice would be and confirmed it. Judas didn't lose his relationship with Jesus; rather, he never found Jesus in the first place. He is called "doomed to destruction" (John 17:12) because he was never saved.

Judas does us a favour if he makes us think a second time about our commitment to God and the presence of God's Spirit within us. Are we true disciples and followers, or uncommitted pretenders? We can choose despair and death, or we can choose repentance, forgiveness, hope, and eternal life. Judas' betrayal sent Jesus to the cross to guarantee that second choice, our only chance. Will we accept Jesus' free gift, or, like Judas, betray him?

Strengths and accomplishments:
- He was chosen as one of the 12 disciples; the only non-Galilean
- He kept the money bag for the expenses of the group
- He was able to recognise the evil in his betrayal of Jesus

Weaknesses and mistakes:
- He was greedy (John 12:6)
- He betrayed Jesus
- He committed suicide instead of seeking forgiveness

Lessons from his life:
- Evil plans and motives leave us open to being used by Satan for even greater evil
- The consequences of evil are so devastating that even small lies and little wrongdoings have serious results
- God's plan and his purposes are worked out even in the worst possible events

Vital statistics:
- Where: Possibly from the town of Kerioth
- Occupation: Disciple of Jesus
- Relative: Father: Simon
- Contemporaries: Jesus, Pilate, Herod, the other 11 disciples

Key verses:
"Then Satan entered Judas, called Iscariot, one of the Twelve. And Judas went to the chief priests and the officers of the temple guard and discussed with them how he might betray Jesus" (Luke 22:3, 4).

Judas' story is told in the Gospels. He is also mentioned in Acts 1:18, 19.

14:3–9 Matthew and Mark placed this event just before the Last Supper, while John placed it a week earlier, just before the Triumphal Entry. It must be remembered that the main purpose of the Gospel writers was not to present an exact chronological account of Christ's life, but to give an accurate record of his message. Matthew and Mark may have chosen to place this event here to contrast the complete devotion of Mary with the betrayal of Judas, the next event in both Gospels.

4Some of those present were saying indignantly to one another, "Why this waste
of perfume? 5It could have been sold for more than a year's wages[a] and the money
given to the poor." And they rebuked her harshly.
6"Leave her alone," said Jesus. "Why are you bothering her? She has done a
beautiful thing to me. 7The poor you will always have with you, and you can help
them any time you want.[e] But you will not always have me. 8She did what she could.
She poured perfume on my body beforehand to prepare for my burial.[f] 9I tell you
the truth, wherever the gospel is preached throughout the world,[g] what she has done
will also be told, in memory of her."

Judas Agrees to Betray Jesus
(208/Matthew 26:14–16; Luke 22:3–6)

10Then Judas Iscariot, one of the Twelve,[h] went to the chief priests to betray Jesus
to them.[i] 11They were delighted to hear this and promised to give him money. So
he watched for an opportunity to hand him over.

Disciples Prepare for the Passover
(209/Matthew 26:17–19; Luke 22:7–13)

12On the first day of the Feast of Unleavened Bread, when it was customary to
sacrifice the Passover lamb,[j] Jesus' disciples asked him, "Where do you want us to
go and make preparations for you to eat the Passover?"
13So he sent two of his disciples, telling them, "Go into the city, and a man carrying
a jar of water will meet you. Follow him. 14Say to the owner of the house he enters,
'The Teacher asks: Where is my guest room, where I may eat the Passover with my

14:7 [e]Dt 15:11
14:8 [f]Jn 19:40
14:9 [g]Mt 24:14; Mk 16:15
14:10 [h]Mk 3:16-19 [i]Mt 10:4
14:12 [j]Ex 12:1-11; Dt 16:1-4; 1Co 5:7

[a] 5 Greek *than three hundred denarii*

14:4, 5 Where Mark says "some of those present", John specifically mentions Judas (John 12:4, 5). Judas' indignation over Mary's act of worship was based not on concern for the poor but on greed. Because Judas was the treasurer of Jesus' ministry and had embezzled funds (John 12:6), he no doubt wanted the perfume sold so that the proceeds could be put into his care.

14:6, 7 Jesus was not saying that we should neglect the poor, nor was he justifying indifference to them. (For Jesus' teaching about the poor, see Matthew 6:2–4; Luke 6:20, 21; 14:13, 21; 18:22.) Jesus was praising Mary for her unselfish act of worship. The essence of worshipping Christ is to regard him with utmost love, respect, and devotion and to be willing to sacrifice to him what is most precious.

14:10 Why would Judas want to betray Jesus? Very likely, Judas expected Jesus to start a political rebellion and overthrow Rome. As treasurer, Judas certainly assumed (as did the other disciples, see 10:35–37) that he would be given an important position in Jesus' new government. But when Jesus praised Mary for pouring out the perfume, thought to be worth a year's salary, Judas finally began to realise that Jesus' kingdom was not physical or political, but spiritual. Judas' greedy desire for money and status could not be fulfilled if he followed Jesus, so he betrayed him in exchange for money and favour from the religious leaders.

14:13 The two men Jesus sent were Peter and John (Luke 22:8).

14:14, 15 Many homes had large upstairs rooms, sometimes with stairways both inside and outside the house. The preparations for the Passover would have included setting the table and buying and preparing the Passover lamb, unleavened bread, sauces, and other ceremonial food and drink.

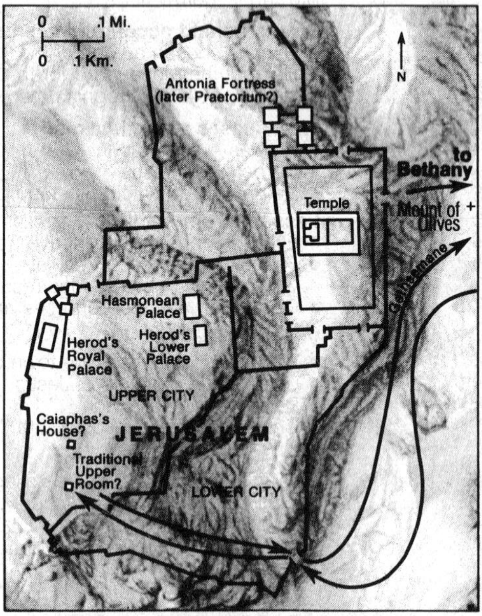

UPPER ROOM AND GETHSEMANE Jesus and the disciples ate the traditional Passover meal in an upper room in the city and then went to the Mount of Olives into a garden called Gethsemane. In the cool of the evening, Jesus prayed for strength to face the trial and suffering ahead.

14:15
[k] Ac 1:13

disciples?' 15He will show you a large upper room,[k] furnished and ready. Make preparations for us there."

16The disciples left, went into the city and found things just as Jesus had told them. So they prepared the Passover.

Jesus and the Disciples Have the Last Supper
(211/Matthew 26:20–30; Luke 22:14–30; John 13:21–30)

17When evening came, Jesus arrived with the Twelve. 18While they were reclining at the table eating, he said, "I tell you the truth, one of you will betray me—one who is eating with me."

MAJOR EVENTS OF PASSION WEEK
From Sunday to Wednesday Jesus spent each night in Bethany, just two miles east of Jerusalem on the opposite slope of the Mount of Olives. He probably stayed at the home of Mary, Martha, and Lazarus. Jesus spent Thursday night praying in the Garden of Gethsemane. Friday and Saturday nights Jesus' body lay in the garden tomb.

Day	*Event*	*References*
Sunday	Triumphal entry into Jerusalem	Matthew 21:1–11 Mark 11:1–10 Luke 19:29–40 John 12:12–19
Monday	Jesus clears the temple	Matthew 21:12, 13 Mark 11:15–17 Luke 19:45, 46
Tuesday	Jesus' authority challenged in the temple	Matthew 21:23–27 Mark 11:27–33 Luke 20:1–8
	Jesus teaches in stories and confronts the Jewish leaders	Matthew 21:28—23:36 Mark 12:1–40 Luke 20:9–47
	Greeks ask to see Jesus	John 12:20–26
	The Olivet Discourse	Matthew 24 Mark 13 Luke 21:5–38
	Judas agrees to betray Jesus	Matthew 26:14–16 Mark 14:10, 11 Luke 22:3–6
Wednesday	The Bible does not say what Jesus did on this day. He probably remained in Bethany with his disciples	
Thursday	The Last Supper	Matthew 26:26–29 Mark 14:22–25 Luke 22:14–20
	Jesus speaks to the disciples in the upper room	John 13—17
	Jesus struggles in Gethsemane	Matthew 26:36–46 Mark 14:32–42 Luke 22:39–46 John 18:1
	Jesus is betrayed and arrested	Matthew 26:47–56 Mark 14:43–52 Luke 22:47–53 John 18:2–12
Friday	Jesus is tried by Jewish and Roman authorities and disowned by Peter	Matthew 26:57—27:2, 11–31 Mark 14:53—15:20 Luke 22:54—23:25 John 18:13—19:16
	Jesus is crucified	Matthew 27:31–56 Mark 15:20–41 Luke 23:26–49 John 19:17–30
Sunday	The resurrection	Matthew 28:1–10 Mark 16:1–11 Luke 24:1–12 John 20:1–18

19 They were saddened, and one by one they said to him, “Surely not I?”
20 “It is one of the Twelve,” he replied, “one who dips bread into the bowl with me.[l]
21 The Son of Man[m] will go just as it is written about him. But woe to that man who
betrays the Son of Man! It would be better for him if he had not been born.”
22 While they were eating, Jesus took bread, gave thanks and broke it,[n] and gave
it to his disciples, saying, “Take it; this is my body.”
23 Then he took the cup, gave thanks and offered it to them, and they all drank from
it.[o]
24 “This is my blood of the[b] covenant,[p] which is poured out for many,” he said
to them. 25 “I tell you the truth, I will not drink again of the fruit of the vine until that
day when I drink it anew in the kingdom of God.”[q]
26 When they had sung a hymn, they went out to the Mount of Olives.[r]

Jesus Again Predicts Peter’s Denial
(222/Matthew 26:31–35)

27 “You will all fall away,” Jesus told them, “for it is written:

> “ ‘I will strike the shepherd,
> and the sheep will be scattered.’[c][s]

28 But after I have risen, I will go ahead of you into Galilee.”[t]
29 Peter declared, “Even if all fall away, I will not.”
30 “I tell you the truth,” Jesus answered, “today—yes, tonight—before the cock
crows twice[d] you yourself will disown me three times.”[u]
31 But Peter insisted emphatically, “Even if I have to die with you,[v] I will never
disown you.” And all the others said the same.

Jesus Agonises in the Garden
(223/Matthew 26:36–46; Luke 22:39–46)

32 They went to a place called Gethsemane, and Jesus said to his disciples, “Sit here
while I pray.” 33 He took Peter, James and John[w] along with him, and he began to
be deeply distressed and troubled. 34 “My soul is overwhelmed with sorrow to the point
of death,”[x] he said to them. “Stay here and keep watch.”
35 Going a little farther, he fell to the ground and prayed that if possible the hour[y]

[b] 24 Some manuscripts *the new* [c] 27 Zech. 13:7 [d] 30 Some early manuscripts do not have *twice*.

14:20 [l] Jn 13:18-27
14:21 [m] Mt 8:20
14:22 [n] Mt 14:19
14:23 [o] 1Co 10:16
14:24 [p] Mt 26:28
14:25 [q] Mt 3:2
14:26 [r] Mt 21:1
14:27 [s] Zec 13:7
14:28 [t] Mk 16:7
14:30 [u] ver 66-72; Lk 22:34; Jn 13:38
14:31 [v] Lk 22:33; Jn 13:37
14:33 [w] Mt 4:21
14:34 [x] Jn 12:27
14:35 [y] ver 41; Mt 26:18

14:19 Judas, the very man who would betray Jesus, was at the table with the others. Judas had already determined to betray Jesus, but in cold-blooded hypocrisy he shared the fellowship of this meal. It is easy to become enraged or shocked by what Judas did; yet professing commitment to Christ and then denying him with one’s life is also betraying him. It is denying Christ’s love to disobey him; it is denying his truth to distrust him; it is denying his deity to reject his authority. Do your words and actions match? If not, consider a change of mind and heart that will protect you from making a terrible mistake.

14:20 It was often the practice to eat from a common bowl. Meat or bread was dipped into a bowl filled with sauce often made from fruit.

14:22-25 Mark records the origin of the Lord’s Supper, also called Communion or Eucharist (thanksgiving), which is still celebrated in worship services today. Jesus and his disciples ate a meal, sang psalms, read Scripture, and prayed. Then Jesus took two traditional parts of the Passover meal, the passing of bread and the drinking of wine, and gave them new meaning as representations of his body and blood. He used the bread and wine to explain the significance of what he was about to do on the cross. For more on the significance of the Last Supper, see 1 Corinthians 11:23–29.

14:24 Jesus’ death for us on the cross seals a new covenant between God and people. The old covenant involved forgiveness of sins through the blood of an animal sacrifice (Exodus 24:6–8). But instead of a spotless lamb on the altar, Jesus offered himself, the spotless Lamb of God, as a sacrifice that would forgive sin once and for all. Jesus was the final sacrifice for sins, and his blood sealed the new agreement between God and us. Now all of us can come to God through Jesus, in full confidence that God will hear us and save us from our sins.

14:26 The hymn they sang was most likely taken from Psalms 115–118, traditionally sung at the Passover meal.

14:27 It’s easy to think that Satan temporarily gained the upper hand in this drama about Jesus’ death. But we see later that God was in control, even in the death of his Son. Satan gained no victory—everything occurred exactly as God had planned.

14:27-31 This was the second time in the same evening that Jesus predicted the disciples’ denial and desertion, which probably explains their strong reaction (14:31). For Jesus’ earlier prediction, see Luke 22:31–34 and John 13:36–38.

14:35, 36 Was Jesus trying to get out of his task? Jesus expressed his true feelings, but he did not deny or rebel against God’s will. He reaffirmed his desire to do what God wanted. Jesus’ prayer highlights the terrible suffering he had to endure—an agony so much more magnified because he had to take on the sins of the whole world. This “cup” was the agony of alienation from God, his Father, at the cross (Hebrews 5:7–9). The sinless Son of God took on our sins and was separated for a while from God so that we could be eternally saved.

might pass from him. 36"*Abba*,[e] Father,"[z] he said, "everything is possible for you. Take this cup[a] from me. Yet not what I will, but what you will."[b]

37Then he returned to his disciples and found them sleeping. "Simon," he said to Peter, "are you asleep? Could you not keep watch for one hour? 38Watch and pray so that you will not fall into temptation.[c] The spirit is willing, but the body is weak."[d]

39Once more he went away and prayed the same thing. 40When he came back, he again found them sleeping, because their eyes were heavy. They did not know what to say to him.

41Returning the third time, he said to them, "Are you still sleeping and resting? Enough! The hour[e] has come. Look, the Son of Man is betrayed into the hands of sinners. 42Rise! Let us go! Here comes my betrayer!"

Jesus Is Betrayed and Arrested
(224/Matthew 26:47–56; Luke 22:47–53; John 18:1–11)

43Just as he was speaking, Judas,[f] one of the Twelve, appeared. With him was a crowd armed with swords and clubs, sent from the chief priests, the teachers of the law, and the elders.

44Now the betrayer had arranged a signal with them: "The one I kiss is the man; arrest him and lead him away under guard." 45Going at once to Jesus, Judas said, "Rabbi!"[g] and kissed him. 46The men seized Jesus and arrested him. 47Then one of those standing near drew his sword and struck the servant of the high priest, cutting off his ear.

48"Am I leading a rebellion," said Jesus, "that you have come out with swords and clubs to capture me? 49Every day I was with you, teaching in the temple courts,[h] and you did not arrest me. But the Scriptures must be fulfilled."[i] 50Then everyone deserted him and fled.[j]

51A young man, wearing nothing but a linen garment, was following Jesus. When they seized him, 52he fled naked, leaving his garment behind.

Caiaphas Questions Jesus
(226/Matthew 26:57–68)

53They took Jesus to the high priest, and all the chief priests, elders and teachers of the law came together. 54Peter followed him at a distance, right into the courtyard of the high priest.[k] There he sat with the guards and warmed himself at the fire.[l]

55The chief priests and the whole Sanhedrin[m] were looking for evidence against Jesus so that they could put him to death, but they did not find any. 56Many testified falsely against him, but their statements did not agree.

14:36 [z] Ro 8:15; Gal 4:6 [a] Mt 20:22 [b] Mt 26:39
14:38 [c] Mt 6:13 [d] Ro 7:22, 23
14:41 [e] ver 35; Mt 26:18
14:43 [f] Mt 10:4
14:45 [g] Mt 23:7
14:49 [h] Mt 26:55 [i] Isa 53:7-12; Mt 1:22
14:50 [j] ver 27
14:54 [k] Mt 26:3 [l] Jn 18:18
14:55 [m] Mt 5:22

e *36* Aramaic for *Father*

14:36 While praying, Jesus was aware of what doing the Father's will would cost him. He understood the suffering he was about to encounter, and he did not want to have to endure the horrible experience. But Jesus prayed, "Not what I will, but what you will." Anything worth having costs something. What does your commitment to God cost you? Be willing to pay the price to gain something worthwhile in the end.

14:38 In times of great stress, we are vulnerable to temptation, even if we have a willing spirit. Jesus gave us an example of what to do to resist: (1) pray to God (14:35); (2) seek support of friends and loved ones (14:33, 37, 40, 41); (3) focus on the purpose God has given us (14:36).

14:43–45 Judas was given a contingent of police and soldiers (John 18:3) in order to seize Jesus and bring him before the religious court for trial. The religious leaders had issued the warrant for Jesus' arrest, and Judas was acting as Jesus' official accuser.

14:47 According to John 18:10, the person who pulled the sword was Peter. Luke 22:51 records that Jesus immediately healed the man's ear and prevented any further bloodshed.

14:50 Just hours earlier, these disciples had vowed never to desert Jesus (14:31).

14:51, 52 Tradition says that this young man may have been John Mark, the writer of this Gospel. The incident is not mentioned in any of the other accounts.

14:53ff This trial by the Sanhedrin had two phases. A small group met at night (John 18:12–24), and then the full Sanhedrin met at daybreak (Luke 22:66–71). They tried Jesus for religious offences such as calling himself the Son of God, which, according to law, was blasphemy. The trial was fixed: these religious leaders had already decided to kill Jesus (Luke 22:2).

14:55 The Romans controlled Israel, but the Jews were given some authority over religious and minor civil disputes. The Jewish ruling body, the Sanhedrin, was made up of 71 of Israel's religious leaders. It was assumed that these men would be just. Instead, they showed great injustice in the trial of Jesus, even to the point of making up lies to use against him (14:57).

57 Then some stood up and gave this false testimony against him: 58 "We heard him
say, 'I will destroy this man-made temple and in three days will build another,[n] not
made by man.' " 59 Yet even then their testimony did not agree.
60 Then the high priest stood up before them and asked Jesus, "Are you not going
to answer? What is this testimony that these men are bringing against you?" 61 But
Jesus remained silent and gave no answer.[o]
Again the high priest asked him, "Are you the Christ,[f] the Son of the Blessed
One?"[p]
62 "I am," said Jesus. "And you will see the Son of Man sitting at the right hand
of the Mighty One and coming on the clouds of heaven."[q]
63 The high priest tore his clothes.[r] "Why do we need any more witnesses?" he
asked. 64 "You have heard the blasphemy. What do you think?"
They all condemned him as worthy of death.[s] 65 Then some began to spit at him;
they blindfolded him, struck him with their fists, and said, "Prophesy!" And the guards
took him and beat him.[t]

Peter Denies Knowing Jesus
(227/Matthew 26:69–75; Luke 22:54–65; John 18:25–27)

66 While Peter was below in the courtyard,[u] one of the servant girls of the high
priest came by. 67 When she saw Peter warming himself,[v] she looked closely at him.
"You also were with that Nazarene, Jesus,"[w] she said.
68 But he denied it. "I don't know or understand what you're talking about,"[x] he
said, and went out into the entrance.[g]
69 When the servant girl saw him there, she said again to those standing around,
"This fellow is one of them." 70 Again he denied it.[y]

[f] 61 Or *Messiah* [g] 68 Some early manuscripts *entrance and the cock crowed*

14:58 [n] Mk 15:29; Jn 2:19
14:61 [o] Isa 53:7; Mt 27:12, 14; Mk 15:5; Lk 23:9; Jn 19:9
[p] Mt 16:16; Jn 4:25, 26
14:62 [q] Rev 1:7
14:63 [r] Lev 10:6; 21:10; Nu 14:6; Ac 14:14
14:64 [s] Lev 24:16
14:65 [t] Mt 16:21
14:66 [u] ver 54
14:67 [v] ver 54
[w] Mk 1:24
14:68 [x] ver 30, 72
14:70 [y] ver 30, 68, 72

14:58 The statement that the false witnesses finally agreed to use as an accusation twisted Jesus' actual words. Jesus did not say, "I will destroy this man-made temple;" he said, "Destroy this temple, and I will raise it again in three days" (John 2:19). Jesus was not talking about Herod's temple, but about his own body.

14:60–64 To the first question, Jesus made no reply because it was based on confusing and erroneous evidence. Not answering was wiser than trying to clarify the fabricated accusations. But if Jesus had refused to answer the second question, it could have been taken as a denial of his mission. Instead, his answer predicted a powerful role reversal. Sitting on the right hand of power, he would come to judge his accusers, and they would have to answer *his* questions (Psalm 110:1; Revelation 20:11–13).

14:63, 64 Of all people, the high priest and members of the Sanhedrin should have recognised the Messiah because they knew the Scriptures thoroughly. Their job was to point people to God, but they were more concerned about preserving their reputations and holding on to their authority. They valued human security more than eternal security.

14:66, 67 Caiaphas' house, where Jesus was tried (14:53), was part of a huge palace with several courtyards. John was apparently acquainted with the high priest, and he was let into the courtyard along with Peter (John 18:15, 16).

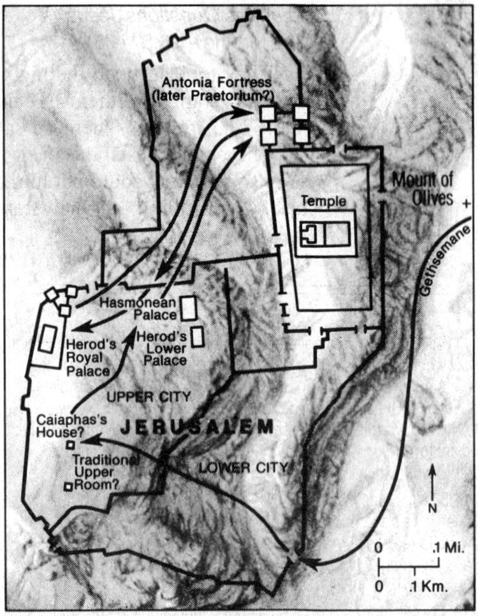

JESUS' TRIAL From Gethsemane, Jesus' trial began at the home of Caiaphas, the high priest. Jesus was then taken to Pilate, the Roman governor. Luke records that Pilate sent him to Herod, who was in Jerusalem—presumably in one of his two palaces (Luke 23:5–12). Herod sent him back to Pilate, who handed Jesus over to be crucified.

14:70 [z] Ac 2:7

After a little while, those standing near said to Peter, "Surely you are one of them,
for you are a Galilean."[z]
71 He began to call down curses on himself, and he swore to them, "I don't know
this man you're talking about."[a]
72 Immediately the cock crowed the second time.[h] Then Peter remembered the word
Jesus had spoken to him: "Before the cock crows twice[i] you will disown me three
times."[b] And he broke down and wept.

14:71 [a] ver 30, 72

14:72 [b] ver 30, 68

The Council of Religious Leaders Condemns Jesus
(228/Matthew 27:1, 2; Luke 22:66–71)

15 Very early in the morning, the chief priests, with the elders, the teachers of the
law[a] and the whole Sanhedrin,[b] reached a decision. They bound Jesus, led
him away and turned him over to Pilate.[c]

15:1 [a] Mt 27:1; Lk 22:66 [b] Mt 5:22 [c] Mt 27:2

Jesus Stands Trial before Pilate
(230/Matthew 27:11–14; Luke 23:1–5; John 18:28–37)

2 "Are you the king of the Jews?"[d] asked Pilate.
"Yes, it is as you say," Jesus replied.
3 The chief priests accused him of many things. 4 So again Pilate asked him, "Aren't
you going to answer? See how many things they are accusing you of."
5 But Jesus still made no reply,[e] and Pilate was amazed.

15:2 [d] ver 9, 12, 18, 26; Mt 2:2

15:5 [e] Mk 14:61

h 72 Some early manuscripts do not have *the second time.* i 72 Some early manuscripts do not have *twice.*

WHY DID JESUS HAVE TO DIE?

The Problem	We have all done things that are wrong, and we have failed to obey God's laws. Because of this, we have been separated from God our Creator. Separation from God is death; but, by ourselves, we can do nothing to become united with God.
Why Jesus Could Help	Jesus was not only a man; he was God's unique Son. Because Jesus never disobeyed God and never sinned, only he can bridge the gap between the sinless God and sinful mankind.
The Solution	Jesus freely offered his life for us, dying on the cross in our place, taking all our wrongdoing upon himself, and saving us from the consequences of sin—including God's judgment and death.
The Results	Jesus took our past, present, and future sins upon himself so that we could have new life. Because all our wrongdoing is forgiven, we are reconciled to God. Furthermore, Jesus' resurrection from the dead is the proof that his substitutionary sacrifice on the cross was acceptable to God, and his resurrection has become the source of new life for whoever believes that Jesus is the Son of God. All who believe in him may have this new life and live it in union with him.

14:71 Peter's curse was more than just a common swear word. He was making the strongest denial he could think of by denying with an oath that he knew Jesus. He was saying, in effect, "May God strike me dead if I'm lying."

14:71 It is easy to get angry at the Sanhedrin and the Roman governor for their injustice in condemning Jesus, but Peter and the rest of the disciples also contributed to Jesus' pain by deserting him (14:50). While most of us may not be like the Jewish and Roman leaders, we are like the disciples because all of us have been guilty of denying Christ as Lord in vital areas of our lives. We may pride ourselves that we have not committed certain sins, but we are all guilty of sin. Don't try to excuse yourself by pointing at others whose sins seem worse than yours.

15:1 Why did the Jewish leaders send Jesus to Pilate, the Roman governor? The Romans had taken away the Jews' right to inflict capital punishment; so in order for Jesus to be condemned to death, he had to be sentenced by a Roman leader. The Jewish leaders wanted Jesus executed on a cross, a method of death that they believed brought a curse from God (see Deuteronomy 21:23). They hoped to persuade the people that Jesus was cursed, not blessed, by God.

15:3, 4 The Jewish leaders had to fabricate new accusations against Jesus when they brought him before Pilate. The charge of blasphemy would mean nothing to the Roman governor, so they accused Jesus of three other crimes: (1) encouraging the people not to pay their taxes to Rome, (2) claiming he was a king—"the king of the Jews", and (3) causing riots all over the countryside. Tax evasion, treason, and insurrection—all these would be cause for Pilate's concern (see also Luke 23:2).

15:5 Why didn't Jesus answer Pilate's questions? It would have been futile to answer, and the time had come to give his life to save the world. Jesus had no reason to try to prolong the trial or save himself. His was the ultimate example of self-assurance and peace, which no ordinary criminal could imitate. Nothing would stop him from completing the work he had come to earth to do (Isaiah 53:7).

Pilate Hands Jesus Over to Be Crucified

(232/Matthew 27:15–26; Luke 23:13–25; John 18:38 – 19:16)

6Now it was the custom at the Feast to release a prisoner whom the people
requested. 7A man called Barabbas was in prison with the insurrectionists who had
committed murder in the uprising. 8The crowd came up and asked Pilate to do for
them what he usually did.
9"Do you want me to release to you the king of the Jews?"[f] asked Pilate, 10knowing
it was out of envy that the chief priests had handed Jesus over to him. 11But the chief
priests stirred up the crowd to have Pilate release Barabbas[g] instead.
12"What shall I do, then, with the one you call the king of the Jews?" Pilate asked
them.
13"Crucify him!" they shouted.
14"Why? What crime has he committed?" asked Pilate.
But they shouted all the louder, "Crucify him!"
15Wanting to satisfy the crowd, Pilate released Barabbas to them. He had Jesus
flogged,[h] and handed him over to be crucified.

15:9 [f]ver 2
15:11 [g]Ac 3:14
15:15 [h]Isa 53:6

Roman Soldiers Mock Jesus

(233/Matthew 27:27–31)

16The soldiers led Jesus away into the palace[i] (that is, the Praetorium) and called
together the whole company of soldiers. 17They put a purple robe on him, then twisted
together a crown of thorns and set it on him. 18And they began to call out to him,
"Hail, king of the Jews!"[j] 19Again and again they struck him on the head with a staff
and spat on him. Falling on their knees, they paid homage to him. 20And when they
had mocked him, they took off the purple robe and put his own clothes on him. Then
they led him out[k] to crucify him.

15:16 [i]Jn 18:28, 33; 19:9
15:18 [j]ver 2
15:20 [k]Heb 13:12

15:7 Barabbas was arrested for his part in a rebellion against the Roman government, and, although he had committed a murder, he may have been a hero among the Jews. The fiercely independent Jews hated to be ruled by pagan Romans. They hated paying taxes to support the despised government and its gods. Most of the Roman authorities who had to settle Jewish disputes hated the Jews in return. The time was ripe for rebellion.

15:8 This crowd was most likely a group of people loyal to the Jewish leaders. But where were the disciples and the crowds who days earlier had shouted, "Hosanna in the highest" (11:10)? Jesus' sympathisers were afraid of the Jewish leaders, so they went into hiding. Another possibility is that the multitude included many people who were in the Palm Sunday parade, but who turned against Jesus when they saw that he was not going to be an earthly conqueror and their deliverer from Rome.

15:10 The Jews hated Pilate, but they went to him for the favour of condemning Jesus to crucifixion. Pilate could see that this was a frame-up. Why else would these people, who hated him and the Roman empire he represented, ask him to convict of treason and give the death penalty to one of their fellow Jews?

15:13 Crucifixion was the Roman penalty for rebellion. Only slaves or those who were not Roman citizens could be crucified. If Jesus died by crucifixion, he would die the death of a rebel and slave, not of the king he claimed to be. This is just what the Jewish religious leaders wanted, and the reason they whipped the mob into a frenzy. In addition, crucifixion would put the responsibility for killing Jesus on the Romans, and thus the crowds could not blame the religious leaders.

15:14, 15 Who was guilty of Jesus' death? In reality, everyone was at fault. The disciples deserted him in terror. Peter denied that he ever knew Jesus. Judas betrayed him. The crowds who had followed him stood by and did nothing. Pilate tried to blame the crowds. The religious leaders actively promoted Jesus' death. The Roman soldiers tortured him. If you had been there, watching these trials, what would your response have been?

15:15 The region of Judea where Pilate ruled as governor was little more than a hot and dusty outpost of the Roman empire. Because Judea was so far from Rome, Pilate was given just a small army. His primary job was to keep peace. We know from historical records that Pilate had already been warned about other uprisings in his region. Although he may have seen no guilt in Jesus and no reason to condemn him to death, Pilate wavered when the Jews in the crowd threatened to report him to Caesar (John 19:12). Such a report, accompanied by a riot, could cost him his position and hopes for advancement.

15:15 Although Jesus was innocent according to Roman law, Pilate caved in to political pressure. He abandoned what he knew was right. Trying to anticipate the Jewish leaders, Pilate gave a decision that would please everyone while keeping himself safe. When we lay aside God's clear statements of right and wrong and make decisions based on the preferences of our audience, we fall into compromise and lawlessness. God promises to honour those who do right, not those who make everyone happy.

15:19 The soldiers "paid homage to him"; in other words, they mocked Jesus by pretending to worship him.

15:21
[l]Mt 27:32
[m]Ro 16:13
[n]Mt 27:32; Lk 23:26

15:23
[o]ver 36; Ps 69:21; Pr 31:6

Jesus Is Led Away to Be Crucified
(234/Matthew 27:32–34; Luke 23:26–31; John 19:17)

21 A certain man from Cyrene,[l] Simon, the father of Alexander and Rufus,[m] was
passing by on his way in from the country, and they forced him to carry the cross.[n]
22 They brought Jesus to the place called Golgotha (which means The Place of the
Skull). 23 Then they offered him wine mixed with myrrh,[o] but he did not take it. 24 And

PILATE

In Jesus' day, any death sentence had to be approved by the Roman official in charge of the administrative district. Pontius Pilate was governor of the province of Judea, where Jerusalem was located. When the Jewish leaders had Jesus in their power and wanted to kill him, they had to obtain Pilate's permission. So it happened that early one morning Pilate found a crowd at his door demanding a man's death.

Pilate's relationship with the Jews had always been stormy. His Roman toughness and fairness had been weakened by cynicism, compromises, and mistakes. On several occasions his actions had deeply offended the religious leaders. The resulting riots and chaos must have made Pilate wonder what he had got himself into. He was trying to control people who treated their Roman conquerors without respect. Jesus' trial was another episode in Pilate's ongoing problems.

For Pilate, there was never a doubt about Jesus' innocence. Three separate times he declared Jesus not guilty. He couldn't understand what made these people want to kill Jesus, but his fear of the pressure the Jews would place on him made him decide to allow Jesus' crucifixion. Because of the people's threat to inform the emperor that Pilate hadn't eliminated a rebel against Rome, Pilate went against what he knew was right. In desperation, he chose to do wrong.

We share a common humanity with Pilate. At times we know the right and choose the wrong. He had his moment in history and now we have ours. What have we done with our opportunities and responsibilities? What judgment have we passed on Jesus?

Strength and accomplishment:
- Roman governor of Judea

Weaknesses and mistakes:
- He failed in his attempt to rule a people who were defeated militarily but never dominated by Rome
- His constant political struggles made him a cynical and uncaring compromiser, susceptible to pressure
- Although he realised Jesus was innocent, he bowed to the public demand for his execution

Lessons from his life:
- Great evil can happen when truth is at the mercy of political pressures
- Resisting the truth leaves a person without purpose or direction

Vital statistics:
- Where: Judea
- Occupation: Roman governor of Judea
- Relative: Wife: unnamed
- Contemporaries: Jesus, Caiaphas, Herod

Key verses:
" 'What is truth?' Pilate asked. With this he went out again to the Jews and said, 'I find no basis for a charge against him. But it is your custom for me to release to you one prisoner at the time of the Passover. Do you want me to release "the king of the Jews"?' " (John 18:38, 39).

Pilate's story is told in the Gospels. He is also mentioned in Acts 3:13; 4:27; 13:28; 1 Timothy 6:13.

15:21 Colonies of Jews existed outside Judea. Simon had made a Passover pilgrimage to Jerusalem all the way from Cyrene in North Africa. His sons, Alexander and Rufus, are mentioned here probably because they became well known later in the early church (Romans 16:13).

15:24 Casting lots was a way of making a decision by chance, like throwing dice or drawing straws. The soldiers cast lots to decide who would receive Jesus' clothing. Roman soldiers had the right to take for themselves the clothing of those crucified. This act fulfilled the prophecy of Psalm 22:18.

they crucified him. Dividing up his clothes, they cast lots[p] to see what each would
get.

Jesus Is Placed on the Cross
(235/Matthew 27:35–44; Luke 23:32–43; John 19:18–27)

25 It was the third hour when they crucified him. 26 The written notice of the charge
against him read: THE KING OF THE JEWS.[q] 27 They crucified two robbers with him,
one on his right and one on his left.[a] 29 Those who passed by hurled insults at him,
shaking their heads[r] and saying, "So! You who are going to destroy the temple and
build it in three days,[s] 30 come down from the cross and save yourself!"
31 In the same way the chief priests and the teachers of the law mocked him[t] among
themselves. "He saved others," they said, "but he can't save himself! 32 Let this
Christ,[b][u] this King of Israel,[v] come down now from the cross, that we may see and
believe." Those crucified with him also heaped insults on him.

Jesus Dies on the Cross
(236/Matthew 27:45–56; Luke 23:44–49; John 19:28–37)

33 At the sixth hour darkness came over the whole land until the ninth hour.[w] 34 And
at the ninth hour Jesus cried out in a loud voice, "*Eloi, Eloi, lama sabach-
thani?*"—which means, "My God, my God, why have you forsaken me?"[c][x]

a *27* Some manuscripts *left,* [28] *and the scripture was fulfilled which says, "He was counted with the lawless ones"* (Isaiah 53:12) b *32* Or *Messiah* c *34* Psalm 22:1

15:24 [p]Ps 22:18
15:26 [q]ver 2
15:29 [r]Ps 22:7; 109:25 [s]Mk 14:58; Jn 2:19
15:31 [t]Ps 22:7
15:32 [u]Mk 14:61 [v]ver 2
15:33 [w]Am 8:9
15:34 [x]Ps 22:1

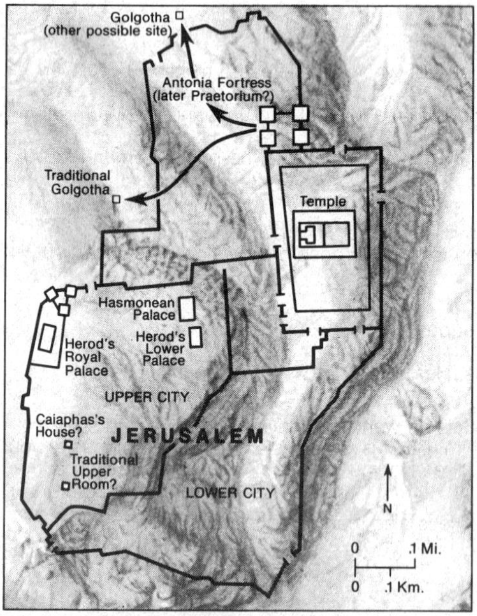

JESUS' ROUTE TO GOLGOTHA After being sentenced by Pilate, Jesus was taken from the Praetorium to a place outside the city, Golgotha, for crucifixion.

15:25 Crucifixion was a feared and shameful form of execution. The victim was forced to carry his cross along the longest possible route to the crucifixion site as a warning to bystanders. There were several shapes for crosses and several different methods of crucifixion. Jesus was nailed to the cross; condemned men were sometimes tied to their crosses with ropes. In either case, death came by suffocation as the person lost strength and the weight of the body made breathing more and more difficult.

15:26 A sign stating the condemned man's crime was often placed on a cross as a warning. Because Jesus was never found guilty, the only accusation placed on his sign was the "crime" of being King of the Jews.

15:27 Luke records that one of these robbers repented before his death, and Jesus promised that criminal that he would be with him in paradise (Luke 23:39–43).

15:31 Jesus could have saved himself, but he endured this suffering because of his love for us. He could have chosen not to take the pain and humiliation; he could have killed those who mocked him—but he suffered through it all because he loved even his enemies. We had a significant part in the drama that afternoon because our sins were on the cross too. Jesus died on that cross for us, and the penalty for our sins was paid by his death. The only adequate response we can make is to confess our sin and freely accept the fact that Jesus paid for it so we wouldn't have to. Don't insult God with indifference towards the greatest act of genuine love in history.

15:32 When James and John had asked Jesus for the places of honour next to him in his kingdom, Jesus had told them that they didn't know what they were asking (10:35–39). Here, as Jesus was preparing to inaugurate his kingdom through his death, the places on his right and on his left were taken by dying men—criminals. As Jesus explained to his two power-hungry disciples, a person who wants to be close to Jesus must be prepared to suffer and die as he himself was doing. The way to the kingdom is the way of the cross. If we want the glory of the kingdom, we must be willing to be united with the crucified Christ.

15:36 [y]ver 23; Ps 69:21
15:37 [z]Jn 19:30
15:38 [a]Heb 10:19, 20
15:39 [b]ver 45 [c]Mk 1:1, 11; 9:7; Mt 4:3
15:40 [d]Ps 38:11 [e]Mk 16:1; Lk 24:10; Jn 19:25
15:41 [f]Mt 27:55, 56; Lk 8:2, 3
15:42 [g]Mt 27:62; Jn 19:31
15:43 [h]Mt 5:22 [i]Mt 3:2; Lk 2:25, 38
15:45 [j]ver 39
15:46 [k]Mk 16:3
15:47 [l]ver 40

35 When some of those standing near heard this, they said, "Listen, he's calling
Elijah."
36 One man ran, filled a sponge with wine vinegar,[y] put it on a stick, and offered
it to Jesus to drink. "Now leave him alone. Let's see if Elijah comes to take him
down," he said.
37 With a loud cry, Jesus breathed his last.[z]
38 The curtain of the temple was torn in two from top to bottom.[a] 39 And when the
centurion,[b] who stood there in front of Jesus, heard his cry and[d] saw how he died,
he said, "Surely this man was the Son[e] of God!"[c]
40 Some women were watching from a distance.[d] Among them were Mary Magdalene, Mary the mother of James the younger and of Joses, and Salome.[e] 41 In Galilee
these women had followed him and cared for his needs. Many other women who had
come up with him to Jerusalem were also there.[f]

Jesus Is Laid in the Tomb
(237/Matthew 27:57–61; Luke 23:50–56; John 19:38–42)

42 It was Preparation Day (that is, the day before the Sabbath).[g] So as evening
approached, 43 Joseph of Arimathea, a prominent member of the Council,[h] who was
himself waiting for the kingdom of God,[i] went boldly to Pilate and asked for Jesus'
body. 44 Pilate was surprised to hear that he was already dead. Summoning the
centurion, he asked him if Jesus had already died. 45 When he learned from the
centurion[j] that it was so, he gave the body to Joseph. 46 So Joseph bought some linen
cloth, took down the body, wrapped it in the linen, and placed it in a tomb cut out
of rock. Then he rolled a stone against the entrance of the tomb.[k] 47 Mary Magdalene
and Mary the mother of Joses[l] saw where he was laid.

d *39* Some manuscripts do not have *heard his cry and.* **e** *39* Or *a son*

15:34 Jesus did not ask this question in surprise or despair. He was quoting the first line of Psalm 22. The whole psalm is a prophecy expressing the deep agony of the Messiah's death for the world's sin. Jesus knew that he would be temporarily separated from God the moment he took upon himself the sins of the world. This separation was what he had dreaded as he prayed in Gethsemane. The physical agony was horrible, but the spiritual alienation from God was the ultimate torture.

15:37 Jesus' loud cry may have been his last words, "It is finished" (John 19:30).

15:38 A heavy curtain hung in front of the temple room called the Most Holy Place, a place reserved by God for himself. Symbolically, the curtain separated the holy God from sinful people. The room was entered only once a year, on the Day of Atonement, by the high priest as he made a sacrifice to gain forgiveness for the sins of all the people. When Jesus died, the curtain was torn in two, showing that his death for our sins had opened up the way for us to approach our holy God. And it was torn from top to bottom, showing that *God* had opened the way. Read Hebrews 9 for a more complete explanation.

15:42ff The Sabbath began at sunset on Friday and ended at sunset on Saturday. Jesus died just a few hours before sundown on Friday. It was against Jewish law to do physical work or to travel on the Sabbath. It was also against Jewish law to let a dead body remain exposed overnight (Deuteronomy 21:23). Joseph came to bury Jesus' body before the Sabbath began. If Jesus had died on the Sabbath when Joseph was unavailable, his body would have been taken down by the Romans. Had the Romans taken Jesus' body, no Jews could have confirmed his death, and opponents could have disputed his resurrection.

15:42, 43 After Jesus died on the cross, Joseph of Arimathea asked for his body and then sealed it in a new tomb. Although an honoured member of the Sanhedrin, Joseph was a secret disciple of Jesus. Not all the Jewish leaders hated Jesus. Joseph risked his reputation to give a proper burial to his Lord. It is frightening to risk one's reputation even for what is right. If your Christian witness endangers your reputation, remember Joseph. Today he is remembered with admiration in the Christian church. How many other members of the Jewish Sanhedrin can you name?

15:44 Pilate was surprised that Jesus had died so quickly, so he asked an official to verify the report. Today, in an effort to deny the resurrection, there are those who say that Jesus didn't really die. His death, however, was confirmed by the centurion, Pilate, Joseph of Arimathea, the religious leaders, and the women who witnessed his burial. Jesus suffered actual physical death on the cross.

15:46 This tomb was probably a man-made cave hewn from a hill. It was large enough to walk into. Joseph wrapped Jesus' body, placed it in the tomb, and rolled a heavy stone across the entrance. The religious leaders also watched where Jesus was buried. They stationed guards by the tomb and sealed the stone to make sure that no-one would steal Jesus' body and claim he had risen from the dead (Matthew 27:62–66).

15:47 These women could do very little. They couldn't speak before the Sanhedrin in Jesus' defence; they couldn't appeal to Pilate; they couldn't stand against the crowds; they couldn't overpower the Roman guards. But they did what they could. They stayed at the cross when the disciples had fled; they followed Jesus' body to its tomb; and they prepared spices for his body. Because these women used the opportunities they had, they were the first to witness the resurrection. God blessed their devotion and diligence. As believers, we should take advantage of the opportunities we have and do what we *can* for Christ, instead of worrying about what we *cannot* do.

Jesus Rises from the Dead
(239/Matthew 28:1–7; Luke 24:1–12; John 20:1–9)

16 When the Sabbath was over, Mary Magdalene, Mary the mother of James, and
Salome bought spices[a] so that they might go to anoint Jesus' body. 2Very early
on the first day of the week, just after sunrise, they were on their way to the tomb
3and they asked each other, "Who will roll the stone away from the entrance of the
tomb?"[b]
4But when they looked up, they saw that the stone, which was very large, had been
rolled away. 5As they entered the tomb, they saw a young man dressed in a white
robe[c] sitting on the right side, and they were alarmed.
6"Don't be alarmed," he said. "You are looking for Jesus the Nazarene,[d] who was
crucified. He has risen! He is not here. See the place where they laid him. 7But go,

16:1 [a]Lk 23:56; Jn 19:39, 40
16:3 [b]Mk 15:46
16:5 [c]Jn 20:12
16:6 [d]Mk 1:24

EVIDENCE THAT JESUS ACTUALLY DIED AND ROSE AGAIN
This evidence demonstrates Jesus' uniqueness in history and proves that he is God's Son. No-one else was able to predict his own resurrection and then accomplish it.

Proposed Explanations for Empty Tomb	*Evidence against These Explanations*	*References*
Jesus was only unconscious and later revived.	A Roman soldier told Pilate that Jesus was dead.	Mark 15:44, 45
	The Roman soldiers did not break Jesus' legs, because he had already died, and one of them pierced Jesus' side with a spear.	John 19:32–34
	Joseph of Arimathea and Nicodemus wrapped Jesus' body and placed it in the tomb.	John 19:38–40
The women made a mistake and went to the wrong tomb.	Mary Magdalene and Mary the mother of Joses saw Jesus placed in the tomb.	Matthew 27:59–61 Mark 15:47 Luke 23:55
	On Sunday morning Peter and John also went to the same tomb.	John 20:3–9
Unknown thieves stole Jesus' body.	The tomb was sealed and guarded by Roman soldiers.	Matthew 27:65, 66
The disciples stole Jesus' body.	The disciples were ready to die for their faith. Stealing Jesus' body would have been admitting that their faith was meaningless.	Acts 12:2
	The tomb was guarded and sealed.	Matthew 27:66
The religious leaders stole Jesus' body to produce it later.	If the religious leaders had taken Jesus' body, they would have produced it to stop the rumours of his resurrection.	None

16:1, 2 The women purchased the spices on Saturday evening after the Sabbath had ended so they could go to the tomb early the next morning and anoint Jesus' body as a sign of love, devotion, and respect. Bringing spices to the tomb was like bringing flowers to a grave today.

16:4 The angels did not roll away the stone so Jesus could get out, but so others could get in and see for themselves that Jesus had indeed risen from the dead, just as he said.

16:5 Mark says that one angel met the women at the tomb, while Luke mentions two angels. These accounts are not contradictory. Each Gospel writer chose to highlight different details as he explained the same story, just as eyewitnesses to a news story may each highlight a different aspect of that event. Mark probably emphasised only the angel who spoke. The unique emphasis of each Gospel shows that the four accounts were written independently. This should give us confidence that all four are true and reliable.

16:6 The resurrection is vitally important for many reasons: (1) Jesus kept his promise to rise from the dead, so we can believe he will keep all his other promises. (2) The resurrection ensures that the ruler of God's eternal kingdom will be the living Christ, not just an idea, hope, or dream. (3) Christ's resurrection gives us the assurance that we too will be resurrected. (4) The power of God that brought Christ's body back from the dead is available to us to bring our morally and spiritually dead selves back to life so that we can change and grow (1 Corinthians 15:12–19). (5) The resurrection provides the substance of the church's witness to the world. We do not merely tell lessons from the life of a good teacher; we proclaim the reality of the resurrection of Jesus Christ.

16:7 The angel made special mention of Peter to show that, in spite of Peter's denials, Jesus had not disowned and deserted him. Jesus had great responsibilities for Peter to fulfil in the church that was not yet born.

16:7 The angel told the disciples to meet Jesus in Galilee "as he told you" (see 14:28). This is where Jesus had called most of them and had said they would become "fishers of men" (Matthew 4:19), and it would be where this mission would be restated (John 21). But the disciples, filled with fear, remained behind locked doors in Jerusalem (John 20:19). Jesus met them first in Jerusalem (Luke 24:36) and later in Galilee (John 21). Then he returned to Jeru-

16:7
[e]Jn 21:1-23
[f]Mk 14:28

16:9
[g]Jn 20:11-18

16:11
[h]ver 13, 14; Lk 24:11

16:12
[i]Lk 24:13-32

16:14
[j]Lk 24:36-43

16:15
[k]Mt 28:18-20; Lk 24:47, 48

16:16
[l]Jn 3:16, 18, 36; Ac 16:31

16:17
[m]Mk 9:38; Lk 10:17; Ac 5:16; 8:7; 16:18; 19:13-16
[n]Ac 2:4; 10:46; 19:6; 1Co 12:10, 28, 30

16:18
[o]Lk 10:19; Ac 28:3-5
[p]Ac 6:6

tell his disciples and Peter, 'He is going ahead of you into Galilee. There you will see him,[e] just as he told you.' "[f]

8 Trembling and bewildered, the women went out and fled from the tomb. They said nothing to anyone, because they were afraid.

[The most reliable early manuscripts and other ancient witnesses do not have Mark 16:9–20.]

Jesus Appears to Mary Magdalene
(240/John 20:10–18)

9 When Jesus rose early on the first day of the week, he appeared first to Mary
Magdalene,[g] out of whom he had driven seven demons. 10 She went and told those
who had been with him and who were mourning and weeping. 11 When they heard
that Jesus was alive and that she had seen him, they did not believe it.[h]

Jesus Appears to Two Believers Travelling on the Road
(243/Luke 24:13–35)

12 Afterwards Jesus appeared in a different form to two of them while they were
walking in the country.[i] 13 These returned and reported it to the rest; but they did not
believe them either.

Jesus Appears to the Disciples Including Thomas
(245/John 20:24–31)

14 Later Jesus appeared to the Eleven as they were eating; he rebuked them for their lack of faith and their stubborn refusal to believe those who had seen him after he had risen.[j]

Jesus Gives the Great Commission
(248/Matthew 28:16–20)

15 He said to them, "Go into all the world and preach the good news to all creation.[k]
16 Whoever believes and is baptised will be saved, but whoever does not believe will
be condemned.[l] 17 And these signs will accompany those who believe: In my name
they will drive out demons;[m] they will speak in new tongues;[n] 18 they will pick up
snakes[o] with their hands; and when they drink deadly poison, it will not hurt them
at all; they will place their hands on[p] sick people, and they will get well."

---

salem where he ascended into heaven from the Mount of Olives (Acts 1:12).

16:13 When the two finally realised who Jesus was, they rushed back to Jerusalem. It's not enough to read about Christ as a personality or to study his teachings. You must also believe he is God, trust him to save you, and accept him as Lord of your life. This is the difference between knowing Jesus and knowing about him. Only when you know Christ will you be motivated to share with others what he has done for you.

16:15 Jesus told his disciples to go into all the world, telling everyone that he had paid the penalty for sin and that those who believe in him can be forgiven and live eternally with God. Christian disciples today in all parts of the world are preaching this gospel to people who haven't heard about Christ. The driving power that carries missionaries around the world and sets Christ's church in motion is the faith that comes from the resurrection. Do you ever feel as though you don't have the skill or determination to be a witness for Christ? You must personally realise that Jesus rose from the dead and lives for you today. As you grow in your relationship with Christ, he will give you both the opportunities and the inner strength to tell his message.

16:16 It is not the water of baptism that saves, but God's grace accepted through faith in Christ. Because of Jesus' response to the criminal on the cross who died with him, we know it is possible to be saved without being baptised (Luke 23:43). Baptism alone, without faith, does not automatically bring a person to heaven. Those who refuse to believe will be condemned, regardless of whether or not they have been baptised.

16:18 There are times when God intervenes miraculously to protect his followers. Occasionally he gives them special powers. Paul handled a snake safely (Acts 28:5), and the disciples healed the sick (Matthew 10:1; Acts 3:7, 8). This does not mean, however, that we should test God by putting ourselves in dangerous situations.

Jesus Ascends into Heaven
(250/Luke 24:50–53)

19 After the Lord Jesus had spoken to them, he was taken up into heaven[q] and he
sat at the right hand of God.[r] 20 Then the disciples went out and preached everywhere,
and the Lord worked with them and confirmed his word by the signs that accompanied
it.

16:19
[q] Lk 24:50, 51; Jn 6:62; Ac 1:9-11; 1Ti 3:16
[r] Ps 110:1; Ro 8:34; Col 3:1; Heb 1:3; 12:2

16:19 When Jesus ascended into heaven, his physical presence left the disciples (Acts 1:9). Jesus' sitting at God's right hand signifies the completion of his work, his authority as God, and his coronation as King.

16:20 Mark's Gospel emphasises Christ's power as well as his servanthood. Jesus' life and teaching turn the world upside down. The world sees power as a way to gain control over others. But Jesus, with all authority and power in heaven and earth, chose to serve others. He held children in his arms, healed the sick, washed the disciples' feet, and died for the sins of the world. Following Jesus means receiving this same power to serve. As believers, we are called to be servants of Christ. As Christ served, so we are to serve.

KEY PLACES IN LUKE

Luke begins his account in the temple in Jerusalem, giving us the background for the birth of John the Baptist, then moves on to the town of Nazareth and the story of Mary, chosen to be Jesus' mother (1:26ff). As a result of Caesar's call for a census, Mary and Joseph had to travel to Bethlehem, where Jesus was born in fulfilment of prophecy (2:1ff). Jesus grew up in Nazareth and began his earthly ministry by being baptised by John (3:21, 22) and tempted by Satan (4:1ff). Much of his ministry focused on Galilee—he set up his "home" in Capernaum (4:31ff) and from there he taught throughout the region (8:1ff). Later he visited the Gerasene region, where he healed a demon-possessed man (8:36ff). He fed more than 5,000 people with one lunch on the shores of the Sea of Galilee near Bethsaida (9:10ff). Jesus always travelled to Jerusalem for the major festivals, and he enjoyed visiting friends in nearby Bethany (10:38ff). He healed ten men with leprosy on the border between Galilee and Samaria (17:11), and helped a dishonest tax collector in Jericho turn his life around (19:1ff). The little villages of Bethphage and Bethany on the Mount of Olives were Jesus' resting places during his last days on earth. He was crucified outside Jerusalem's walls, but he would rise again. Two men on the road leading to Emmaus were among the first to see the resurrected Christ (24:13ff).

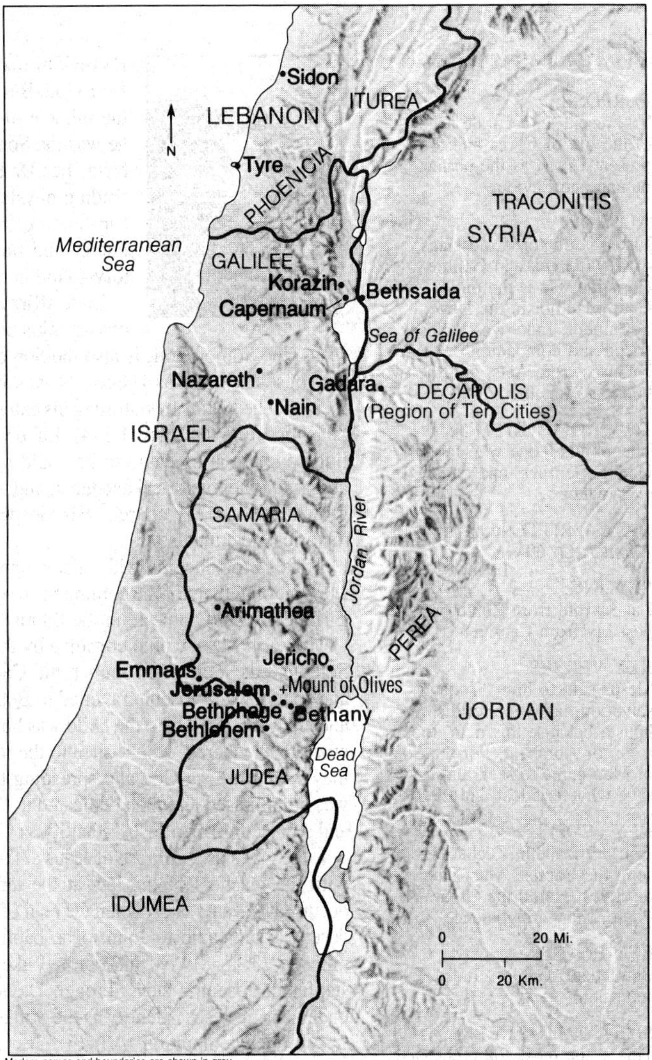

Modern names and boundaries are shown in grey.

LUKE

Herod the Great begins to rule 37 B.C.	Jesus is born 6/5 B.C.	Escape to Egypt 5/4 B.C.	Herod the Great dies 4 B.C.	Return to Nazareth 4/3 B.C.	Jesus visits temple as a boy A.D. 6/7

VITAL STATISTICS

PURPOSE:
To present an accurate account of the life of Christ and to present Christ as the perfect human and Saviour

AUTHOR:
Luke—a doctor (Colossians 4:14), a Greek and Gentile Christian. He is the only known Gentile author in the New Testament. Luke was a close friend and companion of Paul. He also wrote Acts, and the two books go together.

TO WHOM WRITTEN:
Theophilus ("one who loves God"), Gentiles, and people everywhere

DATE WRITTEN:
About A.D. 60

SETTING:
Luke wrote from Rome or possibly from Caesarea.

KEY VERSES:
"Jesus said to him, 'Today salvation has come to this house, because this man, too, is a son of Abraham. For the Son of Man came to seek and to save what was lost'" (19:9, 10).

KEY PEOPLE:
Jesus, Elizabeth, Zechariah, John the Baptist, Mary, the disciples, Herod the Great, Pilate, Mary Magdalene

KEY PLACES:
Bethlehem, Galilee, Judea, Jerusalem

SPECIAL FEATURES:
This is the most comprehensive Gospel. The general vocabulary and diction show that the author was educated. He makes frequent references to illnesses and diagnoses. Luke stresses Jesus' relationships with people; emphasises prayer, miracles, and angels; records inspired hymns of praise; and gives a prominent place to women. Most of 9:51—18:35 is not found in any other Gospel.

EVERY birth is a miracle, and every child is a gift from God. But nearly 20 centuries ago, there was the miracle of miracles. A baby was born, but he was the Son of God. The Gospels tell of this birth, but Dr Luke, as though he were the attending physician, provides most of the details surrounding this awesome occasion. With divine Father and human mother, Jesus entered history—God in the flesh.

Luke affirms Jesus' divinity, but the real emphasis of his book is to show Jesus' humanity—Jesus, the Son of God, is also the Son of Man. As a doctor, Luke was a man of science, and as a Greek, he was a man of detail. It is not surprising, then, that he begins by outlining his extensive research and explaining that he is reporting the facts (1:1–4). Luke was also a close friend and travelling companion of Paul, so he could interview the other disciples, had access to other historical accounts, and was an eyewitness to the birth and growth of the early church. His Gospel and book of Acts are reliable, historical documents.

Luke's story begins with angels appearing to Zechariah and then to Mary, telling them of the coming births of their sons. From Zechariah and Elizabeth would come John the Baptist, who would prepare the way for Christ. And Mary would conceive by the Holy Spirit and bear Jesus, the Son of God. Soon after John's birth, Caesar Augustus declared a census, and so Mary and Joseph travelled to Bethlehem, the town of David, their ancient ancestor. There the child was born. Angels announced the joyous event to shepherds, who rushed to the manger. When the shepherds left, they were praising God and spreading the news. Eight days later, Jesus was circumcised and then dedicated to God in the temple, where Simeon and Anna confirmed Jesus' identity as the Saviour, their Messiah.

Luke gives us a glimpse of Jesus at the age of 12—discussing theology with the teachers of the law at the temple (2:41–52). The next event occurred 18 years later, when we read of John the Baptist preaching in the desert. Jesus came to John to be baptised before beginning his public ministry (3:1–38). At this point, Luke traces Jesus' genealogy on his stepfather Joseph's side, through David and Abraham back to Adam, underscoring Jesus' identity as the Son of Man.

After the temptation (4:1–13), Jesus returned to Galilee to preach, teach, and heal (4:14—21:38). During this time, he began gathering his group of 12 disciples (5:1–10, 27–29). Later Jesus commissioned the disciples and sent them out to proclaim the kingdom of God. When they returned, Jesus revealed to them his mission, his true identity, and what it means to be his disciple (9:18–62). His mission would take him to Jerusalem (9:51–53), where he would be rejected, tried, and crucified.

While Jesus carried his own cross to Golgotha, some women in Jerusalem wept for him, but Jesus told them to weep for themselves and for their children (23:28). But Luke's Gospel does not end in sadness. It concludes with the thrilling account of Jesus' resurrection from the dead, his appearances to the disciples, and his promise to send the Holy Spirit (24:1–53). Read Luke's beautifully written and accurate account of the life of Jesus, Son of Man and Son of God. Then praise God for sending the Saviour for all people—our risen and triumphant Lord.

Tiberius Caesar becomes emperor 14	*John's ministry begins 26*	*Jesus begins his ministry 26/27*	*Jesus chooses twelve disciples 28*	*Jesus feeds 5,000 29*	*Jesus is crucified, rises again, and ascends 30*

THE BLUEPRINT

A. BIRTH AND PREPARATION OF JESUS, THE SAVIOUR (1:1—4:13)	From an infant who could do nothing on his own, Jesus grew to become completely able to fulfil his mission on earth. He was fully human, developing in all ways like us. Yet he remained fully God. He took no shortcuts and was not isolated from the pressures and temptations of life. There are no shortcuts for us either as we prepare for a life of service to God.
B. MESSAGE AND MINISTRY OF JESUS, THE SAVIOUR (4:14—21:38) 1. Jesus' ministry in Galilee 2. Jesus' ministry on the way to Jerusalem 3. Jesus' ministry in Jerusalem	Jesus taught great crowds of people, especially through parables, which are stories with great truths. But only those with ears to hear will understand. We should pray that God's Spirit would help us to understand the implications of these truths for our lives so we can become more and more like Jesus.
C. DEATH AND RESURRECTION OF JESUS, THE SAVIOUR (22:1—24:53)	The Saviour of the world was arrested and executed. But death could not destroy him, and Jesus came back to life and ascended to heaven. In Luke's careful, historical account, we receive the facts about Jesus' resurrection. We must not only believe that these facts are true, but we must also trust Christ as our Saviour. It is shortsighted to neglect the facts, but how sad it is to accept the facts and neglect the forgiveness that Jesus offers to each of us.

MEGATHEMES

THEME	EXPLANATION	IMPORTANCE
Jesus Christ, the Saviour	Luke describes how God's Son entered human history. Jesus lived as the perfect example of a human. After a perfect ministry, he provided a perfect sacrifice for our sin so we could be saved.	Jesus is our perfect leader and Saviour. He offers forgiveness to all who will accept him as Lord of their lives and believe that what he says is true.
History	Luke was a medical doctor and historian. He put great emphasis on dates and details, connecting Jesus to events and people in history.	Luke gives details so that we can believe in the reliability of the history of Jesus' life. Even more importantly, we can believe with certainty that Jesus is God.
People	Jesus was deeply interested in people and relationships. He showed warm concern for his followers and friends—men, women, and children.	Jesus' love for people is good news for everyone. His message is for all people in every nation. Each one of us has an opportunity to respond to him in faith.
Compassion	As a perfect human, Jesus showed tender sympathy to the poor, the despised, the hurt, and the sinful. No-one was rejected or ignored by him.	Jesus is more than an idea or teacher—he cares for you. Only this kind of deep love can satisfy your need.
Holy Spirit	The Holy Spirit was present at Jesus' birth, baptism, ministry, and resurrection. As a perfect example for us, Jesus lived in dependence on the Holy Spirit.	The Holy Spirit was sent by God as confirmation of Jesus' authority. The Holy Spirit is given to enable people to live for Christ. By faith we can have the Holy Spirit's presence and power to witness and to serve.

A. BIRTH AND PREPARATION OF JESUS, THE SAVIOUR (1:1–4:13)

Luke gives us the most detailed account of Jesus' birth. In describing Jesus' birth, childhood, and development, Luke lifts up the humanity of Jesus. Our Saviour was the ideal human. Fully prepared, the ideal human was now ready to live the perfect life.

Luke's Purpose in Writing

(1)

1 Many have undertaken to draw up an account of the things that have been
fulfilled[a] among us, 2just as they were handed down to us by those who from
the first[a] were eye-witnesses[b] and servants of the word.[c] 3Therefore, since I myself
have carefully investigated everything from the beginning, it seemed good also to me
to write an orderly account[d] for you, most excellent[e] Theophilus,[f] 4so that you may
know the certainty of the things you have been taught.[g]

An Angel Promises the Birth of John to Zechariah

(4)

5In the time of Herod king of Judea[h] there was a priest named Zechariah, who
belonged to the priestly division of Abijah;[i] his wife Elizabeth was also a descendant
of Aaron. 6Both of them were upright in the sight of God, observing all the Lord's
commandments and regulations blamelessly.[j] 7But they had no children, because
Elizabeth was barren; and they were both well on in years.
8Once when Zechariah's division was on duty and he was serving as priest before
God,[k] 9he was chosen by lot, according to the custom of the priesthood, to go into
the temple of the Lord and burn incense.[l] 10And when the time for the burning of
incense came, all the assembled worshippers were praying outside.[m]
11Then an angel[n] of the Lord appeared to him, standing at the right side of the altar

a *1* Or *been surely believed*

1:2 [a]Mk 1:1; Jn 15:27; Ac 1:21, 22 [b]Heb 2:3; 1Pe 5:1; 2Pe 1:16; 1Jn 1:1 [c]Mk 4:14

1:3 [d]Ac 11:4 [e]Ac 24:3; 26:25 [f]Ac 1:1

1:4 [g]Jn 20:31

1:5 [h]Mt 2:1 [i]1Ch 24:10

1:6 [j]Ge 7:1; 1Ki 9:4

1:8 [k]1Ch 24:19; 2Ch 8:14

1:9 [l]Ex 30:7, 8; 1Ch 23:13; 2Ch 29:11

1:10 [m]Lev 16:17

1:11 [n]Ac 5:19

1:1, 2 Luke tells Jesus' story from Luke's unique perspective of a Gentile, a physician, and the first historian of the early church. Though not an eyewitness of Jesus' ministry, Luke is nevertheless concerned that eyewitness accounts be preserved accurately and that the foundations of Christian belief be transmitted intact to the next generation. In Luke's Gospel are many of Jesus' parables. In addition, more than any other Gospel, it gives specific instances of Jesus' concern for women.

1:1–4 There was a lot of interest in Jesus, and many people had written firsthand accounts about him. Luke may have used these accounts and all other available resources as material for an accurate and complete account of Jesus' life, teachings, and ministry. Because truth was important to Luke, he relied heavily on eyewitness accounts. Christianity doesn't say, "Close your eyes and believe," but rather, "Try it out for yourself." The Bible encourages you to investigate its claims thoroughly (John 1:46; 21:24; Acts 17:11, 12), because your conclusion about Jesus is a life-and-death matter.

1:3 *Theophilus* means "one who loves God". The book of Acts, also written by Luke, is likewise addressed to Theophilus. This preface may be a general dedication to all Christian readers. Theophilus may have been Luke's patron who helped to finance the book's writing. More likely, Theophilus was a Roman acquaintance of Luke's with a strong interest in the new Christian religion.

1:3, 4 As a medical doctor, Luke knew the importance of being thorough. He used his skills in observation and analysis to thoroughly investigate the stories about Jesus. His diagnosis? The gospel of Jesus Christ is true! You can read Luke's account of Jesus' life with confidence that it was written by a clear thinker and a thoughtful researcher. Because the gospel is founded on historical truth, our spiritual growth must involve careful, disciplined, and thorough investigation of God's word so that we can understand how God has acted in history. If this kind of study is not part of your life, find a pastor, teacher, or even a book to help you get started and to guide you in this important part of Christian growth.

1:5 This was Herod the Great, confirmed by the Roman Senate as king of the Jews. Only half Jewish himself and eager to please his Roman superiors, Herod expanded and beautified the Jerusalem temple – but he placed a Roman eagle over the entrance. When he helped the Jews, it was for political purposes and not because he cared about their God. Herod the Great later ordered a massacre of infants in a futile attempt to kill the infant Jesus, whom some were calling the new "king of the Jews" (Matthew 2:16–18).

1:5 A Jewish priest was a minister of God who worked at the temple managing its upkeep, teaching the people the Scriptures, and directing the worship services. At this time there were about 20,000 priests throughout the country – far too many to minister in the temple at one time. Therefore the priests were divided into 24 separate groups of about 1,000 each, according to David's directions (1 Chronicles 24:3–19).

Zechariah was a member of the Abijah division, on duty this particular week. Each morning a priest was to enter the Holy Place in the temple and burn incense. Lots were cast to decide who would enter the sacred room, and one day the lot fell to Zechariah. But it was not by chance that Zechariah was on duty and that he was chosen that day to enter the Holy Place – perhaps a once-in-a-lifetime opportunity. God was guiding the events of history to prepare the way for Jesus to come to earth.

1:6 Zechariah and Elizabeth didn't merely go through the motions in following God's laws; they backed up their outward compliance with inward obedience. Unlike the religious leaders whom Jesus called hypocrites, Zechariah and Elizabeth did not stop with the letter of the law. Their obedience was from the heart, and that is why they are called "upright in the sight of God".

1:9 Incense was burned in the temple twice daily. When the people saw the smoke from the burning incense, they prayed. The smoke drifting heavenward symbolised their prayers ascending to God's throne.

1:11, 12 Angels are spirit beings who live in God's presence and do his will. Only two angels are mentioned by name in Scripture –

1:11 [o]Ex 30:1-10
1:12 [p]Jdg 6:22, 23
1:13 [q]ver 30 [r]ver 60, 63
1:14 [s]ver 58
1:15 [t]Nu 6:3 [u]Jer 1:5; Gal 1:15

of incense.[o] 12When Zechariah saw him, he was startled and was gripped with fear.[p]
13But the angel said to him: "Do not be afraid,[q] Zechariah; your prayer has been
heard. Your wife Elizabeth will bear you a son, and you are to give him the name
John.[r] 14He will be a joy and delight to you, and many will rejoice because of his
birth,[s] 15for he will be great in the sight of the Lord. He is never to take wine or
other fermented drink,[t] and he will be filled with the Holy Spirit even from birth.[b][u]

[b] *15* Or *from his mother's womb*

ZECHARIAH

Zechariah was told before anyone else that God was setting in motion his own visit to earth. Zechariah and his wife, Elizabeth, were known for their personal holiness. They were well suited to do a special work for God. But they shared the pain of not having children, and in Jewish culture this was considered as not having God's blessing. Zechariah and Elizabeth were old, and they had stopped even asking for children.

This trip to the temple in Jerusalem for Zechariah's turn on duty had included an unexpected blessing. Zechariah was chosen to be the priest who would enter the Holy Place to offer incense to God for the people. Suddenly, much to his surprise and terror, he found himself face to face with an angel. The angel's message was too good to be true! But Zechariah did not respond to the news of the coming Saviour as much as he expressed doubts about his own ability to father the child the angel promised him. His age spoke more loudly than God's promise. As a result, God prevented Zechariah from speaking until the promise became reality.

The record of the prayer in Luke 1 is our last glimpse of Zechariah. Like so many of God's most faithful servants, he passed quietly from the scene once his part was done. He becomes our hero for those times when we doubt God and yet are willing to obey. We gain hope from Zechariah's story that God can do great things through anyone who is available to him.

Strengths and accomplishments:
- Known as a righteous man
- Was a priest before God
- One of the few people to be directly addressed by an angel
- Fathered John the Baptist

Weakness and mistake:
- Momentarily doubted the angel's promise of a son because of his own old age

Lessons from his life:
- Physical limitations do not limit God
- God accomplishes his will, sometimes in unexpected ways

Vital statistics:
- Occupation: Priest
- Relatives: Wife: Elizabeth. Son: John the Baptist

Key verses:
"Both of them were upright in the sight of God, observing all the Lord's commandments and regulations blamelessly. But they had no children, because Elizabeth was barren; and they were both well on in years" (Luke 1:6, 7).

Zechariah's story is told in Luke 1.

Michael and Gabriel – but there are many who act as God's messengers. Here, Gabriel (1:19) delivered a special message to Zechariah. This was not a dream or a vision. The angel appeared in visible form and spoke audible words to the priest.

1:13 Zechariah, while burning incense on the altar, was also praying, perhaps for a son or for the coming of the Messiah. In either case, his prayer was answered. He would soon have a son, who would prepare the way for the Messiah. God answers prayer in his own way and in his own time. He worked in an "impossible" situation – Zechariah's wife was barren – to bring about the fulfilment of all the prophecies concerning the Messiah. If we want to have our prayers answered, we must be open to what God can do in impossible situations. And we must wait for God to work in his way, in his time.

1:13 *John* means "the LORD is gracious", and *Jesus* means "the LORD saves". Both names were prescribed by God, not chosen by human parents. Throughout the Gospels, God acts graciously and saves his people. He will not withhold salvation from anyone who sincerely comes to him.

1:15 John was set apart for special service to God. He may have been forbidden to drink wine as part of the Nazirite vow, an ancient vow of consecration to God (see Numbers 6:1–8). Samson (Judges 13) was under the Nazirite vow, and Samuel may have been also (1 Samuel 1:11).

1:15 This is Luke's first mention of the Holy Spirit, the third person of the Trinity; Luke refers to the Holy Spirit more than any other Gospel writer. Because Luke also wrote the book of Acts, we know he was thoroughly informed about the work of the Holy Spirit. Luke recognised and emphasised the Holy Spirit's work in directing the founding of Christianity and in guiding the early church. The presence of the Spirit is God's gift given to the entire church at Pentecost. Prior to that, God's Spirit was given to the faithful for special tasks. We need the Holy Spirit's help to do God's work effectively.

16Many of the people of Israel will he bring back to the Lord their God. 17And he
will go on before the Lord,[v] in the spirit and power of Elijah,[w] to turn the hearts
of the fathers to their children[x] and the disobedient to the wisdom of the righteous—to
make ready a people prepared for the Lord."
18Zechariah asked the angel, "How can I be sure of this? I am an old man and my
wife is well on in years."[y]
19The angel answered, "I am Gabriel.[z] I stand in the presence of God, and I have
been sent to speak to you and to tell you this good news. 20And now you will be silent
and not able to speak[a] until the day this happens, because you did not believe my
words, which will come true at their proper time."
21Meanwhile, the people were waiting for Zechariah and wondering why he stayed
so long in the temple. 22When he came out, he could not speak to them. They realised
he had seen a vision in the temple, for he kept making signs[b] to them but remained
unable to speak.
23When his time of service was completed, he returned home. 24After this his wife
Elizabeth became pregnant and for five months remained in seclusion. 25"The Lord
has done this for me," she said. "In these days he has shown his favour and taken
away my disgrace[c] among the people."

An Angel Promises the Birth of Jesus to Mary
(5)

26In the sixth month, God sent the angel Gabriel[d] to Nazareth,[e] a town in Galilee,
27to a virgin pledged to be married to a man named Joseph,[f] a descendant of David.
The virgin's name was Mary. 28The angel went to her and said, "Greetings, you who
are highly favoured! The Lord is with you."
29Mary was greatly troubled at his words and wondered what kind of greeting this
might be. 30But the angel said to her, "Do not be afraid,[g] Mary, you have found

1:17 [v]ver 76 [w]Mt 11:14 [x]Mal 4:5, 6
1:18 [y]ver 34; Ge 17:17
1:19 [z]ver 26; Mt 18:10; Da 8:16; 9:21
1:20 [a]Eze 3:26
1:22 [b]ver 62
1:25 [c]Ge 30:23; Isa 4:1
1:26 [d]ver 19 [e]Mt 2:23
1:27 [f]Mt 1:16, 18, 20; Lk 2:4
1:30 [g]ver 13; Mt 14:27

1:17 John's role was to be almost identical to that of an Old Testament prophet—to encourage people to turn away from sin and back to God. John is often compared to the great prophet Elijah, who was known for standing up to evil rulers (Malachi 4:5; Matthew 11:14; 17:10–13). See Elijah's Profile in 1 Kings 18.

1:17 In preparing people for the Messiah's arrival, John would do "heart transplants". He would take stony hearts and exchange them for hearts that were soft, pliable, trusting, and open to change. (See Ezekiel 11:19, 20 and 36:25–29 for more on "heart transplants".) Are you as open to God as you should be? Or do you need a change of heart?

1:18 When told he would have a son, Zechariah doubted the angel's word. From Zechariah's human perspective, his doubts were understandable—but with God, anything is possible. Although Zechariah and Elizabeth were past the age of childbearing, God gave them a child. It is easy to doubt or misunderstand what God wants to do in our lives. Even God's people sometimes make the mistake of trusting their intellect or experience rather than God. When tempted to think that one of God's promises is impossible, remember his work throughout history. God's power is not confined by narrow perspective or bound by human limitations. Trust him completely.

1:20 Zechariah thought it incredible that he and his wife, at their old age, could conceive a child. But what God promises, he delivers. And God delivers *on time!* You can have complete confidence that God will keep his promises. Their fulfilment may not be the next day, but they will be "at their proper time". If you are waiting for God to answer some request or to fill some need, remain patient. No matter how impossible God's promises may seem, what he has said in his word will come true at the right time.

1:21 The people were waiting outside for Zechariah to come out and pronounce the customary blessing upon them as found in Numbers 6:24–26.

1:25 Zechariah and Elizabeth were both faithful people, and yet they were suffering. Some Jews at that time did not believe in a bodily resurrection, so their hope of immortality was in their children. In addition, children cared for their parents in their old age and added to the family's financial security and social status. Children were considered a blessing, and childlessness was seen as a curse. Zechariah and Elizabeth had been childless for many years, and at this time they were too old to expect any change in their situation. They felt humiliated and hopeless. But God was waiting for the right time to encourage them and take away their disgrace.

1:26 Gabriel appeared not only to Zechariah and to Mary but also to the prophet Daniel more than 500 years earlier (Daniel 8:15–17; 9:21). Each time Gabriel appeared, he brought important messages from God.

1:26 Nazareth, Joseph's and Mary's home town, was a long way from Jerusalem, the centre of Jewish life and worship. Located on a major trade route, Nazareth was frequently visited by Gentile merchants and Roman soldiers. It was known for its independent and aloof attitude. Jesus was born in Bethlehem but grew up in Nazareth. Nevertheless, the people of Nazareth would reject him as the Messiah (4:22–30).

1:27, 28 Mary was young, poor, female—all characteristics that, to the people of her day, would make her seem unusable by God for any major task. But God chose Mary for one of the most important acts of obedience he has ever demanded of anyone. You may feel that your ability, experience, or education makes you an unlikely candidate for God's service. Don't limit God's choices. He can use you if you trust him.

1:30, 31 God's favour does not automatically bring instant success or fame. His blessing on Mary, the honour of being the mother of the Messiah, would lead to much pain: her peers would ridicule her; her fiancé would come close to leaving her; her son would be rejected and murdered. But through her son would come the world's only hope, and this is why Mary has been praised by

1:31 [h]Isa 7:14; Mt 1:21, 25; Lk 2:21
1:32 [i]ver 35, 76; Mk 5:7
1:33 [j]Mt 28:18 [k]Da 2:44; 7:14, 27; Mic 4:7; Heb 1:8
1:35 [l]Mt 1:18 [m]ver 32, 76 [n]Mk 1:24 [o]Mt 4:3
1:37 [p]Mt 19:26

favour with God. 31 You will be with child and give birth to a son, and you are to give
him the name Jesus.[h] 32 He will be great and will be called the Son of the Most High.[i]
The Lord God will give him the throne of his father David, 33 and he will reign over
the house of Jacob for ever; his kingdom[j] will never end."[k]
34 "How will this be," Mary asked the angel, "since I am a virgin?"
35 The angel answered, "The Holy Spirit will come upon you,[l] and the power of
the Most High[m] will overshadow you. So the holy one[n] to be born will be called[c]
the Son of God.[o] 36 Even Elizabeth your relative is going to have a child in her old
age, and she who was said to be barren is in her sixth month. 37 For nothing is
impossible with God."[p]
38 "I am the Lord's servant," Mary answered. "May it be to me as you have said."
Then the angel left her.

c 35 Or *So the child to be born will be called holy,*

GOD'S UNUSUAL METHODS
One of the best ways to understand God's willingness to communicate to people is to note the various methods, some of them quite unexpected, that he has used to give his message. Following is a sample of his methods and the people he contacted.

Person/Group	*Method*	*Reference*
Jacob, Zechariah, Mary, Shepherds	Angels	Genesis 32:22–32; Luke 1:13, 30; 2:10
Jacob, Joseph, a baker, a cupbearer, Pharaoh, Isaiah, Joseph, the Magi	Dreams	Genesis 28:10–22; 37:5–10; 40:5; 41:7, 8; Isaiah 1:1; Matthew 1:20; 2:12, 13
Belshazzar	Writing on the wall	Daniel 5:5–9
Balaam	Talking donkey	Numbers 22:21–35
People of Israel	Pillar of cloud and fire	Exodus 13:21, 22
Jonah	Being swallowed by a fish	Jonah 2
Abraham, Moses, Jesus at his baptism, Paul	Verbally	Genesis 12:1–4; Exodus 7:8; Matthew 3:13–17; Acts 18:9
Moses	Fire	Exodus 3:2
Us	God's Son	Hebrews 1:1, 2

countless generations as the young girl who "found favour with God". Her submission was part of God's plan to bring about our salvation. If sorrow weighs you down and dims your hope, think of Mary and wait patiently for God to finish working out his plan.

1:31–33 *Jesus*, a Greek form of the Hebrew name *Joshua*, was a common name meaning "the LORD saves". Just as Joshua had led Israel into the promised land (see Joshua 1:1, 2), so Jesus would lead his people into eternal life. The symbolism of his name was not lost on the people of his day, who took names seriously and saw them as a source of power. In Jesus' name people were healed, demons were banished, and sins were forgiven.

1:32, 33 Centuries earlier, God had promised David that David's kingdom would last for ever (2 Samuel 7:16). This promise was fulfilled in the coming of Jesus, a direct descendant of David, whose reign will continue throughout eternity.

1:34 The birth of Jesus to a virgin is a miracle that many people find hard to believe. These three facts can aid our faith: (1) Luke was a medical doctor, and he knew perfectly well how babies are made. It would have been just as hard for him to believe in a virgin birth as it is for us, and yet he reports it as fact. (2) Luke was a painstaking researcher who based his Gospel on eyewitness accounts. Tradition holds that he talked with Mary about the events he recorded in the first two chapters. This is Mary's story, not a fictional invention. (3) Christians and Jews, who worship God as the Creator of the universe, should believe that God has the power to create a child in a virgin's womb.

1:35 Jesus was born without the sin that entered the world through Adam. He was born holy, just as Adam was created sinless. In contrast to Adam, who disobeyed God, Jesus obeyed God and was thus able to face sin's consequences in our place and make us acceptable to God (Romans 5:14–19).

1:38 A young unmarried girl who became pregnant risked disaster. Unless the father of the child agreed to marry her, she would probably remain unmarried for life. If her own father rejected her, she could be forced into begging or prostitution in order to earn her living. And Mary, with her story about being made pregnant by the Holy Spirit, risked being considered crazy as well. Still Mary said, despite the possible risks, "May it be to me as you have said." When Mary said that, she didn't know about the tremendous opportunity she would have. She only knew that God was asking her to serve him, and she willingly obeyed. Don't wait to see the bottom line before offering your life to God. Offer yourself willingly, even when the outcome seems disastrous.

1:38 God's announcement of a child to be born was met with various responses throughout Scripture. Sarah, Abraham's wife, laughed (Genesis 18:9–15). Zechariah doubted (Luke 1:18). By contrast, Mary submitted. She believed the angel's words and agreed to bear the child, even under humanly impossible circumstances. God is able to do the impossible. Our response to his demands should not be laughter or doubt, but willing acceptance.

Mary Visits Elizabeth
(6)

39At that time Mary got ready and hurried to a town in the hill country of Judea,[q]
40where she entered Zechariah's home and greeted Elizabeth. 41When Elizabeth heard
Mary's greeting, the baby leaped in her womb, and Elizabeth was filled with the Holy
Spirit. 42In a loud voice she exclaimed: "Blessed are you among women,[r] and blessed
is the child you will bear! 43But why am I so favoured, that the mother of my Lord
should come to me? 44As soon as the sound of your greeting reached my ears, the
baby in my womb leaped for joy. 45Blessed is she who has believed that what the Lord
has said to her will be accomplished!"

46And Mary said:

"My soul glorifies the Lord[s]
47 and my spirit rejoices in God my Saviour,[t]
48for he has been mindful
of the humble state of his servant.[u]
From now on all generations will call me blessed,[v]
49 for the Mighty One has done great things[w] for me—
holy is his name.[x]
50His mercy extends to those who fear him,
from generation to generation.[y]
51He has performed mighty deeds with his arm;[z]
he has scattered those who are proud in their inmost thoughts.
52He has brought down rulers from their thrones
but has lifted up the humble.
53He has filled the hungry with good things[a]
but has sent the rich away empty.
54He has helped his servant Israel,
remembering to be merciful[b]
55to Abraham and his descendants[c] for ever,
even as he said to our fathers."

56Mary stayed with Elizabeth for about three months and then returned home.

John the Baptist Is Born
(7)

57When it was time for Elizabeth to have her baby, she gave birth to a son. 58Her
neighbours and relatives heard that the Lord had shown her great mercy, and they
shared her joy.
59On the eighth day they came to circumcise[d] the child, and they were going to

1:39 [q]ver 65
1:42 [r]Jdg 5:24
1:46 [s]Ps 34:2, 3
1:47 [t]1Ti 1:1; 2:3
1:48 [u]Ps 138:6 [v]Lk 11:27
1:49 [w]Ps 71:19 [x]Ps 111:9
1:50 [y]Ex 20:6; Ps 103:17
1:51 [z]Ps 98:1; Isa 40:10
1:53 [a]Ps 107:9
1:54 [b]Ps 98:3
1:55 [c]Ge 17:19; Ps 132:11; Gal 3:16
1:59 [d]Ge 17:12; Lev 12:3; Lk 2:21; Php 3:5

1:41–43 Apparently the Holy Spirit told Elizabeth that Mary's child was the Messiah because Elizabeth called her young relative "the mother of my Lord" as she greeted her. As Mary rushed off to visit her relative, she must have been wondering if the events of the last few days were real. Elizabeth's greeting must have strengthened her faith. Mary's pregnancy may have seemed impossible, but her wise relative believed in the Lord's faithfulness and rejoiced in Mary's blessed condition.

1:42, 43 Even though she herself was pregnant with a long-awaited son, Elizabeth could have envied Mary, whose son would be even greater than her own. Instead she was filled with joy that the mother of her Lord would visit her. Have you ever envied people whom God has apparently singled out for special blessing? A cure for jealousy is to rejoice with those people, realising that God uses his people in ways best suited to his purpose.

1:46–55 This song is often called the *Magnificat*, the first word in the Latin translation of this passage. Mary's song has often been used as the basis for choral music and hymns. Like Hannah, the mother of Samuel (1 Samuel 2:1–10), Mary glorified God in song for what he was going to do for the world through her. Notice that in both songs, God is pictured as a champion of the poor, the oppressed, and the despised.

1:48 When Mary said, "From now on all generations will call me blessed," was she being proud? No, she was recognising and accepting the gift God had given her. If Mary had denied her incredible position, she would have been throwing God's blessing back at him. Pride is refusing to accept God's gifts or taking credit for what God has done; humility is accepting the gifts and using them to praise and serve God. Don't deny, belittle, or ignore your gifts. Thank God for them and use them to his glory.

1:54, 55 God kept his promise to Abraham to be merciful to God's people for ever (Genesis 22:16–18). Christ's birth fulfilled the promise, and Mary understood this. She was not surprised when her special son eventually announced that he was the Messiah. She had known Jesus' mission from before his birth. Some of God's promises to Israel are found in 2 Samuel 22:50, 51; Psalms 89:2–4; 103:17, 18; Micah 7:18–20.

1:56 Because travel was not easy, long visits were customary. Mary must have been a great help to Elizabeth, who was experiencing the discomforts of a first pregnancy in old age.

1:60 [e]ver 13, 63
1:62 [f]ver 22
1:63 [g]ver 13, 60
1:64 [h]ver 20
1:65 [i]ver 39
1:66 [j]Ge 39:2; Ac 11:21
1:67 [k]Joel 2:28
1:68 [l]Ps 72:18 [m]Ps 111:9; Lk 7:16
1:69 [n]1Sa 2:1, 10; Ps 18:2; 89:17; 132:17; Eze 29:21 [o]Mt 1:1
1:70 [p]Jer 23:5
1:72 [q]Mic 7:20 [r]Ps 105:8, 9; 106:45; Eze 16:60
1:73 [s]Ge 22:16-18
1:74 [t]Heb 9:14
1:75 [u]Eph 4:24

name him after his father Zechariah, 60but his mother spoke up and said, "No! He
is to be called John."[e]
61They said to her, "There is no-one among your relatives who has that name."
62Then they made signs[f] to his father, to find out what he would like to name the
child. 63He asked for a writing tablet, and to everyone's astonishment he wrote, "His
name is John."[g] 64Immediately his mouth was opened and his tongue was loosed,
and he began to speak,[h] praising God. 65The neighbours were all filled with awe,
and throughout the hill country of Judea[i] people were talking about all these things.
66Everyone who heard this wondered about it, asking, "What then is this child going
to be?" For the Lord's hand was with him.[j]
67His father Zechariah was filled with the Holy Spirit and prophesied:[k]

68"Praise be to the Lord, the God of Israel,[l]
because he has come and has redeemed his people.[m]
69He has raised up a horn[d][n] of salvation for us
in the house of his servant David[o]
70(as he said through his holy prophets of long ago),[p]
71salvation from our enemies
and from the hand of all who hate us—
72to show mercy to our fathers[q]
and to remember his holy covenant,[r]
73 the oath he swore to our father Abraham:[s]
74to rescue us from the hand of our enemies,
and to enable us to serve him[t] without fear
75 in holiness and righteousness[u] before him all our days.

d 69 *Horn* here symbolises strength.

DOUBTERS IN THE BIBLE

Doubter	*Doubtful Moment*	*Reference*
Abraham	When God told him he would be a father in old age	Genesis 17:17
Sarah	When she heard she would be a mother in old age	Genesis 18:12
Moses	When God told him to return to Egypt to lead the people	Exodus 3:10–15
Israelites	Whenever they faced difficulties in the desert	Exodus 16:1–3
Gideon	When told he would be a judge and leader	Judges 6:14–23
Zechariah	When told he would be a father in old age	Luke 1:18
Thomas	When told Jesus had risen from the dead	John 20:24, 25

Many of the people God used to accomplish great things started out as real doubters. With all of them, God showed great patience. Honest doubt was not a bad starting point as long as they didn't stay there. How great a part does doubt have in your willingness to trust God?

1:59 The circumcision ceremony was an important event to the family of a Jewish baby boy. God commanded circumcision when he was beginning to form his holy nation (Genesis 17:4–14), and he reaffirmed it through Moses (Leviticus 12:1–3). This ceremony was a time of joy when friends and family members celebrated the baby's becoming part of God's covenant nation.

1:59 Family lines and family names were important to the Jews. The people naturally assumed the child would receive Zechariah's name or at least a family name. Thus they were surprised that both Elizabeth and Zechariah wanted to name the boy John, as the angel had told them to do (see 1:13).

1:62 Zechariah's relatives talked to him by gestures, because he was apparently deaf as well as speechless and had not heard what his wife had said.

1:67–79 Zechariah praised God with his first words after months of silence. In a song that is often called the *Benedictus* after the first words in the Latin translation of this passage, Zechariah prophesied the coming of a Saviour who would redeem his people, and he predicted that his son John would prepare the Messiah's way. All the Old Testament prophecies were coming true—no wonder Zechariah praised God! The Messiah would come in Zechariah's lifetime, and his son had been chosen to pave the way.

1:71 The Jews were eagerly awaiting the Messiah, but they thought he would come to save them from the powerful Roman empire. They were ready for a military Saviour, but not for a peaceful Messiah who would conquer sin.

1:72, 73 This was God's promise to Abraham to bless all peoples through him (see Genesis 12:3). It would be fulfilled through the Messiah, Abraham's descendant.

76And you, my child, will be called a prophet[v] of the Most
High;[w]
for you will go on before the Lord to prepare the way for
him,[x]
77to give his people the knowledge of salvation
through the forgiveness of their sins,[y]
78because of the tender mercy of our God,
by which the rising sun[z] will come to us from heaven
79to shine on those living in darkness
and in the shadow of death,[a]
to guide our feet into the path of peace."

80And the child grew and became strong in spirit;[b] and he lived in the desert until
he appeared publicly to Israel.

Jesus Is Born in Bethlehem
(9)

2 In those days Caesar Augustus[a] issued a decree that a census should be taken
of the entire Roman world.[b] (2This was the first census that took place while
Quirinius was governor of Syria.)[c] 3And everyone went to his own town to register.
4So Joseph also went up from the town of Nazareth in Galilee to Judea, to Bethlehem[d] the town of David, because he belonged to the house and line of David. 5He
went there to register with Mary, who was pledged to be married to him and was
expecting a child. 6While they were there, the time came for the baby to be born, 7and

1:76 [v]Mt 11:9 [w]ver 32, 35 [x]ver 17; Mal 3:1
1:77 [y]Jer 31:34; Mk 1:4
1:78 [z]Mal 4:2
1:79 [a]Isa 9:2; 59:9; Mt 4:16; Ac 26:18
1:80 [b]Lk 2:40, 52
2:1 [a]Lk 3:1; Mt 22:17 [b]Mt 24:14
2:2 [c]Mt 4:24
2:4 [d]Jn 7:42

1:76 Zechariah had just recalled hundreds of years of God's sovereign work in history, beginning with Abraham and going on into eternity. Then, in tender contrast, he personalised the story. His son had been chosen for a key role in the drama of the ages. Although God has unlimited power, he chooses to work through frail humans who begin as helpless babies. Don't minimise what God can do through those who are faithful to him.

1:80 Why did John live out in the desert? Prophets used the isolation of the uninhabited desert to enhance their spiritual growth and to focus their message on God. By being in the desert, John remained separate from the economic and political powers so that he could aim his message against them. He also remained separate from the hypocritical religious leaders of his day. His message was different from theirs, and his life proved it.

2:1 Luke is the only Gospel writer who related the events he recorded to world history. His account was addressed to a predominantly Greek audience that would have been interested in and familiar with the political situation. Palestine was under the rule of the Roman empire; Emperor Caesar Augustus, the first Roman emperor, was in charge. The Roman rulers, considered to be like gods, stood in contrast to the tiny baby in a manger who was truly God in the flesh.

2:1 A Roman census (registration) was taken to aid military conscription or tax collection. The Jews didn't have to serve in the Roman army, but they could not avoid paying taxes. Augustus' decree went out in God's perfect timing and according to God's perfect plan to bring his Son into the world.

2:3–6 The government forced Joseph to make a long trip just to pay his taxes. His fiancée, who had to go with him, was going to have a baby any moment. But when they arrived in Bethlehem, they couldn't even find a place to stay. When we do God's will, we are not guaranteed a comfortable life. But we are promised that everything, even our discomfort, has meaning in God's plan.

2:4 God controls all history. By the decree of Emperor Augustus, Jesus was born in the very town prophesied for his birth (Micah 5:2), even though his parents did not live there.

2:4 Joseph and Mary were both descendants of David. The Old Testament is filled with prophecies that the Messiah would be born

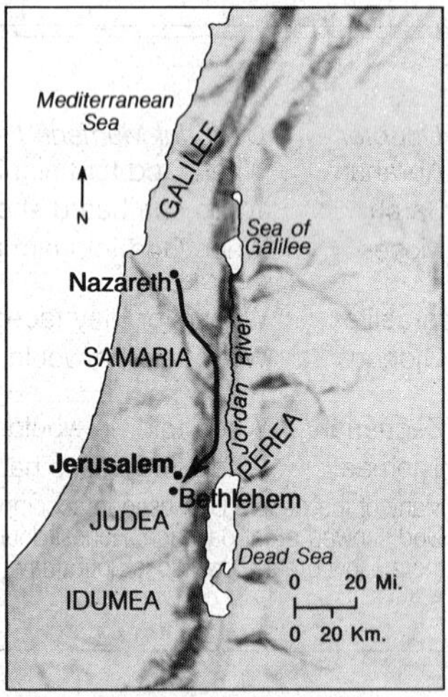

THE JOURNEY TO BETHLEHEM
Caesar's decree for a census of the entire Roman empire made it necessary for Joseph and Mary to leave their home town, Nazareth, and journey the 70 miles to the Judean village of Bethlehem.

in David's royal line (see, for example, Isaiah 11:1; Jeremiah 33:15; Ezekiel 37:24; Hosea 3:5).

2:7 Bands of cloth were used to keep a baby warm and give it a sense of security. These cloths were believed to protect its internal organs. The custom of wrapping infants this way is still practised in many Middle-Eastern countries.

2:7 This mention of the manger is the basis for the traditional belief that Jesus was born in a stable. Stables were often caves with feeding troughs (mangers) carved into the rock walls. Despite popular Christmas card pictures, the surroundings were dark and dirty. This was not the atmosphere the Jews expected as the birthplace of the Messiah King. They thought their promised Messiah would be born in royal surroundings. We should not limit God by our expectations. He is at work wherever he is needed in our sin-darkened and dirty world.

2:9 [e]Lk 1:11; Ac 5:19

2:10 [f]Mt 14:27

2:11 [g]Mt 1:21; Jn 4:42; Ac 5:31 [h]Mt 1:16; 16:16, 20; Jn 11:27; Ac 2:36

2:12 [i]1Sa 2:34; 2Ki 19:29; Isa 7:14

2:14 [j]Lk 1:79; Ro 5:1; Eph 2:14, 17

she gave birth to her firstborn, a son. She wrapped him in cloths and placed him in a manger, because there was no room for them in the inn.

Shepherds Visit Jesus
(10)

8 And there were shepherds living out in the fields near by, keeping watch over their
flocks at night. 9 An angel[e] of the Lord appeared to them, and the glory of the Lord
shone around them, and they were terrified. 10 But the angel said to them, "Do not
be afraid.[f] I bring you good news of great joy that will be for all the people. 11 Today
in the town of David a Saviour[g] has been born to you; he is Christ[a][h] the Lord. 12 This
will be a sign[i] to you: You will find a baby wrapped in cloths and lying in a manger."
13 Suddenly a great company of the heavenly host appeared with the angel, praising
God and saying,

14 "Glory to God in the highest,
and on earth peace[j] to men on whom his favour rests."

15 When the angels had left them and gone into heaven, the shepherds said to one

a *11* Or *Messiah.* "The Christ" (Greek) and "the Messiah" (Hebrew) both mean "the Anointed One"; also in verse 26.

TO FEAR OR NOT TO FEAR

Person	*Reference*
Abraham	Genesis 15:1
Moses	Numbers 21:34 Deuteronomy 3:2
Joshua	Joshua 8:1
Jeremiah	Lamentations 3:57
Daniel	Daniel 10:12, 19
Zechariah	Luke 1:13
Mary	Luke 1:30
Shepherds	Luke 2:10
Peter	Luke 5:10
Paul	Acts 27:23, 24
John	Revelation 1:17, 18

People in the Bible who were confronted by God or his angels all had one consistent response—fear. To each of them, God's response was always the same—don't be afraid. As soon as they sensed that God accepted them and wanted to communicate with them, their fear subsided. He had given them freedom to be his friends. Has he given you the same freedom?

2:7 Although our first picture of Jesus is as a baby in a manger, it must not be our last. The Christ-child in the manger has been made into a beautiful Christmas scene, but we cannot leave him there. This tiny, helpless baby lived an amazing life, died for us, ascended to heaven, and will come back to this earth as King of kings. Christ will rule the world and judge all people according to their decisions about him. Do you still picture Jesus as a baby in a manger—or is he your Lord? Make sure you don't underestimate Jesus. Let him grow up in your life.

2:8 God continued to reveal his Son, but not to those we might expect. Luke records that Jesus' birth was announced to shepherds in the fields. These may have been the shepherds who supplied the lambs for the temple sacrifices that were performed for the forgiveness of sin. Here the angels invited these shepherds to greet the Lamb of God (John 1:36), who would take away the sins of the whole world for ever.

2:8–15 What a birth announcement! The shepherds were terrified, but their fear turned to joy as the angels announced the Messiah's birth. First the shepherds ran to see the baby; then they spread the word. Jesus is *your* Messiah, *your* Saviour. Do you look forward to meeting him in prayer and in his word each day? Have you discovered a Lord so wonderful that you can't help sharing your joy with your friends?

2:9, 10 The greatest event in history had just happened! The Messiah had been born! For ages the Jews had waited for this, and when it finally occurred, the announcement came to humble shepherds. The good news about Jesus is that he comes to all, including the plain and the ordinary. He comes to anyone with a heart humble enough to accept him. Whoever you are, whatever you do, you can have Jesus in your life. Don't think you need extraordinary qualifications—he accepts you as you are.

2:11–14 Some of the Jews were waiting for a saviour to deliver them from Roman rule; others hoped the Christ (Messiah) would deliver them from physical ailments. But Jesus, while healing their illnesses and establishing a spiritual kingdom, delivered them from sin. His work is more far-reaching than anyone could imagine. Christ paid the price for sin and opened the way to peace with God. He offers us more than temporary political or physical changes—he offers us new hearts that will last for eternity.

2:14 The story of Jesus' birth resounds with music that has inspired composers for 2,000 years. The angels' song is an all-time favourite. Often called the *Gloria* after its first word in the Latin translation, it is the basis of modern choral works, traditional Christmas carols, and ancient liturgical chants.

another, "Let's go to Bethlehem and see this thing that has happened, which the Lord
has told us about."
16 So they hurried off and found Mary and Joseph, and the baby, who was lying
in the manger. 17 When they had seen him, they spread the word concerning what had
been told them about this child, 18 and all who heard it were amazed at what the
shepherds said to them. 19 But Mary treasured up all these things and pondered them
in her heart.[k] 20 The shepherds returned, glorifying and praising God[l] for all the
things they had heard and seen, which were just as they had been told.

Mary and Joseph Bring Jesus to the Temple

(11)

21 On the eighth day, when it was time to circumcise him,[m] he was named Jesus,
the name the angel had given him before he had been conceived.[n]
22 When the time of their purification according to the Law of Moses[o] had been
completed, Joseph and Mary took him to Jerusalem to present him to the Lord 23 (as
it is written in the Law of the Lord, "Every firstborn male is to be consecrated to the
Lord"[b]),[p] 24 and to offer a sacrifice in keeping with what is said in the Law of the
Lord: "a pair of doves or two young pigeons".[c][q]
25 Now there was a man in Jerusalem called Simeon, who was righteous and
devout.[r] He was waiting for the consolation of Israel,[s] and the Holy Spirit was upon
him. 26 It had been revealed to him by the Holy Spirit that he would not die before
he had seen the Lord's Christ. 27 Moved by the Spirit, he went into the temple courts.
When the parents brought in the child Jesus to do for him what the custom of the Law
required,[t] 28 Simeon took him in his arms and praised God, saying:

> 29 "Sovereign Lord, as you have promised,[u]
> you now dismiss[d] your servant in peace.[v]
> 30 For my eyes have seen your salvation,[w]
> 31 which you have prepared in the sight of all people,
> 32 a light for revelation to the Gentiles
> and for glory to your people Israel."[x]

33 The child's father and mother marvelled at what was said about him. 34 Then
Simeon blessed them and said to Mary, his mother:[y] "This child is destined to cause
the falling[z] and rising of many in Israel, and to be a sign that will be spoken against,

[b] *23* Exodus 13:2,12 [c] *24* Lev. 12:8 [d] *29* *Or promised, / now dismiss*

2:19 [k] ver 51
2:20 [l] Mt 9:8
2:21 [m] Lk 1:59 [n] Lk 1:31
2:22 [o] Lev 12:2-8
2:23 [p] Ex 13:2, 12, 15; Nu 3:13
2:24 [q] Lev 12:8
2:25 [r] Lk 1:6 [s] ver 38; Isa 52:9; Lk 23:51
2:27 [t] ver 22
2:29 [u] ver 26 [v] Ac 2:24
2:30 [w] Isa 52:10; Lk 3:6
2:32 [x] Isa 42:6; 49:6; Ac 13:47; 26:23
2:34 [y] Mt 12:46 [z] Isa 8:14; Mt 21:44; 1Co 1:23; 2Co 2:16; 1Pe 2:7, 8

2:21–24 Jewish families went through several ceremonies soon after a baby's birth: (1) *Circumcision.* Every boy was circumcised and named on the eighth day after birth (Leviticus 12:3; Luke 1:59, 60). Circumcision symbolised the Jews' separation from Gentiles and their unique relationship with God (see the second note on 1:59). (2) *Redemption of the firstborn.* A firstborn son was presented to God one month after birth (Exodus 13:2, 11–16; Numbers 18:15, 16). The ceremony included buying back – "redeeming" – the child from God through an offering. Thus the parents acknowledged that the child belonged to God, who alone has the power to give life. (3) *Purification of the mother.* For 40 days after the birth of a son and 80 days after the birth of a daughter, the mother was ceremonially unclean and could not enter the temple. At the end of her time of separation, the parents were to bring a lamb for a burnt offering and a dove or pigeon for a sin offering. The priest would sacrifice these animals and declare her to be clean. If a lamb was too expensive, the parents could bring a second dove or pigeon instead. This is what Mary and Joseph did.

Jesus was God's Son, but his family carried out these ceremonies according to God's law. Jesus was not born above the law; instead, he fulfilled it perfectly.

2:28–32 When Mary and Joseph brought Jesus to the temple to be consecrated to God, they met an old man who told them what their child would become. Simeon's song is often called the *Nunc Dimittis*, because these are the first words of its Latin translation. Simeon could die in peace because he had seen the Messiah.

2:32 The Jews were well acquainted with the Old Testament prophecies that spoke of the Messiah's blessings to their nation. They did not always give equal attention to the prophecies saying that he would bring salvation to the entire world, not just the Jews (see, for example, Isaiah 49:6). Many thought that Christ had come to save only his own people. Luke made sure his Greek audience understood that Christ had come to save *all* who believe, Gentiles as well as Jews.

2:33 Joseph and Mary "marvelled" (were amazed) for three reasons: Simeon said that Jesus was a gift from God; Simeon recognised Jesus as the Messiah; and Simeon said Jesus would be a light to the entire world. This was at least the second time that Mary had been greeted with a prophecy about her son; the first time was when Elizabeth welcomed her as the mother of her Lord (1:42–45).

2:34, 35 Simeon prophesied that Jesus would have a paradoxical effect on Israel. Some would fall because of him (see Isaiah 8:14, 15), while others would rise (see Malachi 4:2). With Jesus, there would be no neutral ground: people would either joyfully accept him or totally reject him. As Jesus' mother, Mary would be grieved by the widespread rejection he would face. This is the first note of sorrow in Luke's Gospel.

2:36
[a]Ac 21:9

2:37
[b]1Ti 5:9
[c]Ac 13:3; 14:23; 1Ti 5:5

2:38
[d]ver 25; Isa 40:2; Lk 1:68; 24:21

35so that the thoughts of many hearts will be revealed. And a sword will pierce your
own soul too."
36There was also a prophetess,[a] Anna, the daughter of Phanuel, of the tribe of
Asher. She was very old; she had lived with her husband seven years after her
marriage, 37and then was a widow until she was eighty-four.[e][b] She never left the
temple but worshipped night and day, fasting and praying.[c] 38Coming up to them
at that very moment, she gave thanks to God and spoke about the child to all who
were looking forward to the redemption of Jerusalem.[d]
39When Joseph and Mary had done everything required by the Law of the Lord,

[e] *37* Or *widow for eighty-four years*

ELIZABETH

In societies like Israel, in which a woman's value was largely measured by her ability to bear children, to be aging and without children often led to personal hardship and public shame. For Elizabeth, a childless old age was a painful and lonely time during which she remained faithful to God.

Both Elizabeth and Zechariah came from priestly families. For two weeks each year, Zechariah had to go to the temple in Jerusalem to attend to his priestly duties. After one of those trips, Zechariah returned home excited, but speechless. He had to write down his good news, because he couldn't give it any other way. And what a wonderful surprise he had for his wife—their faded dream would become an exciting reality! Soon Elizabeth became pregnant, and she knew her child was a long-hoped-for gift from God.

News travelled fast among the family. Seventy miles to the north, in Nazareth, Elizabeth's relative, Mary, also unexpectedly became pregnant. Within days of the angel's message that she would bear the Messiah, Mary went to visit Elizabeth. They were instantly bound together by the unique gifts God had given them. Elizabeth knew that Mary's son would be even greater than her own, for John would be the messenger for Mary's son.

When the baby was born, Elizabeth insisted on his God-given name: John. Zechariah's written agreement freed his tongue, and everyone in town wondered what would become of this obviously special child.

Elizabeth whispered her praise as she cared for God's gift. Knowing about Mary must have made her marvel at God's timing. Things had worked out even better than she could have planned. We too need to remember that God is in control of every situation. When did you last pause to recognise God's timing in the events of your life?

Strengths and accomplishments:
- Known as a deeply spiritual woman
- Showed no doubts about God's ability to fulfil his promise
- Mother of John the Baptist
- The first woman besides Mary to hear of the coming Saviour

Lessons from her life:
- God does not forget those who have been faithful to him
- God's timetable and methods do not have to conform to what we expect

Vital statistics:
- Occupation: Housewife
- Relatives: Husband: Zechariah. Son: John the Baptist. Relative: Mary
- Contemporaries: Joseph, Herod the Great

Key verses:
"But why am I so favoured, that the mother of my Lord should come to me? As soon as the sound of your greeting reached my ears, the baby in my womb leaped for joy. Blessed is she who has believed that what the Lord has said to her will be accomplished!" (Luke 1:43–45).

Elizabeth's story is told in Luke 1:5–80.

2:36 Although Simeon and Anna were very old, they had never lost their hope that they would see the Messiah. Led by the Holy Spirit, they were among the first to bear witness to Jesus. In the Jewish culture, elders were respected, so because of Simeon's and Anna's age, their prophecies carried extra weight. Our society, however, values youthfulness over wisdom, and potential contributions by the elderly are often ignored. As Christians, we should reverse those values wherever we can. Encourage older people to share their wisdom and experience. Listen carefully when they speak. Offer them your friendship and help them find ways to continue to serve God.

2:36, 37 Anna was called a prophetess, indicating that she was unusually close to God. Prophets did not necessarily predict the future. Their main role was to speak for God, proclaiming his truth.

2:39 Did Mary and Joseph return immediately to Nazareth, or did they remain in Bethlehem for a time (as implied in Matthew 2)? Apparently there is a gap of several years between verses 38 and 39—ample time for them to find a place to live in Bethlehem, flee to Egypt to escape Herod's wrath, and return to Nazareth when it was safe to do so.

they returned to Galilee to their own town of Nazareth.[e] 40 And the child grew and
became strong; he was filled with wisdom, and the grace of God was upon
him.[f]

Jesus Speaks with the Religious Teachers
(15)

41 Every year his parents went to Jerusalem for the Feast of the Passover.[g] 42 When
he was twelve years old, they went up to the Feast, according to the custom. 43 After
the Feast was over, while his parents were returning home, the boy Jesus stayed behind
in Jerusalem, but they were unaware of it. 44 Thinking he was in their company, they
travelled on for a day. Then they began looking for him among their relatives and
friends. 45 When they did not find him, they went back to Jerusalem to look for him.
46 After three days they found him in the temple courts, sitting among the teachers,
listening to them and asking them questions. 47 Everyone who heard him was amazed[h]
at his understanding and his answers. 48 When his parents saw him, they were astonished. His mother[i] said to him, "Son, why have you treated us like this? Your father[j]
and I have been anxiously searching for you."
49 "Why were you searching for me?" he asked. "Didn't you know I had to be
in my Father's house?"[k] 50 But they did not understand what he was saying to
them.[l]
51 Then he went down to Nazareth with them[m] and was obedient to them. But his

2:39 [e]ver 51; Mt 2:23
2:40 [f]ver 52; Lk 1:80
2:41 [g]Ex 23:15; Dt 16:1-8
2:47 [h]Mt 7:28
2:48 [i]Mt 12:46 [j]Lk 3:23; 4:22
2:49 [k]Jn 2:16
2:50 [l]Mk 9:32
2:51 [m]ver 39; Mt 2:23

2:40 Jesus was filled with wisdom, which is not surprising since he stayed in close contact with his heavenly Father. James 1:5 says God gives wisdom generously to all who ask. Like Jesus, we can grow in wisdom by walking with God.

2:41, 42 According to God's law, every male was required to go to Jerusalem three times a year for the great festivals (Deuteronomy 16:16). In the spring, the Passover was celebrated, followed immediately by the week-long Feast of Unleavened Bread. Passover commemorated the night of the Jews' escape from Egypt when God had killed the Egyptian firstborn but had passed over Israelite homes (see Exodus 12:21–36). Passover was the most important of the three annual festivals.

2:43–45 At age 12, Jesus was considered almost an adult, and so he didn't spend a lot of time with his parents during the feast. Those who attended these feasts often travelled in caravans for protection from robbers along the Palestine roads. It was customary for the women and children to travel at the front of the caravan, with the men bringing up the rear. A 12-year-old boy conceivably could have been in either group, and both Mary and Joseph assumed Jesus was with the other one. But when the caravan left Jerusalem, Jesus stayed behind, absorbed in his discussion with the religious leaders.

2:46, 47 The temple courts were famous throughout Judea as a place of learning. The apostle Paul studied in Jerusalem, perhaps in the temple courts, under Gamaliel, one of its foremost teachers (Acts 22:3). At the time of the Passover, the greatest rabbis of the land would assemble to teach and to discuss great truths among themselves. The coming Messiah would no doubt have been a popular discussion topic, for everyone was expecting him soon. Jesus would have been eager to listen and to ask probing questions. It was not his youth, but the depth of his wisdom, that astounded these teachers.

2:48 Mary had to let go of her child and let him become a man, God's Son, the Messiah. Afraid that she hadn't been careful enough with this God-given child, she searched frantically for him. But she was looking for a boy, not the young man who was in the temple astounding the religious leaders with his questions. It is hard to let go of people or projects we have nurtured. It is both sweet and painful to see our children as adults, our students as teachers, our subordinates as managers, our inspirations as institutions. But when the time comes to step back and let go, we must do so in spite of the hurt. Then our protégés can exercise their wings, take flight, and soar to the heights God intended for them.

2:49, 50 This is the first mention of Jesus' awareness that he was God's Son. But even though he knew his real Father, he did not reject his earthly parents. He went back to Nazareth with them and lived under their authority for another 18 years. God's people do not despise human relationships or family responsibilities. If the Son of God obeyed his human parents, how much more should we honour our family members! Don't use commitment to God's work to justify neglecting your family.

2:50 Jesus' parents didn't understand what he meant about his Father's house. They didn't realise he was making a distinction between his earthly father and his heavenly Father. Jesus knew that he had a unique relationship with God. Although Mary and Joseph knew he was God's Son, they didn't understand what his mission would involve. Besides, they had to bring him up, along with his brothers and sisters (Matthew 13:55, 56), as a normal child. They knew he was unique, but they did not know what was going on in his mind.

2:52 The Bible does not record any events of the next 18 years of Jesus' life, but Jesus was undoubtedly learning and maturing. As the oldest in a large family, he assisted Joseph in his carpentry work. Joseph may have died during this time, leaving Jesus to provide for the family. The normal routines of daily life gave Jesus a solid understanding of the Judean people.

2:52 The second chapter of Luke shows us that although Jesus was unique, he had a normal childhood and adolescence. In terms

mother treasured all these things in her heart.[n]
52 And Jesus grew in wisdom and
stature, and in favour with God and men.[o]

2:51 [n] ver 19
2:52 [o] ver 40; 1Sa 2:26; Lk 1:80

MARY

Motherhood is a painful privilege. Young Mary of Nazareth had the unique privilege of being mother to the very Son of God. Yet the pains and pleasures of her motherhood can be understood by mothers everywhere. Mary was the only human present at Jesus' birth who also witnessed his death. She saw him arrive as her baby son, and she watched him die as her Saviour.

Until Gabriel's unexpected visit, Mary's life was quite satisfactory. She had recently become engaged to a carpenter, Joseph, and was anticipating married life. But her life was about to change for ever.

Angels don't usually make appointments before visiting. As if she were being congratulated for winning the grand prize in a contest she had never entered, Mary found the angel's greeting puzzling and his presence frightening. What she heard next was the news almost every woman in Israel hoped to hear—that her child would be the Messiah, God's promised Saviour. Mary did not doubt the message, but rather asked how pregnancy would be possible. Gabriel told her the baby would be God's Son. Her answer was the one God waits in vain to hear from so many other people: "I am the Lord's servant. . . . May it be to me as you have said" (Luke 1:38). Later, her song of joy shows us how well she knew God, for her thoughts were filled with his words from the Old Testament.

Within a few weeks of his birth, Jesus was taken to the temple to be dedicated to God. There Joseph and Mary were met by two devout people, Simeon and Anna, who recognised the child as the Messiah and praised God. Simeon directed some words to Mary that must have come to her mind many times in the years that followed: "A sword will pierce your own soul" (Luke 2:35). A big part of her painful privilege of motherhood would be to see her son rejected and crucified by the people he came to save.

We can imagine that even if she had known all she would suffer as Jesus' mother, Mary would still have given the same response. Are you, like Mary, available to be used by God?

Strengths and accomplishments:
- The mother of Jesus, the Messiah
- The one human who was with Jesus from birth to death
- Willing to be available to God
- Knew and applied Old Testament Scriptures

Lessons from her life:
- God's best servants are often ordinary people available to him
- God's plans involve extraordinary events in ordinary people's lives
- A person's character is revealed by his or her response to the unexpected

Vital statistics:
- Where: Nazareth, Bethlehem
- Occupation: Housewife
- Relatives: Husband: Joseph. Relatives: Zechariah and Elizabeth. Children: Jesus, James, Joseph, Judas, Simon, and daughters

Key verse:
" 'I am the Lord's servant,' Mary answered. 'May it be to me as you have said.' Then the angel left her" (Luke 1:38).

Mary's story is told throughout the Gospels. She is also mentioned in Acts 1:14.

of development, he went through the same progression we do. He grew physically and mentally, he related to other people, and he was loved by God. A full human life is not unbalanced. It was important to Jesus—and it should be important to all believers—to develop fully and harmoniously in each of these key areas: physical, mental, social, and spiritual.

John the Baptist Prepares the Way for Jesus
(16/Matthew 3:1–12; Mark 1:1–8)

3 In the fifteenth year of the reign of Tiberius Caesar—when Pontius Pilate[a] was
governor of Judea, Herod[b] tetrarch of Galilee, his brother Philip tetrarch of Iturea
and Traconitis, and Lysanias tetrarch of Abilene—2 during the high priesthood of
Annas and Caiaphas,[c] the word of God came to John[d] son of Zechariah[e] in the
desert. 3 He went into all the country around the Jordan, preaching a baptism of
repentance for the forgiveness of sins.[f] 4 As is written in the book of the words of
Isaiah the prophet:

"A voice of one calling in the desert,
'Prepare the way for the Lord,
make straight paths for him.
5 Every valley shall be filled in,
every mountain and hill made low.
The crooked roads shall become straight,
the rough ways smooth.
6 And all mankind will see God's salvation.' "[a][g]

7 John said to the crowds coming out to be baptised by him, "You brood of vipers![h]
Who warned you to flee from the coming wrath?[i] 8 Produce fruit in keeping with
repentance. And do not begin to say to yourselves, 'We have Abraham as our
father.'[j] For I tell you that out of these stones God can raise up children for Abraham.
9 The axe is already at the root of the trees, and every tree that does not produce good
fruit will be cut down and thrown into the fire."[k]
10 "What should we do then?"[l] the crowd asked.

[a] 6 Isaiah 40:3–5

3:1 [a] Mt 27:2 [b] Mt 14:1
3:2 [c] Mt 26:3; Jn 18:13; Ac 4:6 [d] Mt 3:1 [e] Lk 1:13
3:3 [f] ver 16; Mk 1:4
3:6 [g] Isa 40:3-5; Ps 98:2; Isa 42:16; 52:10; Lk 2:30
3:7 [h] Mt 12:34; 23:33 [i] Ro 1:18
3:8 [j] Isa 51:2; Lk 19:9; Jn 8:33, 39; Ac 13:26; Ro 4:1, 11, 12, 16, 17; Gal 3:7
3:9 [k] Mt 3:10
3:10 [l] ver 12, 14; Ac 2:37; 16:30

3:1 Tiberius, the Roman emperor, ruled from A.D. 14 to 37. Pilate was the Roman governor responsible for the province of Judea; Herod (Antipas) and Philip were half brothers and sons of the cruel Herod the Great, who had been dead more than 20 years. Antipas, Philip, Pilate, and Lysanias apparently had equal powers in governing their separate territories. All were subject to Rome and responsible for keeping peace in their respective lands.

3:2 Under Jewish law there was only one high priest. He was appointed from Aaron's line, and he held his position for life. By this time, however, the religious system had been corrupted, and the Roman government was appointing its own religious leaders to maintain greater control over the Jews. Apparently the Roman authorities had deposed the Jewish-appointed Annas and had replaced him with Annas' son-in-law, Caiaphas. Nevertheless, Annas retained his title (see Acts 4:6) and probably also much of the power it carried. Because the Jews believed the high priest's position to be for life, they would have continued to call Annas their high priest.

3:2 This is John the Baptist, whose birth story is told in chapter 1. See his Profile in John 1.

3:2 Pilate, Herod, and Caiaphas were the most powerful leaders in Palestine, but they were upstaged by a desert prophet from rural Judea. God chose to speak through the loner John the Baptist, who has gone down in history as greater than any of the rulers of his day. How often we judge people by our culture's standards—power, wealth, beauty—and miss the truly great people through whom God works! Greatness is not measured by what you have, but by your faith in God. Like John, give yourself entirely to God so God's power can work through you.

3:3 Repentance has two sides—turning away from sins and turning towards God. To be truly repentant, we must do both. We can't just say we believe and then live any way we choose (see 3:7, 8), and neither can we simply live a morally correct life without a personal relationship with God, because that cannot bring forgiveness from sin. Determine to rid your life of any sins God points out, and put your trust in him alone to guide you.

3:4, 5 In John's day, before a king took a trip, messengers would tell those he was planning to visit to prepare the roads for him. Similarly John told his listeners to make their lives ready so the Lord could come to them. To prepare for Jesus' coming to us, we must focus on him, listen to his words, and respond obediently to his directions.

3:6 This book was written to a non-Jewish audience. Luke quoted from Isaiah to show that salvation is for all people, not just the Jews (Isaiah 40:3–5; 52:10). John the Baptist called all mankind to prepare to meet Jesus. That includes you, no matter what your standing is with religious organisations and authorities. Don't let feelings of being an outsider cause you to hold back. No-one who wants to follow Jesus is an outsider in God's kingdom.

3:7 What motivates your faith—fear of the future, or a desire to be a better person in a better world? Some people wanted to be baptised by John so they could escape eternal punishment, but they didn't turn to God for salvation. John had harsh words for such people. He knew that God values reformation above ritual. Is your faith motivated by a desire for a new, changed life, or is it only like a vaccination or insurance policy against possible disaster?

3:8 Many of John's hearers were shocked when he said that being Abraham's descendants was not enough for God. The religious leaders relied more on their family lines than on their faith for their standing with God. For them, religion was inherited. But a personal relationship with God is not handed down from parents to children. Everyone has to make his or her own commitment. Don't rely on someone else's faith for your salvation. Put your own faith in Jesus, and then exercise it every day.

3:8, 9 Confession of sins and a changed life are inseparable. Faith without deeds is dead (James 2:14–26). Jesus' harshest words were to the respectable religious leaders who lacked the desire for real change. They wanted to be known as religious authorities, but they didn't want to change their hearts and minds. Thus their lives were unproductive. Repentance must be tied to action, or it isn't real. Following Jesus means more than saying the right words; it means acting on what he says.

3:11 [m]Isa 58:7
3:12 [n]Lk 7:29
3:13 [o]Lk 19:8
3:14 [p]Ex 23:1; Lev 19:11
3:15 [q]Mt 3:1 [r]Jn 1:19, 20; Ac 13:25
3:16 [s]ver 3; Mk 1:4 [t]Jn 1:26, 33; Ac 1:5; 11:16; 19:4
3:17 [u]Isa 30:24 [v]Mt 13:30; 25:41
3:19 [w]ver 1
3:20 [x]Mt 14:3, 4; Mk 6:17-18

11 John answered, "The man with two tunics should share with him who has none,
and the one who has food should do the same."[m]
12 Tax collectors also came to be baptised.[n] "Teacher," they asked, "what should
we do?"
13 "Don't collect any more than you are required to,"[o] he told them.
14 Then some soldiers asked him, "And what should we do?"
He replied, "Don't extort money and don't accuse people falsely[p]—be content
with your pay."
15 The people were waiting expectantly and were all wondering in their hearts if
John[q] might possibly be the Christ.[b] [r] 16 John answered them all, "I baptise you
with[c] water.[s] But one more powerful than I will come, the thongs of whose sandals
I am not worthy to untie. He will baptise you with the Holy Spirit and with fire.[t]
17 His winnowing fork[u] is in his hand to clear his threshing-floor and to gather the
wheat into his barn, but he will burn up the chaff with unquenchable fire."[v] 18 And
with many other words John exhorted the people and preached the good news to them.

Herod Puts John in Prison
(26)

19 But when John rebuked Herod[w] the tetrarch because of Herodias, his brother's
wife, and all the other evil things he had done, 20 Herod added this to them all: He
locked John up in prison.[x]

b *15* Or *Messiah* **c** *16* Or *in*

3:11–14 John's message demanded at least three specific responses: (1) share what you have with those who need it, (2) whatever your job is, do it well and with fairness, and (3) be content with what you're earning. John had no time to address comforting messages to those who lived careless or selfish lives—he was calling the people to right living. What changes can you make in sharing what you have, doing your work honestly and well, and being content?

3:12 Tax collectors were notorious for their dishonesty. Romans gathered funds for their government by farming out the collection privilege. Tax collectors earned their own living by adding a sizable sum—whatever they could get away with—to the total and keeping this money for themselves. Unless the people revolted and risked Roman retaliation, they had to pay whatever was demanded. Obviously they hated the tax collectors, who were generally dishonest, greedy, and ready to betray their own countrymen for cold cash. Yet, said John, God would accept even these men; God desires to pour out mercy on those who confess, and then to give strength to live changed lives.

3:12–14 John's message took root in unexpected places—among the poor, the dishonest, and even the hated occupation army. These people were painfully aware of their needs. Too often we confuse respectability with right living. They are not the same. Respectability can even hinder right living if it keeps us from seeing our need for God. If you had to choose, would you protect your character or your reputation?

3:14 These soldiers were the Roman troops sent to keep peace in this distant province. Many of them oppressed the poor and used their power to take advantage of all the people. John called them to repent and change their ways.

3:15 There had not been a prophet in Israel for more than 400 years. It was widely believed that when the Messiah came, prophecy would reappear (Joel 2:28, 29; Malachi 3:1; 4:5). When John burst onto the scene, the people were excited. He was obviously a great prophet, and they were sure that the eagerly awaited age of the Messiah had come. Some, in fact, thought John himself was the Messiah. John spoke like the prophets of old, saying that the people must turn from their sin to avoid punishment and turn to God to experience his mercy and approval. This is a message for all times and places, but John spoke it with particular urgency—he was preparing the people for the coming Messiah.

3:16 John's baptism with water symbolised the washing away of sins. His baptism tied in with his message of repentance and reformation. Jesus' baptism with fire includes the power needed to do God's will. The baptism with the Holy Spirit was fulfilled at Pentecost (Acts 2) when the Holy Spirit came upon believers in the form of tongues of fire, empowering them to proclaim Jesus' resurrection in many languages. The baptism with fire also symbolises the work of the Holy Spirit in bringing God's judgment on those who refuse to repent.

3:17 John warned of impending judgment by comparing those who refuse to live for God to chaff, the useless outer husk of the grain. By contrast, he compared those who repent and reform their lives to the nourishing wheat itself. The winnowing fork was a pitchfork used to toss wheat so that the kernels would separate from the blades. Those who refuse to be used by God will be discarded because they have no value in furthering God's work. Those who repent and believe, however, hold great value in God's eyes because they are beginning a new life of productive service for him.

3:19, 20 In these two verses Luke flashes forward to continue his explanation about John the Baptist. See the Harmony of the Gospels for the chronological order of events.

3:19, 20 This is Herod Antipas (see Mark 6 for his Profile). Herodias was Herod's niece and also his brother's wife. She treacherously plotted John the Baptist's death (Matthew 14:1–12). The Herods were a murderous and deceitful family. Rebuking a tyrannical Roman official who could imprison and execute him was extremely dangerous, yet that is what John did. Herod seemingly had the last word, but the story is not finished. At the last judgment, Herod, not John, will be the one in danger.

John Baptises Jesus
(17/Matthew 3:13–17; Mark 1:9–11)

21 When all the people were being baptised, Jesus was baptised too. And as he was
praying,[y] heaven was opened 22 and the Holy Spirit descended on him[z] in bodily
form like a dove. And a voice came from heaven: "You are my Son,[a] whom I love;
with you I am well pleased."[b]

The Ancestors of Jesus
(3/Matthew 1:1–17)

23 Now Jesus himself was about thirty years old when he began his ministry.[c] He
was the son, so it was thought, of Joseph,[d]

the son of Heli, 24 the son of Matthat,
the son of Levi, the son of Melki,
the son of Jannai, the son of Joseph,
25 the son of Mattathias, the son of Amos,
the son of Nahum, the son of Esli,
the son of Naggai, 26 the son of Maath,
the son of Mattathias, the son of Semein,
the son of Josech, the son of Joda,
27 the son of Joanan, the son of Rhesa,
the son of Zerubbabel,[e] the son of Shealtiel,
the son of Neri, 28 the son of Melki,
the son of Addi, the son of Cosam,
the son of Elmadam, the son of Er,
29 the son of Joshua, the son of Eliezer,
the son of Jorim, the son of Matthat,
the son of Levi, 30 the son of Simeon,
the son of Judah, the son of Joseph,
the son of Jonam, the son of Eliakim,
31 the son of Melea, the son of Menna,
the son of Mattatha, the son of Nathan,[f]
the son of David, 32 the son of Jesse,
the son of Obed, the son of Boaz,

3:21 [y]Mt 14:23; Mk 1:35; 6:46; Lk 5:16; 6:12; 9:18, 28; 11:1
3:22 [z]Isa 42:1; Jn 1:32, 33; Ac 10:38 [a]Mt 3:17 [b]Mt 3:17
3:23 [c]Mt 4:17; Ac 1:1 [d]Lk 1:27
3:27 [e]Mt 1:12
3:31 [f]2Sa 5:14; 1Ch 3:5

3:21 Luke emphasises Jesus' human nature. Jesus was born to humble parents, a birth unannounced except to shepherds and foreigners. This baptism recorded here was the first public declaration of Jesus' ministry. Instead of going to Jerusalem and identifying with the established religious leaders, Jesus went to a river and identified himself with those who were repenting of sin. When Jesus, at age 12, visited the temple, he understood his mission (2:49). Eighteen years later, at his baptism, he began carrying it out. And as Jesus prayed, God spoke and confirmed his decision to act. God was breaking into human history through Jesus the Christ.

3:21, 22 If baptism was a sign of repentance from sin, why did Jesus ask to be baptised? Several explanations are often given: (1) Jesus' baptism was one step in fulfilling his earthly mission of identifying with our humanity and sin; (2) by endorsing the rite of baptism, Jesus was giving us an example to follow; (3) Jesus was announcing the beginning of his public ministry; (4) Jesus was being baptised for the sins of the nation. The Holy Spirit's appearance in the form of a dove showed that God's plan for salvation was centred in Jesus. Jesus was the perfect human who didn't need baptism for repentance, but he was baptised anyway on our behalf.

3:21, 22 This is one of several places in Scripture where all the members of the Trinity are mentioned – Father, Son, and Holy Spirit. In the traditional words of the church, the one God exists in three persons but one substance, co-eternal and co-equal. No amount of explanation can adequately portray the power and intricacy of this unique relationship. There are no perfect analogies in nature because there is no other relationship like the Trinity.

3:23 Imagine the Saviour of the world working in a rural carpenter's shop until he was 30 years old! It seems incredible that Jesus would have been content to remain in Nazareth all that time, but he patiently trusted the Father's timing for his life and ministry. Thirty was the prescribed age for priests to begin their ministry (Numbers 4:3). Joseph was 30 years old when he began serving the king of Egypt (Genesis 41:46), and David was 30 years old when he began to reign over Judah (2 Samuel 5:4). Age 30, then, was a good time to begin an important task in the Jewish culture. Like Jesus, we need to resist the temptation to jump ahead before receiving the Spirit's direction. Are you waiting and wondering what your next step should be? Don't jump ahead – trust God's timing.

3:23 Heli may have been Joseph's father-in-law. If that were the case, this would be Mary's genealogy that Luke may have received personally from her. It is fitting that Luke would show Mary's genealogy because of the prominence he gives women in his Gospel.

3:23–38 Matthew's genealogy goes back to Abraham and shows that Jesus was related to all Jews (Matthew 1). Luke's genealogy goes back to Adam, showing that Jesus is related to all human beings. This is consistent with Luke's picture of Jesus as the Saviour of the whole world.

3:33 [g]Ru 4:18-22; 1Ch 2:10-12
3:34 [h]Ge 11:24, 26
3:36 [i]Ge 11:12 [j]Ge 5:28-32
3:38 [k]Ge 5:1, 2, 6-9

the son of Salmon,[d] the son of Nahshon,
33the son of Amminadab, the son of Ram,[e]
the son of Hezron, the son of Perez,[g]
the son of Judah, 34the son of Jacob,
the son of Isaac, the son of Abraham,
the son of Terah, the son of Nahor,[h]
35the son of Serug, the son of Reu,
the son of Peleg, the son of Eber,
the son of Shelah, 36the son of Cainan,
the son of Arphaxad,[i] the son of Shem,
the son of Noah, the son of Lamech,[j]
37the son of Methuselah, the son of Enoch,
the son of Jared, the son of Mahalalel,
the son of Kenan, 38the son of Enosh,
the son of Seth, the son of Adam,
the son of God.[k]

4:1 [a]ver 14, 18 [b]Lk 3:3, 21 [c]Lk 2:27
4:2 [d]Ex 34:28; 1Ki 19:8

Satan Tempts Jesus in the Desert
(18/Matthew 4:1–11; Mark 1:12, 13)

4 Jesus, full of the Holy Spirit,[a] returned from the Jordan[b] and was led by the
Spirit[c] in the desert, 2where for forty days[d] he was tempted by the devil. He
ate nothing during those days, and at the end of them he was hungry.

d *32* Some early manuscripts *Sala* **e** *33* Some manuscripts *Amminadab, the son of Admin, the son of Arni*; other manuscripts vary widely.

4:1 Sometimes we feel that if the Holy Spirit leads us, it will always be "beside quiet waters" (Psalm 23:2). But that is not necessarily true. He led Jesus into the desert for a long and difficult time of testing, and he may also lead us into difficult situations. When facing trials, first make sure you haven't brought them on yourself through sin or unwise choices. If you find no sin to confess or unwise behaviour to change, then ask God to strengthen you for your test. Finally, be careful to follow faithfully wherever the Holy Spirit leads.

4:1 Temptation will often come after a high point in our spiritual lives or ministries (see 1 Kings 18; 19 for Elijah's story of great victory followed by despair). Remember that Satan chooses the times for his attacks. We need to be on our guard in times of victory just as much as in times of discouragement. See the third note on Matthew 4:1ff for a comment on how Satan tempts us when we're vulnerable.

4:1, 2 The devil, who tempted Adam and Eve in the garden, also tempted Jesus in the desert. Satan is a real being, a created but rebellious fallen angel, and not a symbol or an idea. He constantly fights against God and those who follow and obey God. Jesus was a prime target for the devil's temptations. Satan succeeded with Adam and Eve, and he hoped to succeed with Jesus too.

4:1–13 Knowing and obeying God's word is an effective weapon against temptation, the only *offensive* weapon provided in the Christian's "armour" (Ephesians 6:17). Jesus used Scripture to counter Satan's attacks, and you can too. But to use it effectively you must have faith in God's promises, because Satan also knows Scripture and is adept at twisting it to suit his purpose. Obeying the Scriptures is more important than simply having a verse to quote, so read them daily and apply them to your life. Then your "sword" will always be sharp.

4:2 Why was it necessary for Jesus to be tempted? First, temptation is part of the human experience. For Jesus to be fully human, for him to understand us completely, he had to face temptation (see Hebrews 4:15). Second, Jesus had to undo Adam's work. Adam, though created perfect, gave in to temptation and passed sin on to the whole human race. Jesus, by contrast, resisted Satan. His victory offers salvation to all of Adam's descendants (see Romans 5:12–19).

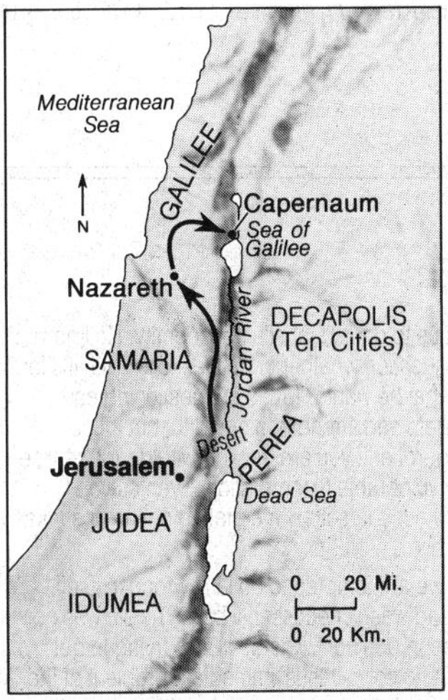

JESUS' TEMPTATION AND RETURN TO GALILEE
Jesus was tempted by Satan in the rough Desert of Judea before returning to his boyhood home, Nazareth. John's Gospel tells of Jesus' journeys in Galilee, Samaria, and Judea (see John 1–4) before he moved to Capernaum to set up his base of operations (see Matthew 4:12, 13).

3The devil said to him, "If you are the Son of God, tell this stone to become bread."
4Jesus answered, "It is written: 'Man does not live on bread alone.'[a]"[e]
5The devil led him up to a high place and showed him in an instant all the kingdoms
of the world.[f] 6And he said to him, "I will give you all their authority and splendour,
for it has been given to me,[g] and I can give it to anyone I want to. 7So if you worship
me, it will all be yours."
8Jesus answered, "It is written: 'Worship the Lord your God and serve him
only.'[b]"[h]
9The devil led him to Jerusalem and had him stand on the highest point of the
temple. "If you are the Son of God," he said, "throw yourself down from here. 10For
it is written:

> " 'He will command his angels concerning you
> to guard you carefully;
> 11they will lift you up in their hands,
> so that you will not strike your foot against a stone.'[c]"[i]

12Jesus answered, "It says: 'Do not put the Lord your God to the test.'[d]"[j]
13When the devil had finished all this tempting,[k] he left him[l] until an opportune
time.

B. MESSAGE AND MINISTRY OF JESUS, THE SAVIOUR (4:14—21:38)

Luke accurately records the actions and teachings of Christ, helping us to understand the way of salvation. There is much unique material in Luke, especially the parables of Jesus. Jesus came to teach us how to live and how to find salvation. How carefully, then, we should study the words and life of our Saviour.

1. Jesus' ministry in Galilee

Jesus Preaches in Galilee

(30/Matthew 4:12–17; Mark 1:14, 15; John 4:43–45)

14Jesus returned to Galilee[m] in the power of the Spirit, and news about him spread
through the whole countryside.[n] 15He taught in their synagogues,[o] and everyone
praised him.

[a] *4* Deut. 8:3 [b] *8* Deut. 6:13 [c] *11* Psalm 91:11,12 [d] *12* Deut. 6:16

4:4 [e]Dt 8:3
4:5 [f]Mt 24:14
4:6 [g]Jn 12:31; 14:30; 1Jn 5:19
4:8 [h]Dt 6:13
4:11 [i]Ps 91:11, 12
4:12 [j]Dt 6:16
4:13 [k]Heb 4:15 [l]Jn 14:30
4:14 [m]Mt 4:12 [n]Mt 9:26
4:15 [o]Mt 4:23

4:3 Satan may tempt us to doubt Christ's true identity. He knows that once we begin to question whether or not Jesus is God, it's far easier to get us to do what he wants. Times of questioning can help us sort out our beliefs and strengthen our faith, but those times can also be dangerous. If you are dealing with doubt, realise that you are especially vulnerable to temptation. Even as you search for answers, protect yourself by meditating on the unshakable truths of God's word.

4:3 Sometimes what we are tempted to do isn't wrong in itself. Turning stones into bread wasn't necessarily bad. The sin was not in the act but in the reason behind it. The devil was trying to get Jesus to take a shortcut, to solve Jesus' immediate problem at the expense of his long-term goals, to seek comfort at the sacrifice of his discipline. Satan often works that way—persuading us to take action, even right action, for the wrong reason or at the wrong time. The fact that something is not wrong in itself does not mean that it is good for you at a given time. Many people sin by attempting to fulfil legitimate desires outside of God's will or ahead of his timetable. First ask, "Is the Holy Spirit leading me to do this? Or is Satan trying to get me off the track?"

4:3ff Often we are tempted not through our weaknesses, but through our strengths. The devil tempted Jesus where he was strong. Jesus had power over stones, the kingdoms of the world, and even angels, and Satan wanted him to use that power without regard to his mission. When we give in to the devil and wrongly use our strengths, we become proud and self-reliant. Trusting in our own powers, we feel little need of God. To avoid this trap, we must realise that all our strengths are God's gifts to us, and we must dedicate those strengths to his service.

4:6, 7 The devil arrogantly hoped to succeed in his rebellion against God by diverting Jesus from his mission and winning his worship. "This world is mine, not God's," he was saying, "and if you hope to do anything worthwhile here, you'd better recognise that fact." Jesus didn't argue with Satan about who owns the world, but Jesus refused to validate Satan's claim by worshipping him. Jesus knew that he would redeem the world through giving up his life on the cross, not through making an alliance with a corrupt angel.

4:9–11 Here the devil misinterpreted Scripture. The intention of Psalm 91 is to show God's protection of his people, not to incite them to use God's power for sensational or foolish displays.

Jesus Is Rejected at Nazareth
(32)

16 He went to Nazareth,[p] where he had been brought up, and on the Sabbath day
he went into the synagogue,[q] as was his custom. And he stood up to read. 17 The scroll
of the prophet Isaiah was handed to him. Unrolling it, he found the place where it
is written:

18 "The Spirit of the Lord is on me,[r]
because he has anointed me
to preach good news to the poor.
He has sent me to proclaim freedom for the prisoners
and recovery of sight for the blind,
to release the oppressed,
19 to proclaim the year of the Lord's favour."[e][s]

20 Then he rolled up the scroll, gave it back to the attendant and sat down.[t] The
eyes of everyone in the synagogue were fastened on him, 21 and he began by saying
to them, "Today this scripture is fulfilled in your hearing."
22 All spoke well of him and were amazed at the gracious words that came from his
lips. "Isn't this Joseph's son?" they asked.[u]
23 Jesus said to them, "Surely you will quote this proverb to me: 'Physician, heal
yourself! Do here in your home town[v] what we have heard that you did in Capernaum.' "[w]
24 "I tell you the truth," he continued, "no prophet is accepted in his home town.[x]
25 I assure you that there were many widows in Israel in Elijah's time, when the sky
was shut for three and a half years and there was a severe famine throughout the land.[y]
26 Yet Elijah was not sent to any of them, but to a widow in Zarephath in the region
of Sidon.[z] 27 And there were many in Israel with leprosy[f] in the time of Elisha the
prophet, yet not one of them was cleansed—only Naaman the Syrian."[a]
28 All the people in the synagogue were furious when they heard this. 29 They got
up, drove him out of the town,[b] and took him to the brow of the hill on which the
town was built, in order to throw him down the cliff. 30 But he walked right through
the crowd and went on his way.[c]

4:16 [p] Mt 2:23 [q] Mt 13:54
4:18 [r] Jn 3:34
4:19 [s] Isa 61:1, 2; Lev 25:10
4:20 [t] ver 17; Mt 26:55
4:22 [u] Mt 13:54, 55; Jn 6:42; 7:15
4:23 [v] ver 16 [w] Mk 1:21-28; 2:1-12
4:24 [x] Mt 13:57; Jn 4:44
4:25 [y] 1Ki 17:1; 18:1; Jas 5:17, 18
4:26 [z] 1Ki 17:8-16; Mt 11:21
4:27 [a] 2Ki 5:1-14
4:29 [b] Nu 15:35; Ac 7:58; Heb 13:12
4:30 [c] Jn 8:59; 10:39

[e] *19* Isaiah 61:1,2 [f] *27* The Greek word was used for various diseases affecting the skin—not necessarily leprosy.

4:13 Christ's defeat of the devil in the desert was decisive but not final. Throughout his ministry, Jesus would confront Satan in many forms. Too often we see temptation as once and for all. In reality, we need to be constantly on guard against the devil's ongoing attacks. Where are you most susceptible to temptation right now? How are you preparing to withstand it?

4:16 Synagogues were very important in Jewish religious life. During the exile when the Jews no longer had their temple, synagogues were established as places of worship on the Sabbath and as schools for young boys during the week. Synagogues continued to exist even after the temple was rebuilt. A synagogue could be set up in any town where there were at least ten Jewish families. It was administered by one leader and an assistant. At the synagogue, the leader would often invite a visiting rabbi to read from the Scriptures and to teach.

4:16 Jesus went to the synagogue "as was his custom". Even though he was the perfect Son of God, and his local synagogue undoubtedly left much to be desired, Jesus attended services every week. His example makes our excuses for not attending church sound weak and self-serving. Make regular worship a part of your life.

4:17–21 Jesus was quoting from Isaiah 61:1, 2. Isaiah pictures the deliverance of Israel from exile in Babylon as a Year of Jubilee when all debts are cancelled, all slaves are freed, and all property is returned to original owners (Leviticus 25). But the release from Babylonian exile had not brought the fulfilment the people had expected; they were still a conquered and oppressed people. So Isaiah must have been referring to a future Messianic age. Jesus boldly announced, "Today this scripture is fulfilled in your hearing." Jesus was proclaiming himself as the One who would bring this good news to pass, but in a way that the people would not yet be able to grasp.

4:24 Even Jesus himself was not accepted as a prophet in his home town. Many people have a similar attitude—an expert is anyone who carries a briefcase and comes from more than 50 miles away. Don't be surprised when your Christian life and faith are not easily understood or accepted by those who know you well.

4:28 Jesus' remarks filled the people of Nazareth with rage because he was saying that God sometimes chose to reach Gentiles rather than Jews. Jesus implied that his hearers were as unbelieving as the citizens of the northern kingdom of Israel in the days of Elijah and Elisha, a time notorious for its great wickedness.

Jesus Teaches with Great Authority
(34/Mark 1:21–28)

31 Then he went down to Capernaum,[d] a town in Galilee, and on the Sabbath began
to teach the people. 32 They were amazed at his teaching,[e] because his message had
authority.[f]
33 In the synagogue there was a man possessed by a demon, an evil[g] spirit. He cried
out at the top of his voice, 34 "Ha! What do you want with us,[g] Jesus of Nazareth?[h]
Have you come to destroy us? I know who you are[i]—the Holy One of God!"[j]
35 "Be quiet!" Jesus said sternly.[k] "Come out of him!" Then the demon threw the
man down before them all and came out without injuring him.
36 All the people were amazed[l] and said to each other, "What is this teaching? With
authority[m] and power he gives orders to evil spirits and they come out!" 37 And the
news about him spread throughout the surrounding area.[n]

Jesus Heals Peter's Mother-in-Law and Many Others
(35/Matthew 8:14–17; Mark 1:29–34)

38 Jesus left the synagogue and went to the home of Simon. Now Simon's mother-in-
law was suffering from a high fever, and they asked Jesus to help her. 39 So he bent
over her and rebuked[o] the fever, and it left her. She got up at once and began to wait
on them.
40 When the sun was setting, the people brought to Jesus all who had various kinds
of sickness, and laying his hands on each one,[p] he healed them.[q] 41 Moreover,
demons came out of many people, shouting, "You are the Son of God!"[r] But he
rebuked[s] them and would not allow them to speak,[t] because they knew he was the
Christ.[h]

Jesus Preaches throughout Galilee
(36/Matthew 4:23–25; Mark 1:35–39)

42 At daybreak Jesus went out to a solitary place. The people were looking for him
and when they came to where he was, they tried to keep him from leaving them. 43 But

[g] 33 Greek *unclean*; also in verse 36 [h] 41 Or *Messiah*

4:31 [d] ver 23; Mt 4:13
4:32 [e] Mt 7:28 [f] ver 36; Mt 7:29
4:34 [g] Mt 8:29 [h] Mk 1:24 [i] Jas 2:19 [j] ver 41; Mk 1:24
4:35 [k] ver 39, 41; Mt 8:26; Lk 8:24
4:36 [l] Mt 7:28 [m] ver 32; Mt 7:29; Mt 10:1
4:37 [n] ver 14; Mt 9:26
4:39 [o] ver 35, 41
4:40 [p] Mk 5:23 [q] Mt 4:23
4:41 [r] Mt 4:3 [s] ver 35 [t] Mt 8:4

4:31 Jesus had recently moved to Capernaum from Nazareth (Matthew 4:13). Capernaum was a thriving city with great wealth as well as great decadence. Because it was the headquarters for many Roman troops, word about Jesus could spread all over the Roman empire.

4:31 Why was Jesus allowed to teach in the synagogues? Jesus was taking advantage of the policy of allowing visitors to teach. Itinerant rabbis were always welcome to speak to those gathered each Sabbath in the synagogues. The apostle Paul also profited from this practice (see Acts 13:5; 14:1).

4:33 A man possessed by a demon was in the synagogue where Jesus was teaching. This man made his way into the place of worship and verbally abused Jesus. It is naive to think that we will be sheltered from evil in the church. Satan is happy to invade our presence wherever and whenever he can. But Jesus' authority is much greater than Satan's; and where Jesus is present, demons cannot stay for long.

4:34–36 The people were amazed at Jesus' authority to drive out demons—evil spirits ruled by Satan and sent to harass people and tempt them to sin. Demons are fallen angels who have joined Satan in rebellion against God. Demons can cause a person to become mute, deaf, blind, or insane. Jesus faced many demons during his time on earth, and he always exerted authority over them. Not only did the evil spirit leave this man; Luke records that the man was not even injured.

4:36 Evil permeates our world, and it is no wonder that people are often fearful. But Jesus' power is far greater than Satan's. The first step towards conquering fear of evil is to recognise Jesus' authority and power. He has overcome all evil, including Satan himself.

4:39 Jesus healed Simon's (Peter's) mother-in-law so completely that not only did the fever leave, but her strength was restored, and immediately she got up and took care of others' needs. What a beautiful attitude of service she showed! God gives us health so that we may serve others.

4:40 The people came to Jesus when the sun was setting because this was the Sabbath (4:31), their day of rest. Sabbath lasted from sunset on Friday to sunset on Saturday. The people didn't want to break the law that prohibited travel on the Sabbath, so they waited until the Sabbath hours were over before coming to Jesus. Then, as Luke the physician notes, they came with all kinds of diseases, and Jesus healed each one.

4:41 Why didn't Jesus want the demons to reveal who he was? (1) Jesus commanded them to remain silent to show his authority over them. (2) Jesus wanted his listeners to believe he was the Messiah because of his words, not because of the demons' words. (3) Jesus was going to reveal his identity according to God's timetable, and he would not be pushed by Satan's evil plans. The demons called Jesus "Son of God" or "the Holy One of God" (4:35) because they knew he was the Christ. But Jesus was going to show himself to be the suffering servant before he became the great King. To reveal his identity as King too soon would stir up the crowds with the wrong expectations of what he had come to do.

4:42 Jesus had to get up very early just to get some time alone. If Jesus needed solitude for prayer and refreshment, how much more is this true for us? Don't become so busy that life turns into a flurry of activity leaving no room for quiet fellowship alone with God. No matter how much you have to do, you should always have time for prayer.

he said, "I must preach the good news of the kingdom of God[u] to the other towns
also, because that is why I was sent." 44 And he kept on preaching in the synagogues
of Judea.[i][v]

Jesus Provides a Miraculous Catch of Fish
(37)

5 One day as Jesus was standing by the Lake of Gennesaret,[a] with the people
crowding round him and listening to the word of God,[a] 2 he saw at the water's
edge two boats, left there by the fishermen, who were washing their nets. 3 He got
into one of the boats, the one belonging to Simon, and asked him to put out a little
from shore. Then he sat down and taught the people from the boat.[b]

4 When he had finished speaking, he said to Simon, "Put out into deep water, and
let down[b] the nets for a catch."[c]

5 Simon answered, "Master,[d] we've worked hard all night and haven't caught
anything.[e] But because you say so, I will let down the nets."

6 When they had done so, they caught such a large number of fish that their nets
began to break.[f] 7 So they signalled to their partners in the other boat to come and
help them, and they came and filled both boats so full that they began to sink.

8 When Simon Peter saw this, he fell at Jesus' knees and said, "Go away from me,
Lord; I am a sinful man!"[g] 9 For he and all his companions were astonished at the
catch of fish they had taken, 10 and so were James and John, the sons of Zebedee,
Simon's partners.

Then Jesus said to Simon, "Don't be afraid;[h] from now on you will catch men."
11 So they pulled their boats up on shore, left everything and followed him.[i]

Jesus Heals a Man with Leprosy
(38/Matthew 8:1–4; Mark 1:40–45)

12 While Jesus was in one of the towns, a man came along who was covered with
leprosy.[c][j] When he saw Jesus, he fell with his face to the ground and begged him,
"Lord, if you are willing, you can make me clean."

4:43 [u]Mt 3:2
4:44 [v]Mt 4:23
5:1 [a]Mk 4:14; Heb 4:12
5:3 [b]Mt 13:2
5:4 [c]Jn 21:6
5:5 [d]Lk 8:24, 45; 9:33, 49; 17:13 [e]Jn 21:3
5:6 [f]Jn 21:11
5:8 [g]Ge 18:27; Job 42:6; Isa 6:5
5:10 [h]Mt 14:27
5:11 [i]ver 28; Mt 4:19
5:12 [j]Mt 8:2

i *44* Or *the land of the Jews*; some manuscripts *Galilee* a *1* That is, Sea of Galilee b *4* The Greek verb is plural.
c *12* The Greek word was used for various diseases affecting the skin—not necessarily leprosy.

4:43 The kingdom of God was good news! It was good news to the Jews because they had been awaiting the coming of the promised Messiah ever since the Babylonian captivity. It is good news for us also because it means freedom from slavery to sin and selfishness. The kingdom of God is here and now because the Holy Spirit lives in the hearts of believers. Yet it is also in the future because Jesus will return to reign over a perfect kingdom where sin and evil no longer exist.

5:1 The Lake of Gennesaret was also known as the Sea of Galilee or the Sea of Tiberias.

5:2 Fishermen on the Sea of Galilee used nets, often bell-shaped nets with lead weights around the edges. A net would be thrown flat onto the water, and the lead weights would cause it to sink around the fish. Then the fishermen would pull on a cord, drawing the net around the fish. Nets had to be kept in good condition, so they were washed to remove weeds and then mended.

5:8 Simon (Peter) was awestruck at this miracle, and his first response was to feel his own insignificance in comparison to this man's greatness. Peter knew that Jesus had healed the sick and driven out demons, but he was amazed that Jesus cared about his day-to-day routine and understood his needs. God is interested not only in saving us, but also in helping us in our daily activities.

5:11 There are two requirements for coming to God. Like Peter, we must recognise our own sinfulness. Then, like these fishermen, we must realise that we can't save ourselves. If we know that we need help, and if we know that Jesus is the only one who can help us, we will be ready to leave everything and follow him.

5:11 This was the disciples' second call. After the first call (Matthew 4:18–22; Mark 1:16–20), Peter, Andrew, James, and John had gone back to fishing. They continued to watch Jesus, however, as he established his authority in the synagogue, healed the sick, and drove out demons. Here he also established his authority in their lives—he met them on their level and helped them in their work. From this point on, they left their nets and remained with Jesus. For us, following Jesus means more than just acknowledging him as Saviour. We must leave our past behind and commit our future to him.

5:12 Leprosy was a feared disease because there was no known cure for it, and some forms of it were highly contagious. Leprosy had a similar emotional impact and terror associated with it as AIDS does today. (Sometimes called Hansen's disease, leprosy still exists today in a less contagious form that can be treated.) The priests monitored the disease, banishing lepers who were in a contagious stage to prevent the spread of infection and readmitting lepers whose disease was in remission. Because leprosy destroys the nerve endings, lepers would often unknowingly damage their fingers, toes, and noses. This man with leprosy had an advanced case, so he undoubtedly had lost much bodily tissue. Still, he believed that Jesus could heal every trace of the disease.

13 Jesus reached out his hand and touched the man. "I am willing," he said. "Be
clean!" And immediately the leprosy left him.
14 Then Jesus ordered him, "Don't tell anyone,[k] but go, show yourself to the priest
and offer the sacrifices that Moses commanded[l] for your cleansing, as a testimony
to them."
15 Yet the news about him spread all the more,[m] so that crowds of people came to
hear him and to be healed of their sicknesses.
16 But Jesus often withdrew to lonely
places and prayed.[n]

Jesus Heals a Paralysed Man
(39/Matthew 9:1–8; Mark 2:1–12)

17 One day as he was teaching, Pharisees and teachers of the law,[o] who had come
from every village of Galilee and from Judea and Jerusalem, were sitting there. And
the power of the Lord was present for him to heal the sick.[p]
18 Some men came
carrying a paralytic on a mat and tried to take him into the house to lay him before
Jesus.
19 When they could not find a way to do this because of the crowd, they went
up on the roof and lowered him on his mat through the tiles into the middle of the
crowd, right in front of Jesus.
20 When Jesus saw their faith, he said, "Friend, your sins are forgiven."[q]
21 The Pharisees and the teachers of the law began thinking to themselves, "Who
is this fellow who speaks blasphemy? Who can forgive sins but God alone?"[r]
22 Jesus knew what they were thinking and asked, "Why are you thinking these
things in your hearts?
23 Which is easier: to say, 'Your sins are forgiven,' or to say,
'Get up and walk'?
24 But that you may know that the Son of Man[s] has authority on
earth to forgive sins. . . ." He said to the paralysed man, "I tell you, get up, take your
mat and go home."
25 Immediately he stood up in front of them, took what he had been
lying on and went home praising God.
26 Everyone was amazed and gave praise to
God.[t] They were filled with awe and said, "We have seen remarkable things today."

Jesus Eats with Sinners at Matthew's House
(40/Matthew 9:9–13; Mark 2:13–17)

27 After this, Jesus went out and saw a tax collector by the name of Levi sitting at
his tax booth. "Follow me,"[u] Jesus said to him,
28 and Levi got up, left everything
and followed him.[v]

5:14 [k] Mt 8:4 [l] Lev 14:2-32
5:15 [m] Mt 9:26
5:16 [n] Mt 14:23; Lk 3:21
5:17 [o] Mt 15:1; Lk 2:46 [p] Mk 5:30; Lk 6:19
5:20 [q] Lk 7:48, 49
5:21 [r] Isa 43:25
5:24 [s] Mt 8:20
5:26 [t] Mt 9:8
5:27 [u] Mt 4:19
5:28 [v] ver 11; Mt 4:19

5:13 Lepers were considered untouchable because people feared contracting their disease. Yet Jesus reached out and touched the leper to heal him. We may consider certain people who are diseased or disabled to be untouchable or repulsive. We must not be afraid to reach out and touch them with God's love. Whom do you know that needs God's touch of love?

5:16 People were flocking to hear Jesus preach and to have their diseases healed, but Jesus made sure he often withdrew to quiet, solitary places to pray. Many things clamour for our attention, and we often run ourselves into the ground attending to them. Like Jesus, however, we should take time to withdraw to a quiet and deserted place to pray. Strength comes from God, and we can only be strengthened by spending time with him.

5:17 The religious leaders spent much time defining and discussing the huge body of religious tradition that had been accumulating for more than 400 years since the Jews' return from exile. They were so concerned with these man-made traditions, in fact, that they often lost sight of Scripture. Here these leaders felt threatened because Jesus challenged their sincerity and because the people were flocking to him.

5:18, 19 In Bible times, houses were built of stone and had flat roofs made of mud mixed with straw. Outside stairways led to the roof. These men carried their friend up the stairs to the roof where they took apart as much of the mud and straw mixture as was necessary to lower him in front of Jesus.

5:18–20 It wasn't the paralytic's faith that impressed Jesus, but the faith of his friends. Jesus responded to their faith and healed the man. For better or worse, our faith affects others. We cannot make another person a Christian, but we can do much through our words, actions, and love to give him or her a chance to respond. Look for opportunities to bring your friends to the living Christ.

5:21 When Jesus told the paralytic his sins were forgiven, the Jewish leaders accused Jesus of blasphemy—claiming to be God or to do what only God can do. In Jewish law, blasphemy was punishable by death (Leviticus 24:16). In labelling Jesus' claim to forgive sins blasphemous, the religious leaders showed they did not understand that Jesus *is* God, and he has God's power to heal both the body and the soul. Forgiveness of sins was a sign that the Messianic age had come (Isaiah 40:2; Joel 2:32; Micah 7:18, 19; Zechariah 13:1).

5:27 For more about Levi (who was also named Matthew), the disciple and author of the Gospel of Matthew, see his Profile in Matthew 9.

5:28, 29 Levi responded as Jesus would want all his followers to do—he followed his Lord immediately, and he called his friends together to meet him too. Levi left a lucrative, though probably dishonest, tax-collecting business to follow Jesus. Then he held a reception for his fellow tax collectors and other notorious "sinners" so they could meet Jesus too. Levi, who left behind a material fortune in order to gain a spiritual fortune, was proud to be associated with Jesus.

29 Then Levi held a great banquet for Jesus at his house, and a large crowd of tax
collectors[w] and others were eating with them. 30 But the Pharisees and the teachers
of the law who belonged to their sect[x] complained to his disciples, "Why do you eat
and drink with tax collectors and 'sinners'?"[y]
31 Jesus answered them, "It is not the healthy who need a doctor, but the sick. 32 I
have not come to call the righteous, but sinners to repentance."[z]

Religious Leaders Ask Jesus about Fasting
(41/Matthew 9:14–17; Mark 2:18–22)

33 They said to him, "John's disciples[a] often fast and pray, and so do the disciples
of the Pharisees, but yours go on eating and drinking."
34 Jesus answered, "Can you make the guests of the bridegroom[b] fast while he is
with them? 35 But the time will come when the bridegroom will be taken from them;[c]
in those days they will fast."
36 He told them this parable: "No-one tears a patch from a new garment and sews
it on an old one. If he does, he will have torn the new garment, and the patch from
the new will not match the old. 37 And no-one pours new wine into old wineskins. If
he does, the new wine will burst the skins, the wine will run out and the wineskins
will be ruined. 38 No, new wine must be poured into new wineskins. 39 And no-one
after drinking old wine wants the new, for he says, 'The old is better.' "

The Disciples Pick Wheat on the Sabbath
(45/Matthew 12:1–8; Mark 2:23–28)

6 One Sabbath Jesus was going through the cornfields, and his disciples began to
pick some ears of corn, rub them in their hands and eat the grain.[a] 2 Some of
the Pharisees asked, "Why are you doing what is unlawful on the Sabbath?"[b]
3 Jesus answered them, "Have you never read what David did when he and his
companions were hungry?[c] 4 He entered the house of God, and taking the consecrated
bread, he ate what is lawful only for priests to eat.[d] And he also gave some to his
companions." 5 Then Jesus said to them, "The Son of Man[e] is Lord of the Sabbath."

5:29 [w]Lk 15:1
5:30 [x]Ac 23:9 [y]Mt 9:11
5:32 [z]Jn 3:17
5:33 [a]Lk 7:18; Jn 1:35; 3:25, 26
5:34 [b]Jn 3:29
5:35 [c]Lk 9:22; 17:22; Jn 16:5-7
6:1 [a]Dt 23:25
6:2 [b]Mt 12:2
6:3 [c]1Sa 21:6
6:4 [d]Lev 24:5, 9
6:5 [e]Mt 8:20

5:30–32 The Pharisees wrapped their sin in respectability. They made themselves appear good by publicly doing good deeds and pointing at the sins of others. Jesus chose to spend time not with these proud, self-righteous religious leaders, but with people who sensed their own sin and knew that they were not good enough for God. In order to come to God, we must repent; and in order to renounce our sin, we must recognise it for what it is.

5:35 Jesus knew his death was coming. After that time, fasting would be in order. Although he was fully human, Jesus knew he was God and knew why he had come – to die for the sins of the world.

5:36–39 "Wineskins" were goatskins sewed together at the edges to form watertight bags. Because new wine expands as it ages, it had to be put in new, pliable wineskins. A used skin, having become more rigid, would burst and spill the wine. Like old wineskins, the Pharisees were too rigid to accept Jesus, who could not be contained in their traditions or rules. Christianity required new approaches, new traditions, new structures. Our church meetings and ministries should not be so structured that they have no room for a fresh touch of the Spirit, a new method, or a new idea. We, too, must be careful that our hearts do not become so rigid that they prevent us from accepting the new way of thinking that Christ brings. We need to keep our hearts pliable so we can accept Jesus' life-changing message.

6:1, 2 In Jewish legal tradition, there were 39 categories of activities forbidden on the Sabbath – and harvesting was one of them. The teachers of the law even went so far as to describe different methods of harvesting. One method was to rub the heads of grain between the hands, as the disciples were doing here. God's law said farmers were to leave the edges of their fields unploughed so travellers and the poor could eat from this bounty (Deuteronomy 23:25), so the disciples were not guilty of stealing grain. Neither were they breaking the Sabbath by doing their daily work on it. In fact, though they may have been violating the Pharisees' rules, they were not breaking any divine law.

6:2 The Pharisees thought their religious system had all the answers. They could not accept Jesus because he did not fit into their system. We could miss Christ for the same reason. Beware of thinking that you or your church has all the answers. No religious system is big enough to contain Christ completely or to fulfil perfectly all his desires for the world.

6:3–5 Each week 12 consecrated loaves of bread, representing the 12 tribes of Israel, were placed on a table in the temple. This bread was called the bread of the Presence. After its use in the temple, it was to be eaten only by priests. Jesus, accused of Sabbath-breaking, referred to a well-known story about David (1 Samuel 21:1–6). On one occasion, when fleeing from Saul, David and his men ate this consecrated bread. Their need was more important than ceremonial regulations. Jesus was appealing to the same principle: human need is more important than human regulations and rules. By comparing himself and his disciples with David and his men, Jesus was saying, "If you condemn me, you must also condemn David."

6:5 When Jesus said he was "Lord of the Sabbath", he meant that he had the authority to overrule the Pharisees' traditions and regulations because he had created the Sabbath. The Creator is always greater than the creation.

Jesus Heals a Man's Hand on the Sabbath
(46/Matthew 12:9–14; Mark 3:1–6)

6On another Sabbath[f] he went into the synagogue and was teaching, and a man was there whose right hand was shrivelled. 7The Pharisees and the teachers of the law were looking for a reason to accuse Jesus, so they watched him closely[g] to see if he would heal on the Sabbath.[h] 8But Jesus knew what they were thinking[i] and said to the man with the shrivelled hand, "Get up and stand in front of everyone." So he got up and stood there.

9Then Jesus said to them, "I ask you, which is lawful on the Sabbath: to do good or to do evil, to save life or to destroy it?"

10He looked round at them all, and then said to the man, "Stretch out your hand." He did so, and his hand was completely restored. 11But they were furious[j] and began to discuss with one another what they might do to Jesus.

Jesus Selects the Twelve Disciples
(48/Mark 3:13–19)

12One of those days Jesus went out to a mountainside to pray, and spent the night praying to God.[k] 13When morning came, he called his disciples to him and chose twelve of them, whom he also designated apostles:[l] 14Simon (whom he named Peter), his brother Andrew, James, John, Philip, Bartholomew, 15Matthew,[m] Thomas, James son of Alphaeus, Simon who was called the Zealot, 16Judas son of James, and Judas Iscariot, who became a traitor.

Jesus Gives the Beatitudes
(49/Matthew 5:1–12)

17He went down with them and stood on a level place. A large crowd of his disciples was there and a great number of people from all over Judea, from Jerusalem, and from the coast of Tyre and Sidon,[n] 18who had come to hear him and to be healed of their diseases. Those troubled by evil[a] spirits were cured, 19and the people all tried to touch him,[o] because power was coming from him and healing them all.[p]

20Looking at his disciples, he said:

a 18 Greek *unclean*

6:6
[f] ver 1

6:7
[g] Mt 12:10
[h] Mt 12:2

6:8
[i] Mt 9:4

6:11
[j] Jn 5:18

6:12
[k] Lk 3:21

6:13
[l] Mk 6:30

6:15
[m] Mt 9:9

6:17
[n] Mt 4:25;
Mt 11:21;
Mk 3:7, 8

6:19
[o] Mt 9:20
[p] Mt 14:36;
Mk 5:30;
Lk 5:17

6:6, 7 According to the tradition of the religious leaders, no healing could be done on the Sabbath. Healing, they argued, was practising medicine, and a person could not practise his or her profession on the Sabbath. It was more important for the religious leaders to protect their laws than to free a person from painful suffering.

6:11 Jesus' enemies were furious. Not only had he read their minds; he also flouted their laws and exposed the hatred in their hearts. It is ironic that it was their hatred, combined with their zeal for the law, that drove them to plot murder — an act that was clearly against the law.

6:12 The Gospel writers note that before every important event in Jesus' life, he took time to go off by himself and pray. This time Jesus was preparing to choose his inner circle, the 12 disciples. Make sure that all your important decisions are grounded in prayer.

6:13 Jesus had many *disciples* (learners), but he chose only 12 *apostles* (messengers). The apostles were his inner circle, to whom he gave special training and whom he sent out with his own authority. These were the men who started the Christian church. In the Gospels these 12 men are usually called the disciples, but in the book of Acts they are called apostles.

6:13–16 Jesus selected "ordinary" men with a mixture of backgrounds and personalities to be his disciples. Today, God calls "ordinary" people together to build his church, teach salvation's message, and serve others out of love. Alone we may feel unqualified to serve Christ effectively, but together we make up a group strong enough to serve God in any way. Ask for patience to accept the diversity of people in your church, and build on the variety of strengths represented in your group.

6:14–16 The disciples are not always listed by the same names. For example, Peter is sometimes called Simon or Cephas. Matthew is also known as Levi. Bartholomew is thought to be the same person as Nathanael (John 1:45). Judas the son of James is also called Thaddaeus.

6:19 Once word of Jesus' healing power spread, crowds gathered just to touch him. For many, he had become a symbol of good fortune, a lucky charm, or a magician. Instead of desiring God's pardon and love, they only wanted physical healing or a chance to see spectacular events. Some people still see God as a cosmic magician and consider prayer as a way to get God to do his tricks. But God is not a magician — he is the Master. Prayer is not a way for us to control God; it is a way for us to put ourselves under his control.

6:20ff This may be Luke's account of the sermon that Matthew records in Matthew 5 – 7, or it may be that Jesus gave similar sermons on several different occasions. Some believe that this was not one sermon, but a composite based on Jesus' customary teachings.

6:20–23 These verses are called the *Beatitudes,* from the Latin word meaning "blessing". They describe what it means to be Christ's follower; they are standards of conduct; they contrast kingdom values with worldly values, showing what Christ's followers can expect from the world and what God will give them; they contrast fake piety with true humility; and finally, they show how Old Testament expectations are fulfilled in God's kingdom.

"Blessed are you who are poor,
for yours is the kingdom of God.[q]
21 Blessed are you who hunger now,
for you will be satisfied.[r]
Blessed are you who weep now,
for you will laugh.[s]
22 Blessed are you when men hate you,
when they exclude you[t] and insult you[u]
and reject your name as evil,
because of the Son of Man.[v]

23 "Rejoice in that day and leap for joy,[w] because great is your reward in heaven.
For that is how their fathers treated the prophets.[x]

24 "But woe to you who are rich,[y]
for you have already received your comfort.[z]
25 Woe to you who are well fed now,
for you will go hungry.[a]
Woe to you who laugh now,
for you will mourn and weep.[b]
26 Woe to you when all men speak well of you,
for that is how their fathers treated the false prophets.[c]

Jesus Teaches about Loving Enemies
(57/Matthew 5:43–48)

27 "But I tell you who hear me: Love your enemies, do good to those who hate you,[d]
28 bless those who curse you, pray for those who ill-treat you.[e] 29 If someone strikes
you on one cheek, turn to him the other also. If someone takes your cloak, do not
stop him from taking your tunic. 30 Give to everyone who asks you, and if anyone takes
what belongs to you, do not demand it back.[f] 31 Do to others as you would have them
do to you.[g]
32 "If you love those who love you, what credit is that to you?[h] Even 'sinners' love
those who love them. 33 And if you do good to those who are good to you, what credit
is that to you? Even 'sinners' do that. 34 And if you lend to those from whom you expect
repayment, what credit is that to you?[i] Even 'sinners' lend to 'sinners', expecting
to be repaid in full. 35 But love your enemies, do good to them,[j] and lend to them
without expecting to get anything back. Then your reward will be great, and you will
be sons[k] of the Most High,[l] because he is kind to the ungrateful and wicked. 36 Be
merciful,[m] just as your Father[n] is merciful.

6:20 [q] Mt 25:34
6:21 [r] Isa 55:1, 2; Mt 5:6 [s] Isa 61:2, 3; Mt 5:4; Rev 7:17
6:22 [t] Jn 9:22; 16:2 [u] Isa 51:7 [v] Jn 15:21
6:23 [w] Mt 5:12 [x] Mt 5:12
6:24 [y] Jas 5:1 [z] Lk 16:25
6:25 [a] Isa 65:13 [b] Pr 14:13
6:26 [c] Mt 7:15
6:27 [d] ver 35; Mt 5:44; Ro 12:20
6:28 [e] Mt 5:44
6:30 [f] Dt 15:7, 8, 10; Pr 21:26
6:31 [g] Mt 7:12
6:32 [h] Mt 5:46
6:34 [i] Mt 5:42
6:35 [j] ver 27 [k] Ro 8:14 [l] Mk 5:7
6:36 [m] Jas 2:13 [n] Mt 5:48; 6:1; Lk 11:2; 12:32; Ro 8:15; Eph 4:6; 1Pe 1:17; 1Jn 1:3; 3:1

6:21 Some believe that the hunger about which Jesus spoke is a hunger for righteousness (Matthew 5:6). Others say this is physical hunger. In any case, in a nation where riches were seen as a sign of God's favour, Jesus startled his hearers by pronouncing blessings on the hungry. In doing so, however, he was in line with an ancient tradition. The Old Testament is filled with texts proclaiming God's concern for the poor and needy. See, for example, 1 Samuel 2:5; Psalm 146:7; Isaiah 58:6, 7; and Jesus' own mother's prayer in Luke 1:53.

6:24 If you are trying to find fulfilment only through riches, wealth may be the only reward you will ever get—and it does not last. We should not seek comfort now at the expense of eternal life.

6:26 There were many false prophets in Old Testament times. They were praised by kings and crowds because their predictions—prosperity and victory in war—were exactly what the people wanted to hear. But popularity is no guarantee of truth, and human flattery does not bring God's approval. Sadness lies ahead for those who chase after the crowd's praise rather than God's truth.

6:27 The Jews despised the Romans because they oppressed God's people, but Jesus told the people to love these enemies. Such words turned many away from Christ. But Jesus wasn't talking about having affection for enemies; he was talking about an act of the will. You can't "fall into" this kind of love—it takes conscious effort. Loving our enemies means acting in their best interests. We can pray for them, and we can think of ways to help them. Jesus loved the whole world, even though the world was in rebellion against God. Jesus asks us to follow his example by loving our enemies. Grant your enemies the same respect and rights as you desire for yourself.

6:35 Love means action. One way to put love to work is to take the initiative in meeting specific needs. This is easy to do with people who love us, people whom we trust; but love means doing this even to those who dislike us or plan to hurt us. The money we give others should be considered a gift, not a high-interest loan that will help us more than them. Give as though you are giving to God.

Jesus Teaches about Criticizing Others
(63/Matthew 7:1–6)

37"Do not judge, and you will not be judged.[o] Do not condemn, and you will not
be condemned. Forgive, and you will be forgiven.[p] 38Give, and it will be given to
you. A good measure, pressed down, shaken together and running over, will be poured
into your lap.[q] For with the measure you use, it will be measured to you."[r]
39He also told them this parable: "Can a blind man lead a blind man? Will they not
both fall into a pit?[s] 40A student is not above his teacher, but everyone who is fully
trained will be like his teacher.[t]
41"Why do you look at the speck of sawdust in your brother's eye and pay no
attention to the plank in your own eye? 42How can you say to your brother, 'Brother,
let me take the speck out of your eye,' when you yourself fail to see the plank in your
own eye? You hypocrite, first take the plank out of your eye, and then you will see
clearly to remove the speck from your brother's eye.

Jesus Teaches about Fruit in People's Lives
(66/Matthew 7:15–20)

43"No good tree bears bad fruit, nor does a bad tree bear good fruit. 44Each tree
is recognised by its own fruit.[u] People do not pick figs from thorn-bushes, or grapes
from briers. 45The good man brings good things out of the good stored up in his heart,
and the evil man brings evil things out of the evil stored up in his heart. For out of
the overflow of his heart his mouth speaks.[v]

Jesus Teaches about Those Who Build Houses on Rock and Sand
(67/Matthew 7:21–29)

46"Why do you call me, 'Lord, Lord,'[w] and do not do what I say?[x] 47I will show
you what he is like who comes to me and hears my words and puts them into practice.[y]
48He is like a man building a house, who dug down deep and laid the foundation on
rock. When the flood came, the torrent struck that house but could not shake it,
because it was well built. 49But the one who hears my words and does not put them
into practice is like a man who built a house on the ground without a foundation. The
moment the torrent struck that house, it collapsed and its destruction was complete."

6:37 [o]Mt 7:1 [p]Mt 6:14
6:38 [q]Ps 79:12; Isa 65:6, 7 [r]Mt 7:2; Mk 4:24
6:39 [s]Mt 15:14
6:40 [t]Mt 10:24; Jn 13:16
6:44 [u]Mt 12:33
6:45 [v]Pr 4:23; Mt 12:34, 35; Mk 7:20
6:46 [w]Jn 13:13 [x]Mal 1:6; Mt 7:21
6:47 [y]Lk 8:21; 11:28; Jas 1:22-25

6:37, 38 A forgiving spirit demonstrates that a person has received God's forgiveness. Jesus uses the picture of measuring grain in a basket to ensure the full amount. If we are critical rather than compassionate, we will also receive criticism. If we treat others generously, graciously, and compassionately, however, these qualities will come back to us in full measure. We are to love others, not judge them.

6:39, 40 Make sure you're following the right teachers and leaders, because you will go no farther than they do. Look for leaders who will show you more about faith and whose guidance you can trust.

6:41 Jesus doesn't mean we should ignore wrongdoing, but we should not be so worried about others' sins that we overlook our own. We often rationalise our sins by pointing out the same mistakes in others. What kinds of specks in others' eyes are the easiest for you to criticise? Remember your own "planks" when you feel like criticising, and you may find that you have less to say.

6:42 We should not be so afraid of the label *hypocrite* that we stand still in our Christian life, hiding our faith and making no attempts to grow. A person who tries to do right but often fails is not a hypocrite. Neither are those who fulfil their duty even when they don't feel like doing it – it is often necessary and good to set aside our desires in order to do what needs doing. It is not hypocrisy to be weak in faith. A hypocrite is a person who puts on religious behaviour in order to gain attention, approval, acceptance, or admiration from others.

6:45 Jesus reminds us that our speech and actions reveal the true underlying beliefs, attitudes, and motivations. The good impressions we try to make cannot last if our hearts are deceptive. What is in your heart will come out in your speech and behaviour.

6:46–49 Obeying God is like building a house on a strong, solid foundation that stands firm when storms come. When life is calm, our foundations don't seem to matter. But when crises come, our foundations are tested. Be sure your life is built on the solid foundation of knowing and trusting Jesus Christ.

6:49 Why would people build a house without a foundation? Perhaps to save time and avoid the hard work of preparing a stone foundation. Possibly because the waterfront scenery is more attractive or because beach houses have higher social status than cliff houses. Perhaps because they want to join their friends who have already settled in sandy areas. Maybe because they haven't heard about the violent storms coming, or because they have discounted the reports, or for some reason they think disaster can't happen to them. Whatever their reason, those with no foundation are shortsighted, and they will be sorry. When you find yourself listening but not obeying, what are your reasons?

7:1 [a]Mt 7:28

A Roman Centurion Demonstrates Faith
(68/Matthew 8:5–13)

7 When Jesus had finished saying all this[a] in the hearing of the people, he entered
Capernaum. 2 There a centurion's servant, whom his master valued highly, was
sick and about to die. 3 The centurion heard of Jesus and sent some elders of the Jews
to him, asking him to come and heal his servant. 4 When they came to Jesus, they
pleaded earnestly with him, "This man deserves to have you do this, 5 because he loves
our nation and has built our synagogue." 6 So Jesus went with them.
He was not far from the house when the centurion sent friends to say to him: "Lord,
don't trouble yourself, for I do not deserve to have you come under my roof. 7 That
is why I did not even consider myself worthy to come to you. But say the word, and
my servant will be healed.[b] 8 For I myself am a man under authority, with soldiers
under me. I tell this one, 'Go', and he goes; and that one, 'Come', and he comes.
I say to my servant, 'Do this', and he does it."
9 When Jesus heard this, he was amazed at him, and turning to the crowd following
him, he said, "I tell you, I have not found such great faith even in Israel." 10 Then
the men who had been sent returned to the house and found the servant well.

7:7 [b]Ps 107:20

Jesus Raises a Widow's Son from the Dead
(69)

11 Soon afterwards, Jesus went to a town called Nain, and his disciples and a large
crowd went along with him. 12 As he approached the town gate, a dead person was
being carried out—the only son of his mother, and she was a widow. And a large
crowd from the town was with her. 13 When the Lord[c] saw her, his heart went out
to her and he said, "Don't cry."

7:13 [c]ver 19; Lk 10:1; 13:15; 17:5; 22:61; 24:34; Jn 11:2

7:2 A *centurion* was a Roman army officer in charge of 100 men. This man came to Jesus not as a last resort or magic charm, but because he believed Jesus was sent from God. Apparently the centurion recognised that the Jews possessed God's message for mankind—it is recorded that he loved the nation and built the synagogue. Thus, in his time of need, it was natural for him to turn to Jesus.

7:3 Why did the centurion send Jewish elders to Jesus instead of going himself? Since he was well aware of the Jewish hatred for Roman soldiers, he may not have wanted to interrupt a Jewish gathering. As an army captain, he daily delegated work and sent groups on missions, so this was how he chose to get his message to Jesus.

7:3 Matthew 8:5 says the Roman centurion visited Jesus himself, while Luke 7:3 says he sent Jewish elders to present his request to Jesus. In dealing with the messengers, Jesus was dealing with the centurion. For his Jewish audience, Matthew emphasised the man's faith. For his Gentile audience, Luke highlighted the good relationship between the Jewish elders and the Roman centurion.

7:9 The Roman centurion didn't come to Jesus, and he didn't expect Jesus to come to him. Just as this officer did not need to be present to have his orders carried out, so Jesus didn't need to be present to heal. The centurion's faith was especially amazing because he was a Gentile who had not been brought up to know a loving God.

7:11–15 The widow's situation was serious. She had lost her husband, and here her only son was dead—her last means of support. The crowd of mourners would go home, and she would be left penniless and alone. The widow was probably past the age of childbearing and would not marry again. Unless a relative came to her aid, her future was bleak. She would be an easy prey for swindlers, and she would likely be reduced to begging for food. In fact, as Luke repeatedly emphasises, this woman was just the kind of person Jesus had come to help—and help her he did. Jesus has the power to bring hope out of any tragedy.

7:11–17 This story illustrates salvation. The whole world was dead in sin (Ephesians 2:1), just as the widow's son was dead. Being dead, we could do nothing to help ourselves—we couldn't even ask for help. But God had compassion on us, and he sent Jesus to raise us to life with him (Ephesians 2:4–7). The dead man did not earn his second chance at life, and we cannot earn our new life in Christ. But we can accept God's gift of life, praise God for it, and use our lives to do his will.

7:12 Honouring the dead was important in Jewish tradition. A funeral procession—the relatives of the dead person following the body that was wrapped and carried on a kind of stretcher—would make its way through town, and bystanders would be expected to join the procession. In addition, hired mourners would cry aloud and draw attention to the procession. The family's mourning would continue for 30 days.

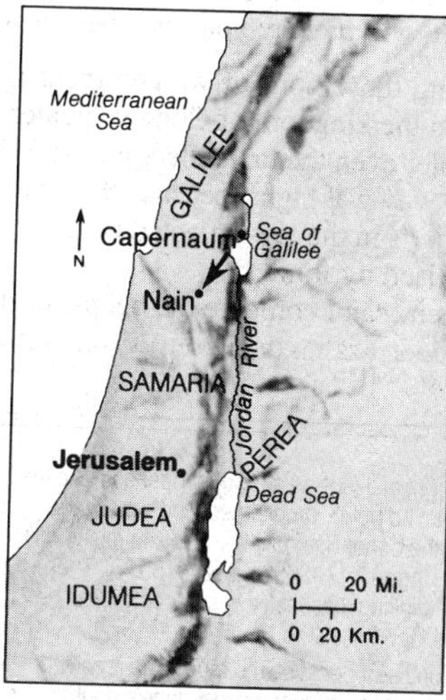

JESUS RAISES A WIDOW'S SON
Jesus travelled to Nain and met a funeral procession leaving the village. A widow's only son had died, leaving her virtually helpless, but Jesus brought the young man back to life. This miracle, recorded only in Luke, reveals Jesus' compassion for people's needs.

14 Then he went up and touched the coffin, and those carrying it stood still. He said,
"Young man, I say to you, get up!"[d] 15 The dead man sat up and began to talk, and
Jesus gave him back to his mother.
16 They were all filled with awe[e] and praised God.[f] "A great prophet[g] has
appeared among us," they said. "God has come to help his people."[h] 17 This news
about Jesus spread throughout Judea[a] and the surrounding country.[i]

Jesus Eases John's Doubt
(70/Matthew 11:1–19)

18 John's[j] disciples[k] told him about all these things. Calling two of them, 19 he sent
them to the Lord to ask, "Are you the one who was to come, or should we expect
someone else?"
20 When the men came to Jesus, they said, "John the Baptist sent us to you to ask,
'Are you the one who was to come, or should we expect someone else?' "
21 At that very time Jesus cured many who had diseases, sicknesses[l] and evil
spirits, and gave sight to many who were blind. 22 So he replied to the messengers,
"Go back and report to John what you have seen and heard: The blind receive sight,
the lame walk, those who have leprosy[b] are cured, the deaf hear, the dead are raised,
and the good news is preached to the poor.[m] 23 Blessed is the man who does not fall
away on account of me."
24 After John's messengers left, Jesus began to speak to the crowd about John:
"What did you go out into the desert to see? A reed swayed by the wind? 25 If not,
what did you go out to see? A man dressed in fine clothes? No, those who wear
expensive clothes and indulge in luxury are in palaces. 26 But what did you go out to
see? A prophet?[n] Yes, I tell you, and more than a prophet. 27 This is the one about
whom it is written:

> " 'I will send my messenger ahead of you,
> who will prepare your way before you.'[c][o]

28 I tell you, among those born of women there is no-one greater than John; yet the
one who is least in the kingdom of God[p] is greater than he."
(29 All the people, even the tax collectors, when they heard Jesus' words, acknowledged that God's way was right, because they had been baptised by John.[q] 30 But the
Pharisees and experts in the law[r] rejected God's purpose for themselves, because they
had not been baptised by John.)
31 "To what, then, can I compare the people of this generation? What are they like?

a *17 Or the land of the Jews* b *22* The Greek word was used for various diseases affecting the skin—not necessarily leprosy. c *27* Mal. 3:1

7:14 [d]Mt 9:25; Mk 1:31; Lk 8:54; Jn 11:43; Ac 9:40
7:16 [e]Lk 1:65 [f]Mt 9:8 [g]ver 39; Mt 21:11 [h]Lk 1:68
7:17 [i]Mt 9:26
7:18 [j]Mt 3:1 [k]Lk 5:33
7:21 [l]Mt 4:23
7:22 [m]Isa 29:18, 19; 35:5, 6; 61:1, 2; Lk 4:18
7:26 [n]Mt 11:9
7:27 [o]Mal 3:1; Mt 11:10; Mk 1:2
7:28 [p]Mt 3:2
7:29 [q]Mt 21:32; Mk 1:5; Lk 3:12
7:30 [r]Mt 22:35

7:16 The people thought of Jesus as a prophet because, like the Old Testament prophets, he boldly proclaimed God's message and sometimes raised the dead. Both Elijah and Elisha raised children from the dead (1 Kings 17:17–24; 2 Kings 4:18–37). The people were correct in thinking that Jesus was a prophet, but he was much more—he is God himself.

7:18–23 John was confused because the reports he received about Jesus were unexpected and incomplete. John's doubts were natural, and Jesus didn't rebuke him for them. Instead, Jesus responded in a way that John would understand: Jesus explained that he had accomplished what the Messiah was supposed to accomplish. God can handle our doubts, and he welcomes our questions. Do you have questions about Jesus—about who he is or what he expects of you? Admit them to yourself and to God, and begin looking for answers. Only as you face your doubts honestly can you begin to resolve them.

7:20–22 The proofs listed here for Jesus' being the Messiah are significant. They consist of observable deeds, not theories—actions that Jesus' contemporaries saw and reported for us to read today. The prophets had said that the Messiah would do these very acts (see Isaiah 35:5, 6; 61:1). These physical proofs helped John—and will help all of us—to recognise who Jesus is.

7:28 Of all people, no-one fulfilled his God-given purpose better than John. Yet in God's kingdom, all who come after John have a greater spiritual heritage because they have clearer knowledge of the purpose of Jesus' death and resurrection. John was the last to function like the Old Testament prophets, the last to prepare the people for the coming Messianic age. Jesus was not contrasting the man John with individual Christians; he was contrasting life before Christ with life in the fulness of Christ's kingdom.

7:29, 30 The tax collectors (who embodied evil in most people's minds) and common people heard John's message and repented. In contrast, the Pharisees and experts in the law—religious leaders—rejected his words. Wanting to live their own way, they justified their own point of view and refused to listen to other ideas. Rather than trying to force your plans on God, try to discover his plan for you.

7:31–35 The religious leaders hated anyone who spoke the truth and exposed their own hypocrisy, and they did not bother to be consistent in their fault-finding. They criticised John the Baptist because he fasted and drank no wine; they criticised Jesus because he ate heartily and drank wine with tax collectors and "sinners". Their real objection to both men, of course, had nothing to do with

7:33 [s]Lk 1:15

32They are like children sitting in the market-place and calling out to each other:

> " 'We played the flute for you,
> and you did not dance;
> we sang a dirge,
> and you did not cry.'

7:34 [t]Lk 5:29, 30; 15:1, 2

33For John the Baptist came neither eating bread nor drinking wine,[s] and you say,
'He has a demon.' 34The Son of Man came eating and drinking, and you say, 'Here
is a glutton and a drunkard, a friend of tax collectors and "sinners".'[t] 35But wisdom
is proved right by all her children."

7:39 [u]ver 16; Mt 21:11

A Sinful Woman Anoints Jesus' Feet
(72)

36Now one of the Pharisees invited Jesus to have dinner with him, so he went to
the Pharisee's house and reclined at the table. 37When a woman who had lived a sinful
life in that town learned that Jesus was eating at the Pharisee's house, she brought
an alabaster jar of perfume, 38and as she stood behind him at his feet weeping, she
began to wet his feet with her tears. Then she wiped them with her hair, kissed them
and poured perfume on them.

7:44 [v]Ge 18:4; 19:2; 43:24; Jdg 19:21; Jn 13:4-14; 1Ti 5:10

39When the Pharisee who had invited him saw this, he said to himself, "If this man
were a prophet,[u] he would know who is touching him and what kind of woman she
is—that she is a sinner."

40Jesus answered him, "Simon, I have something to tell you."

"Tell me, teacher," he said.

7:45 [w]Lk 22:47, 48; Ro 16:16

41"Two men owed money to a certain money-lender. One owed him five hundred
denarii,[d] and the other fifty. 42Neither of them had the money to pay him back, so
he cancelled the debts of both. Now which of them will love him more?"

43Simon replied, "I suppose the one who had the bigger debt cancelled."

"You have judged correctly," Jesus said.

7:46 [x]Ps 23:5; Ecc 9:8

44Then he turned towards the woman and said to Simon, "Do you see this woman?
I came into your house. You did not give me any water for my feet,[v] but she wet
my feet with her tears and wiped them with her hair. 45You did not give me a kiss,[w]
but this woman, from the time I entered, has not stopped kissing my feet. 46You did
not put oil on my head,[x] but she has poured perfume on my feet. 47Therefore, I tell
you, her many sins have been forgiven—for she loved much. But he who has been
forgiven little loves little."

7:48 [y]Mt 9:2

48Then Jesus said to her, "Your sins are forgiven."[y]

d *41* A denarius was a coin worth about a day's wages.

---

dietary habits. What the Pharisees and experts in the law couldn't stand was being exposed for their hypocrisy.

7:33, 34 The Pharisees weren't troubled by their inconsistency towards John the Baptist and Jesus. They were good at justifying their "wisdom". Most of us can find compelling reasons to do or believe whatever suits our purposes. If we do not examine our ideas in the light of God's truth, however, we may be just as obviously self-serving as the Pharisees.

7:35 Wisdom's children were the followers of Jesus and John. These followers lived changed lives. Their righteous living demonstrated the wisdom that Jesus and John taught.

7:36 A similar incident occurred later in Jesus' ministry (see Matthew 26:6–13; Mark 14:3–9; John 12:1–11).

7:37 Alabaster jars were carved, expensive, and beautiful.

7:38 Although the woman was not an invited guest, she entered the house anyway and knelt behind Jesus at his feet. In Jesus' day, it was customary to recline while eating. Dinner guests would lie on couches with their heads near the table, propping themselves up on one elbow and stretching their feet out behind them. The woman could easily anoint Jesus' feet without approaching the table.

7:44ff Again Luke contrasts the Pharisees with sinners—and again the sinners come out on top. Simon had committed several social errors in neglecting to wash Jesus' feet (a courtesy extended to guests because sandalled feet got very dirty), anoint his head with oil, and offer him the kiss of greeting. Did Simon perhaps feel that he was too good to treat Jesus as an equal? The sinful woman, by contrast, lavished tears, expensive perfume, and kisses on her Saviour. In this story it is the grateful prostitute, and not the stingy religious leader, whose sins were forgiven. Although it is God's grace through faith that saves us, and not acts of love or generosity, this woman's act demonstrated her true faith, and Jesus honoured her faith.

7:47 Overflowing love is the natural response to forgiveness and the appropriate consequence of faith. But only those who realise the depth of their sin can appreciate the complete forgiveness God offers them. Jesus has rescued all of his followers, whether they were once extremely wicked or conventionally good, from eternal death. Do you appreciate the wideness of God's mercy? Are you grateful for his forgiveness?

49 The other guests began to say among themselves, "Who is this who even forgives
sins?"
50 Jesus said to the woman, "Your faith has saved you;[z] go in peace."[a]

7:50 [z]Mt 9:22; Mk 5:34; Lk 8:48 [a]Ac 15:33

Women Accompany Jesus and the Disciples
(73)

8 After this, Jesus travelled about from one town and village to another, proclaiming the good news of the kingdom of God.[a] The Twelve were with him, 2 and
also some women who had been cured of evil spirits and diseases: Mary (called
Magdalene)[b] from whom seven demons had come out; 3 Joanna the wife of Chuza,
the manager of Herod's[c] household; Susanna; and many others. These women were
helping to support them out of their own means.

8:1 [a]Mt 4:23
8:2 [b]Mt 27:55, 56
8:3 [c]Mt 14:1

Jesus Tells the Parable of the Four Soils
(77/Matthew 13:1–9; Mark 4:1–9)

4 While a large crowd was gathering and people were coming to Jesus from town
after town, he told this parable: 5 "A farmer went out to sow his seed. As he was
scattering the seed, some fell along the path; it was trampled on, and the birds of the
air ate it up. 6 Some fell on rock, and when it came up, the plants withered because
they had no moisture. 7 Other seed fell among thorns, which grew up with it and
choked the plants. 8 Still other seed fell on good soil. It came up and yielded a crop,
a hundred times more than was sown."
When he said this, he called out, "He who has ears to hear, let him hear."[d]

8:8 [d]Mt 11:15

Jesus Explains the Parable of the Four Soils
(78/Matthew 13:10–23; Mark 4:10–25)

9 His disciples asked him what this parable meant. 10 He said, "The knowledge of
the secrets of the kingdom of God has been given to you,[e] but to others I speak in
parables, so that,

" 'though seeing, they may not see;
though hearing, they may not understand.'[a][f]

11 "This is the meaning of the parable: The seed is the word of God.[g] 12 Those along

8:10 [e]Mt 13:11 [f]Isa 6:9; Mt 13:13, 14
8:11 [g]Heb 4:12

[a] *10* Isaiah 6:9

7:49, 50 The Pharisees believed that only God could forgive sins, so they wondered why this man Jesus was saying that the woman's sins were forgiven. They did not grasp the fact that Jesus was indeed God.

8:2, 3 Jesus lifted women up from the agony of degradation and servitude to the joy of fellowship and service. In Jewish culture, women were not supposed to learn from rabbis. By allowing these women to travel with him, Jesus was showing that all people are equal under God. These women supported Jesus' ministry with their own money. They owed a great debt to him because he had driven demons out of some and had healed others.

8:2, 3 Here we catch a glimpse of a few of the people behind the scenes in Jesus' ministry. The ministry of those in the foreground is often supported by those whose work is less visible but just as essential. Offer your resources to God, whether or not you will be on centre stage.

8:4 Jesus often communicated spiritual truth through *parables*—short stories or descriptions that take a familiar object or situation and give it a startling new twist. By linking the known with the hidden and forcing listeners to think, parables can point to spiritual truths. A parable compels listeners to discover the truth for themselves, and it conceals the truth from those too lazy or dull to understand it. In reading Jesus' parables, we must be careful not to read too much into them. Most have only one point and one meaning.

8:5 Why would a farmer allow precious seed to land on the path, on rocks, or among thorns? This is not an irresponsible farmer scattering seeds at random. He is using the acceptable method of sowing a large field—tossing it by handfuls as he walks through the field. His goal is to get as much seed as possible to take root in good soil, but there is inevitable waste as some falls or is blown into less productive areas. That some of the seed produced no crop was not the fault of the faithful farmer or of the seed. The yield depended on the condition of the soil where the seed fell. It is our responsibility to spread the seed (God's message), but we should not give up when some of our efforts fail. Remember, not every seed falls on good soil.

8:10 Why didn't the crowds understand Jesus' words? Perhaps they were looking for a military leader or a political Messiah and could not fit his gentle teaching style into their preconceived idea. Perhaps they were afraid of pressure from religious leaders and did not want to look too deeply into Jesus' words. God told Isaiah that people would hear without understanding and see without perceiving (Isaiah 6:9), and that kind of reaction confronted Jesus. The parable of the sower was an accurate picture of the people's reaction to the rest of his parables.

8:11–15 "Path" people, like many of the religious leaders, refused to believe God's message. "Rock" people, like many in the crowds who followed Jesus, believed his message but never got around to doing anything about it. "Thorn patch" people, overcome by worries and the lure of materialism, left no room in their lives for God. "Good soil" people, in contrast to all the other groups, fol-

8:13 [h]Mt 11:6 the path are the ones who hear, and then the devil comes and takes away the word
from their hearts, so that they may not believe and be saved. 13Those on the rock are
the ones who receive the word with joy when they hear it, but they have no root. They
8:14 [i]Mt 19:23; 1Ti 6:9, 10, 17 believe for a while, but in the time of testing they fall away.[h] 14The seed that fell
among thorns stands for those who hear, but as they go on their way they are choked
by life's worries, riches[i] and pleasures, and they do not mature. 15But the seed on
good soil stands for those with a noble and good heart, who hear the word, retain it,
8:16 [j]Mt 5:15; Mk 4:21; Lk 11:33 and by persevering produce a crop.

16"No-one lights a lamp and hides it in a jar or puts it under a bed. Instead, he puts
it on a stand, so that those who come in can see the light.[j] 17For there is nothing
hidden that will not be disclosed, and nothing concealed that will not be known or
brought out into the open.[k] 18Therefore consider carefully how you listen. Whoever
8:17 [k]Mt 10:26; Mk 4:22; Lk 12:2 has will be given more; whoever does not have, even what he thinks he has will be
taken from him."[l]

Jesus Describes His True Family
(76/Matthew 12:46–50; Mark 3:31–35)

8:18 [l]Mt 13:12; 25:29; Lk 19:26 19Now Jesus' mother and brothers came to see him, but they were not able to get
near him because of the crowd. 20Someone told him, "Your mother and brothers[m]
are standing outside, wanting to see you."

21He replied, "My mother and brothers are those who hear God's word and put it
8:20 [m]Jn 7:5 into practice."[n]

Jesus Calms the Storm
(87/Matthew 8:23–27; Mark 4:35–41)

8:21 [n]Lk 6:47; 11:28; Jn 14:21 22One day Jesus said to his disciples, "Let's go over to the other side of the lake."
So they got into a boat and set out. 23As they sailed, he fell asleep. A squall came

---

JESUS AND WOMEN

Jesus talks to a Samaritan woman at the well	John 4:1–26
Jesus raises a widow's son from the dead	Luke 7:11–17
A sinful woman anoints Jesus' feet	Luke 7:36–50
The adulterous woman	John 8:1–11
The group of women travels with Jesus	Luke 8:1–3
Jesus visits Mary and Martha	Luke 10:38–42
Jesus heals a crippled woman	Luke 13:10–17
Jesus heals the daughter of a Gentile woman	Mark 7:24–30
Weeping women follow Jesus on his way to the cross	Luke 23:27–31
Jesus' mother and other women gather at the cross	John 19:25–27
Jesus appears to Mary Magdalene	Mark 16:9–11
Jesus appears to other women after his resurrection	Matthew 28:8–10

As a non-Jew recording the words and works of Jesus' life, Luke demonstrates a special sensitivity to other "outsiders" with whom Jesus came into contact. For instance, Luke records five events involving women that are not mentioned in the other Gospels. In first-century Jewish culture, women were usually treated as second-class citizens with few of the rights men had. But Jesus crossed those barriers, and Luke showed the special care Jesus had for women. Jesus treated all people with equal respect. The above passages tell of his encounters with women.

---

lowed Jesus no matter what the cost. Which type of soil are you?

8:16, 17 When the light of the truth about Jesus illuminates us, it is our duty to shine that light to help others. Our witness for Christ should be public, not hidden. We should not keep the benefits for ourselves alone but pass them on to others. In order to be helpful, we need to be well placed. Seek opportunities to be there when unbelievers need help.

8:18 Applying God's word helps us grow. This is a principle of growth in physical, mental, and spiritual life. For example, a muscle, when exercised, will grow stronger, but an unused muscle will grow weak and flabby. If you are not growing stronger, you are growing weaker; it is impossible for you to stand still. How are you using what God has taught you?

8:21 Jesus' true family are those who hear *and* obey his words. Hearing without obeying is not enough. As Jesus loved his mother (see John 19:25–27), so he loves us. Christ offers us an intimate family relationship with him.

8:23 The Sea of Galilee (actually a large lake) is even today the scene of fierce storms, sometimes with waves as high as 20 feet. Jesus' disciples were not frightened without cause. Even though several of them were expert fishermen and knew how to handle a boat, their peril was real.

down on the lake, so that the boat was being swamped, and they were in great danger. 8:24 [o]Lk 5:5
24 The disciples went and woke him, saying, "Master, Master,[o] we're going to [p]Lk 4:35, 39, 41 [q]Ps 107:29;
drown!" Jnh 1:15
He got up and rebuked[p] the wind and the raging waters; the storm subsided, and
all was calm.[q] 25 "Where is your faith?" he asked his disciples.
In fear and amazement they asked one another, "Who is this? He commands even
the winds and the water, and they obey him."

Jesus Sends the Demons into a Herd of Pigs
(88/Matthew 8:28–34; Mark 5:1–20)

26 They sailed to the region of the Gerasenes,[b] which is across the lake from
Galilee. 27 When Jesus stepped ashore, he was met by a demon-possessed man from
the town. For a long time this man had not worn clothes or lived in a house, but had 8:28
lived in the tombs. 28 When he saw Jesus, he cried out and fell at his feet, shouting [r]Mt 8:29 [s]Mk 5:7
at the top of his voice, "What do you want with me,[r] Jesus, Son of the Most High
God?[s] I beg you, don't torture me!" 29 For Jesus had commanded the evil[c] spirit to
come out of the man. Many times it had seized him, and though he was chained hand
and foot and kept under guard, he had broken his chains and had been driven by the
demon into solitary places.
30 Jesus asked him, "What is your name?"
"Legion," he replied, because many demons had gone into him. 31 And they begged
him repeatedly not to order them to go into the Abyss.[t]
32 A large herd of pigs was feeding there on the hillside. The demons begged Jesus
to let them go into them, and he gave them permission. 33 When the demons came out 8:31 [t]Rev 9:1, 2, 11;
11:7; 17:8; 20:1, 3

[b] 26 Some manuscripts *Gadarenes*; other manuscripts *Gergesenes*; also in verse 37 [c] 29 Greek *unclean*

HEALING A DEMON-POSSESSED MAN
As he travelled through Galilee, Jesus told many parables and met many people, as recorded in Matthew and Mark. Later, from Capernaum, Jesus and the disciples set out in a boat, only to encounter a fierce storm. Jesus calmed the storm and, when they came ashore, exorcised a "legion" of demons.

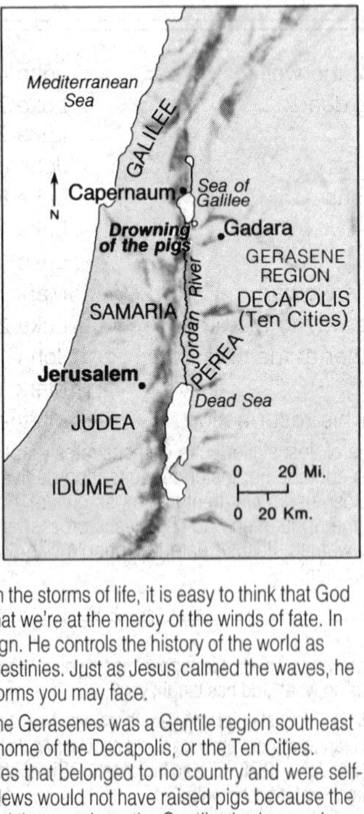

8:25 When caught in the storms of life, it is easy to think that God has lost control and that we're at the mercy of the winds of fate. In reality, God is sovereign. He controls the history of the world as well as our personal destinies. Just as Jesus calmed the waves, he can calm whatever storms you may face.

8:26 The region of the Gerasenes was a Gentile region southeast of the Sea of Galilee, home of the Decapolis, or the Ten Cities. These were Greek cities that belonged to no country and were self-governing. Although Jews would not have raised pigs because the Jewish religion labelled them unclean, the Gentiles had no such aversion.

8:27, 28 These demons recognised Jesus and his authority immediately. They knew who Jesus was and what his great power could do to them. Demons, Satan's messengers, are powerful and destructive. Still active today, they attempt to distort and destroy people's relationship with God. Demons and demon-possession are real. It is vital that believers recognise the power of Satan and his demons, but we shouldn't let curiosity lead us to get involved with demonic forces (Deuteronomy 18:10–12). Demons are powerless against those who trust in Jesus. If we resist the devil, he will leave us alone (James 4:7).

8:29–31 The demons begged Jesus to spare them from the Abyss, which is also mentioned in Revelation 9:1 and 20:1–3 as the place of confinement for Satan and his messengers. The demons, of course, knew all about this place of confinement, and they didn't want to go there.

8:30 The demon's name was Legion. A legion was the largest unit in the Roman army, having between 3,000 and 6,000 soldiers. The man was possessed by not one, but many demons.

8:33 Why didn't Jesus just destroy these demons—or send them to the Abyss? Because the time for such work had not yet come. He healed many people of the destructive effects of demon-possession, but he did not yet destroy demons. The same question could be asked today—why doesn't Jesus stop all the evil in the world? His time for that has not yet come. But it will come. The book of Revelation portrays the future victory of Jesus over Satan, his demons, and all evil.

8:33–37 The demons destroyed the pigs, which hurt the finances of those tending the pigs, but can pigs and money compare with a human life? A man had been freed from the devil's power, but the people thought only about their livestock. People have always tended to value financial gain above needy people. Throughout history, most wars have been fought to protect economic interests. Much injustice and oppression, both at home and abroad, is the direct result of some individual's or company's urge to get rich. People are continually being sacrificed to the god of money. Don't think more highly of "pigs" than of people. Think carefully about how your decisions will affect other human beings, and be willing to choose a simpler life-style if it will keep other people from being harmed.

of the man, they went into the pigs, and the herd rushed down the steep bank into
the lake[u] and was drowned.
34 When those tending the pigs saw what had happened, they ran off and reported
this in the town and countryside, 35 and the people went out to see what had happened.
When they came to Jesus, they found the man from whom the demons had gone out,
sitting at Jesus' feet,[v] dressed and in his right mind; and they were afraid. 36 Those
who had seen it told the people how the demon-possessed[w] man had been cured.
37 Then all the people of the region of the Gerasenes asked Jesus to leave them,[x]
because they were overcome with fear. So he got into the boat and left.
38 The man from whom the demons had gone out begged to go with him, but Jesus
sent him away, saying, 39 "Return home and tell how much God has done for you."
So the man went away and told all over the town how much Jesus had done for him.

Jesus Heals a Bleeding Woman and Restores a Girl to Life
(89/Matthew 9:18–26; Mark 5:21–43)

40 Now when Jesus returned, a crowd welcomed him, for they were all expecting
him. 41 Then a man named Jairus, a ruler of the synagogue,[y] came and fell at Jesus'
feet, pleading with him to come to his house 42 because his only daughter, a girl of
about twelve, was dying.
As Jesus was on his way, the crowds almost crushed him. 43 And a woman was there
who had been subject to bleeding[z] for twelve years,**d** but no-one could heal her.
44 She came up behind him and touched the edge of his cloak,[a] and immediately her
bleeding stopped.
45 "Who touched me?" Jesus asked.
When they all denied it, Peter said, "Master,[b] the people are crowding and pressing
against you."
46 But Jesus said, "Someone touched me;[c] I know that power has gone out from
me."[d]
47 Then the woman, seeing that she could not go unnoticed, came trembling and fell
at his feet. In the presence of all the people, she told why she had touched him and
how she had been instantly healed. 48 Then he said to her, "Daughter, your faith has
healed you.[e] Go in peace."[f]
49 While Jesus was still speaking, someone came from the house of Jairus, the
synagogue ruler.[g] "Your daughter is dead," he said. "Don't bother the teacher any
more."
50 Hearing this, Jesus said to Jairus, "Don't be afraid; just believe, and she will be
healed."

8:33 [u]ver 22, 23
8:35 [v]Lk 10:39
8:36 [w]Mt 4:24
8:37 [x]Ac 16:39
8:41 [y]ver 49; Mk 5:22
8:43 [z]Lev 15:25-30
8:44 [a]Mt 9:20
8:45 [b]Lk 5:5
8:46 [c]Mt 14:36; Mk 3:10 [d]Lk 5:17; 6:19
8:48 [e]Mt 9:22 [f]Ac 15:33
8:49 [g]ver 41

d *43* Many manuscripts *years, and she had spent all she had on doctors*

8:38, 39 Often Jesus asked those he healed to be quiet about the healing, but he urged this man to return to his family and tell them what God had done for him. Why? (1) Jesus knew the man would be an effective witness to those who knew his previous condition and could attest to the miraculous healing. (2) Jesus wanted to expand his ministry by introducing his message into this Gentile area. (3) Jesus knew that the Gentiles, since they were not expecting a Messiah, would not divert his ministry by trying to crown him king. When God touches your life, don't be afraid to share the wonderful events with your family and friends.

8:41 The synagogue was the local centre of worship. The synagogue ruler was responsible for administration, building maintenance, and worship supervision. It would have been quite unusual for a respected synagogue ruler to fall at the feet of an itinerant preacher and beg him to heal his daughter. Jesus honoured this man's humble faith (8:50, 54–56).

8:43–48 Many people surrounded Jesus as he made his way towards Jairus' house. It was virtually impossible to get through the multitude, but one woman fought her way desperately through the crowd in order to touch Jesus. As soon as she did so, she was healed. What a difference there is between the crowds that are curious about Jesus and the few who reach out and touch him! Today, many people are vaguely familiar with Jesus, but nothing in their lives is changed or bettered by this passing acquaintance. It is only faith that releases God's healing power. Are you just curious about God, or do you reach out to him in faith, knowing that his mercy will bring healing to your body, soul, and spirit?

8:45 It isn't that Jesus didn't know who had touched him; it's that he wanted the woman to step forward and identify herself. Jesus wanted to teach her that his cloak did not contain magical properties, but that her faith in him had healed her. He may also have wanted to teach the crowds a lesson. According to Jewish law, a man who touched a menstruating woman became ceremonially unclean (Leviticus 15:19–28). This was true whether her bleeding was normal or, as in this woman's case, the result of illness. To protect themselves from such defilement, Jewish men carefully avoided touching, speaking to, or even looking at women. By contrast, Jesus proclaimed to hundreds of people that this "unclean" woman had touched him—and then he healed her. In Jesus' mind, this suffering woman was not to be overlooked. As God's creation, she deserved attention and respect.

51When he arrived at the house of Jairus, he did not let anyone go in with him except
Peter, John and James,[h] and the child's father and mother. 52Meanwhile, all the
people were wailing and mourning[i] for her. "Stop wailing," Jesus said. "She is not
dead but asleep."[j]
53They laughed at him, knowing that she was dead. 54But he took her by the hand
and said, "My child, get up!"[k] 55Her spirit returned, and at once she stood up. Then
Jesus told them to give her something to eat. 56Her parents were astonished, but he
ordered them not to tell anyone what had happened.[l]

8:51 [h]Mt 4:21
8:52 [i]Lk 23:27 [j]Mt 9:24; Jn 11:11, 13
8:54 [k]Lk 7:14
8:56 [l]Mt 8:4

Jesus Sends Out the Twelve Disciples
(93/Matthew 10:1–16; Mark 6:7–13)

9 When Jesus had called the Twelve together, he gave them power and authority
to drive out all demons[a] and to cure diseases,[b] 2and he sent them out to preach
the kingdom of God[c] and to heal the sick. 3He told them: "Take nothing for the
journey—no staff, no bag, no bread, no money, no extra tunic.[d] 4Whatever house
you enter, stay there until you leave that town. 5If people do not welcome you, shake
the dust off your feet when you leave their town, as a testimony against them."[e] 6So
they set out and went from village to village, preaching the gospel and healing people
everywhere.

9:1 [a]Mt 10:1 [b]Mt 4:23; Lk 5:17
9:2 [c]Mt 3:2
9:3 [d]Lk 10:4; 22:35
9:5 [e]Mt 10:14

Herod Kills John the Baptist
(95/Matthew 14:1–12; Mark 6:14–29)

7Now Herod[f] the tetrarch heard about all that was going on. And he was perplexed,
because some were saying that John[g] had been raised from the dead,[h] 8others that
Elijah had appeared,[i] and still others that one of the prophets of long ago had come
back to life.[j] 9But Herod said, "I beheaded John. Who, then, is this I hear such things
about?" And he tried to see him.[k]

9:7 [f]Mt 14:1 [g]Mt 3:1 [h]ver 19
9:8 [i]Mt 11:14 [j]ver 19; Jn 1:21
9:9 [k]Lk 23:8

8:56 Jesus told the parents not to talk about their daughter's healing because he knew the facts would speak for themselves. Besides, Jesus was concerned for his ministry. He did not want to be known as just a miracle worker; he wanted people to listen to his words that would heal their broken spiritual lives.

9:1–10 Note Jesus' methods of leadership. He empowered his disciples (9:1), gave them specific instructions so they knew what to do (9:3, 4), told them how to deal with tough times (9:5), and held them accountable (9:10). As you lead others, study the Master Leader's pattern. Which of these elements do you need to incorporate into your leadership?

9:2 Jesus announced his kingdom by both preaching and healing. If he had limited himself to preaching, people might have seen his kingdom as spiritual only. On the other hand, if he had healed without preaching, people might not have realised the spiritual importance of his mission. Most of his listeners expected a Messiah who would bring wealth and power to their nation; they preferred material benefits to spiritual discernment. The truth about Jesus is that he is both God and man, both spiritual and physical; and the salvation that he offers is both for the soul and the body. Any group or teaching that emphasises soul at the expense of body, or body at the expense of soul, is in danger of distorting Jesus' Good News.

9:3, 4 Why were the disciples instructed to depend on others while they went from town to town preaching the gospel? Their purpose was to blanket Judea with Jesus' message, and by travelling light they could move quickly. Their dependence on others had other good effects as well: (1) it clearly showed that the Messiah had not come to offer wealth to his followers; (2) it forced the disciples to rely on God's power and not on their own provision; (3) it involved the villagers and made them more eager to hear the message. This was an excellent approach for the disciples' short-term mission; it was not intended, however, to be a permanent way of life for them.

9:4 The disciples were told to stay in only one home in each town because they were not to offend their hosts by moving to a home that was more comfortable or socially prominent. To remain in one home was not a burden for the host, because the disciples' stay in each community was short.

9:5 Shaking the dust of unaccepting towns from their feet had deep cultural implications. Pious Jews would do this after passing through Gentile cities to show their separation from Gentile practices. If the disciples shook the dust of a *Jewish* town from their feet, it would show their separation from Jews who rejected their Messiah. This action also showed that the disciples were not responsible for how the people responded to their message. Neither are we responsible if we have carefully and truthfully presented Christ, but our message is rejected. Like the disciples, we must move on to others whom God desires to reach.

9:7 For more information on Herod, also known as Herod Antipas, see his Profile in Mark 6.

9:7, 8 It was so difficult for the people to accept Jesus as the Son of God that they tried to come up with other solutions—most of which sound quite unbelievable to us. Many thought that he must be someone who had come back to life, perhaps John the Baptist or another prophet. Some suggested that he was Elijah, the great prophet who did not die but was taken to heaven in a chariot of fire (2 Kings 2:1–11). Very few found the correct answer, as Peter did (9:20). For many people today, it is still not easy to accept Jesus as the fully human yet fully divine Son of God. People are still trying to find alternative explanations—a great prophet, a radical political leader, a self-deceived rabble-rouser. None of these explanations can account for Jesus' miracles or, especially, his glorious resurrection—so these realities too have to be explained away. In the end, the attempts to explain away Jesus are far more difficult to believe than the truth.

9:9 For the story of how Herod had John beheaded, see Mark 6:14–29.

Jesus Feeds Five Thousand
(96/Matthew 14:13–21; Mark 6:30–44; John 6:1–15)

10When the apostles[l] returned, they reported to Jesus what they had done. Then he took them with him and they withdrew by themselves to a town called Bethsaida,[m] 11but the crowds learned about it and followed him. He welcomed them and spoke to them about the kingdom of God,[n] and healed those who needed healing.

12Late in the afternoon the Twelve came to him and said, "Send the crowd away so they can go to the surrounding villages and countryside and find food and lodging, because we are in a remote place here."

13He replied, "You give them something to eat."

They answered, "We have only five loaves of bread and two fish—unless we go and buy food for all this crowd." 14(About five thousand men were there.)

But he said to his disciples, "Make them sit down in groups of about fifty each." 15The disciples did so, and everybody sat down. 16Taking the five loaves and the two fish and looking up to heaven, he gave thanks and broke them.[o] Then he gave them to the disciples to set before the people. 17They all ate and were satisfied, and the disciples picked up twelve basketfuls of broken pieces that were left over.

Peter Says Jesus Is the Messiah
(109/Matthew 16:13–20; Mark 8:27–30)

18Once when Jesus was praying[p] in private and his disciples were with him, he asked them, "Who do the crowds say I am?"

19They replied, "Some say John the Baptist;[q] others say Elijah; and still others, that one of the prophets of long ago has come back to life."[r]

20"But what about you?" he asked. "Who do you say I am?"

Peter answered, "The Christ[a] of God."[s]

Jesus Predicts His Death the First Time
(110/Matthew 16:21–28; Mark 8:31–9:1)

21Jesus strictly warned them not to tell this to anyone.[t] 22And he said, "The Son of Man[u] must suffer many things[v] and be rejected by the elders, chief priests and teachers of the law,[w] and he must be killed[x] and on the third day[y] be raised to life."[z]

[a] *20 Or Messiah*

9:10 [l] Mk 6:30 [m] Mt 11:21
9:11 [n] ver 2; Mt 3:2
9:16 [o] Mt 14:19
9:18 [p] Lk 3:21
9:19 [q] Mt 3:1 [r] ver 7, 8
9:20 [s] Jn 1:49; 6:66-69; 11:27
9:21 [t] Mt 16:20; Mk 8:30
9:22 [u] Mt 8:20 [v] Mt 16:21 [w] Mt 27:1, 2 [x] Ac 2:23; 3:13 [y] Mt 16:21 [z] Mt 16:21

9:10, 11 Jesus had tried to slip quietly away from the crowds, but they found out where he was going and followed him. Instead of showing impatience at this interruption, Jesus welcomed the people and ministered to their needs. How do you see people who interrupt your schedule—as nuisances, or as the reason for your life and ministry?

9:11 The kingdom of God was a focal point of Jesus' teaching. He explained that it was not just a future kingdom; it was among them, embodied in him, the Messiah. Even though the kingdom will not be complete until Jesus comes again in glory, we do not have to wait to taste it. The kingdom of God begins in the hearts of those who believe in Jesus (17:21). It is as present with us today as it was with the Judeans almost 2,000 years ago.

9:13, 14 When the disciples expressed concern about where the crowd of thousands would eat, Jesus offered a surprising solution—"You give them something to eat." The disciples protested, focusing their attention on what they didn't have (food and money). Do you think God would ask you to do something that you and he together couldn't handle? Don't let your lack of resources blind you to seeing God's power.

9:16, 17 Why did Jesus bother to feed these people? He could just as easily have sent them on their way. But Jesus does not ignore needs. He is concerned with every aspect of our lives—the physical as well as the spiritual. As we work to bring wholeness to people's lives, we must never ignore the fact that all of us have both physical and spiritual needs. It is impossible to minister effectively to one type of need without considering the other.

9:18–20 The Christian faith goes beyond knowing what others believe. It requires us to hold beliefs for ourselves. When Jesus asks, "Who do you say I am?" he wants us to take a stand. Who do *you* say Jesus is?

9:21 Jesus told his disciples not to tell anyone that he was the Christ because at this point they didn't fully understand the significance of that confession—nor would anyone else. Everyone still expected the Messiah to come as a conquering king. But even though Jesus was the Messiah, he still had to suffer, be rejected by the leaders, be killed, and rise from the dead. When the disciples saw all this happen to Jesus, they would understand what the Messiah had come to do. Only then would they be equipped to share the gospel around the world.

9:22 This was the turning point in Jesus' instruction to his disciples. From then on he began teaching clearly and specifically what they could expect, so that they would not be surprised when it happened. He explained that he would not *now* be the conquering Messiah because he first had to suffer, die, and rise again. But one day he would return in great glory to set up his eternal kingdom.

23Then he said to them all: "If anyone would come after me, he must deny himself
and take up his cross daily and follow me.[a] 24For whoever wants to save his life will
lose it, but whoever loses his life for me will save it.[b] 25What good is it for a man
to gain the whole world, and yet lose or forfeit his very self? 26If anyone is ashamed
of me and my words, the Son of Man will be ashamed of him[c] when he comes in
his glory and in the glory of the Father and of the holy angels.[d] 27I tell you the truth,
some who are standing here will not taste death before they see the kingdom of God."

Jesus Is Transfigured on the Mountain
(111/Matthew 17:1–13; Mark 9:2–13)

28About eight days after Jesus said this, he took Peter, John and James[e] with him
and went up onto a mountain to pray.[f] 29As he was praying, the appearance of his
face changed, and his clothes became as bright as a flash of lightning. 30Two men,
Moses and Elijah, 31appeared in glorious splendour, talking with Jesus. They spoke
about his departure,[g] which he was about to bring to fulfilment at Jerusalem. 32Peter
and his companions were very sleepy,[h] but when they became fully awake, they saw
his glory and the two men standing with him. 33As the men were leaving Jesus, Peter
said to him, "Master,[i] it is good for us to be here. Let us put up three shelters – one
for you, one for Moses and one for Elijah." (He did not know what he was saying.)
34While he was speaking, a cloud appeared and enveloped them, and they were
afraid as they entered the cloud. 35A voice came from the cloud, saying, "This is my
Son, whom I have chosen;[j] listen to him."[k] 36When the voice had spoken, they

9:23 [a]Mt 10:38; Lk 14:27
9:24 [b]Jn 12:25
9:26 [c]Mt 10:33; Lk 12:9; 2Ti 2:12 [d]Mt 16:27
9:28 [e]Mt 4:21 [f]Lk 3:21
9:31 [g]2Pe 1:15
9:32 [h]Mt 26:43
9:33 [i]Lk 5:5
9:35 [j]Isa 42:1 [k]Mt 3:17

9:23 Christians follow their Lord by imitating his life and obeying his commands. To take up the cross meant to carry your own cross to the place where you would be killed. Many Galileans had been killed that way by the Romans. Applied to the disciples, it meant to identify completely with Christ's message, even if it meant death. We must deny our selfish desires to use our time and money our own way and to choose our own direction in life without regard to Christ. Following Christ is costly now, but in the long run, it is well worth the pain and effort.

9:23–26 People are willing to pay a high price for something they value. Is it any surprise that Jesus would demand this much commitment from his followers? There are at least three conditions that must be met by people who want to follow Jesus. We must be willing to deny self, to take up our crosses, and to follow him. Anything less is superficial lip service.

9:24, 25 If this present life is most important to you, you will do everything you can to protect it. You will not want to do anything that might endanger your safety, health, or comfort. By contrast, if following Jesus is most important, you may find yourself in unsafe, unhealthy, and uncomfortable places. You will risk death, but you will not fear it because you know that Jesus will raise you to eternal life. Nothing material can compensate for the loss of eternal life. Jesus' disciples are not to use their lives on earth for their own pleasure – they should spend their lives serving God and people.

9:26 Luke's Greek audience would have found it difficult to understand a God who could die, just as Jesus' Jewish audience would have been perplexed by a Messiah who would let himself be captured. Both would be ashamed of Jesus if they did not look past his death to his glorious resurrection and second coming. Then they would see Jesus not as a loser but as the Lord of the universe, who through his death brought salvation to all people.

9:27 When Jesus said some would not die without seeing the kingdom, he was referring (1) to Peter, James, and John, who would witness the transfiguration eight days later, or in a broader sense (2) to all who would witness the resurrection and ascension, or (3) to all who would take part in the spread of the church after Pentecost. Jesus' listeners were not going to have to wait for another, future Messiah – the kingdom was among them, and it would soon come in power.

9:29, 30 Jesus took Peter, James, and John to the top of a mountain to show them who he really was – not just a great prophet, but God's own Son. Moses, representing the law, and Elijah, representing the prophets, appeared with Jesus. Then God's voice singled out Jesus as the long-awaited Messiah who possessed divine authority. Jesus would fulfil both the Law and the Prophets (Matthew 5:17).

9:33 When Peter suggested making three shelters, he may have been thinking of the Feast of Tabernacles, where shelters were set up to commemorate the exodus, God's deliverance from slavery in Egypt. Peter wanted to keep Moses and Elijah with them. But this was not what God wanted. Peter's desire to build shelters for Jesus, Moses, and Elijah may also show his understanding that real faith is built on three cornerstones: the law, the prophets, and Jesus. But Peter grew in his understanding, and eventually he would write of Jesus as the "chosen and precious cornerstone" of the church (1 Peter 2:6).

9:33 Peter, James, and John experienced a wonderful moment on the mountain, and they didn't want to leave. Sometimes we too have such an inspiring experience that we want to stay where we are – away from the reality and problems of our daily lives. Knowing that struggles await us in the valley encourages us to linger on the mountaintop. Yet staying on top of a mountain prohibits our ministering to others. Instead of becoming spiritual giants, we would soon become dwarfed by our self-centredness. We need times of retreat and renewal, but only so we can return to minister to the world. Our faith must make sense off the mountain as well as on it.

9:35 As God's Son, Jesus has God's power and authority; thus his words should be our final authority. If a person's teaching is true, it will agree with Jesus' teachings. Test everything you hear against Jesus' words, and you will not be led astray. Don't be hasty to seek advice and guidance from merely human sources and thereby neglect Christ's message.

9:35 God clearly identified Jesus as his Son before saying that Peter and the others were to listen to Jesus and not to their own ideas and desires. The ability to follow Jesus comes from confidence about who he is. If we believe he is God's Son, then we will surely want to do what he says.

9:36 [l]Mt 17:9
9:41 [m]Dt 32:5
9:44 [n]ver 22
9:45 [o]Mk 9:32
9:46 [p]Lk 22:24
9:47 [q]Mt 9:4
9:48 [r]Mt 10:40 [s]Mk 9:35
9:49 [t]Lk 5:5
9:50 [u]Mt 12:30; Lk 11:23

found that Jesus was alone. The disciples kept this to themselves, and told no-one at
that time what they had seen.[l]

Jesus Heals a Demon-Possessed Boy
(112/Matthew 17:14–21; Mark 9:14–29)

37 The next day, when they came down from the mountain, a large crowd met him.
38 A man in the crowd called out, "Teacher, I beg you to look at my son, for he is
my only child. 39 A spirit seizes him and he suddenly screams; it throws him into
convulsions so that he foams at the mouth. It scarcely ever leaves him and is destroying
him. 40 I begged your disciples to drive it out, but they could not."
41 "O unbelieving and perverse generation,"[m] Jesus replied, "how long shall I stay
with you and put up with you? Bring your son here."
42 Even while the boy was coming, the demon threw him to the ground in a
convulsion. But Jesus rebuked the evil[b] spirit, healed the boy and gave him back to
his father. 43 And they were all amazed at the greatness of God.

Jesus Predicts His Death the Second Time
(113/Matthew 17:22, 23; Mark 9:30–32)

While everyone was marvelling at all that Jesus did, he said to his disciples,
44 "Listen carefully to what I am about to tell you: The Son of Man is going to be
betrayed into the hands of men."[n] 45 But they did not understand what this meant.
It was hidden from them, so that they did not grasp it,[o] and they were afraid to ask
him about it.

The Disciples Argue about Who Would Be the Greatest
(115/Matthew 18:1–6; Mark 9:33–37)

46 An argument started among the disciples as to which of them would be the
greatest.[p] 47 Jesus, knowing their thoughts,[q] took a little child and made him stand
beside him. 48 Then he said to them, "Whoever welcomes this little child in my name
welcomes me; and whoever welcomes me welcomes the one who sent me.[r] For he
who is least among you all—he is the greatest."[s]

The Disciples Forbid Another to Use Jesus' Name
(116/Mark 9:38–41)

49 "Master,"[t] said John, "we saw a man driving out demons in your name and we
tried to stop him, because he is not one of us."
50 "Do not stop him," Jesus said, "for whoever is not against you is for you."[u]

[b] *42* Greek *unclean*

9:37–39 As the disciples came down from the mountain with Jesus, they passed from a reassuring experience of God's presence to a frightening experience of evil. The beauty they had just seen must have made the ugliness seem even uglier. As our spiritual vision improves and allows us to see and understand God better, we will also be able to see and understand evil better. We would be overcome by its horror if we did not have Jesus with us to take us through it safely.

9:40 Why couldn't the disciples drive out the evil spirit? For a possible answer, see the note on Mark 9:18.

9:45, 46 The disciples didn't understand Jesus' words about his death. They still thought of Jesus as only an earthly king, and they were concerned about their places in the kingdom he would set up. So they ignored Jesus' words about his death and began arguing about who would be the greatest.

9:48 Our care for others is a measure of our greatness. How much concern do you show to others? This is a vital question that can accurately measure your greatness in God's eyes. How have you expressed your care for others lately, especially the helpless, the needy, the poor—those who can't return your love and concern? Your honest answer to that question will give you a good idea of your real greatness.

9:49, 50 The disciples were jealous. Nine of them together were unable to drive out a single evil spirit (9:40), but when they saw a man who was not one of their group driving out demons, they told him to stop. Our pride is hurt when someone else succeeds where we have failed, but Jesus says there is no room for such jealousy in the spiritual warfare of his kingdom. Share Jesus' open-arms attitude to Christian workers outside your group.

2. Jesus' ministry on the way to Jerusalem

Jesus Teaches about the Cost of Following Him
(122/Matthew 8:18–22)

51 As the time approached for him to be taken up to heaven,[v] Jesus resolutely set
out for Jerusalem.[w] 52 And he sent messengers on ahead, who went into a Samaritan[x]
village to get things ready for him; 53 but the people there did not welcome him,
because he was heading for Jerusalem. 54 When the disciples James and John[y] saw
this, they asked, "Lord, do you want us to call fire down from heaven to destroy
them?"[c][z] 55 But Jesus turned and rebuked them, 56 and[d] they went to another village.
57 As they were walking along the road,[a] a man said to him, "I will follow you
wherever you go."
58 Jesus replied, "Foxes have holes and birds of the air have nests, but the Son of
Man[b] has nowhere to lay his head."
59 He said to another man, "Follow me."[c]
But the man replied, "Lord, first let me go and bury my father."
60 Jesus said to him, "Let the dead bury their own dead, but you go and proclaim
the kingdom of God."[d]
61 Still another said, "I will follow you, Lord; but first let me go back and say
good-bye to my family."[e]
62 Jesus replied, "No-one who puts his hand to the plough and looks back is fit for
service in the kingdom of God."

Jesus Sends Out Seventy-two Messengers
(130)

10 After this the Lord[a] appointed seventy-two[a] others[b] and sent them two by
two[c] ahead of him to every town and place where he was about to go.[d] 2 He
told them, "The harvest is plentiful, but the workers are few. Ask the Lord of the
harvest, therefore, to send out workers into his harvest field.[e] 3 Go! I am sending you

9:51 [v]Mk 16:19 [w]Lk 13:22; 17:11; 18:31; 19:28
9:52 [x]Mt 10:5
9:54 [y]Mt 4:21 [z]2Ki 1:10, 12
9:57 [a]ver 51
9:58 [b]Mt 8:20
9:59 [c]Mt 4:19
9:60 [d]Mt 3:2
9:61 [e]1Ki 19:20
10:1 [a]Lk 7:13 [b]Lk 9:1, 2, 51, 52 [c]Mk 6:7 [d]Mt 10:1
10:2 [e]Mt 9:37, 38; Jn 4:35

c *54* Some manuscripts *them, even as Elijah did* **d** *55,56* Some manuscripts *them. And he said, "You do not know what kind of spirit you are of, for the Son of Man did not come to destroy men's lives, but to save them."* 56 *And* **a** *1* Some manuscripts *seventy*; also in verse 17

9:51 Although Jesus knew he would face persecution and death in Jerusalem, he was determined to go there. That kind of resolve should characterise our lives too. When God gives us a course of action, we must move steadily towards our destination, no matter what potential hazards await us there.

9:53 After Assyria invaded Israel, the northern kingdom, and resettled it with its own people (2 Kings 17:24–41), the mixed race that developed became known as the Samaritans. "Purebred" Jews hated these "half-breeds", and the Samaritans in turn hated the Jews. So many tensions arose between the two peoples that Jewish travellers between Galilee and southern Judea often walked around rather than through Samaritan territory, even though this lengthened their trip considerably. Jesus held no such prejudices, and he sent messengers ahead to get things ready in a Samaritan village. But the village refused to welcome these Jewish travellers.

9:54 When James and John were rejected by the Samaritan village, they didn't want to stop at shaking the dust from their feet (9:5). They wanted to retaliate by calling down fire from heaven on the people, as Elijah did on the servants of a wicked king of Israel (2 Kings 1). When others reject or scorn us, we too may feel like retaliating. We must remember that judgment belongs to God, and we must not expect him to use his power to carry out our personal vendettas.

9:59 Luke does not tell us whether the father is already dead or whether he's terminally ill. It seems likely that if the father were dead, the son would have been fulfilling the burial duties. Jesus was proclaiming that true discipleship requires instant action. Jesus did not teach people to forsake responsibilities to family, but he often gave commands to people in light of their real motives. Perhaps this man wanted to delay following Christ and used his father as an excuse. There is a cost to following Jesus, and each of us must be ready to serve, even when it requires sacrifice.

9:62 What does Jesus want from us? Total dedication, not half-hearted commitment. We can't pick and choose among Jesus' ideas and follow him selectively; we have to accept the cross along with the crown, judgment as well as mercy. We must count the cost and be willing to abandon everything else that has given us security. With our focus on Jesus, we should allow nothing to distract us from the manner of living that he calls good and true.

10:1, 2 Far more than 12 people had been following Jesus. Here Jesus designated a group of 72 to prepare a number of towns for Jesus' later visit. These disciples were not unique in their qualifications. They were not better educated, more capable, or of higher status than other followers of Jesus. What equipped them for this mission was their awareness of Jesus' power and their vision to reach all the people. It is important to dedicate our skills to God's kingdom, but we must also be equipped with his power and have a clear vision of what he wants us to do.

10:2 Jesus was sending 36 teams of two to reach the multitudes. These teams were not to try to do the job without help; rather, they were to ask God for more workers. Some people, as soon as they understand the gospel, want to go to work immediately contacting unsaved people. This story suggests a different approach: begin by mobilising people to pray. And before praying for unsaved people, pray that other concerned disciples will join you in reaching out to them.

10:2 In Christian service, there is no unemployment. God has work enough for everyone. Don't just sit back and watch others work—look for ways to help with the harvest.

10:3 [f]Mt 10:16

out like lambs among wolves.[f] 4Do not take a purse or bag or sandals; and do not
greet anyone on the road.
5"When you enter a house, first say, 'Peace to this house.' 6If a man of peace is
there, your peace will rest on him; if not, it will return to you. 7Stay in that house,
eating and drinking whatever they give you, for the worker deserves his wages.[g] Do
not move around from house to house.

10:7 [g]Mt 10:10; 1Co 9:14; 1Ti 5:18

JAMES

Jesus singled out three of his 12 disciples for special training. James, his brother John, and Peter made up this inner circle. Each eventually played a key role in the early church. Peter became a great speaker, John became a major writer, and James was the first of the 12 disciples to die for the faith.

The fact that his name is always mentioned before John's indicates that James was the older brother. Zebedee, their father, owned a fishing business where they worked along with Peter and Andrew. When Peter, Andrew, and John left Galilee to see John the Baptist, James stayed back with the boats and fishing nets. Later, when Jesus called them, James was as eager as his partners to follow.

James enjoyed being in the inner circle of Jesus' disciples, but he misunderstood Jesus' purpose. He and his brother even tried to secure their role in Jesus' kingdom by asking Jesus to promise them each a special position. Like the other disciples, James had a limited view of what Jesus was doing on earth, picturing only an earthly kingdom that would overthrow Rome and restore Israel's former glory. But above all, James wanted to be with Jesus. He had found the right leader, even though he was still on the wrong timetable. It took Jesus' death and resurrection to correct his view.

James was the first of the 12 disciples to die for the gospel. He was willing to die because he knew Jesus had conquered death, the doorway to eternal life. Our expectations about life will be limited if this life is all we can see. Jesus promised eternal life to those willing to trust him. If we believe this promise, he will give us the courage to stand for him even during dangerous times.

Strengths and accomplishments:

- One of the 12 disciples
- One of a special inner circle of three with Peter and John
- First of the 12 disciples to be killed for his faith

Weaknesses and mistakes:

- Two outbursts from James indicate struggles with temper (Luke 9:54) and selfishness (Mark 10:37). Both times, he and his brother, John, spoke as one

Lesson from his life:

- Loss of life is not too heavy a price to pay for following Jesus

Vital statistics:

- Where: Galilee
- Occupations: Fisherman, disciple
- Relatives: Father: Zebedee. Mother: Salome. Brother: John
- Contemporaries: Jesus, Pilate, Herod Agrippa

Key verses:

"Then James and John, the sons of Zebedee, came to him. 'Teacher,' they said, 'we want you to do for us whatever we ask.' 'What do you want me to do for you?' he asked. They replied, 'Let one of us sit at your right and the other at your left in your glory' " (Mark 10:35–37).

James' story is told in the Gospels. He is also mentioned in Acts 1:13 and 12:2.

10:3 Jesus said he was sending his disciples out "like lambs among wolves". They would have to be careful because they would surely meet with opposition. We too are sent into the world like lambs among wolves. Be alert, and remember to face your enemies not with aggression but with love and gentleness. A dangerous mission requires sincere commitment.

10:7 Jesus' direction to stay in one house avoided certain problems. Shifting from house to house could offend the families who first took them in. Some families might begin to compete for the disciples' presence, and some might think they weren't good enough to hear their message. If the disciples appeared not to appreciate the hospitality offered them, the town might not accept Jesus when he followed them there. In addition, by staying in one place, the disciples did not have to worry continually about finding good accommodation. They could settle down and do their appointed task.

10:7 Jesus told his disciples to accept hospitality graciously because their work entitled them to it. Ministers of the gospel deserve to be supported, and it is our responsibility to make sure they have what they need. There are several ways to encourage those who serve God in his church. First, see that they have an adequate salary. Second, see that they are supported emotionally; plan a time to express appreciation for something they have done. Third, lift their spirits with special surprises from time to time. Our ministers deserve to know we are giving to them cheerfully and generously.

8"When you enter a town and are welcomed, eat what is set before you.[h] 9Heal
the sick who are there and tell them, 'The kingdom of God[i] is near you.' 10But when
you enter a town and are not welcomed, go into its streets and say, 11'Even the dust
of your town that sticks to our feet we wipe off against you.[j] Yet be sure of this:
The kingdom of God is near.'[k] 12I tell you, it will be more bearable on that day for
Sodom[l] than for that town.[m]
13"Woe to you,[n] Korazin! Woe to you, Bethsaida! For if the miracles that were
performed in you had been performed in Tyre and Sidon, they would have repented
long ago, sitting in sackcloth[o] and ashes. 14But it will be more bearable for Tyre and
Sidon at the judgment than for you. 15And you, Capernaum,[p] will you be lifted up
to the skies? No, you will go down to the depths.[b]
16"He who listens to you listens to me; he who rejects you rejects me; but he who
rejects me rejects him who sent me."[q]

The Seventy-two Messengers Return
(131)

17The seventy-two[r] returned with joy and said, "Lord, even the demons submit
to us in your name."[s]
18He replied, "I saw Satan[t] fall like lightning from heaven.[u] 19I have given you
authority to trample on snakes[v] and scorpions and to overcome all the power of the
enemy; nothing will harm you. 20However, do not rejoice that the spirits submit to
you, but rejoice that your names are written in heaven."[w]
21At that time Jesus, full of joy through the Holy Spirit, said, "I praise you, Father,
Lord of heaven and earth, because you have hidden these things from the wise and
learned, and revealed them to little children.[x] Yes, Father, for this was your good
pleasure.
22"All things have been committed to me by my Father.[y] No-one knows who the
Son is except the Father, and no-one knows who the Father is except the Son and those
to whom the Son chooses to reveal him."[z]
23Then he turned to his disciples and said privately, "Blessed are the eyes that see

[b] 15 Greek *Hades*

10:8 [h] 1Co 10:27
10:9 [i] Mt 3:2; 10:7
10:11 [j] Mt 10:14; Mk 6:11 [k] ver 9
10:12 [l] Mt 10:15 [m] Mt 11:24
10:13 [n] Lk 6:24-26 [o] Rev 11:3
10:15 [p] Mt 4:13
10:16 [q] Mt 10:40; Jn 13:20
10:17 [r] ver 1 [s] Mk 16:17
10:18 [t] Mt 4:10 [u] Isa 14:12; Rev 9:1; 12:8, 9
10:19 [v] Mk 16:18; Ac 28:3-5
10:20 [w] Ex 32:32; Ps 69:28; Da 12:1; Php 4:3; Heb 12:23; Rev 13:8; 20:12; 21:27
10:21 [x] 1Co 1:26-29
10:22 [y] Mt 28:18 [z] Jn 1:18

10:8, 9 Jesus gave two rules for the disciples to follow as they travelled. They were to eat what was set before them—that is, they were to accept hospitality without being choosy—and they were to heal the sick. Because of the healings, people would be willing to listen to the gospel.

10:12 Sodom was an evil city that God destroyed because of its great sinfulness (Genesis 19). The city's name is often used to symbolise wickedness and immorality. Sodom will suffer at judgment day, but cities who saw the Messiah and rejected him will suffer even more.

10:13 Korazin was a city near the Sea of Galilee, probably about two miles north of Capernaum. Tyre and Sidon were cities destroyed by God as punishment for their wickedness (see Ezekiel 26–28).

10:15 Capernaum was Jesus' base for his Galilean ministry. The city was located at an important crossroads used by traders and the Roman army, so a message proclaimed in Capernaum was likely to go far. But many people of Capernaum did not understand Jesus' miracles or believe his teaching, and the city was included among those who would be judged for rejecting him.

10:17–20 The disciples had seen tremendous results as they ministered in Jesus' name and with his authority. They were elated by the victories they had witnessed, and Jesus shared their enthusiasm. He helped them get their priorities right, however, by reminding them of their most important victory—that their names were written in heaven. This honour was more important than any of their accomplishments. As we see God's wonders at work in and through us, we should not lose sight of the greatest wonder of all—our heavenly citizenship.

10:18, 19 Jesus may have been looking ahead to his victory over Satan at the cross. John 12:31, 32 indicates that Satan would be judged and driven out at the time of Jesus' death. On the other hand, Jesus may have been warning his disciples against pride. Perhaps he was referring to Isaiah 14:12–17, which begins, "How you have fallen from heaven, O morning star, son of the dawn!" Some interpreters identify this verse with Satan and explain that Satan's pride led to all the evil we see on earth today. To Jesus' disciples, who were thrilled with their power over evil spirits ("snakes and scorpions"), he may have been giving this stern warning: "Yours is the kind of pride that led to Satan's downfall. Be careful!"

10:21 Jesus thanked God that spiritual truth was for everyone, and not just for the elite. Many of life's rewards seem to go to the intelligent, the rich, the good-looking, or the powerful, but the kingdom of God is equally available to all, regardless of position or abilities. We come to Jesus not through strength or brains, but through childlike trust. Jesus is not opposed to engaging in scholarly pursuits; he is opposed to spiritual pride (being wise in one's own eyes). Join Jesus in thanking God that we all have equal access to him. Trust in God's grace, not in your personal qualifications, for your citizenship in the kingdom.

10:22 Christ's mission was to reveal God the Father to people. His words brought difficult ideas down to earth. He explained God's love through parables, teachings, and, most of all, his life. By examining Jesus' actions, principles, and attitudes, we can understand God more clearly.

10:23, 24 The disciples had a fantastic opportunity—they were eyewitnesses of Christ, the Son of God. But for many months they took Jesus for granted, not really listening to him or obeying him.

what you see. 24For I tell you that many prophets and kings wanted to see what you
see but did not see it, and to hear what you hear but did not hear it."[a]

Jesus Tells the Parable of the Good Samaritan
(132)

25On one occasion an expert in the law stood up to test Jesus. "Teacher," he asked,
"what must I do to inherit eternal life?"[b]
26"What is written in the Law?" he replied. "How do you read it?"
27He answered: " 'Love the Lord your God with all your heart and with all your
soul and with all your strength and with all your mind';**[c]**[c] and, 'Love your neighbour
as yourself.'**[d]**"[d]
28"You have answered correctly," Jesus replied. "Do this and you will live."[e]
29But he wanted to justify himself,[f] so he asked Jesus, "And who is my neighbour?"
30In reply Jesus said: "A man was going down from Jerusalem to Jericho, when
he fell into the hands of robbers. They stripped him of his clothes, beat him and went
away, leaving him half-dead. 31A priest happened to be going down the same road,
and when he saw the man, he passed by on the other side.[g] 32So too, a Levite, when
he came to the place and saw him, passed by on the other side. 33But a Samaritan,[h]
as he travelled, came where the man was; and when he saw him, he took pity on him.
34He went to him and bandaged his wounds, pouring on oil and wine. Then he put
the man on his own donkey, brought him to an inn and took care of him. 35The next
day he took out two silver coins**[e]** and gave them to the innkeeper. 'Look after him,'
he said, 'and when I return, I will reimburse you for any extra expense you may have.'

10:24 [a]1Pe 1:10-12
10:25 [b]Mt 19:16; Lk 18:18
10:27 [c]Dt 6:5 [d]Lev 19:18; Mt 5:43
10:28 [e]Lev 18:5; Ro 7:10
10:29 [f]Lk 16:15
10:31 [g]Lev 21:1-3
10:33 [h]Mt 10:5

c *27* Deut. 6:5 **d** *27* Lev. 19:18 **e** *35* Greek *two denarii*

A COLLECTION OF ATTITUDES

To the expert in the law, the wounded man was a subject to discuss.

To the robbers, the wounded man was someone to use and exploit.

To the religious men, the wounded man was a problem to be avoided.

To the innkeeper, the wounded man was a customer to serve for a fee.

To the Samaritan, the wounded man was a human being worth being cared for and loved.

To Jesus, all of them and all of us were worth dying for.

Confronting the needs of others brings out various attitudes in us. Jesus used the story of the good but despised Samaritan to make clear what attitude was acceptable to him. If we are honest, we will often find ourselves in the place of the expert in the law, needing to learn again who our neighbour is. Note these different attitudes towards the wounded man.

We also have a privileged position, with knowledge of 2,000 years of church history, availability of the Bible in hundreds of languages and translations, and access to many excellent pastors and speakers. Yet often we take these for granted. Remember, with privilege comes responsibility. Because we are privileged to know so much about Christ, we must be careful to follow him.

10:24 Old Testament men of God such as David and the prophet Isaiah made many God-inspired predictions that Jesus fulfilled. As Peter later wrote, these prophets wondered what their words meant and when they would be fulfilled (1 Peter 1:10–13). In Jesus' words, they "wanted to see what you see" – the coming of God's kingdom.

10:27 This expert in the law was quoting Deuteronomy 6:5 and Leviticus 19:18. He correctly understood that the law demanded total devotion to God and love for one's neighbour. Jesus talked more about these laws elsewhere (see Matthew 19:16–22 and Mark 10:17–22).

10:27–37 The law expert treated the wounded man as a topic for discussion; the robbers, as an object to exploit; the priest, as a problem to avoid; and the Levite, as an object of curiosity. Only the Samaritan treated him as a person to love.

10:27–37 From the parable we learn three principles about loving our neighbour: (1) lack of love is often easy to justify, even though it is never right; (2) our neighbour is anyone of any race, creed, or social background who is in need; and (3) love means acting to meet the person's need. Wherever you live, there are needy people close by. There is no good reason for refusing to help.

10:33 There was deep hatred between Jews and Samaritans. The Jews saw themselves as pure descendants of Abraham, while the Samaritans were a mixed race produced when Jews from the northern kingdom intermarried with other peoples after Israel's exile. To this law expert, the person least likely to act correctly would be the Samaritan. In fact, he could not bear to say "Samaritan" in answer to Jesus' question. This "expert's" attitude betrayed his lack of the very thing that he had earlier said the law commanded – love.

36"Which of these three do you think was a neighbour to the man who fell into the
hands of robbers?"
37The expert in the law replied, "The one who had mercy on him."
Jesus told him, "Go and do likewise."

Jesus Visits Mary and Martha
(133)

38As Jesus and his disciples were on their way, he came to a village where a woman
named Martha[i] opened her home to him. 39She had a sister called Mary,[j] who sat
at the Lord's feet[k] listening to what he said. 40But Martha was distracted by all the
preparations that had to be made. She came to him and asked, "Lord, don't you care[l]
that my sister has left me to do the work by myself? Tell her to help me!"
41"Martha, Martha," the Lord answered, "you are worried[m] and upset about many
things, 42but only one thing is needed.[f][n] Mary has chosen what is better, and it will
not be taken away from her."

Jesus Teaches His Disciples about Prayer
(134)

11 One day Jesus was praying[a] in a certain place. When he finished, one of his
disciples said to him, "Lord,[b] teach us to pray, just as John taught his disciples."
2He said to them, "When you pray, say:

" 'Father,[a]
hallowed be your name,
your kingdom[c] come.[b]
3Give us each day our daily bread.
4Forgive us our sins,
for we also forgive everyone who sins against us.[c][d]
And lead us not into temptation.' "[d][e]

5Then he said to them, "Suppose one of you has a friend, and he goes to him at

10:38 [i]Jn 11:1; 12:2
10:39 [j]Jn 11:1; 12:3 [k]Lk 8:35
10:40 [l]Mk 4:38
10:41 [m]Mt 6:25-34; Lk 12:11, 22
10:42 [n]Ps 27:4
11:1 [a]Lk 3:21 [b]Jn 13:13
11:2 [c]Mt 3:2
11:4 [d]Mt 18:35; Mk 11:25 [e]Mt 26:41; Jas 1:13

[f] 42 Some manuscripts *but few things are needed—or only one* [a] 2 Some manuscripts *Our Father in heaven* [b] 2 Some manuscripts *come. May your will be done on earth as it is in heaven.* [c] 4 Greek *everyone who is indebted to us* [d] 4 Some manuscripts *temptation but deliver us from the evil one*

10:38–42 Mary and Martha both loved Jesus. On this occasion they were both serving him. But Martha thought Mary's style of serving was inferior to hers. She didn't realise that in her desire to serve, she was actually neglecting her guest. Are you so busy doing things *for* Jesus that you're not spending any time *with* him? Don't let your service become self-serving.

10:41, 42 Jesus did not blame Martha for being concerned about household chores. He was only asking her to set priorities. It is possible for service to Christ to degenerate into mere busy work that is no longer full of devotion to God.

11:1–4 Notice the order in this prayer. First Jesus praised God; then he made his requests. Praising God first puts us in the right frame of mind to tell him about our needs. Too often our prayers are more like shopping lists than conversations.

11:2–13 These verses focus on three aspects of prayer: its content (11:2–4), our persistence (11:5–10), and God's faithfulness (11:11–13).

11:3 God's provision is daily, not all at once. We cannot store it up and then cut off communication with God. And we dare not be self-satisfied. If you are running low on strength, ask yourself—how long have I been away from the Source?

11:4 When Jesus taught his disciples to pray, he made forgiveness the cornerstone of their relationship with God. God has forgiven our sins; we must now forgive those who have wronged us. To remain unforgiving shows we have not understood that we ourselves deeply need to be forgiven. Think of some people who have wronged you. Have you forgiven them? How will God deal with you if he treats you as you treat others?

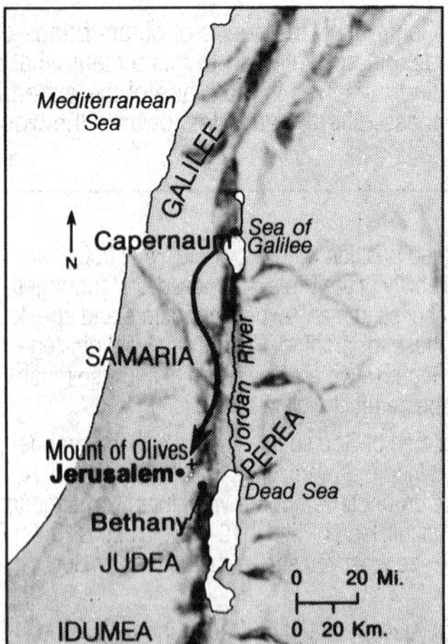

JESUS VISITS MARY AND MARTHA
After teaching throughout Galilee, Jesus returned to Jerusalem for the Feast of Tabernacles (John 7:2). He spoke in Jerusalem and then visited his friends Mary and Martha in the tiny village of Bethany on the slope of the Mount of Olives.

11:8 Persistence, or boldness, in prayer overcomes our insen-

11:8 [f]Lk 18:1-6
11:9 [g]Mt 7:7

midnight and says, 'Friend, lend me three loaves of bread, 6because a friend of mine
on a journey has come to me, and I have nothing to set before him.'
7"Then the one inside answers, 'Don't bother me. The door is already locked, and
my children are with me in bed. I can't get up and give you anything.' 8I tell you,
though he will not get up and give him the bread because he is his friend, yet because
of the man's boldness[e] he will get up and give him as much as he needs.[f]
9"So I say to you: Ask and it will be given to you;[g] seek and you will find; knock
and the door will be opened to you. 10For everyone who asks receives; he who seeks
finds; and to him who knocks, the door will be opened.

[e] 8 Or *persistence*

MARTHA

Many older brothers and sisters have an irritating tendency to take charge, a habit developed while growing up. We can easily see this pattern in Martha, the older sister of Mary and Lazarus. She was used to being in control.

The fact that Martha, Mary, and Lazarus are remembered for their hospitality takes on added significance when we note that hospitality was a social requirement in their culture. It was considered shameful to turn anyone away from your door. Apparently Martha's family met this requirement very well.

Martha worried about details. She wished to please, to serve, to do the right thing—but she often succeeded in making everyone around her uncomfortable. Perhaps as the oldest she feared shame if her home did not measure up to expectations. She tried to do everything she could to make sure that wouldn't happen. As a result, she found it hard to relax and enjoy her guests, and even harder to accept Mary's lack of co-operation in all the preparations. Martha's frustration was so intense that she finally asked Jesus to settle the matter. He gently corrected her attitude and showed her that her priorities, though good, were not the best. The personal attention she gave her guests should be more important than the comforts she tried to provide for them.

Later, following her brother Lazarus' death, Martha could hardly help being herself. When she heard Jesus was finally coming, she rushed out to meet him and expressed her inner conflict of disappointment and hope. Jesus pointed out that her hope was too limited. He was not only Lord beyond death, he was Lord over death—the resurrection and the life! Moments later, Martha again spoke without thinking, pointing out that four-day-old corpses are well on their way to decomposition. Her awareness of details sometimes kept her from seeing the whole picture, but Jesus was consistently patient with her.

In our last picture of Martha, she is once again serving a meal to Jesus and his disciples. She has not stopped serving. But the Bible records her silence this time. She has begun to learn what her younger sister already knew—that worship begins with silence and listening.

Strengths and accomplishments:
- Known as a hospitable homemaker
- Believed in Jesus with growing faith
- Had a strong desire to do everything exactly right

Weaknesses and mistakes:
- Expected others to agree with her priorities
- Was overly concerned with details
- Tended to feel sorry for herself when her efforts were not recognised
- Limited Jesus' power to this life

Lessons from her life:
- Getting caught up in details can make us forget the main reasons for our actions
- There is a proper time to listen to Jesus and a proper time to work for him

Vital statistics:
- Where: Bethany
- Relatives: Sister: Mary. Brother: Lazarus

Key verse:
"But Martha was distracted by all the preparations that had to be made. She came to him and asked, 'Lord, don't you care that my sister has left me to do the work by myself? Tell her to help me!' " (Luke 10:40).

Martha's story is told in Luke 10:38–42 and John 11:17–45.

---

sitivity, not God's. To practise persistence does more to change our hearts and minds than his, and it helps us understand and express the intensity of our need. Persistence in prayer helps us recognise God's work.

11"Which of you fathers, if your son asks for[f] a fish, will give him a snake instead?
12Or if he asks for an egg, will give him a scorpion? 13If you then, though you are
evil, know how to give good gifts to your children, how much more will your Father
in heaven give the Holy Spirit to those who ask him!"

Jesus Answers Hostile Accusations
(135)

14Jesus was driving out a demon that was mute. When the demon left, the man who
had been mute spoke, and the crowd was amazed.[h] 15But some of them said, "By
Beelzebub,[g][i] the prince of demons, he is driving out demons."[j] 16Others tested him
by asking for a sign from heaven.[k]
17Jesus knew their thoughts[l] and said to them: "Any kingdom divided against itself
will be ruined, and a house divided against itself will fall. 18If Satan[m] is divided
against himself, how can his kingdom stand? I say this because you claim that I drive
out demons by Beelzebub. 19Now if I drive out demons by Beelzebub, by whom do
your followers drive them out? So then, they will be your judges. 20But if I drive out
demons by the finger of God,[n] then the kingdom of God[o] has come to you.
21"When a strong man, fully armed, guards his own house, his possessions are safe.
22But when someone stronger attacks and overpowers him, he takes away the armour
in which the man trusted and divides up the spoils.
23"He who is not with me is against me, and he who does not gather with me,
scatters.[p]
24"When an evil[h] spirit comes out of a man, it goes through arid places seeking
rest and does not find it. Then it says, 'I will return to the house I left.' 25When it
arrives, it finds the house swept clean and put in order. 26Then it goes and takes seven
other spirits more wicked than itself, and they go in and live there. And the final
condition of that man is worse than the first."[q]
27As Jesus was saying these things, a woman in the crowd called out, "Blessed is
the mother who gave you birth and nursed you."[r]

11:14 [h]Mt 9:32, 33
11:15 [i]Mk 3:22 [j]Mt 9:34
11:16 [k]Mt 12:38
11:17 [l]Mt 9:4
11:18 [m]Mt 4:10
11:20 [n]Ex 8:19 [o]Mt 3:2
11:23 [p]Mt 12:30; Mk 9:40; Lk 9:50
11:26 [q]2Pe 2:20
11:27 [r]Lk 23:29

[f] *11* Some manuscripts *for bread, will give him a stone; or if he asks for* [g] *15* Greek *Beezeboul* or *Beelzeboul*; also in verses 18 and 19 [h] *24* Greek *unclean*

11:13 Even though good fathers make mistakes, they treat their children well. How much better our perfect heavenly Father treats his children! The most important gift he could ever give us is the Holy Spirit (Acts 2:1–4), whom he promised to give all believers after his death, resurrection, and return to heaven (John 15:26).

11:14–23 A similar and possibly separate event is reported in Matthew 12:22–45 and Mark 3:20–30. The event described by Luke happened in Judea while the other took place in Galilee. According to Luke, Jesus spoke to the crowds; in Matthew and Mark, he accused the Pharisees.

11:15–20 There are two common interpretations of these verses. (1) Some of the Pharisees' followers drove out demons. If this was so, the Pharisees' accusations were becoming more desperate. To accuse Jesus of being empowered by Beelzebub, the prince of demons (or Satan himself), because Jesus was driving out demons was also to say that the Pharisees' own followers were doing Satan's work. Jesus turned the religious leaders' accusation against them. (2) Another possibility is that the Pharisees' followers were *not* driving out demons; and even if they tried, they did not succeed. Jesus first dismissed their claim as absurd (Why would the devil drive out his own demons?). Then he engaged in a little irony ("By whom do your followers drive them out?"). Finally he concluded that his work of driving out demons proves that the kingdom of God has arrived.

Satan, who had controlled the kingdom of this world for thousands of years, was now being controlled and overpowered by Jesus and the kingdom of heaven. Jesus' kingdom began to come into power at Jesus' birth, grew as he resisted the desert temptations, established itself through his teachings and healings, blossomed in victory at his resurrection and at Pentecost, and will become permanent and universal at his second coming. Though these two interpretations may differ, they arrive at the same conclusion – the kingdom of God has arrived with the coming of Jesus Christ.

11:21, 22 Jesus may have been referring to Isaiah 49:24–26. Regardless of how great Satan's power is, Jesus is stronger still. He will bind Satan and dispose of him for eternity (see Revelation 20:2, 10).

11:23 How does this verse relate to 9:50: "Whoever is not against you is for you"? In the earlier passage, Jesus was talking about a person who was driving out demons in Jesus' name. Those who fight evil, he was saying, are on the same side as one driving out demons in Jesus' name. Here, by contrast, he was talking about the conflict between God and the devil. In this battle, if a person is not on God's side, he or she is on Satan's. There is no neutral ground. Because God has already won the battle, why be on the losing side? If you're not actively for Christ, you are against him.

11:24–26 Jesus was illustrating an unfortunate human tendency – our desire to reform often does not last long. In Israel's history, almost as soon as a good king would pull down idols, a bad king would set them up again. It is not enough to be emptied of evil; we must then be filled with the power of the Holy Spirit to accomplish God's new purpose in our lives (see also Matthew 12:43–45; Galatians 5:22).

11:27, 28 Jesus was speaking to people who put extremely high value on family ties. Their genealogies were important guarantees that they were part of God's chosen people. A man's value came from his ancestors, and a woman's value came from the sons she bore. Jesus' response to the woman meant that a person's obedience to God is more important than his or her place on the family

28He replied, "Blessed rather are those who hear the word of God[s] and obey it."[t]

Jesus Warns against Unbelief
(136)

29As the crowds increased, Jesus said, "This is a wicked generation. It asks for a
miraculous sign,[u] but none will be given it except the sign of Jonah.[v] 30For as Jonah
was a sign to the Ninevites, so also will the Son of Man be to this generation. 31The
Queen of the South will rise at the judgment with the men of this generation and
condemn them; for she came from the ends of the earth to listen to Solomon's
wisdom,[w] and now one[i] greater than Solomon is here. 32The men of Nineveh will
stand up at the judgment with this generation and condemn it; for they repented at the
preaching of Jonah,[x] and now one greater than Jonah is here.

Jesus Teaches about the Light Within
(137)

33"No-one lights a lamp and puts it in a place where it will be hidden, or under a
bowl. Instead he puts it on its stand, so that those who come in may see the light.[y]
34Your eye is the lamp of your body. When your eyes are good, your whole body
also is full of light. But when they are bad, your body also is full of darkness. 35See
to it, then, that the light within you is not darkness. 36Therefore, if your whole body
is full of light, and no part of it dark, it will be completely lighted, as when the light
of a lamp shines on you."

Jesus Criticises the Religious Leaders
(138)

37When Jesus had finished speaking, a Pharisee invited him to eat with him; so he
went in and reclined at the table.[z] 38But the Pharisee, noticing that Jesus did not first
wash before the meal,[a] was surprised.
39Then the Lord[b] said to him, "Now then, you Pharisees clean the outside of the
cup and dish, but inside you are full of greed and wickedness.[c] 40You foolish
people![d] Did not the one who made the outside make the inside also? 41But give what
is inside ⌊the dish⌋[j] to the poor,[e] and everything will be clean for you.[f]

[i] *31* Or *something*; also in verse 32 [j] *41* Or *what you have*

11:28 [s]Heb 4:12 [t]Pr 8:32; Lk 6:47; 8:21; Jn 14:21
11:29 [u]ver 16; Mt 12:38 [v]Jnh 1:17; Mt 16:4
11:31 [w]1Ki 10:1; 2Ch 9:1
11:32 [x]Jnh 3:5
11:33 [y]Mt 5:15; Mk 4:21; Lk 8:16
11:37 [z]Lk 7:36; 14:1
11:38 [a]Mk 7:3, 4
11:39 [b]Lk 7:13 [c]Mt 23:25, 26; Mk 7:20-23
11:40 [d]Lk 12:20; 1Co 15:36
11:41 [e]Lk 12:33 [f]Ac 10:15

---

tree. The patient work of consistent obedience is even more important than the honour of bearing a respected son.

11:29, 30 What was the sign of Jonah? God had asked Jonah to preach repentance to the Gentiles (non-Jews). Jesus was affirming Jonah's message. Salvation is not only for Jews, but for all people. Matthew 12:40 adds another explanation: Jesus would die and rise after three days, just as the prophet Jonah was rescued after three days in the belly of the great fish.

11:29–32 The cruel, warlike men of Nineveh, capital of Assyria, repented when Jonah preached to them – and Jonah did not even care about them. The pagan Queen of the South (Sheba) praised the God of Israel when she heard Solomon's wisdom, and Solomon was full of faults. By contrast, Jesus, the perfect Son of God, had come to people that he loved dearly – but they rejected him. Thus God's chosen people made themselves more liable to judgment than either a notoriously wicked nation or a powerful pagan queen. Compare 10:12–15 where Jesus says the evil cities of Sodom, Tyre, and Sidon will be judged less harshly than the cities in Judea and Galilee that rejected Jesus' message.

11:31, 32 The Ninevites and the Queen of the South had turned to God with far less evidence than Jesus was giving his listeners – and far less than we have today. We have eyewitness reports of the risen Jesus, the continuing power of the Holy Spirit unleashed at Pentecost, easy access to the Bible, and knowledge of 2,000 years of Christ's acts through his church. With the knowledge and insight available to us, our response to Christ ought to be even more complete and wholehearted.

11:33–36 The lamp is Christ; the eye represents spiritual understanding and insight. Evil desires make the eye less sensitive and blot out the light of Christ's presence. If you have a hard time seeing God at work in the world and in your life, check your vision. Are any sinful desires blinding you to Christ?

11:37–39 This washing was done not for health reasons, but as a symbol of washing away any contamination from touching anything unclean. Not only did the Pharisees make a public show of their washing, but they also commanded everyone else to follow a practice originally intended only for the priests.

11:41 The Pharisees loved to think of themselves as "clean", but their stinginess towards God and the poor proved that they were not as clean as they thought. How do you use the resources God has entrusted to you? Are you generous in meeting the needs around you? Your generosity reveals much about the purity of your heart.

42"Woe to you Pharisees, because you give God a tenth[g] of your mint, rue and
all other kinds of garden herbs, but you neglect justice and the love of God.[h] You
should have practised the latter without leaving the former undone.[i]
43"Woe to you Pharisees, because you love the most important seats in the synagogues and greetings in the market-places.[j]
44"Woe to you, because you are like unmarked graves,[k] which men walk over
without knowing it."
45One of the experts in the law[l] answered him, "Teacher, when you say these
things, you insult us also."
46Jesus replied, "And you experts in the law, woe to you, because you load people
down with burdens they can hardly carry, and you yourselves will not lift one finger
to help them.[m]
47"Woe to you, because you build tombs for the prophets, and it was your forefathers who killed them. 48So you testify that you approve of what your forefathers
did; they killed the prophets, and you build their tombs.[n] 49Because of this, God in
his wisdom[o] said, 'I will send them prophets and apostles, some of whom they will
kill and others they will persecute.'[p] 50Therefore this generation will be held responsible for the blood of all the prophets that has been shed since the beginning of the
world, 51from the blood of Abel[q] to the blood of Zechariah,[r] who was killed between
the altar and the sanctuary. Yes, I tell you, this generation will be held responsible
for it all.[s]
52"Woe to you experts in the law, because you have taken away the key to
knowledge. You yourselves have not entered, and you have hindered those who were
entering."[t]
53When Jesus left there, the Pharisees and the teachers of the law began to oppose
him fiercely and to besiege him with questions, 54waiting to catch him in something
he might say.[u]

11:42 [g]Lk 18:12 [h]Dt 6:5; Mic 6:8 [i]Mt 23:23
11:43 [j]Mt 23:6, 7; Mk 12:38-39; Lk 14:7; 20:46
11:44 [k]Mt 23:27
11:45 [l]Mt 22:35
11:46 [m]Mt 23:4
11:48 [n]Mt 23:29-32; Ac 7:51-53
11:49 [o]1Co 1:24, 30; Col 2:3 [p]Mt 23:34
11:51 [q]Ge 4:8 [r]2Ch 24:20, 21 [s]Mt 23:35, 36
11:52 [t]Mt 23:13
11:54 [u]Mt 12:10; Mk 12:13

11:42 It is easy to rationalise not helping others because we have already given to the church, but a person who follows Jesus should share with needy neighbours. While tithing is important to the life of the church, our compassion must not stop there. Where we can help, we should help.

11:42–52 Jesus criticised the Pharisees and the experts in the law harshly because they (1) washed their outsides but not their insides, (2) remembered to give a tenth of even their garden herbs, but neglected justice, (3) loved praise and attention, (4) loaded people down with burdensome religious demands, (5) would not accept the truth about Jesus, and (6) prevented others from believing the truth as well. They went wrong by focusing on outward appearances and ignoring the inner condition of their hearts. We do the same when our service comes from a desire to be seen rather than from a pure heart and out of a love for others. People may sometimes be fooled, but God isn't. Don't be a Christian on the outside only. Bring your inner life under God's control, and your outer life will naturally reflect him.

11:44 The Old Testament laws said a person who touched a grave was unclean (Numbers 19:16). Jesus accused the Pharisees of making others unclean by their spiritual rottenness. Like unmarked graves hidden in a field, the Pharisees corrupted everyone who came in contact with them.

11:46 These "burdens" were the details the Pharisees had added to God's law. To the commandment, "Remember the Sabbath day by keeping it holy" (Exodus 20:8), for example, they had added instructions regarding how far a person could walk on the Sabbath, which kinds of knots could be tied, and how much weight could be carried. Healing a person was considered unlawful work on the Sabbath, although rescuing a trapped animal was permitted (14:5). No wonder Jesus condemned their additions to the law.

11:49 God's prophets have been persecuted and murdered throughout history. But this generation was rejecting more than a human prophet – they were rejecting God himself. This quotation is not from the Old Testament. Jesus, the greatest Prophet of all, was directly giving them God's message.

11:51 Abel's death is recorded in Genesis 4:8. For more about him, see his Profile in Genesis 6. Zechariah's death is recorded in 2 Chronicles 24:20–22 (the last book in the Hebrew canon). Why would all these sins come upon this particular generation? Because they were rejecting the Messiah himself, the One to whom all their history and prophecy were pointing.

11:52 How did the law experts take away the "key to knowledge"? Through their erroneous interpretations of Scripture and their added man-made rules, they made God's truth hard to understand and practise. On top of that, these men were bad examples, arguing their way out of the demanding rules they placed on others. Caught up in a religion of their own making, they could no longer lead the people to God. They had closed the door of God's love to the people and had thrown away the key.

11:53, 54 The teachers of the law and the Pharisees hoped to arrest Jesus for blasphemy, heresy, and lawbreaking. They were enraged by Jesus' words about them, but they couldn't arrest him for merely speaking words. They had to find a legal way to get rid of Jesus.

12:1 [a]Mt 16:6, 11, 12; Mk 8:15

12:2 [b]Mk 4:22; Lk 8:17

12:4 [c]Jn 15:14, 15

12:5 [d]Heb 10:31

12:7 [e]Mt 10:30 [f]Mt 12:12

12:8 [g]Lk 15:10

12:9 [h]Mk 8:38; 2Ti 2:12

12:10 [i]Mt 8:20 [j]Mt 12:31, 32; Mk 3:28-29; 1Jn 5:16

12:11 [k]Mt 10:17, 19; Mk 13:11; Lk 21:12, 14

12:12 [l]Ex 4:12; Mt 10:20; Mk 13:11; Lk 21:15

Jesus Speaks against Hypocrisy
(139)

12 Meanwhile, when a crowd of many thousands had gathered, so that they were
trampling on one another, Jesus began to speak first to his disciples, saying:
"Be on your guard against the yeast of the Pharisees, which is hypocrisy.[a] 2 There
is nothing concealed that will not be disclosed, or hidden that will not be made
known.[b] 3 What you have said in the dark will be heard in the daylight, and what you
have whispered in the ear in the inner rooms will be proclaimed from the roofs.
4 "I tell you, my friends,[c] do not be afraid of those who kill the body and after that
can do no more. 5 But I will show you whom you should fear: Fear him who, after
the killing of the body, has power to throw you into hell. Yes, I tell you, fear him.[d]
6 Are not five sparrows sold for two pennies?[a] Yet not one of them is forgotten by
God. 7 Indeed, the very hairs of your head are all numbered.[e] Don't be afraid; you
are worth more than many sparrows.[f]
8 "I tell you, whoever acknowledges me before men, the Son of Man will also
acknowledge him before the angels of God.[g] 9 But he who disowns me before men
will be disowned[h] before the angels of God. 10 And everyone who speaks a word
against the Son of Man[i] will be forgiven, but anyone who blasphemes against the
Holy Spirit will not be forgiven.[j]
11 "When you are brought before synagogues, rulers and authorities, do not worry
about how you will defend yourselves or what you will say,[k] 12 for the Holy Spirit
will teach you at that time what you should say."[l]

Jesus Tells the Parable of the Rich Fool
(140)

13 Someone in the crowd said to him, "Teacher, tell my brother to divide the
inheritance with me."
14 Jesus replied, "Man, who appointed me a judge or an arbiter between you?"

a *6* Greek *two assaria*

12:1, 2 As Jesus watched the huge crowds waiting to hear him, he warned his disciples against hypocrisy – trying to appear good when one's heart is far from God. The Pharisees could not keep their attitudes hidden for ever. Their selfishness would act like yeast, and soon they would expose themselves for what they really were – power-hungry impostors, not devoted religious leaders. It is easy to be angry at the blatant hypocrisy of the Pharisees, but each of us must resist the temptation to settle for the appearance of respectability when our hearts are far from God.

12:4, 5 Fear of opposition or ridicule can weaken our witness for Christ. Often we cling to peace and comfort, even at the cost of our walk with God. Jesus reminds us here that we should fear God, who controls eternal, not merely temporal, consequences. Don't allow fear of a person or group to keep you from standing up for Christ.

12:7 Our true value is God's estimate of our worth, not our peers'. Other people evaluate and categorise us according to how we perform, what we achieve, and how we look. But God cares for us, as he does for all of his creatures, because we belong to him. So we can face life without fear.

12:8, 9 We disown Jesus when we (1) hope no-one will think we are Christians, (2) decide *not* to speak up for what is right, (3) are silent about our relationship with God, (4) blend into society, (5) accept our culture's non-Christian values. By contrast, we acknowledge him when we (1) live moral, upright, Christ-honouring lives, (2) look for opportunities to share our faith with others, (3) help others in need, (4) take a stand for justice, (5) love others, (6) acknowledge our loyalty to Christ, (7) use our lives and resources to carry out his desires rather than our own.

12:10 Jesus said that blasphemy against the Holy Spirit is unforgivable. This has worried many sincere Christians, but it does not need to. The unforgivable sin means attributing to Satan the work that the Holy Spirit accomplishes (see the notes on Matthew 12:31, 32; Mark 3:28, 29). Thus it is deliberate and ongoing rejection of the Holy Spirit's work and even of God himself. A person who has committed this sin has shut himself or herself off from God so thoroughly that he or she is unaware of any sin at all. A person who fears having committed it shows, by his or her very concern, that he or she has not sinned in this way.

12:11, 12 The disciples knew they could never dominate a religious dispute with the well-educated Jewish leaders. Nevertheless, they would not be left unprepared. Jesus promised that the Holy Spirit would supply the needed words. The disciples' testimony might not make them look impressive, but it would still point out God's work in the world through Jesus' life. We need to pray for opportunities to speak for God, and then trust him to help us with our words. This promise of the Spirit's help, however, does not compensate for lack of preparation. Remember that these disciples had three years of teaching and practical application. We too must study God's word. Then God will bring his truths to mind when we most need them, helping us present them in the most effective way.

12:13ff Problems like this were often brought to rabbis for them to settle. Jesus' response, though not directly to the topic, is not a change of subject. Rather, Jesus is pointing to a higher issue – a correct attitude towards the accumulation of wealth. Life is more than material goods; far more important is our relationship with God. Jesus put his finger on this questioner's heart. When we bring problems to God in prayer, he often does the same – showing us how we need to change and grow in our attitude towards the problem. This answer is often not the one we were looking for, but it is more effective in helping us trace God's hand in our lives.

15Then he said to them, "Watch out! Be on your guard against all kinds of greed; a
man's life does not consist in the abundance of his possessions."[m]
16And he told them this parable: "The ground of a certain rich man produced a good
crop. 17He thought to himself, 'What shall I do? I have no place to store my crops.'
18"Then he said, 'This is what I'll do. I will tear down my barns and build bigger
ones, and there I will store all my grain and my goods. 19And I'll say to myself, "You
have plenty of good things laid up for many years. Take life easy; eat, drink and be
merry." '
20"But God said to him, 'You fool![n] This very night your life will be demanded
from you.[o] Then who will get what you have prepared for yourself?'[p]
21"This is how it will be with anyone who stores up things for himself but is not
rich towards God."[q]

Jesus Warns about Worry
(141)

22Then Jesus said to his disciples: "Therefore I tell you, do not worry about your
life, what you will eat; or about your body, what you will wear. 23Life is more than
food, and the body more than clothes. 24Consider the ravens: They do not sow or reap,
they have no storeroom or barn; yet God feeds them.[r] And how much more valuable
you are than birds! 25Who of you by worrying can add a single hour to his life?[b]
26Since you cannot do this very little thing, why do you worry about the rest?
27"Consider how the lilies grow. They do not labour or spin. Yet I tell you, not
even Solomon in all his splendour[s] was dressed like one of these. 28If that is how
God clothes the grass of the field, which is here today, and tomorrow is thrown into
the fire, how much more will he clothe you, O you of little faith![t] 29And do not set
your heart on what you will eat or drink; do not worry about it. 30For the pagan world
runs after all such things, and your Father[u] knows that you need them.[v] 31But seek
his kingdom,[w] and these things will be given to you as well.[x]
32"Do not be afraid,[y] little flock, for your Father has been pleased to give you the
kingdom.[z] 33Sell your possessions and give to the poor.[a] Provide purses for yourselves that will not wear out, a treasure in heaven[b] that will not be exhausted, where
no thief comes near and no moth destroys.[c] 34For where your treasure is, there your
heart will be also.[d]

b *25 Or single cubit to his height*

12:15 [m]Job 20:20; 31:24; Ps 62:10
12:20 [n]Jer 17:11; Lk 11:40 [o]Job 27:8 [p]Ps 39:6; 49:10
12:21 [q]ver 33
12:24 [r]Job 38:41; Ps 147:9
12:27 [s]1Ki 10:4-7
12:28 [t]Mt 6:30
12:30 [u]Lk 6:36 [v]Mt 6:8
12:31 [w]Mt 3:2 [x]Mt 19:29
12:32 [y]Mt 14:27 [z]Mt 25:34
12:33 [a]Mt 19:21; Ac 2:45 [b]Mt 6:20 [c]Jas 5:2
12:34 [d]Mt 6:21

12:15 Jesus says that the good life has nothing to do with being wealthy, so be on guard against greed (desire for what we don't have). This is the exact opposite of what society usually says. Advertisers spend millions on enticing us to think that if we buy more and more of their products, we will be happier, more fulfilled, more comfortable. How do you respond to the constant pressure to buy? Learn to tune out expensive enticements and concentrate instead on the truly good life – living in a relationship with God and doing his work.

12:16–21 The rich man in Jesus' story died before he could begin to use what was stored in his big barns. Planning for retirement – preparing for life *before* death – is wise, but neglecting life *after* death is disastrous. If you accumulate wealth only to benefit yourself, with no concern for helping others, you will enter eternity empty-handed.

12:18–20 Why do you save money? To retire? To buy more expensive cars or toys? To be secure? Jesus challenges us to think beyond earthbound goals and to use what we have been given for God's kingdom. Faith, service, and obedience are the way to become rich towards God.

12:22–34 Jesus commands us not to worry. But how can we avoid it? Only faith can free us from the anxiety caused by greed and covetousness. It is good to work and plan responsibly; it is bad to dwell on all the ways our planning could go wrong. Worry is pointless because it can't fill any of our needs; worry is foolish because the Creator of the universe loves us and knows what we need. He promises to meet all our real needs, but not necessarily all our desires.

12:31 Seeking the kingdom of God means making Jesus the Lord and King of your life. He must control every area – your work, play, plans, relationships. Is the kingdom only one of your many concerns, or is it central to all you do? Are you holding back any areas of your life from God's control? As Lord and Creator, he wants to help provide what you need as well as guide how you use what he provides.

12:33 Money seen as an end in itself quickly traps us and cuts us off from both God and the needy. The key to using money wisely is to see how much we can use for God's purposes, not how much we can accumulate for ourselves. Does God's love touch your wallet? Does your money free you to help others? If so, you are storing up lasting treasures in heaven. If your financial goals and possessions hinder you from giving generously, loving others, or serving God, sell what you must to bring your life into perspective.

12:34 If you concentrate your money in your business, your thoughts will centre on making the business profitable. If you direct it towards other people, you will become concerned with their welfare. Where do you put your time, money, and energy? What do you think about most? How should you change the way you use your resources in order to reflect kingdom values more accurately?

12:37 [e]Mt 24:42, 46; 25:13 [f]Mt 20:28
12:39 [g]Mt 6:19; 1Th 5:2; 2Pe 3:10; Rev 3:3; 16:15
12:40 [h]Mk 13:33; Lk 21:36
12:42 [i]Lk 7:13
12:46 [j]ver 40
12:47 [k]Dt 25:2
12:48 [l]Lev 5:17; Nu 15:27-30
12:50 [m]Mk 10:38 [n]Jn 19:30
12:53 [o]Mic 7:6; Mt 10:21

Jesus Warns about Preparing for His Coming (142)

35 "Be dressed ready for service and keep your lamps burning, 36 like men waiting
for their master to return from a wedding banquet, so that when he comes and knocks
they can immediately open the door for him. 37 It will be good for those servants whose
master finds them watching when he comes.[e] I tell you the truth, he will dress himself
to serve, will have them recline at the table and will come and wait on them.[f] 38 It
will be good for those servants whose master finds them ready, even if he comes in
the second or third watch of the night. 39 But understand this: If the owner of the house
had known at what hour the thief[g] was coming, he would not have let his house be
broken into. 40 You also must be ready,[h] because the Son of Man will come at an
hour when you do not expect him."
41 Peter asked, "Lord, are you telling this parable to us, or to everyone?"
42 The Lord[i] answered, "Who then is the faithful and wise manager, whom the
master puts in charge of his servants to give them their food allowance at the proper
time? 43 It will be good for that servant whom the master finds doing so when he
returns. 44 I tell you the truth, he will put him in charge of all his possessions. 45 But
suppose the servant says to himself, 'My master is taking a long time in coming,' and
he then begins to beat the menservants and maidservants and to eat and drink and get
drunk. 46 The master of that servant will come on a day when he does not expect him
and at an hour he is not aware of.[j] He will cut him to pieces and assign him a place
with the unbelievers.
47 "That servant who knows his master's will and does not get ready or does not
do what his master wants will be beaten with many blows.[k] 48 But the one who does
not know and does things deserving punishment will be beaten with few blows.[l]
From everyone who has been given much, much will be demanded; and from the one
who has been entrusted with much, much more will be asked.

Jesus Warns about Coming Division (143)

49 "I have come to bring fire on the earth, and how I wish it were already kindled!
50 But I have a baptism[m] to undergo, and how distressed I am until it is completed![n]
51 Do you think I came to bring peace on earth? No, I tell you, but division. 52 From
now on there will be five in one family divided against each other, three against two
and two against three. 53 They will be divided, father against son and son against
father, mother against daughter and daughter against mother, mother-in-law against
daughter-in-law and daughter-in-law against mother-in-law."[o]

12:35–40 Jesus repeatedly said that he would leave this world but would return at some future time (see Matthew 24; 25; John 14:1–3). He also said that a kingdom is being prepared for his followers. Many Greeks envisioned this as a heavenly, idealised, spiritual kingdom. Jews—like Isaiah and John, the writer of Revelation—saw it as a restored earthly kingdom.

12:40 Christ's return at an unexpected time is not a trap, a trick by which God hopes to catch us off guard. In fact, God is delaying his return so more people will have the opportunity to follow him (see 2 Peter 3:9). Before Christ's return, we have time to live out our beliefs and to reflect Jesus' love as we relate to others.

People who are ready for their Lord's return are (1) not hypocritical, but sincere (12:1), (2) not fearful, but ready to witness (12:4–9), (3) not worried, but trusting (12:25, 26), (4) not greedy, but generous (12:34), (5) not lazy, but diligent (12:37). May your life be more like Christ's so that when he comes, you will be ready to greet him joyfully.

12:42–44 Jesus promises a reward for those who have been faithful to the Master. While we sometimes experience immediate and material rewards for our obedience to God, this is not always the case. If so, we would be tempted to boast about our achievements and do good only for what we get. Jesus said that if we look for rewards now, we will lose them later (see Mark 8:36). Our heavenly rewards will be the most accurate reflection of what we have done on earth, and they will be far greater than we can imagine.

12:48 Jesus has told us how to live until he comes: we must watch for him, work diligently, and obey his commands. Such attitudes are especially necessary for leaders. Watchful and faithful leaders will be given increased opportunities and responsibilities. The more resources, talents, and understanding we have, the more we are responsible to use them effectively. God will not hold us responsible for gifts he has not given us, but all of us have enough gifts and duties to keep us busy until Jesus comes.

12:50 The "baptism" to which Jesus referred was his coming crucifixion. Jesus was dreading the physical pain, of course, but even worse would be the spiritual pain of complete separation from God that would accompany his death for the sins of the world.

12:51–53 In these strange and unsettling words, Jesus revealed that his coming often results in conflict. He demands a response, so intimate groups may be torn apart when some choose to follow him and others refuse to do so. There is no middle ground with Jesus. Loyalties must be declared and commitments made, sometimes to the point of severing other relationships. Are you willing to risk losing your family's approval in order to gain eternal life?

Jesus Warns about the Future Crisis
(144)

[54]He said to the crowd: "When you see a cloud rising in the west, immediately you
say, 'It's going to rain,' and it does.[p] [55]And when the south wind blows, you say,
'It's going to be hot,' and it is. [56]Hypocrites! You know how to interpret the appearance of the earth and the sky. How is it that you don't know how to interpret this
present time?[q]
[57]"Why don't you judge for yourselves what is right? [58]As you are going with your
adversary to the magistrate, try hard to be reconciled to him on the way, or he may
drag you off to the judge, and the judge turn you over to the officer, and the officer
throw you into prison.[r] [59]I tell you, you will not get out until you have paid the last
penny."[c] [s]

Jesus Calls the People to Repent
(145)

13 Now there were some present at that time who told Jesus about the Galileans
whose blood Pilate[a] had mixed with their sacrifices. [2]Jesus answered, "Do you
think that these Galileans were worse sinners than all the other Galileans because they
suffered this way?[b] [3]I tell you, no! But unless you repent, you too will all perish.
[4]Or those eighteen who died when the tower in Siloam[c] fell on them—do you think
they were more guilty than all the others living in Jerusalem? [5]I tell you, no! But unless
you repent,[d] you too will all perish."
[6]Then he told this parable: "A man had a fig-tree, planted in his vineyard, and he
went to look for fruit on it, but did not find any.[e] [7]So he said to the man who took
care of the vineyard, 'For three years now I've been coming to look for fruit on this
fig-tree and haven't found any. Cut it down![f] Why should it use up the soil?'
[8]" 'Sir,' the man replied, 'leave it alone for one more year, and I'll dig round it
and fertilise it. [9]If it bears fruit next year, fine! If not, then cut it down.' "

Jesus Heals the Crippled Woman
(146)

[10]On a Sabbath Jesus was teaching in one of the synagogues,[g] [11]and a woman was
there who had been crippled by a spirit for eighteen years.[h] She was bent over and
could not straighten up at all. [12]When Jesus saw her, he called her forward and said
to her, "Woman, you are set free from your infirmity." [13]Then he put his hands on
her,[i] and immediately she straightened up and praised God.

[c] 59 Greek *lepton*

12:54 [p]Mt 16:2
12:56 [q]Mt 16:3
12:58 [r]Mt 5:25
12:59 [s]Mt 5:26; Mk 12:42
13:1 [a]Mt 27:2
13:2 [b]Jn 9:2, 3
13:4 [c]Jn 9:7, 11
13:5 [d]Mt 3:2; Ac 2:38
13:6 [e]Isa 5:2; Jer 8:13; Mt 21:19
13:7 [f]Mt 3:10
13:10 [g]Mt 4:23
13:11 [h]ver 16
13:13 [i]Mk 5:23

12:54–57 For most of recorded history, the world's principal occupation was farming. The farmer depended directly on the weather for his livelihood. He needed just the right amounts of sun and rain—not too much, not too little—to make his living, and he grew skilled at interpreting natural signs. Jesus was announcing an earthshaking event that would be much more important than the year's crops—the coming of God's kingdom. Like a downpour or a sunny day, there were signs that the kingdom would soon arrive. But Jesus' hearers, though skilled at interpreting weather signs, were intentionally ignoring the signs of the times.

13:1–5 Pilate may have killed the Galileans because he thought they were rebelling against Rome; those killed by the tower of Siloam may have been working for the Romans on an aqueduct there. The Pharisees, who were opposed to using force to deal with Rome, would have said that the Galileans deserved to die for rebelling. The Zealots, a group of anti-Roman terrorists, would have said the aqueduct workers deserved to die for co-operating. Jesus said that neither the Galileans nor the workers should be blamed for their calamity. And instead of blaming others, everyone should look to his or her own day of judgment.

13:5 Whether a person is killed in a tragic accident or miraculously survives is not a measure of righteousness. Everyone has to die; that's part of being human. But not everyone needs to stay dead. Jesus promises that those who believe in him will not perish but have eternal life (John 3:16).

13:6–9 In the Old Testament, a fruitful tree was often used as a symbol of godly living (see, for example, Psalm 1:3 and Jeremiah 17:7, 8). Jesus pointed out what would happen to the other kind of tree—the kind that took valuable time and space and still produced nothing for the patient gardener. This was one way Jesus warned his listeners that God would not tolerate for ever their lack of productivity. (Luke 3:9 records John the Baptist's version of the same message.) Have you been enjoying God's special treatment without giving anything in return? If so, respond to the Gardener's patient care, and begin to bear the fruit God has created you to produce.

13:10–17 Why was healing considered work? The religious leaders saw healing as part of a doctor's profession, and practising one's profession on the Sabbath was prohibited. The synagogue ruler could not see beyond the law to Jesus' compassion in healing this crippled woman. Jesus shamed him and the other leaders by pointing out their hypocrisy. They would untie their animals and care for them, but they refused to rejoice when a human being was freed from Satan's bondage.

14Indignant because Jesus had healed on the Sabbath,[j] the synagogue ruler[k] said
to the people, "There are six days for work.[l] So come and be healed on those days,
not on the Sabbath."
15The Lord answered him, "You hypocrites! Doesn't each of you on the Sabbath
untie his ox or donkey from the stall and lead it out to give it water?[m] 16Then should
not this woman, a daughter of Abraham,[n] whom Satan[o] has kept bound for eighteen
long years, be set free on the Sabbath day from what bound her?"
17When he said this, all his opponents were humiliated,[p] but the people were
delighted with all the wonderful things he was doing.

Jesus Teaches about the Kingdom of God
(147)

18Then Jesus asked, "What is the kingdom of God[q] like?[r] What shall I compare
it to? 19It is like a mustard seed, which a man took and planted in his garden. It grew
and became a tree,[s] and the birds of the air perched in its branches."[t]
20Again he asked, "What shall I compare the kingdom of God to? 21It is like yeast
that a woman took and mixed into a large amount[a] of flour until it worked all through
the dough."[u]

Jesus Teaches about Entering the Kingdom
(153)

22Then Jesus went through the towns and villages, teaching as he made his way
to Jerusalem.[v] 23Someone asked him, "Lord, are only a few people going to be
saved?"
He said to them, 24"Make every effort to enter through the narrow door,[w] because
many, I tell you, will try to enter and will not be able to. 25Once the owner of the

13:14 [j]Mt 12:2; Lk 14:3 [k]Mk 5:22 [l]Ex 20:9
13:15 [m]Lk 14:5
13:16 [n]Lk 3:8; 19:9 [o]Mt 4:10
13:17 [p]Isa 66:5
13:18 [q]Mt 3:2 [r]Mt 13:24
13:19 [s]Lk 17:6 [t]Mt 13:32
13:21 [u]1Co 5:6
13:22 [v]Lk 9:51
13:24 [w]Mt 7:13

[a] *21* Greek *three satas* (probably about ⅗ bushel or 22 litres)

SEVEN SABBATH MIRACLES

Jesus sends a demon out of a man	Mark 1:21–28
Jesus heals Peter's mother-in-law	Mark 1:29–31
Jesus heals a lame man by Bethesda Pool	John 5:1–18
Jesus heals a man with a shrivelled hand	Mark 3:1–6
Jesus restores a crippled woman	Luke 13:10–17
Jesus heals a man with dropsy	Luke 14:1–6
Jesus heals a man born blind	John 9:1–16

Over the centuries, the Jewish religious leaders had added rule after rule to God's law. For example, God's law said the Sabbath is a day of rest (Exodus 20:10, 11). But the religious leaders added to that law, creating one that said, "You cannot heal on the Sabbath" because that is "work". Seven times Jesus healed people on the Sabbath. In doing this, he was challenging these religious leaders to look beneath their rules to their true purpose—to honour God by helping those in need. Would God have been pleased if Jesus had ignored these people?

13:15, 16 The Pharisees hid behind their own set of laws to avoid love's obligations. We too can use the letter of the law to rationalise away our obligation to care for others (for example, by tithing regularly and then refusing to help a needy neighbour). But people's needs are more important than rules and regulations. Take time to help others, even if doing so might compromise your public image.

13:16 In our fallen world, disease and disability are common. Their causes are many and often multiple—inadequate nutrition, contact with a source of infection, lowered defences, and even direct attack by Satan. Whatever the immediate cause of our illness, we can trace its original source to Satan, the author of all the evil in our world. The good news is that Jesus is more powerful than any devil or any disease. He often brings physical healing in this life; and when he returns, he will put an end to all disease and disability.

13:18–21 The general expectation among Jesus' hearers was that the Messiah would come as a great king and leader, freeing the nation from Rome and restoring Israel's former glory. But Jesus said his kingdom was beginning quietly. Like the tiny mustard seed that grows into an enormous tree, or the spoonful of yeast that makes the bread dough double in size, the kingdom of God would eventually push outward until the whole world was changed.

13:22 This is the second time Luke reminds us that Jesus was intentionally going to Jerusalem (the other time is in 9:51). Jesus knew he was on his way to die, but he continued preaching to large crowds. The prospect of death did not deter Jesus from his mission.

13:24, 25 Finding salvation requires more concentrated effort than most people are willing to put forth. Obviously we cannot save ourselves—there is no way we can work ourselves into God's favour. The effort we must put out "to enter through the narrow door" is earnestly desiring to know Jesus and diligently striving to follow him whatever the cost. We dare not put off making this decision because the door will not stay open for ever.

house gets up and closes the door, you will stand outside knocking and pleading, 'Sir,
open the door for us.'
"But he will answer, 'I don't know you or where you come from.'[x]
26"Then you will say, 'We ate and drank with you, and you taught in our streets.'
27"But he will reply, 'I don't know you or where you come from. Away from me,
all you evildoers!'[y]
28"There will be weeping there, and gnashing of teeth,[z] when you see Abraham,
Isaac and Jacob and all the prophets in the kingdom of God, but you yourselves thrown
out. 29People will come from east and west[a] and north and south, and will take their
places at the feast in the kingdom of God. 30Indeed there are those who are last who
will be first, and first who will be last."[b]

Jesus Grieves over Jerusalem
(154)

31At that time some Pharisees came to Jesus and said to him, "Leave this place and
go somewhere else. Herod[c] wants to kill you."
32He replied, "Go tell that fox, 'I will drive out demons and heal people today and
tomorrow, and on the third day I will reach my goal.'[d] 33In any case, I must keep
going today and tomorrow and the next day—for surely no prophet[e] can die outside
Jerusalem!
34"O Jerusalem, Jerusalem, you who kill the prophets and stone those sent to you,
how often I have longed to gather your children together, as a hen gathers her chicks
under her wings,[f] but you were not willing! 35Look, your house is left to you
desolate.[g] I tell you, you will not see me again until you say, 'Blessed is he who
comes in the name of the Lord.'[b]"[h]

Jesus Heals a Man with Dropsy
(155)

14 One Sabbath, when Jesus went to eat in the house of a prominent Pharisee,[a]
he was being carefully watched.[b] 2There in front of him was a man suffering
from dropsy. 3Jesus asked the Pharisees and experts in the law,[c] "Is it lawful to heal
on the Sabbath or not?"[d] 4But they remained silent. So taking hold of the man, he
healed him and sent him away.

b *35* Psalm 118:26

13:25 [x]Mt 7:23; 25:10-12
13:27 [y]Mt 7:23; 25:41
13:28 [z]Mt 8:12
13:29 [a]Mt 8:11
13:30 [b]Mt 19:30
13:31 [c]Mt 14:1
13:32 [d]Heb 2:10
13:33 [e]Mt 21:11
13:34 [f]Mt 23:37
13:35 [g]Jer 12:17; 22:5 [h]Ps 118:26; Mt 21:9; Lk 19:38
14:1 [a]Lk 7:36; 11:37 [b]Mt 12:10
14:3 [c]Mt 22:35 [d]Mt 12:2

13:26, 27 The kingdom of God will not necessarily be populated with the people we expect to find there. Some perfectly respectable religious leaders claiming allegiance to Jesus will not be there because secretly they were morally corrupt.

13:27 The people were eager to know who would be in God's kingdom. Jesus explained that although many people know something about God, only a few have acknowledged their sins and accepted his forgiveness. Just listening to Jesus' words or admiring his miracles is not enough—we must turn from sin and trust in God to save us.

13:29 God's kingdom will include people from every part of the world. Israel's rejection of Jesus as Messiah would not stop God's plan. True Israel includes all people who believe in God. This was an important fact for Luke to stress as he was directing his Gospel to a Gentile audience (see also Romans 4:16–25; Galatians 3:6–9).

13:30 There will be many surprises in God's kingdom. Some who are despised now will be greatly honoured then; some influential people here will be left outside the gates. Many "great" people on this earth (in God's eyes) are virtually ignored by the rest of the world. What matters to God is not a person's earthly popularity, status, wealth, heritage, or power, but his or her commitment to Christ. How do your values match what the Bible tells you to value? Put God in first place, and you will join people from all over the world who will take their places at the feast in the kingdom of heaven.

13:31–33 The Pharisees weren't interested in protecting Jesus from danger. They were trying to trap him themselves. The Pharisees urged Jesus to leave because they wanted to stop him from going to Jerusalem, not because they feared Herod. But Jesus' life, work, and death were not to be determined by Herod or the Pharisees. His life was planned and directed by God himself, and his mission would unfold in God's time and according to God's plan.

13:33, 34 Why was Jesus focusing on Jerusalem? Jerusalem, the city of God, symbolised the entire nation. It was Israel's largest city and the nation's spiritual and political capital, and Jews from around the world visited it frequently. But Jerusalem had a history of rejecting God's prophets (1 Kings 19:10; 2 Chronicles 24:19; Jeremiah 2:30; 26:20–23), and it would reject the Messiah just as it had rejected his forerunners.

14:1–6 Earlier Jesus had been invited to a Pharisee's home for discussion (7:36). This time a prominent Pharisee invited Jesus to his home specifically to trap him into saying or doing something for which he could be arrested. It may be surprising to see Jesus on the Pharisees' turf after he had denounced them so many times. But he was not afraid to face them, even though he knew that their purpose was to trick him into breaking their laws.

5 Then he asked them, "If one of you has a son[a] or an ox that falls into a well on
the Sabbath day, will you not immediately pull him out?"[e] 6 And they had nothing
to say.

Jesus Teaches about Seeking Honour
(156)

7 When he noticed how the guests picked the places of honour at the table,[f] he told
them this parable: 8 "When someone invites you to a wedding feast, do not take the
place of honour, for a person more distinguished than you may have been invited. 9 If
so, the host who invited both of you will come and say to you, 'Give this man your
seat.' Then, humiliated, you will have to take the least important place. 10 But when
you are invited, take the lowest place, so that when your host comes, he will say to
you, 'Friend, move up to a better place.' Then you will be honoured in the presence
of all your fellow guests. 11 For everyone who exalts himself will be humbled, and
he who humbles himself will be exalted."[g]

12 Then Jesus said to his host, "When you give a luncheon or dinner, do not invite
your friends, your brothers or relatives, or your rich neighbours; if you do, they may
invite you back and so you will be repaid. 13 But when you give a banquet, invite the
poor, the crippled, the lame, the blind,[h] 14 and you will be blessed. Although they
cannot repay you, you will be repaid at the resurrection of the righteous."[i]

Jesus Tells the Parable of the Great Feast
(157)

15 When one of those at the table with him heard this, he said to Jesus, "Blessed
is the man who will eat at the feast[j] in the kingdom of God."[k]

16 Jesus replied: "A certain man was preparing a great banquet and invited many
guests. 17 At the time of the banquet he sent his servant to tell those who had been
invited, 'Come, for everything is now ready.'

18 "But they all alike began to make excuses. The first said, 'I have just bought a
field, and I must go and see it. Please excuse me.'

19 "Another said, 'I have just bought five yoke of oxen, and I'm on my way to try
them out. Please excuse me.'

14:5 [e] Lk 13:15
14:7 [f] Lk 11:43
14:11 [g] Mt 23:12; Lk 18:14
14:13 [h] ver 21
14:14 [i] Ac 24:15
14:15 [j] Isa 25:6; Mt 26:29; Lk 13:29; Rev 19:9 [k] Mt 3:2

[a] *5* Some manuscripts *donkey*

14:2 Luke, the physician, identifies this man's disease – he was suffering from *dropsy*, an abnormal accumulation of fluid in bodily tissues and cavities.

14:7–11 Jesus advised people not to rush for the best places at a feast. People today are just as eager to raise their social status, whether by being with the right people, dressing for success, or driving the right car. Whom do you try to impress? Rather than aiming for prestige, look for a place where you can serve. If God wants you to serve on a wider scale, he will invite you to take a higher place.

14:7–14 Jesus taught two lessons here. First, he spoke to the guests, telling them not to seek places of honour. Service is more important in God's kingdom than status. Second, he told the host not to be exclusive about whom he invites. God opens his kingdom to everyone.

14:11 How can we humble ourselves? Some people try to give the appearance of humility in order to manipulate others. Others think that humility means putting themselves down. Truly humble people compare themselves only with Christ, realise their sinfulness, and understand their limitations. On the other hand, they also recognise their gifts and strengths and are willing to use them as Christ directs. Humility is not self-degradation; it is realistic assessment and commitment to serve.

14:15–24 The man sitting at the table with Jesus saw the glory of God's kingdom, but he did not yet understand how to get in. In Jesus' story, many people turned down the invitation to the banquet because the timing was inconvenient. We too can resist or delay responding to God's invitation, and our excuses may sound reasonable – work duties, family responsibilities, financial needs, or whatever they may be. Nevertheless, God's invitation is the most important event in our lives, no matter how inconveniently it may be timed. Are you making excuses to avoid responding to God's call? Jesus reminds us that the time will come when God will cancel his invitation and offer it to others – then it will be too late to get into the banquet.

14:16ff It was customary to send two invitations to a party – the first to announce the event, the second to tell the guests that everything was ready. The guests in Jesus' story insulted the host by making excuses when he issued the second invitation. In Israel's history, God's first invitation came from Moses and the prophets; the second came from his Son. The religious leaders accepted the first invitation. They believed that God had called them to be his people, but they insulted God by refusing to accept his Son. Thus, as the master in the story sent his servant into the streets to invite the needy to his banquet, so God sent his Son to the whole world of needy people to tell them that God's kingdom had arrived and was ready for them.

14:16ff In this chapter we read Jesus' words against seeking status, and in favour of hard work and even suffering. Let us not lose sight of the end result of all our humility and self-sacrifice – a joyous banquet with our Lord! God never asks us to suffer for the sake of suffering. He never asks us to give up something good unless he plans to replace it with something even better. Jesus is not calling us to join him in a labour camp but in a feast – the wedding supper of the Lamb (Revelation 19:6–9), when God and his beloved church will be joined for ever.

20"Still another said, 'I have just got married, so I can't come.'
21"The servant came back and reported this to his master. Then the owner of the
house became angry and ordered his servant, 'Go out quickly into the streets and alleys
of the town and bring in the poor, the crippled, the blind and the lame.'[l]
22" 'Sir,' the servant said, 'what you ordered has been done, but there is still room.'
23"Then the master told his servant, 'Go out to the roads and country lanes and make
them come in, so that my house will be full. 24I tell you, not one of those men who
were invited will get a taste of my banquet.' "[m]

Jesus Teaches about the Cost of Being a Disciple
(158)

25Large crowds were travelling with Jesus, and turning to them he said: 26"If anyone
comes to me and does not hate his father and mother, his wife and children, his
brothers and sisters—yes, even his own life—he cannot be my disciple.[n] 27And
anyone who does not carry his cross and follow me cannot be my disciple.[o]
28"Suppose one of you wants to build a tower. Will he not first sit down and estimate
the cost to see if he has enough money to complete it? 29For if he lays the foundation
and is not able to finish it, everyone who sees it will ridicule him, 30saying, 'This
fellow began to build and was not able to finish.'
31"Or suppose a king is about to go to war against another king. Will he not first
sit down and consider whether he is able with ten thousand men to oppose the one
coming against him with twenty thousand? 32If he is not able, he will send a delegation
while the other is still a long way off and will ask for terms of peace. 33In the same
way, any of you who does not give up everything he has cannot be my disciple.[p]
34"Salt is good, but if it loses its saltiness, how can it be made salty again?[q] 35It
is fit neither for the soil nor for the manure heap; it is thrown out.[r]
"He who has ears to hear, let him hear."[s]

Jesus Tells the Parable of the Lost Sheep
(159)

15 Now the tax collectors[a] and "sinners" were all gathering round to hear him.
2But the Pharisees and the teachers of the law muttered, "This man welcomes
sinners, and eats with them."[b]
3Then Jesus told them this parable:[c] 4"Suppose one of you has a hundred sheep

14:21 [l]ver 13
14:24 [m]Mt 21:43; Ac 13:46
14:26 [n]Mt 10:37; Jn 12:25
14:27 [o]Mt 10:38; Lk 9:23
14:33 [p]Php 3:7, 8
14:34 [q]Mk 9:50
14:35 [r]Mt 5:13 [s]Mt 11:15
15:1 [a]Lk 5:29
15:2 [b]Mt 9:11
15:3 [c]Mt 13:3

14:27 Jesus' audience was well aware of what it meant to carry one's own cross. When the Romans led a criminal to his execution site, he was forced to carry the cross on which he would die. This showed his submission to Rome and warned observers that they had better submit too. Jesus spoke this teaching to get the crowds to think through their enthusiasm for him. He encouraged those who were superficial either to go deeper or to turn back. Following Christ means total submission to him—perhaps even to the point of death.

14:28–30 When a builder doesn't count the cost or estimates it inaccurately, his building may be left half completed. Will your Christian life be only half built and then abandoned because you did not count the cost of commitment to Jesus? What are those costs? Christians may face loss of social status or wealth. They may have to give up control over their money, their time, or their career. They may be hated, separated from their family, and even put to death. Following Christ does not mean a trouble-free life. We must carefully count the cost of becoming Christ's disciples so that we will know what we are getting into and won't be tempted later to turn back.

14:34 Salt can lose its flavour. When it gets wet and then dries, nothing is left but a tasteless residue. Many Christians blend into the world and avoid the cost of standing up for Christ. But Jesus says if Christians lose their distinctive saltiness, they become worthless. Just as salt flavours and preserves food, we are to preserve the good in the world, help keep it from spoiling, and bring new flavour to life. This requires careful planning, willing sacrifice, and unswerving commitment to Christ's kingdom. Being "salty" is not easy, but if a Christian fails in this function, he or she fails to represent Christ in the world. How salty are you?

15:2 Why were the Pharisees and teachers of the law bothered that Jesus associated with these people? The religious leaders were always careful to stay "clean" according to Old Testament law. In fact, they went well beyond the law in their avoidance of certain people and situations and in their ritual washings. By contrast, Jesus took their concept of "cleanness" lightly. He risked defilement by touching those who had leprosy and by neglecting to wash in the Pharisees' prescribed manner, and he showed complete disregard for their sanctions against associating with certain classes of people. He came to offer salvation to sinners, to show that God loves them. Jesus didn't worry about the accusations. Instead he continued going to those who needed him, regardless of the effect these rejected people might have on his reputation. What keeps you away from people who need Christ?

15:3–6 It may seem foolish for the shepherd to leave 99 sheep to go in search of just one. But the shepherd knew that the 99 would be safe in the fold, whereas the lost sheep was in danger. Because each sheep was of high value, the shepherd knew that it was worthwhile to search diligently for the lost one. God's love for each individual is so great that he seeks each one out and rejoices when he or she is "found". Jesus associated with sinners because he wanted to bring the lost sheep—people considered beyond

and loses one of them. Does he not leave the ninety-nine in the open country and go
after the lost sheep until he finds it?[d] 5 And when he finds it, he joyfully puts it on
his shoulders 6 and goes home. Then he calls his friends and neighbours together and
says, 'Rejoice with me; I have found my lost sheep.'[e] 7 I tell you that in the same
way there will be more rejoicing in heaven over one sinner who repents than over
ninety-nine righteous persons who do not need to repent.[f]

Jesus Tells the Parable of the Lost Coin
(160)

8 "Or suppose a woman has ten silver coins[a] and loses one. Does she not light a
lamp, sweep the house and search carefully until she finds it? 9 And when she finds
it, she calls her friends and neighbours together and says, 'Rejoice with me; I have
found my lost coin.'[g] 10 In the same way, I tell you, there is rejoicing in the presence
of the angels of God over one sinner who repents."[h]

Jesus Tells the Parable of the Lost Son
(161)

11 Jesus continued: "There was a man who had two sons.[i] 12 The younger one said
to his father, 'Father, give me my share of the estate.'[j] So he divided his property[k]
between them.

13 "Not long after that, the younger son got together all he had, set off for a distant
country and there squandered his wealth[l] in wild living. 14 After he had spent
everything, there was a severe famine in that whole country, and he began to be in
need. 15 So he went and hired himself out to a citizen of that country, who sent him
to his fields to feed pigs.[m] 16 He longed to fill his stomach with the pods that the pigs
were eating, but no-one gave him anything.

17 "When he came to his senses, he said, 'How many of my father's hired men have
food to spare, and here I am starving to death! 18 I will set out and go back to my father
and say to him: Father, I have sinned[n] against heaven and against you. 19 I am no
longer worthy to be called your son; make me like one of your hired men.' 20 So he
got up and went to his father.

"But while he was still a long way off, his father saw him and was filled with
compassion for him; he ran to his son, threw his arms around him and kissed him.[o]

15:4 [d]Ps 23; 119:176; Jer 31:10; Eze 34:11-16; Lk 5:32; 19:10
15:6 [e]ver 9
15:7 [f]ver 10
15:9 [g]ver 6
15:10 [h]ver 7
15:11 [i]Mt 21:28
15:12 [j]Dt 21:17 [k]ver 30
15:13 [l]ver 30; Lk 16:1
15:15 [m]Lev 11:7
15:18 [n]Lev 26:40; Mt 3:2
15:20 [o]Ge 45:14, 15; 46:29; Ac 20:37

[a] 8 Greek *ten drachmas*, each worth about a day's wages

---

hope—the gospel of God's kingdom. Before you were a believer, God sought you; and his love is still seeking those who are yet lost.

15:4, 5 We may be able to understand a God who would forgive sinners who come to him for mercy. But a God who tenderly searches for sinners and then joyfully forgives them must possess an extraordinary love! This is the kind of love that prompted Jesus to come to earth to search for lost people and save them. This is the kind of extraordinary love that God has for you. If you feel far from God, don't despair. He is seaching for you.

15:8–10 Palestinian women received ten silver coins as a wedding gift. Besides their monetary value, these coins held sentimental value like that of a wedding ring, and to lose one would be extremely distressing. Just as a woman would rejoice at finding her lost coin or ring, so the angels would rejoice over a repentant sinner. Each individual is precious to God. He grieves over every loss and rejoices whenever one of his children is found and brought into the kingdom. Perhaps we would have more joy in our churches if we shared Jesus' love and concern for the lost.

15:12 The younger son's share of the estate would have been one-third, with the older son receiving two-thirds (Deuteronomy 21:17). In most cases he would have received this at his father's death, although fathers sometimes chose to divide up their inheritance early and retire from managing their estates. What is unusual here is that the younger one initiated the division of the estate. This showed arrogant disregard for his father's authority as head of the family.

15:15, 16 According to Moses' law, pigs were unclean animals (Leviticus 11:2–8; Deuteronomy 14:8). This meant that pigs could not be eaten or used for sacrifices. To protect themselves from defilement, Jews would not even touch pigs. For a Jew to stoop to feeding pigs was a great humiliation, and for this young man to eat food that the pigs had touched was to be degraded beyond belief. The younger son had truly sunk to the depths.

15:17 The younger son, like many who are rebellious and immature, wanted to be free to live as he pleased, and he had to hit rock bottom before he came to his senses. It often takes great sorrow and tragedy to cause people to look to the only One who can help them. Are you trying to live life your own way, selfishly pushing aside any responsibility or commitment that gets in your way? Stop and look before you hit rock bottom. You will save yourself and your family much grief.

15:20 In the two preceding stories, the seekers actively looked for the coin and the sheep, which could not return by themselves. In this story, the father watched and waited. He was dealing with a human being with a will of his own, but he was ready to greet his son if he returned. In the same way, God's love is constant and patient and welcoming. He will search for us and give us opportunities to respond, but he will not force us to come to him. Like the father in this story, God waits patiently for us to come to our senses.

21“The son said to him, ‘Father, I have sinned against heaven and against you.[p]
I am no longer worthy to be called your son.’[b]
22“But the father said to his servants, ‘Quick! Bring the best robe[q] and put it on
him. Put a ring on his finger[r] and sandals on his feet. 23Bring the fattened calf and
kill it. Let’s have a feast and celebrate. 24For this son of mine was dead and is alive
again;[s] he was lost and is found.’ So they began to celebrate.[t]
25“Meanwhile, the older son was in the field. When he came near the house, he
heard music and dancing. 26So he called one of the servants and asked him what was
going on. 27‘Your brother has come,’ he replied, ‘and your father has killed the
fattened calf because he has him back safe and sound.’
28“The older brother became angry[u] and refused to go in. So his father went out
and pleaded with him. 29But he answered his father, ‘Look! All these years I’ve been
slaving for you and never disobeyed your orders. Yet you never gave me even a young
goat so I could celebrate with my friends. 30But when this son of yours who has
squandered your property[v] with prostitutes[w] comes home, you kill the fattened calf
for him!’
31“ ‘My son,’ the father said, ‘you are always with me, and everything I have is
yours. 32But we had to celebrate and be glad, because this brother of yours was dead
and is alive again; he was lost and is found.’ ”[x]

Jesus Tells the Parable of the Shrewd Manager
(162)

16 Jesus told his disciples: “There was a rich man whose manager was accused
of wasting his possessions.[a] 2So he called him in and asked him, ‘What is this
I hear about you? Give an account of your management, because you cannot be
manager any longer.’
3“The manager said to himself, ‘What shall I do now? My master is taking away
my job. I’m not strong enough to dig, and I’m ashamed to beg—4I know what I’ll
do so that, when I lose my job here, people will welcome me into their houses.’
5“So he called in each one of his master’s debtors. He asked the first, ‘How much
do you owe my master?’
6“ ‘Eight hundred gallons[a] of olive oil,’ he replied.
“The manager told him, ‘Take your bill, sit down quickly, and make it four
hundred.’
7“Then he asked the second, ‘And how much do you owe?’
“ ‘A thousand bushels[b] of wheat,’ he replied.
“He told him, ‘Take your bill and make it eight hundred.’
8“The master commended the dishonest manager because he had acted shrewdly.
For the people of this world[b] are more shrewd[c] in dealing with their own kind than

15:21 [p]Ps 51:4
15:22 [q]Zec 3:4; Rev 6:11 [r]Ge 41:42
15:24 [s]Eph 2:1, 5; 5:14; 1Ti 5:6 [t]ver 32
15:28 [u]Jnh 4:1
15:30 [v]ver 12, 13 [w]Pr 29:3
15:32 [x]ver 24; Mal 3:17
16:1 [a]Lk 15:13, 30
16:8 [b]Ps 17:14 [c]Ps 18:26

[b] *21* Some early manuscripts *son. Make me like one of your hired men.* [a] *6* Greek *one hundred batous* (probably about 3 kilolitres) [b] *7* Greek *one hundred korous* (probably about 35 kilolitres)

15:24 The sheep was lost because it may have foolishly wandered away (15:4); the coin was lost through no fault of its own (15:8); and the son left out of selfishness (15:12). God’s great love reaches out and finds sinners no matter why or how they got lost.

15:25–31 It was hard for the older brother to accept his younger brother when he returned, and it is just as difficult to accept “younger brothers” today. People who repent after leading notoriously sinful lives are often held in suspicion; churches are sometimes unwilling to admit them to membership. Instead, we should rejoice like the angels in heaven when an unbeliever repents and turns to God. Like the father, accept repentant sinners wholeheartedly and give them the support and encouragement that they need to grow in Christ.

15:30 In the story of the lost son, the father’s response is contrasted with the older brother’s. The father forgave because he was filled with love. The son refused to forgive because he was bitter about the injustice of it all. His resentment rendered him just as lost to the father’s love as his younger brother had been. Don’t let anything keep you from forgiving others. If you are refusing to forgive people, you are missing a wonderful opportunity to experience joy and share it with others. Make your joy grow: forgive somebody who has hurt you.

15:32 In Jesus’ story, the older brother represented the Pharisees, who were angry and resentful that sinners were being welcomed into God’s kingdom. After all, the Pharisees must have thought, we have sacrificed and done *so much* for God. How easy it is to resent God’s gracious forgiveness of others whom we consider to be far worse sinners than ourselves. But when our self-righteousness gets in the way of rejoicing when others come to Jesus, we are no better than the Pharisees.

16:1–8 Our use of money is a good test of the lordship of Christ. (1) Let us use our resources wisely because they belong to God, and not to us. (2) Money can be used for good or evil; let us use ours for good. (3) Money has a lot of power, so we must use it carefully and thoughtfully. (4) We must use our material goods in a way that will foster faith and obedience (see 12:33, 34).

are the people of the light.[d] 9I tell you, use worldly wealth[e] to gain friends for
yourselves, so that when it is gone, you will be welcomed into eternal dwellings.[f]
10"Whoever can be trusted with very little can also be trusted with much,[g] and
whoever is dishonest with very little will also be dishonest with much. 11So if you
have not been trustworthy in handling worldly wealth,[h] who will trust you with true
riches? 12And if you have not been trustworthy with someone else's property, who
will give you property of your own?
13"No servant can serve two masters. Either he will hate the one and love the other,
or he will be devoted to the one and despise the other. You cannot serve both God
and Money."[i]
14The Pharisees, who loved money,[j] heard all this and were sneering at Jesus.[k]
15He said to them, "You are the ones who justify yourselves[l] in the eyes of men,
but God knows your hearts.[m] What is highly valued among men is detestable in God's
sight.
16"The Law and the Prophets were proclaimed until John.[n] Since that time, the
good news of the kingdom of God is being preached,[o] and everyone is forcing his
way into it. 17It is easier for heaven and earth to disappear than for the least stroke
of a pen to drop out of the Law.[p]
18"Anyone who divorces his wife and marries another woman commits adultery,
and the man who marries a divorced woman commits adultery.[q]

Jesus Tells about the Rich Man and the Beggar
(163)

19"There was a rich man who was dressed in purple and fine linen and lived in
luxury every day.[r] 20At his gate was laid a beggar[s] named Lazarus, covered with
sores 21and longing to eat what fell from the rich man's table.[t] Even the dogs came
and licked his sores.
22"The time came when the beggar died and the angels carried him to Abraham's

16:8 [d]Jn 12:36; Eph 5:8; 1Th 5:5
16:9 [e]ver 11, 13 [f]Mt 19:21; Lk 12:33
16:10 [g]Mt 25:21, 23; Lk 19:17
16:11 [h]ver 9, 13
16:13 [i]ver 9, 11; Mt 6:24
16:14 [j]1Ti 3:3 [k]Lk 23:35
16:15 [l]Lk 10:29 [m]1Sa 16:7; Rev 2:23
16:16 [n]Mt 11:12, 13 [o]Mt 4:23
16:17 [p]Mt 5:18
16:18 [q]Mt 5:31, 32; 19:9; Mk 10:11; Ro 7:2, 3; 1Co 7:10, 11
16:19 [r]Eze 16:49
16:20 [s]Ac 3:2
16:21 [t]Mt 15:27

16:9 We are to make wise use of the financial opportunities we have, not to earn heaven, but so that heaven ("eternal dwellings") will be a welcome experience for those we help. If we use our money to help those in need or to help others find Christ, our earthly investment will bring eternal benefit. When we obey God's will, the unselfish use of possessions will follow.

16:10, 11 Our integrity often meets its match in money matters. God calls us to be honest even in small details we could easily rationalise away. Heaven's riches are far more valuable than earthly wealth. But if we are not trustworthy with our money here (no matter how much or little we have), we will be unfit to handle the vast riches of God's kingdom. Don't let your integrity slip in small matters, and it will not fail you in crucial decisions either.

16:13 Money has the power to take God's place in your life. It can become your master. How can you tell if you are a slave to Money? (1) Do you think and worry about it frequently? (2) Do you give up doing what you should do or would like to do in order to make more money? (3) Do you spend a great deal of your time caring for your possessions? (4) Is it hard for you to give money away? (5) Are you in debt?

Money is a hard master and a deceptive one. Wealth promises power and control, but often it cannot deliver. Great fortunes can be made – and lost – overnight, and no amount of money can provide health, happiness, or eternal life. How much better it is to let God be your Master. His servants have peace of mind and security, both now and for ever.

16:14 Because the Pharisees loved money, they took exception to Jesus' teaching. We live in an age that measures people's worth by how much money they make. Do we laugh at Jesus' warnings against serving Money? Do we try to explain them away? Do we apply them to someone else – the Pharisees, for example? Unless we take Jesus' statements seriously, we may be acting like Pharisees ourselves.

16:15 The Pharisees acted piously to get praise from others, but God knew what was in their hearts. They considered their wealth to be a sign of God's approval. God detested their wealth because it caused them to abandon true spirituality. Though prosperity may earn people's praise, it must never substitute for devotion and service to God.

16:16, 17 John the Baptist's ministry was the dividing line between the Old and New Testaments (John 1:15–18). With the arrival of Jesus came the realisation of all the prophets' hopes. Jesus emphasised that his kingdom fulfilled the law (the Old Testament); it did not cancel it (Matthew 5:17). His was not a new system but the culmination of the old. The same God who worked through Moses was working through Jesus.

16:18 Most religious leaders of Jesus' day permitted a man to divorce his wife for nearly any reason. Jesus' teaching about divorce went beyond Moses' (Deuteronomy 24:1–4). Stricter than any of the then-current schools of thought, Jesus' teachings shocked his hearers (see Matthew 19:10) just as they shake today's readers. Jesus says in no uncertain terms that marriage is a lifetime commitment. To leave your spouse for another person may be legal, but it is adultery in God's eyes. As you think about marriage, remember that God intends it to be a permanent commitment.

16:19–31 The Pharisees considered wealth to be a proof of a person's righteousness. Jesus startled them with this story where a diseased beggar is rewarded and a rich man is punished. The rich man did not go to hell because of his wealth but because he was selfish, refusing to feed Lazarus, take him in, or care for him. The rich man was hardhearted in spite of his great blessings. The amount of money we have is not as important as the way we use it. What is your attitude towards your money and possessions? Do you hoard them selfishly, or do you use them to help others?

16:20 This Lazarus should not be confused with the Lazarus whom Jesus raised from the dead in John 11.

side. The rich man also died and was buried. 23In hell,[c] where he was in torment,
he looked up and saw Abraham far away, with Lazarus by his side. 24So he called
to him, 'Father Abraham,[u] have pity on me and send Lazarus to dip the tip of his
finger in water and cool my tongue, because I am in agony in this fire.'[v]
25"But Abraham replied, 'Son, remember that in your lifetime you received your
good things, while Lazarus received bad things,[w] but now he is comforted here and
you are in agony.[x] 26And besides all this, between us and you a great chasm has been
fixed, so that those who want to go from here to you cannot, nor can anyone cross
over from there to us.'
27"He answered, 'Then I beg you, father, send Lazarus to my father's house, 28for
I have five brothers. Let him warn them,[y] so that they will not also come to this place
of torment.'
29"Abraham replied, 'They have Moses[z] and the Prophets;[a] let them listen to
them.'
30" 'No, father Abraham,'[b] he said, 'but if someone from the dead goes to them,
they will repent.'
31"He said to him, 'If they do not listen to Moses and the Prophets, they will not
be convinced even if someone rises from the dead.' "

Jesus Tells about Forgiveness and Faith
(164)

17 Jesus said to his disciples: "Things that cause people to sin[a] are bound to come,
but woe to that person through whom they come.[b] 2It would be better for him
to be thrown into the sea with a millstone tied round his neck than for him to cause
one of these little ones[c] to sin.[d] 3So watch yourselves.
"If your brother sins, rebuke him,[e] and if he repents, forgive him.[f] 4If he sins
against you seven times in a day, and seven times comes back to you and says, 'I
repent,' forgive him."[g]
5The apostles[h] said to the Lord,[i] "Increase our faith!"
6He replied, "If you have faith as small as a mustard seed,[j] you can say to this
mulberry tree, 'Be uprooted and planted in the sea,' and it will obey you.[k]
7"Suppose one of you had a servant ploughing or looking after the sheep. Would
he say to the servant when he comes in from the field, 'Come along now and sit down
to eat'? 8Would he not rather say, 'Prepare my supper, get yourself ready and wait
on me[l] while I eat and drink; after that you may eat and drink'? 9Would he thank

[c] 23 Greek *Hades*

16:24 [u]ver 30; Lk 3:8 [v]Mt 5:22
16:25 [w]Ps 17:14 [x]Lk 6:21, 24, 25
16:28 [y]Ac 2:40; 20:23; 1Th 4:6
16:29 [z]Lk 24:27, 44; Jn 5:45-47; Ac 15:21 [a]Lk 4:17; Jn 1:45
16:30 [b]ver 24; Lk 3:8
17:1 [a]Mt 5:29 [b]Mt 18:7
17:2 [c]Mk 10:24; Lk 10:21 [d]Mt 5:29
17:3 [e]Mt 18:15 [f]Eph 4:32; Col 3:13
17:4 [g]Mt 18:21, 22
17:5 [h]Mk 6:30 [i]Lk 7:13
17:6 [j]Mt 13:31; 17:20; Lk 13:19 [k]Mt 21:21; Mk 9:23
17:8 [l]Lk 12:37

16:29–31 The rich man thought that his five brothers would surely believe a messenger who had been raised from the dead. But Jesus said that if they did not believe Moses and the prophets, who spoke constantly of the duty to care for the poor, not even a resurrection would convince them. Notice the irony in Jesus' statement; on his way to Jerusalem to die, he was fully aware that even when he had risen from the dead, most of the religious leaders would not accept him. They were set in their ways, and neither Scripture nor God's Son himself would shake them loose.

17:1–3 Jesus may have been directing this warning at the religious leaders who taught their converts their own hypocritical ways (see Matthew 23:15). They were perpetuating an evil system. A person who teaches others has a solemn responsibility (James 3:1). Like physicians, a teacher should keep this ancient oath in mind: "First, do no harm."

17:3, 4 To rebuke does not mean to point out every sin we see; it means to bring sin to a person's attention with the purpose of restoring him or her to God and to fellow humans. When you feel you must rebuke another Christian for a sin, check your attitudes before you speak. Do you love the person? Are you willing to forgive? Unless rebuke is tied to forgiveness, it will not help the sinning person.

17:5, 6 The disciples' request was genuine; they wanted the faith necessary for such radical forgiveness. But Jesus didn't directly answer their question because the amount of faith is not as important as its genuineness. What is faith? It is total dependence on God and a willingness to do his will. Faith is not something we use to put on a show for others. It is complete and humble obedience to God's will, readiness to do whatever he calls us to do. The amount of faith isn't as important as the right kind of faith – faith in our all-powerful God.

17:6 A mustard seed is small, but it is alive and growing. Like a tiny seed, a small amount of genuine faith in God will take root and grow. Almost invisible at first, it will begin to spread, first under the ground and then visibly. Although each change will be gradual and imperceptible, soon this faith will have produced major results that will uproot and destroy competing loyalties. We don't need more faith; a tiny seed of faith is enough, if it is alive and growing.

17:7–10 If we have obeyed God, we have only done our duty and we should regard it as a privilege. Do you sometimes feel that you deserve extra credit for serving God? Remember, obedience is not something extra we do; it is our duty. Jesus is not rendering our service as meaningless or useless, nor is he doing away with rewards. He is attacking unwarranted self-esteem and spiritual pride.

the servant because he did what he was told to do? 10 So you also, when you have done everything you were told to do, should say, 'We are unworthy servants; we have only done our duty.' "[m]

Jesus Heals Ten Men with Leprosy (169)

11 Now on his way to Jerusalem,[n] Jesus travelled along the border between Samaria and Galilee.[o] 12 As he was going into a village, ten men who had leprosy[a][p] met him. They stood at a distance[q] 13 and called out in a loud voice, "Jesus, Master,[r] have pity on us!"

14 When he saw them, he said, "Go, show yourselves to the priests."[s] And as they went, they were cleansed.

15 One of them, when he saw he was healed, came back, praising God[t] in a loud voice. 16 He threw himself at Jesus' feet and thanked him—and he was a Samaritan.[u]

17 Jesus asked, "Were not all ten cleansed? Where are the other nine? 18 Was no-one found to return and give praise to God except this foreigner?" 19 Then he said to him, "Rise and go; your faith has made you well."[v]

Jesus Teaches about the Coming of the Kingdom of God (170)

20 Once, having been asked by the Pharisees when the kingdom of God would come,[w] Jesus replied, "The kingdom of God does not come with your careful observation, 21 nor will people say, 'Here it is,' or 'There it is,'[x] because the kingdom of God is within[b] you."

22 Then he said to his disciples, "The time is coming when you will long to see one of the days of the Son of Man,[y] but you will not see it.[z] 23 Men will tell you, 'There

17:10 [m] 1Co 9:16
17:11 [n] Lk 9:51 [o] Lk 9:51, 52; Jn 4:3, 4
17:12 [p] Mt 8:2 [q] Lev 13:45, 46
17:13 [r] Lk 5:5
17:14 [s] Lev 14:2; Mt 8:4
17:15 [t] Mt 9:8
17:16 [u] Mt 10:5
17:19 [v] Mt 9:22
17:20 [w] Mt 3:2
17:21 [x] ver 23
17:22 [y] Mt 8:20 [z] Mt 9:15; Lk 5:35

[a] *12* The Greek word was used for various diseases affecting the skin—not necessarily leprosy. [b] *21* Or *among*

17:11–14 People who had leprosy were required to try to stay away from other people and to announce their presence if they had to come near. Sometimes leprosy went into remission. If a leper thought his leprosy had gone away, he was supposed to present himself to a priest who could declare him clean (Leviticus 14). Jesus sent the ten lepers to the priest *before* they were healed—and they went! They responded in faith, and Jesus healed them on the way. Is your trust in God so strong that you act on what he says even before you see evidence that it will work?

17:16 Jesus healed all ten lepers, but only one returned to thank him. It is possible to receive God's great gifts with an ungrateful spirit—nine of the ten men did so. Only the thankful man, however, learned that his faith had played a role in his healing; and only grateful Christians grow in understanding God's grace. God does not demand that we thank him, but he is pleased when we do so. And he uses our responsiveness to teach us more about himself.

17:16 Not only was this man a leper, he was also a Samaritan—a race despised by the Jews as idolatrous half-breeds (see the note on 10:33). Once again Luke is pointing out that God's grace is for everybody.

17:20, 21 The Pharisees asked when God's kingdom would come, not knowing that it had already arrived. The kingdom of God is not like an earthly kingdom with geographical boundaries. Instead, it begins with the work of God's Spirit in people's lives and in relationships. Still today we must resist looking to institutions or events for evidence of the progress of God's kingdom. Instead, we should look for what God is doing in people's hearts.

17:23, 24 Many will claim to be the Messiah and many will claim that Jesus has returned—and people will believe them. Jesus warns us never to take such reports seriously, no matter how convincing they may sound. When Jesus returns, his power and presence will be evident to everyone. No-one will need to spread the message because all will see for themselves.

17:23–36 Life will be going on as usual on the day Christ returns. There will be no warning. Most people will be going about their everyday tasks, indifferent to the demands of God. They will be as surprised by Christ's return as the people in Noah's day were by the flood (Genesis 6–8) or the people in Lot's day by the destruction of Sodom (Genesis 19). We don't know the time of Christ's return, but we do know that he is coming. He may come today, tomorrow, or centuries in the future. Whenever he comes, we must be morally and spiritually ready. Live as if Jesus were returning today.

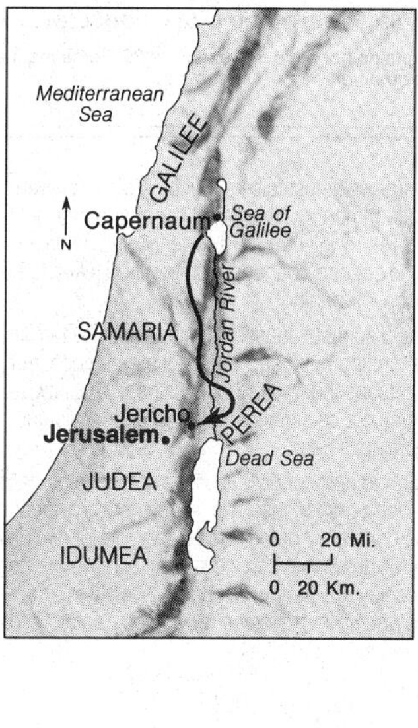

LAST TRIP FROM GALILEE
Jesus left Galilee for the last time—he would not return before his death. He passed through Samaria, met and healed ten men who had leprosy, and continued to Jerusalem. He spent some time east of the Jordan (Mark 10:1) before going to Jericho (19:1).

he is!' or 'Here he is!' Do not go running off after them.[a] 24For the Son of Man in
his day[c] will be like the lightning,[b] which flashes and lights up the sky from one
end to the other. 25But first he must suffer many things[c] and be rejected[d] by this
generation.[e]
26"Just as it was in the days of Noah,[f] so also will it be in the days of the Son
of Man. 27People were eating, drinking, marrying and being given in marriage up to
the day Noah entered the ark. Then the flood came and destroyed them all.
28"It was the same in the days of Lot.[g] People were eating and drinking, buying
and selling, planting and building. 29But the day Lot left Sodom, fire and sulphur
rained down from heaven and destroyed them all.
30"It will be just like this on the day the Son of Man is revealed.[h] 31On that day
no-one who is on the roof of his house, with his goods inside, should go down to get
them. Likewise, no-one in the field should go back for anything.[i] 32Remember Lot's
wife![j] 33Whoever tries to keep his life will lose it, and whoever loses his life will
preserve it.[k] 34I tell you, on that night two people will be in one bed; one will be
taken and the other left. 35Two women will be grinding grain together; one will be
taken and the other left."[d] [l]
37"Where, Lord?" they asked.
He replied, "Where there is a dead body, there the vultures will gather."[m]

Jesus Tells the Parable of the Persistent Widow
(171)

18 Then Jesus told his disciples a parable to show them that they should always
pray and not give up.[a] 2He said: "In a certain town there was a judge who
neither feared God nor cared about men. 3And there was a widow in that town who
kept coming to him with the plea, 'Grant me justice[b] against my adversary.'
4"For some time he refused. But finally he said to himself, 'Even though I don't
fear God or care about men, 5yet because this widow keeps bothering me, I will see
that she gets justice, so that she won't eventually wear me out with her coming!' "[c]
6And the Lord[d] said, "Listen to what the unjust judge says. 7And will not God
bring about justice for his chosen ones, who cry out[e] to him day and night? Will he
keep putting them off? 8I tell you, he will see that they get justice, and quickly.
However, when the Son of Man[f] comes,[g] will he find faith on the earth?"

Jesus Tells the Parable of Two Men Who Prayed
(172)

9To some who were confident of their own righteousness[h] and looked down on
everybody else,[i] Jesus told this parable: 10"Two men went up to the temple to pray,[j]
one a Pharisee and the other a tax collector. 11The Pharisee stood up[k] and prayed

17:23 [a]Mt 24:23; Mk 13:21; Lk 21:8
17:24 [b]Mt 24:27
17:25 [c]Mt 16:21 [d]Lk 9:22; 18:32 [e]Mk 13:30; Lk 21:32
17:26 [f]Ge 7:6-24
17:28 [g]Ge 19:1-28
17:30 [h]Mt 10:23; 16:27; 24:3, 27, 37, 39; 25:31; 1Co 1:7; 1Th 2:19; 2Th 1:7; 2:8; 2Pe 3:4; Rev 1:7
17:31 [i]Mt 24:17, 18; Mk 13:15-16
17:32 [j]Ge 19:26
17:33 [k]Jn 12:25
17:35 [l]Mt 24:41
17:37 [m]Mt 24:28
18:1 [a]Isa 40:31; Lk 11:5-8; Ac 1:14; Ro 12:12; Eph 6:18; Col 4:2; 1Th 5:17
18:3 [b]Isa 1:17
18:5 [c]Lk 11:8
18:6 [d]Lk 7:13
18:7 [e]Ex 22:23; Ps 88:1; Rev 6:10
18:8 [f]Mt 8:20 [g]Mt 16:27
18:9 [h]Lk 16:15 [i]Isa 65:5
18:10 [j]Ac 3:1
18:11 [k]Mt 6:5; Mk 11:25

c *24* Some manuscripts do not have *in his day.* **d** *35* Some manuscripts *left.* 36 *Two men will be in the field; one will be taken and the other left.*

17:26–35 Jesus warned against false security. We are to abandon the values and attachments of this world in order to be ready for Christ's return. His return will happen suddenly, and when he comes, there will be no second chances. Some will be taken to be with him; the rest will be left behind.

17:37 To answer the disciples' question, Jesus quoted a familiar proverb. One vulture circling overhead does not mean much, but a gathering of vultures means that a dead body is nearby. Likewise, one sign of the end may not be significant, but when many signs occur, the second coming is near.

18:1 To persist in prayer and not give up does not mean endless repetition or painfully long prayer sessions. Always praying means keeping our requests constantly before God as we live for him day by day, believing he will answer. When we live by faith, we are not to give up. God may delay answering, but his delays always have good reasons. As we persist in prayer we grow in character, faith, and hope.

18:3 Widows and orphans were among the most vulnerable of all God's people, and both Old Testament prophets and New Testament apostles insisted that these needy people be properly cared for. See, for example, Exodus 22:22–24; Isaiah 1:17; 1 Timothy 5:3; James 1:27.

18:6, 7 If unjust judges respond to constant pressure, how much more will a great and loving God respond to us. If we know he loves us, we can believe he will hear our cries for help.

18:10 The people who lived near Jerusalem often went to the temple to pray. The temple was the centre of their worship.

18:11–14 The Pharisee did not go to the temple to pray to God but to announce to all within earshot how good he was. The tax collector went recognising his sin and begging for mercy. Self-righteousness is dangerous. It leads to pride, causes a person to despise others, and prevents him or her from learning anything from God. The tax collector's prayer should be our prayer because we all need God's mercy every day. Don't let pride in your achievements cut you off from God.

about[a] himself: 'God, I thank you that I am not like other men—robbers, evildoers,
adulterers—or even like this tax collector. 12I fast[l] twice a week and give a tenth[m]
of all I get.'
13"But the tax collector stood at a distance. He would not even look up to heaven,
but beat his breast[n] and said, 'God, have mercy on me, a sinner.'[o]
14"I tell you that this man, rather than the other, went home justified before God.
For everyone who exalts himself will be humbled, and he who humbles himself will
be exalted."[p]

Jesus Blesses Little Children
(174/Matthew 19:13–15; Mark 10:13–16)

15People were also bringing babies to Jesus to have him touch them. When the
disciples saw this, they rebuked them. 16But Jesus called the children to him and said,
"Let the little children come to me, and do not hinder them, for the kingdom of God
belongs to such as these. 17I tell you the truth, anyone who will not receive the
kingdom of God like a little child[q] will never enter it."

Jesus Speaks to the Rich Young Man
(175/Matthew 19:16–30; Mark 10:17–31)

18A certain ruler asked him, "Good teacher, what must I do to inherit eternal life?"[r]
19"Why do you call me good?" Jesus answered. "No-one is good—except God
alone. 20You know the commandments: 'Do not commit adultery, do not murder, do
not steal, do not give false testimony, honour your father and mother.'[b]"[s]
21"All these I have kept since I was a boy," he said.
22When Jesus heard this, he said to him, "You still lack one thing. Sell everything
you have and give to the poor,[t] and you will have treasure in heaven.[u] Then come,
follow me."
23When he heard this, he became very sad, because he was a man of great wealth.
24Jesus looked at him and said, "How hard it is for the rich to enter the kingdom of
God![v] 25Indeed, it is easier for a camel to go through the eye of a needle than for
a rich man to enter the kingdom of God."
26Those who heard this asked, "Who then can be saved?"

a *11* Or *to* b *20* Exodus 20:12–16; Deut. 5:16–20

18:12 l Isa 58:3; Mt 9:14 m Mal 3:8; Lk 11:42
18:13 n Isa 66:2; Jer 31:19; Lk 23:48 o Lk 5:32; 1Ti 1:15
18:14 p Mt 23:12; Lk 14:11
18:17 q Mt 11:25; 18:3
18:18 r Lk 10:25
18:20 s Ex 20:12-16; Dt 5:16-20; Ro 13:9
18:22 t Ac 2:45 u Mt 6:20
18:24 v Pr 11:28

18:15–17 It was customary for a mother to bring her children to a rabbi for a blessing, and that is why these mothers gathered around Jesus. The disciples, however, thought the children were unworthy of the Master's time—less important than whatever else he was doing. But Jesus welcomed them, because little children have the kind of faith and trust needed to enter God's kingdom. It is important that we introduce our children to Jesus and that we ourselves approach him with childlike attitudes of acceptance, faith, and trust.

18:18ff This ruler sought reassurance, some way of knowing for sure that he had eternal life. He wanted Jesus to measure and grade his qualifications, or to give him some task he could do to assure his own immortality. So Jesus gave him a task—the one thing the rich ruler knew he could not do. "Who then can be saved?" the bystanders asked. "No-one can, by his or her own achievements," Jesus' answer implied. "What is impossible with men is possible with God." Salvation cannot be earned—it is God's gift (see Ephesians 2:8–10).

18:18, 19 Jesus' question to the ruler who came and called him "Good teacher" was, in essence, "Do you know who I am?" Undoubtedly the man did not catch the implications of Jesus' reply—that the man was right in calling him good because Jesus truly is God.

18:22, 23 This man's wealth made his life comfortable and gave him power and prestige. When Jesus told him to sell everything he owned, Jesus was touching the very basis of his security and identity. The man did not understand that he would be even more secure if he followed Jesus than he was with all his wealth. Jesus does not ask all believers to sell everything they have, although this may be his will for some. He does ask us all, however, to get rid of anything that has become more important than God. If your basis for security has shifted from God to what you own, it would be better for you to get rid of those possessions.

18:24–27 Because money represents power, authority, and success, it is often difficult for wealthy people to realise their need and their powerlessness to save themselves. The rich in talent or intelligence suffer the same difficulty. Unless God reaches down into their lives, they will not come to him. Jesus surprised some of his hearers by offering salvation to the poor; he may surprise some people today by offering it to the rich. It is difficult for a self-sufficient person to realise his or her need and come to Jesus, but "What is impossible with men is possible with God".

18:26–30 Peter and the other disciples had paid a high price—leaving their homes and jobs—to follow Jesus. But Jesus reminded Peter that following him has its benefits as well as its sacrifices. Any believer who has had to give up something to follow Christ will be paid back in this life as well as in the next. For example, if you must give up a secure job, you will find that God offers a secure relationship with himself now and for ever. If you must give up your family's approval, you will gain the love of the family of God. The disciples had begun to pay the price of following Jesus, and Jesus said they would be rewarded. Don't dwell on what you have given up; think about what you have gained and give thanks for it. You can never outgive God.

[27]Jesus replied, "What is impossible with men is possible with God."[w]
[28]Peter said to him, "We have left all we had to follow you!"[x]
[29]"I tell you the truth," Jesus said to them, "no-one who has left home or wife or
brothers or parents or children for the sake of the kingdom of God [30]will fail to receive
many times as much in this age and, in the age to come,[y] eternal life."[z]

Jesus Predicts His Death the Third Time
(177/Matthew 20:17–19; Mark 10:32–34)

[31]Jesus took the Twelve aside and told them, "We are going up to Jerusalem,[a] and
everything that is written by the prophets[b] about the Son of Man[c] will be fulfilled.
[32]He will be turned over to the Gentiles.[d] They will mock him, insult him, spit on
him, flog him[e] and kill him.[f] [33]On the third day[g] he will rise again."[h]
[34]The disciples did not understand any of this. Its meaning was hidden from them,
and they did not know what he was talking about.[i]

Jesus Heals a Blind Beggar
(179/Matthew 20:29–34; Mark 10:46–52)

[35]As Jesus approached Jericho,[j] a blind man was sitting by the roadside begging.
[36]When he heard the crowd going by, he asked what was happening. [37]They told him,
"Jesus of Nazareth is passing by."[k]
[38]He called out, "Jesus, Son of David,[l] have mercy[m] on me!"
[39]Those who led the way rebuked him and told him to be quiet, but he shouted all
the more, "Son of David, have mercy on me!"[n]
[40]Jesus stopped and ordered the man to be brought to him. When he came near,
Jesus asked him, [41]"What do you want me to do for you?"
"Lord, I want to see," he replied.
[42]Jesus said to him, "Receive your sight; your faith has healed you."[o] [43]Immedi-
ately he received his sight and followed Jesus, praising God. When all the people saw
it, they also praised God.[p]

Jesus Brings Salvation to Zacchaeus' Home
(180)

19 Jesus entered Jericho[a] and was passing through. [2]A man was there by the name
of Zacchaeus; he was a chief tax collector and was wealthy. [3]He wanted to see
who Jesus was, but being a short man he could not, because of the crowd. [4]So he
ran ahead and climbed a sycamore-fig[b] tree to see him, since Jesus was coming that
way.[c]
[5]When Jesus reached the spot, he looked up and said to him, "Zacchaeus, come

18:27 [w]Mt 19:26
18:28 [x]Mt 4:19
18:30 [y]Mt 12:32 [z]Mt 25:46
18:31 [a]Lk 9:51 [b]Ps 22; Isa 53 [c]Mt 8:20
18:32 [d]Lk 23:1 [e]Mt 16:21 [f]Ac 2:23
18:33 [g]Mt 16:21 [h]Mt 16:21
18:34 [i]Mk 9:32; Lk 9:45
18:35 [j]Lk 19:1
18:37 [k]Lk 19:4
18:38 [l]ver 39; Mt 9:27 [m]Mt 17:15; Lk 18:13
18:39 [n]ver 38
18:42 [o]Mt 9:22
18:43 [p]Mt 9:8; Lk 13:17
19:1 [a]Lk 18:35
19:4 [b]1Ki 10:27; 1Ch 27:28; Isa 9:10 [c]Lk 18:37

18:31–34 Some predictions about what would happen to Jesus are found in Psalm 41:9 (betrayal); Psalm 22:16–18 and Isaiah 53:4–7 (crucifixion); Psalm 16:10 (resurrection). The disciples didn't understand Jesus, apparently because they focused on what he said about his death and ignored what he said about his resurrection. Even though Jesus spoke plainly, they would not grasp the significance of his words until they saw the risen Christ face to face.

18:35 Beggars often waited along the roads near cities, because that was where they were able to contact the most people. Usually disabled in some way, beggars were unable to earn a living. Medical help was not available for their problems, and people tended to ignore their obligation to care for the needy (Leviticus 25:35–38). Thus beggars had little hope of escaping their degrading way of life. But this blind beggar took hope in the Messiah. He shamelessly cried out for Jesus' attention, and Jesus said that his faith allowed him to see. No matter how desperate your situation may seem, if you call out to Jesus in faith, he will help you.

18:38 The blind man called Jesus "Son of David", a title for the Messiah (Isaiah 11:1–3). This means that he understood Jesus to be the long-awaited Messiah. A poor and blind beggar could *see* that Jesus was the Messiah, while the religious leaders who saw his miracles were blinded to his identity and refused to recognise him as the Messiah.

19:1–10 To finance their great world empire, the Romans levied heavy taxes on all nations under their control. The Jews opposed these taxes because they supported a secular government and its pagan gods, but they were still forced to pay. Tax collectors were among the most unpopular people in Israel. Jews by birth, they chose to work for Rome and were considered traitors. Besides, it was common knowledge that tax collectors were making themselves rich by "milking" their fellow Jews. No wonder the people muttered when Jesus went home with the tax collector Zacchaeus. But despite the fact that Zacchaeus was both a cheater and a turncoat, Jesus loved him; and in response, the little tax collector was converted. In every society, certain groups of people are considered "untouchable" because of their political views, their immoral behaviour, or their life-style. We should not give in to social pressure to avoid these people. Jesus loves them, and they need to hear his Good News.

19:7 [d]Mt 9:11

19:8 [e]Lk 7:13 [f]Lk 3:12, 13 [g]Ex 22:1; Lev 6:4, 5; Nu 5:7; 2Sa 12:6

19:9 [h]Lk 3:8; 13:16; Ro 4:16; Gal 3:7

19:10 [i]Eze 34:12, 16; Jn 3:17

19:11 [j]Mt 3:2 [k]Lk 17:20; Ac 1:6

19:13 [l]Mk 13:34

down immediately. I must stay at your house today." 6So he came down at once and
welcomed him gladly.
7All the people saw this and began to mutter, "He has gone to be the guest of a
'sinner'."[d]
8But Zacchaeus stood up and said to the Lord,[e] "Look, Lord! Here and now I give
half of my possessions to the poor, and if I have cheated anybody out of anything,[f]
I will pay back four times the amount."[g]
9Jesus said to him, "Today salvation has come to this house, because this man, too,
is a son of Abraham.[h] 10For the Son of Man came to seek and to save what was
lost."[i]

Jesus Tells the Parable of the King's Ten Servants
(181)

11While they were listening to this, he went on to tell them a parable, because he
was near Jerusalem and the people thought that the kingdom of God[j] was going to
appear at once.[k] 12He said: "A man of noble birth went to a distant country to have
himself appointed king and then to return. 13So he called ten of his servants[l] and gave
them ten minas.[a] 'Put this money to work,' he said, 'until I come back.'
14"But his subjects hated him and sent a delegation after him to say, 'We don't want
this man to be our king.'
15"He was made king, however, and returned home. Then he sent for the servants
to whom he had given the money, in order to find out what they had gained with it.
16"The first one came and said, 'Sir, your mina has earned ten more.'

a *13* A mina was about three months' wages.

GOSPEL ACCOUNTS FOUND ONLY IN LUKE

1:5–80	Special events leading up to birth of John the Baptist and Jesus
2:1–52	Events from Jesus' childhood
3:19, 20	Herod puts John in prison
4:16–30	Jesus is rejected at Nazareth
5:1–11	Jesus provides a miraculous catch of fish
7:11–17	Jesus raises a widow's son from the dead
7:36–50	A sinful woman anoints Jesus' feet
8:1–3	Women travel with Jesus
10:1–18:14	Events, miracles, and teachings during the months prior to Christ's death
19:1–27	Jesus meets Zacchaeus and later tells the parable of the king's ten servants
23:6–12	Jesus' trial before Herod
24:44–49	Some of Jesus' last words before his ascension

19:8 Judging from the crowd's reaction to him, Zacchaeus must have been a very crooked tax collector. But after he met Jesus, he realised that his life needed straightening out. By giving to the poor and making restitution – with generous interest – to those he had cheated, Zacchaeus demonstrated inward change by outward action. It is not enough to follow Jesus in your head or heart alone. You must show your faith by changed behaviour. Has your faith resulted in action? What changes do you need to make?

19:9, 10 When Jesus said Zacchaeus was a son of Abraham and yet was lost, he must have shocked his hearers in at least two ways. They would not have liked to acknowledge that this unpopular tax collector was a fellow son of Abraham, and they would not have wished to admit that sons of Abraham could be lost. But a person is not saved by a good heritage or condemned by a bad one; faith is more important than genealogy. Jesus still loves to bring the lost into his kingdom, no matter what their background or previous way of life. Through faith, the lost can be forgiven and made new.

19:11ff The people still hoped for a political leader who would set up an earthly kingdom and get rid of Roman domination. Jesus' parable showed that his kingdom would not take this form right away. First he would go away for a while, and his followers would need to be faithful and productive during his absence. Upon his return, Jesus would inaugurate a kingdom more powerful and just than anything they could expect.

19:11ff This story showed Jesus' followers what they were to do during the time between Jesus' departure and his second coming. Because we live in that time period, it applies directly to us. We have been given excellent resources to build and expand God's kingdom. Jesus expects us to use these talents so that they multiply and the kingdom grows. He asks each of us to account for what we do with his gifts. While awaiting the coming of the kingdom of God in glory, we must do Christ's work.

17" 'Well done, my good servant!'[m] his master replied. 'Because you have been
trustworthy in a very small matter, take charge of ten cities.'[n]
18"The second came and said, 'Sir, your mina has earned five more.'
19"His master answered, 'You take charge of five cities.'
20"Then another servant came and said, 'Sir, here is your mina; I have kept it laid
away in a piece of cloth. 21I was afraid of you, because you are a hard man. You take
out what you did not put in and reap what you did not sow.'[o]
22"His master replied, 'I will judge you by your own words,[p] you wicked servant!
You knew, did you, that I am a hard man, taking out what I did not put in, and reaping
what I did not sow?[q] 23Why then didn't you put my money on deposit, so that when
I came back, I could have collected it with interest?'
24"Then he said to those standing by, 'Take his mina away from him and give it
to the one who has ten minas.'
25" 'Sir,' they said, 'he already has ten!'
26"He replied, 'I tell you that to everyone who has, more will be given, but as for
the one who has nothing, even what he has will be taken away.[r] 27But those enemies
of mine who did not want me to be a king over them—bring them here and kill them
in front of me.' "

3. Jesus' ministry in Jerusalem

Jesus Rides into Jerusalem on a Donkey

(183/Matthew 21:1–11; Mark 11:1–11; John 12:12–19)

28After Jesus had said this, he went on ahead, going up to Jerusalem.[s] 29As he
approached Bethphage and Bethany[t] at the hill called the Mount of Olives,[u] he sent
two of his disciples, saying to them, 30"Go to the village ahead of you, and as you
enter it, you will find a colt tied there, which no-one has ever ridden. Untie it and
bring it here. 31If anyone asks you, 'Why are you untying it?' tell him, 'The Lord
needs it.' "
32Those who were sent ahead went and found it just as he had told them.[v] 33As
they were untying the colt, its owners asked them, "Why are you untying the colt?"
34They replied, "The Lord needs it."
35They brought it to Jesus, threw their cloaks on the colt and put Jesus on it. 36As
he went along, people spread their cloaks[w] on the road.
37When he came near the place where the road goes down the Mount of Olives,[x]

19:17 [m]Pr 27:18 [n]Lk 16:10
19:21 [o]Mt 25:24
19:22 [p]2Sa 1:16; Job 15:6 [q]Mt 25:26
19:26 [r]Mt 13:12; 25:29; Lk 8:18
19:28 [s]Mk 10:32; Lk 9:51
19:29 [t]Mt 21:17 [u]Mt 21:1
19:32 [v]Lk 22:13
19:36 [w]2Ki 9:13
19:37 [x]Mt 21:1

19:20–27 Why was the king so hard on this man who had not increased the money? He punished the man because (1) he didn't share his master's interest in the kingdom; (2) he didn't trust his master's intentions; (3) his only concern was for himself, and (4) he did nothing to use the money. Like the king in this story, God has given you gifts to use for the benefit of his kingdom. Do you want the kingdom to grow? Do you trust God to govern it fairly? Are you as concerned for others' welfare as you are for your own? Are you willing to use faithfully what he has entrusted to you?

19:30–35 By this time Jesus was extremely well known. Everyone coming to Jerusalem for the Passover feast had heard of him, and, for a time, the popular mood was favourable towards him. "The Lord needs it" was all the disciples had to say, and the colt's owners gladly turned their animal over to them.

19:35–38 Christians celebrate this event on Palm Sunday. The people lined the road, praising God, waving palm branches, and throwing their cloaks in front of the colt as it passed before them. "Long live the King" was the meaning behind their joyful shouts, because they knew that Jesus was intentionally fulfilling the prophecy in Zechariah 9:9: "See, your king comes to you, righteous and having salvation, gentle and riding on a donkey, on a colt, the foal of a donkey." To announce that he was indeed the Messiah, Jesus chose a *time* when all Israel would be gathered at Jerusalem, a *place* where huge crowds could see him, and a *way* of proclaiming his mission that was unmistakable. The people went wild. They were sure their liberation was at hand.

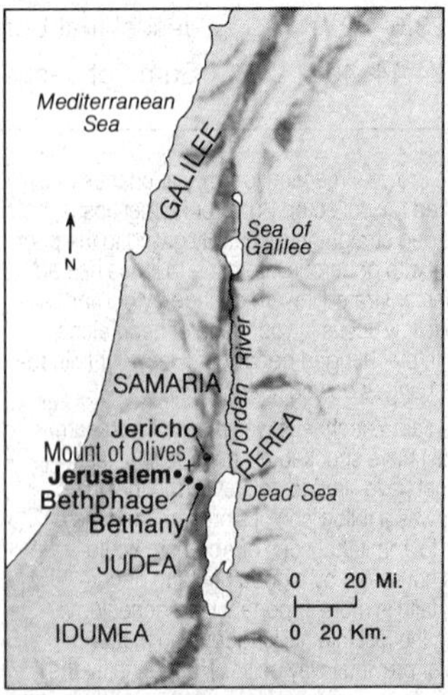

LAST WEEK IN JERUSALEM
As they approached Jerusalem from Jericho (19:1), Jesus and the disciples came to the villages of Bethany and Bethphage, nestled on the eastern slope of the Mount of Olives, only a few miles outside Jerusalem. Jesus stayed in Bethany during the nights of that last week, entering Jerusalem during the day.

the whole crowd of disciples began joyfully to praise God in loud voices for all the
miracles they had seen:

> 38“Blessed is the king who comes in the name of the Lord!”[b][y]
>
> “Peace in heaven and glory in the highest!”[z]

39Some of the Pharisees in the crowd said to Jesus, “Teacher, rebuke your disciples!”[a]
40“I tell you,” he replied, “if they keep quiet, the stones will cry out.”[b]
41As he approached Jerusalem and saw the city, he wept over it[c] 42and said, “If
you, even you, had only known on this day what would bring you peace—but now
it is hidden from your eyes. 43The days will come upon you when your enemies will
build an embankment against you and encircle you and hem you in on every side.[d]
44They will dash you to the ground, you and the children within your walls.[e] They
will not leave one stone on another,[f] because you did not recognise the time of God’s
coming[g] to you.”

Jesus Clears the Temple Again
(184/Matthew 21:12–17; Mark 11:12–19)

45Then he entered the temple area and began driving out those who were selling.
46“It is written,” he said to them, “ ‘My house will be a house of prayer’;[c][h] but you
have made it ‘a den of robbers’.[d]”[i]
47Every day he was teaching at the temple.[j] But the chief priests, the teachers of
the law and the leaders among the people were trying to kill him.[k] 48Yet they could
not find any way to do it, because all the people hung on his words.

Religious Leaders Challenge Jesus’ Authority
(189/Matthew 21:23–27; Mark 11:27–33)

20 One day as he was teaching the people in the temple courts[a] and preaching
the gospel,[b] the chief priests and the teachers of the law, together with the
elders, came up to him. 2“Tell us by what authority you are doing these things,” they
said. “Who gave you this authority?”[c]
3He replied, “I will also ask you a question. Tell me, 4John’s baptism[d]—was it
from heaven, or from men?”
5They discussed it among themselves and said, “If we say, ‘From heaven’, he will

b *38* Psalm 118:26 c *46* Isaiah 56:7 d *46* Jer. 7:11

19:38 [y]Ps 118:26; Lk 13:35 [z]Lk 2:14
19:39 [a]Mt 21:15, 16
19:40 [b]Hab 2:11
19:41 [c]Isa 22:4; Lk 13:34, 35
19:43 [d]Isa 29:3; Jer 6:6; Eze 4:2; 26:8; Lk 21:20
19:44 [e]Ps 137:9 [f]Mt 24:2; Mk 13:2; Lk 21:6 [g]1Pe 2:12
19:46 [h]Isa 56:7 [i]Jer 7:11
19:47 [j]Mt 26:55 [k]Mt 12:14; Mk 11:18
20:1 [a]Mt 26:55 [b]Lk 8:1
20:2 [c]Jn 2:18; Ac 4:7; 7:27
20:4 [d]Mk 1:4

19:38 The people who were praising God for giving them a king had the wrong idea about Jesus. They expected him to be a national leader who would restore their nation to its former glory, and thus they were deaf to the words of their prophets and blind to Jesus' real mission. When it became apparent that Jesus was not going to fulfil their hopes, many people would turn against him.

19:39, 40 The Pharisees thought the crowd's words were sacrilegious and blasphemous. They didn't want someone challenging their power and authority, and they didn't want a revolt that would bring the Roman army down on them. So they asked Jesus to keep his people quiet. But Jesus said that if the people were quiet, the stones would immediately cry out. Why? Not because Jesus was setting up a powerful political kingdom, but because he was establishing God's eternal kingdom, a reason for the greatest celebration of all.

19:41–44 The Jewish leaders had rejected their King (19:47). They had gone too far. They had refused God's offer of salvation in Jesus Christ when they were visited by God himself ("the time of God's coming"), and soon their nation would suffer. God did not turn away from the Jewish people who obeyed him, however. He continues to offer salvation to the people he loves, both Jews and Gentiles. Eternal life is within your reach—accept it while the opportunity is still offered.

19:43, 44 About 40 years after Jesus said these words, they came true. In A.D. 66, the Jews revolted against Roman control. Three years later Titus, son of the Emperor Vespasian, was sent to crush the rebellion. Roman soldiers attacked Jerusalem and broke through the northern wall but still couldn't take the city. Finally they laid siege to it, and in A.D. 70 they were able to enter the severely weakened city and burn it. Six hundred thousand Jews were killed during Titus' onslaught.

19:47 Who were the "leaders among the people"? This group probably included wealthy leaders in politics, commerce, and law. They had several reasons for wanting to get rid of Jesus. He had damaged business in the temple by driving the merchants out. In addition, he was preaching against injustice, and his teachings often favoured the poor over the rich. Further, his great popularity was in danger of attracting Rome's attention, and the leaders of Israel wanted as little as possible to do with Rome.

20:1–8 This group of leaders wanted to get rid of Jesus, so they tried to trap him with their question. If Jesus would answer that his authority came from God—if he stated openly that he was the Messiah and the Son of God—they would accuse him of blasphemy and bring him to trial. Jesus did not let himself be caught. Instead, he turned the question on them. Thus he exposed their motives and avoided their trap.

ask, 'Why didn't you believe him?' 6But if we say, 'From men', all the people[e] will
stone us, because they are persuaded that John was a prophet."[f]
7So they answered, "We don't know where it was from."
8Jesus said, "Neither will I tell you by what authority I am doing these things."

Jesus Tells the Parable of the Wicked Tenants
(191/Matthew 21:33–46; Mark 12:1–12)

9He went on to tell the people this parable: "A man planted a vineyard,[g] rented
it to some farmers and went away for a long time.[h] 10At harvest time he sent a servant
to the tenants so they would give him some of the fruit of the vineyard. But the tenants
beat him and sent him away empty-handed. 11He sent another servant, but that one
also they beat and treated shamefully and sent away empty-handed. 12He sent still a
third, and they wounded him and threw him out.
13"Then the owner of the vineyard said, 'What shall I do? I will send my son, whom
I love;[i] perhaps they will respect him.'
14"But when the tenants saw him, they talked the matter over. 'This is the heir,'
they said. 'Let's kill him, and the inheritance will be ours.' 15So they threw him out
of the vineyard and killed him.
"What then will the owner of the vineyard do to them? 16He will come and kill those
tenants[j] and give the vineyard to others."
When the people heard this, they said, "May this never be!"
17Jesus looked directly at them and asked, "Then what is the meaning of that which
is written:

" 'The stone the builders rejected
has become the capstone'[a, b]?[k]

18Everyone who falls on that stone will be broken to pieces, but he on whom it falls
will be crushed."[l]
19The teachers of the law and the chief priests looked for a way to arrest him[m]
immediately, because they knew he had spoken this parable against them. But they
were afraid of the people.[n]

Religious Leaders Question Jesus about Paying Taxes
(193/Matthew 22:15–22; Mark 12:13–17)

20Keeping a close watch on him, they sent spies, who pretended to be honest. They
hoped to catch Jesus in something he said[o] so that they might hand him over to the
power and authority of the governor.[p] 21So the spies questioned him: "Teacher, we
know that you speak and teach what is right, and that you do not show partiality but
teach the way of God in accordance with the truth.[q] 22Is it right for us to pay taxes
to Caesar or not?"

a 17 Or *cornerstone* b 17 Psalm 118:22

20:6 e Lk 7:29 f Mt 11:9
20:9 g Isa 5:1-7 h Mt 25:14
20:13 i Mt 3:17
20:16 j Lk 19:27
20:17 k Ps 118:22; Ac 4:11
20:18 l Isa 8:14, 15
20:19 m Lk 19:47 n Mk 11:18
20:20 o Mt 12:10 p Mt 27:2
20:21 q Jn 3:2

20:9–16 The characters in this story are easily identified. Even the religious leaders understood it. The owner of the vineyard is God; the vineyard is Israel; the tenants are the religious leaders; the servants are the prophets and priests God sent to Israel; the son is the Messiah, Jesus; and the others are the Gentiles. Jesus' parable indirectly answered the religious leaders' question about his authority; it also showed them that he knew about their plan to kill him.

20:17–19 Quoting Psalm 118:22, Jesus showed the unbelieving leaders that even their rejection of the Messiah had been prophesied in Scripture. Ignoring the capstone, or cornerstone, was dangerous. A person could be tripped or crushed (judged and punished). Jesus' comments were veiled, but the religious leaders had no trouble interpreting them. They immediately wanted to arrest him.

20:20–26 Jesus turned his enemies' attempt to trap him into a powerful lesson: As God's followers, we have legitimate obligations to both God and the government. But it is important to keep our priorities straight. When the two authorities conflict, our duty to God must always come before our duty to the government.

20:21 These spies, pretending to be honest men, flattered Jesus before asking him their trick question, hoping to catch him off guard. But Jesus knew what they were trying to do and stayed out of their trap. Beware of flattery. With God's help, you can detect it and avoid the trap that often follows.

20:22 This was a loaded question. The Jews were enraged at having to pay taxes to Rome, thus supporting the pagan government and its gods. They hated the system that allowed tax collectors to charge exorbitant rates and keep the extra for themselves. If Jesus said they should pay taxes, they would call him a traitor to their nation and their religion. But if he said they should not, they could report him to Rome as a rebel. Jesus' questioners thought they had him this time, but he outwitted them again.

20:25 [r]Lk 23:2; Ro 13:7

23He saw through their duplicity and said to them, 24"Show me a denarius. Whose
portrait and inscription are on it?"
25"Caesar's," they replied.
He said to them, "Then give to Caesar what is Caesar's,[r] and to God what is
God's."

20:27 [s]Ac 4:1 [t]Ac 23:8; 1Co 15:12

26They were unable to trap him in what he had said there in public. And astonished
by his answer, they became silent.

Religious Leaders Question Jesus about the Resurrection
(194/Matthew 22:23–33; Mark 12:18–27)

20:28 [u]Dt 25:5

27Some of the Sadducees,[s] who say there is no resurrection,[t] came to Jesus with
a question. 28"Teacher," they said, "Moses wrote for us that if a man's brother dies
and leaves a wife but no children, the man must marry the widow and have children
for his brother.[u] 29Now there were seven brothers. The first one married a woman
and died childless. 30The second 31and then the third married her, and in the same
way the seven died, leaving no children. 32Finally, the woman died too. 33Now then,
at the resurrection whose wife will she be, since the seven were married to her?"

20:35 [v]Mt 12:32

34Jesus replied, "The people of this age marry and are given in marriage. 35But
those who are considered worthy of taking part in that age[v] and in the resurrection
from the dead will neither marry nor be given in marriage, 36and they can no longer
die; for they are like the angels. They are God's children,[w] since they are children
of the resurrection. 37But in the account of the bush, even Moses showed that the dead
rise, for he calls the Lord 'the God of Abraham, and the God of Isaac, and the God
of Jacob'.[c][x] 38He is not the God of the dead, but of the living, for to him all are
alive."

20:36 [w]Jn 1:12; 1Jn 3:1-2

20:37 [x]Ex 3:6

39Some of the teachers of the law responded, "Well said, teacher!" 40And no-one
dared to ask him any more questions.[y]

Religious Leaders Cannot Answer Jesus' Question
(196/Matthew 22:41–46; Mark 12:35–37)

20:40 [y]Mt 22:46; Mk 12:34

41Then Jesus said to them, "How is it that they say the Christ[d] is the Son of
David?[z] 42David himself declares in the Book of Psalms:

" 'The Lord said to my Lord:
"Sit at my right hand

20:41 [z]Mt 1:1

[c] *37* Exodus 3:6 [d] *41* Or *Messiah*

20:24 The denarius was the usual pay for one day's work.

20:27–38 The Sadducees, a group of conservative religious leaders, honoured only the Pentateuch – Genesis to Deuteronomy – as Scripture. Furthermore, they did not believe in a resurrection of the dead because they could find no mention of it in those books. The Sadducees decided to try their hand at tricking Jesus, so they brought him a question that had always stumped the Pharisees. After addressing their question about marriage, Jesus answered their *real* question about resurrection. Basing his answer on the writings of Moses – an authority they respected – he upheld belief in resurrection.

20:34, 35 Jesus' statement does not mean that people will not recognise their partners in heaven. It simply means that we must not think of heaven as an extension of life as we now know it. Our relationships in this life are limited by time, death, and sin. We don't know everything about our resurrection life, but Jesus affirms that relationships will be different from what we are used to here and now.

20:37, 38 The Sadducees came to Jesus with a trick question. Not believing in the resurrection, they wanted Jesus to say something they could refute. Even so, Jesus did not ignore or belittle their question. He answered it, and then he went beyond it to the real issue. When people ask you tough religious questions – "How can a loving God allow people to starve?" "If God knows what I'm going to do, do I have any free choice?" – follow Jesus' example. First answer the question to the best of your ability; then look for the real issue – hurt over a personal tragedy, for example, or difficulty in making a decision. Often the spoken question is only a test, not of your ability to answer hard questions, but of your willingness to listen and care.

20:41–44 The Pharisees and Sadducees had asked their questions. Then Jesus turned the tables and asked them a question that went right to the heart of the matter – what they thought about the Messiah's identity. The Pharisees knew that the Messiah would be a descendant of David, but they did not understand that he would be more than a human descendant – he was God in the flesh. Jesus quoted from Psalm 110:1 to show that David knew that the Messiah would be both human and divine. The Pharisees expected only a human ruler to restore Israel's greatness as in the days of David and Solomon.

The central issue of life is what we believe about Jesus. Other spiritual questions are irrelevant unless we first decide to believe that Jesus is who he said he is. The Pharisees and Sadducees could not do this. They remained confused over Jesus' identity.

43until I make your enemies
a footstool for your feet." '[e][a]

44David calls him 'Lord'. How then can he be his son?" 20:43 [a]Ps 110:1; Mt 22:44

Jesus Warns against the Religious Leaders
(197/Matthew 23:1–12; Mark 12:38–40)

45While all the people were listening, Jesus said to his disciples, 46"Beware of the 20:46 [b]Lk 11:43
teachers of the law. They like to walk around in flowing robes and love to be greeted
in the market-places and have the most important seats in the synagogues and the
places of honour at banquets.[b] 47They devour widows' houses and for a show make
lengthy prayers. Such men will be punished most severely."

A Poor Widow Gives All She Has
(200/Mark 12:41–44) 21:1 [a]Mt 27:6; Jn 8:20

21 As he looked up, Jesus saw the rich putting their gifts into the temple treasury.[a] 2He also saw a poor widow put in two very small copper coins.[a] 3"I
tell you the truth," he said, "this poor widow has put in more than all the others. 4All
these people gave their gifts out of their wealth; but she out of her poverty put in all
she had to live on."[b] 21:4 [b]2Co 8:12

[e] *43* Psalm 110:1 [a] *2* Greek *two lepta*

20:45–47 The teachers of the law loved the benefits associated with their position, and they sometimes cheated the poor in order to get even more benefits. Every job has its rewards, but gaining rewards should never become more important than doing the job faithfully. God will punish people who use their position of responsibility to cheat others. Whatever resources you have been given, use them to help others and not just yourself.

20:47 How strange to think that the teachers of the law would receive the worst punishment. But behind their appearance of holiness and respectability, they were arrogant, crafty, selfish, and uncaring. Jesus exposed their evil hearts. He showed that despite their pious words, they were neglecting God's laws and doing as they pleased. Religious deeds do not cancel sin. Jesus said that God's most severe judgment awaited these teachers because they should have been living examples of mercy and justice.

21:1, 2 Jesus was in the area of the temple called the court of women. The treasury was located there or in an adjoining walkway. In this area were seven boxes in which worshippers could deposit their temple tax and six boxes for freewill offerings like the one this woman gave. Not only was she poor; as a widow she had few resources for making money. Her small gift was a sacrifice, but she gave it willingly.

21:1–4 This widow gave all she had to live on, in contrast to the way most of us handle our money. When we consider giving a certain percentage of our income a great accomplishment, we resemble those who gave "out of their wealth". Here, Jesus was admiring generous and sacrificial giving. As believers, we should consider increasing our giving—whether of money, time, or talents—to a point beyond convenience or safety.

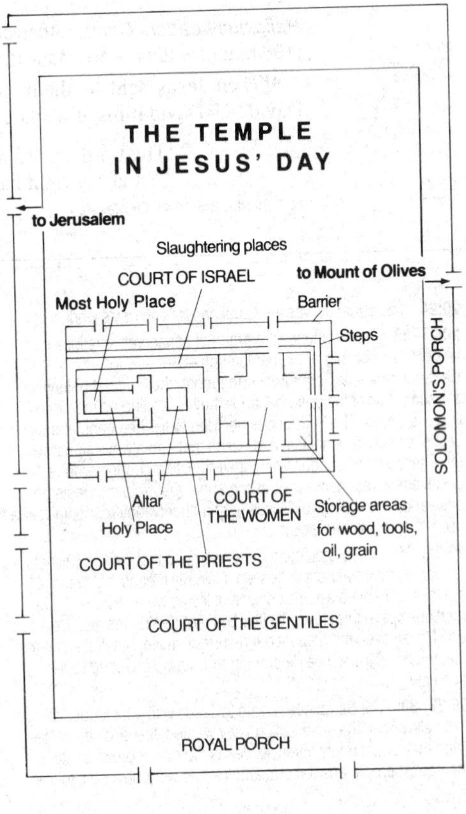

Jesus Tells about the Future
(201/Matthew 24:1–25; Mark 13:1–23)

5Some of his disciples were remarking about how the temple was adorned with
beautiful stones and with gifts dedicated to God. But Jesus said, 6"As for what you
see here, the time will come when not one stone will be left on another;[c] every one
of them will be thrown down."
7"Teacher," they asked, "when will these things happen? And what will be the sign
that they are about to take place?"
8He replied: "Watch out that you are not deceived. For many will come in my name,
claiming, 'I am he,' and 'The time is near.' Do not follow them.[d] 9When you hear
of wars and revolutions, do not be frightened. These things must happen first, but the
end will not come right away."
10Then he said to them: "Nation will rise against nation, and kingdom against
kingdom.[e] 11There will be great earthquakes, famines and pestilences in various
places, and fearful events and great signs from heaven.[f]
12"But before all this, they will lay hands on you and persecute you. They will
deliver you to synagogues and prisons, and you will be brought before kings and
governors, and all on account of my name. 13This will result in your being witnesses
to them.[g] 14But make up your mind not to worry beforehand how you will defend
yourselves.[h] 15For I will give you[i] words and wisdom that none of your adversaries
will be able to resist or contradict. 16You will be betrayed even by parents, brothers,
relatives and friends,[j] and they will put some of you to death. 17All men will hate
you because of me.[k] 18But not a hair of your head will perish.[l] 19By standing firm
you will gain life.[m]
20"When you see Jerusalem being surrounded by armies,[n] you will know that its
desolation is near. 21Then let those who are in Judea flee to the mountains, let those
in the city get out, and let those in the country not enter the city.[o] 22For this is the
time of punishment[p] in fulfilment[q] of all that has been written. 23How dreadful it
will be in those days for pregnant women and nursing mothers! There will be great
distress in the land and wrath against this people. 24They will fall by the sword and
will be taken as prisoners to all the nations. Jerusalem will be trampled[r] on by the
Gentiles until the times of the Gentiles are fulfilled.

21:6 [c]Lk 19:44
21:8 [d]Lk 17:23
21:10 [e]2Ch 15:6; Isa 19:2
21:11 [f]Isa 29:6; Joel 2:30
21:13 [g]Php 1:12
21:14 [h]Lk 12:11
21:15 [i]Lk 12:12
21:16 [j]Lk 12:52, 53
21:17 [k]Jn 15:21
21:18 [l]Mt 10:30
21:19 [m]Mt 10:22
21:20 [n]Lk 19:43
21:21 [o]Lk 17:31
21:22 [p]Isa 63:4; Da 9:24-27; Hos 9:7 [q]Mt 1:22
21:24 [r]Isa 5:5; 63:18; Da 8:13; Rev 11:2

21:5, 6 The temple the disciples were admiring was not Solomon's temple—that had been destroyed by the Babylonians in the seventh century B.C. This temple had been built by Ezra after the return from exile in the sixth century B.C., desecrated by the Seleucids in the second century B.C., reconsecrated by the Maccabees soon afterwards, and enormously expanded by Herod the Great over a 46-year period. It was a beautiful, imposing structure with a significant history, but Jesus said that it would be completely destroyed. This happened in A.D. 70 when the Roman army burned Jerusalem.

21:7ff Jesus did not leave his disciples unprepared for the difficult years ahead. He warned them about false messiahs, natural disasters, and persecutions; but he assured them that he would be with them to protect them and make his kingdom known through them. In the end, Jesus promised that he would return in power and glory to save them. Jesus' warnings and promises to his disciples also apply to us as we look forward to his return.

21:12, 13 These persecutions soon began. Luke recorded many of them in the book of Acts. Paul wrote from prison that he suffered gladly because it helped him know Christ better and do Christ's work for the church (Philippians 3:10; Colossians 1:24). The early church thrived despite intense persecution. In fact, late in the second century the church father Tertullian wrote, "The blood of Christians is seed," because opposition helped spread Christianity.

21:14–19 Jesus warned that in the coming persecutions his followers would be betrayed by their family members and friends. Christians of every age have had to face this possibility. It is reassuring to know that even when we feel completely abandoned, the Holy Spirit will stay with us. He will comfort us, protect us, and give us the words we need. This assurance can give us the courage and hope to stand firm for Christ no matter how difficult the situation.

21:18 Jesus was *not* saying that believers would be exempt from physical harm or death during the persecutions. Remember that most of the disciples were martyred. Rather he was saying that none of his followers would suffer spiritual or eternal loss. On earth, everyone will die, but believers in Jesus will be saved for eternal life.

21:24 The "times of the Gentiles" began with Babylon's destruction of Jerusalem in 586 B.C. and the exile of the Jewish people. Israel was no longer an independent nation but was under the control of Gentile rulers. In Jesus' day, Israel was governed by the Roman empire, and a Roman general would destroy the city in A.D. 70. Jesus was saying that the domination of God's people by his enemies would continue until God decided to end it. The "times of the Gentiles" refers not just to the repeated destructions of Jerusalem, but also to the continuing and mounting persecution of God's people until the end.

Jesus Tells about His Return
(202/Matthew 24:26–35; Mark 13:24–31)

25 "There will be signs in the sun, moon and stars. On the earth, nations will be in
anguish and perplexity at the roaring and tossing of the sea.[s] 26 Men will faint from
terror, apprehensive of what is coming on the world, for the heavenly bodies will be
shaken.[t] 27 At that time they will see the Son of Man[u] coming in a cloud[v] with power
and great glory. 28 When these things begin to take place, stand up and lift up your
heads, because your redemption is drawing near."[w]
29 He told them this parable: "Look at the fig-tree and all the trees. 30 When they
sprout leaves, you can see for yourselves and know that summer is near. 31 Even so,
when you see these things happening, you know that the kingdom of God[x] is near.
32 "I tell you the truth, this generation[b][y] will certainly not pass away until all these
things have happened. 33 Heaven and earth will pass away, but my words will never
pass away.[z]

Jesus Tells about Remaining Watchful
(203/Matthew 24:36–51; Mark 13:32–37)

34 "Be careful, or your hearts will be weighed down with dissipation, drunkenness
and the anxieties of life,[a] and that day will close on you unexpectedly[b] like a trap.
35 For it will come upon all those who live on the face of the whole earth. 36 Be always
on the watch, and pray[c] that you may be able to escape all that is about to happen,
and that you may be able to stand before the Son of Man."
37 Each day Jesus was teaching at the temple,[d] and each evening he went out[e] to
spend the night on the hill called the Mount of Olives,[f] 38 and all the people came
early in the morning to hear him at the temple.[g]

C. DEATH AND RESURRECTION OF JESUS, THE SAVIOUR (22:1 – 24:53)

The perfect man was a high ideal in Greek culture. Written with Greeks in mind, Luke's Gospel shows how Jesus was the perfect man given as the perfect sacrifice for the sin of all mankind. Christ is the ideal human—the perfect model for us to follow. We must stand in awe of his character, which met humanity's highest ideals as well as God's demand for an atonement for sin. He is, at one and the same time, our model and our Saviour.

Religious Leaders Plot to Kill Jesus
(207/Matthew 26:1–5; Mark 14:1, 2)
Judas Agrees to Betray Jesus
(208/Matthew 26:14–16; Mark 14:10, 11)

22 Now the Feast of Unleavened Bread, called the Passover, was approaching,[a]
2 and the chief priests and the teachers of the law were looking for some way
to get rid of Jesus,[b] for they were afraid of the people. 3 Then Satan[c] entered Judas,

[b] *32 Or race*

21:25 [s] 2Pe 3:10, 12
21:26 [t] Mt 24:29
21:27 [u] Mt 8:20 [v] Rev 1:7
21:28 [w] Lk 18:7
21:31 [x] Mt 3:2
21:32 [y] Lk 11:50; 17:25
21:33 [z] Mt 5:18
21:34 [a] Mk 4:19 [b] Lk 12:40, 46; 1Th 5:2-7
21:36 [c] Mt 26:41
21:37 [d] Mt 26:55 [e] Mk 11:19 [f] Mt 21:1
21:38 [g] Jn 8:2
22:1 [a] Jn 11:55
22:2 [b] Mt 12:14
22:3 [c] Mt 4:10; Jn 13:2

21:28 The picture of the coming persecutions and natural disasters is gloomy, but ultimately it is a cause not for worry but for great joy. When believers see these events happening, they will know that the return of their Messiah is near, and they can look forward to his reign of justice and peace. Rather than being terrified by what is happening in our world, we should confidently await Christ's return to bring justice and restoration to his people.

21:34–36 Jesus told the disciples to keep a constant watch for his return. Although nearly 2,000 years have passed since he spoke these words, their truth remains: Christ is coming again, and we need to watch and be spiritually fit. This means working faithfully at the tasks God has given us. Don't let your mind and spirit be dulled by careless living, drinking, or the foolish pursuit of pleasure. Don't let life's anxieties overburden you, so that you will be ready to move at God's command.

21:36 Only days after telling the disciples to pray that they might escape persecution, Jesus himself asked God to spare him the agonies of the cross, if that was God's will (22:41, 42). It is abnormal to *want* to suffer, but as Jesus' followers we are willing to suffer if by doing so we can help build God's kingdom. We have two wonderful promises to help us as we suffer: God will always be with us (Matthew 28:20), and he will one day rescue us and give us eternal life (Revelation 21:1–4).

22:1 All Jewish males over the age of 12 were required to go to Jerusalem for the Passover festival, followed by a seven-day festival called the Feast of Unleavened Bread. For these feasts, Jews from all over the Roman empire converged on Jerusalem to celebrate one of the most important events in their history. To learn more about the Passover and the Feast of Unleavened Bread, see the first note on Mark 14:1.

22:3 Satan's part in the betrayal of Jesus does not remove any of the responsibility from Judas. Disillusioned because Jesus was talking about dying rather than about setting up his kingdom, Judas may have been trying to force Jesus' hand and make him use

called Iscariot,[d] one of the Twelve. 4 And Judas went to the chief priests and the
officers of the temple guard[e] and discussed with them how he might betray Jesus.
5 They were delighted and agreed to give him money.[f] 6 He consented, and watched
for an opportunity to hand Jesus over to them when no crowd was present.

Disciples Prepare for the Passover
(209/Matthew 26:17–19; Mark 14:12–16)

7 Then came the day of Unleavened Bread on which the Passover lamb had to be
sacrificed.[g] 8 Jesus sent Peter and John,[h] saying, "Go and make preparations for us
to eat the Passover."
9 "Where do you want us to prepare for it?" they asked.
10 He replied, "As you enter the city, a man carrying a jar of water will meet you.
Follow him to the house that he enters, 11 and say to the owner of the house, 'The
Teacher asks: Where is the guest room, where I may eat the Passover with my
disciples?' 12 He will show you a large upper room, all furnished. Make preparations
there."
13 They left and found things just as Jesus had told them.[i] So they prepared the
Passover.

Jesus and the Disciples Have the Last Supper
(211/Matthew 26:20–30; Mark 14:17–26; John 13:21–30)

14 When the hour came, Jesus and his apostles[j] reclined at the table.[k] 15 And he
said to them, "I have eagerly desired to eat this Passover with you before I suffer.[l]
16 For I tell you, I will not eat it again until it finds fulfilment in the kingdom of
God."[m]
17 After taking the cup, he gave thanks and said, "Take this and divide it among
you. 18 For I tell you I will not drink again of the fruit of the vine until the kingdom
of God comes."
19 And he took bread, gave thanks and broke it,[n] and gave it to them, saying, "This
is my body given for you; do this in remembrance of me."

22:3 [d] Mt 10:4
22:4 [e] ver 52; Ac 4:1; 5:24
22:5 [f] Zec 11:12
22:7 [g] Ex 12:18-20; Dt 16:5-8; Mk 14:12
22:8 [h] Ac 3:1, 11; 4:13, 19; 8:14
22:13 [i] Lk 19:32
22:14 [j] Mk 6:30 [k] Mt 26:20; Mk 14:17, 18
22:15 [l] Mt 16:21
22:16 [m] Lk 14:15; Rev 19:9
22:19 [n] Mt 14:19

---

his power to prove he was the Messiah. Or perhaps Judas, not understanding Jesus' mission, no longer believed that Jesus was God's chosen one. (For more information on Judas, see his Profile in Mark 14.) Whatever Judas thought, Satan assumed that Jesus' death would end Jesus' mission and thwart God's plan. Like Judas, he did not know that Jesus' death and resurrection were the most important parts of God's plan all along.

22:7, 8 The Passover meal included the sacrifice of a lamb because of the association with the Jews' exodus from Egypt. When the Jews were getting ready to leave, God told them to kill a lamb and paint its blood on the door-frames of their houses. They were then to prepare the meat for food. Peter and John had to buy and prepare the lamb as well as the unleavened bread, herbs, wine, and other ceremonial food.

22:10 Ordinarily women, not men, went to the well and brought home the water. So this man would have stood out in the crowd.

22:14–18 The Passover commemorated Israel's escape from Egypt when the blood of a lamb painted on their door-frames saved their firstborn sons from death. This event foreshadowed Jesus' work on the cross. As the spotless Lamb of God, his blood would be spilled in order to save his people from the penalty of death brought by sin.

22:17, 20 Luke mentions two cups of wine, while Matthew and Mark mention only one. In the traditional Passover meal, the wine is served four times. Christ spoke the words about his body and his blood when he offered the fourth and last cup.

22:17–20 Christians differ in their interpretation of the meaning of the commemoration of the Lord's Supper. There are three main views: (1) the bread and wine actually become Christ's body and blood; (2) the bread and wine remain unchanged, yet Christ is spiritually present by faith in and through them; (3) the bread and wine, which remain unchanged, are lasting memorials of Christ's sacrifice. No matter which view they favour, all Christians agree that the Lord's Supper commemorates Christ's death on the cross for our sins and points to the coming of his kingdom in glory. When we partake of it, we show our deep gratitude for Christ's work on our behalf, and our faith is strengthened.

22:19 Jesus asked the disciples to eat the broken bread "in remembrance of me". He wanted them to remember his sacrifice, the basis for forgiveness of sins, and also his friendship that they could continue to enjoy through the work of the Holy Spirit. Although the exact meaning of Communion has been strongly debated throughout church history, Christians still take bread and wine in remembrance of their Lord and Saviour, Jesus Christ. Do not neglect participating in the Lord's Supper. Let it remind you of what Christ did for you.

20In the same way, after the supper he took the cup, saying, "This cup is the new
covenant[o] in my blood, which is poured out for you. 21But the hand of him who is
going to betray me is with mine on the table.[p] 22The Son of Man[q] will go as it has
been decreed,[r] but woe to that man who betrays him." 23They began to question
among themselves which of them it might be who would do this.
24Also a dispute arose among them as to which of them was considered to be
greatest.[s] 25Jesus said to them, "The kings of the Gentiles lord it over them; and those
who exercise authority over them call themselves Benefactors. 26But you are not to
be like that. Instead, the greatest among you should be like the youngest,[t] and the
one who rules like the one who serves.[u] 27For who is greater, the one who is at the
table or the one who serves? Is it not the one who is at the table? But I am among
you as one who serves.[v] 28You are those who have stood by me in my trials. 29And
I confer on you a kingdom,[w] just as my Father conferred one on me, 30so that you
may eat and drink at my table in my kingdom[x] and sit on thrones, judging the twelve
tribes of Israel.[y]

Jesus Predicts Peter's Denial
(212/John 13:31–38)

31"Simon, Simon, Satan has asked[z] to sift you**[a]** as wheat.[a] 32But I have prayed
for you,[b] Simon, that your faith may not fail. And when you have turned back,
strengthen your brothers."[c]
33But he replied, "Lord, I am ready to go with you to prison and to death."[d]
34Jesus answered, "I tell you, Peter, before the cock crows today, you will deny
three times that you know me."
35Then Jesus asked them, "When I sent you without purse, bag or sandals,[e] did
you lack anything?"
"Nothing," they answered.
36He said to them, "But now if you have a purse, take it, and also a bag; and if
you don't have a sword, sell your cloak and buy one. 37It is written: 'And he was
numbered with the transgressors';**[b]**[f] and I tell you that this must be fulfilled in me.
Yes, what is written about me is reaching its fulfilment."

a *31* The Greek is plural. **b** *37* Isaiah 53:12

22:20 [o]Ex 24:8; Isa 42:6; Jer 31:31-34; Zec 9:11; 2Co 3:6; Heb 8:6; 9:15
22:21 [p]Ps 41:9
22:22 [q]Mt 8:20 [r]Ac 2:23; 4:28
22:24 [s]Mk 9:34; Lk 9:46
22:26 [t]1Pe 5:5 [u]Mk 9:35; Lk 9:48
22:27 [v]Mt 20:28; Lk 12:37
22:29 [w]Mt 25:34; 2Ti 2:12
22:30 [x]Lk 14:15 [y]Mt 19:28
22:31 [z]Job 1:6-12 [a]Am 9:9
22:32 [b]Jn 17:9, 15; Ro 8:34 [c]Jn 21:15-17
22:33 [d]Jn 11:16
22:35 [e]Mt 10:9, 10; Lk 9:3; 10:4
22:37 [f]Isa 53:12

22:20 In Old Testament times, God agreed to forgive people's sins if they brought animals for the priests to sacrifice. When this sacrificial system was inaugurated, the agreement between God and man was sealed with the blood of animals (Exodus 24:8). But animal blood did not in itself remove sin (only God can forgive sin), and animal sacrifices had to be repeated day by day and year after year. Jesus instituted a "new covenant" or agreement between humans and God. Under this new covenant, Jesus would die in the place of sinners. Unlike the blood of animals, his blood (because he is God) would truly remove the sins of all who put their faith in him. And Jesus' sacrifice would never have to be repeated; it would be good for all eternity (Hebrews 9:23–28). The prophets looked forward to this new covenant that would fulfil the old sacrificial agreement (Jeremiah 31:31–34), and John the Baptist called Jesus "the Lamb of God, who takes away the sin of the world" (John 1:29).

22:21 From the accounts of Mark and John we know that the betrayer was Judas Iscariot. Although the other disciples were confused by Jesus' words, Judas knew what he meant.

22:24 The most important event in human history was about to take place, and the disciples were still arguing about their prestige in the kingdom! Looking back, we say, "This was no time to worry about status." But the disciples, wrapped up in their own concerns, did not perceive what Jesus had been trying to tell them about his approaching death and resurrection. What are your major concerns today? Twenty years from now, as you look back, will these worries look petty and inappropriate? Take your eyes off yourself and get ready for Christ's coming into human history for the second time.

22:24–27 The world's system of leadership is very different from leadership in God's kingdom. Worldly leaders are often selfish and arrogant as they claw their way to the top. (Some kings in the ancient world gave themselves the title "Benefactor".) But among Christians, the leader is to be the one who *serves* best. There are different styles of leadership – some lead through public speaking, some through administering, some through relationships – but every Christian leader needs a servant's heart. Ask the people you lead how you can serve them better.

22:31, 32 Satan wanted to crush Simon Peter and the other disciples like grains of wheat. He hoped to find only chaff and blow it away. But Jesus assured Peter that his faith, although it would falter, would not be destroyed. It would be renewed, and Peter would become a powerful leader.

22:33, 34 Jesus predicted that Judas would betray him, and he said that calamity awaited the traitor (22:22). Jesus then predicted that Peter would deny that he knew Jesus, but later Peter would repent and receive a commission to feed Jesus' lambs (John 21:15). Betraying and denying – one is just about as bad as the other. But the two men had entirely different fates because one repented.

22:35–38 Here Jesus reversed his earlier advice regarding how to travel (9:3). The disciples were to bring bags, money, and swords. They would be facing hatred and persecution and would need to be prepared. When Jesus said "That is enough," he may have meant it was not time to think of using swords. In either case,

22:39 [g]Lk 21:37 [h]Mt 21:1
22:40 [i]Mt 6:13
22:41 [j]Lk 18:11
22:42 [k]Mt 20:22 [l]Mt 26:39
22:43 [m]Mt 4:11; Mk 1:13
22:46 [n]ver 40

38The disciples said, "See, Lord, here are two swords."
"That is enough," he replied.

Jesus Agonises in the Garden
(223/Matthew 26:36–46; Mark 14:32–42)

39Jesus went out as usual[g] to the Mount of Olives,[h] and his disciples followed
him. 40On reaching the place, he said to them, "Pray that you will not fall into
temptation."[i] 41He withdrew about a stone's throw beyond them, knelt down[j] and
prayed, 42"Father, if you are willing, take this cup[k] from me; yet not my will, but
yours be done."[l] 43An angel from heaven appeared to him and strengthened him.[m]
44And being in anguish, he prayed more earnestly, and his sweat was like drops of
blood falling to the ground.[c]
45When he rose from prayer and went back to the disciples, he found them asleep,
exhausted from sorrow. 46"Why are you sleeping?" he asked them. "Get up and pray
so that you will not fall into temptation."[n]

[c] *44* Some early manuscripts do not have verses 43 and 44.

JESUS' TRIAL
Jesus' trial was actually a series of hearings, carefully controlled to accomplish the death of Jesus. The verdict was already decided, but certain "legal" procedures were necessary. A lot of effort went into condemning and crucifying an innocent man. Jesus went through an unfair trial in our place so that we would not have to face a fair trial and receive the well-deserved punishment for our sins.

Event	*Probable reasons*	*References*
Trial before Annas (powerful ex-high priest)	Although no longer the high priest, he may still have wielded much power	John 18:13–23
Trial before Caiaphas (the ruling high priest)	To gather evidence for the full council hearing to follow	Matthew 26:57–68 Mark 14:53–65 Luke 22:54, 63–65 John 18:24
Trial before the council (Sanhedrin)	Formal religious trial and condemnation to death	Matthew 27:1 Mark 15:1 Luke 22:66–71
Trial before Pilate (highest Roman authority)	All death sentences needed Roman approval	Matthew 27:2, 11–14 Mark 15:1–5 Luke 23:1–6 John 18:28–38
Trial before Herod (ruler of Galilee)	A courteous and guilt-sharing act by Pilate because Jesus was from Galilee, Herod's district	Luke 23:7–12
Trial before Pilate	Pilate's last effort to avoid condemning an obviously innocent man	Matthew 27:15–26 Mark 15:6–15 Luke 23:13–25 John 18:39—19:16

mention of a sword vividly communicated the trials they were soon to face.

22:39 The Mount of Olives was located just to the east of Jerusalem. Jesus went up the southwestern slope to an olive grove called Gethsemane, which means "oil press".

22:40 Jesus asked the disciples to pray that they would not fall into temptation because he knew that he would soon be leaving them. Jesus also knew that they would need extra strength to face the temptations ahead – temptations to run away or to deny their relationship with him. They were about to see Jesus die. Would they still think he was the Messiah? The disciples' strongest temptation would undoubtedly be to think they had been deceived.

22:41, 42 Was Jesus trying to get out of his mission? It is never wrong to express our true feelings to God. Jesus exposed his dread of the coming trials, but he also reaffirmed his commitment to do what God wanted. The cup he spoke of meant the terrible agony he knew he would endure – not only the horror of the crucifixion but, even worse, the total separation from God that he would have to experience in order to die for the world's sins.

22:44 Only Luke tells us that Jesus' sweat resembled drops of blood. Jesus was in extreme agony, but he did not give up or give in. He went ahead with the mission for which he had come.

22:46 These disciples were asleep. How tragic it is that many Christians act as if they are sound asleep when it comes to devotion to Christ and service for him. Don't be found insensitive to or unprepared for Christ's work.

Jesus Is Betrayed and Arrested
(224/Matthew 26:47–56; Mark 14:43–52; John 18:1–11)

47While he was still speaking a crowd came up, and the man who was called Judas,
one of the Twelve, was leading them. He approached Jesus to kiss him, 48but Jesus
asked him, "Judas, are you betraying the Son of Man with a kiss?"
49When Jesus' followers saw what was going to happen, they said, "Lord, should
we strike with our swords?"[o] 50And one of them struck the servant of the high priest,
cutting off his right ear.
51But Jesus answered, "No more of this!" And he touched the man's ear and healed
him.
52Then Jesus said to the chief priests, the officers of the temple guard,[p] and the
elders, who had come for him, "Am I leading a rebellion, that you have come with
swords and clubs? 53Every day I was with you in the temple courts,[q] and you did
not lay a hand on me. But this is your hour[r]—when darkness reigns."[s]

Peter Denies Knowing Jesus
(227/Matthew 26:69–75; Mark 14:66–72; John 18:25–27)

54Then seizing him, they led him away and took him into the house of the high
priest.[t] Peter followed at a distance.[u] 55But when they had kindled a fire in the
middle of the courtyard and had sat down together, Peter sat down with them. 56A
servant girl saw him seated there in the firelight. She looked closely at him and said,
"This man was with him."
57But he denied it. "Woman, I don't know him," he said.
58A little later someone else saw him and said, "You also are one of them."
"Man, I am not!" Peter replied.

22:49
[o]ver 38

22:52
[p]ver 4

22:53
[q]Mt 26:55
[r]Jn 12:27
[s]Mt 8:12; Jn 1:5; 3:20

22:54
[t]Mt 26:57; Mk 14:53
[u]Mt 26:58; Mk 14:54; Jn 18:15

22:47 A kiss was and still is the traditional greeting among men in certain parts of the world. In this case, it was also the agreed-upon signal to point out Jesus (Matthew 26:48). It is ironic that a gesture of greeting would be the means of betrayal. It was a hollow gesture because of Judas' treachery. Have any of your religious practices become empty gestures? We still betray Christ when our acts of service or giving are insincere or carried out merely for show.

22:50 We learn from the Gospel of John that the man who cut off the servant's ear was Peter (John 18:10).

22:53 The religious leaders had not arrested Jesus in the temple for fear of a riot. Instead, they came secretly at night, under the influence of the prince of darkness, Satan himself. Although it looked as if Satan was getting the upper hand, everything was proceeding according to God's plan. It was time for Jesus to die.

22:54 Jesus was immediately taken to the high priest's house, even though this was the middle of the night. The Jewish leaders were in a hurry—they wanted to complete the execution before the Sabbath and get on with the Passover celebration. This residence was a palace with outer walls enclosing a courtyard where servants and soldiers warmed themselves around a fire.

22:55 Peter's experiences in the next few hours would change his life. He would change from a halfhearted follower to a repentant disciple, and finally to the kind of person Christ could use to build his church. For more information on Peter, see his Profile in Matthew 27.

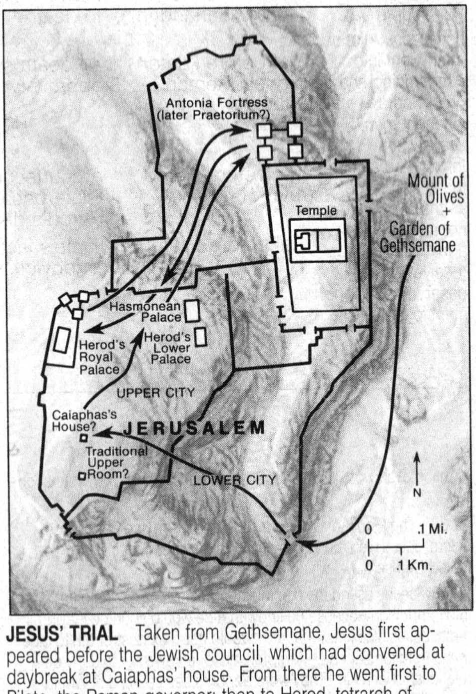

JESUS' TRIAL Taken from Gethsemane, Jesus first appeared before the Jewish council, which had convened at daybreak at Caiaphas' house. From there he went first to Pilate, the Roman governor; then to Herod, tetrarch of Galilee, who was visiting in Jerusalem; and back to Pilate, who, in desperation, sentenced Jesus to die.

22:59 [v]Lk 23:6
22:61 [w]Lk 7:13 [x]ver 34
22:65 [y]Mt 16:21
22:66 [z]Mt 5:22 [a]Mt 27:1; Mk 15:1
22:68 [b]Lk 20:3-8
22:69 [c]Mk 16:19
22:70 [d]Mt 4:3 [e]Mt 27:11; Lk 23:3
23:1 [a]Mt 27:2; Mk 15:1; Jn 18:28
23:2 [b]ver 14 [c]Lk 20:22 [d]Jn 19:12
23:4 [e]ver 14, 22, 41; Mt 27:23; Jn 18:38; 1Ti 6:13; 2Co 5:21
23:5 [f]Mk 1:14

59 About an hour later another asserted, "Certainly this fellow was with him, for he
is a Galilean."[v]
60 Peter replied, "Man, I don't know what you're talking about!" Just as he was
speaking, the cock crowed. 61 The Lord[w] turned and looked straight at Peter. Then
Peter remembered the word the Lord had spoken to him: "Before the cock crows today,
you will disown me three times."[x] 62 And he went outside and wept bitterly.
63 The men who were guarding Jesus began mocking and beating him. 64 They
blindfolded him and demanded, "Prophesy! Who hit you?" 65 And they said many
other insulting things to him.[y]

The Council of Religious Leaders Condemns Jesus
(228/Matthew 27:1, 2; Mark 15:1)

66 At daybreak the council[z] of the elders of the people, both the chief priests and
teachers of the law, met together,[a] and Jesus was led before them. 67 "If you are the
Christ,"**[d]** they said, "tell us."
Jesus answered, "If I tell you, you will not believe me, 68 and if I asked you, you
would not answer.[b] 69 But from now on, the Son of Man will be seated at the right
hand of the mighty God."[c]
70 They all asked, "Are you then the Son of God?"[d]
He replied, "You are right in saying I am."[e]
71 Then they said, "Why do we need any more testimony? We have heard it from
his own lips."

Jesus Stands Trial before Pilate
(230/Matthew 27:11–14; Mark 15:2–5; John 18:28–37)

23 Then the whole assembly rose and led him off to Pilate.[a] 2 And they began
to accuse him, saying, "We have found this man subverting our nation.[b] He
opposes payment of taxes to Caesar[c] and claims to be Christ,**[a]** a king."[d]
3 So Pilate asked Jesus, "Are you the king of the Jews?"
"Yes, it is as you say," Jesus replied.
4 Then Pilate announced to the chief priests and the crowd, "I find no basis for a
charge against this man."[e]
5 But they insisted, "He stirs up the people all over Judea**[b]** by his teaching. He
started in Galilee[f] and has come all the way here."

d *67* Or *Messiah* **a** *2* Or *Messiah*; also in verses 35 and 39 **b** *5* Or *over the land of the Jews*

22:62 Peter wept bitterly, not only because he realised that he had denied his Lord, the Messiah, but also because he had turned away from a very dear friend, a person who had loved and taught him for three years. Peter had said that he would *never* disown Christ, despite Jesus' prediction (Mark 14:29–31; Luke 22:33, 34). But when frightened, he went against all he had boldly promised. Unable to stand up for his Lord for even 12 hours, he had failed as a disciple and as a friend. We need to be aware of our own breaking points and not become overconfident or self-sufficient. If we fail him, we must remember that Christ can use those who recognise their failure. From this humiliating experience Peter learned much that would help him later when he assumed leadership of the young church.

22:70 Jesus in effect agreed that he was the Son of God when he simply turned the high priest's question around by saying, "You are right in saying I am." And Jesus identified himself with God by using a familiar title for God found in the Old Testament: "I am" (Exodus 3:14). The high priest recognised Jesus' claim and accused him of blasphemy. For any other human this claim would have been blasphemy, but in this case it was true. Blasphemy, the sin of claiming to be God or of attacking God's authority and majesty in any way, was punishable by death. The Jewish leaders had the evidence they wanted.

23:1 Pilate was the Roman governor of Judea, where Jerusalem was located. He seemed to take special pleasure in harassing the Jews. For example, Pilate had taken money from the temple treasury and had used it to build an aqueduct. And he had insulted the Jewish religion by bringing imperial images into the city. As Pilate well knew, such acts could backfire. If the people were to lodge a formal complaint against his administration, Rome might remove him from his post. Pilate was already beginning to feel insecure in his position when the Jewish leaders brought Jesus to trial. Would he continue to badger the Jews and risk his political future, or would he give in to their demands and condemn a man who, he was quite sure, was innocent? That was the question facing Pilate that spring Friday morning nearly 2,000 years ago. For more about Pilate, see his Profile in Mark 15.

Jesus Stands Trial before Herod
(231)

6On hearing this, Pilate asked if the man was a Galilean.[g] 7When he learned that
Jesus was under Herod's jurisdiction, he sent him to Herod,[h] who was also in
Jerusalem at that time.
8When Herod saw Jesus, he was greatly pleased, because for a long time he had
been wanting to see him.[i] From what he had heard about him, he hoped to see him
perform some miracle. 9He plied him with many questions, but Jesus gave him no
answer.[j] 10The chief priests and the teachers of the law were standing there, vehe-
mently accusing him. 11Then Herod and his soldiers ridiculed and mocked him.
Dressing him in an elegant robe,[k] they sent him back to Pilate. 12That day Herod
and Pilate became friends[l]—before this they had been enemies.

Pilate Hands Jesus Over to Be Crucified
(232/Matthew 27:15–26; Mark 15:6–15; John 18:38—19:16)

13Pilate called together the chief priests, the rulers and the people, 14and said to
them, "You brought me this man as one who was inciting the people to rebellion. I
have examined him in your presence and have found no basis for your charges against
him.[m] 15Neither has Herod, for he sent him back to us; as you can see, he has done
nothing to deserve death. 16Therefore, I will punish him[n] and then release him."[c]
18With one voice they cried out, "Away with this man! Release Barabbas to us!"[o]
(19Barabbas had been thrown into prison for an insurrection in the city, and for
murder.)

[c] 16 Some manuscripts *him.*" 17*Now he was obliged to release one man to them at the Feast.*

23:6 [g]Lk 22:59
23:7 [h]Mt 14:1; Lk 3:1
23:8 [i]Lk 9:9
23:9 [j]Mk 14:61
23:11 [k]Mk 15:17-19; Jn 19:2, 3
23:12 [l]Ac 4:27
23:14 [m]ver 4
23:16 [n]ver 22; Mt 27:26; Jn 19:1; Ac 16:37; 2Co 11:23, 24
23:18 [o]Ac 3:13, 14

23:7 Herod, also called Herod Antipas, was in Jerusalem that weekend for the Passover celebration. (This was the Herod who killed John the Baptist.) Pilate hoped to pass Jesus over to Herod because he knew that Jesus had lived and worked in Galilee. But Herod was not much help. He was curious about Jesus and enjoyed making fun of him. But when Herod sent Jesus back to Pilate, it was with the verdict of "not guilty". For more about Herod Antipas, see his Profile in Mark 6.

23:12 Herod was the part-Jewish ruler of Galilee and Perea. Pilate was the Roman governor of Judea and Samaria. Those four provinces, together with several others, had been united under Herod the Great. But when Herod died in 4 B.C., the kingdom was divided among his sons, each of whom was called "tetrarch" (meaning "ruler of a fourth part of a region"). Archelaus, the son who had received Judea and Samaria, was removed from office within ten years, and his provinces were then ruled by a succession of Roman governors, of whom Pilate was the fifth.

Herod Antipas had two advantages over Pilate: he came from a hereditary, part-Jewish monarchy, and he had held his position much longer. But Pilate had two advantages over Herod: he was a Roman citizen and an envoy of the emperor, and his position was created to replace that of Herod's ineffective half brother. It is not surprising that the two men were uneasy near each other. Jesus' trial, however, brought them together. Because Pilate had recognised Herod's authority over Galilee, Herod stopped feeling threatened by the Roman politician. And because neither man knew what to do in this predicament, their common problem united them.

23:13–25 Pilate wanted to release Jesus, but the crowd loudly demanded his death; so Pilate sentenced Jesus to die. No doubt Pilate did not want to risk losing his position, which may already have been shaky, by allowing a riot to occur in his province. As a politician, he knew the importance of compromise, and he saw Jesus more as a political threat than as a human being with rights and dignity.

When the stakes are high, it is difficult to stand up for what is right, and it is easy to see our opponents as problems to be solved rather than as people to be respected. Had Pilate been a man of real courage, he would have released Jesus no matter what the consequences. But the crowd roared, and Pilate buckled. We are like Pilate when we know what is right, but decide not to do it. When you have a difficult decision to make, don't discount the effects of peer pressure. Realise beforehand that the right decision could have unpleasant consequences: social rejection, career derailment, public ridicule. Then think of Pilate and resolve to stand up for what is right no matter what other people pressure you to do.

23:15 Jesus was tried six times, by both Jewish and Roman authorities, but he was never convicted of a crime deserving death. Even when condemned to execution, he had been convicted of no crime. Today, no-one can find fault in Jesus. But just like Pilate, Herod, and the religious leaders, many still refuse to acknowledge him as Lord.

23:18, 19 Barabbas had been part of a rebellion against the Roman government (Mark 15:7). As a political insurgent, he was no doubt a hero among some of the Jews. How ironic it is that Barabbas, who was released, was guilty of the very crime Jesus was accused of (23:14).

23:18, 19 Who was Barabbas? Jewish men had names that identified them with their fathers. Simon Peter, for example, is called Simon son of Jonah (Matthew 16:17). Barabbas is never identified by his given name, and this name is not much help either—*barabbas* means "son of *Abba*" (or "son of daddy"). He could have been anybody's son—and that's just the point. Barabbas, son of an unnamed father, committed a crime. Because Jesus died in his place, this man was set free. We too are sinners and criminals who have broken God's holy law. Like Barabbas, we deserve to die. But Jesus has died in our place, for our sins, and we have been set free. We don't have to be "very important people" to accept our freedom in Christ. In fact, thanks to Jesus, God adopts us all as his

23:22
[p]ver 16

23:26
[q]Mt 27:32
[r]Mk 15:21; Jn 19:17

23:27
[s]Lk 8:52

23:28
[t]Lk 19:41-44; 21:23, 24

23:29
[u]Mt 24:19

23:30
[v]Hos 10:8; Isa 2:19; Rev 6:16

23:31
[w]Eze 20:47

20 Wanting to release Jesus, Pilate appealed to them again. 21 But they kept shouting,
"Crucify him! Crucify him!"
22 For the third time he spoke to them: "Why? What crime has this man committed?
I have found in him no grounds for the death penalty. Therefore I will have him
punished and then release him."[p]
23 But with loud shouts they insistently demanded that he be crucified, and their
shouts prevailed. 24 So Pilate decided to grant their demand. 25 He released the man
who had been thrown into prison for insurrection and murder, the one they asked for,
and surrendered Jesus to their will.

Jesus Is Led Away to Be Crucified
(234/Matthew 27:32–34; Mark 15:21–24; John 19:17)

26 As they led him away, they seized Simon from Cyrene,[q] who was on his way
in from the country, and put the cross on him and made him carry it behind Jesus.[r]
27 A large number of people followed him, including women who mourned and
wailed[s] for him. 28 Jesus turned and said to them, "Daughters of Jerusalem, do not
weep for me; weep for yourselves and for your children.[t] 29 For the time will come
when you will say, 'Blessed are the barren women, the wombs that never bore and
the breasts that never nursed!'[u] 30 Then

> " 'they will say to the mountains, "Fall on us!"
> and to the hills "Cover us!" '[d][v]

31 For if men do these things when the tree is green, what will happen when it is
dry?"[w]

[d] *30* Hosea 10:8

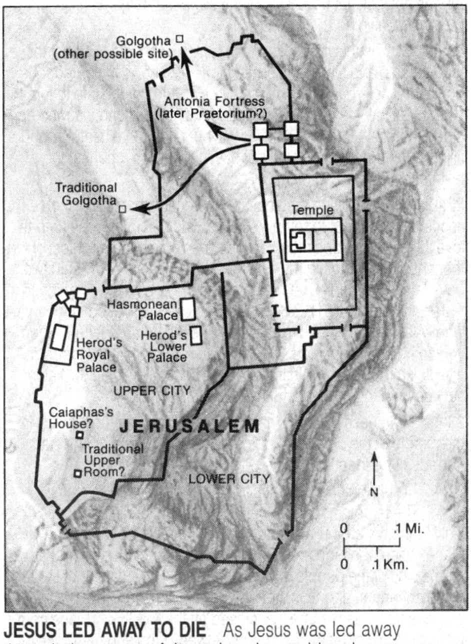

JESUS LED AWAY TO DIE As Jesus was led away through the streets of Jerusalem, he could no longer carry his cross, and Simon of Cyrene was given the burden. Jesus was crucified, along with common criminals, on a hill outside Jerusalem.

own sons and daughters and gives us the right to call him *Abba*—"daddy" (see Galatians 4:4–6).

23:22 When Pilate said he would have Jesus "punished", he was referring to a punishment that could have killed Jesus. The usual procedure was to bare the upper half of the victim's body and tie his hands to a pillar before whipping him with a three-pronged whip. The number of lashes was determined by the severity of the crime; up to 40 were permitted under Jewish law. After being flogged, Jesus also endured other agonies as recorded in Matthew and Mark. He was slapped, struck with fists, and mocked. A crown of thorns was placed on his head, and he was beaten with a stick and stripped before being hung on the cross.

23:23, 24 Pilate did not want to give Jesus the death sentence. He thought the Jewish leaders were simply jealous men who wanted to get rid of a rival. When they threatened to report Pilate to Caesar (John 19:12), however, Pilate became frightened. Historical records indicate that Pilate had already been warned by Roman authorities about tensions in this region. The last thing he needed was a riot in Jerusalem at Passover time, when the city was crowded with Jews from all over the empire. So Pilate turned Jesus over to the mob to do with as they pleased.

23:27–29 Luke alone mentions the tears of the Jewish women while Jesus was being led through the streets to his execution. Jesus told them not to weep for him but for themselves. He knew that in only about 40 years, Jerusalem and the temple would be destroyed by the Romans.

23:31 This proverb is difficult to interpret. Some feel it means: if the innocent Jesus (green tree) suffered at the hands of the Romans, what would happen to the guilty Jews (dry tree)?

Jesus Is Placed on the Cross
(235/Matthew 27:35–44; Mark 15:25–32; John 19:18–27)

32Two other men, both criminals, were also led out with him to be executed.[x]
33When they came to the place called the Skull, there they crucified him, along with
the criminals—one on his right, the other on his left. 34Jesus said, "Father,[y] forgive
them, for they do not know what they are doing."[e][z] And they divided up his clothes
by casting lots.[a]
35The people stood watching, and the rulers even sneered at him.[b] They said,
"He saved others; let him save himself if he is the Christ of God, the Chosen
One."[c]
36The soldiers also came up and mocked him.[d] They offered him wine vinegar[e]
37and said, "If you are the king of the Jews,[f] save yourself."
38There was a written notice above him, which read: THIS IS THE KING OF THE
JEWS.[g]
39One of the criminals who hung there hurled insults at him: "Aren't you the Christ?
Save yourself and us!"[h]
40But the other criminal rebuked him. "Don't you fear God," he said, "since you
are under the same sentence? 41We are punished justly, for we are getting what our
deeds deserve. But this man has done nothing wrong."[i]
42Then he said, "Jesus, remember me when you come into your kingdom.[f][j]"
43Jesus answered him, "I tell you the truth, today you will be with me in paradise."[k]

[e] *34* Some early manuscripts do not have this sentence. [f] *42* Some manuscripts *come with your kingly power*

23:32 [x]Isa 53:12; Mt 27:38; Mk 15:27; Jn 19:18
23:34 [y]Mt 11:25 [z]Mt 5:44 [a]Ps 22:18
23:35 [b]Ps 22:17 [c]Isa 42:1
23:36 [d]Ps 22:7 [e]Ps 69:21; Mt 27:48
23:37 [f]Lk 4:3, 9
23:38 [g]Mt 2:2
23:39 [h]ver 35, 37
23:41 [i]ver 4
23:42 [j]Mt 16:27
23:43 [k]2Co 12:3, 4; Rev 2:7

23:32, 33 The place called the Skull, or Golgotha, was probably a hill outside Jerusalem along a main road. The Romans executed people publicly as examples to others.

23:32, 33 When James and John asked Jesus for the places of honour next to him in his kingdom, he told them they didn't know what they were asking (Mark 10:35–39). Here, as Jesus was preparing to inaugurate his kingdom through his death, the places on his right and on his left were taken by dying men—criminals. As Jesus explained to his two position-conscious disciples, a person who wants to be close to Jesus must be prepared to suffer and die. The way to the kingdom is the way of the cross.

23:34 Jesus asked God to forgive the people who were putting him to death—Jewish leaders, Roman politicians and soldiers, bystanders—and God answered that prayer by opening up the way of salvation even to Jesus' murderers. The Roman centurion and soldiers who witnessed the crucifixion said, "Surely he was the Son of God" (Matthew 27:54). Soon many priests were converted to the Christian faith (Acts 6:7). Because we are all sinners, we all played a part in putting Jesus to death. The gospel—the Good News—is that God is gracious. He will forgive us and give us new life through his Son.

23:34 Roman soldiers customarily divided up the clothing of executed criminals among themselves. When they cast lots for Jesus' clothes, they fulfilled the prophecy in Psalm 22:18.

23:38 This sign was meant to be ironic. A king, stripped and executed in public view, had obviously lost his kingdom for ever. But Jesus, who turns the world's wisdom upside down, was just coming into his kingdom. His death and resurrection would strike the deathblow to Satan's rule and would establish Christ's eternal authority over the earth. Few people reading the sign that bleak afternoon understood its real meaning, but the sign was absolutely true. All was not lost. Jesus is King of the Jews—and the Gentiles, and the whole universe.

23:39–43 As this man was about to die, he turned to Christ for forgiveness, and Christ accepted him. This shows that our deeds don't save us—our faith in Christ does. It is never too late to turn to God. Even in his misery, Jesus had mercy on this criminal who decided to believe in him. Our lives will be much more useful and fulfilling if we turn to God early, but even those who repent at the very last moment will be with God in paradise.

23:42, 43 The dying criminal had more faith than the rest of Jesus' followers put together. Although the disciples continued to love Jesus, their hopes for the kingdom were shattered. Most of them had gone into hiding. As one of his followers sadly said two days later, "We had hoped that he was the one who was going to redeem Israel" (24:21). By contrast, the criminal looked at the man who was dying next to him and said, "Jesus, remember me when you come into your kingdom." By all appearances, the kingdom was finished. How awe-inspiring is the faith of this man who alone saw beyond the present shame to the coming glory!

23:44 Darkness covered the entire land for about three hours in the middle of the day. All nature seemed to mourn over the stark tragedy of the death of God's Son.

23:45 This significant event symbolised Christ's work on the cross. The temple had three parts: the courts for all the people; the Holy Place, where only priests could enter; and the Most Holy Place, where the high priest alone could enter once a year to atone for the sins of the people. It was in the Most Holy Place that the ark of the covenant, and God's presence with it, rested. The curtain that was torn was the one that closed off the Most Holy Place from view. At Christ's death, the barrier between God and man was split in two. Now all people can approach God directly through Christ (Hebrews 9:1–14; 10:19–22).

Jesus Dies on the Cross
(236/Matthew 27:45–56; Mark 15:33–41; John 19:28–37)

44It was now about the sixth hour, and darkness came over the whole land until the
ninth hour,[l] 45for the sun stopped shining. And the curtain of the temple[m] was torn
in two.[n] 46Jesus called out with a loud voice,[o] "Father, into your hands I commit
my spirit."[p] When he had said this, he breathed his last.[q]
47The centurion, seeing what had happened, praised God[r] and said, "Surely this
was a righteous man." 48When all the people who had gathered to witness this sight
saw what took place, they beat their breasts[s] and went away. 49But all those who
knew him, including the women who had followed him from Galilee,[t] stood at a
distance,[u] watching these things.

Jesus Is Laid in the Tomb
(237/Matthew 27:57–61; Mark 15:42–47; John 19:38–42)

50Now there was a man named Joseph, a member of the Council, a good and upright
man, 51who had not consented to their decision and action. He came from the Judean
town of Arimathea and he was waiting for the kingdom of God.[v] 52Going to Pilate,
he asked for Jesus' body. 53Then he took it down, wrapped it in linen cloth and placed
it in a tomb cut in the rock, one in which no-one had yet been laid. 54It was Preparation
Day,[w] and the Sabbath was about to begin.
55The women who had come with Jesus from Galilee[x] followed Joseph and saw
the tomb and how his body was laid in it. 56Then they went home and prepared
spices and perfumes.[y] But they rested on the Sabbath in obedience to the commandment.[z]

Jesus Rises from the Dead
(239/Matthew 28:1–7; Mark 16:1–8; John 20:1–9)

24 On the first day of the week, very early in the morning, the women took the
spices they had prepared[a] and went to the tomb. 2They found the stone rolled
away from the tomb, 3but when they entered, they did not find the body of the Lord
Jesus.[b] 4While they were wondering about this, suddenly two men in clothes that
gleamed like lightning[c] stood beside them. 5In their fright the women bowed down
with their faces to the ground, but the men said to them, "Why do you look for the

23:44 [l]Am 8:9
23:45 [m]Ex 26:31-33; Heb 9:3, 8 [n]Heb 10:19, 20
23:46 [o]Mt 27:50 [p]Ps 31:5; 1Pe 2:23 [q]Jn 19:30
23:47 [r]Mt 9:8
23:48 [s]Lk 18:13
23:49 [t]Lk 8:2 [u]Ps 38:11
23:51 [v]Lk 2:25, 38
23:54 [w]Mt 27:62
23:55 [x]ver 49
23:56 [y]Mk 16:1; Lk 24:1 [z]Ex 12:16; 20:10
24:1 [a]Lk 23:56
24:3 [b]ver 23, 24
24:4 [c]Jn 20:12

23:50–52 Joseph of Arimathea was a wealthy and honoured member of the Jewish Council. He was also a secret disciple of Jesus (John 19:38). The disciples who had publicly followed Jesus fled, but Joseph boldly took a stand that could cost him dearly. He cared enough about Jesus to ask for his body so he could give it a proper burial.

23:53 The tomb was likely a man-made cave cut out of one of the many limestone hills in the area around Jerusalem. Such a tomb was large enough to walk into. After burial, a large stone would have been rolled across the entrance (John 20:1).

23:55 The Galilean women followed Joseph to the tomb, so they knew exactly where to find Jesus' body when they returned after the Sabbath with their spices and perfumes. These women could not do "great" things for Jesus – they were not permitted to stand up before the Jewish council or the Roman governor and testify on his behalf – but they did what they could. They stayed at the cross when most of the disciples had fled, and they got ready to anoint their Lord's body. Because of their devotion, they were the first to know about the resurrection. As believers, we may feel we can't do much for Jesus. But we are called to take advantage of the opportunities given us, doing what we *can* do and not worrying about what we cannot do.

24:1 The women brought spices to the tomb as we would bring flowers – as a sign of love and respect. The women went home and kept Sabbath as the law required, from sunset Friday to sunset Saturday, before gathering up their spices and perfumes and returning to the tomb.

24:1–9 The two angels (appearing as "men in clothes that gleamed like lightning") asked the women why they were looking in a tomb for someone who was alive. Often we run into people who are looking for God among the dead. They study the Bible as a mere historical document and go to church as if going to a memorial service. But Jesus is not among the dead – he lives! He reigns in the hearts of Christians, and he is the head of his church. Do you look for Jesus among the living? Do you expect him to be active in the world and in the church? Look for signs of his power – they are all around you.

24:4 We learn from Matthew and John that these two men in gleaming clothes were angels. When angels appeared to people, they looked like humans.

living among the dead? 6He is not here; he has risen! Remember how he told you,
while he was still with you in Galilee:[d] 7'The Son of Man[e] must be delivered into
the hands of sinful men, be crucified and on the third day be raised again.' "[f] 8Then
they remembered his words.[g]
9When they came back from the tomb, they told all these things to the Eleven and
to all the others. 10It was Mary Magdalene, Joanna, Mary the mother of James, and
the others with them[h] who told this to the apostles.[i] 11But they did not believe[j]
the women, because their words seemed to them like nonsense. 12Peter, however, got
up and ran to the tomb. Bending over, he saw the strips of linen lying by themselves,[k]
and he went away,[l] wondering to himself what had happened.

Jesus Appears to Two Believers Travelling on the Road
(243/Mark 16:12, 13)

13Now that same day two of them were going to a village called Emmaus, about
seven miles[a] from Jerusalem.[m] 14They were talking with each other about everything
that had happened. 15As they talked and discussed these things with each other, Jesus
himself came up and walked along with them;[n] 16but they were kept from recognising
him.[o]
17He asked them, "What are you discussing together as you walk along?"
They stood still, their faces downcast. 18One of them, named Cleopas,[p] asked him,

a *13* Greek *sixty stadia* (about 11 kilometres)

24:6 [d]Mt 17:22, 23; Mk 9:30-31; Lk 9:22; 24:44
24:7 [e]Mt 8:20 [f]Mt 16:21
24:8 [g]Jn 2:22
24:10 [h]Lk 8:1-3 [i]Mk 6:30
24:11 [j]Mk 16:11
24:12 [k]Jn 20:3-7 [l]Jn 20:10
24:13 [m]Mk 16:12
24:15 [n]ver 36
24:16 [o]Jn 20:14; 21:4
24:18 [p]Jn 19:25

24:6, 7 The angels reminded the women that Jesus had accurately predicted all that had happened to him (9:22, 44; 18:31–33).

24:6, 7 The resurrection of Jesus from the dead is the central fact of Christian history. On it, the church is built; without it, there would be no Christian church today. Jesus' resurrection is unique. Other religions have strong ethical systems, concepts about paradise and the afterlife, and various holy scriptures. Only Christianity has a God who became human, literally died for his people, and was raised again in power and glory to rule his church for ever.

Why is the resurrection so important? (1) Because Christ was raised from the dead, we know that the kingdom of heaven has broken into earth's history. Our world is now headed for redemption, not disaster. God's mighty power is at work destroying sin, creating new lives, and preparing us for Jesus' second coming. (2) Because of the resurrection, we know that death has been conquered, and we too will be raised from the dead to live for ever with Christ. (3) The resurrection gives authority to the church's witness in the world. Look at the early evangelistic sermons in the book of Acts: the apostles' most important message was the proclamation that Jesus Christ had been raised from the dead! (4) The resurrection gives meaning to the church's regular feast, the Lord's Supper. Like the disciples on the Emmaus Road, we break bread with our risen Lord, who comes in power to save us. (5) The resurrection helps us find meaning even in great tragedy. No matter what happens to us as we walk with the Lord, the resurrection gives us hope for the future. (6) The resurrection assures us that Christ is alive and ruling his kingdom. He is not legend; he is alive and real. (7) God's power that brought Jesus back from the dead is available to us so that we can live for him in an evil world.

Christians can look very different from one another, and they can hold widely varying beliefs about politics, life-style, and even theology. But one central belief unites and inspires all true Christians—Jesus Christ rose from the dead! (For more on the importance of the resurrection, see 1 Corinthians 15:12–58.)

24:11, 12 People who hear about the resurrection for the first time may need time before they can comprehend this amazing story. Like the disciples, they may pass through four stages of belief. (1) At first, they may think it is a fairy tale, impossible to believe. (2) Like Peter, they may check out the facts but still be puzzled about what happened. (3) Only when they encounter Jesus personally will they be able to accept the fact of the resurrection. (4) Then, as they commit themselves to Jesus and devote their lives to serving him, they will begin fully to understand the reality of his presence with them.

24:12 From John 20:3, 4, we learn that another disciple ran to the tomb with Peter. That other disciple was almost certainly John, the author of the fourth Gospel.

24:13ff The two disciples returning to Emmaus at first missed the significance of history's greatest event because they were too focused on their disappointments and problems. In fact, they didn't recognise Jesus when he was walking beside them. To compound the problem, they were walking in the wrong direction—away from the fellowship of believers in Jerusalem. We are likely to miss Jesus and withdraw from the strength found in other believers

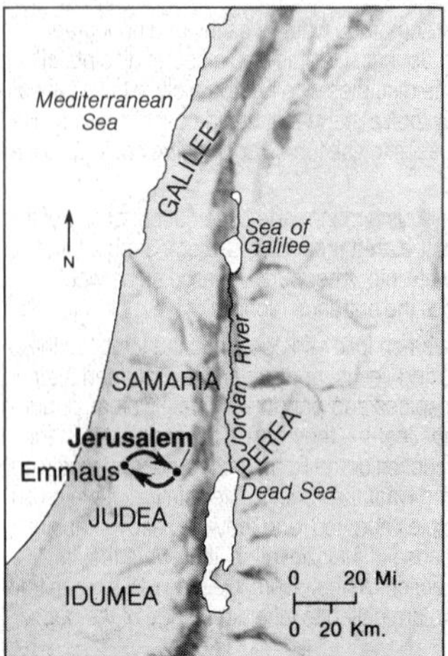

ON THE ROAD TO EMMAUS
After Jesus' death, two of his followers were walking from Jerusalem back towards Emmaus when a stranger joined them. After dinner in Emmaus, Jesus revealed himself to these men and then disappeared. They immediately returned to Jerusalem to tell the disciples the good news that Jesus was alive!

"Are you only a visitor to Jerusalem and do not know the things that have happened
there in these days?"
19"What things?" he asked.
"About Jesus of Nazareth,"[q] they replied. "He was a prophet,[r] powerful in word
and deed before God and all the people. 20The chief priests and our rulers[s] handed
him over to be sentenced to death, and they crucified him; 21but we had hoped that
he was the one who was going to redeem Israel.[t] And what is more, it is the third
day[u] since all this took place. 22In addition, some of our women amazed us.[v] They
went to the tomb early this morning 23but didn't find his body. They came and told
us that they had seen a vision of angels, who said he was alive. 24Then some of our
companions went to the tomb and found it just as the women had said, but him they
did not see."[w]
25He said to them, "How foolish you are, and how slow of heart to believe all that
the prophets have spoken! 26Did not the Christ[b] have to suffer these things and then
enter his glory?"[x] 27And beginning with Moses[y] and all the Prophets,[z] he explained
to them what was said in all the Scriptures concerning himself.[a]
28As they approached the village to which they were going, Jesus acted as if he were
going further. 29But they urged him strongly, "Stay with us, for it is nearly evening;
the day is almost over." So he went in to stay with them.
30When he was at the table with them, he took bread, gave thanks, broke it[b] and
began to give it to them. 31Then their eyes were opened and they recognised him,[c]
and he disappeared from their sight. 32They asked each other, "Were not our hearts
burning within us[d] while he talked with us on the road and opened the Scriptures[e]
to us?"
33They got up and returned at once to Jerusalem. There they found the Eleven and

24:19 [q]Mk 1:24 [r]Mt 21:11
24:20 [s]Lk 23:13
24:21 [t]Lk 1:68; 2:38; 21:28 [u]Mt 16:21
24:22 [v]ver 1-10
24:24 [w]ver 12
24:26 [x]Heb 2:10; 1Pe 1:11
24:27 [y]Ge 3:15; Nu 21:9; Dt 18:15 [z]Isa 7:14; 9:6; 40:10, 11; 53; Eze 34:23; Da 9:24; Mic 7:20; Mal 3:1 [a]Jn 1:45
24:30 [b]Mt 14:19
24:31 [c]ver 16
24:32 [d]Ps 39:3 [e]ver 27, 45

b *26* Or *Messiah*; also in verse 46

---

when we become preoccupied with our dashed hopes and frustrated plans. Only when we are looking for Jesus in our midst will we experience the power and help he can bring.

24:18 The news about Jesus' crucifixion had spread throughout Jerusalem. Because this was Passover week, Jewish pilgrims visiting the city from all over the Roman empire now knew about his death. This was not a small, insignificant event, affecting only the disciples – the whole nation was interested.

24:21 The disciples from Emmaus were counting on Jesus to redeem Israel – that is, to rescue the nation from its enemies. Most Jews believed that the Old Testament prophecies pointed to a military and political Messiah; they didn't realise that the Messiah had come to redeem people from slavery to sin. When Jesus died, therefore, they lost all hope. They didn't understand that Jesus' death offered the greatest hope possible.

24:24 These disciples knew that the tomb was empty but didn't understand that Jesus had risen, and they were filled with sadness. Despite the women's witness, which was verified by other disciples, and despite the biblical prophecies of this very event, they still didn't believe. Today the resurrection still catches people by surprise. In spite of 2,000 years of evidence and witness, many people refuse to believe. What more will it take? For these disciples it took the living, breathing Jesus in their midst. For many people today, it takes the presence of living, breathing Christians.

24:25 Why did Jesus call these disciples foolish? Even though they well knew the biblical prophecies, they failed to understand that Christ's suffering was his path to glory. They could not understand why God did not intervene to save Jesus from the cross. They were so caught up in the world's admiration of political power and military might that they were unprepared for the reversal of values in God's kingdom – that the last will be first, and that life grows out of death. The world has not changed its values: a suffering servant is no more popular today than 2,000 years ago. But we not only have the witness of the Old Testament prophets; we also have the witness of the New Testament apostles and the history of the Christian church all pointing to Jesus' victory over death. Will we step outside the values of our culture and put our faith in Jesus? Or will we foolishly continue to be baffled by his Good News?

24:25–27 After the two disciples had explained their sadness and confusion, Jesus responded by going to Scripture and applying it to his ministry. When we are puzzled by questions or problems, we too can go to Scripture and find authoritative help. If we, like these two disciples, do not understand what the Bible means, we can turn to other believers who know the Bible and have the wisdom to apply it to our situation.

24:27 Beginning with the promised offspring in Genesis (Genesis 3:15) and going through the suffering servant in Isaiah (Isaiah 53), the pierced one in Zechariah (Zechariah 12:10), and the messenger of the covenant in Malachi (Malachi 3:1), Jesus reintroduced these disciples to the Old Testament. Christ is the thread woven through all the Scriptures, the central theme that binds them together. Following are several key passages Jesus may have mentioned on this walk to Emmaus: Genesis 3; 12; Psalms 22; 69; 110; Isaiah 53; Jeremiah 31; Zechariah 9; 13; Malachi 3.

24:33, 34 Paul also mentions that Jesus appeared to Peter alone (1 Corinthians 15:5). This appearance is not further described in the Gospels. Jesus showed individual concern for Peter because Peter felt completely unworthy after disowning his Lord. But Peter repented, and Jesus approached him and forgave him. Soon God would use Peter in building Christ's church (see the first half of the book of Acts).

those with them, assembled together 34and saying, "It is true! The Lord has risen and
has appeared to Simon."[f] 35Then the two told what had happened on the way, and
how Jesus was recognised by them when he broke the bread.[g]

Jesus Appears to the Disciples Behind Locked Doors
(244/John 20:19–23)

36While they were still talking about this, Jesus himself stood among them and said
to them, "Peace be with you."[h]
37They were startled and frightened, thinking they saw a ghost.[i] 38He said to them,
"Why are you troubled, and why do doubts rise in your minds? 39Look at my hands
and my feet. It is I myself! Touch me and see;[j] a ghost does not have flesh and bones,
as you see I have."
40When he had said this, he showed them his hands and feet. 41And while they still
did not believe it because of joy and amazement, he asked them, "Do you have
anything here to eat?" 42They gave him a piece of broiled fish, 43and he took it and
ate it in their presence.[k]

Jesus Appears to the Disciples in Jerusalem
(249)

44He said to them, "This is what I told you while I was still with you:[l] Everything
must be fulfilled[m] that is written about me in the Law of Moses,[n] the Prophets and
the Psalms."[o]
45Then he opened their minds so they could understand the Scriptures. 46He told
them, "This is what is written: The Christ will suffer and rise from the dead on the
third day, 47and repentance and forgiveness of sins will be preached in his name[p]
to all nations,[q] beginning at Jerusalem. 48You are witnesses[r] of these things. 49I am
going to send you what my Father has promised;[s] but stay in the city until you have
been clothed with power from on high."

Jesus Ascends into Heaven
(250/Mark 16:19, 20)

50When he had led them out to the vicinity of Bethany,[t] he lifted up his hands

24:34 [f]1Co 15:5
24:35 [g]ver 30, 31
24:36 [h]Jn 20:19, 21, 26; 14:27
24:37 [i]Mk 6:49
24:39 [j]Jn 20:27; 1Jn 1:1
24:43 [k]Ac 10:41
24:44 [l]Lk 9:45; 18:34 [m]Mt 16:21; Lk 9:22, 44; 18:31-33; 22:37 [n]ver 27 [o]Ps 2; 16; 22; 69; 72; 110; 118
24:47 [p]Ac 5:31; 10:43; 13:38 [q]Mt 28:19
24:48 [r]Ac 1:8; 2:32; 5:32; 13:31; 1Pe 5:1
24:49 [s]Jn 14:16; Ac 1:4
24:50 [t]Mt 21:17

24:36–43 Jesus' body wasn't just a figment of the imagination or the appearance of a ghost – the disciples touched him, and he ate food. On the other hand, his body wasn't merely a restored human body like Lazarus' (John 11) – he was able to appear and disappear. Jesus' resurrected body was immortal. This is the kind of body we will be given at the resurrection of the dead (see 1 Corinthians 15:42–50).

24:44 Many days may have elapsed between verses 43 and 44 because Jesus and his followers travelled to Galilee and back before he returned to heaven (Matthew 28:16; John 21). In his second book, Acts, Luke makes it clear that Jesus spent 40 days with his disciples between his resurrection and ascension.

24:44–46 The Law of Moses, the Prophets, and the Psalms is a way to describe the entire Old Testament. In other words, the entire Old Testament points to the Messiah. For example, his role as prophet was foretold in Deuteronomy 18:15–20; his sufferings were prophesied in Psalm 22 and Isaiah 53; his resurrection was predicted in Psalm 16:9–11 and Isaiah 53:10, 11.

24:45 Jesus opened these people's minds to understand the Scriptures. The Holy Spirit does this in our lives today when we study the Bible. Have you ever wondered how to understand a difficult Bible passage? Besides reading surrounding passages, asking other people, and consulting reference works, pray that the Holy Spirit will open your mind to understand, giving you the needed insight to put God's word into action in your life.

24:47 Luke wrote to the Greek-speaking world. He wanted them to know that Christ's message of God's love and forgiveness should go to all the world. We must never ignore the worldwide scope of Christ's gospel. God wants all the world to hear the Good News of salvation.

24:50–53 As the disciples stood and watched, Jesus began rising into the air, and soon he disappeared into heaven. Seeing Jesus leave must have been frightening, but the disciples knew that Jesus would keep his promise to be with them through the Holy Spirit. This same Jesus, who lived with the disciples, who died and was buried, and who rose from the dead, loves us and promises to be with us always. We can get to know him better through studying the Scriptures, praying, and allowing the Holy Spirit to make us more like Jesus.

24:51 Jesus' physical presence left the disciples when he returned to heaven (Acts 1:9), but the Holy Spirit soon came to comfort them and empower them to spread the gospel of salvation (Acts 2:1–4). Today Jesus' work of salvation is completed, and he is sitting at God's right hand, where he has authority over heaven and earth.

24:53 Luke's Gospel portrays Jesus as the perfect example of a life lived according to God's plan – as a child living in obedience to his parents and yet amazing the religious leaders in the temple, as an adult serving God and others through preaching and healing, and finally as a condemned man suffering without complaint.

24:51
[u] 2Ki 2:11
24:53
[v] Ac 2:46

and blessed them. 51 While he was blessing them, he left them and was taken up into
heaven.[u] 52 Then they worshipped him and returned to Jerusalem with great joy.
53 And they stayed continually at the temple,[v] praising God.

This emphasis was well suited to Luke's Greek audience, who placed high value on being an example and improving oneself, and who often discussed the meaning of perfection. The Greeks, however, had a difficult time understanding the spiritual importance of the physical world. To them, the spiritual was always more important than the physical. To help them understand the God-man who united the spiritual and the physical, Luke emphasised that Jesus was not a phantom human but a real human being who healed people and fed them because he was concerned with their physical health as well as the state of their souls.

As believers living according to God's plan, we too should obey our Lord in every detail as we seek to restore people's bodies and souls to the health and salvation God has in store for them. If we want to know how to live a perfect life, we can look to Jesus as our example.

JOHN

Herod the Great begins to rule 37 B.C.	*Jesus is born 6/5 B.C.*	*Escape to Egypt 5/4 B.C.*	*Herod the Great dies 4 B.C.*	*Return to Nazareth 4/3 B.C.*	*Judea becomes Roman province A.D. 6*

VITAL STATISTICS

PURPOSE:
To prove conclusively that Jesus is the Son of God and that all who believe in him will have eternal life.

AUTHOR:
John the apostle, son of Zebedee, brother of James, called a "Son of Thunder"

TO WHOM WRITTEN:
New Christians and searching non-Christians

DATE WRITTEN:
Probably A.D. 85–90

SETTING:
Written after the destruction of Jerusalem in A.D. 70 and before John's exile to the island of Patmos

KEY VERSES:
"Jesus did many other miraculous signs in the presence of his disciples, which are not recorded in this book. But these are written that you may believe that Jesus is the Christ, the Son of God, and that by believing you may have life in his name" (20:30, 31).

KEY PEOPLE:
Jesus, John the Baptist, the disciples, Mary, Martha, Lazarus, Jesus' mother, Pilate, Mary Magdalene

KEY PLACES:
Judean countryside, Samaria, Galilee, Bethany, Jerusalem

SPECIAL FEATURES:
Of the eight miracles recorded, six are unique (among the Gospels) to John, as is the "Upper Room Discourse" (chapters 14—17). Over 90 per cent of John is unique to his Gospel— John does not contain a genealogy or any record of Jesus' birth, childhood, temptation, transfiguration, appointment of the disciples, nor any account of Jesus' parables, ascension, or Great Commission.

HE SPOKE, and galaxies whirled into place, stars burned the heavens, and planets began orbiting their suns—words of awesome, unlimited, unleashed power. He spoke again, and the waters and lands were filled with plants and creatures, running, swimming, growing, and multiplying—words of animating, breathing, pulsing life. Again he spoke, and man and woman were formed, thinking, speaking, and loving —words of personal and creative glory. Eternal, infinite, unlimited—he was, is, and always will be the Maker and Lord of all that exists.

And then he came in the flesh to a speck in the universe called planet earth. The mighty Creator became a part of the creation, limited by time and space and susceptible to aging, sickness, and death. But love propelled him, and so he came to rescue and save those who were lost and to give them the gift of eternity. He is *the Word;* he is Jesus, the Christ.

It is this truth that the apostle John brings to us in this book. John's Gospel is not a life of Christ; it is a powerful argument for the incarnation, a conclusive demonstration that Jesus was, and is, the very heaven-sent Son of God and the only source of eternal life.

John discloses Christ's identity with his very first words, "In the beginning was the Word, and the Word was with God, and the Word was God. He was with God in the beginning" (1:1, 2); and the rest of the book continues the theme. John, the eyewitness, chose eight of Christ's miracles (or signs, as he calls them), to reveal Christ's divine/human nature and his life-giving mission. These signs are (1) turning water to wine (2:1–11), (2) healing the official's son (4:46–54), (3) healing the invalid at Bethesda (5:1–9), (4) feeding the 5,000 with just a few loaves and fish (6:1–14), (5) walking on the water (6:15–21), (6) restoring sight to the blind man (9:1–41), (7) raising Lazarus from the dead (11:1–44), and, after the resurrection, (8) giving the disciples an overwhelming catch of fish (21:1–14).

In every chapter Jesus' deity is revealed. And Jesus' true identity is underscored through the titles he is given—Word, the One and Only, Lamb of God, Son of God, true bread, life, resurrection, vine. And the formula is "I am." When Jesus uses this phrase, he affirms his preexistence and eternal deity. Jesus says, *I am* the bread of life (6:35); *I am* the light of the world (8:12; 9:5); *I am* the gate (10:7); *I am* the good shepherd (10:11, 14); *I am* the resurrection and the life (11:25); *I am* the way and the truth and the life (14:6); and *I am* the true vine (15:1).

The greatest sign, of course, is the resurrection, and John provides a stirring eyewitness account of finding the empty tomb. Then he records various post-resurrection appearances by Jesus.

John, the devoted follower of Christ, has given us a personal and powerful look at Jesus Christ, the eternal Son of God. As you read his story, commit yourself to believe in and follow him.

Tiberius Caesar becomes emperor 14	Pontius Pilate appointed governor 26	Jesus begins his ministry 26/27	Jesus and Nicodemus 27	Jesus chooses twelve disciples 28	Jesus feeds 5,000 29	Jesus is crucified, rises again, and ascends 30

THE BLUEPRINT

A. BIRTH AND PREPARATION OF JESUS, THE SON OF GOD (1:1—2:11)

John makes it clear that Jesus is not just a man; he is the eternal Son of God. He is the light of the world because he offers this gift of eternal life to all mankind. How blind and foolish to call Jesus nothing more than an unusually good man or moral teacher. Yet we sometimes act as if this were true when we casually toss around his words and go about living our own way. If Jesus is the eternal Son of God, we should pay attention to his divine identity and life-giving message.

B. MESSAGE AND MINISTRY OF JESUS, THE SON OF GOD (2:12—12:50)

1. Jesus encounters belief and unbelief from the people
2. Jesus encounters conflict with the religious leaders
3. Jesus encounters crucial events in Jerusalem

Jesus meets with individuals, preaches to great crowds, trains his disciples, and debates with the religious leaders. The message that he is the Son of God receives a mixed reaction. Some worship him, some are puzzled, some shrink back, and some move to silence him. We see the same varied reactions today. Times have changed, but people's hearts remain hard. May we see ourselves in these encounters Jesus had with people, and may our response be to worship and follow him.

C. DEATH AND RESURRECTION OF JESUS, THE SON OF GOD (13:1—21:25)

1. Jesus teaches his disciples
2. Jesus completes his mission

Jesus carefully instructed the disciples how to continue to believe even after his death, yet they could not take it in. After he died and the first reports came back that Jesus was alive, the disciples could not believe it. Thomas is especially remembered as one who refused to believe even when he heard the eyewitness accounts from other disciples. May we not be like Thomas, demanding a physical face-to-face encounter, but may we accept the eyewitness testimony of the disciples that John has recorded in this Gospel.

MEGATHEMES

THEME	EXPLANATION	IMPORTANCE
Jesus Christ, Son of God	John shows us that Jesus is unique as God's special Son, yet he is fully God. Because he is fully God, Jesus is able to reveal God to us clearly and accurately.	Because Jesus is God's Son, we can perfectly trust what he says. By trusting him, we can gain an open mind to understand God's message and fulfil his purpose in our lives.
Eternal Life	Because Jesus is God, he lives for ever. Before the world began, he lived with God, and he will reign for ever with him. In John we see Jesus revealed in power and magnificence even before his resurrection.	Jesus offers eternal life to us. We are invited to begin living in a personal, eternal relationship with him that begins now. Although we must grow old and die, by trusting him we can have a new life that lasts for ever.
Belief	John records eight specific signs, or miracles, that show the nature of Jesus' power and love. We see his power over everything created, and we see his love of all people. These signs encourage us to believe in him.	Believing is active, living, and continuous trust in Jesus as God. When we believe in his life, his words, his death, and his resurrection, we are cleansed from sin and receive power to follow him. But we must respond to him by believing.
Holy Spirit	Jesus taught his disciples that the Holy Spirit would come after he ascended from earth. The Holy Spirit would then indwell, guide, counsel, and comfort those who follow Jesus. Through the Holy Spirit, Christ's presence and power are multiplied in all who believe.	Through God's Holy Spirit we are drawn to him in faith. We must know the Holy Spirit to understand all Jesus taught. We can experience Jesus' love and guidance as we allow the Holy Spirit to do his work in us.

Resurrection	On the third day after he died, Jesus rose from the dead. This was verified by his disciples and many eyewitnesses. This reality changed the disciples from frightened deserters to dynamic leaders in the new church. This fact is the foundation of the Christian faith.	We can be changed as the disciples were and have confidence that our bodies will one day be raised to live with Christ for ever. The same power that raised Christ to life can give us the ability to follow Christ each day.

KEY PLACES IN JOHN

John's story begins as John the Baptist ministers near Bethany on the other side of the Jordan (1:28ff). Jesus also begins his ministry, talking to some of the men who would later become his 12 disciples. Jesus' ministry in Galilee began with a visit to a wedding in Cana (2:1ff). Then he went to Capernaum, which became his new home (2:12). He journeyed to Jerusalem for the special feasts (2:13) and there met with Nicodemus, a religious leader (3:1ff). When Jesus left Judea, he travelled through Samaria and ministered to the Samaritans (4:1ff). Jesus did miracles in Galilee (4:46ff) and in Judea and Jerusalem (5:1ff). We follow him as he fed 5,000 near Bethsaida beside the Sea of Galilee (Sea of Tiberias) (6:1ff), walked on the water to his frightened disciples (6:16ff), preached through Galilee (7:1), returned to Jerusalem (7:2ff), preached beyond the Jordan in Perea (10:40), raised Lazarus from the dead in Bethany (11:1ff), and finally entered Jerusalem for the last time to celebrate the Passover with his disciples and give them key teachings about what was to come and how they should act. His last hours before his crucifixion were spent in the city (13:1ff), in the Garden of Gethsemane (18:1ff), and finally in various buildings in Jerusalem during his trial (18:12ff). He would be crucified, but he would rise again as he had promised.

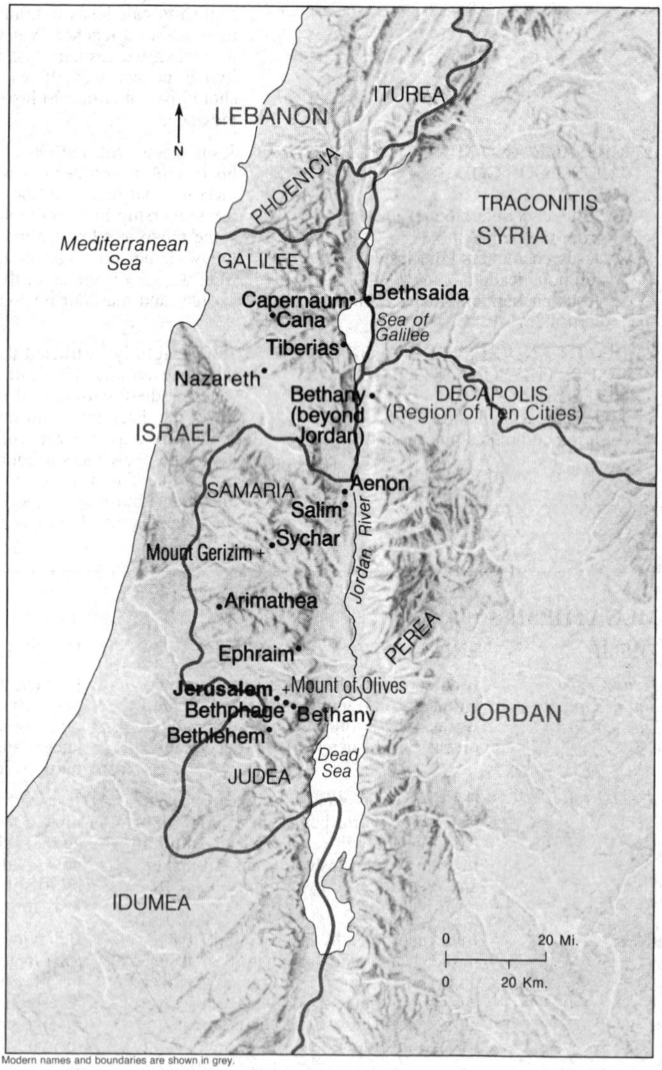

Modern names and boundaries are shown in grey.

A. BIRTH AND PREPARATION OF JESUS, THE SON OF GOD (1:1 – 2:11)

In this Gospel, John provides clear evidence that Jesus is the Son of God and that by believing in him we may have eternal life. John also provides unique material about Jesus' birth. He did not come into being when he was born, because he is eternal.

God Became a Human Being

(2)

1 In the beginning was the Word,[a] and the Word was with God,[b] and the Word
was God.[c] 2He was with God in the beginning.[d]
3Through him all things were made; without him nothing was made that has been
made.[e] 4In him was life,[f] and that life was the light[g] of men. 5The light shines
in the darkness, but the darkness has not understood**[a]** it.[h]
6There came a man who was sent from God; his name was John.[i] 7He came as
a witness to testify[j] concerning that light, so that through him all men might
believe.[k] 8He himself was not the light; he came only as a witness to the light. 9The
true light[l] that gives light to every man[m] was coming into the world.**[b]**
10He was in the world, and though the world was made through him,[n] the world
did not recognise him. 11He came to that which was his own, but his own did not
receive him. 12Yet to all who received him, to those who believed[o] in his name,[p]

a 5 Or *darkness, and the darkness has not overcome* **b** 9 Or *This was the true light that gives light to every man who comes into the world*

1:1 [a]Rev 19:13 [b]Jn 17:5; 1Jn 1:2 [c]Php 2:6
1:2 [d]Ge 1:1
1:3 [e]1Co 8:6; Col 1:16; Heb 1:2
1:4 [f]Jn 5:26; 11:25; 14:6 [g]Jn 8:12
1:5 [h]Jn 3:19
1:6 [i]Mt 3:1
1:7 [j]ver 15, 19, 32 [k]ver 12
1:9 [l]1Jn 2:8 [m]Isa 49:6
1:10 [n]Heb 1:2
1:12 [o]ver 7 [p]1Jn 3:23

1:1 What Jesus taught and what he did are tied inseparably to who he is. John shows Jesus as fully human and fully God. Although Jesus took upon himself full humanity and lived as a man, he never ceased to be the eternal God who has always existed, the Creator and Sustainer of all things, and the source of eternal life. This is the truth about Jesus, and the foundation of all truth. If we cannot or do not believe this basic truth, we will not have enough faith to trust our eternal destiny to him. That is why John wrote this Gospel – to build faith and confidence in Jesus Christ so that we may believe that he truly was and is the Son of God (20:30, 31).

1:1 John wrote to believers everywhere, both Jews and non-Jews (Gentiles). As one of Jesus' 12 disciples, John was an eyewitness, so his story is accurate. His book is not a biography (like the book of Luke); it is a thematic presentation of Jesus' life. Many in John's original audience had a Greek background. Greek culture encouraged worship of many mythological gods, whose supernatural characteristics were as important to Greeks as genealogies were to Jews. John shows that Jesus is not only different from but superior to these gods of mythology.

1:1ff What does John mean by *the Word? The Word* was a term used by theologians and philosophers, both Jews and Greeks, in many different ways. In Hebrew Scripture, *the Word* was an agent of creation (Psalm 33:6), the source of God's message to his people through the prophets (Hosea 1:2), and God's law, his standard of holiness (Psalm 119:11). In Greek philosophy, *the Word* was the principle of reason that governed the world, or the thought still in the mind, while in Hebrew thought, *the Word* was another expression for God. John's description shows clearly that he is speaking of Jesus (see especially 1:14) – a human being he knew and loved, but at the same time the Creator of the universe, the ultimate revelation of God, the living picture of God's holiness, the One in whom "all things hold together" (Colossians 1:17). To Jewish readers, "the Word was God" was blasphemous. To Greek readers, "the Word became flesh" (1:14) was unthinkable. To John, this new understanding of the Word was gospel, the Good News of Jesus Christ.

1:3 When God created, he made something from nothing. Because we are created beings, we have no basis for pride. Remember that you exist only because God made you, and you have special gifts only because God gave them to you. With God you are something valuable and unique; apart from God you are nothing, and if you try to live without him, you will be abandoning the purpose for which you were made.

1:3–5 Do you ever feel that your life is too complex for God to understand? Remember, God created the entire universe, and nothing is too difficult for him. God created you; he is alive today, and his love is bigger than any problem you may face.

1:4, 5 "The darkness has not understood it" means the darkness of evil never has and never will overcome or extinguish God's light. Jesus Christ is the Creator of life, and his life brings light to mankind. In his light, we see ourselves as we really are (sinners in need of a Saviour). When we follow Jesus, the true Light, we can avoid walking blindly and falling into sin. He lights the path ahead of us so we can see how to live. He removes the darkness of sin from our lives. Have you allowed the light of Christ to shine into your life? Let Christ guide your life, and you'll never need to stumble in darkness.

1:6–8 In this book, the name *John* refers to John the Baptist. For more information on John the Baptist, see his Profile in this chapter.

1:8 We, like John the Baptist, are not the source of God's light; we merely reflect that light. Jesus Christ is the true Light; he helps us see our way to God and shows us how to walk along that way. But Christ has chosen to reflect his light through his followers to an unbelieving world, perhaps because unbelievers are not able to bear the full blazing glory of his light first-hand. The word *witness* indicates our role as reflectors of Christ's light. We are never to present ourselves as the light to others, but are always to point them to Christ, the Light.

1:10, 11 Although Christ created the world, the people he created didn't recognise him (1:10). Even the people chosen by God to prepare the rest of the world for the Messiah rejected him (1:11), although the entire Old Testament pointed to his coming.

1:12, 13 All who welcome Jesus Christ as Lord of their lives are reborn spiritually, receiving new life from God. Through faith in Christ, this new birth changes us from the inside out – rearranging our attitudes, desires, and motives. Being born makes you physically alive and places you in your parents' family (1:13). Being born of God makes you spiritually alive and puts you in God's family (1:12). Have you asked Christ to make you a new person? This fresh start in life is available to all who believe in Christ.

he gave the right to become children of God[q]—13children born not of natural
descent,[c] nor of human decision or a husband's will, but born of God.[r]
14The Word became flesh[s] and made his dwelling among us. We have seen his
glory, the glory of the One and Only,[d] who came from the Father, full of grace and
truth.[t]
15John testifies[u] concerning him. He cries out, saying, "This was he of whom I
said, 'He who comes after me has surpassed me because he was before me.' "[v]
16From the fulness[w] of his grace we have all received one blessing after another. 17For
the law was given through Moses;[x] grace and truth came through Jesus Christ.[y]
18No-one has ever seen God,[z] but God the One and Only,[e,f][a] who is at the Father's
side, has made him known.

John the Baptist Declares His Mission
(19)

19Now this was John's testimony when the Jews[b] of Jerusalem sent priests and
Levites to ask him who he was. 20He did not fail to confess, but confessed freely,
"I am not the Christ."[g][c]
21They asked him, "Then who are you? Are you Elijah?"[d]
He said, "I am not."
"Are you the Prophet?"[e]
He answered, "No."
22Finally they said, "Who are you? Give us an answer to take back to those who
sent us. What do you say about yourself?"
23John replied in the words of Isaiah the prophet, "I am the voice of one calling
in the desert,[f] 'Make straight the way for the Lord.'[h] "[g]
24Now some Pharisees who had been sent 25questioned him, "Why then do you
baptise if you are not the Christ, nor Elijah, nor the Prophet?"

1:12 [q]Gal 3:26
1:13 [r]Jn 3:6; Jas 1:18; 1Pe 1:23; 1Jn 3:9
1:14 [s]Gal 4:4; Php 2:7, 8; 1Ti 3:16; Heb 2:14 [t]Jn 14:6
1:15 [u]ver 7 [v]ver 30; Mt 3:11
1:16 [w]Eph 1:23; Col 1:19
1:17 [x]Jn 7:19 [y]ver 14
1:18 [z]Ex 33:20; Jn 6:46; Col 1:15; 1Ti 6:16 [a]Jn 3:16, 18; 1Jn 4:9
1:19 [b]Jn 2:18; 5:10, 16; 6:41, 52
1:20 [c]Jn 3:28; Lk 3:15, 16
1:21 [d]Mt 11:14 [e]Dt 18:15
1:23 [f]Mt 3:1 [g]Isa 40:3

c *13* Greek *of bloods* **d** *14* Or *the Only Begotten* **e** *18* Or *the Only Begotten* **f** *18* Some manuscripts *but the only* (or *only begotten*) *Son* **g** *20* Or *Messiah.* "The Christ" (Greek) and "the Messiah" (Hebrew) both mean "the Anointed One"; also in verse 25. **h** *23* Isaiah 40:3

1:14 "The Word became flesh" means becoming human. By doing so, Christ became (1) *the perfect teacher*—in Jesus' life we see how God thinks and therefore how we should think (Philippians 2:5–11); (2) *the perfect example*—as a model of what we are to become, he shows us how to live and gives us the power to live that way (1 Peter 2:21); (3) *the perfect sacrifice*—Jesus came as a sacrifice for all sins, and his death satisfied God's requirements for the removal of sin (Colossians 1:15–23).

1:14 "The One and Only, who came from the Father" means Jesus is God's only and unique Son. The emphasis is on unique. Jesus is one of a kind and enjoys a relationship with God unlike all believers who are called "children" and said to be "born of God".

1:14 When Christ was born, God became a man. He was not part man and part God; he was completely human and completely divine (Colossians 2:9). Before Christ came, people could know God partially. After Christ came, people could know God fully because he became visible and tangible in Christ. Christ is the perfect expression of God in human form. The two most common errors people make about Jesus are to minimise his humanity or to minimise his divinity. Jesus is both God and man.

1:17 Law and grace are both aspects of God's nature that he uses in dealing with us. Moses emphasised God's law and justice, while Jesus Christ came to highlight God's mercy, love, and forgiveness. Moses could only be the giver of the law, while Christ came to fulfil the law (Matthew 5:17). The nature and will of God were revealed in the law; now the nature and will of God are revealed in Jesus Christ. Rather than coming through cold stone tablets, God's revelation ("truth") now comes through a person's life. As we get to know Christ better, our understanding of God will increase.

1:18 God communicated through various people in the Old Testament, usually prophets who were told to give specific messages. But no-one ever *saw* God. "God the One and Only" is a title showing that Jesus is both God and the Father's unique Son. In Christ, God revealed his nature and essence in a way that could be seen and touched. In Christ, God became a man who lived on earth.

1:19 The priests and Levites were respected religious leaders in Jerusalem. Priests served in the temple, and Levites assisted them. The leaders that came to see John were Pharisees (1:24), a group that both John the Baptist and Jesus often denounced. Many of them outwardly obeyed God's laws to look pious, while inwardly their hearts were filled with pride and greed. The Pharisees believed that their own oral traditions were just as important as God's inspired word. For more information on the Pharisees, see the charts in Matthew 3 and Mark 2.

These leaders came to see John the Baptist for several reasons: (1) Their duty as guardians of the faith caused them to want to investigate any new preaching (Deuteronomy 13:1–5; 18:20–22). (2) They wanted to find out if John had the credentials of a prophet. (3) John had quite a following, and it was growing. They were probably jealous and wanted to see why this man was so popular.

1:21–23 In the Pharisees' minds, there were four options regarding John the Baptist's identity: he was (1) the prophet foretold by Moses (Deuteronomy 18:15), (2) Elijah (Malachi 4:5), (3) the Messiah, or (4) a false prophet. John denied being the first three personages. Instead he called himself, in the words of the Old Testament prophet Isaiah, "A voice of one calling: 'In the desert prepare the way for the LORD' " (Isaiah 40:3). The leaders kept pressing John to say who he was because people were expecting the Messiah to come (Luke 3:15). But John emphasised only *why* he had come—to prepare the way for the Messiah. The Pharisees missed the point. They wanted to know who John was, but John wanted them to know who Jesus was.

1:27
[h]ver 15, 30

1:28
[i]Jn 3:26; 10:40

26"I baptise with[l] water," John replied, "but among you stands one you do not
know. 27He is the one who comes after me,[h] the thongs of whose sandals I am not
worthy to untie."
28This all happened at Bethany on the other side of the Jordan,[i] where John was
baptising.

[l] *26* Or *in*; also in verses 31 and 33

JOHN THE BAPTIST

There's no getting round it—John the Baptist was unique. He wore odd clothes and ate strange food and preached an unusual message to the Judeans who went out to the wastelands to see him.

But John did not aim at uniqueness for its own sake. Instead, he aimed at obedience. He knew he had a specific role to play in the world—announcing the coming of the Saviour—and he put all his energies into this task. Luke tells us that John was in the desert when God's word of direction came to him. John was ready and waiting. The angel who had announced John's birth to Zechariah had made it clear this child was to be a Nazirite—one set apart for God's service. John remained faithful to that calling.

This wild-looking man had no power or position in the Jewish political system, but he spoke with almost irresistible authority. People were moved by his words because he spoke the truth, challenging them to turn from their sins and baptising them as a symbol of their repentance. They responded by the hundreds. But even as people crowded to him, he pointed beyond himself, never forgetting that his main role was to announce the coming of the Saviour.

The words of truth that moved many to repentance goaded others to resistance and resentment. John even challenged Herod to admit his sin. Herodias, the woman Herod had married illegally, decided to get rid of this desert preacher. Although she was able to have him killed, she was not able to stop his message. The One John had announced was already on the move. John had accomplished his mission.

God has given each of us a purpose for living, and we can trust him to guide us. John did not have the complete Bible as we know it today, but he focused his life on the truth he knew from the available Old Testament Scriptures. Likewise we can discover in God's word the truths he wants us to know. And as these truths work in us, others will be drawn to him. God can use you in a way he can use no-one else. Let him know your willingness to follow him today.

Strengths and accomplishments:
- The God-appointed messenger to announce the arrival of Jesus
- A preacher whose theme was repentance
- A fearless confronter
- Known for his remarkable lifestyle
- Uncompromising

Lessons from his life:
- God does not guarantee an easy or safe life to those who serve him
- Doing what God desires is the greatest possible life investment
- Standing for the truth is more important than life itself

Vital statistics:
- Where: Judea
- Occupation: Prophet
- Relatives: Father: Zechariah. Mother: Elizabeth. Distant relative: Jesus
- Contemporaries: Herod, Herodias

Key verse:
"I tell you the truth: Among those born of women there has not risen anyone greater than John the Baptist; yet he who is least in the kingdom of heaven is greater than he" (Matthew 11:11).

John's story is told in all four Gospels. His coming was predicted in Isaiah 40:3 and Malachi 4:5; and he is mentioned in Acts 1:5, 22; 10:37; 11:16; 13:24, 25; 18:25; 19:3, 4.

1:25, 26 John was baptising Jews. The Essenes (a strict, monastic sect of Judaism) practised baptism for purification, but normally only non-Jews (Gentiles) were baptised when they converted to Judaism. When the Pharisees questioned John's authority to baptise, they were asking who gave John the right to treat God's chosen people like Gentiles. John said, "I baptise with water"—he was merely helping the people perform a symbolic act of repentance. But soon one would come who would truly *forgive* sins, something only the Son of God—the Messiah—could do.

1:27 John the Baptist said he was not even worthy to be Christ's slave, to perform the humble task of unfastening his shoes. But according to Luke 7:28, Jesus said that John was the greatest of all prophets. If such a great person felt inadequate even to be Christ's slave, how much more should we lay aside our pride to serve Christ! When we truly understand who Christ is, our pride and self-importance melt away.

John the Baptist Proclaims Jesus As the Messiah
(20)

29The next day John saw Jesus coming towards him and said, "Look, the Lamb of
God,[j] who takes away the sin of the world! 30This is the one I meant when I said,
'A man who comes after me has surpassed me because he was before me.'[k] 31I myself
did not know him, but the reason I came baptising with water was that he might be
revealed to Israel."
32Then John gave this testimony: "I saw the Spirit come down from heaven as a
dove and remain on him.[l] 33I would not have known him, except that the one who
sent me to baptise with water[m] told me, 'The man on whom you see the Spirit come
down and remain is he who will baptise with the Holy Spirit.'[n] 34I have seen and
I testify that this is the Son of God."[o]

The First Disciples Follow Jesus
(21)

35The next day John[p] was there again with two of his disciples. 36When he saw
Jesus passing by, he said, "Look, the Lamb of God!"[q]
37When the two disciples heard him say this, they followed Jesus. 38Turning round,
Jesus saw them following and asked, "What do you want?"
They said, "Rabbi"[r] (which means Teacher), "where are you staying?"
39"Come," he replied, "and you will see."
So they went and saw where he was staying, and spent that day with him. It was
about the tenth hour.

1:29 [j]ver 36; Isa 53:7; 1Pe 1:19; Rev 5:6
1:30 [k]ver 15, 27
1:32 [l]Mt 3:16; Mk 1:10
1:33 [m]Mk 1:4 [n]Mt 3:11; Mk 1:8
1:34 [o]ver 49; Mt 4:3
1:35 [p]Mt 3:1
1:36 [q]ver 29
1:38 [r]ver 49; Mt 23:7

1:29 Every morning and evening, a lamb was sacrificed in the temple for the sins of the people (Exodus 29:38–42). Isaiah 53:7 prophesied that the Messiah, God's servant, would be led to the slaughter like a lamb. To pay the penalty for sin, a life had to be given – and God chose to provide the sacrifice himself. The sins of the world were removed when Jesus died as the perfect sacrifice. This is the way our sins are forgiven (1 Corinthians 5:7). The "sin of the world" means everyone's sin, the sin of each individual. Jesus paid the price of *your* sin by his death. You can receive forgiveness by confessing your sin to him and asking for his forgiveness.

1:30 Although John the Baptist was a well-known preacher who attracted large crowds, he was content for Jesus to take the higher place. This is true humility, the basis for greatness in preaching, teaching, or any other work we do for Christ. When you are content to do what God wants you to do and let Jesus Christ be honoured for it, God will do great things through you.

1:31–34 At Jesus' baptism, John the Baptist had declared Jesus to be the Messiah. At that time God had given John a sign to show him that Jesus truly had been sent from God (1:33). John and Jesus were related (see Luke 1:36), so John probably knew who he was. But it wasn't until Jesus' baptism that John understood that Jesus was the Messiah. Jesus' baptism is described in Matthew 3:13–17; Mark 1:9–11; and Luke 3:21, 22.

1:33 John the Baptist's baptism with water was preparatory, because it was for repentance and symbolised the washing away of sins. Jesus, by contrast, would baptise with the Holy Spirit. He would send the Holy Spirit upon all believers, empowering them to live and to teach the message of salvation. This outpouring of the Spirit came after Jesus had risen from the dead and ascended into heaven (see 20:22; Acts 2).

1:34 John the Baptist's job was to point people to Jesus, their long-awaited Messiah. Today people are looking for someone to give them security in an insecure world. Our job is to point them to Christ and to show that he is the one whom they seek.

11:35ff These new disciples used several names for Jesus: Lamb of God (1:36), Rabbi (1:38), Messiah (1:41), Son of God (1:49), and King of Israel (1:49). As they got to know Jesus, their appreciation of him grew. The more time we spend getting to know Christ, the more we will understand and appreciate who he is. We may be drawn to him for his teaching, but we will come to know him as the Son of God. Although these disciples made this verbal shift in a few days, they would not fully understand Jesus until three years later (Acts 2). What they so easily professed had to be worked out in experience. We may find that words of faith come easily, but deep appreciation of Christ comes with living by faith.

1:37 One of the two disciples was Andrew (1:40). The other was probably John, the writer of this book. Why did these disciples leave John the Baptist? Because that's what John wanted them to do – he was pointing the way to Jesus, the one John had prepared them to follow. These were Jesus' first disciples, along with Simon Peter (1:42) and Nathanael (1:45).

1:38 When the two disciples began to follow Jesus, he asked them, "What do you want?" Following Christ is not enough; we must follow him for the right reasons. To follow Christ for our own purposes would be asking Christ to follow us – to align with us to support and advance our cause, not his. We must examine our motives for following him. Are we seeking his glory or ours?

1:40–42 Andrew accepted John the Baptist's testimony about Jesus and immediately went to tell his brother, Simon, about him. There was no question in Andrew's mind that Jesus was the Messiah. Not only did he tell his brother, he was also eager to introduce others to Jesus (see 6:8, 9; 12:22).

1:42 Jesus saw not only who Simon was, but who he would become. That is why he gave him a new name – Cephas in Aramaic,

1:41
[s]Jn 4:25
1:42
[t]Ge 17:5, 15
[u]Mt 16:18
1:43
[v]Mt 10:3;
Jn 6:5-7; 12:21, 22;
14:8, 9
[w]Mt 4:19
1:44
[x]Mt 11:21;
Jn 12:21
1:45
[y]Jn 21:2
[z]Lk 24:27
[a]Lk 24:27
[b]Mt 2:23;
Mk 1:24
[c]Lk 3:23
1:46
[d]Jn 7:41, 42, 52
1:47
[e]Ro 9:4, 6
[f]Ps 32:2
1:49
[g]ver 38;
Mt 23:7
[h]ver 34;
Mt 4:3
[i]Mt 2:2; 27:42;
Jn 12:13
1:51
[j]Mt 3:16
[k]Ge 28:12
[l]Mt 8:20

40 Andrew, Simon Peter's brother, was one of the two who heard what John had
said and who had followed Jesus. 41 The first thing Andrew did was to find his brother
Simon and tell him, "We have found the Messiah" (that is, the Christ).[s] 42 And he
brought him to Jesus.
Jesus looked at him and said, "You are Simon son of John. You will be called[t]
Cephas" (which, when translated, is Peter[j]).[u]
43 The next day Jesus decided to leave for Galilee. Finding Philip,[v] he said to him,
"Follow me."[w]
44 Philip, like Andrew and Peter, was from the town of Bethsaida.[x] 45 Philip found
Nathanael[y] and told him, "We have found the one Moses wrote about in the
Law,[z] and about whom the prophets also wrote[a]—Jesus of Nazareth,[b] the son of
Joseph."[c]
46 "Nazareth! Can anything good come from there?"[d] Nathanael asked.
"Come and see," said Philip.
47 When Jesus saw Nathanael approaching, he said of him, "Here is a true Israelite,[e] in whom there is nothing false."[f]
48 "How do you know me?" Nathanael asked.
Jesus answered, "I saw you while you were still under the fig-tree before Philip
called you."
49 Then Nathanael declared, "Rabbi,[g] you are the Son of God;[h] you are the King
of Israel."[i]
50 Jesus said, "You believe[k] because I told you I saw you under the fig-tree. You
shall see greater things than that." 51 He then added, "I tell you[l] the truth, you[l] shall
see heaven open,[j] and the angels of God ascending and descending[k] on the Son of
Man."[l]

[j] *42* Both *Cephas* (Aramaic) and *Peter* (Greek) mean *rock.* [k] *50* Or *Do you believe . . . ?* [l] *51* The Greek is plural.

Peter in Greek (the name means "a rock"). Peter is not presented as rock-solid throughout the Gospels, but he became a solid rock in the days of the early church, as we learn in the book of Acts. By giving Simon a new name, Jesus introduced a change in character. For more on Simon Peter, see his Profile in Matthew 27.

1:46 Nazareth was despised by the Jews because a Roman army garrison was located there. Some have speculated that an aloof attitude or a poor reputation in morals and religion on the part of the people of Nazareth led to Nathanael's harsh comment. Nathanael's hometown was Cana, about four miles from Nazareth.

1:46 When Nathanael heard that the Messiah was from Nazareth, he was surprised. Philip responded, "Come and see." Fortunately for Nathanael, he went to meet Jesus and became a disciple. If he had stuck to his prejudice without investigating further, he would have missed the Messiah! Don't let people's stereotypes about Christ cause them to miss his power and love. Invite them to come and see who Jesus really is.

1:47–49 Jesus knew about Nathanael before the two ever met. Jesus also knows what we are really like. An honest person will feel comfortable with the thought that Jesus knows him or her through and through. A dishonest person will feel uncomfortable. You can't pretend to be something you're not. God knows the real you and wants *you* to follow him.

1:51 This is a reference to Jacob's dream recorded in Genesis 28:12. As the unique God-man, Jesus would be the ladder between heaven and earth. Jesus is not saying that this would be a physical experience (that they would see the ladder with their eyes) like the transfiguration, but that they would have spiritual insight into Jesus' true nature and purpose for coming.

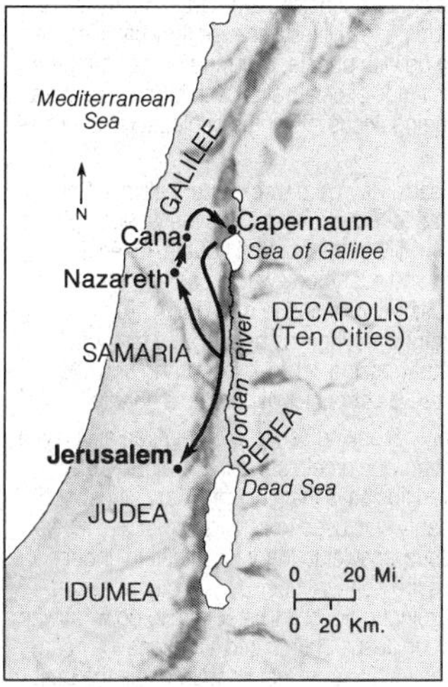

JESUS' FIRST TRAVELS
After his baptism by John in the Jordan River and temptation by Satan in the desert (see the map in Mark 1), Jesus returned to Galilee. He visited Nazareth, Cana, and Capernaum, and then returned to Jerusalem for the Passover.

Jesus Turns Water into Wine
(22)

2 On the third day a wedding took place at Cana in Galilee.[a] Jesus' mother[b] was
there, 2and Jesus and his disciples had also been invited to the wedding. 3When
the wine was gone, Jesus' mother said to him, "They have no more wine."
4"Dear woman,[c] why do you involve me?"[d] Jesus replied. "My time[e] has not
yet come."
5His mother said to the servants, "Do whatever he tells you."[f]
6Nearby stood six stone water jars, the kind used by the Jews for ceremonial
washing,[g] each holding from twenty to thirty gallons.[a]
7Jesus said to the servants, "Fill the jars with water"; so they filled them to the
brim.
8Then he told them, "Now draw some out and take it to the master of the
banquet."
They did so, 9and the master of the banquet tasted the water that had been turned
into wine.[h] He did not realise where it had come from, though the servants who had
drawn the water knew. Then he called the bridegroom aside 10and said, "Everyone
brings out the choice wine first and then the cheaper wine after the guests have had
too much to drink; but you have saved the best till now."
11This, the first of his miraculous signs,[i] Jesus performed at Cana in Galilee. He
thus revealed his glory,[j] and his disciples put their faith in him.[k]
12After this he went down to Capernaum[l] with his mother and brothers[m] and his
disciples. There they stayed for a few days.

a 6 Greek *two to three metretes* (probably about 75 to 115 litres)

2:1 [a]Jn 4:46; 21:2 [b]Mt 12:46
2:4 [c]Jn 19:26 [d]Mt 8:29 [e]Mt 26:18; Jn 7:6
2:5 [f]Ge 41:55
2:6 [g]Mk 7:3, 4; Jn 3:25
2:9 [h]Jn 4:46
2:11 [i]ver 23; Jn 3:2; 4:48; 6:2, 14, 26, 30; 12:37; 20:30 [j]Jn 1:14 [k]Ex 14:31
2:12 [l]Mt 4:13 [m]Mt 12:46

2:1, 2 Jesus was on a mission to save the world, the greatest mission in the history of mankind. Yet he took time to attend a wedding and take part in its festivities. We may be tempted to think we should not take time out from our "important" work for social occasions. But maybe these social occasions are part of our mission. Jesus valued these wedding festivities because they involved people, and Jesus came to be with people. Our mission can often be accomplished in joyous times of celebration with others. Bring balance to your life by bringing Jesus into times of pleasure as well as times of work.

2:1–3 Weddings in Jesus' day were week-long festivals. Banquets would be prepared for many guests, and the week would be spent celebrating the new life of the married couple. Often the whole town was invited, and everybody would come – it was considered an insult to refuse an invitation to a wedding. To accommodate many people, careful planning was needed. To run out of wine was more than embarrassing; it broke the strong unwritten laws of hospitality. Jesus was about to respond to a heartfelt need.

2:4 Mary was probably not asking Jesus to do a miracle; she was simply hoping that her son would help solve this major problem and find some wine. Tradition says that Joseph, Mary's husband, was dead, so she probably was used to asking for her son's help in certain situations. Jesus' answer to Mary is difficult to understand, but maybe that is the point. Although Mary did not understand what Jesus was going to do, she trusted him to do what was right. Those who believe in Jesus but run into situations they cannot understand must continue to trust that he will work in the best way.

2:5 Mary submitted to Jesus' way of doing things. She recognised that Jesus was more than her human son – he was the Son of God. When we bring our problems to Christ, we may think we know how he should take care of them. But he may have a completely different plan. Like Mary, we should submit and allow him to deal with the problem as he sees best.

2:6 The six stone water jars were normally used for ceremonial washing. When full, the pots would hold 20 to 30 gallons. According to the Jews' ceremonial law, people became symbolically unclean by touching objects of everyday life. Before eating, the Jews would pour water over their hands to cleanse themselves of any bad influences associated with what they had touched.

2:10 People look everywhere but to God for excitement and meaning. For some reason, they expect God to be dull and lifeless. Just as the wine Jesus made was the best, so life in him is better than life on our own. Why wait until everything else runs out before trying God? Why save the best until last?

2:11 When the disciples saw Jesus' miracle, they believed. The miracle showed his power over nature and revealed the way he would go about his ministry – helping others, speaking with authority, and being in personal touch with people.

2:11 Miracles are not merely superhuman events, but events that demonstrate God's power. Almost every miracle Jesus did was a renewal of fallen creation – restoring sight, making the lame walk, even restoring life to the dead. Believe in Christ not because he is a superman but because he is the God who continues his creation, even in those of us who are poor, weak, crippled, orphaned, blind, deaf, or with some other desperate need for re-creation.

2:12 Capernaum became Jesus' home base during his ministry in Galilee. Located on a major trade route, it was an important city in the region, with a Roman garrison and a customs station. At Capernaum, Matthew was called to be a disciple (Matthew 9:9). The city was also the home of several other disciples (Matthew 4:13–19) and a high-ranking government official (4:46). It had at least one major synagogue. Although Jesus made this city his base of operations in Galilee, he condemned it for the people's unbelief (Matthew 11:23; Luke 10:15).

B. MESSAGE AND MINISTRY OF JESUS, THE SON OF GOD (2:12–12:50)

John stresses the deity of Christ. He gives us seven miracles that serve as signs that Jesus is the Messiah. In this section he records Jesus describing himself as the bread of life, the water of life, the light of the world, the door, and the good shepherd. John provides teachings of Jesus found nowhere else. This is the most theological of the four Gospels.

1. Jesus encounters belief and unbelief from the people

Jesus Clears the Temple

(23)

13 When it was almost time for the Jewish Passover,[n] Jesus went up to Jerusalem.[o]
14 In the temple courts he found men selling cattle, sheep and doves, and others sitting
at tables exchanging money. 15 So he made a whip out of cords, and drove all from
the temple area, both sheep and cattle; he scattered the coins of the money-changers
and overturned their tables. 16 To those who sold doves he said, "Get these out of here!
How dare you turn my Father's house[p] into a market!"
17 His disciples remembered that it is written: "Zeal for your house will consume
me."[b][q]
18 Then the Jews demanded of him, "What miraculous sign can you show us to prove
your authority to do all this?"[r]
19 Jesus answered them, "Destroy this temple, and I will raise it again in three
days."[s]
20 The Jews replied, "It has taken forty-six years to build this temple, and you are

2:13 [n] Jn 11:55 [o] Dt 16:1-6; Lk 2:41
2:16 [p] Lk 2:49
2:17 [q] Ps 69:9
2:18 [r] Mt 12:38
2:19 [s] Mt 26:61; 27:40; Mk 14:58; 15:29

[b] *17* Psalm 69:9

2:13 The Passover celebration took place yearly at the temple in Jerusalem. Every Jewish male was expected to make a pilgrimage to Jerusalem during this time (Deuteronomy 16:16). This was a week-long festival – the Passover was one day, and the Feast of Unleavened Bread lasted the rest of the week. The entire week commemorated the freeing of the Jews from slavery in Egypt (Exodus 12:1–13).

2:13 Jerusalem was both the religious and the political seat of Palestine, and the place where the Messiah was expected to arrive. The temple was located there, and many Jewish families from all over the world would travel to Jerusalem during the key feasts. The temple was on an imposing site, a hill overlooking the city. Solomon had built the first temple on this same site almost 1,000 years earlier (949 B.C.), but his temple had been destroyed by the Babylonians (2 Kings 25). The temple was rebuilt in 515 B.C., and Herod the Great had enlarged and remodelled it.

2:14 The temple area was always crowded during Passover with thousands of out-of-town visitors. The religious leaders crowded it even further by allowing money changers and merchants to set up booths in the court of the Gentiles. They rationalised this practice as a convenience for the worshippers and as a way to make money for temple upkeep. But the religious leaders did not seem to care that the court of the Gentiles was so full of merchants that foreigners found it difficult to worship. And worship was the main purpose for visiting the temple. No wonder Jesus was angry!

2:14 The temple tax had to be paid in local currency, so foreigners had to have their money changed. But the money changers often would charge exorbitant exchange rates. The people also were required to make sacrifices for sins. Because of the long journey, many could not bring their own animals. Some who brought animals would have them rejected for imperfections. So animal merchants would do a flourishing business in the temple courtyard. The price of sacrificial animals was much higher in the temple area than elsewhere. Jesus was angry at the dishonest, greedy practices of the money changers and merchants, and he particularly disliked their presence on the temple grounds. They were making a mockery of God's house of worship.

2:14ff John records this first clearing, or cleansing, of the temple. A second clearing occurred at the end of Jesus' ministry, about three years later, and that event is recorded in Matthew 21:12–17; Mark 11:12–19; Luke 19:45–48.

2:14–16 God's temple was being misused by people who had turned it into a marketplace. They had forgotten, or didn't care, that God's house is a place of worship, not a place for making a profit. Our attitude towards the church is wrong if we see it as a place for personal contacts or business advantage. Make sure you attend church to worship God.

2:15, 16 Jesus was obviously angry at the merchants who exploited those who had come to God's house to worship. There is a difference between uncontrolled rage and righteous indignation – yet both are called anger. We must be very careful how we use the powerful emotion of anger. It is right to be angry about injustice and sin; it is wrong to be angry over trivial personal offences.

2:15, 16 Jesus made a whip and chased out the money changers. Does his example permit us to use violence against wrongdoers? Certain authority is granted to some, but not to all. For example, the authority to use weapons and restrain people is granted to police officers, but not to the general public. The authority to imprison people is granted to judges, but not to individual citizens. Jesus had God's authority, something we cannot have. While we want to live like Christ, we should never try to claim his authority where it has not been given to us.

2:17 Jesus took the evil acts in the temple as an insult against God, and thus he did not deal with them halfheartedly. He was consumed with righteous anger against such flagrant disrespect for God.

2:19, 20 The Jews understood Jesus to mean the temple out of which he had just driven the merchants and money changers. This was the temple Zerubbabel had built over 500 years earlier, but Herod the Great had begun remodelling it, making it much larger and far more beautiful. It had been 46 years since this remodelling had started (20 B.C.), and it still wasn't completely finished. They understood Jesus' words to mean that this imposing building could be torn down and rebuilt in three days, and they were startled.

going to raise it in three days?" 21 But the temple he had spoken of was his body.[t]
22 After he was raised from the dead, his disciples recalled what he had said.[u] Then
they believed the Scripture and the words that Jesus had spoken.
23 Now while he was in Jerusalem at the Passover Feast,[v] many people saw the
miraculous signs he was doing and believed in his name.[c] 24 But Jesus would not
entrust himself to them, for he knew all men. 25 He did not need man's testimony about
man, for he knew what was in a man.[w]

Nicodemus Visits Jesus at Night
(24)

3 Now there was a man of the Pharisees named Nicodemus,[a] a member of the
Jewish ruling council.[b] 2 He came to Jesus at night and said, "Rabbi, we know
you are a teacher who has come from God. For no-one could perform the miraculous
signs[c] you are doing if God were not with him."[d]
3 In reply Jesus declared, "I tell you the truth, no-one can see the kingdom of God
unless he is born again."[a] [e]
4 "How can a man be born when he is old?" Nicodemus asked. "Surely he cannot
enter a second time into his mother's womb to be born!"
5 Jesus answered, "I tell you the truth, no-one can enter the kingdom of God unless
he is born of water and the Spirit.[f] 6 Flesh gives birth to flesh, but the Spirit[b] gives

c 23 Or *and believed in him* **a** 3 Or *born from above*; also in verse 7 **b** 6 Or *but spirit*

2:21 [t] 1Co 6:19

2:22 [u] Lk 24:5-8; Jn 12:16; 14:26

2:23 [v] ver 13

2:25 [w] Mt 9:4; Jn 6:61, 64; 13:11

3:1 [a] Jn 7:50; 19:39 [b] Lk 23:13

3:2 [c] Jn 9:16, 33 [d] Ac 2:22; 10:38

3:3 [e] Jn 1:13; 1Pe 1:23

3:5 [f] Tit 3:5

2:21, 22 Jesus was not talking about the temple made of stones, but about his body. His listeners didn't realise it, but Jesus was greater than the temple (Matthew 12:6). His words would take on meaning for his disciples after his resurrection. That Christ so perfectly fulfilled this prediction became the strongest proof for his claims to be God.

2:23–25 The Son of God knows all about human nature. Jesus was well aware of the truth of Jeremiah 17:9, which states, "The heart is deceitful above all things and beyond cure. Who can understand it?" Jesus was discerning, and he knew that the faith of some followers was superficial. Some of the same people claiming to believe in Jesus at this time would later yell "Crucify him!" It's easy to believe when it is exciting and everyone else believes the same way. But keep your faith firm even when it isn't popular to follow Christ.

3:1 Nicodemus was a Pharisee and a member of the ruling council (called the Sanhedrin). The Pharisees were a group of religious leaders whom Jesus and John the Baptist often criticised for being hypocrites (see the note on Matthew 3:7 for more on the Pharisees). Most Pharisees were intensely jealous of Jesus because he undermined their authority and challenged their views. But Nicodemus was searching, and he believed that Jesus had some answers. A learned teacher himself, he came to Jesus to be taught. No matter how intelligent and well educated you are, you must come to Jesus with an open mind and heart so he can teach you the truth about God.

3:1ff Nicodemus came to Jesus personally, although he could have sent one of his assistants. He wanted to examine Jesus for himself to separate fact from rumour. Perhaps Nicodemus was afraid of what his peers, the Pharisees, would say about his visit, so he came after dark. Later, when he understood that Jesus was truly the Messiah, he spoke up boldly in his defence (7:50, 51). Like Nicodemus, we must examine Jesus for ourselves – others cannot do it for us. Then, if we believe he is who he says, we will want to speak up for him.

3:3 What did Nicodemus know about the kingdom? From the Bible he knew it would be ruled by God, it would be restored on earth, and it would incorporate God's people. Jesus revealed to this devout Pharisee that the kingdom would come to the whole world (3:16), not just the Jews, and that Nicodemus wouldn't be a part of it unless he was personally born again (3:5). This was a revolutionary concept: the kingdom is personal, not national or ethnic, and its entrance requirements are repentance and spiritual rebirth. Jesus later taught that God's kingdom has *already begun* in the hearts of believers (Luke 17:21). It will be fully realised when Jesus returns again to judge the world and abolish evil for ever (Revelation 21; 22).

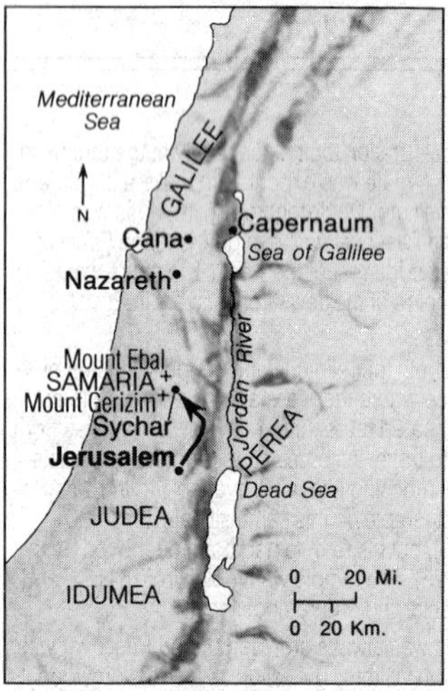

THE VISIT IN SAMARIA
Jesus went to Jerusalem for the Passover, cleared the temple, and talked with Nicodemus, a religious leader, about eternal life. He then left Jerusalem and travelled in Judea. On his way to Galilee, he visited Sychar and other villages in Samaria. Unlike most Jews of the day, he did not try to avoid the region of Samaria.

3:5, 6 "Of water and the Spirit" could refer to (1) the contrast between physical birth (water) and spiritual birth (Spirit), or (2) being regenerated by the Spirit and signifying that rebirth by Christian baptism. The water may also represent the cleansing action of God's Holy Spirit (Titus 3:5). Nicodemus undoubtedly would have been familiar with God's promise in Ezekiel 36:25, 26. Jesus was explaining the importance of a spiritual rebirth, saying that people don't enter the kingdom by living a better life, but by being spiritually reborn.

3:6 Who is the Holy Spirit? God is three persons in one – the Father, the Son, and the Holy Spirit. God became a man in Jesus so that Jesus could die for our sins. Jesus rose from the dead to offer salvation to all people through spiritual renewal and rebirth.

3:6 [g]Jn 1:13; 1Co 15:50
3:9 [h]Jn 6:52, 60
3:10 [i]Lk 2:46
3:11 [j]Jn 1:18; 7:16, 17 [k]ver 32
3:13 [l]Pr 30:4; Ac 2:34; Eph 4:8-10

birth to spirit.[g] 7You should not be surprised at my saying, 'You[c] must be born
again.' 8The wind blows wherever it pleases. You hear its sound, but you cannot tell
where it comes from or where it is going. So it is with everyone born of the Spirit."
9"How can this be?"[h] Nicodemus asked.
10"You are Israel's teacher,"[i] said Jesus, "and do you not understand these things?
11I tell you the truth, we speak of what we know,[j] and we testify to what we have
seen, but still you people do not accept our testimony.[k] 12I have spoken to you of
earthly things and you do not believe; how then will you believe if I speak of heavenly
things? 13No-one has ever gone into heaven[l] except the one who came from

c *7* The Greek is plural.

NICODEMUS

God specialises in finding and changing people we consider out of reach. It took a while for Nicodemus to come out of the dark, but God was patient with this "undercover" believer.

Afraid of being discovered, Nicodemus made an appointment to see Jesus at night. Daylight conversations between Pharisees and Jesus tended to be antagonistic, but Nicodemus really wanted to learn. He probably got a lot more than he expected—a challenge to a new life! We know very little about Nicodemus, but we know that he left that evening's encounter a changed man. He came away with a whole new understanding of both God and himself.

Nicodemus next appears as part of the Jewish council. As the group discussed ways to eliminate Jesus, Nicodemus raised the question of justice. Although his objection was overruled, he had spoken up. He had begun to change.

Our last picture of Nicodemus shows him joining Joseph of Arimathea in asking for Jesus' body in order to provide for its burial. Realising what he was risking, Nicodemus was making a bold move. He was continuing to grow.

God looks for steady growth, not instant perfection. How well does your present level of spiritual growth match up to how long you have known Jesus?

Strengths and accomplishments:
- One of the few religious leaders who believed in Jesus
- A member of the powerful Jewish council
- A Pharisee who was attracted by Jesus' character and miracles
- Joined with Joseph of Arimathea in burying Jesus

Weakness and mistake:
- Limited by his fear of being publicly exposed as Jesus' follower

Lessons from his life:
- Unless we are born again, we can never be part of the kingdom of God
- God is able to change those we might consider unreachable
- God is patient, but persistent
- If we are available, God can use us

Vital statistics:
- Where: Jerusalem
- Occupation: Religious leader
- Contemporaries: Jesus, Annas, Caiaphas, Pilate, Joseph of Arimathea

Key verse:
" 'How can a man be born when he is old?' Nicodemus asked. 'Surely he cannot enter a second time into his mother's womb to be born!' " (John 3:4).

Nicodemus' story is told in John 3:1–21; 7:50–52; and 19:39, 40.

When Jesus ascended into heaven, his physical presence left the earth, but he promised to send the Holy Spirit so that his spiritual presence would still be among mankind (see Luke 24:49). The Holy Spirit first became available to all believers at Pentecost (Acts 2). Whereas in Old Testament days the Holy Spirit empowered specific individuals for specific purposes, now all believers have the power of the Holy Spirit available to them. For more on the Holy Spirit, read 14:16–28; Romans 8:9; 1 Corinthians 12:13; and 2 Corinthians 1:22.

3:8 Jesus explained that we cannot control the work of the Holy Spirit. He works in ways we cannot predict or understand. Just as you did not control your physical birth, so you cannot control your spiritual birth. It is a gift from God through the Holy Spirit (Romans 8:16; 1 Corinthians 2:10–12; 1 Thessalonians 1:5, 6).

3:10, 11 This Jewish teacher of the Bible knew the Old Testament thoroughly, but he didn't understand what it said about the Messiah. Knowledge is not salvation. You should know the Bible, but even more important, you should understand the God whom the Bible reveals and the salvation that God offers.

heaven[m] — the Son of Man.[d] 14Just as Moses lifted up the snake in the desert,[n] so
the Son of Man must be lifted up,[o] 15that everyone who believes[p] in him may have
eternal life.[e]
16"For God so loved[q] the world that he gave his one and only Son,[f] that whoever
believes in him shall not perish but have eternal life.[r] 17For God did not send his
Son into the world[s] to condemn the world, but to save the world through him.[t]
18Whoever believes in him is not condemned,[u] but whoever does not believe stands
condemned already because he has not believed in the name of God's one and only
Son.[g][v] 19This is the verdict: Light[w] has come into the world, but men loved darkness
instead of light because their deeds were evil. 20Everyone who does evil hates the
light, and will not come into the light for fear that his deeds will be exposed.[x] 21But
whoever lives by the truth comes into the light, so that it may be seen plainly that
what he has done has been done through God."[h]

John the Baptist Tells More about Jesus
(25)

22After this, Jesus and his disciples went out into the Judean countryside, where
he spent some time with them, and baptised.[y] 23Now John also was baptising at
Aenon near Salim, because there was plenty of water, and people were constantly
coming to be baptised. 24(This was before John was put in prison.)[z] 25An argument
developed between some of John's disciples and a certain Jew[i] over the matter of
ceremonial washing.[a] 26They came to John and said to him, "Rabbi,[b] that man who
was with you on the other side of the Jordan — the one you testified[c] about — well,
he is baptising, and everyone is going to him."
27To this John replied, "A man can receive only what is given him from heaven.

d *13* Some manuscripts *Man, who is in heaven* **e** *15* Or *believes may have eternal life in him* **f** *16* Or *his only begotten Son* **g** *18* Or *God's only begotten Son* **h** *21* Some interpreters end the quotation after verse 15.
i *25* Some manuscripts *and certain Jews*

3:13 [m]Jn 6:38, 42
3:14 [n]Nu 21:8, 9 [o]Jn 8:28; 12:32
3:15 [p]ver 16, 36
3:16 [q]Ro 5:8; Eph 2:4; 1Jn 4:9, 10 [r]ver 36; Jn 6:29, 40; 11:25, 26
3:17 [s]Jn 6:29, 57; 10:36; 11:42; 17:8, 21; 20:21 [t]Jn 12:47; 1Jn 4:14
3:18 [u]Jn 5:24 [v]1Jn 4:9
3:19 [w]Jn 1:4; 8:12
3:20 [x]Eph 5:11, 13
3:22 [y]Jn 4:2
3:24 [z]Mt 4:12; 14:3
3:25 [a]Jn 2:6
3:26 [b]Mt 23:7 [c]Jn 1:7

3:14, 15 When the Israelites were wandering in the desert, God sent a plague of snakes to punish the people for their rebellious attitudes. Those doomed to die from snakebite could be healed by obeying God's command to look up at the elevated bronze snake and by believing that God would heal them if they did (see Numbers 21:8, 9). Similarly, our salvation happens when we look up to Jesus, believing he will save us. God has provided this way for us to be healed of sin's deadly bite.

3:16 The entire gospel comes to a focus in this verse. God's love is not static or self-centred; it reaches out and draws others in. Here God sets the pattern of true love, the basis for all love relationships — when you love someone dearly, you are willing to give freely to the point of self-sacrifice. God paid dearly with the life of his Son, the highest price he could pay. Jesus accepted our punishment, paid the price for our sins, and then offered us the new life that he had bought for us. When we share the gospel with others, our love must be like Jesus' — willingly giving up our own comfort and security so that others might join us in receiving God's love.

3:16 Some people are repulsed by the idea of eternal life because their lives are miserable. But eternal life is not an extension of a person's miserable, mortal life; eternal life is God's life embodied in Christ given to all believers now as a guarantee that they will live for ever. In eternal life there is no death, sickness, enemy, evil, or sin. When we don't know Christ, we make choices as though this life is all we have. In reality, this life is just the introduction to eternity. Receive this new life by faith and begin to evaluate all that happens from an eternal perspective.

3:16 To "believe" is more than intellectual agreement that Jesus is God. It means to put our trust and confidence in him that he alone can save us. It is to put Christ in charge of our present plans and eternal destiny. Believing is both trusting his words as reliable, and relying on him for the power to change. If you have never trusted Christ, let this promise of everlasting life be yours — and believe.

3:18 People often try to protect themselves from their fears by putting their faith in something they do or have: good deeds, skill or intelligence, money or possessions. But only God can save us from the one thing that we really need to fear — eternal condemnation. We believe in God by recognising the insufficiency of our own efforts to find salvation and by asking him to do his work in us. When Jesus talks about unbelievers, he means those who reject or ignore him completely, not those who have momentary doubts.

3:19–21 Many people don't want their lives exposed to God's light because they are afraid of what will be revealed. They don't want to be changed. Don't be surprised when these same people are threatened by your desire to obey God and do what is right, because they are afraid that the light in you may expose some of the darkness in their lives. Rather than giving in to discouragement, keep praying that they will come to see how much better it is to live in light than in darkness.

3:25ff Some people look for points of disagreement so they can sow seeds of discord, discontent, and doubt. John the Baptist ended this theological argument by focusing on his devotion to Christ. It is divisive to try to force others to believe our way. Instead, let's witness about what Christ has done for us. How can anyone argue with us about that?

3:26 John the Baptist's disciples were disturbed because people were following Jesus instead of John. It is easy to grow jealous of the popularity of another person's ministry. But we must remember that our true mission is to influence people to follow Christ, not us.

3:27 Why did John the Baptist continue to baptise after Jesus came onto the scene? Why didn't he become a disciple too? John explained that because God had given him his work, he had to continue it until God called him to do something else. John's main purpose was to point people to Christ. Even with Jesus beginning his own ministry, John could still turn people to Jesus.

28You yourselves can testify that I said, 'I am not the Christ[j] but am sent ahead of
him.'[d] 29The bride belongs to the bridegroom.[e] The friend who attends the bridegroom waits and listens for him, and is full of joy when he hears the bridegroom's
voice. That joy is mine, and it is now complete.[f] 30He must become greater; I must
become less.
31"The one who comes from above[g] is above all; the one who is from the earth
belongs to the earth, and speaks as one from the earth.[h] The one who comes from
heaven is above all. 32He testifies to what he has seen and heard,[i] but no-one accepts
his testimony.[j] 33The man who has accepted it has certified that God is truthful. 34For
the one whom God has sent[k] speaks the words of God, for God[k] gives the Spirit[l]
without limit. 35The Father loves the Son and has placed everything in his hands.[m]
36Whoever believes in the Son has eternal life,[n] but whoever rejects the Son will not
see life, for God's wrath remains on him."[l]

Jesus Talks to a Woman at the Well
(27)

4 The Pharisees heard that Jesus was gaining and baptising more disciples than
John,[a] 2although in fact it was not Jesus who baptised, but his disciples. 3When
the Lord learned of this, he left Judea[b] and went back once more to Galilee.
4Now he had to go through Samaria. 5So he came to a town in Samaria called
Sychar, near the plot of ground Jacob had given to his son Joseph.[c] 6Jacob's well
was there, and Jesus, tired as he was from the journey, sat down by the well. It was
about the sixth hour.
7When a Samaritan woman came to draw water, Jesus said to her, "Will you give
me a drink?" 8(His disciples had gone into the town[d] to buy food.)
9The Samaritan woman said to him, "You are a Jew and I am a Samaritan[e] woman.

j *28* Or *Messiah* k *34* Greek *he* l *36* Some interpreters end the quotation after verse 30.

3:28 [d]Jn 1:20, 23
3:29 [e]Mt 9:15 [f]Jn 16:24; 17:13; Php 2:2; 1Jn 1:4; 2Jn 12
3:31 [g]ver 13 [h]Jn 8:23; 1Jn 4:5
3:32 [i]Jn 8:26; 15:15 [j]ver 11
3:34 [k]ver 17 [l]Mt 12:18; Lk 4:18; Ac 10:38
3:35 [m]Mt 28:18; Jn 5:20, 22; 17:2
3:36 [n]ver 15; Jn 5:24; 6:47
4:1 [a]Jn 3:22, 26
4:3 [b]Jn 3:22
4:5 [c]Ge 33:19; 48:22; Jos 24:32
4:8 [d]ver 5, 39
4:9 [e]Mt 10:5; Lk 9:52, 53

3:30 John's willingness to decrease in importance shows unusual humility. Pastors and other Christian leaders can be tempted to focus more on the success of their ministries than on Christ. Beware of those who put more emphasis on their own achievements than on God's kingdom.

3:31–35 Jesus' testimony was trustworthy because he had come from heaven and was speaking of what he had seen there. His words were the very words of God. Your whole spiritual life depends on your answer to one question, "Who is Jesus Christ?" If you accept Jesus as only a prophet or teacher, you have to reject his teaching, for he claimed to be God's Son, even God himself. The heartbeat of John's Gospel is the dynamic truth that Jesus Christ is God's Son, the Messiah, the Saviour, who was from the beginning and will continue to live for ever. This same Jesus has invited us to accept him and live with him eternally. When we understand who Jesus is, we are compelled to believe what he said.

3:34 God's Spirit was upon Jesus without limit or measure. Thus Jesus was the highest revelation of God to humanity (Hebrews 1:2).

3:36 Jesus says that those who believe in him *have* (not *will have*) everlasting life. To receive eternal life is to join in God's life, which by nature is eternal. Thus, eternal life begins at the moment of spiritual rebirth.

3:36 John, the author of this Gospel, has been demonstrating that Jesus is the true Son of God. Jesus sets before us the greatest choice in life. We are responsible to decide today whom we will obey (Joshua 24:15), and God wants us to choose him and life (Deuteronomy 30:15–20). The wrath of God is God's final judgment and rejection of the sinner. To put off the choice is to choose not to follow Christ. Indecision is a fatal decision.

4:1–3 Already opposition was rising against Jesus, especially from the Pharisees. They resented Jesus' popularity as well as his message, which challenged much of their teachings. Because Jesus was just beginning his ministry, it wasn't yet time to confront these leaders openly; so he left Jerusalem and travelled north towards Galilee.

4:4 After the northern kingdom, with its capital at Samaria, fell to the Assyrians, many Jews were deported to Assyria, and foreigners were brought in to settle the land and help keep the peace (2 Kings 17:24). The intermarriage between those foreigners and the remaining Jews resulted in a mixed race, impure in the opinion of Jews who lived in the southern kingdom. Thus the pure Jews hated this mixed race called Samaritans because they felt that their fellow Jews who had intermarried had betrayed their people and nation. The Samaritans had set up an alternative centre for worship on Mount Gerizim (4:20) to parallel the temple at Jerusalem, but it had been destroyed 150 years earlier. The Jews did everything they could to avoid travelling through Samaria. But Jesus had no reason to live by such cultural restrictions. The route through Samaria was shorter, and that was the route he took.

4:5–7 Jacob's well was on the property originally owned by Jacob (Genesis 33:18, 19). It was not a spring-fed well, but a well into which water seeped from rain and dew, collecting at the bottom. Wells were almost always located outside the city along the main road. Twice each day, morning and evening, women came to draw water. This woman came at noon, however, probably to avoid meeting people who knew her reputation. Jesus gave this woman an extraordinary message about fresh and pure water that would quench her spiritual thirst for ever.

4:7–9 This woman (1) was a Samaritan, a member of the hated mixed race, (2) was known to be living in sin, and (3) was in a public place. No respectable Jewish man would talk to a woman under such circumstances. But Jesus did. The gospel is for every person, no matter what his or her race, social position, or past sins. We must be prepared to share this gospel at any time and in any place. Jesus crossed all barriers to share the gospel, and we who follow him must do no less.

How can you ask me for a drink?" (For Jews do not associate with Samaritans.[a])
10 Jesus answered her, "If you knew the gift of God and who it is that asks you for
a drink, you would have asked him and he would have given you living water."[f]
11 "Sir," the woman said, "you have nothing to draw with and the well is deep.
Where can you get this living water? 12 Are you greater than our father Jacob, who
gave us the well[g] and drank from it himself, as did also his sons and his flocks and
herds?"
13 Jesus answered, "Everyone who drinks this water will be thirsty again, 14 but
whoever drinks the water I give him will never thirst.[h] Indeed, the water I give him
will become in him a spring of water[i] welling up to eternal life."[j]
15 The woman said to him, "Sir, give me this water so that I won't get thirsty[k] and
have to keep coming here to draw water."
16 He told her, "Go, call your husband and come back."
17 "I have no husband," she replied.
Jesus said to her, "You are right when you say you have no husband. 18 The fact
is, you have had five husbands, and the man you now have is not your husband. What
you have just said is quite true."
19 "Sir," the woman said, "I can see that you are a prophet.[l] 20 Our fathers worshipped on this mountain,[m] but you Jews claim that the place where we must worship
is in Jerusalem."[n]
21 Jesus declared, "Believe me, woman, a time is coming[o] when you will worship
the Father neither on this mountain nor in Jerusalem.[p] 22 You Samaritans worship
what you do not know;[q] we worship what we do know, for salvation is from the
Jews.[r] 23 Yet a time is coming and has now come[s] when the true worshippers will
worship the Father in spirit[t] and truth, for they are the kind of worshippers the Father
seeks. 24 God is spirit,[u] and his worshippers must worship in spirit and in truth."
25 The woman said, "I know that Messiah" (called Christ)[v] "is coming. When he
comes, he will explain everything to us."
26 Then Jesus declared, "I who speak to you am he."[w]

[a] 9 Or *do not use dishes Samaritans have used*

4:10 [f] Isa 44:3; Jer 2:13; Zec 14:8; Jn 7:37, 38; Rev 21:6; 22:1, 17
4:12 [g] ver 6
4:14 [h] Jn 6:35 [i] Jn 7:38 [j] Mt 25:46
4:15 [k] Jn 6:34
4:19 [l] Mt 21:11
4:20 [m] Dt 11:29; Jos 8:33 [n] Lk 9:53
4:21 [o] Jn 5:28; 16:2 [p] Mal 1:11; 1Ti 2:8
4:22 [q] 2Ki 17:28-41 [r] Isa 2:3; Ro 3:1, 2; 9:4, 5
4:23 [s] Jn 5:25; 16:32 [t] Php 3:3
4:24 [u] Php 3:3
4:25 [v] Mt 1:16
4:26 [w] Jn 8:24; 9:35-37

4:10 What did Jesus mean by "living water"? In the Old Testament, many verses speak of thirsting after God as one thirsts for water (Psalm 42:1; Isaiah 55:1; Jeremiah 2:13; Zechariah 13:1). God is called the fountain of life (Psalm 36:9) and the spring of living water (Jeremiah 17:13). In saying he would bring living water that could for ever quench a person's thirst for God, Jesus was claiming to be the Messiah. Only the Messiah could give this gift that satisfies the soul's desire.

4:13–15 Many spiritual functions parallel physical functions. As our bodies hunger and thirst, so do our souls. But our souls need *spiritual* food and water. The woman confused the two kinds of water, perhaps because no-one had ever talked with her about her spiritual hunger and thirst before. We would not think of depriving our bodies of food and water when they hunger or thirst. Why then should we deprive our souls? The living Word, Jesus Christ, and the written word, the Bible, can satisfy our hungry and thirsty souls.

4:15 The woman mistakenly believed that if she received the water Jesus offered, she would not have to return to the well each day. She was interested in Jesus' message because she thought it could make her life easier. But if that were always the case, people would accept Christ's message for the wrong reasons. Christ did not come to take away challenges, but to change us on the inside and to empower us to deal with problems from God's perspective.

4:15 The woman did not immediately understand what Jesus was talking about. It takes time to accept something that changes the very foundations of your life. Jesus allowed the woman time to ask questions and put pieces together for herself. Sharing the gospel will not always have immediate results. When you ask people to let Jesus change their lives, give them time to weigh the matter.

4:16–20 When this woman discovered that Jesus knew all about her private life, she quickly changed the subject. Often people become uncomfortable when the conversation is too close to home, and they try to talk about something else. As we witness, we should gently guide the conversation back to Christ. His presence exposes sin and makes people squirm, but only Christ can forgive sins and give new life.

4:20–24 The woman brought up a popular theological issue – the correct place to worship. But her question was a smoke screen to keep Jesus away from her deepest need. Jesus directed the conversation to a much more important point: the *location* of worship is not nearly as important as the *attitude* of the worshippers.

4:21–24 "God is spirit" means he is not a physical being limited to one place. He is present everywhere and he can be worshipped anywhere, at any time. It is not where we worship that counts, but how we worship. Is your worship genuine and true? Do you have the Holy Spirit's help? How does the Holy Spirit help us worship? The Holy Spirit prays for us (Romans 8:26), teaches us the words of Christ (14:26), and tells us we are loved (Romans 5:5).

4:22 When Jesus said, "salvation is from the Jews," he meant that only through the Jewish Messiah would the whole world find salvation. God had promised that through the Jewish race the whole earth would be blessed (Genesis 12:3). The Old Testament prophets had called the Jews to be a light to the other nations of the world, bringing them to a knowledge of God; and they had predicted the Messiah's coming. The woman at the well may have known of these passages and was expecting the Messiah, but she didn't realise that she was talking to him!

4:27
[x] ver 8

4:29
[y] ver 17, 18
[z] Mt 12:23;
Jn 7:26, 31

4:31
[a] Mt 23:7

4:32
[b] Job 23:12;
Mt 4:4;
Jn 6:27

4:34
[c] Mt 26:39;
Jn 6:38; 17:4; 19:30
[d] Jn 19:30

4:35
[e] Mt 9:37;
Lk 10:2

4:36
[f] Ro 1:13
[g] Mt 25:46

4:37
[h] Job 31:8;
Mic 6:15

4:39
[i] ver 5
[j] ver 29

4:42
[k] Lk 2:11;
1Jn 4:14

4:43
[l] ver 40

4:44
[m] Mt 13:57;
Lk 4:24

4:45
[n] Jn 2:23

Jesus Tells about the Spiritual Harvest
(28)

27 Just then his disciples returned[x] and were surprised to find him talking with a
woman. But no-one asked, "What do you want?" or "Why are you talking with her?"
28 Then, leaving her water jar, the woman went back to the town and said to the
people, 29 "Come, see a man who told me everything I ever did.[y] Could this be the
Christ?"[b][z] 30 They came out of the town and made their way towards him.
31 Meanwhile his disciples urged him, "Rabbi,[a] eat something."
32 But he said to them, "I have food to eat[b] that you know nothing about."
33 Then his disciples said to each other, "Could someone have brought him food?"
34 "My food," said Jesus, "is to do the will[c] of him who sent me and to finish his
work.[d] 35 Do you not say, 'Four months more and then the harvest'? I tell you, open
your eyes and look at the fields! They are ripe for harvest.[e] 36 Even now the reaper
draws his wages, even now he harvests[f] the crop for eternal life,[g] so that the sower
and the reaper may be glad together. 37 Thus the saying 'One sows and another reaps'[h]
is true. 38 I sent you to reap what you have not worked for. Others have done the hard
work, and you have reaped the benefits of their labour."

Many Samaritans Believe in Jesus
(29)

39 Many of the Samaritans from that town[i] believed in him because of the woman's
testimony, "He told me everything I ever did."[j] 40 So when the Samaritans came to
him, they urged him to stay with them, and he stayed two days. 41 And because of
his words many more became believers.
42 They said to the woman, "We no longer believe just because of what you said;
now we have heard for ourselves, and we know that this man really is the Saviour
of the world."[k]

Jesus Preaches in Galilee
(30/Matthew 4:12–17; Mark 1:14, 15; Luke 4:14, 15)

43 After the two days[l] he left for Galilee. 44 (Now Jesus himself had pointed out
that a prophet has no honour in his own country.)[m] 45 When he arrived in Galilee, the
Galileans welcomed him. They had seen all that he had done in Jerusalem at the
Passover Feast,[n] for they also had been there.

b *29* Or *Messiah*

4:34 The "food" about which Jesus was speaking was his spiritual nourishment. It includes more than Bible study, prayer, and attending church. Spiritual nourishment also comes from doing God's will and helping to bring his work of salvation to completion. We are nourished not only by what we take in, but also by what we give out for God. In 17:4, Jesus refers to completing God's work on earth.

4:35 Sometimes Christians excuse themselves from witnessing by saying that their family or friends aren't ready to believe. Jesus, however, makes it clear that around us a continual harvest waits to be reaped. Don't let Jesus find you making excuses. Look around. You will find people ready to hear God's word.

4:36–38 The wages Jesus offers are the joy of working for him and seeing the harvest of believers. These wages come to sower and reaper alike because both find joy in seeing new believers come into Christ's kingdom. The phrase "others have done the hard work" (4:38) may refer to the Old Testament prophets and to John the Baptist, who paved the way for the gospel.

4:39 The Samaritan woman immediately shared her experience with others. Despite her reputation, many took her invitation and came out to meet Jesus. Perhaps there are sins in our past of which we're ashamed. But Christ changes us. As people see these changes, they become curious. Use these opportunities to introduce them to Christ.

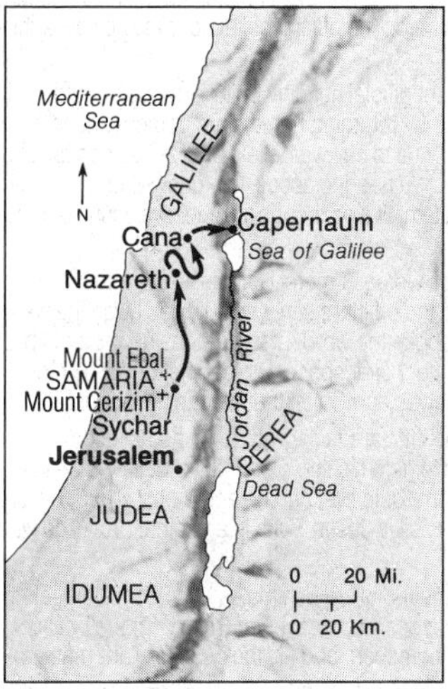

JESUS RETURNS TO GALILEE
Jesus stayed in Sychar for two days, then went on to Galilee. He visited Nazareth and various towns in Galilee before arriving in Cana. From there he spoke the word of healing and a government official's son in Capernaum was healed. The Gospel of Matthew tells us Jesus then settled in Capernaum (Matthew 4:12, 13).

Jesus Heals a Government Official's Son
(31)

46Once more he visited Cana in Galilee, where he had turned the water into wine.[o]
And there was a certain royal official whose son lay sick at Capernaum. 47When this
man heard that Jesus had arrived in Galilee from Judea,[p] he went to him and begged
him to come and heal his son, who was close to death.
48"Unless you people see miraculous signs and wonders,"[q] Jesus told him, "you
will never believe."
49The royal official said, "Sir, come down before my child dies."
50Jesus replied, "You may go. Your son will live."
The man took Jesus at his word and departed. 51While he was still on the way, his
servants met him with the news that his boy was living. 52When he enquired as to
the time when his son got better, they said to him, "The fever left him yesterday at
the seventh hour."
53Then the father realised that this was the exact time at which Jesus had said to
him, "Your son will live." So he and all his household[r] believed.
54This was the second miraculous sign[s] that Jesus performed, having come from
Judea to Galilee.

Jesus Heals a Lame Man by the Pool
(42)

5 Some time later, Jesus went up to Jerusalem for a feast of the Jews. 2Now there
is in Jerusalem near the Sheep Gate[a] a pool, which in Aramaic[b] is called
Bethesda[a] and which is surrounded by five covered colonnades. 3Here a great number
of disabled people used to lie—the blind, the lame, the paralysed.[b] 5One who was
there had been an invalid for thirty-eight years. 6When Jesus saw him lying there and

[a] *2* Some manuscripts *Bethzatha*; other manuscripts *Bethsaida* [b] *3* Some less important manuscripts *paralysed—and they waited for the moving of the waters. 4From time to time an angel of the Lord would come down and stir up the waters. The first one into the pool after each such disturbance would be cured of whatever disease he had.*

4:46 [o]Jn 2:1-11
4:47 [p]ver 3, 54
4:48 [q]Da 4:2, 3; Jn 2:11; Ac 2:43; 14:3; Ro 15:19; 2Co 12:12; Heb 2:4
4:53 [r]Ac 11:14
4:54 [s]ver 48; Jn 2:11
5:2 [a]Ne 3:1; 12:39 [b]Jn 19:13, 17, 20; 20:16; Ac 21:40; 22:2; 26:14

4:46–49 This royal official was probably an officer in Herod's service. He had walked 20 miles to see Jesus and addressed him as "Sir", putting himself under Jesus even though he had legal authority over Jesus.

4:48 This miracle was more than a favour to one official; it was a sign to all the people. John's Gospel was written to all mankind to urge faith in Christ. Here a government official had faith that Jesus could do what he claimed. The official believed; *then* he saw a miraculous sign.

4:50 This government official not only believed Jesus could heal; he also obeyed Jesus by returning home, thus demonstrating his faith. It isn't enough for us to say we believe that Jesus can take care of our problems. We need to act as if he can. When you pray about a need or problem, live as though you believe Jesus can do what he says.

4:51 Jesus' miracles were not mere illusions, the product of wishful thinking. Although the official's son was 20 miles away, he was healed when Jesus spoke the word. Distance was no problem because Christ has mastery over space. We can never put so much space between ourselves and Christ that he can no longer help us.

4:53 Notice how the official's faith grew. First, he believed enough to ask Jesus to help his son. Second, he believed Jesus' assurance that his son would live, and he acted on it. Third, he and his whole house believed in Jesus. Faith is a gift that grows as we use it.

5:1 Three feasts required all Jewish males to come to Jerusalem: (1) the Feast of Passover and Unleavened Bread, (2) the Feast of Weeks (also called Pentecost), and (3) the Feast of Tabernacles.

5:6 After 38 years, this man's problem had become a way of life. No one had ever helped him. He had no hope of ever being healed and no desire to help himself. The man's situation looked hopeless. But no matter how trapped you feel in your infirmities, God can minister to your deepest needs. Don't let a problem or hardship cause you to lose hope. God may have special work for you to do in spite of your condition, or even because of it. Many have ministered effectively to hurting people because they have triumphed over their own hurts.

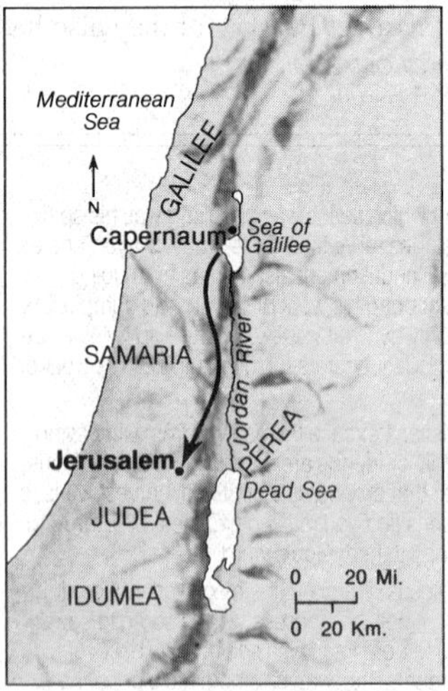

JESUS TEACHES IN JERUSALEM
Between chapters four and five of John, Jesus ministered throughout Galilee, especially in Capernaum. He had been calling certain men to follow him, but it wasn't until after this trip to Jerusalem (5:1) that he chose his 12 disciples from among them.

learned that he had been in this condition for a long time, he asked him, “Do you want
to get well?”
7“Sir,” the invalid replied, “I have no-one to help me into the pool when the water
is stirred. While I am trying to get in, someone else goes down ahead of me.”
8Then Jesus said to him, “Get up! Pick up your mat and walk.”[c] 9At once the man
was cured; he picked up his mat and walked.
The day on which this took place was a Sabbath,[d] 10and so the Jews[e] said to the
man who had been healed, “It is the Sabbath; the law forbids you to carry your mat.”[f]
11But he replied, “The man who made me well said to me, ‘Pick up your mat and
walk.’ ”
12So they asked him, “Who is this fellow who told you to pick it up and walk?”
13The man who was healed had no idea who it was, for Jesus had slipped away
into the crowd that was there.
14Later Jesus found him at the temple and said to him, “See, you are well again.
Stop sinning[g] or something worse may happen to you.” 15The man went away and
told the Jews[h] that it was Jesus who had made him well.
16So, because Jesus was doing these things on the Sabbath, the Jews persecuted
him. 17Jesus said to them, “My Father is always at his work[i] to this very day, and
I, too, am working.” 18For this reason the Jews tried all the harder to kill him;[j] not
only was he breaking the Sabbath, but he was even calling God his own Father, making
himself equal with God.[k]

Jesus Claims to Be God’s Son
(43)

19Jesus gave them this answer: “I tell you the truth, the Son can do nothing by
himself;[l] he can do only what he sees his Father doing, because whatever the Father
does the Son also does. 20For the Father loves the Son[m] and shows him all he does.
Yes, to your amazement he will show him even greater things than these.[n] 21For just
as the Father raises the dead and gives them life,[o] even so the Son gives life[p] to whom
he is pleased to give it. 22Moreover, the Father judges no-one, but has entrusted all
judgment to the Son,[q] 23that all may honour the Son just as they honour the Father.
He who does not honour the Son does not honour the Father, who sent him.[r]
24“I tell you the truth, whoever hears my word and believes him who sent me has
eternal life and will not be condemned;[s] he has crossed over from death to life.[t]

5:8 [c] Mt 9:5, 6; Mk 2:11; Lk 5:24
5:9 [d] Jn 9:14
5:10 [e] ver 16 [f] Ne 13:15-22; Jer 17:21; Mt 12:2
5:14 [g] Mk 2:5; Jn 8:11
5:15 [h] Jn 1:19
5:17 [i] Jn 9:4; 14:10
5:18 [j] Jn 7:1 [k] Jn 10:30, 33; 19:7
5:19 [l] ver 30; Jn 8:28
5:20 [m] Jn 3:35 [n] Jn 14:12
5:21 [o] Ro 4:17; 8:11 [p] Jn 11:25
5:22 [q] ver 27; Jn 9:39; Ac 10:42; 17:31
5:23 [r] Lk 10:16; 1Jn 2:23
5:24 [s] Jn 3:18 [t] 1Jn 3:14

5:10 According to the Pharisees, carrying a mat on the Sabbath was work and was therefore unlawful. It did not break an Old Testament law, but the Pharisees' *interpretation* of God's command to "remember the Sabbath day by keeping it holy" (Exodus 20:8). This was just one of hundreds of rules they had added to the Old Testament law.

5:10 A man who hadn't walked for 38 years had been healed, but the Pharisees were more concerned about their petty rules than the life and health of a human being. It is easy to get so caught up in our man-made structures and rules that we forget the people involved. Are your guidelines for living God-made or man-made? Are they helping people, or have they become needless stumbling blocks?

5:14 This man had been lame, or paralysed, and suddenly he could walk. This was a great miracle. But he needed an even greater miracle – to have his sins forgiven. The man was delighted to be physically healed, but he had to turn from his sins and seek God's forgiveness to be spiritually healed. God's forgiveness is the greatest gift you will ever receive. Don't neglect his gracious offer.

5:16 The Jewish leaders saw both a mighty miracle of healing and a broken rule. They threw the miracle aside as they focused their attention on the broken rule, because the rule was more important to them than the miracle. God is prepared to work in our lives, but we can shut out his miracles by limiting our views about how he works.

5:17 If God stopped every kind of work on the Sabbath, nature would fall into chaos, and sin would overrun the world. Genesis 2:2 says that God rested on the seventh day, but this can't mean that he stopped doing good. Jesus wanted to teach that when the opportunity to do good presents itself, it should not be ignored, even on the Sabbath.

5:17ff Jesus was identifying himself with God, his Father. There could be no doubt as to his claim to be God. Jesus does not leave us the option to believe in God while ignoring God's Son (5:23). The Pharisees also called God their Father, but they realised Jesus was claiming a unique relationship with him. In response to Jesus' claim, the Pharisees had two choices: to believe him, or to accuse him of blasphemy. They chose the second.

5:19–23 Because of his unity with God, Jesus lived as God wanted him to live. Because of our identification with Jesus, we must honour him and live as he wants us to live. The questions "What would Jesus do?" and "What would Jesus have me do?" may help us make the right choices.

5:24 "Eternal life" – living for ever with God – begins when you accept Jesus Christ as Saviour. At that moment, new life begins in you (2 Corinthians 5:17). It is a completed transaction. You will still face physical death, but when Christ returns again, your body will be resurrected to live for ever (1 Corinthians 15).

25I tell you the truth, a time is coming and has now come[u] when the dead will hear[v]
the voice of the Son of God and those who hear will live. 26For as the Father has life
in himself, so he has granted the Son to have life in himself. 27And he has given him
authority to judge[w] because he is the Son of Man.
28"Do not be amazed at this, for a time is coming[x] when all who are in their graves
will hear his voice 29and come out—those who have done good will rise to live, and
those who have done evil will rise to be condemned.[y] 30By myself I can do nothing;[z]
I judge only as I hear, and my judgment is just,[a] for I seek not to please myself but
him who sent me.[b]

Jesus Supports His Claim
(44)

31"If I testify about myself, my testimony is not valid.[c] 32There is another who
testifies in my favour,[d] and I know that his testimony about me is valid.
33"You have sent to John and he has testified[e] to the truth. 34Not that I accept
human testimony;[f] but I mention it that you may be saved. 35John was a lamp that
burned and gave light,[g] and you chose for a time to enjoy his light.
36"I have testimony weightier than that of John.[h] For the very work that the Father
has given me to finish, and which I am doing,[i] testifies that the Father has sent me.[j]
37And the Father who sent me has himself testified concerning me.[k] You have never
heard his voice nor seen his form,[l] 38nor does his word dwell in you,[m] for you do
not believe the one he sent.[n] 39You diligently study[c] the Scriptures[o] because you
think that by them you possess eternal life. These are the Scriptures that testify about
me,[p] 40yet you refuse to come to me to have life.
41"I do not accept praise from men,[q] 42but I know you. I know that you do not
have the love of God in your hearts. 43I have come in my Father's name, and you
do not accept me; but if someone else comes in his own name, you will accept him.
44How can you believe if you accept praise from one another, yet make no effort to
obtain the praise that comes from the only God?[d][r]
45"But do not think I will accuse you before the Father. Your accuser is Moses,[s]
on whom your hopes are set.[t] 46If you believed Moses, you would believe me, for
he wrote about me.[u] 47But since you do not believe what he wrote, how are you going
to believe what I say?"[v]

[c] *39* Or *Study diligently* (the imperative) [d] *44* Some early manuscripts *the Only One*

5:25 [u] Jn 4:23 [v] Jn 8:43, 47
5:27 [w] ver 22; Ac 10:42; 17:31
5:28 [x] Jn 4:21
5:29 [y] Da 12:2; Mt 25:46
5:30 [z] ver 19 [a] Jn 8:16 [b] Mt 26:39; Jn 4:34; 6:38
5:31 [c] Jn 8:14
5:32 [d] ver 37; Jn 8:18
5:33 [e] Jn 1:7
5:34 [f] 1Jn 5:9
5:35 [g] 2Pe 1:19
5:36 [h] 1Jn 5:9 [i] Jn 14:11; 15:24 [j] Jn 3:17; 10:25
5:37 [k] Jn 8:18 [l] Dt 4:12; 1Ti 1:17; Jn 1:18
5:38 [m] 1Jn 2:14 [n] Jn 3:17
5:39 [o] Ro 2:17, 18 [p] Lk 24:27, 44; Ac 13:27
5:41 [q] ver 44
5:44 [r] Ro 2:29
5:45 [s] Jn 9:28 [t] Ro 2:17
5:46 [u] Ge 3:15; Lk 24:27, 44; Ac 26:22
5:47 [v] Lk 16:29, 31

5:25 In saying that the dead will hear his voice, Jesus was talking about the spiritually dead who hear, understand, and accept him. Those who accept Jesus, the Word, will have eternal life. Jesus was also talking about the physically dead. He raised several dead people while he was on earth, and at his second coming all the "dead in Christ" will rise to meet him (1 Thessalonians 4:16).

5:26 God is the source and Creator of life, for there is no life apart from God, here or hereafter. The life in us is a gift from him (see Deuteronomy 30:20; Psalm 36:9). Because Jesus is eternally existent with God, the Creator, he too is "the life" (14:6) through whom we may live eternally (see 1 John 5:11).

5:27 The Old Testament mentioned three signs of the coming Messiah. In this chapter, John shows that Jesus has fulfilled all three signs. All power and authority are given to him as the Son of Man (cf. 5:27 with Daniel 7:13, 14). The lame and sick are healed (cf. 5:20, 26 with Isaiah 35:6; Jeremiah 31:8, 9). The dead are raised to life (cf. 5:21, 28 with Deuteronomy 32:39; 1 Samuel 2:6; 2 Kings 5:7).

5:29 Those who have rebelled against Christ will be resurrected too, but to hear God's judgment against them and to be sentenced to eternity apart from him. There are those who wish to live well on earth, ignore God, and then see death as final rest. Jesus does not allow unbelieving people to see death as the end of it all. There is a judgment to face.

5:31ff Jesus claimed to be equal with God (5:18), to give eternal life (5:24), to be the source of life (5:26), and to judge sin (5:27). These statements make it clear that Jesus was claiming to be divine—an almost unbelievable claim, but one that was supported by another witness, John the Baptist.

5:39, 40 The religious leaders knew what the Bible said but failed to apply its words to their lives. They knew the teachings of the Scriptures but failed to see the Messiah to whom the Scriptures pointed. They knew the rules but missed the Saviour. Entrenched in their own religious system, they refused to let the Son of God change their lives. Don't become so involved in "religion" that you miss Christ.

5:41 Whose praise do you seek? The religious leaders enjoyed great prestige in Israel, but their stamp of approval meant nothing to Jesus. He was concerned about God's approval. This is a good principle for us. If even the highest officials in the world approve of our actions and God does not, we should be concerned. But if God approves, even though others don't, we should be content.

5:45 The Pharisees prided themselves on being the true followers of their ancestor Moses. They were trying to follow every one of his laws to the letter, and they even added some of their own. Jesus' warning that Moses would accuse them stung them to fury. Moses wrote about Jesus (Genesis 3:15; Numbers 21:9; 24:17; Deuteronomy 18:15), yet the religious leaders refused to believe Jesus when he came.

6:2
[a]Jn 2:11

6:3
[b]ver 15

6:4
[c]Jn 2:13; 11:55

Jesus Feeds Five Thousand

(96/Matthew 14:13–21; Mark 6:30–44; Luke 9:10–17)

6 Some time after this, Jesus crossed to the far shore of the Sea of Galilee (that is,
the Sea of Tiberias), 2and a great crowd of people followed him because they saw
the miraculous signs[a] he had performed on the sick. 3Then Jesus went up on a
mountainside[b] and sat down with his disciples. 4The Jewish Passover Feast[c] was
near.
5When Jesus looked up and saw a great crowd coming towards him, he said to

THE CLAIMS OF CHRIST

Those who read the life of Christ are faced with one unavoidable question—was Jesus God? Part of any reasonable conclusion has to include the fact that he did claim to be God. We have no other choice but to agree or disagree with his claim. Eternal life is at stake in the choice.

Jesus claimed to be:	*Matthew*	*Mark*	*Luke*	*John*
the fulfilment of Old Testament prophecies	5:17; 14:33; 16:16, 17; 26:31, 53–56; 27:43	14:21, 61, 62	4:16–21; 7:18–23; 18:31; 22:37; 24:44	2:22; 5:45–47; 6:45; 7:40; 10:34–36; 13:18; 15:25; 20:9
the Son of Man	8:20; 12:8; 16:27; 19:28; 20:18, 19; 24:27, 44; 25:31; 26:2, 45, 64	8:31, 38; 9:9; 10:45; 14:41	6:22; 7:33, 34; 12:8; 17:22; 18:8, 31; 19:10; 21:36	1:51; 3:13, 14; 6:27, 53; 12:23, 34
the Son of God	11:27; 14:33; 16:16, 17; 27:43	3:11, 12; 14:61, 62	8:28; 10:22	1:18; 3:35, 36; 5:18–26; 6:40; 10:36; 11:4; 17:1; 19:7
the Messiah/ the Christ	23:9, 10; 26:63, 64	8:29, 30	4:41; 23:1, 2; 24:25–27	4:25, 26; 10:24, 25; 11:27
Teacher/Master	26:18			13:13, 14
One with authority to forgive		2:1–12	7:48, 49	
Lord		5:19		13:13, 14; 20:28
Saviour			19:10	3:17; 10:9

JESUS WALKS ON THE WATER

Jesus fed the 5,000 on a hill near the Sea of Galilee at Bethsaida. The disciples set out across the sea towards Capernaum. But they encountered a storm—and Jesus came to them walking on the water! The boat anchored at Gennesaret (Mark 6:53); from there they went back to Capernaum.

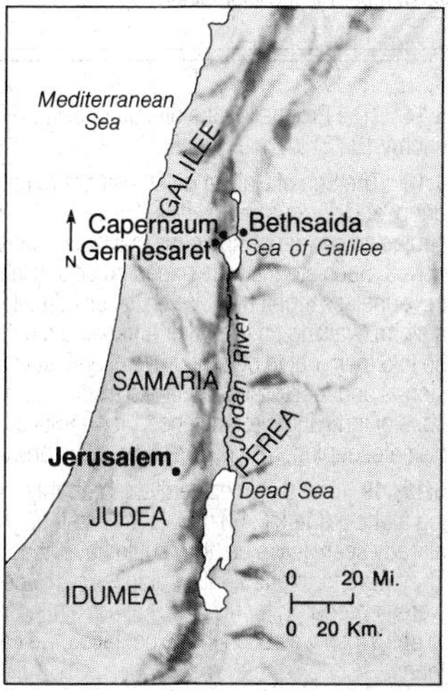

6:5 If anyone knew where to get food, it would have been Philip because he was from Bethsaida, a town about nine miles away (1:44). Jesus was testing Philip to strengthen his faith. By asking for a human solution (knowing that there was none), Jesus highlighted the powerful and miraculous act that he was about to perform.

6:5–7 When Jesus asked Philip where they could buy a great amount of bread, Philip started assessing the probable cost. Jesus wanted to teach him that financial resources are not the most important ones. We can limit what God does in us by assuming what is and is not possible. Is there some impossible task that you believe God wants you to do? Don't let your estimate of what can't be done keep you from taking on the task. God can do the miraculous; trust him to provide the resources.

Philip,[d] "Where shall we buy bread for these people to eat?" 6He asked this only to
test him, for he already had in mind what he was going to do.
7Philip answered him, "Eight months' wages[a] would not buy enough bread for
each one to have a bite!"
8Another of his disciples, Andrew, Simon Peter's brother,[e] spoke up, 9"Here is
a boy with five small barley loaves and two small fish, but how far will they go among
so many?"[f]
10Jesus said, "Make the people sit down." There was plenty of grass in that place,
and the men sat down, about five thousand of them. 11Jesus then took the loaves, gave
thanks,[g] and distributed to those who were seated as much as they wanted. He did
the same with the fish.
12When they had all had enough to eat, he said to his disciples, "Gather the pieces
that are left over. Let nothing be wasted." 13So they gathered them and filled twelve
baskets with the pieces of the five barley loaves left over by those who had eaten.
14After the people saw the miraculous sign[h] that Jesus did, they began to say,
"Surely this is the Prophet who is to come into the world."[i] 15Jesus, knowing that
they intended to come and make him king[j] by force, withdrew again to a mountain
by himself.[k]

6:5 [d]Jn 1:43
6:8 [e]Jn 1:40
6:9 [f]2Ki 4:43
6:11 [g]ver 23; Mt 14:19
6:14 [h]Jn 2:11 [i]Dt 18:15, 18; Mt 11:3; 21:11
6:15 [j]Jn 18:36 [k]Mt 14:23; Mk 6:46

Jesus Walks on Water
(97/Matthew 14:22–33; Mark 6:45–52)

16When evening came, his disciples went down to the lake, 17where they got into
a boat and set off across the lake for Capernaum. By now it was dark, and Jesus had
not yet joined them. 18A strong wind was blowing and the waters grew rough. 19When
they had rowed three or three and a half miles,[b] they saw Jesus approaching the boat,
walking on the water;[l] and they were terrified. 20But he said to them, "It is I; don't
be afraid."[m] 21Then they were willing to take him into the boat, and immediately the
boat reached the shore where they were heading.

6:19 [l]Job 9:8
6:20 [m]Mt 14:27

Jesus Is the True Bread from Heaven
(99)

22The next day the crowd that had stayed on the opposite shore of the lake[n] realised
that only one boat had been there, and that Jesus had not entered it with his disciples,
but that they had gone away alone.[o] 23Then some boats from Tiberias[p] landed near
the place where the people had eaten the bread after the Lord had given thanks.[q]
24Once the crowd realised that neither Jesus nor his disciples were there, they got into
the boats and went to Capernaum in search of Jesus.
25When they found him on the other side of the lake, they asked him, "Rabbi,[r]
when did you get here?"

6:22 [n]ver 2 [o]ver 15-21
6:23 [p]ver 1 [q]ver 11
6:25 [r]Mt 23:7

[a] 7 Greek *two hundred denarii* [b] 19 Greek *rowed twenty-five or thirty stadia* (about 5 or 6 kilometres)

6:8, 9 The disciples are contrasted with the youngster who brought what he had. They certainly had more resources than the boy, but they knew they didn't have enough, so they didn't give anything at all. The boy gave what little he had, and it made all the difference. If we offer nothing to God, he will have nothing to use. But he can take what little we have and turn it into something great.

6:8, 9 In performing his miracles, Jesus usually preferred to work through people. Here he took what a young child offered and used it to accomplish one of the most spectacular miracles recorded in the Gospels. Age is no barrier to Christ. Never think you are too young or old to be of service to him.

6:13 There is a lesson in the leftovers. God gives in abundance. He takes whatever we can offer him in time, ability, or resources and multiplies its effectiveness beyond our wildest expectations. If you take the first step in making yourself available to God, he will show you how greatly you can be used to advance the work of his kingdom.

6:14 "The Prophet" is the one prophesied by Moses (Deuteronomy 18:15).

6:18 The Sea of Galilee is 650 feet below sea level, 150 feet deep, and surrounded by hills. These physical features make it subject to sudden windstorms that would cause extremely high waves. Such storms were expected on this lake, but they were nevertheless frightening. When Jesus came to the disciples during a storm, walking on the water (three and a half miles from shore), he told them not to be afraid. We often face spiritual and emotional storms and feel tossed about like a small boat on a big lake. In spite of terrifying circumstances, if we trust our lives to Christ for his safekeeping, he will give us peace in any storm.

6:18, 19 The disciples, terrified, probably thought they were seeing a ghost (Mark 6:49). But if they had thought about all they had already seen Jesus do, they could have accepted this miracle. They were frightened—they didn't expect Jesus to come, and they weren't prepared for his help. Faith is a mind-set that *expects* God to act. When we act on this expectation, we can overcome our fears.

26 Jesus answered, "I tell you the truth, you are looking for me,[s] not because you
saw miraculous signs[t] but because you ate the loaves and had your fill. 27 Do not work
for food that spoils, but for food that endures[u] to eternal life,[v] which the Son of
Man[w] will give you. On him God the Father has placed his seal[x] of approval."
28 Then they asked him, "What must we do to do the works God requires?"
29 Jesus answered, "The work of God is this: to believe[y] in the one he has sent."[z]
30 So they asked him, "What miraculous sign[a] then will you give that we may see
it and believe you?[b] What will you do? 31 Our forefathers ate the manna[c] in the
desert; as it is written: 'He gave them bread from heaven to eat.'[c]"[d]
32 Jesus said to them, "I tell you the truth, it is not Moses who has given you the
bread from heaven, but it is my Father who gives you the true bread from heaven.
33 For the bread of God is he who comes down from heaven[e] and gives life to the
world."
34 "Sir," they said, "from now on give us this bread."[f]
35 Then Jesus declared, "I am the bread of life.[g] He who comes to me will never
go hungry, and he who believes in me will never be thirsty.[h] 36 But as I told you,
you have seen me and still you do not believe. 37 All that the Father gives me[i] will
come to me, and whoever comes to me I will never drive away. 38 For I have come
down from heaven not to do my will but to do the will of him who sent me.[j] 39 And
this is the will of him who sent me, that I shall lose none of all that he has given me,[k]
but raise them up at the last day.[l] 40 For my Father's will is that everyone who looks
to the Son and believes in him shall have eternal life,[m] and I will raise him up at the
last day."

The Jews Disagree That Jesus Is from Heaven (100)

41 At this the Jews began to grumble about him because he said, "I am the bread
that came down from heaven." 42 They said, "Is this not Jesus, the son of Joseph,[n]
whose father and mother we know?[o] How can he now say, 'I came down from
heaven'?"[p]
43 "Stop grumbling among yourselves," Jesus answered. 44 "No-one can come to me
unless the Father who sent me draws him,[q] and I will raise him up at the last day.

c *31* Exodus 16:4; Neh. 9:15; Psalm 78:24,25

6:26 [s] ver 24 [t] ver 30; Jn 2:11
6:27 [u] Isa 55:2 [v] ver 54; Mt 25:46; Jn 4:14 [w] Mt 8:20 [x] Ro 4:11; 1Co 9:2; 2Co 1:22; Eph 1:13; 4:30; 2Ti 2:19; Rev 7:3
6:29 [y] 1Jn 3:23 [z] Jn 3:17
6:30 [a] Jn 2:11 [b] Mt 12:38
6:31 [c] Nu 11:7-9 [d] Ex 16:4, 15; Ne 9:15; Ps 78:24; 105:40
6:33 [e] ver 50
6:34 [f] Jn 4:15
6:35 [g] ver 48, 51 [h] Jn 4:14
6:37 [i] ver 39; Jn 17:2, 6, 9, 24
6:38 [j] Jn 4:34; 5:30
6:39 [k] Jn 10:28; 17:12; 18:9 [l] ver 40, 44, 54
6:40 [m] Jn 3:15, 16
6:42 [n] Lk 4:22 [o] Jn 7:27, 28 [p] ver 38, 62
6:44 [q] ver 65; Jer 31:3; Jn 12:32

6:26 Jesus criticised the people who followed him only for the physical and temporal benefits and not for the satisfying of their spiritual hunger. Many people use religion to gain prestige, comfort, or even political votes. But those are self-centred motives. True believers follow Jesus simply because they know he has the truth and his way is the way to live.

6:28, 29 Many sincere seekers for God are puzzled about what he wants them to do. The religions of the world are mankind's attempts to answer this question. But Jesus' reply is brief and simple: we must believe on him whom God has sent. Satisfying God does not come from the work we *do,* but from whom we *believe.* The first step is accepting that Jesus is who he claims to be. All spiritual development is built on this affirmation. Declare to Jesus, "You are the Christ, the Son of the living God" (Matthew 16:16), and embark on a life of belief that is satisfying to your Creator.

6:35 People eat bread to satisfy physical hunger and to sustain physical life. We can satisfy spiritual hunger and sustain spiritual life only by a right relationship with Jesus Christ. No wonder he called himself the bread of life. But bread must be eaten to sustain life, and Christ must be invited into our daily walk to sustain spiritual life.

6:37, 38 Jesus did not work independently of God the Father, but in union with him. This should give us even more assurance of being welcomed into God's presence and being protected by him. Jesus' purpose was to do the will of God, not to satisfy Jesus' human desires. When we follow Jesus, we should have the same purpose.

6:39 Jesus said he would not lose even one person whom the Father had given him. Thus anyone who makes a sincere commitment to believe in Jesus Christ as Saviour is secure in God's promise of eternal life. Christ will not let his people be overcome by Satan and lose their salvation (see also 17:12; Philippians 1:6).

6:40 Those who put their faith in Christ will be resurrected from physical death to eternal life with God when Christ comes again (see 1 Corinthians 15:52; 1 Thessalonians 4:16).

6:41 When John says *Jews,* he is referring to the Jewish leaders who were hostile to Jesus, not to Jews in general. John himself was a Jew, and so was Jesus.

6:41 The religious leaders grumbled because they could not accept Jesus' claim of divinity. They saw him only as a carpenter from Nazareth. They refused to believe that Jesus was God's divine Son, and they could not tolerate his message. Many people reject Christ because they say they cannot believe he is the Son of God. In reality, the demands that Christ makes for their loyalty and obedience are what they can't accept. So to protect themselves from the message, they reject the messenger.

6:44 God, not man, plays the most active role in salvation. When someone chooses to believe in Jesus Christ as Saviour, he or she does so only in response to the urging of God's Holy Spirit. God does the urging; then we decide whether or not to believe. Thus no-one can believe in Jesus without God's help.

45 It is written in the Prophets: 'They will all be taught by God.'[d][r] Everyone who
listens to the Father and learns from him comes to me. 46 No-one has seen the Father
except the one who is from God;[s] only he has seen the Father. 47 I tell you the truth,
he who believes has everlasting life. 48 I am the bread of life.[t] 49 Your forefathers ate
the manna in the desert, yet they died.[u] 50 But here is the bread that comes down from
heaven,[v] which a man may eat and not die. 51 I am the living bread that came down
from heaven. If anyone eats of this bread, he will live for ever. This bread is my flesh,
which I will give for the life of the world."[w]

52 Then the Jews began to argue sharply among themselves,[x] "How can this man
give us his flesh to eat?"

53 Jesus said to them, "I tell you the truth, unless you eat the flesh of the Son of
Man[y] and drink his blood, you have no life in you. 54 Whoever eats my flesh and
drinks my blood has eternal life, and I will raise him up at the last day.[z] 55 For my
flesh is real food and my blood is real drink. 56 Whoever eats my flesh and drinks my
blood remains in me, and I in him.[a] 57 Just as the living Father sent me[b] and I live
because of the Father, so the one who feeds on me will live because of me. 58 This
is the bread that came down from heaven. Your forefathers ate manna and died, but
he who feeds on this bread will live for ever."[c] 59 He said this while teaching in the
synagogue in Capernaum.

Many Disciples Desert Jesus
(101)

60 On hearing it, many of his disciples[d] said, "This is a hard teaching. Who can
accept it?"

61 Aware that his disciples were grumbling about this, Jesus said to them, "Does
this offend you?[e] 62 What if you see the Son of Man ascend to where he was before![f]
63 The Spirit gives life;[g] the flesh counts for nothing. The words I have spoken to you
are spirit[e] and they are life. 64 Yet there are some of you who do not believe." For
Jesus had known[h] from the beginning which of them did not believe and who would
betray him. 65 He went on to say, "This is why I told you that no-one can come to
me unless the Father has enabled him."[i]

d *45* Isaiah 54:13 **e** *63* Or *Spirit*

6:45 [r] Isa 54:13; Jer 31:33, 34; Heb 8:10, 11; 10:16
6:46 [s] Jn 1:18; 5:37; 7:29
6:48 [t] ver 35, 51
6:49 [u] ver 31, 58
6:50 [v] ver 33
6:51 [w] Heb 10:10
6:52 [x] Jn 7:43; 9:16; 10:19
6:53 [y] Mt 8:20
6:54 [z] ver 39
6:56 [a] Jn 15:4-7; 1Jn 3:24; 4:15
6:57 [b] Jn 3:17
6:58 [c] ver 49-51; Jn 3:36
6:60 [d] ver 66
6:61 [e] Mt 11:6
6:62 [f] Mk 16:19; Jn 3:13; 17:5
6:63 [g] 2Co 3:6
6:64 [h] Jn 2:25
6:65 [i] ver 37, 44

6:45 Jesus was alluding to an Old Testament view of the Messianic kingdom in which all people are taught directly by God (Isaiah 54:13; Jeremiah 31:31–34). He was stressing the importance of not merely hearing, but learning. We are taught by God through the Bible, our experiences, the thoughts the Holy Spirit brings, and relationships with other Christians. Are you open to God's teaching?

6:47 *Believes* as used here means "continues to believe". We do not believe merely once; we keep on believing in and trusting Jesus.

6:47ff The religious leaders frequently asked Jesus to prove to them why he was better than the prophets they already had. Jesus here referred to the manna that Moses had given their ancestors in the desert (see Exodus 16). This bread was physical and temporal. The people ate it, and it sustained them for a day. But they had to get more bread every day, and this bread could not keep them from dying. Jesus, who is much greater than Moses, offers himself as the spiritual bread from heaven that satisfies completely and leads to eternal life.

6:51 How can Jesus give us his flesh as bread to eat? To eat living bread means to accept Christ into our lives and become united with him. We are united with Christ in two ways: (1) by believing in his death (the sacrifice of his flesh) and resurrection and (2) by devoting ourselves to living as he requires, depending on his teaching for guidance and trusting in the Holy Spirit for power.

6:56 This was a shocking message – to eat flesh and drink blood sounded cannibalistic. The idea of drinking any blood, let alone human blood, was repugnant to the religious leaders because the law forbade it (Leviticus 17:10, 11). Jesus was not talking about literal blood, of course. He was saying that his life had to become their own, but they could not accept this concept. The apostle Paul later used the body and blood imagery in talking about communion (see 1 Corinthians 11:23–26).

6:63, 65 The Holy Spirit gives spiritual life; without the work of the Holy Spirit we cannot even see our need for new life (14:17). All spiritual renewal begins and ends with God. He reveals truth to us, lives within us, and then enables us to respond to that truth.

6:66 Why did Jesus' words cause many of his followers to desert him? (1) They may have realised that he wasn't going to be the conquering Messiah-King they expected. (2) He refused to give in to their self-centred requests. (3) He emphasised faith, not deeds. (4) His teachings were difficult to understand, and some of his words were offensive. As we grow in our faith, we may be tempted to turn away because Jesus' lessons are difficult. Will your response be to give up, ignore certain teachings, or reject Christ? Instead, ask God to show you what the teachings mean and how they apply to your life. Then have the courage to act on God's truth.

6:67 There is no middle ground with Jesus. When he asked the disciples if they would also leave, he was showing that they could either accept or reject him. Jesus was not trying to repel people with his teachings. He was simply telling the truth. The more the

66From this time many of his disciples[j] turned back and no longer followed him.
67"You do not want to leave too, do you?" Jesus asked the Twelve.[k]
68Simon Peter answered him,[l] "Lord, to whom shall we go? You have the words
of eternal life. 69We believe and know that you are the Holy One of God."[m]
70Then Jesus replied, "Have I not chosen you,[n] the Twelve? Yet one of you is a
devil!"[o] 71(He meant Judas, the son of Simon Iscariot, who, though one of the
Twelve, was later to betray him.)

2. Jesus encounters conflict with the religious leaders

Jesus' Brothers Ridicule Him

(121)

7 After this, Jesus went around in Galilee, purposely staying away from Judea
because the Jews[a] there were waiting to take his life.[b] 2But when the Jewish
Feast of Tabernacles[c] was near, 3Jesus' brothers[d] said to him, "You ought to leave
here and go to Judea, so that your disciples may see the miracles you do. 4No-
one who wants to become a public figure acts in secret. Since you are doing these
things, show yourself to the world." 5For even his own brothers did not believe in
him.[e]
6Therefore Jesus told them, "The right time[f] for me has not yet come; for you any
time is right. 7The world cannot hate you, but it hates me[g] because I testify that what
it does is evil.[h] 8You go to the Feast. I am not yet[a] going up to this Feast, because
for me the right time[i] has not yet come." 9Having said this, he stayed in Galilee.

Jesus Teaches Openly at the Temple

(123)

10However, after his brothers had left for the Feast, he went also, not publicly, but
in secret. 11Now at the Feast the Jews were watching for him[j] and asking, "Where
is that man?"
12Among the crowds there was widespread whispering about him. Some said, "He
is a good man."

a 8 Some early manuscripts do not have *yet.*

6:66 [j]ver 60
6:67 [k]Mt 10:2
6:68 [l]Mt 16:16
6:69 [m]Mk 8:29; Lk 9:20
6:70 [n]Jn 15:16, 19 [o]Jn 13:27
7:1 [a]Jn 1:19 [b]Jn 5:18
7:2 [c]Lev 23:34; Dt 16:16
7:3 [d]Mt 12:46
7:5 [e]Mk 3:21
7:6 [f]Mt 26:18
7:7 [g]Jn 15:18, 19 [h]Jn 3:19, 20
7:8 [i]ver 6
7:11 [j]Jn 11:56

---

people heard Jesus' real message, the more they divided into two camps—the honest seekers who wanted to understand more, and those who rejected Jesus because they didn't like what they had heard.

6:67, 68 After many of Jesus' followers had deserted him, he asked the 12 disciples if they were also going to leave. Peter replied, "To whom shall we go?" In his straightforward way, Peter answered for all of us—there is no other way. Though there are many philosophies and self-styled authorities, Jesus alone has the words of eternal life. People look everywhere for eternal life and miss Christ, the only source. Stay with him, especially when you are confused or feel alone.

6:70 In response to Jesus' message, some people left; others stayed and truly believed; and some, like Judas, stayed but tried to use Jesus for personal gain. Many people today turn away from Christ. Others pretend to follow, going to church for status, approval of family and friends, or business contacts. But there are only two real responses to Jesus—you either accept him or reject him. How have you responded to Christ?

6:71 For more information on Judas, see his Profile in Mark 14.

7:2 The Feast of Tabernacles is described in Leviticus 23:33ff. This event occurred in October, about six months after the Passover celebration mentioned in John 6:2–5. The feast commemorated the days when the Israelites wandered in the desert and lived in booths (Leviticus 23:43).

7:3–5 Jesus' brothers had a difficult time believing in him. Some of these brothers would eventually become leaders in the church (James, for example), but for several years they were embarrassed by Jesus. After Jesus died and rose again, they finally believed. We today have every reason to believe because we have the full record of Jesus' miracles, death, and resurrection. We also have the evidence of what the gospel has done in people's lives through the centuries. Don't miss this opportunity to believe in God's Son.

7:7 Because the world hated Jesus, we who follow him can expect that many people will hate us as well. If circumstances are going too well, ask if you are following Christ as you should. We can be grateful when life goes well, but we must make sure it is not at the cost of following Jesus halfheartedly or not at all.

7:10 Jesus came with the greatest gift ever offered, so why did he often act secretly? The religious leaders hated him, and many would refuse his gift of salvation, no matter what he said or did. The more Jesus taught and worked publicly, the more these leaders would cause trouble for him and his followers. So it was necessary for Jesus to teach and work as quietly as possible. Many people today have the privilege of teaching, preaching, and worshipping publicly with little persecution. These believers should be grateful and make the most of their opportunities to proclaim the gospel.

Others replied, "No, he deceives the people."[k] 13 But no-one would say anything
publicly about him for fear of the Jews.[l]
14 Not until halfway through the Feast did Jesus go up to the temple courts and begin
to teach.[m] 15 The Jews[n] were amazed and asked, "How did this man get such
learning[o] without having studied?"[p]
16 Jesus answered, "My teaching is not my own. It comes from him who sent me.[q]
17 If anyone chooses to do God's will, he will find out[r] whether my teaching comes
from God or whether I speak on my own. 18 He who speaks on his own does so to
gain honour for himself,[s] but he who works for the honour of the one who sent him
is a man of truth; there is nothing false about him. 19 Has not Moses given you the
law?[t] Yet not one of you keeps the law. Why are you trying to kill me?"[u]
20 "You are demon-possessed,"[v] the crowd answered. "Who is trying to kill you?"
21 Jesus said to them, "I did one miracle, and you are all astonished. 22 Yet, because
Moses gave you circumcision[w] (though actually it did not come from Moses, but from
the patriarchs),[x] you circumcise a child on the Sabbath. 23 Now if a child can be
circumcised on the Sabbath so that the law of Moses may not be broken, why are you
angry with me for healing the whole man on the Sabbath? 24 Stop judging by mere
appearances, and make a right judgment."[y]
25 At that point some of the people of Jerusalem began to ask, "Isn't this the man
they are trying to kill? 26 Here he is, speaking publicly, and they are not saying a word
to him. Have the authorities[z] really concluded that he is the Christ?[b] 27 But we know
where this man is from;[a] when the Christ comes, no-one will know where he is from."
28 Then Jesus, still teaching in the temple courts,[b] cried out, "Yes, you know me,
and you know where I am from.[c] I am not here on my own, but he who sent me is
true.[d] You do not know him, 29 but I know him[e] because I am from him and he sent
me."
30 At this they tried to seize him, but no-one laid a hand on him,[f] because his time
had not yet come. 31 Still, many in the crowd put their faith in him.[g] They said, "When
the Christ comes, will he do more miraculous signs[h] than this man?"

b *26* Or *Messiah*; also in verses 27, 31, 41 and 42

7:12 [k] ver 40, 43
7:13 [l] Jn 9:22; 12:42; 19:38
7:14 [m] ver 28; Mt 26:55
7:15 [n] Jn 1:19 [o] Ac 26:24 [p] Mt 13:54
7:16 [q] Jn 3:11; 14:24
7:17 [r] Ps 25:14; Jn 8:43
7:18 [s] Jn 5:41; 8:50, 54
7:19 [t] Jn 1:17 [u] ver 1; Mt 12:14
7:20 [v] Jn 8:48; 10:20
7:22 [w] Lev 12:3 [x] Ge 17:10-14
7:24 [y] Isa 11:3, 4; Jn 8:15
7:26 [z] ver 48
7:27 [a] Mt 13:55; Lk 4:22
7:28 [b] ver 14 [c] Jn 8:14 [d] Jn 8:26, 42
7:29 [e] Mt 11:27
7:30 [f] ver 32, 44; Jn 10:39
7:31 [g] Jn 8:30 [h] Jn 2:11

7:13 The religious leaders had a great deal of power over the common people. Apparently these leaders couldn't do much to Jesus at this time, but they threatened anyone who might publicly support him. Excommunication from the synagogue was one of the reprisals for believing in Jesus (9:22). To a Jew, this was a severe punishment.

7:13 Everyone was talking about Jesus! But when it came time to speak up for him in public, no-one said a word. All were afraid. Fear can stifle our witness. Although many people talk about Christ in church, when it comes to making a public statement about their faith, they are often embarrassed. Jesus says that he will acknowledge us before God if we acknowledge him before others (Matthew 10:32). Be courageous! Speak up for Christ!

7:16–18 Those who attempt to know God's will and do it will know intuitively that Jesus was telling the truth about himself. Have you ever listened to religious speakers and wondered if they were telling the truth? Test them: (1) their words should agree with, not contradict, the Bible; (2) their words should point to God and his will, not to themselves.

7:19 The Pharisees spent their days trying to achieve holiness by keeping the meticulous rules that they had added to God's laws. Jesus' accusation that they didn't keep Moses' laws stung them deeply. In spite of their pompous pride in themselves and their rules, they did not even fulfil a legalistic religion, for they were living far below what the law of Moses required. Murder was certainly against the law. Jesus' followers should do *more* than the moral law requires, not by adding to its requirements, but by going beyond and beneath the mere do's and don't's of the law to the spirit of the law.

7:20 Most of the people were probably not aware of the plot to kill Jesus (5:18). There was a small group looking for the right opportunity to kill him, but most were still trying to decide what they believed about him.

7:21–23 According to Moses' law, circumcision was to be performed eight days after a baby's birth (Genesis 17:9–14; Leviticus 12:3). This rite was carried out on all Jewish males to demonstrate their identity as part of God's covenant people. If the eighth day after birth was a Sabbath, the circumcision would still be performed (even though it was considered work). While the religious leaders allowed certain exceptions to Sabbath laws, they allowed none to Jesus, who was simply showing mercy to those who needed healing.

7:26 This chapter shows the many reactions people had toward Jesus. They called him a good man (7:12), a deceiver (7:12), a demon-possessed man (7:20), the Christ (7:26), and the Prophet (7:40). We must make up our own minds about who Jesus is, knowing that whatever we decide will have eternal consequences.

7:27 There was a popular tradition that the Messiah would simply appear. But those who believed this tradition were ignoring the Scriptures that clearly predicted the Messiah's birthplace (Micah 5:2).

7:33
[i]Jn 13:33; 16:16
[j]Jn 16:5, 10, 17, 28
7:34
[k]Jn 8:21; 13:33
7:35
[l]Jas 1:1
[m]Jn 12:20; 1Pe 1:1
7:37
[n]Lev 23:36
[o]Isa 55:1; Rev 22:17
7:38
[p]Isa 58:11
[q]Jn 4:10
[r]Jn 4:14
7:39
[s]Joel 2:28; Ac 2:17, 33
[t]Jn 20:22
[u]Jn 12:23; 13:31, 32
7:40
[v]Mt 21:11; Jn 1:21
7:41
[w]ver 52; Jn 1:46
7:42
[x]Mt 1:1
[y]Mic 5:2; Mt 2:5, 6; Lk 2:4
7:43
[z]Jn 9:16; 10:19
7:44
[a]ver 30
7:46
[b]Mt 7:28
7:47
[c]ver 12
7:48
[d]Jn 12:42
7:50
[e]Jn 3:1; 19:39

Religious Leaders Attempt to Arrest Jesus
(124)

32 The Pharisees heard the crowd whispering such things about him. Then the chief
priests and the Pharisees sent temple guards to arrest him.
33 Jesus said, "I am with you for only a short time,[i] and then I go to the one who
sent me.[j] 34 You will look for me, but you will not find me; and where I am, you
cannot come."[k]
35 The Jews said to one another, "Where does this man intend to go that we cannot
find him? Will he go where our people live scattered[l] among the Greeks,[m] and teach
the Greeks? 36 What did he mean when he said, 'You will look for me, but you will
not find me,' and 'Where I am, you cannot come'?"
37 On the last and greatest day of the Feast,[n] Jesus stood and said in a loud voice,
"If anyone is thirsty, let him come to me and drink.[o] 38 Whoever believes in me, as[c]
the Scripture has said,[p] streams of living water[q] will flow from within him."[r] 39 By
this he meant the Spirit,[s] whom those who believed in him were later to receive.[t]
Up to that time the Spirit had not been given, since Jesus had not yet been glorified.[u]
40 On hearing his words, some of the people said, "Surely this man is the Prophet."[v]
41 Others said, "He is the Christ."
Still others asked, "How can the Christ come from Galilee?[w] 42 Does not the
Scripture say that the Christ will come from David's family[d][x] and from Bethlehem,[y]
the town where David lived?" 43 Thus the people were divided[z] because of Jesus.
44 Some wanted to seize him, but no-one laid a hand on him.[a]
45 Finally the temple guards went back to the chief priests and Pharisees, who asked
them, "Why didn't you bring him in?"
46 "No-one ever spoke the way this man does,"[b] the guards declared.
47 "You mean he has deceived you also?"[c] the Pharisees retorted. 48 "Has any of
the rulers or of the Pharisees believed in him?[d] 49 No! But this mob that knows nothing
of the law—there is a curse on them."
50 Nicodemus,[e] who had gone to Jesus earlier and who was one of their own
number, asked, 51 "Does our law condemn a man without first hearing him to find out
what he is doing?"

c *37, 38* Or *If anyone is thirsty, let him come to me. / And let him drink, 38 who believes in me. / As*
d *42* Greek *seed*

7:37 Jesus' words, "come to me and drink", alluded to the theme of many Bible passages that talk about the Messiah's life-giving blessings (Isaiah 12:2, 3; 44:3, 4; 58:11). In promising to give the Holy Spirit to all who believed, Jesus was claiming to be the Messiah, for that was something only the Messiah could do.

7:38 Jesus used the term *living water* in 4:10 to indicate eternal life. Here he uses the term to refer to the Holy Spirit. The two go together: wherever the Holy Spirit is accepted, he brings eternal life. Jesus teaches more about the Holy Spirit in chapters 14–16. The Holy Spirit empowered Jesus' followers at Pentecost (Acts 2) and has since been available to all who believe in Jesus as Saviour.

7:40–44 The crowd was asking questions about Jesus. Some believed, others were hostile, and others disqualified Jesus as the Messiah because he was from Nazareth, not Bethlehem (Micah 5:2). But he *was* born in Bethlehem (Luke 2:1–7), although he grew up in Nazareth. If they had looked more carefully, they would not have jumped to the wrong conclusions. When you search for God's truth, make sure you look carefully and thoughtfully at the Bible with an open heart and mind. Don't jump to conclusions before knowing more of what the Bible says.

7:44–46 Although the Romans ruled Palestine, they gave the Jewish religious leaders authority over minor civil and religious affairs. The religious leaders supervised their own temple guards and gave the officers power to arrest anyone causing a disturbance or breaking any of their ceremonial laws. Because these leaders had developed hundreds of trivial laws, it was almost impossible for anyone, even the leaders themselves, not to break, neglect, or ignore at least a few of them some of the time. But these temple guards couldn't find one reason to arrest Jesus. And as they listened to Jesus to try to find evidence, they couldn't help hearing the wonderful words he said.

7:46–49 The Jewish leaders saw themselves as an elite group that alone had the truth, and they resisted the truth about Christ because it wasn't *theirs* to begin with. It is easy to think that we have the truth and that those who disagree with us do not have any truth at all. But God's truth is available to everyone. Don't copy the Pharisees' self-centred and narrow attitude.

7:50–52 This passage offers additional insight into Nicodemus, the Pharisee who visited Jesus at night (chapter 3). Apparently Nicodemus had become a secret believer. Since most of the Pharisees hated Jesus and wanted to kill him, Nicodemus risked his reputation and high position when he spoke up for Jesus. His statement was bold, and the Pharisees immediately became suspicious. After Jesus' death, Nicodemus brought spices for his body (19:39). That is the last time he is mentioned in Scripture.

7:51 Nicodemus confronted the Pharisees with their failure to keep their own laws. The Pharisees were losing ground—the temple guards came back impressed by Jesus (7:46), and one of the Pharisees' own, Nicodemus, was defending him. With their hypocritical motives being exposed and their prestige slowly eroding, they began to move to protect themselves. Pride would interfere with their ability to reason, and soon they would become obsessed with getting rid of Jesus just to save face. What was good and right no longer mattered.

52They replied, "Are you from Galilee, too? Look into it, and you will find that
a prophet[e] does not come out of Galilee."[f]

7:52 [f]ver 41

[The earliest and most reliable manuscripts and other ancient witnesses do not have John 7:53–8:11.]

8:1 [a]Mt 21:1

Jesus Forgives an Adulterous Woman
(125)

53Then each went to his own home.
8 But Jesus went to the Mount of Olives.[a] 2At dawn he appeared again in the
temple courts, where all the people gathered round him, and he sat down to teach
them.[b] 3The teachers of the law and the Pharisees brought in a woman caught in
adultery. They made her stand before the group 4and said to Jesus, "Teacher, this
woman was caught in the act of adultery. 5In the Law Moses commanded us to stone
such women.[c] Now what do you say?" 6They were using this question as a trap,[d]
in order to have a basis for accusing him.[e]
But Jesus bent down and started to write on the ground with his finger. 7When they
kept on questioning him, he straightened up and said to them, "If any one of you is
without sin, let him be the first to throw a stone[f] at her."[g] 8Again he stooped down
and wrote on the ground.
9At this, those who heard began to go away one at a time, the older ones first, until
only Jesus was left, with the woman still standing there. 10Jesus straightened up and
asked her, "Woman, where are they? Has no-one condemned you?"
11"No-one, sir," she said.
"Then neither do I condemn you,"[h] Jesus declared. "Go now and leave your life
of sin."[i]

8:2 [b]ver 20; Mt 26:55
8:5 [c]Lev 20:10; Dt 22:22
8:6 [d]Mt 22:15, 18 [e]Mt 12:10
8:7 [f]Dt 17:7 [g]Ro 2:1, 22
8:11 [h]Jn 3:17 [i]Jn 5:14

Jesus Is the Light of the World
(126)

12When Jesus spoke again to the people, he said, "I am[j] the light of the world.[k]
Whoever follows me will never walk in darkness, but will have the light of life."[l]

8:12 [j]Jn 6:35 [k]Jn 1:4; 12:35 [l]Pr 4:18; Mt 5:14

[e] *52* Two early manuscripts *the Prophet*

8:3–6 The Jewish leaders had already disregarded the law by arresting the woman without the man. The law required that both parties to adultery be stoned (Leviticus 20:10; Deuteronomy 22:22). The leaders were using the woman as a trap so they could trick Jesus. If Jesus said the woman should not be stoned, they would accuse him of violating Moses' law. If he urged them to execute her, they would report him to the Romans, who did not permit the Jews to carry out their own executions (18:31).

8:7 This is a significant statement about judging others. Because Jesus upheld the legal penalty for adultery, stoning, he could not be accused of being against the law. But by saying that only a sinless person could throw the first stone, he highlighted the importance of compassion and forgiveness. When others are caught in sin, are you quick to pass judgment? To do so is to act as though you have never sinned. It is God's role to judge, not ours. Our role is to show forgiveness and compassion.

8:8 It is uncertain whether Jesus was merely ignoring the accusers by writing on the ground, listing their sins, or writing out the Ten Commandments.

8:9 When Jesus said that only someone who had not sinned should throw the first stone, the leaders slipped quietly away, from oldest to youngest. Evidently the older men were more aware of their sins than the younger. Age and experience often temper youthful self-righteousness. But whatever your age, take an honest look at your life. Recognise your sinful nature, and look for ways to help others rather than hurt them.

8:11 Jesus didn't condemn the woman accused of adultery, but neither did he ignore or condone her sin. He told her to leave her life of sin. Jesus stands ready to forgive any sin in your life, but confession and repentance mean a change of heart. With God's help we can accept Christ's forgiveness and stop our wrongdoing.

8:12 To understand what Jesus meant by *the light of the world,* see the note on 1:4, 5.

8:12 Jesus was speaking in the part of the temple where the offerings were put (8:20), where candles burned to symbolise the pillar of fire that led the people of Israel through the desert (Exodus 13:21, 22). In this context, Jesus called himself the light of the world. The pillar of fire represented God's presence, protection, and guidance. Jesus brings God's presence, protection, and guidance. Is he the light of *your* world?

8:12 What does it mean to follow Christ? As a soldier follows his captain, so we should follow Christ, our commander. As a slave follows his master, so we should follow Christ, our Lord. As we follow the advice of a trusted counsellor, so we should follow Jesus' commands to us in Scripture. As we follow the laws of our nation, so we should follow the laws of the kingdom of heaven.

13 The Pharisees challenged him, "Here you are, appearing as your own witness;
your testimony is not valid."[m]
14 Jesus answered, "Even if I testify on my own behalf, my testimony is valid, for
I know where I came from and where I am going.[n] But you have no idea where I
come from[o] or where I am going. 15 You judge by human standards;[p] I pass judgment
on no-one.[q] 16 But if I do judge, my decisions are right, because I am not alone. I
stand with the Father, who sent me.[r] 17 In your own Law it is written that the
testimony of two men is valid.[s] 18 I am one who testifies for myself; my other witness
is the Father, who sent me."[t]
19 Then they asked him, "Where is your father?"
"You do not know me or my Father,"[u] Jesus replied. "If you knew me, you would
know my Father also."[v] 20 He spoke these words while teaching[w] in the temple area
near the place where the offerings were put.[x] Yet no-one seized him, because his time
had not yet come.[y]

Jesus Warns of Coming Judgment
(127)

21 Once more Jesus said to them, "I am going away, and you will look for me, and
you will die[z] in your sin. Where I go, you cannot come."[a]
22 This made the Jews ask, "Will he kill himself? Is that why he says, 'Where I go,
you cannot come'?"
23 But he continued, "You are from below; I am from above. You are of this world;
I am not of this world.[b] 24 I told you that you would die in your sins; if you do not
believe that I am ⌊the one I claim to be⌋,[a][c] you will indeed die in your sins."
25 "Who are you?" they asked.
"Just what I have been claiming all along," Jesus replied. 26 "I have much to say
in judgment of you. But he who sent me is reliable,[d] and what I have heard from
him I tell the world."[e]
27 They did not understand that he was telling them about his Father. 28 So Jesus said,
"When you have lifted up the Son of Man,[f] then you will know that I am ⌊the one
I claim to be⌋ and that I do nothing on my own but speak just what the Father has taught
me. 29 The one who sent me is with me; he has not left me alone,[g] for I always do
what pleases him."[h] 30 Even as he spoke, many put their faith in him.[i]

Jesus Speaks about God's True Children
(128)

31 To the Jews who had believed him, Jesus said, "If you hold to my teaching,[j]
you are really my disciples. 32 Then you will know the truth, and the truth will set you
free."[k]
33 They answered him, "We are Abraham's descendants[b][l] and have never been
slaves of anyone. How can you say that we shall be set free?"

a *24* Or *I am he*; also in verse 28 b *33* Greek *seed*; also in verse 37

8:13 m Jn 5:31
8:14 n Jn 13:3; 16:28 o Jn 7:28; 9:29
8:15 p Jn 7:24 q Jn 3:17
8:16 r Jn 5:30
8:17 s Dt 17:6; Mt 18:16
8:18 t Jn 5:37
8:19 u Jn 16:3 v Jn 14:7; 1Jn 2:23
8:20 w Mt 26:55 x Mk 12:41 y Mt 26:18; Jn 7:30
8:21 z Eze 3:18 a Jn 7:34; 13:33
8:23 b Jn 3:31; 17:14
8:24 c Jn 4:26; 13:19
8:26 d Jn 7:28 e Jn 3:32; 15:15
8:28 f Jn 3:14; 5:19; 12:32
8:29 g ver 16; Jn 16:32 h Jn 4:34; 5:30; 6:38
8:30 i Jn 7:31
8:31 j Jn 15:7; 2Jn 9
8:32 k Ro 8:2; Jas 2:12
8:33 l ver 37, 39; Mt 3:9

8:13, 14 The Pharisees thought Jesus was either a lunatic or a liar. Jesus provided them with a third alternative: he was telling the truth. Because most of the Pharisees refused to consider the third alternative, they never recognised him as Messiah and Lord. If you are seeking to know who Jesus is, do not close any door before looking through it honestly. Only with an open mind will you know the truth that he is Messiah and Lord.

8:13–18 The Pharisees argued that Jesus' claim was legally invalid because he had no other witnesses. Jesus responded that his confirming witness was God himself. Jesus and the Father made two witnesses, the number required by the law (Deuteronomy 19:15).

8:20 The temple treasury was located in the court of women. In this area, 13 collection boxes were set up to receive money offerings. Seven of the boxes were for the temple tax; the other six were for freewill offerings. On another occasion, a widow placed her money in one of these boxes, and Jesus taught a profound lesson from her action (Luke 21:1–4).

8:24 People will die in their sins if they reject Christ, because they are rejecting the only way to be rescued from sin. Sadly, many are so taken up with the values of this world that they are blind to the priceless gift Christ offers. Where are you looking? Don't focus on this world's values and miss what is most valuable – eternal life with God.

8:32 Jesus himself is the truth that sets us free (8:36). He is the source of truth, the perfect standard of what is right. He frees us from the consequences of sin, from self-deception, and from deception by Satan. He shows us clearly the way to eternal life with God. Thus Jesus does not give us freedom to do what we want, but freedom to follow God. As we seek to serve God, Jesus' perfect truth frees us to be all that God meant us to be.

[34]Jesus replied, "I tell you the truth, everyone who sins is a slave to sin.[m] [35]Now
a slave has no permanent place in the family, but a son belongs to it for ever.[n] [36]So
if the Son sets you free, you will be free indeed. [37]I know you are Abraham's
descendants. Yet you are ready to kill me,[o] because you have no room for my word.
[38]I am telling you what I have seen in the Father's presence,[p] and you do what you
have heard from your father."[c]
[39]"Abraham is our father," they answered.
"If you were Abraham's children,"[q] said Jesus, "then you would[d] do the things
Abraham did. [40]As it is, you are determined to kill me, a man who has told you the
truth that I heard from God.[r] Abraham did not do such things. [41]You are doing the
things your own father does."[s]
"We are not illegitimate children," they protested. "The only Father we have is God
himself."[t]
[42]Jesus said to them, "If God were your Father, you would love me,[u] for I came
from God[v] and now am here. I have not come on my own;[w] but he sent me.[x] [43]Why
is my language not clear to you? Because you are unable to hear what I say. [44]You
belong to your father, the devil,[y] and you want to carry out your father's desire.[z]
He was a murderer from the beginning, not holding to the truth, for there is no truth
in him. When he lies, he speaks his native language, for he is a liar and the father
of lies.[a] [45]Yet because I tell the truth,[b] you do not believe me! [46]Can any of you
prove me guilty of sin? If I am telling the truth, why don't you believe me? [47]He who
belongs to God hears what God says.[c] The reason you do not hear is that you do not
belong to God."

Jesus States He Is Eternal
(129)

[48]The Jews answered him, "Aren't we right in saying that you are a Samaritan[d]
and demon-possessed?"[e]
[49]"I am not possessed by a demon," said Jesus, "but I honour my Father and you
dishonour me. [50]I am not seeking glory for myself;[f] but there is one who seeks it,
and he is the judge. [51]I tell you the truth, if anyone keeps my word, he will never
see death."[g]
[52]At this the Jews exclaimed, "Now we know that you are demon-possessed!
Abraham died and so did the prophets, yet you say that if anyone keeps your word,
he will never taste death. [53]Are you greater than our father Abraham?[h] He died, and
so did the prophets. Who do you think you are?"

c *38 Or presence. Therefore do what you have heard from the Father.* **d** *39* Some early manuscripts *"If you are Abraham's children," said Jesus, "then*

8:34 [m]Ro 6:16; 2Pe 2:19
8:35 [n]Gal 4:30
8:37 [o]ver 39, 40
8:38 [p]Jn 5:19, 30; 14:10, 24
8:39 [q]ver 37; Ro 9:7; Gal 3:7
8:40 [r]ver 26
8:41 [s]ver 38, 44 [t]Isa 63:16; 64:8
8:42 [u]1Jn 5:1 [v]Jn 16:27; 17:8 [w]Jn 7:28 [x]Jn 3:17
8:44 [y]1Jn 3:8 [z]ver 38, 41 [a]Ge 3:4
8:45 [b]Jn 18:37
8:47 [c]Jn 18:37; 1Jn 4:6
8:48 [d]Mt 10:5 [e]ver 52; Jn 7:20
8:50 [f]ver 54; Jn 5:41
8:51 [g]Jn 11:26
8:53 [h]Jn 4:12

8:34, 35 Sin has a way of enslaving us, controlling us, dominating us, and dictating our actions. Jesus can free you from this slavery that keeps you from becoming the person God created you to be. If sin is restraining, mastering, or enslaving you, Jesus can break its power over your life.

8:41 Jesus made a distinction between hereditary children and *true* children. The religious leaders were hereditary children of Abraham (founder of the Jewish nation) and therefore claimed to be children of God. But their actions showed them to be true children of Satan, for they lived under Satan's guidance. True children of Abraham (faithful followers of God) would not act as they did. Your church membership and family connections will not make you a true child of God. Your true father is the one you imitate and obey.

8:43 The religious leaders were unable to understand because they refused to listen. Satan used their stubbornness, pride, and prejudices to keep them from believing in Jesus.

8:44, 45 The attitudes and actions of these leaders clearly identified them as followers of Satan. They may not have been conscious of this, but their hatred of truth, their lies, and their murderous intentions indicated how much control the devil had over them. They were his tools in carrying out his plans; they spoke the very same language of lies. Satan still uses people to obstruct God's work (Genesis 4:8; Romans 5:12; 1 John 3:12).

8:46 No-one could accuse Jesus of a single sin. People who hated him and wanted him dead scrutinised his behaviour but could find nothing wrong. Jesus proved he was God in the flesh by his sinless life. He is the only perfect example for us to follow.

8:46, 47 In a number of places Jesus intentionally challenged his listeners to test him. He welcomed those who wanted to question his claims and character as long as they were willing to follow through on what they discovered. Jesus' challenge clarifies the two most frequent reasons that people miss when encountering him: (1) they never accept his challenge to test him, or (2) they test him but are not willing to believe what they discover. Have you made either of those mistakes?

8:51 To keep Jesus' word means to hear his words and obey them. When Jesus says those who obey won't die, he is talking about spiritual death, not physical death. Even physical death, however, will eventually be overcome. Those who follow Christ will be raised to live eternally with him.

8:54
[i]ver 50
[j]Jn 16:14; 17:1, 5

8:55
[k]ver 19
[l]Jn 7:28, 29
[m]Jn 15:10

8:56
[n]ver 37, 39
[o]Mt 13:17; Heb 11:13

8:58
[p]Jn 1:2; 17:5, 24
[q]Ex 3:14

8:59
[r]Lev 24:16; Jn 10:31; 11:8
[s]Jn 12:36

9:2
[a]Mt 23:7
[b]ver 34; Lk 13:2; Ac 28:4
[c]Eze 18:20
[d]Ex 20:5; Job 21:19

9:3
[e]Jn 11:4

9:4
[f]Jn 11:9; 12:35

9:5
[g]Jn 1:4; 8:12; 12:46

9:6
[h]Mk 7:33; 8:23

9:7
[i]ver 11; 2Ki 5:10; Lk 13:4
[j]Isa 35:5; Jn 11:37

9:8
[k]Ac 3:2, 10

9:11
[l]ver 7

54Jesus replied, "If I glorify myself,[i] my glory means nothing. My Father, whom
you claim as your God, is the one who glorifies me.[j] 55Though you do not know
him,[k] I know him.[l] If I said I did not, I would be a liar like you, but I do know
him and keep his word.[m] 56Your father Abraham[n] rejoiced at the thought of seeing
my day; he saw it[o] and was glad."

57"You are not yet fifty years old," the Jews said to him, "and you have seen
Abraham!"

58"I tell you the truth," Jesus answered, "before Abraham was born,[p] I am!"[q] 59At
this, they picked up stones to stone him,[r] but Jesus hid himself,[s] slipping away from
the temple grounds.

Jesus Heals the Man Who Was Born Blind
(148)

9 As he went along, he saw a man blind from birth. 2His disciples asked
him, "Rabbi,[a] who sinned,[b] this man[c] or his parents,[d] that he was born
blind?"

3"Neither this man nor his parents sinned," said Jesus, "but this happened so that
the work of God might be displayed in his life.[e] 4As long as it is day,[f] we must
do the work of him who sent me. Night is coming, when no-one can work. 5While
I am in the world, I am the light of the world."[g]

6Having said this, he spat[h] on the ground, made some mud with the saliva, and
put it on the man's eyes. 7"Go," he told him, "wash in the Pool of Siloam"[i] (this
word means Sent). So the man went and washed, and came home seeing.[j]

8His neighbours and those who had formerly seen him begging asked, "Isn't this
the same man who used to sit and beg?"[k] 9Some claimed that he was.

Others said, "No, he only looks like him."

But he himself insisted, "I am the man."

10"How then were your eyes opened?" they demanded.

11He replied, "The man they call Jesus made some mud and put it on my eyes.
He told me to go to Siloam and wash. So I went and washed, and then I could
see."[l]

12"Where is this man?" they asked him.

"I don't know," he said.

8:56 God told Abraham, the father of the Jewish nation, that through him all nations would be blessed (Genesis 12:1–7; 15:1–21). Abraham had been able to see this through the eyes of faith. Jesus, a descendant of Abraham, blessed all people through his death, resurrection, and offer of salvation.

8:58 This is one of the most powerful statements uttered by Jesus. When he said that he existed before Abraham was born, he undeniably proclaimed his divinity. Not only did Jesus say that he existed before Abraham; he also applied God's holy name (*I Am*—Exodus 3:14) to himself. This claim demands a response. It cannot be ignored. The Jewish leaders tried to stone Jesus for blasphemy because he claimed equality with God. But Jesus *is* God. How have you responded to Jesus, the Son of God?

8:59 In accordance with the law given in Leviticus 24:16, the religious leaders were ready to stone Jesus for claiming to be God. They well understood what Jesus was claiming, and because they didn't believe he was God, they charged him with blasphemy. It is ironic that *they* were really the blasphemers, cursing and attacking the very God they claimed to serve!

9:1ff In chapter 9, we see four different reactions to Jesus. The neighbours revealed surprise and scepticism; the Pharisees showed disbelief and prejudice; the parents believed but kept quiet for fear of excommunication; and the healed man showed consistent, growing faith.

9:2, 3 A common belief in Jewish culture was that calamity or suffering was the result of some great sin. But Christ used this man's suffering to teach about faith and to glorify God. We live in a fallen world where good behaviour is not always rewarded and bad behaviour not always punished. Therefore, innocent people sometimes suffer. If God took suffering away whenever we asked, we would follow him for comfort and convenience, not out of love and devotion. Regardless of the reasons for our suffering, Jesus has the power to help us deal with it. When you suffer from a disease, tragedy, or disability, try not to ask, "Why did this happen to me?" or "What did I do wrong?" Instead, ask God to give you strength for the trial and a clearer perspective on what is happening.

9:7 The pool of Siloam was built by Hezekiah. His workers constructed an underground tunnel from a spring outside the city walls to carry water into the city. Thus the people could always get water without fear of being attacked. This was especially important during times of siege (see 2 Kings 20:20; 2 Chronicles 32:30).

Religious Leaders Question the Blind Man
(149)

13They brought to the Pharisees the man who had been blind. 14Now the day on which Jesus had made the mud and opened the man's eyes was a Sabbath.[m] 15Therefore the Pharisees also asked him how he had received his sight.[n] "He put mud on my eyes," the man replied, "and I washed, and now I see."

16Some of the Pharisees said, "This man is not from God, for he does not keep the Sabbath."[o]

But others asked, "How can a sinner do such miraculous signs?" So they were divided.[p]

17Finally they turned again to the blind man, "What have you to say about him? It was your eyes he opened."

The man replied, "He is a prophet."[q]

18The Jews[r] still did not believe that he had been blind and had received his sight until they sent for the man's parents. 19"Is this your son?" they asked. "Is this the one you say was born blind? How is it that now he can see?"

20"We know he is our son," the parents answered, "and we know he was born blind. 21But how he can see now, or who opened his eyes, we don't know. Ask him. He is of age; he will speak for himself." 22His parents said this because they were afraid of the Jews,[s] for already the Jews had decided that anyone who acknowledged that Jesus was the Christ**[a]** would be put out[t] of the synagogue.[u] 23That was why his parents said, "He is of age; ask him."[v]

24A second time they summoned the man who had been blind. "Give glory to God,"**[b]** [w] they said. "We know this man is a sinner."[x]

25He replied, "Whether he is a sinner or not, I don't know. One thing I do know. I was blind but now I see!"

26Then they asked him, "What did he do to you? How did he open your eyes?"

27He answered, "I have told you already[y] and you did not listen. Why do you want to hear it again? Do you want to become his disciples, too?"

28Then they hurled insults at him and said, "You are this fellow's disciple! We are disciples of Moses![z] 29We know that God spoke to Moses, but as for this fellow, we don't even know where he comes from."[a]

30The man answered, "Now that is remarkable! You don't know where he comes from, yet he opened my eyes. 31We know that God does not listen to sinners. He listens to the godly man who does his will.[b] 32Nobody has ever heard of opening the eyes of a man born blind. 33If this man were not from God,[c] he could do nothing."

34To this they replied, "You were steeped in sin at birth;[d] how dare you lecture us!" And they threw him out.[e]

Jesus Teaches about Spiritual Blindness
(150)

35Jesus heard that they had thrown him out, and when he found him, he said, "Do you believe in the Son of Man?"

36"Who is he, sir?" the man asked. "Tell me so that I may believe in him."[f]

a *22* Or *Messiah* **b** *24* A solemn charge to tell the truth (see Joshua 7:19)

9:14 [m]Jn 5:9
9:15 [n]ver 10
9:16 [o]Mt 12:2 [p]Jn 6:52; 7:43; 10:19
9:17 [q]Mt 21:11
9:18 [r]Jn 1:19
9:22 [s]Jn 7:13 [t]ver 34; Lk 6:22 [u]Jn 12:42; 16:2
9:23 [v]ver 21
9:24 [w]Jos 7:19 [x]ver 16
9:27 [y]ver 15
9:28 [z]Jn 5:45
9:29 [a]Jn 8:14
9:31 [b]Ge 18:23-32; Ps 34:15, 16; 66:18; 145:19, 20; Pr 15:29; Isa 1:15; 59:1, 2; Jn 15:7; Jas 5:16-18; 1Jn 5:14, 15
9:33 [c]ver 16; Jn 3:2
9:34 [d]ver 2 [e]ver 22, 35; Isa 66:5
9:36 [f]Ro 10:14

9:13–17 While the Pharisees conducted investigations and debated about Jesus, people were being healed and lives were being changed. The Pharisees' scepticism was based not on insufficient evidence, but on jealousy of Jesus' popularity and his influence on the people.

9:14–16 The Jewish Sabbath, Saturday, was the weekly holy day of rest. The Pharisees had made a long list of specific do's and don't's regarding the Sabbath. Kneading the clay and healing the man were considered work and therefore were forbidden. Jesus may have purposely made the clay in order to emphasise his teaching about the Sabbath – that it is right to care for others' needs even if it involves working on a day of rest.

9:25 By now the man who had been blind had heard the same questions over and over. He did not know how or why he was healed, but he knew that his life had been miraculously changed, and he was not afraid to tell the truth. You don't need to know all the answers in order to share Christ with others. It is important to tell them how he has changed your life. Then trust that God will use your words to help others believe in him too.

9:28, 34 The man's new faith was severely tested by some of the authorities. He was cursed and evicted from the synagogue. Persecution may come when you follow Jesus. You may lose friends; you may even lose your life. But no-one can ever take away the eternal life that Jesus gives you.

37 Jesus said, "You have now seen him; in fact, he is the one speaking with you."[g]
38 Then the man said, "Lord, I believe," and he worshipped him.[h]
39 Jesus said, "For judgment[i] I have come into this world,[j] so that the blind will
see[k] and those who see will become blind."[l]
40 Some Pharisees who were with him heard him say this and asked, "What? Are
we blind too?"[m]
41 Jesus said, "If you were blind, you would not be guilty of sin; but now that you
claim you can see, your guilt remains.[n]

Jesus Is the Good Shepherd
(151)

10 "I tell you the truth, the man who does not enter the sheep pen by the gate,
but climbs in by some other way, is a thief and a robber. 2 The man who enters
by the gate is the shepherd of his sheep.[a] 3 The watchman opens the gate for him,
and the sheep listen to his voice.[b] He calls his own sheep by name and leads them
out. 4 When he has brought out all his own, he goes on ahead of them, and his sheep
follow him because they know his voice. 5 But they will never follow a stranger; in
fact, they will run away from him because they do not recognise a stranger's voice."
6 Jesus used this figure of speech,[c] but they did not understand what he was telling
them.
7 Therefore Jesus said again, "I tell you the truth, I am the gate for the sheep. 8 All
who ever came before me[d] were thieves and robbers, but the sheep did not listen to
them. 9 I am the gate; whoever enters through me will be saved.[a] He will come in
and go out, and find pasture. 10 The thief comes only to steal and kill and destroy; I
have come that they may have life, and have it to the full.
11 "I am the good shepherd.[e] The good shepherd lays down his life for the sheep.[f]
12 The hired hand is not the shepherd who owns the sheep. So when he sees the wolf
coming, he abandons the sheep and runs away.[g] Then the wolf attacks the flock and
scatters it. 13 The man runs away because he is a hired hand and cares nothing for the
sheep.
14 "I am the good shepherd;[h] I know my sheep[i] and my sheep know me— 15 just
as the Father knows me and I know the Father[j]—and I lay down my life for the sheep.
16 I have other sheep[k] that are not of this sheep pen. I must bring them also. They
too will listen to my voice, and there shall be one flock[l] and one shepherd.[m] 17 The

a 9 Or *kept safe*

9:37 [g] Jn 4:26
9:38 [h] Mt 28:9
9:39 [i] Jn 5:22; [j] Jn 3:19; [k] Lk 4:18; [l] Mt 13:13
9:40 [m] Ro 2:19
9:41 [n] Jn 15:22, 24
10:2 [a] ver 11, 14
10:3 [b] ver 4, 5, 14, 16, 27
10:6 [c] Jn 16:25
10:8 [d] Jer 23:1, 2
10:11 [e] ver 14; Isa 40:11; Eze 34:11-16, 23; Heb 13:20; 1Pe 5:4; Rev 7:17; [f] Jn 15:13; 1Jn 3:16
10:12 [g] Zec 11:16, 17
10:14 [h] ver 11; [i] ver 27
10:15 [j] Mt 11:27
10:16 [k] Isa 56:8; [l] Jn 11:52; Eph 2:11-19; [m] Eze 37:24; 1Pe 2:25

9:38 The longer this man experienced his new life through Christ, the more confident he became in the one who had healed him. He gained not only physical sight but also spiritual sight as he recognised Jesus first as a prophet (9:17), then as his Lord. When you turn to Christ, you begin to see him differently. The longer you walk with him, the better you will understand who he is. Peter tells us to "grow in the grace and knowledge of our Lord and Saviour Jesus Christ" (2 Peter 3:18). If you want to know more about Jesus, keep walking with him.

9:40, 41 The Pharisees were shocked that Jesus thought they were spiritually blind. Jesus countered by saying that it was only blindness (stubbornness and stupidity) that could excuse their behaviour. To those who remained open and recognised how sin had truly blinded them from knowing the truth, he gave spiritual understanding and insight. But he rejected those who had become complacent, self-satisfied, and blind.

10:1 At night, sheep were often gathered into a sheep pen to protect them from thieves, weather, or wild animals. The sheep pens were caves, sheds, or open areas surrounded by walls made of stones or branches. The shepherd often slept in the pen to protect the sheep. Just as a shepherd cares for his sheep, Jesus, the Good Shepherd, cares for his flock (those who follow him). The prophet Ezekiel, in predicting the coming of the Messiah, called him a shepherd (Ezekiel 34:23).

10:7 In the sheep pen, the shepherd functioned as a gate, letting the sheep in and protecting them. Jesus is the gate to God's salvation for us. He offers access to safety and security. Christ is our protector. Some people resent that Jesus is the gate, the only way of access to God. But Jesus is God's Son—why should we seek any other way or want to customise a different approach to God? (See also the notes on 14:6.)

10:10 In contrast to the thief who takes life, Jesus gives life. The life he gives right now is abundantly richer and fuller. It is eternal, yet it begins immediately. Life in Christ is lived on a higher plane because of his overflowing forgiveness, love, and guidance. Have you taken Christ's offer of life?

10:11, 12 A hired hand tends the sheep for money, while the shepherd does it for love. The shepherd owns the sheep and is committed to them. Jesus is not merely doing a job; he is committed to love us and even lay down his life for us. False teachers and false prophets do not have this commitment.

10:16 The "other sheep" were non-Jews. Jesus came to save Gentiles as well as Jews. This is an insight into his worldwide mission—to die for the sins of the world. People tend to want to restrict God's blessings to their own group, but Jesus refuses to be limited by the fences we build.

10:17, 18 Jesus' death and resurrection, as part of God's plan for the salvation of the world, were under God's full control. No one could kill Jesus without his consent.

reason my Father loves me is that I lay down my life[n]—only to take it up again.
18 No-one takes it from me, but I lay it down of my own accord.[o] I have authority
to lay it down and authority to take it up again. This command I received from my
Father."[p]
19 At these words the Jews were again divided.[q] 20 Many of them said, "He is
demon-possessed[r] and raving mad.[s] Why listen to him?"
21 But others said, "These are not the sayings of a man possessed by a demon.[t]
Can a demon open the eyes of the blind?"[u]

Religious Leaders Surround Jesus at the Temple (152)

22 Then came the Feast of Dedication[b] at Jerusalem. It was winter, 23 and Jesus was
in the temple area walking in Solomon's Colonnade.[v] 24 The Jews[w] gathered round
him, saying, "How long will you keep us in suspense? If you are the Christ,[c] tell
us plainly."[x]
25 Jesus answered, "I did tell you,[y] but you do not believe. The miracles I do in
my Father's name speak for me,[z] 26 but you do not believe because you are not my
sheep.[a] 27 My sheep listen to my voice; I know them,[b] and they follow me.[c] 28 I
give them eternal life, and they shall never perish; no-one can snatch them out of my
hand.[d] 29 My Father, who has given them to me,[e] is greater than all;[d][f] no-one can
snatch them out of my Father's hand. 30 I and the Father are one."[g]
31 Again the Jews picked up stones to stone him,[h] 32 but Jesus said to them, "I have
shown you many great miracles from the Father. For which of these do you stone me?"
33 "We are not stoning you for any of these," replied the Jews, "but for blasphemy,
because you, a mere man, claim to be God."[i]
34 Jesus answered them, "Is it not written in your Law,[j] 'I have said you are

b 22 That is, Hanukkah c 24 Or *Messiah* d 29 Many early manuscripts *What my Father has given me is greater than all*

10:17 [n]ver 11, 15, 18
10:18 [o]Mt 26:53 [p]Jn 15:10; Php 2:8; Heb 5:8
10:19 [q]Jn 7:43; 9:16
10:20 [r]Jn 7:20 [s]Mk 3:21
10:21 [t]Mt 4:24 [u]Ex 4:11; Jn 9:32, 33
10:23 [v]Ac 3:11; 5:12
10:24 [w]Jn 1:19 [x]Jn 16:25, 29
10:25 [y]Jn 8:58 [z]Jn 5:36
10:26 [a]Jn 8:47
10:27 [b]ver 14 [c]ver 4
10:28 [d]Jn 6:39
10:29 [e]Jn 17:2, 6, 24 [f]Jn 14:28
10:30 [g]Jn 17:21-23
10:31 [h]Jn 8:59
10:33 [i]Lev 24:16; Jn 5:18
10:34 [j]Jn 8:17; Ro 3:19

10:19, 20 If Jesus had been merely a man, his claims to be God would have proven him insane. But his miracles proved his words true—he really was God. The Jewish leaders could not see beyond their own prejudices, and they looked at Jesus only from a human perspective—Jesus confined in a human box. But Jesus was not limited by their restricted vision.

10:22, 23 The Feast of Dedication commemorated the cleansing of the temple under Judas Maccabeus in 165 B.C. after Antiochus Epiphanes had defiled it by sacrificing a pig on the altar of burnt offering. The feast was celebrated toward the end of December. This is also the present-day Feast of Lights called Hanukkah.

10:23 Solomon's Colonnade was a roofed walkway supported by large stone columns, just inside the walls of the temple courtyard.

10:24 Many people asking for proof do so for the wrong reasons. Most of these questioners didn't want to follow Jesus in the way that he wanted to lead them. They hoped that Jesus would declare himself Messiah for perverted reasons. They, along with the disciples and everyone else in the Jewish nation, would have been delighted to have him drive out the Romans. Many of them didn't think he was going to do that, however. These doubters hoped he would identify himself so they could accuse him of telling lies (as the Pharisees did in 8:13).

10:28, 29 Just as a shepherd protects his sheep, Jesus protects his people from eternal harm. While believers can expect to suffer on earth, Satan cannot harm their souls or take away their eternal life with God. There are many reasons to be afraid here on earth because this is the devil's domain (1 Peter 5:8). But if you choose to follow Jesus, he will give you everlasting safety.

10:30 This is the clearest statement of Jesus' divinity he ever made. Jesus and his Father are not the same person, but they are one in essence and nature. Thus Jesus is not merely a good teacher—he is God. His claim to be God was unmistakable. The religious leaders wanted to kill him because their laws said that anyone claiming to be God should die. Nothing could persuade them that Jesus' claim was true.

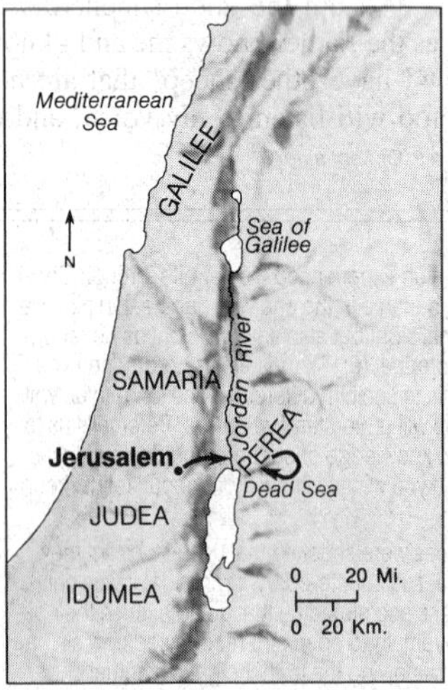

MINISTRY BEYOND THE JORDAN
Jesus had been in Jerusalem for the Feast of Tabernacles (7:2); then he preached in various towns, probably in Judea, before returning to to Jerusalem for the Feast of Dedication. He again angered the religious leaders, who tried to arrest him, but he left the city and went beyond the Jordan to preach.

10:31 The Jewish leaders attempted to carry out the directive found in Leviticus 24:16 regarding those who blaspheme (claim to be God). They intended to stone Jesus.

10:34-36 Jesus referred to Psalm 82:6, where the Israelite rulers and judges are called "gods" (see also Exodus 4:16; 7:1). If God called the Israelite leaders gods because they were agents of God's revelation and will, how could it be blasphemy for Jesus to call himself the Son of God? Jesus was rebuking the religious lead-

10:34
kPs 82:6
10:36
lJer 1:5
mJn 6:69
nJn 3:17
oJn 5:17, 18
10:37
pver 25; Jn 15:24
10:38
qJn 14:10, 11, 20; 17:21
10:39
rJn 7:30
sLk 4:30; Jn 8:59
10:40
tJn 1:28
10:41
uJn 2:11; 3:30
vJn 1:26, 27, 30, 34
10:42
wJn 7:31
11:1
aMt 21:17
bLk 10:38
11:2
cMk 14:3; Lk 7:38; Jn 12:3
11:3
dver 5, 36

gods'[e]?[k] 35If he called them 'gods', to whom the word of God came—and the
Scripture cannot be broken—36what about the one whom the Father set apart[l] as his
very own[m] and sent into the world?[n] Why then do you accuse me of blasphemy
because I said, 'I am God's Son'?[o] 37Do not believe me unless I do what my Father
does.[p] 38But if I do it, even though you do not believe me, believe the miracles, that
you may know and understand that the Father is in me, and I in the Father."[q] 39Again
they tried to seize him,[r] but he escaped their grasp.[s]
40Then Jesus went back across the Jordan[t] to the place where John had been
baptising in the early days. Here he stayed 41and many people came to him. They said,
"Though John never performed a miraculous sign,[u] all that John said about this man
was true."[v] 42And in that place many believed in Jesus.[w]

3. Jesus encounters crucial events in Jerusalem

Lazarus Becomes Ill and Dies

(165)

11 Now a man named Lazarus was sick. He was from Bethany,[a] the village of
Mary and her sister Martha.[b] 2This Mary, whose brother Lazarus now lay sick,
was the same one who poured perfume on the Lord and wiped his feet with her hair.[c]
3So the sisters sent word to Jesus, "Lord, the one you love[d] is sick."
4When he heard this, Jesus said, "This sickness will not end in death. No, it is for

e *34* Psalm 82:6

THE NAMES OF JESUS In different settings, Jesus gave himself names that pointed to special roles he was ready to fulfil for people. Some of these refer back to the Old Testament promises of the Messiah. Others were ways to help people understand him.

Reference	*Name*	*Significance*
6:27	Son of Man	Jesus' favourite reference to himself. It emphasised his humanity—but the way he used it, it was a claim to divinity.
6:35	Bread of life	Refers to his life-giving role—that he is the only source of eternal life.
8:12	Light of the world	Light is a symbol of spiritual truth. Jesus is the universal answer for man's need of spiritual truth.
10:7	Gate for the sheep	Jesus is the only way into God's kingdom.
10:11	Good shepherd	Jesus appropriated the prophetic images of the Messiah pictured in the Old Testament. This is a claim to divinity, focusing on Jesus' love and guidance.
11:25	The resurrection and the life	Not only is Jesus the source of life, he is the power over death.
14:6	The way and the truth and the life	Jesus is the method, the message, and the meaning for all people. With this title he summarised his purpose in coming to earth.
15:1	The vine	This title has an important second part, "you are the branches." As in so many of his other names, Jesus reminds us that just as branches gain life from the vine and cannot live apart from it, so we are completely dependent on Christ for spiritual life.

ers, because he is the Son of God in a unique, unparalleled relationship of oneness with the Father.

10:35 "The Scripture cannot be broken" is a clear statement of the truth of the Bible. If we accept Christ as Lord, we also must accept his testimony to the Bible as God's Word.

11:1 The village of Bethany was located about two miles east of Jerusalem on the road to Jericho. It was near enough to Jerusalem for Jesus and the disciples to be in danger, but far enough away so as not to attract attention prematurely.

11:3 As their brother grew very sick, Mary and Martha turned to Jesus for help. They believed in his ability to help because they had seen his miracles. We too know of Jesus' miracles, both from Scripture and through changed lives we have seen. When we need extraordinary help, Jesus offers extraordinary resources. We should not hesitate to ask him for assistance.

11:4 Any trial a believer faces can ultimately bring glory to God because God can bring good out of any bad situation (Genesis 50:20; Romans 8:28). When trouble comes, do you grumble, complain, and blame God, or do you see your problems as opportunities to honour him?

God's glory[e] so that God's Son may be glorified through it." 5Jesus loved Martha
and her sister and Lazarus. 6Yet when he heard that Lazarus was sick, he stayed where
he was two more days.
7Then he said to his disciples, "Let us go back to Judea."[f]
8"But Rabbi,"[g] they said, "a short while ago the Jews tried to stone you,[h] and
yet you are going back there?"
9Jesus answered, "Are there not twelve hours of daylight? A man who walks by
day will not stumble, for he sees by this world's light.[i] 10It is when he walks by night
that he stumbles, for he has no light."
11After he had said this, he went on to tell them, "Our friend[j] Lazarus has fallen
asleep;[k] but I am going there to wake him up."
12His disciples replied, "Lord, if he sleeps, he will get better." 13Jesus had been
speaking of his death, but his disciples thought he meant natural sleep.[l]
14So then he told them plainly, "Lazarus is dead, 15and for your sake I am glad
I was not there, so that you may believe. But let us go to him."
16Then Thomas[m] (called Didymus) said to the rest of the disciples, "Let us also
go, that we may die with him."

Jesus Comforts Mary and Martha
(166)

17On his arrival, Jesus found that Lazarus had already been in the tomb for four
days.[n] 18Bethany[o] was less than two miles[a] from Jerusalem, 19and many Jews had
come to Martha and Mary to comfort them in the loss of their brother.[p] 20When
Martha heard that Jesus was coming, she went out to meet him, but Mary stayed at
home.[q]
21"Lord," Martha said to Jesus, "if you had been here, my brother would not have
died.[r] 22But I know that even now God will give you whatever you ask."[s]
23Jesus said to her, "Your brother will rise again."
24Martha answered, "I know he will rise again in the resurrection[t] at the last day."
25Jesus said to her, "I am the resurrection and the life.[u] He who believes in me

a *18* Greek *fifteen stadia* (about 3 kilometres)

11:4 [e]ver 40; Jn 9:3
11:7 [f]Jn 10:40
11:8 [g]Mt 23:7 [h]Jn 8:59; 10:31
11:9 [i]Jn 9:4; 12:35
11:11 [j]ver 3 [k]Ac 7:60
11:13 [l]Mt 9:24
11:16 [m]Mt 10:3; Jn 14:5; 20:24-28; 21:2; Ac 1:13
11:17 [n]ver 6, 39
11:18 [o]ver 1
11:19 [p]ver 31; Job 2:11
11:20 [q]Lk 10:38-42
11:21 [r]ver 32, 37
11:22 [s]ver 41, 42; Jn 9:31
11:24 [t]Da 12:2; Jn 5:28, 29; Ac 24:15
11:25 [u]Jn 1:4

JESUS RAISES LAZARUS
Jesus had been preaching in the villages beyond the Jordan, probably in Perea, when he received the news of Lazarus' sickness. Jesus did not leave immediately, but waited two days before returning to Judea. He knew Lazarus would be dead when he arrived in Bethany, but he was going to do a great miracle.

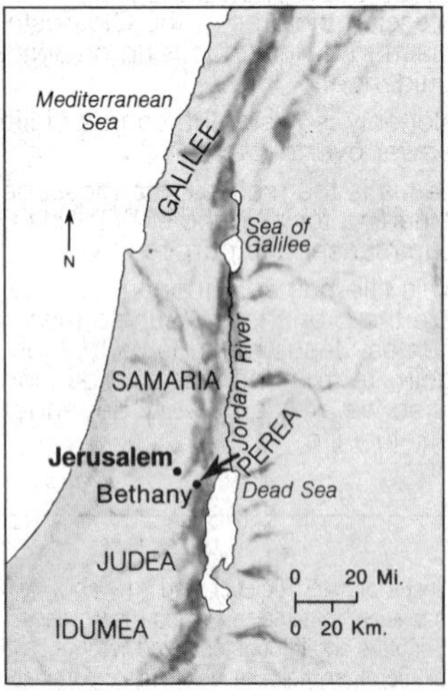

11:5-7 Jesus loved this family and often stayed with them. He knew their pain but did not respond immediately. His delay had a specific purpose. God's timing, especially his delays, may make us think he is not answering or is not answering the way we want. But he will meet all our needs according to his perfect schedule and purpose (Philippians 4:19). Patiently await his timing.

11:9, 10 *Day* symbolises the knowledge of God's will, and *night,* the absence of this knowledge. When we move ahead in darkness, we will be likely to stumble.

11:14, 15 If Jesus had been with Lazarus during the final moments of Lazarus's sickness, he might have healed him rather than let him die. But Lazarus died so that Jesus' power over death could be shown to his disciples and others. The raising of Lazarus was an essential display of his power, and the resurrection from the dead is a crucial belief of Christian faith. Jesus not only raised himself from the dead (10:18), but he has the power to raise others.

11:16 We often remember Thomas as "the doubter", because he doubted Jesus' resurrection. But here he demonstrated love and courage. The disciples knew the dangers of going with Jesus to Jerusalem, and they tried to talk him out of it. Thomas merely expressed what all of them felt. When their objections failed, they were willing to go and even die with Jesus. They may not have understood why Jesus would be killed, but they were loyal. There are unknown dangers in doing God's work. It is wise to consider the high cost of being Jesus' disciple.

11:25, 26 Jesus has power over life and death as well as power to forgive sins. This is because he is the Creator of life (see John 14:6). He who *is* life can surely restore life. Whoever believes in Christ has a spiritual life that death cannot conquer or diminish in any way. When we realise his power and how wonderful his offer to us really is, how can we help but commit our lives to him! To those of us who believe, what wonderful assurance and certainty we have: "Because I live, you also will live" (14:19).

will live, even though he dies; 26and whoever lives and believes in me will never die.
Do you believe this?"
27"Yes, Lord," she told him, "I believe that you are the Christ,[b][v] the Son of
God,[w] who was to come into the world."[x]
28And after she had said this, she went back and called her sister Mary aside. "The
Teacher[y] is here," she said, "and is asking for you." 29When Mary heard this, she
got up quickly and went to him. 30Now Jesus had not yet entered the village, but was
still at the place where Martha had met him.[z] 31When the Jews who had been with
Mary in the house, comforting her,[a] noticed how quickly she got up and went out,
they followed her, supposing she was going to the tomb to mourn there.
32When Mary reached the place where Jesus was and saw him, she fell at his feet
and said, "Lord, if you had been here, my brother would not have died."[b]
33When Jesus saw her weeping, and the Jews who had come along with her also
weeping, he was deeply moved[c] in spirit and troubled.[d] 34"Where have you laid
him?" he asked.
"Come and see, Lord," they replied.
35Jesus wept.[e]
36Then the Jews said, "See how he loved him!"[f]
37But some of them said, "Could not he who opened the eyes of the blind man[g]
have kept this man from dying?"[h]

Jesus Raises Lazarus from the Dead
(167)

38Jesus, once more deeply moved,[i] came to the tomb. It was a cave with a stone
laid across the entrance.[j] 39"Take away the stone," he said.
"But, Lord," said Martha, the sister of the dead man, "by this time there is a bad
odour, for he has been there four days."[k]
40Then Jesus said, "Did I not tell you that if you believed,[l] you would see the glory
of God?"[m]
41So they took away the stone. Then Jesus looked up[n] and said, "Father,[o] I thank
you that you have heard me. 42I knew that you always hear me, but I said this for
the benefit of the people standing here,[p] that they may believe that you sent me."[q]
43When he had said this, Jesus called in a loud voice, "Lazarus, come out!"[r] 44The
dead man came out, his hands and feet wrapped with strips of linen,[s] and a cloth
around his face.[t]
Jesus said to them, "Take off the grave clothes and let him go."

Religious Leaders Plot to Kill Jesus
(168)

45Therefore many of the Jews who had come to visit Mary,[u] and had seen what
Jesus did,[v] put their faith in him.[w] 46But some of them went to the Pharisees and

[b] *27* Or *Messiah*

11:27 [v]Lk 2:11 [w]Mt 16:16 [x]Jn 6:14
11:28 [y]Mt 26:18; Jn 13:13
11:30 [z]ver 20
11:31 [a]ver 19
11:32 [b]ver 21
11:33 [c]ver 38 [d]Jn 12:27
11:35 [e]Lk 19:41
11:36 [f]ver 3
11:37 [g]Jn 9:6, 7 [h]ver 21, 32
11:38 [i]ver 33 [j]Mt 27:60; Lk 24:2; Jn 20:1
11:39 [k]ver 17
11:40 [l]ver 23-25 [m]ver 4
11:41 [n]Jn 17:1 [o]Mt 11:25
11:42 [p]Jn 12:30 [q]Jn 3:17
11:43 [r]Lk 7:14
11:44 [s]Jn 19:40 [t]Jn 20:7
11:45 [u]ver 19 [v]Jn 2:23 [w]Ex 14:31; Jn 7:31

11:27 Martha is best known for being too busy to sit down and talk with Jesus (Luke 10:38–42). But here we see her as a woman of deep faith. Her statement of faith is exactly the response that Jesus wants from us.

11:33–38 John stresses that we have a God who cares. This portrait contrasts with the Greek concept of God that was popular in that day – a God with no emotions and no messy involvement with humans. Here we see many of Jesus' emotions – compassion, indignation, sorrow, even frustration. He often expressed deep emotion, and we must never be afraid to reveal our true feelings to him. He understands them, for he experienced them. Be honest, and don't try to hide anything from your Saviour. He cares.

11:35 When Jesus saw the weeping and wailing, he too wept openly. Perhaps he empathised with their grief, or perhaps he was troubled at their unbelief. In either case, Jesus showed that he cares enough for us to weep with us in our sorrow.

11:38 Tombs at this time were usually caves carved in the limestone rock of a hillside. A tomb was often large enough for people to walk inside. Several bodies would be placed in one tomb. After burial, a large stone was rolled across the entrance to the tomb.

11:44 Jesus raised others from the dead, including Jairus' daughter (Matthew 9:18–26; Mark 5:41, 42; Luke 8:40–56) and a widow's son (Luke 7:11–15).

11:45–53 Even when confronted point-blank with the power of Jesus' deity, some refused to believe. These eyewitnesses not only rejected Jesus; they plotted his murder. They were so hardened that they preferred to reject God's Son rather than admit that they were wrong. Beware of pride. If we allow it to grow, it can lead us into enormous sin.

told them what Jesus had done. 47Then the chief priests and the Pharisees[x] called a
meeting[y] of the Sanhedrin.[z]
"What are we accomplishing?" they asked. "Here is this man performing many
miraculous signs.[a] 48If we let him go on like this, everyone will believe in him, and
then the Romans will come and take away both our place[c] and our nation."
49Then one of them, named Caiaphas,[b] who was high priest that year,[c] spoke up,
"You know nothing at all! 50You do not realise that it is better for you that one man
die for the people than that the whole nation perish."[d]
51He did not say this on his own, but as high priest that year he prophesied that
Jesus would die for the Jewish nation, 52and not only for that nation but also for the
scattered children of God, to bring them together and make them one.[e] 53So from
that day on they plotted to take his life.[f]
54Therefore Jesus no longer moved about publicly among the Jews.[g] Instead he
withdrew to a region near the desert, to a village called Ephraim, where he stayed with
his disciples.
55When it was almost time for the Jewish Passover,[h] many went up from the
country to Jerusalem for their ceremonial cleansing[i] before the Passover. 56They kept
looking for Jesus,[j] and as they stood in the temple area they asked one another, "What
do you think? Isn't he coming to the Feast at all?" 57But the chief priests and Pharisees
had given orders that if anyone found out where Jesus was, he should report it so that
they might arrest him.

A Woman Anoints Jesus with Perfume
(182/Matthew 26:6–13; Mark 14:3–9)

12 Six days before the Passover,[a] Jesus arrived at Bethany,[b] where Lazarus
lived, whom Jesus had raised from the dead. 2Here a dinner was given in Jesus'
honour. Martha served,[c] while Lazarus was among those reclining at the table with
him. 3Then Mary took about a pint[a] of pure nard, an expensive perfume;[d] she poured
it on Jesus' feet and wiped his feet with her hair.[e] And the house was filled with the
fragrance of the perfume.
4But one of his disciples, Judas Iscariot, who was later to betray him,[f] objected,
5"Why wasn't this perfume sold and the money given to the poor? It was worth a year's
wages."[b] 6He did not say this because he cared about the poor but because he was

[c] 48 Or *temple* [a] 3 Greek *a litra* (probably about 0.5 litre) [b] 5 Greek *three hundred denarii*

11:47 [x]ver 57 [y]Mt 26:3 [z]Mt 5:22 [a]Jn 2:11
11:49 [b]Mt 26:3 [c]ver 51; Jn 18:13, 14
11:50 [d]Jn 18:14
11:52 [e]Isa 49:6; Jn 10:16
11:53 [f]Mt 12:14
11:54 [g]Jn 7:1
11:55 [h]Ex 12:13, 23, 27; Mt 26:1, 2; Mk 14:1; Jn 13:1 [i]2Ch 30:17, 18
11:56 [j]Jn 7:11
12:1 [a]Jn 11:55 [b]Mt 21:17
12:2 [c]Lk 10:38-42
12:3 [d]Mk 14:3 [e]Jn 11:2
12:4 [f]Mt 10:4

TIME WITH THE DISCIPLES
Lazarus' return to life became the last straw for the religious leaders, who were bent on killing Jesus. So Jesus stopped his public ministry and took his disciples away from Jerusalem to Ephraim. From there they returned to Galilee for a while (see the map in Luke 17.)

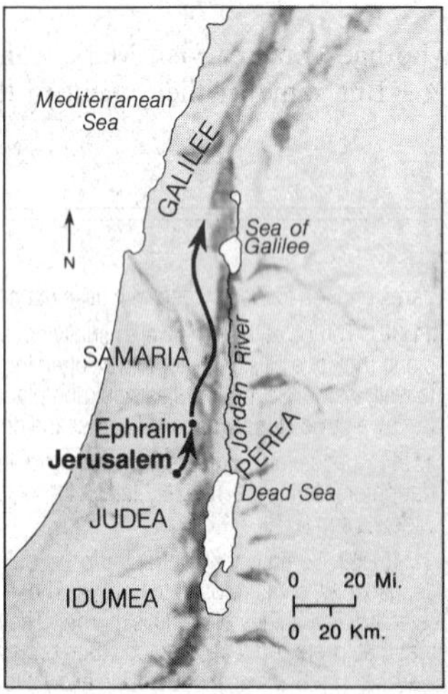

11:48 The Jewish leaders knew that if they didn't stop Jesus, the Romans would discipline them. Rome gave partial freedom to the Jews as long as they were quiet and obedient. Jesus' miracles often caused a disturbance. The leaders feared that Rome's displeasure would bring additional hardship to their nation.

11:51 John regarded Caiaphas' statement as a prophecy. As high priest, Caiaphas was used by God to explain Jesus' death even though Caiaphas didn't realise what he was doing.

12:3 Pure nard was a fragrant ointment imported from the mountains of India. Thus it was very expensive. The amount Mary used was worth a year's wages.

12:4–6 Judas often dipped into the disciples' money bag for his own use. Quite likely, Jesus knew what Judas was doing (2:24, 25; 6:64), but never did or said anything about it. Similarly, when we choose the way of sin, God may not immediately do anything to stop us, but this does not mean he approves of our actions. What we deserve will come.

12:5, 6 Judas used a pious phrase to hide his true motives. But Jesus knew what was in his heart. Judas' life had become a lie, and the devil was entering him (13:27). Satan is the father of lies, and a lying character opens the door to his influence. Jesus' knowledge of us should make us want to keep our actions consistent with our words. Because we have nothing to fear with him, we should have nothing to hide.

12:6 [g]Jn 13:29
12:7 [h]Jn 19:40
12:8 [i]Dt 15:11
12:9 [j]Jn 11:43, 44

a thief; as keeper of the money bag,[g] he used to help himself to what was put into
it.
7"Leave her alone," Jesus replied. "⌞It was intended⌟ that she should save this
perfume for the day of my burial.[h] 8You will always have the poor among you,[i]
but you will not always have me."
9Meanwhile a large crowd of Jews found out that Jesus was there and came, not
only because of him but also to see Lazarus, whom he had raised from the dead.[j]

CAIAPHAS

Caiaphas was the leader of the religious group called the Sadducees. Educated and wealthy, they were politically influential in the nation. As the elite group, they were on fairly good terms with Rome. They hated Jesus because he endangered their secure lifestyles and taught a message they could not accept. A kingdom in which leaders *served* had no appeal to them.

Caiaphas' usual policy was to remove any threats to his power by whatever means necessary. For Caiaphas, whether Jesus should die was not in question; the only point to be settled was *when* his death should take place. Not only did Jesus have to be captured and tried; the Jewish council also needed Roman approval before they could carry out the death sentence. Caiaphas' plans were unexpectedly helped by Judas' offer to betray Christ.

Caiaphas did not realise that his schemes were actually part of a wonderful plan God was carrying out. Caiaphas' willingness to sacrifice another man to preserve his own security was clearly selfish. By contrast, Jesus' willingness to die for us was a clear example of loving self-sacrifice. Caiaphas thought he had won the battle as Jesus hung on the cross, but he did not count on the resurrection!

Caiaphas' mind was closed. He couldn't accept the resurrection even when the evidence was overwhelming, and he attempted to silence those whose lives had been for ever changed by the risen Christ (Matthew 28:12, 13). Caiaphas represents those people who will not believe because they think it will cost them too much to accept Jesus as Lord. They choose the fleeting power, prestige, and pleasures of this life instead of the eternal life God offers those who receive his Son. What is your choice?

Strength and accomplishment:
- High priest for 18 years

Weaknesses and mistakes:
- One of those most directly responsible for Jesus' death
- Used his office as a means to power and personal security
- Planned Jesus' capture, carried out his illegal trial, pressured Pilate to approve the crucifixion, attempted to prevent the resurrection, and later tried to cover up the fact of the resurrection
- Kept up religious appearances while compromising with Rome
- Involved in the later persecution of Christians

Lessons from his life:
- God uses even the twisted motives and actions of his enemies to bring about his will
- When we cover selfish motives with spiritual objectives and words, God still sees our intentions

Vital statistics:
- Where: Jerusalem
- Occupation: High priest
- Relative: Father-in-law: Annas
- Contemporaries: Jesus, Pilate, Herod Antipas

Key verses:
"Then one of them, named Caiaphas, who was high priest that year, spoke up, 'You know nothing at all! You do not realise that it is better for you that one man die for the people than that the whole nation perish' " (John 11:49, 50).

12:7, 8 This act and Jesus' response to it do not teach us to ignore the poor so we can spend money extravagantly for Christ. This was a unique act for a specific occasion – an anointing that anticipated Jesus' burial and a public declaration of faith in him as Messiah. Jesus' words should have taught Judas a valuable lesson about the worth of money. Unfortunately, Judas did not take heed; soon he would sell his Master's life for 30 pieces of silver.

10So the chief priests made plans to kill Lazarus as well, 11for on account of him[k]
many of the Jews were going over to Jesus and putting their faith in him.[l]

Jesus Rides into Jerusalem on a Donkey
(183/Matthew 21:1–11; Mark 11:1–11; Luke 19:28–44)

12The next day the great crowd that had come for the Feast heard that Jesus was
on his way to Jerusalem. 13They took palm branches and went out to meet him,
shouting,

"Hosanna!"[c]

"Blessed is he who comes in the name of the Lord!"[d][m]

"Blessed is the King of Israel!"[n]

14Jesus found a young donkey and sat upon it, as it is written,

15"Do not be afraid, O Daughter of Zion;
see, your king is coming,
seated on a donkey's colt."[e][o]

16At first his disciples did not understand all this.[p] Only after Jesus was glorified[q]
did they realise that these things had been written about him and that they had done
these things to him.
17Now the crowd that was with him[r] when he called Lazarus from the tomb and
raised him from the dead continued to spread the word. 18Many people, because they
had heard that he had given this miraculous sign,[s] went out to meet him. 19So the
Pharisees said to one another, "See, this is getting us nowhere. Look how the whole
world has gone after him!"[t]

Jesus Explains Why He Must Die
(185)

20Now there were some Greeks[u] among those who went up to worship at the Feast.
21They came to Philip, who was from Bethsaida[v] in Galilee, with a request. "Sir,"
they said, "we would like to see Jesus." 22Philip went to tell Andrew; Andrew and
Philip in turn told Jesus.
23Jesus replied, "The hour has come for the Son of Man to be glorified.[w] 24I tell

12:11 [k]ver 17, 18; Jn 11:45 [l]Jn 7:31
12:13 [m]Ps 118:25, 26 [n]Jn 1:49
12:15 [o]Zec 9:9
12:16 [p]Mk 9:32 [q]Jn 2:22; 7:39; 14:26
12:17 [r]Jn 11:42
12:18 [s]ver 11
12:19 [t]Jn 11:47, 48
12:20 [u]Jn 7:35; Ac 11:20
12:21 [v]Mt 11:21; Jn 1:44
12:23 [w]Jn 13:32; 17:1

c *13* A Hebrew expression meaning "Save!" which became an exclamation of praise **d** *13* Psalm 118:25,26
e *15* Zech. 9:9

12:10, 11 The chief priests' blindness and hardness of heart caused them to sink ever deeper into sin. They rejected the Messiah and planned to kill him, and then plotted to murder Lazarus as well. One sin leads to another. From the Jewish leaders' point of view, they could accuse Jesus of blasphemy because he claimed equality with God. But Lazarus had done nothing of the kind. They wanted Lazarus dead simply because he was a living witness to Jesus' power. This is a warning to us to avoid sin. Sin leads to more sin, a downward spiral that can be stopped only by repentance and the power of the Holy Spirit to change our behaviour.

12:13 Jesus began his last week on earth by riding into Jerusalem on a donkey under a canopy of palm branches, with crowds hailing him as their king. To announce that he was indeed the Messiah, Jesus chose a *time* when all Israel would be gathered at Jerusalem, a *place* where huge crowds could see him, and a *way* of proclaiming his mission that was unmistakable. On Palm Sunday we celebrate Jesus' Triumphal Entry into Jerusalem.

12:13 The people who were praising God for giving them a king had the wrong idea about Jesus. They were sure he would be a national leader who would restore their nation to its former glory, and thus they were deaf to the words of their prophets and blind to Jesus' real mission. When it became apparent that Jesus was not going to fulfil their hopes, many people turned against him.

12:16 After Jesus' resurrection, the disciples understood for the first time many of the prophecies that they had missed along the way. Jesus' words and actions took on new meaning and made more sense. In retrospect, the disciples saw how Jesus had led them into a deeper and better understanding of his truth. Stop now and think about the events in your life leading up to where you are now. How has God led you to this point? As you grow older, you will look back and see God's involvement more clearly than you do now.

12:18 The people flocked to Jesus because they had heard about his great miracle in raising Lazarus from the dead. Their adoration was short-lived and their commitment shallow, for in a few days they would do nothing to stop his crucifixion. Devotion based only on curiosity or popularity fades quickly.

12:20, 21 These Greeks probably were converts to the Jewish faith. They may have gone to Philip because, though he was a Jew, he had a Greek name.

12:23–25 This is a beautiful picture of the necessary sacrifice of Jesus. Unless a kernel of wheat is buried in the ground, it will not become a blade of wheat producing many more seeds. Jesus had to die to pay the penalty for our sin, but also to show his power over death. His resurrection proves he has eternal life. Because Jesus is God, Jesus can give this same eternal life to all who believe in him.

12:24 [x] 1Co 15:36 12:25 [y] Mt 10:39; Mk 8:35; Lk 14:26 12:26 [z] Jn 14:3; 17:24; 2Co 5:8 12:27 [a] Mt 26:38, 39; Jn 11:33, 38; 13:21 [b] Mt 11:25 [c] ver 23 12:28 [d] Mt 3:17 12:30 [e] Jn 11:42 12:31 [f] Jn 16:11 [g] Jn 14:30; 16:11

you the truth, unless a grain of wheat falls to the ground and dies,[x] it remains only
a single seed. But if it dies, it produces many seeds. 25The man who loves his life
will lose it, while the man who hates his life in this world will keep it[y] for eternal
life. 26Whoever serves me must follow me; and where I am, my servant also will be.[z]
My Father will honour the one who serves me.
27"Now my heart is troubled,[a] and what shall I say? 'Father,[b] save me from this
hour'?[c] No, it was for this very reason I came to this hour. 28Father, glorify your
name!"
Then a voice came from heaven,[d] "I have glorified it, and will glorify it again."
29The crowd that was there and heard it said it had thundered; others said an angel
had spoken to him.
30Jesus said, "This voice was for your benefit,[e] not mine. 31Now is the time for
judgment on this world;[f] now the prince of this world[g] will be driven out. 32But

GREAT EXPECTATIONS
Wherever he went, Jesus exceeded people's expectations.

What was expected	*What Jesus did*	*Reference*
A man looked for healing	Jesus also forgave his sins	Mark 2:1–12
The disciples were expecting an ordinary day of fishing	They found the Saviour	Luke 5:1–11
A widow was resigned to burying her dead son	Jesus restored her son to life	Luke 7:11–17
The religious leaders wanted a miracle	Jesus offered them the Creator of miracles	Matthew 12:38–45
A woman who wanted to be healed touched Jesus	Jesus helped her see it was her faith that had healed her	Mark 5:25–34
The disciples thought the crowd should be sent home because there was no food	Jesus used a small meal to feed thousands, and there were leftovers!	John 6:1–15
The crowds looked for a political leader to set up a new kingdom to overthrow Rome's control	Jesus offered them an eternal, spiritual kingdom to overthrow sin's control	A theme throughout the Gospels
The disciples wanted to eat the Passover meal with Jesus, their Master	Jesus washed their feet, showing that he was also their servant	John 13:1–20
The religious leaders wanted Jesus killed and got their wish	But Jesus rose from the dead!	John 11:53; 19:30; 20:1–29

12:25 We must be so committed to living for Christ that we "hate" our lives by comparison. This does not mean that we long to die or that we are careless or destructive with the life God has given, but that we are willing to die if doing so will glorify Christ. We must disown the tyrannical rule of our own self-centredness. By laying aside our striving for advantage, security, and pleasure, we can serve God lovingly and freely. Releasing control of our lives and transferring control to Christ bring eternal life and genuine joy.

12:26 Many believed that Jesus came for the Jews only. But when Jesus said, "Whoever serves me must follow me," he was talking to these Greeks as well. No matter who the sincere seekers are, Jesus welcomes them. His message is for everyone. Don't allow social or racial differences to become barriers to the gospel. Take the Good News to all people.

12:27 Jesus knew his crucifixion lay ahead, and because he was human he dreaded it. He knew he would have to take the sins of the world on himself, and he knew this would separate him from his Father. He wanted to be delivered from this horrible death, but he knew that God sent him into the world to die for our sins, in our place. Jesus said no to his human desires in order to obey his Father and glorify him. Although we will never have to face such a difficult and awesome task, we are still called to obedience. Whatever the Father asks, we should do his will and bring glory to his name.

12:31 The prince of this world is Satan, an angel who rebelled against God. Satan is real, not symbolic, and is constantly working against God and those who obey him. Satan tempted Eve in the garden and persuaded her to sin; he tempted Jesus in the desert and did not persuade him to fall (Matthew 4:1–11). Satan has great power, but people can be delivered from his reign of spiritual darkness because of Christ's victory on the cross. Satan is powerful, but Jesus is much more powerful. Jesus' resurrection shattered Satan's deathly power (Colossians 1:13, 14). To overcome Satan we need faithful allegiance to God's word, determination to stay away from sin, and the support of other believers.

12:32–34 The crowd could not believe what Jesus was saying about the Messiah. They were waving palm branches for a victorious Messiah who would set up a political, earthly kingdom that would never end. From their reading of certain Scriptures, they thought the Messiah would never die (Psalms 89:35, 36; 110:4; Isaiah 9:7). Other passages, however, showed that he would (Isaiah 53:5–9). Jesus' words did not mesh with their concept of the Messiah. First he had to suffer and die – then he would one day set up his eternal kingdom. What kind of Messiah, or Saviour, are you seeking? Beware of trying to force Jesus into your own mould – he won't fit.

I, when I am lifted up from the earth,[h] will draw all men to myself."[i] 33He said
this to show the kind of death he was going to die.[j]
34The crowd spoke up, "We have heard from the Law that the Christ[f] will remain
for ever,[k] so how can you say, 'The Son of Man[l] must be lifted up'?[m] Who is this
'Son of Man'?"
35Then Jesus told them, "You are going to have the light[n] just a little while longer.
Walk while you have the light,[o] before darkness overtakes you.[p] The man who walks
in the dark does not know where he is going. 36Put your trust in the light while you
have it, so that you may become sons of light."[q] When he had finished speaking,
Jesus left and hid himself from them.[r]

Most of the People Do Not Believe in Jesus
(186)

37Even after Jesus had done all these miraculous signs[s] in their presence, they still
would not believe in him. 38This was to fulfil the word of Isaiah the prophet:

"Lord, who has believed our message
and to whom has the arm of the Lord been revealed?"[g][t]

39For this reason they could not believe, because, as Isaiah says elsewhere:

40"He has blinded their eyes
and deadened their hearts,
so they can neither see with their eyes,
nor understand with their hearts,
nor turn — and I would heal them."[h][u]

41Isaiah said this because he saw Jesus' glory[v] and spoke about him.[w]
42Yet at the same time many even among the leaders believed in him.[x] But because
of the Pharisees[y] they would not confess their faith for fear they would be put out
of the synagogue;[z] 43for they loved praise from men more than praise from God.[a]

Jesus Summarises His Message
(187)

44Then Jesus cried out, "When a man believes in me, he does not believe in me
only, but in the one who sent me.[b] 45When he looks at me, he sees the one who sent
me.[c] 46I have come into the world as a light,[d] so that no-one who believes in me
should stay in darkness.
47"As for the person who hears my words but does not keep them, I do not judge
him. For I did not come to judge the world, but to save it.[e] 48There is a judge for

[f] *34* Or *Messiah* [g] *38* Isaiah 53:1 [h] *40* Isaiah 6:10

12:32 [h]ver 34; Jn 3:14; 8:28 [i]Jn 6:44
12:33 [j]Jn 18:32
12:34 [k]Ps 110:4; Isa 9:7; Eze 37:25; Da 7:14 [l]Mt 8:20 [m]Jn 3:14
12:35 [n]ver 46 [o]Eph 5:8 [p]1Jn 2:11
12:36 [q]Lk 16:8 [r]Jn 8:59
12:37 [s]Jn 2:11
12:38 [t]Isa 53:1; Ro 10:16
12:40 [u]Isa 6:10; Mt 13:13, 15
12:41 [v]Isa 6:1-4 [w]Lk 24:27
12:42 [x]ver 11; Jn 7:48 [y]Jn 7:13 [z]Jn 9:22
12:43 [a]Jn 5:44
12:44 [b]Mt 10:40; Jn 5:24
12:45 [c]Jn 14:9
12:46 [d]Jn 1:4; 3:19; 8:12; 9:5
12:47 [e]Jn 3:17

12:35, 36 Jesus said he would be with them in person for only a short time, and they should take advantage of his presence while they had it. Like a light shining in a dark place, he would point out the way they should walk. If they walked in his light, they would become "sons of light", revealing the truth and pointing people to God. As Christians, we are to be Christ's light bearers, letting his light shine through us. How brightly is your light shining? Can others see Christ in your actions?

12:37, 38 Jesus had performed many miracles, but most people still didn't believe in him. Likewise, many today won't believe despite all God does. Don't be discouraged if your witness for Christ doesn't turn as many to him as you'd like. Your job is to continue as a faithful witness. You are responsible to reach out to others, but they are responsible for their own decisions.

12:39–41 People in Jesus' time, like those in the time of Isaiah, would not believe despite the evidence (12:37). As a result, God hardened their hearts. Does that mean God intentionally prevented these people from believing in him? No, he simply confirmed their own choices. After a lifetime of resisting God, they had become so set in their ways that they wouldn't even try to understand Jesus' message. For such people, it is virtually impossible to come to God — their hearts have been permanently hardened. Other instances of hardened hearts because of constant stubbornness are recorded in Exodus 9:12, Romans 1:24–28, and 2 Thessalonians 2:8–12.

12:42, 43 Along with those who refused to believe, many believed but refused to admit it. This is just as bad, and Jesus had strong words for such people (see Matthew 10:32, 33). People who will not take a stand for Jesus are afraid of rejection or ridicule. Many Jewish leaders wouldn't admit to faith in Jesus because they feared excommunication from the synagogue (which was their livelihood) and loss of their prestigious place in the community. But the praise of others is fickle and short-lived. We should be much more concerned about God's eternal acceptance than about the temporary approval of other people.

12:45 We often wonder what God is like. How can we know the Creator when he doesn't make himself visible? Jesus said plainly that those who see him see God, because he *is* God. If you want to know what God is like, study the person and words of Jesus Christ.

12:48 The purpose of Jesus' first mission on earth was not to

12:48
[f]Jn 5:45

the one who rejects me and does not accept my words; that very word which I spoke
will condemn him[f] at the last day. 49For I did not speak of my own accord, but the
Father who sent me commanded me[g] what to say and how to say it. 50I know that
his command leads to eternal life. So whatever I say is just what the Father has told
me to say."

12:49
[g]Jn 14:31

C. DEATH AND RESURRECTION OF JESUS, THE SON OF GOD (13:1–21:25)

John begins his Gospel with eternity and ends with Jesus coming to earth again. He features Jesus teaching his disciples privately just before his arrest and death. We see, clearly, the deep love Jesus has for the believer, and the peace that comes from faith. Knowing the love Jesus has for believers, we too should believe and allow Jesus to forgive our sins. Only then will we experience peace in a world filled with turmoil.

13:1
[a]Jn 11:55
[b]Jn 12:23
[c]Jn 16:28

1. Jesus teaches his disciples

Jesus Washes the Disciples' Feet

(210)

13 It was just before the Passover Feast.[a] Jesus knew that the time had come[b]
for him to leave this world and go to the Father.[c] Having loved his own who
were in the world, he now showed them the full extent of his love.[a]

13:3
[d]Mt 28:18
[e]Jn 8:42; 16:27, 28, 30

2The evening meal was being served, and the devil had already prompted Judas
Iscariot, son of Simon, to betray Jesus. 3Jesus knew that the Father had put all things
under his power,[d] and that he had come from God[e] and was returning to God; 4so
he got up from the meal, took off his outer clothing, and wrapped a towel round his
waist. 5After that, he poured water into a basin and began to wash his disciples' feet,[f]
drying them with the towel that was wrapped round him.

13:5
[f]Lk 7:44

6He came to Simon Peter, who said to him, "Lord, are you going to wash my feet?"
7Jesus replied, "You do not realise now what I am doing, but later you will
understand."[g]
8"No," said Peter, "you shall never wash my feet."
Jesus answered, "Unless I wash you, you have no part with me."

13:7
[g]ver 12

9"Then, Lord," Simon Peter replied, "not just my feet but my hands and my head
as well!"
10Jesus answered, "A person who has had a bath needs only to wash his feet; his
whole body is clean. And you are clean,[h] though not every one of you." 11For he
knew who was going to betray him, and that was why he said not every one was clean.

13:10
[h]Jn 15:3

a *1* Or *he loved them to the last*

---

judge people, but to show them the way to find salvation and eternal life. When he comes again, one of his main purposes will be to judge people for how they lived on earth. Christ's words that we would *not* accept and obey will condemn us. On the day of judgment, those who accepted Jesus and lived his way will be raised to eternal life (1 Corinthians 15:51–57; 1 Thessalonians 4:15–18; Revelation 21:1–8), and those who rejected Jesus and lived any way they pleased will face eternal punishment (Revelation 20:11–15). Decide now which side you'll be on, for the consequences of your decision last for ever.

13:1 Jesus knew he would be betrayed by one of his disciples, disowned by another, and deserted by all of them for a time. Still "he now showed them the full extent of his love". God knows us completely, as Jesus knew his disciples (2:24, 25; 6:64). He knows the sins we have committed and the ones we will yet commit. Still, he loves us. How do you respond to that kind of love?

13:1ff Chapters 13–17 tell us what Jesus said to his disciples on the night before his death. These words were all spoken in one evening when, with only the disciples as his audience, he gave final instructions to prepare them for his death and resurrection, events that would change their lives for ever.

13:1–3 For more information on Judas Iscariot, see his Profile in Mark 14.

13:1–17 Jesus was the model servant, and he showed his servant attitude to his disciples. Washing guests' feet was a job for a household servant to carry out when guests arrived. But Jesus wrapped a towel around his waist, as the lowliest slave would do, and washed and dried his disciples' feet. If even he, God in the flesh, is willing to serve, we his followers must also be servants, willing to serve in any way that glorifies God. Are you willing to follow Christ's example of serving? Whom can you serve today? There is a special blessing for those who not only agree that humble service is Christ's way, but who also follow through and do it (13:17).

13:6, 7 Imagine being Peter and watching Jesus wash the others' feet, all the while moving closer to you. Seeing his Master behave like a slave must have confused Peter. He still did not understand Jesus' teaching that to be a leader, a person must be a servant. This is not a comfortable passage for leaders who find it hard to serve those beneath them. How do you treat those who work under you (whether children, employees, or volunteers)?

12 When he had finished washing their feet, he put on his clothes and returned to
his place. "Do you understand what I have done for you?" he asked them. 13 "You
call me 'Teacher'[i] and 'Lord',[j] and rightly so, for that is what I am. 14 Now that
I, your Lord and Teacher, have washed your feet, you also should wash one another's
feet.[k] 15 I have set you an example that you should do as I have done for you.[l] 16 I
tell you the truth, no servant is greater than his master,[m] nor is a messenger greater
than the one who sent him. 17 Now that you know these things, you will be blessed
if you do them.[n]
18 "I am not referring to all of you;[o] I know those I have chosen.[p] But this is to
fulfil the scripture: 'He who shares my bread[q] has lifted up his heel[r] against me.'[b][s]
19 "I am telling you now before it happens, so that when it does happen you will
believe[t] that I am He.[u] 20 I tell you the truth, whoever accepts anyone I send accepts
me; and whoever accepts me accepts the one who sent me."[v]

Jesus and the Disciples Have the Last Supper
(211/Matthew 26:20–30; Mark 14:17–26; Luke 22:14–30)

21 After he had said this, Jesus was troubled in spirit[w] and testified, "I tell you the
truth, one of you is going to betray me."[x]
22 His disciples stared at one another, at a loss to know which of them he meant.
23 One of them, the disciple whom Jesus loved,[y] was reclining next to him. 24 Simon
Peter motioned to this disciple and said, "Ask him which one he means."
25 Leaning back against Jesus, he asked him, "Lord, who is it?"[z]
26 Jesus answered, "It is the one to whom I will give this piece of bread when I have
dipped it in the dish." Then, dipping the piece of bread, he gave it to Judas Iscariot,
son of Simon. 27 As soon as Judas took the bread, Satan entered into him.[a]
"What you are about to do, do quickly," Jesus told him, 28 but no-one at the meal
understood why Jesus said this to him. 29 Since Judas had charge of the money,[b] some
thought Jesus was telling him to buy what was needed for the Feast, or to give
something to the poor. 30 As soon as Judas had taken the bread, he went out. And it
was night.[c]

Jesus Predicts Peter's Denial
(212/Luke 22:31–38)

31 When he was gone, Jesus said, "Now is the Son of Man glorified[d] and God is
glorified in him.[e] 32 If God is glorified in him,[c] God will glorify the Son in himself,[f]
and will glorify him at once.
33 "My children, I will be with you only a little longer. You will look for me, and
just as I told the Jews, so I tell you now: Where I am going, you cannot come.[g]
34 "A new command[h] I give you: Love one another.[i] As I have loved you, so you

b *18* Psalm 41:9 **c** *32* Many early manuscripts do not have *If God is glorified in him.*

13:13 [i] Jn 11:28 [j] Lk 6:46; 1Co 12:3; Php 2:11
13:14 [k] 1Pe 5:5
13:15 [l] Mt 11:29
13:16 [m] Mt 10:24; Lk 6:40; Jn 15:20
13:17 [n] Mt 7:24, 25; Lk 11:28; Jas 1:25
13:18 [o] ver 10 [p] Jn 15:16, 19 [q] Mt 26:23 [r] Jn 6:70 [s] Ps 41:9
13:19 [t] Jn 14:29; 16:4 [u] Jn 8:24
13:20 [v] Mt 10:40; Lk 10:16
13:21 [w] Jn 12:27 [x] Mt 26:21
13:23 [y] Jn 19:26; 20:2; 21:7, 20
13:25 [z] Jn 21:20
13:27 [a] Lk 22:3
13:29 [b] Jn 12:6
13:30 [c] Lk 22:53
13:31 [d] Jn 7:39 [e] Jn 14:13; 17:4; 1Pe 4:11
13:32 [f] Jn 17:1
13:33 [g] Jn 7:33, 34
13:34 [h] 1Jn 2:7-11; 3:11 [i] Lev 19:18; 1Th 4:9; 1Pe 1:22

13:12ff Jesus did not wash his disciples' feet just to get them to be nice to each other. His far greater goal was to extend his mission on earth after he was gone. These men were to move into the world serving God, serving each other, and serving all people to whom they took the message of salvation.

13:22 Judas was not the obvious betrayer. After all, he was the one the disciples trusted to keep the money (12:6; 13:29).

13:26 The honoured guest at a meal was often singled out like this.

13:27 Satan's part in the betrayal of Jesus does not remove any of the responsibility from Judas. Disillusioned because Jesus was talking about dying rather than setting up his kingdom, Judas may have been trying to force Jesus' hand and make him use his power to prove he was the Messiah. Or perhaps Judas, not understanding Jesus' mission, no longer believed Jesus was God's chosen one. Whatever Judas thought, Satan assumed that Jesus' death would end his mission and thwart God's plan. Like Judas, Satan did not know that Jesus' death was the most important part of God's plan all along.

13:27–38 John describes these few moments in clear detail. We can see that Jesus knew exactly what was going to happen. He knew about Judas and about Peter, but he did not change the situation, nor did he stop loving them. In the same way, Jesus knows exactly what you will do to hurt him. Yet he still loves you unconditionally and will forgive you whenever you ask for it. Judas couldn't understand this, and his life ended tragically. Peter understood, and despite his shortcomings, his life ended triumphantly because he never let go of his faith in the One who loved him.

13:34 To love others was not a new commandment (see Leviticus 19:18), but to love others as much as Christ loved others was revolutionary. Now we are to love others based on Jesus' sacrificial love for us. Such love will not only bring unbelievers to Christ; it will also keep believers strong and united in a world hostile to God. Jesus was a living example of God's love, as we are to be living examples of Jesus' love.

13:34, 35 Jesus says that our Christlike love will show we are his disciples. Do people see petty bickering, jealousy, and division in your church? Or do they know you are Jesus'

13:34 [j]Jn 15:12; Eph 5:2; 1Jn 4:10, 11
13:35 [k]1Jn 3:14; 4:20
13:36 [l]ver 33; Jn 14:2 [m]Jn 21:18, 19; 2Pe 1:14
13:38 [n]Jn 18:27

must love one another.[j] 35By this all men will know that you are my disciples, if
you love one another."[k]
36Simon Peter asked him, "Lord, where are you going?"
Jesus replied, "Where I am going, you cannot follow now,[l] but you will follow
later."[m]
37Peter asked, "Lord, why can't I follow you now? I will lay down my life for you."
38Then Jesus answered, "Will you really lay down your life for me? I tell you the
truth, before the cock crows, you will disown me three times![n]

JOHN

Being loved is the most powerful motivation in the world! Our ability to love is often shaped by our experience of love. We usually love others as we have been loved.

Some of the greatest statements about God's loving nature were written by a man who experienced God's love in a unique way. John, Jesus' disciple, expressed his relationship to the Son of God by calling himself "the disciple whom Jesus loved" (John 21:20). Although Jesus' love is clearly communicated in all the Gospels, in John's Gospel it is a central theme. Because his own experience of Jesus' love was so strong and personal, John was sensitive to those words and actions of Jesus that illustrated how the One who *is* love loved others.

Jesus knew John fully and loved him fully. He gave John and his brother James the nickname "Sons of Thunder", perhaps from an occasion when the brothers asked Jesus for permission to "call fire down from heaven" (Luke 9:54) on a village that had refused to welcome Jesus and the disciples. In John's Gospel and letters, we see the great God of love, while the thunder of God's justice bursts from the pages of Revelation.

Jesus confronts each of us as he confronted John. We cannot know the depth of Jesus' love unless we are willing to face the fact that he knows us completely. Otherwise we are fooled into believing he must love the people we pretend to be, not the sinners we actually are. John and all the disciples convince us that God is able and willing to accept us as we are. Being aware of God's love is a great motivator for change. His love is not given in exchange for our efforts; his love frees us to really live. Have you accepted that love?

Strengths and accomplishments:
- Before following Jesus, one of John the Baptist's disciples
- One of the 12 disciples and, with Peter and James, one of the inner three, closest to Jesus
- Wrote five New Testament books: the Gospel of John; 1, 2, and 3 John; and Revelation

Weaknesses and mistakes:
- Along with James, shared a tendency to outbursts of selfishness and anger
- Asked for a special position in Jesus' kingdom

Lessons from his life:
- Those who realise how much they are loved are able to love much
- When God changes a life, he does not take away personality characteristics, but puts them to effective use in his service

Vital statistics:
- Occupations: Fisherman, disciple
- Relatives: Father: Zebedee. Mother: Salome. Brother: James
- Contemporaries: Jesus, Pilate, Herod

Key verses:
"Dear friends, I am not writing you a new command but an old one, which you have had since the beginning. This old command is the message you have heard. Yet I am writing you a new command; its truth is seen in him and you, because the darkness is passing and the true light is already shining" (1 John 2:7, 8).

John's story is told throughout the Gospels, Acts, and Revelation.

---

followers by your love for one another?

13:35 Love is more than simply warm feelings; it is an attitude that reveals itself in action. How can we love others as Jesus loves us? By helping when it's not convenient, by giving when it hurts, by devoting energy to others' welfare rather than our own, by absorbing hurts from others without complaining or fighting back. This kind of loving is hard to do. That is why people notice when you do it and know you are empowered by a supernatural source. The Bible has another beautiful description of love in 1 Corinthians 13.

13:37, 38 Peter proudly told Jesus that he was ready to die for him. But Jesus corrected him. He knew Peter would deny that he knew Jesus that very night to protect himself (18:25–27). In our enthusiasm, it is easy to make promises, but God knows the extent of our commitment. Paul tells us not to think of ourselves more highly than we ought (Romans 12:3). Instead of bragging, demonstrate your commitment step by step as you grow in your knowledge of God's word and in your faith.

Jesus Is the Way to the Father
(213)

14 "Do not let your hearts be troubled.[a] Trust in God;[**a**] trust also in me. 2 In my
Father's house are many rooms; if it were not so, I would have told you. I am
going there[b] to prepare a place for you. 3 And if I go and prepare a place for you,
I will come back and take you to be with me that you also may be where I am.[c] 4 You
know the way to the place where I am going."
5 Thomas[d] said to him, "Lord, we don't know where you are going, so how can
we know the way?"
6 Jesus answered, "I am the way[e] and the truth and the life.[f] No-one comes to
the Father except through me. 7 If you really knew me, you would know[**b**] my Father
as well.[g] From now on, you do know him and have seen him."
8 Philip said, "Lord, show us the Father and that will be enough for us."
9 Jesus answered: "Don't you know me, Philip, even after I have been among you
such a long time? Anyone who has seen me has seen the Father.[h] How can you say,
'Show us the Father'? 10 Don't you believe that I am in the Father, and that the Father
is in me?[i] The words I say to you are not just my own.[j] Rather, it is the Father,
living in me, who is doing his work. 11 Believe me when I say that I am in the Father
and the Father is in me; or at least believe on the evidence of the miracles themselves.[k]
12 I tell you the truth, anyone who has faith[l] in me will do what I have been doing.[m]
He will do even greater things than these, because I am going to the Father. 13 And
I will do whatever you ask[n] in my name, so that the Son may bring glory to the Father.
14 You may ask me for anything in my name, and I will do it.

Jesus Promises the Holy Spirit
(214)

15 "If you love me, you will obey what I command.[o] 16 And I will ask the Father,
and he will give you another Counsellor[p] to be with you for ever—17 the Spirit of

a *1* Or *You trust in God* **b** *7* Some early manuscripts *If you really have known me, you will know*

14:1 [a]ver 27
14:2 [b]Jn 13:33, 36
14:3 [c]Jn 12:26
14:5 [d]Jn 11:16
14:6 [e]Jn 10:9 [f]Jn 11:25
14:7 [g]Jn 8:19
14:9 [h]Jn 12:45; Col 1:15; Heb 1:3
14:10 [i]Jn 10:38 [j]Jn 5:19
14:11 [k]Jn 5:36; 10:38
14:12 [l]Mt 21:21 [m]Lk 10:17
14:13 [n]Mt 7:7
14:15 [o]ver 21, 23; Jn 15:10; 1Jn 5:3
14:16 [p]Jn 15:26; 16:7

14:1–3 Jesus' words show that the way to eternal life, though unseen, is secure—as secure as your trust in Jesus. He has already prepared the way to eternal life. The only issue that may still be unsettled is your willingness to believe.

14:2, 3 There are few verses in Scripture that describe eternal life, but these few verses are rich with promises. Here Jesus says, "I am going there to prepare a place for you," and "I will come back." We can look forward to eternal life because Jesus has promised it to all who believe in him. Although the details of eternity are unknown, we need not fear because Jesus is preparing for us and will spend eternity with us.

14:5, 6 This is one of the most basic and important passages in Scripture. How can we know the way to God? Only through Jesus. Jesus is the way because he is both God and man. By uniting our lives with his, we are united with God. Trust Jesus to take you to the Father, and all the benefits of being God's child will be yours.

14:6 Jesus says he is the *only* way to God the Father. Some people may argue that this way is too narrow. In reality, it is wide enough for the whole world, if the world chooses to accept it. Instead of worrying about how limited it sounds to have only one way, we should be saying, "Thank you, God, for providing a sure way to get to you!"

14:6 As the *way,* Jesus is our path to the Father. As the *truth,* he is the reality of all God's promises. As the *life,* he joins his divine life to ours, both now and eternally.

14:9 Jesus is the visible, tangible image of the invisible God. He is the complete revelation of what God is like. Jesus explained to Philip, who wanted to see the Father, that to know Jesus is to know God. The search for God, for truth and reality, ends in Christ. (See also Colossians 1:15; Hebrews 1:1–4.)

14:12, 13 Jesus is not saying that his disciples would do more amazing miracles—after all, raising the dead is about as amazing as you can get. Rather, the disciples, working in the power of the Holy Spirit, would carry the gospel of God's kingdom out of Palestine and into the whole world.

14:14 When Jesus says we can ask for anything, we must remember that our asking must be in his name—that is, according to God's character and will. God will not grant requests contrary to his nature or his will, and we cannot use his name as a magic formula to fulfil our selfish desires. If we are sincerely following God and seeking to do his will, then our requests will be in line with what he wants, and he will grant them. (See also 15:16; 16:23.)

14:15, 16 Jesus was soon going to leave the disciples, but he would remain with them. How could this be? The Counsellor—the Spirit of God himself—would come after Jesus was gone to care for and guide the disciples. The regenerating power of the Spirit came on the disciples just before Jesus' ascension (20:22), and the Spirit was poured out on all the believers at Pentecost (Acts 2), shortly after Jesus ascended to heaven. The Holy Spirit is the very presence of God within us and all believers, helping us live as God wants and building Christ's church on earth. By faith we can appropriate the Spirit's power each day.

14:16 The word translated *Counsellor* combines the ideas of comfort and counsel. The Holy Spirit is a powerful person on our side, working for and with us.

14:17ff The following chapters teach these truths about the Holy Spirit: he will be with us for ever (14:16); the world at large cannot accept him (14:17); he lives with us and in us (14:17); he teaches us (14:26); he reminds us of Jesus' words (14:26; 15:26); he convicts us of sin, shows us God's righteousness, and announces God's judgment on evil (16:8); he guides into truth and gives insight into future events (16:13); he brings glory to Christ (16:14). The Holy Spirit has been active among people from the beginning

14:17 [q]Jn 15:26; 16:13; 1Jn 4:6 [r]1Co 2:14
14:18 [s]ver 3, 28
14:19 [t]Jn 7:33, 34; 16:16 [u]Jn 6:57
14:20 [v]Jn 10:38
14:21 [w]1Jn 5:3 [x]1Jn 2:5
14:22 [y]Lk 6:16; Ac 1:13 [z]Ac 10:41
14:23 [a]ver 15 [b]1Jn 2:24; Rev 3:20
14:24 [c]Jn 7:16
14:26 [d]Jn 15:26; 16:7 [e]Ac 2:33 [f]Jn 16:13; 1Jn 2:20, 27 [g]Jn 2:22
14:27 [h]Jn 16:33
14:28 [i]ver 2-4, 18 [j]Jn 5:18 [k]Jn 10:29
14:29 [l]Jn 13:19; 16:4
14:30 [m]Jn 12:31
14:31 [n]Jn 10:18; 12:49

truth.[q] The world cannot accept him,[r] because it neither sees him nor knows him.
But you know him, for he lives with you and will be[c] in you. 18 I will not leave you
as orphans; I will come to you.[s] 19 Before long, the world will not see me any more,
but you will see me.[t] Because I live, you also will live.[u] 20 On that day you will
realise that I am in my Father,[v] and you are in me, and I am in you. 21 Whoever has
my commands and obeys them, he is the one who loves me.[w] He who loves me will
be loved by my Father,[x] and I too will love him and show myself to him."
22 Then Judas[y] (not Judas Iscariot) said, "But, Lord, why do you intend to show
yourself to us and not to the world?"[z]
23 Jesus replied, "If anyone loves me, he will obey my teaching.[a] My Father will
love him, and we will come to him and make our home with him.[b] 24 He who does
not love me will not obey my teaching. These words you hear are not my own; they
belong to the Father who sent me.[c]
25 "All this I have spoken while still with you. 26 But the Counsellor,[d] the Holy
Spirit, whom the Father will send in my name,[e] will teach you all things[f] and will
remind you of everything I have said to you.[g] 27 Peace I leave with you; my peace
I give you.[h] I do not give to you as the world gives. Do not let your hearts be troubled
and do not be afraid.
28 "You heard me say, 'I am going away and I am coming back to you.'[i] If you
loved me, you would be glad that I am going to the Father,[j] for the Father is greater
than I.[k] 29 I have told you now before it happens, so that when it does happen you
will believe.[l] 30 I will not speak with you much longer, for the prince of this world[m]
is coming. He has no hold on me, 31 but the world must learn that I love the Father
and that I do exactly what my Father has commanded me.[n]
"Come now; let us leave.

c *17* Some early manuscripts *and is*

---

of time, but after Pentecost (Acts 2) he came to live in all believers. Many people are unaware of the Holy Spirit's activities, but to those who hear Christ's words and understand the Spirit's power, the Spirit gives a whole new way to look at life.

14:18 When Jesus said, "I will come to you," he meant it. Although Jesus ascended to heaven, he sent the Holy Spirit to live in believers, and to have the Holy Spirit is to have Jesus himself.

14:19–21 Sometimes people wish they knew the future so they could prepare for it. God has chosen not to give us this knowledge. He alone knows what will happen, but he tells us all we need to know to *prepare* for the future. When we live by his standards, he will not leave us; he will come to us, he will be in us, and he will show himself to us. God knows what will happen and, because he will be with us through it all, we need not fear. We don't have to know the future to have faith in God; we have to have faith in God to be secure about the future.

14:21 Jesus said that his followers show their love for him by obeying him. Love is more than lovely words; it is commitment and conduct. If you love Christ, then prove it by obeying what he says in his word.

14:22, 23 Because the disciples were still expecting Jesus to establish an earthly kingdom and overthrow Rome, they found it hard to understand why he did not tell the world at large that he was the Messiah. Not everyone, however, could understand Jesus' message. Ever since Pentecost, the gospel of the kingdom has been proclaimed in the whole world, and yet not everyone is receptive to it. Jesus saves the deepest revelations of himself for those who love and obey him.

14:26 Jesus promised the disciples that the Holy Spirit would help them remember what he had been teaching them. This promise ensures the validity of the New Testament. The disciples were eyewitnesses of Jesus' life and teachings, and the Holy Spirit helped them remember without taking away their individual perspectives. We can be confident that the Gospels are accurate records of what Jesus taught and did (see 1 Corinthians 2:10–14). The Holy Spirit can help us in the same way. As we study the Bible, we can trust him to plant truth in our mind, convince us of God's will, and remind us when we stray from it.

14:27 The end result of the Holy Spirit's work in our lives is deep and lasting peace. Unlike worldly peace, which is usually defined as the absence of conflict, this peace is confident assurance in any circumstance; with Christ's peace, we have no need to fear the present or the future. If your life is full of stress, allow the Holy Spirit to fill you with Christ's peace (see Philippians 4:6, 7 for more on experiencing God's peace).

14:27–29 Sin, fear, uncertainty, doubt, and numerous other forces are at war within us. The peace of God moves into our hearts and lives to restrain these hostile forces and offer comfort in place of conflict. Jesus says he will give us that peace if we are willing to accept it from him.

14:28 As God the Son, Jesus willingly submits to God the Father. On earth, Jesus also submitted to many of the physical limitations of his humanity (Philippians 2:6).

14:30, 31 Although Satan, the prince of this world, was unable to overpower Jesus (Matthew 4), he still had the arrogance to try. Satan's power exists only because God allows him to act. But because Jesus is sinless, Satan has no power over him. If we obey Jesus and align ourselves closely with God's purposes, Satan can have no power over us.

14:31 "Come now; let us leave" suggests that chapters 15 – 17 may have been spoken en route to the Garden of Gethsemane. Another view is that Jesus was asking the disciples to get ready to leave the upper room, but they did not actually do so until 18:1.

Jesus Teaches about the Vine and the Branches
(215)

15 "I am the true vine,[a] and my Father is the gardener. 2He cuts off every branch
in me that bears no fruit, while every branch that does bear fruit he prunes[a]
so that it will be even more fruitful. 3You are already clean because of the word I have
spoken to you.[b] 4Remain in me, and I will remain in you.[c] No branch can bear fruit
by itself; it must remain in the vine. Neither can you bear fruit unless you remain in
me.
5"I am the vine; you are the branches. If a man remains in me and I in him, he will
bear much fruit;[d] apart from me you can do nothing. 6If anyone does not remain in
me, he is like a branch that is thrown away and withers; such branches are picked up,
thrown into the fire and burned.[e] 7If you remain in me and my words remain in you,
ask whatever you wish, and it will be given you.[f] 8This is to my Father's glory,[g]
that you bear much fruit, showing yourselves to be my disciples.[h]
9"As the Father has loved me,[i] so have I loved you. Now remain in my love. 10If
you obey my commands,[j] you will remain in my love, just as I have obeyed my
Father's commands and remain in his love. 11I have told you this so that my joy may
be in you and that your joy may be complete.[k] 12My command is this: Love each
other as I have loved you.[l] 13Greater love has no-one than this, that he lay down
his life for his friends.[m] 14You are my friends[n] if you do what I command.[o] 15I no
longer call you servants, because a servant does not know his master's business.
Instead, I have called you friends, for everything that I learned from my Father I have
made known to you.[p] 16You did not choose me, but I chose you and appointed you[q]
to go and bear fruit—fruit that will last. Then the Father will give you whatever you
ask in my name. 17This is my command: Love each other.[r]

a *2* The Greek for *prunes* also means *cleans*.

15:1 [a] Isa 5:1-7
15:3 [b] Jn 13:10; 17:17; Eph 5:26
15:4 [c] Jn 6:56; 1Jn 2:6
15:5 [d] ver 16
15:6 [e] ver 2
15:7 [f] Mt 7:7
15:8 [g] Mt 5:16 [h] Jn 8:31
15:9 [i] Jn 17:23, 24, 26
15:10 [j] Jn 14:15
15:11 [k] Jn 17:13
15:12 [l] Jn 13:34
15:13 [m] Jn 10:11; Ro 5:7, 8
15:14 [n] Lk 12:4 [o] Mt 12:50
15:15 [p] Jn 8:26
15:16 [q] Jn 6:70; 13:18
15:17 [r] ver 12

15:1 The grapevine is a prolific plant; a single vine bears many grapes. In the Old Testament, grapes symbolised Israel's fruitfulness in doing God's work on the earth (Psalm 80:8; Isaiah 5:1–7; Ezekiel 19:10–14). In the Passover meal, the fruit of the vine symbolised God's goodness to his people.

15:1ff Christ is the vine, and God is the gardener who cares for the branches to make them fruitful. The branches are all those who claim to be followers of Christ. The fruitful branches are true believers who by their living union with Christ produce much fruit. But those who become unproductive—those who turn back from following Christ after making a superficial commitment—will be separated from the vine. Unproductive followers are as good as dead and will be cut off and tossed aside.

15:2, 3 Jesus makes a distinction between two kinds of pruning: (1) separating and (2) cutting back branches. Fruitful branches are cut back to promote growth. In other words, God must sometimes discipline us to strengthen our character and faith. But branches that don't bear fruit are cut off at the trunk because not only are they worthless, but they often infect the rest of the tree. People who won't bear fruit for God or who try to block the efforts of God's followers will be cut off from his life-giving power.

15:5 Fruit is not limited to soulwinning. In this chapter, answered prayer, joy, and love are mentioned as fruit (15:7, 11, 12). Galatians 5:22–24 and 2 Peter 1:5–8 describe additional fruit: qualities of Christian character.

15:5, 6 Remaining in Christ means (1) believing that he is God's Son (1 John 4:15), (2) receiving him as Saviour and Lord (John 1:12), (3) doing what God says (1 John 3:24), (4) continuing to believe the gospel (1 John 2:24), and (5) relating in love to the community of believers, Christ's body (John 15:12).

15:5–8 Many people try to be good, honest people who do what is right. But Jesus says that the only way to live a truly good life is to stay close to him, like a branch attached to the vine. Apart from Christ our efforts are unfruitful. Are you receiving the nourishment and life offered by Christ, the vine? If not, you are missing a special gift he has for you.

15:8 When a vine bears "much fruit", God is glorified, for daily he sent the sunshine and rain to make the crops grow, and constantly he nurtured each tiny plant and prepared it to blossom. What a moment of glory for the Lord of the harvest when the harvest is brought into the barns, mature and ready for use! He made it all happen! This farming analogy shows how God is glorified when people come into a right relationship with him and begin to "bear much fruit" in their lives.

15:11 When things are going well, we feel elated. When hardships come, we sink into depression. But true joy transcends the rolling waves of circumstance. Joy comes from a consistent relationship with Jesus Christ. When our lives are intertwined with his, he will help us walk through adversity without sinking into debilitating lows and manage prosperity without moving into deceptive highs. The joy of living with Jesus Christ daily will keep us level-headed, no matter how high or low our circumstances.

15:12, 13 We are to love each other as Jesus loved us, and he loved us enough to give his life for us. We may not have to die for someone, but there are other ways to practice sacrificial love: listening, helping, encouraging, giving. Think of someone in particular who needs this kind of love today. Give all the love you can, and then try to give a little more.

15:15 Because Jesus Christ is Lord and Master, he should call us servants; instead he calls us friends. How comforting and reassuring to be chosen as Christ's friends. Because he is Lord and Master, we owe him our unqualified obedience, but most of all, Jesus asks us to obey him because we love him.

15:16 Jesus made the first choice—to love and to die for us, to invite us to live with him for ever. We make the next choice—to accept or reject his offer. Without *his* choice, we would have no choice to make.

15:17 Christians will get plenty of hatred from the world; from each other we need love and support. Do you allow small problems to get in the way of loving other believers? Jesus commands

Jesus Warns about the World's Hatred
(216)

18“If the world hates you,[s] keep in mind that it hated me first. 19If you belonged
to the world, it would love you as its own. As it is, you do not belong to the world,
but I have chosen you[t] out of the world. That is why the world hates you.[u]
20Remember the words I spoke to you: ‘No servant is greater than his master.’[b][v]
If they persecuted me, they will persecute you also.[w] If they obeyed my teaching,
they will obey yours also. 21They will treat you this way because of my name,[x] for
they do not know the One who sent me.[y] 22If I had not come and spoken to them,
they would not be guilty of sin. Now, however, they have no excuse for their sin.[z]
23He who hates me hates my Father as well. 24If I had not done among them what
no-one else did,[a] they would not be guilty of sin. But now they have seen these
miracles, and yet they have hated both me and my Father. 25But this is to fulfil what
is written in their Law: ‘They hated me without reason.’[c][b]
26“When the Counsellor[c] comes, whom I will send to you from the Father,[d] the
Spirit of truth[e] who goes out from the Father, he will testify about me.[f] 27And you
also must testify,[g] for you have been with me from the beginning.[h]

16 “All this[a] I have told you so that you will not go astray.[b] 2They will put you
out of the synagogue;[c] in fact, a time is coming when anyone who kills you
will think he is offering a service to God.[d] 3They will do such things because they
have not known the Father or me.[e] 4I have told you this, so that when the time comes
you will remember[f] that I warned you. I did not tell you this at first because I was
with you.

Jesus Teaches about the Holy Spirit
(217)

5“Now I am going to him who sent me,[g] yet none of you asks me, ‘Where are
you going?’[h] 6Because I have said these things, you are filled with grief. 7But I tell
you the truth: It is for your good that I am going away. Unless I go away, the
Counsellor[i] will not come to you; but if I go, I will send him to you.[j] 8When he
comes, he will convict the world of guilt[a] in regard to sin and righteousness and
judgment: 9in regard to sin,[k] because men do not believe in me; 10in regard to
righteousness,[l] because I am going to the Father, where you can see me no longer;
11and in regard to judgment, because the prince of this world[m] now stands condemned.

15:18 [s]1Jn 3:13
15:19 [t]ver 16 [u]Jn 17:14
15:20 [v]Jn 13:16 [w]2Ti 3:12
15:21 [x]Mt 10:22 [y]Jn 16:3
15:22 [z]Jn 9:41; Ro 1:20
15:24 [a]Jn 5:36
15:25 [b]Ps 35:19; 69:4
15:26 [c]Jn 14:16 [d]Jn 14:26 [e]Jn 14:17 [f]1Jn 5:7
15:27 [g]Lk 24:48; 1Jn 1:2; 4:14 [h]Lk 1:2
16:1 [a]Jn 15:18-27 [b]Mt 11:6
16:2 [c]Jn 9:22 [d]Isa 66:5; Ac 26:9, 10; Rev 6:9
16:3 [e]Jn 15:21; 17:25; 1Jn 3:1
16:4 [f]Jn 13:19
16:5 [g]Jn 7:33 [h]Jn 13:36; 14:5
16:7 [i]Jn 14:16, 26; 15:26 [j]Jn 7:39
16:9 [k]Jn 15:22
16:10 [l]Ac 3:14; 7:52; 1Pe 3:18
16:11 [m]Jn 12:31

[b] *20* John 13:16 [c] *25* Psalms 35:19; 69:4 [a] *8* Or *will expose the guilt of the world*

---

that you love them, and he will give you the strength to do it.

15:26 Once again Jesus offers hope. The Holy Spirit gives strength to endure the unreasonable hatred and evil in our world and the hostility many have towards Christ. This is especially comforting for those facing persecution.

15:26 Jesus uses two names for the Holy Spirit – *Counsellor* and *Spirit of truth.* The word *Counsellor* conveys the helping, encouraging, and strengthening work of the Spirit. *Spirit of truth* points to the teaching, illuminating, and reminding work of the Spirit. The Holy Spirit ministers to both the head and the heart, and both dimensions are important.

16:1–16 In his last moments with his disciples, Jesus (1) warned them about further persecution, (2) told them where, when, and why he was going, and (3) assured them that they would not be left alone, but that the Spirit would come. Jesus knew what lay ahead, and he did not want the disciples' faith shaken or destroyed. God wants you to know you are not alone. You have the Holy Spirit to comfort you, teach you truth, and help you.

16:2 Saul (who later became Paul), under the authority of the high priest, went through the land hunting down and persecuting Christians, convinced that he was doing the right thing (Acts 9:1, 2; 26:9–11).

16:5 Although the disciples had asked Jesus about his death (13:36; 14:5), they had never wondered about its meaning. They were mostly concerned about themselves. If Jesus went away, what would become of them?

16:7 Unless Jesus did what he came to do, there would be no gospel. If he did not die, he could not remove our sins; he could not rise again and defeat death. If he did not go back to the Father, the Holy Spirit would not come. Christ's presence on earth was limited to one place at a time. His leaving meant he could be present to the whole world through the Holy Spirit.

16:8–11 Three important tasks of the Holy Spirit are (1) convicting the world of its sin and calling it to repentance, (2) revealing the standard of God's righteousness to anyone who believes, because Christ would no longer be physically present on earth, and (3) demonstrating Christ's judgment over Satan.

16:9 According to Jesus, not believing in him is *sin.*

16:10, 11 Christ's death on the cross made a personal relationship with God available to us. When we confess our sin, God declares us righteous and delivers us from judgment for our sins.

12“I have much more to say to you, more than you can now bear.[n] 13But when
he, the Spirit of truth,[o] comes, he will guide you into all truth.[p] He will not speak
on his own; he will speak only what he hears, and he will tell you what is yet to come.
14He will bring glory to me by taking from what is mine and making it known to you.
15All that belongs to the Father is mine.[q] That is why I said the Spirit will take from
what is mine and make it known to you.

Jesus Teaches about Using His Name in Prayer
(218)

16“In a little while[r] you will see me no more, and then after a little while you will
see me.”[s]
17Some of his disciples said to one another, “What does he mean by saying, ‘In
a little while you will see me no more, and then after a little while you will see me,’[t]
and ‘Because I am going to the Father’?”[u] 18They kept asking, “What does he mean
by ‘a little while’? We don’t understand what he is saying.”
19Jesus saw that they wanted to ask him about this, so he said to them, “Are you
asking one another what I meant when I said, ‘In a little while you will see me no
more, and then after a little while you will see me’? 20I tell you the truth, you will
weep and mourn[v] while the world rejoices. You will grieve, but your grief will turn
to joy.[w] 21A woman giving birth to a child has pain[x] because her time has come;
but when her baby is born she forgets the anguish because of her joy that a child is
born into the world. 22So with you: Now is your time of grief,[y] but I will see you
again[z] and you will rejoice, and no-one will take away your joy. 23In that day you
will no longer ask me anything. I tell you the truth, my Father will give you whatever
you ask in my name.[a] 24Until now you have not asked for anything in my name. Ask
and you will receive, and your joy will be complete.[b]
25“Though I have been speaking figuratively,[c] a time is coming[d] when I will no
longer use this kind of language but will tell you plainly about my Father. 26In that
day you will ask in my name.[e] I am not saying that I will ask the Father on your
behalf. 27No, the Father himself loves you because you have loved me[f] and have
believed that I came from God. 28I came from the Father and entered the world; now
I am leaving the world and going back to the Father.”[g]
29Then Jesus’ disciples said, “Now you are speaking clearly and without figures
of speech.[h] 30Now we can see that you know all things and that you do not even need
to have anyone ask you questions. This makes us believe that you came from God.”
31“You believe at last!”**b** Jesus answered. 32“But a time is coming,[i] and has come,
when you will be scattered,[j] each to his own home. You will leave me all alone.
Yet I am not alone, for my Father is with me.[k]

b *31* Or *“Do you now believe?”*

16:12 [n]Mk 4:33
16:13 [o]Jn 14:17 [p]Jn 14:26
16:15 [q]Jn 17:10
16:16 [r]Jn 7:33 [s]Jn 14:18-24
16:17 [t]ver 16 [u]ver 5
16:20 [v]Lk 23:27 [w]Jn 20:20
16:21 [x]Isa 26:17; 1Th 5:3
16:22 [y]ver 6 [z]ver 16
16:23 [a]Mt 7:7; Jn 15:16
16:24 [b]Jn 3:29; 15:11
16:25 [c]Mt 13:34; Jn 10:6 [d]ver 2
16:26 [e]ver 23, 24
16:27 [f]Jn 14:21, 23
16:28 [g]Jn 13:3
16:29 [h]ver 25
16:32 [i]ver 2, 25 [j]Mt 26:31 [k]Jn 8:16, 29

16:13 The truth into which the Holy Spirit guides us is the truth about Christ. The Spirit also helps us through patient practice to discern right from wrong.

16:13 Jesus said the Holy Spirit would tell them “what is yet to come” – the nature of their mission, the opposition they would face, and the final outcome of their efforts. They didn’t fully understand these promises until the Holy Spirit came after Jesus’ death and resurrection. Then the Holy Spirit revealed truths to the disciples that they wrote down in the books that now form the New Testament.

16:16 Jesus was referring to his death, now only a few hours away, and his resurrection three days later.

16:20 What a contrast between the disciples and the world! The world rejoiced as the disciples wept, but the disciples would see him again (in three days) and rejoice. The world’s values are often the opposite of God’s values. This can cause Christians to feel like misfits. But even if life is difficult now, one day we will rejoice. Keep your eye on the future and on God’s promises!

16:23–27 Jesus is talking about a new relationship between the believer and God. Previously, people approached God through priests. After Jesus’ resurrection, any believer could approach God directly. A new day has dawned and now all believers are priests, talking with God personally and directly (see Hebrews 10:19–23). We approach God, not because of our own merit, but because Jesus, our great high priest, has made us acceptable to God.

16:30 The disciples believed Jesus’ words because they were convinced that he knew everything. But their belief was only a first step towards the great faith they would receive when the Holy Spirit came to live in them.

16:31–33 As Christians, we should expect continuing tension with an unbelieving world that is “out of sync” with Christ, his gospel, and his people. At the same time, we can expect our relationship with Christ to produce peace and comfort because we are “in sync” with him.

16:32 The disciples scattered after Jesus was arrested (see Mark 14:50).

33“I have told you these things, so that in me you may have peace.[l] In this world
you will have trouble.[m] But take heart! I have overcome[n] the world.”

Jesus Prays for Himself
(219)

17 After Jesus said this, he looked towards heaven[a] and prayed:

“Father, the time has come. Glorify your Son, that your Son may glorify you.[b]
2For you granted him authority over all people that he might give eternal life to
all those you have given him.[c] 3Now this is eternal life: that they may know
you, the only true God, and Jesus Christ, whom you have sent.[d] 4I have brought
you glory[e] on earth by completing the work you gave me to do.[f] 5And now,
Father, glorify me in your presence with the glory I had with you[g] before the
world began.[h]

Jesus Prays for His Disciples
(220)

6“I have revealed you[a][i] to those whom you gave me[j] out of the world. They
were yours; you gave them to me and they have obeyed your word. 7Now they know
that everything you have given me comes from you. 8For I gave them the words you
gave me[k] and they accepted them. They knew with certainty that I came from you,[l]
and they believed that you sent me.[m] 9I pray for them.[n] I am not praying for the
world, but for those you have given me, for they are yours. 10All I have is yours, and
all you have is mine.[o] And glory has come to me through them. 11I will remain in
the world no longer, but they are still in the world,[p] and I am coming to you.[q] Holy
Father, protect them by the power of your name—the name you gave me—so that
they may be one[r] as we are one.[s] 12While I was with them, I protected them and
kept them safe by that name you gave me. None has been lost[t] except the one doomed
to destruction[u] so that Scripture would be fulfilled.

13“I am coming to you now, but I say these things while I am still in the world,
so that they may have the full measure of my joy[v] within them. 14I have given them
your word and the world has hated them,[w] for they are not of the world any more
than I am of the world.[x] 15My prayer is not that you take them out of the world but
that you protect them from the evil one.[y] 16They are not of the world, even as I am

[a] 6 Greek *your name*; also in verse 26

16:33 [l]Jn 14:27 [m]Jn 15:18-21 [n]Ro 8:37; 1Jn 4:4
17:1 [a]Jn 11:41 [b]Jn 12:23; 13:31, 32
17:2 [c]ver 6, 9, 24; Da 7:14; Jn 6:37, 39
17:3 [d]ver 8, 18, 21, 23, 25; Jn 3:17
17:4 [e]Jn 13:31 [f]Jn 4:34
17:5 [g]Php 2:6 [h]Jn 1:2
17:6 [i]ver 26 [j]ver 2; Jn 6:37, 39
17:8 [k]ver 14, 26 [l]Jn 16:27 [m]ver 3, 18, 21, 23, 25; Jn 3:17
17:9 [n]Lk 22:32
17:10 [o]Jn 16:15
17:11 [p]Jn 13:1 [q]Jn 7:33 [r]ver 21-23 [s]Jn 10:30
17:12 [t]Jn 6:39 [u]Jn 6:70
17:13 [v]Jn 3:29
17:14 [w]Jn 15:19 [x]Jn 8:23
17:15 [y]Mt 5:37

16:33 Jesus summed up all he had told them this night, tying together themes from 14:27–29; 16:1–4; and 16:9–11. With these words he told his disciples to take courage. In spite of the inevitable struggles they would face, they would not be alone. Jesus does not abandon us to our struggles either. If we remember that the ultimate victory has already been won, we can claim the peace of Christ in the most troublesome times.

17:1ff This entire chapter is Jesus' prayer. From it, we learn that the world is a tremendous battleground where the forces under Satan's power and those under God's authority are at war. Satan and his forces are motivated by bitter hatred for Christ and his forces. Jesus prayed for his disciples, including those of us who follow him today. He prayed that God would keep his chosen believers safe from Satan's power, setting them apart and making them pure and holy, uniting them through his truth.

17:3 How do we get eternal life? Jesus tells us clearly here—by knowing God the Father himself through his Son, Jesus Christ. Eternal life requires entering into a personal relationship with God in Jesus Christ. When we admit our sin and turn away from it, Christ's love lives in us by the Holy Spirit.

17:5 Before Jesus came to earth, he was one with God. At this point, when his mission on earth was almost finished, Jesus was asking his Father to restore him to his original place of honour and authority. Jesus' resurrection and ascension—and Stephen's dying exclamation (Acts 7:56)—attest that Jesus did return to his exalted position at the right hand of God.

17:10 What did Jesus mean when he said "glory has come to me through them"? God's glory is the revelation of his character and presence. The lives of Jesus' disciples reveal his character, and he is present to the world through them. Does your life reveal Jesus' character and presence?

17:11 Jesus was asking that the disciples be united in harmony and love as the Father, Son, and Holy Spirit are united—the strongest of all unions. (See the notes on 17:21–23.)

17:12 Judas was the "one doomed to destruction", who was lost because he betrayed Jesus (see Psalm 41:9).

17:13 Joy is a common theme in Christ's teachings—he wants us to be joyful (see 15:11; 16:24, 33). The key to immeasurable joy is living in intimate contact with Christ, the source of all joy. When we do, we will experience God's special care and protection and see the victory God brings even when defeat seems certain.

17:14 The world hates Christians because Christians' values differ from the world's. Because Christ's followers don't co-operate with the world by joining in their sin, they are living accusations against the world's immorality. The world follows Satan's agenda, and Satan is the avowed enemy of Jesus and his people.

not of it.[z] 17Sanctify[b] them by the truth; your word is truth.[a] 18As you sent me into
the world,[b] I have sent them into the world.[c] 19For them I sanctify myself, that they
too may be truly sanctified.

Jesus Prays for Future Believers
(221)

20"My prayer is not for them alone. I pray also for those who will believe in me
through their message, 21that all of them may be one, Father, just as you are in me
and I am in you.[d] May they also be in us so that the world may believe that you have
sent me.[e] 22I have given them the glory that you gave me, that they may be one as
we are one:[f] 23I in them and you in me. May they be brought to complete unity to
let the world know that you sent me[g] and have loved them[h] even as you have loved
me.

24"Father, I want those you have given me to be with me where I am,[i] and to see
my glory,[j] the glory you have given me because you loved me before the creation
of the world.[k]

25"Righteous Father, though the world does not know you,[l] I know you, and they
know that you have sent me.[m] 26I have made you known to them,[n] and will continue
to make you known in order that the love you have for me may be in them[o] and that
I myself may be in them."

2. Jesus completes his mission

Jesus Is Betrayed and Arrested
(224/Matthew 26:47–56; Mark 14:43–52; Luke 22:47–53)

18 When he had finished praying, Jesus left with his disciples and crossed the
Kidron Valley.[a] On the other side there was an olive grove,[b] and he and his
disciples went into it.[c]

2Now Judas, who betrayed him, knew the place, because Jesus had often met there
with his disciples.[d] 3So Judas came to the grove, guiding[e] a detachment of soldiers
and some officials from the chief priests and Pharisees.[f] They were carrying torches,
lanterns and weapons.

4Jesus, knowing all that was going to happen to him,[g] went out and asked them,
"Who is it you want?"[h]

5"Jesus of Nazareth," they replied.

"I am he," Jesus said. (And Judas the traitor was standing there with them.) 6When
Jesus said, "I am he," they drew back and fell to the ground.

7Again he asked them, "Who is it you want?"[i]

And they said, "Jesus of Nazareth."

8"I told you that I am he," Jesus answered. "If you are looking for me, then let these
men go." 9This happened so that the words he had spoken would be fulfilled: "I have
not lost one of those you gave me."[a][j]

b *17* Greek *hagiazo* (*set apart for sacred use* or *make holy*); also in verse 19 **a** *9* John 6:39

17:16 [z]ver 14
17:17 [a]Jn 15:3
17:18 [b]ver 3, 8, 21, 23, 25 [c]Jn 20:21
17:21 [d]Jn 10:38 [e]ver 3, 8, 18, 23, 25; Jn 3:17
17:22 [f]Jn 14:20
17:23 [g]Jn 3:17 [h]Jn 16:27
17:24 [i]Jn 12:26 [j]Jn 1:14 [k]ver 5; Mt 25:34
17:25 [l]Jn 15:21; 16:3 [m]ver 3, 8, 18, 21, 23; Jn 3:17; 7:29; 16:27
17:26 [n]ver 6 [o]Jn 15:9
18:1 [a]2Sa 15:23 [b]ver 26 [c]Mt 26:36
18:2 [d]Lk 21:37; 22:39
18:3 [e]Ac 1:16 [f]ver 12
18:4 [g]Jn 6:64; 13:1, 11 [h]ver 7
18:7 [i]ver 4
18:9 [j]Jn 17:12

17:17 A follower of Christ becomes sanctified (set apart for sacred use, cleansed and made holy) through believing and obeying the word of God (Hebrews 4:12). He or she has already accepted forgiveness through Christ's sacrificial death (Hebrews 7:26, 27). But daily application of God's word has a purifying effect on our minds and hearts. Scripture points out sin, motivates us to confess, renews our relationship with Christ, and guides us back to the right path.

17:18 Jesus didn't ask God to take believers *out* of the world but instead to use them *in* the world. Because Jesus sends us into the world, we should not try to escape from the world, nor should we avoid all relationships with non-Christians. We are called to be salt and light (Matthew 5:13–16), and we are to do the work that God sent us to do.

17:20 Jesus prayed for all who would follow him, including you and others you know. He prayed for unity (17:11), protection from the evil one (17:15), and sanctity (holiness) (17:17). Knowing that Jesus prayed for us should give us confidence as we work for his kingdom.

17:21–23 Jesus' great desire for his disciples was that they would become one. He wanted them unified as a powerful witness to the reality of God's love. Are you helping to unify the body of Christ, the church? You can pray for other Christians, avoid gossip, build others up, work together in humility, give your time and money, exalt Christ, and refuse to get sidetracked arguing over divisive matters.

17:21–23 Jesus prayed for unity among the believers based on the believers' unity with him and the Father. Christians can know unity among themselves if they are living in union with God. For example, each branch living in union with the vine is united with all other branches doing the same.

18:11 [k]Mt 20:22
18:12 [l]ver 3
18:13 [m]ver 24; Mt 26:3
18:14 [n]Jn 11:49-51
18:15 [o]Mt 26:3 [p]Mt 26:58; Mk 14:54; Lk 22:54

10 Then Simon Peter, who had a sword, drew it and struck the high priest's servant,
cutting off his right ear. (The servant's name was Malchus.)
11 Jesus commanded Peter, "Put your sword away! Shall I not drink the cup[k] the
Father has given me?"

Annas Questions Jesus
(225)

12 Then the detachment of soldiers with its commander and the Jewish officials[l]
arrested Jesus. They bound him 13 and brought him first to Annas, who was the
father-in-law of Caiaphas,[m] the high priest that year. 14 Caiaphas was the one who
had advised the Jews that it would be good if one man died for the people.[n]
15 Simon Peter and another disciple were following Jesus. Because this disciple was
known to the high priest,[o] he went with Jesus into the high priest's courtyard,[p] 16 but
Peter had to wait outside at the door. The other disciple, who was known to the high
priest, came back, spoke to the girl on duty there and brought Peter in.
17 "You are not one of his disciples, are you?" the girl at the door asked Peter.

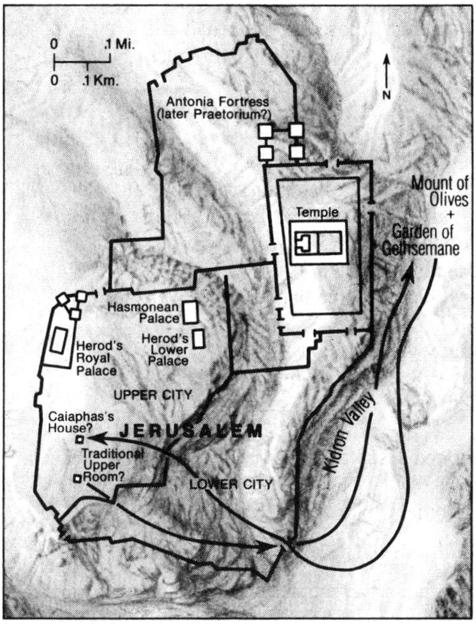

BETRAYAL IN THE GARDEN After eating the Passover meal in the upper room, Jesus and his disciples went to Gethsemane, where Judas led the temple guard to arrest Jesus. Jesus was then taken to Caiaphas' house for his first of many trials.

18:3 The officials from the chief priests and Pharisees were probably members of the temple guard; they were Jews given authority by the religious leaders to make arrests for minor infractions. The soldiers may have been a small contingent of Roman soldiers who did not participate in the arrest but accompanied the temple guard to make sure matters didn't get out of control.

18:4, 5 John does not record Judas's kiss of greeting (Matthew 26:49; Mark 14:45; Luke 22:47, 48), but Judas's kiss marked a turning point for the disciples. With Jesus' arrest, each one's life would be radically different. For the first time, Judas openly betrayed Jesus before the other disciples. For the first time, Jesus' loyal disciples ran away from him (Matthew 26:56). The band of disciples would undergo severe testing before they were transformed from hesitant followers to dynamic leaders.

18:6 The men may have been startled by the boldness of Jesus' question, or by the words "I am he", a declaration of his divinity (Exodus 3:14). Or perhaps they were overcome by his obvious power and authority.

18:10, 11 Trying to protect Jesus, Peter pulled a sword and wounded the high priest's servant. But Jesus told Peter to put away his sword and allow God's plan to unfold. At times it is tempting to take matters into our own hands, to force the issue. Most often such moves lead to sin. Instead we must trust God to work out his plan. Think of it—if Peter had had his way, Jesus would not have gone to the cross, and God's plan of redemption would have been thwarted.

18:11 The cup means the suffering, isolation, and death that Jesus would have to endure in order to atone for the sins of the world.

18:12, 13 Jesus was immediately taken to the high priest's residence, even though this was the middle of the night. The religious leaders were in a hurry—they wanted to complete the execution before the Sabbath and get on with the Passover celebration. This residence was a palace whose outer walls enclosed a courtyard where servants and soldiers would warm themselves around a fire.

18:13 Both Annas and Caiaphas had been high priests. Annas was Israel's high priest from A.D. 6 to 15, when he was deposed by Roman rulers. Caiaphas, Annas' son-in-law, was appointed high priest from A.D. 18 to 36/37. According to Jewish law, the office of high priest was held for life. Many Jews therefore still considered Annas the high priest and still called him by that title. But although Annas retained much authority among the Jews, Caiaphas made the final decisions.

Both Caiaphas and Annas cared more about their political ambitions than about their responsibility to lead the people to God. Though religious leaders, they had become evil. As the nation's spiritual leaders, they should have been sensitive to God's revelation. They should have known that Jesus was the Messiah about whom the Scriptures spoke, and they should have pointed the people to him. But when deceitful men and women pursue evil, they want to eliminate all opposition. Instead of honestly evaluating Jesus' claims based on their knowledge of Scripture, these religious leaders sought to further their own selfish ambitions and were even willing to kill God's Son, if that's what it took, to do it.

18:15, 16 The other disciple is probably John, the author of this Gospel. He knew the high priest and identified himself to the girl at the door. Because of his connections, John got himself and Peter into the courtyard. But Peter refused to identify himself as Jesus' follower. Peter's experiences in the next few hours would change his life. For more information about Peter, see his Profile in Matthew 27.

He replied, "I am not."[q]
18It was cold, and the servants and officials stood round a fire[r] they had made to
keep warm. Peter also was standing with them, warming himself.[s]
19Meanwhile, the high priest questioned Jesus about his disciples and his teaching.
20"I have spoken openly to the world," Jesus replied. "I always taught in synagogues[t] or at the temple,[u] where all the Jews come together. I said nothing in
secret.[v] 21Why question me? Ask those who heard me. Surely they know what I
said."
22When Jesus said this, one of the officials[w] near by struck him in the face.[x] "Is
this the way you answer the high priest?" he demanded.
23"If I said something wrong," Jesus replied, "testify as to what is wrong. But if
I spoke the truth, why did you strike me?"[y] 24Then Annas sent him, still bound, to
Caiaphas[z] the high priest.[b]

Peter Denies Knowing Jesus

(227/Matthew 26:69–75; Mark 14:66–72; Luke 22:54–65)

25As Simon Peter stood warming himself,[a] he was asked, "You are not one of his
disciples, are you?"
He denied it, saying, "I am not."[b]
26One of the high priest's servants, a relative of the man whose ear Peter had cut
off,[c] challenged him, "Didn't I see you with him in the olive grove?"[d] 27Again Peter
denied it, and at that moment a cock began to crow.[e]

Jesus Stands Trial before Pilate

(230/Matthew 27:11–14; Mark 15:2–5; Luke 23:1–5)

28Then the Jews led Jesus from Caiaphas to the palace of the Roman governor.[f]
By now it was early morning, and to avoid ceremonial uncleanness the Jews did not
enter the palace;[g] they wanted to be able to eat the Passover.[h] 29So Pilate came out
to them and asked, "What charges are you bringing against this man?"
30"If he were not a criminal," they replied, "we would not have handed him over
to you."
31Pilate said, "Take him yourselves and judge him by your own law."
"But we have no right to execute anyone," the Jews objected. 32This happened so
that the words Jesus had spoken indicating the kind of death he was going to die[i]
would be fulfilled.
33Pilate then went back inside the palace,[j] summoned Jesus and asked him, "Are
you the king of the Jews?"[k]
34"Is that your own idea," Jesus asked, "or did others talk to you about me?"

b *24* Or *(Now Annas had sent him, still bound, to Caiaphas the high priest.)*

18:17 [q]ver 25
18:18 [r]Jn 21:9 [s]Mk 14:54, 67
18:20 [t]Mt 4:23 [u]Mt 26:55 [v]Jn 7:26
18:22 [w]ver 3 [x]Mt 16:21; Jn 19:3
18:23 [y]Mt 5:39; Ac 23:2-5
18:24 [z]ver 13; Mt 26:3
18:25 [a]ver 18 [b]ver 17
18:26 [c]ver 10 [d]ver 1
18:27 [e]Jn 13:38
18:28 [f]Mt 27:2; Mk 15:1; Lk 23:1 [g]ver 33; Jn 19:9 [h]Jn 11:55
18:32 [i]Mt 20:19; 26:2; Jn 3:14; 8:28; 12:32, 33
18:33 [j]ver 28, 29; Jn 19:9 [k]Lk 23:3; Mt 2:2

18:19ff During the night, Jesus had a pre-trial hearing before Annas before he was taken to Caiaphas and the entire Sanhedrin (Mark 14:53–65). The religious leaders knew they had no grounds for charging Jesus, so they tried to build evidence against him by using false witnesses (Mark 14:55–59).

18:22-27 We can easily get angry at the Sanhedrin for their injustice in condemning Jesus, but we must remember that Peter and the rest of the disciples also contributed to Jesus' pain by deserting and disowning him (Matthew 26:56, 75). While most of us are not like the religious leaders, we are all like the disciples, for all of us have been guilty of denying that Christ is Lord in vital areas of our lives or of keeping secret our identity as believers in times of pressure. Don't excuse yourself by pointing at others whose sins seem worse than yours. Instead, come to Jesus for forgiveness and healing.

18:25 The other three Gospels say that Peter's three denials happened near a fire in the courtyard ouside Caiaphas's palace. John places the first denial outside Annas' home and the other two denials outside Caiaphas' home. This was very likely the same courtyard. The high priest's residence was large, and Annas and Caiaphas undoubtedly lived near each other.

18:25-27 Imagine standing outside while Jesus, your Lord and Master, is questioned. Imagine watching this man, whom you have come to believe is the long-awaited Messiah, being abused and beaten. Naturally Peter was confused and afraid. It is a serious sin to disown Christ, but Jesus forgave Peter (21:15–17). No sin is too great for Jesus to forgive if you are truly repentant. He will forgive even your worst sin if you turn from it and ask his pardon.

18:27 This fulfilled Jesus' words to Peter after he promised he would never disown him (Mark 14:31; John 13:38).

18:28 By Jewish law, entering the house of a Gentile would cause a Jewish person to be ceremonially defiled. As a result, he could not take part in worship at the temple or celebrate the feasts until he was restored to a state of "cleanness". Afraid of being defiled, these men stayed outside the house where they had taken Jesus for trial. They kept the ceremonial requirements of their religion while harbouring murder and treachery in their hearts.

THE SIX STAGES OF JESUS' TRIAL
Although Jesus' trial lasted less than 18 hours, he was taken to six different hearings.

BEFORE JEWISH AUTHORITIES	Preliminary Hearing before Annas (John 18:12–24)	Because the office of high priest was for life, Annas was still the "official" high priest in the eyes of the Jews, even though the Romans had appointed another. Thus Annas still carried much weight among the Sanhedrin.
	Hearing before Caiaphas (Matthew 26:57–68)	Like the hearing before Annas, this hearing was conducted at night in secrecy. It was full of illegalities that made a mockery of justice (see the chart in Matthew 28).
	Trial before the Sanhedrin (Matthew 27:1, 2)	Just after daybreak, 70 members of the Jewish council met to rubber-stamp their approval of the previous hearings to make them appear legal. The purpose of this trial was not to determine justice, but to justify their own preconceptions of Jesus' guilt.
BEFORE ROMAN AUTHORITIES	First Hearing before Pilate (Luke 23:1–5)	The religious leaders had condemned Jesus to death on religious grounds, but only the Roman government could grant the death penalty. Thus, they took Jesus to Pilate, the Roman governor, and accused him of treason and rebellion, crimes for which the Roman government gave the death penalty. Pilate saw at once that Jesus was innocent, but he was afraid about the uproar being caused by the religious leaders.
	Hearing before Herod (Luke 23:6–12)	Because Jesus' home was in the region of Galilee, Pilate sent Jesus to Herod Agrippa, the ruler of Galilee, who was in Jerusalem for the Passover celebration. Herod was eager to see Jesus do a miracle, but when Jesus remained silent, Herod wanted nothing to do with him and sent him back to Pilate.
	Last Hearing before Pilate (Luke 23:13–25)	Pilate didn't like the religious leaders. He wasn't interested in condemning Jesus because he knew Jesus was innocent. However, he knew that another uprising in his district might cost him his job. First he tried to compromise with the religious leaders by having Jesus beaten, an illegal action in itself. But finally he gave in and handed Jesus over to be executed. Pilate's self-interest was stronger than his sense of justice.

18:29 This Roman governor, Pilate, was in charge of Judea (the region where Jerusalem was located) from A.D. 26 to 36. Pilate was unpopular with the Jews because he had raided the temple treasuries for money to build an aqueduct. He did not like the Jews, but when Jesus, the King of the Jews, stood before him, Pilate found him innocent.

18:30 Pilate knew what was going on; he knew that the religious leaders hated Jesus, and he did not want to act as their executioner. They could not sentence him to death themselves—permission had to come from a Roman leader. But Pilate initially refused to sentence Jesus without sufficient evidence. Jesus' life became a pawn in a political power struggle.

18:31ff Pilate made four attempts to deal with Jesus: (1) he tried to put the responsibility on someone else (18:31); (2) he tried to find a way of escape so he could release Jesus (18:39); (3) he tried to compromise by having Jesus flogged rather than handing him over to die (19:1–3); and (4) he tried a direct appeal to the sympathy of the accusers (19:15). Everyone has to decide what to do with Jesus. Pilate tried to let everyone else decide for him—and in the end, he lost.

18:32 This prediction is recorded in Matthew 20:19. Crucifixion was a common method of execution for criminals who were not Roman citizens.

18:34 If Pilate was asking this question in his role as the Roman governor, he would have been inquiring whether Jesus was setting up a rebel government. But the Jews were using the word *king* to mean their religious ruler, the Messiah. Israel was a captive nation, under the authority of the Roman empire. A rival king might have threatened Rome; a Messiah could have been a purely religious leader.

35"Am I a Jew?" Pilate replied. "It was your people and your chief priests who
handed you over to me. What is it you have done?"
36Jesus said, "My kingdom[l] is not of this world. If it were, my servants would
fight to prevent my arrest by the Jews.[m] But now my kingdom is from another
place."[n]
37"You are a king, then!" said Pilate.
Jesus answered, "You are right in saying I am a king. In fact, for this reason I was
born, and for this I came into the world, to testify to the truth.[o] Everyone on the side
of truth listens to me."[p]

18:36 [l]Mt 3:2 [m]Mt 26:53 [n]Lk 17:21; Jn 6:15

18:37 [o]Jn 3:32 [p]Jn 8:47; 1Jn 4:6

Pilate Hands Jesus Over to Be Crucified
(232/Matthew 27:15–26; Mark 15:6–15; Luke 23:13–25)

38"What is truth?" Pilate asked. With this he went out again to the Jews and said,
"I find no basis for a charge against him.[q] 39But it is your custom for me to release
to you one prisoner at the time of the Passover. Do you want me to release 'the king
of the Jews'?"
40They shouted back, "No, not him! Give us Barabbas!" Now Barabbas had taken
part in a rebellion.[r]

18:38 [q]Lk 23:4; Jn 19:4, 6

18:40 [r]Ac 3:14

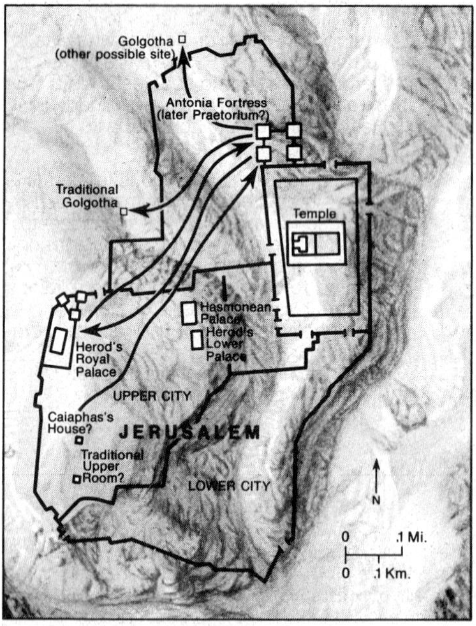

JESUS' TRIAL AND CRUCIFIXION Jesus was taken from trial before the Jewish Sanhedrin to trial before the Roman governor, Pilate, in Pilate's palace. Pilate sent him to Herod (Luke 23:5–12), but Herod just returned Jesus to Pilate. Responding to threats from the mob, Pilate finally turned Jesus over to be crucified.

18:36, 37 Pilate asked Jesus a straightforward question, and Jesus answered clearly. Jesus is a king, but one whose kingdom is not of this world. There seems to have been no question in Pilate's mind that Jesus spoke the truth and was innocent of any crime. It also seems apparent that while recognising the truth, Pilate chose to reject it. It is a tragedy when we fail to recognise the truth. It is a greater tragedy when we recognise the truth but fail to heed it.

18:38 Pilate was cynical; he thought that all truth was relative. To many government officials, truth was whatever the majority of people agreed with or whatever helped advance their own personal power and political goals. When there is no basis for truth, there is no basis for moral right and wrong. Justice becomes whatever works or whatever helps those in power. In Jesus and his word we have a standard for truth and for our moral behaviour.

18:40 Barabbas was a rebel against Rome and, although he had committed murder, he was probably a hero among the Jews. The Jews hated being governed by Rome and paying taxes to the despised government. Barabbas, who had led a rebellion and failed, was released instead of Jesus, the only One who could truly help Israel. For more on Barabbas, see the note on Luke 23:18, 19.

19:1ff To grasp the full picture of Jesus' crucifixion, read John's perspective along with the other three accounts in Matthew 27, Mark 15, and Luke 23. Each writer adds meaningful details, but each has the same message—Jesus died on the cross, in fulfilment of Old Testament prophecy, so that we could be saved from our sins and given eternal life.

19:1–3 Flogging could have killed Jesus. The usual procedure was to bare the upper half of the victim's body and tie his hands to a pillar before whipping him with a three-pronged whip. The number of lashes was determined by the severity of the crime; up to 40 were permitted under Jewish law (Deuteronomy 25:3). After being flogged, Jesus also endured other agonies recorded here and in the other Gospels.

19:2–5 The soldiers went beyond their orders to whip Jesus—they also mocked his claim to royalty by placing a crown on his head and a royal robe on his shoulders.

19:1
[a]Dt 25:3; Isa 50:6; 53:5; Mt 27:26
19:3
[b]Mt 27:29
[c]Jn 18:22
19:4
[d]Jn 18:38
[e]ver 6; Lk 23:4
19:5
[f]ver 2
19:6
[g]Ac 3:13
[h]ver 4; Lk 23:4

19 Then Pilate took Jesus and had him flogged.[a] 2The soldiers twisted together
a crown of thorns and put it on his head. They clothed him in a purple robe
3and went up to him again and again, saying, "Hail, king of the Jews!"[b] And they
struck him in the face.[c]
4Once more Pilate came out and said to the Jews, "Look, I am bringing him out[d]
to you to let you know that I find no basis for a charge against him."[e] 5When Jesus
came out wearing the crown of thorns and the purple robe,[f] Pilate said to them, "Here
is the man!"
6As soon as the chief priests and their officials saw him, they shouted, "Crucify!
Crucify!"
But Pilate answered, "You take him and crucify him.[g] As for me, I find no basis
for a charge against him."[h]

MARY MAGDALENE

The absence of women among the 12 disciples has bothered a few people. But it is clear that there were many women among Jesus' followers. It is also clear that Jesus did not treat women as others in his culture did; he treated them with dignity, as people of worth.

Mary of Magdala was an early follower of Jesus who certainly deserves to be called a disciple. An energetic, impulsive, caring woman, she not only travelled with Jesus, but also contributed to the needs of the group. She was present at the crucifixion and was on her way to anoint Jesus' body on Sunday morning when she discovered the empty tomb. Mary was the first to see Jesus after his resurrection.

Mary Magdalene is a heartwarming example of thankful living. Her life was miraculously freed by Jesus when he drove seven demons out of her. In every glimpse we have of her, she was acting out her appreciation for the freedom Christ had given her. That freedom allowed her to stand under Christ's cross when all the disciples except John were hiding in fear. After Jesus' death, she intended to give his body every respect. Like the rest of Jesus' followers, she never expected his bodily resurrection—but she was overjoyed to discover it.

Mary's faith was not complicated, but it was direct and genuine. She was more eager to believe and obey than to understand everything. Jesus honoured her childlike faith by appearing to her first and by entrusting her with the first message of his resurrection.

Strengths and accomplishments:
- Contributed to the needs of Jesus and his disciples
- One of the few faithful followers present at Jesus' death on the cross
- First to see the risen Christ

Weakness and mistake:
- Jesus had to drive seven demons out of her

Lessons from her life:
- Those who are obedient grow in understanding
- Women are vital to Jesus' ministry
- Jesus relates to women as he created them—as equal reflectors of God's image

Vital statistics:
- Where: Magdala
- Occupation: We are not told, but she seems to have been wealthy
- Contemporaries: Jesus, the 12 disciples, Mary, Martha, Lazarus, Jesus' mother Mary

Key verse:
"When Jesus rose early on the first day of the week, he appeared first to Mary Magdalene, out of whom he had driven seven demons" (Mark 16:9).

Mary Magdalene's story is told in Matthew 27, 28; Mark 15, 16; Luke 23, 24; and John 19, 20. She is also mentioned in Luke 8:2.

7 The Jews insisted, "We have a law, and according to that law he must die,[i]
because he claimed to be the Son of God."[j]
8 When Pilate heard this, he was even more afraid, 9 and he went back inside the
palace.[k] "Where do you come from?" he asked Jesus, but Jesus gave him no
answer.[l] 10 "Do you refuse to speak to me?" Pilate said. "Don't you realise I have
power either to free you or to crucify you?"
11 Jesus answered, "You would have no power over me if it were not given to you
from above.[m] Therefore the one who handed me over to you[n] is guilty of a greater
sin."
12 From then on, Pilate tried to set Jesus free, but the Jews kept shouting, "If you
let this man go, you are no friend of Caesar. Anyone who claims to be a king[o] opposes
Caesar."
13 When Pilate heard this, he brought Jesus out and sat down on the judge's seat[p]
at a place known as the Stone Pavement (which in Aramaic[q] is Gabbatha). 14 It was
the day of Preparation[r] of Passover Week, about the sixth hour.[s]
"Here is your king,"[t] Pilate said to the Jews.
15 But they shouted, "Take him away! Take him away! Crucify him!"
"Shall I crucify your king?" Pilate asked.
"We have no king but Caesar," the chief priests answered.
16 Finally Pilate handed him over to them to be crucified.[u]

Jesus Is Led Away to Be Crucified
(234/Matthew 27:32–34; Mark 15:21–24; Luke 23:26–31)
Jesus Is Placed on the Cross
(235/Matthew 27:35–44; Mark 15:25–32; Luke 23:32–43)

So the soldiers took charge of Jesus. 17 Carrying his own cross,[v] he went out to
the place of the Skull[w] (which in Aramaic[x] is called Golgotha). 18 Here they crucified
him, and with him two others[y]—one on each side and Jesus in the middle.
19 Pilate had a notice prepared and fastened to the cross. It read: JESUS OF NA-

19:7 [i]Lev 24:16 [j]Mt 26:63-66; Jn 5:18; 10:33
19:9 [k]Jn 18:33 [l]Mk 14:61
19:11 [m]Ro 13:1 [n]Jn 18:28-30; Ac 3:13
19:12 [o]Lk 23:2
19:13 [p]Mt 27:19 [q]Jn 5:2
19:14 [r]Mt 27:62 [s]Mk 15:25 [t]ver 19, 21
19:16 [u]Mt 27:26; Mk 15:15; Lk 23:25
19:17 [v]Ge 22:6; Lk 14:27; 23:26 [w]Lk 23:33 [x]Jn 5:2
19:18 [y]Lk 23:32

19:7 The truth finally came out—the religious leaders had not brought Jesus to Pilate because he was causing rebellion against Rome, but because they thought he had broken their religious laws. Blasphemy, one of the most serious crimes in Jewish law, deserved the death penalty. Accusing Jesus of blasphemy would give credibility to their case in the eyes of Jews; accusing Jesus of treason would give credibility to their case in the eyes of the Romans. They didn't care which accusation Pilate listened to, as long as he would co-operate with them in killing Jesus.

19:10 Throughout the trial we see that Jesus was in control, not Pilate or the religious leaders. Pilate vacillated, the Jewish leaders reacted out of hatred and anger, but Jesus remained composed. He knew the truth, he knew God's plan, and he knew the reason for his trial. Despite the pressure and persecution, Jesus remained unmoved. It was really Pilate and the religious leaders who were on trial, not Jesus. When you are questioned or ridiculed because of your faith, remember that while you may be on trial before your accusers, they are on trial before God.

19:11 When Jesus said the man who delivered him to Pilate was guiltier than Pilate, he was not excusing Pilate for reacting to the political pressure placed on him. Pilate was responsible for his decision about Jesus. Caiaphas and the other religious leaders were guilty of a greater sin because they premeditated Jesus' murder.

19:12, 13 These words pressured Pilate into allowing Jesus to be crucified. As Roman governor of the area, Pilate was expected to keep the peace. Because Rome could not afford to keep large numbers of troops in the outlying regions, they maintained control by crushing rebellions immediately with brute force. Pilate was afraid that reports to Caesar of insurrection in his region would cost Pilate his job and perhaps even his life. When we face a tough decision, we can take the easy way out, or we can stand for what is right regardless of the cost. If we know the good we ought to do and don't do it, we sin (James 4:17).

19:13 The Stone Pavement was part of the Tower of Antonia bordering the northwest corner of the temple complex.

19:15 The Jewish leaders were so desperate to get rid of Jesus that, despite their intense hatred for Rome, they shouted, "We have no king but Caesar." How ironic that they feigned allegiance to Rome while rejecting their own Messiah! Their own words condemned them, for God was to be their only true King, and they had abandoned every trace of loyalty to him. The priests had truly lost their reasons for existence—instead of turning people to God, they claimed allegiance to Rome in order to kill their Messiah.

19:17 This place called *Golgotha,* "the skull", was probably a hill outside Jerusalem along a main road. Many executions took place here so the Romans could use them as an example to the people.

19:18 Crucifixion was a Roman form of execution. The condemned man was forced to carry his cross along a main road to the execution site, as a warning to the people. Types of crosses and methods of crucifixion varied. Jesus was nailed to his cross; some people were tied with ropes. Death came by suffocation because the weight of the body made breathing difficult as the victim lost strength. Crucifixion was a hideously slow and painful death.

19:19 This sign was meant to be ironic. A king, stripped nearly naked and executed in public view, had obviously lost his kingdom for ever. But Jesus, who turns the world's wisdom upside down, was just coming into his kingdom. His death and resurrection would strike the deathblow to Satan's rule and would establish Jesus' eternal authority over the earth. Few people reading the sign that bleak afternoon understood its real meaning, but the sign was absolutely true. All was not lost. Jesus was King of the Jews—and the Gentiles, and the whole universe.

ZARETH,[z] THE KING OF THE JEWS.[a] 20Many of the Jews read this sign, for the place
where Jesus was crucified was near the city,[b] and the sign was written in Aramaic,
Latin and Greek. 21The chief priests of the Jews protested to Pilate, "Do not write
'The King of the Jews', but that this man claimed to be king of the Jews."[c]
22Pilate answered, "What I have written, I have written."
23When the soldiers crucified Jesus, they took his clothes, dividing them into four
shares, one for each of them, with the undergarment remaining. This garment was
seamless, woven in one piece from top to bottom.
24"Let's not tear it," they said to one another. "Let's decide by lot who will get
it."

This happened that the scripture might be fulfilled[d] which said,

> "They divided my garments among them
> and cast lots for my clothing."[a][e]

So this is what the soldiers did.
25Near the cross[f] of Jesus stood his mother,[g] his mother's sister, Mary the wife
of Clopas, and Mary Magdalene.[h] 26When Jesus saw his mother[i] there, and the
disciple whom he loved[j] standing near by, he said to his mother, "Dear woman, here
is your son," 27and to the disciple, "Here is your mother." From that time on, this
disciple took her into his home.

Jesus Dies on the Cross

(236/Matthew 27:45–56; Mark 15:33–41; Luke 23:44–49)

28Later, knowing that all was now completed,[k] and so that the Scripture would
be fulfilled,[l] Jesus said, "I am thirsty." 29A jar of wine vinegar[m] was there, so they
soaked a sponge in it, put the sponge on a stalk of the hyssop plant, and lifted it to
Jesus' lips. 30When he had received the drink, Jesus said, "It is finished."[n] With that,
he bowed his head and gave up his spirit.
31Now it was the day of Preparation,[o] and the next day was to be a special Sabbath.
Because the Jews did not want the bodies left on the crosses[p] during the Sabbath,
they asked Pilate to have the legs broken and the bodies taken down. 32The soldiers

[a] *24* Psalm 22:18

19:19 [z]Mk 1:24 [a]ver 14, 21
19:20 [b]Heb 13:12
19:21 [c]ver 14
19:24 [d]ver 28, 36, 37; Mt 1:22 [e]Ps 22:18
19:25 [f]Mt 27:55, 56; Mk 15:40, 41; Lk 23:49 [g]Mt 12:46 [h]Lk 24:18
19:26 [i]Mt 12:46 [j]Jn 13:23
19:28 [k]ver 30; Jn 13:1 [l]ver 24, 36, 37
19:29 [m]Ps 69:21
19:30 [n]Lk 12:50; Jn 17:4
19:31 [o]ver 14, 42 [p]Dt 21:23; Jos 8:29; 10:26, 27

19:20 The placard was written in three languages: Aramaic for the native Jews, Latin for the Roman occupation forces, and Greek for foreigners and Jews visiting from other lands.

19:23, 24 Roman soldiers in charge of crucifixions customarily took for themselves the clothes of the condemned men. They divided Jesus' clothing, casting lots to determine who would get his seamless garment, the most valuable piece of clothing. This fulfilled the prophecy in Psalm 22:18.

19:25–27 Even while dying on the cross, Jesus was concerned about his family. He instructed John to care for Mary, Jesus' mother. Our families are precious gifts from God, and we should value and care for them under all circumstances. Neither Christian work nor key responsibilities in any job or position excuse us from caring for our families. What can you do today to show your love for your family?

19:27 Jesus asked his close friend John, the writer of this Gospel, to care for Jesus' mother, Mary, whose husband, Joseph, must have been dead by this time. Why didn't Jesus assign this task to his brothers? As the oldest son, Jesus entrusted his mother to a person who stayed with him at the cross – and that was John.

19:29 This vinegar was a cheap wine that the Roman soldiers drank while waiting for those crucified to die.

19:30 Until this time, a complicated system of sacrifices had atoned for sins. Sin separates people from God, and only through the sacrifice of an animal, a substitute, could people be forgiven and become clean before God. But people sin continually, so frequent sacrifices were required. Jesus, however, became the final and ultimate sacrifice for sin. The word *finished* is the same as "paid in full". Jesus came to *finish* God's work of salvation (4:34; 17:4), to pay the full penalty for our sins. With his death, the complex sacrificial system ended because Jesus took all sin upon himself. Now we can freely approach God because of what Jesus did for us. Those who believe in Jesus' death and resurrection can live eternally with God and escape the penalty that comes from sin.

19:31 It was against God's law to leave the body of a dead person exposed overnight (Deuteronomy 21:23), and it was also against the law to work after sundown on Friday, when the Sabbath began. This is why the religious leaders urgently wanted to get Jesus' body off the cross and buried by sundown.

19:31–35 These Romans were experienced soldiers. They knew from many previous crucifixions whether a man was dead or alive. There was no question that Jesus was dead when they checked him, so they decided not to break his legs as they had done to the other victims. Piercing his side and seeing the sudden flow of blood and water (indicating that the sac surrounding the heart and the heart itself had been pierced) was further proof of his death. Some people say Jesus didn't really die, that he only fainted – and that's how he came back to life. But we have the witness of an impartial party, the Roman soldiers, that Jesus died on the cross (see Mark 15:44, 45).

19:32 The Roman soldiers would break victims' legs to hasten the death process. When a person hung on a cross, death came by suffocation, but the victim could push against the cross with his legs to hold up his body and keep breathing. With broken legs, he would suffocate almost immediately.

therefore came and broke the legs of the first man who had been crucified with Jesus,
and then those of the other.[q] 33But when they came to Jesus and found that he was
already dead, they did not break his legs. 34Instead, one of the soldiers pierced[r] Jesus'
side with a spear, bringing a sudden flow of blood and water.[s] 35The man who saw
it[t] has given testimony, and his testimony is true.[u] He knows that he tells the truth,
and he testifies so that you also may believe. 36These things happened so that the
scripture would be fulfilled:[v] "Not one of his bones will be broken,"[b][w] 37and, as
another scripture says, "They will look on the one they have pierced."[c][x]

Jesus Is Laid in the Tomb
(237/Matthew 27:57–61; Mark 15:42–47; Luke 23:50–56)

38Later, Joseph of Arimathea asked Pilate for the body of Jesus. Now Joseph was
a disciple of Jesus, but secretly because he feared the Jews. With Pilate's permission,
he came and took the body away. 39He was accompanied by Nicodemus,[y] the man
who earlier had visited Jesus at night. Nicodemus brought a mixture of myrrh and
aloes, about seventy-five pounds.[d] 40Taking Jesus' body, the two of them wrapped
it, with the spices, in strips of linen.[z] This was in accordance with Jewish burial
customs.[a] 41At the place where Jesus was crucified, there was a garden, and in the
garden a new tomb, in which no-one had ever been laid. 42Because it was the Jewish
day of Preparation[b] and since the tomb was near by,[c] they laid Jesus there.

Jesus Rises from the Dead
(239/Matthew 28:1–7; Mark 16:1–8; Luke 24:1–12)

20 Early on the first day of the week, while it was still dark, Mary Magdalene[a]
went to the tomb and saw that the stone had been removed from the entrance.[b]
2So she came running to Simon Peter and the other disciple, the one Jesus loved,[c]
and said, "They have taken the Lord out of the tomb, and we don't know where they
have put him!"[d]

3So Peter and the other disciple started for the tomb.[e] 4Both were running, but the
other disciple outran Peter and reached the tomb first. 5He bent over and looked in[f]
at the strips of linen[g] lying there but did not go in. 6Then Simon Peter, who was
behind him, arrived and went into the tomb. He saw the strips of linen lying there,
7as well as the burial cloth that had been around Jesus' head.[h] The cloth was folded

[b] *36* Exodus 12:46; Num. 9:12; Psalm 34:20 [c] *37* Zech. 12:10 [d] *39* Greek *a hundred litrai* (about 34 kilograms)

19:32 [q] ver 18
19:34 [r] Zec 12:10 [s] 1Jn 5:6, 8
19:35 [t] Lk 24:48 [u] Jn 15:27; 21:24
19:36 [v] ver 24, 28, 37; Mt 1:22 [w] Ex 12:46; Nu 9:12; Ps 34:20
19:37 [x] Zec 12:10; Rev 1:7
19:39 [y] Jn 3:1; 7:50
19:40 [z] Lk 24:12; Jn 11:44; 20:5, 7 [a] Mt 26:12
19:42 [b] ver 14, 31 [c] ver 20, 41
20:1 [a] ver 18; Jn 19:25 [b] Mt 27:60, 66
20:2 [c] Jn 13:23 [d] ver 13
20:3 [e] Lk 24:12
20:5 [f] ver 11 [g] Jn 19:40
20:7 [h] Jn 11:44

19:34, 35 The graphic details of Jesus' death are especially important in John's record because he was an eyewitness.

19:36, 37 Jesus died as the lambs for the Passover meal were being slain. Not a bone was to be broken in these sacrificial lambs (Exodus 12:46; Numbers 9:12). Jesus, the Lamb of God, was the perfect sacrifice for the sins of the world (1 Corinthians 5:7).

19:38, 39 Four people were changed in the process of Jesus' death. The criminal, dying on the cross beside Jesus, asked Jesus to include him in his kingdom (Luke 23:39–43). The Roman centurion proclaimed that surely Jesus was the Son of God (Mark 15:39). Joseph and Nicodemus, members of the Jewish council and secret followers of Jesus (7:50–52), came out of hiding. These men were changed more by Jesus' death than by his life. They realised who Jesus was, and that realisation brought out their belief, proclamation, and action. When confronted with Jesus and his death, we should be changed – to believe, proclaim, and act.

19:38–42 Joseph of Arimathea and Nicodemus were secret followers of Jesus. They were afraid to make this allegiance known because of their positions in the Jewish community. Joseph was a leader and honoured member of the Jewish council. Nicodemus, also a member of the council, had come to Jesus by night (3:1) and later tried to defend him before the other religious leaders (7:50–52). Yet they risked their reputations to provide for Jesus' burial. Are you a secret believer? Do you hide your faith from your friends and fellow workers? This is an appropriate time to step out of hiding and let others know whom you follow.

19:42 This tomb was probably a cave carved out of the stone hillside. It was large enough for a person to walk into, so Joseph and Nicodemus carried Jesus' body into it. A large stone was rolled in front of the entrance.

19:42 As they buried Jesus, Nicodemus and Joseph had to hurry to avoid working on the Sabbath, which began Friday evening at sundown.

20:1 Other women came to the tomb along with Mary Magdalene. The other Gospel accounts give their names. For more information on Mary Magdalene, see her Profile in chapter 19.

20:1 The stone was not rolled away from the entrance to the tomb so Jesus could get out. He could have left easily without moving the stone. It was rolled away so others could get *in* and see that Jesus was gone.

20:1ff People who hear about the resurrection for the first time may need time before they can comprehend this amazing story. Like Mary and the disciples, they may pass through four stages of belief. (1) At first, they may think the story is a fabrication, impossible to believe (20:2). (2) Like Peter, they may check out the facts and still be puzzled about what happened (20:6). (3) Only when they encounter Jesus personally are they able to accept the fact of the resurrection (20:16). (4) Then, as they commit themselves to the risen Lord and devote their lives to serving him, they begin to understand fully the reality of his presence with them (20:28).

20:8 [i] ver 4
20:9 [j] Mt 22:29
[k] Lk 24:26, 46

up by itself, separate from the linen. 8Finally the other disciple, who had reached the
tomb first,[i] also went inside. He saw and believed. 9(They still did not understand
from Scripture[j] that Jesus had to rise from the dead.)[k]

THOMAS

Thomas, so often remembered as "Doubting Thomas", deserves to be respected for his faith. He was a doubter, but his doubts had a purpose—he wanted to know the truth. Thomas did not idolise his doubts; he gladly believed when given reasons to do so. He expressed his doubts fully and had them answered completely. Doubting was only his way of responding, not his way of life.

Although our glimpses of Thomas are brief, his character comes through with consistency. He struggled to be faithful to what he knew, despite what he felt. At one point, when it was plain to everyone that Jesus' life was in danger, only Thomas put into words what most were feeling, "Let us also go, that we may die with him" (John 11:16). He didn't hesitate to follow Jesus.

We don't know why Thomas was absent the first time Jesus appeared to the disciples after the resurrection, but he was reluctant to believe their witness to Christ's resurrection. Not even ten friends could change his mind!

We can doubt without having to live a doubting way of life. Doubt encourages rethinking. Its purpose is more to sharpen the mind than to change it. Doubt can be used to pose the question, get an answer, and push for a decision. But doubt was never meant to be a permanent condition. Doubt is one foot lifted, poised to step forwards or backwards. There is no motion until the foot comes down.

When you experience doubt, take encouragement from Thomas. He didn't stay in his doubt, but allowed Jesus to bring him to belief. Take encouragement also from the fact that countless other followers of Christ have struggled with doubts. The answers God gave them may help you too. Don't settle into doubts, but move on from them to decision and belief. Find another believer with whom you can share your doubts. Silent doubts rarely find answers.

Strengths and accomplishments:
- One of Jesus' 12 disciples
- Intense both in doubt and belief
- Was a loyal and honest man

Weaknesses and mistakes:
- Along with the others, abandoned Jesus at his arrest
- Refused to believe the others' claims to have seen Christ and demanded proof
- Struggled with a pessimistic outlook

Lessons from his life:
- Jesus does not reject doubts that are honest and directed towards belief
- Better to doubt out loud than to disbelieve in silence

Vital statistics:
- Where: Galilee, Judea, Samaria
- Occupation: Disciple of Jesus
- Contemporaries: Jesus, other disciples, Herod, Pilate

Key verses:
"Then he said to Thomas, 'Put your finger here; see my hands. Reach out your hand and put it into my side. Stop doubting and believe.' Thomas answered, 'My Lord and my God!' " (John 20:27, 28).

Thomas' story is told in the Gospels. He is also mentioned in Acts 1:13.

20:7 The graveclothes were left as if Jesus had passed right through them. The headpiece was still rolled up in the shape of a head, and it was at about the right distance from the wrappings that had enveloped Jesus' body. A grave robber couldn't possibly have made off with Jesus' body and left the linens as if they were still shaped around it.

20:9 As further proof that the disciples did not fabricate this story, we find that Peter and John were surprised that Jesus was not in the tomb. When John saw the graveclothes looking like an empty cocoon from which Jesus had emerged, he believed that Jesus had risen. It wasn't until after they had seen the empty tomb that they remembered what the Scriptures and Jesus had said—he would die, but he would also rise again!

20:9 Jesus' resurrection is the key to the Christian faith. Why? (1) Just as he said, Jesus rose from the dead. We can be confident, therefore, that he will accomplish all he has promised. (2) Jesus' bodily resurrection shows us that the living Christ, not a false prophet or impostor, is ruler of God's eternal kingdom. (3) We can be certain of our own resurrection because Jesus was resurrected. Death is not the end—there is future life. (4) The divine power that brought Jesus back to life is now available to us to bring our spiritually dead selves back to life. (5) The resurrection is the basis for the church's witness to the world.

Jesus Appears to Mary Magdalene
(240/Mark 16:9–11)

10Then the disciples went back to their homes, 11but Mary stood outside the tomb
crying. As she wept, she bent over to look into the tomb[l] 12and saw two angels in
white,[m] seated where Jesus' body had been, one at the head and the other at the foot.
13They asked her, "Woman, why are you crying?"[n]
"They have taken my Lord away," she said, "and I don't know where they have
put him."[o] 14At this, she turned round and saw Jesus standing there,[p] but she did
not realise that it was Jesus.[q]
15"Woman," he said, "why are you crying?[r] Who is it you are looking for?"
Thinking he was the gardener, she said, "Sir, if you have carried him away, tell
me where you have put him, and I will get him."
16Jesus said to her, "Mary."
She turned towards him and cried out in Aramaic,[s] "Rabboni!"[t] (which means
Teacher).
17Jesus said, "Do not hold on to me, for I have not yet returned to the Father. Go
instead to my brothers[u] and tell them, 'I am returning to my Father[v] and your Father,
to my God and your God.' "
18Mary Magdalene[w] went to the disciples[x] with the news: "I have seen the Lord!"
And she told them that he had said these things to her.

Jesus Appears to the Disciples behind Locked Doors
(244/Luke 24:36–43)

19On the evening of that first day of the week, when the disciples were together,
with the doors locked for fear of the Jews,[y] Jesus came and stood among them and
said, "Peace[z] be with you!"[a] 20After he said this, he showed them his hands and
side.[b] The disciples were overjoyed[c] when they saw the Lord.
21Again Jesus said, "Peace be with you![d] As the Father has sent me,[e] I am sending
you."[f] 22And with that he breathed on them and said, "Receive the Holy Spirit.[g]
23If you forgive anyone his sins, they are forgiven; if you do not forgive them, they
are not forgiven."[h]

Jesus Appears to the Disciples Including Thomas
(245/Mark 16:14)

24Now Thomas[i] (called Didymus), one of the Twelve, was not with the disciples
when Jesus came. 25So the other disciples told him, "We have seen the Lord!"

20:11 [l]ver 5
20:12 [m]Mt 28:2, 3; Mk 16:5; Lk 24:4; Ac 5:19
20:13 [n]ver 15 [o]ver 2
20:14 [p]Mt 28:9; Mk 16:9 [q]Lk 24:16; Jn 21:4
20:15 [r]ver 13
20:16 [s]Jn 5:2 [t]Mt 23:7
20:17 [u]Mt 28:10 [v]Jn 7:33
20:18 [w]ver 1 [x]Lk 24:10, 22, 23
20:19 [y]Jn 7:13 [z]Jn 14:27 [a]ver 21, 26; Lk 24:36-39
20:20 [b]Lk 24:39, 40; Jn 19:34 [c]Jn 16:20, 22
20:21 [d]ver 19 [e]Jn 3:17 [f]Mt 28:19; Jn 17:18
20:22 [g]Jn 7:39; Ac 2:38; 8:15-17; 19:2; Gal 3:2
20:23 [h]Mt 16:19; 18:18
20:24 [i]Jn 11:16

20:17 Mary did not want to lose Jesus again. She had not yet understood the resurrection. Perhaps she thought this was his promised second coming (14:3). But Jesus did not want to be detained at the tomb. If he did not ascend to heaven, the Holy Spirit could not come. Both he and Mary had important work to do.

20:18 Mary didn't recognise Jesus at first. Her grief had blinded her; she couldn't see him because she didn't expect to see him. Then he spoke her name, and immediately she recognised him. Imagine the love that flooded her heart when she heard her Saviour saying her name. Jesus is near you, and he is calling your name. Can you, like Mary, regard him as your Lord?

20:18 Mary did not meet the risen Christ until she had discovered the empty tomb. She responded with joy and obedience by going to tell the disciples. We cannot meet Christ until we discover that he is indeed alive, that his tomb is empty. Are you filled with joy by this good news, and do you share it with others?

20:21 Jesus again identified himself with his Father. He told the disciples by whose authority he did his work. Then he passed to his disciples the job of spreading the gospel of salvation around the world. Whatever God has asked you to do, remember: (1) your authority comes from God, and (2) Jesus has demonstrated by words and actions how to accomplish the job he has given you. As the Father sent Jesus, Jesus sends his followers . . . and you.

20:22 This may have been a special filling of the Holy Spirit for the disciples, a foretaste of what all believers would experience from the time of Pentecost (Acts 2) and for ever after. To do God's work, we need the guidance and power of the Holy Spirit. We must avoid trying to do his work in our own strength.

20:22 There is life in the breath of God. Man was created but did not come alive until God breathed into him the breath of life (Genesis 2:7). God's first breath made man different from all other forms of creation. Now, through the breath of Jesus, God imparted eternal, spiritual life. With this in-breathing came the power to do God's will on earth.

20:23 Jesus was giving the disciples their Spirit-powered and Spirit-guided mission – to preach the Good News about Jesus so people's sins might be forgiven. The disciples did not have the power to forgive sins (only God can forgive sins), but Jesus gave them the privilege of telling new believers that their sins *have been* forgiven because they have accepted Jesus' message (see the notes on Matthew 16:19 and 18:18). All believers have this same privilege. We can announce the forgiveness of sin with certainty when we ourselves find repentance and faith.

20:24–29 Have you ever wished you could actually see Jesus, touch him, and hear his words? Are there times you want to sit down with him and get his advice? Thomas wanted Jesus' physical

20:25 [j]ver 20 [k]Mk 16:11
20:26 [l]Jn 14:27 [m]ver 21
20:27 [n]ver 25; Lk 24:40
20:29 [o]Jn 3:15 [p]1Pe 1:8
20:30 [q]Jn 2:11 [r]Jn 21:25
20:31 [s]Jn 3:15; 19:35 [t]Mt 4:3 [u]Mt 25:46
21:1 [a]Jn 20:19, 26 [b]Jn 6:1
21:2 [c]Jn 11:16 [d]Jn 1:45 [e]Jn 2:1 [f]Mt 4:21
21:3 [g]Lk 5:5

But he said to them, "Unless I see the nail marks in his hands and put my finger
where the nails were, and put my hand into his side,[j] I will not believe it."[k]
26 A week later his disciples were in the house again, and Thomas was with them.
Though the doors were locked, Jesus came and stood among them and said, "Peace[l]
be with you!"[m] 27 Then he said to Thomas, "Put your finger here; see my hands. Reach
out your hand and put it into my side. Stop doubting and believe."[n]
28 Thomas said to him, "My Lord and my God!"
29 Then Jesus told him, "Because you have seen me, you have believed;[o] blessed
are those who have not seen and yet have believed."[p]
30 Jesus did many other miraculous signs[q] in the presence of his disciples, which
are not recorded in this book.[r] 31 But these are written that you may**[a]** believe[s] that
Jesus is the Christ, the Son of God,[t] and that by believing you may have life in his
name.[u]

Jesus Appears to the Disciples While Fishing
(246)

21 Afterwards Jesus appeared again to his disciples,[a] by the Sea of Tiberias.**[a]**[b]
It happened this way: 2 Simon Peter, Thomas[c] (called Didymus), Nathanael[d]
from Cana in Galilee,[e] the sons of Zebedee,[f] and two other disciples were together.
3 "I'm going out to fish," Simon Peter told them, and they said, "We'll go with you."
So they went out and got into the boat, but that night they caught nothing.[g]

a *31* Some manuscripts *may continue to* **a** *1* That is, Sea of Galilee

JESUS' APPEARANCES AFTER HIS RESURRECTION

Mary Magdalene	Mark 16:9–11; John 20:10–18
The other women at the tomb	Matthew 28:8–10
Peter in Jerusalem	Luke 24:34; 1 Corinthians 15:5
The two travellers on the road	Mark 16:12, 13
Ten disciples behind closed doors	Mark 16:14; Luke 24:36–43; John 20:19–25
All the disciples, with Thomas (excluding Judas Iscariot)	John 20:26–31; 1 Corinthians 15:5
Seven disciples while fishing	John 21:1–14
Eleven disciples on the mountain	Matthew 28:16–20
A crowd of 500	1 Corinthians 15:6
Jesus' brother James	1 Corinthians 15:7
Those who watched Jesus ascend into heaven	Luke 24:44–49; Acts 1:3–8

The truth of Christianity rests heavily on the resurrection. If Jesus rose from the grave, who saw him? How trustworthy were the witnesses? Those who claimed to have seen the risen Jesus went on to turn the world upside down. Most of them also died for being followers of Christ. People rarely die for half-hearted belief. These are the people who saw Jesus risen from the grave.

presence. But God's plan is wiser. He has not limited himself to one physical body; he wants to be present with you at all times. Even now he is with you in the form of the Holy Spirit. You can talk to him, and you can find his words to you in the pages of the Bible. He can be as real to you as he was to Thomas.

20:25–28 Jesus wasn't hard on Thomas for his doubts. Despite his scepticism, Thomas was still loyal to the believers and to Jesus himself. Some people need to doubt before they believe. If doubt leads to questions, questions lead to answers, and the answers are accepted, then doubt has done good work. It is when doubt becomes stubbornness and stubbornness becomes a life-style that doubt harms faith. When you doubt, don't stop there. Let your doubt deepen your faith as you continue to search for the answer.

20:27 Jesus' resurrected body was unique. It was not the same kind of flesh and blood Lazarus had when he came back to life. Jesus' body was no longer subject to the same laws of nature as before his death. He could appear in a locked room; yet he was not a ghost or apparition because he could be touched and could eat. Jesus' resurrection was *literal* and *physical*—he was not a disembodied spirit.

20:29 Some people think they would believe in Jesus if they could see a definite sign or miracle. But Jesus says we are blessed if we can believe without seeing. We have all the proof we need in the words of the Bible and the testimony of believers. A physical appearance would not make Jesus any more real to us than he is now.

20:30, 31 To understand the life and mission of Jesus more fully, all we need to do is study the Gospels. John tells us that his Gospel records only a few of the many events in Jesus' life on earth. But the gospel includes everything we need to know to believe that Jesus is the Christ, the Son of God, through whom we receive eternal life.

21:1ff This chapter tells how Jesus commissioned Peter. Perhaps Peter needed special encouragement after his denial—he may have felt completely worthless. Verses 1–14 set the scene for Jesus' conversation with Peter.

4 Early in the morning, Jesus stood on the shore, but the disciples did not realise
that it was Jesus.[h]
5 He called out to them, "Friends, haven't you any fish?"
"No," they answered.
6 He said, "Throw your net on the right side of the boat and you will find some."
When they did, they were unable to haul the net in because of the large number of
fish.[i]
7 Then the disciple whom Jesus loved[j] said to Peter, "It is the Lord!" As soon as
Simon Peter heard him say, "It is the Lord," he wrapped his outer garment around
him (for he had taken it off) and jumped into the water. 8 The other disciples followed
in the boat, towing the net full of fish, for they were not far from shore, about a
hundred yards.[b] 9 When they landed, they saw a fire[k] of burning coals there with
fish on it,[l] and some bread.
10 Jesus said to them, "Bring some of the fish you have just caught."
11 Simon Peter climbed aboard and dragged the net ashore. It was full of large fish,
153, but even with so many the net was not torn. 12 Jesus said to them, "Come and
have breakfast." None of the disciples dared ask him, "Who are you?" They knew
it was the Lord. 13 Jesus came, took the bread and gave it to them, and did the same
with the fish.[m] 14 This was now the third time Jesus appeared to his disciples[n] after
he was raised from the dead.

Jesus Talks with Peter
(247)

15 When they had finished eating, Jesus said to Simon Peter, "Simon son of John,
do you truly love me more than these?"
"Yes, Lord," he said, "you know that I love you."[o]
Jesus said, "Feed my lambs."[p]
16 Again Jesus said, "Simon son of John, do you truly love me?"
He answered, "Yes, Lord, you know that I love you."
Jesus said, "Take care of my sheep."[q]
17 The third time he said to him, "Simon son of John, do you love me?"
Peter was hurt because Jesus asked him the third time, "Do you love me?"[r] He
said, "Lord, you know all things;[s] you know that I love you."
Jesus said, "Feed my sheep.[t] 18 I tell you the truth, when you were younger you
dressed yourself and went where you wanted; but when you are old you will stretch
out your hands, and someone else will dress you and lead you where you do not want
to go." 19 Jesus said this to indicate the kind of death[u] by which Peter would glorify
God.[v] Then he said to him, "Follow me!"
20 Peter turned and saw that the disciple whom Jesus loved[w] was following them.
(This was the one who had leaned back against Jesus at the supper and had said, "Lord,

21:4 [h] Lk 24:16; Jn 20:14
21:6 [i] Lk 5:4-7
21:7 [j] Jn 13:23
21:9 [k] Jn 18:18 [l] ver 10, 13
21:13 [m] ver 9
21:14 [n] Jn 20:19, 26
21:15 [o] Mt 26:33, 35; Jn 13:37 [p] Lk 12:32
21:16 [q] Mt 2:6; Ac 20:28; 1Pe 5:2, 3
21:17 [r] Jn 13:38 [s] Jn 16:30 [t] ver 16
21:19 [u] Jn 12:33; 18:32 [v] 2Pe 1:14
21:20 [w] ver 7; Jn 13:23

b 8 Greek *about two hundred cubits* (about 90 metres)

21:7 Only John ("the disciple whom Jesus loved") recognised Jesus in the dim morning light, undoubtedly because Jesus had performed a similar miracle earlier (Luke 5:1–11).

21:15–17 In this beach scene, Jesus led Peter through an experience that would remove the cloud of his denial. Peter had disowned Jesus three times. Three times Jesus asked Peter if he loved him. When Peter answered yes, Jesus told him to feed his sheep. It is one thing to say you love Jesus, but the real test is willingness to serve him. Peter had repented, and here Jesus was asking him to commit his life. Peter's life changed when he finally realised who Jesus was. His occupation changed from fisherman to evangelist; his identity changed from impetuous to "rock"; and his relationship to Jesus changed – he was forgiven, and he finally understood the significance of Jesus' words about his death and resurrection.

21:15–17 Jesus asked Peter three times if he loved him. The first time Jesus said, "Do you truly love (Greek *agape:* volitional, self-sacrificial love) me more than these?" The second time, Jesus focused on Peter alone and still used the word translated into Greek, *agape.* The third time, Jesus used the word translated into Greek, *phileo* (signifying affection, affinity, or brotherly love) and asked, in effect, "Are you even my friend?" Each time Peter responded with the word translated into Greek as *phileo.* Jesus doesn't settle for quick, superficial answers. He has a way of getting to the heart of the matter. Peter had to face his true feelings and motives when Jesus confronted him. How would you respond if Jesus asked you, "Do you truly love me?" Do you really love Jesus? Are you even his friend?

21:18, 19 This was a prediction of Peter's death by crucifixion. Tradition indicates that Peter was crucified for his faith – upside down because he did not feel worthy of dying as his Lord did. Despite what Peter's future held, Jesus told him to follow him. We may be uncertain and fearful about our future. But if we know God is in control, we can confidently follow Christ.

21:20
[x]Jn 13:25

21:22
[y]Mt 16:27; 1Co 4:5; Rev 2:25
[z]ver 19

21:23
[a]Ac 1:16

21:24
[b]Jn 15:27
[c]Jn 19:35

21:25
[d]Jn 20:30

who is going to betray you?")[x] 21 When Peter saw him, he asked, "Lord, what about
him?"
22 Jesus answered, "If I want him to remain alive until I return,[y] what is that to
you? You must follow me."[z] 23 Because of this, the rumour spread among the
brothers[a] that this disciple would not die. But Jesus did not say that he would not
die; he only said, "If I want him to remain alive until I return, what is that to you?"
24 This is the disciple who testifies to these things[b] and who wrote them down. We
know that his testimony is true.[c]
25 Jesus did many other things as well.[d] If every one of them were written down,
I suppose that even the whole world would not have room for the books that would
be written.

21:21, 22 Peter asked Jesus how John would die. Jesus replied that Peter should not concern himself with that. We tend to compare our lives to others, whether to rationalise our own level of devotion to Christ or to question God's justice. Jesus responds to us as he did to Peter: "What is that to you? You must follow me."

21:23 Early church history reports that after John spent several years as an exile on the island of Patmos, he returned to Ephesus where he died as an old man, near the end of the first century.

21:25 John's stated purpose for writing his Gospel was to show that Jesus was the Son of God. He clearly and systematically presented the evidence for Jesus' claims. When evidence is presented in the courtroom, those who hear it must make a choice. Those who read the Gospel of John must also make a choice—is Jesus the Son of God, or isn't he? You are the jury. The evidence has been clearly presented. You must decide. Read John's Gospel and believe!

250 EVENTS IN THE LIFE OF CHRIST/ A HARMONY OF THE GOSPELS

All four books in the Bible that tell the story of Jesus Christ—Matthew, Mark, Luke, and John—stand alone, emphasising a unique aspect of Jesus' life. But when these are blended into one complete account, or harmonised, we gain new insights into the life of Christ.

This harmony combines the four Gospels into a single chronological account of Christ's life on earth. It includes every chapter and verse of each Gospel, leaving nothing out.

The harmony is divided into 250 events. The title of each event is identical to the title found in the corresponding Gospel. Parallel passages found in more than one Gospel have identical titles, helping you to identify them quickly.

Each of the 250 events in the harmony is numbered. The number of the event corresponds to the number next to the title in the Bible text. When reading one of the Gospel accounts, you will notice, at times, that some numbers are missing or out of sequence. The easiest way to locate these events is to refer to the harmony.

In addition, if you are looking for a particular event in the life of Christ, the harmony can help you locate it more rapidly than searching through all four Gospels. Each of the 250 events has a distinctive title relating to the main emphasis of the passage to help you locate and remember the events.

This harmony will help you to visualise better the travels of Jesus, study the four Gospels comparatively, and appreciate the unity of their message.

I. BIRTH AND PREPARATION OF JESUS CHRIST

		Matthew	*Mark*	*Luke*	*John*
1	Luke's purpose in writing			1:1–4	
2	God became a human being				1:1–18
3	The ancestors of Jesus	1:1–17		3:23–38	
4	An angel promises the birth of John to Zechariah			1:5–25	
5	An angel promises the birth of Jesus to Mary			1:26–38	
6	Mary visits Elizabeth			1:39–56	
7	John the Baptist is born			1:57–80	
8	An angel appears to Joseph	1:18–25			
9	Jesus is born in Bethlehem			2:1–7	
10	Shepherds visit Jesus			2:8–20	
11	Mary and Joseph bring Jesus to the temple			2:21–40	
12	Visitors arrive from eastern lands	2:1–12			
13	The escape to Egypt	2:13–18			
14	The return to Nazareth	2:19–23			
15	Jesus speaks with the religious teachers			2:41–52	
16	John the Baptist prepares the way for Jesus	3:1–12	1:1–8	3:1–18	
17	John baptises Jesus	3:13–17	1:9–11	3:21, 22	
18	Satan tempts Jesus in the desert	4:1–11	1:12, 13	4:1–13	
19	John the Baptist declares his mission				1:19–28

	Matthew	Mark	Luke	John
20 John the Baptist proclaims Jesus as the Messiah				1:29–34
21 The first disciples follow Jesus				1:35–51
22 Jesus turns water into wine				2:1–12

II. MESSAGE AND MINISTRY OF JESUS CHRIST

	Matthew	Mark	Luke	John
23 Jesus clears the temple				2:12–25
24 Nicodemus visits Jesus at night				3:1–21
25 John the Baptist tells more about Jesus				3:22–36
26 Herod puts John in prison			3:19, 20	
27 Jesus talks to a woman at the well				4:1–26
28 Jesus tells about the spiritual harvest				4:27–38
29 Many Samaritans believe in Jesus				4:39–42
30 Jesus preaches in Galilee	4:12–17	1:14, 15	4:14, 15	4:43–45
31 Jesus heals a government official's son				4:46–54
32 Jesus is rejected at Nazareth			4:16–30	
33 Four fishermen follow Jesus	4:18–22	1:16–20		
34 Jesus teaches with great authority		1:21–28	4:31–37	
35 Jesus heals Peter's mother-in-law and many others	8:14–17	1:29–34	4:38–41	
36 Jesus preaches throughout Galilee	4:23–25	1:35–39	4:42–44	
37 Jesus provides a miraculous catch of fish			5:1–11	
38 Jesus heals a man with leprosy	8:1–4	1:40–45	5:12–16	
39 Jesus heals a paralysed man	9:1–8	2:1–12	5:17–26	
40 Jesus eats with sinners at Matthew's house	9:9–13	2:13–17	5:27–32	
41 Religious leaders ask Jesus about fasting	9:14–17	2:18–22	5:33–39	
42 Jesus heals a lame man by the pool				5:1–18
43 Jesus claims to be God's Son				5:19–30
44 Jesus supports his claim				5:31–47
45 The disciples pick wheat on the Sabbath	12:1–8	2:23–28	6:1–5	
46 Jesus heals a man's hand on the Sabbath	12:9–14	3:1–6	6:6–11	
47 Large crowds follow Jesus	12:15–21	3:7–12		
48 Jesus selects the twelve disciples		3:13–19	6.12–16	
49 Jesus gives the Beatitudes	5:1–12		6:17–26	
50 Jesus teaches about salt and light	5:13–16			
51 Jesus teaches about the law	5:17–20			
52 Jesus teaches about anger	5:21–26			
53 Jesus teaches about lust	5:27–30			
54 Jesus teaches about divorce	5:31, 32			
55 Jesus teaches about vows	5:33–37			
56 Jesus teaches about retaliation	5:38–42			
57 Jesus teaches about loving enemies	5:43–48		6:27–36	
58 Jesus teaches about giving to the needy	6:1–4			
59 Jesus teaches about prayer	6:5–15			
60 Jesus teaches about fasting	6:16–18			
61 Jesus teaches about money	6:19–24			
62 Jesus teaches about worry	6:25–34			
63 Jesus teaches about criticising others	7:1–6		6:37–42	
64 Jesus teaches about asking, seeking, knocking	7:7–12			
65 Jesus teaches about the way to heaven	7:13, 14			
66 Jesus teaches about fruit in people's lives	7:15–20		6:43–45	
67 Jesus teaches about those who build houses on rock and sand	7:21–29		6:46–49	
68 A Roman centurion demonstrates faith	8:5–13		7:1–10	
69 Jesus raises a widow's son from the dead			7:11–17	
70 Jesus eases John's doubt	11:1–19		7:18–35	
71 Jesus promises rest for the soul	11:20–30			
72 A sinful woman anoints Jesus' feet			7:36–50	
73 Women accompany Jesus and the disciples			8:1–3	
74 Religious leaders accuse Jesus of being under Satan's power	12:22–37	3:20–30		

	Matthew	Mark	Luke	John
75 Religious leaders ask Jesus for a miracle	12:38–45			
76 Jesus describes his true family	12:46–50	3:31–35	8:19–21	
77 Jesus tells the parable of the four soils	13:1–9	4:1–9	8:4–8	
78 Jesus explains the parable of the four soils	13:10–23	4:10–25	8:9–18	
79 Jesus tells the parable of the growing seed		4:26–29		
80 Jesus tells the parable of the weeds	13:24–30			
81 Jesus tells the parable of the mustard seed	13:31, 32	4:30–34		
82 Jesus tells the parable of the yeast	13:33–35			
83 Jesus explains the parable of the weeds	13:36–43			
84 Jesus tells the parable of hidden treasure	13:44			
85 Jesus tells the parable of the pearl merchant	13:45, 46			
86 Jesus tells the parable of the fishing net	13:47–52			
87 Jesus calms the storm	8:23–27	4:35–41	8:22–25	
88 Jesus sends the demons into a herd of pigs	8:28–34	5:1–20	8:26–39	
89 Jesus heals a bleeding woman and restores a girl to life	9:18–26	5:21–43	8:40–56	
90 Jesus heals the blind and mute	9:27–34			
91 The people of Nazareth refuse to believe	13:53–58	6:1–6		
92 Jesus urges the disciples to pray for workers	9:35–38			
93 Jesus sends out the twelve disciples	10:1–16	6:7–13	9:1–6	
94 Jesus prepares the disciples for persecution	10:17–42			
95 Herod kills John the Baptist	14:1–12	6:14–29	9:7–9	
96 Jesus feeds five thousand	14:13–21	6:30–44	9:10–17	6:1–15
97 Jesus walks on water	14:22–33	6:45–52		6:16–21
98 Jesus heals all who touch him	14:34–36	6:53–56		
99 Jesus is the true bread from heaven				6:22–40
100 The Jews disagree that Jesus is from heaven				6:41–59
101 Many disciples desert Jesus				6:60–71
102 Jesus teaches about inner purity	15:1–20	7:1–23		
103 Jesus sends a demon out of a girl	15:21–28	7:24–30		
104 The crowd marvels at Jesus' healings	15:29–31	7:31–37		
105 Jesus feeds four thousand	15:32–39	8:1–10		
106 Religious leaders ask for a sign in the sky	16:1–4	8:11–13		
107 Jesus warns against wrong teaching	16:5–12	8:14–21		
108 Jesus restores sight to a blind man		8:22–26		
109 Peter says Jesus is the Messiah	16:13–20	8:27–30	9:18–20	
110 Jesus predicts his death the first time	16:21–28	8:31–9:1	9:21–27	
111 Jesus is transfigured on the mountain	17:1–13	9:2–13	9:28–36	
112 Jesus heals a demon-possessed boy	17:14–21	9:14–29	9:37–43	
113 Jesus predicts his death the second time	17:22, 23	9:30–32	9:44, 45	
114 Peter finds the coin in the fish's mouth	17:24–27			
115 The disciples argue about who would be the greatest	18:1–6	9:33–37	9:46–48	
116 The disciples forbid another to use Jesus' name		9:38–41	9:49, 50	
117 Jesus warns against temptation	18:7–9	9:42–50		
118 Jesus warns against looking down on others	18:10–14			
119 Jesus teaches how to treat a believer who sins	18:15–20			
120 Jesus tells the parable of the unforgiving debtor	18:21–35			
121 Jesus' brothers ridicule him				7:1–9
122 Jesus teaches about the cost of following him	8:18–22		9:51–62	
123 Jesus teaches openly at the temple				7:10–31
124 Religious leaders attempt to arrest Jesus				7:32–52
125 Jesus forgives an adulterous woman				7:53–8:11
126 Jesus is the light of the world				8:12–20
127 Jesus warns of coming judgment				8:21–30
128 Jesus speaks about God's true children				8:31–47
129 Jesus states he is eternal				8:48–59
130 Jesus sends out seventy-two messengers			10:1–16	
131 The seventy-two messengers return			10:17–24	
132 Jesus tells the parable of the Good Samaritan			10:25–37	
133 Jesus visits Mary and Martha			10:38–42	
134 Jesus teaches his disciples about prayer			11:1–13	
135 Jesus answers hostile accusations			11:14–28	
136 Jesus warns against unbelief			11:29–32	

	Matthew	Mark	Luke	John
137 Jesus teaches about the light within			11:33–36	
138 Jesus criticises the religious leaders			11:37–54	
139 Jesus speaks against hypocrisy			12:1–12	
140 Jesus tells the parable of the rich fool			12:13–21	
141 Jesus warns about worry			12:22–34	
142 Jesus warns about preparing for his coming			12:35–48	
143 Jesus warns about coming division			12:49–53	
144 Jesus warns about the future crisis			12:54–59	
145 Jesus calls the people to repent			13:1–9	
146 Jesus heals the crippled woman			13:10–17	
147 Jesus teaches about the kingdom of God			13:18–21	
148 Jesus heals the man who was born blind				9:1–12
149 Religious leaders question the blind man				9:13–34
150 Jesus teaches about spiritual blindness				9:35–41
151 Jesus is the Good Shepherd				10:1–21
152 Religious leaders surround Jesus at the temple				10:22–42
153 Jesus teaches about entering the kingdom			13:22–30	
154 Jesus grieves over Jerusalem			13:31–35	
155 Jesus heals a man with dropsy			14:1–6	
156 Jesus teaches about seeking honour			14:7–14	
157 Jesus tells the parable of the great feast			14:15–24	
158 Jesus teaches about the cost of being a disciple			14:25–35	
159 Jesus tells the parable of the lost sheep			15:1–7	
160 Jesus tells the parable of the lost coin			15:8–10	
161 Jesus tells the parable of the lost son			15:11–32	
162 Jesus tells the parable of the shrewd manager			16:1–18	
163 Jesus tells about the rich man and the beggar			16:19–31	
164 Jesus tells about forgiveness and faith			17:1–10	
165 Lazarus becomes ill and dies				11:1–16
166 Jesus comforts Mary and Martha				11:17–37
167 Jesus raises Lazarus from the dead				11:38–44
168 Religious leaders plot to kill Jesus				11:45–57
169 Jesus heals ten men with leprosy			17:11–19	
170 Jesus teaches about the coming of the kingdom of God			17:20–37	
171 Jesus tells the parable of the persistent widow			18:1–8	
172 Jesus tells the parable of two men who prayed			18:9–14	
173 Jesus teaches about marriage and divorce	19:1–12	10:1–12		
174 Jesus blesses little children	19:13–15	10:13–16	18:15–17	
175 Jesus speaks to the rich young man	19:16–30	10:17–31	18:18–30	
176 Jesus tells the parable of the workers paid equally	20:1–16			
177 Jesus predicts his death the third time	20:17–19	10:32–34	18:31–34	
178 Jesus teaches about serving others	20:20–28	10:35–45		
179 Jesus heals a blind beggar	20:29–34	10:46–52	18:35–43	
180 Jesus brings salvation to Zacchaeus' home			19:1–10	
181 Jesus tells the parable of the king's ten servants			19:11–27	
182 A woman anoints Jesus with perfume	26:6–13	14:3–9		12:1–11
183 Jesus rides into Jerusalem on a donkey	21:1–11	11:1–11	19:28–44	12:12–19
184 Jesus clears the temple again	21:12–17	11:12–19	19:45–48	
185 Jesus explains why he must die				12:20–36
186 Most of the people do not believe in Jesus				12:37–43
187 Jesus summarises his message				12:44–50
188 Jesus says the disciples can pray for anything	21:18–22	11:20–26		
189 Religious leaders challenge Jesus' authority	21:23–27	11:27–33	20:1–8	
190 Jesus tells the parable of the two sons	21:28–32			
191 Jesus tells the parable of the wicked tenants	21:33–46	12:1–12	20:9–19	
192 Jesus tells the parable of the wedding feast	22:1–14			
193 Religious leaders question Jesus about paying taxes	22:15–22	12:13–17	20:20–26	
194 Religious leaders question Jesus about the resurrection	22:23–33	12:18–27	20:27–40	
195 Religious leaders question Jesus about the greatest commandment	22:34–40	12:28–34		
196 Religious leaders cannot answer Jesus' question	22:41–46	12:35–37	20:41–44	

	Matthew	Mark	Luke	John
197 Jesus warns against the religious leaders	23:1–12	12:38–40	20:45–47	
198 Jesus condemns the religious leaders	23:13–36			
199 Jesus grieves over Jerusalem again	23:37–39			
200 A poor widow gives all she has		12:41–44	21:1–4	
201 Jesus tells about the future	24:1–25	13:1–23	21:5–24	
202 Jesus tells about his return	24:26–35	13:24–31	21:25–33	
203 Jesus tells about remaining watchful	24:36–51	13:32–37	21:34–38	
204 Jesus tells the parable of the ten bridesmaids	25:1–13			
205 Jesus tells the parable of the loaned money	25:14–30			
206 Jesus tells about the final judgment	25:31–46			

III. DEATH AND RESURRECTION OF JESUS CHRIST

	Matthew	Mark	Luke	John
207 Religious leaders plot to kill Jesus	26:1–5	14:1, 2	22:1, 2	
208 Judas agrees to betray Jesus	26:14–16	14:10, 11	22:3–6	
209 Disciples prepare for the Passover	26:17–19	14:12–16	22:7–13	
210 Jesus washes the disciples' feet				13:1–20
211 Jesus and the disciples have the Last Supper	26:20–30	14:17–26	22:14–30	13:21–30
212 Jesus predicts Peter's denial			22:31–38	13:31–38
213 Jesus is the way to the Father				14:1–14
214 Jesus promises the Holy Spirit				14:15–31
215 Jesus teaches about the vine and the branches				15:1–17
216 Jesus warns about the world's hatred				15:18—16:4
217 Jesus teaches about the Holy Spirit				16:5–15
218 Jesus teaches about using his name in prayer				16:16–33
219 Jesus prays for himself				17:1–5
220 Jesus prays for his disciples				17:6–19
221 Jesus prays for future believers				17:20–26
222 Jesus again predicts Peter's denial	26:31–35	14:27–31		
223 Jesus agonises in the garden	26:36–46	14:32–42	22:39–46	
224 Jesus is betrayed and arrested	26:47–56	14:43–52	22:47–53	18:1–11
225 Annas questions Jesus				18:12–24
226 Caiaphas questions Jesus	26:57–68	14:53–65		
227 Peter denies knowing Jesus	26:69–75	14:66–72	22:54–65	18:25–27
228 The council of religious leaders condemns Jesus	27:1, 2	15:1	22:66–71	
229 Judas kills himself	27:3–10			
230 Jesus stands trial before Pilate	27:11–14	15:2–5	23:1–5	18:28–37
231 Jesus stands trial before Herod			23:6–12	
232 Pilate hands Jesus over to be crucified	27:15–26	15:6–15	23:13–25	18:38—19:16
233 Roman soldiers mock Jesus	27:27–31	15:16–20		
234 Jesus is led away to be crucified	27:32–34	15:21–24	23:26–31	19:17
235 Jesus is placed on the cross	27:35–44	15:25–32	23:32–43	19:18–27
236 Jesus dies on the cross	27:45–56	15:33–41	23:44–49	19:28–37
237 Jesus is laid in the tomb	27:57–61	15:42–47	23:50–56	19:38–42
238 Guards are posted at the tomb	27:62–66			
239 Jesus rises from the dead	28:1–7	16:1–8	24:1–12	20:1–9
240 Jesus appears to Mary Magdalene		16:9–11		20:10–18
241 Jesus appears to the women	28:8–10			
242 Religious leaders bribe the guards	28:11–15			
243 Jesus appears to two believers travelling on the road		16:12, 13	24:13–35	
244 Jesus appears to the disciples behind locked doors			24:36–43	20:19–23
245 Jesus appears to the disciples including Thomas		16:14		20:24–31
246 Jesus appears to the disciples while fishing				21:1–14
247 Jesus talks with Peter				21:15–25

	Matthew	Mark	Luke	John
248 Jesus gives the Great Commission	28:16–20	16:15–18		
249 Jesus appears to the disciples in Jerusalem			24:44–49	
250 Jesus ascends into heaven		16:19, 20	24:50–53	

THE PARABLES OF JESUS

I. Teaching Parables

A. About the Kingdom of God
1. The Soils (Matthew 13:3–8; Mark 4:4–8; Luke 8:5–8)
2. The Weeds (Matthew 13:24–30)
3. The Mustard Seed (Matthew 13:31, 32; Mark 4:30–32; Luke 13:18, 19)
4. The Yeast (Matthew 13:33; Luke 13:20, 21)
5. The Treasure (Matthew 13:44)
6. The Pearl (Matthew 13:45, 46)
7. The Fishing Net (Matthew 13:47–50)
8. The Growing Wheat (Mark 4:26–29)

B. About Service and Obedience
1. The Workers in the Harvest (Matthew 20:1–16)
2. The Loaned Money (Matthew 25:14–30)
3. The Nobleman's Servants (Luke 19:11–27)
4. The Servant's Role (Luke 17:7–10)

C. About Prayer
1. The Friend at Midnight (Luke 11:5–8)
2. The Unjust Judge (Luke 18:1–8)

D. About Neighbours
1. The Good Samaritan (Luke 10:30–37)

E. About Humility
1. The Wedding Feast (Luke 14:7–11)
2. The Proud Pharisee and the Corrupt Tax Collector (Luke 18:9–14)

F. About Wealth
1. The Rich Fool (Luke 12:16–21)
2. The Great Feast (Luke 14:16–24)
3. The Shrewd Manager (Luke 16:1–9)

II. Gospel Parables

A. About God's Love
1. The Lost Sheep (Matthew 18:12–14; Luke 15:3–7)
2. The Lost Coin (Luke 15:8–10)
3. The Lost Son (Luke 15:11–32)

B. About Thankfulness
1. The Forgiven Debts (Luke 7:41–43)

III. Parables of Judgment and the Future

A. About Christ's Return
1. The Ten Virgins (Matthew 25:1–13)
2. The Wise and Faithful Servants (Matthew 24:45–51; Luke 12:42–48)
3. The Travelling Owner of the House (Mark 13:34–37)

B. About God's Values
1. The Two Sons (Matthew 21:28–32)
2. The Wicked Tenants (Matthew 21:33, 34; Mark 12:1–9; Luke 20:9–16)
3. The Unproductive Fig Tree (Luke 13:6–9)
4. The Marriage Feast (Matthew 22:1–14)
5. The Unforgiving Servant (Matthew 18:23–35)

JESUS' MIRACLES

John and the other Gospel writers were able to record only a fraction of the people who were touched and healed by Jesus. But enough of Jesus' words and works have been saved so that we also might be able to know him and be his disciples in this day. There follows a listing of the miracles that are included in the Gospels. They were supernatural events that pointed people to God, and they were acts of love by One who is love.

	Matthew	*Mark*	*Luke*	*John*
Five thousand people are fed	14:15–21	6:35–44	9:12–17	6:5–14
Calming the storm	8:23–27	4:35–41	8:22–25	
Demons sent into the pigs	8:28–34	5:1–20	8:26–39	
Jairus' daughter raised	9:18–26	5:22–24, 35–43	8:41, 42, 49–56	
A sick woman is healed	9:20–22	5:25–34	8:43–48	
Jesus heals a paralytic	9:1–8	2:1–12	5:17–26	
A leper is healed at Gennesaret	8:1–4	1:40–45	5:12–15	
Peter's mother-in-law healed	8:14–17	1:29–31	4:38, 39	
A shrivelled hand is restored	12:9–13	3:1–5	6:6–11	
A boy with an evil spirit is healed	17:14–21	9:14–29	9:37–42	
Jesus walks on the water	14:22–33	6:45–52		6:17–21
Blind Bartimaeus receives sight	20:29–34	10:46–52	18:35–43	
A girl is freed from a demon	15:21–28	7:24–30		
Four thousand are fed	15:32–38	8:1–9		
Cursing the fig tree	21:18–22	11:12–14, 20–24		
A centurion's servant is healed	8:5–13		7:1–10	
An evil spirit is sent out of a man		1:23–27	4:33–36	
A mute demoniac is healed	12:22		11:14	
Two blind men find sight	9:27–31			
Jesus heals the mute man	9:32, 33			
A coin in a fish's mouth	17:24–27			
A deaf and mute man is healed		7:31–37		
A blind man sees at Bethsaida		8:22–26		
The first miraculous catch of fish			5:1–11	
A widow's son is raised			7:11–16	
A crippled woman is healed			13:10–17	
Jesus heals a sick man			14:1–6	
Ten lepers are healed			17:11–19	
Jesus restores a man's ear			22:49–51	
Jesus turns water into wine				2:1–11
An official's son is healed at Cana				4:46–54
A lame man is healed				5:1–16
Jesus heals a man born blind				9:1–7
Lazarus is raised from the dead				11:1–45
The second miraculous catch of fish				21:1–14

COMPARISON OF THE FOUR GOSPELS

All four Gospels present the life and teachings of Jesus. Each book, however, focuses on a unique facet of Jesus and his character. To understand more about the specific characteristics of Jesus, read any one of the four Gospels.

	Matthew	*Mark*	*Luke*	*John*
Jesus is . . .	The promised King	The Servant of God	The Son of Man	The Son of God
The original readers were . . .	Jews	Gentiles, Romans	Greeks	Christians throughout the world
Significant themes . . .	Jesus is the Messiah because he fulfilled Old Testament prophecy	Jesus backed up his words with action	Jesus was God but also fully human	Belief in Jesus is required for salvation
Character of the writer . . .	Teacher	Storyteller	Historian	Theologian
Greatest emphasis is on . . .	Jesus' sermons and words	Jesus' miracles and actions	Jesus' humanity	The principles of Jesus' teaching

MESSIANIC PROPHECIES AND FULFILMENTS
For the Gospel writers, one of the main reasons for believing in Jesus was the way his life fulfiled the Old Testament prophecies about the Messiah. Following is a list of some of the main prophecies.

	Old Testament Prophecies	*New Testament Fulfilment*
1. Messiah was to be born in Bethlehem	Micah 5:2	Matthew 2:1–6 Luke 2:1–20
2. Messiah was to be born of a virgin	Isaiah 7:14	Matthew 1:18–25 Luke 1:26–38
3. Messiah was to be a prophet like Moses	Deuteronomy 18:15, 18, 19	John 7:40
4. Messiah was to enter Jerusalem in triumph	Zechariah 9:9	Matthew 21:1–9 John 12:12–16
5. Messiah was to be rejected by his own people	Isaiah 53:1, 3 Psalm 118:22	Matthew 26:3, 4 John 12:37–43 Acts 4:1–12
6. Messiah was to be betrayed by one of his followers	Psalm 41:9	Matthew 26:14–16, 47–50 Luke 22:19–23
7. Messiah was to be tried and condemned	Isaiah 53:8	Luke 23:1–25 Matthew 27:1, 2
8. Messiah was to be silent before his accusers	Isaiah 53:7	Matthew 27:12–14 Mark 15:3–4, Luke 23:8–10
9. Messiah was to be struck and spat on by his enemies	Isaiah 50:6	Matthew 26:67 Matthew 27:30 Mark 14:65
10. Messiah was to be mocked and insulted	Psalm 22:7, 8	Matthew 27:39–44 Luke 23:11, 35
11. Messiah was to die by crucifixion	Psalm 22:14, 16, 17	Matthew 27:31 Mark 15:20, 25
12. Messiah was to suffer with criminals and pray for his enemies	Isaiah 53:12	Matthew 27:38 Mark 15:27, 28 Luke 23:32–34
13. Messiah was to be given vinegar and gall	Psalm 69:21	Matthew 27:34 John 19:28–30
14. Others were to cast lots for Messiah's garments	Psalm 22:18	Matthew 27:35 John 19:23, 24
15. Messiah's bones were not to be broken	Exodus 12:46	John 19:31–36
16. Messiah was to die as a sacrifice for sin	Isaiah 53:5, 6, 8, 10, 11, 12	John 1:29; 11:49–52 Acts 10:43; 13:38, 39
17. Messiah was to be raised from the dead	Psalm 16:10	Acts 2:22–32 Matthew 28:1–10
18. Messiah is now at God's right hand	Psalm 110:1	Mark 16:19 Luke 24:50, 51

ACTS

Jesus crucified; Pentecost; church begun A.D. 30	*Stephen martyred; Paul's conversion 35*	*Paul returns to Tarsus 38*	*Barnabas goes to find Paul 43*	*James martyred; Peter in prison 44*	*Paul's first missionary journey 46-48*	*Jerusalem Council 50*	*Paul's second missionary journey 50-52*

VITAL STATISTICS

PURPOSE:
To give an accurate account of the birth and growth of the Christian church

AUTHOR:
Luke (a Gentile physician)

TO WHOM WRITTEN:
Theophilus and all lovers of God

DATE WRITTEN:
Between A.D. 63 and 70

SETTING:
Acts is the connecting link between Christ's life and the life of the church, between the Gospels and the Letters

KEY VERSE:
"But you will receive power when the Holy Spirit comes on you; and you will be my witnesses in Jerusalem, and in all Judea and Samaria, and to the ends of the earth" (1:8).

KEY PEOPLE:
Peter, John, James, Stephen, Philip, Paul, Barnabas, Cornelius, James (Jesus' brother), Timothy, Lydia, Silas, Titus, Apollos, Agabus, Ananias, Felix, Festus, Agrippa, Luke

KEY PLACES:
Jerusalem, Samaria, Lydda, Joppa, Antioch, Cyprus, Pisidian Antioch, Iconium, Lystra, Derbe, Philippi, Thessalonica, Berea, Athens, Corinth, Ephesus, Caesarea, Malta, Rome

SPECIAL FEATURES:
Acts is a sequel to the Gospel of Luke. Because Acts ends so abruptly, Luke may have planned to write a third book, continuing the story.

WITH a flick of the fingers, friction occurs and a spark leaps from match to tinder. A small flame burns the edges and grows, fuelled by wood and air. Heat builds, and soon the kindling is licked by orange-red tongues. Higher and wider it spreads, consuming the wood. The flame has become a fire.

Nearly 2,000 years ago, a match was struck in Palestine. At first, just a few in that corner of the world were touched and warmed; but the fire spread beyond Jerusalem and Judea out to the world and to all people. Acts provides an eyewitness account of the flame and fire—the birth and spread of the church. Beginning in Jerusalem with a small group of disciples, the message travelled across the Roman empire. Empowered by the Holy Spirit, this courageous band preached, taught, healed, and demonstrated love in synagogues, schools, homes, marketplaces, and courtrooms, and on streets, hills, ships, and desert roads—wherever God sent them, lives and history were changed.

Written by Luke as a sequel to his Gospel, Acts is an accurate historical record of the early church. But Acts is also a theological book, with lessons and living examples of the work of the Holy Spirit, church relationships and organisation, the implications of grace, and the law of love. And Acts is an apologetic work, building a strong case for the validity of Christ's claims and promises.

The book of Acts begins with the outpouring of the promised Holy Spirit and the commencement of the proclamation of the gospel of Jesus Christ. This Spirit-inspired evangelism began in Jerusalem and eventually spread to Rome, covering most of the Roman empire. The gospel first went to the Jews; but they, as a nation, rejected it. A remnant of Jews, of course, gladly received the good news. But the continual rejection of the gospel by the vast majority of the Jews led to the ever-increasing proclamation of the gospel to the Gentiles. This was according to Jesus' plan: the gospel was to go from Jerusalem, to Judea, to Samaria, and to the ends of the earth (1:8). This, in fact, is the pattern that the Acts narrative follows. The glorious proclamation began in Jerusalem (chapters 1—7), went to Judea and Samaria (chapter 8 and following), and to the countries beyond Judea (11:19; 13:4 and on to the end of Acts). The second half of Acts is focused primarily on Paul's missionary journeys to many countries north of the Mediterranean Sea. He, with his companions, took the gospel first to the Jews and then to the Gentiles. Some of the Jews believed, and many of the Gentiles received the good news with joy. New churches were started, and new believers began to grow in the Christian life.

As you read Acts, put yourself in the place of the disciples—feel with them as they are filled with the Holy Spirit, and thrill with them as they see thousands respond to the gospel message. Sense their commitment as they give every ounce of talent and treasure to Christ. And as you read, watch the Spirit-led boldness of these first-century believers, who through suffering and in the face of death take every opportunity to tell of their crucified and risen Lord. Then decide to be a 20th-century version of those men and women of God.

Paul's third missionary journey 53-57	Nero becomes emperor 54	Paul imprisoned in Caesarea 57-59	Paul's journey to Rome 59	Paul released from prison 62	Paul martyred 67?	Rome destroys Jerusalem 70

THE BLUEPRINT

A. PETER'S MINISTRY (1:1—12:25)
1. Establishment of the church
2. Expansion of the church

After the resurrection of Jesus Christ, Peter preached boldly and performed many miracles. Peter's actions demonstrate vividly the source and effects of Christian power. Because of the Holy Spirit, God's people were empowered so they could accomplish their tasks. The Holy Spirit is still available to empower believers today. We should turn to the Holy Spirit to give us the strength, courage, and insight to accomplish our work for God.

B. PAUL'S MINISTRY (13:1—28:31)
1. First missionary journey
2. The council at Jerusalem
3. Second missionary journey
4. Third missionary journey
5. Paul on trial

Paul's missionary adventures show us the progress of Christianity. The gospel could not be confined to one corner of the world. This was a faith that offered hope to all humanity. We too should venture forth and share in this heroic task to witness for Christ in all the world.

MEGATHEMES

THEME	EXPLANATION	IMPORTANCE
Church Beginnings	Acts is the history of how Christianity was founded and organised and solved its problems. The community of believers began by faith in the risen Christ and in the power of the Holy Spirit, who enabled them to witness, to love, and to serve.	New churches are continually being founded. By faith in Jesus Christ and through the power of the Holy Spirit, the church can be a vibrant agent for change. As we face new problems, Acts gives important remedies for solving them.
Holy Spirit	The church did not start or grow by its own power or enthusiasm. The disciples were empowered by God's Holy Spirit. He was the promised Counsellor and Guide sent when Jesus went to heaven.	The Holy Spirit's work demonstrated that Christianity was supernatural. Thus the church became more Holy Spirit-conscious than problem-conscious. By faith, any believer can claim the Holy Spirit's power to do Christ's work.
Church Growth	Acts presents the history of a dynamic, growing community of believers from Jerusalem to Syria, Africa, Asia, and Europe. In the first century, Christianity spread from believing Jews to non-Jews in 39 cities and 30 countries, islands, or provinces.	When the Holy Spirit works, there is movement, excitement, and growth. He gives us the motivation, energy, and ability to get the gospel to the whole world. How are you fitting into God's plan for expanding Christianity? What is your place in this movement?
Witnessing	Peter, John, Philip, Paul, Barnabas, and thousands more witnessed to their new faith in Christ. By personal testimony, preaching, or defence before authorities, they told the story with boldness and courage to groups of all sizes.	We are God's people, chosen to be part of his plan to reach the world. In love and by faith, we can have the Holy Spirit's help as we witness or preach. Witnessing is also beneficial to us because it strengthens our faith as we confront those who challenge it.
Opposition	Through imprisonment, beatings, plots, and riots, Christians were persecuted by both Jews and Gentiles. But the opposition became a catalyst for the spread of Christianity. Growth during times of oppression showed that Christianity was not the work of humans, but of God.	God can work through any opposition. When severe treatment from hostile unbelievers comes, realise that it has come because you have been a faithful witness and you have looked for the opportunity to present the good news about Christ. Seize the opportunities that opposition brings.

KEY PLACES IN ACTS

Modern names and boundaries are shown in grey

The apostle Paul, whose missionary journeys fill much of this book, travelled tremendous distances as he tirelessly spread the gospel across much of the Roman empire. His combined trips, by land and ship, equal more than 13,000 airline miles.

1 **Judea** Jesus ascended to heaven from the Mount of Olives outside Jerusalem, and his followers returned to the city to await the infilling of the Holy Spirit, which occurred at Pentecost. Peter gave a powerful sermon that was heard by Jews from across the empire. The Jerusalem church grew, but Stephen was martyred for his faith by Jewish leaders who did not believe in Jesus (1:1–7:59).

2 **Samaria** After Stephen's death, persecution of Christians intensified, but it caused the believers to leave Jerusalem and spread the gospel to other cities in the empire. Philip took the gospel into Samaria, and even to a man from Ethiopia (8:1–40).

3 **Syria** Paul (Saul) began his story as a persecutor of Christians, only to be met by Jesus himself on the road to Damascus. He became a believer, but his new faith caused opposition, so he returned to Tarsus, his home, for safety. Barnabas sought out Paul in Tarsus and brought him to the church in Antioch in Syria, where they worked together. Meanwhile, Peter had received a vision that led him to Caesarea, where he presented the gospel to a Gentile family, who became believers (9:1–12:25).

4 **Cyprus and Galatia** Paul and Barnabas were dedicated by the church in Antioch in Syria for God's work of spreading the gospel to other cities. They set off on their first missionary journey through Cyprus and Galatia (13:1–14:28).

5 **Jerusalem** Controversy between Jewish Christians and Gentile Christians over the matter of keeping the law led to a special council, with delegates from the churches in Antioch and Jerusalem meeting in Jerusalem. Together, they resolved the conflict and the news was taken back to Antioch (15:1–35).

6 **Macedonia** Barnabas travelled to Cyprus while Paul took a second missionary journey. He revisited the churches in Galatia and headed towards Ephesus, but the Holy Spirit said no. He then turned north towards Bithynia and Pontus, but again was told not to go. He then received the "Macedonian call", and followed the Spirit's direction into the cities of Macedonia (15:36–17:14).

7 **Achaia** Paul travelled from Macedonia to Athens and Corinth in Achaia, then travelled by ship to Ephesus before returning to Caesarea, Jerusalem, and finally back to Antioch (17:15–18:22).

8 **Ephesus** Paul's third missionary journey took him back through Cilicia and Galatia, this time straight to Ephesus in Asia. He visited other cities in Asia before going back to Macedonia and Achaia. He returned to Jerusalem by ship, despite his knowledge that arrest awaited him there (18:23–23:30).

9 **Caesarea** Paul was arrested in Jerusalem and taken to Antipatris, then on to Caesarea under Roman guard. Paul always took advantage of any opportunity to share the gospel, and he did so before many Gentile leaders. Because Paul appealed to Caesar, he began the long journey to Rome (23:31–26:32).

10 **Rome** After storms, stopovers in Crete, and shipwreck on the island of Malta, Paul arrived in Sicily, and finally in Italy, where he travelled by land, under guard, to his long-awaited destination, Rome, the capital of the empire (27:1–28:31).

1:1
[a]Lk 1:1-4
[b]Lk 3:23

1:2
[c]ver 9, 11; Mk 16:19
[d]Mt 28:19, 20
[e]Mk 6:30
[f]Jn 13:18

1:3
[g]Mt 28:17; Lk 24:34, 36; Jn 20:19, 26; 21:1, 14; 1Co 15:5-7

1:4
[h]Lk 24:49; Jn 14:16; Ac 2:33

A. PETER'S MINISTRY (1:1 – 12:25)

The book of Acts begins where the Gospels leave off, reporting on the actions of the apostles and the work of the Holy Spirit. Beginning in Jerusalem, the church is established and grows rapidly, then faces intense persecution, which drives the believers out into the surrounding areas. Through this dispersion, Samaritans and Gentiles hear the good news and believe.

1. Establishment of the church

Jesus Taken Up Into Heaven

1 In my former book,[a] Theophilus, I wrote about all that Jesus began to do and
to teach[b] 2until the day he was taken up to heaven,[c] after giving instructions[d]
through the Holy Spirit to the apostles[e] he had chosen.[f] 3After his suffering, he
showed himself to these men and gave many convincing proofs that he was alive. He
appeared to them[g] over a period of forty days and spoke about the kingdom of God.
4On one occasion, while he was eating with them, he gave them this command: "Do
not leave Jerusalem, but wait for the gift my Father promised, which you have heard
me speak about.[h] 5For John baptised with[a] water, but in a few days you will be
baptised with the Holy Spirit."

[a] 5 Or *in*

1:1 The book of Acts continues the story Luke began in his Gospel, covering the 30 years after Jesus was taken up into heaven. During that short time the church was established, and the gospel of salvation was taken throughout the world, even to the capital of the Roman empire. Those preaching the gospel, though ordinary people with human frailties and limitations, were empowered by the Holy Spirit to take the Good News "all over the world" (17:6). Throughout the book of Acts we learn about the nature of the church and how we today are also to go about turning our world upside down.

1:1 Luke's former book was the Gospel of Luke; that book was also addressed to Theophilus, whose name means "one who loves God". (See note on Luke 1:3.)

1:1ff Verses 1–11 are the bridge between the events recorded in the Gospels and the events marking the beginning of the church. Jesus spent 40 days teaching his disciples, and they were changed drastically. Before, they had argued with each other, deserted their Lord, and one (Peter) even lied about knowing Jesus. Here, in a series of meetings with the living, resurrected Christ, the disciples had many questions answered. They became convinced about the resurrection, learned about the kingdom of God, and learned about their power source – the Holy Spirit. By reading the Bible, we can sit with the resurrected Christ in his school of discipleship. By believing in him, we can receive his power through the Holy Spirit to be new people. By joining with other Christians in Christ's church, we can take part in doing his work on earth.

1:1-3 Luke says that the disciples were eyewitnesses to all that had happened to Jesus Christ – his life before his crucifixion ("suffering"), and the 40 days after his resurrection as he taught them more about the kingdom of God. Today there are still people who doubt Jesus' resurrection. But Jesus appeared to the disciples on many occasions after his resurrection, proving that he was alive. Look at the change the resurrection made in the disciples' lives. At Jesus' death, they scattered – they were disillusioned, and they feared for their lives. After seeing the resurrected Christ, they were fearless and risked everything to spread the Good News about him around the world. They faced imprisonment, beatings, rejection, and martyrdom, yet they never compromised their mission. These men would not have risked their lives for something they knew was a fraud. They knew Jesus was raised from the dead, and the early church was fired with their enthusiasm to tell others. It is important to know this so we can have confidence in their testimony. Twenty centuries later we can still be confident that our faith is based on fact.

1:3 Jesus explained that with his coming, the kingdom of God was inaugurated. When he returned to heaven, God's kingdom would remain in the hearts of all believers through the presence of the Holy Spirit. But the kingdom of God will not be fully realised until Jesus Christ comes again to judge all people and remove all evil from the world. Before that time, believers are to work to spread God's kingdom across the world. The book of Acts records how this work was begun. What the early church started, we must continue.

1:4, 5 The *Trinity* is a description of the unique relationship of God the Father, the Son, and the Holy Spirit. If Jesus had stayed on earth, his physical presence would have limited the spread of the gospel, because physically he could be in only one place at a time. After Christ was taken up into heaven, he would be spiritually present everywhere through the Holy Spirit. The Holy Spirit was sent so that God would be with and within his followers after Christ returned to heaven. The Spirit would comfort them, guide them to know his truth, remind them of Jesus' words, give them the right words to say, and fill them with power (see John 14 – 16).

1:5 At Pentecost (2:1–4) the Holy Spirit was made available to all who believed in Jesus. We receive the Holy Spirit (are baptised by him) when we receive Jesus Christ. The baptism of the Holy Spirit must be understood in the light of his total work in Christians.

(1) The Spirit marks the beginning of the Christian experience. We cannot belong to Christ without his Spirit (Romans 8:9); we cannot be united to Christ without his Spirit (1 Corinthians 6:17); we cannot be adopted as his children without his Spirit (Romans 8:14–17; Galatians 4:6, 7); we cannot be in the body of Christ except by baptism by the Spirit (1 Corinthians 12:13).

(2) The Spirit is the power of our new lives. He begins a lifelong process of change as we become more like Christ (Galatians 3:3; Philippians 1:6). When we receive Christ by faith, we begin an immediate personal relationship with God. The Holy Spirit works in us to help us become like Christ.

(3) The Spirit unites the Christian community in Christ (Ephesians 2:19–22). The Holy Spirit can be experienced by all, and he works through all (1 Corinthians 12:11; Ephesians 4:4).

6 So when they met together, they asked him, "Lord, are you at this time going to
restore[i] the kingdom to Israel?"
7 He said to them: "It is not for you to know the times or dates the Father has set
by his own authority.[j] 8 But you will receive power when the Holy Spirit comes on
you;[k] and you will be my witnesses[l] in Jerusalem, and in all Judea and Samaria,[m]
and to the ends of the earth."[n]
9 After he said this, he was taken up[o] before their very eyes, and a cloud hid him
from their sight.
10 They were looking intently up into the sky as he was going, when suddenly two
men dressed in white[p] stood beside them. 11 "Men of Galilee,"[q] they said, "why do
you stand here looking into the sky? This same Jesus, who has been taken from you
into heaven, will come back[r] in the same way you have seen him go into heaven."

Matthias Chosen to Replace Judas

12 Then they returned to Jerusalem[s] from the hill called the Mount of Olives,[t] a
Sabbath day's walk[b] from the city. 13 When they arrived, they went upstairs to the
room[u] where they were staying. Those present were Peter, John, James and Andrew;
Philip and Thomas, Bartholomew and Matthew; James son of Alphaeus and Simon
the Zealot, and Judas son of James.[v] 14 They all joined together constantly in prayer,[w]
along with the women[x] and Mary the mother of Jesus, and with his brothers.[y]
15 In those days Peter stood up among the believers[c] (a group numbering about a

1:6 [i]Mt 17:11
1:7 [j]Mt 24:36
1:8 [k]Ac 2:1-4 [l]Lk 24:48 [m]Ac 8:1-25 [n]Mt 28:19
1:9 [o]ver 2
1:10 [p]Lk 24:4; Jn 20:12
1:11 [q]Ac 2:7 [r]Mt 16:27
1:12 [s]Lk 24:52 [t]Mt 21:1
1:13 [u]Ac 9:37; 20:8 [v]Mt 10:2-4; Mk 3:16-19; Lk 6:14-16
1:14 [w]Ac 2:42; 6:4 [x]Lk 23:49, 55 [y]Mt 12:46

[b] *12* That is, about 3/4 of a mile (about 1,100 metres) [c] *15* Greek *brothers*

1:6 During the years of Jesus' ministry on earth, the disciples continually wondered about his kingdom. When would it come? What would their role be? In the traditional view, the Messiah would be an earthly conqueror who would free Israel from Rome. But the kingdom Jesus spoke about was first of all a *spiritual* kingdom established in the hearts and lives of believers (Luke 17:21). God's presence and power dwell in believers in the person of the Holy Spirit.

1:6, 7 Like other Jews, the disciples chafed under their Roman rulers. They wanted Jesus to free Israel from Roman power and then become their king. Jesus replied that God the Father sets the timetable for all events – worldwide, national, and personal. If you want changes that God isn't making immediately, don't become impatient. Instead, trust God's timetable.

1:8 Power from the Holy Spirit is not limited to strength beyond the ordinary – that power also involves courage, boldness, confidence, insight, ability, and authority. The disciples would need all these gifts to fulfil their mission. If you believe in Jesus Christ, you can experience the power of the Holy Spirit in your life.

1:8 Jesus promised the disciples that they would receive power to witness after they received the Holy Spirit. Notice the progression: (1) they would receive the Holy Spirit, (2) he would give them power, and (3) they would witness with extraordinary results. Often we try to reverse the order and witness by our own power and authority. Witnessing is not showing what we can do for God. It is showing and telling what God has done for us.

1:8 Jesus had instructed his disciples to witness to people of all nations about him (Matthew 28:19, 20). But they were told to wait first for the Holy Spirit (Luke 24:49). God has important work for you to do for him, but you must do it by the power of the Holy Spirit. We often like to get on with the job, even if it means running ahead of God. But waiting is sometimes part of God's plan. Are you waiting and listening for God's complete instructions, or are you running ahead of his plans? We need God's timing and power to be truly effective.

1:8 This verse describes a series of ever-widening circles. The gospel was to spread, geographically, from Jerusalem, into Judea and Samaria, and finally to the whole world. It would begin with the devout Jews in Jerusalem and Samaria, spread to the mixed race in Samaria, and finally be offered to the Gentiles in the uttermost parts of the earth. God's gospel has not reached its final destination if someone in your family, your workplace, your school, or your community hasn't heard about Jesus Christ. Make sure that you are contributing in some way to the ever-widening circle of God's loving message.

1:9 It was important for the disciples to see Jesus taken up into heaven. Then they knew without a doubt that he was God and that his home was in heaven.

1:9–11 After 40 days with his disciples (1:3), Jesus returned to heaven. The two men dressed in white were angels who proclaimed to the disciples that one day Jesus would return in the same way he went – bodily and visibly. History is not haphazard or cyclical; it is moving towards a specific point – the return of Jesus to judge and rule over the earth. We should be ready for his sudden return (1 Thessalonians 5:2), not by standing around "looking into the sky", but by working hard to share the gospel so that others will be able to share in God's great blessings.

1:12, 13 After Christ was taken up into heaven, the disciples immediately returned to Jerusalem and had a prayer meeting. Jesus had said they would be baptised with the Holy Spirit in a few days, so they waited and prayed. When you face a difficult task, an important decision, or a baffling dilemma, don't rush into the work and just hope it comes out the way it should. Instead, your first step should be to pray for the Holy Spirit's power and guidance.

1:13 A "Zealot" could mean anyone zealous for the Jewish law. The Zealots may have been a radical political party working for the violent overthrow of Roman rule in Israel.

1:14 At this time, Jesus' brothers were with the disciples. During Jesus' lifetime, they did not believe he was the Messiah (John 7:5), but his resurrection must have convinced them. Jesus' special appearance to James, one of his brothers, may have been an especially significant event in their conversion (see 1 Corinthians 15:7).

1:15–26 This was the first church business meeting. The small group of 11 had already grown to more than 120. The main order of business was to appoint a new disciple, or apostle, as the 12 were now called. While the apostles waited, they were doing what they could – praying, seeking God's guidance, and getting organized. Waiting for God to work does not mean sitting around doing nothing. We must do what we can, while we can, as long as we don't run ahead of God.

1:16
[z]ver 20
[a]Jn 13:18

1:17
[b]Jn 6:70, 71
[c]ver 25

1:18
[d]Mt 26:14, 15
[e]Mt 27:3-10

1:20
[f]Ps 69:25
[g]Ps 109:8

1:22
[h]Mk 1:4
[i]ver 8

1:24
[j]Ac 6:6; 14:23
[k]1Sa 16:7;
Jer 17:10;
Ac 15:8;
Rev 2:23

1:26
[l]Ac 2:14

2:1
[a]Lev 23:15, 16;
Ac 20:16
[b]Ac 1:14

2:2
[c]Ac 4:31

hundred and twenty) 16 and said, "Brothers, the Scripture had to be fulfilled[z] which
the Holy Spirit spoke long ago through the mouth of David concerning Judas,[a] who
served as guide for those who arrested Jesus — 17 he was one of our number[b] and
shared in this ministry."[c]
18 (With the reward[d] he got for his wickedness, Judas bought a field;[e] there he
fell headlong, his body burst open and all his intestines spilled out. 19 Everyone in
Jerusalem heard about this, so they called that field in their language Akeldama, that
is, Field of Blood.)
20 "For," said Peter, "it is written in the Book of Psalms,

> " 'May his place be deserted;
> let there be no-one to dwell in it,'[d][f]

and,

> " 'May another take his place of leadership.'[e][g]

21 Therefore it is necessary to choose one of the men who have been with us the whole
time the Lord Jesus went in and out among us, 22 beginning from John's baptism[h]
to the time when Jesus was taken up from us. For one of these must become a witness[i]
with us of his resurrection."
23 So they proposed two men: Joseph called Barsabbas (also known as Justus) and
Matthias. 24 Then they prayed,[j] "Lord, you know everyone's heart.[k] Show us which
of these two you have chosen 25 to take over this apostolic ministry, which Judas left
to go where he belongs." 26 Then they cast lots, and the lot fell to Matthias; so he was
added to the eleven apostles.[l]

The Holy Spirit Comes at Pentecost

2 When the day of Pentecost[a] came, they were all together[b] in one place. 2 Suddenly a sound like the blowing of a violent wind came from heaven and filled
the whole house where they were sitting.[c] 3 They saw what seemed to be tongues of

d *20* Psalm 69:25 **e** *20* Psalm 109:8

1:16, 17 How could someone who had been with Jesus daily betray him? Judas received the same calling and teaching as everyone else. But he chose to reject Christ's warning as well as his offers of mercy. Judas hardened his heart and joined in the plot with Jesus' enemies to put him to death. Judas remained unrepentant to the end, and he finally committed suicide. Although Jesus predicted this would happen, it was Judas's choice. Those privileged to be *close* to the truth are not necessarily *committed* to the truth. See Judas's Profile in Mark 14 for more information on his life.

1:18 Matthew says that Judas hanged himself (Matthew 27:5); Acts says that he fell. The traditional explanation is that when Judas hanged himself, the rope or branch broke, Judas fell, and his body burst open.

1:21, 22 There were many who consistently followed Jesus throughout his ministry on earth. The 12 disciples were his inner circle, but others shared the disciples' deep love for and commitment to Jesus.

1:21–25 The apostles had to choose a replacement for Judas Iscariot. They outlined specific criteria for making the choice. When the "finalists" had been chosen, the apostles prayed, asking God to guide the selection process. This gives us a good example of how to proceed when we are making important decisions. Set up criteria consistent with the Bible, examine the alternatives, and pray for wisdom and guidance to reach a wise decision.

1:26 The disciples became *apostles. Disciple* means follower or learner, and *apostle* means messenger or missionary. These men now had the special assignment of spreading the Good News of Jesus' death and resurrection.

2:1 Held 50 days after Passover, Pentecost was also called the Feast of Weeks. It was one of three major annual feasts (Deuteronomy 16:16), a festival of thanksgiving for the harvested crops. Jesus was crucified at Passover time, and he ascended 40 days after his resurrection. The Holy Spirit came 50 days after the resurrection, ten days after the ascension. Jews of many nations gathered in Jerusalem for this festival. Thus Peter's speech (2:14ff) was given to an international audience, and it resulted in a worldwide harvest of new believers — the first converts to Christianity.

2:3, 4 This was a fulfilment of John the Baptist's words about the Holy Spirit's baptising with fire (Luke 3:16), and of the prophet Joel's words about the outpouring of the Holy Spirit (Joel 2:28, 29).

Why tongues of fire? Tongues symbolise speech and the communication of the gospel. Fire symbolises God's purifying presence, which burns away the undesirable elements of our lives and sets our hearts aflame to ignite the lives of others. On Mount Sinai, God confirmed the validity of the Old Testament law with fire from heaven (Exodus 19:16–18). At Pentecost, God confirmed the validity of the Holy Spirit's ministry by sending fire. At Mount Sinai, fire had come down on one place; at Pentecost, fire came down on many believers, symbolising that God's presence is now available to all who believe in him.

2:3, 4 God made his presence known to this group of believers in a spectacular way — violent wind, fire, and his Holy Spirit. Would you like God to reveal himself to you in such recognisable ways? He may do so, but be wary of forcing your expectations on God. In 1 Kings 19:10–13, Elijah also needed a message from God. There was a great wind, then an earthquake, and finally a fire. But God's message came in a "gentle whisper". God may use dramatic methods to work in your life — or he may speak in gentle whispers. Wait patiently and always listen.

fire that separated and came to rest on each of them. 4All of them were filled with
the Holy Spirit and began to speak in other tongues[a][d] as the Spirit enabled them.
5Now there were staying in Jerusalem God-fearing[e] Jews from every nation under
heaven. 6When they heard this sound, a crowd came together in bewilderment,
because each one heard them speaking in his own language. 7Utterly amazed,[f] they
asked: "Are not all these men who are speaking Galileans?[g] 8Then how is it that each
of us hears them in his own native language? 9Parthians, Medes and Elamites;
residents of Mesopotamia, Judea and Cappadocia,[h] Pontus[i] and Asia,[j] 10Phrygia[k]
and Pamphylia,[l] Egypt and the parts of Libya near Cyrene;[m] visitors from Rome
11(both Jews and converts to Judaism); Cretans and Arabs—we hear them declaring
the wonders of God in our own tongues!" 12Amazed and perplexed, they asked one
another, "What does this mean?"
13Some, however, made fun of them and said, "They have had too much wine."[b][n]

Peter Addresses the Crowd

14Then Peter stood up with the Eleven, raised his voice and addressed the crowd:
"Fellow Jews and all of you who live in Jerusalem, let me explain this to you; listen
carefully to what I say. 15These men are not drunk, as you suppose. It's only nine
in the morning![o] 16No, this is what was spoken by the prophet Joel:

17" 'In the last days, God says,
I will pour out my Spirit on all people.[p]
Your sons and daughters will prophesy,[q]
your young men will see visions,
your old men will dream dreams.
18Even on my servants, both men and women,
I will pour out my Spirit in those days,
and they will prophesy.[r]
19I will show wonders in the heaven above
and signs on the earth below,
blood and fire and billows of smoke.
20The sun will be turned to darkness

2:4 [d]Mk 16:17; 1Co 12:10
2:5 [e]Ac 8:2
2:7 [f]ver 12 [g]Ac 1:11
2:9 [h]1Pe 1:1 [i]Ac 18:2 [j]Ac 16:6; Ro 16:5; 1Co 16:19; 2Co 1:8
2:10 [k]Ac 16:6; 18:23 [l]Ac 13:13; 15:38 [m]Mt 27:32
2:13 [n]1Co 14:23
2:15 [o]1Th 5:7
2:17 [p]Isa 44:3; Jn 7:37-39; Ac 10:45 [q]Ac 21:9
2:18 [r]Ac 21:9-12

a *4* Or *languages*; also in verse 11 **b** *13* Or *sweet wine*

2:4–11 These people literally spoke in other languages—a miraculous attention-getter for the international crowd gathered in town for the feast. All the nationalities represented recognised their own languages being spoken. But more than miraculous speaking drew people's attention; they saw the presence and power of the Holy Spirit. The apostles continued to minister in the power of the Holy Spirit wherever they went.

2:7, 8 Christianity is not limited to any race or group of people. Christ offers salvation to all people without regard to nationality. Visitors in Jerusalem were surprised to hear the apostles and other believers speaking in languages other than their own, the languages of other nationalities, but they need not have been. God works all kinds of miracles to spread the gospel, using many languages as he calls all kinds of people to become his followers. No matter what your race, colour, nationality, or language, God speaks to you. Are you listening?

2:9–11 Why are all these places mentioned? This is a list of many lands from which Jews came to the festivals in Jerusalem. These Jews were not living in Palestine because they had been dispersed throughout the world through captivities and persecutions. Very likely, some of the Jews who responded to Peter's message returned to their homelands with God's Good News of salvation. Thus God prepared the way for the spread of the gospel. As you read Acts, you will see how the way was often prepared for Paul and other messengers by people who became believers at Pentecost. The church at Rome, for example, was probably begun by such Jewish believers.

2:14 Peter had been an unstable leader during Jesus' ministry, letting his bravado be his downfall, even denying that he knew Jesus (John 18:15–18, 25–27). But Christ had forgiven and restored him (John 21). This was a new Peter, humble but bold. His confidence came from the Holy Spirit, who made him a powerful and dynamic speaker. Have you ever felt as if you've made such bad mistakes that God could never forgive and use you? No matter what sins you have committed, God promises to forgive you and make you useful for his kingdom. Allow him to forgive you and use you effectively to serve him.

2:14ff Peter tells the people why they should listen to the testimony of the believers: because the Old Testament prophecies had been entirely fulfilled in Jesus (2:14–21), because Jesus is the Messiah (2:25–36), and because the risen Christ could change their lives (2:37–40).

2:15 Peter answered accusations that they were all drunk (2:13) by saying it was much too early in the day for that.

2:16–21 Not everything mentioned in Joel 2:28, 29 was happening that particular morning. The "last days" include all the days between Christ's first and second comings, and is another way of saying "from now on". "The great and glorious day of the Lord" (2:20) denotes the whole Christian age. Even Moses yearned for the Lord to put his Spirit on everyone (Numbers 11:29). At Pentecost the Holy Spirit was released throughout the entire world—to men, women, slaves, Jews, Gentiles. Now *everyone* can receive the Spirit. This was a revolutionary thought for first-century Jews.

A JOURNEY THROUGH THE BOOK OF ACTS

Beginning with a brief summary of Jesus' last days on earth with his disciples, his ascension, and the selection of a replacement for Judas Iscariot, Luke moves quickly to his subject—the spread of the gospel and the growth of the church. Pentecost, highlighted by the filling of the Holy Spirit (2:1–13) and Peter's powerful sermon (2:14–42), was the beginning. Then the Jerusalem church grew daily through the bold witness of Peter and John and the love of the believers (2:43—4:37). The infant church was not without problems, however, with external opposition (resulting in imprisonment, beatings, and death) and internal deceit and complaining. Greek-speaking Jewish believers were appointed to help with the administration of the church to free the apostles to preach. Stephen and Philip were among the first deacons, and Stephen became the church's first martyr (5:1—8:3).

Instead of stopping Christianity, opposition and persecution served as catalysts for its spread because the believers took the message with them wherever they fled (8:4). Soon there were converts throughout Samaria and even in Ethiopia (8:5–40). At this point, Luke introduces us to a bright young Jew, zealous for the law and intent on ridding Judaism of the Jesus heresy. But on the way to Damascus to capture believers, Saul was converted when he was confronted in person by the risen Christ (9:1–9). Through the ministry of Ananias and the sponsorship of Barnabas, Saul (Paul) was welcomed into the fellowship and then sent to Tarsus for safety (9:10–30).

Meanwhile, the church continued to thrive throughout Judea, Galilee, and Samaria. Luke recounts Peter's preaching and how Peter healed Aeneas in Lydda and Dorcas in Joppa (9:31–43). While in Joppa, Peter learned through a vision that he could take the gospel to the "unclean" Gentiles. Peter understood, and he faithfully shared the truth with Cornelius, whose entire household became believers (chapter 10). This was startling news to the Jerusalem church; but when Peter told his story, they praised God for his plan for *all* people to hear the good news (11:1–18). This pushed the church into even wider circles as the message was preached to Greeks in Antioch, where Barnabas went to encourage the believers and find Saul (11:20–26).

To please the Jewish leaders, Herod joined in the persecution of the Jerusalem church, killing James (John's brother) and imprisoning Peter. But God freed Peter, and Peter walked from prison to a prayer meeting on his behalf at John Mark's house (chapter 12).

Here Luke shifts the focus to Paul's ministry. Commissioned by the Antioch church for a missionary tour (13:1–3), Paul and Barnabas took the gospel to Cyprus and south Galatia with great success (13:4—14:28). But the Jewish-Gentile controversy still smouldered, and with so many Gentiles responding to Christ, the controversy threatened to divide the church. So a council met in Jerusalem to rule on the relationship of Gentile Christians to the Old Testament laws. After hearing both sides, James (Jesus' brother and the leader of the Jerusalem church) resolved the issue and sent messengers to the churches with the decision (15:1–31).

After the council, Paul and Silas preached in Antioch. Then they left for Syria and Cilicia as Barnabas and Mark sailed for Cyprus (15:36–41). On this second missionary journey, Paul and Silas travelled throughout Macedonia and Achaia, establishing churches in Philippi, Thessalonica, Berea, Corinth, and Ephesus before returning to Antioch (16:1—18:21). Luke also tells of the ministry of Apollos (18:24–28).

On Paul's third missionary trip he travelled through Galatia, Phrygia, Macedonia, and Achaia, encouraging and teaching the believers (19:1—21:9). During this time, he felt compelled to go to Jerusalem; and although he was warned by Agabus and others of impending imprisonment (21:10–12), he continued his journey in that direction.

While in Jerusalem, Paul was accosted in the temple by an angry mob and taken into protective custody by the Roman commander (21:17—22:29). Now we see Paul as a prisoner and on trial before the Jewish Sanhedrin (23:1–9), Governor Felix (23:23—24:27), and Festus and Agrippa (25:1—26:32). In each case, Paul gave a strong and clear witness for his Lord.

Because Paul appealed to Caesar, however, he was sent to Rome for the final hearing of his case. But on the way the ship was destroyed in a storm, and the sailors and prisoners had to swim ashore. Even in this circumstance Paul shared his faith (27:1—28:10). Eventually the journey continued and Paul arrived in Rome, where he was held under house arrest while awaiting trial (28:11–31).

Luke ends Acts abruptly with the encouraging word that Paul had freedom in his captivity to talk to visitors and guards: "Boldly and without hindrance he preached the kingdom of God and taught about the Lord Jesus Christ" (28:31).

and the moon to blood[s]
before the coming of the great and glorious day of the Lord.
21 And everyone who calls
on the name of the Lord will be saved.'[c] [t]

22 "Men of Israel, listen to this: Jesus of Nazareth was a man accredited by God to
you by miracles, wonders and signs,[u] which God did among you through him,[v] as
you yourselves know. 23 This man was handed over to you by God's set purpose and
foreknowledge;[w] and you, with the help of wicked men,[d] put him to death by nailing
him to the cross.[x] 24 But God raised him from the dead,[y] freeing him from the agony
of death, because it was impossible for death to keep its hold on him.[z] 25 David said
about him:

" 'I saw the Lord always before me.
Because he is at my right hand,
I will not be shaken.
26 Therefore my heart is glad and my tongue rejoices;
my body also will live in hope,
27 because you will not abandon me to the grave,
nor will you let your Holy One see decay.[a]
28 You have made known to me the paths of life;
you will fill me with joy in your presence.'[e]

29 "Brothers, I can tell you confidently that the patriarch[b] David died and was
buried,[c] and his tomb is here[d] to this day. 30 But he was a prophet and knew that
God had promised him on oath that he would place one of his descendants on his
throne.[e] 31 Seeing what was ahead, he spoke of the resurrection of the Christ,[f] that
he was not abandoned to the grave, nor did his body see decay.[f] 32 God has raised
this Jesus to life,[g] and we are all witnesses[h] of the fact. 33 Exalted[i] to the right hand
of God,[j] he has received from the Father[k] the promised Holy Spirit[l] and has poured
out[m] what you now see and hear. 34 For David did not ascend to heaven, and yet he
said,

" 'The Lord said to my Lord:
"Sit at my right hand
35 until I make your enemies
a footstool for your feet." '[g] [n]

36 "Therefore let all Israel be assured of this: God has made this Jesus, whom you
crucified, both Lord and Christ."[o]
37 When the people heard this, they were cut to the heart and said to Peter and the
other apostles, "Brothers, what shall we do?"[p]
38 Peter replied, "Repent and be baptised,[q] every one of you, in the name of Jesus

[c] *21* Joel 2:28–32 [d] *23* Or *of those not having the law* (that is, Gentiles) [e] *28* Psalm 16:8–11 [f] *31* Or *Messiah.* "The Christ" (Greek) and "the Messiah" (Hebrew) both mean "the Anointed One"; also in verse 36. [g] *35* Psalm 110:1

2:20 [s]Mt 24:29
2:21 [t]Ro 10:13
2:22 [u]Jn 4:48; Ac 10:38 [v]Jn 3:2
2:23 [w]Lk 22:22; Ac 3:18; 4:28 [x]Lk 24:20; Ac 3:13
2:24 [y]ver 32; 1Co 6:14; 2Co 4:14; Eph 1:20; Col 2:12; Heb 13:20; 1Pe 1:21 [z]Jn 20:9
2:27 [a]ver 31; Ac 13:35
2:29 [b]Ac 7:8, 9 [c]Ac 13:36; 1Ki 2:10 [d]Ne 3:16
2:30 [e]2Sa 7:12; Ps 132:11
2:31 [f]Ps 16:10
2:32 [g]ver 24 [h]Ac 1:8
2:33 [i]Php 2:9 [j]Mk 16:19 [k]Ac 1:4 [l]Jn 7:39; 14:26 [m]Ac 10:45
2:35 [n]Ps 110:1; Mt 22:44
2:36 [o]Lk 2:11
2:37 [p]Lk 3:10, 12, 14
2:38 [q]Ac 8:12, 16, 36, 38; 22:16

2:23 Everything that happened to Jesus was under God's control. His plans were never disrupted by the Roman government or the Jewish officials. This was especially comforting to those facing oppression during the time of the early Christian church.

2:24 Peter began with a public proclamation of the resurrection at a time when it could be verified by many witnesses. This was a powerful statement, because many of the people listening to Peter's words had been in Jerusalem 50 days earlier at Passover and may have seen or heard about the crucifixion and resurrection of this "great teacher". Jesus' resurrection was the ultimate sign that what he said about himself was true. Without the resurrection, we would have no reason to believe in Jesus (1 Corinthians 15:14).

2:25–32 Peter quoted from Psalm 16:8–11 – a psalm written by David. He explained that David was not writing about himself, because David died and was buried (2:29). Instead, he wrote as a prophet (2:30) who spoke of the Messiah who would be resurrected. The audience understood "decay" (2:27) to mean the grave. The emphasis here is that Jesus' body was *not* left to decay but was in fact resurrected and glorified.

2:33 He "has poured out what you now see and hear" could be paraphrased, "gave Jesus the authority to send the Holy Spirit, with the results you are seeing and hearing today".

2:37 After Peter's powerful, Spirit-filled message, the people were deeply moved and asked, "What shall we do?" This is the basic question we must ask. It is not enough to be sorry for our sins – we must let God forgive them, and then we must live like forgiven people. Has God spoken to you through his word or through the words of another believer? Like Peter's audience, ask God what you should do, and then obey.

2:38, 39 If you want to follow Christ, you must "repent and be

2:38 [r]Lk 24:47; Ac 3:19
2:39 [s]Isa 44:3 [t]Ac 10:45; Eph 2:13
2:40 [u]Dt 32:5
2:42 [v]Ac 1:14
2:43 [w]Ac 5:12
2:44 [x]Ac 4:32
2:45 [y]Mt 19:21
2:46 [z]Lk 24:53; Ac 5:21, 42 [a]Ac 20:7
2:47 [b]Ro 14:18 [c]ver 41; Ac 5:14
3:1 [a]Lk 22:8 [b]Ac 2:46 [c]Ps 55:17
3:2 [d]Ac 14:8 [e]Lk 16:20 [f]Jn 9:8
3:6 [g]ver 16; Ac 4:10

Christ for the forgiveness of your sins.[r] And you will receive the gift of the Holy
Spirit. 39The promise is for you and your children[s] and for all who are far off[t]—for
all whom the Lord our God will call."
40With many other words he warned them; and he pleaded with them, "Save
yourselves from this corrupt generation."[u] 41Those who accepted his message were
baptised, and about three thousand were added to their number that day.

The Fellowship of the Believers

42They devoted themselves to the apostles' teaching and to the fellowship, to the
breaking of bread and to prayer.[v] 43Everyone was filled with awe, and many wonders
and miraculous signs were done by the apostles.[w] 44All the believers were together
and had everything in common.[x] 45Selling their possessions and goods, they gave
to anyone as he had need.[y] 46Every day they continued to meet together in the temple
courts.[z] They broke bread[a] in their homes and ate together with glad and sincere
hearts, 47praising God and enjoying the favour of all the people.[b] And the Lord added
to their number[c] daily those who were being saved.

Peter Heals the Crippled Beggar

3 One day Peter and John[a] were going up to the temple[b] at the time of prayer—at
three in the afternoon.[c] 2Now a man crippled from birth[d] was being carried to
the temple gate[e] called Beautiful, where he was put every day to beg[f] from those
going into the temple courts. 3When he saw Peter and John about to enter, he asked
them for money. 4Peter looked straight at him, as did John. Then Peter said, "Look
at us!" 5So the man gave them his attention, expecting to get something from them.
6Then Peter said, "Silver or gold I do not have, but what I have I give you. In the
name of Jesus Christ of Nazareth,[g] walk." 7Taking him by the right hand, he helped

---

baptised". To repent means to *turn from* sin, changing the direction of your life from selfishness and rebellion against God's laws. At the same time, you must *turn to* Christ, depending on him for forgiveness, mercy, guidance, and purpose. We cannot save ourselves—only God can save us. Baptism identifies us with Christ and with the community of believers. It is a condition of discipleship and a sign of faith.

2:40–43 About 3,000 people became new believers when Peter preached the Good News about Christ. These new Christians were united with the other believers, taught by the apostles, and included in the prayer meetings and fellowship. New believers in Christ need to be in groups where they can learn God's word, pray, and mature in the faith. If you have just begun a relationship with Christ, seek out other believers for fellowship, prayer, and teaching. This is the way to grow.

2:42 "Breaking of bread" refers to communion services that were celebrated in remembrance of Jesus and were patterned after the Last Supper that Jesus had with his disciples before his death (Matthew 26:26–29).

2:44 Recognising the other believers as brothers and sisters in the family of God, the Christians in Jerusalem shared all they had so that all could benefit from God's gifts. It is tempting—especially if we have material wealth—to cut ourselves off from one another, each taking care of his or her own interests, each providing for and enjoying his or her own little piece of the world. But as part of God's spiritual family, it is our responsibility to help one another in every way possible. God's family works best when its members work together.

2:46 A common misconception about the first Christians (who were Jews) was that they rejected the Jewish religion. But these believers saw Jesus' message and resurrection as the fulfilment of everything they knew and believed from the Old Testament. The Jewish believers at first did not separate from the rest of the Jewish community. They still went to the temple and synagogues for worship and instruction in the Scriptures. But their belief in Jesus created great friction with Jews who didn't believe that Jesus was the Messiah. Thus, believing Jews were forced to meet in private homes for communion, prayer, and teaching about Christ. By the end of the first century, many of these Jewish believers were excommunicated from their synagogues.

2:47 A healthy Christian community attracts people to Christ. The Jerusalem church's zeal for worship and brotherly love was contagious. A healthy, loving church will grow in numbers. What are you doing to make your church the kind of place that will attract others to Christ?

3:1 The Jews observed three times of prayer—morning (9:00 a.m.), afternoon (3:00 p.m.), and evening (sunset). At these times devout Jews and Gentiles who believed in God often went to the temple to pray. Peter and John were going to the temple at 3:00 p.m.

3:2 The gate called Beautiful was an entrance to the temple, not to the city. It was one of the favoured entrances, and many people passed through it on their way to worship. The crippled man was begging where he would be seen by the most people.

3:2 Giving money to beggars was considered praiseworthy in the Jewish religion. So the beggar wisely placed himself where pious people might see him on their way to worship at the temple.

3:5, 6 The crippled man asked for money, but Peter gave him something much better—the use of his legs. We often ask God to solve a small problem, but he wants to give us a whole new life and help for *all* our problems. When we ask God for help, he may say, "I've got something even better for you." Ask God for what you want, but don't be surprised when he gives you what you really *need.*

3:6 "In the name of Jesus Christ" means "by the authority of Jesus Christ". The apostles were doing this healing through the Holy Spirit's power, not their own.

3:7–10 In his excitement, the formerly crippled man began to jump and walk around. He also praised God! And then others were also awed by God's power. Don't forget to thank people who help you, but also remember to praise God for his care and protection.

him up, and instantly the man's feet and ankles became strong. 8 He jumped to his
feet and began to walk. Then he went with them into the temple courts, walking and
jumping,[h] and praising God. 9 When all the people[i] saw him walking and praising
God, 10 they recognised him as the same man who used to sit begging at the temple
gate called Beautiful,[j] and they were filled with wonder and amazement at what had
happened to him.

Peter Speaks to the Onlookers

11 While the beggar held on to Peter and John,[k] all the people were astonished and
came running to them in the place called Solomon's Colonnade.[l] 12 When Peter saw
this, he said to them: "Men of Israel, why does this surprise you? Why do you stare
at us as if by our own power or godliness we had made this man walk? 13 The God
of Abraham, Isaac and Jacob, the God of our fathers,[m] has glorified his servant Jesus.
You handed him over to be killed, and you disowned him before Pilate,[n] though he
had decided to let him go.[o] 14 You disowned the Holy[p] and Righteous One[q] and
asked that a murderer be released to you.[r] 15 You killed the author of life, but God
raised him from the dead.[s] We are witnesses of this. 16 By faith in the name of Jesus,
this man whom you see and know was made strong. It is Jesus' name and the faith
that comes through him that has given this complete healing to him, as you can all
see.

17 "Now, brothers, I know that you acted in ignorance,[t] as did your leaders.[u] 18 But
this is how God fulfilled what he had foretold[v] through all the prophets,[w] saying that
his Christ[a] would suffer.[x] 19 Repent, then, and turn to God, so that your sins may
be wiped out,[y] that times of refreshing may come from the Lord, 20 and that he may
send the Christ, who has been appointed for you—even Jesus. 21 He must remain in
heaven[z] until the time comes for God to restore everything,[a] as he promised long

a 18 Or *Messiah*; also in verse 20

3:8 [h] Ac 14:10
3:9 [i] Ac 4:16, 21
3:10 [j] ver 2
3:11 [k] Lk 22:8 [l] Jn 10:23; Ac 5:12
3:13 [m] Ac 5:30 [n] Mt 27:2 [o] Lk 23:4
3:14 [p] Mk 1:24; Ac 4:27 [q] Ac 7:52 [r] Mk 15:11; Lk 23:18-25
3:15 [s] Ac 2:24
3:17 [t] Lk 23:34 [u] Ac 13:27
3:18 [v] Ac 2:23 [w] Lk 24:27 [x] Ac 17:2, 3; 26:22, 23
3:19 [y] Ac 2:38
3:21 [z] Ac 1:11 [a] Mt 17:11

3:11 Solomon's Colonnade was a covered porch or entrance with columns.

3:11ff Peter had an audience, and he capitalised on the opportunity to share Jesus Christ. He clearly presented his message by telling (1) who Jesus is, (2) how the Jews had rejected him, (3) why their rejection was fatal, and (4) what they needed to do to change the situation. Peter told the crowd that they still had a choice; God still offered them the opportunity to believe and receive Jesus as their Messiah and as their Lord. Displays of God's mercy and grace, such as the healing of this crippled man, often create teachable moments. Pray to have courage like Peter to see these opportunities and to use them to speak up for Christ.

3:13, 14 Pilate had decided to release Jesus, but the people had clamoured to have Barabbas, a murderer, released instead (see John 19:1–16). When Peter said "You handed him over to be killed", he meant it literally. Jesus' trial and death had occurred right there in Jerusalem only weeks earlier. It wasn't an event of the distant past—most of these people had heard about it, and some may very well have taken part in condemning Jesus.

3:15 The religious leaders thought they had put an end to Jesus when they crucified him. But their confidence was shaken when Peter told them that Jesus was alive again and that this time they could not harm him. Peter's message emphasised that (1) the people and their religious leaders killed Jesus (3:17), (2) God brought him back to life, and (3) the apostles were witnesses to this fact. After pointing out the sin and injustice of these leaders, Peter showed the significance of the resurrection, God's triumph and power over death.

3:16 Jesus, not the apostles, received the glory for the healing of the crippled man. In those days a man's name represented his character; it stood for his authority and power. By using Jesus' name, Peter showed who gave him the authority and power to heal. The apostles did not emphasise what *they* could do, but what God could do through them. Jesus' name is not to be used as magic—it must be used in faith. When we pray in Jesus' name, we must remember that it is Christ himself, not merely the sound of his name, who gives our prayers their power.

3:18 These prophecies are found in Psalm 22 and Isaiah 50:6 and Isaiah 53. Peter was explaining the kind of Messiah God had sent to earth. The Jews expected a great ruler, not a suffering servant.

3:19 John the Baptist prepared the way for Jesus by preaching repentance. The apostles' message of salvation also included the call to repentance—acknowledging personal sin and turning away from it. Many people want the benefits of being identified with Christ without admitting their own disobedience and turning from sin. The key to forgiveness is confessing your sin and turning from it (see 2:38).

3:19, 20 When we repent, God promises not only to wipe out our sins, but to bring spiritual refreshment. Repentance may at first seem painful because it is hard to give up certain sins. But God will give you a better way. As Hosea promised, "Let us acknowledge the LORD; let us press on to acknowledge him. As surely as the sun rises, he will appear; he will come to us like the winter rains, like the spring rains that water the earth" (Hosea 6:3). Do you feel a need to be refreshed?

3:21 The time when God will "restore everything" refers to the second coming, the Last Judgment, and the removal of sin from the world.

3:21, 22 Most Jews thought that Joshua was this prophet predicted by Moses (Deuteronomy 18:15). Peter was saying that the prophet was Jesus Christ. Peter wanted to show them that their long-awaited Messiah had come! He and all the apostles were calling the Jewish nation to realise what they had done to their Messiah, to repent, and to believe. From this point on in Acts, we see many Jews rejecting the gospel. So the message went also to the Gentiles, many of whom were open to receive Jesus.

3:21 [b]Lk 1:70
3:22 [c]Dt 18:15, 18; Ac 7:37
3:23 [d]Dt 18:19
3:24 [e]Lk 24:27
3:25 [f]Ac 2:39 [g]Ro 9:4, 5 [h]Ge 12:3; 22:18; 26:4; 28:14
3:26 [i]ver 22; Ac 2:24 [j]Ac 13:46; Ro 1:16
4:1 [a]Lk 22:4 [b]Mt 3:7
4:2 [c]Ac 17:18
4:3 [d]Ac 5:18
4:4 [e]Ac 2:41
4:5 [f]Lk 23:13
4:6 [g]Mt 26:3; Lk 3:2
4:8 [h]ver 5; Lk 23:13
4:9 [i]Ac 3:6

ago through his holy prophets.[b] 22For Moses said, 'The Lord your God will raise up
for you a prophet like me from among your own people; you must listen to everything
he tells you.[c] 23Anyone who does not listen to him will be completely cut off from
among his people.'[b][d]
24"Indeed, all the prophets[e] from Samuel on, as many as have spoken, have
foretold these days. 25And you are heirs[f] of the prophets and of the covenant[g] God
made with your fathers. He said to Abraham, 'Through your offspring all peoples on
earth will be blessed.'[c][h] 26When God raised up[i] his servant, he sent him first[j] to
you to bless you by turning each of you from your wicked ways."

Peter and John Before the Sanhedrin

4 The priests and the captain of the temple guard[a] and the Sadducees[b] came up
to Peter and John while they were speaking to the people. 2They were greatly
disturbed because the apostles were teaching the people and proclaiming in Jesus the
resurrection of the dead.[c] 3They seized Peter and John, and because it was evening,
they put them in jail[d] until the next day. 4But many who heard the message believed,
and the number of men grew[e] to about five thousand.
5The next day the rulers,[f] elders and teachers of the law met in Jerusalem. 6Annas
the high priest was there, and so were Caiaphas,[g] John, Alexander and the other men
of the high priest's family. 7They had Peter and John brought before them and began
to question them: "By what power or what name did you do this?"
8Then Peter, filled with the Holy Spirit, said to them: "Rulers and elders of the
people![h] 9If we are being called to account today for an act of kindness shown to
a cripple[i] and are asked how he was healed, 10then know this, you and all the people

b *23* Deut. 18:15,18,19 **c** *25* Gen. 22:18; 26:4

3:24 The prophet Samuel lived during the transition between the judges and the kings of Israel, and he was seen as the first in a succession of prophets. He anointed David king, founding David's royal line, from which the Messiah eventually came. All the prophets pointed to a future Messiah. For more on Samuel, see his Profile in 1 Samuel 8.

3:25 God promised Abraham that he would bless the world through Abraham's descendants, the Jewish race (Genesis 12:3), from which the Messiah would come. God intended the Jewish nation to be a separate and holy nation that would teach the world about God, introduce the Messiah, and then carry on his work in the world. After the days of Solomon, the nation gave up its mission to tell the world about God. Here too, in apostolic times as well as in the time Jesus spent on earth, Israel rejected its Messiah.

4:1 These priests may have been chief priests, who had special influence and were often close relatives of the high priests. The captain of the temple guard was the leader of the guards who were set around the temple to ensure order. The Sadducees were members of a small but powerful Jewish religious sect that did not believe in the resurrection of the dead. They were the religious leaders who stood to gain financially by co-operating with the Romans. Most of those who engineered and carried out Jesus' arrest and crucifixion were from these three groups.

4:2, 3 Peter and John spoke to the people during the afternoon prayer time. The Sadducees moved in quickly to investigate. Because they did not believe in the resurrection, they were understandably disturbed with what the apostles were saying. Peter and John were refuting one of their fundamental beliefs and thus threatening their authority as religious teachers. Even though the nation was under Roman rule, the Sadducees had almost unlimited power over the temple grounds. Thus they were able to arrest Peter and John for no other reason than teaching something that contradicted their beliefs.

4:3 Not often will sharing the gospel send us to jail as it did Peter and John. Still, we run risks in trying to win others to Christ. We might be willing to face a night in jail if it would bring 5,000 people to Christ, but shouldn't we also be willing to suffer for the sake of even one? What do you risk in witnessing – rejection, persecution? Whatever the risks, realise that nothing done for God is ever wasted.

4:5, 6 The rulers, elders, and teachers of the law made up the Jewish council – the same council that had condemned Jesus to death (Luke 22:66). It had 70 members plus the current high priest, who presided over the group. The Sadducees held a majority in this ruling group. These were the wealthy, intellectual, and powerful men of Jerusalem. Jesus' followers stood before this council just as he had.

4:6 Annas had been deposed as high priest by the Romans, who then appointed Caiaphas, Annas' son-in-law, in his place. But because the Jews considered the office of high priest a lifetime position, they still called Annas by that title and gave him respect and authority within the council. Annas and Caiaphas had played significant roles in Jesus' trial (John 18:24, 28). It did not please them that the man they thought they had sacrificed for the good of the nation (John 11:49–51) had followers who were just as persistent and who promised to be just as troublesome as he was.

4:7 The council asked Peter and John by what power they had healed the man (3:6, 7) and by what authority they preached (3:12–26). The actions and words of Peter and John threatened these religious leaders who, for the most part, were more interested in their reputations and positions than in God. Through the help of the Holy Spirit (Mark 13:11), Peter spoke boldly before the council, actually putting the council on trial by showing them that the One they had crucified had risen again. Instead of being defensive, the apostles went on the offensive, boldly speaking out for God and presenting the gospel to these leaders.

of Israel: It is by the name of Jesus Christ of Nazareth, whom you crucified but whom
God raised from the dead,[j] that this man stands before you healed. 11He is

> " 'the stone you builders rejected,
> which has become the capstone.'[a,b][k]

12Salvation is found in no-one else, for there is no other name under heaven given
to men by which we must be saved."[l]
13When they saw the courage of Peter and John[m] and realised that they were
unschooled, ordinary men,[n] they were astonished and they took note that these men
had been with Jesus. 14But since they could see the man who had been healed standing
there with them, there was nothing they could say. 15So they ordered them to withdraw
from the Sanhedrin[o] and then conferred together. 16"What are we going to do with
these men?"[p] they asked. "Everybody living in Jerusalem knows they have done an
outstanding miracle,[q] and we cannot deny it. 17But to stop this thing from spreading
any further among the people, we must warn these men to speak no longer to anyone
in this name."
18Then they called them in again and commanded them not to speak or teach at all
in the name of Jesus.[r] 19But Peter and John replied, "Judge for yourselves whether
it is right in God's sight to obey you rather than God.[s] 20For we cannot help speaking
about what we have seen and heard."
21After further threats they let them go. They could not decide how to punish them,
because all the people[t] were praising God[u] for what had happened. 22For the man
who was miraculously healed was over forty years old.

The Believers' Prayer

23On their release, Peter and John went back to their own people and reported all
that the chief priests and elders had said to them. 24When they heard this, they raised
their voices together in prayer to God. "Sovereign Lord," they said, "you made the
heaven and the earth and the sea, and everything in them. 25You spoke by the Holy
Spirit through the mouth of your servant, our father David:[v]

> " 'Why do the nations rage
> and the peoples plot in vain?
> 26The kings of the earth take their stand
> and the rulers gather together

a *11* Or *cornerstone* b *11* Psalm 118:22

4:10 [j]Ac 2:24
4:11 [k]Ps 118:22; Isa 28:16; Mt 21:42
4:12 [l]Mt 1:21; Ac 10:43; 1Ti 2:5
4:13 [m]Lk 22:8 [n]Mt 11:25
4:15 [o]Mt 5:22
4:16 [p]Jn 11:47 [q]Ac 3:6-10
4:18 [r]Ac 5:40
4:19 [s]Ac 5:29
4:21 [t]Ac 5:26 [u]Mt 9:8
4:25 [v]Ac 1:16

4:11 The capstone unites the two sides of an arch and holds it together. Peter said that the Jews rejected Jesus, but now Christ has become the capstone of the church (Psalm 118:22; Mark 12:10; 1 Peter 2:7). Without him there would be no church, because it wouldn't be able to stand.

4:12 Many people react negatively to the fact that there is no other name than that of Jesus to call on for salvation. Yet this is not something the church decided; it is the specific teaching of Jesus himself (John 14:6). If God designated Jesus to be the Saviour of the world, no-one else can be his equal. Christians are to be open-minded on many issues, but not on how we are saved from sin. No other religious teacher could die for our sins; no other religious teacher came to earth as God's only Son; no other religious teacher rose from the dead. Our focus should be on Jesus, whom God offered as the way to have an eternal relationship with himself. There is no other name or way!

4:13 Knowing that Peter and John were unschooled, the council was amazed at what being with Jesus had done for them. A changed life convinces people of Christ's power. One of your greatest testimonies is the difference others see in your life and attitudes since you have believed in Christ.

4:13–18 Although the evidence was overwhelming and irrefutable (changed lives and a healed man), the religious leaders refused to believe in Christ and continued to try to suppress the truth. Don't be surprised if some people reject you and your positive witness for Christ. When minds are closed, even the clearest presentation of the facts can't open them. But don't give up either. Pray for those people and continue to spread the gospel.

4:20 We sometimes may be afraid to share our faith in Christ because people might feel uncomfortable and might reject us. But Peter and John's zeal for the Lord was so strong that they could not keep quiet, even when threatened. If your courage to witness for God has weakened, pray that your boldness may increase. Remember Jesus' promise, "Whoever acknowledges me before men, I will also acknowledge him before my Father in heaven" (Matthew 10:32).

4:24–30 Notice how the believers prayed. First they praised God; then they told God their specific problem and asked for his help. They did not ask God to remove the problem, but to help them deal with it. This is a model for us to follow when we pray. We may ask God to remove our problems, and he may choose to do so. But we must recognise that often he will leave the problem in place and give us the strength and courage to deal with it.

against the Lord
and against his Anointed One.'[c,d][w]

[27]Indeed Herod[x] and Pontius Pilate[y] met together with the Gentiles and the people[e]
of Israel in this city to conspire against your holy servant Jesus,[z] whom you anointed.
[28]They did what your power and will had decided beforehand should happen.[a]
[29]Now, Lord, consider their threats and enable your servants to speak your word with
great boldness.[b] [30]Stretch out your hand to heal and perform miraculous signs and
wonders[c] through the name of your holy servant Jesus."[d]
[31]After they prayed, the place where they were meeting was shaken.[e] And they
were all filled with the Holy Spirit and spoke the word of God boldly.[f]

The Believers Share Their Possessions

[32]All the believers were one in heart and mind. No-one claimed that any of his
possessions was his own, but they shared everything they had.[g] [33]With great power
the apostles continued to testify[h] to the resurrection[i] of the Lord Jesus, and much
grace was upon them all. [34]There were no needy persons among them. For from time
to time those who owned lands or houses sold them,[j] brought the money from the
sales [35]and put it at the apostles' feet,[k] and it was distributed to anyone as he had
need.[l]
[36]Joseph, a Levite from Cyprus, whom the apostles called Barnabas[m] (which means
Son of Encouragement), [37]sold a field he owned and brought the money and put it
at the apostles' feet.[n]

Ananias and Sapphira

5 Now a man named Ananias, together with his wife Sapphira, also sold a piece
of property. [2]With his wife's full knowledge he kept back part of the money for
himself, but brought the rest and put it at the apostles' feet.[a]

c *26* That is, Christ or Messiah **d** *26* Psalm 2:1,2 **e** *27* The Greek is plural.

4:26 [w]Ps 2:1, 2; Da 9:25; Lk 4:18; Ac 10:38; Heb 1:9
4:27 [x]Mt 14:1 [y]Mt 27:2; Lk 23:12 [z]ver 30
4:28 [a]Ac 2:23
4:29 [b]ver 13, 31; Ac 9:27; 14:3; Php 1:14
4:30 [c]Jn 4:48 [d]ver 27
4:31 [e]Ac 2:2 [f]ver 29
4:32 [g]Ac 2:44
4:33 [h]Lk 24:48 [i]Ac 1:22
4:34 [j]Mt 19:21; Ac 2:45
4:35 [k]ver 37; Ac 5:2 [l]Ac 2:45; 6:1
4:36 [m]Ac 9:27; 1Co 9:6
4:37 [n]ver 35; Ac 5:2
5:2 [a]Ac 4:35, 37

4:27 This Herod was Herod Antipas, appointed by the Romans to rule over the territory of Galilee. For more information on Herod, see his Profile in Mark 6. Pontius Pilate was the Roman governor over Judea. He bowed to pressure from the crowd and sentenced Jesus to death. For more information on Pilate, see his Profile in Mark 15.

4:28 God is the sovereign Lord of all events who rules history to fulfil his purpose. What his will determines, his power carries out. No army, government, or council can stand in God's way.

4:29–31 Boldness is not reckless impulsiveness. Boldness requires courage to press on through our fears and do what we know is right. How can we be more bold? Like the disciples, we need to pray with others for that courage. To gain boldness, you can (1) pray for the power of the Holy Spirit to give you courage, (2) look for opportunities in your family and neighbourhood to talk about Christ, (3) realise that rejection, social discomfort, and embarrassment are not necessarily persecution, and (4) start where you are by being bolder in small ways.

4:32 Differences of opinion are inevitable among human personalities and can actually be helpful, if handled well. But spiritual unity is essential—loyalty, commitment, and love for God and his word. Without spiritual unity, the church could not survive. Paul wrote the letter of 1 Corinthians to urge the church in Corinth towards greater unity.

4:32 None of these Christians felt that what they had was their own, and so they were able to give and share, eliminating poverty among them. They would not let a brother or sister suffer when others had plenty. How do you feel about your possessions? We should adopt the attitude that everything we have comes from God, and we are only sharing what is already his.

4:32–35 The early church was able to share possessions and property as a result of the unity brought by the Holy Spirit working in and through the believers' lives. This way of living is different from communism because (1) the sharing was voluntary; (2) it didn't involve *all* private property, but only as much as was needed; (3) it was not a membership requirement in order to be a part of the church. The spiritual unity and generosity of these early believers attracted others to them. This organisational structure is not a biblical command, but it offers vital principles for us to follow.

4:36 Barnabas (Joseph) was a respected leader of the church. He was a Levite by birth, a member of the Jewish tribe that carried out temple duties. But his family had moved to Cyprus, so Barnabas didn't serve in the temple. He travelled with Paul on Paul's first missionary journey (13:1ff). For more information on Barnabas, see his Profile in chapter 13.

5:1ff In Acts 5:1—8:3 we see both internal and external problems facing the early church. Inside, there was dishonesty (5:1–11) and administrative headaches (6:1–7). Outside, the church was being pressured by persecution. While church leaders were careful and sensitive in dealing with the internal problems, there was not much they could do to prevent the external pressures. Through it all, the leaders kept their focus on what was most important—spreading the gospel of Jesus Christ.

3Then Peter said, "Ananias, how is it that Satan[b] has so filled your heart[c] that
you have lied to the Holy Spirit[d] and have kept for yourself some of the money you
received for the land? 4Didn't it belong to you before it was sold? And after it was
sold, wasn't the money at your disposal? What made you think of doing such a thing?
You have not lied to men but to God."
5When Ananias heard this, he fell down and died.[e] And great fear[f] seized all who
heard what had happened. 6Then the young men came forward, wrapped up his
body,[g] and carried him out and buried him.
7About three hours later his wife came in, not knowing what had happened. 8Peter
asked her, "Tell me, is this the price you and Ananias got for the land?"
"Yes," she said, "that is the price."[h]
9Peter said to her, "How could you agree to test the Spirit of the Lord?[i] Look!
The feet of the men who buried your husband are at the door, and they will carry you
out also."
10At that moment she fell down at his feet and died.[j] Then the young men came
in and, finding her dead, carried her out and buried her beside her husband. 11Great
fear[k] seized the whole church and all who heard about these events.

The Apostles Heal Many

12The apostles performed many miraculous signs and wonders[l] among the people.
And all the believers used to meet together[m] in Solomon's Colonnade.[n] 13No-one
else dared join them, even though they were highly regarded by the people.[o] 14Never-
theless, more and more men and women believed in the Lord and were added to their
number. 15As a result, people brought the sick into the streets and laid them on beds
and mats so that at least Peter's shadow might fall on some of them as he passed by.[p]
16Crowds gathered also from the towns around Jerusalem, bringing their sick and
those tormented by evil[a] spirits, and all of them were healed.[q]

The Apostles Persecuted

17Then the high priest and all his associates, who were members of the party[r] of
the Sadducees,[s] were filled with jealousy. 18They arrested the apostles and put them

a *16* Greek *unclean*

5:3 [b]Mt 4:10 [c]Jn 13:2, 27 [d]ver 9
5:5 [e]ver 10 [f]ver 11
5:6 [g]Jn 19:40
5:8 [h]ver 2
5:9 [i]ver 3
5:10 [j]ver 5
5:11 [k]ver 5; Ac 19:17
5:12 [l]Ac 2:43 [m]Ac 4:32 [n]Ac 3:11
5:13 [o]Ac 2:47; 4:21
5:15 [p]Ac 19:12
5:16 [q]Mk 16:17
5:17 [r]Ac 15:5 [s]Ac 4:1

5:3 Even after the Holy Spirit had come, the believers were not immune to Satan's temptations. Although Satan was defeated by Christ at the cross, he was still actively trying to make the believers stumble – as he does today (Ephesians 6:12; 1 Peter 5:8). Satan's overthrow is inevitable, but it will not occur until the last days, when Christ returns to judge the world (Revelation 20:10).

5:3ff The sin Ananias and Sapphira committed was not stinginess or holding back part of the money – it was their choice whether or not to sell the land and how much to give. Their sin was lying to God and God's people – saying they gave the whole amount but holding back some for themselves and trying to make themselves appear more generous than they really were. This act was judged harshly because dishonesty, greed, and covetousness are destructive in a church, preventing the Holy Spirit from working effectively. All lying is bad, but when we lie to try to deceive God and his people about our relationship with him, we destroy our testimony about Christ.

5:11 God's judgment on Ananias and Sapphira produced shock and fear among the believers, making them realise how seriously God regards sin in the church.

5:12 Solomon's Colonnade was part of the temple complex built by King Herod the Great in an attempt to strengthen his relationship with the Jews. A colonnade is an entrance or porch supported by columns. Jesus taught and performed miracles in the temple many times. When the apostles went to the temple, they were undoubtedly in close proximity to the same religious leaders who had conspired to put Jesus to death.

5:13 Although many people greatly respected the apostles, they did not dare join them in the temple or work beside them. Some may have been afraid to face the same kind of persecution the apostles had just faced (4:17), while others may have feared a similar fate as the one that fell on Ananias and Sapphira.

5:14 What makes Christianity attractive? It is easy to be drawn to churches because of activities, good speakers, size, beautiful facilities, or fellowship. People were attracted to the early church by expressions of God's power at work, the generosity, sincerity, honesty, and unity of the members, and the character of the leaders. Have our standards slipped? God wants to add believers to his church, not just newer and better schemes or larger and fancier facilities.

5:15 People who passed within Peter's shadow were healed, not by Peter's shadow, but by God's power working through Peter.

5:16 What did these miraculous healings do for the early church? (1) They attracted new believers. (2) They confirmed the truth of the apostles' teaching. (3) They demonstrated that the power of the Messiah who had been crucified and risen was now with his followers.

5:17 The religious leaders were jealous – Peter and the apostles were already commanding more respect than they had ever received. The difference, however, was that the religious leaders demanded respect and reverence for themselves; the apostles' goal was to bring respect and reverence to God. The apostles were respected not because they demanded it, but because they deserved it.

5:17, 18 The apostles experienced power to do miracles, great boldness in preaching, and God's presence in their lives, yet they

in the public jail.[t] 19But during the night an angel[u] of the Lord opened the doors
of the jail[v] and brought them out. 20"Go, stand in the temple courts," he said, "and
tell the people the full message of this new life."[w]
21At daybreak they entered the temple courts, as they had been told, and began to
teach the people.
When the high priest and his associates[x] arrived, they called together the Sanhedrin[y]—the full assembly of the elders of Israel—and sent to the jail for the apostles.
22But on arriving at the jail, the officers did not find them there. So they went back
and reported, 23"We found the jail securely locked, with the guards standing at the
doors; but when we opened them, we found no-one inside." 24On hearing this report,
the captain of the temple guard and the chief priests[z] were puzzled, wondering what
would come of this.
25Then someone came and said, "Look! The men you put in jail are standing in the
temple courts teaching the people." 26At that, the captain went with his officers and
brought the apostles. They did not use force, because they feared that the people[a]
would stone them.
27Having brought the apostles, they made them appear before the Sanhedrin[b] to
be questioned by the high priest. 28"We gave you strict orders not to teach in this
name,"[c] he said. "Yet you have filled Jerusalem with your teaching and are determined to make us guilty of this man's blood."[d]
29Peter and the other apostles replied: "We must obey God rather than men![e] 30The
God of our fathers[f] raised Jesus from the dead[g]—whom you had killed by hanging
him on a tree.[h] 31God exalted him to his own right hand[i] as Prince and Saviour[j]
that he might give repentance and forgiveness of sins to Israel.[k] 32We are witnesses
of these things,[l] and so is the Holy Spirit,[m] whom God has given to those who obey
him."
33When they heard this, they were furious[n] and wanted to put them to death. 34But
a Pharisee named Gamaliel,[o] a teacher of the law,[p] who was honoured by all the
people, stood up in the Sanhedrin and ordered that the men be put outside for a little
while. 35Then he addressed them: "Men of Israel, consider carefully what you intend
to do to these men. 36Some time ago Theudas appeared, claiming to be somebody,
and about four hundred men rallied to him. He was killed, all his followers were
dispersed, and it all came to nothing. 37After him, Judas the Galilean appeared in the
days of the census[q] and led a band of people in revolt. He too was killed, and all

5:18 [t]Ac 4:3
5:19 [u]Mt 1:20; Lk 1:11; Ac 8:26; 27:23 [v]Ac 16:26
5:20 [w]Jn 6:63, 68
5:21 [x]Ac 4:5, 6 [y]ver 27, 34, 41; Mt 5:22
5:24 [z]Ac 4:1
5:26 [a]Ac 4:21
5:27 [b]Mt 5:22
5:28 [c]Ac 4:18 [d]Mt 23:35; 27:25; Ac 2:23, 36; 3:14, 15; 7:52
5:29 [e]Ac 4:19
5:30 [f]Ac 3:13 [g]Ac 2:24 [h]Ac 10:39; 13:29; Gal 3:13; 1Pe 2:24
5:31 [i]Ac 2:33 [j]Lk 2:11 [k]Mt 1:21; Lk 24:47; Ac 2:38
5:32 [l]Lk 24:48 [m]Jn 15:26
5:33 [n]Ac 2:37; 7:54
5:34 [o]Ac 22:3 [p]Lk 2:46
5:37 [q]Lk 2:1, 2

were not free from hatred and persecution. They were arrested, put in jail, beaten, and slandered by community leaders. Faith in God does not make troubles disappear; it makes troubles appear less frightening because it puts them in the right perspective. Don't expect everyone to react favourably when you share something as dynamic as your faith in Christ. Some will be jealous, afraid, or threatened. Expect some negative reactions, and remember that you must be more concerned about serving God than about the reactions of people (see 5:29).

5:21 The "full assembly of the elders of Israel" refers to the entire group, the 70 men of the council (also called the Sanhedrin). This was going to be no small trial. The religious leaders would do anything to stop these apostles from challenging their authority, threatening their secure position, and exposing their hypocritical motives to the people.

5:21 The temple at daybreak was a busy place. Many people stopped at the temple to pray and worship at sunrise. The apostles were already there, ready to tell them the good news of new life in Jesus Christ.

5:21 Suppose someone threatened to kill you if you didn't stop talking about God. You might be tempted to keep quiet. But after being threatened by powerful leaders, arrested, jailed, and miraculously released, the apostles went back to preaching. This was nothing less than God's power working through them (4:13)! When we are convinced of the truth of Christ's resurrection and have experienced the presence and power of his Holy Spirit, we can have the confidence to speak out for Christ.

5:29 The apostles knew their priorities. While we should try to live at peace with everyone (Romans 12:18), conflict with the world and its authorities is sometimes inevitable for a Christian (John 15:18). There will be situations where you cannot obey both God and man. Then you must obey God and trust his word. Let Jesus' words in Luke 6:22 encourage you: "Blessed are you when men hate you, when they exclude you and insult you and reject your name as evil, because of the Son of Man."

5:34 The Pharisees were the other major party in the Jewish council with the Sadducees (5:17). The Pharisees were the strict keepers of the law—not only God's law, but hundreds of other rules they had added to God's law. They were careful about outward purity, but many had hearts full of impure motives. Jesus confronted the Pharisees often during his ministry on earth.

5:34 Gamaliel was an unexpected ally for the apostles, although he probably did not support their teachings. He was a distinguished member of the council and a teacher. While Gamaliel may have saved the apostles' lives, his real intentions probably were to prevent a division in the council and to avoid arousing the Romans. The apostles were popular among the people, and killing them might start a riot. Gamaliel's advice to the council gave the apostles some breathing room to continue their work. The council decided to wait, hoping that this would all fade away harmlessly. They couldn't have been more wrong. Ironically, Paul, later one of the greatest apostles, was one of Gamaliel's students (22:3).

his followers were scattered. 38 Therefore, in the present case I advise you: Leave these
men alone! Let them go! For if their purpose or activity is of human origin, it will
fail.[r] 39 But if it is from God, you will not be able to stop these men; you will only
find yourselves fighting against God."[s]
40 His speech persuaded them. They called the apostles in and had them flogged.[t]
Then they ordered them not to speak in the name of Jesus, and let them go.
41 The apostles left the Sanhedrin, rejoicing[u] because they had been counted worthy
of suffering disgrace for the Name.[v] 42 Day after day, in the temple courts[w] and from
house to house, they never stopped teaching and proclaiming the good news that Jesus
is the Christ.[b]

The Choosing of the Seven

6 In those days when the number of disciples was increasing,[a] the Grecian Jews[b]
among them complained against the Hebraic Jews because their widows[c] were
being overlooked in the daily distribution of food.[d] 2 So the Twelve gathered all the
disciples together and said, "It would not be right for us to neglect the ministry of the
word of God in order to wait on tables. 3 Brothers,[e] choose seven men from among
you who are known to be full of the Spirit and wisdom. We will turn this responsibility
over to them 4 and will give our attention to prayer[f] and the ministry of the word."
5 This proposal pleased the whole group. They chose Stephen,[g] a man full of faith
and of the Holy Spirit;[h] also Philip,[i] Procorus, Nicanor, Timon, Parmenas, and
Nicolas from Antioch, a convert to Judaism. 6 They presented these men to the
apostles, who prayed[j] and laid their hands on them.[k]

b *42* Or *Messiah*

5:38 [r]Mt 15:13
5:39 [s]Pr 21:30; Ac 7:51; 11:17
5:40 [t]Mt 10:17
5:41 [u]Mt 5:12 [v]Jn 15:21
5:42 [w]Ac 2:46
6:1 [a]Ac 2:41 [b]Ac 9:29 [c]Ac 9:39, 41 [d]Ac 4:35
6:3 [e]Ac 1:16
6:4 [f]Ac 1:14
6:5 [g]ver 8; Ac 11:19 [h]Ac 11:24 [i]Ac 8:5-40; 21:8
6:6 [j]Ac 1:24; 8:17; 13:3; 2Ti 1:6 [k]Nu 8:10; Ac 9:17; 1Ti 4:14

5:39 Gamaliel presented some sound advice about reacting to religious movements. Unless disciples in these groups endorse obviously dangerous doctrines or practices, it is often wiser to be tolerant rather than repressive. Sometimes only time will tell if they are merely the work of humans or if God is trying to say something through them. The next time a group promotes differing religious ideas, consider Gamaliel's advice, just in case you "find yourselves fighting against God".

5:40–42 Peter and John were warned repeatedly not to preach, but they continued in spite of the threats. We, too, should live as Christ has asked us to, sharing our faith no matter what the cost. We may not be beaten or thrown in jail, but we may be ridiculed, ostracised, or slandered. To what extent are you willing to suffer for the sake of sharing the gospel with others?

5:41 Have you ever thought of persecution as a blessing, as something worth rejoicing about? This beating suffered by Peter and John was the first time any of the apostles had been physically abused for their faith. These men knew how Jesus had suffered, and they praised God that he had allowed them to be persecuted like their Lord. If you are mocked or persecuted for your faith, it isn't because you're doing something wrong, but because God has counted you "worthy of suffering disgrace for the Name".

5:42 Home Bible studies are not new. As the believers needed to grow in their new faith, home Bible studies met their needs, as well as serving as a means to introduce new people to the Christian faith. During later times of persecution, meeting in homes became the primary method of passing on Bible knowledge. Christians throughout the world still use this approach when under persecution and as a way to build up believers.

6:1 When we read the descriptions of the early church – the miracles, the sharing and generosity, the fellowship – we may wish we could have been a part of this "perfect" church. In reality, the early church had problems just as we do today. No church has ever been or will ever be perfect until Christ and his followers are united at his second coming. All churches have problems. If your church's shortcomings distress you, ask yourself: "Would a perfect church allow me to be a member?" Then do what you can to make your church better. A church does not have to be perfect to be faithful.

6:1ff Another internal problem developed in the early church. The Hebraic Jews, native Jewish Christians, spoke Aramaic, a Semitic language. The Grecian Jews, Greek-speaking Christians, were probably Jews from other lands who were converted at Pentecost. The Greek-speaking Christians complained that their widows were being unfairly treated. This favouritism was probably not intentional, but was more likely caused by the language barrier. To correct the situation, the apostles put seven respected Greek-speaking men in charge of the food distribution scheme. This solved the problem and allowed the apostles to keep their focus on teaching and preaching the Good News about Jesus.

6:2 "The Twelve" are the 11 original disciples and Matthias, who was chosen to replace Judas Iscariot (1:26).

6:2–4 As the early church increased in size, so did its needs. One great need was to organise the distribution of food to the poor. The apostles needed to focus on preaching, so they chose others to administer the food scheme. Each person has a vital part to play in the life of the church (see 1 Corinthians 12). If you are in a position of leadership and find yourself overwhelmed by responsibilities, determine *your* God-given abilities and priorities and then find others to help. If you are not in leadership, you have gifts that can be used by God in various areas of the church's ministry. Offer these gifts in service to him.

6:3 This administrative task was not taken lightly. Notice the requirements for the men who were to handle the food scheme: full of the Holy Spirit and wisdom. People who carry heavy responsibilities and work closely with others should have these qualities. We must look for spiritually mature and wise men and women to lead our churches.

6:4 The apostles' priorities were correct. The ministry of the word should never be neglected because of administrative burdens. Pastors should not try, or be expected to try, to do everything. Instead, the work of the church should be spread out among its members.

6:6 Spiritual leadership is serious business and must not be taken lightly by the church or its leaders. In the early church, the

7 So the word of God spread.[l] The number of disciples in Jerusalem increased
rapidly, and a large number of priests became obedient to the faith.

Stephen Seized

8 Now Stephen, a man full of God's grace and power, did great wonders and
miraculous signs[m] among the people. 9 Opposition arose, however, from members of
the Synagogue of the Freedmen (as it was called) — Jews of Cyrene[n] and Alexandria
as well as the provinces of Cilicia[o] and Asia.[p] These men began to argue with
Stephen, 10 but they could not stand up against his wisdom or the Spirit by whom he
spoke.[q]
11 Then they secretly[r] persuaded some men to say, "We have heard Stephen speak
words of blasphemy against Moses and against God."[s]
12 So they stirred up the people and the elders and the teachers of the law. They
seized Stephen and brought him before the Sanhedrin.[t] 13 They produced false
witnesses, who testified, "This fellow never stops speaking against this holy place[u]
and against the law. 14 For we have heard him say that this Jesus of Nazareth will
destroy this place and change the customs Moses handed down to us."[v]
15 All who were sitting in the Sanhedrin[w] looked intently at Stephen, and they saw
that his face was like the face of an angel.

Stephen's Speech to the Sanhedrin

7 Then the high priest asked him, "Are these charges true?"
2 To this he replied: "Brothers and fathers,[a] listen to me! The God of glory[b]
appeared to our father Abraham while he was still in Mesopotamia, before he lived
in Haran.[c] 3 'Leave your country and your people,' God said, 'and go to the land I
will show you.'[a][d]
4 "So he left the land of the Chaldeans and settled in Haran. After the death of his
father, God sent him to this land where you are now living.[e] 5 He gave him no
inheritance here, not even a foot of ground. But God promised him that he and his
descendants after him would possess the land,[f] even though at that time Abraham
had no child. 6 God spoke to him in this way: 'Your descendants will be strangers in
a country not their own, and they will be enslaved and ill-treated for four hundred

a *3* Gen. 12:1

6:7 [l] Ac 12:24; 19:20
6:8 [m] Jn 4:48
6:9 [n] Mt 27:32 [o] Ac 15:23, 41; 22:3; 23:34 [p] Ac 2:9
6:10 [q] Lk 21:15
6:11 [r] 1Ki 21:10 [s] Mt 26:59-61
6:12 [t] Mt 5:22
6:13 [u] Ac 21:28
6:14 [v] Ac 15:1; 21:21; 26:3; 28:17
6:15 [w] Mt 5:22
7:2 [a] Ac 22:1 [b] Ps 29:3 [c] Ge 11:31; 15:7
7:3 [d] Ge 12:1
7:4 [e] Ge 12:5
7:5 [f] Ge 12:7; 17:8; 26:3

---

chosen men were ordained or commissioned (set apart by prayer and laying on of hands) by the apostles. Laying hands on someone, an ancient Jewish practice, was a way to set a person apart for special service (see Numbers 27:23; Deuteronomy 34:9).

6:7 Jesus had told the apostles that they were to witness first in Jerusalem (1:8). In a short time, their message had infiltrated the entire city and all levels of society. Even some priests were being converted, an obvious violation of the wishes of the council that would endanger their position.

6:7 The word of God spread like ripples on a pond where, from a single centre, each wave touches the next, spreading wider and farther. The gospel still spreads this way today. You don't have to change the world single-handedly – it is enough just to be part of the wave, touching those around you, who in turn will touch others until all have felt the movement. Don't ever feel that your part is insignificant or unimportant.

6:8–10 The most important prerequisite for any kind of Christian service is to be filled with faith and the power of the Holy Spirit. By the Spirit's power, Stephen was a wise servant (6:3), miracle worker (6:8), and evangelist (6:10). By the Spirit's power, you can exercise the gifts God has given you.

6:9 The Freedmen was a group of Jewish slaves who had been freed by Rome and had formed their own synagogue in Jerusalem.

6:11 These men lied about Stephen, causing him to be arrested and brought before the Jewish council. The Sadducees, the dominant party in the council, accepted and studied only the writings of Moses (Genesis through Deuteronomy). In their view, to speak blasphemy against Moses was a crime. But from Stephen's speech (chapter 7), we learn that this accusation was false. Stephen based his review of Israel's history on Moses' writings.

6:14 When Stephen was brought before the Sanhedrin (the council of religious leaders), the accusation against him was the same as the religious leaders had used against Jesus (Matthew 26:59–61). The group falsely accused Stephen of wanting to change Moses' customs, because they knew that the Sadducees, who controlled the council, believed *only* in Moses' laws.

7:1 This high priest was probably Caiaphas, the same man who had earlier questioned and condemned Jesus (John 18:24).

7:2ff Stephen launched into a long speech about Israel's relationship with God. From Old Testament history he showed that the Jews had constantly rejected God's message and his prophets, and that this council had rejected the Messiah, God's Son. He made three main points: (1) Israel's history is the history of God's acts in the world; (2) people worshipped God long before there was a temple, because God does not live in a temple; (3) Jesus' death was just one more example of Israel's rebellion against and rejection of God.

7:2ff Stephen didn't really defend himself. Instead, he took the offensive, seizing the opportunity to summarise his teaching about Jesus. Stephen was accusing these religious leaders of failing to obey God's laws – the laws they prided themselves in following so meticulously. This was the same accusation that Jesus had levelled against them. When we witness for Christ, we don't need to be on the defensive. Instead we can simply share our faith.

years.[g] 7But I will punish the nation they serve as slaves,' God said, 'and afterwards
they will come out of that country and worship me in this place.'[b][h] 8Then he gave
Abraham the covenant of circumcision.[i] And Abraham became the father of Isaac
and circumcised him eight days after his birth.[j] Later Isaac became the father of
Jacob,[k] and Jacob became the father of the twelve patriarchs.[l]
9"Because the patriarchs were jealous of Joseph,[m] they sold him as a slave into
Egypt.[n] But God was with him[o] 10and rescued him from all his troubles. He gave
Joseph wisdom and enabled him to gain the goodwill of Pharaoh king of Egypt; so
he made him ruler over Egypt and all his palace.[p]
11"Then a famine struck all Egypt and Canaan, bringing great suffering, and our
fathers could not find food.[q] 12When Jacob heard that there was grain in Egypt, he
sent our fathers on their first visit.[r] 13On their second visit, Joseph told his brothers
who he was,[s] and Pharaoh learned about Joseph's family. 14After this, Joseph sent
for his father Jacob and his whole family,[t] seventy-five in all.[u] 15Then Jacob went
down to Egypt, where he and our fathers died.[v] 16Their bodies were brought back
to Shechem and placed in the tomb that Abraham had bought from the sons of Hamor
at Shechem for a certain sum of money.[w]
17"As the time drew near for God to fulfil his promise to Abraham, the number of
our people in Egypt greatly increased.[x] 18Then another king, who knew nothing about
Joseph, became ruler of Egypt.[y] 19He dealt treacherously with our people and
oppressed our forefathers by forcing them to throw out their newborn babies so that
they would die.[z]
20"At that time Moses was born, and he was no ordinary child.[c] For three months
he was cared for in his father's house.[a] 21When he was placed outside, Pharaoh's
daughter took him and brought him up as her own son.[b] 22Moses was educated in
all the wisdom of the Egyptians[c] and was powerful in speech and action.
23"When Moses was forty years old, he decided to visit his fellow Israelites. 24He
saw one of them being ill-treated by an Egyptian, so he went to his defence and
avenged him by killing the Egyptian. 25Moses thought that his own people would
realise that God was using him to rescue them, but they did not. 26The next day Moses
came upon two Israelites who were fighting. He tried to reconcile them by saying,
'Men, you are brothers; why do you want to hurt each other?'
27"But the man who was ill-treating the other pushed Moses aside and said, 'Who
made you ruler and judge over us? 28Do you want to kill me as you killed the Egyptian
yesterday?'[d] 29When Moses heard this, he fled to Midian, where he settled as a
foreigner and had two sons.[d]
30"After forty years had passed, an angel appeared to Moses in the flames of a
burning bush in the desert near Mount Sinai. 31When he saw this, he was amazed at
the sight. As he went over to look more closely, he heard the Lord's voice:[e] 32'I am
the God of your fathers, the God of Abraham, Isaac and Jacob.'[e] Moses trembled
with fear and did not dare to look.[f]
33"Then the Lord said to him, 'Take off your sandals; the place where you are
standing is holy ground.[g] 34I have indeed seen the oppression of my people in Egypt.
I have heard their groaning and have come down to set them free. Now come, I will
send you back to Egypt.'[f][h]
35"This is the same Moses whom they had rejected with the words, 'Who made you

b *7* Gen. 15:13,14 **c** *20* Or *was fair in the sight of God* **d** *28* Exodus 2:14 **e** *32* Exodus 3:6
f *34* Exodus 3:5,7,8,10

7:6 [g]Ex 12:40
7:7 [h]Ex 3:12
7:8 [i]Ge 17:9-14 [j]Ge 21:2-4 [k]Ge 25:26 [l]Ge 29:31-35; 30:5-13, 17-24; 35:16-18, 22-26
7:9 [m]Ge 37:4, 11 [n]Ge 37:28; Ps 105:17 [o]Ge 39:2, 21, 23
7:10 [p]Ge 41:37-43
7:11 [q]Ge 41:54
7:12 [r]Ge 42:1, 2
7:13 [s]Ge 45:1-4
7:14 [t]Ge 45:9, 10 [u]Ge 46:26, 27; Ex 1:5; Dt 10:22
7:15 [v]Ge 46:5-7; 49:33; Ex 1:6
7:16 [w]Ge 23:16-20; 33:18, 19; 50:13; Jos 24:32
7:17 [x]Ex 1:7; Ps 105:24
7:18 [y]Ex 1:8
7:19 [z]Ex 1:10-22
7:20 [a]Ex 2:2; Heb 11:23
7:21 [b]Ex 2:3-10
7:22 [c]1Ki 4:30; Isa 19:11
7:29 [d]Ex 2:11-15
7:31 [e]Ex 3:1-4
7:32 [f]Ex 3:6
7:33 [g]Ex 3:5; Jos 5:15
7:34 [h]Ex 3:7-10

7:8 Circumcision was a sign of the promise or covenant made between God, Abraham, and the entire nation of Israel (Genesis 17:9–13). Because Stephen's speech summarised Israel's history, he summarised how this covenant fared during that time. Stephen pointed out that God had always kept his side of the promise, but Israel had failed again and again to uphold its end. Although the Jews in Stephen's day still circumcised their baby boys, they failed to obey God. The people's hearts were far from God. Their lack of faith and lack of obedience meant that they had failed to keep their part of the covenant.

7:17 Stephen's review of Jewish history gives a clear testimony of God's faithfulness and sovereignty. Despite the continued failures of his chosen people and the swirling world events, God was working out his plan. When faced by a confusing array of circumstances, remember that: (1) God is in control – nothing surprises him; (2) this world is not all there is – it will pass away, but God is eternal; (3) God is just, and he will make things right – punishing the wicked and rewarding the faithful; (4) God wants to use you (like Joseph, Moses, and Stephen) to make a difference in the world.

7:35 [i]ver 27
7:36 [j]Ex 12:41; 33:1 [k]Ex 14:21
7:37 [l]Dt 18:15, 18; Ac 3:22
7:38 [m]ver 53

ruler and judge?'[i] He was sent to be their ruler and deliverer by God himself, through
the angel who appeared to him in the bush. 36He led them out of Egypt[j] and did
wonders and miraculous signs in Egypt, at the Red Sea[g][k] and for forty years in the
desert.
37"This is that Moses who told the Israelites, 'God will send you a prophet like me
from your own people.'[h][l] 38He was in the assembly in the desert, with the angel[m]

[g] 36 That is, Sea of Reeds [h] 37 Deut. 18:15

STEPHEN

Around the world, the gospel has most often taken root in places prepared by the blood of martyrs. Before people can *give* their lives for the gospel, however, they must first *live* their lives for the gospel. One way God trains his servants is to place them in insignificant positions. Their desire to serve Christ is translated into the reality of serving others. Stephen was an effective administrator and messenger before becoming a martyr.

Stephen was named among the managers of food distribution in the early church. Long before violent persecution broke out against Christians, there was already social ostracism. Jews who accepted Jesus as Messiah were usually cut off from their families. As a result, the believers depended on each other for support. The sharing of homes, food, and resources was both a practical and necessary mark of the early church. Eventually, the number of believers made it necessary to organise the sharing. People were being overlooked. There were complaints. Those chosen to help manage were chosen for their integrity, wisdom, and sensitivity to God.

Stephen, besides being a good administrator, was also a powerful speaker. When confronted in the temple by various antagonistic groups, Stephen's logic in responding was convincing. This is clear from the defence he made before the council. He presented a summary of the Jews' own history and made powerful applications that stung his listeners. During his defence Stephen must have known he was speaking his own death sentence. Members of the council could not stand to have their evil motives exposed. They stoned him to death while he prayed for their forgiveness. His final words show how much like Jesus he had become in a short time. His death had a lasting impact on young Saul (Paul) of Tarsus, who would move from being a violent persecutor of Christians to being one of the greatest champions of the gospel the church has known.

Stephen's life is a continual challenge to all Christians. Because he was the first to die for the faith, his sacrifice raises questions: How many risks do we take in being Jesus' followers? Would we be willing to die for him? Are we really willing to live for him?

Strengths and accomplishments:
- One of seven leaders chosen to supervise food distribution to the needy in the early church
- Known for his spiritual qualities of faith, wisdom, grace, and power, and for the Spirit's presence in his life
- Outstanding leader, teacher, and debater
- First to give his life for the gospel

Lessons from his life:
- Striving for excellence in small assignments prepares one for greater responsibilities
- Real understanding of God always leads to practical and compassionate actions towards people

Vital statistics:
- Church responsibilities: Deacon—distributing food to the needy
- Contemporaries: Paul, Caiaphas, Gamaliel, the apostles

Key verses:
"While they were stoning him, Stephen prayed, 'Lord Jesus, receive my spirit.' Then he fell on his knees and cried out, 'Lord, do not hold this sin against them.' When he had said this, he fell asleep" (Acts 7:59, 60).

Stephen's story is told in Acts 6:3—8:2. He is also mentioned in Acts 11:19; 22:20.

7:37 The Jews originally thought this "prophet" was Joshua. But Moses was prophesying about the coming Messiah (Deuteronomy 18:15). Peter also quoted this verse in referring to the Messiah (3:22).

7:38 Stephen used the word "ekklesia" (translated "assembly") to describe the congregation or people of God in the desert. This word means "called out ones" and was used by the first-century Christians to describe their own community or "assembly". Stephen's point was that the giving of the law through Moses to the Jews was the sign of the covenant. By *obedience*, then, they would continue to be God's covenant people. But because they disobeyed (7:39), they broke the covenant and forfeited their right to be the chosen people.

7:38 From Galatians 3:19 and Hebrews 2:2, it appears that God had given the law to Moses through angels. Exodus 31:18 says God wrote the Ten Commandments himself ("inscribed by the finger of God"). Apparently God used angelic messengers as mediators to deliver his law to Moses.

who spoke to him on Mount Sinai, and with our fathers;[n] and he received living
words[o] to pass on to us.[p]
39"But our fathers refused to obey him. Instead, they rejected him and in their hearts
turned back to Egypt.[q] 40They told Aaron, 'Make us gods who will go before us.
As for this fellow Moses who led us out of Egypt — we don't know what has happened
to him!'[i][r] 41That was the time they made an idol in the form of a calf. They brought
sacrifices to it and held a celebration in honour of what their hands had made.[s] 42But
God turned away[t] and gave them over to the worship of the heavenly bodies.[u] This
agrees with what is written in the book of the prophets:

" 'Did you bring me sacrifices and offerings
for forty years in the desert, O house of Israel?
43You have lifted up the shrine of Molech
and the star of your god Rephan,
the idols you made to worship.
Therefore I will send you into exile'[j][v] beyond Babylon.

44"Our forefathers had the tabernacle of the Testimony[w] with them in the desert.
It had been made as God directed Moses, according to the pattern he had seen.[x]
45Having received the tabernacle, our fathers under Joshua brought it with them when
they took the land from the nations God drove out before them.[y] It remained in the
land until the time of David, 46who enjoyed God's favour and asked that he might
provide a dwelling-place for the God of Jacob.[k][z] 47But it was Solomon who built
the house for him.
48"However, the Most High does not live in houses made by men.[a] As the prophet
says:

49" 'Heaven is my throne,
and the earth is my footstool.[b]
What kind of house will you build for me?
says the Lord.
Or where will my resting place be?
50Has not my hand made all these things?'[l][c]

51"You stiff-necked people,[d] with uncircumcised hearts[e] and ears! You are just
like your fathers: You always resist the Holy Spirit! 52Was there ever a prophet your
fathers did not persecute?[f] They even killed those who predicted the coming of the
Righteous One. And now you have betrayed and murdered him[g] — 53you who have
received the law that was put into effect through angels[h] but have not obeyed it."

The Stoning of Stephen

54When they heard this, they were furious[i] and gnashed their teeth at him. 55But
Stephen, full of the Holy Spirit, looked up to heaven and saw the glory of God, and

[i] 40 Exodus 32:1 [j] 43 Amos 5:25–27 [k] 46 Some early manuscripts *the house of Jacob* [l] 50 Isaiah 66:1,2

7:38 [n]Ex 19:17 [o]Dt 32:45-47; Heb 4:12 [p]Ro 3:2
7:39 [q]Nu 14:3, 4
7:40 [r]Ex 32:1, 23
7:41 [s]Ex 32:4-6; Ps 106:19, 20; Rev 9:20
7:42 [t]Jos 24:20; Isa 63:10 [u]Jer 19:13
7:43 [v]Am 5:25-27
7:44 [w]Ex 38:21 [x]Ex 25:8, 9, 40
7:45 [y]Jos 3:14-17; 18:1; 23:9; 24:18; Ps 44:2
7:46 [z]2Sa 7:8-16; Ps 132:1-5
7:48 [a]1Ki 8:27; 2Ch 2:6
7:49 [b]Mt 5:34, 35
7:50 [c]Isa 66:1, 2
7:51 [d]Ex 32:9; 33:3, 5 [e]Lev 26:41; Dt 10:16; Jer 4:4; 9:26
7:52 [f]2Ch 36:16; Mt 5:12 [g]Ac 3:14;
7:53 1Th 2:15 [h]ver 38; Gal 3:19; Heb 2:2
7:54 [i]Ac 5:33

7:42 The *heavenly bodies* refers to their practice of worshipping deities associated with stars and planets.

7:43 Here Stephen gave more details of the idolatry referred to in 7:40. These were idols worshipped by Israel during their desert wanderings (Exodus 32:4). Molech was the god associated with child sacrifice, and Rephan was an Egyptian god. Amos also names Assyrian deities worshipped by Israel (Amos 5:25–27).

7:44–50 Stephen had been accused of speaking against the temple (6:13). Although he recognised the importance of the temple, he knew that it was not more important than God. God is not limited; he doesn't live only in a house of worship, but wherever hearts of faith are open to receive him (Isaiah 66:1, 2). Solomon knew this when he prayed at the dedication of the temple (2 Chronicles 6:18). God wants to live in us. Is he living in you?

7:52 Indeed many prophets were persecuted and killed: Uriah (Jeremiah 26:20–23); Jeremiah (Jeremiah 38:1–6); Isaiah (tradition says he was killed by King Manasseh; see 2 Kings 21:16); Amos (Amos 7:10–13); Zechariah (not the author of the Bible book, but the son of Jehoiada the priest, 2 Chronicles 24:20–22); Elijah (1 Kings 19:1, 2). Jesus also told a parable about how the Jews had constantly rejected God's messages and persecuted his messengers (Luke 20:9–19). The Righteous One refers to the Messiah.

7:55–58 Stephen saw the glory of God, and Jesus the Messiah standing at God's right hand. Stephen's words are similar to Jesus' words spoken before the council (Matthew 26:64; Mark 14:62; Luke 22:69). Stephen's vision supported Jesus' claim and angered the Jewish leaders who had condemned Jesus to death for blasphemy. They would not tolerate Stephen's words, so they dragged him out and killed him. People may not kill us for witnessing about Christ, but they will let us know they don't want to hear the truth and will often try to silence us. Keep honouring God in your con-

Jesus standing at the right hand of God.[j] 56"Look," he said, "I see heaven open[k]
and the Son of Man[l] standing at the right hand of God."
57At this they covered their ears and, yelling at the top of their voices, they all
rushed at him, 58dragged him out of the city[m] and began to stone him.[n] Meanwhile,
the witnesses laid their clothes[o] at the feet of a young man named Saul.[p]
59While they were stoning him, Stephen prayed, "Lord Jesus, receive my spirit."[q]
60Then he fell on his knees[r] and cried out, "Lord, do not hold this sin against them."[s]
When he had said this, he fell asleep.

8 And Saul[a] was there, giving approval to his death.

2. Expansion of the church

The Church Persecuted and Scattered

On that day a great persecution broke out against the church at Jerusalem, and all
except the apostles were scattered[b] throughout Judea and Samaria.[c] 2Godly men
buried Stephen and mourned deeply for him. 3But Saul[d] began to destroy the
church.[e] Going from house to house, he dragged off men and women and put them
in prison.

Philip in Samaria

4Those who had been scattered[f] preached the word wherever they went.[g]
5Philip[h] went down to a city in Samaria and proclaimed the Christ[a] there. 6When

a 5 Or *Messiah*

7:55 [j]Mk 16:19
7:56 [k]Mt 3:16 [l]Mt 8:20
7:58 [m]Lk 4:29 [n]Lev 24:14, 16; Dt 13:9 [o]Ac 22:20 [p]Ac 8:1
7:59 [q]Ps 31:5; Lk 23:46
7:60 [r]Ac 9:40 [s]Mt 5:44
8:1 [a]Ac 7:58 [b]Ac 11:19 [c]Ac 9:31
8:3 [d]Ac 7:58 [e]Ac 22:4, 19; 26:10, 11; 1Co 15:9; Gal 1:13, 23; Php 3:6; 1Ti 1:13
8:4 [f]ver 1 [g]Ac 15:35
8:5 [h]Ac 6:5

THE EFFECTS OF STEPHEN'S DEATH

Stephen's death was not in vain. Below are some of the events that were by-products (either directly or indirectly) of the persecution that began with Stephen's martyrdom.

1. Philip's evangelistic tour (Acts 8:4–40)
2. Paul's (Saul's) conversion (Acts 9:1–30)
3. Peter's missionary tour (Acts 9:32—11:18)
4. The church in Antioch in Syria founded (Acts 11:19ff)

duct and words; though many may turn against you and your message, some will follow Christ. Remember, Stephen's death made a profound impact on Paul, who later became the world's greatest missionary. Even those who oppose you now may later turn to Christ.

7:58 Saul is also called Paul (see 13:9), the great missionary who wrote many of the letters in the New Testament. Saul was his Hebrew name; Paul, his Greek name, was used as he began his ministry to the Gentiles. When Luke introduces him, Paul was hating and persecuting Jesus' followers. This is a great contrast to the Paul about whom Luke will write for most of the rest of the book of Acts—a devoted follower of Christ and a gifted gospel preacher. Paul was uniquely qualified to talk to the Jews about Jesus because he had once persecuted those who believed in Jesus, and he understood how the opposition felt. Paul is a powerful example of how no-one is beyond God's power to reach and change.

7:59 The penalty for blasphemy, speaking irreverently about God, was death by stoning (Leviticus 24:14). The religious leaders, who were furious, had Stephen stoned without a trial. They did not understand that Stephen's words were true, because they were not seeking the truth. They only wanted support for their own views.

7:60 As Stephen died, he spoke words very similar to Jesus' words on the cross (Luke 23:34). The early believers were glad to suffer as Jesus had suffered because that meant they were counted worthy (5:41). Stephen was ready to suffer like Jesus, even to the point of asking forgiveness for his murderers. Such a forgiving response comes only from the Holy Spirit. The Spirit can also help us respond as Stephen did with love for our enemies (Luke 6:27). How would you react if someone hurt you because of what you believed?

8:1–4 Persecution forced the Christians out of Jerusalem and into Judea and Samaria—thus fulfilling the second part of Jesus' command (see 1:8). The persecution helped spread the gospel. God would bring great results from the believers' suffering.

8:4 Persecution forced the believers out of their homes in Jerusalem, and along with them went the gospel. Sometimes we have to become uncomfortable before we'll move. We may not want to experience it, but discomfort may be the best thing for us because God may be working through our hurts. When you are tempted to complain about uncomfortable or painful circumstances, stop and ask if God might be preparing you for a special task.

8:5 This is not the apostle Philip (see John 1:43, 44), but a Greek-speaking Jew, "full of the Spirit and wisdom" (6:3), who was one of the seven deacons chosen to help with the food distribution scheme in the church (6:5).

8:5 Israel had been divided into three main regions—Galilee in the north, Samaria in the middle, and Judea in the south. The city of Samaria (in the region of Samaria) had been the capital of the northern kingdom of Israel in the days of the divided kingdom, before it was conquered by Assyria in 722 B.C. During that war, the Assyrian king took many captives, leaving only the poorest people in the land and resettling it with foreigners. These foreigners intermarried with the Jews who were left, and the mixed race became known as Samaritans. The Samaritans were considered half-breeds by the "pure" Jews in the southern kingdom of Judah, and there was intense hatred between the two groups. But Jesus himself went into Samaria (John 4), and he commanded his followers to spread the gospel there (1:8).

the crowds heard Philip and saw the miraculous signs he did, they all paid close 8:7 [i]Mk 16:17
attention to what he said. 7With shrieks, evil[b] spirits came out of many,[i] and many [j]Mt 4:24
paralytics and cripples were healed.[j] 8So there was great joy in that city.

Simon the Sorcerer

9Now for some time a man named Simon had practised sorcery[k] in the city and 8:9 [k]Ac 13:6 [l]Ac 5:36
amazed all the people of Samaria. He boasted that he was someone great,[l] 10and all
the people, both high and low, gave him their attention and exclaimed, "This man
is the divine power known as the Great Power."[m] 11They followed him because he 8:10 [m]Ac 14:11; 28:6

[b] 7 Greek *unclean*

MISSIONARIES OF THE NEW TESTAMENT AND THEIR JOURNEYS

Name	*Journey's Purpose*	*Scripture Reference in Acts*
Philip	One of the first to preach the gospel outside Jerusalem	8:4–40
Peter and John	Visited new Samaritan believers to encourage them	8:14–25
Paul (journey to Damascus)	Set out to capture Christians but was captured by Christ	9:1–25
Peter	Led by God to one of the first Gentile families to become Christians—Cornelius' family	9:32—10:48
Barnabas	Went to Antioch as an encourager; travelled on to Troas to bring Paul back to Jerusalem from Antioch	11:25–30
Barnabas, Paul, John Mark	Left Antioch for Cyprus, Pamphylia, and Galatia on the first missionary journey	13:1—14:28
Barnabas and John Mark	After a break with Paul, they left Antioch for Cyprus	15:36–41
Paul, Silas, Timothy, Luke	Left Antioch to revisit churches in Galatia, then travelled on to Asia, Macedonia, and Achaia on a second missionary journey	15:36—18:22
Apollos	Left Alexandria for Ephesus; learned the complete gospel story from Priscilla and Aquila; preached in Athens and Corinth	18:24–28
Paul, Timothy, Erastus	Third major missionary journey revisiting churches in Galatia, Asia, Macedonia, and Achaia	18:23; 19:1—21:14

PHILIP'S MINISTRY
To escape persecution in Jerusalem, Philip fled to Samaria, where he continued preaching the gospel. While he was there, an angel commanded him to meet an Ethiopian official on the road between Jerusalem and Gaza. The man became a believer before continuing on to Ethiopia. Philip then went from Azotus to Caesarea.

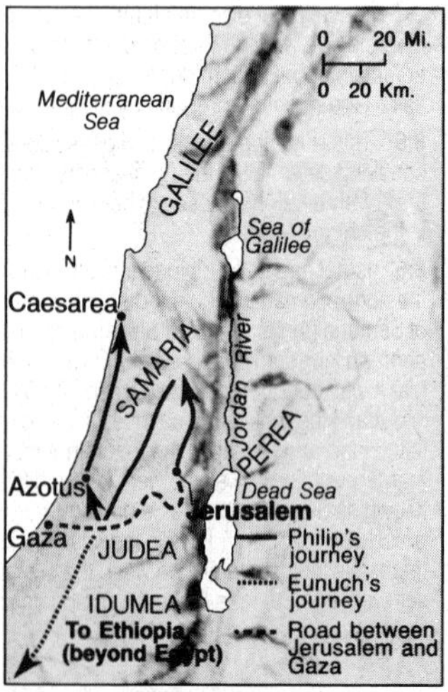

8:7 Jesus encountered and drove out many demons during his ministry on earth. Demons, or evil spirits, are ruled by Satan. Most scholars believe that they are fallen angels who joined Satan in his rebellion against God, and who can cause a person to be mute, deaf, blind, or insane. Demons also tempt people to sin. Although they can be powerful, they are not able to read our minds and cannot be everywhere at once. Demons are real and active, but Jesus has authority over them; and he gave this authority to his followers. Although Satan is allowed to work in our world, God is in complete control. He can drive demons out and end their destructive work in people's lives. Eventually Satan and his demons will be thrown into the lake of fire, for ever ending their evil work in the world (Revelation 20:10).

8:9–11 In the days of the early church, sorcerers and magicians were numerous and influential. They worked wonders, performed healings and exorcisms, and practised astrology. Their wonders may simply have been magic tricks, or the sorcerers may have been empowered by Satan (Matthew 24:24; 2 Thessalonians 2:9). Simon had done so many wonders that some even thought that he was the Messiah; but his powers did not come from God (see 8:18–24).

8:14 Peter and John were sent to Samaria to find out whether or not the Samaritans were truly becoming believers. The Jewish

had amazed them for a long time with his magic. 12But when they believed Philip as
he preached the good news of the kingdom of God[n] and the name of Jesus Christ,
they were baptised,[o] both men and women. 13Simon himself believed and was
baptised. And he followed Philip everywhere, astonished by the great signs and
miracles[p] he saw.
14When the apostles in Jerusalem heard that Samaria[q] had accepted the word
of God, they sent Peter and John[r] to them. 15When they arrived, they prayed for
them that they might receive the Holy Spirit,[s] 16because the Holy Spirit had not yet
come upon any of them;[t] they had simply been baptised into[c] the name of the Lord
Jesus.[u] 17Then Peter and John placed their hands on them,[v] and they received the Holy
Spirit.
18When Simon saw that the Spirit was given at the laying on of the apostles' hands,
he offered them money 19and said, "Give me also this ability so that everyone on
whom I lay my hands may receive the Holy Spirit."
20Peter answered: "May your money perish with you, because you thought you
could buy the gift of God with money![w] 21You have no part or share in this ministry,
because your heart is not right[x] before God. 22Repent of this wickedness and pray
to the Lord. Perhaps he will forgive you for having such a thought in your heart. 23For
I see that you are full of bitterness and captive to sin."
24Then Simon answered, "Pray to the Lord for me[y] so that nothing you have said
may happen to me."
25When they had testified and proclaimed the word of the Lord, Peter and John
returned to Jerusalem, preaching the gospel in many Samaritan villages.[z]

Philip and the Ethiopian

26Now an angel[a] of the Lord said to Philip, "Go south to the road—the desert
road—that goes down from Jerusalem to Gaza." 27So he started out, and on his way
he met an Ethiopian[d][b] eunuch,[c] an important official in charge of all the treasury
of Candace, queen of the Ethiopians. This man had gone to Jerusalem to worship,[d]
28and on his way home was sitting in his chariot reading the book of Isaiah the prophet.

8:12 [n]Ac 1:3 [o]Ac 2:38
8:13 [p]ver 6; Ac 19:11
8:14 [q]ver 1 [r]Lk 22:8
8:15 [s]Ac 2:38
8:16 [t]Ac 19:2 [u]Mt 28:19; Ac 2:38
8:17 [v]Ac 6:6
8:20 [w]2Ki 5:16; Da 5:17; Mt 10:8; Ac 2:38
8:21 [x]Ps 78:37
8:24 [y]Ex 8:8; Nu 21:7; 1Ki 13:6
8:25 [z]ver 40
8:26 [a]Ac 5:19
8:27 [b]Ps 68:31; 87:4; Zep 3:10 [c]Isa 56:3-5 [d]1Ki 8:41-43; Jn 12:20

c *16* Or *in* **d** *27* That is, from the upper Nile region

---

Christians, even the apostles, were still unsure whether Gentiles (non-Jews) and half-Jews could receive the Holy Spirit. It wasn't until Peter's experience with Cornelius (chapter 10) that the apostles became fully convinced that the Holy Spirit was for all people. It was John who had asked Jesus if they should call fire down from heaven to burn up a Samaritan village that refused to welcome them (Luke 9:51–55). Here he and Peter went to the Samaritans to pray with them.

8:15–17 This was a crucial moment for the spread of the gospel and for the growth of the church. Peter and John had to go to Samaria to help keep this new group of believers from becoming separated from other believers. When Peter and John saw the Lord working in these people, they were assured that the Holy Spirit worked through *all* believers—Gentiles and mixed races as well as "pure" Jews.

8:15–17 Many scholars believe that God chose to have a dramatic filling of his Spirit as a sign at this special moment in history—the spread of the gospel into Samaria through the powerful, effective preaching of believers. Normally, the Holy Spirit enters a person's life at conversion. This was a special event. The pouring out of the Spirit would happen again with Cornelius and his family (10:44–47), a sign that the uncircumcised Gentiles could receive the gospel.

8:18–23 "Everything has a price" seems to be true in our world of bribes, wealth, and materialism. Simon thought he could buy the Holy Spirit's power, but Peter harshly rebuked him. The only way to receive God's power is to do what Peter told Simon to do—turn from sin, ask God for forgiveness, and be filled with his Spirit. No amount of money can buy salvation, forgiveness of sin, or God's power. These are only gained by repentance and belief in Christ as Saviour.

8:24 The last time a parent or friend rebuked you, were you hurt, angry, or defensive? Learn a lesson from Simon and his reaction to what Peter told him. He exclaimed, "Pray to the Lord for me." If you are rebuked for a serious mistake, it is for your good. Admit your error, repent quickly, and ask for prayer.

8:26 Philip was having a successful preaching ministry to great crowds in Samaria (8:5–8), but he obediently left that ministry to travel on a desert road. Because Philip went where God sent him, Ethiopia was opened up to the gospel. Follow God's leading, even if it seems like a demotion. At first you may not understand his plans, but the results will prove that God's way is right.

8:27 Ethiopia was located in Africa south of Egypt. The eunuch was obviously very dedicated to God because he had travelled such a long distance to worship in Jerusalem. The Jews had contact with Ethiopia (known as Cush) in ancient days (Psalm 68:31; Jeremiah 38:7), so this man may have been a Gentile convert to Judaism. Because he was in charge of the treasury of Ethiopia, this man's conversion brought Christianity into the power structures of another government. This is the beginning of the witness "to the ends of the earth" (1:8). See the prophecy in Isaiah 56:3–5 for words about foreigners and eunuchs.

29The Spirit told[e] Philip, "Go to that chariot and stay near it."
30Then Philip ran up to the chariot and heard the man reading Isaiah the prophet.
"Do you understand what you are reading?" Philip asked.
31"How can I," he said, "unless someone explains it to me?" So he invited Philip
to come up and sit with him.
32The eunuch was reading this passage of Scripture:

"He was led like a sheep to the slaughter,
and as a lamb before the shearer is silent,
so he did not open his mouth.
33In his humiliation he was deprived of justice.
Who can speak of his descendants?
For his life was taken from the earth."[e][f]

34The eunuch asked Philip, "Tell me, please, who is the prophet talking about,
himself or someone else?" 35Then Philip began[g] with that very passage of Scripture[h]
and told him the good news about Jesus.
36As they travelled along the road, they came to some water and the eunuch said,
"Look, here is water. Why shouldn't I be baptised?"[f][i] 38And he gave orders to stop
the chariot. Then both Philip and the eunuch went down into the water and Philip
baptised him. 39When they came up out of the water, the Spirit of the Lord suddenly
took Philip away,[j] and the eunuch did not see him again, but went on his way
rejoicing. 40Philip, however, appeared at Azotus and travelled about, preaching the
gospel in all the towns[k] until he reached Caesarea.[l]

Saul's Conversion

9 Meanwhile, Saul was still breathing out murderous threats against the Lord's
disciples.[a] He went to the high priest 2and asked him for letters to the synagogues
in Damascus, so that if he found any there who belonged to the Way,[b] whether men

e *33* Isaiah 53:7,8 **f** *36* Some late manuscripts *baptised?" 37Philip said, "If you believe with all your heart, you may." The eunuch answered, "I believe that Jesus Christ is the Son of God."*

8:29 [e]Ac 10:19; 11:12; 13:2; 20:23; 21:11
8:33 [f]Isa 53:7, 8
8:35 [g]Mt 5:2 [h]Lk 24:27; Ac 17:2; 18:28; 28:23
8:36 [i]Ac 10:47
8:39 [j]1Ki 18:12; 2Ki 2:16; Eze 3:12, 14; 8:3; 11:1, 24; 43:5; 2Co 12:2
8:40 [k]ver 25 [l]Ac 10:1, 24; 12:19; 21:8, 16; 23:23, 33; 25:1, 4, 6, 13
9:1 [a]Ac 8:3
9:2 [b]Ac 19:9, 23; 22:4; 24:14, 22

8:29–35 Philip found the Ethiopian man reading Scripture. Taking advantage of this opportunity to explain the gospel, Philip asked the man if he understood what he was reading. Philip (1) followed the Spirit's leading, (2) began the discussion from where the man was (immersed in the prophecies of Isaiah), and (3) explained how Jesus Christ fulfilled Isaiah's prophecies. When we share the gospel, we should start where the other person's concerns are focused. Then we can bring the gospel to bear on those concerns.

8:30, 31 The eunuch asked Philip to explain a passage of Scripture that he did not understand. When we have trouble understanding the Bible, we should ask others to help us. We must never let our insecurity or pride get in the way of understanding God's word.

8:35 Some think that the Old Testament is not relevant today, but Philip led this man to faith in Jesus Christ by using the Old Testament. Jesus Christ is found in the pages of both the Old and New Testaments. God's entire word is applicable to all people in all ages. Don't avoid or neglect to use the Old Testament. It too is God's word.

8:38 Baptism was a sign of identification with Christ and with the Christian community. Although there were no witnesses besides Philip, it was still important for the eunuch to take this step.

8:39, 40 Why was Philip suddenly transported to a different city? This miraculous sign showed the urgency of bringing the Gentiles to belief in Christ. Azotus is Ashdod, one of the ancient Philistine capitals. Philip probably lived in Caesarea for the next 20 years (21:8).

9:2 Saul (later called Paul) was so zealous for his Jewish beliefs that he began a persecution campaign against anyone who believed in Christ ("who belonged to the Way"). Why would the Jews in Jerusalem want to persecute Christians as far away as Damascus? There are several possibilities: (1) to seize the Christians who had fled, (2) to prevent the spread of Christianity to other major cities, (3) to keep the Christians from causing any trouble with Rome, (4) to advance Saul's career and build his reputation as a true Pharisee, zealous for the law, (5) to unify the factions of Judaism by giving them a common enemy.

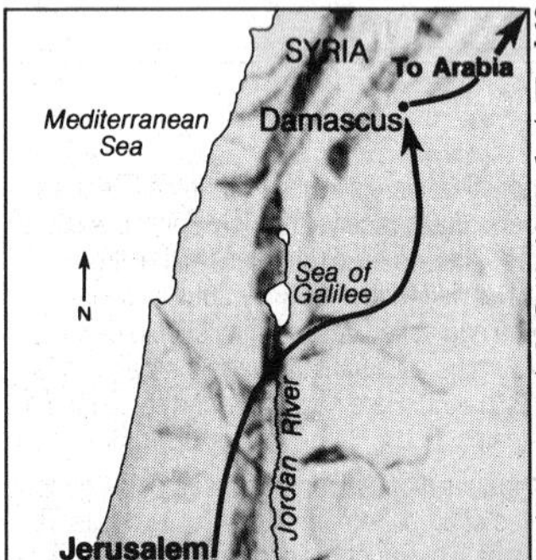

SAUL TRAVELS TO DAMASCUS
Many Christians fled Jerusalem when persecution began after Stephen's death, seeking refuge in other cities and countries. Saul tracked them down, even travelling 150 miles to Damascus in Syria to bring Christians back in chains to Jerusalem. But as he neared the ancient city, he discovered that God had other plans for him (9:15).

9:3 [c]1Co 15:8

9:6 [d]ver 16

or women, he might take them as prisoners to Jerusalem. 3As he neared Damascus
on his journey, suddenly a light from heaven flashed around him.[c] 4He fell to the
ground and heard a voice say to him, "Saul, Saul, why do you persecute me?"
5"Who are you, Lord?" Saul asked.
"I am Jesus, whom you are persecuting," he replied. 6"Now get up and go into the
city, and you will be told what you must do."[d]

PHILIP

Jesus' last words to his followers were a command to take the gospel everywhere, but they seemed reluctant to leave Jerusalem. It took intense persecution to scatter the believers from Jerusalem and into Judea and Samaria, where Jesus had instructed them to go. Philip, one of the deacons in charge of food distribution, left Jerusalem and, like most Jewish Christians, spread the gospel wherever he went; but unlike most of them, he did not limit his audience to other Jews. He went directly to Samaria, the last place many Jews would go, due to age-old prejudice.

The Samaritans responded in large numbers. When word got back to Jerusalem, Peter and John were sent to evaluate Philip's ministry. They quickly became involved themselves, seeing firsthand God's acceptance of those who previously were considered unacceptable.

In the middle of all this success and excitement, God directed Philip out to the desert for an appointment with an Ethiopian eunuch, another foreigner, who had been in Jerusalem. Philip went immediately. His effectiveness in sharing the gospel with this man placed a Christian in a significant position in a distant country, and may well have had an effect on an entire nation.

Philip ended up in Caesarea, where events allowed him to be Paul's host many years later. Paul, who as the leading persecutor of the Christians had been instrumental in pushing Philip and others out of Jerusalem, had himself become an effective believer. The conversion of the Gentiles begun by Philip was continued across the entire Roman empire by Paul.

Whether or not you are a follower of Christ, Philip's life presents a challenge. To those still outside the gospel, he is a reminder that the gospel is for you also. To those who have accepted Christ, he is a reminder that we are not free to disqualify anyone from hearing about Jesus. How much like Philip would your neighbours say you are?

Strengths and accomplishments:
- One of the seven organisers of food distribution in the early church
- Became an evangelist, one of the first travelling missionaries
- One of the first to obey Jesus' command to take the gospel to all people
- A careful student of the Bible who could explain its meaning clearly

Lessons from his life:
- God finds great and various uses for those willing to obey wholeheartedly
- The gospel is universal good news
- The whole Bible, not just the New Testament, helps us understand more about Jesus
- Both mass response (the Samaritans) and individual response (the man from Ethiopia) to the gospel are valuable

Vital statistics:
- Occupations: Deacon, evangelist
- Relatives: Four daughters
- Contemporaries: Paul, Stephen, the apostles

Key verse:
"Then Philip began with that very passage of Scripture and told him the good news about Jesus" (Acts 8:35).

Philip's story is told in Acts 6:1–7; 8:5–40; 21:8–10.

9:2–5 As Saul travelled to Damascus, pursuing Christians, he was confronted by the risen Christ and brought face to face with the truth of the gospel. Sometimes God breaks into a life in a spectacular manner, and sometimes conversion is a quiet experience. Beware of people who insist that you must have a particular type of conversion experience. The right way to come to faith in Jesus is whatever way God brings *you.*

9:3 Damascus, a key commercial city, was located about 175 miles north-east of Jerusalem in the Roman province of Syria. Several trade routes linked Damascus to other cities throughout the Roman world. Saul may have thought that by stamping out Christianity in Damascus, he could prevent its spread to other areas.

9:3–5 Paul refers to this experience as the start of his new life in Christ (1 Corinthians 9:1; 15:8; Galatians 1:15, 16). At the centre of this wonderful experience was Jesus Christ. Paul did not see a vision; he saw the risen Christ himself (9:17). Paul acknowledged Jesus as Lord, confessed his own sin, surrendered his life to Christ, and resolved to obey him. True conversion comes from a personal encounter with Jesus Christ and leads to a new life in relationship with him.

9:5 Saul thought he was pursuing heretics, but he was persecuting Jesus himself. Anyone who persecutes believers today is also guilty of persecuting Jesus (see Matthew 25:40, 45), because believers are the body of Christ on earth.

7The men travelling with Saul stood there speechless; they heard the sound[e] but
did not see anyone.[f] 8Saul got up from the ground, but when he opened his eyes he
could see nothing. So they led him by the hand into Damascus. 9For three days he
was blind, and did not eat or drink anything.
10In Damascus there was a disciple named Ananias. The Lord called to him in a
vision,[g] "Ananias!"

9:7 [e]Jn 12:29 [f]Da 10:7; Ac 22:9
9:10 [g]Ac 10:3, 17, 19

GREAT ESCAPES IN THE BIBLE

Who escaped	*Reference*	*What happened*	*What the escape accomplished*	*Application*
Jacob	Genesis 31:1–55	Left his father-in-law, Laban, after almost 20 years of service	Allowed Jacob to return home for Isaac's death and for reconciliation with Esau, his brother	A time away from home often puts the really important things into perspective
Moses	Exodus 2:11–15	Fled Egypt after killing an Egyptian in defence of a fellow Israelite	Saved his own life and began another part of God's training	God fits even our mistakes into his plan
Israelites	Exodus 12:28–42	Escaped Egypt after 430 years, most of that time in slavery	God confirmed his choice of Abraham's descendants	God will not forget his promises
Spies	Joshua 2:1–24	Escaped searchers in Jericho by hiding in Rahab's house	Prepared the destruction of Jericho and preserved Rahab, who would become one of David's ancestors—as well as an ancestor of Jesus	God's plan weaves lives together in a pattern beyond our understanding
Ehud	Judges 3:15–30	Assassinated the Moabite King Eglon, but escaped undetected	Broke the control of Moab over Israel and began 80 years of peace	Punishments by God are often swift and deadly
Samson	Judges 16:1–3	Escaped a locked city by ripping the gates from their hinges	Merely postponed Samson's self-destruction because of his lack of self-control	Without dependence on God and his guidance, even great ability is wasted
Elijah	1 Kings 19:1–18	Fled into the desert out of fear of Queen Jezebel	Preserved Elijah's life, but also displayed his human weakness	Even at moments of real success, our personal weaknesses are our greatest challenges
Saul (Paul)	Acts 9:23–25	Lowered over the wall in a basket to get out of Damascus	Saved this new Christian for great service to God	God has a purpose for every life, which leads to a real adventure for those willing to co-operate
Peter	Acts 12:1–11	Freed from prison by an angel	Saved Peter for God's further plans for his life	God can use extraordinary means to carry out his plan—often when we least expect it
Paul and Silas	Acts 16:22–40	Chains loosened and doors opened by an earthquake, but they chose not to leave the prison	Pointed out the powerlessness of humans before God	When our dependence and attention are focused on God rather than our problems, he is able to offer help in unexpected ways

13"Lord," Ananias answered, "I have heard many reports about this man and all
the harm he has done to your saints[j] in Jerusalem.[k] 14And he has come here with
authority from the chief priests[l] to arrest all who call on your name."
15But the Lord said to Ananias, "Go! This man is my chosen instrument[m] to carry
my name before the Gentiles[n] and their kings[o] and before the people of Israel. 16I
will show him how much he must suffer for my name."[p]
17Then Ananias went to the house and entered it. Placing his hands on[q] Saul, he
said, "Brother Saul, the Lord—Jesus, who appeared to you on the road as you were
coming here—has sent me so that you may see again and be filled with the Holy
Spirit." 18Immediately, something like scales fell from Saul's eyes, and he could see
again. He got up and was baptised, 19and after taking some food, he regained his
strength.

Saul in Damascus and Jerusalem

Saul spent several days with the disciples[r] in Damascus.[s] 20At once he began to
preach in the synagogues[t] that Jesus is the Son of God.[u] 21All those who heard him
were astonished and asked, "Isn't he the man who caused havoc in Jerusalem among
those who call on this name?[v] And hasn't he come here to take them as prisoners
to the chief priests?"[w] 22Yet Saul grew more and more powerful and baffled the Jews
living in Damascus by proving that Jesus is the Christ.[a][x]
23After many days had gone by, the Jews conspired to kill him, 24but Saul learned
of their plan.[y] Day and night they kept close watch on the city gates in order to kill
him. 25But his followers took him by night and lowered him in a basket through an
opening in the wall.[z]
26When he came to Jerusalem,[a] he tried to join the disciples, but they were all
afraid of him, not believing that he really was a disciple. 27But Barnabas[b] took him
and brought him to the apostles. He told them how Saul on his journey had seen the
Lord and that the Lord had spoken to him,[c] and how in Damascus he had preached

a 22 Or *Messiah*

9:13 [j]ver 32; Ro 1:7; 16:2, 15 [k]Ac 8:3
9:14 [l]ver 2, 21
9:15 [m]Ac 13:2; Ro 1:1; Gal 1:15 [n]Ro 11:13; 15:15, 16; Gal 2:7, 8; Eph 3:7, 8 [o]Ac 25:22, 23; 26:1
9:16 [p]Ac 20:23; 21:11; 2Co 11:23-27
9:17 [q]Ac 6:6
9:19 [r]Ac 11:26 [s]Ac 26:20
9:20 [t]Ac 13:5, 14 [u]Mt 4:3
9:21 [v]Ac 8:3 [w]Gal 1:13, 23
9:22 [x]Ac 18:5, 28
9:24 [y]Ac 20:3, 19
9:25 [z]1Sa 19:12; 2Co 11:32, 33
9:26 [a]Ac 22:17; 26:20; Gal 1:17, 18
9:27 [b]Ac 4:36 [c]ver 3-6

9:13, 14 "Not him, Lord; that's impossible. He could never become a Christian!" In essence, that's what Ananias said when God told him of Saul's conversion. After all, Saul had pursued believers to their death. Despite these understandable feelings, Ananias obeyed God and ministered to Saul. We must not limit God—he can do anything. We must obey and follow God's leading, even when he leads us to difficult people and places.

9:15, 16 Faith in Christ brings great blessings but often great suffering too. Paul would suffer for his faith (see 2 Corinthians 11:23–27). God calls us to commitment, not to comfort. He promises to be with us *through* suffering and hardship, not to spare us from them.

9:17 Ananias found Saul, as he had been instructed, and greeted him as "Brother Saul". Ananias feared this meeting because Saul had come to Damascus to capture the believers and take them as prisoners to Jerusalem (9:2). But in obedience to the Holy Spirit, Ananias greeted Saul lovingly. It is not always easy to show love to others, especially when we are afraid of them or doubt their motives. Nevertheless, we must follow Jesus' command (John 13:34) and Ananias's example, showing loving acceptance to other believers.

9:17, 18 Although there is no mention of a special filling of the Holy Spirit for Saul, his changed life and subsequent accomplishments bear strong witness to the Holy Spirit's presence and power in his life. Evidently, the Holy Spirit filled Saul when he received his sight and was baptised. See the second note on 8:15–17 for more on the filling of the Holy Spirit.

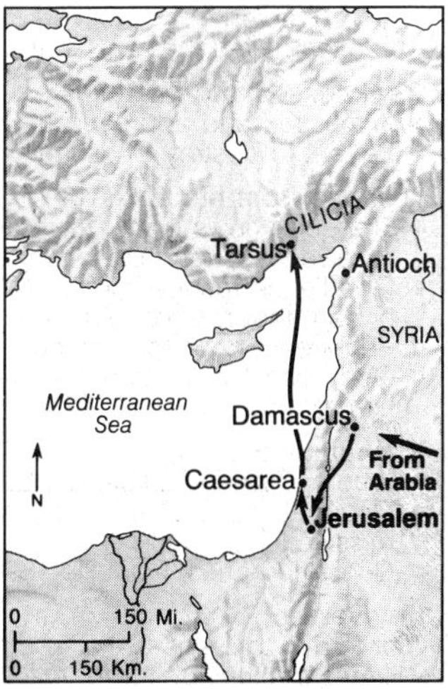

SAUL'S RETURN TO TARSUS
At least three years elapsed between Acts 9:22 and 9:26. After time alone in Arabia (see Galatians 1:16–18), Saul (Paul) returned to Damascus and then to Jerusalem. The apostles were reluctant to believe that this former persecutor could have become one of them. He escaped to Caesarea, where he caught a ship and returned to Tarsus.

9:20 Immediately after receiving his sight and spending some time with the believers in Damascus, Saul went to the synagogue to tell the Jews about Jesus Christ. Some Christians counsel new believers to wait until they are thoroughly grounded in their faith before attempting to share the gospel. Saul took time alone to learn

9:11 [h] ver 30; Ac 21:39; 22:3
9:12 [i] Mk 5:23

"Yes, Lord," he answered.
11The Lord told him, "Go to the house of Judas on Straight Street and ask for a
man from Tarsus[h] named Saul, for he is praying. 12In a vision he has seen a man
named Ananias come and place his hands on[i] him to restore his sight."

PAUL

No person, apart from Jesus himself, shaped the history of Christianity like the apostle Paul. Even before he was a believer, his actions were significant. His frenzied persecution of Christians following Stephen's death got the church started in obeying Christ's final command to take the gospel worldwide. Paul's personal encounter with Jesus changed his life. He never lost his fierce intensity, but from then on it was channelled for the gospel.

Paul was very religious. His training under Gamaliel was the finest available. His intentions and efforts were sincere. He was a good Pharisee, who knew the Bible and sincerely believed that this Christian movement was dangerous to Judaism. Thus Paul hated the Christian faith and persecuted Christians without mercy.

Paul got permission to travel to Damascus to capture Christians and bring them back to Jerusalem. But God stopped him in his hurried tracks on the Damascus road. Paul personally met Jesus Christ, and his life was never again the same.

Until Paul's conversion, little had been done about carrying the gospel to non-Jews. Philip had preached in Samaria and to an Ethiopian man; Cornelius, a Gentile, was converted under Peter; and in Antioch in Syria, some Greeks had joined the believers. When Barnabas was sent from Jerusalem to check on this situation, he went to Tarsus to find Paul and bring him to Antioch, and together they worked among the believers there. They were then sent on a missionary journey, the first of three Paul would take, that would carry the gospel across the Roman empire.

The thorny issue of whether Gentile believers had to obey Jewish laws before they could become Christians caused many problems in the early church. Paul worked hard to convince the Jews that Gentiles were acceptable to God, but he spent even more time convincing the Gentiles that they were acceptable to God. The lives Paul touched were changed and challenged by meeting Christ through him.

God did not waste any part of Paul—his background, his training, his citizenship, his mind, or even his weaknesses. Are you willing to let God do the same for you? You will never know all he can do with you until you allow him to have all that you are!

Strengths and accomplishments:
- Transformed by God from a persecutor of Christians to a preacher for Christ
- Preached for Christ throughout the Roman empire on three missionary journeys
- Wrote letters to various churches, which became part of the New Testament
- Was never afraid to face an issue head-on and deal with it
- Was sensitive to God's leading and, despite his strong personality, always did as God directed
- Is often called the apostle to the Gentiles

Weaknesses and mistakes:
- Witnessed and approved of Stephen's stoning
- Set out to destroy Christianity by persecuting Christians

Lessons from his life:
- The good news is that forgiveness and eternal life are a gift of God's grace received through faith in Christ and available to all people
- Obedience results from a relationship with God, but obedience will never create or earn that relationship
- Real freedom doesn't come until we no longer have to prove our freedom
- God does not waste our time—he will use our past and present so we may serve him with our future

Vital statistics:
- Where: Born in Tarsus, but became a world traveller for Christ
- Occupations: Trained as a Pharisee, learned the tentmaking trade, served as a missionary
- Contemporaries: Gamaliel, Stephen, the apostles, Luke, Barnabas, Timothy

Key verses:
"For to me, to live is Christ and to die is gain. If I am to go on living in the body, this will mean fruitful labour for me. Yet what shall I choose? I do not know! I am torn between the two: I desire to depart and be with Christ, which is better by far; but it is more necessary for you that I remain in the body" (Philippians 1:21–24).

Paul's story is told in Acts 7:58—28:31 and throughout his New Testament letters.

9:27
[d]ver 20, 22
9:29
[e]Ac 6:1
[f]2Co 11:26
9:30
[g]Ac 1:16
[h]Ac 8:40
[i]ver 11
9:31
[j]Ac 8:1
9:32
[k]ver 13
9:34
[l]Ac 3:6, 16; 4:10
9:35
[m]1Ch 5:16; 27:29;
Isa 33:9; 35:2; 65:10
[n]Ac 11:21
9:36
[o]Jos 19:46;
2Ch 2:16;
Ezr 3:7;
Jnh 1:3;
Ac 10:5

fearlessly in the name of Jesus.[d] 28So Saul stayed with them and moved about freely
in Jerusalem, speaking boldly in the name of the Lord. 29He talked and debated with
the Grecian Jews,[e] but they tried to kill him.[f] 30When the brothers[g] learned of this,
they took him down to Caesarea[h] and sent him off to Tarsus.[i]
31Then the church throughout Judea, Galilee and Samaria[j] enjoyed a time of
peace. It was strengthened; and encouraged by the Holy Spirit, it grew in numbers,
living in the fear of the Lord.

Aeneas and Dorcas

32As Peter travelled about the country, he went to visit the saints[k] in Lydda.
33There he found a man named Aeneas, a paralytic who had been bedridden for eight
years. 34"Aeneas," Peter said to him, "Jesus Christ heals you.[l] Get up and tidy up
your mat." Immediately Aeneas got up. 35All those who lived in Lydda and Sharon[m]
saw him and turned to the Lord.[n]
36In Joppa[o] there was a disciple named Tabitha (which, when translated, is

---

about Jesus before beginning his worldwide ministry, but he did not wait to witness. Although we should not rush into a ministry unprepared, we do not need to wait before telling others what has happened to us.

9:21, 22 Saul's arguments were powerful because he was a brilliant scholar. But what was more convincing was his changed life. People knew that what he taught was real because they could see the evidence in the way he lived. It is important to know what the Bible teaches and how to defend the faith, but your words should be backed up with a changed life.

9:23 According to Galatians 1:17, 18, Paul left Damascus and travelled to Arabia, the desert region just south-east of Damascus, where he lived for three years. It is unclear whether his three-year stay occurred between verses 22 and 23, or between verses 25 and 26. Some commentators say that "many days" could mean a long period of time. They suggest that when Paul returned to Damascus, the governor under Aretas ordered his arrest (2 Corinthians 11:32), in an effort to keep the peace with influential Jews.

The other possibility is that Paul's night escape occurred during his first stay in Damascus, just after his conversion, when the Pharisees were especially upset over his defection from their ranks. He would have fled to Arabia to spend time alone with God and to let the Jewish religious leaders cool down. Regardless of which theory is correct, there was a period of at least three years between Paul's conversion (9:3–6) and his trip to Jerusalem (9:26).

9:26, 27 It is difficult to change your reputation, and Saul had a terrible reputation with the Christians. But Barnabas, a Jewish convert (mentioned in 4:36), became the bridge between Saul and the apostles. New Christians (especially those with tarnished reputations) need sponsors, people who will come alongside, encourage, teach, and introduce them to other believers. Find ways that you can become a Barnabas to new believers.

9:27 Galatians 1:18, 19 explains that Paul was in Jerusalem only 15 days and that he met only with Peter and James.

9:29, 30 In these short sentences we can see two characteristics of Paul, even as a new believer in Christ: He was bold, and he stirred up controversy. These would characterise Paul's ministry for the rest of his life. The Grecian Jews were Greek-speaking Jews.

9:30 Saul's visit to Tarsus helped to quiet conflicts with the Jews and allowed him time to prove his commitment. After Saul, the most zealous persecutor, was converted, the church enjoyed a brief time of peace. "Brothers" refers to fellow Christians, members of God's family.

9:36 The important harbour city of Joppa sits 125 feet above sea level overlooking the Mediterranean Sea. Joppa was the town into which the cedars of Lebanon had been floated to be shipped to Jerusalem and used in the temple construction (2 Chronicles 2:16; Ezra 3:7). The prophet Jonah left the port of Joppa on his ill-fated trip (Jonah 1:3).

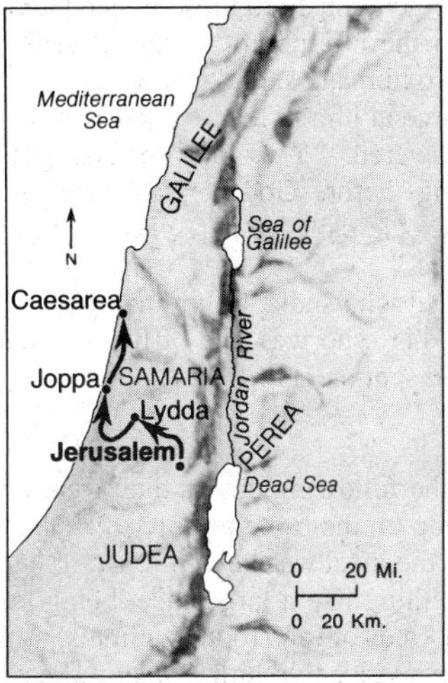

PETER'S MINISTRY
Peter travelled to the ancient cross-roads town of Lydda, where he healed crippled Aeneas. The believers in Joppa, an old port city, sent for him after a wonderful woman had died. Peter went and brought her back to life. While in Joppa, Peter had a vision that led him to take the gospel to Cornelius, a Gentile, in Caesarea.

9:36–42 Dorcas made an enormous impact on her community by "always doing good and helping the poor", by making robes and other clothing (9:39). When she died, the room was filled with mourners, very likely many of the people she had helped. And when she was brought back to life, the news raced through the town. God uses great preachers like Peter and Paul, but he also uses those who have gifts of kindness like Dorcas. Rather than wishing you had other gifts, make good use of the gifts God has given you.

Dorcas[b]), who was always doing good[p] and helping the poor. 37About that time she
became sick and died, and her body was washed and placed in an upstairs room.[q]
38Lydda was near Joppa; so when the disciples[r] heard that Peter was in Lydda, they
sent two men to him and urged him, "Please come at once!"
39Peter went with them, and when he arrived he was taken upstairs to the room.
All the widows[s] stood around him, crying and showing him the robes and other
clothing that Dorcas had made while she was still with them.
40Peter sent them all out of the room;[t] then he got down on his knees[u] and prayed.
Turning towards the dead woman, he said, "Tabitha, get up." She opened her eyes,
and seeing Peter she sat up. 41He took her by the hand and helped her to her feet.
Then he called the believers and the widows and presented her to them alive. 42This
became known all over Joppa, and many people believed in the Lord. 43Peter stayed
in Joppa for some time with a tanner named Simon.[v]

Cornelius Calls for Peter

10 At Caesarea[a] there was a man named Cornelius, a centurion in what was
known as the Italian Regiment. 2He and all his family were devout and God-
fearing;[b] he gave generously to those in need and prayed to God regularly. 3One day
at about three in the afternoon[c] he had a vision.[d] He distinctly saw an angel[e] of
God, who came to him and said, "Cornelius!"
4Cornelius stared at him in fear. "What is it, Lord?" he asked.
The angel answered, "Your prayers and gifts to the poor have come up as a
memorial offering[f] before God.[g] 5Now send men to Joppa[h] to bring back a man
named Simon who is called Peter. 6He is staying with Simon the tanner,[i] whose
house is by the sea."
7When the angel who spoke to him had gone, Cornelius called two of his servants
and a devout soldier who was one of his attendants. 8He told them everything that
had happened and sent them to Joppa.[j]

Peter's Vision

9About noon the following day as they were on their journey and approaching the
city, Peter went up on the roof[k] to pray. 10He became hungry and wanted something
to eat, and while the meal was being prepared, he fell into a trance.[l] 11He saw heaven
opened and something like a large sheet being let down to earth by its four corners.
12It contained all kinds of four-footed animals, as well as reptiles of the earth and birds
of the air. 13Then a voice told him, "Get up, Peter. Kill and eat."

b *36* Both *Tabitha* (Aramaic) and *Dorcas* (Greek) mean *gazelle*.

9:36 [p] 1Ti 2:10; Tit 3:8
9:37 [q] Ac 1:13
9:38 [r] Ac 11:26
9:39 [s] Ac 6:1
9:40 [t] Mt 9:25 [u] Lk 22:41; Ac 7:60
9:43 [v] Ac 10:6
10:1 [a] Ac 8:40
10:2 [b] ver 22, 35; Ac 13:16, 26
10:3 [c] Ac 3:1 [d] Ac 9:10 [e] Ac 5:19
10:4 [f] Mt 26:13 [g] Rev 8:4
10:5 [h] Ac 9:36
10:6 [i] Ac 9:43
10:8 [j] Ac 9:36
10:9 [k] Mt 24:17
10:10 [l] Ac 22:17

9:43 In Joppa, Peter stayed at the home of Simon, a tanner. Tanners made animal hides into leather. It is significant that Peter was at Simon's house, because tanning involved contact with dead animals, and Jewish law considered it an "unclean" job. Peter was already beginning to break down his prejudice against people who were not of his kind and customs that did not adhere to Jewish religious traditions.

10:1 This Caesarea, sometimes called Palestinian Caesarea, was located on the coast of the Mediterranean Sea, 32 miles north of Joppa. The largest and most important port city on the Mediterranean in Palestine, it served as the capital of the Roman province of Judea. This was the first city to have Gentile Christians and a non-Jewish church.

10:1 This Roman officer was a *centurion,* a commander of 100 soldiers. Although stationed in Caesarea, Cornelius would probably return soon to Rome. Thus his conversion was a major stepping-stone for spreading the gospel to the empire's capital city.

10:2 "What will happen to the heathen who have never heard about Christ?" This question is often asked about God's justice. Cornelius wasn't a believer in Christ, but he was seeking God, and he was reverent and generous. Therefore God sent Peter to tell Cornelius about Christ. Cornelius is an example that God "rewards those who earnestly seek him" (Hebrews 11:6). Those who sincerely seek God will find him! God made Cornelius' knowledge complete.

10:4 God saw Cornelius' sincere faith. His prayers and generous giving were a "memorial offering before God", a sacrificial offering to the Lord. God answers the sincere prayers of those who seek him by sending the right person or the right information at the right time.

10:12 According to Jewish law, certain foods were forbidden to be eaten (see Leviticus 11). The food laws made it difficult for Jews to eat with Gentiles without risking defilement. In fact, the Gentiles themselves were often seen as "unclean". Peter's vision meant that he should not look upon the Gentiles as inferior people whom God would not redeem. Before having the vision, Peter would have thought that a Gentile Roman officer could not accept Christ. Afterwards, he understood that it was his responsibility to go with the messengers into a Gentile home and tell Cornelius the Good News of salvation in Jesus Christ.

14“Surely not, Lord!”[m] Peter replied. “I have never eaten anything impure or
unclean.”[n]
15The voice spoke to him a second time, “Do not call anything impure that God
has made clean.”[o]
16This happened three times, and immediately the sheet was taken back to heaven.
17While Peter was wondering about the meaning of the vision, the men sent by
Cornelius[p] found out where Simon’s house was and stopped at the gate. 18They called
out, asking if Simon who was known as Peter was staying there.
19While Peter was still thinking about the vision, the Spirit said[q] to him, “Simon,
three[a] men are looking for you. 20So get up and go downstairs. Do not hesitate to
go with them, for I have sent them.”[r]
21Peter went down and said to the men, “I’m the one you’re looking for. Why have
you come?”
22The men replied, “We have come from Cornelius the centurion. He is a righteous
and God-fearing man,[s] who is respected by all the Jewish people. A holy angel told

10:14 [m]Ac 9:5 [n]Lev 11:4-8, 13-20; 20:25; Dt 14:3-20; Eze 4:14
10:15 [o]Mt 15:11; Ro 14:14, 17, 20; 1Co 10:25; 1Ti 4:3, 4; Tit 1:15
10:17 [p]ver 7, 8
10:19 [q]Ac 8:29
10:20 [r]Ac 15:7-9
10:22 [s]ver 2

a *19* One early manuscript *two*; other manuscripts do not have the number.

CORNELIUS

The early days of Christianity were exciting as God’s Spirit moved and people’s lives were changed. Converts were pouring in from surprising backgrounds. Even the dreaded Saul (Paul) became a Christian, and non-Jews were responding to the good news about Jesus. Among the first of these was the Roman centurion, Cornelius.

Because of frequent outbreaks of violence, Roman soldiers had to be stationed to keep peace throughout Israel. But most Romans, hated as conquerors, did not get on well in the nation. As an army officer, Cornelius was in a difficult position. He represented Rome, but his home was in Caesarea. During his years in Israel, he had himself been conquered by the God of Israel. He had a reputation as a godly man who put his faith into action, and he was respected by the Jews.

Four significant aspects of Cornelius’ character are noted in Acts. He actively sought God, he revered God, he was generous in meeting other people’s needs, and he prayed. God told him to send for Peter, because Peter would give him more knowledge about the God he was already seeking to please.

When Peter entered Cornelius’ home, Peter broke a whole list of Jewish rules. Peter confessed he wasn’t comfortable, but here was an eager audience and he couldn’t hold back his message. He had no sooner started sharing the gospel when God gave overwhelming approval by filling that Roman family with his Holy Spirit. Peter saw he had no choice but to baptise them and welcome them as equals in the growing Christian church. Another step had been taken in carrying the gospel to the whole world.

Cornelius is a welcome example of God’s willingness to use extraordinary means to reach those who desire to know him. He does not play favourites, and he does not hide from those who want to find him. God sent his Son because he loves the whole world—and that includes Peter, Cornelius, and you.

Strengths and accomplishments:
- A godly and generous Roman
- Although an officer in the occupying army, he seems to have been well-respected by the Jews
- He responded to God and encouraged his family to do the same
- His conversion helped the young church realise that the good news was for all people, both Jews and Gentiles

Lessons from his life:
- God reaches those who want to know him
- The gospel is open to all people
- There are people everywhere eager to believe
- When we are willing to seek the truth and be obedient to the light God gives us, God will reward us richly

Vital statistics:
- Where: Caesarea
- Occupation: Roman centurion
- Contemporaries: Peter, Philip, the apostles

Key verse:
“He and all his family were devout and God-fearing; he gave generously to those in need and prayed to God regularly” (Acts 10:2).

Cornelius’ story is told in Acts 10:1—11:18.

him to have you come to his house so that he could hear what you have to say."[t]
23Then Peter invited the men into the house to be his guests.

Peter at Cornelius' House

The next day Peter started out with them, and some of the brothers[u] from Joppa
went along.[v] 24The following day he arrived in Caesarea.[w] Cornelius was expecting
them and had called together his relatives and close friends. 25As Peter entered the
house, Cornelius met him and fell at his feet in reverence. 26But Peter made him get
up. "Stand up," he said, "I am only a man myself."[x]
27Talking with him, Peter went inside and found a large gathering of people. 28He
said to them: "You are well aware that it is against our law for a Jew to associate with
a Gentile or visit him.[y] But God has shown me that I should not call any man impure
or unclean.[z] 29So when I was sent for, I came without raising any objection. May
I ask why you sent for me?"
30Cornelius answered: "Four days ago I was in my house praying at this hour, at
three in the afternoon. Suddenly a man in shining clothes stood before me 31and said,
'Cornelius, God has heard your prayer and remembered your gifts to the poor. 32Send
to Joppa for Simon who is called Peter. He is a guest in the home of Simon the tanner,
who lives by the sea.' 33So I sent for you immediately, and it was good of you to come.
Now we are all here in the presence of God to listen to everything the Lord has
commanded you to tell us."
34Then Peter began to speak: "I now realise how true it is that God does not show
favouritism[a] 35but accepts men from every nation who fear him and do what is
right.[b] 36You know the message God sent to the people of Israel, telling the good
news[c] of peace[d] through Jesus Christ, who is Lord of all.[e] 37You know what has
happened throughout Judea, beginning in Galilee after the baptism that John
preached—38how God anointed[f] Jesus of Nazareth with the Holy Spirit and power,
and how he went around doing good and healing[g] all who were under the power of
the devil, because God was with him.[h]
39"We are witnesses[i] of everything he did in the country of the Jews and in
Jerusalem. They killed him by hanging him on a tree,[j] 40but God raised him from
the dead[k] on the third day and caused him to be seen. 41He was not seen by all the
people,[l] but by witnesses whom God had already chosen—by us who ate[m] and drank
with him after he rose from the dead. 42He commanded us to preach to the people[n]
and to testify that he is the one whom God appointed as judge of the living and the
dead.[o] 43All the prophets testify about him[p] that everyone[q] who believes in him
receives forgiveness of sins through his name."
44While Peter was still speaking these words, the Holy Spirit came on[r] all who
heard the message. 45The circumcised believers who had come with Peter[s] were

10:22 [t]Ac 11:14
10:23 [u]Ac 1:16 [v]ver 45; Ac 11:12
10:24 [w]Ac 8:40
10:26 [x]Ac 14:15; Rev 19:10
10:28 [y]Jn 4:9; 18:28; Ac 11:3 [z]Ac 15:8, 9
10:34 [a]Dt 10:17; 2Ch 19:7; Job 34:19; Ro 2:11; Gal 2:6; Eph 6:9; Col 3:25; 1Pe 1:17
10:35 [b]Ac 15:9
10:36 [c]Ac 13:32 [d]Lk 2:14 [e]Mt 28:18; Ro 10:12
10:38 [f]Ac 4:26 [g]Mt 4:23 [h]Jn 3:2
10:39 [i]Lk 24:48 [j]Ac 5:30
10:40 [k]Ac 2:24
10:41 [l]Jn 14:17, 22 [m]Lk 24:43; Jn 21:13
10:42 [n]Mt 28:19, 20 [o]Jn 5:22; Ac 17:31; Ro 14:9; 2Co 5:10; 2Ti 4:1; 1Pe 4:5
10:43 [p]Isa 53:11 [q]Ac 15:9
10:44 [r]Ac 8:15, 16; 11:15; 15:8
10:45 [s]ver 23

10:26 This act of worship could have caused Peter to become arrogant. After all, a Roman centurion was bowing before him. Instead, Peter pointed Cornelius to Christ. We too should remember our mortality whenever we are flattered or honoured, and use the opportunity to give glory to God.

10:34, 35 Perhaps the greatest barrier to the spread of the gospel in the first century was the Jewish-Gentile conflict. Most of the early believers were Jewish, and to them it was scandalous even to think of associating with Gentiles. But God told Peter to take the gospel to a Roman, and Peter obeyed despite his background and personal feelings. (Later Peter struggled with this again—see Galatians 2:11–14.) God was making it clear that the Good News of Christ is for everyone! We should not allow any barrier—language, culture, prejudice, geography, economic level, or educational level—to keep us from telling others about Christ.

10:35 In every nation there are hearts restless for God, ready to receive the gospel—but someone must take it to them. Seeking God is not enough—people must find him. How then shall seekers find God without someone to point the way? Is God asking you to show someone the way to him? (See Romans 10:14, 15.)

10:37–43 Peter's brief and powerful sermon contains a concise statement of the gospel: Jesus' perfect life of servanthood; his death on the cross; his resurrection, personally witnessed and experienced by Peter; Jesus' fulfilment of the Scriptures; and the necessity of personal faith in him. A sermon or witness for Christ does not need to be long to be effective. It should be Spirit-led and should centre on Christ, the way and the truth and the life.

10:43 Two examples of prophets testifying about Jesus and his forgiveness of sins are Isaiah 52:13–53:12 and Ezekiel 36:25, 26.

10:45 Cornelius and Peter were very different people. Cornelius was wealthy, a Gentile, and a military man. Peter was a Jewish fisherman turned preacher. But God's plan included both of them. In Cornelius' house that day, a new chapter in Christian history was written as a Jewish Christian leader and a Gentile Christian convert each discovered something significant about God at work in the other person. Cornelius needed Peter and his gospel to know the way to salvation. Peter needed Cornelius and his salvation experience to know that Gentiles were included in God's plan. You and another believer may also need each other to understand how God works!

astonished that the gift of the Holy Spirit had been poured out[t] even on the Gentiles.[u]
46 For they heard them speaking in tongues[b][v] and praising God.
Then Peter said, 47 "Can anyone keep these people from being baptised with
water?[w] They have received the Holy Spirit just as we have."[x] 48 So he ordered that
they be baptised in the name of Jesus Christ.[y] Then they asked Peter to stay with them
for a few days.

Peter Explains His Actions

11 The apostles and the brothers[a] throughout Judea heard that the Gentiles also
had received the word of God. 2 So when Peter went up to Jerusalem, the
circumcised believers[b] criticised him 3 and said, "You went into the house of uncircumcised men and ate with them."[c]
4 Peter began and explained everything to them precisely as it had happened: 5 "I
was in the city of Joppa praying, and in a trance I saw a vision.[d] I saw something
like a large sheet being let down from heaven by its four corners, and it came down
to where I was. 6 I looked into it and saw four-footed animals of the earth, wild beasts,
reptiles, and birds of the air. 7 Then I heard a voice telling me, 'Get up, Peter. Kill
and eat.'
8 "I replied, 'Surely not, Lord! Nothing impure or unclean has ever entered my
mouth.'
9 "The voice spoke from heaven a second time, 'Do not call anything impure that
God has made clean.'[e] 10 This happened three times, and then it was pulled up to
heaven again.
11 "Right then three men who had been sent to me from Caesarea stopped at the
house where I was staying. 12 The Spirit told[f] me to have no hesitation about going
with them.[g] These six brothers also went with me, and we entered the man's house.
13 He told us how he had seen an angel appear in his house and say, 'Send to Joppa
for Simon who is called Peter. 14 He will bring you a message through which you and
all your household[h] will be saved.'
15 "As I began to speak, the Holy Spirit came on[i] them as he had come on us at
the beginning.[j] 16 Then I remembered what the Lord had said: 'John baptised with[a]
water, but you will be baptised with the Holy Spirit.'[k] 17 So if God gave them the

b *46* Or *other languages* **a** *16* Or *in*

10:45 [t]Ac 2:33, 38 [u]Ac 11:18
10:46 [v]Mk 16:17
10:47 [w]Ac 8:36 [x]Ac 11:17
10:48 [y]Ac 2:38; 8:16
11:1 [a]Ac 1:16
11:2 [b]Ac 10:45
11:3 [c]Ac 10:25, 28; Gal 2:12
11:5 [d]Ac 10:9-32; 9:10
11:9 [e]Ac 10:15
11:12 [f]Ac 8:29 [g]Ac 15:9; Ro 3:22
11:14 [h]Jn 4:53; Ac 16:15, 31-34; 1Co 1:11, 16
11:15 [i]Ac 10:44 [j]Ac 2:4
11:16 [k]Mk 1:8; Ac 1:5

10:45 "The circumcised believers" could be translated, "the Jewish believers" (see also 11:2).

10:47, 48 In this case, the people were baptised *after* they received the Holy Spirit, publicly declaring their allegiance to Christ and identification with the Christian community.

10:48 Cornelius wanted Peter to stay with him for several days. He was a new believer and realised his need for teaching and fellowship. Are you as eager to learn more about Christ? Recognise your need to be with more mature Christians, and strive to learn from them.

11:1 A Gentile was anyone who was not a Jew; the Jewish believers are sometimes referred to as "the circumcised believers" (11:2). Most Jewish believers thought that God offered salvation only to the Jews because God had given his law to them (Exodus 19; 20). A group in Jerusalem believed that Gentiles could be saved, but only if they followed all the Jewish laws and traditions – in essence, if they became Jews. Both were mistaken. God chose the Jews and taught them his laws so they could bring the message of salvation to *all* people (see Genesis 12:3; Psalm 22:27; Isaiah 42:4; 49:6; 56:3–7; 60:1–3; Jeremiah 16:19–21; Zechariah 2:11; Malachi 1:11; Romans 15:9–12).

11:2–18 When Peter brought the news of Cornelius' conversion back to Jerusalem, the believers were shocked that Peter had eaten with Gentiles. After they heard the whole story, however, they praised God (11:18). Their reactions teach us how to handle disagreements with other Christians. Before judging the behaviour of fellow believers, it is important to listen to them. The Holy Spirit may have something important to teach us through them.

11:8 God had promised throughout Scripture that he would reach the nations. This began with his general promise to Abraham (Genesis 12:3; 18:18) and became very specific in Malachi's statement: "My name will be great among the nations, from the rising to the setting of the sun" (Malachi 1:11). But this was an extremely difficult truth for Jews, even Jewish believers, to accept. The Jewish believers understood how certain prophecies were fulfilled in Christ, but they overlooked other Old Testament teachings. Too often we are inclined to accept only the parts of God's word that appeal to us and support our own agendas, ignoring the teachings we don't like. We must accept all of God's word as absolute truth.

11:12ff Peter's defence for eating with Gentiles was a simple restatement of what happened. He brought six witnesses with him to back him up, and then he quoted Jesus' promise about the coming of the Holy Spirit (11:16). These Gentiles' lives had been changed, and that was all the evidence Peter and the other believers needed. Changed lives are an equally powerful evidence today.

11:16 Jesus had also demonstrated clearly that he and his message were for all people. He preached in Samaria (John 4:1–42); in the region of the Gerasenes, populated by Greeks (Mark 5:1–20); and he even reached out to Romans (Luke 7:1–10). The apostles shouldn't have been surprised that they were called to do the same.

same gift as he gave us,[l] who believed in the Lord Jesus Christ, who was I to think
that I could oppose God?"
18 When they heard this, they had no further objections and praised God, saying,
"So then, God has granted even the Gentiles repentance unto life."[m]

The Church in Antioch

19 Now those who had been scattered by the persecution in connection with Stephen[n] travelled as far as Phoenicia, Cyprus and Antioch,[o] telling the message only
to Jews. 20 Some of them, however, men from Cyprus[p] and Cyrene,[q] went to Antioch
and began to speak to Greeks also, telling them the good news about the Lord Jesus.
21 The Lord's hand was with them,[r] and a great number of people believed and turned
to the Lord.[s]
22 News of this reached the ears of the church at Jerusalem, and they sent Barnabas[t]
to Antioch. 23 When he arrived and saw the evidence of the grace of God,[u] he was
glad and encouraged them all to remain true to the Lord with all their hearts.[v] 24 He
was a good man, full of the Holy Spirit and faith, and a great number of people were
brought to the Lord.[w]
25 Then Barnabas went to Tarsus[x] to look for Saul, 26 and when he found him, he
brought him to Antioch. So for a whole year Barnabas and Saul met with the church
and taught great numbers of people. The disciples[y] were called Christians first[z] at
Antioch.
27 During this time some prophets[a] came down from Jerusalem to Antioch. 28 One

11:17 [l]Ac 10:45, 47
11:18 [m]Ro 10:12, 13; 2Co 7:10
11:19 [n]Ac 8:1, 4 [o]ver 26, 27; Ac 13:1; 18:22; Gal 2:11
11:20 [p]Ac 4:36 [q]Mt 27:32
11:21 [r]Lk 1:66 [s]Ac 2:47
11:22 [t]Ac 4:36
11:23 [u]Ac 13:43; 14:26; 20:24 [v]Ac 14:22
11:24 [w]ver 21; Ac 5:14
11:25 [x]Ac 9:11
11:26 [y]Ac 6:1, 2; 13:52 [z]Ac 26:28; 1Pe 4:16
11:27 [a]Ac 13:1; 15:32; 1Co 12:28, 29; Eph 4:11

11:18 The intellectual questions ended and the theological discussion stopped with the report that God had given the Holy Spirit to the Gentiles. This was a turning point for the early church. They had to accept those whom God had chosen, even if they were Gentiles. But joy over the conversion of Gentiles was not unanimous. This continued to be a struggle for some Jewish Christians throughout the first century.

11:19–21 When the church accepted Peter's testimony that the gospel was also for Gentiles, Christianity exploded into Gentile areas, and large numbers became believers. The seeds of this missionary work had been sown after Stephen's death when many believing Jews were persecuted and scattered, settling in faraway cities and spreading the gospel.

11:20, 21 It was in Antioch that Christianity was launched on its worldwide mission and where the believers aggressively preached to the Gentiles (non-Jews who did not worship God). Philip had preached in Samaria, but the Samaritans were part Jewish (8:5); Peter preached to Cornelius, but he already worshipped God (10:2). Believers who were scattered after the outbreak of persecution in Jerusalem spread the gospel to other Jews in the lands they fled to (11:19). At this time, the believers began actively sharing the Good News with Gentiles.

11:22 With the exception of Jerusalem, Antioch of Syria played a more important role in the early church than any other city. After Rome and Alexandria, Antioch was the largest city in the Roman world. In Antioch, the first Gentile church was founded, and there the believers were first called Christians (11:26). Paul used the city as his home base during his missionary journeys. Antioch was the centre of worship for several pagan cults that promoted much sexual immorality and other forms of evil common to pagan religions. It was also a vital commercial centre – the gateway to the eastern world. Antioch was a key city both to Rome and to the early church.

11:22–26 Barnabas gives us a wonderful example of how to help new Christians. He demonstrated strong faith; he ministered joyfully with kindness and encouragement; he taught new believers further lessons about God (see 9:26–30). Remember Barnabas when you see new believers, and think of ways to help them grow in their faith.

11:25 Saul had been sent to his home in Tarsus for protection

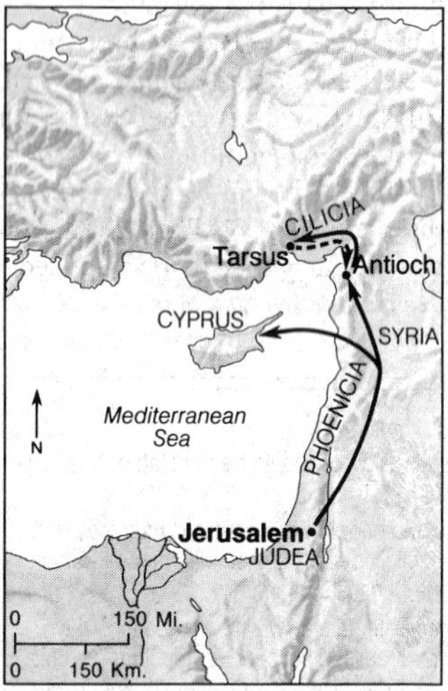

BARNABAS AND SAUL IN ANTIOCH
Persecution scattered the believers into Phoenicia, Cyprus, and Antioch, and the gospel went with them. Most spoke only to Jews, but in Antioch, some Gentiles were converted. The church sent Barnabas to investigate, and he was pleased with what he found. Barnabas went to Tarsus to bring Saul (Paul) back to Antioch.

after his conversion caused an uproar among the Jewish leaders in Jerusalem (9:26–30). He stayed there for several years before Barnabas brought him to help the church at Antioch.

11:26 The young church at Antioch was a curious mixture of Jews (who spoke Greek or Aramaic) and Gentiles. It is significant that this is the first place where the believers were called Christians (or "Christ-ones"), because all they had in common was Christ – not race, culture, or even language. Christ can cross all boundaries and unify all people.

11:26 Barnabas and Saul stayed at Antioch for a full year, teaching the new believers. They could have left for other cities, but they saw the importance of follow-through and training. Have you helped someone believe in God? Spend time teaching and encouraging that person. Are you a new believer? Remember, you are just beginning your Christian life. Your faith needs to grow and mature through consistent Bible study and teaching.

11:27, 28 Prophets were found not only in the Old Testament,

11:28
[b]Ac 21:10
[c]Mt 24:14
[d]Ac 18:2

11:29
[e]ver 26
[f]Ro 15:26; 2Co 9:2
[g]Ac 1:16

11:30
[h]Ac 14:23
[i]Ac 12:25

12:2
[a]Mt 4:21

12:3
[b]Ac 24:27
[c]Ex 12:15; 23:15

12:5
[d]Eph 6:18

12:6
[e]Ac 21:33

12:7
[f]Ac 5:19
[g]Ac 16:26

of them, named Agabus,[b] stood up and through the Spirit predicted that a severe
famine would spread over the entire Roman world.[c] (This happened during the reign
of Claudius.)[d] 29 The disciples,[e] each according to his ability, decided to provide
help[f] for the brothers[g] living in Judea. 30 This they did, sending their gift to the
elders[h] by Barnabas and Saul.[i]

Peter's Miraculous Escape From Prison

12 It was about this time that King Herod arrested some who belonged to the
church, intending to persecute them. 2 He had James, the brother of John,[a] put
to death with the sword. 3 When he saw that this pleased the Jews,[b] he proceeded
to seize Peter also. This happened during the Feast of Unleavened Bread.[c] 4 After
arresting him, he put him in prison, handing him over to be guarded by four squads
of four soldiers each. Herod intended to bring him out for public trial after the
Passover.

5 So Peter was kept in prison, but the church was earnestly praying to God for
him.[d]

6 The night before Herod was to bring him to trial, Peter was sleeping between
two soldiers, bound with two chains,[e] and sentries stood guard at the entrance. 7 Suddenly an angel[f] of the Lord appeared and a light shone in the cell. He struck Peter
on the side and woke him up. "Quick, get up!" he said, and the chains fell off Peter's
wrists.[g]

8 Then the angel said to him, "Put on your clothes and sandals." And Peter did so.
"Wrap your cloak around you and follow me," the angel told him. 9 Peter followed

---

but also in the early church. Their role was to present God's will to the people and to instruct them in God's word. Sometimes, like Agabus, they also had the gift of predicting the future.

11:28, 29 There were serious food shortages during the reign of the Roman emperor Claudius (A.D. 41–54) because of a drought that had extended across much of the Roman empire for many years. It is significant that the church in Antioch assisted the church in Jerusalem. The daughter church had grown enough to be able to help the established church.

11:29 The people of Antioch were motivated to give generously because they cared about the needs of others. This is the "cheerful" giving that the Bible commends (2 Corinthians 9:7). Reluctant giving reflects a lack of concern for people. Focus your concern on the needy, and you will be motivated to give.

11:30 Elders were appointed to manage the affairs of the congregation. At this point, not much is known about their responsibilities, but it appears that their main role was to respond to the believers' needs.

12:1 This King Herod was Herod Agrippa I, the son of Aristobulus and grandson of Herod the Great. His sister was Herodias, who was responsible for the death of John the Baptist (see Mark 6:17–28). Herod Agrippa I was partly Jewish. The Romans had appointed him to rule over most of Palestine, including the territories of Galilee, Perea, Judea, and Samaria. He persecuted the Christians in order to please the Jewish leaders who opposed them, hoping that would solidify his position. Agrippa I died suddenly in A.D. 44 (see 12:20–23). His death was also recorded by the historian Josephus.

12:2 James and John were two of the original 12 disciples who followed Jesus. They had asked Jesus for special recognition in his kingdom (Mark 10:35–40). Jesus said that to be a part of his kingdom would mean suffering with Jesus (drink from the same cup – Mark 10:38, 39). James and John did indeed suffer – Herod executed James, and later John was exiled (see Revelation 1:9).

12:2–11 Why did God allow James to die and yet miraculously save Peter? Life is full of difficult questions like this. Why is one child physically disabled and another child athletically gifted? Why do people die seemingly before realising their potential? These are questions we cannot possibly answer in this life because we do not see all that God sees. He has chosen to allow evil in this world for a time. But we can trust God's leading because he has promised to destroy all evil eventually. In the meantime, we know that God will help us use our suffering to strengthen us and glorify him. For more on this question, see the notes on Job 1:1ff; 2:10; 3:23–26.

12:3 Peter was arrested during the Feast of Unleavened Bread, the week-long festival directly following Passover. This was a strategic move, since more Jews were in the city than usual, and Herod could impress the most people.

12:5 Herod's plan undoubtedly was to execute Peter, but the believers were praying for Peter's safety. The earnest prayer of the church significantly affected the outcome of these events. Prayer changes things, so pray often and with confidence.

12:7 God sent an angel to rescue Peter. Angels are God's messengers. They are divinely created beings with supernatural powers, and they sometimes take on human appearance in order to talk to people. Angels should not be worshipped, because they are not divine. They are God's servants, just as we are.

him out of the prison, but he had no idea that what the angel was doing was really
happening; he thought he was seeing a vision.[h] 10 They passed the first and second
guards and came to the iron gate leading to the city. It opened for them by itself,[i]
and they went through it. When they had walked the length of one street, suddenly
the angel left him.
11 Then Peter came to himself[j] and said, "Now I know without a doubt that the
Lord sent his angel and rescued me[k] from Herod's clutches and from everything the
Jewish people were anticipating."
12 When this had dawned on him, he went to the house of Mary the mother of John,
also called Mark,[l] where many people had gathered and were praying.[m] 13 Peter
knocked at the outer entrance, and a servant girl named Rhoda came to answer the
door.[n] 14 When she recognised Peter's voice, she was so overjoyed[o] she ran back
without opening it and exclaimed, "Peter is at the door!"
15 "You're out of your mind," they told her. When she kept insisting that it was so,
they said, "It must be his angel."[p]
16 But Peter kept on knocking, and when they opened the door and saw him, they
were astonished. 17 Peter motioned with his hand[q] for them to be quiet and described
how the Lord had brought him out of prison. "Tell James[r] and the brothers[s] about
this," he said, and then he left for another place.
18 In the morning, there was no small commotion among the soldiers as to what had
become of Peter. 19 After Herod had a thorough search made for him and did not find
him, he cross-examined the guards and ordered that they be executed.[t]

Herod's Death

Then Herod went from Judea to Caesarea[u] and stayed there a while. 20 He had been
quarrelling with the people of Tyre and Sidon;[v] they now joined together and sought
an audience with him. Having secured the support of Blastus, a trusted personal
servant of the king, they asked for peace, because they depended on the king's country
for their food supply.[w]
21 On the appointed day Herod, wearing his royal robes, sat on his throne and
delivered a public address to the people. 22 They shouted, "This is the voice of a god,

12:9 [h]Ac 9:10
12:10 [i]Ac 5:19; 16:26
12:11 [j]Lk 15:17 [k]Ps 34:7; Da 3:28; 6:22; 2Co 1:10; 2Pe 2:9
12:12 [l]ver 25; Ac 15:37, 39; Col 4:10; Phm 24; 1Pe 5:13 [m]ver 5
12:13 [n]Jn 18:16, 17
12:14 [o]Lk 24:41
12:15 [p]Mt 18:10
12:17 [q]Ac 13:16; 19:33; 21:40 [r]Ac 15:13 [s]Ac 1:16
12:19 [t]Ac 16:27 [u]Ac 8:40
12:20 [v]Mt 11:21 [w]1Ki 5:9, 11; Eze 27:17

12:12 John Mark wrote the Gospel of Mark. His mother's house was large enough to accommodate a meeting of many believers. An upstairs room in this house may have been the location of Jesus' last supper with his disciples (Luke 22:8ff).

12:13–15 The prayers of the group of believers were answered, even as they prayed. But when the answer arrived at the door, they didn't believe it. We should be people of faith who believe that God answers the prayers of those who seek his will. When you pray, believe you'll get an answer. And when the answer comes, don't be surprised; be thankful!

12:17 This James was Jesus' brother, who became a leader in the Jerusalem church (15:13; Galatians 1:19). The James who was killed (12:2) was John's brother and one of the original 12 disciples.

12:19 Under Roman law, guards who allowed a prisoner to escape were subject to the same punishment the prisoner was to receive. Thus these 16 guards were sentenced to death.

12:19 The Jews considered Jerusalem their capital, but the Romans made Caesarea their headquarters in Palestine. That is where Herod Agrippa I lived.

12:20 These coastal cities, Tyre and Sidon, were free and self-governing but economically dependent on Judea (see the map in the introduction to Acts for their location). We don't know why Herod had quarrelled with them, but now representatives from those cities were trying to appease him through his personal servant.

12:23 Herod died a horrible death accompanied by intense pain; he was literally eaten alive, from the inside out, by worms. To be eaten by worms was considered to be one of the most disgraceful ways to die. Pride is a serious sin, and in this case, God chose to punish it immediately. God does not immediately punish all sin, but he *will* bring all to judgment (Hebrews 9:27). Accept Christ's offer of forgiveness today. No one can afford to wait.

12:25 John Mark was Barnabas' cousin (Colossians 4:10). His mother, Mary, often opened her home to the apostles (12:12), so John Mark would have been exposed to most of the great men and teachings of the early church. Later, John Mark joined Paul and Barnabas on their first missionary journey, but for unknown reasons, he left them in the middle of the trip. John Mark was criticised by Paul for abandoning the mission (15:37–39), but he wrote the Gospel of Mark and was later acclaimed by Paul as a vital help in the growth of the early church (2 Timothy 4:11).

12:23 [x]1Sa 25:38; 2Sa 24:16, 17
12:24 [y]Ac 6:7; 19:20
12:25 [z]Ac 4:36 [a]Ac 11:30 [b]ver 12

not of a man." 23Immediately, because Herod did not give praise to God, an angel
of the Lord struck him down,[x] and he was eaten by worms and died.
24But the word of God continued to increase and spread.[y]
25When Barnabas[z] and Saul had finished their mission,[a] they returned from[a]
Jerusalem, taking with them John, also called Mark.[b]

[a] *25* Some manuscripts *to*

HEROD AGRIPPA I

For good or evil, families have lasting and powerful influence on their children. Traits and qualities are passed on to the next generation, and often the mistakes and sins of the parents are repeated by the children. Four generations of the Herod family are mentioned in the Bible. Each leader left his evil mark: Herod the Great murdered Bethlehem's children; Herod Antipas was involved in Jesus' trial and John the Baptist's execution; Herod Agrippa I murdered the apostle James; and Herod Agrippa II was one of Paul's judges.

Herod Agrippa I related fairly well to his Jewish subjects. Because he had a Jewish grandmother of royal blood (Mariamne), he was grudgingly accepted by the people. Although as a youth he had been temporarily imprisoned by the emperor Tiberias, he was now trusted by Rome and got on well with the emperors Caligula and Claudius.

An unexpected opportunity for Herod to gain new favour with the Jews was created by the Christian movement. Gentiles began to be accepted into the church in large numbers. Many Jews had been tolerating this new movement as a sect within Judaism, but its rapid growth alarmed them. Persecution of Christians was revived, and even the apostles were not spared. James was killed, and Peter was thrown into prison.

But soon, Herod made a fatal error. During a visit to Caesarea, the people called him a god, and he accepted their praise. Herod was immediately struck with a painful disease, and he died within a week.

Like his grandfather, uncle, and son after him, Herod Agrippa I came close to the truth but missed it. Because religion was important only as an aspect of politics, he had no reverence and no qualms about taking praise that only God should receive. His mistake is a common one. Whenever we are proud of our own abilities and accomplishments, not recognising them as gifts from God, we repeat Herod's sin.

Strengths and accomplishments:
- Capable administrator and negotiator
- Managed to maintain good relations with the Jews in his region and with Rome

Weaknesses and mistakes:
- Arranged the murder of the apostle James
- Imprisoned Peter with plans to execute him
- Allowed the people to praise him as a god

Lessons from his life:
- Those who set themselves against God are doomed to ultimate failure
- There is great danger in accepting praise that only God deserves
- Family traits can influence children towards great good or great evil

Vital statistics:
- Where: Jerusalem
- Occupation: Roman-appointed king of the Jews
- Relatives: Grandfather: Herod the Great. Father: Aristobulus. Uncle: Herod Antipas. Sister: Herodias. Wife: Cypros. Son: Herod Agrippa II. Daughters: Bernice, Mariamne, Drusilla
- Contemporaries: Emperors Tiberias, Caligula, and Claudius. James, Peter, the apostles.

Key verse:
"Immediately, because Herod did not give praise to God, an angel of the Lord struck him down, and he was eaten by worms and died" (Acts 12:23).

Herod Agrippa I's story is told in Acts 12:1–23.

B. PAUL'S MINISTRY (13:1 – 28:31)

The book focuses now on the ministry to the Gentiles and the spread of the church around the world, and Paul replaces Peter as the central figure in the book. Paul completes three missionary journeys and ends up being imprisoned in Jerusalem and transported to Rome. The book of Acts ends abruptly, showing that the history of the church is not yet complete. We are to be a part of the sequel.

1. First missionary journey

Barnabas and Saul Sent Off

13 In the church at Antioch[a] there were prophets[b] and teachers: Barnabas,[c]
Simeon called Niger, Lucius of Cyrene, Manaen (who had been brought up with
Herod[d] the tetrarch) and Saul. 2While they were worshipping the Lord and fasting,
the Holy Spirit said,[e] "Set apart for me Barnabas and Saul for the work[f] to which
I have called them."[g] 3So after they had fasted and prayed, they placed their hands
on them[h] and sent them off.[i]

On Cyprus

4The two of them, sent on their way by the Holy Spirit,[j] went down to Seleucia and sailed from there to Cyprus.[k] 5When they arrived at Salamis, they proclaimed the word of God in the Jewish synagogues.[l] John[m] was with them as their
helper.
6They travelled through the whole island until they came to Paphos. There they met
a Jewish sorcerer[n] and false prophet[o] named Bar-Jesus, 7who was an attendant of
the proconsul,[p] Sergius Paulus. The proconsul, an intelligent man, sent for Barnabas
and Saul because he wanted to hear the word of God. 8But Elymas the sorcerer[q] (for
that is what his name means) opposed them and tried to turn the proconsul[r] from the
faith.[s] 9Then Saul, who was also called Paul, filled with the Holy Spirit,[t] looked
straight at Elymas and said, 10"You are a child of the devil[u] and an enemy of
everything that is right! You are full of all kinds of deceit and trickery. Will you never
stop perverting the right ways of the Lord?[v] 11Now the hand of the Lord is against
you.[w] You are going to be blind, and for a time you will be unable to see the light
of the sun."
Immediately mist and darkness came over him, and he groped about, seeking
someone to lead him by the hand. 12When the proconsul[x] saw what had happened,
he believed, for he was amazed at the teaching about the Lord.

13:1 [a]Ac 11:19 [b]Ac 11:27 [c]Ac 4:36; 11:22-26 [d]Mt 14:1
13:2 [e]Ac 8:29 [f]Ac 14:26 [g]Ac 22:21
13:3 [h]Ac 6:6 [i]Ac 14:26
13:4 [j]ver 2, 3 [k]Ac 4:36
13:5 [l]Ac 9:20 [m]Ac 12:12
13:6 [n]Ac 8:9 [o]Mt 7:15
13:7 [p]ver 8, 12; Ac 19:38
13:8 [q]Ac 8:9 [r]ver 7 [s]Ac 6:7
13:9 [t]Ac 4:8
13:10 [u]Mt 13:38; Jn 8:44 [v]Hos 14:9
13:11 [w]Ex 9:3; 1Sa 5:6, 7; Ps 32:4
13:12 [x]ver 7

13:1 What variety there is in the church! The common thread among these five men was their deep faith in Christ. We must never exclude anyone whom Christ has called to follow him.

13:2, 3 The church set apart Barnabas and Saul to the work God had for them. To *set apart* means to dedicate for a special purpose. We too should dedicate our pastors, missionaries, and Christian workers for their tasks. We can also dedicate ourselves to use our time, money, and talents for God's work. Ask God what he wants you to set apart for him.

13:2, 3 This was the beginning of Paul's first missionary journey. The church was involved in sending Paul and Barnabas, but it was God's plan. Why did Paul and Barnabas go where they did? (1) The Holy Spirit led them. (2) They followed the communication routes of the Roman empire – this made travel easier. (3) They visited key population and cultural centres to reach as many people as possible. (4) They went to cities with synagogues, speaking first to the Jews in hopes that they would see Jesus as the Messiah and help spread the Good News to everyone.

13:4 Located in the Mediterranean Sea, the island of Cyprus, with a large Jewish population, was Barnabas' home. Their first stop was in familiar territory.

13:6, 7 A proconsul was a high Roman official. Here he functioned as the governor of the island. Such leaders often kept private sorcerers. Bar-Jesus realised that if Sergius Paulus believed in Jesus, he would soon be out of a job.

13:9, 10 Here is where Saul is first called Paul.

13:10 The Holy Spirit led Paul to confront Bar-Jesus with his sin. There is a time to be nice and a time to confront. Ask God to show you the difference and to give you the courage to do what is right.

13:13 No reason is given why John Mark left Paul and Barnabas. Some suggestions are: (1) he was homesick; (2) he resented the change in leadership from Barnabas (his cousin) to Paul; (3) he became ill (an illness that may have affected all of them – see Galatians 4:13); (4) he was unable to withstand the rigours and dangers of the missionary journey; (5) he may have planned to go only that far but had not communicated this to Paul and Barnabas. Paul implicitly accused John Mark of lacking courage and commitment, refusing to take him along on another journey (see 15:37, 38). It is clear from Paul's later letters, however, that he grew to respect Mark (Colossians 4:10), and that he needed Mark in his work (2 Timothy 4:11).

13:13 [y]ver 6 [z]Ac 12:12
13:14 [a]Ac 14:19, 21 [b]Ac 16:13 [c]Ac 9:20

In Pisidian Antioch

13From Paphos,[y] Paul and his companions sailed to Perga in Pamphylia, where
John[z] left them to return to Jerusalem. 14From Perga they went on to Pisidian
Antioch.[a] On the Sabbath[b] they entered the synagogue[c] and sat down. 15After the

JOHN MARK

Mistakes are effective teachers. Their consequences have a way of making lessons painfully clear. But those who learn from their mistakes are likely to develop wisdom. John Mark was a good learner who just needed some time and encouragement.

Mark was eager to do the right thing, but he had trouble staying with a task. In his Gospel, Mark mentions a young man (probably referring to himself) who fled in such fear during Jesus' arrest that he left his clothes behind. This tendency to run was to reappear later when Paul and Barnabas took him as their assistant on their first missionary journey. At their second stop, Mark left them and returned to Jerusalem. It was a decision Paul did not easily accept. In preparing for their second journey two years later, Barnabas again suggested Mark as a travelling companion, but Paul flatly refused. As a result, the team was divided. Barnabas took Mark with him, and Paul chose Silas. Barnabas was patient with Mark, and the young man repaid his investment. Paul and Mark were later reunited, and the older apostle became a close friend of the young disciple.

Mark was a valuable companion to three early Christian leaders—Barnabas , Paul, and Peter. The material in Mark's Gospel seems to have come mostly from Peter. Mark's role as a serving assistant allowed him to be an observer. He heard Peter's accounts of the years with Jesus over and over again, and he was one of the first to put Jesus' life in writing.

Barnabas played a key role in Mark's life. He stood beside the young man despite his failure, giving him patient encouragement. Mark challenges us to learn from our mistakes and appreciate the patience of others. Is there a Barnabas in your life whom you need to thank for his or her encouragement to you?

Strengths and accomplishments:
- Wrote the Gospel of Mark
- He and his mother provided their home as one of the main meeting places for the Christians in Jerusalem
- Persisted beyond his youthful mistakes
- Was an assistant and travelling companion to three of the greatest early missionaries

Weaknesses and mistakes:
- Probably the nameless young man described in the Gospel of Mark who fled in panic when Jesus was arrested
- Left Paul and Barnabas for unknown reasons during the first missionary journey

Lessons from his life:
- Personal maturity usually comes from a combination of time and mistakes
- Mistakes are not usually as important as what can be learned from them
- Effective living is not measured as much by what we accomplish as by what we overcome in order to accomplish it
- Encouragement can change a person's life

Vital statistics:
- Where: Jerusalem
- Occupations: Missionary-in-training, Gospel writer, travelling companion
- Relatives: Mother: Mary. Cousin: Barnabas
- Contemporaries: Paul, Peter, Timothy, Luke, Silas

Key verse:
"Only Luke is with me. Get Mark and bring him with you, because he is helpful to me in my ministry" (Paul writing in 2 Timothy 4:11).

John Mark's story is told in Acts 12:23—13:13 and 15:36–39. He is also mentioned in Colossians 4:10; 2 Timothy 4:11; Philemon 24; 1 Peter 5:13.

13:14 This is Pisidian Antioch, not the Antioch of Syria where there was already a flourishing church (11:26). This Antioch, in the region of Pisidia, was a hub of good roads and trade, with a large Jewish population.

13:14 When they went to a new city to witness for Christ, Paul and Barnabas went first to the synagogue. The Jews who were

reading from the Law[d] and the Prophets, the synagogue rulers sent word to them,
saying, "Brothers, if you have a message of encouragement for the people, please
speak."
16Standing up, Paul motioned with his hand[e] and said: "Men of Israel and you
Gentiles who worship God, listen to me! 17The God of the people of Israel chose our
fathers; he made the people prosper during their stay in Egypt, with mighty power
he led them out of that country,[f] 18he endured their conduct[a][g] for about forty years
in the desert,[h] 19he overthrew seven nations in Canaan[i] and gave their land to his
people[j] as their inheritance. 20All this took about 450 years.
"After this, God gave them judges[k] until the time of Samuel the prophet.[l] 21Then
the people asked for a king,[m] and he gave them Saul[n] son of Kish, of the tribe of
Benjamin,[o] who ruled for forty years. 22After removing Saul,[p] he made David their
king.[q] He testified concerning him: 'I have found David son of Jesse a man after my
own heart;[r] he will do everything I want him to do.'
23"From this man's descendants[s] God has brought to Israel the Saviour[t] Jesus,[u]
as he promised.[v] 24Before the coming of Jesus, John preached repentance and
baptism to all the people of Israel.[w] 25As John was completing his work,[x] he said:

a *18* Some manuscripts *and cared for them*

13:15 [d]Ac 15:21
13:16 [e]Ac 12:17
13:17 [f]Ex 6:6, 7
13:18 [g]Dt 1:31 [h]Ac 7:36
13:19 [i]Dt 7:1 [j]Jos 19:51
13:20 [k]Jdg 2:16 [l]1Sa 3:19, 20
13:21 [m]1Sa 8:5, 19 [n]1Sa 10:1 [o]1Sa 9:1, 2
13:22 [p]1Sa 15:23, 26 [q]1Sa 16:13 [r]1Sa 13:14
13:23 [s]Mt 1:1 [t]Lk 2:11 [u]Mt 1:21 [v]ver 32
13:24 [w]Mk 1:4
13:25 [x]Ac 20:24

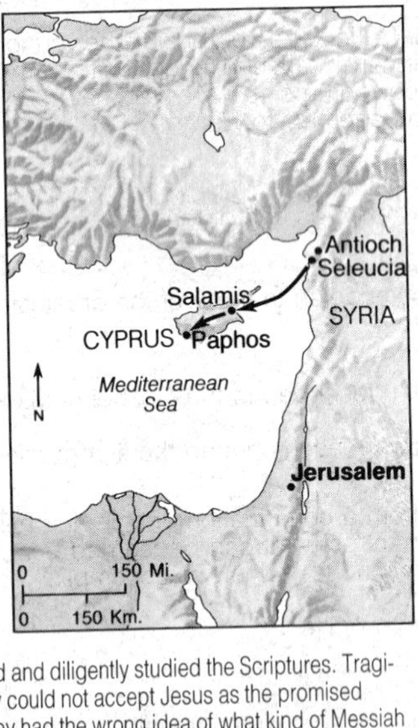

MINISTRY IN CYPRUS The leaders of the church in Antioch chose Paul and Barnabas to take the gospel westward. Along with John Mark, they boarded ship at Seleucia and set out across the Mediterranean for Cyprus. They preached in Salamis, the largest city, and went across the island to Paphos.

there believed in God and diligently studied the Scriptures. Tragically, however, many could not accept Jesus as the promised Messiah because they had the wrong idea of what kind of Messiah he would be. He was not, as they desired, a military king who would overthrow Rome's control, but a servant king who would defeat sin in people's hearts. (Only later, when Christ returns, will he judge the nations of the world.) Paul and Barnabas did not separate themselves from the synagogues but tried to show clearly that the very Scriptures the Jews studied pointed to Jesus.

13:14, 15 What happened in a synagogue service? First the *Shema* was recited (this is Deuteronomy 6:4, which Jews repeated several times daily). Certain prayers were spoken; then there was a reading from the law (the books of Genesis to Deuteronomy), a reading from the prophets intending to illustrate the law, and a sermon. The synagogue leader decided who was to lead the service and give the sermon. A different person was chosen to lead each week. Since it was customary for the synagogue leader to invite visiting rabbis to speak, Paul and Barnabas usually had an open door when they first went to a synagogue. But as soon as they spoke about Jesus as Messiah, the door would slam shut. They were usually not invited back by the religious leaders, and sometimes they were thrown out of town!

13:16ff Paul's message to the Jews in the synagogue in Antioch began with an emphasis on God's covenant with Israel. This was a point of agreement, because all Jews were proud to be God's chosen people. Then Paul went on to explain how the gospel fulfilled the covenant. Some Jews found this message hard to swallow.

13:23–31 Paul began where his listeners were and then introduced them to Christ. Because Paul was speaking to devout Jews, he began with the covenant, Abraham, David, and other familiar themes. Later, when speaking to the Greek philosophers in Athens (17:22–32), he would begin by talking about what he had observed in their city. In both cases, however, he centred the sermon around Christ and emphasised the resurrection. When you share the Good News, begin where your audience is—then tell them about Christ.

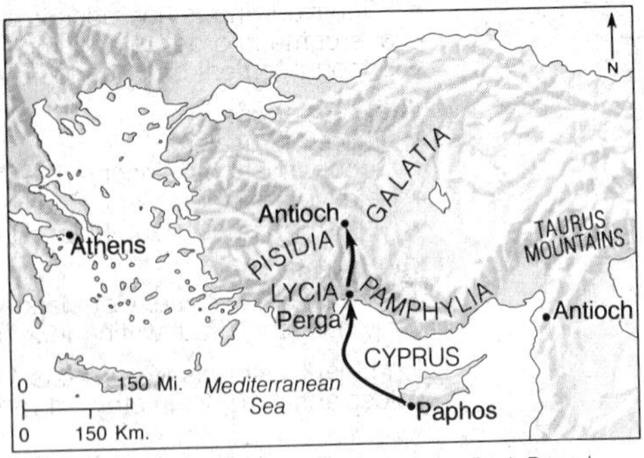

MINISTRY IN PAMPHYLIA AND GALATIA Paul, Barnabas, and John Mark left Paphos and landed at Perga in the humid region of Pamphylia, a narrow strip of land between the sea and the Taurus Mountains. John Mark left them in Perga, but Paul and Barnabas travelled up the steep road into the higher elevation of Pisidia in Galatia. When the Jews rejected his message, Paul preached to Gentiles, and the Jews drove Paul and Barnabas out of the Pisidian city of Antioch.

13:25
[y]Jn 1:20
[z]Jn 1:27
13:26
[a]Ac 4:12
13:27
[b]Ac 3:17
[c]Lk 24:27
13:28
[d]Mt 27:20-25
13:29
[e]Lk 18:31
[f]Ac 5:30
[g]Lk 23:53
13:30
[h]Mt 28:6

'Who do you think I am? I am not that one.[y] No, but he is coming after me, whose
sandals I am not worthy to untie.'[z]
26"Brothers, children of Abraham, and you God-fearing Gentiles, it is to us that
this message of salvation[a] has been sent. 27The people of Jerusalem and their rulers
did not recognise Jesus,[b] yet in condemning him they fulfilled the words of the
prophets[c] that are read every Sabbath. 28Though they found no proper ground for
a death sentence, they asked Pilate to have him executed.[d] 29When they had carried
out all that was written about him,[e] they took him down from the tree[f] and laid him
in a tomb.[g] 30But God raised him from the dead,[h] 31and for many days he was seen

---

BARNABAS

Every group needs an "encourager", because everyone needs encouragement at one time or another. However, the value of encouragement is often missed because it tends to be private rather than public. In fact, people most need encouragement when they feel most alone. A man named Joseph was such an encourager that he earned the nickname "Son of Encouragement", or Barnabas, from the Jerusalem Christians.

Barnabas was drawn to people he could encourage, and he was a great help to those around him. It is delightful that wherever Barnabas encouraged Christians, non-Christians flocked to become believers!

Barnabas' actions were crucial to the early church. In a way, we can thank him for most of the New Testament. God used his relationship with Paul at one point and with Mark at another to keep these two men going when either might have failed. Barnabas did wonders with encouragement!

When Paul arrived in Jerusalem for the first time following his conversion, the local Christians were understandably reluctant to welcome him. They thought his story was a trick to capture more Christians. Only Barnabas proved willing to risk his life to meet with Paul and then convince the others that their former enemy was now a vibrant believer in Jesus. We can only wonder what might have happened to Paul without Barnabas.

It was Barnabas who encouraged Mark to go with him and Paul to Antioch. Mark joined them on their first missionary journey, but decided during the trip to return home. Later, Barnabas wanted to invite Mark to join them for another journey, but Paul would not agree. As a result, the partners went separate ways, Barnabas with Mark and Paul with Silas. This actually doubled the missionary effort. Barnabas' patient encouragement was confirmed by Mark's eventual effective ministry. Paul and Mark were later reunited in missionary efforts.

As Barnabas' life shows, we are rarely in a situation where there isn't someone we can encourage. Our tendency, however, is to criticise instead. It may be important at times to point out someone's shortcomings, but before we have the right to do this, we must build that person's trust through encouragement. Are you prepared to encourage those with whom you come in contact today?

Strengths and accomplishments:
- One of the first to sell possessions to help the Christians in Jerusalem
- First to travel with Paul as a missionary team
- Was an encourager, as his nickname shows, and thus one of the most quietly influential people in the early days of Christianity
- Called an apostle, although not one of the original 12

Weakness and mistake:
- With Peter, temporarily stayed aloof from Gentile believers until Paul corrected him

Lessons from his life:
- Encouragement is one of the most effective ways to help
- Sooner or later, true obedience to God will involve risk
- There is always someone who needs encouragement

Vital statistics:
- Where: Cyprus, Jerusalem, Antioch
- Occupations : Missionary, teacher
- Relatives: Aunt: Mary. Cousin: John Mark
- Contemporaries: Peter, Silas, Paul, Herod Agrippa I

Key verses:
"When he arrived and saw the evidence of the grace of God, he was glad and encouraged them all to remain true to the Lord with all their hearts. He was a good man, full of the Holy Spirit and faith, and a great number of people were brought to the Lord" (Acts 11:23, 24).

Barnabas' story is told in Acts 4:36, 37; 9:27—15:39. He is also mentioned in 1 Corinthians 9:6; Galatians 2:1, 9, 13; Colossians 4:10.

by those who had travelled with him from Galilee to Jerusalem.[i] They are now his
witnesses[j] to our people.
32"We tell you the good news:[k] What God promised our fathers[l] 33he has fulfilled
for us, their children, by raising up Jesus. As it is written in the second Psalm:

> " 'You are my Son;
> today I have become your Father.'[b,c][m]

34The fact that God raised him from the dead, never to decay, is stated in these words:

> " 'I will give you the holy and sure blessings promised to
> David.'[d][n]

35So it is stated elsewhere:

> " 'You will not let your Holy One see decay.'[e][o]

36"For when David had served God's purpose in his own generation, he fell asleep;
he was buried with his fathers[p] and his body decayed. 37But the one whom God raised
from the dead did not see decay.
38"Therefore, my brothers, I want you to know that through Jesus the forgiveness
of sins is proclaimed to you.[q] 39Through him everyone who believes is justified from
everything you could not be justified from by the law of Moses.[r] 40Take care that
what the prophets have said does not happen to you:

> 41" 'Look, you scoffers,
> wonder and perish,
> for I am going to do something in your days
> that you would never believe,
> even if someone told you.'[f]"[s]

42As Paul and Barnabas were leaving the synagogue,[t] the people invited them to
speak further about these things on the next Sabbath. 43When the congregation was
dismissed, many of the Jews and devout converts to Judaism followed Paul and
Barnabas, who talked with them and urged them to continue in the grace of God.[u]
44On the next Sabbath almost the whole city gathered to hear the word of the Lord.
45When the Jews saw the crowds, they were filled with jealousy and talked abusively[v]
against what Paul was saying.[w]
46Then Paul and Barnabas answered them boldly: "We had to speak the word of
God to you first.[x] Since you reject it and do not consider yourselves worthy of eternal
life, we now turn to the Gentiles.[y] 47For this is what the Lord has commanded us:

> " 'I have made you[g] a light for the Gentiles,[z]
> that you[g] may bring salvation to the ends of the earth.'[h]"[a]

48When the Gentiles heard this, they were glad and honoured the word of the Lord;
and all who were appointed for eternal life believed.
49The word of the Lord spread through the whole region. 50But the Jews incited

b 33 Or *have begotten you* c 33 Psalm 2:7 d 34 Isaiah 55:3 e 35 Psalm 16:10 f 41 Hab. 1:5 g 47 The Greek is singular. h 47 Isaiah 49:6

13:31 i Mt 28:16 j Lk 24:48
13:32 k Ac 5:42 l Ac 26:6; Ro 4:13
13:33 m Ps 2:7
13:34 n Isa 55:3
13:35 o Ps 16:10; Ac 2:27
13:36 p 1Ki 2:10; Ac 2:29
13:38 q Lk 24:47; Ac 2:38
13:39 r Ro 3:28
13:41 s Hab 1:5
13:42 t ver 14
13:43 u Ac 11:23; 14:22
13:45 v Ac 18:6; 1Pe 4:4; Jude 10 w 1Th 2:16
13:46 x ver 26; Ac 3:26 y Ac 18:6; 22:21; 28:28
13:47 z Lk 2:32 a Isa 49:6

13:38, 39 This is the Good News of the gospel: that forgiveness of sins and freedom from guilt are available through faith in Christ to all people – including *you*. Have you received this forgiveness? Are you refreshed by it each day?

13:42–45 The Jewish leaders undoubtedly brought theological arguments against Paul and Barnabas, but Luke tells us that the real reason for their hostility was that "they were filled with jealousy". When we see others succeeding where we haven't, or receiving the affirmation we crave, it is hard to rejoice with them. Jealousy is our natural reaction. But how tragic it is when our own jealous feelings make us try to stop God's work. If a work is God's work, rejoice in it – no matter who is doing it.

13:46 Why was it necessary for the gospel to go first to the Jews? God planned that through the Jewish nation *all* the world would come to know God (Genesis 12:3). Paul, a Jew himself, loved his people (Romans 9:1–5) and wanted to give them every opportunity to join him in proclaiming God's salvation. Unfortunately, many Jews did not recognise Jesus as Messiah, and they did not understand that God was offering salvation to anyone, Jew or Gentile, who comes to him through faith in Christ.

13:47 God had planned for Israel to be this light (Isaiah 49:6). Through Israel came Jesus, the light of the nations (Luke 2:32). This light would spread out and enlighten the Gentiles.

13:50 Instead of accepting the truth, the Jewish leaders stirred up opposition and ran Paul and Barnabas out of town. When confronted by a disturbing truth, people often turn away and refuse to

13:50 [b]1Th 2:16
13:51 [c]Mt 10:14; Ac 18:6 [d]Ac 14:1, 19, 21; 2Ti 3:11
14:1 [a]Ac 13:51
14:3 [b]Ac 4:29 [c]Jn 4:48; Heb 2:4
14:4 [d]Ac 17:4, 5
14:5 [e]ver 19
14:6 [f]Mt 10:23
14:7 [g]Ac 16:10 [h]ver 15, 21
14:8 [i]Ac 3:2
14:9 [j]Mt 9:28, 29
14:10 [k]Ac 3:8
14:11 [l]Ac 8:10; 28:6

the God-fearing women of high standing and the leading men of the city. They stirred
up persecution against Paul and Barnabas, and expelled them from their region.[b] 51 So
they shook the dust from their feet[c] in protest against them and went to Iconium.[d]
52 And the disciples were filled with joy and with the Holy Spirit.

In Iconium

14 At Iconium[a] Paul and Barnabas went as usual into the Jewish synagogue.
There they spoke so effectively that a great number of Jews and Gentiles
believed. 2 But the Jews who refused to believe stirred up the Gentiles and poisoned
their minds against the brothers. 3 So Paul and Barnabas spent considerable time there,
speaking boldly[b] for the Lord, who confirmed the message of his grace by enabling
them to do miraculous signs and wonders.[c] 4 The people of the city were divided;
some sided with the Jews, others with the apostles.[d] 5 There was a plot afoot among
the Gentiles and Jews, together with their leaders, to ill-treat them and stone them.[e]
6 But they found out about it and fled[f] to the Lycaonian cities of Lystra and Derbe
and to the surrounding country, 7 where they continued to preach[g] the good news.[h]

In Lystra and Derbe

8 In Lystra there sat a man crippled in his feet, who was lame from birth[i] and had
never walked. 9 He listened to Paul as he was speaking. Paul looked directly at him,
saw that he had faith to be healed[j] 10 and called out, "Stand up on your feet!" At that,
the man jumped up and began to walk.[k]

11 When the crowd saw what Paul had done, they shouted in the Lycaonian language, "The gods have come down to us in human form!"[l] 12 Barnabas they called
Zeus, and Paul they called Hermes because he was the chief speaker. 13 The priest of
Zeus, whose temple was just outside the city, brought bulls and wreaths to the city
gates because he and the crowd wanted to offer sacrifices to them.

---

listen. When God's Spirit points out needed changes in our lives, we must listen to him. Otherwise we may be pushing the truth so far away that it no longer affects us.

13:51 Often Jews would shake the dust off their feet when leaving a Gentile town, on the way back to their own land. This symbolised cleansing themselves from the contamination of those who did not worship God. For Paul and Barnabas to do this to Jews demonstrated that Jews who reject the gospel are not truly part of Israel and are no better than pagans.

13:51 Jesus had told his disciples to shake from their feet the dust of any town that would not accept or listen to them (Mark 6:11). The disciples were not to blame if the message was rejected, as long as they had faithfully presented it. When we share Christ carefully and sensitively, God does not hold us responsible for the other person's decision.

14:3, 4 We may wish we could perform a miraculous act that would convince everyone once and for all that Jesus is the Lord. But we see here that even if we could perform a miracle, it wouldn't convince everyone. God gave these men power to do great wonders as confirmation of the message of grace, but people were still divided. Don't spend your time and energy wishing for miracles. Sow your seeds of Good News on the best ground you can find in the best way you can, and leave the convincing to the Holy Spirit.

14:6 Iconium (14:1), Lystra, and Derbe were three cities Paul visited in the southern part of the region of Galatia. Paul probably wrote a letter to these churches – the letter to the Galatians – because many Jewish Christians were claiming that non-Jewish Christians couldn't be saved unless they followed Jewish laws and customs. Paul's letter refuted this and brought the believers back to a right understanding of faith in Jesus (see Galatians 3:3, 5). Paul may have written his letter soon after leaving the region (see the note on 14:28).

14:11 "The Lycaonian language" refers to their local dialect.

14:11, 12 Zeus and Hermes (also known as Jupiter and Mercury) were two popular gods in the Roman world. People from Lystra claimed that these gods had once visited their city. According to legend, no-one offered them hospitality except an old couple, so Zeus and Hermes killed the rest of the people and rewarded the old couple. When the citizens of Lystra saw the miracles of Paul and Barnabas, they assumed that the gods were revisiting them. Remembering the story of what had happened to the previous citizens, they immediately honoured Paul and Barnabas and showered them with gifts.

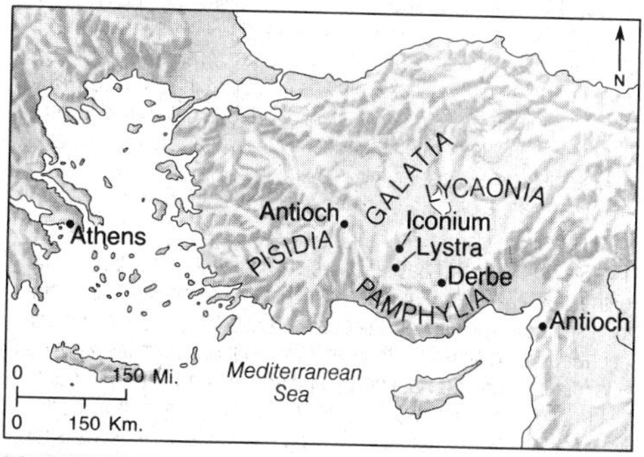

CONTINUED MINISTRY IN GALATIA Paul and Barnabas, thrown out of Antioch in Pisidia, descended the mountains, going east into Lycaonia. They went first to Iconium, a commercial centre on the road between Asia and Syria. After preaching there, they had to flee to Lystra, 25 miles south. Paul was stoned in Lystra, but he and Barnabas travelled the 50 miles to Derbe, a border town. The pair then boldly retraced their steps.

14But when the apostles Barnabas and Paul heard of this, they tore their clothes[m]
and rushed out into the crowd, shouting: 15"Men, why are you doing this? We too
are only men,[n] human like you. We are bringing you good news,[o] telling you to
turn from these worthless things[p] to the living God,[q] who made heaven and earth[r]
and sea and everything in them.[s] 16In the past, he let[t] all nations go their own way.[u]
17Yet he has not left himself without testimony:[v] He has shown kindness by giving
you rain from heaven and crops in their seasons;[w] he provides you with plenty of food
and fills your hearts with joy." 18Even with these words, they had difficulty keeping
the crowd from sacrificing to them.
19Then some Jews[x] came from Antioch and Iconium[y] and won the crowd over.
They stoned Paul[z] and dragged him outside the city, thinking he was dead. 20But
after the disciples[a] had gathered round him, he got up and went back into the city.
The next day he and Barnabas left for Derbe.

The Return to Antioch in Syria

21They preached the good news in that city and won a large number of disciples.
Then they returned to Lystra, Iconium[b] and Antioch, 22strengthening the disciples
and encouraging them to remain true to the faith.[c] "We must go through many
hardships[d] to enter the kingdom of God," they said. 23Paul and Barnabas appointed
elders[a][e] for them in each church and, with prayer and fasting,[f] committed them
to the Lord,[g] in whom they had put their trust. 24After going through Pisidia, they
came into Pamphylia, 25and when they had preached the word in Perga, they went
down to Attalia.
26From Attalia they sailed back to Antioch,[h] where they had been committed to
the grace of God[i] for the work they had now completed.[j] 27On arriving there, they
gathered the church together and reported all that God had done through them[k] and
how he had opened the door[l] of faith to the Gentiles. 28And they stayed there a long
time with the disciples.

a 23 Or *Barnabas ordained elders*; or *Barnabas had elders elected*

14:14 [m]Mk 14:63
14:15 [n]Ac 10:26 [o]Ac 13:32 [p]1Th 1:9 [q]Mt 16:16 [r]Ge 1:1; [s]Ps 146:6;
14:16 [t]Ac 17:30 [u]Ps 81:12; Mic 4:5
14:17 [v]Ac 17:27; Ro 1:20 [w]Dt 11:14; Job 5:10; Ps 65:10
14:19 [x]Ac 13:45 [y]Ac 13:51 [z]2Co 11:25; 2Ti 3:11
14:20 [a]ver 22, 28; Ac 11:26
14:21 [b]Ac 13:51
14:22 [c]Ac 11:23; 13:43 [d]Jn 16:33; 1Th 3:3; 2Ti 3:12
14:23 [e]Ac 11:30; Tit 1:5 [f]Ac 13:3 [g]Ac 20:32
14:26 [h]Ac 11:19 [i]Ac 15:40 [j]Ac 13:1, 3
14:27 [k]Ac 15:4, 12; 21:19 [l]1Co 16:9; 2Co 2:12; Col 4:3; Rev 3:8

14:15–18 Responding to the people of Lystra, Paul and Barnabas reminded them that God never leaves himself "without testimony". Rain and crops, for example, are evidence of his goodness. Later Paul wrote that this evidence in nature leaves people without an excuse for unbelief (Romans 1:20). When in doubt about God, look around and you will see abundant evidence that he is at work in our world.

14:18, 19 Only days after the people in Lystra had thought that Paul and Barnabas were gods and wanted to offer sacrifices to them, they stoned Paul and left him for dead. That's human nature. Jesus understood how fickle crowds can be (John 2:24, 25). When many people approve of us, we feel good, but that should never cloud our thinking or affect our decisions. We should not live to please the crowd—especially in our spiritual lives. Be like Jesus. Know the nature of the crowd and don't put your trust in it. Put your trust in God alone.

14:18–20 Paul and Barnabas were persistent in their preaching of the Good News, considering the cost to themselves to be nothing in comparison with obedience to Christ. They had just narrowly escaped being stoned in Iconium (14:1–7), but Jews from Antioch and Iconium tracked Paul down, stoned him, and left him for dead. But Paul got up and went back into the city to preach the Good News. That's true commitment! Being a disciple of Christ calls for total commitment. As Christians, we no longer belong to ourselves but to our Lord, for whom we are called to suffer.

14:21, 22 Paul and Barnabas returned to visit the believers in all the cities where they had recently been threatened and physically attacked. These men knew the dangers they faced, yet they believed that they had a responsibility to encourage the new believers. No matter how inconvenient or uncomfortable the task may seem, we must always support new believers who need our help and encouragement. It was not convenient or comfortable for Jesus to go to the cross for us!

14:23 Part of the reason that Paul and Barnabas risked their lives to return to these cities was to organise the churches' leadership. They were not just following up on a loosely knit group; they were helping the believers get organised with spiritual leaders who could help them grow. Churches grow under Spirit-led leaders, both laypersons and pastors. Pray for your church leaders and support them; and if God puts his finger on you, humbly accept the responsibility of a leadership role in your church.

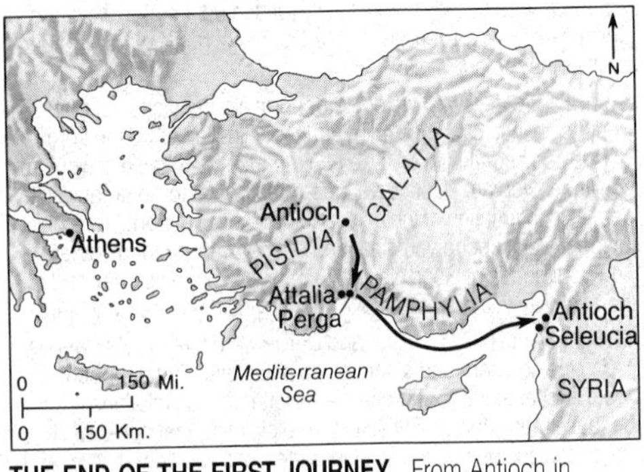

THE END OF THE FIRST JOURNEY From Antioch in Pisidia, Paul and Barnabas went down the mountains back to Pamphylia on the coast. Stopping first in Perga, where they had landed, they went west to Attalia, the main port that sent goods from Asia to Syria and Egypt. There they found a ship bound for Seleucia, the port of Antioch in Syria. This ended their first missionary journey.

15:1
[a] ver 24; Gal 2:12
[b] ver 5; Gal 5:2, 3
[c] Ac 6:14

15:2
[d] Gal 2:2
[e] Ac 11:30

15:3
[f] Ac 14:27

15:4
[g] ver 12; Ac 14:27

15:8
[h] Ac 1:24
[i] Ac 10:44, 47

15:9
[j] Ac 10:28, 34; 11:12
[k] Ac 10:43

15:10
[l] Mt 23:4; Gal 5:1

2. The council at Jerusalem

15 Some men[a] came down from Judea to Antioch and were teaching the brothers:
"Unless you are circumcised,[b] according to the custom taught by Moses,[c] you
cannot be saved." 2 This brought Paul and Barnabas into sharp dispute and debate with
them. So Paul and Barnabas were appointed, along with some other believers, to go
up to Jerusalem[d] to see the apostles and elders[e] about this question. 3 The church
sent them on their way, and as they travelled through Phoenicia and Samaria, they
told how the Gentiles had been converted.[f] This news made all the brothers very glad.
4 When they came to Jerusalem, they were welcomed by the church and the apostles
and elders, to whom they reported everything God had done through them.[g]
5 Then some of the believers who belonged to the party of the Pharisees stood up
and said, "The Gentiles must be circumcised and required to obey the law of Moses."
6 The apostles and elders met to consider this question. 7 After much discussion,
Peter got up and addressed them: "Brothers, you know that some time ago God made
a choice among you that the Gentiles might hear from my lips the message of the
gospel and believe. 8 God, who knows the heart,[h] showed that he accepted them by
giving the Holy Spirit to them,[i] just as he did to us. 9 He made no distinction between
us and them,[j] for he purified their hearts by faith.[k] 10 Now then, why do you try
to test God by putting on the necks of the disciples a yoke[l] that neither we nor our

---

14:28 Paul probably wrote his letter to the Galatians while he was staying in Antioch (A.D. 48 or 49) after completing his first missionary journey. There are several theories as to what part of Galatia Paul was addressing, but most agree that Iconium, Lystra, and Derbe were part of that region for whom the letter is intended. Galatians was probably written before the Jerusalem council (Acts 15), because in the letter the question of whether Gentile believers should be required to follow Jewish law was not yet resolved. The council met to solve that problem.

15:1 The real problem for the Jewish Christians was not whether Gentiles could be saved, but whether Gentiles had to adhere to the laws of Moses. The test of following these laws was circumcision. The Jewish Christians were worried because soon there would be more Gentile than Jewish Christians. And they were afraid of weakening moral standards among believers if they did not follow Jewish laws. Paul, Barnabas, and the other church leaders believed that the Old Testament law was very important, but it was not a prerequisite to salvation. The law cannot save; only by grace through faith in Jesus Christ can a person be saved.

15:1ff The delegates to the council at Jerusalem came from the churches in Jerusalem and Antioch. The conversion of Gentiles was raising an urgent question for the early church – do the Gentiles have to adhere to the laws of Moses and other Jewish traditions to be saved? One group of Jewish Christians insisted that following the law, including submitting to the rite of circumcision, was necessary for salvation. The Gentiles, however, did not think they needed to become Jewish first in order to become Christians. So Paul and Barnabas discussed this problem with the leaders of the church. The council upheld the convictions expressed by Paul and Barnabas that following the Jewish laws, including being circumcised, was not essential for salvation.

15:2 The question of whether the Gentile believers should obey the Law of Moses to be saved was an important one. The controversy intensified largely due to the success of the new Gentile churches. The conservatives in the Jerusalem church were led by converted Pharisees (15:5) who preferred a legalistic religion to one based on faith alone. If the conservatives had won, the Gentiles would have been required to be circumcised and converted to Judaism. This would have seriously confined Christianity to simply being another sect within Judaism. There is something of a "Pharisee" in each one of us. We may unwittingly mistake upholding tradition, structure, and legal requirements for obeying God. Make sure the gospel brings freedom and life to those you are trying to reach.

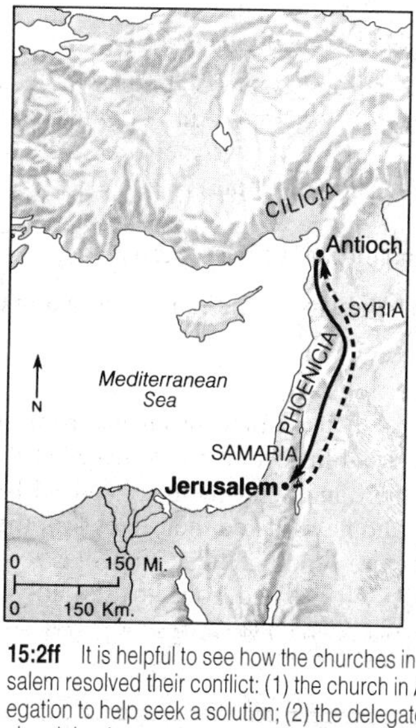

THE JERUSALEM COUNCIL
A dispute arose when some Judeans taught that Gentile believers had to be circumcised to be saved. Paul and Barnabas went to Jerusalem to discuss this situation with the leaders there. After the Jerusalem council made its decision, Paul and Barnabas returned to Antioch with the news.

15:2ff It is helpful to see how the churches in Antioch and Jerusalem resolved their conflict: (1) the church in Antioch sent a delegation to help seek a solution; (2) the delegates met with the church leaders to give their reports and set another date to continue the discussion; (3) Paul and Barnabas gave their report; (4) James summarised the reports and drew up the decision; (5) everyone agreed to abide by the decision; (6) the council sent a letter with delegates back to Antioch to report the decision.

This is a wise way to handle conflicts within the church. Problems must be confronted, and all sides of the argument must be given a fair hearing. The discussion should be held in the presence of leaders who are spiritually mature and trustworthy to make wise decisions. Everyone should then abide by the decisions.

15:10 If the law was a yoke that the Jews could not bear, how did having the law help them throughout their history? Paul wrote that the law was a guide that pointed out their sins so they could repent and return to God and right living (see Galatians 3:24, 25). It was, and still is, impossible to obey the law completely.

fathers have been able to bear? 11No! We believe it is through the grace[m] of our Lord
Jesus that we are saved, just as they are."
12The whole assembly became silent as they listened to Barnabas and Paul telling
about the miraculous signs and wonders[n] God had done among the Gentiles through
them.[o] 13When they finished, James[p] spoke up: "Brothers, listen to me. 14Simon[a]
has described to us how God at first showed his concern by taking from the Gentiles
a people for himself. 15The words of the prophets are in agreement with this, as it
is written:

16" 'After this I will return
and rebuild David's fallen tent.
Its ruins I will rebuild,
and I will restore it,
17that the remnant of men may seek the Lord,
and all the Gentiles who bear my name,
says the Lord, who does these things'[b][q]
18 that have been known for ages.[c]

19"It is my judgment, therefore, that we should not make it difficult for the Gentiles
who are turning to God. 20Instead we should write to them, telling them to abstain
from food polluted by idols,[r] from sexual immorality,[s] from the meat of strangled
animals and from blood.[t] 21For Moses has been preached in every city from the
earliest times and is read in the synagogues on every Sabbath."[u]

The Council's Letter to Gentile Believers

22Then the apostles and elders, with the whole church, decided to choose some of
their own men and send them to Antioch with Paul and Barnabas. They chose Judas
(called Barsabbas) and Silas,[v] two men who were leaders among the brothers. 23With
them they sent the following letter:

The apostles and elders, your brothers,

To the Gentile believers in Antioch,[w] Syria and Cilicia:[x]

Greetings.[y]

24We have heard that some went out from us without our authorisation and
disturbed you, troubling your minds by what they said.[z] 25So we all agreed to
choose some men and send them to you with our dear friends Barnabas and
Paul—26men who have risked their lives[a] for the name of our Lord Jesus Christ.
27Therefore we are sending Judas and Silas to confirm by word of mouth what
we are writing. 28It seemed good to the Holy Spirit[b] and to us not to burden

a *14* Greek *Simeon*, a variant of *Simon*; that is, Peter b *17* Amos 9:11,12 c *17,18* Some manuscripts *things'— / 18known to the Lord for ages is his work*

15:11 [m]Ro 3:24; Eph 2:5-8
15:12 [n]Jn 4:48 [o]Ac 14:27
15:13 [p]Ac 12:17
15:17 [q]Am 9:11, 12
15:20 [r]1Co 8:7-13; 10:14-28; Rev 2:14, 20 [s]1Co 10:7, 8 [t]ver 29; Ge 9:4; Lev 3:17; Dt 12:16, 23
15:21 [u]Ac 13:15; 2Co 3:14, 15
15:22 [v]ver 27, 32, 40
15:23 [w]ver 1 [x]ver 41 [y]Ac 23:25, 26; Jas 1:1
15:24 [z]ver 1; Gal 1:7; 5:10
15:26 [a]Ac 9:23-25; 14:19
15:28 [b]Ac 5:32

15:13 This James is Jesus' brother. He became the leader of the church in Jerusalem and wrote the book of James.

15:14 Simon is another name for Peter.

15:20, 21 James's judgment was that Gentile believers did not have to be circumcised, but they should stay away from food polluted by idols, from sexual immorality (a common part of idol worship), and from eating meat of strangled animals and from consuming blood (reflecting the biblical teaching that the life is in the blood—Leviticus 17:14). If Gentile Christians would abstain from these practices, they would please God and get along better with their Jewish brothers and sisters in Christ. Of course, there were other actions inappropriate for believers, but the Jews were especially concerned about these four. This compromise helped the church grow unhindered by the cultural differences of Jews and Gentiles. When we share our message across cultural and economic boundaries, we must be sure that the requirements for faith we set up are God's, not people's.

15:22 Apostleship was not a church office but a position and function based on specific gifts. Elders were appointed to lead and manage the church. In this meeting, apostles submitted to the judgment of an elder—James, Jesus' brother.

15:22 Later Silas accompanied Paul on Paul's second missionary journey in place of Barnabas, who visited different cities with John Mark.

15:23–29 This letter answered their questions and brought great joy to the Gentile Christians in Antioch (15:31). Beautifully written, it appeals to the Holy Spirit's guidance and explains what is to be done as though the readers already knew it. It is helpful when believers learn to be careful not only in what they say, but also in how they say it. We may be correct in our content, but we can lose our audience by our tone of voice or by our attitude.

15:29 [c] ver 20; Ac 21:25

you with anything beyond the following requirements: 29 You are to abstain from
food sacrificed to idols, from blood, from the meat of strangled animals and from
sexual immorality.[c] You will do well to avoid these things.

Farewell.

15:33 [d] Mk 5:34; Ac 16:36; 1Co 16:11

30 The men were sent off and went down to Antioch, where they gathered the church
together and delivered the letter. 31 The people read it and were glad for its encouraging
message. 32 Judas and Silas, who themselves were prophets, said much to encourage
and strengthen the brothers. 33 After spending some time there, they were sent off by
the brothers with the blessing of peace[d] to return to those who had sent them.[d] 35 But
Paul and Barnabas remained in Antioch, where they and many others taught and
preached[e] the word of the Lord.

15:35 [e] Ac 8:4

d *33* Some manuscripts *them,* [34] *but Silas decided to remain there*

THE FIRST CHURCH CONFERENCE

Group	*Position*	*Reasons*
Judaisers (some Jewish Christians)	Gentiles must become Jewish first to be eligible for salvation	1. They were devout, practising Jews who found it difficult to set aside a tradition of gaining merit with God by keeping the law 2. They thought grace was too easy for the Gentiles 3. They were afraid of seeming too non-Jewish in the practice of their new faith—which could lead to death 4. The demands on the Gentiles were a way of maintaining control and authority in the movement
Gentile Christians	Faith in Christ as Saviour is the only requirement for salvation	1. To submit to Jewish demands would be to doubt what God had already done for them by grace alone 2. They resisted exchanging a system of Jewish rituals for their pagan rituals—neither of which had power to save 3. They sought to obey Christ by baptism (rather than by circumcision) as a sign of their new faith
Peter and James	Faith is the only requirement, but there must be evidence of change by rejecting the old lifestyle	1. They tried to distinguish between what was true from God's word and what was just human tradition 2. They had Christ's command to preach to all the world 3. They wanted to preserve unity 4. They saw that Christianity could never survive as just a sect within Judaism

As long as most of the first Christians were Jewish, there was little difficulty in welcoming new believers; however, Gentiles (non-Jews) began to accept Jesus' offer of salvation. The evidence in their lives and the presence of God's Spirit in them showed that God was accepting them. Some of the early Christians believed that non-Jewish Christians needed to meet certain conditions before they could be worthy to accept Christ. The issue could have destroyed the church, so a conference was called in Jerusalem and the issue was formally settled there, although it continued to be a problem for many years following. Above is an outline of the three points of view at the conference.

15:31 The debate over circumcision could have split the church, but Paul, Barnabas, and the Jews in Antioch made the right decision—they sought counsel from the church leaders and from God's word. Our differences should be settled the same way, by seeking wise counsel and abiding by the decisions. Don't let disagreements divide you from other believers. Third-party assistance is a sound method for resolving problems and preserving unity.

3. Second missionary journey

Disagreement Between Paul and Barnabas

36 Some time later Paul said to Barnabas, "Let us go back and visit the brothers in
all the towns[f] where we preached the word of the Lord and see how they are doing."
37 Barnabas wanted to take John, also called Mark,[g] with them, 38 but Paul did not
think it wise to take him, because he had deserted them[h] in Pamphylia and had not
continued with them in the work. 39 They had such a sharp disagreement that they
parted company. Barnabas took Mark and sailed for Cyprus, 40 but Paul chose Silas[i]
and left, commended by the brothers to the grace of the Lord.[j] 41 He went through
Syria[k] and Cilicia,[l] strengthening the churches.[m]

Timothy Joins Paul and Silas

16 He came to Derbe and then to Lystra,[a] where a disciple named Timothy[b]
lived, whose mother was a Jewess and a believer, but whose father was a Greek.
2 The brothers[c] at Lystra and Iconium[d] spoke well of him. 3 Paul wanted to take him
along on the journey, so he circumcised him because of the Jews who lived in that
area, for they all knew that his father was a Greek.[e] 4 As they travelled from town
to town, they delivered the decisions reached by the apostles and elders[f] in Jerusalem[g] for the people to obey.[h] 5 So the churches were strengthened[i] in the faith
and grew daily in numbers.

Paul's Vision of the Man of Macedonia

6 Paul and his companions travelled throughout the region of Phrygia[j] and Galatia,[k] having been kept by the Holy Spirit from preaching the word in the province
of Asia.[l] 7 When they came to the border of Mysia, they tried to enter Bithynia, but

15:36 [f] Ac 13:4, 13, 14, 51; 14:1, 6, 24, 25
15:37 [g] Ac 12:12
15:38 [h] Ac 13:13
15:40 [i] ver 22 [j] Ac 11:23
15:41 [k] ver 23 [l] Ac 6:9 [m] Ac 16:5
16:1 [a] Ac 14:6 [b] Ac 17:14; 18:5; 19:22; Ro 16:21; 1Co 4:17; 2Co 1:1, 19; 1Th 3:2, 6; 1Ti 1:2, 18; 2Ti 1:2, 5, 6
16:2 [c] ver 40 [d] Ac 13:51
16:3 [e] Gal 2:3
16:4 [f] Ac 11:30 [g] Ac 15:2 [h] Ac 15:28, 29
16:5 [i] Ac 9.31; 15:41
16:6 [j] Ac 18:23 [k] Ac 18:23; Gal 1:2; 3:1 [l] Ac 2:9

15:36–39 Paul and Barnabas disagreed sharply over Mark. Paul didn't want to take him along because he had left them earlier (13:13). This disagreement caused the two great preachers to form two teams, opening up two missionary endeavours instead of one. God works even through conflict and disagreements. Later, Mark became vital to Paul's ministry (Colossians 4:10). Christians do not always agree, but problems can be solved by agreeing to disagree and letting God work his will.

15:40 Paul's second missionary journey, this time with Silas as his partner, began approximately three years after his first one ended. The two visited many of the cities covered on Paul's first journey, plus others. This journey laid the groundwork for the church in Greece.

15:40 Silas had been involved in the Jerusalem council and was one of the two men chosen to represent the Jerusalem church by taking the letter and decision back to Antioch (15:22). Paul, from the Antioch church, chose Silas, from the Jerusalem church, and they travelled together to many cities to spread the Good News. This teamwork demonstrated the church's unity after the decision at the Jerusalem council.

16:1 Timothy is the first second-generation Christian mentioned in the New Testament. His mother, Eunice, and grandmother, Lois (2 Timothy 1:5), had become believers and had faithfully influenced him for the Lord. Although Timothy's father was apparently not a Christian, the faithfulness of Timothy's mother and grandmother prevailed. Never underestimate the far-reaching consequences of raising one small child to love the Lord.

16:2, 3 Timothy and his mother, Eunice, were from Lystra. Eunice had probably heard Paul's preaching when he was there during his first missionary journey (14:6–18). Timothy was the son of a Jewish mother and Greek father—to the Jews, a half-breed like a Samaritan. So Paul asked Timothy to be circumcised to remove some of the stigma he may have had with Jewish believers. Timothy was not required to be circumcised (the Jerusalem council had decided that—chapter 15), but he voluntarily did this to overcome any barriers to his witness for Christ. Sometimes we need to go beyond the minimum requirements in order to help our audience receive our testimony.

16:6 We don't know how the Holy Spirit told Paul that he and his companions should not go into Asia. It may have been through a prophet, a vision, an inner conviction, or some other circumstance. To know God's will does not mean we must hear his voice. He leads in different ways. When seeking God's will, (1) make sure your plan is in harmony with God's word; (2) ask mature Christians for their advice; (3) check your own motives—are you seeking to do what you want or what you think God wants?—and (4) pray for God to open and close the doors as he desires.

16:7–9 The "Spirit of Jesus" is another name for the Holy Spirit.

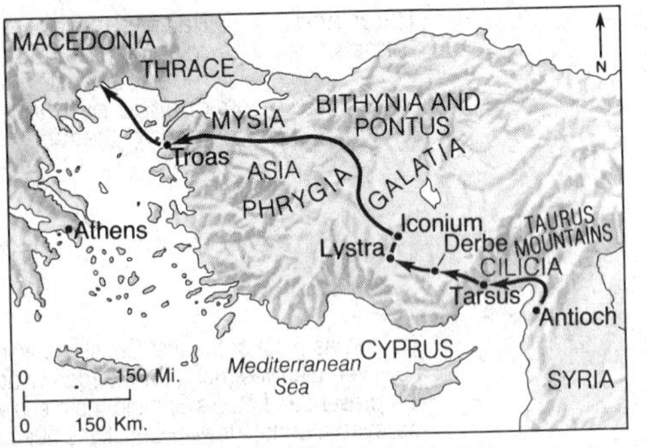

THE SECOND JOURNEY BEGINS Paul and Silas set out on a second missionary journey to visit the cities Paul had preached in earlier. This time they set out by land rather than sea, travelling the Roman road through Cilicia and the Cilician Gates—a gorge through the Taurus Mountains—then northwest towards Derbe, Lystra, and Iconium. The Spirit told them not to go into Asia, so they turned northward towards Bithynia. Again the Spirit said no, so they turned west through Mysia to the harbour city of Troas.

16:7 [m]Ro 8:9; Gal 4:6
16:8 [n]ver 11; 2Co 2:12; 2Ti 4:13
16:9 [o]Ac 9:10 [p]Ac 20:1, 3
16:10 [q]ver 10-17 [r]Ac 14:7
16:11 [s]ver 8
16:12 [t]Ac 20:6; Php 1:1; 1Th 2:2 [u]ver 9
16:13 [v]Ac 13:14
16:14 [w]Rev 1:11 [x]Lk 24:45
16:15 [y]Ac 11:14
16:16 [z]ver 13 [a]Dt 18:11; 1Sa 28:3, 7

the Spirit of Jesus[m] would not allow them to. 8So they passed by Mysia and went
down to Troas.[n] 9During the night Paul had a vision[o] of a man of Macedonia[p]
standing and begging him, "Come over to Macedonia and help us." 10After Paul had
seen the vision, we[q] got ready at once to leave for Macedonia, concluding that God
had called us to preach the gospel[r] to them.

Lydia's Conversion in Philippi

11From Troas[s] we put out to sea and sailed straight for Samothrace, and the next
day on to Neapolis. 12From there we travelled to Philippi,[t] a Roman colony and the
leading city of that district of Macedonia.[u] And we stayed there several days.
13On the Sabbath[v] we went outside the city gate to the river, where we expected
to find a place of prayer. We sat down and began to speak to the women who had
gathered there. 14One of those listening was a woman named Lydia, a dealer in purple
cloth from the city of Thyatira,[w] who was a worshipper of God. The Lord opened
her heart[x] to respond to Paul's message. 15When she and the members of her
household[y] were baptised, she invited us to her home. "If you consider me a believer
in the Lord," she said, "come and stay at my house." And she persuaded us.

Paul and Silas in Prison

16Once when we were going to the place of prayer,[z] we were met by a slave girl
who had a spirit[a] by which she predicted the future. She earned a great deal of money

---

The Holy Spirit had closed the door twice for Paul, so Paul must have wondered which geographical direction to take in spreading the gospel. Then, in a vision (16:9), Paul was given definite direction, and he and his companions obediently travelled into Macedonia. The Holy Spirit guides us to the right places, but he also guides us away from the wrong places. As we seek God's will, it is important to know what God wants us to do and where he wants us to go, but it is equally important to know what God does not want us to do and where he does not want us to go.

16:10 The use of the pronoun *we* indicates that Luke, the author of the Gospel of Luke and of this book, joined Paul, Silas, and Timothy on their journey. He was an eyewitness to most of the remaining incidents in this book.

16:12 Philippi was the key city in the region of Macedonia (northern Greece today). Paul founded a church during this visit (A.D. 50–51). Later Paul wrote a letter to the church, the book of Philippians, probably from a prison in Rome (A.D. 61). The letter was personal and tender, showing Paul's deep love for and friendship with the believers there. In it he thanked them for a gift they had sent, alerted them to a coming visit by Timothy and Epaphroditus, urged the church to clear up any disunity, and encouraged the believers not to give in to persecution.

16:13 Inscribed on the arches outside the city of Philippi was a prohibition against bringing an unrecognised religion into the city; therefore, this prayer meeting was held outside the city, beside the river.

16:13, 14 After following the Holy Spirit's leading into Macedonia, Paul made his first evangelistic contact with a small group of women. Paul never allowed gender or cultural boundaries to keep him from preaching the gospel. He preached to these women, and Lydia, an influential merchant, believed. This opened the way for ministry in that region. God often worked in and through women in the early church.

16:14 Lydia was a dealer in purple cloth, so she was probably wealthy. Purple cloth was valuable and expensive. It was often worn as a sign of nobility or royalty.

16:14ff Luke highlights the stories of three individuals who became believers through Paul's ministry in Philippi: Lydia, the influential businesswoman (16:14), the demon-possessed slave girl (16:16–18), and the jailer (16:27–30). The gospel was affecting all strata of society, just as it does today.

16:15 Why was Lydia's household baptised after Lydia responded in faith to the gospel? Baptism was a public sign of identification with Christ and the Christian community. Although not all members of her household may have chosen to follow Christ (we don't know), it was now a Christian home.

16:16 This girl's fortune-telling ability came from evil spirits. Fortune-telling was a common practice in Greek and Roman culture. There were many superstitious methods by which people thought they could foretell future events, from interpreting omens in nature to communicating with the spirits of the dead. This young slave girl had an evil spirit, and she made her master rich by interpreting signs and telling people their fortunes. The master was exploiting her unfortunate condition for personal gain.

PAUL TRAVELS TO MACEDONIA At Troas, Paul received the Macedonian call (16:9), and he, Silas, Timothy, and Luke boarded a ship. They sailed to the island of Samothrace, then on to Neapolis, the port for the city of Philippi. Philippi sat on the Egnatian Way, a main transportation artery connecting the eastern provinces with Italy.

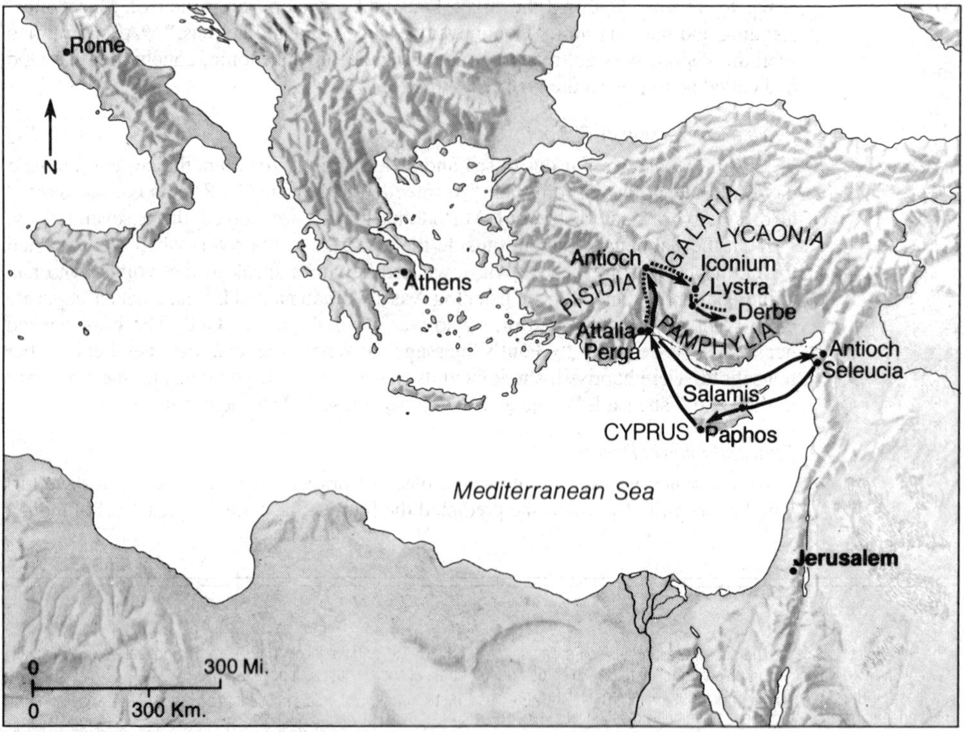

PAUL'S FIRST MISSIONARY JOURNEY (ACTS 13:1—14:28)

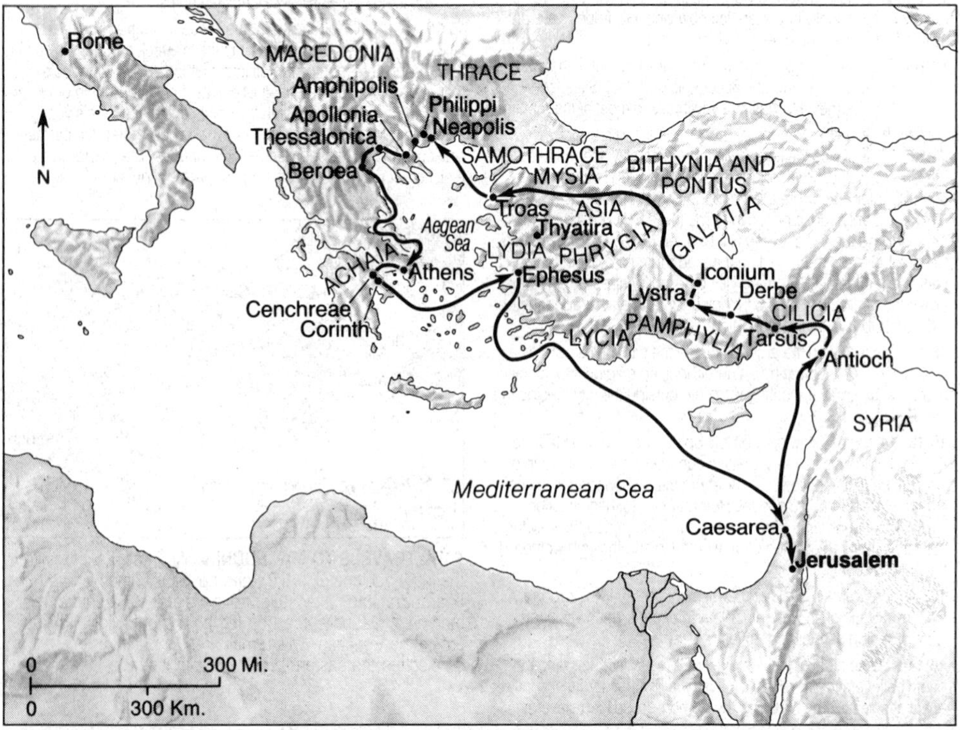

PAUL'S SECOND MISSIONARY JOURNEY (ACTS 15:36—18:22)

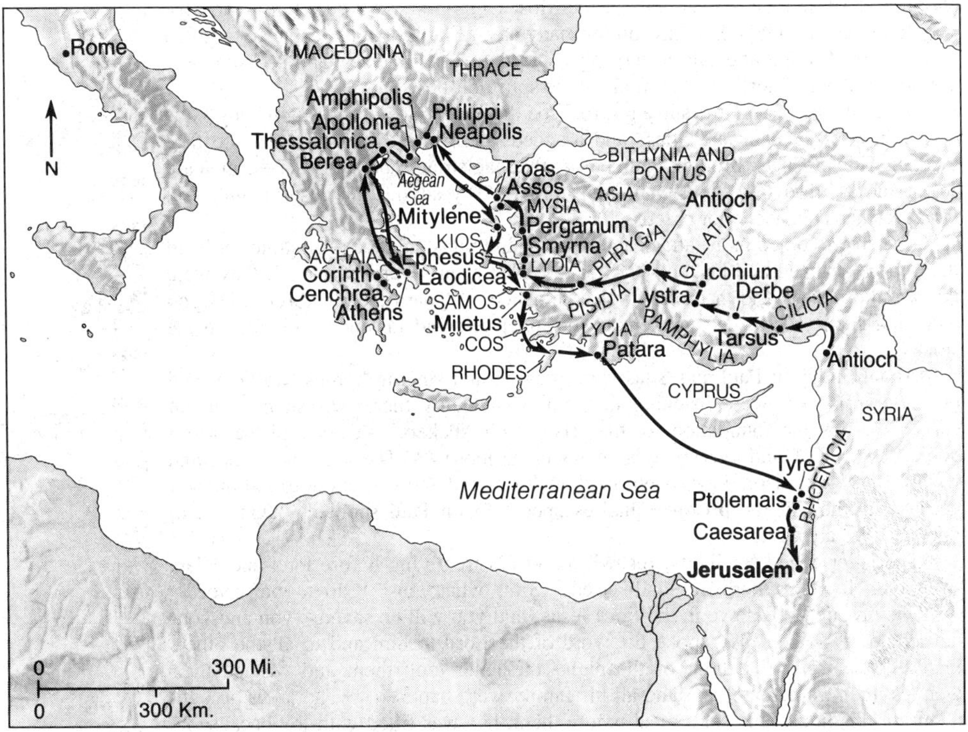

PAUL'S THIRD MISSIONARY JOURNEY (ACTS 18:23—21:16)

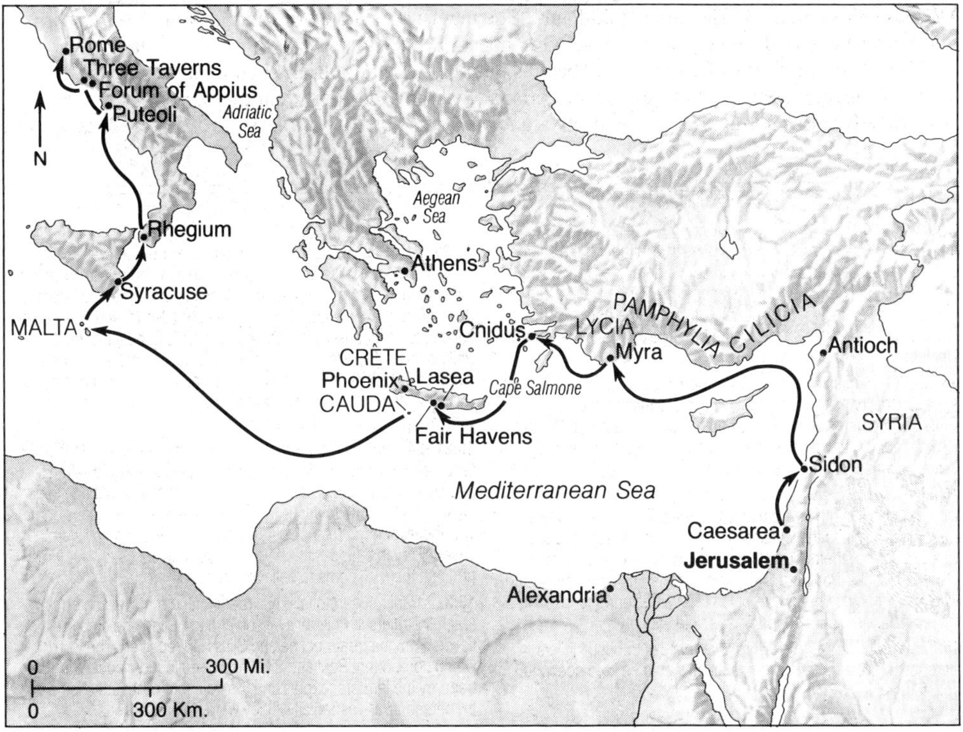

PAUL'S JOURNEY TO ROME (ACTS 21:17—28:31)

for her owners by fortune-telling. 17 This girl followed Paul and the rest of us,
shouting, "These men are servants of the Most High God,[b] who are telling you the
way to be saved." 18 She kept this up for many days. Finally Paul became so troubled
that he turned round and said to the spirit, "In the name of Jesus Christ I command
you to come out of her!" At that moment the spirit left her.[c]
19 When the owners of the slave girl realised that their hope of making money[d] was
gone, they seized Paul and Silas[e] and dragged[f] them into the market-place to face
the authorities. 20 They brought them before the magistrates and said, "These men are
Jews, and are throwing our city into an uproar[g] 21 by advocating customs unlawful
for us Romans[h] to accept or practise."[i]
22 The crowd joined in the attack against Paul and Silas, and the magistrates ordered
them to be stripped and beaten.[j] 23 After they had been severely flogged, they were
thrown into prison, and the jailer[k] was commanded to guard them carefully. 24 Upon
receiving such orders, he put them in the inner cell and fastened their feet in the
stocks.[l]
25 About midnight Paul and Silas were praying and singing hymns[m] to God, and
the other prisoners were listening to them. 26 Suddenly there was such a violent
earthquake that the foundations of the prison were shaken.[n] At once all the prison
doors flew open,[o] and everybody's chains came loose.[p] 27 The jailer woke up, and
when he saw the prison doors open, he drew his sword and was about to kill himself
because he thought the prisoners had escaped.[q] 28 But Paul shouted, "Don't harm
yourself! We are all here!"
29 The jailer called for lights, rushed in and fell trembling before Paul and Silas.
30 He then brought them out and asked, "Sirs, what must I do to be saved?"[r]
31 They replied, "Believe in the Lord Jesus, and you will be saved—you and your
household."[s] 32 Then they spoke the word of the Lord to him and to all the others
in his house. 33 At that hour of the night[t] the jailer took them and washed their
wounds; then immediately he and all his family were baptised. 34 The jailer brought
them into his house and set a meal before them; he[u] was filled with joy because he
had come to believe in God—he and his whole family.
35 When it was daylight, the magistrates sent their officers to the jailer with the order:
"Release those men." 36 The jailer[v] told Paul, "The magistrates have ordered that you
and Silas be released. Now you can leave. Go in peace."[w]
37 But Paul said to the officers: "They beat us publicly without a trial, even though
we are Roman citizens,[x] and threw us into prison. And now do they want to get rid
of us quietly? No! Let them come themselves and escort us out."

16:17 [b] Mk 5:7
16:18 [c] Mk 16:17
16:19 [d] ver 16; Ac 19:25, 26 [e] Ac 15:22 [f] Ac 8:3; 17:6; 21:30; Jas 2:6
16:20 [g] Ac 17:6
16:21 [h] ver 12 [i] Est 3:8
16:22 [j] 2Co 11:25; 1Th 2:2
16:23 [k] ver 27, 36
16:24 [l] Job 13:27; 33:11; Jer 20:2, 3; 29:26
16:25 [m] Eph 5:19
16:26 [n] Ac 4:31 [o] Ac 12:10 [p] Ac 12:7
16:27 [q] Ac 12:19
16:30 [r] Ac 2:37
16:31 [s] Ac 11:14
16:33 [t] ver 25
16:34 [u] Ac 11:14
16:36 [v] ver 23, 27 [w] Ac 15:33
16:37 [x] Ac 22:25-29

16:17, 18 What the slave girl said was true, although the source of her knowledge was a demon. Why did a demon announce the truth about Paul, and why did this annoy Paul? If Paul accepted the demon's words, he would appear to be linking the gospel with demon-related activities. This would damage his message about Christ. Truth and evil do not mix.

16:22–25 Paul and Silas were stripped, beaten, and placed in stocks in the inner cell. Despite this dismal situation, they praised God, praying and singing as the other prisoners listened. No matter what our circumstances, we should praise God. Others may come to Christ because of our example.

16:24 Stocks were made of two boards joined with iron clamps, leaving holes just big enough for the ankles. The prisoner's legs were placed across the lower board, and then the upper board was closed over them. Sometimes both wrists and ankles were placed in stocks. Paul and Silas, who had committed no crime and who were peaceful men, were put in stocks designed for holding the most dangerous prisoners in absolute security.

16:27 The jailer drew his sword to kill himself because jailers were responsible for their prisoners and would be held accountable for their escape.

16:30, 31 Paul and Silas' reputation in Philippi was well known. When the jailer realised his own true condition and need, he risked everything to find the answer. The Christian Good News of salvation is simply expressed: Believe in the Lord Jesus, and you will be saved (see Romans 10:9; 1 Corinthians 12:3; Ephesians 2:8, 9; Philippians 2:11). When we recognise Jesus as Lord and trust in him with our entire life, salvation is assured to us. If you have never trusted in Jesus to save you, do so quickly. Your life can be filled with joy, just as the jailer's was (16:34).

16:31–34 Paul and Silas took the family unit seriously. So the offer of salvation was made to the jailer's entire household—family and servants. Yet it was not the jailer's faith that saved them; they all needed to come to Jesus in faith and believe in him in the same way the jailer had. Yet his entire family did believe and all were saved. Pray that God will use you to introduce Jesus to your family and that they will come to believe in him.

16:37 Paul refused to take his freedom and run. He wanted to teach the rulers in Philippi a lesson and to protect the other believers from the treatment he and Silas had received. The word would spread that Paul and Silas had been found innocent and freed by the leaders, expressing the truth that believers should not be persecuted—especially if they were Roman citizens.

16:38
[y]Ac 22:29
16:39
[z]Mt 8:34
16:40
[a]ver 14
[b]ver 2;
Ac 1:16

38 The officers reported this to the magistrates, and when they heard that Paul and
Silas were Roman citizens, they were alarmed.[y] 39 They came to appease them and
escorted them from the prison, requesting them to leave the city.[z] 40 After Paul
and Silas came out of the prison, they went to Lydia's house,[a] where they met with
the brothers[b] and encouraged them. Then they left.

SILAS

The lives of the first Christian missionaries can be described with many words, but "boring" is not one of them. There were days of great excitement as men and women who had never heard of Jesus responded to the gospel. There were dangerous journeys over land and sea. Health risks and hunger were part of the daily routine. And there was open and hostile resistance to Christianity in many cities. Silas was one of the first missionaries, and he found out that serving Jesus Christ was certainly not boring!

Silas' name appears in Acts at the end of the first church council on the Jewish/Gentile problem. The majority of early Christians were Jews who realised that Jesus was the fulfilment of God's Old Testament promises to his people; however, the universal application of those promises had been overlooked. Thus, many felt that becoming Jewish was a prerequisite to becoming a Christian. The idea that God could accept a Gentile pagan was too incredible. But Gentiles began to accept Christ as Saviour, and the transformation of their lives and the presence of God's Spirit confirmed their conversions. Some Jews were still reluctant though, and insisted these new Christians take on various Jewish customs. The issue came to a boiling point at the Jerusalem meeting, but was peacefully resolved. Silas was one of the representatives from Jerusalem sent with Paul and Barnabas back to Antioch with an official letter of welcome and acceptance to the Gentile Christians. Having fulfilled this mission, Silas returned to Jerusalem. Within a short time, however, he was back in Antioch at Paul's request to join him on his second missionary journey.

Paul, Silas, and Timothy began a far-ranging ministry that included some exciting adventures. Paul and Silas spent a night singing in a Philippian jail after being severely beaten. An earthquake, the loosing of their chains, and the resulting panic led to the conversion of their jailer. Later, they narrowly missed another beating in Thessalonica, prevented by an evening escape. In Berea there was more trouble, but Silas and Timothy stayed to teach the young believers while Paul travelled on to Athens. The team was finally reunited in Corinth. In each place they visited, they left behind a small group of Christians.

Silas leaves the story as suddenly as he entered it. Peter mentions him as the co-author of 1 Peter, but we do not know when he joined Peter. He was an effective believer before leaving Jerusalem, and he doubtless continued to minister after his work with Paul was completed. He took advantage of opportunities to serve God and was not discouraged by the setbacks and opposition he met along the way. Silas, though not the most famous of the early missionaries, was certainly a hero worth imitating.

Strengths and accomplishments:
- A leader in the Jerusalem church
- Represented the church in carrying the "acceptance letter" prepared by the Jerusalem council to the Gentile believers in Antioch
- Was closely associated with Paul from the second missionary journey onwards
- When in jail with Paul in Philippi, sang songs of praise to God
- Worked as a writing secretary for both Paul and Peter

Lessons from his life:
- Partnership is a significant part of effective ministry
- God never guarantees that his servants will not suffer
- Obedience to God will often mean giving up what makes us feel secure

Vital statistics:
- Where: Roman citizen living in Jerusalem
- Occupation: One of the first career missionaries
- Contemporaries: Paul, Timothy, Peter, Mark, Barnabas

Key verses:
"So we all agreed to choose some men and send them to you with our dear friends Barnabas and Paul—men who have risked their lives for the name of our Lord Jesus Christ. Therefore we are sending Judas and Silas to confirm by word of mouth what we are writing" (Acts 15:25–27).

Silas' story is told in Acts 15:22—19:10. He is also mentioned in 2 Corinthians 1:19; 1 Thessalonians 1:1; 2 Thessalonians 1:1; 1 Peter 5:12.

16:38 Roman citizenship carried with it certain privileges. These Philippian authorities were alarmed because it was illegal to whip a Roman citizen. In addition, every citizen had the right to a fair trial—which Paul and Silas had not been given.

In Thessalonica

17 When they had passed through Amphipolis and Apollonia, they came to Thessalonica,[a] where there was a Jewish synagogue. 2As his custom was, Paul
went into the synagogue,[b] and on three Sabbath[c] days he reasoned with them from
the Scriptures,[d] 3explaining and proving that the Christ**[a]** had to suffer[e] and rise from
the dead.[f] "This Jesus I am proclaiming to you is the Christ,"**[a]**[g] he said. 4Some
of the Jews were persuaded and joined Paul and Silas,[h] as did a large number of
God-fearing Greeks and not a few prominent women.
5But the Jews were jealous; so they rounded up some bad characters from the
market-place, formed a mob and started a riot in the city.[i] They rushed to Jason's[j]
house in search of Paul and Silas in order to bring them out to the crowd.**[b]** 6But when
they did not find them, they dragged[k] Jason and some other brothers before the city
officials, shouting: "These men who have caused trouble all over the world[l] have
now come here,[m] 7and Jason has welcomed them into his house. They are all defying
Caesar's decrees, saying that there is another king, one called Jesus."[n] 8When they
heard this, the crowd and the city officials were thrown into turmoil. 9Then they put
Jason[o] and the others on bail and let them go.

In Berea

10As soon as it was night, the brothers sent Paul and Silas away to Berea.[p] On
arriving there, they went to the Jewish synagogue. 11Now the Bereans were of more

a 3 Or *Messiah* **b** 5 Or *the assembly of the people*

17:1 [a]ver 11, 13; Php 4:16; 1Th 1:1; 2Th 1:1; 2Ti 4:10
17:2 [b]Ac 9:20 [c]Ac 13:14 [d]Ac 8:35
17:3 [e]Lk 24:26; Ac 3:18 [f]Lk 24:46 [g]Ac 9:22; 18:28
17:4 [h]Ac 15:22
17:5 [i]ver 13; 1Th 2:16 [j]Ro 16:21
17:6 [k]Ac 16:19 [l]Mt 24:14 [m]Ac 16:20
17:7 [n]Lk 23:2; Jn 19:12
17:9 [o]ver 5
17:10 [p]ver 13; Ac 20:4

17:1 Thessalonica was one of the wealthiest and most influential cities in Macedonia. This is the first city Paul visited where his teachings attracted a large group of socially prominent citizens. The church he planted grew quickly, but in A.D. 50–51, Paul was forced out of the city by a mob (17:5, 6, 10). Paul later sent Timothy back to Thessalonica to see how the Christians were doing. Soon afterwards, Paul wrote two letters to the Thessalonian believers (1 and 2 Thessalonians), encouraging them to remain faithful and to refuse to listen to false teachers who tried to refute their beliefs.

17:1, 2 A synagogue, a group of Jews who gathered for teaching and prayer, could be established wherever there were ten Jewish males. Paul's regular practice was to preach in synagogues as long as the Jews allowed it. Often those who weren't Jews would come to these services and hear Paul's preaching. For a description of a synagogue service, see the note on 13:14, 15.

17:2, 3 When Paul spoke in the synagogues, he wisely began by talking about Old Testament writings and explaining how the Messiah fulfilled them, moving from the known to the unknown. This is a good strategy for us. When we witness for Christ, we should begin where people are, affirming the truth they do know, and then we can present Christ, the One who is truth.

17:5 The Jewish leaders didn't refute the theology of Paul and Silas, but they were jealous of the popularity of these itinerant preachers. Their motives for causing the riot were rooted in personal jealousy, not doctrinal purity.

17:6 We don't know much about Jason except that he evidently was the local host and sponsor of Paul and Silas; thus he took the heat for all the problems. Jason is just one of many "unsung heroes" who faithfully played their part to help spread the gospel. Because of Jason's courage, Paul and Silas were able to minister more effectively. You may not receive much attention (in fact you may receive only grief) for your service for Christ. But God wants to use you. Lives will be changed because of your courage and faithfulness.

17:6 What a reputation these early Christians had! The power of the gospel revolutionised lives, broke down all social barriers, threw open prison doors, caused people to care deeply for one another, and stirred them to worship God. Our world needs to be turned upside down, to be transformed. The gospel is not in the business of merely improving church schemes and encouraging good conduct, but of dynamically transforming lives. Take courage and ask God how you can help spread his Good News all over *your* world.

MINISTRY IN MACEDONIA
Luke stayed in Philippi while Paul, Silas, and Timothy continued on the Egnatian Way to Amphipolis, Apollonia, and Thessalonica. But trouble arose in Thessalonica, and they fled to Berea. When their enemies from Thessalonica pursued them, Paul set out by sea to Athens, leaving Silas and Timothy to encourage the believers.

17:7 The Jewish leaders had difficulty manufacturing an accusation that would be heard by the city government. The Romans did not care about theological disagreements between the Jews and these preachers. Treason, however, was a serious offence in the Roman empire. Although Paul and Silas were not advocating rebellion against Roman law, their loyalty to another king sounded suspicious.

17:8, 9 Jason put up money to buy their freedom. By doing so, he promised that the trouble would cease or his own property and possibly his own life would be taken.

17:11 How do you evaluate sermons and teachings? The people in Berea opened the Scriptures for themselves and searched for truths to verify or disprove the message they heard. Always compare what you hear with what the Bible says. A preacher or teacher

17:11 [q]ver 1 [r]Lk 16:29; Jn 5:39
17:14 [s]Ac 15:22 [t]Ac 16:1
17:15 [u]ver 16, 21, 22; Ac 18:1; 1Th 3:1 [v]Ac 18:5
17:17 [w]Ac 9:20
17:18 [x]ver 31, 32; Ac 4:2
17:19 [y]ver 22 [z]Mk 1:27

noble character than the Thessalonians,[q] for they received the message with great
eagerness and examined the Scriptures[r] every day to see if what Paul said was true.
12 Many of the Jews believed, as did also a number of prominent Greek women and
many Greek men.
13 When the Jews in Thessalonica learned that Paul was preaching the word of God
at Berea, they went there too, agitating the crowds and stirring them up. 14 The brothers
immediately sent Paul to the coast, but Silas[s] and Timothy[t] stayed at Berea. 15 The
men who escorted Paul brought him to Athens[u] and then left with instructions for
Silas and Timothy to join him as soon as possible.[v]

In Athens

16 While Paul was waiting for them in Athens, he was greatly distressed to see that
the city was full of idols. 17 So he reasoned in the synagogue[w] with the Jews and the
God-fearing Greeks, as well as in the market-place day by day with those who
happened to be there. 18 A group of Epicurean and Stoic philosophers began to dispute
with him. Some of them asked, "What is this babbler trying to say?" Others remarked,
"He seems to be advocating foreign gods." They said this because Paul was preaching
the good news about Jesus and the resurrection.[x] 19 Then they took him and brought
him to a meeting of the Areopagus,[y] where they said to him, "May we know what
this new teaching[z] is that you are presenting? 20 You are bringing some strange ideas
to our ears, and we want to know what they mean." 21 (All the Athenians and the
foreigners who lived there spent their time doing nothing but talking about and
listening to the latest ideas.)
22 Paul then stood up in the meeting of the Areopagus and said: "Men of Athens!

THE BOOKS OF THE NEW TESTAMENT: WHEN WERE THEY WRITTEN?

Book	Approximate Date	Book	Approximate Date
Galatians	49	Jude	65
James	49	1 Timothy	64
1, 2 Thessalonians	51/52	1 Peter	64/65
1, 2 Corinthians	55	Titus	64
Romans	57	Acts	66/68
Mark	58/60	2 Peter	66/68
Ephesians	60	2 Timothy	66/67
Colossians	60	Hebrews	68/70
Philemon	60	John	85
Philippians	61	1, 2, 3 John	85/90
Matthew	61/64	Revelation	95
Luke	61/64		

who gives God's true message will never contradict or explain away anything that is found in God's word.

17:15 Athens, with its magnificent buildings and many gods, was a centre for Greek culture, philosophy, and education. Philosophers and educated men were always ready to hear something new, so they invited Paul to speak to them at the meeting of the Areopagus (17:18, 19).

17:18 The Epicureans and Stoics were the dominant philosophers in Greek culture. The Epicureans believed that seeking happiness or pleasure was the primary goal of life. By contrast, the Stoics placed thinking above feeling and tried to live in harmony with nature and reason, suppressing their desire for pleasure. Thus they were very disciplined.

17:19 For a time the Council or Court (here called the Areopagus) met on a low hill in Athens near the Acropolis. As Paul stood there and spoke about the one true God, his audience could look down on the city and see the many idols representing gods that Paul knew were worthless.

17:22 Paul was well prepared to speak to this group. He came from Tarsus, an educational centre, and had the training and knowledge to present his beliefs clearly and persuasively. Paul was a rabbi, taught by the finest scholar of his day, Gamaliel, and he had spent much of his life thinking and reasoning through the Scriptures.

It is not enough to teach or preach with conviction. Like Paul, we must be prepared. The more we know about the Bible, what it means, and how to apply it to our lives, the more convincing our words will be. This does not mean that we should avoid presenting the gospel until we feel adequately prepared. We should work with what we know, but always want to know more in order to reach more people and answer their questions and arguments more effectively.

17:22ff Paul's address is a good example of how to communicate the gospel. Paul did not begin by reciting Jewish history, as he usually did, for this would have been meaningless to his Greek audience. He began by building a case for the one true God, using examples they understood (17:22, 23). Then he established common ground by emphasising what they agreed on about God (17:24–29). Finally he moved his message to the person of Christ, centring on the resurrection (17:30, 31). When you witness to others, you can use Paul's approach: use examples, establish common ground, and then move people towards a decision about Jesus Christ.

I see that in every way you are very religious. 23For as I walked around and looked
carefully at your objects of worship, I even found an altar with this inscription: TO
AN UNKNOWN GOD. Now what you worship as something unknown[a] I am going to
proclaim to you.
24"The God who made the world and everything in it[b] is the Lord of heaven and
earth[c] and does not live in temples built by hands.[d] 25And he is not served by human
hands, as if he needed anything, because he himself gives all men life and breath and
everything else.[e] 26From one man he made every nation of men, that they should
inhabit the whole earth; and he determined the times set for them and the exact places
where they should live.[f] 27God did this so that men would seek him and perhaps reach
out for him and find him, though he is not far from each one of us.[g] 28'For in him
we live and move and have our being.'[h] As some of your own poets have said, 'We
are his offspring.'
29"Therefore since we are God's offspring, we should not think that the divine being
is like gold or silver or stone—an image made by man's design and skill.[i] 30In the
past God overlooked[j] such ignorance,[k] but now he commands all people everywhere
to repent.[l] 31For he has set a day when he will judge[m] the world with justice[n] by
the man he has appointed.[o] He has given proof of this to all men by raising him from
the dead."[p]
32When they heard about the resurrection of the dead,[q] some of them sneered, but
others said, "We want to hear you again on this subject." 33At that, Paul left the
Council. 34A few men became followers of Paul and believed. Among them was
Dionysius, a member of the Areopagus,[r] also a woman named Damaris, and a
number of others.

In Corinth

18 After this, Paul left Athens[a] and went to Corinth.[b] 2There he met a Jew named
Aquila, a native of Pontus, who had recently come from Italy with his wife
Priscilla,[c] because Claudius[d] had ordered all the Jews to leave Rome. Paul went to
see them, 3and because he was a tentmaker as they were, he stayed and worked with
them.[e] 4Every Sabbath[f] he reasoned in the synagogue, trying to persuade Jews and
Greeks.
5When Silas[g] and Timothy[h] came from Macedonia,[i] Paul devoted himself
exclusively to preaching, testifying to the Jews that Jesus was the Christ.[a][j] 6But

a 5 Or *Messiah*; also in verse 28

17:23 [a]Jn 4:22
17:24 [b]Isa 42:5; Ac 14:15 [c]Dt 10:14 [d]Ac 7:48
17:25 [e]Isa 42:5
17:26 [f]Dt 32:8
17:27 [g]Dt 4:7
17:28 [h]Job 12:10; Da 5:23
17:29 [i]Isa 40:18-20; Ro 1:23
17:30 [j]Ac 14:16; Ro 3:25 [k]ver 23; 1Pe 1:14 [l]Lk 24:47; Tit 2:11, 12
17:31 [m]Mt 10:15 [n]Ps 9:8; 96:13; 98:9 [o]Ac 10:42 [p]Ac 2:24
17:32 [q]ver 18, 31
17:34 [r]ver 19, 22
18:1 [a]Ac 17:15 [b]Ac 19:1; 1Co 1:2; 2Co 1:1, 23; 2Ti 4:20
18:2 [c]Ro 16:3; 1Co 16:19; 2Ti 4:19 [d]Ac 11:28
18:3 [e]Ac 20:34; 1Co 4:12; 1Th 2:9; 2Th 3:8
18:4 [f]Ac 13:14
18:5 [g]Ac 15:22 [h]Ac 16:1 [i]Ac 16:9; 17:14, 15 [j]Ac 17:3

17:23 The Athenians had built an idol to the unknown god for fear of missing blessings or receiving punishment. Paul's opening statement to the men of Athens was about their unknown god. Paul was not endorsing this god, but using the inscription as a point of entry for his witness to the one true God.

17:23 Paul explained the one true God to these educated men of Athens; although these men were, in general, very religious, they did not know God. Today we have a "Christian" society, but to most people, God is still unknown. We need to proclaim who he is and make it clear what he did for all mankind through his Son Jesus Christ. We cannot assume that even religious people around us truly know Jesus or understand the importance of faith in him.

17:27, 28 God is known in his creation, and he is close to every one of us. But he is not trapped in his creation—he is transcendent. God is the Creator, not the creation. This means that God is sovereign and in control, while at the same time he is close and personal. Let the Creator of the universe rule your life.

17:30, 31 Paul did not leave his message unfinished. He confronted his listeners with Jesus' resurrection and its meaning to all people—either blessing or punishment. The Greeks had no concept of judgment. Most of them preferred worshipping many gods instead of just one, and the concept of resurrection was unbelievable and offensive to them. Paul did not hold back the truth, however, no matter what they might think of it. Paul often changed his approach to fit his audience, but he never changed his basic message.

17:32–34 Paul's speech received a mixed reaction: some sneered, some kept searching for more information, and a few believed. Don't hesitate to tell others about Christ because you fear that some will not believe you. Don't expect a unanimously positive response to your witnessing. Even if only a few believe, it's worth the effort.

18:1 Corinth was the political and commercial centre of Greece, surpassing Athens in importance. It had a reputation for great wickedness and immorality. A temple to Aphrodite—goddess of love and war—had been built on the large hill behind the city. In this popular religion, people worshipped the goddess by giving money to the temple and taking part in sexual acts with male and female temple prostitutes. Paul found Corinth a challenge and a great ministry opportunity. Later, he would write a series of letters to the Corinthians dealing in part with the problems of immorality. First and Second Corinthians are two of those letters.

18:2, 3 Each Jewish boy learned a trade and tried to earn his living with it. Paul and Aquila had been trained in tentmaking, cutting and sewing the woven cloth of goats' hair into tents. Tents were used to house soldiers, and so these tents may have been sold to the Roman army. As a tentmaker, Paul was able to go wherever God led him, carrying his livelihood with him. The word "tentmaker" in Greek was also used to describe a leather worker.

18:6
[k]Ac 13:45
[l]2Sa 1:16;
Eze 18:13; 33:4
[m]Ac 20:26
[n]Ac 13:46
18:7
[o]Ac 16:14
18:8
[p]1Co 1:14
[q]Mk 5:22
[r]Ac 11:14
18:10
[s]Mt 28:20

when the Jews opposed Paul and became abusive,[k] he shook out his clothes in protest
and said to them, "Your blood be on your own heads![l] I am clear of my responsibility.[m] From now on I will go to the Gentiles."[n]
7Then Paul left the synagogue and went next door to the house of Titius Justus,
a worshipper of God.[o] 8Crispus,[p] the synagogue ruler,[q] and his entire household[r]
believed in the Lord; and many of the Corinthians who heard him believed and were
baptised.
9One night the Lord spoke to Paul in a vision: "Do not be afraid; keep on speaking,
do not be silent. 10For I am with you,[s] and no-one is going to attack and harm you,

LUKE

One of the essential qualities of a good doctor is compassion. People need to know that their doctor cares. Even if he or she doesn't know what is wrong or isn't sure what to do, real concern is always a doctor's good medicine. Doctor Luke was a person of compassion.

Although we know few facts about his life, Luke has left us a strong impression of himself by what he wrote. In his Gospel, he emphasises Jesus Christ's compassion. He vividly recorded both the power demonstrated by Christ's life and the care with which Christ treated people. Luke highlighted the relationships Jesus had with women. His writing in Acts is full of sharp verbal pictures of real people caught up in the greatest events of history.

Luke was also a doctor. He had a travelling medical practice as Paul's companion. Since the gospel was often welcomed with whips and stones, the doctor was undoubtedly seldom without patients. It is even possible that Paul's "thorn in the flesh" was some kind of physical ailment that needed Luke's regular attention. Paul deeply appreciated Luke's skills and faithfulness.

God also made special use of Luke as the historian of the early church. Repeatedly, the details of Luke's descriptions have been proved accurate. The first words in his Gospel indicate his interest in the truth.

Luke's compassion reflected his Lord's. Luke's skill as a doctor helped Paul. His passion for the facts as he recorded the life of Christ, the spread of the early church, and the lives of Christianity's missionaries gives us dependable sources for the basis of our faith. He accomplished all this while staying out of the spotlight. Perhaps his greatest example is the challenge to greatness even when we are not the centre of attention.

Strengths and accomplishments:
- A humble, faithful, and useful companion of Paul
- A well-educated and trained physician
- A careful and exact historian
- Writer of both the Gospel of Luke and the book of Acts

Lessons from his life:
- The words we leave behind will be a lasting picture of who we are
- Even the most successful person needs the personal care of others
- Excellence is shown by how we work when no-one is noticing

Vital statistics:
- Where: Probably met Paul in Troas
- Occupations: Doctor, historian, travelling companion
- Contemporaries: Paul, Timothy, Silas, Peter

Key verses:
"Many have undertaken to draw up an account of the things that have been fulfilled among us, just as they were handed down to us by those who from the first were eye-witnesses and servants of the word. Therefore, since I myself have carefully investigated everything from the beginning, it seemed good also to me to write an orderly account for you, most excellent Theophilus, so that you may know the certainty of the things you have been taught" (Luke 1:1–4).

Luke includes himself in the *we* sections of Acts 16—28. He is also mentioned in Luke 1:3; Acts 1:1; Colossians 4:14; 2 Timothy 4:11; Philemon 24.

18:6 Paul told the Jews he had done all he could for them. Because they rejected Jesus as their Messiah, he would go to the Gentiles, who would be more receptive.

18:10 In a vision, Christ told Paul that he had many people in Corinth. Sometimes we can feel alone or isolated, especially when we see wickedness all around us and when we are persecuted for our faith. Usually, however, there are others in the neighbourhood or community who also follow Christ. Ask God to lead you to them.

18:10, 11 Others who became Christians in Corinth were Phoebe (Romans 16:1—Cenchrea was the port city of Corinth), Tertius (Romans 16:22), Erastus (Romans 16:23), Quartus (Romans 16:23), Chloe (1 Corinthians 1:11), Gaius (1 Corinthians 1:14), Stephanas and his household (1 Corinthians 16:15), Fortunatus (1 Corinthians 16:17), and Achaicus (1 Corinthians 16:17).

because I have many people in this city." 11So Paul stayed for a year and a half,
teaching them the word of God.
12While Gallio was proconsul of Achaia,[t] the Jews made a united attack on Paul
and brought him into court. 13"This man," they charged, "is persuading the people
to worship God in ways contrary to the law."
14Just as Paul was about to speak, Gallio said to the Jews, "If you Jews were making
a complaint about some misdemeanour or serious crime, it would be reasonable for
me to listen to you. 15But since it involves questions about words and names and your
own law[u]—settle the matter yourselves. I will not be a judge of such things." 16So
he had them ejected from the court. 17Then they all turned on Sosthenes[v] the
synagogue ruler and beat him in front of the court. But Gallio showed no concern
whatever.

Priscilla, Aquila and Apollos

18Paul stayed on in Corinth for some time. Then he left the brothers[w] and sailed
for Syria, accompanied by Priscilla and Aquila. Before he sailed, he had his hair cut
off at Cenchrea[x] because of a vow he had taken.[y] 19They arrived at Ephesus,[z] where
Paul left Priscilla and Aquila. He himself went into the synagogue and reasoned with
the Jews. 20When they asked him to spend more time with them, he declined. 21But
as he left, he promised, "I will come back if it is God's will."[a] Then he set sail from
Ephesus. 22When he landed at Caesarea,[b] he went up and greeted the church and then
went down to Antioch.[c]

4. Third missionary journey

23After spending some time in Antioch, Paul set out from there and travelled from
place to place throughout the region of Galatia[d] and Phrygia, strengthening all the
disciples.[e]
24Meanwhile a Jew named Apollos,[f] a native of Alexandria, came to Ephesus. He
was a learned man, with a thorough knowledge of the Scriptures. 25He had been
instructed in the way of the Lord, and he spoke with great fervour[b][g] and taught about
Jesus accurately, though he knew only the baptism of John.[h] 26He began to speak
boldly in the synagogue. When Priscilla and Aquila heard him, they invited him to
their home and explained to him the way of God more adequately.

b 25 Or *with fervour in the Spirit*

18:12 [t]ver 27
18:15 [u]Ac 23:29; 25:11, 19
18:17 [v]1Co 1:1
18:18 [w]Ac 1:16 [x]Ro 16:1 [y]Nu 6:2, 5, 18; Ac 21:24
18:19 [z]ver 21, 24; 1Co 15:32
18:21 [a]Ro 1:10; 1Co 4:19; Jas 4:15
18:22 [b]Ac 8:40 [c]Ac 11:19
18:23 [d]Ac 16:6 [e]Ac 14:22; 15:32, 41
18:24 [f]Ac 19:1; 1Co 1:12; 3:5, 6, 22; 4:6; 16:12; Tit 3:13
18:25 [g]Ro 12:11 [h]Ac 19:3

18:11 During the year and a half that Paul stayed in wicked Corinth, he established a church and wrote two letters to the believers in Thessalonica (the books of 1 and 2 Thessalonians). Although Paul had been in Thessalonica for only a short time (17:1–15), he commended the believers there for their loving deeds, strong faith, and endurance inspired by hope. While encouraging them to stay away from immorality, he dealt with the themes of salvation, suffering, and the second coming of Jesus Christ. Paul told them to continue to work hard while they awaited Christ's return.

18:12 Gallio was proconsul of Achaia (modern Greece) and the brother of Seneca the philosopher. He came to power in A.D. 51–52.

18:13 Paul was charged with promoting a religion not approved by Roman law. This charge amounted to treason. Paul was not encouraging obedience to a human king other than Caesar (see 17:7), nor was he speaking against the Roman empire. Instead he was speaking about Christ's eternal kingdom.

18:14–16 This was an important judicial decision for the spread of the gospel in the Roman empire. Judaism was a recognised religion under Roman law. As long as Christians were seen as part of Judaism, the court refused to hear cases brought against them. If they had claimed to be a new religion, they could easily have been outlawed by the government. In effect Gallio was saying, "I don't understand all your terminology and finer points of theology. Handle the matter yourself and don't bother me."

18:17 Crispus had been the ruler of the synagogue, but he and his family were converted and joined the Christians (18:8). Sosthenes was chosen to take his place. The mob could have been Greeks venting their feelings against the Jews for causing turmoil, or the crowd may have included some Jews. In any case, they beat Sosthenes for losing the case and leaving the synagogue worse off than before. A person named Sosthenes is mentioned in 1 Corinthians 1:1, and many believe this was the same man who, in time, became a convert and a companion of Paul.

18:18 This vow Paul took was probably a temporary Nazirite vow that ended with shaving of the head and offering the hair as a sacrifice (Numbers 6:18).

18:22 This verse marks the end of Paul's second missionary journey and the beginning of the third, which lasted from A.D. 53–57. Leaving the church at Antioch (his home base), Paul headed towards Ephesus, but along the way he revisited the churches in Galatia and Phrygia (18:23). The heart of this trip was a lengthy stay (two to three years) in Ephesus. Before returning to Jerusalem, he also visited believers in Macedonia and Greece.

18:24–26 Apollos had heard only what John the Baptist had said about Jesus (see Luke 3:1–18), so his message was not the complete story. John focused on repentance from sin, the first step. But the whole message is to repent from sin and then believe in Christ. Apollos did not know about Jesus' life, crucifixion, and resurrection. Nor did he know about the coming of the Holy Spirit. Priscilla and Aquila explained the way of salvation to him.

18:27
[i]ver 12
[j]ver 18

27When Apollos wanted to go to Achaia,[i] the brothers[j] encouraged him and wrote
to the disciples there to welcome him. On arriving, he was a great help to those who
by grace had believed. 28For he vigorously refuted the Jews in public debate, proving
from the Scriptures[k] that Jesus was the Christ.[l]

18:28
[k]Ac 17:2
[l]ver 5;
Ac 9:22

Paul in Ephesus

19 While Apollos was at Corinth,[a] Paul took the road through the interior and
arrived at Ephesus.[b] There he found some disciples 2and asked them, "Did you
receive the Holy Spirit when[a] you believed?"

They answered, "No, we have not even heard that there is a Holy Spirit."

3So Paul asked, "Then what baptism did you receive?"

"John's baptism," they replied.

19:1
[a]Ac 18:1
[b]Ac 18:19

a 2 Or *after*

MINISTRY IN CORINTH AND EPHESUS
Paul left Athens and travelled on to Corinth, one of the greatest commercial centres of the empire, located on a narrow neck of land offering direct passage between the Aegean and Adriatic seas. When Paul left from the port of Corinth at Cenchrea, he visited Ephesus. He then travelled to Caesarea, from where he went on to Jerusalem to report on his trip before returning to Antioch.

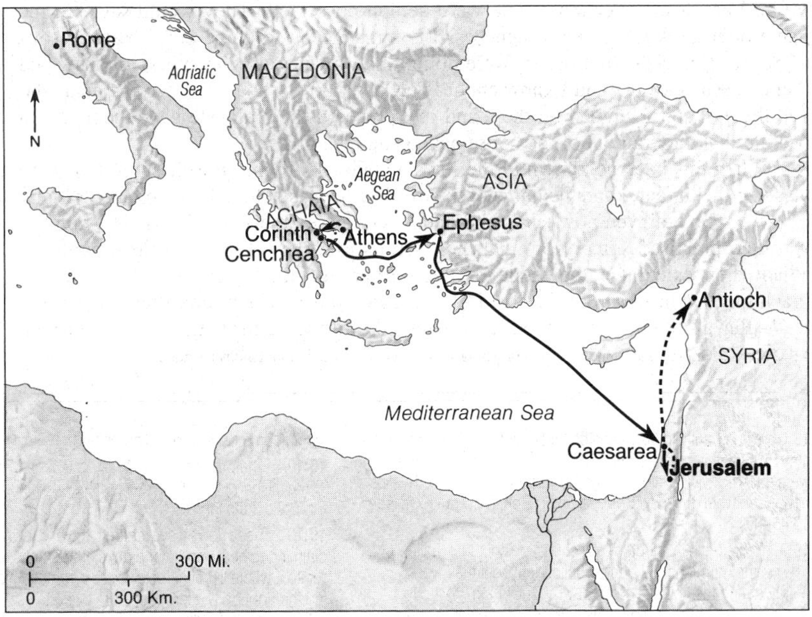

18:27, 28 Apollos was from Alexandria in Egypt, the second most important city in the Roman empire, and the home of a great university. There was a thriving Jewish population in Alexandria. Apollos was a scholar, orator, and debater; and after his knowledge about Christ was made more complete, God greatly used these gifts to strengthen and encourage the church. Reason is a powerful tool in the right hands and in the right situation. Apollos used the gift of reason to convince many in Greece of the truth of the gospel. You don't have to turn off your mind when you turn to Christ. If you have an ability in logic or debate, use it to bring others to God.

18:27, 28 Not all the work of a minister or missionary is drudgery, setback, or suffering. Chapter 18 is triumphant, showing victories in key cities and the addition of exciting new leaders such as Priscilla, Aquila, and Apollos to the church. Rejoice in the victories Christ brings, and don't let the hazards create a negative mindset.

19:1 Ephesus was the capital and leading business centre of the Roman province of Asia (part of present-day Turkey). A hub of sea and land transportation, it ranked with Antioch in Syria and Alexandria in Egypt as one of the great cities on the Mediterranean Sea. Paul stayed in Ephesus for a little over two years. There he wrote his first letter to the Corinthians to counter several problems the church in Corinth was facing. Later, while imprisoned in Rome, Paul wrote a letter to the Ephesian church (the book of Ephesians).

19:2–4 John's baptism was a sign of repentance from sin only, not a sign of new life in Christ. Like Apollos (18:24–26), these Ephesian believers needed further instruction on the message and ministry of Jesus Christ. They believed in Jesus as the Messiah, but they did not understand the significance of his death and resurrection or the work of the Holy Spirit. Becoming a Christian involves turning from sin (repentance) and turning to Christ (faith). These "believers" were incomplete.

In the book of Acts, believers received the Holy Spirit in a variety of ways. Usually the Holy Spirit would fill a person as soon as he or she professed faith in Christ. Here that filling happened later because these disciples' knowledge was incomplete. God was confirming to these believers, who did not initially know about the Holy Spirit, that they were a part of the church. The Holy Spirit's filling endorsed them as believers.

Pentecost was the formal outpouring of the Holy Spirit on the church. The other outpourings in the book of Acts were God's way of uniting new believers to the church. The mark of the true church is not merely right doctrine, but right actions, the true evidence of the Holy Spirit's work.

4Paul said, "John's baptism was a baptism of repentance. He told the people to
believe in the one coming after him, that is, in Jesus."[c] 5On hearing this, they were
baptised into[b] the name of the Lord Jesus. 6When Paul placed his hands on them,[d]
the Holy Spirit came on them,[e] and they spoke in tongues[c][f] and prophesied. 7There
were about twelve men in all.
8Paul entered the synagogue[g] and spoke boldly there for three months, arguing
persuasively about the kingdom of God.[h] 9But some of them[i] became obstinate; they
refused to believe and publicly maligned the Way.[j] So Paul left them. He took the
disciples[k] with him and had discussions daily in the lecture hall of Tyrannus. 10This
went on for two years,[l] so that all the Jews and Greeks who lived in the province
of Asia[m] heard the word of the Lord.
11God did extraordinary miracles[n] through Paul, 12so that even handkerchiefs and
aprons that had touched him were taken to the sick, and their illnesses were cured[o]
and the evil spirits left them.
13Some Jews who went around driving out evil spirits[p] tried to invoke the name
of the Lord Jesus over those who were demon-possessed. They would say, "In the
name of Jesus,[q] whom Paul preaches, I command you to come out." 14Seven sons
of Sceva, a Jewish chief priest, were doing this. 15 ⌞One day⌟ the evil spirit answered
them, "Jesus I know, and I know about Paul, but who are you?" 16Then the man who
had the evil spirit jumped on them and overpowered them all. He gave them such a
beating that they ran out of the house naked and bleeding.
17When this became known to the Jews and Greeks living in Ephesus,[r] they were
all seized with fear,[s] and the name of the Lord Jesus was held in high honour. 18Many
of those who believed now came and openly confessed their evil deeds. 19A number
who had practised sorcery brought their scrolls together and burned them publicly.
When they calculated the value of the scrolls, the total came to fifty thousand
drachmas.[d] 20In this way the word of the Lord spread widely and grew in power.[t]
21After all this had happened, Paul decided to go to Jerusalem,[u] passing through

[b] 5 Or *in* [c] 6 Or *other languages* [d] 19 A drachma was a silver coin worth about a day's wages.

19:4 [c]Jn 1:7; Ac 13:24, 25
19:6 [d]Ac 6:6; 8:17 [e]Ac 2:4 [f]Mk 16:17; Ac 10:46
19:8 [g]Ac 9:20 [h]Ac 1:3; 28:23
19:9 [i]Ac 14:4 [j]ver 23; Ac 9:2 [k]ver 30; Ac 11:26
19:10 [l]Ac 20:31 [m]ver 22, 26, 27
19:11 [n]Ac 8:13
19:12 [o]Ac 5:15
19:13 [p]Mt 12:27 [q]Mk 9:38
19:17 [r]Ac 18:19 [s]Ac 5:5, 11
19:20 [t]Ac 6:7; 12:24
19:21 [u]Ac 20:16, 22; Ro 15:25

19:6 When Paul laid his hands on these disciples, they received the Holy Spirit, just as the disciples did at Pentecost, and there were outward, visible signs of the Holy Spirit's presence. This also happened when the Holy Spirit came on Gentiles (non-Jews, see 10:45–47).

19:9 Paul spoke in a lecture hall at this school. Such halls were used in the morning for teaching philosophy, but they were empty during the hot part of the day (about 11 a.m. to 4 p.m.). Because many people did not work during those hours, they would come to hear Paul's preaching.

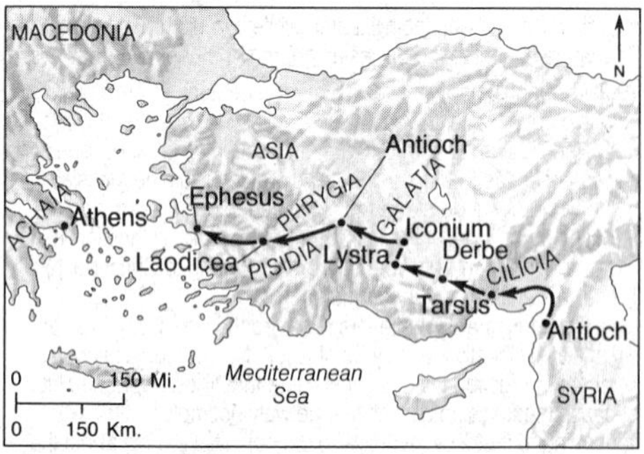

PAUL MAKES A THIRD JOURNEY What prompted Paul's third journey may have been the need to correct any misunderstandings in the churches Paul had planted. So he hurried north, then west, returning to many of the cities he had previously visited. This time, however, he stayed on a more direct westward route towards Ephesus.

19:10 "The province of Asia" refers to Asia Minor or modern-day Turkey. During this time, Paul and his co-workers spread the gospel throughout the land.

19:13 These Jews travelled from town to town making a living by claiming to heal people and drive out demons. Often they would recite a whole list of names in their incantation to be sure of including the right deity. Here they were trying to use Jesus' name in an effort to match Paul's power.

19:13–16 Many Ephesians engaged in exorcism and occult practices for profit (see 19:18, 19). The sons of Sceva were impressed by Paul's work, whose power to drive out demons came from God's Holy Spirit, not from witchcraft, and was obviously more powerful than theirs. They discovered, however, that no-one can control or duplicate God's power. These men were calling on the name of Jesus without knowing the person. The power to change people comes from Christ. It cannot be tapped by reciting his name like a magic charm. God works his power only through those he chooses.

19:18, 19 Ephesus was a centre for black magic and other occult practices. The people made up magical formulas to give them wealth, happiness, and success in marriage. Superstition and sorcery were commonplace. God clearly forbids such practices (Deuteronomy 18:9–13). You cannot be a believer and hold on to the occult, black magic, or sorcery. Once you begin to dabble in these areas, it is extremely easy to become obsessed by them because Satan is very powerful. But God's power is even greater (1 John 4:4; Revelation 20:10). If you are mixed up in the occult, learn a lesson from the Ephesians and get rid of anything that could keep you trapped in such practices.

19:21 Why did Paul say he had to go to Rome? Wherever he went, he could see Rome's influence. Paul wanted to take the mes-

19:21
[v]Ac 16:9
[w]Ac 18:12
[x]Ro 15:24, 28
19:22
[y]Ac 13:5
[z]Ac 16:1
[a]Ro 16:23;
2Ti 4:20
[b]ver 10, 26, 27
19:23
[c]Ac 9:2

Macedonia[v] and Achaia.[w] "After I have been there," he said, "I must visit Rome
also."[x] 22He sent two of his helpers,[y] Timothy[z] and Erastus,[a] to Macedonia, while
he stayed in the province of Asia[b] a little longer.

The Riot in Ephesus

23About that time there arose a great disturbance about the Way.[c] 24A silversmith
named Demetrius, who made silver shrines of Artemis, brought in no little business
for the craftsmen. 25He called them together, along with the workmen in related

AQUILA, PRISCILLA

Some couples know how to make the most of life. They complement each other, capitalise on each other's strengths, and form an effective team. Their united efforts affect those around them. Aquila and Priscilla were such a couple. They are never mentioned separately in the Bible. In marriage and ministry, they were together.

Priscilla and Aquila met Paul in Corinth during his second missionary journey. They had just been expelled from Rome by Emperor Claudius' decree against Jews. Their home was as movable as the tents they made to support themselves. They opened their home to Paul, and he joined them in tentmaking. He shared with them his wealth of spiritual wisdom.

Priscilla and Aquila made the most of their spiritual education. They listened carefully to sermons and evaluated what they heard. When they heard Apollos speak, they were impressed by his ability, but realised that his information was not complete. Instead of open confrontation, the couple quietly took Apollos home and shared with him what he needed to know. Until then, Apollos had only John the Baptist's message about Christ. Priscilla and Aquila told him about Jesus' life, death, and resurrection, and the reality of God's indwelling Spirit. He continued to preach powerfully—but now with the full story.

As for Priscilla and Aquila, they went on using their home as a warm place for training and worship. Back in Rome years later, they hosted one of the house churches that developed.

In an age when the focus is mostly on what happens *between* husband and wife, Aquila and Priscilla are an example of what can happen *through* husband and wife. Their effectiveness together speaks about their relationship with each other. Their hospitality opened the doorway of salvation to many. The Christian home is still one of the best tools for spreading the gospel. Do guests find Christ in your home?

Strengths and accomplishments:
- Outstanding husband/wife team who ministered in the early church
- Supported themselves by tentmaking while serving Christ
- Close friends of Paul
- Explained to Apollos the full message of Christ

Lessons from their lives:
- Couples can have an effective ministry together
- The home is a valuable tool for evangelism
- Every believer needs to be well educated in the faith, whatever his or her role in the church

Vital statistics:
- Where: Originally from Rome, moved to Corinth, then Ephesus
- Occupation: Tentmakers
- Contemporaries: Emperor Claudius, Paul, Timothy, Apollos

Key verses:
"Greet Priscilla and Aquila, my fellow-workers in Christ Jesus. They risked their lives for me. Not only I but all the churches of the Gentiles are grateful to them" (Romans 16:3, 4).

Their story is told in Acts 18. They are also mentioned in Romans 16:3–5; 1 Corinthians 16:19; 2 Timothy 4:19.

sage of Christ to the world's centre of influence and power.

19:22 Paul mentions Timothy in more detail in the books of 1 and 2 Timothy. Erastus was a committed follower of Christ who was not only Paul's helpful assistant, but also Corinth's director of public works (see Romans 16:23).

19:23 "The Way" refers to those who followed the way of Christ—the Christians.

19:24 Artemis was a goddess of fertility. She was represented by a carved female figure with many breasts. A large statue of her (which was said to have come from heaven, 19:35) was in the great temple at Ephesus. That temple was one of the wonders of the ancient world. The festival of Artemis involved wild orgies and carousing. Obviously the religious and commercial life of Ephesus reflected the city's worship of this pagan deity.

19:25–27 When Paul preached in Ephesus, Demetrius and his fellow craftsmen did not quarrel with his doctrine. Their anger boiled because his preaching threatened their profits. They made silver statues of the Ephesian goddess Artemis. The craftsmen knew that if people started believing in God and discarding the idols, their livelihood would suffer.

trades, and said: "Men, you know we receive a good income from this business.[d]
26 And you see and hear how this fellow Paul has convinced and led astray large
numbers of people here in Ephesus[e] and in practically the whole province of Asia.
He says that man-made gods are no gods at all.[f] 27 There is danger not only that our
trade will lose its good name, but also that the temple of the great goddess Artemis
will be discredited, and the goddess herself, who is worshipped throughout the
province of Asia and the world, will be robbed of her divine majesty."
28 When they heard this, they were furious and began shouting: "Great is Artemis
of the Ephesians!"[g] 29 Soon the whole city was in an uproar. The people seized
Gaius[h] and Aristarchus,[i] Paul's travelling companions from Macedonia,[j] and
rushed as one man into the theatre. 30 Paul wanted to appear before the crowd, but the
disciples would not let him. 31 Even some of the officials of the province, friends of
Paul, sent him a message begging him not to venture into the theatre.
32 The assembly was in confusion: Some were shouting one thing, some another.[k]
Most of the people did not even know why they were there. 33 The Jews pushed
Alexander to the front, and some of the crowd shouted instructions to him. He
motioned[l] for silence in order to make a defence before the people. 34 But when they
realised he was a Jew, they all shouted in unison for about two hours: "Great is Artemis
of the Ephesians!"
35 The city clerk quietened the crowd and said: "Men of Ephesus,[m] doesn't all the
world know that the city of Ephesus is the guardian of the temple of the great Artemis
and of her image, which fell from heaven? 36 Therefore, since these facts are undeni-
able, you ought to be quiet and not do anything rash. 37 You have brought these men
here, though they have neither robbed temples[n] nor blasphemed our goddess. 38 If,
then, Demetrius and his fellow craftsmen have a grievance against anybody, the courts
are open and there are proconsuls.[o] They can press charges. 39 If there is anything
further you want to bring up, it must be settled in a legal assembly. 40 As it is, we
are in danger of being charged with rioting because of today's events. In that case we
would not be able to account for this commotion, since there is no reason for it."
41 After he had said this, he dismissed the assembly.

Through Macedonia and Greece

20 When the uproar had ended, Paul sent for the disciples[a] and, after encouraging
them, said good-bye and set out for Macedonia.[b] 2 He travelled through that
area, speaking many words of encouragement to the people, and finally arrived in

19:25 [d] Ac 16:16, 19, 20

19:26 [e] Ac 18:19 [f] Dt 4:28; Ps 115:4; Isa 44:10-20; Jer 10:3-5; Ac 17:29; 1Co 8:4; Rev 9:20

19:28 [g] Ac 18:19

19:29 [h] Ac 20:4; Ro 16:23; 1Co 1:14 [i] Ac 20:4; 27:2; Col 4:10; Phm 24 [j] Ac 16:9

19:32 [k] Ac 21:34

19:33 [l] Ac 12:17

19:35 [m] Ac 18:19

19:37 [n] Ro 2:22

19:38 [o] Ac 13:7, 8, 12

20:1 [a] Ac 11:26 [b] Ac 16:9

19:27 Demetrius' strategy for stirring up a riot was to appeal to his fellow workmen's love of money and then to encourage them to hide their greed behind the mask of patriotism and religious loyalty. The rioters couldn't see the selfish motives for their rioting – instead they saw themselves as heroes for the sake of their land and beliefs.

19:29 Paul often sought others to help him in his work. On this occasion, his travelling companions were Aristarchus (who would accompany him on other journeys; see 20:3, 4 and 27:1, 2), and Gaius (probably not the same Gaius mentioned in Romans 16:23 or 1 Corinthians 1:14).

19:30 Paul wanted to go to the theatre to speak up and defend his companions, but the other believers wouldn't let him go, fearing for his safety.

19:31 These officials of the province were government officials, responsible for the religious and political order of the region. Paul's message had reached all levels of society, crossing all social barriers and giving Paul friends in high places.

19:33, 34 The mob had become anti-Jewish as well as anti-Christian. This Alexander may have been pushed forward by the Jews as a spokesman to explain that the Jews had no part in the Christian community, and thus were not involved in the economic problem of the silversmiths.

19:38 A proconsul served as a civil magistrate or governor of a Roman province.

19:40 The city of Ephesus was under the domination of the Roman empire. The main responsibility of the local city leaders was simply to maintain peace and order. If they failed to control the people, Rome would remove the appointed officials from office. The entire town could also be put under martial law, taking away many civic freedoms.

19:41 The riot in Ephesus convinced Paul that it was time to move on. But it also showed that the law still provided some protection for Christians as they challenged the worship of the goddess Artemis and the most idolatrous religion in Asia.

20:1–3 While in Greece, Paul spent much of his time in Corinth. From there he wrote the letter to the Romans. Although Paul had not yet been to Rome, believers had already started a church there (2:10; 18:2). Paul wrote to tell the church that he planned to visit the Roman believers. The letter to the Romans is a theological essay on the meaning of faith and salvation, an explanation of the relation between Jews and Gentiles in Christ, and a list of practical guidelines for the church.

20:3
[c]ver 19;
[d]Ac 16:9
20:4
[e]Ac 19:29
[f]Ac 17:1
[g]Ac 19:29
[h]Ac 16:1
[i]Eph 6:21;

Greece, 3where he stayed three months. Because the Jews made a plot against him[c]
just as he was about to sail for Syria, he decided to go back through Macedonia.[d]
4He was accompanied by Sopater son of Pyrrhus from Berea, Aristarchus[e] and
Secundus from Thessalonica,[f] Gaius[g] from Derbe, Timothy[h] also, and Tychicus[i]

APOLLOS

Some people have an amazing natural talent for public speaking. Some even have a great message to go with it. When Apollos arrived in Ephesus shortly after Paul's departure, he made an immediate impact. He spoke boldly in public, interpreting and applying the Old Testament Scriptures effectively. He debated with opponents of Christianity forcefully and effectively. It didn't take long for him to be noticed by Priscilla and Aquila.

The couple quickly realised that Apollos did not have the whole story. His preaching was based on the Old Testament and John the Baptist's message. He was probably urging people to repent and prepare for the coming Messiah. Priscilla and Aquila took him home with them and brought him up to date on all that had happened. As they told him of the life of Jesus, his death and resurrection, and the coming of the Holy Spirit, Apollos must have seen scripture after scripture become clear. He was filled with new energy and boldness now that he had the complete gospel.

Apollos next decided to travel to Achaia. His friends in Ephesus were able to send with him a glowing letter of introduction. He quickly became the verbal champion of the Christians in Corinth, debating with the opponents of the gospel in public. As often happens, Apollos' abilities eventually created a problem. Some of the Corinthians began to follow Apollos rather than his message. Paul had to confront the Corinthians about their divisiveness. They had been forming little groups named after their favourite preacher. Apollos left Corinth and hesitated to return. Paul wrote warmly of Apollos as a fellow minister who had "watered" the seeds of the gospel that Paul had planted in Corinth. Paul last mentions Apollos briefly to Titus. Apollos was still a travelling representative of the gospel who deserved Titus' help.

Although his natural abilities could have made him proud, Apollos proved himself willing to learn. God used Priscilla and Aquila, fresh from months of learning from Paul, to give Apollos the complete gospel. Because Apollos did not hesitate to be a student, he became an even better teacher. How much does your willingness to learn affect God's efforts to help you become all he wants you to be?

Strengths and accomplishments:
- A gifted and persuasive preacher and apologist in the early church
- Willing to be taught
- One of the possible candidates for the unknown author of Hebrews

Lessons from his life:
- Effective communication of the gospel includes an accurate message delivered with God's power
- A clear verbal defence of the gospel can be a real encouragement to believers, while convincing non-believers of its truth

Vital statistics:
- Where: From Alexandria in Egypt
- Occupations: Travelling preacher, apologist
- Contemporaries: Priscilla, Aquila, Paul

Key verses:
"He had been instructed in the way of the Lord, and he spoke with great fervour and taught about Jesus accurately, though he knew only the baptism of John. He began to speak boldly in the synagogue. When Priscilla and Aquila heard him, they invited him to their home and explained to him the way of God more adequately" (Acts 18:25, 26).

Apollos' story is told in Acts 18:24–28; 19:1. He is also mentioned in 1 Corinthians 1:12; 3:4–6, 22; 4:1, 6; 16:12; Titus 3:13.

20:4 These men who were travelling with Paul represented churches that Paul had started in Asia. Each man was carrying an offering from his home church to be given to the believers in Jerusalem. By having each man deliver the gift, the gifts had a personal touch, and the unity of the believers was strengthened. This was also an effective way to teach the church about giving, because the men were able to report back to their churches the way God was working through their giving. Paul discussed this gift in one of his letters to the Corinthian church (see 2 Corinthians 8:1–21).

and Trophimus[j] from the province of Asia. 5These men went on ahead and waited
for us[k] at Troas.[l] 6But we sailed from Philippi[m] after the Feast of Unleavened Bread, and five days later joined the others at Troas,[n] where we stayed seven
days.

Eutychus Raised From the Dead at Troas

7On the first day of the week[o] we came together to break bread. Paul spoke to the
people and, because he intended to leave the next day, kept on talking until midnight.
8There were many lamps in the upstairs room[p] where we were meeting. 9Seated in
a window was a young man named Eutychus, who was sinking into a deep sleep as
Paul talked on and on. When he was sound asleep, he fell to the ground from the third
storey and was picked up dead. 10Paul went down, threw himself on the young man[q]
and put his arms around him. "Don't be alarmed," he said. "He's alive!"[r] 11Then
he went upstairs again and broke bread[s] and ate. After talking until daylight, he left.
12The people took the young man home alive and were greatly comforted.

Paul's Farewell to the Ephesian Elders

13We went on ahead to the ship and sailed for Assos, where we were going to take
Paul aboard. He had made this arrangement because he was going there on foot.
14When he met us at Assos, we took him aboard and went on to Mitylene. 15The next
day we set sail from there and arrived off Kios. The day after that we crossed over
to Samos, and on the following day arrived at Miletus.[t] 16Paul had decided to sail

20:4 [j]Ac 21:29; 2Ti 4:20
20:5 [k]Ac 16:10 [l]Ac 16:8
20:6 [m]Ac 16:12 [n]Ac 16:8
20:7 [o]1Co 16:2; Rev 1:10
20:8 [p]Ac 1:13
20:10 [q]1Ki 17:21; 2Ki 4:34 [r]Mt 9:23, 24
20:11 [s]ver 7
20:15 [t]ver 17; 2Ti 4:20

THROUGH MACEDONIA AND ACHAIA
A riot in Ephesus sent Paul to Troas, then through Macedonia to the region of Achaia. In Achaia he went to Corinth to deal with problems there. Paul had planned to sail from there straight to Antioch in Syria, but a plot against his life was discovered. So he retraced his steps through Macedonia.

PAUL TRAVELS FROM TROAS TO MILETUS
From Troas, Paul travelled overland to Assos, then boarded a ship to Mitylene and Samos on its way to Miletus. He summoned the elders of the Ephesian church to say farewell to them, because he knew he would probably not see them again.

20:5, 6 The use of *us* and *we* shows that this is where Luke again joins the group. The last *we* was in chapter 16.

20:6 Jewish believers celebrated the Passover (which was immediately followed by the Feast of Unleavened Bread) according to Moses' instructions (see Exodus 12:43–51) even if they couldn't be at Jerusalem for the occasion.

20:8, 9 The "many lamps" were candles in lanterns. The combination of the heat from the candles and the gathered number of people in an upstairs room probably made the room very warm. This no doubt helped Eutychus fall asleep, as well as the fact that Paul spoke for a long time. Eutychus was probably somewhere in the range of 8–14 years old (the age of a "young man").

20:16 Paul had missed attending the Passover in Jerusalem, so he was especially interested in arriving on time for Pentecost, which was 50 days after Passover. He was carrying with him gifts for the Jerusalem believers from churches in Asia and Greece (see Romans 15:25, 26; 1 Corinthians 16:1ff; 2 Corinthians 8; 9). The Jerusalem church was experiencing difficult times. Paul may have been anxious to deliver this gift to the believers at Pentecost because it was a day of celebration and thanksgiving to God for his provision.

past Ephesus[u] to avoid spending time in the province of Asia, for he was in a hurry
to reach Jerusalem,[v] if possible, by the day of Pentecost.[w]
17 From Miletus, Paul sent to Ephesus for the elders[x] of the church. 18 When they
arrived, he said to them: "You know how I lived the whole time I was with you,[y]
from the first day I came into the province of Asia. 19 I served the Lord with great
humility and with tears, although I was severely tested by the plots of the Jews.[z]
20 You know that I have not hesitated to preach anything[a] that would be helpful to
you but have taught you publicly and from house to house. 21 I have declared to both
Jews[b] and Greeks that they must turn to God in repentance[c] and have faith in our
Lord Jesus.[d]
22 "And now, compelled by the Spirit, I am going to Jerusalem,[e] not knowing what
will happen to me there. 23 I only know that in every city the Holy Spirit warns me[f]
that prison and hardships are facing me.[g] 24 However, I consider my life worth
nothing to me,[h] if only I may finish the race and complete the task[i] the Lord Jesus
has given me[j]—the task of testifying to the gospel of God's grace.
25 "Now I know that none of you among whom I have gone about preaching the
kingdom will ever see me again.[k] 26 Therefore, I declare to you today that I am
innocent of the blood of all men.[l] 27 For I have not hesitated to proclaim to you the
whole will of God.[m] 28 Keep watch over yourselves and all the flock of which the Holy
Spirit has made you overseers.**a**[n] Be shepherds of the church of God,**b** which he
bought with his own blood. 29 I know that after I leave, savage wolves[o] will come
in among you and will not spare the flock.[p] 30 Even from your own number men will
arise and distort the truth in order to draw away disciples[q] after them. 31 So be on
your guard! Remember that for three years[r] I never stopped warning each of you night
and day with tears.[s]
32 "Now I commit you to God[t] and to the word of his grace, which can build you
up and give you an inheritance[u] among all those who are sanctified.[v] 33 I have not
coveted anyone's silver or gold or clothing.[w] 34 You yourselves know that these hands
of mine have supplied my own needs and the needs of my companions.[x] 35 In
everything I did, I showed you that by this kind of hard work we must help the weak,
remembering the words the Lord Jesus himself said: 'It is more blessed to give than
to receive.' "
36 When he had said this, he knelt down with all of them and prayed.[y] 37 They all

a *28* Traditionally *bishops* **b** *28* Many manuscripts *of the Lord*

20:16 [u] Ac 18:19 [v] Ac 19:21 [w] Ac 2:1; 1Co 16:8
20:17 [x] Ac 11:30
20:18 [y] Ac 18:19-21; 19:1-41
20:19 [z] ver 3
20:20 [a] ver 27
20:21 [b] Ac 18:5 [c] Ac 2:38 [d] Ac 24:24; 26:18;
20:22 [e] ver 16
20:23 [f] Ac 21:4 [g] Ac 9:16
20:24 [h] Ac 21:13 [i] 2Co 4:1 [j] Gal 1:1
20:25 [k] ver 38
20:26 [l] Ac 18:6
20:27 [m] ver 20
20:28 [n] 1Pe 5:2
20:29 [o] Mt 7:15 [p] ver 28
20:30 [q] Ac 11:26
20:31 [r] Ac 19:10 [s] ver 19
20:32 [t] Ac 14:23 [u] Eph 1:14; Col 1:12; 3:24; Heb 9:15; 1Pe 1:4 [v] Ac 26:18
20:33 [w] 1Sa 12:3
20:34 [x] Ac 18:3
20:36 [y] Ac 21:5

20:18–21 The way of the believer is not an easy road; being a Christian does not solve or remove all problems. Paul served humbly and "with tears", but he never quit, never gave up. The message of salvation was so important that he never missed an opportunity to share it. And although he preached his message in different ways to fit different audiences, the message remained the same—turning away from sin and turning to Christ by faith. The Christian life will have its rough times, its tears, and its sorrows, as well as its joys, but we should always be ready to tell others what good things God has done for us. His blessings far outweigh life's difficulties.

20:22 "Compelled by the Spirit" could be paraphrased, "drawn irresistibly by the Holy Spirit".

20:23 The Holy Spirit showed Paul that he would be imprisoned and experience suffering. Even knowing this, Paul did not shrink from fulfilling his mission. His strong character was a good example to the Ephesian elders, some of whom would also suffer for Christ.

20:24 We often feel that life is a failure unless we're getting a lot out of it: recognition, fun, money, success. But Paul considered life worth *nothing* unless he used it for God's work. What he put *into* life was far more important than what he got out. Which is more important to you—what you get out of life, or what you put into it?

20:24 Single-mindedness is a quality needed by anyone who wishes to do God's work. Paul was a single-minded person, and the most important goal of his life was to tell others about Christ (Philippians 3:7–13). It is no wonder that Paul was the greatest missionary who ever lived. God is looking for more men and women who focus on that one great task God has given them to do.

20:31, 36–38 Paul's relationship with these believers is a beautiful example of Christian fellowship. He had cared for them and loved them, even cried over their needs. They responded with love and care for him and sorrow over his leaving. They had prayed together and comforted one another. Like Paul, you can build strong relationships with other Christians by sharing, caring, grieving, rejoicing, and praying with them. You will gather others around you only by giving yourself away to them.

20:33 Paul was satisfied with whatever he had, wherever he was, as long as he could do God's work. Examine your attitudes towards wealth and comfort. If you focus more on what you don't have than on what you do have, it's time to re-examine your priorities and put God's work back in first place.

20:34 Paul was a tentmaker, and he supported himself with this trade. Paul worked not in order to become rich, but to be free from being dependent on anyone. He supported himself and others who travelled with him (he also mentions this in some of his letters; see Philippians 4:11–13; 1 Thessalonians 2:9).

20:35 These words of Jesus are not recorded in the Gospels. Obviously, not all of Jesus' words were written down (John 21:25); this saying may have been passed on orally through the apostles.

wept as they embraced him and kissed him.[z] 38 What grieved them most was his
statement that they would never see his face again.[a] Then they accompanied him to
the ship.

On to Jerusalem

21 After we[a] had torn ourselves away from them, we put out to sea and sailed
straight to Cos. The next day we went to Rhodes and from there to Patara. 2 We
found a ship crossing over to Phoenicia,[b] went on board and set sail. 3 After sighting
Cyprus and passing to the south of it, we sailed on to Syria. We landed at Tyre, where
our ship was to unload its cargo. 4 Finding the disciples[c] there, we stayed with them
seven days. Through the Spirit[d] they urged Paul not to go on to Jerusalem. 5 But when
our time was up, we left and continued on our way. All the disciples and their wives
and children accompanied us out of the city, and there on the beach we knelt to pray.[e]
6 After saying good-bye to each other, we went aboard the ship, and they returned
home.

7 We continued our voyage from Tyre[f] and landed at Ptolemais, where we greeted
the brothers[g] and stayed with them for a day. 8 Leaving the next day, we reached
Caesarea[h] and stayed at the house of Philip[i] the evangelist,[j] one of the Seven. 9 He
had four unmarried daughters who prophesied.[k]

10 After we had been there a number of days, a prophet named Agabus[l] came down
from Judea. 11 Coming over to us, he took Paul's belt, tied his own hands and feet
with it and said, "The Holy Spirit says, 'In this way the Jews of Jerusalem will bind[m]
the owner of this belt and will hand him over to the Gentiles.' "[n]

12 When we heard this, we and the people there pleaded with Paul not to go up to
Jerusalem. 13 Then Paul answered, "Why are you weeping and breaking my heart? I
am ready not only to be bound, but also to die[o] in Jerusalem for the name of the Lord
Jesus."[p] 14 When he would not be dissuaded, we gave up and said, "The Lord's will
be done."

15 After this, we got ready and went up to Jerusalem. 16 Some of the disciples from
Caesarea[q] accompanied us and brought us to the home of Mnason, where we were
to stay. He was a man from Cyprus[r] and one of the early disciples.

5. Paul on trial

Paul's Arrival at Jerusalem

17 When we arrived at Jerusalem, the brothers received us warmly.[s] 18 The next day
Paul and the rest of us went to see James,[t] and all the elders[u] were present. 19 Paul
greeted them and reported in detail what God had done among the Gentiles[v] through
his ministry.[w]

20 When they heard this, they praised God. Then they said to Paul: "You see,
brother, how many thousands of Jews have believed, and all of them are zealous[x]
for the law.[y] 21 They have been informed that you teach all the Jews who live among

20:37 [z] Lk 15:20
20:38 [a] ver 25
21:1 [a] Ac 16:10
21:2 [b] Ac 11:19
21:4 [c] Ac 11:26 [d] ver 11; Ac 20:23
21:5 [e] Ac 20:36
21:7 [f] Ac 12:20 [g] Ac 1:16
21:8 [h] Ac 8:40 [i] Ac 6:5; 8:5-40 [j] Eph 4:11; 2Ti 4:5
21:9 [k] Lk 2:36; Ac 2:17
21:10 [l] Ac 11:28
21:11 [m] ver 33 [n] 1Ki 22:11
21:13 [o] Ac 20:24 [p] Ac 9:16
21:16 [q] Ac 8:40 [r] ver 3, 4
21:17 [s] Ac 15:4
21:18 [t] Ac 15:13 [u] Ac 11:30
21:19 [v] Ac 14:27 [w] Ac 1:17
21:20 [x] Ac 22:3; Ro 10:2; Gal 1:14 [y] Ac 15:1, 5

21:4 Did Paul disobey the Holy Spirit by going to Jerusalem? No. More likely, the Holy Spirit warned these believers about the suffering that Paul would face in Jerusalem. They drew the conclusion that he should not go there because of that danger. This is supported by 21:10–12 where the local believers, after hearing that Paul would be turned over to the Romans, begged him to turn back.

21:8 This is the Philip mentioned in 6:5 and 8:26–40.

21:9 Obviously the gift of prophecy was given to both men and women. Women actively participated in God's work (2:17; Philippians 4:3). Other women who prophesied include Miriam (Exodus 15:20), Deborah (Judges 4:4), Huldah (2 Kings 22:14), Noadiah (Nehemiah 6:14), Isaiah's wife (Isaiah 8:3), and Anna (Luke 2:36–38).

21:10 Fifteen years earlier, Agabus had predicted the famine in Jerusalem (11:27–29).

21:13, 14 Paul knew he would be imprisoned in Jerusalem. Although his friends pleaded with him to not go there, he knew that he had to because God wanted him to. No-one enjoys pain, but a faithful disciple wants above all else to please God. Our desire to please God should overshadow our desire to avoid hardship and suffering. When we really want to do God's will, we must accept all that comes with it – even the pain. Then we can say with Paul, "The Lord's will be done."

21:18 James, Jesus' brother, was the leader of the Jerusalem church (15:13–21; Galatians 1:19; 2:9). He was called an apostle even though he wasn't one of the original 12 who followed Jesus.

21:21 The Jerusalem council (Acts 15) had settled the issue of circumcision of Gentile believers. Evidently there was a rumour that Paul had gone far beyond their decision, even forbidding Jews to circumcise their children. This, of course, was not true, and so Paul willingly submitted to Jewish custom to show that he was not working against the council's decision and that he was still Jewish in his lifestyle. Sometimes we must go the second mile to avoid offend-

the Gentiles to turn away from Moses,[z] telling them not to circumcise their children[a]
or live according to our customs.[b] 22What shall we do? They will certainly hear that
you have come, 23so do what we tell you. There are four men with us who have made
a vow.[c] 24Take these men, join in their purification rites[d] and pay their expenses,
so that they can have their heads shaved.[e] Then everybody will know there is no truth
in these reports about you, but that you yourself are living in obedience to the law.
25As for the Gentile believers, we have written to them our decision that they should
abstain from food sacrificed to idols, from blood, from the meat of strangled animals
and from sexual immorality."[f]
26The next day Paul took the men and purified himself along with them. Then he
went to the temple to give notice of the date when the days of purification would end
and the offering would be made for each of them.[g]

Paul Arrested

27When the seven days were nearly over, some Jews from the province of Asia saw
Paul at the temple. They stirred up the whole crowd and seized him,[h] 28shouting,

21:21 [z]ver 28 [a]Ac 15:19-21; 1Co 7:18, 19 [b]Ac 6:14

21:23 [c]Ac 18:18

21:24 [d]ver 26; Ac 24:18 [e]Ac 18:18

21:25 [f]Ac 15:20, 29

21:26 [g]Nu 6:13-20; Ac 24:18

21:27 [h]Ac 24:18; 26:21

PAUL RETURNS TO JERUSALEM The ship sailed from Miletus to Cos, Rhodes, and Patara. Paul and his companions then boarded a cargo ship bound for Phoenicia. They passed Cyprus and anchored at Tyre, then Ptolemais, and finally Caesarea, where Paul disembarked and returned by land to Jerusalem.

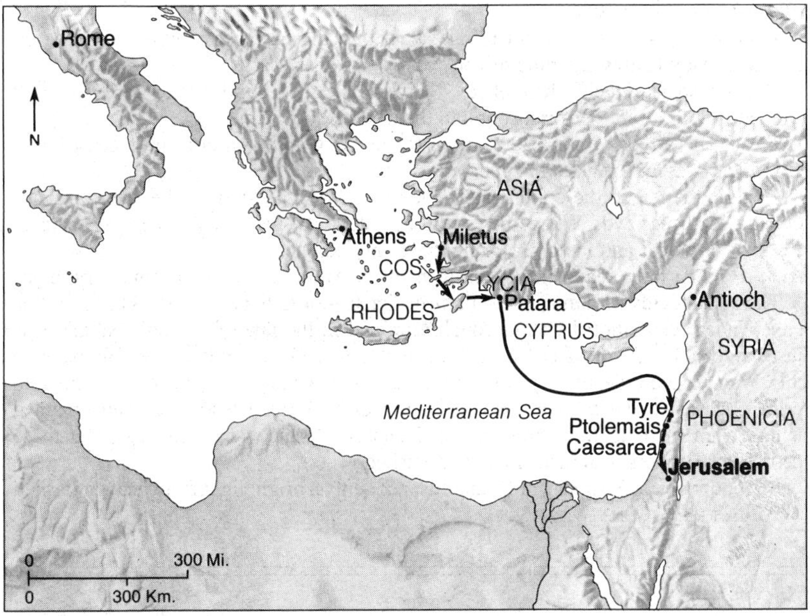

ing others, especially when doing so would hinder God's work.

21:23, 24 Evidently these four men had made a religious vow. Because Paul was going to participate with them in the vow (apparently he was asked to pay for some of the required expenses), he would need to take part in the purification ceremony for entering the temple (Numbers 6:9–20). Paul submitted himself to this Jewish custom to keep the peace in the Jerusalem church. Although Paul was a man of strong convictions, he was willing to compromise on non-essential points, becoming all things to all people so that he might save some (1 Corinthians 9:19–23). Often a church is split over disagreements about minor issues or traditions. Like Paul, we should remain firm on Christian essentials but flexible on non-essentials. Of course, no-one should violate his or her true convictions, but sometimes we need to exercise the gift of mutual submission for the sake of the gospel.

21:23, 24 There are two ways to think of the Jewish laws. Paul rejected one way and accepted the other. (1) Paul rejected the idea that the Old Testament laws bring salvation to those who keep them. Our salvation is freely given by God's gracious act. We receive salvation through faith. The laws are of no value for salvation except to show us our sin. (2) Paul accepted the view that the Old Testament laws prepare us for and teach us about the coming of Jesus Christ. Christ fulfilled the law and released us from its burden of guilt. But the law still teaches us many valuable principles and gives us guidelines for grateful living. Paul was not observing the laws in order to be saved. He was simply keeping the laws as custom to avoid offending those he wished to reach with the gospel (see Romans 3:21–31; 7:4–6; 13:9, 10). For more on the law, see Galatians 3:23–29; 4:21–31, and the chart in Galatians 4.

21:28, 29 These Jews knew how effective Paul's work had been in Asia. Their strategy was to discredit Paul so that his work would be weakened. Be alert when you hear accusations against God's workers. Someone may be trying to discredit them or to hinder their work. Keep an open mind and pray for the workers. They will be strengthened by your support.

"Men of Israel, help us! This is the man who teaches all men everywhere against our
people and our law and this place. And besides, he has brought Greeks into the temple
area and defiled this holy place."[i] 29(They had previously seen Trophimus[j] the
Ephesian[k] in the city with Paul and assumed that Paul had brought him into the temple
area.)
30The whole city was aroused, and the people came running from all directions.
Seizing Paul,[l] they dragged him[m] from the temple, and immediately the gates were
shut. 31While they were trying to kill him, news reached the commander of the Roman
troops that the whole city of Jerusalem was in an uproar. 32He at once took some
officers and soldiers and ran down to the crowd. When the rioters saw the commander
and his soldiers, they stopped beating Paul.[n]
33The commander came up and arrested him and ordered him to be bound[o] with
two[p] chains.[q] Then he asked who he was and what he had done. 34Some in the crowd
shouted one thing and some another,[r] and since the commander could not get at the
truth because of the uproar, he ordered that Paul be taken into the barracks.[s] 35When
Paul reached the steps,[t] the violence of the mob was so great he had to be carried
by the soldiers. 36The crowd that followed kept shouting, "Away with him!"[u]

Paul Speaks to the Crowd

37As the soldiers were about to take Paul into the barracks,[v] he asked the commander, "May I say something to you?"
"Do you speak Greek?" he replied. 38"Aren't you the Egyptian who started a revolt
and led four thousand terrorists out into the desert[w] some time ago?"[x]
39Paul answered, "I am a Jew, from Tarsus[y] in Cilicia,[z] a citizen of no ordinary
city. Please let me speak to the people."
40Having received the commander's permission, Paul stood on the steps and motioned[a] to the crowd. When they were all silent, he said to them in Aramaic[a]:[b]
22 1"Brothers and fathers,[a] listen now to my defence."
2When they heard him speak to them in Aramaic,[b] they became very quiet.
Then Paul said: 3"I am a Jew,[c] born in Tarsus[d] of Cilicia, but brought up in this
city. Under[e] Gamaliel[f] I was thoroughly trained in the law of our fathers[g] and was
just as zealous[h] for God as any of you are today. 4I persecuted[i] the followers of
this Way to their death, arresting both men and women and throwing them into
prison,[j] 5as also the high priest and all the Council[k] can testify. I even obtained
letters from them to their brothers[l] in Damascus,[m] and went there to bring these
people as prisoners to Jerusalem to be punished.
6"About noon as I came near Damascus, suddenly a bright light from heaven flashed

a *40* Or possibly *Hebrew*; also in 22:2

21:28 [i]Mt 24:15; Ac 24:5, 6
21:29 [j]Ac 20:4 [k]Ac 18:19
21:30 [l]Ac 26:21 [m]Ac 16:19
21:32 [n]Ac 23:27
21:33 [o]ver 11 [p]Ac 12:6 [q]Ac 20:23; Eph 6:20; 2Ti 2:9
21:34 [r]Ac 19:32 [s]ver 37; Ac 23:10, 16, 32
21:35 [t]ver 40
21:36 [u]Lk 23:18; Jn 19:15; Ac 22:22
21:37 [v]ver 34
21:38 [w]Mt 24:26 [x]Ac 5:36
21:39 [y]Ac 9:11 [z]Ac 22:3
21:40 [a]Ac 12:17 [b]Jn 5:2
22:1 [a]Ac 7:2
22:2 [b]Ac 21:40
22:3 [c]Ac 21:39 [d]Ac 9:11 [e]Lk 10:39 [f]Ac 5:34 [g]Ac 26:5 [h]Ac 21:20
22:4 [i]Ac 8:3 [j]ver 19, 20
22:5 [k]Lk 22:66 [l]Ac 13:26 [m]Ac 9:2

21:31 Because Jerusalem was under Roman control, an uproar in the city would be investigated by Roman authorities. The commander of the troops at this time was Claudius Lysias (23:26). This commander was head of a cohort (a special group, part of a legion) of Roman soldiers. He was the senior Roman official in Jerusalem.

21:37, 38 By speaking in Greek, Paul showed that he was a cultured, educated man and not just a common rebel starting riots in the streets. The language grabbed the commander's attention and gave Paul protection and the opportunity to give his defence.

21:37, 38 The historian Josephus wrote of an Egyptian who led a revolt of 4,000 people in Jerusalem in A.D. 54 and then disappeared. The commander assumed that Paul was this rebel.

21:40 – 22:2 Paul was probably speaking in Aramaic, the common language among Palestinian Jews. He used Aramaic not only to communicate in the language of his listeners, but also to show that he was a devout Jew and had respect for the Jewish laws and customs. Paul spoke Greek to the Roman officials and Aramaic to the Jews. To minister to people more effectively, use their language.

22:3 Gamaliel was the most honoured rabbi of the first century. He was well known and respected as an expert on religious law and as a voice for moderation (5:34). Paul was showing his credentials as a well-educated man trained under the most respected Jewish rabbi.

22:3 By saying that at one time he was as zealous for God as any of his listeners, Paul was acknowledging their sincere motives behind their desire to kill him and recognising that he would have done the same to Christian leaders a few years earlier. Paul always tried to establish a common point of contact with his audience before launching into a full-scale defence of Christianity. When you witness for Christ, first identify yourself with your audience. They are much more likely to listen if they feel a common bond with you.

22:6ff After gaining a hearing and establishing common ground with his audience, Paul gave his testimony. He shared how he had come to faith in Christ. Sound reasoning is good, but it is also important to share simply what Christ has done in our lives. But no matter how we present the message, not everyone will accept it, as Paul knew. We must faithfully and responsibly present the gospel, and leave the results to God.

around me.[n] 7I fell to the ground and heard a voice say to me, 'Saul! Saul! Why do
you persecute me?'
8" 'Who are you, Lord?' I asked.
" 'I am Jesus of Nazareth, whom you are persecuting,' he replied. 9My companions
saw the light,[o] but they did not understand the voice[p] of him who was speaking to
me.
10" 'What shall I do, Lord?' I asked.
" 'Get up,' the Lord said, 'and go into Damascus. There you will be told all that
you have been assigned to do.'[q] 11My companions led me by the hand into Damascus,
because the brilliance of the light had blinded me.[r]
12"A man named Ananias came to see me.[s] He was a devout observer of the law
and highly respected by all the Jews living there.[t] 13He stood beside me and said,
'Brother Saul, receive your sight!' And at that very moment I was able to see him.
14"Then he said: 'The God of our fathers[u] has chosen you to know his will and
to see[v] the Righteous One[w] and to hear words from his mouth. 15You will be his
witness[x] to all men of what you have seen and heard. 16And now what are you waiting
for? Get up, be baptised[y] and wash your sins away,[z] calling on his name.'[a]
17"When I returned to Jerusalem[b] and was praying at the temple, I fell into a
trance[c] 18and saw the Lord speaking. 'Quick!' he said to me. 'Leave Jerusalem
immediately, because they will not accept your testimony about me.'
19" 'Lord,' I replied, 'these men know that I went from one synagogue to another
to imprison[d] and beat[e] those who believe in you. 20And when the blood of your
martyr**a** Stephen was shed, I stood there giving my approval and guarding the clothes
of those who were killing him.'[f]
21"Then the Lord said to me, 'Go; I will send you far away to the Gentiles.' "[g]

Paul the Roman Citizen

22The crowd listened to Paul until he said this. Then they raised their voices and
shouted, "Rid the earth of him![h] He's not fit to live!"[i]
23As they were shouting and throwing off their cloaks[j] and flinging dust into the
air,[k] 24the commander ordered Paul to be taken into the barracks.[l] He directed[m]
that he be flogged and questioned in order to find out why the people were shouting
at him like this. 25As they stretched him out to flog him, Paul said to the centurion
standing there, "Is it legal for you to flog a Roman citizen who hasn't even been found
guilty?"[n]
26When the centurion heard this, he went to the commander and reported it. "What
are you going to do?" he asked. "This man is a Roman citizen."
27The commander went to Paul and asked, "Tell me, are you a Roman citizen?"
"Yes, I am," he answered.
28Then the commander said, "I had to pay a big price for my citizenship."
"But I was born a citizen," Paul replied.
29Those who were about to question him withdrew immediately. The commander
himself was alarmed when he realised that he had put Paul, a Roman citizen,[o] in
chains.

a *20* Or *witness*

22:6 [n]Ac 9:3
22:9 [o]Ac 26:13 [p]Ac 9:7
22:10 [q]Ac 16:30
22:11 [r]Ac 9:8
22:12 [s]Ac 9:17 [t]Ac 10:22
22:14 [u]Ac 3:13 [v]1Co 9:1; 15:8 [w]Ac 7:52
22:15 [x]Ac 23:11; 26:16
22:16 [y]Ac 2:38 [z]Heb 10:22 [a]Ro 10:13
22:17 [b]Ac 9:26 [c]Ac 10:10
22:19 [d]ver 4; Ac 8:3 [e]Mt 10:17
22:20 [f]Ac 7:57-60; 8:1
22:21 [g]Ac 9:15; 13:46
22:22 [h]Ac 21:36 [i]Ac 25:24
22:23 [j]Ac 7:58 [k]2Sa 16:13
22:24 [l]Ac 21:34 [m]ver 29
22:25 [n]Ac 16:37
22:29 [o]ver 24, 25; Ac 16:38

22:21, 22 These people listened intently to Paul, but the word *Gentile* brought out all their anger and exposed their pride. They were supposed to be a light to the Gentiles, telling them about the one true God. But they had renounced that mission by becoming separatist and exclusive. God's plan, however, would not be thwarted; the Gentiles were hearing the Good News through Jewish Christians such as Paul and Peter.

22:25–28 Paul's question stopped the centurion because, by law, a Roman citizen could not be punished until he had been proven guilty of a crime. Paul was born a Roman citizen, whereas the commander had purchased his citizenship. Buying citizenship was a common practice and a good source of income for the Roman government. Bought citizenship was considered inferior to citizenship by birth.

Before the Sanhedrin

30The next day, since the commander wanted to find out exactly why Paul was being
accused by the Jews,[p] he released him[q] and ordered the chief priests and all the
Sanhedrin[r] to assemble. Then he brought Paul and had him stand before them.
23 Paul looked straight at the Sanhedrin[a] and said, "My brothers,[b] I have
fulfilled my duty to God in all good conscience[c] to this day." 2At this the high
priest Ananias[d] ordered those standing near Paul to strike him on the mouth.[e] 3Then
Paul said to him, "God will strike you, you whitewashed wall![f] You sit there to judge
me according to the law, yet you yourself violate the law by commanding that I be
struck!"[g]
4Those who were standing near Paul said, "You dare to insult God's high priest?"
5Paul replied, "Brothers, I did not realise that he was the high priest; for it is written:
'Do not speak evil about the ruler of your people.'**[a]**"[h]
6Then Paul, knowing that some of them were Sadducees and the others Pharisees,
called out in the Sanhedrin, "My brothers,[i] I am a Pharisee,[j] the son of a Pharisee.
I stand on trial because of my hope in the resurrection of the dead."[k] 7When he said
this, a dispute broke out between the Pharisees and the Sadducees, and the assembly
was divided. 8(The Sadducees say that there is no resurrection,[l] and that there are
neither angels nor spirits, but the Pharisees acknowledge them all.)
9There was a great uproar, and some of the teachers of the law who were Pharisees[m]
stood up and argued vigorously. "We find nothing wrong with this man,"[n] they said.
"What if a spirit or an angel has spoken to him?"[o] 10The dispute became so violent
that the commander was afraid Paul would be torn to pieces by them. He ordered the
troops to go down and take him away from them by force and bring him into the
barracks.[p]
11The following night the Lord stood near Paul and said, "Take courage![q] As you
have testified about me in Jerusalem, so you must also testify in Rome."[r]

The Plot to Kill Paul

12The next morning the Jews formed a conspiracy and bound themselves with an
oath not to eat or drink until they had killed Paul.[s] 13More than forty men were
involved in this plot. 14They went to the chief priests and elders and said, "We have
taken a solemn oath not to eat anything until we have killed Paul.[t] 15Now then, you
and the Sanhedrin[u] petition the commander to bring him before you on the pretext
of wanting more accurate information about his case. We are ready to kill him before
he gets here."
16But when the son of Paul's sister heard of this plot, he went into the barracks[v]
and told Paul.

a *5* Exodus 22:28

22:30 [p]Ac 23:28 [q]Ac 21:33 [r]Mt 5:22
23:1 [a]Ac 22:30 [b]Ac 22:5 [c]Ac 24:16; 1Co 4:4; 2Co 1:12; 2Ti 1:3; Heb 13:18
23:2 [d]Ac 24:1 [e]Jn 18:22
23:3 [f]Mt 23:27 [g]Lev 19:15; Dt 25:1, 2; Jn 7:51
23:5 [h]Ex 22:28
23:6 [i]Ac 22:5 [j]Ac 26:5; Php 3:5 [k]Ac 24:15, 21; 26:8
23:8 [l]Mt 22:23
23:9 [m]Mk 2:16 [n]ver 29; Ac 25:25; 26:31 [o]Ac 22:7, 17, 18
23:10 [p]Ac 21:34
23:11 [q]Ac 18:9 [r]Ac 19:21; 28:23
23:12 [s]ver 14, 21, 30; Ac 25:3
23:14 [t]ver 12
23:15 [u]ver 1; Ac 22:30
23:16 [v]ver 10; Ac 21:34

22:30 Paul used his times of persecution as an opportunity to witness. Even his enemies were creating a platform for him to address the entire Sanhedrin (Jewish council). If we are sensitive to the Holy Spirit's leading, we will see increased opportunities to share our faith, even in the face of opposition.

23:2–5 Josephus, a respected first-century historian, described Ananias as profane, greedy, and hot-tempered. Paul's outburst came as a result of the illegal command that Ananias had given. Ananias had violated Jewish law by assuming that Paul was guilty without a trial and ordering his punishment (see Deuteronomy 19:15). Paul didn't recognise Ananias as the high priest, probably because Ananias' command broke the law he was pledged to represent. As Christians, we are to represent Christ. When those around us say, "I didn't know you were a Christian," we have failed to represent him as we should. We are not merely Christ's followers; we are his representatives to others.

23:6–8 The Sadducees and Pharisees were two groups of religious leaders, but with strikingly different beliefs. The Pharisees believed in a bodily resurrection, but the Sadducees did not. The Sadducees adhered only to Genesis through Deuteronomy, which contain no explicit teaching on resurrection. Paul's words moved the debate away from himself and towards their festering controversy about the resurrection. The Jewish council was split.

23:6–8 Paul's sudden insight that the council was a mixture of Sadducees and Pharisees is an example of the power that Jesus promised to believers (Mark 13:9–11). God will help us when we are under fire for our faith. Like Paul, we should always be ready to present our testimony. The Holy Spirit will give us power to speak boldly.

23:14, 15 When the Pharisee/Sadducee controversy died down, the religious leaders refocused their attention on Paul. To these leaders, politics and position had become more important than God. They were ready to plan another murder, just as they had done with Jesus. But as always, God was in control.

23:16 This is the only biblical reference to Paul's family. Some scholars believe that Paul's family had disowned Paul when he became a Christian. Paul wrote of having suffered the loss of everything for Christ (Philippians 3:8). Paul's nephew was able to see Paul, even though Paul was in protective custody, because Roman prisoners were accessible to their relatives and friends who could

23:18 [w]Eph 3:1

[17]Then Paul called one of the centurions and said, "Take this young man to the
commander; he has something to tell him." [18]So he took him to the commander.
The centurion said, "Paul, the prisoner,[w] sent for me and asked me to bring this
young man to you because he has something to tell you."

23:20 [x]ver 1 [y]ver 14, 15

[19]The commander took the young man by the hand, drew him aside and asked,
"What is it you want to tell me?"
[20]He said: "The Jews have agreed to ask you to bring Paul before the Sanhedrin[x]
tomorrow on the pretext of wanting more accurate information about him.[y] [21]Don't
give in to them, because more than forty[z] of them are waiting in ambush for him.
They have taken an oath not to eat or drink until they have killed him.[a] They are
ready now, waiting for your consent to their request."
[22]The commander dismissed the young man and cautioned him, "Don't tell anyone
that you have reported this to me."

23:21 [z]ver 13 [a]ver 12, 14

Paul Transferred to Caesarea

23:23 [b]Ac 8:40 [c]ver 33

[23]Then he called two of his centurions and ordered them, "Get ready a detachment
of two hundred soldiers, seventy horsemen and two hundred spearmen**b** to go to
Caesarea[b] at nine tonight.[c] [24]Provide mounts for Paul so that he may be taken safely
to Governor Felix."[d]
[25]He wrote a letter as follows:

23:24 [d]ver 26, 33; Ac 24:1-3, 10; 25:14

b *23* The meaning of the Greek for this word is uncertain.

UNSUNG HEROES IN ACTS
When we think of the success of the early church, we often think of the work of the apostles. But the church could have died if it hadn't been for the unsung heroes, the men and women who through some small but committed act moved the church forward.

Hero	*Reference*	*Heroic action*
Crippled man	3:9–12	After his healing, he praised God. With the crowds gathering to see what had happened, Peter used the opportunity to tell many about Jesus.
Five deacons	6:2–5	Everyone has heard of Stephen and many know of Philip, but there were five other men chosen to be deacons. They not only laid the foundation for service in the church, but their hard work also gave the apostles the time they needed to preach the gospel.
Ananias	9:10–19	He had the responsibility of being the first to demonstrate Christ's love to Saul (Paul) after his conversion.
Cornelius	10:30–35	His example showed Peter that the gospel was for *all* people, Jews and Gentiles.
Rhoda	12:13–15	Her persistence brought Peter inside Mary's home where he would be safe.
James	15:13–21	He took command of the Jerusalem council and had the courage and discernment to help form a decision that would affect literally millions of Christians over many generations.
Lydia	16:13–15	She opened her home to Paul, from which he led many to Christ and founded a church in Philippi.
Jason	17:5–9	He risked his life for the gospel by allowing Paul to stay in his home. He stood up for what was true and right, even though he faced persecution for it.
Paul's nephew	23:16–24	He saved Paul's life by telling officials of a murder plot.
Julius	27:1, 43	He spared Paul when the other soldiers wanted to kill him.

bring them food and other amenities.

23:16–22 It is easy to overlook children, assuming that they aren't old enough to do much for the Lord. But a young boy played an important part in protecting Paul's life. God can use anyone, of any age, who is willing to yield to him. Jesus made it clear that children are important (Matthew 18:2–6). Give children the importance God gives them.

23:23, 24 The Roman commander ordered Paul to be sent to Caesarea. Jerusalem was the seat of Jewish government, but Caesarea was the Roman headquarters for the area. God works in amazing and amusing ways. There were many ways God could have used to get Paul to Caesarea, but he chose to use the Roman army to deliver Paul from his enemies. God's ways are not our ways. Ours are limited; his are not. Don't limit God by asking him to respond your way. When God intervenes, anything can happen, so much more and so much better than you could ever anticipate.

26Claudius Lysias,

To His Excellency,[e] Governor Felix:

Greetings.[f]

27This man was seized by the Jews and they were about to kill him,[g] but I
came with my troops and rescued him,[h] for I had learned that he is a Roman
citizen.[i] 28I wanted to know why they were accusing him, so I brought him to
their Sanhedrin.[j] 29I found that the accusation had to do with questions about
their law,[k] but there was no charge against him[l] that deserved death or imprisonment. 30When I was informed[m] of a plot[n] to be carried out against the man,
I sent him to you at once. I also ordered his accusers[o] to present to you their
case against him.

31So the soldiers, carrying out their orders, took Paul with them during the night
and brought him as far as Antipatris. 32The next day they let the cavalry[p] go on with
him, while they returned to the barracks.[q] 33When the cavalry[r] arrived in Caesarea,[s] they delivered the letter to the governor[t] and handed Paul over to him. 34The
governor read the letter and asked what province he was from. Learning that he was
from Cilicia,[u] 35he said, "I will hear your case when your accusers[v] get here." Then
he ordered that Paul be kept under guard[w] in Herod's palace.

The Trial Before Felix

24 Five days later the high priest Ananias[a] went down to Caesarea with some of
the elders and a lawyer named Tertullus, and they brought their charges[b]
against Paul before the governor.[c] 2When Paul was called in, Tertullus presented his
case before Felix: "We have enjoyed a long period of peace under you, and your
foresight has brought about reforms in this nation. 3Everywhere and in every way,
most excellent[d] Felix, we acknowledge this with profound gratitude. 4But in order
not to weary you further, I would request that you be kind enough to hear us briefly.
5"We have found this man to be a troublemaker, stirring up riots[e] among the Jews[f]
all over the world. He is a ringleader of the Nazarene[g] sect[h] 6and even tried to

23:26 [e]Lk 1:3; Ac 24:3; 26:25 [f]Ac 15:23
23:27 [g]Ac 21:32 [h]Ac 21:33 [i]Ac 22:25-29
23:28 [j]Ac 22:30
23:29 [k]Ac 18:15; 25:19 [l]ver 9; Ac 26:31
23:30 [m]ver 20, 21 [n]Ac 20:3 [o]ver 35; Ac 24:19; 25:16
23:32 [p]ver 23 [q]Ac 21:34
23:33 [r]ver 23, 24 [s]Ac 8:40 [t]ver 26
23:34 [u]Ac 6:9; 21:39
23:35 [v]ver 30; Ac 24:19; 25:16 [w]Ac 24:27
24:1 [a]Ac 23:2 [b]Ac 23:30, 35 [c]Ac 23:24
24:3 [d]Lk 1:3; Ac 23:26; 26:25
24:5 [e]Ac 16:20; 17:6 [f]Ac 21:28 [g]Mk 1:24 [h]ver 14; Ac 26:5; 28:22

23:26 Felix was the Roman governor or procurator of Judea from A.D. 52 to 59. This was the same position Pontius Pilate had held. While the Jews were given much freedom to govern themselves, the governor ran the army, kept the peace, and gathered the taxes.

23:26 How did Luke know what was written in the letter from Claudius Lysias? In his concern for historical accuracy, Luke used many sources to make sure that his writings were correct (see Luke 1:1–4). This letter was probably read aloud in court when Paul came before Felix to answer the Jews' accusations. Also, because Paul was a Roman citizen, a copy may have been given to him as a courtesy.

24:1 The accusers arrived – Ananias the high priest; Tertullus the lawyer; and several Jewish leaders. They travelled 60 miles to Caesarea, the Roman centre of government, to bring their false accusations against Paul. Their murder plot had failed (23:12–15), but they persisted in trying to kill him. This attempt at murder was both premeditated and persistent.

24:2ff Tertullus was a special orator called to present the religious leaders' case before the Roman governor. He made three accusations against Paul: (1) he was a troublemaker, stirring up riots among the Jews around the world; (2) he was the ringleader of an unrecognised religious sect, which was against Roman law; and (3) he had tried to desecrate the temple. The religious leaders hoped that these accusations would persuade Felix to execute Paul in order to keep the peace in Palestine.

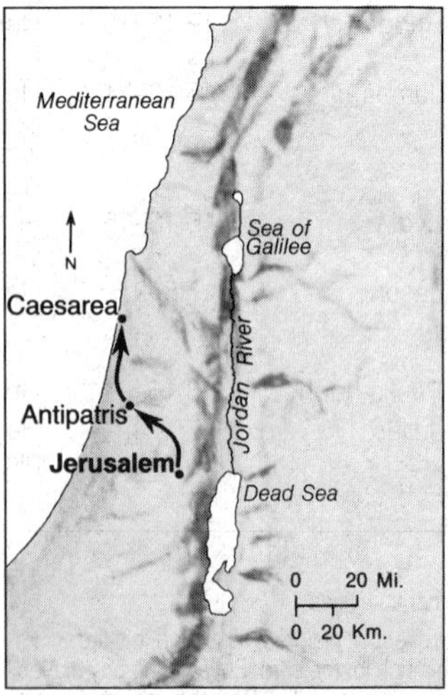

IMPRISONMENT IN CAESAREA
Paul brought news of his third journey to the elders of the Jerusalem church, who rejoiced at his ministry. But Paul's presence soon stirred up the Jews, who persuaded the Romans to arrest him. A plot to kill Paul was uncovered, so Paul was taken by night to Antipatris, and then transferred to the provincial prison in Caesarea.

24:5 While the charge that Paul was a troublemaker was insulting to Paul, it was too vague to be a substantial legal charge. The Nazarene sect referred to the Christians – named here after Jesus' home town of Nazareth.

desecrate the temple;[i] so we seized him. 8 By[a] examining him yourself you will be
able to learn the truth about all these charges we are bringing against him."
9 The Jews joined in the accusation,[j] asserting that these things were true.
10 When the governor[k] motioned for him to speak, Paul replied: "I know that for
a number of years you have been a judge over this nation; so I gladly make my defence.
11 You can easily verify that no more than twelve days[l] ago I went up to Jerusalem
to worship. 12 My accusers did not find me arguing with anyone at the temple,[m] or
stirring up a crowd[n] in the synagogues or anywhere else in the city. 13 And they cannot
prove to you the charges they are now making against me.[o] 14 However, I admit that
I worship the God of our fathers[p] as a follower of the Way,[q] which they call a sect.[r]
I believe everything that agrees with the Law and that is written in the Prophets,[s]
15 and I have the same hope in God as these men, that there will be a resurrection[t]
of both the righteous and the wicked.[u] 16 So I strive always to keep my conscience
clear[v] before God and man.
17 "After an absence of several years, I came to Jerusalem to bring my people gifts
for the poor[w] and to present offerings. 18 I was ceremonially clean[x] when they found
me in the temple courts doing this. There was no crowd with me, nor was I involved
in any disturbance.[y] 19 But there are some Jews from the province of Asia, who ought
to be here before you and bring charges if they have anything against me.[z] 20 Or these
who are here should state what crime they found in me when I stood before the
Sanhedrin — 21 unless it was this one thing I shouted as I stood in their presence: 'It
is concerning the resurrection of the dead that I am on trial before you today.' "[a]
22 Then Felix, who was well acquainted with the Way, adjourned the proceedings.
"When Lysias the commander comes," he said, "I will decide your case." 23 He
ordered the centurion to keep Paul under guard[b] but to give him some freedom[c] and
permit his friends to take care of his needs.[d]
24 Several days later Felix came with his wife Drusilla, who was a Jewess. He sent
for Paul and listened to him as he spoke about faith in Christ Jesus.[e] 25 As Paul
discoursed on righteousness, self-control[f] and the judgment[g] to come, Felix was
afraid and said, "That's enough for now! You may leave. When I find it convenient,
I will send for you." 26 At the same time he was hoping that Paul would offer him a
bribe, so he sent for him frequently and talked with him.
27 When two years had passed, Felix was succeeded by Porcius Festus,[h] but
because Felix wanted to grant a favour to the Jews,[i] he left Paul in prison.[j]

[a] 6–8 Some manuscripts *him and wanted to judge him according to our law. 7 But the commander, Lysias, came and with the use of much force snatched him from our hands 8 and ordered his accusers to come before you. By*

24:6 [i] Ac 21:28
24:9 [j] 1Th 2:16
24:10 [k] Ac 23:24
24:11 [l] Ac 21:27; ver 1
24:12 [m] Ac 25:8; 28:17 [n] ver 18
24:13 [o] Ac 25:7
24:14 [p] Ac 3:13 [q] Ac 9:2 [r] ver 5 [s] Ac 26:6, 22; 28:23
24:15 [t] Ac 23:6; 28:20 [u] Da 12:2; Jn 5:28, 29
24:16 [v] Ac 23:1
24:17 [w] Ac 11:29, 30; Ro 15:25-28, 31; 1Co 16:1-4, 15; 2Co 8:1-4; Gal 2:10
24:18 [x] Ac 21:26 [y] ver 12
24:19 [z] Ac 23:30
24:21 [a] Ac 23:6
24:23 [b] Ac 23:35 [c] Ac 28:16 [d] Ac 23:16; 27:3
24:24 [e] Ac 20:21
24:25 [f] Gal 5:23; 2Pe 1:6 [g] Ac 10:42
24:27 [h] Ac 25:1, 4, 9, 14 [i] Ac 12:3; 25:9 [j] Ac 23:35; 25:14

24:10ff Tertullus and the religious leaders seemed to have a strong argument against Paul, but Paul refuted their accusations point by point. Paul was also able to present the gospel message through his defence. Paul's accusers were unable to present specific evidence to support their general accusations. For example, Paul was accused of starting trouble among the Jews in the province of Asia (24:18, 19), but the Jews in the province of Asia (western Turkey) were not present to confirm this. This is another example of Paul using every opportunity to witness for Christ (see 24:14, 24).

24:22 Felix had been governor for six years and would have known about the Christians ("the Way"), a topic of conversation among the Roman leaders. The Christians' peaceful lifestyles had already proven to the Romans that Christians didn't go around starting riots.

24:25 Paul's talk with Felix became so personal that Felix grew fearful. Felix, like Herod Antipas (Mark 6:17, 18), had taken another man's wife. Paul's words were interesting until they focused on "righteousness, self-control, and the judgment to come". Many people will be glad to discuss the gospel with you as long as it doesn't touch their lives too personally. When it does, some will resist or run. But this is what the gospel is all about – God's power to change lives. The gospel is not effective until it moves from principles and doctrine into a life-changing dynamic. When someone resists or runs from your witness, you have undoubtedly succeeded in making the gospel personal.

24:27 Felix lost his job as governor and was called back to Rome. Porcius Festus took over as governor in late 59 or early 60. He was more just than Felix, who had kept Paul in prison for two years, in hopes that perhaps Paul would bribe him, and that by detaining Paul, the Jews would be kept happy. When Festus came into office, he immediately ordered Paul's trial to resume.

24:27 The Jews were in the majority, and the Roman political leaders wanted to defer to them to help keep the peace. Paul seemed to incite problems among the Jews everywhere he went. By keeping him in prison, Felix left office on good terms with the Jews.

The Trial Before Festus

25 Three days after arriving in the province, Festus went up from Caesarea[a] to
Jerusalem, 2where the chief priests and Jewish leaders appeared before him and
presented the charges against Paul.[b] 3They urgently requested Festus, as a favour to
them, to have Paul transferred to Jerusalem, for they were preparing an ambush to
kill him along the way. 4Festus answered, "Paul is being held[c] at Caesarea, and I
myself am going there soon. 5Let some of your leaders come with me and press
charges against the man there, if he has done anything wrong."
6After spending eight or ten days with them, he went down to Caesarea, and the
next day he convened the court[d] and ordered that Paul be brought before him. 7When
Paul appeared, the Jews who had come down from Jerusalem stood around him,
bringing many serious charges against him,[e] which they could not prove.[f]
8Then Paul made his defence: "I have done nothing wrong against the law of the
Jews or against the temple[g] or against Caesar."
9Festus, wishing to do the Jews a favour,[h] said to Paul, "Are you willing to go
up to Jerusalem and stand trial before me there on these charges?"[i]
10Paul answered: "I am now standing before Caesar's court, where I ought to be
tried. I have not done any wrong to the Jews, as you yourself know very well. 11If,
however, I am guilty of doing anything deserving death, I do not refuse to die. But
if the charges brought against me by these Jews are not true, no-one has the right to
hand me over to them. I appeal to Caesar!"[j]
12After Festus had conferred with his council, he declared: "You have appealed to
Caesar. To Caesar you will go!"

Festus Consults King Agrippa

13A few days later King Agrippa and Bernice arrived at Caesarea[k] to pay their
respects to Festus. 14Since they were spending many days there, Festus discussed
Paul's case with the king. He said: "There is a man here whom Felix left as a
prisoner.[l] 15When I went to Jerusalem, the chief priests and elders of the Jews
brought charges against him[m] and asked that he be condemned.
16"I told them that it is not the Roman custom to hand over any man before he has
faced his accusers and has had an opportunity to defend himself against their
charges.[n] 17When they came here with me, I did not delay the case, but convened
the court the next day and ordered the man to be brought in.[o] 18When his accusers
got up to speak, they did not charge him with any of the crimes I had expected.
19Instead, they had some points of dispute[p] with him about their own religion[q] and
about a dead man named Jesus whom Paul claimed was alive. 20I was at a loss how
to investigate such matters; so I asked if he would be willing to go to Jerusalem and
stand trial there on these charges.[r] 21When Paul made his appeal to be held over for
the Emperor's decision, I ordered him to be held until I could send him to Caesar."[s]
22Then Agrippa said to Festus, "I would like to hear this man myself."
He replied, "Tomorrow you will hear him."[t]

25:1 [a] Ac 8:40
25:2 [b] ver 15; Ac 24:1
25:4 [c] Ac 24:23
25:6 [d] ver 17
25:7 [e] Mk 15:3; Lk 23:2, 10; Ac 24:5, 6 [f] Ac 24:13
25:8 [g] Ac 6:13; 24:12; 28:17
25:9 [h] Ac 24:27 [i] ver 20
25:11 [j] ver 21, 25; Ac 26:32; 28:19
25:13 [k] Ac 8:40
25:14 [l] Ac 24:27
25:15 [m] ver 2; Ac 24:1
25:16 [n] ver 4, 5; Ac 23:30
25:17 [o] ver 6, 10
25:19 [p] Ac 18:15; 23:29 [q] Ac 17:22
25:20 [r] ver 9
25:21 [s] ver 11, 12
25:22 [t] Ac 9:15

25:1–9 Although two years had passed, the Jewish leaders were still looking for a way to kill Paul. They told Festus about Paul and tried to convince him to hold the trial in Jerusalem (so they could prepare an ambush). But God and Paul thwarted their schemes again.

25:10, 11 Every Roman citizen had the right to appeal to Caesar. This didn't mean that Caesar himself would hear the case, but that the citizen's case would be tried by the highest courts in the empire. Festus saw Paul's appeal as a way to send him out of the country and thus pacify the Jews. Paul wanted to go to Rome to preach the gospel (Romans 1:10), and he knew that his appeal would give him the opportunity. To go to Rome as a prisoner was better than not to go there at all.

25:11 Paul knew that he was innocent of the charges against him and could appeal to Caesar's judgment. He knew his rights as a Roman citizen and as an innocent person. Paul had met his responsibilities as a Roman, and so he had the opportunity to claim Rome's protection. The good reputation and clear conscience that result from our walk with God can help us remain guiltless before God and blameless before the world.

25:13 This was Herod Agrippa II, son of Herod Agrippa I, and a descendant of Herod the Great. He had power over the temple, controlled the temple treasury, and could appoint and remove the high priest. Bernice was the sister of Herod Agrippa II. She married her uncle, Herod Chalcis, became a mistress to her brother Agrippa II, and then became mistress to the emperor Vespasian's son, Titus. Here Agrippa and Bernice were making an official visit to Festus. Agrippa, of Jewish descent, could help clarify Paul's case for Roman governor. Agrippa and Festus were anxious to co-operate in governing their neighbouring territories.

25:19 Even though Festus knew little about Christianity, he somehow sensed that the resurrection was central to Christian belief.

Paul Before Agrippa

23The next day Agrippa and Bernice[u] came with great pomp and entered the
audience room with the high ranking officers and the leading men of the city. At the
command of Festus, Paul was brought in. 24Festus said: "King Agrippa, and all who
are present with us, you see this man! The whole Jewish community[v] has petitioned
me about him in Jerusalem and here in Caesarea, shouting that he ought not to live
any longer.[w] 25I found he had done nothing deserving of death,[x] but because he made
his appeal to the Emperor[y] I decided to send him to Rome. 26But I have nothing
definite to write to His Majesty about him. Therefore I have brought him before all
of you, and especially before you, King Agrippa, so that as a result of this investigation
I may have something to write. 27For I think it is unreasonable to send on a prisoner
without specifying the charges against him."

26 Then Agrippa said to Paul, "You have permission to speak for yourself."[a]
So Paul motioned with his hand and began his defence: 2"King Agrippa, I
consider myself fortunate to stand before you today as I make my defence against all
the accusations of the Jews, 3and especially so because you are well acquainted with
all the Jewish customs[b] and controversies.[c] Therefore, I beg you to listen to me
patiently.

4"The Jews all know the way I have lived ever since I was a child,[d] from the
beginning of my life in my own country, and also in Jerusalem. 5They have known
me for a long time[e] and can testify, if they are willing, that according to the strictest
sect of our religion, I lived as a Pharisee.[f] 6And now it is because of my hope[g] in
what God has promised our fathers[h] that I am on trial today. 7This is the promise
our twelve tribes[i] are hoping to see fulfilled as they earnestly serve God day and
night.[j] O King, it is because of this hope that the Jews are accusing me.[k] 8Why
should any of you consider it incredible that God raises the dead?[l]

9"I too was convinced[m] that I ought to do all that was possible to oppose[n] the name
of Jesus of Nazareth.[o] 10And that is just what I did in Jerusalem. On the authority
of the chief priests I put many of the saints[p] in prison,[q] and when they were put to
death, I cast my vote against them.[r] 11Many a time I went from one synagogue to
another to have them punished,[s] and I tried to force them to blaspheme. In my
obsession against them, I even went to foreign cities to persecute them.

12"On one of these journeys I was going to Damascus with the authority and
commission of the chief priests. 13About noon, O King, as I was on the road, I saw
a light from heaven, brighter than the sun, blazing around me and my companions.
14We all fell to the ground, and I heard a voice[t] saying to me in Aramaic,[a] 'Saul,
Saul, why do you persecute me? It is hard for you to kick against the goads.'
15"Then I asked, 'Who are you, Lord?'

" 'I am Jesus, whom you are persecuting,' the Lord replied. 16'Now get up and
stand on your feet.[u] I have appeared to you to appoint you as a servant and as a witness
of what you have seen of me and what I will show you.[v] 17I will rescue you[w] from
your own people and from the Gentiles.[x] I am sending you to them 18to open their
eyes[y] and turn them from darkness to light,[z] and from the power of Satan to God,
so that they may receive forgiveness of sins[a] and a place among those who are
sanctified by faith in me.'[b]

19"So then, King Agrippa, I was not disobedient to the vision from heaven. 20First

a *14* Or *Hebrew*

25:23 [u]ver 13; Ac 26:30
25:24 [v]ver 2, 3, 7 [w]Ac 22:22
25:25 [x]Ac 23:9 [y]ver 11
26:1 [a]Ac 9:15; 25:22
26:3 [b]ver 7; Ac 6:14 [c]Ac 25:19
26:4 [d]Gal 1:13, 14; Php 3:5
26:5 [e]Ac 22:3 [f]Ac 23:6; Php 3:5
26:6 [g]Ac 23:6; 24:15; 28:20 [h]Ac 13:32; Ro 15:8
26:7 [i]Jas 1:1 [j]1Th 3:10; 1Ti 5:5 [k]ver 2
26:8 [l]Ac 23:6
26:9 [m]1Ti 1:13 [n]Jn 16:2 [o]Jn 15:21
26:10 [p]Ac 9:13 [q]Ac 8:3; 9:2, 14, 21 [r]Ac 22:20
26:11 [s]Mt 10:17
26:14 [t]Ac 9:7
26:16 [u]Eze 2:1; Da 10:11 [v]Ac 22:14, 15
26:17 [w]Jer 1:8, 19 [x]Ac 9:15
26:18 [y]Isa 35:5 [z]Isa 42:7, 16; Eph 5:8; Col 1:13; 1Pe 2:9 [a]Lk 24:47; Ac 2:38 [b]Ac 20:21, 32

25:23ff Paul was in prison, but that didn't stop him from making the most of his situation. Military officers and prominent city leaders met in the palace room with Agrippa to hear this case. Paul saw this new audience as yet another opportunity to present the gospel. Rather than complain about your present situation, look for ways to use every opportunity to serve God and share him with others. Your problems may be opportunities in disguise.

26:3ff This speech is a good example of Paul's powerful oratory. Beginning with a compliment to Agrippa, he told his story, including the resurrection of Christ, and the royal audience was spellbound.

26:14 An oxgoad was a sharp stick used to prod cattle. "It is hard for you to kick against the goads" (oxgoads) means, "You are only hurting yourself."

26:17, 18 Paul took every opportunity to remind his audience that the Gentiles have an equal share in God's inheritance. This inheritance is the promise and blessing of the covenant that God made with Abraham (see Ephesians 2:19; 1 Peter 1:3, 4). Paul's mission was to preach the Good News to the Gentiles.

to those in Damascus,[c] then to those in Jerusalem[d] and in all Judea, and to the
Gentiles[e] also, I preached that they should repent[f] and turn to God and prove their
repentance by their deeds.[g] 21 That is why the Jews seized me[h] in the temple courts
and tried to kill me.[i] 22 But I have had God's help to this very day, and so I stand
here and testify to small and great alike. I am saying nothing beyond what the prophets
and Moses said would happen[j]— 23 that the Christ[b] would suffer and, as the first to
rise from the dead,[k] would proclaim light to his own people and to the Gentiles."[l]
24 At this point Festus interrupted Paul's defence. "You are out of your mind,[m]
Paul!" he shouted. "Your great learning[n] is driving you insane."
25 "I am not insane, most excellent[o] Festus," Paul replied. "What I am saying is
true and reasonable. 26 The king is familiar with these things,[p] and I can speak freely
to him. I am convinced that none of this has escaped his notice, because it was not
done in a corner. 27 King Agrippa, do you believe the prophets? I know you do."
28 Then Agrippa said to Paul, "Do you think that in such a short time you can
persuade me to be a Christian?"[q]
29 Paul replied, "Short time or long—I pray God that not only you but all who are
listening to me today may become what I am, except for these chains."[r]
30 The king rose, and with him the governor and Bernice[s] and those sitting with
them. 31 They left the room, and while talking with one another, they said, "This man
is not doing anything that deserves death or imprisonment."[t]
32 Agrippa said to Festus, "This man could have been set free[u] if he had not
appealed to Caesar."[v]

Paul Sails for Rome

27 When it was decided that we[a] would sail for Italy,[b] Paul and some other
prisoners were handed over to a centurion named Julius, who belonged to the
Imperial Regiment.[c] 2 We boarded a ship from Adramyttium about to sail for ports
along the coast of the province of Asia,[d] and we put out to sea. Aristarchus,[e] a
Macedonian[f] from Thessalonica,[g] was with us.
3 The next day we landed at Sidon;[h] and Julius, in kindness to Paul,[i] allowed him
to go to his friends so they might provide for his needs.[j] 4 From there we put out to
sea again and passed to the lee of Cyprus because the winds were against us.[k] 5 When
we had sailed across the open sea off the coast of Cilicia[l] and Pamphylia, we landed
at Myra in Lycia. 6 There the centurion found an Alexandrian ship[m] sailing for Italy[n]
and put us on board. 7 We made slow headway for many days and had difficulty
arriving off Cnidus. When the wind did not allow us to hold our course,[o] we sailed
to the lee of Crete,[p] opposite Salmone. 8 We moved along the coast with difficulty
and came to a place called Fair Havens, near the town of Lasea.

[b] 23 Or *Messiah*

26:20 [c] Ac 9:19-25 [d] Ac 9:26-29; 22:17-20 [e] Ac 9:15; 13:46 [f] Ac 3:19 [g] Mt 3:8; Lk 3:8
26:21 [h] Ac 21:27, 30 [i] Ac 21:31
26:22 [j] Lk 24:27, 44; Ac 10:43; 24:14
26:23 [k] 1Co 15:20, 23; Col 1:18; Rev 1:5 [l] Lk 2:32
26:24 [m] Jn 10:20; 1Co 4:10 [n] Jn 7:15
26:25 [o] Ac 23:26
26:26 [p] ver 3
26:28 [q] Ac 11:26
26:29 [r] Ac 21:33
26:30 [s] Ac 25:23
26:31 [t] Ac 23:9
26:32 [u] Ac 28:18 [v] Ac 25:11
27:1 [a] Ac 16:10 [b] Ac 18:2; 25:12, 25 [c] Ac 10:1
27:2 [d] Ac 2:9 [e] Ac 19:29 [f] Ac 16:9 [g] Ac 17:1
27:3 [h] Mt 11:21 [i] ver 43 [j] Ac 24:23; 28:16
27:4 [k] ver 7
27:5 [l] Ac 6:9
27:6 [m] Ac 28:11 [n] ver 1
27:7 [o] ver 4 [p] ver 12, 13, 21

26:24 Paul was risking his life for a message that was offensive to the Jews and unbelievable to the Gentiles. Jesus received the same response to his message (Mark 3:21; John 10:20). To a worldly, materialistic mind, it seems insane to risk so much to gain what seems to be so little. But as you follow Christ, you soon discover that temporary possessions look so small next to even the smallest eternal reward.

26:26 Paul was appealing to the *facts*—people were still alive who had heard Jesus and seen his miracles; the empty tomb could still be seen; and the Christian message was turning the world upside down (17:6). The history of Jesus' life and the early church are facts that are still open for us to examine. We still have eyewitness accounts of Jesus' life recorded in the Bible as well as historical and archaeological records of the early church to study. Examine the events and facts as verified by many witnesses. Strengthen your faith with the truth of these accounts.

26:28, 29 Agrippa responded to Paul's presentation with a sarcastic remark. Paul didn't react to the brush-off, but made a personal appeal to which he hoped all his listeners would respond. Paul's response is a good example for us as we tell others about God's plan of salvation. A sincere personal appeal or personal testimony can show the depth of our concern and break through hardened hearts.

26:28, 29 Paul's heart is revealed here in his words: he was more concerned for the salvation of these strangers than for the removal of his own chains. Ask God to give you a burning desire to see others come to Christ—a desire so strong that it overshadows your problems.

27:1, 2 Use of the pronoun *we* indicates that Luke accompanied Paul on this journey. Aristarchus is the man who was dragged into the theatre at the beginning of the riot in Ephesus (19:29; 20:4; Philemon 24).

27:1–3 Julius, a hardened Roman centurion, was assigned to guard Paul. Obviously he had to remain close to Paul at all times. Through this contact, Julius developed a respect for Paul. He gave Paul a certain amount of freedom (27:3) and later spared his life (27:43). Would your character stand close scrutiny?

27:9 [q]Lev 16:29-31; 23:27-29; Nu 29:7

9Much time had been lost, and sailing had already become dangerous because by
now it was after the Fast.[a][q] So Paul warned them, 10"Men, I can see that our voyage
is going to be disastrous and bring great loss to ship and cargo, and to our own lives
also."[r] 11But the centurion, instead of listening to what Paul said, followed the advice
of the pilot and of the owner of the ship. 12Since the harbour was unsuitable to winter
in, the majority decided that we should sail on, hoping to reach Phoenix and winter
there. This was a harbour in Crete, facing both south-west and north-west.

27:10 [r]ver 21

The Storm

13When a gentle south wind began to blow, they thought they had obtained what
they wanted; so they weighed anchor and sailed along the shore of Crete. 14Before
very long, a wind of hurricane force,[s] called the "north-easter", swept down from
the island. 15The ship was caught by the storm and could not head into the wind; so
we gave way to it and were driven along. 16As we passed to the lee of a small island
called Cauda, we were hardly able to make the lifeboat secure. 17When the men had

27:14 [s]Mk 4:37

[a] *9* That is, the Day of Atonement (Yom Kippur)

HEROD AGRIPPA II

Like great-grandfather, like grandfather, like father, like son—this tells the story of Herod Agrippa II. He inherited the effects of generations of powerful men with flawed personalities. Each son followed his father in weaknesses, mistakes, and missed opportunities. Each generation had a confrontation with God, but each failed to realise the importance of the decision. Herod Agrippa's great-uncle, Herod Antipas, actually met Jesus during his trial, but failed to see Jesus for who he was. Agrippa II heard the gospel from Paul, but considered the message mild entertainment. He found it humorous that Paul actually tried to convince him to become a Christian.

Like so many before and after, Agrippa II stopped within hearing distance of the kingdom of God. He left himself without excuse. He heard the gospel but decided it wasn't worth responding to personally. Unfortunately, his mistake isn't uncommon. Many who read his story will also not believe. Their problem, like his, is not really that the gospel isn't convincing or that they don't need to know God personally; it is that they choose not to respond.

What has been your response to the gospel? Has it turned your life around and given you the hope of eternal life, or has it been a message to resist or reject? Perhaps it has just been entertainment. It may seem like too great a price to give God control of your life, but it is an even greater price by far to live eternally apart from him because you have chosen not to be his child.

Strengths and accomplishments:
- Last of the Herod dynasty that ruled parts of Palestine from 40 B.C. to A.D. 100
- Continued his father's success in mediating between Rome and Palestine
- Continued the family tradition of building and improving cities

Weaknesses and mistakes:
- Was not convinced by the gospel and consciously rejected it
- Carried on an incestuous relationship with his sister Bernice

Lessons from his life:
- Families pass on both positive and negative influences to children
- There are no guarantees of multiple opportunities to respond to God

Vital statistics:
- Occupation: Ruler of northern and eastern Palestine
- Relatives: Great-grandfather: Herod the Great. Father: Herod Agrippa I. Great-uncle: Herod Antipas. Sister: Bernice, Drusilla
- Contemporaries: Paul, Felix, Festus, Peter, Luke

Key verse:
"Then Agrippa said to Paul, 'Do you think that in such a short time you can persuade me to be a Christian?' " (Acts 26:28).

Herod Agrippa II's story is told in Acts 25:13—26:32.

27:9 The "Fast" was the Day of Atonement. Sailors in ancient times had no compasses and navigated by the stars. Overcast weather made sailing almost impossible and very dangerous. Sailing was doubtful in September and impossible by November. This event occurred in October (A.D. 59).

27:12 Although this was not the best time to sail, the pilot and the owner of the ship didn't want to spend the winter in Lasea, and so the pilot took a chance. At first the winds and weather were favourable, but then the deadly storm arose.

27:17 The measures they took to survive included passing ropes under the ship to hold it together. Syrtis was on the northern coast of Africa.

hoisted it aboard, they passed ropes under the ship itself to hold it together. Fearing
that they would run aground[t] on the sand-bars of Syrtis, they lowered the sea anchor
and let the ship be driven along. 18We took such a violent battering from the storm
that the next day they began to throw the cargo overboard.[u] 19On the third day, they
threw the ship's tackle overboard with their own hands. 20When neither sun nor stars
appeared for many days and the storm continued raging, we finally gave up all hope
of being saved.
21After the men had gone a long time without food, Paul stood up before them and
said: "Men, you should have taken my advice[v] not to sail from Crete;[w] then you
would have spared yourselves this damage and loss. 22But now I urge you to keep
up your courage,[x] because not one of you will be lost; only the ship will be destroyed.
23Last night an angel[y] of the God whose I am and whom I serve[z] stood beside me[a]
24and said, 'Do not be afraid, Paul. You must stand trial before Caesar;[b] and God
has graciously given you the lives of all who sail with you.'[c] 25So keep up your
courage,[d] men, for I have faith in God that it will happen just as he told me.[e]
26Nevertheless, we must run aground[f] on some island."[g]

The Shipwreck

27On the fourteenth night we were still being driven across the Adriatic[b] Sea, when
about midnight the sailors sensed they were approaching land. 28They took soundings
and found that the water was one hundred and twenty feet[c] deep. A short time later
they took soundings again and found it was ninety feet[d] deep. 29Fearing that we would
be dashed against the rocks, they dropped four anchors from the stern and prayed for
daylight. 30In an attempt to escape from the ship, the sailors let the lifeboat[h] down
into the sea, pretending they were going to lower some anchors from the bow. 31Then
Paul said to the centurion and the soldiers, "Unless these men stay with the ship, you
cannot be saved."[i] 32So the soldiers cut the ropes that held the lifeboat and let it fall
away.
33Just before dawn Paul urged them all to eat. "For the last fourteen days," he said,
"you have been in constant suspense and have gone without food — you haven't eaten
anything. 34Now I urge you to take some food. You need it to survive. Not one of
you will lose a single hair from his head."[j] 35After he said this, he took some bread
and gave thanks to God in front of them all. Then he broke it[k] and began to eat.
36They were all encouraged[l] and ate some food themselves. 37Altogether there were
276 of us on board. 38When they had eaten as much as they wanted, they lightened
the ship by throwing the grain into the sea.[m]
39When daylight came, they did not recognise the land, but they saw a bay with
a sandy beach,[n] where they decided to run the ship aground if they could. 40Cutting
loose the anchors,[o] they left them in the sea and at the same time untied the ropes
that held the rudders. Then they hoisted the foresail to the wind and made for the
beach. 41But the ship struck a sand-bar and ran aground. The bow stuck fast and would
not move, and the stern was broken to pieces by the pounding of the surf.[p]
42The soldiers planned to kill the prisoners to prevent any of them from swimming
away and escaping. 43But the centurion wanted to spare Paul's life[q] and kept them
from carrying out their plan. He ordered those who could swim to jump overboard

b *27* In ancient times the name referred to an area extending well south of Italy. **c** *28* Greek *twenty orguias* (about 37 metres) **d** *28* Greek *fifteen orguias* (about 27 metres)

27:17 [t]ver 26, 39
27:18 [u]ver 19, 38; Jnh 1:5
27:21 [v]ver 10 [w]ver 7
27:22 [x]ver 25, 36
27:23 [y]Ac 5:19 [z]Ro 1:9 [a]Ac 18:9; 23:11; 2Ti 4:17
27:24 [b]Ac 23:11 [c]ver 44
27:25 [d]ver 22, 36 [e]Ro 4:20, 21
27:26 [f]ver 17, 39 [g]Ac 28:1
27:30 [h]ver 16
27:31 [i]ver 24
27:34 [j]Mt 10:30
27:35 [k]Mt 14:19
27:36 [l]ver 22, 25
27:38 [m]ver 18; Jnh 1:5
27:39 [n]Ac 28:1
27:40 [o]ver 29
27:41 [p]2Co 11:25
27:43 [q]ver 3

27:21 Why would Paul talk to the crew this way? Paul was not taunting them with an "I told you so", but was reminding them that, with God's guidance, he had predicted this very problem (27:10). In the future, they listened to him (27:30–32) and their lives were spared because of it.

27:27 The Adriatic Sea referred to the central part of the Mediterranean Sea between Italy, Crete, and the northern coast of Africa.

27:28 Soundings were made by throwing a weighted, marked line into the water. When the lead hit the bottom, sailors could tell the depth of the water from the marks on the rope.

27:42, 43 The soldiers would pay with their own lives if any of their prisoners escaped. Their instinctive reaction was to kill the prisoners so they wouldn't get away. Julius, the centurion, was impressed with Paul and wanted to save his life. Julius was the highest ranking official and therefore he could make this decision. This act preserved Paul for his later ministry in Rome and fulfilled Paul's prediction that all the people on the ship would be saved (27:22).

27:44 [r]ver 22, 31

first and get to land. 44 The rest were to get there on planks or on pieces of the ship.
In this way everyone reached land in safety.[r]

28:1 [a]Ac 16:10 [b]Ac 27:26, 39
28:4 [c]Mk 16:18 [d]Lk 13:2, 4
28:5 [e]Lk 10:19
28:6 [f]Ac 14:11
28:8 [g]Jas 5:14, 15 [h]Ac 9:40

Ashore on Malta

28 Once safely on shore, we[a] found out that the island[b] was called Malta. 2 The
islanders showed us unusual kindness. They built a fire and welcomed us all
because it was raining and cold. 3 Paul gathered a pile of brushwood and, as he put
it on the fire, a viper, driven out by the heat, fastened itself on his hand. 4 When the
islanders saw the snake hanging from his hand,[c] they said to each other, "This man
must be a murderer; for though he escaped from the sea, Justice has not allowed him
to live."[d] 5 But Paul shook the snake off into the fire and suffered no ill effects.[e]
6 The people expected him to swell up or suddenly fall dead, but after waiting a long
time and seeing nothing unusual happen to him, they changed their minds and said
he was a god.[f]
7 There was an estate near by that belonged to Publius, the chief official of the island.
He welcomed us to his home and for three days entertained us hospitably. 8 His father
was sick in bed, suffering from fever and dysentery. Paul went in to see him and, after
prayer,[g] placed his hands on him and healed him.[h] 9 When this had happened, the
rest of the sick on the island came and were cured. 10 They honoured us in many ways
and when we were ready to sail, they furnished us with the supplies we needed.

PAUL'S JOURNEY TO ROME

One of Paul's most important journeys was to Rome, but he didn't get there the way he expected. It turned out to be more of a legal journey than a missionary journey because, through a series of legal trials and transactions, Paul was delivered to Rome where his presentation of the gospel would penetrate even the walls of the emperor's palace. Sometimes when our plans don't work out as we want them to, they work out even better than we expected.

Reference	*What happened*
21:30–34	When Paul arrived in Jerusalem, a riot broke out. Seeing the riot, Roman soldiers put Paul into protective custody. Paul asked for a chance to defend himself to the people. His speech was interrupted by the crowd when he told about what God was doing in the lives of Gentiles.
22:24, 25	A Roman commander ordered a beating to get a confession from Paul. Paul claimed Roman citizenship and escaped the whip.
22:30	Paul was brought before the Jewish Sanhedrin. Because of his Roman citizenship, he was rescued from the religious leaders who wanted to kill him.
23:10	The Roman commander put Paul back under protective custody.
23:21–24	Due to a plot to kill Paul, the commander transferred him to Caesarea, which was under Governor Felix's control.
23:35	Paul was in prison until the Jews arrived to accuse him. Paul defended himself before Felix.
24:25, 26	Paul was in prison for two years, speaking occasionally to Felix and Drusilla.
24:27	Felix was replaced by Festus.
25:1, 10	New accusations were brought against Paul—Jews wanted him back in Jerusalem for a trial. Paul claimed his right to a hearing before Caesar.
25:12	Festus promised to send him to Rome.
25:13, 14	Festus discussed Paul's case with Herod Agrippa II.
26:1	Agrippa and Festus heard Paul speak. Paul again told his story.
26:24–28	Agrippa interrupted with a sarcastic rejection of the gospel.
26:30–32	Group consensus was that Paul was guilty of nothing and could have been released if he had not appealed to Rome.
27:1, 2	Paul left for Rome, courtesy of the Roman empire.

28:1 The island of Malta is 60 miles south of Sicily. It had excellent harbours and was ideally located for trade.

28:2 The islanders on Malta were of Phoenician ancestry.

28:3 God had promised safe passage to Paul (27:23–25), and he would let nothing stop his servant. The poisonous viper that bit Paul was unable to harm him. Our lives are in God's hands, to continue on or to come to an end in his good timing. God still had work for Paul to do.

28:6 These people were very superstitious and believed in many gods. When they saw that Paul was unhurt by the poisonous viper, they thought he was a god. A similar assessment is reported in 14:11–18.

28:7, 8 Paul continued to minister to others, even as a shipwrecked prisoner. On this trip alone, his centurion, the chief official of Malta, and many others were affected. It is no wonder that the gospel spread like wildfire.

Arrival at Rome

[11]After three months we put out to sea in a ship that had wintered in the island.
It was an Alexandrian ship[i] with the figurehead of the twin gods Castor and Pollux.
[12]We put in at Syracuse and stayed there three days. [13]From there we set sail and
arrived at Rhegium. The next day the south wind came up, and on the following day
we reached Puteoli. [14]There we found some brothers[j] who invited us to spend a week
with them. And so we came to Rome. [15]The brothers[k] there had heard that we were
coming, and they travelled as far as the Forum of Appius and the Three Taverns to
meet us. At the sight of these men Paul thanked God and was encouraged. [16]When
we got to Rome, Paul was allowed to live by himself, with a soldier to guard him.[l]

28:11 [i]Ac 27:6
28:14 [j]Ac 1:16
28:15 [k]Ac 1:16
28:16 [l]Ac 24:23; 27:3

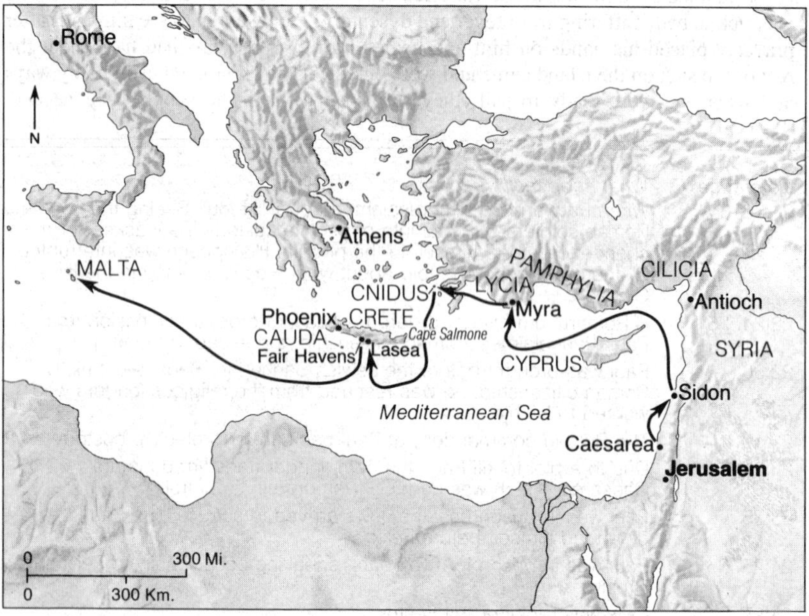

THE TRIP TOWARDS ROME
Paul began his 2,000-mile trip to Rome at Caesarea. To avoid the open seas, the ship followed the coastline. At Myra, Paul was put on a vessel bound for Italy. It arrived with difficulty at Cnidus, then went to Crete, docking at the port of Fair Havens. The next stop was Phoenix, but the ship was blown south around the island of Cauda, then drifted for two weeks until it was shipwrecked on the island of Malta.

28:15 Where did the Roman believers come from? The gospel message had spread to Rome by various methods. Many Jews who lived in Rome visited Jerusalem for religious festivals. Some were present at Pentecost (2:10), believed in Jesus, and brought the message back to Rome. Also, Paul had written his letter to the Romans before he visited there.

28:15 The Forum of Appius was a town about 43 miles south of Rome; Three Taverns was located about 35 miles south of Rome. A *tavern* was a shop, or a place that provided food and lodging for travellers. The Christians openly went to meet Paul and encourage him.

28:17 The decree of Claudius expelling Jews from Rome (18:2) must have been temporary, because Jewish leaders were back in Rome.

28:17–20 Paul wanted to preach the gospel in Rome, and he eventually got there – in chains, through shipwreck, and after many trials. Although he may have wished for an easier passage, he knew that God had blessed him greatly in allowing him to meet the believers in Rome and preach the message to both Jews and Gentiles in that great city. In all things, God worked for Paul's good (Romans 8:28). You can trust him to do the same for you. God may not make you comfortable or secure, but he will provide the opportunity to do his work.

28:22 Christians were denounced everywhere by the Romans because they were seen as a threat to the Roman establishment. They believed in one God, whereas the Romans had many gods, including Caesar. The Christians were committed to an authority higher than Caesar.

28:23 Paul used the Old Testament to teach the Jews that Jesus was the Messiah, the fulfilment of God's promises. The book of Romans, written ten years earlier, reveals the ongoing dialogue that Paul had with the Jews in Rome.

28:17 [m]Ac 25:2 [n]Ac 22:5 [o]Ac 25:8 [p]Ac 6:14
28:18 [q]Ac 22:24 [r]Ac 26:31, 32 [s]Ac 23:9
28:19 [t]Ac 25:11
28:20 [u]Ac 26:6, 7 [v]Ac 21:33
28:21 [w]Ac 22:5
28:22 [x]Ac 24:5, 14
28:23 [y]Ac 19:8 [z]Ac 17:3 [a]Ac 8:35
28:24 [b]Ac 14:4
28:27 [c]Ps 119:70 [d]Isa 6:9, 10
28:28 [e]Lk 2:30 [f]Ac 13:46

Paul Preaches at Rome Under Guard

17 Three days later he called together the leaders of the Jews.[m] When they had
assembled, Paul said to them: "My brothers,[n] although I have done nothing against
our people[o] or against the customs of our ancestors,[p] I was arrested in Jerusalem
and handed over to the Romans. 18 They examined me[q] and wanted to release me,[r]
because I was not guilty of any crime deserving death.[s] 19 But when the Jews
objected, I was compelled to appeal to Caesar[t]—not that I had any charge to bring
against my own people. 20 For this reason I have asked to see you and talk with you.
It is because of the hope of Israel[u] that I am bound with this chain."[v]
21 They replied, "We have not received any letters from Judea concerning you, and
none of the brothers[w] who have come from there has reported or said anything bad
about you. 22 But we want to hear what your views are, for we know that people
everywhere are talking against this sect."[x]
23 They arranged to meet Paul on a certain day, and came in even larger numbers
to the place where he was staying. From morning till evening he explained and
declared to them the kingdom of God[y] and tried to convince them about Jesus[z] from
the Law of Moses and from the Prophets.[a] 24 Some were convinced by what he said,
but others would not believe.[b] 25 They disagreed among themselves and began to
leave after Paul had made this final statement: "The Holy Spirit spoke the truth to your
forefathers when he said through Isaiah the prophet:

26 " 'Go to this people and say,
"You will be ever hearing but never understanding;
you will be ever seeing but never perceiving."
27 For this people's heart has become calloused;[c]
they hardly hear with their ears,
and they have closed their eyes.
Otherwise they might see with their eyes,
hear with their ears,
understand with their hearts
and turn, and I would heal them.'[a][d]

28 "Therefore I want you to know that God's salvation[e] has been sent to the
Gentiles,[f] and they will listen!"[b]

[a] *27* Isaiah 6:9,10 [b] *28* Some manuscripts *listen!" 29 After he said this, the Jews left, arguing vigorously among themselves.*

PAUL ARRIVES IN ROME
The shipwreck occurred on Malta, where the ship's company spent three months. Finally another ship gave them passage for the 100 miles to Syracuse, capital of Sicily, then on to Rhegium, finally dropping anchor at Puteoli. Paul was taken along the Appian Way to the Forum of Appius, and to the Three Taverns before arriving in Rome.

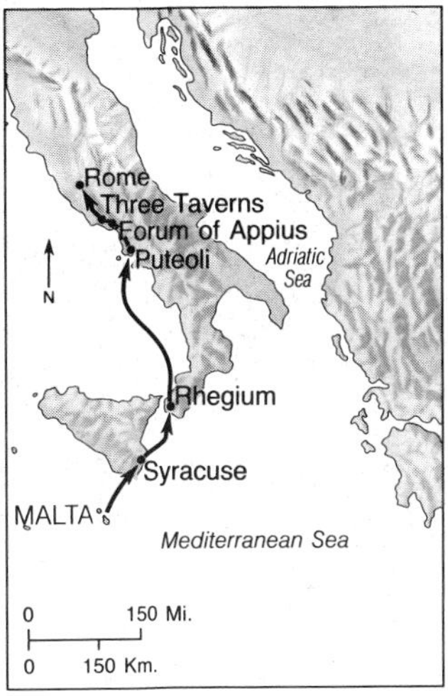

28:30 While Paul was under house arrest, he did more than speak to the Jews. He wrote letters, commonly called his Prison Letters, to the Ephesians, Colossians, and Philippians. He also wrote personal letters, such as the one to Philemon. Luke was with Paul in Rome (2 Timothy 4:11). Timothy often visited him (Philippians 1:1; Colossians 1:1; Philemon 1), as did Tychicus (Ephesians 6:21), Epaphroditus (Philippians 4:18), and Mark (Colossians 4:10). Paul witnessed to the whole Roman guard (Philippians 1:13) and was involved with the Roman believers.

30For two whole years Paul stayed there in his own rented house and welcomed all
who came to see him. 31Boldly and without hindrance he preached the kingdom of
God[g] and taught about the Lord Jesus Christ.

28:31 [g] ver 23; Mt 4:23

28:30 Tradition says that Paul was released after two years of house arrest in Rome and then set off on a fourth missionary journey. Some reasons for this tradition are as follows: (1) Luke does not give us an account of his trial before Caesar, and Luke was a detailed chronicler; (2) the prosecution had two years to bring the case to trial, and time may have run out; (3) in his letter to the Philippians, written during his imprisonment in Rome, Paul implied that he would soon be released and would do further travelling; (4) Paul mentions several places where he intended to take the gospel, but he never visited those places in his first three journeys; and (5) early Christian literature talks plainly about other travels by Paul.

It may be that during Paul's time of freedom, he continued to travel extensively, even going to Spain (see Romans 15:24, 28) and back to the churches in Greece. The books of 1 Timothy and Titus were written during this time. Later, Paul was imprisoned again, probably in Rome, where he wrote his last letter (2 Timothy).

28:31 Why does the book of Acts end here and so abruptly? The book is not about the life of Paul, but about the spread of the gospel, and that has been clearly presented. God apparently thought it was not necessary for someone to write an additional book describing the continuing history of the early church. Now that the gospel had been preached and established at the centre of trade and government, it would spread across the world.

28:31 The book of Acts deals with the history of the Christian church and its expansion in ever-widening circles touching Jerusalem, Antioch, Ephesus, and Rome – the most influential cities in the Western world. Acts also shows the mighty miracles and testimonies of the heroes and martyrs of the early church – Peter, Stephen, James, Paul. All the ministry was prompted and held together by the Holy Spirit working in the lives of ordinary people – merchants, travellers, slaves, jailers, church leaders, males, females, Gentiles, Jews, rich, poor. Many unsung heroes of the faith continued the work, through the Holy Spirit, in succeeding generations, changing the world with a changeless message – that Jesus Christ is Saviour and Lord for all who call on him. Today we can be the unsung heroes in the continuing story of the spread of the gospel. It is that same message that we Christians are to take to our world so that many more may hear and believe.

ROMANS

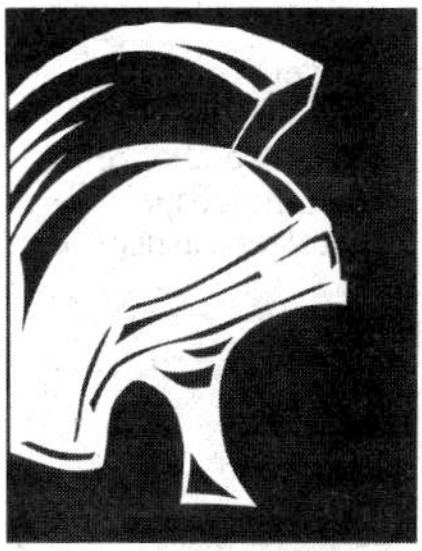

KNOWLEDGEABLE and experienced, the lawyer makes his case. Calling key witnesses to the stand, he presents the evidence. After discrediting the testimonies of witnesses for the defence by skilfully cross-examining them, he concludes with an airtight summary and stirring challenge for the jury. The announced verdict is no surprise. "Guilty" states the jury; and justice is served.

The apostle Paul was intelligent, articulate, and committed to his calling. Like a skilled lawyer, he presented the case for the gospel clearly and forthrightly in his letter to the believers in Rome.

Paul had heard of the church at Rome, but he had never been there, nor had any of the other apostles. Evidently the church had been begun by Jews who had come to faith during Pentecost (Acts 2). They spread the faith on their return to Rome, and the church grew.

Although many barriers separated them, Paul felt a bond with these Romans. They were his brothers and sisters in Christ, and he longed to see them face to face. He had never met most of the believers there, yet he loved them. He sent this letter to introduce himself and to make a clear declaration of the faith.

After a brief introduction, Paul presents the facts of the gospel (1:3) and declares his allegiance to it (1:16, 17). He continues by building an airtight case for the lostness of mankind and the necessity for God's intervention (1:18—3:20).

Then Paul presents the good news—salvation is available to all, regardless of a person's identity, sin, or heritage. We are saved by *grace* (unearned, undeserved favour from God) through *faith* (complete trust) in Christ and his finished work. Through him we can stand before God justified, "not guilty" (3:21—5:21). With this foundation Paul moves directly into a discussion of the freedom that comes from being saved—freedom from the power of sin (6:1–23), freedom from the domination of the law (7:1–25), freedom to become like Christ and discover God's limitless love (8:1–39).

Speaking directly to his Jewish brothers and sisters, Paul shares his concern for them and explains how they fit into God's plan (9:1—11:12). God has made the way for Jews and Gentiles to be united in the body of Christ—both groups can praise God for his wisdom and love (11:13–36).

Paul explains what it means to live in complete submission to Christ—using spiritual gifts to serve others (12:3–8), genuinely loving others (12:9–21), and being good citizens (13:1–14). Freedom must be guided by love as we build each other up in the faith, being sensitive and helpful to those who are weak (14:1—15:4). Paul stresses unity, especially between Gentiles and Jews (15:5–13). He concludes by reviewing his reasons for writing, outlining his personal plans (15:22–33), greeting his friends, and giving a few final thoughts and greetings from his travelling companions (16:1–27).

As you read Romans, re-examine your commitment to Christ and reconfirm your relationships with other believers in Christ's body.

VITAL STATISTICS

PURPOSE:
To introduce Paul to the Romans and to give a sample of his message before he arrives in Rome

AUTHOR:
Paul

TO WHOM WRITTEN:
The Christians in Rome and believers everywhere

DATE WRITTEN:
About A.D. 57, from Corinth, as Paul was preparing for his visit to Jerusalem.

SETTING:
Apparently Paul had finished his work in the east, and he planned to visit Rome on his way to Spain after first bringing a collection to Jerusalem for the poor Christians there (15:23–28). The Roman church was mostly Jewish but also contained a great number of Gentiles.

KEY VERSE:
"Therefore, since we have been justified through faith, we have peace with God through our Lord Jesus Christ" (5:1).

KEY PEOPLE:
Paul, Phoebe

KEY PLACE:
Rome

SPECIAL FEATURES:
Paul wrote Romans as an organised and carefully presented statement of his faith—it does not have the form of a typical letter. He does, however, spend considerable time greeting people in Rome at the end of the letter.

THE BLUEPRINT

A. WHAT TO BELIEVE (1:1—11:36) 1. Sinfulness of mankind 2. Forgiveness of sin through Christ 3. Freedom from sin's grasp 4. Israel's past, present, and future	Paul clearly sets forth the foundations of the Christian faith. All people are sinful; Christ died to forgive sin; we are made right with God through faith; this begins a new life with a new relationship with God. Like a sports team that constantly reviews the basics, we will be greatly helped in our faith by keeping close to these foundations. If we study Romans carefully, we will never be at a loss to know what to believe.
B. HOW TO BEHAVE (12:1—16:27) 1. Personal responsibility 2. Personal notes	Paul gives clear, practical guidelines for the believers in Rome. The Christian life is not abstract theology unconnected with life, but it has practical implications that will affect how we choose to behave each day. It is not enough merely to know the gospel; we must let it transform our lives and let God impact every aspect of our lives.

MEGATHEMES

THEME	EXPLANATION	IMPORTANCE
Sin	Sin means refusing to do God's will and failing to do all that God wants. Since Adam's rebellion against God, our nature is to disobey him. Our sin cuts us off from God. Sin causes us to want to live our own way rather than God's way. Because God is morally perfect, just, and fair, he is right to condemn sin.	Each person has sinned, either by rebelling against God or by ignoring his will. No matter what our background or how hard we try to live good and moral lives, we cannot earn salvation or remove our sin. Only Christ can save us.
Salvation	Our sin points out our need to be forgiven and cleansed. Although we don't deserve it, God, in his kindness, reached out to love and forgive us. He provides the way for us to be saved. Christ's death paid the penalty for our sin.	It is good news that God saves us from our sin. But we must believe in Jesus Christ and believe that he forgave our sin in order to enter into a wonderful new relationship with God.
Growth	By God's power, believers are sanctified—made holy. This means we are set apart from sin, enabled to obey and to become more like Christ. When we are growing in our relationship with Christ, the Holy Spirit frees us from the demands of the law and from fear of judgment.	Because we are free from sin's control, the law's demands, and fear of God's punishment, we can grow in our relationship with Christ. By trusting in the Holy Spirit and allowing him to help us, we can overcome sin and temptation.
Sovereignty	God oversees and cares about his people—past, present, and future. God's ways of dealing with people are always fair. Because God is in charge of all creation, he can save whomever he wills.	Because of God's mercy, both Jews and Gentiles can be saved. We must all respond to his mercy and accept his gracious offer of forgiveness. Because he is sovereign, let him reign in your heart.
Service	When our purpose is to give credit to God for his love, power, and perfection in all we do, we can serve him properly. Serving him unifies all believers and enables them to show love and sensitivity to others.	None of us can be fully Christlike by ourselves—it takes the entire body of Christ to express Christ fully. By actively and vigorously building up other believers, Christians can be a symphony of service to God.

1:1
[a]1Co 1:1
[b]Ac 9:15
[c]2Co 11:7

A. WHAT TO BELIEVE (1:1–11:36)

Paul begins his message to the Romans by vividly portraying the sinfulness of all mankind, explaining how forgiveness is available through faith in Christ, and showing what believers experience in life through their new faith. In this section, we learn of the centrality of faith to becoming a Christian and to living the Christian life. Apart from faith, we have no hope in life.

1:2
[d]Gal 3:8

1. Sinfulness of mankind

1 Paul, a servant of Christ Jesus, called to be an apostle[a] and set apart[b] for the
gospel of God[c]—2the gospel he promised beforehand through his prophets in
the Holy Scriptures[d] 3regarding his Son, who as to his human nature[e] was a
descendant of David, 4and who through the Spirit[a] of holiness was declared with
power to be the Son of God,[b] by his resurrection from the dead: Jesus Christ our Lord.

1:3
[e]Jn 1:14

a 4 Or *who as to his spirit* **b** 4 Or *was appointed to be the Son of God with power*

THE GOSPEL GOES TO ROME
When Paul wrote his letter to the church in Rome, he had not yet been there, but he had taken the gospel "from Jerusalem all the way around to Illyricum" (15:19). He planned to visit and preach in Rome one day, and hoped to continue to take the gospel further west—even to Spain.

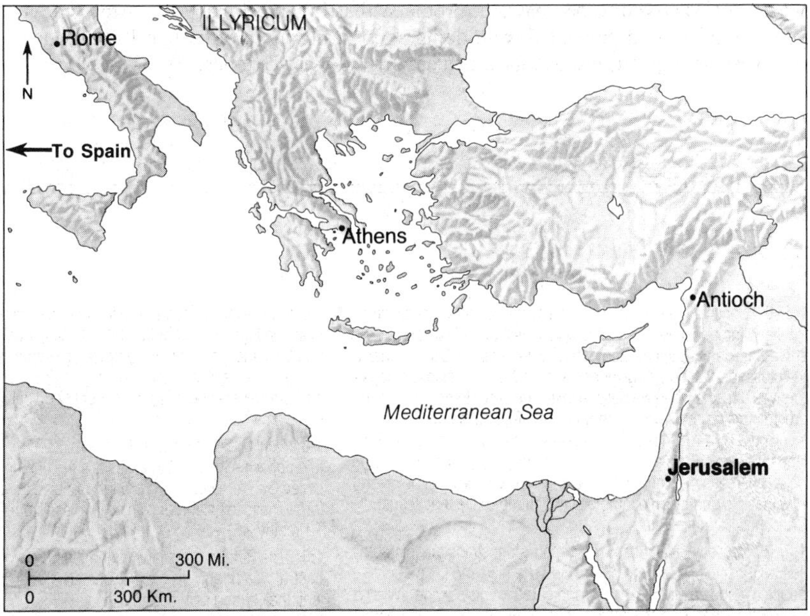

1:1 Paul wrote this letter to the church in Rome. Neither he nor the other church leaders, James and Peter, had yet been to Rome. Most likely, the Roman church had been established by believers who had been at Jerusalem for Pentecost (Acts 2:10) and travellers who had heard the Good News in other places and had brought it back to Rome (for example, Priscilla and Aquila, Acts 18:2; Romans 16:3–5). Paul wrote the letter to the Romans during his ministry in Corinth (at the end of his third missionary journey just before returning to Jerusalem; Acts 20:3; Romans 15:25) to encourage the believers and to express his desire to visit them someday (within three years he would). The Roman church had no New Testament because the Gospels were not yet being circulated in their final written form. Thus, this letter may well have been the first piece of Christian literature the Roman believers had seen. Written to both Jewish and Gentile Christians, the letter to the Romans is a systematic presentation of the Christian faith.

1:1 When Paul, a devout Jew who had at first persecuted the Christians, became a believer, God used him to spread the gospel throughout the world. Although it was as a prisoner, Paul did eventually preach in Rome (Acts 28), perhaps even to Caesar himself. Paul's Profile is found in Acts 9.

1:1 Paul humbly calls himself a servant of Jesus Christ and an apostle ("one who is sent"). For a Roman citizen—which Paul was—to choose to be a servant was unthinkable. But Paul chose to be completely dependent on and obedient to his beloved Master. What is your attitude toward Christ, your Master? Our willingness to serve and obey Jesus Christ enables us to be useful and usable servants to do work for him—work that really matters.

1:2 Some of the prophecies predicting the Good News regarding Jesus Christ are Genesis 12:3; Psalms 16:10; 40:6–10; 118:22; Isaiah 11:1ff; Zechariah 9:9–11; 12:10; Malachi 4:1–6.

1:3, 4 Paul states that Jesus is the Son of God, the promised Messiah, and the resurrected Lord. Paul calls Jesus a descendant of King David to emphasise that Jesus truly had fulfilled the Old Testament Scriptures predicting that the Messiah would come from David's line. With this statement of faith, Paul declares his agreement with the teaching of all Scripture and of the apostles.

1:3–5 Here Paul summarises the Good News about Jesus Christ, who (1) came as a human by natural descent, (2) was part of the Jewish royal line through David, (3) died and was raised from the dead, and (4) opened the door for God's grace and kindness to be poured out on us. The book of Romans is an expansion of these themes.

5Through him and for his name's sake, we received grace and apostleship to call
people from among all the Gentiles[f] to the obedience that comes from faith.[g] 6And
you also are among those who are called to belong to Jesus Christ.[h]

7To all in Rome who are loved by God[i] and called to be saints:

Grace and peace to you from God our Father and from the Lord Jesus Christ.[j]

Paul's Longing to Visit Rome

8First, I thank my God through Jesus Christ for all of you,[k] because your faith is
being reported all over the world.[l] 9God, whom I serve[m] with my whole heart in
preaching the gospel of his Son, is my witness[n] how constantly I remember you 10in
my prayers at all times; and I pray that now at last by God's will the way may be
opened for me to come to you.[o]
11I long to see you[p] so that I may impart to you some spiritual gift to make you
strong—12that is, that you and I may be mutually encouraged by each other's faith.
13I do not want you to be unaware, brothers, that I planned many times to come to
you (but have been prevented from doing so until now)[q] in order that I might have
a harvest among you, just as I have had among the other Gentiles.

1:5 [f] Ac 9:15 [g] Ac 6:7
1:6 [h] Rev 17:14
1:7 [i] Ro 8:39 [j] 1Co 1:3
1:8 [k] 1Co 1:4 [l] Ro 16:19
1:9 [m] 2Ti 1:3 [n] Php 1:8
1:10 [o] Ro 15:32
1:11 [p] Ro 15:23
1:13 [q] Ro 15:22, 23

1:5, 6 Christians have both privilege and a great responsibility. Paul and the apostles received forgiveness ("grace") as an undeserved privilege. But they also received the responsibility to share the message of God's forgiveness with others. God also graciously forgives our sins when we believe in him as Lord. In doing this, we are committing ourselves to begin a new life. Paul's new life also involved a God-given responsibility—to witness about God's Good News to the world as a missionary. God may or may not call you to be an overseas missionary, but he does call you (and all believers) to witness to and be an example of the changed life that Jesus Christ has begun in you.

1:6, 7 Paul says that those who become Christians are invited by Jesus Christ to (1) become part of God's family, and (2) be holy people ("to be saints", set apart, dedicated for his service). What a wonderful expression of what it means to be a Christian! In being reborn into God's family we have the greatest experience of love and the greatest inheritance. Because of all that God has done for us, we strive to be his holy people.

1:6–12 Paul showed his love for the Roman Christians by expressing God's love for them and his own gratitude and prayers for them. To have an effect on people's lives, you first need to love them and believe in them. Paul's passion to teach these people began with his love for them. Thank God for your Christian brothers and sisters, and let them know how deeply you care for them.

1:7 Rome was the capital of the Roman empire that had spread over most of Europe, North Africa, and the Near East. In New Testament times, Rome was experiencing a golden age. The city was wealthy, literary, and artistic. It was a cultural centre, but it was also morally decadent. The Romans worshipped many pagan gods, and even some of the emperors were worshipped. In stark contrast to the Romans, the followers of Christ believed in only one God and lived by his high moral standards.

1:7 Christianity was at odds with the Romans' dependence on military strength. Many Romans were naively pragmatic, believing that any means to accomplish the intended task was good. And for them, nothing worked better than physical might. The Romans trusted in their strong military power to protect them against all enemies. Christians in every age need to be reminded that God is the only permanent source of our security and salvation, and at the same time he is "our Father"!

1:8 Paul uses the phrase "I thank my God through Jesus Christ" to emphasise the point that Christ is the one and only mediator between God and humans. Through Christ, God sends his love and forgiveness to us; through Christ, we send our thanks to God (see 1 Timothy 2:5).

1:8 The Roman Christians, at the Western world's political power centre, were highly visible. Fortunately, their reputation was excellent; their strong faith was making itself known around the world. When people talk about your congregation or your denomination, what do they say? Are their comments accurate? Would you rather they noticed other features? What is the best way to get the public to recognise your faith?

1:9, 10 When you pray continually about a concern, don't be surprised at how God answers. Paul prayed to visit Rome so he could teach the Christians there. When he finally arrived in Rome, it was as a prisoner (see Acts 28:16). Paul prayed for a safe trip, and he did arrive safely—after getting arrested, slapped in the face, shipwrecked, and bitten by a poisonous snake. God's ways of answering our prayers are often far from what we expect. When you pray sincerely, God will answer—although sometimes with timing and in ways you do not expect.

1:11, 12 Paul prayed for the chance to visit these Christians so that he could encourage them with his gift of faith and be encouraged by theirs. As God's missionary, he could help them understand the meaning of the Good News about Jesus. As God's devoted people, they could offer him fellowship and comfort. When Christians gather, everyone should give *and* receive. Our mutual faith gives us a common language and a common purpose for encouraging one another.

1:13 By the end of his third missionary journey, Paul had travelled through Syria, Galatia, Asia, Macedonia, and Achaia. The churches in these areas were made up mostly of Gentile believers.

1:14
[r]1Co 9:16
1:15
[s]Ro 15:20
1:16
[t]2Ti 1:8
[u]1Co 1:18
[v]Ac 3:26
[w]Ro 2:9, 10
1:17
[x]Ro 3:21
[y]Gal 3:11

14 I am bound[r] both to Greeks and non-Greeks, both to the wise and the foolish.
15 That is why I am so eager to preach the gospel also to you who are at Rome.[s]
16 I am not ashamed of the gospel,[t] because it is the power of God[u] for the
salvation of everyone who believes: first for the Jew,[v] then for the Gentile.[w] 17 For
in the gospel a righteousness from God is revealed,[x] a righteousness that is by faith
from first to last,[c] just as it is written: "The righteous will live by faith."[d][y]

[c] 17 Or *is from faith to faith* [d] 17 Hab. 2:4

FAITH

Faith is a word with many meanings. It can mean faithfulness (Matthew 24:45). It can mean absolute trust, as shown by some of the people who came to Jesus for healing (Luke 7:2–10). It can mean confident hope (Hebrews 11:1). Or, as James points out, it can even mean a barren belief that does not result in good deeds (James 2:14–26). What does Paul mean when, in Romans, he speaks of saving faith?

We must be very careful to understand faith as Paul uses the word, because he ties faith so closely to salvation. It is *not* something we must do in order to earn salvation—if that were true, then faith would be just one more deed, and Paul clearly states that human deeds can never save us (Galatians 2:16). Instead, faith is a gift God gives us *because* he is saving us (Ephesians 2:8). It is God's grace, not our faith, that saves us. In his mercy, however, when he saves us he gives us faith—a relationship with his Son that helps us become like him. Through the faith he gives us, he carries us from death into life (John 5:24).

Even in Old Testament times, grace, not deeds, was the basis of salvation. As Hebrews points out, "it is impossible for the blood of bulls and goats to take away sins" (10:4). God intended for his people to look beyond the animal sacrifices to him, but all too often they, instead, put their confidence in fulfilling the requirements of the law—that is, performing the required sacrifices. When Jesus triumphed over death, he cancelled the charges against us and opened the way to the Father (Colossians 2:12–15). Because he is merciful, he offers us faith. How tragic if we turn faith into a deed and try to develop it on our own! We can never come to God through our own faith, any more than his Old Testament people could come through their own sacrifices. Instead, we must accept his gracious offer with thanksgiving and allow him to plant the seed of faith within us.

1:14 By "Greeks and non-Greeks", Paul was referring to those of the Greek culture and those not of the Greek culture. "The wise and the foolish" refers to educated and uneducated people. What was Paul's obligation? After his experience with Christ on the road to Damascus (Acts 9), his whole life was consumed with spreading the Good News of salvation. His obligation was to Christ for being his Saviour, and he was obligated to the entire world. He met his obligation by proclaiming Christ's salvation to *all* people—both Jews and Gentiles, across all cultural, social, racial, and economic lines. We also are obligated to Christ because he took on the punishment we deserve for our sin. Although we cannot repay Christ for all he has done, we can demonstrate our gratitude by showing his love to others.

1:16 Paul was not ashamed because his message was the gospel of Christ, the Good News. It was a message of salvation, it had life-changing power, and it was for everyone. When you are tempted to be ashamed, remember what the Good News is all about. If you focus on God and on what God is doing in the world rather than on your own inadequacy, you won't be ashamed or embarrassed.

1:16 Why did the message go to the Jews first? They had been God's special people for more than 2,000 years, ever since God chose Abraham and promised great blessings to his descendants (Genesis 12:1–3). God did not choose the Jews because they deserved to be chosen (Deuteronomy 7:7, 8; 9:4–6), but because he wanted to show his love and mercy to them, teach them, and prepare them to welcome his Messiah into the world. God chose them, not to play favourites, but so that they would tell the world about his plan of salvation.

For centuries the Jews had been learning about God by obeying his laws, keeping his feasts, and living according to his moral principles. Often they would forget God's promises and requirements; often they would have to be disciplined; but still they had a precious heritage of belief in the one true God. Of all the people on earth, the Jews should have been the most ready to welcome the Messiah and to understand his mission and message—and some of them were (see Luke 2:25, 36–38). Of course, the disciples and the great apostle Paul were faithful Jews who recognised in Jesus God's most precious gift to the human race.

1:16 Jews and Christians alike stood against the idolatrous Roman religions, and Roman officials often confused the two groups. This was especially easy to do since the Christian church in Rome could have been originally composed of Jewish converts who had attended the Feast of Pentecost (see Acts 2:1ff). By the time Paul wrote this letter to the Romans, however, many Gentiles had joined the church. The Jews and the Gentiles needed to know the relationship between Judaism and Christianity.

1:17 The gospel shows us both how righteous God is in his plan for us to be saved, and also how we may be made fit for eternal life. By trusting Christ, our relationship with God is made right. "From first to last" God declares us to be righteous because of faith and faith alone.

1:17 Paul is quoting Habakkuk 2:4. Habakkuk may have understood "will live" to mean this present life only. But Paul extends this statement to include eternal life. As we trust God, we are saved; we find life both now and for ever.

God's Wrath Against Mankind

18The wrath of God[z] is being revealed from heaven against all the godlessness and
wickedness of men who suppress the truth by their wickedness, 19since what may be
known about God is plain to them, because God has made it plain to them.[a] 20For
since the creation of the world God's invisible qualities—his eternal power and divine
nature—have been clearly seen, being understood from what has been made,[b] so that
men are without excuse.
21For although they knew God, they neither glorified him as God nor gave thanks
to him, but their thinking became futile and their foolish hearts were darkened.[c]
22Although they claimed to be wise, they became fools[d] 23and exchanged the glory
of the immortal God for images[e] made to look like mortal man and birds and animals
and reptiles.
24Therefore God gave them over[f] in the sinful desires of their hearts to sexual

1:18 [z]Eph 5:6; Col 3:6
1:19 [a]Ac 14:17
1:20 [b]Ps 19:1-6
1:21 [c]Jer 2:5; Eph 4:17, 18
1:22 [d]1Co 1:20, 27
1:23 [e]Ps 106:20; Jer 2:11; Ac 17:29
1:24 [f]Eph 4:19

1:18 Why is God angry at sinful people? Because they have substituted the truth about him with a fantasy of their own imagination (1:25). They have stifled the truth God naturally reveals to all people in order to believe anything that supports their own self-centred lifestyles. God cannot tolerate sin because his nature is morally perfect. He cannot ignore or condone such wilful rebellion. God wants to remove the sin and restore the sinner—and he is able to, as long as the sinner does not stubbornly distort or reject the truth. But his anger erupts against those who persist in sinning. Make sure you are not pursuing a fantasy rather than the true God. Don't suppress the truth about him merely to protect your own lifestyle.

1:18ff Romans 1:18–3:20 develops Paul's argument that no-one can claim by their own efforts or merit to be good in God's sight—not the masses, not the Romans, not even the Jews. All people everywhere deserve God's condemnation for their sin.

1:18–20 Does anyone have an excuse for not believing in God? The Bible answers an emphatic *no.* God has revealed what he is like in and through his creation. Every person, therefore, either accepts or rejects God. Don't be fooled. When the day comes for God to judge your response to him, no excuses will be accepted. Begin today to give your devotion and worship to him.

1:18–20 In these verses, Paul answers a common objection: How could a loving God send anyone to hell, especially someone who has never heard about Christ? In fact, says Paul, God has revealed himself plainly in the creation to *all* people. And yet people reject even this basic knowledge of God. Also, everyone has an inner sense of what God requires, but they choose not to live up to it. Put another way, people's moral standards are always better than their behaviour. If people suppress God's truth in order to live their own way, they have no excuse. They know the truth, and they will have to endure the consequences of ignoring it.

1:18–20 Some people wonder why we need missionaries if people can know about God through nature (the creation). The answer: (1) Although people know that God exists, they suppress that truth by their wickedness and thus refuse a relationship with him. Missionaries sensitively expose their error and point them to a new beginning. (2) Although people may believe there is a God, they refuse to commit themselves to him. Missionaries help persuade them, both through loving words and caring actions. (3) Missionaries convince people who reject God of the dangerous consequences of their actions. (4) Missionaries help the church obey the Great Commission of our Lord (Matthew 28:19, 20). (5) Most important, though nature reveals God, people need to be told about Jesus and how, through him, they can have a personal relationship with God.

Knowing that God exists is not enough. People must learn that God is loving. They must understand what he did to demonstrate his love for us (5:8). They must be shown how to accept God's forgiveness of their sins. (See also 10:14, 15.)

1:20 What kind of God does nature reveal? Nature shows us a God of might, intelligence, and intricate detail; a God of order and beauty; a God who controls powerful forces. That is *general* revelation. Through *special* revelation (the Bible and the coming of Jesus), we learn about God's love and forgiveness, and the promise of eternal life. God has graciously given us both sources that we might fully believe in him.

1:20 God reveals his divine nature and personal qualities through creation, even though creation's testimony has been distorted by the fall. Adam's sin resulted in a divine curse upon the whole natural order (Genesis 3:17–19); thorns and thistles were an immediate result, and natural disasters have been common from Adam's day to ours. In Romans 8:19–21, Paul says that nature itself is eagerly awaiting its own redemption from the effects of sin (see Revelation 22:3).

1:21–23 How could intelligent people turn to idolatry? Idolatry begins when people reject what they know about God. Instead of looking to him as the Creator and sustainer of life, they see themselves as the centre of the universe. They soon invent "gods" that are convenient projections of their own selfish plans and decrees. These gods may be wooden figures, but they may also be goals or things we pursue such as money, power, or comfort. They may even be misrepresentations of God himself—making God in our image, instead of the reverse. The common denominator is this—idolaters worship the things God made rather than God himself. Is there anything you feel you can't live without? Is there any priority greater than God? Do you have a dream you would sacrifice everything to realise? Does God take first place? Do you worship God or idols of your own making?

1:21–32 Paul clearly portrays the inevitable downward spiral into sin. First, people reject God; next, they make up their own ideas of what a god should be and do; then they fall into sin—sexual sin, greed, hatred, envy, murder, strife, deceit, malice, gossip. Finally, they grow to hate God and encourage others to do so. God does not cause this steady progression towards evil. Rather, when people reject him, he allows them to live as they choose. God gives them over or permits them to experience the natural consequences of their sin. Once caught in the downward spiral, no-one can pull himself or herself out. Sinners must trust Christ alone to put them on the path of escape.

1:23 When Paul says that men exchanged the glory of the immortal God for images of birds, animals, and reptiles, he seems to deliberately state man's wickedness in the terms used in the Genesis narrative of Adam's fall (see Genesis 1:20–26). When we worship the creature instead of the Creator, we lose sight of our own identity as those who are higher than the animals—made in the image of God.

1:24–32 These people chose to reject God, and God allowed them to do it. God does not usually stop us from making choices that are against his will. He lets us declare our supposed independence from him, even though he knows that in time we will become slaves to our own rebellious choices—we will lose our freedom not to sin. Does life without God look like freedom to you? Look more closely. There is no worse slavery than slavery to sin.

impurity for the degrading of their bodies with one another.[g] 25They exchanged the
truth of God for a lie,[h] and worshipped and served created things[i] rather than the
Creator — who is for ever praised.[j] Amen.
26Because of this, God gave them over[k] to shameful lusts.[l] Even their women
exchanged natural relations for unnatural ones.[m] 27In the same way the men also
abandoned natural relations with women and were inflamed with lust for one another.
Men committed indecent acts with other men, and received in themselves the due
penalty for their perversion.[n]
28Furthermore, since they did not think it worth while to retain the knowledge of
God, he gave them over[o] to a depraved mind, to do what ought not to be done. 29They
have become filled with every kind of wickedness, evil, greed and depravity. They
are full of envy, murder, strife, deceit and malice. They are gossips,[p] 30slanderers,
God-haters, insolent, arrogant and boastful; they invent ways of doing evil; they
disobey their parents;[q] 31they are senseless, faithless, heartless,[r] ruthless. 32Al-
though they know God's righteous decree that those who do such things deserve
death,[s] they not only continue to do these very things but also approve[t] of those
who practise them.

God's Righteous Judgment

2 You, therefore, have no excuse,[a] you who pass judgment on someone else, for
at whatever point you judge the other, you are condemning yourself, because you
who pass judgment do the same things.[b] 2Now we know that God's judgment against
those who do such things is based on truth. 3So when you, a mere man, pass judgment
on them and yet do the same things, do you think you will escape God's judgment?

1:24 [g]1Pe 4:3
1:25 [h]Isa 44:20 [i]Jer 10:14 [j]Ro 9:5
1:26 [k]ver 24, 28 [l]1Th 4:5 [m]Lev 18:22, 23
1:27 [n]Lev 18:22; 20:13
1:28 [o]ver 24, 26
1:29 [p]2Co 12:20
1:30 [q]2Ti 3:2
1:31 [r]2Ti 3:3
1:32 [s]Ro 6:23 [t]Ps 50:18; Lk 11:48; Ac 8:1; 22:20
2:1 [a]Ro 1:20 [b]2Sa 12:5-7; Mt 7:1, 2

1:25 People tend to believe lies that reinforce their own selfish, personal beliefs. Today, more than ever, we need to be careful about the input we allow to form our beliefs. With TV, music, films, and the rest of the media often presenting sinful lifestyles and unwholesome values, we find ourselves constantly bombarded by attitudes and beliefs that are totally opposed to the Bible. Be careful about what you allow to form your opinions. The Bible is the only standard of truth. Evaluate all other opinions in the light of its teachings.

1:26, 27 God's plan for natural sexual relationships is his ideal for his creation. Unfortunately, sin distorts the natural use of God's gifts. Sin often means not only denying God, but also denying the way we are made. When people say that any sex act is acceptable as long as nobody gets hurt, they are fooling themselves. In the long run (and often in the short run), sin hurts people — individuals, families, whole societies. How sad it is that people who worship the things God made instead of the Creator so often distort and destroy the very things they claim to value!

1:26, 27 Homosexuality (to exchange or abandon natural relations of sex) was as widespread in Paul's day as it is in ours. Many pagan practices encouraged it. God is willing to receive anyone who comes to him in faith, and Christians should love and accept others no matter what their background. Yet, homosexuality is strictly forbidden in Scripture (Leviticus 18:22). Homosexuality is considered an acceptable practice by many in our world today — even by some churches. But society does not set the standard for God's law. Many homosexuals believe that their desires are normal and that they have a right to express them. But God does not obligate nor encourage us to fulfil all our desires (even normal ones). Those desires that violate his laws must be controlled.

If you have these desires, you can and must resist acting upon them. Consciously avoid places or activities you know will kindle temptations of this kind. Don't underestimate the power of Satan to tempt you, nor the potential for serious harm if you yield to these temptations. Remember, God can and will forgive sexual sins just as he forgives other sins. Surrender yourself to the grace and mercy of God, asking him to show you the way out of sin and into the light of his freedom and his love. Prayer, Bible study, and strong support in a Christian church can help you to gain strength to resist these powerful temptations. If you are already deeply involved in homosexual behaviour, seek help from a trustworthy, professional, pastoral counsellor.

1:32 How were these people aware of God's death penalty? Human beings, created in God's image, have a basic moral nature and a conscience. This truth is understood beyond religious circles. Psychologists, for example, say that the rare person who has no conscience has a serious personality disorder that is extremely difficult to treat. Most people instinctively know when they do wrong — but they may not care. Some people will even risk an early death for the freedom to indulge their desires now. "I know it's wrong, but I really want it," they say; or, "I know it's dangerous, but it's worth the risk." For such people, part of the "fun" is going against God's law, the community's moral standards, common sense, or their own sense of right and wrong. But deep down inside they know that sin deserves the punishment of death (6:23).

2:1 Whenever we find ourselves feeling justifiably angry about someone's sin, we should be careful. We need to speak out against sin, but we must do so in a spirit of humility. Often the sins we notice most clearly in others are the ones that have taken root in us. If we look closely at ourselves, we may find that we are committing the same sins in more socially acceptable forms. For example, a person who gossips may be very critical of others who gossip about him or her.

2:1ff When Paul's letter was read in the Roman church, no doubt many heads nodded as he condemned idol worshippers, homosexual practices, and violent people. But what surprise his listeners must have felt when he turned on them and said in effect, "You have no excuse. You are just as bad!" Paul was emphatically stressing that *nobody* is good enough to save himself or herself. If we want to avoid punishment and live eternally with Christ, all of us, whether we have been murderers and molesters or whether we have been honest, hardworking, solid citizens, must depend totally on God's grace. Paul is not discussing whether some sins are worse than others. Any sin is enough to lead us to depend on Jesus Christ for salvation and eternal life. We have all sinned repeatedly, and there is no way apart from Christ to be saved from sin's consequences.

4 Or do you show contempt for the riches[c] of his kindness,[d] tolerance[e] and patience,[f] not realising that God's kindness leads you towards repentance?[g]
5 But because of your stubbornness and your unrepentant heart, you are storing up
wrath against yourself for the day of God's wrath, when his righteous judgment[h] will
be revealed. 6 God "will give to each person according to what he has done".[a][i] 7 To
those who by persistence in doing good seek glory, honour[j] and immortality,[k] he
will give eternal life. 8 But for those who are self-seeking and who reject the truth and
follow evil,[l] there will be wrath and anger. 9 There will be trouble and distress for
every human being who does evil: first for the Jew, then for the Gentile;[m] 10 but glory,
honour and peace for everyone who does good: first for the Jew, then for the Gentile.[n]
11 For God does not show favouritism.[o]
12 All who sin apart from the law will also perish apart from the law, and all who
sin under the law[p] will be judged by the law. 13 For it is not those who hear the law
who are righteous in God's sight, but it is those who obey[q] the law who will be
declared righteous. 14 (Indeed, when Gentiles, who do not have the law, do by nature
things required by the law,[r] they are a law for themselves, even though they do not
have the law, 15 since they show that the requirements of the law are written on their
hearts, their consciences also bearing witness, and their thoughts now accusing, now
even defending them.) 16 This will take place on the day when God will judge men's
secrets[s] through Jesus Christ,[t] as my gospel[u] declares.

The Jews and the Law

17 Now you, if you call yourself a Jew; if you rely on the law and brag about your
relationship to God;[v] 18 if you know his will and approve of what is superior because
you are instructed by the law; 19 if you are convinced that you are a guide for the blind,
a light for those who are in the dark, 20 an instructor of the foolish, a teacher of infants,
because you have in the law the embodiment of knowledge and truth — 21 you, then,
who teach others, do you not teach yourself? You who preach against stealing, do you
steal?[w] 22 You who say that people should not commit adultery, do you commit

a *6* Psalm 62:12; Prov. 24:12

2:4 c Ro 9:23; Eph 1:7, 18; 2:7 d Ro 11:22 e Ro 3:25 f Ex 34:6 g 2Pe 3:9
2:5 h Jude 6
2:6 i Ps 62:12; Mt 16:27
2:7 j ver 10 k 1Co 15:53, 54
2:8 l 2Th 2:12
2:9 m 1Pe 4:17
2:10 n ver 9
2:11 o Ac 10:34
2:12 p Ro 3:19; 1Co 9:20, 21
2:13 q Jas 1:22, 23, 25
2:14 r Ac 10:35
2:16 s Ecc 12:14 t Ac 10:42 u Ro 16:25
2:17 v ver 23; Mic 3:11; Ro 9:4
2:21 w Mt 23:3, 4

2:4 In his kindness, God holds back his judgment, giving people time to repent. It is easy to mistake God's patience for approval of the wrong way we are living. Self-evaluation is difficult, and it is even more difficult to expose our conduct to God and let him tell us where we need to change. But as Christians we must pray constantly that God will point out our sins, so that he can heal them. Unfortunately, we are more likely to be amazed at God's patience with others than humbled by his patience with us.

2:5–11 Although God does not usually punish us immediately for sin, his eventual judgment is certain. We don't know exactly when it will happen, but we know that no-one will escape that final encounter with the Creator. For more on judgment, see John 12:48 and Revelation 20:11–15.

2:7 Paul says that those who patiently and persistently *do* God's will find eternal life. He is not contradicting his previous statement that salvation comes by faith alone (1:16, 17). We are not saved by good deeds, but when we commit our lives fully to God, we want to please him and do his will. As such, our good deeds are a grateful *response* to what God has done, not a prerequisite to earning his grace.

2:12–15 People are condemned not for what they don't know, but for what they do with what they know. Those who know God's written word and his law will be judged by them. Those who have never seen a Bible still know right from wrong, and they will be judged because they did not keep even those standards that their own consciences dictated. Our modern-day sense of fair play and the rights of the individual often balks at God's judgment. But keep in mind that people violate the very standards they create for themselves.

2:12–15 If you travelled around the world, you would find evidence in every society and culture of God's moral law. For example, all cultures prohibit murder, and yet in all societies that law has been broken. We belong to a stubborn race. We know what's right, but we insist on doing what's wrong. It is not enough to know what's right; we must also do it. Admit to yourself and to God that you fit the human pattern and frequently fail to live up to your own standards (much more to God's standards). That's the first step to forgiveness and healing.

2:17ff Paul continues to argue that all stand guilty before God. After describing the fate of the unbelieving, pagan Gentiles, he moves to that of the religiously privileged. Despite their knowledge of God's will, they are guilty because they too have refused to live by their beliefs. Those of us who have grown up in Christian families are the religiously privileged of today. Paul's condemnation applies to us if we do not live up to what we know.

2:21, 22 Paul explained to the Jews that they needed to teach *themselves,* not others, by their law. They knew the law so well that they had learned how to excuse their own actions while criticising others. But the law is more than legalistic minimum requirements — it is a guideline for living according to God's will. It is also a reminder that we cannot please God without a proper relationship with him. As Jesus pointed out, even withholding what rightfully belongs to someone else is stealing (Mark 7:9–13), and looking on another person with lustful, adulterous intent is adultery (Matthew 5:27, 28). Before we accuse others, we must look at ourselves and see if that sin, in any form, exists within us.

2:21–27 These verses are a scathing criticism of hypocrisy. It is much easier to tell others how to behave than to behave properly ourselves. It is easier to say the right words than to allow them to take root in our lives. Do you ever advise others to do something you are unwilling to do yourself? Make sure that your actions match your words.

2:22 [x]Ac 19:37 2:23 [y]ver 17 2:24 [z]Isa 52:5; Eze 36:22 2:25 [a]Gal 5:3 [b]Jer 4:4 2:26 [c]Ro 8:4 [d]1Co 7:19 2:27 [e]Mt 12:41, 42 2:28 [f]Mt 3:9; Jn 8:39; Ro 9:6, 7 [g]Gal 6:15 2:29 [h]Php 3:3; Col 2:11 [i]Ro 7:6 [j]Jn 5:44; 1Co 4:5; 2Co 10:18; 1Th 2:4; 1Pe 3:4 3:2 [a]Dt 4:8; Ps 147:19 3:3 [b]Heb 4:2 [c]2Ti 2:13 3:4 [d]Jn 3:33 [e]Ps 116:11 [f]Ps 51:4

adultery? You who abhor idols, do you rob temples?[x] 23You who brag about the
law,[y] do you dishonour God by breaking the law? 24As it is written: "God's name
is blasphemed among the Gentiles because of you."[b][z]
25Circumcision has value if you observe the law,[a] but if you break the law, you
have become as though you had not been circumcised.[b] 26If those who are not
circumcised keep the law's requirements,[c] will they not be regarded as though they
were circumcised?[d] 27The one who is not circumcised physically and yet obeys the
law will condemn you[e] who, even though you have the[c] written code and circumcision, are a law-breaker.
28A man is not a Jew if he is only one outwardly,[f] nor is circumcision merely
outward and physical.[g] 29No, a man is a Jew if he is one inwardly; and circumcision
is circumcision of the heart, by the Spirit,[h] not by the written code.[i] Such a man's
praise is not from men, but from God.[j]

God's Faithfulness

3 What advantage, then, is there in being a Jew, or what value is there in circumcision? 2Much in every way! First of all, they have been entrusted with the very
words of God.[a]
3What if some did not have faith?[b] Will their lack of faith nullify God's faithfulness?[c] 4Not at all! Let God be true,[d] and every man a liar.[e] As it is written:

> "So that you may be proved right when you speak
> and prevail when you judge."[a][f]

[b] *24* Isaiah 52:5; Ezek. 36:22 [c] *27* Or *who, by means of a* [a] *4* Psalm 51:4

SALVATION'S WAY

Romans 3:23	Everyone has sinned.
Romans 6:23	The penalty for our sin is death.
Romans 5:8	Jesus Christ died for sin.
Romans 10:8–10	To be forgiven for our sin, we must believe and confess that Jesus is Lord. Salvation comes through Jesus Christ.

2:24 If you claim to be one of God's people, your life should reflect what God is like. When you disobey God, you dishonour his name. People may even blaspheme or profane God's name because of you. What do people think about God from watching your life?

2:25–29 *Circumcision* refers to the sign of God's special covenant with his people. Submitting to this rite was required for all Jewish males (Genesis 17:9–14). According to Paul, being a Jew (being circumcised) meant nothing if the person didn't obey God's laws. On the other hand, the Gentiles (the uncircumcised) would receive God's love and approval if they kept the law's requirements. Paul goes on to explain that a real Jew (one who pleases God) is not someone who has been circumcised (a Jew "outwardly") but someone whose heart is right with God and obeys him (a Jew "inwardly").

2:28, 29 To be a Jew meant you were in God's family, an heir to all his promises. Yet Paul made it clear that membership in God's family is based on internal, not external, qualities. All whose hearts are right with God are real Jews – that is, part of God's family (see also Galatians 3:7). Attending church or being baptised, confirmed, or accepted for membership is not enough, just as submitting to circumcision was not enough for the Jews. God desires our heartfelt devotion and obedience. (See also Deuteronomy 10:16; Jeremiah 4:4 for more on "circumcision of the heart".)

3:1ff In this chapter Paul contends that everyone stands guilty before God. Paul has dismantled the common excuses of people who refuse to admit they are sinners: (1) "There is no God" or "I follow my conscience" – 1:18–32; (2) "I'm not as bad as other people" – 2:1–16; (3) "I'm a church member" or "I'm a religious person" – 2:17–29. No-one will be exempt from God's judgment on sin. Every person must accept that he or she is sinful and condemned before God. Only then can we understand and receive God's wonderful gift of salvation.

3:1ff What a depressing picture Paul is painting! All of us – pagan Gentiles, humanitarians, and religious people – are condemned by our own actions. The law, which God gave to show the way to live, holds up our evil deeds to public view. Is there any hope for us? Yes, says Paul. The law condemns us, it is true, but the law is not the basis of our hope. God himself is. He, in his righteousness and wonderful love, offers us eternal life. We receive our salvation not through law but through faith in Jesus Christ. We do not – cannot – earn it; we accept it as a gift from our loving heavenly Father.

3:2 The Jewish nation had many advantages. (1) They were entrusted with God's laws ("the very words of God", Exodus 19, 20; Deuteronomy 4:8). (2) They were the race through whom the Messiah came to earth (Isaiah 11:1–10; Matthew 1:1–17). (3) They were the beneficiaries of covenants with God himself (Genesis 17:1–16; Exodus 19:3–6). But these privileges did not make them better than anyone else (see 3:9). In fact, because of them the Jews were even more responsible to live up to God's requirements.

5 But if our unrighteousness brings out God's righteousness more clearly, what shall
we say? That God is unjust in bringing his wrath on us? (I am using a human
argument.)[g] 6 Certainly not! If that were so, how could God judge the world?[h]
7 Someone might argue, "If my falsehood enhances God's truthfulness and so increases
his glory,[i] why am I still condemned as a sinner?" 8 Why not say—as we are being
slanderously reported as saying and as some claim that we say—"Let us do evil that
good may result"?[j] Their condemnation is deserved.

No One Is Righteous

9 What shall we conclude then? Are we any better?[b] Not at all! We have already
made the charge that Jews and Gentiles alike are all under sin.[k] 10 As it is written:

"There is no-one righteous, not even one;
11 there is no-one who understands,
no-one who seeks God.
12 All have turned away,
they have together become worthless;
there is no-one who does good,
not even one."[c] [l]
13 "Their throats are open graves;
their tongues practise deceit."[d] [m]
"The poison of vipers is on their lips."[e] [n]
14 "Their mouths are full of cursing and bitterness."[f] [o]
15 "Their feet are swift to shed blood;
16 ruin and misery mark their ways,
17 and the way of peace they do not know."[g]
18 "There is no fear of God before their eyes."[h] [p]

19 Now we know that whatever the law says,[q] it says to those who are under the
law,[r] so that every mouth may be silenced and the whole world held accountable to
God. 20 Therefore no-one will be declared righteous in his sight by observing the law;[s]
rather, through the law we become conscious of sin.[t]

2. Forgiveness of sin through Christ

Righteousness Through Faith

21 But now a righteousness from God,[u] apart from law, has been made known, to
which the Law and the Prophets testify.[v] 22 This righteousness from God comes

3:5 [g]Ro 6:19; Gal 3:15
3:6 [h]Ge 18:25
3:7 [i]ver 4
3:8 [j]Ro 6:1
3:9 [k]ver 19, 23; Gal 3:22
3:12 [l]Ps 14:1-3
3:13 [m]Ps 5:9 [n]Ps 140:3
3:14 [o]Ps 10:7
3:18 [p]Ps 36:1
3:19 [q]Jn 10:34 [r]Ro 2:12
3:20 [s]Ac 13:39; Gal 2:16 [t]Ro 7:7
3:21 [u]Ro 1:17; 9:30 [v]Ac 10:43

b 9 Or *worse* c 12 Psalms 14:1–3; 53:1–3; Eccles. 7:20 d 13 Psalm 5:9 e 13 Psalm 140:3 f 14 Psalm 10:7
g 17 Isaiah 59:7,8 h 18 Psalm 36:1

3:5–8 Some may think they don't have to worry about sin because (1) it's God's job to forgive; (2) God is so loving that he won't judge us; (3) sin isn't so bad—it teaches us valuable lessons, or (4) we need to stay in touch with the culture around us. It is far too easy to take God's grace for granted. But God cannot overlook sin. Sinners, no matter how many excuses they make, will have to answer to God for their sin.

3:10–12 Paul is referring to Psalm 14:1–3. "There is no-one righteous" means "no-one is innocent". Every person is valuable in God's eyes because God created us in his image and he loves us. But no-one is righteous (that is, no-one can earn right standing with God). Though valuable, we have fallen into sin. But God, through Jesus his Son, has redeemed us and offers to forgive us if we return to him in faith.

3:10–18 Paul uses these Old Testament references to show that humanity in general, in its present sinful condition, is unacceptable before God. Have you ever thought to yourself, "Well, I'm not too bad. I'm a pretty good person"? Look at these verses and see if any of them apply to you. Have you ever lied? Have you ever hurt someone's feelings by your words or tone of voice? Are you bitter towards anyone? Do you become angry with those who strongly disagree with you? In thought, word, and deed you, like everyone else in the world, stand guilty before God. We must remember who we are in his sight—alienated sinners. Don't deny that you are a sinner. Instead, allow your desperate need to point you towards Christ.

3:19 The last time someone accused you of wrongdoing, what was your reaction? Denial, argument, and defensiveness? The Bible tells us the world stands silent and accountable before Almighty God. No excuses or arguments are left. Have you reached the point with God where you are ready to drop your defences and await his decision? If you haven't, stop now and admit your sin to him. If you have, the following verses are truly good news for you!

3:20, 31 In these verses we see two functions of God's law. First, it shows us where we go wrong. Because of the law, we know that we are helpless sinners and that we must come to Jesus Christ for mercy. Second, the moral code revealed in the law can serve to guide our actions by holding up God's moral standards. We do not earn salvation by keeping the law (no-one except Christ ever kept or could keep God's law perfectly), but we do please God when our lives conform to his revealed will for us.

3:22
[w]Ro 9:30
[x]Ro 10:12; Gal 3:28; Col 3:11
3:24
[y]Ro 4:16
[z]Eph 1:7, 14 Heb 9:12
3:25
[a]1Jn 4:10
[b]Heb 9:12, 14
[c]Ac 17:30
3:27
[d]Ro 2:17, 23; 4:2; 1Co 1:29-31
3:28
[e]ver 20, 21; Ac 13:39
3:29
[f]Ro 9:24
3:30
[g]Gal 3:8

through faith[w] in Jesus Christ to all who believe. There is no difference,[x] 23 for all
have sinned and fall short of the glory of God, 24 and are justified freely by his grace[y]
through the redemption[z] that came by Christ Jesus. 25 God presented him as a sacrifice
of atonement,[i][a] through faith in his blood.[b] He did this to demonstrate his justice,
because in his forbearance he had left the sins committed beforehand unpunished[c]
26 — he did it to demonstrate his justice at the present time, so as to be just and the
one who justifies those who have faith in Jesus.
27 Where, then, is boasting?[d] It is excluded. On what principle? On that of observing the law? No, but on that of faith. 28 For we maintain that a man is justified by faith
apart from observing the law.[e] 29 Is God the God of Jews only? Is he not the God
of Gentiles too? Yes, of Gentiles too,[f] 30 since there is only one God, who will justify
the circumcised by faith and the uncircumcised through that same faith.[g] 31 Do we,
then, nullify the law by this faith? Not at all! Rather, we uphold the law.

[i] 25 *Or as the one who would turn aside his wrath, taking away sin*

CRUCIAL CONCEPTS IN ROMANS

ELECTION Romans 9:10–13	God's choice of an individual or group for a specific purpose or destiny.
JUSTIFICATION Romans 4:25; 5:18	God's act of declaring us "not guilty" for our sins.
PROPITIATION Romans 3:25	The removal of God's punishment for sin through the perfect sacrifice of Jesus Christ.
REDEMPTION Romans 3:24; 8:23	Jesus Christ has paid the price so we can go free. The price of sin is death; Jesus paid the price.
SANCTIFICATION Romans 5:2; 15:16	Becoming more and more like Jesus Christ through the work of the Holy Spirit.
GLORIFICATION Romans 8:18, 19, 30	The ultimate state of the believer after death when he or she becomes like Christ (1 John 3:2).

3:21–29 After all this bad news about our sinfulness and God's condemnation, Paul gives the wonderful news. There is a way to be declared not guilty – by trusting Jesus Christ to take away our sins. Trusting means putting our confidence in Christ to forgive our sins, to make us right with God, and to empower us to live the way he taught us. God's solution is available to all of us regardless of our background or past behaviour.

3:23 Some sins seem bigger than others because their obvious consequences are much more serious. Murder, for example, seems to us to be worse than hatred, and adultery seems worse than lust. But this does not mean that because we do lesser sins we deserve eternal life. All sin makes us sinners, and all sin cuts us off from our holy God. All sin, therefore, leads to death (because it disqualifies us from living with God), regardless of how great or small it seems. Don't minimise "little" sins or overrate "big" sins. They all separate us from God, but they all can be forgiven.

3:24 *Justified* means to be declared not guilty. When a judge in a court of law declares the defendant not guilty, all the charges are removed from his record. Legally, it is as if the person had never been accused. When God forgives our sins, our record is wiped clean. From his perspective, it is as though we had never sinned.

3:24 Redemption refers to Christ setting sinners free from slavery to sin. In Old Testament times, a person's debts could result in his being sold as a slave. The next of kin could redeem him – buy his freedom. Christ purchased our freedom and the price was his life.

3:25 Christ is our sacrifice of atonement. In other words, he died in our place, for our sins. God is justifiably angry at sinners. They have rebelled against him and cut themselves off from his life-giving power. But God declares Christ's death to be the appropriate, designated sacrifice for our sin. Christ then stands in our place, having paid the penalty of death for our sin, and he completely satisfies God's demands. His sacrifice brings pardon, deliverance, and freedom.

3:25 What happened to people who lived before Christ came and died for sin? If God condemned them, was he being unfair? If he saved them, was Christ's sacrifice unnecessary? Paul shows that God forgave all human sin at the cross of Jesus. Old Testament believers looked forward in faith to Christ's coming and were saved, even though they did not know Jesus' name or the details of his earthly life. Unlike the Old Testament believers, you know about the God who loved the world so much that he gave his own Son (John 3:16). Have you put your trust in him?

3:27, 28 Most religions prescribe specific duties that must be performed to make a person acceptable to a god. Christianity is unique in teaching that the good deeds we do will not make us right with God. No amount of human achievement or progress in personal development will close the gap between God's moral perfection and our imperfect daily performance. Good deeds are important, but they will not earn us eternal life. We are saved only by trusting in what God has done for us (see Ephesians 2:8–10).

3:28 Why does God save us by faith alone? (1) Faith eliminates the pride of human effort, because faith is not a deed that we do. (2) Faith exalts what God has done, not what people do. (3) Faith admits that we can't keep the law or measure up to God's standards – we need help. (4) Faith is based on our relationship with God, not our performance for God.

3:31 There were some misunderstandings between the Jewish and Gentile Christians in Rome. Worried Jewish Christians were asking Paul, "Does faith wipe out everything Judaism stands for? Does it cancel our Scriptures, put an end to our customs, declare that God is no longer working through us?" (This is essentially the question used to open chapter 3.) "Absolutely not!" says Paul. When we understand the way of salvation through faith, we understand the Jewish religion better. We know why Abraham was chosen, why the law was given, why God worked patiently with Israel for centuries. Faith does not wipe out the Old Testament. Rather, it makes God's dealings with the Jewish people understandable. In chapter 4, Paul will expand on this theme (see also 5:20, 21; 8:3, 4; 13:9, 10; Galatians 3:24–29; and 1 Timothy 1:8 for more on this concept).

Abraham Justified by Faith

4 What then shall we say that Abraham, our forefather, discovered in this matter?
2 If, in fact, Abraham was justified by works, he had something to boast
about—but not before God.[a] 3 What does the Scripture say? "Abraham believed God,
and it was credited to him as righteousness."[a][b]
4 Now when a man works, his wages are not credited to him as a gift,[c] but as an
obligation. 5 However, to the man who does not work but trusts God who justifies the
wicked, his faith is credited as righteousness. 6 David says the same thing when he
speaks of the blessedness of the man to whom God credits righteousness apart from
works:

7 "Blessed are they
whose transgressions are forgiven,
whose sins are covered.
8 Blessed is the man
whose sin the Lord will never count against him."[b][d]

9 Is this blessedness only for the circumcised, or also for the uncircumcised?[e] We
have been saying that Abraham's faith was credited to him as righteousness.[f] 10 Under
what circumstances was it credited? Was it after he was circumcised, or before? It
was not after, but before! 11 And he received the sign of circumcision, a seal of the
righteousness that he had by faith while he was still uncircumcised.[g] So then, he is
the father[h] of all who believe[i] but have not been circumcised, in order that righteousness might be credited to them. 12 And he is also the father of the circumcised who
not only are circumcised but who also walk in the footsteps of the faith that our father
Abraham had before he was circumcised.
13 It was not through law that Abraham and his offspring received the promise[j] that
he would be heir of the world,[k] but through the righteousness that comes by faith.
14 For if those who live by law are heirs, faith has no value and the promise is
worthless,[l] 15 because law brings wrath.[m] And where there is no law there is no
transgression.[n]
16 Therefore, the promise comes by faith, so that it may be by grace[o] and may be

[a] *3* Gen. 15:6; also in verse 22 [b] *8* Psalm 32:1,2

4:2 [a] 1Co 1:31
4:3 [b] ver 5, 9, 22; Ge 15:6; Gal 3:6; Jas 2:23
4:4 [c] Ro 11:6
4:8 [d] Ps 32:1, 2; 2Co 5:19
4:9 [e] Ro 3:30 [f] ver 3
4:11 [g] Ge 17:10, 11 [h] ver 16, 17; Lk 19:9 [i] Ro 3:22
4:13 [j] Gal 3:16, 29 [k] Ge 17:4-6
4:14 [l] Gal 3:18
4:15 [m] Ro 7:7-25; 1Co 15:56; 2Co 3:7; Gal 3:10; Ro 7:12 [n] Ro 3:20; 7:7
4:16 [o] Ro 3:24

4:1–3 The Jews were proud to be called children of Abraham. Paul uses Abraham as a good example of someone who was saved by faith. By emphasising faith, Paul is not saying that God's laws are unimportant (4:13) but that it is impossible to be saved simply by obeying them. For more about Abraham, see his Profile in Genesis 18.

4:4 This verse means that if a person could earn right standing with God by being good, the granting of that gift wouldn't be a free act; it would be an obligation. Our self-reliance is futile; all we can do is cast ourselves on God's mercy and grace.

4:5 When some people learn that they are saved by God through faith, they start to worry. "Do I have enough faith?" they wonder. "Is my faith strong enough to save me?" These people miss the point. It is Jesus Christ who saves us, not *our* feelings or actions, and he is strong enough to save us no matter how weak our faith is. Jesus offers us salvation as a gift because he loves us, not because we have earned it through our powerful faith. What, then, is the role of faith? Faith is believing and trusting in Jesus Christ, and reaching out to accept his wonderful gift of salvation.

4:6–8 What can we do to get rid of guilt? King David was guilty of terrible sins—adultery, murder, lying—and yet he experienced the joy of forgiveness. We too can have this joy when we (1) stop denying our guilt and recognise that we have sinned, (2) admit our guilt to God and ask for his forgiveness, and (3) let go of our guilt and believe that God has forgiven us. This can be difficult when a sin has taken root and grown over many years, when it is very serious, or when it involves others. We must remember that Jesus is willing and able to forgive every sin. In view of the tremendous price he paid on the cross, it is arrogant to think that any of our sins are too great for him to cover. Even though our faith is weak, our conscience is sensitive, and our memory haunts us, God's word declares that sins confessed are sins forgiven (1 John 1:9).

4:10 Circumcision was a sign to others and a personal seal or certification for the Jews that they were God's special people. Circumcision of all Jewish boys set the Jewish people apart from the nations who worshipped other gods; thus it was a very important ceremony. God gave the blessing and the command for this ceremony to Abraham (Genesis 17:9–14).

4:10–12 Rituals did not earn any reward for Abraham; he had been blessed long before the circumcision ceremony was introduced. Abraham found favour with God by faith alone, before he was circumcised. Genesis 12:1–4 tells of God's call to Abraham when he was 75 years old; the circumcision ceremony was introduced when he was 99 (Genesis 17:1–14). Ceremonies and rituals serve as reminders of our faith, and they instruct new and younger believers. But we should not think that they give us any special merit before God. They are outward signs and seals that demonstrate inward belief and trust. The focus of our faith should be on Christ and his saving actions, not on our own actions.

4:16 Paul explains that Abraham had pleased God through Abraham's faith alone, before he had ever heard about the rituals that would become so important to the Jewish people. We too are saved by faith plus nothing. It is not by loving God and doing good that we are saved; neither is it by faith plus love or by faith plus

4:16 [p]Ro 15:8
4:17 [q]Ge 17:5 [r]Jn 5:21 [s]Isa 48:13 [t]1Co 1:28
4:18 [u]ver 17 [v]Ge 15:5
4:19 [w]Heb 11:11, 12 [x]Ge 17:17 [y]Ge 18:11
4:20 [z]Mt 9:8
4:21 [a]Ge 18:14; Heb 11:19
4:22 [b]ver 3
4:24 [c]Ro 15:4; 1Co 9:10; 10:11 [d]Ro 10:9 [e]Ac 2:24
4:25 [f]Isa 53:5, 6; Ro 5:6, 8
5:1 [a]Ro 3:28
5:2 [b]Eph 2:18 [c]1Co 15:1 [d]Heb 3:6

guaranteed[p] to all Abraham's offspring—not only to those who are of the law but
also to those who are of the faith of Abraham. He is the father of us all. 17As it is
written: "I have made you a father of many nations."[c][q] He is our father in the sight
of God, in whom he believed—the God who gives life[r] to the dead and calls[s] things
that are not[t] as though they were.
18Against all hope, Abraham in hope believed and so became the father of many
nations,[u] just as it had been said to him, "So shall your offspring be."[d][v] 19Without
weakening in his faith, he faced the fact that his body was as good as dead[w]—since
he was about a hundred years old[x]—and that Sarah's womb was also dead.[y] 20Yet
he did not waver through unbelief regarding the promise of God, but was strengthened
in his faith and gave glory to God,[z] 21being fully persuaded that God had power to
do what he had promised.[a] 22This is why "it was credited to him as righteousness."[b]
23The words "it was credited to him" were written not for him alone, 24but also for
us,[c] to whom God will credit righteousness—for us who believe in him[d] who raised
Jesus our Lord from the dead.[e] 25He was delivered over to death for our sins[f] and
was raised to life for our justification.

Peace and Joy

5 Therefore, since we have been justified through faith,[a] we[a] have peace with
God through our Lord Jesus Christ, 2through whom we have gained access[b] by
faith into this grace in which we now stand.[c] And we[a] rejoice in the hope[d] of the

c *17* Gen. 17:5 d *18* Gen. 15:5 a *1, 2* Or *let us*

WHAT WE HAVE AS CHILDREN

What we have as Adam's children	*What we have as God's children*
Ruin 5:9	Rescue 5:8
Sin 5:12, 15, 21	Righteousness 5:18
Death 5:12, 16, 21	Eternal life 5:17, 21
Separation from God 5:18	Relationship with God 5:11, 19
Disobedience 5:12, 19	Obedience 5:19
Judgment 5:18	Deliverance 5:10, 11
Law 5:20	Grace 5:20

good deeds. We are saved only through faith in Christ, trusting him to forgive all our sins. For more on Abraham, see his Profile in Genesis 17.

4:17 The promise (or covenant) God gave Abraham stated that Abraham would be the father of many nations (Genesis 17:2–4) and that the entire world would be blessed through him (Genesis 12:3). This promise was fulfilled in Jesus Christ. Jesus was from Abraham's line, and truly the whole world was blessed through him.

4:21 Abraham never doubted that God would fulfil his promise. Abraham's life was marked by mistakes, sins, and failures as well as by wisdom and goodness, but he consistently trusted God. His faith was strengthened by the obstacles he faced, and his life was an example of faith in action. If he had looked only at his own resources for subduing Canaan and founding a nation, he would have given up in despair. But Abraham looked to God, obeyed him, and waited for God to fulfil his word.

4:25 When we believe, an exchange takes place. We give Christ our sins, and he gives us his righteousness and forgiveness (see 2 Corinthians 5:21). There is nothing we can do to earn this. Only through Christ can we receive God's righteousness. What an incredible bargain this is for us! But sadly, many still choose to pass up this gift to continue "enjoying" their sin.

5:1 We now have peace *with God,* which may differ from peaceful feelings such as calmness and tranquility. Peace with God means that we have been reconciled with him. There is no more hostility between us, no sin blocking our relationship with him. Peace with God is possible only because Jesus paid the price for our sins through his death on the cross.

5:1–5 These verses introduce a section that contains some difficult concepts. To understand the next four chapters, it helps to keep in mind the two-sided reality of the Christian life. On the one hand, we are complete in Christ (our acceptance with him is secure). On the other hand, we are growing in Christ (we are becoming more and more like him). At one and the same time we have the status of kings and the duties of slaves. We feel both the presence of Christ and the pressure of sin. We enjoy the peace that comes from being made right with God, but we still face daily problems that often help us grow. If we remember these two sides of the Christian life, we will not grow discouraged as we face temptations and problems. Instead, we will learn to depend on the power available to us from Christ, who lives in us by the Holy Spirit.

5:2 Paul states that, as believers, we now stand in a place of highest privilege ("this grace in which we now stand"). Not only has God declared us not guilty; he has drawn us close to himself. Instead of being enemies, we have become his friends—in fact, his own children (John 15:15; Galatians 4:5).

5:2–5 As Paul states clearly in 1 Corinthians 13:13, faith, hope, and love are at the heart of the Christian life. Our relationship with God begins with *faith,* which helps us realise that we are delivered from our past by Christ's death. *Hope* grows as we learn all that God has in mind for us; it gives us the promise of the future. And God's *love* fills our lives and gives us the ability to reach out to others.

glory of God. 3Not only so, but we[b] also rejoice in our sufferings,[e] because we know
that suffering produces perseverance;[f] 4perseverance, character; and character, hope.
5And hope[g] does not disappoint us, because God has poured out his love into our
hearts by the Holy Spirit,[h] whom he has given us.
6You see, at just the right time,[i] when we were still powerless, Christ died for
the ungodly.[j] 7Very rarely will anyone die for a righteous man, though for a good
man someone might possibly dare to die. 8But God demonstrates his own love for us
in this: While we were still sinners, Christ died for us.[k]
9Since we have now been justified by his blood,[l] how much more shall we be saved
from God's wrath[m] through him! 10For if, when we were God's enemies,[n] we were
reconciled[o] to him through the death of his Son, how much more, having been
reconciled, shall we be saved through his life![p] 11Not only is this so, but we also
rejoice in God through our Lord Jesus Christ, through whom we have now received
reconciliation.

Death Through Adam, Life Through Christ

12Therefore, just as sin entered the world through one man,[q] and death through
sin,[r] and in this way death came to all men, because all sinned—13for before the
law was given, sin was in the world. But sin is not taken into account when there is
no law.[s] 14Nevertheless, death reigned from the time of Adam to the time of Moses,
even over those who did not sin by breaking a command, as did Adam, who was a
pattern of the one to come.[t]
15But the gift is not like the trespass. For if the many died by the trespass of the

[b] 3 *Or let us*

5:3 [e]Mt 5:12 [f]Jas 1:2, 3
5:5 [g]Php 1:20 [h]Ac 2:33
5:6 [i]Gal 4:4 [j]Ro 4:25
5:8 [k]Jn 15:13; 1Pe 3:18
5:9 [l]Ro 3:25 [m]Ro 1:18
5:10 [n]Ro 11:28; Col 1:21 [o]2Co 5:18, 19; Col 1:20, 22 [p]Ro 8:34
5:12 [q]ver 15, 16, 17; 1Co 15:21, 22 [r]Ge 2:17; 3:19; Ro 6:23
5:13 [s]Ro 4:15
5:14 [t]1Co 15:22, 45

5:3, 4 For first-century Christians, suffering was the rule rather than the exception. Paul tells us that in the future we will *become,* but until then we must *overcome.* This means we will experience difficulties that help us grow. We rejoice in suffering not because we like pain or deny its tragedy, but because we know God is using life's difficulties and Satan's attacks to build our character. The problems that we run into will develop our perseverance—which in turn will strengthen our character, deepen our trust in God, and give us greater confidence about the future. You probably find your patience tested in some way every day. Thank God for those opportunities to grow, and deal with them in his strength (see also James 1:2–4; 1 Peter 1:6, 7).

5:5, 6 All three members of the Trinity are involved in salvation. The Father loved us so much that he sent his Son to bridge the gap between us (John 3:16). The Father and the Son send the Holy Spirit to fill our lives with love and to enable us to live by his power (Acts 1:8). With all this loving care, how can we do less than serve him completely!

5:6 We were weak and helpless because we could do nothing on our own to save ourselves. Someone had to come and rescue us. Not only did Christ come at a good time in history; he came at exactly the right time—according to God's own schedule. God controls all history, and he controlled the timing, methods, and results of Jesus' death.

5:8 *While we were still sinners*—these are amazing words. God sent Jesus Christ to die for us, not because we were good enough, but because he loved us. Whenever you feel uncertain about God's love for you, remember that he loved you even before you turned to him. If God loved you when you were a rebel, he can surely strengthen you, now that you love him in return.

5:9, 10 The love that caused Christ to die is the same love that sends the Holy Spirit to live in us and guide us every day. The power that raised Christ from the dead is the same power that saved you and is available to you in your daily life. Be assured that, having begun a life with Christ, you have a reserve of power and love to call on each day, for help to meet every challenge or trial. You can pray for God's power and love as you need it.

5:11 God is holy, and he will not be associated with sin. All people are sinful and so they are separated from God. In addition, all sin deserves punishment. Instead of punishing us with the death we deserve, however, Christ took our sins upon himself and took our punishment by dying on the cross. Now we can "rejoice in God". Through faith in *Christ's* work, we become close to God (reconciled) rather than being enemies and outcasts.

5:12 How can we be declared guilty for something Adam did thousands of years ago? Many feel it isn't right for God to judge us because of Adam's sin. Yet each of us confirms our solidarity with Adam by our own sins each day. We are made of the same stuff and are prone to rebel, and we are judged for the sins *we* commit. Because we are sinners, it isn't fairness we need—it's mercy.

5:13, 14 Paul has shown that keeping the law does not bring salvation. Here he adds that breaking the law is not what brings death. Death is the result of Adam's sin and of the sins we all commit, even if they don't resemble Adam's. Paul reminds his readers that for thousands of years the law had not yet been explicitly given, and yet people died. The law was added, he explains in 5:20, to help people see their sinfulness, to show them the seriousness of their offences, and to drive them to God for mercy and pardon. This was true in Moses' day, and it is still true today. Sin is a deep discrepancy between who we are and who we were created to be. The law points out our sin and places the responsibility for it squarely on our shoulders. But the law offers no remedy. When we are convicted of sin, we must turn to Jesus Christ for healing.

5:14 Adam is a *pattern;* he is the counterpart of Christ. Just as Adam was a representative of created humanity, so is Christ the representative of a new spiritual humanity.

5:15–19 We were all born into Adam's physical family—the family line that leads to certain death. All of us have reaped the results of Adam's sin. We have inherited his guilt, a sinful nature (the tendency to sin), and God's punishment. Because of Jesus, however, we can trade judgment for forgiveness. We can trade our sin for Jesus' righteousness. Christ offers us the opportunity to be born into his spiritual family—the family line that begins with forgiveness and leads to eternal life. If we do nothing, we have death through Adam; but if we come to God by faith, we have life through Christ. Which family line do you now belong to?

5:15 [u]ver 12, 18, 19 [v]Ac 15:11
5:17 [w]ver 12
5:18 [x]ver 12 [y]Ro 4:25
5:19 [z]ver 12 [a]Php 2:8
5:20 [b]Ro 7:7, 8; Gal 3:19 [c]1Ti 1:13, 14
5:21 [d]ver 12, 14
6:1 [a]ver 15; Ro 3:5, 8
6:2 [b]Col 3:3, 5; 1Pe 2:24
6:3 [c]Mt 28:19
6:4 [d]Col 2:12 [e]Ro 7:6; Gal 6:15; Eph 4:22-24; Col 3:10

one man,[u] how much more did God's grace and the gift that came by the grace of
the one man, Jesus Christ,[v] overflow to the many!
16 Again, the gift of God is not
like the result of the one man's sin: The judgment followed one sin and brought
condemnation, but the gift followed many trespasses and brought justification.
17 For
if, by the trespass of the one man, death[w] reigned through that one man, how much
more will those who receive God's abundant provision of grace and of the gift of
righteousness reign in life through the one man, Jesus Christ.

18 Consequently, just as the result of one trespass was condemnation for all men,[x]
so also the result of one act of righteousness was justification[y] that brings life for all
men.
19 For just as through the disobedience of the one man[z] the many were made
sinners, so also through the obedience[a] of the one man the many will be made
righteous.

20 The law was added so that the trespass might increase.[b] But where sin increased,
grace increased all the more,[c]
21 so that, just as sin reigned in death,[d] so also grace
might reign through righteousness to bring eternal life through Jesus Christ our Lord.

3. Freedom from sin's grasp

Dead to Sin, Alive in Christ

6 What shall we say, then? Shall we go on sinning, so that grace may increase?[a]
2 By no means! We died to sin;[b] how can we live in it any longer?
3 Or don't you
know that all of us who were baptised[c] into Christ Jesus were baptised into his death?
4 We were therefore buried with him through baptism into death in order that, just as
Christ was raised from the dead[d] through the glory of the Father, we too may live
a new life.[e]

WHAT HAS GOD DONE ABOUT SIN?

He has given us . . .		Principle	Importance
New life	6:2, 3	Sin's power is broken.	We can be certain that sin's power is broken.
	6:4	Sin-loving nature is buried.	
	6:6	You are no longer under sin's control.	
New nature	6:5	Now you share his new life.	We can see ourselves as unresponsive to the old power and alive to the new.
	6:11	Look upon your old self as dead; instead be alive to God.	
New freedom	6:12	Do not let sin control you.	We can commit ourselves to obey Christ in perfect freedom.
	6:13	Give yourselves completely to God.	
	6:14	You are free.	
	6:16	You can choose your own master.	

5:17 What a promise this is to those who love Christ! We can reign over sin's power, over death's threats, and over Satan's attacks. Eternal life is ours now and for ever. In the power and protection of Jesus Christ, we can overcome temptation. See 8:17 for more on our privileged position in Christ.

5:20 As a sinner, separated from God, you see his law from below, as a ladder to be climbed to get to God. Perhaps you have repeatedly tried to climb it, only to fall to the ground every time you have advanced one or two rungs. Or perhaps the sheer height of the ladder seems so overwhelming that you have never even started up. In either case, what relief you should feel to see Jesus offering with open arms to lift you above the ladder of the law, to take you directly to God! Once Jesus lifts you into God's presence, you are free to obey – out of love, not necessity, and through God's power, not your own. You know that if you stumble, you will not fall back to the ground. Instead, you will be caught and held in Christ's loving arms.

6:1 – 8:39 This section deals with *sanctification* – the change God makes in our lives as we grow in the faith. Chapter 6 explains that believers are free from sin's control. Chapter 7 discusses the continuing struggle believers have with sin. Chapter 8 describes how we can have victory over sin.

6:1, 2 If God loves to forgive, why not give him more to forgive? If forgiveness is guaranteed, do we have the freedom to sin as much as we want? Paul's forceful answer is *By no means!* Such an attitude – deciding ahead of time to take advantage of God – shows that a person does not understand the seriousness of sin. God's forgiveness does not make sin less serious; his Son's death for sin shows us the dreadful seriousness of sin. Jesus paid with his life so we could be forgiven. The availability of God's mercy must not become an excuse for careless living and moral laxness.

6:1–4 In the church of Paul's day, immersion was the usual form of baptism – that is, new Christians were completely "buried" in water. They understood this form of baptism to symbolise the death and burial of the old way of life. Coming up out of the water symbolised resurrection to new life with Christ. If we think of our old, sinful life as dead and buried, we have a powerful motive to resist sin. We can consciously choose to treat the desires and temptations of the old nature as if they were dead. Then we can continue to enjoy our wonderful new life with Jesus (see Galatians 3:27 and Colossians 2:12 and 3:1–4 for more on this concept).

5 If we have been united with him like this in his death, we will certainly also be
united with him in his resurrection.[f] 6 For we know that our old self[g] was crucified
with him[h] so that the body of sin[i] might be done away with,[a] that we should no
longer be slaves to sin—7 because anyone who has died has been freed from sin.
8 Now if we died with Christ, we believe that we will also live with him. 9 For we
know that since Christ was raised from the dead,[j] he cannot die again; death no longer
has mastery over him.[k] 10 The death he died, he died to sin[l] once for all; but the
life he lives, he lives to God.
11 In the same way, count yourselves dead to sin[m] but alive to God in Christ Jesus.
12 Therefore do not let sin reign in your mortal body so that you obey its evil desires.
13 Do not offer the parts of your body to sin, as instruments of wickedness,[n] but rather
offer yourselves to God, as those who have been brought from death to life; and offer
the parts of your body to him as instruments of righteousness.[o] 14 For sin shall not
be your master, because you are not under law,[p] but under grace.[q]

Slaves to Righteousness

15 What then? Shall we sin because we are not under law but under grace? By no
means! 16 Don't you know that when you offer yourselves to someone to obey him
as slaves, you are slaves to the one whom you obey—whether you are slaves to sin,[r]
which leads to death,[s] or to obedience, which leads to righteousness? 17 But thanks
be to God[t] that, though you used to be slaves to sin, you wholeheartedly obeyed the
form of teaching[u] to which you were entrusted. 18 You have been set free from sin[v]
and have become slaves to righteousness.
19 I put this in human terms[w] because you are weak in your natural selves. Just as
you used to offer the parts of your body in slavery to impurity and to ever-increasing
wickedness, so now offer them in slavery to righteousness[x] leading to holiness.
20 When you were slaves to sin,[y] you were free from the control of righteousness.
21 What benefit did you reap at that time from the things you are now ashamed of?

a *6* Or *be rendered powerless*

6:5 [f]2Co 4:10; Php 3:10, 11
6:6 [g]Eph 4:22; Col 3:9 [h]Gal 2:20; Col 2:12, 20 [i]Ro 7:24
6:9 [j]Ac 2:24 [k]Rev 1:18
6:10 [l]ver 2
6:11 [m]ver 2
6:13 [n]ver 16, 19; Ro 7:5 [o]Ro 12:1; 1Pe 2:24
6:14 [p]Gal 5:18 [q]Ro 3:24
6:16 [r]Jn 8:34; 2Pe 2:19 [s]ver 23
6:17 [t]Ro 1:8; 2Co 2:14 [u]2Ti 1:13
6:18 [v]ver 7, 22; Ro 8:2
6:19 [w]Ro 3:5 [x]ver 13
6:20 [y]ver 16

6:5ff We can enjoy our new life in Christ because we are united with him in his death and resurrection. Our evil desires, our bondage to sin, and our love of sin died with him. Now, united by faith with him in his resurrection life, we have unbroken fellowship with God and freedom from sin's hold on us. For more on the difference between our new life in Christ and our old sinful nature, read Ephesians 4:21–24 and Colossians 3:3–15.

6:6 The power and penalty of sin died with Christ on the cross. Our "old self", our sinful nature, died once and for all, so we are freed from its power. The "body of sin" is not the human body, but our rebellious sin-loving nature inherited from Adam. Though our body willingly co-operates with our sinful nature, we must not regard the body as evil. It is the sin in us that is evil. And it is this power of sin at work in our body that is defeated. Paul has already stated that through faith in Christ we stand acquitted, "not guilty" before God. Here Paul emphasises that we need no longer live under sin's power. God does not take us out of the world or make us robots—we will still feel like sinning, and sometimes we will sin. The difference is that before we were saved we were slaves to our sinful nature, but now we can choose to live for Christ (see Galatians 2:20).

6:8 Because of Christ's death and resurrection, his followers need never fear death. That assurance frees us to enjoy fellowship with him and to do his will. This will affect all our activities—work and worship, play, Bible study, quiet times, and times of caring for others. When you know that you don't have to fear death, you will experience a new vigour in life.

6:11 "Count yourselves dead to sin" means that we should regard our old sinful nature as dead and unresponsive to sin. Because of our union and identification with Christ, we are no longer obligated to carry out those old motives, desires, and goals. So let us consider ourselves to be what God has in fact made us. We have a new start, and the Holy Spirit will help us become in our daily experience what Christ has declared us to be.

6:14, 15 If we're no longer under the law but under grace, are we now free to sin and disregard the Ten Commandments? Paul says, "By no means". When we were under the law, sin was our master—the law does not justify us or help us overcome sin. But now that we are bound to Christ, he is our Master, and he gives us power to do good rather than evil.

6:16–18 In certain skilled crafts, an apprentice works under a master, who trains, shapes, and moulds his apprentice in the finer points of his craft. All people choose a master and pattern themselves after him. Without Jesus, we would have no choice—we would have to apprentice ourselves to sin, and the results would be guilt, suffering, and separation from God. Thanks to Jesus, however, we can now choose God as our Master. Following him, we can enjoy new life and learn how to work for him. Are you still serving your first master, sin? Or have you apprenticed yourself to God?

6:17 To obey wholeheartedly means to give yourself fully to God, to love him "with all your heart and with all your soul and with all your mind" (Matthew 22:37). And yet so often our efforts to know and obey God's commands can best be described as "half-hearted". How do you rate your heart's obedience? God wants to give you the power to obey him with all your heart.

6:17 The "form of teaching" delivered to them is the Good News that Jesus died for their sins and was raised to give them new life. Many believe that this refers to the early church's statement of faith found in 1 Corinthians 15:1–11.

6:19–22 It is impossible to be neutral. Every person has a master—either God or sin. A Christian is not someone who cannot sin, but someone who is no longer a slave to sin. He or she belongs to God.

Those things result in death![z] 22But now that you have been set free from sin[a] and
have become slaves to God,[b] the benefit you reap leads to holiness, and the result
is eternal life. 23For the wages of sin is death,[c] but the gift of God is eternal life[d]
in[b] Christ Jesus our Lord.

An Illustration From Marriage

7 Do you not know, brothers[a]—for I am speaking to men who know the law—that
the law has authority over a man only as long as he lives? 2For example, by law
a married woman is bound to her husband as long as he is alive, but if her husband
dies, she is released from the law of marriage.[b] 3So then, if she marries another man
while her husband is still alive, she is called an adulteress. But if her husband dies,
she is released from that law and is not an adulteress, even though she marries another
man.

4So, my brothers, you also died to the law[c] through the body of Christ,[d] that you
might belong to another, to him who was raised from the dead, in order that we might
bear fruit to God. 5For when we were controlled by the sinful nature,[a] the sinful
passions aroused by the law[e] were at work in our bodies,[f] so that we bore fruit for
death. 6But now, by dying to what once bound us, we have been released from the
law so that we serve in the new way of the Spirit, and not in the old way of the written
code.[g]

Struggling With Sin

7What shall we say, then? Is the law sin? Certainly not! Indeed I would not have
known what sin was except through the law.[h] For I would not have known what
coveting really was if the law had not said, "Do not covet."[b][i] 8But sin, seizing the
opportunity afforded by the commandment,[j] produced in me every kind of covetous

b *23* Or *through* a *5* Or *the flesh*; also in verse 25 b *7* Exodus 20:17; Deut. 5:21

6:21 [z]ver 23
6:22 [a]ver 18 [b]1Co 7:22; 1Pe 2:16
6:23 [c]Ge 2:17; Ro 5:12; Gal 6:7, 8; Jas 1:15 [d]Mt 25:46
7:1 [a]Ro 1:13
7:2 [b]1Co 7:39
7:4 [c]Ro 8:2; Gal 2:19 [d]Col 1:22
7:5 [e]Ro 7:7-11 [f]Ro 6:13
7:6 [g]Ro 2:29; 2Co 3:6
7:7 [h]Ro 3:20; 4:15 [i]Ex 20:17; Dt 5:21
7:8 [j]ver 11

6:23 You are free to choose between two masters, but you are not free to manipulate the consequences of your choice. Each of the two masters pays with his own kind of currency. The currency of sin is death. That is all you can expect or hope for in life without God. Christ's currency is eternal life—new life with God that begins on earth and continues for ever with God. What choice have you made?

6:23 Eternal life is a free gift from God. If it is a gift, then it is not something that we earn, nor something that must be paid back. Consider the foolishness of someone who receives a gift given out of love and then offers to pay for it. A gift cannot be purchased by the recipient. A more appropriate response to a loved one who offers a gift is graceful acceptance with gratitude. Our salvation is a gift of God, not something of our own doing (Ephesians 2:8, 9). He saved us because of his mercy, not because of any righteous things that we have done (Titus 3:5). How much more we should accept with thanksgiving the gift that God has freely given to us.

7:1ff Paul shows that the law is powerless to save the sinner (7:7–14), the lawkeeper (7:15–22), and even the person with a new nature (7:23–25). The sinner is condemned by the law; the lawkeeper can't live up to it; and the person with the new nature finds his or her obedience to the law sabotaged by the effects of the old nature. Once again, Paul declares that salvation cannot be found by obeying the law. No matter who we are, only Jesus Christ can set us free.

7:2–6 Paul uses marriage to illustrate our relationship to the law. When a spouse dies, the law of marriage no longer applies. Because we have died with Christ, the law can no longer condemn us. We rose again when Christ was resurrected and, as new people, we "belong" to Christ. His Spirit enables us to produce good fruit for God. We now serve not by obeying a set of rules, but out of renewed hearts and minds that overflow with love for God.

7:4 When a person dies to the old life and belongs to Christ, a new life begins. An unbeliever's mindset is centred on his or her own personal gratification. Those who don't follow Christ have only their own self-determination as their source of power. By contrast, God is at the centre of a Christian's life. God supplies the power for the Christian's daily living. Believers find that their whole way of looking at the world changes when they come to Christ.

7:6 Some people try to earn their way to God by keeping a set of rules (obeying the Ten Commandments, attending church faithfully, or doing good deeds), but all they earn for their efforts is frustration and discouragement. However, because of Christ's sacrifice, the way to God is already open, and we can become his children simply by putting our faith in him. No longer trying to reach God by keeping rules, we can become more and more like Jesus as we live with him day by day. Let the Holy Spirit turn your eyes away from your own performance and towards Jesus. He will free you to serve him out of love and gratitude. This is living "in the new way of the Spirit".

7:6 Keeping the rules, laws, and customs of Christianity doesn't save us. Even if we could keep our actions pure, we would still be doomed because our hearts and minds are perverse and rebellious. Like Paul, we can find no relief in the synagogue or church until we look to Jesus Christ himself for our salvation—which he gives us freely. When we do come to Jesus, we are flooded with relief and gratitude. Will we keep the rules any better? Most likely, but we will be motivated by love and gratitude, not by the desire to get God's approval. We will not be merely submitting to an external code, but willingly and lovingly seeking to do God's will.

desire. For apart from law, sin is dead.[k] 9Once I was alive apart from law; but when
the commandment came, sin sprang to life and I died. 10I found that the very
commandment that was intended to bring life[l] actually brought death. 11For sin,
seizing the opportunity afforded by the commandment, deceived me,[m] and through
the commandment put me to death. 12So then, the law is holy, and the commandment
is holy, righteous and good.[n]

13Did that which is good, then, become death to me? By no means! But in order
that sin might be recognised as sin, it produced death in me through what was good,
so that through the commandment sin might become utterly sinful.

14We know that the law is spiritual; but I am unspiritual,[o] sold[p] as a slave to sin.
15I do not understand what I do. For what I want to do I do not do, but what I hate
I do.[q] 16And if I do what I do not want to do, I agree that the law is good.[r] 17As
it is, it is no longer I myself who do it, but it is sin living in me.[s] 18I know that nothing
good lives in me, that is, in my sinful nature.[c][t] For I have the desire to do what
is good, but I cannot carry it out. 19For what I do is not the good I want to do; no,
the evil I do not want to do—this I keep on doing.[u] 20Now if I do what I do not want
to do, it is no longer I who do it, but it is sin living in me that does it.[v]

21So I find this law at work:[w] When I want to do good, evil is right there with me.
22For in my inner being[x] I delight in God's law;[y] 23but I see another law at work
in the members of my body, waging war[z] against the law of my mind and making
me a prisoner of the law of sin at work within my members. 24What a wretched man

c *18* *Or my flesh*

7:8 [k]Ro 4:15; 1Co 15:56
7:10 [l]Lev 18:5; Lk 10:26-28
7:11 [m]Ge 3:13
7:12 [n]1Ti 1:8
7:14 [o]1Co 3:1 [p]1Ki 21:20, 25; 2Ki 17:17
7:15 [q]ver 19; Gal 5:17
7:16 [r]ver 12
7:17 [s]ver 20
7:18 [t]ver 25
7:19 [u]ver 15
7:20 [v]ver 17
7:21 [w]ver 23, 25
7:22 [x]Eph 3:16 [y]Ps 1:2
7:23 [z]Gal 5:17; Jas 4:1; 1Pe 2:11

7:9–11 Where there is no law, there is no sin, because people cannot know that their actions are sinful unless a law forbids those actions. God's law makes people realise that they are sinners doomed to die, yet it offers no help. Sin is real, and it is dangerous. Imagine a sunny day at the beach. You plunge into the sea; then you notice a sign on the pier: "No swimming. Sharks in water." Your day is ruined. Is it the sign's fault? Are you angry with the people who put it up? The law is like the sign. It is essential, and we are grateful for it—but it doesn't get rid of the sharks.

7:11, 12 Sin deceives people by misusing the law. The law was holy, expressing God's nature and will for people. In the Garden of Eden (Genesis 3), the serpent deceived Eve by taking her focus off the freedom she had and putting it on the one restriction God had made. Ever since then, we have all been rebels. Sin looks good to us precisely because God has said it is wrong. Instead of paying attention to his warnings, we use them as a "to do" list. When we are tempted to rebel, we need to look at the law from a wider perspective—in the light of God's grace and mercy. If we focus on his great love for us, we will understand that he only restricts us from actions and attitudes that ultimately will harm us.

7:14 "I am unspiritual, sold as a slave to sin" may be a reference to the old nature that seeks to rebel and be independent of God. If I, being a Christian, try to struggle with sin in my own strength, I am slipping into the grasp of sin's power.

7:15 Paul shares three lessons that he learned in trying to deal with his old sinful desires. (1) Knowledge is not the answer (7:9). Paul felt fine as long as he did not understand what the law demanded. When he learned the truth, he knew he was doomed. (2) Self-determination (struggling in one's own strength) doesn't succeed (7:15). Paul found himself sinning in ways that weren't even attractive to him. (3) Becoming a Christian does not stamp out all sin and temptation from a person's life (7:22–25).

Being born again takes a moment of faith, but becoming like Christ is a lifelong process. Paul compares Christian growth to a strenuous race or fight (1 Corinthians 9:24–27; 2 Timothy 4:7). Thus, as Paul has been emphasising since the beginning of this letter, *no-one* in the world is innocent; no-one deserves to be saved—not the pagan who doesn't know God's laws, not the Christian or Jew who knows them and tries to keep them. All of us must depend totally on the work of Christ for our salvation. We cannot earn it by our good behaviour.

7:15 This is more than the cry of one desperate man—it describes the experience of any Christian struggling against sin or trying to please God by keeping rules and laws without the Spirit's help. We must never underestimate the power of sin. We must never attempt to fight it in our own strength. Satan is a crafty tempter, and we have an amazing ability to make excuses. Instead of trying to overcome sin with human willpower, we must take hold of the tremendous power of Christ that is available to us. This is God's provision for victory over sin—he sends the Holy Spirit to live in us and give us power. And when we fall, he lovingly reaches out to help us up.

7:17–20 "The devil made me do it." "I didn't do it; the sin in me did it." These sound like good excuses, but we are responsible for our actions. We must never use the power of sin or Satan as an excuse, because they are defeated enemies. Without Christ's help, sin is stronger than we are, and sometimes we are unable to defend ourselves against its attacks. That is why we should never stand up to sin all alone. Jesus Christ, who has conquered sin once and for all, promises to fight by our side. If we look to him for help, we will not have to give in to sin.

7:23–25 The "law at work in the members of my body" is the sin deep within us. This is our vulnerability to sin; it refers to everything within us that is more loyal to our old way of selfish living than to God.

7:23–25 This inward struggle with sin was as real for Paul as it is for us. From Paul we learn what to do about it. Whenever Paul felt lost, he would return to the beginning of his spiritual life, remembering that he had already been freed by Jesus Christ. When you feel confused and overwhelmed by sin's appeal, follow Paul's example: thank God that he has given you freedom through Jesus Christ. Let the reality of Christ's power lift you up to real victory over sin.

7:24 [a]Ro 6:6; 8:2
8:1 [a]ver 34 [b]ver 39; Ro 16:3
8:2 [c]1Co 15:45 [d]Ro 6:18 [e]Ro 7:4
8:3 [f]Ac 13:39; Heb 7:18 [g]Php 2:7 [h]Heb 2:14, 17
8:4 [i]Gal 5:16
8:5 [j]Gal 5:19-21 [k]Gal 5:22-25
8:6 [l]Gal 6:8
8:7 [m]Jas 4:4
8:9 [n]1Co 6:19; Gal 4:6 [o]Jn 14:17; 1Jn 4:13
8:10 [p]Gal 2:20; Eph 3:17; Col 1:27
8:11 [q]Ac 2:24 [r]Jn 5:21

I am! Who will rescue me from this body of death?[a] 25 Thanks be to God — through
Jesus Christ our Lord!
So then, I myself in my mind am a slave to God's law, but in the sinful nature a
slave to the law of sin.

Life Through the Spirit

8 Therefore, there is now no condemnation[a] for those who are in Christ Jesus,[a][b]
2 because through Christ Jesus the law of the Spirit of life[c] set me free[d] from
the law of sin[e] and death. 3 For what the law was powerless[f] to do in that it was
weakened by the sinful nature,[b] God did by sending his own Son in the likeness of
sinful man[g] to be a sin offering.[c][h] And so he condemned sin in sinful man,[d] 4 in
order that the righteous requirements of the law might be fully met in us, who do not
live according to the sinful nature but according to the Spirit.[i]
5 Those who live according to the sinful nature have their minds set on what that
nature desires;[j] but those who live in accordance with the Spirit have their minds set
on what the Spirit desires.[k] 6 The mind of sinful man[e] is death, but the mind
controlled by the Spirit is life[l] and peace; 7 the sinful mind[f] is hostile to God.[m] It
does not submit to God's law, nor can it do so. 8 Those controlled by the sinful nature
cannot please God.
9 You, however, are controlled not by the sinful nature but by the Spirit, if the Spirit
of God lives in you.[n] And if anyone does not have the Spirit of Christ,[o] he does
not belong to Christ. 10 But if Christ is in you,[p] your body is dead because of sin,
yet your spirit is alive because of righteousness. 11 And if the Spirit of him who raised
Jesus from the dead[q] is living in you, he who raised Christ from the dead will also
give life to your mortal bodies[r] through his Spirit, who lives in you.
12 Therefore, brothers, we have an obligation — but it is not to the sinful nature, to
live according to it. 13 For if you live according to the sinful nature, you will die; but

a *1* Some later manuscripts *Jesus, who do not live according to the sinful nature but according to the Spirit,*
b *3* Or *the flesh*; also in verses 4, 5, 8, 9, 12 and 13 **c** *3* Or *man, for sin* **d** *3* Or *in the flesh* **e** *6* Or *mind set on the flesh* **f** *7* Or *the mind set on the flesh*

8:1 "Not guilty; let him go free" — what would those words mean to you if you were in the condemned cell? The fact is that the whole human race *is* condemned–justly so for repeatedly breaking God's holy law. Without Jesus we would have no hope at all. But thank God! He has declared us not guilty and has offered us freedom from sin and power to do his will.

8:2 This Spirit of life is the Holy Spirit. He was present at the creation of the world (Genesis 1:2), and he is the power behind the rebirth of every Christian. He gives us the power we need to live the Christian life. For more about the Holy Spirit, read the notes on John 3:6; Acts 1:3; 1:4, 5; 1–5.

8:3 Jesus gave himself as a *sacrifice* ("sin offering") for our sins. In Old Testament times, animal sacrifices were continually offered at the temple. The sacrifices showed the Israelites the seriousness of sin: blood had to be shed before sins could be pardoned (see Leviticus 17:11). But animal blood could not really remove sins (Hebrews 10:4). The sacrifices could only point to Jesus' sacrifice, which paid the penalty for all sins.

8:5, 6 Paul divides people into two categories — those who let themselves be controlled by their sinful natures, and those who follow after the Holy Spirit. All of us would be in the first category if Jesus hadn't offered us a way out. Once we have said yes to Jesus, we will want to continue following him, because his way brings life and peace. Daily we must consciously choose to centre our lives on God. Use the Bible to discover God's guidelines, and then follow them. In every perplexing situation ask yourself, "What would Jesus want me to do?" When the Holy Spirit points out what is right, do it eagerly. For more on our sinful natures versus our new life in Christ, see 6:6–8, Ephesians 4:22–24; Colossians 3:3–15.

8:9 Have you ever worried about whether or not you really are a Christian? A Christian is anyone who has the Spirit of God living in him or her. If you have sincerely trusted Christ for your salvation and acknowledged him as Lord, then the Holy Spirit has come into your life, and you are a Christian. You won't know that the Holy Spirit has come if you are waiting for a certain feeling; you will know he has come because Jesus promised he would. When the Holy Spirit is working within you, you will believe that Jesus Christ is God's Son and that eternal life comes through him (1 John 5:5); you will begin to act as Christ directs (Romans 8:5; Galatians 5:22, 23); you will find help in your daily problems and in your praying (Romans 8:26, 27); you will be empowered to serve God and do his will (Acts 1:8; Romans 12:6ff); and you will become part of God's plan to build up his church (Ephesians 4:12, 13).

8:11 The Holy Spirit is God's promise or guarantee of eternal life for those who believe in him. The Spirit is in us now by faith, and by faith we are certain to live with Christ for ever. See Romans 8:23; 1 Corinthians 6:14; 2 Corinthians 4:14; 1 Thessalonians 4:14.

8:13 "Put to death the misdeeds of the body" means to regard as dead the power of sin in your body (see 6:11; Galatians 5:24). When we regard sin's appeal as dead and lifeless, we can ignore temptation when it comes.

if by the Spirit you put to death the misdeeds of the body, you will live,[s] 14because
those who are led by the Spirit of God[t] are sons of God.[u] 15For you did not receive
a spirit that makes you a slave again to fear,[v] but you received the Spirit of sonship.[g]
And by him we cry, "*Abba*,[h] Father."[w] 16The Spirit himself testifies with our spirit[x]
that we are God's children. 17Now if we are children, then we are heirs[y]—heirs of
God and co-heirs with Christ, if indeed we share in his sufferings in order that we
may also share in his glory.[z]

Future Glory

18I consider that our present sufferings are not worth comparing with the glory that
will be revealed in us.[a] 19The creation waits in eager expectation for the sons of God
to be revealed. 20For the creation was subjected to frustration, not by its own choice,
but by the will of the one who subjected it,[b] in hope 21that[i] the creation itself will
be liberated from its bondage to decay[c] and brought into the glorious freedom of the
children of God.

22We know that the whole creation has been groaning[d] as in the pains of childbirth
right up to the present time. 23Not only so, but we ourselves, who have the firstfruits
of the Spirit,[e] groan[f] inwardly as we wait eagerly[g] for our adoption as sons, the
redemption of our bodies. 24For in this hope we were saved.[h] But hope that is seen
is no hope at all. Who hopes for what he already has? 25But if we hope for what we
do not yet have, we wait for it patiently.

26In the same way, the Spirit helps us in our weakness. We do not know what we
ought to pray for, but the Spirit himself intercedes for us[i] with groans that words
cannot express. 27And he who searches our hearts[j] knows the mind of the Spirit,
because the Spirit intercedes for the saints in accordance with God's will.

8:13 [s]Gal 6:8
8:14 [t]Gal 5:18 [u]Jn 1:12; Rev 21:7
8:15 [v]2Ti 1:7; Heb 2:15 [w]Mk 14:36; Gal 4:5, 6
8:16 [x]Eph 1:13
8:17 [y]Ac 20:32; Gal 4:7 [z]1Pe 4:13
8:18 [a]2Co 4:17; 1Pe 4:13
8:20 [b]Ge 3:17-19
8:21 [c]Ac 3:21; 2Pe 3:13; Rev 21:1
8:22 [d]Jer 12:4
8:23 [e]2Co 5:5 [f]2Co 5:2, 4 [g]Gal 5:5
8:24 [h]1Th 5:8
8:26 [i]Eph 6:18
8:27 [j]Rev 2:23

[g] *15* Or *adoption* [h] *15* Aramaic for *Father* [i] *20,21* Or *subjected it in hope.* [21]*For*

8:14–17 Paul uses adoption or "sonship" to illustrate the believer's new relationship with God. In Roman culture, the adopted person lost all rights in his old family and gained all the rights of a legitimate child in his new family. He became a full heir to his new father's estate. Likewise, when a person becomes a Christian, he or she gains all the privileges and responsibilities of a child in God's family. One of these outstanding privileges is being led by the Spirit (see Galatians 4:5, 6). We may not always feel as though we belong to God, but the Holy Spirit is our witness. His inward presence reminds us of who we are and encourages us with God's love (5:5).

8:14–17 We are no longer cringing and fearful slaves; instead, we are the Master's children. What a privilege! Because we are God's children, we share in great treasures as co-heirs. God has already given us his best gifts: his Son, forgiveness, and eternal life; and he encourages us to ask him for whatever we need.

8:17 There is a price for being identified with Jesus. Along with the great treasures, Paul mentions the suffering that Christians must face. What kinds of suffering are we to endure? For first-century believers, there was economic and social persecution, and some even faced death. We too must pay a price for following Jesus. In many parts of today's world, Christians face pressures just as severe as those faced by Christ's first followers. Even in countries where Christianity is tolerated or encouraged, Christians must not become complacent. To live as Jesus did—serving others, giving up one's own rights, resisting pressures to conform to the world—always exacts a price. Nothing we suffer, however, can compare to the great price that Jesus paid to save us.

8:19–22 Sin has caused all creation to fall from the perfect state in which God created it. So the world is subject to frustration and bondage to decay so that it cannot fulfil its intended purpose. One day all creation will be liberated and transformed. Until that time it waits in eager expectation for the resurrection of God's children.

8:19–22 Christians see the world as it is—physically decaying and spiritually infected with sin. But Christians do not need to be pessimistic, because they have hope for future glory. They look forward to the new heaven and new earth that God has promised, and they wait for God's new order that will free the world of sin, sickness, and evil. In the meantime, Christians go with Christ into the world where they heal people's bodies and souls and fight the evil effects of sin in the world.

8:23 We will be resurrected with bodies, glorified bodies like the body Christ now has in heaven (see 1 Corinthians 15:25–58). We have the "firstfruits", the first installment or down payment of the Holy Spirit as a guarantee of our resurrection life (see 2 Corinthians 1:22; 5:5; Ephesians 1:14).

8:24, 25 It is natural for children to trust their parents, even though parents sometimes fail to keep their promises. Our heavenly Father, however, never makes promises he won't keep. Nevertheless, his plan may take more time than we expect. Rather than acting like impatient children as we wait for God's will to unfold, we should place our confidence in God's goodness and wisdom.

8:24, 25 In Romans, Paul presents the idea that salvation is past, present, and future. It is past because we *were* saved the moment we believed in Jesus Christ as Saviour (3:21–26; 5:1–11; 6:1–11, 22, 23); our new life (eternal life) begins at that moment. And it is present because we *are being* saved; this is the process of sanctification (see the note on 6:1–8:39). But at the same time, we have not fully received all the benefits and blessings of salvation that will be ours when Christ's new kingdom is completely established. That's our future salvation. While we can be confident of our salvation, we still look ahead with hope and trust towards that complete change of body and personality that lies beyond this life, when we will be like Christ (1 John 3:2).

8:26, 27 As a believer, you are not left to your own resources to cope with problems. Even when you don't know the right words to pray, the Holy Spirit prays with and for you, and God answers. With God helping you pray, you don't need to be afraid to come before him. Ask the Holy Spirit to intercede for you "in accordance with God's will". Then, when you bring your requests to God, trust that he will always do what is best.

8:28
[k]1Co 1:9;
2Ti 1:9
8:29
[l]Ro 11:2
[m]Eph 1:5, 11
[n]1Co 15:49;
2Co 3:18;
Php 3:21;
1Jn 3:2
8:30
[o]Eph 1:5, 11
[p]1Co 6:11
[q]Ro 9:23
8:31
[r]Ro 4:1
[s]Ps 118:6
8:32
[t]Jn 3:16;
Ro 4:25; 5:8
8:33
[u]Isa 50:8, 9
8:34
[v]Ro 5:6-8
[w]Mk 16:19
[x]Heb 7:25; 9:24;
1Jn 2:1
8:35
[y]1Co 4:11
8:36
[z]Ps 44:22;
2Co 4:11
8:37
[a]1Co 15:57
[b]Gal 2:20;
Rev 1:5; 3:9
8:38
[c]Eph 1:21;
1Pe 3:22
8:39
[d]Ro 5:8

More Than Conquerors

28 And we know that in all things God works for the good of those who love him,[j]
who[k] have been called[k] according to his purpose. 29 For those God foreknew[l] he
also predestined[m] to be conformed to the likeness of his Son,[n] that he might be the
firstborn among many brothers. 30 And those he predestined,[o] he also called; those
he called, he also justified;[p] those he justified, he also glorified.[q]

31 What, then, shall we say in response to this?[r] If God is for us, who can be against
us?[s] 32 He who did not spare his own Son,[t] but gave him up for us all—how will
he not also, along with him, graciously give us all things? 33 Who will bring any
charge[u] against those whom God has chosen? It is God who justifies. 34 Who is he
that condemns? Christ Jesus, who died[v]—more than that, who was raised to life—is
at the right hand of God[w] and is also interceding for us.[x] 35 Who shall separate us
from the love of Christ? Shall trouble or hardship or persecution or famine or nakedness or danger or sword?[y] 36 As it is written:

> "For your sake we face death all day long;
> we are considered as sheep to be slaughtered."[l][z]

37 No, in all these things we are more than conquerors[a] through him who loved us.[b]
38 For I am convinced that neither death nor life, neither angels nor demons,[m] neither
the present nor the future, nor any powers,[c] 39 neither height nor depth, nor anything
else in all creation, will be able to separate us from the love of God[d] that is in Christ
Jesus our Lord.

j *28* Some manuscripts *And we know that all things work together for good to those who love God*
k *28* Or *works together with those who love him to bring about what is good—with those who*
l *36* Psalm 44:22
m *38* Or *not heavenly rulers*

8:28 God works in "all things"—not just isolated incidents—for our good. This does not mean that all that happens to us is good. Evil is prevalent in our fallen world, but God is able to turn every circumstance around for our long-range good. Note that God is not working to make us happy, but to fulfil his purpose. Note also that this promise is not for everybody. It can be claimed only by those who love God and are called according to his purpose. Those who are "called" are those the Holy Spirit convinces and enables to receive Christ. Such people have a new perspective on life, a new mindset. They trust in God, not life's treasures; they look for their security in heaven, not on earth; they learn to accept, not resent, pain and persecution because God is with them.

8:29 God's ultimate goal for us is to make us like Christ (1 John 3:2). As we become more and more like him, we discover our true selves, the persons we were created to be. How can we be conformed to Christ's likeness? By reading and heeding the word, by studying his life on earth through the Gospels, by being filled with his Spirit, and by doing his work in the world.

8:29, 30 Some believe these verses mean that before the beginning of the world, God chose certain people to receive his gift of salvation. They point to verses like Ephesians 1:11 that says we are "predestined according to the plan of him who works out everything in conformity with the purpose of his will". Others believe that God *foreknew* those who would respond to him and upon those he set his mark (predestined). What is clear is that God's *purpose* for people was not an afterthought; it was settled before the foundation of the world. People are to serve and honour God. If you have believed in Christ, you can rejoice in the fact that God has always known you. God's love is eternal. His wisdom and power are supreme. He will guide and protect you until one day you stand in his presence.

8:30 *Called* means summoned or invited. For more on justification and glorification, see the chart in chapter 3.

8:31–34 Do you ever think that because you aren't good enough for God, he will not save you? Do you ever feel as if salvation is for everyone else but you? Then these verses are especially for you. If God gave his Son for you, he isn't going to hold back the gift of salvation! If Christ gave his life for you, he isn't going to turn around and condemn you! He will not withhold anything you need to live for him. The book of Romans is more than a theological explanation of God's redeeming grace—it is a letter of comfort and confidence addressed to you.

8:34 Paul says that Jesus is interceding for us in heaven. God has acquitted us and has removed our sin and guilt, so it is Satan, not God, who accuses us. When he does, Jesus, the advocate for our defence, stands at God's right hand to present our case. For more on the concept of Christ as our advocate, see the notes on Hebrews 4:14; 4:15.

8:35, 36 These words were written to a church that would soon undergo terrible persecution. In just a few years, Paul's hypothetical situations would turn into painful realities. This passage reaffirms God's profound love for his people. No matter what happens to us, no matter where we are, we can never be lost to his love. Suffering should not drive us away from God, but help us to identify with him further and allow his love to reach us and heal us.

8:35–39 These verses contain one of the most comforting promises in all Scripture. Believers have always had to face hardships in many forms: persecution, illness, imprisonment, even death. These could cause them to fear that they have been abandoned by Christ. But Paul exclaims that it is *impossible* to be separated from Christ. His death for us is proof of his unconquerable love. Nothing can stop Christ's constant presence with us. God tells us how great his love is so that we will feel totally secure in him. If we believe these overwhelming assurances, we will not be afraid.

8:38 *Powers* are unseen forces of evil in the universe, forces like Satan and his fallen angels (see Ephesians 6:12). In Christ we are super-conquerors, and his love will protect us from any such forces.

4. Israel's past, present, and future

God's Sovereign Choice

9 I speak the truth in Christ—I am not lying,[a] my conscience confirms[b] it in the
Holy Spirit—2I have great sorrow and unceasing anguish in my heart. 3For I
could wish that I myself[c] were cursed[d] and cut off from Christ for the sake of my
brothers, those of my own race,[e] 4the people of Israel. Theirs is the adoption as
sons;[f] theirs the divine glory, the covenants,[g] the receiving of the law,[h] the temple
worship[i] and the promises.[j] 5Theirs are the patriarchs, and from them is traced the
human ancestry of Christ,[k] who is God over all,[l] for ever praised![a][m] Amen.
6It is not as though God's word had failed. For not all who are descended from Israel
are Israel.[n] 7Nor because they are his descendants are they all Abraham's children.
On the contrary, "It is through Isaac that your offspring will be reckoned."[b][o] 8In
other words, it is not the natural children who are God's children,[p] but it is the
children of the promise who are regarded as Abraham's offspring. 9For this was how
the promise was stated: "At the appointed time I will return, and Sarah will have a
son."[c][q]
10Not only that, but Rebekah's children had one and the same father, our father
Isaac.[r] 11Yet, before the twins were born or had done anything good or bad—in order
that God's purpose[s] in election might stand: 12not by works but by him who
calls—she was told, "The older will serve the younger."[d][t] 13Just as it is written:
"Jacob I loved, but Esau I hated."[e][u]
14What then shall we say? Is God unjust? Not at all![v] 15For he says to Moses,

> "I will have mercy on whom I have mercy,
> and I will have compassion on whom I have compassion."[f][w]

16It does not, therefore, depend on man's desire or effort, but on God's mercy.[x] 17For
the Scripture says to Pharaoh: "I raised you up for this very purpose, that I might
display my power in you and that my name might be proclaimed in all the earth."[g][y]
18Therefore God has mercy on whom he wants to have mercy, and he hardens whom
he wants to harden.[z]
19One of you will say to me:[a] "Then why does God still blame us? For who resists
his will?"[b] 20But who are you, O man, to talk back to God? "Shall what is formed
say to him who formed it,[c] 'Why did you make me like this?' "[h][d] 21Does not the

[a] *5* Or *Christ, who is over all. God be for ever praised!* Or *Christ. God who is over all be for ever praised!*
[b] *7* Gen. 21:12 [c] *9* Gen. 18:10,14 [d] *12* Gen. 25:23 [e] *13* Mal. 1:2,3 [f] *15* Exodus 33:19 [g] *17* Exodus 9:16
[h] *20* Isaiah 29:16; 45:9

9:1 [a]2Co 11:10; Gal 1:20; 1Ti 2:7 [b]Ro 1:9
9:3 [c]Ex 32:32 [d]1Co 12:3; 16:22 [e]Ro 11:14
9:4 [f]Ex 4:22 [g]Ge 17:2; Ac 3:25; Eph 2:12 [h]Ps 147:19 [i]Heb 9:1 [j]Ac 13:32
9:5 [k]Mt 1:1-16 [l]Jn 1:1 [m]Ro 1:25
9:6 [n]Ro 2:28, 29; Gal 6:16
9:7 [o]Ge 21:12; Heb 11:18
9:8 [p]Ro 8:14
9:9 [q]Ge 18:10, 14
9:10 [r]Ge 25:21
9:11 [s]Ro 8:28
9:12 [t]Ge 25:23
9:13 [u]Mal 1:2, 3
9:14 [v]2Ch 19:7
9:15 [w]Ex 33:19
9:16 [x]Eph 2:8
9:17 [y]Ex 9:16
9:18 [z]Ex 4:21
9:19 [a]Ro 11:19 [b]2Ch 20:6; Da 4:35
9:20 [c]Isa 64:8 [d]Isa 29:16

9:1–3 Paul expressed concern for his Jewish "brothers" by saying that he would willingly take their punishment if that could save them. While the only one who can save us is Christ, Paul showed a rare depth of love. Like Jesus, he was willing to sacrifice for others. How concerned are you for those who don't know Christ? Are you willing to sacrifice your time, money, energy, comfort, and safety to see them come to faith in Jesus?

9:4 The Jews viewed God's choosing of Israel in the Old Testament as being like adoption. They were undeserving and without rights as natural children. Yet God adopted them and granted them the status of his sons and daughters.

9:6 God's word in the form of beautiful covenant promises came to Abraham. Covenant people, the true children of Abraham, are not just his biological descendants. They are all those who trust in God and in what Jesus Christ has done for them. (See also 2:29; Galatians 3:7.)

9:11 The Jews were proud of the fact that their lineage came from Isaac, whose mother was Sarah (Abraham's legitimate wife), rather than Ishmael, whose mother was Hagar (Sarah's maidservant). Paul asserts that no-one can claim to be chosen by God because of his or her heritage or good deeds. God freely chooses to save whomever he wills. The doctrine of election teaches that it is God's sovereign choice to save us by his goodness and mercy, and not by our own merit.

9:12–14 Was it right for God to choose Jacob, the younger, to be over Esau? In Malachi 1:2, 3, the statement "I have loved Jacob, but Esau I have hated" refers to the nations of Israel and Edom rather than to the individual brothers. God chose Jacob to continue the family line of the faithful because he knew his heart was for God. But he did not exclude Esau from knowing and loving him. Keep in mind the kind of God we worship: he is sovereign; he is not arbitrary; in all things he works for our good; he is trustworthy; he will save all who believe in him. When we understand these qualities of God, we know that his choices are good even if we don't understand all his reasons.

9:17, 18 Paul quotes from Exodus 9:16, where God foretold how Pharaoh would be used to declare God's power. Paul uses this argument to show that salvation was God's proper work, not man's. God's judgment on Pharaoh's sin was to harden his heart, to confirm his disobedience, so that the consequences of his rebellion would be his own punishment.

9:21 With this illustration, Paul is not saying that some of us are worth more than others, but simply that the Creator has control over the created object. The created object, therefore, has no right to demand anything from its Creator—its very existence depends on him. Keeping this perspective removes any temptation to have pride in personal achievement.

potter have the right to make out of the same lump of clay some pottery for noble purposes and some for common use?[e]

22 What if God, choosing to show his wrath and make his power known, bore with great patience[f] the objects of his wrath—prepared for destruction? 23 What if he did this to make the riches of his glory[g] known to the objects of his mercy, whom he prepared in advance for glory[h]— 24 even us, whom he also called,[i] not only from the Jews but also from the Gentiles?[j] 25 As he says in Hosea:

> "I will call them 'my people' who are not my people;
> and I will call her 'my loved one' who is not my loved one,"[i][k]

26 and,

> "It will happen that in the very place where it was said to them,
> 'You are not my people,'
> they will be called 'sons of the living God'."[j][l]

27 Isaiah cries out concerning Israel:

> "Though the number of the Israelites be like the sand by the sea,[m]
> only the remnant will be saved.[n]
> 28 For the Lord will carry out
> his sentence on earth with speed and finality."[k][o]

29 It is just as Isaiah said previously:

> "Unless the Lord Almighty[p]
> had left us descendants,
> we would have become like Sodom,
> we would have been like Gomorrah."[l][q]

Israel's Unbelief

30 What then shall we say? That the Gentiles, who did not pursue righteousness, have obtained it, a righteousness that is by faith;[r] 31 but Israel, who pursued a law of righteousness,[s] has not attained it.[t] 32 Why not? Because they pursued it not by faith but as if it were by works. They stumbled over the "stumbling-stone".[u] 33 As it is written:

> "See, I lay in Zion a stone that causes men to stumble
> and a rock that makes them fall,
> and the one who trusts in him will never be put to shame."[m][v]

i *25* Hosea 2:23 j *26* Hosea 1:10 k *28* Isaiah 10:22,23 l *29* Isaiah 1:9 m *33* Isaiah 8:14; 28:16

9:21 e 2Ti 2:20
9:22 f Ro 2:4
9:23 g Ro 2:4; h Ro 8:30
9:24 i Ro 8:28; j Ro 3:29
9:25 k Hos 2:23; 1Pe 2:10
9:26 l Hos 1:10
9:27 m Ge 22:17; Hos 1:10; n Ro 11:5
9:28 o Isa 10:22, 23
9:29 p Jas 5:4; q Isa 1:9; Dt 29:23; Isa 13:19; Jer 50:40
9:30 r Ro 1:17; 10:6; Gal 2:16; Php 3:9; Heb 11:7
9:31 s Isa 51:1; Ro 10:2, 3; t Gal 5:4
9:32 u 1Pe 2:8
9:33 v Isa 28:16; Ro 10:11

9:25, 26 About seven hundred years before Jesus' birth, Hosea told of God's intention to restore his people. Paul applies Hosea's message to God's intention to bring Gentiles into his family after the Jews rejected his plan. Verse 25 is a quotation from Hosea 2:23 and verse 26 is from Hosea 1:10.

9:27–29 Isaiah prophesied that only a small number—a remnant—of God's original people, the Jews, would be saved. Paul saw this happening in every city where he preached. Even though he went to the Jews first, relatively few ever accepted the message. Verses 27 and 28 are based on Isaiah 10:22, 23; and 9:29 is from Isaiah 1:9.

9:31–33 Sometimes we are like these people, trying to get right with God by keeping his laws. We may think that attending church, doing church work, giving offerings, and being nice will be enough. After all, we've played by the rules, haven't we? But Paul's words sting—this approach never succeeds. Paul explains that God's plan is not for those who try to earn his favour by being good; it is for those who realise that they can never be good enough and so must depend on Christ. We can be saved only by putting our faith in what Jesus Christ has done. If we do that, we will never be "put to shame" or be disappointed.

9:32 The Jews had a worthy goal—to honour God. But they tried to achieve it the wrong way—by rigid and painstaking obedience to the law. Thus some of them became more dedicated to the law than to God. They thought that if they kept the law, God would have to accept them as his people. But God cannot be controlled. The Jews did not see that their Scriptures, the Old Testament, taught salvation by faith, and not by human effort (see Genesis 15:6).

9:32 The "stumbling-stone" was Jesus. The Jews did not believe in him, because he didn't meet their expectations for the Messiah. Some people still stumble over Christ because salvation by faith doesn't make sense to them. They would rather try to earn their way to God, or else they expect God simply to overlook their sins. Others stumble over Christ because his values are the opposite of the world's. He asks for humility, and many are unwilling to humble themselves before him. He requires obedience, and many refuse to put their wills at his disposal.

10 Brothers, my heart's desire and prayer to God for the Israelites is that they may
be saved. 2 For I can testify about them that they are zealous[a] for God, but their
zeal is not based on knowledge. 3 Since they did not know the righteousness that comes
from God and sought to establish their own, they did not submit to God's righteousness.[b] 4 Christ is the end of the law[c] so that there may be righteousness for everyone
who believes.[d]
5 Moses describes in this way the righteousness that is by the law: "The man who
does these things will live by them."[a][e] 6 But the righteousness that is by faith[f] says:
"Do not say in your heart, 'Who will ascend into heaven?'[b]"[g] (that is, to bring Christ
down) 7 "or 'Who will descend into the deep?'[c]" (that is, to bring Christ up from the
dead). 8 But what does it say? "The word is near you; it is in your mouth and in your
heart,"[d][h] that is, the word of faith we are proclaiming: 9 That if you confess[i] with
your mouth, "Jesus is Lord," and believe in your heart that God raised him from the
dead,[j] you will be saved. 10 For it is with your heart that you believe and are justified,
and it is with your mouth that you confess and are saved. 11 As the Scripture says,
"Anyone who trusts in him will never be put to shame."[e][k] 12 For there is no difference
between Jew and Gentile[l]—the same Lord is Lord of all[m] and richly blesses all who
call on him, 13 for, "Everyone who calls on the name of the Lord[n] will be saved."[f][o]
14 How, then, can they call on the one they have not believed in? And how can they
believe in the one of whom they have not heard? And how can they hear without
someone preaching to them? 15 And how can they preach unless they are sent? As it
is written, "How beautiful are the feet of those who bring good news!"[g][p]
16 But not all the Israelites accepted the good news. For Isaiah says, "Lord, who
has believed our message?"[h][q] 17 Consequently, faith comes from hearing the message,[r] and the message is heard through the word of Christ.[s] 18 But I ask: Did they
not hear? Of course they did:

[a] *5* Lev. 18:5 [b] *6* Deut. 30:12 [c] *7* Deut. 30:13 [d] *8* Deut. 30:14 [e] *11* Isaiah 28:16 [f] *13* Joel 2:32
[g] *15* Isaiah 52:7 [h] *16* Isaiah 53:1

10:2 [a] Ac 21:20
10:3 [b] Ro 1:17
10:4 [c] Gal 3:24; Ro 7:1-4 [d] Ro 3:22
10:5 [e] Lev 18:5; Ne 9:29; Eze 20:11, 13, 21; Ro 7:10
10:6 [f] Ro 9:30 [g] Dt 30:12
10:8 [h] Dt 30:14
10:9 [i] Mt 10:32; Lk 12:8 [j] Ac 2:24
10:11 [k] Isa 28:16; Ro 9:33
10:12 [l] Ro 3:22, 29 [m] Ac 10:36
10:13 [n] Ac 2:21 [o] Joel 2:32
10:15 [p] Isa 52:7; Na 1:15
10:16 [q] Isa 53:1; Jn 12:38
10:17 [r] Gal 3:2, 5 [s] Col 3:16

10:1 What will happen to the Jewish people who believe in God but not in Christ? Since they believe in the same God, won't they be saved? If that were true, Paul would not have worked so hard and sacrificed so much to teach them about Christ. Because Jesus is the most complete revelation of God, we cannot fully know God apart from Christ; and because God appointed Jesus to bring God and man together, we cannot come to God by another path. The Jews, like everyone else, can find salvation only through Jesus Christ (John 14:6; Acts 4:12). Like Paul, we should wish that all Jews might be saved. We should pray for them and lovingly share the Good News with them.

10:3–5 Rather than living by faith in God, the Jews established customs and traditions (in addition to God's law) to try to make themselves acceptable in God's sight. But human effort, no matter how sincere, can never substitute for the righteousness God offers us by faith. The only way to *earn* salvation is to be perfect—and that is impossible. We can only hold out our empty hands and receive salvation as a gift.

10:4 Christ is the "end of the law" in two ways. He fulfils the purpose and goal of the law (Matthew 5:17) in that he perfectly exemplified God's desires on earth. But he is also the termination of the law because in comparison to Christ, the law is powerless to save.

10:5 In order to be saved by the law, a person would have to live a perfect life, not sinning once. Why did God give the law when he knew people couldn't keep it? According to Paul, one reason the law was given was to show people how guilty they are (Galatians 3:19). The law was a shadow of Christ—that is, the sacrificial system educated the people so that when the true sacrifice came, they would be able to understand his work (Hebrews 10:1–4). The system of ceremonial laws was to last until the coming of Christ. The law, including animal sacrifices, points to Christ.

10:6–8 Paul adapts Moses' farewell challenge from Deuteronomy 30:11–14 to apply to Christ. Christ has provided our salvation through his incarnation (coming to earth) and resurrection (coming back from the dead). God's salvation is right in front of us. He will come to us wherever we are. All we need to do is respond and accept his gift of salvation. The *deep* as used here refers to the grave or Hades, the place of the dead.

10:8–12 Have you ever been asked, "How do I become a Christian?" These verses give you the beautiful answer—salvation is as close as your own mouth and heart. People think it must be a complicated process, but it is not. If we believe in our hearts and say with our mouths that Christ is the risen Lord, we will be saved.

10:11 This verse must be read in context. Paul is not saying Christians will never be put to shame or be disappointed. There will be times when people will let us down and when circumstances will take a turn for the worse. Paul is saying that God will keep his side of the bargain—those who call on him will be saved. God will never fail to provide righteousness to those who believe.

10:14, 15 We must take God's great message of salvation to others so that they can respond to the Good News. How will your loved ones and neighbours hear it unless someone tells them? Is God calling you to take a part in making his message known in your community? Think of one person who needs to hear the Good News, and think of something you can do to help him or her hear it. Then take that step as soon as possible.

10:18–20 Many Jews who looked for the Messiah refused to believe in him when he came. God offered his salvation to the Gentiles ("those who are not a nation" and "a nation that has no understanding"); thus many Gentiles who didn't even know about a Messiah found and believed in him. Some religious people are spiritually blind, while those who have never been in a church are sometimes the most responsive to God's message. Because appearances are deceiving, and we can't see into people's hearts, beware of judging beforehand who will respond to the gospel and who will not.

10:18 [t]Ps 19:4; Mt 24:14; Col 1:6, 23; 1Th 1:8

"Their voice has gone out into all the earth,
their words to the ends of the world."[i][t]

19Again I ask: Did Israel not understand? First, Moses says,

10:19 [u]Ro 11:11, 14 [v]Dt 32:21

"I will make you envious[u] by those who are not a nation;
I will make you angry by a nation that has no
understanding."[j][v]

10:20 [w]Isa 65:1; Ro 9:30

20And Isaiah boldly says,

"I was found by those who did not seek me;
I revealed myself to those who did not ask for me."[k][w]

10:21 [x]Isa 65:2

21But concerning Israel he says,

"All day long I have held out my hands
to a disobedient and obstinate people."[l][x]

11:1 [a]1Sa 12:22; Jer 31:37 [b]2Co 11:22 [c]Php 3:5

The Remnant of Israel

11 I ask then: Did God reject his people? By no means![a] I am an Israelite myself,
a descendant of Abraham,[b] from the tribe of Benjamin.[c] 2God did not reject
his people, whom he foreknew.[d] Don't you know what the Scripture says in the
passage about Elijah — how he appealed to God against Israel: 3"Lord, they have killed
your prophets and torn down your altars; I am the only one left, and they are trying
to kill me"[a]?[e] 4And what was God's answer to him? "I have reserved for myself
seven thousand who have not bowed the knee to Baal."[b][f] 5So too, at the present
time there is a remnant[g] chosen by grace. 6And if by grace, then it is no longer by
works;[h] if it were, grace would no longer be grace.[c]
7What then? What Israel sought so earnestly it did not obtain,[i] but the elect did.
The others were hardened,[j] 8as it is written:

11:2 [d]Ro 8:29

11:3 [e]1Ki 19:10, 14

11:4 [f]1Ki 19:18

11:5 [g]Ro 9:27

11:6 [h]Ro 4:4

11:7 [i]Ro 9:31 [j]ver 25; Ro 9:18

"God gave them a spirit of stupor,
eyes so that they could not see
and ears so that they could not hear,[k]
to this very day."[d][l]

11:8 [k]Mt 13:13-15 [l]Dt 29:4; Isa 29:10

9And David says:

"May their table become a snare and a trap,
a stumbling-block and a retribution for them.
10May their eyes be darkened so they cannot see,
and their backs be bent for ever."[e][m]

11:10 [m]Ps 69:22, 23

i *18* Psalm 19:4 j *19* Deut. 32:21 k *20* Isaiah 65:1 l *21* Isaiah 65:2 a *3* 1 Kings 19:10,14 b *4* 1 Kings 19:18 c *6* Some manuscripts *by grace. But if by works, then it is no longer grace; if it were, work would no longer be work.* d *8* Deut. 29:4; Isaiah 29:10 e *10* Psalm 69:22,23

11:1ff In this chapter Paul points out that not *all* Jews have rejected God's message of salvation. There is still a faithful remnant (11:5). Paul himself, after all, was a Jew, and so were Jesus' disciples and nearly all of the early Christian missionaries.

11:2 Elijah was a great reforming prophet who challenged the northern kingdom of Israel to repent. See his Profile in 1 Kings 18 for more information.

11:2 God chose the Jews ("his people, whom he foreknew") to be the people through whom the rest of the world could find salvation. But this did not mean the entire Jewish nation would be saved; only those who were faithful to God (the remnant) were considered true Jews (11:5). We are saved through faith in Christ, not because we are part of a nation, religion, or family. On whom or on what are you depending for salvation?

11:6 Do you think it's easier for God to love you when you're good? Do you secretly suspect that God chose you because you deserved it? Do you think some people's behaviour is so bad that God couldn't possibly save them? If you ever think this way, you don't entirely understand that salvation is by grace, a free gift. It cannot be earned, in whole or in part; it can only be accepted with thankfulness and praise.

11:7 "The others were hardened" was God's punishment for their sin. It was a confirmation of their own stubbornness. In judging them, God removed their ability to see and hear, and to repent; thus they would experience the consequences of their rebellion.

11:8–10 These verses describe the punishment for hardened hearts predicted by the prophet Isaiah (Isaiah 6:9–13). If people refuse to hear God's Good News, they will eventually be unable to understand it. Paul saw this happening in the Jewish congregations he visited on his missionary journeys. (Verse 8 is based on Deuteronomy 29:4 and Isaiah 29:10. Verses 9 and 10 are from Psalm 69:22, 23.)

Ingrafted Branches

11Again I ask: Did they stumble so as to fall beyond recovery? Not at all![n] Rather,
because of their transgression, salvation has come to the Gentiles[o] to make Israel
envious.[p] 12But if their transgression means riches for the world, and their loss means
riches for the Gentiles,[q] how much greater riches will their fulness bring!
13I am talking to you Gentiles. Inasmuch as I am the apostle to the Gentiles,[r] I
make much of my ministry 14in the hope that I may somehow arouse my own people
to envy[s] and save[t] some of them. 15For if their rejection is the reconciliation[u] of
the world, what will their acceptance be but life from the dead?[v] 16If the part of the
dough offered as firstfruits[w] is holy, then the whole batch is holy; if the root is holy,
so are the branches.
17If some of the branches have been broken off,[x] and you, though a wild olive
shoot, have been grafted in among the others[y] and now share in the nourishing
sap from the olive root, 18do not boast over those branches. If you do, consider
this: You do not support the root, but the root supports you.[z] 19You will say
then, "Branches were broken off so that I could be grafted in." 20Granted. But
they were broken off because of unbelief, and you stand by faith.[a] Do not be arrogant,[b] but be afraid.[c] 21For if God did not spare the natural branches, he will not spare
you either.
22Consider therefore the kindness[d] and sternness of God: sternness to those who
fell, but kindness to you, provided that you continue[e] in his kindness. Otherwise,
you also will be cut off.[f] 23And if they do not persist in unbelief, they will be grafted

11:11 [n]ver 1 [o]Ac 13:46 [p]Ro 10:19
11:12 [q]ver 25
11:13 [r]Ac 9:15
11:14 [s]Ro 10:19 [t]1Co 1:21
11:15 [u]Ro 5:10 [v]Lk 15:24, 32
11:16 [w]Lev 23:10, 17; Nu 15:18-21
11:17 [x]Jer 11:16; Jn 15:2 [y]Ac 2:39; Eph 2:11-13
11:18 [z]Jn 4:22
11:20 [a]1Co 10:12 [b]1Ti 6:17 [c]1Pe 1:17
11:22 [d]Ro 2:4 [e]1Co 15:2; Heb 3:6 [f]Jn 15:2

11:11ff Paul had a vision of a church where all Jews and Gentiles would be united in their love of God and in obedience to Christ. While respecting God's law, this ideal church would look to Christ alone for salvation. A person's ethnic background and social status would be irrelevant (see Galatians 3:28) – what mattered would be his or her faith in Christ.

But Paul's vision has not yet been realised. Many Jewish people rejected the gospel. They depended on their heritage for salvation, and they did not have the heart of obedience that was so important to the Old Testament prophets and to Paul. Once Gentiles became dominant in many of the Christian churches, they began rejecting Jews and even persecuting them. Unfortunately, this practice has recurred through the centuries.

True Christians should not persecute others. Both Gentiles and Jews have done so much to damage the cause of the God they claim to serve that Paul's vision often seems impossible to fulfil. Yet God chose the Jews, just as he chose the Gentiles, and he is still working to unite Jew and Gentile in a new Israel, a new Jerusalem, ruled by his Son (see Ephesians 2:11–22).

11:13–15 Paul was appointed as a missionary to the Gentiles. He reminded his Jewish brothers of this fact, hoping that they too would want to be saved. The Jews had been rejected, and thus Gentiles were being offered salvation. But when a Jew comes to Christ, there is great rejoicing, as if a dead person had come back to life.

11:17–24 Speaking to Gentile Christians, Paul warns them not to feel superior because God rejected some Jews. Abraham's faith is like the root of a productive tree, and the Jewish people are the tree's natural branches. Because of faithlessness, the Jews were the broken branches. Gentile believers have been grafted into the tree like a wild olive shoot. Both Jews and Gentiles share the tree's nourishment based on faith in God; neither can rest on heritage or culture for salvation.

11:22 "Continue in his kindness" refers to steadfast perseverance in faith. Steadfastness is a proof of the reality of faith and a by-product of salvation, not a means to it.

11:26 Some say the phrase "And so all Israel will be saved" means that the majority of Jews in the final generation before Christ's return will turn to Christ for salvation. Others say that Paul is using the term *Israel* for the "spiritual" nation of Israel made up of everyone – Jew and Gentile – who has received salvation through faith in Christ. Thus *all Israel* (or all believers) will receive God's promised gift of salvation. Still others say that *all Israel* means Israel as a whole will have a role in Christ's kingdom. Their identity as a people won't be discarded. God chose the nation of Israel, and he has never rejected it. He also chose the church, through Jesus Christ, and he will never reject it either. This does not mean, of course, that all Jews or all church members will be saved. It is possible to belong to a nation or to an organisation without ever responding in faith. But just because some people have rejected Christ does not mean that God stops working with either Israel or the church. He continues to offer salvation freely to all. Still others say that the phrase "and so" means "in this way" or "this is how", referring to the necessity of faith in Christ.

in, for God is able to graft them in again.[g] 24After all, if you were cut out of an olive
tree that is wild by nature, and contrary to nature were grafted into a cultivated olive
tree, how much more readily will these, the natural branches, be grafted into their own
olive tree!

All Israel Will Be Saved

25I do not want you to be ignorant[h] of this mystery,[i] brothers, so that you may
not be conceited:[j] Israel has experienced a hardening[k] in part until the full number
of the Gentiles has come in.[l] 26And so all Israel will be saved, as it is written:

"The deliverer will come from Zion;
he will turn godlessness away from Jacob.
27And this is[f] my covenant with them
when I take away their sins."[g][m]

28As far as the gospel is concerned, they are enemies[n] on your account; but as far
as election is concerned, they are loved on account of the patriarchs,[o] 29for God's
gifts and his call[p] are irrevocable.[q] 30Just as you who were at one time disobedient[r]
to God have now received mercy as a result of their disobedience, 31so they too have
now become disobedient in order that they too may now[h] receive mercy as a result
of God's mercy to you. 32For God has bound all men over to disobedience[s] so that
he may have mercy on them all.

Doxology

33Oh, the depth of the riches[t] of the wisdom and[i] knowledge of
God![u]
How unsearchable his judgments,
and his paths beyond tracing out![v]
34"Who has known the mind of the Lord?
Or who has been his counsellor?"[j][w]
35"Who has ever given to God,
that God should repay him?"[k][x]
36For from him and through him and to him are all things.[y]
To him be the glory for ever! Amen.[z]

f *27* Or *will be* **g** *27* Isaiah 59:20,21; 27:9; Jer. 31:33,34 **h** *31* Some manuscripts do not have *now.*
i *33* Or *riches and the wisdom and the* **j** *34* Isaiah 40:13 **k** *35* Job 41:11

11:23 [g]2Co 3:16
11:25 [h]Ro 1:13 [i]Ro 16:25 [j]Ro 12:16 [k]ver 7; Ro 9:18 [l]Lk 21:24
11:27 [m]Isa 27:9; Heb 8:10, 12
11:28 [n]Ro 5:10 [o]Dt 7:8; 10:15; Ro 9:5
11:29 [p]Ro 8:28 [q]Heb 7:21
11:30 [r]Eph 2:2
11:32 [s]Ro 3:9
11:33 [t]Ro 2:4 [u]Ps 92:5 [v]Job 11:7
11:34 [w]Isa 40:13, 14; Job 15:8; 36:22; 1Co 2:16
11:35 [x]Job 35:7
11:36 [y]1Co 8:6; Col 1:16; Heb 2:10 [z]Ro 16:27

11:28–32 In this passage Paul shows how the Jews and the Gentiles benefit each other. Whenever God shows mercy to one group, the other shares the blessing. In God's original plan, the Jews would be the source of God's blessing to the Gentiles (see Genesis 12:3). When the Jews neglected this mission, God blessed the Gentiles anyway through the Jewish Messiah. He still maintained his love for the Jews because of his promises to Abraham, Isaac, and Jacob ("on account of the patriarchs"). But someday the faithful Jews will share in God's mercy. God's plans will not be thwarted: he will "have mercy on them all". For a beautiful picture of Jews and Gentiles experiencing rich blessings, see Isaiah 60.

11:29 The privileges and invitation of God given to Israel can never be withdrawn.

11:33 This doxology is a prayer of praise to God for the wisdom of his plan. Although God's method and means are beyond our comprehension, God himself is not arbitrary. He governs the universe and our lives in perfect wisdom, justice, and love.

11:34, 35 The implication of these questions is that no-one has fully understood the mind of the Lord. No one has been his counsellor. And God owes nothing to any one of us. Isaiah and Jeremiah asked similar questions to show that we are unable to give advice to God or criticise his ways (Isaiah 40:13; Jeremiah 23:18). God alone is the possessor of absolute power and absolute wisdom.

11:36 In the final analysis, all of us are absolutely dependent on God. He is the source of all things, including ourselves. He is the power that sustains and rules the world that we live in. And God works out all things to bring glory to himself. The all-powerful God deserves our praise.

B. HOW TO BEHAVE (12:1 – 16:27)

Moving from the theological to the practical, Paul gives guidelines for living as a redeemed people in a fallen world. We are to give ourselves to Christ as living sacrifices, obey the government, love our neighbours, and take special care of those who are weak in the faith. He closes with personal remarks. Throughout this section, we learn how to live our faith each day.

1. Personal responsibility

Living Sacrifices

12 Therefore, I urge you,[a] brothers, in view of God's mercy, to offer your bodies
as living sacrifices,[b] holy and pleasing to God—this is your spiritual[a] act of
worship. 2 Do not conform[c] any longer to the pattern of this world,[d] but be transformed by the renewing of your mind.[e] Then you will be able to test and approve
what God's will is[f]—his good, pleasing and perfect will.
3 For by the grace given me[g] I say to every one of you: Do not think of yourself
more highly than you ought, but rather think of yourself with sober judgment, in
accordance with the measure of faith God has given you. 4 Just as each of us has one
body with many members, and these members do not all have the same function,[h]
5 so in Christ we who are many form one body,[i] and each member belongs to all the
others. 6 We have different gifts,[j] according to the grace given us. If a man's gift
is prophesying, let him use it in proportion to his[b] faith.[k] 7 If it is serving, let him
serve; if it is teaching, let him teach;[l] 8 if it is encouraging, let him encourage;[m] if

a 1 Or *reasonable* b 6 Or *in agreement with the*

12:1 [a] Eph 4:1 [b] Ro 6:13, 16, 19; 1Pe 2:5
12:2 [c] 1Pe 1:14 [d] 1Jn 2:15 [e] Eph 4:23 [f] Eph 5:17
12:3 [g] Ro 15:15; Gal 2:9; Eph 4:7
12:4 [h] 1Co 12:12-14; Eph 4:16
12:5 [i] 1Co 10:17
12:6 [j] 1Co 7:7; 12:4, 8-10 [k] 1Pe 4:10, 11
12:7 [l] Eph 4:11
12:8 [m] Ac 15:32

12:1 When sacrificing an animal according to God's law, a priest would kill the animal, cut it in pieces, and place it on the altar. Sacrifice was important, but even in the Old Testament God made it clear that obedience from the heart was much more important (see 1 Samuel 15:22; Psalm 40:6; Amos 5:21–24). God wants us to offer ourselves, not animals, as *living* sacrifices—daily laying aside our own desires to follow him, putting all our energy and resources at his disposal and trusting him to guide us. We do this out of gratitude that our sins have been forgiven.

12:1, 2 God has good, pleasing, and perfect plans for his children. He wants us to be transformed people with renewed minds, living to honour and obey him. Because he wants only what is best for us, and because he gave his Son to make our new lives possible, we should joyfully give ourselves as living sacrifices for his service.

12:2 Christians are called to "not conform any longer to the pattern of this world", with its behaviour and customs that are usually selfish and often corrupting. Many Christians wisely decide that much worldly behaviour is off limits for them. Our refusal to conform to this world's values, however, must go even deeper than the level of behaviour and customs—it must be firmly planted in our minds—"be transformed by the renewing of your mind". It is possible to avoid most worldly customs and still be proud, covetous, selfish, stubborn, and arrogant. Only when the Holy Spirit renews, re-educates, and redirects our minds are we truly transformed (see 8:5).

12:3 Healthy self-esteem is important because some of us think too little of ourselves; on the other hand, some of us overestimate ourselves. The key to an honest and accurate evaluation is knowing the basis of our self-worth—our identity in Christ. Apart from him, we aren't capable of very much by eternal standards; in him, we are valuable and capable of worthy service. Evaluating yourself by the worldly standards of success and achievement can cause you to think too much about your worth in the eyes of others and thus miss your true value in God's eyes.

12:4, 5 Paul uses the concept of the human body to teach how Christians should live and work together. Just as the parts of the body function under the direction of the brain, so Christians are to work together under the command and authority of Jesus Christ (see 1 Corinthians 12:12–31; Ephesians 4:1–16).

12:4–8 God gives us gifts so we can build up his church. To use them effectively, we must (1) realise that all gifts and abilities come from God; (2) understand that not everyone has the same gifts; (3) know who we are and what we do best; (4) dedicate our gifts to God's service and not to our personal success; (5) be willing to utilise our gifts wholeheartedly, not holding back anything from God's service.

12:6 God's gifts differ in nature, power, and effectiveness according to his wisdom and graciousness, not according to our faith. The "measure of faith" (12:3) or the "proportion to his faith" means that God will give spiritual power necessary and appropriate to carry out each responsibility. We cannot, by our own effort or willpower, drum up more faith and thus be more effective teachers or servants. These are God's gifts to his church, and he gives faith and power as he wills. Our role is to be faithful and to seek ways to serve others with what Christ has given us.

12:6 *Prophesying* in Scripture is not always predicting the future. Often it means preaching God's messages (1 Corinthians 14:1–3).

12:6–8 Look at this list of gifts and imagine the kinds of people who would have each gift. Prophets are often bold and articulate. Servers (those in ministry) are faithful and loyal. Teachers are clear thinkers. Encouragers know how to motivate others. Givers are generous and trusting. Leaders are good organisers and managers. Those who show mercy are caring people who are happy to give their time to others. It would be difficult for one person to embody all these gifts. An assertive prophet would not usually make a good counsellor, and a generous giver might fail as a leader. When you identify your own gifts (and this list is far from complete), ask how you can use them to build up God's family. At the same time, realise that your gifts can't do the work of the church all alone. Be thankful for people whose gifts are completely different from yours. Let your strengths balance their weaknesses, and be grateful that their abilities make up for your deficiencies. Together you can build Christ's church.

12:8
[n]2Co 9:5-13
12:9
[o]1Ti 1:5
12:10
[p]Heb 13:1
[q]Php 2:3
12:11
[r]Ac 18:25
12:12
[s]Ro 5:2
[t]Heb 10:32, 36
12:13
[u]1Ti 3:2
12:14
[v]Mt 5:44
12:15
[w]Job 30:25
12:16
[x]Ro 15:5
[y]Jer 45:5;
Ro 11:25
12:17
[z]Pr 20:22
[a]2Co 8:21
12:18
[b]Mk 9:50;
Ro 14:19
12:19
[c]Lev 19:18;
Pr 20:22; 24:29
[d]Dt 32:35
12:20
[e]Pr 25:21, 22;
Mt 5:44;
Lk 6:27

it is contributing to the needs of others, let him give generously;[n] if it is leadership,
let him govern diligently; if it is showing mercy, let him do it cheerfully.

Love

9Love must be sincere.[o] Hate what is evil; cling to what is good. 10Be devoted
to one another in brotherly love.[p] Honour one another above yourselves.[q] 11Never
be lacking in zeal, but keep your spiritual fervour,[r] serving the Lord. 12Be joyful
in hope,[s] patient in affliction,[t] faithful in prayer. 13Share with God's people who
are in need. Practise hospitality.[u]

14Bless those who persecute you;[v] bless and do not curse. 15Rejoice with those
who rejoice; mourn with those who mourn.[w] 16Live in harmony with one another.[x]
Do not be proud, but be willing to associate with people of low position.[c] Do not
be conceited.[y]

17Do not repay anyone evil for evil.[z] Be careful to do what is right in the eyes
of everybody.[a] 18If it is possible, as far as it depends on you, live at peace with
everyone.[b] 19Do not take revenge,[c] my friends, but leave room for God's wrath,
for it is written: "It is mine to avenge; I will repay,"[d][d] says the Lord. 20On the
contrary:

> "If your enemy is hungry, feed him;
> if he is thirsty, give him something to drink.
> In doing this, you will heap burning coals on his head."[e][e]

21Do not be overcome by evil, but overcome evil with good.

c *16* Or *willing to do menial work* d *19* Deut. 32:35 e *20* Prov. 25:21,22

12:9 Most of us have learned how to pretend to love others – how to speak kindly, avoid hurting their feelings, and appear to take an interest in them. We may even be skilled in pretending to feel moved with compassion when we hear of others' needs, or to become indignant when we learn of injustice. But God calls us to real and sincere love that goes far beyond pretence and politeness. Sincere love requires concentration and effort. It means helping others become better people. It demands our time, money, and personal involvement. No individual has the capacity to express love to a whole community, but the body of Christ in your town does. Look for people who need your love, and look for ways you and your fellow believers can love your community for Christ.

12:10 We can honour others in one of two ways. One involves ulterior motives. We honour our bosses so they will reward us, our employees so they will work harder, the wealthy so they will contribute to our cause, the powerful so they will use their power for us and not against us. God's other way involves love. As Christians, we honour people because they have been created in God's image, because they are our brothers and sisters in Christ, and because they have a unique contribution to make to Christ's church. Does God's way of honouring others sound too difficult for your competitive nature? Why not try to outdo one another in showing honour? Put others first!

12:13 Christian hospitality differs from social entertaining. Entertaining focuses on the host – the home must be spotless; the food must be well prepared and abundant; the host must appear relaxed and good-natured. Hospitality, by contrast, focuses on the guests. Their needs – whether for a place to stay, nourishing food, a listening ear, or acceptance – are the primary concern. Hospitality can happen in a messy home. It can happen around a dinner table where the main dish is canned soup. It can even happen while the host and the guest are doing chores together. Don't hesitate to offer hospitality just because you are too tired, too busy, or not wealthy enough to entertain.

12:17–21 These verses summarise the core of Christian living. If we love someone the way Christ loves us, we will be willing to forgive. If we have experienced God's grace, we will want to pass it on to others. And remember, grace is *undeserved* favour. By giving an enemy a drink, we're not excusing his misdeeds. We're recognising him, forgiving him, and loving him in spite of his sins – just as Christ did for us.

12:19–21 In this day of constant lawsuits and incessant demands for legal rights, Paul's command sounds almost impossible. When someone hurts you deeply, instead of giving him what he deserves, Paul says to befriend him. Why does Paul tell us to forgive our enemies? (1) Forgiveness may break a cycle of retaliation and lead to mutual reconciliation. (2) It may make the enemy feel ashamed and change his or her ways. (3) By contrast, repaying evil for evil hurts you just as much as it hurts your enemy. Even if your enemy never repents, forgiving him or her will free you of a heavy load of bitterness.

12:19–21 Forgiveness involves both attitudes and actions. If you find it difficult to *feel* forgiving toward someone who has hurt you, try responding with kind actions. If appropriate, tell this person that you would like to heal your relationship. Lend a helping hand. Send him or her a gift. Smile at him or her. Many times you will discover that right actions lead to right feelings.

12:20 What does it mean to "heap burning coals" on someone's head? This may refer to an Egyptian tradition of carrying a pan of burning charcoal on one's head as a public act of repentance. By referring to this proverb, Paul was saying that we should treat our enemies with kindness so that they will become ashamed and turn from their sins. The best way to get rid of enemies is to turn them into friends.

Submission to the Authorities

13 Everyone must submit himself to the governing authorities,[a] for there is no
authority except that which God has established.[b] The authorities that exist
have been established by God. 2Consequently, he who rebels against the authority is
rebelling against what God has instituted, and those who do so will bring judgment
on themselves. 3For rulers hold no terror for those who do right, but for those who
do wrong. Do you want to be free from fear of the one in authority? Then do what
is right and he will commend you.[c] 4For he is God's servant to do you good. But
if you do wrong, be afraid, for he does not bear the sword for nothing. He is God's
servant, an agent of wrath to bring punishment on the wrongdoer.[d] 5Therefore, it is
necessary to submit to the authorities, not only because of possible punishment but
also because of conscience.
6This is also why you pay taxes, for the authorities are God's servants, who give
their full time to governing. 7Give everyone what you owe him: If you owe taxes,
pay taxes;[e] if revenue, then revenue; if respect, then respect; if honour, then honour.

Love, for the Day Is Near

8Let no debt remain outstanding, except the continuing debt to love one another,
for he who loves his fellow-man has fulfilled the law.[f] 9The commandments, "Do
not commit adultery," "Do not murder," "Do not steal," "Do not covet,"**a**[g] and
whatever other commandment there may be, are summed up in this one rule: "Love
your neighbour as yourself."**b**[h] 10Love does no harm to its neighbour. Therefore love
is the fulfilment of the law.[i]
11And do this, understanding the present time. The hour has come[j] for you to wake
up from your slumber,[k] because our salvation is nearer now than when we first
believed. 12The night is nearly over; the day is almost here.[l] So let us put aside the

a *9* Exodus 20:13–15,17; Deut. 5:17–19,21 **b** *9* Lev. 19:18

13:1 [a]Tit 3:1; 1Pe 2:13, 14 [b]Da 2:21; Jn 19:11
13:3 [c]1Pe 2:14
13:4 [d]1Th 4:6
13:7 [e]Mt 17:25; 22:17, 21; Lk 23:2
13:8 [f]ver 10; Jn 13:34; Gal 5:14; Col 3:14
13:9 [g]Ex 20:13-15, 17; Dt 5:17-19, 21 [h]Lev 19:18; Mt 19:19
13:10 [i]ver 8; Mt 22:39, 40
13:11 [j]1Co 7:29-31; 10:11 [k]Eph 5:14; 1Th 5:5, 6
13:12 [l]1Jn 2:8

13:1 Are there times when we should not submit to the government? We should never allow government to force us to disobey God. Jesus and his apostles never disobeyed the government for personal reasons; when they disobeyed, it was in order to follow their higher loyalty to God. Their disobedience was not cheap: they were threatened, beaten, thrown into jail, tortured, and executed for their convictions. Like them, if we are compelled to disobey, we must be ready to accept the consequences.

13:1ff Christians understand Romans 13 in different ways. All Christians agree that we are to live at peace with the state as long as the state allows us to live by our religious convictions. For hundreds of years, however, there have been at least three interpretations of how we are to do this.

(1) Some Christians believe that the state is so corrupt that Christians should have as little to do with it as possible. Although they should be good citizens as long as they can do so without compromising their beliefs, they should not work for the government, vote in elections, or serve in the armed forces.

(2) Others believe that God has given the state authority in certain areas and the church authority in others. Christians can be loyal to both and can work for either. They should not, however, confuse the two. In this view, church and state are concerned with two totally different spheres – the spiritual and the physical – and thus complement each other but do not work together.

(3) Still others believe that Christians have a responsibility to make the state better. They can do this politically, by electing Christian or other high-principled leaders. They can also do this morally, by serving as an influence for good in society. In this view, church and state ideally work together for the good of all.

None of these views advocate rebelling against or refusing to obey the government's laws or regulations unless those laws clearly require you to violate the moral standards revealed by God. Wherever we find ourselves, we must be responsible citizens, as well as responsible Christians.

13:3, 4 When civil rulers are unjust, upright people are afraid. In these verses, Paul is talking about officials who are doing their duty. When these officials are just, people who are doing right have nothing to fear.

13:8 Why is love for others called a debt? We are permanently in debt to Christ for the lavish love he has poured out on us. The only way we can even begin to repay this debt is by loving others in turn. Because Christ's love will always be infinitely greater than ours, we will always have the obligation to love our neighbours.

13:9 Somehow many of us have got the idea that self-love is wrong. But if this were the case, it would be pointless to love our neighbours as ourselves. But Paul explains what he means by self-love. Even if you have low self-esteem, you probably don't willingly let yourself go hungry. You clothe yourself reasonably well. You make sure there's a roof over your head if you can. You try not to let yourself be cheated or injured. And you get angry if someone tries to ruin your marriage. This is the kind of love we need to have for our neighbours. Do we see that others are fed, clothed, and housed as well as they can be? Are we concerned about issues of social justice? Loving others as ourselves means to be actively working to see that their needs are met. Interestingly, people who focus on others rather than on themselves rarely suffer from low self-esteem.

13:10 Christians must obey the law of love, which supersedes both religious and civil laws. How easy it is to excuse our indifference to others merely because we have no legal obligation to help them, and even to justify harming them if our actions are technically legal! But Jesus does not leave loopholes in the law of love. Whenever love demands it, we are to go beyond human legal requirements and imitate the God of love. See James 2:8, 9; 4:11 and 1 Peter 2:16, 17 for more about this law of love.

13:12–14 The *night* refers to the present evil time. The *day* refers to the time of Christ's return. Some people are surprised that Paul lists dissension and jealousy with the gross and obvious sins of or-

deeds of darkness[m] and put on the armour[n] of light. 13Let us behave decently, as
in the daytime, not in orgies and drunkenness, not in sexual immorality and debauchery, not in dissension and jealousy.[o] 14Rather, clothe yourselves with the Lord Jesus
Christ,[p] and do not think about how to gratify the desires of the sinful nature.[c]

The Weak and the Strong

14 Accept him whose faith is weak,[a] without passing judgment on disputable
matters. 2One man's faith allows him to eat everything, but another man, whose
faith is weak, eats only vegetables. 3The man who eats everything must not look down
on[b] him who does not, and the man who does not eat everything must not condemn[c]
the man who does, for God has accepted him. 4Who are you to judge someone else's
servant?[d] To his own master he stands or falls. And he will stand, for the Lord is
able to make him stand.

5One man considers one day more sacred than another;[e] another man considers
every day alike. Each one should be fully convinced in his own mind. 6He who regards
one day as special, does so to the Lord. He who eats meat, eats to the Lord, for he
gives thanks to God;[f] and he who abstains, does so to the Lord and gives thanks to
God. 7For none of us lives to himself alone[g] and none of us dies to himself alone.
8If we live, we live to the Lord; and if we die, we die to the Lord. So, whether we
live or die, we belong to the Lord.[h]

9For this very reason, Christ died and returned to life[i] so that he might be the Lord

13:12 [m]Eph 5:11 [n]Eph 6:11, 13
13:13 [o]Gal 5:20, 21
13:14 [p]Gal 3:27; 5:16; Eph 4:24
14:1 [a]Ro 15:1; 1Co 8:9-12
14:3 [b]Lk 18:9 [c]Col 2:16
14:4 [d]Jas 4:12
14:5 [e]Gal 4:10
14:6 [f]Mt 14:19; 1Co 10:30, 31; 1Ti 4:3, 4
14:7 [g]2Co 5:15; Gal 2:20
14:8 [h]Php 1:20
14:9 [i]Rev 1:18

[c] *14* Or *the flesh*

---

gies, drunkenness, and sexual immorality. Like Jesus in his Sermon on the Mount (Matthew 5 – 7), Paul considers attitudes as important as actions. Just as hatred leads to murder, so jealousy leads to strife and lust to adultery. When Christ returns, he wants to find his people clean on the inside as well as on the outside.

13:14 How do we clothe ourselves with the Lord Jesus Christ? First we identify with Christ by being baptised (Galatians 3:27). This shows our solidarity with other Christians and with the death, burial, and resurrection of Jesus Christ. Second, we exemplify the qualities Jesus showed while he was here on earth (love, humility, truth, service). In a sense, we role-play what Jesus would do in our situation (see Ephesians 4:24–32; Colossians 3:10–17). We also must not give our desires any opportunity to lead us into sin. Avoid those situations that open the door to gratifying sinful desires.

14:1 Who is weak in faith and who is strong? We are all weak in some areas and strong in others. Our faith is strong in an area if we can survive contact with sinners without falling into their patterns. It is weak in an area if we must avoid certain activities, people, or places in order to protect our spiritual life. It is important to take stock in order to find out our strengths and weaknesses. Whenever in doubt, we should ask, "Can I do that without sinning? Can I influence others for good, rather than being influenced by them?"

In areas of strength, we should not fear being defiled by the world; rather we should go and serve God. In areas of weakness, we need to be cautious. If we have a strong faith but shelter it, we are not doing Christ's work in the world. If we have a weak faith but expose it, we are being extremely foolish.

14:1 This verse assumes there will be differences of opinion in the church (disputable matters). Paul says we are not to quarrel about issues that are matters of opinion. Differences should not be feared or avoided, but accepted and handled with love. Don't expect everyone, even in the best possible church, to agree on every subject. Through sharing ideas we can come to a fuller understanding of what the Bible teaches. Accept, listen to, and respect others. Differences of opinion need not cause division. They can be a source of learning and richness in our relationships.

14:1ff What is weak faith? Paul is speaking about immature faith that has not yet developed the muscle it needs to stand against external pressures. For example, if a person who once worshipped idols were to become a Christian, he might understand perfectly well that Christ saved him through faith and that idols have no real power. Still, because of his past associations, he might be badly shaken if he knowingly ate meat that had been used in idol worship as part of a pagan ritual. If a person who once worshipped God on the required Jewish holy days were to become a Christian, he might well know that Christ saved him through faith, not through his keeping of the law. Still, when the feast days came, he might feel empty and unfaithful if he didn't dedicate those days to God.

Paul responds to both weak brothers in love. Both are acting according to their consciences, but their honest scruples do not need to be made into rules for the church. Certainly some issues are central to the faith and worth fighting for – but many are based on individual differences and should not be legislated. Our principle should be: In essentials, unity; in non-essentials, liberty; in everything, love.

14:2 Eating "everything" may refer to freedom from dietary restrictions, or it may refer to eating meat offered to idols, while the person weaker in the faith eats only vegetables and refuses to eat meat that has been offered to idols. But how would Christians end up eating meat that had been offered to idols? The ancient system of sacrifice was at the centre of the religious, social, and domestic life of the Roman world. After a sacrifice was presented to a god in a pagan temple, only part of it was burned. The remainder was often sent to the market to be sold. Thus a Christian might easily – even unknowingly – buy such meat in the market-place or eat it at the home of a friend. Should a Christian question the source of his meat? Some thought there was nothing wrong with eating meat that had been offered to idols because idols were worthless and phony. Others carefully checked the source of their meat or gave up meat altogether, in order to avoid a guilty conscience. The problem was especially acute for Christians who had once been idol worshippers. For them, such a strong reminder of their pagan days might weaken their new-found faith. Paul also deals with this problem in 1 Corinthians 8.

of both the dead and the living.[j] 10You, then, why do you judge your brother? Or
why do you look down on your brother? For we will all stand before God's judgment
seat.[k] 11It is written:

> " 'As surely as I live,' says the Lord,
> 'Every knee will bow before me;
> every tongue will confess to God.' "[a][l]

12So then, each of us will give an account of himself to God.[m]
13Therefore let us stop passing judgment[n] on one another. Instead, make up your
mind not to put any stumbling-block or obstacle in your brother's way. 14As one who
is in the Lord Jesus, I am fully convinced that no food[b] is unclean in itself.[o] But
if anyone regards something as unclean, then for him it is unclean.[p] 15If your brother
is distressed because of what you eat, you are no longer acting in love.[q] Do not by
your eating destroy your brother for whom Christ died.[r] 16Do not allow what you
consider good to be spoken of as evil.[s] 17For the kingdom of God is not a matter
of eating and drinking,[t] but of righteousness, peace and joy in the Holy Spirit,[u]
18because anyone who serves Christ in this way is pleasing to God and approved by
men.[v]
19Let us therefore make every effort to do what leads to peace[w] and to mutual
edification.[x] 20Do not destroy the work of God for the sake of food.[y] All food is
clean, but it is wrong for a man to eat anything that causes someone else to stumble.[z]
21It is better not to eat meat or drink wine or to do anything else that will cause your
brother to fall.[a]
22So whatever you believe about these things keep between yourself and God.
Blessed is the man who does not condemn[b] himself by what he approves. 23But the
man who has doubts[c] is condemned if he eats, because his eating is not from faith;
and everything that does not come from faith is sin.

15 We who are strong ought to bear with the failings of the weak[a] and not to please
ourselves. 2Each of us should please his neighbour for his good,[b] to build him
up.[c] 3For even Christ did not please himself[d] but, as it is written: "The insults of

a *11* Isaiah 45:23 b *14* Or *that nothing*

14:9 [j]2Co 5:15
14:10 [k]2Co 5:10
14:11 [l]Isa 45:23; Php 2:10, 11
14:12 [m]Mt 12:36; 1Pe 4:5
14:13 [n]Mt 7:1
14:14 [o]Ac 10:15 [p]1Co 8:7
14:15 [q]Eph 5:2 [r]1Co 8:11
14:16 [s]1Co 10:30
14:17 [t]1Co 8:8 [u]Ro 15:13
14:18 [v]2Co 8:21
14:19 [w]Ps 34:14; Ro 12:18; Heb 12:14 [x]Ro 15:2; 2Co 12:19
14:20 [y]ver 15 [z]1Co 8:9-12
14:21 [a]1Co 8:13
14:22 [b]1Jn 3:21
14:23 [c]ver 5
15:1 [a]Ro 14:1; Gal 6:1, 2; 1Th 5:14
15:2 [b]1Co 10:33 [c]Ro 14:19
15:3 [d]2Co 8:9

14:10–12 Each person is accountable to Christ, not to others. While the church must be uncompromising in its stand against activities that are expressly forbidden by Scripture (adultery, homosexuality, murder, theft), it should not create additional rules and regulations and give them equal standing with God's law. Many times Christians base their moral judgments on opinion, personal dislikes, or cultural bias rather than on the word of God. When they do this, they show that their own faith is weak—they do not think that God is powerful enough to guide his children. When we stand before God's court of justice ("judgment seat"), we won't be worried about what our Christian neighbour has done (see 2 Corinthians 5:10).

14:13 Both strong and weak Christians can cause their brothers and sisters to stumble. The strong but insensitive Christian may flaunt his or her freedom and intentionally offend others' consciences. The scrupulous but weak Christian may try to fence others in with petty rules and regulations, thus causing dissension. Paul wants his readers to be both strong in the faith and sensitive to others' needs. Because we are all strong in some areas and weak in others, we need constantly to monitor the effects of our behaviour on others.

14:13ff Some Christians use an invisible weaker brother to support their own opinions, prejudices, or standards. "You must live by these standards," they say, "or you will be offending the weaker brother." In truth, the person would often be offending no-one but the speaker. While Paul urges us to be sensitive to those whose faith may be harmed by our actions, we should not sacrifice our liberty in Christ just to satisfy the selfish motives of those who are trying to force their opinions on us. Neither fear them nor criticise them, but follow Christ as closely as you can.

14:14 At the Jerusalem council (Acts 15), the Jewish church in Jerusalem asked the Gentile church in Antioch not to eat meat that had been sacrificed to idols. Paul was at the Jerusalem council, and he accepted this request not because he felt that eating such meat was wrong in itself, but because this practice would deeply offend many Jewish believers. Paul did not think the issue was worth dividing the church over; his desire was to promote unity.

14:20, 21 Sin is not just a private matter. Everything we do affects others, and we have to think of them constantly. God created us to be interdependent, not independent. We who are strong in our faith must, without pride or condescension, treat others with love, patience, and self-restraint.

14:23 We try to steer clear of actions forbidden by Scripture, of course, but sometimes Scripture is silent. Then we should follow our consciences. "Everything that does not come from faith is sin" means that to go against a conviction will leave a person with a guilty or uneasy conscience. When God shows us that something is wrong for us, we should avoid it. But we should not look down on other Christians who exercise their freedom in those areas.

15:2 If we merely set out to please our neighbours, we will be people-pleasers. Paul was opposed to that (see Galatians 1:10). But we are to set aside wilfulness and self-pleasing actions for the sake of building others up for good. Our Christian convictions must not be a disguise for coldhearted treatment of our brothers and sisters.

those who insult you have fallen on me."[a][e] 4 For everything that was written in the
past was written to teach us,[f] so that through endurance and the encouragement of
the Scriptures we might have hope.
5 May the God who gives endurance and encouragement give you a spirit of unity[g]
among yourselves as you follow Christ Jesus, 6 so that with one heart and mouth you
may glorify the God and Father[h] of our Lord Jesus Christ.
7 Accept one another,[i] then, just as Christ accepted you, in order to bring praise
to God. 8 For I tell you that Christ has become a servant of the Jews[b][j] on behalf of
God's truth, to confirm the promises[k] made to the patriarchs 9 so that the Gentiles[l]
may glorify God[m] for his mercy, as it is written:

> "Therefore I will praise you among the Gentiles;
> I will sing hymns to your name."[c][n]

10 Again, it says,

> "Rejoice, O Gentiles, with his people."[d][o]

11 And again,

> "Praise the Lord, all you Gentiles,
> and sing praises to him, all you peoples."[e][p]

12 And again, Isaiah says,

> "The Root of Jesse[q] will spring up,
> one who will arise to rule over the nations;
> the Gentiles will hope in him."[f][r]

13 May the God of hope fill you with all joy and peace[s] as you trust in him, so that
you may overflow with hope by the power of the Holy Spirit.[t]

2. Personal notes

Paul the Minister to the Gentiles

14 I myself am convinced, my brothers, that you yourselves are full of goodness,[u]
complete in knowledge[v] and competent to instruct one another. 15 I have written to
you quite boldly on some points, as if to remind you of them again, because of the
grace God gave me[w] 16 to be a minister of Christ Jesus to the Gentiles[x] with the
priestly duty of proclaiming the gospel of God,[y] so that the Gentiles might become
an offering[z] acceptable to God, sanctified by the Holy Spirit.
17 Therefore I glory in Christ Jesus[a] in my service to God.[b] 18 I will not venture
to speak of anything except what Christ has accomplished through me in leading the
Gentiles[c] to obey God[d] by what I have said and done — 19 by the power of signs and
miracles,[e] through the power of the Spirit.[f] So from Jerusalem[g] all the way round
to Illyricum, I have fully proclaimed the gospel of Christ. 20 It has always been my

15:3 [e]Ps 69:9
15:4 [f]Ro 4:23, 24
15:5 [g]Ro 12:16; 1Co 1:10
15:6 [h]Rev 1:6
15:7 [i]Ro 14:1
15:8 [j]Mt 15:24; Ac 3:25, 26 [k]2Co 1:20
15:9 [l]Ro 3:29 [m]Mt 9:8 [n]2Sa 22:50; Ps 18:49
15:10 [o]Dt 32:43
15:11 [p]Ps 117:1
15:12 [q]Rev 5:5 [r]Isa 11:10; Mt 12:21
15:13 [s]Ro 14:17 [t]ver 19; 1Co 2:4; 1Th 1:5
15:14 [u]Eph 5:9 [v]2Pe 1:12
15:15 [w]Ro 12:3
15:16 [x]Ac 9:15; Ro 11:13 [y]Ro 1:1 [z]Isa 66:20
15:17 [a]Php 3:3 [b]Heb 2:17
15:18 [c]Ac 15:12; 21:19; Ro 1:5 [d]Ro 16:26
15:19 [e]Jn 4:48; Ac 19:11 [f]ver 13 [g]Ac 22:17-21

a *3* Psalm 69:9 **b** *8* Greek *circumcision* **c** *9* 2 Samuel 22:50; Psalm 18:49 **d** *10* Deut. 32:43 **e** *11* Psalm 117:1 **f** *12* Isaiah 11:10

15:4 The knowledge of the Scriptures affects our attitude towards the present and the future. The more we know about what God has done in years past, the greater the confidence we have about what he will do in the days ahead. We should read our Bibles diligently to increase our trust that God's will is best for us.

15:5–7 To accept Jesus' lordship in all areas of life means to share his values and his perspective. Just as we take Jesus' view on the authority of Scripture, the nature of heaven, and the resurrection, we are to have his attitude of love towards other Christians as well (have a "spirit of unity"). As we grow in faith and come to know Jesus better, we will become more capable of maintaining this attitude of loving unity throughout each day. Christ's attitude is explained in more detail in Philippians 2.

15:8 This verse means that Jesus came to bring the truth to the Jews and to show that God is true to his promises.

15:12 The *Root of Jesse* refers to Christ as the heir from the family line of Jesse, David's father (1 Samuel 16:1).

15:17 Paul did not glory in what he had done, but in what God had done through him. Being proud of God's work is not a sin – it is worship. If you are not sure whether your pride is selfish or holy, ask yourself this question: Are you just as proud of what God is doing through other people as of what he is doing through you?

15:19 Illyricum was a Roman territory on the Adriatic Sea between present-day Italy and Greece. It covered much the same territory as present-day Yugoslavia. See the map in chapter 1.

15:20–22 Paul wanted to visit the church at Rome, but he had delayed his visit because he had heard many good reports about the believers there and he knew they were doing well on their own. It was more important for him to preach in areas that had not yet heard the Good News.

ambition to preach the gospel where Christ was not known, so that I would not be
building on someone else's foundation.[h] 21Rather, as it is written:

> "Those who were not told about him will see,
> and those who have not heard will understand."[g] [i]

22This is why I have often been hindered from coming to you.[j]

Paul's Plan to Visit Rome

23But now that there is no more place for me to work in these regions, and since
I have been longing for many years to see you,[k] 24I plan to do so when I go to Spain.[l]
I hope to visit you while passing through and to have you assist me on my journey
there, after I have enjoyed your company for a while. 25Now, however, I am on my
way to Jerusalem[m] in the service[n] of the saints there. 26For Macedonia[o] and
Achaia[p] were pleased to make a contribution for the poor among the saints in
Jerusalem. 27They were pleased to do it, and indeed they owe it to them. For if the
Gentiles have shared in the Jews' spiritual blessings, they owe it to the Jews to share
with them their material blessings.[q] 28So after I have completed this task and have
made sure that they have received this fruit, I will go to Spain and visit you on the
way. 29I know that when I come to you,[r] I will come in the full measure of the
blessing of Christ.
30I urge you, brothers, by our Lord Jesus Christ and by the love of the Spirit,[s]
to join me in my struggle by praying to God for me.[t] 31Pray that I may be rescued[u]
from the unbelievers in Judea and that my service in Jerusalem may be acceptable to
the saints there, 32so that by God's will[v] I may come to you[w] with joy and together
with you be refreshed.[x] 33The God of peace[y] be with you all. Amen.

Personal Greetings

16 I commend[a] to you our sister Phoebe, a servant[a] of the church in Cenchrea.[b]
2I ask you to receive her in the Lord[c] in a way worthy of the saints and to give
her any help she may need from you, for she has been a great help to many people,
including me.

g *21* Isaiah 52:15 a *1* Or *deaconess*

15:20 [h]2Co 10:15, 16
15:21 [i]Isa 52:15
15:22 [j]Ro 1:13
15:23 [k]Ac 19:21; Ro 1:10, 11
15:24 [l]ver 28
15:25 [m]Ac 19:21 [n]Ac 24:17
15:26 [o]Ac 16:9; 2Co 8:1 [p]Ac 18:12
15:27 [q]1Co 9:11
15:29 [r]Ro 1:10, 11
15:30 [s]Gal 5:22 [t]2Co 1:11; Col 4:12
15:31 [u]2Th 3:2
15:32 [v]Ac 18:21 [w]Ro 1:10, 13 [x]1Co 16:18
15:33 [y]Ro 16:20; 2Co 13:11; Php 4:9; 1Th 5:23; Heb 13:20
16:1 [a]2Co 3:1 [b]Ac 18:18
16:2 [c]Php 2:29

15:23, 24 Paul was referring to the completion of his work in Corinth, the city from which he most likely wrote this letter. Most of Paul's three-month stay in Achaia (see Acts 20:3) was probably spent in Corinth. He believed that he had accomplished what God wanted him to do there, and he was looking forward to taking the gospel to new lands west of Rome. When Paul eventually went to Rome, however, it was as a prisoner (see Acts 28). Tradition says that Paul was released for a time, and that he used this opportunity to go to Spain to preach the Good News. This journey is not mentioned in the book of Acts.

15:27 If the Gentiles had received the gospel ("spiritual blessings") originally from Jerusalem, surely they would want to offer financial help ("material blessings").

15:28 Paul's future plan was to go to Spain because Spain was at the very western end of the civilised world. He wanted to extend Christianity there. Also, Spain had many great minds and influential leaders in the Roman world (Lucan, Martial, Hadrian), and perhaps Paul thought Christianity would advance greatly in such an atmosphere.

15:30 Too often we view prayer as a time for comfort, reflection, or making our requests known to God. But here Paul urges believers to join in his struggle by means of prayer. Prayer is also a weapon in all believers' armour as we intercede for others who join in the fight against Satan. Do your prayers reflect that urgency?

15:33 This phrase sounds like it should signal the end of the book, and it does pronounce the end of Paul's teaching. He concludes his letter, then, with personal greetings and remarks.

16:1, 2 Phoebe was known as a servant (the Greek word used here is often translated "deaconess") and a helper. Apparently she was a wealthy person who helped support Paul's ministry. Phoebe was highly regarded in the church, and she may have delivered this letter from Corinth to Rome. This provides evidence that women had important roles in the early church. Cenchrea, the town where Phoebe lived, was the eastern port of Corinth, six miles from the city centre.

16:3 Priscilla and Aquila were a married couple who had become Paul's close friends. They, along with all other Jews, had been expelled from Rome by the emperor (Acts 18:2, 3) and had moved to Corinth. There they met Paul and invited him to live with them. They were Christians before they met Paul, and probably told him much about the Roman church. Like Paul, Priscilla and Aquila were missionaries. They helped believers in Ephesus (Acts 18:18–28), in Rome when they were allowed to return, and again at Ephesus (2 Timothy 4:19).

3Greet Priscilla[b] and Aquila,[d] my fellow-workers in Christ Jesus.[e] 4They risked
their lives for me. Not only I but all the churches of the Gentiles are grateful to
them.
5Greet also the church that meets at their house.[f]
Greet my dear friend Epenetus, who was the first convert[g] to Christ in the province
of Asia.
6Greet Mary, who worked very hard for you.
7Greet Andronicus and Junias, my relatives[h] who have been in prison with me. They
are outstanding among the apostles, and they were in Christ before I was.
8Greet Ampliatus, whom I love in the Lord.
9Greet Urbanus, our fellow-worker in Christ,[i] and my dear friend Stachys.
10Greet Apelles, tested and approved in Christ.
Greet those who belong to the household of Aristobulus.
11Greet Herodion, my relative.[j]
Greet those in the household of Narcissus who are in the Lord.
12Greet Tryphena and Tryphosa, those women who work hard in the Lord.
Greet my dear friend Persis, another woman who has worked very hard in the Lord.
13Greet Rufus, chosen in the Lord, and his mother, who has been a mother to me,
too.
14Greet Asyncritus, Phlegon, Hermes, Patrobas, Hermas and the brothers with them.
15Greet Philologus, Julia, Nereus and his sister, and Olympas and all the saints[k] with
them.[l]
16Greet one another with a holy kiss.[m]
All the churches of Christ send greetings.

17I urge you, brothers, to watch out for those who cause divisions and put obstacles
in your way that are contrary to the teaching you have learned.[n] Keep away from
them.[o] 18For such people are not serving our Lord Christ, but their own appetites.[p]
By smooth talk and flattery they deceive[q] the minds of naïve people. 19Everyone has
heard[r] about your obedience, so I am full of joy over you; but I want you to be wise
about what is good, and innocent about what is evil.[s]
20The God of peace[t] will soon crush[u] Satan under your feet.
The grace of our Lord Jesus be with you.[v]
21Timothy,[w] my fellow-worker, sends his greetings to you, as do Lucius,[x] Jason[y]
and Sosipater, my relatives.[z]
22I, Tertius, who wrote down this letter, greet you in the Lord.
23Gaius, whose hospitality I and the whole church here enjoy, sends you his
greetings.
Erastus,[a] who is the city's director of public works, and our brother Quartus send
you their greetings.[c]

16:3 [d]Ac 18:2 [e]ver 7, 9, 10
16:5 [f]1Co 16:19; Col 4:15; Phm 2 [g]1Co 16:15
16:7 [h]ver 11, 21
16:9 [i]ver 3
16:11 [j]ver 7, 21
16:15 [k]ver 2 [l]ver 14
16:16 [m]1Co 16:20; 2Co 13:12; 1Th 5:26
16:17 [n]Gal 1:8, 9; 1Ti 1:3; 6:3 [o]2Th 3:6, 14; 2Jn 10
16:18 [p]Php 3:19 [q]Col 2:4
16:19 [r]Ro 1:8 [s]Mt 10:16; 1Co 14:20
16:20 [t]Ro 15:33 [u]Ge 3:15 [v]1Th 5:28
16:21 [w]Ac 16:1 [x]Ac 13:1 [y]Ac 17:5 [z]ver 7, 11
16:23 [a]Ac 19:22

b *3* Greek *Prisca,* a variant of *Priscilla* **c** *23* Some manuscripts *their greetings. 24May the grace of our Lord Jesus Christ be with all of you. Amen.*

16:5ff Paul's personal greetings went to Romans and Greeks, Jews and Gentiles, men and women, prisoners and prominent citizens. The church's base was broad: it crossed cultural, social, and economic lines. From this list we learn that the Christian community was mobile. Though Paul had not yet been to Rome, he had met these people in other places on his journeys.

16:7 The fact that Andronicus and Junias were "outstanding among the apostles" could mean they had distinguished themselves as apostles. They may have been a husband and wife team. Paul's references to them as relatives (see also 16:21) could mean that they were from the same tribe as Paul.

16:17–20 When we read books or listen to sermons, we should check the content of what is written or said and not be fooled by smooth style. Christians who study God's word will not be fooled, even though superficial listeners may easily be taken in. For an example of believers who carefully checked God's word, see Acts 17:10–12.

16:21 Timothy was a key person in the growth of the early church, travelling with Paul on his second missionary journey (Acts 16:1–3). Later Paul wrote two letters to him as he worked to strengthen the churches in Ephesus – 1 and 2 Timothy. See his Profile in the book of 1 Timothy.

25Now to him who is able[b] to establish you by my gospel[c] and the proclamation
of Jesus Christ, according to the revelation of the mystery[d] hidden for long ages past,
26but now revealed and made known through the prophetic writings by the command
of the eternal God, so that all nations might believe and obey him—27to the only wise
God be glory for ever through Jesus Christ! Amen.[e]

16:25 [b]Eph 3:20 [c]Ro 2:16 [d]Eph 1:9; Col 1:26, 27

16:27 [e]Ro 11:36

16:25–27 Paul exclaims that it is wonderful to be alive when the mystery, God's secret—his way of saving the Gentiles—is becoming known throughout the world! All the Old Testament prophecies were coming true, and God was using Paul as his instrument to tell this Good News.

16:25–27 As Jerusalem was the centre of Jewish life, Rome was the world's political, religious, social, and economic centre. There the major governmental decisions were made, and from there the gospel spread to the ends of the earth. The church in Rome was a cosmopolitan mixture of Jews, Gentiles, slaves, free people, men, women, Roman citizens, and world travellers; therefore, it had potential for both great influence and great conflict.

Paul had not yet been to Rome to meet all the Christians there, and, of course, he has not yet met us. We too live in a cosmopolitan setting with the entire world open to us. We also have the potential for both widespread influence and wrenching conflict. We should listen carefully to and apply Paul's teaching about unity, service, and love.

1 CORINTHIANS

ON A BED of grass, a chameleon's skin turns green. On the earth, it becomes brown. The animal changes to match the environment. Many creatures blend into nature with God-given camouflage suits to aid their survival. It's natural to fit in and adapt to the environment. But followers of Christ are *new creations,* born from above and changed from within, with values and lifestyles that confront the world and clash with accepted morals. True believers don't blend in very well.

The Christians in Corinth were struggling with their environment. Surrounded by corruption and every conceivable sin, they felt the pressure to adapt. They knew they were free in Christ, but what did this freedom mean? How should they view idols or sexuality? What should they do about marriage, women in the church, and the gifts of the Spirit? These were more than theoretical questions—the church was being undermined by immorality and spiritual immaturity. The believers' faith was being tried in the crucible of immoral Corinth, and some of them were failing the test.

Paul heard of their struggles and wrote this letter to address their problems, heal their divisions, and answer their questions. Paul confronted them with their sin and their need for corrective action and clear commitment to Christ.

After a brief introduction (1:1–9), Paul immediately turns to the question of unity (1:10—4:21). He emphasises the clear and simple gospel message around which all believers should rally; he explains the role of church leaders; and he urges them to grow up in their faith.

Paul then deals with the immorality of certain church members and the issue of lawsuits among Christians (5:1—6:8). He tells them to exercise church discipline and to settle their internal matters themselves. Because so many of the problems in the Corinthian church involved sex, Paul denounces sexual sin in the strongest possible terms (6:9–20).

Next Paul answers some questions that the Corinthians had. Because prostitution and immorality were pervasive, marriages in Corinth were in a shambles, and Christians weren't sure how to react. Paul gives pointed and practical answers (7:1–40). Concerning the question of meat sacrificed to idols, Paul suggests that we show complete commitment to Christ and sensitivity to other believers, especially weaker brothers and sisters (8:1—11:2).

Paul goes on to talk about worship, and he carefully explains the role of women, the Lord's Supper, and spiritual gifts (11:3—14:39). Sandwiched in the middle of this section is his magnificent description of the greatest gift—love (chapter 13). Then Paul concludes with a discussion of the resurrection (15:1–58), some final thoughts, greetings, and a benediction (16:1–24).

In this letter Paul confronted the Corinthians about their sins and shortcomings. And 1 Corinthians calls all Christians to be careful not to blend in with the world and accept its values and lifestyles. We must live Christ-centred, blameless, loving lives that make a difference for God. As you read 1 Corinthians, examine your values in the light of complete commitment to Christ.

VITAL STATISTICS

PURPOSE:
To identify problems in the Corinthian church, to offer solutions, and to teach the believers how to live for Christ in a corrupt society

AUTHOR:
Paul

TO WHOM WRITTEN:
The church in Corinth, and Christians everywhere

DATE WRITTEN:
About A.D. 55, near the end of Paul's three-year ministry in Ephesus, during his third missionary journey

SETTING:
Corinth was a major cosmopolitan city, a seaport and major trade centre—the most important city in Achaia. It was also filled with idolatry and immorality. The church was largely made up of Gentiles. Paul had established this church on his second missionary journey.

KEY VERSE:
"I appeal to you, brothers, in the name of our Lord Jesus Christ, that all of you agree with one another so that there may be no divisions among you and that you may be perfectly united in mind and thought" (1:10).

KEY PEOPLE:
Paul, Timothy, members of Chloe's household

KEY PLACES:
Worship meetings in Corinth

SPECIAL FEATURES:
This is a strong, straightforward letter.

THE BLUEPRINT

A. PAUL ADDRESSES CHURCH PROBLEMS (1:1—6:20) 1. Divisions in the church 2. Disorder in the church	Without Paul's presence, the Corinthian church had fallen into divisiveness and disorder. This resulted in many problems, which Paul addressed squarely. We must be concerned for unity and order in our local churches, but we should not mistake inactivity for order and cordiality for unity. We too must squarely address problems in our churches.
B. PAUL ANSWERS CHURCH QUESTIONS (7:1—16:24) 1. Instruction on Christian marriage 2. Instruction on Christian freedom 3. Instruction on public worship 4. Instruction on the resurrection	The Corinthians had sent Paul a list of questions, and he answered them in a way meant to correct abuses in the church and to show how important it is that they live what they believe. Paul gives us a Christian approach to problem-solving. He analysed the problem thoroughly to uncover the underlying issue and then highlighted the biblical values that should guide our actions.

MEGATHEMES

THEME	EXPLANATION	IMPORTANCE
Loyalties	The Corinthians were rallying around various church leaders and teachers—Peter, Paul, and Apollos. These loyalties led to intellectual pride and created a spirit of division in the church.	Our loyalty to human leaders or human wisdom must never divide Christians into camps. We must care for our fellow believers, not fight with them. Your allegiance must be to Christ. Let him lead you.
Immorality	Paul received a report of uncorrected sexual sin in the church at Corinth. The people had grown indifferent to immorality. Others had misconceptions about marriage. We are to live morally, keeping our bodies ready to serve God at all times.	Christians must never compromise with sinful ideas and practices. We should not blend in with people around us. You must live up to God's standard of morality and not condone immoral behaviour even if society accepts it.
Freedom	Paul taught freedom of choice on practices not expressly forbidden in Scripture. Some believers felt certain actions—like eating the meat of animals used in pagan rituals—were corrupt by association. Others felt free to participate in such actions without feeling that they had sinned.	We are free in Christ, yet we must not abuse our Christian freedom by being inconsiderate and insensitive to others. We must never encourage others to do wrong because of something we have done. Let love guide your behaviour.
Worship	Paul addressed disorder in worship. People were taking the Lord's Supper without first confessing sin. There was misuse of spiritual gifts and confusion over women's roles in the church.	Worship must be carried out properly and in an orderly manner. Everything we do to worship God should be done in a manner worthy of his high honour. Make sure that worship is harmonious, useful, and edifying to all believers.
Resurrection	Some people denied that Christ rose from the dead. Others felt that people would not physically be resurrected. Christ's resurrection assures us that we will have new, living bodies after we die. The hope of the resurrection forms the secret of Christian confidence.	Since we will be raised again to life after we die, our lives are not in vain. We must stay faithful to God in our morality and our service. We are to live today knowing we will spend eternity with Christ.

1:1
[a]Ro 1:1;
Eph 1:1
[b]2Co 1:1
[c]Ac 18:17

A. PAUL ADDRESSES CHURCH PROBLEMS (1:1 – 6:20)

Through various sources, Paul had received reports of problems in the Corinthian church, including jealousy, divisiveness, sexual immorality, and failure to discipline members. Churches today must also address the problems they face. We can learn a great deal by observing how Paul handled these delicate situations.

1 Paul, called to be an apostle[a] of Christ Jesus by the will of God,[b] and our brother
Sosthenes,[c]

1:2
[d]Ac 18:1
[e]Ro 1:7

2 To the church of God in Corinth,[d] to those sanctified in Christ Jesus and called[e]

CORINTH AND EPHESUS
Paul wrote this letter to Corinth during his three-year visit to Ephesus on his third missionary journey. The two cities sat across from each other on the Aegean Sea – both were busy and important ports. Titus may have carried this letter from Ephesus to Corinth (2 Corinthians 12:18).

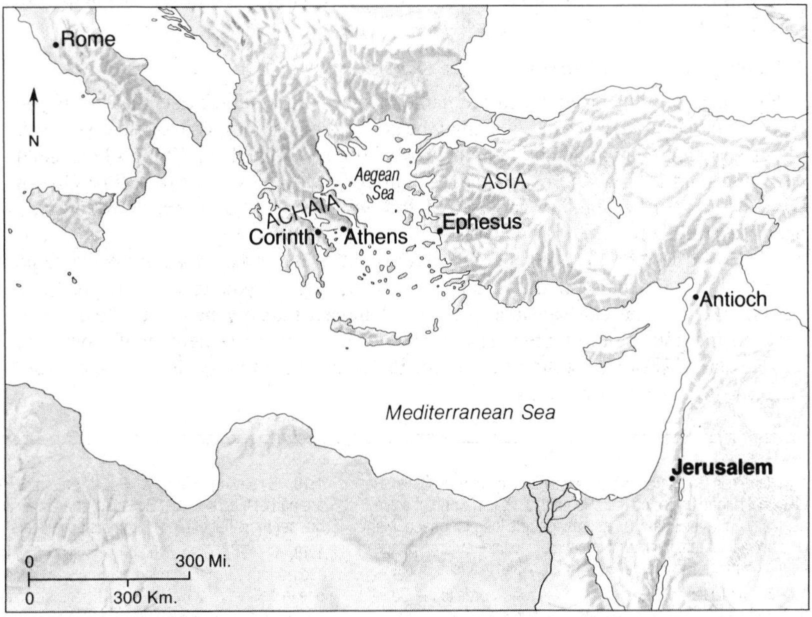

1:1 Paul wrote this letter to the church in Corinth while he was visiting Ephesus during his third missionary journey (Acts 19:1 – 20:1). Corinth and Ephesus faced each other across the Aegean Sea. Paul knew the Corinthian church well because he had spent 18 months in Corinth during his second missionary journey (Acts 18:1–18). While in Ephesus, he had heard about problems in Corinth (1:11). About the same time, a delegation from the Corinthian church had visited Paul to ask his advice about their conflicts (16:17). Paul's purpose for writing was to correct those problems and to answer questions church members had asked in a previous letter (7:1).

1:1 Paul was given a special calling from God to preach about Jesus Christ. Each Christian has a job to do, a role to take, or a contribution to make. One assignment may seem more spectacular than another, but all are necessary to carry out God's greater plans for his church and for his world (12:12–27). Be available to God by placing your gifts at his service. Then as you discover what he calls you to do, be ready to do it.

1:1 Sosthenes may have been Paul's secretary who wrote down this letter as Paul dictated it. He was probably the Jewish synagogue leader in Corinth (Acts 18:17) who had been beaten during an attack on Paul, and then later became a believer. Sosthenes was well known to the members of the Corinthian church, and so Paul included his familiar name in the opening of the letter.

1:2 Corinth, a giant cultural melting pot with a great diversity of wealth, religions, and moral standards, had a reputation for being fiercely independent and as decadent as any city in the world. The Romans had destroyed Corinth in 146 B.C. after a rebellion. But in 46 B.C., the Roman Emperor Julius Caesar rebuilt it because of its strategic seaport. By Paul's day (A.D. 50), the Romans had made Corinth the capital of Achaia (present-day Greece). It was a large city, offering Rome great profits through trade as well as the military protection of its ports. But the city's prosperity made it ripe for all sorts of corruption. Idolatry flourished, and there were more than a dozen pagan temples employing at least a thousand prostitutes. Corinth's reputation was such that prostitutes in other cities began to be called "Corinthian girls".

1:2 A personal invitation makes a person feel wanted and welcome. We are "called to be holy". God personally invites us to be citizens of his eternal kingdom. But Jesus Christ, God's Son, is the only one who can bring us into this glorious kingdom because he is the only one who removes our sins. *Sanctified* means that we are chosen or set apart by Christ for his service. We accept God's invitation by accepting his Son, Jesus Christ, and by trusting in the work he did on the cross to forgive our sins.

1:2 By including a salutation to "all those everywhere who call on the name of our Lord Jesus Christ", Paul is making it clear that this is not a private letter. Although it deals with specific issues facing the church at Corinth, all believers can learn from it. The Corinthian church included a great cross-section of believers – wealthy merchants, common labourers, former temple prostitutes, and middle class families. Because of the wide diversity of people and backgrounds, Paul takes great pains to stress the need for both spiritual unity and Christlike character.

to be holy, together with all those everywhere who call on the name of our Lord Jesus
Christ—their Lord and ours:

3Grace and peace to you from God our Father and the Lord Jesus Christ.[f]

Thanksgiving

4I always thank God for you[g] because of his grace given you in Christ Jesus. 5For
in him you have been enriched[h] in every way—in all your speaking and in all your
knowledge[i]—6because our testimony[j] about Christ was confirmed in you. 7There-
fore you do not lack any spiritual gift as you eagerly wait for our Lord Jesus Christ
to be revealed.[k] 8He will keep you strong to the end, so that you will be blameless[l]
on the day of our Lord Jesus Christ. 9God, who has called you into fellowship with
his Son Jesus Christ our Lord,[m] is faithful.[n]

1. Divisions in the church

10I appeal to you, brothers, in the name of our Lord Jesus Christ, that all of you
agree with one another so that there may be no divisions among you and that you may
be perfectly united in mind and thought. 11My brothers, some from Chloe's household
have informed me that there are quarrels among you. 12What I mean is this: One of
you says, "I follow Paul";[o] another, "I follow Apollos";[p] another, "I follow Cephas";**[a]**[q] still another, "I follow Christ."

13Is Christ divided? Was Paul crucified for you? Were you baptised into**[b]** the name
of Paul?[r] 14I am thankful that I did not baptise any of you except Crispus[s] and
Gaius,[t] 15so no-one can say that you were baptised into my name. (16Yes, I also
baptised the household of Stephanas;[u] beyond that, I don't remember if I baptised
anyone else.) 17For Christ did not send me to baptise,[v] but to preach the gospel—not

a *12* That is, Peter **b** *13* Or *in*; also in verse 15

1:3 [f]Ro 1:7
1:4 [g]Ro 1:8
1:5 [h]2Co 9:11 [i]2Co 8:7
1:6 [j]Rev 1:2
1:7 [k]Php 3:20; Tit 2:13; 2Pe 3:12
1:8 [l]1Th 3:13
1:9 [m]1Jn 1:3 [n]Isa 49:7; 1Th 5:24
1:12 [o]1Co 3:4, 22 [p]Ac 18:24 [q]Jn 1:42
1:13 [r]Mt 28:19
1:14 [s]Ac 18:8; Ro 16:23 [t]Ac 19:29
1:16 [u]1Co 16:15
1:17 [v]Jn 4:2

1:3 Grace is God's free gift of salvation given to us in Christ. Receiving it brings us peace (see Romans 5:1). In a world of noise, confusion, and relentless pressures, people long for peace. Many give up the search, thinking it impossible to find, but true peace of heart and mind is available to us through faith in Jesus Christ.

1:4–6 In this letter, Paul wrote some strong words to the Corinthians, but he began on a positive note of thanksgiving. He affirmed their privilege of belonging to the Lord and receiving his grace, the power God gave them to speak out for him and understand his truth, and the reality of their spiritual gifts. When we must correct others, it helps to begin by affirming what God has already accomplished in them.

1:7 The Corinthian church members had all the spiritual gifts they needed to live the Christian life, to witness for Christ, and to stand against the paganism and immorality of Corinth. But instead of using what God had given them, they were arguing over which gifts were more important. Paul addresses this issue in depth in chapters 12–14.

1:7–9 Paul guaranteed the Corinthian believers that God would consider them "blameless" when Christ returns (see Ephesians 1:7–10). This guarantee was not because of their great gifts or their shining performance, but because of what Jesus Christ accomplished for them through his death and resurrection. *All* who believe in the Lord Jesus will be considered blameless when Jesus Christ returns (see also 1 Thessalonians 3:13; Hebrews 9:28). If you have faith in Christ, even if it is weak, you *are* and *will be* saved.

1:10 Paul founded the church in Corinth on his second missionary journey. Eighteen months after he left, arguments and divisions arose, and some church members slipped back into an immoral life-style. Paul wrote this letter to address the problems, to clear up confusion about right and wrong, and to remove the immorality among them. The Corinthian people had a reputation for jumping from fad to fad; Paul wanted to keep Christianity from degenerating into just another fad.

1:10 By saying "brothers", Paul is emphasising that all Christians are part of God's family. Believers share a unity that runs even deeper than that of blood brothers and sisters.

1:10, 11 To "agree with one another", allow for "no divisions" and "be perfectly united in mind and thought" does not require everyone to believe exactly the same. There is a difference between having opposing viewpoints and being divisive. A group of people will not completely agree on every issue, but they can work together harmoniously if they agree on what truly matters—Jesus Christ is Lord of all. In your church, speak and behave in a way that will reduce arguments and increase harmony. Petty differences should never divide Christians.

1:12ff In this large and diverse Corinthian church, the believers favoured different preachers. Because there was as yet no written New Testament, the believers depended heavily on preaching and teaching for spiritual insight into the meaning of the Old Testament. Some followed Paul, who had founded their church; some who had heard Peter (Cephas) in Jerusalem followed him; while others listened only to Apollos, an eloquent and popular preacher who had had a dynamic ministry in Corinth (Acts 18:24; 19:1). Although these three preachers were united in their message, their personalities attracted different people. At this time the church was in danger of dividing. By mentioning Jesus Christ ten times in the first ten verses, Paul makes it clear who it is all preachers and teachers should emphasise. God's message is much more important than any human messenger.

1:12, 13 Paul wondered whether the Corinthians' quarrels had "divided" Christ. This is a graphic picture of what happens when the church (the body of Christ) is divided. With the many churches and styles of worship available today, we could get caught up in the same game of "my preacher is better than yours"! To do so would divide Christ again. But Christ is not divided, and his true followers should not allow anything to divide them. Don't let your appreciation for any teacher, preacher, or author lead you into intellectual pride. Our allegiance must be to Christ and to the unity that he desires.

1:17
[w]1Co 2:1, 4, 13
1:18
[x]2Co 2:15
[y]Ro 1:16
1:19
[z]Isa 29:14
1:20
[a]Isa 19:11, 12
[b]Job 12:17;
Ro 1:22
1:22
[c]Mt 12:38
1:23
[d]Lk 2:34;
Gal 5:11
[e]1Co 2:14
1:24
[f]Ro 8:28
[g]ver 30;
Col 2:3
1:25
[h]ver 18
[i]2Co 13:4

with words of human wisdom,[w] lest the cross of Christ be emptied of its power.

Christ the Wisdom and Power of God

18 For the message of the cross is foolishness to those who are perishing,[x] but to
us who are being saved it is the power of God.[y] 19 For it is written:

> "I will destroy the wisdom of the wise;
> the intelligence of the intelligent I will frustrate."[c][z]

20 Where is the wise man?[a] Where is the scholar? Where is the philosopher of this
age? Has not God made foolish[b] the wisdom of the world? 21 For since in the wisdom
of God the world through its wisdom did not know him, God was pleased through
the foolishness of what was preached to save those who believe. 22 Jews demand
miraculous signs[c] and Greeks look for wisdom, 23 but we preach Christ crucified: a
stumbling-block[d] to Jews and foolishness[e] to Gentiles, 24 but to those whom God
has called,[f] both Jews and Greeks, Christ the power of God and the wisdom of God.[g]
25 For the foolishness[h] of God is wiser than man's wisdom, and the weakness[i] of
God is stronger than man's strength.

c *19* Isaiah 29:14

HIGHLIGHTS OF 1 CORINTHIANS		
	The Meaning of the Cross 1:18—2:16	Be considerate of one another because of what Christ has done for us. There is no place for pride or a know-it-all attitude. We are to have the mind of Christ.
	The Story of the Last Supper 11:23–29	The Last Supper is a time of reflection on Christ's final words to his disciples before he died on the cross; we must celebrate this in an orderly and correct manner.
	The Poem of Love 13:1–13	Love is to guide all we do. We have different gifts, abilities, likes, dislikes—but we are called, without exception, to love.
	The Christian's Destiny 15:42–58	We are promised by Christ, who died for us, that, as he came back to life after death, so our perishable bodies will be exchanged for heavenly bodies. Then we will live and reign with Christ.

1:17 When Paul said that Christ didn't send him to baptise, he wasn't minimising the importance of baptism. Baptism was commanded by Jesus himself (Matthew 28:19) and practised by the early church (Acts 2:41). Paul was emphasising that no one person should do everything. Paul's gift was preaching, and that's what he did. Christian ministry should be a team effort; no preacher or teacher is a complete link between God and people, and no individual can do all that the apostles did. We must be content with the contribution God has given us to make, and carry it out wholeheartedly. (For more on different gifts, see chapters 12 and 13.)

1:17 Some speakers use impressive words, but they are weak on content. Paul stressed solid content and practical help for his listeners. He wanted them to be impressed with his *message,* not just his style (see 2:1–5). You don't need to be a great speaker with a large vocabulary to share the gospel effectively. The persuasive power is in the story, not the story-teller. Paul was not against those who carefully prepare what they say (see 2:6), but against those who try to impress others only with their own knowledge or speaking ability.

1:19 Paul summarises Isaiah 29:14 to emphasise a point Jesus often made: God's way of thinking is not like the world's way (normal human wisdom). And God offers eternal life, which the world can never give. We can spend a lifetime accumulating human wisdom and yet never learn how to have a personal relationship with God. We must come to the crucified and risen Christ to receive eternal life and the joy of a personal relationship with our Saviour.

1:22–24 Many Jews considered the Good News of Jesus Christ to be foolish, because they thought the Messiah would be a conquering king accompanied by signs and miracles. Jesus had not restored David's throne as they expected. Besides, he was executed as a criminal, and how could a criminal be a saviour? Greeks, too, considered the gospel foolish: they did not believe in a bodily resurrection; they did not see in Jesus the powerful characteristics of their mythological gods; and they thought no reputable person would be crucified. To them, death was defeat, not victory.

The Good News of Jesus Christ still sounds foolish to many. Our society worships power, influence, and wealth. Jesus came as a humble, poor servant, and he offers his kingdom to those who have faith, not to those who do all kinds of good deeds to try to earn his gifts. This looks foolish to the world, but Christ is our power, the only way we can be saved. Knowing Christ personally is the greatest wisdom anyone could have.

1:25 The message of Christ's death for sins sounds foolish to those who don't believe. Death seems to be the end of the road, the ultimate weakness. But Jesus did not stay dead. His resurrection demonstrated his power even over death. And he will save us from eternal death and give us everlasting life if we trust him as Saviour and Lord. This sounds so simple that many people won't accept it. They try other ways to obtain eternal life (being good, being wise, etc). But all their attempts will not work. The "foolish" people who simply accept Christ's offer are actually the wisest of all, because they alone will live eternally with God.

26Brothers, think of what you were when you were called. Not many of you were
wise by human standards; not many were influential; not many were of noble birth.
27But God chose[j] the foolish[k] things of the world to shame the wise; God chose the
weak things of the world to shame the strong. 28He chose the lowly things of this world
and the despised things—and the things that are not[l]—to nullify the things that are,
29so that no-one may boast before him.[m] 30It is because of him that you are in Christ
Jesus, who has become for us wisdom from God—that is, our righteousness,[n]
holiness and redemption.[o] 31Therefore, as it is written: "Let him who boasts boast
in the Lord."[d][p]

2 When I came to you, brothers, I did not come with eloquence or superior
wisdom[a] as I proclaimed to you the testimony about God.[a] 2For I resolved to
know nothing while I was with you except Jesus Christ and him crucified.[b] 3I came
to you[c] in weakness and fear, and with much trembling. 4My message and my
preaching were not with wise and persuasive words, but with a demonstration of the
Spirit's power,[d] 5so that your faith might not rest on men's wisdom, but on God's
power.[e]

Wisdom From the Spirit

6We do, however, speak a message of wisdom among the mature,[f] but not the
wisdom of this age[g] or of the rulers of this age, who are coming to nothing. 7No,
we speak of God's secret wisdom, a wisdom that has been hidden and that God
destined for our glory before time began. 8None of the rulers of this age understood
it, for if they had, they would not have crucified the Lord of glory.[h] 9However, as
it is written:

"No eye has seen,
no ear has heard,
no mind has conceived
what God has prepared for those who love him"[b][i]—

10but God has revealed[j] it to us by his Spirit.[k]

d *31* Jer. 9:24 a *1* Some manuscripts *as I proclaimed to you God's mystery* b *9* Isaiah 64:4

1:27 [j]Jas 2:5 [k]ver 20
1:28 [l]Ro 4:17
1:29 [m]Eph 2:9
1:30 [n]Jer 23:5, 6; 2Co 5:21 [o]Ro 3:24; Eph 1:7, 14
1:31 [p]Jer 9:23, 24; 2Co 10:17
2:1 [a]1Co 1:17
2:2 [b]Gal 6:14; 1Co 1:23
2:3 [c]Ac 18:1-18
2:4 [d]Ro 15:19
2:5 [e]2Co 4:7; 6:7
2:6 [f]Eph 4:13; Php 3:15; Heb 5:14 [g]1Co 1:20
2:8 [h]Ac 7:2; Jas 2:1
2:9 [i]Isa 64:4; 65:17
2:10 [j]Mt 13:11; Eph 3:3, 5 [k]Jn 14:26

1:27 Is Christianity against rational thinking? Christians clearly do believe in using their minds to weigh the evidence and make wise choices. Paul is declaring that no amount of human knowledge can replace or bypass Christ's work on the cross. If it could, Christ would be accessible only to the intellectually gifted and well educated, and not to ordinary people or to children.

1:28–31 Paul continues to emphasise that the way to receive salvation is so simple that *any* person who wants to can understand it. Skill and wisdom do not get a person into God's kingdom—simple faith does—so no-one can boast that his or her achievements helped him or her secure eternal life. Salvation is totally from God through Jesus' death. There is *nothing* we can do to earn our salvation; we need only accept what Jesus has already done for us.

1:30 God is the source of and the reason for our personal and living relationship with Christ. Our union and identification with Christ results in our having God's wisdom and knowledge (Colossians 2:3), possessing right standing with God (*righteousness,* 2 Corinthians 5:21), being holy (1 Thessalonians 4:3–7), and having the penalty for our sins paid by Jesus (*redemption,* Mark 10:45).

2:1 Paul is referring to his first visit to Corinth during his second missionary journey (A.D. 51), when he founded the church (Acts 18:1ff).

2:1–5 A brilliant scholar, Paul could have overwhelmed his listeners with intellectual arguments. Instead he shared the simple message of Jesus Christ by allowing the Holy Spirit to guide his words. In sharing the gospel with others, we should follow Paul's example and keep our message simple and basic. The Holy Spirit will give power to our words and use them to bring glory to Jesus.

2:4 Paul's confidence was not in his keen intellect or speaking ability but in his knowledge that the Holy Spirit was helping and guiding him. Paul is not denying the importance of study and preparation for preaching—he had a thorough education in the Scriptures. Effective preaching must combine studious preparation with reliance on the work of the Holy Spirit. Don't use Paul's statement as an excuse for not studying or preparing.

2:7 God's "secret wisdom . . . that has been hidden" was his offer of salvation to all people. Originally unknown to humanity, this plan became crystal clear when Jesus rose from the dead. His resurrection proved that he had power over sin and death and could offer us this power as well (see also 1 Peter 1:10–12 and the first note on Romans 16:25–27). God's plan, however, is still hidden to unbelievers because they either refuse to accept it, choose to ignore it, or simply haven't heard about it.

2:8 Jesus was misunderstood and rejected by those whom the world considered wise and great. He was put to death by the rulers in Palestine—the high priest, King Herod, Pilate, and the Pharisees and Sadducees. Jesus' rejection by these rulers had been predicted in Isaiah 53:3 and Zechariah 12:10, 11.

2:9 We cannot imagine all that God has in store for us, both in this life and for eternity. He will create a new heaven and a new earth (Isaiah 65:17; Revelation 21:1), and we will live with him for ever. Until then, his Holy Spirit comforts and guides us. Knowing the wonderful and eternal future that awaits us gives us hope and courage to press on in this life, to endure hardship, and to avoid giving in to temptation. This world is not all there is. The best is yet to come.

2:10 The "deep things of God" refers to God's unfathomable nature and his wonderful plan—Jesus' death and resurrection—

2:11
[l]Jer 17:9
[m]Pr 20:27

2:12
[n]Ro 8:15
[o]1Co 1:20, 27

2:13
[p]1Co 1:17

2:14
[q]1Co 1:18

2:16
[r]Isa 40:13
[s]Jn 15:15

3:1
[a]1Co 2:15
[b]Ro 7:14;
1Co 2:14
[c]Heb 5:13

3:2
[d]Heb 5:12-14;
1Pe 2:2
[e]Jn 16:12

3:3
[f]1Co 1:11;
Gal 5:20

3:4
[g]1Co 1:12

3:6
[h]Ac 18:4-11

3:8
[i]Ps 62:12

3:9
[j]2Co 6:1
[k]Isa 61:3
[l]Eph 2:20-22;
1Pe 2:5

The Spirit searches all things, even the deep things of God. 11 For who among men
knows the thoughts of a man[l] except the man's spirit[m] within him? In the same way
no-one knows the thoughts of God except the Spirit of God. 12 We have not received
the spirit[n] of the world[o] but the Spirit who is from God, that we may understand
what God has freely given us. 13 This is what we speak, not in words taught us by
human wisdom[p] but in words taught by the Spirit, expressing spiritual truths in
spiritual words.[c] 14 The man without the Spirit does not accept the things that come
from the Spirit of God, for they are foolishness[q] to him, and he cannot understand
them, because they are spiritually discerned. 15 The spiritual man makes judgments
about all things, but he himself is not subject to any man's judgment:

16 "For who has known the mind of the Lord
that he may instruct him?"[d][r]

But we have the mind of Christ.[s]

On Divisions in the Church

3 Brothers, I could not address you as spiritual[a] but as worldly[b]—mere infants[c]
in Christ. 2 I gave you milk, not solid food,[d] for you were not yet ready for it.[e]
Indeed, you are still not ready. 3 You are still worldly. For since there is jealousy and
quarrelling[f] among you, are you not worldly? Are you not acting like mere men?
4 For when one says, "I follow Paul," and another, "I follow Apollos,"[g] are you not
mere men?

5 What, after all, is Apollos? And what is Paul? Only servants, through whom you
came to believe—as the Lord has assigned to each his task. 6 I planted the seed,[h]
Apollos watered it, but God made it grow. 7 So neither he who plants nor he who waters
is anything, but only God, who makes things grow. 8 The man who plants and the man
who waters have one purpose, and each will be rewarded according to his own
labour.[i] 9 For we are God's fellow-workers;[j] you are God's field,[k] God's building.[l]

c *13* Or *Spirit, interpreting spiritual truths to spiritual men* **d** *16* Isaiah 40:13

---

and to the promise of salvation, revealed only to those who believe that what God says is true. Those who believe in Christ's death and resurrection and put their faith in him will know all they need to know to be saved. This knowledge, however, can't be grasped by even the wisest people unless they accept God's message. All who reject God's message are foolish, no matter how wise the world thinks they are.

2:13 Paul's words are authoritative because their source was the Holy Spirit. Paul was not merely giving his own personal views or his personal impression of what God had said. Under the inspiration of the Holy Spirit, he wrote the very thoughts and words of God.

2:14, 15 Non-Christians cannot understand God, and they cannot grasp the concept that God's Spirit lives in believers. Don't expect most people to approve of or understand your decision to follow Christ. It all seems so silly to them. Just as a tone-deaf person cannot appreciate fine music, the person who rejects God cannot understand God's beautiful message. With the lines of communication broken, he or she won't be able to hear what God is saying to him or her.

2:15, 16 No one can comprehend God (Romans 11:34), but through the guidance of the Holy Spirit, believers have insight into some of God's plans, thoughts, and actions—they, in fact, have the "mind of Christ". Through the Holy Spirit we can begin to know God's thoughts, talk with him, and expect his answers to our prayers. Are you spending enough time with Christ to have his very mind in you? An intimate relationship with Christ comes only from spending time consistently in his presence and in his word. Read Philippians 2:5ff for more on the mind of Christ.

3:1–3 Paul called the Corinthians infants in the Christian life because they were not yet spiritually healthy and mature. The proof was that they quarrelled like children, allowing divisions to distract them. Immature Christians are "worldly", controlled by their own desires; mature believers are in tune with God's desires. How much influence do your desires have on your life? Your goal should be to let God's desires be yours. Being controlled by your own desires will stunt your growth.

3:6 Paul planted the seed of the gospel message in people's hearts. He was a missionary pioneer; he brought the message of salvation. Apollos' role was to water—to help the believers grow stronger in the faith. Paul founded the church in Corinth, and Apollos built on that foundation. Tragically, the believers in Corinth had split into factions, pledging loyalty to different teachers (see 1:11–13). After the preachers' work is completed, God keeps making Christians grow. Our leaders should certainly be respected, but we should never place them on pedestals that create barriers between people or set them up as substitutes for Christ.

3:7–9 God's work involves many different individuals with a variety of gifts and abilities. There are no superstars in this task, only team members performing their own special roles. We can become useful members of God's team by setting aside our desires to receive glory for what we do. Don't seek the praise that comes from people—it is comparatively worthless. Instead, seek approval from God.

10By the grace God has given me,[m] I laid a foundation[n] as an expert builder, and
someone else is building on it. But each one should be careful how he builds. 11For
no-one can lay any foundation other than the one already laid, which is Jesus Christ.[o]
12If any man builds on this foundation using gold, silver, costly stones, wood, hay
or straw, 13his work will be shown for what it is,[p] because the Day[q] will bring it
to light. It will be revealed with fire, and the fire will test the quality of each man's
work. 14If what he has built survives, he will receive his reward. 15If it is burned up,
he will suffer loss; he himself will be saved, but only as one escaping through the
flames.[r]
16Don't you know that you yourselves are God's temple[s] and that God's Spirit lives
in you? 17If anyone destroys God's temple, God will destroy him; for God's temple
is sacred, and you are that temple.
18Do not deceive yourselves. If any one of you thinks he is wise[t] by the standards
of this age, he should become a "fool" so that he may become wise. 19For the wisdom
of this world is foolishness[u] in God's sight. As it is written: "He catches the wise
in their craftiness";[a][v] 20and again, "The Lord knows that the thoughts of the wise
are futile."[b][w] 21So then, no more boasting about men![x] All things are yours,[y]
22whether Paul or Apollos or Cephas[c][z] or the world or life or death or the present
or the future[a]—all are yours, 23and you are of Christ,[b] and Christ is of God.

Apostles of Christ

4 So then, men ought to regard us as servants of Christ and as those entrusted[a]
with the secret things[b] of God. 2Now it is required that those who have been
given a trust must prove faithful. 3I care very little if I am judged by you or by any
human court; indeed, I do not even judge myself. 4My conscience is clear, but that
does not make me innocent.[c] It is the Lord who judges me. 5Therefore judge
nothing[d] before the appointed time; wait till the Lord comes. He will bring to light

a *19* Job 5:13 **b** *20* Psalm 94:11 **c** *22* That is, Peter

3:10 [m]Ro 12:3 [n]Ro 15:20
3:11 [o]Isa 28:16; Eph 2:20
3:13 [p]1Co 4:5 [q]2Th 1:7-10
3:15 [r]Jude 23
3:16 [s]1Co 6:19; 2Co 6:16
3:18 [t]Isa 5:21; 1Co 8:2
3:19 [u]1Co 1:20, 27 [v]Job 5:13
3:20 [w]Ps 94:11
3:21 [x]1Co 4:6 [y]Ro 8:32
3:22 [z]1Co 1:12 [a]Ro 8:38
3:23 [b]1Co 15:23; 2Co 10:7; Gal 3:29
4:1 [a]1Co 9:17; Tit 1:7 [b]Ro 16:25
4:4 [c]Ro 2:13
4:5 [d]Mt 7:1, 2; Ro 2:1

3:10, 11 The foundation of the church—of all believers—is Jesus Christ. Paul laid this foundation (by preaching Christ) when he began the church at Corinth. Whoever builds the church—officers, teachers, preachers, parents, and others—must build with high quality materials (right doctrine and right living, 3:12ff) that meet God's standards. Paul is not criticising Apollos, but challenging future church leaders to have sound preaching and teaching.

3:10–17 In the church built on Jesus Christ, each church member would be mature, spiritually sensitive, and doctrinally sound. However, the Corinthian church was filled with those whose work was "wood, hay or straw", members who were immature, insensitive to one another, and vulnerable to wrong doctrine (3:1–4). No wonder they had so many problems. Local church members should be deeply committed to Christ. Can your Christian character stand the test?

3:11 A building is only as solid as its foundation. The foundation of our lives is Jesus Christ; he is our base, our reason for being. Everything we are and do must fit into the pattern provided by him. Are you building your life on the only real and lasting foundation, or are you building on a faulty foundation such as wealth, security, success, or fame?

3:13–15 Two sure ways to destroy a building are to tamper with the foundation and to build with inferior materials. The church must be built on Christ, not on any other person or principle. Christ will evaluate each minister's contribution to the life of the church, and the day of judgment ("the Day") will reveal the sincerity of each person's work. God will determine whether or not they have been faithful to Jesus' instructions. Good work will be rewarded; unfaithful or inferior work will be discounted. The builder "will be saved, but only as one escaping through the flames" means that unfaithful workers will be saved, but like people escaping from a burning building. All their possessions (accomplishments) will be lost.

3:16, 17 Just as our bodies are the "temple of the Holy Spirit" (6:19), the local church or Christian community is God's temple. Just as the Jews' temple in Jerusalem was not to be destroyed, the church is not to be spoiled and ruined by divisions, controversy, or other sins as members come together to worship God.

3:18–21 Paul was not telling the Corinthian believers to neglect the pursuit of knowledge. He was warning them that if worldly wisdom holds them back from God, it is not wisdom at all. God's way of thinking is far more valuable, even though it may seem foolish to the world (1:27). The Corinthians were using so-called worldly wisdom to evaluate their leaders and teachers. Their pride made them value the presentation of the message more than its content.

3:22 Paul says that both life and death are ours. While non-believers are victims of life, swept along by its current and wondering if there is meaning to it, believers can use life well because they understand its true purpose. Non-believers can only fear death. For believers, however, death holds no terrors because Christ has conquered all fears (see 1 John 4:18). Death is only the beginning of eternal life with God.

4:1, 2 Paul urged the Corinthians to think of him, Peter (Cephas), and Apollos not as leaders of factions, but as servants of Christ entrusted with the secret things of God (see the note on 2:7). A servant does what his master tells him to do. We must do what God tells us to do in the Bible and through his Holy Spirit. Each day God presents us with needs and opportunities that challenge us to do what we know is right.

4:5 It is tempting to judge fellow Christians, evaluating whether or not they are good followers of Christ. But only God knows a person's heart, and he is the only one with the right to judge. Paul's warning to the Corinthians should also warn us. We are to confront those who are sinning (see 5:12, 13), but we must not judge who is a better servant for Christ. When you judge someone, you invariably consider yourself better—and that is arrogant.

what is hidden in darkness and will expose the motives of men's hearts. At that time
each will receive his praise from God.[e]
6 Now, brothers, I have applied these things to myself and Apollos for your benefit,
so that you may learn from us the meaning of the saying, "Do not go beyond what
is written."[f] Then you will not take pride in one man over against another.[g] 7 For
who makes you different from anyone else? What do you have that you did not
receive?[h] And if you did receive it, why do you boast as though you did not?
8 Already you have all you want! Already you have become rich![i] You have
become kings—and that without us! How I wish that you really had become kings
so that we might be kings with you! 9 For it seems to me that God has put us apostles
on display at the end of the procession, like men condemned to die[j] in the arena.
We have been made a spectacle[k] to the whole universe, to angels as well as to men.
10 We are fools for Christ,[l] but you are so wise in Christ![m] We are weak, but you
are strong![n] You are honoured, we are dishonoured! 11 To this very hour we go hungry
and thirsty, we are in rags, we are brutally treated, we are homeless.[o] 12 We work
hard with our own hands.[p] When we are cursed, we bless;[q] when we are persecuted,
we endure it; 13 when we are slandered, we answer kindly. Up to this moment we have
become the scum of the earth, the refuse[r] of the world.
14 I am not writing this to shame you, but to warn you, as my dear children.[s] 15 Even
though you have ten thousand guardians in Christ, you do not have many fathers, for
in Christ Jesus I became your father through the gospel.[t] 16 Therefore I urge you to
imitate me.[u] 17 For this reason I am sending to you Timothy, my son[v] whom I love,
who is faithful in the Lord. He will remind you of my way of life in Christ Jesus,
which agrees with what I teach everywhere in every church.[w]
18 Some of you have become arrogant, as if I were not coming to you. 19 But I will
come to you very soon,[x] if the Lord is willing,[y] and then I will find out not only
how these arrogant people are talking, but what power they have. 20 For the kingdom
of God is not a matter of talk but of power. 21 What do you prefer? Shall I come to
you with a whip,[z] or in love and with a gentle spirit?

4:5 [e] Ro 2:29
4:6 [f] 1Co 1:19, 31; 3:19, 20 [g] 1Co 1:12
4:7 [h] Jn 3:27; Ro 12:3, 6
4:8 [i] Rev 3:17, 18
4:9 [j] Ro 8:36 [k] Heb 10:33
4:10 [l] 1Co 1:18; Ac 17:18 [m] 1Co 3:18 [n] 1Co 2:3
4:11 [o] Ro 8:35; 2Co 11:23-27
4:12 [p] Ac 18:3 [q] 1Pe 3:9
4:13 [r] La 3:45
4:14 [s] 1Th 2:11
4:15 [t] 1Co 9:12, 14, 18, 23
4:16 [u] 1Co 11:1; Php 3:17; 1Th 1:6; 2Th 3:7, 9
4:17 [v] 1Ti 1:2 [w] 1Co 7:17
4:19 [x] 2Co 1:15, 16 [y] Ac 18:21
4:21 [z] 2Co 1:23; 13:2, 10

4:6, 7 How easy it is for us to become attached to a spiritual leader. When someone has helped us, it's natural to feel loyalty. But Paul warns against having such pride in our favourite leaders that we cause divisions in the church. Any true spiritual leader is a representative of Christ and has nothing to offer that God hasn't given him or her. Don't let your loyalty cause strife, slander, or broken relationships. Make sure that your deepest loyalties are to Christ and not to his human agents. Those who spend more time debating church leadership than declaring Christ's message don't have Christ as their top priority.

4:6–13 The Corinthians had split into various cliques, each following its favourite preacher (Paul, Apollos, Peter, etc). Each clique really believed it was the only one to have the whole truth, and thus felt spiritually proud. But Paul told the groups not to boast about being tied to a particular preacher because each preacher was simply a humble servant who had suffered for the same message of salvation in Jesus Christ. No preacher of God has more status than another.

4:15 In Paul's day, a guardian was a slave who was assigned as a special tutor and caretaker of a child. Paul was portraying his special affection for the Corinthians (greater than a slave) and his special role (more than a caretaker). In an attempt to unify the church, Paul appealed to his relationship with them. By *father,* he meant he was the church's founder. Because he started the church, he could be trusted to have its best interests at heart. Paul's tough words were motivated by love—like the love a good father has for his children (see also 1 Thessalonians 2:11).

4:16 Paul told the Corinthians to imitate him. He was able to make this statement because he walked close to God, spent time in God's word and in prayer, and was aware of God's presence in his life at all times. God was Paul's example; therefore, Paul's life could be an example to other Christians. Paul wasn't expecting others to imitate everything he did, but they should imitate those aspects of his beliefs and conduct that were modelling Christ's way of living.

4:17 Timothy had travelled with Paul on Paul's second missionary journey (see Acts 16:1–3) and was a key person in the growth of the early church. Timothy may have delivered this letter to Corinth, but more likely he arrived there shortly after the letter came (see 16:10). Timothy's role was to see that Paul's advice was received, read, and implemented. Then he was to return to Paul and report on the church's progress.

4:18–20 Some people talk a lot about faith, but that's all it is—talk. They may know all the right words to say, but their lives don't reflect God's power. Paul says that the kingdom of God is to be *lived,* not just discussed. There is a big difference between knowing the right words and living them out. Don't be content to have the right answers about Christ. Let your life show that God's power is really working in you.

4:19 It is not known whether Paul ever returned to Corinth, but it is likely. In 2 Corinthians 2:1, he writes that he decided not to make "another painful visit", implying that he had had a previous painful confrontation with the Corinthian believers (see 2 Corinthians 12:14; 13:1; and the note on 2 Corinthians 2:1).

2. Disorder in the church

Expel the Immoral Brother!

5 It is actually reported that there is sexual immorality among you, and of a kind
that does not occur even among pagans: A man has his father's wife.[a] 2And you
are proud! Shouldn't you rather have been filled with grief[b] and have put out of your
fellowship the man who did this? 3Even though I am not physically present, I am with
you in spirit.[c] And I have already passed judgment on the one who did this, just as
if I were present. 4When you are assembled in the name of our Lord Jesus[d] and I
am with you in spirit, and the power of our Lord Jesus is present, 5hand this man over[e]
to Satan, so that the sinful nature[a] may be destroyed and his spirit saved on the day
of the Lord.

6Your boasting is not good.[f] Don't you know that a little yeast[g] works through
the whole batch of dough?[h] 7Get rid of the old yeast that you may be a new batch
without yeast—as you really are. For Christ, our Passover lamb, has been sacrificed.[i]
8Therefore let us keep the Festival, not with the old yeast, the yeast of malice and
wickedness, but with bread without yeast,[j] the bread of sincerity and truth.

9I have written to you in my letter not to associate[k] with sexually immoral
people—10not at all meaning the people of this world[l] who are immoral, or the
greedy and swindlers, or idolaters. In that case you would have to leave this world.
11But now I am writing to you that you must not associate with anyone who calls
himself a brother but is sexually immoral or greedy, an idolater[m] or a slanderer, a
drunkard or a swindler. With such a man do not even eat.

12What business is it of mine to judge those outside[n] the church? Are you not to
judge those inside?[o] 13God will judge those outside. "Expel the wicked man from
among you."[b][p]

a 5 Or *that his body*; or *that the flesh* b 13 Deut. 17:7; 19:19; 21:21; 22:21,24; 24:7

5:1 [a]Lev 18:8; Dt 22:30
5:2 [b]2Co 7:7-11
5:3 [c]Col 2:5
5:4 [d]2Th 3:6
5:5 [e]1Ti 1:20
5:6 [f]Jas 4:16 [g]Mt 16:6, 12 [h]Gal 5:9
5:7 [i]Mk 14:12; 1Pe 1:19
5:8 [j]Ex 12:14, 15; Dt 16:3
5:9 [k]Eph 5:11; 2Th 3:6, 14
5:10 [l]1Co 10:27
5:11 [m]1Co 10:7, 14
5:12 [n]Mk 4:11 [o]ver 3-5; 1Co 6:1-4
5:13 [p]Dt 13:5

5:1ff The church must discipline flagrant sin among its members—such sins, left unchecked, can polarise and paralyse a church. The correction, however, should never be vengeful. Instead, it should be given to help bring about a cure. There was a specific sin in the church, but the Corinthian believers had refused to deal with it. In this case, a man was having an affair with his mother (or stepmother), and the church members were trying to ignore the situation. Paul was telling the church that it had a responsibility to maintain the standards of morality found in God's commandments. God tells us not to judge others. But he also tells us not to tolerate flagrant sin because leaving that sin undisciplined will have a dangerous influence on other believers (5:6).

5:5 To "hand this man over to Satan" means to exclude him from the fellowship of believers. Without the spiritual support of Christians, this man would be left alone with his sin and Satan, and perhaps this emptiness would drive him to repentance. "That the sinful nature may be destroyed" states the hope that the experience would bring him to God to destroy his sinful nature through repentance. *Sinful nature* could mean his body or flesh (see the NIV text note). This alternative translation would imply that Satan would afflict him physically and thus bring him to God. Putting someone out of the church should be a last resort in disciplinary action. It should not be done out of vengeance, but out of love, just as parents punish children to correct and restore them. The church's role should be to help, not hurt, offenders, motivating them to repent of their sins and to return to the fellowship of the church.

5:6 Paul was writing to those who wanted to ignore this church problem. They didn't realise that allowing public sin to exist in the church affects all its members. Paul does not expect anyone to be sinless—all believers struggle with sin daily. Instead, he is speaking against those who deliberately sin, feel no guilt, and refuse to repent. This kind of sin cannot be tolerated in the church because it affects others. We have a responsibility to other believers. Yeast makes bread dough rise. A little bit affects the whole batch. Blatant sins, left uncorrected, confuse and divide the congregation. While believers should encourage, pray for, and build up one another, they must also be intolerant of sin that jeopardises the spiritual health of the church.

5:7, 8 As the Hebrews prepared for their exodus from slavery in Egypt, they were commanded to prepare bread without yeast because they didn't have time to wait for it to rise. And because yeast was also a symbol of sin, they were commanded to sweep all of it out of the house (Exodus 12:15; 13:7). Christ is our Passover lamb, the perfect sacrifice for our sin. Because he has delivered us from the slavery of sin, we should have nothing to do with the sins of the past ("old yeast").

5:9 Paul is referring to an earlier letter to the Corinthian church, often called the lost letter because it has not been preserved.

5:10, 11 Paul makes it clear that we should not disassociate ourselves from unbelievers—otherwise, we could not carry out Christ's command to tell them about salvation (Matthew 28:18–20). But we are to distance ourselves from the person who claims to be a Christian, yet indulges in sins explicitly forbidden in Scripture and then rationalises his or her actions. By rationalising sin, a person harms others for whom Christ died and dims the image of God in himself or herself. A church that includes such people is hardly fit to be the light of the world. To do so would distort the picture of Christ it presents to the world. Church leaders must be ready to correct, in love, for the sake of spiritual unity.

5:12 The Bible consistently tells us not to criticise people by gossiping or making rash judgments. At the same time, however, we are to judge and deal with sin that can hurt others. Paul's instructions should not be used to handle trivial matters or to take revenge; nor should they be applied to individual problems between believers. These verses are instructions for dealing with open sin in the church, with a person who claims to be a Christian and yet who sins without remorse. The church is to confront and discipline such a person in love. Also see the notes on 4:5 and 5:1ff.

6:1
[a]Mt 18:17

6:2
[b]Mt 19:28; Lk 22:30

6:5
[c]1Co 4:14
[d]Ac 1:15

6:6
[e]2Co 6:14, 15

6:7
[f]Mt 5:39, 40

6:8
[g]1Th 4:6

6:9
[h]Gal 5:21
[i]1Co 15:33; Jas 1:16

Lawsuits Among Believers

6 If any of you has a dispute with another, dare he take it before the ungodly for
judgment instead of before the saints?[a] 2Do you not know that the saints will
judge the world?[b] And if you are to judge the world, are you not competent to judge
trivial cases? 3Do you not know that we will judge angels? How much more the things
of this life! 4Therefore, if you have disputes about such matters, appoint as judges
even men of little account in the church![a] 5I say this to shame you.[c] Is it possible
that there is nobody among you wise enough to judge a dispute between believers?[d]
6But instead, one brother goes to law against another—and this in front of unbelievers![e]

7The very fact that you have lawsuits among you means you have been completely
defeated already. Why not rather be wronged? Why not rather be cheated?[f] 8Instead,
you yourselves cheat and do wrong, and you do this to your brothers.[g]

9Do you not know that the wicked will not inherit the kingdom of God?[h] Do not
be deceived:[i] Neither the sexually immoral nor idolaters nor adulterers nor male
prostitutes nor homosexual offenders 10nor thieves nor the greedy nor drunkards nor
slanderers nor swindlers will inherit the kingdom of God. 11And that is what some

a 4 *Or matters, do you appoint as judges men of little account in the church?*

CHURCH DISCIPLINE
The church, at times, must exercise discipline towards members who have sinned. But church discipline must be handled carefully, straightforwardly, and lovingly.

Situations	*Steps* (Matthew 18:15–17)
Unintentional error and/or private sin Public sin and/or that done flagrantly and arrogantly	1. Go to the brother or sister, show the fault to him or her in private. 2. If he/she does not listen, go with one or two witnesses. 3. If he/she refuses to listen, take the matter before the church.

After these steps have been carried out, the next steps are:

1. Remove the one in error from the fellowship (1 Corinthians 5:2–13).
2. The church gives united disapproval, but forgiveness and comfort are in order if he/she chooses to repent (2 Corinthians 2:5–8).
3. Do not associate with the disobedient person; and if you must, speak to him/her as one who needs a warning (2 Thessalonians 3:14, 15).
4. After two warnings, reject the person from the fellowship (Titus 3:10).

6:1–6 In chapter 5, Paul explained what to do with open immorality in the congregation. In chapter 6, he teaches how the congregation should handle smaller problems between believers. Society has set up a legal system where disagreements can be resolved in courts. But Paul declares that disagreeing Christians should not have to go to a secular court to resolve their differences. As Christians, we have the Holy Spirit and the mind of Christ, so why should we turn to those who lack God's wisdom? Because of all that we have been given as believers, and because of the authority that we will have in the future to judge the world and the angels, we should be able to deal with disputes among ourselves. The *saints* are believers. See John 5:22 and Revelation 3:21 for more on judging the world. Judging angels is mentioned in 2 Peter 2:4 and Jude 6.

6:6–8 Why did Paul say that Christians should not take their disagreements to unbelivers in secular courts? (1) If the judge and jury are not Christians, they are not likely to be sensitive to Christian values. (2) The basis for going to court is often revenge; this should never be a Christian's motive. (3) Lawsuits make the church look bad, causing unbelievers to focus on its problems rather than on its purpose.

6:9–11 Paul is describing characteristics of unbelievers. He doesn't mean that idolaters, adulterers, male prostitutes, homosexuals, thieves, greedy people, drunkards, slanderers or swindlers are automatically and irrevocably excluded from heaven. Christians come out of all kinds of different backgrounds, including these. They may still struggle with evil desires, but they should not continue in these practices. In 6:11, Paul clearly states that even those who sin in these ways can have their lives changed by Christ. However, those who say that they are Christians but persist in these practices with no sign of remorse will not inherit the kingdom of God. Such people need to re-evaluate their lives to see if they truly believe in Christ.

6:9–11 In a permissive society it is easy for Christians to overlook or tolerate some forms of immoral behaviour (greed, drunkenness, etc) while remaining outraged at others (homosexuality, thievery). We must not participate in sin or condone it in any way, nor may we be selective about what we condemn or excuse. Staying away from more "acceptable" forms of sin is difficult, but it is no harder for us than it was for the Corinthians. God expects his followers in any age to have high standards.

6:11 Paul emphasises God's action in making believers new people. The three aspects of God's work are all part of our salvation: our sins were washed away, we were set apart for special use ("sanctified"), and we were pronounced not guilty ("justified") for our sins.

of you were.[j] But you were washed,[k] you were sanctified,[l] you were justified in
the name of the Lord Jesus Christ and by the Spirit of our God.

Sexual Immorality

12“Everything is permissible for me” — but not everything is beneficial.[m] “Everything is permissible for me” — but I will not be mastered by anything. 13“Food for the
stomach and the stomach for food” — but God will destroy them both.[n] The body is
not meant for sexual immorality, but for the Lord, and the Lord for the body. 14By
his power God raised the Lord from the dead, and he will raise us also.[o] 15Do you
not know that your bodies are members of Christ himself?[p] Shall I then take the
members of Christ and unite them with a prostitute? Never! 16Do you not know that
he who unites himself with a prostitute is one with her in body? For it is said, “The
two will become one flesh.”[b][q] 17But he who unites himself with the Lord is one with
him in spirit.[r]
18Flee from sexual immorality.[s] All other sins a man commits are outside his body,
but he who sins sexually sins against his own body.[t] 19Do you not know that your
body is a temple[u] of the Holy Spirit, who is in you, whom you have received from
God? You are not your own;[v] 20you were bought at a price.[w] Therefore honour God
with your body.

b *16* Gen. 2:24

6:11 [j]Eph 2:2 [k]Ac 22:16 [l]1Co 1:2
6:12 [m]1Co 10:23
6:13 [n]Col 2:22
6:14 [o]Ro 6:5; Eph 1:19, 20
6:15 [p]Ro 12:5
6:16 [q]Ge 2:24; Mt 19:5; Eph 5:31
6:17 [r]Jn 17:21-23; Gal 2:20
6:18 [s]2Co 12:21; 1Th 4:3, 4; Heb 13:4 [t]Ro 6:12
6:19 [u]Jn 2:21 [v]Ro 14:7, 8
6:20 [w]Ac 20:28; 1Co 7:23; 1Pe 1:18, 19; Rev 5:9

6:12 Apparently the church had been quoting and misapplying the words “everything is permissible for me”. Some Christians in Corinth were excusing their sins by saying that (1) Christ had taken away all sin, and so they had complete freedom to live as they pleased, or (2) what they were doing was not strictly forbidden by Scripture. Paul answered both these excuses. (1) While Christ has taken away our sin, this does not give us freedom to go on doing what we know is wrong. The New Testament specifically forbids many sins (see 6:9, 10) that were originally prohibited in the Old Testament (see Romans 12:9–21; 13:8–10). (2) Some actions are not sinful in themselves, but they are not appropriate because they can control our lives and lead us away from God. (3) Some actions may hurt others. Anything we do that hurts rather than helps others is not right.

6:12, 13 Many of the world’s religions teach that the soul or spirit is important but the body is not; and Christianity has sometimes been influenced by these ideas. In truth, however, Christianity takes very seriously the realm of the physical. We worship a God who created a physical world and pronounced it good. He promises us a new earth where real people have transformed physical lives — not a pink cloud where disembodied souls listen to harp music. At the heart of Christianity is the story of God himself taking on flesh and blood and coming to live with us, offering both physical healing and spiritual restoration.

We humans, like Adam, are a combination of dust and spirit. Just as our spirits affect our bodies, so our physical bodies affect our spirits. We cannot commit sin with our bodies without damaging our souls because our bodies and souls are inseparably joined. In the new earth we will have resurrection bodies that are not corrupted by sin. Then we will enjoy the fullness of our salvation.

6:12, 13 Freedom is a mark of the Christian faith — freedom from sin and guilt, and freedom to use and enjoy anything that comes from God. But Christians should not abuse this freedom and hurt themselves or others. Drinking too much leads to alcoholism, gluttony leads to obesity. Be careful that what God has allowed you to enjoy doesn’t grow into a bad habit that controls you. For more about Christian freedom and everyday behaviour, read chapter 8.

6:13 Sexual immorality is a temptation that is always before us. In movies and on television, sex outside marriage is treated as a normal, even desirable, part of life, while marriage is often shown as confining and joyless. We can even be looked down on by others if we are suspected of being pure. But God does not forbid sexual sin just to be difficult. He knows its power to destroy us physically and spiritually. No-one should underestimate the power of sexual immorality. It has devastated countless lives and destroyed families, churches, communities, and even nations. God wants to protect us from damaging ourselves and others, and so he offers to fill us — our loneliness, our desires — with himself.

6:15–17 This teaching about sexual immorality and prostitutes was especially important for the Corinthian church because the temple of the love goddess Aphrodite was in Corinth. This temple employed more than a thousand prostitutes as priestesses, and sex was part of the worship ritual. Paul clearly stated that Christians are to have no part in sexual immorality, even if it is acceptable and popular in our culture.

6:18 Christians are free to be all they can be for God, but they are not free *from* God. God created sex to be a beautiful and essential ingredient of marriage, but sexual sin — sex outside the marriage relationship — *always* hurts someone. It hurts God because it shows that we prefer following our own desires instead of the leading of the Holy Spirit. It hurts others because it violates the commitment so necessary to a relationship. It often brings disease to our bodies. And it deeply affects our personalities, which respond in anguish when we harm ourselves physically and spiritually.

6:19, 20 What did Paul mean when he said that our bodies belong to God? Many people say they have the right to do whatever they want with their own bodies. Although they think that this is freedom, they are really enslaved to their own desires. When we become Christians, the Holy Spirit fills and lives in us. Therefore, we no longer own our bodies. “Bought at a price” refers to slaves purchased at auction. Christ’s death freed us from sin, but also obligates us to his service. If you live in a building owned by someone else, you try not to violate the building’s rules. Because your body belongs to God, you must not violate his standards for living.

7:1
[a]ver 8, 26

7:3
[b]Ex 21:10;
1Pe 3:7

7:5
[c]Ex 19:15;
1Sa 21:4, 5
[d]Mt 4:10
[e]1Th 3:5

7:6
[f]2Co 8:8

7:7
[g]ver 8;
1Co 9:5
[h]Mt 19:11, 12;
Ro 12:6;
1Co 12:4, 11

7:8
[i]ver 1, 26

7:9
[j]1Ti 5:14

7:10
[k]Mal 2:14-16;
Mt 5:32; 19:3-9;
Mk 10:11;
Lk 16:18

B. PAUL ANSWERS CHURCH QUESTIONS (7:1 – 16:24)

After discussing disorder in the church, Paul moves to the list of questions that the Corinthians had sent him, including subjects of marriage, singleness, eating meat offered to idols, propriety in worship, orderliness in the Lord's Supper, spiritual gifts, and the resurrection. Questions that plague churches today are remarkably similar to these, so we can receive specific guidance in these areas from the letter.

1. Instruction on Christian marriage

7 Now for the matters you wrote about: It is good for a man not to marry.[a][a] 2But
since there is so much immorality, each man should have his own wife, and each
woman her own husband. 3The husband should fulfil his marital duty to his wife,[b]
and likewise the wife to her husband. 4The wife's body does not belong to her alone
but also to her husband. In the same way, the husband's body does not belong to him
alone but also to his wife. 5Do not deprive each other except by mutual consent and
for a time,[c] so that you may devote yourselves to prayer. Then come together again
so that Satan[d] will not tempt you[e] because of your lack of self-control. 6I say this
as a concession, not as a command.[f] 7I wish that all men were as I am.[g] But each
man has his own gift from God; one has this gift, another has that.[h]
8Now to the unmarried and the widows I say: It is good for them to stay unmarried,
as I am.[i] 9But if they cannot control themselves, they should marry,[j] for it is better
to marry than to burn with passion.
10To the married I give this command (not I, but the Lord): A wife must not separate
from her husband.[k] 11But if she does, she must remain unmarried or else be reconciled to her husband. And a husband must not divorce his wife.

a *1* Or *"It is good for a man not to have sexual relations with a woman."*

7:1 The Corinthians had written to Paul, asking him several questions relating to the Christian life and problems in the church. The first question was whether it was good to be married. Paul answers this and other questions in the remainder of this letter.

7:1ff Christians in Corinth were surrounded by sexual temptation. The city had a reputation even among pagans for sexual immorality and religious prostitution. It was to this kind of society that Paul delivered these instructions on sex and marriage. The Corinthians needed special, specific instructions because of their culture's immoral standards. For more on Paul's teaching about marriage, see Ephesians 5.

7:3–5 Sexual temptations are difficult to withstand because they appeal to the normal and natural desires that God has given us. Marriage provides God's way to satisfy these natural sexual desires and to strengthen the partners against temptation. Married couples have the responsibility to care for each other; therefore, husbands and wives should not withhold themselves sexually from one another, but should fulfil each other's needs and desires. (See also the note on 10:13.)

7:3–11 The Corinthian church was in turmoil because of the immorality of the culture around them. Some Greeks, in rejecting immorality, rejected sex and marriage altogether. The Corinthian Christians wondered if this was what they should do also, so they asked Paul several questions: "Because sex is perverted, shouldn't we also abstain in marriage"? "If my spouse is unsaved, should I seek a divorce"? "Should unmarried people and widows remain unmarried"? Paul answered many of these questions by saying, "For now, stay put. Be content in the situation where God has placed you. If you're married, don't seek to be single. If you're single, don't seek to be married. Live God's way, one day at a time, and he will show you what to do".

7:4 Spiritually, our bodies belong to God when we become Christians because Jesus Christ bought us by paying the price to release us from sin (see 6:19, 20). Physically, our bodies belong to our spouses because God designed marriage so that, through the union of husband and wife, the two become one (Genesis 2:24). Paul stressed complete equality in sexual relationships. Neither male nor female should seek dominance or autonomy.

7:7 Both marriage and singleness are gifts from God. One is not morally better than the other, and both are valuable to accomplishing God's purposes. It is important for us, therefore, to accept our present situation. When Paul said he wished that all people were like him (i.e., unmarried), he was expressing his desire that more people would devote themselves *completely* to the ministry without the added concerns of spouse and family, as he had done. He was not criticising marriage – after all, it is God's created way of providing companionship and populating the earth.

7:9 Sexual pressure is not the best motive for getting married, but it is better to marry the right person than to "burn with passion". Many new believers in Corinth thought that all sex was wrong, and so engaged couples were deciding not to get married. In this passage, Paul was telling couples who wanted to marry that they should not frustrate their normal sexual drives by avoiding marriage. This does not mean, however, that people who have trouble controlling themselves should marry the first person who comes along. It is better to deal with the pressure of desire than to deal with an unhappy marriage.

12To the rest I say this (I, not the Lord):[l] If any brother has a wife who is not a
believer and she is willing to live with him, he must not divorce her. 13And if a woman
has a husband who is not a believer and he is willing to live with her, she must not
divorce him. 14For the unbelieving husband has been sanctified through his wife, and
the unbelieving wife has been sanctified through her believing husband. Otherwise
your children would be unclean, but as it is, they are holy.[m]
15But if the unbeliever leaves, let him do so. A believing man or woman is not
bound in such circumstances; God has called us to live in peace.[n] 16How do you
know, wife, whether you will save[o] your husband?[p] Or, how do you know, husband,
whether you will save your wife?
17Nevertheless, each one should retain the place in life that the Lord assigned to
him and to which God has called him.[q] This is the rule I lay down in all the
churches.[r] 18Was a man already circumcised when he was called? He should not
become uncircumcised. Was a man uncircumcised when he was called? He should
not be circumcised.[s] 19Circumcision is nothing and uncircumcision is nothing.[t]
Keeping God's commands is what counts. 20Each one should remain in the situation
which he was in when God called him.[u] 21Were you a slave when you were called?
Don't let it trouble you—although if you can gain your freedom, do so. 22For he who
was a slave when he was called by the Lord is the Lord's freedman;[v] similarly, he
who was a free man when he was called is Christ's slave.[w] 23You were bought at

7:12 [l]ver 6, 10; 2Co 11:17
7:14 [m]Mal 2:15
7:15 [n]Ro 14:19; 1Co 14:33
7:16 [o]Ro 11:14 [p]1Pe 3:1
7:17 [q]Ro 12:3 [r]1Co 4:17; 14:33; 2Co 8:18; 11:28
7:18 [s]Ac 15:1, 2
7:19 [t]Ro 2:25-27; Gal 5:6; 6:15; Col 3:11
7:20 [u]ver 24
7:22 [v]Jn 8:32, 36; Phm 16 [w]Eph 6:6

7:12 Paul's *command* about the permanence of marriage (7:10) comes from the Old Testament (Genesis 2:24) and from Jesus (Mark 10:2–12). His *suggestion* in this verse is based on God's command, and Paul applies it to the situation the Corinthians were facing. Paul ranked the command above the suggestion because one is an eternal principle while the other is a specific application. Nevertheless, for people in similar situations, Paul's suggestion is the best advice they will get. Paul was a man of God, an apostle, and he had the mind of Christ.

7:12–14 Because of their desire to serve Christ, some people in the Corinthian church thought they ought to divorce their pagan spouses and marry Christians. But Paul affirmed the marriage commitment. God's ideal is for marriages to stay together—even when one spouse is not a believer. The Christian spouse should try to win the other to Christ. It would be easy to rationalise leaving; however, Paul makes a strong case for staying with the unbelieving spouse and being a positive influence on the marriage. Paul, like Jesus, believed that marriage is permanent (see Mark 10:1–9).

7:14 The blessings that flow to believers don't stop there, but extend to others. God regards the marriage as "sanctified" (set apart for his use) by the presence of one Christian spouse. The other does not receive salvation automatically, but is helped by this relationship. The children of such a marriage are to be regarded as "holy" (because of God's blessing on the family unit) until they are old enough to decide for themselves.

7:15, 16 This verse is misused by some as a loophole to get out of marriage. But Paul's statements were given to encourage the Christian spouse to try to get along with the unbeliever and make the marriage work. If, however, the unbelieving spouse insisted on leaving, Paul said to let him or her go. The only alternative would be for the Christian to deny his or her faith to preserve the marriage, and that would be worse than dissolving the marriage. Paul's chief purpose in writing this was to urge the married couples to seek unity, not separation (see 7:17; 1 Peter 3:1, 2).

7:17 Apparently the Corinthians were ready to make wholesale changes without thinking through the ramifications. Paul was writing to say that people should be Christians where they are. You can do God's work and demonstrate your faith *anywhere*. If you became a Christian after marriage, and your spouse is not a believer, remember that you don't have to be married to a Christian to live for Christ. Don't assume that you are in the wrong place, or stuck with the wrong person. You may be just where God wants you (see 7:20).

7:18, 19 The ceremony of circumcision was an important part of the Jews' relationship with God. In fact, before Christ came, circumcision was commanded by God for those who claimed to follow him (Genesis 17:9–14). But after Christ's death, circumcision was no longer necessary (Acts 15; Romans 4:9–11; Galatians 5:2–4; Colossians 2:11). Pleasing God and obeying him is more important than observing traditional ceremonies.

7:20 Often we are so concerned about what we *could* be doing for God somewhere else that we miss great opportunities right where we are. Paul says that when someone becomes a Christian, he or she should usually continue with the work he or she has previously been doing—provided it isn't immoral or unethical. Every job can become Christian work when you realise that the purpose of your life is to honour, serve, and speak out for Christ. Because God has placed you where you are, look carefully for opportunities to serve him there.

7:23 Slavery was common throughout the Roman empire. Some Christians in the Corinthian church were undoubtedly slaves. Paul said that although the Christian slaves were slaves to other human beings, they were free from the power of sin in their lives. People today are slaves to sin until they commit their lives to Christ, who alone can conquer sin's power. Sin, pride, and fear no longer have any claim over us, just as a slave owner no longer has power over the slaves he has sold. The Bible says we become Christ's slaves when we become Christians (Romans 6:18), but this actually means we gain our freedom, because sin no longer controls us.

7:26 Paul probably foresaw the impending persecution that the Roman government would soon bring upon Christians. He gave this practical advice because being unmarried would mean less suffering and more freedom to throw one's life into the cause of Christ (7:29), even to the point of fearlessly dying for him. Paul's advice reveals his single-minded devotion to spreading the Good News.

a price;[x] do not become slaves of men. 24Brothers, each man, as responsible to God,
should remain in the situation God called him to.[y]
25Now about virgins: I have no command from the Lord,[z] but I give a judgment
as one who by the Lord's mercy[a] is trustworthy. 26Because of the present crisis, I
think that it is good for you to remain as you are.[b] 27Are you married? Do not seek
a divorce. Are you unmarried? Do not look for a wife. 28But if you do marry, you
have not sinned; and if a virgin marries, she has not sinned. But those who marry will
face many troubles in this life, and I want to spare you this.
29What I mean, brothers, is that the time is short.[c] From now on those who have
wives should live as if they had none; 30those who mourn, as if they did not; those
who are happy, as if they were not; those who buy something, as if it were not theirs
to keep; 31those who use the things of the world, as if not engrossed in them. For this
world in its present form is passing away.[d]
32I would like you to be free from concern. An unmarried man is concerned about
the Lord's affairs[e]—how he can please the Lord. 33But a married man is concerned
about the affairs of this world—how he can please his wife—34and his interests are
divided. An unmarried woman or virgin is concerned about the Lord's affairs: Her
aim is to be devoted to the Lord in both body and spirit.[f] But a married woman is
concerned about the affairs of this world—how she can please her husband. 35I am
saying this for your own good, not to restrict you, but that you may live in a right
way in undivided[g] devotion to the Lord.
36If anyone thinks he is acting improperly towards the virgin he is engaged to, and
if she is getting on in years and he feels he ought to marry, he should do as he wants.
He is not sinning.[h] They should get married. 37But the man who has settled the matter
in his own mind, who is under no compulsion but has control over his own will, and
who has made up his mind not to marry the virgin—this man also does the right thing.
38So then, he who marries the virgin does right,[i] but he who does not marry her does
even better.[b]
39A woman is bound to her husband as long as he lives.[j] But if her husband dies,
she is free to marry anyone she wishes, but he must belong to the Lord.[k] 40In my
judgment,[l] she is happier if she stays as she is—and I think that I too have the Spirit
of God.

7:23 [x]1Co 6:20
7:24 [y]ver 20
7:25 [z]ver 6; 2Co 8:8 [a]2Co 4:1; 1Ti 1:13, 16
7:26 [b]ver 1, 8
7:29 [c]ver 31; Ro 13:11, 12
7:31 [d]1Jn 2:17
7:32 [e]1Ti 5:5
7:34 [f]Lk 2:37
7:35 [g]Ps 86:11
7:36 [h]ver 28
7:38 [i]Heb 13:4
7:39 [j]Ro 7:2, 3 [k]2Co 6:14
7:40 [l]ver 25

b *36–38* Or 36*If anyone thinks he is not treating his daughter properly, and if she is getting on in years, and he feels she ought to marry, he should do as he wants. He is not sinning. He should let her get married.* 37*But the man who has settled the matter in his own mind, who is under no compulsion but has control over his own will, and who has made up his mind to keep the virgin unmarried—this man also does the right thing.* 38*So then, he who gives his virgin in marriage does right, but he who does not give her in marriage does even better.*

7:28 Many people naively think that marriage will solve all their problems. Here are some problems marriage won't solve: (1) loneliness, (2) sexual temptation, (3) satisfaction of one's deepest emotional needs, (4) elimination of life's difficulties. Marriage alone does not hold two people together, but commitment does—commitment to Christ and to each other despite conflicts and problems. As wonderful as it is, marriage does not automatically solve every problem. Whether married or single, we must be content with our situation and focus on Christ, not on loved ones, to help address our problems.

7:29 Paul urges all believers to make the most of their time before Christ's return. Every person in every generation should have this sense of urgency about telling the Good News to others. Life is short—there's not much time!

7:29–31 Paul urges believers not to regard marriage, home, or financial security as the ultimate goals of life. As much as possible, we should live unhindered by the cares of this world, not getting involved with burdensome mortgages, budgets, investments, or debts that might keep us from doing God's work. A married man or woman, as Paul points out (7:33, 34), must take care of earthly responsibilities—but they should make every effort to keep them modest and manageable.

7:32–34 Some single people feel tremendous pressure to be married. They think their lives can be complete only with a spouse. But Paul underlines one advantage of being single—the potential of a greater focus on Christ and his work. If you are unmarried, use your special opportunity to serve Christ whole-heartedly.

7:38 When Paul says the unmarried person does even better, he is talking about the potential time available for service to God. The single person does not have the responsibility of caring for a spouse and raising a family. Singleness, however, does not ensure service to God—involvement in service depends on the commitment of the individual.

7:40 Paul's advice comes from the Holy Spirit, who guides and equips both single and married people to fulfil their roles.

2. Instruction on Christian freedom

Food Sacrificed to Idols

8 Now about food sacrificed to idols:[a] We know that we all possess knowledge.[a][b] Knowledge puffs up, but love builds up. 2The man who thinks he knows
something[c] does not yet know as he ought to know.[d] 3But the man who loves God
is known by God.[e]
4So then, about eating food sacrificed to idols:[f] We know that an idol is nothing
at all in the world[g] and that there is no God but one.[h] 5For even if there are so-called
gods,[i] whether in heaven or on earth (as indeed there are many "gods" and many
"lords"), 6yet for us there is but one God, the Father,[j] from whom all things came[k]
and for whom we live; and there is but one Lord,[l] Jesus Christ, through whom all
things came[m] and through whom we live.
7But not everyone knows this. Some people are still so accustomed to idols that
when they eat such food they think of it as having been sacrificed to an idol, and since
their conscience is weak,[n] it is defiled. 8But food does not bring us near to God;[o]
we are no worse if we do not eat, and no better if we do.
9Be careful, however, that the exercise of your freedom does not become a
stumbling-block[p] to the weak.[q] 10For if anyone with a weak conscience sees you
who have this knowledge eating in an idol's temple, won't he be emboldened to eat
what has been sacrificed to idols? 11So this weak brother, for whom Christ died, is
destroyed[r] by your knowledge. 12When you sin against your brothers[s] in this way
and wound their weak conscience, you sin against Christ. 13Therefore, if what I eat
causes my brother to fall into sin, I will never eat meat again, so that I will not cause
him to fall.[t]

The Rights of an Apostle

9 Am I not free? Am I not an apostle?[a] Have I not seen Jesus our Lord?[b] Are
you not the result of my work in the Lord?[c] 2Even though I may not be an apostle
to others, surely I am to you! For you are the seal[d] of my apostleship in the Lord.
3This is my defence to those who sit in judgment on me. 4Don't we have the right
to food and drink?[e] 5Don't we have the right to take a believing wife[f] along with

a 1 Or *"We all possess knowledge," as you say*

8:1 [a]Ac 15:20 [b]Ro 15:14
8:2 [c]1Co 3:18 [d]1Co 13:8, 9, 12; 1Ti 6:4
8:3 [e]Ro 8:29; Gal 4:9
8:4 [f]ver 1, 7, 10 [g]1Co 10:19 [h]Dt 6:4; Eph 4:6
8:5 [i]2Th 2:4
8:6 [j]Mal 2:10 [k]Ro 11:36 [l]Eph 4:5 [m]Jn 1:3
8:7 [n]Ro 14:14; 1Co 10:28
8:8 [o]Ro 14:17
8:9 [p]Gal 5:13 [q]Ro 14:1
8:11 [r]Ro 14:15, 20
8:12 [s]Mt 18:6
8:13 [t]Ro 14:21
9:1 [a]2Co 12:12 [b]1Co 15:8 [c]1Co 3:6; 4:15
9:2 [d]2Co 3:2, 3
9:4 [e]1Th 2:6
9:5 [f]1Co 7:7, 8

8:1 Meat bought in the market-place was likely to have been symbolically offered to an idol in one of the many pagan temples. Animals were brought to a temple, killed before an idol as part of a pagan religious ceremony, and eaten at a feast in the idol's temple or taken to butchers who sold the meat in the market-place. The believers wondered if by eating such meat, they were somehow participating in the worship of pagan idols.

8:1–3 Love is more important than knowledge. Knowledge can make us look good and feel important, but we can all too easily develop an arrogant, know-it-all attitude. Many people with strong opinions are unwilling to listen to and learn from God and others. We can obtain God's knowledge only by loving him (see James 3:17, 18). And we can know and be known by God only when we model him by showing love (1 John 4:7, 8).

8:4–9 Paul addressed these words to believers who weren't bothered by eating meat that had been sacrificed to idols. Although idols were phony, and the pagan ritual of sacrificing to them was meaningless, eating such meat offended Christians with more sensitive consciences. Paul said, therefore, that if a weaker or less mature believer misunderstood their actions, they should, out of consideration, avoid eating meat offered to idols.

8:10–13 Christian freedom does not mean that anything goes. It means that our salvation is not determined by good deeds or legalistic rules, but by the free gift of God (Ephesians 2:8, 9). Christian freedom, then, is inseparably tied to Christian responsibility. New believers are often very sensitive to what is right or wrong, what they should or shouldn't do. Some actions may be perfectly all right for us to do, but may harm a Christian brother or sister who is still young in the faith and learning what the Christian life is all about. We must be careful not to offend a sensitive or younger Christian or, by our example, to cause him or her to sin. When we love others, our freedom should be less important to us than strengthening the faith of a brother or sister in Christ.

9:1 Some Corinthians were questioning Paul's authority and rights as an apostle, so Paul gave his credentials – he actually saw and talked with the resurrected Christ, who called him to be an apostle (see Acts 9:3–18). Such credentials make the advice he gives in this letter more persuasive. In 2 Corinthians 10 – 13, Paul defends his apostleship in greater detail.

9:1 Changed lives were the evidence that God was using Paul. Does your faith have an impact on others? You can be a life-changer, helping others grow spiritually, if you dedicate yourself to being used by God and letting him make you effective.

9:4ff Paul uses himself as an illustration of giving up personal rights. Paul had the right to hospitality, to be married, and to be paid for his work. But he willingly gave up these rights to win people to Christ. When your focus is on living for Christ, your rights become comparatively unimportant.

9:4–10 Jesus said that workers deserve their wages (Luke 10:7). Paul echoes this thought and urges the church to be sure to pay their Christian workers. We have the responsibility to care for our pastors, teachers, and other spiritual leaders. It is our duty to see that those who serve us in the ministry are fairly and adequately compensated.

9:5 The brothers of Jesus attained leadership status in the church at Jerusalem. James (one of the "Lord's brothers"), for ex-

us, as do the other apostles and the Lord's brothers[g] and Cephas?[a] 6Or is it only I and Barnabas[h] who must work for a living?

7Who serves as a soldier at his own expense? Who plants a vineyard[i] and does not eat of its grapes? Who tends a flock and does not drink of the milk? 8Do I say this merely from a human point of view? Doesn't the Law say the same thing? 9For it is written in the Law of Moses: "Do not muzzle an ox while it is treading out the grain."[b][j] Is it about oxen that God is concerned?[k] 10Surely he says this for us, doesn't he? Yes, this was written for us,[l] because when the ploughman ploughs and the thresher threshes, they ought to do so in the hope of sharing in the harvest.[m] 11If we have sown spiritual seed among you, is it too much if we reap a material harvest from you?[n] 12If others have this right of support from you, shouldn't we have it all the more?

But we did not use this right.[o] On the contrary, we put up with anything rather than hinder[p] the gospel of Christ. 13Don't you know that those who work in the temple get their food from the temple, and those who serve at the altar share in what is offered on the altar?[q] 14In the same way, the Lord has commanded that those who preach the gospel should receive their living from the gospel.[r]

15But I have not used any of these rights.[s] And I am not writing this in the hope that you will do such things for me. I would rather die than have anyone deprive me of this boast.[t] 16Yet when I preach the gospel, I cannot boast, for I am compelled to preach.[u] Woe to me if I do not preach the gospel! 17If I preach voluntarily, I have a reward;[v] if not voluntarily, I am simply discharging the trust committed to me.[w] 18What then is my reward? Just this: that in preaching the gospel I may offer it free of charge,[x] and so not make use of my rights in preaching it.

19Though I am free[y] and belong to no man, I make myself a slave to everyone,[z] to win as many as possible.[a] 20To the Jews I became like a Jew, to win the Jews.[b] To those under the law I became like one under the law (though I myself am not under the law), so as to win those under the law. 21To those not having the law I became

[a] 5 That is, Peter [b] 9 Deut. 25:4

9:5 [g] Mt 12:46
9:6 [h] Ac 4:36
9:7 [i] Dt 20:6; Pr 27:18
9:9 [j] Dt 25:4; 1Ti 5:18 [k] Dt 22:1-4
9:10 [l] Ro 4:23, 24 [m] 2Ti 2:6
9:11 [n] Ro 15:27
9:12 [o] Ac 18:3 [p] 2Co 11:7-12
9:13 [q] Lev 6:16, 26; Dt 18:1
9:14 [r] Mt 10:10; 1Ti 5:18
9:15 [s] Ac 18:3 [t] 2Co 11:9, 10
9:16 [u] Ro 1:14; Ac 9:15
9:17 [v] 1Co 3:8, 14 [w] Gal 2:7; Col 1:25
9:18 [x] 2Co 11:7; 12:13
9:19 [y] ver 1 [z] Gal 5:13 [a] Mt 18:15; 1Pe 3:1
9:20 [b] Ac 16:3; 21:20-26; Ro 11:14

STRONGER/ WEAKER BELIEVERS

Advice to:	
Stronger believer	Don't be proud of your maturity; don't flaunt your freedom. Act in love so you do not cause a weaker believer to stumble.
Weaker believer	Although you may not feel the same freedom in some areas as in others, take your time, pray to God, but do not force others to adhere to your stipulations. You would hinder other believers by making up rules and standards for how everyone ought to behave. Make sure your convictions are based on God's word, and are not simply an expression of your opinions.
Pastors and leaders	Teach correctly from God's word, helping Christians understand what is right and wrong in God's eyes, and helping them see that they can have varied opinions on other issues and still be unified. Don't allow potential problems to get out of hand, causing splits and divisions.

Paul advises those who are more mature in the faith about how they must care about their brothers and sisters in Christ who have more tender consciences; those "weaker" brothers and sisters are advised concerning their growth; and pastors and leaders are instructed on how to deal with the conflicts that could easily arise between these groups.

ample, led the way to an agreement at the Jerusalem council in Acts 15, and wrote the book of James.

9:13 As part of their pay, priests in the temple would receive a portion of the offerings as their food (see Numbers 18:8–24).

9:16 Preaching the gospel was Paul's gift and calling, and he said he couldn't stop preaching even if he wanted to. Paul was driven by the desire to do what God wanted, using his gifts for God's glory. What special gifts has God given you? Are you motivated, like Paul, to honour God with your gifts?

9:19–27 In 9:19–22 Paul asserts that he has freedom to do anything; in 9:24–27 he emphasises a life of strict discipline. The Christian life involves both freedom and discipline. The goals of Paul's life were to glorify God and bring people to Christ. Thus he stayed free of any philosophical position or material entanglement that might side-track him, while he strictly disciplined himself to carry out his goal. For Paul, both freedom and discipline were important tools to be used in God's service.

like one not having the law[c] (though I am not free from God's law but am under
Christ's law), so as to win those not having the law. 22 To the weak I became weak,
to win the weak. I have become all things to all men[d] so that by all possible means
I might save some.[e] 23 I do all this for the sake of the gospel, that I may share in its
blessings.
24 Do you not know that in a race all the runners run, but only one gets the prize?
Run[f] in such a way as to get the prize. 25 Everyone who competes in the games goes
into strict training. They do it to get a crown that will not last; but we do it to get
a crown that will last for ever.[g] 26 Therefore I do not run like a man running aimlessly;
I do not fight like a man beating the air. 27 No, I beat my body[h] and make it my slave
so that after I have preached to others, I myself will not be disqualified for the prize.

Warnings From Israel's History

10 For I do not want you to be ignorant of the fact, brothers, that our forefathers
were all under the cloud[a] and that they all passed through the sea.[b] 2 They were
all baptised into Moses in the cloud and in the sea. 3 They all ate the same spiritual
food 4 and drank the same spiritual drink; for they drank from the spiritual rock[c] that
accompanied them, and that rock was Christ. 5 Nevertheless, God was not pleased with
most of them; their bodies were scattered over the desert.[d]
6 Now these things occurred as examples[a] to keep us from setting our hearts on evil
things as they did. 7 Do not be idolaters,[e] as some of them were; as it is written: "The
people sat down to eat and drink and got up to indulge in pagan revelry."[b][f] 8 We
should not commit sexual immorality, as some of them did—and in one day twenty-
three thousand of them died.[g] 9 We should not test the Lord, as some of them
did—and were killed by snakes.[h] 10 And do not grumble, as some of them did[i]—and
were killed[j] by the destroying angel.[k]
11 These things happened to them as examples and were written down as warnings
for us, on whom the fulfilment of the ages has come.[l] 12 So, if you think you are
standing firm,[m] be careful that you don't fall! 13 No temptation has seized you except

[a] *6* Or *types*; also in verse 11 [b] *7* Exodus 32:6

9:21 [c] Ro 2:12, 14
9:22 [d] 1Co 10:33 [e] Ro 11:14
9:24 [f] Gal 2:2; 2Ti 4:7; Heb 12:1
9:25 [g] Jas 1:12; Rev 2:10
9:27 [h] Ro 8:13
10:1 [a] Ex 13:21 [b] Ex 14:22, 29
10:4 [c] Ex 17:6; Nu 20:11; Ps 78:15
10:5 [d] Nu 14:29; Heb 3:17
10:7 [e] ver 14 [f] Ex 32:4, 6, 19
10:8 [g] Nu 25:1-9
10:9 [h] Nu 21:5, 6
10:10 [i] Nu 16:41 [j] Nu 16:49 [k] Ex 12:23
10:11 [l] Ro 13:11
10:12 [m] Ro 11:20

9:22, 23 Paul gives several important principles for ministry: (1) find common ground with those you contact; (2) avoid a know-it-all attitude; (3) make others feel accepted; (4) be sensitive to their needs and concerns; and (5) look for opportunities to tell them about Christ. These principles are just as valid for us as they were for Paul.

9:24–27 Winning a race requires purpose and discipline. Paul uses this illustration to explain that the Christian life takes hard work, self-denial, and gruelling preparation. As Christians, we are running towards our heavenly reward. The essential disciplines of prayer, Bible study, and worship equip us to run with vigour and stamina. Don't merely observe from the grandstand; don't just turn out to jog a couple of laps each morning. Train diligently—your spiritual progress depends upon it.

9:25 At times we must even give up something good in order to do what God wants. Each person's special duties determine the discipline and denial that he or she must accept. Without a goal, discipline is nothing but self-punishment. With the goal of pleasing God, our denial seems like nothing compared to the eternal, imperishable reward that will be ours.

9:27 When Paul says he might be disqualified, he does not mean that he could lose his salvation, but rather that he could lose his privilege of telling others about Christ. It is easy to tell others how to live and then not to take our own advice. We must be careful to practise what we preach.

10:1ff In chapter 9 Paul used himself as an example of a mature Christian who disciplines himself to better serve God. In chapter 10, he uses Israel as an example of spiritual immaturity, shown in their over-confidence and lack of self-discipline.

10:1–5 The cloud and the sea mentioned here refer to Israel's escape from slavery in Egypt when God led them by a cloud and brought them safely through the Red Sea (Exodus 14). The spiritual food and drink are the miraculous provisions God gave as they travelled through the desert (Exodus 15; 16).

10:2 "Baptised into Moses" means that just as we are united in Christ by baptism, so the Israelites were united under Moses' leadership in the events of the exodus.

10:7–10 The incident referred to in 10:7 is when the Israelites made a golden calf and worshipped it in the desert (Exodus 32). The incident in 10:8 is recorded in Numbers 25:1–9 when the Israelites worshipped Baal of Peor and engaged in sexual immorality with Moabite women. The reference in 10:9 is to the Israelites' complaint about their food (Numbers 21:5, 6). They put the Lord to the test by seeing how far they could go. In 10:10, Paul refers to when the people complained against Moses and Aaron, and the plague that resulted (Numbers 14:2, 36; 16:41–50). The destroying angel is referred to in Exodus 12:23.

10:11 Today's pressures make it easy to ignore or forget the lessons of the past. But Paul cautions us to remember the lessons the Israelites learned about God so we can avoid repeating their errors. The key to remembering is to study the Bible regularly so that these lessons remind us of how God wants us to live. We need not repeat their mistakes!

10:13 In a culture filled with moral depravity and sin-inducing pressures, Paul gave strong encouragement to the Corinthians about temptation. He said: (1) wrong desires and temptations happen to everyone, so don't feel you've been singled out; (2) others have resisted temptation, and so can you; (3) any temptation can be resisted because God will help you resist it. God helps you resist temptation by helping you (1) recognise those people and situations that give you trouble, (2) run from anything you know is

10:13 [n] 1Co 1:9 [o] 2Pe 2:9
10:16 [p] Mt 26:26-28
10:17 [q] Ro 12:5; 1Co 12:27
10:18 [r] Lev 7:6, 14, 15
10:19 [s] 1Co 8:4
10:20 [t] Dt 32:17; Ps 106:37; Rev 9:20
10:21 [u] 2Co 6:15, 16
10:22 [v] Dt 32:16, 21 [w] Ecc 6:10; Isa 45:9

what is common to man. And God is faithful;[n] he will not let you be tempted beyond
what you can bear.[o] But when you are tempted, he will also provide a way out so
that you can stand up under it.

Idol Feasts and the Lord's Supper

14 Therefore, my dear friends, flee from idolatry. 15 I speak to sensible people; judge
for yourselves what I say. 16 Is not the cup of thanksgiving for which we give thanks
a participation in the blood of Christ? And is not the bread that we break a participation
in the body of Christ?[p] 17 Because there is one loaf, we, who are many, are one
body,[q] for we all partake of the one loaf.
18 Consider the people of Israel: Do not those who eat the sacrifices[r] participate
in the altar? 19 Do I mean then that a sacrifice offered to an idol is anything, or that
an idol is anything?[s] 20 No, but the sacrifices of pagans are offered to demons,[t] not
to God, and I do not want you to be participants with demons. 21 You cannot drink
the cup of the Lord and the cup of demons too; you cannot have a part in both the
Lord's table and the table of demons.[u] 22 Are we trying to arouse the Lord's jealousy?[v] Are we stronger than he?[w]

WHY WE DON'T GIVE UP

Perseverance, persistence, the prize! The Christian life was never promised as an easy way to live; instead, Paul constantly reminds us that we must have a purpose and a plan because times will be difficult and Satan will attack. But we never persevere without the promise of a prize—a promise God will keep.

Reference	*The Purpose*	*The Plan*	*The Prize*
1 Corinthians 9:24–27	• Run to get the prize • Run straight to the goal	• Deny yourself whatever is potentially harmful • Discipline your body, training it	• A crown that will last for ever
Galatians 6:7–10	• Don't become weary in doing good • Don't get discouraged and give up • Do good to everyone	• Sow to please the Spirit	• Reap eternal life
Ephesians 6:10–20	• Put on the full armour of God • Pray on all occasions	• Use all the pieces of God's armour provided for you	• Taking our stand against the devil's schemes
Philippians 3:12–14	• Press on towards the day when you will be all God wants you to be	• Forget the past, strain towards what is ahead	• The prize for which God calls us heavenward
2 Timothy 2:1–13	• Entrust these great truths to people who will teach them to others • Be strong in Christ's grace, even when your faith is faltering	• Endure hardship like a soldier, and don't get involved in worldly affairs • Follow the Lord's rules, as an athlete must do in order to win • Work hard, like a farmer who tends his crops for the harvest	• We will live with Christ; we will reign with him • He always remains faithful to us and always carries out his promises

wrong, (3) choose to do only what is right, (4) pray for God's help, and (5) seek friends who love God and can offer help when you are tempted. Running from a tempting situation is your first step on the way to victory (see 2 Timothy 2:22).

10:14 Idol worship was the major expression of religion in Corinth. There were several pagan temples in the city, and they were very popular. The statues of wood or stone were not evil in themselves, but people gave them credit for what only God could do, such as provide good weather, crops, and children. Idolatry is still a serious problem today, but it takes a different form. We don't put our trust in statues of wood and stone, but in paper money and plastic cards. Trusting anything for what God alone provides is idolatry. Our modern idols are those symbols of power, pleasure, or prestige that we so highly regard. When we understand contemporary parallels to idolatry, Paul's words to "flee from idolatry" become much more meaningful.

10:16–21 The idea of unity and fellowship with God through eating a sacrifice was strong in Judaism and Christianity as well as in paganism. In Old Testament days, when a Jew offered a sacrifice, he ate a part of that sacrifice as a way of restoring his unity with God, against whom he had sinned (Deuteronomy 12:17, 18). Similarly, Christians participate in Christ's once-for-all sacrifice when they eat the bread and drink the wine symbolising his body and blood. Recent converts from paganism could not help being affected if they knowingly ate with pagans in their feasts the meat offered to idols.

10:21 As followers of Christ we must give him our total allegiance. We cannot, as Paul explains, have a part in "both the Lord's table and the table of demons". Eating at the Lord's table means communing with Christ and identifying with his death. Eating at the demons' table means identifying with Satan by worshipping or promoting pagan (or evil) activities. Are you trying to lead two lives, following the desires of both Christ and the crowd? The Bible says that you can't do both at the same time.

The Believer's Freedom

23"Everything is permissible"—but not everything is beneficial.[x] "Everything is
permissible"—but not everything is constructive. 24Nobody should seek his own
good, but the good of others.[y]
25Eat anything sold in the meat market without raising questions of conscience,[z]
26for, "The earth is the Lord's, and everything in it."[c][a]
27If some unbeliever invites you to a meal and you want to go, eat whatever is put
before you[b] without raising questions of conscience. 28But if anyone says to you,
"This has been offered in sacrifice," then do not eat it, both for the sake of the man
who told you and for conscience' sake[d][c]—29the other man's conscience, I mean,
not yours. For why should my freedom[d] be judged by another's conscience? 30If I
take part in the meal with thankfulness, why am I denounced because of something
I thank God for?[e]
31So whether you eat or drink or whatever you do, do it all for the glory of God.[f]
32Do not cause anyone to stumble,[g] whether Jews, Greeks or the church of
God[h]—33even as I try to please everybody in every way.[i] For I am not seeking my
11 own good but the good of many, so that they may be saved.[j] 1Follow my
example,[a] as I follow the example of Christ.

3. Instruction on public worship

Propriety in Worship

2I praise you[b] for remembering me in everything[c] and for holding to the teachings,[a] just as I passed them on to you.[d]

c *26* Psalm 24:1 d *28* Some manuscripts *conscience' sake, for "the earth is the Lord's and everything in it"*
a *2* Or *traditions*

10:23 [x]1Co 6:12
10:24 [y]ver 33; Ro 15:1, 2; 1Co 13:5; Php 2:4, 21
10:25 [z]Ac 10:15; 1Co 8:7
10:26 [a]Ps 24:1
10:27 [b]Lk 10:7
10:28 [c]1Co 8:7, 10-12
10:29 [d]Ro 14:16; 1Co 9:1, 19
10:30 [e]Ro 14:6
10:31 [f]Col 3:17; 1Pe 4:11
10:32 [g]Ac 24:16 [h]Ac 20:28
10:33 [i]Ro 15:2; 1Co 9:22
10:33 [j]Ro 11:14
11:1 [a]1Co 4:16
11:2 [b]ver 17, 22 [c]1Co 4:17 [d]1Co 15:2, 3; 2Th 2:15

10:23, 24 Sometimes it's hard to know when to defer to the weaker believer. Paul gives a simple rule of thumb to help in making the decision—we should be sensitive and gracious. While some actions may not be wrong, they may not be in the best interest of others. While we have freedom in Christ, we shouldn't exercise our freedom at the cost of hurting a Christian brother or sister. We are not to consider only ourselves, but we must be sensitive to others. For more on the proper attitude towards a weaker believer, see the notes on 8:10–13 and Romans 14.

10:25–27 Paul gave one answer to the dilemma—to buy whatever meat is sold at the market without asking whether it was offered to idols. It doesn't matter anyway, and no-one's conscience would be troubled. When we become too worried about our every action, we become legalistic and cannot enjoy life. Everything belongs to God, and he has given us all things to enjoy. If we know something is a problem, then we can deal with it, but we don't need to go looking for problems.

10:28–33 Why should we be limited by another person's conscience? Simply because we are to do all things for God's glory, even our eating and drinking. Nothing we do should cause another believer to stumble. We do what is best for others, so that they might be saved. On the other hand, Christians should not make a career out of being the weaker person with over-sensitive consciences. Christian leaders and teachers should carefully teach about the freedom we have in matters not expressly forbidden by Scripture.

10:31 God's love must so permeate our motives that all we do will be for his glory. Keep this as a guiding principle by asking, "Is this action glorifying God?" or "How can I honour God through this action?"

10:33 Paul's criterion for all his actions was not what he liked best, but what was best for those around him. The opposite attitude would be: (1) being insensitive and doing what we want, no matter who is hurt by it; (2) being over-sensitive and doing nothing, for fear that someone may be displeased; (3) being a "yes person" by going along with everything, trying to gain approval from people rather than from God. In this age of "me first" and "looking out for number one", Paul's startling statement is a good standard. If we make the good of others one of our primary goals, we will develop a serving attitude that pleases God.

11:1 Why did Paul say, "Follow my example"? Paul wasn't being arrogant—he did not think of himself as sinless. At this time, however, the Corinthian believers did not know much about the life and ministry of Christ. Paul could not tell them to imitate Jesus, because the Gospels had not yet been written, so they did not know what Jesus was like. The best way to point these new Christians to Christ was to point them to a Christian whom they trusted (see also Galatians 4:12; Philippians 3:17; 1 Thessalonians 1:6; 2:14; 2 Thessalonians 3:7, 9). Paul had been in Corinth almost two years and had built a relationship of trust with many of these new believers.

11:2ff In this section Paul's main concern is irreverence in worship. We need to read it in the context of the situation in Corinth. The matter of wearing hats or head coverings, although seemingly insignificant, had become a big problem because two cultural backgrounds were colliding. Jewish women always covered their heads in worship. For a woman to uncover her head in public was a sign of loose morals. On the other hand, Greek women may have been used to worshipping without head coverings.

In this letter Paul had already spoken about divisions and disorder in the church. Both are involved in this issue. Paul's solution comes from his desire for unity among church members and for appropriateness in the worship service. He accepted God's sovereignty in creating the rules for relationships.

11:2–16 This section focuses primarily on proper attitudes and conduct in worship, not on the marriage relationship or on the role of women in the church. While Paul's specific instructions may be cultural (women covering their heads in worship), the principles behind his specific instructions are timeless, principles like respect for spouse, reverence and appropriateness in worship, and focus of all of life on God. If anything you do can easily offend members and divide the church, then change your ways to promote church unity. Thus Paul told the women who were not wearing head coverings to wear them, not because it was a Scriptural command, but because it kept the congregation from dividing over a petty issue that served only to take people's minds off Christ.

11:3 [e]Eph 1:22 [f]Ge 3:16; Eph 5:23 [g]1Co 3:23
11:5 [h]Ac 21:9 [i]Dt 21:12
11:7 [j]Ge 1:26; Jas 3:9
11:8 [k]Ge 2:21-23; 1Ti 2:13
11:9 [l]Ge 2:18
11:12 [m]Ro 11:36

3 Now I want you to realise that the head of every man is Christ,[e] and the head
of the woman is man,[f] and the head of Christ is God.[g] 4 Every man who prays or
prophesies with his head covered dishonours his head. 5 And every woman who prays
or prophesies[h] with her head uncovered dishonours her head—it is just as though her
head were shaved.[i] 6 If a woman does not cover her head, she should have her hair
cut off; and if it is a disgrace for a woman to have her hair cut or shaved off, she should
cover her head. 7 A man ought not to cover his head,**[b]** since he is the image[j] and
glory of God; but the woman is the glory of man. 8 For man did not come from woman,
but woman from man;[k] 9 neither was man created for woman, but woman for man.[l]
10 For this reason, and because of the angels, the woman ought to have a sign of
authority on her head.

11 In the Lord, however, woman is not independent of man, nor is man independent
of woman. 12 For as woman came from man, so also man is born of woman. But
everything comes from God.[m] 13 Judge for yourselves: Is it proper for a woman to
pray to God with her head uncovered? 14 Does not the very nature of things teach you

b *4-7* Or *4 Every man who prays or prophesies with long hair dishonours his head. 5 And every woman who prays or prophesies with no covering of hair, on her head dishonours her head—she is just like one of the "shorn women". 6 If a woman has no covering, let her be for now with short hair, but since it is a disgrace for a woman to have her hair shorn or shaved, she should grow it again. 7 A man ought not to have long hair*

MAKING CHOICES IN SENSITIVE ISSUES

If I choose one course of action:

... does it help my witness for Christ? (9:19–22)
... am I motivated by a desire to help others to know Christ? (9:23; 10:33)
... does it help me do my best? (9:25)
... is it against a specific command in Scripture and would thus cause me to sin? (10:12)
... is it the best and most beneficial course of action? (10:23, 33)
... am I thinking only of myself, or do I truly care about the other person? (10:24)
... am I acting lovingly or selfishly? (10:28–31)
... does it glorify God? (10:31)
... will it cause someone else to sin? (10:32)

All of us make hundreds of choices every day. Most choices have no right or wrong attached to them—like what we wear or what we eat. But we always face decisions that carry a little more weight. We don't want to do wrong, and we don't want to cause others to do wrong, so how can we make such decisions?

11:3 In the phrase, "the head of the woman is man", *head* is not used to indicate control or supremacy, but rather, "the source of". Because man was created first, the woman derives her existence from man, as man does from Christ and Christ from God. Evidently Paul was correcting some excesses in worship that the emancipated Corinthian women were engaging in.

11:3 Submission is a key element in the smooth functioning of any business, government, or family. God ordained submission in certain relationships to prevent chaos. It is essential to understand that submission is not surrender, withdrawal, or apathy. It does not mean inferiority, because God created all people in his image and because all have equal value. Submission is mutual commitment and co-operation.

Thus God calls for submission among *equals*. He did not make the man superior; he made a way for the man and woman to work together. Jesus Christ, although equal with God the Father, submitted to him to carry out the plan for salvation. Likewise, although equal to man under God, the wife should submit to her husband for the sake of their marriage and family. Submission between equals is submission by choice, not by force. We serve God in these relationships by willingly submitting to others in our church, to our spouses, and to our government leaders.

11:9–11 God created lines of authority in order for his created world to function smoothly. Although there must be lines of authority, even in marriage, there should *not* be lines of superiority. God created men and women with unique and complementary characteristics. One sex is not better than the other. We must not let the issue of authority and submission become a wedge to destroy oneness in marriage. Instead, we should use our unique gifts to strengthen our marriages and to glorify God.

11:10 "Because of the angels, the woman ought to have a sign of authority on her head" may mean that the woman should wear a covering on her head as a sign that she is under the man's authority. This is a fact even the angels understand as they observe Christians in worship. See the note on 11:2ff for an explanation of head coverings.

11:14, 15 In talking about head coverings and length of hair, Paul is saying that believers should look and behave in ways that are honourable within their own culture. In many cultures long hair on men is considered appropriate and masculine. In Corinth, it was thought to be a sign of male prostitution in the pagan temples. And women with short hair were labelled prostitutes. Paul was saying that in the Corinthian culture, Christian women should keep their hair long. If short hair on women was a sign of prostitution, then a Christian woman with short hair would find it even more difficult to be a believable witness for Jesus Christ. Paul wasn't saying we should adopt all the practices of our culture, but that we should avoid appearances and behaviour that detract from our ultimate goal of being believable witnesses for Jesus Christ while demonstrating our Christian faith.

that if a man has long hair, it is a disgrace to him, 15but that if a woman has long
hair, it is her glory? For long hair is given to her as a covering. 16If anyone wants
to be contentious about this, we have no other practice — nor do the churches of God.[n]

The Lord's Supper

17In the following directives I have no praise for you,[o] for your meetings do more
harm than good. 18In the first place, I hear that when you come together as a church,
there are divisions[p] among you, and to some extent I believe it. 19No doubt there
have to be differences among you to show which of you have God's approval.[q]
20When you come together, it is not the Lord's Supper you eat, 21for as you eat, each
of you goes ahead without waiting for anybody else.[r] One remains hungry, another
gets drunk. 22Don't you have homes to eat and drink in? Or do you despise the church
of God[s] and humiliate those who have nothing?[t] What shall I say to you? Shall I
praise you[u] for this? Certainly not!
23For I received from the Lord[v] what I also passed on to you:[w] The Lord Jesus,
on the night he was betrayed, took bread, 24and when he had given thanks, he broke
it and said, "This is my body, which is for you; do this in remembrance of me." 25In
the same way, after supper he took the cup, saying, "This cup is the new covenant[x]
in my blood;[y] do this, whenever you drink it, in remembrance of me." 26For
whenever you eat this bread and drink this cup, you proclaim the Lord's death until
he comes.

11:16 [n] 1Co 7:17
11:17 [o] ver 2, 22
11:18 [p] 1Co 1:10-12; 3:3
11:19 [q] 1Jn 2:19
11:21 [r] 2Pe 2:13; Jude 12
11:22 [s] 1Co 10:32 [t] Jas 2:6 [u] ver 2, 17
11:23 [v] Gal 1:12 [w] 1Co 15:3
11:25 [x] Lk 22:20 [y] 1Co 10:16

11:17–34 The Lord's Supper (11:20) is a visible representation of the Good News of the death of Christ for our sins. It reminds us of Christ's death and the glorious hope of his return. Our participation in it strengthens our faith through fellowship with Christ and with other believers.

11:19 Paul allows that there might be differences among church members. When they develop into self-willed divisions, they are destructive to the congregation. Those who cause division only serve to highlight those who are genuine believers.

11:21, 22 When the Lord's Supper was celebrated in the early church, it included a feast or fellowship meal followed by the celebration of Communion. In the church in Corinth, the fellowship meal had become a time when some ate and drank excessively while others went hungry. There was little sharing and caring. This certainly did not demonstrate the unity and love that should characterise the church, nor was it a preparation for Communion. Paul condemned these actions and reminded the church of the real purpose of the Lord's Supper.

11:24, 25 What does the Lord's Supper mean? The early church remembered that Jesus instituted the Lord's Supper on the night of the Passover meal (Luke 22:13–20). Just as Passover celebrated deliverance from slavery in Egypt, so the Lord's Supper celebrates deliverance from sin by Christ's death.

Christians pose several different possibilities for what Christ meant when he said, "This is my body". (1) Some believe that the wine and bread actually become Christ's physical blood and body. (2) Others believe that the bread and wine remain unchanged, but Christ is spiritually present with the bread and wine. (3) Still others believe that the bread and wine symbolise Christ's body and blood. Christians generally agree, however, that participating in the Lord's Supper is an important element in the Christian faith and that Christ's presence, however we understand it, strengthens us spiritually.

11:25 What is this new covenant? In the old covenant, people could approach God only through the priests and the sacrificial system. Jesus' death on the cross ushered in the new covenant or agreement between God and us. Now all people can personally approach God and communicate with him. The people of Israel first entered into this agreement after their exodus from Egypt (Exodus 24), and it was designed to point to the day when Jesus Christ would come. The new covenant completes, rather than replaces, the old covenant, fulfilling everything the old covenant looked forward to (see Jeremiah 31:31–34). Eating the bread and drinking the cup shows that we are remembering Christ's death for us and renewing our commitment to serve him.

11:25 Jesus said, "Do this, whenever you drink it, in remembrance of me." How do we remember Christ in the Lord's Supper? By thinking about what he did and why he did it. If the Lord's Supper becomes just a ritual or a pious habit, it no longer remembers Christ, and it loses its significance.

11:27ff Paul gives specific instructions on how the Lord's Supper should be observed. (1) We should take the Lord's Supper thoughtfully because we are proclaiming that Christ died for our sins (11:26). (2) We should take it worthily, with due reverence and respect (11:27). (3) We should examine ourselves for any unconfessed sin or resentful attitude (11:28). We are to be properly prepared, based on our belief in and love for Christ. (4) We should be considerate of others (11:33), waiting until everyone is there and then eating in an orderly and unified manner.

11:27–34 When Paul said that no-one should take the Lord's Supper in an unworthy manner, he was speaking to the church members who were rushing into it without thinking of its meaning. Those who did so were "guilty of sinning against the body and blood of the Lord". Instead of honouring his sacrifice, they were sharing in the guilt of those who crucified Christ. In reality, *no-one* is worthy to take the Lord's Supper. We are all sinners saved by grace. This is why we should prepare ourselves for Communion through healthy introspection, confession of sin, and resolution of differences with others. These actions remove the barriers that affect our relationship with Christ and with other believers. Awareness of your sin should not keep you away from Communion but should drive you to participate in it.

11:29 "Without recognising the body of the Lord" means not understanding what the Lord's Supper means and not distinguishing it from a normal meal. Those who do so condemn themselves (see 11:27).

11:27
[z]Heb 10:29
11:28
[a]2Co 13:5
11:31
[b]Ps 32:5; 1Jn 1:9
11:32
[c]Ps 94:12; Heb 12:7-10; Rev 3:19
11:34
[d]ver 21
[e]ver 22
[f]1Co 4:19
12:1
[a]Ro 1:11; 1Co 14:1, 37
12:2
[b]Eph 2:11, 12; 1Pe 4:3
[c]Ps 115:5; Jer 10:5; Hab 2:18, 19; 1Th 1:9
12:3
[d]Ro 9:3
[e]Jn 13:13
[f]1Jn 4:2, 3
12:4
[g]Ro 12:4-8; Eph 4:11; Heb 2:4
12:6
[h]Eph 4:6
12:7
[i]Eph 4:12
12:8
[j]1Co 2:6
[k]2Co 8:7
12:9
[l]Mt 17:19, 20; 2Co 4:13
[m]ver 28, 30
12:10
[n]Gal 3:5
[o]1Jn 4:1
[p]Mk 16:17
12:11
[q]ver 4

27 Therefore, whoever eats the bread or drinks the cup of the Lord in an unworthy
manner will be guilty of sinning against the body and blood of the Lord.[z] 28 A man
ought to examine himself[a] before he eats of the bread and drinks of the cup. 29 For
anyone who eats and drinks without recognising the body of the Lord eats and drinks
judgment on himself. 30 That is why many among you are weak and sick, and a number
of you have fallen asleep. 31 But if we judged ourselves, we would not come under
judgment.[b] 32 When we are judged by the Lord, we are being disciplined[c] so that
we will not be condemned with the world.
33 So then, my brothers, when you come together to eat, wait for each other. 34 If
anyone is hungry,[d] he should eat at home,[e] so that when you meet together it may
not result in judgment.
And when I come[f] I will give further directions.

Spiritual Gifts

12 Now about spiritual gifts,[a] brothers, I do not want you to be ignorant. 2 You
know that when you were pagans,[b] somehow or other you were influenced and
led astray to mute idols.[c] 3 Therefore I tell you that no-one who is speaking by the
Spirit of God says, "Jesus be cursed,"[d] and no-one can say, "Jesus is Lord,"[e] except
by the Holy Spirit.[f]
4 There are different kinds of gifts, but the same Spirit.[g] 5 There are different kinds
of service, but the same Lord. 6 There are different kinds of working, but the same
God[h] works all of them in all men.
7 Now to each one the manifestation of the Spirit is given for the common good.[i]
8 To one there is given through the Spirit the message of wisdom,[j] to another the
message of knowledge[k] by means of the same Spirit, 9 to another faith[l] by the same
Spirit, to another gifts of healing[m] by that one Spirit, 10 to another miraculous powers,[n] to another prophecy, to another distinguishing between spirits,[o] to another
speaking in different kinds of tongues,[a][p] and to still another the interpretation of
tongues.[a] 11 All these are the work of one and the same Spirit,[q] and he gives them
to each one, just as he determines.

[a] *10* Or *languages*; also in verse 28

11:30 "Fallen asleep" is another way of describing death. That some of the people had died may have been a special supernatural judgment on the Corinthian church. This type of disciplinary judgment highlights the seriousness of the Communion service. The Lord's Supper is not to be taken lightly; this new covenant cost Jesus his life. It is not a meaningless ritual, but a sacrament given by Christ to help strengthen our faith.

11:34 People should come to this meal desiring to fellowship with other believers and prepare for the Lord's Supper to follow, not to fill up on a big dinner. "If anyone is hungry, he should eat at home" means that they should eat dinner beforehand, so as to come to the fellowship meal in the right frame of mind.

12:1ff The spiritual gifts given to each person by the Holy Spirit are special abilities that are to be used to minister to the needs of the body of believers. This chapter is not an exhaustive list of spiritual gifts (see Romans 12; Ephesians 4; 1 Peter 4:10, 11 for more examples). There are many gifts, some people have different gifts, some people have more than one gift, and one gift is not superior to another. All spiritual gifts come from the Holy Spirit, and their purpose is to build up Christ's body, the church.

12:1ff Instead of building up and unifying the Corinthian church, the issue of spiritual gifts was splitting it. Spiritual gifts had become symbols of spiritual power, causing rivalries because some people thought they were more "spiritual" than others because of their gifts. This was a terrible misuse of spiritual gifts because their purpose is always to help the church function more effectively, not to divide it. We can be divisive if we insist on using our gift our own way without being sensitive to others. We must never use gifts as a means of manipulating others or serving our own self-interest.

12:3 Anyone can claim to speak for God, and the world is full of false teachers. Paul gives us a test to help us discern whether or not a messenger is really from God: does he or she confess Christ as Lord? Don't naively accept the words of all who claim to speak for God; test their credentials by finding out what they teach about Christ.

12:9 All Christians have faith. Some, however, have the spiritual gift of faith, which is an unusual measure of trust in the Holy Spirit's power.

12:10, 11 "Prophecy" is not just a prediction about the future; it can also mean preaching God's word with power. "Distinguishing between spirits" means the ability to discern whether a person who claims to speak for God is actually doing so, or is speaking by an evil spirit. (Paul discusses tongues and their interpretation in more detail in chapter 14.) No matter what gift(s) a person has, each gift is given by the Holy Spirit. The Holy Spirit decides which gifts each one of us should have. We are responsible to use and sharpen our gifts, but we can take no credit for what God has freely given us.

One Body, Many Parts

12The body is a unit, though it is made up of many parts; and though all its parts
are many, they form one body.[r] So it is with Christ.[s] 13For we were all baptised
by[b] one Spirit[t] into one body—whether Jews or Greeks, slave or free[u]—and we
were all given the one Spirit to drink.[v]
14Now the body is not made up of one part but of many. 15If the foot should say,
"Because I am not a hand, I do not belong to the body," it would not for that reason
cease to be part of the body. 16And if the ear should say, "Because I am not an eye,
I do not belong to the body," it would not for that reason cease to be part of the body.
17If the whole body were an eye, where would the sense of hearing be? If the whole
body were an ear, where would the sense of smell be? 18But in fact God has arranged[w]
the parts in the body, every one of them, just as he wanted them to be.[x] 19If they
were all one part, where would the body be? 20As it is, there are many parts, but one
body.[y]
21The eye cannot say to the hand, "I don't need you!" And the head cannot say to
the feet, "I don't need you!" 22On the contrary, those parts of the body that seem to
be weaker are indispensable, 23and the parts that we think are less honourable we treat
with special honour. And the parts that are unpresentable are treated with special
modesty, 24while our presentable parts need no special treatment. But God has
combined the members of the body and has given greater honour to the parts that
lacked it, 25so that there should be no division in the body, but that its parts should
have equal concern for each other. 26If one part suffers, every part suffers with it; if
one part is honoured, every part rejoices with it.
27Now you are the body of Christ,[z] and each one of you is a part of it.[a] 28And
in the church[b] God has appointed first of all apostles,[c] second prophets, third
teachers, then workers of miracles, also those having gifts of healing,[d] those able to
help others, those with gifts of administration,[e] and those speaking in different kinds
of tongues.[f] 29Are all apostles? Are all prophets? Are all teachers? Do all work
miracles? 30Do all have gifts of healing? Do all speak in tongues?[c][g] Do all interpret?
31But eagerly desire[d][h] the greater gifts.

b *13* Or *with*; or *in* **c** *30* Or *other languages* **d** *31* Or *But you are eagerly desiring*

12:12 [r]Ro 12:5 [s]ver 27
12:13 [t]Eph 2:18 [u]Gal 3:28; Col 3:11 [v]Jn 7:37-39
12:18 [w]ver 28 [x]ver 11
12:20 [y]ver 12, 14
12:27 [z]Eph 1:23; 4:12; Col 1:18, 24 [a]Ro 12:5
12:28 [b]1Co 10:32 [c]Eph 4:11 [d]ver 9 [e]Ro 12:6-8 [f]ver 10
12:30 [g]ver 10
12:31 [h]1Co 14:1, 39

12:12 Paul compares the body of Christ to a human body. Each part has a specific function that is necessary to the body as a whole. The parts are different for a purpose, and in their differences they must work together. Christians must avoid two common errors: (1) being too proud of their abilities, or (2) thinking they have nothing to give to the body of believers. Instead of comparing ourselves to one another, we should use our different gifts, together, to spread the Good News of salvation.

12:13 The church is composed of many types of people from a variety of backgrounds with a multitude of gifts and abilities. It is easy for these differences to divide people, as was the case in Corinth. But despite the differences, all believers have one thing in common—faith in Christ. On this essential truth the church finds unity. All believers are baptised by one Holy Spirit into one body of believers, the church. We don't lose our individual identities, but we have an overriding oneness in Christ. When a person becomes a Christian, the Holy Spirit takes up residence, and he or she is born into God's family. "We were all given the one Spirit to drink" means that the same Holy Spirit completely fills our innermost beings. As members of God's family, we may have different interests and gifts, but we have a common goal.

12:14–24 Using the analogy of the body, Paul emphasises the importance of each church member (see the note on 12:12). If a seemingly insignificant part is taken away, the whole body becomes less effective. Thinking that your gift is more important than someone else's is an expression of spiritual pride. We should not look down on those who seem unimportant, and we should not be jealous of others who have impressive gifts. Instead, we should use the gifts we have been given and encourage others to use theirs. If we don't, the body of believers will be less effective.

12:25, 26 What is your response when a fellow Christian is honoured? How do you respond when someone is suffering? We are called to rejoice with those who rejoice and weep with those who weep (Romans 12:15). Too often, unfortunately, we are jealous of those who rejoice and apathetic towards those who weep. Believers are in the world together—there is no such thing as private or individualistic Christianity. We shouldn't stop with enjoying only our own relationship with God; we need to get involved in the lives of others.

12:30 Paul discusses the subject of speaking in and interpreting tongues in more detail in chapter 14.

12:31 The greater gifts are those that are more beneficial to the body of Christ. Paul has already made it clear that one gift is not superior to another, but he urges the believers to discover how they can serve Christ's body with the gifts God has given them. Your spiritual gifts are not for your own self-advancement. They were given to you for serving God and enhancing the spiritual growth of the body of believers.

13:1
[a]ver 8
13:2
[b]1Co 14:2
[c]1Co 12:9
[d]Mt 17:20; 21:21
13:3
[e]Mt 6:2
[f]Da 3:28
13:4
[g]1Th 5:14
13:5
[h]1Co 10:24
13:6
[i]2Th 2:12
[j]2Jn 4;
3Jn 3, 4
13:8
[k]ver 2
[l]ver 1
13:9
[m]ver 12;
1Co 8:2
13:10
[n]Php 3:12
13:12
[o]Ge 32:30;
2Co 5:7;
1Jn 3:2
[p]1Co 8:3
13:13
[q]Gal 5:5, 6
[r]1Co 16:14
14:1
[a]1Co 16:14
[b]ver 39;
1Co 12:31
[c]1Co 12:1
14:2
[d]Mk 16:17
[e]1Co 13:2
14:3
[f]ver 4, 5, 12, 17, 26;
Ro 14:19
14:4
[g]Mk 16:17
[h]1Co 13:2

Love

And now I will show you the most excellent way.
13 If I speak in the tongues[a][a] of men and of angels, but have not love, I am only
a resounding gong or a clanging cymbal. 2If I have the gift of prophecy and
can fathom all mysteries[b] and all knowledge, and if I have a faith[c] that can move
mountains,[d] but have not love, I am nothing. 3If I give all I possess to the poor[e]
and surrender my body to the flames,[b][f] but have not love, I gain nothing.
4Love is patient,[g] love is kind. It does not envy, it does not boast, it is not proud.
5It is not rude, it is not self-seeking,[h] it is not easily angered, it keeps no record of
wrongs. 6Love does not delight in evil[i] but rejoices with the truth.[j] 7It always
protects, always trusts, always hopes, always perseveres.
8Love never fails. But where there are prophecies,[k] they will cease; where there
are tongues,[l] they will be stilled; where there is knowledge, it will pass away. 9For
we know in part[m] and we prophesy in part, 10but when perfection comes,[n] the
imperfect disappears. 11When I was a child, I talked like a child, I thought like a child,
I reasoned like a child. When I became a man, I put childish ways behind me. 12Now
we see but a poor reflection as in a mirror; then we shall see face to face.[o] Now I
know in part; then I shall know fully, even as I am fully known.[p]
13And now these three remain: faith, hope and love.[q] But the greatest of these is
love.[r]

Gifts of Prophecy and Tongues

14 Follow the way of love[a] and eagerly desire[b] spiritual gifts,[c] especially the
gift of prophecy. 2For anyone who speaks in a tongue[a][d] does not speak to
men but to God. Indeed, no-one understands him; he utters mysteries[e] with his
spirit.[b] 3But everyone who prophesies speaks to men for their strengthening,[f]
encouragement and comfort. 4He who speaks in a tongue[g] edifies himself, but he who
prophesies[h] edifies the church. 5I would like every one of you to speak in tongues,[c]

a *1* Or *languages* **b** *3* Some early manuscripts *body that I may boast* **a** *2* Or *another language*; also in verses 4, 13, 14, 19, 26 and 27 **b** *2* Or *by the Spirit* **c** *5* Or *other languages*; also in verses 6, 18, 22, 23 and 39

13:1ff In chapter 12 Paul gave evidence of the Corinthians' lack of love in the utilisation of spiritual gifts; chapter 13 defines real love; and chapter 14 shows how love works. Love is more important than all the spiritual gifts exercised in the church body. Great faith, acts of dedication or sacrifice, and miracle-working power produce very little without love. Love makes our actions and gifts useful. Although people have different gifts, love is available to everyone.

13:4–7 Our society confuses love and lust. Unlike lust, God's kind of love is directed outward towards others, not inward towards ourselves. It is utterly unselfish. This kind of love goes against our natural inclinations. It is possible to practise this love only if God helps us set aside our own desires and instincts, so that we can give love while expecting nothing in return. Thus the more we become like Christ, the more love we will show to others.

13:10 God gives us spiritual gifts for our lives on earth in order to build up, serve, and strengthen fellow Christians. The spiritual gifts are for the church. In eternity, we will be made perfect and complete and will be in the very presence of God. We will no longer need the spiritual gifts, so they will come to an end.

13:12 Paul offers a glimpse into the future to give us hope that one day we will be complete when we see God face to face. This truth should strengthen our faith – we don't have all the answers now, but one day we will. Someday we will see Christ in person and be able to see with God's perspective.

13:13 In morally corrupt Corinth, love had become a mixed-up term with little meaning. Today people are still confused about love. Love is the greatest of all human qualities, and it is an attribute of God himself (1 John 4:8). Love involves unselfish service to others; to show it gives evidence that you care. *Faith* is the foundation and content of God's message; *hope* is the attitude and focus; *love* is the action. When faith and hope are in line, you are free to love completely because you understand how God loves.

14:1 Prophecy may involve predicting future events, but its main purpose is to communicate God's message to people, providing insight, warning, correction, and encouragement.

14:2 The gift of speaking in a tongue was a concern of the Corinthian church because the use of the gift had caused disorder in worship. Speaking in tongues is a legitimate gift of the Holy Spirit, but the Corinthian believers were using it as a sign of spiritual superiority rather than as a means to spiritual unity. Spiritual gifts are beneficial only when they are properly used to help everyone in the church. We should not exercise them only to make *ourselves* feel good.

14:2ff Paul makes several points about speaking in tongues: (1) it is a spiritual gift from God (14:2); (2) it is a desirable gift even though it isn't a requirement of faith (12:28–31); (3) it is less important than prophecy and teaching (14:4). Although Paul himself spoke in tongues, he stresses prophecy (preaching) because it benefits the whole church, while speaking in tongues primarily benefits the speaker. Public worship must be understandable and edifying to the whole church.

14:5–12 As musical instruments must play each note in order for the music to be clear, so Paul says words preached in the hearers' language are more clear and helpful. There are many languages in the world (14:10), and people who speak different languages can rarely understand each other. It is the same with speaking in tongues. Although this gift is helpful to many people in private worship, and helpful in public worship with interpretation, Paul says he would rather speak five words that his hearers can understand than 10,000 that they cannot (14:19).

but I would rather have you prophesy.[i] He who prophesies is greater than one who
speaks in tongues,[d] unless he interprets, so that the church may be edified.
6Now, brothers, if I come to you and speak in tongues, what good will I be to you,
unless I bring you some revelation[j] or knowledge or prophecy or word of instruction?[k]
7Even in the case of lifeless things that make sounds, such as the flute or harp,
how will anyone know what tune is being played unless there is a distinction in the
notes? 8Again, if the trumpet does not sound a clear call, who will get ready for
battle?[l] 9So it is with you. Unless you speak intelligible words with your tongue,
how will anyone know what you are saying? You will just be speaking into the air.
10Undoubtedly there are all sorts of languages in the world, yet none of them is without
meaning. 11If then I do not grasp the meaning of what someone is saying, I am a
foreigner to the speaker, and he is a foreigner to me. 12So it is with you. Since you
are eager to have spiritual gifts, try to excel in gifts that build up the church.
13For this reason anyone who speaks in a tongue should pray that he may interpret
what he says. 14For if I pray in a tongue, my spirit prays, but my mind is unfruitful.
15So what shall I do? I will pray with my spirit, but I will also pray with my mind;
I will sing[m] with my spirit, but I will also sing with my mind. 16If you are praising
God with your spirit, how can one who finds himself among those who do not
understand[e] say "Amen"[n] to your thanksgiving,[o] since he does not know what you
are saying? 17You may be giving thanks well enough, but the other man is not edified.
18I thank God that I speak in tongues more than all of you. 19But in the church I
would rather speak five intelligible words to instruct others than ten thousand words
in a tongue.
20Brothers, stop thinking like children.[p] In regard to evil be infants,[q] but in your
thinking be adults. 21In the Law[r] it is written:

"Through men of strange tongues
and through the lips of foreigners
I will speak to this people,
but even then they will not listen to me,"[f][s]

says the Lord.

22Tongues, then, are a sign, not for believers but for unbelievers; prophecy,[t]
however, is for believers, not for unbelievers. 23So if the whole church comes together
and everyone speaks in tongues, and some who do not understand[g] or some unbelievers
come in, will they not say that you are out of your mind?[u] 24But if an unbeliever
or someone who does not understand[h] comes in while everybody is prophesying, he
will be convinced by all that he is a sinner and will be judged by all, 25and the secrets
of his heart will be laid bare. So he will fall down and worship God, exclaiming, "God
is really among you!"[v]

Orderly Worship

26What then shall we say, brothers? When you come together, everyone[w] has a
hymn,[x] or a word of instruction,[y] a revelation, a tongue or an interpretation. All

[d] *5* Or *other languages*; also in verses 6, 18, 22, 23 and 39 [e] *16* Or *among the enquirers* [f] *21* Isaiah 28:11,12
[g] *23* Or *some enquirers* [h] *24* Or *or some enquirer*

14:5 [i] Nu 11:29
14:6 [j] ver 26; Eph 1:17 [k] Ro 6:17
14:8 [l] Nu 10:9; Jer 4:19
14:15 [m] Eph 5:19; Col 3:16
14:16 [n] Dt 27:15-26; 1Ch 16:36; Ne 8:6; Ps 106:48; Rev 5:14; 7:12 [o] 1Co 11:24
14:20 [p] Eph 4:14; Heb 5:12, 13; 1Pe 2:2 [q] Ro 16:19
14:21 [r] Jn 10:34 [s] Isa 28:11, 12
14:22 [t] ver 1
14:23 [u] Ac 2:13
14:25 [v] Isa 45:14; Zec 8:23
14:26 [w] 1Co 12:7-10 [x] Eph 5:19 [y] ver 6

14:13–20 If a person has the gift of speaking in tongues, he should also pray for the gift of knowing what he has said (interpretation) so he can tell people afterwards. This way, the entire church will be edified by this gift.

14:15 There is a proper place for the intellect in Christianity. In praying and singing, both the mind and the spirit are to be fully engaged. When we sing, we should also think about the meaning of the words. When we pour out our feelings to God in prayer, we should not turn off our capacity to think. True Christianity is neither barren intellectualism nor thoughtless emotionalism. See also Ephesians 1:17, 18; Philippians 1:9–11; Colossians 1:9.

14:22–25 The way the Corinthians were speaking in tongues was helping no-one because believers did not understand what was being said, and unbelievers thought that the people speaking in tongues were crazy. Speaking in tongues was supposed to be a *sign* to unbelievers (as it was in Acts 2). After speaking in tongues, believers were supposed to explain what was said and give the credit to God. The unsaved people would then be convinced of a spiritual reality and motivated to look further into the Christian faith. While this is one way to reach unbelievers, Paul says that clear preaching is usually better (14:5).

14:26ff Everything done in worship services must be beneficial to the worshippers. This principle touches every aspect – singing, preaching, and the exercise of spiritual gifts. Those contributing to the service (singers, speakers, readers) must have love as their

14:26
[z]Ro 14:19
14:29
[a]1Co 12:10
14:32
[b]1Jn 4:1
14:33
[c]ver 40
[d]Ac 9:13
14:34
[e]1Ti 2:11, 12
[f]Ge 3:16
14:37
[g]2Co 10:7
[h]1Jn 4:6
14:39
[i]1Co 12:31
14:40
[j]ver 33
15:1
[a]Ro 2:16
15:2
[b]Ro 1:16
[c]Ro 11:22
15:3
[d]Gal 1:12
[e]1Co 11:23
[f]Isa 53:5;
1Pe 2:24
[g]Lk 24:27;
Ac 26:22, 23
15:4
[h]Ac 2:24
[i]Mt 16:21
[j]Ac 2:25, 30, 31
15:5
[k]Lk 24:34
[l]Mk 16:14
15:7
[m]Lk 24:33, 36, 37;
Ac 1:3, 4

of these must be done for the strengthening[z] of the church. 27If anyone speaks in a
tongue, two—or at the most three—should speak, one at a time, and someone must
interpret. 28If there is no interpreter, the speaker should keep quiet in the church and
speak to himself and God.
29Two or three prophets should speak, and the others should weigh carefully what
is said.[a] 30And if a revelation comes to someone who is sitting down, the first speaker
should stop. 31For you can all prophesy in turn so that everyone may be instructed
and encouraged. 32The spirits of prophets are subject to the control of prophets.[b]
33For God is not a God of disorder[c] but of peace.
As in all the congregations of the saints,[d] 34women should remain silent in the
churches. They are not allowed to speak, but must be in submission,[e] as the Law[f]
says. 35If they want to enquire about something, they should ask their own husbands
at home; for it is disgraceful for a woman to speak in the church.
36Did the word of God originate with you? Or are you the only people it has
reached? 37If anybody thinks he is a prophet[g] or spiritually gifted, let him acknowledge that what I am writing to you is the Lord's command.[h] 38If he ignores this, he
himself will be ignored.[i]
39Therefore, my brothers, be eager[i] to prophesy, and do not forbid speaking in
tongues. 40But everything should be done in a fitting and orderly[j] way.

4. Instruction on the resurrection

The Resurrection of Christ

15 Now, brothers, I want to remind you of the gospel[a] I preached to you, which
you received and on which you have taken your stand. 2By this gospel you are
saved,[b] if you hold firmly[c] to the word I preached to you. Otherwise, you have
believed in vain.
3For what I received[d] I passed on to you[e] as of first importance:[a] that Christ
died for our sins[f] according to the Scriptures,[g] 4that he was buried, that he was
raised[h] on the third day[i] according to the Scriptures,[j] 5and that he appeared to
Peter,[b][k] and then to the Twelve.[l] 6After that, he appeared to more than five hundred of the brothers at the same time, most of whom are still living, though some
have fallen asleep. 7Then he appeared to James, then to all the apostles,[m] 8and

[i] *38* Some manuscripts *If he is ignorant of this, let him be ignorant* [a] *3* Or *you at the first* [b] *5* Greek *Cephas*

chief motivation, speaking useful words or participating in a way that will strengthen the faith of other believers.

14:33 In worship, everything must be done in harmony and with order. Even when the gifts of the Holy Spirit are being exercised, there is no excuse for disorder. When there is chaos, the church is not allowing God to work among believers as he would like.

14:34, 35 Does this mean that women should not speak in church services today? It is clear from 11:5 that women prayed and prophesied in public worship. It is also clear in chapters 12–14 that women are given spiritual gifts and are encouraged to exercise them in the body of Christ. Women have much to contribute and can participate in worship services.

In the Corinthian culture, women were not allowed to confront men in public. Apparently some of the women who had become Christians thought that their Christian freedom gave them the right to question the men in public worship. This was causing division in the church. In addition, women of that day did not receive formal religious education as did the men. Women may have been raising questions in the worship services that could have been answered at home without disrupting the services. Paul was asking the women not to flaunt their Christian freedom during worship. The purpose of Paul's words was to promote unity, not to teach about women's role in the church.

14:40 Worship is vital to the life of an individual and to the whole church. Our church services should be conducted in an orderly way so that we can worship, be taught, and be prepared to serve God. Those who are responsible for planning worship should make sure it has order and direction rather than chaos and confusion.

15:2 Most churches contain people who do not yet believe. Some are moving in the direction of belief, and others are simply pretending. Imposters, however, are not to be removed (see Matthew 13:28, 29), for that is the Lord's work alone. The Good News about Jesus Christ will save us *if* we firmly believe it and faithfully follow it.

15:5–8 There will always be people who say that Jesus didn't rise from the dead. Paul assures us that many people saw Jesus after his resurrection: Peter; the disciples (the Twelve); more than 500 Christian believers (most of whom were still alive when Paul wrote this, although some had died); James (Jesus' brother); all the apostles; and finally Paul himself. The resurrection is an historical fact. Don't be discouraged by doubters who deny the resurrection. Be filled with hope because of the knowledge that one day you, and they, will see the living proof when Christ returns. (For more evidence on the resurrection, see the chart in Mark 16.)

15:7 This James is Jesus' brother, who at first did not believe that Jesus was the Messiah (John 7:5). After seeing the resurrected Christ, he became a believer and ultimately a leader of the church in Jerusalem (Acts 15:13). James wrote the New Testament book of James.

15:8, 9 Paul's most important credential to be an apostle was that he was an eye-witness of the risen Christ (see Acts 9:3–6). "Abnormally born" means that his was a special case. The other apostles saw Christ in the flesh. Paul was in the next generation of believers—yet Christ appeared to him.

last of all he appeared to me also,[n] as to one abnormally born.
9For I am the least of the apostles[o] and do not even deserve to be called an apostle,
because I persecuted[p] the church of God. 10But by the grace of God I am what I am,
and his grace to me[q] was not without effect. No, I worked harder than all of
them[r]—yet not I, but the grace of God that was with me.[s] 11Whether, then, it was
I or they, this is what we preach, and this is what you believed.

The Resurrection of the Dead

12But if it is preached that Christ has been raised from the dead, how can some of
you say that there is no resurrection of the dead?[t] 13If there is no resurrection of the
dead, then not even Christ has been raised. 14And if Christ has not been raised,[u] our
preaching is useless and so is your faith. 15More than that, we are then found to be
false witnesses about God, for we have testified about God that he raised Christ from
the dead.[v] But he did not raise him if in fact the dead are not raised. 16For if the dead
are not raised, then Christ has not been raised either. 17And if Christ has not been
raised, your faith is futile; you are still in your sins.[w] 18Then those also who have
fallen asleep in Christ are lost. 19If only for this life we have hope in Christ, we are
to be pitied more than all men.[x]
20But Christ has indeed been raised from the dead,[y] the firstfruits[z] of those who
have fallen asleep.[a] 21For since death came through a man,[b] the resurrection of the
dead comes also through a man. 22For as in Adam all die, so in Christ all will be made
alive.[c] 23But each in his own turn: Christ, the firstfruits;[d] then, when he comes,[e]
those who belong to him. 24Then the end will come, when he hands over the
kingdom[f] to God the Father after he has destroyed all dominion, authority and
power.[g] 25For he must reign until he has put all his enemies under his feet.[h] 26The
last enemy to be destroyed is death.[i] 27For he "has put everything under his feet".[c][j]
Now when it says that "everything" has been put under him, it is clear that this does

[c] 27 Psalm 8:6

15:8 [n]Ac 9:3-6, 17; 1Co 9:1
15:9 [o]Eph 3:8; 1Ti 1:15 [p]Ac 8:3
15:10 [q]Ro 12:3 [r]2Co 11:23 [s]Php 2:13
15:12 [t]Ac 17:32; 23:8; 2Ti 2:18
15:14 [u]1Th 4:14
15:15 [v]Ac 2:24
15:17 [w]Ro 4:25
15:19 [x]1Co 4:9
15:20 [y]1Pe 1:3 [z]ver 23; Ac 26:23; Rev 1:5 [a]ver 6, 18
15:21 [b]Ro 5:12
15:22 [c]Ro 5:14-18
15:23 [d]ver 20 [e]ver 52
15:24 [f]Da 7:14, 27 [g]Ro 8:38
15:25 [h]Ps 110:1; Mt 22:44
15:26 [i]2Ti 1:10; Rev 20:14; 21:4
15:27 [j]Ps 8:6

15:9, 10 As a zealous Pharisee, Paul had been an enemy of the Christian church—even to the point of capturing and persecuting believers (see Acts 9:1–3). Thus he felt unworthy to be called an apostle of Christ. Though undoubtedly the most influential of the apostles, Paul was deeply humble. He knew that he had worked hard and accomplished much, but only because God had poured kindness and grace upon him. True humility is not convincing yourself that you are worthless, but recognising God's work in you. It is having God's perspective on who you are and acknowledging his grace in developing your abilities.

15:10 Paul wrote of working harder than the other apostles. This was not an arrogant boast because he knew that his power came from God and that it really didn't matter who worked hardest. Because of his prominent position as a Pharisee, Paul's conversion made him the object of even greater persecution than the other apostles; thus he had to work harder to preach the same message.

15:12ff Most Greeks did not believe that people's bodies would be resurrected after death. They saw the afterlife as something that happened only to the soul. According to Greek philosophers, the soul was the real person, imprisoned in a physical body, and at death the soul was released. There was no immortality for the body, but the soul entered an eternal state. Christianity, by contrast, affirms that the body and soul will be united after resurrection. The church at Corinth was in the heart of Greek culture. Thus many believers had a difficult time believing in a bodily resurrection. Paul wrote this part of his letter to clear up this confusion about the resurrection.

15:13–18 The resurrection of Christ is the centre of the Christian faith. Because Christ rose from the dead as he promised, we know that what he said is true—he is God. Because he rose, we have certainty that our sins are forgiven. Because he rose, he lives and represents us to God. Because he rose and defeated death, we know we will also be raised.

15:19 Why does Paul say believers should be pitied if there were only earthly value to Christianity? In Paul's day, Christianity often brought a person persecution, ostracism from family, and, in many cases, poverty. There were few tangible benefits from being a Christian in that society. It was certainly not a step up the social or career ladder. Even more important, however, is the fact that if Christ had not been resurrected from death, Christians could not be forgiven for their sins and would have no hope of eternal life.

15:20 Firstfruits were the first part of the harvest that faithful Jews brought to the temple as an offering (Leviticus 23:10ff). Although Christ was not the first to rise from the dead (he raised Lazarus and others), he was the first never to die again. He is the forerunner for us, the proof of our eventual resurrection to eternal life.

15:21 Death came into the world as a result of Adam and Eve's sin. In Romans 5:12–21, Paul explained why Adam's sin brought sin to all people, how death and sin spread to all humans because of this first sin, and the parallel between Adam's death and Christ's death.

15:24–28 This is not a chronological sequence of events, and no specific time for these events is given. Paul's point is that the resurrected Christ will conquer all evil, including death. See Revelation 20:14 for words about the final destruction of death.

15:25–28 Although God the Father and God the Son are equal, each has a special work to do and an area of sovereign control (15:28). Christ is not inferior to the Father, but his work is to defeat all evil on earth. First he defeated sin and death on the cross, and in the final days, he will defeat Satan and all evil. World events may seem out of control and justice may seem scarce. But God is in control, allowing evil to remain for a time until he sends Jesus to earth again. Then Christ will present to God a perfect new world.

not include God himself, who put everything under Christ.[k] 28When he has done this,
then the Son himself will be made subject to him who put everything under him,[l]
so that God may be all in all.[m]
29Now if there is no resurrection, what will those do who are baptised for the dead?
If the dead are not raised at all, why are people baptised for them? 30And as for us,
why do we endanger ourselves every hour?[n] 31I die every day[o]—I mean that,
brothers—just as surely as I glory over you in Christ Jesus our Lord. 32If I fought
wild beasts[p] in Ephesus[q] for merely human reasons, what have I gained? If the dead
are not raised,

"Let us eat and drink,
for tomorrow we die."[d][r]

33Do not be misled: "Bad company corrupts good character." 34Come back to your
senses as you ought, and stop sinning; for there are some who are ignorant of God—I
say this to your shame.

The Resurrection Body

35But someone may ask,[s] "How are the dead raised? With what kind of body will
they come?"[t] 36How foolish![u] What you sow does not come to life unless it dies.[v]
37When you sow, you do not plant the body that will be, but just a seed, perhaps of
wheat or of something else. 38But God gives it a body as he has determined, and to
each kind of seed he gives its own body.[w] 39All flesh is not the same: Men have one
kind of flesh, animals have another, birds another and fish another. 40There are also
heavenly bodies and there are earthly bodies; but the splendour of the heavenly bodies
is one kind, and the splendour of the earthly bodies is another. 41The sun has one kind
of splendour, the moon another and the stars another; and star differs from star in
splendour.
42So will it be[x] with the resurrection of the dead. The body that is sown is
perishable, it is raised imperishable; 43it is sown in dishonour, it is raised in glory;[y]
it is sown in weakness, it is raised in power; 44it is sown a natural body, it is raised
a spiritual body.[z]
If there is a natural body, there is also a spiritual body. 45So it is written: "The first
man Adam became a living being";[e][a] the last Adam,[b] a life-giving spirit.[c] 46The
spiritual did not come first, but the natural, and after that the spiritual. 47The first man

d *32* Isaiah 22:13 **e** *45* Gen. 2:7

15:27 [k]Mt 28:18
15:28 [l]Php 3:21 [m]1Co 3:23
15:30 [n]2Co 11:26
15:31 [o]Ro 8:36
15:32 [p]2Co 1:8 [q]Ac 18:19 [r]Isa 22:13; Lk 12:19
15:35 [s]Ro 9:19 [t]Eze 37:3
15:36 [u]Lk 11:40 [v]Jn 12:24
15:38 [w]Ge 1:11
15:42 [x]Da 12:3; Mt 13:43
15:43 [y]Php 3:21; Col 3:4
15:44 [z]ver 50
15:45 [a]Ge 2:7 [b]Ro 5:14 [c]Jn 5:21; Ro 8:2

15:29 Some believers were baptised on behalf of others who had died unbaptised. Nothing more is known about this practice, but it obviously affirms a belief in resurrection. Paul is not promoting baptism for the dead; he is illustrating his argument that the resurrection is a reality.

15:30–34 If death ended it all, enjoying the moment would be all that matters. But Christians know that there is life beyond the grave and that our life on earth is only a preparation for our life that will never end. What you do today matters for eternity. In light of eternity, sin is a foolish gamble.

15:31, 32 "I die every day" refers to Paul's daily exposure to danger. There is no evidence that Paul actually "fought wild beasts in Ephesus", but rather he was referring to the savage opposition he had faced.

15:33 Keeping company with those who deny the resurrection could corrupt good Christian character. Don't let your relationships with unbelievers lead you away from Christ or cause your faith to waver.

15:35ff Paul launches into a discussion about what our resurrected bodies will be like. If you could select your own body, what kind would you choose—strong, athletic, beautiful? Paul explains that we will be recognised in our resurrected bodies, yet they will be better than we can imagine, for they will be made to live for ever. We will still have our own personalities and individualities, but these will be perfected through Christ's work. The Bible does not reveal everything that our resurrected bodies will be able to do, but we know they will be perfect, without sickness or disease (see Philippians 3:21).

15:35ff Paul compares the resurrection of our bodies with the growth in a garden. Seeds placed in the ground don't grow unless they "die" first. The plant that grows looks very different from the seed because God gives it a new "body". There are different kinds of bodies—people, animals, fish, birds. Even the angels in heaven have bodies that are different in beauty and glory. Our resurrected bodies will be very different in some ways, but not all, from our earthly bodies.

15:42–44 Our present bodies are perishable and prone to decay. Our resurrection bodies will be transformed. These spiritual bodies will not be limited by the laws of nature. This does not necessarily mean we'll be superpeople, but our bodies will be different from and more capable than our present earthly bodies. Our spiritual bodies will not be weak, will never get sick, and will never die.

15:45 The "last Adam" refers to Christ. Because Christ rose from the dead, he is a life-giving spirit. This means that he entered into a new form of existence (see the note on 2 Corinthians 3:17). He is the source of the spiritual life that will result in our resurrection. Christ's new glorified human body now suits his new glorified life—just as Adam's human body was suitable to his natural life. When we are resurrected, God will give us a transformed, eternal body suited to our new eternal life.

was of the dust of the earth,[d] the second man from heaven.[e] 48As was the earthly
man, so are those who are of the earth; and as is the man from heaven, so also are
those who are of heaven.[f] 49And just as we have borne the likeness of the earthly
man,[g] so shall we[f] bear the likeness of the man from heaven.[h]
50I declare to you, brothers, that flesh and blood[i] cannot inherit the kingdom of
God, nor does the perishable inherit the imperishable. 51Listen, I tell you a mystery:[j]
We will not all sleep, but we will all be changed[k]—52in a flash, in the twinkling of
an eye, at the last trumpet. For the trumpet will sound,[l] the dead[m] will be raised
imperishable, and we will be changed. 53For the perishable must clothe itself with the
imperishable,[n] and the mortal with immortality. 54When the perishable has been
clothed with the imperishable, and the mortal with immortality, then the saying that
is written will come true: "Death has been swallowed up in victory."[g][o]

55"Where, O death, is your victory?
Where, O death, is your sting?"[h][p]

56The sting of death is sin,[q] and the power of sin is the law.[r] 57But thanks be to
God![s] He gives us the victory through our Lord Jesus Christ.[t]
58Therefore, my dear brothers, stand firm. Let nothing move you. Always give
yourselves fully to the work of the Lord,[u] because you know that your labour in the
Lord is not in vain.

The Collection for God's People

16 Now about the collection[a] for God's people:[b] Do what I told the Galatian[c]
churches to do. 2On the first day of every week,[d] each one of you should set
aside a sum of money in keeping with his income, saving it up, so that when I come
no collections will have to be made.[e] 3Then, when I arrive, I will give letters of
introduction to the men you approve[f] and send them with your gift to Jerusalem. 4If
it seems advisable for me to go also, they will accompany me.

Personal Requests

5After I go through Macedonia, I will come to you[g]—for I will be going through
Macedonia.[h] 6Perhaps I will stay with you awhile, or even spend the winter, so that
you can help me on my journey,[i] wherever I go. 7I do not want to see you now and
make only a passing visit; I hope to spend some time with you, if the Lord permits.[j]
8But I will stay on at Ephesus[k] until Pentecost,[l] 9because a great door for effective
work has opened to me,[m] and there are many who oppose me.

f *49* Some early manuscripts *so let us* g *54* Isaiah 25:8 h *55* Hosea 13:14

15:47 d Ge 2:7; 3:19 e Jn 3:13, 31
15:48 f Php 3:20, 21
15:49 g Ge 5:3 h Ro 8:29
15:50 i Jn 3:3, 5
15:51 j 1Co 13:2 k Php 3:21
15:52 l Mt 24:31 m Jn 5:25
15:53 n 2Co 5:2, 4
15:54 o Isa 25:8; Rev 20:14
15:55 p Hos 13:14
15:56 q Ro 5:12 r Ro 4:15
15:57 s 2Co 2:14 t Ro 8:37
15:58 u 1Co 16:10
16:1 a Ac 24:17 b Ac 9:13 c Ac 16:6
16:2 d Ac 20:7 e 2Co 9:4, 5
16:3 f 2Co 8:18, 19
16:5 g 1Co 4:19 h Ac 19:21
16:6 i Ro 15:24
16:7 j Ac 18:21
16:8 k Ac 18:19 l Ac 2:1
16:9 m Ac 14:27

15:50–53 We all face limitations. Those who have physical, mental, or emotional disabilities are especially aware of this. Some may be blind, but they can see a new way to live. Some may be deaf, but they can hear God's Good News. Some may be lame, but they can walk in God's love. In addition, they have the encouragement that those disabilities are only temporary. Paul tells us that we all will be given new bodies when Christ returns and that these bodies will be without disabilities, never to die or become sick. This can give us hope in our suffering.

15:51, 52 "We will not all sleep" means that Christians alive at that day will not have to die but will be transformed immediately. A trumpet blast will usher in the new heaven and earth. The Jews would understand the significance of this because trumpets were always blown to signal the start of great festivals and other extraordinary events (Numbers 10:10).

15:54–56 Satan seemed to be victorious in the Garden of Eden (Genesis 3) and at the cross of Jesus. But God turned Satan's apparent victory into defeat when Jesus Christ rose from the dead (Colossians 2:15; Hebrews 2:14, 15). Thus death is no longer a source of dread or fear. Christ overcame it, and one day we will also. The law will no longer make sinners out of us who cannot keep it. Death has been defeated, and we have hope beyond the grave.

15:58 Paul says that because of the resurrection, nothing we do is in vain. Sometimes we hesitate to do good because we don't see any results. But if we can maintain a heavenly perspective, we will understand that we often will not see the good that results from our efforts. If we truly believe that Christ has won the ultimate victory, that fact must affect the way we live right now. Don't let discouragement over an apparent lack of results keep you from working. Do the good that you have opportunity to do, knowing that your work will have eternal results.

16:1ff Paul had just said that no good deed is ever in vain (15:58). In this chapter he mentions some practical deeds that have value for all Christians.

16:1–4 The Christians in Jerusalem were suffering from poverty and famine, so Paul was collecting money for them (Romans 15:25–31; 2 Corinthians 8:4; 9:1ff). He suggested that believers set aside a certain amount each week and give it to the church until he arrived to take it on to Jerusalem. Paul had planned to go straight to Corinth from Ephesus, but he changed his mind (2 Corinthians 1; 2). When he finally arrived, he took the gift and delivered it to the Jerusalem church (Acts 21:18; 24:17).

16:10 [n]Ac 16:1 [o]1Co 15:58 **16:11** [p]1Ti 4:12 [q]Ac 15:33 **16:12** [r]Ac 18:24; 1Co 1:12 **16:13** [s]Gal 5:1; Php 1:27; 1Th 3:8; 2Th 2:15 [t]Eph 6:10 **16:14** [u]1Co 14:1 **16:15** [v]1Co 1:16 [w]Ro 16:5 [x]Ac 18:12 **16:16** [y]Heb 13:17 **16:17** [z]2Co 11:9; Php 2:30 **16:18** [a]Phm 7 [b]Php 2:29 **16:19** [c]Ac 18:2 [d]Ro 16:5 **16:20** [e]Ro 16:16 **16:21** [f]Gal 6:11; Col 4:18

10 If Timothy[n] comes, see to it that he has nothing to fear while he is with you,
for he is carrying on the work of the Lord,[o] just as I am. 11 No-one, then, should refuse
to accept him.[p] Send him on his way in peace[q] so that he may return to me. I am
expecting him along with the brothers.
12 Now about our brother Apollos:[r] I strongly urged him to go to you with the
brothers. He was quite unwilling to go now, but he will go when he has the opportunity.
13 Be on your guard; stand firm[s] in the faith; be men of courage; be strong.[t] 14 Do
everything in love.[u]
15 You know that the household of Stephanas[v] were the first converts[w] in Achaia,[x]
and they have devoted themselves to the service of the saints. I urge you, brothers,
16 to submit[y] to such as these and to everyone who joins in the work, and labours at
it. 17 I was glad when Stephanas, Fortunatus and Achaicus arrived, because they have
supplied what was lacking from you.[z] 18 For they refreshed[a] my spirit and yours also.
Such men deserve recognition.[b]

Final Greetings

19 The churches in the province of Asia send you greetings. Aquila and Priscilla**[a]**[c]
greet you warmly in the Lord, and so does the church that meets at their house.[d] 20 All
the brothers here send you greetings. Greet one another with a holy kiss.[e]
21 I, Paul, write this greeting in my own hand.[f]

a *19* Greek *Prisca*, a variant of *Priscilla*

PHYSICAL AND RESURRECTION BODIES

Physical Bodies	*Resurrection Bodies*
Perishable	Imperishable
Sown in dishonour	Raised in glory
Sown in weakness	Raised in power
Natural	Spiritual
From the dust	From heaven

We all have bodies—each looks different, each has different strengths and weaknesses. But as physical, earthly bodies, they are all alike. All believers are promised life after death and bodies like Christ's (15:49), resurrection bodies.

16:10, 11 Paul was sending Timothy ahead to Corinth. Paul respected Timothy and had worked closely with him (Philippians 2:22; 1 Timothy 1:2). Although Timothy was young, Paul encouraged the Corinthian church to welcome him because he was doing the Lord's work. God's work is not limited by age. Paul wrote two personal letters to Timothy that have been preserved in the Bible (1 and 2 Timothy).

16:12 Apollos, who had preached in Corinth, was doing evangelistic work in Greece (see Acts 18:24–28; 1 Corinthians 3:3ff). Apollos didn't go to Corinth right away, partly because he knew of the factions there and didn't want to cause any more divisions.

16:13, 14 As the Corinthians awaited Paul's next visit, they were directed to (1) be on their guard against spiritual dangers, (2) stand firm in the faith, (3) behave courageously, (4) be strong, and (5) do everything with kindness and in love. Today, as we wait for the return of Christ, we should follow the same instructions.

16:19 Aquila and Priscilla were tentmakers (or leather workers) whom Paul had met in Corinth (Acts 18:1–3). They followed Paul to Ephesus and lived there with him, helping to teach others about Jesus (Romans 16:3–5). Many in the Corinthian church would have known this Christian couple. They are also mentioned in Acts 18:18, 26; Romans 16:3; 2 Timothy 4:19.

16:20 Kissing was a normal way of greeting each other in Paul's day. Paul encouraged the "holy kiss" as a way to greet Christians, and a way to help break down the divisions in this church.

16:21 Paul had a helper, or secretary, who wrote down this letter while he dictated. Paul wrote the final words, however, in his own handwriting. This is similar to adding a handwritten postscript (P.S.) to a typewritten letter. It also served to verify that this was a genuine letter from the apostle, and not a forgery.

22If anyone does not love the Lord[g]—a curse[h] be on him. Come, O Lord![b][i]
23The grace of the Lord Jesus be with you.[j]
24My love to all of you in Christ Jesus. Amen.[c]

b 22 In Aramaic the expression *Come, O Lord* is *Marana tha.* c 24 Some manuscripts do not have *Amen.*

16:22
g Eph 6:24
h Ro 9:3
i Rev 22:20

16:23
j Ro 16:20

16:22 The Lord Jesus Christ is coming back to earth again. To Paul, this was a glad hope, the very best he could look forward to. He was not afraid of seeing Christ—he could hardly wait! Do you share Paul's eager anticipation? Those who love Christ are looking forward to that wonderful time of his return (Titus 2:13). To those who did not love the Lord, however, Paul says, let them be cursed.

16:24 The church at Corinth was a church in trouble. Paul lovingly and forcefully confronted their problems and pointed them back to Christ. He dealt with divisions and conflicts, selfishness, inconsiderate use of freedom, disorder in worship, misuse of spiritual gifts, and wrong attitudes about the resurrection.

In every church, there are enough problems to create tensions and divisions. We should not ignore or gloss over problems in our churches or in our lives. Instead, like Paul, we should deal with problems head on as they arise. The lesson for us in 1 Corinthians is that unity and love in a church are far more important than leaders and labels.

2 CORINTHIANS

SLITHERING through the centuries, the serpent whispers his smooth-tongued promises, beguiling, deceiving, and tempting—urging men and women to reject God and to follow Satan. Satan's emissaries have been many—false prophets contradicting God's ancient spokesmen, "pious" leaders hurling blasphemous accusations, and heretical teachers infiltrating churches. And the deception continues. Our world is filled with cults, "isms", and ideologies, all claiming to provide the way to God.

Paul constantly struggled with those who would mislead God's people, and he poured his life into spreading the good news to the uttermost parts of the world. During three missionary trips and other travels, he proclaimed Christ, made converts, and established churches. But often young believers were easy prey for false teachers. False teachers were a constant threat to the gospel and the early church. So Paul had to spend much time warning and correcting these new Christians.

The church at Corinth was weak. Surrounded by idolatry and immorality, they struggled with their Christian faith and lifestyle. Through personal visits and letters, Paul tried to instruct them in the faith, resolve their conflicts, and solve some of their problems. First Corinthians was sent to deal with specific moral issues in the church and to answer questions about sex, marriage, and tender consciences. That letter confronted the issues directly and was well received by most. But there were false teachers who denied Paul's authority and slandered him. Paul then wrote 2 Corinthians to defend his position and to denounce those who were twisting the truth.

This must have been a difficult letter for Paul to write because he had to list his credentials as an apostle. Paul was reluctant to do so as a humble servant of Christ, but he knew it was necessary. Paul also knew that most of the believers in Corinth had taken his previous words to heart and were beginning to mature in their faith. He affirmed their commitment to Christ.

The letter begins with Paul reminding his readers of (1) his relationship to them—Paul had always been honest and straightforward with them (1:12–14), (2) his itinerary—he was planning to visit them again (1:15—2:3), and (3) his previous letter (2:4–11). Paul then moves directly to the subject of false teachers (2:17), and he reviews his ministry among the Corinthians to demonstrate the validity of his message and to urge them not to turn away from the truth (3:1—7:16).

Paul next turns to the issue of collecting money for the poor Christians in Jerusalem. He tells them how others have given, and he urges them to show their love in a tangible way as well (8:1—9:15). Paul then gives a strong defence of his authority as a genuine apostle while pointing out the deceptive influence of the false apostles (10:1—13:13).

As you read this intensely personal letter, listen to Paul's words of love and exhortation, and be committed to the truth of God's word and prepared to reject all false teaching.

VITAL STATISTICS

PURPOSE:
To affirm Paul's ministry, defend his authority as an apostle, and refute the false teachers in Corinth

AUTHOR:
Paul

TO WHOM WRITTEN:
The church in Corinth, and Christians everywhere

DATE WRITTEN:
About A.D. 55–57, from Macedonia

SETTING:
Paul had already written three letters to the Corinthians (two are now lost). In 1 Corinthians (the second of these letters), he used strong words to correct and teach. Most of the church had responded in the right spirit; there were, however, those who were denying Paul's authority and questioning his motives.

KEY VERSE:
"We are therefore Christ's ambassadors, as though God were making his appeal through us. We implore you on Christ's behalf: Be reconciled to God" (5:20).

KEY PEOPLE:
Paul, Timothy, Titus, false teachers

KEY PLACES:
Corinth, Jerusalem

SPECIAL FEATURES:
This is an intensely personal and autobiographical letter.

THE BLUEPRINT

1. Paul explains his actions (1:1—2:11)
2. Paul defends his ministry (2:12—7:16)
3. Paul defends the collection (8:1—9:15)
4. Paul defends his authority (10:1—13:13)

In responding to the attacks on his character and authority, Paul explains the nature of Christian ministry and, as an example, openly shares about his ministry. This is an important letter for all who wish to be involved in any kind of Christian ministry, because it has much to teach us about how we should handle our ministries today. Like Paul, those involved in ministry should be blameless, sincere, confident, caring, open, and willing to suffer for the sake of Christ.

MEGATHEMES

THEME	EXPLANATION	IMPORTANCE
Trials	Paul experienced great suffering, persecution, and opposition in his ministry. He even struggled with a personal weakness—a "thorn in the flesh". Through it all, Paul affirmed God's faithfulness.	God is faithful. His strength is sufficient for any trial. When trials come, they keep us from pride and teach us dependence on God. He comforts us so we can comfort others.
Church Discipline	Paul defends his role in church discipline. Neither immorality nor false teaching could be ignored. The church was to be neither too lax nor too severe in administering discipline. The church was to restore the corrected person when he or she repented.	The goal of all discipline in the church should be correction, not vengeance. For churches to be effective, they must confront and solve problems, not ignore them. In everything, we must act in love.
Hope	To encourage the Corinthians as they faced trials, Paul reminded them that they would receive new bodies in heaven. This would be a great victory in contrast to their present suffering.	To know we will receive new bodies offers us hope. No matter what adversity we face, we can keep going. Our faithful service will result in triumph.
Giving	Paul organised a collection of funds for the poor in the Jerusalem church. Many of the Asian churches gave money. Paul explains and defends his beliefs about giving, and he urges the Corinthians to follow through on their previous commitment.	Like the Corinthians, we should follow through on our financial commitments. Our giving must be generous, sacrificial, well planned, and based on need. Our generosity not only helps those in need but enables them to thank God.
Sound Doctrine	False teachers were challenging Paul's ministry and authority as an apostle. Paul asserts his authority in order to preserve correct Christian doctrine. His sincerity, his love for Christ, and his concern for the people were his defence.	We should share Paul's concern for correct teaching in our churches. But in so doing, we must share his motivation—love for Christ and people—and his sincerity.

1. Paul explains his actions

1 Paul, an apostle of Christ Jesus by the will of God,[a] and Timothy our brother,
To the church of God[b] in Corinth, together with all the saints throughout Achaia:[c]
2Grace and peace to you from God our Father and the Lord Jesus Christ.[d]

1:1 [a]1Co 1:1; Eph 1:1; Col 1:1; 2Ti 1:1 [b]1Co 10:32 [c]Ac 18:12
1:2 [d]Ro 1:7

1:1 Paul visited Corinth on his second missionary journey and founded a church there (Acts 18:1ff). He later wrote several letters to the believers in Corinth, two of which are included in the Bible. Paul's first letter to the Corinthians is lost (1 Corinthians 5:9–11), his second letter to them is our book of 1 Corinthians, his third letter is lost (2:6–9; 7:12), and his fourth letter is our book of 2 Corinthians. This letter was written less than a year after 1 Corinthians.

Paul wrote 1 Corinthians to deal with divisions in the church. When his advice was not taken and their problems weren't solved, Paul visited Corinth a second time. That visit was painful both for Paul and for the church (2:1). He then planned a third visit, but delayed it and wrote 2 Corinthians instead. After writing 2 Corinthians, Paul visited Corinth once more (Acts 20:2, 3).

1:1 Paul had great respect for Timothy (see also Philippians 2:19, 20; 1 Timothy 1:2), one of his travelling companions (Acts 16:1–3). Timothy had accompanied Paul to Corinth on his second missionary journey, and Paul had recently sent him there to minister (1 Corinthians 4:17; 16:10). Timothy's report to Paul about the crisis in the Corinthian church prompted Paul to make an unplanned visit to

The God of All Comfort

3Praise be to the God and Father of our Lord Jesus Christ,[e] the Father of compassion and the God of all comfort, 4who comforts us[f] in all our troubles, so that we
can comfort those in any trouble with the comfort we ourselves have received from
God. 5For just as the sufferings of Christ flow over into our lives,[g] so also through
Christ our comfort overflows. 6If we are distressed, it is for your comfort and
salvation;[h] if we are comforted, it is for your comfort, which produces in you patient
endurance of the same sufferings we suffer. 7And our hope for you is firm, because
we know that just as you share in our sufferings,[i] so also you share in our comfort.
8We do not want you to be uninformed, brothers, about the hardships we suffered[j]
in the province of Asia. We were under great pressure, far beyond our ability to
endure, so that we despaired even of life. 9Indeed, in our hearts we felt the sentence
of death. But this happened that we might not rely on ourselves but on God,[k] who
raises the dead. 10He has delivered us from such a deadly peril,[l] and he will deliver
us. On him we have set our hope that he will continue to deliver us, 11as you help
us by your prayers.[m] Then many will give thanks[n] on our**[a]** behalf for the gracious
favour granted us in answer to the prayers of many.

a *11* Many manuscripts *your*

1:3 [e]Eph 1:3; 1Pe 1:3
1:4 [f]2Co 7:6, 7, 13
1:5 [g]2Co 4:10; Col 1:24
1:6 [h]2Co 4:15
1:7 [i]Ro 8:17
1:8 [j]1Co 15:32
1:9 [k]Jer 17:5, 7
1:10 [l]Ro 15:31
1:11 [m]Ro 15:30; Php 1:19 [n]2Co 4:15

DIFFERENCES BETWEEN 1 AND 2 CORINTHIANS
The two letters to the Corinthian church that are found in the Bible are very different, with different tones and focuses.

1 Corinthians	*2 Corinthians*
Practical	Personal
Focuses on the character of the Corinthian church	Focuses on Paul as he bares his soul and tells of his love for the Corinthian church
Deals with questions on marriage, freedom, spiritual gifts, and order in the church	Deals with the problem of false teachers, whereby Paul defends his authority and the truth of his message
Paul instructs in matters concerning the church's well-being	Paul gives his testimony because he knows that acceptance of his advice is vital to the church's well-being
Contains advice to help the church combat the pagan influences in the wicked city of Corinth	Contains testimony to help the church combat the havoc caused by false teachers

the church to deal with the problem in person (see 2:1). For more information on Timothy, see his Profile in 1 Timothy.

1:1 The Romans had made Corinth the capital of Achaia (the southern half of present-day Greece). The city was a flourishing trade centre because of its seaport. With the thousands of merchants and sailors who disembarked there each year, it had developed a reputation as one of the most immoral cities in the ancient world; its many pagan temples encouraged the practice of sexual immorality along with idol worship. In fact, the Greek word "to Corinthianize" came to mean "to practice sexual immorality". A Christian church in the city would face many pressures and conflicts. For more information on Corinth, see the first note on 1 Corinthians 1:2.

1:3–5 Many think that when God comforts us, our troubles should go away. But if that were always so, people would turn to God only out of a desire to be relieved of pain and not out of love for him. We must understand that being *comforted* can also mean receiving strength, encouragement, and hope to deal with our troubles. The more we suffer, the more comfort God gives us. If you are feeling overwhelmed, allow God to comfort you. Remember that every trial you endure will help you comfort other people who are suffering similar troubles.

1:5 The "sufferings of Christ" are those afflictions we experience as we do Christ's ministry. At the same time, Christ suffers with his people, since they are united with him. In Acts 9:4, 5 Christ asked Paul why he was persecuting him. This implies that Christ suffered with the early Christians when they were persecuted.

1:6, 7 Paul explains that he and his companions suffered greatly for bringing "comfort and salvation" to the Corinthians. But just as God comforted Paul, God would also comfort the Corinthian believers when they suffered for their faith. He would give them the strength to endure.

1:8–10 Paul does not give details about their hardships in Asia, although his accounts of all three missionary journeys record many difficult trials he faced (Acts 13:2 – 14:28; Acts 15:40 – 21:17). He does write that they felt that they were going to die, and realised that they could do nothing to help themselves – they simply had to rely on God.

1:8–10 We often depend on our own skills and abilities when life seems easy, but we turn to God when we feel unable to help ourselves. Depending on God is a realisation of our own powerlessness without him and our need for his constant touch in our lives. God is our source of power, and we receive his help by keeping in touch with him. With this attitude of dependence, problems will drive us to God rather than away from him. Learn how to rely on God daily.

1:11 Paul requested prayer for himself and his companions as they travelled to spread God's message. Pray for pastors, teachers, missionaries, and others who are spreading the gospel. Satan will challenge anyone making a real difference for God.

Paul's Change of Plans

12 Now this is our boast: Our conscience[o] testifies that we have conducted ourselves
in the world, and especially in our relations with you, in the holiness and sincerity[p]
that are from God. We have done so not according to worldly wisdom[q] but according
to God's grace. 13 For we do not write to you anything you cannot read or understand.
And I hope that, 14 as you have understood us in part, you will come to understand
fully that you can boast of us just as we will boast of you in the day of the Lord Jesus.[r]
15 Because I was confident of this, I planned to visit you[s] first so that you might
benefit twice.[t] 16 I planned to visit you on my way[u] to Macedonia and to come back
to you from Macedonia, and then to have you send me on my way to Judea. 17 When
I planned this, did I do it lightly? Or do I make my plans in a worldly manner[v] so
that in the same breath I say, "Yes, yes" and "No, no"?
18 But as surely as God is faithful,[w] our message to you is not "Yes" and "No".
19 For the Son of God, Jesus Christ, who was preached among you by me and Silas[b]
and Timothy, was not "Yes" and "No", but in him it has always[x] been "Yes." 20 For
no matter how many promises[y] God has made, they are "Yes" in Christ. And so
through him the "Amen"[z] is spoken by us to the glory of God. 21 Now it is God who
makes both us and you stand firm in Christ. He anointed[a] us, 22 set his seal of
ownership on us, and put his Spirit in our hearts as a deposit, guaranteeing what is
to come.[b]
23 I call God as my witness[c] that it was in order to spare you[d] that I did not return
to Corinth. 24 Not that we lord it over[e] your faith, but we work with you for your
2 joy, because it is by faith you stand firm.[f] 1 So I made up my mind that I would
not make another painful visit to you.[a] 2 For if I grieve you,[b] who is left to make
me glad but you whom I have grieved? 3 I wrote as I did[c] so that when I came I should
not be distressed[d] by those who ought to make me rejoice. I had confidence[e] in all

b *19* Greek *Silvanus*, a variant of *Silas*

1:12 [o]Ac 23:1 [p]2Co 2:17 [q]1Co 2:1, 4, 13
1:14 [r]1Co 1:8
1:15 [s]1Co 4:19 [t]Ro 1:11, 13; 15:29
1:16 [u]1Co 16:5-7
1:17 [v]2Co 10:2, 3
1:18 [w]1Co 1:9
1:19 [x]Heb 13:8
1:20 [y]Ro 15:8 [z]1Co 14:16
1:21 [a]1Jn 2:20, 27
1:22 [b]2Co 5:5
1:23 [c]Ro 1:9; Gal 1:20 [d]1Co 4:21; 2Co 2:1, 3; 13:2, 10
1:24 [e]1Pe 5:3
1:24 [f]Ro 11:20; 1Co 15:1
2:1 [a]2Co 1:23
2:2 [b]2Co 7:8
2:3 [c]2Co 7:8, 12 [d]2Co 12:21 [e]2Co 8:22; Gal 5:10

1:12–14 Paul knew the importance of holiness and sincerity in word and action, especially in a situation as in Corinth, where constructive criticism was necessary. So Paul did not come with impressive human knowledge (worldly wisdom). God wants us to be real and transparent in all our relationships. If we aren't, we may end up lowering ourselves to spreading rumours, gossiping, and second-guessing.

1:15–17 Paul had recently made a brief, unscheduled visit to Corinth that was very painful for him and the church (see 2:1). After that visit, he told the church when he would return. But Paul changed his original travel plans. Instead of sailing from Ephesus to Corinth before going to Macedonia, he travelled from Ephesus directly to Macedonia, where he wrote a letter to the Corinthians that caused him much anguish and them much sorrow (7:8, 9). He had made his original plans thinking that the church would have solved its problems. When the time came for Paul's scheduled trip to Corinth, however, the crisis had not been fully resolved (although progress was being made in some areas; 7:11–16). So he wrote a letter instead (2:3, 4; 7:8) because another visit may have only made matters worse. Thus Paul stayed away from Corinth because he was concerned over the church's unity, not because he was fickle.

1:17–20 Paul's change of plans caused some of his accusers to say that he couldn't be trusted, hoping to undermine his authority. Paul said that he was not the type of person to say "yes" when he means "no". Paul explained that it was not indecision but concern for their feelings that forced him to change his plans. The reason for his trip – to bring joy (1:24) – could not be accomplished with the present crisis. Paul didn't want to visit them only to rebuke them severely (1:23). Just as the Corinthians could trust God to keep his promises, they could trust Paul as God's representative to keep his. He would still visit them, but at a better time.

1:19, 20 All of God's promises of what the Messiah would be like are fulfilled in Christ ("in him it has always been 'Yes' "). Jesus was completely faithful in his ministry; he never sinned (1 Peter 3:18); he faithfully died for us (Hebrews 2:9); and now he faithfully intercedes for us (Romans 8:34; Hebrews 4:14, 15). Because Jesus Christ is faithful, Paul wanted to be faithful in his ministry.

1:21, 22 Paul mentions two gifts God gives when we become believers: (1) a *seal of ownership* to show who our Master is, and (2) the Holy Spirit, who guarantees that we belong to him and will receive all his benefits (Ephesians 1:13, 14). The Holy Spirit guarantees that salvation is ours now, and that we will receive so much more when Christ returns. The great comfort and power the Holy Spirit gives in this life is a foretaste or down payment ("deposit") of the benefits of our eternal life in God's presence. With the privilege of belonging to God comes the responsibility of identifying ourselves as his faithful servants. Don't be ashamed to let others know that you are his.

1:23 The Corinthian church had written to Paul with questions about their faith (see 1 Corinthians 7:1). In response, Paul had written 1 Corinthians. But the church did not follow his instructions.

Paul had planned to visit them again, but instead he wrote a letter that caused sorrow (7:8, 9) to give them another chance to change their ways. He didn't want to visit and repeat the same advice for the same problems. He wrote the emotional letter to encourage them to follow the advice that he had already given in previous letters and visits.

2:1 Paul's phrase, "another painful visit", indicates that he had already made one difficult trip to Corinth (see the notes on 1:1; 1:15–17) since founding the church. Paul had gone there to deal with those in the church who had been attacking and undermining his authority as an apostle of Jesus Christ, thus confusing other believers.

2:3 Paul's last letter, referred to here, was not the book of 1 Corinthians, but a letter written between 1 and 2 Corinthians, just after his unplanned, painful visit (2:1). Paul refers to this letter again in 7:8.

of you, that you would all share my joy. 4For I wrote to you[f] out of great distress
and anguish of heart and with many tears, not to grieve you but to let you know the
depth of my love for you.

Forgiveness for the Sinner

5If anyone has caused grief,[g] he has not so much grieved me as he has grieved
all of you, to some extent—not to put it too severely. 6The punishment[h] inflicted
on him by the majority is sufficient for him. 7Now instead, you ought to forgive and
comfort him,[i] so that he will not be overwhelmed by excessive sorrow. 8I urge you,
therefore, to reaffirm your love for him. 9The reason I wrote to you was to see if you
would stand the test and be obedient in everything.[j] 10If you forgive anyone, I also
forgive him. And what I have forgiven—if there was anything to forgive—I have
forgiven in the sight of Christ for your sake, 11in order that Satan[k] might not outwit
us. For we are not unaware of his schemes.[l]

2. Paul defends his ministry

Ministers of the New Covenant

12Now when I went to Troas[m] to preach the gospel of Christ[n] and found that the
Lord had opened a door[o] for me, 13I still had no peace of mind,[p] because I did not
find my brother Titus[q] there. So I said good-bye to them and went on to Macedonia.
14But thanks be to God,[r] who always leads us in triumphal procession in Christ
and through us spreads everywhere the fragrance[s] of the knowledge of him. 15For
we are to God the aroma of Christ among those who are being saved and those who
are perishing.[t] 16To the one we are the smell of death;[u] to the other, the fragrance
of life. And who is equal to such a task?[v] 17Unlike so many, we do not peddle the

2:4 [f]2Co 7:8, 12
2:5 [g]1Co 5:1, 2
2:6 [h]1Co 5:4, 5
2:7 [i]Gal 6:1; Eph 4:32
2:9 [j]2Co 10:6
2:11 [k]Mt 4:10 [l]Lk 22:31; 2Co 4:4; 1Pe 5:8, 9
2:12 [m]Ac 16:8 [n]Ro 1:1 [o]Ac 14:27
2:13 [p]2Co 7:5 [q]2Co 7:6, 13; 12:18
2:14 [r]Ro 6:17 [s]Eph 5:2; Php 4:18
2:15 [t]1Co 1:18
2:16 [u]Lk 2:34 [v]2Co 3:5, 6

2:4 Paul did not enjoy reprimanding his friends and fellow believers, but he cared enough about the Corinthians to confront them with their wrong-doing. Proverbs 27:6 says: "Wounds from a friend can be trusted, but an enemy multiplies kisses". Sometimes our friends make choices that we know are wrong. If we ignore their behaviour and let them continue in it, we won't be showing love to them. We show love by honestly sharing our concerns in order to help these friends do and be their very best for God. When we don't make any move to help, we show that we are more concerned about being well liked than about what will happen to them.

2:5–11 Paul explained that it was time to forgive the man who had been punished by the church and had subsequently repented. He needed forgiveness, acceptance, and comfort. Satan would gain an advantage if they permanently separated this man from the congregation rather than forgiving and restoring him. This may have been the man who had required the disciplinary action described in 1 Corinthians 5, or he may have been the chief opponent of Paul who had caused Paul the anguish described in 2:1–11. The sorrowful letter had finally brought about the repentance of the Corinthians (7:8–14), and their discipline of the man had led to his repentance. Church discipline should seek restoration. Two mistakes in church discipline should be avoided—being too lenient and not correcting mistakes, or being too harsh and not forgiving the sinner. There is a time to confront and a time to comfort.

2:11 We use church discipline to help keep the church pure and to help wayward people repent. But Satan tries to harm the church by tempting it to use discipline in an unforgiving way. This causes those exercising discipline to become proud of their purity, and it causes the person who is being disciplined to become bitter and perhaps leave the church entirely. We must remember that our purpose in discipline is to *restore* a person to the fellowship, not to destroy him or her. We must be cautious that personal anger is not vented under the guise of church discipline.

2:13 Titus was a Greek convert whom Paul greatly loved and trusted (the book of Titus is a letter that Paul wrote to him). Titus was one of the men responsible for collecting the money for the poverty-stricken Jerusalem church (8:6). Paul may also have sent Titus with the sorrowful letter. On his way to Macedonia, Paul was supposed to meet Titus in Troas. When Paul didn't find him there, he was worried for Titus's safety and left Troas to search for him in Macedonia. There Paul found him (7:6), and the good news that Paul received (7:8–16) led to this letter. Paul would send Titus back to Corinth with this letter (8:16, 17).

2:14ff In the middle of discussing his unscheduled trip to Macedonia, Paul thanked God for his ministry, his relationship with the Corinthian believers, and the way God had used him to help others wherever he went, despite difficulties (2:14–7:4). In 7:5, Paul resumed his story of his trip to Macedonia.

2:14–16 In a Roman triumphal procession, the Roman general would display his treasures and captives amidst a cloud of incense burned for the gods. To the victors, the aroma was sweet; to the captives in the parade, it was the smell of slavery and death. When Christians preach the gospel, it is good news to some and repulsive news to others. Believers recognise the life-giving fragrance of the message. To non-believers, however, it smells foul, like death—their own.

2:16, 17 Paul asks "who is equal" to the task of representing Christ? Our adequacy is always from God (1 Corinthians 15:10; 2 Corinthians 3:5). He has already commissioned and sent us (see Matthew 28:18–20). He has given us the Holy Spirit to enable us to speak with Christ's power. He keeps his eye on us, protecting us as we work for him. So, if we realise that God makes us competent and useful, we can overcome our feelings of inadequacy. Serving Christ, therefore, requires that we focus on what he can do through us, not on what we can't do by ourselves.

2:17 Some preachers in Paul's day were "pedlars" of God's word, preaching without understanding God's message or caring about what happened to their listeners. They weren't concerned about furthering God's kingdom—they just wanted money. Today there are still religious teachers who care only about money, and not about truth. Those who truly speak for God should have sincerity and integrity, and should never preach for selfish reasons (1 Timothy 6:5–10).

word of God for profit.[w] On the contrary, in Christ we speak before God with
sincerity,[x] like men sent from God.[y]

3 Are we beginning to commend ourselves[a] again? Or do we need, like some
people, letters of recommendation[b] to you or from you? 2You yourselves are our
letter, written on our hearts, known and read by everybody.[c] 3You show that you
are a letter from Christ, the result of our ministry, written not with ink but with the
Spirit of the living God, not on tablets of stone[d] but on tablets of human hearts.[e]
4Such confidence[f] as this is ours through Christ before God. 5Not that we are
competent in ourselves to claim anything for ourselves, but our competence comes
from God.[g] 6He has made us competent as ministers of a new covenant[h]—not of
the letter but of the Spirit; for the letter kills, but the Spirit gives life.[i]

The Glory of the New Covenant

7Now if the ministry that brought death, which was engraved in letters on stone,
came with glory, so that the Israelites could not look steadily at the face of Moses
because of its glory,[j] fading though it was, 8will not the ministry of the Spirit be
even more glorious? 9If the ministry that condemns men[k] is glorious, how much more
glorious is the ministry that brings righteousness![l] 10For what was glorious has no
glory now in comparison with the surpassing glory. 11And if what was fading away
came with glory, how much greater is the glory of that which lasts!
12Therefore, since we have such a hope, we are very bold.[m] 13We are not like
Moses, who would put a veil over his face[n] to keep the Israelites from gazing at it
while the radiance was fading away. 14But their minds were made dull,[o] for to this
day the same veil remains when the old covenant[p] is read.[q] It has not been removed,
because only in Christ is it taken away. 15Even to this day when Moses is read, a veil
covers their hearts. 16But whenever anyone turns to the Lord,[r] the veil is taken
away.[s] 17Now the Lord is the Spirit,[t] and where the Spirit of the Lord is, there is

2:17 [w] 2Co 4:2 [x] 1Co 5:8 [y] 2Co 1:12
3:1 [a] 2Co 5:12; 12:11 [b] Ac 18:27
3:2 [c] 1Co 9:2
3:3 [d] Ex 24:12 [e] Pr 3:3; Jer 31:33; Eze 11:19
3:4 [f] Eph 3:12
3:5 [g] 1Co 15:10
3:6 [h] Lk 22:20 [i] Jn 6:63
3:7 [j] Ex 34:29-35
3:9 [k] ver 7 [l] Ro 1:17; 3:21, 22
3:12 [m] Eph 6:19
3:13 [n] ver 7; Ex 34:33
3:14 [o] Ro 11:7, 8 [p] Ac 13:15 [q] ver 6
3:16 [r] Ro 11:23 [s] Ex 34:34
3:17 [t] Isa 61:1, 2

3:1–3 Some false teachers had started carrying forged letters of recommendation to authenticate their authority. In no uncertain terms, Paul stated that he needed no such letters. The believers to whom Paul and his companions had preached were enough of a recommendation. Paul did use letters of introduction, however, many times. He wrote them on behalf of Phoebe (Romans 16:1, 2) and Timothy (1 Corinthians 16:10, 11). These letters helped Paul's trusted companions and friends find a welcome in various churches.

3:3 Paul uses powerful imagery from famous Old Testament passages predicting the promised day of new hearts and new beginnings for God's people (see Jeremiah 31:33; Ezekiel 11:19; 36:26). No human minister can take credit for this process of conversion. It is the work of God's Spirit. We do not become believers by following some manual or using some technique. Our conversion is a result of God's implanting his Spirit in our hearts, giving us new power to live for him.

3:4, 5 Paul was not boasting; he gave God the credit for all his accomplishments. While the false teachers boasted of their own power and prestige, Paul expressed his humility before God. No-one can claim to be adequate without God's help. No-one is competent to carry out the responsibilities of God's calling in his or her own strength. Without the Holy Spirit's enabling, our natural talent can carry us only so far. As Christ's witnesses, we need the character and special strength that only God gives.

3:6 "The letter kills, but the Spirit gives life" means that trying to be saved by keeping the Old Testament laws will end in death. Only by believing in the Lord Jesus Christ can a person receive eternal life through the Holy Spirit. No-one but Jesus has ever fulfilled the law perfectly, and thus the whole world is condemned to death. The law makes people realise their sin, but it cannot give life. Under the new covenant, which means promise or agreement, eternal life comes from the Holy Spirit. The Spirit gives new life to all who believe in Christ. The moral law (Ten Commandments) still points out sin and shows us how to obey God, but forgiveness comes only through the grace and mercy of Christ (see Romans 7:10–8:2).

3:7–11 Paul contrasts the glory of the Ten Commandments with the glory of the life-giving Spirit. If the law that leads to death, was glorious, how much more glorious is God's plan to give us life through his Spirit! The sacrifice of Jesus Christ is far superior to the Old Testament system of sacrifice (see Hebrews 8; 10 for a more complete discussion). If Christianity is superior to the Judaism of the Old Testament, which was the highest form of religion on earth, it will surely be superior to any other religion we may come across. Because God's plan is wonderful by comparison to any other, we dare not reject it or treat it casually.

3:9 Paul is saying that if the old covenant had its glory (and certainly it did), just imagine how glorious the new covenant is. The law was wonderful because, although it condemned us, it pointed us to Christ. But in the new covenant, the law and the promise are fulfilled. Christ has come – by faith we can be justified (made right with God)!

3:13–18 When Moses came down Mount Sinai with the Ten Commandments, his face glowed from being in God's presence (Exodus 34:29–35). Moses had to put on a veil to keep the people from being terrified by the brightness of his face. Paul adds that this veil kept them from seeing the radiance fade away. Moses and his veil illustrate the fading of the old system and the veiling of the people's minds and understanding by their pride, hardness of heart, and refusal to repent. The veil kept them from understanding the references to Christ in the Scriptures. When anyone becomes a Christian, Christ removes the veil (3:16), giving eternal life and freedom from trying to be saved by keeping laws. And without the veil, we can be like mirrors reflecting God's glory.

3:17 Those who were trying to be saved by keeping the Old Testament law were soon tied up in rules and ceremonies. But now, through the Holy Spirit, God provides freedom from sin and con-

3:17 [u]Jn 8:32
3:18 [v]1Co 13:12 [w]2Co 4:4, 6 [x]Ro 8:29
4:1 [a]1Co 7:25
4:2 [b]1Co 4:5 [c]2Co 2:17 [d]2Co 5:11
4:3 [e]2Co 2:12 [f]2Co 3:14 [g]1Co 1:18
4:4 [h]Jn 12:31 [i]2Co 3:14
4:5 [j]1Co 1:13 [k]1Co 9:19

freedom.[u] 18And we, who with unveiled faces all reflect[a][v] the Lord's glory,[w] are
being transformed into his likeness[x] with ever-increasing glory, which comes from
the Lord, who is the Spirit.

Treasures in Jars of Clay

4 Therefore, since through God's mercy[a] we have this ministry, we do not lose
heart. 2Rather, we have renounced secret and shameful ways;[b] we do not use
deception, nor do we distort the word of God.[c] On the contrary, by setting forth the
truth plainly we commend ourselves to every man's conscience[d] in the sight of God.
3And even if our gospel[e] is veiled,[f] it is veiled to those who are perishing.[g] 4The
god[h] of this age has blinded[i] the minds of unbelievers, so that they cannot see the
light of the gospel of the glory of Christ, who is the image of God. 5For we do not
preach ourselves,[j] but Jesus Christ as Lord, and ourselves as your servants[k] for

[a] *18* Or *contemplate*

PAUL SEARCHES FOR TITUS
Paul had searched for Titus, hoping to meet him in Troas and receive news about the Corinthian church. When he did not find Titus in Troas, he went on to Macedonia (2:13), most likely to Philippi, where he found Titus.

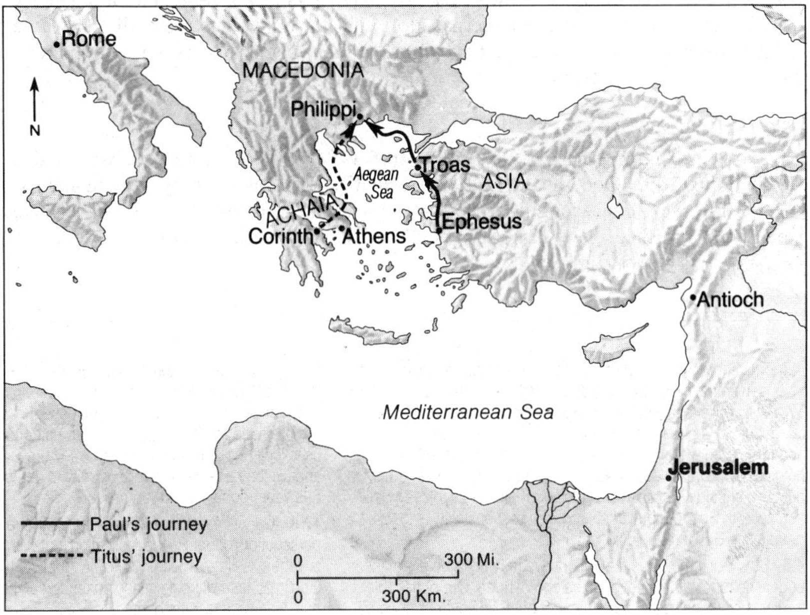

demnation (Romans 8:1). When we trust Christ to save us, he removes our heavy burden of trying to please him and our guilt for failing to do so. By trusting Christ we are loved, accepted, forgiven, and freed to live for him. "Where the Spirit of the Lord is, there is freedom".

3:18 The glory that the Spirit imparts to the believer is more excellent and lasts longer than the glory that Moses experienced. By gazing at the nature of God with unveiled minds, we can be more like him. In the gospel, we see the truth about Christ, and it transforms us morally as we understand and apply it. Through learning about Christ's life, we can understand how wonderful God is and what he is really like. As our knowledge deepens, the Holy Spirit helps us to change. Becoming Christlike is a progressive experience (see Romans 8:29; Galatians 4:19; Philippians 3:21; 1 John 3:2). The more closely we follow Christ, the more we will be like him.

4:2 Preachers, teachers, and anyone else who talks about Jesus Christ must remember that they stand in God's presence – he hears every word. When you tell people about Christ, be careful not to distort the message to please your audience. Proclaim the truth of God's word.

4:3, 4 The gospel is open and revealed to everyone, except to those who refuse to believe. Satan is "the god of this age". His work is to deceive, and he has blinded those who don't believe in Christ (see 11:14, 15). The allure of money, power, and pleasure blinds people to the light of Christ's gospel. Those who reject Christ and prefer their own pursuits have unknowingly made Satan their god.

4:5 The focus of Paul's preaching was Christ and not himself. When you witness, tell people about what Christ has done, and not about your abilities and accomplishments. People must be introduced to Christ, not to you. And if you hear someone preaching himself or his own ideas rather than Christ, beware – he is a false teacher.

4:5 Paul willingly served the Corinthian church even though the people must have deeply disappointed him. Serving people requires a sacrifice of time and personal desires. Being Christ's follower means serving others, even when they do not measure up to our expectations.

Jesus' sake. 6For God, who said, "Let light shine out of darkness,"[a] [l] made his light
shine in our hearts[m] to give us the light of the knowledge of the glory of God in the
face of Christ.
7But we have this treasure in jars of clay[n] to show that this all-surpassing power
is from God[o] and not from us. 8We are hard pressed on every side,[p] but not crushed;
perplexed, but not in despair; 9persecuted,[q] but not abandoned;[r] struck down, but
not destroyed.[s] 10We always carry around in our body the death of Jesus, so that the
life of Jesus may also be revealed in our body.[t] 11For we who are alive are always
being given over to death for Jesus' sake,[u] so that his life may be revealed in our
mortal body. 12So then, death is at work in us, but life is at work in you.[v]
13It is written: "I believed; therefore I have spoken."[b] [w] With that same spirit of
faith we also believe and therefore speak, 14because we know that the one who raised
the Lord Jesus from the dead will also raise us with Jesus[x] and present us with you
in his presence.[y] 15All this is for your benefit, so that the grace that is reaching more
and more people may cause thanksgiving[z] to overflow to the glory of God.
16Therefore we do not lose heart. Though outwardly we are wasting away, yet
inwardly[a] we are being renewed[b] day by day. 17For our light and momentary
troubles are achieving for us an eternal glory that far outweighs them all.[c] 18So we
fix our eyes not on what is seen, but on what is unseen.[d] For what is seen is temporary,
but what is unseen is eternal.

Our Heavenly Dwelling

5 Now we know that if the earthly[a] tent[b] we live in is destroyed, we have a
building from God, an eternal house in heaven, not built by human hands.
2Meanwhile we groan,[c] longing to be clothed with our heavenly dwelling,[d] 3because
when we are clothed, we will not be found naked. 4For while we are in this tent, we

[a] *6* Gen. 1:3 [b] *13* Psalm 116:10

4:6 [l]Ge 1:3 [m]2Pe 1:19
4:7 [n]Job 4:19; 2Co 5:1 [o]1Co 2:5
4:8 [p]2Co 7:5
4:9 [q]Jn 15:20 [r]Heb 13:5 [s]Ps 37:24
4:10 [t]Ro 6:5
4:11 [u]Ro 8:36
4:12 [v]2Co 13:9
4:13 [w]Ps 116:10
4:14 [x]1Th 4:14 [y]Eph 5:27
4:15 [z]2Co 1:11
4:16 [a]Ro 7:22 [b]Col 3:10
4:17 [c]Ro 8:18; 1Pe 1:6, 7
4:18 [d]Ro 8:24; Heb 11:1
5:1 [a]1Co 15:47 [b]2Pe 1:13, 14
5:2 [c]ver 4; Ro 8:23 [d]1Co 15:53, 54

4:7 The supremely valuable message of salvation in Jesus Christ has been entrusted by God to frail and fallible human beings ("jars of clay"). Paul's focus, however, was not on the perishable container but on its priceless contents – God's power dwelling in us. Though we are weak, God uses us to spread his Good News, and he gives us power to do his work. Knowing that the power is his, not ours, should keep us from pride and motivate us to keep daily contact with God, our power source. Our responsibility is to let people see God through us.

4:8–12 Paul reminds us that though we may think we are at the end of the rope, we are never at the end of hope. Our perishable bodies are subject to sin and suffering, but God never abandons us. Because Christ has won the victory over death, we have eternal life. All our risks, humiliations, and trials are opportunities for Christ to demonstrate his power and presence in and through us.

4:15–18 Paul had faced sufferings, trials, and distress as he preached the Good News. But he knew that they would one day be over, and he would obtain God's rest and rewards. As we face great troubles, it's easy to focus on the pain rather than on our ultimate goal. Just as athletes concentrate on the finish line and ignore their discomfort, we too must focus on the reward for our faith and the joy that lasts for ever. No matter what happens to us in this life, we have the assurance of eternal life, when all suffering will end and all sorrow will flee away (Isaiah 35:10).

4:16 It is easy to lose heart and give up. We have all faced problems in our relationships or in our work that have caused us to want to think about laying down the tools and walking away. Rather than giving up when persecution wore him down, Paul concentrated on experiencing the inner strength from the Holy Spirit (Ephesians 3:16). Don't let fatigue, pain, or criticism force you off the job. Renew your commitment to serving Christ. Don't forsake your eternal reward because of the intensity of today's pain. Your very weakness allows the resurrection power of Christ to strengthen you moment by moment.

4:17 Our troubles should not diminish our faith or disillusion us. We should realise that there is a purpose in our suffering. Problems and human limitations have several benefits: (1) they remind us of Christ's suffering for us; (2) they keep us from pride; (3) they cause us to look beyond this brief life; (4) they prove our faith to others; and (5) they give God the opportunity to demonstrate his power. See your troubles as opportunities!

4:18 Our ultimate hope when we are experiencing terrible illness, persecution, or pain is the realisation that this life is not all there is – there is life after death! Knowing that we will live for ever with God in a place without sin and suffering can help us live above the pain that we face in this life.

5:1–10 Paul contrasts our earthly bodies ("earthly tent") and our future resurrection bodies ("a building from God, an eternal house in heaven, not built by human hands"). Paul clearly states that our present bodies make us groan, but when we die we will not be spirits without bodies ("be found naked"). We will have new bodies that will be perfect for our everlasting life.

Paul wrote as he did because the church at Corinth was in the heart of Greek culture, and many believers had difficulty with the concept of bodily resurrection. Greeks did not believe in a bodily resurrection. Most saw the afterlife as something that happened only to the soul, with the real person imprisoned in a physical body. They believed that at death the soul is released – there is no immortality for the body, and the soul enters an eternal state. But the Bible teaches that the body and soul are not permanently separated.

Paul describes our resurrected bodies in more detail in 1 Corinthians 15:46–58. We will still have personalities and recognisable characteristics in our resurrected bodies, but through Christ's work, our bodies will be better than we can imagine. The Bible does not tell us everything about our resurrected bodies, but we know they will be perfect, without sickness, disease, or pain (see Philippians 3:21; Revelation 21:4).

5:4 [e]1Co 15:53, 54
5:5 [f]Ro 8:23; 2Co 1:22
5:7 [g]1Co 13:12
5:8 [h]Php 1:23
5:9 [i]Ro 14:18
5:10 [j]Mt 16:27; Ro 14:10; Eph 6:8
5:11 [k]Heb 10:31; Jude 23 [l]2Co 4:2
5:12 [m]2Co 3:1 [n]2Co 1:14
5:13 [o]2Co 11:1, 16, 17
5:14 [p]Gal 2:20
5:15 [q]Ro 14:7-9
5:16 [r]2Co 11:18
5:17 [s]Gal 6:15 [t]Isa 65:17; Rev 21:4, 5
5:18 [u]Ro 5:10; Col 1:20
5:19 [v]Ro 4:8
5:20 [w]2Co 6:1; Eph 6:20

groan and are burdened, because we do not wish to be unclothed but to be clothed
with our heavenly dwelling,[e] so that what is mortal may be swallowed up by life.
5 Now it is God who has made us for this very purpose and has given us the Spirit
as a deposit, guaranteeing what is to come.[f]
6 Therefore we are always confident and know that as long as we are at home in
the body we are away from the Lord. 7 We live by faith, not by sight.[g] 8 We are
confident, I say, and would prefer to be away from the body and at home with the
Lord.[h] 9 So we make it our goal to please him,[i] whether we are at home in the body
or away from it. 10 For we must all appear before the judgment seat of Christ, that
each one may receive what is due to him[j] for the things done while in the body,
whether good or bad.

The Ministry of Reconciliation

11 Since, then, we know what it is to fear the Lord,[k] we try to persuade men. What
we are is plain to God, and I hope it is also plain to your conscience.[l] 12 We are not
trying to commend ourselves to you again,[m] but are giving you an opportunity to take
pride in us,[n] so that you can answer those who take pride in what is seen rather than
in what is in the heart. 13 If we are out of our mind,[o] it is for the sake of God; if we
are in our right mind, it is for you. 14 For Christ's love compels us, because we are
convinced that one died for all, and therefore all died.[p] 15 And he died for all, that
those who live should no longer live for themselves[q] but for him who died for them
and was raised again.
16 So from now on we regard no-one from a worldly[r] point of view. Though we
once regarded Christ in this way, we do so no longer. 17 Therefore, if anyone is in
Christ, he is a new creation;[s] the old has gone, the new has come![t] 18 All this is from
God, who reconciled us to himself through Christ[u] and gave us the ministry of
reconciliation: 19 that God was reconciling the world to himself in Christ, not counting
men's sins against them.[v] And he has committed to us the message of reconciliation.
20 We are therefore Christ's ambassadors,[w] as though God were making his appeal
through us. We implore you on Christ's behalf: Be reconciled to God. 21 God made

---

5:5 The Holy Spirit within us is our guarantee that God will give us everlasting bodies at the resurrection (1:22). We have eternity in us now! This truth should give us great courage and patience to endure anything we might experience.

5:6–8 Paul was not afraid to die, because he was confident of spending eternity with Christ. Of course, facing the unknown may cause us anxiety, and leaving loved ones hurts deeply, but if we believe in Jesus Christ, we can share Paul's hope and confidence of eternal life with Christ.

5:8 For those who believe in Christ, death is only a prelude to eternal life with God. We will continue to live. Let this hope give you confidence and inspire you to faithful service.

5:9, 10 While eternal life is a free gift given on the basis of God's grace (Ephesians 2:8, 9), each of us will still be judged by Christ. This judgment will reward us for how we have lived. God's gracious gift of salvation does not free us from the requirement for faithful obedience. All Christians must give account for how they have lived (see Matthew 16:27; Romans 14:10–12; 1 Corinthians 3:10–15).

5:12 Those who "take pride in what is seen rather than in what is in the heart" are the false preachers (see 2:17) who were concerned only about getting ahead in this world. They were preaching the gospel for money and popularity, while Paul and his companions were preaching out of concern for eternity. You can identify false preachers by finding out what really motivates them. If they are more concerned about themselves than about Christ, avoid them and their message.

5:13–15 Everything that Paul and his companions did was to honour God. Christ's love controlled their lives. Because Christ died for us, we also are dead to our old lives. Like Paul, we should no longer live to please ourselves; we should spend our lives pleasing Christ, who died for us and rose from the grave.

5:17 Christians are brand-new people on the *inside.* The Holy Spirit gives them new life, and they are not the same any more. We are not reformed, rehabilitated, or re-educated – we are re-created (new creations), living in vital union with Christ (Colossians 2:6, 7). At conversion we are not merely turning over a new leaf; we are beginning a new life under a new Master.

5:18, 19 God brings us back to himself (reconciles us) by blotting out our sins (see also Ephesians 2:13–18) and making us righteous. We are no longer God's enemies, or strangers or foreigners to him, when we trust in Christ. Because we have been reconciled to God, we have the privilege of encouraging others to do the same, and thus we are those who have the "ministry of reconciliation".

5:20 An ambassador is an official representative on behalf of one country to another. As believers, we are Christ's ambassadors, sent with his message of reconciliation to the world. An ambassador of reconciliation has an important responsibility. We dare not take this responsibility lightly. How well are you fulfilling your commission as Christ's ambassador?

5:21 When we trust in Christ, we make an exchange – our sin for his righteousness. Our sin was poured into Christ at his crucifixion. His righteousness is poured into us at our conversion. This is what Christians mean by Christ's atonement for sin. In the world, bartering works only when two people exchange goods of relatively equal value. But God offers to trade his righteousness for our sin – something of immeasurable worth for something completely worthless. How grateful we should be for his kindness to us.

him who had no sin[x] to be sin[a] for us, so that in him we might become the
righteousness of God.[y]

6 As God's fellow-workers[a] we urge you not to receive God's grace in vain. 2For
he says,

> "In the time of my favour I heard you,
> and in the day of salvation I helped you."[a b]

I tell you, now is the time of God's favour, now is the day of salvation.

Paul's Hardships

3We put no stumbling-block in anyone's path,[c] so that our ministry will not be
discredited. 4Rather, as servants of God we commend ourselves in every way: in great
endurance; in troubles, hardships and distresses; 5in beatings, imprisonments[d] and
riots; in hard work, sleepless nights and hunger;[e] 6in purity, understanding, patience
and kindness; in the Holy Spirit[f] and in sincere love; 7in truthful speech[g] and in the
power of God; with weapons of righteousness[h] in the right hand and in the left;
8through glory and dishonour,[i] bad report and good report; genuine, yet regarded
as impostors;[j] 9known, yet regarded as unknown; dying,[k] and yet we live on;[l]
beaten, and yet not killed; 10sorrowful, yet always rejoicing;[m] poor, yet making many
rich;[n] having nothing, and yet possessing everything.[o]
11We have spoken freely to you, Corinthians, and opened wide our hearts to you.[p]
12We are not withholding our affection from you, but you are withholding yours from
us. 13As a fair exchange — I speak as to my children[q] — open wide your hearts also.

Do Not Be Yoked With Unbelievers

14Do not be yoked together[r] with unbelievers. For what do righteousness and
wickedness have in common? Or what fellowship can light have with darkness?[s]
15What harmony is there between Christ and Belial?[b] What does a believer[t] have
in common with an unbeliever? 16What agreement is there between the temple of God
and idols? For we are the temple[u] of the living God. As God has said: "I will live
with them and walk among them, and I will be their God, and they will be my
people."[c v]

a *21* Or *be a sin offering* a *2* Isaiah 49:8 b *15* Greek *Beliar*, a variant of *Belial* c *16* Lev. 26:12; Jer. 32:38; Ezek. 37:27

5:21 [x]Heb 4:15; 1Pe 2:22, 24; 1Jn 3:5 [y]Ro 1:17
6:1 [a]1Co 3:9; 2Co 5:20
6:2 [b]Isa 49:8
6:3 [c]Ro 14:13, 20; 1Co 9:12; 10:32
6:5 [d]2Co 11:23-25 [e]1Co 4:11
6:6 [f]1Th 1:5
6:7 [g]2Co 4:2 [h]2Co 10:4; Eph 6:10-18
6:8 [i]1Co 4:10 [j]Mt 27:63
6:9 [k]Ro 8:36 [l]2Co 1:8-10; 4:10, 11
6:10 [m]2Co 7:4 [n]2Co 8:9 [o]Ro 8:32; 1Co 3:21
6:11 [p]2Co 7:3
6:13 [q]1Co 4:14
6:14 [r]1Co 5:9, 10 [s]Eph 5:7, 11; 1Jn 1:6
6:15 [t]Ac 5:14
6:16 [u]1Co 3:16 [v]Lev 26:12; Jer 32:38; Eze 37:27

6:1 How could the Corinthian believers toss aside God's message ("receive God's grace in vain")? Perhaps they were doubting Paul and his words, confused by the false teachers who taught a different message. The people heard God's message, but did not let it affect what they said and did. How often does God's message reach you in vain?

6:2 God offers salvation to all people. Many people put off a decision for Christ, thinking that there will be a better time – but they could easily miss their opportunity altogether. There is no time like the present to receive God's forgiveness. Don't let anything hold you back from coming to Christ.

6:3 In everything he did, Paul always considered what his actions communicated about Jesus Christ. If you are a believer, you are a minister for God. In the course of each day, non-Christians observe you. Don't let your careless or undisciplined actions be another person's excuse for rejecting Christ.

6:7 See Romans 13:2; 2 Corinthians 10:3–5; and Ephesians 6:10–18 for more about the weapons of righteousness. Weapons for the right hand are offensive weapons; those for the left hand are defensive. No soldier is fully prepared for battle without both.

6:8–10 What a difference it makes to know Jesus! He cares for us in spite of what the world thinks. Christians don't have to give in to public opinion and pressure. Paul stood faithful to God whether people praised him or condemned him. He remained active, joyous, and content in the most difficult hardships. Don't let circumstances or people's expectations control you. Be firm as you stand true to God, and refuse to compromise his standards for living.

6:11–13 "Opened wide our hearts to you" and "not withholding our affection from you" mean that Paul had told the Corinthian believers his true feelings for them, clearly revealing how much he loved them. The Corinthians were reacting coldly to Paul's words, but Paul explained that his harsh words came from his love for them. It is easy to react against those whom God has placed over us in leadership, rather than to accept their exhortations as a sign of their love for us. We need an open rather than a closed heart towards God's messengers.

6:14–18 Paul urges believers not to form binding relationships with non-believers, because this might weaken their Christian commitment, integrity, or standards. It would be a mismatch. Earlier, Paul had explained that this did not mean isolating oneself from non-believers (see 1 Corinthians 5:9, 10). Paul even tells Christians to stay with their non-believing spouses (1 Corinthians 7:12, 13). Paul wants believers to be active in their witness for Christ to non-believers, but they should not lock themselves into personal or business relationships that could cause them to compromise the faith. Believers should do everything in their power to avoid situations that could force them to divide their loyalties.

6:15 Belial is a name that Paul uses for Satan. For those who have discovered God's light, there can be no fellowship or compromise with the darkness (1 Corinthians 10:20, 21).

6:17 [w]Rev 18:4 [x]Isa 52:11

6:18 [y]Isa 43:6

7:1 [a]2Co 6:17, 18

7:2 [b]2Co 6:12, 13

7:3 [c]2Co 6:11, 12

7:4 [d]2Co 6:10

7:5 [e]2Co 2:13 [f]2Co 4:8 [g]Dt 32:25

7:6 [h]2Co 1:3, 4 [i]ver 13; 2Co 2:13

7:8 [j]2Co 2:2, 4

7:10 [k]Ac 11:18

17"Therefore come out from them[w]
and be separate,
says the Lord.
Touch no unclean thing,
and I will receive you."[d][x]
18"I will be a Father to you,
and you will be my sons and daughters,[y]
says the Lord Almighty."[e]

7 Since we have these promises,[a] dear friends, let us purify ourselves from
everything that contaminates body and spirit, perfecting holiness out of reverence
for God.

Paul's Joy

2Make room for us in your hearts.[b] We have wronged no-one, we have corrupted
no-one, we have exploited no-one. 3I do not say this to condemn you; I have said
before that you have such a place in our hearts[c] that we would live or die with you.
4I have great confidence in you; I take great pride in you. I am greatly encouraged;
in all our troubles my joy knows no bounds.[d]
5For when we came into Macedonia,[e] this body of ours had no rest, but we were
harassed at every turn[f]—conflicts on the outside, fears within.[g] 6But God, who
comforts the downcast,[h] comforted us by the coming of Titus,[i] 7and not only by
his coming but also by the comfort you had given him. He told us about your longing
for me, your deep sorrow, your ardent concern for me, so that my joy was greater
than ever.
8Even if I caused you sorrow by my letter,[j] I do not regret it. Though I did regret
it—I see that my letter hurt you, but only for a little while—9yet now I am happy,
not because you were made sorry, but because your sorrow led you to repentance.
For you became sorrowful as God intended and so were not harmed in any way by
us. 10Godly sorrow brings repentance that leads to salvation[k] and leaves no regret,

d *17* Isaiah 52:11; Ezek. 20:34,41 e *18* 2 Samuel 7:14; 7:8

PRINCIPLES OF CONFRONTATION IN 2 CORINTHIANS

Method	*Reference*
Be firm and bold	7:9; 10:2
Affirm all you see that is good	7:4
Be accurate and honest	7:14; 8:21
Know the facts	11:22–27
Follow up after the confrontation	7:13; 12:14
Be gentle after being firm	7:15; 13:11–13
Speak words that reflect Christ's message, not your own ideas	10:3; 10:12, 13; 12:19
Use discipline only when all else fails	13:2

Sometimes rebuke is necessary, but it must be used with caution. The purpose of any rebuke, confrontation, or discipline is to help people, not hurt them.

6:17 Separation from the world involves more than keeping our distance from sinners; it means staying close to God (see 7:1, 2). It involves more than avoiding entertainment that leads to sin; it extends into how we spend our time and money. There is no way to separate ourselves totally from all sinful influences. Nevertheless, we are to resist the sin around us, without either giving up or giving in.

7:1 Purifying ourselves is a twofold action: turning *away* from sin, and turning *towards* God. "Perfecting holiness" means that the Corinthians were to have nothing to do with paganism. They were to make a clean break with their past and give themselves to God alone.

7:5 Here Paul resumed the story that he left in 2:13, where he said he went to Macedonia to look for Titus. Though Paul still had many problems and hardships to face, he still found comfort and joy in the progress of the ministry.

7:8ff "My letter" refers to the third letter (now lost) that Paul had written to the Corinthians. Apparently it had caused the people to begin to change. For an explanation of the chronology of Paul's letters to Corinth, see the first note on 1:1.

7:10 "Godly sorrow brings repentance that leads to salvation" refers to the sorrow for our sins that results in changed behaviour. Many people are sorry only for the effects of their sins or for being caught ("worldly sorrow"). Compare Peter's remorse and repentance with Judas' bitterness and act of suicide. Both disowned Christ. One repented and was restored to faith and service; the other took his own life.

but worldly sorrow brings death. 11See what this godly sorrow has produced in you:
what earnestness, what eagerness to clear yourselves, what indignation, what alarm,
what longing, what concern,[l] what readiness to see justice done. At every point you
have proved yourselves to be innocent in this matter. 12So even though I wrote to
you,[m] it was not on account of the one who did the wrong[n] or of the injured party,
but rather that before God you could see for yourselves how devoted to us you are.
13By all this we are encouraged.
In addition to our own encouragement, we were especially delighted to see how
happy Titus[o] was, because his spirit has been refreshed by all of you. 14I had boasted
to him about you,[p] and you have not embarrassed me. But just as everything we said
to you was true, so our boasting about you to Titus[q] has proved to be true as well.
15And his affection for you is all the greater when he remembers that you were all
obedient,[r] receiving him with fear and trembling.[s] 16I am glad I can have complete
confidence in you.[t]

3. Paul defends the collection

Generosity Encouraged

8 And now, brothers, we want you to know about the grace that God has given the
Macedonian[a] churches. 2Out of the most severe trial, their overflowing joy and
their extreme poverty welled up in rich generosity. 3For I testify that they gave as much
as they were able,[b] and even beyond their ability. Entirely on their own, 4they
urgently pleaded with us for the privilege of sharing in this service[c] to the saints.[d]
5And they did not do as we expected, but they gave themselves first to the Lord and
then to us in keeping with God's will. 6So we urged[e] Titus,[f] since he had earlier
made a beginning, to bring also to completion[g] this act of grace on your part. 7But
just as you excel in everything[h]—in faith, in speech, in knowledge,[i] in complete
earnestness and in your love for us**a**—see that you also excel in this grace of giving.
8I am not commanding you,[j] but I want to test the sincerity of your love by
comparing it with the earnestness of others. 9For you know the grace of our Lord Jesus
Christ,[k] that though he was rich, yet for your sakes he became poor,[l] so that you
through his poverty might become rich.
10And here is my advice[m] about what is best for you in this matter: Last year you

7:11 [l]ver 7
7:12 [m]ver 8; 2Co 2:3, 9 [n]1Co 5:1, 2
7:13 [o]ver 6; 2Co 2:13
7:14 [p]ver 4 [q]ver 6
7:15 [r]2Co 2:9 [s]Php 2:12
7:16 [t]2Co 2:3
8:1 [a]Ac 16:9
8:3 [b]1Co 16:2
8:4 [c]Ac 24:17 [d]Ro 15:25; 2Co 9:1
8:6 [e]ver 17; 2Co 12:18 [f]ver 16, 23 [g]ver 10, 11
8:7 [h]2Co 9:8 [i]1Co 1:5
8:8 [j]1Co 7:6
8:9 [k]2Co 13:14 [l]Mt 20:28; Php 2:6-8
8:10 [m]1Co 7:25, 40

a 7 Some manuscripts *in our love for you*

7:11 It is difficult to be confronted with our sin, and even more difficult to get rid of sin. Paul praised the Corinthians for clearing up an especially troublesome situation (see the note on 2:5–11). Do you tend to be defensive when confronted? Don't let pride keep you from admitting your sins. Accept correction as a tool for your growth, and do all you can to correct problems that are pointed out to you.

8:1ff Paul, writing from Macedonia, hoped that news of the generosity of these churches would encourage the Corinthian believers and motivate them to solve their problems and unite in fellowship.

8:2–5 During his third missionary journey, Paul had collected money for the impoverished believers in Jerusalem. The churches in Macedonia—Philippi, Thessalonica, and Berea—had given money even though they were poor, and they had given more than Paul expected. This was sacrificial giving—they were poor themselves, but they wanted to help. The point of giving is not so much the amount we give, but why and how we give. God does not want gifts given grudgingly. Instead, he wants us to give as these churches did—out of dedication to Christ, love for fellow believers, the joy of helping those in need, as well as the fact that it was simply the good and right thing to do. How well does your giving measure up to the standards set by the Macedonian churches?

8:3–6 The kingdom of God spreads through believers' concern and eagerness to help others. Here we see several churches joining to help others beyond their own circle of friends and their own city. Explore ways that you might link up with a ministry outside your city, either through your church or through a Christian organisation. By joining with other believers to do God's work, you increase Christian unity and help the kingdom grow.

8:7, 8 The Corinthian believers excelled in everything—they had faith, good preaching (speech), much knowledge, much earnestness, much love. Paul wanted them to also be leaders in giving. Giving is a natural response of love. Paul did not order the Corinthians to give, but he encouraged them to prove that their love was sincere. When you love someone, you want to give him or her your time and attention and to provide for his or her needs. If you refuse to help, your love is not as genuine as you say.

8:9 There is no evidence that Jesus was any poorer than most first-century Palestinians; rather, Jesus became poor by giving up his rights as God and becoming human. In his incarnation God voluntarily became man—the wholly human person, Jesus of Nazareth. As a man, Jesus was subject to place, time, and other human limitations. He did not give up his eternal power when he became human, but he did set aside his glory and his rights (see the note on Philippians 2:5–7). In response to the Father's will, he limited his power and knowledge. Christ became "poor" when he became human, because he set aside so much. Yet by doing so, he made us "rich" because we received salvation and eternal life.

What made Jesus' humanity unique was his freedom from sin. In his full humanity, we can see everything about God's character that can be conveyed in human terms. The incarnation is explained further in these Bible passages: John 1:1–14; Romans 1:2–5; Philippians 2:6–11; 1 Timothy 3:16; Hebrews 2:14; 1 John 1:1–3.

8:10 [n]1Co 16:2, 3; 2Co 9:2
8:11 [o]2Co 9:2
8:12 [p]Mk 12:43, 44; Lk 21:3
8:14 [q]2Co 9:12
8:15 [r]Ex 16:18
8:16 [s]2Co 2:14 [t]Rev 17:17 [u]2Co 2:13
8:17 [v]ver 6
8:18 [w]2Co 12:18 [x]1Co 7:17 [y]2Co 2:12
8:19 [z]1Co 16:3, 4 [a]ver 11, 12
8:21 [b]Ro 12:17; 14:18
8:23 [c]Phm 17 [d]Php 2:25 [e]ver 18, 22
8:24 [f]2Co 7:4, 14; 9:2

were the first not only to give but also to have the desire to do so.[n] 11Now finish
the work, so that your eager willingness[o] to do it may be matched by your completion
of it, according to your means. 12For if the willingness is there, the gift is acceptable
according to what one has,[p] not according to what he does not have.
13Our desire is not that others might be relieved while you are hard pressed, but
that there might be equality. 14At the present time your plenty will supply what they
need,[q] so that in turn their plenty will supply what you need. Then there will be
equality, 15as it is written: "He who gathered much did not have too much, and he
who gathered little did not have too little."[b][r]

Titus Sent to Corinth

16I thank God,[s] who put into the heart[t] of Titus[u] the same concern I have for
you. 17For Titus not only welcomed our appeal, but he is coming to you with much
enthusiasm and on his own initiative.[v] 18And we are sending along with him the
brother[w] who is praised by all the churches[x] for his service to the gospel.[y] 19What
is more, he was chosen by the churches to accompany us[z] as we carry the offering,
which we administer in order to honour the Lord himself and to show our eagerness
to help.[a] 20We want to avoid any criticism of the way we administer this liberal gift.
21For we are taking pains to do what is right, not only in the eyes of the Lord but
also in the eyes of men.[b]
22In addition, we are sending with them our brother who has often proved to us in
many ways that he is zealous, and now even more so because of his great confidence
in you. 23As for Titus, he is my partner[c] and fellow-worker[d] among you; as for our
brothers,[e] they are representatives of the churches and an honour to Christ. 24There-
fore show these men the proof of your love and the reason for our pride in you,[f] so
that the churches can see it.

b *15* Exodus 16:18

NEEDS OF A FUND-RAISING PROJECT

Information	8:4
Definite purpose	8:4
Readiness and willingness	9:7
Dedication	8:5
Leadership	8:7
Enthusiasm	8:7, 8, 11
Persistence	8:2ff
Honesty and integrity	8:21
Accountability	9:3
Someone to keep it moving	8:18–22

The topic of fund-raising is not one to be avoided or one that should embarrass us, but all fund-raising efforts should be planned and conducted responsibly.

8:10–15 The Corinthian church had money, and apparently they had planned to collect money for the Jerusalem churches a year previously (see also 9:2). Paul challenges them to act on their plans. Four principles of giving emerge here: (1) your willingness to give cheerfully is more important than the amount you give; (2) you should strive to fulfil your financial commitments; (3) if you give to others in need, they will, in turn, help you when you are in need; (4) you should give as a response to Christ, not for anything you can get out of it. How you give reflects your devotion to Christ.

8:12 How do you decide how much to give? What about differences in the financial resources Christians have? Paul gives the Corinthian church several principles to follow: (1) each person should follow through on previous promises (8:10, 11; 9:3); (2) each person should give as much as he or she is able (8:12; 9:6); (3) each person must make up his or her own mind how much to give (9:7); and (4) each person should give in proportion to what God has given him or her (9:10). God gives to us so that we can give to others.

8:12 Paul says that we should give of what we have, not what we don't have. Sacrificial giving must be responsible. Paul wants believers to give generously, but not to the extent that those who depend on the givers (their families, for example) must go without having their basic needs met. Give until it hurts, but don't give so that it hurts your family and/or relatives who need your financial support.

8:18–21 Another "brother" was travelling with Paul and Titus, a man who was elected by the churches to take also the large financial gift to Jerusalem. Paul explained that by travelling together there could be no suspicion and people would know that the gift was being handled honestly. The church did not need to worry that the bearers of the collection would misuse the money.

9 There is no need[a] for me to write to you about this service to the saints.[b] [2]For
I know your eagerness to help, and I have been boasting[c] about it to the
Macedonians, telling them that since last year[d] you in Achaia[e] were ready to give;
and your enthusiasm has stirred most of them to action. [3]But I am sending the brothers
in order that our boasting about you in this matter should not prove hollow, but that
you may be ready, as I said you would be.[f] [4]For if any Macedonians[g] come with
me and find you unprepared, we — not to say anything about you — would be ashamed
of having been so confident. [5]So I thought it necessary to urge the brothers to visit
you in advance and finish the arrangements for the generous gift you had promised.
Then it will be ready as a generous gift,[h] not as one grudgingly given.[i]

Sowing Generously

[6]Remember this: Whoever sows sparingly will also reap sparingly, and whoever
sows generously will also reap generously.[j] [7]Each man should give what he has
decided in his heart to give,[k] not reluctantly or under compulsion,[l] for God loves
a cheerful giver.[m] [8]And God is able[n] to make all grace abound to you, so that in
all things at all times, having all that you need,[o] you will abound in every good work.
[9]As it is written:

> "He has scattered abroad his gifts to the poor;
> his righteousness endures for ever."[a][p]

[10]Now he who supplies seed to the sower and bread for food[q] will also supply and
increase your store of seed and will enlarge the harvest of your righteousness.[r] [11]You
will be made rich[s] in every way so that you can be generous on every occasion, and
through us your generosity will result in thanksgiving to God.[t]

[12]This service that you perform is not only supplying the needs[u] of God's people
but is also overflowing in many expressions of thanks to God.[v] [13]Because of the
service[w] by which you have proved yourselves, men will praise God[x] for the
obedience that accompanies your confession of the gospel of Christ,[y] and for your
generosity in sharing with them and with everyone else. [14]And in their prayers for
you their hearts will go out to you, because of the surpassing grace God has given
you. [15]Thanks be to God[z] for his indescribable gift![a]

4. Paul defends his authority

10 By the meekness and gentleness[a] of Christ, I appeal to you — I, Paul,[b] who
am "timid" when face to face with you, but "bold" when away! [2]I beg you that
when I come I may not be as bold[c] as I expect to be towards some people
who think that we live by the standards of this world. [3]For though we live in the world,

[a] *9* Psalm 112:9

9:1 [a]1Th 4:9 [b]2Co 8:4
9:2 [c]2Co 7:4, 14 [d]2Co 8:10 [e]Ac 18:12
9:3 [f]1Co 16:2
9:4 [g]Ro 15:26
9:5 [h]Php 4:17 [i]2Co 12:17, 18
9:6 [j]Pr 11:24, 25; 22:9; Gal 6:7, 9
9:7 [k]Ex 25:2; 2Co 8:12 [l]Dt 15:10 [m]Ro 12:8
9:8 [n]Eph 3:20 [o]Php 4:19
9:9 [p]Ps 112:9
9:10 [q]Isa 55:10 [r]Hos 10:12
9:11 [s]1Co 1:5 [t]2Co 1:11
9:12 [u]2Co 8:14 [v]2Co 1:11
9:13 [w]2Co 8:4 [x]Mt 9:8 [y]2Co 2:12
9:15 [z]2Co 2:14 [a]Ro 5:15, 16
10:1 [a]Mt 11:29 [b]Gal 5:2
10:2 [c]1Co 4:21; 2Co 13:2, 10

9:3–5 Paul reminded the Corinthians to fulfil the commitment that they had already made (see also 8:10–12). They had said that they would collect a financial gift to send to the church in Jerusalem. Paul was sending a few men ahead of him to make sure their gift was ready, so it would be a real gift and not look like people had to give under pressure at the last minute ("ready as a generous gift, not as one grudgingly given"). He was holding them accountable to keep their promise, so that neither Paul nor the Corinthians would be embarrassed.

9:6–8 People may hesitate to give generously to God if they worry about having enough money left over to meet their own needs. Paul assured the Corinthians that God was able to meet their needs. The person who gives only a little will receive only a little in return. Don't let a lack of faith keep you from giving freely and generously.

9:7 Our attitude when we give is more important than the amount we give. We don't have to be embarrassed if we can give only a small gift. God is concerned about *how* we give from the resources we have (see Mark 12:41–44). According to that standard, the giving of the Macedonian churches would be difficult to match (8:3).

9:10 God gives us resources to use and invest for him. Paul uses the illustration of seed to explain that the resources God gives us are not to be hidden, foolishly devoured, or thrown away. Instead, they should be cultivated in order to produce more crops. When we invest what God has given us in his work, he will provide us with even more to give in his service.

9:12–15 Paul emphasises the spiritual rewards for those who give generously to God' s work. We should not expect to become wealthy through giving. Those who receive your gifts will be helped, will praise God, and will pray for you. As you bless others, you will be blessed.

10:1, 2 Paul's opponents questioned his authority. From 7:8–16 we know that the majority of Corinthian believers sided with Paul. However, a minority continued to slander him, saying that he was bold in his letters but had no authority in person. Chapters 10 – 13 are Paul's response to this charge.

10:3–6 We, like Paul, are merely weak humans, but we don't need to use human plans and methods to win our battles. God's mighty weapons are available to us as we fight against Satan's "strongholds". The Christian must choose whose methods to use,

10:4 [d]2Co 6:7 [e]1Co 2:5 [f]Jer 1:10; 2Co 13:10
10:5 [g]Isa 2:11, 12; 1Co 1:19 [h]2Co 9:13
10:6 [i]2Co 2:9; 7:15
10:7 [j]Jn 7:24 [k]1Co 1:12; 3:23; 14:37 [l]2Co 11:23
10:8 [m]2Co 13:10
10:10 [n]1Co 2:3; Gal 4:13, 14 [o]1Co 1:17
10:12 [p]2Co 3:1
10:13 [q]ver 15, 16
10:14 [r]1Co 3:6 [s]2Co 2:12
10:15 [t]Ro 15:20 [u]2Th 1:3
10:16 [v]Ac 19:21
10:17 [w]Jer 9:24; 1Co 1:31
10:18 [x]ver 12 [y]Ro 2:29; 1Co 4:5

we do not wage war as the world does. 4The weapons we fight with[d] are not the
weapons of the world. On the contrary, they have divine power[e] to demolish strongholds.[f] 5We demolish arguments and every pretension that sets itself up against the
knowledge of God,[g] and we take captive every thought to make it obedient[h] to
Christ. 6And we will be ready to punish every act of disobedience, once your
obedience is complete.[i]

7You are looking only on the surface of things.[a][j] If anyone is confident that he
belongs to Christ,[k] he should consider again that we belong to Christ just as much
as he.[l] 8For even if I boast somewhat freely about the authority the Lord gave us
for building you up rather than pulling you down,[m] I will not be ashamed of it. 9I
do not want to seem to be trying to frighten you with my letters. 10For some say, "His
letters are weighty and forceful, but in person he is unimpressive[n] and his speaking
amounts to nothing."[o] 11Such people should realise that what we are in our letters
when we are absent, we will be in our actions when we are present.

12We do not dare to classify or compare ourselves with some who commend
themselves.[p] When they measure themselves by themselves and compare themselves
with themselves, they are not wise. 13We, however, will not boast beyond proper
limits, but will confine our boasting to the field God has assigned to us,[q] a field that
reaches even to you. 14We are not going too far in our boasting, as would be the case
if we had not come to you, for we did get as far as you[r] with the gospel of Christ.[s]
15Neither do we go beyond our limits by boasting of work done by others.[b][t] Our
hope is that, as your faith continues to grow,[u] our area of activity among you will
greatly expand, 16so that we can preach the gospel in the regions beyond you.[v] For
we do not want to boast about work already done in another man's territory. 17But,
"Let him who boasts boast in the Lord."[c][w] 18For it is not the one who commends
himself[x] who is approved, but the one whom the Lord commends.[y]

a *7* Or *Look at the obvious facts* **b** *13–15* Or 13*We, however, will not boast about things that cannot be measured, but we will boast according to the standard of measurement that the God of measure has assigned us—a measurement that relates even to you.* 14. . . 15*Neither do we boast about things that cannot be measured in regard to the work done by others.* **c** *17* Jer. 9:24

God's or the world's. Paul assures us that God's mighty weapons—prayer, faith, hope, love, God's word, the Holy Spirit—are powerful and effective (see Ephesians 6:13–18)! These weapons can break down the proud human arguments against God and the walls that Satan builds to keep people from finding God. When dealing with the pride that keeps people from a relationship with Christ, we may be tempted to use our own methods. But nothing can break down these barriers like God's weapons.

10:5 Paul uses military terminology to describe this warfare against sin and Satan. God must be the commander in chief—even our thoughts must be submitted to his control as we live for him.

10:7–9 Those who opposed Paul portrayed him as weak and powerless, but Paul reminded the Corinthians that he claimed the power and authority of Christ. False teachers were encouraging the believers to ignore Paul, but Paul explained that the words in his letters were to be taken seriously. Paul had authority because he and his companions were the first to bring the Good News to Corinth (10:14). On the basis of this authority over them, Paul wrote to them to help them grow.

10:10 Some said that Paul's speaking amounted to nothing. Greece was known for its eloquent and persuasive orators. Evidently, some were judging Paul by comparing him to other speakers they had heard, and Paul was perhaps not the most powerful preacher (although he was an excellent debater). But Paul responded obediently to God's call and thus introduced Christianity to the Roman empire. Moses and Jeremiah also had problems with speaking (see Exodus 4:10–12; Jeremiah 1:6). Preaching ability is not the first prerequisite of a great leader!

10:12, 13 Paul criticised the false teachers who were trying to prove their goodness by comparing themselves with others rather than with God's standards. When we compare ourselves with others, we may feel pride because we think we're better. But when we measure ourselves against God's standards, it becomes obvious that we have no basis for pride. Don't worry about other people's accomplishments. Instead, continually ask: How does my life measure up to what God wants? How does my life compare to Jesus Christ?

10:17, 18 When we do something well, we want to tell others and be recognised. But recognition is dangerous—it can lead to inflated pride. How much better it is to seek the praise of God rather than the praise of people. Then, when we receive praise, we will be free to give God the credit. What should you change about the way you live in order to receive God's commendation?

Paul and the False Apostles

11 I hope you will put up with[a] a little of my foolishness;[b] but you are already
doing that. 2I am jealous for you with a godly jealousy. I promised you to one
husband,[c] to Christ, so that I might present you[d] as a pure virgin to him. 3But I am
afraid that just as Eve was deceived by the serpent's cunning,[e] your minds may
somehow be led astray from your sincere and pure devotion to Christ. 4For if someone
comes to you and preaches a Jesus other than the Jesus we preached,[f] or if you receive
a different spirit[g] from the one you received, or a different gospel[h] from the one you
accepted, you put up with it easily enough. 5But I do not think I am in the least inferior
to those "super-apostles".[i] 6I may not be a trained speaker,[j] but I do have knowledge.[k] We have made this perfectly clear to you in every way.
7Was it a sin[l] for me to lower myself in order to elevate you by preaching the
gospel of God to you free of charge?[m] 8I robbed other churches by receiving support
from them[n] so as to serve you. 9And when I was with you and needed something,
I was not a burden to anyone, for the brothers who came from Macedonia supplied
what I needed. I have kept myself from being a burden to you[o] in any way, and will
continue to do so. 10As surely as the truth of Christ is in me,[p] nobody in the regions
of Achaia[q] will stop this boasting[r] of mine. 11Why? Because I do not love you? God
knows I do![s] 12And I will keep on doing what I am doing in order to cut the ground
from under those who want an opportunity to be considered equal with us in the things
they boast about.
13For such men are false apostles,[t] deceitful[u] workmen, masquerading as apostles
of Christ.[v] 14And no wonder, for Satan himself masquerades as an angel of light.

11:1 [a]ver 4, 19, 20; Mt 17:17 [b]ver 16, 17, 21; 2Co 5:13
11:2 [c]Hos 2:19; Eph 5:26, 27 [d]2Co 4:14
11:3 [e]Ge 3:1-6, 13; Jn 8:44
11:4 [f]1Co 3:11 [g]Ro 8:15 [h]Gal 1:6-9
11:5 [i]2Co 12:11
11:6 [j]1Co 1:17 [k]Eph 3:4
11:7 [l]2Co 12:13 [m]1Co 9:18
11:8 [n]Php 4:15, 18
11:9 [o]2Co 12:13, 14, 16
11:10 [p]Ro 9:1 [q]Ac 18:12 [r]1Co 9:15
11:11 [s]2Co 12:15
11:13 [t]2Pe 2:1 [u]Tit 1:10 [v]Rev 2:2

11:1 Paul asked the Corinthian believers to bear with him as he talked a little "foolishness". In other words, Paul felt foolish rehearsing his credentials as a preacher of the gospel (11:16–21). But he thought that he had to do this in order to silence the false teachers (11:13).

11:2 Paul was anxious that the church's love should be for Christ alone, just as a pure virgin saves her love for one man only. By "virgin" he meant one who was unaffected by false doctrine.

11:3 The Corinthians' sincere and pure devotion to Christ was being threatened by false teaching. Paul did not want the believers to lose their single-minded love for Christ. Keeping Christ first in our lives can be very difficult when we have so many distractions threatening to sidetrack our faith. Just as Eve lost her focus by listening to the serpent, we too can lose our focus by letting our lives become overcrowded and confused. Is there anything that weakens your commitment to keep Christ first in your life? How can you minimize the distractions that threaten your devotion to him?

11:3, 4 The Corinthian believers fell for smooth talk and messages that sounded good and seemed to make sense. Today there are many false teachings that seem to make sense. Don't believe someone simply because he or she sounds like an authority or says words you like to hear. Search the Bible and check his or her teachings against God's Word. The Bible should be your authoritative guide. Don't listen to any "authoritative preacher" who contradicts God's Word.

11:4 The false teachers distorted the truth about Jesus and ended up preaching a different Jesus, a different spirit than the Holy Spirit, and a different gospel than God's way of salvation. Because the Bible is God's infallible Word, those who teach anything different from what it says are both mistaken and misleading.

11:5 Paul was saying that these marvellous teachers ("super-apostles") were no better than he was. They may have been more eloquent speakers, but they spoke lies and were servants of Satan.

11:6 Paul, a brilliant thinker, was not a trained, spellbinding speaker. Although his ministry was effective (see Acts 17), he had not been trained in the Greek schools of oratory and speechmaking, as many of the false teachers probably had been. Paul believed in a simple presentation of the gospel (see 1 Corinthians 1:17), and some people thought this showed simple-mindedness. Thus Paul's speaking performance was often used against him by false teachers. In all our teaching and preaching, content is far more important than the presentation. A simple, clear presentation that helps listeners understand will be of great value.

11:7 The Corinthians may have thought that preachers could be judged by how much money they demanded. A good speaker would charge a large sum, a fair speaker would be a little cheaper, and a poor speaker would speak for free. The false teachers may have argued that because Paul asked no fee for his preaching, he must have been an amateur, with little authority or competence. Believers today must be careful not to assume that every speaker who is well known and demands a large fee is superior at explaining and applying God's word.

11:7–12 Paul could have asked the Corinthian church for financial support. Jesus himself taught that those who minister for God should be supported by the people to whom they minister (Matthew 10:10). But Paul thought that asking for support in Corinth might be misunderstood. There were many false teachers who hoped to make a good profit from preaching (2:17), and Paul might look like one of them. Paul separated himself completely from those false teachers.

11:14, 15 One Jewish writing (the Apocalypse of Moses) says that the story of Eve's temptation includes Satan masquerading as an angel. Paul may have been thinking of this story, or he could have been referring to Satan's typical devices. In either case, nothing could be more deceitful than Satan, the prince of darkness (Ephesians 6:12; Colossians 1:13), disguising himself as an angel of light. In the same way, when the false teachers were claiming to represent Christ as servants of righteousness, they were lying shamelessly.

11:14, 15 Satan and his servants can deceive us by appearing to be attractive, good, and moral. Many unsuspecting people follow smooth-talking, Bible-quoting leaders into cults that alienate them from their families and lead them into the practice of immorality and deceit. Don't be fooled by external appearances. Our impressions alone are not accurate indicators of who is or isn't a

11:15 [w]Php 3:19
11:16 [x]ver 1
11:17 [y]1Co 7:12, 25
11:18 [z]Php 3:3, 4
11:19 [a]1Co 4:10
11:20 [b]Gal 2:4
11:21 [c]2Co 10:1, 10

15 It is not surprising, then, if his servants masquerade as servants of righteousness.
Their end will be what their actions deserve.[w]

Paul Boasts About His Sufferings

16 I repeat: Let no-one take me for a fool.[x] But if you do, then receive me just as
you would a fool, so that I may do a little boasting. 17 In this self-confident boasting
I am not talking as the Lord would,[y] but as a fool. 18 Since many are boasting in the
way the world does, I too will boast.[z] 19 You gladly put up with fools since you are
so wise![a] 20 In fact, you even put up with anyone who enslaves you[b] or exploits you
or takes advantage of you or pushes himself forward or slaps you in the face. 21 To
my shame I admit that we were too weak[c] for that!
What anyone else dares to boast about—I am speaking as a fool—I also dare to

PAUL'S CREDENTIALS

One of Paul's biggest problems with the church in Corinth was his concern that they viewed him as no more than a blustering preacher; thus, they were not taking seriously his advice in his letters and on his visits. Paul addressed this attitude in the letter of 2 Corinthians, pointing out his credentials as an apostle of Christ and why the Corinthians should take his advice.

1:1; 1:21; 4:1	Commissioned by God
1:18; 4:2	Spoke truthfully
1:12	Acted in holiness, sincerity, and dependence on God alone in his dealings with them
1:13, 14	Was straightforward and sincere in his letters
1:22	Had God's Holy Spirit
2:4; 6:11; 11:11	Loved the Corinthian believers
2:17	Spoke with sincerity and Christ's power
3:2, 3	Worked among them and changed their lives
3:4; 12:6	Lived as an example to the believers
4:1, 16	Did not lose heart
4:2	Taught the Bible with integrity
4:5	Had Christ as the centre of his message
4:8–12; 6:4, 5, 9, 10	Endured persecution as he taught the good news
5:18–20	Was Christ's ambassador, called to tell the good news
6:3, 4	Tried to live an exemplary life so others would not be kept from God
6:6	Led a pure life, understood the gospel, and displayed patience with the Corinthians
6:7	Was truthful and filled with God's power
6:8	Stood true to God first and always
7:2; 11:7–9	Never corrupted or exploited anyone
8:20, 21	Handled their offering for the Jerusalem believers in a responsible, blameless manner
10:1–6	Used God's weapons, not his own, for God's work
10:7, 8	Was confident that he belonged to Christ
10:12, 13	Would boast not in himself but in the Lord
10:14, 15	Had authority because he taught them the good news
11:23–33	Endured pain and danger as he fulfilled his calling
12:2–4	Was blessed with an astounding vision
12:7–10	Was constantly humbled by a "thorn in the flesh" that God refused to take away
12:12	Did miracles among them
12:19	Was always motivated to strengthen others spiritually
13:4	Was filled with God's power
13:5, 6	Passed the test
13:9	Was always concerned that his spiritual children become mature believers

true follower of Christ; so it helps to ask these questions: (1) Do the teachings confirm Scripture (Acts 17:11)? (2) Does the teacher affirm and proclaim that Jesus Christ is God who came into the world as a man to save people from their sins (1 John 4:1–3)? (3) Is the teacher's life-style consistent with Biblical morality (Matthew 12:33–37)?

boast about.[d] 22 Are they Hebrews? So am I.[e] Are they Israelites? So am I.[f] Are
they Abraham's descendants? So am I. 23 Are they servants of Christ? (I am out of
my mind to talk like this.) I am more. I have worked much harder,[g] been in prison
more frequently,[h] been flogged more severely, and been exposed to death again and
again. 24 Five times I received from the Jews the forty lashes[i] minus one. 25 Three
times I was beaten with rods,[j] once I was stoned,[k] three times I was shipwrecked,
I spent a night and a day in the open sea, 26 I have been constantly on the move. I
have been in danger from rivers, in danger from bandits, in danger from my own
countrymen,[l] in danger from Gentiles; in danger in the city,[m] in danger in the
country, in danger at sea; and in danger from false brothers.[n] 27 I have laboured and
toiled and have often gone without sleep; I have known hunger and thirst and have
often gone without food;[o] I have been cold and naked. 28 Besides everything else,
I face daily the pressure of my concern for all the churches. 29 Who is weak, and I
do not feel weak? Who is led into sin, and I do not inwardly burn?
30 If I must boast, I will boast of the things that show my weakness.[p] 31 The God
and Father of the Lord Jesus, who is to be praised for ever,[q] knows that I am not
lying. 32 In Damascus the governor under King Aretas had the city of the Damascenes
guarded in order to arrest me.[r] 33 But I was lowered in a basket from a window in
the wall and slipped through his hands.[s]

Paul's Vision and His Thorn

12 I must go on boasting.[a] Although there is nothing to be gained, I will go on
to visions and revelations[b] from the Lord. 2 I know a man in Christ who
fourteen years ago was caught up[c] to the third heaven.[d] Whether it was in the body
or out of the body I do not know—God knows.[e] 3 And I know that this man—whether
in the body or apart from the body I do not know, but God knows—4 was caught up
to paradise.[f] He heard inexpressible things, things that man is not permitted to tell.
5 I will boast about a man like that, but I will not boast about myself, except about
my weaknesses. 6 Even if I should choose to boast, I would not be a fool,[g] because
I would be speaking the truth. But I refrain, so no-one will think more of me than
is warranted by what I do or say.
7 To keep me from becoming conceited because of these surpassingly great revela-

11:21 [d] Php 3:4
11:22 [e] Php 3:5 [f] Ro 9:4
11:23 [g] 1Co 15:10 [h] Ac 16:23; 2Co 6:4, 5
11:24 [i] Dt 25:3
11:25 [j] Ac 16:22 [k] Ac 14:19
11:26 [l] Ac 9:23; 14:5 [m] Ac 21:31 [n] Gal 2:4
11:27 [o] 1Co 4:11, 12; 2Co 6:5
11:30 [p] 1Co 2:3
11:31 [q] Ro 9:5
11:32 [r] Ac 9:24
11:33 [s] Ac 9:25
12:1 [a] 2Co 11:16, 30 [b] ver 7
12:2 [c] Ac 8:39 [d] Eph 4:10 [e] 2Co 11:11
12:4 [f] Lk 23:43; Rev 2:7
12:6 [g] 2Co 11:16

11:22, 23 Paul presented his credentials to counteract the charges that the false teachers were making against him. He felt foolish boasting like this, but his list of credentials would silence any doubts about his authority. Paul wanted to keep the Corinthians from slipping under the spell of the false teachers and turning away from the gospel. Paul also gave a list of his credentials in his letter to the Philippians (see Philippians 3:4–8).

11:23–29 Paul was angry that the false teachers had impressed and deceived the Corinthians (11:13–15). Therefore, he had to re-establish his credibility and authority by listing the trials he had endured in his service for Christ. Some of these trials are recorded in the book of Acts (Acts 14:19; 16:22–24). Because Paul wrote this letter during his third missionary journey (Acts 18:23–21:17), his trials weren't over. He would experience yet further difficulties and humiliations for the cause of Christ (see Acts 21:30–33; 22:24–30). Paul was sacrificing his life for the gospel, something the false teachers would never do. The trials and hurts we experience for Christ's sake build our character, demonstrate our faith, and prepare us for further service to the Lord.

11:25 Sea travel was not as safe as it is today. Paul had been shipwrecked three times, and he would face another accident on his voyage to Rome (see Acts 27). By this time, Paul had probably made at least eight or nine voyages.

11:28, 29 Not only did Paul face beatings and dangers, he also carried the daily concern for the young churches, worrying that they were staying true to the gospel and free from false teachings and inner strife. Paul was concerned for individuals in the churches he served. If God has placed you in a position of leadership and authority, treat people with Paul's kind of empathy and concern.

11:32–33 King Aretas, king of the Nabateans (Edomites) from 9 B.C. to A.D. 40, had appointed a governor to oversee the Nabatean segment of the population in Damascus. Somehow the Jews in Damascus had been able to enlist this governor to help them try to capture Paul (see Acts 9:22–25). Paul gave a "for instance" here, describing his escape from Damascus in a basket lowered from a window in the city wall. Paul recounted this incident to show what he had endured for Christ. The false teachers couldn't make such claims.

12:2, 3 Paul continued his "boasting" by telling about visions and revelations he had received from the Lord. "I know a man in Christ" means that he was speaking about himself. He explained that he didn't know if he was taken up in his body or in his spirit, but he was in paradise ("the third heaven"). This incident cannot be positively identified with a recorded event in Paul's career, although some think this may have been when he was stoned and left for dead (Acts 14:19, 20). Paul told about this incident to show that he had been uniquely touched by God.

12:7, 8 We don't know what Paul's thorn in the flesh was, because he doesn't tell us. Some have suggested that it was malaria, epilepsy, or a disease of the eyes (see Galatians 4:13–15). Whatever the case, it was a chronic and debilitating problem, which at times kept him from working. This thorn was a hindrance to his ministry, and he prayed for its removal; but God refused. Paul was a very self-sufficient person, so this thorn must have been difficult

tions, there was given me a thorn in my flesh,[h] a messenger of Satan, to torment me.
8Three times I pleaded with the Lord to take it away from me.[i] 9But he said to me,
"My grace is sufficient for you, for my power[j] is made perfect in weakness."
Therefore I will boast all the more gladly about my weaknesses, so that Christ's power
may rest on me. 10That is why, for Christ's sake, I delight in weaknesses, in insults,
in hardships,[k] in persecutions,[l] in difficulties. For when I am weak, then I am
strong.[m]

Paul's Concern for the Corinthians

11I have made a fool of myself,[n] but you drove me to it. I ought to have been
commended by you, for I am not in the least inferior to the "super-apostles",[o] even
though I am nothing.[p] 12The things that mark an apostle – signs, wonders and
miracles[q] – were done among you with great perseverance. 13How were you inferior
to the other churches, except that I was never a burden to you?[r] Forgive me this
wrong![s]
14Now I am ready to visit you for the third time,[t] and I will not be a burden to
you, because what I want is not your possessions but you. After all, children should
not have to save up for their parents,[u] but parents for their children.[v] 15So I will
very gladly spend for you everything I have and expend myself as well.[w] If I love
you more, will you love me less? 16Be that as it may, I have not been a burden to
you.[x] Yet, crafty fellow that I am, I caught you by trickery! 17Did I exploit you
through any of the men I sent you? 18I urged[y] Titus to go to you and I sent our
brother[z] with him. Titus did not exploit you, did he? Did we not act in the same spirit
and follow the same course?
19Have you been thinking all along that we have been defending ourselves to you?
We have been speaking in the sight of God[a] as those in Christ; and everything we
do, dear friends, is for your strengthening.[b] 20For I am afraid that when I come[c]
I may not find you as I want you to be, and you may not find me as you want me
to be.[d] I fear that there may be quarrelling,[e] jealousy, outbursts of anger, factions,[f]
slander, gossip,[g] arrogance and disorder.[h] 21I am afraid that when I come again my
God will humble me before you, and I will be grieved[i] over many who have sinned
earlier[j] and have not repented of the impurity, sexual sin and debauchery in which
they have indulged.

12:7 [h]Nu 33:55
12:8 [i]Mt 26:39, 44
12:9 [j]Php 4:13
12:10 [k]2Co 6:4 [l]Ro 5:3; 2Th 1:4 [m]2Co 13:4
12:11 [n]2Co 11:1 [o]2Co 11:5 [p]1Co 15:9, 10
12:12 [q]Jn 4:48
12:13 [r]1Co 9:12, 18 [s]2Co 11:7
12:14 [t]2Co 13:1 [u]1Co 4:14, 15 [v]Pr 19:14
12:15 [w]Php 2:17; 1Th 2:8
12:16 [x]2Co 11:9
12:18 [y]2Co 8:6, 16 [z]2Co 8:18
12:19 [a]Ro 9:1 [b]2Co 10:8
12:20 [c]2Co 2:1-4 [d]1Co 4:21 [e]1Co 1:11; 3:3 [f]Gal 5:20 [g]Ro 1:29 [h]1Co 14:33
12:21 [i]2Co 2:1, 4 [j]2Co 13:2

---

for him. It kept Paul humble, reminded him of his need for constant contact with God, and benefited those around him as they saw God at work in his life.

12:9 Although God did not remove Paul's physical affliction, he promised to demonstrate his power in Paul. The fact that God's power is displayed in weak people should give us courage. Though we recognise our limitations, we will not congratulate ourselves and rest at that. Instead, we will turn to God to seek pathways for effectiveness. We must rely on God for our effectiveness rather than simply on our own energy, effort, or talent. Our weakness not only helps develop Christian character; it also deepens our worship, because in admitting our weakness, we affirm God's strength.

12:10 When we are strong in abilities or resources, we are tempted to do God's work on our own, and that can lead to pride. When we are weak, allowing God to fill us with *his* power, then we are stronger than we could ever be on our own. God does not intend for us to seek to be weak, passive, or ineffective – life provides enough hindrances and setbacks without us creating them. When those obstacles come, we must depend on God. Only his power will make us effective for him and will help us do work that has lasting value.

12:11–15 Paul was not merely revealing his feelings; he was defending his authority as an apostle of Jesus Christ. Paul was hurt that the church in Corinth doubted and questioned him, so he defended himself for the cause of the gospel, not to satisfy his ego. When you are "put on trial", do you think only about saving your reputation or are you more concerned about what people will think about Christ?

12:13 Paul explained that the only thing he did for the other churches that he didn't do in Corinth was to become a burden – to ask the believers to feed and house him. When he said, "Forgive me this wrong", he was clearly being sarcastic. He actually did more for the Corinthians than for any other church, but still they misunderstood him.

12:14 Paul had founded the church in Corinth on his first visit there (Acts 18:1). He subsequently made a second visit (2:1). He was planning what would be his third visit (see also 13:1). Paul explained that, as before, he didn't want to be paid, fed, or housed; he only wanted the believers to be nourished with the spiritual food he would feed them.

12:16–19 Although Paul asked nothing of the Corinthian believers, some doubters were still saying that Paul must have been crafty and made money from them somehow. But Paul again explained that everything he did for the believers was for their edification, not to enrich himself.

12:20, 21 After reading this catalogue of sins, it is hard to believe that these are the people that Paul said possessed great gifts and excelled as leaders (8:7). Paul feared that the practices of wicked Corinth had invaded the congregation. He wrote sternly, hoping that they would straighten out their lives before he arrived. We must live differently from unbelievers, not letting secular society dictate how we are to treat others. Don't let culture invade your practises at church.

Final Warnings

13 This will be my third visit to you.[a] "Every matter must be established by the
testimony of two or three witnesses."[a][b] 2I already gave you a warning when
I was with you the second time. I now repeat it while absent: On my return I will not
spare[c] those who sinned earlier[d] or any of the others, 3since you are demanding proof
that Christ is speaking through me.[e] He is not weak in dealing with you, but is
powerful among you. 4For to be sure, he was crucified in weakness,[f] yet he lives
by God's power.[g] Likewise, we are weak[h] in him, yet by God's power we will live
with him to serve you.
5Examine yourselves[i] to see whether you are in the faith; test yourselves.[j] Do
you not realise that Christ Jesus is in you[k]—unless, of course, you fail the test? 6And
I trust that you will discover that we have not failed the test. 7Now we pray to God
that you will not do anything wrong. Not that people will see that we have stood the
test but that you will do what is right even though we may seem to have failed. 8For
we cannot do anything against the truth, but only for the truth. 9We are glad whenever
we are weak but you are strong; and our prayer is for your perfection.[l] 10This is why
I write these things when I am absent, that when I come I may not have to be harsh
in my use of authority—the authority the Lord gave me for building you up, not for
tearing you down.[m]

Final Greetings

11Finally, brothers,[n] good-bye. Aim for perfection, listen to my appeal, be of one
mind, live in peace.[o] And the God of love and peace[p] will be with you.
12Greet one another with a holy kiss.[q] 13All the saints send their greetings.[r]
14May the grace of the Lord Jesus Christ,[s] and the love of God,[t] and the
fellowship of the Holy Spirit[u] be with you all.

a *1* Deut. 19:15

13:1 [a] 2Co 12:14 [b] Dt 19:15; Mt 18:16
13:2 [c] 2Co 1:23 [d] 2Co 12:21
13:3 [e] Mt 10:20; 1Co 5:4
13:4 [f] Php 2:7, 8; 1Pe 3:18 [g] Ro 1:4; 6:4 [h] ver 9
13:5 [i] 1Co 11:28 [j] Jn 6:6 [k] Ro 8:10
13:9 [l] ver 11
13:10 [m] 2Co 10:8
13:11 [n] 1Th 4:1; 2Th 3:1 [o] Mk 9:50 [p] Ro 15:33; Eph 6:23
13:12 [q] Ro 16:16
13:13 [r] Php 4:22
13:14 [s] Ro 16:20; 2Co 8:9 [t] Ro 5:5; Jude 21 [u] Php 2:1

13:2 When Paul arrived the third time in Corinth, he would not be lenient towards unrepentant sinners. His actions could include (1) confronting and publicly denouncing their behaviour; (2) exercising church discipline by calling them before the church leaders; or (3) excommunicating them from the church.

13:5 The Corinthians were called to examine and test themselves to see if they really were Christians. Just as we get physical check-ups, Paul urges us to give ourselves spiritual check-ups. We should look for a growing awareness of Christ's presence and power in our lives. Only then will we know if we are true Christians or merely imposters. If we're not taking active steps to grow closer to God, we are drawing further away from him.

13:8, 9 Just as parents want their children to grow into mature adults, so Paul wanted the Corinthians to grow into mature believers. As we share the gospel, our goal should not be merely to see others profess faith or begin attending church, but to see them become mature in their faith. Don't set your sights too low.

13:11 Paul's closing words—what he wanted the Corinthians to remember about the needs facing their church—are still fitting for the church today. When these qualities are not present, there are problems that must be dealt with. These traits do not come to a church by glossing over problems, conflicts, and difficulties. They are not produced by neglect, denial, withdrawal, or bitterness. They are the by-products of the extremely hard work of solving problems. Just as Paul and the Corinthians had to hammer out difficulties to bring peace, so we must *apply* the principles of God's word and not just hear them.

13:14 Paul's farewell blessing invokes all three members of the Trinity—Father (God), Son (Lord Jesus Christ), and Holy Spirit. Although the term *Trinity* is not explicitly used in Scripture, verses such as this one show that it was believed and experienced through knowing God's grace, love, and fellowship. See Luke 1:35—the angel Gabriel's announcement of Jesus' birth to Mary; Matthew 3:17—the Father's voice was heard at the baptism of Jesus; and Matthew 28:19—Jesus' commission to the disciples.

13:14 Paul was dealing with an on-going problem in the Corinthian church. He could have refused to communicate until they cleared up their situation, but he loved them and reached out to them again with the love of Christ. Love, however, means that sometimes we must confront those we care about. Both authority and personal concern are needed in dealing with people who are ruining their lives with sin. But there are several wrong approaches in confronting others, and these can further break relationships rather than heal them. We can be legalistic and blast people away with the laws they should be obeying. We can turn away from them because we don't want to face the situation. We can isolate them by gossiping about their problem and turning others against them as well. Or, like Paul, we can seek to build relationships by taking a better approach—sharing, communicating, and caring. This is a difficult approach that can drain us emotionally, but it is the best way for the other person, and it is the only Christlike way to deal with others' sin.

GALATIANS

A FAMILY, executing their carefully planned escape at midnight, dashing for the border . . . a man standing outside prison walls, gulping fresh air, awash in the new sun . . . a young woman with every trace of the ravaging drug gone from her system . . . they are FREE! With fresh anticipation, they can begin life anew.

Whether fleeing oppression, stepping out of prison, or breaking a strangling habit, freedom means life. There is nothing so exhilarating as knowing that the past is forgotten and that new options await. People yearn to be free.

The book of Galatians is the charter of Christian freedom. In this profound letter, Paul proclaims the reality of our liberty in Christ—freedom from the law and the power of sin, and freedom to serve our living Lord.

Most of the first converts and early leaders in the church were Jewish Christians who proclaimed Jesus as their Messiah. As Jewish Christians, they struggled with a dual identity: their Jewishness constrained them to be strict followers of the law; their newfound faith in Christ invited them to celebrate a holy liberty. They wondered how Gentiles (non-Jews) could be part of the kingdom of heaven.

This controversy tore the early church. Judaisers—an extremist Jewish faction within the church—taught that Gentile Christians had to submit to Jewish laws and traditions *in addition to* believing in Christ. As a missionary to the Gentiles, Paul had to confront this issue many times.

Galatians was written, therefore, to refute the Judaisers and to call believers back to the pure gospel. The good news is for all people—Jews and Gentiles alike. Salvation is by God's grace through faith in Christ Jesus *and nothing else*. Faith in Christ means true freedom.

After a brief introduction (1:1–5), Paul addresses those who were accepting the Judaiser's perverted gospel (1:6–9). He summarises the controversy, including his personal confrontation with Peter and other church leaders (1:10—2:16). He then demonstrates that salvation is by faith alone by alluding to his conversion (2:17–21), appealing to his readers' own experience of the gospel (3:1–5), and showing how the Old Testament teaches about grace (3:6–20). Next, he explains the purpose of God's laws and the relationship between law, God's promises, and Christ (3:21—4:31).

Having laid the foundation, Paul builds his case for Christian liberty. We are saved by faith, not by keeping the law (5:1–12); our freedom means that we are free to love and serve one another, not to do wrong (5:13–26); and Christians should carry each other's burdens and be kind to each other (6:1–10). In 6:11–18, Paul takes the pen into his own hand and shares his final thoughts.

As you read Galatians, try to understand this first-century conflict between grace and law, faith and deeds, but also be aware of modern parallels. Like Paul, defend the truth of the gospel and reject all those who would add to or twist this truth. You are *free* in Christ—step into the light and celebrate!

VITAL STATISTICS

PURPOSE:
To refute the Judaisers (who taught that Gentile believers must obey the Jewish law in order to be saved), and to call Christians to faith and freedom in Christ

AUTHOR:
Paul

TO WHOM WRITTEN:
The churches in southern Galatia founded on Paul's first missionary journey (including Iconium, Lystra, Derbe), and Christians everywhere

DATE WRITTEN:
About A.D. 49, from Antioch, prior to the Jerusalem council (A.D. 50)

SETTING:
The most pressing controversy in the early church was the relationship of new believers, particularly Gentiles, to the Jewish laws. This was especially a problem for the converts and for the young churches that Paul had founded on his first missionary journey. Paul wrote to correct this problem. Later, at the council in Jerusalem, the conflict was officially resolved by the church leaders.

KEY VERSE:
"It is for freedom that Christ has set us free. Stand firm, then, and do not let yourselves be burdened again by a yoke of slavery" (5:1).

KEY PEOPLE:
Paul, Peter, Barnabas, Titus, Abraham, false teachers

KEY PLACES:
Galatia, Jerusalem

SPECIAL FEATURES:
This letter is not addressed to any specific body of believers and was probably circulated to several churches in Galatia.

THE BLUEPRINT

1. Authenticity of the gospel (1:1–2:21)
2. Superiority of the gospel (3:1–4:31)
3. Freedom of the gospel (5:1–6:18)

In response to attacks from false teachers, Paul wrote to defend his apostleship and to defend the authority of the gospel. The Galatians were beginning to turn from faith to legalism. The struggle between the gospel and legalism is still a crisis. Many today would have us return to trying to earn God's favour through following rituals or obeying a set of rules. As Christians, we are not boxed in, but set free. To preserve our freedom, we must stay close to Christ and resist any who promote subtle ways of trying to earn our salvation.

MEGATHEMES

THEME	EXPLANATION	IMPORTANCE
Law	A group of Jewish teachers insisted that non-Jewish believers must obey Jewish law and traditional rules. They believed a person was saved by following the law of Moses (with emphasis on circumcision, the sign of the covenant), in addition to faith in Christ. Paul opposed them by showing that the law can't save anyone.	We can't be saved by keeping the Old Testament law, even the Ten Commandments. The law served as a guide to point out our need to be forgiven. Christ fulfilled the obligations of the law for us. We must turn to him to be saved. He alone can make us right with God.
Faith	We are saved from God's judgment and penalty for sin by God's gracious gift to us. We receive salvation by faith—trusting in him—not in anything else. Becoming a Christian is in no way based on our initiative, wise choice, or good character. We can be right with God only by believing in him.	Your acceptance by God comes through believing in Christ alone. You must never add to or twist this truth. We are saved by faith, not by the good that we do. Have you placed your whole trust and confidence in Christ? He alone can forgive you and bring you into a relationship with God.
Freedom	Galatians is our charter of Christian freedom. We are not under the jurisdiction of Jewish laws and traditions, nor under the authority of Jerusalem. Faith in Christ brings true freedom from sin and from the futile attempt to be right with God by keeping the law.	We are free in Christ, and yet freedom is a privilege. We are not free to disobey Christ or practise immorality, but we are free to serve the risen Christ. Let us use our freedom to love and to serve, not to do wrong.
Holy Spirit	We become Christians through the work of the Holy Spirit. He brings new life; even our faith to believe is a gift from him. The Holy Spirit instructs, guides, leads, and gives us power. He ends our bondage to evil desires, and he creates in us love, joy, peace, and many other wonderful changes.	When the Holy Spirit leads us, he produces his fruit in us. Just as we are saved by faith, not deeds, we also grow by faith. By believing, we can have the Holy Spirit within us, helping us live for Christ. Obey Christ by following the Holy Spirit's leading.

1. Authenticity of the gospel

1 Paul, an apostle—sent not from men nor by man, but by Jesus Christ[a] and God
the Father, who raised him from the dead[b]—2and all the brothers with me,[c]

To the churches in Galatia:[d]

1:1 [a]Ac 9:15 [b]Ac 2:24
1:2 [c]Php 4:21 [d]Ac 16:6; 1Co 16:1

1:1 Paul and Barnabas had just completed their first missionary journey (Acts 13:2–14:28). They had visited Iconium, Lystra, and Derbe, cities in the Roman province of Galatia (present-day Turkey). Upon returning to Antioch, Paul was accused by some Jewish Christians of diluting Christianity to make it more appealing to Gentiles. These Jewish Christians disagreed with Paul's statements that Gentiles did not have to follow many of the religious laws that the Jews had obeyed for centuries. Some of Paul's accusers had even followed him to those Galatian cities and had told the Gentile converts they had to be circumcised and follow all the Jewish laws and customs in order to be saved. According to these men, Gentiles had to first become Jews in order to become Christians.

In response to this threat, Paul wrote this letter to the Galatian churches. In it, he explains that following the Old Testament laws or the Jewish laws will not bring salvation. A person is saved by grace through faith. Paul wrote this letter about A.D. 49, shortly be-

1:3
[e]Ro 1:7
1:4
[f]Mt 20:28; Ro 4:25; Gal 2:20
[g]Php 4:20
1:5
[h]Ro 11:36
1:6
[i]Gal 5:8

3Grace and peace to you from God our Father and the Lord Jesus Christ,[e]
4who gave himself for our sins[f] to rescue us from the present evil age, according
to the will of our God and Father,[g] 5to whom be glory for ever and ever.
Amen.[h]

No Other Gospel

6I am astonished that you are so quickly deserting the one who called[i] you by the

CITIES IN GALATIA
Paul visited several cities in Galatia on each of his three missionary journeys. On his first journey he went through Antioch in Pisidia, Iconium, Lystra, and Derbe, and then retraced his steps; on his second journey he went by land from Antioch in Syria through the four cities in Galatia; on his third journey he also went through those cities on the main route to Ephesus.

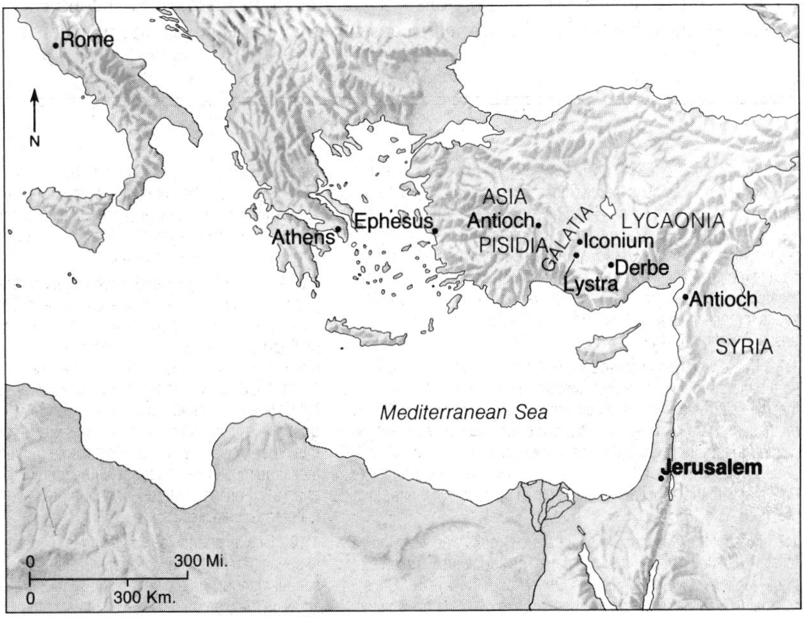

fore the meeting of the Jerusalem council, which settled the law versus grace controversy (Acts 15).

1:1 Paul was called to be an apostle by Jesus Christ and God the Father. He presented his credentials at the very outset of this letter because some people in Galatia were questioning his authority.

1:1 For more information about Paul's life, see his Profile in Acts 9. Paul had been a Christian for about 15 years at this time.

1:2 In Paul's time, *Galatia* was the Roman province located in the centre section of present-day Turkey. Much of the region rests on a large and fertile plateau, and large numbers of people had moved to the region because of its favourable agriculture. One of Paul's goals during his missionary journeys was to visit regions with large population centres in order to reach as many people as possible.

1:3–5 God's plan all along was to save us by Jesus' death. We have been rescued from the power of this present evil age – a world ruled by Satan and full of cruelty, tragedy, temptation, and deception. Being rescued from this evil age doesn't mean that we are taken out of it, but that we are no longer enslaved by it. You were saved to live for God. Does your life reflect your gratitude for being rescued? Have you transferred your loyalty from this world to Christ?

1:6 Some people were preaching "a different gospel". They were teaching that to be saved, Gentile believers had to follow Jewish laws and customs, especially the rite of circumcision. Faith in Christ was not enough. This message undermined the truth of the good news that salvation is a gift, not a reward for certain deeds. Jesus Christ has made this gift available to all people, not just to Jews. Beware of people who say that we need more than simple faith in Christ to be saved. When people set up additional requirements for salvation, they deny the power of Christ's death on the cross (see 3:1–5).

grace of Christ and are turning to a different gospel[j]— 7which is really no gospel at
all. Evidently some people are throwing you into confusion[k] and are trying to pervert
the gospel of Christ. 8But even if we or an angel from heaven should preach a gospel
other than the one we preached to you,[l] let him be eternally condemned![m] 9As we
have already said, so now I say again: If anybody is preaching to you a gospel other
than what you accepted,[n] let him be eternally condemned!
10Am I now trying to win the approval of men, or of God? Or am I trying to
please men?[o] If I were still trying to please men, I would not be a servant of
Christ.

Paul Called by God

11I want you to know, brothers,[p] that the gospel I preached is not something that
man made up. 12I did not receive it from any man,[q] nor was I taught it; rather, I
received it by revelation[r] from Jesus Christ.
13For you have heard of my previous way of life in Judaism,[s] how intensely I
persecuted the church of God and tried to destroy it.[t] 14I was advancing in Judaism

1:6 [j]2Co 11:4
1:7 [k]Ac 15:24; Gal 5:10
1:8 [l]2Co 11:4 [m]Ro 9:3
1:9 [n]Ro 16:17
1:10 [o]Ro 2:29; 1Th 2:4
1:11 [p]1Co 15:1
1:12 [q]ver 1 [r]ver 16
1:13 [s]Ac 26:4, 5 [t]Ac 8:3

1:7 There is only one way given to us by God to be forgiven of sin—through believing in Jesus Christ as Saviour and Lord. No other person, method, or ritual can give eternal life. Attempting to be open-minded and tolerant, some people assert that all religions are equally valid paths to God. In a free society, people have the right to their religious opinions, but this doesn't guarantee that their ideas are right. God does not accept man-made religion as a substitute for faith in Jesus Christ. He has provided just one way—Jesus Christ (John 14:6).

1:7 Those who had confused the Galatian believers and perverted the gospel were zealous Jewish Christians who believed that the Old Testament practices such as circumcision and dietary restrictions were required of all believers. Because these teachers wanted to turn the Gentile Christians into Jews, they were called *Judaisers.* Some time after the letter to the Galatians was sent, Paul met with the apostles in Jerusalem to discuss this matter further (see Acts 15).

1:7 Most of the Galatian Christians were Greeks who were unfamiliar with Jewish laws and customs. The Judaisers were an extreme faction of Jewish Christians. Both groups believed in Christ, but their life-styles differed considerably. We do not know why the Judaisers may have travelled no small distance to teach their mistaken notions to the new Gentile converts. They may have been motivated by (1) a sincere wish to integrate Judaism with the new Christian faith, (2) a sincere love for their Jewish heritage, or (3) a jealous desire to destroy Paul's authority. Whether or not these Judaisers were sincere, their teaching threatened these new churches and had to be countered. When Paul called their teaching a perversion of the gospel, he was not rejecting everything Jewish. He himself was a Jew who worshipped in the temple and attended the religious festivals. But he was concerned that *nothing* get in the way of the simple truth of his message—that salvation, for Jews and Gentiles alike, is through faith in Jesus Christ alone.

1:7 A twisting of the truth is more difficult to spot than an outright lie. The Judaisers were twisting the truth about Christ. They claimed to follow him, but they denied that Jesus' work on the cross was sufficient for salvation. There will always be people who pervert the Good News. Either they do not understand what the Bible teaches, or they are uncomfortable with the truth as it stands. How can we tell when people are twisting the truth? Before accepting the teachings of any group, find out what the group teaches about Jesus Christ. If their teaching does not match the truth in God's word, then it is perverted.

1:8, 9 Paul strongly denounced the Judaisers' perversion of the gospel of Christ. He said that even if an angel from heaven comes preaching another message, that angel should be "eternally condemned". If an angel came preaching another message, he would not be from heaven, no matter what he looked like. In 2 Corinthians 11:14, 15, Paul warned that Satan masquerades as an angel of light. Here he invoked a curse on any angel who spreads a false gospel—a fitting response to an emissary of hell. Paul extended that curse to include himself if he should pervert the gospel. His message must never change, for the truth of the gospel never changes. Paul used strong language because he was dealing with a life-and-death issue.

1:10 Do you spend your life trying to please everybody? Paul had to speak harshly to the Christians in Galatia because they were in serious danger. He did not apologise for his straightforward words, knowing that he could not serve Christ faithfully if he allowed the Galatian Christians to remain on the wrong track. Whose approval are you seeking—others' or God's? Pray for the courage to seek God's approval above anyone else's.

1:11ff Why should the Galatians have listened to Paul instead of the Judaisers? Paul answered this implicit question by furnishing his credentials: his message was received directly from Christ (1:12); he had been an exemplary Jew (1:13, 14); he had had a special conversion experience (1:15, 16; see also Acts 9:1–9); he had been confirmed and accepted in his ministry by the other apostles (1:18, 19; 2:1–9). Paul also presented his credentials to the Corinthian and Philippian churches (2 Corinthians 11; 12; Philippians 3:4–9).

1:12 We do not know the details of this revelation. Paul is referring to something other than his experience on the road to Damascus. His point is that his words are more than his own speculations or ideas.

1:13, 14 Paul had been one of the most religious Jews of his day, scrupulously keeping the law and relentlessly persecuting Christians (see Acts 9:1, 2). Before his conversion Paul had been even more zealous for the law than the Judaisers. He had surpassed his contemporaries in religious knowledge and practice. Paul had been sincere in his zeal—but wrong. When he met Jesus Christ, his life changed. He then directed all his energies towards building up the Christian church.

1:14 [u]Mt 15:2
1:15 [v]Isa 49:1, 5; Jer 1:5 [w]Ac 9:15
1:16 [x]Gal 2:9 [y]Mt 16:17
1:18 [z]Ac 9:22, 23 [a]Ac 9:26, 27
1:19 [b]Mt 13:55
1:20 [c]Ro 9:1
1:21 [d]Ac 6:9
1:22 [e]1Th 2:14
1:23 [f]Ac 6:7
1:24 [g]Mt 9:8

beyond many Jews of my own age and was extremely zealous for the traditions of
my fathers.[u] 15But when God, who set me apart from birth[a][v] and called me[w] by
his grace, was pleased 16to reveal his Son in me so that I might preach him among
the Gentiles,[x] I did not consult any man,[y] 17nor did I go up to Jerusalem to see those
who were apostles before I was, but I went immediately into Arabia and later returned
to Damascus.
18Then after three years,[z] I went up to Jerusalem[a] to get acquainted with Peter[b]
and stayed with him fifteen days. 19I saw none of the other apostles—only James,[b]
the Lord's brother. 20I assure you before God that what I am writing to you is no lie.[c]
21Later I went to Syria and Cilicia.[d] 22I was personally unknown to the churches of
Judea[e] that are in Christ. 23They only heard the report: "The man who formerly
persecuted us is now preaching the faith[f] he once tried to destroy." 24And they praised
God[g] because of me.

a *15* Or *from my mother's womb* b *18* Greek *Cephas*

THE MARKS OF THE TRUE GOSPEL AND OF FALSE GOSPELS

Marks of a false gospel	
2:21	Treats Christ's death as meaningless
3:12	Says people must obey the law in order to be saved
4:10	Tries to find favour with God by observing certain rituals
5:4	Counts on keeping laws to erase sin

Marks of the true gospel	
1:11, 12	Teaches that the source of the gospel is God
2:20	Knows that life is obtained through death; we trust in the God who loved us and died for us so that we might die to sin and live for him
3:14	Explains that all believers have the Holy Spirit through faith
3:21, 22	Declares that we cannot be saved by keeping laws; the only way of salvation is through faith in Christ, which is available to all
3:26–28	Says that all believers are one in Christ, so there is no basis for discrimination of any kind
5:24, 25	Proclaims that we are free from the grip of sin and that the Holy Spirit's power fills and guides us

1:14 The word *Judaism* refers not only to nationality but also to religion. To be fully Jewish, a person must have descended from Abraham. In addition, a faithful Jew adhered to the Jewish laws. *Gentiles* (1:16) are non-Jews, whether in nationality or religion. In Paul's day, Jews thought of all Gentiles as pagans. Jews avoided Gentiles, believing that contact with Gentiles brought spiritual corruption. Although Gentiles could become Jews in religion by undergoing circumcision and by following Jewish laws and customs, they were never fully accepted.

Many Jews had difficulty understanding that God's message is for Jews and Gentiles alike. Some Jews thought that Gentiles had to become Jews before they could become Christians. But God planned to save both Jews and Gentiles. He had revealed this plan through Old Testament prophets (see, for example, Genesis 12:3; Isaiah 42:6; 66:19), and he had fulfilled it through Jesus Christ; he was proclaiming it to the Gentiles through Paul.

1:15, 16 Because God was guiding his ministry, Paul wasn't doing anything that God hadn't already planned and given him power to do. Similarly, God told Jeremiah that God had called him, even before he was born, to do special work for God (Jeremiah 1:5). God knows you intimately as well, and he chose you to be his even before you were born (see Psalm 139). He wants you to draw close to him and to fulfil the purpose he has for your life.

1:15–24 Paul tells of his conversion to show that his message came directly from God. God commissioned him to preach the Good News to the Gentiles. After his call, Paul did not consult anyone; instead he spent three years in Arabia. Then he spoke with Peter and James, but he had no other contact with Jewish Christians for several more years. During those years, Paul preached to the Gentiles the message God had given him. His Good News did not come from human insight; it came from God.

1:18 This was Paul's first visit to Jerusalem as a Christian, as recorded in Acts 9:26–30.

1:21 Because of opposition in Jerusalem (see Acts 9:29, 30), Paul had gone to Syria and Cilicia. In those remote areas, he had no opportunity to receive instruction from the apostles.

1:24 Paul's changed life had brought praise from those who saw him or heard about him. His new life had astonished them. They had praised God because only God could have turned this zealous persecutor of Christians into a Christian himself. We may not have had as dramatic a change as Paul, but still our new lives should honour God in every way. When people look at you, do they recognise that God has made changes in you? If not, perhaps you are not living as you should.

Paul Accepted by the Apostles

2 Fourteen years later I went up again to Jerusalem,[a] this time with Barnabas. I
took Titus along also. 2 I went in response to a revelation and set before them the
gospel that I preach among the Gentiles.[b] But I did this privately to those who seemed
to be leaders, for fear that I was running or had run my race[c] in vain. 3 Yet not even
Titus,[d] who was with me, was compelled to be circumcised, even though he was a
Greek.[e] 4 ⌊This matter arose⌋ because some false brothers[f] had infiltrated our ranks
to spy on[g] the freedom[h] we have in Christ Jesus and to make us slaves. 5 We did
not give in to them for a moment, so that the truth of the gospel[i] might remain with
you.
6 As for those who seemed to be important[j]—whatever they were makes no
difference to me; God does not judge by external appearance[k]—those men added
nothing to my message. 7 On the contrary, they saw that I had been entrusted with the
task[l] of preaching the gospel to the Gentiles,[a][m] just as Peter[n] had been to the
Jews.[b] 8 For God, who was at work in the ministry of Peter as an apostle[o] to the Jews,
was also at work in my ministry as an apostle to the Gentiles. 9 James, Peter[c][p] and
John, those reputed to be pillars,[q] gave me and Barnabas[r] the right hand of fellowship when they recognised the grace given to me.[s] They agreed that we should go
to the Gentiles, and they to the Jews. 10 All they asked was that we should continue
to remember the poor,[t] the very thing I was eager to do.

[a] 7 Greek *uncircumcised* [b] 7 Greek *circumcised*; also in verses 8 and 9 [c] 9 Greek *Cephas*; also in verses 11 and 14

2:1 [a] Ac 15:2
2:2 [b] Ac 15:4, 12 [c] 1Co 9:24; Php 2:16
2:3 [d] 2Co 2:13 [e] Ac 16:3; 1Co 9:21
2:4 [f] 2Co 11:26 [g] Jude 4 [h] Ac 15:1; Gal 5:1, 13
2:5 [i] ver 14
2:6 [j] Gal 6:3 [k] Ac 10:34
2:7 [l] 1Th 2:4; 1Ti 1:11 [m] Ac 9:15 [n] ver 9, 11, 14
2:8 [o] Ac 1:25
2:9 [p] ver 7, 11, 14 [q] 1Ti 3:15 [r] Ac 4:36 [s] Ro 12:3
2:10 [t] Ac 24:17

2:1 Paul was converted around A.D. 35. The 14 years he mentions are probably calculated from the time of his conversion. Therefore, this trip to Jerusalem was not his first. Most likely, he made his first trip to Jerusalem around A.D. 38 (see Acts 9:26–30), and other trips to Jerusalem in approximately A.D. 44 (Acts 11:29, 30; Galatians 2:1–10), A.D. 49/50 (Acts 15), A.D. 52 (Acts 18:22, where *the church* refers to the church in Jerusalem), and A.D. 57 (Acts 21:15ff). Paul probably visited Jerusalem on several other occasions as well.

2:1 Barnabas and Titus were two of Paul's close friends. Barnabas and Paul visited Galatia together on their first missionary journey. Paul wrote a personal letter to Titus, a faithful believer and church leader serving on the island of Crete (see the book of Titus). For more information on Barnabas, see his Profile in Acts 13. For more information on Titus, see the letter Paul wrote to him in the New Testament.

2:1 After his conversion, Paul spent many years preparing for the ministry to which God had called him. This preparation period included time alone with God (1:16, 17), as well as time conferring with other Christians. Often new Christians, in their zeal, want to begin a full-time ministry without investing the necessary time studying the Bible and learning from qualified teachers. We need not wait to share Christ with our friends, but we may need more preparation before embarking on a special ministry, whether volunteer or paid. While we wait for God's timing, we should continue to study, learn, and grow.

2:2 God told Paul, through a revelation, to confer with the church leaders in Jerusalem about the message he was preaching to the Gentiles, so they would understand and approve of what he was doing. The essence of Paul's message to both Jews and Gentiles was that God's salvation is offered to all people regardless of race, sex, nationality, wealth, social standing, educational level, or anything else. Anyone can be forgiven by trusting in Christ (see Romans 10:8–13).

2:2, 3 Even though God had specifically sent him to the Gentiles (Acts 9:15, 16), Paul needed to discuss his gospel message with the leaders of the Jerusalem church (Acts 15). This meeting prevented a major split in the church, and it formally acknowledged the apostles' approval of Paul's preaching. Sometimes we avoid conferring with others because we fear that problems or arguments may develop. Instead, we should openly discuss our plans and actions with friends, counsellors, and advisers. Good communication helps everyone understand the situation better, it reduces gossip, and it builds unity in the church.

2:3–5 When Paul took Titus, a Greek Christian, to Jerusalem, the Judaisers (false brothers) said that Titus should be circumcised. Paul adamantly refused to give in to their demands. The apostles agreed that circumcision was an unnecessary rite for Gentile converts. Several years later, Paul circumcised Timothy, another Greek Christian (Acts 16:3). Unlike Titus, however, Timothy was half Jewish. Paul did not deny Jews the right to be circumcised; he was simply saying that Gentiles should not be asked to become Jews before becoming Christians.

2:4 These false brothers were most likely from the party of the Pharisees (Acts 15:5). These were the strictest religious leaders of Judaism, some of whom had been converted. We don't know if these were representatives of well-meaning converts or of those trying to pervert Christianity. Most commentators agree that neither Peter nor James had any part in this conspiracy.

2:5 We normally think of taking a stand against those who might lead us into immoral behaviour, but Paul had to take a hard line against the most "moral" of people. We must not give in to those who make the keeping of man-made standards a condition for salvation, even when such people are morally upright or in respected positions.

2:6 It's easy to rate people on the basis of their official status and to be intimidated by powerful people. But Paul was not intimidated by "those who seemed to be important" because all believers are equal in Christ. We should show respect for our spiritual leaders, but our ultimate allegiance must be to Christ. We are to serve him with our whole being. God doesn't rate us according to our status; he looks at the attitude of our hearts (1 Samuel 16:7).

2:7–9 The church leaders ("pillars")—James, Peter, and John—realised that God was using Paul to reach the Gentiles, just as Peter was being used so greatly to reach the Jews. After hearing Paul's message, they gave Paul and Barnabas their approval ("the right hand of fellowship") to continue working among the Gentiles.

2:10 The apostles were referring to the poor of Jerusalem. While many Gentile converts were financially comfortable, the Jerusalem church had suffered from the effects of a severe famine in Palestine (see Acts 11:28–30) and was struggling. So on his journeys, Paul had gathered funds for the Jewish Christians (Acts 24:17; Ro-

Paul Opposes Peter

11When Peter[u] came to Antioch,[v] I opposed him to his face, because he was
clearly in the wrong. 12Before certain men came from James, he used to eat with the
Gentiles.[w] But when they arrived, he began to draw back and separate himself from
the Gentiles because he was afraid of those who belonged to the circumcision group.[x]
13The other Jews joined him in his hypocrisy, so that by their hypocrisy even Barnabas[y] was led astray.
14When I saw that they were not acting in line with the truth of the gospel,[z] I said
to Peter[a] in front of them all, "You are a Jew, yet you live like a Gentile and not
like a Jew.[b] How is it, then, that you force Gentiles to follow Jewish customs?
15"We who are Jews by birth[c] and not 'Gentile sinners'[d] 16know that a man is
not justified by observing the law, but by faith in Jesus Christ.[e] So we, too, have

2:11 [u]ver 7, 9, 14 [v]Ac 11:19
2:12 [w]Ac 11:3 [x]Ac 11:2
2:13 [y]ver 1; Ac 4:36
2:14 [z]ver 5 [a]ver 7, 9, 11 [b]Ac 10:28
2:15 [c]Php 3:4, 5 [d]1Sa 15:18
2:16 [e]Ac 13:39; Ro 9:30

JUDAISERS VERSUS PAUL

What the Judaisers said about Paul	*Paul's defence*
They said he was perverting the truth.	He received his message from Christ himself (1:11, 12).
They said he was a traitor to the Jewish faith.	Paul was one of the most dedicated Jews of his time. Yet, in the midst of one of his most zealous acts, God transformed him through a revelation of the good news about Jesus (1:13–16; Acts 9:1–30).
They said he compromised and watered down his message for the Gentiles.	The other apostles declared that the message Paul preached was the true gospel (2:1–10).
They said he was disregarding the law of Moses.	Far from degrading the law, Paul puts the law in its proper place. He says it shows people where they have sinned, and it points them to Christ (3:19–29).

As the debate raged between the Gentile Christians and the Judaisers, Paul found it necessary to write to the churches in Galatia. The Judaisers were trying to undermine Paul's authority, and they taught a false gospel. In reply, Paul defended his authority as an apostle and the truth of his message. The debate over Jewish laws and Gentile Christians was officially resolved at the Jerusalem council (Acts 15), yet it continued to be a point of contention after that time.

---

mans 15:25–29; 1 Corinthians 16:1–4; 2 Corinthians 8). The need for believers to care for the poor is a constant theme in Scripture. But often we do nothing, caught up in meeting our own needs and desires. Perhaps we don't see enough poverty to remember the needs of the poor. The world is filled with poor people, here and in other countries. What can you do to help?

2:11 Antioch in Syria (distinguished from Antioch in Pisidia) was a major trade centre in the ancient world. Heavily populated by Greeks, it eventually became a strong Christian centre. In Antioch the believers were first called Christians (Acts 11:26). Antioch in Syria became the headquarters for the Gentile church and was Paul's base of operations.

2:11ff The Judaisers accused Paul of watering down the gospel to make it easier for Gentiles to accept, while Paul accused the Judaisers of nullifying the truth of the gospel by adding conditions to it. The basis of salvation was the issue – is salvation through Christ alone, or does it come through Christ *and* adherence to the law? The argument came to a climax when Peter, Paul, the Judaisers, and some Gentile Christians all gathered together in Antioch to share a meal. Peter probably thought that by staying away from the Gentiles, he was promoting harmony – he did not want to offend James and the Jewish Christians. James had a very prominent position and presided over the Jerusalem council (Acts 15). But Paul charged that Peter's action violated the gospel. By joining the Judaisers, Peter was implicitly supporting their claim that Christ was not sufficient for salvation. Compromise is an important element in getting on with others, but we should never compromise the truth of God's word. If we feel we have to change our Christian beliefs to match those of our companions, we are on dangerous ground.

2:11, 12 Although Peter was a leader of the church, he was acting like a hypocrite. He knew better, yet he was driven by fear of what James and the others would think. Proverbs 29:25 says, "Fear of man will prove to be a snare." Paul knew that he had to confront Peter before his actions damaged the church. So, Paul publicly opposed Peter. Note, however, that Paul did not go to the other leaders, nor did he write letters to the churches telling them not to follow Peter's example. Instead, he opposed Peter face to face. Sometimes sincere Christians, even Christian leaders, make mistakes. And it may take other sincere Christians to get them back on track. If you are convinced that someone is doing harm to himself/herself or the church, try the direct approach. There is no place for backstabbing in the body of Christ.

2:15, 16 If observing the Jewish laws cannot justify us, why should we still obey the Ten Commandments and other Old Testament laws? We know that Paul was not saying the law is bad, because in another letter he wrote, "The law is holy" (Romans 7:12). Instead, he is saying that the law can never make us acceptable to God. The law still has an important role to play in the life of a Christian. The law: (1) guards us from sin by giving us standards for behaviour; (2) convicts us of sin, leaving us the opportunity to ask for God's forgiveness; (3) drives us to trust in the sufficiency of Christ, because we can never keep the Ten Commandments perfectly. The law cannot possibly save us. But after we have become Christians, it can guide us to live as God requires.

put our faith in Christ Jesus that we may be justified by faith in Christ and not by
observing the law, because by observing the law no-one will be justified.
17“If, while we seek to be justified in Christ, it becomes evident that we ourselves
are sinners,[f] does that mean that Christ promotes sin? Absolutely not![g] 18If I rebuild
what I destroyed, I prove that I am a law-breaker. 19For through the law I died to the
law[h] so that I might live for God.[i] 20I have been crucified with Christ[j] and I no
longer live, but Christ lives in me.[k] The life I live in the body, I live by faith in the
Son of God,[l] who loved me[m] and gave himself for me.[n] 21I do not set aside the
grace of God, for if righteousness could be gained through the law,[o] Christ died for
nothing!”[d]

2. Superiority of the gospel

Faith or Observance of the Law

3 You foolish Galatians! Who has bewitched you?[a] Before your very eyes Jesus
Christ was clearly portrayed as crucified.[b] 2I would like to learn just one thing
from you: Did you receive the Spirit by observing the law, or by believing what you
heard?[c] 3Are you so foolish? After beginning with the Spirit, are you now trying to
attain your goal by human effort? 4Have you suffered so much for nothing—if it really
was for nothing? 5Does God give you his Spirit and work miracles[d] among you
because you observe the law, or because you believe what you heard?
6Consider Abraham: “He believed God, and it was credited to him as righteousness.”[a][e] 7Understand, then, that those who believe[f] are children of Abraham. 8The

d *21* Some interpreters end the quotation after verse 14. a *6* Gen. 15:6

2:17 [f]ver 15 [g]Gal 3:21
2:19 [h]Ro 7:4 [i]Ro 6:10, 11, 14; 2Co 5:15
2:20 [j]Ro 6:6 [k]1Pe 4:2 [l]Mt 4:3 [m]Ro 8:37 [n]Gal 1:4
2:21 [o]Gal 3:21
3:1 [a]Gal 5:7 [b]1Co 1:23
3:2 [c]Ro 10:17
3:5 [d]1Co 12:10
3:6 [e]Ge 15:6; Ro 4:3
3:7 [f]ver 9

2:17–19 Through studying the Old Testament Scriptures, Paul realised that he could not be saved by obeying God's laws. The prophets knew that God's plan of salvation did not rest on keeping the law (see the chart in chapter 4 for references). Because we have all been infected by sin, we cannot keep God's laws perfectly. Fortunately, God has provided a way of salvation that depends on Jesus Christ, not on our own efforts. Even though we know this truth, we must guard against the temptation of using service, good deeds, charitable giving, or any other effort as a substitute for faith.

2:20 How have we been crucified with Christ? *Legally,* God looks at us as if we had died with Christ. Because our sins died with him, we are no longer condemned (Colossians 2:13–15). *Relationally,* we have become one with Christ, and his experiences are ours. Our Christian life began when, in unity with him, we died to our old life (see Romans 6:5–11). *In our daily life,* we must regularly crucify sinful desires that keep us from following Christ. This too is a kind of dying with him (Luke 9:23–25).

And yet the focus of Christianity is not dying, but living. Because we have been crucified with Christ, we have also been raised with him (Romans 6:5). *Legally,* we have been reconciled with God (2 Corinthians 5:19) and are free to grow into Christ's likeness (Romans 8:29). And *in our daily life,* we have Christ's resurrection power as we continue to fight sin (Ephesians 1:19, 20). We are no longer alone, for Christ lives in us—he is our power for living and our hope for the future (Colossians 1:27).

2:21 Believers today may still be in danger of acting as if Christ died for nothing. How? By replacing Jewish legalism with their own brand of Christian legalism, they are giving people extra laws to obey. By believing they can earn God's favour by what they do, they are not trusting completely in Christ's work on the cross. By struggling to appropriate God's power to change them (sanctification), they are not resting in God's power to save them (justification). If we could be saved by being good, then Christ did not have to die. But the cross is the only way to salvation.

3:1 The Galatian believers had become fascinated by the false teachers' arguments, almost as though they had been bewitched. Magic was common in Paul's day (Acts 8:9–11; 13:6, 7). Magicians used both optical illusions and Satan's power to perform miracles, and people were drawn into the magician's mysterious rites without recognising their dangerous source.

3:2, 3 The believers in Galatia, some of whom may have been in Jerusalem at Pentecost and received the Holy Spirit there, knew that they hadn't received God's Spirit by obeying the Jewish laws. Paul stressed that just as they began their Christian lives in the power of the Spirit, so they should grow by the Spirit's power. The Galatians had taken a step backward when they had decided to insist on keeping the Jewish laws. We must realise that we grow spiritually because of God's work in us by his Spirit, not by following special rules.

3:5 The Galatians knew that they had received the Holy Spirit when they believed, not when they obeyed the law. People still feel insecure in their faith, because faith alone seems too easy. People still try to get closer to God by following rules. While certain disciplines (Bible study, prayer) and service may help us grow, they must not take the place of the Holy Spirit in us or become ends in themselves. By asking these questions, Paul hoped to get the Galatians to focus again on Christ as the foundation of their faith.

3:5 The Holy Spirit gives Christians great power to live for God. Some Christians want more than this. They want to live in a state of perpetual excitement. The tedium of everyday living leads them to conclude that something is wrong spiritually. Often the Holy Spirit's greatest work is teaching us to persist, to keep on doing what is right even when it no longer seems interesting or exciting. The Galatians quickly turned from Paul's Good News to the teachings of the newest teachers in town; what they needed was the Holy Spirit's gift of persistence. If the Christian life seems ordinary, you may need the Spirit to stir you up. Every day offers a challenge to live for Christ.

3:6–9 The main argument of the Judaisers was that Gentiles had to become Jews in order to become Christians. Paul exposed the flaw in this argument by showing that real children of Abraham are those who have faith, not those who keep the law. Abraham himself was saved by his faith (Genesis 15:6). All believers in every age and from every nation share Abraham's blessing. This is a comforting promise to us, a great heritage for us, and a solid foundation for living.

Scripture foresaw that God would justify the Gentiles by faith, and announced the
gospel in advance to Abraham: "All nations will be blessed through you."[b][g] 9So
those who have faith[h] are blessed along with Abraham, the man of faith.
10All who rely on observing the law are under a curse, for it is written: "Cursed
is everyone who does not continue to do everything written in the Book of the
Law."[c][i] 11Clearly no-one is justified before God by the law, because, "The righteous will live by faith."[d][j] 12The law is not based on faith; on the contrary, "The
man who does these things will live by them."[e][k] 13Christ redeemed us from the curse
of the law[l] by becoming a curse for us, for it is written: "Cursed is everyone who
is hung on a tree."[f][m] 14He redeemed us in order that the blessing given to Abraham
might come to the Gentiles through Christ Jesus,[n] so that by faith we might receive
the promise of the Spirit.[o]

The Law and the Promise

15Brothers, let me take an example from everyday life. Just as no-one can set aside
or add to a human covenant that has been duly established, so it is in this case. 16The
promises were spoken to Abraham and to his seed.[p] The Scripture does not say "and
to seeds", meaning many people, but "and to your seed",[g] meaning one person, who
is Christ. 17What I mean is this: The law, introduced 430 years[q] later, does not set
aside the covenant previously established by God and thus do away with the promise.

3:8 [g]Ge 12:3; Ac 3:25
3:9 [h]ver 7; Ro 4:16
3:10 [i]Dt 27:26; Jer 11:3
3:11 [j]Hab 2:4; Gal 2:16; Heb 10:38
3:12 [k]Lev 18:5; Ro 10:5
3:13 [l]Gal 4:5 [m]Dt 21:23; Ac 5:30
3:14 [n]Ro 4:9, 16 [o]ver 2; Joel 2:28; Ac 2:33
3:16 [p]Lk 1:55; Ro 4:13, 16
3:17 [q]Ge 15:13, 14; Ex 12:40

b *8* Gen. 12:3; 18:18; 22:18 **c** *10* Deut. 27:26 **d** *11* Hab. 2:4 **e** *12* Lev. 18:5 **f** *13* Deut. 21:23 **g** *16* Gen. 12:7; 13:15; 24:7

WHAT IS THE LAW?
Part of the Jewish law included those laws found in the Old Testament. When Paul says that non-Jews (Gentiles) are no longer bound by these laws, he is not saying that the Old Testament laws do not apply to us today. He is saying certain types of laws may not apply to us. In the Old Testament there were three categories of laws:

Ceremonial law	This kind of law relates specifically to Israel's worship (see, for example, Leviticus 1:1–13). Its primary purpose was to point forward to Jesus Christ. Therefore, these laws were no longer necessary after Jesus' death and resurrection. While we are no longer bound by ceremonial laws, the principles behind them—to worship and love a holy God—still apply. The Jewish Christians often accused the Gentile Christians of violating the ceremonial law.
Civil law	This type of law dictated Israel's daily living (see Deuteronomy 24:10, 11, for example). Because modern society and culture are so radically different, some of these guidelines cannot be followed specifically. But the principles behind the commands should guide our conduct. At times, Paul asked Gentile Christians to follow some of these laws, not because they had to, but in order to promote unity.
Moral law	This sort of law is the direct command of God—for example, the Ten Commandments (Exodus 20:1–17). It requires strict obedience. It reveals the nature and will of God, and it still applies to us today. We are to obey this moral law not to obtain salvation, but to live in ways pleasing to God.

3:10 Paul quoted Deuteronomy 27:26 to prove that, contrary to what the Judaisers claimed, the law cannot justify and save—it can only condemn. Breaking even one commandment brings a person under condemnation. And because everyone has broken the commandments, everyone stands condemned. The law can do nothing to reverse the condemnation (Romans 3:20–24). But Christ took the curse of the law upon himself when he hung on the cross. He did this so we wouldn't have to bear our own punishment. The only condition is that we accept Christ's death on our behalf as the means to be saved (Colossians 1:20–23).

3:11 Trying to be right with God ("justified") by our own effort doesn't work. Good intentions such as "I'll do better next time" or "I'll never do that again" usually end in failure. Paul points to Habakkuk's declaration (Habakkuk 2:4) that by trusting God—believing in his provision for our sins and living each day in his power—we can break this cycle of failure.

3:17 God kept his promise to Abraham (Genesis 17:7, 8)—he has not revoked it, though thousands of years have passed. He saved Abraham through his faith, and he blessed the world through Abraham by sending the Messiah as one of Abraham's descendants. Circumstances may change, but God remains constant and does not break his promises. He has promised to forgive our sins through Jesus Christ, and we can be sure that he will do so.

18For if the inheritance depends on the law, then it no longer depends on a promise;[r]
but God in his grace gave it to Abraham through a promise.
19What, then, was the purpose of the law? It was added because of transgressions[s]
until the Seed[t] to whom the promise referred had come. The law was put into effect
through angels[u] by a mediator.[v] 20A mediator,[w] however, does not represent just
one party; but God is one.
21Is the law, therefore, opposed to the promises of God? Absolutely not![x] For if
a law had been given that could impart life, then righteousness would certainly have
come by the law.[y] 22But the Scripture declares that the whole world is a prisoner of
sin,[z] so that what was promised, being given through faith in Jesus Christ, might be
given to those who believe.
23Before this faith came, we were held prisoners[a] by the law, locked up until faith
should be revealed. 24So the law was put in charge to lead us to Christ[h][b] that we
might be justified by faith.[c] 25Now that faith has come, we are no longer under the
supervision of the law.

Sons of God

26You are all sons of God[d] through faith in Christ Jesus, 27for all of you who were
baptised into Christ[e] have clothed yourselves with Christ.[f] 28There is neither Jew
nor Greek, slave nor free,[g] male nor female, for you are all one in Christ Jesus.[h]
29If you belong to Christ,[i] then you are Abraham's seed, and heirs according to the
promise.[j]

4 What I am saying is that as long as the heir is a child, he is no different from
a slave, although he owns the whole estate. 2He is subject to guardians and
trustees until the time set by his father. 3So also, when we were children, we were

h *24* Or *charge until Christ came*

3:18 [r]Ro 4:14
3:19 [s]Ro 5:20 [t]ver 16 [u]Ac 7:53 [v]Ex 20:19
3:20 [w]Heb 8:6; 9:15; 12:24
3:21 [x]Gal 2:17 [y]Gal 2:21
3:22 [z]Ro 3:9-19; 11:32
3:23 [a]Ro 11:32
3:24 [b]Ro 10:4 [c]Gal 2:16
3:26 [d]Ro 8:14
3:27 [e]Mt 28:19; Ro 6:3 [f]Ro 13:14
3:28 [g]Col 3:11 [h]Jn 10:16; 17:11; Eph 2:14, 15
3:29 [i]1Co 3:23 [j]ver 16

3:18, 19 The law has two functions. On the positive side, it reveals the nature and will of God and shows people how to live. On the negative side, it points out people's sins and shows them that it is impossible to please God by trying to obey all his laws completely. God's promise to Abraham dealt with Abraham's faith; the law focuses on actions. The covenant with Abraham shows that faith is the only way to be saved; the law shows how to obey God in grateful response. Faith does not annul the law; but the more we know God, the more we see how sinful we are. Then we are driven to depend on our faith in Christ alone for our salvation.

3:19, 20 When God gave his promise to Abraham, he did it by himself alone, without angels or Moses as mediators. Although it is not mentioned in Exodus, Jews believed that the Ten Commandments had been given to Moses by angels (Stephen referred to this in his speech, see Acts 7:38, 53). Paul was showing the superiority of salvation and growth by faith over trying to be saved by keeping the Jewish laws. Christ is the best and only way given by God for us to come to him (1 Timothy 2:5).

3:21, 22 Before faith in Christ delivered us, we were imprisoned by sin, beaten down by past mistakes, and choked by desires that we knew were wrong. God knew we were sin's prisoners, but he provided a way of escape – faith in Jesus Christ. Without Christ, everyone is held in sin's grasp, and only those who place their faith in Christ ever get out of it. Look to Christ – he is reaching out to set you free.

3:24, 25 "The supervision of the law" is like the supervision given by a tutor to a young child. We no longer need that kind of supervision. The law teaches us the *need* for salvation; God's grace *gives* us that salvation. The Old Testament still applies today. In it, God reveals his nature, his will for humanity, his moral laws, and his guidelines for living. But we cannot be saved by keeping that law; we must trust in Christ.

3:26, 27 In Roman society, a youth coming of age laid aside the robe of childhood and put on a new toga. This represented his move into adult citizenship with full rights and responsibilities. Paul combined this cultural understanding with the concept of baptism. By becoming Christians and being baptised, the Galatian believers were becoming spiritually grown up and ready to take on the privileges and responsibilities of the more mature. Paul was saying that they had laid aside the old clothes of the law, and were putting on Christ's new robe of righteousness (see 2 Corinthians 5:21; Ephesians 4:23, 24).

3:28 Some Jewish males greeted each new day by praying, "Lord, I thank you that I am not a Gentile, a slave, or a woman." The role of women was enhanced by Christianity. Faith in Christ transcends these differences and makes all believers one in Christ. Make sure you do not impose distinctions that Christ has removed. Because all believers are his heirs, no-one is more privileged than or superior to anyone else.

3:28 It's our natural inclination to feel uncomfortable around people who are different from us and to gravitate towards those who are similar to us. But when we allow our differences to separate us from our fellow believers, we are disregarding clear biblical teaching. Make a point of seeking out and appreciating people who are not just like you and your friends. You may find that you have a lot in common with them.

3:29 The original promise to Abraham was intended for the whole world, not just for Abraham's descendants (see Genesis 12:3). All believers participate in this promise and are blessed as children of Abraham.

4:3–7 The "basic principles of the world" are the elementary stages of religious practice, whether in the Jewish or pagan religion. Paul uses the illustration of slavery to show that before Christ came and died for sins, people were in bondage to the law. Thinking they could be saved by it, they became enslaved to trying – and failing – to keep it. But we who were once slaves are now God's very own children who have an intimate relationship with him. Because of Christ, there is no reason to be afraid of God. We can come boldly into his presence, knowing that he will welcome us as his family members.

4:3
[a]Gal 2:4
[b]Col 2:8, 20
4:4
[c]Mk 1:15
[d]Jn 1:14
[e]Lk 2:27
4:5
[f]Jn 1:12
4:6
[g]Ro 5:5

in slavery[a] under the basic principles of the world.[b] 4But when the time had fully
come,[c] God sent his Son, born of a woman,[d] born under law,[e] 5to redeem those
under law, that we might receive the full rights[f] of sons. 6Because you are sons, God
sent the Spirit of his Son into our hearts,[g] the Spirit who calls out, *"Abba,*[a]

[a] 6 Aramaic for *Father*

THREE DISTORTIONS OF CHRISTIANITY

Almost from the beginning there were forces at work within Christianity that could have destroyed or sidetracked the movement. Of these, three created many problems then and have continued to reappear in other forms even today. The three aberrations are contrasted to true Christianity.

Group	*Their definition of a Christian*	*Their genuine concern*	*The danger*	*Application question*
Judaised Christianity	Christians are Jews who have recognised Jesus as the promised Saviour. Therefore any Gentile desiring to become a Christian must first become a Jew.	Having a high regard for the Scriptures and God's choice of Jews as his people, they did not want to see God's commands overlooked or broken.	Tends to add human traditions and standards to God's law. Also subtracts from the Scriptures God's clear concern for all nations.	Do you appreciate God's choice of a unique people through whom he offered forgiveness and eternal life to all peoples?
Legalised Christianity	Christians are those who live by a long list of "don'ts". God's favour is earned by good behaviour.	Recognised that real change brought about by God should lead to changes in behaviour.	Tends to make God's love something to earn rather than to accept freely. Would reduce Christianity to a set of impossible rules and transform the good news into bad news.	As important as change in action is, can you see that God may be desiring different changes in you than in others?
Lawless Christianity	Christians live above the law. They need no guidelines. God's word is not as important as our personal sense of God's guidance.	Recognised that forgiveness from God cannot be based on our ability to live up to his perfect standards. It must be received by faith as a gift made possible by Christ's death on the cross.	Forgets that Christians are still human and fail consistently when trying to live only by what they "feel" God wants.	Do you recognise the ongoing need for God's expressed commands as you live out your gratitude for his great salvation?
True Christianity	Christians are those who believe inwardly and outwardly that Jesus' death has allowed God to offer them forgiveness and eternal life as a gift. They have accepted that gift through faith and are seeking to live a life of obedient gratitude for what God has done for them.	Christianity is both private and public, with heart-belief and mouth-confession. Our relationship to God and the power he provides result in obedience. Having received the gift of forgiveness and eternal life, we are now daily challenged to live that life with his help.	Avoids the above dangers.	How would those closest to you describe your Christianity? Do they think you live *so* that God will accept you or do they know that you live *because* God has accepted you in Christ?

4:4 "When the time had fully come", God sent Jesus to earth to die for our sins. For centuries the Jews had been wondering when their Messiah would come – but God's timing was perfect. We may sometimes wonder if God will ever respond to our prayers. But we must never doubt him or give up hope. At the right time he will respond. Are you waiting for God's timing? Trust his judgment and trust that he has your best interests in mind.

4:4, 5 Jesus was born of a woman – he was human. He was born as a Jew – he was subject to God's law and fulfilled it perfectly. Thus Jesus was the perfect sacrifice because, although he was fully human, he never sinned. His death bought freedom for us who were enslaved to sin so that we could be adopted into God's family.

4:5–7 Under Roman law, an adopted child was guaranteed all legal rights to his father's property, even if he was formerly a slave. He was not a second-class son; he was equal to all other sons, biological or adopted, in his father's family. *Abba* is an Aramaic word for father. It was used by Christ in his prayer in Mark 14:36. As adopted children of God, we share with Jesus all rights to God's resources. As God's heirs, we can claim what he has provided for us – our full identity as his children (see Romans 8:15–17).

Father."[h] 7So you are no longer a slave, but a son; and since you are a son, God has
made you also an heir.[i]

Paul's Concern for the Galatians

8Formerly, when you did not know God,[j] you were slaves to those who by nature
are not gods.[k] 9But now that you know God—or rather are known by God[l]—how
is it that you are turning back to those weak and miserable principles? Do you wish
to be enslaved[m] by them all over again?[n] 10You are observing special days and
months and seasons and years![o] 11I fear for you, that somehow I have wasted my
efforts on you.[p]

12I plead with you, brothers,[q] become like me, for I became like you. You have
done me no wrong. 13As you know, it was because of an illness[r] that I first preached
the gospel to you. 14Even though my illness was a trial to you, you did not treat me
with contempt or scorn. Instead, you welcomed me as if I were an angel of God, as
if I were Christ Jesus himself.[s] 15What has happened to all your joy? I can testify
that, if you could have done so, you would have torn out your eyes and given them
to me. 16Have I now become your enemy by telling you the truth?[t]

17Those people are zealous to win you over, but for no good. What they want is
to alienate you ⌞from us⌟, so that you may be zealous for them. 18It is fine to be zealous,
provided the purpose is good, and to be so always and not just when I am with you.[u]
19My dear children,[v] for whom I am again in the pains of childbirth until Christ is
formed in you,[w] 20how I wish I could be with you now and change my tone, because
I am perplexed about you!

Hagar and Sarah

21Tell me, you who want to be under the law, are you not aware of what the law
says? 22For it is written that Abraham had two sons, one by the slave woman[x] and
the other by the free woman.[y] 23His son by the slave woman was born in the ordinary
way;[z] but his son by the free woman was born as the result of a promise.[a]

24These things may be taken figuratively, for the women represent two covenants.
One covenant is from Mount Sinai and bears children who are to be slaves: This is
Hagar. 25Now Hagar stands for Mount Sinai in Arabia and corresponds to the present

4:6 [h]Ro 8:15, 16
4:7 [i]Ro 8:17
4:8 [j]1Co 1:21; Eph 2:12; 1Th 4:5 [k]2Ch 13:9; Isa 37:19
4:9 [l]1Co 8:3 [m]ver 3 [n]Col 2:20
4:10 [o]Ro 14:5
4:11 [p]1Th 3:5
4:12 [q]Gal 6:18
4:13 [r]1Co 2:3
4:14 [s]Mt 10:40
4:16 [t]Am 5:10
4:18 [u]ver 13, 14
4:19 [v]1Co 4:15 [w]Eph 4:13
4:22 [x]Ge 16:15 [y]Ge 21:2
4:23 [z]Ro 9:7, 8 [a]Ge 18:10-14; Heb 11:11

4:13, 14 Paul's illness was a sickness that he was enduring while he visited the Galatian churches. The world is often callous to people's pain and misery. Paul commended the Galatians for not scorning him, even though his condition was a trial to them (he didn't explain what was wrong with him). Such caring was what Jesus meant when he called us to serve the homeless, hungry, sick, and imprisoned as if they were Jesus himself (Matthew 25:34–40). Do you avoid those in pain or those facing difficulty—or are you willing to care for them as if they were Jesus Christ himself?

4:15 Have you lost your joy? Paul sensed that the Galatians had lost the joy of their salvation because of legalism. Legalism can take away joy because (1) it makes people feel guilty rather than loved; (2) it produces self-hatred rather than humility; (3) it stresses performance over relationship; (4) it points out how far short we fall rather than how far we've come because of what Christ did for us. If you feel guilty and inadequate, check your focus. Are you living by faith in Christ or by trying to live up to the demands and expectations of others?

4:16 Paul did not gain great popularity when he rebuked the Galatians for turning away from their first faith in Christ. Human nature hasn't changed much—we still get angry when we're scolded. But don't write off someone who challenges you. There may be truth in what he or she says. Receive his or her words with humility; carefully think them over. If you discover that you need to change an attitude or action, take steps to do it.

4:17 "Those people" refers to false teachers who claimed to be religious authorities and experts in Judaism and Christianity. Appealing to the believers' desire to do what was right, they drew quite a following. Paul said, however, that they were wrong and that their motives were selfish. False teachers are often respectable and persuasive. That is why all teachings should be checked against the Bible.

4:19 Paul led many people to Christ and helped them mature spiritually. Perhaps one reason for his success as a spiritual father was the deep concern he felt for his spiritual children; he compared his pain over their faithlessness to the pain of childbirth. We should have the same intense care for those to whom we are spiritual parents. When you lead people to Christ, remember to stand by them to help them grow.

4:21ff People are saved because of their faith in Christ, not because of what they do. Paul contrasted those who are enslaved to the law (represented by Hagar, the slave woman) with those who are free from the law (represented by Sarah, the free woman). Hagar's abuse of Sarah (Genesis 16:4) was like the persecution that the Gentile Christians were suffering from the Judaisers who insisted on keeping the law in order to be saved. Eventually Sarah triumphed because God kept his promise to give her a son, just as those who worship Christ in faith will also triumph.

4:24 Paul explained that what happened to Sarah and Hagar is an allegory or picture of the relationship between God and mankind. Paul was using a type of argument that was common in his day and that was probably being used against him by his opponents.

4:26 [b]Heb 12:22; Rev 3:12
4:27 [c]Isa 54:1
4:29 [d]ver 23 [e]Ge 21:9
4:30 [f]Ge 21:10
5:1 [a]Jn 8:32 [b]1Co 16:13 [c]Ac 15:10; Gal 2:4
5:2 [d]Ac 15:1
5:3 [e]Gal 3:10

city of Jerusalem, because she is in slavery with her children. 26But the Jerusalem that
is above[b] is free, and she is our mother. 27For it is written:

> "Be glad, O barren woman,
> who bears no children;
> break forth and cry aloud,
> you who have no labour pains;
> because more are the children of the desolate woman
> than of her who has a husband."[b][c]

28Now you, brothers, like Isaac, are children of promise. 29At that time the son born
in the ordinary way[d] persecuted the son born by the power of the Spirit.[e] It is the
same now. 30But what does the Scripture say? "Get rid of the slave woman and her
son, for the slave woman's son will never share in the inheritance with the free
woman's son."[c][f] 31Therefore, brothers, we are not children of the slave woman,
but of the free woman.

3. Freedom of the gospel

Freedom in Christ

5 It is for freedom that Christ has set us free.[a] Stand firm,[b] then, and do not let
yourselves be burdened again by a yoke of slavery.[c]
2Mark my words! I, Paul, tell you that if you let yourselves be circumcised,[d] Christ
will be of no value to you at all. 3Again I declare to every man who lets himself be
circumcised that he is required to obey the whole law.[e] 4You who are trying to be

b *27* Isaiah 54:1 **c** *30* Gen. 21:10

VICES AND VIRTUES
The Bible mentions many specific actions and attitudes that are either right or wrong. Look at the list included here. Are there a number of characteristics from the wrong column that are influencing you?

VICES
(Neglecting God and others)
Sexual immorality *(Galatians 5:19)*
Impurity *(Galatians 5:19)*
Lust *(Colossians 3:5)*
Hatred *(Galatians 5:20)*
Discord *(Galatians 5:20)*
Jealousy *(Galatians 5:20)*
Anger *(Galatians 5:20)*
Selfish ambition *(Galatians 5:20)*
Dissension *(Galatians 5:20)*
Arrogance *(2 Corinthians 12:20; Galatians 5:20)*
Envy *(Galatians 5:21)*
Murder *(Revelation 22:12–16)*
Idolatry *(Galatians 5:20; Ephesians 5:5)*
Witchcraft *(Galatians 5:20)*
Drunkenness *(Galatians 5:21)*
Wild living *(Luke 15:13; Galatians 5:21)*
Cheating *(1 Corinthians 6:8)*
Adultery *(1 Corinthians 6:9, 10)*
Homosexuality *(1 Corinthians 6:9, 10)*
Greed *(1 Corinthians 6:9, 10; Ephesians 5:5)*
Stealing *(1 Corinthians 6:9, 10)*
Lying *(Revelation 22:12–16)*

VIRTUES
(The by-products of living for God)
Love *(Galatians 5:22)*
Joy *(Galatians 5:22)*
Peace *(Galatians 5:22)*
Patience *(Galatians 5:22)*
Kindness *(Galatians 5:22)*
Goodness *(Galatians 5:22)*
Faithfulness *(Galatians 5:22)*
Gentleness *(Galatians 5:23)*
Self-control *(Galatians 5:23)*

5:1 Christ died to set us free from sin and from a long list of laws and regulations. Christ came to set us free – not free to do whatever we want because that would lead us back into slavery to our selfish desires. Rather, thanks to Christ, we are now free and able to do what was impossible before – to live unselfishly. Those who appeal to their freedom so that they can have their own way or indulge their own desires are falling back into sin. But it is also wrong to put a burden of lawkeeping on Christians. We must stand against those who would enslave us with rules, methods, or special conditions for being saved or growing in Christ.

5:2–4 Trying to be saved by keeping the law and being saved by grace are two entirely different approaches. "Christ will be of no value to you at all" means that Christ's provision for our salvation will not help us if we are trying to save ourselves. Obeying the law does not make it any easier for God to save us. All we can do is accept his gracious gift through faith. Our deeds of service must never be used to try to earn God's love or favour.

5:3, 4 Circumcision was a symbol of having the right background and doing everything required by religion. No amount of work, discipline, or moral behaviour can save us. If a person were counting on finding favour with God by being circumcised, he would also have to obey the rest of God's law completely. Trying to save ourselves by keeping all God's laws only separates us from God.

justified by law have been alienated from Christ; you have fallen away from grace.[f]
5But by faith we eagerly await through the Spirit the righteousness for which we
hope.[g] 6For in Christ Jesus neither circumcision nor uncircumcision has any value.[h]
The only thing that counts is faith expressing itself through love.[i]
7You were running a good race.[j] Who cut in on you[k] and kept you from obeying
the truth? 8That kind of persuasion does not come from the one who calls you.[l] 9"A
little yeast works through the whole batch of dough."[m] 10I am confident[n] in the Lord
that you will take no other view.[o] The one who is throwing you into confusion[p] will
pay the penalty, whoever he may be. 11Brothers, if I am still preaching circumcision,
why am I still being persecuted?[q] In that case the offence[r] of the cross has been
abolished. 12As for those agitators,[s] I wish they would go the whole way and
emasculate themselves!
13You, my brothers, were called to be free. But do not use your freedom to indulge
the sinful nature;[a][t] rather, serve one another[u] in love. 14The entire law is summed
up in a single command: "Love your neighbour as yourself."[b][v] 15If you keep
on biting and devouring each other, watch out or you will be destroyed by each
other.

Life by the Spirit

16So I say, live by the Spirit,[w] and you will not gratify the desires of the sinful
nature.[x] 17For the sinful nature desires what is contrary to the Spirit, and the Spirit

5:4 [f]Heb 12:15; 2Pe 3:17
5:5 [g]Ro 8:23, 24
5:6 [h]1Co 7:19 [i]1Th 1:3
5:7 [j]1Co 9:24 [k]Gal 3:1
5:8 [l]Ro 8:28; Gal 1:6
5:9 [m]1Co 5:6
5:10 [n]2Co 2:3 [o]Php 3:15 [p]Gal 1:7
5:11 [q]Gal 4:29; 6:12 [r]1Co 1:23
5:12 [s]ver 10
5:13 [t]1Co 8:9; 1Pe 2:16 [u]1Co 9:19; Eph 5:21
5:14 [v]Lev 19:18; Mt 22:39
5:16 [w]Ro 8:2, 4-6, 9, 14 [x]ver 24

a *13* Or *the flesh*; also in verses 16, 17, 19 and 24 b *14* Lev. 19:18

OUR WRONG DESIRES VERSUS THE FRUIT OF THE SPIRIT
The will of the Holy Spirit is in constant opposition to our sinful desires. The two are on opposite sides of the spiritual battle.

Our wrong desires are:	*The fruit of the Spirit is:*
Evil	Good
Destructive	Productive
Easy to ignite	Difficult to ignite
Difficult to stifle	Easy to stifle
Self-centred	Self-giving
Oppressive and possessive	Liberating and nurturing
Decadent	Uplifting
Sinful	Holy
Deadly	Abundant life

5:6 We are saved by faith, not by deeds. But love for others and for God is the response of those whom God has forgiven. God's forgiveness is complete, and Jesus said that those who are forgiven much love much (Luke 7:47). Because faith expresses itself through love, you can check your love for others as a way to monitor your faith.

5:9 A little yeast causes a whole lump of dough to rise. It only takes one wrong person to infect all the others.

5:11 Persecution proved that Paul was preaching the true gospel. If he had taught what the false teachers were teaching, no-one would be offended. But because he was teaching the truth, he was persecuted by both Jews and Judaisers. Have friends or loved ones rejected you because you have taken a stand for Christ? Jesus said not to be surprised if the world hates you, because it hated him (John 15:18, 19). Just as Paul continued to faithfully proclaim the message about Christ, you should continue doing the ministry God has given you – in spite of the obstacles others may put in your way.

5:13 Paul distinguishes between freedom to sin and freedom to serve. Freedom or licence to sin is no freedom at all, because it enslaves you to Satan, others, or your own sinful nature. Christians, by contrast, should not be slaves to sin, because they are free to do right and to glorify God through loving service to others.

5:14, 15 When we are not motivated by love, we become critical of others. We stop looking for good in them and see only their faults. Soon the unity of believers is broken. Have you talked behind someone's back? Have you focused on others' shortcomings instead of their strengths? Remind yourself of Jesus' command to love others as you love yourself (Matthew 22:39). When you begin to feel critical of someone, make a list of that person's positive qualities. If there are problems that need to be addressed, it is better to confront in love than to gossip.

5:16–18 If your desire is to have the qualities listed in 5:22, 23, then you know that the Holy Spirit is leading you. At the same time, be careful not to confuse your subjective feelings with the Spirit's leading. Being led by the Holy Spirit involves the desire to hear, the readiness to obey God's word, and the sensitivity to discern between your feelings and his promptings. Live each day controlled and guided by the Holy Spirit. Then the words of Christ will be in your mind, the love of Christ will be behind your actions, and the power of Christ will help you control your selfish desires.

5:17 Paul describes the two forces conflicting within us – the Holy Spirit and the sinful nature (our evil desires or inclinations that stem from our bodies; see also 5:16, 19, 24). Paul is not saying that these forces are equal – the Holy Spirit is infinitely stronger. But if we rely on our own wisdom, we will make wrong choices. If we try to follow the Spirit by our own human effort, we will fail. Our only way to freedom from our evil desires is through the empowering of the Holy Spirit (see Romans 8:9; Ephesians 4:23, 24; Colossians 3:3–8).

5:17
[y]Ro 8:5-8
[z]Ro 7:15-23
5:18
[a]Ro 6:14; 1Ti 1:9
5:19
[b]1Co 6:18
5:21
[c]Ro 13:13
5:22
[d]Mt 7:16-20; Eph 5:9
[e]Col 3:12-15
5:23
[f]Ac 24:25
5:24
[g]Ro 6:6
[h]ver 16, 17
5:26
[i]Php 2:3
6:1
[a]1Co 2:15
6:2
[b]Ro 15:1; Jas 2:8
6:3
[c]Ro 12:3; 1Co 8:2
6:6
[d]1Co 9:11, 14
6:7
[e]1Co 6:9
[f]2Co 9:6
6:8
[g]Job 4:8; Hos 8:7

what is contrary to the sinful nature.[y] They are in conflict with each other, so that
you do not do what you want.[z] 18 But if you are led by the Spirit, you are not under
law.[a]
19 The acts of the sinful nature are obvious: sexual immorality,[b] impurity and
debauchery; 20 idolatry and witchcraft; hatred, discord, jealousy, fits of rage, selfish
ambition, dissensions, factions 21 and envy; drunkenness, orgies, and the like.[c] I warn
you, as I did before, that those who live like this will not inherit the kingdom of God.
22 But the fruit[d] of the Spirit is love,[e] joy, peace, patience, kindness, goodness,
faithfulness, 23 gentleness and self-control.[f] Against such things there is no law.
24 Those who belong to Christ Jesus have crucified the sinful nature[g] with its passions
and desires.[h] 25 Since we live by the Spirit, let us keep in step with the Spirit. 26 Let
us not become conceited,[i] provoking and envying each other.

Doing Good to All

6 Brothers, if someone is caught in a sin, you who are spiritual[a] should restore
him gently. But watch yourself, or you also may be tempted. 2 Carry each other's
burdens, and in this way you will fulfil the law of Christ.[b] 3 If anyone thinks he is
something[c] when he is nothing, he deceives himself. 4 Each one should test his own
actions. Then he can take pride in himself, without comparing himself to somebody
else, 5 for each one should carry his own load.
6 Anyone who receives instruction in the word must share all good things with his
instructor.[d]
7 Do not be deceived:[e] God cannot be mocked. A man reaps what he sows.[f] 8 The
one who sows to please his sinful nature, from that nature[a] will reap destruction;[g]

[a] 8 *Or his flesh, from the flesh*

5:19–21 We all have evil desires, and we can't ignore them. In order for us to follow the Holy Spirit's guidance, we must deal with them decisively (crucify them – 5:24). These desires include obvious sins such as sexual immorality and witchcraft. They also include less obvious sins such as selfish ambition, hatred, and jealousy. Those who ignore such sins or refuse to deal with them reveal that they have not received the gift of the Spirit that leads to a transformed life.

5:22, 23 The fruit of the Spirit is the spontaneous work of the Holy Spirit in us. The Spirit produces these character traits that are found in the nature of Christ. They are the by-products of Christ's control – we can't obtain them by *trying* to get them without his help. If we want the fruit of the Spirit to grow in us, we must join our lives to his (see John 15:4, 5). We must know him, love him, remember him, and imitate him. As a result, we will fulfil the intended purpose of the law – to love God and our neighbours. Which of these qualities do you want the Spirit to produce in you?

5:23 Because the God who sent the law also sent the Spirit, the by-products of the Spirit-filled life are in perfect harmony with the intent of God's law. A person who exhibits the fruit of the Spirit fulfils the law far better than a person who observes the rituals but has little love in his or her heart.

5:24 In order to accept Christ as Saviour, we need to turn from our sins and willingly nail our sinful nature to the cross. This doesn't mean, however, that we will never see traces of its evil desires again. As Christians we still have the capacity to sin, but we have been set free from sin's power over us and no longer have to give in to it. We must daily commit our sinful tendencies to God's control, daily crucify them, and moment by moment draw on the Spirit's power to overcome them (see 2:20; 6:14).

5:25 God is interested in every part of our lives, not just the spiritual part. As we live by the Holy Spirit's power, we need to submit every aspect of our lives to God – emotional, physical, social, intellectual, vocational. Paul says that because we're saved, we should live like it! The Holy Spirit is the source of your new life, so keep in step with his leading. Don't let anything or anyone else determine your values and standards in any area of your life.

5:26 Everyone needs a certain amount of approval from others. But those who go out of their way to secure honours or to win popularity with a lot of people become conceited and show they are not following the Holy Spirit's leading. Those who look to God for approval won't need to envy others. Because we are God's sons and daughters, we have his Holy Spirit as the loving guarantee of his approval.

6:1–3 No Christian should ever think that he or she is totally independent and doesn't need help from others, and no-one should feel excused from the task of helping others. The body of Christ – the church – functions only when the members work together for the common good. Do you know someone who needs help? Is there a Christian brother or sister who needs correction or encouragement? Humbly and gently reach out to that person (John 13:34, 35).

6:4 When you do your very best, you feel good about the results. There is no need to compare yourself with others. People make comparisons for many reasons. Some point out others' flaws in order to feel better about themselves. Others simply want reassurance that they are doing well. When you are tempted to compare, look at Jesus Christ. His example will inspire you to do your very best, and his loving acceptance will comfort you when you fall short of your expectations.

6:6 Paul says that students should take care of the material needs of their teachers (1 Corinthians 9:7–12). It is easy to receive the benefit of good Bible teaching and then to take our spiritual leaders for granted, ignoring their financial and physical needs. We should care for our teachers, not grudgingly or reluctantly, but with a generous spirit, showing honour and appreciation for all they have done (1 Timothy 5:17, 18).

6:7, 8 It would certainly be a surprise if you planted corn and potatoes came up. It's a natural law to reap what we sow. It's true in other areas too. If you gossip about your friends, you will lose their friendship. Every action has results. If you plant to please your own desires, you'll reap a crop of sorrow and evil. If you plant to please God, you'll reap joy and everlasting life. What kind of seeds are you sowing?

the one who sows to please the Spirit, from the Spirit will reap eternal life.[h] 9Let
us not become weary in doing good,[i] for at the proper time we will reap a harvest
if we do not give up.[j] 10Therefore, as we have opportunity, let us do good[k] to all
people, especially to those who belong to the family[l] of believers.

Not Circumcision but a New Creation

11See what large letters I use as I write to you with my own hand![m]
12Those who want to make a good impression outwardly are trying to compel you
to be circumcised.[n] The only reason they do this is to avoid being persecuted[o] for
the cross of Christ. 13Not even those who are circumcised obey the law,[p] yet they
want you to be circumcised that they may boast about your flesh.[q] 14May I never
boast except in the cross of our Lord Jesus Christ, through which[b] the world has been
crucified to me, and I to the world.[r] 15Neither circumcision nor uncircumcision
means anything;[s] what counts is a new creation.[t] 16Peace and mercy to all who
follow this rule, even to the Israel of God.
17Finally, let no-one cause me trouble, for I bear on my body the marks[u] of Jesus.
18The grace of our Lord Jesus Christ[v] be with your spirit,[w] brothers. Amen.

b *14* Or *whom*

6:8 [h] Jas 3:18
6:9 [i] 1Co 15:58 [j] Rev 2:10
6:10 [k] Pr 3:27 [l] Eph 2:19
6:11 [m] 1Co 16:21
6:12 [n] Ac 15:1 [o] Gal 5:11
6:13 [p] Ro 2:25 [q] Php 3:3
6:14 [r] Ro 6:2, 6
6:15 [s] 1Co 7:19 [t] 2Co 5:17
6:17 [u] Isa 44:5; 2Co 1:5
6:18 [v] Ro 16:20 [w] 2Ti 4:22

6:9, 10 It is discouraging to continue to do right and receive no word of thanks or see no tangible results. But Paul challenged the Galatians and he challenges us to keep on doing good and to trust God for the results. In due time, we will reap a harvest of blessing.

6:11 Up to this point, Paul had probably dictated the letter to a scribe. Here he takes the pen into his own hand to write his final, personal greetings. Paul did this in other letters as well, to add emphasis to his words and to validate that the letter was genuine.

6:13 Some of the Judaisers were emphasising circumcision as proof of holiness – but ignoring the other Jewish laws. People often choose a certain principle or prohibition and make it the measure of faith. Some may abhor drunkenness but ignore gluttony. Others may despise promiscuity but tolerate prejudice. The Bible in its entirety is our rule of faith and practice. We cannot pick and choose the mandates we will follow.

6:14 The world is full of enticements. Daily we are confronted with subtle cultural pressures and overt propaganda. The only way to escape these destructive influences is to ask God to help crucify our interest in them, just as Paul did. How much do the interests of this world matter to you? (See 2:20 and 5:24 for more on this concept.)

6:15 It is easy to get caught up with the externals. Beware of those who emphasise actions that we should or shouldn't do, with no concern for the inward condition of the heart. Living a good life without an inward change leads to a shallow or empty spiritual walk. What matters to God is that we be completely changed from the inside out (2 Corinthians 5:17).

6:18 Paul's letter to the Galatians boldly declares the freedom of the Christian. Doubtless these early Christians in Galatia wanted to grow in the Christian life, but they were being misled by those who said this could be done only by keeping certain Jewish laws.

How strange it would be for a prisoner who had been set free to walk back into his or her cell and refuse to leave! How strange for an animal, released from a trap, to go back inside it! How sad for a believer to be freed from the bondage of sin, only to return to rigid conformity to a set of rules and regulations!

If you believe in Jesus Christ, you have been set free. Instead of going back into some form of slavery, whether to legalism or to sin, use your freedom to live for Christ and serve him as he desires.

EPHESIANS

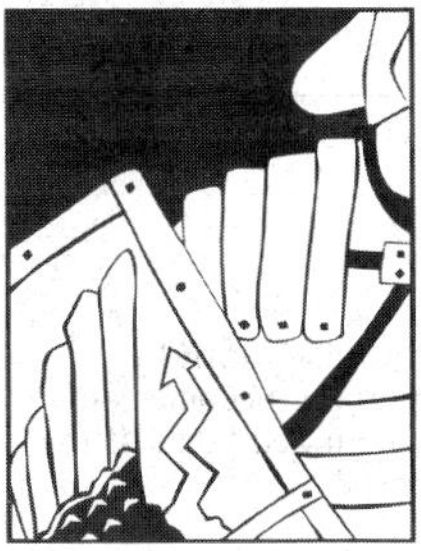

OUR CHURCHES come in all styles and shapes—secret meetings in homes; wide-open gatherings in amphitheatres; worship services packing thousands into a sanctuary while an overflow crowd watches on closed circuit television. Buildings will vary, but the church is not confined to four walls. The church of Jesus Christ is *people*, his people, of every race and nation who love Christ and are committed to serving him.

The "church age" began at Pentecost (Acts 2). Born in Jerusalem, the church spread rapidly through the ministry of the apostles and the early believers. Fanned by persecution, the gospel flame then spread to other cities and nations. On three courageous journeys, Paul and his associates established local assemblies in scores of Gentile cities.

One of the most prominent of those churches was at Ephesus. It was established in A.D. 53 on Paul's homeward journey to Jerusalem. But Paul returned a year later, on his third missionary trip, and stayed there for three years, preaching and teaching with great effectiveness (Acts 19:1–20). At another time, Paul met with the Ephesian elders, and he sent Timothy to serve as their leader (1 Timothy 1:3). Just a few years later, Paul was sent as a prisoner to Rome. In Rome, he was visited by messengers from various churches, including Tychicus of Ephesus. Paul wrote this letter to the church and sent it with Tychicus. Not written to counteract heresy or to confront any specific problem, Ephesians is a letter of encouragement. In it Paul describes the nature and appearance of the church, and he challenges believers to function as the living body of Christ on earth.

After a warm greeting (1:1, 2), Paul affirms the nature of the church—the glorious fact that believers in Christ have been showered with God's kindness (1:3–8), chosen for greatness (1:9–12), marked with the Holy Spirit (1:13, 14), filled with the Spirit's power (1:15–23), freed from sin's curse and bondage (2:1–10), and brought near to God (2:11–18). As part of God's "household", we stand with the prophets, apostles, Jews, Gentiles, and Christ himself (2:19—3:13). Then, as though overcome with emotion by remembering all that God has done, Paul challenges the Ephesians to live close to Christ, and he breaks into spontaneous praise (3:14–21).

Paul then turns his attention to the implications of being in the body of Christ, the church. Believers should have unity in their commitment to Christ and their use of spiritual gifts (4:1–16). They should have the highest moral standards (4:17—6:9). For the individual, this means rejecting pagan practices (4:17—5:20), and for the family, this means mutual submission and love (5:21—6:9).

Paul then reminds them that the church is in a constant battle with the forces of darkness and that they should use every spiritual weapon at their disposal (6:10–17). He concludes by asking for their prayers, commissioning Tychicus, and giving a benediction (6:18–24).

As you read this masterful description of the church, thank God for the diversity and unity in his family, pray for your brothers and sisters across the world, and draw close to those in your local church.

VITAL STATISTICS

PURPOSE:
To strengthen the believers in Ephesus in their Christian faith by explaining the nature and purpose of the church, the body of Christ

AUTHOR:
Paul

TO WHOM WRITTEN:
The church at Ephesus, and all believers everywhere

DATE WRITTEN:
About A.D. 60, from Rome, during Paul's imprisonment there

SETTING:
The letter was not written to confront any heresy or problem in the churches. It was sent with Tychicus to strengthen and encourage the churches in the area. Paul had spent over three years with the Ephesian church. As a result, he was very close to them. Paul met with the elders of the Ephesian church at Miletus (Acts 20:17–38)—a meeting that was filled with great sadness because he was leaving them for what he thought would be the last time. Because there are no specific references to people or problems in the Ephesian church and because the words "at Ephesus" (1:1) are not present in some early manuscripts, Paul may have intended this to be a circular letter to be read to all the churches in the area.

KEY VERSES:
"There is one body and one Spirit—just as you were called to one hope when you were called—one Lord, one faith, one baptism; one God and Father of all, who is over all and through all and in all" (4:4–6).

KEY PEOPLE:
Paul, Tychicus

SPECIAL FEATURES:
Several pictures of the church are presented: body, temple, mystery, new man, bride, and soldier. This letter was probably distributed to many of the early churches.

THE BLUEPRINT

1. Unity in Christ (1:1—3:21)
2. Unity in the body of Christ (4:1—6:24)

In this letter, Paul explains the wonderful things that we have received through Christ and refers to the church as a body, a temple, a bride, and a soldier. These all illustrate unity of purpose and show how each individual member is a part that must work together with all the other parts. In our own lives, we should work to eradicate all backbiting, gossip, criticism, jealousy, anger, and bitterness, because these are barriers to unity in the church.

MEGATHEMES

THEME	EXPLANATION	IMPORTANCE
God's Purpose	According to God's eternal, loving plan, he directs, carries out, and sustains our salvation.	When we respond to Christ's love by trusting in him, his purpose becomes our mission. Have you committed yourself to fulfilling God's purpose?
Christ the Centre	Christ is exalted as the central meaning of the universe and the focus of history. He is the head of the body, the church. He is the Creator and Sustainer of all creation.	Because Christ is central to everything, his power must be central in us. Begin by placing all your priorities under his control.
Living Church	Paul describes the nature of the church. The church, under Christ's control, is a living body, a family, a dwelling. God gives believers special abilities by his Holy Spirit to build the church.	We are part of Christ's body, and we must live in vital union with him. Our conduct must be consistent with this living relationship. Use your God-given abilities to equip believers for service. Fulfil your role in the living church.
New Family	Because God through Christ paid our penalty for sin and forgave us, we have been reconciled—brought near to him. We are a new society, a new family. Being united with Christ means we are to treat one another as family members.	We are one family in Christ, so there should be no barriers, no divisions, no basis for discrimination. We all belong to him, so we should live in harmony with one another.
Christian Conduct	Paul encourages all Christians to wise, dynamic Christian living, for with privileges goes family responsibility. As a new community, we are to live by Christ's new standards.	God provides his Holy Spirit to enable us to live his way. To utilise the Spirit's power, we must lay aside our evil desires and draw on the power of his new life. Submit your will to Christ, and seek to love others.

1. Unity in Christ

1 Paul, an apostle[a] of Christ Jesus by the will of God,[b]

1:1 [a]1Co 1:1 [b]2Co 1:1 [c]Col 1:2

To the saints in Ephesus,[a] the faithful[b][c] in Christ Jesus:

2 Grace and peace to you from God our Father and the Lord Jesus Christ.[d]

1:2 [d]Ro 1:7

a *1* Some early manuscripts do not have *in Ephesus.* b *1* Or *believers who are*

1:1 Paul wrote this letter to the Ephesian believers and all other believers to give them in-depth teaching about how to nurture and maintain the unity of the church. He wanted to put this important information in written form because he was in prison for preaching the gospel and could not visit the churches himself. The words "in Ephesus" are not present in some early manuscripts (see the NIV text note). Therefore, this was very likely a circular letter—it was first sent to Ephesus and then circulated to neighbouring local churches. Paul mentions no particular problems or local situations, and he offers no personal greetings.

1:1 Paul had been a Christian for nearly 30 years. He had made three missionary trips and established churches all around the Mediterranean Sea. When he wrote Ephesians, Paul was under house arrest in Rome (see Acts 28:16ff). Though a prisoner, he

1:3
[e]2Co 1:3
[f]Eph 2:6; 3:10; 6:12
1:4
[g]Eph 5:27; Col 1:22
[h]Eph 4:2, 15, 16
1:5
[i]Ro 8:29, 30
[j]1Co 1:21

Spiritual Blessings in Christ

3Praise be to the God and Father of our Lord Jesus Christ,[e] who has blessed us
in the heavenly realms[f] with every spiritual blessing in Christ. 4For he chose us in
him before the creation of the world to be holy and blameless[g] in his sight. In love[h]
5he[c] predestined[i] us to be adopted as his sons through Jesus Christ, in accordance
with his pleasure[j] and will—6to the praise of his glorious grace, which he has freely

c 4,5 Or *sight in love. 5He*

LOCATION OF EPHESUS
Ephesus was a strategic city, ranking in importance with Alexandria in Egypt and Antioch in Syria as a port. It lay on the most western edge of Asia Minor (modern-day Turkey), the most important port on the Aegean Sea on the main route from Rome to the east.

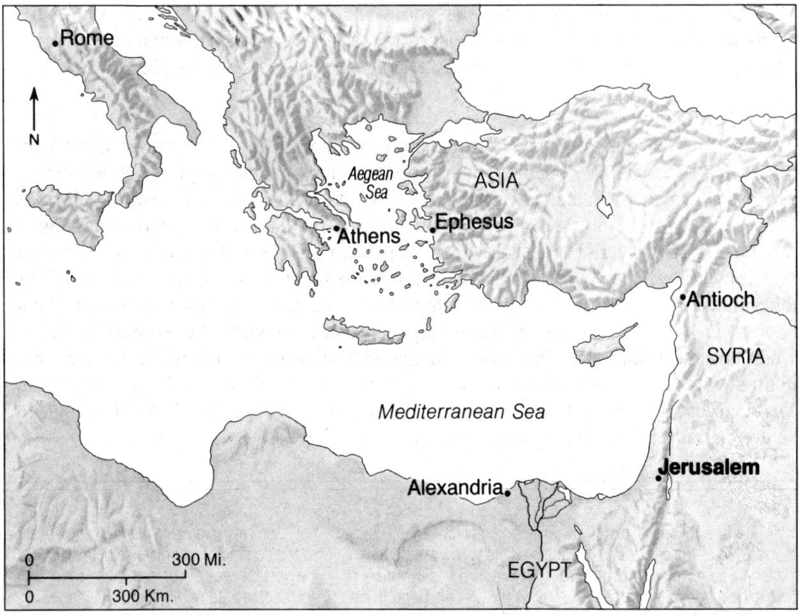

was free to have visitors and write letters. For more information on Paul, see his Profile in Acts 9.

1:1 Ephesus was one of the five major cities in the Roman empire, along with Rome, Corinth, Antioch, and Alexandria. Paul first visited Ephesus on his second missionary journey (Acts 18:19–21). During his third missionary journey, he stayed there for almost three years (Acts 19). Paul later met again with the elders of the Ephesian church at Miletus (Acts 20:16–38). Ephesus was a commercial, political, and religious centre for all of Asia Minor. The temple to the Greek goddess Artemis (Diana is her Roman equivalent) was located there.

1:1 "Faithful in Christ Jesus"—what an excellent reputation! Such a label would be an honour for any believer. What would it take for others to characterize you as faithful to Christ Jesus? Hold fast to your faith, one day at a time; faithfully obey God, even in the details of life. Then, like the Ephesians, you will be known as a person who is faithful to the Lord.

1:3 "Who has blessed us in the heavenly realms with every spiritual blessing" means that in Christ we have all the benefits of knowing God—being chosen for salvation, being adopted as his children, forgiveness, insight, the gifts of the Spirit, power to do God's will, the hope of living for ever with Christ. Because we have an intimate relationship with Christ, we can enjoy these blessings now. The *heavenly realms* means that these blessings are eternal, not temporal. The blessings come from Christ's spiritual realm, not the earthly realm of the goddess Artemis. Other references to the heavenly realms in this letter include 1:20; 2:6; 3:10. Such passages reveal Christ in his victorious, exalted role as ruler of all.

1:4 Paul says that God "chose us in him" to emphasise that salvation depends totally on God. We are not saved because we deserve it, but because God is gracious and freely gives salvation. We did not influence God's decision to save us; he saved us according to his plan. Thus there is no way we can take credit for our salvation or allow room for pride. The mystery of salvation originated in the timeless mind of God long before we existed. It is hard to understand how God could accept us. But because of Christ, we are holy and blameless in his sight. God chose us, and when we belong to him through Jesus Christ, God looks at us as if we had never sinned. All we can do is express our thanks for his wonderful love.

1:5 "Predestined" means marked out beforehand. This is another way of saying that salvation is God's work and not our own doing. In his infinite love, God has adopted us as his own children. Through Jesus' sacrifice, he has brought us into his family and made us heirs along with Jesus (Romans 8:17). In Roman law, adopted children had the same rights and privileges as biological children, even if they had been slaves. Paul uses this term to show how strong our relationship to God is. Have you entered into this loving relationship with God? For more on the meaning of adoption, see Galatians 4:5–7.

1:6 "Freely given us in the One he loves" means that God graciously accepts us (though we don't deserve it) now that we belong to his dearly loved Son.

given us in the One he loves.[k] 7In him we have redemption[l] through his blood, the
forgiveness of sins, in accordance with the riches of God's grace 8that he lavished on
us with all wisdom and understanding. 9And he[d] made known to us the mystery[m]
of his will according to his good pleasure, which he purposed in Christ, 10to be put
into effect when the times will have reached their fulfilment[n] — to bring all things in
heaven and on earth together under one head, even Christ.[o]

11In him we were also chosen,[e] having been predestined according to the plan of
him who works out everything in conformity with the purpose[p] of his will, 12in order
that we, who were the first to hope in Christ, might be for the praise of his glory.[q]
13And you also were included in Christ when you heard the word of truth,[r] the gospel
of your salvation. Having believed, you were marked in him with a seal,[s] the
promised Holy Spirit, 14who is a deposit guaranteeing our inheritance[t] until the
redemption of those who are God's possession — to the praise of his glory.

Thanksgiving and Prayer

15For this reason, ever since I heard about your faith in the Lord Jesus and your
love for all the saints,[u] 16I have not stopped giving thanks for you,[v] remembering
you in my prayers. 17I keep asking that the God of our Lord Jesus Christ, the glorious
Father,[w] may give you the Spirit[f] of wisdom[x] and revelation, so that you may know
him better. 18I pray also that the eyes of your heart may be enlightened[y] in order that
you may know the hope to which he has called you, the riches of his glorious
inheritance in the saints, 19and his incomparably great power for us who believe. That
power[z] is like the working of his mighty strength,[a] 20which he exerted in Christ
when he raised him from the dead[b] and seated him at his right hand in the heavenly
realms, 21far above all rule and authority, power and dominion, and every title[c] that
can be given, not only in the present age but also in the one to come. 22And God placed

[d] *8, 9* Or *us. With all wisdom and understanding, 9he* [e] *11* Or *were made heirs* [f] *17* Or *a spirit*

1:6 [k]Mt 3:17
1:7 [l]Ro 3:24
1:9 [m]Ro 16:25
1:10 [n]Gal 4:4 [o]Col 1:20
1:11 [p]Eph 3:11; Heb 6:17
1:12 [q]ver 6, 14
1:13 [r]Col 1:5 [s]Eph 4:30
1:14 [t]Ac 20:32
1:15 [u]Col 1:4
1:16 [v]Ro 1:8
1:17 [w]Jn 20:17 [x]Col 1:9
1:18 [y]Ac 26:18; 2Co 4:6
1:19 [z]Col 1:29 [a]Eph 6:10
1:20 [b]Ac 2:24
1:21 [c]Php 2:9, 10

1:7 To speak of Jesus' blood was an important first-century way of speaking of Christ's death. His death points to two wonderful truths – redemption and forgiveness. *Redemption* was the price paid to gain freedom for a slave (Leviticus 25:47–54). Through his death, Jesus paid the price to release us from slavery to sin. *Forgiveness* was granted in Old Testament times on the basis of the shedding of animals' blood (Leviticus 17:11). Now we are forgiven on the basis of the shedding of Jesus' blood – he died as the perfect and final sacrifice. (See also Romans 5:9; Ephesians 2:13; Colossians 1:20; Hebrews 9:22; 1 Peter 1:19.)

1:7, 8 Grace is God's voluntary and loving favour given to those he saves. We can't earn salvation, nor do we deserve it. No religious, intellectual, or moral effort can gain it, because it comes only from God's mercy and love. Without God's grace, no person can be saved. To receive it, we must acknowledge that we cannot save ourselves, that only God can save us, and that our only way to receive this loving favour is through faith in Christ.

1:9, 10 God was not intentionally keeping his plan a secret ("the mystery of his will"), but his plan for the world could not be fully understood until Christ rose from the dead. His purpose for sending Christ was to unite Jews and Gentiles in one body with Christ as the head. Many people still do not understand God's plan; but when the time is right ("when the times will have reached their fulfilment"), he will bring us together to be with him for ever. Then everyone will understand. On that day, all people will bow to Jesus as Lord, either because they love him or because they fear his power (see Philippians 2:10, 11).

1:11 God's purpose is to offer salvation to the world, just as he planned to do long ago. God is sovereign; he is in charge. When your life seems chaotic, rest in this truth: Jesus is Lord, and God is in control. God's purpose to save you cannot be thwarted, no matter what evil Satan may bring.

1:13, 14 The Holy Spirit is God's seal that we belong to him and his deposit guaranteeing that he will do what he has promised. The Holy Spirit is like a down payment, a deposit, a validating signature on the contract. The presence of the Holy Spirit in us demonstrates the genuineness of our faith, proves that we are God's children, and secures eternal life for us. His power works in us to transform us now, and what we experience now is a taste of the total change we will experience in eternity.

1:16, 17 Paul prayed that the Ephesians would know Christ better. Christ is our model, and the more we know of him, the more we will be like him. Study Jesus' life in the Gospels to see what he was like on earth nearly 2,000 years ago, and get to know him in prayer now. Personal knowledge of Christ will change your life.

1:18 The hope we have is not a vague feeling that the future will be positive, but it is complete assurance of certain victory through God. This complete certainty comes to us through the Holy Spirit who is working in us. For more on hope, see Romans 8:23, 24; Ephesians 4:4; Colossians 1:5; 1 Thessalonians 1:3; 1 Peter 3:15.

1:19, 20 The world fears the power of the atom, yet we belong to the God of the universe who not only created that atomic power but also raised Jesus Christ from the dead. God's incomparably great power is available to help you. There is nothing too difficult for him.

1:20–22 Having been raised from the dead, Christ is now the head of the church, the ultimate authority over the world. Jesus is the Messiah, God's Anointed One, the One Israel longed for, the One who would set their broken world right. As Christians we can be confident that God has won the final victory and is in control of everything. We need not fear any dictator or nation, or even death or Satan himself. The contract has been signed and sealed; we are waiting just a short while for delivery. Paul says, in Romans 8:37–39, that nothing can separate us from God and his love.

1:22, 23 *Fulness* refers to Christ filling the church with gifts and blessings. The church should be the full expression of Christ, who himself fills everything (see 3:19). When reading Ephesians, it is important to remember that it was written primarily to the entire

1:22
[d] Mt 28:18
[e] Eph 4:15; 5:23

all things under his feet[d] and appointed him to be head[e] over everything for the
church, 23which is his body, the fulness of him who fills everything in every way.

2:1
[a] ver 5; Col 2:13

2:2
[b] Col 3:7
[c] Jn 12:31; Eph 6:12
[d] Eph 5:6

2:3
[e] Gal 5:16

Made Alive in Christ

2 As for you, you were dead in your transgressions and sins,[a] 2in which you used
to live[b] when you followed the ways of this world and of the ruler of the kingdom
of the air,[c] the spirit who is now at work in those who are disobedient.[d] 3All of us
also lived among them at one time, gratifying the cravings of our sinful nature[a][e]
and following its desires and thoughts. Like the rest, we were by nature objects of
wrath. 4But because of his great love for us, God, who is rich in mercy, 5made us

a 3 Or *our flesh*

OUR TRUE IDENTITY IN CHRIST

Romans 3:24	We are justified (declared "not guilty" of sin).
Romans 8:1	No condemnation awaits us.
Romans 8:2	We are set free from the law of sin and death.
1 Corinthians 1:2	We are sanctified and made acceptable in Jesus Christ.
1 Corinthians 1:30	We are righteous and holy in Christ.
1 Corinthians 15:22	We will be made alive at the resurrection.
2 Corinthians 5:17	We are a new creation.
2 Corinthians 5:21	We receive God's righteousness.
Galatians 3:28	We are one in Christ with all other believers.
Ephesians 1:3	We are blessed with every spiritual blessing in Christ.
Ephesians 1:4	We are holy, blameless, and covered with God's love.
Ephesians 1:5, 6	We are adopted as God's children.
Ephesians 1:7	Our sins are taken away, and we are forgiven.
Ephesians 1:10, 11	We will be brought under Christ's headship.
Ephesians 1:13	We are marked as belonging to God by the Holy Spirit.
Ephesians 2:6	We have been raised up to sit with Christ in glory.
Ephesians 2:10	We are God's work of art.
Ephesians 2:13	We have been brought near to God.
Ephesians 3:6	We share in the promise in Christ.
Ephesians 3:12	We can come with freedom and confidence into God's presence.
Ephesians 5:29, 30	We are members of Christ's body, the church.
Colossians 2:10	We have been given fulness in Christ.
Colossians 2:11	We are set free from our sinful nature.
2 Timothy 2:10	We will have eternal glory.

church, not merely to an individual. Christ is the head and we are the body of his church (Paul uses this metaphor in Romans 12:4, 5; 1 Corinthians 12:12–27; and Colossians 3:15 as well as throughout the book of Ephesians). The image of the body shows the church's unity. Each member is involved with all the others as they go about doing Christ's work on earth. We should not attempt to work, serve, or worship merely on our own. We need the entire body.

2:2 "The ruler of the kingdom of the air" was understood by Paul's readers to mean Satan. They believed that Satan and the evil spiritual forces inhabited the region between earth and sky. Satan is thus pictured as ruling an evil spiritual kingdom – the demons and those who are against Christ. *Satan* means "the accuser". He is also called the devil (4:27). In the resurrection, Christ was victorious over Satan and his power. Therefore, Jesus Christ is the permanent ruler of the whole world; Satan is only the temporary ruler of the part of the world that chooses to follow him.

2:3 The fact that all people, without exception, commit sin proves that without Christ we have a sinful nature. We are lost in sin and cannot save ourselves. Does this mean only Christians do good? Of course not – many people do good to others. On a relative scale, many are moral, kind, and law-abiding. Comparing these people to criminals, we would say that they are very good indeed. But on God's absolute scale, *no-one* is good enough to earn salvation ("you were dead in your transgressions and sins", 2:1). Only through being united with Christ's perfect life can we become good in God's sight. "Objects of wrath" refers to those who are to receive God's wrath because of their rejection of Christ.

2:4, 5 In the previous verses Paul wrote about our old sinful nature (2:1–3). Here Paul emphasises that we do not need to live any longer under sin's power. The penalty of sin and its power over us were miraculously destroyed by Christ on the cross. Through faith in Christ we stand acquitted, or not guilty, before God (Romans 3:21, 22). God does not take us out of the world or make us robots – we will still feel like sinning, and sometimes we will sin. The difference is that before we became Christians, we were dead in sin and were slaves to our sinful nature. But now we are alive with Christ (see also Galatians 2:20).

alive with Christ even when we were dead in transgressions[f]—it is by grace you have
been saved.[g] 6And God raised us up with Christ and seated us with him[h] in the
heavenly realms[i] in Christ Jesus, 7in order that in the coming ages he might show
the incomparable riches of his grace, expressed in his kindness[j] to us in Christ Jesus.
8For it is by grace you have been saved,[k] through faith—and this not from yourselves, it is the gift of God—9not by works,[l] so that no-one can boast.[m] 10For we
are God's workmanship, created[n] in Christ Jesus to do good works,[o] which God
prepared in advance for us to do.

One in Christ

11Therefore, remember that formerly you who are Gentiles by birth and called
"uncircumcised" by those who call themselves "the circumcision" (that done in the
body by the hands of men)[p]—12remember that at that time you were separate from
Christ, excluded from citizenship in Israel and foreigners to the covenants of the
promise,[q] without hope[r] and without God in the world. 13But now in Christ Jesus
you who once were far away have been brought near[s] through the blood of Christ.[t]
14For he himself is our peace, who has made the two one[u] and has destroyed the
barrier, the dividing wall of hostility, 15by abolishing in his flesh[v] the law with its
commandments and regulations.[w] His purpose was to create in himself one[x] new man
out of the two, thus making peace, 16and in this one body to reconcile both of them
to God through the cross,[y] by which he put to death their hostility. 17He came and
preached peace to you who were far away and peace to those who were near.[z] 18For
through him we both have access[a] to the Father[b] by one Spirit.[c]

2:5 [f] ver 1 [g] Ac 15:11
2:6 [h] Eph 1:20 [i] Eph 1:3
2:7 [j] Tit 3:4
2:8 [k] ver 5
2:9 [l] 2Ti 1:9 [m] 1Co 1:29
2:10 [n] Eph 4:24 [o] Tit 2:14
2:11 [p] Col 2:11
2:12 [q] Gal 3:17 [r] 1Th 4:13
2:13 [s] Ac 2:39 [t] Col 1:20
2:14 [u] 1Co 12:13
2:15 [v] Col 1:21, 22 [w] Col 2:14 [x] Gal 3:28
2:16 [y] Col 1:20, 22
2:17 [z] Ps 148:14; Isa 57:19
2:18 [a] Eph 3:12 [b] Col 1:12 [c] 1Co 12:13

2:6 Because of Christ's resurrection, we know that our bodies will also be raised from the dead (1 Corinthians 15:2–23) and that we have been given the power to live as Christians now (1:19). These ideas are combined in Paul's image of sitting with Christ in "the heavenly realms" (see the note on 1:3). Our eternal life with Christ is certain because we are united in his powerful victory.

2:8, 9 When someone gives you a gift, do you say, "That's very nice—now how much do I owe you?"? No, the appropriate response to a gift is "Thank you". Yet how often Christians, even after they have been given the gift of salvation, feel obligated to try to work their way to God. Because our salvation and even our faith are gifts, we should respond with gratitude, praise, and joy.

2:8–10 We become Christians through God's unmerited grace, not as the result of any effort, ability, intelligent choice, or act of service on our part. However, out of gratitude for this free gift, we will seek to help and serve others with kindness, love, and gentleness, and not merely to please ourselves. While no action or work we do can help us obtain salvation, God's intention is that our salvation will result in acts of service. We are not saved merely for our own benefit but to serve Christ and build up the church (4:12).

2:10 We are God's workmanship (work of art, masterpiece). Our salvation is something only God can do. It is his powerful, creative work in us. If God considers us his works of art, we dare not treat ourselves or others with disrespect or as inferior work.

2:11–13 Pious Jews ("the circumcision") considered all non-Jews (the "uncircumcised") ceremonially unclean. They thought of themselves as pure and clean because of their national heritage and religious ceremonies. Paul pointed out that Jews and Gentiles alike were unclean before God and needed to be cleansed by Christ. In order to realise how great a gift salvation is, we need to remember our former natural, unclean condition. Have you ever felt separate, excluded, hopeless? These verses are for you. No-one is alienated from Christ's love or from the body of believers.

2:11–13 Jews and Gentiles alike could be guilty of spiritual pride—Jews for thinking their faith and traditions elevated them above everyone else, Gentiles for trusting in their achievements, power, or position. Spiritual pride blinds us to our own faults and magnifies the faults of others. Be careful not to become proud of your salvation. Instead, humbly thank God for what he has done, and encourage others who might be struggling in their faith.

2:11–16 Before Christ's coming, Gentiles and Jews kept apart from one another. Jews considered Gentiles beyond God's saving power and therefore without hope. Gentiles resented Jewish claims. Christ revealed the total sinfulness of both Jews and Gentiles, and then he offered his salvation to both. Only Christ breaks down the walls of prejudice, reconciles all believers to God, and unifies us in one body.

2:14ff Christ has destroyed the barriers people build between themselves. Because these walls have been removed, we can have real unity with people who are not like us. This is true reconciliation. Because of Christ's death, we are all one (2:14); our hostility against each other has been put to death (2:16); we can all have access to the Father by the Holy Spirit (2:18); we are no longer foreigners or aliens to God (2:19); and we are all being built into a holy temple with Christ as our chief cornerstone (2:20, 21).

2:14–22 There are many barriers that can divide us from other Christians: age, appearance, intelligence, political persuasion, economic status, race, theological perspective. One of the best ways to stifle Christ's love is to be friendly with only those people that we like. Fortunately, Christ has knocked down the barriers and has unified all believers in one family. His cross should be the focus of our unity. The Holy Spirit helps us look beyond the barriers to the unity we are called to enjoy.

2:15 By his death, Christ ended the angry resentment between Jews and Gentiles, caused by the Jewish laws that favoured the Jews and excluded the Gentiles. Christ died to abolish that whole system of Jewish laws. Then he took the two groups that had been opposed to each other and made them parts of himself. "One new man" means that Christ made a single entity or person out of the two. Thus he fused all believers together to become one in himself.

2:17, 18 The Jews were near to God because they already knew of him through the Scriptures and worshipped him in their religious ceremonies. The Gentiles were far away because they knew little or nothing about God. Because neither group could be saved by good deeds, knowledge, or sincerity, both needed to hear about the salvation available through Jesus Christ. Both Jews and Gentiles are now free to come to God through Christ. You have been brought near to him (2:13).

2:19
[d]ver 12
[e]Php 3:20
[f]Gal 6:10
2:20
[g]Mt 16:18; Rev 21:14
[h]1Pe 2:4-8
2:21
[i]1Co 3:16, 17
3:1
[a]Ac 23:18; Eph 4:1
3:2
[b]Col 1:25
3:3
[c]Ro 16:25
[d]1Co 2:10
3:4
[e]2Co 11:6
3:5
[f]Ro 16:26
3:6
[g]Gal 3:29
[h]Eph 2:15, 16
3:7
[i]1Co 3:5
[j]Eph 1:19
3:8
[k]1Co 15:9

19Consequently, you are no longer foreigners and aliens,[d] but fellow-citizens[e]
with God's people and members of God's household,[f] 20built on the foundation[g]
of the apostles and prophets, with Christ Jesus himself as the chief cornerstone.[h] 21In
him the whole building is joined together and rises to become a holy temple[i] in the
Lord. 22And in him you too are being built together to become a dwelling in which
God lives by his Spirit.

Paul the Preacher to the Gentiles

3 For this reason I, Paul, the prisoner[a] of Christ Jesus for the sake of you Gentiles—
2Surely you have heard about the administration of God's grace that was given to
me[b] for you, 3that is, the mystery[c] made known to me by revelation,[d] as I have
already written briefly. 4In reading this, then, you will be able to understand my
insight[e] into the mystery of Christ, 5which was not made known to men in other
generations as it has now been revealed by the Spirit to God's holy apostles and
prophets.[f] 6This mystery is that through the gospel the Gentiles are heirs[g] together
with Israel, members together of one body,[h] and sharers together in the promise in
Christ Jesus.
7I became a servant of this gospel[i] by the gift of God's grace given me through
the working of his power.[j] 8Although I am less than the least of all God's people,[k]
this grace was given me: to preach to the Gentiles the unsearchable riches of Christ,

OUR LIVES BEFORE AND AFTER CHRIST

Before	*After*
Dead in transgressions	Made alive with Christ
Objects of wrath	Shown God's mercy and given salvation
Followed the ways of the world	Stand for Christ and truth
God's enemies	God's children
Enslaved to Satan	Free in Christ to love, serve, and sit with him
Followed our evil thoughts and desires	Raised up with Christ to glory

2:19–22 A church building is sometimes called God's house. In reality, God's household is not a building, but a group of people. He lives in us and shows himself to a watching world through us. People can see that God is love and that Christ is Lord as we live in harmony with each other and in accordance with what God says in his word. We are citizens of God's kingdom and members of his household.

2:20 What does it mean to be built on the foundation of the apostles and prophets? It means that the church is not built on modern ideas, but rather on the spiritual heritage given to us by the early apostles and prophets of the Christian church.

3:1 Paul was under house arrest in Rome for preaching about Christ. The religious leaders in Jerusalem, who felt threatened by Christ's teachings and didn't believe he was the Messiah, pressured the Romans to arrest Paul and bring him to trial for treason and for causing rebellion among the Jews. Paul had appealed for his case to be heard by the emperor, and he was awaiting trial (see Acts 28:16–31). Even though he was under arrest, Paul maintained his firm belief that God was in control of all that happened to him. Do circumstances make you wonder if God has lost control of this world? Like Paul, remember that no matter what happens, God directs the world's affairs.

3:2, 3 "The administration of God's grace" means the special stewardship, trust, or commitment that Paul had been given. He had been assigned the special work of preaching the Good News to the Gentiles, God's great plan shown to Paul in a revelation. "As I have already written briefly" may refer to a previous letter that was not preserved by the church, or it may refer to an earlier part of this letter (especially 1:9ff; 2:11ff).

3:5, 6 God's plan was hidden from previous generations, not because God wanted to keep something from his people, but because he would reveal it to everyone in his perfect timing. God planned to have Jews and Gentiles comprise one body, the church. It was known in the Old Testament that the Gentiles would receive salvation (Isaiah 49:6); but it was never revealed in the Old Testament that all Gentile and Jewish believers would become equal in the body of Christ. Yet this equality was accomplished when Jesus destroyed the "dividing wall" and created the "one new man" (2:14, 15).

3:7 When Paul became a servant of the gospel, God gave him the ability to share effectively the gospel of Christ. You may not be an apostle or even an evangelist, but God will give you opportunities to tell others about Christ. And with the opportunities he will provide the ability, courage, and power. Whenever an opportunity presents itself, make yourself available to God as his servant. As you focus on the other person and his or her needs, God will communicate your caring attitude. Your words will be natural, loving, and compelling.

3:8 When Paul describes himself as "less than the least of all God's people", he means that without God's help, he would never be able to do God's work. Yet God chose him to share the gospel with the Gentiles and gave him the power to do it. If we feel that our role is minor, we may be right—except that we have forgotten what a difference God makes. How does God want to use you? Draw on his power, do your part, and faithfully perform the special role God has called you to play in his plan.

9and to make plain to everyone the administration of this mystery,[l] which for ages
past was kept hidden in God, who created all things. 10His intent was that now,
through the church, the manifold wisdom of God[m] should be made known[n] to the
rulers and authorities[o] in the heavenly realms, 11according to his eternal purpose
which he accomplished in Christ Jesus our Lord. 12In him and through faith in him
we may approach God[p] with freedom and confidence.[q] 13I ask you, therefore, not
to be discouraged because of my sufferings for you, which are your glory.

A Prayer for the Ephesians

14For this reason I kneel[r] before the Father, 15from whom his whole family[a] in
heaven and on earth derives its name. 16I pray that out of his glorious riches he may
strengthen you with power[s] through his Spirit in your inner being,[t] 17so that Christ
may dwell in your hearts[u] through faith. And I pray that you, being rooted[v] and
established in love, 18may have power, together with all the saints, to grasp how wide
and long and high and deep[w] is the love of Christ, 19and to know this love that
surpasses knowledge — that you may be filled[x] to the measure of all the fulness of
God.[y]
20Now to him who is able[z] to do immeasurably more than all we ask or imagine,
according to his power that is at work within us, 21to him be glory in the church and
in Christ Jesus throughout all generations, for ever and ever! Amen.[a]

2. Unity in the body of Christ

4 As a prisoner[a] for the Lord, then, I urge you to live a life worthy[b] of the calling
you have received. 2Be completely humble and gentle; be patient, bearing with
one another[c] in love.[d] 3Make every effort to keep the unity[e] of the Spirit through

a *15* Or *whom all fatherhood*

3:9 [l]Ro 16:25
3:10 [m]1Co 2:7 [n]1Pe 1:12 [o]Eph 1:21
3:12 [p]Eph 2:18 [q]Heb 4:16
3:14 [r]Php 2:10
3:16 [s]Col 1:11 [t]Ro 7:22
3:17 [u]Jn 14:23 [v]Col 1:23
3:18 [w]Job 11:8, 9
3:19 [x]Col 2:10 [y]Eph 1:23
3:20 [z]Ro 16:25
3:21 [a]Ro 11:36
4:1 [a]Eph 3:1 [b]Php 1:27; Col 1:10
4:2 [c]Col 3:12, 13 [d]Eph 1:4
4:3 [e]Col 3:14

3:9 "The administration of this mystery" refers to the way God's great plan is carried out through the church and to Paul's work to demonstrate and teach God's great purpose in Christ (see 3:2).

3:10 The "rulers and authorities in the heavenly realms" are either angels who are witnesses to these events (see 1 Peter 1:12), or hostile spiritual forces opposed to God (2:2; 6:12).

3:12 It is an awesome privilege to be able to approach God with freedom and confidence. Most of us would be apprehensive in the presence of a powerful ruler. But thanks to Christ, by faith we can enter directly into God's presence through prayer. We know we'll be welcomed with open arms because we are God's children through our union with Christ. Don't be afraid of God. Talk with him about everything. He is waiting to hear from you.

3:13 Why should Paul's suffering make the Ephesians feel honoured ("which are your glory")? If Paul had not preached the gospel, he would not be in jail — but then the Ephesians would not have heard the Good News and been converted either. Just as a mother endures the pain of childbirth in order to bring new life into the world, Paul endured the pain of persecution in order to bring new believers to Christ. Obeying Christ is never easy. He calls you to take up your cross and follow him (Matthew 16:24) — that is, to be willing to endure pain so that God's message of salvation can reach the entire world. We should feel honoured that others have suffered and sacrificed for us so that we might reap the benefit.

3:14, 15 The family of God includes all who have believed in him in the past, all who believe in the present, and all who will believe in the future. We are all a family because we have the same Father. He is the source of all creation, the rightful owner of everything. God promises his love and power to his family, the church (3:16–21). If we want to receive God's blessings, it is important that we stay in contact with other believers in the body of Christ. Those who isolate themselves from God's family and try to go it alone cut themselves off from God's power.

3:17–19 God's love is total, says Paul. It reaches every corner of our experience. It is *wide* — it covers the breadth of our own experience, and it reaches out to the whole world. God's love is *long* — it continues the length of our lives. It is *high* — it rises to the heights of our celebration and elation. His love is *deep* — it reaches to the depths of discouragement, despair, and even death. When you feel shut out or isolated, remember that you can never be lost to God's love. For another prayer about God's immeasurable and inexhaustible love, see Paul's words in Romans 8:38, 39.

3:19 "The fulness of God" is fully expressed only in Christ (Colossians 2:9, 10). In union with Christ and through his empowering Spirit, we are complete. We have all the fulness of God available to us. But we must appropriate that fulness through faith and through prayer as we daily live for him. Paul's prayer for the Ephesians is also for you. You can ask the Holy Spirit to fill every aspect of your life to the fullest.

3:20, 21 This *doxology* — prayer of praise to God — ends Part One of Ephesians. In the first section, Paul described the timeless role of the church. In Part Two (chapters 4 – 6), he will explain how church members should live in order to bring about the unity God wants. As in most of his books, Paul first lays a doctrinal foundation and then makes practical applications of the truths he has presented.

4:1, 2 God has chosen us to be Christ's representatives on earth. In the light of this truth, Paul challenges us to live lives worthy of the calling we have received — the awesome privilege of being called Christ's very own. This includes being humble, gentle, patient, understanding, and peaceful. People are watching your life. Can they see Christ in you? How well are you doing as his representative?

4:1–6 "There is one body," says Paul. Unity does not just happen; we have to work at it. Often differences among people can lead to division, but this should not be true in the church. Instead of concentrating on what divides us, we should remember what unites us: *one* body, *one* Spirit, *one* hope, *one* Lord, *one* faith, *one* baptism, *one* God! Have you learned to appreciate people who are different from you? Can you see how their differing gifts and viewpoints can help the church as it does God's work? Learn to enjoy

4:4 [f]1Co 12:13
4:6 [g]Ro 11:36
4:7 [h]1Co 12:7, 11 [i]Ro 12:3
4:8 [j]Col 2:15 [k]Ps 68:18
4:11 [l]1Co 12:28 [m]Ac 21:8
4:12 [n]1Co 12:27
4:13 [o]ver 3, 5

the bond of peace. 4 There is one body and one Spirit[f]—just as you were called to
one hope when you were called—5 one Lord, one faith, one baptism; 6 one God and
Father of all, who is over all and through all and in all.[g]
7 But to each one of us[h] grace has been given[i] as Christ apportioned it. 8 This is
why it[a] says:

> "When he ascended on high,
> he led captives[j] in his train
> and gave gifts to men."[b][k]

9 (What does "he ascended" mean except that he also descended to the lower, earthly
regions?[c] 10 He who descended is the very one who ascended higher than all the
heavens, in order to fill the whole universe.) 11 It was he who gave some to be
apostles,[l] some to be prophets, some to be evangelists,[m] and some to be pastors and
teachers, 12 to prepare God's people for works of service, so that the body of Christ[n]
may be built up 13 until we all reach unity[o] in the faith and in the knowledge of the

[a] 8 Or *God* [b] 8 Psalm 68:18 [c] 9 Or *the depths of the earth*

THE ONENESS OF ALL BELIEVERS

Believers are one in:	*Our unity is experienced in:*
Body	The fellowship of believers—the church
Spirit	The Holy Spirit, who activates the fellowship
Hope	That glorious future to which we are all called
Lord	Christ, to whom we all belong
Faith	Our singular commitment to Christ
Baptism	Baptism—the sign of entry into the church
God	God, who is our Father who keeps us for eternity

Too often believers are separated because of minor differences in doctrine. But Paul here shows those areas where Christians must agree to attain true unity. When believers have this unity of spirit, petty differences should never be allowed to dissolve that unity.

the way we members of Christ's body complement one another. (See 1 Corinthians 12:12, 13 for more on this thought.)

4:2 No-one is ever going to be perfect here on earth, so we must accept and love other Christians in spite of their faults. When we see faults in fellow believers, we should be patient and gentle. Is there someone whose actions or personality really annoy you? Rather than dwelling on that person's weaknesses or looking for faults, pray for him or her. Then do even more—spend time together and see if you can learn to like him or her.

4:3 To build unity is one of the Holy Spirit's important roles. He leads, but we have to be willing to be led and to do our part to keep the peace. We do that by focusing on God, not on ourselves. For more about who the Holy Spirit is and what he does, see the notes on John 3:6; Acts 1:5; and Ephesians 1:13, 14.

4:4–7 All believers in Christ belong to one body; all are united under one head, Christ himself (see 1 Corinthians 12:12–26). Each believer has God-given abilities that can strengthen the whole body. Your special ability may seem small or large, but it is yours to use in God's service. Ask God to use your unique gifts to contribute to the strength and health of the body of believers.

4:6 God is *over all*—this shows his overruling care (transcendence). He is *through all and in all*—this shows his active presence in the world and in the lives of believers (immanence). Any view of God that violates either his transcendence or his immanence does not paint a true picture of God.

4:8 In Psalm 68:18, God is pictured as a conqueror marching to the gates and taking tribute from the fallen city. Paul uses that picture to teach that Christ, in his crucifixion and resurrection, was victorious over Satan. When Christ ascended to heaven, he gave gifts to the church, some of which Paul discusses in 4:11–13.

4:9 The "lower, earthly regions" may be (1) the earth itself (lowly by comparison to heaven), (2) the grave, or (3) Hades (many believe Hades is the resting place of souls between death and resurrection). However we understand it, Christ is Lord of the whole universe, past, present, and future. Nothing or no-one is hidden from him. The Lord of all came to earth and faced death to rescue all people. No-one is beyond his reach.

4:11, 12 Our oneness in Christ does not destroy our individuality. The Holy Spirit has given each Christian special gifts for building up the church. Now that we have these gifts, it is crucial to use them. Are you spiritually mature, exercising the gifts God has given you? If you know what your gifts are, look for opportunities to serve. If you don't know, ask God to show you, perhaps with the help of your minister or Christian friends. Then, as you begin to recognise your special area of service, use your gifts to strengthen and encourage the church.

4:12, 13 God has given his church an enormous responsibility—to make disciples in every nation (Matthew 28:18–20). This involves preaching, teaching, healing, nurturing, giving, administering, building, and many other tasks. If we had to fulfil this command as individuals, we might as well give up without trying—it would be impossible. But God calls us as members of his body. Some of us can do one task; some can do another. Together we can obey God more fully than any of us could alone. It is a human tendency to overestimate what we can do by ourselves and to underestimate what we can do as a group. But as the body of Christ, we can accomplish more together than we would dream possible working by ourselves. Working together, the church can express the fulness of Christ (see the note on 3:19).

Son of God and become mature,[p] attaining to the whole measure of the fulness of
Christ.
14 Then we will no longer be infants,[q] tossed back and forth by the waves,[r] and
blown here and there by every wind of teaching and by the cunning and craftiness of
men in their deceitful scheming.[s] 15 Instead, speaking the truth in love, we will in
all things grow up into him who is the Head,[t] that is, Christ. 16 From him the whole
body, joined and held together by every supporting ligament, grows[u] and builds itself
up in love, as each part does its work.

Living as Children of Light

17 So I tell you this, and insist on it in the Lord, that you must no longer live as
the Gentiles do, in the futility of their thinking.[v] 18 They are darkened in their
understanding[w] and separated from the life of God[x] because of the ignorance that
is in them due to the hardening of their hearts.[y] 19 Having lost all sensitivity,[z] they
have given themselves over[a] to sensuality[b] so as to indulge in every kind of impurity,
with a continual lust for more.
20 You, however, did not come to know Christ that way. 21 Surely you heard of him
and were taught in him in accordance with the truth that is in Jesus. 22 You were taught,
with regard to your former way of life, to put off[c] your old self,[d] which is being
corrupted by its deceitful desires; 23 to be made new in the attitude of your minds;[e]
24 and to put on the new self,[f] created to be like God in true righteousness and
holiness.[g]
25 Therefore each of you must put off falsehood and speak truthfully[h] to his
neighbour, for we are all members of one body.[i] 26 "In your anger do not sin"[d]: Do
not let the sun go down while you are still angry, 27 and do not give the devil a foothold.
28 He who has been stealing must steal no longer, but must work,[j] doing something
useful with his own hands,[k] that he may have something to share with those in need.[l]

d *26* Psalm 4:4

4:13 [p]Col 1:28
4:14 [q]1Co 14:20 [r]Jas 1:6 [s]Eph 6:11
4:15 [t]Eph 1:22
4:16 [u]Col 2:19
4:17 [v]Ro 1:21
4:18 [w]Ro 1:21 [x]Eph 2:12 [y]2Co 3:14
4:19 [z]1Ti 4:2 [a]Ro 1:24 [b]Col 3:5
4:22 [c]1Pe 2:1 [d]Ro 6:6
4:23 [e]Col 3:10
4:24 [f]Ro 6:4 [g]Eph 2:10
4:25 [h]Zec 8:16 [i]Ro 12:5
4:28 [j]Ac 20:35 [k]1Th 4:11 [l]Lk 3:11

4:14–16 Christ is the truth (John 14:6), and the Holy Spirit who guides the church is the Spirit of truth (John 16:13). Satan, by contrast, is the father of lies (John 8:44). As followers of Christ, we must be committed to the truth. This means both that our words should be honest and that our actions should reflect Christ's integrity. Speaking the truth in love is not always easy, convenient, or pleasant, but it is necessary if the church is going to do Christ's work in the world.

4:15, 16 Some Christians fear that any mistake will destroy their witness for the Lord. They see their own weaknesses, and they know that many non-Christians seem to have stronger characters than they do. How can we grow up into Christ? The answer is that Christ forms us into a body – into a group of individuals who are united in their purpose and in their love for one another and for the Lord. If an individual stumbles, the rest of the group is there to pick him or her up and help him or her walk with God again. If an individual sins, he or she can find restoration through the church (Galatians 6:1) even as the rest of the body continues to witness to God's truth. As part of Christ's body, do you reflect part of Christ's character and carry out your special role in his work?

4:17 Living "in the futility of their thinking" refers to the natural tendency of human beings to think their way away from God. Intellectual pride, rationalisations, and excuses all keep people from God. Don't be surprised if people can't grasp the gospel. The gospel will seem foolish to those who forsake faith and rely on their own understanding.

4:17–24 People should be able to see a difference between Christians and non-Christians because of the way Christians live. We are to live as children of light (5:8). Paul told the Ephesians to leave behind the old life of sin, since they were followers of Christ. Living the Christian life is a process. Although we have a new nature, we don't automatically think all good thoughts and express all right attitudes when we become new people in Christ. But if we keep listening to God, we will be changing all the time. As you look back over the last year, do you see a process of change for the better in your thoughts, attitudes, and actions? Although change may be slow, it comes as you trust God to change you. For more about our new nature as believers, see Romans 6:6; 8:9; Galatians 5:16–26; Colossians 3:3–8.

4:22–24 Our old way of life before we believed in Christ is completely in the past. We should put it behind us like old clothes to be thrown away. This is both a once-for-all decision when we decide to accept Christ's gift of salvation (2:8–10) and also a daily conscious commitment. We are not to be driven by desire and impulse. We must put on the new role, head in the new direction, and have the new way of thinking that the Holy Spirit gives.

4:25 Lying to each other disrupts unity by creating conflicts and destroying trust. It tears down relationships and leads to open warfare in a church.

4:26, 27 The Bible doesn't tell us that we shouldn't feel angry, but it points out that it is important to handle our anger properly. If vented thoughtlessly, anger can hurt others and destroy relationships. If bottled up inside, it can cause us to become bitter and destroy us from within. Paul tells us to deal with our anger immediately in a way that builds relationships rather than destroys them. If we nurse our anger, we will give Satan an opportunity to divide us. Are you angry with someone right now? What can you do to resolve your differences? Don't let the day end before you begin to work on mending your relationship.

4:28–32 We can grieve the Holy Spirit by the way we live. Paul warns us against unwholesome language, bitterness, improper use of anger, brawling, slander, and bad attitudes towards others. Instead of acting that way, we should be forgiving, just as God has forgiven us. Are you grieving or pleasing God with your attitudes and actions? Act in love towards your brothers and sisters in Christ, just as God acted in love by sending his Son to die for your sins.

29 Do not let any unwholesome talk come out of your mouths,[m] but only what is
helpful for building others up according to their needs, that it may benefit those who
listen. 30 And do not grieve the Holy Spirit of God,[n] with whom you were sealed for
the day of redemption.[o] 31 Get rid of all bitterness, rage and anger, brawling and
slander, along with every form of malice.[p] 32 Be kind and compassionate to one
another, forgiving each other, just as in Christ God forgave you.[q]

5 Be imitators of God,[a] therefore, as dearly loved children 2 and live a life of love,
just as Christ loved us and gave himself up for us[b] as a fragrant offering and
sacrifice to God.[c]

3 But among you there must not be even a hint of sexual immorality, or of any kind
of impurity, or of greed,[d] because these are improper for God's holy people. 4 Nor
should there be obscenity, foolish talk or coarse joking, which are out of place, but
rather thanksgiving.[e] 5 For of this you can be sure: No immoral, impure or greedy
person—such a man is an idolater[f]—has any inheritance in the kingdom of Christ
and of God.[a][g] 6 Let no-one deceive you with empty words, for because of such things
God's wrath[h] comes on those who are disobedient. 7 Therefore do not be partners with
them.

8 For you were once[i] darkness, but now you are light in the Lord. Live as children
of light[j] 9 (for the fruit[k] of the light consists in all goodness, righteousness and truth)
10 and find out what pleases the Lord. 11 Have nothing to do with the fruitless deeds
of darkness, but rather expose them. 12 For it is shameful even to mention what the
disobedient do in secret. 13 But everything exposed by the light[l] becomes visible,
14 for it is light that makes everything visible. This is why it is said:

> "Wake up, O sleeper,[m]
> rise from the dead,[n]
> and Christ will shine on you."[o]

15 Be very careful, then, how you live—not as unwise but as wise, 16 making the
most of every opportunity,[p] because the days are evil.[q] 17 Therefore do not be

[a] 5 Or *kingdom of the Christ and God*

4:29 [m] Col 3:8
4:30 [n] 1Th 5:19 [o] Ro 8:23
4:31 [p] Col 3:8
4:32 [q] Mt 6:14, 15
5:1 [a] Lk 6:36
5:2 [b] Gal 1:4 [c] 2Co 2:15; Heb 7:27
5:3 [d] Col 3:5
5:4 [e] ver 20
5:5 [f] Col 3:5 [g] 1Co 6:9
5:6 [h] Ro 1:18
5:8 [i] Eph 2:2 [j] Lk 16:8
5:9 [k] Gal 5:22
5:13 [l] Jn 3:20, 21
5:14 [m] Ro 13:11 [n] Jn 5:25 [o] Isa 60:1
5:16 [p] Col 4:5 [q] Eph 6:13

4:30 The Holy Spirit within us is a seal or guarantee that we belong to God. For more on this thought, see the note on 1:13, 14.

4:32 This is Christ's law of forgiveness as taught in the Gospels (Matthew 6:14, 15; 18:35; Mark 11:25). We also see it in the Lord's Prayer—"Forgive us our debts, as we also have forgiven our debtors." God does not forgive us *because* we forgive others, but solely because of his great mercy. As we come to understand his mercy, however, we will want to be like him. Having received forgiveness, we will pass it on to others. Those who are unwilling to forgive have not become one with Christ, who was willing to forgive even those who crucified him (Luke 23:34).

5:1, 2 Just as children imitate their parents, we should imitate Christ. His great love for us led him to sacrifice himself so that we might live. Our love for others should be of the same kind—a love that goes beyond affection to self-sacrificing service.

5:4 Obscenity and coarse joking are so common that we begin not to notice them. Paul cautions, however, that improper language should have no place in the Christian's conversation because it does not reflect God's gracious presence in us. How can we praise God and remind others of his goodness when we are speaking coarsely?

5:5–7 Paul is not forbidding all contact with unbelievers. Jesus taught his followers to befriend sinners and lead them to him (Luke 5:30–32). Instead, Paul is speaking against condoning the lifestyle of people who make excuses for bad behaviour and recommend its practice to others—whether they are in the church or outside of it. Such people can quickly pollute the church and endanger its unity and purpose. We must befriend unbelievers if we are to lead them to Christ, but we must be wary of those who are viciously evil, immoral, or opposed to all that Christianity stands for. Such people are more likely to influence us for evil than we are likely to influence them for good.

5:8 As children of light, your actions should reflect your faith. You should live above reproach morally so that you will reflect God's goodness to others. Jesus stressed this truth in the Sermon on the Mount (Matthew 5:15, 16).

5:10–14 It is important to avoid the "fruitless deeds of darkness" (any pleasure or activity that results in sin), but we must go even further. Paul instructs us to expose these deeds, because our silence may be interpreted as approval. God needs people who will take a stand for what is right. Christians must lovingly speak out for what is true and right.

5:14 This is not a direct quote from Scripture but was probably taken from a hymn well known to the Ephesians. The hymn seems to have been based on Isaiah 26:19; 51:17; 52:1; 60:1; and Malachi 4:2. Paul was appealing to the Ephesians to wake up and realise the dangerous condition into which some of them had been slipping.

5:15, 16 By saying "the days are evil", Paul was communicating his sense of urgency because of evil's pervasiveness. We need the same sense of urgency because our days are also difficult. We must keep our standards high, act wisely, and do good whenever we can.

foolish, but understand what the Lord's will is.[r] 18 Do not get drunk on wine,[s] which
leads to debauchery. Instead, be filled with the Spirit.[t] 19 Speak to one another with
psalms, hymns and spiritual songs.[u] Sing and make music in your heart to the Lord,
20 always giving thanks[v] to God the Father for everything, in the name of our Lord
Jesus Christ.
21 Submit to one another[w] out of reverence for Christ.

Wives and Husbands

22 Wives, submit to your husbands[x] as to the Lord.[y] 23 For the husband is the head
of the wife as Christ is the head of the church,[z] his body, of which he is the Saviour.
24 Now as the church submits to Christ, so also wives should submit to their husbands
in everything.
25 Husbands, love your wives,[a] just as Christ loved the church and gave himself
up for her[b] 26 to make her holy, cleansing[b] her by the washing[c] with water through
the word, 27 and to present her to himself as a radiant church, without stain or wrinkle
or any other blemish, but holy and blameless.[d] 28 In this same way, husbands ought
to love their wives[e] as their own bodies. He who loves his wife loves himself. 29 After
all, no-one ever hated his own body, but he feeds and cares for it, just as Christ does
the church — 30 for we are members of his body.[f] 31 "For this reason a man will leave

b 26 Or *having cleansed*

5:17 [r] Ro 12:2; 1Th 4:3
5:18 [s] Pr 20:1 [t] Lk 1:15
5:19 [u] Ac 16:25; Col 3:16
5:20 [v] Ps 34:1
5:21 [w] Gal 5:13
5:22 [x] Ge 3:16; 1Pe 3:1, 5, 6 [y] Eph 6:5
5:23 [z] 1Co 11:3; Eph 1:22
5:25 [a] Col 3:19 [b] ver 2
5:26 [c] Ac 22:16
5:27 [d] Eph 1:4; Col 1:22
5:28 [e] ver 25
5:30 [f] 1Co 12:27

5:18 Paul contrasts getting drunk with wine, which produces a temporary "high", to being filled with the Spirit, which produces lasting joy. Getting drunk with wine is associated with the old way of life and its selfish desires. In Christ, we have a better joy, higher and longer lasting, to cure our depression, monotony, or tension. We should not be concerned with how much of the Holy Spirit we have, but how much of us the Holy Spirit has. Submit yourself daily to his leading and draw constantly on his power.

5:20 When you feel down, you may find it difficult to give thanks. Take heart – in all things God works for our good if we love him and are called according to his purpose (Romans 8:28). Thank God, not for your problems, but for the strength he is building in you through the difficult experiences of your life. You can be sure that God's perfect love will see you through.

5:21, 22 Submitting to another person is an often misunderstood concept. It does not mean becoming a doormat. Christ – at whose name "every knee should bow, in heaven and on earth and under the earth" (Philippians 2:10) – submitted his will to the Father, and we honour Christ by following his example. When we submit to God, we become more willing to obey his command to submit to others, that is, to subordinate our rights to theirs. In a marriage relationship, both husband and wife are called to submit. For the wife, this means willingly following her husband's leadership in Christ. For the husband, it means putting aside his own interests in order to care for his wife. Submission is rarely a problem in homes where both partners have a strong relationship with Christ and where each is concerned for the happiness of the other.

5:22–24 In Paul's day, women, children, and slaves were to submit to the head of the family – slaves would submit until they were freed, male children until they grew up, and women and girls their whole lives. Paul emphasised the equality of all believers in Christ (Galatians 3:28), but he did not suggest overthrowing Roman society to achieve it. Instead, he counselled all believers to submit to one another by choice – wives to husbands and also husbands to wives; slaves to masters and also masters to slaves; children to parents and also parents to children. This kind of mutual submission preserves order and harmony in the family while it increases love and respect among family members.

5:22–24 Although some people have distorted Paul's teaching on submission by giving unlimited authority to husbands, we cannot get around it – Paul told wives to submit to their husbands. The fact that a teaching is not popular is no reason to discard it. According to the Bible, the man is the spiritual head of the family, and his wife should acknowledge his leadership. But real spiritual leadership involves service. Just as Christ served the disciples, even to the point of washing their feet, so the husband is to serve his wife. A wise and Christ-honouring husband will not take advantage of his leadership role, and a wise and Christ-honouring wife will not try to undermine her husband's leadership. Either approach causes disunity and friction in marriage.

5:22–28 Why did Paul tell wives to submit and husbands to love? Perhaps Christian women, newly freed in Christ, found submission difficult; perhaps Christian men, used to the Roman custom of giving unlimited power to the head of the family, were not used to treating their wives with respect and love. Of course both husbands and wives should submit to each other (5:21), just as both should love each other.

5:25ff Some Christians have thought that Paul was negative about marriage because of the counsel he gave in 1 Corinthians 7:32–38. These verses in Ephesians, however, show a high view of marriage. Here marriage is not a practical necessity or a cure for lust, but a picture of the relationship between Christ and his church! Why the apparent difference? Paul's counsel in 1 Corinthians was designed for a state of emergency during a time of persecution and crisis. Paul's counsel to the Ephesians is more the biblical ideal for marriage. Marriage, for Paul, is a holy union, a living symbol, a precious relationship that needs tender, self-sacrificing care.

5:25–30 Paul devotes twice as many words to telling husbands to love their wives as to telling wives to submit to their husbands. How should a man love his wife? (1) He should be willing to sacrifice everything for her. (2) He should make her well-being of primary importance. (3) He should care for her as he cares for his own body. No wife needs to fear submitting to a man who treats her in this way.

5:26, 27 Christ's death sanctifies and cleanses the church. He cleanses us from the old ways of sin and sets us apart for his special sacred service (Hebrews 10:29; 13:12). Christ cleansed the church by the "washing" of baptism. Through baptism we are prepared for entrance into the church just as ancient Near Eastern brides were prepared for marriage by a ceremonial bath. It is God's word that cleanses us (John 17:17; Titus 3:5).

5:31–33 The union of husband and wife merges two people in such a way that little can affect one without also affecting the other. Oneness in marriage does not mean losing your personality in the personality of the other. Instead, it means caring for your partner

his father and mother and be united to his wife, and the two will become one
flesh."[c][g] 32This is a profound mystery—but I am talking about Christ and the
church. 33However, each one of you also must love his wife[h] as he loves himself,
and the wife must respect her husband.

Children and Parents

6 Children, obey your parents in the Lord, for this is right.[a] 2"Honour your father
and mother"—which is the first commandment with a promise—3"that it may
go well with you and that you may enjoy long life on the earth."[a][b]
4Fathers, do not exasperate your children;[c] instead, bring them up in the training
and instruction of the Lord.[d]

Slaves and Masters

5Slaves, obey your earthly masters with respect[e] and fear, and with sincerity of
heart,[f] just as you would obey Christ.[g] 6Obey them not only to win their favour when
their eye is on you, but like slaves of Christ, doing the will of God from your heart.
7Serve wholeheartedly, as if you were serving the Lord, not men,[h] 8because you
know that the Lord will reward everyone for whatever good he does,[i] whether he
is slave or free.
9And masters, treat your slaves in the same way. Do not threaten them, since you
know that he who is both their Master and yours[j] is in heaven, and there is no
favouritism with him.

[c] *31* Gen. 2:24 [a] *3* Deut. 5:16

5:31 [g]Ge 2:24; Mt 19:5; 1Co 6:16
5:33 [h]ver 25
6:1 [a]Col 3:20
6:3 [b]Ex 20:12
6:4 [c]Col 3:21 [d]Ge 18:19; Dt 6:7
6:5 [e]1Ti 6:1 [f]Col 3:22 [g]Eph 5:22
6:7 [h]Col 3:23
6:8 [i]Col 3:24
6:9 [j]Job 31:13, 14

---

as you care for yourself, learning to anticipate his or her needs, helping the other person become all he or she can be. The creation story tells of God's plan that husband and wife should be one (Genesis 2:24), and Jesus also referred to this plan (Matthew 19:4–6).

6:1, 2 There is a difference between obeying and honouring. To obey means to do as one is told; to honour means to respect and love. Children are not commanded to disobey God in obeying their parents. Adult children are not asked to be subservient to domineering parents. Children are to obey while under their parents' care, but the responsibility to honour parents is for life.

6:1–4 If our faith in Christ is real, it will usually prove itself at home, in our relationships with those who know us best. Children and parents have a responsibility to each other. Children should honour their parents even if the parents are demanding and unfair. Parents should care gently for their children, even if the children are disobedient and unpleasant. Ideally, of course, Christian parents and Christian children will relate to each other with thoughtfulness and love. This will happen if both parents and children put the others' interests above their own—that is, if they submit to one another.

6:3 Some societies honour their elders. They respect their wisdom, defer to their authority, and pay attention to their comfort and happiness. This is how Christians should act. Where elders are respected, long life is a blessing, not a burden to them.

6:4 The purpose of parental discipline is to help children grow, not to exasperate and provoke them to anger or discouragement (see also Colossians 3:21). Parenting is not easy—it takes lots of patience to raise children in a loving, Christ-honouring manner. But frustration and anger should not be causes for discipline. Instead, parents should act in love, treating their children as Jesus treats the people he loves. This is vital to children's development and to their understanding of what Christ is like.

6:5 Slaves played a significant part in this society. There were several million of them in the Roman empire at this time. Because many slaves and owners had become Christians, the early church had to deal straightforwardly with the question of master/slave relations. Paul's statement neither condemns nor condones slavery. Instead, it tells masters and slaves how to live together in Christian households. In Paul's day, women, children, and slaves had few rights. In the church, however, they had freedoms that society denied them. Paul tells husbands, parents, and masters to be caring.

6:6–8 Paul's instructions encourage responsibility and integrity on the job. Christian employees should do their jobs as if Jesus Christ were their supervisor. And Christian employers should treat their employees fairly and with respect. Can you be trusted to do your best, even when the boss is not around? Do you work hard and with enthusiasm? Do you treat your employees as people, not machines? Remember that no matter whom you work for, and no matter who works for you, the One you ultimately should want to please is your Father in heaven.

6:9 Although Christians may be at different levels in earthly society, we are all equal before God. He does not play favourites; no-one is more important than anyone else. Paul's letter to Philemon stresses the same point: Philemon, the master, and Onesimus, his slave, were brothers in Christ.

The Armour of God

10 Finally, be strong in the Lord[k] and in his mighty power.[l] 11 Put on the full
armour of God[m] so that you can take your stand against the devil's schemes. 12 For
our struggle is not against flesh and blood, but against the rulers, against the authorities,[n] against the powers[o] of this dark world and against the spiritual forces of evil
in the heavenly realms.[p] 13 Therefore put on the full armour of God, so that when
the day of evil comes, you may be able to stand your ground, and after you have done
everything, to stand. 14 Stand firm then, with the belt of truth buckled round your
waist,[q] with the breastplate of righteousness in place,[r] 15 and with your feet fitted
with the readiness that comes from the gospel of peace.[s] 16 In addition to all this, take
up the shield of faith,[t] with which you can extinguish all the flaming arrows of the
evil one. 17 Take the helmet of salvation[u] and the sword of the Spirit, which is the
word of God.[v] 18 And pray in the Spirit on all occasions[w] with all kinds of prayers

6:10 [k] 1Co 16:13 [l] Eph 1:19
6:11 [m] Ro 13:12
6:12 [n] Eph 1:21 [o] Ro 8:38 [p] Eph 1:3
6:14 [q] Isa 11:5 [r] Isa 59:17
6:15 [s] Isa 52:7
6:16 [t] 1Jn 5:4
6:17 [u] Isa 59:17 [v] Heb 4:12
6:18 [w] Lk 18:1

GOD'S ARMOUR FOR US

We are engaged in a spiritual battle—all believers find themselves subject to Satan's attacks because they are no longer on Satan's side. Thus, Paul tells us to use *every piece* of God's armour to resist Satan's attacks and to stand true to God in the midst of those attacks.

Piece of Armour	*Use*	*Application*
Belt	Truth	Satan fights with lies, and sometimes his lies *sound* like truth; but only believers have God's truth, which can defeat Satan's lies.
Breastplate	Righteousness	Satan often attacks our hearts—the seat of our emotions, self-worth, and trust. God's righteousness is the breastplate that protects our hearts and ensures his approval. He approves of us because he loves us and sent his Son to die for us.
Footwear	Readiness to spread the good news	Satan wants us to think that telling others the good news is a worthless and hopeless task—the size of the task is too big and the negative responses are too much to handle. But the footwear God gives us is the motivation to continue to proclaim the true peace that is available in God—news everyone needs to hear.
Shield	Faith	What *we* see are Satan's attacks in the form of insults, setbacks, and temptations. But the shield of faith protects us from Satan's flaming arrows. With God's perspective, we can see beyond our circumstances and know that ultimate victory is ours.
Helmet	Salvation	Satan wants to make us doubt God, Jesus, and our salvation. The helmet protects our minds from doubting God's saving work for us.
Sword	The Spirit, the word of God	The sword is the only weapon of *offence* in this list of armour. There are times when we need to take the offensive against Satan. When we are tempted, we need to trust in the truth of God's word.

6:10–17 In the Christian life we battle against rulers and authorities (the powerful evil forces of fallen angels headed by Satan, who is a vicious fighter, see 1 Peter 5:8). To withstand their attacks, we must depend on God's strength and use every piece of his armour. Paul is not only giving this counsel to the church, the body of Christ, but to all individuals within the church. The whole body needs to be armed. As you do battle against "the powers of this dark world", fight in the strength of the church, whose power comes from the Holy Spirit.

6:12 These who are not "flesh and blood" are demons over whom Satan has control. They are not mere fantasies—they are very real. We face a powerful army whose goal is to defeat Christ's church. When we believe in Christ, these beings become our enemies, and they try every device to turn us away from him and back to sin. Although we are assured of victory, we must engage in the struggle until Christ returns, because Satan is constantly battling against all who are on the Lord's side. We need supernatural power to defeat Satan, and God has provided this by giving us his Holy Spirit within us and his armour surrounding us. If you feel discouraged, remember Jesus' words to Peter: "On this rock I will build my church, and the gates of Hades will not overcome it" (Matthew 16:18).

6:18 How can anyone pray on all occasions? One way is to make quick, brief prayers your habitual response to every situation you meet throughout the day. Another way is to order your life around God's desires and teachings so that your very life becomes a prayer. You don't have to isolate yourself from other people and from daily work in order to pray constantly. You can make prayer your life and your life a prayer while living in a world that needs God's powerful influence. "Praying for all the saints" means praying for all believers in Christ; so pray for the Christians you know

6:18
[x]Mt 26:41; Php 1:4
6:19
[y]1Th 5:25
[z]Ac 4:29; 2Co 3:12
6:20
[a]2Co 5:20
[b]Ac 21:33
6:21
[c]Ac 20:4
6:22
[d]Col 4:7-9
6:23
[e]Gal 6:16; 1Pe 5:14

and requests.[x] With this in mind, be alert and always keep on praying for all the saints.
19Pray also for me,[y] that whenever I open my mouth, words may be given me so that I will fearlessly[z] make known the mystery of the gospel,
20for which I am an ambassador[a] in chains.[b] Pray that I may declare it fearlessly, as I should.

Final Greetings

21Tychicus,[c] the dear brother and faithful servant in the Lord, will tell you everything, so that you also may know how I am and what I am doing.
22I am sending him to you for this very purpose, that you may know how we are,[d] and that he may encourage you.
23Peace[e] to the brothers, and love with faith from God the Father and the Lord Jesus Christ.
24Grace to all who love our Lord Jesus Christ with an undying love.

---

and for the church around the world.

6:19, 20 Undiscouraged and undefeated, Paul wrote powerful letters of encouragement from prison. Paul did not ask the Ephesians to pray that his chains would be removed, but that he would continue to speak fearlessly for Christ in spite of them. God can use us in any circumstance to do his will. Even as we pray for a change in our circumstances, we should also pray that God will accomplish his plan through us right where we are. Knowing God's eternal purpose for us will help us through the difficult times.

6:21 Tychicus is also mentioned in Acts 20:4, Colossians 4:7, 2 Timothy 4:12, and Titus 3:12.

6:24 This letter was written to the church at Ephesus, but it was also meant for circulation among other churches. In this letter, Paul highlights the supremacy of Christ, gives information on both the nature of the church and on how church members should live, and stresses the unity of all believers—male, female, parent, child, master, slave—regardless of sex, nationality, or social rank. The home and the church are difficult places to live the Christian life, because our real self comes through to those who know us well. Close relationships between imperfect people can lead to trouble—or to increased faith and deepened dependence on God. We can build unity in our churches through willing submission to Christ's leadership and humble service to one another.

PHILIPPIANS

VITAL STATISTICS

PURPOSE:
To thank the Philippians for the gift they had sent Paul and to strengthen these believers by showing them that true joy comes from Jesus Christ alone

AUTHOR:
Paul

TO WHOM WRITTEN:
All the Christians at Philippi, and all believers everywhere

DATE WRITTEN:
About A.D. 61, from Rome during Paul's imprisonment there

SETTING:
Paul and his companions began the church at Philippi on his second missionary journey (Acts 16:11–40). This was the first church established on the European continent. The Philippian church had sent a gift with Epaphroditus (one of their members) to be delivered to Paul (4:18). Paul was in a Roman prison at the time. He wrote this letter to thank them for their gift and to encourage them in their faith.

KEY VERSE:
"Rejoice in the Lord always. I will say it again: Rejoice!" (4:4).

KEY PEOPLE:
Paul, Timothy, Epaphroditus, Euodia, and Syntyche

KEY PLACE:
Philippi

THE WORD *happiness* evokes visions of unwrapping gifts on Christmas morning, strolling hand in hand with the one you love, being surprised on your birthday, responding with unbridled laughter to a comedian, or taking a holiday in an exotic location. Everyone wants to be happy; we make chasing this elusive ideal a lifelong pursuit: spending money, collecting things, and searching for new experiences. But if happiness depends on our circumstances, what happens when the toys rust, loved ones die, health deteriorates, money is stolen, and the party's over? Often happiness flees and despair sets in.

In contrast to *happiness* stands *joy*. Running deeper and stronger, joy is the quiet, confident assurance of God's love and work in our lives—that he will be there no matter what! Happiness depends on happenings, but joy depends on Christ.

Philippians is Paul's joy letter. The church in that Macedonian city had been a great encouragement to Paul. The Philippian believers had enjoyed a very special relationship with Paul, so he wrote them a personal expression of his love and affection. They had brought him great joy (4:1). Philippians is also a joyful book because it emphasises the real joy of the Christian life. The concept of *rejoicing* or *joy* appears sixteen times in four chapters, and the pages radiate this positive message, culminating in the exhortation to "Rejoice in the Lord always. I will say it again: Rejoice!" (4:4).

In a life dedicated to serving Christ, Paul had faced excruciating poverty, abundant wealth, and everything in between. He even wrote this joyful letter from prison. Whatever the circumstances, Paul had learned to be content (4:11, 12), finding real joy as he focused all of his attention and energy on knowing Christ (3:8) and obeying him (3:12, 13).

Paul's desire to know Christ above all else is wonderfully expressed in the following words: "What is more, I consider everything a loss compared to the surpassing greatness of knowing Christ Jesus my Lord, for whose sake I have lost all things. I consider them rubbish, that I may gain Christ and be found in him. . . . I want to know Christ and the power of his resurrection and the fellowship of sharing in his sufferings, becoming like him in his death" (3:8–10). May we share Paul's aspiration and seek to know Jesus Christ more and more. Rejoice with Paul in Philippians, and rededicate yourself to finding joy in Christ.

THE BLUEPRINT

1. Joy in suffering (1:1–30)
2. Joy in serving (2:1–30)
3. Joy in believing (3:1–4:1)
4. Joy in giving (4:2–23)

Although Paul was writing from prison, joy is a dominant theme in this letter. The secret of his joy is grounded in his relationship with Christ. People today desperately want to be happy but are tossed and turned by daily successes, failures, and inconveniences. Christians are to be joyful in every circumstance, even when things are going badly, even when we feel like complaining, even when no-one else is joyful. Christ still reigns, and we still know him, so we can rejoice at all times.

MEGATHEMES

THEME	EXPLANATION	IMPORTANCE
Humility	Christ showed true humility when he laid aside his rights and privileges as God to become human. He poured out his life to pay the penalty we deserve. Laying aside self-interest is essential to all our relationships.	We are to take Christ's attitude in serving others. We must renounce personal recognition and merit. When we give up our self-interest, we can serve with joy, love, and kindness.
Self-sacrifice	Christ suffered and died so that we might have eternal life. With courage and faithfulness, Paul sacrificed himself for the ministry. He preached the gospel even while he was in prison.	Christ gives us power to lay aside our personal needs and concerns. To utilise his power, we must imitate those leaders who show self-denying concern for others. We dare not be self-centred.
Unity	In every church, in every generation, there are divisive influences (issues, loyalties, and conflicts). In the midst of hardships, it is easy to turn on one another. Paul encouraged the Philippians to agree with one another, stop complaining, and work together.	As believers, we should contend against a common enemy, not against one another. When we are unified in love, Christ's strength is most abundant. Keep before you the ideals of teamwork, consideration for others, and unselfishness.
Christian Living	Paul shows us how to live successful Christian lives. We can become mature by being so identified with Christ that his attitude of humility and self-sacrifice rules us. Christ is both our source of power and our guide.	Developing our character begins with God's work in us. But growth also requires discipline, obedience, and relentless concentration on our part.
Joy	Believers can have profound contentment, serenity, and peace no matter what happens. This joy comes from knowing Christ personally and from depending on his strength rather than our own.	We can have joy, even in hardship. Joy does not come from outward circumstances but from inward strength. As Christians, we must not rely on what we have or what we experience to give us joy, but on Christ within us.

1. Joy in suffering

1 Paul and Timothy,[a] servants of Christ Jesus,

To all the saints[b] in Christ Jesus at Philippi,[c] together with the overseers[a][d] and
deacons:[e]

2Grace and peace to you from God our Father and the Lord Jesus Christ.[f]

Thanksgiving and Prayer

3I thank my God every time I remember you.[g] 4In all my prayers for all of you,
I always pray[h] with joy 5because of your partnership[i] in the gospel from the first
day[j] until now, 6being confident of this, that he who began a good work in you will
carry it on to completion until the day of Christ Jesus.[k]
7It is right[l] for me to feel this way about all of you, since I have you in my heart;[m]
for whether I am in chains[n] or defending[o] and confirming the gospel, all of you share
in God's grace with me. 8God can testify[p] how I long for all of you with the affection
of Christ Jesus.
9And this is my prayer: that your love[q] may abound more and more in knowledge

a 1 Traditionally *bishops*

1:1
[a]Ac 16:1; 2Co 1:1
[b]Ac 9:13
[c]Ac 16:12
[d]1Ti 3:1
[e]1Ti 3:8
1:2
[f]Ro 1:7
1:3
[g]Ro 1:8
1:4
[h]Ro 1:10
1:5
[i]Ac 2:42; Php 4:15
[j]Ac 16:12-40
1:6
[k]ver 10; 1Co 1:8
1:7
[l]2Pe 1:13
[m]2Co 7:3
[n]ver 13, 14, 17; Ac 21:33
[o]ver 16
1:8
[p]Ro 1:9
1:9
[q]1Th 3:12

1:1 This is a personal letter to the Philippians, not intended for general circulation to all the churches as was the letter to the Ephesians. Paul wanted to thank the believers for helping him when he had a need. He also wanted to tell them why he could be full of joy despite his imprisonment and forthcoming trial. In this uplifting letter, Paul counselled the Philippians about humility and unity and warned them about potential problems.

1:1 On Paul's first missionary journey, he visited towns close to his headquarters in Antioch of Syria. On his second and third journeys, he travelled even farther. Because of the great distance between the congregations that Paul had founded, he could no longer personally oversee them all. Thus he was compelled to write letters to teach and encourage the believers. Fortunately, Paul had a staff of volunteers (including Timothy, Mark, and Epaphras) who personally delivered these letters and often remained with the congregations for a while to teach and encourage them.

1:1 For more information on Paul, see his Profile in Acts 9. Timothy's Profile is found in 1 Timothy 6.

1:1 The Roman colony of Philippi was located in northern Greece (called Macedonia in Paul's day). Philip II of Macedon (the father of Alexander the Great) took the town from ancient Thrace in about 357 B.C., enlarged and strengthened it, and gave it his name. This thriving commercial centre sat at the crossroads between Europe and Asia. In about A.D. 50, Paul, Silas, Timothy, and Luke crossed the Aegean Sea from Asia Minor and landed at Philippi (Acts 16:11–40). The church in Philippi consisted mostly of Gentile (non-Jewish) believers. Because they were not familiar with the Old Testament, Paul did not specifically quote any Old Testament passages in this letter.

1:1 Overseers (bishops or pastors) and deacons led the early Christian churches. The qualifications and duties of the overseers are explained in detail in 1 Timothy 3:1–7 and Titus 1:5–9. The qualifications and duties of deacons are spelled out in 1 Timothy 3:8–13. The saints are all those who believe in Christ.

1:4 This is the first of many times Paul used the word *joy* in his letter. The Philippians were remembered with joy and thanksgiving whenever Paul prayed. By helping Paul, they were helping Christ's cause. The Philippians were willing to be used by God for whatever he wanted them to do. When others think about you, what comes to their minds? Are you remembered with joy by them? Do your acts of kindness lift up others?

1:4, 5 The Philippians first heard the gospel about ten years earlier when Paul and his companions visited Philippi (during Paul's second missionary journey) and founded the church there.

1:5 When Paul said that the Philippians were partners in the gospel, he was pointing out their valuable contribution in spreading God's message. They contributed through their practical help when Paul was in Philippi, and through their financial support when he was in prison. As we help our ministers, missionaries, and evangelists through prayer, hospitality, and financial donations, we become partners with them.

1:6 The God who began a good work in us continues it throughout our lifetime and will finish it when we meet him face to face. God's work *for* us began when Christ died on the cross in our place. His work *in* us began when we first believed. Now the Holy Spirit lives in us, enabling us to be more like Christ every day. Paul is describing the process of Christian growth and maturity that began when we accepted Jesus and continues until Christ returns.

1:6 Do you sometimes feel as though you're not making progress in your spiritual life? When God starts a project, he completes it! As with the Philippians, God will help you grow in grace until he has completed his work in your life. When you are discouraged, remember that God won't give up on you. He promises to finish the work he has begun. When you feel incomplete, unfinished, or distressed by your shortcomings, remember God's promise and provision. Don't let your present condition rob you of the joy of knowing Christ or keep you from growing closer to him.

1:7 When he said, "in chains", Paul was probably referring to his imprisonment in Philippi, recorded in Acts 16:22–36. In verses 13 and 14, Paul speaks of his Roman imprisonment. Wherever Paul was, even in prison, he faithfully preached the Good News. Remember Paul's inspiring example when hindrances, small or large, slow down your work for God.

1:7, 8 Have you ever longed to see a friend with whom you share fond memories? Paul had such a longing to see the Christians at Philippi. His love and affection for them was based not merely on past experiences, but also on the unity that comes when believers draw upon Christ's love. All Christians are part of God's family and thus share equally in the transforming power of his love. Do you feel a deep love for fellow Christians, friends and strangers alike? Let Christ's love motivate you to love other Christians and to express that love in your actions towards them.

1:9 Often the best way to influence someone is to pray for him or her. Paul's prayer for the Philippians was that they would be unified in love. Their love was to result in greater knowledge of Christ and deeper insight (moral discernment). Their love was not based on feelings but on what Christ had done for them. As you grow in Christ's love, your heart and mind must grow together. Are your love and insight growing?

1:10 [r] ver 6; 1Co 1:8
1:11 [s] Jas 3:18
1:13 [t] ver 7, 14, 17
1:14 [u] ver 7, 13, 17

and depth of insight, 10so that you may be able to discern what is best and may be
pure and blameless until the day of Christ,[r] 11filled with the fruit of righteousness[s]
that comes through Jesus Christ — to the glory and praise of God.

Paul's Chains Advance the Gospel

12Now I want you to know, brothers, that what has happened to me has really served
to advance the gospel. 13As a result, it has become clear throughout the whole palace
guard[b] and to everyone else that I am in chains[t] for Christ. 14Because of my
chains,[u] most of the brothers in the Lord have been encouraged to speak the word
of God more courageously and fearlessly.

b 13 Or *whole palace*

LOCATION OF PHILIPPI
Philippi sat on the Egnatian Way, the main transportation route in Macedonia, an extension of the Appian Way, which joined the eastern empire with Italy.

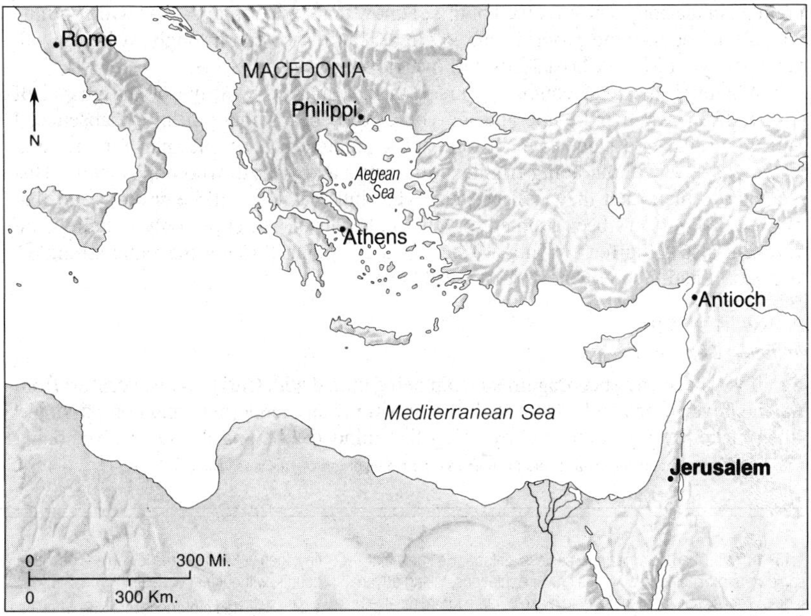

1:10 Paul prayed that the Philippian believers would "discern what is best" — in other words, that they would have the ability to differentiate between right and wrong, good and bad, vital and trivial. We ought to pray for moral discernment so we can maintain our Christian morals and values. Hebrews 5:14 emphasises the need for discernment.

1:10 The "day of Christ" refers to the time when God will judge the world through Jesus Christ. We should live each day as though he could return at any moment.

1:11 The "fruit of righteousness" includes all of the character traits flowing from a right relationship with God. There is no other way for us to gain this fruit of righteousness than through Christ. See Galatians 5:22, 23 for the "fruit of the Spirit".

1:12–14 Being imprisoned would cause many people to become bitter or to give up, but Paul saw it as one more opportunity to spread the Good News of Christ. Paul realised that his current circumstances weren't as important as what he did with them. Turning a bad situation into a good one, he reached out to the Roman soldiers who made up the palace guard and encouraged those Christians who were afraid of persecution. We may not be in prison, but we still have plenty of opportunities to be discouraged — times of indecision, financial burdens, family conflict, church conflict, or the loss of our jobs. How we act in such situations will reflect what we believe. Like Paul, look for ways to demonstrate your faith even in bad situations. Whether or not the situation improves, your faith will grow stronger.

1:13 How did Paul end up in chains in a Roman prison? While he was visiting Jerusalem, some Jews had him arrested for preaching the gospel, but he appealed to Caesar to hear his case (Acts 21:15 – 25:12). He was then escorted by soldiers to Rome, where he was placed under house arrest while awaiting trial — not a trial for breaking civil law, but for proclaiming the Good News of Christ. At that time, the Roman authorities did not consider this to be a serious charge. A few years later, however, Rome would take a different view of Christianity and make every effort to stamp it out of existence. Paul's house arrest allowed him some degree of freedom. He could have visitors, continue to preach, and write letters such as this one. A brief record of Paul's time in Rome is found in Acts 28:11–31. The "whole palace guard" refers to the Praetorian guard, the elite troops housed in the emperor's palace.

1:14 When we speak fearlessly for Christ, or live faithfully for him during difficult situations, we encourage others to do the same. Be an encouragement by the way that you live.

15 It is true that some preach Christ out of envy and rivalry, but others out of
goodwill. 16 The latter do so in love, knowing that I am put here for the defence of
the gospel.[v] 17 The former preach Christ out of selfish ambition,[w] not sincerely,
supposing that they can stir up trouble for me while I am in chains.[c][x] 18 But what
does it matter? The important thing is that in every way, whether from false motives
or true, Christ is preached. And because of this I rejoice.
Yes, and I will continue to rejoice, 19 for I know that through your prayers[y] and
the help given by the Spirit of Jesus Christ,[z] what has happened to me will turn out
for my deliverance.[d] 20 I eagerly expect[a] and hope that I will in no way be ashamed,
but will have sufficient courage[b] so that now as always Christ will be exalted in my
body,[c] whether by life or by death.[d] 21 For to me, to live is Christ[e] and to die is
gain. 22 If I am to go on living in the body, this will mean fruitful labour for me. Yet
what shall I choose? I do not know! 23 I am torn between the two: I desire to depart[f]
and be with Christ,[g] which is better by far; 24 but it is more necessary for you that
I remain in the body. 25 Convinced of this, I know that I will remain, and I will continue
with all of you for your progress and joy in the faith, 26 so that through my being with
you again your joy in Christ Jesus will overflow on account of me.
27 Whatever happens, conduct yourselves in a manner worthy[h] of the gospel of
Christ. Then, whether I come and see you or only hear about you in my absence, I
will know that you stand firm[i] in one spirit, contending[j] as one man for the faith
of the gospel 28 without being frightened in any way by those who oppose you. This
is a sign to them that they will be destroyed, but that you will be saved—and that
by God. 29 For it has been granted to you[k] on behalf of Christ not only to believe on
him, but also to suffer[l] for him, 30 since you are going through the same struggle[m]
you saw[n] I had, and now hear[o] that I still have.

2. Joy in serving

Imitating Christ's Humility

2 If you have any encouragement from being united with Christ, if any comfort from
his love, if any fellowship with the Spirit,[a] if any tenderness and compassion,[b]
2 then make my joy complete[c] by being like-minded,[d] having the same love, being

c *16,17* Some late manuscripts have verses 16 and 17 in reverse order. **d** *19* Or *salvation*

1:16 [v]ver 7, 12
1:17 [w]Php 2:3 [x]ver 7, 13, 14
1:19 [y]2Co 1:11 [z]Ac 16:7
1:20 [a]Ro 8:19 [b]ver 14 [c]1Co 6:20 [d]Ro 14:8
1:21 [e]Gal 2:20
1:23 [f]2Ti 4:6 [g]Jn 12:26; 2Co 5:8
1:27 [h]Eph 4:1 [i]1Co 16:13 [j]Jude 3
1:29 [k]Mt 5:11, 12 [l]Ac 14:22
1:30 [m]Col 2:1; 1Th 2:2 [n]Ac 16:19-40 [o]ver 13
2:1 [a]2Co 13:14 [b]Col 3:12
2:2 [c]Jn 3:29 [d]Php 4:2

1:15–18 Paul had an amazingly selfless attitude. He knew that some were preaching to build their own reputations, taking advantage of Paul's imprisonment to try to make a name for themselves. Regardless of the motives of these preachers, Paul rejoiced that the gospel was being preached. Some Christians serve for the wrong reasons. Paul wouldn't condone, nor does God excuse, their motives, but we should be glad if God uses their message, regardless of their motives.

1:19–21 This was not Paul's final imprisonment in Rome. But he didn't know that. Awaiting trial, he knew he could either be released or executed. However, he trusted Christ to work it out for his deliverance. Paul's prayer was that when he stood trial, he would speak courageously for Christ and not be timid or ashamed. Whether he lived or died, he wanted to exalt Christ. As it turned out, he was released from this imprisonment but arrested again two or three years later. Only faith in Christ could sustain Paul in such adversity.

1:20, 21 To those who don't believe in God, life on earth is all there is, and so it is natural for them to strive for this world's values—money, popularity, power, pleasure, and prestige. For Paul, however, to live meant to develop eternal values and to tell others about Christ, who alone could help them see life from an eternal perspective. Paul's whole purpose in life was to speak out boldly for Christ and to become more like him. Thus Paul could confidently say that dying would be even better than living, because in death he would be removed from worldly troubles, and he would see Christ face to face (1 John 3:2, 3). If you're not ready to die, then you're not ready to live. Make certain of your eternal destiny; then you will be free to serve—devoting your life to what really counts, without fear of death.

1:24 Paul had a purpose for living when he served the Philippians and others. We also need a purpose for living that goes beyond providing for our own physical needs. Whom can you serve or help? What is your purpose for living?

1:27 Paul encourages the believers to be unified, as they "stand firm in one spirit, contending as one man for the faith". How sad that much time and effort is lost in some churches by fighting against one another instead of uniting against the real opposition! It takes a courageous church to resist in-fighting and to maintain the common purpose of serving Christ.

1:29 Paul considered it a privilege to suffer for Christ. We do not by nature consider suffering a privilege. Yet when we suffer, if we faithfully represent Christ, our message and example affect us and others for good (see Acts 5:41). Suffering has these additional benefits: (1) it takes our eyes off earthly comforts; (2) it weeds out superficial believers; (3) it strengthens the faith of those who endure; (4) it serves as an example to others who may follow us. When we suffer for our faith, it doesn't mean that we have done something wrong. In fact, the opposite is often true—it verifies that we have been faithful. Use suffering to build your character. Don't resent it or let it tear you down.

1:30 Throughout his life Paul suffered for spreading the gospel. Like the Philippians, we are in conflict with anyone who would discredit the saving message of Christ. All true believers are in this fight together, uniting against the same enemy for a common cause.

2:2 [e]Ro 12:16
2:3 [f]Gal 5:26 [g]Ro 12:10; 1Pe 5:5
2:5 [h]Mt 11:29
2:6 [i]Jn 1:1 [j]Jn 5:18
2:7 [k]Mt 20:28 [l]Jn 1:14; Heb 2:17
2:8 [m]Mt 26:39; Jn 10:18; Heb 5:8
2:9 [n]Ac 2:33; Heb 2:9 [o]Eph 1:20, 21
2:10 [p]Ro 14:11

one[e] in spirit and purpose. 3Do nothing out of selfish ambition or vain conceit,[f] but
in humility consider others better than yourselves.[g] 4Each of you should look not only
to your own interests, but also to the interests of others.
5Your attitude should be the same as that of Christ Jesus:[h]

6Who, being in very nature[a] God,[i]
did not consider equality with God[j] something to be grasped,
7but made himself nothing,
taking the very nature[b] of a servant,[k]
being made in human likeness.[l]
8And being found in appearance as a man,
he humbled himself
and became obedient to death[m]—even death on a cross!
9Therefore God exalted him[n] to the highest place
and gave him the name that is above every name,[o]
10that at the name of Jesus every knee should bow,[p]

[a] 6 Or *in the form of* [b] 7 Or *the form*

2:1–5 Many people—even Christians—live only to make a good impression on others or to please themselves. But "selfish ambition or vain conceit" brings discord. Paul therefore stressed spiritual unity, asking the Philippians to love one another and to be one in spirit and purpose. When we work together, caring for the problems of others as if they were our problems, we demonstrate Christ's example of putting others first, and we experience unity. Don't be so concerned about making a good impression or meeting your own needs that you strain relationships in God's family.

2:3 Selfish ambition can ruin a church, but genuine humility can build it. Being humble involves having a true perspective about ourselves (see Romans 12:3). It does not mean that we should put ourselves down. Before God, we are sinners, saved only by God's grace, but we *are* saved and therefore have great worth in God's kingdom. We are to lay aside selfishness and treat others with respect and common courtesy. Considering others' interests as more important than our own links us with Christ, who was a true example of humility.

2:4 Philippi was a cosmopolitan city. The composition of the church reflected great diversity, with people from a variety of backgrounds and walks of life. Acts 16 gives us some indication of the diverse makeup of this church. The church included Lydia, a Jewish convert from Asia and a wealthy businesswoman (Acts 16:14); the slave girl (Acts 16:16, 17), probably a native Greek; and the jailer serving this colony of the empire, probably a Roman (Acts 16:25–36). With so many different backgrounds among the members, unity must have been difficult to maintain. Although there is no evidence of division in the church, its unity had to be safeguarded (3:2; 4:2). Paul encourages us to guard against any selfishness, prejudice, or jealousy that might lead to dissension. Showing genuine interest in others is a positive step forward in maintaining unity among believers.

2:5 Jesus Christ was humble, willing to give up his rights in order to obey God and serve people. Like Christ, we should have a servant's attitude, serving out of love for God and for others, not out of guilt or fear. Remember, you can choose your attitude. You can approach life expecting to be served, or you can look for opportunities to serve others. See Mark 10:45 for more on Christ's attitude of servanthood.

2:5–7 The *incarnation* was the act of the pre-existent Son of God voluntarily assuming a human body and human nature. Without ceasing to be God, he became a human being, the man called Jesus. He did not give up his deity to become human, but he set aside the right to his glory and power. In submission to the Father's will, Christ limited his power and knowledge. Jesus of Nazareth was subject to place, time, and many other human limitations. What made his humanity unique was his freedom from sin. In his full humanity, Jesus showed us everything about God's character that can be conveyed in human terms. The incarnation is explained further in these passages: John 1:1–14; Romans 1:2–5; 2 Corinthians 8:9; 1 Timothy 3:16; Hebrews 2:14; and 1 John 1:1–3.

2:5–11 These verses are probably from a hymn sung by the early Christian church. The passage holds many parallels to the prophecy of the suffering servant in Isaiah 53. As a hymn, it was not meant to be a complete statement about the nature and work of Christ. Several key characteristics of Jesus Christ, however, are praised in this passage: (1) Christ has always existed with God; (2) Christ is equal to God because he *is* God (John 1:1ff; Colossians 1:15–19); (3) though Christ is God, he became a man in order to fulfil God's plan of salvation for all people; (4) Christ did not just have the appearance of being a man—he actually became human to identify with our sins; (5) Christ voluntarily laid aside his divine rights and privileges out of love for his Father; (6) Christ died on the cross for our sins so we wouldn't have to face eternal death; (7) God glorified Christ because of his obedience; (8) God raised Christ to his original position at the Father's right hand, where he will reign for ever as our Lord and Judge. How can we do anything less than praise Christ as our Lord and dedicate ourselves to his service!

2:5–11 Often people excuse selfishness, pride, or evil by claiming their rights. They think, "I can cheat in this test; after all, I deserve to pass," or "I can spend all this money on myself—I worked hard for it," or "I can have an abortion; I have a right to control my own body." But as believers, we should have a different attitude, one that enables us to lay aside our rights in order to serve others. If we say we follow Christ, we must also say we want to live as he lived. We should develop his attitude of humility as we serve, even when we are not likely to get recognition for our efforts. Are you selfishly clinging to your rights, or are you willing to serve?

2:8 Death on a cross (crucifixion) was the form of capital punishment that Romans used for notorious criminals. It was excruciatingly painful and humiliating. Prisoners were nailed or tied to a cross and left to die. Death might not come for several days, and it usually came by suffocation when the weight of the weakened body made breathing more and more difficult. Jesus died as one who was cursed (Galatians 3:13). How amazing that the perfect man should die this most shameful death so that we would not have to face eternal punishment!

2:9–11 At the last judgment even those who are condemned will recognise Jesus' authority and right to rule. People can choose to regard Jesus as Lord now as a step of willing and loving commitment, or be forced to acknowledge him as Lord when he returns. Christ may return at any moment. Are you prepared to meet him?

in heaven and on earth and under the earth,[q]
11and every tongue confess that Jesus Christ is Lord,[r]
to the glory of God the Father.

Shining as Stars

12Therefore, my dear friends, as you have always obeyed—not only in my presence, but now much more in my absence—continue to work out your salvation with
fear and trembling,[s] 13for it is God who works in you[t] to will and to act according
to his good purpose.
14Do everything without complaining[u] or arguing, 15so that you may become
blameless and pure, children of God[v] without fault in a crooked and depraved
generation,[w] in which you shine like stars in the universe 16as you hold out[c] the word
of life—in order that I may boast on the day of Christ that I did not run or labour for
nothing.[x] 17But even if I am being poured out like a drink offering[y] on the sacrifice[z]
and service coming from your faith, I am glad and rejoice with all of you. 18So you
too should be glad and rejoice with me.

Timothy and Epaphroditus

19I hope in the Lord Jesus to send Timothy to you soon,[a] that I also may be cheered
when I receive news about you. 20I have no-one else like him,[b] who takes a genuine
interest in your welfare. 21For everyone looks out for his own interests,[c] not those
of Jesus Christ. 22But you know that Timothy has proved himself, because as a son
with his father[d] he has served with me in the work of the gospel. 23I hope, therefore,
to send him as soon as I see how things go with me.[e] 24And I am confident[f] in the
Lord that I myself will come soon.
25But I think it is necessary to send back to you Epaphroditus, my brother, fellow-

c *16* Or *hold on to*

2:10 [q]Mt 28:18
2:11 [r]Jn 13:13
2:12 [s]2Co 7:15
2:13 [t]Ezr 1:5
2:14 [u]1Co 10:10; 1Pe 4:9
2:15 [v]Mt 5:45, 48; Eph 5:1 [w]Ac 2:40
2:16 [x]1Th 2:19
2:17 [y]2Ti 4:6 [z]Ro 15:16
2:19 [a]ver 23
2:20 [b]1Co 16:10
2:21 [c]1Co 10:24; 13:5
2:22 [d]1Co 4:17; 1Ti 1:2
2:23 [e]ver 19
2:24 [f]Php 1:25

2:12 "Therefore" ties this verse to the previous section. "Work out your salvation", in light of the preceding exhortation to unity, may mean that the entire church was to work together to rid themselves of divisions and discord. The Philippian Christians needed to be especially careful to obey Christ, now that Paul wasn't there to continually remind them about what was right. We too must be careful about what we believe and how we live, especially when we are on our own. In the absence of cherished Christian leaders, we must focus our attention and devotion even more on Christ so that we won't be sidetracked.

2:13 What do we do when we don't feel like obeying? God has not left us alone in our struggles to do his will. He wants to come alongside us and be within us to help. God helps us *want* to obey him and then gives us the *power* to do what he wants. The secret to a changed life is to submit to God's control and let him work. Next time, ask God to help you *want* to do his will.

2:13 To be like Christ, we must train ourselves to think like Christ. To change our desires to be more like Christ's, we need the power of the indwelling Spirit (1:19), the influence of faithful Christians, obedience to God's word (not just exposure to it), and sacrificial service. Often it is in *doing* God's will that we gain the *desire* to do it (see 4:8, 9). Do what he wants and trust him to change your desires.

2:14–16 Why are complaining and arguing so harmful? If all that people know about a church is that its members constantly argue, complain, and gossip, they get a false impression of Christ and the gospel. Belief in Christ should unite those who trust him. If your church is always complaining and arguing, it lacks the unifying power of Jesus Christ. Stop arguing with other Christians or complaining about people and conditions within the church and let the world see Christ.

2:14–16 Our lives should be characterised by moral purity, patience, and peacefulness, so that we will "shine like stars" in a dark and depraved world. A transformed life is an effective witness to the power of God's word. Are you shining brightly, or are you clouded by complaining and arguing? Shine out for God.

2:17 The drink offering was an important part of the sacrificial system of the Jews (for an explanation, see Numbers 28:7). Because this church had little Jewish background, the drink offering may refer to the wine poured out to pagan deities prior to important public events. Paul regarded his life as a sacrifice.

2:17 Even if he had to die, Paul was content, knowing that he had helped the Philippians live for Christ. When you're totally committed to serving Christ, sacrificing to build the faith of others brings a joyous reward.

2:19 Timothy was with Paul in Rome when Paul wrote this letter. He travelled with Paul on his second missionary journey when the church at Philippi was begun. For more information on Timothy, see his Profile in 1 Timothy.

2:21 Paul observed that most believers are too preoccupied with their own needs to spend time working for Christ. Don't let your schedule and concerns crowd out your Christian service to and love for others.

2:22 Just as a skilled workman trains an apprentice, Paul was preparing Timothy to carry on the ministry in his absence. Who are you apprenticing for God's work? For more information, see Timothy's Profile in 1 Timothy.

2:23 Paul was in prison (either awaiting his trial or its verdict) for preaching about Christ. He was telling the Philippians that when he learned of the court's decision, he would send Timothy to them with the news and that he was ready to accept whatever came (1:21–26).

2:25 Epaphroditus delivered money from the Philippians to Paul; then he returned with this thank-you letter to Philippi. Epaphroditus may have been an elder in Philippi (2:25–30; 4:18) who, while staying with Paul, became ill (2:27, 30). After Epaphroditus recovered, he returned home. He is mentioned only in Philippians.

2:25 [g]Php 4:3 [h]Phm 2 [i]Php 4:18
2:26 [j]Php 1:8
2:29 [k]1Co 16:18; 1Ti 5:17
2:30 [l]1Co 16:17
3:2 [a]Ps 22:16, 20
3:3 [b]Ro 2:28, 29; Gal 6:15; Col 2:11
3:5 [c]Lk 1:59 [d]2Co 11:22 [e]Ro 11:1 [f]Ac 23:6
3:6 [g]Ac 8:3 [h]Ro 10:5
3:7 [i]Mt 13:44; Lk 14:33

worker[g] and fellow-soldier,[h] who is also your messenger, whom you sent to take
care of my needs.[i] 26For he longs for all of you[j] and is distressed because you heard
he was ill. 27Indeed he was ill, and almost died. But God had mercy on him, and not
on him only but also on me, to spare me sorrow upon sorrow. 28Therefore I am all
the more eager to send him, so that when you see him again you may be glad and
I may have less anxiety. 29Welcome him in the Lord with great joy, and honour men
like him,[k] 30because he almost died for the work of Christ, risking his life to make
up for the help you could not give me.[l]

3. Joy in believing

No Confidence in the Flesh

3 Finally, my brothers, rejoice in the Lord! It is no trouble for me to write the same
things to you again, and it is a safeguard for you.
2Watch out for those dogs,[a] those men who do evil, those mutilators of the flesh.
3For it is we who are the circumcision,[b] we who worship by the Spirit of God, who
glory in Christ Jesus, and who put no confidence in the flesh—4though I myself have
reasons for such confidence.
If anyone else thinks he has reasons to put confidence in the flesh, I have more:
5circumcised[c] on the eighth day, of the people of Israel,[d] of the tribe of Benjamin,[e]
a Hebrew of Hebrews; in regard to the law, a Pharisee;[f] 6as for zeal, persecuting the
church;[g] as for legalistic righteousness,[h] faultless.
7But whatever was to my profit I now consider loss[i] for the sake of Christ. 8What
is more, I consider everything a loss compared to the surpassing greatness of know-

---

2:29, 30 The world honours those who are intelligent, beautiful, rich, and powerful. What kind of people should the church honour? Paul indicates that we should honour those who give their lives for the sake of Christ, going where we cannot go ourselves. Our missionaries do that for us today by providing ministry where we are not able to go.

3:1 As a safeguard, Paul reviewed the basics with these believers. The Bible is our safeguard both morally and theologically. When we read it individually and publicly in church, it alerts us to corrections we need to make in our thoughts, attitudes, and actions.

3:2, 3 These "dogs" and "men who do evil" were very likely *Judaisers*—Jewish Christians who wrongly believed that it was essential for Gentiles to follow all the Old Testament Jewish laws, especially submission to the rite of circumcision, in order to receive salvation. Many Judaisers were motivated by spiritual pride. Because they had invested so much time and effort in keeping their laws, they couldn't accept the fact that all their efforts couldn't bring them a step closer to salvation.

Paul criticised the Judaisers because they looked at Christianity backwards—thinking that what they *did* (*circumcision*—cutting or mutilating the flesh) made them believers rather than the free gift of grace given by Christ. What believers do is a *result* of faith, not a *prerequisite* to faith. This had been confirmed by the early church leaders at the Jerusalem council 11 years earlier (Acts 15). Who are the Judaisers of our day? They are those who say that people must add something else to simple faith. No person should add anything to Christ's offer of salvation by grace through faith.

3:2, 3 It is easy to place more emphasis on religious effort ("confidence in the flesh") than on internal faith, but God values the attitude of our hearts above all else. Don't judge people's spirituality by their fulfilment of duties or by their level of human activity. And don't think that you will satisfy God by feverishly doing his work. God notices all you do for him and will reward you for it, but only if it comes as a loving response to his free gift of salvation.

3:4–6 At first glance, it looks like Paul is boasting about his achievements. But he is actually doing the opposite, showing that human achievements, no matter how impressive, cannot earn a person salvation and eternal life with God. Paul had impressive credentials: upbringing, nationality, family background, inheritance, orthodoxy, activity, and morality (see 2 Corinthians 11; Galatians 1:13–24, for more of his credentials). However, his conversion to faith in Christ (Acts 9) wasn't based on what he had done, but on God's grace. Paul did not depend on his deeds to please God because even the most impressive credentials fall short of God's holy standards. Are you depending on Christian parents, church affiliation, or just being good to make you right with God? Credentials, accomplishments, or reputation cannot earn salvation. Salvation comes only through faith in Christ.

3:5 Paul belonged to the tribe of Benjamin, a heritage greatly esteemed among the Jews. From this tribe had come Israel's first king, Saul (1 Samuel 10:20–24). The tribes of Benjamin and Judah were the only two tribes to return to Israel after the exile (Ezra 4:1). Paul was also a Pharisee, a member of a very devout Jewish sect that scrupulously kept its own numerous rules in addition to the laws of Moses. Jewish listeners would have been impressed by both of these credentials.

3:6 Why did Paul, a devout Jewish leader, persecute the church? Agreeing with the leaders of the religious establishment, Paul thought that Christianity was heretical and blasphemous. Because Jesus did not meet his expectations of what the Messiah would be like, Paul assumed that Jesus' claims were false—and therefore wicked. In addition, he saw Christianity as a political menace because it threatened to disrupt the fragile harmony between the Jews and the Roman government.

3:7 When Paul spoke of his "profit", he was referring to his credentials, credits, and successes. After showing that he could beat the Judaisers at their own game (being proud of who they were and what they had done), Paul showed that it was the wrong game. Be careful of considering past achievements so important that they get in the way of your relationship with Christ.

3:8 After Paul considered everything he had accomplished in his life, he said that it was all "a loss" when compared with the greatness of knowing Christ. This is a profound statement about values: a person's relationship with Christ is more important than anything else. To know Christ should be our ultimate goal. Consider your values. Do you place anything above your relationship with Christ? If your priorities are wrong, how will you change them?

ing[j] Christ Jesus my Lord, for whose sake I have lost all things. I consider them
rubbish, that I may gain Christ 9and be found in him, not having a righteousness of
my own that comes from the law,[k] but that which is through faith in Christ—the
righteousness that comes from God and is by faith.[l] 10I want to know Christ and the
power of his resurrection and the fellowship of sharing in his sufferings,[m] becoming
like him in his death,[n] 11and so, somehow, to attain to the resurrection[o] from the
dead.

Pressing on Toward the Goal

12Not that I have already obtained all this, or have already been made perfect,[p]
but I press on to take hold[q] of that for which Christ Jesus took hold of me.[r]
13Brothers, I do not consider myself yet to have taken hold of it. But one thing I do:
Forgetting what is behind[s] and straining towards what is ahead, 14I press on[t] towards
the goal to win the prize for which God has called[u] me heavenwards in Christ Jesus.
15All of us who are mature[v] should take such a view of things.[w] And if on some
point you think differently, that too God will make clear to you. 16Only let us live
up to what we have already attained.
17Join with others in following my example,[x] brothers, and take note of those who
live according to the pattern we gave you. 18For, as I have often told you before and
now say again even with tears,[y] many live as enemies of the cross of Christ.[z] 19Their
destiny is destruction, their god is their stomach,[a] and their glory is in their shame.[b]
Their mind is on earthly things.[c] 20But our citizenship[d] is in heaven.[e] And we

3:8 [j]Eph 4:13; 2Pe 1:2
3:9 [k]Ro 10:5 [l]Ro 9:30
3:10 [m]Ro 8:17 [n]Ro 6:3-5
3:11 [o]Rev 20:5, 6
3:12 [p]1Co 13:10 [q]1Ti 6:12 [r]Ac 9:5, 6
3:13 [s]Lk 9:62
3:14 [t]Heb 6:1 [u]Ro 8:28
3:15 [v]1Co 2:6 [w]Gal 5:10
3:17 [x]1Co 4:16; 1Pe 5:3
3:18 [y]Ac 20:31 [z]Gal 6:12
3:19 [a]Ro 16:18 [b]Ro 6:21 [c]Ro 8:5, 6
3:20 [d]Eph 2:19 [e]Col 3:1

3:9 No amount of lawkeeping, self-improvement, discipline, or religious effort can make us right with God. Righteousness comes only from God. We are made righteous (receive right standing with him) by trusting in Christ. He exchanges our sin and shortcomings for his complete righteousness. See 2 Corinthians 5:21 for more on Christ's gift of righteousness.

3:9, 10 Paul gave up everything—family, friendship, and freedom—in order to know Christ and his resurrection power. We too have access to this knowledge and this power, but we may have to make sacrifices to enjoy it fully. What are you willing to give up in order to know Christ? A busy timetable in order to set aside a few minutes each day for prayer and Bible study? Your friends' approval? Some of your plans or pleasures? Whatever it is, knowing Christ is more than worth the sacrifice.

3:10 When we are united with Christ by trusting in him, we experience the power that raised him from the dead. That same mighty power will help us live morally renewed and regenerated lives. But before we can walk in newness of life, we must also die to sin. Just as the resurrection gives us Christ's power to live for him, his crucifixion marks the death of our old sinful nature. We can't know the victory of the resurrection without personally applying the crucifixion.

3:11 When Paul wrote, "somehow, to attain to the resurrection" he was not implying uncertainty or doubt. He was unsure of the way that he would meet God, whether by execution or by natural death. He did not doubt that he would be raised, but attainment of it was within God's power and not his own.

3:11 Just as Christ was exalted after his resurrection, so we will one day share Christ's glory (Revelation 22:1–7). Paul knew that he might die soon, but he had faith that he would be raised to life again.

3:12–14 Paul says that his goal is to know Christ, to be like Christ, and to be all Christ has in mind for him. This goal absorbs all Paul's energy. This is a helpful example for us. We should not let anything take our eyes off our goal—knowing Christ. With the single-mindedness of an athlete in training, we must lay aside everything harmful and forsake anything that may distract us from being effective Christians. What is holding you back?

3:13, 14 Paul had reason to forget what was behind—he had held the coats of those who stoned Stephen, the first Christian martyr (Acts 7:57, 58, Paul is called Saul here). We have all done things for which we are ashamed, and we live in the tension of what we have been and what we want to be. Because our hope is in Christ, however, we can let go of past guilt and look forward to what God will help us become. Don't dwell on your past. Instead, grow in the knowledge of God by concentrating on your relationship with him *now.* Realise that you are forgiven, and then move on to a life of faith and obedience. Look forward to a fuller and more meaningful life because of your hope in Christ.

3:15, 16 Sometimes trying to live a perfect Christian life can be so difficult that it leaves us drained and discouraged. We may feel so far from perfect that we can never please God with our lives. Paul used *perfect* (3:12) to mean mature or complete, not flawless in every detail. Those who are mature should press on in the Holy Spirit's power, knowing that Christ will reveal and fill in any discrepancy between what we are and what we should be. Christ's provision is no excuse for lagging devotion, but it provides relief and assurance for those who feel driven.

3:16 Christian maturity involves acting on the guidance that you have already received. We can always make excuses that we still have so much to learn. The instruction for us is to live up to what we already know and live out what we have already learned. We do not have to be sidetracked by an unending search for truth.

3:17 Paul challenged the Philippians to pursue Christlikeness by following Paul's own pattern or example. This did not mean, of course, that they should copy everything he did; he had just stated that he was not perfect (3:12). But as he focused his life on being like Christ, so should they. The Gospels may not yet have been in circulation, so Paul could not tell them to read the Bible to see what Christ was like. Therefore he urged them to imitate him. That Paul could tell people to follow his example is a testimony to his character. Can you do the same? What kind of follower would a new Christian become if he or she imitated you?

3:17–21 Paul criticised not only the Judaisers (see the first note on 3:2, 3), but also the self-indulgent Christians, people who claim to be Christians but don't live up to Christ's model of servanthood

3:20
[f]1Co 1:7

3:21
[g]Eph 1:19
[h]1Co 15:43-53
[i]Col 3:4

4:1
[a]Php 1:8
[b]1Co 16:13; Php 1:27

4:2
[c]Php 2:2

eagerly await a Saviour from there, the Lord Jesus Christ,[f] 21 who, by the power[g]
that enables him to bring everything under his control, will transform our lowly
bodies[h] so that they will be like his glorious body.[i]
4 Therefore, my brothers, you whom I love and long for,[a] my joy and crown, that
is how you should stand firm[b] in the Lord, dear friends!

4. Joy in giving

Exhortations

2 I plead with Euodia and I plead with Syntyche to agree with each other[c] in the
Lord. 3 Yes, and I ask you, loyal yokefellow,[a] help these women who have contended
at my side in the cause of the gospel, along with Clement and the rest of my
fellow-workers, whose names are in the book of life.

[a] 3 Or *loyal Syzygus*

THREE STAGES OF PERFECTION

1. Perfect Relationship	We are perfect because of our eternal union with the infinitely perfect Christ. When we become his children, we are declared "not guilty", and thus righteous, because of what Christ, God's beloved Son, has done for us. This perfection is absolute and unchangeable, and it is this perfect relationship that guarantees that we will one day be "completely perfect" (below). See Colossians 2:8–10; Hebrews 10:8–14.
2. Perfect Progress	We can grow and mature spiritually as we continue to trust Christ, learn more about him, draw closer to him, and obey him. Our progress is changeable (in contrast to our relationship, above) because it depends on our daily walk—at times in life we mature more than at other times. But we are growing towards perfection if we "press on" (Philippians 3:12). These good deeds do not perfect us; rather, as God perfects us, we do good deeds for him. See Philippians 3:1–15.
3. Completely Perfect	When Christ returns to take us into his eternal kingdom, we will be glorified and made completely perfect. See Philippians 3:20, 21.

All phases of perfection are grounded in faith in Christ and what he has done, not what we can do for him. We cannot perfect ourselves; only God can work in and through us to "carry it on to completion until the day of Christ Jesus" (1:6).

and self-sacrifice. These people satisfy their own desires before even thinking about the needs of others. Freedom in Christ does not mean freedom to be selfish. It means taking every opportunity to serve and to become the best person you can be.

3:20 Citizens of Philippi had the same rights and privileges as the citizens of Rome, because Philippi was a Roman colony. Likewise, we Christians will one day experience all the special privileges of our heavenly citizenship, because we belong to Christ. Let us not be so tied to this life that we would be sorry to see Christ return.

3:21 The phrase "lowly bodies" does not imply any negative attitude towards the human body. However, the bodies we will receive when we are raised from the dead will be glorious, like Christ's resurrected body. Those who struggle with pain, physical limitations, or disabilities can have wonderful hope in the resurrection. For a more detailed discussion of our new bodies, see 1 Corinthians 15:35ff and 2 Corinthians 5:1–10.

4:1 How do we "stand firm in the Lord"? This refers to what Paul has just taught in 3:20, 21. The way to stand firm is to keep our eyes on Christ, to remember that this world is not our home, and to focus on the fact that Christ will bring everything under his control.

4:2, 3 Paul did not warn the Philippian church of doctrinal errors, but he did address some relational problems. These two women had been workers for Christ in the church. Their broken relationship was no small matter, because many had become believers through their efforts. It is possible to believe in Christ, work hard for his kingdom, and yet have broken relationships with others who are committed to the same cause. But there is no excuse for remaining unreconciled. Do you need to be reconciled to someone today?

4:3 The identity of this "loyal yokefellow" remains a mystery. It could be Epaphroditus, the bearer of this letter, or a comrade of Paul in prison. It could also be someone named Syzygus, another way to understand the word for yokefellow.

4:3 Those "whose names are in the book of life" are all who are marked for salvation through their faith in Christ (see also Luke 10:17–20; Revelation 20:11–15).

4Rejoice in the Lord always. I will say it again: Rejoice![d] 5Let your gentleness
be evident to all. The Lord is near.[e] 6Do not be anxious about anything,[f] but in
everything, by prayer and petition, with thanksgiving, present your requests to God.[g]

4:4 [d]Php 3:1
4:5 [e]Jas 5:8, 9
4:6 [f]Mt 6:25-34 [g]Eph 6:18

TRAINING FOR THE CHRISTIAN LIFE

As a great amount of training is needed for athletic activities, so we must train diligently for the Christian life. Such training takes time, dedication, energy, continued practice, and vision. We must all commit ourselves to the Christian life, but we must first know the rules as prescribed in God's word (2 Timothy 2:5).

Reference	*Metaphors*	*Training*	*Our Goal as Believers*
1 Corinthians 9:24–27	Race	Go into strict training in order to get the prize.	We train ourselves to run the race of life. So we keep our eyes on Christ—the goal—and don't get sidetracked or slowed down. When we do this, we will win a reward in Christ's kingdom.
Philippians 3:13, 14	Race	Focus all your energies towards winning the race.	Living the Christian life demands all of our energy. We can forget the past and strain for the goal because we know Christ promises eternity with him at the race's end.
1 Timothy 4:7–10	Exercise	Spiritual exercise will help you grow in faith and character.	As we must repeat exercises to tone our bodies, so we must steadily repeat spiritual exercises to be spiritually fit. When we do this, we will be better Christians, living in accordance with God's will. Such a life will attract others to Christ and pay dividends in this present life and the next.
2 Timothy 4:7, 8	Fight Race	Fighting the good fight and persevering to the end.	The Christian life is a fight against evil forces from without and temptation from within. If we stay true to God through it all, he promises an end, a rest, and a crown.

4:4 It seems strange that a man in prison would be telling a church to rejoice. But Paul's attitude teaches us an important lesson: our inner attitudes do not have to reflect our outward circumstances. Paul was full of joy because he knew that no matter what happened to him, Jesus Christ was with him. Several times in this letter, Paul urged the Philippians to be joyful, probably because they needed to hear this. It's easy to get discouraged about unpleasant circumstances or to take unimportant events too seriously. If you haven't been joyful lately, you may not be looking at life from the right perspective.

4:4, 5 Ultimate joy comes from Christ dwelling within us. Christ is near, and at his second coming we will fully realise this ultimate joy. He who lives within us will fulfil his final purposes for us.

4:5 We are to be gentle (reasonable, fair minded, and charitable) to those outside the church, and not just to fellow believers. This means we are not to seek revenge against those who treat us unfairly, nor are we to be too vocal about our personal rights.

4:6, 7 Imagine never being "anxious about anything"! It seems like an impossibility—we all have worries at work, in our homes, at school. But Paul's advice is to turn our worries into prayers. Do you want to worry less? Then pray more! Whenever you start to worry, stop and pray.

4:7 God's peace is different from the world's peace (see John 14:27). True peace is not found in positive thinking, in the absence of conflict, or in good feelings. It comes from knowing that God is in control. Our citizenship in Christ's kingdom is sure, our destiny is set, and we can have victory over sin. Let God's peace guard your heart against anxiety.

4:8 What we put into our minds determines what comes out in our words and actions. Paul tells us to program our minds with thoughts that are true, noble, right, pure, lovely, admirable, excellent, and praiseworthy. Do you have problems with impure thoughts and daydreams? Examine what you are putting into your mind through television, books, conversations, films, and magazines. Replace harmful input with wholesome material. Above all, read God's word and pray. Ask God to help you focus your mind on what is good and pure. It takes practice, but it can be done.

4:9 It's not enough to hear or read the word of God, or even to know it well. We must also put it into practice. How easy it is to listen to a sermon and forget what the preacher said. How easy it is to read the Bible and not think about how to live differently. How easy it is to debate what a passage means and not live out that meaning. Exposure to God's word is not enough. It must lead to obedience.

7 And the peace of God,[h] which transcends all understanding, will guard your hearts
and your minds in Christ Jesus.
8 Finally, brothers, whatever is true, whatever is noble, whatever is right, whatever
is pure, whatever is lovely, whatever is admirable — if anything is excellent or praiseworthy — think about such things. 9 Whatever you have learned or received or heard
from me, or seen in me — put it into practice.[i] And the God of peace[j] will be with
you.

Thanks for Their Gifts

10 I rejoice greatly in the Lord that at last you have renewed your concern for me.[k]
Indeed, you have been concerned, but you had no opportunity to show it. 11 I am not
saying this because I am in need, for I have learned to be content[l] whatever the
circumstances. 12 I know what it is to be in need, and I know what it is to have plenty.
I have learned the secret of being content in any and every situation, whether well
fed or hungry,[m] whether living in plenty or in want.[n] 13 I can do everything through
him who gives me strength.[o]
14 Yet it was good of you to share[p] in my troubles. 15 Moreover, as you Philippians
know, in the early days[q] of your acquaintance with the gospel, when I set out from
Macedonia, not one church shared with me in the matter of giving and receiving,
except you only;[r] 16 for even when I was in Thessalonica,[s] you sent me aid again
and again when I was in need.[t] 17 Not that I am looking for a gift, but I am looking
for what may be credited to your account.[u] 18 I have received full payment and even
more; I am amply supplied, now that I have received from Epaphroditus[v] the gifts
you sent. They are a fragrant[w] offering, an acceptable sacrifice, pleasing to God.
19 And my God will meet all your needs[x] according to his glorious riches[y] in Christ
Jesus.
20 To our God and Father[z] be glory for ever and ever. Amen.[a]

4:7 [h] Isa 26:3; Jn 14:27; Col 3:15
4:9 [i] Php 3:17 [j] Ro 15:33
4:10 [k] 2Co 11:9
4:11 [l] 1Ti 6:6, 8
4:12 [m] 1Co 4:11 [n] 2Co 11:9
4:13 [o] 2Co 12:9
4:14 [p] Php 1:7
4:15 [q] Php 1:5 [r] 2Co 11:8, 9
4:16 [s] Ac 17:1 [t] 1Th 2:9
4:17 [u] 1Co 9:11, 12
4:18 [v] Php 2:25 [w] 2Co 2:14
4:19 [x] Ps 23:1; 2Co 9:8 [y] Ro 2:4
4:20 [z] Gal 1:4 [a] Ro 11:36

4:10 In 1 Corinthians 9:11–18, Paul wrote that he didn't accept gifts from the Corinthian church because he didn't want to be accused of preaching only for money. But Paul maintained that it was a church's responsibility to support God's ministers (1 Corinthians 9:14). He accepted the Philippians' gift because they gave it willingly and because he was in need.

4:10–14 Are you content in any circumstances you face? Paul knew how to be content whether he had plenty or whether he was in need. The secret was drawing on Christ's power for strength. Do you have great needs, or are you discontented because you don't have what you want? Learn to rely on God's promises and Christ's power to help you be content. If you always want more, ask God to remove that desire and teach you contentment in every circumstance. He will supply all your needs, but in a way that he knows is best for you (see the note on 4:19 for more on God supplying our needs).

4:12, 13 Paul was content because he could see life from God's point of view. He focused on what he was supposed to *do,* not what he felt he should *have.* Paul had his priorities straight, and he was grateful for everything God had given him. Paul had detached himself from the non-essentials so that he could concentrate on the eternal. Often the desire for more or better possessions is really a longing to fill an empty place in a person's life. To what are you drawn when you feel empty inside? How can you find true contentment? The answer lies in your perspective, your priorities, and your source of power.

4:13 Can we really do everything? The power we receive in union with Christ is sufficient to do his will and to face the challenges that arise from our commitment to doing it. He does not grant us superhuman ability to accomplish anything we can imagine without regard to his interests. As we contend for the faith we will face troubles, pressures, and trials. As they come, ask Christ to strengthen you.

4:14 The Philippians shared in Paul's financial support while he was in prison.

4:17 When we give to those in need, there is not only benefit to the receiver, but we are benefited as well. It was not the Philippians' gift, but their spirit of love and devotion that Paul appreciated most.

4:18 Paul was not referring to a sin offering but to a thank offering, "a fragrant offering, an acceptable sacrifice, pleasing to God" (Leviticus 7:12–15 contains the instructions for thank offerings). Although the Greek and Roman Christians were not Jews, and they had not offered sacrifices according to the Old Testament laws, they were well acquainted with the pagan rituals of offering sacrifices.

4:19 We can trust that God will always meet our needs. Whatever we need on earth he will always supply, even if it is the courage to face death as Paul did. Whatever we need in heaven he will supply. We must remember, however, the difference between our wants and our needs. Most people want to feel good and avoid discomfort or pain. We may not get all that we want. By trusting in Christ, our attitudes and appetites can change from wanting everything to accepting his provision and power to live for him.

Final Greetings

21 Greet all the saints in Christ Jesus. The brothers who are with me[b] send greetings.
22 All the saints[c] send you greetings, especially those who belong to Caesar's household.
23 The grace of the Lord Jesus Christ[d] be with your spirit. Amen.[b]

b *23* Some manuscripts do not have *Amen.*

4:21 [b]Gal 1:2
4:22 [c]Ac 9:13
4:23 [d]Ro 16:20

4:22 There were many Christians in Rome; some were even in Caesar's household. Perhaps Paul, while awaiting trial, was making converts of the Roman civil service! Paul sent greetings from these Roman Christians to the believers at Philippi. The gospel had spread to all strata of society, linking people who had no other bond but Christ. The Roman Christians and the Philippian Christians were brothers and sisters because of their unity in Christ. Believers today are also linked to others across cultural, economic, and social barriers. Because all believers are brothers and sisters in Christ, let us live like God's true family.

4:23 In many ways the Philippian church was a model congregation. It was made up of many different kinds of people who were learning to work together. But Paul recognised that problems could arise, so in his thank-you letter he prepared the Philippians for difficulties that could crop up within a body of believers. Though a prisoner in Rome, Paul had learned the true secret of joy and peace—imitating Christ and serving others. By focusing our minds on Christ we will learn unity, humility, joy, and peace. We will also be motivated to live for him. We can live confidently for him because we have "the grace of the Lord Jesus Christ" with us.

COLOSSIANS

REMOVE the head coach, and the team flounders; break the fuel pipe, and the car won't run; unplugged, the electrical appliance has no power; without the head, the body dies. Whether for leadership, power, or life, connections are vital!

Colossians is a book of connections. Writing from prison in Rome, Paul combated false teachings, which had infiltrated the Colossian church. The problem was "syncretism", combining ideas from other philosophies and religions (such as paganism, strains of Judaism, and Greek thought) with Christian truth. The resulting heresy later became known as "Gnosticism", emphasising special knowledge (*gnosis* in Greek) and denying Christ as God and Saviour. To combat this devious error, Paul stressed Christ's deity—his connection with the Father—and his sacrificial death on the cross for sin. Only by being connected with Christ through faith can anyone have eternal life and only through a continuing connection with him can anyone have power for living. Christ is God incarnate and the *only* way to forgiveness and peace with God the Father. Paul also emphasised believers' connections with each other as Christ's body on earth.

Paul's introduction to the Colossians includes a greeting, a note of thanksgiving, and a prayer for spiritual wisdom and strength for these brothers and sisters in Christ (1:1–12). He then moves into a doctrinal discussion of the person and work of Christ (1:13–23), stating that Christ is the "image of the invisible God" (1:15), the Creator (1:16), the "head of the body, the church" (1:18), and the "beginning and the firstborn from among the dead" (1:18). His death on the cross makes it possible for us to stand in the presence of God (1:22).

Paul then explains how the world's teachings are totally empty when compared with God's plan, and he challenges the Colossians to reject shallow answers and to live in union with Christ (1:24—2:23).

Against this theological backdrop, Paul turns to practical considerations—what the divinity, death, and resurrection of Jesus should mean to all believers (3:1—4:6). Because our eternal destiny is sure, heaven should fill our thoughts (3:1–4), sexual impurity and other worldly lusts should not be named among us (3:5–8), and truth, love, and peace should mark our lives (3:9–15). Our love for Christ should also translate into love for others—friends, fellow believers, spouses, children, parents, slaves, and masters (3:16—4:1). We should constantly communicate with God through prayer (4:2–4), and we should take every opportunity to tell others the good news (4:5, 6). In Christ we have everything we need for salvation and for living the Christian life.

Paul had probably never visited Colosse, so he concludes this letter with personal comments about their common Christian associations, providing a living lesson of the connectedness of the body of Christ.

Read Colossians as a book for an embattled church in the first century, but read it also for its timeless truths. Gain a fresh appreciation for Christ as the *fulness* of God and the *only* source for living the Christian life. Know that he is your leader, head, and power source, and make sure of your connection to him.

VITAL STATISTICS

PURPOSE:
To combat errors in the church and to show that believers have everything they need in Christ

AUTHOR:
Paul

TO WHOM WRITTEN:
The church at Colosse, a city in Asia Minor, and all believers everywhere

DATE WRITTEN:
About A.D. 60, during Paul's imprisonment in Rome

SETTING:
Paul had never visited Colosse—evidently the church had been founded by Epaphras and other converts from Paul's missionary travels. The church, however, had been infiltrated by religious relativism, with some believers attempting to combine elements of paganism and secular philosophy with Christian doctrine. Paul confronts these false teachings and affirms the sufficiency of Christ.

KEY VERSES:
"For in Christ all the fulness of the Deity lives in bodily form, and you have been given fulness in Christ, who is the head over every power and authority" (2:9, 10).

KEY PEOPLE:
Paul, Timothy, Tychicus, Onesimus, Aristarchus, Mark, Epaphras

KEY PLACES:
Colosse, Laodicea (4:15, 16)

SPECIAL FEATURES:
Christ is presented as having absolute supremacy and sole sufficiency. Colossians has similarities to Ephesians, probably because it was written at about the same time, but it has a different emphasis.

THE BLUEPRINT

1. What Christ has done (1:1—2:23)
2. What Christians should do (3:1—4:18)

In this letter Paul clearly teaches that Christ has paid for sin, that Christ has reconciled us to God, and that Christ gives us the pattern and the power to grow spiritually. Because Christ is the exact likeness of God, when we learn what he is like, we see what we need to become. Since Christ is Lord over all creation, we should crown him Lord over our lives. Since Christ is the head of the body, his church, we should nurture our vital connection to him.

MEGATHEMES

THEME	EXPLANATION	IMPORTANCE
Christ is God	Jesus Christ is God in the flesh, Lord of all creation, and Lord of the new creation. He is the expressed reflection of the invisible God. He is eternal, pre-existent, omnipotent, equal with the Father. He is supreme and complete.	Because Christ is supreme, our lives must be Christ-centred. To recognise him as God means to regard our relationship with him as most vital and to make his interests our top priority.
Christ Is Head of the Church	Because Christ is God, he is the head of the church, his true believers. Christ is the founder, the leader, and the highest authority on earth. He requires first place in all our thoughts and activities.	To acknowledge Christ as our head, we must welcome his leadership in all we do or think. No person, group, or church can regard any loyalty as more critical than that of loyalty to Christ.
Union with Christ	Because our sin has been forgiven and we have been reconciled to God, we have a union with Christ that can never be broken. In our faith connection with him, we identify with his death, burial, and resurrection.	We should live in constant contact and communication with God. When we do, we all will be unified with Christ and with one another.
Man-made Religion	False teachers were promoting a heresy that stressed self-made rules (legalism). They also sought spiritual growth by discipline of the body (asceticism) and visions (mysticism). This search created pride in their self-centred efforts.	We must not cling to our own ideas and try to blend them into Christianity. Nor should we let our hunger for a more fulfilling Christian experience cause us to trust in a teacher, a group, or a system of thought more than in Christ himself. Christ is our hope and our true source of wisdom.

1. What Christ has done

1 Paul, an apostle[a] of Christ Jesus by the will of God,[b] and Timothy our brother, **1:1** [a]1Co 1:1 [b]2Co 1:1

2 To the holy and faithful[a] brothers in Christ at Colosse:

Grace[c] and peace to you from God our Father.[b][d] **1:2** [c]Col 4:18 [d]Ro 1:7

Thanksgiving and Prayer

3 We always thank God,[e] the Father of our Lord Jesus Christ, when we pray for **1:3** [e]Ro 1:8

[a] 2 Or *believing* [b] 2 Some manuscripts *Father and the Lord Jesus Christ*

1:1 Colossians, along with Philippians, Ephesians, and Philemon, is called a *Prison Letter* because Paul wrote it from prison in Rome. This prison was actually a house where Paul was kept under close guard at all times (probably chained to a soldier) but given certain freedoms not offered to most prisoners. He was allowed to write letters and to see any visitors he wanted to see.

1:1 Paul was an apostle "by the will of God". Paul would often establish his credentials as chosen and sent by God because he had not been one of the original 12 disciples. *Apostle* means chosen and sent by God as a missionary or ambassador. *By the will of God* means that he was appointed; this was not just a matter of his own personal aspirations.

1:1 Paul mentions Timothy in other New Testament letters as well: 2 Corinthians, Philippians, 1 and 2 Thessalonians, and Philemon. Paul also wrote two letters to Timothy (1 and 2 Timothy). For more information on these men, two of the greatest missionaries of the early church, see Paul's Profile in Acts 9 and Timothy's Profile in 1 Timothy.

1:2 The city of Colosse was 100 miles east of Ephesus on the Lycus River. It was not as influential as the nearby city of Laodicea,

1:4
[f]Gal 5:6
[g]Eph 1:15
1:5
[h]Tit 1:2
[i]1Pe 1:4
1:6
[j]Ro 10:18
[k]Jn 15:16

you, 4 because we have heard of your faith in Christ Jesus and of the love[f] you have
for all the saints[g]— 5 the faith and love that spring from the hope[h] that is stored up
for you in heaven[i] and that you have already heard about in the word of truth, the
gospel 6 that has come to you. All over the world[j] this gospel is bearing fruit[k] and
growing, just as it has been doing among you since the day you heard it and understood

THE COLOSSIAN HERESY
Paul answered the various tenets of the Colossian heresy that threatened the church. This heresy was a "mixed bag", containing elements from several different heresies, some of which contradicted each other (as the chart shows).

The Heresy	*Reference*	*Paul's Answer*
Spirit is good; matter is evil.	1:15–20	God created heaven and earth for his glory.
One must follow ceremonies, rituals, and restrictions in order to be saved or perfected.	2:11, 16–23; 3:11	These were only shadows that ended when Christ came. He is all you need to be saved.
One must deny the body and live in strict asceticism.	2:20–23	Asceticism is no help in conquering evil thoughts and desires; instead, it leads to pride.
Angels must be worshipped.	2:18	Angels are not to be worshipped; Christ alone is worthy of worship.
Christ could not be both human and divine.	1:15–20; 2:2, 3	Christ is God in the flesh; he is the eternal One, head of the body, first in everything, supreme.
One must obtain "secret knowledge" in order to be saved or perfected—and this was not available to everyone.	2:2, 18	God's secret is Christ, and he has been revealed to all.
One must adhere to human wisdom, tradition, and philosophies.	2:4, 8–10; 3:15–17	By themselves, these can be misleading and shallow because they have human origin; instead, we should remember what Christ taught and follow his words as our ultimate authority.
It is even better to combine aspects of several religions.	2:10	You have everything when you have Christ; he is all-sufficient.
There is nothing wrong with immorality.	3:1–11	Get rid of sin and evil because you have been chosen by God to live a new life as a representative of the Lord Jesus.

but as a trading centre it was a crossroads for ideas and religions. Colosse had a large Jewish population – many Jews had fled there when they were forced out of Jerusalem under the persecutions of Antiochus III and IV, almost 200 years before Christ. The church in Colosse had been founded by Epaphras (1:7), one of Paul's converts. Paul had not yet visited this church. His purpose in writing was to refute heretical teachings about Christ that had been causing confusion among the Christians there.

1:2, 3 Letters in Paul's day would frequently begin with identifying the writer and the readers, followed by a greeting of peace. Paul would usually add Christian elements to his greetings, reminding his readers of his call by God to spread the gospel, emphasising that the authority for his words came from God, and giving thanks for God's blessings.

1:4, 5 Throughout this letter Paul combats a heresy similar to *Gnosticism* (see the notes on 1:9–14; 1:15-23; 2:4ff). Gnostics believed that it took special knowledge to be accepted by God; for them, even for those who claimed to be Christians, Christ alone was not the way of salvation (1:20). In his introductory comments, therefore, Paul commended the Colossians for their faith, love, and hope – three main emphases of Christianity (1 Corinthians 13:13). He deliberately omitted the word *knowledge* because of the "special knowledge" aspect of the heresy. It is not *what* we know that brings salvation, but *whom* we know. Knowing Christ is knowing God.

1:5 When Paul says that our hope is stored up in heaven, he is emphasising the security of the believer. Because we know that our future destination and salvation are sure, we are free to live for Christ and love others (1 Peter 1:3, 4). When you find yourself doubting or wavering in your faith or love, remember your destination – heaven.

1:6 Wherever Paul went, he preached the gospel – to Gentile audiences, to hostile Jewish leaders, and even to his Roman guards. Whenever people believed in the message that Paul spoke, they were changed. God's word is not just for our information, it is for our transformation! Becoming a Christian means beginning a whole new relationship with God, not just turning over a new leaf or determining to do right. New believers have a changed purpose, direction, attitude, and behaviour. They are no longer seeking to serve themselves, but they are bearing fruit for God. How is the gospel reaching others through your life?

God's grace in all its truth. 7You learned it from Epaphras,[l] our dear fellow-servant, 1:7 [l]Phm 23
who is a faithful minister[m] of Christ on our[c] behalf, 8and who also told us of your [m]Col 4:7
love in the Spirit.[n] 1:8 [n]Ro 15:30
9For this reason, since the day we heard about you,[o] we have not stopped praying 1:9 [o]Eph 1:15
for you and asking God to fill you with the knowledge of his will[p] through all spiritual [p]Eph 5:17
wisdom and understanding.[q] 10And we pray this in order that you may live a life [q]Eph 1:17
worthy[r] of the Lord and may please him in every way: bearing fruit in every good 1:10 [r]Eph 4:1
work, growing in the knowledge of God, 11being strengthened with all power[s] 1:11 [s]Eph 3:16
according to his glorious might so that you may have great endurance and patience,[t] [t]Eph 4:2
and joyfully 12giving thanks to the Father,[u] who has qualified you[d] to share in the 1:12 [u]Eph 5:20 [v]Ac 20:32

c 7 Some manuscripts *your* d 12 Some manuscripts *us*

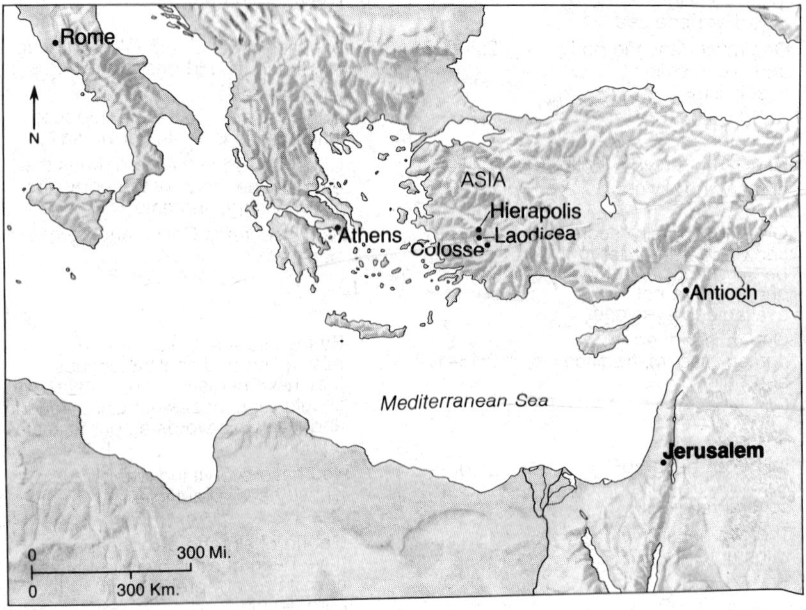

LOCATION OF COLOSSE
Paul had no doubt been through Laodicea on his third missionary journey, as it lay on the main route to Ephesus, but he had never been to Colosse. Though a large city with a significant population, Colosse was smaller and less important than the nearby cities of Laodicea and Hierapolis.

1:7 Epaphras had founded the church at Colosse while Paul was living in Ephesus (Acts 19:10). Epaphras may have been converted in Ephesus, and then he returned to Colosse, his home-town. For some reason, he visited Rome and, while there, told Paul about the problem with the Colossian heresy. This prompted Paul to write this letter. Epaphras is also mentioned in Philemon 23 (the Colossian church met in Philemon's house).

1:8 Because of their love for one another, Christians can have an impact that goes far beyond their neighbourhoods and communities. Christian love comes from the Holy Spirit (see Galatians 5:22). The Bible speaks of it as an action and attitude, not just an emotion. Love is a by-product of our new life in Christ (see Romans 5:5; 1 Corinthians 13). Christians have no excuse for not loving, because Christian love is a decision to *act* in the best interests of others.

1:9–14 Paul was exposing a heresy in the Colossian church that was similar to *Gnosticism* (see the note on 2:4ff for more information). Gnostics valued the accumulation of knowledge, but Paul pointed out that knowledge in itself is empty. To be worth anything, it must lead to a changed life and right living. His prayer for the Colossians has two dimensions: (1) that they might be filled with the knowledge of God's will through all spiritual wisdom and understanding, and (2) that they would bear fruit in every good work, growing in the knowledge of God. Knowledge is not merely to be accumulated; it should give us direction for living. Paul wanted the Colossians to be wise, but he also wanted them to *use* their knowledge. Knowledge of God is not a secret that only a few can discover; it is open to everyone. God wants us to learn more about him, and also to put belief into practice by helping others.

1:9–14 Sometimes we wonder how to pray for missionaries and other leaders we have never met. Paul had never met the Colossians, but he faithfully prayed for them. His prayers teach us how to pray for others, whether we know them or not. We can request that they (1) understand God's will, (2) gain spiritual wisdom, (3) please and honour God, (4) bear good fruit, (5) grow in the knowledge of God, (6) be filled with God's strength, (7) have great endurance and patience, (8) stay full of Christ's joy, and (9) give thanks always. All believers have these same basic needs. When you don't know how to pray for someone, use Paul's prayer pattern for the Colossians.

1:12–14 Paul lists five benefits God gives all believers through Christ: (1) he made us qualified to share his inheritance (see also 2 Corinthians 5:21); (2) he rescued us from Satan's dominion of darkness and made us his children (see also 2:15); (3) he brought us into his eternal kingdom (see also Ephesians 1:5, 6); (4) he redeemed us—bought our freedom from sin and judgment (see also Hebrews 9:12); and (5) he forgave all our sins (see also Ephesians 1:7). Thank God for what you have received in Christ.

inheritance[v] of the saints in the kingdom of light. 13For he has rescued us from the
dominion of darkness[w] and brought us into the kingdom[x] of the Son he loves,[y] 14in
whom we have redemption,[e][z] the forgiveness of sins.[a]

The Supremacy of Christ

15He is the image[b] of the invisible God,[c] the firstborn over all creation. 16For by
him all things were created:[d] things in heaven and on earth, visible and invisible,
whether thrones or powers or rulers or authorities;[e] all things were created by him
and for him.[f] 17He is before all things,[g] and in him all things hold together. 18And
he is the head[h] of the body, the church; he is the beginning and the firstborn from
among the dead,[i] so that in everything he might have the supremacy. 19For God was
pleased[j] to have all his fulness[k] dwell in him, 20and through him to reconcile[l] to

e *14* A few late manuscripts *redemption through his blood*

1:13
[w] Ac 26:18
[x] 2Pe 1:11
[y] Mt 3:17
1:14
[z] Ro 3:24
[a] Eph 1:7
1:15
[b] 2Co 4:4
[c] Jn 1:18
1:16
[d] Jn 1:3
[e] Eph 1:20, 21
[f] Ro 11:36
1:17
[g] Jn 1:2
1:18
[h] Eph 1:22
[i] Rev 1:5
1:19
[j] Eph 1:5
[k] Jn 1:16
1:20
[l] 2Co 5:18

HOW TO PRAY FOR OTHER CHRISTIANS
How many people in your life could be touched if you prayed in this way?

1. Be thankful for their faith and changed lives (1:3)
2. Ask God to help them know what he wants them to do (1:9)
3. Ask God to give them deep spiritual understanding (1:9)
4. Ask God to help them live for him (1:10)
5. Ask God to give them more knowledge of himself (1:10)
6. Ask God to give them strength for endurance (1:11)
7. Ask God to fill them with joy, strength, and thankfulness (1:11)

1:13 The Colossians feared the unseen forces of darkness, but Paul says that true believers have been transferred from darkness to light, from slavery to freedom, from guilt to forgiveness, and from the power of Satan to the power of God. We have been rescued from a rebel kingdom to serve the rightful King. Our conduct should reflect our new allegiance.

1:15, 16 This is one of the strongest statements about the divine nature of Christ found anywhere in the Bible. Jesus is not only equal to God (Philippians 2:6), he *is* God (John 10:30, 38; 12:45; 14:1–11); as the image of the invisible God, he is the exact representation of God. He not only reflects God, but he reveals God to us (John 1:18; 14:9); as the firstborn over all creation, he has all the priority and authority of the firstborn prince in a king's household. He came from heaven, not from the dust of the earth (1 Corinthians 15:47), and he is Lord of all (Romans 9:5; 10:11–13; Revelation 1:5; 17:14). He is completely holy (Hebrews 7:26–28; 1 Peter 1:19; 2:22; 1 John 3:5), and he has authority to judge the world (Romans 2:16; 2 Corinthians 5:10; 2 Timothy 4:1). Therefore, Christ is supreme over all creation, including the spirit world. We, like the Colossian believers, must believe in the deity of Jesus Christ (that Jesus is God) or our Christian faith is hollow, misdirected, and meaningless. This is a central truth of Christianity.

1:15–23 In the Colossian church there were several misconceptions about Christ that Paul directly refuted: (1) Believing that matter is evil, false teachers argued that God would not have come to earth as a true human being in bodily form. Paul stated that Christ is the image—the exact likeness—of God, and is himself God, and yet he died on the cross as a human being. (2) They believed that God did not create the world, because he would not have created evil. Paul proclaimed that Jesus Christ, who was also God in the flesh, is the Creator of both heaven and earth. (3) They said that Christ was not the unique Son of God, but rather one of many intermediaries between God and people. Paul explained that Christ existed before anything else and is the firstborn of those resurrected. (4) They refused to see Christ as the source of salvation, insisting that people could find God only through special and secret knowledge. In contrast Paul openly proclaimed the way of salvation to be through Christ alone. Paul continued to bring the argument back to Christ. When we share the gospel, we too must keep the focus on Christ.

1:16 Because the false teachers believed that the physical world was evil, they thought that God himself could not have created it. If Christ were God, they reasoned, he would be in charge only of the spiritual world. But Paul explained that all the rulers, powers, thrones, and authorities of both the spiritual and physical worlds were created by and are under the authority of Christ himself. This includes not only the government but also the spiritual world that the heretics were so concerned about. Christ has no equal and no rival. He is the Lord of all.

1:17 God is not only the Creator of the world, but he is also its Sustainer. In him, everything is held together, protected, and prevented from disintegrating into chaos. Because Christ is the Sustainer of all life, none of us is independent from him. We are all his servants who must daily trust him to protect us, care for us, and sustain us.

1:18 Christ is the "firstborn from among the dead". Jesus was raised from death, and his resurrection proves his lordship over the material world. All who trust in Christ will also defeat death and rise again to live eternally with him (1 Corinthians 15:20; 1 Thessalonians 4:14). Because of Christ's death on the cross, he has been exalted and elevated to the status that was rightfully his (see Philippians 2:5–11). Because Christ is spiritually supreme in the universe, surely we should give him first place in all our thoughts and activities. See the second note on Luke 24:6, 7 for more about the significance of Christ's resurrection.

1:19 By this statement, Paul was refuting the Greek idea that Jesus could not be human and divine at the same time. Christ is fully human; he is also fully divine. Christ has always been God and always will be God. When we have Christ we have all of God in human form. Don't diminish any aspect of Christ—either his humanity or his divinity.

1:20 Christ's death provided a way for all people to come to God. It cleared away the sin that keeps us from having a right relationship with our Creator. This does not mean that everyone has been saved, but that the way has been cleared for anyone who will trust Christ to be saved. We can have peace with God and be reconciled to him by accepting Christ, who died in our place. Is there a distance between you and the Creator? Be reconciled to God. Come to him through Christ.

himself all things, whether things on earth or things in heaven,[m] by making peace
through his blood,[n] shed on the cross.
21 Once you were alienated from God and were enemies[o] in your minds[p] because
of[f] your evil behaviour. 22 But now he has reconciled you by Christ's physical body[q]
through death to present you holy in his sight, without blemish and free from accusation[r]—23 if you continue in your faith, established[s] and firm, not moved from the
hope[t] held out in the gospel. This is the gospel that you heard and that has been
proclaimed to every creature under heaven,[u] and of which I, Paul, have become a
servant.[v]

Paul's Labour for the Church

24 Now I rejoice in what was suffered for you, and I fill up in my flesh what is still
lacking in regard to Christ's afflictions,[w] for the sake of his body, which is the church.
25 I have become its servant[x] by the commission God gave me[y] to present to you
the word of God in its fulness—26 the mystery[z] that has been kept hidden for ages
and generations, but is now disclosed to the saints. 27 To them God has chosen to make
known[a] among the Gentiles the glorious riches of this mystery, which is Christ in
you, the hope of glory.
28 We proclaim him, admonishing[b] and teaching everyone with all wisdom,[c] so
that we may present everyone perfect[d] in Christ. 29 To this end I labour,[e] struggling[f]
with all his energy, which so powerfully works in me.[g]

2 I want you to know how much I am struggling[a] for you and for those at
Laodicea,[b] and for all who have not met me personally. 2 My purpose is that they
may be encouraged in heart[c] and united in love, so that they may have the full riches

[f] 21 *Or minds, as shown by*

1:20 [m] Eph 1:10 [n] Eph 2:13
1:21 [o] Ro 5:10 [p] Eph 2:3
1:22 [q] Ro 7:4 [r] Eph 5:27
1:23 [s] Eph 3:17 [t] ver 5 [u] Ro 10:18 [v] ver 25; 1Co 3:5
1:24 [w] 2Co 1:5
1:25 [x] ver 23 [y] Eph 3:2
1:26 [z] Ro 16:25
1:27 [a] Mt 13:11
1:28 [b] Col 3:16 [c] 1Co 2:6, 7 [d] Eph 5:27
1:29 [e] 1Co 15:10 [f] Col 2:1 [g] Eph 1:19
2:1 [a] Col 1:29; 4:12 [b] Rev 1:11
2:2 [c] Col 4:8

1:21 Because we were alienated from God, we were strangers to his way of thinking and were "enemies in our minds". Sin corrupted our way of thinking about God. Wrong thinking leads to sin, which further perverts and destroys our thoughts about him. When we were out of harmony with God, our natural condition was to be totally hostile to his standards. See Romans 1:21–32 for more on the perverted thinking of unbelievers.

1:21, 22 *No-one* is good enough to save himself or herself. If we want to live eternally with Christ, we must depend totally on God's grace. This is true whether we have been murderers or honest, hardworking citizens. We have all sinned repeatedly, and *any* sin is enough to cause us to come to Jesus Christ for salvation and eternal life. Apart from Christ, there is no way for our sin to be forgiven and removed.

1:22 In order to answer the accusation that Jesus was only a spirit and not a true human being, Paul explained that Jesus' physical body actually died. Jesus suffered death fully as a human so that we could be assured that he died in our place. Jesus faced death as God so we can be assured that his sacrifice was complete and that he truly removed our sin.

1:22, 23 The way to be free from sin is to trust Jesus Christ to take it away. We must remain "established and firm" in the truth of the gospel, putting our confidence in Jesus alone to forgive our sins, to make us right with God, and to empower us to live the way he desires. When a judge in a court of law declares the defendant not guilty, the person has been acquitted of all the accusations or charges. Legally, it is as if he or she had never been accused. When God forgives our sins, our record is wiped clean. From his perspective, it is as though we had never sinned. God's solution is available to you. No matter what you have done or what you have been like, God's forgiveness is for you.

1:24 When Paul says, "I fill up in my flesh what is still lacking in regard to Christ's afflictions," he does not mean that Christ's suffering was inadequate to save him, nor does he mean that there is a predetermined amount of suffering that must be paid by all believers. Paul could be saying that suffering is unavoidable in bringing the Good News of Christ to the world. It is called Christ's suffering, because all Christians are related to Christ. When we suffer, Christ feels it with us. But this suffering can be endured joyfully because it changes lives and brings people into God's kingdom (see 1 Peter 4:1, 2, 12–19). For more about how Paul could rejoice despite his suffering, see the note on Philippians 1:29.

1:26, 27 The false teachers in the Colossian church believed that spiritual perfection was a secret and hidden plan that only a few privileged people could discover. Their secret plan was meant to be exclusive. Paul said that he was proclaiming the word of God in its fulness, not just a part of the plan. He also called God's plan a "mystery that has been kept hidden for ages and generations", not in the sense that only a few would understand, but because it was hidden until Christ came. Through Christ it was made open to all. God's secret plan is "Christ in you, the hope of glory"—God planned to have his Son, Jesus Christ, live in the hearts of all who believe in him—even Gentiles like the Colossians. Do you know Christ? He is not hidden if you will come to him.

1:28, 29 The word *perfect* means mature or complete, not flawless. Paul wanted to see each believer mature spiritually. Like Paul, we must work wholeheartedly like an athlete, but we should not strive in our own strength alone. We have the power of God's Spirit working in us. We can learn and grow daily, motivated by love, and not by fear or pride, knowing that God gives the energy to become mature.

1:28, 29 Christ's message is for everyone; so everywhere Paul and Timothy went they brought the Good News to all who would listen. An effective presentation of the gospel includes *admonishing* (warning) and teaching. The warning is that without Christ, people are doomed to eternal separation from God. The teaching is that salvation is available through faith in Christ. As Christ works in you, tell others about him, warning and teaching them in love. Who do you know that needs to hear this message?

2:1 Laodicea was located a few miles northwest of Colosse. Like the church at Colosse, the Laodicean church was probably founded by one of Paul's converts while Paul was staying in Ephesus (Acts 19:10). The city was a wealthy centre of trade and commerce, but later Christ would criticise the believers at Laodicea for

2:3 [d]Ro 11:33; 1Co 1:24, 30
2:4 [e]Ro 16:18
2:5 [f]1Th 2:17 [g]1Co 14:40 [h]1Pe 5:9
2:6 [i]Col 1:10
2:7 [j]Eph 3:17
2:8 [k]1Ti 6:20 [l]Gal 4:3

of complete understanding, in order that they may know the mystery of God, namely,
Christ, 3 in whom are hidden all the treasures of wisdom and knowledge.[d] 4 I tell you
this so that no-one may deceive you by fine-sounding arguments.[e] 5 For though I am
absent from you in body, I am present with you in spirit[f] and delight to see how
orderly[g] you are and how firm[h] your faith in Christ is.

Freedom From Human Regulations Through Life With Christ

6 So then, just as you received Christ Jesus as Lord,[i] continue to live in him,
7 rooted[j] and built up in him, strengthened in the faith as you were taught, and
overflowing with thankfulness.
8 See to it that no-one takes you captive through hollow and deceptive philosophy,[k]
which depends on human tradition and the basic principles of this world[l] rather than
on Christ.
9 For in Christ all the fulness of the Deity lives in bodily form, 10 and you have been

SALVATION THROUGH FAITH

	Religion by Self-effort	*Salvation by Faith*
Goal	Please God by our own good deeds	Trust in Christ and then live to please God
Means	Practice, diligent service, discipline, and obedience, in hope of reward	Confess, submit, and commit yourself to Christ's control
Power	Good, honest effort through self-determination	The Holy Spirit in us helps us do good work for Christ's kingdom
Control	Self-motivation; self-control	Christ in me; I in Christ
Results	Chronic guilt, apathy, depression, failure, constant desire for approval	Joy, thankfulness, love, guidance, service, forgiveness

Salvation by faith in Christ sounds too easy for many people. They would rather think that they have done something to save themselves. Their religion becomes one of self-effort that leads either to disappointment or pride, but finally to eternal death. Christ's simple way is the only way, and it alone leads to eternal life.

their lukewarm commitment (Revelation 3:14–22). The fact that Paul wanted this letter to be passed on to the Laodicean church (4:16) indicates that false teaching may have spread there as well. Paul was counting on ties of love to bring the churches together to stand against this heresy and to encourage each other to remain true to God's plan of salvation in Christ. Our churches should be encouraging, unified communities committed to carrying out Christ's work.

2:4ff The problem that Paul was combatting in the Colossian church was similar to *Gnosticism* (from the Greek word for *knowledge*). This *heresy* (a teaching contrary to biblical doctrine) undermined Christianity in several basic ways: (1) It insisted that important secret knowledge was hidden from most believers; Paul, however, said that Christ provides all the knowledge we need. (2) It taught that the body was evil; Paul countered that God himself lived in a body – that is, he was embodied in Jesus Christ. (3) It contended that Christ only seemed to be human, but was not; Paul insisted that Jesus is fully human and fully God.

Gnosticism became fashionable in the second century. Even in Paul's day, these ideas sounded attractive to many, and exposure to such teachings could easily seduce a church that didn't know Christian doctrine well. Similar teachings still pose significant problems for many in the church today. We combat heresy by becoming thoroughly acquainted with God's word through personal study and sound Bible teaching.

2:6, 7 Receiving Christ as Lord of your life is the beginning of life with Christ. But you must continue to follow his leadership by being rooted, built up, and strengthened in the faith. Christ wants to guide you and help you with your daily problems. You can live for Christ by (1) committing your life and submitting your will to him (Romans 12:1, 2); (2) seeking to learn from him, his life, and his teachings (3:16); and (3) recognising the Holy Spirit's power in you (Acts 1:8; Galatians 5:22).

2:7 Paul uses the illustration of our being rooted in Christ. Just as plants draw nourishment from the soil through their roots, so we draw our life-giving strength from Christ. The more we draw our strength from him, the less we will be fooled by those who falsely claim to have life's answers. If Christ is our strength, we will be free from human regulations.

2:8 Paul writes against any philosophy of life based only on human ideas and experiences. Paul himself was a gifted philosopher, so he is not condemning philosophy. He is condemning teaching that credits humanity, not Christ, with being the answer to life's problems. That approach becomes a false religion. There are many man-made approaches to life's problems that totally disregard God. To resist heresy you must use your mind, keep your eyes on Christ, and study God's word.

2:9 Again Paul asserts Christ's deity. "In Christ all the fulness of the Deity lives in bodily form" means that all of God was in Christ's human body. When we have Christ we have everything we need for salvation and right living. See the note on 1:15, 16 for more on the divine nature of Christ.

2:10 When we know Jesus Christ, we don't need to seek God by means of other religions, cults, or unbiblical philosophies as the Colossians were doing. Christ alone holds the answers to the true meaning of life, because he *is* life. Christ is the unique source of knowledge and power for the Christian life. No Christian needs anything in addition to what Christ has provided to be saved. We are complete in him.

given fulness in Christ, who is the Head[m] over every power and authority. 11In him
you were also circumcised,[n] in the putting off of the sinful nature,[a][o] not with a
circumcision done by the hands of men but with the circumcision done by Christ,
12having been buried with him in baptism and raised with him[p] through your faith
in the power of God, who raised him from the dead.[q]
13When you were dead in your sins[r] and in the uncircumcision of your sinful
nature,[b] God made you[c] alive with Christ. He forgave us all our sins, 14having
cancelled the written code, with its regulations,[s] that was against us and that stood
opposed to us; he took it away, nailing it to the cross.[t] 15And having disarmed the
powers and authorities,[u] he made a public spectacle of them, triumphing over them[v]
by the cross.[d]
16Therefore do not let anyone judge you[w] by what you eat or drink,[x] or with regard
to a religious festival,[y] a New Moon celebration[z] or a Sabbath day.[a] 17These are
a shadow of the things that were to come;[b] the reality, however, is found in Christ.

a *11* Or *the flesh* **b** *13* Or *your flesh* **c** *13* Some manuscripts *us* **d** *15* Or *them in him*

2:10
[m]Eph 1:22
2:11
[n]Ro 2:29; Php 3:3
[o]Gal 5:24
2:12
[p]Ro 6:5
[q]Ac 2:24
2:13
[r]Eph 2:1, 5
2:14
[s]Eph 2:15
[t]1Pe 2:24
2:15
[u]Eph 6:12
[v]Lk 10:18
2:16
[w]Ro 14:3, 4
[x]Ro 14:17
[y]Ro 14:5
[z]1Ch 23:31
[a]Gal 4:10
2:17
[b]Heb 8:5

2:11 Jewish males were circumcised as a sign of the Jews' covenant with God (Genesis 17:9–14). With the death of Christ, circumcision was no longer necessary. So now our commitment to God is written on our hearts, not our bodies. Christ sets us free from our evil desires by a spiritual operation, not a bodily one. God removes the old nature and gives us a new nature.

2:11, 12 In this passage, circumcision is related to baptism; therefore, some see baptism as the New Testament sign of the covenant, identifying the person with the covenant community. Baptism parallels the death, burial, and resurrection of Christ, and it also portrays the death and burial of our sinful old way of life followed by resurrection to new life in Christ. Remembering that our old sinful life is dead and buried with Christ gives us a powerful motive to resist sin. Not wanting the desires of our past to come back to power again, we can consciously choose to treat our desires as if they were dead. Then we can continue to enjoy our wonderful new life with Christ (see Galatians 3:27 and Colossians 3:1–4).

2:13–15 Before we believed in Christ, our nature was evil. We disobeyed, rebelled, and ignored God (even at our best, we did not love him with all our heart, soul, and mind). The Christian, however, has a new nature. God has crucified the old rebellious nature (Romans 6:6) and replaced it with a new loving nature (3:9, 10). The penalty of sin died with Christ on the cross. God has declared us not guilty, and we need no longer live under sin's power. God does not take us out of the world or make us robots – we will still feel like sinning, and sometimes we will sin. The difference is that before we were saved, we were slaves to our sinful nature; but now we are free to live for Christ (see Galatians 2:20).

2:14 The written code that was cancelled was the legal demands of the Old Testament law. The law opposed us by its demands for payment for our sin. Though no-one can be saved by merely keeping that code, the moral truths and principles in the Old Testament still teach and guide today.

2:14 We can enjoy our new life in Christ because we have joined him in his death and resurrection. Our evil desires, our bondage to sin, and our love of sin died with him. Now, joining him in his resurrection life, we may have unbroken fellowship with God and freedom from sin. Our debt for sin has been paid in full; our sins are swept away and forgotten by God; and we can be clean and new. For more on the difference between our new life in Christ and our old sinful nature, read Ephesians 4:23, 24 and Colossians 3:3–15.

2:15 Who are these powers and authorities? Several suggestions have been made, including (1) demonic powers, (2) the gods of the powerful nations, (3) angels (highly regarded by the heretical teachers), or (4) the government of Rome. These powers and authorities were probably not the demonic forces in 2:10. More likely they are the angels who were mediators of the law (Galatians 3:19). The Colossian false teachers were encouraging worship of angels. But at his death, Christ surpassed the position and authority of any angel. So rather than fear angels or worship them, we are to view them as deposed rulers. Paul meant no disrespect towards angels, but he showed that they are not to be compared with Jesus Christ. Some scholars believe these powers are the powers of Rome. By his resurrection, Christ stripped the power away from a world empire that seemed temporarily to defeat him.

2:16 "What you eat or drink" probably refers to the Jewish dietary laws. The festivals mentioned are Jewish holy days celebrated annually, monthly (New Moon), and weekly (the Sabbath). These rituals distinguished the Jews from their pagan neighbours. Failure to observe them could be easily noticed by those who were keeping track of what others did. But we should not let ourselves be judged by the opinions of others, because Christ has set us free.

2:16, 17 Paul told the Colossian Christians not to let others criticise their diet or their religious ceremonies. Instead of outward observance, believers should focus on faith in Christ alone. Our worship, traditions and ceremonies can help bring us close to God, but we should never criticise fellow Christians whose traditions and ceremonies differ from ours. More important than how we worship is that we worship Christ. Don't let anyone judge you. You are responsible to Christ.

2:17 Old Testament laws, holidays, and feasts pointed towards Christ. Paul calls them a "shadow" of the reality that was to come – Christ himself. When Christ came, he dispelled the shadow. If we have Christ, we have what we need to know and please God.

2:18 The false teachers were proud of their humility! This false humility brought attention and praise to themselves rather than to God. True humility means seeing ourselves as we really are from God's perspective, and acting accordingly. People today practise false humility when they talk negatively about themselves so that others will think they are spiritual. False humility is self-centred; true humility is God-centred.

2:18 [c]ver 23 [d]Php 3:14
2:19 [e]Eph 1:22 [f]Eph 4:16
2:20 [g]Gal 4:3, 9 [h]ver 14, 16
2:22 [i]1Co 6:13 [j]Isa 29:13; Mt 15:9; Tit 1:14

18 Do not let anyone who delights in false humility[c] and the worship of angels
disqualify you for the prize.[d] Such a person goes into great detail about what he has
seen, and his unspiritual mind puffs him up with idle notions.
19 He has lost connection
with the Head,[e] from whom the whole body, supported and held together by its
ligaments and sinews, grows as God causes it to grow.[f]
20 Since you died with Christ to the basic principles of this world,[g] why, as though
you still belonged to it, do you submit to its rules:[h]
21 "Do not handle! Do not taste!
Do not touch!"?
22 These are all destined to perish[i] with use, because they are based
on human commands and teachings.[j]
23 Such regulations indeed have an appearance
of wisdom, with their self-imposed worship, their false humility and their harsh
treatment of the body, but they lack any value in restraining sensual indulgence.

FROM DEATH TO LIFE

The Bible uses many illustrations to teach what happens when we choose to let Jesus be Lord of our lives. Following are some of the most vivid pictures:

1. Because Christ died for us, we have been crucified with him.	Romans 6:2–13; 7:4–6 2 Corinthians 5:14 Galatians 2:20; 5:24; 6:14 Colossians 2:20; 3:3–5 1 Peter 2:24
2. Our old, rebellious nature died with Christ.	Romans 6:6; 7:4–6 Colossians 3:9, 10
3. Christ's resurrection guarantees our new life now and eternal life with him later.	Romans 6:4, 11 Colossians 2:12, 13; 3:1, 3

This process is acted out in baptism (Colossians 2:12), based on our faith in Christ: (1) The old sinful nature dies (crucified); (2) We are ready to receive a new life (buried); (3) Christ gives us new life (resurrected).

2:18 The false teachers were claiming that God was far away and could be approached only through various levels of angels. They taught that people had to worship angels in order, eventually, to reach God. This is unscriptural; the Bible teaches that angels are God's servants, and it forbids worshipping them (Exodus 20:3, 4; Revelation 22:8, 9). As you grow in your Christian faith, let God's word be your guide, not the opinions of other people.

2:18 The expression "unspiritual mind" means that these people had a self-made religion. The false teachers were trying to deny the significance of the body by saying that it was evil, but their desire for attention from others showed that, in reality, they were obsessed with the physical realm.

2:19 The fundamental problem with the false teachers was that they were not connected to Christ, the Head of the body of believers. If they had been joined to him, they could not have taught false doctrine or lived immorally. Anyone who teaches about God without being connected to him by faith should not be trusted.

2:20 The "basic principles" are the beliefs of pagans. See 2:8 for more on Paul's view of non-Christian philosophy.

2:20; 3:1 How do we die with Christ, and how are we raised with him? When a person becomes a Christian, he or she is given new life through the power of the Holy Spirit. See the notes on 2:11, 12 and 2:13–15 for further information.

2:20–23 People should be able to see a difference between the way Christians and non-Christians live. Still, we should not expect instant maturity in new Christians. Christian growth is a lifelong process. Although we have a new nature, we don't automatically think all good thoughts and have all pure attitudes when we become new people in Christ. But if we keep listening to God, we will be changing all the time. As you look over the last year, what changes for the better have you seen in your thoughts and attitudes? Change may be slow, but your life will change significantly if you trust God to change you.

2:20–23 We cannot reach up to God by following rules of self-denial, by observing rituals, or by practising religion. Paul isn't saying all rules are bad (see the note on Galatians 2:15, 16). But no keeping of laws or rules will earn salvation. The Good News is that God reaches down to human beings, and he asks for our response. Man-made religions focus on human effort; Christianity focuses on Christ's work. Believers must put aside sinful desires, but doing so is the by-product of our new life in Christ, not the reason for our new life. Our salvation does not depend on our own discipline and rule-keeping, but on the power of Christ's death and resurrection.

2:22, 23 We can guard against man-made religions by asking these questions about any religious group: (1) Does it stress man-made rules and taboos rather than God's grace? (2) Does it foster a critical spirit towards others, or does it exercise discipline discreetly and lovingly? (3) Does it stress formulas, secret knowledge, or special visions more than the word of God? (4) Does it elevate self-righteousness, honouring those who keep the rules, rather than elevating Christ? (5) Does it neglect Christ's universal church, claiming to be an elite group? (6) Does it teach humiliation of the body as a means to spiritual growth rather than focusing on the growth of the whole person? (7) Does it disregard the family rather than holding it in high regard as the Bible does?

2:23 To the Colossians, the discipline demanded by the false teachers seemed good, and legalism still attracts many people today. Following a long list of religious rules requires strong self-discipline and can make a person appear moral, but religious rules cannot change a person's heart. Only the Holy Spirit can do that.

2. What Christians should do

Rules for Holy Living

3 Since, then, you have been raised with Christ, set your hearts on things above,
where Christ is seated at the right hand of God. 2 Set your minds on things above,
not on earthly things.[a] 3 For you died,[b] and your life is now hidden with Christ in
God. 4 When Christ, who is your[a] life, appears,[c] then you also will appear with him
in glory.[d]
5 Put to death, therefore, whatever belongs to your earthly nature: sexual immorality, impurity, lust, evil desires and greed,[e] which is idolatry.[f] 6 Because of these,
the wrath of God[g] is coming.[b] 7 You used to walk in these ways, in the life you once
lived.[h] 8 But now you must rid yourselves[i] of all such things as these: anger, rage,
malice, slander[j] and filthy language from your lips.[k] 9 Do not lie to each other,[l]
since you have taken off your old self with its practices 10 and have put on the new
self, which is being renewed[m] in knowledge in the image of its Creator.[n] 11 Here there
is no Greek or Jew,[o] circumcised or uncircumcised,[p] barbarian, Scythian, slave or
free,[q] but Christ is all,[r] and is in all.
12 Therefore, as God's chosen people, holy and dearly loved, clothe yourselves with
compassion, kindness, humility,[s] gentleness and patience.[t] 13 Bear with each
other[u] and forgive whatever grievances you may have against one another. Forgive

3:2 [a]Php 3:19, 20
3:3 [b]Ro 6:2;
3:4 [c]1Co 1:7 [d]1Jn 3:2
3:5 [e]Eph 5:3 [f]Eph 5:5
3:6 [g]Ro 1:18
3:7 [h]Eph 2:2
3:8 [i]Eph 4:22 [j]Eph 4:31 [k]Eph 4:29
3:9 [l]Eph 4:22, 25
3:10 [m]Ro 12:2; Eph 4:23 [n]Eph 2:10
3:11 [o]Ro 10:12 [p]1Co 7:19 [q]Gal 3:28 [r]Eph 1:23
3:12 [s]Php 2:3 [t]Gal 5:22, 23
3:13 [u]Eph 4:2

[a] 4 Some manuscripts *our* [b] 6 Some early manuscripts *coming on those who are disobedient*

3:1ff In chapter 2, Paul exposed the wrong reasons for self-denial. In chapter 3, he explains true Christian behaviour – putting on the new self by accepting Christ and regarding the earthly nature as dead. We change our moral and ethical behaviour by letting Christ live within us, so that he can shape us into what we *should* be.

3:1, 2 Setting our hearts on things above means striving to put heaven's priorities into daily practice. Setting our minds on things above means concentrating on the eternal rather than the temporal. See Philippians 4:9 and Colossians 3:15 for more on Christ's rule in our hearts and minds.

3:2, 3 "For you died" means that we should have as little desire for this world as a dead person would have. The Christian's real home is where Christ lives (John 14:2, 3). This truth gives us a different perspective on our lives here on earth. To "set your minds on things above" means to look at life from God's perspective and to seek what he desires. This is the antidote to materialism; we gain the proper perspective on material goods when we take God's view of them. The more we regard the world around us as God does, the more we will live in harmony with him. We must not become too attached to what is only temporary.

3:3 What does it mean that a believer's life is "hidden with Christ"? *Hidden* means concealed and safe. This is not only a future hope, but an accomplished fact right now. Our service and conduct do not earn our salvation, but they are results of our salvation. Take heart that your salvation is sure, and live each day for Christ.

3:4 Christ gives us power to live for him now, and he gives us hope for the future – he will return. In the rest of this chapter Paul explains how Christians should act *now* in order to be prepared for Christ's return.

3:5 We should consider ourselves dead and unresponsive to sexual immorality, impurity, lust, evil desires, and greed. Just like diseased limbs of a tree, these practices must be cut off before they destroy us. We must make a conscious, daily decision to remove anything that supports or feeds these desires and to rely on the Holy Spirit's power.

3:6 The "wrath of God" refers to God's judgment on these kinds of behaviour, culminating with future and final punishment of evil. When tempted to sin, remember that you must one day stand before God.

3:8–10 We must rid ourselves of all evil practices and immorality. Then we can commit ourselves to what Christ teaches. Paul was appealing to the commitment the believers had made and urging them to remain true to their confession of faith. They were to rid themselves of the old life and "put on" the new way of living given by Christ and guided by the Holy Spirit. If you have made such a commitment to Christ, are you remaining true to it?

3:9 Lying to one another disrupts unity by destroying trust. It tears down relationships and may lead to serious conflict in a church. So don't exaggerate statistics, pass on rumours or gossip, or say things to build up your own image. Be committed to telling the truth.

3:10 What does it mean to "put on the new self"? It means that your conduct should match your faith. If you are a Christian, you should act like it. To be a Christian means more than just making good resolutions and having good intentions; it means taking the right actions. This is a straightforward step that is as simple as putting on your clothes.

3:10 Every Christian is in a continuing education programme. The more we know of Christ and his work, the more we are being changed to be like him. Because this process is lifelong, we must never stop learning and obeying. There is no justification for drifting along, but there is an incentive to find the rich treasures of growing in him. It takes practice, ongoing review, patience, and concentration to keep in line with his will.

3:11 The Christian church should have no barriers of nationality, race, education level, social standing, wealth, gender, religion, or power. Christ breaks down all barriers and accepts all people who come to him. Nothing should keep us from telling others about Christ or accepting into our fellowship any and all believers (Ephesians 2:14, 15). Christians should be building bridges, not walls.

3:12–17 Paul offers a strategy to help us live for God day by day: (1) imitate Christ's compassionate, forgiving attitude (3:12, 13); (2) let love guide your life (3:14); (3) let the peace of Christ rule in your heart (3:15); (4) always be thankful (3:15); (5) keep God's word in you at all times (3:16); (6) live as Jesus Christ's representative (3:17).

3:13 The key to forgiving others is remembering how much God has forgiven you. Is it difficult for you to forgive someone who has wronged you a little when God has forgiven you so much? Realising God's infinite love and forgiveness can help you love and forgive others.

3:13 [v]Eph 4:32
3:14 [w]1Co 13:1-13 [x]Eph 4:3
3:15 [y]Jn 14:27
3:16 [z]Ro 10:17 [a]Col 1:28 [b]Eph 5:19
3:17 [c]1Co 10:31 [d]Eph 5:20
3:18 [e]Eph 5:22

as the Lord forgave you.[v] 14And over all these virtues put on love,[w] which binds
them all together in perfect unity.[x]
15Let the peace of Christ[y] rule in your hearts, since as members of one body you
were called to peace. And be thankful. 16Let the word of Christ[z] dwell in you richly
as you teach and admonish one another with all wisdom,[a] and as you sing psalms,
hymns and spiritual songs with gratitude in your hearts to God.[b] 17And whatever you
do,[c] whether in word or deed, do it all in the name of the Lord Jesus, giving thanks[d]
to God the Father through him.

Rules for Christian Households

18Wives, submit to your husbands,[e] as is fitting in the Lord.
19Husbands, love your wives and do not be harsh with them.
20Children, obey your parents in everything, for this pleases the Lord.
21Fathers, do not embitter your children, or they will become discouraged.
22Slaves, obey your earthly masters in everything; and do it, not only when their
eye is on you and to win their favour, but with sincerity of heart and reverence for

SINS VERSUS SIGNS OF LOVE

Sins of Sexual Attitude and Behaviour	*Sins of Speech*	*Signs of Love*
Evil desires	Anger expressed	Compassion
Sexual immorality	Malice	Kindness
Impurity	Slander	Humility
Lust	Filthy language	Patience
Greed	Lying	Gentleness
		Forgiveness

In Colossians 3:5 Paul tells us to put to death the things found in list 1. In 3:8 he tells us to rid ourselves of the things found in list 2. In 3:12 we're told to practise the things found in list 3. List 1 deals with sins of sexual attitudes and behaviour—they are particularly destructive because of what they do to destroy any group or church. List 2 deals with sins of speech—these are the relationship-breakers. List 3 contains the relationship-builders, which we are to express as members of Christ's body.

3:14 All the virtues that Paul encourages us to develop are perfectly bound together by love. As we clothe ourselves with these virtues, the last garment we are to put on is love, which holds all of the others in place. To practise any list of virtues without practising love will lead to distortion, fragmentation, and stagnation (1 Corinthians 13:3).

3:14, 15 Christians should live in peace. To live in peace does not mean that suddenly all differences of opinion are eliminated, but it does require that loving Christians work together despite their differences. Such love is not a feeling, but a decision to meet others' needs (see 1 Corinthians 13). To live in love leads to peace between individuals and among the members of the body of believers. Do problems in your relationships with other Christians cause open conflicts or mutual silence? Consider what you can do to heal those relationships with love.

3:15 The word *rule* comes from the language of athletics: Paul tells us to let Christ's peace be umpire or referee in our hearts. Our hearts are the centre of conflict because there our feelings and desires clash—our fears and hopes, distrust and trust, jealousy and love. How can we deal with these constant conflicts and live as God wants? Paul explains that we must decide between conflicting elements by using the rule of peace—which choice will promote peace in our souls and in our churches? For more on the peace of Christ, see Philippians 4:9.

3:16 Although the early Christians had access to the Old Testament and freely used it, they did not yet have the New Testament or any other Christian books to study. Their stories and teachings about Christ were memoriszed and passed on from person to person. Sometimes the teachings were set to music, and so music became an important part of Christian worship and education.

3:17 Doing "all in the name of the Lord Jesus" means bringing honour to Christ in every aspect and activity of daily living. As a Christian, you represent Christ at all times—wherever you go and whatever you say. What impression do people have of Christ when they see or talk with you? What changes would you make in your life in order to honour Christ?

3:18—4:1 Paul gives rules for three sets of household relationships: (1) husbands and wives, (2) parents and children, and (3) masters and slaves. In each case there is mutual responsibility to submit and love, to obey and encourage, to work hard and be fair. Examine your family and work relationships. Do you relate to others as God intended? See Ephesians 5:21—6:9 for similar instructions.

3:19 Christian marriage involves mutual submission, subordinating our personal desires for the good of the loved one, and submitting ourselves to Christ as Lord. For more on submission, see the notes on Ephesians 5:21–33.

3:20, 21 Children must be handled with care. They need firm discipline administered in love. Don't alienate them by nagging, deriding, or destroying their self-respect so that they lose heart.

3:22—4:1 Paul does not condemn or condone slavery, but explains that Christ transcends all divisions between people. Slaves are told to work hard as though their master were Christ himself (3:22–25); but masters should be just and fair (4:1). Perhaps Paul was thinking specifically of Onesimus and Philemon—the slave and master whose conflict lay behind the letter to Philemon (see the book of Philemon). Philemon was a slave owner in the Colossian church, and Onesimus had been his slave (4:9).

the Lord. 23Whatever you do, work at it with all your heart, as working for the Lord,
not for men, 24since you know that you will receive an inheritance[f] from the Lord
as a reward. It is the Lord Christ you are serving. 25Anyone who does wrong will be
repaid for his wrong, and there is no favouritism.[g]

4 Masters, provide your slaves with what is right and fair, because you know that
you also have a Master in heaven.

Further Instructions

2Devote yourselves to prayer,[a] being watchful and thankful. 3And pray for us, too,
that God may open a door[b] for our message, so that we may proclaim the mystery
of Christ, for which I am in chains.[c] 4Pray that I may proclaim it clearly, as I should.
5Be wise[d] in the way you act towards outsiders;[e] make the most of every opportunity.[f] 6Let your conversation be always full of grace,[g] seasoned with salt,[h] so that
you may know how to answer everyone.[i]

Final Greetings

7Tychicus[j] will tell you all the news about me. He is a dear brother, a faithful
minister and fellow-servant[k] in the Lord. 8I am sending him to you for the express
purpose that you may know about our[a] circumstances and that he may encourage your
hearts.[l] 9He is coming with Onesimus,[m] our faithful and dear brother, who is one
of you. They will tell you everything that is happening here.
10My fellow-prisoner Aristarchus[n] sends you his greetings, as does Mark, the

a 8 Some manuscripts *that he may know about your*

3:24 [f]Ac 20:32
3:25 [g]Ac 10:34
4:2 [a]Lk 18:1
4:3 [b]Ac 14:27 [c]Eph 6:19, 20
4:5 [d]Eph 5:15 [e]Mk 4:11 [f]Eph 5:16
4:6 [g]Eph 4:29 [h]Mk 9:50 [i]1Pe 3:15
4:7 [j]Ac 20:4 [k]Eph 6:21, 22
4:8 [l]Eph 6:21, 22
4:9 [m]Phm 10
4:10 [n]Ac 19:29

RULES OF SUBMISSION

Wives, submit to your husbands (3:18).	*Husbands,* love your wives and don't be harsh with them (3:19).
Children, obey your parents (3:20).	*Parents,* don't embitter your children so that they become discouraged (3:21).
Slaves, obey your masters (3:22).	*Masters,* be just and fair towards your slaves (4:1).
(*Employees,* work hard for your employers.)	(*Employers,* be just and fair with your employees.)

The New Testament includes many instructions concerning relationships. Most people read these instructions for the other person and ignore the ones that apply to themselves. But you can't control another person's behaviour, only your own. Start by following your own instructions and not insisting on the obedience of others first.

3:23 Since the creation, God has given us work to do. If we could regard our work as an act of worship or service to God, such an attitude would take some of the drudgery and boredom out of it. We could work without complaining or resentment if we would treat our job problems as the cost of discipleship.

4:1 Masters were to provide what was right and fair. Similarly today, employers should pay fair wages and treat their employees justly. And leaders should take care of their volunteers and not abuse them. If you have responsibility over others, make sure you do what is right and fair – you are accountable to your Master in heaven.

4:2 Have you ever grown tired of praying for something or someone? Paul says we should "devote" ourselves to prayer and be "watchful" in prayer. Our persistence is an expression of our faith that God answers our prayers. Faith shouldn't die if the answers come slowly, for the delay may be God's way of working his will in our lives. When you feel tired of praying, know that God is present, always listening, always answering – maybe not in ways you had hoped, but in ways that he knows are best.

4:3 The "mystery of Christ" is Christ's Good News of salvation, the gospel. The whole focus of Paul's life was to tell others about Christ, explaining and preaching this wonderful mystery.

4:4 Paul asked for prayer that he could proclaim the Good News about Christ clearly, and we can request prayer to do the same. No matter what approach to evangelism we use, whether emphasising lifestyle and example or whether building relationships, we should never obscure the message of the gospel.

4:5 We should be wise in our contacts with non-Christians ("outsiders"), making the most of our opportunities to tell them the Good News of salvation. What opportunities do you have?

4:6 When we tell others about Christ, it is important always to be gracious in what we say. No matter how much sense the message makes, we lose our effectiveness if we are not courteous. Just as we like to be respected, we must respect others if we want them to listen to what we have to say. "Seasoned with salt" means that what we say should be "tasty" and should encourage further dialogue.

4:7 Tychicus was one of Paul's personal representatives and probably the bearer of the letters to the Colossians and Ephesians (see also Ephesians 6:21, 22). He accompanied Paul to Jerusalem with the collection for the church (Acts 20:4).

4:10 Aristarchus was a Thessalonian who accompanied Paul on his third missionary journey. He was with Paul in the riot at Ephesus (Acts 19:29). He and Tychicus were with Paul in Greece (Acts 20:4). Aristarchus went to Rome with Paul (Acts 27:2). Mark started out with Paul and Barnabas on their first missionary journey (Acts 12:25), but he left in the middle of the trip for unknown reasons (Acts 13:13). Barnabas and Mark were relatives, and when Paul re-

4:10 [o]Ac 4:36
4:12 [p]Col 1:7 [q]Ro 15:30 [r]1Co 2:6
4:13 [s]Col 2:1
4:14 [t]2Ti 4:11 [u]2Ti 4:10
4:15 [v]Ro 16:5
4:16 [w]2Th 3:14
4:17 [x]Phm 2 [y]2Ti 4:5
4:18 [z]1Co 16:21 [a]Heb 13:3 [b]1Ti 6:21; 2Ti 4:22; Tit 3:15; Heb 13:25

cousin of Barnabas.[o] (You have received instructions about him; if he comes to you,
welcome him.) 11 Jesus, who is called Justus, also sends greetings. These are the only
Jews among my fellow-workers for the kingdom of God, and they have proved a
comfort to me. 12 Epaphras,[p] who is one of you and a servant of Christ Jesus, sends
greetings. He is always wrestling in prayer for you,[q] that you may stand firm in all
the will of God, mature[r] and fully assured. 13 I vouch for him that he is working hard
for you and for those at Laodicea[s] and Hierapolis. 14 Our dear friend Luke,[t] the
doctor, and Demas[u] send greetings. 15 Give my greetings to the brothers at Laodicea,
and to Nympha and the church in her house.[v]

16 After this letter has been read to you, see that it is also read[w] in the church of
the Laodiceans and that you in turn read the letter from Laodicea.

17 Tell Archippus:[x] "See to it that you complete the work you have received in the
Lord."[y]

18 I, Paul, write this greeting in my own hand.[z] Remember[a] my chains. Grace be
with you.[b]

---

fused to take Mark on another journey, Barnabas and Mark journeyed together to preach the Good News (Acts 15:37–41). Mark also worked with Peter (Acts 12:12, 13; 1 Peter 5:13). Later, Mark and Paul were reconciled (Philemon 24). Mark wrote the Gospel of Mark. His Profile is in Acts 12.

4:12 Epaphras founded the Colossian church (see the note on 1:7), and his report to Paul in Rome caused Paul to write this letter. Epaphras was a hero of the Colossian church, one of the believers who helped keep the church together despite growing troubles. His earnest prayers for the believers show his deep love and concern for them.

4:13 Laodicea was located a few miles northwest of Colosse; Hierapolis was about five miles north of Laodicea. See the note on 2:1 for more about Laodicea.

4:14 Luke spent much time with Paul, not only accompanying him on most of his third missionary journey, but sitting with him in the prison at Rome. Luke wrote the Gospel of Luke and the book of Acts. His Profile is in Acts 17. Demas was faithful for a while, but then he deserted Paul, having "loved this world" (2 Timothy 4:10).

4:15 The early Christians often met in homes. Church buildings were not common until the third century.

4:16 Some suggest that the letter from Laodicea may be the book of Ephesians, because the letter to the Ephesians was circulated to all the churches in Asia Minor. It is also possible that there was a special letter to the Laodiceans, of which we have no record today. Paul wrote several letters that have been lost (see, for example, 2 Corinthians 2:3 and note).

4:17 Paul's letter to Philemon is also addressed to Archippus (Philemon 2). Paul called him a "fellow-soldier". He may have been a Roman soldier who had become a member of the Colossian church, or he may have been Philemon's son.

4:17 Paul encouraged Archippus to make sure that he completed the work he had received in the Lord. There are many ways for us to leave our work unfinished. We can easily get sidetracked morally, we can become exhausted and stop, we can become frustrated and give up, or we can let it slide and leave it up to others. We should see to it that we finish God's assignments, completing the work we have received.

4:18 Paul usually dictated his letters to a scribe, and then often ended with a short note in his own handwriting (see also 1 Corinthians 16:21; Galatians 6:11). This assured the recipients that false teachers were not writing letters in Paul's name. It also gave the letters a personal touch.

4:18 To understand the letter to the Colossians, we need to know that the church was facing pressure from a heresy that promised deeper spiritual life through secret knowledge (an early form of Gnosticism). The false teachers were destroying faith in Christ by undermining Christ's humanity and divinity.

Paul makes it clear in Colossians that Christ alone is the source of our spiritual life, the Head of the body of believers. Christ is Lord of both the physical and spiritual worlds. The path to deeper spiritual life is not through religious duties, special knowledge, or secrets; it is only through a clear connection with the Lord Jesus Christ. We must never let anything come between us and our Saviour.

1 THESSALONIANS

VITAL STATISTICS

PURPOSE:
To strengthen the Thessalonian Christians in their faith and give them the assurance of Christ's return

AUTHOR:
Paul

TO WHOM WRITTEN:
The church at Thessalonica, and all believers everywhere

DATE WRITTEN:
About A.D. 51 from Corinth; one of Paul's earliest letters

SETTING:
The church at Thessalonica was very young, having been established only two or three years before this letter was written. The Thessalonian Christians needed to mature in their faith. In addition, there was a misunderstanding concerning Christ's second coming—some thought Christ would return immediately, and thus they were confused when their loved ones died because they expected Christ to return beforehand. Also, believers were being persecuted.

KEY VERSE:
"We believe that Jesus died and rose again and so we believe that God will bring with Jesus those who have fallen asleep in him" (4:14).

KEY PEOPLE:
Paul, Timothy, Silas

KEY PLACE:
Thessalonica

SPECIAL FEATURES:
Paul received from Timothy a favourable report about the Thessalonians. However, Paul wrote this letter to correct their misconceptions about the resurrection and the second coming of Christ.

SLOWLY they walk, one by one, scattering the leaves and trampling the grass under measured and heavy steps. The minister's words still echoing in their minds, they hear workmen moving towards the terrible place, preparing to cover the coffin of their loved one. Death, the enemy, has torn the bonded relationships of family and friends, leaving only memories . . . and tears . . . and loneliness.

But like a golden shaft of sun piercing the winter sky, a singular truth shatters the oppressive gloom—death is not the end! Christ is the victor over death, and there is hope of the resurrection through him.

As with every member of the human family, first-century Christians came face to face with their mortality. Many of them met early deaths at the hands of those who hated Christ and all allied with him. Whether at the hands of zealous Jews (like Paul before his conversion), angry Greeks, or ruthless Roman authorities, persecution included stonings, beatings, crucifixions, torture, and death. To be a follower of Christ meant to give up everything.

Paul established the church in Thessalonica during his second missionary journey (in about A.D. 51). He wrote this letter a short time later to encourage the young believers there. He wanted to assure them of his love, to praise them for their faithfulness during persecution, and to remind them of their hope—the sure return of their Lord and Saviour.

Paul begins this letter with a note of affirmation, thanking God for the strong faith and good reputation of the Thessalonians (1:1–10). Then Paul reviews their relationship—how he and his companions brought the gospel to them (2:1–12), how they accepted the message (2:13–16), and how he longed to be with them again (2:17–20). Because of his concern, Paul sent Timothy to encourage them in their faith (3:1–13).

Paul then presents the core of his message—exhortation and comfort. He challenges them to please God in their daily living by avoiding sexual immorality (4:1–8), loving each other (4:9, 10), and living as good citizens in a sinful world (4:11, 12).

Paul comforts the Thessalonians by reminding them of the hope of the resurrection (4:13–18). Then he warns them to be prepared at all times, for Jesus Christ could return at any moment. When Christ returns, those Christians who are alive and those who have died will be raised to new life (5:1–11).

Paul then gives the Thessalonians a handful of reminders on how to prepare themselves for the second coming—warn the idle (5:14), encourage the timid (5:14), help the weak (5:14), be patient with everyone (5:14), be kind to everyone (5:15), be joyful always (5:16), pray continually (5:17), give thanks (5:18), test everything that is taught (5:20, 21), and avoid evil (5:22). Paul concludes his letter with two benedictions and a request for prayer.

As you read this letter, listen carefully to Paul's practical advice for Christian living. And when burdened by grief and overwhelmed by sorrow, take hope in the reality of Christ's return, the resurrection, and eternal life!

THE BLUEPRINT

1. Faithfulness to the Lord (1:1—3:13)
2. Watchfulness for the Lord (4:1—5:28)

Paul and his companions were faithful to bring the gospel to the Thessalonians in the midst of persecution. The Thessalonians had only recently become Christians, and yet they had remained faithful to the Lord, despite the fact that the apostles were not with them. Others have been faithful in bringing God's word to us. We must remain faithful and live in the expectation that Christ will return at any time.

MEGATHEMES

THEME	EXPLANATION	IMPORTANCE
Persecution	Paul and the new Christians at Thessalonica experienced persecution because of their faith in Christ. We can expect trials and troubles as well. We need to stand firm in our faith in the midst of trials, being strengthened by the Holy Spirit.	The Holy Spirit helps us to remain strong in faith, able to show genuine love to others and maintain our moral character even when we are being persecuted, slandered, or oppressed.
Paul's Ministry	Paul expressed his concern for this church even while he was being slandered. Paul's commitment to sharing the gospel in spite of difficult circumstances is a model we should follow.	Paul not only delivered his message, but gave of himself. In our ministries, we must become like Paul—faithful and bold, yet sensitive and self-sacrificing.
Hope	One day all believers, both those who are alive and those who have died, will be united with Christ. To those Christians who die before Christ's return, there is hope—the hope of the resurrection of the body.	If we believe in Christ, we will live with him for ever. All those who belong to Jesus Christ—from throughout history—will be present with him at his second coming. We can be confident that we will be with loved ones who have trusted in Christ.
Being Prepared	No-one knows the time of Christ's return. We are to live moral and holy lives, ever watchful for his coming. Believers must not neglect daily responsibilities, but always work and live to please the Lord.	The gospel is not only what we believe, but also what we must live. The Holy Spirit leads us in faithfulness, so we can avoid lust and fraud. Live as though you expect Christ's return at any time. Don't be caught unprepared.

1. Faithfulness to the Lord

1 Paul, Silas[a] and Timothy,[a]

To the church of the Thessalonians[b] in God the Father and the Lord Jesus Christ:

Grace and peace to you.[b][c]

Thanksgiving for the Thessalonians' Faith

2We always thank God for all of you,[d] mentioning you in our prayers. 3We
continually remember before our God and Father your work produced by faith,[e] your
labour prompted by love, and your endurance inspired by hope in our Lord Jesus
Christ.
4For we know, brothers loved by God, that he has chosen you, 5because our
gospel[f] came to you not simply with words, but also with power, with the Holy Spirit
and with deep conviction. You know how we lived among you for your sake. 6You
became imitators of us[g] and of the Lord; in spite of severe suffering,[h] you welcomed
the message with the joy given by the Holy Spirit.[i] 7And so you became a model
to all the believers in Macedonia and Achaia. 8The Lord's message rang out from you
not only in Macedonia and Achaia—your faith in God has become known everywhere.[j] Therefore we do not need to say anything about it, 9for they themselves
report what kind of reception you gave us. They tell how you turned to God from
idols[k] to serve the living and true God, 10and to wait for his Son from heaven, whom
he raised from the dead[l]—Jesus, who rescues us from the coming wrath.[m]

a *1* Greek *Silvanus,* a variant of *Silas* **b** *1* Some early manuscripts *you from God our Father and the Lord Jesus Christ*

1:1 [a]Ac 16:1; 2Th 1:1 [b]Ac 17:1 [c]Ro 1:7
1:2 [d]Ro 1:8
1:3 [e]2Th 1:11
1:5 [f]2Th 2:14
1:6 [g]1Co 4:16 [h]Ac 17:5-10 [i]Ac 13:52
1:8 [j]Ro 1:8; 10:18
1:9 [k]1Co 12:2; Gal 4:8
1:10 [l]Ac 2:24 [m]Ro 5:9

1:1 Paul and his companions probably arrived in Thessalonica in the early summer of A.D. 50. They planted the first Christian church in that city, but had to leave in a hurry because their lives were threatened (Acts 17:1–10). At the first opportunity, probably when he stopped at Corinth, Paul sent Timothy back to Thessalonica to see how the new believers were doing. Timothy returned to Paul with good news: the Christians in Thessalonica were remaining firm in the faith and were unified. But the Thessalonians did have some questions about their new faith. Paul had not had time to answer all their questions during his brief visit, and in the meantime, other questions had arisen. So Paul wrote this letter to answer their questions and to commend them on their faithfulness to Christ.

1:1 For more information on Paul, see his Profile in Acts 9. Timothy's Profile is in 1 Timothy. Silas accompanied Paul on his second missionary journey (Acts 15:36—17:15). He helped Paul establish the church in Thessalonica (Acts 17:1–9). He is also mentioned in 2 Corinthians 1:19, 2 Thessalonians 1:1, and in 1 Peter 5:12. Silas' Profile is found in Acts 16.

1:1 Thessalonica was the capital and largest city (about 200,000 population) of the Roman province of Macedonia. The most important Roman highway (the Egnatian Way)—extending from Rome all the way to the Orient—went through Thessalonica. This highway, along with the city's thriving harbour, made Thessalonica one of the wealthiest and most flourishing trade centres in the Roman empire. Recognised as a free city, Thessalonica was allowed self-rule and was exempted from most of the restrictions placed by Rome on other cities in the empire. However, with its international flavour came many pagan religions and cultural influences that challenged the faith of the young Christians there.

1:3 The Thessalonians had stood firm when they were persecuted (1:6; 3:1–4, 7, 8). Paul commended these young Christians for their work produced by faith, labour prompted by love, and endurance inspired by hope. These characteristics are the marks of effective Christians in any age.

1:5 The gospel came "with power"; it had a powerful effect on the Thessalonians. Whenever the Bible is heard and obeyed, lives are changed! Christianity is more than a collection of interesting facts; it is the power of God to every one who believes. What has God's power done in your life since you first believed?

1:5 The Holy Spirit changes people when they believe the gospel. When we tell others about Christ, we must depend on the Holy Spirit to open their eyes and convince them that they need salvation. God's power changes people—not our cleverness or persuasion. Without the work of the Holy Spirit, our words are meaningless. The Holy Spirit not only convicts people of sin but also assures them of the truth of the gospel. (For more information on the Holy Spirit, see John 14:23–26; 15:26, 27; and the notes on John 3:6 and Acts 1:5.)

1:5 Paul wrote, "You know how we lived among you for your sake." The Thessalonians could see that what Paul, Silas, and Timothy were preaching was true because these men lived it. Does your life confirm or contradict what you say you believe?

1:6 The message of salvation, though welcomed with great joy, brought the Thessalonians severe suffering because it led to persecution from both Jews and Gentiles (3:2–4; Acts 17:5). Having believed the gospel message and accepted new life in Christ, apparently many Thessalonians believed that they would be protected from death until Christ returned. Then, when believers began to die under persecution, some Thessalonian Christians started to question their faith. Many of Paul's comments throughout this letter were addressed to these people, as he explained what happens when believers die (see 4:13ff).

1:9, 10 All of us should respond to the Good News as the Thessalonians did: *turn* to God, *serve* God, and *wait* for his Son, Christ, to return from heaven. We should turn from sin to God because Christ is coming to judge the earth. We should be fervent in our service because we have little time before Christ returns. We should be prepared for Christ to return because we don't know when he will come.

1:10 Paul emphasised Christ's second coming throughout this book. Because the Thessalonian church was being persecuted, Paul encouraged them to look forward to the deliverance that Christ would bring. A believer's hope is in the return of Jesus, our great God and Saviour (Titus 2:13). Our perspective on life remains incomplete without this hope. Just as surely as Christ was raised

2:1
[a]1Th 1:5, 9
2:2
[b]Ac 16:22; Php 1:30
2:3
[c]2Co 2:17
2:4
[d]Gal 2:7
[e]Gal 1:10
2:5
[f]Ac 20:33
[g]Ro 1:9
2:6
[h]1Co 9:1, 2
2:7
[i]ver 11

Paul's Ministry in Thessalonica

2 You know, brothers, that our visit to you[a] was not a failure. 2We had previously
suffered[b] and been insulted in Philippi, as you know, but with the help of our
God we dared to tell you his gospel in spite of strong opposition. 3For the appeal we
make does not spring from error or impure motives,[c] nor are we trying to trick you.
4On the contrary, we speak as men approved by God to be entrusted with the gospel.[d]
We are not trying to please men[e] but God, who tests our hearts. 5You know we never
used flattery, nor did we put on a mask to cover up greed[f]—God is our witness.[g]
6We were not looking for praise from men, not from you or anyone else.
As apostles[h] of Christ we could have been a burden to you, 7but we were gentle
among you, like a mother caring for her little children.[i] 8We loved you so much that

LOCATION OF THESSALONICA Paul visited Thessalonica on his second and third missionary journeys. It was a seaport and trade centre located on the Egnatian Way, a busy international route. Paul probably wrote his two letters to the Thessalonians from Corinth.

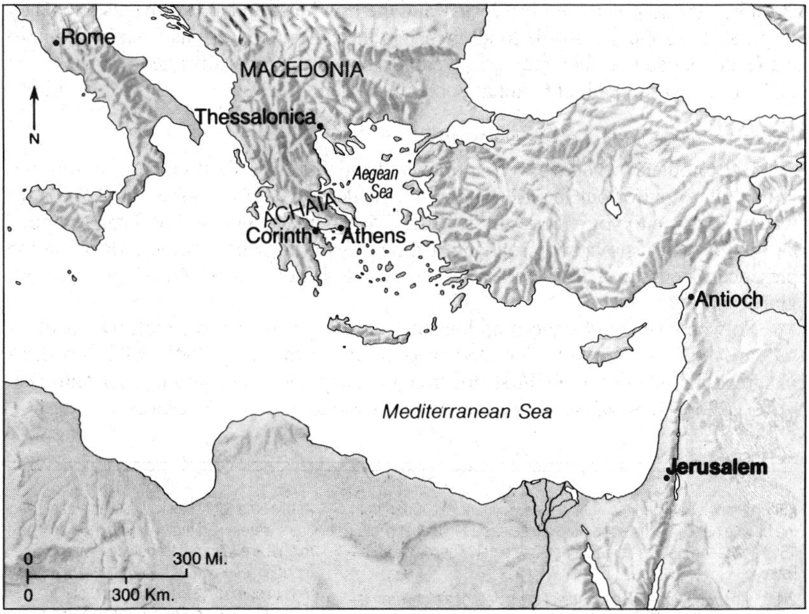

from the dead and ascended into heaven, he will return (Acts 1:11).

2:1 "Our visit to you" refers to Paul's first visit to Thessalonica (see Acts 17:1–9).

2:2 The Thessalonians knew that Paul had been imprisoned in Philippi just prior to coming to Thessalonica (see Acts 16:11–17:1). Fear of imprisonment did not keep Paul from preaching the gospel. If God wants us to do something, he will give us the strength and courage to do it despite any obstacles that may come our way.

2:3 This pointed statement may be a response to accusations from the Jewish leaders who had stirred up the crowds (Acts 17:5). Paul did not seek money, fame, or popularity by sharing the gospel. He demonstrated the sincerity of his motives by showing that he and Silas had suffered for sharing the gospel in Philippi. People become involved in ministry for a variety of reasons, not all of them good or pure. When their bad motives are exposed, all of Christ's work suffers. When you get involved in ministry, do so out of love for Christ and others.

2:4–8 In trying to persuade people, we may be tempted to alter our position just enough to make our message more palatable or to use flattery or praise. Paul never changed his *message* to make it more acceptable, but he did tailor his *methods* to each audience. Although our presentation must be altered to be appropriate to the situation, the truth of the gospel must never be compromised.

2:5 It's sickening to hear a person "butter up" someone. Flattery is empty, and it is a false cover-up for a person's real intentions. Christians should not be flatterers. Those who proclaim God's truth have a special responsibility to be honest. Are you honest and straightforward in your words and actions? Or do you tell people what they want to hear in order to get what you want or to get ahead?

2:6–8 When Paul was with the Thessalonians, he didn't flatter them, didn't seek their praise, and didn't become a burden to them. He and Silas completely focused their efforts on presenting God's message of salvation to the Thessalonians. This was important! The Thessalonian believers had their lives changed by God, not Paul; it was Christ's message they believed, not Paul's. When we witness for Christ, our focus should not be on the impressions we make. As true ministers of Christ, we should point to him, not to ourselves.

2:7 Gentleness is often overlooked as a personal trait in our society. Power and assertiveness gain more respect, even though noone likes to be bullied. Gentleness is love in action—being considerate, meeting the needs of others, allowing time for the other person to talk, and being willing to learn. It is an essential trait for both men and women. Maintain a gentle attitude in your relationships with others.

we were delighted to share with you not only the gospel of God but our lives as well,[j]
because you had become so dear to us. 9 Surely you remember, brothers, our toil and
hardship; we worked[k] night and day in order not to be a burden to anyone[l] while
we preached the gospel of God to you.
10 You are witnesses,[m] and so is God, of how holy,[n] righteous and blameless we
were among you who believed. 11 For you know that we dealt with each of you as a
father deals with his own children,[o] 12 encouraging, comforting and urging you to live
lives worthy[p] of God, who calls you into his kingdom and glory.
13 And we also thank God continually[q] because, when you received the word of
God,[r] which you heard from us, you accepted it not as the word of men, but as it
actually is, the word of God, which is at work in you who believe. 14 For you, brothers,
became imitators of God's churches in Judea,[s] which are in Christ Jesus: You
suffered from your own countrymen[t] the same things those churches suffered from
the Jews, 15 who killed the Lord Jesus[u] and the prophets[v] and also drove us out. They
displease God and are hostile to all men 16 in their effort to keep us from speaking to
the Gentiles[w] so that they may be saved. In this way they always heap up their sins
to the limit.[x] The wrath of God has come upon them at last.[a]

Paul's Longing to See the Thessalonians

17 But, brothers, when we were torn away from you for a short time (in person, not
in thought),[y] out of our intense longing we made every effort to see you.[z] 18 For we
wanted to come to you—certainly I, Paul, did, again and again—but Satan[a] stopped
us.[b] 19 For what is our hope, our joy, or the crown[c] in which we will glory[d] in the
presence of our Lord Jesus when he comes?[e] Is it not you? 20 Indeed, you are our
glory[f] and joy.

3 So when we could stand it no longer,[a] we thought it best to be left by ourselves
in Athens.[b] 2 We sent Timothy, who is our brother and God's fellow-worker[a]
in spreading the gospel of Christ, to strengthen and encourage you in your faith, 3 so

a *16* Or *them fully* a *2* Some manuscripts *brother and fellow-worker*; other manuscripts *brother and God's servant*

2:8 [j]2Co 12:15; 1Jn 3:16
2:9 [k]Ac 18:3 [l]2Th 3:8
2:10 [m]1Th 1:5 [n]2Co 1:12
2:11 [o]ver 7; 1Co 4:14
2:12 [p]Eph 4:1
2:13 [q]1Th 1:2 [r]Heb 4:12
2:14 [s]Gal 1:22 [t]Ac 17:5; 2Th 1:4
2:15 [u]Ac 2:23 [v]Mt 5:12
2:16 [w]Ac 13:45, 50 [x]Mt 23:32
2:17 [y]1Co 5:3; Col 2:5 [z]1Th 3:10
2:18 [a]Mt 4:10 [b]Ro 1:13; 15:22
2:19 [c]Php 4:1 [d]2Co 1:14 [e]Mt 16:27; 1Th 3:13
2:20 [f]2Co 1:14
3:1 [a]ver 5 [b]Ac 17:15

2:9 Although Paul had the right to receive financial support from the people he taught, he supported himself as a tentmaker (Acts 18:3) so that he wouldn't be a burden to the new Thessalonian believers.

2:11 No loving father would neglect the safety of his children, allowing them to walk into circumstances that might be harmful or fatal. In the same way, we must take new believers under our wing until they are mature enough to stand firm in their faith. We must help new Christians become strong enough to influence others for the sake of the gospel.

2:11, 12 By his words and example, Paul encouraged the Thessalonians to live in such a way that would be worthy of God. Is there anything about your daily life that would embarrass God? What do people think of God from watching you?

2:13 In the New Testament, *the word of God* usually refers to the preaching of the gospel, the Old Testament, or Jesus Christ himself. Today we often apply it only to the Bible. Remember that Jesus Christ himself is the Word (John 1:1).

2:14 Just as the Jewish Christians in Jerusalem were persecuted by other Jews, so the Gentile Christians in Thessalonica were persecuted by their fellow Gentiles. Persecution is discouraging, especially when it comes from your own people. When you take a stand for Christ, you may face opposition, disapproval, and ridicule from your neighbours, friends, and even family members.

2:14 When Paul refers to the Jews, he is talking about certain Jews who opposed his preaching of the gospel. He does not mean all Jews. Many of Paul's converts were Jewish. Paul himself was a Jew (2 Corinthians 11:22).

2:15, 16 Why were so many Jews opposed to Christianity? (1) Although the Jewish religion had been declared legal by the Roman government, it still had a tenuous relationship with the government. At this time, Christianity was viewed as a sect of Judaism. The Jews were afraid that reprisals levelled against the Christians might be expanded to include them. (2) The Jewish leaders thought Jesus was a false prophet, and they didn't want his teachings to spread. (3) They feared that if many Jews were drawn away, their own political position might be weakened. (4) They were proud of their special status as God's chosen people, and they resented the fact that Gentiles could be full members within the Christian church.

2:18 Satan is real. He is called "the god of this age" (2 Corinthians 4:4) and "the ruler of the kingdom of the air" (Ephesians 2:2). We don't know exactly what hindered Paul from returning to Thessalonica—opposition, illness, travel complications, or a direct attack by Satan—but Satan worked in some way to keep him away. Many of the difficulties that prevent us from accomplishing God's work can be attributed to Satan (see Ephesians 6:12).

2:20 The ultimate reward for Paul's ministry was not money, prestige, or fame, but new believers whose lives had been changed by God through the preaching of the gospel. This was why he longed to see them. No matter what ministry God has given to you, your highest reward and greatest joy should be those who come to believe in Christ and are growing in him.

3:1–3 Some think that troubles are always caused by sin or a lack of faith. Trials may be a part of God's plan for believers. Experiencing problems and persecutions can build character (James 1:2–4), perseverance (Romans 5:3–5), and sensitivity towards others who also face trouble (2 Corinthians 1:3–7). Problems are unavoidable for God's people. Your troubles may be a sign of effective Christian living.

3:1–4 Because Paul could not return to Thessalonica (2:18), he sent Timothy as his representative. According to Acts 17:10, Paul

that no-one would be unsettled by these trials. You know quite well that we were
destined for them.[c] 4In fact, when we were with you, we kept telling you that we
would be persecuted. And it turned out that way, as you well know.[d] 5For this reason,
when I could stand it no longer,[e] I sent to find out about your faith. I was afraid that
in some way the tempter[f] might have tempted you and our efforts might have been
useless.[g]

Timothy's Encouraging Report

6But Timothy has just now come to us from you[h] and has brought good news about
your faith and love.[i] He has told us that you always have pleasant memories of us
and that you long to see us, just as we also long to see you. 7Therefore, brothers, in
all our distress and persecution we were encouraged about you because of your faith.
8For now we really live, since you are standing firm[j] in the Lord. 9How can we thank
God enough for you[k] in return for all the joy we have in the presence of our God
because of you? 10Night and day we pray[l] most earnestly that we may see you again[m]
and supply what is lacking in your faith.
11Now may our God and Father himself and our Lord Jesus clear the way for us
to come to you. 12May the Lord make your love increase and overflow for each other[n]
and for everyone else, just as ours does for you. 13May he strengthen your hearts so
that you will be blameless[o] and holy in the presence of our God and Father when
our Lord Jesus comes[p] with all his holy ones.

2. Watchfulness for the Lord

Living to Please God

4 Finally, brothers,[a] we instructed you how to live in order to please God,[b] as
in fact you are living. Now we ask you and urge you in the Lord Jesus to do this
more and more. 2For you know what instructions we gave you by the authority of the
Lord Jesus.
3It is God's will that you should be sanctified: that you should avoid sexual

3:3 [c]Ac 9:16; 14:22
3:4 [d]1Th 2:14
3:5 [e]ver 1 [f]Mt 4:3 [g]Gal 2:2; Php 2:16
3:6 [h]Ac 18:5 [i]1Th 1:3
3:8 [j]1Co 16:13
3:9 [k]1Th 1:2
3:10 [l]2Ti 1:3 [m]1Th 2:17
3:12 [n]1Th 4:9, 10
3:13 [o]1Co 1:8 [p]1Th 2:19
4:1 [a]2Co 13:11 [b]2Co 5:9

---

left Thessalonica and went to Berea. When trouble broke out in Berea, some Christians took Paul to Athens, while Silas and Timothy stayed behind (Acts 17:13–15). Then Paul directed Silas and Timothy to join him in Athens. Later Paul sent Timothy to encourage the Thessalonian Christians to be strong in their faith in the face of persecution and other troubles.

3:4 Some people turn to God with the hope of escaping suffering on earth. But God doesn't promise that. Instead he gives us power to grow through our sufferings. The Christian life involves obedience to Christ despite temptations and hardships.

3:5 Satan ("the tempter") is the most powerful of the evil spirits. His power can affect both the spiritual world (Ephesians 2:1–3; 6:10–12) and the physical world (2 Corinthians 12:7–10). Satan even tempted Jesus (Matthew 4:1–11). But Jesus defeated Satan when he died on the cross for our sins and rose again to bring us new life. At the proper time God will overthrow Satan for ever (Revelation 20:7–10).

3:7, 8 During persecution or pressure, believers should encourage one another. Christians who stand firm in the Lord encourage both ministers and teachers (who can see the benefit of their work in those who remain faithful), and also those who are new in their faith (who can learn from the steadfastness of the mature).

3:9, 10 It brings great joy to a Christian to see another person come to faith in Christ and mature in that faith. Paul experienced this joy countless times. He thanked God for those who had come to know Christ and for their strong faith. He also prayed for their continued growth. If there are new Christians who have brought you joy, thank God for them and support them as they continue to grow in the faith.

3:11 Paul wanted to return to Thessalonica. We have no record that he was able to do so; but when he was travelling through Asia on his third journey, he was joined by Aristarchus and Secundus, who were from Thessalonica (Acts 20:4, 5).

3:11–13 "When our Lord Jesus comes with all his holy ones" refers to the second coming of Christ when he will establish his eternal kingdom. At that time, Christ will gather all believers, those who have died and those who are alive, into one united family under his rule. All believers from all times, including these Thessalonians, will be with Christ in his kingdom.

3:12 If we are full of God's love, it will overflow to others. It's not enough merely to be courteous to others; we must actively and persistently show love to them. Our love should be growing continually. If your capacity to love has remained unchanged for some time, ask God to fill you again with his never-ending supply. Then look for opportunities to express his love.

4:1–8 Sexual standards were very low in the Roman empire, and in many societies today they are not any higher. The temptation to engage in sexual intercourse outside the marriage relationship has always been powerful. Giving in to that temptation can have disastrous results. Sexual sins always hurt someone: individuals, families, businesses, churches. Besides the physical consequences, there are also spiritual consequences. For more on why sexual sin is so harmful, see the note on 1 Corinthians 6:18.

4:1–8 Sexual desires and activities must be placed under Christ's control. God created sex for procreation and pleasure, and as an expression of love between a husband and wife. Sexual experience must be limited to the marriage relationship to avoid hurting ourselves, our relationship to God, and our relationships with others.

4:3 Being *sanctified* or made holy is the process of living the Christian life. The Holy Spirit works in us, conforming us into the image of Christ (Romans 8:29).

immorality;[c] 4that each of you should learn to control his own body[a][d] in a way that
is holy and honourable, 5not in passionate lust[e] like the heathen,[f] who do not know
God; 6and that in this matter no-one should wrong his brother or take advantage of
him.[g] The Lord will punish men for all such sins,[h] as we have already told you and
warned you. 7For God did not call us to be impure, but to live a holy life.[i] 8Therefore,
he who rejects this instruction does not reject man but God, who gives you his Holy
Spirit.[j]
9Now about brotherly love[k] we do not need to write to you,[l] for you yourselves
have been taught by God to love each other.[m] 10And in fact, you do love all the
brothers throughout Macedonia.[n] Yet we urge you, brothers, to do so more and
more.[o]
11Make it your ambition to lead a quiet life, to mind your own business and to work
with your hands,[p] just as we told you, 12so that your daily life may win the respect
of outsiders[q] and so that you will not be dependent on anybody.

The Coming of the Lord

13Brothers, we do not want you to be ignorant about those who fall asleep, or to
grieve like the rest of men, who have no hope.[r] 14We believe that Jesus died and
rose again and so we believe that God will bring with Jesus those who have fallen
asleep in him.[s] 15According to the Lord's own word, we tell you that we who are
still alive, who are left till the coming of the Lord, will certainly not precede those
who have fallen asleep.[t] 16For the Lord himself will come down from heaven, with
a loud command, with the voice of the archangel and with the trumpet call of God,[u]
and the dead in Christ will rise first.[v] 17After that, we who are still alive and are left[w]
will be caught up together with them in the clouds[x] to meet the Lord in the air. And
so we will be with the Lord[y] for ever. 18Therefore encourage each other with these
words.

5 Now, brothers, about times and dates[a] we do not need to write to you,[b] 2for
you know very well that the day of the Lord[c] will come like a thief in the night.[d]
3While people are saying, "Peace and safety", destruction will come on them suddenly, as labour pains on a pregnant woman, and they will not escape.
4But you, brothers, are not in darkness[e] so that this day should surprise you like
a thief. 5You are all sons of the light and sons of the day. We do not belong to the

a 4 Or *learn to live with his own wife*; or *learn to acquire a wife*

4:3 [c]1Co 6:18
4:4 [d]1Co 7:2, 9
4:5 [e]Ro 1:26 [f]Eph 4:17
4:6 [g]1Co 6:8 [h]Heb 13:4
4:7 [i]Lev 11:44; 1Pe 1:15
4:8 [j]Ro 5:5; Gal 4:6
4:9 [k]Ro 12:10 [l]1Th 5:1 [m]Jn 13:34
4:10 [n]1Th 1:7 [o]1Th 3:12
4:11 [p]Eph 4:28; 2Th 3:10-12
4:12 [q]Mk 4:11
4:13 [r]Eph 2:12
4:14 [s]1Co 15:18
4:15 [t]1Co 15:52
4:16 [u]Mt 24:31 [v]1Co 15:23; 2Th 2:1
4:17 [w]1Co 15:52 [x]Ac 1:9; Rev 11:12 [y]Jn 12:26
5:1 [a]Ac 1:7 [b]1Th 4:9
5:2 [c]1Co 1:8 [d]2Pe 3:10
5:4 [e]Ac 26:18; 1Jn 2:8

4:11, 12 There is more to Christian living than simply loving other Christians. We must be responsible in all areas of life. Some of the Thessalonian Christians had adopted a life of idleness, depending on others for handouts. Some Greeks looked down on manual labour. So Paul told the Thessalonians to work hard and live a quiet life. You can't be effective in sharing your faith with others if they don't respect you. Whatever you do, do it faithfully and be a positive force in society.

4:13ff The Thessalonians were wondering why many of their fellow believers had fallen asleep (died) and what would happen to them when Christ returned. Paul wanted the Thessalonians to understand that death is not the end of the story. When Christ returns, all believers – dead and alive – will be reunited, never to suffer or die again.

4:15 What does Paul mean when he says, "according to the Lord's own word"? Either this was something that the Lord had revealed directly to Paul, or it was a teaching of Jesus that had been passed along orally by the apostles and other Christians.

4:15–18 Knowing exactly *when* the dead will be raised, in relation to the other events at the second coming, is not as important as knowing why Paul wrote these words – to challenge believers to comfort and encourage one another when loved ones die. This passage can be a great comfort when any believer dies. The same love that should unite believers in this life (4:9) will unite believers when Christ returns and reigns for eternity.

4:15–18 Because Jesus Christ came back to life, so will all believers. All Christians, including those living when Christ returns, will live with Christ for ever. Therefore, we need not despair when loved ones die or world events take a tragic turn. God will turn our tragedies to triumphs, our poverty to riches, our pain to glory, and our defeat to victory. All believers throughout history will stand reunited in God's very presence, safe and secure. As Paul comforted the Thessalonians with the promise of the resurrection, so we should comfort and reassure each other with this great hope.

4:16 An *archangel* is a high or holy angel appointed to a special task. Michael is the only archangel mentioned in the New Testament (see Jude 9).

5:1 "Times and dates" refers to the knowledge of what will happen in the future, specifically to the return of Christ.

5:1–3 Efforts to determine the date of Christ's return are foolish. Don't be misled by anyone who claims to know. We are told here that no-one knows and that even believers will be surprised. The Lord will return suddenly and unexpectedly, warns Paul, so be ready! Because no-one knows when Jesus will come back to earth, we should be ready at all times. Suppose he were to return today. How would he find you living? Are you ready to meet him? Live each day prepared to welcome Christ.

5:2 The "day of the Lord" is a future time when God will intervene directly and dramatically in world affairs. Predicted and discussed often in the Old Testament (Isaiah 13:6–12; Joel 2:28–32; Zephaniah 1:14–18), the day of the Lord will include both punishment and blessing. Christ will judge sin and set up his eternal kingdom.

5:6 [f]Ro 13:11
5:7 [g]Ac 2:15; 2Pe 2:13
5:8 [h]Eph 6:14 [i]Ro 8:24 [j]Eph 6:17
5:9 [k]2Th 2:13, 14
5:10 [l]2Co 5:15
5:12 [m]1Ti 5:17; Heb 13:17
5:13 [n]Mk 9:50
5:14 [o]2Th 3:6, 7, 11 [p]Ro 14:1
5:15 [q]1Pe 3:9 [r]Gal 6:10; Eph 4:32
5:16 [s]Php 4:4
5:19 [t]Eph 4:30
5:20 [u]1Co 14:1-40
5:21 [v]1Co 14:29; 1Jn 4:1

night or to the darkness. 6So then, let us not be like others, who are asleep,[f] but let
us be alert and self-controlled. 7For those who sleep, sleep at night, and those who
get drunk, get drunk at night.[g] 8But since we belong to the day, let us be self-
controlled, putting on faith and love as a breastplate,[h] and the hope of salvation[i]
as a helmet.[j] 9For God did not appoint us to suffer wrath but to receive salvation
through our Lord Jesus Christ.[k] 10He died for us so that, whether we are awake or
asleep, we may live together with him.[l] 11Therefore encourage one another and build
each other up, just as in fact you are doing.

Final Instructions

12Now we ask you, brothers, to respect those who work hard among you, who are
over you in the Lord[m] and who admonish you. 13Hold them in the highest regard in
love because of their work. Live in peace with each other.[n] 14And we urge you,
brothers, warn those who are idle,[o] encourage the timid, help the weak,[p] be patient
with everyone. 15Make sure that nobody pays back wrong for wrong,[q] but always
try to be kind to each other[r] and to everyone else.
16Be joyful always;[s] 17pray continually; 18give thanks in all circumstances, for this
is God's will for you in Christ Jesus.
19Do not put out the Spirit's fire;[t] 20do not treat prophecies[u] with contempt. 21Test
everything.[v] Hold on to the good. 22Avoid every kind of evil.

THE EVENTS OF CHRIST'S RETURN

1. Christ will return visibly, with a loud command.
2. There will be an unmistakable cry from an angel.
3. There will be a trumpet fanfare such as has never been heard.
4. Believers in Christ who are dead will rise from their graves.
5. Believers who are alive will be caught up in the clouds to meet Christ.

While Christians have often disagreed about what events will lead up to the return of Christ, there has been less disagreement about what will happen once Christ does return.

5:8 For more about the Christian's armour, see Ephesians 6:13–17.

5:9–11 As you near the end of a long race, your legs ache, your throat burns, and your whole body cries out for you to stop. This is when friends and fans are most valuable. Their encouragement helps you push through the pain to the finish line. In the same way, Christians are to encourage one another. A word of encouragement offered at the right moment can be the difference between finishing well and collapsing along the way. Look around you. Be sensitive to others' need for encouragement, and offer supportive words or actions.

5:12 "Those who work hard among you, who are over you in the Lord" probably refers to elders and deacons in the church.

5:12, 13 How can you show respect to and hold in the "highest regard" your pastor and other church leaders? Express your appreciation, tell them how you have been helped by their leadership and teaching, and thank them for their ministry in your life. If you say nothing, how will they know where you stand? Remember, they need and deserve your support and love.

5:14 Don't loaf around with the idle; warn them. Don't yell at the timid and weak; encourage and help them. At times it's difficult to distinguish between idleness and timidity. Two people may be doing nothing – one out of laziness and the other out of shyness or fear of doing something wrong. The key to ministry is sensitivity: sensing the condition of each person and offering the appropriate remedy for each situation. You can't help effectively until you know the problem. You can't apply the medicine until you know where the wound is.

5:16–18 Our joy, prayers, and thankfulness should not fluctuate with our circumstances or feelings. Obeying these three commands – be joyful, pray continually, and give thanks – often goes against our natural inclinations. When we make a conscious decision to do what God says, however, we will begin to see people in a new perspective. When we do God's will, we will find it easier to be joyful and thankful.

5:17 We cannot spend all our time on our knees, but it is possible to have a prayerful attitude at all times. This attitude is built upon acknowledging our dependence on God, realising his presence within us, and determining to obey him fully. Then we will find it natural to pray frequent, spontaneous, short prayers. A prayerful attitude is not a substitute for regular times of prayer but should be an outgrowth of those times.

5:18 Paul was not teaching that we should thank God *for* everything that happens to us, but *in* everything. Evil does not come from God, so we should not thank him for it. But when evil strikes, we can still be thankful for God's presence and for the good that he will accomplish through the distress.

5:19 By warning us not to "put out the Spirit's fire", Paul means that we should not ignore or toss aside the gifts the Holy Spirit gives. Here, he mentions prophecy (5:20); in 1 Corinthians 14:39, he mentions tongues. Sometimes spiritual gifts are controversial, and they may cause division in a church. Rather than trying to solve the problems, some Christians prefer to smother the gifts. This impoverishes the church. We should not stifle the Holy Spirit's work in anyone's life but encourage the full expression of these gifts to benefit the whole body of Christ.

5:20, 21 We shouldn't make fun of those who don't agree with what we believe ("treat prophecies with contempt"), but we should always "test everything", checking their words against the Bible. We are on dangerous ground if we scoff at a person who speaks the truth. Instead we should carefully check out what people say, accepting what is true and rejecting what is false.

5:22–24 As Christians, we cannot avoid every kind of evil because we live in a sinful world. We can, however, make sure that we don't give evil a foothold by avoiding tempting situations and concentrating on obeying God.

23May God himself, the God of peace,[w] sanctify you through and through. May
your whole spirit, soul and body be kept blameless at the coming of our Lord Jesus
Christ. 24The one who calls you is faithful[x] and he will do it.

25Brothers, pray for us.[y] 26Greet all the brothers with a holy kiss.[z] 27I charge you
before the Lord to have this letter read to all the brothers.[a]
28The grace of our Lord Jesus Christ be with you.[b]

5:23 [w]Ro 15:33
5:24 [x]1Co 1:9
5:25 [y]Eph 6:19
5:26 [z]Ro 16:16
5:27 [a]Col 4:16
5:28 [b]Ro 16:20

CHECKLIST FOR ENCOURAGERS

The command to encourage others is found throughout the Bible. In 5:11–23, Paul gives many specific examples of how we can encourage others.

Reference	*Example*	*Suggested application*
5:11	Build each other up.	Point out to someone a quality you appreciate in him or her.
5:12	Respect leaders.	Look for ways to co-operate.
5:13	Hold leaders in highest regard.	Hold back your next critical comment about those in positions of responsibility. Say "thank you" to your leaders for their efforts.
5:13	Live in peace.	Search for ways to get on with others.
5:14	Warn the idle.	Challenge someone to join you in a project.
5:14	Encourage the timid.	Encourage those who are timid by reminding them of God's promises.
5:14	Help the weak.	Support those who are weak by loving them and praying for them.
5:14	Be patient.	Think of a situation that tries your patience and plan in advance how you can stay calm.
5:15	Resist revenge.	Instead of planning to get even with those who mistreat you, do good to them.
5:16	Be joyful.	Remember that even in the midst of turmoil, God is in control.
5:17	Pray continually.	God is always with you—talk to him.
5:18	Give thanks.	Make a list of all the gifts God has given you, giving thanks to God for each one.
5:19	Do not put out the Spirit's fire.	Co-operate with the Spirit the next time he prompts you to participate in a Christian meeting.
5:20	Do not treat prophecies with contempt.	Receive God's word from those who speak for him.
5:22	Avoid every kind of evil.	Avoid situations where you will be drawn into temptation.
5:23	Count on God's constant help.	Realise that the Christian life is to be lived not in our own strength but through God's power.

5:23 The spirit, soul, and body refer not so much to the distinct parts of a person as to the entire being of a person. This expression is Paul's way of saying that God must be involved in *every* aspect of our lives. It is wrong to think that we can separate our spiritual lives from everything else, obeying God only in some ethereal sense or living for him only one day each week. Christ must control *all* of us, not just a "religious" part.

5:27 For every Christian to hear this letter, it had to be read in a public meeting—there were not enough copies to circulate. Paul wanted to make sure that everyone had the opportunity to hear his message because he was answering important questions and offering needed encouragement.

5:28 The Thessalonian church was young, and they needed help and encouragement. Both the persecution they faced and the temptations of their pagan culture were potential problems for these new Christians. Paul wrote, therefore, to strengthen their faith and bolster their resistance to persecution and temptation. We too have a responsibility to help new believers, and to make sure that they continue in their faith and don't become sidetracked by wrong beliefs or practices. First Thessalonians can better equip us to help our brothers and sisters in Christ.

2 THESSALONIANS

"BUT I thought he said . . ." "I'm sure he meant . . ." "It is clear to me that we should . . ." "I disagree. I think we must . . ."

Effective communication is difficult; often the message sent is *not* the message received in the home, marketplace, neighbourhood, or church. Even when clearly stated or written, words can be misinterpreted and misunderstood, especially when filtered through the sieve of prejudices and preconceptions.

Paul faced this problem with the Thessalonians. He had written to them earlier to help them grow in the faith, comforting and encouraging them by affirming the reality of Christ's return. Just a few months later, however, word came from Thessalonica that some had misunderstood Paul's teaching about the second coming. His announcement that Christ could come at any moment had caused some to stop working and just wait, rationalising their idleness by pointing to Paul's teaching. Adding fuel to this fire was the continued persecution of the church. Many felt that indeed this must be the "day of the Lord".

Responding quickly, Paul sent a second letter to this young church. In it he gave further instruction concerning the second coming and the day of the Lord (2:1, 2). This letter, therefore, continues the subject of 1 Thessalonians and is a call to continued courage and consistent conduct.

The letter begins with Paul's trademark—a personal greeting and a statement of thanksgiving for their faith (1:1–3). He mentions their perseverance in spite of their persecution and trials (1:4) and uses this situation to broach the subject of Christ's return. At that time, Christ will vindicate the righteous who endure and will punish the wicked (1:5–12).

Paul then directly answers the misunderstanding concerning the timing of the events of the end times. He tells them not to listen to rumours and reports that the day of the Lord has already begun (2:1, 2), because a number of events must occur before Christ returns (2:3–12). Meanwhile, they should stand firm for Christ's truth (2:13–15), receive God's encouragement and hope (2:16, 17), pray for strength and for the spread of the Lord's message (3:1–5), and warn those who are idle (3:6–15). Paul ends with personal greetings and a benediction (3:16–18).

Almost 2,000 years later, we stand much closer to the time of Christ's return; but we also would be wrong to see his imminent appearance as an excuse for idle waiting and heavenward gazing. Being prepared for his coming means spreading the gospel, reaching out to those in need, and building the church, his body. As you read 2 Thessalonians, then, see clearly the reality of his return and your responsibility to live for him until that day.

VITAL STATISTICS

PURPOSE:
To clear up the confusion about the second coming of Christ

AUTHOR:
Paul

TO WHOM WRITTEN:
The church at Thessalonica, and all believers everywhere

DATE WRITTEN:
About A.D. 51 or 52, a few months after 1 Thessalonians, from Corinth

SETTING:
Many in the church were confused about the timing of Christ's return. Because of mounting persecution, they thought the day of the Lord must be imminent, and they interpreted Paul's first letter to say that the second coming would be at any moment. In the light of this misunderstanding, many persisted in being idle and disorderly, with the excuse of waiting for Christ's return.

KEY VERSE:
"May the Lord direct your hearts into God's love and Christ's perseverance" (3:5).

KEY PEOPLE:
Paul, Silas, Timothy

KEY PLACE:
Thessalonica

SPECIAL FEATURES:
This is a follow-up letter to 1 Thessalonians. In this letter, Paul indicates various events that must precede the second coming of Christ.

THE BLUEPRINT

1. The bright hope of Christ's return (1:1—2:17)
2. Living in the light of Christ's return (3:1–18)

Paul wrote to encourage those who were facing persecution and to correct a misunderstanding about the timing of Christ's return. The teaching about the Lord's return promoted idleness in this young church. The imminent coming of Christ should never make us idle; we should be even more busy—living purely, using our time well, and working for his kingdom. We must work not only during easy times when it is convenient, but also during difficult times. Christians must patiently watch for Christ's return, and work for him while we wait.

MEGATHEMES

THEME	EXPLANATION	IMPORTANCE
Persecution	Paul encouraged the church to persevere in spite of troubles and trials. God will bring victory to his faithful followers and judge those who persecute them.	God promises to reward our faith by giving us his power and helping us to bear persecution. Suffering for our faith will strengthen us to serve Christ. We must be faithful to him.
Christ's Return	Since Paul had said that the Lord could come at any moment, some of the Thessalonian believers had stopped working in order to wait for Christ.	Christ will return and bring total victory to all who trust in him. If we are ready, we need not be concerned about *when* he will return. We should stand firm, keep working, and wait for Christ.
Great Rebellion	Before Christ's return, there will be a great rebellion against God led by the man of lawlessness (the antichrist). God will remove all the restraints on evil before he brings judgment on the rebels. The antichrist will attempt to deceive many.	We should not be afraid when we see evil increase. God is in control, no matter how evil the world becomes. God guards us during Satan's attacks. We can have victory over evil by remaining faithful to God.
Persistence	Because church members had stopped working and become disorderly and disobedient, Paul chastised them for their idleness. He called them to show courage and true Christian conduct.	We must never get so tired of doing right that we give up. We can be persistent by making the most of our time and talent. Our endurance will be rewarded.

1. The bright hope of Christ's return

1 Paul, Silas[a] and Timothy,[a]

To the church of the Thessalonians in God our Father and the Lord Jesus Christ:

2 Grace and peace to you from God the Father and the Lord Jesus Christ.[b]

a 1 Greek *Silvanus*, a variant of *Silas*

1:1 [a] Ac 16:1; 1Th 1:1
1:2 [b] Ro 1:7

1:1 Paul wrote this letter from Corinth less than a year after he wrote 1 Thessalonians. He and his companions, Timothy and Silas, had visited Thessalonica on Paul's second missionary journey (Acts 17:1–10). They established the church there, but Paul had to leave suddenly because of persecution. This prompted him to write his first letter (1 Thessalonians), which contains words of comfort and encouragement. Paul then heard how the Thessalonians had responded to this letter. The good news was that they were continuing to grow in their faith. But the bad news was that false teachings about Christ's return were spreading, leading many to leave their jobs and wait for the end of the world. So Paul wrote to them again. While the purpose of Paul's first letter was to comfort the Thessalonians with the assurance of Christ's second coming, the purpose of his second letter is to correct false teaching about the second coming.

1:1 Paul, Silas, and Timothy were together in Corinth (Acts 18:5). Paul wrote this letter on behalf of all three of them. Paul often included Timothy as a co-sender of his letters (see Philippians 1:1; Colossians 1:1; 1 Thessalonians 1:1). For more information about Paul, see his Profile in Acts 9. Timothy's Profile is found in 1 Timothy, and Silas' Profile is in Acts 16.

1:1 Thessalonica was the capital and largest city of the Roman

1:3 [c]1Th 3:12
1:4 [d]2Co 7:14 [e]1Th 1:3 [f]1Th 2:14
1:5 [g]Php 1:28
1:6 [h]Col 3:25; Rev 6:10

Thanksgiving and Prayer

3We ought always to thank God for you, brothers, and rightly so, because your faith
is growing more and more, and the love every one of you has for each other is
increasing.[c] 4Therefore, among God's churches we boast[d] about your perseverance
and faith[e] in all the persecutions and trials you are enduring.[f]
5All this is evidence[g] that God's judgment is right, and as a result you will be
counted worthy of the kingdom of God, for which you are suffering. 6God is just:
He will pay back trouble to those who trouble you[h] 7and give relief to you who are
troubled, and to us as well. This will happen when the Lord Jesus is revealed from

LOCATION OF THESSALONICA
After Paul visited Thessalonica on his second missionary journey, he went on to Berea, Athens, and Corinth (Acts 17, 18). From Corinth, Paul wrote his two letters to the Thessalonian church.

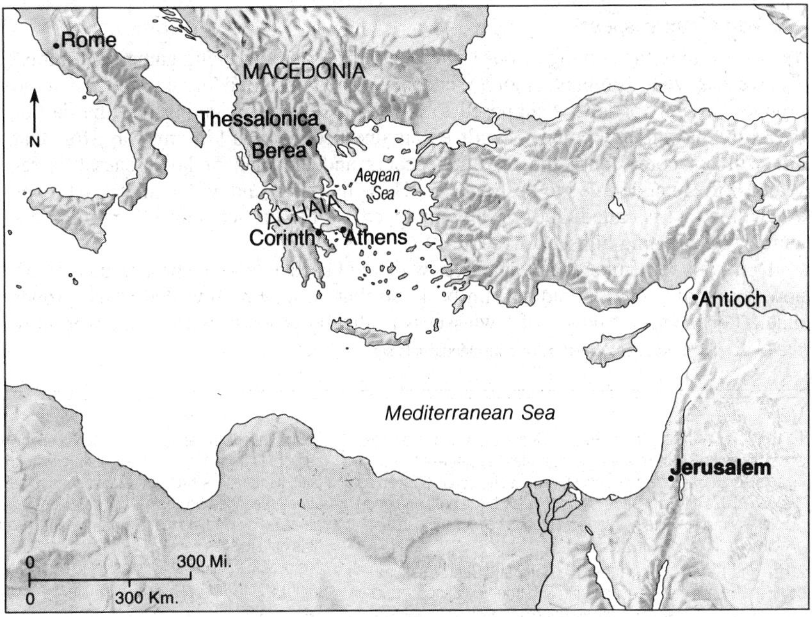

province of Macedonia. The most important Roman highway—extending from Rome to the Orient—went through Thessalonica. This highway, along with the city's thriving harbour, made Thessalonica one of the wealthiest and most flourishing trade centres in the Roman empire. Recognised as a free city, Thessalonica was allowed self-rule and was exempted from most of the restrictions placed by Rome on other cities. Because of this open climate, however, the city had many pagan religions and cultural influences that challenged the Christians' faith.

1:3 Regardless of the contents of Paul's letters, his style was affirming. Paul began most of his letters by stating what he most appreciated about his readers and the joy he felt because of their faith in God. We too should look for ways to encourage and build up other believers.

1:4 The keys to surviving persecution and trials are perseverance and faith. When we are faced with crushing troubles, we can have faith that God is using our trials for our good and for his glory. Knowing that God is fair and just will give us patience in our suffering because we know that he has not forgotten us. In God's perfect timing, he will relieve our suffering and punish those who persecute us. Can you trust God's timing?

1:4–6 Paul had been persecuted during his first visit to Thessalonica (Acts 17:5–9). No doubt those who had responded to his message and had become Christians were continuing to be persecuted by both Jews and Gentiles. In Paul's first letter to the Thessalonians, he said that Christ's return would bring deliverance from persecution and judgment on the persecutors. But this caused the people to expect Christ's return right away to rescue and vindicate them. So Paul had to point out that while waiting for God's kingdom, believers could and should learn perseverance and faith from their suffering.

1:5 As we live for Christ, we will experience troubles because we are trying to be God's people in a perverse world. Some people say that troubles are the result of sin or lack of faith, but Paul teaches that they may be a part of God's plan for believers. Our problems can help us look upward and forward, instead of inward (Mark 13:35, 36; Philippians 3:13, 14); they can build strong character (Romans 5:3, 4); and they can provide us with opportunities to comfort others who are also struggling (2 Corinthians 1:3–5). Your troubles may be an indication that you are taking a stand for Christ.

1:5–7 There are two dimensions to the relief mentioned by Paul. We can gain relief in knowing that our sufferings are strengthening us, making us ready for Christ's kingdom. We can also gain relief in the fact that one day everyone will stand before God; at that time, wrongs will be righted, judgment will be pronounced, and evil will be terminated.

1:7–9 The "everlasting destruction" that Paul describes is the lake of fire (see Revelation 20:14)—the place of eternal separation from God. Those people who are separated from God in eternity no longer have any hope of salvation.

heaven in blazing fire with his powerful angels.[i] 8He will punish those who do not
know God[j] and do not obey the gospel of our Lord Jesus.[k] 9They will be punished
with everlasting destruction[l] and shut out from the presence of the Lord and from
the majesty of his power[m] 10on the day[n] he comes to be glorified[o] in his holy people
and to be marvelled at among all those who have believed. This includes you, because
you believed our testimony to you.[p]
11With this in mind, we constantly pray for you, that our God may count you
worthy[q] of his calling, and that by his power he may fulfil every good purpose of
yours and every act prompted by your faith.[r] 12We pray this so that the name of our
Lord Jesus may be glorified in you,[s] and you in him, according to the grace of our
God and the Lord Jesus Christ.[b]

The Man of Lawlessness

2 Concerning the coming of our Lord Jesus Christ and our being gathered to him,[a]
we ask you, brothers, 2not to become easily unsettled or alarmed by some
prophecy, report or letter[b] supposed to have come from us, saying that the day of
the Lord[c] has already come. 3Don't let anyone deceive you[d] in any way, for ⌊that
day will not come⌋ until the rebellion occurs and the man of lawlessness[a] is revealed,[e] the man doomed to destruction. 4He will oppose and will exalt himself over
everything that is called God[f] or is worshipped, so that he sets himself up in God's
temple, proclaiming himself to be God.[g]
5Don't you remember that when I was with you I used to tell you these things? 6And
now you know what is holding him back, so that he may be revealed at the proper
time. 7For the secret power of lawlessness is already at work; but the one who now

b *12* Or *God and Lord, Jesus Christ* **a** *3* Some manuscripts *sin*

1:7 [i]1Th 4:16; Jude 14
1:8 [j]Gal 4:8 [k]Ro 2:8
1:9 [l]Php 3:19; 2Pe 3:7 [m]2Th 2:8
1:10 [n]1Co 3:13 [o]Jn 17:10 [p]1Co 1:6
1:11 [q]ver 5 [r]1Th 1:3
1:12 [s]Php 2:9-11
2:1 [a]Mk 13:27; 1Th 4:15-17
2:2 [b]2Th 3:17 [c]1Co 1:8
2:3 [d]Eph 5:6-8 [e]Da 7:25; 8:25; 11:36; Rev 13:5, 6
2:4 [f]1Co 8:5 [g]Isa 14:13, 14; Eze 28:2

1:11, 12 Our "calling" from God, as Christians, is to become like Christ (Romans 8:29). This is a gradual, lifelong process that will be completed when we see Christ face to face (1 John 3:2). To be "worthy" of this calling means to *want* to do what is right and good (as Christ would). We're not perfect yet, but we're moving in that direction as God works in us.

2:1ff Paul describes the end of the world and Christ's second coming. He says that great suffering and trouble lie ahead, but evil will not prevail, because Christ will return to judge all people. Although Paul presents a few signs of the end times, his emphasis, like Jesus' (Mark 13), is the need for each person to prepare for Christ's return by living aright day by day. If we are ready, we won't have to be concerned about the preceding events or the timing of Christ's return. God controls all events. (See 1 Thessalonians 4 and 5 for Paul's earlier teaching on this subject.)

2:1, 2 In the Bible, the *day of the Lord* is used in two ways: it can mean the end times (beginning with Christ's birth and continuing until today), and it can mean the final judgment day (in the future). Because some false teachers were saying that judgment day had come, many believers were waiting expectantly for their vindication and for relief from suffering. But judgment day had not yet come; other events would have to happen first.

2:2 "Prophecy, report, or letter" could refer to the fact that false teaching had come from: (1) someone claiming to have had a divine revelation; (2) someone passing on a teaching as though it were from Paul; or (3) someone distributing a letter supposedly written by Paul.

2:3 Throughout history there have been individuals who epitomised evil and who were hostile to everything Christ stands for (see 1 John 2:18; 4:3; 2 John 7). These antichrists have lived in every generation and will continue to work their evil. Then just before Christ's second coming, "the man of lawlessness . . . the man doomed to destruction", a completely evil man, will arise. He will be Satan's tool, equipped with Satan's power (2:9). This lawless man will be *the* antichrist.

It is dangerous, however, to label any person as the antichrist and to try to predict Christ's coming based on that assumption. Paul mentions the antichrist, not so we might identify him specifically, but so we might be ready for anything that threatens our faith. If our faith is strong, we don't need to be afraid of what lies ahead, because we know that this lawless man has already been defeated by God, no matter how powerful he becomes or how terrible our situation seems. God is in control, and he will be victorious over the antichrist. Our task is to be prepared for Christ's return and to spread the gospel so that even more people will also be prepared.

2:3ff When Paul first wrote to the Thessalonians, they were in danger of losing hope in the second coming. Then they shifted to the opposite extreme – some of them thought that Jesus would be coming at any minute. Paul tried to restore the balance by describing certain events that would happen before Christ's return.

2:6, 7 Who holds back the lawless one? We do not know for certain. Three possibilities have been suggested: (1) government and law, which help to curb evil; (2) the ministry and activity of the church and the effects of the gospel; or (3) the Holy Spirit. The Bible is not clear on who this restrainer is, only that he will not restrain for ever. But we should not fear this time when the restraint is removed – God is far stronger than the man of lawlessness, and God will save his people.

2:7 "The secret power of lawlessness is already at work" means that the work that this antichrist will do is already going on. *Secret* means something no-one can discover, but something God will reveal. *Lawlessness* is the hidden, subtle, underlying force from which all sin springs. Civilisation still has a veneer of decency through law enforcement, education, science, and reason. Although we are horrified by criminal acts, we have yet to see the real horror of complete lawlessness. This will happen when "the one who now holds it back [possibly the Holy Spirit]. . . is taken out of the way". Why will God allow this to happen? To show people and nations their own sinfulness, and to show them by bitter experience the true alternative to the lordship of Christ. People totally without God can act no better than vicious animals. Lawlessness, to a certain extent, is already going on, but the man of lawlessness has not yet been revealed.

holds it back will continue to do so till he is taken out of the way. 8 And then the lawless
one will be revealed, whom the Lord Jesus will overthrow with the breath of his
mouth[h] and destroy by the splendour of his coming. 9 The coming of the lawless one
will be in accordance with the work of Satan displayed in all kinds of counterfeit
miracles, signs and wonders,[i] 10 and in every sort of evil that deceives those who are
perishing.[j] They perish because they refused to love the truth and so be saved. 11 For
this reason God sends them[k] a powerful delusion so that they will believe the lie 12 and
so that all will be condemned who have not believed the truth but have delighted in
wickedness.[l]

Stand Firm

13 But we ought always to thank God for you, brothers loved by the Lord, because
from the beginning God chose you[b][m] to be saved[n] through the sanctifying work of
the Spirit[o] and through belief in the truth. 14 He called you to this through our gospel,
that you might share in the glory of our Lord Jesus Christ. 15 So then, brothers, stand
firm[p] and hold to the teachings[c] we passed on to you,[q] whether by word of mouth
or by letter.

16 May our Lord Jesus Christ himself and God our Father, who loved us[r] and by
his grace gave us eternal encouragement and good hope, 17 encourage[s] your hearts
and strengthen[t] you in every good deed and word.

2. Living in the light of Christ's return

Request for Prayer

3 Finally, brothers,[a] pray for us[b] that the message of the Lord[c] may spread
rapidly and be honoured, just as it was with you. 2 And pray that we may be
delivered from wicked and evil men,[d] for not everyone has faith. 3 But the Lord is
faithful,[e] and he will strengthen and protect you from the evil one.[f] 4 We have
confidence[g] in the Lord that you are doing and will continue to do the things we
command. 5 May the Lord direct your hearts[h] into God's love and Christ's perseverance.

b *13* Some manuscripts *because God chose you as his firstfruits* **c** *15* Or *traditions*

2:8 [h]Isa 11:4; Rev 19:15
2:9 [i]Mt 24:24; Jn 4:48
2:10 [j]1Co 1:18
2:11 [k]Ro 1:28
2:12 [l]Ro 1:32
2:13 [m]Eph 1:4 [n]1Th 5:9 [o]1Pe 1:2
2:15 [p]1Co 16:13 [q]1Co 11:2
2:16 [r]Jn 3:16
2:17 [s]1Th 3:2 [t]2Th 3:3
3:1 [a]1Th 4:1 [b]1Th 5:25 [c]1Th 1:8
3:2 [d]Ro 15:31
3:3 [e]1Co 1:9 [f]Mt 5:37
3:4 [g]2Co 2:3
3:5 [h]1Ch 29:18

2:9 This lawless one will use "counterfeit miracles, signs, and wonders" to deceive and draw a following. Miracles from God can help strengthen our faith and lead people to Christ, but not all miracles are necessarily from God. Christ's miracles were significant, not just because of their power, but because of their purpose—to help, to heal, and to point us to God. The man of lawlessness will have power to do amazing things, but his power will be from Satan. He will use this power to destroy and to lead people away from God and towards himself. If any so-called religious personality draws attention only to himself or herself, his or her work is not from God.

2:10–12 This man of lawlessness with his power and miracles will deceive those who have refused to believe God's truth. God gives people freedom to turn their backs on him and believe Satan's lies. If they say no to the truth, they will experience the consequences of their sin.

2:13 Paul consistently taught that salvation begins and ends with God. We can do nothing to be saved on our own merit—we must accept God's gift of salvation (see the note on Ephesians 1:4). There is no other way to receive forgiveness from sin. Paul is encouraging the Thessalonian believers by reminding them that they were chosen by God from the beginning. *Sanctification* is the process of Christian growth through which the Holy Spirit makes us like Christ (Romans 8:29). See the note on 1:11, 12.

2:14 God worked through Paul and his companions to tell the Good News so that people could share in Christ's glory. It may seem strange that God works through us—fallible, unfaithful, untrustworthy human creatures. But he has given us the fantastic privilege of accomplishing his great mission—telling the world how to find salvation.

2:15 Paul knew that the Thessalonians would face pressure from persecutions, false teachers, worldliness, and apathy to waver from the truth and to leave the faith. So he urged them to "stand firm" and hold on to the truth they had been taught both through his letters and in person. We too may face persecution, false teachings, worldliness, and apathy. We should hold on to the truth of Christ's teachings because our lives depend on it. Never forget the reality of Christ's life and love!

3:1–3 Beneath the surface of the routine of daily life, a fierce struggle among invisible spiritual powers is being waged. Our main defence is prayer that God will protect us from the evil one and that he will strengthen us. (See also comments on Ephesians 6:10–19 concerning our armour for spiritual warfare.) The following guidelines can help you prepare for and survive satanic attacks: (1) take the threat of spiritual attack seriously; (2) pray for strength and help from God; (3) study the Bible to recognise Satan's style and tactics; (4) memorise Scripture so it will be a source of help no matter where you are; (5) associate with those who speak the truth; and (6) practise what you are taught by spiritual leaders.

Warning Against Idleness

6In the name of the Lord Jesus Christ,[i] we command you, brothers, to keep away
from[j] every brother who is idle[k] and does not live according to the teaching[a] you
received from us.[l] 7For you yourselves know how you ought to follow our example.[m] We were not idle when we were with you, 8nor did we eat anyone's food without
paying for it. On the contrary, we worked[n] night and day, labouring and toiling so
that we would not be a burden to any of you. 9We did this, not because we do not
have the right to such help,[o] but in order to make ourselves a model for you to
follow.[p] 10For even when we were with you,[q] we gave you this rule: "If a man will
not work,[r] he shall not eat."

11We hear that some among you are idle. They are not busy; they are busybodies.[s]
12Such people we command and urge in the Lord Jesus Christ[t] to settle down and
earn the bread they eat.[u] 13And as for you, brothers, never tire of doing what is
right.[v]

14If anyone does not obey our instruction in this letter, take special note of him.
Do not associate with him,[w] in order that he may feel ashamed. 15Yet do not regard
him as an enemy, but warn him as a brother.[x]

Final Greetings

16Now may the Lord of peace[y] himself give you peace at all times and in every
way. The Lord be with all of you.[z]

17I, Paul, write this greeting in my own hand,[a] which is the distinguishing mark
in all my letters. This is how I write.

18The grace of our Lord Jesus Christ be with you all.[b]

[a] 6 *Or tradition*

3:6 [i]1Co 5:4 [j]Ro 16:17 [k]ver 7, 11 [l]1Co 11:2
3:7 [m]1Co 4:16
3:8 [n]Ac 18:3; Eph 4:28
3:9 [o]1Co 9:4-14 [p]ver 7
3:10 [q]1Th 3:4 [r]1Th 4:11
3:11 [s]ver 6, 7; 1Ti 5:13
3:12 [t]1Th 4:1 [u]1Th 4:11; Eph 4:28
3:13 [v]Gal 6:9
3:14 [w]ver 6
3:15 [x]Gal 6:1; 1Th 5:14
3:16 [y]Ro 15:33 [z]Ru 2:4
3:17 [a]1Co 16:21
3:18 [b]Ro 16:20

3:6–10 Paul was writing here about the person who is lazy. Paul explained that when he and his companions were in Thessalonica, they worked hard, buying what they needed rather than becoming a burden to any of the believers. The rule they followed was, "If a man will not work, he shall not eat." There's a difference between leisure and laziness. Relaxation and recreation provide a necessary and much needed balance to our lives; but when it is time to work, Christians should jump right in. We should make the most of our talent and time, doing all we can to provide for ourselves and our dependants. Rest when you should be resting, and work when you should be working.

3:6–15 Some people in the Thessalonian church were falsely teaching that because Christ would return any day, people should set aside their responsibilities, leave work, do no future planning, and just wait for the Lord. But their lack of activity only led them into sin. They became a burden to the church, which was supporting them; they wasted time that could have been used for helping others; and they became "busybodies" (3:11). These church members may have thought that they were being more spiritual by not working, but Paul tells them to be responsible and get back to work. Being ready for Christ means obeying him in every area of life. Because we know that Christ is coming, we must live in such a way that our faith and our daily practice will please him when he arrives.

3:11, 12 A "busybody" is a gossip. An idle person who doesn't work ends up filling his or her time with less than helpful activities, like gossip. Rumours and hearsay are tantalising, exciting to hear, and make us feel like insiders. But they tear people down. If you often find your nose in other people's business, you may be underemployed. Look for a task to do for Christ or for your family, and get to work.

3:14, 15 Paul counselled the church to stop supporting financially and associating with those who persisted in their idleness. Hunger and loneliness can be very effective ways to make the idle person become productive. Paul was not advising coldness or cruelty, but the kind of tough love that a person would show a brother or sister.

3:18 The book of 2 Thessalonians is especially meaningful for those who are being persecuted or are under pressure because of their faith. In chapter 1 we are told what suffering can do for us. In chapter 2 we are assured of final victory. In chapter 3 we are encouraged to continue living responsibly in spite of difficult circumstances. Christ's return is more than a doctrine; it is a promise. It is not just for the future; it has a vital impact on how we live now.

1 TIMOTHY

WITHOUT trying, we model our values. Parents in particular demonstrate to their children what they consider important and valuable. "Like father, like son" is not just a well-worn cliché; it is a truth repeated in our homes. And experience proves that children often follow the lifestyles of their parents, repeating their successes and mistakes.

Timothy is a prime example of one who was influenced by godly relatives. His mother Eunice and grandmother Lois were Jewish believers who helped shape his life and promote his spiritual growth (2 Timothy 1:5; 3:15). The first "second generation" Christian mentioned in the New Testament, Timothy became Paul's protégé and pastor of the church at Ephesus. As a young minister, Timothy faced all sorts of pressures, conflicts, and challenges from the church and his surrounding culture. To counsel and encourage Timothy, Paul sent this very personal letter.

Paul wrote 1 Timothy in about A.D. 64, probably just prior to his final Roman imprisonment. Because he had appealed to Caesar, Paul was sent as a prisoner to Rome (see Acts 25—28). Most scholars believe that Paul was released in about A.D. 62 (possibly because the "statute of limitations" had expired), and that during the next few years he was able to travel. During this time, he wrote 1 Timothy and Titus. Soon, however, Emperor Nero began his campaign to eliminate Christianity. It is believed that during this time Paul was imprisoned again and eventually executed. During this second Roman imprisonment, Paul wrote 2 Timothy. Titus and the two letters to Timothy comprise what are called the "Pastoral Letters".

Paul's first letter to Timothy affirms their relationship (1:2). Paul begins his fatherly advice, warning Timothy about false teachers (1:3–11) and urging him to hold on to his faith in Christ (1:12–20). Next, Paul considers public worship, emphasising the importance of prayer (2:1–7) and order in church meetings (2:8–15). This leads to a discussion of the qualifications of church leaders—overseers and deacons. Here Paul lists specific criteria for each office (3:1–16).

Paul speaks again about false teachers, telling Timothy how to recognise them and respond to them (4:1–16). Next, he gives practical advice on pastoral care to the young and old (5:1, 2), widows (5:3–16), elders (5:17–25), and slaves (6:1, 2). Paul concludes by exhorting Timothy to guard his motives (6:3–10), to stand firm in his faith (6:11, 12), to live above reproach (6:13–16), and to minister faithfully (6:17–21).

The letter holds many lessons. If you are a church leader, take note of Paul's relationship with this young disciple—his careful counsel and guidance. Measure yourself against the qualifications that Paul gives for overseers and deacons. If you are young in the faith, follow the example of godly Christian leaders like Timothy, who imitated Paul's life. If you are a parent, remind yourself of the profound effect a Christian home can have on family members—a faithful mother and grandmother led Timothy to Christ, and Timothy's ministry helped change the world.

VITAL STATISTICS

PURPOSE:
To give encouragement and instruction to Timothy, a young leader

AUTHOR:
Paul

TO WHOM WRITTEN:
Timothy, young church leaders, and all believers everywhere

DATE WRITTEN:
About A.D. 64, from Rome or Macedonia (possibly Philippi), probably just prior to Paul's final imprisonment in Rome

SETTING:
Timothy was one of Paul's closest companions. Paul had sent Timothy to the church at Ephesus to counter the false teaching that had arisen there (1 Timothy 1:3, 4). Timothy probably served for a time as a leader in the church at Ephesus. Paul hoped to visit Timothy (3:14, 15; 4:13), but in the meantime, he wrote this letter to give Timothy practical advice about the ministry.

KEY VERSE:
"Don't let anyone look down on you because you are young, but set an example for the believers in speech, in life, in love, in faith and in purity" (4:12).

KEY PEOPLE:
Paul, Timothy

KEY PLACE:
Ephesus

SPECIAL FEATURES:
This is a personal letter and a handbook of church administration and discipline.

THE BLUEPRINT

1. Instructions on right belief (1:1–20)
2. Instructions for the church (2:1—3:16)
3. Instructions for leaders (4:1—6:21)

Paul advised Timothy on such practical topics as qualifications for church leaders, public worship, confronting false teaching, and how to treat various groups of people within the church. Right belief and right behaviour are critical for anyone who desires to lead or serve effectively in the church. We should all believe rightly, participate in church actively, and minister to one another lovingly.

MEGATHEMES

THEME	EXPLANATION	IMPORTANCE
Sound Doctrine	Paul instructed Timothy to preserve the Christian faith by teaching sound doctrine and modelling right living. Timothy had to oppose false teachers who were leading church members away from belief in salvation by faith in Jesus Christ alone.	We must know the truth in order to defend it. We must cling to the belief that Christ came to save us. We should stay away from those who twist the words of the Bible for their own purposes.
Public Worship	Prayer in public worship must be done with a proper attitude towards God and fellow believers.	Christian character must be evident in every aspect of worship. We must rid ourselves of any anger, resentment, or offensive behaviour that might disrupt worship or damage church unity.
Church Leadership	Paul gives specific instructions concerning the qualifications for church leaders so that the church might honour God and operate smoothly.	Church leaders must be wholly committed to Christ. If you are a new or young Christian, don't be anxious to become a leader in the church. Seek to develop your Christian character first. Be sure to seek God, not your own ambition.
Personal Discipline	It takes discipline to be a leader in the church. Timothy, like all pastors, had to guard his motives, minister faithfully, and live above reproach. Any pastor must keep morally and spiritually fit.	To stay in good spiritual shape, you must discipline yourself to study God's word and to obey it. Put your spiritual abilities to work!
Caring Church	The church has a responsibility to care for the needs of all its members, especially the sick, the poor, and the widowed. Caring must go beyond good intentions.	Caring for the family of believers demonstrates our Christlike attitude and exhibits genuine love to non-believers.

1. Instructions on right belief

1 Paul, an apostle of Christ Jesus by the command of God[a] our Saviour and of
Christ Jesus our hope,[b]

2 To Timothy[c] my true son[d] in the faith:

Grace, mercy and peace from God the Father and Christ Jesus our Lord.

1:1 [a]Tit 1:3 [b]Col 1:27
1:2 [c]Ac 16:1 [d]2Ti 1:2; Tit 1:4

1:1 This letter was written to Timothy in A.D. 64 or 65, after Paul's first imprisonment in Rome (Acts 28:16–31). Apparently Paul had been out of prison for several years, and during that time he had revisited many churches in Asia and Macedonia. When he and Timothy returned to Ephesus, they found widespread false teaching in the church. Paul had warned the Ephesian elders to be on guard against the false teachers who inevitably would come after he had left (Acts 20:17–31). Paul sent Timothy to lead the Ephesian church while he moved on to Macedonia. From there Paul wrote this letter of encouragement and instruction to help Timothy deal with the difficult situation in the Ephesian church. Later, Paul was arrested again and brought back to a Roman prison.

1:1 Paul calls himself an *apostle,* meaning *one who is sent.* Paul was sent by Jesus Christ to bring the message of salvation to the Gentiles (Acts 9:1–20). For more information on Paul, see his Profile in Acts 9.

1:1 How was Paul an apostle "by the command of God"? In Acts 13:2, the Holy Spirit, through the prophets, said, "Set apart for me Barnabas and Saul [Paul] for the work to which I have called them." From Romans 16:25, 26 and Titus 1:3 it is obvious that Paul regarded his commission as directly from God.

1:3
[e]Ac 18:19
[f]Gal 1:6, 7

1:4
[g]1Ti 4:7; Tit 1:14
[h]1Ti 6:4

1:5
[i]2Ti 2:22
[j]2Ti 1:5

1:8
[k]Ro 7:12

1:9
[l]Gal 3:19

1:10
[m]2Ti 4:3; Tit 1:9

1:11
[n]Gal 2:7

1:12
[o]Php 4:13

1:13
[p]Ac 8:3

Warning Against False Teachers of the Law

3As I urged you when I went into Macedonia, stay there in Ephesus[e] so that you
may command certain men not to teach false doctrines[f] any longer 4nor to devote
themselves to myths[g] and endless genealogies. These promote controversies[h] rather
than God's work—which is by faith. 5The goal of this command is love, which comes
from a pure heart[i] and a good conscience and a sincere faith.[j] 6Some have wandered
away from these and turned to meaningless talk. 7They want to be teachers of the law,
but they do not know what they are talking about or what they so confidently affirm.
8We know that the law is good[k] if one uses it properly. 9We also know that law[a]
is made not for the righteous but for lawbreakers and rebels,[l] the ungodly and sinful,
the unholy and irreligious; for those who kill their fathers or mothers, for murderers,
10for adulterers and perverts, for slave traders and liars and perjurers—and for
whatever else is contrary to the sound doctrine[m] 11that conforms to the glorious gospel
of the blessed God, which he entrusted to me.[n]

The Lord's Grace to Paul

12I thank Christ Jesus our Lord, who has given me strength,[o] that he considered
me faithful, appointing me to his service. 13Even though I was once a blasphemer and
a persecutor[p] and a violent man, I was shown mercy because I acted in ignorance

[a] 9 Or *that the law*

1:3, 4 Paul first visited Ephesus on his second missionary journey (Acts 18:19–21). Later, on his third missionary journey, he stayed there for almost three years (Acts 19; 20). Ephesus, along with Rome, Corinth, Antioch, and Alexandria, was one of the major cities in the Roman empire. It was a centre for the commerce, politics, and religions of Asia Minor, and the location of the temple dedicated to the goddess Artemis (Diana).

1:3, 4 The church at Ephesus may have been plagued by the same heresy that was threatening the church at Colosse—the teaching that to be acceptable to God, a person had to discover certain hidden knowledge and had to worship angels (Colossians 2:8, 18). Thinking that it would aid in their salvation, some Ephesians constructed mythical stories based on Old Testament history or genealogies. The false teachers were motivated by their own interests rather than Christ's. They embroiled the church in endless and irrelevant questions and controversies, taking precious time away from the study of the truth. Today we could also enter into worthless and irrelevant discussions, but such disputes quickly crowd out the life-changing message of Christ. Stay away from religious speculation and pointless theological arguments. Such exercises may seem harmless at first, but they have a way of sidetracking us from the central message of the gospel—the person and work of Jesus Christ. And they expend time we should use to share the gospel with others. You should avoid anything that keeps you from doing God's work.

1:3–11 There are many leaders and authorities today who demand allegiance, some of whom would even have us turn from Christ to follow them. When they seem to know the Bible, their influence can be dangerously subtle. How can you recognise false teaching? (1) It promotes controversies instead of helping people come to Jesus (1:4). (2) It is often initiated by those whose motivation is to make a name for themselves (1:7). (3) It will be contrary to the true teaching of the Scriptures (1:6, 7; 4:1–3). To protect yourself from the deception of false teachers, you should learn what the Bible teaches and remain steadfast in your faith in Christ alone.

1:5 The false teachers were motivated by a spirit of curiosity and a desire to gain power and prestige. By contrast, genuine Christian teachers are motivated by sincere faith and a desire to do what is right. It may be exciting to impress people with our great knowledge, but high status based on falsehood is ultimately empty.

1:6 Arguing about details of the Bible can send us off on interesting but irrelevant tangents and cause us to miss the intent of God's message. The false teachers at Ephesus constructed vast speculative systems and then argued about the minor details of their wholly imaginary ideas. We should allow nothing to distract us from the Good News of salvation in Jesus Christ, the main point of Scripture. We should know what the Bible says, apply it to our lives daily, and teach it to others. When we do this, we will be able to evaluate all teachings in the light of the central truth about Jesus. Don't focus on the minute details of the Bible to the exclusion of the main point God is teaching you.

1:7 Paul was writing against those who were engaging in philosophical speculation based on the Pentateuch (the first five books of the Old Testament, written by Moses).

1:7–11 The false teachers wanted to become famous as teachers of God's law, but they didn't even understand the law's purpose. The law was not meant to give believers a list of commands for every occasion, but to show unbelievers their sin and bring them to God. For more of what Paul taught about our relationship to law, see Romans 5:20, 21; 13:9, 10; Galatians 3:24–29.

1:10 "Perverts" may refer to homosexuals. There are those who attempt to legitimise homosexuality as an acceptable alternative life-style. Even some Christians say people have a right to choose their sexual preference. But the Bible specifically calls homosexual behaviour sin (see Leviticus 18:22; Romans 1:18–32; 1 Corinthians 6:9–11). We must be careful, however, to condemn only the practice, and not the people. Those who commit homosexual acts are not to be feared, ridiculed, or hated. They can be forgiven and their lives can be transformed. The church should be a haven of forgiveness and healing for repentant homosexuals without compromising its stance against homosexual behaviour. For more on this subject see the notes on Romans 1:26, 27.

1:12–17 People can feel so guilt-ridden by their past that they think God could never forgive and accept them. But consider Paul's past. He had scoffed at the teachings of Jesus ("a blasphemer") and hunted down and murdered God's people ("a persecutor and a violent man") before coming to faith in Christ (Acts 9:1–9). God forgave Paul and used Paul mightily for his kingdom. No matter how shameful your past, God can forgive and use you as well.

and unbelief.[q] 14The grace of our Lord was poured out on me abundantly,[r] along
with the faith and love that are in Christ Jesus.[s]
15Here is a trustworthy saying[t] that deserves full acceptance: Christ Jesus came
into the world to save sinners—of whom I am the worst. 16But for that very reason
I was shown mercy[u] so that in me, the worst of sinners, Christ Jesus might display
his unlimited patience as an example for those who would believe on him and receive
eternal life. 17Now to the King[v] eternal, immortal, invisible,[w] the only God, be
honour and glory for ever and ever. Amen.[x]
18Timothy, my son, I give you this instruction in keeping with the prophecies once
made about you,[y] so that by following them you may fight the good fight,[z] 19holding
on to faith and a good conscience. Some have rejected these and so have shipwrecked
their faith.[a] 20Among them are Hymenaeus[b] and Alexander,[c] whom I have handed
over to Satan[d] to be taught not to blaspheme.

2. Instructions for the church

Instructions on Worship

2 I urge, then, first of all, that requests, prayers, intercession and thanksgiving be
made for everyone—2for kings and all those in authority,[a] that we may live
peaceful and quiet lives in all godliness and holiness. 3This is good, and pleases God
our Saviour, 4who wants[b] all men[c] to be saved and to come to a knowledge of the
truth.[d] 5For there is one God[e] and one mediator[f] between God and men, the man

1:13 [q]Ac 26:9
1:14 [r]Ro 5:20 [s]2Ti 1:13
1:15 [t]1Ti 3:1; 2Ti 2:11; Tit 3:8
1:16 [u]ver 13
1:17 [v]Rev 15:3 [w]Col 1:15 [x]Ro 11:36
1:18 [y]1Ti 4:14 [z]2Ti 2:3
1:19 [a]1Ti 6:21
1:20 [b]2Ti 2:17 [c]2Ti 4:14 [d]1Co 5:5
2:2 [a]Ezr 6:10; Ro 13:1
2:4 [b]Eze 18:23, 32 [c]Tit 2:11 [d]2Ti 2:25
2:5 [e]Ro 3:29, 30 [f]Gal 3:20

1:14 We may feel that our faith in God and our love for Christ and for others is inadequate. But we can be confident that Christ will help our faith and love grow as our relationship with him deepens.

1:15 Here Paul summarises the Good News: Jesus came into the world to save sinners, and no sinner is beyond his saving power. (See Luke 5:32 for Jesus' purpose for being on earth.) Jesus didn't come merely to show us how to live a better life or to challenge us to be better people. He came to offer us salvation that leads to eternal life. Have you accepted his offer?

1:15 Paul calls himself "the worst" of sinners. We think of Paul as a great hero of the faith, but Paul never saw himself that way, because he remembered his life before he met Christ. The more Paul understood God's grace, the more he was aware of his own sinfulness. Humility and gratitude should mark the life of every Christian. Never forget that you too are a sinner saved by grace.

1:17 This verse is a typical doxology given by Paul as a natural, emotional response to these reflections about the mercy of God. Paul was so moved by God's love that he was able to praise God spontaneously.

1:18 Paul highly valued the gift of prophecy (1 Corinthians 14:1). Through prophecy important messages of warning and encouragement came to the church. Just as pastors are ordained and set apart for ministry in church today, Timothy had been set apart for ministry when elders laid their hands on him (see 4:14). Apparently at this ceremony, several believers had prophesied about Timothy's gifts and strengths. These words from the Lord must have encouraged Timothy throughout his ministry.

1:19 How can you hold on to a good conscience? Treasure your faith in Christ more than anything else and do what you know is right. Each time you deliberately ignore your conscience, you are hardening your heart. Over a period of time your capacity to tell right from wrong will diminish. As you walk with God, he will speak to you through your conscience, letting you know the difference between right and wrong. Be sure to act on those inner tugs so that you do what is right—then your conscience will remain clear.

1:20 We don't know who Alexander was—he may have been an associate of Hymenaeus. Hymenaeus' error is explained in 2 Timothy 2:17, 18. He weakened people's faith by teaching that the resurrection had already occurred. Paul says that he handed Hymenaeus over to Satan, meaning that Paul had removed him from the fellowship of the church. Paul did this so that Hymenaeus would see his error and repent. The ultimate purpose of this punishment was correction. The church today is too often lax in disciplining Christians who deliberately sin. Deliberate disobedience should be responded to quickly and sternly to prevent the entire congregation from being affected. But discipline must be done in a way that tries to bring the offender back to Christ and into the loving embrace of the church. The definition of discipline includes these words: strengthening, purifying, training, correcting, perfecting. Condemnation, suspicion, withholding of forgiveness, or permanent exile should not be a part of church discipline.

2:1–4 Although God is all-powerful and all-knowing, he has chosen to let us help him change the world through our prayers. How this works is a mystery to us because of our limited understanding, but it is a reality. Paul urges us to pray for each other and for our leaders in government. Our earnest prayers will have powerful results (James 5:16).

2:2 Paul's command to pray for kings was remarkable considering that Nero, a notoriously cruel ruler, was emperor at this time (A.D. 54–68). When Paul wrote this letter, persecution was a growing threat to believers. Later, when Nero needed a scapegoat for the great fire that destroyed much of Rome in A.D. 64, he blamed the Roman Christians so as to take the focus off himself. Then persecution erupted throughout the Roman empire. Not only were Christians denied certain privileges in society, some were even publicly butchered, burned, or fed to animals.

2:2 When our lives are going along peacefully and quietly, it is difficult to remember to pray for those in authority, because we often take good government for granted. It's easier to remember to pray when we experience problems. But we should pray for those in authority around the world so that their societies will be conducive to the spread of the gospel.

2:4 Both Peter and Paul said that God wants all to be saved (see 2 Peter 3:9). This does not mean that all *will* be saved, because the Bible makes it clear that many reject Christ (Matthew 25:31–46; John 12:44–50; Hebrews 10:26–29). The gospel message has a universal scope; it is not directed only to people of one race, one sex, or one national background. God loves the whole world and sent his Son to save sinners. Never assume that anyone is outside God's mercy or beyond the reach of his offer of salvation.

2:5, 6 We human beings are separated from God by sin, and

TIMOTHY

Painful lessons are usually doorways to new opportunities. Even the apostle Paul had much to learn. Shortly after his disappointing experience with John Mark, Paul recruited another eager young man, Timothy, to be his assistant. Paul's intense personality may have been too much for John Mark to handle. It could easily have created the same problem for Timothy. But Paul seems to have learned a lesson in patience from his old friend Barnabas. As a result, Timothy became a "son" to Paul.

Timothy probably became a Christian after Paul's first missionary visit to Lystra (Acts 16:1–5). Timothy already had solid Jewish training in the Scriptures from his mother and grandmother. By Paul's second visit, Timothy had grown into a respected disciple of Jesus. He did not hesitate to join Paul and Silas on their journey. His willingness to be circumcised as an adult is clearly a mark of his commitment. (Timothy's mixed Greek/Jewish background could have created problems on their missionary journeys, because many of their audiences would be made up of Jews who were concerned about the strict keeping of this tradition. Timothy's submission to the rite of circumcision helped to avoid that potential problem.)

Beyond the tensions created by his mixed racial background, Timothy seemed to struggle with a naturally timid character and a sensitivity to his youthfulness. Unfortunately, many who share Timothy's character traits are quickly written off as too great a risk to deserve much responsibility. By God's grace, Paul saw great potential in Timothy. Paul demonstrated his confidence in Timothy by entrusting him with important responsibilities. Paul sent Timothy as his personal representative to Corinth during a particularly tense time (1 Corinthians 4:14–17). Although Timothy was apparently ineffective in that difficult mission, Paul did not give up on him. Timothy continued to travel with Paul.

Our last pictures of Timothy come from the most personal letters in the New Testament: 1 and 2 Timothy. The aging apostle Paul was near the end of his life, but his burning desire to continue his mission had not dimmed. Paul was writing to one of his closest friends—they had travelled, suffered, cried, and laughed together. They shared the intense joy of seeing people respond to the good news and the agonies of seeing the gospel rejected and distorted. Paul left Timothy in Ephesus to oversee the young church there (1 Timothy 1:3, 4). He wrote to encourage Timothy and give him needed direction. These letters have provided comfort and help to countless other "Timothys" through the years. When you face a challenge that seems beyond your abilities, read 1 and 2 Timothy, and remember that others have shared your experience.

Strengths and accomplishments:
- Became a believer after Paul's first missionary journey and joined him for his other two journeys
- Was a respected Christian in his home town
- Was Paul's special representative on several occasions
- Received two personal letters from Paul
- Probably knew Paul better than any other person, becoming like a son to Paul

Weaknesses and mistakes:
- Struggled with a timid and reserved nature
- Allowed others to look down on his youthfulness
- Was apparently unable to correct some of the problems in the church at Corinth when Paul sent him there

Lessons from his life:
- Youthfulness should not be an excuse for ineffectiveness
- Our inadequacies and inabilities should not keep us from being available to God

Vital statistics:
- Where: Lystra
- Occupations: Missionary, pastor
- Relatives: Mother: Eunice. Grandmother: Lois. Greek father
- Contemporaries: Paul, Silas, Luke, Mark, Peter, Barnabas

Key verses:
"I have no-one else like him [Timothy], who takes a genuine interest in your welfare. For everyone looks out for his own interests, not those of Jesus Christ. But you know that Timothy has proved himself, because as a son with his father he has served with me in the work of the gospel" (Philippians 2:20–22).

Timothy's story is told in Acts, starting in chapter 16. He is also mentioned in Romans 16:21; 1 Corinthians 4:17; 16:10, 11; 2 Corinthians 1:1, 19; Philippians 1:1; 2:19–23; Colossians 1:1; 1 Thessalonians 1:1–10; 2:3, 4; 3:2–6; 1 and 2 Timothy; Philemon 1; Hebrews 13:23.

---

only one person in the universe is our mediator and can stand between us and God and bring us together again—Jesus, who is both God and man. Jesus' sacrifice brought new life to all people. Have you let him bring you to the Father?

Christ Jesus, 6who gave himself as a ransom for all men — the testimony[g] given in
its proper time.[h] 7And for this purpose I was appointed a herald and an apostle — I
am telling the truth, I am not lying — and a teacher[i] of the true faith to the Gentiles.[j]
8I want men everywhere to lift up holy hands[k] in prayer, without anger or disputing.
9I also want women to dress modestly, with decency and propriety, not with braided
hair or gold or pearls or expensive clothes,[l] 10but with good deeds, appropriate for
women who profess to worship God.
11A woman should learn in quietness and full submission.[m] 12I do not permit a
woman to teach or to have authority over a man; she must be silent. 13For Adam was
formed first, then Eve.[n] 14And Adam was not the one deceived; it was the woman
who was deceived and became a sinner.[o] 15But women[a] will be saved[b] through
childbearing — if they continue in faith, love[p] and holiness with propriety.

[a] 15 Greek *she* [b] 15 Or *restored*

2:6 [g] 1Co 1:6 [h] 1Ti 6:15
2:7 [i] 2Ti 1:11 [j] Ac 9:15; Eph 3:7, 8
2:8 [k] Ps 134:2; Lk 24:50
2:9 [l] 1Pe 3:3
2:11 [m] 1Co 14:34
2:13 [n] Ge 2:7, 22; 1Co 11:8
2:14 [o] Ge 3:1-6, 13; 2Co 11:3
2:15 [p] 1Ti 1:14

2:6 Jesus gave his life as a ransom for our sin (Mark 10:45). A ransom was the price paid to release a slave from captivity. Jesus, our mediator, gave his life in exchange for ours. By his death, he paid our penalty for sin.

2:7 Paul describes himself as a herald or preacher. He was given the special privilege of announcing the gospel to the Gentiles. He gives his credentials as an apostle in 1 Corinthians 15:7–11.

2:8 Besides displeasing God, anger and strife make prayer difficult. That is why Jesus said that we should interrupt our prayers, if necessary, to make peace with others (Matthew 5:23, 24). God wants us to obey him immediately and thoroughly. Our goal should be to have a right relationship with God and also with others.

2:9, 10 Apparently some Christian women were trying to gain respect by looking beautiful rather than by becoming Christlike in character. Some may have thought that they could win unbelieving husbands to Christ through their appearance (see Peter's counsel to such women in 1 Peter 3:1–6). It is not unscriptural for a woman to want to be attractive. Beauty, however, begins inside a person. A gentle, modest, loving character gives a light to the face that cannot be duplicated by the best cosmetics and jewellery in the world. A carefully groomed and well-decorated exterior is artificial and cold unless inner beauty is present.

2:9–15 To understand these verses, we must understand the situation in which Paul and Timothy worked. In first-century Jewish culture, women were not allowed to study. When Paul said that women should *learn* in quietness and full submission, he was offering them an amazing new opportunity. Paul did not want the Ephesian women to teach because they didn't yet have enough knowledge or experience. The Ephesian church had a particular problem with false teachers. Evidently the women were especially susceptible to the false teachings (2 Timothy 3:1–9), because they did not yet have enough biblical knowledge to discern the truth. In addition, some of the women were apparently flaunting their newfound Christian freedom by wearing inappropriate clothing (2:9). Paul was telling Timothy not to put anyone (in this case, women) into a position of leadership who was not yet mature in the faith (see 5:22). The same principle applies to churches today (see the note on 3:6).

2:12 Some interpret this passage to mean that women should never teach in the assembled church; however, commentators point out that Paul did not forbid women from ever teaching. Paul's commended co-worker, Priscilla, taught Apollos, the great preacher (Acts 18:24–26). In addition, Paul frequently mentioned other women who held positions of responsibility in the church. Phoebe worked in the church (Romans 16:1). Mary, Tryphena, and Tryphosa were the Lord's workers (Romans 16:6, 12), as were Euodia and Syntyche (Philippians 4:2). Paul was very likely prohibiting the Ephesian women, not all women, from teaching (see the note on 2:9–15).

2:12 In Paul's reference to women being silent, the word *silent* expresses an attitude of quietness and composure. (A different Greek word is usually used to convey "complete silence".) In addition, Paul himself acknowledges that women publicly prayed and prophesied (1 Corinthians 11:5). Apparently, however, the women in the Ephesian church were abusing their newly acquired Christian freedom. Because these women were new converts, they did not yet have the necessary experience, knowledge, or Christian maturity to teach those who already had extensive scriptural education.

2:13, 14 In previous letters Paul had discussed male/female roles in marriage (Ephesians 5:21–33; Colossians 3:18, 19). Here he talks about male/female roles within the church. Some scholars see these verses about Adam and Eve as an illustration of what was happening in the Ephesian church. Just as Eve had been deceived in the Garden of Eden, so the women in the church were being deceived by false teachers. And just as Adam was the first human created by God, so the men in the church in Ephesus should be the first to speak and teach, because they had more training. This view, then, stresses that Paul's teaching here is not universal, but applies to churches with similar problems. Other scholars, however, contend that the roles Paul points out are God's design for his created order – God established these roles to maintain harmony in both the family and the church.

2:14 Paul is not excusing Adam for his part in the fall (Genesis 3:6, 7, 17–19). On the contrary, in his letter to the Romans Paul places the primary blame for humanity's sinful nature on Adam (Romans 5:12–21).

2:15 There are several ways to understand the phrase, being "saved through childbearing": (1) Man sinned and so men were condemned to painful labour. Woman sinned and so women were condemned to pain in childbearing. Both men and women, however, can be saved through trusting Christ and obeying him. (2) Women who fulfil their God-given roles are demonstrating true commitment and obedience to Christ. One of the most important roles for a wife and mother is to care for her family. (3) The childbearing mentioned here refers to the birth of Jesus Christ. Women (and men) are saved spiritually because of the most important birth, that of Christ himself. (4) From the lessons learned through the trials of childbearing, women can develop qualities that teach them about love, trust, submission, and service.

3:1
[a]1Ti 1:15
[b]Ac 20:28
3:2
[c]Tit 1:6-8
[d]Ro 12:13
[e]2Ti 2:24
3:3
[f]2Ti 2:24
[g]Heb 13:5; 1Pe 5:2
3:4
[h]Tit 1:6
3:5
[i]1Co 10:32
3:6
[j]1Ti 6:4
3:7
[k]2Ti 2:26
3:8
[l]Php 1:1
[m]Tit 2:3
3:9
[n]1Ti 1:19
3:11
[o]2Ti 3:3; Tit 2:3
3:12
[p]ver 4
3:15
[q]ver 5; Eph 2:21
3:16
[r]Ro 16:25

Overseers and Deacons

3 Here is a trustworthy saying:[a] If anyone sets his heart on being an overseer,**[a]**[b] he desires a noble task. 2 Now the overseer must be above reproach,[c] the husband of but one wife, temperate, self-controlled, respectable, hospitable,[d] able to teach,[e] 3 not given to drunkenness, not violent but gentle, not quarrelsome,[f] not a lover of money.[g] 4 He must manage his own family well and see that his children obey him with proper respect.[h] 5 (If anyone does not know how to manage his own family, how can he take care of God's church?)[i] 6 He must not be a recent convert, or he may become conceited[j] and fall under the same judgment as the devil. 7 He must also have a good reputation with outsiders, so that he will not fall into disgrace and into the devil's trap.[k]

8 Deacons,[l] likewise, are to be men worthy of respect, sincere, not indulging in much wine,[m] and not pursuing dishonest gain. 9 They must keep hold of the deep truths of the faith with a clear conscience.[n] 10 They must first be tested; and then if there is nothing against them, let them serve as deacons.

11 In the same way, their wives**[b]** are to be women worthy of respect, not malicious talkers[o] but temperate and trustworthy in everything.

12 A deacon must be the husband of but one wife and must manage his children and his household well.[p] 13 Those who have served well gain an excellent standing and great assurance in their faith in Christ Jesus.

14 Although I hope to come to you soon, I am writing you these instructions so that, 15 if I am delayed, you will know how people ought to conduct themselves in God's household, which is the church[q] of the living God, the pillar and foundation of the truth. 16 Beyond all question, the mystery[r] of godliness is great:

a *1* Traditionally *bishop*; also in verse 2 **b** *11* Or *way, deaconesses*

3:1 To be a church leader ("overseer") is a heavy responsibility because the church belongs to the living God. Church leaders should not be elected because they are popular, nor should they be allowed to push their way to the top. Instead they should be chosen by the church because of their respect for the truth, both in what they believe and in how they live.

3:1–13 The word *overseer* can refer to a pastor, church leader, or presiding elder. It is good to want to be a spiritual leader, but the standards are high. Paul enumerates some of the qualifications here. Do you hold a position of spiritual leadership, or would you like to be a leader one day? Check yourself against Paul's standard of excellence. Those with great responsibility must meet high expectations.

3:1–13 The lists of qualifications for church office show that living a blameless and pure life requires effort and self-discipline. All believers, even if they never plan to be church leaders, should strive to follow these guidelines because they are consistent with what God says is true and right. The strength to live according to God's will comes from Christ.

3:2 When Paul says that each overseer should have only one wife, he is prohibiting both polygamy and promiscuity. This does not prohibit an unmarried person from becoming an elder or a widowed elder from remarrying.

3:4, 5 Christian workers and volunteers sometimes make the mistake of thinking their work is so important that they are justified in ignoring their families. Spiritual leadership, however, must begin at home. If a man is not willing to care for, discipline, and teach his children, he is not qualified to lead the church. Don't allow your volunteer activities to detract from your family responsibilities.

3:6 New believers should become secure and strong in the faith before taking leadership roles in the church. Too often, when the church is desperate for workers, new believers are placed in positions of responsibility prematurely. New faith needs time to mature. New believers should have a place of service, but they should not be put into leadership positions until they are firmly grounded in their faith, with a solid Christian life-style and a knowledge of the word of God.

3:6, 7 Younger believers who are selected for office need to beware of the damaging effects of pride. Pride can seduce our emotions and cloud our reason. It can make those who are immature susceptible to the influence of unscrupulous people. Pride and conceit were the devil's downfall, and he uses pride to trap others.

3:8–13 *Deacon* means "one who serves". This position was possibly begun by the apostles in the Jerusalem church (Acts 6:1–6) to care for the physical needs of the congregation, especially the needs of the Greek-speaking widows. Deacons were leaders in the church, and their qualifications resemble those of the overseers. In some churches today, the office of deacon has lost its importance. New Christians are often asked to serve in this position, but that is not the New Testament pattern. Paul says that potential deacons should first be tested before they are asked to serve.

3:11 *Wives* can refer to women helpers or deaconesses. It could also mean wives of deacons, or female leaders of the church (such as Phoebe, the deaconess mentioned in Romans 16:1). In either case, Paul expected the behaviour of prominent women in the church to be just as responsible and blameless as that of prominent men.

3:16 In this short hymn, Paul affirms the humanity and divinity of Christ. By so doing he reveals the heart of the gospel, "the mystery of godliness" (the secret of how we become godly). "Appeared in a body"—Jesus was a man; Jesus' incarnation is the basis of our being right with God. "Was vindicated by the Spirit"—Jesus' resurrection showed that the Holy Spirit's power was in him (Romans 8:11). "Was seen by angels" and "was taken up in glory"—Jesus is divine. We can't please God on our own; we must depend on Christ. As a man, Jesus lived a perfect life, and so he is a perfect example of how to live. As God, Jesus gives us the power to do what is right. It is possible to live a godly life—through following Christ.

He[c] appeared in a body,[d][s]
was vindicated by the Spirit,
was seen by angels,
was preached among the nations,[t]
was believed on in the world,
was taken up in glory.[u]

3. Instructions for leaders

Instructions to Timothy

4 The Spirit[a] clearly says that in later times[b] some will abandon the faith and
follow deceiving spirits[c] and things taught by demons. 2Such teachings come
through hypocritical liars, whose consciences have been seared as with a hot iron.[d]
3They forbid people to marry[e] and order them to abstain from certain foods,[f] which
God created[g] to be received with thanksgiving[h] by those who believe and who know
the truth. 4For everything God created is good,[i] and nothing is to be rejected if it
is received with thanksgiving, 5because it is consecrated by the word of God and
prayer.
6If you point these things out to the brothers, you will be a good minister of Christ
Jesus, brought up in the truths of the faith[j] and of the good teaching that you have
followed. 7Have nothing to do with godless myths and old wives' tales;[k] rather, train
yourself to be godly. 8For physical training is of some value, but godliness has value
for all things,[l] holding promise for both the present life[m] and the life to come.
9This is a trustworthy saying[n] that deserves full acceptance 10(and for this we
labour and strive), that we have put our hope in the living God, who is the Saviour
of all men, and especially of those who believe.
11Command and teach these things.[o] 12Don't let anyone look down on you because
you are young, but set an example[p] for the believers in speech, in life, in love, in
faith[q] and in purity. 13Until I come, devote yourself to the public reading of Scripture,

c *16* Some manuscripts *God* d *16* Or *in the flesh*

3:16 [s]Jn 1:14 [t]Col 1:23 [u]Mk 16:19
4:1 [a]Jn 16:13 [b]2Ti 3:1 [c]2Th 2:3
4:2 [d]Eph 4:19
4:3 [e]Heb 13:4 [f]Col 2:16 [g]Ge 1:29 [h]Ro 14:6
4:4 [i]Ro 14:14-18
4:6 [j]1Ti 1:10
4:7 [k]2Ti 2:16
4:8 [l]1Ti 6:6 [m]Ps 37:9, 11; Mk 10:29, 30
4:9 [n]1Ti 1:15
4:11 [o]1Ti 5:7; 6:2
4:12 [p]Tit 2:7; 1Pe 5:3 [q]1Ti 1:14

4:1 The "later times" began with Christ's resurrection and will continue until his return when he will set up his kingdom and judge all humanity.

4:1, 2 False teachers were and still are a threat to the church. Jesus and the apostles repeatedly warned against them (see, for example, Mark 13:21–23; Acts 20:28–31; 2 Thessalonians 2:1–12; 2 Peter 3:3–7). The danger that Timothy faced in Ephesus seems to have come from certain people in the church who were following some Greek philosophers who taught that the body was evil and that only the soul mattered. The false teachers refused to believe that the God of creation was good, because his very contact with the physical world would have soiled him. Though these Greek-influenced church members honoured Jesus, they could not believe he was truly human. Paul knew that their teachings, if left unchecked, would greatly distort Christian truth.

It is not enough that a teacher appears to know what he is talking about, is disciplined and moral, or says that he is speaking for God. If his words contradict the Bible, his teaching is false. Like Timothy, we must guard against any teaching that causes believers to dilute or reject any aspect of their faith. Such false teaching can be very direct or extremely subtle.

4:1–5 Paul said the false teachers were hypocritical liars who encouraged people to follow "deceiving spirits and things taught by demons". Satan deceives people by offering a clever imitation of the real thing. The false teachers gave stringent rules (such as forbidding people to marry or to eat certain foods). This made them appear self-disciplined and righteous. Their strict disciplines for the body, however, could not remove sin (see Colossians 2:20–23). We must not be unduly impressed by a teacher's style or credentials; we must look to his teaching about Jesus Christ. His conclusions about Christ show the source of his message.

4:4, 5 In opposition to the false teachers, Paul affirmed that everything God created is good (see Genesis 1). We should ask for God's blessing on his created gifts that give us pleasure and thank him for them. This doesn't mean that we should abuse what God has made (for example, gluttony abuses God's gift of good food, lust abuses God's gift of love, and murder abuses God's gift of life). Instead of abusing, we should enjoy these gifts by using them to serve and honour God. Have you thanked God for the good gifts he has given? Are you using the gifts in ways pleasing to you *and* to God?

4:7–10 Are you in shape both physically and spiritually? In our society, much emphasis is placed on physical fitness, but spiritual health (godliness) is even more important. Our physical health is susceptible to disease and injury, but faith can sustain us through these tragedies. To train ourselves to be godly, we must develop our faith by using our God-given abilities in the service of the church (see 4:14–16). Are you developing your spiritual muscles?

4:10 Christ is the Saviour for all, but his salvation becomes effective only for those who trust him.

4:12 Timothy was a young pastor. It would have been easy for older Christians to look down on him because of his youth. He had to earn the respect of his elders by setting an example in his speech, life, love, faith, and purity. Regardless of your age, God can use you. Whether you are young or old, don't think of your age as a handicap. Live so others can see Christ in you.

4:13 The Scripture that Paul mentions is in fact the Old Testament. We must make sure to emphasise the entire Bible, both the Old and the New Testaments. There are rich rewards in studying the people, events, prophecies, and principles of the Old Testament.

4:14 [r] 1Ti 1:18 [s] Ac 6:6; 2Ti 1:6
5:1 [a] Tit 2:2 [b] Lev 19:32 [c] Tit 2:6
5:3 [d] ver 5, 16
5:4 [e] Eph 6:1, 2 [f] 1Ti 2:3
5:5 [g] ver 3, 16 [h] 1Co 7:34; 1Pe 3:5 [i] Lk 2:37
5:6 [j] Lk 15:24
5:7 [k] 1Ti 4:11
5:8 [l] 2Pe 2:1; Jude 4; Tit 1:16

to preaching and to teaching. 14 Do not neglect your gift, which was given you through
a prophetic message[r] when the body of elders laid their hands on you.[s]
15 Be diligent in these matters; give yourself wholly to them, so that everyone may
see your progress. 16 Watch your life and doctrine closely. Persevere in them, because
if you do, you will save both yourself and your hearers.

Advice About Widows, Elders and Slaves

5 Do not rebuke an older man[a] harshly,[b] but exhort him as if he were your father.
Treat younger men[c] as brothers, 2 older women as mothers, and younger women
as sisters, with absolute purity.
3 Give proper recognition to those widows who are really in need.[d] 4 But if a widow
has children or grandchildren, these should learn first of all to put their religion into
practice by caring for their own family and so repaying their parents and grandparents,[e] for this is pleasing to God.[f] 5 The widow who is really in need[g] and left
all alone puts her hope in God[h] and continues night and day to pray[i] and to ask God
for help. 6 But the widow who lives for pleasure is dead even while she lives.[j] 7 Give
the people these instructions,[k] too, so that no-one may be open to blame. 8 If anyone
does not provide for his relatives, and especially for his immediate family, he has
denied[l] the faith and is worse than an unbeliever.
9 No widow may be put on the list of widows unless she is over sixty, has been

---

4:14 Timothy's commission as a church leader was confirmed by prophecy (see also 1:18) and by the laying on of hands by the elders of the church. He was not a self-appointed leader. If you aspire to church leadership, seek the counsel of mature Christians who know you well and who will hold you accountable.

4:14, 15 As a young leader in a church that had a lot of problems, Timothy may have felt intimidated. But the elders and prophets encouraged him and charged him to use his spiritual gift responsibly. Highly skilled and talented athletes lose their abilities if their muscles aren't toned by constant use, and we will lose our spiritual gifts if we don't put them to work. Our talents are improved by exercise, but failing to use them causes them to waste away from lack of practice and nourishment. What gifts and abilities has God given you? Use them regularly in serving God and others. (See Romans 12:1–8; 2 Timothy 1:6–8 for more on using well the abilities God has given us.)

4:16 We know the importance of watching our lives closely. We must be on constant guard against falling into sin that can so easily destroy us. Yet we must watch what we believe ("doctrine") just as closely. Wrong beliefs can quickly lead us into sin and heresy. We should be on guard against those who would persuade us that how we live is more important than what we believe. We should persevere in both.

5:2 Men in the ministry can avoid improper attitudes towards women by treating them as family members. If men see women as fellow members in God's family, they will protect them and help them grow spiritually.

5:3ff Paul wanted Christian families to be as self-supporting as possible. He insisted that children and grandchildren take care of the widows in their families (5:4); he suggested that younger widows remarry and start new families (5:14); and he ordered the church not to support lazy members who refused to work (2 Thessalonians 3:10). Nevertheless, when necessary, the believers pooled their resources (Acts 2:44–47); they gave generously to help disaster-ridden churches (1 Corinthians 16:1–4); and they took care of a large number of widows (Acts 6:1–6). The church has always had limited resources, and it has always had to balance financial responsibility with generosity. It only makes sense for members to work as hard as they can and to be as independent as possible, so they can adequately care for themselves and for less fortunate members. When church members are both responsible and generous, everyone's needs will be met.

5:3–5 Because there were no pensions, no social security, no life insurance, and few honourable jobs for women, widows were usually unable to support themselves. The responsibility for caring for the helpless naturally falls first on their families, the people whose lives are most closely linked with theirs. Paul stresses the importance of families caring for the needs of widows, and not leaving it to the church – so the church can care for those widows who have no families. A widow who had no children or other family members to support her was doomed to poverty. From the beginning, the church took care of its widows, who in turn gave valuable service to the church.

The church should support those who have no families and should also help the elderly, young, disabled, ill, or poverty-stricken with their emotional and spiritual needs. Often families who are caring for their own helpless members have heavy burdens. They may need extra money, a listening ear, a helping hand, or a word of encouragement. Interestingly, those who are helped often turn around and help others, turning the church into more of a caring community. Don't wait for people to ask. Take the initiative and look for ways to serve them.

5:8 Almost everyone has relatives, family of some kind. Family relationships are so important in God's eyes, Paul says, that a person who neglects his or her family responsibilities has denied the faith. Are you doing your part to meet the needs of those included in your family circle?

5:9–16 Apparently some older widows had been "put on the list of widows", meaning that they had taken a vow committing themselves to work for the church in exchange for financial support. Paul lists a few qualifications for these church workers – these widows should be at least 60 years old, should have been faithful to their husbands, and should be well known for their kind deeds. Younger widows should not be included in this group because they might desire to marry again and thus have to break their pledge (5:11, 12).

Three out of four wives today are eventually widowed, and many of the older women in our churches have lost their husbands. Does your church provide an avenue of service for these women? Could you help match their gifts and abilities with your church's needs? Often their maturity and wisdom can be of great service in the church.

faithful to her husband,[a] 10and is well known for her good deeds,[m] such as bringing
up children, showing hospitality, washing the feet[n] of the saints, helping those in
trouble[o] and devoting herself to all kinds of good deeds.
11As for younger widows, do not put them on such a list. For when their sensual
desires overcome their dedication to Christ, they want to marry. 12Thus they bring
judgment on themselves, because they have broken their first pledge. 13Besides, they
get into the habit of being idle and going about from house to house. And not only
do they become idlers, but also gossips and busybodies,[p] saying things they ought
not to. 14So I counsel younger widows to marry,[q] to have children, to manage their
homes and to give the enemy no opportunity for slander.[r] 15Some have in fact already
turned away to follow Satan.[s]
16If any woman who is a believer has widows in her family, she should help them
and not let the church be burdened with them, so that the church can help those widows
who are really in need.[t]
17The elders[u] who direct the affairs of the church well are worthy of double
honour,[v] especially those whose work is preaching and teaching. 18For the Scripture
says, "Do not muzzle the ox while it is treading out the grain,"[b][w] and "The worker
deserves his wages."[c][x] 19Do not entertain an accusation against an elder[y] unless
it is brought by two or three witnesses.[z] 20Those who sin are to be rebuked[a] publicly,
so that the others may take warning.[b]
21I charge you, in the sight of God and Christ Jesus[c] and the elect angels, to keep
these instructions without partiality, and to do nothing out of favouritism.
22Do not be hasty in the laying on of hands,[d] and do not share in the sins of
others.[e] Keep yourself pure.
23Stop drinking only water, and use a little wine[f] because of your stomach and
your frequent illnesses.
24The sins of some men are obvious, reaching the place of judgment ahead of them;
the sins of others trail behind them. 25In the same way, good deeds are obvious, and
even those that are not cannot be hidden.

a *9* Or *has had but one husband* b *18* Deut. 25:4 c *18* Luke 10:7

5:10 [m]Ac 9:36; 1Ti 6:18; 1Pe 2:12 [n]Lk 7:44 [o]ver 16
5:13 [p]2Th 3:11
5:14 [q]1Co 7:9 [r]1Ti 6:1
5:15 [s]Mt 4:10
5:16 [t]ver 3-5
5:17 [u]Ac 11:30 [v]Php 2:29; 1Th 5:12
5:18 [w]Dt 25:4; 1Co 9:7-9 [x]Lk 10:7; Lev 19:13; Dt 24:14, 15; Mt 10:10; 1Co 9:14
5:19 [y]Ac 11:30 [z]Mt 18:16
5:20 [a]2Ti 4:2; Tit 1:13 [b]Dt 13:11
5:21 [c]1Ti 6:13; 2Ti 4:1
5:22 [d]Ac 6:6 [e]Eph 5:11
5:23 [f]1Ti 3:8

5:10 "Washing the feet of the saints" means to help and serve other believers with humility, following the example of Jesus, who washed the feet of his disciples at the Last Supper (John 13:1–17).

5:15 "Turned away to follow Satan" refers to the immoral conduct that identified these women with their pagan neighbours.

5:17, 18 Faithful church leaders should be supported and appreciated. Too often they are targets for criticism because the congregation has unrealistic expectations. How do you treat your church leaders? Do you enjoy finding fault, or do you show your appreciation? Do they receive enough financial support to allow them to live without worry and to provide for the needs of their families? Jesus and Paul emphasised the importance of supporting those who lead and teach us (see Galatians 6:6 and the notes on Luke 10:7 and 1 Corinthians 9:4–10).

5:17, 18 Preaching and teaching are closely related. Preaching is proclaiming the word of God and confronting listeners with the truth of Scripture. Teaching is explaining the truth in Scripture, helping learners understand difficult passages, and helping them apply God's word to daily life. Paul says that these elders are worthy of double honour. Unfortunately, however, we often take them for granted by not providing adequately for their needs or by subjecting them to heavy criticism. Think of how you can honour your preachers and teachers.

5:19–21 Church leaders are not exempt from sin, faults, and mistakes. But they are often criticised for the wrong reasons—minor imperfections, failure to meet someone's expectations, personality clashes. Thus Paul said that accusations should not even be heard unless two or three witnesses confirm them. Sometimes church leaders should be confronted about their behaviour, and sometimes they should be rebuked. But all rebuking must be done fairly and lovingly, and for the purpose of restoration.

5:21 "Elect angels" are all those angels who did not rebel against God like Satan did.

5:21 We must be constantly on guard against favouritism, against giving preferential treatment to some and ignoring others. We live in a society that plays favourites. It's easy to give special treatment to those who are gifted, intelligent, rich, or beautiful without realising what we are doing. Make sure you honour people for who they are in Christ, not for who they are in the world.

5:22 Paul says that a church should never be hasty about choosing its leaders, especially the pastor, because we may overlook major problems or sins. It is a serious responsibility to choose church leaders. They must have strong faith and be morally upright, having the qualities described in 3:1–13 and Titus 1:5–9. Not everyone who wants to be a church leader is eligible. Be certain of an applicant's qualifications before asking him or her to take a leadership position.

5:23 It is unclear why Paul gave this advice to Timothy. Perhaps contaminated water had led to Timothy's indigestion and so he should stop drinking only water. Whatever the reason, this statement is not an invitation to overindulgence or alcoholism.

5:24, 25 Paul instructs Timothy to choose church leaders carefully because sometimes their sins are not obvious and it takes time for them to be revealed. Church leaders should live lives that are above reproach.

6:1 [a]Eph 6:5; Tit 2:9; 1Pe 2:18 [b]Tit 2:5, 8
6:2 [c]Phm 16 [d]1Ti 4:11
6:3 [e]1Ti 1:3 [f]1Ti 1:10
6:4 [g]2Ti 2:14
6:5 [h]Tit 1:15
6:6 [i]Php 4:11; Heb 13:5 [j]1Ti 4:8
6:7 [k]Job 1:21; Ecc 5:15
6:8 [l]Heb 13:5
6:9 [m]Pr 15:27 [n]1Ti 3:7
6:10 [o]1Ti 3:3 [p]Jas 5:19
6:11 [q]2Ti 3:17 [r]2Ti 2:22
6:12 [s]1Co 9:25, 26; 1Ti 1:18 [t]Php 3:12
6:13 [u]Jn 18:33-37 [v]1Ti 5:21
6:15 [w]1Ti 1:11 [x]1Ti 1:17 [y]Rev 17:14; 19:16
6:16 [z]1Ti 1:17 [a]Jn 1:18

6 All who are under the yoke of slavery should consider their masters worthy of
full respect,[a] so that God's name and our teaching may not be slandered.[b]
2Those who have believing masters are not to show less respect for them because they
are brothers.[c] Instead, they are to serve them even better, because those who benefit
from their service are believers, and dear to them. These are the things you are to teach
and urge on them.[d]

Love of Money

3If anyone teaches false doctrines[e] and does not agree to the sound instruction[f]
of our Lord Jesus Christ and to godly teaching, 4he is conceited and understands
nothing. He has an unhealthy interest in controversies and quarrels about words[g] that
result in envy, strife, malicious talk, evil suspicions 5and constant friction between
men of corrupt mind, who have been robbed of the truth[h] and who think that godliness
is a means to financial gain.
6But godliness with contentment[i] is great gain.[j] 7For we brought nothing into the
world, and we can take nothing out of it.[k] 8But if we have food and clothing, we
will be content with that.[l] 9People who want to get rich[m] fall into temptation and
a trap[n] and into many foolish and harmful desires that plunge men into ruin and
destruction. 10For the love of money[o] is a root of all kinds of evil. Some people, eager
for money, have wandered from the faith[p] and pierced themselves with many griefs.

Paul's Charge to Timothy

11But you, man of God,[q] flee from all this, and pursue righteousness, godliness,
faith, love,[r] endurance and gentleness. 12Fight the good fight[s] of the faith. Take
hold of[t] the eternal life to which you were called when you made your good
confession in the presence of many witnesses. 13In the sight of God, who gives life
to everything, and of Christ Jesus, who while testifying before Pontius Pilate[u] made
the good confession, I charge you[v] 14to keep this command without spot or blame
until the appearing of our Lord Jesus Christ, 15which God will bring about in his own
time—God, the blessed[w] and only Ruler,[x] the King of kings and Lord of lords,[y]
16who alone is immortal[z] and who lives in unapproachable light, whom no-one has
seen or can see.[a] To him be honour and might for ever. Amen.

6:1, 2 In Paul's culture there was a great social and legal gulf separating masters and slaves. But as Christians, masters and slaves became spiritual equals, brothers and sisters in Christ Jesus (Galatians 3:28). Paul did not speak against the institution of slavery, but he gave guidelines for Christian slaves and Christian masters. His counsel for the master/slave relationship can be applied to the employer/employee relationship today. Employees should work hard, showing respect for their employers. In turn, employers should be fair (Ephesians 6:5–9; Colossians 3:22–25). Our work should reflect our faithfulness to and love for Christ.

6:3–5 Paul told Timothy to stay away from those who just wanted to make money from preaching, and from those who strayed from the sound teachings of the gospel into quarrels that caused strife in the church. A person's understanding of the finer points of theology should not become the basis for lording it over others or for making money. Stay away from people who just want to argue.

6:6 This statement is the key to spiritual growth and personal fulfilment. We should honour God and centre our desires on him ("godliness", see Matthew 6:33), and we should be content with what God is doing in our lives (see Philippians 4:11–13).

6:6–10 Despite overwhelming evidence to the contrary, most people still believe that money brings happiness. Rich people craving greater riches can be caught in an endless cycle that only ends in ruin and destruction. How can you keep away from the love of money? Paul gives us some guidelines: (1) realise that one day riches will all be gone (6:7, 17); (2) be content with what you have (6:8); (3) monitor what you are willing to do to get more money (6:9, 10); (4) love people more than money (6:11); (5) love God's work more than money (6:11); (6) freely share what you have with others (6:18). (See Proverbs 30:7–9 for more on avoiding the love of money.)

6:8 It is often helpful to distinguish between *needs* and *wants*. We may have all we need to live but let ourselves become anxious and discontented over what we merely want. Like Paul, we can choose to be content without having all that we want. The only alternative is to be a slave to our desires.

6:10 Greed leads to all kinds of evil: marriage problems, robbery, blowups in partnerships. To master greed, you must control it at its root. Get rid of the desire to be rich.

6:11, 12 Paul uses active and forceful verbs to describe the Christian life: flee, pursue, fight, take hold. Some think Christianity is a passive religion that advocates waiting for God to act. But we must have an *active* faith, obeying God with courage and doing what we know is right. Is it time for action on your part? Don't wait—get going!

6:13 Jesus' trial before Pilate is recorded in the Gospels: Matthew 27:11–26; Mark 15:1–15; Luke 23:1–25; John 18:28–19:16.

6:13–16 Paul concludes with a charge to Timothy to keep "this command", referring to the commands Christ has given to his church, or perhaps to Timothy's promise to serve Christ. Timothy's own confession of faith is compared with Christ's before Pilate.

17Command those who are rich in this present world not to be arrogant nor to put
their hope in wealth,[b] which is so uncertain, but to put their hope in God,[c] who richly
provides us with everything for our enjoyment.[d] 18Command them to do good, to
be rich in good deeds,[e] and to be generous and willing to share.[f] 19In this way they
will lay up treasure for themselves[g] as a firm foundation for the coming age, so that
they may take hold of the life that is truly life.
20Timothy, guard what has been entrusted[h] to your care. Turn away from godless
chatter[i] and the opposing ideas of what is falsely called knowledge, 21which some
have professed and in so doing have wandered from the faith.[j]
Grace be with you.[k]

6:17 [b]Lk 12:20, 21 [c]1Ti 4:10 [d]Ac 14:17
6:18 [e]1Ti 5:10 [f]Ro 12:8, 13
6:19 [g]Mt 6:20
6:20 [h]2Ti 1:12, 14 [i]2Ti 2:16
6:21 [j]2Ti 2:18 [k]Col 4:18

6:17–19 Ephesus was a wealthy city, and the Ephesian church probably had many wealthy members. Paul advised Timothy to deal with any potential problems by teaching that having riches carries great responsibility. Those who have money must be generous, and they must not be arrogant just because they have a lot to give. They must be careful not to put their hope in money instead of in the living God for their security. Even if we don't have material wealth, we can be rich in good deeds. No matter how poor we are, we have something to share with someone.

6:21 The book of 1 Timothy provides guiding principles for local churches, including rules for public worship and qualifications for overseers (elders, pastors), deacons, and special church workers (widows). Paul tells the church leaders to correct incorrect doctrine and to deal lovingly and fairly with all people in the church. The church is not organised simply for the sake of organisation, but so that Christ can be honoured and glorified. While studying these guidelines, don't lose sight of what is most important in the life of the church – knowing God, working together in loving harmony, and taking God's Good News to the world.

2 TIMOTHY

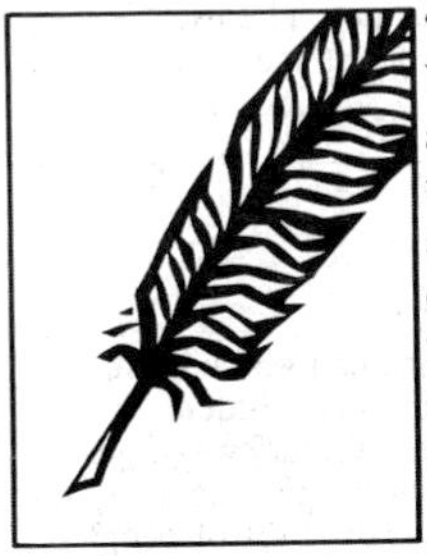

"FAMOUS last words" is more than a cliché. When notable men and women of influence are about to die, the world waits to hear their final words of insight and wisdom. Then those quotes are repeated worldwide. This is also true with a dying loved one. Gathered at his or her side, the family strains to hear every whispered syllable of blessing, encouragement, and advice, knowing that this will be the final message.

One of the most knowledgeable, influential, and beloved men of history is the apostle Paul. And we have his famous last words.

Paul was facing death. He was not dying of a disease in a sterile hospital with loved ones gathered nearby. He was very much alive, but his condition was terminal. Convicted as a follower of Jesus of Nazareth, Paul lay in a cold Roman prison, cut off from the world, with just a visitor or two and his writing materials. Paul knew that soon he would be executed (4:6), and so he wrote his final thoughts to his "son" Timothy, passing to him the torch of leadership, reminding him of what was truly important, and encouraging him in the faith. Imagine how Timothy must have read and reread every word—this was the last message from his beloved mentor, Paul. Because of the situation and the recipient, this is the most intimate and moving of all Paul's letters, and his last.

Paul's introduction is tender, and the love he has for Timothy exudes from every phrase (1:1–5). He then reminds Timothy of the qualities necessary for a faithful minister of Jesus Christ (1:6—2:13). Timothy should remember his call and use his gifts with boldness (1:6–12), keep to the truth (1:13–18), prepare others to follow him in the ministry (2:1, 2), be disciplined and ready to endure hardship (2:3–7), and keep his eyes and mind focused on Christ (2:8–13). Paul challenges Timothy to hold to sound doctrine, reject error and avoid godless chatter, correctly handle the word of truth (2:14–19), and keep his life pure (2:20–26).

Next, Paul warns Timothy of the opposition that he and other believers would face in the last days from self-centred people who use the church for their own gain and who teach false doctrines (3:1–9). Paul tells Timothy to be prepared for these unfaithful people by remembering his example (3:10, 11), understanding the real source of the opposition (3:12, 13), and finding strength and power in the word of God (3:14–17). Then Paul gives Timothy a stirring charge—to preach the word (4:1–4) and to fulfil his ministry until the end (4:5–8).

Paul concludes with personal requests and items of information. In these final words, he reveals his loneliness and his strong love for his brothers and sisters in Christ (4:9–22).

There has never been another person like Paul, the missionary apostle. He was a man of deep faith, undying love, constant hope, tenacious conviction, and profound insight. And he was inspired by the Holy Spirit to give us God's message. As you read 2 Timothy, know that you are reading the last words of this great man of God—last words to Timothy and to all who would claim to follow Christ. Recommit yourself to stand courageously for the truth, knowing the word and being empowered by the Holy Spirit.

VITAL STATISTICS

PURPOSE:
To give final instructions and encouragement to Timothy, pastor of the church at Ephesus

AUTHOR:
Paul

TO WHOM WRITTEN:
Timothy, and all Christians everywhere

DATE WRITTEN:
About A.D. 66 or 67, from prison in Rome. After a year or two of freedom, Paul was arrested again and executed under Emperor Nero.

SETTING:
Paul was virtually alone in prison; only Luke was with him. Paul wrote this letter to pass the torch to the new generation of church leaders. He also asked for visits from his friends and for his scrolls, especially the parchments—possibly parts of the Old Testament, the Gospels, and other biblical manuscripts.

KEY VERSE:
"Do your best to present yourself to God as one approved, a workman who does not need to be ashamed and who correctly handles the word of truth" (2:15).

KEY PEOPLE:
Paul, Timothy, Luke, Mark, and others

KEY PLACES:
Rome, Ephesus

SPECIAL FEATURES:
Because this is Paul's last letter, it reveals his heart and his priorities—sound doctrine, steadfast faith, confident endurance, and enduring love.

THE BLUEPRINT

1. Foundations of Christian service (1:1—2:26)
2. Difficult times for Christian service (3:1—4:22)

Paul gives helpful advice to Timothy to remain solidly grounded in Christian service and to endure suffering during the difficult days to come. It is easy for us to serve Christ for the wrong reasons: because it is exciting, rewarding, or personally enriching. Without a proper foundation, however, we will find it easy to give up during difficult times. All believers need a strong foundation for their service, because Christian service does not get easier as we grow older, and it will become no easier as the time of Christ's return grows closer.

MEGATHEMES

THEME	EXPLANATION	IMPORTANCE
Boldness	In the face of opposition and persecution, Timothy was to carry out his ministry without fear or shame. Paul urged him to utilise boldly the gifts of preaching and teaching that the Holy Spirit had given him.	The Holy Spirit helps us to be wise and strong. God honours our confident testimony even when we suffer. To get over our fear of what people might say or do, we must take our eyes off of people and look only to God.
Faithfulness	Christ was faithful to all of us in dying for our sin. Paul was a faithful minister even when he was in prison. Paul urged Timothy to maintain not only sound doctrine but also loyalty, diligence, and endurance.	We can count on opposition, suffering, and hardship as we serve Christ. But this shows that our faithfulness is having an effect on others. As we trust Christ, he counts us worthy to suffer, and he will give us the strength we need to be steadfast.
Preaching and Teaching	Paul and Timothy were active in preaching and teaching the good news about Jesus Christ. Paul encouraged Timothy not only to carry the torch of truth but also to train others, passing on to them sound doctrine and enthusiasm for Christ's mission.	We must prepare people to transmit God's word to others so that they in turn might pass it on. Does your church carefully train others to teach?
Error	In the final days before Christ returns, there will be false teachers, spiritual deviants, and heretics. The remedy for error is to have a solid programme for teaching Christians.	Because of deception and false teaching, we must be disciplined and ready to reject error. Know the word of God as your sure defence against error and confusion.

1. Foundations of Christian service

1 Paul, an apostle of Christ Jesus by the will of God,[a] according to the promise
of life that is in Christ Jesus,[b]

2To Timothy,[c] my dear son:[d]

Grace, mercy and peace from God the Father and Christ Jesus our Lord.

Encouragement to Be Faithful

3I thank God,[e] whom I serve, as my forefathers did, with a clear conscience, as
night and day I constantly remember you in my prayers.[f] 4Recalling your tears,[g]

1:1 [a]2Co 1:1 [b]Eph 3:6; 1Ti 6:19
1:2 [c]Ac 16:1 [d]1Ti 1:2
1:3 [e]Ro 1:8 [f]Ro 1:10
1:4 [g]Ac 20:37

1:1 This letter has a sombre tone. Paul was imprisoned for the last time, and he knew he would soon die. Unlike Paul's first imprisonment in Rome, when he was in a house (Acts 28:16, 23, 30) where he continued to teach, this time he was probably confined to a cold dungeon, awaiting his death (4:6–8). Emperor Nero had begun a major persecution in A.D. 64 as part of his plan to pass the blame for the great fire of Rome from himself to the Christians. This persecution spread across the empire and included social ostracism, public torture, and murder. As Paul was waiting to die, he wrote a letter to his dear friend Timothy, a younger man who was like a son to him (1:2). Written in approximately A.D. 66/67, these are the last words we have from Paul.

1:2 Paul's second letter to Timothy was written about two to four years after his first letter. Timothy had been Paul's travelling companion on the second and third missionary journeys, and Paul had left him in Ephesus to help the church there (1 Timothy 1:3, 4). For more information on Timothy, see his Profile in 1 Timothy. For more information on the great missionary, Paul, see his Profile in Acts 9.

1:3 Paul constantly prayed for Timothy, his friend, his fellow traveller, his son in the faith, and a strong leader in the Christian

1:4 [h]2Ti 4:9
1:5 [i]1Ti 1:5 [j]Ac 16:1
1:6 [k]1Ti 4:14
1:7 [l]Ro 8:15
1:8 [m]Mk 8:38; Ro 1:16 [n]Eph 3:1 [o]2Ti 2:3, 9; 4:5
1:9 [p]Ro 8:28
1:10 [q]Eph 1:9 [r]1Co 15:26, 54
1:11 [s]1Ti 2:7
1:12 [t]1Ti 6:20 [u]ver 18
1:13 [v]Tit 1:9 [w]1Ti 1:14
1:14 [x]Ro 8:9

I long to see you,[h] so that I may be filled with joy. 5 I have been reminded of your
sincere faith,[i] which first lived in your grandmother Lois and in your mother Eunice[j]
and, I am persuaded, now lives in you also. 6 For this reason I remind you to fan into
flame the gift of God, which is in you through the laying on of my hands.[k] 7 For God
did not give us a spirit of timidity,[l] but a spirit of power, of love and of self-discipline.
8 So do not be ashamed[m] to testify about our Lord, or ashamed of me his prisoner.[n]
But join with me in suffering for the gospel,[o] by the power of God, 9 who has saved
us and called[p] us to a holy life — not because of anything we have done but because
of his own purpose and grace. This grace was given us in Christ Jesus before the
beginning of time, 10 but it has now been revealed[q] through the appearing of our
Saviour, Christ Jesus, who has destroyed death[r] and has brought life and immortality
to light through the gospel. 11 And of this gospel I was appointed a herald and an
apostle and a teacher.[s] 12 That is why I am suffering as I am. Yet I am not ashamed,
because I know whom I have believed, and am convinced that he is able to guard[t]
what I have entrusted to him for that day.[u]
13 What you heard from me, keep[v] as the pattern of sound teaching, with faith and
love in Christ Jesus.[w] 14 Guard the good deposit that was entrusted to you — guard it
with the help of the Holy Spirit who lives in us.[x]

---

church. Although the two men were separated from each other, their prayers provided a source of mutual encouragement. We too should pray consistently for others, especially for those who do God's work.

1:4 We don't know when Paul and Timothy last parted, but it was probably when Paul was arrested and taken to Rome for his second imprisonment. The tears they shed at parting revealed the depth of their relationship.

1:5 Timothy's mother and grandmother, Eunice and Lois, were early Christian converts, possibly through Paul's ministry in their home city, Lystra (Acts 16:1). They had communicated their strong Christian faith to Timothy, even though his father was probably not a believer. Don't hide your light at home: our families are fertile fields for planting gospel seeds. Let your parents, children, spouse, brothers, and sisters know of your faith in Jesus, and be sure they see Christ's love, helpfulness, and joy in you.

1:6 At the time of his ordination, Timothy had received special gifts of the Spirit to enable him to serve the church (see 1 Timothy 4:14). In telling Timothy to "fan into flame the gift of God", Paul was encouraging him to persevere. Timothy did not need new revelations or new gifts; he needed the courage and self-discipline to hang on to the truth and to use the gifts he had already received (see 1:13, 14). If Timothy would step out boldly in faith and proclaim the gospel once again, the Holy Spirit would go with him and give him power. When you use the gifts God has given you, you will find that God will give you the power you need.

1:6 Clearly Timothy's spiritual gift had been given to him when Paul and the elders had laid their hands on him and set him apart for ministry (see 1 Timothy 4:14). God gives all Christians gifts to use to build up the body of Christ (see 1 Corinthians 12:4–31), and he gives special gifts to some through church leaders, who serve as God's instruments.

1:6, 7 Timothy was experiencing great opposition to his message and to himself as a leader. His youth, his association with Paul, and his leadership had come under fire from believers and non-believers alike. Paul urged him to be bold. When we allow people to intimidate us, we neutralise our effectiveness for God. The power of the Holy Spirit can help us overcome our fear of what some might say or do to us, so that we can continue to do God's work.

1:7 Paul mentions three characteristics of the effective Christian leader: power, love, and self-discipline. These are available to us because the Holy Spirit lives in us. Follow his leading each day so that your life will more fully exhibit these characteristics. See Galatians 5:22, 23 for a list of the by-products of the Holy Spirit living in us.

1:8 In this time of mounting persecution, Timothy may have been afraid to continue preaching the gospel. His fears were based on fact, because believers were being arrested and executed. Paul told Timothy to expect suffering — Timothy, like Paul, would be jailed for preaching the gospel (Hebrews 13:23). But Paul promised Timothy that God would give him strength and that he would be ready when it was his turn to suffer. Even when there is no persecution, it can be difficult to share our faith in Christ. Fortunately we, like Paul and Timothy, can call on the Holy Spirit to give us courage. Don't be ashamed to testify.

1:9, 10 In these verses Paul gives a brief summary of the gospel. God loves us, called us, and sent Christ to die for us. We can have eternal life through faith in him, because he broke the power of death with his resurrection. We do not deserve to be saved, but God offers us salvation anyway. What we must do is believe in him and accept his offer.

1:12 Paul was in prison, but that did not stop his ministry. He carried it on through others like Timothy. Paul had lost all his material possessions, but he would never lose his faith. He trusted God to use him regardless of his circumstances. If your situation looks bleak, give your concerns to Christ. He will guard your faith and safely guard all you have entrusted to him until the day of his return. For more on our security in Christ, see Romans 8:38, 39.

1:12 The phrase "guard what I have entrusted to him" could mean: (1) Paul knew that God would guard the souls of those converted through his preaching; (2) Paul trusted God to guard his own soul until Christ's second coming; or (3) Paul was confident that, though he was in prison and facing death, God would carry out the gospel ministry through others such as Timothy. Paul may have expressed his confidence to encourage Timothy, who was undoubtedly discouraged by the problems in Ephesus and fearful of persecution. Even in prison, Paul knew that God was still in control. No matter what setbacks or problems we face, we can trust fully in God.

1:13, 14 Timothy was in a time of transition. He had been Paul's bright young helper; soon he would be on his own as leader of a church in a difficult environment. Although his responsibilities were changing, Timothy was not without help. He had everything he needed to face the future, if he would hold on tightly to the Lord's resources. When you are facing difficult transitions, it is good to follow Paul's advice to Timothy and look back at your experience. Who is the foundation of your faith? How can you build on that foundation? What gifts has the Holy Spirit given you? Use the gifts you have already been given.

15 You know that everyone in the province of Asia has deserted me,[y] including
Phygelus and Hermogenes.
16 May the Lord show mercy to the household of Onesiphorus,[z] because he often
refreshed me and was not ashamed of my chains. 17 On the contrary, when he was in
Rome, he searched hard for me until he found me. 18 May the Lord grant that he will
find mercy from the Lord on that day! You know very well in how many ways he
helped me[a] in Ephesus.

2 You then, my son, be strong[a] in the grace that is in Christ Jesus. 2 And the things
you have heard me say[b] in the presence of many witnesses[c] entrust to reliable
men who will also be qualified to teach others. 3 Endure hardship with us like a good
soldier[d] of Christ Jesus. 4 No-one serving as a soldier gets involved in civilian
affairs – he wants to please his commanding officer. 5 Similarly, if anyone competes
as an athlete, he does not receive the victor's crown[e] unless he competes according
to the rules. 6 The hardworking farmer should be the first to receive a share of the crops.
7 Reflect on what I am saying, for the Lord will give you insight into all this.
8 Remember Jesus Christ, raised from the dead,[f] descended from David.[g] This is
my gospel,[h] 9 for which I am suffering[i] even to the point of being chained like a
criminal. But God's word is not chained. 10 Therefore I endure everything[j] for the
sake of the elect, that they too may obtain the salvation that is in Christ Jesus, with
eternal glory.[k]
11 Here is a trustworthy saying:

> If we died with him,
> we will also live with him;[l]
> 12 if we endure,

1:15 [y] 2Ti 4:10, 11, 16
1:16 [z] 2Ti 4:19
1:18 [a] Heb 6:10
2:1 [a] Eph 6:10
2:2 [b] 2Ti 1:13 [c] 1Ti 6:12
2:3 [d] 1Ti 1:18
2:5 [e] 1Co 9:25
2:8 [f] Ac 2:24 [g] Mt 1:1 [h] Ro 2:16
2:9 [i] Ac 9:16
2:10 [j] Col 1:24 [k] 2Co 4:17
2:11 [l] Ro 6:2-11

1:15, 16 Nothing more is known about Phygelus and Hermogenes, who evidently opposed Paul's ministry. These men serve as a warning that even leaders can fall. Onesiphorus was mentioned as a positive example in contrast to these men.

2:1 How can someone be strong in grace? Grace means undeserved favour. Just as we are saved by grace (Ephesians 2:8, 9), we should live by grace (Colossians 2:6). This means trusting completely in Christ and *his* power, and not trying to live for Christ in our strength alone. Receive and utilise Christ's power. He will give you the strength to do his work.

2:2 If the church were consistently to follow this advice, it would expand geometrically as well-taught believers would teach others and commission them, in turn, to teach still others. Disciples need to be equipped to pass on their faith; our work is not done until new believers are able to make disciples of others (see Ephesians 4:12, 13).

2:3–7 As Timothy preached and taught, he would face suffering, but he should be able to endure. Paul used a comparison with soldiers, athletes, and farmers who must discipline themselves and be willing to sacrifice to achieve the results they want. Like soldiers, we have to give up worldly security and endure rigorous discipline. Like athletes, we must train hard and follow the rules. Like farmers, we must work extremely hard and be patient. But we keep going despite suffering because of the thought of victory, the vision of winning, and the hope of harvest. We will see that our suffering is worthwhile when we achieve our goal of glorifying God, winning people to Christ, and one day living eternally with him.

2:7 Paul told Timothy to reflect on his words, and God would give him insight. God speaks through the Bible, his word, but we need to be open and receptive to him. As you read the Bible, ask God to show you his timeless truths and the application to your life. Then consider what you have read by thinking it through and meditating on it. God will give you understanding.

2:8 False teachers were a problem in Ephesus (see Acts 20:29, 30; 1 Timothy 1:3–11). At the heart of false teaching is an incorrect view of Christ. In Timothy's day many asserted that Christ was divine but not human – God but not man. These days we often hear that Jesus was human but not divine – man but not God. Either view destroys the good news that Jesus Christ has taken our sins on himself and has reconciled us to God. In this verse, Paul firmly states that Jesus is fully man ("descended from David") and fully God ("raised from the dead"). This is an important doctrine for all Christians. For more on this key concept see the note on Philippians 2:5–7.

2:9 Paul was in chains in prison because of the gospel he preached. The truth about Jesus is no more popular in our day than in Paul's, but it still reaches receptive hearts. When Paul said that Jesus was God, he angered the Jews who had condemned Jesus for blasphemy; but many Jews became followers of Christ (1 Corinthians 1:24). He angered the Romans who worshipped the emperor as god; but even some in Caesar's household turned to Jesus (Philippians 4:22). When Paul said Jesus was human, he angered the Greeks who thought divinity was soiled if it had any contact with humanity; still many Greeks accepted the faith (Acts 11:20, 21). The truth that Jesus is one person with two united natures has never been easy to understand, but it is being believed by people every day. Despite the opposition, continue to proclaim Christ. Some will listen and believe.

2:10 When Paul says "obtain the salvation", is he contradicting grace? Salvation is not something that can be earned, as Paul taught in Ephesians 2:8, 9. Paul is referring to being faithful to the end, not to a way to earn salvation.

2:11–13 This is probably an early Christian hymn. God is faithful to his children, and although we may suffer great hardships here, God promises that someday we will live eternally with him. What will this involve? It means believers will live in Christ's kingdom, and that we will share in the administration of that kingdom. This truth comforted Paul as he went through suffering and death. Are you facing hardships? Don't turn away from God – he promises you a wonderful future with him. For more information about living eternally with God, see Matthew 16:24–27; 19:28–30; Luke 22:28–30; Romans 5:17; 6:8; 8:10, 11, 17; 1 Corinthians 15:42–58; Colossians 3:3, 4; 1 Thessalonians 4:13–18; Revelation 3:21; 21:1 – 22:21.

2:12 [m]Ro 8:17; 1Pe 4:13 [n]Mt 10:33
2:13 [o]Nu 23:19; Ro 3:3
2:14 [p]1Ti 6:4
2:15 [q]Eph 1:13; Jas 1:18
2:16 [r]Tit 3:9
2:17 [s]1Ti 1:20
2:18 [t]1Ti 1:19
2:19 [u]Isa 28:16 [v]Jn 10:14 [w]1Co 1:2
2:20 [x]Ro 9:21
2:21 [y]2Ti 3:17
2:22 [z]1Ti 1:14; 6:11 [a]1Ti 1:5

we will also reign with him.[m]
If we disown him,
he will also disown us;[n]
13 if we are faithless,
he will remain faithful,[o]
for he cannot disown himself.

A Workman Approved by God

14 Keep reminding them of these things. Warn them before God against quarrelling
about words;[p] it is of no value, and only ruins those who listen. 15 Do your best to
present yourself to God as one approved, a workman who does not need to be ashamed
and who correctly handles the word of truth.[q] 16 Avoid godless chatter,[r] because
those who indulge in it will become more and more ungodly. 17 Their teaching will
spread like gangrene. Among them are Hymenaeus[s] and Philetus, 18 who have
wandered away from the truth. They say that the resurrection has already taken place,
and they destroy the faith of some.[t] 19 Nevertheless, God's solid foundation stands
firm,[u] sealed with this inscription: "The Lord knows those who are his,"[a][v] and,
"Everyone who confesses the name of the Lord[w] must turn away from wickedness."
20 In a large house there are articles not only of gold and silver, but also of wood
and clay; some are for noble purposes and some for ignoble.[x] 21 If a man cleanses
himself from the latter, he will be an instrument for noble purposes, made holy, useful
to the Master and prepared to do any good work.[y]
22 Flee the evil desires of youth, and pursue righteousness, faith, love[z] and peace,
along with those who call on the Lord out of a pure heart.[a] 23 Don't have anything
to do with foolish and stupid arguments, because you know they produce quarrels.

a *19* Num. 16:5 (see Septuagint)

2:13 Jesus is faithful. He will stay by our side even when we have endured so much that we seem to have no faith left. We may be faithless at times, but Jesus is faithful to his promise to be with us "to the very end of the age" (Matthew 28:20). Refusing Christ's help will break our communication with God, but he will never turn his back on us even though we may turn our backs on him.

2:14–16 Paul urged Timothy to remind the believers not to argue over unimportant details ("quarrelling about words") or have foolish discussions ("godless chatter") because such arguments are confusing, useless, and even harmful. False teachers loved to cause strife and divisions by their meaningless quibbling over unimportant details (see 1 Timothy 6:3–5). To handle the word of truth correctly, we must study what the word of God says so we can understand what it means.

2:15 Because God will examine what kind of workers we have been for him, we should build our lives on his word and build his word into our lives – it alone tells us how to live for him and serve him. Believers who ignore the Bible will certainly be ashamed at the judgment. Consistent and diligent study of God's word is vital; otherwise we will be lulled into neglecting God and our true purpose for living.

2:16 In important areas of Christian teaching, we must carefully work through our disagreements. But when we bicker long hours over words and theories that are not central to the Christian faith and life, we only provoke anger and hurt feelings. Even if "godless chatter" reaches a resolution, it gains little ground for the kingdom. Learning and discussing are not bad unless they keep believers constantly focusing on false doctrine or unhelpful trivialities. Don't let anything keep you from your work for and service to God.

2:17, 18 Hymenaeus was also mentioned in 1 Timothy 1:20. Paul had handed Hymenaeus over to Satan because his false teaching concerning the resurrection was destroying some people's faith.

2:18 The false teachers were denying the resurrection of the body. They believed that when a person became a Christian, he or she was spiritually reborn, and that was the only resurrection there would ever be. To them, resurrection was symbolic and spiritual, not physical. Paul clearly taught, however, that believers will be resurrected after they die, and that their bodies as well as their souls will live eternally with Christ (1 Corinthians 15:35ff; 2 Corinthians 5:1–10; 1 Thessalonians 4:15–18). We cannot shape the doctrines of Scripture to match our opinions. If we do, we are putting ourselves above God. Instead, our beliefs should be consistent with God's word.

2:19 False teachers still spout lies. Some distort the truth, some dilute it, and some simply delete it by saying that God's truth no longer applies. But no matter how many people follow the liars, the solid foundation of God's truth never changes, is never shaken, and will never fade. When we follow God's truth, he will never forsake us.

2:20, 21 Here Paul urged Timothy to be the kind of person Christ could use for his noblest purposes. Don't settle for less than God's highest and best. Allow God to use you as an instrument of his will.

2:22 Running away is sometimes considered cowardly. But wise people realise that removing themselves physically from temptation can often be the most courageous action to take. Timothy, a young man, was warned to flee anything that produced evil thoughts. Do you have a recurring temptation that is difficult to resist? Remove yourself physically from any situation that stimulates your desire to sin. Knowing when to run is as important in spiritual battle as knowing when and how to fight. (See also 1 Timothy 6:11.)

2:23–26 As a teacher, Timothy helped those who were confused about the truth. Paul's advice to Timothy, and to all who teach God's truth, is to be kind and gentle, patiently and courteously explaining the truth. Good teaching never promotes quarrels or foolish arguments. Whether you are teaching Sunday school, leading a Bible study, or preaching in church, remember to listen to people's questions and treat them respectfully, while avoiding foolish debates. If you do this, those who oppose you will be more willing to hear what you have to say and perhaps turn from their error.

24 And the Lord's servant must not quarrel; instead, he must be kind to everyone, able
to teach, not resentful.[b] 25 Those who oppose him he must gently instruct, in the hope
that God will grant them repentance leading them to a knowledge of the truth,[c] 26 and
that they will come to their senses and escape from the trap of the devil,[d] who has
taken them captive to do his will.

2. Difficult times for Christian service

Godlessness in the Last Days

3 But mark this: There will be terrible times in the last days.[a] 2 People will be lovers
of themselves, lovers of money,[b] boastful, proud,[c] abusive, disobedient to their
parents,[d] ungrateful, unholy, 3 without love, unforgiving, slanderous, without self-
control, brutal, not lovers of the good, 4 treacherous, rash, conceited,[e] lovers of
pleasure rather than lovers of God — 5 having a form of godliness but denying its
power. Have nothing to do with them.
6 They are the kind who worm their way[f] into homes and gain control over
weak-willed women, who are loaded down with sins and are swayed by all kinds of
evil desires, 7 always learning but never able to acknowledge the truth. 8 Just as Jannes
and Jambres opposed Moses,[g] so also these men oppose[h] the truth — men of depraved minds,[i] who, as far as the faith is concerned, are rejected. 9 But they will not
get very far because, as in the case of those men,[j] their folly will be clear to everyone.

Paul's Charge to Timothy

10 You, however, know all about my teaching,[k] my way of life, my purpose, faith,
patience, love, endurance, 11 persecutions, sufferings — what kinds of things happened
to me in Antioch,[l] Iconium and Lystra, the persecutions I endured.[m] Yet the Lord
rescued me from all of them.[n] 12 In fact, everyone who wants to live a godly life in
Christ Jesus will be persecuted,[o] 13 while evil men and impostors will go from bad
to worse,[p] deceiving and being deceived. 14 But as for you, continue in what you have

2:24 [b] 1Ti 3:2, 3
2:25 [c] 1Ti 2:4
2:26 [d] 1Ti 3:7
3:1 [a] 1Ti 4:1
3:2 [b] 1Ti 3:3 [c] Ro 1:30 [d] Ro 1:30
3:4 [e] 1Ti 3:6
3:6 [f] Jude 4
3:8 [g] Ex 7:11 [h] Ac 13:8 [i] 1Ti 6:5
3:9 [j] Ex 7:12
3:10 [k] 1Ti 4:6
3:11 [l] Ac 13:14, 50 [m] 2Co 11:23-27 [n] Ps 34:19
3:12 [o] Ac 14:22
3:13 [p] 2Ti 2:16

3:1 Paul's reference to the "last days" reveals his sense of urgency. The last days began after Jesus' resurrection when the Holy Spirit came upon the believers at Pentecost. The "last days" will continue until Christ's second coming. This means that *we* are living in the last days. So we should make the most of the time that God has given us (Ephesians 5:16; Colossians 4:5).

3:1ff In many parts of the world today it is not especially difficult to be a Christian — people aren't jailed for reading the Bible or executed for preaching Christ. But Paul's descriptive list of behaviour in the last days describes our society — even, unfortunately, the behaviour of many Christians. Check your life against Paul's list. Don't give in to society's pressures. Don't settle for comfort without commitment. Stand up against evil by living as God would have his people live.

3:5 The "form" or appearance of godliness includes going to church, knowing Christian doctrine, using Christian clichés, and following a community's Christian traditions. Such practices can make a person look good, but if the inner attitudes of belief, love, and worship are lacking, the outer appearance is meaningless. Paul warns us not to be deceived by people who only appear to be Christians. It may be difficult to distinguish them from true Christians at first, but their daily behaviour will give them away. The characteristics described in 3:2–4 are unmistakable.

3:6, 7 Because of their cultural background, women in the Ephesian church had had no formal religious training. They enjoyed their new freedom to study Christian truths, but their eagerness to learn made them a target for false teachers. Paul warned Timothy to watch out for men who would take advantage of these women. New believers need to grow in their knowledge of the word, because ignorance can make them vulnerable to deception.

3:7 This verse is not opposing study and learning; it is warning about ineffective learning. It is possible to be a perpetual student and never graduate to putting theory into practice. But honest seekers and true students look for answers. Remember this as you study God's word. Seek to find God's truth and will for your life.

3:8, 9 According to tradition, Jannes and Jambres were two of the magicians who counterfeited Moses' miracles before Pharaoh (Exodus 7:11, 12). Paul explained that just as Moses exposed and defeated them (Exodus 8:18, 19), God would overthrow the false teachers who were plaguing the Ephesian church.

3:9 Sin has consequences, and no-one will get away with it for ever. Live each day as if your actions will one day be known to everyone. Now is the time to change anything you wouldn't want revealed later.

3:11 In Lystra, Timothy's home town, Paul had been stoned and left for dead (Acts 14:19); and this was only one incident among many. In 2 Corinthians 11:23–33 Paul summarised his lifetime of suffering for the sake of the gospel. Paul mentioned his suffering here to contrast his experience with that of the pleasure-seeking false teachers.

3:12 In this charge, Paul told Timothy that people who obey God and live for Christ will be persecuted. Don't be surprised when people misunderstand, criticise, and even try to hurt you because of what you believe and how you live. Don't give up. Continue to live as you know you should. God is the only one you need to please.

3:13 Don't expect false teachers and evil people to reform and change on their own. Left alone, they will go from bad to worse. If you have the opportunity, correct them so as to bring them back to faith in Christ. Fight for the truth, especially to protect younger Christians.

3:14 Besieged by false teachers and the inevitable pressures of a growing ministry, Timothy could easily have abandoned his faith or modified his doctrine. Once again Paul counselled Timothy to look to his past, and to hold to the basic teachings about Jesus that are eternally true. Like Timothy, we are surrounded by false

learned and have become convinced of, because you know those from whom you
learned it,[q] 15 and how from infancy[r] you have known the holy Scriptures,[s] which
are able to make you wise[t] for salvation through faith in Christ Jesus. 16 All Scripture
is God-breathed[u] and is useful for teaching,[v] rebuking, correcting and training in
righteousness, 17 so that the man of God[w] may be thoroughly equipped for every good
work.[x]

4 In the presence of God and of Christ Jesus, who will judge the living and the
dead,[a] and in view of his appearing and his kingdom, I give you this charge:[b]
2 Preach[c] the Word;[d] be prepared in season and out of season; correct, rebuke[e] and
encourage—with great patience and careful instruction. 3 For the time will come when
men will not put up with sound doctrine.[f] Instead, to suit their own desires, they will
gather around them a great number of teachers to say what their itching ears want to
hear. 4 They will turn their ears away from the truth and turn aside to myths.[g] 5 But
you, keep your head in all situations, endure hardship,[h] do the work of an evangelist,[i] discharge all the duties of your ministry.

6 For I am already being poured out like a drink offering,[j] and the time has come
for my departure.[k] 7 I have fought the good fight,[l] I have finished the race,[m] I have

3:14 [q] 2Ti 1:13
3:15 [r] 2Ti 1:5 [s] Jn 5:39 [t] Ps 119:98, 99
3:16 [u] 2Pe 1:20, 21 [v] Ro 4:23, 24
3:17 [w] 1Ti 6:11 [x] 2Ti 2:21
4:1 [a] Ac 10:42 [b] 1Ti 5:21
4:2 [c] 1Ti 4:13 [d] Gal 6:6 [e] 1Ti 5:20;
4:3 [f] 1Ti 1:10
4:4 [g] 1Ti 1:4
4:5 [h] 2Ti 1:8 [i] Ac 21:8
4:6 [j] Php 2:17 [k] Php 1:23
4:7 [l] 1Ti 1:18 [m] 1Co 9:24

---

teachings. But we must not allow our society to distort or crowd out God's eternal truth. Spend time every day reflecting on the foundation of your Christian faith found in God's word, the great truths that build up your life.

3:15 Timothy was one of the first second-generation Christians: he became a Christian not because an evangelist preached a powerful sermon, but because his mother and grandmother taught him the holy Scriptures when he was a small child (1:5). A parent's work is vitally important. At home and in church, we should realise that teaching small children is both an opportunity and a responsibility. Jesus wanted little children to come to him (Matthew 19:13–15). Like Timothy's mother and grandmother, Eunice and Lois, do your part in leading children to Christ.

3:15 For Timothy, the "holy Scriptures" were the Old Testament—Genesis to Malachi. The Old Testament is important because it points to Jesus Christ. At the same time, faith in Christ makes the whole Bible intelligible.

3:16 The Bible is not a collection of stories, fables, myths, or merely human ideas about God. It is not a human book. Through the Holy Spirit, God revealed his person and plan to certain believers, who wrote down his message for his people (2 Peter 1:20, 21). This process is known as *inspiration*. The writers wrote from their own personal, historical, and cultural contexts. Although they used their own minds, talents, language, and style, they wrote what God wanted them to write. Scripture is completely trustworthy because God was in control of its writing. Its words are entirely authoritative for our faith and lives. The Bible is "God-breathed". Read it, and use its teachings to guide your conduct.

3:16, 17 The whole Bible is God's inspired word. Because it is inspired and trustworthy, we should *read* it and *apply* it to our lives. The Bible is our standard for testing everything else that claims to be true. It is our safeguard against false teaching and our source of guidance for how we should live. It is our only source of knowledge about how we can be saved. God wants to show you what is true and equip you to live for him. How much time do you spend in God's word? Read it regularly to discover God's truth and to become confident in your life and faith. Develop a plan for reading the whole Bible, not just the familiar passages.

3:17 In our zeal for the *truth* of Scripture, we must never forget its *purpose*—to equip us to do good. We should not study God's word simply to increase our knowledge or to prepare us to win arguments. We should study the Bible so that we will know how to do Christ's work in the world. Our knowledge of God's word is not useful unless it strengthens our faith and leads us to do good.

4:1, 2 It was important for Timothy to preach the gospel so that the Christian faith could spread throughout the world. We believe in Christ today because people like Timothy were faithful to their mission. It is still vitally important for believers to spread the gospel. Half the people who have ever lived are alive today, and most of them do not know Christ. He is coming soon, and he wants to find his faithful believers ready for him. It may be inconvenient to take a stand for Christ or to tell others about his love, but preaching the word of God is the most important responsibility the church and its members have been given. Be prepared for, courageous in, and sensitive to God-given opportunities to tell the Good News.

4:2 "Be prepared in season and out of season" means to always be ready to serve God in any situation, whether or not it is convenient. Be sensitive to the opportunities God gives you.

4:2 Paul told Timothy to "correct, rebuke and encourage". It is difficult to accept correction, to be told we have to change. But no matter how much the truth hurts, we must be willing to listen to it so we can more fully obey God.

4:5 To keep cool when you are jarred and jolted by people or circumstances, don't react quickly. In any work of ministry that you undertake, keeping your head makes you morally alert to temptation, resistant to pressure, and vigilant when facing heavy responsibility.

4:5–8 As he neared the end of his life, Paul could confidently say he had been faithful to his call. Thus he faced death calmly, knowing that he would be rewarded by Christ. Is your life preparing you for death? Do you share Paul's confident expectation of meeting Christ? The good news is that the heavenly reward is not just for giants of the faith, like Paul, but for all who are eagerly looking forward to Jesus' second coming. Paul gave these words to encourage Timothy, and us, that no matter how difficult the fight seems—keep fighting. When we are with Jesus Christ, we will discover that it was all worth it.

4:6 A drink offering consisted of wine poured out on an altar as a sacrifice to God (see Genesis 35:14; Exodus 29:41). Its fragrance was considered pleasing to God. Paul viewed his life as an offering to God.

kept the faith. 8 Now there is in store for me[n] the crown of righteousness, which the
Lord, the righteous Judge, will award to me on that day[o]—and not only to me, but
also to all who have longed for his appearing.

Personal Remarks

9 Do your best to come to me quickly, 10 for Demas,[p] because he loved this world,[q]
has deserted me and has gone to Thessalonica. Crescens has gone to Galatia,[r] and
Titus to Dalmatia. 11 Only Luke[s] is with me.[t] Get Mark[u] and bring him with you,
because he is helpful to me in my ministry. 12 I sent Tychicus[v] to Ephesus. 13 When
you come, bring the cloak that I left with Carpus at Troas, and my scrolls, especially
the parchments.

14 Alexander[w] the metalworker did me a great deal of harm. The Lord will repay
him for what he has done.[x] 15 You too should be on your guard against him, because
he strongly opposed our message.

16 At my first defence, no-one came to my support, but everyone deserted me. May
it not be held against them.[y] 17 But the Lord stood at my side[z] and gave me strength,
so that through me the message might be fully proclaimed and all the Gentiles might
hear it.[a] And I was delivered from the lion's mouth. 18 The Lord will rescue me from
every evil attack[b] and will bring me safely to his heavenly kingdom. To him be glory
for ever and ever. Amen.[c]

Final Greetings

19 Greet Priscilla[a] and Aquila[d] and the household of Onesiphorus. 20 Erastus[e]
stayed in Corinth, and I left Trophimus[f] sick in Miletus. 21 Do your best to get here

a *19* Greek *Prisca*, a variant of *Priscilla*

4:8 [n]Col 1:5 [o]2Ti 1:12
4:10 [p]Col 4:14 [q]1Jn 2:15 [r]Ac 16:6
4:11 [s]Col 4:14 [t]2Ti 1:15 [u]Ac 12:12
4:12 [v]Ac 20:4
4:14 [w]Ac 19:33 [x]Ro 12:19
4:16 [y]Ac 7:60
4:17 [z]Ac 23:11 [a]Ac 9:15
4:18 [b]Ps 121:7 [c]Ro 11:36
4:19 [d]Ac 18:2
4:20 [e]Ac 19:22 [f]Ac 20:4

4:8 In Roman athletic games, a laurel wreath was given to the winners. A symbol of triumph and honour, it was the most coveted prize in ancient Rome. This is probably what Paul was referring to when he spoke of a "crown". But his would be a crown of righteousness. See 2 Corinthians 5:10 and the note on Matthew 19:27 for more on the rewards awaiting us for our faith and deeds. Although Paul would not receive an earthly reward, he would be rewarded in heaven. Whatever we may face—discouragement, persecution, or death—we know our reward is with Christ in heaven.

4:9, 10 Paul was virtually alone and probably lonely. No-one had been there at his trial to speak in his defence (4:16), and Demas had left the faith (4:10). Only Luke had returned (4:11).

4:10 Demas had been one of Paul's co-workers (Colossians 4:14; Philemon 24), but he had deserted Paul because he "loved this world". In other words, Demas loved worldly values and worldly pleasures. There are two ways to love the world. God loves the world as he created it and as it could be if it were rescued from evil. Others, like Demas, love the world as it is, sin and all. Do you love the world as it could be if justice were done, the hungry were fed, and people loved one another? Or do you love what the world has to offer—wealth, power, pleasure—even if gaining it means hurting people and neglecting the work God has given you to do?

4:11 Crescens and Titus had left, but not for the same reasons as Demas. Paul did not criticise or condemn them.

4:11, 12 Mentioning Demas reminded Paul of more faithful co-workers. Only Luke was with Paul, and Paul was feeling lonely. Tychicus, one of his most trusted companions (Acts 20:4; Ephesians 6:21; Colossians 4:7; Titus 3:12), had already left for Ephesus. Paul missed his young helpers Timothy and Mark. Mark had left Paul and Barnabas on the first missionary journey, and this had greatly upset Paul (Acts 13:13; 15:36–41). But later Mark proved to be a worthy helper, and Paul recognised him as a good friend and trusted Christian leader (Colossians 4:10; Philemon 24). Mark wrote the Gospel of Mark.

4:13 Paul's arrest probably occurred so suddenly that he was not allowed to return home to gather his personal belongings. Because he was a prisoner in a damp and chilly dungeon, Paul asked Timothy to bring him his cloak. Even more than the cloak, Paul wanted his parchments. These may have included parts of the Old Testament, the Gospels, copies of his own letters, or other important documents.

4:14, 15 Alexander may have been a witness against Paul at his trial. He may have been the Alexander mentioned in 1 Timothy 1:20.

4:17 With his mentor in prison and his church in turmoil, Timothy was probably not feeling very brave. Paul may have been subtly telling Timothy that the Lord had called Timothy to preach, and would give him the courage to continue to do so. God always gives us the strength to do what he has commanded. This strength may not be evident, however, until we step out in faith and actually begin doing the task.

4:17 Some have seen this as a reference to Nero throwing Christians to the lions in the Coliseum. More likely, it is Paul's way of describing his deliverance at his first defence (see, for example, Psalm 22:21; Daniel 6:22).

4:18 Here Paul was affirming his belief in eternal life after death. Paul knew the end was near, and he was ready for it. Paul was confident in God's power even as he faced death. Anyone facing a life and death struggle can be comforted knowing that God will bring each believer safely through death to his heavenly kingdom.

4:19, 20 Priscilla and Aquila were fellow Christian leaders with whom Paul had lived and worked (Acts 18:2, 3). Onesiphorus visited and encouraged Paul in jail. Erastus was one of Paul's trusted companions (Acts 19:22), as was Trophimus (Acts 20:4; 21:29).

4:19–22 Paul ended the final chapter in his book and in his life by greeting those who were closest to him. Although Paul had spent most of his life travelling, he had developed close and lasting friendships. Too often, we rush through our days, barely touching anyone's life. Like Paul, take time to weave your life into others through deep relationships.

4:21
[g] ver 9
4:22
[h] Gal 6:18;
[i] Col 4:18

before winter.[g] Eubulus greets you, and so do Pudens, Linus, Claudia and all the brothers.
22 The Lord be with your spirit.[h] Grace be with you.[i]

4:22 As Paul reached the end of his life, he could look back and know he had been faithful to God's call. Now it was time to pass the torch to the next generation, preparing leaders to take his place so that the world would continue to hear the life-changing message of Jesus Christ. Timothy was Paul's living legacy, a product of Paul's faithful teaching, discipleship, and example. Because of Paul's work with many believers, including Timothy, the world is full of believers today who are also carrying on the work. What legacy will you leave behind? Whom are you training to carry on your work? It is our responsibility to do all we can do to keep the gospel message alive for the next generation.

TITUS

VITAL STATISTICS

PURPOSE:
To advise Titus in his responsibility of supervising the churches on the island of Crete

AUTHOR:
Paul

TO WHOM WRITTEN:
Titus, a Greek, probably converted to Christ through Paul's ministry (he had become Paul's special representative to the island of Crete), and all believers everywhere

DATE WRITTEN:
About A.D. 64, around the same time 1 Timothy was written; probably from Macedonia when Paul travelled between his Roman imprisonments

SETTING:
Paul sent Titus to organise and oversee the churches on Crete. This letter tells Titus how to do this job.

KEY VERSE:
"The reason I left you in Crete was that you might straighten out what was left unfinished and appoint elders in every town, as I directed you" (1:5).

KEY PEOPLE:
Paul, Titus

KEY PLACES:
Crete, Nicopolis

SPECIAL FEATURES:
Titus is very similar to 1 Timothy with its instructions to church leaders.

THE VACUUM produced when a strong leader departs can devastate a movement, organisation, or institution. Having been dependent on his or her skill, style, and personality, associates and subordinates flounder or vie for control. Soon efficiency and vitality are lost, and decline and demise follow. Often this pattern is repeated in churches. Great speakers and teachers gather a following, and soon a church is flourishing. It is alive, vital, and effective. Lives are being changed and people led into the kingdom. But when this catalyst leaves or dies, with him or her goes the drive and the heart of the organisation.

People flocked to hear Paul's teaching. Educated, articulate, motivated, and filled with the Holy Spirit, this man of faith faithfully proclaimed the good news throughout the Roman empire—lives were changed and churches begun. But Paul knew that the church must be built on Christ, not on a person. And he knew that eventually he would not be there to build, encourage, discipline, and teach. So he trained young pastors to assume leadership in the church after he was gone. Paul urged them to centre their lives and preaching on the word of God (2 Timothy 3:16, 17) and to train others to carry on the ministry (2 Timothy 2:2).

Titus was a Greek believer. Taught and nurtured by Paul, he stood before the leaders of the church in Jerusalem as a living example of what Christ was doing among the Gentiles (Galatians 2:1–3). Like Timothy, he was one of Paul's trusted travelling companions and closest friends. Later he became Paul's special ambassador (2 Corinthians 7:5–16) and eventually the overseer of the churches on Crete (Titus 1:5). Slowly and carefully, Paul developed Titus into a mature Christian and a responsible leader. The letter to Titus was a step in this discipleship process. As with Timothy, Paul told Titus how to organise and lead the churches.

Paul begins with a longer than usual greeting and introduction, outlining the leadership progression—Paul's ministry (1:1–3), Titus' responsibilities (1:4, 5), and those leaders whom Titus would appoint and train (1:5). Paul then lists pastoral qualifications (1:6–9) and contrasts faithful overseers with the false leaders and teachers (1:10–16).

Next, Paul emphasises the importance of good deeds in the life of the Christian, telling Titus how to relate to the various age groups in the church (2:2–6). He urges Titus to be a good example of a mature believer (2:7, 8) and to teach with courage and conviction (2:9–15). He then discusses the general responsibilities of Christians in society—Titus should remind the people of these (3:1–8), and he should avoid divisive arguments (3:9–11). Paul concludes with a few matters of itinerary and personal greetings (3:12–15).

Paul's letter to Titus is brief, but it is an important link in the discipleship process—helping a young man grow into leadership in the church. As you read this pastoral letter, you will gain insight into the organisation and life of the early church, and you will find principles for structuring contemporary churches. But you should also see how to be a responsible Christian leader. Read the letter to Titus and determine, like Paul, to train men and women to lead and teach others.

THE BLUEPRINT

1. Leadership in the church (1:1–16)
2. Right living in the church (2:1–15)
3. Right living in society (3:1–15)

Paul calls for church order and right living on an island known for laziness, gluttony, lying, and evil. The Christians are to be self-disciplined as individuals, and they must be orderly as people who form one body, the church. We need to obey this message in our day when discipline is not respected or rewarded by our society. Although others may not appreciate our efforts, we must live upright lives, obey the government, and control our speech. We should live together peacefully in the church and be living examples of our faith to contemporary society.

MEGATHEMES

THEME	EXPLANATION	IMPORTANCE
A Good Life	The good news of salvation is that we can't be saved by living a good life; we are saved only by faith in Jesus Christ. But the gospel transforms people's lives so that they eventually perform good deeds. Our service won't save us, but we are saved to serve.	A good life is a witness to the gospel's power. As Christians, we must have commitment and discipline to serve. Are you putting your faith into action by serving others?
Character	Titus' responsibility in Crete was to appoint elders to maintain proper organisation and discipline, so Paul listed the qualities needed for the eldership. Their conduct in their homes revealed their fitness for service in the church.	It's not enough to be educated or to have a loyal following to be Christ's kind of leader. You must have self-control, spiritual and moral fitness, and Christian character. Who you are is just as important as what you can do.
Church Relationships	Church teaching must relate to various groups. Older Christians were to teach and to be examples to younger men and women. People of every age and group have a lesson to learn and a role to play.	Right living and right relationship go along with right doctrine. Treat relationships with other believers as an outgrowth of your faith.
Citizenship	Christians must be good citizens in society, not just in church. Believers must obey the government and work honestly.	How you fulfil your civic duties is a witness to the watching world. Your community life should reflect Christ's love as much as your church life does.

1. Leadership in the church

1 Paul, a servant of God[a] and an apostle of Jesus Christ for the faith of God's elect
and the knowledge of the truth[b] that leads to godliness—2a faith and knowledge
resting on the hope of eternal life,[c] which God, who does not lie, promised before
the beginning of time,[d] 3and at his appointed season[e] he brought his word to light[f]
through the preaching entrusted to me[g] by the command of God our Saviour,[h]

4To Titus,[i] my true son in our common faith:

Grace and peace from God the Father and Christ Jesus our Saviour.

Titus' Task on Crete

5The reason I left you in Crete[j] was that you might straighten out what was left
unfinished and appoint**a** elders[k] in every town, as I directed you. 6An elder must
be blameless,[l] the husband of but one wife, a man whose children believe and are
not open to the charge of being wild and disobedient. 7Since an overseer**b**[m] is
entrusted with God's work,[n] he must be blameless—not overbearing, not quick-tempered, not given to drunkenness, not violent, not pursuing dishonest gain.[o]
8Rather he must be hospitable,[p] one who loves what is good,[q] who is self-controlled,
upright, holy and disciplined. 9He must hold firmly[r] to the trustworthy message as
it has been taught, so that he can encourage others by sound doctrine[s] and refute those
who oppose it.
10For there are many rebellious people, mere talkers[t] and deceivers, especially

a *5* Or *ordain* **b** *7* Traditionally *bishop*

1:1 [a]Ro 1:1 [b]1Ti 2:4
1:2 [c]2Ti 1:1 [d]2Ti 1:9
1:3 [e]1Ti 2:6 [f]2Ti 1:10 [g]1Ti 1:11 [h]Lk 1:47
1:4 [i]2Co 2:13
1:5 [j]Ac 27:7 [k]Ac 11:30
1:6 [l]1Ti 3:2
1:7 [m]1Ti 3:1 [n]1Co 4:1 [o]1Ti 3:3, 8
1:8 [p]1Ti 3:2 [q]2Ti 3:3
1:9 [r]1Ti 1:19 [s]1Ti 1:10
1:10 [t]1Ti 1:6

1:1 Paul wrote this letter between his first and second imprisonments in Rome (before he wrote 2 Timothy) to guide Titus in working with the churches on the island of Crete. Paul had visited Crete with Titus and had left him there to minister (1:5). There was a strong pagan influence on this small island because Crete may have been a training centre for Roman soldiers. Therefore, the church in Crete needed strong Christian leadership.

1:1 In one short phrase, Paul gives us insight into his reason for living. He calls himself a servant of God—that is, one who was committed to obeying God. This obedience led him to spend his life telling others about Christ. How would you describe your purpose in life? To what are you devoted? For more information on Paul, see his Profile in Acts 9.

1:1 Paul called himself "an apostle". Even though Paul was not one of the original 12, he was specially called by God to bring the Good News to the Gentiles (see Acts 9:1–16 for an account of his call). The word *apostle* means messenger or missionary. "God's elect" refers to God's choice of his people, the church.

1:2 Apparently lying was commonplace in Crete (1:12). Paul made it clear at the start that God does not lie. The foundation of our faith is trust in God's character. Because God *is* truth, he is the *source* of all truth, and he cannot lie. Believing in him leads to *godliness,* living a God-honouring life-style (1:1). The eternal life that God has promised will be ours, because he keeps his promises. Build your faith on the foundation of a trustworthy God who never lies.

1:3 God is called "our Saviour", as is Jesus Christ (1:4). "God" here refers to the Father. Jesus did the work of salvation by dying for our sins and, therefore, he is our Saviour. God planned the work of salvation, and he forgives our sins. Both the Father and the Son acted to save us from our sins.

1:4 Titus, a Greek, was one of Paul's most trusted and dependable co-workers. Paul sent Titus to Corinth on several special missions to help the church in its troubles (2 Corinthians 7; 8). Paul and Titus also travelled together to Jerusalem (Galatians 2:3) and Crete (1:5). Paul left Titus in Crete to lead the new churches springing up on the island. Titus is last mentioned by Paul in 2 Timothy 4:10, Paul's last recorded letter. Titus had leadership ability, so Paul gave him leadership responsibility, urging him to use his abilities well.

1:5 Crete, a small island in the Mediterranean Sea, had a large population of Jews. The churches there were probably founded by Cretan Jews who had been in Jerusalem at Pentecost (Acts 2:11) more than 30 years before Paul wrote this letter.

1:5 The unfinished work refers to establishing correct teaching and appointing elders in every town.

1:5 Paul had appointed elders in various churches during his journeys (Acts 14:23). He could not stay in each church, but he knew that these new churches needed strong spiritual leadership. The men chosen were to lead the churches by teaching sound doctrine, helping believers mature spiritually, and equipping them to live for Jesus Christ despite opposition.

1:5–9 Paul briefly described some qualifications that the elders or overseers should have. Paul had given Timothy a similar set of instructions for the church in Ephesus (see 1 Timothy 3:1–7; 5:22). Notice that most of the qualifications involve character, not knowledge or skill. A person's life-style and relationships provide a window into his or her character. Consider these qualifications as you evaluate a person for a position of leadership in your church. It is important to have leaders who can effectively preach God's word, but it is even more important to have those who can live out God's word and be examples for others to follow.

1:10 "The circumcision group" were the *Judaisers,* Jews who taught that the Gentiles had to obey all the Jewish laws before they could become Christians. This regulation confused new Christians and caused problems in many churches where Paul had preached the Good News. Paul wrote letters to several churches to help them understand that Gentile believers did not have to become Jews first in order to be Christians—God accepts anyone who comes to him in faith (see Romans 1:17; Galatians 3:2–7). Although the Jerusalem council had dealt with this issue (see Acts 15), devout Jews who refused to believe in Jesus still tried to cause problems in the Christian churches. Church leaders must be alert and take action on anything that divides Christians.

1:10–14 Paul warned Titus to be on the lookout for people who teach wrong doctrines and lead others into error. Some false

1:10 [u]11:2
1:11 [v]2Ti 3:6
1:12 [w]Ac 17:28 [x]Ac 2:11
1:13 [y]2Co 13:10 [z]Tit 2:2
1:14 [a]1Ti 1:4 [b]Col 2:22
1:15 [c]Ro 14:14, 23
1:16 [d]1Jn 2:4

those of the circumcision group.[u] 11They must be silenced, because they are ruining
whole households[v] by teaching things they ought not to teach—and that for the sake
of dishonest gain. 12Even one of their own prophets[w] has said, "Cretans[x] are always
liars, evil brutes, lazy gluttons." 13This testimony is true. Therefore, rebuke[y] them
sharply, so that they will be sound in the faith[z] 14and will pay no attention to Jewish
myths[a] or to the commands[b] of those who reject the truth. 15To the pure, all things
are pure, but to those who are corrupted and do not believe, nothing is pure.[c] In fact,
both their minds and consciences are corrupted. 16They claim to know God, but by
their actions they deny him.[d] They are detestable, disobedient and unfit for doing
anything good.

TITUS GOES TO CRETE
Tradition says that after Paul was released from prison in Rome (before his second and final Roman imprisonment), he and Titus travelled together for a while. They stopped in Crete, and when it was time for Paul to go, he left Titus behind to help the churches there.

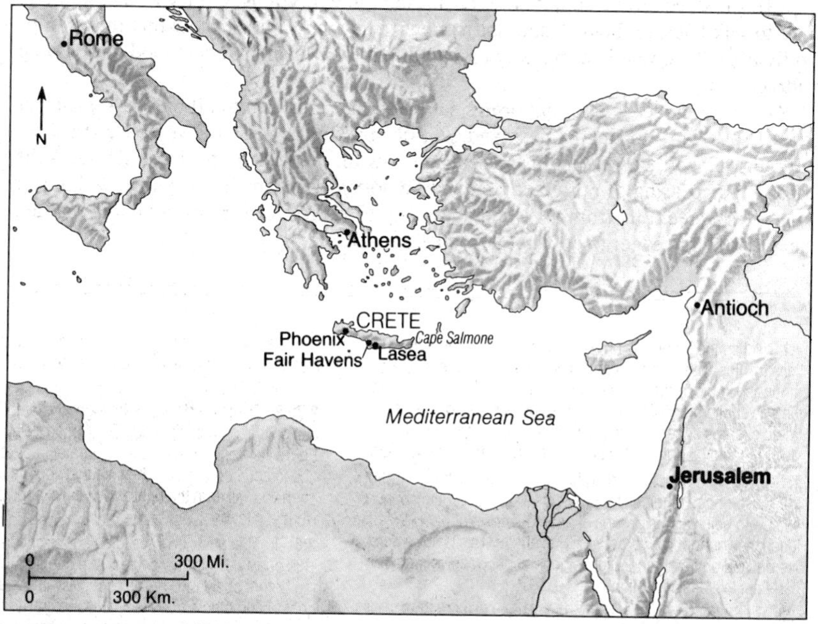

teachers are simply confused—they speak their misguided opinions without checking them against the Bible. Others have evil motives—they pretend to be Christians only because they can get more money ("dishonest gain"), additional business, or a feeling of power from being a leader in the church. Jesus and the apostles repeatedly warned against false teachers (see Mark 13:22; Acts 20:29; 2 Thessalonians 2:3–12; 2 Peter 3:3–7) because their teachings attack the foundations of truth and integrity upon which the Christian faith is built. You can recognise false teachers because they will (1) focus more attention on themselves than on Christ; (2) ask you to do something that will compromise or dilute your faith; (3) play down the divine nature of Christ or the inspiration of the Bible; or (4) urge believers to make decisions based more on human judgment than on prayer and biblical guidelines.

1:12 Paul was quoting a line from a poem by Epimenides, a poet and philosopher who had lived in Crete 600 years earlier. Some Cretans had a bad reputation and were known for lying. Paul used this familiar phrase to make the point that Titus' ministry and leadership were very much needed.

1:15 Some people see good all around them, while others see nothing but evil. What is the difference? Our souls become filters through which we perceive goodness or evil. The pure (those who have Christ in control of their lives) learn to see goodness and purity even in this evil world. But corrupt and unbelieving people find evil in everything because their evil minds and hearts colour even the good they see and hear. Whatever you choose to fill your mind with will affect the way you think and act. Turn your thoughts to God and his word, and you will discover more and more goodness, even in this evil world. A mind filled with good has little room for what is evil (see Philippians 4:8).

1:16 Many people claim to know God. How can we know if they really do? We will not know for certain in this life, but a glance at their life-styles will quickly tell us what they value and whether they have ordered their lives around kingdom priorities. Our conduct speaks volumes about what we believe (see 1 John 2:4–6). What do people know about God and about your faith by watching your life?

2. Right living in the church

What Must Be Taught to Various Groups

2 You must teach what is in accord with sound doctrine.[a] 2 Teach the older men
to be temperate, worthy of respect, self-controlled, and sound in faith,[b] in love
and in endurance.
3 Likewise, teach the older women to be reverent in the way they live, not to be
slanderers or addicted to much wine,[c] but to teach what is good. 4 Then they can train
the younger women to love their husbands and children, 5 to be self-controlled and
pure, to be busy at home, to be kind, and to be subject to their husbands,[d] so that
no-one will malign the word of God.[e]
6 Similarly, encourage the young men[f] to be self-controlled. 7 In everything set
them an example[g] by doing what is good. In your teaching show integrity, seriousness
8 and soundness of speech that cannot be condemned, so that those who oppose you
may be ashamed because they have nothing bad to say about us.[h]
9 Teach slaves to be subject to their masters in everything,[i] to try to please them,
not to talk back to them, 10 and not to steal from them, but to show that they can be
fully trusted, so that in every way they will make the teaching about God our Saviour
attractive.[j]
11 For the grace of God that brings salvation has appeared to all men.[k] 12 It teaches
us to say "No" to ungodliness and worldly passions,[l] and to live self-controlled,
upright and godly lives[m] in this present age, 13 while we wait for the blessed hope — the
glorious appearing of our great God and Saviour, Jesus Christ,[n] 14 who gave himself
for us to redeem us from all wickedness and to purify for himself a people that are
his very own,[o] eager to do what is good.[p]

2:1 a 1Ti 1:10
2:2 b Tit 1:13
2:3 c 1Ti 3:8
2:5 d Eph 5:22; e 1Ti 6:1
2:6 f 1Ti 5:1
2:7 g 1Ti 4:12
2:8 h 1Pe 2:12
2:9 i Eph 6:5
2:10 j Mt 5:16
2:11 k 1Ti 2:4
2:12 l Tit 3:3; m 2Ti 3:12
2:13 n 2Pe 1:1
2:14 o Ex 19:5; p Eph 2:10

2:1 Notice the emphasis on "sound doctrine" in Paul's instructions to Titus. This is the *content* of our faith. Believers must be grounded in the truths of the Bible — then they won't be swayed by the powerful oratory of false teachers, the possible devastation of tragic circumstances, or the pull of emotions. Learn the Bible, study theology, apply biblical principles, and *do* what you learn.

2:1–8 Having people of all ages in the church makes it strong, but it also brings potential for problems. Paul gave Titus counsel on how to help various groups of people. The older people should teach the younger by words *and* by example. This is how values are passed on from generation to generation. Does your church carry out this basic function?

2:2, 5 Self-control was an important aspect in early Christianity. The Christian community was made up of people from differing backgrounds and viewpoints, making conflict inevitable. Christians existed in a pagan and often hostile world. To stay above reproach, men and women needed wisdom and discernment to be discreet, and to master their wills, tongues, and passions so that Christ would not be dishonoured. How's your self-control?

2:3–5 Women who were new Christians were to learn how to have harmony in the home by watching older women who had been Christians for some time. We have the same need today. Younger wives and mothers should learn to live in a Christian manner — loving their husbands and caring for their children — through observing exemplary women of God. If you are of an age or position where people look up to you, make sure that your example is motivating younger believers to live in a way that honours God.

2:6 This advice given to young men was very important. In ancient Greek society, the role of the husband/father was not viewed as a nurturing role, but merely as a functional one. Many young men today have been brought up in families where fathers have neglected their responsibilities to their wives and children. Husbands and fathers who are good examples of Christian living are important role models for young men who need to *see* how it is done.

2:7 When Paul encouraged Titus, and through Titus other young men, to be serious, he wanted them to be reverent and purposeful. Christianity should never be intentionally boring or gloomy. Don't let the seriousness of the gospel cause you to repel others by your grim disposition.

2:7, 8 Paul urged Titus to be a good example to those around him so that others might see Titus' good deeds and imitate him. Paul's life would give his words greater impact. If you want someone to act a certain way, be sure that you live that way yourself. Then you will earn the right to be heard, and your life will reinforce what you teach.

2:8 Paul counselled Titus to be above criticism in how he taught. This quality of integrity comes from careful Bible study and listening before speaking. This is especially important when teaching or confronting others about spiritual or moral issues. If we are impulsive, unreasonable, and confusing, we are likely to start arguments rather than to convince people of the truth.

2:9, 10 Slavery was common in Paul's day. Paul did not condemn slavery in any of his letters, but he advised slaves and masters to be loving and responsible in their conduct (see also Ephesians 6:5–9). The standards set by Paul can help any employee/employer relationship. Employees should always do their best work and be trustworthy, not just when the employer is watching. Businesses lose millions a year to employee theft and time-wasting. If all Christian employees would follow Paul's advice at work, what a transformation it would make!

2:11–14 The power to live as a Christian comes from the Holy Spirit. Because Christ died and rescued us from sin, we are free from sin's control. God gives us the power and understanding to live according to his will and to do good. Then we will look forward to Christ's wonderful return with eager expectation and hope.

2:12 It is not enough to renounce sin and evil desires; we must also live actively for God. To fight against lust we must say no to temptation, but we must also say yes to active service for Christ.

2:14 Christ's redeeming us opens the way for him to purify us. *Redeem* means to purchase our release from the captivity of sin with a ransom (see Mark 10:45 for more on Christ as our ransom). We are not only free from the sentence of death for our sin, but we are also purified from sin's influence as we grow in Christ.

15 These, then, are the things you should teach. Encourage and rebuke with all
authority. Do not let anyone despise you.

3. Right living in society

Doing What Is Good

3 Remind the people to be subject to rulers and authorities,[a] to be obedient, to be
ready to do whatever is good,[b] 2 to slander no-one,[c] to be peaceable and
considerate, and to show true humility towards all men.
3 At one time we too were foolish, disobedient, deceived and enslaved by all kinds
of passions and pleasures. We lived in malice and envy, being hated and hating one
another. 4 But when the kindness[d] and love of God our Saviour appeared,[e] 5 he saved
us, not because of righteous things we had done,[f] but because of his mercy. He saved
us through the washing of rebirth and renewal[g] by the Holy Spirit, 6 whom he poured
out on us[h] generously through Jesus Christ our Saviour, 7 so that, having been justified
by his grace,[i] we might become heirs[j] having the hope[k] of eternal life.[l] 8 This is
a trustworthy saying.[m] And I want you to stress these things, so that those who have
trusted in God may be careful to devote themselves to doing what is good.[n] These
things are excellent and profitable for everyone.
9 But avoid foolish controversies and genealogies and arguments and quarrels[o]
about the law, because these are unprofitable and useless. 10 Warn a divisive person
once, and then warn him a second time. After that, have nothing to do with
him.[p] 11 You may be sure that such a man is warped and sinful; he is self-
condemned.

Final Remarks

12 As soon as I send Artemas or Tychicus[q] to you, do your best to come to me at
Nicopolis, because I have decided to winter there.[r] 13 Do everything you can to help

3:1 [a]Ro 13:1 [b]2Ti 2:21
3:2 [c]Eph 4:31; 2Ti 2:24
3:4 [d]Eph 2:7 [e]Tit 2:11
3:5 [f]Eph 2:9 [g]Ro 12:2
3:6 [h]Ro 5:5
3:7 [i]Ro 3:24 [j]Ro 8:17 [k]Ro 8:24 [l]Tit 1:2
3:8 [m]1Ti 1:15 [n]Tit 2:14
3:9 [o]1Ti 1:4; 2Ti 2:14
3:10 [p]Ro 16:17
3:12 [q]Ac 20:4 [r]2Ti 4:9, 21

2:15 Paul told Titus to teach the Scriptures as well as to live them. We must also teach, encourage, and correct others when necessary. It is easy to feel afraid when others are older, more influential in the community, or wealthier. Like Titus, we should not let ourselves be threatened when we are trying to minister to others or provide leadership in the church.

3:1, 2 As Christians, our first allegiance is to Jesus as Lord, but we must obey our government and its leaders as well. Christians are not above the law. Obeying the civil law is only the beginning of our Christian responsibility; we must do what we can to be good citizens. In a democracy, this means participation and willingness to serve. (See Acts 5:29 and Romans 13:1ff for more on the Christian's attitude towards government.)

3:3 Following a life of pleasure and giving in to every sensual desire leads to slavery. Many think freedom consists in doing anything they want. But this path leads to a slavish addiction to sensual gratification. A person is no longer free, but is a slave to what his or her body dictates (2 Peter 2:19). Christ frees us from the desires and control of sin. Have you been released?

3:3–8 Paul summarised what Christ does for us when he saves us. We move from a life full of sin to one where we are led by God's Holy Spirit. *All* our sins, not merely some, are washed away. Washing refers to the water of baptism, which is a sign of salvation. In becoming a Christian, the believer acknowledges Christ as Lord and recognises Christ's saving work. We gain eternal life with *all* its treasures. We have *renewal* by the Holy Spirit, and he continually renews our hearts. None of this occurs because we earned or deserved it; it is all God's gift.

3:4–6 All three persons of the Trinity are mentioned in these verses because all three participate in the work of salvation. Based upon the redemptive work of his Son, the Father forgives and sends the Holy Spirit to wash away our sins and continually renew us.

3:9 Paul warned Titus, as he warned Timothy, not to get involved in foolish and unprofitable arguments (2 Timothy 2:14). This does not mean we should refuse to study, discuss, and examine different interpretations of difficult Bible passages. Paul is warning against petty quarrels, not honest discussion that leads to wisdom. As foolish arguments develop, it is best to turn the discussion back to a helpful direction or politely excuse yourself.

3:9 The false teachers were basing their heresies on genealogies and speculations about the law (see 1 Timothy 1:3, 4). Similar to the methods used by false teachers in Ephesus and Colosse, they were building their case on genealogies of angels. We should avoid false teachers, not even bothering to react to their pretentious positions. Our overreaction can sometimes give more attention to their points of view.

3:9–11 A person must be warned when he or she is causing division that threatens the unity of the church. This warning should not be a heavy-handed action, but it is intended to correct the individual's divisive nature and restore him or her to fellowship. A person who refuses to be corrected should be put outside the fellowship. As Paul said, that person is "self-condemned"—he or she is sinning and knows it. (See also Matthew 18:15–18 and 2 Thessalonians 3:14, 15 for help in handling such problems in the church.)

3:12 The city of Nicopolis was on the western coast of Greece. Artemas or Tychicus would take over Titus' work on the island of Crete so Titus could meet Paul in Nicopolis. Tychicus was one of Paul's trusted companions (Acts 20:4; Ephesians 6:21; Colossians 4:7). Titus would have to leave soon because sea travel was dangerous in the winter months.

3:13 Apollos was a famous Christian preacher. A native of Alexandria in North Africa, he became a Christian in Ephesus and was trained by Aquila and Priscilla (Acts 18:24–28; 1 Corinthians 1:12).

Zenas the lawyer and Apollos[s] on their way and see that they have everything they
need. 14Our people must learn to devote themselves to doing what is good,[t] in order
that they may provide for daily necessities and not live unproductive lives.
15Everyone with me sends you greetings. Greet those who love us in the faith.[u]
Grace be with you all.[v]

3:13 [s]Ac 18:24
3:14 [t]ver 8
3:15 [u]1Ti 1:2 [v]Col 4:18

3:15 The letters of Paul to Titus and Timothy are his last writings and mark the end of his life and ministry. These letters are rich treasures for us today because they give vital information for church leadership. They provide a strong model for elders, pastors, and other Christian leaders as they develop younger leaders to carry on the work, following Paul's example of preparing Timothy and Titus to carry on his ministry. For practical guidelines on church leadership and problem solving, carefully study the principles found in these letters.

PHILEMON

AT THE FOREMAN'S signal, the giant ball is released, and with dynamite force and a reverberating crash, it meets the wall, snapping bricks like twigs and scattering pieces of mortar. Repeatedly, the powerful pendulum works, and soon the barrier has been reduced to rubble. Then it is carted away so that construction can begin.

Life has many walls and fences that divide, separate, and compartmentalise. Not made of wood or stone, they are personal obstructions, blocking people from each other and from God. But Christ came as the great wall remover, tearing down the sin partition that separates us from God and blasting the barriers that keep us from each other. His death and resurrection opened the way to eternal life to bring all who believe into the family of God (see Ephesians 2:14–18).

Roman, Greek, and Jewish cultures were littered with barriers, as society assigned people to classes and expected them to stay in their place—men and women, slave and free, rich and poor, Jews and Gentiles, Greeks and barbarians, pious and pagan. But with the message of Christ, the walls came down, and Paul could declare, "Here there is no Greek or Jew, circumcised or uncircumcised, barbarian, Scythian, slave or free, but Christ is all, and is in all" (Colossians 3:11).

This life-changing truth forms the backdrop for the letter to Philemon. One of three personal letters in the Bible, the letter to Philemon is Paul's personal plea for a slave. Onesimus "belonged" to Philemon, a member of the Colossian church and Paul's friend. But Onesimus, the slave, had stolen from his master and run away. He ran to Rome where he met Paul, and there he responded to the good news and came to faith in Christ (verse 10). So Paul writes to Philemon and reintroduces Onesimus to him, explaining that he is sending him back, not just as a slave but as a brother (verses 11, 12, 16). Tactfully he asks Philemon to accept and forgive his brother (verses 10, 14, 15, 20). The barriers of the past and the new ones erected by Onesimus' desertion and theft should divide them no longer—they are one in Christ.

This small book is a masterpiece of grace and tact and a profound demonstration of the power of Christ and of true Christian fellowship in action. What barriers are in your home, neighbourhood, and church? What separates you from fellow believers—race? status? wealth? education? personality? As with Philemon, God calls you to seek unity, breaking down those walls and embracing your brothers and sisters in Christ.

VITAL STATISTICS

PURPOSE:
To convince Philemon to forgive his runaway slave, Onesimus, and to accept him as a brother in the faith

AUTHOR:
Paul

TO WHOM WRITTEN:
Philemon, who was probably a wealthy member of the Colossian church, and all believers

DATE WRITTEN:
About A.D. 60, during Paul's first imprisonment in Rome, at about the same time Ephesians and Colossians were written

SETTING:
Slavery was very common in the Roman empire, and evidently some Christians had slaves. Paul does not condemn the institution of slavery in his writings, but he makes a radical statement by calling this slave Philemon's brother in Christ.

KEY VERSES:
"Perhaps the reason he was separated from you for a little while was that you might have him back for good—no longer as a slave, but better than a slave, as a dear brother. He is very dear to me but even dearer to you, both as a man and as a brother in the Lord" (verses 15, 16).

KEY PEOPLE:
Paul, Philemon, Onesimus

KEY PLACES:
Colosse, Rome

SPECIAL FEATURES:
This is a private, personal letter to a friend

THE BLUEPRINT

1. Paul's appreciation of Philemon (1–7)
2. Paul's appeal for Onesimus (8–25)

Paul pleads on behalf of Onesimus, a runaway slave. Paul's intercession for him illustrates what Christ has done for us. As Paul interceded for a slave, so Christ intercedes for us, slaves to sin. As Onesimus was reconciled to Philemon, so we are reconciled to God through Christ. As Paul offered to pay the debts of a slave, so Christ paid our debt of sin. Like Onesimus, we must return to God our Master and serve him.

MEGATHEMES

THEME	EXPLANATION	IMPORTANCE
Forgiveness	Philemon was Paul's friend and the legal owner of the slave, Onesimus. Paul asked him not to punish Onesimus, but to forgive and restore him as a new Christian brother.	Christian relationships must be full of forgiveness and acceptance. Can you forgive those who have wronged you?
Barriers	Slavery was widespread in the Roman empire, but no-one is lost to God or beyond his love. Slavery was a barrier between people, but Christian love and fellowship are to overcome such barriers.	In Christ we are one family. No walls of racial, economic or political differences should separate us. Let Christ work through you to remove barriers between Christian brothers and sisters.
Respect	Paul was a friend of both Philemon and Onesimus. He had the authority as an apostle to tell Philemon what to do. Yet Paul chose to appeal to his friend in Christian love rather than to order him what to do.	Tactful persuasion accomplishes a great deal more than commands when dealing with people. Remember to exhibit courtesy and respect in your relationships.

1. Paul's appreciation of Philemon

1 Paul, a prisoner[a] of Christ Jesus, and Timothy our brother,[b]

To Philemon our dear friend and fellow-worker,[c] 2 to Apphia our sister, to Archippus[d] our fellow-soldier[e] and to the church that meets in your home:[f]

3 Grace to you and peace from God our Father and the Lord Jesus Christ.

1:1 [a] ver 9, 23; Eph 3:1 [b] 2Co 1:1 [c] Php 2:25
1:2 [d] Col 4:17 [e] Php 2:25 [f] Ro 16:5

1 Paul wrote this letter from Rome in about A.D. 60, when he was under house arrest (see Acts 28:30, 31). Onesimus was a domestic slave who belonged to Philemon, a wealthy man and a member of the church in Colosse. Onesimus had run away from Philemon and had made his way to Rome where he met Paul, who apparently led him to Christ (verse 10). Paul convinced Onesimus that running from his problems wouldn't solve them, and he persuaded Onesimus to return to his master. Paul wrote this letter to Philemon to ask him to be reconciled to his runaway slave.

1 For more information on Paul's life, see his Profile in Acts 9. Timothy's name is included with Paul's in 2 Corinthians, 1 Thessalonians, 2 Thessalonians, Philippians, Colossians, and Philemon—the last three of these letters are from a group known as the "Prison Letters". Timothy was one of Paul's trusted companions; Paul wrote two letters to him—1 and 2 Timothy.

1 Philemon was a Greek landowner living in Colosse. He had been converted under Paul's ministry, and the Colossian church met in his home. Onesimus was one of Philemon's slaves.

2 Apphia may have been Philemon's wife. Archippus may have been Philemon's son, or perhaps an elder in the Colossian church. In either case, Paul included him as a recipient of the letter, possibly so Archippus could read the letter with Philemon and encourage him to take Paul's advice.

2 The early churches would often meet in people's homes. Because of sporadic persecutions and the great expense involved, church buildings were generally not constructed at this time.

Thanksgiving and Prayer

4 I always thank my God[g] as I remember you in my prayers, 5 because I hear about
your faith in the Lord Jesus and your love for all the saints.[h] 6 I pray that you may
be active in sharing your faith, so that you will have a full understanding of every good
thing we have in Christ. 7 Your love has given me great joy and encouragement,[i]
because you, brother, have refreshed[j] the hearts of the saints.

2. Paul's appeal for Onesimus

8 Therefore, although in Christ I could be bold and order you to do what you ought
to do, 9 yet I appeal to you on the basis of love. I then, as Paul—an old man and now
also a prisoner[k] of Christ Jesus— 10 I appeal to you for my son[l] Onesimus,[a][m] who
became my son while I was in chains. 11 Formerly he was useless to you, but now
he has become useful both to you and to me.

12 I am sending him—who is my very heart—back to you. 13 I would have liked
to keep him with me so that he could take your place in helping me while I am in
chains for the gospel. 14 But I did not want to do anything without your consent, so
that any favour you do will be spontaneous and not forced.[n] 15 Perhaps the reason
he was separated from you for a little while was that you might have him back for
good— 16 no longer as a slave, but better than a slave, as a dear brother.[o] He is very
dear to me but even dearer to you, both as a man and as a brother in the Lord.

17 So if you consider me a partner,[p] welcome him as you would welcome me. 18 If
he has done you any wrong or owes you anything, charge it to me. 19 I, Paul, am
writing this with my own hand. I will pay it back—not to mention that you owe me
your very self. 20 I do wish, brother, that I may have some benefit from you in the
Lord; refresh[q] my heart in Christ. 21 Confident[r] of your obedience, I write to you,
knowing that you will do even more than I ask.

22 And one thing more: Prepare a guest room for me, because I hope to be[s] restored
to you in answer to your prayers.[t]

a *10 Onesimus* means *useful.*

1:4 g Ro 1:8
1:5 h Eph 1:15; Col 1:4
1:7 i 2Co 7:4, 13; j ver 20
1:9 k ver 1, 23
1:10 l 1Co 4:15; m Col 4:9
1:14 n 2Co 9:7; 1Pe 5:2
1:16 o Mt 23:8; 1Ti 6:2
1:17 p 2Co 8:23
1:20 q ver 7
1:21 r 2Co 2:3
1:22 s Php 1:25; 2:24; t 2Co 1:11

4–7 Paul reflected on Philemon's faith and love. Philemon had opened his heart and his home to the church. We should do likewise, opening ourselves and our homes to others, offering Christian fellowship to refresh people's hearts.

8, 9 Because Paul was an elder and an apostle, he could have used his authority with Philemon, commanding him to deal kindly with his runaway slave. But Paul based his request not on his own authority, but on Philemon's Christian commitment. Paul wanted Philemon's heartfelt, not grudging, obedience. When you know something is right and you have the power to demand it, do you appeal to your authority or to the other person's commitment? Here Paul provides a good example of how to deal with a possible conflict between Christian friends.

10 A master had the legal right to kill a runaway slave, so Onesimus feared for his life. Paul wrote this letter to Philemon to help him understand his new relationship with Onesimus. Onesimus was now a Christian brother, not a mere possession. "Who became my son" means that Onesimus had become a Christian.

10ff From his prison cell, Paul had led Onesimus to the Lord. Paul asked Philemon to forgive his runaway slave who had become a Christian, and even going beyond forgiveness, to accept Onesimus as a brother. As Christians, we should forgive as we have been forgiven (Matthew 6:12; Ephesians 4:31, 32). True forgiveness means that we treat the one we've forgiven as we would want to be treated. Is there someone you say you have forgiven, but who still needs your kindness?

11–15 *Onesimus* means "useful". Paul used a play on words, saying that Onesimus had not been much use to Philemon in the past, but had become very useful to both Philemon and Paul. Although Paul wanted to keep Onesimus with him, he was sending Onesimus back, requesting that Philemon accept him not only as a forgiven runaway servant, but also as a brother in Christ.

15, 16 Slavery was widespread throughout the Roman empire. In these early days, Christians did not have the political power to change the slavery system. Paul didn't condemn or condone slavery, but he worked to transform relationships. The gospel begins to change social structures by changing the *people* within those structures. (See also 1 Corinthians 7:20–24; Ephesians 6:5–9; Colossians 3:22–4:1 for more on master/slave relationships.)

16 What a difference Onesimus' status as a Christian made in his relationship to Philemon. He was no longer merely a slave, but he was also a brother. That meant that both Onesimus and Philemon were members of God's family—equals in Christ. A Christian's status as a member of God's family transcends all other distinctions among believers. Do you look down on any fellow Christians? Remember, they are your equals before Christ (Galatians 3:28). How you treat your brothers and sisters in Christ's family reflects your true Christian commitment.

17–19 Paul genuinely loved Onesimus. Paul showed his love by personally guaranteeing payment for any stolen goods or wrongs for which Onesimus might be responsible. Paul's investment in the life of this new believer certainly encouraged and strengthened Onesimus' faith. Are there young believers who need you to demonstrate such self-sacrifice towards them? Be grateful when you can invest in the lives of others, helping them with Bible study, prayer, encouragement, support, and friendship.

19 Philemon owed himself to Paul, meaning that Paul had led Philemon to Christ. Because Paul was Philemon's spiritual father, he was hoping that Philemon would feel a debt of gratitude that he would repay by accepting Onesimus with a spirit of forgiveness.

22 Paul was released from prison soon after writing this letter, but the Bible doesn't say whether or not he returned to Colosse.

23 Epaphras,[u] my fellow-prisoner in Christ Jesus, sends you greetings. 24 And so
do Mark,[v] Aristarchus,[w] Demas[x] and Luke, my fellow-workers.
25 The grace of the Lord Jesus Christ be with your spirit.[y]

1:23
[u] Col 1:7
1:24
[v] Ac 12:12
[w] Ac 19:29
[x] Col 4:14
1:25
[y] 2Ti 4:22

---

23 Epaphras was well known to the Colossians because he had founded the church there (Colossians 1:7). He was a hero to this church, helping to hold it together in spite of growing persecution and struggles with false doctrine. His report to Paul about the problems in Colosse had prompted Paul to write his letter to the Colossians. Epaphras' greetings to and prayers for the Colossian Christians reveal his deep love for them (Colossians 4:12, 13). He may have been in prison with Paul for preaching the gospel.

24 Mark, Aristarchus, Demas, and Luke are also mentioned in Colossians 4:10, 14. Mark had accompanied Paul and Barnabas on their first missionary journey (Acts 12:25ff). Mark also wrote the Gospel of Mark. Luke had accompanied Paul on his third missionary journey and was the writer of the Gospel of Luke and the book of Acts. Demas had been faithful to Paul for a while but then deserted him (see 2 Timothy 4:10).

25 Paul urged Philemon to be reconciled to his slave, receiving him as a brother and fellow member of God's family. *Reconciliation* means re-establishing relationship. Christ has reconciled us to God and to others. Many barriers come between people – race, social status, sex, personality differences – but Christ can break down these barriers. Jesus Christ changed Onesimus' relationship to Philemon from slave to brother. Christ can transform our most hopeless relationships into deep and loving friendships.

HEBREWS

CONSCIENTIOUS consumers shop for value, the best products for their money. Wise parents desire only the best for their children, nourishing their growing bodies, minds, and spirits. Individuals with integrity seek the best investment of time, talents, and treasures. In every area, to settle for less would be wasteful, foolish, and irresponsible. Yet it is a natural pull to move towards what is convenient and comfortable.

Judaism was not second-rate or easy. Divinely designed, it was the best religion, expressing true worship and devotion to God. The commandments, the rituals, and the prophets described God's promises and revealed the way to forgiveness and salvation. But Christ came, fulfilling the Law and the Prophets, conquering sin, shattering all barriers to God, and freely providing eternal life.

This message was difficult for Jews to accept. Although they had sought the Messiah for centuries, they were entrenched in thinking and worshipping in traditional forms. Following Jesus seemed to repudiate their marvellous heritage and their profound Scriptures. With caution and questions they listened to the gospel, but many rejected it and sought to eliminate this "heresy". Those who did accept Jesus as the Messiah often found themselves slipping back into familiar routines, trying to live a hybrid faith.

Hebrews is a masterful document written to Jews who were evaluating Jesus or struggling with this new faith. The message of Hebrews is that Jesus is better, Christianity is superior, Christ is supreme and completely sufficient for salvation.

Hebrews begins by emphasising that the old (Judaism) and the new (Christianity) are both religions revealed by God (1:1–3). In the doctrinal section that follows (1:4—10:18), the writer shows how Jesus is superior to angels (1:4—2:18), superior to their leaders (3:1–4:13), and superior to their priests (4:14—7:28). Christianity surpasses Judaism because it has a better covenant (8:1–13), a better sanctuary (9:1–10), and a more sufficient sacrifice for sins (9:11—10:18).

Having established the superiority of Christianity, the writer moves on to the practical implications of following Christ. The readers are exhorted to hold on to their new faith, encourage each other, and look forward to Christ's return (10:19–25). They are warned about the consequences of rejecting Christ's sacrifice (10:26–31) and reminded of the rewards for faithfulness (10:32–39). Then the author explains how to live by faith, giving illustrations of the faithful men and women in Israel's history (11:1–40) and giving encouragement and exhortation for daily living (12:1–17). This section ends by comparing the old covenant with the new (12:18–29). The writer concludes with moral exhortations (13:1–17), a request for prayer (13:18, 19), and a benediction and greetings (13:20–25).

Whatever you are considering as the focus of life, Christ is better. He is the perfect revelation of God, the final and complete sacrifice for sin, the compassionate and understanding mediator, and the *only* way to eternal life. Read Hebrews and begin to see history and life from God's perspective. Then give yourself unreservedly and completely to Christ. Don't settle for anything less.

VITAL STATISTICS

PURPOSE:
To present the sufficiency and superiority of Christ

AUTHOR:
Paul, Luke, Barnabas, Apollos, Silas, Philip, Priscilla, and others have been suggested because the name of the author is not given in the biblical text itself. Whoever it was speaks of Timothy as "brother" (13:23).

TO WHOM WRITTEN:
Hebrew Christians (perhaps second-generation Christians, see 2:3) who may have been considering a return to Judaism, perhaps because of immaturity, stemming from a lack of understanding of biblical truths; and all believers in Christ.

DATE WRITTEN:
Probably before the destruction of the temple in Jerusalem in A.D. 70, because the religious sacrifices and ceremonies are referred to in the book, but no mention is made of the temple's destruction

SETTING:
These Jewish Christians were probably undergoing fierce persecution, socially and physically, both from Jews and from Romans. Christ had not returned to establish his kingdom, and the people needed to be reassured that Christianity was true and that Jesus was indeed the Messiah.

KEY VERSE:
"The Son is the radiance of God's glory and the exact representation of his being, sustaining all things by his powerful word. After he had provided purification for sins, he sat down at the right hand of the Majesty in heaven" (1:3).

KEY PEOPLE:
Old Testament men and women of faith (chapter 11)

SPECIAL FEATURES:
Although Hebrews is called a "letter" (13:22), it has the form and the content of a sermon

THE BLUEPRINT

A. THE SUPERIORITY OF CHRIST (1:1—10:18) 1. Christ is greater than the angels 2. Christ is greater than Moses 3. Christ is greater than the Old Testament priesthood 4. The new covenant is greater than the old	The superiority of Christ over everyone and everything is clearly demonstrated by the author. Christianity supersedes all other religions and can never be surpassed. Where can one find anything better than Christ? Living in Christ is having the best there is in life. All competing religions are deceptions or cheap imitations.
B. THE SUPERIORITY OF FAITH (10:19—13:25)	Jews who had become Christians in the first century were tempted to fall back into Judaism because of uncertainty, the security of custom, and persecution. Today believers are also tempted to fall back into legalism, fulfilling minimum religious requirements rather than pressing on in genuine faith. We must strive to live by faith each day.

MEGATHEMES

THEME	EXPLANATION	IMPORTANCE
Christ Is Superior	Hebrews reveals Jesus' true identity as God. Jesus is the ultimate authority. He is greater than any religion or any angel. He is superior to any Jewish leader (such as Abraham, Moses, or Joshua) and superior to any priest. He is the complete revelation of God.	Jesus alone can forgive your sin. He has secured your forgiveness and salvation by his death on the cross. You can find peace with God and real meaning for life by believing in Christ. Don't accept any alternative to or substitute for him.
High Priest	In the Old Testament, the high priest represented the Jews before God. Jesus Christ links us with God. There is no other way to reach God. Because Jesus Christ lived a sinless life, he is the perfect substitute to die for our sin. He is our perfect representative with God.	Jesus guarantees our access to God the Father. He intercedes for us so we can boldly come to the Father with our needs. When we are weak, we can come confidently to God for forgiveness and ask for his help.
Sacrifice	Christ's sacrifice was the ultimate fulfilment of all that the Old Testament sacrifices represented—God's forgiveness for sin. Because Christ is the perfect sacrifice for our sin, our sins are completely forgiven—past, present, and future.	Christ removed sin, which barred us from God's presence and fellowship. But we must accept his sacrifice for us. By believing in him we are no longer guilty, but cleansed and made whole. His sacrifice clears the way for us to have eternal life.
Maturity	Though we are saved from sin when we believe in Christ, we are given the task of going on and growing in our faith. Through our relationship with Christ we can live blameless lives, be set aside for his special use, and develop maturity.	The process of maturing in our faith takes time. Daily commitment and service produce maturity. When we are mature in our faith, we are not easily swayed or shaken by temptations or worldly concerns.
Faith	Faith is confident trust in God's promises. God's greatest promise is that we can be saved through Jesus.	If you trust in Jesus Christ for your complete salvation, he will transform you completely. A life of obedience and complete trust is pleasing to God.
Endurance	Faith enables Christians to face trials. Genuine faith includes the commitment to stay true to God when we are under fire. Endurance builds character and leads to victory.	You can have victory in your trials if you don't give up or turn your back on Christ. Stay true to Christ and pray for endurance.

1:1
[a] Jn 9:29; Heb 2:2, 3
[b] Ac 2:30
[c] Nu 12:6, 8

1:2
[d] Ps 2:8
[e] Jn 1:3

1:3
[f] Jn 1:14
[g] Col 1:17
[h] Heb 7:27
[i] Mk 16:19

1:4
[j] Eph 1:21; Php 2:9, 10

A. THE SUPERIORITY OF CHRIST (1:1 – 10:18)

The relationship of Christianity to Judaism was a critical issue in the early church. The author clears up confusion by carefully explaining how Christ is superior to angels, Moses, and high priests. The new covenant is shown to be far superior to the old. This can be of great encouragement to us and it can help us to avoid drifting away from our faith in Christ.

1. Christ is greater than the angels

1 In the past God spoke[a] to our forefathers through the prophets[b] at many times
and in various ways,[c] 2but in these last days he has spoken to us by his Son,
whom he appointed heir[d] of all things, and through whom[e] he made the universe.
3The Son is the radiance of God's glory[f] and the exact representation of his being,
sustaining all things[g] by his powerful word. After he had provided purification for
sins,[h] he sat down at the right hand of the Majesty in heaven.[i] 4So he became as
much superior to the angels as the name he has inherited is superior to theirs.[j]
5For to which of the angels did God ever say,

CHRIST AND THE ANGELS

Hebrews passage	*Old Testament passage*	*How Christ is superior to angels*
1:5, 6	Psalm 2:7	Christ is called "Son" of God, a title never given to an angel.
1:7, 14	Psalm 104:4	Angels are important, but are still only servants under God.
1:8, 9	Psalm 45:6	Christ's kingdom is for ever.
1:10	Psalm 102:25	Christ is the Creator of the world.
1:13	Psalm 110:1	Christ is given unique honour by God.

The writer of Hebrews quotes from the Old Testament repeatedly in demonstrating Christ's greatness in comparison to the angels. This audience of first-century Jewish Christians had developed an imbalanced belief in angels and their role. Christ's lordship is affirmed without disrespect to God's valued angelic messengers.

1:1 The book of Hebrews describes in detail how Jesus Christ not only fulfils the promises and prophecies of the Old Testament, but how Jesus Christ is better than everything in the Jewish system of thought. The Jews accepted the Old Testament, but most of them rejected Jesus as the long-awaited Messiah. The recipients of this letter seem to have been Jewish Christians. They were well-versed in Scripture, and they had professed faith in Christ. Whether through doubt, persecution, or false teaching, however, they may have been in danger of giving up their Christian faith and returning to Judaism.

The authorship of this book is uncertain. Several names have been suggested, including Luke, Barnabas, Apollos, Priscilla, and Paul. Most scholars do not believe that Paul was the author, because the writing style of Hebrews is quite different from that of his letters. In addition, Paul identified himself in his other letters and appealed to his authority as an apostle, whereas this writer of Hebrews, who never gives his or her name, appeals to eyewitnesses of Jesus' ministry for authority. Nevertheless, the author of Hebrews evidently knew Paul well. Hebrews was probably written by one of Paul's close associates who often heard him preach.

1:1, 2 God used many approaches to send his messages to people in Old Testament times. He spoke to Isaiah in visions (Isaiah 6), to Jacob in a dream (Genesis 28:10–22), and to Abraham and Moses personally (Genesis 18; Exodus 31:18). Jewish people familiar with these stories would not have found it hard to believe that God was still revealing his will, but it was astonishing for them to think that God had revealed *himself* by speaking through his Son, Jesus Christ. Jesus is the fulfilment and culmination of God's revelation through the centuries. When we know him, we have all we need to be saved from our sin and to have a perfect relationship with God.

1:2, 3 Not only is Jesus the exact representation of God, but he is God himself – the very God who spoke in Old Testament times. He is eternal; he worked with the Father in creating the world (John 1:3; Colossians 1:16). He is the full revelation of God. You can have no clearer view of God than by looking at Christ. Jesus Christ is the complete expression of God in a human body.

1:3 The book of Hebrews links God's saving power with his creative power. In other words, the power that brought the universe into being and that keeps it operating is the very power that removes (provides purification for) our sins. How mistaken we would be ever to think that God couldn't forgive us. No sin is too big for the Ruler of the universe to handle. He can and will forgive us when we come to him through his Son. That Jesus *sat down* means that the work was complete. Christ's sacrifice was final.

1:4 The name Jesus inherited that is superior is "Son of God". This name given to him by his Father is greater than the names and titles of the angels.

1:4ff False teachers in many of the early churches taught that God could be approached only through angels. Instead of worshipping God directly, followers of these heretics revered angels. Hebrews clearly denounces such teaching as false. Some thought of Jesus as the highest angel of God. But Jesus is not a superior angel; and, in any case, angels are not to be worshipped (see Colossians 2:18; Revelation 19:1–10). We should not regard any intermediaries or authorities as greater than Christ. Jesus is God. He alone deserves our worship.

1:5, 6 Jesus is God's firstborn Son. In Jewish families the firstborn son held the place of highest privilege and responsibility. The Jewish Christians reading this message would understand that as God's firstborn, Jesus was superior to any created being.

"You are my Son;
today I have become your Father"[a,b]?[k]

Or again,

"I will be his Father,
and he will be my Son"[c]?[l]

6 And again, when God brings his firstborn into the world,[m] he says,

"Let all God's angels worship him."[d][n]

7 In speaking of the angels he says,

"He makes his angels winds,
his servants flames of fire."[e][o]

8 But about the Son he says,

"Your throne, O God, will last for ever and ever,
and righteousness will be the sceptre of your kingdom.
9 You have loved righteousness and hated wickedness;
therefore God, your God, has set you above your
companions[p]
by anointing you with the oil[q] of joy."[f]

10 He also says,

"In the beginning, O Lord, you laid the foundations of the earth,
and the heavens are the work of your hands.
11 They will perish, but you remain;
they will all wear out like a garment.[r]
12 You will roll them up like a robe;
like a garment they will be changed.
But you remain the same,[s]
and your years will never end."[g][t]

13 To which of the angels did God ever say,

"Sit at my right hand
until I make your enemies
a footstool[u] for your feet"[h]?[v]

14 Are not all angels ministering spirits[w] sent to serve those who will inherit salvation?[x]

a *5* Or *have begotten you* b *5* Psalm 2:7 c *5* 2 Samuel 7:14; 1 Chron. 17:13 d *6* Deut. 32:43 (see Dead Sea Scrolls and Septuagint) e *7* Psalm 104:4 f *9* Psalm 45:6,7 g *12* Psalm 102:25–27 h *13* Psalm 110:1

1:5
k Ps 2:7
l 2Sa 7:14

1:6
m Heb 10:5
n Dt 32:43 (LXX and DSS) Ps 97:7

1:7
o Ps 104:4

1:9
p Php 2:9
q Isa 61:1, 3

1:11
r Isa 34:4

1:12
s Heb 13:8
t Ps 102:25-27

1:13
u Jos 10:24; Heb 10:13
v Ps 110:1

1:14
w Ps 103:20
x Heb 5:9

1:10–12 The author of Hebrews quotes Psalm 102:25–27. In the quotation, he regards God as the speaker and applies the words to the Son Jesus. The earth and the heavens rolled up like a robe reveals that the earth is not permanent or indestructible (a position held by many Greek and Roman philosophies). Jesus' authority is established over all of creation, so we dare not treat any created object or earthly resource as more important than he is.

1:11, 12 Because the readers of Hebrews had experienced the rejection of their fellow Jews, they often felt isolated. Many were tempted to exchange the changeless Christ for their familiar old faith. The writer of Hebrews warned them not to do this: Christ is ...nly security in a changing world. Whatever may happen in this ...Christ remains for ever changeless. If we trust him, we are absolutely secure, because we stand on the firmest foundation in the universe – Jesus Christ. A famous hymn captures this truth: "On Christ the solid rock I stand, all other ground is sinking sand."

1:12 What does it mean that Christ is changeless ("you remain the same")? It means that Christ's character will never change. He persistently shows his love to us. He is always fair, just, and merciful to us who are so undeserving. Be thankful that Christ is changeless – he will always help you when you need it and offer forgiveness when you fall.

1:14 Angels are God's messengers, spiritual beings created by God and under his authority (Colossians 1:16). They have several functions: serving believers (1:14), protecting the helpless (Matthew 18:10), proclaiming God's messages (Revelation 14:6–12), and executing God's judgment (Acts 12:1–23; Revelation 20:1–3).

2:2
[a]Heb 1:1
[b]Dt 33:2; Ac 7:53
[c]Heb 10:28

2:3
[d]Heb 10:29
[e]Heb 1:2
[f]Lk 1:2

2:4
[g]Jn 4:48
[h]1Co 12:4
[i]Eph 1:5

2:6
[j]Job 7:17

2:8
[k]Ps 8:4-6; 1Co 15:25

2:9
[l]Ac 2:33; 3:13; Php 2:9
[m]Php 2:7-9
[n]Jn 3:16; 2Co 5:15

Warning to Pay Attention

2 We must pay more careful attention, therefore, to what we have heard, so that
we do not drift away. 2 For if the message spoken[a] by angels[b] was binding, and
every violation and disobedience received its just punishment,[c] 3 how shall we escape
if we ignore such a great salvation?[d] This salvation, which was first announced by
the Lord,[e] was confirmed to us by those who heard him.[f] 4 God also testified to it
by signs, wonders and various miracles,[g] and gifts of the Holy Spirit[h] distributed
according to his will.[i]

Jesus Made Like His Brothers

5 It is not to angels that he has subjected the world to come, about which we are
speaking. 6 But there is a place where someone has testified:

"What is man that you are mindful of him,
  the son of man that you care for him?[j]
7 You made him a little[a] lower than the angels;
  you crowned him with glory and honour
8 and put everything under his feet."[b][k]

In putting everything under him, God left nothing that is not subject to him. Yet at
present we do not see everything subject to him. 9 But we see Jesus, who was made
a little lower than the angels, now crowned with glory and honour[l] because he
suffered death,[m] so that by the grace of God he might taste death for everyone.[n]

[a] *7* Or *him for a little while*; also in verse 9 [b] *8* Psalm 8:4–6

LESSONS FROM CHRIST'S HUMANITY

Christ is the perfect human	leader	and he wants to lead you
	model	and he is worth imitating
	sacrifice	and he died for you
	conqueror	and he conquered death to give you eternal life
	High Priest	and he is merciful, loving, and understanding

God, in Christ, became a living, breathing human being. Hebrews points out many reasons why this is so important.

2:1–3 The author called his readers to pay attention to the truth they had heard so that they wouldn't drift away into false teachings. Paying careful attention is hard work. It involves focusing our minds, bodies, and senses. Listening to Christ means not merely hearing, but also obeying (see James 1:22–25). We must listen carefully and be ready to carry out his instructions.

2:2, 3 "The message spoken by angels" refers to the teaching that angels, as messengers for God, had brought the law to Moses (see Galatians 3:19). A central theme of Hebrews is that Christ is infinitely greater than all other proposed ways to God. The author was saying that the faith of his Jewish readers was good, but faith must point to Christ. Just as Christ is greater than angels, so Christ's message is more important than theirs. No-one will escape God's punishment if he or she is indifferent to the salvation offered by Christ.

2:3 Eyewitnesses to Jesus' ministry had handed down his teachings to the readers of this book. These readers were second-generation believers who had not seen Christ in the flesh. They are like us; we have not seen Jesus personally. We base our belief in Jesus on the eyewitness accounts recorded in the Bible. See John 20:29 for Jesus' encouragement to those who believe without ever having seen him.

2:4 "God also testified to it" continues the thought from 2:3. Those who had heard Jesus speak and then had passed on his words also had the truth of their words confirmed by "signs, wonders and various miracles, and gifts of the Holy Spirit". In the book of Acts, miracles and gifts of the Spirit authenticated the gospel wherever it was preached (see Acts 9:31–42; 14:1–20). Paul, who discussed spiritual gifts in Romans 12, 1 Corinthians 12 – 14, and Ephesians 4, taught that their purpose is to build up the church, making it strong and mature. When we see the gifts of the Spirit in an individual or congregation, we know that God is truly present. As we receive God's gifts, we should thank him for them and put them to use in the church.

2:8, 9 God put Jesus in charge of everything, and Jesus revealed himself to us. We do not yet see Jesus reigning on earth, but we can picture him in his heavenly glory. When you are confused by present events and anxious about the future, remember Jesus' true position and authority. He is Lord of all, and one day he will rule on earth as he does now in heaven. This truth can give stability to your decisions day by day.

2:9, 10 God's grace to us led Christ to his death. Jesus did not come into the world to gain status or political power, but to suffer and die so that we could have eternal life ("bringing many sons to glory"). If it is difficult for us to identify with Christ's servant attitude, perhaps we need to evaluate our own motives. Are we more interested in power or participation, domination or service, getting or giving?

10In bringing many sons to glory, it was fitting that God, for whom and through
whom everything exists,[o] should make the author of their salvation perfect through
suffering.[p] 11Both the one who makes men holy and those who are made holy[q] are
of the same family. So Jesus is not ashamed to call them brothers.[r] 12He says,

"I will declare your name to my brothers;
in the presence of the congregation I will sing your
praises."[c][s]

13And again,

"I will put my trust in him."[d][t]

And again he says,

"Here am I, and the children God has given me."[e][u]

14Since the children have flesh and blood, he too shared in their humanity[v] so that
by his death he might destroy[w] him who holds the power of death—that is, the
devil[x]— 15and free those who all their lives were held in slavery by their fear[y] of
death. 16For surely it is not angels he helps, but Abraham's descendants. 17For this
reason he had to be made like his brothers[z] in every way, in order that he might
become a merciful[a] and faithful high priest[b] in service to God,[c] and that he might
make atonement for[f] the sins of the people. 18Because he himself suffered when he
was tempted, he is able to help those who are being tempted.[d]

2. Christ is greater than Moses

3 Therefore, holy brothers,[a] who share in the heavenly calling, fix your thoughts
on Jesus, the apostle and high priest[b] whom we confess.[c] 2He was faithful to
the one who appointed him, just as Moses was faithful in all God's house.[d] 3Jesus

2:10 [o]Ro 11:36 [p]Lk 24:26; Heb 7:28
2:11 [q]Heb 10:10 [r]Mt 28:10; Jn 20:17
2:12 [s]Ps 22:22
2:13 [t]Isa 8:17 [u]Isa 8:18; Jn 10:29
2:14 [v]Jn 1:14 [w]1Co 15:54-57; 2Ti 1:10 [x]1Jn 3:8
2:15 [y]2Ti 1:7
2:17 [z]Php 2:7 [a]Heb 5:2 [b]Heb 4:14, 15; 7:26, 28 [c]Heb 5:1
2:18 [d]Heb 4:15
3:1 [a]Heb 2:11 [b]Heb 2:17 [c]Heb 4:14
3:2 [d]Nu 12:7

[c] *12* Psalm 22:22 [d] *13* Isaiah 8:17 [e] *13* Isaiah 8:18 [f] *17* Or *and that he might turn aside God's wrath, taking away*

2:10 How was Jesus made perfect through suffering? Jesus' suffering made him a perfect leader, or pioneer, of our salvation (see the notes on 5:8 and 5:9). Jesus did not need to suffer for his own salvation, because he was God in human form. His perfect obedience (which led him down the road of suffering) demonstrates that he was the complete sacrifice for us. Through suffering, Jesus completed the work necessary for our own salvation. Our suffering can make us more sensitive servants of God. People who have known pain are able to reach out with compassion to others who hurt. If you have suffered, ask God how your experience can be used to help others.

2:11–13 We who have been set apart for God's service, cleansed, and made holy (sanctified) by Jesus now have the same Father he has, so he has made us his brothers and sisters. Various psalms look forward to Christ and his work in the world. Here the writer quotes a portion of Psalm 22, a Messianic psalm. Because God has adopted all believers as his children, Jesus calls them his brothers and sisters.

2:14, 15 Jesus had to become human ("flesh and blood") so that he could die and rise again, in order to destroy the devil's power over death (Romans 6:5–11). Only then could Christ deliver those who had lived in constant fear of death, and free them to live for him. When we belong to God, we need not fear death, because we know that death is only the doorway into eternal life (1 Corinthians 15).

2:14, 15 Christ's death and resurrection set us free from the fear of death because death has been defeated. Every person must die b... ath is not the end; instead, it is the doorway to a new ... dread death should have the opportunity to know the ... rist's victory brings. How can you share this truth with ... you?

... e Old Testament, the high priest was the mediator between God and his people. His job was to regularly offer animal sacrifices according to the law and to intercede with God for forgiveness for the people's sins. Jesus Christ is now our high priest. He came to earth as a human being; therefore, he understands our weaknesses and shows mercy to us. He has *once and for all* paid the penalty for our sins by his own sacrificial death (atonement), and he can be depended on to restore our broken relationship with God. We are released from sin's domination over us when we commit ourselves fully to Christ, trusting completely in what he has done for us (see the note on 4:14 for more about Jesus as the great high priest).

2:18 Knowing that Christ suffered pain and faced temptation helps us face our trials. Jesus understands our struggles because he faced them as a human being. We can trust Christ to help us survive suffering and overcome temptation. When you face trials, go to Jesus for strength and patience. He understands your needs and is able to help (see 4:14–16).

3:1 This verse would have been especially meaningful to Jewish Christians. For Jews, the highest human authority was the high priest. For Christians, the highest human authorities were God's apostles. Jesus, God's apostle (meaning "one who is sent") and high priest, is the ultimate authority in the church.

3:1–6 The author uses different pictures to explain Jesus' relationship to believers: he is (1) the apostle ("one who is sent") of God, to whom we should listen; (2) our high priest, through whom we come to God the Father; and (3) the ruler of God's house ("faithful as a son over God's house"), whom we should obey. The Bible is filled with different names for and pictures of Jesus Christ, and each one reveals something more about his nature and ministry. What do these images teach you about your relationship with Christ?

3:2, 3 To the Jewish people, Moses was a great hero; he had led

3:5 [e]Ex 14:31 [f]ver 2; Nu 12:7
3:6 [g]Heb 1:2 [h]1Co 3:16 [i]Ro 11:22 [j]Ro 5:2
3:7 [k]Heb 9:8
3:9 [l]Ac 7:36
3:11 [m]Heb 4:3, 5 [n]Ps 95:7-11
3:13 [o]Heb 10:24, 25 [p]Eph 4:22
3:14 [q]ver 6
3:15 [r]ver 7, 8; Ps 95:7, 8

has been found worthy of greater honour than Moses, just as the builder of a house
has greater honour than the house itself. 4 For every house is built by someone, but
God is the builder of everything. 5 Moses was faithful as a servant[e] in all God's
house,[f] testifying to what would be said in the future. 6 But Christ is faithful as a son[g]
over God's house. And we are his house,[h] if we hold on[i] to our courage and the
hope[j] of which we boast.

Warning Against Unbelief

7 So, as the Holy Spirit says:[k]

"Today, if you hear his voice,
8 do not harden your hearts
as you did in the rebellion,
during the time of testing in the desert,
9 where your fathers tested and tried me
and for forty years saw what I did.[l]
10 That is why I was angry with that generation,
and I said, 'Their hearts are always going astray,
and they have not known my ways.'
11 So I declared on oath in my anger,
'They shall never enter my rest.'[m]"[a][n]

12 See to it, brothers, that none of you has a sinful, unbelieving heart that turns away
from the living God. 13 But encourage one another daily,[o] as long as it is called Today,
so that none of you may be hardened by sin's deceitfulness.[p] 14 We have come to share
in Christ if we hold firmly[q] till the end the confidence we had at first. 15 As has just
been said:

"Today, if you hear his voice,
do not harden your hearts
as you did in the rebellion."[b][r]

a *11* Psalm 95:7–11 **b** *15* Psalm 95:7,8

---

their ancestors, the Israelites, from Egyptian bondage to the border of the promised land. He had also written the first five books of the Old Testament, and he was the prophet through whom God had given the law; therefore, Moses was the greatest prophet in the Scriptures. But Jesus is worthy of greater honour as the central figure of faith than Moses, who was merely a human servant. Jesus is more than human; he is God himself (1:3). As Moses led the people of Israel out of Egyptian bondage, so Christ leads us out of sin's slavery. Why settle for Moses, the author of Hebrews asks, when you can have Jesus Christ, who appointed Moses?

3:5 Moses was faithful to God's calling not only to deliver Israel but also to prepare the way for the Messiah ("testifying to what would be said in the future"). All the Old Testament believers also served to prepare the way. Thus, knowing the Old Testament is the best foundation for understanding the New Testament. In reading the Old Testament, we see (1) how God used people to accomplish his purposes, (2) how God used events and personalities to illustrate important truths, (3) how, through prophets, God announced the Messiah, and (4) how, through the system of sacrifices, God prepared people to understand the Messiah's work. If you include the Old Testament in your regular Bible reading, the New Testament will grow clearer and more meaningful to you.

3:6 Because Christ lives in us as believers, we can remain courageous and hopeful to the end. We are not saved by being steadfast and firm in our faith, but our courage and hope do reveal that our faith is real. Without this enduring faithfulness, we could easily be blown away by the winds of temptation, false teaching, or persecution. (See also 3:14.)

3:7–15 In many places, the Bible warns us not to "harden" our hearts. This means stubbornly setting ourselves against God so that we are no longer able to turn to him for forgiveness. The Israelites became hardhearted when they disobeyed God's command to conquer the promised land (here called "the rebellion", see Numbers 13; 14; 20; and Psalm 95). Be careful to obey God's word, and do not allow your heart to become hardened.

3:11 God's *rest* has several meanings in Scripture: (1) the seventh day of creation and the weekly Sabbath commemorating it (Genesis 2:2; Hebrews 4:4–9); (2) the promised land of Canaan (Deuteronomy 12:8–12; Psalm 95); (3) peace with God now because of our relationship with Christ through faith (Matthew 12:28; Hebrews 4:1, 3, 8–11); and (4) our future eternal life with Christ (Hebrews 4:8–11). All of these meanings were probably familiar to the Jewish Christian readers of Hebrews.

3:12–14 Our hearts turn away from the living God when we stubbornly refuse to believe him. If we persist in our unbelief, God will eventually leave us alone in our sin. But God can give us new hearts, new desires, and new spirits (Ezekiel 36:22–27). To prevent having an unbelieving heart, stay in fellowship with other believers, talk daily about your mutual faith, be aware of the deceitfulness of sin (it attracts but also destroys), and encourage each other with love and concern.

3:15–19 The Israelites failed to enter the promised land because they did not believe in God's protection, and they did not believe that God would help them conquer the giants in the land (see Numbers 14; 15). So God sent them into the desert to wander for 40 years. This was an unhappy alternative to the wonderful gift he had planned for them. Lack of trust in God always prevents us from receiving his best.

16 Who were they who heard and rebelled? Were they not all those Moses led out
of Egypt?[s] 17 And with whom was he angry for forty years? Was it not with those
who sinned, whose bodies fell in the desert?[t] 18 And to whom did God swear that
they would never enter his rest[u] if not to those who disobeyed?[c][v] 19 So we see that
they were not able to enter, because of their unbelief.[w]

A Sabbath-Rest for the People of God

4 Therefore, since the promise of entering his rest still stands, let us be careful that
none of you be found to have fallen short of it.[a] 2 For we also have had the gospel
preached to us, just as they did; but the message they heard was of no value to them,
because those who heard did not combine it with faith.[a][b] 3 Now we who have
believed enter that rest, just as God has said,

> "So I declared on oath in my anger,
> 'They shall never enter my rest.' "[b][c]

And yet his work has been finished since the creation of the world. 4 For somewhere
he has spoken about the seventh day in these words: "And on the seventh day God
rested from all his work."[c][d] 5 And again in the passage above he says, "They shall
never enter my rest."[e]
6 It still remains that some will enter that rest, and those who formerly had the gospel
preached to them did not go in, because of their disobedience.[f] 7 Therefore God again
set a certain day, calling it Today, when a long time later he spoke through David,
as was said before:

> "Today, if you hear his voice,
> do not harden your hearts."[d][g]

8 For if Joshua had given them rest,[h] God would not have spoken[i] later about another
day. 9 There remains, then, a Sabbath-rest for the people of God; 10 for anyone who
enters God's rest also rests from his own work, just as God did from his.[j] 11 Let us,
therefore, make every effort to enter that rest, so that no-one will fall by following
their example of disobedience.[k]
12 For the word of God[l] is living and active.[m] Sharper than any double-edged

c *18* Or *disbelieved* **a** *2* Many manuscripts *because they did not share in the faith of those who obeyed*
b *3* Psalm 95:11; also in verse 5 **c** *4* Gen. 2:2 **d** *7* Psalm 95:7,8

3:16 [s]Nu 14:2
3:17 [t]Nu 14:29; Ps 106:26
3:18 [u]Nu 14:20-23 [v]Heb 4:6
3:19 [w]Jn 3:36
4:1 [a]Heb 12:15
4:2 [b]1Th 2:13
4:3 [c]Ps 95:11; Heb 3:11
4:4 [d]Ge 2:2, 3; Ex 20:11
4:5 [e]Ps 95:11
4:6 [f]Heb 3:18
4:7 [g]Ps 95:7, 8; Heb 3:7, 8, 15
4:8 [h]Jos 22:4 [i]Heb 1:1
4:10 [j]ver 4
4:11 [k]Heb 3:18
4:12 [l]1Pe 1:23 [m]Jer 23:29

4:1–3 Some of the Jewish Christians who received this letter may have been on the verge of turning back from their promised rest in Christ, just as the people in Moses' day had turned back from the promised land. In both cases, the difficulties of the present moment overshadowed the reality of God's promise, and the people doubted that God would fulfil his promises. When we trust our own efforts instead of Christ's power, we too are in danger of turning back. Our own efforts are never adequate; only Christ can see us through.

4:2 The Israelites of Moses' day illustrate a problem facing many who fill our churches today. They know a great deal about Christ, but they do not know him personally—they don't combine their knowledge with faith. Let the Good News about Christ benefit your life. Believe in him and then act on what you know. Trust in Christ and do what he says.

4:4 God rested on the seventh day, not because he was tired, but to indicate the completion of creation. The world was perfect, and God was well satisfied with it. This rest is a foretaste of our eternal joy when creation will be renewed and restored, every mark of sin will be removed, and the world will be made perfect again. Our Sabbath-rest in Christ begins when we trust him to complete hi[illegible] and perfect work in us (see the note on 3:11).

[illegible]d had given the Israelites the opportunity to enter Ca-[illegible]y disobeyed and failed to enter (Numbers 13; 14). [illegible]rs us the opportunity to enter his ultimate place of [illegible]s us to come to Christ. To enter his rest, you must believe that God has this relationship in mind for you; you must stop trying to create it; you must trust in Christ for it; and you must determine to obey him. *Today* is the best time to find peace with God. Tomorrow may be too late.

4:8–11 God wants us to enter his rest. For the Israelites of Moses' time, this rest was the earthly rest to be found in the promised land. For Christians, it is peace with God now and eternal life on a new earth later. We do not need to wait for the next life to enjoy God's rest and peace; we may have it daily now! Our daily rest in the Lord will not end with death, but will become an eternal rest in the place that Christ is preparing for us (John 14:1–4).

4:11 If Jesus has provided for our rest through faith, why must we "make every effort to enter that rest"? This is not the struggle of doing good in order to obtain salvation, nor is it a mystical struggle to overcome selfishness. It refers to making every effort to appreciate and benefit from what God has already provided. Salvation is not to be taken for granted; to appropriate the gift God offers requires decision and commitment.

4:12 The word of God is not simply a collection of words from God, a vehicle for communicating ideas; it is living, life-changing, and dynamic as it works in us. With the incisiveness of a surgeon's knife, God's word reveals who we are and what we are not. It penetrates the core of our moral and spiritual life. It discerns what is within us, both good and evil. The demands of God's word require decisions. We must not only listen to the word; we must also let it shape our lives.

4:12
[n]Eph 6:17; Rev 1:16
[o]1Co 14:24, 25

4:13
[p]Ps 33:13-15

4:14
[q]Heb 6:20
[r]Heb 3:1

4:15
[s]Heb 2:18
[t]2Co 5:21

5:1
[a]Heb 8:3
[b]Heb 7:27

5:2
[c]Heb 2:18
[d]Heb 7:28

5:3
[e]Heb 7:27; 9:7

5:4
[f]Ex 28:1

5:5
[g]Jn 8:54
[h]Heb 1:1
[i]Ps 2:7

sword,[n] it penetrates even to dividing soul and spirit, joints and marrow; it judges
the thoughts and attitudes of the heart.[o] 13Nothing in all creation is hidden from God's
sight.[p] Everything is uncovered and laid bare before the eyes of him to whom we
must give account.

3. Christ is greater than the Old Testament priesthood

Jesus the Great High Priest

14Therefore, since we have a great high priest who has gone through the heavens,[e][q] Jesus the Son of God, let us hold firmly to the faith we profess.[r] 15For we
do not have a high priest who is unable to sympathise with our weaknesses, but we
have one who has been tempted in every way, just as we are[s]—yet was without sin.[t]
16Let us then approach the throne of grace with confidence, so that we may receive
mercy and find grace to help us in our time of need.

5 Every high priest is selected from among men and is appointed to represent them
in matters related to God, to offer gifts and sacrifices[a] for sins.[b] 2He is able
to deal gently with those who are ignorant and are going astray,[c] since he himself
is subject to weakness.[d] 3This is why he has to offer sacrifices for his own sins, as
well as for the sins of the people.[e]
4No-one takes this honour upon himself; he must be called by God, just as Aaron
was.[f] 5So Christ also did not take upon himself the glory[g] of becoming a high priest.
But God said[h] to him,

"You are my Son;
today I have become your Father."[a,b][i]

[e] 14 Or *gone into heaven* [a] 5 Or *have begotten you* [b] 5 Psalm 2:7

THE CHOICES OF MATURITY
One way to evaluate spiritual maturity is by looking at the choices we make. The writer of Hebrews notes many of the ways those choices change with personal growth.

Mature choices	*Versus*	*Immature choices*
Teaching others	rather than . . .	just being taught.
Developing depth of understanding	rather than . . .	struggling with the basics.
Self-evaluation	rather than . . .	self-criticism.
Seeking unity	rather than . . .	promoting disunity.
Desiring spiritual challenges	rather than . . .	desiring entertainment.
Careful study and observation	rather than . . .	opinions and halfhearted efforts.
Active faith	rather than . . .	cautious apathy and doubt.
Confidence	rather than . . .	fear.
Feelings and experiences evaluated in the light of God's Word	rather than . . .	experiences evaluated according to feelings.

4:13 Nothing can be hidden from God. He knows about everyone everywhere, and everything about us is wide open to his all-seeing eyes. God sees all we do and knows all we think. Even when we are unaware of his presence, he is there. When we try to hide from him, he sees us. We can have no secrets from God. It is comforting to realise that although God knows us intimately, he still loves us.

4:14 Christ is superior to the priests, and his priesthood is superior to their priesthood. To the Jews, the high priest was the highest religious authority in the land. He alone entered the Holy of Holies in the temple once a year to make atonement for the sins of the whole nation (Leviticus 16). Like the high priest, Jesus mediates between God and us. As humanity's representative, he intercedes for us before God. As God's representative, he assures us of God's forgiveness. Jesus has more authority than the Jewish high priests because he is truly God and truly man. Unlike the high priest who could go before God only once a year, Christ is always at God's right hand, interceding for us. He is always available to hear us when we pray.

4:15 Jesus is like us because he experienced a full range of temptations throughout his life as a human being. We can be comforted knowing that Jesus faced temptation—he can sympathise with us. We can be encouraged knowing that Jesus faced temptation without giving in to sin. He shows us that we do not have to sin when facing the seductive lure of temptation. Jesus is the only perfect human being who has ever lived.

4:16 Prayer is our approach to God, and we are to come "with confidence". Some Christians approach God meekly with heads hung low, afraid to ask him to meet their needs. Others pray flippantly, giving little thought to what they say. Come with reverence because he is your King. But also come with bold assurance because he is your Friend and Counsellor.

5:4–6 This chapter stresses both Christ's divine appointment and his humanity. The writer uses two Old Testament verses to show Christ's divine appointment—Psalms 2:7 and 110:4. At the time this book was written, the Romans selected the high priest in Jerusalem. In the Old Testament, however, God chose Aaron, and only Aaron's descendants could be high priests. Christ, like Aaron, was chosen and called by God.

6And he says in another place,

"You are a priest for ever,
in the order of Melchizedek."[c][j]

7During the days of Jesus' life on earth, he offered up prayers and petitions with
loud cries and tears[k] to the one who could save him from death, and he was heard
because of his reverent submission.[l] 8Although he was a son, he learned obedience
from what he suffered[m] 9and, once made perfect,[n] he became the source of eternal
salvation for all who obey him 10and was designated by God to be high priest[o] in
the order of Melchizedek.[p]

Warning Against Falling Away

11We have much to say about this, but it is hard to explain because you are slow
to learn. 12In fact, though by this time you ought to be teachers, you need someone
to teach you the elementary truths[q] of God's word all over again. You need milk,
not solid food![r] 13Anyone who lives on milk, being still an infant,[s] is not acquainted
with the teaching about righteousness. 14But solid food is for the mature,[t] who by
constant use have trained themselves to distinguish good from evil.[u]

6 Therefore let us leave[a] the elementary teachings[b] about Christ and go on to
maturity, not laying again the foundation of repentance from acts that lead to
death,[a][c] and of faith in God, 2instruction about baptisms,[d] the laying on of hands,[e]
the resurrection of the dead,[f] and eternal judgment. 3And God permitting,[g] we will
do so.

4It is impossible for those who have once been enlightened,[h] who have tasted the
heavenly gift,[i] who have shared in the Holy Spirit,[j] 5who have tasted the goodness

c 6 Psalm 110:4 a 1 Or *from useless rituals*

5:6 [j]Ps 110:4; Heb 7:17, 21
5:7 [k]Mt 27:46, 50 [l]Mk 14:36
5:8 [m]Php 2:8
5:9 [n]Heb 2:10
5:10 [o]ver 5 [p]ver 6
5:12 [q]Heb 6:1 [r]1Co 3:2; 1Pe 2:2
5:13 [s]1Co 14:20
5:14 [t]1Co 2:6 [u]Isa 7:15
6:1 [a]Php 3:12-14 [b]Heb 5:12 [c]Heb 9:14
6:2 [d]Jn 3:25 [e]Ac 6:6 [f]Ac 17:18, 32
6:3 [g]Ac 18:21
6:4 [h]Heb 10:32 [i]Eph 2:8 [j]Gal 3:2

5:6 Melchizedek was a priest of Salem (now called Jerusalem). His Profile is found in Genesis 16. Melchizedek's position is explained in Hebrews 7.

5:7 Jesus was in great agony as he prepared to face death (Luke 22:41–44). Although Jesus cried out to God, asking to be delivered, he was prepared to suffer humiliation, separation from his Father, and death in order to do God's will. At times we will undergo trials, not because we want to suffer, but because we want to obey God. Let Jesus' obedience sustain and encourage you in times of trial. You will be able to face anything if you know that Jesus Christ is with you.

5:7 Have you ever felt that God didn't hear your prayers? Be sure you are praying with reverent submission, willing to do what God wants. God responds to his obedient children.

5:8 Jesus' human life was not a script that he passively followed. It was a life that he chose freely (John 10:17, 18). It was a continuous process of making the will of God the Father his own. Jesus chose to obey, even though obedience led to suffering and death. Because Jesus obeyed perfectly, even under great trial, he can help us obey, no matter how difficult obedience seems to be.

5:9 Christ was always morally perfect. By obeying, he demonstrated his perfection to us, not to God or to himself. In the Bible, *perfection* usually means completeness or maturity. By sharing our experience of suffering, Christ shared our human experience completely. He is now able to offer eternal salvation to those who obey him. See Philippians 2:5–11 for Christ's attitude as he took on human form.

5:12, 13 These Jewish Christians were immature. Some of them should have been teaching others, but they had not even applied the basics to their own lives. They were reluctant to move beyond age-ol[illegible]aditions, established doctrines, and discussion of the ba-[illegible]ouldn't be able to understand the high-priestly role of [illegible] they moved out of their comfortable position, cut [illegible] Jewish ties, and stopped trying to blend in with their culture. Commitment to Christ moves people out of their comfort zones.

5:12–14 In order to grow from infant Christians to mature Christians, we must learn discernment. We must train our consciences, our senses, our minds, and our bodies to distinguish good from evil. Can you recognise temptation before it traps you? Can you tell the difference between a correct use of Scripture and a mistaken one?

5:14 Our capacity to feast on deeper knowledge of God ("solid food") is determined by our spiritual growth. Too often we want God's banquet before we are spiritually capable of digesting it. As you grow in the Lord and put into practice what you have learned, your capacity to understand will also grow.

6:1, 2 Certain elementary teachings are essential for all believers to understand. Those basics include the importance of faith, the foolishness of trying to be saved by good deeds, the meaning of baptism and spiritual gifts, and the facts of resurrection and eternal life. To go on to maturity in our understanding, we need to move beyond (but not away from) the elementary teachings to a more complete understanding of the faith. And this is what the author intends for them to do (6:3). Mature Christians should be teaching new Christians the basics. Then, acting on what they know, the mature will learn even more from God's word.

6:3 These Christians needed to move beyond the basics of their faith to an understanding of Christ as the perfect high priest and the fulfilment of all the Old Testament prophecies. Rather than arguing about the respective merits of Judaism and Christianity, they needed to depend on Christ and live effectively for him.

6:4–6 In the first century, a pagan who investigated Christianity and then went back to paganism made a clean break with the church. But for Jewish Christians who decided to return to Judaism, the break was less obvious. Their life-style remained relatively unchanged. But by deliberately turning away from Christ, they were cutting themselves off from God's forgiveness. Those who persevere in believing are true saints; those who continue to reject Christ are unbelievers, no matter how well they behave.

6:6
k 2Pe 2:21; 1Jn 5:16

of the word of God and the powers of the coming age, 6if they fall away, to be brought
back to repentance,[k] because[b] to their loss they are crucifying the Son of God all
over again and subjecting him to public disgrace.

b 6 Or *repentance while*

ABRAHAM IN THE NEW TESTAMENT

Abraham was an ancestor of Jesus Christ	Matthew 1:1, 2, 17; Luke 3:23, 34	Jesus Christ was human; he was born into the line of Abraham, whom God had chosen to be the father of a great nation through which the whole world would be blessed. We are blessed because of what Jesus Christ, Abraham's descendant, did for us.
Abraham was the father of the Jewish nation	Matthew 3:9; Luke 3:8; Acts 13:26; Romans 4:1; 11:1; 2 Corinthians 11:22; Hebrews 6:13, 14	God wanted to set apart a nation for himself, a nation that would tell the world about him. He began with a man of faith who, though old and childless, believed God's promise of innumerable descendants. We can trust God to do the impossible when we have faith.
Abraham, because of his faith, now sits in the kingdom with Christ.	Matthew 8:11; Luke 13:28; 16:23–31	Abraham followed God, and now he is enjoying his reward—eternity with God. We will one day meet Abraham, because we have been promised eternity as well.
God *is* Abraham's God; thus Abraham is alive with God	Matthew 22:32; Mark 12:26; Luke 20:37; Acts 7:32	As Abraham lives for ever, we will live for ever, because we, like Abraham, have chosen the life of faith.
Abraham received great promises from God	Luke 1:55, 72, 73; Acts 3:25; 7:17, 18; Galatians 3:6, 14–16; Hebrews 6:13–15	Many of the promises God made to Abraham seemed impossible to be realised, but Abraham trusted God. The promises to believers in God's word also seem too incredible to believe, but we can trust God to keep all his promises.
Abraham followed God	Acts 7:2–8; Hebrews 11:8, 17–19	Abraham followed God's leading from his homeland to an unknown territory, which became the Jews' promised land. When we follow God, even before he makes all his plans clear to us, we will never be disappointed.
God blessed Abraham because of his faith	Romans 4; Galatians 3:6–9, 14–29; Hebrews 11:8, 17–19; James 2:21–24	Abraham showed faith in times of disappointment, trial, and testing. Because of Abraham's faith, God counted him righteous and called him his "friend". God accepts us because of our faith.
Abraham is the father of all those who come to God by faith	Romans 9:6–8; Galatians 3:6–9, 14–29	The Jews are Abraham's children, and Christ was his descendant. We are Christ's brothers and sisters; thus all believers are Abraham's children and God's children. Abraham was righteous because of his faith; we are made righteous through faith in Christ. The promises made to Abraham apply to us because of Christ.

6:6 This verse points to the danger of the Hebrew Christians returning to Judaism and thus committing apostasy. Some apply this verse today to superficial believers who renounce their Christianity, or to unbelievers who come close to salvation and then turn away. Either way, those who reject Christ will not be saved. Christ died once for all. He will not be crucified again. Apart from his cross, there is no other possible way of salvation. However, the author does not indicate that his readers were in danger of renouncing Christ (see 6:9). He is warning against hardness of heart that would make repentance inconceivable for the sinner.

7Land that drinks in the rain often falling on it and that produces a crop useful to
those for whom it is farmed receives the blessing of God. 8But land that produces
thorns and thistles is worthless and is in danger of being cursed.[l] In the end it will
be burned.
9Even though we speak like this, dear friends,[m] we are confident of better things
in your case—things that accompany salvation. 10God is not unjust; he will not forget
your work and the love you have shown him as you have helped his people and
continue to help them.[n] 11We want each of you to show this same diligence to the
very end, in order to make your hope[o] sure. 12We do not want you to become lazy,
but to imitate[p] those who through faith and patience[q] inherit what has been promised.[r]

The Certainty of God's Promise

13When God made his promise to Abraham, since there was no-one greater for him
to swear by, he swore by himself,[s] 14saying, "I will surely bless you and give you
many descendants."[c][t] 15And so after waiting patiently, Abraham received what was
promised.[u]
16Men swear by someone greater than themselves, and the oath confirms what is
said and puts an end to all argument.[v] 17Because God wanted to make the unchanging[w] nature of his purpose very clear to the heirs of what was promised,[x] he
confirmed it with an oath. 18God did this so that, by two unchangeable things in which
it is impossible for God to lie,[y] we who have fled to take hold of the hope[z] offered
to us may be greatly encouraged. 19We have this hope as an anchor for the soul, firm
and secure. It enters the inner sanctuary behind the curtain,[a] 20where Jesus, who went
before us, has entered on our behalf.[b] He has become a high priest[c] for ever, in the
order of Melchizedek.[d]

Melchizedek the Priest

7 This Melchizedek was king of Salem and priest of God Most High.[a] He met
Abraham returning from the defeat of the kings and blessed him,[b] 2and Abraham
gave him a tenth of everything. First, his name means "king of righteousness"; then
also, "king of Salem" means "king of peace". 3Without father or mother, without

c *14* Gen. 22:17

6:8 [l]Ge 3:17, 18; Isa 5:6
6:9 [m]1Co 10:14
6:10 [n]Mt 10:40, 42; 25:40; 1Th 1:3
6:11 [o]Heb 3:6
6:12 [p]Heb 13:7 [q]2Th 1:4; Jas 1:3; Rev 13:10 [r]Heb 10:36
6:13 [s]Ge 22:16; Lk 1:73
6:14 [t]Ge 22:17
6:15 [u]Ge 21:5
6:16 [v]Ex 22:11
6:17 [w]Ps 110:4 [x]Heb 11:9
6:18 [y]Nu 23:19; Tit 1:2 [z]Heb 3:6
6:19 [a]Lev 16:2; Heb 9:2, 3, 7
6:20 [b]Heb 4:14 [c]Heb 2:17 [d]Heb 5:6
7:1 [a]Mk 5:7 [b]Ge 14:18-20

6:7, 8 Land that produces a good crop receives loving care, but land that produces thorns and thistles has to be burned so the farmer can start again. An unproductive Christian life falls under God's condemnation. We are not saved by deeds or conduct, but what we do is the *evidence* of our faith.

6:10 It's easy to get discouraged, thinking that God has forgotten us. But God is never unjust. He never forgets or overlooks our hard work for him. You may not be receiving rewards and acclaim right now, but God knows your efforts of love and ministry. Let God's love for you and his intimate knowledge of your service for him bolster you as you face disappointment and rejection here on earth.

6:11, 12 Hope keeps the Christian from becoming lazy or feeling bored. Like an athlete, train hard and run well, remembering the reward that lies ahead (Philippians 3:14).

6:15 Abraham waited patiently—it was 25 years from the time God had promised him a son (Genesis 17:16) to Isaac's birth (Genesis 21:1–3). Because our trials and temptations are often so intense, they seem to last for an eternity. Both the Bible and the testimony of mature Christians encourage us to wait for God to act in his timing, even when our needs seem too great to wait any longer.

6:17 God's promises are unchanging and trustworthy because God is unchanging and trustworthy. When promising Abraham a son, God took an oath in his own name. The oath was as good as God's name, and God's name was as good as his divine nature.

6:18, 19 These two unchangeable things are God's nature and his promise. God embodies all truth; therefore, he cannot lie. Because God is truth, you can be secure in his promises; you don't need to wonder if he will change his plans. Our hope is secure and immovable, anchored in God, just as a ship's anchor holds firmly to the seabed. To the true seeker who comes to God in belief, God gives an unconditional promise of acceptance. When you ask God with openness, honesty, and sincerity to save you from your sins, *he will do it.* This truth should give you encouragement, assurance, and confidence.

6:19, 20 This curtain hung across the entrance from the Holy Place to the Most Holy Place, the two innermost rooms of the temple. This curtain prevented anyone from entering, gazing into, or even catching a fleeting glimpse of the interior of the Most Holy Place (see also 9:1–8). The high priest could enter there only once a year to stand before God's presence and atone for the sins of the entire nation. But Christ is in God's presence at all times, not just once a year, as the high priest who can continually intercede for us.

7:2ff The writer of Hebrews uses this story from Genesis 14:18–20 to show that Christ is even greater than Abraham, father of the Jewish nation, and Levi (Abraham's descendant). Therefore, the Jewish priesthood (made up of Levi's descendants) was inferior to Melchizedek's priesthood (a type of Christ's priesthood).

7:3–10 Melchizedek was a priest of God Most High (see the note on Genesis 14:18 and his Profile in Genesis 16). He is said to remain a priest for ever (see also Psalm 110:4), because his priesthood has no record of beginning or ending—he was a priest of

genealogy,[c] without beginning of days or end of life, like the Son of God[d] he remains
a priest for ever.
4Just think how great he was: Even the patriarch[e] Abraham gave him a tenth of
the plunder![f] 5Now the law requires the descendants of Levi who become priests to
collect a tenth from the people[g]—that is, their brothers—even though their brothers
are descended from Abraham. 6This man, however, did not trace his descent from
Levi, yet he collected a tenth from Abraham and blessed[h] him who had the promises.[i] 7And without doubt the lesser person is blessed by the greater. 8In the one case,
the tenth is collected by men who die; but in the other case, by him who is declared
to be living.[j] 9One might even say that Levi, who collects the tenth, paid the tenth
through Abraham, 10because when Melchizedek met Abraham, Levi was still in the
body of his ancestor.

Jesus Like Melchizedek

11If perfection could have been attained through the Levitical priesthood (for on the
basis of it the law was given to the people),[k] why was there still need for another
priest to come[l]—one in the order of Melchizedek,[m] not in the order of Aaron? 12For
when there is a change of the priesthood, there must also be a change of the law. 13He
of whom these things are said belonged to a different tribe,[n] and no-one from that
tribe has ever served at the altar.[o] 14For it is clear that our Lord descended from
Judah,[p] and in regard to that tribe Moses said nothing about priests. 15And what we
have said is even more clear if another priest like Melchizedek appears, 16one who
has become a priest not on the basis of a regulation as to his ancestry but on the basis
of the power of an indestructible life. 17For it is declared:

> "You are a priest for ever,
> in the order of Melchizedek."[a][q]

18The former regulation is set aside because it was weak and useless[r] 19(for the
law made nothing perfect),[s] and a better hope is introduced, by which we draw near
to God.[t]
20And it was not without an oath! Others became priests without any oath, 21but
he became a priest with an oath when God said to him:

> "The Lord has sworn
> and will not change his mind:[u]
> 'You are a priest for ever.' "[b][v]

22Because of this oath, Jesus has become the guarantee of a better covenant.[w]
23Now there have been many of those priests, since death prevented them from
continuing in office; 24but because Jesus lives for ever, he has a permanent priest-

a *17* Psalm 110:4 b *21* Psalm 110:4

7:3 [c]ver 6 [d]Mt 4:3
7:4 [e]Ac 2:29 [f]Ge 14:20
7:5 [g]Nu 18:21, 26
7:6 [h]Ge 14:19, 20 [i]Ro 4:13
7:8 [j]Heb 5:6; 6:20
7:11 [k]ver 18, 19; Heb 8:7 [l]Heb 10:1 [m]ver 17
7:13 [n]ver 11 [o]ver 14
7:14 [p]Isa 11:1; Mt 1:3; Lk 3:33
7:17 [q]Ps 110:4; ver 21; Heb 5:6
7:18 [r]Ro 8:3
7:19 [s]Ac 13:39; Ro 3:20; Heb 9:9 [t]Heb 4:16
7:21 [u]1Sa 15:29 [v]Ps 110:4
7:22 [w]Heb 8:6

God in Salem (Jerusalem) long before the nation of Israel and the regular priesthood began.

7:7 The "lesser person is blessed by the greater" means a person who has the power to bless is always greater than the person whom he or she blesses.

7:11–17 Jesus' high-priestly role was superior to that of any priest of Levi, because the Messiah was a priest of a higher order (Psalm 110:4). If the Jewish priests and their laws had been able to save people, why would God need to send Christ as a priest, who came not from the tribe of Levi (the priestly tribe), but from the tribe of Judah? The animal sacrifices had to be repeated, and they offered only temporary forgiveness; but Christ's sacrifice was offered once, and it offers total and permanent forgiveness. Under the new covenant, the Levitical priesthood was cancelled in favour of Christ's role as high priest. Because Christ is our high priest, we need to pay attention to him. No minister, leader, or Christian friend can substitute for Christ's work and for his role in our salvation.

7:18, 19 The law was not intended to save people, but to point out sin (see Romans 3:20; 5:20) and to point towards Christ (see Galatians 3:24, 25). Salvation comes through Christ, whose sacrifice brings forgiveness for our sins. Being ethical, working diligently to help others, and giving to charitable causes are all commendable, but all of our good deeds cannot save us or make us right with God. There is a "better hope".

7:22–24 This "better covenant" is also called the new covenant or testament. It is new and better because it allows us to go directly to God through Christ. We no longer need to rely on sacrificed animals and mediating priests to obtain God's forgiveness. This new covenant is better because, while all human priests die, Christ lives for ever. Priests and sacrifices could not save people, but Christ truly saves. You have access to Christ. He is available to you, but do you go to him with your needs?

hood.[x] 25Therefore he is able to save completely[c] those who come to God[y] through
him, because he always lives to intercede for them.[z]
26Such a high priest meets our need—one who is holy, blameless, pure, set apart
from sinners,[a] exalted above the heavens.[b] 27Unlike the other high priests, he does
not need to offer sacrifices[c] day after day, first for his own sins,[d] and then for the
sins of the people. He sacrificed for their sins once for all[e] when he offered himself.[f]
28For the law appoints as high priests men who are weak;[g] but the oath, which came
after the law, appointed the Son,[h] who has been made perfect[i] for ever.

4. The new covenant is greater than the old

The High Priest of a New Covenant

8 The point of what we are saying is this: We do have such a high priest,[a] who
sat down at the right hand of the throne of the Majesty in heaven, 2and who serves
in the sanctuary, the true tabernacle[b] set up by the Lord, not by man.
3Every high priest is appointed to offer both gifts and sacrifices,[c] and so it was
necessary for this one also to have something to offer.[d] 4If he were on earth, he would
not be a priest, for there are already men who offer the gifts prescribed by the law.[e]
5They serve at a sanctuary that is a copy[f] and shadow[g] of what is in heaven. This
is why Moses was warned[h] when he was about to build the tabernacle: "See to it that
you make everything according to the pattern shown you on the mountain."[a][i] 6But
the ministry Jesus has received is as superior to theirs as the covenant[j] of which he
is mediator[k] is superior to the old one, and it is founded on better promises.
7For if there had been nothing wrong with that first covenant, no place would have
been sought for another.[l] 8But God found fault with the people and said:[b]

> "The time is coming, declares the Lord,
> when I will make a new covenant[m]
> with the house of Israel
> and with the house of Judah.

[c] *25* Or *for ever* [a] *5* Exodus 25:40 [b] *8* Some manuscripts may be translated *fault and said to the people.*

7:24 [x]ver 28
7:25 [y]ver 19 [z]Ro 8:34
7:26 [a]2Co 5:21 [b]Heb 4:14
7:27 [c]Heb 5:1 [d]Heb 5:3 [e]Heb 9:12, 26, 28 [f]Eph 5:2; Heb 9:14, 28
7:28 [g]Heb 5:2 [h]Heb 1:2 [i]Heb 2:10
8:1 [a]Heb 2:17
8:2 [b]Heb 9:11, 24
8:3 [c]Heb 5:1 [d]Heb 9:14
8:4 [e]Heb 5:1
8:5 [f]Heb 9:23 [g]Col 2:17; Heb 10:1 [h]Heb 11:7; 12:25 [i]Ex 25:40
8:6 [j]Lk 22:20 [k]Heb 7:22
8:7 [l]Heb 7:11, 18
8:8 [m]Jer 31:31

7:25 No-one can add to what Jesus did to save us; our past, present, and future sins are all forgiven, and Jesus is with the Father as a sign that our sins are forgiven. If you are a Christian, remember that Christ has paid the price for your sins once and for all. (See also 9:24–28.)

7:25 As our high priest, Christ is our advocate, the mediator between us and God. He looks after our interests and intercedes for us with God. The Old Testament high priest went before God once a year to plead for the forgiveness of the nation's sins; Christ makes perpetual intercession before God for us. Christ's continuous presence in heaven with the Father assures us that our sins have been paid for and forgiven (see Romans 8:33, 34; Hebrews 2:17, 18; 4:15, 16; 9:24). This wonderful assurance frees us from guilt and from fear of failure.

7:27 In Old Testament times when animals were sacrificed, they were cut into pieces, the parts were washed, the fat was burned, the blood was sprinkled, and the meat was boiled. Blood was demanded as atonement for sins, and God accepted animal blood to cover the people's sins (Leviticus 17:11). Because of the sacrificial system, the Israelites were generally aware that sin costs someone something and that they themselves were sinful. Many people take Christ's work on the cross for granted. They don't realise how costly it was for Jesus to secure our forgiveness—it cost him his life and painful, temporary separation from his Father (Matthew 27:46; 1 Peter 1:18, 19).

7:27 Because Jesus died *once for all,* he brought the sacrificial system to an end. He forgave sins—past, present, and future. The Jews did not need to go back to the old system because Christ, the perfect sacrifice, completed the work of redemption. You don't have to look for another way to have your sins forgiven—Christ was the final sacrifice for you.

7:28 As we better understand the Jewish sacrificial system, we see that Jesus' death served as the perfect atonement for our sins. His death brings us eternal life. How callous, how cold, how stubborn it would be to refuse God's greatest gift.

8:4 Under the old Jewish system, priests were chosen only from the tribe of Levi, and sacrifices were offered daily on the altar for forgiveness of sins (see 7:12–14). This system would not have allowed Jesus to be a priest, because he was from the tribe of Judah. But his perfect sacrifice ended all need for further priests and sacrifices.

The use of the present tense, "there are already men who offer the gifts" indicates that this book was written before A.D. 70 when the temple in Jerusalem was destroyed, ending the sacrifices.

8:5 The pattern for the tabernacle built by Moses was given by God. It was a pattern of the spiritual reality of Christ's sacrifice, and thus it looked forward to the future reality. There is no tabernacle in heaven of which the earthly one is a copy, but rather the earthly tabernacle was an expression of eternal, theological principles. Because the temple at Jerusalem had not yet been destroyed, using the worship system there as an example would have had a great impact on this original audience.

8:8–12 This passage is a quotation of Jeremiah 31:31–34, which compares the new covenant with the old. The old covenant was the covenant of law between God and Israel. The new and better way is the covenant of grace—Christ's offer to forgive our sins and bring us to God through his sacrificial death. This covenant is new in extent—it goes beyond Israel and Judah to include all the Gentile nations. It is new in application because it is written on our hearts and in our minds. It offers a new way to forgiveness, not through animal sacrifice but through faith. Have you entered into this new covenant and begun walking in the better way?

8:9 [n]Ex 19:5, 6
8:10 [o]2Co 3:3; Heb 10:16 [p]Zec 8:8
8:11 [q]Isa 54:13; Jn 6:45
8:12 [r]Heb 10:17 [s]Jer 31:31-34
8:13 [t]2Co 5:17

9It will not be like the covenant
I made with their forefathers[n]
when I took them by the hand
to lead them out of Egypt,
because they did not remain faithful to my covenant,
and I turned away from them,
declares the Lord.
10This is the covenant I will make with the house of Israel
after that time, declares the Lord.
I will put my laws in their minds
and write them on their hearts.[o]
I will be their God,
and they will be my people.[p]
11No longer will a man teach his neighbour,
or a man his brother, saying, 'Know the Lord,'
because they will all know me,[q]
from the least of them to the greatest.
12For I will forgive their wickedness
and will remember their sins no more.[r]"[c][s]

13By calling this covenant "new", he has made the first one obsolete;[t] and what is obsolete and ageing will soon disappear.

c *12* Jer. 31:31–34

THE OLD AND NEW COVENANTS

Like pointing out the similarities and differences between the photograph of a person and the actual person, the writer of Hebrews shows the connection between the old Mosaic covenant and the new messianic covenant. He proves that the old covenant was a shadow of the real Christ.

The Old Covenant under Moses	*The New Covenant in Christ*	*Application*
Gifts and sacrifices by those guilty of sin	Self-sacrifice by the guiltless Christ	Christ died for you
Focused on a physical building where one goes to worship	Focuses on the reign of Christ in the hearts of believers	God is directly involved in your life
A shadow	A reality	Not temporal, but eternal
Limited promises	Limitless promises	We can trust God's promises to us
Failed agreement by people	Faithful agreement by Christ	Christ has kept the agreement where people couldn't
External standards and rules	Internal standards—a new heart	God sees both actions and motives—we are accountable to God, not rules
Limited access to God	Unlimited access to God	God is personally available
Based on fear	Based on love and forgiveness	Forgiveness keeps our failures from destroying the agreement
Legal cleansing	Personal cleansing	God's cleansing is complete
Continual sacrifice	Conclusive sacrifice	Christ's sacrifice was perfect and final
Obey the rules	Serve the living God	We have a relationship, not regulations
Forgiveness earned	Forgiveness freely given	We have true and complete forgiveness
Repeated yearly	Completed by Christ's death	Christ's death can be applied to your sin
Human effort	God's grace	Initiated by God's love for you
Available to some	Available to all	Available to you

8:10 If our hearts are not changed, following God's rules will be unpleasant and difficult. We will rebel against being told how to live. The Holy Spirit, however, gives us new desires, helping us *want* to obey God (see Philippians 2:12, 13). With new hearts, we find that serving God is our greatest joy.

8:10, 11 Under God's new covenant, God's law is inside us. It is no longer an external set of rules and principles. The Holy Spirit reminds us of Christ's words, activates our consciences, influences our motives and desires, and makes us want to obey. Now doing God's will is something we desire with all our heart and mind.

Worship in the Earthly Tabernacle

9 Now the first covenant had regulations for worship and also an earthly sanctuary.[a] 2A tabernacle[b] was set up. In its first room were the lampstand,[c] the
table[d] and the consecrated bread;[e] this was called the Holy Place. 3Behind the second
curtain was a room called the Most Holy Place,[f] 4which had the golden altar of
incense[g] and the gold-covered ark of the covenant.[h] This ark contained the gold jar
of manna,[i] Aaron's staff that had budded,[j] and the stone tablets of the covenant.
5Above the ark were the cherubim of the Glory,[k] overshadowing the atonement
cover.**[a]** But we cannot discuss these things in detail now.
6When everything had been arranged like this, the priests entered regularly[l] into
the outer room to carry on their ministry. 7But only the high priest entered[m] the inner
room, and that only once a year,[n] and never without blood, which he offered for
himself[o] and for the sins the people had committed in ignorance. 8The Holy Spirit
was showing[p] by this that the way[q] into the Most Holy Place had not yet been
disclosed as long as the first tabernacle was still standing. 9This is an illustration for
the present time, indicating that the gifts and sacrifices being offered[r] were not able
to clear the conscience of the worshipper. 10They are only a matter of food[s] and
drink[t] and various ceremonial washings—external regulations[u] applying until the
time of the new order.

The Blood of Christ

11When Christ came as high priest[v] of the good things that are already here,**[b]**[w]
he went through the greater and more perfect tabernacle[x] that is not man-made, that
is to say, not a part of this creation. 12He did not enter by means of the blood of goats
and calves;[y] but he entered the Most Holy Place[z] once for all[a] by his own blood,
having obtained eternal redemption. 13The blood of goats and bulls and the ashes of
a heifer[b] sprinkled on those who are ceremonially unclean sanctify them so that they
are outwardly clean. 14How much more, then, will the blood of Christ, who through
the eternal Spirit[c] offered himself unblemished to God, cleanse our consciences[d]
from acts that lead to death,**[c]**[e] so that we may serve the living God!
15For this reason Christ is the mediator[f] of a new covenant, that those who are
called may receive the promised eternal inheritance—now that he has died as a ransom
to set them free from the sins committed under the first covenant.[g]
16In the case of a will,**[d]** it is necessary to prove the death of the one who made
it, 17because a will is in force only when somebody has died; it never takes effect while

a *5* Traditionally *the mercy seat* **b** *11* Some early manuscripts *are to come* **c** *14* Or *from useless rituals*
d *16* Same Greek word as *covenant*; also in verse 17

9:1 [a]Ex 25:8
9:2 [b]Ex 25:8, 9 [c]Ex 25:31-39 [d]Ex 25:23-29 [e]Lev 24:5-8
9:3 [f]Ex 26:31-33
9:4 [g]Ex 30:1-5 [h]Ex 25:10-22 [i]Ex 16:32, 33 [j]Nu 17:10
9:5 [k]Ex 25:17-19
9:6 [l]Nu 28:3
9:7 [m]Lev 16:11-19 [n]Lev 16:34 [o]Heb 5:2, 3
9:8 [p]Heb 3:7 [q]Jn 14:6; Heb 10:19, 20
9:9 [r]Heb 5:1
9:10 [s]Lev 11:2-23 [t]Col 2:16 [u]Heb 7:16
9:11 [v]Heb 2:17 [w]Heb 10:1 [x]Heb 8:2
9:12 [y]Heb 10:4 [z]ver 24 [a]Heb 7:27
9:13 [b]Nu 19:9, 17, 18
9:14 [c]1Pe 3:18 [d]Tit 2:14; Heb 10:2, 22 [e]Heb 6:1
9:15 [f]1Ti 2:5 [g]Heb 7:22

9:5 *Cherubim* are mighty angels.

9:6–8 The high priest could enter the Most Holy Place (9:3; or the "inner room", 9:7), the innermost room of the tabernacle, one day each year to atone for the nation's sins. The Most Holy Place was a small room that contained the ark of the covenant (a gold-covered chest containing the original stone tablets on which the Ten Commandments were written, a jar of manna, and Aaron's staff). The top of the chest served as the "atonement cover" (the altar) on which the blood would be sprinkled by the high priest on the Day of Atonement. The Most Holy Place was the most sacred spot on earth for the Jews. Only the high priest could enter—the other priests and the common people were forbidden to come into the room. Their only access to God was through the high priest, who would offer a sacrifice and use the animal's blood to atone first for his own sins and then for the people's sins (see also 10:19).

9:10 The people had to keep the Old Testament dietary laws and ceremonial cleansing laws until Christ came with God's new and better way.

9:12 This imagery comes from the Day of Atonement rituals described in Leviticus 16. *Redemption* refers to the process of paying the price (ransom) to free a slave. Through his own death, Christ freed us from the slavery of sin for ever.

9:12–14 Though you know Christ, you may believe that you have to work hard to make yourself good enough for God. But rules and rituals have never cleansed people's hearts. By Jesus' blood alone (1) we have our consciences cleansed, (2) we are freed from death's sting and can live to serve God, and (3) we are freed from sin's power. If you are carrying a load of guilt because you are finding that you can't be good enough for God, take another look at Jesus' death and what it means for you. Christ can heal your conscience and deliver you from the frustration of trying to earn God's favour.

9:13, 14 When the people sacrificed animals, God considered the people's faith and obedience, cleansed them from sin, and made them *ceremonially* acceptable according to Old Testament law. But Christ's sacrifice transforms our lives and hearts and makes us clean on the inside. His sacrifice is infinitely more effective than animal sacrifices. No barrier of sin or weakness on our part can stifle his forgiveness.

9:15 People in Old Testament times were saved through Christ's sacrifice, although that sacrifice had not yet happened. In offering unblemished animal sacrifices, they were anticipating Christ's coming and his death for sin. There was no point in returning to the sacrificial system now that Christ had come and had become the final, perfect sacrifice.

the one who made it is living. 18This is why even the first covenant was not put into
effect without blood.[h] 19When Moses had proclaimed every commandment of the law
to all the people, he took the blood of calves, together with water, scarlet wool and
branches of hyssop, and sprinkled the scroll and all the people.[i] 20He said, "This
is the blood of the covenant, which God has commanded you to keep."[e][j] 21In the
same way, he sprinkled with the blood both the tabernacle and everything used in its
ceremonies. 22In fact, the law requires that nearly everything be cleansed with
blood,[k] and without the shedding of blood there is no forgiveness.[l]
23It was necessary, then, for the copies[m] of the heavenly things to be purified with
these sacrifices, but the heavenly things themselves with better sacrifices than these.
24For Christ did not enter a man-made sanctuary that was only a copy of the true one;[n]
he entered heaven itself, now to appear for us in God's presence. 25Nor did he enter
heaven to offer himself again and again, the way the high priest enters the Most Holy
Place[o] every year with blood that is not his own.[p] 26Then Christ would have had
to suffer many times since the creation of the world.[q] But now he has appeared once
for all[r] at the end of the ages to do away with sin by the sacrifice of himself. 27Just
as man is destined to die once,[s] and after that to face judgment,[t] 28so Christ was
sacrificed once to take away the sins of many people; and he will appear a second
time,[u] not to bear sin,[v] but to bring salvation to those who are waiting for him.[w]

Christ's Sacrifice Once for All

10 The law is only a shadow[a] of the good things[b] that are coming—not the
realities themselves.[c] For this reason it can never, by the same sacrifices
repeated endlessly year after year, make perfect[d] those who draw near to worship.
2If it could, would they not have stopped being offered? For the worshippers would
have been cleansed once for all, and would no longer have felt guilty for their sins.
3But those sacrifices are an annual reminder of sins,[e] 4because it is impossible for
the blood of bulls and goats[f] to take away sins.

e *20* Exodus 24:8

9:18 [h]Ex 24:6-8
9:19 [i]Ex 24:6-8
9:20 [j]Ex 24:8; Mt 26:28
9:22 [k]Lev 8:15 [l]Lev 17:11
9:23 [m]Heb 8:5
9:24 [n]Heb 8:2
9:25 [o]Heb 10:19 [p]ver 7, 8
9:26 [q]Heb 4:3 [r]Heb 7:27
9:27 [s]Ge 3:19 [t]2Co 5:10
9:28 [u]Tit 2:13 [v]1Pe 2:24 [w]1Co 1:7
10:1 [a]Heb 8:5 [b]Heb 9:11 [c]Heb 9:23 [d]Heb 7:19
10:3 [e]Heb 9:7
10:4 [f]Heb 9:12, 13

9:22 Why does forgiveness require the shedding of blood? This is no arbitrary decree on the part of a bloodthirsty God, as some have suggested. There is no greater symbol of life than blood; blood keeps us alive. Jesus shed his blood—gave his life—for our sins so that we wouldn't have to experience spiritual death, eternal separation from God. Jesus is the source of life, not death. He gave his own life to pay our penalty for us so that we might live. After shedding his blood for us, Christ rose from the grave and proclaimed victory over sin and death.

9:23 In a way that we don't fully understand, the earthly tabernacle was a copy and symbol of heavenly realities. This purification of the heavenly things can best be understood as referring to Christ's spiritual work for us in heaven (see the note on 8:5).

9:24 Among references to priests, tabernacles, sacrifices, and other ideas unfamiliar to us, we come to this description of Christ as our mediator, appearing in God's presence on our behalf. We can relate to this role and be encouraged by it. Christ is on our side at God's side. He is our Lord and Saviour. He is not there to convince or remind God that our sins are forgiven, but to present both our needs and our service for him as an offering (see 7:25).

9:24–28 All people die physically, but Christ died so that we would not have to die spiritually. We can have wonderful confidence in his saving work for us, doing away with sin—past, present, and future. He has forgiven our past sin—when he died on the cross, he sacrificed himself once for all (9:26); he has given us the Holy Spirit to help us deal with present sin; he appears for us now in heaven as our high priest (9:24); and he promises to return (9:28) and raise us to eternal life in a world where sin will be banished.

9:26 The "end of the ages" refers to the time of Christ's coming to earth in fulfilment of the Old Testament prophecies. Christ ushered in the new era of grace and forgiveness. We are still living in the "end of the ages". The day of the Lord has begun and will be completed at Christ's return.

10:3 When people gathered for the offering of sacrifices on the Day of Atonement, they were reminded of their sins, and they undoubtedly felt guilty all over again. What they needed most was forgiveness—the permanent, powerful, sin-destroying forgiveness we have from Christ. When we confess a sin to him, we need never think of it again. Christ has forgiven us, and the sin no longer exists. See 1 John 1:9.

10:4 Animal sacrifices could not take away sins; they provided only a temporary way to deal with sin until Jesus came to deal with sin permanently. How, then, were people forgiven in Old Testament times? Because Old Testament believers were following God's command to offer sacrifices, he graciously forgave them when, by faith, they made their sacrifices. But that practice looked forward to Christ's perfect sacrifice. Christ's way was superior to the Old Testament way because the old way only pointed to what Christ would do to take away sins.

5Therefore, when Christ came into the world,[g] he said:

"Sacrifice and offering you did not desire,
but a body you prepared for me;[h]
6with burnt offerings and sin offerings
you were not pleased.
7Then I said, 'Here I am—it is written about me in the scroll[i]—
I have come to do your will, O God.' "[a][j]

8First he said, "Sacrifices and offerings, burnt offerings and sin offerings you did not
desire, nor were you pleased with them"[k] (although the law required them to be
made). 9Then he said, "Here I am, I have come to do your will."[l] He sets aside the
first to establish the second. 10And by that will, we have been made holy[m] through
the sacrifice of the body[n] of Jesus Christ once for all.[o]
11Day after day every priest stands and performs his religious duties; again and
again he offers the same sacrifices,[p] which can never take away sins.[q] 12But when
this priest had offered for all time one sacrifice for sins, he sat down at the right hand
of God. 13Since that time he waits for his enemies to be made his footstool,[r]
14because by one sacrifice he has made perfect[s] for ever those who are being made
holy.
15The Holy Spirit also testifies[t] to us about this. First he says:

16"This is the covenant I will make with them
after that time, says the Lord.
I will put my laws in their hearts,
and I will write them on their minds."[b][u]

17Then he adds:

"Their sins and lawless acts
I will remember no more."[c][v]

18And where these have been forgiven, there is no longer any sacrifice for sin.

[a] *7* Psalm 40:6–8 (see Septuagint) [b] *16* Jer. 31:33 [c] *17* Jer. 31:34

10:5 [g]Heb 1:6 [h]1Pe 2:24
10:7 [i]Jer 36:2 [j]Ps 40:6-8
10:8 [k]ver 5, 6; Mk 12:33
10:9 [l]ver 7
10:10 [m]Jn 17:19 [n]Heb 2:14; 1Pe 2:24 [o]Heb 7:27
10:11 [p]Heb 5:1 [q]ver 1, 4
10:13 [r]Heb 1:13
10:14 [s]ver 1
10:15 [t]Heb 3:7
10:16 [u]Jer 31:33; Heb 8:10
10:17 [v]Heb 8:12

10:5–10 This quotation is not cited in any other New Testament book. However, it is a central teaching of the Old Testament that God desires obedience and a right heart, not empty compliance to the sacrifice system (see the chart in Hosea 7). The writer of Hebrews applies to Christ the words of the psalmist in Psalm 40:6–8. Christ came to offer his body on the cross for us as a sacrifice that is completely acceptable to God. God's new and living way for us to please him is not by keeping laws or even by abstaining from sin. It is by coming to him in faith to be forgiven, and then following him in loving obedience.

10:5–10 The costly sacrifice of an animal's life impressed upon the sinner the seriousness of his or her own sin before God. Because Jesus shed his own blood for us, his sacrifice is infinitely greater than any Old Testament offering. Considering the immeasurable gift he gave us, we should respond by giving him our devotion and service.

10:9 Setting aside the first system in order to establish a far better one meant doing away with the system of sacrifices contained in the ceremonial law. It didn't mean eliminating God's *moral* law (the Ten Commandments). The ceremonial law prepared people for Christ's coming. With Christ's death and resurrection, that system was no longer needed. And through Christ we can fulfil the moral law as we let him live in us.

10:11, 12 Christ's work is contrasted with the work of the Jewish priests. The priests' work was never finished, so they always had to stand and offer sacrifices; Christ's sacrifice (dying in our place) is finished, so he is seated. The priests repeated the sacrifices often; Christ sacrificed once for all. The sacrifice system couldn't completely remove sin; Christ's sacrifice effectively cleansed us.

10:12 If the Jewish readers of this book were to return to the old Jewish system, they would be implying that Christ's sacrifice wasn't enough to forgive their sins. Adding anything to his sacrifice or taking anything from it denies its validity. Any system to gain salvation through good deeds is essentially rejecting the significance of Christ's death and spurning the Holy Spirit's work. Beware of anyone who tells you that Christ's sacrifice still leaves you incomplete or that something else is needed to make you acceptable to God. When we believe in Christ, he makes us completely right with God. Our loving relationship leads us to follow him in willing obedience and service. He is pleased with our service, but we cannot be saved by our good deeds.

10:14 We have been made perfect, yet we are "being made holy". Through his death and resurrection, Christ, once for all, made his believers perfect in God's sight. At the same time, he is making them holy (progressively cleansed and set apart for his special use) in their daily pilgrimage here. We should not be surprised, ashamed, or shocked that we still need to grow. God is not finished with us. We can encourage this growth process by deliberately applying Scripture to all areas of our lives, by accepting the discipline and guidance Christ provides, and by giving him control of our desires and goals.

10:17 The writer concludes his argument with this powerful statement that God will remember our sins no more. Christ forgives completely, so there is no need to confess our past sins repeatedly. As believers, we can be confident that the sins we confess and renounce are forgiven and forgotten.

10:19 [w]Eph 2:18; Heb 9:8, 12, 25
10:20 [x]Heb 9:8 [y]Heb 9:3
10:21 [z]Heb 2:17
10:22 [a]Heb 7:19 [b]Eze 36:25; Heb 9:14
10:23 [c]Heb 3:6 [d]1Co 1:9
10:25 [e]Ac 2:42 [f]Heb 3:13
10:26 [g]Nu 15:30; 2Pe 2:20
10:27 [h]Isa 26:11; 2Th 1:7; Heb 9:27
10:28 [i]Dt 17:6, 7; Heb 2:2
10:29 [j]Heb 6:6 [k]Mt 26:28 [l]Eph 4:30; Heb 6:4 [m]Heb 2:3
10:30 [n]Dt 32:35; Ro 12:19 [o]Dt 32:36
10:31 [p]Mt 16:16
10:32 [q]Heb 6:4 [r]Php 1:29, 30
10:33 [s]1Co 4:9 [t]Php 4:14; 1Th 2:14
10:34 [u]Heb 13:3 [v]Heb 11:16

B. THE SUPERIORITY OF FAITH (10:19 – 13:25)

Moving from argument to instruction, the author cites many examples of those who have demonstrated faith throughout history. Living by faith is far better than merely fulfilling rituals and rules. This can challenge us to grow in faith and to live in obedience to God each day.

A Call to Persevere

19 Therefore, brothers, since we have confidence to enter the Most Holy Place[w] by the blood of Jesus, 20 by a new and living way[x] opened for us through the curtain,[y] that is, his body, 21 and since we have a great priest[z] over the house of God, 22 let us draw near to God[a] with a sincere heart in full assurance of faith, having our hearts sprinkled to cleanse us from a guilty conscience[b] and having our bodies washed with pure water. 23 Let us hold unswervingly to the hope[c] we profess, for he who promised is faithful.[d] 24 And let us consider how we may spur one another on towards love and good deeds. 25 Let us not give up meeting together,[e] as some are in the habit of doing, but let us encourage one another[f]—and all the more as you see the Day approaching.

26 If we deliberately keep on sinning[g] after we have received the knowledge of the truth, no sacrifice for sins is left, 27 but only a fearful expectation of judgment and of raging fire[h] that will consume the enemies of God. 28 Anyone who rejected the law of Moses died without mercy on the testimony of two or three witnesses.[i] 29 How much more severely do you think a man deserves to be punished who has trampled the Son of God under foot,[j] who has treated as an unholy thing the blood of the covenant[k] that sanctified him, and who has insulted the Spirit[l] of grace?[m] 30 For we know him who said, "It is mine to avenge; I will repay,"[d][n] and again, "The Lord will judge his people."[e][o] 31 It is a dreadful thing to fall into the hands of the living God.[p]

32 Remember those earlier days after you had received the light,[q] when you stood your ground in a great contest in the face of suffering.[r] 33 Sometimes you were publicly exposed to insult and persecution;[s] at other times you stood side by side with those who were so treated.[t] 34 You sympathised with those in prison[u] and joyfully accepted the confiscation of your property, because you knew that you yourselves had better and lasting possessions.[v]

35 So do not throw away your confidence; it will be richly rewarded. 36 You need

d *30* Deut. 32:35 **e** *30* Deut. 32:36; Psalm 135:14

10:19 The Most Holy Place in the temple was sealed from view by a curtain (10:20). Only the high priest could enter this holy room, and he did so only once a year on the Day of Atonement when he offered the sacrifice for the nation's sins. But Jesus' death removed the curtain, and all believers may walk into God's presence at any time (see also 6:19, 20).

10:22–25 We have significant privileges associated with our new life in Christ: (1) we have personal access to God through Christ and can draw near to him without an elaborate system (10:22); (2) we may grow in faith, overcome doubts and questions, and deepen our relationship with God (10:23); (3) we may enjoy encouragement from one another (10:24); (4) we may worship together (10:25).

10:25 To neglect Christian meetings is to give up the encouragement and help of other Christians. We gather together to share our faith and to strengthen one another in the Lord. As we get closer to the "Day" when Christ will return, we will face many spiritual struggles, and even times of persecution. Anti-Christian forces will grow in strength. Difficulties should never be excuses for missing church services. Rather, as difficulties arise, we should make an even greater effort to be faithful in attendance.

10:26 When people deliberately reject Christ's offer of salvation, they reject God's most precious gift. They ignore the leading of the Holy Spirit, the one who communicates to us God's saving love. This warning was given to Jewish Christians who were tempted to reject Christ for Judaism, but it applies to anyone who rejects Christ for another religion or, having understood Christ's atoning work, deliberately turns away from it (see also Numbers 15:30, 31 and Mark 3:28–30). The point is that there is no other acceptable sacrifice for sin than the death of Christ on the cross. If someone deliberately rejects the sacrifice of Christ after clearly understanding the gospel teaching about it, then there is no way for that person to be saved, because God has not provided any other name under heaven by which we can be saved (see Acts 4:12).

10:31 This judgment is for those who have rejected God's mercy. For those who accept Christ's love and accept his salvation, the coming judgment is no cause for worry. Being saved through his grace, they have nothing to fear (see 1 John 4:18).

10:32–36 Hebrews encourages believers to persevere in their Christian faith and conduct when facing persecution and pressure. We don't usually think of suffering as good for us, but it can build our character and our patience. During times of great stress, we may feel God's presence more clearly and find help from Christians we never thought would care. Knowing that Jesus is with us in our suffering and that he will return one day to put an end to all pain helps us grow in our faith and our relationship with him (see Romans 5:3–5).

10:35–38 The writer encourages his readers not to abandon their faith in times of persecution, but to show by their endurance that their faith is real. Faith means resting in what Christ has done for us in the past, but it also means trusting him for what he will do for us in the present and in the future (see Romans 8:12–25; Galatians 3:10–13).

to persevere[w] so that when you have done the will of God, you will receive what he
has promised. 37For in just a very little while,

> "He who is coming[x] will come and will not delay.[y]
> 38 But my righteous one[f] will live by faith.[z]
> And if he shrinks back,
> I will not be pleased with him."[g]

39But we are not of those who shrink back and are destroyed, but of those who believe
and are saved.

By Faith

11 Now faith is being sure of what we hope for and certain of what we do not see.[a]
2This is what the ancients were commended for.[b]
3By faith we understand that the universe was formed at God's command,[c] so that
what is seen was not made out of what was visible.
4By faith Abel offered God a better sacrifice than Cain did. By faith he was
commended as a righteous man, when God spoke well of his offerings.[d] And by faith
he still speaks, even though he is dead.[e]
5By faith Enoch was taken from this life, so that he did not experience death; he
could not be found, because God had taken him away.[f] For before he was taken,
he was commended as one who pleased God. 6And without faith it is impossible to
please God, because anyone who comes to him[g] must believe that he exists and that
he rewards those who earnestly seek him.
7By faith Noah, when warned about things not yet seen, in holy fear built an ark[h]
to save his family.[i] By his faith he condemned the world and became heir of the
righteousness that comes by faith.
8By faith Abraham, when called to go to a place he would later receive as his
inheritance,[j] obeyed and went,[k] even though he did not know where he was going.
9By faith he made his home in the promised land[l] like a stranger in a foreign country;
he lived in tents,[m] as did Isaac and Jacob, who were heirs with him of the same

10:36 [w]Lk 21:19; Heb 12:1
10:37 [x]Mt 11:3 [y]Rev 22:20
10:38 [z]Ro 1:17; Gal 3:11
11:1 [a]Ro 8:24; 2Co 4:18
11:2 [b]ver 4, 39
11:3 [c]Ge 1; Jn 1:3; 2Pe 3:5
11:4 [d]Ge 4:4; 1Jn 3:12 [e]Heb 12:24
11:5 [f]Ge 5:21-24
11:6 [g]Heb 7:19
11:7 [h]Ge 6:13-22 [i]1Pe 3:20
11:8 [j]Ge 12:7 [k]Ge 12:1-4; Ac 7:2-4
11:9 [l]Ac 7:5 [m]Ge 12:8; 18:1, 9

f *38* One early manuscript *But the righteous* g *38* Hab. 2:3,4

11:1 Do you remember how you felt when you were very young and your birthday approached? You were excited and anxious. You knew you would certainly receive gifts and other special treats. But some things would be a surprise. Birthdays combine assurance and anticipation, and so does faith! Faith is the conviction based on past experience that God's new and fresh surprises will surely be ours.

11:1 Two words describe faith: *sure* and *certain.* These two qualities need a secure beginning and ending point. The beginning point of faith is believing in God's character – he *is* who he says. The end point is believing in God's promises – he will *do* what he says. When we believe that God will fulfil his promises even though we don't see those promises materialising yet, we demonstrate true faith (see John 20:24–31).

11:3 God called the universe into existence out of nothing; he declared that it was to be, and it was. Our faith is in the God who created the entire universe by his word. God's word has awesome power. When he speaks, do you listen and respond? How can you better prepare yourself to respond to God's word?

11:4 Cain and Abel were Adam and Eve's first two sons. Abel offered a sacrifice that pleased God, while Cain's sacrifice was unacceptable. Abel's Profile is found in Genesis 6. Cain's Profile is in Genesis 7. Abel's sacrifice (an animal substitute) was more acceptable to God, both because it was a blood sacrifice and, most important, because of Abel's attitude when he offered it.

11:6 Believing that God exists is only the beginning; even the demons believe that much (James 2:19, 20). God will not settle for mere acknowledgment of his existence. He wants a personal, dynamic relationship with you that will transform your life. Those who seek God will find that they are rewarded with his intimate presence.

11:6 Sometimes we wonder about the fate of those who haven't heard of Christ and have not even had a Bible to read. God assures us that all who honestly seek him – who act in faith on the knowledge of God that they possess – will be rewarded. When you tell others the gospel, encourage them to be honest and diligent in their search for truth. Those who hear the gospel are responsible for what they have heard (see 2 Corinthians 6:1, 2).

11:7 Noah experienced rejection because he was different from his neighbours. God commanded him to build a huge boat in the middle of dry land, and although God's command seemed foolish, Noah obeyed. Noah's obedience made him appear strange to his neighbours, just as the new beliefs of Jewish Christians undoubtedly made them stand out. As you obey God, don't be surprised if others regard you as "different". Your obedience makes their disobedience stand out. Remember, if God asks you to do something, he will give you the necessary strength to carry out that task. For more information on Noah, see his Profile in Genesis 8.

11:8–10 Abraham's life was filled with faith. At God's command, he left home and went to another land – obeying without question (Genesis 12:1ff). He believed the covenant that God made with him (Genesis 12:2, 3; 13:14–16; 15:1–6). In obedience to God, Abraham was even willing to sacrifice his son Isaac (Genesis 22:1–19). Do not be surprised if God asks you to give up secure, familiar surroundings in order to carry out his will. For further information on Abraham, see his Profile in Genesis 18.

promise.[n] 10 For he was looking forward to the city[o] with foundations,[p] whose
architect and builder is God.
11 By faith Abraham, even though he was past age—and Sarah herself was barren[q]—was enabled to become a father[r] because he[a] considered him faithful who
had made the promise. 12 And so from this one man, and he as good as dead,[s] came
descendants as numerous as the stars in the sky and as countless as the sand on the
seashore.[t]
13 All these people were still living by faith when they died. They did not receive
the things promised;[u] they only saw them and welcomed them from a distance.[v] And
they admitted that they were aliens and strangers on earth.[w] 14 People who say such
things show that they are looking for a country of their own. 15 If they had been
thinking of the country they had left, they would have had opportunity to return.[x]
16 Instead, they were longing for a better country—a heavenly one.[y] Therefore God
is not ashamed[z] to be called their God,[a] for he has prepared a city[b] for them.
17 By faith Abraham, when God tested him, offered Isaac as a sacrifice.[c] He who
had received the promises was about to sacrifice his one and only son, 18 even though
God had said to him, "It is through Isaac that your offspring[b] will be reckoned."[c][d]
19 Abraham reasoned that God could raise the dead,[e] and figuratively speaking, he
did receive Isaac back from death.
20 By faith Isaac blessed Jacob and Esau in regard to their future.[f]
21 By faith Jacob, when he was dying, blessed each of Joseph's sons,[g] and worshipped as he leaned on the top of his staff.
22 By faith Joseph, when his end was near, spoke about the exodus of the Israelites
from Egypt and gave instructions about his bones.[h]
23 By faith Moses' parents hid him for three months after he was born,[i] because
they saw he was no ordinary child, and they were not afraid of the king's edict.[j]

a *11* Or *By faith even Sarah, who was past age, was enabled to bear children because she* **b** *18* Greek *seed*
c *18* Gen. 21:12

11:9 [n]Heb 6:17
11:10 [o]Heb 12:22; 13:14 [p]Rev 21:2, 14
11:11 [q]Ge 17:17-19; 18:11-14 [r]Ge 21:2
11:12 [s]Ro 4:19 [t]Ge 22:17
11:13 [u]ver 39 [v]Mt 13:17 [w]Ge 23:4; Ps 39:12; 1Pe 1:17
11:15 [x]Ge 24:6-8
11:16 [y]2Ti 4:18 [z]Mk 8:38 [a]Ex 3:6, 15 [b]Heb 13:14
11:17 [c]Ge 22:1-10; Jas 2:21
11:18 [d]Ge 21:12; Ro 9:7
11:19 [e]Ro 4:21
11:20 [f]Ge 27:27-29, 39, 40
11:21 [g]Ge 48:1, 8-22
11:22 [h]Ge 50:24, 25; Ex 13:19
11:23 [i]Ex 2:2 [j]Ex 1:16, 22

11:11, 12 Sarah was Abraham's wife. They were unable to have children through many years of their marriage. God promised Abraham a son, but Sarah doubted that she could become pregnant in her old age. At first she laughed, but afterwards, she believed (Genesis 18). For more information on Sarah, see her Profile in Genesis 19.

11:13 That we are "aliens and strangers" may be an awareness forced on us by circumstances. It may come late in life or as the result of difficult times. But this world is not our home. We cannot live here for ever (see also 1 Peter 1:1). It is best for us not to be so attached to this world's desires and possessions that we can't move out at God's command.

11:13–16 These people of faith died without receiving all that God had promised, but they never lost their vision of heaven ("a better country—a heavenly one"). Many Christians become frustrated and defeated because their needs, wants, expectations, and demands are not immediately met when they believe in Christ. They become impatient and want to give up. Are you discouraged because the achievement of your goal seems far away? Take courage from these heroes of faith who lived and died without seeing the fruit of their faith on earth and yet continued to believe (see 11:36–39).

11:17–19 Abraham was willing to give up his son when God commanded him to do so (Genesis 22:1–19). God did not let Abraham take Isaac's life, because God had given the command in order to test Abraham's faith. Instead of taking Abraham's son, God gave Abraham a whole nation of descendants through Isaac. If you are afraid to trust God with your most prized possession, dream, or person, pay attention to Abraham's example. Because Abraham was willing to give up everything for God, he received back more than he could have imagined. What we receive, however, is not always immediate, or in the form of material possessions. Material things should be among the least satisfying of rewards. Our best and greatest rewards await us in eternity.

11:20 Isaac was the son who had been promised to Abraham and Sarah in their old age. It was through Isaac that God fulfilled his promise to eventually give Abraham countless descendants. Isaac had twin sons, Jacob and Esau. God chose the younger son, Jacob, through whom to continue the fulfilment of his promise to Abraham. For more information on Isaac, see his Profile in Genesis 22.

11:21 Jacob was Isaac's son and Abraham's grandson. Jacob's sons became the fathers of Israel's 12 tribes. Even when Jacob (also called "Israel") was dying in a strange land, he believed the promise that Abraham's descendants would be like the sand on the seashore and that Israel would become a great nation (Genesis 48:1–22). True faith helps us see beyond the grave. For more information on Jacob and Esau, see their Profiles in Genesis 26 and 27.

11:22 Joseph, one of Jacob's sons, was sold into slavery by his jealous brothers (Genesis 37). Eventually, Joseph was sold again, this time to an official of the Pharaoh of Egypt. Because of Joseph's faithfulness to God, however, he was given a top-ranking position in Egypt. Although Joseph could have used that position to build a personal empire, he remembered God's promise to Abraham. After he had been reconciled to his brothers, Joseph brought his family to be near him and requested that his bones be taken to the promised land when the Jews eventually left Egypt (Genesis 50:24, 25). Faith means trusting in God and doing what he wants, regardless of the circumstances or consequences. For more information on Joseph, see his Profile in Genesis 37.

11:23 Moses' parents trusted God to protect their son's life. They were not merely proud parents; they were believers who had faith that God would care for him. As a parent, have you trusted God enough to take care of your children? God has a plan for every person, and your important task is to pray for your children and prepare them to do the work God has planned for them to do. Faith allows us to entrust even our children to God.

24 By faith Moses, when he had grown up, refused to be known as the son of
Pharaoh's daughter.[k] 25 He chose to be ill-treated[l] along with the people of God
rather than to enjoy the pleasures of sin for a short time. 26 He regarded disgrace[m] for
the sake of Christ as of greater value than the treasures of Egypt, because he was
looking ahead to his reward.[n] 27 By faith he left Egypt,[o] not fearing the king's anger;
he persevered because he saw him who is invisible. 28 By faith he kept the Passover
and the sprinkling of blood, so that the destroyer of the firstborn would not touch the
firstborn of Israel.[p]
29 By faith the people passed through the Red Sea[d] as on dry land; but when the
Egyptians tried to do so, they were drowned.[q]
30 By faith the walls of Jericho fell, after the people had marched around them for
seven days.[r]
31 By faith the prostitute Rahab, because she welcomed the spies, was not killed with
those who were disobedient.[e][s]
32 And what more shall I say? I do not have time to tell about Gideon, Barak,[t]
Samson, Jephthah, David,[u] Samuel[v] and the prophets, 33 who through faith conquered kingdoms,[w] administered justice, and gained what was promised; who shut
the mouths of lions,[x] 34 quenched the fury of the flames, and escaped the edge of the
sword; whose weakness was turned to strength;[y] and who became powerful in battle
and routed foreign armies.[z] 35 Women received back their dead, raised to life again.[a]
Others were tortured and refused to be released, so that they might gain a better
resurrection. 36 Some faced jeers and flogging,[b] while still others were chained and
put in prison.[c] 37 They were stoned;[f][d] they were sawn in two; they were put to death
by the sword.[e] They went about in sheepskins and goatskins,[f] destitute, persecuted
and ill-treated — 38 the world was not worthy of them. They wandered in deserts and
mountains, and in caves[g] and holes in the ground.
39 These were all commended[h] for their faith, yet none of them received what had

[d] 29 That is, Sea of Reeds [e] 31 Or *unbelieving* [f] 37 Some early manuscripts *stoned; they were put to the test;*

11:24 [k]Ex 2:10, 11
11:25 [l]ver 37
11:26 [m]Heb 13:13 [n]Heb 10:35
11:27 [o]Ex 12:50, 51
11:28 [p]Ex 12:21-23
11:29 [q]Ex 14:21-31
11:30 [r]Jos 6:12-20
11:31 [s]Jos 2:1, 9-14; 6:22-25; Jas 2:25
11:32 [t]Jdg 4-5 [u]1Sa 16:1, 13 [v]1Sa 1:20
11:33 [w]2Sa 7:11; 8:1-3 [x]Da 6:22
11:34 [y]2Ki 20:7 [z]Jdg 15:8
11:35 [a]1Ki 17:22, 23
11:36 [b]Jer 20:2 [c]Ge 39:20
11:37 [d]2Ch 24:21 [e]1Ki 19:10 [f]2Ki 1:8
11:38 [g]1Ki 18:4
11:39 [h]ver 2, 4

11:24–28 Moses became one of Israel's greatest leaders, a prophet and a lawgiver. But when he was born, his people were slaves in Egypt, and the Egyptian officials had ordered that all Hebrew baby boys were to be killed. Moses was spared, however, and Pharaoh's daughter brought Moses up in Pharaoh's own household (Exodus 1; 2)! It took faith for Moses to give up his place in the palace, but he could do it because he saw the fleeting nature of great wealth and prestige. It is easy to be deceived by the temporary benefits of wealth, popularity, status, and achievement, and to be blind to the long-term benefits of God's kingdom. Faith helps us look beyond the world's value system to see the eternal values of God's kingdom. For more information on Moses, see his Profile in Exodus 14.

11:31 When Joshua planned the conquest of Jericho, he sent spies to investigate the fortifications of the city. The spies met Rahab, who had two points against her – she was a Gentile and a prostitute. But she showed that she had faith in God by welcoming the spies and by trusting God to spare her and her family when the city was destroyed. Faith helps us turn around and do what is right regardless of our past or the disapproval of others. For more information on Rahab, see her Profile in Joshua 3.

11:32–35 The Old Testament records the lives of the various people who experienced these great victories. Joshua and Deborah conquered kingdoms (the book of Joshua; Judges 4; 5). Nehemiah administered justice (the book of Nehemiah). Daniel was saved from the mouths of lions (Daniel 6). Shadrach, Meshach, and Abednego were kept from harm in the furious flames of a fiery furnace (Daniel 3). Elijah escaped the edge of the swords of evil Queen Jezebel's henchmen (1 Kings 19:2ff). Hezekiah regained strength after sickness (2 Kings 20). Gideon was powerful in battle (Judges 7). A widow's son was brought back to life by the prophet Elisha (2 Kings 4:8–37).

We, too, can experience victory through faith in Christ. Our victories over oppressors may be like those of the Old Testament saints, but more likely, our victories will be directly related to the role God wants us to play. Even though our bodies deteriorate and die, we will live for ever because of Christ. In the promised resurrection, even death will be defeated and Christ's victory will be made complete.

11:32–40 These verses summarise the lives of other great men and women of faith. Some experienced outstanding victories, even over the threat of death. But others were severely mistreated, tortured, and even killed. Having a steadfast faith in God does not guarantee a happy, carefree life. On the contrary, our faith almost guarantees us some form of abuse from the world. While we are on earth, we may never see the purpose of our suffering. But we know that God will keep his promises to us. Do you believe that God will keep his promises to you?

11:35–39 Many think that pain is the exception in the Christian life. When suffering occurs, they say, "Why me?" They feel as though God has deserted them, or perhaps they accuse him of not being as dependable as they thought. In reality, however, we live in an evil world filled with suffering, even for believers. But God is still in control. He allows some Christians to become martyrs for the faith, and he allows others to survive persecution. Rather than asking, "Why me?" it is much more helpful to ask, "Why not me?" Our faith and the values of this world are on a collision course. If we expect pain and suffering to come, we will not be shocked when it does. But we can also take comfort in knowing that Jesus also suffered. He understands our fears, our weaknesses, and our disappointments (see 2:16–18; 4:14–16). He promised never to leave us (Matthew 28:18–20), and he intercedes on our behalf (7:24, 25). In times of pain, persecution, or suffering we should trust confidently in Christ.

11:39, 40 Hebrews 11 has been called faith's hall of fame. No doubt the author surprised his readers by this conclusion: these

been promised.[i] 40God had planned something better for us so that only together with
us would they be made perfect.

God Disciplines His Sons

12 Therefore, since we are surrounded by such a great cloud of witnesses, let us
throw off everything that hinders and the sin that so easily entangles, and let
us run[a] with perseverance[b] the race marked out for us. 2Let us fix our eyes on Jesus,
the author and perfecter of our faith, who for the joy set before him endured the
cross,[c] scorning its shame,[d] and sat down at the right hand of the throne of God.
3Consider him who endured such opposition from sinful men, so that you will not
grow weary[e] and lose heart.

4In your struggle against sin, you have not yet resisted to the point of shedding your
blood.[f] 5And you have forgotten that word of encouragement that addresses you as
sons:

"My son, do not make light of the Lord's discipline,
and do not lose heart when he rebukes you,
6because the Lord disciplines those he loves,[g]
and he punishes everyone he accepts as a son."[a][h]

7Endure hardship as discipline; God is treating you as sons.[i] For what son is not
disciplined by his father? 8If you are not disciplined (and everyone undergoes discipline),[j] then you are illegitimate children and not true sons. 9Moreover, we have all
had human fathers who disciplined us and we respected them for it. How much more
should we submit to the Father of our spirits[k] and live![l] 10Our fathers disciplined
us for a little while as they thought best; but God disciplines us for our good, that we
may share in his holiness.[m] 11No discipline seems pleasant at the time, but painful.
Later on, however, it produces a harvest of righteousness and peace[n] for those who
have been trained by it.

12Therefore, strengthen your feeble arms and weak knees![o] 13"Make level paths
for your feet,"[b][p] so that the lame may not be disabled, but rather healed.[q]

[a] *6* Prov. 3:11,12 [b] *13* Prov. 4:26

11:39 [i]ver 13
12:1 [a]1Co 9:24 [b]Heb 10:36
12:2 [c]Php 2:8, 9 [d]Heb 13:13
12:3 [e]Gal 6:9
12:4 [f]Heb 10:32-34
12:6 [g]Ps 94:12; Rev 3:19 [h]Pr 3:11, 12
12:7 [i]Dt 8:5
12:8 [j]1Pe 5:9
12:9 [k]Nu 16:22 [l]Isa 38:16
12:10 [m]2Pe 1:4
12:11 [n]Isa 32:17; Jas 3:17, 18
12:12 [o]Isa 35:3
12:13 [p]Pr 4:26 [q]Gal 6:1

---

mighty Jewish heroes did not receive God's total reward, because they died before Christ came. In God's plan, they and the Christian believers (who were also enduring much testing) would be rewarded together. Once again Hebrews shows that Christianity offers a better way than Judaism.

11:40 There is a solidarity among believers (see 12:23). Old and New Testament believers will be glorified together. Not only are we one in the body of Christ with all those alive, but we are also one with all those who ever lived. It takes all of us to be perfect in him.

12:1 This "great cloud of witnesses" is composed of the people described in chapter 11. Their faithfulness is a constant encouragement to us. We do not struggle alone, and we are not the first to struggle with the problems we face. Others have run the race and won, and their witness stirs us to run and win also. What an inspiring heritage we have!

12:1–4 The Christian life involves hard work. It requires us to give up whatever endangers our relationship with God, to run patiently, and to struggle against sin with the power of the Holy Spirit. To live effectively, we must keep our eyes on Jesus. We will stumble if we look away from him to stare at ourselves or at the circumstances surrounding us. We should be running for Christ, not ourselves, and we must always keep him in sight.

12:3 When we face hardship and discouragement, it is easy to lose sight of the big picture. But we're not alone; there is help. Many have already made it through life, enduring far more difficult circumstances than we have experienced. Suffering is the training ground for Christian maturity. It develops our patience and makes our final victory sweet.

12:4 These readers were facing difficult times of persecution, but none of them had yet died for their faith. Because they were still alive, the writer urged them to continue to run their race. Just as Christ did not give up, neither should they.

12:5–11 Who loves his child more—the father who allows the child to do what will harm him, or the one who corrects, trains, and even punishes the child to help him learn what is right? It's never pleasant to be corrected and disciplined by God, but his discipline is a sign of his deep love for us. When God corrects you, see it as proof of his love and ask him what he is trying to teach you.

12:11 We may respond to discipline in several ways: (1) we can accept it with resignation; (2) we can accept it with self-pity, thinking we really don't deserve it; (3) we can be angry and resentful towards God; or (4) we can accept it gratefully, as the appropriate response we owe a loving Father.

12:12, 13 God is not only a disciplining parent but also a demanding coach who pushes us to our limits and requires our lives to be disciplined. Although we may not feel strong enough to push on to victory, we will be able to accomplish it as we follow Christ and draw on his strength. Then we can use our growing strength to help those around us who are weak and struggling.

12:12, 13 The word *therefore* is a clue that what follows is important! We must not live with only our own survival in mind. Others will follow our example, and we have a responsibility to them if we are living for Christ, as we claim to be. Does your example make it easier for others to believe in and follow Christ, and to mature in him? Or would those who follow you end up confused and misled?

Warning Against Refusing God

14 Make every effort to live in peace with all men[r] and to be holy;[s] without
holiness no-one will see the Lord.[t] 15 See to it that no-one misses the grace of God[u]
and that no bitter root grows up to cause trouble and defile many. 16 See that no-one
is sexually immoral, or is godless like Esau, who for a single meal sold his inheritance
rights as the oldest son.[v] 17 Afterwards, as you know, when he wanted to inherit this
blessing, he was rejected. He could bring about no change of mind, though he sought
the blessing with tears.[w]
18 You have not come to a mountain that can be touched and that is burning with
fire; to darkness, gloom and storm;[x] 19 to a trumpet blast[y] or to such a voice speaking
words that those who heard it begged that no further word be spoken to them,[z]
20 because they could not bear what was commanded: "If even an animal touches the
mountain, it must be stoned."[c][a] 21 The sight was so terrifying that Moses said, "I
am trembling with fear."[d]
22 But you have come to Mount Zion, to the heavenly Jerusalem,[b] the city[c] of the
living God. You have come to thousands upon thousands of angels in joyful assembly,
23 to the church of the firstborn, whose names are written in heaven.[d] You have come
to God, the judge of all men,[e] to the spirits of righteous men made perfect,[f] 24 to
Jesus the mediator of a new covenant, and to the sprinkled blood that speaks a better
word than the blood of Abel.[g]
25 See to it that you do not refuse him who speaks. If they did not escape when they
refused him who warned[h] them on earth, how much less will we, if we turn away
from him who warns us from heaven?[i] 26 At that time his voice shook the earth,[j]
but now he has promised, "Once more I will shake not only the earth but also the
heavens."[e][k] 27 The words "once more" indicate the removing of what can be
shaken[l]—that is, created things—so that what cannot be shaken may remain.
28 Therefore, since we are receiving a kingdom that cannot be shaken,[m] let us be
thankful, and so worship God acceptably with reverence and awe,[n] 29 for our "God
is a consuming fire."[f][o]

[c] *20* Exodus 19:12,13 [d] *21* Deut. 9:19 [e] *26* Haggai 2:6 [f] *29* Deut. 4:24

12:14 [r]Ro 14:19 [s]Ro 6:22 [t]Mt 5:8
12:15 [u]Gal 5:4; Heb 3:12
12:16 [v]Ge 25:29-34
12:17 [w]Ge 27:30-40
12:18 [x]Ex 19:12-22; Dt 4:11
12:19 [y]Ex 20:18 [z]Ex 20:19; Dt 5:5, 25
12:20 [a]Ex 19:12, 13
12:22 [b]Gal 4:26 [c]Heb 11:10
12:23 [d]Lk 10:20 [e]Ps 94:2 [f]Php 3:12
12:24 [g]Ge 4:10; Heb 11:4
12:25 [h]Heb 8:5; 11:7 [i]Heb 2:2, 3
12:26 [j]Ex 19:18 [k]Hag 2:6
12:27 [l]1Co 7:31; 2Pe 3:10
12:28 [m]Da 2:44 [n]Heb 13:15
12:29 [o]Dt 4:24

12:14 The readers were familiar with the ceremonial cleansing ritual that prepared them for worship, and they knew that they had to be holy or clean in order to enter the temple. Sin always blocks our vision of God; so if we want to see God, we must renounce sin and obey him (see Psalm 24:3, 4). Holiness is coupled with living in peace. A right relationship with God leads to right relationships with fellow believers. Although we will not always feel loving towards all other believers, we must pursue peace as we become more Christlike.

12:15 Like a small root that grows into a great tree, bitterness springs up in our hearts and overshadows even our deepest Christian relationships. A "bitter root" comes when we allow disappointment to grow into resentment, or when we nurse grudges over past hurts. Bitterness brings with it jealousy, dissension, and immorality. When the Holy Spirit fills us, however, he can heal the hurt that causes bitterness.

12:16, 17 Esau's story shows us that mistakes and sins sometimes have lasting consequences (Genesis 25:29–34; 27:36). Even repentance and forgiveness do not always eliminate sin's consequences. How often do you make decisions based on what you want now, rather than on what you need in the long run? Evaluate the long-term effects of your decisions and actions.

12:18–24 What a contrast between the people's terrified approach to God at Mount Sinai and their joyful approach at Mount Zion! What a difference Jesus has made! Before Jesus came, God seemed distant and threatening. After Jesus came, God welcomes us through Christ into his presence. Accept God's invitation!

12:22 As Christians, we are citizens of the heavenly Jerusalem right now; because Christ rules our lives, the Holy Spirit is always with us, and we experience close fellowship with other believers. The full and ultimate rewards and reality of the heavenly Jerusalem are depicted in Revelation 21.

12:27–29 Eventually the world will crumble, and only God's kingdom will last. Those who follow Christ are part of this unshakable kingdom, and they will withstand the shaking, sifting, and burning. When we feel unsure about the future, we can take confidence from these verses. No matter what happens here, our future is built on a solid foundation that cannot be destroyed. Don't put your confidence in what will be destroyed; instead, build your life on Christ and his unshakable kingdom. (See Matthew 7:24–29 for the importance of building on a solid foundation.)

12:29 There is a big difference between the flame of a candle and the roaring blast of a forest fire. We cannot even stand near a raging fire. Even with sophisticated fire-fighting equipment, a consuming fire is often beyond human control. God is not within our control either. We cannot force him to do anything for us through our prayers. He cannot be contained. Yet, he is a God of compassion. He has saved us from sin, and he will save us from death. But everything that is worthless and sinful will be consumed by the fire of his wrath. Only what is good, dedicated to God, and righteous will remain.

13:1
[a]Ro 12:10;
1Pe 1:22

13:2
[b]Mt 25:35
[c]Ge 18:1-33

13:3
[d]Mt 25:36;
Col 4:18

13:4
[e]1Co 6:9

13:5
[f]Php 4:11
[g]Dt 31:6, 8;
Jos 1:5

13:7
[h]ver 17, 24
[i]Heb 6:12

13:8
[j]Heb 1:12

13:9
[k]Eph 4:14
[l]Col 2:7
[m]Col 2:16

13:10
[n]1Co 9:13; 10:18

13:11
[o]Ex 29:14;
Lev 16:27

13:12
[p]Jn 19:17

Concluding Exhortations

13 Keep on loving each other as brothers.[a] 2 Do not forget to entertain strangers,[b]
for by so doing some people have entertained angels without knowing it.[c]
3 Remember those in prison[d] as if you were their fellow-prisoners, and those who are
ill-treated as if you yourselves were suffering.
4 Marriage should be honoured by all, and the marriage bed kept pure, for God will
judge the adulterer and all the sexually immoral.[e] 5 Keep your lives free from the love
of money and be content with what you have,[f] because God has said,

"Never will I leave you;
never will I forsake you."[a][g]

6 So we say with confidence,

"The Lord is my helper; I will not be afraid.
What can man do to me?"[b]

7 Remember your leaders,[h] who spoke the word of God to you. Consider the
outcome of their way of life and imitate[i] their faith. 8 Jesus Christ is the same
yesterday and today and for ever.[j]
9 Do not be carried away by all kinds of strange teachings.[k] It is good for our hearts
to be strengthened[l] by grace, not by ceremonial foods,[m] which are of no value to
those who eat them. 10 We have an altar from which those who minister at the
tabernacle have no right to eat.[n]
11 The high priest carries the blood of animals into the Most Holy Place as a sin
offering, but the bodies are burned outside the camp.[o] 12 And so Jesus also suffered
outside the city gate[p] to make the people holy through his own blood. 13 Let us, then,

a *5* Deut. 31:6 **b** *6* Psalm 118:6,7

13:1–5 Real love for others produces tangible actions: (1) kindness to strangers (13:2); (2) empathy for those who are in prison and those who have been mistreated (13:3); (3) respect for your marriage vows (13:4); and (4) contentment with what you have (13:5). Make sure that your love runs deep enough to affect your hospitality, empathy, fidelity, and contentment.

13:2 Three Old Testament people "entertained angels without knowing it": (1) Abraham (Genesis 18:1ff), (2) Gideon (Judges 6:11ff), and (3) Manoah (Judges 13:2ff). Some people say they cannot be hospitable because their homes are not large enough or nice enough. But even if you have no more than a table and two chairs in a rented room, there are people who would be grateful to spend time in your home. Are there visitors to your church with whom you could share a meal? Do you know single people who would enjoy an evening of conversation? Is there any way your home could meet the needs of travelling missionaries? Hospitality simply means making other people feel comfortable and at home.

13:3 We are to have empathy for those in prison, especially for (but not limited to) Christians imprisoned for their faith. Jesus said that his true followers would represent him as they visit those in prison (Matthew 25:36).

13:5 How can we learn to be content? Strive to live with less rather than desiring more; give away out of your abundance rather than accumulating more; relish what you have rather than resent what you're missing. See God's love expressed in what he has provided, and remember that money and possessions will all pass away. (See Philippians 4:11 for more on contentment, and 1 John 2:17 for the futility of earthly desires.)

13:5, 6 We become content when we realise God's sufficiency for our needs. Christians who become materialistic are saying by their actions that God can't take care of them – or at least that he won't take care of them the way they want. Insecurity can lead to the love of money, whether we are rich or poor. The only antidote is to trust God to meet all our needs.

13:7 If you are a Christian, you owe much to others who have taught you and modelled for you what you needed to know about the gospel and Christian living. Continue following the good examples of those who have invested themselves in you by investing your life through evangelism, service, and Christian education.

13:8 Though human leaders have much to offer, we must keep our eyes on Christ, our ultimate leader. Unlike any human leaders, he will never change. Christ has been and will be the same for ever. In a changing world we can trust our unchanging Lord.

13:9 Apparently some were teaching that keeping the Old Testament ceremonial laws and rituals (such as not eating certain foods) was important to salvation. But these laws were useless for conquering a person's evil thoughts and desires (Colossians 2:23). The laws could influence conduct, but they could not change the heart. Lasting changes in conduct begin when the Holy Spirit lives in each person.

13:13 The Jewish Christians were being ridiculed and persecuted by Jews who didn't believe in Jesus the Messiah. Most of the book of Hebrews tells them how Christ is greater than the sacrificial system. Here the writer drives home the point of his lengthy argument: It may be necessary to leave the "camp" and suffer with Christ. To be outside the camp meant to be unclean – in the days of the exodus, those who were ceremonially unclean had to stay outside the camp. But Jesus suffered humiliation and uncleanness outside the Jerusalem gates on their behalf. The time had come for Jewish Christians to declare their loyalty to Christ above any other loyalty, to choose to follow the Messiah whatever suffering that might entail. They needed to move outside the safe confinement of their past, their traditions, and their ceremonies to live for Christ. What holds you back from complete loyalty to Jesus Christ?

go to him outside the camp, bearing the disgrace he bore.[q] 14For here we do not have
an enduring city, but we are looking for the city that is to come.[r]
15Through Jesus, therefore, let us continually offer to God a sacrifice[s] of
praise — the fruit of lips[t] that confess his name. 16And do not forget to do good and
to share with others,[u] for with such sacrifices[v] God is pleased.
17Obey your leaders and submit to their authority. They keep watch over you[w] as
men who must give an account. Obey them so that their work will be a joy, not a
burden, for that would be of no advantage to you.
18Pray for us.[x] We are sure that we have a clear conscience[y] and desire to live
honourably in every way. 19I particularly urge you to pray so that I may be restored
to you soon.[z]
20May the God of peace,[a] who through the blood of the eternal covenant[b]
brought back from the dead[c] our Lord Jesus, that great Shepherd of the sheep,[d]
21equip you with everything good for doing his will, and may he work in us[e] what is
pleasing to him,[f] through Jesus Christ, to whom be glory for ever and ever.
Amen.[g]

22Brothers, I urge you to bear with my word of exhortation, for I have written you
only a short letter.[h]
23I want you to know that our brother Timothy[i] has been released. If he arrives
soon, I will come with him to see you.
24Greet all your leaders[j] and all God's people. Those from Italy[k] send you their
greetings.
25Grace be with you all.[l]

13:13 [q]Heb 11:26
13:14 [r]Php 3:20; Heb 12:22
13:15 [s]1Pe 2:5 [t]Hos 14:2
13:16 [u]Ro 12:13 [v]Php 4:18
13:17 [w]Isa 62:6; Ac 20:28
13:18 [x]1Th 5:25 [y]Ac 23:1
13:19 [z]Phm 22
13:20 [a]Ro 15:33 [b]Isa 55:3; Eze 37:26; Zec 9:11 [c]Ac 2:24 [d]Jn 10:11
13:21 [e]Php 2:13 [f]1Jn 3:22 [g]Ro 11:36
13:22 [h]1Pe 5:12
13:23 [i]Ac 16:1
13:24 [j]ver 7, 17 [k]Ac 18:2
13:25 [l]Col 4:18

13:14 We should not be attached to this world, because all that we are and have here is temporary. Only our relationship with God and our service to him will last. Don't store up your treasures here; store them in heaven (Matthew 6:19–21).

13:15, 16 Since these Jewish Christians, because of their witness to the Messiah, no longer worshipped with other Jews, they should consider praise and acts of service their sacrifices – ones they could offer anywhere, anytime. This must have reminded them of the prophet Hosea's words, "Forgive all our sins and receive us graciously, that we may offer the fruit of our lips" (Hosea 14:2). A "sacrifice of praise" today would include thanking Christ for his sacrifice on the cross and telling others about it. Acts of kindness and sharing are particularly pleasing to God, even when they go unnoticed by others.

13:17 The task of church leaders is to help people mature in Christ. Co-operative followers greatly ease the burden of leadership. Does your conduct give your leaders reason to report joyfully about you?

13:18, 19 The writer recognises the need for prayer. Christian leaders are especially vulnerable to criticism from others, pride (if they succeed), depression (if they fail), and Satan's constant efforts to destroy their work for God. They desperately need our prayers! For whom should you pray regularly?

13:21 This verse includes two significant results of Christ's death and resurrection. God works in us to make us the kind of people that would please him, and he equips us to do the kind of *work* that would please him. Let God change you from within and then use you to help others.

13:23 We have no record of Timothy's imprisonment, but we know that he had been in prison because it states here that he had been released. For more about Timothy, see his Profile in 1 Timothy 2.

13:24, 25 Hebrews is a call to Christian maturity. It was addressed to first-century Jewish Christians, but it applies to Christians of any age or background. Christian maturity means making Christ the beginning and end of our faith. To grow in maturity, we must centre our lives on him, not depending on religious ritual, not falling back into sin, not trusting in ourselves, and not letting anything come between us and Christ. Christ is sufficient and superior.

JAMES

"MIRACULOUS!" . . . "Revolutionary!" . . . "Greatest ever!" We are inundated by a flood of extravagant claims as we flip through television channels or magazine pages. The messages leap out at us. The products assure us that they are new, improved, fantastic, and capable of changing our lives. For only a few pounds, we can have "cleaner clothes", "whiter teeth", "glamorous hair", and "tastier food". Cars, perfume, diet drinks, and mouthwash are guaranteed to bring happiness, friends, and the good life. And just before an election, no-one can match the politicians' promises. But talk is cheap, and too often we soon realise that the boasts were hollow, quite far from the truth.

"Jesus is the answer!" . . . "Believe in God!" . . . "Follow me to church!" Christians also make great claims but are often guilty of belying them with their actions. Professing to trust God and to be his people, they cling tightly to the world and its values. Possessing all the right answers, they contradict the gospel with their lives.

With energetic style and crisp, well-chosen words, James confronts this conflict head-on. It is not enough to talk the Christian faith, he says; we must live it. "What good is it, my brothers, if a man claims to have faith but has no deeds? Can such faith save him?" (2:14). The proof of the reality of our faith is a changed life.

Genuine faith will inevitably produce good deeds. This is the central theme of James' letter, around which he supplies practical advice on living the Christian life.

James begins his letter by outlining some general characteristics of the Christian life (1:1–27). Next, he exhorts Christians to act justly in society (2:1–13). He follows this practical advice with a theological discourse on the relationship between faith and action (2:14–26). Then James shows the importance of controlling one's speech (3:1–12). In 3:13–18, James distinguishes two kinds of wisdom, earthly and heavenly. Then he encourages his readers to turn from evil desires and obey God (4:1–12). James reproves those who trust in their own plans and possessions (4:13—5:6). Finally, he exhorts his readers to be patient with each other (5:7–11), to be straightforward in their promises (5:12), to pray for each other (5:13–18), and to help each other remain faithful to God (5:19, 20).

This letter could be seen as a how-to book on Christian living. Confrontation, challenge, and a call to commitment await you in its pages. Read James and become a *doer* of the word (1:22–25).

VITAL STATISTICS

PURPOSE:
To expose hypocritical practices and to teach right Christian behaviour

AUTHOR:
James, Jesus' brother, a leader in the Jerusalem church

TO WHOM WRITTEN:
First-century Jewish Christians residing in Gentile communities outside Palestine, and all Christians everywhere

DATE WRITTEN:
Probably A.D. 49, prior to the Jerusalem council held in A.D. 50

SETTING:
This letter expresses James' concern for persecuted Christians who were once part of the Jerusalem church

KEY VERSE:
"But someone will say, 'You have faith; I have deeds.' Show me your faith without deeds, and I will show you my faith by what I do" (2:18).

THE BLUEPRINT

1. Genuine religion (1:1–27)
2. Genuine faith (2:1—3:12)
3. Genuine wisdom (3:13—5:20)

James wrote to Jewish Christians who had been scattered throughout the Mediterranean world because of persecution. In their hostile surroundings they were tempted to let intellectual agreement pass for true faith. This letter can have rich meaning for us as we are reminded that genuine faith transforms lives. We are encouraged to put our faith into action. It is easy to say we have faith, but true faith will produce loving actions towards others.

MEGATHEMES

THEME	EXPLANATION	IMPORTANCE
Living Faith	James wants believers not only to hear the truth, but also to do it. He contrasts empty faith (claims without conduct) with faith that works. Commitment to love and to serve is evidence of true faith.	Living faith makes a difference. Make sure your faith is more than just a statement—it should also result in action. Seek ways of putting your faith to work.
Trials	In the Christian life there are trials and temptations. Successfully overcoming these adversities produces maturity and strong character.	Don't resent troubles when they come. Pray for wisdom; God will supply all that you will need to face persecution or adversity. He will give you patience and keep you strong in times of trial.
Law of Love	We are saved by God's gracious mercy, not by keeping the law. But Christ gave us a special command, "Love your neighbour as yourself" (Matthew 19:19). We are to love and serve those around us.	Keeping the law of love shows that our faith is vital and real. When we show love to others, we are overcoming our own selfishness.
Wise Speech	Wisdom shows itself in speech. We are responsible for the destructive results of our talk. The wisdom of God that helps control the tongue can help control all our actions.	Accepting God's wisdom will affect your speech. Your words will convey true humility and lead to peace. Think before you speak and allow God to give you self-control.
Wealth	James taught Christians not to compromise with worldly attitudes about wealth. Because the glory of wealth fades, Christians should store up God's treasures through sincere service. Christians must not show partiality to the wealthy, nor be prejudiced against the poor.	All of us are accountable for how we use what we have. We should not hoard wealth, but be generous towards others. In addition, we should not be impressed by the wealthy nor look down on those who are poor.

1. Genuine religion

1 James,[a] a servant of God[b] and of the Lord Jesus Christ,

To the twelve tribes[c] scattered[d] among the nations:

Greetings.

1:1 [a]Ac 15:13 [b]Tit 1:1 [c]Ac 26:7 [d]Dt 32:26; Jn 7:35; 1Pe 1:1

Trials and Temptations

2Consider it pure joy, my brothers, whenever you face trials of many kinds,[e]
3because you know that the testing of your faith develops perseverance. 4Perseverance

1:2 [e]Mt 5:12; 1Pe 1:6

1:1 The writer of this letter, a leader of the church in Jerusalem (see Acts 12:17; 15:13), was James, Jesus' brother, not James the apostle. The book of James was one of the earliest letters, probably written before A.D. 50. After Stephen was martyred (Acts 7:55—8:3), persecution increased, and Christians in Jerusalem were scattered throughout the Roman world. There were thriving Jewish-Christian communities in Rome, Alexandria, Cyprus, and cities in Greece and Asia Minor. Because these early believers did not have the support of established Christian churches, James wrote to them as a concerned leader, to encourage them in their faith during those difficult times.

1:2, 3 James doesn't say *if* you face trials, but *whenever* you face them. He assumes that we will have trials and that it is possible to profit from them. The point is not to pretend to be happy when we face pain, but to have a positive outlook ("consider it pure joy") because of what trials can produce in our lives. James tells us to turn our hardships into times of learning. Tough times can teach us perseverance. For other passages dealing with perseverance

1:5
[f]1Ki 3:9, 10; Pr 2:3-6
[g]Mt 7:7
1:6
[h]Mk 11:24
1:8
[i]Jas 4:8
1:10
[j]1Co 7:31; 1Pe 1:24
1:11
[k]Ps 102:4, 11
[l]Isa 40:6-8
1:12
[m]1Co 9:25
[n]Jas 2:5

must finish its work so that you may be mature and complete, not lacking anything.
5 If any of you lacks wisdom, he should ask God,[f] who gives generously to all without
finding fault, and it will be given to him.[g] 6 But when he asks, he must believe and
not doubt,[h] because he who doubts is like a wave of the sea, blown and tossed by
the wind. 7 That man should not think he will receive anything from the Lord; 8 he is
a double-minded man,[i] unstable in all he does.

9 The brother in humble circumstances ought to take pride in his high position. 10 But
the one who is rich should take pride in his low position, because he will pass away
like a wild flower.[j] 11 For the sun rises with scorching heat and withers[k] the plant;
its blossom falls and its beauty is destroyed.[l] In the same way, the rich man will fade
away even while he goes about his business.

12 Blessed is the man who perseveres under trial, because when he has stood the
test, he will receive the crown of life[m] that God has promised to those who love him.[n]

CHAPTER SUMMARY

Chapter 1	Confident Stand	What a Christian has
Chapter 2	Compassionate Service	What a Christian does
Chapter 3	Careful Speech	What a Christian says
Chapter 4	Contrite Submission	What a Christian feels
Chapter 5	Concerned Sharing	What a Christian gives

(also called patience and steadfastness), see Romans 2:7; 5:3–5; 8:24, 25; 2 Corinthians 6:3–7; 2 Peter 1:2–9.

1:2–4 We can't really know the depth of our character until we see how we react under pressure. It is easy to be kind to others when everything is going well, but can we still be kind when others are treating us unfairly? God wants to make us mature and complete, not to keep us from all pain. Instead of complaining about our struggles, we should see them as opportunities for growth. Thank God for promising to be with you in rough times. Ask him to help you solve your problems or to give you the strength to endure them. Then be patient. God will not leave you alone with your problems; he will stay close and help you grow.

1:5 By *wisdom,* James is talking not only about knowledge, but about the ability to make wise decisions in difficult circumstances. Whenever we need wisdom, we can pray to God, and he will generously supply what we need. Christians don't have to grope around in the dark, hoping to stumble upon answers. We can ask for God's wisdom to guide our choices.

1:5 *Wisdom* means practical discernment. It begins with respect for God, leads to right living, and results in increased ability to tell right from wrong. God is willing to give us this wisdom, but we will be unable to receive it if our goals are self-centred instead of God-centered. To learn God's will, we need to read his word and ask him to show us how to obey it. Then we must do what he tells us.

1:6 To "believe and not doubt" means not only believing in the existence of God, but also believing in his loving care. It includes relying on God and expecting that he will hear and answer when we pray. We must put away our critical attitude when we come to him. God does not grant every thoughtless or selfish request. We must have confidence that God will align our desires with his purposes. For more on this concept, read the note on Matthew 21:22.

1:6 A mind that wavers is not completely convinced that God's way is best. It treats God's word like any human advice, and it retains the option to disobey. It vacillates between allegiance to subjective feelings, the world's ideas, and God's commands. If your faith is new, weak, or struggling, remember that you can trust God. Then be loyal to him. To stabilise your wavering or doubtful mind, commit yourself wholeheartedly to God.

1:6–8 If you have ever seen the constant rolling of huge waves at sea, you know how restless they are — subject to the forces of wind, gravity, and tide. Doubt leaves a person as unsettled as the restless waves. If you want to stop being tossed about, rely on God to show you what is best for you. Ask him for wisdom, and trust that he will give it to you. Then your decisions will be sure and solid.

1:9 Christians who aren't in high positions in this world should be glad, because they are great in the Lord's eyes. This "brother in humble circumstances" is a person without status or wealth. Such people are often overlooked, even in our churches today, but they are not overlooked by God.

1:9–11 The poor should be glad that riches mean nothing to God; otherwise these people would be considered unworthy. The rich should be glad that money means nothing to God, because money is easily lost. We find true wealth by developing our spiritual life, not by developing our financial assets. God is interested in what is lasting (our souls), not in what is temporary (our money and possessions). See Mark 4:18, 19 for Jesus' words on this subject. Strive to treat each person as Christ would treat him or her.

1:10, 11 If wealth, power, and status mean nothing to God, why do we attribute so much importance to them and so much honour to those who possess them? Do your material possessions give you goals and your only reason for living? If they were gone, what would be left? What you have in your heart, not your bank account, matters to God and endures for eternity.

1:12 The crown of life is like the victory wreath given to winning athletes (see 1 Corinthians 9:25). God's crown of life is not glory and honour here on earth, but the reward of eternal life — living with God for ever. The way to be in God's winners' circle is by loving him and staying faithful even under pressure.

1:12–15 Temptation comes from evil desires inside us, not from God. It begins with an evil thought and becomes sin when we dwell on the thought and allow it to become an action. Like a snowball rolling downhill, sin grows more destructive the more we let it have its way. The best time to stop a temptation is before it is too strong or moving too fast to control. See Matthew 4:1–11; 1 Corinthians 10:13; and 2 Timothy 2:22 for more about escaping temptation.

13 When tempted, no-one should say, "God is tempting me." For God cannot be
tempted by evil, nor does he tempt anyone; 14 but each one is tempted when, by his
own evil desire, he is dragged away and enticed. 15 Then, after desire has conceived,
it gives birth to sin;[o] and sin, when it is full-grown, gives birth to death.[p]
16 Don't be deceived,[q] my dear brothers.[r] 17 Every good and perfect gift is from
above,[s] coming down from the Father of the heavenly lights, who does not change[t]
like shifting shadows. 18 He chose to give us birth[u] through the word of truth, that
we might be a kind of firstfruits[v] of all he created.

Listening and Doing

19 My dear brothers, take note of this: Everyone should be quick to listen, slow to
speak[w] and slow to become angry, 20 for man's anger does not bring about the
righteous life that God desires. 21 Therefore, get rid of[x] all moral filth and the evil
that is so prevalent, and humbly accept the word planted in you,[y] which can save
you.
22 Do not merely listen to the word, and so deceive yourselves. Do what it says.
23 Anyone who listens to the word but does not do what it says is like a man who looks
at his face in a mirror 24 and, after looking at himself, goes away and immediately
forgets what he looks like. 25 But the man who looks intently into the perfect law that
gives freedom,[z] and continues to do this, not forgetting what he has heard, but doing
it—he will be blessed in what he does.[a]
26 If anyone considers himself religious and yet does not keep a tight rein on his
tongue,[b] he deceives himself and his religion is worthless. 27 Religion that God our
Father accepts as pure and faultless is this: to look after[c] orphans and widows[d] in
their distress and to keep oneself from being polluted by the world.[e]

1:15 [o]Job 15:35; Ps 7:14 [p]Ro 6:23
1:16 [q]1Co 6:9 [r]ver 19
1:17 [s]Jn 3:27 [t]Nu 23:19; Mal 3:6
1:18 [u]Jn 1:13 [v]Eph 1:12; Rev 14:4
1:19 [w]Pr 10:19
1:21 [x]Eph 4:22 [y]Eph 1:13
1:25 [z]Jas 2:12 [a]Jn 13:17
1:26 [b]Ps 34:13; 1Pe 3:10
1:27 [c]Mt 25:36 [d]Isa 1:17, 23 [e]Ro 12:2

1:13, 14 People who live for God often wonder why they still have temptations. Does God tempt them? God *tests* people, but he does not *tempt* them by trying to seduce them into sin. God allows Satan to tempt people, however, in order to refine their faith and to help them grow in their dependence on Christ. We can resist the temptation to sin by turning to God for strength and choosing to obey his word.

1:13–15 It is easy to blame others and make excuses for evil thoughts and wrong actions. Excuses include (1) it's the other person's fault; (2) I couldn't help it; (3) everybody's doing it; (4) it was just a mistake; (5) nobody's perfect; (6) the devil made me do it; (7) I was pressured into it; (8) I didn't know it was wrong; (9) God is tempting me. A person who makes excuses is trying to shift the blame from himself or herself to something or someone else. A Christian, on the other hand, accepts responsibility for his or her wrongs, confesses them, and asks God for forgiveness.

1:17 The Bible often compares goodness with light and evil with darkness. For other passages where God is pictured as light, see Psalm 27:1, Isaiah 60:19–22, John 1:1–14.

1:18 First-century Christians were the first generation to believe in Jesus Christ as Messiah. James called them "a kind of firstfruits of all he created". The Jewish leaders would be well aware of the practice of offering the first crops to ripen just prior to harvest as an act of worship, and also as a blessing on the rest of the harvest (see Deuteronomy 26:9–11). In 1 Corinthians 15:20, Paul refers to Christ as the firstfruits of those who have died.

1:19 When we talk too much and listen too little, we communicate to others that we think our ideas are much more important than theirs. James wisely advises us to reverse this process. Put a mental stopwatch on your conversations and keep track of how much you talk and how much you listen. When people talk to you, do they feel that their viewpoints and ideas have value?

1:19, 20 These verses speak of anger that erupts when our egos are bruised – "*I* am hurt"; "*My* opinions are not being heard". When injustice and sin occur, we *should* become angry because others are being hurt. But we should not become angry when we fail to win an argument or when we feel offended or neglected. Selfish anger never helps anybody.

1:21 James advises us to get rid of all that is wrong in our lives and "humbly accept" the salvation message we have received ("the word planted in you"), because it alone can save us.

1:22–25 It is important to listen to what God's word says, but it is much more important to obey it, to *do* what it says. We can measure the effectiveness of our Bible study time by the effect it has on our behaviour and attitudes. Do you put into action what you have studied?

1:25 It seems paradoxical that a law could give us freedom, but God's law points out sin in us and gives us the opportunity to ask for God's forgiveness (see Romans 7:7, 8). As Christians, we are saved by God's grace, and salvation frees us from sin's control. As believers, we are free to live as God created us to live. Of course, this does not mean that we are free to do as we please (see 1 Peter 2:16). We are now free to obey God.

1:26 See the notes in chapter 3 for more on taming the tongue. No matter how spiritual we may think we are, we could all control our speech more effectively.

1:27 In the first century, orphans and widows had very little means of economic support. Unless a family member was willing to care for them, they were reduced to begging, selling themselves as slaves, or starving. By caring for these powerless people, the church put God's word into practice. When we give with no hope of receiving in return, we show what it means to serve others.

1:27 To keep ourselves from being polluted by the world, we need to commit ourselves to Christ's ethical and moral system, not the world's. We are not to adapt to the world's value system, which is based on money, power, and pleasure. True faith means nothing if we are contaminated with such values.

2. Genuine faith

Favourite Forbidden

2 My brothers, as believers in our glorious[a] Lord Jesus Christ, don't show favouritism.[b] 2Suppose a man comes into your meeting wearing a gold ring and fine
clothes, and a poor man in shabby clothes also comes in. 3If you show special attention
to the man wearing fine clothes and say, "Here's a good seat for you," but say to the
poor man, "You stand there" or "Sit on the floor by my feet," 4have you not
discriminated among yourselves and become judges[c] with evil thoughts?
5Listen, my dear brothers:[d] Has not God chosen those who are poor in the eyes
of the world[e] to be rich in faith[f] and to inherit the kingdom he promised those who
love him?[g] 6But you have insulted the poor.[h] Is it not the rich who are exploiting
you? Are they not the ones who are dragging you into court?[i] 7Are they not the ones
who are slandering the noble name of him to whom you belong?
8If you really keep the royal law found in Scripture, "Love your neighbour as
yourself,"[a][j] you are doing right. 9But if you show favouritism,[k] you sin and are

[a] *8* Lev. 19:18

2:1 [a] 1Co 2:8 [b] Lev 19:15
2:4 [c] Jn 7:24
2:5 [d] Jas 1:16, 19 [e] 1Co 1:26-28 [f] Lk 12:21 [g] Jas 1:12
2:6 [h] 1Co 11:22 [i] Ac 8:3
2:8 [j] Lev 19:18
2:9 [k] ver 1

SHOWING FAVOURITISM
Why it is wrong to show favouritism to the wealthy:

1. It is inconsistent with Christ's teachings.
2. It results from evil thoughts.
3. It insults people made in God's image.
4. It is a by-product of selfish motives.
5. It goes against the biblical definition of love.
6. It shows a lack of mercy to those less fortunate.
7. It is hypocritical.
8. It is sin.

2:1ff In this chapter James argues against favouritism and for the necessity of good deeds. He presents three principles of faith: (1) Commitment is an essential part of faith. You cannot be a Christian simply by affirming the right doctrines or agreeing with biblical facts (2:19). You must commit your mind and heart to Christ. (2) Right actions are the natural by-products of true faith. A genuine Christian will have a changed life (2:18). (3) Faith without good deeds doesn't do anybody any good – it is useless (2:14–17). James' teachings are consistent with Paul's teaching that we receive salvation by faith alone. Paul emphasises the purpose of faith – to bring salvation. James emphasises the results of faith – a changed life.

2:1–7 James condemns acts of favouritism. Often we treat a well-dressed, impressive-looking person better than someone who looks shabby. We do this because we would rather identify with successful people than with apparent failures. The irony, as James reminds us, is that the supposed winners may have gained their impressive life-style at our expense. In addition, the rich find it difficult to identify with the Lord Jesus, who came as a humble servant. Are you easily impressed by status, wealth, or fame? Are you partial to the "haves" while ignoring the "have nots"? This attitude is sinful. God views all people as equals, and if he favours anyone, it is the poor and the powerless. We should follow his example.

2:2–4 Why is it wrong to judge a person by his or her economic status? Wealth may indicate intelligence, wise decisions, and hard work. On the other hand, it may mean only that a person had the good fortune of being born into a wealthy family. Or it can even be the sign of greed, dishonesty, and selfishness. By honouring someone just because he or she dresses well, we are making appearance more important than character. Sometimes we do this because (1) poverty makes us uncomfortable; we don't want to face our responsibilities to those who have less than we do; (2) we want to be wealthy too, and we hope to use the rich person as a means to that end; (3) we want the rich person to join our church and help support it financially. All these motives are selfish; they view neither the rich nor the poor person as a human being in need of fellowship. If we say that Christ is our Lord, then we must live as he requires, showing no favouritism and loving all people regardless of whether they are rich or poor.

2:2–4 We are often partial to the rich because we mistakenly assume that riches are a sign of God's blessing and approval. But God does not promise us earthly rewards or riches; in fact, Christ calls us to be ready to suffer for him and give up everything in order to hold on to eternal life (Matthew 6:19–21; 19:28–30; Luke 12:14–34; Romans 8:15–21; 1 Timothy 6:17–19). We will have untold riches in eternity if we are faithful in our present life (Luke 6:35; John 12:23–25; Galatians 6:7–10; Titus 3:4–8).

2:5 When James speaks about the poor, he is talking about those who have no money and also about those whose simple values are despised by much of our affluent society. Perhaps the "poor" people prefer serving to managing, human relationships to financial security, peace to power. This does not mean that the poor will automatically go to heaven and the rich to hell. Poor people, however, are usually more aware of their powerlessness. Thus it is often easier for them to acknowledge their need for salvation. One of the greatest barriers to salvation for the rich is pride. For the poor, bitterness can often bar the way to acceptance of salvation.

2:8 The *royal law* is the law of our great King Jesus Christ, who said, "Love each other as I have loved you" (John 15:12). This law, originally summarised in Leviticus 19:18, is the basis for all the laws of how people should relate to one another. Christ reinforced this truth in Matthew 22:37–40, and Paul taught it in Romans 13:8 and Galatians 5:14.

2:8, 9 We must treat all people as we would want to be treated. We should not ignore the rich, because then we would be withholding our love. But we must not favour them for what they can do for us, while ignoring the poor who can offer us seemingly so little in return.

convicted by the law as law-breakers.[l] 10For whoever keeps the whole law and yet
stumbles at just one point is guilty of breaking all of it.[m] 11For he who said, "Do not
commit adultery,"[b][n] also said, "Do not murder."[c][o] If you do not commit adultery
but do commit murder, you have become a law-breaker.
12Speak and act as those who are going to be judged by the law that gives freedom,[p]
13because judgment without mercy will be shown to anyone who has not been
merciful.[q] Mercy triumphs over judgment!

Faith and Deeds

14What good is it, my brothers, if a man claims to have faith but has no deeds?[r]
Can such faith save him? 15Suppose a brother or sister is without clothes and daily
food.[s] 16If one of you says to him, "Go, I wish you well; keep warm and well fed,"
but does nothing about his physical needs, what good is it?[t] 17In the same way, faith
by itself, if it is not accompanied by action, is dead.
18But someone will say, "You have faith; I have deeds."
Show me your faith without deeds,[u] and I will show you my faith by what I do.[v]
19You believe that there is one God.[w] Good! Even the demons believe that[x]—and
shudder.
20You foolish man, do you want evidence that faith without deeds is useless?[d][y]
21Was not our ancestor Abraham considered righteous for what he did when he offered
his son Isaac on the altar?[z] 22You see that his faith and his actions were working
together,[a] and his faith was made complete by what he did.[b] 23And the scripture
was fulfilled that says, "Abraham believed God, and it was credited to him as
righteousness,"[e][c] and he was called God's friend.[d] 24You see that a person is
justified by what he does and not by faith alone.
25In the same way, was not even Rahab the prostitute considered righteous for what
she did when she gave lodging to the spies and sent them off in a different direction?[e]
26As the body without the spirit is dead, so faith without deeds is dead.[f]

b *11* Exodus 20:14; Deut. 5:18 **c** *11* Exodus 20:13; Deut. 5:17 **d** *20* Some early manuscripts *dead*
e *23* Gen. 15:6

2:9 [l]Dt 1:17
2:10 [m]Mt 5:19; Gal 3:10
2:11 [n]Ex 20:14; Dt 5:18 [o]Ex 20:13; Dt 5:17
2:12 [p]Jas 1:25
2:13 [q]Mt 5:7; 18:32-35
2:14 [r]Mt 7:26; Jas 1:22-25
2:15 [s]Mt 25:35, 36
2:16 [t]1Jn 3:17, 18
2:18 [u]Ro 3:28 [v]Jas 3:13
2:19 [w]Dt 6:4 [x]Mt 8:29; Lk 4:34
2:20 [y]ver 17, 26
2:21 [z]Ge 22:9, 12
2:22 [a]Heb 11:17 [b]1Th 1:3
2:23 [c]Ge 15:6; Ro 4:3 [d]2Ch 20:7; Isa 41:8
2:25 [e]Heb 11:31
2:26 [f]ver 17, 20

2:10 Christians must not use this verse to justify sinning. We dare not say: "Because I can't keep every demand of God, why even try?" James reminds us that if we've broken just one law, we are sinners. We can't decide to keep part of God's law and ignore the rest. You can't break the law a little bit; if you have broken it at all, you need Christ to pay for your sin. Measure yourself, not someone else, against God's standards. Ask for forgiveness where you need it, and then renew your effort to put your faith into practice.

2:12 As Christians we are saved by God's free gift (grace) through faith, not by keeping the law. But as Christians, we are also required to obey Christ. The apostle Paul taught "for we must all appear before the judgment seat of Christ" (2 Corinthians 5:10) to be judged for our conduct. God's grace does not cancel our duty to obey him; it gives our obedience a new basis. The law is no longer an external set of rules, but it is a "law that gives freedom"—one we joyfully and willingly carry out, because we love God and because we have the power of his Holy Spirit to carry it out (see 1:25).

2:13 Only God in his mercy can forgive our sins. We can't earn forgiveness by forgiving others. But when we withhold forgiveness from others after having received it ourselves, we show that we don't understand or appreciate God's mercy towards us (see Matthew 6:14, 15; 18:21ff; Ephesians 4:31, 32).

2:14 When someone claims to have faith, what he or she may have is intellectual assent—agreement with a set of Christian teachings—and as such it would be incomplete faith. True faith transforms our conduct as well as our thoughts. If our lives remain unchanged, we don't truly believe the truths we claim to believe.

2:17 We cannot earn our salvation by serving and obeying God. But such actions show that our commitment to God is real. Deeds of loving service are not a substitute for, but rather a verification of, our faith in Christ.

2:18 At first glance, this verse seems to contradict Romans 3:28, "man is justified by faith apart from observing the law". Deeper investigation, however, shows that the teachings of James and Paul are not at odds. While it is true that our good deeds can never earn salvation, true faith always results in a changed life and good deeds. Paul speaks against those who try to be saved by deeds instead of true faith; James speaks against those who confuse mere intellectual assent with true faith. After all, even demons know who Jesus is, but they don't obey him (2:19). True faith involves a commitment of your whole self to God.

2:21–24 James says that Abraham was "considered righteous" for what he *did*. Paul says he was justified because he *believed* God (Romans 4:1–5). James and Paul are not contradicting but complementing each other. Let's not conclude that the truth is a blending of these two statements. We are not justified by what we do in any way. True faith always results in deeds, but the deeds do not justify us. Faith brings us salvation; active obedience demonstrates that our faith is genuine.

2:25 Rahab lived in Jericho, a city the Israelites conquered as they entered the promised land (Joshua 2). When Israel's spies came to the city, she hid them and helped them escape. In this way she demonstrated faith in God's purpose for Israel. As a result, she and her family were saved when the city was destroyed. Hebrews 11:31 lists Rahab among the heroes of faith.

Taming the Tongue

3 Not many of you should presume to be teachers, my brothers, because you know
that we who teach will be judged more strictly. 2We all stumble[a] in many ways.
If anyone is never at fault in what he says,[b] he is a perfect man,[c] able to keep his
whole body in check.[d]
3When we put bits into the mouths of horses to make them obey us, we can turn
the whole animal.[e] 4Or take ships as an example. Although they are so large and are
driven by strong winds, they are steered by a very small rudder wherever the pilot
wants to go. 5Likewise the tongue is a small part of the body, but it makes great
boasts.[f] Consider what a great forest is set on fire by a small spark. 6The tongue also
is a fire,[g] a world of evil among the parts of the body. It corrupts the whole person,[h]
sets the whole course of his life on fire, and is itself set on fire by hell.
7All kinds of animals, birds, reptiles and creatures of the sea are being tamed and
have been tamed by man, 8but no man can tame the tongue. It is a restless evil, full
of deadly poison.[i]
9With the tongue we praise our Lord and Father, and with it we curse men, who
have been made in God's likeness.[j] 10Out of the same mouth come praise and
cursing. My brothers, this should not be. 11Can both fresh water and salt[a] water flow
from the same spring? 12My brothers, can a fig-tree bear olives, or a grapevine bear
figs?[k] Neither can a salt spring produce fresh water.

3. Genuine wisdom

Two Kinds of Wisdom

13Who is wise and understanding among you? Let him show it[l] by his good life,
by deeds done in the humility that comes from wisdom. 14But if you harbour bitter
envy and selfish ambition[m] in your hearts, do not boast about it or deny the truth.[n]
15Such "wisdom" does not come down from heaven[o] but is earthly, unspiritual, of
the devil.[p] 16For where you have envy and selfish ambition, there you find disorder
and every evil practice.
17But the wisdom that comes from heaven[q] is first of all pure; then peace-loving,

[a] *11* Greek *bitter* (see also verse 14)

3:2 [a] 1Ki 8:46; Jas 2:10 [b] 1Pe 3:10 [c] Mt 12:37 [d] Jas 1:26
3:3 [e] Ps 32:9
3:5 [f] Ps 12:3, 4
3:6 [g] Pr 16:27 [h] Mt 15:11, 18, 19
3:8 [i] Ps 140:3; Ro 3:13
3:9 [j] Ge 1:26, 27; 1Co 11:7
3:12 [k] Mt 7:16
3:13 [l] Jas 2:18
3:14 [m] ver 16 [n] Jas 5:19
3:15 [o] Jas 1:17 [p] 1Ti 4:1
3:17 [q] 1Co 2:6

3:1 Teaching was a highly valued and respected profession in Jewish culture, and many Jews who embraced Christianity wanted to become teachers. James warned that although it is good to aspire to teach, the teachers' responsibility is great because their words and example affect others' spiritual lives. If you are in a teaching or leadership role, how are you affecting those you lead?

3:2, 3 What you say and what you *don't* say are both important. Proper speech is not only saying the right words at the right time, but it is also controlling your desire to say what you shouldn't. Examples of an untamed tongue include gossiping, putting others down, bragging, manipulating, false teaching, exaggerating, complaining, flattering, and lying. Before you speak, ask, "Is what I want to say true? Is it necessary? Is it kind?"

3:6 James compares the damage the tongue can do to a raging fire—the tongue's wickedness has its source in hell itself. The uncontrolled tongue can do terrible damage. Satan uses the tongue to divide people and pit them against one another. Idle and hateful words are damaging because they spread destruction quickly, and no-one can stop the results once they are spoken. We dare not be careless with what we say, thinking we can apologise later, because even if we do, the scars remain. A few words spoken in anger can destroy a relationship that took years to build. Before you speak, remember that words are like fire—you can neither control nor reverse the damage they can do.

3:8 If no human being can control the tongue, why bother trying? Even if we may not achieve perfect control of our tongues, we can still learn enough control to reduce the damage our words can do. It is better to fight a fire than to go around starting new ones! Remember that we are not fighting the tongue's fire in our own strength. The Holy Spirit will give us increasing power to monitor and control what we say, so that when we are offended, the Spirit will remind us of God's love, and we won't react in a hateful manner. When we are criticised, the Spirit will heal the hurt, and we won't lash out.

3:9–12 Our contradictory speech often puzzles us. At times our words are right and pleasing to God, but at other times they are violent and destructive. Which of these speech patterns reflects our true identity? The tongue gives us a picture of our basic human nature. We were made in God's image, but we have also fallen into sin. God works to change us from the inside out. When the Holy Spirit purifies a heart, he gives self-control so that the person will speak words that please God.

3:13–18 Have you ever known anyone who claimed to be wise but who acted foolishly? True wisdom can be measured by the depth of a person's character. Just as you can identify a tree by the type of fruit it produces, you can evaluate your wisdom by the way you act. Foolishness leads to disorder, but wisdom leads to peace and goodness. Are you tempted to escalate the conflict, pass on the gossip, or fan the fire of discord? Careful, winsome speech and wise, loving words are the seeds of peace. God loves peacemakers (Matthew 5:9).

3:14, 15 "Bitter envy and selfish ambition" are inspired by the devil. It is easy for us to be drawn into wrong desires by the pressures of society and sometimes even by well-meaning Christians. By listening to the advice: "Assert yourself", "Go for it", "Set high goals", we can be drawn into greed and destructive competitiveness. Seeking God's wisdom delivers us from the need to compare ourselves to others and to want what they have.

considerate, submissive, full of mercy[r] and good fruit, impartial and sincere.[s]
18 Peacemakers who sow in peace raise a harvest of righteousness.[t]

Submit Yourselves to God

4 What causes fights and quarrels[a] among you? Don't they come from your desires
that battle[b] within you? 2 You want something but don't get it. You kill and covet,
but you cannot have what you want. You quarrel and fight. You do not have, because
you do not ask God. 3 When you ask, you do not receive,[c] because you ask with wrong
motives,[d] that you may spend what you get on your pleasures.
4 You adulterous people, don't you know that friendship with the world[e] is hatred
towards God?[f] Anyone who chooses to be a friend of the world becomes an enemy
of God.[g] 5 Or do you think Scripture says without reason that the spirit he caused to
live in us envies intensely?[a] 6 But he gives us more grace. That is why Scripture says:

> "God opposes the proud
> but gives grace to the humble."[b][h]

7 Submit yourselves, then, to God. Resist the devil,[i] and he will flee from you.
8 Come near to God and he will come near to you.[j] Wash your hands,[k] you sinners,
and purify your hearts, you double-minded.[l] 9 Grieve, mourn and wail. Change your
laughter to mourning and your joy to gloom.[m] 10 Humble yourselves before the Lord,
and he will lift you up.
11 Brothers, do not slander one another.[n] Anyone who speaks against his brother
or judges him[o] speaks against the law and judges it. When you judge the law, you
are not keeping it,[p] but sitting in judgment on it. 12 There is only one Lawgiver and
Judge, the one who is able to save and destroy.[q] But you—who are you to judge your
neighbour?[r]

[a] 5 Or *that God jealously longs for the spirit that he made to live in us*; or *that the Spirit he caused to live in us longs jealously* [b] 6 Prov. 3:34

3:17 [r] Lk 6:36 [s] Ro 12:9
3:18 [t] Pr 11:18; Isa 32:17
4:1 [a] Tit 3:9 [b] Ro 7:23
4:3 [c] Ps 18:41 [d] 1Jn 3:22; 5:14
4:4 [e] Jas 1:27 [f] 1Jn 2:15 [g] Jn 15:19
4:6 [h] Ps 138:6; Pr 3:34; Mt 23:12
4:7 [i] Eph 4:27; 1Pe 5:6-9
4:8 [j] 2Ch 15:2 [k] Isa 1:16 [l] Jas 1:8
4:9 [m] Lk 6:25
4:11 [n] 1Pe 2:1 [o] Mt 7:1 [p] Jas 1:22
4:12 [q] Mt 10:28 [r] Ro 14:4

4:1–3 Conflicts and disputes among believers are always harmful. James explains that these quarrels result from evil desires battling within us—we want more possessions, more money, higher status, more recognition. When we want badly enough to fulfil these desires, we fight in order to do so. Instead of aggressively grabbing what we want, we should submit ourselves to God, ask God to help us get rid of our selfish desires, and trust him to give us what we really need.

4:2, 3 James mentions the most common problems in prayer: not asking, asking for the wrong things, asking for the wrong reasons. Do you talk to God at all? When you do, what do you talk about? Do you ask only to satisfy your desires? Do you seek God's approval for what you already plan to do? Your prayers will become powerful when you allow God to change your desires so that they perfectly correspond to his will for you (1 John 3:21, 22).

4:3, 4 There is nothing wrong with wanting a pleasurable life. God gives us good gifts that he wants us to enjoy (1:17; Ephesians 4:7; 1 Timothy 4:4, 5). But having friendship with the world involves seeking pleasure at others' expense or at the expense of obeying God. Pleasure that keeps us from pleasing God is sinful; pleasure from God's rich bounty is good.

4:4–6 The cure for evil desires is humility (see Proverbs 16:18, 19; 1 Peter 5:5, 6). Pride makes us self-centred and leads us to conclude that we deserve all we can see, touch, or imagine. It creates greedy appetites for far more than we need. We can be released from our self-centred desires by humbling ourselves before God, realising that all we really need is his approval. When the Holy Spirit fills us, we see that this world's seductive attractions are only cheap substitutes for what God has to offer.

4:5 This verse may mean that because of our fallen nature, we have a tendency towards envy. James is not quoting a specific verse or passage—he is summing up a teaching of Scripture. See Romans 6:6–8 and Galatians 5:17–21 for more on the human tendency towards envy and discontent.

4:7 Although God and the devil are at war, we don't have to wait until the end to see who will win. God has *already* defeated Satan (Revelation 12:10–12), and when Christ returns, the devil and all he stands for will be eliminated for ever (Revelation 20:10–15). Satan is here now, however, and he is trying to win us over to his evil cause. With the Holy Spirit's power, we can resist the devil, and he will flee from us.

4:7–10 How can you come near to God? James gives five ways: (1) *Submit to God* (4:7). Yield to his authority and will, commit your life to him and his control, and be willing to follow him. (2) *Resist the devil* (4:7). Don't allow Satan to entice and tempt you. (3) *Wash your hands . . . and purify your hearts* (that is, lead a pure life) (4:8). Be cleansed from sin, replacing your desire to sin with your desire to experience God's purity. (4) *Grieve and mourn and wail* in sincere sorrow for your sins (4:9). Don't be afraid to express deep heartfelt sorrow for what you have done. (5) *Humble yourself before the Lord,* and he will lift you up (4:10; 1 Peter 5:6).

4:10 Humbling ourselves means recognising that our worth comes from God alone. To be humble involves working with his power according to his guidance, not with our own independent effort. Although we do not deserve God's favour, he reaches out to us in love and gives us worth and dignity, despite our human shortcomings.

4:11, 12 Jesus summarised the law as love for God and neighbour (Matthew 22:37–40), and Paul said that love demonstrated towards a neighbour would fully satisfy the law (Romans 13:6–10). When we fail to love, we are actually breaking God's law. Examine your attitude and actions towards others. Do you build people up or tear them down? When you're ready to criticise someone, remember God's law of love and say something good instead. Saying something beneficial to others will cure you of finding fault and increase your ability to obey God's law of love.

4:13 [s]Pr 27:1
4:14 [t]Job 7:7; Ps 102:3
4:15 [u]Ac 18:21
4:16 [v]1Co 5:6
4:17 [w]Lk 12:47; Jn 9:41
5:1 [a]Lk 6:24
5:2 [b]Job 13:28; Mt 6:19, 20
5:3 [c]ver 7, 8
5:4 [d]Lev 19:13 [e]Dt 24:15 [f]Ro 9:29
5:5 [g]Am 6:1 [h]Jer 12:3; 25:34
5:6 [i]Heb 10:38

Boasting About Tomorrow

13Now listen, you who say, "Today or tomorrow we will go to this or that city,
spend a year there, carry on business and make money."[s] 14Why, you do not even
know what will happen tomorrow. What is your life? You are a mist that appears for
a little while and then vanishes.[t] 15Instead, you ought to say, "If it is the Lord's
will,[u] we will live and do this or that." 16As it is, you boast and brag. All such
boasting is evil.[v] 17Anyone, then, who knows the good he ought to do and doesn't
do it, sins.[w]

Warning to Rich Oppressors

5 Now listen, you rich people,[a] weep and wail because of the misery that is coming
upon you. 2Your wealth has rotted, and moths have eaten your clothes.[b] 3Your
gold and silver are corroded. Their corrosion will testify against you and eat your flesh
like fire. You have hoarded wealth in the last days.[c] 4Look! The wages you failed
to pay the workmen[d] who mowed your fields are crying out against you. The cries[e]
of the harvesters have reached the ears of the Lord Almighty.[f] 5You have lived on
earth in luxury and self-indulgence. You have fattened yourselves[g] in the day of
slaughter.[a][h] 6You have condemned and murdered innocent men,[i] who were not
opposing you.

a *5* Or *yourselves as in a day of feasting*

SPEECH	*When our speech is motivated by:*	*It is full of:*
	Satan	Bitter envy Selfish ambition Earthly concerns and desires Unspiritual thoughts and ideas Disorder Evil
	God and his wisdom	Mercy Love for others Peace Consideration for others Submission Sincerity, impartiality Righteousness

---

4:13–16 It is good to have goals, but goals will disappoint us if we leave God out of them. There is no point in making plans as though God does not exist, because the future is in his hands. What would you like to be doing ten years from now? One year from now? Tomorrow? How will you react if God steps in and re-arranges your plans? Plan ahead, but hold your plans loosely. Put God's desires at the centre of your planning; he will never disappoint you.

4:14 Life is short no matter how many years we live. Don't be deceived into thinking that you have lots of remaining time to live for Christ, to enjoy your loved ones, or to do what you know you should. Live for God today! Then, no matter when your life ends, you will have fulfilled God's plan for you.

4:17 We tend to think that *doing* wrong is sin. But James tells us that sin is also *not* doing right. (These two kinds of sin are sometimes called sins of commission and sins of omission.) It is a sin to lie; it can also be a sin to know the truth and not tell it. It is a sin to speak evil of someone; it is also a sin to avoid him or her when you know he or she needs your friendship. We should be willing to help as the Holy Spirit guides us. If God has directed you to do a kind act, to render a service, or to restore a relationship, do it. You will experience a renewed and refreshed vitality in your Christian faith.

5:1–6 James proclaims the worthlessness of riches, not the worthlessness of the rich. Today's money will be worthless when Christ returns, so we should spend our time accumulating the kind of treasures that will be worthwhile in God's eternal kingdom. Money is not the problem; Christian leaders need money to live and to support their families; missionaries need money to help them spread the gospel; churches need money to do their work effectively. It is the *love* of money that leads to evil (1 Timothy 6:10) and causes some people to oppress others in order to get more. This is a warning to all Christians who are tempted to adopt worldly standards rather than God's standards (Romans 12:1, 2) as well as an encouragement to all those who are oppressed by the rich. Also read Matthew 6:19–21 to see what Jesus says about riches.

5:6 *Innocent men* were defenceless people, probably poor labourers. Poor people who could not pay their debts were thrown in prison or forced to sell all their possessions. At times, they were even forced to sell their family members into slavery. With no opportunity to work off their debts, poor people often died of starvation. God called this murder. Hoarding money, exploiting employees, and living self-indulgently will not escape God's notice.

Patience in Suffering

7Be patient, then, brothers, until the Lord's coming. See how the farmer waits for
the land to yield its valuable crop and how patient he is for the autumn and spring
rains.[j] 8You too, be patient and stand firm, because the Lord's coming is near.[k]
9Don't grumble against each other, brothers,[l] or you will be judged. The Judge[m]
is standing at the door![n]
10Brothers, as an example of patience in the face of suffering, take the prophets[o]
who spoke in the name of the Lord. 11As you know, we consider blessed[p] those who
have persevered. You have heard of Job's perseverance[q] and have seen what the Lord
finally brought about.[r] The Lord is full of compassion and mercy.[s]
12Above all, my brothers, do not swear—not by heaven or by earth or by anything
else. Let your "Yes" be yes, and your "No", no, or you will be condemned.[t]

The Prayer of Faith

13Is any one of you in trouble? He should pray.[u] Is anyone happy? Let him sing
songs of praise.[v] 14Is any one of you sick? He should call the elders of the church
to pray over him and anoint him with oil[w] in the name of the Lord. 15And the prayer
offered in faith will make the sick person well; the Lord will raise him up. If he has
sinned, he will be forgiven. 16Therefore confess your sins[x] to each other and pray
for each other so that you may be healed.[y] The prayer of a righteous man is powerful
and effective.[z]
17Elijah was a man just like us.[a] He prayed earnestly that it would not rain, and
it did not rain on the land for three and a half years.[b] 18Again he prayed, and the
heavens gave rain, and the earth produced its crops.[c]
19My brothers, if one of you should wander from the truth[d] and someone should

5:7 [j]Dt 11:14; Jer 5:24
5:8 [k]Ro 13:11; 1Pe 4:7
5:9 [l]Jas 4:11 [m]1Co 4:5; 1Pe 4:5 [n]Mt 24:33
5:10 [o]Mt 5:12
5:11 [p]Mt 5:10 [q]Job 1:21, 22; 2:10 [r]Job 42:10, 12-17 [s]Nu 14:18
5:12 [t]Mt 5:34-37
5:13 [u]Ps 50:15 [v]Col 3:16
5:14 [w]Mk 6:13
5:16 [x]Mt 3:6 [y]1Pe 2:24 [z]Jn 9:31
5:17 [a]Ac 14:15 [b]1Ki 17:1; Lk 4:25
5:18 [c]1Ki 18:41-45
5:19 [d]Jas 3:14

5:7, 8 The farmer must wait patiently for his crops to grow; he cannot hurry the process. But he does not take the summer off and hope that all goes well in the fields. There is much work to do to ensure a good harvest. In the same way, we must wait patiently for Christ's return. We cannot make him come back any sooner. But while we wait, there is much work that we can do to advance God's kingdom. Both the farmer and the Christian must live by faith, looking towards the future reward for their labours. Don't live as if Christ will never come. Work faithfully to build his kingdom—the King *will* come when the time is right.

5:9 When things go wrong, we tend to grumble against and blame others for our miseries (see the second note on Genesis 3:11–13). Blaming others is easier than admitting our share of the responsibility, but it can be both destructive and sinful. Before you judge others for their shortcomings, remember that Christ the Judge will come to evaluate each of us (Matthew 7:1–5; 25:31–46). He will not let us get away with shifting the blame to others.

5:10, 11 Many prophets suffered and were persecuted, such as Moses, Elijah, and Jeremiah. For a complete list of those persecuted, see the chart in 2 Chronicles 19. For more on the topic of suffering, see the notes on Job 1:1ff; 2:10; 3:23–26; 4:7, 8; 42:17; and Job's Profile in Job 2.

5:12 A person with a reputation for exaggeration or lying often can't get anyone to believe him on his word alone. Christians should never become like that. Always be honest so that others will believe your simple yes or no. By avoiding lies, half-truths, and omissions of the truth, you will become known as a trustworthy person.

5:14, 15 James is referring to someone who is incapacitated physically. In Scripture, oil was both a medicine (see the parable of the Good Samaritan in Luke 10:30–37) and a symbol of the Spirit of God (as used in anointing kings, see 1 Samuel 16:1–13). Thus oil can represent both the medical and the spiritual spheres of life. Christians should not separate the physical and the spiritual—Jesus Christ is Lord over both the body and the spirit.

5:14, 15 People in the church are not alone. Members of Christ's body should be able to count on others for support and prayer, especially when they are sick or suffering. The elders should be on call to respond to the illness of any member, and the church should stay alert to pray for the needs of all its members.

5:15 "The prayer offered in faith" does not refer to the faith of the sick person, but to the faith of the people praying. God heals, faith doesn't, and all prayers are subject to God's will. But our prayers are part of God's healing process. That is why God often waits for our prayers of faith before intervening to heal a person.

5:16 Christ has made it possible for us to go directly to God for forgiveness. But confessing our sins to each other still has an important place in the life of the church. (1) If we have sinned against an individual, we must ask him or her to forgive us. (2) If our sin has affected the church, we must confess it publicly. (3) If we need loving support as we struggle with a sin, we should confess that sin to those who are able to provide that support. (4) If, after confessing a private sin to God, we still don't feel his forgiveness, we may wish to confess that sin to a fellow believer and hear him or her assure us of God's pardon. In Christ's kingdom, every believer is a priest to other believers (1 Peter 2:9).

5:16–18 The Christian's most powerful resource is communion with God through prayer. The results are often greater than we thought were possible. Some people see prayer as a last resort to be tried when all else fails. This approach is backward. Prayer should come first. Because God's power is infinitely greater than ours, it only makes sense to rely on it—especially because God encourages us to do so.

5:17 For more about the great prophet Elijah, read his Profile in 1 Kings 18.

5:19, 20 Clearly this person who has wandered from the truth is a believer who has fallen into sin—one who is no longer living a life consistent with his or her beliefs. Christians disagree over whether or not it is possible for people to lose their salvation, but all agree that those who move away from their faith are in serious trouble and need to repent. James urges Christians to help backsliders return to God. By taking the initiative, praying for the person, and acting in love, we can meet the person where he or she is and

5:19 [e]Mt 18:15 5:20 [f]Ro 11:14 [g]1Pe 4:8

bring him back,[e] 20remember this: Whoever turns a sinner from the error of his way
will save[f] him from death and cover over a multitude of sins.[g]

FAITH THAT WORKS
James offers a larger number of similarities to the Sermon on the Mount than any other book in the New Testament. James relied heavily on Jesus' teachings.

Lesson	*Reference*
When your life is full of difficulties and persecutions, be glad. A reward awaits you.	James 1:2 Matthew 5:10–12
You are to be perfect, mature, and complete, not lacking anything.	James 1:4 Matthew 5:48
Ask God, and he will answer.	James 1:5; 5:15 Matthew 7:7–12
Those who are humble (who don't amount to much by the world's standards) should rejoice in their position as those whom God loves.	James 1:9 Matthew 5:3
Watch out for your anger . . . it can be dangerous.	James 1:20 Matthew 5:22
Be merciful to others, as God is merciful to you.	James 2:13 Matthew 5:7; 6:14
Your faith must express itself in helping others.	James 2:14–16 Matthew 7:21–23
Blessed are the peacemakers; they sow in peace and reap a harvest of righteousness.	James 3:17, 18 Matthew 5:9
You cannot serve God *and* money, pleasures, or evil. Friendship with the world is hatred towards God.	James 4:4 Matthew 6:24
When we humble ourselves and realise our need for God, he will come to us and lift us up.	James 4:10 Matthew 5:3, 4
Don't slander or speak against others; it speaks against God's command to love one another.	James 4:11 Matthew 7:1, 2
Treasures on earth will only rot and fade away—we must store up eternal treasures in heaven.	James 5:2 Matthew 6:19
Be patient in suffering, as God's prophets were patient.	James 5:10 Matthew 5:12
Be honest in your speech so you can say a simple "yes" or "no" and always be trusted.	James 5:12 Matthew 5:33–37

bring him or her back to God and his forgiveness.

5:20 The book of James emphasises faith in action. Right living is the evidence and result of faith. The church must serve with compassion, speak lovingly and truthfully, live in obedience to God's commands, and love one another. The body of believers ought to be an example of heaven on earth, drawing people to Christ through love for God and each other. If we truly believe God's word, we will *live* it day by day. God's word is not merely something we read or think about, but something we do. Belief, faith, and trust must have hands and feet—ours!

1 PETER

VITAL STATISTICS

PURPOSE:
To offer encouragement to suffering Christians

AUTHOR:
Peter

TO WHOM WRITTEN:
Jewish Christians driven out of Jerusalem and scattered throughout Asia Minor, and all believers everywhere

DATE WRITTEN:
About A.D. 62–64, possibly from Rome

SETTING:
Peter was probably in Rome when the great persecution under Emperor Nero began. (Eventually Peter was executed during this persecution.) Throughout the Roman empire, Christians were being tortured and killed for their faith, and the church in Jerusalem was being scattered throughout the Mediterranean world.

KEY VERSE:
"These have come so that your faith . . . may be proved genuine and may result in praise, glory and honour when Jesus Christ is revealed" (1:7).

KEY PEOPLE:
Peter, Silas, Mark

KEY PLACES:
Jerusalem, Rome, and the regions of Pontus, Galatia, Cappadocia, Asia Minor, and Bithynia

SPECIAL FEATURES:
Peter used several images that were very special to him because Jesus had used them when he revealed certain truths to Peter. Peter's name (which means "rock") had been given to him by Jesus. Peter's conception of the church—a spiritual house composed of living stones built upon Christ as the foundation—came from Christ. Jesus encouraged Peter to care for the church as a shepherd tending the flock. Thus, it is not surprising to see Peter using living stones (2:5–9) and shepherds and sheep (2:25; 5:2, 4) to describe the church.

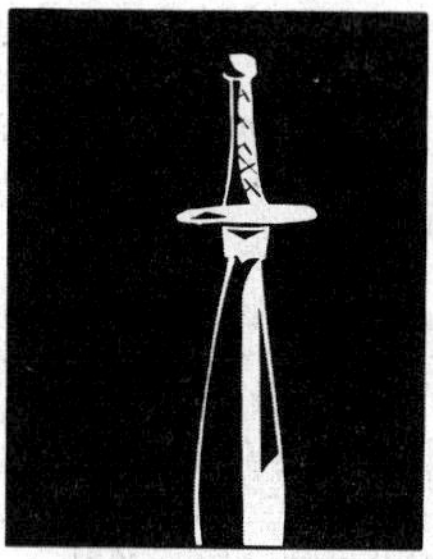

CRUSHED, overwhelmed, devastated, torn—these waves of feelings wash over those who suffer, blinding all vision of hope and threatening to destroy them. Suffering has many forms—physical abuse, debilitating disease, social ostracism, persecution. The pain and anguish tempt a person to turn back, to to give in.

Many first-century followers of Christ were suffering and being abused and persecuted for believing in and obeying Jesus. Beginning in Jerusalem at the hands of their Jewish brothers, the pattern of persecution spread to the rest of the world—wherever Christians gathered—and climaxed when Rome determined to rid the empire of those who would not bow to Caesar . . . the "Christ-ones".

Peter knew persecution firsthand. Beaten and imprisoned, Peter had been threatened often. He had seen fellow Christians die and the church scattered. But he knew Christ, and nothing could shake his confidence in his risen Lord. In this personal context, Peter wrote to the church scattered and suffering for the faith, giving comfort and hope, and urging continued loyalty to Christ.

Peter begins by thanking God for salvation (1:2–6). He explains to his readers that trials will refine their faith (1:7–9). They should believe in spite of their circumstances; for many in past ages believed in God's plan of salvation, even the prophets of old who wrote about it but didn't understand it. But now salvation has been revealed in Christ (1:10–13).

In response to such a great salvation, Peter commands them to live holy lives (1:14–16), reverently to fear and trust God (1:17–21), to be honest and loving (2:1–3), and to become like Christ (2:1–3).

Jesus Christ, as "a chosen and precious cornerstone" upon whom the church is to be built (2:4, 6), is also the stone that was rejected, causing those who are disobedient to stumble and fall (2:7, 8). But the church, built upon this Stone, is to be God's holy priesthood (2:9, 10).

Next, Peter explains how believers should live during difficult times (2:11—4:11). Christians should be above reproach (2:12–17), imitating Christ in all their social roles—masters and servants, husbands and wives, church members and neighbours (2:18—3:17). Christ should be our model for obedience to God in the midst of great suffering (3:18—4:11).

Peter then outlines the right attitude to have about persecution: expect it (4:12), be thankful for the privilege of suffering for Christ (4:13–18), and trust God for deliverance (4:19).

Next, Peter gives some special instructions—elders should care for God's flock (5:1–4), younger men should be submissive to those who are older (5:5, 6), and everyone should trust God and resist Satan (5:7–11).

Peter concludes by introducing Silas and by giving personal greetings from himself, possibly from the church in Rome, and from Mark (5:12–14).

When you suffer for doing what is right, remember that following Christ is a costly commitment. When persecuted for your faith, rejoice that you have been counted worthy to suffer for Christ. He suffered for us; as his followers, we should expect nothing less. As you read 1 Peter, remember that trials will come to refine your faith. When they come, remain faithful to God.

THE BLUEPRINT

1. God's great blessings to his people (1:1—2:10)
2. The conduct of God's people in the midst of suffering (2:11—4:19)
3. The shepherding of God's people in the midst of suffering (5:1–14)

Peter wrote to Jewish Christians who were experiencing persecution for their faith. He wrote to comfort them with the hope of eternal life and to challenge them to continue living holy lives. Those who suffer for being Christians become partners with Christ in his suffering. As we suffer, we must remember that Christ is both our hope in the midst of suffering and our example of how to endure suffering faithfully.

MEGATHEMES

THEME	EXPLANATION	IMPORTANCE
Salvation	Our salvation is a gracious gift from God. God chose us out of his love for us, Jesus died to pay the penalty for our sin, and the Holy Spirit cleansed us from sin when we believed. Eternal life is a wonderful privilege for those who trust in Christ.	Our safety and security are in God. If we experience joy in relationship with Christ now, how much greater will our joy be when he returns and we see him face to face. Such a hope should motivate us to serve Christ with greater commitment.
Persecution	Peter offers faithful believers comfort and hope. We should expect ridicule, rejection, and suffering because we are Christians. Persecution makes us stronger because it refines our faith. We can face persecution victoriously as Christ did, if we rely on him.	Christians still suffer for what they believe. We should expect persecution, but we don't have to be terrified by it. The fact that we will live eternally with Christ should give us the confidence, patience, and hope to stand firm even when we are persecuted.
God's Family	We are privileged to belong to God's family, a community with Christ as the founder and foundation. Everyone in this community is related—we are all brothers and sisters, loved equally by God.	Because Christ is the foundation of our family, we must be devoted, loyal, and faithful to him. By obeying him, we show that we are his children. We must accept the challenge to live differently from the society around us.
Family Life	Peter encouraged the wives of unbelievers to submit to their husbands' authority as a means to winning them to Christ. He urged all family members to treat others with sympathy, love, compassion, and humility.	We must treat our families lovingly. Though it's never easy, willing service is the best way to influence loved ones. To gain the strength we need for self-discipline and submission, we need to pray for God's help.
Judgment	God will judge everyone with perfect justice. We will all face God. He will punish evildoers and those who persecute God's people. Those who love him will be rewarded with life for ever in his presence.	Because all are accountable to God, we can leave judgment of others to him. We must not hate or resent those who persecute us. We should realise that we will be held responsible for how we live each day.

1. God's great blessings to his people

1 Peter, an apostle of Jesus Christ,[a]

To God's elect,[b] strangers in the world, scattered throughout Pontus, Galatia,
Cappadocia, Asia and Bithynia,[c] 2who have been chosen according to the foreknowledge[d] of God the Father, through the sanctifying work of the Spirit,[e] for obedience
to Jesus Christ and sprinkling by his blood:[f]

Grace and peace be yours in abundance.

Praise to God for a Living Hope

3Praise be to the God and Father of our Lord Jesus Christ![g] In his great mercy[h]
he has given us new birth into a living hope through the resurrection of Jesus Christ
from the dead,[i] 4and into an inheritance that can never perish, spoil or fade—kept
in heaven for you,[j] 5who through faith are shielded by God's power[k] until the

1:1 [a]2Pe 1:1 [b]Mt 24:22 [c]Ac 16:7
1:2 [d]Ro 8:29 [e]2Th 2:13 [f]Heb 10:22; 12:24
1:3 [g]2Co 1:3; Eph 1:3 [h]Tit 3:5; Jas 1:18 [i]1Co 15:20
1:4 [j]Col 1:5
1:5 [k]Jn 10:28

1:1 The apostle Peter wrote this letter to encourage believers who would likely face trials and persecution under Emperor Nero. During most of the first century, Christians were not hunted down and killed throughout the Roman empire. They could, however, expect social and economic persecution from three main sources: the Romans, the Jews, and their own families. All would very likely be misunderstood; some would be harassed; a few would be tortured and even put to death.

The legal status of Christians in the Roman empire was unclear. Many Romans still thought of Christians as members of a Jewish sect, and because the Jewish religion was legal, they considered Christianity legal also—as long as Christians complied with the empire's laws. However, if Christians refused to worship the emperor or join the army, or if they were involved in civil disturbances (such as the one in Ephesus recorded in Acts 19:23ff), they might be punished by the civil authorities.

Many Jews did not appreciate being legally associated with Christians. As the book of Acts frequently records, Jews occasionally harmed Christians physically, drove them out of town, or attempted to turn Roman officials against them. Saul, later the great apostle Paul, was an early Jewish persecutor of Christians.

Another source of persecution was the Christian's own family. Under Roman law, the head of the household had absolute authority over all its members. Unless the ruling male became a Christian, the wife, children and servants who were believers might well face extreme hardship. If they were sent away, they would have no place to turn but the church; if they were beaten, no court of law would uphold their interests.

Peter may have been writing especially for new Christians and those planning to be baptised. Peter wanted to warn them about what lay ahead, and they needed his encouraging words to help them face opposition. This letter is still helpful for any Christians facing trials. Many Christians around the world are living under governments more repressive than the Roman empire of the first century. Christians everywhere are subject to misunderstanding, ridicule, and even harassment by unbelieving friends, employers, and family members. None of us is exempt from catastrophe, pain, illness, and death—trials that, like persecution, make us lean heavily on God's grace. For today's readers, as well as for Peter's original audience, the theme of this letter is *hope.*

1:1 Peter (also called Simon and Cephas) was one of the 12 disciples chosen by Jesus (Mark 1:16–18; John 1:42) and, with James and John, was part of the inner group that Jesus singled out for special training and fellowship. Peter was one of the first to recognise Jesus as the Messiah, God's Son, and Jesus gave him a special leadership role in the church (Matthew 16:16–19; Luke 22:31, 32; John 21:15–19). Although during Jesus' trial Peter denied knowing Jesus, Peter repented and became a great apostle. For more information on Peter, see his Profile in Matthew 27.

1:1 This letter is addressed to "God's elect, strangers in the world", or to the Jewish Christians scattered throughout the world as a result of persecution against believers in and around Jerusalem. The first believers and leaders of the early church were Jews. When they became Christians, they didn't give up their Jewish heritage, just as you didn't give up your nationality when you became a follower of Christ. Because of persecution, these believers had been scattered throughout the Roman world (this scattering is described in Acts 8:1–4). Persecution didn't stop the spread of the gospel; instead, persecution served as a way to introduce the Good News to the whole empire. Thus the churches to whom Peter wrote also included Gentile Christians.

1:2 Peter encouraged his readers by this strong declaration that they were *chosen* by God the Father. At one time, only the nation of Israel could claim to be God's chosen people; but through Christ, all believers—Jews and Gentiles—belong to God. Our salvation and security rest in the free and merciful choice of Almighty God; no trials or persecutions can take away the eternal life he gives to those who believe in him.

1:2 This verse mentions all three members of the Trinity—God the Father, God the Son (Jesus Christ), and God the Holy Spirit. All members of the Trinity work to bring about our salvation. The Father chose us before we chose him (Ephesians 1:4). Jesus Christ the Son died for us while we were still sinners (Romans 5:6–10). The Holy Spirit brings us the benefits of salvation and sets us apart (sanctifies us) for God's service (2 Thessalonians 2:13).

1:3 The term *new birth* refers to spiritual birth (regeneration)—the Holy Spirit's act of bringing believers into God's family. Jesus used this concept of new birth when he explained salvation to Nicodemus (see John 3).

1:3–6 Do you need encouragement? Peter's words offer joy and hope in times of trouble, and he bases his confidence on what God has done for us in Christ Jesus. We're called into a *living* hope of eternal life (1:3). Our hope is not only for the future; eternal life begins when we trust Christ and join God's family. No matter what pain or trial we face in this life, we know that it is not our final experience. Eventually we will live with Christ for ever.

1:4 The Jews had looked forward to an inheritance in the promised land of Canaan (Numbers 32:19; Deuteronomy 2:12; 19:9). Christians now look forward to a family inheritance in the eternal city of God. God has reserved the inheritance; it will never fade or decay; it will be unstained by sin. The best part is that *you* have an inheritance if you have trusted Christ as your Saviour.

1:5 God will help us remain true to our faith through whatever difficult times we must face. The "last time" is the judgment day of Christ described in Romans 14:10 and Revelation 20:11–15. We may have to endure trials, persecution, or violent death, but our souls cannot be harmed if we have accepted Christ's gift of salvation. We know we will receive the promised rewards.

1:6
[l]Ro 5:2
[m]1Pe 5:10
[n]Jas 1:2
1:7
[o]Job 23:10; Ps 66:10; Pr 17:3
[p]Jas 1:3
[q]Ro 2:7
1:8
[r]Jn 20:29
1:9
[s]Ro 6:22
1:10
[t]Mt 26:24
[u]Mt 13:17
1:11
[v]2Pe 1:21
1:12
[w]ver 25

coming of the salvation that is ready to be revealed in the last time. 6In this you greatly
rejoice,[l] though now for a little while[m] you may have had to suffer grief in all kinds
of trials.[n] 7These have come so that your faith—of greater worth than gold, which
perishes even though refined by fire[o]—may be proved genuine[p] and may result in
praise, glory and honour when Jesus Christ is revealed.[q] 8Though you have not seen
him, you love him; and even though you do not see him now, you believe in him[r]
and are filled with an inexpressible and glorious joy, 9for you are receiving the goal
of your faith, the salvation of your souls.[s]
10Concerning this salvation, the prophets, who spoke[t] of the grace that was to
come to you, searched intently and with the greatest care,[u] 11trying to find out the
time and circumstances to which the Spirit of Christ[v] in them was pointing when he
predicted the sufferings of Christ and the glories that would follow. 12It was revealed
to them that they were not serving themselves but you, when they spoke of the things
that have now been told you by those who have preached the gospel to you[w] by the
Holy Spirit sent from heaven. Even angels long to look into these things.

THE CHURCHES OF PETER'S LETTER

Peter addressed his letter to the churches located through Bithynia, Pontus, Asia, Galatia, and Cappadocia. Paul had evangelised many of these areas; other areas had churches that were begun by the Jews who were in Jerusalem on the day of Pentecost and heard Peter's powerful sermon (see Acts 2:9–11).

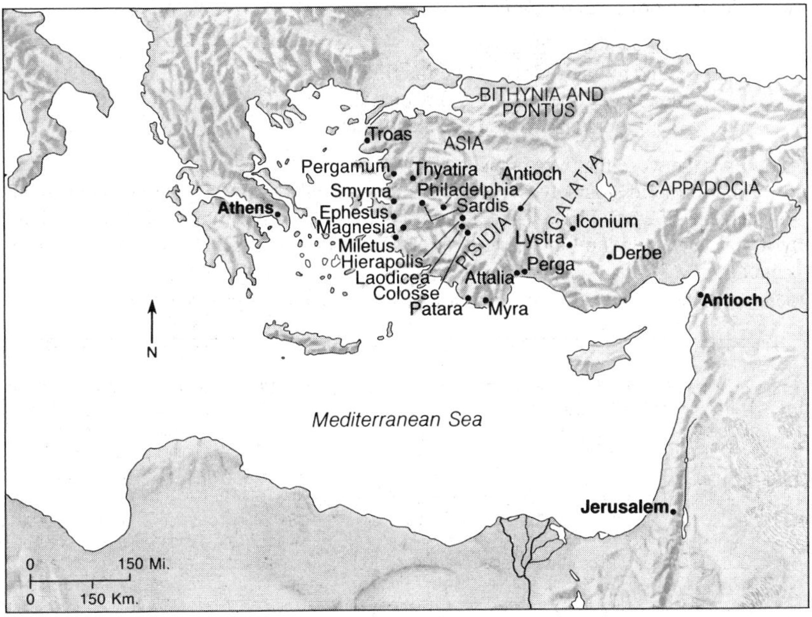

1:6 Why were Christians the target of persecution? (1) They refused to worship the emperor as a god and thus were viewed as atheists and traitors. (2) They refused to worship at pagan temples, so business for these money-making enterprises dropped wherever Christianity took hold. (3) They didn't support the Roman ideals of self, power, and conquest; and the Romans scorned the Christian ideal of self-sacrificing service. (4) They exposed and rejected the horrible immorality of pagan culture.

1:6, 7 Peter mentions suffering several times in this letter: 1:6, 7; 3:13–17; 4:12–19; 5:9. When he speaks of trials, he is not talking about natural disasters or the experience of God's punishments, but the response of an unbelieving world to people of faith. All believers face such trials when they let their light shine into the darkness. We must accept trials as part of the refining process that burns away impurities and prepares us to meet Christ. Trials teach us patience (Romans 5:3, 4; James 1:2, 3) and help us grow to be the kind of people God wants.

1:7 As gold is heated, impurities float to the top and can be skimmed off. Steel is tempered or strengthened by heating it in fire. Likewise, our trials, struggles, and persecutions refine and strengthen our faith, making us useful to God.

1:10–12 Although the plan of salvation was a mystery to the Old Testament prophets, they still suffered persecution, and some even died for God. In contrast, some Jewish Christians who read Peter's letter had seen Jesus for themselves and knew why he came. They based their assurance on Jesus' death and resurrection. With their firsthand knowledge and personal experience of Jesus, their faith could be even stronger than that of the Old Testament prophets.

1:11 The Spirit of Christ is another name for the Holy Spirit. Before Jesus left his ministry on earth to return to heaven, he promised to send the Holy Spirit, the Counsellor, to teach, help, and guide his followers (John 14:15–17, 26; 16:7). The Holy Spirit would tell them all about Jesus and would reveal his glory (John 15:26; 16:14). The Old Testament prophets, writing under the Holy Spirit's inspiration (2 Peter 1:20, 21), described the coming of the Messiah. The New Testament apostles, through the inspiration of the same Spirit, preached the crucified and risen Lord.

Be Holy

13Therefore, prepare your minds for action; be self-controlled; set your hope fully
on the grace to be given you when Jesus Christ is revealed. 14As obedient children,
do not conform[x] to the evil desires you had when you lived in ignorance.[y] 15But
just as he who called you is holy, so be holy in all you do;[z] 16for it is written: "Be
holy, because I am holy."[a][a]
17Since you call on a Father who judges each man's work impartially,[b] live your
lives as strangers here in reverent fear.[c] 18For you know that it was not with
perishable things such as silver or gold that you were redeemed[d] from the empty way
of life handed down to you from your forefathers, 19but with the precious blood of
Christ, a lamb[e] without blemish or defect.[f] 20He was chosen before the creation of
the world,[g] but was revealed in these last times[h] for your sake. 21Through him you
believe in God,[i] who raised him from the dead and glorified him, and so your faith
and hope are in God.
22Now that you have purified[j] yourselves by obeying the truth so that you have
sincere love for your brothers, love one another deeply,[k] from the heart.[b] 23For you
have been born again,[l] not of perishable seed, but of imperishable, through the living
and enduring word of God.[m] 24For,

"All men are like grass,
and all their glory is like the flowers of the field;
the grass withers and the flowers fall,
25 but the word of the Lord stands for ever."[c][n]

And this is the word that was preached to you.

2 Therefore, rid yourselves[a] of all malice and all deceit, hypocrisy, envy, and
slander[b] of every kind. 2Like newborn babies, crave pure spiritual milk,[c] so that
by it you may grow up[d] in your salvation, 3now that you have tasted that the Lord
is good.[e]

[a] *16* Lev. 11:44,45; 19:2; 20:7 [b] *22* Some early manuscripts *from a pure heart* [c] *25* Isaiah 40:6–8

1:14 [x]Ro 12:2 [y]Eph 4:18
1:15 [z]2Co 7:1; 1Th 4:7
1:16 [a]Lev 11:44, 45
1:17 [b]Ac 10:34 [c]Heb 12:28
1:18 [d]Mt 20:28; 1Co 6:20
1:19 [e]Jn 1:29 [f]Ex 12:5
1:20 [g]Eph 1:4 [h]Heb 9:26
1:21 [i]Ro 4:24
1:22 [j]Jas 4:8 [k]Jn 13:34; Heb 13:1
1:23 [l]Jn 1:13 [m]Heb 4:12
1:25 [n]Isa 40:6-8
2:1 [a]Eph 4:22 [b]Jas 4:11
2:2 [c]1Co 3:2 [d]Eph 4:15, 16
2:3 [e]Heb 6:5

1:13 The imminent return of Christ should motivate us to live for him. This means being mentally alert ("prepare your minds for action"), disciplined ("self-controlled"), and focused ("set your hope fully"). Are you ready to meet Christ?

1:14–16 The God of Israel and of the Christian church is holy—he sets the standard for morality. Unlike the Roman gods, he is not warlike, adulterous, or spiteful. Unlike the gods of the pagan cults popular in the first century, he is not bloodthirsty or promiscuous. He is a God of mercy and justice who cares personally for each of his followers. Our holy God expects us to imitate him by following his high moral standards. Like him, we should be both merciful and just; like him, we should sacrifice ourselves for others.

1:15, 16 After people commit their lives to Christ, they usually still feel a pull back to their old ways. Peter tells us to be like our heavenly Father—holy in everything we do. Holiness means being totally devoted or dedicated to God, set aside for his special use and set apart from sin and its influence. We're to be set apart and different, not blending in with the crowd, yet not being different just for the sake of being different. What makes us different are God's qualities in our lives. Our focus and priorities must be his. All this is in direct contrast to our old ways (1:14). We cannot become holy on our own, but God gives us his Holy Spirit to help us obey and to give us power to overcome sin. Don't use the excuse that you can't help slipping into sin. Call on God's power to free you from sin's grip.

1:17 "Reverent fear" is not the fear of a slave for a ruthless master, but the healthy respect of a believer for the all-powerful God. Because God is the Judge of all the earth, we dare not ignore him or treat him casually. We should not assume that our privileged status as God's children gives us freedom to do whatever we want. We should not be spoiled children, but grateful children who love to show respect for our heavenly Father.

1:18, 19 A slave was "redeemed" when someone paid money to buy his or her freedom. God redeemed us from the tyranny of sin, not with money, but with the precious blood of his own Son (Romans 6:6, 7; 1 Corinthians 6:20; Colossians 2:13, 14; Hebrews 9:12). We cannot escape from sin on our own; only the life of God's Son can free us.

1:20 Christ's sacrifice for our sins was not an afterthought, not something God decided to do when the world spun out of control. This plan was set in motion by the all-knowing, eternal God long before the world was created. What a comfort it must have been to Jewish believers to know that Christ's coming and his work of salvation were planned by God long before the world began. This assured them that the law was not being scrapped because it didn't work, but that both the law *and* the coming of Christ were part of God's eternal plan.

1:22 "Sincere love" involves selfless giving; a self-centred person can't truly love. God's love and forgiveness free you to take your eyes off yourselves and to meet others' needs. By sacrificing his life, Christ showed that he truly loves you. Now you can love others by following his example and giving of yourself sacrificially.

1:24, 25 Quoting Isaiah 40:6–8, Peter reminds believers that everything in this life—possessions, accomplishments, people—will eventually fade away and disappear. Only God's will, word, and work are permanent. We must stop grasping the temporary, and begin focusing our time, money, and energy on the permanent—the word of God and our eternal life in Christ.

2:2, 3 One characteristic all children share is that they want to grow up—to be like big brother or sister or like their parents. When we are born again, we become spiritual newborn babies. If we are healthy, we will yearn to grow. How sad it is that some people never grow up. The need for milk is a natural instinct for a baby, and it signals the desire for nourishment that will lead to growth.

2:4 [f]ver 7

The Living Stone and a Chosen People

4As you come to him, the living Stone[f]—rejected by men but chosen by God and
precious to him—5you also, like living stones, are being built[g] into a spiritual house[h]
to be a holy priesthood,[i] offering spiritual sacrifices acceptable to God through Jesus
Christ.[j] 6For in Scripture it says:

2:5 [g]1Co 3:9 [h]1Ti 3:15 [i]Isa 61:6 [j]Php 4:18; Heb 13:15

> "See, I lay a stone in Zion,
> a chosen and precious cornerstone,[k]
> and the one who trusts in him
> will never be put to shame."[a][l]

2:6 [k]Eph 2:20 [l]Isa 28:16

7Now to you who believe, this stone is precious. But to those who do not believe,[m]

> "The stone the builders rejected
> has become the capstone,"[b,c][n]

2:7 [m]2Co 2:16 [n]Ps 118:22

8and,

> "A stone that causes men to stumble
> and a rock that makes them fall."[d][o]

2:8 [o]Isa 8:14; 1Co 1:23 [p]Ro 9:22

They stumble because they disobey the message—which is also what they were
destined for.[p]

2:9 [q]Dt 10:15 [r]Isa 62:12 [s]Ac 26:18

9But you are a chosen people,[q] a royal priesthood, a holy nation,[r] a people
belonging to God, that you may declare the praises of him who called you out of
darkness into his wonderful light.[s] 10Once you were not a people, but now you are
the people of God;[t] once you had not received mercy, but now you have received
mercy.

2:10 [t]Hos 1:9, 10

[a] *6* Isaiah 28:16 [b] *7* Or *cornerstone* [c] *7* Psalm 118:22 [d] *8* Isaiah 8:14

Once we see our need for God's word and begin to find nourishment in Christ, our spiritual appetite will increase, and we will start to mature. How strong is your desire for God's word?

2:4–8 In describing the church as God's spiritual house, Peter drew on several Old Testament texts familiar to his Jewish Christian readers: Psalm 118:22; Isaiah 8:14; 28:16. Peter's readers would have understood the living stones to be Israel; then Peter applied the image of "stone" to Christ. Once again Peter showed that the church does not cancel the Jewish heritage, but fulfils it.

2:4–8 Peter portrays the church as a living, spiritual house, with Christ as the foundation and cornerstone and each believer as a stone. Paul portrays the church as a body, with Christ as the head and each believer as a member (see, for example, Ephesians 4:15, 16). Both pictures emphasise *community.* One stone is not a temple or even a wall; one body part is useless without the others. In our individualistic society, it is easy to forget our interdependence with other Christians. When God calls you to a task, remember that he is also calling others to work with you. Together your individual efforts will be multiplied. Look for those people and join with them to build a beautiful house for God.

2:6 Christians will sometimes be put to shame or face disappointment in this life, but their trust in God is never misplaced. God will not let them down. We can safely put our confidence in him because the eternal life he promises is certain.

2:6–8 No doubt Peter often thought of Jesus' words to him right after he confessed that Jesus was "the Christ, the Son of the living God": "You are Peter, and on this rock I will build my church, and the gates of Hades will not overcome it" (Matthew 16:16–18). What is the stone that really counts in the building of the church? Peter answers: Christ himself. What are the characteristics of Christ, the cornerstone? (1) He is completely trustworthy; (2) he is precious to believers; (3) and, though rejected by some, he is the most important part of the church.

2:8 Jesus Christ is called "the stone that causes men to stumble and a rock that makes them fall". Some will stumble over Christ because they reject him or refuse to believe that he is who he says he is. But Psalm 118:22 says that "the stone the builders rejected has become the capstone", the most important part of God's building, the church. In the same way today, people who refuse to believe in Christ have made the greatest mistake of their lives. They have stumbled over the one person who could save them and give meaning to their lives, and they have fallen into God's hands for judgment.

2:9 Christians sometimes speak of "the priesthood of all believers". In Old Testament times, people did not approach God directly. A priest acted as intermediary between God and sinful human beings. With Christ's victory on the cross, that pattern changed. Now we can come directly into God's presence without fear (Hebrews 4:16), and we are given the responsibility of bringing others to him also (2 Corinthians 5:18–21). When we are united with Christ as members of his body, we join in his priestly work of reconciling God and man.

2:9, 10 People often base their self-concept on their accomplishments. But our relationship with Christ is far more important than our jobs, successes, wealth, or knowledge. We have been chosen by God as his very own, and we have been called to represent him to others. Remember that your value comes from being one of God's children, not from what you can achieve. You have worth because of what *God does,* not because of what you do.

2. The conduct of God's people in the midst of suffering

11 Dear friends, I urge you, as aliens and strangers in the world, to abstain from
sinful desires,[u] which war against your soul.[v] 12 Live such good lives among the
pagans that, though they accuse you of doing wrong, they may see your good deeds[w]
and glorify God[x] on the day he visits us.

Submission to Rulers and Masters

13 Submit yourselves for the Lord's sake to every authority[y] instituted among men:
whether to the king, as the supreme authority, 14 or to governors, who are sent by him
to punish those who do wrong[z] and to commend those who do right.[a] 15 For it is
God's will[b] that by doing good you should silence the ignorant talk of foolish men.[c]
16 Live as free men,[d] but do not use your freedom as a cover-up for evil; live as
servants of God.[e] 17 Show proper respect to everyone: Love the brotherhood of
believers,[f] fear God, honour the king.[g]
18 Slaves, submit yourselves to your masters with all respect,[h] not only to those
who are good and considerate,[i] but also to those who are harsh. 19 For it is commendable if a man bears up under the pain of unjust suffering because he is conscious of
God.[j] 20 But how is it to your credit if you receive a beating for doing wrong and
endure it? But if you suffer for doing good and you endure it, this is commendable
before God.[k] 21 To this[l] you were called, because Christ suffered for you, leaving
you an example,[m] that you should follow in his steps.

> 22 "He committed no sin,
> and no deceit was found in his mouth."[e][n]

23 When they hurled their insults at him, he did not retaliate; when he suffered, he made

[e] *22* Isaiah 53:9

2:11 [u] Gal 5:16 [v] Jas 4:1
2:12 [w] Php 2:15; 1Pe 3:16 [x] Mt 5:16; 9:8
2:13 [y] Ro 13:1
2:14 [z] Ro 13:4 [a] Ro 13:3
2:15 [b] 1Pe 3:17 [c] ver 12
2:16 [d] Jn 8:32 [e] Ro 6:22
2:17 [f] Ro 12:10 [g] Ro 13:7
2:18 [h] Eph 6:5 [i] Jas 3:17
2:19 [j] 1Pe 3:14, 17
2:20 [k] 1Pe 3:17
2:21 [l] Ac 14:22 [m] Mt 16:24
2:22 [n] Isa 53:9

2:11 As believers, we are "aliens and strangers" in this world, because our real home is with God. Heaven is not the pink-cloud-and-harp existence popular in cartoons. Heaven is where God lives. Life in heaven operates according to God's principles and values, and it is eternal and unshakable. Heaven came to earth in the symbolism of the Jewish sanctuary (the tabernacle and temple) where God's presence dwelt. It came in a fuller way in the person of Jesus Christ, "God with us". It permeated the entire world as the Holy Spirit came to live in every believer.

One day, after God judges and destroys all sin, the kingdom of heaven will rule every corner of this earth. John saw this day in a vision, and he cried out, "Now the dwelling of God is with men, and he will live with them. They will be his people, and God himself will be with them and be their God" (Revelation 21:3). Our true loyalty should be to our citizenship in heaven, not to our citizenship here, because the earth will be destroyed. Our loyalty should be to God's truth, his way of life, and his dedicated people. Because we are loyal to God, we will often feel like strangers in a world that would prefer to ignore God.

2:12 Peter's advice sounds like Jesus' in Matthew 5:16: If your actions are above reproach, even hostile people will end up praising God. Peter's readers were scattered among unbelieving Gentiles who were inclined to believe and spread vicious lies about Christians. Attractive, gracious, and upright behaviour on the part of Christians could show these rumours to be false and could even win some of the unsaved critics to the Lord's side. Don't write off people because they misunderstand Christianity; instead, show them Christ by your life. The day may come when those who criticise you will praise God with you.

2:13–17 When Peter told his readers to submit to the civil authorities, he was speaking of the Roman empire under Nero, a notoriously cruel tyrant. Obviously he was not telling believers to compromise their consciences; as Peter had told the high priest years before, "We must obey God rather than men" (Acts 5:29). But in most aspects of daily life, it was possible and desirable for Christians to live according to the law of their land. Today, some Christians live in freedom while others live under repressive governments. All are commanded to co-operate with the rulers as far as conscience will allow. We are to do this "for the Lord's sake"—so that his Good News and his people will be respected. If we are to be persecuted, it should be for obeying God, and not for breaking moral or civil laws. For more about the Christian's relationship to government, see the note on Romans 13:1ff.

2:16 We are free from keeping the law as a way to earn salvation. However we are still to obey, out of gratitude for our free salvation, the teachings of the Ten Commandments, for they are an expression of God's will for us.

2:18–21 Many Christians were household slaves. It would be easy for them to submit to masters who were gentle and kind. But Peter encouraged loyalty and perseverance even in the face of unjust treatment. In the same way, we should submit to our employers, whether they are considerate or harsh. By so doing, we may win them to Christ by our good example. Paul gave similar advice in his letters (see Ephesians 6:5–9; Colossians 3:22–25), as did Jesus (Matthew 5:46; Luke 6:32–36).

2:21, 22 We may suffer for many reasons. Some suffering is the direct result of our own sin; some happens because of our foolishness; and some is the result of living in a fallen world. Peter is writing about suffering that comes as a result of doing good. Christ never sinned, and yet he suffered so that we could be set free. When we follow Christ's example and live for others, we too may suffer. Our goal should be to face suffering as he did—with patience, calmness, and confidence that God is in control of the future.

2:21–25 Peter had learned about suffering from Jesus. He knew that Jesus' suffering was part of God's plan (Matthew 16:21–23; Luke 24:25–27, 44–47) and was intended to save us (Matthew 20:28; 26:28). He also knew that all who follow Jesus must be prepared to suffer (Mark 8:34, 35). Peter learned these truths from Jesus and passed them on to us.

2:23 [o]Isa 53:7 [p]Lk 23:46
2:24 [q]Heb 9:28 [r]Ro 6:2 [s]Isa 53:5; Heb 12:13; Jas 5:16
2:25 [t]Isa 53:6 [u]Jn 10:11
3:1 [a]1Pe 2:18 [b]Eph 5:22 [c]1Co 7:16; 9:19
3:3 [d]Isa 3:18-23; 1Ti 2:9
3:4 [e]Ro 7:22
3:5 [f]1Ti 5:5
3:6 [g]Ge 18:12
3:7 [h]Eph 5:25-33

no threats.[o] Instead, he entrusted himself[p] to him who judges justly. 24He himself
bore our sins[q] in his body on the tree, so that we might die to sins[r] and live for
righteousness; by his wounds you have been healed.[s] 25For you were like sheep going
astray,[t] but now you have returned to the Shepherd[u] and Overseer of your souls.

Wives and Husbands

3 Wives, in the same way be submissive[a] to your husbands[b] so that, if any of
them do not believe the word, they may be won over[c] without words by the
behaviour of their wives, 2when they see the purity and reverence of your lives. 3Your
beauty should not come from outward adornment, such as braided hair and the wearing
of gold jewellery and fine clothes.[d] 4Instead, it should be that of your inner self,[e]
the unfading beauty of a gentle and quiet spirit, which is of great worth in God's sight.
5For this is the way the holy women of the past who put their hope in God[f] used
to make themselves beautiful. They were submissive to their own husbands, 6like
Sarah, who obeyed Abraham and called him her master.[g] You are her daughters if
you do what is right and do not give way to fear.
7Husbands,[h] in the same way be considerate as you live with your wives, and treat

---

SUBMISSION Submission is:		
	Functional	a distinguishing of our roles and the work we are called to do
	Relational	a loving acknowledgment of another's value as a person
	Reciprocal	a mutual, humble co-operation with one another
	Universal	an acknowledgment by the church of the all-encompassing lordship of Jesus Christ

Submission is voluntarily co-operating with anyone out of love and respect for God first, and then secondly, out of love and respect for that person. Submitting to non-believers is difficult, but it is a vital part of leading them to Jesus Christ. We are not called to submit to non-believers to the point that we compromise our relationship with God, but we must look for every opportunity to serve humbly in the power of God's Spirit.

2:24 Christ died for *our* sins, in *our* place, so we would not have to suffer the punishment we deserve. This is called *substitutionary atonement.*

3:1ff When a man became a Christian, he would usually bring his whole family into the church with him (see, for example, the story of the conversion of the Philippian jailer in Acts 16:29–33). By contrast, a woman who became a Christian usually came into the church alone. Under Roman law, the husband and father had absolute authority over all members of his household, including his wife. Demanding her rights as a free woman in Christ could endanger her marriage if her husband disapproved. Peter reassured Christian women who were married to unbelievers that they did not need to preach to their husbands. Under the circumstances, their best approach would be one of loving service: they should show their husbands the kind of self-giving love that Christ showed the church. By being exemplary wives, they would please their husbands. At the very least, the men would then allow them to continue practising their "strange" religion. At best, their husbands would join them and become Christians too.

3:1–7 A changed life speaks loudly and clearly, and it is often the most effective way to influence a family member. Peter instructs Christian wives to develop inner beauty rather than being over concerned about their outward appearance. Their husbands will be won over by their love rather than by their looks. Live your Christian faith quietly and consistently in your home, and your family will see Christ in you.

3:3 We should not be obsessed by fashion, but neither should we be so unconcerned that we do not bother to care for ourselves. Hygiene, neatness, and grooming are important, but even more important are a person's attitude and inner spirit. True beauty begins inside.

3:5 To be *submissive* means to co-operate voluntarily with someone else out of love and respect for God and for that person. Ideally, submission is mutual ("Submit to one another out of reverence for Christ" – Ephesians 5:21). Even when it is one-sided, however, the expression of submission can be an effective Christian strategy. Jesus Christ submitted to death so that we could be saved; we may sometimes have to submit to unpleasant circumstances so that others will see Christ in us. (Christian submission never requires us to disobey God or to participate in what our conscience forbids.) One-sided submission requires tremendous strength. We could not do it without the power of the Holy Spirit working in us.

3:7 When Peter calls women the "weaker" partners, he does not imply moral or intellectual inferiority, but he is recognising women's physical limitations. Women in his day, if unprotected by men, were vulnerable to attack, abuse, and financial disaster. Women's lives may be easier today, but women are still vulnerable to criminal attack and family abuse. And in spite of increased opportunities in the workplace, most women still earn considerably less than most men, and the vast majority of the nations' poor are single mothers and their children. A man who honours his wife as a member of the weaker sex will protect, respect, help, and stay with her. He will not expect her to work full-time outside the home and full-time at home; he will lighten her load wherever he can. He will be sensitive to her needs, and he will relate to her with courtesy, consideration, insight, and tact.

3:7 If a man is not considerate and respectful of his wife, his prayers will be hindered, because a living relationship with God depends on right relationships with others. Jesus said that if you have a problem with a fellow believer, you must make it right with that person before coming to worship (Matthew 5:23, 24). This principle carries over into family relationships. If men use their position to mistreat their wives, their relationship with God will suffer.

them with respect as the weaker partner and as heirs with you of the gracious gift of
life, so that nothing will hinder your prayers.

Suffering for Doing Good

8Finally, all of you, live in harmony with one another; be sympathetic, love as
brothers,[i] be compassionate and humble.[j] 9Do not repay evil with evil[k] or insult
with insult,[l] but with blessing, because to this[m] you were called so that you may
inherit a blessing.[n] 10For,

"Whoever would love life
  and see good days
must keep his tongue from evil
  and his lips from deceitful speech.
11He must turn from evil and do good;
  he must seek peace and pursue it.
12For the eyes of the Lord are on the righteous
  and his ears are attentive to their prayer,
but the face of the Lord is against those who do evil."[a][o]

13Who is going to harm you if you are eager to do good?[p] 14But even if you should
suffer for what is right, you are blessed.[q] "Do not fear what they fear;[b] do not be
frightened."[c][r] 15But in your hearts set apart Christ as Lord. Always be prepared to
give an answer[s] to everyone who asks you to give the reason for the hope that you
have. But do this with gentleness and respect, 16keeping a clear conscience,[t] so that
those who speak maliciously against your good behaviour in Christ may be ashamed
of their slander.[u] 17It is better, if it is God's will,[v] to suffer for doing good[w] than
for doing evil. 18For Christ died for sins[x] once for all, the righteous for the unright-

a *12* Psalm 34:12–16 **b** *14* Or *not fear their threats* **c** *14* Isaiah 8:12

3:8
[i] Ro 12:10
[j] 1Pe 5:5

3:9
[k] Ro 12:17
[l] 1Pe 2:23
[m] 1Pe 2:21
[n] Heb 6:14

3:12
[o] Ps 34:12-16

3:13
[p] Pr 16:7

3:14
[q] 1Pe 2:19, 20; 4:15, 16
[r] Isa 8:12, 13

3:15
[s] Col 4:6

3:16
[t] Heb 13:18
[u] 1Pe 2:12, 15

3:17
[v] 1Pe 2:15
[w] 1Pe 2:20

3:18
[x] 1Pe 2:21

3:8 Peter lists five key elements that should characterise any group of believers: (1) harmony – pursuing the same goals; (2) sympathy – being responsive to others' needs; (3) love – seeing and treating each other as brothers and sisters; (4) compassion – being affectionately sensitive and caring; and (5) humility – being willing to encourage one another and rejoice in each other's successes. These five qualities go a long way towards helping believers serve God effectively.

3:8, 9 Peter developed the qualities of compassion and humility the hard way. In his early days with Christ, these attitudes did not come naturally to his impulsive, strong-willed personality (see Mark 8:31–33; John 13:6–9 for examples of Peter's blustering). But the Holy Spirit changed Peter, moulding his strong personality to God's use, and teaching him tenderness and humility.

3:9 In our fallen world, it is often deemed acceptable by some to tear people down verbally or to get back at them if we feel hurt. Peter, remembering Jesus' teaching to turn the other cheek (Matthew 5:39), encourages his readers to pay back wrongs by praying for the offenders. In God's kingdom, revenge is unacceptable behaviour, as is insulting a person, no matter how indirectly it is done. Rise above getting back at those who hurt you. Instead of reacting angrily to these people, pray for them.

3:10 For more about controlling your tongue, see the notes in James 3:2–18.

3:11 Too often we see peace as merely the absence of conflict, and we think of peacemaking as a passive role. But an effective peacemaker actively pursues peace. He or she builds good relationships, knowing that peace is a by-product of commitment. The peacemaker anticipates problems and deals with them before they occur. When conflicts arise, he or she brings them into the open and deals with them before they grow unmanageable. Making peace can be harder work than waging war, but it results not in death but in life and happiness.

3:14, 15 Rather than fear our enemies, we are to quietly trust in God as the Lord of all. We must believe that Christ is truly in control of all events. When he rules our thoughts and emotions, we cannot be shaken by anything our enemies may do.

3:15 Some Christians believe that faith is a personal matter that should be kept to oneself. It is true that we shouldn't be boisterous or obnoxious in sharing our faith, but we should always be ready to give an answer, gently and respectfully, when asked about our faith, our life-style, or our Christian perspective. Can others see your hope in Christ? Are you prepared to tell them what Christ has done in your life?

3:16 You may not be able to keep people from slandering you, but you can at least stop supplying them with ammunition. As long as you do what is right, their accusations will be empty and will only embarrass them. Keep your conduct above criticism!

3:18–20 The meaning of preaching "to the spirits in prison" is not completely clear, and commentators have explained it in different ways. The traditional interpretation is that Christ, between his death and resurrection, announced salvation to God's faithful followers who had been waiting for their salvation during the whole Old Testament era. Matthew records that when Jesus died, "the bodies of many holy people who had died were raised to life. They came out of the tombs, and after Jesus' resurrection they went into the holy city and appeared to many people" (Matthew 27:52, 53). A few commentators think that this passage says that Christ's Spirit was in Noah as Noah preached to those imprisoned by sin (but now in hell). Still others hold that Christ went to Hades to proclaim his victory and final condemnation to the fallen angels imprisoned there since Noah's day (see 2 Peter 2:4).

In any case, the passage shows that Christ's Good News of salvation and victory is not limited. It has been preached in the past as well as in the present; it has gone to the dead as well as to the living. God has given everyone the opportunity to come to him, but this does not imply a second chance for those who reject Christ in this life.

eous, to bring you to God. He was put to death in the body[y] but made alive by the
Spirit,[z] 19through whom[d] also he went and preached to the spirits in prison[a] 20who
disobeyed long ago when God waited patiently in the days of Noah while the ark was
being built.[b] In it only a few people, eight in all, were saved[c] through water, 21and
this water symbolises baptism that now saves you[d] also — not the removal of dirt from
the body but the pledge[e] of a good conscience towards God. It saves you by the
resurrection of Jesus Christ,[e] 22who has gone into heaven and is at God's right
hand[f] — with angels, authorities and powers in submission to him.[g]

Living for God

4 Therefore, since Christ suffered in his body, arm yourselves also with the same
attitude, because he who has suffered in his body is done with sin. 2As a result,
he does not live the rest of his earthly life for evil human desires,[a] but rather for the
will of God. 3For you have spent enough time in the past[b] doing what pagans choose
to do — living in debauchery, lust, drunkenness, orgies, carousing and detestable
idolatry. 4They think it strange that you do not plunge with them into the same flood
of dissipation, and they heap abuse on you.[c] 5But they will have to give account to
him who is ready to judge the living and the dead.[d] 6For this is the reason the gospel
was preached even to those who are now dead,[e] so that they might be judged
according to men in regard to the body, but live according to God in regard to the
spirit.
7The end of all things is near.[f] Therefore be clear minded and self-controlled so
that you can pray. 8Above all, love each other deeply,[g] because love covers over a
multitude of sins.[h] 9Offer hospitality to one another without grumbling.[i] 10Each one
should use whatever gift he has received to serve others,[j] faithfully[k] administering
God's grace in its various forms. 11If anyone speaks, he should do it as one speaking
the very words of God. If anyone serves, he should do it with the strength God

d *18,19* Or *alive in the spirit,* 19*through which* **e** *21* Or *response*

3:18 [y]Col 1:22; 1Pe 4:1 [z]1Pe 4:6
3:19 [a]1Pe 4:6
3:20 [b]Ge 6:3, 5, 13, 14 [c]Heb 11:7
3:21 [d]Tit 3:5 [e]1Pe 1:3
3:22 [f]Mk 16:19 [g]Ro 8:38
4:2 [a]Ro 6:2
4:3 [b]Eph 2:2
4:4 [c]1Pe 3:16
4:5 [d]Ac 10:42; 2Ti 4:1
4:6 [e]1Pe 3:19
4:7 [f]Ro 13:11
4:8 [g]1Pe 1:22 [h]Pr 10:12
4:9 [i]Php 2:14
4:10 [j]Ro 12:6, 7 [k]1Co 4:2

3:21 Peter says that Noah's salvation *through water* symbolised baptism, a ceremony involving water. In baptism we identify with Jesus Christ, who separates us from the lost and gives us new life. It is not the ceremony that saves us, but faith in Christ's death and resurrection. Baptism is the symbol of the transformation that happens in the hearts of those who believe (Romans 6:3–5; Galatians 3:27; Colossians 2:12). By identifying themselves with Christ through baptism, Peter's readers could resist turning back, even under the pressure of persecution. Public baptism would keep them from the temptation to renounce their faith.

4:1, 2 Some people will do anything to avoid pain. As followers of Christ, however, we should be willing and prepared to do God's will and to suffer for it if necessary. Sin loses its power to defeat us in our suffering if we focus on Christ and what he wants us to do. When our bodies are in pain or our lives are in jeopardy, our real values show up clearly, and sinful pleasures seem less important. If anyone suffers for doing good and still faithfully obeys in spite of suffering, that person has made a clean break with sin.

4:3, 4 A person whose life changes radically at conversion may experience contempt from his or her old friends. He may be scorned not only because he refuses to participate in certain activities, but also because his priorities have changed and he is now heading in the opposite direction. His very life incriminates their sinful activities. Mature Christians should help new believers resist such pressures of opposition by encouraging them to be faithful to Christ. *Dissipation* refers to wasteful expenditure and intemperate pursuit of pleasure, especially drinking to excess.

4:5 The basis of salvation is our belief in Jesus (Acts 16:31), but the basis for judgment is how we have lived. Those who inflict persecution are marked for punishment when they stand before God. Believers have nothing to fear, however, because Jesus will be the final Judge over all (John 5:22; 2 Timothy 4:1).

4:5, 6 Many people in the early church had concerns about life after death. In Thessalonica, Christians worried that loved ones who died before Christ's return might never see Christ (1 Thessalonians 4:13–18). Peter's readers needed to be reminded that the dead (both the faithful and their oppressors) would be judged. The judgment will be perfectly fair, he pointed out, because even the dead have heard the gospel (see also 3:18, 19). The Good News was first announced when Jesus Christ preached on the earth, but it has been operating since before the creation of the world (Ephesians 1:4), and it affects all people, the dead as well as the living.

4:7–9 We should live expectantly because Christ is coming. Getting ready to meet Christ involves continually growing in love for God and for others (see Jesus' summary of the law in Matthew 22:37–40). It is important to pray regularly, and it is also important to reach out to needy people. Your possessions, status, and power will mean nothing in God's kingdom, but you will spend eternity with other people. Invest your time and talents where they will make an eternal difference.

4:9 For more about hospitality, see the note on Romans 12:13.

4:10, 11 Some people, well aware of their abilities, believe that they have the right to use their abilities as they please. Others feel that they have no special talents at all. Peter addresses both groups in these verses. Everyone has some gifts; find yours and use them. All our abilities should be used in serving others; none are for our own exclusive enjoyment. Peter mentions speaking and serving. Paul lists these and other abilities in Romans 12:6–8; 1 Corinthians 12:8–11; Ephesians 4:11.

4:11 How is God praised when we use our abilities? When we use them as he directs, to help others, they will see Jesus in us and praise him for the help they have received. Peter may have been thinking of Jesus' words, "Let your light shine before men, that they may see your good deeds and praise your Father in heaven" (Matthew 5:16).

provides,[l] so that in all things God may be praised[m] through Jesus Christ. To him
be the glory and the power for ever and ever. Amen.

Suffering for Being a Christian

12Dear friends, do not be surprised at the painful trial you are suffering,[n] as though
something strange were happening to you. 13But rejoice that you participate in the
sufferings of Christ, so that you may be overjoyed when his glory is revealed.[o] 14If
you are insulted because of the name of Christ, you are blessed,[p] for the Spirit of
glory and of God rests on you. 15If you suffer, it should not be as a murderer or thief
or any other kind of criminal, or even as a meddler. 16However, if you suffer as a
Christian, do not be ashamed, but praise God that you bear that name.[q] 17For it is
time for judgment to begin with the family of God;[r] and if it begins with us, what
will the outcome be for those who do not obey the gospel of God?[s] 18And,

> "If it is hard for the righteous to be saved,
> what will become of the ungodly and the sinner?"[a][t]

19So then, those who suffer according to God's will should commit themselves to
their faithful Creator and continue to do good.

3. The shepherding of God's people in the midst of suffering

To Elders and Young Men

5 To the elders among you, I appeal as a fellow-elder,[a] a witness[b] of Christ's
sufferings and one who also will share in the glory to be revealed:[c] 2Be shepherds
of God's flock[d] that is under your care, serving as overseers—not because you must,
but because you are willing, as God wants you to be; not greedy for money,[e] but
eager to serve; 3not lording it over[f] those entrusted to you, but being examples[g] to
the flock. 4And when the Chief Shepherd appears, you will receive the crown of
glory[h] that will never fade away.

a *18* Prov. 11:31

4:11 [l]Eph 6:10 [m]1Co 10:31
4:12 [n]1Pe 1:6, 7
4:13 [o]Ro 8:17
4:14 [p]Mt 5:11
4:16 [q]Ac 5:41
4:17 [r]Jer 25:29 [s]2Th 1:8
4:18 [t]Pr 11:31; Lk 23:31
5:1 [a]Ac 11:30 [b]Lk 24:48 [c]1Pe 1:5, 7; Rev 1:9
5:2 [d]Jn 21:16 [e]1Ti 3:3
5:3 [f]Eze 34:4 [g]Php 3:17
5:4 [h]1Co 9:25

4:14–16 Again Peter brings to mind Jesus' words: "Blessed are you when people insult you, persecute you and falsely say all kinds of evil against you because of me" (Matthew 5:11). Christ will send his Spirit to strengthen those who are persecuted for their faith. This does not mean that all suffering is the result of good Christian conduct. Sometimes a person will grumble, "He's just picking on me because I'm a Christian," when it's obvious to everyone else that the person's own unpleasant behaviour is the cause of his or her problems. It may take careful thought or wise counsel to determine the real cause of our suffering. We can be assured, however, that whenever we suffer because of our loyalty to Christ, he will be with us all the way.

4:16 It is not shameful to suffer for being a Christian. When Peter and John were persecuted for preaching the Good News, they rejoiced because such persecution was a mark of God's approval of their work (Acts 5:41). Don't seek out suffering, and don't try to avoid it. Instead, keep on doing what is right regardless of the suffering it might bring.

4:17, 18 This refers not to final judgment but to God's refining discipline (Hebrews 12:7). God often allows believers to sin and then experience the consequences. He does this for several reasons: (1) to show us our potential for sinning, (2) to encourage us to turn from sin and more constantly depend on him, (3) to prepare us to face other, even stronger temptations in the future, and (4) to help us stay faithful and keep on trusting him. If believers need earthly discipline (judgment) from God, how much more will unbelievers receive it? If it is hard for the righteous to be saved (only because of God's mercy), what chance do those have who reject Christ?

4:19 God created the world, and he has faithfully ordered it and kept it since the creation. Because we know that God is faithful, we can count on him to fulfil his promises to us. If God can oversee the forces of nature, surely he can see us through the trials we face.

5:1 Elders were church officers providing supervision, protection, discipline, instruction, and direction for the other believers. *Elder* simply means "older". Both Greeks and Jews gave positions of great honour to wise older men, and the Christian church continued this pattern of leadership. Elders carried great responsibility, and they were expected to be good examples.

5:1, 2 Peter, one of Jesus' 12 disciples, was one of the three who saw Christ's glory at the transfiguration (Mark 9:1–13; 2 Peter 1:16–18). Often the spokesman for the apostles, Peter witnessed Jesus' death and resurrection, preached at Pentecost, and became a pillar of the Jerusalem church. But writing to the elders, he identified himself as a fellow elder, not a superior. He asked them to "be shepherds of God's flock", exactly what Jesus had told him to do (John 21:15–17). Peter was taking his own advice as he worked along with the other elders in caring for God's faithful people. His identification with the elders is a powerful example of Christian leadership, where authority is based on service, not power (Mark 10:42–45).

5:2–5 Peter describes several characteristics of good leaders in the church: (1) they realise they are caring for God's flock, not their own; (2) they lead out of eagerness to serve, not out of obligation; (3) they are concerned for what they can give, not for what they can get; (4) they lead by example, not force. All of us lead others in some way. Whatever our role, our leadership should be in line with these characteristics.

5:4 The Chief Shepherd is Jesus Christ. This refers to his second coming, when he will judge all people.

5:5 [i]Eph 5:21 [j]Pr 3:34; Jas 4:6
5:6 [k]Jas 4:10
5:7 [l]Ps 37:5; Mt 6:25 [m]Heb 13:5
5:8 [n]Job 1:7
5:9 [o]Jas 4:7 [p]Col 2:5 [q]Ac 14:22
5:10 [r]2Co 4:17 [s]2Th 2:17
5:11 [t]Ro 11:36
5:12 [u]2Co 1:19 [v]Heb 13:22
5:13 [w]Ac 12:12
5:14 [x]Ro 16:16 [y]Eph 6:23

5Young men, in the same way be submissive[i] to those who are older. All of you,
clothe yourselves with humility towards one another, because,

> "God opposes the proud
> but gives grace to the humble."[a][j]

6Humble yourselves, therefore, under God's mighty hand, that he may lift you up in
due time.[k] 7Cast all your anxiety on him[l] because he cares for you.[m]
8Be self-controlled and alert. Your enemy the devil prowls around[n] like a roaring
lion looking for someone to devour. 9Resist him,[o] standing firm in the faith,[p]
because you know that your brothers throughout the world are undergoing the same
kind of sufferings.[q]
10And the God of all grace, who called you to his eternal glory[r] in Christ, after
you have suffered a little while, will himself restore you and make you strong,[s] firm
and steadfast. 11To him be the power for ever and ever. Amen.[t]

Final Greetings

12With the help of Silas,[b][u] whom I regard as a faithful brother, I have written to
you briefly,[v] encouraging you and testifying that this is the true grace of God. Stand
fast in it.
13She who is in Babylon, chosen together with you, sends you her greetings, and
so does my son Mark.[w] 14Greet one another with a kiss of love.[x]
Peace[y] to all of you who are in Christ.

a *5* Prov. 3:34 b *12* Greek *Silvanus*, a variant of *Silas*

5:5 Both young and old can benefit from Peter's instructions. Pride often keeps older people from trying to understand young people and keeps young people from listening to those who are older. Peter told both young and old to be humble and to serve each other. Young men should follow the leadership of older men, who should lead by example. Respect those who are older than you, listen to those younger than you, and be humble enough to admit that you can learn from each other.

5:6 We often worry about our position and status, hoping to get proper recognition for what we do. But Peter advises us to remember that God's recognition counts for more than human praise. God is able and willing to bless us according to his timing. Humbly obey God regardless of present circumstances, and in his good time—either in this life or in the next—he will lift you up.

5:7 Carrying your worries, stresses, and daily struggles by yourself shows that you have not trusted God fully with your life. It takes humility, however, to recognise that God cares, to admit your need, and to let others in God's family help you. Sometimes we think that struggles caused by our own sin and foolishness are not God's concern. But when we turn to God in repentance, he will bear the weight even of those struggles. Letting God have your anxieties calls for action, not passivity. Don't submit to circumstances, but to the Lord who controls circumstances.

5:8, 9 Lions attack sick, young, or straggling animals; they choose victims who are alone or not alert. Peter warns us to watch out for Satan when we are suffering or being persecuted. Feeling alone, weak, helpless, and cut off from other believers, so focused on our troubles that we forget to watch for danger, we are especially vulnerable to Satan's attacks. During times of suffering, seek other Christians for support. Keep your eyes on Christ, and resist the devil. Then, says James, "he will flee from you" (James 4:7).

5:10 When we are suffering, we often feel as though our pain will never end. Peter gave these faithful Christians the wider perspective. In comparison with eternity, their suffering would last only "a little while". Some of Peter's readers would be strengthened and delivered in their own lifetimes. Others would be released from their suffering through death. All of God's faithful followers are assured of an eternal life with Christ where there will be no suffering (Revelation 21:4).

5:12 Silas was one of the men chosen to deliver the letter from the Jerusalem council to the church in Antioch (Acts 15:22). He accompanied Paul on his second missionary journey (Acts 15:40–18:11), is mentioned by Paul in the salutation of Paul's letters to the Thessalonians (1 Thessalonians 1:1; 2 Thessalonians 1:1), and ministered with Timothy in Corinth (2 Corinthians 1:19).

5:13 *Babylon* has been broadly understood by believers to be a reference to Rome. Just as the nation of Israel had been under captivity to Babylon, so the Christians as the new Israel were exiles in a foreign land.

5:13 Mark, also called John Mark, was known to many of this letter's readers because he had travelled widely (Acts 12:25–13:13; 15:36–41) and was recognised as a leader in the church (Colossians 4:10; Philemon 24). Mark was probably with the disciples at the time of Jesus' arrest (Mark 14:51, 52). Tradition holds that Peter was Mark's main source of information when Mark wrote his Gospel.

5:14 Peter wrote this letter just before the cruel Emperor Nero began persecuting Christians in Rome and throughout the empire. Afraid for his life, Peter had three times denied even knowing Jesus (John 18:15–27). But here, having learned how to stand firm in an evil world, he encouraged other Christians who were facing persecution for their faith. Peter himself lived by the words he wrote, because he was martyred for his faith. Those who stand for Christ will be persecuted because the world is ruled by Christ's greatest enemy. But just as the small group of early believers stood against persecution, so we must be willing to stand for our faith with the patience, endurance, and courage that Peter exhibited.

2 PETER

VITAL STATISTICS

PURPOSE:
To warn Christians about false teachers and to exhort them to grow in their faith in and knowledge of Christ

AUTHOR:
Peter

TO WHOM WRITTEN:
The church at large, and all believers everywhere

DATE WRITTEN:
About A.D. 67, three years after 1 Peter was written, possibly from Rome

SETTING:
Peter knew that his time on earth was limited (1:13, 14), so he wrote about what was on his heart, warning believers of what would happen when he was gone—especially about the presence of false teachers. He reminded his readers of the unchanging truth of the gospel.

KEY VERSE:
"His divine power has given us everything we need for life and godliness through our knowledge of him who called us by his own glory and goodness" (1:3).

KEY PEOPLE:
Peter, Paul

SPECIAL FEATURES:
The date and destination are uncertain, and the authorship has been disputed. Because of this, 2 Peter was the last book admitted to the canon of the New Testament Scripture. Also, there are similarities between 2 Peter and Jude.

WARNINGS have many forms—lights, signs, sights, sounds, smells, feelings, and written words. With varied focus, their purpose is the same—to advise alertness and caution because of imminent danger. Responses to these warnings will also vary, from disregard and neglect to evasive or corrective action. How a person reacts to a warning is usually determined by the situation and the source. An impending storm is treated differently from an oncoming car, and the counsel of a trusted friend is heeded much more than the flippant remark by a stranger or the fearful guess of a child.

Second Peter is a letter of warning—from an authority none other than the courageous, experienced, and faithful apostle. And it is the last communication from this great warrior of Christ. Soon thereafter he would die, martyred for the faith.

Previously Peter had written to comfort and encourage believers in the midst of suffering and persecution—an external onslaught. But three years later, in this letter containing his last words, he wrote to warn them of an internal attack—complacency and heresy. He spoke of holding fast to the non-negotiable facts of the faith, of growing and maturing in the faith, and of rejecting all who would distort the truth. To follow this advice would ensure Christ-honouring individuals and Christ-centred churches.

After a brief greeting (1:1), Peter gives the antidote for stagnancy and shortsightedness in the Christian life (1:2–11). Then he explains that his days are numbered (1:12–15) and that the believers should listen to his messages and the words of Scripture (1:16–21).

Next, Peter gives a blunt warning about false teachers (2:1–22). They will become prevalent in the last days (2:1, 2), they will do or say anything for money (2:3), they will spurn the things of God (2:2, 10, 11), they will do whatever they feel like doing (2:12–17), they will be proud and boastful (2:18, 19), and they will be judged and punished by God (2:3–10, 20–22).

Peter concludes his brief letter by explaining why he has written it (3:1–18)—to remind them of the words of the prophets and apostles that predicted the coming of false teachers, to give the reasons for the delay in Christ's return (3:1–13), and to encourage them to beware of heresies and to grow in their faith (3:14–18).

Addressed to those who "have received a faith as precious as ours", 2 Peter could have been written to us. Our world is filled with false prophets and teachers who claim to have the truth and who clamour for attention and allegiance. Listen carefully to Peter's message and heed his warning. Determine to grow in your knowledge of Christ and to reject all those who preach anything inconsistent with God's word.

THE BLUEPRINT

1. Guidance for growing Christians (1:1–21)
2. Danger to growing Christians (2:1–22)
3. Hope for growing Christians (3:1–18)

While Peter wrote his first letter to teach about handling persecution (trials from without), he wrote this letter to teach about handling heresy (trials from within). False teachers are often subtly deceitful. Believers today must still be vigilant against falling into false doctrine, heresy, and cult activity. This letter gives us clues to help detect false teaching.

MEGATHEMES

THEME	EXPLANATION	IMPORTANCE
Diligence	If our faith is real, it will be evident in our faithful behaviour. If people are diligent in Christian growth, they won't backslide or be deceived by false teachers.	Growth is essential. It begins with faith and culminates in love for others. To keep growing we need to know God, keep on following him, and remember what he taught us. We must remain diligent in faithful obedience and Christian growth.
False Teachers	Peter warns the church to beware of false teachers. These teachers were proud of their position, promoted sexual sin, and advised against keeping the Ten Commandments. Peter countered them by pointing to the Spirit-inspired Scriptures as our authority.	Christians need discernment to be able to resist false teachers. God can rescue us from their lies if we stay true to his word, the Bible, and reject those who distort the truth.
Christ's Return	One day Christ will create a new heaven and earth where we will live for ever. As Christians, our hope is in this promise. But with Christ's return comes his judgment on all who refuse to believe.	The cure for complacency, lawlessness, and heresy is found in the confident assurance that Christ will return. God is still giving unbelievers time to repent. To be ready, Christians must keep on trusting and resist the pressure to give up waiting for Christ's return.

1:1
[a] Ro 1:1
[b] 1Pe 1:1
[c] Ro 3:21-26
[d] Tit 2:13

1. Guidance for growing Christians

1 Simon Peter, a servant[a] and apostle of Jesus Christ,[b]

To those who through the righteousness[c] of our God and Saviour Jesus Christ[d]
have received a faith as precious as ours:

1:2
[e] Php 3:8

2Grace and peace be yours in abundance through the knowledge of God and of
Jesus our Lord.[e]

1:1 Peter's first letter was written just before the time that the Roman Emperor Nero began his persecution of Christians. This letter was written two or three years later (between A.D. 66–68), after persecution had intensified. First Peter was a letter of encouragement to the Christians who suffered, but 2 Peter focuses on the church's internal problems, especially on the false teachers who were causing people to doubt their faith and turn away from Christianity. Second Peter combats their heresies by denouncing the evil motives of the false teachers and reaffirming Christianity's truths – the authority of Scripture, the primacy of faith, and the certainty of Christ's return.

1:2 Many believers want an abundance of God's grace and peace, but they are unwilling to put forth the effort to get to know him better through Bible study and prayer. To enjoy the privileges God offers us freely, we have "the knowledge of God and of Jesus our Lord".

Making One's Calling and Election Sure

3 His divine power[f] has given us everything we need for life and godliness through
our knowledge of him who called us[g] by his own glory and goodness. 4 Through these
he has given us his very great and precious promises,[h] so that through them you may
participate in the divine nature[i] and escape the corruption in the world caused by evil
desires.[j]
5 For this very reason, make every effort to add to your faith goodness; and to
goodness, knowledge;[k] 6 and to knowledge, self-control;[l] and to self-control, perseverance; and to perseverance, godliness;[m] 7 and to godliness, brotherly kindness;
and to brotherly kindness, love.[n] 8 For if you possess these qualities in increasing
measure, they will keep you from being ineffective and unproductive[o] in your
knowledge of our Lord Jesus Christ. 9 But if anyone does not have them, he is
short-sighted and blind,[p] and has forgotten that he has been cleansed from his past
sins.[q]
10 Therefore, my brothers, be all the more eager to make your calling and election
sure. For if you do these things, you will never fall,[r] 11 and you will receive a rich
welcome into the eternal kingdom of our Lord and Saviour Jesus Christ.

Prophecy of Scripture

12 So I will always remind you of these things,[s] even though you know them and
are firmly established in the truth you now have. 13 I think it is right to refresh your
memory as long as I live in the tent of this body,[t] 14 because I know that I will soon
put it aside,[u] as our Lord Jesus Christ has made clear to me.[v] 15 And I will make
every effort to see that after my departure[w] you will always be able to remember these
things.
16 We did not follow cleverly invented stories when we told you about the power

1:3 [f] 1Pe 1:5 [g] 1Th 2:12
1:4 [h] 2Co 7:1 [i] Eph 4:24; Heb 12:10; 1Jn 3:2 [j] 2Pe 2:18-20
1:5 [k] Col 2:3
1:6 [l] Ac 24:25 [m] ver 3
1:7 [n] 1Th 3:12
1:8 [o] Jn 15:2; Tit 3:14
1:9 [p] 1Jn 2:11 [q] Eph 5:26
1:10 [r] 2Pe 3:17
1:12 [s] Php 3:1; 1Jn 2:21
1:13 [t] 2Co 5:1, 4
1:14 [u] 2Ti 4:6 [v] Jn 21:18, 19
1:15 [w] Lk 9:31

1:3, 4 The power to grow doesn't come from within us, but from God. Because we don't have the resources to be truly godly, God allows us to "participate in the divine nature" in order to keep us from sin and help us live for him. When we are born again, God by his Spirit empowers us with his own moral goodness. See John 3:6; 14:17–23; 2 Corinthians 5:21; and 1 Peter 1:22, 23.

1:5–9 Faith must be more than belief in certain facts; it must result in action, growth in Christian character, and the practice of moral discipline, or it will die away (James 2:14–17). Peter lists several of faith's actions: learning to know God better, developing perseverance, doing God's will, loving others. These actions do not come automatically; they require hard work. They are not optional; all of them must be a continual part of the Christian life. We don't finish one and start on the next, but we work on them all together. God empowers and enables us, but he also gives us the responsibility to learn and to grow. We should not be surprised at or resentful of the process.

1:6 False teachers were saying that self-control was not needed because deeds do not help the believer anyway (2:19). It is true that deeds cannot save us, but it is absolutely false to think they are unimportant. We are saved so that we can grow to resemble Christ and so that we can serve others. God wants to produce his character in us. But to do this, he demands our discipline and effort. As we obey Christ who guides us by his Spirit, we will develop self-control, not only with respect to food and drink, but also with respect to our emotions.

1:9 Our faith must go beyond what we believe; it must become a dynamic part of all we do, resulting in good fruit and spiritual maturity. Salvation does not depend on good deeds, but it results in good deeds. A person who claims to be saved while remaining unchanged does not understand faith or what God has done for him or her.

1:10 Peter wanted to rouse the complacent believers who had listened to the false teachers and believed that because salvation is not based on good deeds they could live any way they wanted. If you truly belong to the Lord, Peter wrote, your hard work will prove it. If you're not working to develop the qualities listed in 1:5–7, maybe you don't belong to him. If you are the Lord's – and your hard work backs up your claim to be chosen by God ("calling and election") – you will never be led astray by the lure of false teaching or glamorous sin.

1:12–15 Outstanding coaches constantly review the basics of the sport with their teams, and good athletes can execute the fundamentals consistently well. We must not neglect the basics of our faith when we go on to study deeper truths. Just as an athlete needs constant practice, we need constant reminders of the fundamentals of our faith and of how we came to believe in the first place. Don't allow yourself to be bored or impatient with messages on the basics of the Christian life. Instead, take the attitude of an athlete who continues to practise and refine the basics even as he or she learns more advanced skills.

1:13, 14 Peter knew that he would die soon. Many years before, Christ had prepared Peter for the kind of death Peter would face (see John 21:18, 19). At this time, Peter knew that his death was at hand. Peter was martyred for the faith in about A.D. 68. According to one tradition, he was crucified upside down, at his own request, because he did not feel worthy to die in the same manner as his Master.

1:16–18 Peter is referring to the transfiguration where Jesus' divine identity was revealed to him and two other disciples, James and John (see Matthew 17:1–8; Mark 9:2–8; Luke 9:28–36).

1:16–21 This section is a strong statement on the inspiration of Scripture. Peter affirms that the Old Testament prophets wrote God's messages. He puts himself and the other apostles in the same category, because they also proclaim God's truth. The Bible is not a collection of fables or human ideas about God. It is God's very words given *through* people *to* people. Peter emphasised his authority as an eyewitness as well as the God-inspired authority of Scripture to prepare the way for his harsh words against the false teachers. If these wicked men were contradicting the apostles and the Bible, their message could not be from God.

and coming of our Lord Jesus Christ, but we were eye-witnesses of his majesty.[x]
17 For he received honour and glory from God the Father when the voice came to him
from the Majestic Glory, saying, "This is my Son, whom I love; with him I am well
pleased."[a][y] 18 We ourselves heard this voice that came from heaven when we were
with him on the sacred mountain.[z]

19 And we have the word of the prophets made more certain, and you will do well
to pay attention to it, as to a light[a] shining in a dark place, until the day dawns and
the morning star[b] rises in your hearts. 20 Above all, you must understand that no
prophecy of Scripture came about by the prophet's own interpretation. 21 For prophecy
never had its origin in the will of man, but men spoke from God[c] as they were carried
along by the Holy Spirit.[d]

2. Danger to growing Christians

False Teachers and Their Destruction

2 But there were also false prophets[a] among the people, just as there will be false
teachers among you.[b] They will secretly introduce destructive heresies, even
denying the sovereign Lord[c] who bought them[d]—bringing swift destruction on
themselves. 2 Many will follow their shameful ways and will bring the way of truth
into disrepute. 3 In their greed these teachers will exploit you[e] with stories they have
made up. Their condemnation has long been hanging over them, and their destruction
has not been sleeping.

4 For if God did not spare angels when they sinned, but sent them to hell,[a] putting
them into gloomy dungeons[b] to be held for judgment;[f] 5 if he did not spare the ancient
world[g] when he brought the flood on its ungodly people, but protected Noah, a
preacher of righteousness, and seven others;[h] 6 if he condemned the cities of Sodom
and Gomorrah by burning them to ashes,[i] and made them an example[j] of what is
going to happen to the ungodly; 7 and if he rescued Lot,[k] a righteous man, who was
distressed by the filthy lives of lawless men[l] 8 (for that righteous man, living among
them day after day, was tormented in his righteous soul by the lawless deeds he saw
and heard)—9 if this is so, then the Lord knows how to rescue godly men from trials[m]
and to hold the unrighteous for the day of judgment, while continuing their punish-

[a] *17* Matt. 17:5; Mark 9:7; Luke 9:35 [a] *4* Greek *Tartarus* [b] *4* Some manuscripts *into chains of darkness*

1:16 [x] Mt 17:1-8
1:17 [y] Mt 3:17
1:18 [z] Mt 17:6
1:19 [a] Ps 119:105 [b] Rev 22:16
1:21 [c] 2Ti 3:16 [d] 2Sa 23:2; Ac 1:16; 1Pe 1:11
2:1 [a] Dt 13:1-3 [b] 1Ti 4:1 [c] Jude 4 [d] 1Co 6:20
2:3 [e] 2Co 2:17; 1Th 2:5
2:4 [f] Jude 6; Rev 20:1, 2
2:5 [g] 2Pe 3:6 [h] Heb 11:7; 1Pe 3:20
2:6 [i] Ge 19:24, 25 [j] Nu 26:10; Jude 7
2:7 [k] Ge 19:16 [l] 2Pe 3:17
2:9 [m] 1Co 10:13

1:19 Christ is the "morning star", and when he returns, he will shine in his full glory. Until that day we have Scripture as a light and the Holy Spirit to illuminate Scripture for us and guide us as we seek the truth. For more on Christ as the morning star, see Luke 1:78; Ephesians 5:14; Revelation 2:28; 22:16.

1:20, 21 "Men spoke from God as they were carried along by the Holy Spirit" means that Scripture did not come from the creative work of the prophets' own invention or interpretation. God inspired the writers, so their message is authentic and reliable. God used the talents, education, and cultural background of each writer (they were not mindless robots); and God co-operated with the writers in such a way as to ensure that the message he intended was faithfully communicated in the very words they wrote.

2:1 Jesus had told the disciples that false teachers would come (Matthew 24:11; Mark 13:22, 23). Peter had heard these words, and at this time he was seeing them come true. Just as false prophets had contradicted the true prophets in Old Testament times (see, for example, Jeremiah 23:16–40; 28:1–17), telling people only what they wanted to hear, so false teachers were twisting Christ's teachings and the words of his apostles. These teachers were belittling the significance of Jesus' life, death, and resurrection. Some claimed that Jesus couldn't be God; others claimed that he couldn't have been a real man. These teachers allowed and even encouraged all kinds of wrong and immoral acts, especially sexual sin. We must be careful to avoid false teachers today. Any book, tape series, or TV message must be evaluated according to God's word. Beware of special meanings or interpretations that belittle Christ or his work.

2:3 Teachers should be paid by the people they teach, but these false teachers were attempting to make more money by distorting the truth and saying what people wanted to hear. They were more interested in making money than in teaching truth. Peter and Paul both condemned greedy, lying teachers (see 1 Timothy 6:5). Before you send money to any cause, evaluate it carefully. Is the teacher or preacher clearly serving God or promoting his/her own interests? Will the money be used to promote valid ministry, or will it merely finance further promotions?

2:4–6 If God did not spare angels, or people who lived before the flood, or the citizens of Sodom and Gomorrah, he would not spare these false teachers. Some people would have us believe that God will save all people because he is so loving. But it is foolish to think that he will cancel the last judgment. These three examples should warn us clearly that God judges sin and that unrepentant sinners cannot escape.

2:7–9 Just as God rescued Lot from Sodom, so he is able to rescue us from the temptations and trials we face in a wicked world. Lot was not sinless, but he put his trust in God and was spared when Sodom was destroyed. For more information on Lot, see his Profile in Genesis 14. God will also judge those who cause the temptations and trials, so we need never worry about justice being done.

ment.[c] 10This is especially true of those who follow the corrupt desire[n] of the sinful
nature[d] and despise authority.
Bold and arrogant, these men are not afraid to slander celestial beings;[o] 11yet even
angels, although they are stronger and more powerful, do not bring slanderous
accusations against such beings in the presence of the Lord.[p] 12But these men
blaspheme in matters they do not understand. They are like brute beasts, creatures of
instinct, born only to be caught and destroyed, and like beasts they too will perish.[q]
13They will be paid back with harm for the harm they have done. Their idea of
pleasure is to carouse in broad daylight.[r] They are blots and blemishes, revelling in
their pleasures while they feast with you.[e][s] 14With eyes full of adultery, they never
stop sinning; they seduce[t] the unstable; they are experts in greed[u]—an accursed
brood![v] 15They have left the straight way and wandered off to follow the way of
Balaam[w] son of Beor, who loved the wages of wickedness. 16But he was rebuked
for his wrongdoing by a donkey—a beast without speech—who spoke with a man's
voice and restrained the prophet's madness.[x]
17These men are springs without water[y] and mists driven by a storm. Blackest
darkness is reserved for them.[z] 18For they mouth empty, boastful words[a] and, by
appealing to the lustful desires of sinful human nature, they entice people who are just
escaping from those who live in error. 19They promise them freedom, while they
themselves are slaves of depravity—for a man is a slave to whatever has mastered
him.[b] 20If they have escaped the corruption of the world by knowing[c] our Lord and
Saviour Jesus Christ and are again entangled in it and overcome, they are worse off
at the end than they were at the beginning.[d] 21It would have been better for them
not to have known the way of righteousness, than to have known it and then to turn
their backs on the sacred command that was passed on to them.[e] 22Of them the
proverbs are true: "A dog returns to its vomit,"[f][f] and, "A sow that is washed goes
back to her wallowing in the mud."

3. Hope for growing Christians

The Day of the Lord

3 Dear friends, this is now my second letter to you. I have written both of them
as reminders[a] to stimulate you to wholesome thinking. 2I want you to recall the
words spoken in the past by the holy prophets and the command given by our Lord
and Saviour through your apostles.

[c] 9 Or *unrighteous for punishment until the day of judgment* [d] 10 Or *the flesh* [e] 13 Some manuscripts *in their love feasts* [f] 22 Prov. 26:11

2:10 [n]2Pe 3:3 [o]Jude 8
2:11 [p]Jude 9
2:12 [q]Jude 10
2:13 [r]Ro 13:13 [s]1Co 11:20, 21; Jude 12
2:14 [t]ver 18 [u]ver 3 [v]Eph 2:3
2:15 [w]Nu 22:4-20; Jude 11
2:16 [x]Nu 22:21-30
2:17 [y]Jude 12 [z]Jude 13
2:18 [a]Jude 16
2:19 [b]Jn 8:34; Ro 6:16
2:20 [c]2Pe 1:2 [d]Mt 12:45
2:21 [e]Heb 6:4-6
2:22 [f]Pr 26:11
3:1 [a]2Pe 1:13

2:10–12 The *celestial beings* may be angels, all the glories of the unseen world, or more probably, fallen angels. A similar passage is found in Jude 8–10. Whoever they are, the false teachers slandered the spiritual realities they did not understand, taking Satan's power lightly and claiming to have the ability to judge evil. Many in our world today mock the supernatural. They deny the reality of the spiritual world and claim that only what can be seen and felt is real. Like the false teachers of Peter's day, they are fools who will be proved wrong in the end. Don't take Satan and his supernatural powers of evil lightly, and don't become arrogant about how defeated he will be. Although Satan will be destroyed completely, he is at work now trying to render Christians complacent and ineffective.

2:13, 14 The feast may have been part of the celebration of the Lord's Supper. The feast was a full meal that ended with Communion. The false teachers, although they were sinning openly, took part in these meals with everyone else in the church. In one of the greatest of hypocritical acts, they attended a sacred feast designed to promote love and unity among believers, while at the same time they gossiped and slandered those who disagreed with their opinions. As Paul told the Corinthians, "Therefore, whoever eats the bread or drinks the cup of the Lord in an unworthy manner will be guilty of sinning against the body and blood of the Lord" (1 Corinthians 11:27). These men were guilty of more than false teaching and promoting evil pleasures; they were guilty of leading others away from God's Son, Jesus.

2:15 Balaam was hired by a pagan king to curse Israel. He did what God told him to do for a time (Numbers 22–24), but eventually his evil motives and desire for money won out (Numbers 25:1–3; 31:16). Like the false teachers of Peter's day, Balaam used religion for personal advancement, a sin that God does not take lightly.

2:19 A person is a slave to whatever controls him or her. Many believe that freedom means doing anything we want. But no-one is ever completely free in that sense. If we refuse to follow God, we will follow our own sinful desires and become enslaved to what our bodies want. If we submit our lives to Christ, he will free us from slavery to sin. Christ frees us to serve him, a freedom that results in our ultimate good.

2:20–22 Peter is speaking of a person who has learned about Christ and how to be saved, and has even been positively influenced by Christians, but then rejects the truth and returns to his or her sin. This person is worse off than before, because he or she has rejected the only way out of sin, the only way of salvation. Like a person sinking in quicksand who refuses to grab the rope thrown to him or her, the one who turns away from Christ casts aside his or her only means of escape (see the note on Luke 11:24–26).

3:3
[b]1Ti 4:1
[c]2Pe 2:10; Jude 18
3:4
[d]Isa 5:19; Eze 12:22; Mt 24:48
[e]Mk 10:6
3:5
[f]Ge 1:6, 9; Heb 11:3
[g]Ps 24:2
3:6
[h]Ge 7:21, 22
3:7
[i]ver 10, 12; 2Th 1:7
3:8
[j]Ps 90:4
3:9
[k]Hab 2:3; Heb 10:37
[l]Ro 2:4
[m]1Ti 2:4
3:10
[n]Lk 12:39; 1Th 5:2
[o]Mt 24:35; Rev 21:1
3:12
[p]1Co 1:7
[q]Ps 50:3
[r]ver 10
3:13
[s]Isa 65:17; 66:22; Rev 21:1
3:14
[t]1Th 3:13
3:15
[u]Ro 2:4
[v]ver 9
[w]Eph 3:3
3:16
[x]2Pe 2:14
[y]ver 2

3 First of all, you must understand that in the last days[b] scoffers will come, scoffing
and following their own evil desires.[c] 4 They will say, "Where is this 'coming' he
promised?[d] Ever since our fathers died, everything goes on as it has since the
beginning of creation."[e] 5 But they deliberately forget that long ago by God's word[f]
the heavens existed and the earth was formed out of water and by water.[g] 6 By these
waters also the world of that time was deluged and destroyed.[h] 7 By the same word
the present heavens and earth are reserved for fire,[i] being kept for the day of judgment
and destruction of ungodly men.

8 But do not forget this one thing, dear friends: With the Lord a day is like a thousand
years, and a thousand years are like a day.[j] 9 The Lord is not slow in keeping his
promise,[k] as some understand slowness. He is patient[l] with you, not wanting anyone
to perish, but everyone to come to repentance.[m]

10 But the day of the Lord will come like a thief.[n] The heavens will disappear with
a roar; the elements will be destroyed by fire, and the earth and everything in it will
be laid bare.[a][o]

11 Since everything will be destroyed in this way, what kind of people ought you
to be? You ought to live holy and godly lives 12 as you look forward[p] to the day
of God and speed its coming.[b][q] That day will bring about the destruction of the heavens by fire, and the elements will melt in the heat.[r] 13 But in keeping with his
promise we are looking forward to a new heaven and a new earth,[s] the home of righteousness.

14 So then, dear friends, since you are looking forward to this, make every effort
to be found spotless, blameless[t] and at peace with him. 15 Bear in mind that our Lord's
patience[u] means salvation,[v] just as our dear brother Paul also wrote to you with the
wisdom that God gave him.[w] 16 He writes the same way in all his letters, speaking
in them of these matters. His letters contain some things that are hard to understand,
which ignorant and unstable[x] people distort, as they do the other Scriptures,[y] to their
own destruction.

a *10* Some manuscripts *be burned up* **b** *12* Or *as you wait eagerly for the day of God to come*

3:3, 4 "In the last days" scoffers will say that Jesus is never coming back, but Peter refutes their argument by explaining that God is the master of time. The "last days" is the time between Christ's first and second comings; thus we, like Peter, live in the last days. We must do the work to which God has called us and believe that he will return as he promised.

3:7 In Noah's day the earth was judged by water; at the second coming it will be judged by fire. This fire is described in Revelation 19:20; 20:10–15.

3:8, 9 God may have seemed slow to these believers as they faced persecution every day and longed to be delivered. But God is not slow; he simply works to his own timetable (Psalm 90:4). Jesus is waiting so that more sinners will repent and turn to him. We must not sit and wait for Christ to return, but we should live with the realisation that time is short and that we have important work to do. Be ready to meet Christ any time, even today; yet plan your course of service as though he may not return for many years.

3:10, 11 The day of the Lord is the day of God's judgment on the earth. Here it is used in reference to Christ's return. Christ's second coming will be sudden and terrible for those who do not believe in him. But if we are morally clean and spiritually alert, it won't come as a surprise. For other prophetic pictures of the day of the Lord, see Isaiah 34:4; Joel 3:15, 16; Matthew 24; Mark 13; Luke 21; Revelation 6:12–17. Realising that the earth is going to be burned up, we should put our confidence in what is lasting and eternal and not be bound to earth and its treasures or pursuits. Do you spend more of your time piling up possessions, or striving to develop Christlike character?

3:13 God's purpose for people is not destruction but re-creation (see Isaiah 66:22; Revelation 21; 22). God will purify the heavens and earth with fire; then he will create them anew. We can joyously look forward to the restoration of God's good world.

3:14 We should not become lazy and complacent because Christ has not yet returned. Instead, we should live in eager expectation of his coming. What would you like to be doing when Christ returns? That is how you should be living each day.

3:15, 16 By the time of Peter's writing, Paul's letters already had a widespread reputation. Notice that Peter spoke of Paul's letters as if they were on a level with "the other Scriptures". Already the early church was thinking of Paul's letters as inspired by God.

3:15–18 Peter and Paul had very different backgrounds and personalities, and they preached from different viewpoints. Paul emphasised salvation by grace, not law, while Peter preferred to talk about Christian life and service. The two men did not contradict each other, however, and they always held each other in high esteem. The false teachers intentionally misused Paul's writings by distorting them to condone lawlessness. No doubt this made the teachers popular, because people always like to have their favourite sins justified, but the net effect was to totally destroy Paul's message. Paul may have been thinking of teachers like these when he wrote in Romans 6:15: "What then? Shall we sin because we are not under law but under grace? By no means!" Peter warned his readers to avoid the mistakes of those wicked teachers by growing in the grace and knowledge of Jesus. The better we know Jesus, the less attractive false teaching will be.

17Therefore, dear friends, since you already know this, be on your guard[z] so that
you may not be carried away by the error[a] of lawless men and fall from your secure
position.[b] 18But grow in the grace and knowledge of our Lord and Saviour Jesus
Christ.[c] To him be glory both now and for ever! Amen.

3:17
[z]1Co 10:12
[a]2Pe 2:18
[b]Rev 2:5

3:18
[c]2Pe 1:11

3:18 Peter concludes this brief letter as he began, by urging his readers to grow in the grace and knowledge of the Lord and Saviour Jesus Christ – to get to know him better and better. This is the most important step in refuting false teachers. No matter where we are in our spiritual journey, no matter how mature we are in our faith, the sinful world will always challenge our faith. We still have much room for growth. If every day we find some way to draw closer to Christ, we will be prepared to stand for truth in any and all circumstances.

1 JOHN

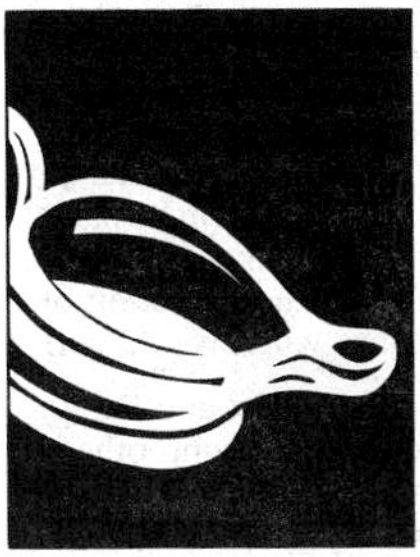

"A GOOD MAN . . . yes . . . perhaps one of the best who ever lived . . . but just a man," say many. Others disagree, claiming that he suffered from delusions of grandeur—a "messiah complex". And the argument rages over the true identity of this man called Jesus. Suggestions have ranged from "simple teacher" to "egomaniac" and "misguided fool". Whoever he was, all would agree that Jesus left his mark on history.

Hearing these discussions, even Christians can begin to wonder and doubt. Is Jesus really God? Did he come to save sinners like us? Does God care about me?

John's first letter was written to dispel doubts and to build assurance by presenting a clear picture of Christ. Entering history, Jesus was and is God in the flesh and God in focus—seen, heard, and touched by the author of this letter, John the apostle. John walked and talked with Jesus, saw him heal, heard him teach, watched him die, met him arisen, and saw him ascend. John knew God—he had lived with him and had seen him work. And John enjoyed fellowship with the Father and the Son all the days of his life.

The elder statesman in the church, John wrote this letter to his "dear children". In it he presented God as light, as love, and as life. He explained in simple and practical terms what it means to have fellowship with God.

At the same time, false teachers had entered the church, denying the incarnation of Christ. John wrote to correct their serious errors. So, John's letter is a model for us to follow as we combat modern heresies.

John opens this letter by giving his credentials as an eyewitness of the incarnation and by stating his reason for writing (1:1–4). He then presents God as "light", symbolising absolute purity and holiness (1:5–7), and he explains how believers can walk in God's light and have fellowship with him (1:8–10) with Christ as their defender (2:1, 2). John urges them to obey Christ fully and to love all the members of God's family (2:3–17). He warns his readers of "antichrists" and the antichrist who will try to lead them away from the truth (2:18–29).

In the next section, John presents God as "love"—giving, dying, forgiving, and blessing (3:1—4:21). God *is* love, and because God loves us, he calls us his children and makes us like Christ (3:1, 2). This truth should motivate us to live close to him (3:3–6). We can be sure of our family relationship with God when our lives are filled with good deeds and love for others (3:7–24). Again, John warns of false teachers who twist the truth. We should reject these false teachers (4:1–6) as we continue to live in God's love (4:7–21).

In the last section, John presents God as "life" (5:1–21). God's life is in his Son. To have his Son is to have eternal life.

Do you know God? Do you know Christ? Do you know that you have eternal life? This letter was written to help you know the reality of God in your life through faith in Christ, to assure you that you have eternal life, and to encourage you to remain in fellowship with the God who is light and love. Read this letter written by one overwhelmed by God's love, and with renewed confidence, pass on his love to others.

VITAL STATISTICS

PURPOSE:
To reassure Christians in their faith and to counter false teachings

AUTHOR:
The apostle John

TO WHOM WRITTEN:
The letter is untitled and was written to no particular church. It was sent as a pastoral letter to several Gentile congregations. It was also written to all believers everywhere.

DATE WRITTEN:
Probably between A.D. 85 and 90, from Ephesus

SETTING:
John was an older man and perhaps the only surviving apostle at this time. He had not yet been banished to the island of Patmos, where he would live in exile. As an eyewitness of Christ, he wrote authoritatively to give this new generation of believers assurance and confidence in God and in their faith.

KEY VERSE:
"I write these things to you who believe in the name of the Son of God so that you may know that you have eternal life" (5:13).

KEY PEOPLE:
John, Jesus

SPECIAL FEATURES:
John is the apostle of love, and love is mentioned throughout this letter. There are a number of similarities between this letter and John's Gospel—in vocabulary, style, and main ideas. John uses brief statements and simple words, and he features sharp contrasts—light and darkness, truth and error, God and Satan, life and death, love and hate.

THE BLUEPRINT

1. God is light (1:1—2:27)
2. God is love (2:28—4:21)
3. God is life (5:1–21)

John wrote about the most vital aspects of faith so that readers would know Christian truth from error. He emphasises the basics of faith so that we can be confident in our faith. In our dark world, God is light. In our cold world, God brings the warmth of love. In our dying world, God brings life. When we lack confidence, these truths bring us certainty.

MEGATHEMES

THEME	EXPLANATION	IMPORTANCE
Sin	Even Christians sin. Sin requires God's forgiveness, and Christ's death provides it for us. Determining to live according to God's standards in the Bible shows that our lives are being transformed.	We cannot deny our sinful nature, maintain that we are "above" sinning, or minimise the consequences of sin in our relationship with God. We must resist the attraction of sin, yet we must confess when we do sin.
Love	Christ commands us to love others as he loved us. This love is evidence that we are truly saved. God is the Creator of love; he cares that his children love each other.	Love means putting others first and being unselfish. Love is action—showing others we care—not just saying it. To show love we must give sacrificially of our time and money to meet the needs of others.
Family of God	We become God's children by believing in Christ. God's life in us enables us to love our fellow family members.	How we treat others shows who our Father is. Live as a faithful, loving family member.
Truth and Error	Teaching that the physical body does not matter, false teachers encouraged believers to throw off moral restraints. They also taught that Christ wasn't really a man and that we must be saved by having some special mystical knowledge. The result was that people became indifferent to sin.	God is truth and light, so the more we get to know him the better we can keep focused on the truth. Don't be led astray by any teaching that denies Christ's deity or humanity. Check the message; test the claims.
Assurance	God is in control of heaven and earth. Because his word is true, we can have assurance of eternal life and victory over sin. By faith we can be certain of our eternal destiny with him.	Assurance of our relationship with God is a promise, but it is also a way of life. We build our confidence by trusting in God's word and in Christ's provision for our sin.

1. God is light

The Word of Life

1 That which was from the beginning,[a] which we have heard, which we have seen
with our eyes,[b] which we have looked at and our hands have touched[c]—this
we proclaim concerning the Word of life. 2The life appeared;[d] we have seen it and
testify to it, and we proclaim to you the eternal life, which was with the Father and
has appeared to us. 3We proclaim to you what we have seen and heard, so that you

1:1 [a]Jn 1:2 [b]Jn 1:14; 2Pe 1:16 [c]Jn 20:27

1:2 [d]Jn 1:1-4; 1Ti 3:16

1:1 This letter was written by John, one of Jesus' original 12 disciples. He was probably "the disciple whom Jesus loved" (John 21:20) and, along with Peter and James, he had a special relationship with Jesus. This letter was written between A.D. 85–90 from Ephesus, before John's exile to the island of Patmos (see Revelation 1:9). Jerusalem had been destroyed in A.D. 70, and Christians were scattered throughout the empire. By the time John wrote this letter, Christianity had been around for more than a generation. It had faced and survived severe persecution. The main problem confronting the church at this time was declining commitment: many believers were conforming to the world's standards, failing to stand up for Christ, and compromising their faith. False teachers were plentiful, and they were accelerating the church's downward slide away from the Christian faith.

John wrote this letter to put believers back on track, to show the difference between light and darkness (truth and error), and to encourage the church to grow in genuine love for God and for one another. He also wrote to assure true believers that they possessed eternal life and to help them know that their faith was genuine—so they could enjoy all the benefits of being God's children. For more about John, see his Profile in John 13.

1:1–5 John opens his first letter to the churches like the way in which he began his Gospel, emphasising that Christ ("the Word of life") is eternal, that God came into the world as a human, that he, John, was an eyewitness to Jesus' life, and that Jesus brings light and life.

1:3 As an eyewitness to Jesus' ministry, John was qualified to teach the truth about him. The readers of this letter had not seen and heard Jesus themselves, but they could trust that what John wrote was accurate. We are like those second- and third-

1:3 [e]1Co 1:9
1:4 [f]1Jn 2:1 [g]Jn 3:29
1:5 [h]1Jn 3:11
1:6 [i]2Co 6:14 [j]Jn 3:19-21
1:7 [k]Heb 9:14; Rev 1:5
1:8 [l]Pr 20:9; Jas 3:2 [m]1Jn 2:4

also may have fellowship with us. And our fellowship is with the Father and with his
Son, Jesus Christ.[e] 4We write this[f] to make our[a] joy complete.[g]

Walking in the Light

5This is the message we have heard[h] from him and declare to you: God is light;
in him there is no darkness at all. 6If we claim to have fellowship with him yet walk
in the darkness,[i] we lie and do not live by the truth.[j] 7But if we walk in the light,
as he is in the light, we have fellowship with one another, and the blood of Jesus,
his Son, purifies us from all[b] sin.[k]
8If we claim to be without sin,[l] we deceive ourselves and the truth is not in us.[m]

a *4* Some manuscripts *your* **b** *7* Or *every*

JOHN COUNTERS FALSE TEACHINGS

John counters two major threads in the false teachings of the heretics in this letter:

1:6, 8, 10	They denied the reality of sin. John says that if we continue in sin, we can't claim to belong to God. If we say we have no sin, we are only fooling ourselves and refusing to accept the truth.
2:22; 4:1–3	They denied that Jesus was the Messiah—God in the flesh. John said that if we believe that Jesus was God incarnate and trust him for our salvation, we are children of God.

---

generation Christians. Though we have not personally seen, heard, or touched Jesus, we have the New Testament record of his eyewitnesses, and we can trust that they spoke the truth about him. See John 20:29.

1:3, 4 John writes about having fellowship with other believers. There are three principles behind true Christian fellowship. First, our fellowship is grounded in the testimony of God's word. Without this underlying strength, togetherness is impossible. Second, it is mutual, depending on the unity of believers. Third, it is renewed daily through the Holy Spirit. True fellowship combines social and spiritual interaction, and it is made possible only through a living relationship with Christ.

1:5, 6 Light represents what is good, pure, true, holy, and reliable. Darkness represents what is sinful and evil. The statement "God is light" means that God is perfectly holy and true and that he alone can guide us out of the darkness of sin. Light is also related to truth in that light exposes whatever exists, whether it is good or bad. In the dark, good and evil look alike; in the light, they can be clearly distinguished. Just as darkness cannot exist in the presence of light, sin cannot exist in the presence of a holy God. If we want to have a relationship with God, we must put aside our sinful ways of living. To claim that we belong to him but then to go out and live for ourselves is hypocrisy. Christ will expose and judge such deceit.

1:6 Here John was confronting the first of three claims of the false teachers: that we can have fellowship with God and still walk in darkness. False teachers who thought that the physical body was evil or worthless taught one of two approaches to behaviour: either they insisted on denying bodily desires through rigid discipline, or they approved of gratifying every physical lust because the body was going to be destroyed anyway. Obviously the second approach was more popular! Here John is saying that no-one can claim to be a Christian and still live in evil and immorality. We can't love God and court sin at the same time.

1:7 How does Jesus' blood purify us from every sin? In Old Testament times, believers symbolically transferred their sins to an animal, which they then sacrificed (see a description of this ceremony in Leviticus 4). The animal died in their place to pay for their sin and to allow them to continue living in God's favour. God graciously forgave them because of their faith in him, and because they obeyed his commandments concerning the sacrifice. Those sacrifices anticipated the day when Christ would completely remove sin. Real cleansing from sin came with Jesus, the "Lamb of God, who takes away the sin of the world" (John 1:29). Sin, by its very nature, brings death—that is a fact as certain as the law of gravity. Jesus did not die for his own sins; he had none. Instead, by a transaction that we may never fully understand, he died for the sins of the world. When we commit our lives to Christ and thus identify ourselves with him, his death becomes ours. He has paid the penalty for our sins, and his blood has purified us. Just as Christ rose from the grave, we rise to a new life of fellowship with him (Romans 6:4).

1:8 Here John was attacking the second claim of the false teachers: that people had no natural tendency towards sin, that they were "without sin", and that they were then incapable of sinning. This idea is at best self-deception and at worst a bald-faced lie. The false teachers refused to take sin seriously. They wanted to be considered Christians, but they saw no need to confess and repent. The death of Christ did not mean much to them because they didn't think they needed it. Instead of repenting and being purified by Christ's blood, they were encouraging sin among believers. In this life we are always capable of sinning, so we should never let down our guard.

1:8–10 The false teachers not only denied that sin breaks our fellowship with God (1:6) and that they had a sinful nature (1:8), but they also denied that their conduct involved any sin at all (1:10). That was a lie that ignored one basic truth: all people are sinners by nature and by practice. At conversion all our sins are forgiven—past, present, and future. Yet even after we become Christians, we still sin and still need to confess. This kind of confession is not offered to gain God's acceptance, but to remove the barrier to fellowship that our sin has put between us and him. It is difficult, however, for many people to admit their faults and shortcomings, even to God. It takes humility and honesty to recognise our weaknesses, and most of us would rather pretend that we are strong. But we need not fear revealing our sins to God—he knows them already. He will not push us away, no matter what we've done. Instead he will draw us to himself.

9If we confess our sins, he is faithful and just and will forgive us our sins[n] and purify
us from all unrighteousness. 10If we claim we have not sinned, we make him out to
be a liar[o] and his word has no place in our lives.[p]

2 My dear children,[a] I write this to you so that you will not sin. But if anybody
does sin, we have one who speaks to the Father in our defence[b]—Jesus Christ,
the Righteous One. 2He is the atoning sacrifice for our sins,[c] and not only for ours
but also for**a** the sins of the whole world.
3We know that we have come to know him if we obey his commands.[d] 4The man
who says, "I know him," but does not do what he commands is a liar, and the truth
is not in him.[e] 5But if anyone obeys his word,[f] God's love**b** is truly made complete
in him.[g] This is how we know we are in him: 6Whoever claims to live in him must
walk as Jesus did.[h]
7Dear friends, I am not writing you a new command but an old one, which you
have had since the beginning.[i] This old command is the message you have heard.
8Yet I am writing you a new command;[j] its truth is seen in him and you, because
the darkness is passing[k] and the true light[l] is already shining.[m]
9Anyone who claims to be in the light but hates his brother is still in the darkness.

a *2 Or He is the one who turns aside God's wrath, taking away our sins, and not only ours but also* **b** *5* Or *word, love for God*

1:9 *n* Ps 32:5; 51:2
1:10 *o* 1Jn 5:10 *p* 1Jn 2:14
2:1 *a* ver 12, 13, 28 *b* Ro 8:34; Heb 7:25
2:2 *c* Ro 3:25
2:3 *d* Jn 14:15
2:4 *e* 1Jn 1:6, 8
2:5 *f* Jn 14:21, 23 *g* 1Jn 4:12
2:6 *h* Mt 11:29; 1Pe 2:21
2:7 *i* 1Jn 3:11, 23; 2Jn 5, 6
2:8 *j* Jn 13:34 *k* Ro 13:12 *l* Jn 1:9 *m* Eph 5:8; 1Th 5:5

1:9 Confession is supposed to free us to enjoy fellowship with Christ. It should ease our consciences and lighten our cares. But some Christians do not understand how it works. They feel so guilty that they confess the same sins over and over again; then they wonder if they might have forgotten something. Other Christians believe that God forgives them when they confess, but if they died with unconfessed sins, they would be for ever lost. These Christians do not understand that God *wants* to forgive us. He allowed his beloved Son to die just so he could offer us pardon. When we come to Christ, he forgives all the sins we have committed or will ever commit. We don't need to confess the sins of the past all over again, and we don't need to fear that God will reject us if we don't keep our slate perfectly clean. Of course we should continue to confess our sins, but not because failure to do so will make us lose our salvation. Our relationship with Christ is secure. Instead, we should confess so that we can enjoy maximum fellowship and joy with him.

True confession also involves a commitment not to continue in sin. We wouldn't be genuinely confessing our sins to God if we planned to commit them again and just wanted temporary forgiveness. We should also pray for strength to defeat temptation the next time we face it.

1:9 If God has forgiven us for our sins because of Christ's death, why must we confess our sins? In admitting our sins and receiving Christ's cleansing, we are: (1) agreeing with God that our sin truly is sin and that we are willing to turn from it, (2) ensuring that we don't conceal our sins from him and consequently from ourselves, and (3) recognising our tendency to sin and relying on his power to overcome it.

2:1 John uses the address "dear children" in a warm, fatherly way. He is not talking down to his readers but is showing affection for them. At this writing, John was a very old man. He had spent almost all his life in ministry, and many of his readers were indeed his spiritual children.

2:1, 2 To people who are feeling guilty and condemned, John offers reassurance. They know they have sinned, and Satan (called "the accuser" in Revelation 12:10) is demanding the death penalty. When you feel this way, don't give up hope—the best defence lawyer in the universe is pleading your case. Jesus Christ, your advocate, your defender, is the Judge's Son. He has already suffered your penalty in your place. You can't be tried for a cime for which you've already been acquitted. United with Christ, you are as safe as he is. Don't be afraid to ask Christ to plead your case—he has already won it (see Romans 8:33, 34; Hebrews 7:24, 25).

2:2 Jesus Christ is the atoning sacrifice for our sins (see also 4:10). He can stand before God as our mediator because his death satisfied the wrath of God against sin and paid the death penalty for our sin. Thus Christ both satisfies God's requirement and removes our sin. In him we are forgiven and purified.

2:2 Sometimes it is difficult to forgive those who wrong us. Imagine how hard it would be to forgive everyone, no matter what they had done! This is what God has done in Jesus. No-one, no matter what he or she has done, is beyond forgiveness. All a person has to do is turn from his or her sin, receive Christ's forgiveness, and commit his or her life to him.

2:3–6 How can you be sure that you belong to Christ? This passage gives two ways to know: if you do what Christ says and live as Christ wants. What does Christ tell us to do? John answers in 3:23: "to believe in the name of his Son, Jesus Christ, and to love one another". True Christian faith results in loving behaviour; that is why John says that the way we act can give us assurance that we belong to Christ.

2:6 To "walk as Jesus did" or living as Christ did doesn't mean choosing 12 disciples, performing great miracles, and being crucified. We cannot merely copy Christ's life—much of what Jesus did had to do with his identity as God's Son, the fulfilment of his special role in dying for sin, and the cultural context of the first-century Roman world. To walk today as Christ did we must obey his teachings and follow his example of complete obedience to God and loving service to people.

2:7, 8 The commandment to love others is both old and new. It is old because it comes from the Old Testament (Leviticus 19:18). It is new because Jesus interpreted it in a radically new way (John 13:34, 35). In the Christian church, love is not only expressed by showing respect; it is also expressed through self-sacrifice and servanthood (John 15:13). In fact, it can be defined as "selfless giving", reaching beyond friends to enemies and persecutors (Matthew 5:43–48). Love should be the unifying force and the identifying mark of the Christian community. Love is the key to walking in the light, because we cannot grow spiritually while we hate others. Our growing relationship with God will result in growing relationships with others.

2:9–11 Does this mean that if you dislike someone you're not a Christian? These verses are not talking about disliking a disagreeable Christian brother or sister. There will always be people we will not like as much as others. John's words focus on the attitude that causes us to ignore or despise others, to treat them as irritants, competitors, or enemies. Christian love is not a feeling but a choice. We can choose to be concerned with people's well-being and treat them with respect, whether or not we feel affection to-

2:10 [n] 1Jn 3:14
2:11 [o] Jn 12:35
2:13 [p] ver 14
2:14 [q] Eph 6:10 [r] Jn 5:38; 1Jn 1:10 [s] ver 13
2:15 [t] Ro 12:2 [u] Jas 4:4
2:16 [v] Ro 13:14 [w] Pr 27:20

10 Whoever loves his brother lives in the light,[n] and there is nothing in him[c] to make
him stumble. 11 But whoever hates his brother is in the darkness and walks around in
the darkness; he does not know where he is going, because the darkness has blinded
him.[o]

12 I write to you, dear children,
because your sins have been forgiven on account of his name.
13 I write to you, fathers,
because you have known him who is from the beginning.
I write to you, young men,
because you have overcome the evil one.[p]
I write to you, dear children,
because you have known the Father.
14 I write to you, fathers,
because you have known him who is from the beginning.
I write to you, young men,
because you are strong,[q]
and the word of God lives in you,[r]
and you have overcome the evil one.[s]

Do Not Love the World

15 Do not love the world or anything in the world.[t] If anyone loves the world, the
love of the Father is not in him.[u] 16 For everything in the world — the cravings of sinful
man,[v] the lust of his eyes[w] and the boasting of what he has and does — comes not

c *10* Or *it*

A BOOK OF CONTRASTS
One of the distinct features of John's writing style was his habit of noting both sides of a conflict. He wrote to show the difference between real Christianity and anything else. Here are some of his favourite contrasts.

Contrast between:	*Passage*
Light and darkness	1:5
The new command and the old command	2:7, 8
Loving the Father and loving the world	2:15, 16
Christ and antichrist	2:18
Truth and lies	2:20, 21
Children of God and children of the devil	3:1–10
Eternal life and eternal death	3:14
Love and hatred	3:15, 16
True teaching and false teaching	4:1–3
Love and fear	4:18, 19
Having life and not having life	5:11, 12

wards them. If we choose to love others, God will help us express our love.

2:12–14 John was writing to believers of all ages, his "dear children" who had experienced forgiveness through Jesus. The older men ("fathers") were mature in the faith and had a long-standing relationship with Christ. The young men had struggled with Satan's temptations and had won. The boys and girls had learned about Christ and were just beginning their spiritual journey. Each stage of life in the Christian pilgrimage builds upon the one before. As children learn about Christ, they grow in their ability to win battles with temptation. As young adults move from victory to victory, they grow in their relationship with Christ. Older adults, having known Christ for years, have developed the wisdom needed to teach young people and start the cycle all over again. Has your Christian growth reached the maturity level appropriate for your stage in life?

2:15, 16 Some people think that worldliness is limited to external behaviour — the people we associate with, the places we go, the activities we enjoy. Worldliness is also internal because it begins in the heart and is characterised by three attitudes: (1) *the cravings of sinful man* — preoccupation with gratifying physical desires; (2) *the lust of his eyes* — craving and accumulating things, bowing to the god of materialism; and (3) *boasting of what he has and does* — obsession with one's status or importance. When the serpent tempted Eve (Genesis 3:6), he tempted her in these areas. Also, when the devil tempted Jesus in the desert, these were his three areas of attack (see Matthew 4:1–11).

By contrast, God values self-control, a spirit of generosity, and a commitment to humble service. It is possible to give the impression of avoiding worldly pleasures while still harbouring worldly attitudes in one's heart. It is also possible, like Jesus, to love sinners and spend time with them while maintaining a commitment to the values of God's kingdom. What values are most important to you? Do your actions reflect the world's values or God's values?

from the Father but from the world. 17The world and its desires pass away,[x] but the
man who does the will of God lives for ever.

Warning Against Antichrists

18Dear children, this is the last hour; and as you have heard that the antichrist is
coming,[y] even now many antichrists have come.[z] This is how we know it is the last
hour. 19They went out from us,[a] but they did not really belong to us. For if they had
belonged to us, they would have remained with us; but their going showed that none
of them belonged to us.[b]
20But you have an anointing[c] from the Holy One,[d] and all of you know the
truth.[d][e] 21I do not write to you because you do not know the truth, but because you
do know it[f] and because no lie comes from the truth. 22Who is the liar? It is the man
who denies that Jesus is the Christ. Such a man is the antichrist—he denies the Father
and the Son.[g] 23No-one who denies the Son has the Father; whoever acknowledges
the Son has the Father also.[h]
24See that what you have heard from the beginning remains in you. If it does, you
also will remain in the Son and in the Father.[i] 25And this is what he promised
us—even eternal life.
26I am writing these things to you about those who are trying to lead you astray.[j]
27As for you, the anointing[k] you received from him remains in you, and you do not

d *20* Some manuscripts *and you know all things*

2:17 [x]1Co 7:31
2:18 [y]ver 22; 1Jn 4:3; 2Jn 7 [z]1Jn 4:1
2:19 [a]Ac 20:30 [b]1Co 11:19
2:20 [c]2Co 1:21 [d]Mk 1:24 [e]Jn 14:26
2:21 [f]2Pe 1:12; Jude 5
2:22 [g]2Jn 7
2:23 [h]Jn 8:19; 1Jn 4:15
2:24 [i]Jn 14:23
2:26 [j]2Jn 7
2:27 [k]ver 20

2:17 When our attachment to possessions is strong, it's hard to believe that what we want will one day pass away. It may be even harder to believe that the person who does the will of God will live for ever. But this was John's conviction based on the facts of Jesus' life, death, resurrection, and promises. Knowing that this evil world and our desires for its pleasures will end can give us courage to control our greedy, self-indulgent behaviour and to continue doing God's will.

2:18–23 John is talking about the last days, the time between Christ's first and second comings. The first-century readers of 1 John lived in the last days, and so do we. During this time, antichrists (false teachers who pretend to be Christians and who lure weak members away from Christ) will appear. Finally, just before the world ends, one great antichrist will arise (Revelation 13; 19:20; 20:10). We do not need to fear these evil people, however. The Holy Spirit shows us their errors, so we will not be deceived. However, we must teach God's word clearly and carefully to the peripheral, weak members among us so that they won't fall prey to these teachers who "come to you in sheep's clothing, but inwardly they are ferocious wolves" (Matthew 7:15).

2:19 The antichrists were not total strangers to the church; they had once been in the church, but they did not really belong to it. John does not say why they left; it is clear that their reasons for joining in the first place were wrong. Some people may call themselves Christians for less than the best reasons. Perhaps going to church is a family tradition. Maybe they like the social and business contacts they make there. Or possibly going to church is a long-standing habit, and they have never stopped to ask themselves why they do it. What is your main reason for being a Christian? Unless it is a Christ-centred reason, you may not really belong. You don't have to settle for less than the best. You can become personally acquainted with Jesus Christ and become a loyal, trustworthy follower.

2:20 *Anointing* usually refers to the pouring out of special olive oil. Oil was used to consecrate kings and special servants for service (1 Samuel 16:1, 13), and was also used by the church when someone was sick (James 5:14). "You have an anointing from the Holy One" could read, 'The Holy Spirit has been given to you by the Father and the Son." When a person becomes a Christian, he or she receives the Holy Spirit. One way the Holy Spirit helps the believer and the church is by communicating truth. Jesus is the truth (John 14:6), and the Holy Spirit guides believers to him (John 16:13). People who are opposed to Christ are also opposed to his truth, and the Holy Spirit is not working in their lives. When we are led by the Spirit, we can stand against false teachers and the antichrist. Ask the Spirit to guide you each day (see 2:27).

2:22, 23 Apparently the antichrists in John's day were claiming faith in God while denying and opposing Christ. To do so, John firmly states, is impossible. Because Jesus is God's Son and the Messiah, to deny Christ is to reject God's way of revealing himself to the world. A person who accepts Christ as God's Son, however, accepts God the Father at the same time. The two are one and cannot be separated. Many cultists today call themselves Christians, but they deny that Jesus is divine. We must expose these heresies and oppose such teachings so that the weak believers among us do not succumb to their teachings.

2:24 These Christians had heard the gospel, very likely from John himself. They knew that Christ was God's Son, that he died for their sins and was raised to give them new life, and that he would return and establish his kingdom in its fulness. But their fellowship was being infiltrated by teachers who denied these basic doctrines of the Christian faith, and some of the believers were in danger of succumbing to false arguments. John encouraged them to hold on to the Christian truth they heard at the beginning of their walk with Christ. It is important to grow in our knowledge of the Lord, to deepen our understanding through careful study, and to teach these truths to others. But no matter how much we learn, we must never abandon the basic truths about Christ. Jesus will always be God's Son, and his sacrifice for our sins is permanent. No truth will ever contradict these teachings in the Bible.

2:26, 27 Christ had promised to send the Holy Spirit to teach his followers and to remind them of all that Christ had taught (John 14:26). As a result, Christians have the Holy Spirit within them ("the anointing") to keep them from going astray. In addition, they have the God-inspired Scriptures, against which they can test questionable teachings. To stay true to Christ, we must follow his word and his Spirit. Let the Holy Spirit help you discern truth from error. For more about who the Holy Spirit is and what he does, see the notes on John 3:6; Acts 1:5; and Ephesians 1:13, 14.

2:27 Christ lives (remains) in us through the Holy Spirit, and we also live in Christ. This means that we place our total trust in him, rely on him for guidance and strength, and live as he wants us to live. It implies a personal, life-giving relationship. John uses the same idea in John 15:5, where he speaks of Christ as the vine and

2:28 [l]ver 1 [m]1Jn 3:2 [n]1Jn 4:17 [o]1Th 2:19
2:29 [p]1Jn 3:7
3:1 [a]Jn 3:16 [b]Jn 1:12 [c]Jn 16:3
3:2 [d]Ro 8:29; 2Pe 1:4 [e]2Co 3:18
3:3 [f]2Co 7:1; 2Pe 3:13, 14
3:4 [g]1Jn 5:17
3:5 [h]2Co 5:21
3:6 [i]ver 9 [j]3Jn 11 [k]1Jn 2:4
3:7 [l]1Jn 2:1 [m]1Jn 2:26 [n]1Jn 2:29
3:8 [o]Jn 8:44
3:9 [p]Jn 1:13 [q]1Jn 5:18 [r]1Pe 1:23

need anyone to teach you. But as his anointing teaches you about all things and as
that anointing is real, not counterfeit—just as it has taught you, remain in him.

2. God is love

Children of God

28And now, dear children,[l] continue in him, so that when he appears[m] we may
be confident[n] and unashamed before him at his coming.[o]
29If you know that he is righteous,[p] you know that everyone who does what is right
has been born of him.
3 How great is the love[a] the Father has lavished on us, that we should be called
children of God![b] And that is what we are! The reason the world does not know
us is that it did not know him.[c] 2Dear friends, now we are children of God, and what
we will be has not yet been made known. But we know that when he appears,**[a]** we
shall be like him,[d] for we shall see him as he is.[e] 3Everyone who has this hope in
him purifies himself,[f] just as he is pure.
4Everyone who sins breaks the law; in fact, sin is lawlessness.[g] 5But you know
that he appeared so that he might take away our sins. And in him is no sin.[h] 6No-one
who lives in him keeps on sinning.[i] No-one who continues to sin has either seen
him[j] or known him.[k]
7Dear children,[l] do not let anyone lead you astray.[m] He who does what is right
is righteous, just as he is righteous.[n] 8He who does what is sinful is of the devil,[o]
because the devil has been sinning from the beginning. The reason the Son of God
appeared was to destroy the devil's work. 9No-one who is born of God[p] will continue
to sin,[q] because God's seed[r] remains in him; he cannot go on sinning, because he

a *2* Or *when it is made known*

---

his followers as the branches (see also 3:24; 4:15).

2:28, 29 The visible proof of being a Christian is right behaviour. Many people do good deeds but don't have faith in Jesus Christ. Others claim to have faith but rarely produce good deeds. A deficit in either faith or right behaviour will be a cause for shame when Christ returns. Because true faith always results in good deeds, those who claim to have faith *and* who consistently do what is right are true believers. Good deeds cannot produce salvation (see Ephesians 2:8, 9), but they are necessary proof that true faith is actually present (James 2:14–17).

3:1 As believers, our self-worth is based on the fact that God loves us and calls us his children. We are his children *now,* not just sometime in the distant future. Knowing that we are his children should encourage us to live as Jesus did. For other references about being part of God's family, see Romans 8:14–17; Galatians 3:26, 27; 4:6, 7.

3:1ff Verse 1 tells us who we are—members of God's family ("children of God"). Verse 2 tells us who we are becoming—reflections of God. The rest of the chapter tells us what we have as we grow to resemble God: (1) victory over sin (3:4–9); (2) love for others (3:10–18); and (3) confidence before God (3:19–24).

3:2, 3 The Christian life is a process of becoming more and more like Christ (see Romans 8:29). This process will not be complete until we see Christ face to face (1 Corinthians 13:12; Philippians 3:21), but knowing that it is our ultimate destiny should motivate us to purify ourselves. To purify means to keep morally straight, free from the corruption of sin. God also purifies us, but there is action we must take to remain morally fit (see 1 Timothy 5:22; James 4:8; 1 Peter 1:22).

3:4ff There is a difference between committing a sin and continuing to sin. Even the most faithful believers sometimes commit sins, but they do not cherish a particular sin and choose to commit it. A believer who commits a sin repents, confesses, and finds forgiveness. A person who continues to sin, by contrast, is not sorry for what he or she is doing. Thus this person never confesses and never receives forgiveness. Such a person is in opposition to God, no matter what religious claims he or she makes.

3:5 Under the Old Testament sacrifice system, a lamb without blemish was offered as a sacrifice for sin. Jesus is "the Lamb of God, who takes away the sin of the world" (John 1:29). Because Jesus lived a perfect life and sacrificed himself for our sins, we can be completely forgiven (2:2). We can look back to his death for us and know that we need never suffer eternal death (1 Peter 1:18–20).

3:8, 9 We all have areas where temptation is strong and habits are hard to conquer. These weaknesses give the devil a foothold, so we must deal with our areas of vulnerability. If we are struggling with a particular sin, however, these verses are not directed at us, even if for the moment we seem to keep on sinning. John is not talking about people whose victories are still incomplete; he is talking about people who make a practice of sinning and look for ways to justify it.

Three steps are necessary to find victory over prevailing sin: (1) seek the power of the Holy Spirit and God's word; (2) stay away from tempting situations; and (3) seek the help of the body of Christ—be open to their willingness to hold you accountable and to pray for you.

3:9 "No-one who is born of God will continue to sin" means that true believers do not make a practice of sinning, nor do they become indifferent to God's moral law. All believers still sin, but they are working to gain victory over sin. "God's seed remains in him" means that true believers do not make a practice of sinning because God's new life has been born into them.

3:9 We are "born of God" when the Holy Spirit lives in us and gives us Jesus' new life. Being born again is more than a fresh start; it is a rebirth, receiving a new family name based on Christ's death for us. When this happens, God forgives us and totally accepts us; the Holy Spirit gives us new minds and hearts, lives in us, and begins helping us to become like Christ. Our perspective changes too because we have a mind that is renewed day by day by the Holy Spirit (see Romans 12:2; Ephesians 4:22–24). So we must begin to think and act differently. See John 3:1–21 for more on being born again.

has been born of God. 10This is how we know who the children of God are and who
the children of the devil are: Anyone who does not do what is right is not a child of
God; nor is anyone who does not love[s] his brother.

Love One Another

11This is the message you heard[t] from the beginning: We should love one another.[u] 12Do not be like Cain, who belonged to the evil one and murdered his
brother.[v] And why did he murder him? Because his own actions were evil and his
brother's were righteous. 13Do not be surprised, my brothers, if the world hates you.[w]
14We know that we have passed from death to life,[x] because we love our brothers.
Anyone who does not love remains in death.[y] 15Anyone who hates his brother is a
murderer,[z] and you know that no murderer has eternal life in him.[a]
16This is how we know what love is: Jesus Christ laid down his life for us. And
we ought to lay down our lives for our brothers.[b] 17If anyone has material possessions
and sees his brother in need but has no pity on him,[c] how can the love of God be
in him?[d] 18Dear children,[e] let us not love with words or tongue but with actions and
in truth.[f] 19This then is how we know that we belong to the truth, and how we set
our hearts at rest in his presence 20whenever our hearts condemn us. For God is greater
than our hearts, and he knows everything.
21Dear friends, if our hearts do not condemn us, we have confidence before God[g]
22and receive from him anything we ask,[h] because we obey his commands and do
what pleases him.[i] 23And this is his command: to believe[j] in the name of his Son,
Jesus Christ, and to love one another as he commanded us.[k] 24Those who obey his
commands live in him,[l] and he in them. And this is how we know that he lives in
us: We know it by the Spirit he gave us.[m]

Test the Spirits

4 Dear friends, do not believe every spirit, but test the spirits to see whether they
are from God, because many false prophets have gone out into the world.[a] 2This
is how you can recognise the Spirit of God: Every spirit that acknowledges that Jesus

3:10 [s]1Jn 4:8
3:11 [t]1Jn 1:5 [u]Jn 13:34, 35; 2Jn 5
3:12 [v]Ge 4:8
3:13 [w]Jn 15:18, 19; 17:14
3:14 [x]Jn 5:24 [y]1Jn 2:9
3:15 [z]Mt 5:21, 22; Jn 8:44 [a]Gal 5:20, 21
3:16 [b]Jn 15:13
3:17 [c]Dt 15:7, 8 [d]1Jn 4:20
3:18 [e]1Jn 2:1 [f]Eze 33:31; Ro 12:9
3:21 [g]1Jn 5:14
3:22 [h]Mt 7:7 [i]Jn 8:29
3:23 [j]Jn 6:29 [k]Jn 13:34
3:24 [l]1Jn 2:6 [m]1Jn 4:13
4:1 [a]2Pe 2:1; 1Jn 2:18

3:12, 13 Cain killed his brother, Abel, when God accepted Abel's offering and not his (Genesis 4:1–16). Abel's offering showed that Cain was not giving his best to God, and Cain's jealous anger drove him to murder. People who are morally upright expose and shame those who aren't. If we live for God, the world will often hate us, because we make them painfully aware of their immoral way of living.

3:15 John echoes Jesus' teaching that whoever hates another person is a murderer at heart (Matthew 5:21, 22). Christianity is a religion of the heart; outward compliance alone is not enough. Bitterness against someone who has wronged you is an evil cancer within you and will eventually destroy you. Don't let a "bitter root" (Hebrews 12:15) grow in you or your church.

3:16 Real love is an action, not a feeling. It produces selfless, sacrificial giving. The greatest act of love is giving oneself for others. How can we lay down our lives? By serving others with no thought of receiving anything in return. Sometimes it is easier to say we'll die for others than to truly live for them – this involves putting others' desires first. Jesus taught this same principle of love in John 15:13.

3:17, 18 These verses give an example of how to lay down our lives for others – to help those in need. This is strikingly similar to James' teaching (James 2:14–17). How clearly do your actions say you really love others? Are you as generous as you should be with your money, possessions, and time?

3:19, 20 Many are afraid that they don't love others as they should. They feel guilty because they think they are not doing enough to show proper love to Christ. Their consciences bother them. John has these people in mind in this letter. How do we escape the gnawing accusations of our consciences? Not by ignoring them or rationalising our behaviour, but by setting our hearts on God's love. When we feel guilty, we should remind ourselves that God knows our motives as well as our actions. His voice of assurance is stronger than the accusing voice of our conscience. If we are in Christ, he will not condemn us (Romans 8:1; Hebrews 9:14, 15). So if you are living for the Lord but feeling that you are not good enough, remind yourself that God is greater than your conscience.

3:21, 22 If your conscience is clear, you can come to God without fear, confident that your requests will be heard. John reaffirms Jesus' promise that whatever we ask for will be given to us (Matthew 7:7; see also Matthew 21:22; John 9:31; 15:7). You will receive if you obey and do what pleases him because you will then be asking in line with God's will. Of course this does not mean that you can have anything you want, like instant riches. If you are truly seeking God's will, there are some requests you will not make.

3:23 In the Bible, a person's name stands for his or her character. It represents who he or she really is. We are to believe not only in Jesus' words, but also in his very person as the Son of God. Moreover, to believe "in the name" means to model your life on Christ's, to become more like him by uniting yourself with him. And if we are living like Christ, we will "love one another".

3:24 The mutual relationship, living in Christ as he lives in us, shows itself in Christians who keep these three essential commands: (1) believe in Christ, (2) love the brothers and sisters, and (3) live morally upright lives. The Spirit's presence is not only spiritual and mystical, but it is also practical. Our conduct verifies his presence.

4:1, 2 "Do not believe every spirit, but test the spirits" means that we shouldn't believe everything we hear just because someone says it is a message inspired by God. There are many ways to test teachers to see if their message is truly from the Lord. One is to

4:2 [b]Jn 1:14; 1Jn 2:23 [c]1Co 12:3
4:3 [d]1Jn 2:22; 2Jn 7
4:4 [e]Ro 8:31 [f]Jn 12:31
4:5 [g]Jn 15:19
4:6 [h]Jn 8:47 [i]Jn 14:17

Christ has come in the flesh[b] is from God,[c] 3but every spirit that does not acknowledge Jesus is not from God. This is the spirit of the antichrist,[d] which you have heard
is coming and even now is already in the world.
4You, dear children, are from God and have overcome them, because the one who
is in you[e] is greater than the one who is in the world.[f] 5They are from the world[g]
and therefore speak from the viewpoint of the world, and the world listens to them.
6We are from God, and whoever knows God listens to us; but whoever is not from
God does not listen to us.[h] This is how we recognise the Spirit[a] of truth[i] and the
spirit of falsehood.

[a] 6 Or *spirit*

HERESIES

Most of the eyewitnesses to Jesus' ministry had died by the time John composed this letter. Some of the second- or third-generation Christians began to have doubts about what they had been taught about Jesus. Some Christians with a Greek background had a hard time believing that Jesus was human as well as divine, because in Platonic thought the spirit was all-important. The body was only a prison from which one desired to escape. Heresies developed from a uniting of this kind of Platonic thought and Christianity.

A particularly widespread false teaching, later called *Docetism* (from a Greek word meaning "to seem"), held that Jesus was actually a spirit who only appeared to have a body. In reality he cast no shadow and left no footprints; he was God, but not man. Another heretical teaching, related to *Gnosticism* (from a Greek word meaning "knowledge"), held that all physical matter was evil, the spirit was good, and only the intellectually enlightened could enjoy the benefits of religion. Both groups found it hard to believe in a Saviour who was fully human.

John answers these false teachers as an eyewitness to Jesus' life on earth. He saw Jesus, talked with him, touched him—he knew that Jesus was more than a mere spirit. In the very first sentence of his letter, John establishes that Jesus had been alive before the world began and also that he lived as a man among men and women. In other words, he was both divine and human.

Through the centuries, many heretics have denied that Jesus was both God and man. In John's day people had trouble believing he was human; today more people have problems seeing him as God. But Jesus' divine-human nature is the pivotal issue of Christianity. Before you accept what religious teachers say about any topic, listen carefully to what they believe about Jesus. To deny either his divinity or his humanity is to consider him less than Christ, the Saviour.

---

check to see if their words match what God says in the Bible. Other tests include their commitment to the body of believers (2:19), their life-style (3:23, 24), and the fruit of their ministry (4:6). But the most important test of all, says John, is what they believe about Christ. Do they teach that Jesus is fully God and fully man? Our world is filled with voices claiming to speak for God. Give them these tests to see if they are indeed speaking God's truth.

4:1–3 Some people believe everything they read or hear. Unfortunately, many ideas printed and taught are not true. Christians should have faith, but they should not be gullible. Verify every message you hear, even if the person who brings it says it's from God. If the message is truly from God, it will be consistent with Christ's teachings.

4:3 The antichrist will be a person who epitomises all that is evil, and he will be readily received by an evil world. He is more fully described in 2 Thessalonians 2:3–12 and Revelation 13. The "spirit of the antichrist" is already here (see the note on 2:18–23).

4:4 It is easy to be frightened by the wickedness we see all around us and overwhelmed by the problems we face. Evil is obviously much stronger than we are. John assures us, however, that God is even stronger. He will conquer all evil—and his Spirit and his word live in our hearts!

4:6 False teachers are popular with the world because, like the false prophets of the Old Testament, they tell people what they want to hear. John warns that Christians who faithfully teach God's word will not win any popularity contests in the world. People don't want to hear their sins denounced; they don't want to listen to demands that they change their behaviour. A false teacher will be well received by non-Christians.

God's Love and Ours

7 Dear friends, let us love one another,[j] for love comes from God. Everyone who
loves has been born of God and knows God.[k] 8 Whoever does not love does not know
God, because God is love.[l] 9 This is how God showed his love among us: He sent
his one and only Son[b] into the world that we might live through him.[m] 10 This is love:
not that we loved God, but that he loved us[n] and sent his Son as an atoning sacrifice
for[c] our sins.[o] 11 Dear friends, since God so loved us,[p] we also ought to love one
another. 12 No-one has ever seen God;[q] but if we love one another, God lives in us
and his love is made complete in us.[r]
13 We know that we live in him and he in us, because he has given us of his Spirit.[s]
14 And we have seen and testify[t] that the Father has sent his Son to be the Saviour
of the world.[u] 15 If anyone acknowledges that Jesus is the Son of God,[v] God lives
in him and he in God. 16 And so we know and rely on the love God has for us.
God is love.[w] Whoever lives in love lives in God, and God in him.[x] 17 In this way,
love is made complete[y] among us so that we will have confidence on the day of
judgment, because in this world we are like him. 18 There is no fear in love. But perfect
love drives out fear,[z] because fear has to do with punishment. The one who fears
is not made perfect in love.
19 We love because he first loved us.[a] 20 If anyone says, "I love God," yet hates
his brother,[b] he is a liar.[c] For anyone who does not love his brother, whom he has

[b] *9 Or his only begotten Son* [c] *10 Or as the one who would turn aside his wrath, taking away*

4:7 [j] 1Jn 3:11 [k] 1Jn 2:4
4:8 [l] ver 7, 16
4:9 [m] Jn 3:16, 17; 1Jn 5:11
4:10 [n] Ro 5:8, 10 [o] 1Jn 2:2
4:11 [p] Jn 3:16
4:12 [q] Jn 1:18; 1Ti 6:16 [r] 1Jn 2:5
4:13 [s] 1Jn 3:24
4:14 [t] Jn 15:27 [u] Jn 3:17
4:15 [v] Ro 10:9
4:16 [w] ver 8 [x] 1Jn 3:24
4:17 [y] 1Jn 2:5
4:18 [z] Ro 8:15
4:19 [a] ver 10
4:20 [b] 1Jn 2:9 [c] 1Jn 2:4

4:7ff Everyone believes that love is important, but love is usually thought of as a feeling. In reality, love is a choice and an action, as 1 Corinthians 13:4–7 shows. God is the source of our love: he loved us enough to sacrifice his Son for us. Jesus is our example of what it means to love; everything he did in life and death was supremely loving. The Holy Spirit gives us the power to love; he lives in our hearts and makes us more and more like Christ. God's love always involves a choice and an action, and our love should be like his. How well do you display your love for God in the choices you make and the actions you take?

4:8 John says, "God is love," not "Love is God." Our world, with its shallow and selfish view of love, has turned these words around and contaminated our understanding of love. The world thinks that love is what makes a person feel good and that it is all right to sacrifice moral principles and others' rights in order to obtain such "love". But that isn't real love; it is the exact opposite – selfishness. And God is not that kind of "love". Real love is like God, who is holy, just, and perfect. If we truly know God, we will love as he does.

4:9 Jesus is God's *only* Son. While all believers are sons and daughters of God, only Jesus lives in this special unique relationship (see John 1:18; 3:16).

4:9, 10 Love explains (1) why God creates – because he loves, he creates people to love; (2) why God cares – because he loves them, he cares for sinful people; (3) why we are free to choose – God wants a loving response from us; (4) why Christ died – his love for us caused him to seek a solution to the problem of sin; and (5) why we receive eternal life – God's love expresses itself to us for ever.

4:10 Nothing sinful or evil can exist in God's presence. He is absolute goodness. He cannot overlook, condone, or excuse sin as though it never happened. He loves us, but his love does not make him morally lax. If we trust in Christ, however, we will not have to bear the penalty for our sins (1 Peter 2:24). We will be acquitted (Romans 5:18) by his atoning sacrifice.

4:12 If no-one has ever seen God, how can we ever know him? John in his Gospel said, "God the One and Only, who is at the Father's side, has made him known" (John 1:18). Jesus is the complete expression of God in human form and he has revealed God to us. When we love one another, the invisible God reveals himself to others through us, and his love is made complete.

4:12 Some people enjoy being with others. They make friends with strangers easily and are always surrounded by many friends. Other people are shy or reserved. They have a few friends, but they are uncomfortable talking with people they don't know or mingling in crowds. Shy people don't need to become extroverts in order to love others. John isn't telling us *how many* people to love, but *how much* to love the people we already know. Our job is to love faithfully the people God has given us to love, whether there are two or two hundred of them. If God sees that we are ready to love others, he will bring them to us. No matter how shy we are, we don't need to be afraid of the love commandment. God provides us the strength to do what he asks.

4:13 When we become Christians, we receive the Holy Spirit. God's presence in our lives is proof that we really belong to him. He also gives us the power to love (Romans 5:5; 8:9; 2 Corinthians 1:22). Rely on that power as you reach out to others. As you do so, you will gain confidence. See also Romans 8:16.

4:17 The day of judgment is that time when all people will appear before Christ and be held accountable for their actions. With God living in us through Christ, we have no reason to fear this day, because we have been saved from punishment. Instead, we can look forward to the day of judgment, because it will mean the end of sin and the beginning of a face-to-face relationship with Jesus Christ.

4:18 If ever we are afraid of the future, eternity, or God's judgment, we can remind ourselves of God's love. We know that he loves us perfectly (Romans 8:38, 39). We can resolve our fears first by focusing on his immeasurable love for us, and then by allowing him to love others through us. His love will quiet your fears and give you confidence.

4:19 God's love is the source of all human love, and it spreads like fire. In loving his children, God kindles a flame in their hearts. In turn, they love others, who are warmed by God's love through them.

4:20, 21 It is easy to say we love God when that love doesn't cost us anything more than weekly attendance at religious services. But the real test of our love for God is how we treat the people right in front of us – our family members and fellow believers.

seen,[d] cannot love God, whom he has not seen.[e] 21And he has given us this
command: Whoever loves God must also love his brother.[f]

3. God is life

Faith in the Son of God

5 Everyone who believes that Jesus is the Christ[a] is born of God,[b] and everyone
who loves the father loves his child as well.[c] 2This is how we know that we love
the children of God: by loving God and carrying out his commands. 3This is love for
God: to obey his commands.[d] And his commands are not burdensome,[e] 4for everyone born of God overcomes[f] the world. This is the victory that has overcome the
world, even our faith. 5Who is it that overcomes the world? Only he who believes
that Jesus is the Son of God.

6This is the one who came by water and blood[g]—Jesus Christ. He did not come
by water only, but by water and blood. And it is the Spirit who testifies, because the
Spirit is the truth.[h] 7For there are three[i] that testify: 8the[a] Spirit, the water and the
blood; and the three are in agreement. 9We accept man's testimony,[j] but God's
testimony is greater because it is the testimony of God,[k] which he has given about
his Son. 10Anyone who believes in the Son of God has this testimony in his heart.[l]
Anyone who does not believe God has made him out to be a liar,[m] because he has
not believed the testimony God has given about his Son. 11And this is the testimony:
God has given us eternal life, and this life is in his Son.[n] 12He who has the Son has
life; he who does not have the Son of God does not have life.[o]

Concluding Remarks

13I write these things to you who believe in the name of the Son of God[p] so that
you may know that you have eternal life.[q] 14This is the confidence[r] we have in
approaching God: that if we ask anything according to his will, he hears us.[s] 15And
if we know that he hears us—whatever we ask—we know[t] that we have what we
asked of him.

4:20 [d] 1Jn 3:17 [e] ver 12
4:21 [f] Mt 5:43
5:1 [a] 1Jn 2:22 [b] Jn 1:13; 1Jn 2:23 [c] Jn 8:42
5:3 [d] Jn 14:15; 2Jn 6 [e] Mt 11:30
5:4 [f] Jn 16:33
5:6 [g] Jn 19:34 [h] Jn 14:17
5:7 [i] Mt 18:16
5:9 [j] Jn 5:34 [k] Mt 3:16, 17; Jn 8:17, 18
5:10 [l] Ro 8:16; Gal 4:6 [m] Jn 3:33
5:11 [n] Jn 1:4; 1Jn 2:25
5:12 [o] Jn 3:15, 16, 36
5:13 [p] 1Jn 3:23 [q] Jn 20:31; 1Jn 1:1, 2
5:14 [r] 1Jn 3:21 [s] Mt 7:7
5:15 [t] ver 18, 19, 20

a *7,8* Late manuscripts of the Vulgate *testify in heaven: the Father, the Word and the Holy Spirit, and these three are one. 8And there are three that testify on earth: the* (not found in any Greek manuscript before the sixteenth century)

We cannot truly love God while neglecting to love those who are created in his image.

5:1, 2 When we become Christians, we become part of God's family, with fellow believers as our brothers and sisters. It is God who determines who the other family members are, not us. We are simply called to accept and love them. How well do you treat your fellow family members?

5:3, 4 Jesus never promised that obeying him would be easy. But the hard work and self-discipline of serving Christ is no burden to those who love him. And if our load starts to feel heavy, we can always trust Christ to help us bear it (see Matthew 11:28–30).

5:6–8 The phrase "came by water and blood" may refer to Jesus' baptism and his crucifixion. At this time, there was a false teaching in circulation that said Jesus was "the Christ" only between his baptism and his death—that is, he was merely human until he was baptised, at which time "the Christ" then descended upon him but then later left him before his death on the cross. But if Jesus died only as a man, he could not have taken upon himself the sins of the world, and Christianity would be an empty religion. Only an act of God could take away the punishment that we deserve for our sin.

5:7–9 The Gospels twice record God's clear declaration that Jesus was his Son—at Jesus' baptism (Matthew 3:16, 17), and at his transfiguration (Matthew 17:5).

5:12 Whoever believes in God's Son has eternal life. He is all you need. You don't need to *wait* for eternal life, because it begins the moment you believe. You don't need to *work* for it, because it is already yours. You don't need to *worry* about it, because you have been given eternal life by God himself—and it is guaranteed.

5:13 Some people *hope* that they will receive eternal life. John says we can *know* we have it. Our certainty is based on God's promise that he has given us eternal life through his Son. This is true whether you feel close to God or far away from him. Eternal life is not based on feelings, but on facts. You can know that you have eternal life if you believe God's truth. If you're not sure that you are a Christian, ask yourself: "Have I honestly committed my life to him as my Saviour and Lord?" If so, you know by faith that you are indeed a child of God.

5:14, 15 The emphasis here is on God's will, not our will. When we communicate with God, we don't demand what we want; rather we discuss with him what *he* wants for us. If we align our prayers to his will, he will listen; and we can be certain that if he listens, he will give us a definite answer. Start praying with confidence!

16If anyone sees his brother commit a sin that does not lead to death, he should pray
and God will give him life.[u] I refer to those whose sin does not lead to death. There
is a sin that leads to death.[v] I am not saying that he should pray about that.[w] 17All
wrongdoing is sin,[x] and there is sin that does not lead to death.[y]
18We know that anyone born of God does not continue to sin; the one who was born
of God keeps him safe, and the evil one cannot harm him.[z] 19We know that we are
children of God,[a] and that the whole world is under the control of the evil one.[b]
20We know also that the Son of God has come and has given us understanding,[c] so
that we may know him who is true.[d] And we are in him who is true—even in his
Son Jesus Christ. He is the true God and eternal life.[e]
21Dear children, keep yourselves from idols.[f]

5:16
[u]Jas 5:15
[v]Heb 6:4-6; 10:26
[w]Jer 7:16
5:17
[x]1Jn 3:4
[y]1Jn 2:1
5:18
[z]Jn 14:30
5:19
[a]1Jn 4:6
[b]Gal 1:4
5:20
[c]Lk 24:45
[d]Jn 17:3
[e]ver 11
5:21
[f]1Co 10:14; 1Th 1:9

5:16, 17 Commentators differ widely in their thoughts about what this sin that leads to death is, and whether the death it causes is physical or spiritual. Paul wrote that some Christians had died because they took Communion "in an unworthy manner" (1 Corinthians 11:27–30), and Ananias and Sapphira were struck dead when they lied to God (Acts 5:1–11). Blasphemy against the Holy Spirit results in spiritual death (Mark 3:29), and the book of Hebrews describes the spiritual death of the person who turns against Christ (Hebrews 6:4–6). John was probably referring to the people who had left the Christian fellowship and joined the antichrists. By rejecting the only way of salvation, these people were putting themselves out of reach of prayer. In most cases, however, even if we knew what the terrible sin is, we would have no sure way of knowing whether a certain person had committed it. Therefore we should continue praying for our loved ones and for our Christian brothers and sisters, leaving the judgment up to God. Note that John says, "I am not saying that he should pray about that," rather than "You cannot pray about that." He recognised the lack of certainty.

5:18, 19 Christians commit sins, of course, but they ask God to forgive them, and then they continue serving him. God has freed believers from their slavery to Satan, and he keeps them safe from Satan's continued attacks. The rest of the world does not have the Christian's freedom to obey God. Unless they come to Christ in faith, they have no choice but to obey Satan. There is no middle ground; people either belong to God and obey him, or they live under Satan's control.

5:21 An idol is anything that substitutes for the true faith, anything that robs Christ of his full deity and humanity, any human idea that claims to be more authoritative than the Bible, any loyalty that replaces God at the centre of our lives.

5:21 John presents a clear picture of Christ. What we think about Jesus Christ is central to our teaching, preaching, and living. Jesus is the God-man, fully God and fully human at the same time. He came to earth to die in our place for our sins. Through faith in him, we are given eternal life and the power to do his will. What is your answer to the most important question you could ever ask—who is Jesus Christ?

2 JOHN

TRUTH and love are frequently discussed in our world, but seldom practised.

From politicians to salesmen, people conveniently ignore or conceal facts and use words to enhance positions or sell products. Perjury is common, and integrity and credibility are endangered species. Words, twisted in meaning and torn from context, have become mere tools for ego building. It is not surprising that we have to "swear" to tell the truth.

And what about love? Our world is filled with its words—popular songs, greeting cards, agony aunts, and romantic novels shower us with notions and dreams of ethereal, idyllic relationships and feelings. Real love, however, is scarce—selfless giving, caring, sharing, and even dying. We yearn to love and be loved but see few living examples of real love. Plentiful are those who grasp, hoard, and watch out for "number one".

Christ is the antithesis of society's prevailing values, that is, falsehood and self-centredness—for *he is truth and love*, in person. Therefore, all who claim loyalty to him must be committed to these ideals—following the truth and living the truth, reflecting love and acting with love towards one another.

The apostle John had seen Truth and Love firsthand—he had been with Jesus. So affected was this disciple that all of his writings, from the Gospel to the book of Revelation, are filled with this theme—truth and love are vital to the Christian and are inseparable in the Christian life. This letter, his brief letter to a dear friend, is no different. John says to walk in the truth and obey God (verse 4), watch out for deceivers (verse 7), and love God and each other (verse 6).

The letter will take just a few minutes to read, but its message should last a lifetime. As you reflect on these few paragraphs penned by the wise and aged follower of Christ, recommit yourself to being a person of truth, of love, and of obedience.

VITAL STATISTICS

PURPOSE:
To emphasise the basics of following Christ—truth and love—and to warn against false teachers

AUTHOR:
The apostle John

TO WHOM WRITTEN:
To "the chosen lady" and her children—or possibly to a local church, and all believers everywhere

DATE WRITTEN:
About the same time as 1 John, around A.D. 90, from Ephesus

SETTING:
Evidently this woman and her family were involved in one of the churches that John was overseeing—they had developed a strong friendship with John. John was warning her of the false teachers who were becoming prevalent in some of the churches.

KEY VERSE:
"And this is love: that we walk in obedience to his commands. As you have heard from the beginning, his command is that you walk in love " (verse 6).

KEY PEOPLE:
John, the chosen lady, and her children

THE BLUEPRINT

1. Watch out for false teachers (1–11)
2. John's final words (12, 13)

False teachers were a dangerous problem for the church to which John was writing. His warning against showing hospitality to false teachers may sound harsh and unloving to many today. Yet these men were teaching heresy that could seriously harm many believers—for eternity.

MEGATHEMES

THEME	EXPLANATION	IMPORTANCE
Truth	Following God's word, the Bible, is essential to Christian living, because God is truth. Christ's true followers consistently obey his truth.	To be loyal to Christ's teaching we must seek to know the Bible, but we may never twist its message to our own needs or purposes, nor encourage others who misuse it.
Love	Christ's command is for Christians to love one another. This is the basic ingredient of true Christianity.	To obey Christ fully, we must believe his command to love others. Helping, giving, and meeting needs put love into practice.
False Leaders	We must be wary of religious leaders who are not true to Christ's teaching. We should not give them a platform to spread false teaching.	Don't encourage those who are opposed to Christ. Politely remove yourself from association with false leaders. Be aware of what's being taught in your church.

1. Watch out for false teachers

1The elder,[a]

To the chosen[b] lady and her children, whom I love in the truth—and not I only,
but also all who know the truth[c]—2because of the truth,[d] which lives in us[e] and
will be with us for ever:

3Grace, mercy and peace from God the Father and from Jesus Christ,[f] the Father's
Son, will be with us in truth and love.

4It has given me great joy to find some of your children walking in the truth,[g] just
as the Father commanded us. 5And now, dear lady, I am not writing you a new
command but one we have had from the beginning.[h] I ask that we love one another.
6And this is love:[i] that we walk in obedience to his commands. As you have heard
from the beginning, his command is that you walk in love.
7Many deceivers, who do not acknowledge Jesus Christ[j] as coming in the flesh,
have gone out into the world.[k] Any such person is the deceiver and the antichrist.[l]
8Watch out that you do not lose what you have worked for, but that you may be
rewarded fully.[m] 9Anyone who runs ahead and does not continue in the teaching of
Christ does not have God; whoever continues in the teaching has both the Father and
the Son.[n] 10If anyone comes to you and does not bring this teaching, do not take him

1:1 [a] 3Jn 1 [b] Ro 16:13 [c] Jn 8:32
1:2 [d] 2Pe 1:12 [e] 1Jn 1:8
1:3 [f] Ro 1:7
1:4 [g] 3Jn 3, 4
1:5 [h] 1Jn 2:7; 3:11
1:6 [i] 1Jn 2:5
1:7 [j] 1Jn 2:22; 4:2, 3 [k] 1Jn 4:1 [l] 1Jn 2:18
1:8 [m] 1Co 3:8
1:9 [n] 1Jn 2:23

1 The "elder" is John, one of Jesus' 12 disciples and the writer of the Gospel of John, three letters, and the book of Revelation. For more information about John, see his Profile in John 13. This letter was written shortly after 1 John to warn about false teachers. The salutation, "to the chosen lady and her children", could refer to a specific woman, or to a church whose identity is no longer known. John may have written this from Ephesus.

1–4 The "truth" is the truth about Jesus Christ, as opposed to the lies of the false teachers (see 1 John 2:21–23).

5, 6 The statement that Christians should love one another is a recurrent New Testament theme. Yet love for one's neighbour is an old command, first appearing in the third book of Moses (Leviticus 19:18). We can show love in many ways: by avoiding prejudice and discrimination, by accepting people, by listening, helping, giving, serving, and refusing to judge. Knowing God's command is not enough. We must put it into practice, walking "in obedience to his commands". (See also Matthew 22:37–39 and 1 John 2:7, 8.)

7 In John's day, many false teachers taught that spirit was good and matter was evil; therefore, they reasoned that Jesus could not have been both God and man. In strong terms, John warns against this kind of teaching. There are still many false teachers who promote an understanding of Jesus that is not biblical. These teachers are dangerous because they distort the truth and undermine the foundations of Christian faith. They may use the right words but change the meanings. The way your teachers live shows a lot about what they believe about Christ. For more on testing teachers, see 1 John 4:1.

8 To "be rewarded fully" refers not to salvation but to the rewards of loyal service. All who value the truth and persistently hold to it will win their full reward. Those who live for themselves and justify their self-centredness by teaching false doctrines will lose that reward (see Matthew 7:21–23).

10 John instructed the believers not to show hospitality to false teachers. They were to do nothing that would encourage the heretics in their propagation of falsehoods. In addition, if believers were to invite them in, such action would show that they were approving of what the false teachers said and did. It may seem rude to turn people away, even if they are teaching heresy, but how much better it is to be faithful to God than merely courteous to people! John is condemning the support of those who are dedicated to opposing the true teachings of God, not condemning hospitality to unbelievers. John adds that a person who supports a false teacher in any way shares in the teacher's wicked work.

1:10
[o] Ro 16:17

1:11
[p] 1Ti 5:22

1:12
[q] 3Jn 13, 14

1:13
[r] ver 1

into your house or welcome him.[o] 11 Anyone who welcomes him shares[p] in his wicked work.

2. John's final words

12 I have much to write to you, but I do not want to use paper and ink. Instead, I hope to visit you and talk with you face to face,[q] so that our joy may be complete.

13 The children of your chosen[r] sister send their greetings.

13 False teaching is serious business, and we dare not overlook it. It is so serious that John wrote this letter to warn against it. There are so many false teachings in our world that we might be tempted to take many of them lightly. Instead, we should realise the dangers they pose and actively refuse to give heresies any foothold.

3 JOHN

VITAL STATISTICS

PURPOSE:
To commend Gaius for his hospitality and to encourage him in his Christian life

AUTHOR:
The apostle John

TO WHOM WRITTEN:
Gaius, a prominent Christian in one of the churches known to John; and all Christians

DATE WRITTEN:
About A.D. 90, from Ephesus

SETTING:
Church leaders travelled from town to town helping to establish new congregations. They depended on the hospitality of fellow believers. Gaius was one who welcomed these leaders into his home.

KEY VERSE:
"Dear friend, you are faithful in what you are doing for the brothers, even though they are strangers to you" (verse 5).

KEY PEOPLE:
John, Gaius, Diotrephes, Demetrius

By special invitation or with a surprise knock, company arrives and with them comes the promise of dirty floors, extra laundry, washing up, altered schedules, personal expense, and inconvenience. From sharing a meal to providing a bed, *hospitality* costs . . . in time, energy, and money. But how we treat others reflects our true values, what is really important to us. Do we see people as objects or inconveniences, or as unique creations of a loving God? And which is more important to God, a person or a carpet? Perhaps the most effective way to demonstrate God's values and Christ's love to others is to invite and welcome guests into our homes.

For Gaius, hospitality was a habit, and his reputation for friendship and generosity, especially to travelling teachers and missionaries (verse 5), had spread. To affirm and thank Gaius for his Christian lifestyle, and to encourage him in his faith, John wrote this personal note.

John's format for this letter centres around three men—Gaius, the example of one who follows Christ and loves others (verses 1–8); Diotrephes, the self-proclaimed church leader who does not reflect God's values (verses 9–11); and Demetrius, who also follows the truth (verse 12). John encourages Gaius to practise hospitality, continue to walk in the truth, and do what is right.

Although this is a personal letter, we can "look over the shoulder" of Gaius and apply its lessons to our lives. As you read 3 John, with which man do you identify? Are you a Gaius, generously giving to others? A Demetrius, loving the truth? Or a Diotrephes, looking out for yourself and your "things"? Determine to reflect Christ's values in your relationships, opening your home and touching others with his love.

THE BLUEPRINT

1. God's children live by the standards of the gospel
   (1–12)
2. John's final words
   (13–15)

John wrote to commend Gaius, who was taking care of travelling teachers and missionaries, and to warn against people like Diotrephes, who was proud and refused to listen to spiritual leaders in authority. If we are to live in the truth of the gospel, we must look for ways to support pastors, Christian workers, and missionaries today. All Christians should work together to support God's work, both at home and around the world.

MEGATHEMES

THEME	EXPLANATION	IMPORTANCE
Hospitality	John wrote to encourage those who were kind to others. Genuine hospitality for travelling Christian workers was needed then and is still important today.	Faithful Christian teachers and missionaries need our support. Whenever you can extend hospitality to others, it will make you a partner in their ministry.
Pride	Diotrephes not only refused to offer hospitality, but he set himself up as a church boss. Pride disqualified him from being a real leader.	Christian leaders must shun pride and its effects on them. Be careful not to misuse your position of leadership.
Faithfulness	Gaius and Demetrius were commended for their faithful work in the church. They were held up as examples of faithful, selfless servants.	Don't take for granted Christian workers who serve faithfully. Be sure to encourage them so they won't grow weary of serving.

1. God's children live by the standards of the gospel

1:1 [a] 2Jn 1

1The elder,[a]

1:3 [b] ver 5, 10 [c] 2Jn 4

To my dear friend Gaius, whom I love in the truth.

1:4 [d] 1Co 4:15; 1Jn 2:1

1:5 [e] Ro 12:13; Heb 13:2

2Dear friend, I pray that you may enjoy good health and that all may go well with
you, even as your soul is getting along well. 3It gave me great joy to have some
brothers[b] come and tell about your faithfulness to the truth and how you continue
to walk in the truth.[c] 4I have no greater joy than to hear that my children[d] are walking in the truth.
5Dear friend, you are faithful in what you are doing for the brothers, even though
they are strangers to you.[e] 6They have told the church about your love. You will do

1 This letter gives us an important glimpse into the life of the early church. Addressed to Gaius, it is about the need for showing hospitality to travelling preachers and other believers. It also warns against a would-be church dictator.

1 The "elder", John, was one of Jesus' 12 disciples and the writer of the Gospel of John, three letters, and the book of Revelation. For more information about John, see his Profile in John 13. We have no further information about Gaius, but he is someone whom John loved dearly. Perhaps Gaius had shared his home and hospitality with John at some time during John's travels. If so, John would have appreciated his actions, because travelling preachers depended on expressions of hospitality to survive (see Matthew 10:11–16).

2 John was concerned for Gaius's physical *and* spiritual well-being. This was the opposite of the popular heresy that taught the separation of spirit and matter and despised the physical side of life. Today, many people still fall into this way of thinking. This non-Christian attitude logically leads to one of two responses: neglect of the body and physical health, or indulgence of the body's sinful desires. God is concerned for both your body and your soul. As a responsible Christian, you should neither neglect nor indulge yourself, but care for your physical needs and discipline your body so that you are at your best for God's service.

4 John wrote about "my children" because, as a result of his preaching, he was the spiritual father of many, including Gaius.

5 In the church's early days, travelling prophets, evangelists, and teachers ("the brothers") were helped on their way by people like Gaius who housed and fed them. Hospitality is a lost art in many churches today. We would do well to invite more people for meals—fellow church members, young people, travelling missionaries, those in need, visitors. This is an active and much-appreciated way to show your love. In fact it is probably more important today. Because of our individualistic, self-centred society, there are many lonely people who wonder if anyone cares whether they live or die. If you find such a lonely person, show him or her that *you* care!

well to send them on their way in a manner worthy of God. 7 It was for the sake of
the Name[f] that they went out, receiving no help from the pagans.[g] 8 We ought
therefore to show hospitality to such men so that we may work together for the truth.
9 I wrote to the church, but Diotrephes, who loves to be first, will have nothing to
do with us. 10 So if I come,[h] I will call attention to what he is doing, gossiping
maliciously about us. Not satisfied with that, he refuses to welcome the brothers.[i]
He also stops those who want to do so and puts them out of the church.[j]
11 Dear friend, do not imitate what is evil but what is good.[k] Anyone who does
what is good is from God.[l] Anyone who does what is evil has not seen God.[m]
12 Demetrius is well spoken of by everyone[n]—and even by the truth itself. We also
speak well of him, and you know that our testimony is true.[o]

2. John's final words

13 I have much to write to you, but I do not want to do so with pen and ink. 14 I
hope to see you soon, and we will talk face to face.[p]

Peace to you. The friends here send their greetings. Greet the friends there by
name.[q]

1:7 [f] Jn 15:21 [g] Ac 20:33, 35
1:10 [h] 2Jn 12 [i] ver 5 [j] Jn 9:22, 34
1:11 [k] Ps 37:27 [l] 1Jn 2:29 [m] 1Jn 3:6, 9, 10
1:12 [n] 1Ti 3:7 [o] Jn 21:24
1:14 [p] 2Jn 12 [q] Jn 10:3

---

7 The travelling missionaries neither asked for nor accepted anything from non-believers because they didn't want anyone questioning their motives for preaching. God's true preachers do not preach to make money but to express their love for God. It is the church's responsibility to care for Christian workers; this should never be left to non-believers.

7, 8 When you help someone who is spreading the gospel, you are in a very real way a partner in the ministry. This is the other side of the principle in 2 John 10 (see the note there). Not everyone should go to the mission field; those who work for Christ at home are vital to the ministry of those who go and who need support. We can support missionaries by praying for them and by giving them our money, hospitality, and time.

9 This letter to which John refers was neither 1 nor 2 John, but another letter that no longer exists.

9, 10 All we know about Diotrephes is that he wanted to control the church. John denounced (1) his refusal to have anything to do with other spiritual leaders, (2) his slander of the leaders, (3) his bad example in refusing to welcome any gospel teachers, and (4) his attempt to excommunicate those who opposed his leadership. Sins such as pride, jealousy, and slander are still present in the church, and when a leader makes a habit of encouraging sin and discouraging right actions, he must be stopped. If no-one speaks up, great harm can come to the church. We must confront sin in the church; if we try to avoid it, it will continue to grow. A true Christian leader is a servant, not an autocrat!

12 We know nothing about Demetrius except that he may have carried this letter from John to Gaius. The book of Acts mentions an Ephesian silversmith named Demetrius who opposed Paul (Acts 19:24ff), but this is probably another man. In contrast to the corrupt Diotrephes, Demetrius had a high regard for truth. John personified truth as a witness to Demetrius' character and teaching. In other words, if truth could speak, it would speak on Demetrius' behalf. When Demetrius arrived, Gaius certainly opened his home to him.

14 Whereas 2 John emphasises the need to refuse hospitality to false teachers, 3 John urges continued hospitality to those who teach the truth. Hospitality is a strong sign of support for people and their work. It means sharing your resources with them so their stay will be comfortable and their work and travel easier. Actively look for creative ways to show hospitality to God's workers. It may be in the form of a letter of encouragement, a gift, financial support, an open home, or prayer.

JUDE

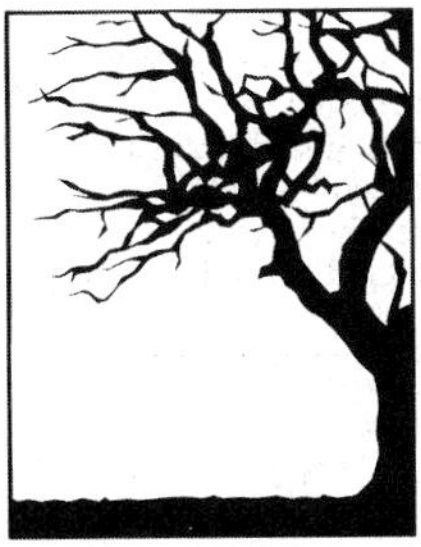

TO PROTECT from harm, to guard from attack, to repulse enemies—for centuries rugged defenders have built walls, launched missiles, and waged wars, expending material and human resources in the battle to save nations and cities. And with total commitment and courageous abandon, individuals have fought for their families. It is a rule of life that we fight for survival, defending with all our strength what is most precious to us, from every real or imagined attack.

God's word and the gift of eternal life have infinite value and have been entrusted to Christ's faithful followers. There are many people who live in opposition to God and his followers. They twist God's truth, seeking to deceive and destroy the unwary. But God's truth must go forth, carried and defended by those who have committed their lives to God's Son. It is an important task, an awesome responsibility, and a profound privilege to have this commission.

This was Jude's message to Christians everywhere. Opposition would come and godless teachers would arise, but Christians should "contend for the faith" (verse 3) by rejecting all falsehood and immorality (verses 4–19), remembering God's mighty acts of rescue and punishment (verses 5–11, 14–16) and the warnings of the apostles (verses 17–19). His readers are to build up their own faith through prayer (verse 20), keeping close to Christ (verse 21), helping others (verses 22, 23), and hating sin (verse 23). Then Jude concludes with a glorious benediction of praise to God (verses 24, 25).

How much do you value God's word, the fellowship of the church, and obedience to Jesus Christ? There are many false teachers waiting to destroy your Christ-centred life, the credibility of God's word, and the unity of the body of Christ. Read Jude and determine to stand firm in your faith and defend God's truth at all costs. *Nothing* is more valuable.

VITAL STATISTICS

PURPOSE:
To remind the church of the need for constant vigilance—to keep strong in the faith and to oppose heresy

AUTHOR:
Jude, brother of Jesus and James

TO WHOM WRITTEN:
Jewish Christians, and all believers everywhere

DATE WRITTEN:
About A.D. 65

SETTING:
From the first century on, the church has been threatened by heresy and false teaching—we must always be on our guard.

KEY VERSE:
"Dear friends, although I was very eager to write to you about the salvation we share, I felt I had to write and urge you to contend for the faith that was once for all entrusted to the saints" (verse 3).

KEY PEOPLE:
Jude, James, Jesus

THE BLUEPRINT

1. The danger of false teachers (1–16)
2. The duty to fight for God's truth (17–25)

Jude wrote to motivate Christians everywhere to action. He wanted them to recognise the dangers of false teaching, to protect themselves and other believers, and to win back those who had already been deceived. Jude was writing against godless teachers who were saying that Christians could do as they pleased without fear of God's punishment. While few teach this heresy openly in the church today, many in the church act as though it were true. This letter contains a warning against living a nominal Christian life.

MEGATHEMES

THEME	EXPLANATION	IMPORTANCE
False Teachers	Jude warns against false teachers and leaders who reject the lordship of Christ, undermine the faith of others, and lead them astray. These leaders and any who follow them will be punished.	We must staunchly defend Christian truth. Make sure that you avoid leaders and teachers who distort the Bible to suit their own purposes. Genuine servants of God will faithfully portray Christ in their words and conduct.
Apostasy	Jude also warns against apostasy—turning away from Christ. We are to remember that God punishes rebellion against him. We must be careful not to drift away from a faithful commitment to Christ.	Those who do not seek to know the truth in God's word are susceptible to apostasy. Christians must guard against any false teachings that would distract them from the truth preached by the apostles and written in God's word.

1. The danger of false teachers

1 Jude,[a] a servant of Jesus Christ and a brother of James,

To those who have been called,[b] who are loved by God the Father and kept by**a**
Jesus Christ:[c]

2 Mercy, peace and love be yours in abundance.[d]

The Sin and Doom of Godless Men

3 Dear friends, although I was very eager to write to you about the salvation we
share,[e] I felt I had to write and urge you to contend[f] for the faith that was once for
all entrusted to the saints. 4 For certain men whose condemnation was written about**b**
long ago have secretly slipped in among you.[g] They are godless men, who change
the grace of our God into a licence for immorality and deny Jesus Christ our only
Sovereign and Lord.[h]
5 Though you already know all this, I want to remind you that the Lord**c** delivered

1:1 [a]Mt 13:55; Ac 1:13 [b]Ro 1:6, 7 [c]Jn 17:12
1:2 [d]2Pe 1:2
1:3 [e]Tit 1:4 [f]1Ti 6:12
1:4 [g]Gal 2:4 [h]Tit 1:16; 2Pe 2:1

a *1* Or *for*; or *in* **b** *4* Or *men who were marked out for condemnation* **c** *5* Some early manuscripts *Jesus*

1 Jude's letter focuses on *apostasy*—when people turn away from God's truth and embrace false teachings. Jude reminded his readers of God's judgment on those who had left the faith in the past. This letter is a warning against false teachers—in this case, probably Gnostic teachers (see the note on Colossians 2:4ff for a description of the Gnostic heresy). Gnostics opposed two of the basic tenets of Christianity—the incarnation of Christ and the call to Christian ethics. Jude wrote to combat these false teachings and to encourage true doctrine and right conduct.

1 Jude was a brother of James, who was one of the leaders in the early church. Both of these men were Jesus' half brothers. Mary was their mother, and Joseph was their father. Although Mary was Jesus' true mother, God was Jesus' true Father.

3 Jude emphasises the important relationship between correct doctrine and true faith. The truth of the Bible must not be compromised, because it gives us the real facts about Jesus and salvation. The Bible is inspired by God and should never be twisted or manipulated; when it is, we can become confused over right and wrong and lose sight of the only path that leads to eternal life. Before writing about salvation, then, Jude felt he had to set his readers back on the right track, calling them back to the basics of their faith. Then the way to salvation would be clearer. *Saints* refers to all believers.

4 Even some of our churches today have false ("godless") teachers who "have secretly slipped in" and are twisting the Bible's teachings to justify their own opinions, life-style, or wrong behaviour. In doing this, they may gain temporary freedom to do as they wish, but they will discover that in distorting Scripture they are playing with fire. God will judge them for excusing, tolerating, and promoting sin.

4 Some people avoid studying the Bible because they think theology is dry and boring. Those who refuse to learn correct doctrine, however, are susceptible to false teaching because they are not fully grounded in God's truth. We must understand the basic doctrines of our faith so that we can recognise false doctrines and prevent wrong teaching from undermining our faith and hurting others.

4 Many first-century false teachers were teaching that Christians could do whatever they liked without fear of God's punishment. They had a light view of God's holiness and his justice. Paul refuted this same kind of false teaching in Romans 6:1–23. Even today, some Christians minimise the sinfulness of sin, believing that how they live has little to do with their faith. But what a person truly believes will show up in how he or she acts. Those who truly have faith will show it by their deep respect for God and their sincere desire to live according to the principles in his word.

5–7 Jude gave three examples of rebellion: (1) the children of Israel—who, although they were delivered from Egypt, refused to trust God and enter the promised land (Numbers 14:26–39); (2) the angels—although they were once pure, holy, and living in God's presence, some gave in to pride and joined Satan to rebel against God (2 Peter 2:4); and (3) the cities of Sodom and Gomorrah—the inhabitants were so full of sin that God wiped them off the face of the earth (Genesis 19:1–29). If the chosen people, angels, and sinful cities were punished, how much more would these false teachers be severely judged?

1:5 [i]Nu 14:29; Ps 106:26
1:6 [j]2Pe 2:4, 9
1:7 [k]Dt 29:23 [l]2Pe 2:6
1:8 [m]2Pe 2:10
1:9 [n]Da 10:13, 21 [o]Zec 3:2
1:10 [p]2Pe 2:12
1:11 [q]Ge 4:3-8; 1Jn 3:12 [r]2Pe 2:15 [s]Nu 16:1-3, 31-35
1:12 [t]2Pe 2:13; 1Co 11:20-22 [u]Pr 25:14; 2Pe 2:17 [v]Eph 4:14 [w]Mt 15:13
1:13 [x]Isa 57:20 [y]Php 3:19 [z]2Pe 2:17
1:14 [a]Ge 5:18, 21-24 [b]Dt 33:2; Da 7:10
1:15 [c]2Pe 2:6-9 [d]1Ti 1:9
1:16 [e]2Pe 2:18
1:17 [f]2Pe 3:2
1:18 [g]1Ti 4:1

his people out of Egypt, but later destroyed those who did not believe.[i] 6 And the
angels who did not keep their positions of authority but abandoned their own
home — these he has kept in darkness, bound with everlasting chains for judgment on
the great Day.[j] 7 In a similar way, Sodom and Gomorrah and the surrounding towns[k]
gave themselves up to sexual immorality and perversion. They serve as an example
of those who suffer the punishment of eternal fire.[l]
8 In the very same way, these dreamers pollute their own bodies, reject authority
and slander celestial beings.[m] 9 But even the archangel Michael,[n] when he was
disputing with the devil about the body of Moses, did not dare to bring a slanderous
accusation against him, but said, "The Lord rebuke you!"[o] 10 Yet these men speak
abusively against whatever they do not understand; and what things they do understand
by instinct, like unreasoning animals — these are the very things that destroy them.[p]
11 Woe to them! They have taken the way of Cain;[q] they have rushed for profit into
Balaam's error;[r] they have been destroyed in Korah's rebellion.[s]
12 These men are blemishes at your love feasts,[t] eating with you without the
slightest qualm — shepherds who feed only themselves. They are clouds without
rain,[u] blown along by the wind;[v] autumn trees, without fruit and uprooted[w] — twice
dead. 13 They are wild waves of the sea,[x] foaming up their shame;[y] wandering stars,
for whom blackest darkness has been reserved for ever.[z]
14 Enoch,[a] the seventh from Adam, prophesied about these men: "See, the Lord
is coming with thousands upon thousands of his holy ones[b] 15 to judge[c] everyone,
and to convict all the ungodly of all the ungodly acts they have done in the ungodly
way, and of all the harsh words ungodly sinners have spoken against him."[d] 16 These
men are grumblers and fault-finders; they follow their own evil desires; they boast[e]
about themselves and flatter others for their own advantage.

2. The duty to fight for God's truth

A Call to Persevere

17 But, dear friends, remember what the apostles of our Lord Jesus Christ foretold.[f]
18 They said to you, "In the last times[g] there will be scoffers who will follow their

7 Many people don't want to believe that God sentences people to "eternal fire" for rejecting him. But this is clearly taught in Scripture. Sinners who don't seek forgiveness from God will face eternal separation from him. Jude gives this warning to all who rebel against, ignore, or reject God.

8 The "celestial beings" here are probably angels. Just as the men of Sodom insulted angels (Genesis 19), these false teachers scoffed at any authority. For information on the danger of insulting even the fallen angels, see the note on 2 Peter 2:10–12.

9 This incident is not recorded in any other place in Scripture. Moses' death is recorded in Deuteronomy 34. Here Jude may have been making use of an ancient book called *The Assumption of Moses*.

10 False teachers claimed that they possessed secret knowledge that gave them authority. Their "knowledge" of God was esoteric — mystical and beyond human understanding. The nature of God *is* beyond our understanding, but God, in his grace, has chosen to reveal himself to us — in his word, and supremely in Jesus Christ. Therefore, we must seek to know all we can about what he has revealed, even though we cannot fully comprehend God with our finite human minds. Beware of those who claim to have all the answers and who belittle what they do not understand.

11 Jude gives three examples of men who did whatever they wanted (verse 10) — Cain, who murdered his brother out of vengeful jealousy (Genesis 4:1–16); Balaam, who prophesied out of greed, not out of obedience to God's command (Numbers 22–24); and Korah, who rebelled against God's divinely appointed leaders, wanting the power for himself (Numbers 16:1–35). These stories illustrate attitudes that are typical of false teachers — pride, selfishness, jealousy, greed, lust for power, and disregard of God's will.

12 When the Lord's Supper was celebrated in the early church, believers ate a full meal before taking part in Communion with the sharing of the bread and wine. The meal was called a "love feast", and it was designed to be a sacred time of fellowship to prepare one's heart for Communion. However, the false teachers were joining these love feasts, becoming "blemishes" in what should have been a time of rejoicing in the Lord. In several of the churches, however, this meal had turned into a time of gluttony and drunken revelry. In Corinth, for example, some people hastily gobbled food while others went hungry (1 Corinthians 11:20–22). No church function should be an occasion for selfishness, gluttony, greed, disorder, or other sins that destroy unity or take one's mind away from the real purpose for gathering together.

12 The false teachers were "twice dead". They were useless "trees" because they weren't producing fruit; because they weren't even believers, they would be rooted up and burned.

14 Enoch is mentioned briefly in Genesis 5:21–24. This quotation is from an apocryphal book called the book of Enoch.

14 Other places where Jesus is mentioned as coming with angels ("holy ones") are Matthew 16:27 and 24:31. Daniel 7:10 speaks of God judging humanity in the presence of ten thousand times ten thousand angels.

17 Other apostles also warned about false teachers — see Acts 20:29; 1 Timothy 4:1; 2 Timothy 3:1–5; 2 Peter 2:1–3; 2 John 7.

18 The *last times* is a common phrase referring to the time between Jesus' first and second comings. We live in the last times.

own ungodly desires."[h] 19 These are the men who divide you, who follow mere
natural instincts and do not have the Spirit.[i]
20 But you, dear friends, build yourselves up[j] in your most holy faith and pray in
the Holy Spirit.[k] 21 Keep yourselves in God's love as you wait[l] for the mercy of our
Lord Jesus Christ to bring you to eternal life.
22 Be merciful to those who doubt; 23 snatch others from the fire and save them;[m]
to others show mercy, mixed with fear—hating even the clothing stained by corrupted
flesh.[n]

Doxology

24 To him who is able[o] to keep you from falling and to present you before his
glorious presence[p] without fault[q] and with great joy—25 to the only God[r] our
Saviour be glory, majesty, power and authority, through Jesus Christ our Lord, before
all ages, now and for evermore![s] Amen.[t]

1:18 [h]2Pe 2:1
1:19 [i]1Co 2:14, 15
1:20 [j]Col 2:7 [k]Eph 6:18
1:21 [l]Tit 2:13; 2Pe 3:12
1:23 [m]Am 4:11; Zec 3:2-5 [n]Rev 3:4
1:24 [o]Ro 16:25 [p]2Co 4:14 [q]Col 1:22
1:25 [r]Jn 5:44; 1Ti 1:17 [s]Heb 13:8 [t]Ro 11:36

---

20 To "pray in the Holy Spirit" means to pray in the power and strength of the Holy Spirit. He prays for us (Romans 8:26, 27), opens our minds to Jesus (John 14:26), and teaches us about him (John 15:26).

21 To "keep yourselves in God's love" means to live close to God and his people, not listening to false teachers who would try to pull you away from him (John 15:9, 10).

22, 23 Effective witnessing saves people from God's judgment. We witness to some through our compassion and kindness; to others we witness as if we were snatching them from the eternal fire. To hate "even the clothing stained by corrupted flesh" means that we are to hate the sin, but we must witness to and love the sinner. Unbelievers, no matter how successful they seem by worldly standards, are lost and in need of salvation. We should not take witnessing lightly—it is a matter of life and death.

23 In trying to find common ground with those to whom we witness, we must be careful not to fall into the quicksand of compromise. When reaching out to others, we must be sure that our own footing is safe and secure. Be careful not to become so much like non-Christians that no-one can tell who you are or what you believe. Influence them for Christ—don't allow them to influence you to sin!

24, 25 As the letter begins, so it ends—with assurance. God keeps believers from falling prey to false teachers. Although false teachers are widespread and dangerous, we don't have to be afraid if we trust God and are rooted and grounded in him.

24, 25 To be sinless and perfect ("without fault") will be the ultimate condition of the believer when he or she finally sees Christ face to face. When Christ appears, and we are given our new bodies, we will be like Christ (1 John 3:2). Coming into Christ's presence will be more wonderful than we could ever imagine!

24, 25 The audience to whom Jude wrote was vulnerable to heresies and to temptations of immoral living. Jude encouraged the believers to remain firm in their faith and trust in God's promises for their future. This was all the more important because they were living in a time of increased apostasy. We too are living in the last days, much closer to the end than were the original readers of this letter. We too are vulnerable to doctrinal error. We too are tempted to give in to sin. Although there is much false teaching around us, we need not be afraid or give up in despair—God can keep us from falling, and he guarantees that if we remain faithful, he will bring us into his presence and give us everlasting joy.

R E V E L A T I O N

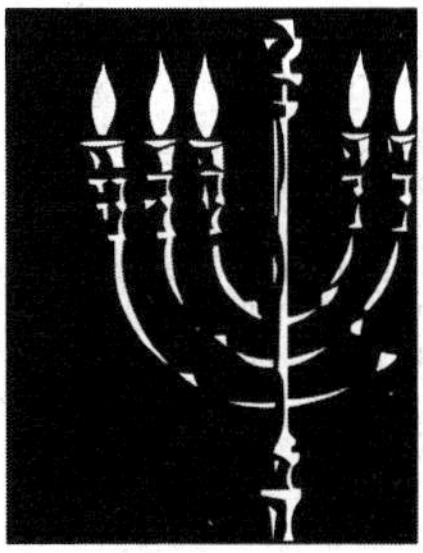

WITH TINY wrinkles and cries, he entered the world and, wrapped in strips of cloth, he slept on a bed of straw. Subject to time and to parents, he grew to manhood in Roman-occupied Palestine, his gentle hands becoming strong and calloused in Joseph's workshop. As a man, he walked through the countryside and city, touching individuals, preaching to crowds, and training 12 men to carry on his work. At every step he was hounded by those seeking to rid the world of his influence. Finally, falsely accused and tried, he was condemned to a disgraceful execution by foreign hands. And he died—spat upon, cursed, pierced by nails, and hung heavenward for all to deride. Jesus, the God-man, gave his life completely so that all might live.

At God's appointed time, the risen and ascended Lord Jesus will burst onto the world scene. Then everyone will know that Jesus is Lord of the universe! Those who love him will rejoice, greeting their Saviour with hearts overflowing into songs of praise. But his enemies will be filled with fear. Allied with Satan, the enemies of Christ will marshal their legions against Christ and his armies. But who can withstand God's wrath? Christ will win the battle and reign victorious for ever! Jesus, the humble suffering Servant, is also the powerful, conquering King and Judge.

Revelation is a book of hope. John, the beloved apostle and eyewitness of Jesus, proclaimed that the victorious Lord would surely return to vindicate the righteous and judge the wicked. But Revelation is also a book of warning. Things were not as they should have been in the churches, so Christ called the members to commit themselves to live in righteousness.

Although Jesus gave this revelation of himself to John nearly 2,000 years ago, it still stands as a comfort and challenge to God's people today. We can take heart as we understand John's vision of hope—Christ will return to rescue his people and settle accounts with all who defy him.

John begins this book by explaining how he received this revelation from God (1:1–20). He then records specific messages from Jesus to the seven churches in Asia (2:1—3:22). Suddenly the scene shifts as a mosaic of dramatic and majestic images bursts into view before John's eyes. This series of visions portrays the future rise of evil, culminating in the antichrist (4:1—18:24). Then follows John's recounting of the triumph of the King of kings, the wedding of the Lamb, the final judgment, and the coming of the new Jerusalem (19:1—22:5). Revelation concludes with the promise of Christ's imminent return (22:6–21), and John breathes a prayer that has been echoed by Christians through the centuries, "Amen. Come, Lord Jesus" (22:20).

As you read the book of Revelation, marvel with John at the wondrous panorama of God's revealed plan. Listen as Christ warns the churches, and root out any sin that blocks your relationship with him. Be full of hope, knowing that God is in control, Christ's victory is assured, and all who trust him will be saved.

VITAL STATISTICS

PURPOSE:
To reveal the full identity of Christ and to give warning and hope to believers

AUTHOR:
The apostle John

TO WHOM WRITTEN:
The seven churches in Asia, and all believers everywhere

DATE WRITTEN:
About A.D. 95, from Patmos

SETTING:
Most scholars believe that the seven churches of Asia to whom John writes were experiencing the persecution that took place under Emperor Domitian (A.D. 90–95). It seems that the Roman authorities had exiled John to the island of Patmos (off the coast of Asia). John, who had been an eyewitness of the incarnate Christ, had a vision of the glorified Christ. God also revealed to him what would take place in the future— judgment and the ultimate triumph of God over evil.

KEY VERSE:
"Blessed is the one who reads the words of this prophecy, and blessed are those who hear it and take to heart what is written in it, because the time is near" (1:3).

KEY PEOPLE:
John, Jesus

KEY PLACES:
Patmos, the seven churches, the new Jerusalem

SPECIAL FEATURES:
Revelation is written in "apocalyptic" form—a type of Jewish literature that uses symbolic imagery to communicate hope (in the ultimate triumph of God) to those in the midst of persecution. The events are ordered according to literary, rather than strictly chronological, patterns.

THE BLUEPRINT

A. LETTERS TO THE CHURCHES (1:1—3:22)	The vision John received opens with instructions for him to write to seven churches. He both commends them for their strengths and warns them about their flaws. Each letter was directed to a church then in existence, but also speaks to conditions in the church throughout history. Both in the church and in our individual lives, we must constantly fight against the temptation to become loveless, immoral, lenient, compromising, lifeless, or casual about our faith. The letters make it clear how our Lord feels about these faults.
B. MESSAGE FOR THE CHURCH (4:1—22:21) 1. Worshipping God in heaven 2. Opening the seven seals 3. Sounding the seven trumpets 4. Observing the great conflict 5. Pouring out the seven plagues 6. Seizing the final victory 7. Making everything new	This revelation is both a warning to Christians who have grown apathetic and an encouragement to those who are faithfully enduring the struggles in this world. It reassures us that good will triumph over evil, gives us hope as we face difficult times, and gives guidance when we are wavering in our faith. Christ's message to the church is a message of hope for all believers in every generation.

MEGATHEMES

THEME	EXPLANATION	IMPORTANCE
God's Sovereignty	God is sovereign. He is greater than any power in the universe. God is not to be compared with any leader, government, or religion. He controls history for the purpose of uniting true believers in loving fellowship with him.	Though Satan's power may temporarily increase, we are not to be led astray. God is all-powerful. He is in control. He will bring his true family safely into eternal life. Because he cares for us, we can trust him with our very lives.
Christ's Return	Christ came to earth as a "Lamb", the symbol of his perfect sacrifice for our sin. He will return as the triumphant "Lion", the rightful ruler and conqueror. He will defeat Satan, settle accounts with all those who reject him, and bring his faithful people into eternity.	Assurance of Christ's return gives suffering Christians the strength to endure. We can look forward to his return as King and Judge. Since no-one knows the time when he will appear, we must be ready at all times by keeping our faith strong.
God's Faithful People	John wrote to encourage the church to resist the demands to worship the Roman emperor. He warns all God's faithful people to be devoted only to Christ. Revelation identifies who the faithful people are and what they should be doing until Christ returns.	You can take your place in the ranks of God's faithful people by believing in Christ. Victory is sure for those who resist temptation and make loyalty to Christ their top priority.
Judgment	One day God's anger towards sin will be fully and completely unleashed. Satan will be defeated with all of his agents. False religion will be destroyed. God will reward the faithful with eternal life, but all who refuse to believe in him will face eternal punishment.	Evil and injustice will not prevail for ever. God's final judgment will put an end to these. We need to be certain of our commitment to Jesus if we want to escape this great final judgment. No-one who rejects Christ will escape God's punishment.
Hope	One day God will create a new heaven and a new earth. All believers will live with him for ever in perfect peace and security. Those who have already died will be raised to life. These promises for the future bring us hope.	Our great hope is that what Christ promises will come true. When we have confidence in our final destination, we can follow Christ with unwavering dedication no matter what we must face. We can be encouraged by hoping in Christ's return.

A. LETTERS TO THE CHURCHES (1:1 – 3:22)

Near the end of his life, John received a vision from Christ, which he recorded for the benefit of the seven churches in Asia and for Christians throughout history. This book contains a beautiful promise of blessing for those who listen to its words and do what it says.

Prologue

1 The revelation of Jesus Christ, which God gave him to show his servants what
must soon take place. He made it known by sending his angel[a] to his servant
John, 2who testifies to everything he saw — that is, the word of God and the testimony
of Jesus Christ.[b] 3Blessed is the one who reads the words of this prophecy, and
blessed are those who hear it and take to heart what is written in it,[c] because the time
is near.

Greetings and Doxology

4John,

To the seven churches in the province of Asia:

Grace and peace to you from him who is, and who was, and who is to come, and

1:1 [a]Rev 22:16
1:2 [b]1Co 1:6; Rev 12:17
1:3 [c]Lk 11:28

1:1 Revelation is a book about the future *and* about the present. It offers future hope to all believers, especially those who have suffered for their faith, by proclaiming Christ's final victory over evil and the reality of eternal life with him. It also gives present guidance as it teaches us about Jesus Christ and how we should live for him now. Through graphic pictures we learn that (1) Jesus Christ is coming again, (2) evil will be judged, and (3) the dead will be raised to judgment, resulting in eternal life or eternal destruction.

1:1 According to tradition, John, the author, was the only one of Jesus' original twelve disciples who was not killed for the faith. He also wrote the Gospel of John and the letters of 1, 2, and 3 John. When he wrote Revelation, John was in exile on the island of Patmos in the Aegean Sea, sent there by the Romans for his witness about Jesus Christ. For more information on John, see his Profile in John 13.

1:1 This book is the revelation *of, concerning,* and *from* Jesus Christ. God gave the revelation of his plan to Jesus Christ, who, in turn, revealed it to John. The book of Revelation unveils Christ's full identity and God's plan for the end of the world, and it focuses on Jesus Christ, his second coming, his victory over evil, and the establishment of his kingdom. As you read and study Revelation, don't focus so much on the timetable of the events or the details of John's imagery that you miss the main message – the infinite love, power, and justice of the Lord Jesus Christ.

1:1 The book of Revelation is *apocalyptic* (meaning uncovered, unveiled, or revealed) in style. This style of ancient literature usually featured spectacular and mysterious imagery, and such literature was written under the name of an ancient hero. John was acquainted with Jewish apocalyptic works, but his book is different in several ways: (1) he uses his own name rather than the name of an ancient hero; (2) he denounces evil and exhorts people to high Christian standards; (3) he offers hope rather than gloom. John was not a psychic attempting to predict the future; he was a prophet of God describing what God had shown him.

1:1 For more about angels, see the note on 5:11.

1:1 Jesus gave his message to John in a vision, allowing John to see and record certain future events so they could be an encouragement to all believers. The vision includes many signs and symbols that convey the essence of what is to happen. What John saw, in most cases, was indescribable, so he used illustrations to show what it was *like*. When reading this symbolic language, we don't have to understand every detail – John himself didn't. Instead, realise that John's imagery shows us that Christ is indeed the glorious and victorious Lord of all.

1:1–3 The book of Revelation reveals future events, but there is not the gloomy pessimism we might expect. The drama of these unfolding events is spectacular, but there is nothing to fear if you are on the winning side. When you think about the future, walk with confidence because Christ, the victor, walks with you.

1:3 Revelation is a book of prophecy that is both *prediction* (foretelling future events) and *proclamation* (preaching about who God is and what he will do). Prophecy is more than telling the future. Behind the predictions are important principles about God's character and promises. As we read, we will get to know God better so that we can trust him completely.

1:3 The typical news reports – filled with violence, scandal, and political haggling – are depressing, and we may wonder where the world is heading. God's plan for the future, however, provides inspiration and encouragement because we know he will intervene in history to conquer evil. John encourages churches to read this book aloud so everyone can hear it, apply it ("take to heart what is written in it"), and be assured of the fact that God will triumph.

1:3 When John says, "the time is near", he is urging his readers to be ready at all times for the Last Judgment and the establishment of God's kingdom. We do not know when these events will occur, but we must always be prepared. They will happen quickly, and there will be no second chance to change sides.

1:4 Jesus told John to write to seven churches that knew and trusted him and had read his earlier letters (see 1:11). The letters were addressed so that they could be read and passed on in a systematic fashion, following the main Roman road clockwise around the province of Asia (now called Turkey).

1:4 The "seven spirits" is another name for the Holy Spirit. The number seven is used throughout Revelation to symbolise completeness and perfection. For more about the Holy Spirit, see the notes on John 3:6 and Acts 1:5.

1:4–6 The Trinity – the Father ("him who is, and who was, and who is to come"), the Holy Spirit ("the seven spirits"), and the Son (Jesus Christ) – is the source of all truth (John 14:6, 17; 1 John 2:27; Revelation 19:11). Thus we can be assured that John's message is reliable and is God's word to us.

from the seven spirits[a][d] before his throne, 5and from Jesus Christ, who is the faithful
witness,[e] the firstborn from the dead,[f] and the ruler of the kings of the earth.[g]

To him who loves us and has freed us from our sins by his blood, 6and has made
us to be a kingdom and priests[h] to serve his God and Father—to him be glory and
power for ever and ever! Amen.[i]

7Look, he is coming with the clouds,[j]
and every eye will see him,
even those who pierced him;
and all the peoples of the earth will mourn[k] because of him.
So shall it be! Amen.

8"I am the Alpha and the Omega,"[l] says the Lord God, "who is, and who was,
and who is to come, the Almighty."[m]

One Like a Son of Man

9I, John, your brother and companion in the suffering[n] and kingdom and patient
endurance[o] that are ours in Jesus, was on the island of Patmos because of the word
of God and the testimony of Jesus. 10On the Lord's Day I was in the Spirit,[p] and
I heard behind me a loud voice like a trumpet,[q] 11which said: "Write on a scroll what
you see and send it to the seven churches:[r] to Ephesus, Smyrna, Pergamum, Thyatira,
Sardis,[s] Philadelphia and Laodicea."
12I turned round to see the voice that was speaking to me. And when I turned I saw
seven golden lampstands,[t] 13and among the lampstands was someone "like a son of

a 4 Or *the sevenfold Spirit*

1:4 [d]Rev 3:1; 4:5
1:5 [e]Rev 3:14 [f]Col 1:18 [g]Rev 17:14
1:6 [h]1Pe 2:5 [i]Ro 11:36
1:7 [j]Da 7:13 [k]Zec 12:10
1:8 [l]Rev 21:6 [m]Rev 4:8
1:9 [n]Php 4:14 [o]2Ti 2:12
1:10 [p]Rev 4:2 [q]Rev 4:1
1:11 [r]ver 4, 20 [s]Rev 3:1
1:12 [t]Ex 25:31-40; Zec 4:2

1:5 Others had risen from the dead—people whom the prophets, Jesus, and the apostles had brought back to life during their ministries—but later those people died again. Jesus was the first who rose from the dead in an imperishable body (1 Corinthians 15:20), never to die again. He is the firstborn from the dead.

1:5, 6 Many hesitate to witness about their faith in Christ because they don't feel the change in their lives has been spectacular enough. But you qualify as a witness for Jesus because of what he has done for you, not because of what you have done for him. Christ demonstrated his great love by setting us free from our sins through his death on the cross ("freed us from our sins by his blood"), guaranteeing us a place in his kingdom, and making us priests to administer God's love to others. The fact that the all-powerful God has offered eternal life to you is nothing short of spectacular.

1:5–7 Jesus is portrayed as an all-powerful King, victorious in battle, glorious in peace. He is not just a humble earthly teacher, he is the glorious God. When you read John's description of the vision, keep in mind that his words are not just good advice; they are truth from the King of kings. Don't just read his words for their interesting and amazing portrayal of the future. Let the truth about Christ penetrate your life, deepen your faith in him, and strengthen your commitment to follow him no matter what the cost.

1:7 John is announcing the return of Jesus to earth (see also Matthew 24; Mark 13; 1 Thessalonians 4:15–18). Jesus' second coming will be *visible* and *victorious.* All people will see him arrive (Mark 13:26), and they will *know* it is Jesus. When he comes, he will conquer evil and judge all people according to their deeds (20:11–15).

1:7 "Those who pierced him" could refer to the Roman soldiers who pierced Jesus' side as he hung on the cross or to the Jews who were responsible for his death. John saw Jesus' death with his own eyes, and he never forgot the horror of it (see John 19:34, 35; see also Zechariah 12:10).

1:8 Alpha and omega are the first and last letters of the Greek alphabet. The Lord God is the beginning and the end. God the Father is the eternal Lord and Ruler of the past, present, and future (see also 4:8; Isaiah 44:6; 48:12–15). Without him you have nothing that is eternal, nothing that can change your life, nothing that can save you from sin. Is the Lord your reason for living, "the Alpha and the Omega" of your life? Honour the One who is the beginning and the end of all existence, wisdom, and power.

1:9 Patmos was a small rocky island in the Aegean Sea, about 50 miles offshore from the city of Ephesus on the Asia Minor coast (see map on page 2291).

1:9 The Christian church was facing severe persecution. Almost all believers were socially, politically, or economically suffering because of this empire-wide persecution, and some were even being killed for their faith. John was exiled to Patmos because he refused to stop preaching the gospel. We may not face persecution for our faith as the early Christians did, but even with our freedom few of us have the courage to share God's word with others. If we hesitate to share our faith during easy times, how will we do during times of persecution?

1:12, 13 The seven golden lampstands are the seven churches in Asia (1:11, 20), and Jesus stands among them. No matter what the churches face, Jesus protects them with his all-encompassing love and reassuring power. Through his Spirit, Jesus Christ is still among the churches today. When a church faces persecution, it should remember Christ's deep love and compassion. When a church is wracked by internal strife and conflict, it should remember Christ's concern for purity and his intolerance of sin.

1:13, 14 This man "like a son of man" is Jesus himself. The title *Son of Man* occurs many times in the New Testament in reference to Jesus as the Messiah. John recognised Jesus because he lived with him for three years and had seen him both as the Galilean preacher and as the glorified Son of God at the transfiguration (Matthew 17:1–8). Here Jesus appears as the mighty Son of Man. His white hair indicates his wisdom and divine nature (see also Daniel 7:9); his blazing eyes symbolise judgment of all evil; the golden sash round his chest reveals him as the high priest who goes into God's presence to obtain forgiveness of sin for those who have believed in him.

man",[b][u] dressed in a robe reaching down to his feet and with a golden sash round
his chest.[v] 14His head and hair were white like wool, as white as snow, and his eyes
were like blazing fire.[w] 15His feet were like bronze glowing in a furnace,[x] and his
voice was like the sound of rushing waters.[y] 16In his right hand he held seven stars,[z]
and out of his mouth came a sharp double-edged sword.[a] His face was like the sun
shining in all its brilliance.
17When I saw him, I fell at his feet[b] as though dead. Then he placed his right hand

1:13 [u]Da 7:13 [v]Da 10:5
1:14 [w]Da 7:9; 10:6
1:15 [x]Da 10:6 [y]Eze 43:2
1:16 [z]Rev 2:1; 3:1 [a]Heb 4:12
1:17 [b]Da 8:17, 18

b *13* Daniel 7:13

A JOURNEY THROUGH THE BOOK OF REVELATION
Revelation is a complex book, and it has baffled interpreters for centuries. We can avoid a great deal of confusion by understanding the literary structure of the book. This approach will allow us to understand the individual scenes within the overall structure of Revelation and keep us from getting unnecessarily bogged down in the details of each vision. John gives hints throughout the book to indicate a change of scene, a change of subject, or a flashback to an earlier scene.

In chapter one, John relates the circumstances that led to the writing of this book (1:1–20). In chapters two and three, Jesus gives special messages to the seven churches of Asia Minor (2:1—3:22).

Suddenly John is caught up into heaven, where he sees a vision of God Almighty on his throne. All of Christ's followers and the heavenly angels are worshipping God (4:1–11). John watches as God gives a scroll with seven seals to the worthy Lamb, Jesus Christ (5:1–14). The Lamb begins to open the seals one by one. As each seal is opened, a new vision appears.

As the first four seals are opened, riders appear on horses of different colours—war, famine, disease, and death are in their path (6:1–8). As the fifth seal is opened, John sees those in heaven who have been martyred for their faith in Christ (6:9–11).

A set of contrasting images appears at the opening of the sixth seal. On one side, there is a huge earthquake, stars falling from the sky, and the sky rolling up like a scroll (6:12–17). On the other side, multitudes are before the great throne, worshipping and praising God and the Lamb (7:1–17).

Finally, the seventh seal is opened (8:1–5), unveiling a series of God's judgments announced by seven angels with seven trumpets. The first four angels bring hail, fire, a burning mountain, and a falling star—the sun and moon are darkened (8:6–13). The fifth trumpet announces the coming of locusts with the power to sting (9:1–12). The sixth trumpet heralds the coming of an army of warriors on horses (9:13–21). In chapter 10:1–11, John is given a little scroll to eat. Following this, John is commanded to measure the temple of God (11:1–2). He sees two witnesses who proclaim God's judgment on the earth for three and a half years (11:3–14).

Finally, the seventh trumpet sounds, calling the rival forces of good and evil to the final battle. On one side is Satan and his forces; on the other side stands Jesus Christ with his forces (11:15—13:18). In the midst of this call to battle, John sees three angels announcing the final judgment (14:6–13). Two angels begin to reap this harvest of judgment on the earth (14:14–20). Following on the heels of these two angels are seven more angels who pour out God's judgment on the earth from seven bowls (15:1—16:21). One of these angels from the group of seven reveals to John a vision of a "great prostitute" called Babylon (symbolising the Roman empire) riding a scarlet beast (17:1–18). After the defeat of Babylon (18:1–24), a great multitude in heaven shouts praise to God for his mighty victory (19:1–10).

The final three chapters of the book of Revelation catalogue the events that finalise Christ's victory over the enemy: Satan's 1,000-year imprisonment (20:1–10), the final judgment (20:11–15), and the creation of a new earth and a new Jerusalem (21:1—22:6). An angel then gives John final instructions concerning the visions John has seen and what to do once he has written them all down (22:7–11).

Revelation concludes with the promise of Christ's imminent return, an offer to drink of the water of life that flows through the great street of the new Jerusalem, and a warning to those who read the book (22:12–21). May we pray with John, "Amen. Come, Lord Jesus" (22:20).

The Bible ends with a message of warning and hope for men and women of every generation. Christ is victorious, and all evil has been done away with. As you read the book of Revelation, marvel at God's grace in the salvation of the saints and his power over the evil forces of Satan, and remember the hope of this victory to come.

1:16 The sword in Jesus' mouth symbolises the power and force of his message. His words of judgment are as sharp as swords (Isaiah 49:2; Hebrews 4:12).

1:17, 18 As the Roman government stepped up its persecution of Christians, John must have wondered if the church could survive and stand against the opposition. But Jesus appeared in glory and splendour, reassuring John that he and his fellow believers had access to God's strength to face these trials. If you are facing difficult problems, remember that the power available to John and the early church is also available to you (see 1 John 4:4).

1:17, 18 Our sins have convicted and sentenced us, but Jesus holds the keys of death and Hades. He alone can free us from eternal bondage to Satan. He alone has the power and authority to set us free from sin's control. Believers don't have to fear Hades or death, because Christ holds the keys to both. All we must do is turn from sin and turn to him in faith. When we attempt to control our lives and disregard God, we set a course that leads directly to hell. But when we place our lives in Christ's hands, he restores us now and resurrects us later to an eternal, peaceful relationship with him.

on me and said: "Do not be afraid. I am the First and the Last.[c] 18I am the Living
One; I was dead,[d] and behold I am alive for ever and ever![e] And I hold the keys
of death and Hades.[f]
19"Write, therefore, what you have seen, what is now and what will take place later.
20The mystery of the seven stars that you saw in my right hand and of the seven golden
lampstands[g] is this: The seven stars are the angels[c] of the seven churches,[h] and the
seven lampstands are the seven churches.[i]

To the Church in Ephesus

2 "To the angel[a] of the church in Ephesus write:

These are the words of him who holds the seven stars in his right hand[a] and
walks among the seven golden lampstands:[b] 2I know your deeds,[c] your hard
work and your perseverance. I know that you cannot tolerate wicked men, that
you have tested[d] those who claim to be apostles but are not, and have found them
false.[e] 3You have persevered and have endured hardships for my name,[f] and
have not grown weary.
4Yet I hold this against you: You have forsaken your first love.[g] 5Remember
the height from which you have fallen! Repent[h] and do the things you did at
first. If you do not repent, I will come to you and remove your lampstand[i] from

c 20 Or *messengers* a 1 Or *messenger*, also in verses 8, 12 and 18

1:17 [c] Isa 41:4; 44:6; 48:12; Rev 22:13
1:18 [d] Ro 6:9 [e] Rev 4:9, 10 [f] Rev 20:1
1:20 [g] Zec 4:2 [h] ver 4, 11 [i] Mt 5:14, 15
2:1 [a] Rev 1:16 [b] Rev 1:12, 13
2:2 [c] Rev 3:1, 8, 15 [d] 1Jn 4:1 [e] 2Co 11:13
2:3 [f] Jn 15:21
2:4 [g] Mt 24:12
2:5 [h] ver 16, 22 [i] Rev 1:20

1:20 Who are the "angels of the seven churches"? Some say that they are angels designated to guard the churches; others say that they are elders or pastors of the local churches. Because the seven letters in chapters 2 and 3 contain reprimands, it is doubtful that these angels are heavenly messengers. If these are earthly leaders or messengers, they are accountable to God for the churches they represent.

2:1 Ephesus was the capital of Asia Minor, a centre of land and sea trade, and, along with Alexandria and Antioch in Syria, one of the three most influential cities in the eastern part of the Roman empire. The temple to Artemis, one of the ancient wonders of the world, was located in this city, and a major industry was the manufacture of images of this goddess (see Acts 19:21–41). Paul ministered in Ephesus for three years and warned the Ephesians that false teachers would come and try to draw people away from the faith (see Acts 20:29–31). False teachers did indeed cause problems in the Ephesian church, but the church resisted them, as we can see from Paul's letter to them (see the book of Ephesians). John spent much of his ministry in this city and knew that they had resisted false teaching (2:2).

2:1 The one who "walks among the seven golden lampstands" (the seven churches) is Jesus (1:11–13). He holds the "seven stars in his right hand" (messengers of the churches), indicating his power and authority over the churches and their leaders. Ephesus had become a large, proud church, and Jesus' message would remind them that he alone is the head of the body of believers.

2:1ff Does God care about your church? If you are tempted to doubt it, look more closely at these seven letters. The Lord of the universe knew each of these churches and its precise situation. In each letter, Jesus told John to write about specific people, places, and events. He praised believers for their successes and told them how to correct their failures. Just as Jesus cared for each of these churches, he cares for yours. He wants it to reach its greatest potential. The group of believers with whom you worship and serve is God's vehicle for changing the world. Take it seriously – God does.

2:2 Over a long period of time, the church in Ephesus had steadfastly refused to tolerate sin among its members. This was not easy in a city noted for immoral sexual practices associated with the worship of the goddess Artemis. We too are living in times of widespread sin and sexual immorality. It is popular to be open-minded towards many types of sin, calling them personal choices or alternative life-styles. But when the body of believers begins to tolerate sin in the church, it is lowering the standards and compromising the church's witness. Remember that God's approval is infinitely more important than the world's.

2:2, 3 Christ commended the church at Ephesus for (1) working hard, (2) persevering, (3) resisting sin, (4) critically examining the claims of false apostles, and (5) enduring hardships without becoming weary. Every church should have these characteristics. But these good efforts should spring from our love for Jesus Christ. Both Jesus and John stressed love for one another as an authentic proof of the gospel (John 13:34; 1 John 3:18, 19). In the battle to maintain sound teaching and moral and doctrinal purity, it is possible to lose a charitable spirit. Prolonged conflict can weaken or destroy our patience and affection. In defending the faith, guard against any structure or rigidity that weakens love.

2:4 Paul had once commended the church at Ephesus for its love for God and others (Ephesians 1:15), but many of the church founders had died, and many of the second-generation believers had lost their zeal for God. They were a busy church – the members did much to benefit themselves and the community – but they were acting out of the wrong motives. Work for God must be motivated by love for God or it will not last.

2:4, 5 Just as when a man and woman fall in love, so also new believers rejoice at their newfound forgiveness. But when we lose sight of the seriousness of sin, we begin to lose the thrill of our forgiveness (see 2 Peter 1:9). In the first steps of your Christian life, you may have had enthusiasm without knowledge. Do you now have knowledge without enthusiasm? Both are necessary if we are to keep love for God intense and untarnished (see Hebrews 10:32, 35). Do you love God with the same fervour as when you were a new Christian?

2:5 For Jesus to "remove your lampstand from its place" would mean the church would cease to be an effective church. Just as the seven-branched candlestick in the temple gave light for the priests to see, the churches were to give light to their surrounding communities. But Jesus warned them that their lights could go out. In fact, Jesus himself would extinguish any light that did not fulfil its purpose. The church had to repent of its sins.

2:6 [j]ver 15

2:7 [k]Mt 11:15; Rev 3:6, 13, 22 [l]Ge 2:9; Rev 22:2, 14, 19 [m]Lk 23:43

2:8 [n]Rev 1:11 [o]Rev 1:17

its place. 6But you have this in your favour: You hate the practices of the
Nicolaitans,[j] which I also hate.
7He who has an ear, let him hear[k] what the Spirit says to the churches. To
him who overcomes, I will give the right to eat from the tree of life,[l] which
is in the paradise[m] of God.

To the Church in Smyrna

8"To the angel of the church in Smyrna[n] write:

These are the words of him who is the First and the Last,[o] who died and came

INTERPRETING THE BOOK OF REVELATION
Over the centuries, four main approaches to interpreting the book of Revelation have developed. Each approach has had capable supporters, but none has proved itself the only way to read this book. However, the most basic application question for each approach can be summarised by asking yourself, "Will this help me become a better follower of Jesus Christ today?"

Approach	*Description*	*Challenge*	*Caution*
PRETERIST VIEW	John is writing to encourage Christians in his own day who are experiencing persecution from the Roman empire.	To gain the same kind of encouragement John's first readers gained from the vivid images of God's sovereignty.	Do not forget that most biblical prophecy has both an immediate and a future application.
FUTURIST VIEW	Except for the first three chapters, John is describing events that will occur at the end of history.	To see in contemporary events many of the characteristics John describes and realise that the end could come at any time.	Do not assume that we have figured out the future, since Jesus said that no-one will know the day of his return before it happens.
HISTORICIST VIEW	The book of Revelation is a presentation of history from John's day until the second coming of Christ and beyond.	To note the consistency of human evil throughout history and recognise that names may change but the rebellion against God has not.	Be careful before identifying current events or leaders as fulfilling aspects of the book of Revelation.
IDEALIST VIEW	The book of Revelation is a symbolic representation of the continual struggle of good and evil. It does not refer to any particular historical events. It is applicable at any point in history.	Read the book to gain insight into the past, to prepare for the future, and to live obediently and confidently in the present.	Do not avoid the book because it is difficult. Try to understand Revelation within its broader literary context.

2:6 The Nicolaitans were believers who compromised their faith in order to enjoy some of the sinful practices of Ephesian society. The name *Nicolaitans* is held by some to be roughly the Greek equivalent of the Hebrew word for "Balaamites". Balaam was a prophet who induced the Israelites to carry out their lustful desires (see 2:14 and Numbers 31:16). When we want to take part in an activity that we know is wrong, we may make excuses to justify our behaviour, saying that it isn't as bad as it seems or that it won't hurt our faith. Christ has strong words for those who look for excuses to sin.

2:6 Through John, Jesus commended the church at Ephesus for hating the wicked practices of the Nicolaitans. Note that they didn't hate the people, just their sinful actions. We should accept and love all people and refuse to tolerate all evil. God cannot tolerate sin, and he expects us to stand against it. The world needs Christians who will stand for God's truth and point people towards right living.

2:7 To overcome is to be victorious by believing in Christ, persevering, remaining faithful, and living as one who follows Christ. Such a life brings great rewards (21:7).

2:7 Two trees were in the Garden of Eden – the tree of life and the tree of the knowledge of good and evil (see Genesis 2:9). Eating from the tree of life brought eternal life with God; eating from the tree of knowledge brought realisation of good and evil. When Adam and Eve ate from the tree of knowledge, they disobeyed God's command. So they were excluded from Eden and barred from eating from the tree of life. Eventually, evil will be destroyed and believers will be brought into a restored paradise. In the new earth, everyone will eat from the tree of life and will live for ever.

2:8 The city of Smyrna was about 25 miles north of Ephesus. It was nicknamed "Port of Asia" because it had an excellent harbour on the Aegean Sea. The church in this city struggled against two hostile forces: a Jewish population strongly opposed to Christianity, and a non-Jewish population that was loyal to Rome and supported emperor worship. Persecution and suffering were inevitable in an environment like this.

to life again.[p] 9I know your afflictions and your poverty—yet you are rich![q]
I know the slander of those who say they are Jews and are not,[r] but are a
synagogue of Satan.[s] 10Do not be afraid of what you are about to suffer. I tell
you, the devil will put some of you in prison to test you,[t] and you will suffer
persecution for ten days.[u] Be faithful,[v] even to the point of death, and I will
give you the crown of life.
11He who has an ear, let him hear what the Spirit says to the churches. He
who overcomes will not be hurt at all by the second death.[w]

To the Church in Pergamum

12"To the angel of the church in Pergamum[x] write:

These are the words of him who has the sharp, double-edged sword.[y] 13I know
where you live—where Satan has his throne. Yet you remain true to my name.
You did not renounce your faith in me,[z] even in the days of Antipas, my faithful
witness, who was put to death in your city—where Satan lives.[a]
14Nevertheless, I have a few things against you:[b] You have people there who
hold to the teaching of Balaam,[c] who taught Balak to entice the Israelites to sin
by eating food sacrificed to idols and by committing sexual immorality.[d] 15Like-
wise you also have those who hold to the teaching of the Nicolaitans.[e] 16Repent
therefore! Otherwise, I will soon come to you and will fight against them with
the sword of my mouth.[f]
17He who has an ear, let him hear what the Spirit says to the churches. To him

2:8 [p]Rev 1:18
2:9 [q]Jas 2:5 [r]Rev 3:9 [s]Mt 4:10
2:10 [t]Rev 3:10 [u]Da 1:12, 14 [v]ver 13
2:11 [w]Rev 20:6, 14; 21:8
2:12 [x]Rev 1:11 [y]Rev 1:16
2:13 [z]Rev 14:12 [a]ver 9, 24
2:14 [b]ver 20 [c]2Pe 2:15 [d]1Co 6:13
2:15 [e]ver 6
2:16 [f]2Th 2:8; Rev 1:16

2:9, 10 Persecution comes from Satan, not from God. Satan, the devil, will cause believers to be thrown into prison and even killed. But believers need not fear death, because it will only result in their receiving the crown of life. Satan may harm their earthly bodies, but he can do them no spiritual harm. The "synagogue of Satan" means that these Jews were serving Satan's purposes, not God's, when they gathered to worship. "Ten days" means that although persecution would be intense, it would be relatively short. It would have a definite beginning and end, and God would remain in complete control.

2:9–11 Pain is part of life, but it is never easy to suffer, no matter what the cause. Jesus commended the church at Smyrna for its faith in suffering. He then encouraged the believers that they need not fear the future if they remained faithful. If you are experiencing difficult times, don't let them turn you away from God. Instead let them draw you towards greater faithfulness. Trust God and remember your heavenly reward (see also 22:12–14).

2:10 Smyrna was famous for its athletic games. A crown was the victory wreath, the trophy for the champion at the games. If we have been faithful, we will receive the prize of victory—eternal life (James 1:12). The message to the Smyrna church was to remain faithful during their suffering because God is in control and his promises are reliable. Jesus never says that by being faithful to him we will avoid troubles, suffering, and persecution. Rather, we must be faithful to him *in* our sufferings. Only then will our faith prove to be genuine. We remain faithful by keeping our eyes on Christ and on what he promises us now and in the future (see Philippians 3:13, 14; 2 Timothy 4:8).

2:11 Believers and unbelievers alike experience physical death. All people will be resurrected, but believers will be resurrected to eternal life with God while unbelievers will be resurrected to be punished with a second death, eternal separation from God (see also 20:14; 21:8, 27; 22:15).

2:12 The city of Pergamum was built on a hill 1,000 feet above the surrounding countryside, creating a natural fortress. It was a sophisticated city, a centre of Greek culture and education, with a 200,000-volume library. But it was also the centre of four cults, and it rivalled Ephesus in its worship of idols. The city's chief god was Asclepius, whose symbol was a serpent, and who was considered the god of healing. People came to Pergamum from all over the world to seek healing from this god.

2:12 Just as the Romans used their swords for authority and judgment, Jesus' sharp, double-edged sword represents God's ultimate authority and judgment. It may also represent God's future separation of believers from unbelievers. Unbelievers cannot experience the eternal rewards of living in God's kingdom.

2:13 As the centre for four idolatrous cults (Zeus, Dionysius, Asclepius, and Athene), Pergamum was called the city "where Satan has his throne". Surrounded by worship of Satan and the Roman emperor as god, the church at Pergamum refused to renounce their faith, even when Satan's worshippers martyred one of their members. Standing firm against the strong pressures and temptations of society is never easy, but the alternative is deadly (2:11).

2:13–15 It was not easy to be a Christian in Pergamum. Believers experienced great pressure to compromise or leave the faith. (For information on the Nicolaitans, see the first note on 2:6.) Nothing is known about Antipas except that he did *not* compromise. He was faithful, and he died for his faith. Apparently, however, some in the church were tolerating those who taught or practised what Christ opposed. Compromise can be defined as a blending of the qualities of two different things or a concession of principles. Co-operate with people as much as you can, but avoid any alliance, partnership, or participation that could lead to immoral practices.

2:14 There is room for differences of opinion among Christians in some areas, but there is no room for heresy and moral impurity. Your town might not participate in idol feasts, but it probably has pornography, sexual sin, cheating, gossiping, and lying. Don't tolerate sin by bowing to the pressure to be open-minded.

2:14–16 Balak was a king who feared the large number of Israelites travelling through his country, so he employed Balaam to pronounce a curse on them. Balaam refused at first, but an offer of money changed his mind (Numbers 22—24). Later Balaam influenced the Israelites to turn to idol worship (Numbers 31:16; also see 2 Peter 2:15; Jude 11). Here Christ rebuked the church for tolerating those who, like Balaam, lead people away from God.

2:16 This sword is God's judgment against rebellious nations (19:15, 21) and all forms of sin. See also the note on 1:16 and the second note on 2:12.

2:17
[g]Jn 6:49, 50
[h]Isa 62:2
[i]Rev 19:12

who overcomes, I will give some of the hidden manna.[g] I will also give him
a white stone with a new name[h] written on it, known only to him who receives
it.[i]

To the Church in Thyatira

2:18
[j]Rev 1:11
[k]Rev 1:14, 15

18"To the angel of the church in Thyatira[j] write:

These are the words of the Son of God, whose eyes are like blazing fire and
whose feet are like burnished bronze.[k] 19I know your deeds,[l] your love and
faith, your service and perseverance, and that you are now doing more than you
did at first.

2:19
[l]ver 2

THE SEVEN CHURCHES
The seven churches were located on a major Roman road. A letter carrier would leave the island of Patmos (where John was exiled), arriving first at Ephesus. He would travel north to Smyrna and Pergamum, turn southeast to Thyatira, and continue on to Sardis, Philadelphia, and Laodicea—the exact order in which the letters were dictated.

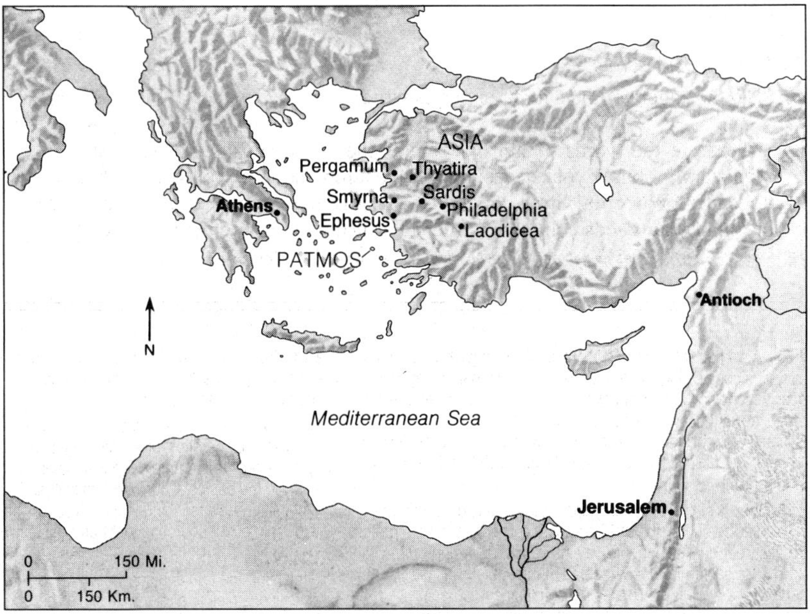

2:17 "Hidden manna" suggests the spiritual nourishment that the faithful believers will receive. As the Israelites travelled towards the promised land, God provided manna from heaven for their physical nourishment (Exodus 16:13–18). Jesus, as the bread of life (John 6:51), provides spiritual nourishment that satisfies our deepest hunger.

2:17 It is unclear what the white stones are or exactly what the names on each will be. Because they relate to the hidden manna, they may be symbols of the believer's eternal nourishment, or eternal life. The stones are significant because each will bear the new name of every person who truly believes in Christ. They are the evidence that a person has been accepted by God and declared worthy to receive eternal life. A person's name represented his or her character. God will give us new names and new hearts.

2:18 Thyatira was a working man's town, with many trade guilds for cloth making, dyeing, and pottery. Lydia, Paul's first convert in Philippi, was a merchant from Thyatira (Acts 16:14). The city was basically secular, with no focus on any particular religion.

2:19 The believers in Thyatira were commended for growing in good deeds. We should not feel satisfied when our church only rejoices in the salvation of its members or in the comfort of gathering for worship. We should grow in love, faith, and acts of service. Because the times are critical, we must spend our days wisely and faithfully.

20Nevertheless, I have this against you: You tolerate that woman Jezebel,[m]
who calls herself a prophetess. By her teaching she misleads my servants into
sexual immorality and the eating of food sacrificed to idols. 21I have given her
time[n] to repent of her immorality, but she is unwilling.[o] 22So I will cast her
on a bed of suffering, and I will make those who commit adultery[p] with her
suffer intensely, unless they repent of her ways. 23I will strike her children dead.
Then all the churches will know that I am he who searches hearts and minds,[q]
and I will repay each of you according to your deeds. 24Now I say to the rest
of you in Thyatira, to you who do not hold to her teaching and have not learned
Satan's so-called deep secrets (I will not impose any other burden on you):[r]
25Only hold on to what you have[s] until I come.

26To him who overcomes and does my will to the end, I will give authority
over the nations[t]—

> 27'He will rule them with an iron sceptre;[u]
> he will dash them to pieces like pottery'[b][v]—

just as I have received authority from my Father. 28I will also give him the
morning star.[w] 29He who has an ear, let him hear[x] what the Spirit says to the
churches.

To the Church in Sardis

3 "To the angel[a] of the church in Sardis write:

These are the words of him who holds the seven spirits[b][a] of God and the
seven stars.[b] I know your deeds;[c] you have a reputation of being alive, but you
are dead.[d] 2Wake up! Strengthen what remains and is about to die, for I have
not found your deeds complete in the sight of my God. 3Remember, therefore,

b *27* Psalm 2:9 **a** *1* Or *messenger*, also in verses 7 and 14 **b** *1* Or *the sevenfold Spirit*

2:20 [m]1Ki 16:31; 21:25; 2Ki 9:7
2:21 [n]Ro 2:4 [o]Rev 9:20
2:22 [p]Rev 17:2; 18:9
2:23 [q]1Sa 16:7; Jer 11:20; Ac 1:24; Ro 8:27
2:24 [r]Ac 15:28
2:25 [s]Rev 3:11
2:26 [t]Ps 2:8; Rev 3:21
2:27 [u]Rev 12:5 [v]Isa 30:14; Jer 19:11
2:28 [w]Rev 22:16
2:29 [x]ver 7
3:1 [a]Rev 1:4 [b]Rev 1:16 [c]Rev 2:2 [d]1Ti 5:6

2:20 A woman in the church in Thyatira was teaching that immorality was not a serious matter for believers. Her name may have been Jezebel, or John may have used the name Jezebel to symbolise the kind of evil she was promoting. Jezebel, a pagan queen of Israel, was considered the most evil woman who ever lived (see 1 Kings 19:1, 2; 21:1–15; 2 Kings 9:7–10, 30–37; and her Profile in 1 Kings 21).

2:20 Why is sexual immorality serious? Sex outside marriage always hurts someone. It hurts God because it shows that we prefer to satisfy our desires our own way instead of according to God's word, or to satisfy them now instead of waiting for his timing. It hurts others because it violates the commitment so necessary to a relationship. It hurts us because it often brings disease to our bodies and adversely affects our personalities. Sexual immorality has tremendous power to destroy families, churches, and communities because it destroys the integrity on which these relationships are built. God wants to protect us from hurting ourselves and others; thus we are to have no part in sexual immorality, even if our culture accepts it.

2:20 In pagan temples, meat was often offered to idols. Then the meat that wasn't burned was sold to shoppers in the temple marketplace. Eating meat offered to idols wasn't wrong in itself, but it could violate the principle of sensitivity towards weaker Christian brothers and sisters who would be bothered by it (see 1 Corinthians 8 and the note on Romans 14:2). Jezebel was obviously more concerned about her own selfish pleasure and freedom than about the needs and concerns of fellow believers.

2:21 Jezebel was unwilling to repent. "Repent" means to change our mind and direction from following our way to following God's way, from sin and its disastrous consequences to God and eternal life. In his mercy, God has given us time to decide to follow him. Only our stubborn wilfulness stands in the way.

2:23 We cannot hide from Christ; he knows what is in our hearts and minds, and still he loves us. The sins we try to hide from God need to be confessed to him.

2:24, 25 The "deep secrets" of Satan were either false teaching advocated by heretics, or secret insights by so-called believers "guaranteed" to promote deeper spiritual life. We should hold tightly to the basics of our Christian faith and view with caution and counsel any new teaching that turns us away from the Bible, the fellowship of our church, or our basic confession of faith.

2:26, 27 Christ says that those who overcome (those who remain faithful until the end and continue to please God) will rule over Christ's enemies and reign with him as he judges evil (see also Psalm 2:8, 9; Isaiah 30:14; Jeremiah 19:11; 1 Corinthians 6:2, 3; Revelation 12:5; 19:15; 20:3, 4 for more about God's judgment).

2:28 Christ is called the morning star in 2:28, 22:16, and 2 Peter 1:19. A morning star appears just before dawn, when the night is coldest and darkest. When the world is at its bleakest point, Christ will burst onto the scene, exposing evil with his light of truth and bringing his promised reward.

3:1 The wealthy city of Sardis was actually in two locations. The older section of the city was on a mountain, and, when its population outgrew the spot, a newer section was built in the valley below.

3:1 The "seven spirits of God" is another name for the Holy Spirit. The seven stars are the messengers, or leaders, of the churches (see 2:1).

3:1 The problem in the Sardis church was not heresy, but spiritual death. In spite of its reputation for being active, Sardis was infested with sin. Its deeds were evil and its clothes soiled. The Spirit has no words of commendation for this church that looked so good on the outside but was so corrupt on the inside.

3:3 The church at Sardis was urged to obey the Christian truth they had heard when they first believed in Christ, to get back to the

3:3
[e]Rev 2:5
[f]2Pe 3:10

3:4
[g]Jude 23
[h]Rev 4:4; 6:11; 7:9, 13, 14

3:5
[i]Rev 20:12
[j]Mt 10:32

3:6
[k]Rev 2:7

3:7
[l]Rev 1:11
[m]1Jn 5:20
[n]Isa 22:22; Mt 16:19

3:8
[o]Ac 14:27
[p]Rev 2:13

3:9
[q]Rev 2:9
[r]Isa 49:23
[s]Isa 43:4

3:10
[t]2Pe 2:9
[u]Rev 2:10
[v]Rev 6:10; 17:8

3:11
[w]Rev 2:25

what you have received and heard; obey it, and repent.[e] But if you do not wake
up, I will come like a thief,[f] and you will not know at what time I will come
to you.
4Yet you have a few people in Sardis who have not soiled their clothes.[g] They
will walk with me, dressed in white,[h] for they are worthy. 5He who overcomes
will, like them, be dressed in white. I will never blot out his name from the book
of life,[i] but will acknowledge his name before my Father[j] and his angels. 6He
who has an ear, let him hear[k] what the Spirit says to the churches.

To the Church in Philadelphia

7"To the angel of the church in Philadelphia[l] write:

These are the words of him who is holy and true,[m] who holds the key of
David.[n] What he opens no-one can shut, and what he shuts no-one can open.
8I know your deeds. See, I have placed before you an open door[o] that no-one
can shut. I know that you have little strength, yet you have kept my word and
have not denied my name.[p] 9I will make those who are of the synagogue of
Satan,[q] who claim to be Jews though they are not, but are liars—I will make
them come and fall down at your feet[r] and acknowledge that I have loved you.[s]
10Since you have kept my command to endure patiently, I will also keep you[t]
from the hour of trial that is going to come upon the whole world to test[u] those
who live on the earth.[v]
11I am coming soon. Hold on to what you have,[w] so that no-one will take your

THE NAMES OF JESUS

Reference	Jesus' name	Reference	Jesus' name
1:8	The Alpha and the Omega	5:5	Root of David
1:8	Lord	5:6	Lamb
1:8	Almighty	7:17	Shepherd
1:13	Son of Man	12:10	Christ
1:17	The First and the Last	19:11	Faithful and True
1:18	The Living One		
2:18	Son of God	19:13	Word of God
3:14	Witness	19:16	King of kings
4:11	Creator	19:16	Lord of lords
5:5	Lion of the tribe of Judah	22:16	The Morning Star

Scattered among the vivid images of the book of Revelation is a large collection of names for Jesus. Each one tells something of his character and highlights a particular aspect of his role within God's plan of redemption.

basics of the faith. It is important to grow in our knowledge of the Lord, to deepen our understanding through careful study. But no matter how much we learn, we must never abandon the basic truths about Jesus. Jesus will always be God's Son, and his sacrifice for our sins is permanent. No new truth from God will ever contradict these biblical teachings.

3:5 To be "dressed in white" means to be set apart for God and made pure. Christ promises future honour and eternal life to those who stand firm in their faith. The names of all believers are registered in the book of life. This book symbolises God's knowledge of who belongs to him. All such people are guaranteed a place in the book of life and are introduced to the hosts of heaven as belonging to Christ (see Luke 12:8, 9).

3:7 Philadelphia was founded by the citizens of Pergamum. The community was built in a border area as a gateway to the central plateau of Asia Minor. Philadelphia's residents kept barbarians out of the region and brought in Greek culture and language. The city was destroyed by an earthquake in A.D. 17, and aftershocks kept the people so worried that most of them lived outside the city limits.

3:7 The key of David represents Christ's authority to open the door of invitation into his future kingdom. After the door is opened, no-one can close it—salvation is assured. Once it is closed, no-one can open it—judgment is certain.

3:10 Some believe that "I will also keep you from the hour of trial" means there will be a future time of great tribulation from which true believers will be spared. Others interpret this to mean that the church will go through the time of tribulation and that God will keep them strong in the midst of it. Still others believe this refers to times of great distress in general, the church's suffering through the ages. Whatever the case, our emphasis should be on patiently obeying God no matter what we may face.

3:11 Christians have differing gifts, abilities, experience, and maturity. God doesn't expect us all to be and act the same, but he does expect us to "hold on" to what we have, to persevere in using our resources for him. The Philadelphians are commended for their effort to obey (3:8) and encouraged to hold tightly to whatever strength they have. You may be a new believer and feel that your faith and spiritual strength are little. Use what you have to live for Christ, and God will commend you.

crown.[x] 12 Him who overcomes I will make a pillar[y] in the temple of my God.
Never again will he leave it. I will write on him the name of my God[z] and the
name of the city of my God, the new Jerusalem,[a] which is coming down out
of heaven from my God; and I will also write on him my new name. 13 He who
has an ear, let him hear what the Spirit says to the churches.

To the Church in Laodicea

14 "To the angel of the church in Laodicea write:

These are the words of the Amen, the faithful and true witness, the ruler of
God's creation.[b] 15 I know your deeds, that you are neither cold nor hot.[c] I wish
you were either one or the other! 16 So, because you are lukewarm—neither hot
nor cold—I am about to spit you out of my mouth. 17 You say, 'I am rich; I have
acquired wealth and do not need a thing.'[d] But you do not realise that you are
wretched, pitiful, poor, blind and naked. 18 I counsel you to buy from me gold
refined in the fire, so that you can become rich; and white clothes to wear, so
that you can cover your shameful nakedness;[e] and salve to put on your eyes,
so that you can see.

19 Those whom I love I rebuke and discipline.[f] So be earnest, and repent.[g]
20 Here I am! I stand at the door[h] and knock. If anyone hears my voice and opens
the door,[i] I will come in[j] and eat with him, and he with me.

21 To him who overcomes, I will give the right to sit with me on my throne,[k]
just as I overcame[l] and sat down with my Father on his throne. 22 He who has
an ear, let him hear[m] what the Spirit says to the churches."

3:11 [x] Rev 2:10
3:12 [y] Gal 2:9; [z] Rev 14:1; 22:4; [a] Rev 21:2, 10
3:14 [b] Col 1:16, 18
3:15 [c] Ro 12:11
3:17 [d] Hos 12:8; 1Co 4:8
3:18 [e] Rev 16:15
3:19 [f] Pr 3:12; Heb 12:5, 6; [g] Rev 2:5
3:20 [h] Mt 24:33; [i] Lk 12:36; [j] Jn 14:23
3:21 [k] Mt 19:28; [l] Rev 5:5
3:22 [m] Rev 2:7

3:12 The new Jerusalem is the future dwelling of the people of God (21:2). We will have a new citizenship in God's future kingdom. Everything will be new, pure, and secure.

3:14 Laodicea was the wealthiest of the seven cities, known for its banking industry, manufacture of wool, and a medical school that produced eye salve. But the city had always had a problem with its water supply. At one time an aqueduct was built to bring water to the city from hot springs. But by the time the water reached the city, it was neither hot nor refreshingly cool—only lukewarm. The church had become as bland as the tepid water that came into the city.

3:15 Lukewarm water makes an unpleasant drink. The church in Laodicea had become lukewarm and thus distasteful and repugnant. The believers didn't take a stand on anything; indifference had led to idleness. By neglecting to do anything for Christ, the church had become hardened and self-satisfied, and it was destroying itself. There is nothing worse than a halfhearted, nominal Christian who is self-sufficient. Don't settle for following God halfway. Let Christ fire up your faith and stir you into action.

3:17 Some believers assume that numerous material possessions are a sign of God's spiritual blessing. Laodicea was a wealthy city, and the church was also wealthy. But what the Laodiceans could see and buy had become more valuable to them than what is unseen and eternal. Wealth, luxury, and ease can make people feel confident, satisfied, and complacent. But no matter how much you possess or how much money you make, you have nothing if you don't have a vital relationship with Christ. How does your current level of wealth affect your spiritual desire? Instead of centring your life primarily on comfort and luxury, find your true riches in Christ.

3:18 Laodicea was known for its great wealth—but Christ told the Laodiceans to buy their gold from him (real spiritual treasures). The city was proud of its cloth and dyeing industries—but Christ told them to purchase white clothes from him (his righteousness). Laodicea prided itself on its precious eye salve that healed many eye problems—but Christ told them to get medicine from him to heal their eyes so they could see the truth (John 9:39). Christ was showing the Laodiceans that true value was not in material possessions, but in a right relationship with God. Their possessions and achievements were valueless compared with the everlasting future of Christ's kingdom.

3:19 God would discipline this lukewarm church unless it turned from its indifference towards him. God's purpose in discipline is not to punish, but to bring people back to him. Are you lukewarm in your devotion to God? God may discipline you to help you out of your uncaring attitude, but he uses only loving discipline. You can avoid God's discipline by drawing near to him again through confession, service, worship, and studying his word. Just as the spark of love can be rekindled in marriage, so the Holy Spirit can reignite our zeal for God when we allow him to work in our hearts.

3:20 The Laodicean church was complacent and rich. They felt self-satisfied, but they didn't have Christ's presence among them. Christ knocked at the door of their hearts, but they were so busy enjoying worldly pleasures that they didn't notice that he was trying to enter. The pleasures of this world—money, security, material possessions—can be dangerous, because their temporary satisfaction makes us indifferent to God's offer of lasting satisfaction. If you find yourself feeling indifferent to church, to God, or to the Bible, you have begun to shut God out of your life. Leave the door of your heart constantly open to God, and you won't need to worry about hearing his knock. Letting him in is your only hope for lasting fulfilment.

3:20 Jesus is knocking on the door of our hearts every time we sense we should turn to him. Jesus wants to have fellowship with us, and he wants us to open up to him. He is patient and persistent in trying to get through to us—not breaking and entering, but knocking. He allows us to decide whether or not to open our lives to him. Do you intentionally keep his life-changing presence and power on the other side of the door?

3:22 At the end of each letter to these churches, the believers were urged to listen and take to heart what was written to them. Although a different message was addressed to each church, all the messages contain warnings and principles for everyone. Which letter speaks most directly to your church? Which has the greatest bearing on your own spiritual condition at this time? How will you respond?

4:1 [a]Rev 1:10 [b]Rev 11:12 [c]Rev 1:19
4:2 [d]Rev 1:10 [e]Isa 6:1; Eze 1:26-28; Da 7:9
4:3 [f]Eze 1:28
4:4 [g]Rev 11:16 [h]Rev 3:4, 5
4:5 [i]Rev 8:5; 16:18 [j]Zec 4:2 [k]Rev 1:4
4:6 [l]Rev 15:2 [m]Eze 1:5
4:7 [n]Eze 1:10; 10:14

B. MESSAGE FOR THE CHURCH (4:1 – 22:21)

Moving from the conditions within the churches in Asia to the future of the universal church, John sees the course of coming events in a way similar to Daniel and Ezekiel. Many of these passages contain clear spiritual teachings, but others seem beyond our ability to understand. The clear teaching of this book is that God will defeat all evil in the end. We must live in obedience to Jesus Christ, the coming Conqueror and Judge.

1. Worshipping God in heaven

The Throne in Heaven

4 After this I looked, and there before me was a door standing open in heaven. And
the voice I had first heard speaking to me like a trumpet[a] said, "Come up here,[b]
and I will show you what must take place after this."[c] 2 At once I was in the Spirit,[d]
and there before me was a throne in heaven[e] with someone sitting on it. 3 And the
one who sat there had the appearance of jasper and carnelian. A rainbow,[f] resembling
an emerald, encircled the throne. 4 Surrounding the throne were twenty-four other
thrones, and seated on them were twenty-four elders.[g] They were dressed in white[h]
and had crowns of gold on their heads. 5 From the throne came flashes of lightning,
rumblings and peals of thunder.[i] Before the throne, seven lamps[j] were blazing.
These are the seven spirits[a][k] of God. 6 Also before the throne there was what looked
like a sea of glass,[l] clear as crystal.
In the centre, around the throne, were four living creatures,[m] and they were covered
with eyes, in front and behind. 7 The first living creature was like a lion, the second
was like an ox, the third had a face like a man, the fourth was like a flying eagle.[n]

a 5 Or *the sevenfold Spirit*

THE LETTERS TO THE SEVEN CHURCHES

Church	*Reference*	*Commendation*	*Rebuke*	*Action*
Ephesus	2:1–7	Hard work, perseverence	Forsaken first love	Remember and repent
Smyrna	2:8–11	Suffered persecution, poverty	None	Don't fear, be faithful
Pergamum	2:12–17	True to faith	Compromise	Repent
Thyatira	2:18–29	Love, faith, service	Immorality	Repent
Sardis	3:1–6	Effective	Superficial	Wake up, repent
Philadelphia	3:7–13	Faithful	None	Hold on
Laodicea	3:14–22	None	Lukewarm	Be earnest and repent

This summary of the letters to the seven churches shows us the qualities our churches should seek and the faults we should avoid.

4:1 Chapters 4 and 5 record glimpses into Christ's glory. Here we see into the throne room of heaven. God is on the throne and orchestrating all the events that John will record. The world is not spinning out of control; the God of creation will carry out his plans as Christ initiates the final battle with the forces of evil. John shows us heaven before showing us earth so that we will not be frightened by future events.

4:1 The voice John had first heard that sounded like a trumpet blast was the voice of Christ (see 1:10, 11).

4:2 Four times in the book of Revelation John says he was "in the Spirit" (1:10; 4:2; 17:3; 21:10). This expression means that the Holy Spirit was giving him a vision – showing him situations and events he could not have seen with mere human eyesight. All true prophecy comes from God through the Holy Spirit (2 Peter 1:20, 21).

4:4 Who are these 24 elders? Because there were 12 tribes of Israel in the Old Testament and 12 apostles in the New Testament, the 24 elders in this vision probably represent all the redeemed of God for all time (both before and after Christ's death and resurrection). They symbolise all those – both Jews and Gentiles – who are now part of God's family. The 24 elders show us that *all* the redeemed of the Lord are worshipping him.

4:5 In Revelation, lightning and thunder are connected with significant events in heaven. They remind us of the lightning and thunder at Mount Sinai when God gave the people his laws (Exodus 19:16). The Old Testament often uses such imagery to reflect God's power and majesty (Psalm 77:18).

4:5 The "seven spirits of God" is another name for the Holy Spirit. See also Zechariah 4:2–6, where the seven lamps are equated with the one Spirit.

4:6 Glass was very rare in New Testament times, and crystal-clear glass was virtually impossible to find (see 1 Corinthians 13:12). The "sea of glass" highlights both the magnificence and holiness of God.

4:6, 7 Just as the Holy Spirit is seen symbolically in the seven lighted lamps, so the "four living creatures" represent the attributes (the qualities and character) of God. These creatures were not real animals. Like the cherubim (the highest order of the angels), they guard God's throne, lead others in worship, and proclaim God's holiness. God's attributes symbolised in the animal-like appearance of these four creatures are majesty and power (the lion), faithfulness (the ox), intelligence (the man), and sovereignty (the eagle). The Old Testament prophet Ezekiel saw four similar creatures in one of his visions (Ezekiel 1:5–10).

8Each of the four living creatures had six wings[o] and was covered with eyes all
around, even under his wings. Day and night they never stop saying:

> "Holy, holy, holy
> is the Lord God Almighty,[p]
> who was, and is, and is to come."[q]

9Whenever the living creatures give glory, honour and thanks to him who sits on the
throne[r] and who lives for ever and ever, 10the twenty-four elders[s] fall down before
him[t] who sits on the throne,[u] and worship him who lives for ever and ever. They
lay their crowns before the throne and say:

> 11"You are worthy, our Lord and God,
> to receive glory and honour and power,[v]
> for you created all things,
> and by your will they were created
> and have their being."[w]

The Scroll and the Lamb

5 Then I saw in the right hand of him who sat on the throne[a] a scroll with writing
on both sides[b] and sealed[c] with seven seals. 2And I saw a mighty angel
proclaiming in a loud voice, "Who is worthy to break the seals and open the scroll?"
3But no-one in heaven or on earth or under the earth could open the scroll or even
look inside it. 4I wept and wept because no-one was found who was worthy to open
the scroll or look inside. 5Then one of the elders said to me, "Do not weep! See, the
Lion[d] of the tribe of Judah, the Root of David,[e] has triumphed. He is able to open
the scroll and its seven seals."

6Then I saw a Lamb,[f] looking as if it had been slain, standing in the centre of the
throne, encircled by the four living creatures and the elders. He had seven horns and
seven eyes,[g] which are the seven spirits[a] of God sent out into all the earth. 7He came
and took the scroll from the right hand of him who sat on the throne.[h] 8And when
he had taken it, the four living creatures and the twenty-four elders fell down before
the Lamb. Each one had a harp[i] and they were holding golden bowls full of incense,
which are the prayers[j] of the saints. 9And they sang a new song:[k]

a 6 *Or the sevenfold Spirit*

4:8 [o]Isa 6:2 [p]Isa 6:3; Rev 1:8 [q]Rev 1:4
4:9 [r]Ps 47:8
4:10 [s]ver 4 [t]Rev 5:8, 14 [u]ver 2
4:11 [v]Rev 5:12 [w]Rev 10:6
5:1 [a]ver 7, 13 [b]Eze 2:9, 10 [c]Isa 29:11; Da 12:4
5:5 [d]Ge 49:9 [e]Isa 11:1, 10; Ro 15:12; Rev 22:16
5:6 [f]Jn 1:29 [g]Zec 4:10
5:7 [h]ver 1
5:8 [i]Rev 14:2 [j]Ps 141:2
5:9 [k]Ps 40:3

4:11 The point of this chapter is summed up in this verse: all creatures in heaven and earth will praise and honour God because he is the Creator and Sustainer of everything.

5:1 In John's day, books were written on scrolls – pieces of papyrus or vellum up to 30 feet long, rolled up and sealed with clay or wax. The scroll that John sees contains the full account of what God has in store for the world. The seven seals indicate the importance of its contents. The seals are located throughout the scroll so that as each one is broken, more of the scroll can be read to reveal another phase of God's plan for the end of the world. Only Christ is worthy to break the seals and open the scroll (5:3–5).

5:1ff Chapter 5 continues the glimpse into heaven begun in chapter 4.

5:5 The Lion, Jesus, proved himself worthy to break the seals and open the scroll by living a perfect life of obedience to God, dying on the cross for the sins of the world, and rising from the dead to show his power and authority over evil and death. Only Christ conquered sin, death, hell, and Satan himself; so only he can be trusted with the world's future. The Root of David refers to Jesus being from David's family line, thus fulfilling the promise of the Messiah in the Old Testament.

5:5, 6 Jesus Christ is pictured as both a Lion (symbolising his authority and power) and a Lamb (symbolising his submission to God's will). One of the elders calls John to look at the Lion, but when John looks he sees a Lamb. Christ the Lamb was the perfect sacrifice for the sins of all mankind; therefore, only he can save us from the terrible events revealed by the scroll. Christ the Lamb won the greatest battle of all. He defeated all the forces of evil by dying on the cross. The role of Christ the Lion will be to lead the battle where Satan is finally defeated (19:19–21). Christ the Lion is victorious because of what Christ the Lamb has already done. We will participate in his victory not because of our effort or goodness, but because he has promised eternal life to all who believe in him.

5:6 John sees the Lamb "looking as if it had been slain"; the wounds inflicted on Jesus' body during his trial and crucifixion could still be seen (see John 20:24–31). Jesus was called the Lamb of God by John the Baptist (John 1:29). In the Old Testament, lambs were sacrificed to atone for sins: the Lamb of God died as the final sacrifice for all sins (see Isaiah 53:7; Hebrews 10:1–12, 18).

5:6 The horns symbolise strength and power (see 1 Kings 22:11; Zechariah 1:18). Although Christ is a sacrificial lamb, he is in no way weak. He was killed, but now he lives in God's strength and power. In Zechariah 4:2–10, the eyes are equated with the seven lamps and the one Spirit.

5:9, 10 People from every nation are praising God before his throne. God's message of salvation and eternal life is not limited to a specific culture, race, or country. Anyone who comes to God in repentance and faith is accepted by him and will be part of his kingdom. Don't allow prejudice or bias to keep you from sharing

5:9
[l] Rev 4:11
[m] Heb 9:12
[n] 1Co 6:20

"You are worthy[l] to take the scroll
and to open its seals,
because you were slain,
and with your blood[m] you purchased[n] men for God
from every tribe and language and people and nation.
10 You have made them to be a kingdom and priests[o] to serve our God,
and they will reign on the earth."

5:10
[o] 1Pe 2:5

EVENTS IN REVELATION DESCRIBED ELSEWHERE IN THE BIBLE

Other Reference	*Revelation Reference*	*Event*
Ezekiel 1:22–28	4:2, 3; 10:1–3	Glowing rainbow around God's throne
Isaiah 53:7	5:6–8	Christ is pictured as a Lamb
Psalm 96	5:9–14	New song
Zechariah 1:7–11; 6:1–8	6:1–8	Horses and riders
Isaiah 2:19–22	6:12; 8:5; 11:13	Earthquake
Joel 2:28–32; Acts 2:14–21	6:12	Moon turns blood red
Mark 13:21–25	6:13	Stars falling from the sky
Isaiah 34:1–4	6:14	Sky rolled up like a scroll
Zephaniah 1:14–18; 1 Thessalonians 5:1–3	6:15–17	God's inescapable wrath
Jeremiah 49:35–39	7:1	Four winds of judgment
Luke 8:26–34	9:1, 2; 17:3–8	Abyss (bottomless pit)
Joel 1:2—2:11	9:3–11	Plague of locusts
Luke 21:20–24	11:1–2	Trampling of the holy city of Jerusalem
Zechariah 4	11:3–6	Two olive trees as witnesses
Daniel 7	13:1–10	A beast coming out of the sea
2 Thessalonians 2:7–14	13:11–15	Wondrous signs and miracles done by the evil beast
Jeremiah 25:15–29	14:9–12	Drinking the cup of God's wrath
Isaiah 21:1–10	18:2, 3	"Babylon" falls
Matthew 22:1–14	19:5–8	Wedding supper of the Lamb
Ezekiel 38, 39	20:7–10	Conflict with Gog and Magog
John 5:19–30	20:11–15	Judging of all people
Ezekiel 37:21–28	21:3	God lives among mankind
Isaiah 25:1–8	21:4	Our tears will be wiped away for ever
Genesis 2:8–14	22:1, 2	Tree of life
1 Corinthians 13:11, 12	22:3–5	We will see God face to face
Daniel 7:18–28	22:5	Believers will reign with God for ever

Christ with others. Christ welcomes all people into his kingdom.

5:9, 10 The song of God's people praises Christ's work. He (1) was slain, (2) purchased them with his blood, (3) gathered them into a kingdom, (4) made them priests, and (5) appointed them to reign on the earth. Jesus has already died and paid the penalty for sin. He is now gathering us into his kingdom and making us priests. In the future we will reign with him. Worship God and praise him for what he has done, what he is doing, and what he will do for all who trust in him. When we realise the glorious future that awaits us, we will find the strength to face our present difficulties.

5:10 The believers' song praises Christ for bringing them into the kingdom and making them kings and priests. While now we are sometimes despised and mocked for our faith (John 15:17–27), in the future we will reign over all the earth (Luke 22:29, 30). Christ's death made all believers priests of God — the channels of blessing between God and mankind (1 Peter 2:5–9).

11Then I looked and heard the voice of many angels, numbering thousands upon
thousands, and ten thousand times ten thousand.[p] They encircled the throne and the
living creatures and the elders. 12In a loud voice they sang:

> "Worthy is the Lamb, who was slain,
> to receive power and wealth and wisdom and strength
> and honour and glory and praise!"[q]

13Then I heard every creature in heaven and on earth and under the earth[r] and on
the sea, and all that is in them, singing:

> "To him who sits on the throne and to the Lamb[s]
> be praise and honour and glory and power,
> for ever and ever!"[t]

14The four living creatures said, "Amen",[u] and the elders fell down and worshipped.[v]

2. Opening the seven seals

The Seals

6 I watched as the Lamb[a] opened the first of the seven seals.[b] Then I heard one
of the four living creatures[c] say in a voice like thunder,[d] "Come!" 2I looked,
and there before me was a white horse![e] Its rider held a bow, and he was given a
crown,[f] and he rode out as a conqueror bent on conquest.[g]
3When the Lamb opened the second seal, I heard the second living creature[h] say,
"Come!" 4Then another horse came out, a fiery red one.[i] Its rider was given power
to take peace from the earth[j] and to make men slay each other. To him was given
a large sword.
5When the Lamb opened the third seal, I heard the third living creature[k] say,
"Come!" I looked, and there before me was a black horse![l] Its rider was holding a
pair of scales in his hand. 6Then I heard what sounded like a voice among the four
living creatures,[m] saying, "A quart[a] of wheat for a day's wages,[b] and three quarts
of barley for a day's wages,[b] and do not damage[n] the oil and the wine!"

a 6 Greek *a choinix* (probably about a litre) b 6 Greek *a denarius*

5:11 [p]Da 7:10; Heb 12:22
5:12 [q]Rev 4:11
5:13 [r]ver 3; Php 2:10 [s]Rev 6:16 [t]1Ch 29:11
5:14 [u]Rev 4:9 [v]Rev 4:10; 19:4
6:1 [a]Rev 5:6 [b]Rev 5:1 [c]Rev 4:6, 7 [d]Rev 14:2; 19:6
6:2 [e]Zec 6:3; Rev 19:11 [f]Zec 6:11; Rev 14:14 [g]Ps 45:4
6:3 [h]Rev 4:7
6:4 [i]Zec 6:2 [j]Mt 10:34
6:5 [k]Rev 4:7 [l]Zec 6:2
6:6 [m]Rev 4:6, 7 [n]Rev 9:4

5:11 Angels are spiritual beings created by God who help carry out his work on earth. They bring messages (Luke 1:26–28), protect God's people (Daniel 6:22), offer encouragement (Genesis 16:7ff), give guidance (Exodus 14:19), bring punishment (2 Samuel 24:16), patrol the earth (Ezekiel 1:9–14), and fight the forces of evil (2 Kings 6:16–18; Revelation 20:1). There are both good and evil angels (12:7), but because evil angels are allied with Satan, they have considerably less power and authority than good angels. Eventually, the main role of the good angels will be to offer continuous praise to God (see also 19:1–3).

5:14 The scene in chapter 5 shows us that only the Lamb, Jesus Christ, is worthy to open the scroll (the events of history). Jesus, not Satan, holds the future. Jesus Christ is in control, and he alone is worthy to set into motion the events of the last days of history.

6:1ff This is the first of three seven-part judgments. The trumpets (chapters 8; 9) and the bowls (chapter 16) are the other two. As each seal is opened, Christ the Lamb sets in motion events that will bring about the end of human history. This scroll is not completely opened until the seventh seal is broken (8:1). The contents of the scroll reveal mankind's depravity and portray God's authority over the events of human history.

6:2ff Four horses appear as the first four seals are opened. The horses represent God's judgment of people's sin and rebellion. God is directing human history – even using his enemies to accomplish his purposes. The four horses are a foretaste of the final judgments yet to come. Some view this chapter as a parallel to the Olivet Discourse (see Matthew 24). The imagery of four horses is also found in Zechariah 6:1–8.

6:2–8 Each of the four horses is a different colour. Some assume that the white horse represents victory and that its rider must be Christ (because Christ later rides to victory on a white horse – 19:11). But because the other three horses relate to judgment and destruction, this rider on a white horse is not likely to be Christ. The four are part of the unfolding judgment of God, and it would be premature for Christ to ride forth as conqueror. The other horses represent different kinds of judgment: red for warfare and bloodshed; black for famine; pale for death. The high prices of wheat and barley illustrate famine conditions. But the worst is yet to come.

6:8 It is not clear whether Hades was on a separate horse than Death or merely rode alongside Death, but the riders described in verses 2–8 are commonly referred to as the four horsemen of the Apocalypse.

[7]When the Lamb opened the fourth seal, I heard the voice of the fourth living
creature[o] say, "Come!" [8]I looked, and there before me was a pale horse![p] Its rider
was named Death, and Hades[q] was following close behind him. They were given
power over a fourth of the earth to kill by sword, famine and plague, and by the wild
beasts of the earth.[r]

[9]When he opened the fifth seal, I saw under the altar[s] the souls of those who had
been slain[t] because of the word of God and the testimony they had maintained.
[10]They called out in a loud voice, "How long,[u] Sovereign Lord, holy and true,[v] until
you judge the inhabitants of the earth and avenge our blood?"[w] [11]Then each of them
was given a white robe,[x] and they were told to wait a little longer, until the number
of their fellow-servants and brothers who were to be killed as they had been was
completed.[y]

[12]I watched as he opened the sixth seal. There was a great earthquake.[z] The sun
turned black[a] like sackcloth made of goat hair, the whole moon turned blood red,
[13]and the stars in the sky fell to earth,[b] as late figs drop from a fig-tree[c] when shaken
by a strong wind. [14]The sky receded like a scroll, rolling up, and every mountain and
island was removed from its place.[d]

[15]Then the kings of the earth, the princes, the generals, the rich, the mighty, and
every slave and every free man hid in caves and among the rocks of the mountains.[e]
[16]They called to the mountains and the rocks, "Fall on us[f] and hide us from the face
of him who sits on the throne and from the wrath of the Lamb! [17]For the great day[g]
of their wrath has come, and who can stand?"[h]

144,000 Sealed

7 After this I saw four angels standing at the four corners of the earth, holding back
the four winds[a] of the earth to prevent any wind from blowing on the land or
on the sea or on any tree. [2]Then I saw another angel coming up from the east, having
the seal of the living God. He called out in a loud voice to the four angels who had
been given power to harm the land and the sea: [3]"Do not harm[b] the land or the sea

6:7 [o]Rev 4:7
6:8 [p]Zec 6:3 [q]Hos 13:14 [r]Jer 15:2, 3; Eze 5:12, 17
6:9 [s]Rev 14:18; 16:7 [t]Rev 20:4
6:10 [u]Zec 1:12 [v]Rev 3:7 [w]Rev 19:2
6:11 [x]Rev 3:4 [y]Heb 11:40
6:12 [z]Rev 16:18 [a]Mt 24:29
6:13 [b]Mt 24:29; Rev 8:10; 9:1 [c]Isa 34:4
6:14 [d]Jer 4:24; Rev 16:20
6:15 [e]Isa 2:10, 19, 21
6:16 [f]Hos 10:8; Lk 23:30
6:17 [g]Zep 1:14, 15; Rev 16:14 [h]Ps 76:7
7:1 [a]Da 7:2
7:3 [b]Rev 6:6

6:8 The four riders are given power over one-fourth of the earth, indicating that God is still limiting his judgment—it is not yet complete. With these judgments there is still time for unbelievers to turn to Christ and away from their sin. In this case, the limited punishment not only demonstrates God's wrath against sin, but also his merciful love in giving people yet another opportunity to turn to him before he brings final judgment.

6:9 The altar represents the altar of sacrifice in the temple, where animals were sacrificed to atone for sins. Instead of the animals' blood at the base of the altar, John saw the souls of martyrs who had died for preaching the gospel. These martyrs were told that still more would lose their lives for their belief in Christ (6:11). In the face of warfare, famine, persecution, and death, Christians will be called on to stand firmly for what they believe. Only those who endure to the end will be rewarded by God (Mark 13:13).

6:9–11 The martyrs are eager for God to bring justice to the earth, but they are told to wait. God is not waiting until a certain number is reached, but he is promising that those who suffer and die for their faith will not be forgotten. Rather, they will be singled out by God for special honour. We may wish for justice immediately, as these martyrs did, but we must be patient. God works according to his own timetable, and he promises justice. No suffering for the sake of God's kingdom, however, is wasted.

6:12 The sixth seal changes the scene back to the physical world. The first five judgments were directed towards specific areas, but this judgment is universal. Everyone will be afraid when the earth itself trembles.

6:15–17 At the sight of God sitting on the throne, all human beings, great and small, will be terrified, calling for the mountains to fall on them so that they will not have to face the judgment of the Lamb. This vivid picture was not intended to frighten believers. For them, the Lamb is a gentle Saviour. But those generals, emperors, or kings who previously showed no fear of God and arrogantly flaunted their unbelief will find that they were wrong, and in that day they will have to face God's wrath. No-one who has rejected God can survive the day of his wrath, but those who belong to Christ will receive a reward rather than punishment. Do you belong to Christ? If so, you need not fear these final days.

7:1ff The sixth seal has been opened, and the people of the earth have tried to hide from God, saying, "Who can stand?" (6:12–17). Just when all hope seems lost, four angels hold back the four winds of judgment until God's people are sealed as his own. Only then will God open the seventh seal (8:1).

7:2 A seal on a scroll or document identified and protected its contents. God places his own seal on his followers, identifying them as his own and guaranteeing his protection over their souls. This shows how valuable we are to him. Our physical bodies may be beaten, maimed, or even destroyed, but *nothing* can harm our souls when we have been sealed by God. See Ephesians 1:13 for the seal of the Holy Spirit.

7:3 God's seal is placed on the foreheads of his servants. This seal is the exact opposite of the mark of the beast explained in 13:16. These two marks place the people in two distinct categories—those owned by God and those owned by Satan.

or the trees until we put a seal on the foreheads[c] of the servants of our God." 4Then
I heard the number[d] of those who were sealed: 144,000[e] from all the tribes of Israel.

7:3
[c]Eze 9:4;
Rev 22:4

5From the tribe of Judah 12,000 were sealed,
from the tribe of Reuben 12,000,
from the tribe of Gad 12,000,
6from the tribe of Asher 12,000,
from the tribe of Naphtali 12,000,
from the tribe of Manasseh 12,000,
7from the tribe of Simeon 12,000,
from the tribe of Levi 12,000,
from the tribe of Issachar 12,000,
8from the tribe of Zebulun 12,000,
from the tribe of Joseph 12,000,
from the tribe of Benjamin 12,000.

7:4
[d]Rev 9:16
[e]Rev 14:1, 3

The Great Multitude in White Robes

9After this I looked and there before me was a great multitude that no-one could
count, from every nation, tribe, people and language,[f] standing before the throne[g]
and in front of the Lamb. They were wearing white robes and were holding palm
branches in their hands. 10And they cried out in a loud voice:

7:9
[f]Rev 5:9
[g]ver 15

"Salvation belongs to our God,[h]
who sits on the throne,
and to the Lamb."

7:10
[h]Ps 3:8;
Rev 12:10; 19:1

11All the angels were standing round the throne and around the elders[i] and the four
living creatures.[j] They fell down on their faces[k] before the throne and worshipped
God, 12saying:

7:11
[i]Rev 4:4
[j]Rev 4:6
[k]Rev 4:10

"Amen!
Praise and glory
and wisdom and thanks and honour
and power and strength
be to our God for ever and ever.
Amen!"[l]

7:12
[l]Rev 5:12-14

7:4–8 The number 144,000 is 12 x 12 x 1,000, symbolising completeness—*all* God's followers will be brought safely to him; not one will be overlooked or forgotten. God seals these believers either by withdrawing them from the earth (this is called the Rapture) or by giving them special strength and courage to make it through this time of great persecution. Even though many believers have to undergo persecution, the seal does not necessarily guarantee protection from physical harm—many will die (see 6:11)—but God will protect them from spiritual harm. No matter what happens, they will be brought to their reward of eternal life. Their destiny is secure. These believers will not fall away from God even though they may undergo intense persecution.

This is not saying that 144,000 individuals must be sealed before the persecution comes, but that when persecution begins, the faithful will have already been sealed (marked by God) and they will remain true to him until the end.

7:4–8 This is a different list from the usual listing of the 12 tribes in the Old Testament, because it is a symbolic list of God's true followers. (1) Judah is mentioned first because Judah is the tribe of both David and Jesus the Messiah (Genesis 49:8–12; Matthew 1:1). (2) Levi had no tribal allotment because of the Levites' work for God in the temple (Deuteronomy 18:1), but here the tribe is given a place as a reward for faithfulness. (3) Dan is not mentioned because it was known for rebellion and idolatry, traits unacceptable for God's followers (Genesis 49:17). (4) The two tribes representing Joseph (usually called Ephraim and Manasseh, after Joseph's sons) are here called Joseph and Manasseh because of Ephraim's rebellion. See Genesis 49 for the story of the beginning of these 12 tribes.

7:9 Who is this great multitude? While some interpreters identify it as the martyrs described in 6:9, it may also be the same group as the 144,000 just mentioned (7:4–8). The 144,000 were sealed by God before the great time of persecution; the great multitude was brought to eternal life, as God had promised. Before, they were being prepared; now, they are victorious. This multitude in heaven is comprised of all those who remained faithful to God throughout the generations. No true believer ever need worry about which group he or she will be in. God includes and protects each of us, and we are guaranteed a place in his presence.

7:10 People try many methods to remove the guilt of sin—good deeds, intellectual pursuits, and even casting blame on others. The multitude in heaven however, praises God, saying that salvation comes from him and from the Lamb. Salvation from sin's penalty can come only through Jesus Christ. Have you had the guilt of sin removed in the only way possible?

7:11 More information about the elders is found in the note on 4:4. The four living creatures are explained further in the note on 4:6, 7.

13Then one of the elders asked me, "These in white robes — who are they, and where
did they come from?"
14I answered, "Sir, you know."
And he said, "These are they who have come out of the great tribulation; they have
washed their robes[m] and made them white in the blood of the Lamb.[n] 15Therefore,

"they are before the throne of God[o]
and serve him[p] day and night in his temple;[q]
and he who sits on the throne will spread his tent over them.[r]
16Never again will they hunger;
never again will they thirst.
The sun will not beat upon them,
nor any scorching heat.[s]
17For the Lamb at the centre of the throne will be their shepherd;[t]
he will lead them to springs of living water.
And God will wipe away every tear from their eyes."[u]

The Seventh Seal and the Golden Censer

8 When he opened the seventh seal,[a] there was silence in heaven for about half
an hour.
2And I saw the seven angels[b] who stand before God, and to them were given seven
trumpets.
3Another angel,[c] who had a golden censer, came and stood at the altar. He was
given much incense to offer, with the prayers of all the saints,[d] on the golden altar[e]
before the throne. 4The smoke of the incense, together with the prayers of the saints,
went up before God[f] from the angel's hand. 5Then the angel took the censer, filled
it with fire from the altar,[g] and hurled it on the earth; and there came peals of
thunder,[h] rumblings, flashes of lightning and an earthquake.[i]

3. Sounding the seven trumpets

The Trumpets

6Then the seven angels who had the seven trumpets[j] prepared to sound them.
7The first angel sounded his trumpet, and there came hail and fire[k] mixed with
blood, and it was hurled down upon the earth. A third[l] of the earth was burned up,
a third of the trees were burned up, and all the green grass was burned up.[m]
8The second angel sounded his trumpet, and something like a huge mountain,[n] all
ablaze, was thrown into the sea. A third[o] of the sea turned into blood,[p] 9a third[q]
of the living creatures in the sea died, and a third of the ships were destroyed.
10The third angel sounded his trumpet, and a great star, blazing like a torch, fell

7:14 [m]Rev 22:14 [n]Heb 9:14; 1Jn 1:7
7:15 [o]ver 9 [p]Rev 22:3 [q]Rev 11:19 [r]Isa 4:5, 6; Rev 21:3
7:16 [s]Isa 49:10
7:17 [t]Ps 23:1; Jn 10:11 [u]Isa 25:8; Rev 21:4
8:1 [a]Rev 6:1
8:2 [b]ver 6-13; Rev 9:1, 13; 11:15
8:3 [c]Rev 7:2 [d]Rev 5:8 [e]Ex 30:1-6; Heb 9:4; Rev 9:13
8:4 [f]Ps 141:2
8:5 [g]Lev 16:12, 13 [h]Rev 4:5 [i]Rev 6:12
8:6 [j]ver 2
8:7 [k]Eze 38:22 [l]ver 7-12; Rev 9:15, 18; 12:4 [m]Rev 9:4
8:8 [n]Jer 51:25 [o]ver 7 [p]Rev 16:3
8:9 [q]ver 7

7:14 "The great tribulation" has been explained in several ways. Some believe it refers to the suffering of believers through the ages; others believe that there is a specific time of intense tribulation yet to come. In either case, these believers come through their times of suffering by remaining loyal to God. Because they remain faithful, God will give them eternal life with him (7:17).

7:14 It is difficult to imagine how blood could make any cloth white, but the blood of Jesus Christ is the world's greatest purifier because it removes the stain of sin. White symbolises sinless perfection or holiness, which can be given to people only by the death of the sinless Lamb of God on our behalf. This is a picture of how we are saved through faith (see Isaiah 1:18; Romans 3:21–26).

7:16, 17 God will provide for his children's needs in their eternal home where there will be no hunger, thirst, or pain, and he will wipe away all tears. When you are suffering or torn apart by sorrow, take comfort in this promise of complete protection and relief.

7:17 In verses 1–8 we see the believers receiving a seal to protect them through a time of great tribulation and suffering; in verses 9–17 we see the believers finally with God in heaven. All who have been faithful through the ages are singing before God's throne. Their tribulations and sorrows are over: no more tears for sin, for all sins are forgiven; no more tears for suffering, for all suffering is over; no more tears for death, for all believers have been resurrected to die no more.

8:1, 2 When the seventh seal is opened, the seven trumpet judgments are revealed. In the same way, the seventh trumpet will announce the seven bowl judgments in 11:15 and 16:1–21. The trumpet judgments, like the seal judgments, are only partial. God's final and complete judgment has not yet come.

8:3 A censer filled with live coals was used in temple worship. Incense was poured on the coals, and the sweet-smelling smoke drifted upwards, symbolising believers' prayers ascending to God (see Exodus 30:7–9).

8:6 The trumpet blasts have three purposes: (1) to warn that judgment is certain, (2) to call the forces of good and evil to battle, and (3) to announce the return of the King, the Messiah. These warnings urge us to make sure our faith is firmly fixed on Christ.

8:7–12 Since only one-third of the earth is destroyed by these trumpet judgments, this is only a partial judgment from God. His full wrath is yet to be unleashed.

from the sky[r] on a third of the rivers and on the springs of water[s]— 11 the name of
the star is Wormwood.[a] A third[t] of the waters turned bitter, and many people died
from the waters that had become bitter.[u]
12 The fourth angel sounded his trumpet, and a third of the sun was struck, a third
of the moon, and a third of the stars, so that a third[v] of them turned dark.[w] A third
of the day was without light, and also a third of the night.
13 As I watched, I heard an eagle that was flying in mid-air[x] call out in a loud voice:
"Woe! Woe! Woe[y] to the inhabitants of the earth, because of the trumpet blasts about
to be sounded by the other three angels!"

9 The fifth angel sounded his trumpet, and I saw a star that had fallen from the sky
to the earth.[a] The star was given the key to the shaft of the Abyss.[b] 2 When he
opened the Abyss, smoke rose from it like the smoke from a gigantic furnace.[c] The
sun and sky were darkened[d] by the smoke from the Abyss. 3 And out of the smoke
locusts[e] came down upon the earth and were given power like that of scorpions[f]
of the earth. 4 They were told not to harm[g] the grass of the earth or any plant or tree,[h]
but only those people who did not have the seal of God on their foreheads.[i] 5 They
were not given power to kill them, but only to torture them for five months.[j] And
the agony they suffered was like that of the sting of a scorpion[k] when it strikes a man.
6 During those days men will seek death, but will not find it; they will long to die,
but death will elude them.[l]
7 The locusts looked like horses prepared for battle.[m] On their heads they wore
something like crowns of gold, and their faces resembled human faces.[n] 8 Their hair
was like women's hair, and their teeth were like lions' teeth.[o] 9 They had breastplates
like breastplates of iron, and the sound of their wings was like the thundering of many
horses and chariots rushing into battle.[p] 10 They had tails and stings like scorpions,
and in their tails they had power to torment people for five months.[q] 11 They had as
king over them the angel of the Abyss,[r] whose name in Hebrew is Abaddon, and
in Greek, Apollyon.[a]
12 The first woe is past; two other woes are yet to come.[s]
13 The sixth angel sounded his trumpet, and I heard a voice coming from the
horns[b][t] of the golden altar that is before God.[u] 14 It said to the sixth angel who had

[a] 11 That is, Bitterness [a] 11 *Abaddon* and *Apollyon* mean *Destroyer.* [b] 13 That is, projections

8:10 [r] Isa 14:12; Rev 6:13; 9:1 [s] Rev 14:7; 16:4
8:11 [t] ver 7 [u] Jer 9:15; 23:15
8:12 [v] ver 7 [w] Ex 10:21-23; Rev 6:12, 13
8:13 [x] Rev 14:6; 19:17 [y] Rev 9:12; 11:14
9:1 [a] Rev 8:10 [b] ver 2, 11; Lk 8:31
9:2 [c] Ge 19:28; Ex 19:18 [d] Joel 2:2, 10
9:3 [e] Ex 10:12-15 [f] ver 5, 10
9:4 [g] Rev 6:6 [h] Rev 8:7 [i] Rev 7:2, 3
9:5 [j] ver 10 [k] ver 3
9:6 [l] Job 3:21; Jer 8:3; Rev 6:16
9:7 [m] Joel 2:4 [n] Da 7:8
9:8 [o] Joel 1:6
9:9 [p] Joel 2:5
9:10 [q] ver 3, 5, 19
9:11 [r] ver 1, 2
9:12 [s] Rev 8:13
9:13 [t] Ex 30:1-3 [u] Rev 8:3

8:11 Wormwood is a plant with a very bitter taste, and it stands for the bitterness of God's judgment.

8:13 Habakkuk used the image of a vulture to symbolise swiftness and destruction (see Habakkuk 1:8). The picture here is of a strong, powerful bird flying over all the earth, warning of the terrors yet to come. While both believers and unbelievers experience the terrors described in verses 7–12, the "inhabitants of the earth" are the unbelievers who will meet spiritual harm through the next three trumpet judgments. God has guaranteed believers protection from spiritual harm (7:2, 3).

8:13 In 6:10, the martyrs call out to God, "How long . . . until you judge the inhabitants of the earth and avenge our blood?" As we see the world's wickedness, we too may cry out to God, "How long?" In the following chapters, the judgment comes at last. We may be distressed and impatient, but God has his plan and his timing, and we must learn to trust him to know what is best. Judgment is coming – be sure of that. Thank God for the time he has given you to turn from sin. Use the available time to work to help others turn to him.

9:1 It is not known whether this "star" that fell from heaven is Satan, a fallen angel, Christ, or a good angel. Most likely it is a good angel, because the key to the shaft of the Abyss (bottomless pit) is normallv held by Christ (1:17, 18), and it was temporarily given to this other being from heaven (see also 20:1). This being, whoever he may be, is still under God's control and authority. The Abyss represents the place of the demons and of Satan, the king of demons (9:11). See also Luke 8:31 for another reference to the Abyss.

9:3 The prophet Joel described a locust plague as a foreshadowing of the "day of the LORD", meaning God's coming judgment (Joel 2:1–10). In the Old Testament, locusts were symbols of destruction because they destroyed vegetation. Here, however, they symbolise an invasion of demons called to torture people who do not believe in God. The limitations placed on the demons (they could only torment people for five months) show that they are under God's authority.

9:3ff Most likely these locusts are demons – evil spirits ruled by Satan who tempt people to sin. They were not created by Satan, because God is the Creator of all; rather, they are fallen angels who joined Satan in his rebellion. God limits what they can do; they can do nothing without his permission. Their main purpose on earth is to prevent, distort, or destroy people's relationship with God. Because they are corrupt and degenerate, their appearance reflects the distortion of their spirits. While it is important to recognise their evil activity so we can stay away from them, we must avoid any curiosity about or involvement with demonic forces or with the occult.

9:11 The locust-demons have a leader whose name in Hebrew and in Greek means *destroyer.* It may be a play on words by John to show that those who worshipped the great god Apollo worshipped only a demon.

9:13 The altar in the temple had four projections, one at each corner, and these were called the horns of the altar (see Exodus 27:2).

9:14 The word "angels" here means fallen angels or demons. These four unidentified demons will be exceedingly evil and de-

the trumpet, "Release the four angels who are bound at the great river Euphrates."[v]
15And the four angels who had been kept ready for this very hour and day and month
and year were released to kill a third of mankind.[w] 16The number of the mounted
troops was two hundred million. I heard their number.[x]
17The horses and riders I saw in my vision looked like this: Their breastplates were
fiery red, dark blue, and yellow as sulphur. The heads of the horses resembled the
heads of lions, and out of their mouths[y] came fire, smoke and sulphur.[z] 18A third
of mankind was killed[a] by the three plagues of fire, smoke and sulphur[b] that came
out of their mouths. 19The power of the horses was in their mouths and in their tails;
for their tails were like snakes, having heads with which they inflict injury.
20The rest of mankind that were not killed by these plagues still did not repent of
the work of their hands;[c] they did not stop worshipping demons,[d] and idols of gold,
silver, bronze, stone and wood—idols that cannot see or hear or walk.[e] 21Nor did
they repent[f] of their murders, their magic arts,[g] their sexual immorality[h] or their
thefts.

The Angel and the Little Scroll

10 Then I saw another mighty angel[a] coming down from heaven. He was robed
in a cloud, with a rainbow above his head; his face was like the sun,[b] and his
legs were like fiery pillars.[c] 2He was holding a little scroll, which lay open in his
hand. He planted his right foot on the sea and his left foot on the land, 3and he gave
a loud shout like the roar of a lion. When he shouted, the voices of the seven thunders[d]
spoke. 4And when the seven thunders spoke, I was about to write; but I heard a voice
from heaven say, "Seal up what the seven thunders have said and do not write it
down."[e]
5Then the angel I had seen standing on the sea and on the land raised his right hand
to heaven.[f] 6And he swore by him who lives for ever and ever, who created the
heavens and all that is in them, the earth and all that is in it, and the sea and all that
is in it,[g] and said, "There will be no more delay![h] 7But in the days when the seventh
angel is about to sound his trumpet, the mystery[i] of God will be accomplished, just
as he announced to his servants the prophets."
8Then the voice that I had heard from heaven[j] spoke to me once more: "Go, take
the scroll that lies open in the hand of the angel who is standing on the sea and on
the land."

9:14 [v]Rev 16:12
9:15 [w]ver 18
9:16 [x]Rev 5:11; 7:4
9:17 [y]Rev 11:5 [z]ver 18
9:18 [a]ver 15 [b]ver 17
9:20 [c]Dt 31:29 [d]1Co 10:20 [e]Ps 115:4-7; 135:15-17; Da 5:23
9:21 [f]Rev 2:21 [g]Rev 18:23 [h]Rev 17:2, 5
10:1 [a]Rev 5:2 [b]Mt 17:2; Rev 1:16 [c]Rev 1:15
10:3 [d]Rev 4:5
10:4 [e]Da 8:26; 12:4, 9; Rev 22:10
10:5 [f]Da 12:7
10:6 [g]Rev 4:11; 14:7 [h]Rev 16:17
10:7 [i]Ro 16:25
10:8 [j]ver 4

structive. But note that they do not have the power to release themselves and do their evil work on earth. Instead, they are held back by God and will be released at a specific time, doing only what he allows them to do.

9:15 Here one-third of all people are killed. In 6:7, 8, one-fourth of mankind was killed. Thus, over half of the people in the world will have been killed by God's great judgments. Even more would have been killed if God had not set limits on the destruction.

9:16 In John's day, this number of mounted troops in an army was inconceivable, but today there are countries and alliances that could easily amass this many soldiers. This huge army, led by the four demons, will be sent out to destroy one-third of the earth's population. But the judgment is still not complete.

9:20, 21 These people were so hard-hearted that even plagues did not drive them to God. People don't usually fall into immorality and evil suddenly—they slip into it a little bit at a time until, hardly realising what has happened, they are irrevocably bogged down in their wicked ways. Any person who allows sin to take root in his or her life can find himself or herself in this predicament. Temptation entertained today becomes sin tomorrow, then a habit the next day, then death and separation from God for ever (see James 1:15). To think you could never become this evil is the first step towards a hard heart. Acknowledge your need to confess your sin before God.

10:1–6 The purpose of this mighty angel is clear—to announce the final judgments on the earth. His right foot on the sea and left foot on the land (10:2) indicate that his words deal with all creation, not just a limited part as did the seal and trumpet judgments. The seventh trumpet (11:15) will usher in the seven bowl judgments, which will bring an end to the present world. When this universal judgment comes, God's truth will prevail.

10:2 We see two scrolls in Revelation. The first contains a revelation of judgments against evil (5:1ff). The contents of the second little scroll are not indicated, but it too may contain a revelation of judgment.

10:4 Throughout history people have wanted to know what would happen in the future, and God reveals some of it in this book. But John was stopped from revealing certain parts of his vision. An angel also told the prophet Daniel that some visions he saw were not to be revealed yet to everyone (Daniel 12:9), and Jesus told his disciples that the time of the end is known by no-one but God (Mark 13:32, 33). God has revealed all we need to know to live for him now. In our desire to be ready for the end, we must not place more emphasis on speculation about the last days than on living for God while we wait.

10:7 When God's plan for human history is completely revealed, all prophecy will be fulfilled. The end of the age will have arrived (see 11:15 and Ephesians 1:9, 10).

9 So I went to the angel and asked him to give me the little scroll. He said to me,
"Take it and eat it. It will turn your stomach sour, but in your mouth it will be as sweet
as honey."[k] 10 I took the little scroll from the angel's hand and ate it. It tasted as sweet
as honey in my mouth, but when I had eaten it, my stomach turned sour. 11 Then I
was told, "You must prophesy[l] again about many peoples, nations, languages and
kings."

The Two Witnesses

11 I was given a reed like a measuring rod[a] and was told, "Go and measure the
temple of God and the altar, and count the worshippers there. 2 But exclude the
outer court;[b] do not measure it, because it has been given to the Gentiles.[c] They
will trample on the holy city[d] for 42 months.[e] 3 And I will give power to my two
witnesses,[f] and they will prophesy for 1,260 days, clothed in sackcloth."[g] 4 These
are the two olive trees[h] and the two lampstands that stand before the Lord of the
earth.[i] 5 If anyone tries to harm them, fire comes from their mouths and devours their
enemies.[j] This is how anyone who wants to harm them must die.[k] 6 These men have
power to shut up the sky so that it will not rain during the time they are prophesying;
and they have power to turn the waters into blood[l] and to strike the earth with every
kind of plague as often as they want.
7 Now when they have finished their testimony, the beast[m] that comes up from the
Abyss will attack them,[n] and overpower and kill them. 8 Their bodies will lie in the
street of the great city, which is figuratively called Sodom[o] and Egypt, where also
their Lord was crucified.[p] 9 For three and a half days men from every people, tribe,
language and nation will gaze on their bodies and refuse them burial.[q] 10 The inhabitants of the earth[r] will gloat over them and will celebrate by sending each other
gifts,[s] because these two prophets had tormented those who live on earth.
11 But after the three and a half days a breath of life from God entered them,[t] and
they stood on their feet, and terror struck those who saw them. 12 Then they heard a
loud voice from heaven saying to them, "Come up here."[u] And they went up to
heaven in a cloud,[v] while their enemies looked on.
13 At that very hour there was a severe earthquake[w] and a tenth of the city collapsed.

10:9 [k]Jer 15:16; Eze 2:8-3:3
10:11 [l]Eze 37:4, 9
11:1 [a]Eze 40:3; Rev 21:15
11:2 [b]Eze 40:17, 20 [c]Lk 21:24 [d]Rev 21:2 [e]Da 7:25; Rev 13:5
11:3 [f]Rev 1:5 [g]Ge 37:34
11:4 [h]Ps 52:8; Jer 11:16; Zec 4:3, 11 [i]Zec 4:14
11:5 [j]2Ki 1:10; Jer 5:14 [k]Nu 16:29, 35
11:6 [l]Ex 7:17, 19
11:7 [m]Rev 13:1-4 [n]Da 7:21
11:8 [o]Isa 1:9 [p]Heb 13:12
11:9 [q]Ps 79:2, 3
11:10 [r]Rev 3:10 [s]Est 9:19, 22
11:11 [t]Eze 37:5, 9, 10, 14
11:12 [u]Rev 4:1 [v]2Ki 2:11; Ac 1:9
11:13 [w]Rev 6:12

10:9, 10 The prophet Ezekiel had a vision in which he was told to eat a scroll filled with judgments against the nation of Israel (Ezekiel 3:1ff). The taste was sweet in his mouth, but the scroll's contents brought destruction – just like the scroll John was told to eat. God's word is sweet to us as believers because it brings encouragement, but it turns our stomach because of the coming judgment we must pronounce on unbelievers.

11:1ff This temple is most likely a symbol of the church (all true believers), because there will be no temple in the new Jerusalem (21:22). John measured the temple to show that God is building walls of protection around his people to spare them from spiritual harm, and that there is a place reserved for all believers who remain faithful to God.

11:2 Those worshipping inside the temple will be protected spiritually, but those outside will face great suffering. This is a way of saying that true believers will be protected through persecution, but those who refuse to believe will be destroyed.

11:3 These two witnesses bear strong resemblance to Moses and Elijah, two of God's mighty prophets. With God's power, Moses called plagues down upon the nation of Egypt (see Exodus 8–11). Elijah defeated the prophets of Baal (1 Kings 18). Both of these men appeared with Christ at his transfiguration (see Matthew 17:1–7).

11:3 In the book of Revelation, numbers are likely to have symbolic rather than literal meanings. The 42 months or 1,260 days equal 3½ years. As half of the perfect number 7, 3½ can indicate incompletion, imperfection, or even evil. Notice the events predicted for this time period: there is trouble (Daniel 12:7), the holy city is trampled (11:2), the woman takes refuge in the desert (12:6), and the devil-inspired beast exercises his authority (13:5). Some commentators link the 3½ years with the period of famine in the days of Elijah (Luke 4:25; James 5:17). Since Malachi predicted the return of Elijah before the Last Judgment (Malachi 4:5), and since the events in Daniel and Revelation pave the way for the second coming, perhaps John was making this connection. It is possible, of course, that the 3½ years are literal. If so, we will clearly recognise when the 3½ years are over! Whether symbolic or literal, however, they indicate that evil's reign will have a definite end.

11:7 This beast could be Satan or an agent of Satan.

11:8, 9 Jerusalem, once the great city and the capital of Israel, is now enemy territory. It is compared with Sodom and with Egypt, both well known for their evil. At the time of John's writing, Jerusalem had been destroyed by the Romans in 70 A.D., nearly a million Jews had been slaughtered, and the temple treasures had been carried off to Rome.

11:10 The whole world rejoices at the deaths of these two witnesses who have caused trouble by saying what the people didn't want to hear – words about their sin, their need for repentance, and the coming punishment. Sinful people hate those who call attention to their sin and who urge them to repent. They hated Christ, and they hate his followers (1 John 3:13). When you obey Christ and take a stand against sin, be prepared to experience the world's hatred. But remember that the great reward awaiting you in heaven far outweighs any suffering that you face now.

Seven thousand people were killed in the earthquake, and the survivors were terrified
and gave glory[x] to the God of heaven.[y]
14The second woe has passed; the third woe is coming soon.[z]

The Seventh Trumpet

15The seventh angel sounded his trumpet,[a] and there were loud voices[b] in heaven,
which said:

"The kingdom of the world has become the kingdom of our Lord
and of his Christ,[c]
and he will reign for ever and ever."[d]

16And the twenty-four elders,[e] who were seated on their thrones before God, fell on
their faces and worshipped God, 17saying:

"We give thanks to you, Lord God Almighty,[f]
the One who is and who was,
because you have taken your great power
and have begun to reign.[g]
18The nations were angry;[h]
and your wrath has come.
The time has come for judging the dead,
and for rewarding your servants the prophets[i]
and your saints and those who reverence your name,
both small and great[j]—
and for destroying those who destroy the earth."

19Then God's temple[k] in heaven was opened, and within his temple was seen the
ark of his covenant. And there came flashes of lightning, rumblings, peals of thunder,
an earthquake and a great hailstorm.[l]

4. Observing the great conflict

The Woman and the Dragon

12 A great and wondrous sign appeared in heaven: a woman clothed with the sun,
with the moon under her feet and a crown of twelve stars on her head. 2She
was pregnant and cried out in pain[a] as she was about to give birth. 3Then another
sign appeared in heaven: an enormous red dragon with seven heads and ten horns[b]
and seven crowns[c] on his heads. 4His tail swept a third[d] of the stars out of the sky

11:13 [x]Rev 14:7 [y]Rev 16:11
11:14 [z]Rev 8:13
11:15 [a]Rev 10:7 [b]Rev 16:17; 19:1 [c]Rev 12:10 [d]Da 2:44; 7:14, 27
11:16 [e]Rev 4:4
11:17 [f]Rev 1:8 [g]Rev 19:6
11:18 [h]Ps 2:1 [i]Rev 10:7 [j]Rev 19:5
11:19 [k]Rev 15:5, 8 [l]Rev 16:21
12:2 [a]Gal 4:19
12:3 [b]Da 7:7, 20; Rev 13:1 [c]Rev 19:12
12:4 [d]Rev 8:7

11:15 The seventh trumpet is sounded, announcing the arrival of the King. There is now no turning back. The coming judgments are no longer partial, but complete in their destruction. God is in control, and he unleashes his full wrath on the evil world that refuses to turn to him (9:20, 21). When his wrath begins, there will be no escape.

11:16 For more on the 24 elders, see the note on 4:4.

11:18 In the Bible, God gives rewards to his people according to what they deserve. Throughout the Old Testament, obedience often brought reward in this life (Deuteronomy 28), but obedience and immediate reward are not always linked. If they were, good people would always be rich, and suffering would always be a sign of sin. If we were quickly rewarded for every faithful deed, we would soon think we were pretty good. Before long, we would be doing many good deeds for purely selfish reasons. While it is true that God will reward us for our earthly deeds (see 20:12), our greatest reward will be eternal life in his presence.

11:19 In Old Testament days, the ark of the covenant was the most sacred treasure of the Israelite nation. For more information about the ark, see the note on Exodus 37:1.

12:1–14:20 The seventh trumpet (11:15) ushers in the bowl judgments (15:1–16:21), but in the intervening chapters (12–14), John sees the conflict between God and Satan. He sees the source of all sin, evil, persecution, and suffering on the earth, and he understands why the great battle between the forces of God and Satan must soon take place. In these chapters the nature of evil is exposed, and Satan is seen in all his wickedness.

12:1–6 The woman represents God's faithful people who have been waiting for the Messiah; the crown of 12 stars represents the 12 tribes of Israel. God set apart the Jews for himself (Romans 9:4, 5), and that nation gave birth to the Messiah. The male child (12:5) is Jesus, born to a devout Jew named Mary (Luke 1:26–33). Evil King Herod immediately tried to destroy the infant Jesus (Matthew 2:13–20). Herod's desire to kill this newborn king, whom he saw as a threat to his throne, was motivated by Satan (the red dragon), who wanted to kill the world's Saviour. The heavenly scene in Revelation 12 shows that Christ's quiet birth in the town of Bethlehem had cosmic significance.

12:3, 4 The enormous red dragon, Satan, has seven heads, ten horns, and seven crowns, representing his power and the kingdoms of the world over which he rules. The stars that plunged to earth with him are usually considered to be the angels who fell with Satan and became his demons. According to Hebrew tradition, one-third of all the angels in heaven fell with Satan. For more on demons, see the notes on 9:3ff and Mark 5:1–20.

and flung them to the earth.[e] The dragon stood in front of the woman who was about
to give birth, so that he might devour her child[f] the moment it was born. 5She gave
birth to a son, a male child, who will rule all the nations with an iron sceptre.[g] And
her child was snatched up to God and to his throne. 6The woman fled into the desert
to a place prepared for her by God, where she might be taken care of for 1,260 days.[h]
7And there was war in heaven. Michael and his angels fought against the dragon,[i]
and the dragon and his angels fought back. 8But he was not strong enough, and they
lost their place in heaven. 9The great dragon was hurled down—that ancient serpent[j]
called the devil,[k] or Satan, who leads the whole world astray.[l] He was hurled to
the earth,[m] and his angels with him.
10Then I heard a loud voice in heaven[n] say:

"Now have come the salvation and the power and the kingdom
of our God,
and the authority of his Christ.
For the accuser of our brothers,[o]
who accuses them before our God day and night,
has been hurled down.
11They overcame him
by the blood of the Lamb[p]
and by the word of their testimony;[q]
they did not love their lives so much
as to shrink from death.[r]
12Therefore rejoice, you heavens[s]
and you who dwell in them!
But woe[t] to the earth and the sea,[u]
because the devil has gone down to you!
He is filled with fury,
because he knows that his time is short."

13When the dragon[v] saw that he had been hurled to the earth, he pursued the

12:4 [e]Da 8:10 [f]Mt 2:16
12:5 [g]Ps 2:9; Rev 2:27
12:6 [h]Rev 11:2
12:7 [i]ver 3
12:9 [j]Ge 3:1-7 [k]Mt 25:41 [l]Rev 20:3, 8, 10 [m]Lk 10:18; Jn 12:31
12:10 [n]Rev 11:15 [o]Job 1:9-11; Zec 3:1
12:11 [p]Rev 7:14 [q]Rev 6:9 [r]Lk 14:26
12:12 [s]Ps 96:11; Isa 49:13; Rev 18:20 [t]Rev 8:13 [u]Rev 10:6
12:13 [v]ver 3

12:6 The desert represents a place of spiritual refuge and protection from Satan. Because God aided the woman's escape into the desert, we can be sure that he offers security to all true believers. Satan always attacks God's people, but God keeps them spiritually secure. Some will experience physical harm, but all will be protected from spiritual harm. God will not let Satan take the souls of God's true followers.

12:6 The 1,260 days (3½ years) is the same length of time that the dragon is allowed to exercise his authority (13:5) and that the holy city is trampled (see the second note on 11:3).

12:7 This event fulfils Daniel 12:1ff. Michael is a high-ranking angel. One of his responsibilities is to guard God's community of believers.

12:7ff Much more happened at Christ's birth, death, and resurrection than most people realise. A war between the forces of good and evil was under way. With Christ's resurrection, Satan's ultimate defeat was assured. Some believe that Satan's fall to earth took place at Jesus' resurrection or ascension and that the 1,260 days (3½ years) is a symbolic way of referring to the time between Christ's first and second comings. Others say that Satan's defeat will occur in the middle of a literal seven-year tribulation period, following the rapture of the church and preceding the second coming of Christ and the beginning of Christ's 1,000-year reign. Whatever the case, we must remember that Christ is victorious—Satan has already been defeated because of Christ's death on the cross (12:10–12).

12:9 The devil is not a symbol or legend; he is very real. Originally Satan was an angel of God, but through his own pride, he became corrupt. The devil is God's enemy, and he constantly tries to hinder God's work, but he is limited by God's power and can do only what he is permitted to do (Job 1:6—2:8). The name *Satan* means "accuser" (12:10). He actively looks for people to attack (1 Peter 5:8, 9). Satan likes to pursue believers who are vulnerable in their faith, who are spiritually weak, or who are isolated from other believers.

Even though God permits the devil to do his work in this world, God is still in control. And Jesus has complete power over Satan—he defeated Satan when he died and rose again for the sins of mankind. One day Satan will be bound for ever, never again to do his evil work (see 20:10).

12:10 Many believe that until this time, Satan still had access to God (see the note on Job 1:7ff). But here his access is for ever barred (see also 9:1). He can no longer accuse people before God (see how Satan made accusations about Job before God in Job 1:6ff).

12:11 The critical blow to Satan came when the Lamb, Jesus Christ, shed his blood for our sins. The victory is won by sacrifice—Christ's death in our place to pay the penalty for our sin, and the sacrifices we make because of our faith in him. As we face the battle with Satan, we should not fear it or try to escape from it, but we should loyally serve Christ, who alone brings victory (see Romans 8:34–39).

12:12 The devil begins to step up his persecution because he knows that "his time is short". We are living in the last days, and Satan's work has become more intense. Even though the devil is very powerful, as we can see by the condition of our world, he is always under God's control. One of the reasons God allows Satan to work evil and bring temptation is so that those who pretend to be Christ's followers will be weeded out from Christ's true believers. Knowing that the last great confrontation with Jesus is near, Satan is desperately trying to recruit as great an enemy force as possible for this final battle.

woman who had given birth to the male child.[w] 14The woman was given the two
wings of a great eagle,[x] so that she might fly to the place prepared for her in the desert,
where she would be taken care of for a time, times and half a time,[y] out of the
serpent's reach. 15Then from his mouth the serpent spewed water like a river, to
overtake the woman and sweep her away with the torrent. 16But the earth helped the
woman by opening its mouth and swallowing the river that the dragon had spewed
out of his mouth. 17Then the dragon was enraged at the woman and went off to make
war[z] against the rest of her offspring[a]—those who obey God's commandments[b]
13 and hold to the testimony of Jesus.[c] 1And the dragon[a] stood on the shore
of the sea.

The Beast out of the Sea

And I saw a beast coming out of the sea.[a] He had ten horns and seven heads,[b]
with ten crowns on his horns, and on each head a blasphemous name.[c] 2The beast
I saw resembled a leopard,[d] but had feet like those of a bear[e] and a mouth like that
of a lion.[f] The dragon gave the beast his power and his throne and great authority.[g]
3One of the heads of the beast seemed to have had a fatal wound, but the fatal wound
had been healed.[h] The whole world was astonished[i] and followed the beast. 4Men
worshipped the dragon because he had given authority to the beast, and they also
worshipped the beast and asked, "Who is like[j] the beast? Who can make war against
him?"

a *1* Some late manuscripts *And I*

12:13 [w]ver 5
12:14 [x]Ex 19:4 [y]Da 7:25
12:17 [z]Rev 11:7 [a]Ge 3:15 [b]Rev 14:12
12:17 [c]Rev 1:2
13:1 [a]Da 7:1-6; Rev 15:2 [b]Rev 12:3 [c]Da 11:36; Rev 17:3
13:2 [d]Da 7:6 [e]Da 7:5 [f]Da 7:4 [g]Rev 16:10
13:3 [h]ver 12, 14 [i]Rev 17:8
13:4 [j]Ex 15:11

SATAN'S WORK IN THE WORLD

12:13	His hatred for Christ
12:17	His hatred for God's people
13:2	His power and authority
13:4	His popularity among unbelievers
13:6	His blasphemy against God
13:7	His war against believers
13:14	His ability to deceive

12:17 While the woman (12:1) represents faithful Jews and the child (12:5) represents Christ, the rest of her offspring could be either Jewish believers or, most likely, all believers.

12:17 The apostle Paul tells us that we are in a spiritual battle (Ephesians 6:10–12). John says that the war is still being waged, but the outcome has already been determined. Satan and his followers have been defeated and will be destroyed. Nevertheless, Satan is battling daily to bring more into his ranks and to keep his own from defecting to God's side. Those who belong to Christ have gone into battle on God's side, and he has guaranteed them victory. God will not lose the war, but we must make certain not to lose the battle for our own souls. Don't waver in your commitment to Christ. A great spiritual battle is being fought, and there is no time for indecision.

13:1 This beast was initially identified with Rome, because the Roman empire, in its early days, encouraged an evil life-style, persecuted believers, and opposed God and his followers. But the beast also symbolises the antichrist—not Satan, but someone under Satan's power and control. This antichrist looks like a combination of the four beasts that Daniel saw centuries earlier in a vision (Daniel 7). As the dragon (12:17) is in opposition to God, so the beast from the sea is against Christ and may be seen as Satan's false messiah. The early Roman empire was strong and also anti-Christ (or against Christ's standards); many other individual powers throughout history have been anti-Christ. Many Christians believe that Satan's evil will culminate in a final antichrist, one who will focus all the powers of evil against Jesus Christ and his followers.

13:1ff Chapter 13 introduces Satan's (the dragon's) two evil accomplices: (1) the beast out of the sea (13:1ff) and (2) the beast out of the earth (13:11ff). Together, the three evil beings form an unholy trinity in direct opposition to the holy Trinity of God the Father, God the Son, and God the Holy Spirit.

When Satan tempted Jesus in the desert, he wanted Jesus to show his power by turning stones into bread, to do miracles by jumping from a high place, and to gain political power by worshipping him (see Matthew 4:1–11). Satan's plan was to rule the world through Jesus, but Jesus refused to do Satan's bidding. Thus Satan turns to the frightening beasts described in Revelation. To the beast out of the sea he gives political power. To the beast out of the earth he gives power to do miracles. Both beasts work together to capture the control of the whole world. This unholy trinity—the dragon, the beast out of the sea, and the false prophet (see 16:13)—unite in a desperate attempt to overthrow God, but their efforts are doomed to failure. See what becomes of them in 19:19–21 and 20:10.

13:3ff Because the beast, the antichrist, is a false messiah, he will be a counterfeit of Christ and will even stage a false resurrection (13:14). People will follow and worship him because they will be amazed by his power and miracles (13:3, 4). He will unite the world under his leadership (13:7, 8), and he will control the world economy (13:16, 17). People are impressed by power and will follow those who display it forcefully or offer it to their followers. But those who follow the beast will only be fooling themselves: he will use his power to manipulate others, to point to himself, and to promote evil plans. God, by contrast, uses his infinitely greater power to love and to build up. Don't be misled by claims of great miracles or reports about a resurrection or reincarnation of someone claiming to be Christ. When Jesus returns, he will reveal himself to everyone (Matthew 24:23–28).

5 The beast was given a mouth to utter proud words and blasphemies[k] and to
exercise his authority for forty-two months.[l] 6 He opened his mouth to blaspheme
God, and to slander his name and his dwelling-place and those who live in heaven.[m]
7 He was given power to make war[n] against the saints and to conquer them. And he
was given authority over every tribe, people, language and nation.[o] 8 All inhabitants
of the earth[p] will worship the beast—all whose names have not been written in the
book of life[q] belonging to the Lamb that was slain from the creation of the world.[b][r]
9 He who has an ear, let him hear.[s]

> 10 If anyone is to go into captivity,
> into captivity he will go.
> If anyone is to be killed[c] with the sword,
> with the sword he will be killed.[t]

This calls for patient endurance and faithfulness[u] on the part of the saints.[v]

The Beast out of the Earth

11 Then I saw another beast, coming out of the earth. He had two horns like a lamb,
but he spoke like a dragon. 12 He exercised all the authority[w] of the first beast on his
behalf,[x] and made the earth and its inhabitants worship the first beast,[y] whose fatal
wound had been healed.[z] 13 And he performed great and miraculous signs,[a] even
causing fire to come down from heaven[b] to earth in full view of men. 14 Because of
the signs[c] he was given power to do on behalf of the first beast, he deceived[d] the
inhabitants of the earth. He ordered them to set up an image in honour of the beast
who was wounded by the sword and yet lived. 15 He was given power to give breath
to the image of the first beast, so that it could speak and cause all who refused to
worship the image to be killed.[e] 16 He also forced everyone, small and great,[f] rich
and poor, free and slave, to receive a mark on his right hand or on his forehead,[g]

b *8* Or *written from the creation of the world in the book of life belonging to the Lamb that was slain* **c** *10* Some manuscripts *anyone kills*

13:5 [k] Da 7:8, 11, 20, 25; 11:36; 2Th 2:4 [l] Rev 11:2
13:6 [m] Rev 12:12
13:7 [n] Da 7:21; Rev 11:7 [o] Rev 5:9
13:8 [p] Rev 3:10 [q] Rev 3:5; 20:12 [r] Mt 25:34
13:9 [s] Rev 2:7
13:10 [t] Jer 15:2; 43:11 [u] Heb 6:12 [v] Rev 14:12
13:12 [w] ver 4 [x] ver 14 [y] Rev 14:9, 11 [z] ver 3
13:13 [a] Mt 24:24 [b] 1Ki 18:38; Rev 20:9
13:14 [c] 2Th 2:9, 10 [d] Rev 12:9
13:15 [e] Da 3:3-6
13:16 [f] Rev 19:5 [g] Rev 14:9

13:5 The power given to the beast will be limited by God. He will allow the beast to exercise authority only for a short time. Even while the beast is in power, God will still be in control (11:15; 12:10–12).

13:7 The beast will conquer God's people and rule over them, but he will not be able to harm them spiritually. He will establish worldwide dominance and demand that everyone worship him. And many *will* worship him—everyone except true believers. Refusal to worship the beast will result in temporary suffering for God's people, but they will be rewarded with eternal life in the end.

13:8 See the note on 3:5 for more information on the book of life.

13:10 In this time of persecution, being faithful to Christ could bring imprisonment and even execution. Some believers will be hurt or killed. But all that the beast and his followers will be able to do to believers is harm them physically; no spiritual harm will come to those whose faith in God is sincere. All believers will enter God's presence perfected and purified by the blood of the Lamb (7:9–17).

13:10 The times of great persecution that John saw will provide an opportunity for believers to exercise patient endurance and faithfulness. The tough times we face right now are also opportunities for spiritual growth. Don't fall into Satan's trap and turn away from God when hard times come. Instead, use those tough times as opportunities for growth.

13:11ff The first beast came out of the sea (13:1), but this second beast comes out of the earth. Later identified as the false prophet (16:13; 19:20), he is a counterfeit of the Holy Spirit. He seems to do good, but the purpose of his miracles is to deceive.

13:14 Throughout the Bible we see miracles performed as proofs of God's power, love, and authority. But here we see counterfeit miracles performed to deceive. This is a reminder of Pharaoh's magicians, who duplicated Moses' signs in Egypt. True signs and miracles point us to Jesus Christ, but miracles alone can be deceptive. That is why we must ask concerning each miracle we see: Is this consistent with what God says in the Bible? The second beast here gains influence through the signs and wonders that he can perform on behalf of the first beast. The second beast orders the people to worship an image in honour of the first beast—a direct flouting of the second commandment (Exodus 20:4–6). Allowing the Bible to guide our faith and actions will keep us from being deceived by false signs, however convincing they appear to be. Any teaching that contradicts God's word is false.

13:16, 17 In every generation, Christians need to maintain a healthy scepticism about society's pleasures and rewards. In our educational, economic, and civic structures, there are incentives and rewards. Co-operating Christians must always support what is good and healthy about our society, but we must stand against sin. In some cases, such as Satan's system described here, the system or structure becomes so evil that there is no way to co-operate with it.

13:16–18 This mark of the beast is designed to mock the seal that God places on his followers (7:2, 3). Just as God marks his people to save them, so Satan's beast marks his people to save them from the persecution that Satan will inflict upon God's followers. Identifying this particular mark is not as important as identifying the purpose of the mark. Those who accept it show their allegiance to Satan, their willingness to operate within the economic system he promotes, and their rebellion against God. To refuse the mark means to commit oneself entirely to God, preferring death to compromising one's faith in Christ.

13:17
[h]Rev 14:9
[i]Rev 14:11; 15:2
13:18
[j]Rev 17:9
[k]Rev 15:2; 21:17
14:1
[a]Rev 5:6
[b]Ps 2:6
[c]Rev 7:4
[d]Rev 3:12
14:2
[e]Rev 1:15
[f]Rev 5:8
14:3
[g]Rev 5:9
[h]ver 1
14:4
[i]2Co 11:2; Rev 3:4
[j]Rev 5:9
[k]Jas 1:18
14:5
[l]Ps 32:2; Zep 3:13
[m]Eph 5:27
14:6
[n]Rev 8:13
[o]Rev 3:10
[p]Rev 13:7
14:7
[q]Rev 15:4
[r]Rev 11:13
[s]Rev 8:10
14:8
[t]Isa 21:9; Jer 51:8
[u]Rev 17:2, 4; 18:3, 9
14:9
[v]Rev 13:14
14:10
[w]Isa 51:17; Jer 25:15
[x]Rev 18:6

17so that no-one could buy or sell unless he had the mark,[h] which is the name of the
beast or the number of his name.[i]
18This calls for wisdom.[j] If anyone has insight, let him calculate the number of
the beast, for it is man's number.[k] His number is 666.

The Lamb and the 144,000

14 Then I looked, and there before me was the Lamb,[a] standing on Mount Zion,[b]
and with him 144,000[c] who had his name and his Father's name[d] written on
their foreheads. 2And I heard a sound from heaven like the roar of rushing waters[e]
and like a loud peal of thunder. The sound I heard was like that of harpists playing
their harps.[f] 3And they sang a new song[g] before the throne and before the four living
creatures and the elders. No-one could learn the song except the 144,000[h] who had
been redeemed from the earth. 4These are those who did not defile themselves with
women, for they kept themselves pure.[i] They follow the Lamb wherever he goes.
They were purchased from among men[j] and offered as firstfruits[k] to God and the
Lamb. 5No lie was found in their mouths;[l] they are blameless.[m]

The Three Angels

6Then I saw another angel flying in mid-air,[n] and he had the eternal gospel to
proclaim to those who live on the earth[o]—to every nation, tribe, language and
people.[p] 7He said in a loud voice, "Fear God[q] and give him glory,[r] because the
hour of his judgment has come. Worship him who made the heavens, the earth, the
sea and the springs of water."[s]
8A second angel followed and said, "Fallen! Fallen is Babylon the Great,[t] which
made all the nations drink the maddening wine of her adulteries."[u]
9A third angel followed them and said in a loud voice: "If anyone worships the beast
and his image[v] and receives his mark on the forehead or on the hand, 10he, too, will
drink of the wine of God's fury,[w] which has been poured full strength into the cup
of his wrath.[x] He will be tormented with burning sulphur in the presence of the holy

---

13:18 The meaning of this number has been discussed more than that of any other part of the book of Revelation. The three sixes have been said to represent many things, including the number of man or the unholy trinity of Satan, the first beast, and the false prophet (16:13). If the number seven is considered to be the perfect number in the Bible, and if three sevens represent complete perfection, then the number 666 falls completely short of perfection. The first readers of this book probably applied the number to the Emperor Nero, who symbolised all the evils of the Roman empire. (The Greek letters of Nero's name represent numbers that total 666.) Whatever specific application the number is given, the number symbolises the worldwide dominion and complete evil of this unholy trinity designed to undo Christ's work and overthrow him.

14:1ff Chapter 13 described the onslaught of evil that will occur when Satan and his helpers control the world. Chapter 14 gives a glimpse into eternity to show believers what awaits them if they endure. The Lamb is the Messiah. Mount Zion, often another name for Jerusalem, the capital of Israel, is contrasted with the worldly empire. The 144,000 represent believers who have endured persecutions on earth and are now ready to enjoy the eternal benefits and blessings of life with God for ever. The three angels contrast the destiny of believers with that of unbelievers.

14:4 These people are true believers whose robes have been washed and made white in Christ's blood (7:14) through his death ("purchased from among men"). In the Old Testament, idolatry was often portrayed as spiritual adultery (see the book of Hosea). Their purity is best understood symbolically, meaning that they are free from involvement with the pagan world system. These believers are spiritually pure; they have remained faithful to Christ, they have followed him exclusively, and they have received God's reward for staying committed to him. "Firstfruits" refers to the act of dedicating the first part of the harvest as holy to God (Exodus 23:19; see also James 1:18).

14:6, 7 Some believe that this is a final, worldwide appeal to all people to recognise the one true God. No-one will have the excuse of never hearing God's truth. Others, however, see this as an announcement of judgment rather than as an appeal. The people of the world have had their chance to proclaim their allegiance to God, and now God's great judgment is about to begin. If you are reading this, you have already heard God's truth. You know that God's final judgment will not be put off for ever. Have you joyfully received the everlasting Good News? Have you confessed your sins and trusted in Christ to save you? If so, you have nothing to fear from God's judgment. The Judge of all the earth is your Saviour!

14:8 Babylon was the name of both an evil city and an immoral empire, a world centre for idol worship. Babylon ransacked Jerusalem and carried the people of Judah into captivity (see 2 Kings 24 and 2 Chronicles 36). Just as Babylon was the Jews' worst enemy, the Roman empire was the worst enemy of the early Christians. John, who probably did not dare speak against Rome openly, applied the name *Babylon* to this enemy of God's people (Rome)—and, by extension, to all God's enemies of all times.

14:9–11 Those who worship the beast, accept his mark on their foreheads, and operate according to his world economic system will ultimately face God's judgment. Our world values money, power, and pleasure over God's leadership. To get what the world values, many people disown God and violate Christian principles. Thus they must drink of the wine of God's wrath (see Psalm 75; Isaiah 51:17).

angels and of the Lamb. 11 And the smoke of their torment rises for ever and ever.[y]
There is no rest day or night for those who worship the beast and his image, or for
anyone who receives the mark of his name." 12 This calls for patient endurance on the
part of the saints[z] who obey God's commandments and remain faithful to Jesus.
13 Then I heard a voice from heaven say, "Write: Blessed are the dead who die in
the Lord[a] from now on."
"Yes," says the Spirit, "they will rest from their labour, for their deeds will follow
them."

14:11 [y] Isa 34:10; Rev 19:3
14:12 [z] Rev 13:10
14:13 [a] 1Co 15:18; 1Th 4:16

The Harvest of the Earth

14 I looked, and there before me was a white cloud, and seated on the cloud was
one "like a son of man"[a][b] with a crown[c] of gold on his head and a sharp sickle
in his hand. 15 Then another angel came out of the temple and called in a loud voice
to him who was sitting on the cloud, "Take your sickle[d] and reap, because the time
to reap has come, for the harvest[e] of the earth is ripe." 16 So he who was seated on
the cloud swung his sickle over the earth, and the earth was harvested.
17 Another angel came out of the temple in heaven, and he too had a sharp sickle.
18 Still another angel, who had charge of the fire, came from the altar and called in
a loud voice to him who had the sharp sickle, "Take your sharp sickle and gather the
clusters of grapes from the earth's vine, because its grapes are ripe." 19 The angel
swung his sickle on the earth, gathered its grapes and threw them into the great
winepress of God's wrath.[f] 20 They were trampled in the winepress[g] outside the
city,[h] and blood flowed out of the press, rising as high as the horses' bridles for a
distance of 1,600 stadia.[b]

14:14 [b] Da 7:13; Rev 1:13 [c] Rev 6:2
14:15 [d] Joel 3:13 [e] Jer 51:33
14:19 [f] Rev 19:15
14:20 [g] Isa 63:3 [h] Heb 13:12; Rev 11:8

5. Pouring out the seven plagues

Seven Angels With Seven Plagues

15 I saw in heaven another great and marvellous sign:[a] seven angels[b] with the
seven last plagues[c]—last, because with them God's wrath is completed. 2 And
I saw what looked like a sea of glass[d] mixed with fire and, standing beside the sea,
those who had been victorious over the beast and his image[e] and over the number
of his name. They held harps given them by God 3 and sang the song of Moses[f] the
servant of God and the song of the Lamb:

15:1 [a] Rev 12:1, 3 [b] Rev 16:1 [c] Lev 26:21
15:2 [d] Rev 4:6 [e] Rev 13:14
15:3 [f] Ex 15:1; Dt 32:4

[a] *14* Daniel 7:13 [b] *20* That is, about 180 miles (about 300 kilometres)

14:11 The ultimate result of sin is unending separation from God. Because human beings are created in God's image with an inborn thirst for fellowship with him, separation from God will be the ultimate torment and misery. Sin always brings misery, but in this life we can choose to repent and restore our relationship with God. In eternity there will no longer be opportunity for repentance. If in this life we choose to be independent of God, in the next life we will be separated from him for ever. Nobody is forced to choose eternal separation from God, and nobody suffers this fate by accident. Jesus invites all of us to open the door of our hearts to him (3:20). If we do this, we will enjoy everlasting fellowship with him.

14:12 This news about God's ultimate triumph should encourage God's people to remain faithful through every trial and persecution. They can do this, God promises, by trusting in Jesus and obeying the commands found in his word. The secret to enduring, therefore, is trust and obedience. Trust God to give you patience to endure even the small trials you face daily; obey him even when obedience is unattractive or dangerous.

14:13 While it is true that money, fame, and belongings can't be taken with us from this life, God's people *can* produce fruit that survives even death. God will remember our love, kindness, and faithfulness, and those who accept Christ through our witness will join us in the new earth. Be sure that your values are in line with God's values, and decide today to produce fruit that lasts for ever.

14:14–16 This is an image of judgment: Christ is separating the faithful from the unfaithful like a farmer harvesting his crops. This is a time of joy for the Christians who have been persecuted and martyred—they will receive their long-awaited reward. Christians should not fear the Last Judgment. Jesus said, "I tell you the truth, whoever hears my word and believes him who sent me has eternal life and will not be condemned; he has crossed over from death to life" (John 5:24).

14:19 A winepress was a large vat or trough where grapes were collected and then crushed. The juice flowed out of a duct that led into a large holding vat. The winepress is often used in the Bible as a symbol of God's wrath and judgment against sin (Isaiah 63:3–6; Lamentations 1:15; Joel 3:12, 13).

14:20 The distance of 1,600 stadia equals about 180 miles, approximately the north-south length of Palestine.

15:1 The seven last plagues are also called the seven bowl judgments. They actually begin in chapter 16. Unlike the previous plagues, these are universal, and they will culminate in the abolition of all evil ("with them God's wrath is completed") and the end of the world.

15:2 This is similar to the "sea of glass" described in 4:6, located before the throne of God. Here it is mixed with fire to represent wrath and judgment. Those who stand beside it are victorious over Satan and his evil beast.

15:3, 4 The song of Moses celebrated Israel's deliverance from Egypt (Exodus 15). The song of the Lamb celebrates the ultimate

15:3 [g]Ps 111:2 [h]Ps 145:17
15:4 [i]Jer 10:7 [j]Isa 66:23
15:5 [k]Rev 11:19 [l]Nu 1:50
15:6 [m]Rev 14:15 [n]ver 1 [o]Rev 1:13
15:7 [p]Rev 4:6
15:8 [q]Isa 6:4 [r]Ex 40:34, 35; 1Ki 8:10, 11; 2Ch 5:13, 14
16:1 [a]Rev 15:1
16:2 [b]Rev 8:7 [c]Ex 9:9-11 [d]Rev 13:15-17
16:3 [e]Ex 7:17-21; Rev 8:8, 9
16:4 [f]Rev 8:10 [g]Ex 7:17-21
16:5 [h]Rev 15:3 [i]Rev 1:4 [j]Rev 15:4
16:6 [k]Isa 49:26; Rev 17:6
16:7 [l]Rev 6:9 [m]Rev 15:3; 19:2
16:8 [n]Rev 8:12 [o]Rev 14:18

"Great and marvellous are your deeds,[g]
  Lord God Almighty.
Just and true are your ways,[h]
  King of the ages.
4 Who will not fear you, O Lord,[i]
  and bring glory to your name?
For you alone are holy.
All nations will come
  and worship before you,[j]
for your righteous acts have been revealed."

5 After this I looked and in heaven the temple,[k] that is, the tabernacle of the
Testimony,[l] was opened. 6 Out of the temple[m] came the seven angels with the seven
plagues.[n] They were dressed in clean, shining linen and wore golden sashes round
their chests.[o] 7 Then one of the four living creatures[p] gave to the seven angels seven
golden bowls filled with the wrath of God, who lives for ever and ever. 8 And the
temple was filled with smoke[q] from the glory of God and from his power, and no-one
could enter the temple[r] until the seven plagues of the seven angels were completed.

The Seven Bowls of God's Wrath

16 Then I heard a loud voice from the temple saying to the seven angels,[a] "Go,
pour out the seven bowls of God's wrath on the earth."
2 The first angel went and poured out his bowl on the land,[b] and ugly and painful
sores[c] broke out on the people who had the mark of the beast and worshipped his
image.[d]
3 The second angel poured out his bowl on the sea, and it turned into blood like that
of a dead man, and every living thing in the sea died.[e]
4 The third angel poured out his bowl on the rivers and springs of water,[f] and they
became blood.[g] 5 Then I heard the angel in charge of the waters say:

"You are just in these judgments,[h]
  you who are and who were,[i] the Holy One,[j]
  because you have so judged;
6 for they have shed the blood of your saints and prophets,
  and you have given them blood to drink[k] as they deserve."

7 And I heard the altar[l] respond:

"Yes, Lord God Almighty,
  true and just are your judgments."[m]

8 The fourth angel[n] poured out his bowl on the sun, and the sun was given power
to scorch people with fire.[o] 9 They were seared by the intense heat and they cursed

---

deliverance of God's people from the power of Satan.

15:5–8 The *tabernacle of Testimony* is a Greek translation for the Hebrew "Tent of Meeting" (see Exodus 40:34, 35). The imagery brings us back to the time of the exodus in the desert when the ark of the covenant (the symbol of God's presence among his people) resided in the tabernacle. The angels coming out of the temple are clothed in clean, shining linen with golden sashes around their chests. Their garments, reminiscent of the high priest's clothing, show that they are free from corruption, immorality, and injustice. The smoke that fills the temple is the manifestation of God's glory and power. There is no escape from this judgment.

15:8 Our eternal reign with Christ won't begin until all evil is destroyed by his judgment. The faithful must wait for his timetable to be revealed.

16:1ff The bowl judgments are God's final and complete judgments on the earth. The end has come. There are many similarities between the bowl judgments and the trumpet judgments (8:6–11:19), but there are three main differences: (1) these judgments are complete whereas the trumpet judgments are partial; (2) the trumpet judgments still give unbelievers the opportunity to repent, but the bowl judgments do not; and (3) mankind is indirectly affected by several of the trumpet judgments but directly attacked by all the bowl judgments.

16:7 The significance of the altar itself responding is that *everyone and everything* will be praising God, acknowledging his righteousness and perfect justice.

16:9–21 We know that the people realise that these judgments come from God because they curse him for sending them. But they still refuse to recognise God's authority and repent of their sins. Christians should not be surprised at the hostility and hardness of heart of unbelievers. Even when the power of God is fully and completely revealed, many will still refuse to repent. If you find yourself ignoring God more and more, turn back to him now before your heart becomes too hard to repent (see the note on 9:20, 21 for more on hard hearts).

the name of God,[p] who had control over these plagues, but they refused to repent[q]
and glorify him.[r]
10The fifth angel poured out his bowl on the throne of the beast,[s] and his kingdom
was plunged into darkness.[t] Men gnawed their tongues in agony 11and cursed[u] the
God of heaven[v] because of their pains and their sores,[w] but they refused to repent
of what they had done.[x]
12The sixth angel poured out his bowl on the great river Euphrates,[y] and its water
was dried up to prepare the way for the kings from the East.[z] 13Then I saw three evil[a]
spirits that looked like frogs; they came out of the mouth of the dragon,[a] out of the
mouth of the beast[b] and out of the mouth of the false prophet.[c] 14They are spirits
of demons[d] performing miraculous signs, and they go out to the kings of the whole
world, to gather them for the battle[e] on the great day of God Almighty.
15"Behold, I come like a thief! Blessed is he who stays awake[f] and keeps his
clothes with him, so that he may not go naked and be shamefully exposed."
16Then they gathered the kings together to the place that in Hebrew[g] is called
Armageddon.[h]
17The seventh angel poured out his bowl into the air,[i] and out of the temple[j] came
a loud voice[k] from the throne, saying, "It is done!"[l] 18Then there came flashes of
lightning, rumblings, peals of thunder[m] and a severe earthquake.[n] No earthquake like
it has ever occurred since man has been on earth,[o] so tremendous was the quake.
19The great city[p] split into three parts, and the cities of the nations collapsed. God
remembered[q] Babylon the Great[r] and gave her the cup filled with the wine of the
fury of his wrath.[s] 20Every island fled away and the mountains could not be found.[t]
21From the sky huge hailstones[u] of about a hundred pounds each fell upon men. And
they cursed God on account of the plague of hail,[v] because the plague was so terrible.

6. Seizing the final victory

The Woman on the Beast

17 One of the seven angels[a] who had the seven bowls[b] came and said to me,
"Come, I will show you the punishment[c] of the great prostitute,[d] who sits on
many waters.[e] 2With her the kings of the earth committed adultery and the inhabitants
of the earth were intoxicated with the wine of her adulteries."[f]
3Then the angel carried me away in the Spirit into a desert.[g] There I saw a woman
sitting on a scarlet beast that was covered with blasphemous names[h] and had seven

a 13 Greek *unclean*

16:9 [p]ver 11, 21 [q]Rev 2:21 [r]Rev 11:13
16:10 [s]Rev 13:2 [t]Rev 9:2
16:11 [u]ver 9, 21 [v]Rev 11:13 [w]ver 2 [x]Rev 2:21
16:12 [y]Rev 9:14 [z]Isa 41:2
16:13 [a]Rev 12:3 [b]Rev 13:1 [c]Rev 19:20
16:14 [d]1Ti 4:1 [e]Rev 17:14
16:15 [f]Lk 12:37
16:16 [g]Rev 9:11 [h]2Ki 23:29, 30
16:17 [i]Eph 2:2 [j]Rev 14:15 [k]Rev 11:15 [l]Rev 21:6
16:18 [m]Rev 4:5 [n]Rev 6:12 [o]Da 12:1
16:19 [p]Rev 17:18 [q]Rev 18:5 [r]Rev 14:8 [s]Rev 14:10
16:20 [t]Rev 6:14
16:21 [u]Rev 11:19 [v]Ex 9:23-25
17:1 [a]Rev 15:1 [b]Rev 21:9 [c]Rev 16:19 [d]Rev 19:2 [e]Jer 51:13
17:2 [f]Rev 14:8; 18:3
17:3 [g]Rev 12:6, 14 [h]Rev 13:1

16:12 The Euphrates River was a natural protective boundary against the empires to the east (Babylon, Assyria, Persia). If it dried up, nothing could hold back invading armies. The armies from the east symbolise unhindered judgment.

16:13, 14 These spirits of demons performing miraculous signs who come out of the mouths of the unholy trinity unite the rulers of the world for battle against God. The imagery of the demons coming out of the mouths of the three evil rulers signifies the verbal enticements and propaganda that will draw many people to their evil cause. For more about demons, see the note on 9:3ff.

16:15 Christ will return unexpectedly (1 Thessalonians 5:1–6), so we must be ready when he returns. We can prepare ourselves by standing firm in temptation and by being committed to God's moral standards. In what ways does your life show either your readiness or your lack of preparation for Christ's return?

16:16 This battlefield called Armageddon is near the city of Megiddo (south-east of the modern port of Haifa), which guarded a large plain in northern Israel. It is a strategic location near a prominent international highway leading north from Egypt through Israel, along the coast, and on to Babylon. Megiddo overlooked the entire plain southward towards Galilee and westward towards the mountains of Gilboa.

16:16 Sinful people will unite to fight against God in a final display of rebellion. Many are already united against Christ and his people—those who stand for truth, peace, justice, and morality. Your personal battle with evil foreshadows the great battle pictured here, where God will meet evil and destroy it once and for all. Be strong and courageous as you battle against sin and evil: you are fighting on the winning side.

16:17–21 For more information on Babylon and what it represents in Revelation, see the note on 14:8. The city's division into three sections is a symbol of its complete destruction.

17:1ff The destruction of Babylon mentioned in 16:17–21 is now described in greater detail. The "great prostitute", called Babylon, represents the early Roman empire with its many gods and the blood of Christian martyrs on its hands. The water stands for either sea commerce or a well-watered (well-provisioned) city. The great prostitute represents the seductiveness of the governmental system that uses immoral means to gain its own pleasure, prosperity, and advantage. In contrast to the prostitute, Christ's bride, the church, is pure and obedient (19:6–9). The wicked city of Babylon contrasts with the heavenly city of Jerusalem (21:10–22:5). The original readers probably rather quickly identified Babylon with Rome, but Babylon also symbolises any system that is hostile to God (see 17:5).

17:3 The scarlet beast is either the dragon of 12:3, or the beast from the sea described in 13:1.

17:3 [i]Rev 12:3
17:4 [j]Rev 18:16 [k]Jer 51:7; Rev 18:6
17:5 [l]Rev 14:8
17:6 [m]Rev 18:24
17:7 [n]ver 5 [o]ver 3
17:8 [p]Rev 13:10 [q]Rev 3:10 [r]Rev 13:8 [s]Rev 13:3
17:9 [t]Rev 13:18
17:11 [u]ver 8
17:12 [v]Rev 12:3 [w]Rev 18:10, 17, 19
17:13 [x]ver 17
17:14 [y]Rev 16:14 [z]1Ti 6:15; Rev 19:16 [a]Mt 22:14
17:15 [b]Isa 8:7 [c]Rev 13:7
17:16 [d]Rev 18:17, 19 [e]Eze 16:37, 39 [f]Rev 19:18 [g]Rev 18:8
17:17 [h]Rev 10:7
17:18 [i]Rev 16:19

heads and ten horns.[i] 4 The woman was dressed in purple and scarlet, and was
glittering with gold, precious stones and pearls.[j] She held a golden cup[k] in her hand,
filled with abominable things and the filth of her adulteries. 5 This title was written
on her forehead:

MYSTERY
BABYLON THE GREAT[l]
THE MOTHER OF PROSTITUTES
AND OF THE ABOMINATIONS OF THE EARTH.

6 I saw that the woman was drunk with the blood of the saints,[m] the blood of those
who bore testimony to Jesus.
When I saw her, I was greatly astonished. 7 Then the angel said to me: "Why are
you astonished? I will explain to you the mystery[n] of the woman and of the beast
she rides, which has the seven heads and ten horns.[o] 8 The beast, which you saw,
once was, now is not, and will come up out of the Abyss and go to his destruction.[p]
The inhabitants of the earth[q] whose names have not been written in the book of life[r]
from the creation of the world will be astonished[s] when they see the beast, because
he once was, now is not, and yet will come.
9 "This calls for a mind with wisdom.[t] The seven heads are seven hills on which
the woman sits. 10 They are also seven kings. Five have fallen, one is, the other has
not yet come; but when he does come, he must remain for a little while. 11 The beast
who once was, and now is not,[u] is an eighth king. He belongs to the seven and is
going to his destruction.
12 "The ten horns[v] you saw are ten kings who have not yet received a kingdom,
but who for one hour[w] will receive authority as kings along with the beast. 13 They
have one purpose and will give their power and authority to the beast.[x] 14 They will
make war[y] against the Lamb, but the Lamb will overcome them because he is Lord
of lords and King of kings[z]—and with him will be his called, chosen[a] and faithful
followers."
15 Then the angel said to me, "The waters[b] you saw, where the prostitute sits, are
peoples, multitudes, nations and languages.[c] 16 The beast and the ten horns you saw
will hate the prostitute. They will bring her to ruin[d] and leave her naked;[e] they will
eat her flesh[f] and burn her with fire.[g] 17 For God has put it into their hearts to
accomplish his purpose by agreeing to give the beast their power to rule, until God's
words are fulfilled.[h] 18 The woman you saw is the great city[i] that rules over the kings
of the earth."

17:6 Throughout history, people have been killed for their faith. Over the last century, millions have been killed by oppressive governments, and many of those victims were believers. The woman's drunkenness shows her pleasure in her evil accomplishments and her false feeling of triumph over the church. But every martyr who has fallen before her sword has only served to strengthen the faith of the church.

17:8 In chapter 12 we met the dragon (Satan). In chapter 13 we saw the beast from the sea and the power he received from Satan. In chapters 14–16 we see God's great judgments. In this chapter, a scarlet beast similar to the beast and the dragon appears as an ally of the great prostitute. The phrase, "was, now is not, and will come" means that the beast was alive, died, and then came back to life. The beast's resurrection symbolises the persistence of evil. This resurgence of evil power will convince many to join forces with the beast, but those who choose the side of evil condemn themselves to the devil's fate—eternal torment.

17:8 For more information on the book of life, see the note on 3:5.

17:9–11 Here John is referring to Rome, the city famous for its seven hills. Many say that this city also symbolised all evil in the world—any person, religion, group, government, or structure that opposed Christ. Whatever view is taken of the seven hills and seven kings, this section indicates the climax of Satan's struggle against God. Evil's power is limited, and its destruction is on the horizon.

17:12 The ten horns represent kings of nations yet to arise. Rome will be followed by other powers. Rome is a good example of how the antichrist's system will work, demanding complete allegiance, and ruling by raw power, oppression, and slavery. Whoever the ten kings are, they will give their power to the antichrist and will make war against the Lamb.

17:16 In a dramatic turn of events, the prostitute's allies turn on her and destroy her. This is how evil operates. Destructive by its very nature, it discards its own adherents when they cease to serve its purposes. An unholy alliance is an uneasy alliance because each partner puts its own interests first.

17:17 No matter what happens, we must trust that God is still in charge, that God overrules all the plans and intrigues of the evil one, and that God's plans will happen just as he says. God even uses people opposed to him as tools to execute his will. Although he allows evil to permeate this present world, the new earth will never know sin.

The Fall of Babylon

18 After this I saw another angel[a] coming down from heaven.[b] He had great
authority, and the earth was illuminated by his splendour.[c] 2With a mighty
voice he shouted:

"Fallen! Fallen is Babylon the Great![d]
She has become a home for demons
and a haunt for every evil[a] spirit,
a haunt for every unclean and detestable bird.[e]
3For all the nations have drunk
the maddening wine of her adulteries.[f]
The kings of the earth committed adultery with her,[g]
and the merchants of the earth grew rich[h] from her excessive
luxuries."[i]

4Then I heard another voice from heaven say:

"Come out of her, my people,[j]
so that you will not share in her sins,
so that you will not receive any of her plagues;
5for her sins are piled up to heaven,[k]
and God has remembered[l] her crimes.
6Give back to her as she has given;
pay her back[m] double for what she has done.
Mix her a double portion from her own cup.[n]
7Give her as much torture and grief
as the glory and luxury she gave herself.[o]
In her heart she boasts,
'I sit as queen; I am not a widow,
and I will never mourn.'[p]
8Therefore in one day[q] her plagues will overtake her:
death, mourning and famine.
She will be consumed by fire,[r]
for mighty is the Lord God who judges her.

9"When the kings of the earth who committed adultery with her[s] and shared her
luxury see the smoke of her burning,[t] they will weep and mourn over her.[u] 10Terri-
fied at her torment, they will stand far off[v] and cry:

[a] 2 Greek *unclean*

18:1 [a]Rev 17:1 [b]Rev 10:1 [c]Eze 43:2

18:2 [d]Rev 14:8 [e]Isa 13:21, 22; Jer 50:39

18:3 [f]Rev 14:8 [g]Rev 17:2 [h]Eze 27:9-25 [i]ver 7, 9

18:4 [j]Isa 48:20; Jer 50:8; 2Co 6:17

18:5 [k]Jer 51:9 [l]Rev 16:19

18:6 [m]Ps 137:8; Jer 50:15, 29 [n]Rev 14:10; 16:19

18:7 [o]Eze 28:2-8 [p]Isa 47:7, 8; Zep 2:15

18:8 [q]ver 10; Isa 47:9; Jer 50:31, 32 [r]Rev 17:16

18:9 [s]Rev 17:2, 4 [t]ver 18; Rev 19:3 [u]Eze 26:17, 18

18:10 [v]ver 15, 17

18:1ff This chapter shows the complete destruction of Babylon, John's metaphorical name for the evil world power and all it represents. Everything that tries to block God's purposes will come to a violent end. For more information on how the book of Revelation uses the name *Babylon*, see the note on 14:8.

18:2, 3 Merchants in the Roman empire grew rich by exploiting the sinful pleasures of their society. Many business people today do the same thing. Businesses and governments are often based on greed, money, and power. Many bright individuals are tempted to take advantage of an evil system to enrich themselves. Christians are warned to stay free from the lure of money, status, and the good life. We are to live according to the values Christ exemplified: service, giving, self-sacrifice, obedience, and truth.

18:4–8 The people of Babylon had lived in luxury and pleasure. The city boasted, "I sit as queen . . . and I will never mourn." The powerful, wealthy people of this world are susceptible to this same attitude. A person who is financially comfortable often feels invulnerable, secure, and in control, feeling no need for God or anyone else. This kind of attitude defies God, and his judgment against it is harsh. We are told to avoid Babylon's sins. If you are financially secure, don't become complacent and deluded by the myth of self-sufficiency. Use your resources to help others and advance God's kingdom.

18:9, 10 Those who are tied to the world's system will lose everything when it collapses. What they have worked for a lifetime to build up will be destroyed in one hour. Those who work only for material rewards will have nothing when they die or when their possessions are destroyed. What can we take with us to the new earth? Our faith, our Christian character, and our relationships with other believers. These are more important than any amount of money, power, or pleasure.

18:9–19 Those who are in control of various parts of the economic system will mourn at Babylon's fall. The political leaders will mourn because they were the overseers of Babylon's wealth and were in a position to enrich themselves greatly. The merchants will mourn because Babylon, the greatest customer for their goods, will be gone. The sea captains will no longer have anywhere to bring their goods because the merchants will have nowhere to sell them. The fall of the evil world system affects all who enjoyed and depended on it. No-one will remain unaffected by Babylon's fall.

18:11–13 This list of various items of merchandise illustrates the extreme materialism of this society. Few of these goods are necessities—most are luxuries. The society had become so self-indulgent that people were willing to use evil means to gratify their desires. Even people had become commodities—the "bodies and souls of men" were sold as slaves to Babylon.

“ ‘Woe! Woe, O great city,[w]
O Babylon, city of power!
In one hour[x] your doom has come!’

11“The merchants[y] of the earth will weep and mourn over her because no-one buys
their cargoes any more[z]—12cargoes of gold, silver, precious stones and pearls; fine
linen, purple, silk and scarlet cloth; every sort of citron wood, and articles of every
kind made of ivory, costly wood, bronze, iron and marble;[a] 13cargoes of cinnamon
and spice, of incense, myrrh and frankincense, of wine and olive oil, of fine flour and
wheat; cattle and sheep; horses and carriages; and bodies and souls of men.[b]
14“They will say, ‘The fruit you longed for is gone from you. All your riches and
splendour have vanished, never to be recovered.’ 15The merchants who sold these
things and gained their wealth from her[c] will stand far off, terrified at her torment.
They will weep and mourn[d] 16and cry out:

“ ‘Woe! Woe, O great city,
dressed in fine linen, purple and scarlet,
and glittering with gold, precious stones and pearls![e]
17In one hour[f] such great wealth has been brought to ruin!’[g]

“Every sea captain, and all who travel by ship, the sailors, and all who earn their
living from the sea,[h] will stand far off. 18When they see the smoke of her burning,
they will exclaim, ‘Was there ever a city like this great city?’[i] 19They will throw dust
on their heads,[j] and with weeping and mourning cry out:

“ ‘Woe! Woe, O great city,
where all who had ships on the sea
became rich through her wealth!
In one hour she has been brought to ruin![k]
20Rejoice over her, O heaven![l]
Rejoice, saints and apostles and prophets!
God has judged her for the way she treated you.’ ”[m]

21Then a mighty angel[n] picked up a boulder the size of a large millstone and threw
it into the sea,[o] and said:

“With such violence
the great city of Babylon will be thrown down,
never to be found again.
22The music of harpists and musicians, flute players and
trumpeters,
will never be heard in you again.[p]
No workman of any trade
will ever be found in you again.
The sound of a millstone
will never be heard in you again.[q]
23The light of a lamp

18:10 [w]ver 16, 19 [x]Rev 17:12
18:11 [y]Eze 27:27 [z]ver 3
18:12 [a]Rev 17:4
18:13 [b]Eze 27:13; 1Ti 1:10
18:15 [c]ver 3 [d]Eze 27:31
18:16 [e]Rev 17:4
18:17 [f]ver 10 [g]Rev 17:16 [h]Eze 27:28-30
18:18 [i]Eze 27:32; Rev 13:4
18:19 [j]Jos 7:6; Eze 27:30 [k]Rev 17:16
18:20 [l]Jer 51:48; Rev 12:12 [m]Rev 19:2
18:21 [n]Rev 5:2 [o]Jer 51:63
18:22 [p]Isa 24:8; Eze 26:13 [q]Jer 25:10

HOW CAN A PERSON KEEP AWAY FROM THE EVIL SYSTEM? Here are some suggestions:

1. People must always be more important than products.
2. Keep away from pride in your own plans and successes.
3. Remember that God's will and word must never be compromised.
4. People must always be considered above the making of money.
5. Do what is right, no matter what the cost.
6. Be involved in businesses that provide worthwhile products or services—not just things that feed the world's desires.

18:11–19 God's people should not live for money, because money will be worthless in eternity. And they should keep on guard constantly against greed, a sin that is always ready to take over their lives.

will never shine in you again.
The voice of bridegroom and bride
will never be heard in you again.[r]
Your merchants were the world's great men.[s]
By your magic spell[t] all the nations were led astray.
24 In her was found the blood of prophets and of the saints,[u]
and of all who have been killed on the earth."[v]

18:23
[r] Jer 7:34; 16:9; 25:10
[s] Isa 23:8
[t] Na 3:4

18:24
[u] Rev 16:6; 17:6
[v] Jer 51:49

Hallelujah!

19 After this I heard what sounded like the roar of a great multitude[a] in heaven shouting:

"Hallelujah!
Salvation[b] and glory and power[c] belong to our God,
2 for true and just are his judgments.
He has condemned the great prostitute
who corrupted the earth by her adulteries.
He has avenged on her the blood of his servants."[d]

3 And again they shouted:

"Hallelujah!
The smoke from her goes up for ever and ever."[e]

4 The twenty-four elders[f] and the four living creatures[g] fell down[h] and worshipped God, who was seated on the throne. And they cried:

"Amen, Hallelujah!"

5 Then a voice came from the throne, saying:

"Praise our God,
all you his servants,[i]
you who fear him,
both small and great!"[j]

6 Then I heard what sounded like a great multitude,[k] like the roar of rushing waters
and like loud peals of thunder, shouting:

"Hallelujah!
For our Lord God Almighty reigns.
7 Let us rejoice and be glad
and give him glory!
For the wedding of the Lamb[l] has come,
and his bride[m] has made herself ready.
8 Fine linen, bright and clean,
was given her to wear."
(Fine linen stands for the righteous acts[n] of the saints.)

9 Then the angel said to me,[o] "Write:[p] 'Blessed are those who are invited to the
wedding supper of the Lamb!' "[q] And he added, "These are the true words of God."[r]

19:1
[a] Rev 11:15
[b] Rev 7:10
[c] Rev 4:11

19:2
[d] Dt 32:43; Rev 6:10

19:3
[e] Isa 34:10; Rev 14:11

19:4
[f] Rev 4:4
[g] Rev 4:6
[h] Rev 5:14

19:5
[i] Ps 134:1
[j] Rev 11:18; 20:12

19:6
[k] Rev 11:15

19:7
[l] Mt 22:2; 25:10; Eph 5:32
[m] Rev 21:2, 9

19:8
[n] Rev 15:4

19:9
[o] ver 10
[p] Rev 1:19
[q] Lk 14:15
[r] Rev 21:5; 22:6

19:1ff Praise is the heartfelt response to God by those who love him. The more you get to know God and realise what he has done, the more you will respond with praise. Praise is at the heart of true worship. Let your praise of God flow out of your realisation of who he is and how much he loves you.

19:1, 2 The identity of this great prostitute is explained in the note on 17:1ff.

19:1–8 A great multitude in heaven initiates the chorus of praise to God for his victory (19:1–3). Then the 24 elders (identified in the note on 4:4) join the chorus (19:4). Finally, the great choir of heaven once again praises God – the wedding of the Lamb has come (19:6–8). See Matthew 25:1–13 where Christ compares the coming of his kingdom to a wedding for which we must be prepared.

19:7, 8 This is the culmination of human history – the judgment of the wicked and the wedding of the Lamb and his bride, the church. The church consists of all faithful believers from all time. The bride's clothing stands in sharp contrast to the gaudy clothing of the great prostitute of 17:4 and 18:16. The bride's clothing is the righteousness of the saints. These righteous acts are not religious deeds done by believers to their merit, but they reflect the work of Christ to save us (7:9, 14).

19:10
[s] Rev 22:8
[t] Ac 10:25, 26; Rev 22:9
[u] Rev 12:17
19:11
[v] Rev 6:2
[w] Rev 3:14
[x] Isa 11:4
19:12
[y] Rev 1:14
[z] Rev 6:2
[a] Rev 2:17
19:13
[b] Isa 63:2, 3
[c] Jn 1:1
19:14
[d] ver 8
19:15
[e] Rev 1:16
[f] Isa 11:4; 2Th 2:8
[g] Ps 2:9; Rev 2:27
[h] Rev 14:20
19:16
[i] ver 12
[j] Rev 17:14
19:17
[k] ver 21
[l] Rev 8:13
[m] Eze 39:17
19:18
[n] Eze 39:18-20
19:19
[o] Rev 16:14, 16
19:20
[p] Rev 16:13
[q] Rev 13:12
[r] Da 7:11; Rev 20:10, 14, 15; 21:8
[s] Rev 14:10
19:21
[t] ver 15
[u] ver 11, 19
[v] ver 17

10 At this I fell at his feet to worship him.[s] But he said to me, "Do not do it! I am
a fellow-servant with you and with your brothers who hold to the testimony of Jesus.
Worship God![t] For the testimony of Jesus[u] is the spirit of prophecy."

The Rider on the White Horse

11 I saw heaven standing open and there before me was a white horse, whose rider[v]
is called Faithful and True.[w] With justice he judges and makes war.[x] 12 His eyes are
like blazing fire,[y] and on his head are many crowns.[z] He has a name written on him
that no-one knows but he himself.[a] 13 He is dressed in a robe dipped in blood,[b] and
his name is the Word of God.[c] 14 The armies of heaven were following him, riding
on white horses and dressed in fine linen,[d] white and clean. 15 Out of his mouth comes
a sharp sword[e] with which to strike down[f] the nations. "He will rule them with an
iron sceptre."**a**[g] He treads the winepress[h] of the fury of the wrath of God Almighty.
16 On his robe and on his thigh he has this name written:[i]

KING OF KINGS AND LORD OF LORDS.[j]

17 And I saw an angel standing in the sun, who cried in a loud voice to all the birds[k]
flying in mid-air,[l] "Come,[m] gather together for the great supper of God, 18 so that
you may eat the flesh of kings, generals, and mighty men, of horses and their riders,
and the flesh of all people,[n] free and slave, small and great."
19 Then I saw the beast and the kings of the earth[o] and their armies gathered together
to make war against the rider on the horse and his army. 20 But the beast was captured,
and with him the false prophet[p] who had performed the miraculous signs on his
behalf.[q] With these signs he had deluded those who had received the mark of the beast
and worshipped his image. The two of them were thrown alive into the fiery lake[r]
of burning sulphur.[s] 21 The rest of them were killed with the sword[t] that came out
of the mouth of the rider on the horse,[u] and all the birds[v] gorged themselves on their
flesh.

a *15* Psalm 2:9

19:10 The angel did not accept John's homage and worship because only God is worthy of worship. Like John, it would be easy for us to become overwhelmed by this prophetic scene. But Jesus is the central focus of God's revelation and his redemptive plan (as announced by the prophets). As you read the book of Revelation, don't get bogged down in all the details of the awesome visions; remember that the overarching theme in all the visions is the ultimate victory of Jesus Christ over evil.

19:11 The name "Faithful and True" contrasts with the faithless and deceitful Babylon described in chapter 18.

19:11–21 John's vision shifts again. Heaven opens and Jesus appears, this time not as a Lamb, but as a warrior on a white horse (symbolising victory). Jesus came first as a Lamb to be a sacrifice for sin, but he will return as a Conqueror and King to execute judgment (2 Thessalonians 1:7–10). Jesus' first coming brought forgiveness; his second will bring judgment. The battle lines have been drawn between God and evil, and the world is waiting for the King to ride onto the field.

19:12 Although Jesus is called "Faithful and True" (19:11), "Word of God" (19:13), and "KING OF KINGS AND LORD OF LORDS" (19:16), this verse implies that no name can do him justice. He is greater than any description or expression the human mind can devise.

19:13 For more about the symbolism of Jesus' clothes being dipped in blood, see the second note on 7:14.

19:16 This title indicates our God's sovereignty. Most of the world is worshipping the beast, the antichrist, whom they believe has all power and authority. Then suddenly out of heaven rides Christ and his army of angels – the "KING OF KINGS AND LORD OF LORDS". His entrance signals the end of the false powers.

19:17 This "great supper of God" is a grim contrast to the wedding supper of the Lamb (19:9). One is a celebration; the other is devastation.

19:19 The beast is identified in the note on 13:1.

19:19–21 The battle lines have been drawn, and the greatest confrontation in the history of the world is about to begin. The beast (the antichrist) and the false prophet have gathered the governments and armies of the earth under the antichrist's rule. The enemy armies believe they have come of their own volition; in reality, God has summoned them to battle in order to defeat them. That they would even presume to fight against God shows how their pride and rebellion have perverted their thinking. There really is no fight, however, because the victory was won when Jesus died on the cross for sin and rose from the dead. Thus the evil leaders are immediately captured and sent to their punishment, and the forces of evil are annihilated.

19:20 The fiery lake of burning sulphur is the final destination of the wicked. This lake is different from the Abyss (bottomless pit) referred to in 9:1. The antichrist and the false prophet are thrown into the fiery lake. Then their leader, Satan himself, will be thrown into that lake (20:10), and finally death and Hades (20:14). Afterwards, everyone whose name is not recorded in the book of life will be thrown into the lake of fire (20:15).

The Thousand Years

20 And I saw an angel coming down out of heaven,[a] having the key[b] to the
Abyss and holding in his hand a great chain. 2 He seized the dragon, that ancient
serpent, who is the devil, or Satan,[c] and bound him for a thousand years.[d] 3 He threw
him into the Abyss, and locked and sealed[e] it over him, to keep him from deceiving
the nations[f] any more until the thousand years were ended. After that, he must be
set free for a short time.

4 I saw thrones[g] on which were seated those who had been given authority to judge.
And I saw the souls of those who had been beheaded[h] because of their testimony for
Jesus and because of the word of God. They had not worshipped the beast[i] or his
image and had not received his mark on their foreheads or their hands.[j] They came
to life and reigned with Christ for a thousand years. 5 (The rest of the dead did not
come to life until the thousand years were ended.) This is the first resurrection.[k]
6 Blessed[l] and holy are those who have part in the first resurrection. The second
death[m] has no power over them, but they will be priests[n] of God and of Christ and
will reign with him[o] for a thousand years.

Satan's Doom

7 When the thousand years are over,[p] Satan will be released from his prison 8 and
will go out to deceive the nations[q] in the four corners of the earth—Gog and
Magog[r]—to gather them for battle.[s] In number they are like the sand on the
seashore.[t] 9 They marched across the breadth of the earth and surrounded[u] the camp
of God's people, the city he loves. But fire came down from heaven[v] and devoured
them. 10 And the devil, who deceived them,[w] was thrown into the lake of burning
sulphur, where the beast and the false prophet had been thrown. They will be
tormented day and night for ever and ever.[x]

20:1 [a]Rev 10:1 [b]Rev 1:18
20:2 [c]Rev 12:9 [d]2Pe 2:4
20:3 [e]Da 6:17 [f]Rev 12:9
20:4 [g]Da 7:9 [h]Rev 6:9 [i]Rev 13:12 [j]Rev 13:16
20:5 [k]Lk 14:14; Php 3:11
20:6 [l]Rev 14:13 [m]Rev 2:11 [n]Rev 1:6 [o]ver 4
20:7 [p]ver 2
20:8 [q]ver 3, 10 [r]Eze 38:2; 39:1 [s]Rev 16:14 [t]Heb 11:12
20:9 [u]Eze 38:9, 16 [v]Eze 38:22; 39:6
20:10 [w]Rev 19:20 [x]Rev 14:10, 11

20:1 The angel and the Abyss (bottomless pit) are explained in the notes on 9:1 and 19:20.

20:2 The dragon, Satan, is discussed in more detail in the notes on 12:3, 4 and 12:9. The dragon is not bound as punishment—that occurs in 20:10—but so that he cannot deceive the nations.

20:2–4 The 1,000 years are often referred to as the *Millennium* (Latin for *1,000 years*). Just how and when this 1,000 years takes place is understood differently among Christian scholars. The three major positions on this issue are called postmillennialism, premillennialism, and amillennialism.

(1) *Postmillennialism* looks for a literal 1,000-year period of peace on earth ushered in by the church. At the end of the 1,000 years, Satan will be unleashed once more, but then Christ will return to defeat him and reign for ever. Christ's second coming will not occur until after the 1,000-year period.

(2) *Premillennialism* also views the 1,000 years as a literal time period, but holds that Christ's second coming initiates his 1,000-year reign and that this reign occurs before the final removal of Satan.

(3) *Amillennialism* understands the 1,000-year period to be symbolic of the time between Christ's ascension and his return. This Millennium is the reign of Christ in the hearts of believers and in his church; thus it is another way of referring to the church age. This period will end with the second coming of Christ.

These different views about the Millennium need not cause division and controversy in the church, because each view acknowledges what is most crucial to Christianity—Christ will return, defeat Satan, and reign for ever! Whatever and whenever the Millennium is, Jesus Christ will unite all believers; therefore, we should not let this issue divide us.

20:3 John doesn't say why God once again sets Satan free, but it is part of God's plan for judging the world. Perhaps it is to expose those who rebel against God in their hearts and confirm those who are truly faithful to God. Whatever the reason, Satan's release results in the final destruction of all evil (20:12–15).

20:4 The beast's mark is explained in the note on 13:16–18.

20:5, 6 Christians hold two basic views concerning this first resurrection. (1) Some believe that the first resurrection is spiritual (in our hearts at salvation), and that the Millennium is our spiritual reign with Christ between his first and second comings. During this time, we are priests of God because Christ reigns in our hearts. In this view, the second resurrection is the bodily resurrection of all people for judgment. (2) Others believe that the first resurrection occurs after Satan has been set aside. It is a physical resurrection of believers who then reign with Christ on the earth for a literal 1,000 years. The second resurrection occurs at the end of this Millennium in order to judge unbelievers who have died.

20:6 The second death is spiritual death—everlasting separation from God (see 21:8).

20:7–9 Gog and Magog symbolise all the forces of evil that band together to battle God. Noah's son, Japheth, had a son named Magog (Genesis 10:2). Ezekiel presents Gog as a leader of forces against Israel (Ezekiel 38; 39).

20:9 This is not a typical battle where the outcome is in doubt during the heat of the conflict. Here there is no contest. Two mighty forces of evil—those of the beast (19:19) and of Satan (20:8)—unite to do battle against God. The Bible uses just two verses to describe each battle—the evil beast and his forces are captured and thrown into the fiery lake (19:20, 21), and fire from heaven devours Satan and his attacking armies (20:9, 10). For God, it is as easy as that. There will be no doubt, no worry, no second thoughts for believers about whether they have chosen the right side. If you are with God, you will experience this tremendous victory with Christ.

20:10 Satan's power is not eternal—he will meet his doom. He began his evil work in mankind at the beginning (Genesis 3:1–6) and continues it today, but he will be destroyed when he is thrown into the lake of burning sulphur. The devil will be released from the Abyss ("his prison", 20:7), but he will never be released from the fiery lake. He will never be a threat to anyone again.

20:11 [y]Rev 4:2
20:12 [z]Da 7:10 [a]Rev 3:5 [b]Jer 17:10; Mt 16:27; Rev 2:23
20:13 [c]Rev 6:8 [d]Isa 26:19
20:14 [e]1Co 15:26
20:15 [f]ver 12
21:1 [a]Isa 65:17; 2Pe 3:13
21:2 [b]Heb 11:10; 12:22; Rev 3:12
21:3 [c]2Co 6:16
21:4 [d]Rev 7:17 [e]1Co 15:26; Rev 20:14 [f]Isa 35:10; 65:19

The Dead Are Judged

11 Then I saw a great white throne[y] and him who was seated on it. Earth and sky
fled from his presence, and there was no place for them. 12 And I saw the dead, great
and small, standing before the throne, and books were opened.[z] Another book was
opened, which is the book of life.[a] The dead were judged according to what they
had done[b] as recorded in the books. 13 The sea gave up the dead that were in it, and
death and Hades[c] gave up the dead[d] that were in them, and each person was judged
according to what he had done. 14 Then death[e] and Hades were thrown into the lake
of fire. The lake of fire is the second death. 15 If anyone's name was not found written
in the book of life,[f] he was thrown into the lake of fire.

7. Making everything new

The New Jerusalem

21 Then I saw a new heaven and a new earth,[a] for the first heaven and the first
earth had passed away, and there was no longer any sea. 2 I saw the Holy City,
the new Jerusalem, coming down out of heaven from God,[b] prepared as a bride
beautifully dressed for her husband. 3 And I heard a loud voice from the throne saying,
"Now the dwelling of God is with men, and he will live with them. They will be his
people, and God himself will be with them and be their God.[c] 4 He will wipe every
tear from their eyes.[d] There will be no more death[e] or mourning or crying or pain,[f]
for the old order of things has passed away."

THE BEGINNING AND THE END
The Bible records for us the beginning of the world and the end of the world. The story of mankind, from beginning to end—from the fall into sin to redemption and God's ultimate victory over evil—is found in the pages of the Bible.

Genesis	*Revelation*
The sun is created	The sun is not needed
Satan is victorious	Satan is defeated
Sin enters the human race	Sin is banished
People run and hide from God	People are invited to live with God for ever
People are cursed	The curse is removed
Tears are shed, with sorrow for sin	No more sin, no more tears or sorrow
The garden and earth are cursed	God's city is glorified, the earth is made new
The fruit from the tree of life is not to be eaten	God's people may eat from the tree of life
Paradise is lost	Paradise is regained
People are doomed to death	Death is defeated, believers live for ever with God

20:12–15 At the judgment, the books are opened. They represent God's judgment, and in them are recorded the deeds of everyone, good or evil. We are not saved by deeds, but deeds are seen as clear evidence of a person's actual relationship with God. The book of life contains the names of those who have put their trust in Christ to save them.

20:14 Death and Hades are thrown into the lake of fire. God's judgment is finished. The lake of fire is the ultimate destination of everything wicked—Satan, the beast, the false prophet, the demons, death, Hades, and all those whose names are not recorded in the book of life because they did not place their faith in Jesus Christ. John's vision does not permit any grey areas in God's judgment. If by faith we have not identified with Christ, confessing him as Lord, there will be no hope, no second chance, no other appeal.

21:1 The earth as we know it will not last for ever, but after God's great judgment, he will create a new earth (see Romans 8:18–21; 2 Peter 3:7–13). God had also promised Isaiah that he would create a new and eternal earth (Isaiah 65:17; 66:22). The sea in John's time was viewed as dangerous and changeable. It was also the source of the beast (13:1). We don't know how the new earth will look or where it will be, but God and his followers—those whose names are written in the book of life—will be united to live there for ever. Will you be there?

21:2, 3 The new Jerusalem is where God lives among his people. Instead of our going up to meet him, he comes down to be with us, just as God became man in Jesus Christ and lived among us (John 1:14). Wherever God reigns, there is peace, security, and love.

21:3, 4 Have you ever wondered what eternity will be like? The "Holy City, the new Jerusalem" is described as the place where God will "wipe every tear from their eyes". For evermore, there will be no death, pain, sorrow, or crying. What a wonderful truth! No matter what you are going through, it's not the last word—God has written the final chapter, and it is about true fulfilment and eternal joy for those who love him. We do not know as much as we would like, but it is enough to know that eternity with God will be more wonderful than we could ever imagine.

5He who was seated on the throne[g] said, "I am making everything new!" Then he
said, "Write this down, for these words are trustworthy and true."[h]
6He said to me: "It is done.[i] I am the Alpha and the Omega,[j] the Beginning and
the End. To him who is thirsty I will give to drink without cost from the spring of
the water of life.[k] 7He who overcomes will inherit all this, and I will be his God and
he will be my son. 8But the cowardly, the unbelieving, the vile, the murderers, the
sexually immoral, those who practise magic arts, the idolaters and all liars[l]—their
place will be in the fiery lake of burning sulphur. This is the second death."[m]
9One of the seven angels who had the seven bowls full of the seven last plagues[n]
came and said to me, "Come, I will show you the bride,[o] the wife of the Lamb."
10And he carried me away[p] in the Spirit[q] to a mountain great and high, and showed
me the Holy City, Jerusalem, coming down out of heaven from God. 11It shone with
the glory of God,[r] and its brilliance was like that of a very precious jewel, like a
jasper, clear as crystal.[s] 12It had a great, high wall with twelve gates, and with twelve
angels at the gates. On the gates were written the names of the twelve tribes of Israel.[t]
13There were three gates on the east, three on the north, three on the south and three
on the west. 14The wall of the city had twelve foundations, and on them were the
names of the twelve apostles of the Lamb.
15The angel who talked with me had a measuring rod[u] of gold to measure the city,
its gates and its walls. 16The city was laid out like a square, as long as it was wide.
He measured the city with the rod and found it to be 12,000 stadia[a] in length, and
as wide and high as it is long. 17He measured its wall and it was 144 cubits[b] thick,[c]
by man's measurement, which the angel was using. 18The wall was made of jasper,[v]
and the city of pure gold, as pure as glass.[w] 19The foundations of the city walls were
decorated with every kind of precious stone.[x] The first foundation was jasper, the
second sapphire, the third chalcedony, the fourth emerald, 20the fifth sardonyx, the
sixth carnelian,[y] the seventh chrysolite, the eighth beryl, the ninth topaz, the tenth
chrysoprase, the eleventh jacinth, and the twelfth amethyst.[d] 21The twelve gates were
twelve pearls, each gate made of a single pearl. The great street of the city was of
pure gold, like transparent glass.[z]
22I did not see a temple[a] in the city, because the Lord God Almighty[b] and the

a *16* That is, about 1,400 miles (about 2,200 kilometres) **b** *17* That is, about 200 feet (about 65 metres)
c *17* Or *high* **d** *20* The precise identification of some of these precious stones is uncertain.

21:5
[g]Rev 4:9; 20:11
[h]Rev 19:9

21:6
[i]Rev 16:17
[j]Rev 1:8; 22:13
[k]Jn 4:10

21:8
[l]1Co 6:9
[m]Rev 2:11

21:9
[n]Rev 15:1, 6, 7
[o]Rev 19:7

21:10
[p]Rev 17:3
[q]Rev 1:10

21:11
[r]Rev 15:8; 22:5
[s]Rev 4:6

21:12
[t]Eze 48:30-34

21:15
[u]Rev 11:1

21:18
[v]ver 11
[w]ver 21

21:19
[x]Isa 54:11, 12

21:20
[y]Rev 4:3

21:21
[z]ver 18

21:22
[a]Jn 4:21, 23
[b]Rev 1:8

21:5 God is the Creator. The Bible begins with the majestic story of his creation of the universe, and it concludes with his creation of a new heaven and a new earth. This is a tremendous hope and encouragement for the believer. When we are with God, with our sins forgiven and our future secure, we will be like Christ. We will be made perfect like him.

21:6 Just as God finished the work of creation (Genesis 2:1–3) and Jesus finished the work of redemption (John 19:30), so the Trinity will finish the entire plan of salvation by inviting the redeemed into a new creation.

21:6 For more about the water of life, see the note on 22:1.

21:7, 8 The "cowardly" are not those who are faint-hearted in their faith or who sometimes doubt or question, but those who turn back from following God. They are not brave enough to stand up for Christ; they are not humble enough to accept his authority over their lives. They are put in the same list as the unbelieving, the vile, the murderers, the liars, the idolaters, the sexually immoral, and those practising magic arts.

People who overcome "stand firm to the end" (Mark 13:13). They will receive the blessings that God promised: (1) eating from the tree of life (2:7), (2) escaping from the lake of fire (the "second death", 2:11), (3) receiving a special name (2:17), (4) having authority over the nations (2:26), (5) being included in the book of life (3:5), (6) being a pillar in God's spiritual temple (3:12), and (7) sitting with Christ on his throne (3:21). Those who can endure the testing of evil and remain faithful will be rewarded by God.

21:8 The lake is explained in the notes on 19:20 and 20:14. The second death is spiritual death, meaning either eternal torment or destruction. In either case, it is permanent separation from God.

21:10ff The rest of the chapter is a stunning description of the new city of God. The vision is symbolic and shows us that our new home with God will defy description. We will not be disappointed by it in any way.

21:12–14 The new Jerusalem is a picture of God's future home for his people. The 12 tribes of Israel (21:12) probably represent all the faithful in the Old Testament; the twelve apostles (21:14) represent the church. Thus, both believing Gentiles and Jews who have been faithful to God will live together in the new earth.

21:15–17 The city's measurements are symbolic of a place that will hold all God's people. These measurements are all multiples of 12, the number for God's people: there were 12 tribes in Israel, and 12 apostles who started the church. The walls are 144 (12 x 12) cubits (200 feet) thick; there are 12 layers in the walls, and 12 gates in the city; and the height, length, and breadth are all the same, 12,000 stadia (1,400 miles). The new Jerusalem is a perfect cube, the same shape as the Most Holy Place in the temple (1 Kings 6:20). These measurements illustrate that this new home will be perfect for us.

21:18–21 The picture of walls made of jewels reveals that the new Jerusalem will be a place of purity and durability—it will last for ever.

21:22–24 The temple, the centre of God's presence among his people, was the primary place of worship. No temple is needed in the new city, however, because God's presence will be every-

21:22 [c]Rev 5:6
21:23 [d]Isa 24:23; 60:19; Rev 22:5
21:24 [e]Isa 60:3, 5
21:25 [f]Isa 60:11 [g]Zec 14:7; Rev 22:5
21:27 [h]Isa 52:1; Joel 3:17; Rev 22:14, 15
22:1 [a]Rev 4:6 [b]Eze 47:1; Zec 14:8
22:2 [c]Rev 2:7 [d]Eze 47:12
22:3 [e]Zec 14:11 [f]Rev 7:15
22:4 [g]Mt 5:8 [h]Rev 14:1
22:5 [i]Rev 21:25 [j]Rev 21:23 [k]Da 7:27; Rev 20:4
22:6 [l]Rev 1:1 [m]Rev 19:9; 21:5 [n]Heb 12:9 [o]ver 16
22:7 [p]Rev 3:11 [q]Rev 1:3

Lamb[c] are its temple.
23 The city does not need the sun or the moon to shine on it,
for the glory of God gives it light,[d] and the Lamb is its lamp.
24 The nations will walk
by its light, and the kings of the earth will bring their splendour into it.[e]
25 On no
day will its gates ever be shut,[f] for there will be no night there.[g]
26 The glory and
honour of the nations will be brought into it.
27 Nothing impure will ever enter it, nor
will anyone who does what is shameful or deceitful,[h] but only those whose names
are written in the Lamb's book of life.

The River of Life

22 Then the angel showed me the river of the water of life, as clear as crystal,[a]
flowing[b] from the throne of God and of the Lamb
2 down the middle of the
great street of the city. On each side of the river stood the tree of life,[c] bearing twelve
crops of fruit, yielding its fruit every month. And the leaves of the tree are for the
healing of the nations.[d]
3 No longer will there be any curse.[e] The throne of God and
of the Lamb will be in the city, and his servants will serve him.[f]
4 They will see his
face,[g] and his name will be on their foreheads.[h]
5 There will be no more night.[i]
They will not need the light of a lamp or the light of the sun, for the Lord God will
give them light.[j] And they will reign for ever and ever.[k]
6 The angel said to me,[l] "These words are trustworthy and true.[m] The Lord, the
God of the spirits of the prophets,[n] sent his angel[o] to show his servants the things
that must soon take place."

Jesus Is Coming

7 "Behold, I am coming soon![p] Blessed[q] is he who keeps the words of the prophecy
in this book."

WHAT WE KNOW ABOUT ETERNITY

Reference	*Description*
John 14:2, 3	A place prepared for us
John 20:19, 26	Unlimited by physical properties (1 Corinthians 15:35–49)
1 John 3:2	We will be like Jesus
1 Corinthians 15	We will have new bodies
1 Corinthians 2:9	Our experience will be wonderful
Revelation 21:1	A new environment
Revelation 21:3	A new experience of God's presence (1 Corinthians 13:12)
Revelation 21:4	New emotions
Revelation 21:4	There will be no more death

The Bible devotes much less space to describing eternity than it does to convincing people that eternal life is available as a free gift from God. Most of the brief descriptions of eternity would be more accurately called hints, since they use terms and ideas from present experience to describe what we cannot fully grasp until we are there ourselves. These references hint at aspects of what our future will be like if we have accepted Christ's gift of eternal life.

---

where. He will be worshipped throughout the city, and nothing will hinder us from being with him.

21:25–27 Not everyone will be allowed into the new Jerusalem, but "only those whose names are written in the Lamb's book of life". (The book of life is explained in the notes on 3:5 and 20:12–15.) Don't think that you will get in because of your background, personality, or good behaviour. Eternal life is available to you only because of what Jesus, the Lamb, has done. Trust him today to secure your citizenship in his new creation.

22:1 The water of life is a symbol of eternal life. Jesus used this same image with the Samaritan woman (John 4:7–14). It pictures the fullness of life with God and the eternal blessings that come when we believe in him and allow him to satisfy our spiritual thirst (see 22:17).

22:2 This tree of life is like the tree of life in the Garden of Eden (Genesis 2:9). After Adam and Eve sinned, they were forbidden to eat from the tree of life because they could not have eternal life as long as they were under sin's control. But because of the forgiveness of sin through the blood of Jesus, there will be no evil or sin in this city. We will be able to eat freely from the tree of life when sin's control over us is destroyed and our eternity with God is secure.

22:2 Why would the nations need to be healed if all evil is gone? John is quoting from Ezekiel 47:12, where water flowing from the temple produces trees with healing leaves. He is not implying that there will be illness in the new earth; he is emphasising that the water of life produces health and strength wherever it goes.

22:3 "No longer will there be any curse" means that nothing accursed will be in God's presence. This fulfils Zechariah's prophecy (see Zechariah 14:11).

8 I, John, am the one who heard and saw these things.[r] And when I had heard and
seen them, I fell down to worship at the feet[s] of the angel who had been showing
them to me. 9 But he said to me, "Do not do it! I am a fellow-servant with you and
with your brothers the prophets and of all who keep the words of this book.[t] Worship
God!"[u]
10 Then he told me, "Do not seal up[v] the words of the prophecy of this book,
because the time is near.[w] 11 Let him who does wrong continue to do wrong; let him
who is vile continue to be vile; let him who does right continue to do right; and let
him who is holy continue to be holy."[x]

12 "Behold, I am coming soon![y] My reward is with me,[z] and I will give to
everyone according to what he has done. 13 I am the Alpha and the Omega,[a] the First
and the Last,[b] the Beginning and the End.[c]
14 "Blessed are those who wash their robes, that they may have the right to the tree
of life[d] and may go through the gates[e] into the city.[f] 15 Outside[g] are the dogs,[h]
those who practise magic arts, the sexually immoral, the murderers, the idolaters and
everyone who loves and practises falsehood.
16 "I, Jesus,[i] have sent my angel to give you[a] this testimony for the churches.[j]
I am the Root[k] and the Offspring of David, and the bright Morning Star."[l]

17 The Spirit[m] and the bride say, "Come!" And let him who hears say, "Come!"
Whoever is thirsty, let him come; and whoever wishes, let him take the free gift of
the water of life.

18 I warn everyone who hears the words of the prophecy of this book: If anyone adds
anything to them,[n] God will add to him the plagues described in this book.[o] 19 And
if anyone takes words away[p] from this book of prophecy, God will take away from
him his share in the tree of life and in the holy city, which are described in this book.

a *16* The Greek is plural.

22:8 [r]Rev 1:1 [s]Rev 19:10
22:9 [t]ver 10, 18, 19 [u]Rev 19:10
22:10 [v]Da 8:26; Rev 10:4 [w]Rev 1:3
22:11 [x]Eze 3:27; Da 12:10
22:12 [y]ver 7, 20 [z]Isa 40:10
22:13 [a]Rev 1:8 [b]Rev 1:17 [c]Rev 21:6
22:14 [d]Rev 2:7 [e]Rev 21:12 [f]Rev 21:27
22:15 [g]1Co 6:9, 10; Gal 5:19-21; Col 3:5, 6 [h]Php 3:2
22:16 [i]Rev 1:1 [j]Rev 1:4 [k]Rev 5:5 [l]2Pe 1:19; Rev 2:28
22:17 [m]Rev 2:7
22:18 [n]Dt 4:2; Pr 30:6 [o]Rev 15:6-16:21
22:19 [p]Dt 4:2

22:8, 9 Hearing or reading an eyewitness account is the next best thing to seeing the event yourself. John witnessed the events reported in Revelation and wrote them down so we could see and believe as he did. If you have read this far, you have seen. Have you also believed?

22:8, 9 The first of the Ten Commandments is "You shall have no other gods before me" (Exodus 20:3). Jesus said that the greatest command of Moses' laws was "Love the Lord your God with all your heart and with all your soul and with all your mind" (Matthew 22:37). Here, at the end of the Bible, this truth is reiterated. The angel instructs John to "worship God"! God alone is worthy of our worship and adoration. He is above all creation, even the angels. Are there people, ideas, goals, or possessions that occupy the central place in your life, crowding God out? Worship *only* God by allowing nothing to distract you from your devotion to him.

22:10, 11 The angel tells John what to do after his vision is over. Instead of sealing up what he has written, as Daniel was commanded to do (Daniel 12:4–12), the book is to be left open so that all can read and understand. Daniel's message was sealed because it was not a message for Daniel's time. But the book of Revelation was a message for John's time, and it is relevant today. As Christ's return gets closer, there is a greater polarisation between God's followers and Satan's followers. We must read the book of Revelation, hear its message, and be prepared for Christ's imminent return.

22:12–14 Those who wash their robes are those who seek to purify themselves from a sinful way of life. They strive daily to remain faithful and ready for Christ's return. This concept is also explained in the second note on 7:14.

22:14 In Eden, Adam and Eve were barred from any access to the tree of life because of their sin (Genesis 3:22–24). In the new earth, God's people will eat from the tree of life because their sins have been removed by Christ's death and resurrection. Those who eat the fruit of this tree will live for ever. If Jesus has forgiven your sins, you will have the right to eat from this tree. For more on this concept, see the first note on 22:2.

22:15 The exact location of these sinners is not known, nor is it relevant. They are outside. They were judged and condemned in 21:7, 8. The emphasis is that nothing evil and no sinner will be in God's presence to corrupt or harm any of the faithful.

22:16 Jesus is both David's "Root" and "Offspring". As the Creator of all, Jesus existed long before David. As a human, however, he was one of David's direct descendants (see Isaiah 11:1–5; Matthew 1:1–17). As the Messiah, he is the "bright Morning Star", the light of salvation to all.

22:17 Both the Holy Spirit and the bride, the church, extend the invitation to all the world to come to Jesus and experience the joys of salvation in Christ.

22:17 When Jesus met the Samaritan woman at the well, he told her of the living water that he could supply (John 4:10–15). This image is used again as Christ invites anyone to come and drink of the water of life. The gospel is unlimited in scope – all people everywhere may come. Salvation cannot be earned, but God gives it freely. We live in a world desperately thirsty for living water, and many are dying of thirst. But it's still not too late. Let us invite everyone to come and drink.

22:18, 19 This warning is given to those who might purposefully distort the message in this book. Moses gave a similar warning in Deuteronomy 4:1–4. We too must handle the Bible with care and great respect so that we do not distort its message, even unintentionally. We should be quick to put its principles into practice in our lives. No human explanation or interpretation of God's word should be elevated to the same authority as the text itself.

22:20
q Rev 1:2
r 1Co 16:22
22:21
s Ro 16:20

20 He who testifies to these things[q] says, "Yes, I am coming soon."
Amen. Come, Lord Jesus.[r]
21 The grace of the Lord Jesus be with God's people.[s] Amen.

22:20 We don't know the day or the hour, but Jesus is coming soon and unexpectedly. This is good news to those who trust him, but a terrible message for those who have rejected him and stand under judgment. *Soon* means at any moment, and we must be ready for him, always prepared for his return. Would Jesus' sudden appearance catch you off guard?

22:21 Revelation closes human history as Genesis opened it – in paradise. But there is one distinct difference in Revelation – evil is gone for ever. Genesis describes Adam and Eve walking and talking with God; Revelation describes people worshipping God face to face. Genesis describes a garden with an evil serpent; Revelation describes a perfect city with no evil. The Garden of Eden was destroyed by sin; but paradise is re-created in the new Jerusalem.

The book of Revelation ends with an urgent request: "Come, Lord Jesus." In a world of problems, persecution, evil, and immorality, Christ calls us to endure in our faith. Our efforts to better our world are important, but their results cannot compare with the transformation that Jesus will bring about when he returns. He alone controls human history, forgives sin, and will re-create the earth and bring lasting peace.

Revelation is, above all, a book of hope. It shows that no matter what happens on earth, God is in control. It promises that evil will not last for ever. And it depicts the wonderful reward that is waiting for all those who believe in Jesus Christ as Saviour and Lord.

TABLE OF WEIGHTS AND MEASURES

	Approximate Biblical Unit	Approximate Imperial Unit	Metric Equivalent
		Weights	
talent	60 minas	75 pounds	34 kilograms
mina	50 shekels	1¼ pounds	0.6 kilogram
shekel	2 bekas	⅖ ounce	11.5 grams
pim	⅔ shekel	¼ ounce	7.7 grams
beka	10 gerahs	⅕ ounce	5.8 grams
gerah		1/50 ounce	0.6 gram
		Length	
cubit		18 inches	0.5 metre
span		9 inches	23 centimetres
handbreadth		3 inches	8 centimetres
		Capacity: Dry Measure	
cor	10 ephahs	6 bushels	220 litres
lethek	5 ephahs	3 bushels	110 litres
ephah	10 omers	⅗ bushel	22 litres
seah	⅓ ephah	13 pints	7.3 litres
omer	1/10 ephah	4 pints	2 litres
cab	1/18 ephah	2 pints	1 litre
		Capacity: Liquid Measure	
bath	1 ephah	5 gallons	22 litres
hin	⅙ bath	7 pints	4 litres
log	1/72 bath	½ pint	0.3 litre

The figures of the table are calculated on the basis of a shekel equalling 11.5 grams, a cubit equalling 18 inches and an ephah equalling 22 litres. It is based upon the best available information, but it is not intended to be mathematically precise; like the measurement equivalents in the footnotes, it merely gives approximate amounts and distances. Weights and measures differed somewhat at various times and places in the ancient world. There is uncertainty particularly about the ephah and the bath; further discoveries may give more light on these units of capacity.

ABBREVIATIONS IN THE INDEX TO NOTES

Following is a list of abbreviations in the Index to Notes:

BOOKS OF THE BIBLE

Genesis	Gn	Isaiah	Is	Romans	Rom
Exodus	Ex	Jeremiah	Jer	1 Corinthians	1 Cor
Leviticus	Lv	Lamentations	Lam	2 Corinthians	2 Cor
Numbers	Nm	Ezekiel	Ez	Galatians	Gal
Deuteronomy	Dt	Daniel	Dn	Ephesians	Eph
Joshua	Jos	Hosea	Hos	Philippians	Phil
Judges	Jgs	Joel	Jl	Colossians	Col
Ruth	Ru	Amos	Am	1 Thessalonians	1 Thes
1 Samuel	1 Sm	Obadiah	Ob	2 Thessalonians	2 Thes
2 Samuel	2 Sm	Jonah	Jon	1 Timothy	1 Tm
1 Kings	1 Kgs	Micah	Mi	2 Timothy	2 Tm
2 Kings	2 Kgs	Nahum	Na	Titus	Ti
1 Chronicles	1 Chr	Habakkuk	Hb	Philemon	Phlm
2 Chronicles	2 Chr	Zephaniah	Zep	Hebrews	Heb
Ezra	Ezr	Haggai	Hg	James	Jas
Nehemiah	Neh	Zechariah	Zec	1 Peter	1 Pt
Esther	Est	Malachi	Mal	2 Peter	2 Pt
Job	Jb	Matthew	Mt	1 John	1 Jn
Psalms	Ps	Mark	Mk	2 John	2 Jn
Proverbs	Prv	Luke	Lk	3 John	3 Jn
Ecclesiastes	Eccl	John	Jn	Jude	Jude
Song of Songs	Song	Acts	Acts	Revelation	Rv

INDEX TO NOTES

This is an index to the notes, charts, maps, and personality profiles in the *Life Application Bible.* Every entry concerning a note has a Bible reference and a page number; every entry concerning a chart, map, or personality profile has a page number. In some instances, a Bible reference is followed by a number in parentheses to indicate that there is more than one note on that particular scripture. For example, Rv 1:1(2) means that the reader should look up the second note with the heading of 1:1 in Revelation. In most cases, the entries follow in Biblical/canonical order (i.e., from Genesis to Revelation). In some cases, however, the entries follow a chronological order – this is especially true with important people in the Bible. Following the general index are special indexes: Index to Charts, Index to Maps, and Index to Personality Profiles. Because of the emphasis on application in the *Life Application Bible,* these indexes are helpful guides for personal and group Bible study, sermon preparation, or teaching.

PREACHERS

PREACHING

PREJUDICE

PREMARITAL SEX

PREMILLENNIALISM

PREPARATION

PRESENCE

PRESENCE, BREAD OF THE

INDEX TO CHARTS

INDEX TO MAPS

Note: maps concerning Jesus' ministry are given in chronological order — see Harmony of the Gospels.

INDEX TO PERSONALITY PROFILES

Jerusalem in New Testament Times

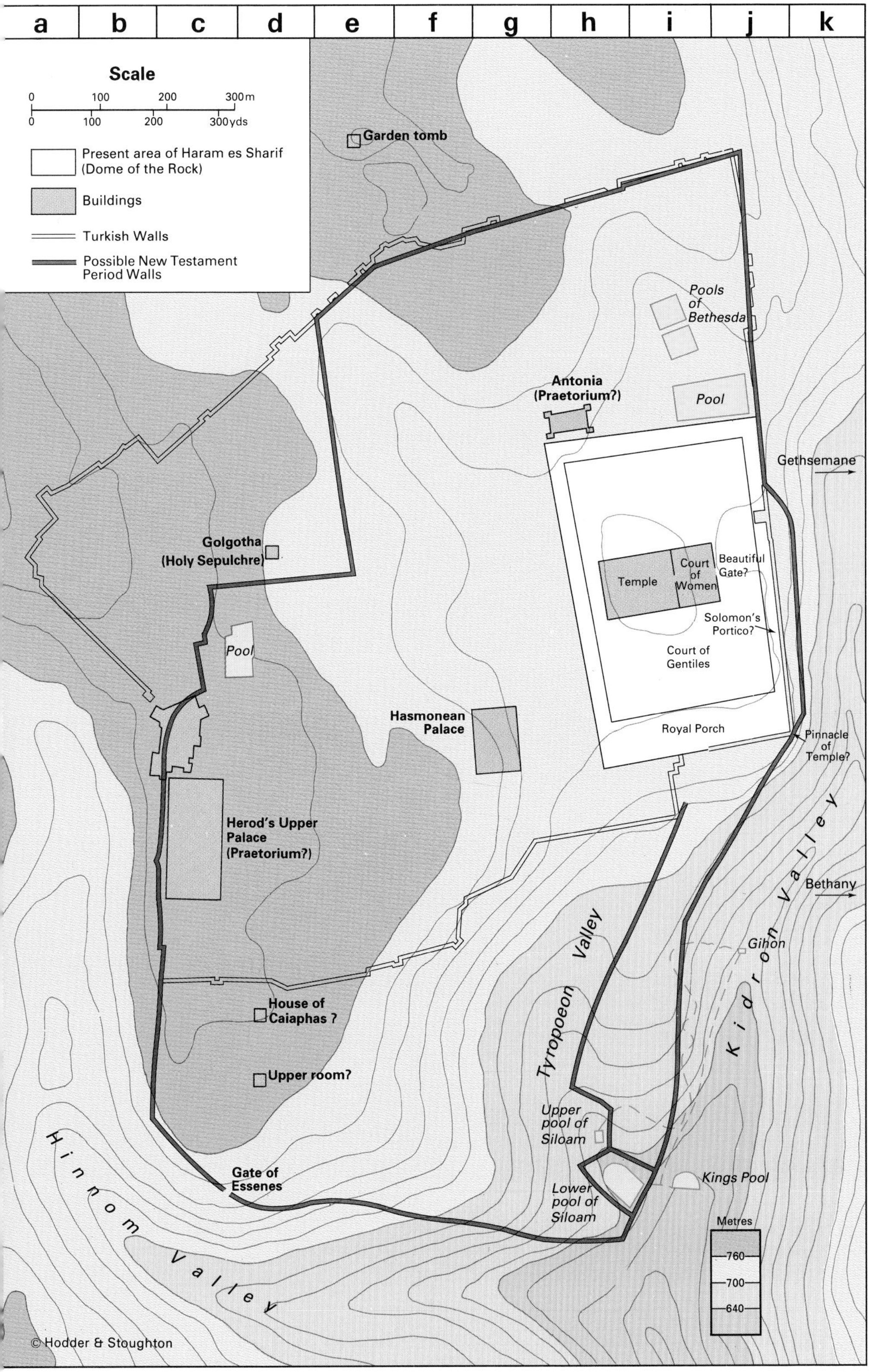

a
b
c
d
e
f
g
h
i
j
k
Scale
0
100
200
300m
0
100
200
300yds
Present area of Haram es Sharif (Dome of the Rock)
Buildings
Turkish Walls
Possible New Testament Period Walls
Garden tomb
Pools of Bethesda
Antonia (Praetorium?)
Pool
Gethsemane
Golgotha (Holy Sepulchre)
Temple
Court of Women
Beautiful Gate?
Solomon's Portico?
Court of Gentiles
Pool
Hasmonean Palace
Royal Porch
Pinnacle of Temple?
Herod's Upper Palace (Praetorium?)
Kidron Valley
Bethany
Tyropoeon Valley
Gihon
House of Caiaphas ?
Upper room?
Upper pool of Siloam
Hinnom Valley
Gate of Essenes
Lower pool of Siloam
Kings Pool
Metres
760
700
640

Palestine in New Testament Times

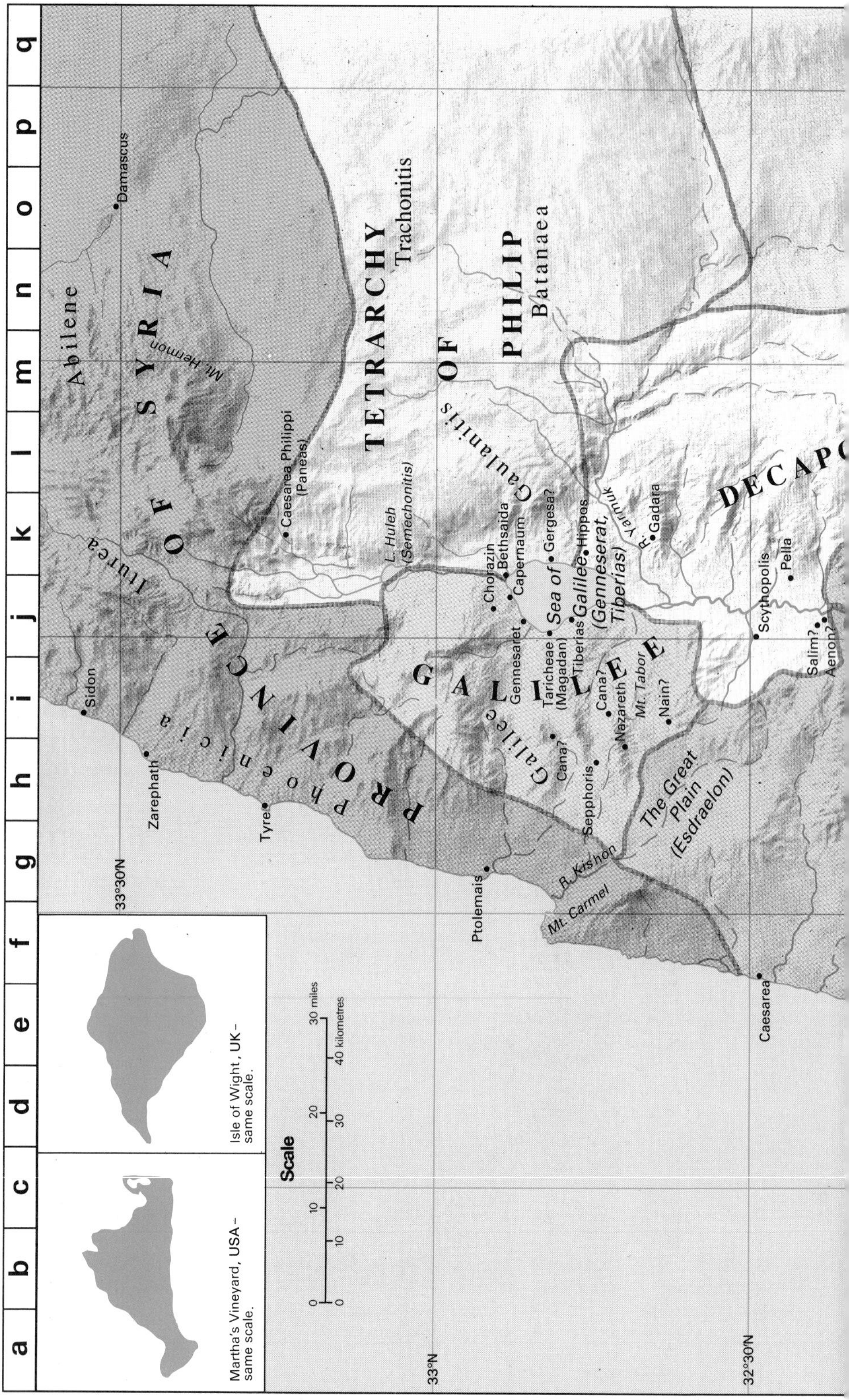